Webster's Seventh New Collegiate Dictionary

A Merriam-Webster

REG. U.S. PAT. OFF.

BASED ON
WEBSTER'S
THIRD
NEW INTERNATIONAL
DICTIONARY

REG. U.S. PAT. OFF.

G. & C. MERRIAM COMPANY, *Publishers*

SPRINGFIELD, MASSACHUSETTS, U.S.A.

Standard Book Numbers:
87779-108-2 (plain)
87779-109-0 (indexed)
87779-110-4 (Fabrikoid)
87779-111-2 (black leather)
87779-112-0 (blue pigskin)
87779-113-9 (brown pigskin)
87779-114-7 (large type)
87779-116-3 (goatskin, slip-cased)

MADE IN THE U.S.A.

R. R. DONNELLEY & SONS COMPANY, THE LAKESIDE PRESS, CHICAGO, ILLINOIS, U.S.A.
COMPOSITORS

RAND McNALLY & COMPANY, CHICAGO, ILLINOIS, U.S.A.
PRINTERS AND BINDERS

CONTENTS

———

Preface 4a

Front Matter

    Explanatory Notes 7a

    Guide to Pronunciation 15a

    Abbreviations Used in this Work 22a

Dictionary of the English Language 1

Back Matter

    Vocabulary of Abbreviations 1042

    Arbitrary Symbols and Proofreaders' Marks 1050

    Proof of Lincoln's Gettysburg Address 1052

    Biographical Names 1053

    Pronouncing Gazetteer 1092

    Forms of Address 1173

    Pronouncing Vocabulary of Common English Given Names 1177

    Vocabulary of Rhymes 1182

    Spelling 1187

    Plurals 1191

    Punctuation 1193

    Compounds 1199

    Capitalization 1204

    Italicization 1205

    Colleges and Universities in the United States and Canada 1206

    Index 1223

PREFACE

HISTORY OF THE COLLEGIATE

WEBSTER'S SEVENTH NEW COLLEGIATE DIC-TIONARY is an entirely new book—newly edited and typeset. It will however have for many persons the characteristics of an old friend. For many years MERRIAM-WEBSTER dictionaries have formed a series in which the unabridged dictionary is the parent work and the COLLEGIATE DICTIONARY the largest abridgment. From each successive revision of the unabridged work new abridged books have sprung. In 1898 the first edition of the COLLEGIATE appeared. Its size, appearance, typography, and above all its wealth of material and scholarly presentation quickly won for it a high place in the regard of both general reader and scholar. In 1910 a second edition appeared, followed by new editions or revisions in 1916 (the third), 1931 (the fourth), 1936 (the fifth), and 1949 (the sixth). This seventh in the COLLEGIATE series incorporates the best of the time-tested features of its predecessors.

SCOPE AND FORMAT

The general content and overall plan of the previous edition have proved so well adapted to the needs of its users that an attempt to change its essential character and form seems inadvisable. The editors feel too that relatively few entires, both in its main vocabulary and in the special sections, can be omitted without loss to the user of WEBSTER'S SEVENTH NEW COLLEGIATE. At the same time many new terms and meanings, many older terms and meanings of increasing importance or frequency, many abbreviations, and many proper names must be added in a new edition. The problem is solved partly by the development of a new dictionary style based upon completely analytical one-phrase definitions throughout and partly by the adoption of a new typeface, Times Roman, introduced to MERRIAM-WEBSTER dictionaries in WEBSTER'S THIRD NEW INTERNATIONAL DICTIO-NARY. This compact and legible face makes possible more words to a line and more lines to a column than in the preceding COLLEGIATE.

THE GENERAL VOCABULARY

The vocabulary of the COLLEGIATE is intended to meet the needs both of the college student and of the general reader seeking clear and accurate but not encyclopedic information. Every entry and every definition of the previous edition has been reviewed, and many of them have been revised to incorporate additional, often new, information or to effect improvements in the former presentation. The definitions are for the most part based on the most recent available information contained in the parent work, WEBSTER'S THIRD NEW INTERNATIONAL DICTIONARY, with such modifications or adaptations as are required by the smaller scope of the COLLEGIATE. Wherever they are needed and as freely as possible within the limitations of the space, phrases and sentences have been given that illustrate the definitions. This COLLEGIATE follows the practice of its predecessors in including only a limited selection of slang, dialect, and obsolete terms and meanings. Since behind the present work are all the vast resources of the THIRD NEW INTERNATIONAL, containing some 450,000 vocabulary entires, the problem is one of selection of terms to be included here. Usefulness is the criterion.

SPECIAL SUBJECTS

The greater emphasis on the technical and scientific vocabulary, which is perhaps the most noticeable difference between recent and earlier COLLEGIATES, has been continued in this COLLEGIATE. The wealth of information prepared by the 200 outside consultants for the THIRD NEW INTERNATIONAL has been freely drawn upon.

TRADEMARKS

Public interest in the status, the pronunciation, and the application of many terms originally coined for use as trademarks makes such terms a matter of lexical concern. In a dictionary of this scope, however, it is possible to include only a limited number of those trademarks most likely to be sought by the average dictionary user. All entries suspected of being trademarks have been checked on the trademark register in the United States Patent Office at Washington, D. C., and those which were thus found to be trademarks are identified as such. The inclusion of a term in this dictionary is not to be taken as an expression of the publishers' opinion as to whether or not it is subject to proprietary rights, but only as an expression of their belief that such a term is of sufficiently general use and interest to warrant its inclusion in a work of this kind. No definition in this dictionary is to be regarded as affecting the validity of any trademark.

PRESENTATION OF MATERIAL

Although the presentation of the material conforms to accepted MERRIAM-WEBSTER dictionary practice and will in general offer no difficulty to most users of this book, occasional details may raise questions requiring precise answer. The edi-

tors have tried to anticipate and answer all such questions in the section of "Explanatory Notes" following this preface. Every user of this book, even the experienced dictionary consulter, will gain much from a reading of these pages.

ORDER OF DEFINITIONS

In general the order of definitions follows the practice of the THIRD NEW INTERNATIONAL, where the earliest ascertainable meaning is placed first and later meanings are arranged in the order shown to be most probable by dated citations and semantic development. This arrangement applies alike to all meanings whether standard, technical, or scientific. The historical order is of especial value to those interested in the development of meanings and offers no difficulty to the user who is merely looking for a particular meaning.

PRONUNCIATION

The pronunciations given in this dictionary are based on those of the THIRD NEW INTERNATIONAL and reflect a large file of transcriptions from actual educated speech in all fields and in all parts of the United States. To make these pronunciations more representative the MERRIAM-WEBSTER pronunciation key has been revised. Many of the symbols of preceding editions have been retained, some with slight alteration, a few substitutions have been made, and some symbols have been dropped altogether. It is still fundamentally a diacritical key that makes use of many of the conventions of English spelling and is based on the principles that every distinct significant sound should have a distinct symbol to represent it and that no sound should be represented in more than one way. The elimination of symbols for all nonsignificant differences in sound makes it possible for transcriptions to convey to speakers in different parts of the English-speaking world sounds proper to their own speech. The new pronunciation alphabet is designed to represent clearly the standard speech of educated Americans. A chart of this key is printed on the front and back inside covers, key lines are printed at the bottom of every other page, and the system is further explained in the "Guide to Pronunciation" in the front matter. This guide has been condensed by Edward Artin, associate editor, from the fuller treatment in the THIRD NEW INTERNATIONAL.

SYNONYMS

Brief articles discriminating from one another words of closely associated meaning have long been a valuable feature of the COLLEGIATE. The articles, adapted from the fuller treatments in WEB-

STER'S DICTIONARY OF SYNONYMS and WEBSTER'S THIRD NEW INTERNATIONAL DICTIONARY, were prepared by Dr. Philip H. Goepp, associate editor.

PICTORIAL ILLUSTRATIONS

The wide scope of illustrations that was a feature of previous editions of the COLLEGIATE has been retained in this new work. Many new illustrations have been especially prepared under the supervision of Mildred A. Mercier, assistant editor. In general the aim has been to include illustrations not for their decorative quality but for their value in clarifying definitions.

SUPPLEMENTARY FEATURES

The supplementary features of the previous edition have been retained, and "Forms of Address" has been added.

The "Pronouncing Gazetteer" gives the spelling, syllabic division, and pronunciation of over ten thousand names and continues to provide information on location, political status or ownership, population, and other statistics (as length of rivers, height of mountains, area of political divisions) in the concise form familiar to users of the COLLEGIATE.

The "Biographical Names" section gives the spelling, pronunciation, given names, dates, nationality, and a brief indication of achievements or sphere of activity for over five thousand persons, ancient and modern, of general interest.

The list of "Colleges and Universities" which has proved to be one of the most often consulted of the special sections of the COLLEGIATE, has been revised and its basis of selection broadened to include a larger number of institutions. The pronunciation and syllabic division of the names of these institutions are given wherever needed.

The list of "Abbreviations" and of "Given Names" have been revised and many entries have been added.

The section of "Arbitrary Symbols", the "Vocabulary of Rhymes", and the several sections treating "Spelling", "Punctuation", "Plurals", "Compounds", "Capitalization", "Italicization", and "Proofreaders' Marks" have been revised and retained.

EDITORIAL STAFF

The editing, checking, proofreading, and similar operations have been carried out by the trained editorial staff of G. & C. MERRIAM COMPANY, many of whom worked not only on the preparation of the previous edition of the COLLEGIATE but also on the WEBSTER'S THIRD NEW INTERNATIONAL. An exhaustive list of staff members who

contributed to this COLLEGIATE, some by performing essential clerical work and others by preparing or reviewing a few definitions, would serve little purpose; but it would be ungracious not to mention the chief participants in various phases of the work. The writing of definitions and production of copy have been under the general supervision of Dr. H. Bosley Woolf, managing editor, assisted by Laverne W. King and Patricia F. Martin. Definitions have been written by Dr. Philip H. Goepp, Dr. Mairé Weir Kay, Hubert P. Kelsey, Dr. Howard G. Rhoads, Dr. Charles R. Sleeth, associate editors; and Dr. Warren B. Austin, Robert B. Costello, Philip W. Cummings, J. Edward Gates, E. Ward Gilman, Dr. Robert J. Quinlan, Thomas H. B. Robertson, and Raymond R. Wilson, assistant editors. Pronunciations have been done by Edward Artin, associate editor, assisted by Elsie Mag, assistant editor, and Harold E. Niergarth, editorial assistant. Etymologies have been under the supervision of Dr. Sleeth and Dr. F. Stuart Crawford, assistant editor, assisted by M. Eluned Roberts, assistant editor, and Betty Meltzer

and Mary Ellen Knight, editorial assistants. Cross-referencing has been under the supervision of Ervina E. Foss, assistant editor, assisted by Grace A. Kellogg, assistant editor, and Eulelah W. Lyon and Doris N. Sherwood, editorial assistants. Proofreading, under the supervision of Mr. Gilman, has been done chiefly by Hubert H. Roe, assistant editor, and by Grace E. Brophy, Robert W. Conboy, James M. Donovan, Peter D. Haraty, Edith M. Lowe, and Gertrude F. New, editorial assistants.

WEBSTER'S SEVENTH NEW COLLEGIATE DICTIONARY represents the results of the collaborative efforts of the permanent MERRIAM-WEBSTER editorial staff. It is the product of the only organization specializing completely in dictionary making with more than 100 years of continuous experience in this field. It is the latest addition to the MERRIAM-WEBSTER series of dictionaries which have served successive generations. We offer it to the user with the conviction that it will serve him well.

PHILIP B. GOVE, *Editor in Chief*

EXPLANATORY NOTES

A careful reading of these explanatory notes will make it easier for the user of this dictionary to comprehend the information contained at each entry. Here are brief explanations of the different typefaces, different labels, significant punctuation, symbols, and other conventions by which this dictionary achieves compactness and comprehensiveness. The chief divisions are:

1.	THE MAIN ENTRY	7.	THE ETYMOLOGY	12.	VERBAL ILLUSTRATIONS
2.	THE PRONUNCIATION	8.	STATUS LABELS	13.	NAMES OF PLANTS AND ANIMALS
3.	FUNCTIONAL LABELS	9.	SUBJECT LABELS	14.	USAGE NOTES
4.	INFLECTIONAL FORMS	10.	THE SYMBOLIC COLON	15.	CROSS-REFERENCES
5.	CAPITALIZATION	11.	SENSE DIVISION	16.	RUN-ON ENTRIES
6.	ATTRIBUTIVE NOUNS				

17.	SYNONYMIES
18.	COMBINING FORMS
19.	THE VOCABULARY ENTRY
20.	PROPER NAMES
21.	ABBREVIATIONS

1. THE MAIN ENTRY

1.1 A heavy black letter or a combination of heavy black letters (**boldface type**) set flush with the left-hand margin of each column of type is a main entry or entry word. The combination consists usually of letters set solid (*about*), of letters separated by one or more spaces (*air line*), or of letters joined by a hyphen (*air-dry*). What follows each such boldface entry in lightface type on the same line and on indented lines below explains and justifies its inclusion in the dictionary. The boldface entry together with this added matter is also called an entry.

1.2 The main entries follow one another in this dictionary in alphabetical order letter by letter. For example, *book of account* follows *bookmobile* as if it were printed *bookofaccount* without spacing. Entry words containing an arabic numeral (*3-D, 1080* "ten-eighty") are alphabetized as if the numeral were spelled out. Entry words derived from proper names beginning with abbreviated forms of *Mac-* (*McCoy*) are alphabetized as if spelled *mac-*. Entries often beginning with *St.* in common usage have the abbreviation spelled out *saint* (*Saint Martin's summer*).

1.3 As an aid to finding an entry, a pair of guide words is printed at the top of each page. These are the first and last words of a sequence of boldface words on one page of the dictionary. Entries alphabetically between the word in the upper left corner and the word in the upper right corner are defined on the same page.

1.4.1 When one entry has exactly the same written form as another that follows it, the two are distinguished by superior numbers (superscripts) preceding each word:

    ¹dead
    ²dead

Sometimes such homographs are related, like the two *deads*, which are different parts of speech derived from the same root. At other times, there is no relationship beyond the accident of spelling:

    ¹can *verb*
    ²can *noun*

Whether homographs are related or not, their order is usually historical: the one first used in English, insofar as the dates can be established, is entered first.

1.4.2 For a homograph that is undefined, see 16.1.1.

1.5 Such superscripts are used only when all the letters, spaces, and hyphens of two or more main entries are identical (except for foreign accent marks). A variation in form calls for a new series of superscripts. In general, words precede word elements made up of the same letters, and lowercase type precedes uppercase type.

1.6 The centered periods within entry words indicate division points at which a hyphen may be put at the end of a written line, thus for *ar·chae·ol·o·gy*:

	ar-
chaeology	archae-
ology	archaeol-
ogy	archaeology
gy	

Such periods are not shown after a single initial letter (*aplomb*, not *a·plomb*) or before a single terminal letter (*ar·ea*, not *ar·e·a*) because printers seldom cut off one letter only. Many printers try to avoid cutting off two letters only, especially at the end. They might divide *ar·cha·ic* into *ar-/chaic* but not into *archa-/ic*. Other words (*April, apron*) that are not often divided in printing do not show a centered period.

1.6.1 A double hyphen ⸗ at the end of a line stands for a hyphen that belongs normally at that point in a hyphened word and should be retained when the word is written out as a unit on one line.

1.7.1 When a main entry is followed by the word *or* and another spelling or form, the two spellings or forms are equal variants, and the first is no more to be preferred than the second, or third, or fourth, if three or four are joined by *or*. Both or all are standard and any one may be used according to personal inclination or personal style preferences:

    ab·er·rance . . . *or* **ab·er·ran·cy**
    cad·die *or* **cad·dy**

If the alphabetical order of variants joined by *or* is reversed, they remain equal variants. The one printed first may be slightly more common but not common enough to justify calling them unequal:

    cad·dis *or* **cad·dice**

1.7.2 When another spelling or form is joined to the first entry by the word *also* instead of *or*, the spelling or form after *also* is a secondary variant and occurs less frequently than the first form:

    wool·ly *also* **wooly** . . . *adj*

The secondary variant belongs to standard usage and may for personal or regional reasons be preferred by some. If there are two secondary variants, the second is joined to the first by *or*. Once the italic *also* is used to signal a secondary variant, all following variants are joined by *or*:

    wool·ly *also* **wool·ie** *or* **wooly** . . . *n*

No evaluation below secondary is implied. Absence of a variant does not mean that there is no variant.

1.7.3 Standard variants not shown with an *or* or *also* are entered at their own places alphabetically whenever their spelling places them alphabetically more than one column away from the main entry. The form of entry is

    loth *var of* LOATH
    rime, rimer, rimester *var of* RHYME, RHYMER, RHYMESTER

in which *var of* stands for "variant of".

2. THE PRONUNCIATION

2.1 The matter between reversed virgules \ \ is the pronunciation in symbols shown in the chart headed "Merriam-Webster Pronunciation Symbols". A hyphen - shows syllable divisions. The hyphens in the respelling for pronunciation often do not correspond with centered periods in the boldface entry. For example, the first

syllable of the pronunciation of *metric* ends with \e\ and the second syllable begins with \t\, but printers usually divide the word between the *t* and the *r*.

2.2 A high-set mark ' indicates primary accent or stress; a low-set mark , indicates a secondary accent:

> **dead·wood** \'ded-,wu̇d\

To facilitate progressive reading, a stress mark stands at the beginning of the syllable to be stressed.

2.3 The presence of variant pronunciations simply indicates that not all educated speakers pronounce the word the same way. A second-place variant is not to be regarded as per se a less desirable variant than the one given first. In fact, it may be used by as many educated speakers as the first variant. A variant which, according to our records, is appreciably less frequent than the variant preceding may be preceded by *also*. Some variant pronunciations (as \'fȯr-ən\ and \'fär-ən\ for *foreign*) are the kind that one speaker uses but another does not for the reason that their dialects are different and that the speech habits of one are different from those of the other. Such variants are labeled in the vocabulary only if parallel examples are rare or nonexistent. Thus *South also* precedes the variant \'gre(ə)t\ at *great*.

2.4 Parentheses mean that whatever is indicated by the symbol or symbols between them is present in the pronunciation of some speakers and absent from the pronunciation of other speakers, or that it is present in some utterances and absent from other utterances of the same speaker, or that its presence or absence is uncertain:

> **hick·o·ry** \'hik-(ə-)rē\
> **sense** \'sen(t)s\
> **com·fort·able** \'kəm(p)(f)-tə-bəl\

Such pronunciations could alternatively have been shown, at greater cost of space, as \'hik-rē, 'hik-ə-rē\ and \'sens, 'sents\. At *comfortable* the parentheses mean that both \p\ and \f\ occur between \m\ and \t\, or \p\ alone, or \f\ alone, or nothing.

2.5 When a word that is at its own alphabetical place has less than a full pronunciation, the missing part is to be supplied from a pronunciation in a preceding entry or within the same pair of reversed virgules:

> **de·ba·cle** \di-'bäk-əl, -'bak-\
> **de·cem·vi·ral** \-və-rəl\

The hyphens before and after \'bak\ indicate that the first part of the pronunciation and the final part are to be taken from the pronunciation just preceding. The pronunciation for the first two syllables of *decemviral* will be found at the entry *decemvir*:

> **de·cem·vir** \di-'sem-vər\

2.6 Open compounds of two or more English words usually have no pronunciation indicated (as at *deadly sin*). Usually only the first word in a sequence of numbered homographs is pronounced if their pronunciations are the same:

> **¹carp** \'kärp\
> **²carp**

²carp has the same pronunciation as *¹carp*. No pronunciation is to be inferred for obsolete words. (In general, words obsolete in their entire range of meaning show a pronunciation only if they occur in Shakespeare.)

2.7 The pronunciation of unpronounced derivatives and compounds at the end of a main entry is a combination of the pronunciation at the main entry and the pronunciation of the suffix or final element as given at its alphabetical place in the vocabulary.

2.8 When a part of two or more variants is common to each, only the varying part of such variants is usually shown. Such partial pronunciations are almost always begun or stopped at a syllable boundary. An exception occurs when a variation of stress is involved. Then a partial pronunciation may be stopped at the stress mark preceding a syllable not shown:

> **er·satz** \'er-,zäts, er-'\
> **di·verse** \dī-'vərs, də-, 'dī-,\

3. FUNCTIONAL LABELS

3.1 An italic label indicating a part of speech or some other functional classification follows the pronunciation or, if no pronunciation is given, the main entry. The eight traditional parts of speech are thus indicated:

ac·tive . . . *adj*	(adjective)
across . . . *adv*	(adverb)
al·though . . . *conj*	(conjunction)
alas . . . *interj*	(interjection)
act . . . *n*	(noun)
across *prep*	(preposition)
he . . . *pron*	(pronoun)
help . . . *vb*	(verb)

3.2 If a verb is both transitive and intransitive, the labels *vt* and *vi* introduce the subdivisions:

> **help** . . . *vb* . . . *vt* . . . ~ *vi*

The character ~ is a boldface swung dash used to stand for the main entry (as *help*) and mark the subdivisions of the verb.
If there is no subdivision, *vt* or *vi* takes the place of *vb:*

> **de·base** . . . *vt*

Definition of a verb as transitive does not preclude intransitive usage, although it may be uncommon. On occasion most transitive verbs get used intransitively.

3.3 Other italicized labels sometimes occurring in the same position as the part-of-speech label are:

audio- *comb form*	(combining form, see 18)
ante- *prefix*	
-ee . . . *n suffix*	
may . . . *verbal auxiliary*	
whoa . . . *v imper*	(imperative verb)
me·thinks . . . *vb impersonal*	(impersonal verb)

Occasionally, two or more functional labels are combined, as *n or adj*.

4. INFLECTIONAL FORMS

4.1 A plural for all standard nouns is shown in this dictionary if it is not formed regularly by adding *-s* or *-es* and changing a final *-y*, if present, to *-i-:*

> **man** . . . *n, pl* **men**
> **mouse** . . . *n, pl* **mice**
> **moth·er–in–law** . . . *n, pl* **mothers–in–law**

4.2 If there are two or more plurals, all are written out in full and are joined by *or* or *also* to indicate whether the forms are equal or secondary variants (see also 1.7.1 and 1.7.2):

> **fish** . . . *n, pl* **fish** *or* **fish·es**
> **court–martial** . . . *n, pl* **courts–martial** *also* **court–martials**
> **fun·gus** . . . *n, pl* **fun·gi** . . . *also* **fun·gus·es**
> **beef** . . . *n, pl* **beefs** . . . *or* **beeves**

4.3 Nouns that are plural in form and regularly used in plural construction are labeled *n pl* (without a comma):

> **en·vi·rons** . . . *n pl*

If the plural form is not always construed as a plural, the label continues with an applicable qualification:

> **ge·net·ics** . . . *n pl but sing in constr*
> **forty winks** *n pl but sing or pl in constr*

in which *sing in constr* stands for "singular in construction" and means that the entry word takes a singular verb.

4.4 An irregular plural form that falls alphabetically more than one column from the main entry is entered at its own alphabetical place:

> **mice** *pl of* MOUSE
> **feet** *pl of* FOOT

Such an entry does not specify whether it is the only plural; it simply tells where to look for relevant information. At *foot* the variant plurals *feet* and *foot* are shown.

4.5 The principal parts of all irregular standard verbs are given in this dictionary. These principal parts, besides the main entry, are the past; the past participle, if different from the past; and the present participle. They are printed in that order in boldface:

see . . . *vb* saw . . . seen . . . see·ing
make . . . *vb* made . . . mak·ing
hit . . . *vb* hit; hit·ting
trap *vb* trapped; trap·ping
chagrin *vt* cha·grined . . . cha·grin·ing
dye *vb* dyed; dye·ing
die . . . *vi* died; dy·ing
volley *vb* vol·leyed; vol·ley·ing
emcee *vb* em·ceed; em·cee·ing
ring *vb* rang . . . rung . . . ring·ing

4.6 Whenever any of the parts has a variant, both are written out in full:

sky *vt* skied *or* skyed; sky·ing
burn . . . *vb* burned . . . *or* burnt . . . burn·ing
show . . . *vb* showed . . . shown . . . *or* showed; show·ing
dwell . . . *vi* dwelt . . . *or* dwelled . . . dwell·ing
im·per·il . . . *vt* im·per·iled *or* im·per·illed; im·per·il·ing *or* im·per·il·ling

4.7 Verbs are considered regular when their past is formed by a terminal *-ed* which is added with no other change except dropping a final *-e* or changing a final *-y* to *-i-*. The principal parts for these verbs are not indicated unless there is some irregularity.

4.8 Principal parts are usually omitted at compounds containing a terminal element or related homograph whose principal parts are shown at its own place. At

over·take . . . *vt*
un·wrap . . . *vt*

the principal parts are not given because they can be found at *take* and *wrap*. Principal parts are often not given at nonstandard terms or at verbs of relatively low frequency.

4.9 An entered principal verb part that falls alphabetically more than one column away from the main entry is found at its own alphabetical place if there is no entry that is a homograph:

rang *past of* RING

4.10 All adjectives and adverbs that have comparatives and superlatives with the suffixes *-er* and *-est* have these forms written out in full in boldface when they are irregular or when they double a final consonant:

red . . . *adj* red·der; red·dest
well *adv* bet·ter . . . best

4.11 Comparatives and superlatives are usually omitted at compounds containing a constituent element whose inflection is regular. At

kind·heart·ed . . . *adj*
un·lucky . . . *adj*

kinderhearted and *unluckiest* are omitted. Similarly the comparatives and superlatives of adverbs are often omitted when an adjective homograph shows them, as at *flat* and *hot*.

4.12 Showing *-er* and *-est* forms does not imply anything more about the use of *more* and *most* with a simple adjective or adverb than that the comparative and superlative degrees can often be expressed in either way (*hotter* or *more hot*, *hottest* or *most hot*).

4.13.1 A form inflected by the addition of an ending that does not add a syllable may be divided at any point where a division is shown in the inflectional base:

mul·let→ *pl* mullet *or* mullets
in·ter·vene→ in·ter·vened→ in·ter·venes

4.13.2 A form inflected by the addition of an ending that adds a syllable may, if the spelling of the base does not change, be divided between the two components, as well as at any point at which a division is shown in the base:

church→ church·es
con·strain→ con·strained→ con·strain·ing→ con·strains
ap·proach→ ap·proached→ ap·proach·ing→ ap·proach·es
re·tort→ re·tort·ed→ re·tort·ing→ re·torts
stout→ stout·er→ stout·est

4.13.3 In a syllable-increased form in which the final consonant of the inflectional base is doubled, a division is made between the doubled consonants:

re·but→ re·but·ted→ re·but·ting→ re·buts

When both of two identical consonants immediately preceding a syllable-increasing ending belong to the inflectional base, a division is made after the second consonant:

bluff·ing

4.13.4 In a syllable-increased form in which a final *e* of the base is dropped before the ending a division is made between the letter that preceded the *e* and the ending:

rate→ rat·ed→ rat·ing
glue→ glu·ing
plague→ plagu·ing
pique→ piqu·ing
gro·tesque→ gro·tesqu·er→ gro·tesqu·est

In syllable-increased forms like those in the last three lines, in which *gu* or *qu*, with *u* silent, appears immediately before the ending, some prefer to divide immediately before the *g* or *q* if it is not immediately preceded by a short vowel or, in the case of *g*, if it is not immediately preceded by *n* (*hᴜ·ran·guing* would suggest the substandard pronunciation \hə-'raŋ-giŋ\):

pi·quing, pla·guing, grotes·quer

5. CAPITALIZATION

5.1 The entries in this dictionary usually begin with a lowercase letter. An initial uppercase letter is shown when a word is almost always capitalized or capitalized more often than not in standard printing practice. Other entries sometimes have an italic label:

often cap = as likely to be capitalized as not; acceptable one way or the other
sometimes cap = more often not capitalized than capitalized; not usually capitalized

The absence of an initial capital or of one of these labels indicates that the word is almost never capitalized except under irrelevant circumstances (as beginning a sentence or being in a list of all-capitalized words):

French *n*
Christian *adj*
french·ify . . . *vt, often cap*
die·sel . . . *n . . . sometimes cap*

5.2 When an entry has more than one letter in question, the form or the label specifies the capitalization required by usage:

French bulldog
black–eyed Su·san
French Canadian
neo–Dar·win·ian . . . *often cap N*

5.3 A word that usually has some of its senses capitalized and some not is labeled to show a variation from the boldface form of entry by applicable use of additional labels:

cap = almost always capitalized or more often capitalized than not
not cap = almost never capitalized
often not cap = acceptable one way or the other

5.4 See also section 20, on "Proper Names".

6. ATTRIBUTIVE NOUNS

6.1 The label *often attrib* in italics added to the label *n* at a main entry indicates that the noun is often used as an adjective equivalent in attributive position before a substantive (as in *air passage, cabbage soup*):

air . . . *n, often attrib*
cab·bage . . . *n, often attrib*
fox . . . *n, pl* fox·es *or* fox *often attrib*
shoul·der . . . *n, often attrib*
va·ca·tion . . . *n, often attrib*

6.2 While any noun is likely to be used attributively sometimes, the label *often attrib* is confined to those having such widespread general frequent attributive use that they could be entered and defined as adjectives or adjectival elements. The label is not used when there is an entered adjective homograph (as *silver, adj*). Also, it is not used at open compounds that may be often used attributively when hyphened (as *X ray* in *X-ray microscope*).

7. THE ETYMOLOGY

7.1 The matter in boldface square brackets preceding the definition is the etymology. Meanings given in roman type within these brackets are not definitions of the main entry. They are meanings of the Middle English, Old English, or non-English words within the brackets. Such etymological meanings may or may not be the same as one or more of the meanings of the main entry. For the meanings of abbreviations in an etymology, see the page headed "Abbreviations Used in This Work".

7.2 It is the purpose of the etymology to trace a main vocabulary entry as far back as possible in English, as to Old English; to tell from what language and what form it came into English; and (except in the case of some words so highly specialized in usage as to be distinctly outside the general vocabulary of English) to trace the pre-English source as far back as possible. These etyma (or a part of them) are printed in italic type.

7.3 The etymology usually gives the Middle English and Old English forms of native words in the manner illustrated by the following examples:

> **earth** . . . *n* [ME *erthe*, fr. OE *eorthe* . . .]
> **day** . . . *n* [ME, fr. OE *dæg* . . .]

7.3.1 When a word is traced back to Middle English but not to Old English, it is found in Middle English but not in the texts that have survived from the Old English period. This is true even though it cannot be shown to have been borrowed from any other language and even though it may have cognates in the other Germanic languages:

> **girl** . . . *n* [ME *gurle, girle* young person of either sex]
> **poke** *vb* [ME *poken*; akin to MD *poken* to poke]

7.3.2 When a word is traced back directly to Old English with no intervening mention of Middle English, it has not survived continuously from Old English times to the present. Rather it died out after the Old English period and has been revived in modern times for its historical or antiquarian interest:

> **ge·mot** *or* **ge·mote** . . . *n* [OE *gemōt* . . .]

7.4 For words borrowed into English from other languages, the etymology gives the language from which the word is borrowed. It gives also the form or a transliteration of the word in that language if the form differs from that in English:

> **etch** . . . *vb* [D *etsen* . . .]
> **flam·boy·ant** . . . *adj* [F . . .]
> **judge** . . . *vb* [ME *juggen*, fr. OF *jugier* . . .]
> **ab·bot** . . . *n* [ME *abbod*, fr. OE, fr. LL *abbat-, abbas* . . .]

7.4.1 In comparatively rare cases the expression "deriv. of" replaces the more usual "fr.". This indicates that one or more intermediate steps has been omitted in tracing the derivation of the form which precedes the expression from the form which follows it:

> **gal·ley** . . . *n* [. . . OF *galie*, deriv. of MGk *galea*]

7.5.1 Usually no etymology is given for words (including open compounds) created in English by the combination of existing constituents or by functional shift from a homograph. This generally indicates that the identity of the constituents is expected to be evident to the user without guidance. Examples:

> **black·fish** . . . *n* 1 : any of numerous dark-colored fishes
> **black·ness** *n* : the quality or state of being black
> **lame** *vt* 1 : to make lame

7.5.2 When a family of words is obviously related to a common English basic word, but differs from it only by containing various easily recognizable suffixes, no etymology is usually given except at the basic word, even though some of the derivatives may have been formed in some other language than English:

> **im·mor·tal** . . . *adj* [ME, fr. L *immortalis* . . .] 1 : exempt from death
> **im·mor·tal·i·ty** . . . *n* : the quality or state of being immortal . . .

Actually the latter word was borrowed into Middle English (via Middle French) from Latin *immortalitas*.

7.6 A considerable part of the technical vocabulary of the sciences and other specialized studies consists of words or word elements that are current in two or more languages, with only such slight modifications as are necessary to adapt them to the structure of the individual language in each case. Many words and word elements of this kind have become sufficiently a part of the general vocabulary of English to require entry even in an abridged dictionary of our language. On account of the vast extent of the relevant published material in many languages and in many scientific and other specialized fields, it is impracticable to ascertain the language of origin of every such term. Yet it would not be accurate to formulate a statement about the origin of any such term in a way that could be interpreted as implying that it was coined in English. Accordingly, whenever a term that is entered in this dictionary belongs recognizably to this class of internationally current terms, and whenever no positive evidence is at hand to show that it was coined in English, the etymology recognizes its international status and the possibility that it originated elsewhere than in English by use of the label ISV (for International Scientific Vocabulary). Examples:

> **en·do·scope** . . . *n* [ISV]
> **hap·loid** . . . *adj* [ISV, fr. Gk *haploeidēs* single . . .] 1 : having the gametic number of chromosomes or half the number characteristic of somatic cells
> **-ene** . . . *n suffix* [ISV, fr. Gk *-ēnē*, fem. of *-enos*, adj. suffix] : unsaturated carbon compound

7.7.1 An etymology beginning with the name of a language (including ME or OE) and not giving the foreign (or Middle English or Old English) form indicates that the foreign (or Middle English or Old English) form is the same as that in present-day English:

> **for** . . . *prep* [ME, fr. OE . . .]
> **au·tom·a·ton** . . . *n* . . . [L, fr. Gk . . .]

7.7.2 An etymology beginning with the name of a language (including ME or OE) and not giving the foreign (or Middle English or Old English) meaning indicates that the foreign (or Middle English or Old English) meaning is the same as that expressed in the first or only definition in the entry:

> **bea·con** . . . *n* [ME *beken*, fr. OE *bēacen* sign . . .] 1 : a signal fire
> **de·note** . . . *vt* [MF *denoter*, fr. L *denotare* . . .] 1 : to serve as an indication of

7.8 When an entry word is derived from an earlier Modern English word now obsolete or so rare that it does not deserve an entry of its own in an abridged dictionary, the meaning of such a word is given in parentheses:

> **bash·ful** . . . *adj* [obs. *bash* (to be abashed)]

7.9 Small superscript figures following words or syllables in an etymology refer in each case to the tone of the word or syllable which they follow. Accordingly they are used only with forms cited from tone languages:

> **sam·pan** . . . *n* [Chin(Pek) *san¹ pan³*, fr. *san¹* three + *pan³* board, plank]
> **voo·doo** . . . *n* [. . . Ewe *vo¹du³* tutelary deity, demon]

7.10 When the source of a word appearing as a main entry is unknown, the expression "origin unknown" is usually used. Only rarely and in exceptional circumstances does absence of an etymology mean that it has not been possible to furnish any informative etymology. This is the case, however, with some ethnic names. More usually it means that no etymology is felt to be necessary. This is the case, for instance, with a very large proportion of the entries identified as variants and with derivatives of the kind mentioned in paragraphs 7.5.1 and 7.5.2.

7.11.1 When a word has been traced back to the earliest language in which it is attested and if this is an Indo-European language, selected cognates in other Indo-European languages (especially Old High German, Latin, and Greek) are usually given where possible. Examples:

> **bench** . . . *n* [ME, fr. OE *benc*; akin to OHG *bank* bench]
> **bear** *vb* . . . [ME *beren*, fr. OE *beran*; akin to OHG *beran* to carry, L *ferre*, Gk *pherein*]
> **equine** . . . *adj* [L *equinus*, fr. *equus* horse; akin to OE *eoh* horse, Gk *hippos*]

7.11.2 Sometimes, however, to avoid space-consuming repetition, the expression "more at" directs the user to

another entry where the cognates are given:

   edict . . . *n* [L *edictum*, fr. neut. of *edictus*, pp. of *edicere* to decree, fr. *e-* + *dicere* to say — more at DICTION]

7.12 Besides the use of "akin to" to denote ordinary cognate relationship (as in several examples in the preceding paragraph) there is in some etymologies a somewhat special use of "akin to" as part of a longer formula "of—origin; akin to—". This longer formula indicates that a word was borrowed from some language belonging to a group of languages, the name of the group being inserted in the blank just before *origin;* that for some reason it is not possible to say with confidence that the word in question is a borrowing of a particular attested word in a particular language of the source group; and that the form cited in the blank after "akin to" is a cognate of the word in question, as attested within the source group. Examples:

   guard . . . *n* [ME *garde*, fr. MF, fr. OF, fr. *garder* to guard, defend, of Gmc origin; akin to OHG *wartēn* to watch, take care — more at WARD]
   cant *n* [ME, prob. fr. MD or ONF; MD, edge, corner, fr. ONF, fr. L *canthus, cantus* iron tire, perh. of Celt origin; akin to W *cant* rim; akin to Gk *kanthos* corner of the eye]

This last example shows the two uses of "akin to" in explicit contrast with each other. The word cited immediately after "of Celt origin; akin to" is a Celtic cognate of the presumed Celtic source word from which the Latin word was borrowed. The word cited after the second "akin to" is a further cognate from another Indo-European language.

8. STATUS LABELS

8.0 A status label in italics sometimes appears before a definition. It provides a degree of usage orientation by identifying the nature of the context in which a word ordinarily occurs. Status labels are of three kinds: temporal, stylistic, and regional.

8.1.1 The temporal label *obs* for "obsolete" means that no evidence of standard use since 1755 has been found:

   en·wheel . . . *vt, obs*
   em·boss . . . *vt* . . . *obs*

obs is a comment on the word being defined, not on the thing denoted by the word. When obsoleteness of the thing is in question, it is implied in the definition (as by *onetime, formerly,* or historical reference):

   ge·mot . . . *n* . . . : a judicial or legislative assembly in England before the Norman conquest
   man·telet . . . *n* . . . : a movable shelter formerly used by besiegers as a protection when attacking

8.1.2 The temporal label *archaic* means standard after 1755 but surviving in the present only sporadically or in special contexts:

   be·like . . . *adv, archaic*
   end·long . . . *adv* . . . *archaic*
   eld . . . *n* . . . 1 *archaic*

archaic is a comment on the word being defined, not on the thing the word represents.

8.2.1 The stylistic label *slang* is used with terms especially appropriate in contexts of extreme informality, having usually a currency not limited to a particular region or area of interest, and composed typically of clipped or shortened forms of extravagant, forced, or facetious figures of speech:

   cork·er . . . *n* . . . *slang*
   lu·lu . . . *n* . . . *slang*
   egg *n* . . . 3 *slang*

There is no completely satisfactory objective test for slang, especially in application to a word out of context. No word is invariably slang, and many standard words can be given slang connotations or used so inappropriately as to become slang.

8.2.2 The stylistic label *substand* for "substandard" indicates status conforming to a pattern of usage that exists throughout the American language community but differs in choice of word or form from that of the prestige group in that community:

   drown . . . *vb* . . . *substand* **drownd·ed**

This label is not regional.

8.2.3 The stylistic label *nonstand* for "nonstandard" is used for a very small number of words that can hardly stand without some status label but are too widely current in reputable context to be labeled *substand:*

   ir·re·gard·less . . . *adj* . . . *nonstand*

8.3.1 The regional label *dial* for "dialect" indicates, when unqualified, a regional pattern too complex for summary labeling, usually because it includes several regional varieties of American English or of American and British English:

   larrup *n, dial*

8.3.2 The combined label *dial Brit* and the combined label *dial Eng* indicate substandard currency in a provincial dialect of the British Commonwealth and in England respectively:

   thir . . . *pron* . . . *dial Brit*
   end *vt* . . . *dial Eng*

8.3.3 A standard word requiring a specified regional restriction in the U.S. will have one of the seven labels *North, NewEng, Midland, South, West, Southwest,* and *Northwest.* These correspond loosely to the areas in Hans Kurath's *Word Geography of the Eastern United States* (1949). Examples:

   bon·ny·clab·ber . . . *n* . . . *North & Midland*
   can·ni·kin . . . *n* . . . *NewEng*
   jay·bird . . . *n, chiefly Midland*
   light·wood . . . *n, chiefly South*
   Cay·use . . . *n* . . . *West*
   ace·quia . . . *n* . . . *Southwest*
   pot·latch . . . *n* . . . *Northwest*

No collective label (as *U.S.*) is used to indicate currency in all regions of the U.S.

8.3.4 A regional label that names a country indicates standard currency in that part of the whole English language area. Examples:

   syne . . . *adv* . . . *chiefly Scot*
   sun·down·er . . . *n, Austral*
   ma·vour·neen . . . *n* . . . *Irish*
   Ca·nuck . . . *n* . . . *chiefly Canad*
   pet·rol . . . *n* . . . *Brit*
   draught *chiefly Brit*

9. SUBJECT LABELS

9.1 A prefixed word or phrase in italics indicates an activity or association in which a word usually has a special meaning not identical with any other meaning it may have apart from the labeled subject:

   dhar·ma . . . *n* . . . 1 *Hinduism* :
   dress . . . *vi* . . . 2 *of a food animal* :
   dressmaker *adj, of women's clothes* :
   ex·og·e·nous . . . *adj* . . . **b** *of disease* :

10. THE SYMBOLIC COLON

10.1 This dictionary uses a boldface character recognizably distinct from the usual roman colon as a linking symbol between the main entry and a definition. It stands for an unexpressed simple predicate that may be read "is being here defined as (or by)". It indicates that the supporting orientation immediately after the main entry is over and thus facilitates a visual jumping from entry word to definition:

   de·bil·i·tate . . . : to impair the strength of
   debt . . . 3 : something owed

10.2 Words that have two or more definitions have two or more symbolic colons. The signal for another definition is another symbolic colon:

   dead . . . *adj* . . . 1 : deprived of life : having died

10.3 If there is no symbolic colon, there is no definition. For what sometimes takes the place of a definition see 14.2, 15.3.

11. SENSE DIVISION

11.1 Boldface arabic numerals separate the senses of a word that has more than a single sense:

> **x** . . . **1** : . . . **2** : . . . **3** :
> **de·camp** . . . *vi* . . . **1** : to break up a camp   **2** : to depart suddenly

11.2 Boldface lowercase letters separate coordinate subsenses of a numbered sense or sometimes of an unnumbered sense:

> **x** . . . **1** : . . . **2 a** : . . . **b** : . . . **c** : . . . **3** :
> **de·cen·cy** . . . *n* . . . **2 a** : the quality or state of being decent . . . **b** : conformity to standards of taste, propriety, or quality
> **x** . . . **1** : . . . **2** : . . . : as **a** : . . . **b** : . . . **c** :
> **hump** . . . *n* . . . **1** : a rounded protuberance: as **a** : HUMPBACK **b** : a fleshy protuberance on the back of an animal . . . **2** : . . .
> **x** . . . : . . . : as **a** : . . . **b** : . . . **c** :
> **wheal** . . . *n* . . . : a suddenly formed elevation of the skin surface: as **a** : WELT **b** : a flat burning or itching eminence . . .
> **x** . . . **1** : . . . **2** : . . . : **a** : . . . **b** : . . . **c** :
> **in·an·i·mate** . . . *adj* . . . **1** : not animate: **a** : not endowed with life or spirit **b** : lacking consciousness or power of motion **2** : . . .

11.2.1 The lightface colon indicates that the definition immediately preceding it binds together or subsumes the coordinate subsenses that follow it:

> **de·ceit·ful** . . . *adj* : having a tendency or disposition to deceive: **a** : not honest . . . **b** : DECEPTIVE, MISLEADING

11.2.2 The word *as* may or may not follow this lightface colon. Its presence indicates that the subsenses following are typical or significant examples which are not exhaustive. Its absence indicates that the subsenses following are exhaustive with respect to evidence for dictionary inclusion.

11.3 Lightface numbers in parentheses indicate a further division of subsenses:

> **x** . . . **1 a** : . . . **b** (1) : . . . (2) : . . . **c** : . . . **2** :
> **drag** . . . *n* . . . **3 a** : something (as a sea anchor) that retards motion **b** (1) : the retarding force acting on a body . . . moving through a fluid . . . parallel and opposite to the direction of motion (2) : friction between engine parts

11.4.1 The system of separating by numbers and letters reflects something of the semantic relationship between various senses of a word. It is only a lexical convenience. It does not evaluate senses or establish an enduring hierarchy of importance among them. The best sense is the one that most aptly fits the context of an actual genuine utterance.

11.4.2 Occasionally a particular semantic relationship between senses is suggested by use of one of four italic sense dividers: *esp* (for *especially*), *specif* (for *specifically*), *also*, or *broadly*.

11.5 The order of senses is historical: the one known to have been first used in English is entered first. This ordering does not imply that each sense has developed from the immediately preceding sense. Sense 1 may give rise to sense 2 and sense 2 to sense 3. As often as not, however, each of several senses derived in independent lines from sense 1 has served as the source of a number of other meanings. Sometimes an arbitrary arrangement or rearrangement is the only reasonable and expedient solution to the problems of ordering senses.

11.6.1 An italic functional label or other information given between a main entry and the etymology of a multisense word applies to all senses and subsenses unless a limiting label (as *pl*) is inserted immediately after a divisional number or letter and before the symbolic colon or unless the label is in any way clearly inapplicable. Examples of limiting labels:

> **li·on** . . . *n, pl* **lions** . . . **1 a** *or pl* **lion** :
> **ep·i·cu·re·an** . . . *adj* **1** *cap* : of or relating to Epicurus or Epicureanism **2** : of, relating to, or suited to an epicure

11.6.2 The etymology also applies to all senses and subsenses unless another etymology in boldface brackets is given after a sense number or letter:

> **deuce** . . . *n* [MF *deus* two . . .] . . . **3** [obs. E *deuce* bad luck]

11.6.3 An italic status label, subject label, or guide phrase does not apply to all the senses of a multisense word. When divisional numbers are present, such a label is inserted after the number:

> **x** *n* **1** *slang* : . . . **2** *slang* :
> **hor·rent** . . . *adj* . . . **1** *archaic* : . . . **2** *archaic* : . .

It then applies to lettered and parenthetically numbered subsenses that follow. It does not apply to succeeding boldface-numbered senses:

> **x** . . . *vt* . . . **2** *obs* **a** : . . . **b** : . . . **3** :
> **im·pugn** . . . *vt* . . . **1** *obs* **a** : ASSAIL **b** : RESIST **2** : . . .

Senses 1a and 1b are both obsolete but not sense 2. If the label falls between a boldface letter and the symbolic colon or between a lightface number in parentheses and the symbolic colon, it applies only to the immediately following sense.

12. VERBAL ILLUSTRATIONS

12.1 The matter enclosed in a pair of angle brackets illustrates an appropriate use of the word in context. The word being illustrated is replaced by a swung dash, which stands for the same form of the word as the main entry, or by a swung dash plus an italicized suffix, which can be added without any change of letters to the form of the main entry. Otherwise the word is written in full and italicized:

> **er·satz** . . . *adj* . . . ⟨~ flour⟩
> **Lu·cul·lan** . . . *adj* . . . **2** : . . . ⟨a ~ feast⟩
> **high-water** *adj* : unusually short ⟨~ pants⟩
> **join** . . . *vt* . . . **4 a** : . . . ⟨~ed us for lunch⟩

12.2.1 A person's name or an italicized title included in the angle brackets acknowledges the authorship or source of a quoted verbal illustration:

> **like** *conj* **1** : in the same way that : AS ⟨they raven down scenery ~ children do sweetmeats —John Keats⟩

12.2.2 Suspension periods . . . indicate an omission in quoted matter. Sometimes spelling, punctuation, or capitalization has been normalized without notation, usually because the brief quotation is so far removed from its original context that such matters are no longer significant and may be actually misleading.

13. NAMES OF PLANTS AND ANIMALS

13.1 A main entry that defines the name of a kind of plant or animal (as rose or lion) is a taxonomic entry. Such entries employ in part a formal codified vocabulary of New Latin names (taxa) that has been developed and used by biologists in accord with international codes of botanical and of zoological nomenclature for the purpose of identifying and indicating the relationships of plants and animals. Names of taxa higher than the genus (as class, order, family) are capitalized plural nouns often used with singular verbs. They are not abbreviated in normal use. The genus is the fundamental taxon. It names a group of closely related kinds of plants (as *Malus*, which includes wild and cultivated apples, crab apples, pears) or animals (as *Felis*, which includes domestic and wild cats, lions, tigers, cougars). It is a capitalized singular noun. Each kind of organism has one and only one correct name under these codes. The name for a species (binomial or species name) consists of a singular capitalized genus name combined with an uncapitalized specific epithet which is an appositive noun, genitive noun, or adjective agreeing in case, number, and gender with the genus name (as in *Rosa setigera*). For a variety or subspecies (a trinomial, variety name, or subspecies name) the name adds a similar varietal or subspecific epithet (as in *Rosa setigera tomentosa*). Taxa in this dictionary are enclosed in parentheses and ordinarily immediately follow the primary orienting noun. Genus names and higher taxa are routinely oriented in rank, while genus names as well as binomials and trinomials are italicized:

> **ba·sid·io·my·cete** . . . *n* . . . : any of a large class (Basidiomycetes) . . .
> **perch** *n* . . . **2** : any of numerous teleost fishes (as of the families Percidae, Centrarchidae, Serranidae) . . .
> **hem·lock** . . . *n* . . . **2** : any of a genus (*Tsuga*) of evergreen coniferous trees . . .
> **rob·in** . . . *n* . . . **1 a** : a small European thrush (*Erithacus rubecola*) . . .

Taxa are used in this dictionary to provide precise technical identifications through which defined terms may be pursued in technical writing. Because of the specialized nature of taxa, they do not have separate entry.

13.2 Taxonomic entries are in general oriented indirectly to higher taxa by other vernaculars (as by *thrush* at *robin* or *alga* at *seaweed*) or by technical adjectives (as by *teleost* at *perch*, *leguminous* at *pea*, or *composite* at *daisy*). Among the higher plants, except the composites and legumes and a few obscure tropical groups, such orientation is by a vernacular family name which is linked at the corresponding taxonomic entry to its technical equivalent:

> **oak** . . . *n* . . . **1** : a tree or shrub (genera *Quercus* or *Lithocarpus*) of the beech family . . .
> **beech** . . . *n* . . . any of a genus (*Fagus* of the family Fagaceae, the beech family) of hardwood trees . . .
> **pars·ley** . . . *n* . . . a southern European annual or biennial herb (*Petroselinum crispum*) of the carrot family . . .
> **car·rot** . . . *n* . . . **1** : a biennial herb (*Daucus carota* of the family Umbelliferae, the carrot family) . . .

13.3 A genus name may be abbreviated to its initial letter whenever it is used more than once in senses not separated by a boldface number:

> **nas·tur·tium** . . . *n* . . . : any of a genus (*Tropaeolum* . . .); *esp* : either of two widely cultivated ornamentals (*T. majus* and *T. minus*)

14. USAGE NOTES

14.1 A usage note is introduced by a lightface dash. Two or more successive usage notes are separated by a semicolon. A usage note provides information about the use of the word being defined and so always modifies the word that is the main entry. It may be in the form of a comment on idiom, syntax, semantic relationship, status, or various other matters:

> **dredge** *vt* . . . — often used with *up*
> **al·le·gro** . . . *adv (or adj)* . . . : . . . — used as a direction in music
> **dreg** . . . *n* . . . **1** . . . — usu. used in pl.

14.2 A usage note may stand in place of a definition and without the symbolic colon. Some function words have little or no semantic content. Most interjections express feelings but otherwise are untranslatable into a meaning that can be substituted. Many other words (as some oaths and imprecations, calls to animals, specialized signals, song refrains, and honorific titles), though genuinely a part of the language, have a usage note instead of a definition:

> **gee** *interj* . . . — used as an introductory expletive or to express surprise or enthusiasm
> **at** . . . *prep* . . . **1** — used as a function word to indicate presence or occurrence in, on, or near
> **ahoy** . . . *interj* . . . — used in hailing ⟨ship ∼⟩

15. CROSS-REFERENCES

15.0 Various word relationships requiring that matter at one place in a dictionary show special awareness of matter at another place are taken care of by a system of cross-references. A sequence of lightface small capitals used anywhere in a definition is identical letter-by-letter with a boldface main entry (or with one of its inflectional forms) at its own alphabetical place. This sequence is a cross-reference; its boldface equivalent elsewhere is what is cross-referred to and is not itself a cross-reference.

15.1 A cross-reference following a lightface dash and beginning with either *see* or *compare* is a directional cross-reference. It explicitly directs one to look somewhere else for further information. It never stands for a definition but (with a few exceptions, as at variant combining forms and numerals) is always appended to one:

> **im·ide** . . . *n* . . . — compare AMIDE
> **eight** . . . *n* . . . **1** — see NUMBER table

15.2 A cross-reference following a symbolic colon is a synonymous cross-reference. It may stand alone as the only definitional matter for a boldface entry or for a sense or subsense of an entry. It may be one of a group of definitions joined in series by symbolic colons. In either case the cross-reference means that the definitions at the entry cross-referred to can be substituted as

definitions for the boldface entry or the sense or subsense at which the cross-reference appears:

> **horse·less carriage** . . . *n* : AUTOMOBILE
> **dec·la·ra·tion** . . . *n* **1** : the act of declaring : ANNOUNCEMENT
> **deck** *vt* . . . **2 a** : to clothe elegantly : ARRAY **b** : DECORATE

15.2.1 Two or more synonymous cross-references are sometimes introduced by a symbolic colon and separated from each other by a comma. This indicates that there are two or more sets of definitions at other entries which can be substituted in various contexts:

> **lay out** *vt* . . . **4** : ARRANGE, DESIGN

15.2.2 A synonymous cross-reference sometimes accounts for a usage note introduced by *called also* at the entry cross-referred to:

> **vir·gule** . . . *n* . . . DIAGONAL 3
> **diagonal** *n* . . . **3** : . . . — called also . . . *virgule*

15.3.1 A cross-reference following an italic *var of* is a cognate cross-reference. It is explained and illustrated in 1.7.3 as applied to standard variants.

15.3.2 A limiting label before the *var of* in a cognate cross-reference indicates in what way an entry word is nonstandard.

> **gie** . . . *chiefly Scot var of* GIVE
> **hern** . . . *dial var of* HERON

15.4 A cross-reference following an italic label identifying an entry as an inflectional form of a singular noun, of an adjective or adverb, or of an infinitive verb is an inflectional cross-reference. These are illustrated in 4.4 and 4.9.

15.5 A cross-reference may or may not be identified by a superscript number before it or by a lightface sense number or letter after it. A synonymous cross-reference to a homograph is not identified by part of speech: nouns refer to nouns, adjectives to adjectives. Cross-references to verbs sometimes distinguish between *vt* and *vi*.

16. RUN-ON ENTRIES

16.1.1 A main entry may be followed, after a lightface dash, by a boldface derivative or compound or by a homograph with a different functional label. This continuation is a run-on entry. Its boldface is always in alphabetical order with respect to the word it is run on to. It has a functional label but no definition:

> **elas·tic** . . . *adj* . . . — **elas·ti·cal·ly** . . . *adv*
> **El·e·at·ic** . . . *adj* . . . — **Eleatic** *n*

16.1.2 An additional run-on entry sometimes follows:

> **er·ro·ne·ous** . . . *adj* . . . — **er·ro·ne·ous·ly** *adv* — **er·ro·ne·ous·ness** *n*

16.2 A main entry may be followed, after a lightface dash, by a boldface phrase containing the main entry word or an inflected form of it. This continuation also is a run-on entry. It often is not in alphabetical order. It may or may not have a functional label but it does have a definition:

> **event** . . . *n* . . . — **in any event** :

16.3 A run-on entry is an independent entry with respect to function and status. Labels at the main entry do not apply unless they are repeated.

17. SYNONYMIES

17.1 Synonymous words are briefly discriminated in a paragraph following the entry of one of the words of a group. This paragraph is a synonymy and is signaled by the boldface abbreviation **syn** indented.

17.2 Words considered in a synonymy refer at their own alphabetical places to its location by running on the boldface letters **syn** and the word:

> **decline** *n* . . . **syn** see DETERIORATION

18. COMBINING FORMS

18.1 A main entry that begins or ends with a hyphen is a word element that forms part of an English compound. The identifying label, besides the hyphen, is *comb form* for "combining form", or, if the element is used only as an affix, the label is *prefix* or *suffix*. A suffix or terminal combining form that always determines syntactic function is further identified by addition of a part-of-speech label (as *adj suffix* or *n comb form*):

> **eo-** *comb form*
> **de-** *prefix*
> **-derm** . . . *n comb form*

18.2 This dictionary enters combining forms for two reasons: (1) to make easier the writing of etymologies of words in which they occur over and over again; and (2) to recognize meaningful elements used in new words that are not yet widely enough found for dictionary inclusion. A compound consisting of a known word and a known combining form is not censurable merely by being absent from the dictionary.

19. THE VOCABULARY ENTRY

19.1 The following definition appears at its own alphabetical place in the dictionary:

> **vocabulary entry** *n* **:** a word (as the noun *book*), hyphened or open compound (as the verb *book-match* or the noun *book review*), word element (as the affix *pro-*), abbreviation (as *agt*), verbalized symbol (as *Na*), or term (as *man in the street*) entered alphabetically in a dictionary for the purpose of definition or identification or expressly included as an inflectional form (as the noun *mice* or the verb *saw*) or as a derived form (as the noun *godlessness* or the adverb *globally*) or related phrase (as *one for the book*) run on at its base word and usu. set in a type (as boldface) readily distinguishable from that of the lightface running text which defines, explains, or identifies the entry

As defined, this term applies to all the entries as they are printed alphabetically (with or without hyphens), all their boldface and italic variants (preceded by *called also*), all the run-on entries, and all inflectional forms written out in boldface.

20. PROPER NAMES

20.1 Names of human beings are not entered as such in the main vocabulary. They are dictionary entries but are not classed as vocabulary entries. They are entered in a separate section of back matter titled "Biographical Names". It contains surname and prenames, pronunciation and syllabic division, dates, epithets, nationality, and occupation.

20.2 Names of places and geographic formations (as rivers and mountains) are not entered as such in the main vocabulary. They are dictionary entries but are not classed as vocabulary entries. They are entered in a separate section of back matter titled "A Pronouncing Gazetteer". It contains name, pronunciation and syllabic division, location by geographic or national relationship, and quantitative data (as population, area, length, or height). Many entries run on derivative adjectives and nouns (as *Cuban*) not given in the main vocabulary.

20.3 Names of institutions of higher education are not entered as such in the main vocabulary. They are dictionary entries but are not classed as vocabulary entries. They are entered in a separate section in the back matter under the title "Colleges and Universities in the United States and Canada". It contains name, pronunciation and syllabic division, location, kind of student body, and earliest date.

20.4 Given names of persons are not entered as such in the main vocabulary. They are dictionary entries but are not classed as vocabulary entries. They are entered in two lists in the back matter under the title "A Pronouncing Vocabulary of Common English Given Names". It contains pronunciation and syllabic division, provenience, and meaning if known.

21. ABBREVIATIONS

21.1 Abbreviations are not included as main entries in the vocabulary but they are classed as vocabulary entries. They are separately alphabetized in a section of back matter titled "Abbreviations". For abbreviations used in the dictionary chiefly as space savers see the separate list "Abbreviations Used in This Work" preceding the first page of the vocabulary.

21.2 Symbols for chemical elements are included alphabetically among the abbreviations in the back matter.

MERRIAM-WEBSTER PRONUNCIATION SYMBOLS

See "Guide to Pronunciation", "Explanatory Notes", 2

ə .... banana, collect, abut

'ə, ˌə humdrum, abut

ᵊ .... immediately preceding \l\, \n\, \m\, \ŋ\, as in battle, mitten, eaten, and sometimes cap and bells \-ᵊm-\, lock and key \-ᵊŋ-\; immediately following \l\, \m\, \r\, as often in French table, prisme, titre

ər .... operation, further, urger

'ər-⎫
    ⎬ as in two different pronunciations
'ə-r⎭ of hurry \'hər-ē, 'hə-rē\

a .... mat, map, mad, gag, snap, patch

ā .... day, fade, date, aorta, drape, cape

ä .... bother, cot, and, with most American speakers, father, cart

à .... father as pronounced by speakers who do not rhyme it with bother

au̇ ... now, loud, out

b .... baby, rib

ch ... chin, nature \'nā-chər\ (actually, this sound is \t\ + \sh\)

d .... did, adder

e .... bet, bed, peck

'ē, ˌē beat, nosebleed, evenly, easy

ē .... easy, mealy

f .... fifty, cuff

g .... go, big, gift

h .... hat, ahead

hw .. whale as pronounced by those who do not have the same pronunciation for both whale and wail

i .... tip, banish, active

ī .... site, side, buy, tripe (actually, this sound is \ä\ + \i\, or \à\ + \i\)

j .... job, gem, edge, join, judge (actually, this sound is \d\ + \zh\)

k .... kin, cook, ache

k̲ .... German ich, Buch

l .... lily, pool

m .... murmur, dim, nymph

n .... no, own

nˌ .... indicates that a preceding vowel or diphthong is pronounced with the nasal passages open, as in French un bon vin blanc \œⁿ-bōⁿ-vaⁿ-bläⁿ\

ŋ ... sing \'siŋ\, singer \'siŋ-ər\, finger \'fiŋ-gər\, ink \'iŋk\, thing \'thiŋ\

ō .... bone, know, beau

ȯ .... saw, all, gnaw

œ .... French bœuf, German Hölle

ō̵e ... French feu, German Höhle

ȯi .... coin, destroy, sawing

p .... pepper, lip

r .... rarity

s .... source, less

sh ... with nothing between, as in shy, mission, machine, special (actually, this is a single sound, not two); with a hyphen between, two sounds as in death's-head \'deths-ˌhed\

t .... tie, attack

th ... with nothing between, as in thin, ether (actually, this is a single sound, not two); with a hyphen between, two sounds as in knighthood \'nīt-ˌhu̇d\

t̲h̲ ... then, either, this (actually, this is a single sound, not two)

ü ... rule, youth, union \'yün-yən\, few \'fyü\

u̇ .... pull, wood, book

ue ... German füllen, hübsch

u̅e ... French rue, German fühlen

v .... vivid, give

w .... we, away; in some words having final \(ˌ)ō\ a variant \ə-w\ occurs before vowels, as in \'fäl-ə-wiŋ\, covered by the variant \ə(-w)\ at the entry word

y .... yard, young, cue \'kyü\, union \'yün-yən\

ʸ .... indicates that during the articulation of the sound represented by the preceding character the front of the tongue has substantially the position it has for the articulation of the first sound of yard, as in French digne \dēnʸ\

yü ... youth, union, cue, few, mute

yu̇ ... curable, fury

z .... zone, raise

zh ... with nothing between, as in vision, azure \'azh-ər\ (actually, this is a single sound, not two); with a hyphen between, two sounds as in gazehound \'gāz-ˌhau̇nd\

For syllable-final \i\, \u̇\, see \i\, \u̇\ in "Guide"

\ .... slant line used in pairs to mark the beginning and end of a transcription: \'pen\

' ..... mark preceding a syllable with primary (strongest) stress: \'pen-mən-ˌship\

ˌ ..... mark preceding a syllable with secondary (next-strongest) stress: \'pen-mən-ˌship\

- ..... mark of syllable division

( ) ... indicate that what is symbolized between is present in some utterances but not in others: \'fak-t(ə-)rē\ at factory =\'fak-tə-rē, 'fak-trē\

A GUIDE TO PRONUNCIATION

\ə\ when a stress mark (' or ‚) stands at the beginning of the syllable in which it occurs, this symbol, called *schwa*, is pronounced as in *bud* or *nut* or the last syllable of *aqueduct;* when the syllable in which it stands is without stress mark, it is pronounced as in the first syllable of *alone* or *occur* or as in the second syllable of *colony* or as in the last syllable of *abbot* or *famous* or *sabbath* or *circus*.

Formerly nearly all phonetic alphabets used for the vowel of *bud* a symbol different from that for the vowel of the second syllable of *abbot*, and some alphabets still do. Some who are familiar only with these alphabets find the use of \ə\ in stressed syllables objectionable when they encounter it for the first time. But use of \ə\ as a symbol for both unstressed and stressed vowel is rapidly increasing, and abandonment of a separate symbol for the vowel of *bud* parallels abandonment of former symbols for half-long a, e, and o in whose stead ā, ē, and ō without stress mark are entirely adequate. With \ə-'bət\ for *abut* compare \'ē-zē\ for *easy*, where the same vowel symbol is used in both a stressed and unstressed syllable.

The sound \ə\ often intrudes between a vowel and a following \l\ or \r\ in words whose orthography has no letter answering to \ə\, as in *eel, aisle, mere, flour*. On the other hand, words often pronounced with \ə\ between a vowel and \l\ or \r\ and written with a letter answering to \ə\ may often or sometimes be pronounced without \ə\, as *denial, betrayal, theory, flower, aeronaut, puerile, diary*.

Many transcribers who record an epenthetic \ə\ before \r\ completely or largely ignore the same epenthesis before \l\ and yet \ə\ is often as distinctly heard in *frailty* as in *realty, cruelty, loyalty*. In spite of the fact that a context favorable to the presence or the absence of \ə\ in *flower* is usually equally favorable to the presence or the absence of \ə\ in *flour*, writers of metered verse usually treat a vowel + \l\ or \r\ of words like *denial* and *flower* as freely either disyllabic or monosyllabic but infrequently treat the vowel + \l\ or \r\ of words like *aisle* and *flour* as disyllabic. Therefore the transcriptions in this book parenthesize \ə\ in both *flower* and *flour* but show a hyphen before the \ə\ of *flower* and no hyphen before the \ə\ of *flour*, thus:

flow·er \'flaὺ(-ə)r\
flour \flaὺ(ə)r\

A variant pronunciation without hyphen before the \ə\ (e.g., \'flaὺ(ə)r\ at *flower*, \di-'nī(ə)l\) is to be understood for all words in whose transcription \(-ə)\ occurs, except in the sequence \ər(-ə)l\ as at *pearl*. Words transcribed with \(-ə)\ before a word-final \l\ or \r\ are more apt to retain the \ə\ before a vowel-initial word following without pause than words transcribed only with \(ə)\ in such position.

For such words as *weary, eerie*, which do not contain any of the orthographic sequences *ir, irr, yr, yrr*, most dictionaries of English show the first vowel as something other than the vowel of *bid* or the first vowel of *mirror, pyrrhic*. American dictionaries have often used for the first syllable of *weary, eerie* the same vowel symbol as for the first syllable of *beady;* \'wē-ri\ or \'wē-rē\, \'ē-ri\ or \'ē-rē\ are indeed often heard from speakers in the deep South. British dictionaries usually show the penult of these words as containing the vowel of the penult of *mirror* and *pyrrhic* but as having, unlike *mirror* and *pyrrhic*, \ə\ between the \i\ and the \r\: \'wiəri\, \'iəri\. Some observers of American speech believe that many American speakers, especially in the region east of the Alleghenies, consistently have, like southern British speakers, \iə\ in the penult of *weary* but only \i\ in the penult of *mirror*. *Webster's Third New International Dictionary* usually shows no more than what may be regarded as the two extremes of variation of words like *weary*, \'wir-\ and \'wēr-\, leaving the third variant, \'wiər-\, to be inferred. In this *Collegiate* the pronunciation for *weary* is the less

space-consuming formula \'wi(ə)r-ē\ (= \'wir-ē, 'wiər-ē\), leaving the variant \'wē-rē\ to be inferred. We do not, however, transcribe \i(ə)\ in all environments in which some transcribers do. For example, \ə\ following the \r\ often seems less conducive than \ē\ or \i\ following the \r\ to \iə\ before the \r\ in American speech. We accordingly show only \i\ in *serum, appearance*, although both apparently usually have \iə\ in southern British speech and the first at least often has \ē\ in the deep South.

Certain disyllables, typically with only one intervocalic r and with a or ai preceding and y or ie following, as *vary, fairy*, are usually shown as having \aə\, \eə\, or \ā\ in their penult and as differing from *very* (with penultimate \e\) and *carry* (with penultimate \a\). The treatment of *vary* and *fairy* in *Webster's Third New International Dictionary* and in this book parallels that of words like *weary* and *eerie*. We are less confident than some observers, however, as to the extent and consistency of the distinction that penultimate \ə\ maintains between words like *weary* and *vary* on the one hand and *mirror, very*, and *carry* on the other. Sentence-final *eerie, vary* in "How utterly eerie!", "They never vary" are more apt to be spoken with an \ə\-final penultimate diphthong in all varieties of American speech than weaker-stressed *very, Larry* of "not very good", "Larry Johnson". But we hear \ə\ in words like *very* and *Larry* also when they are more prominent, as when *Very!* is the whole of a sentence or *Larry* is used vocatively.

No dialect of English appears to contain a class of disyllables that contrasts with disyllables like *fury* in that the penult of the one class has \(y)ύə\ or \(y)ü\ whereas the penult of the other has \ύ\. Words like *fury* have traditionally been transcribed with \ü\ or \ύə\ in the penult. Treatment in this book parallels that for *weary* and *vary*.

For words of the type *glory* the usual transcription in American dictionaries is with \ō\ or \ό\, or both, in the penult. We show both \ō\ and \ό\, and have a degree of misgiving that \(ə)\ might have been justifiable after the first. At least beyond much doubt \'glόr-ē\ is a better transcription than the often shown \'glō-rē\ for most speakers who have \ō\ in the penult, although \'glō-ri\, with more of a diphthongizing \ύ\ ending to the \ō\ and with a more consonantal \r\, is often used in the deep South.

In words of the type *serious, various, furious*, and *glorious*, with antepenultimate rather than penultimate stress, a diphthongizing \ə\, although apparently usual in southern British speech, is rare in most varieties of U.S. speech and is not shown in this book. Thus pairs like *serious* and *Sirius* are rarely distinguished in this country except in the deep South, where *Sirius* has first-syllable \i\ and *serious* may have first syllable \ē\, and the other three-syllable words mentioned have the same vowel as the related two-syllable words.

In three of the four classes of antepenultimate-stress words of which the foregoing statements are made — the classes to which belong *serious, various*, and *glorious*—two successive vowel sounds follow the \r\. Words in which a single vowel sound follows usually do not exhibit the same pronunciation pattern. Compare *imperial* but *imperative, posterior* but *posterity* (*experiment*, however, may have \-'pir-\, especially in less cultivated speech, on the analogy of *experience*), *hilarious* but *hilarity* (the latter never or rarely has \-'lār-\), *victorious* but *priority* (the latter never or rarely has \-'ōr-\). The u of *security*, however, is of the same quality as the u of *curious*.

\ə\ (preceding \l\, \n\, \m\, \ŋ\; for ᵊ following \l\, \m\, \r\, see below \lᵊ\, \mᵊ\, \rᵊ\) printed as a superior character means that a consonant following it is a syllabic consonant, that is, a consonant that immediately follows another consonant without any vowel between, as in the second syllable of *battle* \'bat-ᵊl\, *eaten* \'ēt-ᵊn\, and in one pronunciation of

and as in *cap and bells* \ˌkap-ᵊm-'belz\ and in *lock and key* \ˌläk-ᵊŋ-'kē\.

When the consonant next preceding the \l\ or \n\ of an unstressed syllable is other than \t\, \d\, \s\, \z\, or (before \l\) \n\, there is room for doubt whether the nucleus of the unstressed syllable is syllabic \l\ or \n\ or is \ə\ between the two consonants.

\ᵊ\ immediately following \l\, \m\, \r\ (used only in words borrowed from French) indicates that these sounds are like the *-le*, *-me*, and *-re* respectively of French *table*, *prisme*, *titre*, all of which are one-syllable words when so pronounced. In certain contexts in French and, with speakers who know something of the phonetics of French, in similar contexts in English, words such as these for which the vocabulary may show only \lᵊ\, \mᵊ\, \rᵊ\ have other variants. Illustrative examples, with fully French transcriptions:

table \'tàblᵊ—one syllable; before a pause\
table \'tàb—one syllable; also before a pause; most frequent in rapid or informal speech\
la table est belle \là-tà-ble—bel—four syllables; before a vowel following without pause\
table de bois \tà-blə-də-bwä—four syllables; before a consonant following without pause\
table de bois \tàb-də-bwä—three syllables; also before a consonant following without pause; most frequent in rapid or informal speech and in set phrases\

\'ər-ər\ words like *demurrer* are so transcribed but in rapid speech the last syllable is much weakened or lost.

\a\ as in *mat*, *map*, *mad*, *gag*, *snap*, *patch*. For the vowel part of the words *map*, *mad*, *gag* most dictionaries use the same symbol, although two appreciably different vocalic sounds or sequences are heard from some speakers and three from others. For many speakers and for most items with other speakers the differences are susceptible to the explanation that one word has the sort of \a\ that occurs before \p\, the second the kind of \a\ that occurs before \d\, and the third the kind of \a\ that occurs before \g\. But for some speakers whose two *can*'s of "Let's can what we can" are vocally different such an explanation does not suffice. The number of such otherwise identical pairs consistently occurring in the speech of any one speaker is small enough, however, so that we follow the traditional practice of showing \a\ in *mad* and *gag* as well as in *map*. Words of the type of *vary*, *Carey*, *carious*, discussed in section on \ə\, are reported by observers of the speech of an area having New York City at its northern perimeter and Washington, D.C., at its southern, to have with a high percentage of speakers a stressed vowel like that of *mad*, *maddest* as spoken in the same area and to differ therein from words like *carry*, whose stressed vowel is like that of *map* as spoken in the same area. The discussion at the section on \ə\ provides clues to the identification of such words.

In words in which this dictionary shows only \ar\ some American speakers have \er\ instead, pronouncing both *marry* and *merry* \'mer-ē\.

\ä\, \ȧ\ the symbol \ä\ represents the vowel of *cot* and *cod* in the speech of those who pronounce these words differently from *caught* and *cawed*. The \ä\ of some such speakers may vary appreciably from the \ä\ of other such speakers, the \ä\ of most Americans, for example, being articulated with the lips not or little rounded and being fairly long in duration before certain consonants. The \ä\ of many southern British speakers, on the other hand, is articulated with appreciable lip rounding and is short in duration in all contexts. \ä\ is to be understood, however, as covering all pronunciations of *cot*, *cod* that are different from *caught*, *cawed*.

The symbol \ȧ\ represents the *a* of *cart*, *card*, *father* in the speech of those who have for the *a* a sound different from the sound used for the *o* of *cot*, *cod*, *bother*. Because speakers of American English who have a sound requiring \ȧ\ for its representation are a decided minority, \ȧ\ is sparingly used in vocabulary transcriptions of English words (see last paragraph of this section). In transcriptions of foreign words, as French, \ȧ\ indicates a vowel with an articulation between that of the vowel of English *stack* and that of the most frequent American pronunciation of *stock*. In British and British-dialect pronunciations, as at Scottish *daw*, \ȧ\ indicates a vowel of fairly long duration.

The four words *stalk*, *stork*, *stock*, *stark* conveniently illustrate (with respect to the sound immediately follow-ing the \t\) the variation in the pronunciation of these and rhyming words in the English-speaking world as a whole. With probably most American speakers *stalk* and *stork* have after the \t\ the same vowel, for which our symbol is \ȯ\, and *stock* and *stark* both have after the \t\ the same vowel, different from \ȯ\, for which our symbol is \ä\:

\ȯ\ *stalk*, *stork*   \ä\ *stock*, *stark*

In the vocabulary, these and rhyming words are so transcribed only, and departures from this pattern have to be supplied from the paragraphs that follow.

In southern British speech the grouping for these words is

stalk, *stork*;   *stock*;   *stark*

This grouping has been the traditional one for a long period even in American dictionaries, and symbols of the type \ȯ\, \o\, and \ä\, respectively, have usually been employed. But we strongly feel the desirability of emphasizing the sameness in most American speech of the vowels of *stock* and *stark*, and have no doubt that an *a*-based symbol is much more acceptable in a transcription of *stock* than an *o*-based in a transcription of *stark*. Our vowel symbols for the southern British pronunciation of these words would be

\ȯ\ *stalk*, *stork*   \ä\ *stock*   \ȧ\ *stark*

With many speakers in eastern New England these words group in one of the two following ways:

\ȯ\ *stalk*, *stork*, *stock*   \ä\ *stark*
\ȯ\ *stalk*, *stork*   \ȯ\ or \ä\ *stock*   \ä\ *stark*

In both southern British and eastern New England speech \ȧ\ occurs in a small number of words not having *ar* in the spelling and not shown with an \ȧ\ variant in the vocabulary transcription. The commonest of these are listed below.

In areas of the United States as disparate as western Pennsylvania and the Far West the four words group

\ȯ\ *stork*   \ä\ or \ȯ\ *stalk*, *stock*   \ä\ *stark*

Another grouping, heard in the Southwest, is

\ȯ\ *stalk*, *stork*, *stark*   \ä\ *stock*

With many in the New Orleans area either the grouping is the same or *stark* belongs in a middle group, with articulation between that of *stalk*, *stork* and that of *stock*.

In dialects in which \ȧ\ is to be understood instead of the \ä\ of our transcriptions, \ȧ\ occurs in words of the type of *stark*, *hearken* (in which the sound or sound sequence used for *ar*, *ear* is followed by a consonant), in words of the type of *star* (in which the sound or sound sequence used for *ar* is followed by pause when the word is sentence-final), in derivatives of words like *star* (as *starry*, *starred*), and in words in which *a* of the spelling is followed by a consonant letter other than *r* and is not preceded by *w* or *wh* (thus \ȧ\ may be the value of the *a* in *father*, *calm*, *Chicago* but not of the *a* in *watch*, *what*, *swap*; \ȧ\ does occur, however, in *quaff*, *waft*). \ȧ\ occurs also, with more consistency probably in southern British than in eastern New England speech, in certain words in which \a\ is the usual American vowel and in most of which the vowel is immediately followed by \f\, \th\, \s\ (but not by \sh\), or by \n\ and a consonant. The following words and word constituents are among the most susceptible to the \ȧ\ pronunciation. It is to be understood for all of these items although in the vocabulary it is shown only for the dozen or so in which it occurs with especially high frequency.

advánce, advántage, aft, after, aghást, Alexánder, answer, ask, aunt, avalánche, bask, basket, bath, behalf, blanch, Blanche, blast, branch, brass, calf, can't, cask, casket, cast, caste, caster, castle, castor, chaff, chance, chancel, chancellor, chancery, chandler, chant, clasp, class, craft, daft, dance, disaster, disgráft, draft, draught, enchant, example, fast, fasten, flabbergást, Flanders, flask, France, Frances, Francis, gasp, ghastly, giraffe, glance, glass, graft, grant, -graph, grass, grasp, half, halve, lance, last, lath, laugh, -mand, mask, mast, master, nasty, pass, past, pastor, path, plant, plaster, prance, raft, rafter, ráscal, rasp, raspberry, repast, salve (n), sample, sampler, Sanders(on), shaft, shan't, slander, slant, staff, stanchion, supplant, task, trance, trans-, vántage, vast

\ā-ər\ is frequently the only variant shown or implied for words like *player* but when stress is sufficiently weak, as in *taxpayer*, the variant \e(-)ər\ or even \er\ occurs.

\au̇\ as the sound of *ow* in *now*, *ou* in *loud*, and *ou* in *out*. The first element ranges in value from \a\ through \ȧ\ to \ä\. In eastern Canada and along the Atlantic coast of the U.S. from Virginia to South Carolina a variety that may be symbolized \əu̇\ also occurs before voiceless consonants. \au̇\ is used in the vocabulary for all varieties.

\b\ as in *baby, knob.*

\ch\ based on English orthography, for the sound \t\ followed by the sound \sh\ in the same syllable, as in *chin, pitcher, fixture, exhaustion*. The sounds that come between the two vowels in the words *cha-cha* (dance) and *hotshot* can in both cases be regarded as \t\ followed by \sh\ but as being in the same syllable in the first (\'chä-,chä\) and distributed between the two syllables in the second (\'hät-,shät\).

For words of the type *mention, essential,* and *provincial,* transcriptions of the type \-n-shən\ and \-n-shəl\ have enjoyed a long tradition in dictionaries. At least in American speech and in most common words of this type \t\ almost always intrudes between the \n\ and \sh\, and we transcribe \-n-chən\ and \-n-chəl\.

Words like *picture, capture,* in which a second stop \k\ or \p\ precedes the stop \t\ of the sound complex transcribed \ch\, are usually transcribed with the equivalent of the symbols \-k-tshər\, \-p-tshər\. But these consonantal sequences are frequently simplified to \-k-shər\, \-p-shər\, which are to be understood as variants when not given. The \ksh\, \psh\ sequences are most frequent in the shorter of the two forms that present participles of *-cture* and *-pture* usually have, and the one-stop variants are usually shown for these in the vocabulary.

correctness in pronunciation
the term *correct pronunciation* is often used. Yet it is probable that many who use the term would find it difficult to give a precise and clear definition of the sense in which they use it. When the essential facts are considered, *correctness* of pronunciation must be a flexible term. It is perhaps as accurate a definition as can be made to say that a pronunciation is correct when it is in actual use by a sufficient number of cultivated speakers. This is obviously elastic, depending both on knowledge — never accurately ascertainable — of the number of users, and on judgment as to the cultivation of the speakers.

The standard of English pronunciation, so far as a standard may be said to exist, is the usage that now prevails among the educated and cultured people to whom the language is vernacular; but since somewhat different pronunciations are used by the cultivated in different regions too large to be ignored, we must admit the fact that uniformity of pronunciation is not to be found throughout the English-speaking world, though there is a very large percentage of practical uniformity.

The function of a pronouncing dictionary is to record as far as possible the pronunciations prevailing in the best present usage rather than to attempt to dictate what that usage should be. Insofar as a dictionary may be known and acknowledged as a faithful recorder and interpreter of such usage, so far and no farther may it be appealed to as an authority.

There is a constantly increasing body of technical terms which, being more often written than spoken, are often called "book words". For many of these no accepted usage can properly be said to exist, and their pronunciations must be determined on the analogies of words more often spoken, or according to the accepted rules of pronunciation for the languages from which they are derived.

\d\ as in *dried, deduce.*
\d\ is often lost between \n\ and \z\ as in *mends* and between \l\ and \z\ as *fields*. Such inflected forms are not transcribed or entered simply in order that such loss may be indicated.

diphthongs
diphthongal vowel sequences not shown in the key line or key page

are used in the transcription of some interjections and borrowings from foreign languages, as in \—, 'a(i)\ *eh,* \'leu̇\ *leu.*

dissimilation
often in some words in which one pronunciation variant contains two or more identical or similar sounds another variant lacks one of these sounds, by dissimilation. Thus there is often no first \r\ in *governor* and *surprise,* no second \r\ in *paraphernalia,* no first \n\ in *government,* and no second \l\ in *Wilhelmina.* This tendency for one of such sounds not to appear is so strong that the nonappearance is frequent with the very best of speakers.

The nonappearance of one \r\ in *governor,* etc., is frequent in the speech of those who regularly have \r\ in words like *barn, cure,* and hence is not to be explained in the same way as is the nonappearance of the corresponding \r\ in the speech of *r*-droppers, who usually do not have \r\ in *barn* and usually have \r\ in *cure* only when a vowel sound follows. For *governors,* for example, *r*-droppers usually say \'gəv-ə-nəz\, with neither of the two possible \r\'s present, whereas those who have no first \r\ by dissimilation usually say \'gəv-ə-nərz\. *R*-droppers' pronunciations are not shown in the vocabulary of this dictionary.

divisions in pronunciations
syllables in speech usually happen automatically when sequences of sounds are uttered. Most syllables can be articulated properly by articulating in order the sounds of a transcription that makes no attempt to demarcate the syllables. However, an attempt at complete syllable demarcation has been traditional in American general dictionaries for so long a time that an impression prevails that transcriptions without it are incomplete. Out of deference to this questionable but widely held belief this dictionary attempts complete syllable demarcation. The syllabic indication is in many specific instances, however, prosodic rather than phonetic. A word like *night* is sharply monosyllabic, and a word like *winner* or *Moab* is sharply disyllabic, but words having a vowel sequence of which unstressed \ə\ is the final member fall in between, as the variant of *sower* or *sore* with \ō-ə\, the variant of *sawer* or *sore* with \ȯ-ə\, and the variant of *flower* or *flour* with \au̇-ə\. Phonetically these words are all parallel in that all have variants without the \ə\ and all are ambiguous as to their syllabic content on a strictly phonetic basis. A vowel or vowel sequence with \ə\ alternatively present or absent after it is usually freely treated in verse as either disyllabic or monosyllabic when the spelling contains a letter to which \ə\ is referable and that letter is in turn followed by *r* or *l* (as in *sower, sawer, flower, friar, fryer, real, vial*), but such a vowel item is usually treated as monosyllabic in verse when there is no such letter (as in *sore, reel, vile;* whether *-r* and *-l* words, as *soar* and *real,* with vowel-letter sequences that in other environments are capable of being digraphs, as in *soak, reap,* fall prosodically in the *flower* or the *flour* class is determined largely by etymology). In this dictionary, accordingly, *sore* and *flour* are transcribed \'sō(ə)r, 'sȯ(ə)r\ and \'flau̇(ə)r\, respectively, with no mark of syllable division, whereas *sower, sawer,* and *flower* are transcribed \'sō(-ə)r\, \'sȯ(-ə)r\, and \'flau̇(-ə)r\, respectively, with hyphen. For this last group the variants \'sōər\, \'sȯər\, and \'flau̇ər\, with \ə\ but without the hyphen and hence matching variants given for the first group, are not shown but are to be understood.

An exception to the disyllabic alternative in poetry for transcriptions containing the item \(-ə)\ are such words as *world,* in the transcription of which \(-ə)\ appears between \r\ and \l\ to make it clear that only one of the two values of \ər\ heard in a word like *worry* occurs in these words. Phonetically, however, the \'wər-əld\ alternative is as disyllabic as is a word like *moral.*

\ə\-final vowel sequences in other environments, as in *Goa, riot,* may also vary in syllabic count in poetry but do not raise the transcriptional problems that words with *r* and *l* do (they would if our transcriptions covered the speech of *r*-droppers; compare *Goa, gore*). Words like *Goa* and *riot* are transcribed with an unparenthesized hyphen before the \ə\.

Items like *strawy* and the *-stroy* part of *destroy* also raise a problem of syllable count. In the vocabulary, however, the traditional interpretation of the syllables in these has been followed.

Unanimity of opinion does not exist among linguists and phoneticians as to the extent to which boundaries

between words are recognizable on a purely phonetic basis, without the help of context. It is possible in transcription that does not attempt complete syllable division and that employs a noncommittal placement of stress marks (as over, under, or immediately preceding a vowel) to avoid committing oneself where there is doubt, but in the kind of transcription shown in this dictionary such avoidance is not possible. The placement of our marks of syllable division is based largely on an accumulation of records of syllable divisions heard between the vowels of two consecutive words at a point other than the word boundary. Thus hearing *a never-* . . . as *an ever-* . . ., and vice versa, in the interval that elapses until further context makes the speaker's intent clear (occasionally a speaker's intent is unclear even after the addition of context) is cause for feeling that *a name* and *an aim* are indistinguishable when both have the same first vowel \ə\, as they usually do, and are without context or are in an ambiguous context. Accordingly, the articulation of some sounds and sequences of sounds varies when their distribution at word boundaries having no pause varies whereas the articulation of others does not. Though \n\ seems to sound the same in *a name* and *an aim*, *nt* definitely does not seem to sound in *ten trips* as it does in *tent rips*. Items like \nt\, in vocabulary-transcription practice, can vary in division in phonetic contexts otherwise identical; items like \n\ cannot (two exceptions are noted in the next paragraph). The syllabic placement of items, like \n\, regarded as not subject to variation has been determined thus: a consonant or consonant sequence that can freely begin English words is put with the following vowel if the preceding vowel is long or is unstressed (\in-'d(y)ü-smənt\ *inducement*, \'pā-strē\ *pastry*, \ə-'strin-jənt\ *astringent*); a single such consonant or the first member of such a sequence is put with the preceding vowel if that vowel is short and stressed (\'bəs-mən\ *busman*, \'ves-trē\ *vestry*); of a sequence that cannot freely begin English words such right-hand part as can be is put with the following vowel (\'fər-'strāt\ *first-rate*, \'han-,drit-ən\ *hand-written*). The *freely* here makes necessary several ad hoc decisions, as the division \'yüs-fəl\ *useful* in spite of English *sphere* and division after rather than before the \s\ of \sth\ in *calisthenics*, *esthetic* in spite of English *sthenic*. On the other hand, a few consonant sequences have been made syllable-initial that do not begin thoroughly English words. A two-syllable pronunciation of *admiral* is common but syllable-final \dm\ of the alternative \'adm-rəl\ does not end English words and syllable-initial \mr\ of the alternative \'ad-mrəl\ does not begin English words (the second alternative is shown). \dl\ and \tl\ are placed at the beginning of a syllable when certain consonants precede although the \dl\ and \tl\ sequences do not occur initially in purely English words (\'lan-,dlād-ē\ *landlady*, \'dək-tləs\ *ductless*). In some environments \d\ and \t\ can be formed by merely a closure of the articulating organs involved, but after these certain consonants \d\ and \t\ require a release or explosion to be heard at all and the release takes place through the tongue opening for \l\. If \l\ is in a following syllable then the \d\ or \t\, it appears, necessarily is too.

An occasional departure is made from these practices when there is a variant pronunciation that requires a different division: \'ēz-(ə-)lē\ instead of the longer 'ē-zə-le 'ēz-lē\ at *easily*, \,dō-mes-'tis-ət-ē, də-, ,dä-\ instead of the longer last variant \,däm-,es-\ at *domesticity*. Such liberties are taken only with consonants and consonant sequences regarded as always articulated the same in a given phonetic context. For such differences as \i-'lü-siv\ for *elusive* but \il-'ü-siv\ for *illusive* see the section on \i\.

It has been traditional practice in dictionaries not to show a short vowel as the last sound in a stressed syllable. But the \tr\ of *Patrick* is different with most American speakers from the \tr\ of *pat request*, the \t\ of *atoll* is usually different from the last intervocalic consonant in "not *in* all but *at* all". This dictionary therefore contains such divisions as \'pa-trik\ at *Patrick* and \'a-,tȯl\ at *atoll*.

When no \s\ precedes, \k\ or \p\ before a vowel with less than primary stress is spoken with so much less force than \k\ or \p\ before a vowel with primary stress (compare *microbe* with *crow*) that its syllable initialness is less likely to be felt, and such a \k\ or \p\ could be put with a preceding vowel. However, in contexts the same in sounds and stress the pronunciation seems to be the same whether a word boundary

precedes or follows, and the system evolved for this dictionary calls for such divisions as \'mī-,krōb\ *microbe*, \'ā-prəl\ *April*.

\e\   as in *bet*, *bed*, and the first syllable of *merry*. In words in which this dictionary shows only \ar\ some American speakers have \er\ instead, pronouncing both *merry* and *marry* \'mer-ē\.

\ē\   as in *beat*, *bead*, as in the first syllable of *easy*, and, with most Americans, Canadians, and Australians, as in the second syllable of *easy*. \i\ occurs instead of unstressed \ē\ as in *easy* in some dialects (e.g., southern British and in the southern U.S.).

\ē-ər\   is frequently the only variant shown or implied for words like *freer*, but when stress is sufficiently weak, as in *sightseer*, the variant \i(-)ər\ or even \ir\ occurs.

foreign words this dictionary shows a partially or completely anglicized pronunciation for many foreign words and phrases for which a full foreign pronunciation has traditionally been given in dictionaries. For such entries the full foreign pronunciation, if not alternatively shown, is usually an acceptable variant. The speaker who is sufficiently conversant with the phonetics of a foreign language to be capable and desirous of using the full foreign pronunciation is unlikely to use an English dictionary as a source. In foreign pronunciations all except the simplest indications of length have been avoided. For the same reasons the pronunciations of British dialect words have often been somewhat anglicized. No special symbol, for example, has been used for the vowel that occurs in Scotland and northern England for the vowel of words like *cat*.

French words fully French pronunciations are shown without any stress marks, as is the usual practice of transcribers of French.

\h\   as in *hat*, *ahead*. After voiceless fricatives alone or preceded by another consonant (*household*, *bathhouse*, *fishhook*, *foxhole*, *self-help*), after the voiceless affricate \ch\ (*beachhead*), after the voiceless stop \k\ or \p\ alone or preceded by another consonant (*Lockheed*, *elkhound*, *sinkhole*, *trip hammer*), after the voiceless stop \t\ when preceded by another consonant (*pesthouse*, *priesthood*, *felt hat*), and possibly in British speech after \t\ when not so preceded (*rathole*), an \h\ that would be pronounced if what preceded were omitted has a strong tendency to disappear. Since the variant without \h\ often cannot be shown by simply parenthesizing the \h\ (\'prēst-,hùd, 'prē-,stùd\) it has usually been omitted.

\hw\   used for the *wh* of *whet*, *whale* by speakers whose *whet* and *wet*, *whale* and *wail* are not pronounced the same.

\i\   as in *bit*, *bid*, *here*, *hear*. For \i\ preceding \j\, \g\, \k\, \ŋ\, \sh\, \ch\, \v\ (as in *cabbage*, *pfennig*, *attic*, *riding*, *famish*, *spinach*, *active*) in the same unstressed syllable in the vocabulary, \ē\, not shown, is a frequent variant. Before the same sounds, except possibly \ŋ\, \ə\ is a much less frequent variant.

When in the vocabulary unstressed \i\ is the vowel of the first of two successive syllables and there occurs between it and the following vowel a consonant or consonant sequence that can be pronounced at the beginning of a syllable, \i\ frequently has variants that are not shown but are to be understood, and the range of the variation depends on whether the consonant or sequence is placed in the syllable with the \i\ or is placed in the following syllable. When \i\ is not final in the syllable, \ə\ is to be understood as a variant, as in \il-'ü-siv\ for *illusive*. When \i\ stands at the end of its syllable, \ə\ and \ē\ as well are to be understood as variants, as in \i-'lü-siv\ for *elusive*, unless the \ē\ variant is shown, in which case the \ē\ variant is not to be understood. Thus the \ē\ variant is not to be understood for the first vowel of *Italian*, the transcription for which is \ə-'tal-yən, i-\.

In some dialects of English, as southern British, \i\ is the usual vowel in most words in which this dictionary shows \ə\ answering to *i*, *y*, or *e* in the spelling, as for the *i* of *rabbit*, the *e* of *duchess*, and the *y* of *syllabic*. See the section on \ē\.

\ī\ as in *try, light, guide, aisle*. \ī\ is a diphthong, not a single sound, with heaviest stress on the first element. Its beginning position ranges from the position for the \à\ heard in *ask* in eastern New England to the position for the unrounded \ä\ heard from most U.S. speakers for the vowel of *hot, heart;* its ending position ranges from that for monophthongal \ā\ to that for \i\. In eastern Virginia and in an area of Canada having Toronto as its metropolis, the position of the first element before voiceless consonants is approximately that of the \'ə\ of *nut*. In the southern U.S., the second part of the \ȧi\ or \äi\ variety of the diphthong may disappear, and finally and before voiced consonants, less often before voiceless consonants, the pronunciation may be simply \ȧ\ or unrounded \ä\, as in \'wȧvz\ or \'wävz\ for *wives*.

\iŋ\ when stressed, as in *sing, forefinger*, \āŋ\ and perhaps less often \eŋ\ are variants especially in the southern U.S. These variants are not shown.

\j\ as in *jug*, ba*dge*, *agile*. \j\ is the sequence \d\ and \zh\ pronounced in the same syllable, and is probably different from the \dzh\ that occurs in one pronunciation of *bad gendarme*, although words beginning with \zh\ are so rare in English that there is scant opportunity for the reaching of conclusions on the basis of random listening.

\k̲\ as for *ch* in German *siech* and *Buch;* a non-English voiceless fricative sound, made with the tongue in a range of positions from approximately that of the \k\ in English *keep* to that of the \k\ in English *cool* but without closure.

\l\ as in *leaf, loot, police, allude, feel, fool*. The range of articulation for \l\ in English is fairly wide, but the variations are similar in most contexts in the English-speaking world. An \l\, however, between a preceding stressed vowel and a following unstressed vowel often exhibits a striking dialectal difference that vocabulary transcriptions do not attempt to cover. Most Americans, for example, pronounce *Alice* and *salad* \'al-əs\, \'sal-əd\ whereas in the South these words are widely pronounced \'a-lis\, \'sa-lid\.

\m\ as in *maim, hammer, nymph;* the usual articulation of \m\ is with the lips in contact to form a closure but when an \f\ or \v\ sound immediately precedes or follows, the closure is made by the lower lip against the upper front teeth, as in *nymph, triumph, triumvir, Hoffman*(n). In this dictionary the \m\ of words like *chasm* is treated as forming an extra syllable (\'kaz-əm\). Such pronunciations are the usual ones in prose but other pronunciations occur and are to be understood. Before a vowel in poetry a word like *chasm* fits without jar into a line where a stressed monosyllable is required, since the \m\ can be pronounced at the beginning of the syllable to which the following vowel belongs: *abysm of time* \ə-ˌbiz-məv-'tīm\. Similar pronunciations before a vowel are heard, though less frequently, in prose, especially when the vowel preceding the \m\ has only secondary stress, as in *enthusiasm of the crowd*. In poetry a monosyllabic pronunciation of a word-final vowel and *-sm* is also sometimes required before a pause or a consonant, and before the latter at least may be accomplished by using a pronunciation like that which occurs in some contexts for *-sme* words in French, as in *abysm below* \ə-ˌbizmə-'lō\.

\n\ as in *known, manly, enrage, tenth*.

\ⁿ\ indicates that the preceding vowel is pronounced through the nose, that is, with the velum lowered and the nostrils open at the back.

ng see section on \ŋ\.

\ŋ\ as in *hang* \'haŋ\, *hanger* \'haŋ-ər\, *anger* \'aŋ-gər\, *singer* \'siŋ-ər\, *finger* \'fiŋ-gər\. The sound of the *ng* in *hang* and of the *n* in *anger* is a single sound not the sound \n\ followed by the sound \g\, although the transcription \ng\ for this single sound is used in some of the smaller members of this series to avoid the use of characters that are not letters of the ordinary English alphabet.

\œ\ as in French *bœuf*, German *Hölle;* \œ\ can be approximated by pronouncing \e\ with moderately rounded lips. This and \œ̄\ are variously anglicized in English. In a few words \ō\ is frequent, as in the surname *Loeb*. Among those who do not drop r, \'ər\ is frequently heard, less often \'ə\ (*Köchel*, surname of a musicologist who assigned opus numbers to Mozart's works, is constantly made an exact rhyme of *circle* by announcers for radio classical-music programs). Those who drop r, and some even who do not, often use the same pronunciation as for the *or* of *work*. \'ə(r)\ is frequently the transcription in anglicized pronunciations in this dictionary, as at *diseuse*.

\œ̄\ as in French *feu*, German *Höhle;* \œ̄\ can be approximated by pronouncing \ā\ with strongly rounded lips.

\ȯi\ as in *coin, boy*. In the southern U.S. and chiefly before a consonant in the same word the second element is sometimes lost or replaced by \ə\. It is problematic whether phonetically the sequence of sounds represented by the spelling *strawy* is disyllabic whereas the sequence represented by the *-stroy* of *destroy* is monosyllabic; prosodically however the sequences are usually so treated and the vocabulary puts a parenthesized hyphen in the respelling of *strawy*.

present participles many present participles are pronounced in the vocabulary in order to show such variations as that between the two-syllabled and the three-syllabled pronunciation of *flickering*. In these pronunciations only \iŋ\ is shown for the ending but other variants occur: see the entry *-ing* in the vocabulary.

\r\ as in *rid, arouse, merry* as pronounced by all speakers of standard English, and as in one pronunciation of *carbarn, lizard, bare, murder*. In some dialects, as those of eastern New England, the southeastern U.S., and southern England, words of the type of the last three, in which *r* occurs at the end of a word (often before a silent *e*) or before a consonant, are not, at least in some contexts, pronounced with an \r\. See the section on dissimilation.

\s\ as in *so, less, lesser*. Presenting difficulty is the transcription of the *s* of words like *abstain, teamster, instigate*, which is preceded by a voiced consonant and followed by a voiceless one that starts out like a \z\ but ends up like an \s\. This dictionary follows tradition and transcribes \s\, except when *s* is clearly the final member of a word component, as in *foolscap*. When an *s* of the spelling is followed by letters whose pronunciation is \ch\, as in *mischief, digestion*, both \s\ and \sh\ occur for the *s*. The articulatory position of the vowels \ē\, \i\, \ā\, \e\ is closest to that of \sh\ and the \sh\ variant is limited to words in which one of those four vowels precedes.

semicolon usually a comma separates variant pronunciations, but a semicolon separates a partially transcribed variant on the right of it that is not meant to be read with a variant on the left of it: at *dengue* the semicolon in \'deŋ-gē; 'deŋ-ˌgā, 'den-\ signifies that \'den-\ goes with the \-ˌgā\ variant only.

-sia, -sian as in *magnesia, Andalusia*. For many words ending in *-sia* as many as ten variants for the ending occur: \zhə, zhē-ə, shə, shē-ə, *chiefly Brit* zi-ə, zyə, zhyə, si-ə, syə, shyə\. An especially wide range of variants occurs for many words in *-sian*.

stress the stress shown for words in the vocabulary is usually that borne by the word when it is pronounced by itself without context. In context, however, a word may have a different stress pattern. In particular, adjectives that in isolation are pronounced with a primary stress on a syllable except the first and that have preceding this primary stress a syllable with secondary stress or a vowel followed by two or more consonants, in context (as when they are attributive or sentence-initial) undergo a reduction of the primary stress to secondary; retain a secondary stress that precedes or undergo a change of it to primary; or acquire either a secondary or a primary stress on a preceding syllable on which no stress is indicated in

the vocabulary. When such words are spoken with emphasis, the primary stress may be retained and a second primary stress pronounced ahead of it:

> The therapy was ‚bene'ficial
> The story was fic'titious
> This proved ‚bene‚ficial (or 'bene‚ficial) therapy
> An obviously ‚fic‚titious (or 'fic‚titious) story
> 'Bene‚ficial (or ‚Bene‚ficial or 'Bene'ficial) as the therapy was …
> 'Fic‚titious (or ‚Fic‚titious or 'Fic'titious) though the story is …

Other parts of speech that in isolation have a primary stress on the last syllable may undergo the same kind of stress variation:

> 'Al‚giers (or 'Al'giers), site of the trouble …

symbol names the terms *bar*, *one-dot*, and *two-dot* can be used with the name of a character in this way: \ā\ is "bar a", \t̲h̲\ is "bar t-h", \ȯ\ is "one-dot o", \ü\ is "two-dot u". Symbols with no modifier are *plain:* \a\ is "plain a", \i\ is "plain i" because the dot is not a modifier.

\t\   as in *tights, attend, Atlantic.*
In some positions (as when a stressed vowel precedes and an unstressed vowel follows) the consonant represented by a *t* or *tt* in the spelling is widely pronounced in the U.S. the same as *d* or *dd* would be pronounced in the same context, with resultant leveling of pairs like *latter* and *ladder*. If there were in English in addition to the word *mediator* the three words *metiador*, *mediador*, *metiator*, all with \'ē\ and \‚ā\, many would pronounce all four exactly alike. Such leveling is not indicated in vocabulary transcriptions. Because, however, the consonant sound that causes it can be treated as a syllable-final \d\, the leveling is frequently suggested by placing a \t\ at the end of the syllable containing a preceding vowel rather than at the beginning of the syllable containing a following vowel, as in \'kwōt-ə\ *quota*, \'fāt-ᵊl\ *fatal*. Divisions like \'kwō-tə\, traditional when a long vowel precedes the consonant, are realistic enough for some dialects (e.g., southern British) but are misleading for the usual American pronunciation.
The sound that often makes *latter* and *ladder* the same in pronunciation does not occur in standard speech in words like *enter* (different from *ender*), and yet the traditional division \'en-tər\ is as unrealistic for most American pronunciation, as is \'kwō-tə\. \'ent-ər\ is better, and in fact even in standard rapid speech the \t\ may not be present at all, with consequent leveling of such pairs as *winter, winner.*

\t̲h̲\ , \t̲h̲\   the basic difference between \t̲h̲\ as in *thin, ether* and \t̲h̲\ as in *then, either* is that the first is pronounced without and the second with vibration of the vocal cords.

\ū\   this symbol, used in most diacritical alphabets for the sounds following the \f\ of *few* and often for the sounds between the \f\ and \r\ of *fury*, is replaced in this dictionary by \yü\ and \yu̇\, which are not only phonetically more realistic but also transcriptionally more economical in permitting the showing of two variants by parenthesization, as in \'n(y)ü\ for *new.*

\u̇\   as in *pull, wood, injurious.* \u̇\ is usually shown as the second part or ending position of the diphthong of *loud* but in most articulations a point this high is not reached, the ending position being closer to \ō\. Diphthongs with the same second member and various first members are used by some speakers instead of a vowel + \l\ sequence when what follows the potential \l\ is one of the consonants \b\, \f\, \k\, \m\, \p\, \v\, as in \'seu̇f\ for *self* and \'fiu̇m\ for *film*. Such \u̇\ variants are not shown in the vocabulary.
A \u̇\ that is the last character in an unstressed syllable is to be understood as having multiple value. When a consonant stands at the beginning of the next syllable, \u̇\ equals \ü\, \u̇\, and \ə\, as in \byu̇-'räk-rə-sē\ at *bureaucracy*. When a vowel stands at the beginning of the next syllable, \u̇\ equals \ü\, \u̇\,

and \əw\, as in \yu̇-'än-ə-məs\ at *euonymus* (the division \yə-'wän-ə-məs\ is to be understood for the third variant).

\ü\   as in *rule, moon, few* \'fyü\, *union* \'yün-yən\.
The sequences \lyü\, \syü\, and \zyü\ in the same syllable are rare in American speech and are not shown in this dictionary. They are heard more often in British speech, where they are used in words, most of them of Latin or Greek origin, that have in the spelling a vowel item other than *oo* or *ou*, as *ew* of *lewd*, *eu* of *pseudo*, *u* of *presume*, *ui* of *suit.*

\œ\   as in German *füllen, hübsch;* \œ\ can be approximated by pronouncing \i\ with moderately rounded lips.

\ōœ\   as in French *rue*, German *fühlen;* \ōœ\ can be approximated by pronouncing \ē\ with strongly rounded lips.

\ü-ər\   is frequently the only variant shown or implied for words like *wooer, viewer*, but when stress is sufficiently weak, as in *horseshoer*, the variant \u̇(-)ər\ or even \u̇r\ occurs.

\v\   as in *vote, level, give.* Under the assimilative influence of a following \ᵊm\, the lip-teeth sound \v\ may have as a variant the two-lip sound \b\, as in *give 'em, government*. This variant, not shown in the vocabulary, is widely believed to be confined to substandard speech.

\w\   as in *we, sweep, away.*
Words like *strenuous* and *silhouette* are often transcribed in some such fashion as \'stren-yü-əs\, \‚sil-ü-'et\. But *silhouette* and *Scylla wet* as usually pronounced have the same sounds in them, and in an ambiguous context in which the two would be stressed the same could not usually be distinguished. The simplest way to show this identity is to retain the traditional transcription for *Scylla* and to transcribe *silhouette* \‚sil-ə-'wet\, as this dictionary does.

\wʸ\   as *hu* in French *huile* or *u* in French *nuit.*
\wʸ\ can be approximated by rounding the lips as for \w\ while the tongue makes the articulation for \y\.

\x\   for words of the type of *exact, exult*, in which the sounds that correspond to the *x* of the spelling are preceded by an unstressed and followed by a stressed vowel, the vocabulary usually shows only the value \gz\ for the *x*. For such words some speakers have \ks\ instead.

\y\   as in *yard, yours, European* \‚yu̇r-ə-'pē-ən\, *cue* \'kyü\, *union* \'yün-yən\.

\ʸ\   not a symbol for a sound but a diacritic used in transcriptions of foreign words only to signify a modification of the sound of the preceding symbol by articulating the sound while the tongue is in approximately the position for the sound \y\, with the tip behind the lower front teeth.
Frequently at the end of the articulation of \nʸ\ or \lʸ\ an independent \y\ sound is heard, without anything else accompanying, \nʸy\, \lʸy\, but it is usually considered unnecessary to transcribe this off-glide.

\yü\ , \yu̇\   these two transcriptions replace the ū of previous editions of this dictionary, \yu̇\ occurring before \r\ as in *European* and \yü\ elsewhere as in *unity*. These two transcriptions not only better display the nature of the sounds but also make it possible to show two pronunciations for a word like *new* simply by parenthesizing, \'n(y)ü\.

\z\   as in *zone, freezer, raise.* On the sound of the *s* in words like *abstain, teamster, instigate*, see the section on \s\.

ABBREVIATIONS USED IN THIS WORK

For a more extensive list see "Abbreviations" following the vocabulary

A .... Agricultural
ab .... about
abbr .... abbreviation
abl .... ablative
Acad .... Academy
acc .... accusative
act .... active
A.D. .... anno Domini
adj .... adjective
adv .... adverb
AF .... Anglo-French
Afrik .... Afrikaans
Agric .... Agriculture
Ala .... Alabama
Alb .... Albanian
Alta .... Alberta
alter .... alteration
a.m. .... ante meridiem
Am .... America, American
AmerF ...... American French
AmerInd .... American Indian
AmerSp ..... American Spanish
anc .... ancient, anciently
anthropol .... anthropologist
aor .... aorist
Ar .... Arabic
Aram .... Aramaic
archaeol ..... archaeologist
Ariz .... Arizona
Ark .... Arkansas
Arm .... Armenian
art .... article
Assyr .... Assyrian
astron ...... astronomer, astronomy
attrib .... attributive
atty .... attorney
aug .... augmentative
Austral ..... Australian
Av .... Avestan
AV .... Authorized Version
b .... born
Bab .... Babylonian
bacteriol .... bacteriologist
B.C. .... before Christ, British Columbia
Belg .... Belgian
Beng .... Bengalese
Bib .... Biblical
Braz .... Brazilian
Bret .... Breton
Brit .... Britain, British
bro .... brother
Bulg .... Bulgarian
C .... centigrade, College
Calif .... California
Canad ...... Canadian
CanF .... Canadian French
Cant .... Cantonese
cap .... capital, capitalized
capt .... captain
Catal .... Catalan
caus .... causative
Celt .... Celtic
cen .... central
cent .... century
cgs .... centimeter-gram-second
chem .... chemist
Chin .... Chinese
Co .... company, county
coed .... coeducational
Colo .... Colorado
comb .... combining
compar ..... comparative
Confed ..... Confederate
conj .... conjunction
Conn .... Connecticut
constr ...... construction
contr .... contraction
Copt .... Coptic
Corn .... Cornish
criminol ..... criminologist
d .... died
D .... Dutch
Dan .... Danish
dat .... dative
dau .... daughter
D.C. .... District of Columbia
def .... definite
Del .... Delaware
deriv .... derivative
dial .... dialect
dim .... diminutive
disc .... discovered
Dor .... Doric
Dr .... Doctor
dram .... dramatist
Du .... Dutch
DV .... Douay Version

E .... east, eastern, English
econ .... economist
Ed .... Education
educ .... educator
e.g. .... exempli gratia
EGmc ...... East Germanic
Egypt ...... Egyptian
emp .... emperor
Eng .... England, English
Esk .... Eskimo
esp .... especially
Eth .... Ethiopic
ethnol ...... ethnologist
F .... Fahrenheit, French
fem .... feminine
Finn .... Finnish
fl .... floruit (L, flourished)
Fla .... Florida
Flem .... Flemish
fr .... from
Fr .... French
freq .... frequentative, frequently
Fris .... Frisian
ft .... feet
fut .... future
G .... German
Ga .... Georgia
Gael .... Gaelic
gen .... general, genitive
Ger .... German
Gk .... Greek
Gmc .... Germanic
Goth .... Gothic
gov .... governor
govt .... government
Gr Brit ..... Great Britain
Heb .... Hebrew
hist .... historian
Hitt .... Hittite
Hung .... Hungarian
I .... island
Icel .... Icelandic
IE .... Indo-European
Ill .... Illinois
imit .... imitative
imper .... imperative
incho .... inchoative
Ind .... Indiana
indef .... indefinite
indic .... indicative
infin .... infinitive
Inst .... Institute
instr .... instrumental
interj .... interjection
intrans ..... intransitive
Ion .... Ionic
IrGael ...... Irish Gaelic
irreg .... irregular
ISV .... International Scientific Vocabulary
It, Ital ..... Italian
Jap .... Japanese
Jav .... Javanese
Kans .... Kansas
Ky .... Kentucky
L .... Latin
La .... Louisiana
LaF .... Louisiana French
lat .... latitude
LG .... Low German
LGk .... Late Greek
LHeb .... Late Hebrew
lit .... literally
Lith .... Lithuanian
LL .... Late Latin
loc .... locative
long .... longitude
m .... miles
M .... Mechanical
Man .... Manitoba
manuf ...... manufacturer
masc .... masculine
Mass .... Massachusetts
math .... mathematician
Md .... Maryland
MD .... Middle Dutch
Me .... Maine
ME .... Middle English
Med .... Medical
meteorol .... meteorologist
Mex .... Mexican
MexSp ...... Mexican Spanish
MF .... Middle French
MFlem ...... Middle Flemish
MGk .... Middle Greek
MHG .... Middle High German
Mich .... Michigan
mil .... military
min .... minister
Minn .... Minnesota
MIr .... Middle Irish

Miss .... Mississippi
ML .... Medieval Latin
MLG .... Middle Low German
Mo .... Missouri
modif .... modification
Mont .... Montana
MPer .... Middle Persian
MS .... manuscript
MSw .... Middle Swedish
mt .... mountain
Mt .... Mount
MW .... Middle Welsh
n .... noun
N .... north, northern
N.A.T.O. .... North Atlantic Treaty Organization
naut .... nautical
N.B. .... New Brunswick
N.C. .... North Carolina
NCE .... New Catholic Edition
N.Dak. ..... North Dakota
NE .... northeast, northeastern
Nebr .... Nebraska
neut .... neuter
Nev .... Nevada
NewEng .... New England
Nfld .... Newfoundland
NGk .... New Greek
NGmc ...... North Germanic
N.H. .... New Hampshire
NHeb .... New Hebrew
N.J. .... New Jersey
NL .... New Latin
N.Mex. ..... New Mexico
No .... North
nom .... nominative
nonstand .... nonstandard
Norw .... Norwegian
nov .... novelist
n pl .... noun plural
N.S. .... Nova Scotia
NW .... northwest, northwestern
N.Y. .... New York
NYC .... New York City
N.Z. .... New Zealand
obs .... obsolete
occas .... occasionally
OE .... Old English
OF .... Old French
OFris .... Old Frisian
OHG .... Old High German
OIr .... Old Irish
OIt .... Old Italian
Okla .... Oklahoma
OL .... Old Latin
ON .... Old Norse
ONF .... Old North French
Ont .... Ontario
OPer .... Old Persian
OPg .... Old Portuguese
opp .... opposite
OProv ...... Old Provençal
OPruss ...... Old Prussian
Oreg .... Oregon
orig .... originally
ORuss ...... Old Russian
OS .... Old Saxon
OSlav .... Old Slavic
OSp .... Old Spanish
OSw .... Old Swedish
p .... page
Pa .... Pennsylvania
PaG .... Pennsylvania German
part .... participle
pass .... passive
P.E.I. .... Prince Edward Island
Pek .... Pekingese
Per .... Persian
perf .... perfect
perh .... perhaps
pers .... person
Pg .... Portuguese
philos .... philosopher
physiol ...... physiologist
pl .... plural
p.m. .... post meridiem
Pol .... Polish
polit .... political, politician
pop .... population
Port .... Portuguese
pp .... past participle
P.Q. .... Province of Quebec
prec .... preceding
prep .... preposition
pres .... present, president
prob .... probably

prof .... professor
pron .... pronoun, pronunciation
pronunc ..... pronunciation
Prov .... Provençal
prp .... present participle
Pruss .... Prussian
pseud .... pseudonym
psychol ..... psychologist
Que .... Quebec
R.C. .... Roman Catholic
redupl ...... reduplication
refl .... reflexive
R.I. .... Rhode Island
Rom .... Roman, Romanian
rpm .... revolutions per minute
RSV .... Revised Standard Version
Russ .... Russian
S .... south, southern
Sask .... Saskatchewan
Sc .... Scotch, Scots
S.C. .... South Carolina
Scand .... Scandinavian
ScGael ...... Scottish Gaelic
Sch .... School
Scot .... Scottish
S.Dak .... South Dakota
SE .... southeast, southeastern
secy .... secretary
Sem .... Seminary, Semitic
Serb .... Serbian
Shak .... Shakespeare
sing .... singular
Skt .... Sanskrit
Slav .... Slavic
So .... South
sociol .... sociologist
Sp, Span .... Spanish
specif .... specifically
sp. gr. ...... specific gravity
sq .... square
St .... Saint, Sainte
Ste .... Sainte
subj .... subject
substand .... substandard
Sudan ...... Sudanese
superl .... superlative
Sw, Swed ... Swedish
SW .... southwest, southwestern
syll .... syllable
syn .... synonymy
Tag .... Tagalog
Tech .... Technology
Tenn .... Tennessee
Tex .... Texas
theol .... theologian
Theol .... Theological
Toch .... Tocharian
Toch A ...... Tocharian A
Toch B ...... Tocharian B
trans .... transitive, translation
treas .... treasurer
Turk .... Turkish
U .... University
U.A.R. ...... United Arab Republic
U.N. .... United Nations
US .... United States
USSR .... Union of Soviet Socialist Republics
usu .... usual, usually
v .... verb
Va .... Virginia
var .... variant
vb .... verb
vi .... verb intransitive
VL .... Vulgar Latin
voc .... vocative
vt .... verb transitive
Vt .... Vermont
W .... Welsh, west, western
Wash .... Washington
WGmc ...... West Germanic
Wis .... Wisconsin
W. Va .... West Virginia
Wyo .... Wyoming
zool .... zoologist

22a

A
DICTIONARY
OF
THE ENGLISH LANGUAGE

¹a \'ā\ *n, often cap, often attrib* **1 a :** the first letter of the English alphabet **b :** a graphic representation of this letter **c :** a speech counterpart of orthographic *a* **2 :** the tone A **3 :** a graphic device for reproducing the letter *a* **4 :** one designated *a* esp. as the first in order or class **5 a :** a grade rating a student's work as superior in quality **b :** one graded or rated with an A **6 :** something shaped like the letter A

²a \'ā\ *indefinite article* [ME, fr. OE *ān* one — more at ONE] **1** — used as a function word before singular nouns when the individual in question is unspecified ⟨*a* man overboard⟩ and before number collectives and some numbers ⟨*a* dozen⟩; used before words beginning with a consonant sound **2 a :** ONE ⟨swords all of *a* length⟩ **b :** the same ⟨birds of *a* feather⟩ **3 :** ANY ⟨*a* man who is sick can't work⟩ **4** [by folk etymology fr. ³a] **:** in, to, or for each ⟨twice *a* week⟩

³a \ə\ *prep* [ME, fr. OE *a-, an, on*] *chiefly dial* **:** ON, IN, AT

⁴a \ə, (')a\ *vb* [ME, contr. of *have*] *archaic* **:** HAVE ⟨God ∼ mercy⟩

⁵a \ə\ *prep, archaic* **:** OF ⟨the time ∼ day⟩

¹a- *prefix* [ME, fr. OE] **1 :** on **:** in **:** at ⟨abed⟩ **2 :** in (such) a state or condition ⟨afire⟩ **3 :** in (such) a manner ⟨aloud⟩ **4 :** in the act or process of ⟨gone *a*-hunting⟩

²a- *or* **an-** *prefix* [L & Gk; L, fr. Gk — more at UN-] **:** not **:** without ⟨asexual⟩ — *a-* before consonants other than *h* and sometimes even before *h, an-* before vowels and usu. before *h* ⟨ahistorical⟩ ⟨anastigmatic⟩ ⟨anhydrate⟩

-a *n suffix* [NL, fr. *-a* (as in *magnesia*)] **:** OXIDE ⟨thoria⟩

aard·vark \'ärd-,värk\ *n* [obs. Afrik, fr. Afrik *aard* earth + *vark* pig] **:** a large burrowing nocturnal African mammal (*Orycteropus afer* of the order Tubulidentata) that has extensile tongue, powerful claws, large ears, and heavy tail and feeds on ants and termites

aard·wolf \-,wu̇lf\ *n* [Afrik, fr. *aard* + *wolf*] **:** a maned striped mammal (*Proteles cristata*) of southern and eastern Africa that resembles the related hyenas and feeds chiefly on carrion and insects

Aar·on \'ar-ən, 'er-\ *n* [LL, fr. Gk *Aarōn*, fr. Heb *Ahărōn*] **:** a brother of Moses and high priest of the Hebrews

Aa·ron·ic \a-'rän-ik, e-\ *adj* **1 :** of or stemming from Aaron **2 :** of or relating to the lesser Mormon order of priesthood

Ab \'äb, 'äv, 'óv\ *n* [Heb *Ābh*] **:** the 11th month of the civil year or the 5th month of the ecclesiastical year in the Jewish calendar

ab- *prefix* [ME, fr. OF & L; ME *ab-, abs-, a-*, fr. *ab, a* — more at OF] **:** from **:** away **:** off ⟨abaxial⟩ ⟨abstriction⟩

aba \ə-'bä\ *n* [Ar *'abā'*] **1 :** a fabric woven from the hair of camels or goats **2 :** a loose sleeveless outer garment worn by Arabs

ab·a·ca \,ab-ə-'kä\ *n* [Sp *abacá*, fr. Tag *abaká*] **1 :** a fiber obtained from the leafstalk of a banana (*Musa textilis*) native to the Philippines **2 :** the plant that yields abaca

aback \ə-'bak\ *adv* **1** *archaic* **:** BACKWARD, BACK **2 :** in a position to catch the wind upon the forward surface of a square sail **3 :** by surprise **:** UNAWARES

aba·cus \'ab-ə-kəs, ə-'bak-əs\ *n, pl* **aba·ci** \'ab-ə-,sī, -,kē; ə-'bak-,ī\ *or* **aba·cus·es** [L, fr. Gk *abak-, abax*, lit., slab] **1 :** a slab that forms the uppermost member or division of the capital of a column **2 :** an instrument for performing calculations by sliding counters along rods or in grooves

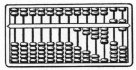

abacus 2

¹abaft \ə-'baft\ *adv* [¹a- + *baft* aft] **:** toward or at the stern **:** AFT

²abaft *prep* **:** to the rear of **:** BEHIND; *specif* **:** toward the stern from

ab·a·lo·ne \,ab-ə-'lō-nē\ *n* [AmerSp *abulón*] **:** any of a genus (*Haliotis*) of rock-clinging gastropod mollusks having a flattened shell of slightly spiral form that is lined with mother-of-pearl and has a row of apertures along its outer edge

¹aban·don \ə-'ban-dən\ *vt* [ME *abandounen*, fr. MF *abandoner*, fr. *abandon*, n., surrender, fr. *a bandon* in one's power] **1 :** to give up with the intent of never again claiming a right or interest in **2 :** to withdraw from often in the face of danger or encroachment ⟨∼ ship⟩ **3 :** to withdraw protection, support, or help from **:** DESERT **4 :** to give (oneself) over to a feeling or emotion without check, restraint, or control **5 a :** to cease from maintaining, practicing or using **b :** to cease intending or attempting to perform — **aban·don·er** *n* — **aban·don·ment** \-mənt\ *n*

syn DESERT, FORSAKE: ABANDON stresses leaving a person or thing entirely at the mercy of someone or something; DESERT implies terminating an occupation, companionship, or guardianship, and often implies culpable leaving of a post of duty; FORSAKE implies a breaking off of a close association by repudiation or renunciation **syn** see in addition RELINQUISH

²abandon *n* **1 :** a thorough yielding to natural impulses **2 :** ENTHUSIASM, EXUBERANCE

aban·doned \ə-'ban-dənd\ *adj* **:** wholly free from restraint and esp moral restraint

à bas \ä-'bä\ [F] **:** down with

abase \ə-'bās\ *vt* [ME *abassen*, fr. MF *abaisser*, fr. *a-* (fr. L *ad-*) + (assumed) VL *bassiare* to lower] **1** *archaic* **:** LOWER, DEPRESS **2 :** DEGRADE, HUMBLE — **abase·ment** \-'bā-smənt\ *n*

syn DEMEAN, DEBASE, DEGRADE, HUMILIATE: ABASE suggests losing or voluntarily yielding up dignity or prestige; DEMEAN implies losing or injuring social standing by an unsuitable act or association; DEBASE implies a deterioration of moral standards or character; DEGRADE suggests the taking of a step downward sometimes in rank but more often on the road to moral degeneration; HUMILIATE implies the severe wounding of one's pride and the causing of deep shame

abash \ə-'bash\ *vt* [ME *abaishen*, fr. (assumed) MF *abaiss-, abair* to astonish, alter. of MF *esbair*, fr. *ex-* + *bair* to yawn — more at ABEYANCE] **:** to destroy the self-possession or self-confidence of **:** DISCONCERT **syn** see EMBARRASS — **abash·ment** \-mənt\ *n*

abate \ə-'bāt\ *vb* [ME *abaten*, fr. OF *abattre* to beat down — more at REBATE] *vt* **1 :** to put an end to **:** NULLIFY ⟨∼ a nuisance⟩ **2 a :** to reduce in degree or intensity **:** DIMINISH **b :** to reduce in value **3 :** DEDUCT, OMIT **4 a :** to beat down or cut away so as to leave a figure in relief **b** *obs* **:** BLUNT **5 :** DEPRIVE ∼ *vi* **1 :** to decrease in force or intensity **:** SUBSIDE **2 a :** to become defeated or become null or void **b :** to decrease in amount or value — **abat·er** *n*

syn SUBSIDE, WANE, EBB: ABATE stresses the idea of progressive diminishing ⟨winds are *abating*⟩ SUBSIDE implies the ceasing of turbulence or agitation ⟨after the panic had *subsided*⟩ WANE suggests the fading or weakening of something good or impressive ⟨*waning* enthusiasm⟩ EBB suggests the receding of something that commonly comes and goes ⟨*ebbing* vitality⟩ **syn** see in addition DECREASE

abate·ment \ə-'bāt-mənt\ *n* **1 :** the act or process of abating **:** the state of being abated **2 :** an amount abated; *esp* **:** a deduction from the full amount of a tax

ab·a·tis \'ab-ə-,tē, 'ab-ət-əs\ *n, pl* **ab·a·tis** \-ə-,tēz\ *or* **ab·a·tis·es** \-ət-ə-səz\ [F, fr. *abattre*] **:** a defensive obstacle formed by felled trees with sharpened branches facing the enemy

A battery *n* **:** a battery used to heat the filaments or cathode heaters of electron tubes

ab·at·toir \'ab-ə-,twär\ *n* [F, fr. *abattre*] **:** SLAUGHTERHOUSE

ab·ax·i·al \(')a-'bak-sē-əl\ *adj* **:** situated out of or directed away from the axis

ab·ba·cy \'ab-ə-sē\ *n* [ME *abbatie*, fr. LL *abbatia*] **:** the office, dignity, jurisdiction, or term of tenure of an abbot

Ab·bas·id \ə-'bas-əd\ *n* **:** a member of a dynasty of caliphs (750–1258) claiming descent from Abbas the uncle of Muhammad

ab·ba·tial \ə-'bā-shəl, a-\ *adj* **:** of or relating to an abbot, abbess, or abbey

ab·bé \a-'bā, 'ab-,ā\ *n* [F, fr. LL *abbat-, abbas*] **:** a member of the French secular clergy in major or minor orders — used as a title

ab·bess \'ab-əs\ *n* [ME *abbesse*, fr. OF, fr. LL *abbatissa*, fem. of *abbat-, abbas*] **:** a woman who is the superior of a convent of nuns

Abbe·vil·li·an \ab-'vil-ē-ən, ,ab-ə-'vil-\ *adj* [*Abbeville*, France] **:** of or relating to an early Paleolithic culture characterized by bifacial stone hand axes

ab·bey \'ab-ē\ *n* [ME, fr. OF *abaïe*, fr. LL *abbatia* abbey, fr. *abbat-, abbas*] **1 a :** a monastery ruled by an abbot **b :** a convent ruled by an abbess **2 :** an abbey church **syn** see CLOISTER

ab·bot \'ab-ət\ *n* [ME *abbod*, fr. OE, fr. LL *abbat-, abbas*, fr. LGk *abbas*, fr. Aram *abbā* father] **:** the superior of an abbey for men

ab·bre·vi·ate \ə-'brē-vē-,āt\ *vt* [ME *abbreviaten*, fr. LL *abbreviatus*, pp. of *abbreviare* — more at ABRIDGE] **:** to make briefer **:** SHORTEN; *specif* **:** to reduce (as a word or phrase) to a written form intended to stand for the whole **syn** see SHORTEN — **ab·bre·vi·a·tor** \-,āt-ər\ *n*

ab·bre·vi·a·tion \ə-,brē-vē-'ā-shən\ *n* **1 :** the act or result of abbreviating **:** ABRIDGMENT **2 :** a shortened form of a word or phrase used esp. in writing in place of the whole

ABC \,ā-(,)bē-'sē\ *n, pl* **ABC's** *or* **ABCs** \-'sēz\ **1 :** ALPHABET — usu. used in pl. **2 a :** the rudiments of reading, writing, and spelling — usu. used in pl. **b :** the rudiments of a subject

ABC soil *n* **:** a soil that has a well-differentiated profile with distinct A-, B-, and C-horizons

ab·di·ca·ble \'ab-di-kə-bəl\ *adj* **:** that may be abdicated

ab·di·cate \'ab-di-,kāt\ *vb* [L *abdicatus*, pp. of *abdicare*, fr. *ab-* + *dicare* to proclaim — more at DICTION] *vt* **:** to relinquish (as sovereign power) formally **:** RENOUNCE ∼ *vi* **:** to renounce a throne, high office, dignity, or function — **ab·di·ca·tion** \,ab-di-'kā-shən\ *n* — **ab·di·ca·tor** \'ab-di-,kāt-ər\ *n*

ə abut; ə kitten; ər further; a back; ā bake; ä cot, cart; aú out; ch chin; e less; ē easy; g gift; i trip; ī life
j joke; ŋ sing; ō flow; ó flaw; ói coin; th thin; th this; ü loot; ú foot; y yet; yü few; yú furious; zh vision

syn RENOUNCE, RESIGN: ABDICATE implies a giving up of sovereign power or sometimes an evading of responsibility such as that of a parent; RENOUNCE may replace it but often implies additionally a sacrifice for a greater end; RESIGN applies to the giving up of an unexpired office or trust

ab·do·men \'ab-də-mən, ab-'dō-mən\ *n* [MF & L; MF, fr. L] **1 :** the part of the body between the thorax and the pelvis; *also* **:** the cavity of this part of the trunk containing the chief viscera **2 :** the posterior section of the body behind the thorax in an arthropod — **ab·dom·i·nal** \ab-'däm-ən-ᵊl\ *adj* — **ab·dom·i·nal·ly** \-ē\ *adv*

ab·dom·i·nous \ab-'däm-ə-nəs\ *adj* [L *abdomin-, abdomen*] **:** big-bellied

ab·duce \ab-'d(y)üs\ *vt* [L *abducere*] **:** ABDUCT

ab·du·cent \ab-'d(y)ü-sᵊnt\ *adj* [L *abducent-, abducens,* prp. of *abducere*] *of a muscle* **:** ABDUCTING

ab·duct \ab-'dəkt\ *vt* [L *abductus,* pp. of *abducere,* lit., to lead away, fr. *ab-* + *ducere* to lead — more at TOW] **1 :** to carry off (a person) by force **2 :** to draw away (as a limb) from a position near or parallel to the median axis of the body; *also* **:** to move apart (similar parts) — **ab·duc·tor** \-'dək-tər\ *n*

ab·duc·tion \ab-'dək-shən\ *n* **1 :** the action of abducting **:** the condition of being abducted **2 :** the unlawful carrying away of a woman for marriage or immoral intercourse

abeam \ə-'bēm\ *adv (or adj)* **:** on a line at right angles to a ship's keel

1abe·ce·dar·i·an \,ā-bē-(,)sē-'der-ē-ən\ *n* [ME *abecedary,* fr. ML *abecedarium* alphabet, fr. LL, neut. of *abecedarius* of the alphabet, fr. the letters *a* + *b* + *c* + *d*] **:** one learning the rudiments of something (as the alphabet)

2abecedarian *adj* **1 a :** of or relating to the alphabet **b :** alphabetically arranged **2 :** RUDIMENTARY

abed \ə-'bed\ *adv (or adj)* **:** in bed

Abel \'ā-bəl\ *n* [LL, fr. Gk, fr. Heb *Hebhel*] **:** a son of Adam and Eve killed by his brother Cain

abele \ə-'bē(ə)l\ *n* [D *abeel,* fr. ONF *abiel,* fr. L *albus* white] **:** a tall Old World poplar (*Populus alba*) with whitish tomentose twigs and leaves

Abe·lian group \ə-,bēl-yən-\ *n* [Niels *Abel* †1829 Norw mathematician] **:** a commutative group

abel·mosk \'ā-bəl-,mäsk\ *n* [deriv. of Ar *abū -l- misk* father of the musk] **:** a bushy herb (*Hibiscus moschatus*) of the mallow family native to tropical Asia and the East Indies whose musky seeds are used in perfumery and in flavoring coffee

Ab·er·deen An·gus \,ab-ər-,dē-'naŋ-gəs\ *n* [*Aberdeen* & *Angus,* counties in Scotland] **:** any of a breed of black hornless beef cattle originating in Scotland

ab·er·rance \a-'ber-ən(t)s\ *or* **ab·er·ran·cy** \-ən-sē\ *n* **:** DEVIATION

1ab·er·rant \a-'ber-ənt\ *adj* [L *aberrant-, aberrans,* prp. of *aberrare* to go astray, fr. *ab-* + *errare* to wander, err] **1 :** straying from the right or normal way **2 :** deviating from the usual or natural type **:** ATYPICAL — **ab·er·rant·ly** *adv*

2aberrant *n* **1 :** an aberrant natural group, individual, or structure **2 :** a person whose behavior departs substantially from the standard

ab·er·ra·tion \,ab-ə-'rā-shən\ *n* [L *aberratus,* pp. of *aberrare*] **1 :** the act of being aberrant esp. from a moral standard or normal state **2 :** failure of a mirror, refracting surface, or lens to produce exact point-to-point correspondence between an object and its image **3 :** unsoundness or disorder of the mind **4 :** a small periodic change of apparent position in heavenly bodies due to the combined effect of the motion of light and the motion of the observer **5 :** an aberrant organ or individual **:** SPORT 5 — **ab·er·ra·tion·al** \-shnəl, -shən-ᵊl\ *adj*

abet \ə-'bet\ *vt* **abet·ted; abet·ting** [ME *abetten,* fr. MF *abeter,* fr. OF, fr. *a-* (fr. L *ad-*) + *beter* to bait, of Gmc origin; akin to OE *bǣtan* to bait] **1 :** ENCOURAGE, INSTIGATE **2 :** to assist in the achievement of a purpose **syn** see INCITE — **abet·ment** \-mənt\ *n* — **abet·tor** *or* **abet·ter** \-'bet-ər\ *n*

ab ex·tra \a-'bek-strə\ *adv* [LL] **:** from without

abey·ance \ə-'bā-ən(t)s\ *n* [MF *abeance* expectation, fr. *abaer* to desire, fr. *a-* + *baer* to yawn, fr. ML *batare*] **1 :** a lapse in succession during which there is no person in whom a title is vested **2 :** temporary inactivity **:** SUSPENSION

abey·ant \ə-'bā-ənt\ *adj* [back-formation fr. *abeyance*] **:** being in abeyance **syn** see LATENT

abhominable *adj, obs* **:** ABOMINABLE

ab·hor \əb-'hȯ(ə)r, ab-\ *vt* **ab·horred; ab·hor·ring** [ME *abhorren,* fr. L *abhorrēre,* fr. *ab-* + *horrēre* to shudder — more at HORROR] **1 :** to regard with extreme repugnance **:** LOATHE **2 :** to turn aside or keep away from esp. in scorn **:** REJECT **syn** see HATE — **ab·hor·rence** \-'hȯr-ən(t)s, -'här-\ *n* — **ab·hor·rer** \-'hȯr-ər\ *n*

ab·hor·rent \-'hȯr-ənt, -'här-\ *adj* [L *abhorrent-, abhorrens,* prp. of *abhorrēre*] **1 a** *archaic* **:** strongly opposed **b :** feeling or showing abhorrence **2 :** not agreeable ⟨~ to their philosophy⟩ **3 :** DETESTABLE **syn** see HATEFUL, REPUGNANT — **ab·hor·rent·ly** *adv*

Abib \ä-'vēv\ *n* [Heb *Ābhībh,* lit., ear of grain] **:** the 1st month of the ancient Hebrew calendar corresponding to Nisan

abid·ance \ə-'bīd-ᵊn(t)s\ *n* **1 :** an act or state of abiding **:** CONTINUANCE **2 :** COMPLIANCE

abide \ə-'bīd\ *vb* **abode** \-'bōd\ *or* **abid·ed; abid·ing** [ME *abiden,* fr. OE *ābīdan,* fr. *ā-,* perfective prefix + *bīdan* to bide; akin to OHG *ir-,* perfective prefix] *vt* **1** *archaic* **:** to wait for **:** AWAIT **2 a :** to endure without yielding **:** WITHSTAND **b :** to bear patiently **:** TOLERATE **3 :** to accept without objection ~ *vi* **1 :** to remain stable or fixed in a state **2 :** to continue in a place **:** SOJOURN **syn** see BEAR, CONTINUE, STAY — **abid·er** *n* — **abide by 1 :** to conform to **2 :** to acquiesce in

abid·ing *adj* **:** ENDURING, PERMANENT

ab·i·gail \'ab-ə-,gāl\ *n* [*Abigail,* servant in *The Scornful Lady,* a play by Francis Beaumont & John Fletcher] **:** a lady's waiting maid

abil·i·ty \ə-'bil-ət-ē\ *n* [ME *abilite,* fr. MF *habilité,* fr. L *habilitat-, habilitas,* fr. *habilis* apt, skillful — more at ABLE] **1 a :** the quality or state of being able; *esp* **:** physical, mental, or legal power to perform **b :** competence in doing **:** SKILL **2 :** natural talent or acquired proficiency **:** APTITUDE

-abil·i·ty *also* **-ibil·i·ty** \ə-'bil-ət-ē\ *n suffix* [ME *-abilite, -ibilite,* fr. MF *-abilité, -ibilité,* fr. L *-abilitas, -ibilitas,* fr. *-abilis, -ibilis* -able + *-tas* -ty] **:** capacity, fitness, or tendency to act or be acted on in a (specified) way ⟨recuper*ability*⟩

ab in·i·tio \,ab-ə-'nish-ē-,ō\ *adv* [L] **:** from the beginning

ab in·tra \a-'bin-trə\ *adv* [NL] **:** from within

abio·gen·e·sis \,ā-,bī-ō-'jen-ə-səs\ *n, pl* **abio·gen·e·ses** \-'jen-ə-,sēz\ [NL, fr. 2*a-* + *bio-* + L *genesis*] **:** the origination of living from lifeless matter — **abio·ge·net·ic** \-ō-jə-'net-ik\ *adj* — **abio·ge·net·i·cal** \-i-kəl\ *adj* — **abio·ge·net·i·cal·ly** \-k(ə-)lē\ *adv* — **abi·og·e·nist** \,ā-(,)bī-'äj-ə-nəst\ *n*

ab·ject \'ab-,jekt, ab-'\ *adj* [ME, fr. L *abjectus,* fr. pp. of *abicere* to cast off, fr. *ab-* + *jacere* to throw — more at JET] **1 :** sunk to a low condition **2 a :** cast down in spirit **:** SERVILE **b :** showing utter resignation **:** HOPELESS **syn** see MEAN — **ab·jec·tion** \ab-'jek-shən\ *n* — **ab·ject·ly** \'ab-,jek-(t)lē, ab-'\ *adv* — **ab·ject·ness** \-,jek(t)-nəs, -'jek(t)-\ *n*

ab·ju·ra·tion \,ab-jə-'rā-shən\ *n* **1 :** the act or process of abjuring **2 :** an oath of abjuring

ab·jure \ab-'jü(ə)r\ *vt* [ME *abjuren,* fr. MF or L; MF *abjurer,* fr. L *abjurare,* fr. *ab-* + *jurare* to swear — more at JURY] **1 a :** to renounce upon oath **b :** to reject solemnly **:** RECANT **2 :** to abstain from **:** AVOID — **ab·jur·er** *n*

syn ABJURE, RENOUNCE, FORSWEAR, RECANT, RETRACT mean to withdraw a vow or given word. ABJURE implies a firm and final rejecting or abandoning often made under oath; RENOUNCE often equals ABJURE but may carry the meaning of disclaim or disown; FORSWEAR may add to ABJURE an implication of perjury or betrayal; RECANT stresses the withdrawing or denying of something professed or taught; RETRACT applies to the withdrawing of a promise, an offer, or an accusation

ab·late \a-'blāt\ *vb* [L *ablatus* (suppletive pp. of *auferre* to remove, fr. *au-* away + *ferre* to carry), fr. *ab-* + *latus,* suppletive pp. of *ferre* — more at UKASE, BEAR, TOLERATE] *vt* **:** to remove by cutting or by erosion, melting, evaporation, or vaporization ~ *vi* **:** to become ablated

ab·la·tion \a-'blā-shən\ *n* **:** the process of ablating; *specif* **:** surgical removal

1ab·la·tive \'ab-lət-iv\ *adj* **:** of, relating to, or constituting a grammatical case expressing typically the relations of separation and source and also frequently such relations as cause or instrument — **ablative** *n*

2ab·la·tive \a-'blāt-iv\ *adj* **:** tending to ablate

ablative absolute \,ab-lət-iv-\ *n* **:** a construction in Latin in which a noun or pronoun and its adjunct both in the ablative case form together an adverbial phrase expressing generally the time, cause, or an attendant circumstance of an action

ab·laut \'äp-,lau̇t, 'ab-\ *n* [G, fr. *ab* away from + *laut* sound] **:** a systematic variation of vowels in the same root or affix or in related roots or affixes esp. in the Indo-European languages that is usu. paralleled by differences in use or meaning (as in *sing, sang, sung, song*)

ablaze \ə-'blāz\ *adj* **1 :** being on fire **2 :** radiant with light or bright color

able \'ā-bəl\ *adj* **abler** \-b(ə-)lər\ **ablest** \-b(ə-)ləst\ [ME, fr. MF, fr. L *habilis* apt, fr. *habēre* to have — more at HABIT] **1 a :** having sufficient power, skill, or resources to accomplish an object **b :** susceptible to action or treatment **2 :** marked by intelligence, knowledge, skill, or competence

syn ABLE, CAPABLE, COMPETENT, QUALIFIED mean having power or fitness for work. ABLE suggests ability above the average as revealed in actual performance; CAPABLE stresses the having of qualities fitting one for work but does not imply outstanding ability; COMPETENT and QUALIFIED imply having the experience or training for adequate performance

-able *also* **-ible** \ə-bəl\ *adj suffix* [ME, fr. OF, fr. L *-abilis, -ibilis,* fr. *-a-, -i-,* verb stem vowels + *-bilis* capable or worthy of] **1 :** capable of, fit for, or worthy of (being so acted upon or toward) — chiefly in adjectives derived from verbs ⟨break*able*⟩ ⟨collect*ible*⟩ **2 :** tending, given, or liable to ⟨knowledge*able*⟩ ⟨perish*able*⟩

Able — a communications code word for the letter *a*

able–bod·ied \,ā-bəl-'bäd-ēd\ *adj* **:** having a sound strong body

able–bodied seaman *n* **:** an experienced deck-department seaman qualified to perform routine duties at sea — called also *able seaman*

abloom \ə-'blüm\ *adj* **:** BLOOMING

ab·lu·tion \ə-'blü-shən, a-'blü-\ *n* [ME, fr. MF or L; MF, fr. L *ablution-, ablutio,* fr. *ablutus,* pp. of *abluere* to wash away, fr. *ab-* + *lavere* to wash — more at LYE] **:** the washing of one's body or part of it (as in a religious rite) — **ab·lu·tion·ary** \-shə-,ner-ē\ *adj*

ably \'ā-blē\ *adv* **:** in an able manner

ABM \,ā-(,)bē-'em\ *n* **:** ANTIBALLISTIC MISSILE

ab·ne·gate \'ab-ni-,gāt\ *vt* [back-formation fr. *abnegation*] **1 :** SURRENDER, RELINQUISH **2 :** DENY, RENOUNCE — **ab·ne·ga·tor** \-,gāt-ər\ *n*

ab·ne·ga·tion \,ab-ni-'gā-shən\ *n* [LL *abnegation-, abnegatio,* fr. L *abnegatus,* pp. of *abnegare* to refute, fr. *ab-* + *negare* to deny — more at NEGATE] **:** DENIAL; *esp* **:** SELF-DENIAL

ab·nor·mal \(')ab-'nȯr-məl\ *adj* [F *anormal,* fr. ML *anormalis,* fr. L *a-* + LL *normalis* normal] **:** deviating from the normal or average; *esp* **:** markedly irregular — **ab·nor·mal·ly** \-mə-lē\ *adv*

ab·nor·mal·i·ty \,ab-(,)nȯr-'mal-ət-ē\ *n* **1 :** the quality or state of being abnormal **2 :** something abnormal

1aboard \ə-'bō(ə)rd, -'bȯ(ə)rd\ *adv* **1 :** on, onto, or within a ship, a railway car, or a passenger vehicle **2 :** ALONGSIDE **3 :** on base

2aboard *prep* **:** ON, ONTO, WITHIN ⟨go ~ ship⟩ ⟨~ a plane⟩

abode \ə-'bōd\ *n* [ME *abod,* fr. *abiden* to abide] **1** *obs* **:** WAIT DELAY **2 :** RESIDENCE, SOJOURN **3 :** the place where one abides **:** HOME

abol·ish \ə-'bäl-ish\ *vt* [ME *abolisshen,* fr. MF *aboliss-,* stem of *abolir,* fr. L *abolēre,* prob. back-formation fr. *abolescere* to disappear, fr. *ab-* + *-olescere* (as in *adolescere* to grow up) — more at ADULT] **1 :** to do away with wholly **:** ANNUL **2 :** to destroy completely — **abol·ish·able** \-ə-bəl\ *adj* — **abol·ish·er** *n* — **abol·ish·ment** \-mənt\ *n*

syn ABOLISH, ANNIHILATE, EXTINGUISH mean to make nonexistent. ABOLISH implies a putting an end chiefly to things that are the outgrowth of law, custom, and conditions of existence; ANNIHILATE may apply to the wiping out of existence of anything material or immaterial; EXTINGUISH implies complete destruction and suggests a gradual means such as stifling, choking, smothering

ab·o·li·tion \,ab-ə-'lish-ən\ *n* [MF, fr. L *abolition-, abolitio,* fr. *abolitus,* pp. of *abolēre*] **1 :** the act of abolishing **:** the state of being abolished **:** ABROGATION; *specif* **:** the abolishing of slavery — **ab·o·li·tion·ary** \-'lish-ə-,ner-ē\ *adj*

ab·o·li·tion·ism \,ab-ə-'lish-ə-,niz-əm\ *n* **:** principles or measures fostering abolition esp. of slavery — **ab·o·li·tion·ist** \-'lish-(ə-)nəst\ *n or adj*

ab·oma·sal \ˌab-ō-ˈmā-səl\ *adj* **:** of or relating to the abomasum

ab·oma·sum \-səm\ *n, pl* **ab·oma·sa** \-sə\ [NL, fr. L *ab-* + *omasum* tripe of a bullock] **:** the fourth or true digestive stomach of a ruminant

A–bomb \ˈā-ˌbäm\ *n* **:** ATOM BOMB — **A–bomb** *vb*

abom·i·na·ble \ə-ˈbäm-(ə-)nə-bəl\ *adj* **1 :** worthy of or causing loathing or hatred **:** DETESTABLE **2 :** quite disagreeable or unpleasant **syn** see HATEFUL — **abom·i·na·bly** \-blē\ *adv*

abominable snow·man \-ˈsnō-mən, -ˌman\ *n, often cap A&S* **:** an animal reported as existing in the high Himalayas and usu. thought to be a bear

abom·i·nate \ə-ˈbäm-ə-ˌnāt\ *vt* [L *abominatus*, pp. of *abominari*, lit., to deprecate as an ill omen, fr. *ab-* + *omin-, omen* omen] **:** to hate or loathe intensely **:** ABHOR **syn** see HATE — **abom·i·na·tor** \-ˌnāt-ər\ *n*

abom·i·na·tion \ə-ˌbäm-ə-ˈnā-shən\ *n* **1 :** something abominable **2 :** extreme disgust and hatred **:** LOATHING

ab·oral \(ˈ)a-ˈbōr-əl, -ˈbȯr-\ *adj* **:** opposite to or away from the mouth — **ab·oral·ly** \-ə-lē\ *adv*

ab·orig·i·nal \ˌab-ə-ˈrij-nəl, -ən-ᵊl\ *adj* **1 :** INDIGENOUS, PRIMITIVE **2 :** of or relating to aborigines **syn** see NATIVE — **ab·orig·i·nal·ly** \-ē\ *adv*

ab·orig·i·ne \ˌab-ə-ˈrij-ə-(ˌ)nē\ *n* [L *aborigines*, pl., fr. *ab origine* from the beginning] **1 :** an indigenous inhabitant esp. as contrasted with an invading or colonizing people **2** *pl* **:** the original fauna and flora of a geographical area

aborn·ing \ə-ˈbȯ(ə)r-niŋ\ *adv* [¹*a-* + E dial. *borning* (birth)] **:** while being born or produced

¹**abort** \ə-ˈbȯ(ə)rt\ *vb* [L *abortare*, fr. *abortus*, pp. of *aboriri* to miscarry, fr. *ab-* + *oriri* to rise, be born — more at RISE] *vi* **1 :** to bring forth premature or stillborn offspring **2 :** to become checked in development so as to remain rudimentary or to shrink away ~ *vt* **1 :** to give birth to prematurely; *also* **:** to terminate the pregnancy of before term **2 :** to terminate prematurely ⟨~ a disease⟩

²**abort** *n* **:** the premature termination of an action, procedure, or mission relating to a rocket or spacecraft ⟨a launch ~⟩

abor·ti·fa·cient \ə-ˌbȯrt-ə-ˈfā-shənt\ *adj* **:** inducing abortion — **abortifacient** *n*

abor·tion \ə-ˈbȯr-shən\ *n* **1 :** the expulsion of a nonviable fetus: as **a :** spontaneous expulsion of a human fetus during the first 12 weeks of gestation — compare MISCARRIAGE **b :** illegal abortion **2 :** MONSTROSITY **3 a :** arrest of development (as of a part or process) resulting in imperfection **b :** a result of such arrest

abor·tion·ist \-sh(ə-)nəst\ *n* **:** a producer of illegal abortions

abor·tive \ə-ˈbȯrt-iv\ *adj* **1** *obs* **:** prematurely born **2 :** FRUITLESS, UNSUCCESSFUL **3 :** imperfectly formed or developed **4 :** tending to abort — **abor·tive·ly** *adv* — **abor·tive·ness** *n*

ABO system \ˌā-(ˌ)bē-ˈō-\ *n* **:** the basic system of antigens of human blood behaving in heredity as an allelic unit to produce any of the four blood groups A, B, AB, or O — called also *ABO group*

abound \ə-ˈbau̇nd\ *vi* [ME *abounden*, fr. MF *abonder*, fr. L *abundare*, fr. *ab-* + *unda* wave — more at WATER] **1 :** to be present in large numbers or in great quantity **2 :** to become copiously supplied ⟨stream ~*ing* in fish⟩

¹**about** \ə-ˈbau̇t\ *adv* [ME, fr. OE *abūtan*, fr. ¹*a-* + *būtan* outside — more at BUT] **1 :** on all sides **:** AROUND **2 a :** in rotation **b :** around the outside **3 a :** APPROXIMATELY **b :** ALMOST ⟨~ starved⟩ **4 :** here and there **5 :** in the vicinity **:** NEAR **6 :** in succession **:** ALTERNATELY ⟨turn ~ is fair play⟩ **7 a :** in the opposite direction ⟨face ~⟩ **b :** in reverse order ⟨the other way ~⟩

²**about** *prep* **1 :** on every side of **:** AROUND **2 a :** in the immediate neighborhood of **:** NEAR **b :** on or near the person of **c :** in the makeup of ⟨a mature wisdom ~ him⟩ **d :** at the command of ⟨has his wits ~ him⟩ **3 a :** engaged in **b :** on the verge of ⟨~ to join the army⟩ **4 :** with regard to **:** CONCERNING **5 :** over or in different parts of

³**about** *adj* **1 :** moving from place to place; *specif* **:** out of bed **2 :** AROUND 2

about–face \ə-ˈbau̇t-ˈfās\ *n* [fr. the imper. phrase *about face*] **1 :** a reversal of direction **2 :** a reversal of attitude or point of view — **about–face** *vi*

about ship *vi* [fr. the imper. phrase *about ship*] **:** TACK

¹**above** \ə-ˈbəv\ *adv* [ME, fr. OE *abufan*, fr. *a-* + *bufan* above, fr. *be-* + *ufan* above; akin to OE *ofer* over] **1 a :** in the sky **:** OVERHEAD **b :** in or to heaven **2 a :** in or to a higher place **b :** higher on the same page or on a preceding page **c :** UPSTAIRS **3 :** in or to a higher rank or number **4** *archaic* **:** in addition **:** BESIDES

²**above** *prep* **1 :** in or to a higher place than **:** OVER **2 a :** superior to (as in rank, quality, or degree) **b :** out of reach of **c :** in preference to **d :** too proud or honorable to stoop to **3 :** exceeding in number, quantity, or size **:** more than

³**above** *n* **:** something that is above

⁴**above** *adj* **:** written or discussed higher on the same page or on a preceding page

¹**above·board** \ə-ˈbəv-ˌbō(ə)rd, -ˌbȯ(ə)rd\ *adv* [fr. the difficulty of cheating at cards when the hands are above the table] **:** in a straightforward manner **:** OPENLY

²**aboveboard** *adj* **:** being without concealment or deception

above·ground \-ˌgrau̇nd\ *adj* **:** located on or above the surface of the ground

ab ovo \a-ˈbō-(ˌ)vō\ *adv* [L, lit., fr. the egg] **:** from the beginning

ab·ra·ca·dab·ra \ˌab-rə-kə-ˈdab-rə\ *n* [LL] **1 :** a magical charm or incantation used to ward off calamity **2 :** unintelligible language

abrad·ant \ə-ˈbrād-ᵊnt\ *n* **:** ABRASIVE

abrade \ə-ˈbrād\ *vb* [L *abradere* to scrape off, fr. *ab-* + *radere* to scrape — more at RAT] *vt* **1 a :** to rub or wear away esp. by friction **:** ERODE **b :** to irritate or roughen by rubbing **2 :** to wear down in spirit **:** IRRITATE ~ *vi* **:** to undergo abrasion — **abrad·er** *n*

Abra·ham \ˈā-brə-ˌham\ *n* [LL, fr. Gk *Abraam*, fr. Heb *ʼAbhrāhām*] **:** an Old Testament patriarch and founder of the Hebrew people

abran·chi·ate \(ˈ)ā-ˈbraŋ-kē-ət\ *adj* **:** lacking gills

abra·sion \ə-ˈbrā-zhən\ *n* [ML *abrasion-, abrasio*, fr. L *abrasus*, pp. of *abradere*] **1 :** a wearing, grinding, or rubbing away by friction **2 :** an abraded area of the skin or mucous membrane

¹**abra·sive** \ə-ˈbrā-siv, -ziv\ *adj* **:** tending to abrade

²**abrasive** *n* **:** a substance used for abrading

ab·re·act \ˌab-rē-ˈakt\ *vt* [part trans. of G *abreagieren*, fr. *ab* away from + *reagieren* to react] **:** to release (a repressed or forgotten emotion) by or as if by verbalization in psychoanalysis — **ab·re·ac·tion** \-ˈak-shən\ *n*

abreast \ə-ˈbrest\ *adv (or adj)* **1 :** beside one another with bodies in line **2 :** up to a particular standard or level esp. of knowledge of recent developments

abridge \ə-ˈbrij\ *vt* [ME *abregen*, fr. MF *abregier*, fr. LL *abbreviare*, fr. L *ad-* + *brevis* short — more at BRIEF] **1 a** *archaic* **:** DEPRIVE **b :** DIMINISH, CURTAIL **2 :** to shorten in duration or extent **3 :** to shorten by omission of words without sacrifice of sense **:** CONDENSE **syn** see SHORTEN — **abridg·er** *n*

abridg·ment *or* **abridge·ment** \ə-ˈbrij-mənt\ *n* **1 a :** the action of abridging **b :** the state of being abridged **2 :** a shortened form of a work retaining the general sense and unity of the original

syn ABRIDGMENT, ABSTRACT, SYNOPSIS, CONSPECTUS, EPITOME mean a condensed treatment. ABRIDGMENT suggests reduction in compass with retention of relative completeness; ABSTRACT applies to a summary of points of a treatise, document, or proposed treatment and usu. has no independent worth; SYNOPSIS implies a skeletal presentation of an argument or a narrative suitable for rapid examination; CONSPECTUS implies a quick overall view of a large detailed subject; EPITOME suggests the briefest possible presentation of a complex whole that still has independent value

abroach \ə-ˈbrōch\ *adj* **1 :** BROACHED, TAPPED **2 :** being in action or agitation **:** ASTIR

abroad \ə-ˈbrȯd\ *adv (or adj)* **1 :** over a wide area **:** WIDELY **2 :** outside of an implied place; *esp* **:** in the open **3 :** beyond the boundaries of a country **4 :** in wide circulation **:** ABOUT **5 :** wide of the mark **:** ASTRAY

ab·ro·gate \ˈab-rə-ˌgāt\ *vt* [L *abrogatus*, pp. of *abrogare*, fr. *ab-* + *rogare* to ask, propose a law — more at RIGHT] **1 :** to abolish by authoritative action **:** ANNUL **2 :** to do away with **syn** see NULLIFY — **ab·ro·ga·tion** \ˌab-rə-ˈgā-shən\ *n*

abrupt \ə-ˈbrəpt\ *adj* [L *abruptus*, fr. pp. of *abrumpere* to break off, fr. *ab-* + *rumpere* to break — more at REAVE] **1 :** broken off; *also* **:** suddenly terminating as if cut or broken off ⟨~ plant filaments⟩ **2 a :** SUDDEN, UNEXPECTED **b :** unceremoniously curt ⟨~ manner⟩ **c :** marked by sudden changes in subject matter **:** DISCONNECTED **3 :** rising or dropping sharply **:** PRECIPITOUS **syn** see PRECIPITATE, STEEP — **abrupt·ly** \ə-ˈbrəp-(t)lē\ *adv* — **abrupt·ness** \ə-ˈbrəp(t)-nəs\ *n*

abrup·tion \ə-ˈbrəp-shən\ *n* **:** a sudden breaking off or away

ab·scess \ˈab-ˌses\ *n* [L *abscessus*, lit., act of going away, fr. *abscessus*, pp. of *abscedere* to go away, fr. *abs-, ab-* + *cedere* to go — more at CEDE] **:** a localized collection of pus surrounded by inflamed tissue — **ab·scessed** \-ˌsest\ *adj*

ab·scise \ab-ˈsīz\ *vb* [L *abscisus*, pp. of *abscidere*, fr. *abs-* + *caedere* to cut — more at CONCISE] *vt* **:** to cut off by abscission ~ *vi* **:** to separate by abscission

ab·scis·sa \ab-ˈsis-ə\ *n* [NL, fr. L, fem. of *abscissus*, pp. of *abscindere* to cut off, fr. *ab-* + *scindere* to cut — more at SHED] **:** the horizontal coordinate of a point in a plane Cartesian coordinate system obtained by measuring parallel to the x-axis

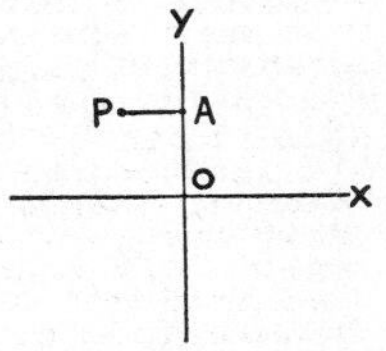

AP abscissa of point *P*

ab·scis·sion \ab-ˈsizh-ən\ *n* [L *abscission-, abscissio*, fr. *abscissus*] **1 :** the act or process of cutting off **:** REMOVAL **2 :** the natural separation of flowers, fruit, or leaves from plants at a special separation layer

ab·scond \ab-ˈskänd\ *vi* [L *abscondere* to hide away, fr. *abs-* + *condere* to store up, conceal — more at CONDIMENT] **:** to depart secretly and hide oneself — **ab·scond·er** *n*

ab·sence \ˈab-sən(t)s\ *n* **1 :** the state of being absent **2 :** WANT, LACK **3 :** inattention to things present

¹**ab·sent** \ˈab-sənt\ *adj* [ME, fr. MF, fr. L *absent-, absens*, prp. of *abesse* to be absent, fr. *ab-* + *esse* to be — more at IS] **1 :** not present or attending **:** MISSING **2 :** not existing **:** LACKING **3 :** INATTENTIVE — **ab·sent·ly** *adv*

²**ab·sent** \ab-ˈsent\ *vt* **:** to keep (oneself) away

ab·sen·tee \ˌab-sən-ˈtē\ *n* **:** one that is absent or that absents himself; *specif* **:** a proprietor that lives away from his estate or business — **absentee** *adj*

absentee ballot *n* **:** a ballot by which an absent voter may vote in advance by mail

ab·sen·tee·ism \ˌab-sən-ˈtē-ˌiz-əm\ *n* **1 :** protracted absence of an owner from his property **2 :** chronic absence from work or other duty

ab·sent·mind·ed \ˌab-sənt-ˈmīn-dəd\ *adj* **:** lost in thought and unaware of one's surroundings or action; *also* **:** given to absence of mind — **ab·sent·mind·ed·ly** *adv* — **ab·sent·mind·ed·ness** *n*

absent voter *n* **:** a qualified voter unavoidably not present to vote in person at the place where he is registered

ab·sinthe *or* **ab·sinth** \ˈab-ˌsin(t)th\ *n* [F *absinthe*, fr. L *absinthium*, fr. Gk *apsinthion*] **1 :** WORMWOOD 1; *esp* **:** a common European wormwood (*Artemisia absinthium*) **2 :** a green liqueur flavored with wormwood or a substitute, anise, and other aromatics

ab·sit omen \ˌab-sət-ˈō-mən\ *interj* [L, may (evil) omen be absent] — used as a mild invocation

ab·so·lute \ˈab-sə-ˌlüt\ *adj* [ME *absolut*, fr. L *absolutus*, fr. pp. of *absolvere*] **1 a :** free from imperfection **:** PERFECT **b :** free from mixture **:** PURE ⟨~ alcohol⟩ **2 :** being, governed by, or characteristic of a ruler or authority completely free from constitutional or other restraint **3 a :** standing apart from a normal or usual syntactical relation with other words or sentence elements ⟨the ~ construction *this being the case* in the sentence "this being the case, let us go"⟩ **b** *of an adjective or possessive pronoun* **:** standing alone without a modified substantive ⟨*blind* in "help the blind" and *ours* in "your work and ours" are ~⟩ **c** *of a verb* **:** having no object in the particular construction under consideration though normally transitive ⟨*kill* in "if looks could kill" is an ~ verb⟩ **4 :** having no restriction, exception, or qualification ⟨an ~ requirement⟩ ⟨~ freedom⟩ **5 :** INDUBITABLE, UNQUESTIONABLE ⟨~ proof⟩ **6 a :** independent of arbitrary standards of measurement **b :** relating to or derived in the simplest manner from the fundamental units of length, mass, and time ⟨~ electric units⟩ **c :** relating to

ə abut; ᵊ kitten; ər further; a back; ā bake; ä cot, cart; au̇ out; ch chin; e less; ē easy; g gift; i trip; ī life
j joke; ŋ sing; ō flow; ȯ flaw; ȯi coin; th thin; t͟h this; ü loot; u̇ foot; y yet; yü few; yu̇ furious; zh vision

the absolute-temperature scale ⟨10° ∼⟩ **7 :** FUNDAMENTAL, ULTIMATE **8 :** perfectly embodying the nature of a thing **9 :** comprising an artistically self-sufficient composition having no external reference ⟨∼ music⟩ **10 :** measuring or representing the distance from an aircraft to the ground or water beneath — **absolute** *n* — **ab·so·lute·ly** \'ab-sə-,lüt-lē, ,ab-sə-'\ *adv* — **ab·so·lute·ness** \-,lüt-nəs, -'lüt-\ *n*

absolute ceiling *n* **:** the maximum height above sea level at which a particular airplane can maintain horizontal flight under standard air conditions

absolute pitch *n* **1 :** the position of a tone in a standard scale independently determined by its rate of vibration **2 :** the ability to sing or name a note asked for or heard

absolute scale *n* **:** a temperature scale based on absolute zero

absolute temperature *n* **:** temperature measured on the absolute scale

absolute value *n* **1 :** the numerical value of a real number irrespective of sign **2 :** the positive square root of the sum of the squares of the real and imaginary parts of a complex number

absolute zero *n* **:** a hypothetical temperature characterized by complete absence of heat and equivalent to approximately −273.16°C or −459.69°F

ab·so·lu·tion \,ab-sə-'lü-shən\ *n* **:** the act of absolving; *specif* **:** a remission of sins pronounced by a priest in the sacrament of penance

ab·so·lut·ism \'ab-sə-,lüt-,iz-əm\ *n* **1 a :** a political theory that absolute power should be vested in one or more rulers **b :** government by an absolute ruler or authority **2 :** advocacy of a rule by absolute standards or principles — **ab·so·lut·ist** \-,lüt-əst\ *n or adj* — **ab·so·lu·tis·tic** \,ab-sə-,lü-'tis-tik\ *adj*

ab·solve \əb-'zälv, -'sälv, -'zȯlv, -'sȯlv\ *vt* [ME *absolven*, fr. L *absolvere*, fr. *ab-* + *solvere* to loosen — more at SOLVE] **1 :** to set free from an obligation or the consequences of guilt **2 :** to remit (a sin) by absolution **syn** see EXCULPATE — **ab·solv·er** *n*

ab·sorb \əb-'sȯ(ə)rb, -'zȯ(ə)rb\ *vt* [MF *absorber*, fr. L *absorbēre*, fr. *ab-* + *sorbēre* to suck up; akin to Gk *rhophein* to suck up] **1 :** ASSIMILATE, INCORPORATE **2 :** to suck or take up or in ⟨a sponge ∼*s* water⟩ **3 :** to engage or engross wholly ⟨∼*ed* in thought⟩ **4 :** to receive without recoil or echo ⟨provided with a sound-*absorbing* surface⟩ **5 :** to take over (a cost) — **ab·sorb·abil·i·ty** \əb-,sȯr-bə-'bil-ət-ē, -,zȯr-\ *n* — **ab·sorb·able** \əb-'sȯr-bə-bəl, -'zȯr-\ *adj* — **ab·sorb·er** *n*

syn ABSORB, IMBIBE, ASSIMILATE mean to take something in so as to become imbued with it. ABSORB may connote a loss of identity in what is taken in or an enrichment of what takes in; IMBIBE implies a drinking in with noticeable or profound effect; ASSIMILATE stresses an incorporation into the substance of the body or mind

ab·sor·ben·cy \əb-'sȯr-bən-sē, -'zȯr-\ *n* **:** the quality or state of being absorbent

ab·sor·bent \-bənt\ *adj* [L *absorbent-*, *absorbens*, prp. of *absorbēre*] **:** having power, capacity, or tendency to absorb ⟨∼ cotton⟩ — **absorbent** *n*

ab·sorb·ing *adj* **:** fully taking attention **:** ENGROSSING — **ab·sorb·ing·ly** \-biŋ-lē\ *adv*

ab·sorp·tion \əb-'sȯrp-shən, -'zȯrp-\ *n* [F & L; F, fr. L *absorption-*, *absorptio*, fr. *absorptus*, pp. of *absorbēre*] **1 a :** the process of absorbing or of being absorbed — compare ADSORPTION **b :** interception esp. of light or sound waves **2 :** entire occupation of the mind — **ab·sorp·tive** \-'sȯrp-tiv, -'zȯrp-\ *adj*

ab·stain \əb-'stān\ *vi* [ME *absteinen*, fr. MF *abstenir*, fr. L *abstinēre*, fr. *abs-*, *ab-* + *tenēre* to hold — more at THIN] **:** to refrain voluntarily from an action **syn** see REFRAIN — **ab·stain·er** *n*

ab·ste·mi·ous \ab-'stē-mē-əs\ *adj* [L *abstemius*, fr. *abs-* + *temetum* mead; akin to L *tenebrae* darkness — more at TEMERITY] **1 :** sparing esp. in eating and drinking **2 :** sparingly used or indulged in ⟨∼ diet⟩ — **ab·ste·mi·ous·ly** *adv*

ab·sten·tion \əb-'sten-chən\ *n* [LL *abstention-*, *abstentio*, fr. L *abstentus*, pp. of *abstinēre*] **:** the act or practice of abstaining — **ab·sten·tious** \-chəs\ *adj*

ab·sti·nence \'ab-stə-nən(t)s\ *n* [ME, fr. OF, fr. L *abstinentia*, fr. *abstinent-*, *abstinens*, prp. of *abstinēre*] **1 :** voluntary forbearance esp. from indulgence of appetite or from eating some foods **:** ABSTENTION **2 :** habitual abstaining from intoxicating beverages — **ab·sti·nent** \-nənt\ *adj* — **ab·sti·nent·ly** *adv*

[1]**ab·stract** \ab-'strakt, 'ab-,\ *adj* [ML *abstractus*, fr. L, pp. of *abstrahere* to draw away, fr. *abs-*, *ab-* + *trahere* to draw — more at DRAW] **1 a :** disassociated from any specific instance ⟨∼ entity⟩ **b :** difficult to understand **:** ABSTRUSE ⟨∼ problems⟩ **c :** IDEAL ⟨∼ justice⟩ **d :** insufficiently factual **:** FORMAL ⟨possessed only an ∼ right⟩ **2 :** expressing a quality apart from an object ⟨*honesty*, *whiteness*, *triangularity* are ∼ words⟩ **3 a :** dealing with a subject in its abstract aspects **:** THEORETICAL **b :** IMPERSONAL, DETACHED **4 :** having only intrinsic form with little or no attempt at pictorial representation ⟨∼ painting⟩ — **ab·stract·ly** \ab-'strak-(t)lē, 'ab-,\ *adv* — **ab·stract·ness** \ab-'strak(t)-nəs, 'ab-,\ *n*

[2]**ab·stract** \'ab-,strakt, *in sense 2 also* ab-'\ *n* [ME, fr. L *abstractus*] **1 :** SUMMARY, EPITOME **2 :** an abstract thing or state **3 :** ABSTRACTION 4 **syn** see ABRIDGMENT

[3]**ab·stract** \ab-'strakt, 'ab-,, *in sense 3 usu* 'ab-,\ *vt* **1 :** REMOVE, SEPARATE **2 :** to consider apart from application to a particular instance **3 :** to make an abstract of **:** SUMMARIZE **4 :** to draw away the attention of **5 :** STEAL, PURLOIN — **ab·strac·tor** *or* **ab·stract·er** *n*

ab·stract·ed \ab-'strak-təd, 'ab-,\ *adj* **:** PREOCCUPIED, ABSENT-MINDED — **ab·stract·ed·ly** *adv* — **ab·stract·ed·ness** *n*

abstract expressionism *n* **:** the theory or practice of freely creating abstractions characterized by sinuous linearity, amorphous shape, and highly decorative surface

ab·strac·tion \ab-'strak-shən\ *n* **1 a :** the act or process of abstracting **:** the state of being abstracted **b (1) :** an abstract idea or term **(2) :** a visionary idea **2 :** absence of mind **3 :** abstract quality or character **4 :** an abstract composition or creation in art

ab·strac·tion·ism \-shə-,niz-əm\ *n* **1 :** the creation of abstractions in art **2 :** the principles or ideals of abstract art — **ab·strac·tion·ist** \-sh(ə-)nəst\ *adj or n*

ab·strac·tive \ab-'strak-tiv\ *adj* **:** relating to, characterized by, or derived by abstraction

ab·strict \ab-'strikt\ *vt* [*ab-* + L *strictus*, pp. of *stringere* to draw tight — more at STRAIN] **:** to cut off in or as if in abstriction

ab·stric·tion \ab-'strik-shən\ *n* **:** the formation of spores by the cutting off of portions of the sporophore through the growth of septa

ab·struse \əb-'strüs, ab-\ *adj* [L *abstrusus*, fr. pp. of *abstrudere* to conceal, fr. *abs-*, *ab-* + *trudere* to push — more at THREAT] **:** difficult to comprehend **:** RECONDITE — **ab·struse·ly** *adv* — **ab·struse·ness** *n*

ab·surd \əb-'sərd, -'zərd\ *adj* [MF *absurde*, fr. L *absurdus*, fr. *ab-* + *surdus* deaf, stupid — more at SURD] **:** ridiculously unreasonable, unsound, or incongruous — **absurd** *n* — **ab·sur·di·ty** \əb-'sərd-ət-ē, -'zərd-\ *n* — **ab·surd·ly** *adv* — **ab·surd·ness** *n*

abu·lia \ā-'b(y)ü-lē-ə\ *n* [NL, fr. [2]*a-* + Gk *boulē* will] **:** abnormal lack of ability to act or to make decisions — **abu·lic** \-lik\ *adj*

abun·dance \ə-'bən-dən(t)s\ *n* **1 :** an ample or overflowing quantity **:** PROFUSION **2 :** AFFLUENCE, WEALTH **3 :** relative degree of plentifulness

abun·dant \ə-'bən-dənt\ *adj* [ME, fr. MF, fr. L *abundant-*, *abundans*, prp. of *abundare* to abound] **:** existing in or possessing abundance **:** ABOUNDING **syn** see PLENTIFUL — **abun·dant·ly** *adv*

abundant year *n* **:** PERFECT YEAR

[1]**abuse** \ə-'byüz\ *vt* [ME *abusen*, fr. MF *abuser*, fr. L *abusus*, pp. of *abuti*, fr. *ab-* + *uti* to use — more at USE] **1 :** to attack in words **:** REVILE **2** *obs* **:** DECEIVE **3 :** to put to a wrong or improper use **4 :** to use so as to injure or damage **:** MALTREAT — **abus·er** *n*

[2]**abuse** \ə-'byüs\ *n* **1 :** a corrupt practice or custom **2 :** improper use or treatment **:** MISUSE **3** *obs* **:** a deceitful act **:** DECEPTION **4 :** abusive language **5 :** physical maltreatment

syn VITUPERATION, INVECTIVE, OBLOQUY, SCURRILITY, BILLINGSGATE: ABUSE stresses harshness and unfairness of verbal attack; VITUPERATION implies fluent and sustained abuse; INVECTIVE implies fully as much vehemence but usu. suggests logical presentation or cogent expression and public attack; OBLOQUY suggests defamation and consequent shame and disgrace; SCURRILITY implies viciousness of attack and coarseness or foulness of language; BILLINGSGATE implies practiced fluency and variety of profane or obscene abuse

abu·sive \ə-'byü-siv, -ziv\ *adj* **1 :** wrongly used **:** PERVERTED **2 a :** characterized by or serving for verbal abuse **b :** physically injurious — **abu·sive·ly** *adv* — **abu·sive·ness** *n*

abut \ə-'bət\ *vb* **abut·ted; abut·ting** [ME *abutten*, partly fr. OF *aboter* to border on, fr. *a-* (fr. L *ad-*) + *bout* blow, end, fr. *boter* to strike; partly fr. OF *abuter* to come to an end, fr. *a-* + *but* end, aim — more at [1]BUTT, [3]BUTT] *vi* **1 :** to touch along a border or with a projecting part ⟨land ∼*s* on the road⟩ **2 a :** to terminate at a point of contact **b :** to lean for support ∼ *vt* **:** to border on **:** TOUCH — **abut·ter** *n*

abu·ti·lon \ə-'byüt-ᵊl-,än\ *n* [NL, genus name, fr. Ar *awbūtīlūn* abutilon] **:** any of a genus (*Abutilon*) of plants of the mallow family with usu. lobed leaves and showy solitary bell-shaped flowers

abut·ment \ə-'bət-mənt\ *n* **:** the action or place of abutting: as **a :** the part of a structure that directly receives thrust or pressure (as of an arch) **b :** an anchorage for the cables of a suspension bridge or aerial railway

abut·tals \ə-'bət-ᵊlz\ *n pl* **:** the boundaries of lands with respect to other contiguous lands or highways by which they are bounded

abut·ting *adj* **:** ADJOINING, BORDERING **syn** see ADJACENT

aby *or* **abye** \ə-'bī\ *vt* [ME *abien*, fr. OE *ābycgan*, fr. *ā-* + *bycgan* to buy — more at ABIDE, BUY] *archaic* **:** to suffer a penalty for

abysm \ə-'biz-əm\ *n* [ME *abime*, fr. OF *abisme*, modif. of LL *abyssus*] **:** ABYSS ⟨the dark backward and ∼ of time—Shak.⟩

abys·mal \ə-'biz-məl\ *adj* **1 a :** having the character of an abyss **:** BOTTOMLESS **b :** immeasurably hopeless or wretched **:** UNENDING **2 :** ABYSSAL **syn** see DEEP — **abys·mal·ly** \-mə-lē\ *adv*

abyss \ə-'bis\ *n* [ME *abissus*, fr. LL *abyssus*, fr. Gk *abyssos*, fr. *abyssos* bottomless, fr. *a-* + *byssos* depth; akin to Gk *bathys* deep — more at BATHY-] **1 :** the bottomless gulf, pit, or chaos of the old cosmogonies **2 a :** an immeasurably deep gulf or great space **b :** intellectual or spiritual profundity; *also* **:** vast moral depravity

abys·sal \ə-'bis-əl\ *adj* **1 :** UNFATHOMABLE **2 :** of or relating to the bottom waters of the ocean depths

Ab·ys·sin·i·an cat \,ab-ə-,sin-ē-ən-, -,sin-yən-\ *n* [*Abyssinia*, kingdom in Africa] **:** any of a breed of small slender cats of African origin with short brownish hair ticked with darker color

ac- — see AD-

aca·cia \ə-'kā-shə\ *n* [NL, genus name, fr. L, acacia tree, fr. Gk *akakia* shittah] **1 :** any of a genus (*Acacia*) of woody leguminous plants of warm regions having the leaves pinnate or reduced to phyllodes, having white or yellow flower clusters, and including some that yield gums or tanning extracts **2 :** GUM ARABIC

ac·a·deme \'ak-ə-,dēm\ *n* [irreg. fr. L *academia*] **1 a :** a place of instruction **b :** academic environment **2 :** ACADEMIC; *esp* **:** PEDANT

[1]**ac·a·dem·ic** \,ak-ə-'dem-ik\ *adj* **1 a :** of, relating to, or associated with an academy or school esp. of higher learning ⟨∼ costume⟩ **b :** very learned but inexperienced in the world of practical reality ⟨∼ thinker⟩ **c :** based on formal study at an institution of learning **2 :** of or relating to literary or art rather than technical or professional studies **3 :** conforming to the traditions or rules of a school (as of literature or art) or an official academy **:** CONVENTIONAL **4 a :** theoretical without having an immediate or practical bearing **:** ABSTRACT ⟨an ∼ question⟩ **b :** having no practical or useful significance — **ac·a·dem·i·cal** \-i-kəl\ *adj* — **ac·a·dem·i·cal·ly** \-k(ə-)lē\ *adv*

[2]**academic** *n* **1 :** a member of an institution of learning **2 :** one that is academic in background, outlook, or methods

ac·a·dem·i·cals \,ak-ə-'dem-i-kəlz\ *n pl* **:** conventional academic dress consisting of cap and gown and sometimes hood

ac·a·de·mi·cian \,ak-əd-ə-'mish-ən, ə-,kad-ə-\ *n* **1 a :** a member of an academy for promoting science, art, or literature **b :** a follower of an artistic or philosophical tradition or a promoter of its ideas **2 :** ACADEMIC

ac·a·dem·i·cism \,ak-ə-'dem-ə-,siz-əm\ *also* **acad·e·mism** \ə-'kad-ə-,miz-əm\ *n* **1 :** academic manner, style, or content **:** FORMALISM **2 :** purely speculative thoughts and attitudes

acad·e·my \ə-'kad-ə-mē\ *n, often attrib* [L *academia*, fr. Gk *Akadēmeia*, fr. *Akadēmeia*, gymnasium where Plato taught, fr. *Akadēmos* Attic mythological hero] **1** *cap* **:** the school of philosophy founded by Plato **2 a :** a school above the elementary level; *esp* **:** a private high school **b :** a high school or college in which special subjects or skills are taught **3 :** a society of learned persons united to advance art, science, or literature **4 :** a body of established opinion in a particular field widely accepted as authoritative

ac·a·leph \'ak-ə-,lef\ *n* [deriv. of Gk *akalēphē* nettle] **:** any of a group (Acalephae) of coelenterates including the jellyfishes, hydroids, and related forms

acanth- *or* **acantho-** *comb form* [NL, fr. Gk *akanth-, akantho-,* fr. *akantha;* akin to ON *ögn* awn — more at AWN] **:** thorn **:** spine ⟨*acanthous*⟩ ⟨*Acanthopterygii*⟩

acan·tho·ceph·a·lan \ə-ˌkan(t)-thə-ˈsef-ə-lən\ *n* [deriv. of *acanth-* + Gk *kephalē* head — more at CEPHALIC] **:** any of a group (Acanthocephala) of intestinal worms with a hooked proboscis that as adults lack a digestive tract and absorb food through the body wall — **acanthocephalan** *adj*

acan·thoid \ə-ˈkan-ˌthȯid\ *adj* **:** resembling a spine **:** SPINOUS

ac·an·thop·ter·yg·i·an \ˌak-ən-ˌthäp-tə-ˈrij-ē-ən\ *n* [deriv. of *acanth-* + Gk *pteryg-, pteryx* wing, fin — more at PTERYGOID] **:** any of a major division (Acanthopterygii) of teleost fishes including most spiny-finned fishes (as basses, perches, mackerels) and some soft-finned fishes — **acanthopterygian** *adj*

acan·thous \ə-ˈkan(t)-thəs\ *adj* **:** SPINOUS

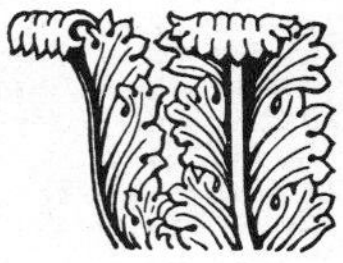

acanthus 2

acan·thus \ə-ˈkan(t)-thəs\ *n, pl* **acan·thus·es** *also* **acan·thi** \-ˈkan-ˌthī\ [NL, genus name, fr. Gk *akanthos* bear's-foot, fr. *akantha*] **1 :** any of a genus (*Acanthus* of the family Acanthaceae, the acanthus family) of prickly herbs of the Mediterranean region **2 :** an ornamentation (as in a Corinthian capital) representing or suggesting the leaves of the acanthus

a cap·pel·la *also* **a ca·pel·la** \ˌäk-ə-ˈpel-ə\ *adv* (*or adj*) [It *a cappella* in chapel style] **:** without instrumental accompaniment

ac·a·ri·a·sis \ˌak-ə-ˈrī-ə-səs\ *n* **:** infestation with or disease caused by mites

ac·a·rid \ˈak-ə-rəd\ *n* **:** any of an order (Acarina) of arachnids including the mites and ticks; *esp* **:** a typical mite (family Acaridae) — **acarid** *adj*

ac·a·roid resin \ˌak-ə-ˌrȯid-\ *n* [NL *acaroides*] **:** an alcohol-soluble resin from Australian grass trees

acar·pel·ous *or* **acar·pel·lous** \(ˈ)ā-ˈkär-pə-ləs\ *adj* **:** having no carpels

acar·pous \(ˈ)ā-ˈkär-pəs\ *adj* [Gk *akarpos,* fr. *a-* + *-karpos* -carpous] **:** not producing fruit **:** STERILE

ac·a·rus \ˈak-ə-rəs\ *n, pl* **ac·a·ri** \-ˌrī\ [NL, genus name, fr. Gk *akari,* a mite] **:** MITE; *esp* **:** one of a formerly extensive genus (*Acarus*)

acat·a·lec·tic \ˌā-ˌkat-ᵊl-ˈek-tik\ *adj* [LL *acatalecticus,* fr. *acatalectus,* fr. Gk *akatalēktos,* fr. *a-* + *katalēgein* to leave off] **:** not defective in the last foot ⟨∼ verse⟩ — **acatalectic** *n*

acau·dal \(ˈ)ā-ˈkȯd-ᵊl\ *or* **acau·date** \-ˈkȯ-ˌdāt\ *adj* **:** lacking a tail

acau·les·cent \ˌā-(ˌ)kȯ-ˈles-ᵊnt\ *or* **acau·line** \(ˈ)ā-ˈkȯ-ˌlīn\ *adj* [*a-* + L *caulis* stem] **:** having no stem or appearing to have none

ac·cede \ak-ˈsēd\ *vi* [ME *acceden,* fr. L *accedere* to go to, be added, fr. *ad-* + *cedere* to go — more at CEDE] **1** *archaic* **:** APPROACH **2 a :** to adhere to an agreement **b :** to express approval or give consent **3 :** to enter upon an office or dignity **syn** see ASSENT

ac·ce·le·ran·do \(ˌ)ä-ˌchel-ə-ˈrän-(ˌ)dō\ *adv* (*or adj*) [It, lit., accelerating, fr. L *accelerandum,* gerund of *accelerare*] **:** gradually faster — used as a direction in music

ac·cel·er·ate \ik-ˈsel-ə-ˌrāt, ak-\ *vb* [L *acceleratus,* pp. of *accelerare,* fr. *ad-* + *celer* swift — more at CELERITY] *vt* **1 :** to bring about at an earlier point of time **2 :** to add to the speed of **3 :** to hasten the ordinary progress or development of **4 a :** to enable (a student) to complete a course in less than usual time **b :** to speed up (a course of study) **5 :** to cause to undergo acceleration ∼ *vi* **1 :** to move faster **2 :** to follow a speeded-up educational program — **ac·cel·er·a·tive** \-ˌrāt-iv\ *adj*

ac·cel·er·a·tion \ik-ˌsel-ə-ˈrā-shən, (ˌ)ak-\ *n* **1 :** the act or process of accelerating **:** the state of being accelerated **2 :** the time rate of change of velocity

acceleration of gravity : the acceleration of a freely falling body under the influence of gravity expressed as the rate of increase of velocity per unit of time with the value at sea level in latitude 45 degrees being 980.616 centimeters per second per second

ac·cel·er·a·tor \ik-ˈsel-ə-ˌrāt-ər, ak-\ *n* **:** one that accelerates: as **a :** a muscle or nerve that speeds the performance of an action **b :** any of several devices for increasing the speed of a motor vehicle engine; *esp* **:** a foot-operated throttle that varies the supply of fuel-air mixture to the combustion chamber **c :** a substance that speeds a chemical reaction **d :** an apparatus for imparting high velocities to charged particles

ac·cel·er·om·e·ter \ik-ˌsel-ə-ˈräm-ət-ər, ak-\ *n* [ISV *acceleration* + *-o-* + *-meter*] **:** an instrument for measuring acceleration or for detecting and measuring vibrations

1ac·cent \ˈak-ˌsent\ *n* [MF, fr. L *accentus,* fr. *ad-* + *cantus* song, fr. *cantus,* pp. of *canere* to sing — more at CHANT] **1 :** a distinctive manner of usu. oral expression: as **a :** the inflection, tone, or choice of words taken to be unique in or highly characteristic of an individual — usu. used in pl. **b :** speech habits typical of the natives or residents of a region or of any other group **2 a :** an articulative effort giving prominence to one syllable over adjacent syllables **b :** the prominence thus given a syllable **3 :** rhythmically significant stress on the syllables of a verse usu. at regular intervals **4** *archaic* **:** UTTERANCE **5 a :** a mark (as ´, `, ˆ) used in writing or printing to indicate a specific sound value, stress, or pitch, to distinguish words otherwise identically spelled, or to indicate that an ordinarily mute vowel should be pronounced **b :** an accented letter **6 a :** greater stress given to one musical tone than to its neighbors **b** (1) **:** the principle of regularly recurring stresses which serve to distribute a succession of pulses into measures (2) **:** special emphasis placed exceptionally upon tones not subject to such accent **c :** ACCENT MARK 2 **7 a :** emphasis laid on a part of an artistic design or composition **b :** a detail or area emphasized; *esp* **:** a small detail in sharp contrast with its surroundings **c :** a substance or object used for emphasis **8 :** a mark placed to the right of a letter or number and usu. slightly above it: **a** (1) **:** a double prime (2) **:** PRIME **b :** a mark used singly with numbers to denote minutes and doubly to denote seconds of time or to denote minutes and seconds of an angle or arc **c :** a mark used singly with numbers to denote feet and doubly to denote inches **9 :** attribution of special importance **:** EMPHASIS

2ac·cent \ˈak-ˌsent, ak-ˈ\ *vt* **1 a :** to utter with accent **:** STRESS **b :** to mark with a written or printed accent **2** *archaic* **:** to give voice to **3 :** to give prominence to or increase the prominence of

accent mark *n* **1 :** ACCENT 5a, 8 **2 a :** one of several symbols used to indicate musical stress **b :** a mark placed after a letter designating a note of music to indicate in which octave the note occurs

ac·cen·tu·al \ak-ˈsench-(ə-)wəl\ *adj* [L *accentus*] **:** of, relating to, or characterized by accent; *specif* **:** based upon accent rather than upon quantity or syllabic recurrence — **ac·cen·tu·al·ly** \-ē\ *adv*

ac·cen·tu·ate \ak-ˈsen-chə-ˌwāt\ *vt* [ML *accentuatus,* pp. of *accentuare,* fr. L *accentus*] **:** ACCENT, EMPHASIZE — **ac·cen·tu·a·tion** \(ˌ)ak-ˌsen-chə-ˈwā-shən\ *n*

ac·cept \ik-ˈsept, ak-\ *vb* [ME *accepten,* fr. MF *accepter,* fr. L *acceptare,* fr. *acceptus,* pp. of *accipere* to receive, fr. *ad-* + *capere* to take — more at HEAVE] *vt* **1 a :** to receive with consent **b :** to be able or designed to take or hold (something applied) **2 :** to give admittance or approval to **3 a :** to endure without protest **b :** to regard as proper, normal, or inevitable **c :** to receive as true **d :** to receive into the mind **:** UNDERSTAND **4 a :** to make a favorable response to **b :** to undertake the responsibility of **5 :** to assume an obligation to pay **6 :** to receive (a legislative report) officially ∼ *vi* **:** to receive favorably something offered — usu. used with *of* **syn** see RECEIVE

ac·cept·abil·i·ty \ik-ˌsep-tə-ˈbil-ət-ē, (ˌ)ak-\ *n* **:** the quality or state of being acceptable

ac·cept·able \ik-ˈsep-tə-bəl, ak-\ *adj* **1 :** capable or worthy of being accepted **:** SATISFACTORY **2 a :** WELCOME, PLEASING **b :** barely adequate — **ac·cept·able·ness** *n* — **ac·cept·ably** \-blē\ *adv*

ac·cep·tance \ik-ˈsep-tən(t)s, ak-\ *n* **1 :** the act of accepting **:** APPROVAL **2 :** the quality or state of being accepted or acceptable **3 :** an agreeing either expressly or by conduct to the act or offer of another so that a contract is concluded and the parties become legally bound **4 a :** the act of accepting a time draft or bill of exchange for payment when due according to the specified terms **b :** an accepted draft or bill of exchange **5 :** ACCEPTATION 2

ac·cep·tant \-tənt\ *adj* **:** willing to accept **:** RECEPTIVE

ac·cep·ta·tion \ˌak-ˌsep-ˈtā-shən\ *n* **1 :** ACCEPTANCE; *esp* **:** favorable reception or approval **2 :** the generally accepted meaning of a word or understanding of a concept **syn** see MEANING

ac·cept·ed *adj* **:** generally approved or used — **ac·cept·ed·ly** *adv*

ac·cept·er \ik-ˈsep-tər, ak-\ *n* **1 :** one that accepts **2 :** ACCEPTOR 2

ac·cep·tive \ak-ˈsep-tiv\ *adj* **1 :** RECEPTIVE **2 :** ACCEPTABLE

ac·cep·tor \ik-ˈsep-tər, ak-\ *n* **1 :** ACCEPTER 1 **2 :** one that accepts an order or a bill of exchange

ac·cess \ˈak-ˌses\ *n* [ME, fr. MF & L; MF *acces* arrival, fr. L *accessus* approach, fr. *accessus,* pp. of *accedere* to approach — more at ACCEDE] **1 a :** ONSET 2 **b :** a fit of intense feeling **:** OUTBURST **2 a :** permission, liberty, or ability to enter, approach, communicate with, or pass to and from or to make use of **b :** a way or means of approach **c :** the action of going to or reaching **3 :** an increase by addition

ac·ces·si·bil·i·ty \(ˌ)ak-ˌses-ə-ˈbil-ət-ē, ik-\ *n* **:** the quality or state of being accessible

ac·ces·si·ble \ik-ˈses-ə-bəl, ak-\ *adj* **1 :** usable for access **2 :** easy of access **3 :** open to influence **4 :** OBTAINABLE — **ac·ces·si·ble·ness** *n* — **ac·ces·si·bly** \-blē\ *adv*

1ac·ces·sion \ik-ˈsesh-ən, ak-\ *n* **1 :** something added **:** ACQUISITION **2 :** the act of becoming joined **:** ADHERENCE **3 a :** increase by something added **b :** acquisition of additional property by growth, increase, or other addition to existing property **4 :** the act of assenting or agreeing **5 a :** a coming near or to **:** APPROACH, ADMITTANCE **b :** the act of coming to high office or a position of honor or power **6 :** a sudden fit or outburst **:** ACCESS — **ac·ces·sion·al** \-ˈsesh-nəl, -ən-ᵊl\ *adj*

2accession *vt* **:** to record in order of acquisition

ac·ces·so·ri·al \ˌak-sə-ˈsōr-ē-əl, -ˈsȯr-\ *adj* **:** of, relating to, or constituting an accession or accessory **:** SUPPLEMENTARY

1ac·ces·so·ry *also* **ac·ces·sa·ry** \ik-ˈses-(ə-)rē, ak-\ *n* **1 a :** a thing of secondary or subordinate importance **:** ADJUNCT **b :** an object or device not essential in itself but adding to the beauty, convenience, or effectiveness of something else **2 a :** a person not actually or constructively present but contributing as an assistant or instigator to the commission of an offense — called also *accessory before the fact* **b :** one who knowing that a crime has been committed aids or shelters the offender with intent to defeat justice — called also *accessory after the fact*

2accessory *adj* **1 :** aiding or contributing in a secondary way **:** SUPPLEMENTARY **2 :** assisting in or contributing to as a subordinate **3 :** present in a minor amount and not essential as a constituent ⟨an ∼ mineral in a rock⟩

accessory fruit *n* **:** a fruit (as apple) of which a conspicuous part consists of tissue other than that of the ripened ovary

ac·ciac·ca·tu·ra \(ˌ)ä-ˌchäk-ə-ˈtür-ə\ *n* [It, lit., crushing] **:** a discordant note sounded with a principal note or chord and immediately released

ac·ci·dence \ˈak-səd-ən(t)s, -sə-ˌden(t)s\ *n* [L *accidentia* inflections of words, nonessential qualities, pl. of *accident-, accidens,* n.] **:** a part of grammar that deals with inflections

ac·ci·dent \ˈak-səd-ənt, -sə-ˌdent\ *n* [ME, fr. MF, fr. L *accident-, accidens* nonessential quality, chance, fr. prp. of *accidere* to happen, fr. *ad-* + *cadere* to fall — more at CHANCE] **1 a :** an event occurring by chance or from unknown causes **b :** lack of intention or necessity **:** CHANCE **c :** an unforeseen or unplanned event **2 a :** an unfortunate event resulting from carelessness, unawareness, ignorance, or unavoidable causes **b :** an unexpected happening causing loss or injury which is not due to any fault or misconduct on the part of the person injured but from the consequences of which he may be entitled to some legal relief **3 :** a nonessential property of an entity or circumstance **4 :** an irregularity of a surface (as of the moon)

1ac·ci·den·tal \ˌak-sə-ˈdent-ᵊl\ *adj* **1 :** arising from extrinsic causes **:** NONESSENTIAL **2 :** occurring by chance or unexpectedly — **ac·ci·den·tal·ly** \-ˈdent-lē, -ᵊl-ē\ *adv* — **ac·ci·den·tal·ness** \-ˈdent-ᵊl-nəs\ *n*

syn FORTUITOUS, CONTINGENT, CASUAL, INCIDENTAL, ADVENTITIOUS: ACCIDENTAL stresses chance; FORTUITOUS so strongly suggests chance that it often connotes entire absence of cause; CONTINGENT suggests possibility of happening but stresses uncertainty and dependence on other future events for existence or occurrence; CASUAL stresses lack of real or apparent premeditation or intent; INCIDENTAL stresses nonessential or secondary character; AD-

VENTITIOUS implies a lack of relation to the original or intrinsic character of a thing ⟨*adventitious* importance⟩
[2]accidental *n* **1 :** a nonessential property **2 a :** a chromatically altered note (as a sharp or flat) foreign to a key indicated by a signature **b :** a prefixed sign indicating an accidental
ac·cip·i·ter \ak-'sip-ət-ər\ *n* [NL, genus name, fr. L, hawk] **:** any of a genus (*Accipiter*) of medium-sized short-winged long-legged hawks with low darting flight; *broadly* **:** a hawk (as of the family Accipitridae, the accipiter family) of similar appearance or habit of flight — **ac·cip·i·trine** \-'sip-ə-,trīn\ *adj or n*
[1]ac·claim \ə-'klām\ *vb* [L *acclamare*, lit., to shout at, fr. *ad-* + *clamare* to shout — more at CLAIM] *vt* **1 :** APPLAUD, PRAISE **2 :** to declare by acclamation **3** *archaic* **:** SHOUT ~ *vi* **:** to shout praise or applause — **ac·claim·er** *n*
[2]acclaim *n* **1 :** the act of acclaiming **2 :** APPLAUSE, PRAISE
ac·cla·ma·tion \,ak-lə-'mā-shən\ *n* [L *acclamation-*, *acclamatio*, fr. *acclamatus*, pp. of *acclamare*] **1 :** a loud eager expression of approval, praise, or assent **2 :** an overwhelming affirmative vote by cheers, shouts, or applause rather than by ballot
ac·cli·mate \ə-'klī-mət, 'ak-lə-,māt\ *vt* [F *acclimater*, fr. *a-* (fr. L *ad-*) + *climat* climate] **:** ACCLIMATIZE — **ac·cli·ma·tion** \,ak-,lī-'mā-shən, ,ak-lə-\ *n*
ac·cli·ma·ti·za·tion \ə-,klī-mət-ə-'zā-shən\ *n* **:** the process or result of acclimatizing
ac·cli·ma·tize \ə-'klī-mə-,tīz\ *vt* **:** to adapt to a new temperature, altitude, climate, environment, or situation ~ *vi* **:** to become acclimatized — **ac·cli·ma·tiz·er** *n*
ac·cliv·i·ty \ə-'kliv-ət-ē\ *n* [L *acclivitas*, fr. *acclivis* ascending, fr. *ad-* + *clivus* slope — more at DECLIVITY] **:** a slope that ascends
ac·co·lade \'ak-ə-,lād\ *n* [F, fr. *accoler* to embrace, fr. (assumed) VL *accollare*, fr. L *ad-* + *collum* neck — more at COLLAR] **1 :** a ceremonial embrace **2 a :** a ceremony or salute to mark the conferring of knighthood **b :** a ceremony marking the recognition of special merit **3 :** a mark of acknowledgment **:** AWARD **4 :** a brace or a line used in music to join two or more staffs carrying simultaneous parts
ac·com·mo·date \ə-'käm-ə-,dāt\ *vb* [L *accommodatus*, pp. of *accommodare*, fr. *ad-* + *commodare* to make fit, fr. *commodus* suitable — more at COMMODE] *vt* **1 :** to make fit, suitable, or congruous **:** ADAPT **2 :** to bring into agreement or concord **:** RECONCILE **3 :** to furnish with something desired, needed, or suited: **a :** to grant a loan to esp. without security **b :** to provide with lodgings **:** HOUSE **c :** to make room for **d :** to hold without crowding or inconvenience ~ *vi* **:** to adapt oneself; *specif* **:** to undergo accommodation **syn** see ADAPT, CONTAIN — **ac·com·mo·da·tive** \-,dāt-iv\ *adj* — **ac·com·mo·da·tive·ness** *n*
ac·com·mo·dat·ing *adj* **:** disposed to be helpful or obliging — **ac·com·mo·dat·ing·ly** \-,dāt-iŋ-lē\ *adv*
ac·com·mo·da·tion \ə-,käm-ə-'dā-shən\ *n* **1 :** something supplied for convenience or to satisfy a need: as **a :** lodging, food, and services or seat, berth, or other space occupied together with services available — usu. used in pl. **b :** a public conveyance (as a train) that stops at all or nearly all points **c :** LOAN **2 :** the act of accommodating **:** the state of being accommodated: as **a :** the provision of what is needed or desired for convenience **b :** ADAPTATION, ADJUSTMENT **c :** an adjustment of differences **:** SETTLEMENT **d :** the automatic adjustment of the eye for seeing at different distances effected chiefly by changes in the convexity of the crystalline lens; *also* **:** the range over which such adjustment is possible — **ac·com·mo·da·tion·al** \-shnəl, -shən-ᵊl\ *adj*
accommodation ladder *n* **:** a light ladder or stairway hung over the side of a ship for ascending from or descending to small boats
accommodation paper *n* **:** a bill, draft, or note made, drawn, accepted, or endorsed by one person for another without consideration to enable that other to raise money or obtain credit thereby
ac·com·mo·da·tor \ə-'käm-ə-,dāt-ər\ *n* **:** one who substitutes for a regularly employed domestic worker
ac·com·pa·ni·ment \ə-'kəmp-(ə-)nē-mənt\ *n* **1 :** a subordinate instrumental or vocal part designed to support or complement a principal voice or instrument **2 :** an addition (as an ornament) intended to give completeness or symmetry **:** COMPLEMENT **3 :** an accompanying situation or occurrence **:** CONCOMITANT
ac·com·pa·nist \ə-'kəmp-(ə-)nəst\ *also* **ac·com·pa·ny·ist** \-'kəmp-(ə-)nē-əst\ *n* **:** one (as a pianist) that plays an accompaniment
ac·com·pa·ny \ə-'kəmp-(ə-)nē\ *vb* [ME *accompanien*, fr. MF *acompaignier*, fr. *a-* (fr. L *ad-*) + *compaing* companion, fr. LL *companio*] *vt* **1 :** to go with or attend as an associate or companion **2 :** to perform an accompaniment to or for **3 a :** to cause to be in association **b :** to be in association with ~ *vi* **:** to perform an accompaniment
syn ACCOMPANY, ATTEND, ESCORT mean to go along with. ACCOMPANY implies closeness of association and with a personal subject usu. equality of status; ATTEND implies a waiting upon in order to serve usu. as a subordinate; ESCORT adds to ACCOMPANY implications of protection, ceremony, or courtesy
ac·com·plice \ə-'käm-pləs, -'kəm-\ *n* [alter. (fr. incorrect division of *a complice*) of *complice*] **:** one associated with another esp. in wrongdoing
ac·com·plish \ə-'käm-plish, -'kəm-\ *vt* [ME *accomplisshen*, fr. MF *acompliss-*, stem of *acomplir*, fr. (assumed) VL *accomplēre*, fr. L *ad-* + *complēre* to fill up — more at COMPLETE] **1 :** to execute fully **:** PERFORM **2 :** to attain to (a measure of time or distance) **:** COVER **3** *archaic* **a :** to equip thoroughly **b :** PERFECT **syn** see PERFORM — **ac·com·plish·able** \-ə-bəl\ *adj*
ac·com·plished *adj* **1 :** COMPLETED, EFFECTED **2 :** complete in acquirements as the result of practice or training; *esp* **:** having many social accomplishments
ac·com·plish·ment \ə-'käm-plish-mənt, -'kəm-\ *n* **1 :** the act of accomplishing **:** COMPLETION **2 :** something accomplished **:** ACHIEVEMENT **3 a :** a quality or ability equipping one for society **b :** a special skill or ability acquired by training or practice **syn** see ACQUIREMENT
[1]ac·cord \ə-'kȯ(ə)rd\ *vb* [ME *accorden*, fr. OF *acorder*, fr. (assumed) VL *accordare*, fr. L *ad-* + *cord-*, *cor* heart — more at HEART] *vt* **1 :** to bring into agreement **:** RECONCILE **2 a :** to grant as suitable or proper **b :** ALLOW **c :** AWARD **d :** ALLOT ~ *vi* **1** *archaic* **:** to arrive at an agreement **2** *obs* **:** to give consent **3 :** to be in harmony **syn** see AGREE, GRANT
[2]accord *n* [ME, fr. OF *acort*, fr. *acorder*] **1 :** AGREEMENT, CONFORMITY **2 :** balanced interrelationship **:** HARMONY **3** *obs* **:** ASSENT **4 :** voluntary or spontaneous impulse to act

ac·cor·dance \ə-'kȯrd-ᵊn(t)s\ *n* **1 :** AGREEMENT, CONFORMITY ⟨in ~ with a rule⟩ **2 :** the act of granting
ac·cor·dant \-ᵊnt\ *adj* **1 :** AGREEING, CONSONANT **2 :** HARMONIOUS — **ac·cor·dant·ly** *adv*
ac·cord·ing as *conj* **1 :** in accord with the way in which **2 a :** depending on how **b :** depending on whether **:** IF
ac·cord·ing·ly \ə-'kȯrd-iŋ-lē\ *adv* **1 :** in accordance **:** CORRESPONDINGLY **2 :** CONSEQUENTLY, SO
according to *prep* **1 :** in conformity with **2 :** as stated or attested by **3 :** depending on
[1]ac·cor·di·on \ə-'kȯrd-ē-ən\ *n* [G *akkordion*, fr. *akkord* chord, fr. F *accord*, fr. OF *acort*] **:** a portable keyboard wind instrument in which the wind is forced past free metallic reeds by means of a hand-operated bellows — **ac·cor·di·on·ist** \-ē-ə-nəst\ *n*

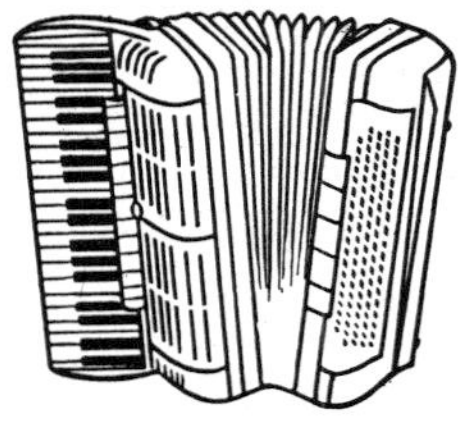
accordion

[2]accordion *adj* **:** folding or creased or hinged to fold like an accordion
[1]ac·cost \ə-'kȯst\ *vt* [MF *accoster*, deriv. of L *ad-* + *costa* rib, side — more at COAST] **:** to approach and speak to **:** speak first to **:** ADDRESS
[2]accost *n*, *archaic* **:** ADDRESS, GREETING
ac·couche·ment \,a-,küsh-'mäⁿ, ə-'küsh-,\ *n* [F] **:** LYING-IN; *esp* **:** PARTURITION
ac·cou·cheur \,a-,kü-'shər\ *n* [F] **:** OBSTETRICIAN
[1]ac·count \ə-'kaunt\ *n* **1** *archaic* **:** RECKONING, COMPUTATION **2 a :** a record of debit and credit entries chronologically posted to a ledger page to cover transactions involving a particular item or a particular person or concern **b :** a statement of transactions during a fiscal period **3 :** a collection of items to be balanced — usu. used in pl. **4 :** a statement of explanation of one's conduct **5 a :** a periodically rendered reckoning listing charged purchases and credits **b :** the patronage involved in establishing or maintaining an account **:** BUSINESS **6 a :** VALUE, IMPORTANCE **b :** ESTEEM, JUDGMENT **7 :** PROFIT, ADVANTAGE **8 a :** a statement or exposition of reasons, causes, grounds, or motives **b :** a reason giving rise to an action or other result **c :** careful thought **:** CONSIDERATION **9 :** a statement of facts or events **:** RELATION **10 :** HEARSAY, REPORT — usu. used in pl. **11 :** a sum of money or its equivalent deposited in the common cash of a bank and subject to withdrawal by the depositor — **on account of :** for the sake of **:** by reason of **:** because of
[2]account *vb* [ME *accounten*, fr. MF *acompter*, fr. *a-* (fr. L *ad-*) + *compter* to count] *vt* **1 :** to give a report on **2 :** to think of as ⟨~*s* himself lucky⟩ ~ *vi* **1 :** to furnish a justifying analysis or explanation — used with *for* **2 a :** to be the sole or primary factor — used with *for* **b :** to bring about the capture or destruction of something ⟨~*ed* for two rabbits⟩
ac·count·abil·i·ty \ə-,kaunt-ə-'bil-ət-ē\ *n* **:** the quality or state of being accountable
ac·count·able \ə-'kaunt-ə-bəl\ *adj* **1 :** subject to giving an account **:** ANSWERABLE **2 :** capable of being accounted for **:** EXPLAINABLE **syn** see RESPONSIBLE — **ac·count·able·ness** *n* — **ac·count·ably** \-blē\ *adv*
ac·coun·tan·cy \ə-'kaunt-ᵊn-sē\ *n* **:** the profession or practice of accounting
ac·coun·tant \ə-'kaunt-ᵊnt\ *n* **1 :** one that gives an account or is accountable **:** RECKONER **2 :** one skilled in the practice of accounting or in charge of public or private accounts — **ac·coun·tant·ship** \-,ship\ *n*
account executive *n* **:** a business executive responsible for the management of a client's account
ac·count·ing *n* **1 :** the system of recording and summarizing business and financial transactions in books and analyzing, verifying, and reporting the results; *also* **:** the underlying body of principles and procedures **2 a :** practical application of accounting **b :** an instance of applying the principles and procedures of accounting
ac·cou·ter *or* **ac·cou·tre** \ə-'küt-ər\ *vt* **ac·cou·ter·ing** *or* **ac·cou·tring** \-'küt-ə-riŋ, -'kü-triŋ\ [F *accoutrer*, fr. MF *acoustrer*, fr. *a-* + *costure* seam, fr. (assumed) VL *consutura*, fr. L *consutus*, pp. of *consuere* to sew together, fr. *com-* + *suere* to sew] **:** to provide with equipment or furnishings **:** fit out **syn** see FURNISH
ac·cou·ter·ment *or* **ac·cou·tre·ment** \ə-'küt-ər-mənt, -'kü-trə-mənt\ *n* **1 :** the act of accoutering **:** the state of being accoutered **2 a :** an article of equipment or dress esp. when used as an accessory **b :** EQUIPMENT, TRAPPINGS; *specif* **:** a soldier's outfit usu. not including clothes and weapons — usu. used in pl.
ac·cred·it \ə-'kred-ət\ *vt* [F *accréditer*, fr. *ad-* + *crédit* credit] **1 :** to put (as by common consent) into a reputable category **2 :** to give official authorization to or approval of: **a :** to provide with credentials; *esp* **:** to send (an envoy) with letters of authorization **b :** to vouch for as in conformity with a standard **c :** to recognize (an educational institution) as maintaining standards that qualify the graduates for admission to higher or more specialized institutions or for professional practice **3 :** CREDIT **syn** see APPROVE — **ac·cred·i·ta·tion** \ə-,kred-ə-'tā-shən\ *n*
ac·crete \ə-'krēt\ *vb* [back-formation fr. *accretion*] *vi* **:** to grow or become attached by accretion ~ *vt* **:** to cause to adhere or become attached
ac·cre·tion \ə-'krē-shən\ *n* [L *accretion-*, *accretio*, fr. *accretus*, pp. of *accrescere*] **1 :** the process of growth or enlargement: **a :** increase by external addition or accumulation **b :** the increase of land by the gradual or imperceptible action of natural forces **2 :** a product of accretion; *esp* **:** an extraneous addition **3 :** coherence of separate particles **:** CONCRETION — **ac·cre·tion·ary** \-shə-,ner-ē\ *adj* — **ac·cre·tive** \ə-'krēt-iv\ *adj*
ac·cru·al \ə-'krü-əl\ *n* **1 :** the action or process of accruing **2 :** something that accrues or has accrued
ac·crue \ə-'krü\ *vb* [ME *acreuen*, prob. fr. MF *acreue* increase, fr. *acreistre* to increase, fr. L *accrescere*, fr. *ad-* + *crescere* to grow — more at CRESCENT] *vi* **1 :** to come into existence as a legally enforceable claim **2 :** to come by way of increase or addition **3 :** to be periodically accumulated whether as an increase or a decrease ~ *vt* **:** ACCUMULATE — **ac·crue·ment** \-mənt\ *n*
ac·cul·tur·ate \ə-'kəl-chə-,rāt\ *vb* [back-formation fr. *acculturation*] **:** to change through acculturation
ac·cul·tur·a·tion \ə-,kəl-chə-'rā-shən\ *n* **:** a process of intercultural borrowing between diverse peoples resulting in new and blended patterns; *esp* **:** modifications in a primitive culture resulting

from contact with an advanced society — **ac·cul·tur·a·tion·al** \-shnəl, -shən-ᵊl\ *adj* — **ac·cul·tur·a·tive** \ə-'kəl-chə-ˌrāt-iv\ *adj*

ac·cu·mu·late \ə-'kyü-myə-ˌlāt\ *vb* [L *accumulatus*, pp. of *accumulare*, fr. *ad-* + *cumulare* to heap up — more at CUMULATE] *vt* **1 :** to heap or pile up **:** AMASS **2 :** COLLECT, GATHER ~ *vi* **:** to increase in quantity or number

ac·cu·mu·la·tion \ə-ˌkyü-myə-'lā-shən\ *n* **1 :** the action or process of accumulating **:** the state of being or having accumulated **2 :** increase or growth by addition esp. when continuous or repeated **3 :** something that has accumulated or has been accumulated

ac·cu·mu·la·tive \ə-'kyü-myə-ˌlāt-iv, -lət-\ *adj* **1 :** CUMULATIVE **2 :** tending or given to accumulation — **ac·cu·mu·la·tive·ly** *adv* — **ac·cu·mu·la·tive·ness** *n*

ac·cu·mu·la·tor \ə-'kyü-myə-ˌlāt-ər\ *n* **:** one that accumulates: as **a :** SHOCK ABSORBER **b** *Brit* **:** STORAGE CELL

ac·cu·ra·cy \'ak-yə-rə-sē\ *n* **1 :** freedom from mistake or error **:** CORRECTNESS **2 a :** conformity to truth or to a standard or model **:** EXACTNESS **b :** degree of conformity of a measure to a standard or a true value

ac·cu·rate \'ak-yə-rət\ *adj* [L *accuratus*, fr. pp. of *accurare* to take care of, fr. *ad-* + *cura* care — more at CURE] **1 :** free from error esp. as the result of care **2 :** conforming exactly to truth or to a standard **:** EXACT **syn** see CORRECT — **ac·cu·rate·ly** \-yə-rət-lē, -yərt-\ *adv* — **ac·cu·rate·ness** \-nəs\ *n*

ac·cursed \ə-'kərst, -'kər-səd\ *or* **ac·curst** \ə-'kərst\ *adj* [ME *acursed*, fr. pp. of *acursen* to consign to destruction with a curse, fr. *a-* (fr. OE *ā-*, perfective prefix) + *cursen* to curse — more at ABIDE] **1 :** being under a curse **2 :** DAMNABLE, DETESTABLE — **ac·curs·ed·ly** \-'kər-səd-lē\ *adv* — **ac·curs·ed·ness** \-'kər-səd-nəs\ *n*

ac·cus·al \ə-'kyü-zəl\ *n* **:** ACCUSATION

ac·cu·sa·tion \ˌak-yə-'zā-shən\ *n* **1 :** the act of accusing **:** the state or fact of being accused **2 :** a charge of wrongdoing **:** ALLEGATION

¹**ac·cu·sa·tive** \ə-'kyü-zət-iv\ *adj* [ME, fr. MF or L; MF *accusatif*, fr. L *accusativus*, fr. *accusatus*, pp. of *accusare*] **1 :** of, relating to, or being the grammatical case that marks the direct object of a verb or the object of any of several prepositions **2 :** ACCUSATORY — **ac·cu·sa·tive·ly** *adv*

²**accusative** *n* **:** the accusative case of a language **:** a form in the accusative case

ac·cu·sa·to·ry \ə-'kyü-zə-ˌtōr-ē, -ˌtȯr-\ *adj* **:** containing, expressing, or tending to accusation

ac·cuse \ə-'kyüz\ *vb* [ME *accusen*, fr. OF *acuser*, fr. L *accusare* to call to account, fr. *ad-* + *causa* lawsuit, cause] *vt* **:** to charge with a fault or offense **:** BLAME ~ *vi* **:** to bring an accusation — **ac·cus·er** \ə-'kyü-zər\ *n* — **ac·cus·ing·ly** \-'kyü-ziŋ-lē\ *adv*

ac·cused *n, pl* **accused :** one charged with an offense; *esp* **:** the defendant in a criminal case

ac·cus·tom \ə-'kəs-təm\ *vt* [ME *accustomen*, fr. MF *acostumer*, fr. *a-* (fr. L *ad-*) + *costume* custom] **:** to make familiar through use or experience **:** HABITUATE

ac·cus·tomed *adj* **1 :** CUSTOMARY, USUAL **2 :** USED, WONT ⟨~ to work⟩ **syn** see USUAL

¹**ace** \'ās\ *n* [ME *as*, fr. OF, fr. L, unit, a copper coin] **1 a :** a die face marked with one spot **b :** a playing card marked in its center with one large pip **c :** a domino end marked with one spot **2 :** a very small amount or degree **:** PARTICLE **3 :** a score won by a single stroke **4 :** a golf score of one stroke on a hole or a hole so made **5 :** a combat pilot who has brought down at least five enemy airplanes **6 :** one that excels at something

²**ace** *vt* **1 :** to score an ace against (an opponent) **2 :** to make (a hole in golf) in one stroke

³**ace** *adj* **:** of first or high rank or quality

-a·ce·ae \'ā-sē-ˌē\ *n pl suffix* [NL, fr. L, fem. pl. of *-aceus* -aceous] **:** plants of the nature of ⟨Rosa*ceae*⟩ — in names of families of plants; formerly in names of orders of plants

acel·da·ma \ə-'sel-də-mə\ *n* [fr. *Aceldama*, field bought by Judas with the money received for betraying Christ (Acts 1:18–19), fr. Gk *Akeldama*, fr. Aram *ḥăqēl dĕmā*, lit., field of blood] **:** a field of bloodshed

acel·lu·lar \(')ā-'sel-yə-lər\ *adj* **:** not made up of cells

acen·tric \(')ā-'sen-trik\ *adj* **:** not centered **:** having no center

-a·ceous \'ā-shəs\ *adj suffix* [L *-aceus*] **1 a :** characterized by **:** full of ⟨set*aceous*⟩ **b :** consisting of ⟨carbon*aceous*⟩ **:** having the nature or form of ⟨sapon*aceous*⟩ **2 a :** of or relating to a group of animals typified by (such) a form ⟨cet*aceous*⟩ or characterized by (such) a feature ⟨crust*aceous*⟩ **b :** of or relating to a plant family typified by (such) a genus ⟨ros*aceous*⟩

aceph·a·lous \(')ā-'sef-ə-ləs\ *adj* [Gk *akephalos*, fr. *a-* + *kephalē* head — more at CEPHALIC] **1 :** lacking a head or having the head reduced **2 :** lacking a governing head or chief

ace·quia \ə-'sā-kē-ə\ *n* [Sp, fr. Ar *as-sāqiyah* the irrigation stream] *Southwest* **:** an irrigation ditch or canal

ac·er·ate \'as-ə-ˌrāt\ *or* **ac·er·ose** \-ˌrōs\ *adj* [L *acer* sharp — more at EDGE] **:** having the form of or a tip like the point of a needle

acerb \ə-'sərb\ *adj* [F or L; F *acerbe*, fr. L *acerbus*, fr. *acer*] **1 :** acid or sour to the taste **2 :** acid in temper, mood, or tone

ac·er·bate \'as-ər-ˌbāt\ *vt* **:** IRRITATE, EXASPERATE

acer·bi·ty \ə-'sər-bət-ē\ *n* **1 :** acidity of taste **2 :** acidity of temper or tone **syn** see ACRIMONY

acer·vate \ə-'sər-vət, 'as-ər-ˌvāt\ *adj* [L *acervatus*, pp. of *acervare* to heap up, fr. *acervus* heap] **:** growing in heaps or closely compacted clusters — **acer·vate·ly** *adv* — **ac·er·va·tion** \ˌas-ər-'vā-shən\ *n*

acet- *or* **aceto-** *comb form* [F & L; F *acét-*, fr. L *acet-*, fr. *acetum*] **:** acetic acid **:** acetic ⟨*acet*yl⟩

ac·e·tab·u·lar \ˌas-ə-'tab-yə-lər\ *adj* **:** of or relating to an acetabulum

ac·e·tab·u·lum \-ləm\ *n, pl* **acetabulums** *or* **ac·e·tab·u·la** \-lə\ [L, fr. *acetum*] **1 a :** the cup-shaped socket in the hipbone **b :** the cavity by which the leg of an insect articulates with the body **2 :** a sucker of an invertebrate (as a trematode or leech)

ac·e·tal \'as-ə-ˌtal\ *n* [G *azetal*, fr. *azet-* acet- + *al*kohal alcohol] **:** any of various compounds characterized by the grouping $>C(OR)_2$ and obtained esp. by heating aldehydes or ketones with alcohols

ac·et·al·de·hyde \ˌas-ə-'tal-də-ˌhīd, ˌas-ət-'al-\ *n* [ISV] **:** a colorless volatile water-soluble liquid aldehyde CH_3CHO used chiefly in organic synthesis

acet·amide \ə-'set-ə-ˌmīd, ˌas-ət-'am-ˌīd\ *n* [G *azetamid*, fr. *azet-* + *amid* amide] **:** a white crystalline amide C_2H_5NO of acetic acid used esp. as a solvent and in organic synthesis

ac·et·an·i·lide *or* **ac·et·an·i·lid** \ˌas-ə-'tan-ᵊl-ˌīd, ˌas-ət-'an-, -ᵊl-əd\ *n* [ISV] **:** a white crystalline compound C_8H_9NO that is derived from aniline and acetic acid and is used esp. to check pain or fever

ac·e·tate \'as-ə-ˌtāt\ *n* **1 :** a salt or ester of acetic acid **2 :** cellulose acetate or one of its products **3 :** a phonograph recording disk made of an acetate or coated with cellulose acetate

ace·tic \ə-'sēt-ik\ *adj* [prob. fr. F *acétique*, fr. L *acetum* vinegar, fr. *acēre* to be sour, fr. *acer* sharp — more at EDGE] **:** of, relating to, or producing acetic acid or vinegar

acetic acid *n* **:** a colorless pungent liquid acid $C_2H_4O_2$ that is the chief acid of vinegar and that is used esp. in synthesis (as of plastics)

ace·ti·fi·ca·tion \ə-ˌsēt-ə-fə-'kā-shən\ *n* **:** the act of acetifying **:** the state of being acetified

ace·ti·fi·er \ə-'sēt-ə-ˌfī(-ə)r\ *n* **:** one that acetifies

ace·ti·fy \-ˌfī\ *vb* **:** to turn into acetic acid or vinegar

ace·to·ace·tic acid \ˌas-ə-tō-ə-ˌsēt-ik-, ə-ˌsēt-ō-\ *n* [part trans. of G *azetessigsäure*, fr. *azet-* acet- + *essigsäure* acetic acid] **:** an unstable acid $C_4H_6O_3$ found in abnormal urine

ac·e·tone \'as-ə-ˌtōn\ *n* [G *azeton*, fr. L *acetum*] **:** a volatile fragrant flammable liquid ketone C_3H_6O used chiefly as a solvent and in organic synthesis and found abnormally in urine — **ac·e·ton·ic** \ˌas-ə-'tän-ik\ *adj*

ac·e·to·phe·net·i·din \ˌas-ə-ˌtō-fə-'net-əd-ən\ *n* [ISV] **:** a white crystalline compound $C_{10}H_{13}NO_2$ that is used to ease pain or fever

ac·e·tose \'as-ə-ˌtōs\ *adj* **:** sour like vinegar **:** ACETOUS

ace·tous \ə-'sēt-əs\ *adj* **:** relating to or producing vinegar; *also* **:** SOUR, VINEGARY

ace·tyl \ə-'sēt-ᵊl, 'as-ət-\ *n* **:** the radical $CH_3CO—$ of acetic acid

acet·y·late \ə-'set-ᵊl-ˌāt\ *or* **acet·y·lize** \-ˌīz\ *vt* **:** to introduce the acetyl radical into (a compound) — **acet·y·la·tion** \ə-ˌset-ᵊl-'ā-shən\ *n*

ace·tyl·cho·line \ə-ˌsēt-ᵊl-'kō-ˌlēn\ *n* [ISV] **:** a compound $C_7H_{17}NO_3$ released at autonomic nerve endings, held to function in the transmission of the nerve impulse, and formed enzymatically in the tissues from choline

acet·y·lene \ə-'set-ᵊl-ən, -ᵊl-ˌēn\ *n* **:** a colorless gaseous hydrocarbon $HC{\equiv}CH$ made esp. by the action of water on calcium carbide and used chiefly in welding and soldering and in organic synthesis — **acet·y·le·nic** \ə-ˌset-ᵊl-'ē-nik, -'en-ik\ *adj*

ac·e·tyl·ic \ˌas-ə-'til-ik\ *adj* **:** of or relating to acetyl

ace·tyl·sa·lic·y·late \ə-ˌsēt-ᵊl-sə-'lis-ə-ˌlāt\ *n* **:** a salt or ester of acetylsalicylic acid

ace·tyl·sal·i·cyl·ic acid \ə-'sēt-ᵊl-ˌsal-ə-ˌsil-ik-\ *n* [ISV] **:** ASPIRIN 1

Acha·tes \ə-'kāt-(ˌ)ēz\ *n* [L] **1 :** a faithful companion of Aeneas in Vergil's *Aeneid* **2 :** a faithful friend

¹**ache** \'āk\ *vi* [ME *aken*, fr. OE *acan*; akin to LG *äken* to hurt] **1 a :** to suffer a usu. dull persistent pain **b :** to become distressed or disturbed (as with anxiety or regret) **c :** to feel compassion **2 :** to become filled with painful yearning

²**ache** *n* **:** a usu. dull persistent pain

achene \ə-'kēn\ *n* [NL *achaenium*, fr. *a-* + Gk *chainein* to yawn — more at YAWN] **:** a small dry indehiscent one-seeded fruit developing from a simple ovary and usu. having a thin pericarp attached to the seed at only one point — **ache·ni·al** \ə-'kē-nē-əl\ *adj*

Ach·er·on \'ak-ə-ˌrän\ *n* [L, fr. Gk *Acherōn*] **1 :** a river in Hades **2 :** the nether world **:** HADES

Acheu·le·an *also* **Acheu·li·an** \ə-'shü-lē-ən\ *adj* [F *Acheuléen*, fr. St. *Acheul*, near Amiens, France] **:** of or relating to a lower Paleolithic culture characterized by bifacial tools with round cutting edges

à che·val \ˌäsh-ə-'väl\ *adv* [F, lit., on horseback] **:** with a part on each side **:** ASTRIDE

achiev·able \ə-'chē-və-bəl\ *adj* **:** capable of being achieved **:** ATTAINABLE

achieve \ə-'chēv\ *vb* [ME *acheven*, fr. MF *achever* to finish, fr. *a-* (fr. L *ad-*) + *chief* end, head — more at CHIEF] *vt* **1 :** to bring to a successful conclusion **:** ACCOMPLISH **2 :** to get as the result of exertion **:** WIN ⟨~ greatness⟩ ~ *vi* **:** to attain a desired end or aim **syn** see PERFORM, REACH

achieve·ment \ə-'chēv-mənt\ *n* **1 :** the act of achieving **:** ACCOMPLISHMENT **2 a :** a result brought about by resolve, persistence, or endeavor **b :** a great or heroic deed **syn** see FEAT

Achil·les \ə-'kil-(ˌ)ēz\ *n* [L, fr. Gk *Achilleus*] **:** a Greek warrior and hero of Homer's *Iliad*

Achilles' heel *n* [fr. the story that Achilles was vulnerable only in the heel] **:** a vulnerable point

Achilles tendon *n* **:** the strong tendon joining the muscles in the calf of the leg to the bone of the heel

achla·myd·e·ous \ˌak-lə-'mid-ē-əs, ˌā-klə-\ *adj* [*a-* + Gk *chlamyd-*, *chlamys* mantle] **:** lacking both calyx and corolla

achlor·hy·dria \ˌā-ˌklōr-'hī-drē-ə, -ˌklȯr-\ *n* [NL, fr. *a-* + *chlor*ine + *hydr*ogen] **:** absence of hydrochloric acid from the gastric juice — **achlor·hy·dric** \-drik\ *adj*

achon·drite \(')ā-'kän-ˌdrīt\ *n* **:** a stony meteorite without rounded grains — **achon·drit·ic** \ˌā-ˌkän-'drit-ik\ *adj*

achon·dro·pla·sia \ˌā-ˌkän-drə-'plā-zh(ē-)ə\ *n* [NL] **:** failure of normal development of cartilage resulting in dwarfism — **achon·dro·plas·tic** \-'plas-tik\ *adj*

achromat- *or* **achromato-** *comb form* [Gk *achrōmatos* colorless, fr. *a-* + *chrōmat-*, *chrōma* color — more at CHROMATIC] **:** achromatic ⟨*achromat*ism⟩

ach·ro·mat·ic \ˌak-rə-'mat-ik\ *adj* **1 :** refracting light without dispersing into its constituent colors **:** giving images practically free from extraneous colors ⟨an ~ telescope⟩ **2 :** not readily colored by the usual staining agents **3 :** possessing no hue **:** NEUTRAL **:** being black, gray, or white **4 :** being without accidentals or modulation **:** DIATONIC — **ach·ro·mat·i·cal·ly** \-i-k(ə-)lē\ *adv*

— **ach·ro·ma·tic·i·ty** \ˌak-rō-mə-'tis-ət-ē\ *n* — **achro·ma·tize** \(ˈ)ā-'krō-mə-ˌtīz\ *vt*
chromatic lens *n* **:** a lens made by combining lenses of different glasses having different focal powers so that the light emerging from the lens forms an image practically free from unwanted colors

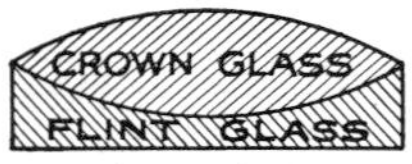

achromatic lens

achro·ma·tin \(ˈ)ā-'krō-mət-ən\ *n* **:** the part of the cell nucleus not readily colored by basic stains — **achro·ma·tin·ic** \ˌā-ˌkrō-mə-'tin-ik\ *adj*
achro·ma·tism \(ˈ)ā-'krō-mə-ˌtiz-əm\ *n* **:** the quality or state of being achromatic
achro·ma·tous \(ˈ)ā-'krō-mət-əs\ *adj* **:** lacking or deficient in color
achy \'ā-kē\ *adj* **:** afflicted with aches
acic·u·la \ə-'sik-yə-lə\ *n, pl* **acic·u·lae** \-ˌlē\ *or* **aciculas** [NL, fr. LL, ornamental pin] **:** a needlelike spine, bristle, or crystal — **acic·u·lar** \-lər\ *adj* — **acic·u·late** \-lət, -ˌlāt\ *adj*
[1]**ac·id** \'as-əd\ *adj* [F or L; F *acide*, fr. L *acidus*, fr. *acēre* to be sour — more at ACETIC] **1 a :** sour, sharp, or biting to the taste **b :** sharp, biting, or sour in manner, disposition, or nature **c :** sharply clear, discerning, or pointed **2 a :** of, relating to, or being an acid; *also* **:** having the reactions or characteristics of an acid **b :** marked by excessive or abnormal concentration of acid **3 :** relating to or made by a process (as in making steel) in which the furnace is lined with acidic material and an acidic slag is used **4 :** rich in silica **syn** see SOUR — **ac·id·ly** *adv* — **ac·id·ness** *n*
[2]**acid** *n* **1 :** a sour substance; *specif* **:** any of various typically water-soluble and sour compounds capable of reacting with a base to form a salt that are hydrogen-containing molecules or ions able to give up a proton to a base or substances able to accept an unshared pair of electrons from a base **2 :** LSD
ac·i·dan·the·ra \ˌas-ə-'dan(t)-thə-rə\ *n* [NL, genus name, fr. Gk *akid-*, *akis* needle + NL *anthera* anther; akin to Gk *akmē* point — more at EDGE] **:** any of a genus (*Acidanthera*) of African herbs of the lily family cultivated for their loose spikes of slender-tubed flowers
ac·id–fast \'as-əd-ˌfast\ *adj* **:** not easily decolorized by acids
ac·id·head \-ˌhed\ *n* **:** an individual who uses LSD
acid·ic \ə-'sid-ik\ *adj* **1 :** acid-forming **2 :** ACID
acid·i·fi·ca·tion \ə-ˌsid-ə-fə-'kā-shən\ *n* **:** the act or process of acidifying
acid·i·fi·er \ə-'sid-ə-ˌfī(-ə)r\ *n* **:** one that acidifies; *esp* **:** a substance used to increase soil acidity
acid·i·fy \ə-'sid-ə-ˌfī\ *vt* **:** to make acid or convert into an acid ~ *vi* **:** to become acid
ac·i·dim·e·ter \ˌas-ə-'dim-ət-ər\ *n* **:** an apparatus for measuring the strength or the amount of acid present in a solution — **acid·i·met·ric** \ə-ˌsid-ə-'me-trik\ *adj* — **ac·i·dim·e·try** \ˌas-ə-'dim-ə-trē\ *n*
acid·i·ty \ə-'sid-ət-ē\ *n* **1 :** the quality, state, or degree of being acid **:** TARTNESS **2 :** HYPERACIDITY
acid·o·phile \ə-'sid-ə-ˌfīl\ *or* **acid·o·phil** \-ˌfil\ *n* **:** an acidophilic substance, tissue, or organism
ac·i·do·phil·ic \ˌas-ə-ˌdō-'fil-ik\ *or* **ac·i·doph·i·lous** \ˌas-ə-'däf-(ə-)ləs\ *adj* **1 :** staining readily with acid stains **2 :** preferring or thriving in a relatively acid environment
ac·i·doph·i·lus milk \ˌas-ə-ˌdäf-(ə-)ləs-\ *n* [NL *Lactobacillus acidophilus*, lit., acidophilic Lactobacillus] **:** milk fermented by any of several bacteria and used therapeutically to change the intestinal flora
ac·i·do·sis \ˌas-ə-'dō-səs\ *n* **:** an abnormal state of reduced alkalinity of the blood and of the body tissues — **ac·i·dot·ic** \-'dät-ik\ *adj*
acid test *n* **:** a severe or crucial test
acid·u·late \ə-'sij-ə-ˌlāt\ *vt* [L *acidulus*] **:** to make acid or slightly acid — **acid·u·la·tion** \ə-ˌsij-ə-'lā-shən\ *n*
acid·u·lent \ə-'sij-ə-lənt\ *adj* [F *acidulant*, fr. prp. of *aciduler* to acidulate, fr. L *acidulus*] **:** ACIDULOUS
acid·u·lous \ə-'sij-ə-ləs\ *adj* [L *acidulus* sourish, fr. *acidus*] **:** acid in taste or manner **:** HARSH **syn** see SOUR
ac·i·nar \'as-ə-nər\ *adj* **:** of or relating to an acinus
ac·i·nous \'as-ə-nəs\ *adj* [F or L; F *acineux*, fr. L *acinosus*, fr. *acinus*] **:** consisting of or containing acini
ac·i·nus \'as-ə-nəs\ *n, pl* **ac·i·ni** \-ˌnī\ [NL, fr. L, berry, berry seed] **:** one of the small sacs in a racemose gland lined with secreting cells
ack–ack \'ak-ˌak\ *n* [Brit. signalmen's telephone pron. of *AA*, abbr. of *antiaircraft*] **:** an antiaircraft gun; *also* **:** antiaircraft fire
ac·knowl·edge \ik-'näl-ij, ak-\ *vt* [*ac-* (as in *accord*) + *knowledge*] **1 :** to own or admit knowledge of **2 :** to recognize the rights, authority, or status of **3 a :** to express gratitude or obligation for **b :** to take notice of **c :** to make known the receipt of **4 :** to recognize as genuine or valid — **ac·knowl·edge·able** \-i-jə-bəl\ *adj*
syn ACKNOWLEDGE, ADMIT, OWN, AVOW, CONFESS mean to disclose against one's will or inclination. ACKNOWLEDGE implies the disclosing of something that has been or might be concealed; ADMIT implies a degree of reluctance to disclose, grant, or concede; OWN implies acknowledging something in close relation to oneself; AVOW implies openly or boldly declaring what one might be expected to be silent about; CONFESS may apply to an admission of a weakness, failure, omission, or guilt
ac·knowl·edged \-ijd\ *adj* **:** generally recognized or accepted — **ac·knowl·edged·ly** \-i-jəd-lē, -ij-dlē\ *adv*
ac·knowl·edg·ment *also* **ac·knowl·edge·ment** \ik-'näl-ij-mənt, ak-\ *n* **1 a :** the act of acknowledging **b :** recognition or favorable notice of an act or achievement **2 :** a thing done or given in recognition of something received **3 :** a declaration or avowal of one's act or of a fact to give it legal validity
aclin·ic line \ˌā-ˌklin-ik-\ *n* **:** an imaginary line roughly parallel to the geographical equator and passing through those points where a magnetic needle has no dip
ac·me \'ak-mē\ *n* [Gk *akmē* point, highest point — more at EDGE] **:** the highest point **:** PEAK **syn** see SUMMIT
ac·ne \'ak-nē\ *n* [Gk *aknē* eruption on the face, MS var. of *akmē*, lit., point] **:** an inflammatory disease involving the oil glands and hair follicles of the skin; *specif* **:** one found chiefly in adolescents and marked by papules or pustules esp. about the face
acock \ə-'käk\ *adv* (*or adj*) **:** in a cocked position
acold \ə-'kōld\ *adj* [ME] *archaic* **:** COLD, CHILLED
ac·o·lyte \'ak-ə-ˌlīt\ *n* [ME *acolite*, fr. OF & ML; OF, fr. ML *acoluthus*, fr. MGk *akolouthos*, fr. Gk, adj., following, fr. *a-*, *ha-* (akin to Gk *homos* same) + *keleuthos* path — more at SAME] **1 :** one who assists the minister in a liturgical service by performing minor duties **2 :** one who attends or assists **:** FOLLOWER
ac·o·nite \'ak-ə-ˌnīt\ *n* **1 :** ACONITUM 1; *esp* **:** a common monkshood (*Aconitum napellus*) **2 :** the dried tuberous root of a monkshood (*Aconitum napellus*) formerly used as a sedative
ac·o·ni·tum \ˌak-ə-'nīt-əm\ *n* [NL, genus name, fr. L, aconitum, fr. Gk *akoniton*] **1 :** any of a genus (*Aconitum*) of usu. bluish flowered poisonous herbs of the crowfoot family — compare MONKSHOOD, WOLFSBANE **2 :** ACONITE 2
acorn \'ā-ˌkò(ə)rn, -kərn\ *n* [ME *akern*, fr. OE *æcern*; akin to MHG *ackeran* acorns collectively, Russ *yagoda* berry] **:** the nut of the oak usu. seated in or surrounded by a hard woody cupule of indurated bracts

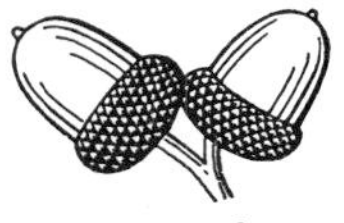
acorns of white oak

acorn tube *n* **:** a very small vacuum tube resembling an acorn in shape and used at extremely high frequencies
acous·tic \ə-'kü-stik\ *adj* [Gk *akoustikos* of hearing, fr. *akouein* to hear — more at HEAR] **:** of or relating to the sense or organs of hearing, to sound, or to the science of sounds: as **a :** deadening sound **b :** operated by or utilizing sound waves — **acous·ti·cal** \-sti-kəl\ *adj* — **acous·ti·cal·ly** \-k(ə-)lē\ *adv*
ac·ous·ti·cian \ˌa-ˌkü-'stish-ən, ə-ˌkü-\ *n* **:** a specialist in acoustics
acous·tics \ə-'kü-stiks\ *n pl but sing or pl in constr* **1 :** a science that deals with the production, control, transmission, reception, and effects of sound **2** *also* **acoustic :** the sum of the qualities that determine the value of an auditorium or other enclosure as to distinct hearing
ac·quaint \ə-'kwānt\ *vt* [ME *aquainten*, fr. OF *acointier*, fr. ML *accognitare*, fr. LL *accognitus*, pp. of *accognoscere* to know perfectly, fr. L *ad-* + *cognoscere* to know — more at COGNITION] **1 :** to cause to know personally **2 :** to make familiar **:** cause to know firsthand **syn** see INFORM
ac·quaint·ance \ə-'kwānt-ᵊn(t)s\ *n* **1 a :** personal knowledge **:** FAMILIARITY **b :** the state of being acquainted **2 a :** the persons with whom one is acquainted **b :** a person whom one knows but who is not a particularly close friend — **ac·quaint·ance·ship** \-ˌship\ *n*
ac·qui·esce \ˌak-wē-'es\ *vi* [F *acquiescer*, fr. L *acquiescere*, fr. *ad-* + *quiescere* to be quiet — more at QUIET] **:** to accept or comply tacitly or passively **syn** see ASSENT
ac·qui·es·cence \ˌak-wē-'es-ᵊn(t)s\ *n* **:** the act of acquiescing **:** the state of being acquiescent
ac·qui·es·cent \ˌak-wē-'es-ᵊnt\ *adj* [L *acquiescent-*, *acquiescens*, prp. of *acquiescere*] **:** acquiescing or disposed to acquiesce — **ac·qui·es·cent·ly** *adv*
ac·quir·able \ə-'kwī-rə-bəl\ *adj* **:** capable of being acquired
ac·quire \ə-'kwī(ə)r\ *vt* [ME *aqueren*, fr. MF *aquerre*, fr. L *acquirere*, fr. *ad-* + *quaerere* to seek, obtain] **1 :** to come into possession of often by some uncertain or unspecified means **2 :** to come to have as a characteristic, trait, or ability (as by sustained effort or through environmental forces) ⟨an *acquired* physical character⟩ **syn** see GET
ac·quire·ment \-mənt\ *n* **1 :** the act of acquiring **2 :** an attainment of mind or body usu. resulting from continued endeavor
syn ACQUIREMENT, ACQUISITION, ATTAINMENT, ACCOMPLISHMENT mean a power or skill won through exertion or effort. ACQUIREMENT suggests the fruit of constant endeavor to cultivate oneself; ACQUISITION stresses eagerness of effort and an inherent value in what is gained; ATTAINMENT suggests a distinguished achievement; ACCOMPLISHMENT implies a socially useful skill
ac·qui·si·tion \ˌak-wə-'zish-ən\ *n* [ME *acquisicioun*, fr. MF or L; MF *acquisition*, fr. L *acquisition-*, *acquisitio*, fr. *acquisitus*, pp. of *acquirere*] **1 :** the act of acquiring **2 :** something acquired or gained **syn** see ACQUIREMENT
ac·quis·i·tive \ə-'kwiz-ət-iv\ *adj* **:** given to or strongly desirous of acquiring and possessing **syn** see COVETOUS — **ac·quis·i·tive·ly** *adv* — **ac·quis·i·tive·ness** *n*
ac·quit \ə-'kwit\ *vt* **ac·quit·ted; ac·quit·ting** [ME *aquiten*, fr. OF *aquiter*, fr. *a-* (fr. L *ad-*) + *quite* free of — more at QUIT] **1 a** *archaic* **:** to pay off (as a claim or debt) **b** *obs* **:** REPAY, REQUITE **2 :** to discharge completely (as from an obligation or accusation) ⟨the court *acquitted* the prisoner⟩ **3 :** to conduct (oneself) usu. satisfactorily ⟨the recruits *acquitted* themselves like veterans⟩ **syn** see BEHAVE, EXCULPATE — **ac·quit·ter** *n*
ac·quit·tal \ə-'kwit-ᵊl\ *n* **:** a setting free from the charge of an offense by verdict, sentence, or other legal process
ac·quit·tance \ə-'kwit-ᵊn(t)s\ *n* **:** a writing evidencing a discharge from an obligation; *esp* **:** RECEIPT
acr- *or* **acro-** *comb form* [MF or Gk; MF *acro-*, fr. Gk *akr-*, *akro-*, fr. *akros* topmost, extreme; akin to Gk *akmē* point — more at EDGE] **1 :** beginning **:** end **:** tip ⟨*acr*onym⟩ **2 a :** top **:** peak **:** summit ⟨*acro*dont⟩ **b :** height ⟨*acro*phobia⟩ **c :** extremity of the body ⟨*acro*cyanosis⟩
acre \'ā-kər\ *n* [ME, fr. OE *æcer*; akin to OHG *ackar* field, L *ager*, Gk *agros*, L *agere* to drive — more at AGENT] **1 a** *archaic* **:** a field esp. of arable or pasture land **b** *pl* **:** LANDS, ESTATE **2 :** any of various units of area; *esp* **:** a unit in the U.S. and England equal to 160 square rods — see MEASURE table **3 :** a broad expanse or great quantity
acre·age \'ā-k(ə-)rij\ *n* **:** area in acres **:** ACRES
acre–foot \'ā-kər-'fu̇t\ *n* **:** the volume (as of irrigation water) that would cover one acre to a depth of one foot
acre–inch \'ā-kə-'rinch\ *n* **:** one twelfth of an acre-foot
ac·rid \'ak-rəd\ *adj* [modif. of L *acr-*, *acer* sharp — more at EDGE] **1 :** sharp and harsh or unpleasantly pungent in taste or odor **:** IRRITATING, CORROSIVE **2 :** bitterly irritating to the feelings — **acrid·i·ty** \a-'krid-ət-ē, ə-\ *n* — **ac·rid·ly** *adv* — **ac·rid·ness** *n*
ac·ri·dine \'ak-rə-ˌdēn\ *n* **:** a colorless crystalline compound $C_{13}H_9N$ occurring in coal tar and important as the parent compound of dyes and pharmaceuticals
ac·ri·fla·vine \ˌak-rə-'flā-ˌvēn\ *n* [*acri*dine + *flavine*] **:** a yellow dye $C_{14}H_{14}N_3Cl$ used as an antiseptic esp. for wounds
ac·ri·mo·ni·ous \ˌak-rə-'mō-nē-əs\ *adj* **:** caustic, biting, or rancorous esp. in feeling, language, or manner — **ac·ri·mo·ni·ous·ly** *adv* — **ac·ri·mo·ni·ous·ness** *n*

ac·ri·mo·ny \'ak-rə-,mō-nē\ *n* [MF or L; MF *acrimonie*, fr. L *acrimonia*, fr. *acr-, acer*] **:** harsh or biting sharpness esp. of words, manner, or disposition
syn ACRIMONY, ACERBITY, ASPERITY mean temper or language marked by angry irritation. ACRIMONY implies bitterness and ill will and the power to sting or blister with verbal attack; ACERBITY suggests sourness as well as bitterness and applies esp. to mood; ASPERITY suggests quickness of temper and sharpness of resentment usu. without bitterness

ac·ro·bat \'ak-rə-,bat\ *n* [F & Gk; F *acrobate*, fr. Gk *akrobatēs*, fr. *akrobatos* walking up high, fr. *akros* + *bainein* to go — more at COME] **1 :** one that performs gymnastic feats requiring skillful control of the body **2 :** one adept at swiftly changing his position — **ac·ro·bat·ic** \,ak-rə-'bat-ik\ *adj* — **ac·ro·bat·i·cal·ly** \-i-k(ə-)lē\ *adv*

ac·ro·bat·ics \,ak-rə-'bat-iks\ *n pl but sing or pl in constr* **1 :** the art, performance, or activity of an acrobat **2 :** any spectacular, showy, or startling performance involving great agility

ac·ro·car·pous \,ak-rə-'kär-pəs\ *adj* [NL *acrocarpus*, fr. Gk *akrokarpos* bearing fruit at the top, fr. *akr-* acr- + *-karpos* -carpous] *of a moss* **:** having the archegonia and hence the capsules terminal on the stem

ac·ro·dont \'ak-rə-,dänt\ *adj* **1** *of teeth* **:** consolidated with the summit of the alveolar ridge without sockets **2 :** having acrodont teeth

acrog·e·nous \ə-'kräj-ə-nəs\ *also* **ac·ro·gen·ic** \,ak-rə-'jen-ik\ *adj* **:** increasing by growth from the summit or apex — **acrog·e·nous·ly** *adv*

acro·le·in \ə-'krō-lē-ən\ *n* [ISV *acr-* (fr. L *acr-, acer*) + L *olēre* to smell — more at ODOR] **:** a colorless irritant pungent liquid aldehyde C_3H_4O obtained by dehydration of glycerol or destructive distillation of fats

ac·ro·me·gal·ic \,ak-rō-mi-'gal-ik\ *adj* **:** exhibiting acromegaly — **acromegalic** *n*

ac·ro·meg·a·ly \,ak-rō-'meg-ə-lē\ *n* [F *acromégalie*, fr. *acr-* + Gk *megal-, megas* large — more at MUCH] **:** chronic hyperpituitarism marked by progressive enlargement of hands, feet, and face

ac·ro·nym \'ak-rə-,nim\ *n* [*acr-* + *-onym* (as in *homonym*)] **:** a word (as *radar, snafu*) formed from the initial letter or letters of each of the successive parts or major parts of a compound term

acrop·e·tal \ə-'kräp-ət-ᵊl\ *adj* [*acr-* + *-petal* (as in *centripetal*)] **:** proceeding from the base toward the apex or from below upward — **acrop·e·tal·ly** \-ᵊl-ē\ *adv*

ac·ro·pho·bia \,ak-rə-'fō-bē-ə\ *n* [NL] **:** abnormal dread of being at a great height

acrop·o·lis \ə-'kräp-ə-ləs\ *n* [Gk *akropolis*, fr. *akr-* acr- + *polis* city] **:** the upper fortified part of an ancient Greek city

[1]**across** \ə-'krȯs\ *adv* [ME *acros*, fr. AF *an crois*, fr. *an* in (fr. L *in*) + *crois* cross, fr. L *crux*] **1 :** in a position reaching from one side to the other **:** CROSSWISE **2 :** to or on the opposite side **3 :** so as to be understandable, acceptable, or successful **:** OVER

[2]**across** *prep* **1 :** to or on the opposite side of **2 :** so as to intersect or pass at an angle **3 :** into an accidental or transitory meeting or contact with ⟨ran ~ an old friend⟩

[3]**across** *adj* **:** CROSSED

across–the–board *adj* **1 :** placed in combination to win, place, or show **2 :** embracing all classes or categories **:** BLANKET

acros·tic \ə-'krȯ-stik\ *n* [MF & Gk; MF *acrostiche*, fr. Gk *akrostichis*, fr. *akr-* acr- + *stichos* line; akin to *steichein* to go — more at STAIR] **1 :** a composition usu. in verse in which sets of letters (as the initial or final letters of the lines) taken in order form a word or phrase or a regular sequence of letters of the alphabet **2 :** ACRONYM **3 :** a series of words of equal length arranged to read the same horizontally or vertically — **acrostic** *adj* — **acros·ti·cal·ly** \-sti-k(ə-)lē\ *adv*

ac·ry·late \'ak-rə-,lāt\ *n* **1 :** a salt or ester of acrylic acid **2 :** ACRYLIC RESIN

acryl·ic \ə-'kril-ik\ *adj* [ISV *acrolein* + *-yl* + *-ic*] **:** relating to acrylic acid or its derivatives — **acrylic** *n*

acrylic acid *n* **:** an unsaturated liquid acid $C_3H_4O_2$ that polymerizes readily

acrylic fiber *n* **:** a synthetic textile fiber made by polymerization of acrylonitrile usu. with other monomers

acrylic resin *n* **:** a glassy thermoplastic made by polymerizing acrylic or methacrylic acid or a derivative of either and used for cast and molded parts or as coatings and adhesives

ac·ry·lo·ni·trile \,ak-rə-lō-'nī-trəl\ *n* **:** a colorless volatile flammable liquid nitrile $CH_2{=}CHCN$ used chiefly in organic synthesis and for polymerization

[1]**act** \'akt\ *n* [ME, partly fr. L *actus* doing, act, fr. *actus*, pp. of *agere* to drive, do; partly fr. L *actum* thing done, record, fr. neut. of *actus*, pp. — more at AGENT] **1 a :** a thing done **:** DEED **b :** something done by a person pursuant to his volition **2 :** a state of real existence rather than possibility **3** *often cap* **:** the formal product of a legislative body **:** STATUTE; *also* **:** a decision or determination of a sovereign, a legislative council, or a court of justice **4 :** the process of doing **5** *often cap* **:** a formal record of something done or transacted **6 a :** one of the principal divisions of a play or opera **b :** one of the successive parts of a variety show or circus **c :** a display of affected insincere behavior **:** PRETENSE **syn** see ACTION

[2]**act** *vt* **1** *obs* **:** ACTUATE, ANIMATE **2 a :** to represent or perform by action esp. on the stage **b :** FEIGN, SIMULATE **c :** IMPERSONATE **3 :** to play the part of as if in a play ⟨~ the man of the world⟩ **4 :** to behave in a manner suitable to ⟨~ your age⟩ ~ *vi* **1 a :** to perform on the stage **b :** to behave as if performing on the stage **:** PRETEND **2 :** to take action **:** MOVE ⟨think before ~*ing*⟩ **3 :** to conduct oneself **:** BEHAVE ⟨~ like a fool⟩ **4 :** to perform a specified function **:** SERVE ⟨trees ~*ing* as a windbreak⟩ **5 :** to produce an effect **:** WORK ⟨wait for a medicine to ~⟩ **6** *of a play* **:** to be capable of being performed **7 :** to give a decision or award — **act·abil·i·ty** \,ak-tə-'bil-ət-ē\ *n* — **act·able** \'ak-tə-bəl\ *adj*

Ac·tae·on \ak-'tē-ən\ *n* [L, fr. Gk *Aktaiōn*] **:** a hunter in classical mythology transformed into a stag and killed by his own hounds for having seen Diana bathing

ac·tin \'ak-tən\ *n* [ISV, fr. L *actus*] **:** a protein of muscle that is active in muscular contraction

actin- *or* **actini-** *or* **actino-** *comb form* [NL, ray, fr. Gk *aktin-, aktino-*, fr. *aktin-, aktis;* akin to OE *ūhte* morning twilight, L *noct-, nox* night — more at NIGHT] **1 a :** having a radiate form ⟨*Actino*myces⟩ **b :** actinian ⟨*actini*form⟩ **2 a :** actinic ⟨*actin*ium⟩ **b :** actinic radiation (as X rays) ⟨*actino*therapy⟩

[1]**act·ing** *adj* **1 :** performing services temporarily or for another ⟨~ president⟩ **2 a :** suitable for stage performance ⟨~ play⟩ **b :** prepared with directions for actors

[2]**acting** *n* **:** the art or practice of representing a character on a stage or before cameras

ac·tin·ia \ak-'tin-ē-ə\ *n, pl* **ac·tin·i·ae** \-ē-,ē\ *or* **ac·tin·i·as** [NL, fr. Gk *aktin-, aktis*] **:** any sea anemone or related animal — **ac·tin·i·an** \-ē-ən\ *adj or n*

ac·tin·ic \ak-'tin-ik\ *adj* **:** of, relating to, or exhibiting actinism — **ac·tin·i·cal·ly** \-i-k(ə-)lē\ *adv*

actinic ray *n* **:** a radiation having marked photochemical action

ac·ti·nide series \'ak-tə-,nīd-\ *n* [ISV] **:** a series of heavy radioactive metallic elements of increasing atomic number beginning with actinium (89) or thorium (90) and ending with element of atomic number 103 — compare PERIODIC TABLE

ac·ti·nism \'ak-tə-,niz-əm\ *n* **:** the property of radiant energy esp. in the visible and ultraviolet spectral regions by which chemical changes are produced

ac·tin·i·um \ak-'tin-ē-əm\ *n* **:** a radioactive trivalent metallic element resembling lanthanum in chemical properties and found esp. in pitchblende — see ELEMENT table

ac·ti·noid \'ak-tə-,nȯid\ *adj* **1 :** resembling a ray (as of a radially symmetrical animal) **2 :** exhibiting radial symmetry

ac·tin·o·lite \ak-'tin-ᵊl-,īt\ *n* **:** a bright or grayish green amphibole occurring in fibrous, radiated, or columnar forms

ac·ti·nom·e·ter \,ak-tə-'näm-ət-ər\ *n* **1 :** an instrument for measuring the direct heating power of the sun's rays **2 :** an instrument for measuring the actinic power of radiant energy or for determining photographic exposure to be given — **ac·ti·no·me·tric** \,ak-tə-nō-'me-trik\ *adj* — **ac·ti·nom·e·try** \,ak-tə-'näm-ə-trē\ *n*

ac·ti·no·mor·phic \,ak-tə-nō-'mȯr-fik\ *also* **ac·ti·no·mor·phous** \-fəs\ *adj* [ISV] **:** being radially symmetrical and capable of division into essentially symmetrical halves by any longitudinal plane passing through the axis — **ac·ti·no·mor·phy** \'ak-tə-nō-,mȯr-fē\ *n*

ac·ti·no·my·ces \,ak-tə-nō-'mī-,sēz\ *n, pl* **actinomyces** [NL, genus name, fr. *actin-* + Gk *mykēt-, mykēs* fungus; akin to Gk *myxa* mucus] **:** any of a genus (*Actinomyces*) of filamentous bacteria including both soil-inhabiting saprophytes and disease-producing parasites — **ac·ti·no·my·ce·tal** \-,mī-'sēt-ᵊl\ *adj*

ac·ti·no·my·cete \,ak-tə-nō-'mī-,sēt, -,mī-'sēt\ *n* [deriv. of Gk *aktin-, aktis* + *mykēt-, mykēs*] **:** any of an order (Actinomycetales) of filamentous or rod-shaped bacteria including the actinomyces and streptomyces — **ac·ti·no·my·ce·tous** \-,mī-'sēt-əs\ *adj*

ac·ti·no·my·cin \,ak-tə-nō-'mīs-ᵊn\ *n* **:** any of various red or yellow-red mostly toxic polypeptide antibiotics isolated from soil bacteria (esp. *Streptomyces antibioticus*)

ac·ti·no·my·co·sis \,ak-tə-nō-,mī-'kō-səs\ *n* **:** infection with or disease caused by actinomycetes; *esp* **:** a chronic disease of cattle, swine, and man characterized by hard granulomatous masses usu. in mouth and jaw — **ac·ti·no·my·cot·ic** \-'kät-ik\ *adj*

ac·ti·non \'ak-tə-,nän\ *n* [NL, fr. *actinium*] **:** a heavy radioactive gaseous element that is an inert gas isotopic with radon and thoron and lives only a few seconds

ac·ti·no·ura·ni·um \,ak-tə-(,)nō-yu̇-'rā-nē-əm\ *n* [NL, fr. *actinium* + *uranium*] **:** the uranium isotope of mass 235

ac·ti·no·zo·an \,ak-tə-nə-'zō-ən\ *n or adj* [*actin-* + Gk *zōion* animal; akin to Gk *zōē* life — more at QUICK] **:** ANTHOZOAN

ac·tion \'ak-shən\ *n* **1 :** a proceeding in a court of justice by which one demands or enforces one's right **2 :** the bringing about of an alteration by force or through a natural agency **3 :** the manner or method of performing: **a :** the deportment of an actor or speaker or his expression by means of attitude, voice, and gesture **b :** the style of movement of the feet and legs (as of a horse) **c :** a function of the body or one of its parts **4 :** an act of will **5 a :** a thing done **:** DEED **b** *pl* **:** BEHAVIOR, CONDUCT **c :** INITIATIVE, ENTERPRISE **6 a** (1) **:** an engagement between troops or ships (2) **:** combat in war **b** (1) **:** an event or series of events forming a literary composition (2) **:** the unfolding of the events of a drama or work of fiction **:** PLOT (3) **:** the movement of incidents in a plot **c :** the combination of circumstances that constitute the subject matter of a painting or sculpture **7 a :** an operating mechanism **b :** the manner in which a mechanism operates
syn ACTION, ACT, DEED mean something done or effected. ACTION often implies a process that involves more than one step, or is continuous, or is capable of repetition; ACT suggests a single accomplishment complete in itself and essentially unique; DEED commonly suggests an act either illustrious or remarkable **syn** see in addition BATTLE

ac·tion·able \'ak-sh(ə-)nə-bəl\ *adj* **:** subject to or affording ground for an action or suit at law — **ac·tion·ably** \-blē\ *adv*

action painting *n* **:** nonrepresentational painting marked esp. by thickly textured surfaces and by the use of improvised techniques (as splattering) to create apparently accidental pictorial effects

ac·ti·vate \'ak-tə-,vāt\ *vt* **:** to make active or more active: as **a** (1) **:** to make (as molecules) reactive or more reactive (2) **:** to convert (as a provitamin) into a biologically active derivative **b :** to make (a substance) radioactive, luminescent, photosensitive, or photoconductive **c :** to treat (as carbon or alumina) esp. so as to improve adsorptive properties **d :** to aerate (sewage) so as to favor the growth of organisms that decompose organic matter **e :** to set up or formally institute (a military unit) with the necessary personnel and equipment ~ *vi* **:** to become active — **ac·ti·va·tor** \'ak-tə-,vāt-ər\ *n*

activated carbon *n* **:** a highly adsorbent powdered or granular carbon made usu. by carbonization and chemical activation and used chiefly for purifying by adsorption — called also *activated charcoal*

ac·ti·va·tion \,ak-tə-'vā-shən\ *n* **:** the act or process of activating

ac·tive \'ak-tiv\ *adj* [ME, fr. MF or L; MF *actif*, fr. L *activus*, fr. *actus*, pp. of *agere* to drive, do — more at AGENT] **1 :** characterized by action rather than by contemplation or speculation **2 :** productive of action or movement **3 a** *of a verb form or voice* **:** asserting that the person or thing represented by the grammatical subject performs the action represented by the verb ⟨*hits* in "he hits the

ball" is ~⟩ **b** *of a verb or verb form* **:** expressing action as distinct from mere existence or state **c** *of a grammatical construction* **:** containing an active verb form **4 :** quick in physical movement **:** LIVELY **5 :** requiring vigorous action or exertion ⟨~ sports⟩ **6 :** having practical operation or results **:** EFFECTIVE ⟨an ~ law⟩ **7 a :** disposed to action **:** ENERGETIC ⟨~ interest⟩ **b :** engaged in an action or activity **:** PARTICIPATING ⟨an ~ club member⟩ **8 :** engaged in full-time service esp. in the armed forces ⟨~ duty⟩ **9 :** marked by present operation, transaction, movement, or use ⟨~ account⟩ ⟨~ titles in a publisher's catalog⟩ ⟨a student's ~ vocabulary⟩ **10 a :** capable of acting or reacting **:** ACTIVATED **b :** tending to progress or increase ⟨~ tuberculosis⟩ **11 :** still eligible to win the pot in poker **12 :** moving down the line **:** visiting in the set — used of couples in contredanses or square dances — **active** *n* — **ac·tive·ly** *adv* — **ac·tive·ness** *n*

ac·tiv·ism \'ak-ti-ˌviz-əm\ *n* **:** a doctrine or practice that emphasizes vigorous action (as the use of force for political ends) — **ac·tiv·ist** \-vəst\ *n or adj* — **ac·tiv·is·tic** \ˌak-ti-'vis-tik\ *adj*

ac·tiv·i·ty \ak-'tiv-ət-ē\ *n* **1 :** the quality or state of being active **2 :** vigorous or energetic action **:** LIVELINESS **3 :** natural or normal function: as **a :** a process that an organism carries on or participates in by virtue of being alive **b :** any similar process actually or potentially involving mental function; *specif* **:** an educational procedure designed to stimulate learning by firsthand experience **4 :** an active force **5 a :** a pursuit in which a person is active **b :** a form of organized, supervised, often extracurricular recreation **6 :** an organizational unit for performing a specific function; *also* **:** its function or duties

act of God : an extraordinary interruption by a natural cause (as a flood or earthquake) of the usual course of events that experience, prescience, or care cannot reasonably foresee or prevent

ac·to·my·o·sin \ˌak-tə-'mī-ə-sən\ *n* [ISV *actin* + *-o-* + *myosin*] **:** a viscous contractile complex of actin and myosin held to be concerned together with adenosine triphosphate in muscular contraction

ac·tor \'ak-tər\ *n* **1 a :** one that acts a part **b :** a theatrical performer **c :** one that behaves as if acting a part **2 :** one that takes part in any affair **:** PARTICIPANT — **ac·tress** \'ak-trəs\ *n*

act out *vt* **:** to express (repressed or unconscious impulses) in overt behavior without awareness or insight esp. during psychoanalytic investigation

ac·tu·al \'ak-ch(-əw)əl, 'aksh-wəl\ *adj* [ME *actuel*, fr. MF, fr. LL *actualis*, fr. L *actus* act] **1** *obs* **:** ACTIVE **2 a :** existing in act and not merely potentially **b :** existing in fact or reality ⟨~ and imagined conditions⟩ **c :** not false or apparent **:** REAL ⟨~ costs⟩ **3 :** present or active at the time **:** CURRENT **syn** see REAL

ac·tu·al·i·ty \ˌak-chə-'wal-ət-ē\ *n* **1 :** the quality or state of being actual **2 :** something that is actual

ac·tu·al·iza·tion \ˌak-ch(ə-w)ə-lə-'zā-shən, ˌaksh-wə-\ *n* **:** the act or process of actualizing **:** REALIZATION

ac·tu·al·ize \'ak-ch(ə-w)ə-ˌlīz, 'aksh-wə-\ *vt* **:** to make actual ~ *vi* **:** to become actual

ac·tu·al·ly \'ak-ch(ə-w)ə-lē, 'aksh-wə-; 'aksh-lē\ *adv* **:** in act or in fact **:** REALLY

ac·tu·ar·i·al \ˌak-chə-'wer-ē-əl\ *adj* **:** of or relating to actuaries **:** relating to statistical calculation esp. of life expectancy — **ac·tu·ar·i·al·ly** \-ē-ə-lē\ *adv*

ac·tu·ary \'ak-chə-ˌwer-ē\ *n* [L *actuarius* shorthand writer, fr. *actum* record — more at ACT] **1** *obs* **:** CLERK, REGISTRAR **2 :** one who calculates insurance and annuity premiums, reserves, and dividends

ac·tu·ate \'ak-chə-ˌwāt\ *vt* [ML *actuatus*, pp. of *actuare*, fr. L *actus* act] **1 :** to put into mechanical action or motion **2 :** to move to action **syn** see MOVE — **ac·tu·a·tion** \ˌak-chə-'wā-shən\ *n*

ac·tu·a·tor \'ak-chə-ˌwāt-ər\ *n* **:** one that actuates; *specif* **:** a mechanism for moving or controlling something indirectly instead of by hand

act up *vi* **:** to act in a way different from that which is normal or expected: as **a :** to behave in an unruly manner **b :** to show off

acu·ity \ə-'kyü-ət-ē\ *n* [MF *acuité*, fr. OF *agüeté*, fr. *agu* sharp, fr. L *acutus*] **:** keenness of perception **:** SHARPNESS

acu·le·ate \ə-'kyü-lē-ət\ *adj* [L *aculeatus* having stings, fr. *aculeus*, dim. of *acus*] **:** having a sting **:** furnished with spines or prickles

acu·men \ə-'kyü-mən\ *n* [L *acumin-*, *acumen*, lit., point, fr. *acuere*] **:** keenness of perception, discernment, or discrimination esp. in practical matters **syn** see DISCERNMENT

[1]**acu·mi·nate** \ə-'kyü-mə-nət\ *adj* **:** tapering to a slender point **:** POINTED

[2]**acu·mi·nate** \-ˌnāt\ *vt* **:** to make sharp or acute ~ *vi* **:** to taper or come to a point — **acu·mi·na·tion** \ə-ˌkyü-mə-'nā-shən\ *n*

acu·punc·ture \'ak-yü-ˌpəŋ(k)-chər\ *n* [L *acus* + E *puncture*] **:** an orig. Chinese practice of puncturing the body to cure disease or relieve pain

acute \ə-'kyüt\ *adj* [L *acutus*, pp. of *acuere* to sharpen, fr. *acus* needle; akin to L *acer* sharp — more at EDGE] **1 :** ending in a sharp point: as **a :** measuring less than 90 degrees ⟨~ angle⟩ **b :** composed of acute angles **2 a :** marked by keen discernment or intellectual perception esp. of subtle distinctions **:** PENETRATING **b :** responsive to slight impressions or stimuli ⟨~ observer⟩ **3 :** of a kind (as in intensity) to act keenly on the senses; *esp* **:** characterized by sharpness or severity ⟨~ pain⟩ **4 :** having a sudden onset, sharp rise, and short course ⟨~ disease⟩ **5 :** seriously demanding urgent attention **:** CRITICAL **6 a** *of an accent mark* **:** having the form ′ **b :** marked with an acute accent **c :** of the variety indicated by an acute accent — **acute·ly** *adv* — **acute·ness** *n*

syn ACUTE, CRITICAL, CRUCIAL mean full of uncertainty as to outcome. ACUTE stresses intensification of need, or symptoms, or conflicting emotions to a culmination or breaking point; CRITICAL adds to ACUTE implications of imminent change, of attendant suspense, and of decisiveness in the outcome; CRUCIAL suggests a dividing of the ways and often a test or trial involving the determination of a future course or direction **syn** see in addition SHARP

acy·clic \(ˈ)ā-'sī-klik, -'sik-lik\ *adj* **1 :** not cyclic; *esp* **:** not disposed in cycles or whorls **2 :** having an open-chain structure; *esp* **:** ALIPHATIC

ac·yl \'as-əl\ *n* [ISV, fr. *acid*] **:** a radical derived usu. from an organic acid by removal of the hydroxyl from all acid groups

ad \'ad\ *n* **:** ADVERTISEMENT 2

ad- *or* **ac-** *or* **af-** *or* **ag-** *or* **al-** *or* **ap-** *or* **as-** *or* **at-** *prefix* [ME, fr. MF, OF & L; MF, fr. OF, fr. L, fr. *ad* — more at AT] **1 :** to **:** towards — usu. *ac-* before *c*, *k*, or *q* ⟨*ac*culturation⟩ and *af-* before *f* and *ag-* before *g* ⟨*ag*grade⟩ and *al-* before *l* ⟨*al*literation⟩ and *ap-* before *p* ⟨*ap*proximal⟩ and *as-* before *s* ⟨*as*suasive⟩ and *at-* before *t* ⟨*at*tune⟩ and *ad-* before other sounds but sometimes *ad-* even before one of the listed consonants ⟨*ad*sorb⟩ **2 :** near **:** adjacent to — in this sense always in the form *ad-* ⟨*ad*renal⟩

-ad \ˌad, əd\ *adv suffix* [L *ad*] **:** in the direction of **:** toward ⟨cephal*ad*⟩

ad·age \'ad-ij\ *n* [MF, fr. L *adagium*, fr. *ad-* + *-agium* (akin to *aio* I say); akin to Gk *ē* he spoke] **:** a saying embodying common observation often in metaphorical form

[1]**ada·gio** \ə-'däj-(ˌ)ō, -'däj-ē-ˌō, -'däzh-\ *adv (or adj)* [It, fr. *ad* to + *agio* ease] **:** in an easy graceful manner **:** SLOWLY — used chiefly as a direction in music

[2]**adagio** *n* **1 :** a musical composition or movement in adagio tempo **2 :** a ballet duet by a man and woman or a mixed trio displaying difficult feats of balance, lifting, or spinning

[1]**Ad·am** \'ad-əm\ *n* [ME, fr. LL, fr. Gk, fr. Heb *Ādhām*] **1 :** the first man and progenitor of the human race **2 :** the unregenerate nature of man — **Adam·ic** \ə-'dam-ik\ *adj* — **Adam·i·cal** \-i-kəl\ *adj*

[2]**Adam** *adj* [Robert *Adam* †1792 & James *Adam* †1794 Sc designers] **:** of or relating to an 18th century style of furniture characterized by straight lines, surface decoration, and conventional designs (as festooned garlands and medallions)

adam–and–eve \ˌad-ə-mən-'(d)ēv\ *n* **:** PUTTYROOT

[1]**ad·a·mant** \'ad-ə-mənt, -ˌmant\ *n* [ME, fr. OF, fr. L *adamant-*, *adamas* hardest metal, diamond, fr. Gk] **1 :** a stone believed to be of impenetrable hardness **2 :** an unbreakable or extremely hard substance

[2]**adamant** *adj* **:** unshakable or immovable esp. in opposition **:** UNYIELDING **syn** see INFLEXIBLE — **ad·a·mant·ly** *adv*

ad·a·man·tine \ˌad-ə-'man-ˌtēn, -ˌtīn, -'mant-ᵊn\ *adj* [ME, fr. L *adamantinus*, fr. Gk *adamantinos*, fr. *adamant-*, *adamas*] **1 :** made of or having the quality of adamant **2 :** rigidly firm **:** UNYIELDING **3 :** resembling the diamond in hardness or luster

Adam's apple *n* **:** the projection in the front of the neck formed by the largest cartilage of the larynx

Adam's needle *n* **:** any of several yuccas

adapt \ə-'dapt\ *vb* [F or L; F *adapter*, fr. L *adaptare*, fr. *ad-* + *aptare* to fit, fr. *aptus* apt, fit] *vt* **:** to make fit (as for a specific or new use or situation) often by modifying ~ *vi* **:** to become adapted

syn ADAPT, ADJUST, ACCOMMODATE, CONFORM, RECONCILE mean to bring one into correspondence with another. ADAPT implies a suiting or fitting by modification and sometimes connotes pliability or readiness; ADJUST implies a bringing into exact or close correspondence often by use of tact or ingenuity; ACCOMMODATE implies a reaching of a state of adjustment or adaptation by yielding or giving in a necessary degree or amount; CONFORM implies a bringing into accord with a pattern, example, or principle; RECONCILE implies the demonstrating of the consistency or congruity of things that seem to be incompatible

adapt·abil·i·ty \ə-ˌdap-tə-'bil-ət-ē\ *n* **:** the quality or state of being adaptable

adapt·able \ə-'dap-tə-bəl\ *adj* **:** capable of being adapted **:** SUITABLE **syn** see PLASTIC

ad·ap·ta·tion \ˌad-ˌap-'tā-shən\ *n* **1 a :** the act or process of adapting **b :** the state of being adapted **2 :** adjustment to environmental conditions: as **a :** adjustment of a sense organ to the intensity or quality of stimulation **b :** modification of an organism or its parts that fits it better for the conditions of its environment **3 :** something that is adapted; *specif* **:** a composition rewritten into a new form — **ad·ap·ta·tion·al** \-shnəl, -shən-ᵊl\ *adj* — **ad·ap·ta·tion·al·ly** \-ē\ *adv*

adapt·er *also* **adapt·or** \ə-'dap-tər\ *n* **1 :** one that adapts **2 a :** a device for connecting two parts (as of different diameters) of an apparatus **b :** an attachment for adapting apparatus for uses not orig. intended

adap·tion \ə-'dap-shən\ *n* **:** ADAPTATION

adap·tive \ə-'dap-tiv\ *adj* **:** showing or having a capacity for or tendency toward adaptation — **adap·tive·ly** *adv*

Adar \ä-'där\ *n* [Heb *Ădhār*] **:** the 6th month of the civil year or the 12th month of the ecclesiastical year in the Jewish calendar

Adar She·ni \ä-ˌdär-shā-'nē\ *n* [Heb *Ădhār Shēnī* second Adar] **:** VEADAR

ad·ax·i·al \(ˈ)a-'dak-sē-əl\ *adj* **:** situated on the same side as or facing the axis (as of an organ)

add \'ad\ *vb* [ME *adden*, fr. L *addere*, fr. *ad-* + *-dere* to put — more at DO] *vt* **1 :** to join or unite so as to increase in number, size, or amount **2 :** to say further **:** APPEND **3 :** to combine (numbers) into an equivalent simple quantity or number ~ *vi* **1 a :** to perform addition **b :** to come together or unite by addition **2 a :** to serve as an addition **b :** to make an addition **:** ENLARGE — **add·able** *or* **add·ible** \'ad-ə-bəl\ *adj*

ad·dax \'ad-ˌaks\ *n* [L] **:** a large light-colored antelope (*Addax nasomaculata*) of No. Africa, Arabia, and Syria

ad·dend \'ad-ˌend, ə-'dend\ *n* [short for *addendum*] **:** a number to be added to another

ad·den·dum \ə-'den-dəm\ *n, pl* **ad·den·da** \-də\ [L, neut. of *addendus*, gerundive of *addere*] **1 :** a thing added **:** ADDITION **2 :** a supplement to a book — sometimes pl. but sing. in constr.

[1]**ad·der** \'ad-ər\ *n* [ME, alter. (by incorrect division of *a naddre*) of *naddre*, fr. OE *nǣdre;* akin to OHG *nātara* adder, L *natrix* water snake] **1 :** the common venomous viper (*Vipera berus*) of Europe; *broadly* **:** a terrestrial viper (family Viperidae) **2 :** any of several No. American snakes (as the hognose snakes) harmless but popularly reputed venomous

[2]**add·er** \'ad-ər\ *n* **:** one that adds

ad·der's–tongue \'ad-ərz-ˌtəŋ\ *n* **1 :** a fern (genus *Ophioglossum*, family Ophioglossaceae) whose fruiting spike resembles a serpent's tongue **2 :** DOGTOOTH VIOLET

[1]**ad·dict** \ə-'dikt\ *vt* [L *addictus*, pp. of *addicere* to favor, fr. *ad-* + *dicere* to say — more at DICTION] **1 :** to devote or surrender (oneself) to something habitually or obsessively; *esp* **:** to accustom (oneself) to the habitual use of a drug **2 :** to induce to use an addictive drug

[2]**ad·dict** \'ad-(ˌ)ikt\ *n* **:** one who is addicted esp. to a drug

ad·dic·tion \ə-'dik-shən\ *n* **:** the quality or state of being addicted; *specif* **:** compulsive use of habit-forming drugs

ad·dic·tive \ə-'dik-tiv\ *adj* **:** causing or characterized by addiction

Ad·di·son's disease \'ad-ə-sənz-\ *n* [Thomas *Addison* †1860 E

physician] **:** a destructive disease marked by deficient secretion of the adrenal cortical hormone and characterized by extreme weakness, loss of weight, low blood pressure, gastrointestinal disturbances, and brownish pigmentation of the skin and mucous membranes

ad·di·tion \ə-'dish-ən\ *n* [ME, fr. MF, fr. L *addition-, additio,* fr. *additus,* pp. of *addere*] **1 :** the result of adding **:** INCREASE **2 :** the act or process of adding **3 :** the operation of combining numbers so as to obtain an equivalent simple quantity **4 :** a part added (as to a building or residential section) **5 :** direct chemical combination of substances into a single product

ad·di·tion·al \ə-'dish-nəl, -'dish-ən-ᵊl\ *adj* **:** existing by way of addition **:** ADDED — **ad·di·tion·al·ly** \-ē\ *adv*

¹**ad·di·tive** \'ad-ət-iv\ *adj* **1 :** admitting, involving, or characterized by addition **2 :** produced by addition — **ad·di·tive·ly** *adv*

²**additive** *n* **:** a substance added to another in relatively small amounts to impart or improve desirable properties or suppress undesirable properties

¹**ad·dle** \'ad-ᵊl\ *adj* [ME *adel* filth, fr. OE *adela;* akin to MLG *adele* liquid manure] **1** *of an egg* **:** ROTTEN **2 :** CONFUSED, MUDDLED

²**addle** *vb* **ad·dling** \'ad-liŋ, -ᵊl-iŋ\ *vt* **:** to throw into confusion **:** CONFOUND ~ *vi* **1 :** to become rotten **:** SPOIL **2 :** to become addled

¹**ad·dress** \ə-'dres\ *vb* [ME *adressen,* fr. MF *adresser,* fr. *a-* (fr. L *ad-*) + *dresser* to arrange — more at DRESS] *vt* **1 a :** DIRECT, AIM **b :** to direct to go **:** SEND **2** *archaic* **:** to make ready; *esp* **:** DRESS **3 :** to direct the efforts or attention of (oneself) **4 a :** to communicate directly **b :** to communicate directly to; *esp* **:** to deliver a formal speech to **5 a :** to mark directions for delivery on ⟨~ a letter⟩ **b :** to consign to the care of another **6 :** to greet by a prescribed form **7 :** to adjust the club preparatory to hitting (a golf ball) ~ *vi, obs* **:** to direct one's speech or attentions — **ad·dress·er** *n*

²**ad·dress** \ə-'dres, 'ad-ˌres\ *n* **1 a** *obs* **:** PREPARATION **b :** skillful readiness **:** ADROITNESS **2 a :** BEARING, DEPORTMENT **b :** the manner of speaking or singing **:** DELIVERY **3 :** dutiful attention esp. in courtship — usu. used in pl. **4 :** a formal communication; *esp* **:** a prepared speech delivered to a special audience or on a special occasion **5 a :** a place where a person or organization may be communicated with **b :** directions for delivery on the outside of an object (as a letter or package) **c :** the designation of place of delivery on a business letter **6 :** a preparatory position of the player and club in golf **7 :** a unit where particular information is stored (as in a computer) **syn** see TACT

ad·dress·ee \ˌad-ˌres-'ē, ə-ˌdres-'ē\ *n* **:** one to whom something is addressed

ad·duce \ə-'d(y)üs\ *vt* [L *adducere,* lit., to lead to, fr. *ad-* + *ducere* to lead — more at TOW] **:** to offer as example, reason, or proof in discussion or analysis — **ad·duc·er** *n*

syn CITE, ADVANCE, ALLEGE: ADDUCE implies offering facts, evidence, or instances as proof of or in support of something stated; CITE implies an adducing of specific instances or authority; ADVANCE implies the presenting not of facts but of a theory or claim or proposal for consideration or acceptance; ALLEGE implies reciting facts intended to be proved but may suggest that proof is not available or possible

ad·du·cent \a-'d(y)üs-ᵊnt\ *adj* [L *adducent-, adducens,* prp. of *adducere*] *of a muscle* **:** ADDUCTING

¹**ad·duct** \ə-'dəkt, a-\ *vt* [L *adductus,* pp. of *adducere*] **:** to draw (as a limb) toward or past the median axis of the body; *also* **:** to bring together (similar parts) ⟨~ the fingers⟩ — **ad·duc·tive** \-'dək-tiv\ *adj* — **ad·duc·tor** \-tər\ *n*

²**ad·duct** \'ad-ˌəkt\ *n* [G *addukt,* fr. L *adductus*] **:** a chemical addition product

ad·duc·tion \ə-'dək-shən, a-\ *n* **1 :** the action of adducting **:** the state of being adducted **2 :** the act or action of adducing or bringing forward

-ade *n suffix* [ME, fr. MF, fr. OProv *-ada,* fr. LL *-ata,* fr. L, fem. of *-atus* -ate] **1 :** act **:** action ⟨block*ade*⟩ **2 :** product; *esp* **:** sweet drink ⟨lime*ade*⟩

-adel·phous \ə-'del-fəs\ *adj comb form* [prob. fr. NL *-adelphus,* fr. Gk *adelphos* brother, fr. *ha-, a-* (akin to *homos* same) + *delphys* womb — more at SAME, DOLPHIN] **:** having (such or so many) stamen fascicles ⟨mon*adelphous*⟩

aden- *or* **adeno-** *comb form* [NL, fr. Gk, fr. *aden-, adēn;* akin to L *inguen* groin, Gk *nephros* kidney] **:** gland ⟨*aden*itis⟩

ad·e·nine \'ad-ᵊn-ˌēn\ *n* **:** a purine base $C_5H_5N_5$ that is a constituent of nucleic acids and various enzyme systems

ad·e·no·car·ci·no·ma \ˌad-ᵊn-(ˌ)ō-ˌkärs-ᵊn-'ō-mə\ *n* [NL] **:** a malignant tumor originating in glandular epithelium — **ad·e·no·car·ci·no·ma·tous** \-'äm-ət-əs, -'ō-mət-\ *adj*

¹**ad·e·noid** \'ad-ᵊn-ˌȯid, 'ad-ˌnȯid\ *or* **ad·e·noi·dal** \ˌad-ᵊn-'ȯid-ᵊl\ *adj* [Gk *adenoeidēs,* fr. *adēn*] **1 :** of, resembling, or relating to glands or glandular or lymphoid tissue **2 a :** of or relating to the adenoids **b** *usu adenoidal* **:** typical or suggestive of adenoid disorder

²**adenoid** *n* **:** an enlarged mass of lymphoid tissue at the back of the pharynx characteristically obstructing breathing — usu. used in pl.

ad·e·no·ma \ˌad-ᵊn-'ō-mə\ *n* **:** a benign tumor of a glandular structure or of glandular origin — **ad·e·nom·a·tous** \-'äm-ət-əs\ *adj*

aden·o·sine \ə-'den-ə-ˌsēn\ *n* [ISV, blend of *adenine & ribose*] **:** a nucleoside $C_{10}H_{13}N_5O_4$ that is a constituent of ribonucleic acid yielding adenine and ribose on hydrolysis

adenosine tri·phos·phate \-ˌtrī-'fäs-ˌfāt\ *n* **:** a derivative of adenosine that occurs in muscle tissue and serves as a source of energy

¹**ad·ept** \'ad-ˌept\ *n* [NL *adeptus,* alchemist who has attained the knowledge of how to change base metals into gold, fr. L, pp. of *adipisci* to attain, fr. *ad-* + *apisci* to reach — more at APT] **:** a highly skilled or well-trained individual **:** EXPERT

²**adept** \ə-'dept\ *adj* **:** thoroughly proficient **:** EXPERT **syn** see PROFICIENT — **adept·ly** \-'dep-(t)lē\ *adv* — **adept·ness** \-'dep(t)-nəs\ *n*

ad·e·qua·cy \'ad-i-kwə-sē\ *n* **:** the quality or state of being adequate

ad·e·quate \-kwət\ *adj* [L *adaequatus,* pp. of *adaequare* to make equal, fr. *ad-* + *aequare* to equal — more at EQUATE] **1 :** sufficient for a specific requirement; *specif* **:** barely sufficient **2 :** lawfully and reasonably sufficient **syn** see SUFFICIENT — **ad·e·quate·ly** *adv* — **ad·e·quate·ness** *n*

ad eun·dem \ˌad-ē-'ən-dəm\ *or* **ad eundem gra·dum** \-'grād-əm\ *adv (or adj)* [NL *ad eundem gradum*] **:** to, in, or of the same rank — used esp. of the honorary granting of standing or a degree by a university to one whose work was done elsewhere

ad·here \ad-'hi(ə)r, əd-\ *vi* [MF or L; MF *adhérer,* fr. L *adhaerēre,* fr. *ad-* + *haerēre* to stick — more at HESITATE] **1 :** to give support or maintain loyalty **2** *obs* **:** to be consistent **:** ACCORD **3 :** to hold fast or stick by or as if by gluing, suction, grasping, or fusing **4 :** to bind oneself to observance **syn** see STICK

ad·her·ence \-'hir-ən(t)s\ *n* **1 :** the act, action, or quality of adhering **2 :** steady or faithful attachment **:** FIDELITY

syn ADHERENCE, ADHESION mean a sticking to or together. ADHERENCE is applied chiefly to mental or moral attachment ⟨*adherence* to principles⟩; ADHESION is commonly restricted to physical attachment ⟨*adhesion* of iron to a magnet⟩

ad·her·end \-'hi(ə)r-ˌend, ˌad-ˌhi(ə)r-'\ *n* [*adhere* + *-end* (as in *addend*)] **:** the surface to which an adhesive adheres; *also* **:** one of the bodies held to another by an adhesive

¹**ad·her·ent** \ad-'hir-ənt, əd-\ *adj* [ME, fr. MF or L; MF *adhérent,* fr. L *adhaerent-, adhaerens,* prp. of *adhaerēre*] **1 :** able or tending to adhere **2 :** connected or associated with esp. by contract **3 :** ADNATE — **ad·her·ent·ly** *adv*

²**adherent** *n* **:** one that adheres: as **a :** a follower of a leader, party, or profession **b :** a believer in or advocate of a particular thing, idea, or church **syn** see FOLLOWER

ad·he·sion \-'hē-zhən\ *n* [F or L; F *adhésion,* fr. L *adhaesion-, adhaesio,* fr. *adhaesus,* pp. of *adhaerēre*] **1 :** steady or firm attachment **:** ADHERENCE **2 :** the action or state of adhering; *specif* **:** a union of bodily parts by growth **3 :** tissues abnormally united by fibrous tissue resulting from an inflammatory process **4 :** agreement to join **5 :** the molecular attraction exerted between the surfaces of bodies in contact **syn** see ADHERENCE — **ad·he·sion·al** \-'hēzh-nəl, -'hē-zhən-ᵊl\ *adj*

¹**ad·he·sive** \-'hē-siv, -ziv\ *adj* **1 :** tending to remain in association or memory **2 :** tending to adhere **:** prepared for adhering **:** STICKY — **ad·he·sive·ly** *adv* — **ad·he·sive·ness** *n*

²**adhesive** *n* **:** an adhesive substance (as glue or cement)

adhesive tape *n* **:** tape coated on one side with an adhesive mixture

ad hoc \(')ad-'häk\ *adv (or adj)* [L, for this] **:** for the particular end or case at hand without consideration of wider application

ad ho·mi·nem \(')ad-'häm-ə-ˌnem\ *adj* [NL, lit., to the man] **:** appealing to a person's feelings or prejudices rather than his intellect

adia·bat·ic \ˌad-ē-ə-'bat-ik, ˌā-ˌdī-ə-\ *adj* [Gk *adiabatos* impassable, fr. *a-* + *diabatos* passable, fr. *diabainein* to go across, fr. *dia-* + *bainein* to go — more at COME] **:** occurring without loss or gain of heat ⟨~ expansion⟩ — **adia·bat·i·cal·ly** \-i-k(ə-)lē\ *adv*

adieu \ə-'d(y)ü\ *n, pl* **adieus** *or* **adieux** \ə-'d(y)üz\ [ME, fr. MF, fr. *a* (fr. L *ad*) + *Dieu* God, fr. L *Deus* — more at AT, DEITY] **:** FAREWELL — often used interjectionally

ad in·fi·ni·tum \ˌad-ˌin-fə-'nīt-əm\ *adv (or adj)* [L] **:** without end or limit

¹**ad in·ter·im** \(')ad-'in-tə-rəm, -ˌrim\ *adv* [L] **:** for the intervening time **:** TEMPORARILY

²**ad interim** *adj* **:** made or serving ad interim

adi·os \ˌad-ē-'ōs, ˌäd-\ *interj* [Sp *adiós,* fr. *a* (fr. L *ad*) + *Dios* God, fr. L *Deus*] — used to express farewell

ad·i·pose \'ad-ə-ˌpōs\ *adj* [NL *adiposus,* fr. L *adip-, adeps* fat, fr. Gk *aleipha;* akin to Gk *lipos* fat — more at LEAVE] **:** of or relating to animal fat **:** FATTY — **ad·i·pos·i·ty** \ˌad-ə-'päs-ət-ē\ *n*

adipose tissue *n* **:** connective tissue in which fat is stored and which has the cells distended by droplets of fat

ad·it \'ad-ət\ *n* [L *aditus* approach, fr. *aditus,* pp. of *adire* to go to, fr. *ad-* + *ire* to go — more at ISSUE] **:** a nearly horizontal passage from the surface in a mine

ad·ja·cen·cy \ə-'jās-ᵊn-sē\ *n* **1 :** something that is adjacent **2 :** the quality or state of being adjacent **:** CONTIGUITY

ad·ja·cent \ə-'jās-ᵊnt\ *adj* [ME, fr. MF or L; MF, fr. L *adjacent-, adjacens,* prp. of *adjacēre* to lie near, fr. *ad-* + *jacēre* to lie; akin to L *jacere* to throw — more at JET] **1 a :** not distant **:** NEARBY **b :** having a common border **:** ABUTTING **c :** immediately preceding or following **2** *of two angles* **:** having a common vertex and side — **ad·ja·cent·ly** *adv*

syn ADJACENT, ADJOINING, CONTIGUOUS, ABUTTING mean being in close proximity. ADJACENT may or may not imply contact but always implies absence of anything of the same kind in between; ADJOINING definitely implies meeting and touching at some point or line; CONTIGUOUS implies having contact on all or most of one side; ABUTTING suggests having a contact with something else at a boundary or dividing line

ad·jec·ti·val \ˌaj-ik-'tī-vəl\ *adj* **1 :** ADJECTIVE **2 :** characterized by the use of adjectives — **ad·jec·ti·val·ly** \-və-lē\ *adv*

¹**ad·jec·tive** \'aj-ik-tiv\ *adj* [ME, fr. MF or LL; MF *adjectif,* fr. LL *adjectivus,* fr. L *adjectus,* pp. of *adjicere* to throw to, fr. *ad-* + *jacere* to throw — more at JET] **1 :** of, relating to, or functioning as an adjective ⟨an ~ clause⟩ **2 :** not standing by itself **:** DEPENDENT **3 :** requiring or employing a mordant ⟨~ dyes⟩ **4 :** PROCEDURAL ⟨~ law⟩ — **ad·jec·tive·ly** *adv*

²**adjective** *n* **:** a word belonging to one of the major form classes in any of numerous languages and typically serving as a modifier of a noun to denote a quality of the thing named, to indicate its quantity or extent, or to specify a thing as distinct from something else

ad·join \ə-'jȯin\ *vb* [ME *adjoinen,* fr. MF *adjoindre,* fr. L *adjungere,* fr. *ad-* + *jungere* to join — more at YOKE] *vt* **1 :** to add or attach by joining **2 :** to lie next to or in contact with ~ *vi* **:** to be close to or in contact with one another

ad·join·ing *adj* **:** touching or bounding at a point or line **syn** see ADJACENT

ad·journ \ə-'jərn\ *vb* [ME *ajournen,* fr. MF *ajourner,* fr. *a-* (fr. L *ad-*) + *jour* day — more at JOURNEY] *vt* **:** to suspend indefinitely or until a later stated time ~ *vi* **:** to suspend a session to another time or place or indefinitely

syn PROROGUE, DISSOLVE: ADJOURN implies suspending deliberations either until an appointed resumption or indefinitely; PRO-

ROGUE and DISSOLVE apply to action by the crown or its representative; PROROGUE implies ending a session so that all bills not enacted are quashed and can be taken up only as new matter at a succeeding session; DISSOLVE implies that the body ceases to exist as presently constituted so that an election must be held if it is to be reconstituted

ad·journ·ment \ə-'jərn-mənt\ *n* **1 :** the act of adjourning **2 :** the state or interval of being adjourned

ad·judge \ə-'jəj\ *vt* [ME *ajugen*, fr. MF *ajugier*, fr. L *adjudicare*, fr. *ad-* + *judicare* to judge — more at JUDGE] **1 a :** to decide or rule upon as a judge **:** ADJUDICATE **b :** to pronounce judicially **:** RULE **2** *archaic* **:** SENTENCE, CONDEMN **3 :** to hold or pronounce to be **:** DEEM **4 :** to award or grant judicially

ad·ju·di·cate \ə-'jüd-i-,kāt\ *vt* [L *adjudicatus*, pp. of *adjudicare*] **:** to hear or try and determine judicially — **ad·ju·di·ca·tive** \-,kāt-iv, -kət-\ *adj* — **ad·ju·di·ca·tor** \-,kāt-ər\ *n*

ad·ju·di·ca·tion \ə-,jüd-i-'kā-shən\ *n* **1 :** the act or process of adjudicating **2 :** a judicial decision or sentence; *specif* **:** a decree in bankruptcy — **ad·ju·di·ca·to·ry** \-'jüd-i-kə-,tōr-ē, -,tȯr-\ *adj*

1**ad·junct** \'aj-,əŋ(k)t\ *n* [L *adjunctum*, fr. neut. of *adjunctus*, pp. of *adjungere*] **1 :** something joined or added to another thing but not essentially a part of it **2 :** a word or word group that qualifies or completes the meaning of another word or other words and is not itself one of the principal structural elements in its sentence **3 :** a person associated with or assisting another — **ad·junc·tive** \a-'jəŋ(k)-tiv\ *adj*

2**adjunct** *adj* **1 :** added or joined as an accompanying object or circumstance **2 :** attached in a subordinate or temporary capacity to a staff — **ad·junct·ly** \'aj-,əŋ(k)-tlē, -,əŋ-klē\ *adv*

ad·junc·tion \a-'jəŋ(k)-shən\ *n* **:** the act or process of adjoining

ad·ju·ra·tion \,aj-ə-'rā-shən\ *n* **1 :** a solemn oath **2 :** an earnest or solemn urging or charging — **ad·jur·a·to·ry** \ə-'jür-ə-,tōr-ē, -,tȯr-\ *adj*

ad·jure \ə-'jü(ə)r\ *vt* [ME *adjuren*, fr. MF & L; MF *ajurer*, fr. L *adjurare*, fr. *ad-* + *jurare* to swear — more at JURY] **1 :** to charge or command solemnly under or as if under oath or penalty of a curse **2 :** to entreat earnestly **:** CHARGE **syn** see BEG

ad·just \ə-'jəst\ *vb* [F *ajuster*, fr. *a-* + *juste* exact, just] *vt* **1 a :** to bring to a more satisfactory state: (1) **:** SETTLE, RESOLVE (2) **:** RECTIFY **b :** to make correspondent or conformable **:** ADAPT **c :** to bring the parts of to a true or more effective relative position **2 :** to reduce to a system **:** REGULATE **3 :** to determine the amount to be paid under an insurance policy in settlement of (a loss) ~ *vi* **:** to adapt or conform oneself **syn** see ADAPT — **ad·just·able** \ə-'jəs-tə-bəl\ *adj* — **ad·just·er** *also* **ad·jus·tor** \-tər\ *n*

ad·just·ment \ə-'jəs(t)-mənt\ *n* **1 :** the act or process of adjusting **2 :** a settlement of a claim or debt in a case in which the amount involved is uncertain or in which full payment is not made **3 :** the state of being adjusted **4 :** a means by which things are adjusted one to another **5 :** a correction or modification to reflect actual conditions — **ad·just·men·tal** \ə-,jəs(t)-'ment-ᵊl\ *adj*

ad·ju·tan·cy \'aj-ət-ən-sē\ *n* **:** the office or rank of an adjutant

ad·ju·tant \'aj-ət-ənt\ *n* [L *adjutant-*, *adjutans*, prp. of *adjutare* to help — more at AID] **1 :** a staff officer in the army, air force, or marine corps assisting the commanding officer and responsible esp. for correspondence **2 :** one who helps **:** ASSISTANT

adjutant bird *n* **:** any of several large upright storks (genus *Leptoptilos*) having the head and neck bare and feeding on carrion or small animals

adjutant general *n, pl* **adjutants general 1 :** the chief administrative officer of an army **2 :** the chief administrative officer of a major military unit (as a division or corps)

1**ad·ju·vant** \'aj-ə-vənt\ *adj* [F or L; F, fr. L *adjuvant-*, *adjuvans*, prp. of *adjuvare* to aid — more at AID] **:** serving to aid or contribute **:** AUXILIARY

2**adjuvant** *n* **:** one that helps or facilitates; *esp* **:** something that enhances the effectiveness of medical treatment

Ad·le·ri·an \ad-'lir-ē-ən\ *adj* [Alfred *Adler* †1937 Austrian psychiatrist] **:** of, relating to, or being a theory and technique of psychotherapy emphasizing the importance of feelings of inferiority, a will to power, and overcompensation in neurotic processes

ad lib \(')ad-'lib\ *adv* [NL *ad libitum*] **:** without restraint or limit

1**ad–lib** \(')ad-'lib\ *adj* **:** spoken or composed extempore

2**ad–lib** *vb* **ad–libbed; ad–lib·bing** *vt* **:** to deliver spontaneously ~ *vi* **:** to improvise lines or a speech

ad li·bi·tum \(')ad-'lib-ət-əm\ *adv* [NL] **:** in accordance with one's wishes — used as a direction in music

ad·man \'ad-,man\ *n* **:** one who writes, solicits, or places advertisements

ad·mea·sure \ad-'mezh-ər, -'mā-zhər\ *vt* [ME *amesuren*, fr. MF *amesurer*, fr. *a-* (fr. L *ad-*) + *mesurer* to measure] **:** to determine the proper share of **:** APPORTION

ad·mea·sure·ment \-mənt\ *n* **1 :** determination and apportionment of shares **2 :** determination or comparison of dimensions **3 :** DIMENSIONS, SIZE

Ad·me·tus \ad-'mēt-əs\ *n* [Gk *Admētos*] **:** the husband of Alcestis

ad·min·is·ter \əd-'min-ə-stər\ *vb* **ad·min·is·ter·ing** \-st(ə-)riŋ\ [ME *administren*, fr. MF *administrer*, fr. L *administrare*, fr. *ad-* + *ministrare* to serve — more at MINISTER] *vt* **1 :** to superintend the execution, use, or conduct of **2 a :** to mete out **:** DISPENSE **b :** to give ritually **c :** to give remedially ~ *vi* **1 :** to perform the office of administrator **2 :** to furnish a benefit **:** MINISTER **3 :** to manage affairs **syn** see EXECUTE — **ad·min·is·tra·ble** \-strə-bəl\ *adj* — **ad·min·is·trant** \-strənt\ *n*

ad·min·is·trate \əd-'min-ə-,strāt\ *vt* [L *administratus*, pp. of *administrare*] **:** ADMINISTER

ad·min·is·tra·tion \-,min-ə-'strā-shən, ad-\ *n* **1 :** the act or process of administering **2 :** performance of executive duties **:** MANAGEMENT **3 :** the execution of public affairs as distinguished from policy making **4 a :** a body of persons who administer **b** *cap* **:** a group constituting the political executive in a presidential government **c :** a governmental agency or board **5 :** the term of office of an administrative officer or body

ad·min·is·tra·tive \əd-,min-ə-,strāt-iv, -strət-\ *adj* **:** of or relating to administration or an administration **:** EXECUTIVE

administrative county *n* **:** a British local administrative unit often not coincident with an older county

ad·min·is·tra·tor \əd-'min-ə-,strāt-ər\ *n* **1 :** a person legally vested with the right of administration of an estate **2 a :** one that administers esp. public affairs **b :** a priest appointed to administer temporarily a diocese or parish — **ad·min·is·tra·trix** \-,min-ə-'strā-triks\ *n*

ad·mi·ra·ble \'ad-m(ə-)rə-bəl\ *adj* **1** *obs* **:** exciting wonder **:** SURPRISING **2 :** deserving the highest esteem **:** EXCELLENT — **ad·mi·ra·ble·ness** *n* — **ad·mi·ra·bly** \-blē\ *adv*

ad·mi·ral \'ad-m(ə-)rəl\ *n* [ME, fr. MF *amiral* admiral & ML *admiralis* emir, *admirallus* admiral, fr. Ar *amīr -al-* commander of the (as in *amīr-al-bahr* commander of the sea)] **1** *archaic* **:** the commander in chief of a navy **2 a :** a naval officer of flag rank **b :** a commissioned officer in the navy ranking above a vice admiral and below a fleet admiral **3** *archaic* **:** FLAGSHIP **4 :** any of several brightly colored butterflies (family Nymphalidae)

admiral of the fleet : the highest-ranking officer of the British navy

ad·mi·ral·ty \'ad-m(ə-)rəl-tē\ *n* **1** *Brit, cap* **:** the executive department or officers having general authority over naval affairs **2 :** the court having jurisdiction of maritime questions; *also* **:** the system of law administered by admiralty courts

ad·mi·ra·tion \,ad-mə-'rā-shən\ *n* **1** *archaic* **:** WONDER **2 :** the object of admiring esteem **3 a :** a feeling of delighted or astonished approbation **b :** the act or process of regarding with admiration

ad·mire \əd-'mī(ə)r\ *vt* [MF *admirer*, fr. L *admirari*, fr. *ad-* + *mirari* to wonder — more at SMILE] **1** *archaic* **:** to marvel at **2 :** to regard with admiration **3 :** to esteem highly **syn** see REGARD — **ad·mir·er** *n*

ad·mis·si·bil·i·ty \əd-,mis-ə-'bil-ət-ē\ *n* **:** the quality or state of being admissible

ad·mis·si·ble \əd-'mis-ə-bəl\ *adj* [F, fr. ML *admissibilis*, fr. L *admissus*, pp. of *admittere*] **1 :** capable of being allowed or conceded **:** PERMISSIBLE ⟨~ conclusions⟩ **2 :** capable of being or worthy to be admitted ⟨~ evidence⟩

ad·mis·sion \əd-'mish-ən\ *n* **1 a :** the granting of an argument or position not fully proved **b :** acknowledgment that a fact or statement is true **2 a :** the act or process of admitting **b :** the state or privilege of being admitted **c :** a fee paid at or for admission **syn** see ADMITTANCE — **ad·mis·sive** \-'mis-iv\ *adj*

ad·mit \əd-'mit\ *vb* **ad·mit·ted; ad·mit·ting** [ME *admitten*, fr. L *admittere*, fr. *ad-* + *mittere* to send — more at SMITE] *vt* **1 a :** to allow scope for **:** PERMIT **b :** to accept as true or valid **2 :** to allow entry ~ *vi* **1 :** to give entrance or access **2 a :** ALLOW, PERMIT **b :** to make acknowledgment **syn** see ACKNOWLEDGE, RECEIVE — **ad·mit·ted·ly** *adv*

ad·mit·tance \əd-'mit-ᵊn(t)s\ *n* **1 a :** permission to enter **b :** ADMISSION **2 :** the reciprocal of the impedance of a circuit

syn ADMITTANCE, ADMISSION mean permitted entrance. ADMITTANCE is usu. applied to mere physical entrance to a locality or a building; ADMISSION applies to entrance or formal acceptance that carries with it rights, privileges, standing, or membership

ad·mix \ad-'miks\ *vt* [back-formation fr. obs. *admixt* mingled with, fr. ME, fr. L *admixtus*] **:** MINGLE, BLEND

ad·mix·ture \ad-'miks-chər\ *n* [L *admixtus*, pp. of *admiscēre* to mix with, fr. *ad-* + *miscēre* to mix — more at MIX] **1 a :** the act of mixing **b :** the fact of being mixed **2 a :** something added by mixing **b :** a product of mixing **:** MIXTURE

ad·mon·ish \ad-'män-ish\ *vt* [ME *admonesten*, fr. MF *admonester*, fr. (assumed) VL *admonestare*, alter. of L *admonēre* to warn, fr. *ad-* + *monēre* to warn — more at MIND] **1 a :** to indicate duties or obligations to **b :** to express warning or disapproval to esp. gently, earnestly, and solicitously **2 :** to give friendly earnest advice or encouragement to **syn** see REPROVE — **ad·mon·ish·er** *n* — **ad·mon·ish·ing·ly** \-iŋ-lē\ *adv* — **ad·mon·ish·ment** \-mənt\ *n*

ad·mo·ni·tion \,ad-mə-'nish-ən\ *n* [ME *amonicioun*, fr. MF *amonition*, fr. L *admonition-*, *admonitio*, fr. *admonitus*, pp. of *admonēre*] **1 :** gentle or friendly reproof **2 :** counsel or warning against fault or oversight

ad·mon·i·to·ry \ad-'män-ə-,tōr-ē, -,tȯr-\ *adj* **:** expressing admonition **:** WARNING

ad·nate \'ad-,nāt\ *adj* [L *adgnatus*, pp. of *adgnasci* to grow on, fr. *ad-* + *nasci* to be born — more at NATION] **:** grown to a usu. unlike part esp. along a margin ⟨an ~ antler⟩ — **ad·na·tion** \ad-'nā-shən\ *n*

ad nau·se·am \ad-'nȯ-zē-əm\ *adv* [L] **:** to a sickening degree

ad·nexa \ad-'nek-sə\ *n pl* [NL, fr. L *annexa*, neut. pl. of *annexus*, pp. of *annectere* to bind to — more at ANNEX] **:** conjoined, subordinate, or associated anatomic parts; *specif* **:** the embryonic membranes and other temporary structures of the embryo — **ad·nex·al** \-səl\ *adj*

ado \ə-'dü\ *n* [ME, fr. *at do*, fr. *at* + *don, do* to do] **1 :** bustling excitement **:** TURMOIL **2 :** TROUBLE, DIFFICULTY **syn** see STIR

ado·be \ə-'dō-bē\ *n, often attrib* [Sp, fr. Ar *aṭ-ṭub* the brick, fr. Copt *tōbe* brick] **1 :** a brick or building material of sun-dried earth and straw **2 :** a heavy clay used in making adobe bricks; *broadly* **:** alluvial or playa clay in desert or arid regions **3 :** a structure made of adobe bricks

ad·o·les·cence \,ad-ᵊl-'es-ᵊn(t)s\ *n* **:** the state or process of growing up; *also* **:** the period of life from puberty to maturity terminating legally at the age of majority

1**ad·o·les·cent** \,ad-ᵊl-'es-ᵊnt\ *n* [F, fr. L *adolescent-*, *adolescens*, prp. of *adolescere* to grow up — more at ADULT] **:** one that is in the state of adolescence

2**adolescent** *adj* **:** of, relating to, or being in adolescence — **ad·o·les·cent·ly** *adv*

Ado·nis \ə-'dän-əs, -'dō-nəs\ *n* [L, fr. Gk *Adōnis*] **:** a beautiful youth loved by Aphrodite

adopt \ə-'däpt\ *vt* [MF or L; MF *adopter*, fr. L *adoptare*, fr. *ad-* + *optare* to choose — more at OPTION] **1 :** to take by choice into a relationship; *specif* **:** to take voluntarily (a child of other parents) as one's own child **2 :** to take up and practice as one's own **3 :** to accept formally and put into effect **4 :** to choose (a textbook) for required study in a course — **adopt·abil·i·ty** \ə-,däp-tə-'bil-ət-ē\ *n* — **adopt·able** \-'däp-tə-bəl\ *adj* — **adopt·er** *n*

syn ADOPT, EMBRACE, ESPOUSE mean to take an opinion, policy, or practice as one's own. ADOPT implies accepting something devised or created by another; EMBRACE implies a ready or happy acceptance; ESPOUSE adds an implication of close attachment to a cause and a sharing of its fortunes for better or worse

adop·tion \ə-'däp-shən\ *n* **:** the act of adopting **:** the state of being adopted

adop·tion·ism *or* **adop·tian·ism** \-shə-,niz-əm\ *n, often cap* **:** the doctrine that Jesus of Nazareth became son of God by adoption — **adop·tion·ist** \-sh(ə-)nəst\ *n, often cap*

adop·tive \ə-'däp-tiv\ *adj* **1 :** of or relating to adoption **2 :** made

or acquired by adoption ⟨~ father⟩ **3 :** tending to adopt — **adop·tive·ly** *adv*

ador·abil·i·ty \ə-ˌdōr-ə-ˈbil-ət-ē, -ˌdȯr-\ *n* **:** the quality of being adorable

ador·able \ə-ˈdōr-ə-bəl, -ˈdȯr-\ *adj* **1 :** worthy of being adored **2 :** extremely charming — **ador·able·ness** *n* — **ador·ably** \-blē\ *adv*

ad·o·ra·tion \ˌad-ə-ˈrā-shən\ *n* **:** the act of adoring **:** the state of being adored

adore \ə-ˈdō(ə)r, -ˈdȯ(ə)r\ *vt* [MF *adorer,* fr. L *adorare,* fr. *ad-* + *orare* to speak, pray — more at ORATION] **1 :** to worship or honor as a deity or as divine **2 :** to regard with reverent admiration and devotion **3 :** to be extremely fond of **syn** see REVERE — **ador·er** *n*

adorn \ə-ˈdȯ(ə)rn\ *vt* [ME *adornen,* fr. MF *adorner,* fr. L *adornare,* fr. *ad-* + *ornare* to furnish — more at ORNATE] **:** to decorate with ornaments **:** BEAUTIFY

syn DECORATE, ORNAMENT, EMBELLISH, BEAUTIFY, DECK, GARNISH: ADORN implies an enhancing by something beautiful in itself; DECORATE suggests relieving plainness or monotony by adding beauty of color or design; ORNAMENT and EMBELLISH imply the adding of something extraneous, ORNAMENT stressing the heightening or setting off of the original, EMBELLISH often stressing the adding of superfluous or adventitious ornament; BEAUTIFY adds to EMBELLISH a suggestion of counterbalancing plainness or ugliness; DECK implies the addition of something that contributes to gaiety, splendor, or showiness; GARNISH suggests decorating with a small final touch for use or service

adorn·ment \-mənt\ *n* **1 :** the action of adorning **:** the state of being adorned **2 :** something that adorns

ad rem \(ˈ)ad-ˈrem\ *adv* [L, to the thing] **:** to the point **:** RELEVANTLY

adren- *or* **adreno-** *comb form* [*adrenal*] **1 :** adrenal glands ⟨*adreno*cortical⟩ **2 :** adrenaline ⟨*adren*ergic⟩

adre·nal \ə-ˈdrēn-ᵊl\ *adj* **1 :** adjacent to the kidneys **2 :** of, relating to, or derived from adrenal glands or secretion

adrenal gland *n* **:** either of a pair of complex endocrine organs near the anterior medial border of the kidney consisting of a mesodermal cortex that produces steroids like sex hormones and hormones concerned esp. with metabolic functions and an ectodermal medulla that produces adrenaline

Adren·a·lin \ə-ˈdren-ᵊl-ən\ *trademark* — used for a preparation of levorotatory epinephrine

adren·a·line \ə-ˈdren-ᵊl-ən\ *n* **:** EPINEPHRINE

ad·ren·er·gic \ˌad-rə-ˈnər-jik\ *adj* [*adren-* + Gk *ergon* work — more at WORK] **1 :** liberating or activated by adrenaline or a substance like adrenaline ⟨an ~ nerve⟩ **2 :** resembling adrenaline

adre·no·cor·ti·cal \ə-ˌdrē-nō-ˈkȯrt-i-kəl\ *adj* **:** of, relating to, or derived from the cortex of the adrenal glands

adre·no·cor·ti·co·tro·phic \ə-ˌdrē-nō-ˌkȯrt-i-kō-ˈträf-ik, -ˈtrō-fik\ *or* **adre·no·cor·ti·co·trop·ic** \-ˈträp-ik\ *adj* **:** acting on or stimulating the adrenal cortex

adrenocorticotrophic hormone *n* **:** a protein hormone of the anterior lobe of the pituitary gland that stimulates the adrenal cortex

adrift \ə-ˈdrift\ *adv* (*or adj*) **1 :** without motive power and without anchor or mooring **2 :** without guidance or purpose

adroit \ə-ˈdrȯit\ *adj* [F, fr. *à droit* properly] **1 :** dexterous in the use of the hands **2 :** marked by shrewdness, craft, or resourcefulness in coping with difficulty or danger **syn** see CLEVER, DEXTEROUS — **adroit·ly** *adv* — **adroit·ness** *n*

ad·sci·ti·tious \ˌad-sə-ˈtish-əs\ *adj* [L *adscitus,* fr. pp. of *adsciscere* to receive, fr. *ad-* + *sciscere* to accept, fr. *scire* to know — more at SCIENCE] **:** derived or acquired from something extrinsic

ad·script \ˈad-ˌskript\ *adj* [L *adscriptus,* pp. of *adscribere* to ascribe] **:** written after ⟨iota ~⟩

ad·sorb \ad-ˈsȯ(ə)rb, -ˈzȯ(ə)rb\ *vt* [*ad-* + *-sorb* (as in *absorb*)] **:** to take up and hold by adsorption — **ad·sorb·able** \-ˈsȯr-bə-bəl, -ˈzȯr-\ *adj*

ad·sor·bate \ad-ˈsȯr-bət, -ˈzȯr-\ *n* **:** an adsorbed substance

ad·sor·bent \-bənt\ *adj* **:** having the capacity or tendency to adsorb — **adsorbent** *n*

ad·sorp·tion \ad-ˈsȯrp-shən, -ˈzȯrp-\ *n* [irreg. fr. *adsorb*] **:** the adhesion in an extremely thin layer of molecules (as of gases, solutes, or liquids) to the surfaces of solid bodies or liquids with which they are in contact — compare ABSORPTION — **ad·sorp·tive** \-ˈsȯrp-tiv, -ˈzȯrp-\ *adj*

ad·u·lar·ia \ˌaj-ə-ˈlar-ē-ə, -ˈler-\ *n* [It *adularia,* fr. F *adulaire,* fr. *Adula,* Swiss mountain group] **:** a transparent or translucent orthoclase

ad·u·late \ˈaj-ə-ˌlāt\ *vt* [back-formation fr. *adulation,* fr. ME, fr. MF, fr. L *adulation-, adulatio,* fr. *adulatus,* pp. of *adulari* to flatter] **:** to flatter or admire excessively or slavishly — **ad·u·la·tion** \ˌaj-ə-ˈlā-shən\ *n* — **ad·u·la·tor** \ˈaj-ə-ˌlāt-ər\ *n* — **ad·u·la·to·ry** \-lə-ˌtōr-ē, -ˌtȯr-\ *adj*

1**adult** \ə-ˈdəlt, ˈad-ˌəlt\ *adj* [L *adultus,* pp. of *adolescere* to grow up, fr. *ad-* + *-olescere* (fr. *alescere* to grow) — more at OLD] **1 :** fully developed and mature **:** GROWN-UP **2 :** of, relating to, or characteristic of adults — **adult·hood** \ə-ˈdəlt-ˌhu̇d\ *n* — **adult·ness** \ə-ˈdəlt-nəs, ˈad-ˌəlt-\ *n*

2**adult** *n* **:** one that is adult; *esp* **:** a human being after an age (as 21) specified by law

adul·ter·ant \ə-ˈdəl-t(ə-)rənt\ *n* **:** an adulterating substance or agent — **adulterant** *adj*

1**adul·ter·ate** \ə-ˈdəl-tə-ˌrāt\ *vt* [L *adulteratus,* pp. of *adulterare,* fr. *ad-* + *alter* other — more at ELSE] **:** to corrupt, debase, or make impure by the addition of a foreign or inferior substance; *esp* **:** to prepare for sale by replacing more valuable with less valuable or inert ingredients in whole or in part — **adul·ter·a·tor** \-ˌrāt-ər\ *n*

2**adul·ter·ate** \ə-ˈdəl-t(ə-)rət\ *adj* **1 :** tainted with adultery **:** ADULTEROUS **2 :** ADULTERATED, SPURIOUS

adul·ter·a·tion \ə-ˌdəl-tə-ˈrā-shən\ *n* **1 :** the process of adulterating **:** the condition of being adulterated **2 :** an adulterated product

adul·ter·er \ə-ˈdəl-tər-ər\ *n* **:** one that commits adultery; *esp* **:** a man who commits adultery

adul·ter·ess \ə-ˈdəl-t(ə-)rəs\ *n* **:** a woman who commits adultery

adul·ter·ine \ə-ˈdəl-tə-ˌrīn, -ˌrēn\ *adj* **1 a :** marked by adulteration **:** SPURIOUS **b :** ILLEGAL **2 :** born of adultery

adul·ter·ous \ə-ˈdəl-t(ə-)rəs\ *adj* **:** relating to, characterized by, or given to adultery — **adul·ter·ous·ly** *adv*

adul·tery \ə-ˈdəl-t(ə-)rē\ *n* [ME, alter. of *avoutrie,* fr. MF, fr. L *adulterium,* fr. *adulter* adulterer, back-formation fr. *adulterare*] **:** voluntary sexual intercourse between a married man and someone other than his wife or between a married woman and someone other than her husband

ad·um·brate \ˈad-əm-ˌbrāt, a-ˈdəm-\ *vt* [L *adumbratus,* pp. of *adumbrare,* fr. *ad-* + *umbra* shadow — more at UMBRAGE] **1 :** to foreshadow vaguely **:** INTIMATE **2 a :** to give a sketchy representation or outline of **b :** to suggest or disclose partially **3 :** SHADE, OBSCURE — **ad·um·bra·tion** \ˌad-(ˌ)əm-ˈbrā-shən\ *n* — **ad·um·bra·tive** \a-ˈdəm-brət-iv\ *adj* — **ad·um·bra·tive·ly** *adv*

adust \ə-ˈdəst\ *adj* [ME, fr. L *adustus,* pp. of *adurere* to set fire to, fr. *ad-* + *urere* to burn — more at EMBER] **1 :** BURNED, SCORCHED **2** *archaic* **:** of a sunburned appearance **3 :** of a gloomy appearance or disposition

ad va·lo·rem \ˌad-və-ˈlōr-əm, -ˈlȯr-\ *adj* [L, according to the value] **:** imposed at a rate percent of the value as stated in an invoice ⟨*ad valorem* tax on goods⟩

1**ad·vance** \əd-ˈvan(t)s\ *vb* [ME *advauncen,* fr. OF *avancier,* fr. (assumed) VL *abantiare,* fr. L *abante* before, fr. *ab-* + *ante* before — more at ANTE-] *vt* **1 :** to bring or move forward **2 :** to accelerate the growth or progress of **:** FORWARD **3 :** to raise to a higher rank **:** PROMOTE **4 :** to supply or furnish in expectation of repayment **5** *archaic* **:** to lift up **:** RAISE **6 :** to bring forward in time: **a :** to make earlier **:** HASTEN **b :** to place later in time **7 :** to bring forward for notice, consideration, or acceptance **:** PROPOSE **8 :** to raise in rate **:** INCREASE ~ *vi* **1 :** to move forward **:** PROCEED **2 :** to make progress **:** INCREASE **3 :** to rise in rank, position, or importance **4 :** to rise in rate or price — **ad·vanc·er** *n*

syn ADVANCE, PROMOTE, FORWARD, FURTHER mean to move or help to move ahead. ADVANCE stresses effective assisting or hastening a process bringing about a desired end; PROMOTE suggests an encouraging or fostering; FORWARD implies an impetus forcing something ahead; FURTHER suggests a removing of obstacles or obstructions in the way of a desired advance **syn** see in addition ADDUCE

2**advance** *n* **1 :** a forward movement **2 :** progress in development **:** IMPROVEMENT **3 :** a rise in price, value, or amount **4 :** a first step or approach made **:** OFFER; *also* **:** a progressive step **5 :** a provision of something (as money or goods) before a return is received; *also* **:** the money or goods supplied — **in advance :** BEFORE, BEFOREHAND

3**advance** *adj* **1 :** made, sent, or furnished ahead of time **2 :** going or situated before

ad·vanced *adj* **1 :** far on in time or course **2 a :** beyond the elementary or introductory **b :** being beyond others in progress or development

ad·vance·ment \əd-ˈvan(t)-smənt\ *n* **1 :** the action of advancing **:** the state of being advanced: **a :** promotion or elevation to a higher rank or position **b :** progression to a higher stage of development **2 :** an advance of money or value

1**ad·van·tage** \əd-ˈvant-ij\ *n* [ME *avantage,* fr. MF, fr. *avant* before, fr. L *abante*] **1 :** superiority of position or condition **2 a :** BENEFIT, GAIN; *esp* **:** benefit resulting from some course of action **b** *obs* **:** INTEREST 3a **3 :** a factor or circumstance of benefit to its possessor **4 :** the first point won in tennis after deuce; *also* **:** the score for it — **to advantage :** so as to produce a favorable impression or effect

2**advantage** *vt* **:** to give an advantage to **:** BENEFIT

ad·van·ta·geous \ˌad-ˌvan-ˈtā-jəs, -vən-\ *adj* **:** giving an advantage **:** FAVORABLE **syn** see BENEFICIAL — **ad·van·ta·geous·ly** *adv* — **ad·van·ta·geous·ness** *n*

ad·vec·tion \ad-ˈvek-shən\ *n* [L *advection-, advectio* act of bringing, fr. *advectus,* pp. of *advehere* to carry to, fr. *ad-* + *vehere* to carry — more at WAY] **:** the horizontal movement of a mass of air that causes changes in temperature or in other physical properties — **ad·vec·tive** \-ˈvek-tiv\ *adj*

Ad·vent \ˈad-ˌvent\ *n* [ME, fr. ML *adventus,* fr. L, arrival, fr. *adventus,* pp.] **1 :** a penitential season beginning four Sundays before Christmas **2 a :** the coming of Christ at the incarnation **b :** SECOND COMING **3** *not cap* **:** COMING, ARRIVAL ⟨~ of spring⟩ **syn** see ARRIVAL

Ad·vent·ism \ˈad-ˌvent-ˌiz-əm, -vənt-\ *n* **1 :** the doctrine that the second coming of Christ and the end of the world are near at hand **2 :** the principles and practices of Seventh-day Adventists — **Ad·vent·ist** \-ˌvent-əst, -vən-təst\ *adj or n*

ad·ven·ti·tia \ˌad-vən-ˈtish-(ē-)ə\ *n* [NL, alter. of L *adventicia,* neut. pl. of *adventicius* coming from outside, fr. *adventus,* pp.] **:** an external chiefly connective tissue covering of an organ; *esp* **:** the external coat of a blood vessel — **ad·ven·ti·tial** \-ˈtish-əl\ *adj*

ad·ven·ti·tious \ˌad-vən-ˈtish-əs\ *adj* [L *adventicius*] **1 :** added extrinsically and not inherent or innate **2 :** arising or occurring sporadically or in other than the usual location **syn** see ACCIDENTAL — **ad·ven·ti·tious·ly** *adv* — **ad·ven·ti·tious·ness** *n*

ad·ven·tive \ad-ˈvent-iv\ *adj* **1 :** introduced but not fully naturalized **2 :** ADVENTITIOUS 2 — **adventive** *n* — **ad·ven·tive·ly** *adv*

Advent Sunday *n* **:** the first Sunday in Advent

1**ad·ven·ture** \əd-ˈven-chər\ *n* [ME *aventure,* fr. OF, fr. (assumed) VL *adventura,* fr. L *adventus,* pp. of *advenire* to arrive, fr. *ad-* + *venire* to come — more at COME] **1 a :** an undertaking involving danger and unknown risks **b :** the encountering of risks **2 :** a remarkable experience **3 :** an enterprise involving financial risk

2**adventure** *vb* **ad·ven·tur·ing** \-ˈvench-(ə-)riŋ\ *vt* **1 :** to expose to danger or loss **:** VENTURE **2 :** to venture upon **:** TRY ~ *vi* **1 :** to proceed despite danger or risk **2 :** to take the risk

ad·ven·tur·er \əd-ˈven-chər-ər\ *n* **:** one that adventures: as **a :** SOLDIER OF FORTUNE **b :** one that engages in risky commercial enterprises for profit

ad·ven·ture·some \əd-ˈven-chər-səm\ *adj* **:** given to incurring risks **:** VENTURESOME

ad·ven·tur·ess \əd-ˈvench-(ə-)rəs\ *n* **:** a female adventurer; *esp* **:** a woman who seeks position or livelihood by questionable means

ad·ven·tur·ism \əd-ˈven-chə-ˌriz-əm\ *n* **:** ill-considered or rash improvisation or experimentation esp. in politics or foreign affairs or in defiance of consistent plans or principles — **ad·ven·tur·ist** \-ˈvench-(ə-)rəst\ *n* — **ad·ven·tur·is·tic** \-ˌven-chə-ˈris-tik\ *adj*

ad·ven·tur·ous \əd-'vench-(ə-)rəs\ *adj* **1 :** disposed to seek adventure or to cope with the new and unknown **2 :** characterized by unknown dangers and risks — **ad·ven·tur·ous·ly** *adv* — **ad·ven·tur·ous·ness** *n*
syn ADVENTUROUS, VENTURESOME, DARING, DAREDEVIL, RASH, RECKLESS, FOOLHARDY mean exposing oneself to danger more than required by good sense. ADVENTUROUS implies a willingness to accept risks but not necessarily imprudence; VENTURESOME applies chiefly to acts and carries a stronger suggestion of imprudence; DARING stresses fearlessness in courting danger; DAREDEVIL stresses ostentation in daring; RASH suggests imprudence and lack of forethought; RECKLESS implies heedlessness of probable consequences; FOOLHARDY suggests a recklessness that is inconsistent with good sense

¹ad·verb \'ad-,vərb\ *n* [MF *adverbe*, fr. L *adverbium*, fr. *ad-* + *verbum* word — more at WORD] **:** a word belonging to one of the major form classes in any of numerous languages, typically serving as a modifier of a verb, an adjective, another adverb, a preposition, a phrase, a clause, or a sentence, and expressing some relation of manner or quality, place, time, degree, number, cause, opposition, affirmation, or denial

²adverb *adj* **:** ADVERBIAL

ad·ver·bi·al \ad-'vər-bē-əl\ *adj* **:** of, relating to, or having the function of an adverb — **ad·ver·bi·al·ly** \-ə-lē\ *adv*

ad ver·bum \(')ad-'vər-bəm\ *adv* [L] **:** to a word **:** VERBATIM

ad·ver·sary \'ad-və(r)-,ser-ē\ *n* **:** one that contends with, opposes, or resists **:** ENEMY **syn** see OPPONENT

ad·ver·sa·tive \əd-'vər-sət-iv\ *adj* **:** expressing antithesis, opposition, or adverse circumstance ⟨the ~ conjunction *but*⟩ — **adversative** *n* — **ad·ver·sa·tive·ly** *adv*

ad·verse \ad-'vərs, 'ad-,\ *adj* [ME, fr. MF *advers*, fr. L *adversus*, pp. of *advertere*] **1 :** acting against or in a contrary direction **:** ANTAGONISTIC **2 :** opposed to one's interests **:** UNFAVORABLE **3 a :** opposite in position **b :** turned toward the stem or axis ⟨~ leaves⟩ — compare AVERSE — **ad·verse·ly** *adv* — **ad·verse·ness** *n*
syn ANTAGONISTIC, COUNTER, COUNTERACTIVE: ADVERSE applies to what is unfavorable, harmful, or detrimental; ANTAGONISTIC usu. implies mutual opposition and either hostility or incompatibility; COUNTER applies to forces coming from opposite directions with resulting conflict or tension; COUNTERACTIVE implies an opposition between two things that nullifies the effect of one or both

ad·ver·si·ty \ad-'vər-sət-ē\ *n* **1 :** a condition of suffering, destitution, or affliction **2 :** a calamitous or disastrous experience **syn** see MISFORTUNE

ad·vert \ad-'vərt\ *vi* [ME *adverten*, fr. MF & L; MF *advertir*, fr. L *advertere*, fr. *ad-* + *vertere* to turn — more at WORTH] **1 :** to pay heed or attention **2 :** to direct attention **:** REFER

ad·ver·tence \ad-'vərt-ᵊns\ *n* **1 :** the action or process of adverting **:** ATTENTION, NOTICE **2 :** ADVERTENCY 1

ad·ver·ten·cy \-ᵊn-sē\ *n* **1 :** the quality or state of being advertent **:** HEEDFULNESS **2 :** ADVERTENCE 1

ad·ver·tent \-ᵊnt\ *adj* [L *advertent-*, *advertens*, prp. of *advertere*] **:** giving attention **:** HEEDFUL — **ad·ver·tent·ly** *adv*

ad·ver·tise \'ad-vər-,tīz\ *vb* [ME *advertisen*, fr. MF *advertiss-*, stem of *advertir*] *vt* **1 :** INFORM, NOTIFY **2 a :** to announce publicly esp. by a printed notice or a broadcast **b :** to call public attention to esp. by emphasizing desirable qualities so as to arouse a desire to buy or patronize **~** *vi* **:** to issue or sponsor advertising — **ad·ver·tis·er** *n*

ad·ver·tise·ment \,ad-vər-'tīz-mənt; əd-'vərt-əz-mənt, -ə-smənt\ *n* **1 :** the act or process of advertising **2 :** a public notice; *esp* **:** one published in the press or broadcast over the air

ad·ver·tis·ing *n* **1 :** the action of calling something to the attention of the public esp. by paid announcements **2 :** ADVERTISEMENTS **3 :** the business of preparing advertisements for publication or broadcast

ad·vice \əd-'vīs\ *n* [ME, fr. OF *avis* opinion, prob. fr. the phrase *ce m'est a vis* that appears to me, part. trans. of L *mihi visum est* it seemed so to me] **1 :** recommendation regarding a decision or course of conduct **:** COUNSEL **2 :** information or notice given **:** INTELLIGENCE
syn COUNSEL: ADVICE implies real or pretended knowledge or experience, often professional or technical, on the part of the one who advises; COUNSEL often stresses the fruit of wisdom or deliberation and may presuppose a weightier occasion, or more authority, or more personal concern on the part of the one giving counsel

ad·vis·abil·i·ty \əd-,vī-zə-'bil-ət-ē\ *n* **:** the quality or state of being advisable

ad·vis·able \əd-'vī-zə-bəl\ *adj* **:** proper to be advised or to be done **:** PRUDENT **syn** see EXPEDIENT — **ad·vis·able·ness** *n* — **ad·vis·ably** \-blē\ *adv*

ad·vise \əd-'vīz\ *vb* [MF *advisen*, fr. OF *aviser*, fr. *avis*] *vt* **1 a :** to give advice to **:** COUNSEL **b :** CAUTION, WARN **c :** RECOMMEND **2 :** to give information or notice to **:** INFORM **~** *vi* **:** to take counsel **:** CONSULT — **ad·vis·er** *or* **ad·vi·sor** \-'vī-zər\ *n*

ad·vised \əd-'vīzd\ *adj* **:** thought out **:** CONSIDERED — **ad·vis·ed·ly** \-'vī-zəd-lē\ *adv*

ad·vise·ment \əd-'vīz-mənt\ *n* **:** careful consideration **:** DELIBERATION

¹ad·vi·so·ry \əd-'vīz-(ə-)rē\ *adj* **1 :** having or exercising power to advise **2 :** containing or giving advice

²advisory *n* **:** a report giving information (as on the weather)

ad·vo·ca·cy \'ad-və-kə-sē\ *n* **:** the act or process of advocating **:** SUPPORT

¹ad·vo·cate \'ad-və-kət, -,kāt\ *n* [ME *advocat*, fr. MF, fr. L *advocatus*, fr. pp. of *advocare* to summon, fr. *ad-* + *vocare* to call — more at VOICE] **1 :** one that pleads the cause of another; *specif* **:** one that pleads the cause of another before a tribunal or judicial court **:** COUNSELOR **2 :** one that defends or maintains a cause or proposal

²ad·vo·cate \-,kāt\ *vt* **:** to plead in favor of **syn** see SUPPORT — **ad·vo·ca·tion** \,ad-və-'kā-shən\ *n* — **ad·vo·ca·tor** \'ad-və-,kāt-ər\ *n*

ad·vow·son \əd-'vaùz-ᵊn\ *n* [ME, fr. OF *avoueson*, fr. ML *advocation-*, *advocatio*, fr. L, act of calling, fr. *advocatus*, pp.] **:** the right in English law of presenting a nominee to a vacant ecclesiastical benefice

ady·nam·ic \,ā-,dī-'nam-ik, ,ad-ə-\ *adj* [Gk *adynamia*, fr. *a-* + *dynamis* power, fr. *dynasthai* to be able] **:** of defective functional or vital powers

ad·y·tum \'ad-ə-təm\ *n*, *pl* **ad·y·ta** \-tə\ [L, fr. Gk *adyton*, neut. of *adytos* not to be entered, fr. *a-* + *dyein* to enter; akin to Skt *upā-du* to put on] **:** the innermost sanctuary in an ancient temple open only to priests **:** SANCTUM

adz *or* **adze** \'adz\ *n* [ME *adse*, fr. OE *adesa*] **:** a cutting tool with a thin arched blade set at right angles to the handle

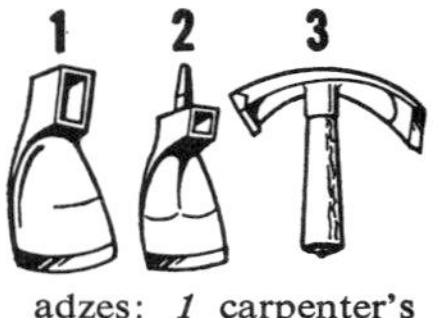

adzes: *1* carpenter's with flat head, *2* ship carpenter's with spur, *3* cooper's

ae \'ā\ *adj* [ME (northern dial.) *a*, alter. of *an*] *chiefly Scot* **:** ONE

ae·cial \'ē-sh(ē-)əl\ *adj* **:** of or relating to an aecium

ae·ci·um \'ē-s(h)ē-əm\ *n*, *pl* **ae·cia** \-ə\ [NL, fr. Gk *aikia* assault, fr. *aeikēs* unseemly, fr. *a-* + *eikōs* seemly, fr. participle of *eikenai* to seem] **:** the fruiting body of a rust fungus in which the first binucleate spores are usu. produced

aë·des \ā-'ēd-(,)ēz\ *n* [NL, genus name, fr. Gk *aēdēs* unpleasant, fr. *a-* + *ēdos* pleasure; akin to Gk *hēdys* sweet — more at SWEET] **:** any of a genus (*Aëdes*) of mosquitoes including the vector of yellow fever, dengue, and other diseases

ae·dile \'ē-,dīl\ *n* [L *aedilis*, fr. *aedes* temple — more at EDIFY] **:** an official in ancient Rome in charge of public works and games, police, and the grain supply

Ae·ge·an \i-'jē-ən\ *adj* [L *Aegaeus*, fr. Gk *Aigaios*] **1 :** of or relating to the arm of the Mediterranean sea east of Greece **2 :** of or relating to the prehistoric civilization of the islands of the Aegean sea and the countries adjacent to it esp. in the Bronze Age

Ae·gir \'ag-ər\ *n* [ON *Ægir*] **:** the god of the sea in Norse mythology

ae·gis \'ē-jəs\ *n* [L, fr. Gk *aigis* goatskin, perh. fr. *aig-*, *aix* goat; akin to Arm *aic* goat] **1 :** a shield or breastplate emblematic of majesty that was orig. associated chiefly with Zeus but later mainly with Athena **2 :** PROTECTION, DEFENSE **3 :** PATRONAGE, SPONSORSHIP

Ae·gis·thus \i-'jis-thəs\ *n* [L, fr. Gk *Aigisthos*] **:** a lover of Clytemnestra

-aemia — see -EMIA

Ae·ne·as \i-'nē-əs\ *n* [L, fr. Gk *Aineias*] **:** a son of Anchises and Aphrodite, defender of Troy, and hero of Vergil's *Aeneid*

Aeneo·lith·ic \ā-,ē-nē-ō-'lith-ik\ *adj* [L *aeneus* of copper or bronze, fr. *aes* copper, bronze — more at ORE] **:** of or relating to a transitional period between the Neolithic and Bronze ages in which some copper was used

¹ae·o·lian \ē-'ō-lē-ən, -'ōl-yən\ *adj* **1** *often cap* **:** of or relating to Aeolus **2 :** giving forth or marked by a soughing sound or musical tone produced by or as if by the wind

²aeolian *var of* EOLIAN

¹Ae·o·lian \ē-'ō-lē-ən, -'ōl-yən\ *adj* **:** of or relating to Aeolis or its inhabitants

²Aeolian *n* **1 :** a member of a group of Greek peoples of Thessaly and Boeotia that colonized Lesbos and the adjacent coast of Asia Minor **2 :** AEOLIC

aeolian harp *n* **:** a box-shaped musical instrument having stretched strings usu. tuned in unison on which the wind produces varying harmonics over the same fundamental tone

¹Ae·ol·ic \ē-'äl-ik\ *adj* **:** ¹AEOLIAN

²Aeolic *n* **:** a group of ancient Greek dialects used by the Aeolians

ae·o·lo·trop·ic \,ē-ə-lō-'träp-ik\ *adj* [Gk *aiolos* variegated] **:** ANISOTROPIC 1 — **ae·o·lot·ro·py** \,ē-ə-'lä-trə-pē\ *n*

Ae·o·lus \'ē-ə-ləs\ *n* [L, fr. Gk *Aiolos*] **:** the god of the winds in classical mythology

ae·on \'ē-ən, 'ē-,än\ *n* [L, fr. Gk *aiōn* — more at AYE] **:** an immeasurably or indefinitely long period of time **:** AGE

ae·o·ni·an \ē-'ō-nē-ən\ *or* **ae·on·ic** \-'än-ik\ *adj* **:** EVERLASTING 2 a(1), 2 b

aer- *or* **aero-** *comb form* [ME *aero-*, fr. MF, fr. L, fr. Gk *aer-*, *aero-*, fr. *aēr*] **1 a :** air **:** atmosphere ⟨aerate⟩ ⟨*aero*biology⟩ **b :** aerial and ⟨*aero*marine⟩ **2 :** gas ⟨*aero*sol⟩ **3 :** aviation ⟨*aero*drome⟩

aer·ate \'a(-ə)r-,āt, 'e(-ə)r-\ *vt* **1 :** to supply (the blood) with oxygen by respiration **2 :** to supply or impregnate with air **3 a :** to combine or charge with gas **b :** to make effervescent — **aer·a·tion** \,a(-ə)r-'ā-shən, ,e(-ə)r-\ *n*

aer·a·tor \'a(-ə)r-,āt-ər, 'e(-ə)r-\ *n* **:** one that aerates; *esp* **:** an apparatus for aerating something (as sewage)

¹ae·ri·al \'ar-ē-əl, 'er-, ā-'ir-ē-əl\ *adj* [L *aerius*, fr. Gk *aerios*, fr. *aēr*] **1 a :** of, relating to, or occurring in the air or atmosphere **b :** consisting of air **c :** existing or growing in the air rather than in the ground or in water **d :** LOFTY **e :** operating or operated overhead on elevated cables or rails **2 :** suggestive of air: as **a :** lacking substance **:** THIN **b :** IMAGINARY, ETHEREAL **3 a :** of or relating to aircraft **b :** designed for use in, taken from, or operating from or against aircraft **c :** effected by means of aircraft — **aer·i·al·ly** \-ə-lē\ *adv*

²aer·i·al \'ar-ē-əl, 'er-\ *n* **1 :** ANTENNA 2 **2 :** FORWARD PASS

aer·i·al·ist \'ar-ē-ə-ləst, 'er-\ *n* **:** one that performs feats in the air or above the ground esp. on the flying trapeze

aerial ladder *n* **:** a mechanically operated extensible fire ladder usu. mounted on a truck

ae·rie \'a(ə)r-ē, 'e(ə)r-, 'i(ə)r-, 'ā-(ə-)rē\ *n* [ML *aerea*, fr. OF *aire*, fr. L *area* area, feeding place for animals] **1 :** the nest of a bird on a cliff or a mountaintop **2** *obs* **:** a brood of birds of prey **3 :** a dwelling on a height

aer·if·er·ous \,a-(ə-)'rif-ə-rəs, ,e-\ *adj* **:** containing or conveying air

aer·i·fi·ca·tion \,ar-ə-fə-'kā-shən, ,er-\ *n* **:** the act of aerifying or of aerating **:** the state of being aerified or aerated

aer·i·form \'ar-ə-,fórm, 'er-\ *adj* **:** having the nature of air **:** GASEOUS

aer·i·fy \-,fī\ *vt* **1 :** AERATE 2 **2 :** to change into an aeriform state and esp. into vapor

aer·i·ly \'ar-ə-lē, 'er-\ *adv* **:** in an aery manner

aero \'a(-ə)r-(,)ō, 'e(-ə)r-\ *adj* [*aero-*] **1 :** of or relating to aircraft or aeronautics **2 :** designed for aerial use

aero·bal·lis·tics \,ar-ō-bə-'lis-tiks, ,er-\ *n pl but sing or pl in constr* **:** the ballistics of the flight of missiles and projectiles in the atmosphere

aer·o·bat·ics \,ar-ə-'bat-iks, ,er-\ *n pl but sing or pl in constr* [blend of *aer-* and *acrobatics*] **:** performance of stunts in an airplane or glider

aer·obe \'a(-ə)r-,ōb, 'e(-ə)r-\ *n* [F *aérobie*, fr. *aér-* aer- + *-bie* (fr. Gk *bios* life) — more at QUICK] **:** an organism (as a bacterium) that lives only in the presence of oxygen

aer·o·bic \ˌa-(ə-)ˈrō-bik, ˌe-\ *adj* **1 :** living, active, or occurring only in the presence of oxygen **2 :** of, relating to, or induced by aerobes — **aer·o·bi·cal·ly** \-bi-k(ə-)lē\ *adv*

aero·bi·o·sis \ˌar-ō-(ˌ)bī-ˈō-səs, ˌer-, -bē-\ *n* **:** life in the presence of air or oxygen — **aero·bi·ot·ic** \-ˈät-ik\ *adj* — **aero·bi·ot·i·cal·ly** \-i-k(ə-)lē\ *adv*

aero·drome \ˈar-ə-ˌdrōm, ˈer-\ *n, Brit* **:** AIRFIELD, AIRPORT

aero·dy·nam·ic \ˌar-ō-(ˌ)dī-ˈnam-ik, ˌer-\ *adj* **:** of or relating to aerodynamics — **aero·dy·nam·i·cal·ly** \-i-k(ə-)lē\ *adv*

aero·dy·nam·i·cist \-ˈnam-ə-səst\ *n* **:** one who specializes in aerodynamics

aero·dy·nam·ics \ˌar-ō-(ˌ)dī-ˈnam-iks, ˌer-\ *n pl but sing or pl in constr* **:** a branch of dynamics that deals with the motion of air and other gaseous fluids and with the forces acting on bodies in motion relative to such fluids

aero·dyne \ˈar-ə-ˌdīn, ˈer-\ *n* [*aerodynamic*] **:** a heavier-than-air aircraft that derives its lift in flight from forces resulting from its motion through the air

aero·em·bo·lism \ˌar-ō-ˈem-bə-ˌliz-əm, ˌer-\ *n* **1 :** a gaseous embolism **2 :** a condition equivalent to caisson disease caused by rapid ascent to high altitudes and resulting exposure to rapidly lowered air pressure — called also *air bends*

aero·gram *or* **aero·gramme** \ˈar-ə-ˌgram, ˈer-\ *n* **:** AIR LETTER

aer·og·ra·pher \ˌa-(ə-)ˈräg-rə-fər, ˌe-\ *n* **:** a navy warrant officer who observes and forecasts weather and surf conditions

aer·og·ra·phy \-fē\ *n* **:** METEOROLOGY

aer·o·lite \ˈar-ə-ˌlīt, ˈer-\ *also* **aero·lith** \-ˌlith\ *n* **:** a stony meteorite — **aer·o·lit·ic** \ˌar-ə-ˈlit-ik, ˌer-\ *adj*

aer·o·log·i·cal \ˌar-ə-ˈläj-i-kəl, ˌer-\ *adj* **:** of or relating to aerology

aer·ol·o·gist \ˌa-(ə-)ˈräl-ə-jəst, ˌe-\ *n* **:** a specialist in aerology

aer·ol·o·gy \-jē\ *n* **1 :** METEOROLOGY **2 :** a branch of meteorology that deals esp. with the air

aero·me·chan·ic \ˌar-ō-mi-ˈkan-ik, ˌer-\ *n* **:** an aircraft mechanic

aero·me·chan·ics \-iks\ *n pl but sing or pl in constr* **:** mechanics that deals with the equilibrium and motion of gases and of solid bodies immersed in them

aero·med·i·cal \ˌar-ō-ˈmed-i-kəl, ˌer-\ *adj* **:** of or relating to aeromedicine

aero·med·i·cine \-ˈmed-ə-sən\ *n* **:** a branch of medicine that deals with the diseases and disturbances arising from flying and the associated physiologic and psychologic problems

aero·me·te·or·o·graph \ˌar-ō-ˌmēt-ē-ˈór-ə-ˌgraf, ˌer-\ *n* **:** METEOROGRAPH; *esp* **:** one adapted for use on an airplane

aer·om·e·ter \ˌa-(ə-)ˈräm-ət-ər, ˌe-\ *n* [prob. fr. F *aéromètre,* fr. *aér-* + *mètre* -meter] **:** an instrument for ascertaining the weight or density of air or other gases

aero·naut \ˈar-ə-ˌnȯt, ˈer-, -ˌnät\ *n* [F *aéronaute,* fr. *aér-* aer- + Gk *nautēs* sailor — more at NAUTICAL] **:** one that operates or travels in an airship or balloon

aero·nau·ti·cal \ˌar-ə-ˈnȯt-i-kəl, ˌer-, -ˈnät-\ *or* **aero·nau·tic** \-ik\ *adj* **:** of or relating to aeronautics — **aero·nau·ti·cal·ly** \-i-k(ə-)lē\ *adv*

aero·nau·tics \-iks\ *n pl but sing in constr* **1 :** a science dealing with the operation of aircraft **2 :** the art or science of flight

aero·neu·ro·sis \ˌar-ō-n(y)u̇-ˈrō-səs, ˌer-\ *n* **:** a functional nervous disorder of airmen caused by emotional stress and characterized by physical symptoms (as restlessness, abdominal pains, and diarrhea)

aero·pause \ˈar-ō-ˌpȯz, ˈer-\ *n* **:** the level above the earth's surface where the atmosphere becomes ineffective for human and aircraft functions

aero·plane \ˈar-ə-ˌplān, ˈer-\ *n, chiefly Brit var of* AIRPLANE

aero·sol \ˈar-ə-ˌsäl, ˈer-, -ˌsȯl\ *n* **:** a suspension of fine solid or liquid particles in gas (as smoke, fog, or an insecticide)

aero·sol·ize \-ˌīz\ *vt* **:** to disperse as an aerosol

aero·space \ˈar-ō-ˌspās, ˈer-\ *n* **:** the earth's atmosphere and the space beyond

aero·sphere \ˈar-ō-ˌsfi(ə)r, ˈer-\ *n* [F *aérosphère,* fr. *aér-* aer- + *sphère* sphere, fr. L *sphaera*] **:** the body of air around the earth

aero·stat \-ˌstat\ *n* [F *aérostat,* fr. *aér-* + *-stat*] **:** an aircraft that embodies one or more containers filled with a gas lighter than air and that is supported chiefly by buoyancy derived from the surrounding air

aero·stat·ics \ˌar-ō-ˈstat-iks, ˌer-\ *n pl but sing or pl in constr* [modif. of NL *aerostatica,* fr. *aer-* + *statica* statics] **:** a branch of statics that deals with the equilibrium of gaseous fluids and of solid bodies immersed in them

aero·ther·mo·dy·nam·ics \ˌar-ō-ˌthər-mə-(ˌ)dī-ˈnam-iks, ˌer-\ *n pl but sing or pl in constr* **:** the thermodynamics of gases and esp. of air

¹aery \ˈa(ə)r-ē, ˈe(ə)r-ē, ˈā-ə-rē\ *adj* [L *aerius* — more at AERIAL] **:** having an aerial quality **:** ETHEREAL

²aery *like* AERIE\ *var of* AERIE

Aes·chy·le·an \ˌes-kə-ˈlē-ən\ *adj* **:** of, relating to, or suggestive of Aeschylus or his tragedies

Aes·cu·la·pi·an \ˌes-kyə-ˈlā-pē-ən\ *adj* [*Aesculapius,* Greco-Roman god of medicine, fr. L, fr. Gk *Asklēpios*] **:** of or relating to Aesculapius or the healing art **:** MEDICAL

Ae·sir \ˈas-ˌi(ə)r\ *n pl* [ON *Æsir,* pl. of *āss* god] **:** the chief gods of the Norse pantheon

Ae·so·pi·an \ē-ˈsō-pē-ən\ *also* **Ae·sop·ic** \-ˈsäp-ik\ *adj* **:** of, relating to, or characteristic of Aesop or his fables

aesthesio- — see ESTHESIO-

aes·thete \ˈes-ˌthēt\ *n* [back-formation fr. *aesthetic*] **:** one having or affecting sensitivity to the beautiful esp. in art

aes·thet·ic \es-ˈthet-ik\ *adj* [G *ästhetisch,* fr. NL *aestheticus,* fr. Gk *aisthētikos* of sense perception, fr. *aisthanesthai* to perceive — more at AUDIBLE] **1 a :** relating to or dealing with aesthetics or the beautiful **b :** ARTISTIC **2 :** appreciative of, responsive to, or zealous about the beautiful **syn** see ARTISTIC — **aes·thet·i·cal** \-i-kəl\ *adj* — **aes·thet·i·cal·ly** \-k(ə-)lē\ *adv* — **aes·the·ti·cian** \ˌes-thə-ˈtish-ən\ *n*

aes·thet·i·cism \es-ˈthet-ə-ˌsiz-əm\ *n* **1 a :** a doctrine that the principles of beauty are basic to other esp. moral principles **b :** the advocacy of artistic and aesthetic autonomy **2 :** devotion to or emphasis on beauty or the cultivation of the arts

aes·thet·ics \es-ˈthet-iks\ *n pl but sing or pl in constr* **1 :** a branch of philosophy dealing with the nature of the beautiful and with judgments concerning beauty **2 :** the description and explanation of artistic phenomena and aesthetic experience by means of other sciences (as psychology, sociology, ethnology, or history)

aes·ti·val \ˈes-tə-vəl\ *adj* [ME *estival,* fr. MF or L; MF, fr. L *aestivalis,* fr. *aestivus* of summer, fr. *aestas* summer — more at EDIFY] **:** of or relating to the summer

aes·ti·vate \ˈes-tə-ˌvāt\ *vi* **:** to pass the summer in a state of torpor

aes·ti·va·tion \ˌes-tə-ˈvā-shən\ *n* **1 :** the state of one that aestivates **2 :** the disposition or method of arrangement of floral parts in a bud

af- — see AD-

afar \ə-ˈfär\ *adv* [ME *afer,* fr. *on fer* at a distance and *of fer* from a distance] **:** from or at a great distance

afeard *or* **afeared** \ə-ˈfi(ə)rd\ *adj* [ME *afered,* fr. OE *āfǣred,* pp. of *āfǣran* to frighten, fr. *ā-,* perfective prefix + *fǣran* to frighten — more at ABIDE, FEAR] *dial* **:** AFRAID

af·fa·bil·i·ty \ˌaf-ə-ˈbil-ət-ē\ *n* **:** the quality or state of being affable **:** SOCIABILITY

af·fa·ble \ˈaf-ə-bəl\ *adj* [MF, fr. L *affabilis,* fr. *affari* to speak to, fr. *ad-* + *fari* to speak — more at BAN] **1 a :** being pleasant and at ease in talking to others **b :** characterized by ease and friendliness **2 :** PLEASANT **syn** see GRACIOUS — **af·fa·bly** \-blē\ *adv*

af·fair \ə-ˈfa(ə)r, -ˈfe(ə)r\ *n* [ME & MF; ME *affaire,* fr. MF, fr. *a faire* to do] **1 a** *pl* **:** commercial, professional, or public business **b :** MATTER, CONCERN **2 :** a procedure, action, or occasion only vaguely specified; *also* **:** an object or collection of objects only vaguely specified **3 a** *also* **af·faire :** a romantic or passionate attachment typically of limited duration **:** LIAISON 1b **b** *or* **affaire :** a matter occasioning public anxiety, controversy, or scandal **:** CASE

af·faire d'hon·neur \ə-ˌfa(ə)r-də-ˈnər, -ˌfe(ə)r-, -(ˌ)dȯ-\ *n, pl* **affaires d'honneur** \-ˌfa(ə)r(z)-, -ˌfe(ə)r(z)-\ [F, lit., affair of honor] **:** a matter involving honor; *specif* **:** DUEL

¹af·fect \ˈaf-ˌekt\ *n* [L *affectus,* fr. *affectus,* pp.] **1** *obs* **:** FEELING, AFFECTION **2 :** the conscious subjective aspect of an emotion considered apart from bodily changes

²af·fect \ə-ˈfekt, a-\ *vb* [MF & L; MF *affecter,* fr. L *affectare,* fr. *affectus,* pp. of *afficere* to influence, fr. *ad-* + *facere* to do — more at DO] *vt* **1** *archaic* **:** to aim at **2 a** *archaic* **:** to have affection for **b :** to be given to **:** FANCY ⟨~ flashy clothes⟩ **3 :** to make a display of liking or using **:** CULTIVATE ⟨~ a worldly manner⟩ **4 :** to put on a pretense of **:** FEIGN ⟨~ indifference, though deeply hurt⟩ **5 :** to tend toward ⟨drops of water ~ roundness⟩ **6 :** FREQUENT ~ *vi, obs* **:** INCLINE 2 **syn** see ASSUME

³af·fect \ə-ˈfekt, a-\ *vt* **1 :** to produce an effect upon **2 :** to produce a material influence upon or alteration in **3 :** to make an impression on **:** INFLUENCE

syn INFLUENCE, TOUCH, IMPRESS, SWAY: AFFECT applies to the acting of a stimulus strong enough to produce a noticeable response or reaction or modification usu. without a radical change; INFLUENCE presupposes an agent or agency that acts so as to change in some degree one's nature, character, or behavior; TOUCH may suggest forceful or emotional stirring, arousing, or impinging on; IMPRESS suggests a deep or lasting effect; SWAY implies the acting of influences that are not resisted or are irresistible, with resulting change in character or course of action

af·fec·ta·tion \ˌaf-ˌek-ˈtā-shən\ *n* **1** *obs* **:** a striving after **2 a :** the act of taking on or displaying an attitude or mode of behavior not natural or not genuine **b :** unnatural speech or conduct **:** ARTIFICIALITY **syn** see POSE

af·fect·ed *adj* **1 :** inclined toward **2 a :** given to affection **b :** assumed artificially or falsely **:** PRETENDED — **af·fect·ed·ly** *adv* — **af·fect·ed·ness** *n*

af·fect·ing *adj* **:** moving the emotions **syn** see MOVING — **af·fect·ing·ly** \-ˈfek-tiŋ-lē\ *adv*

¹af·fec·tion \ə-ˈfek-shən\ *n* [ME, fr. MF *affection,* fr. L *affection-, affectio,* fr. *affectus,* pp.] **1 :** a moderate feeling or emotion **2 :** tender attachment **:** LOVE **3** *obs* **:** PARTIALITY, PREJUDICE **4 :** the feeling aspect of consciousness **5 a :** PROPENSITY, DISPOSITION **b** *archaic* **:** AFFECTATION 2 **syn** see FEELING

²affection *n* **1 :** the action of affecting **:** the state of being affected **2 a (1) :** a bodily condition **(2) :** DISEASE, MALADY **b :** ATTRIBUTE

af·fec·tion·al \ə-ˈfek-shnəl, -shən-ᵊl\ *adj* **:** belonging or relating to the affections — **af·fec·tion·al·ly** \-ē\ *adv*

af·fec·tion·ate \ə-ˈfek-sh(ə-)nət\ *adj* **1** *obs* **:** mentally or emotionally affected or inclined **2 :** having affection or warm regard **:** LOVING **3 :** proceeding from affection **:** TENDER — **af·fec·tion·ate·ly** *adv*

af·fec·tioned \-shənd\ *adj, archaic* **:** DISPOSED

af·fec·tive \a-ˈfek-tiv\ *adj* **1 :** relating to, arising from, or influencing feelings or emotions **:** EMOTIONAL **2 :** expressing emotion — **af·fec·tive·ly** *adv* — **af·fec·tiv·i·ty** \ˌaf-ˌek-ˈtiv-ət-ē\ *n*

af·fen·pin·scher \ˈaf-ən-ˌpin-chər\ *n* [G, fr. *affe* monkey + *pinscher,* a breed of hunting dog] **:** any of a breed of small dogs with a stiff red, gray, or black coat, pointed ears, and bushy eyebrows, chin tuft, and moustache

af·fer·ent \ˈaf-ə-rənt, -ˌer-ənt\ *adj* [L *afferent-, afferens,* prp. of *afferre* to bring to, fr. *ad-* + *ferre* to bear — more at BEAR] **:** bearing or conducting inward; *specif* **:** conveying impulses toward a nerve center — compare EFFERENT — **af·fer·ent·ly** *adv*

¹af·fi·ance \ə-ˈfī-ən(t)s\ *n* [ME, fr. MF, fr. *affier* to pledge, trust, fr. ML *affidare* to pledge, fr. L *ad-* + (assumed) VL *fidare* to trust — more at FIANCÉ] *archaic* **:** TRUST, CONFIDENCE

²affiance *vt* **:** to solemnly promise (oneself or another) in marriage **:** BETROTH

af·fi·ant \ə-ˈfī-ənt\ *n* [MF, fr. prp. of *affier*] **:** one that swears to an affidavit; *broadly* **:** DEPONENT

af·fi·da·vit \ˌaf-ə-ˈdā-vət\ *n* [ML, he has made an oath, fr. *affidare*] **:** a sworn statement in writing made esp. under oath or on affirmation before an authorized magistrate or officer

¹af·fil·i·ate \ə-ˈfil-ē-ˌāt\ *vb* [ML *affiliatus,* pp. of *affiliare* to adopt as a son, fr. L *ad-* + *filius* son — more at FEMININE] *vt* **1 a :** to bring or receive into close connection as a member or branch ⟨*affiliated* organizations⟩ **b :** to associate as a member ⟨~*s* himself with the local club⟩ **2 :** to trace the origin of ~ *vi* **:** to

connect or associate oneself : COMBINE — **af·fil·i·a·tion** \ə-ˌfil-ē-'ā-shən\ *n*

[2]**af·fil·i·ate** \ə-'fil-ē-ət\ *n* : an affiliated person or organization

[1]**af·fine** \ə-'fīn\ *n* [MF *affin*, fr. L *affinis*, fr. *affinis*, adj.] : a relative by marriage

[2]**affine** *adj* [L *affinis*, adj.] : of, relating to, or being a transformation that transforms straight lines into straight lines and parallel lines into parallel lines but may alter distance between points and angles between lines ⟨~ geometry⟩

af·fined \ə-'fīnd\ *adj* **1** : joined in a close relationship : CONNECTED **2** : bound by obligation

af·fin·i·ty \ə-'fin-ət-ē\ *n* [ME *affinite*, fr. MF or L; MF *afinité*, fr. L *affinitas*, fr. *affinis* bordering on, related by marriage, fr. *ad-* + *finis* end, border] **1** : relationship by marriage — compare CONSANGUINITY **2 a** : sympathy marked by community of interest : KINSHIP **b** : ATTRACTION; *esp* : an attractive force between substances or particles that causes them to enter into and remain in chemical combination **c** : a person esp. of the opposite sex having a particular attraction **3 a** : causal connection or relationship : RESEMBLANCE **b** : a relation between biological groups involving resemblance in the whole plan of structure and indicating community of origin **syn** see ATTRACTION, LIKENESS

af·firm \ə-'fərm\ *vb* [ME *affermen*, fr. MF *afermer*, fr. L *affirmare*, fr. *ad-* + *firmare* to make firm, fr. *firmus* firm — more at FIRM] *vt* **1 a** : VALIDATE, CONFIRM **b** : to state positively **2** : to assert as valid or confirmed ~ *vi* **1** : to testify or declare by affirmation **2** : to uphold a judgment or decree of a lower court **syn** see ASSERT — **af·firm·able** \ə-'fər-mə-bəl\ *adj* — **af·fir·mance** \ə-'fər-mən(t)s\ *n*

af·fir·ma·tion \ˌaf-ər-'mā-shən\ *n* **1** : the act of affirming; *also* : something affirmed : ASSERTION **2** : a solemn declaration made under the penalties of perjury by a person who conscientiously declines taking an oath

[1]**af·fir·ma·tive** \ə-'fər-mət-iv\ *adj* **1** : asserting a predicate of a subject **2** : asserting that the fact is so **3** : POSITIVE ⟨~ approach⟩ — **af·fir·ma·tive·ly** *adv*

[2]**affirmative** *n* **1** : an expression (as the word *yes*) of affirmation or assent **2** : an affirmative proposition **3** : the side that upholds the proposition stated in a debate

[1]**af·fix** \ə-'fiks\ *vt* [ML *affixare*, fr. L *affixus*, pp. of *affigere* to fasten to, fr. *ad-* + *figere* to fasten — more at DIKE] **1** : to attach physically : FASTEN ⟨~ a stamp to a letter⟩ **2** : to attach in any way : ADD, APPEND ⟨~ a signature to a document⟩ **3** : IMPRESS ⟨~*ed* his seal⟩ **syn** see FASTEN — **af·fix·a·tion** \ˌaf-ˌik-'sā-shən\ *n*

[2]**af·fix** \'af-ˌiks\ *n* **1** : a sound or sequence of sounds or a letter or sequence of letters occurring as a bound form attached to the beginning or end of a word, base, or phrase or inserted within a word or base and serving to produce a derivative word or an inflectional form **2** : APPENDAGE — **af·fix·al** \-ˌik-səl\ *or* **af·fix·i·al** \a-'fik-sē-əl\ *adj*

af·fla·tus \ə-'flāt-əs\ *n* [L, act of blowing or breathing on, fr. *afflatus*, pp. of *afflare* to blow on, fr. *ad-* + *flare* to blow — more at BLOW] : a divine imparting of knowledge or power : INSPIRATION

af·flict \ə-'flikt\ *vt* [ME *afflicten*, fr. L *afflictus*, pp. of *affligere* to cast down, fr. *ad-* + *fligere* to strike — more at PROFLIGATE] **1** *obs* **a** : HUMBLE **b** : OVERTHROW **2 a** : to distress severely so as to cause continued suffering **b** : TROUBLE, INJURE

syn TRY, TORMENT, TORTURE, RACK, GRILL: AFFLICT is a general term applying to the causing of pain or suffering or of acute annoyance, embarrassment, or any distress; TRY suggests imposing something that puts a strain on the powers of endurance or of self-control; TORMENT suggests persecution or the repeated inflicting of suffering or annoyance; TORTURE adds the implication of causing to writhe with unbearable pain; RACK stresses straining or wrenching; GRILL suggests causing acute discomfort as by long and relentless questioning

af·flic·tion \ə-'flik-shən\ *n* **1** : the state of being afflicted **2** : the cause of continued pain or distress; *also* : great suffering

af·flic·tive \ə-'flik-tiv\ *adj* : causing affliction : DISTRESSING — **af·flic·tive·ly** *adv*

af·flu·ence \'af-ˌlü-ən(t)s, -lə-wən(t)s\ *n* **1 a** : an abundant flow or supply : PROFUSION **b** : abundance of property : WEALTH **2** : a flowing to or toward a point : INFLUX

[1]**af·flu·ent** \'af-ˌlü-ənt, -lə-wənt\ *adj* [ME, fr. MF, fr. L *affluent-*, *affluens*, prp. of *affluere* to flow to, flow abundantly, fr. *ad-* + *fluere* to flow — more at FLUID] **1 a** : flowing in abundance : COPIOUS **b** : having an abundance of goods : WEALTHY **2** : flowing toward **syn** see RICH — **af·flu·ent·ly** *adv*

[2]**affluent** *n* : a tributary stream

af·flux \'af-ˌləks\ *n* [F or L; F, fr. L *affluxus*, pp. of *affluere*] : AFFLUENCE 2

af·ford \ə-'fō(ə)rd, -'fȯ(ə)rd\ *vt* [ME *aforthen*, fr. OE *geforthian* to carry out, fr. *ge-*, perfective prefix + *forthian* to carry out, fr. *forth* — more at CO-, FORTH] **1** : to manage to bear or to bear the cost of without serious loss or detriment ⟨can ~ to be generous⟩ ⟨~ a new coat⟩ **2 a** : YIELD, FURNISH ⟨~*s* an opportunity⟩ **b** : to furnish or offer typically or as an essential concomitant ⟨~*s* a fine view⟩ **syn** see GIVE

af·for·est \a-'fȯr-əst, -'fär-\ *vt* [ML *afforestare*, fr. L *ad-* + ML *forestis* forest — more at FOREST] : to establish forest cover on — **af·for·es·ta·tion** \(ˌ)a-ˌfȯr-ə-'stā-shən, -ˌfär-\ *n*

af·fran·chise \a-'fran-ˌchīz\ *vt* [MF *afranchiss-*, stem of *afranchir*, fr. *a-* (fr. L *ad-*) + *franchir* to free — more at FRANCHISE] : ENFRANCHISE 1

[1]**af·fray** \ə-'frā\ *n* [ME, fr. MF, fr. *affreer* to startle] : FRAY, BRAWL

[2]**affray** *vt* [ME *affraien*, fr. MF *affreer*] *archaic* : STARTLE, FRIGHTEN

af·fri·cate \'af-ri-kət\ *n* [prob. fr. G *affrikata*, fr. L *affricata*, fem. of *affricatus*, pp. of *affricare* to rub against, fr. *ad-* + *fricare* to rub — more at FRICTION] : a stop and its immediately following release through the articulatory position for a continuant nonsyllabic consonant (as the \t\ and \sh\ that are the constituents of the \ch\ in *why choose*) — **af·fric·a·tive** \ə-'frik-ət-iv\ *n or adj*

af·fri·ca·tion \ˌaf-rə-'kā-shən\ *n* : conversion (as of a simple stop sound) into an affricate

[1]**af·fright** \ə-'frīt\ *vt* [fr. ME *afyrht*, *afright* frightened, fr. OE *āfyrht*, pp. of *āfyrhtan* to frighten, fr. *ā-*, perfective prefix + *fyrhtan* to fear; akin to OE *fyrhto* fright — more at ABIDE, FRIGHT] : FRIGHTEN, ALARM

[2]**affright** *n* : sudden and great fear : TERROR

[1]**af·front** \ə-'frənt\ *vt* [ME *afronten*, fr. MF *afronter* to defy, fr. (assumed) VL *affrontare*, fr. L *ad-* + *front-*, *frons* forehead — more at FRONT] **1** : to insult esp. to the face by behavior or language : OFFEND **2 a** : to face in defiance : CONFRONT **b** *obs* : to encounter face to face **3** : to appear directly before **syn** see OFFEND

[2]**affront** *n* **1 a** : a deliberately offensive act or utterance **b** : an offense to one's self-respect **2** *obs* : a hostile encounter

syn INSULT, INDIGNITY: AFFRONT implies a deliberate and usu. open act of disrespect; INSULT implies an attack intended to humiliate or degrade; INDIGNITY suggests an outrageous offense to one's personal dignity

af·fu·sion \a-'fyü-zhən\ *n* [LL *affusion-*, *affusio*, fr. L *affusus*, pp. of *affundere* to pour on, fr. *ad-* + *fundere* to pour — more at FOUND] : an act of pouring a liquid upon

af·ghan \'af-ˌgan, -gən\ *n* [Pashto *afghānī*] **1** *cap* : a native or inhabitant of Afghanistan **2** *cap* : PASHTO **3** : a blanket or shawl of colored wool knitted or crocheted in strips or squares **4** : a Turkoman carpet of large size and long pile woven in geometric designs — **Afghan** *adj*

Afghan hound *n* : a tall slim swift hunting dog native to the Near East with a coat of silky thick hair and a long silky topknot

af·ghani \af-'gan-ē\ *n* [Pashto *afghānī*, lit., Afghan] **1** — see MONEY table **2** : a silver coin no longer in active circulation representing one afghani

afi·cio·na·do \ə-ˌfis-ē-ə-'näd-(ˌ)ō, -ˌfē-sē-ə-, -ˌfish-ə-\ *n* [Sp, fr. pp. of *aficionar* to inspire affection, fr. *afición* affection, fr. L *affection-*, *affectio* — more at AFFECTION] : DEVOTEE, FAN

afield \ə-'fē(ə)ld\ *adv* **1** : to, in, or on the field **2** : away from home or usual surroundings : ABROAD **3** : out of the way : ASTRAY

afire \ə-'fī(ə)r\ *adj* : on fire : BLAZING

aflame \ə-'flām\ *adj* : AFIRE

afloat \ə-'flōt\ *adv (or adj)* [ME *aflot*, fr. OE *on flot*, fr. *on* + *flot*, fr. *flot* deep water, sea; akin to OE *flēotan* to float — more at FLEET] **1 a** : borne on or as if on the water **b** : at sea **2** : free of difficulties : SELF-SUFFICIENT **3 a** : circulating about : RUMORED **b** : ADRIFT **4** : flooded with or submerged under water : AWASH

aflut·ter \ə-'flət-ər\ *adj* **1** : FLUTTERING **2** : nervously excited

afoot \ə-'fu̇t\ *adv (or adj)* **1** : on foot **2 a** : on the move : ASTIR **b** : in progress

afore \ə-'fō(ə)r, -'fȯ(ə)r\ *adv or conj or prep* [ME, fr. OE *onforan*, fr. *on* + *foran* before — more at BEFORE] *chiefly dial* : BEFORE

afore·men·tioned \-ˌmen-chənd\ *adj* : mentioned previously

afore·said \-ˌsed\ *adj* : said or named before or above

afore·thought \-ˌthȯt\ *adj* : PREMEDITATED, DELIBERATE ⟨with malice ~⟩

afore·time \-ˌtīm\ *adv*, *archaic* : FORMERLY

a for·ti·o·ri \ˌä-ˌfȯrt-ē-'ō(ə)r-ē; ā-ˌfȯrt-ē-'ō(ə)r-ˌī, -'ō(ə)r-ē; -'ȯ(ə)r-\ *adv* [NL, lit. fr. the stronger (argument)] : with greater reason or more convincing force — used in drawing a conclusion that is inferred to be even more certain than another

afoul \ə-'fau̇(ə)l\ *adj* : FOULED, TANGLED

afoul of *prep* **1** : in or into collision or entanglement with **2** : in or into conflict with

Afr- *or* **Afro-** *comb form* [L *Afr-*, *Afer*] : African ⟨*Afr*american⟩ : African and ⟨*Afro*-Asiatic⟩

afraid \ə-'frād, *South also* ə-'fre(ə)d\ *adj* [ME *affraied*, fr. pp. of *affraien* to frighten — more at AFFRAY] **1** : filled with fear or apprehension **2** : filled with concern or regret over an unwanted contingency **3** : DISINCLINED, RELUCTANT ⟨~ of hard work⟩ **syn** see FEARFUL

afreet *or* **afrit** \'af-ˌrēt, ə-'frēt\ *n* [Ar *'ifrīt*] : a powerful evil jinn, demon, or monstrous giant in Arabic mythology

afresh \ə-'fresh\ *adv* **1** : with fresh or unabated vigor : ANEW **2** : from a new start : AGAIN

Af·ri·can \'af-ri-kən\ *n* **1** : a native or inhabitant of Africa **2** : an individual of immediate or remote African ancestry; *esp* : NEGRO — **African** *adj*

Af·ri·can·der *or* **Af·ri·kan·der** \ˌaf-ri-'kan-dər\ *n* [Afrik *Afrikaner*, *Afrikaander*, lit., Afrikaner] : any of a breed of tall red large-horned humped southern African cattle used chiefly for meat or draft

Af·ri·can·ist \'af-ri-kə-nəst\ *n* : a specialist in African languages or cultures

African violet *n* : a tropical African plant (*Saintpaulia ionantha*) of the gloxinia family widely grown as a house plant for its velvety fleshy leaves and showy purple, pink, or white flowers

Af·ri·kaans \ˌaf-ri-'kän(t)s, -'känz, ˌaf-ri-ˌ\ *n* [Afrik, fr. *afrikaans*, adj., African, fr. obs. Afrik *afrikanisch*, fr. L *africanus*] : a language developed from 17th century Dutch that is one of the official languages of the Republic of So. Africa

Af·ri·ka·ner \ˌaf-ri-'kän-ər\ *n* [Afrik, lit., African, fr. L *africanus*] : a So. African native of European descent; *esp* : an Afrikaans-speaking descendant of the 17th century Dutch settlers

Af·ro–Amer·i·can \ˌaf-(ˌ)rō-ə-'mer-ə-kən\ *or* **Af·ra·mer·i·can** \ˌaf-rə-'mer-\ *adj* : of or relating to Americans of African and esp. of negroid descent — **Afro–American** *or* **Aframerican** *n*

Af·ro–Asi·at·ic languages \ˌaf-(ˌ)rō-ˌā-zhē-ˌat-ik-\ *n pl* : a family of languages widely distributed over southwestern Asia and northern Africa comprising the Semitic, Egyptian, Berber, Cushitic, and Chad subfamilies

afront *adv*, *obs* : ABREAST

[1]**aft** \'aft\ *adv* [ME *afte* back, fr. OE *æftan* from behind, behind; akin to OE *æfter*] : near, toward, or in the stern of a ship or the tail of an aircraft : ABAFT

[2]**aft** *adj* : REARWARD, [4]AFTER 2

[3]**aft** *Scot var of* OFT

[1]**af·ter** \'af-tər\ *adv* [ME, fr. OE *æfter;* akin to OHG *aftar* after] : following in time or place : AFTERWARD, BEHIND

[2]**after** *prep* **1 a** : behind in place **b** (1) : subsequent to in time or order (2) : subsequent to and in view of ⟨~ all our advice⟩ **2** — used as a function word to indicate the object of a stated or implied action ⟨go ~ gold⟩ **3** : so as to resemble: as **a** : in accordance with **b** : with the same or a derived name **c** : in the characteristic manner of **d** : in imitation of

[3]**after** *conj* : subsequently to the time when

[4]**after** *adj* **1** : later in time : SUBSEQUENT **2** : located toward the stern of a ship or tail of an aircraft : HINDER

af·ter·birth \'af-tər-ˌbərth\ *n* : the placenta and fetal membranes that are expelled after delivery

af·ter·brain \-ˌbrān\ *n* **:** the posterior subdivision of the hindbrain **:** MYELENCEPHALON
af·ter·burn·er \-ˌbər-nər\ *n* **:** an auxiliary burner attached to the tail pipe of a turbojet engine for injecting fuel into the hot exhaust gases and burning it to provide extra thrust
af·ter·care \-ˌke(ə)r, -ˌka(ə)r\ *n* **:** the care, nursing, or treatment of a convalescent patient
af·ter·clap \-ˌklap\ *n* **:** an unexpected usu. untoward event following a supposedly closed affair
af·ter·damp \ˈaf-tər-ˌdamp\ *n* **:** a toxic gas mixture remaining after an explosion of firedamp in mines
af·ter·deck \-ˌdek\ *n* **:** the part of a deck abaft midships
af·ter·ef·fect \ˈaf-tə-rə-ˌfekt\ *n* **1 :** an effect that follows its cause after an interval **2 :** a secondary result (as in the action of a drug) coming on after the subsidence of the first effect
af·ter·glow \ˈaf-tər-ˌglō\ *n* **1 :** a glow remaining where a light has disappeared **2 :** a reflection of past splendor, success, or emotion
af·ter·im·age \ˈaf-tə-ˌrim-ij\ *n* **:** a usu. visual sensation occurring after the external stimulus causing it has ceased to operate
af·ter·life \ˈaf-tər-ˌlīf\ *n* **1 :** an existence after death **2 :** a later period in one's life
af·ter·math \ˈaf-tər-ˌmath\ *n* [[4]*after* + *math* (mowing, crop)] **1 :** a second-growth crop **:** ROWEN **2 :** CONSEQUENCE, RESULT
af·ter·most \-ˌmōst\ *adj* **:** nearest the stern of a ship **:** farthest aft
af·ter·noon \ˌaf-tər-ˈnün\ *n* **1 :** the part of day between noon and sunset **2 :** a relatively late period (as of time or life) — **afternoon** *adj*
af·ter·noons \-ˈnünz\ *adv* **:** in the afternoon repeatedly **:** on any afternoon
af·ter·piece \ˈaf-tər-ˌpēs\ *n* **:** a short usu. comic entertainment performed after a play
af·ter·shaft \-ˌshaft\ *n* **:** an accessory plume arising from the posterior side of the stem of some feathers — **af·ter·shaft·ed** *adj*
af·ter·taste \-ˌtāst\ *n* **:** persistence of a sensation (as of flavor) after the stimulating agent has gone
af·ter·tax \ˌaf-tər-ˌtaks\ *adj* **:** remaining after payment of taxes and esp. income tax
af·ter·thought \ˈaf-tər-ˌthȯt\ *n* **:** an idea occurring later **:** a part, feature, or device not thought of originally
af·ter·time \-ˌtīm\ *n* **:** FUTURE
af·ter·ward \ˈaf-tə(r)-wərd\ *or* **af·ter·wards** \-wərdz\ *adv* **:** at a later or succeeding time **:** SUBSEQUENTLY
af·ter·world \ˈaf-tər-ˌwərld\ *n* **:** a future world **:** a world after death
ag- — see AD-
Ag·a·da \ə-ˈgäd-ə, -ˈgȯd-\ *var of* HAGGADAH
again \ə-ˈgen, -ˈgin\ *adv* [ME, opposite, again fr. OE *ongēan* opposite, back, fr. *on* + *gēn*, *gēan* still, again; akin to OE *gēan-* against, OHG *gegin* against, toward] **1 :** in return **:** BACK **2 :** another time **:** ANEW **3 a :** on the other hand **b :** in the next place **:** FURTHER **4 :** in addition **:** BESIDES
[1]**against** \ə-ˈgen(t)st, -ˈgin(t)st\ *prep* [ME, alter. of *againes*, fr. *again*] **1 a :** directly opposite **:** FACING **b** *obs* **:** exposed to **2 a :** in opposition or hostility to **b :** as a defense or protection from **3 :** compared or contrasted with **4 :** in preparation or provision for **5 a :** in the direction of and into contact with **b :** in contact with **6 :** in a direction opposite to the motion or course of **7 a :** as a counterbalance to **b :** in exchange for **c :** as a charge on **8 :** before the background of
[2]**against** *conj, archaic* **:** in preparation for the time when **:** BEFORE
Ag·a·mem·non \ˌag-ə-ˈmem-ˌnän, -nən\ *n* [L, fr. Gk *Agamemnōn*] **:** a King of Mycenae and leader of the Greeks in the Trojan War
aga·mete \ˌā-gə-ˈmēt, (ˈ)ā-ˈgam-ˌēt\ *n* [ISV, fr. Gk *agametos* unmarried, fr. *a-* + *gamein* to marry — more at GAMETE] **:** an asexual reproductive cell
agam·ic \(ˈ)ā-ˈgam-ik\ *adj* [Gk *agamos* unmarried, fr. *a-* + *gamos* marriage — more at BIGAMY] **:** ASEXUAL, PARTHENOGENETIC — **agam·i·cal·ly** \-i-k(ə-)lē\ *adv*
aga·mo·gen·e·sis \ˌā-ˌgam-ə-ˈjen-ə-səs, ˌag-ə-mō-ˈjen-\ *n* [NL, fr. Gk *agamos* + L *genesis*] **1 :** PARTHENOGENESIS **2 :** asexual reproduction — **aga·mo·ge·net·ic** \-jə-ˈnet-ik\ *adj* — **aga·mo·ge·net·i·cal·ly** \-i-k(ə-)lē\ *adv*
aga·mo·sper·my \(ˈ)ā-ˈgam-ə-ˌspər-mē, ˈag-ə-mō-ˌspər-\ *n* [Gk *agamos* + E *-spermy*] **:** APOGAMY; *specif* **:** apogamy in which sexual union is not completed and the embryo is produced from the innermost layer of the integument
ag·a·pan·thus \ˌag-ə-ˈpan(t)-thəs\ *n* [NL, genus name, fr. Gk *agapē* + *anthos* flower — more at ANTHOLOGY] **:** any of several African plants (genus *Agapanthus*) of the lily family cultivated for their umbels of showy blue or purple flowers
[1]**agape** \ə-ˈgāp *also* -ˈgap\ *adj* **1 :** wide open **:** GAPING **2 :** being in a state of wonder
[2]**aga·pe** \ä-ˈgä-(ˌ)pā, ˈäg-ə-ˌpā\ *n* [LL, fr. Gk *agapē*, lit., love] **1 :** LOVE 3a **2 :** LOVE FEAST
agar \ˈäg-ˌär\ *or* **agar-agar** \ˌäg-ˌär-ˈäg-ˌär\ *n* [Malay *agar-agar*] **1 :** a gelatinous colloidal extractive of a red alga (as of the genera *Gelidium*, *Gracilaria*, and *Eucheuma*) used esp. in culture media or as a gelling and stabilizing agent in foods **2 :** a culture medium containing agar
aga·ric \ˈag-ə-rik, ə-ˈgar-ik\ *n* [L *agaricum*, a fungus, fr. Gk *agarikon*] **1 a :** any of several pore fungi (genus *Fomes*) used esp. in the preparation of punk **b :** the dried fruiting body of a fungus (*F. officinalis*) formerly used in medicine **2 :** any of a family (Agaricaceae) of gill fungi including the common brown-spored edible meadow mushroom
ag·ate \ˈag-ət\ *n, often attrib* [MF, fr. L *achates*, fr. Gk *achatēs*] **1 :** a fine-grained variegated chalcedony having its colors arranged in stripes, blended in clouds, or showing mosslike forms **2 :** something made of or fitted with agate: as **a :** a drawplate used by gold-wire drawers **b :** a bookbinder's burnisher **c :** a playing marble of agate **3 :** a size of type approximately 5½ point
agate line *n* **:** a space one column wide and $\frac{1}{14}$ inch deep used as a unit of measurement in publication advertising
ag·ate·ware \ˈag-ət-ˌwa(ə)r, -ˌwe(ə)r\ *n* **1 :** pottery veined and mottled to resemble agate **2 :** an enameled iron or steel ware for household utensils
aga·ve \ə-ˈgäv-ē\ *n* [NL *Agave*, genus name, fr. L, a daughter of Cadmus, fr. Gk *Agauē*] **:** any of a genus (*Agave*) of plants of the amaryllis family having spiny-margined leaves and flowers in tall spreading panicles and including some cultivated for their fiber or for ornament
agaze \ə-ˈgāz\ *adj* **:** GAZING
[1]**age** \ˈāj\ *n* [ME, fr. OF *aage*, fr. (assumed) VL *aetaticum*, fr. L *aetat-*, *aetas*, fr. *aevum* lifetime — more at AYE] **1 a :** the part of an existence extending from the beginning to any given time **b :** LIFETIME **c :** the time of life at which some particular qualification, power, or capacity arises or rests; *specif* **:** MAJORITY **d :** one of the stages of life **e :** an advanced stage of life **2 a :** the period contemporary with a person's lifetime or with his active life **b :** GENERATION **c :** a long time **3 a :** a period of time in history or in the development of man or in the history of the earth **b :** a period of time in prehistory characterized by the use of artifacts made from a distinctive material **4 :** an individual's development measured in terms of the years requisite for like development of an average individual **syn** see PERIOD
[2]**age** *vb* **aged; ag·ing** *or* **age·ing** *vi* **1 :** to become old **:** show the effects or the characteristics of increasing age **2 a :** to acquire a desirable quality by standing undisturbed for some time **b :** to become mellow or mature **:** RIPEN ~ *vt* **1 :** to cause to become old **2 :** to bring to a state fit for use or to maturity
-age \ij\ *n suffix* [ME, fr. OF, fr. L *-aticum*] **1 :** aggregate **:** collection ⟨track*age*⟩ **2 a :** action **:** process ⟨haul*age*⟩ **b :** cumulative result of ⟨break*age*⟩ **c :** rate of ⟨dos*age*⟩ **3 :** house or place of ⟨orphan*age*⟩ **4 :** state **:** rank ⟨peon*age*⟩ **5 :** fee **:** charge ⟨post*age*⟩
aged \ˈā-jəd, ˈājd; ˈājd *for 1b & 2b*\ *adj* **1 :** grown old: as **a :** of an advanced age **b :** having attained a specified age ⟨a man ~ forty years⟩ **c :** well advanced toward reduction to base level — used of topographic features **2 a :** typical of old age **b :** having acquired a desired quality with age — **aged·ness** *n*
age·less \ˈāj-ləs\ *adj* **1 :** not growing old or showing the effects of age **2 :** TIMELESS, ETERNAL — **age·less·ly** *adv*
age·long \ˈāj-ˌlȯŋ\ *adj* **:** lasting for an age **:** EVERLASTING
agen·cy \ˈā-jən-sē\ *n* **1 :** the capacity, condition, or state of acting or of exerting power **:** OPERATION **2 :** a person or thing through which power is exerted or an end is achieved **:** INSTRUMENTALITY **3 a :** the office or function of an agent **b :** the relationship between a principal and his agent **4 :** an establishment engaged in doing business for another **5 :** an administrative division (as of a government) **syn** see MEAN
agen·da \ə-ˈjen-də\ *n* [L, neut. pl. of *agendum*, gerundive of *agere*] **:** a list, outline, or plan of things to be done **:** PROGRAM
agen·dum \-dəm\ *n, pl* **agenda** *or* **agendums** [L] **:** AGENDA
agene \ˈā-ˌjēn\ *n* [fr. *Agene*, a trademark] **:** nitrogen trichloride
agen·e·sis \(ˈ)ā-ˈjen-ə-səs\ *n* [NL] **:** lack or failure of development (as of a body part)
age·nize \ˈā-jə-ˌnīz\ *vt* **:** to treat (flour) with nitrogen trichloride
agent \ˈā-jənt\ *n* [ME, fr. ML *agent-*, *agens*, fr. L, prp. of *agere* to drive, lead, act, do; akin to ON *aka* to travel in a vehicle, Gk *agein* to drive, lead] **1 a :** something that produces or is capable of producing an effect **:** an active or efficient cause **b :** a chemically, physically, or biologically active principle **2 :** one that acts or exerts power **3 :** a person responsible for his acts **4 :** MEANS, INSTRUMENT **5 :** one who acts for or in the place of another by authority from him: as **a :** a representative, emissary, or official of a government ⟨crown ~⟩ ⟨secret-service ~⟩ **b :** one engaged in undercover activities (as espionage) ⟨secret ~⟩ **syn** see MEAN
agen·tial \ā-ˈjen-chəl\ *adj* **:** of, relating to, or expressive of an agent or agency — **agen·tial·ly** \-chə-lē\ *adv*
agent officer *n* **:** an army officer appointed to disburse funds
agent pro·vo·ca·teur \ˌäzh-ˌäⁿ-prō-ˌväk-ə-ˈtər, ˈā-jənt-\ *n, pl* **agents provocateurs** \ˌäzh-ˌäⁿ-prō-ˌväk-ə-ˈtər, ˈā-jən(t)s-prō-\ [F, lit., provoking agent] **:** one employed to associate himself with members of a group or with suspected persons and by pretended sympathy with their aims or attitudes to incite them to some action that will make them liable to apprehension and punishment
age-old \ˈā-ˈjōld\ *adj* **:** having existed for ages **:** ANCIENT
ag·er·a·tum \ˌaj-ə-ˈrāt-əm\ *n* [NL, genus name, fr. Gk *agēratos* ageless, fr. *a-* + *gēras* old age — more at CORN] **:** any of a large genus (*Ageratum*) of tropical American composite herbs often cultivated for their small showy heads of blue or white flowers; *also* **:** any of several related blue-flowered plants (genus *Eupatorium*)
ag·gior·na·men·to \ə-ˌjȯr-nə-ˈmen-(ˌ)tō\ *n* [It, fr. *aggiornare* to bring up to date, fr. *a* to (fr. L *ad-*) + *giorno* day, fr. LL *diurnum* day — more at JOURNEY] **:** a bringing up to date **:** MODERNIZATION
[1]**ag·glom·er·ate** \ə-ˈgläm-ə-ˌrāt\ *vb* [L *agglomeratus*, pp. of *agglomerare* to heap up, join, fr. *ad-* + *glomer-*, *glomus* ball — more at CLAM] **:** to gather into a ball, mass, or cluster
[2]**ag·glom·er·ate** \-rət\ *adj* **:** AGGLOMERATED; *specif* **:** clustered or growing together but not coherent ⟨an ~ flower head⟩
[3]**ag·glom·er·ate** \-rət\ *n* **1 :** a jumbled mass or collection **2 :** a rock composed of volcanic fragments of various sizes and degrees of angularity
ag·glom·er·a·tion \ə-ˌgläm-ə-ˈrā-shən\ *n* **1 :** the action or process of collecting in a mass **2 :** a heap or cluster of disparate elements — **ag·glom·er·a·tive** \ə-ˈgläm-ə-ˌrāt-iv\ *adj*
[1]**ag·glu·ti·nate** \ə-ˈglüt-ᵊn-ət\ *adj* **:** AGGLUTINATIVE 2
[2]**ag·glu·ti·nate** \-ᵊn-ˌāt\ *vb* [L *agglutinatus*, pp. of *agglutinare* to glue to, fr. *ad-* + *glutinare* to glue, fr. *glutin-*, *gluten* glue — more at GLUTEN] *vt* **1 :** to cause to adhere **:** FASTEN **2 :** to combine into a compound **:** attach to a base as an affix **3 :** to cause to undergo agglutination ~ *vi* **1 :** to unite or combine into a group or mass **2 :** to form words by agglutination
ag·glu·ti·na·tion \ə-ˌglüt-ᵊn-ˈā-shən\ *n* **1 :** the action or process of agglutinating **2 :** a mass or group formed by the union of separate elements **3 :** the formation of derivative or compound words by putting together constituents of which each expresses a single definite meaning **4 :** a reaction in which particles (as red blood cells or bacteria) suspended in a liquid collect into clumps and which occurs esp. as a serologic response to a specific antibody
ag·glu·ti·na·tive \ə-ˈglüt-ᵊn-ˌāt-iv\ *adj* **1 :** ADHESIVE **2 :** characterized by agglutination
ag·glu·ti·nin \ə-ˈglüt-ᵊn-ən\ *n* [ISV *agglutin*ation + *-in*] **:** a substance (as an antibody) producing agglutination
ag·gra·da·tion \ˌag-rə-ˈdā-shən\ *n* **:** a modification of the earth's

surface in the direction of uniformity of grade by deposition
ag·grade \ə-ˈgrād\ *vt* [*ad-* + *grade*] **:** to fill with detrital material
ag·gran·dize \ə-ˈgran-ˌdīz, ˈag-rən-\ *vt* [F *agrandiss-*, stem of *agrandir*, fr. *a-* (fr. L *ad-*) + *grandir* to increase, fr. L *grandire*, fr. *grandis* great] **1 :** to make great or greater **2 :** to make appear great or greater **:** EXAGGERATE — **ag·gran·dize·ment** \ə-ˈgran-dəz-mənt, -ˌdīz-, ˌag-rən-ˈdīz-\ *n* — **ag·gran·diz·er** \ə-ˈgran-ˌdī-zər, ˈag-rən-\ *n*
ag·gra·vate \ˈag-rə-ˌvāt\ *vt* [L *aggravatus*, pp. of *aggravare* to make heavier, fr. *ad-* + *gravare* to burden, fr. *gravis* heavy — more at GRIEVE] **1** *obs* **a :** to make heavy **:** BURDEN **b :** INCREASE **2 :** to make worse, more serious, or more severe **3 a :** EXASPERATE, ANNOY **b :** to produce inflammation in **syn** see INTENSIFY
ag·gra·va·tion \ˌag-rə-ˈvā-shən\ *n* **1 :** the act, action, or result of aggravating; *esp* **:** an increasing in seriousness or severity **2 :** an act or circumstance that intensifies or makes worse **3 :** IRRITATION, PROVOCATION
[1]**ag·gre·gate** \ˈag-ri-gət\ *adj* [ME *aggregat*, fr. L *aggregatus*, pp. of *aggregare* to add to, fr. *ad-* + *greg-*, *grex* flock — more at GREGARIOUS] **:** formed by the collection of units or particles into a body, mass, or amount **:** COLLECTIVE: as **a** (1) **:** clustered in a dense mass or head ⟨an ~ flower⟩ (2) **:** formed from the several ovaries of a single flower **b :** composed of mineral crystals of one or more kinds or of mineral or rock fragments — **ag·gre·gate·ly** *adv* — **ag·gre·gate·ness** *n*
[2]**ag·gre·gate** \-ˌgāt\ *vt* **1 :** to collect or gather into a mass or whole **2 :** to amount in the aggregate to
[3]**ag·gre·gate** \-gət\ *n* **1 :** a mass or body of units or parts somewhat loosely associated with one another **2 :** the whole sum or amount **:** SUM TOTAL **3 a :** an aggregate rock **b :** any of several hard inert materials used for mixing with a cementing material to form concrete, mortar, or plaster **c :** a clustered mass of individual soil particles varied in shape, ranging in size from a microscopic granule to a small crumb, and considered the basic structural unit of soil **4 :** SET 17 **syn** see SUM
ag·gre·ga·tion \ˌag-ri-ˈgā-shən\ *n* **1 a :** the collecting of units or parts into a mass or whole **b :** the condition of being so collected **2 :** a group, body, or mass composed of many distinct parts
ag·gre·ga·tive \ˈag-ri-ˌgāt-iv\ *adj* **:** tending to aggregate
ag·gress \ə-ˈgres\ *vi* **:** to commit aggression
ag·gres·sion \ə-ˈgresh-ən\ *n* [L *aggressus*, pp. of *aggredi* to attack, fr. *ad-* + *gradi* to step, go — more at GRADE] **1 :** an offensive action or procedure **2 :** the practice of making attacks or encroachments; *esp* **:** unprovoked violation by one country of the territorial integrity of another **3 :** aggressive outlook or its manifestation (as in overt forceful action or in mental attitudes)
ag·gres·sive \ə-ˈgres-iv\ *adj* **1 a :** tending toward or practicing aggression **b :** marked by combative readiness **:** MILITANT **2 a :** marked by driving forceful energy or initiative **:** ENTERPRISING **b :** marked by obtrusive energy **:** SELF-ASSERTIVE — **ag·gres·sive·ly** *adv* — **ag·gres·sive·ness** *n*
syn MILITANT, ASSERTIVE, SELF-ASSERTIVE, PUSHING: AGGRESSIVE implies a disposition to dominate often in disregard of others' rights or in determined and energetic pursuit of one's ends; MILITANT also implies a fighting disposition but suggests not self-seeking but devotion to a cause, movement, or principle; ASSERTIVE suggests bold self-confidence in expression of opinion; SELF-ASSERTIVE connotes unpleasant forwardness or brash self-confidence; PUSHING may apply to ambition or enterprise or to snobbish and crude intrusiveness or officiousness
ag·gres·sor \-ər\ *n* **:** one that commits or practices aggression
ag·grieve \ə-ˈgrēv\ *vt* [ME *agreven*, fr. MF *agrever*, fr. L *aggravare* to make heavier] **1 :** to give pain or trouble to **:** DISTRESS **2 :** to inflict injury upon **syn** see WRONG
ag·grieved *adj* **1 :** troubled or distressed in spirit **2 a :** showing grief, injury, or offense **b :** suffering from an infringement or denial of legal rights
aghast \ə-ˈgast\ *adj* [ME *agast*, fr. pp. of *agasten* to frighten, fr. *a-* (perfective prefix) + *gasten* to frighten — more at ABIDE, GAST] **:** struck with terror, amazement, or horror **:** SHOCKED
ag·ile \ˈaj-əl\ *adj* [MF, fr. L *agilis*, fr. *agere* to drive, act — more at AGENT] **1 :** readily able to move quickly and easily **:** NIMBLE **2 :** mentally quick and resourceful — **ag·ile·ly** \-ə(l)-lē\ *adv*
syn NIMBLE, BRISK, SPRY: AGILE implies dexterity and ease in physical or mental actions; NIMBLE stresses lightness and swiftness of action or thought; BRISK suggests liveliness, animation, or vigor of movement sometimes with a suggestion of hurry; SPRY stresses an ability for quick action that is unexpected because of age or known infirmity
agil·i·ty \ə-ˈjil-ət-ē\ *n* **:** the quality or state of being agile **:** NIMBLENESS, DEXTERITY
aging *pres part of* AGE
agio \ˈaj-(ˌ)ō, -ē-ˌō\ *n* [It, alter. of It dial. *lajjë*, fr. MGk *allagion* exchange, fr. Gk *allagē* exchange, fr. *allos* other — more at ELSE] **:** a premium or percentage paid for the exchange of one currency for another; *also* **:** the premium or discount on foreign bills of exchange
agio·tage \ˌazh-ə-ˈtäzh, ˌaj-ə-\ *n* [F, deriv. of It *agio*] **1 :** exchange business **2 :** STOCKJOBBING
ag·i·tate \ˈaj-ə-ˌtāt\ *vb* [L *agitatus*, pp. of *agitare*, freq. of *agere* to drive — more at AGENT] *vt* **1 a** *obs* **:** to give motion to **b :** to move with an irregular, rapid, or violent action **2 :** to excite the mind or feelings of **:** DISTURB **3 a :** to discuss excitedly and earnestly **b :** to stir up public discussion of ~ *vi* **:** to attempt to arouse public feeling **syn** see DISCOMPOSE, SHAKE — **ag·i·tat·ed·ly** *adv*
ag·i·ta·tion \ˌaj-ə-ˈtā-shən\ *n* **:** the act or process of agitating **:** the state of being agitated
ag·i·ta·to \ˌaj-ə-ˈtät-(ˌ)ō\ *adv* (*or adj*) [It, lit., agitated, fr. L *agitatus*] **:** in a restless and agitated manner — used as a direction in music
ag·i·ta·tor \ˈaj-ə-ˌtāt-ər\ *n* **:** one who agitates: as **a :** one who stirs up public feeling on political or other issues **b :** an implement or apparatus for stirring or shaking
Agla·ia \ə-ˈglā-(y)ə, -ˈglī-ə\ *n* [L, fr. Gk] **:** one of the three Graces
agleam \ə-ˈglēm\ *adj* **:** GLEAMING
ag·let \ˈag-lət\ *n* [ME *aglet*, fr. MF *aguillette*, *aiguillette*, dim. of *aguille*, *aiguille* needle, fr. LL *acicula*, *acucula* ornamental pin, dim. of L *acus* needle, pin — more at ACUTE] **1 :** the plain or ornamental tag covering the ends of a lace or point **2 :** any of various ornamental studs, cords, or pins worn on clothing
agley \ə-ˈglā, -ˈglē\ *adv* [Sc, lit., squintingly, fr. [1]*a-* + *gley* to squint] *chiefly Scot* **:** AWRY, WRONG
aglit·ter \ə-ˈglit-ər\ *adj* **:** GLITTERING
aglow \ə-ˈglō\ *adj* **:** GLOWING
ag·nail \ˈag-ˌnāl\ *n* [ME, corn on the foot or toe, fr. OE *angnægl*, fr. *ang-* (akin to *enge* tight, painful) + *nægl* metal nail — more at ANGER, NAIL] **:** a sore or inflammation about a fingernail or toenail; *also* **:** HANGNAIL
[1]**ag·nate** \ˈag-ˌnāt\ *n* [L *agnatus*, fr. pp. of *agnasci* to be born in addition to, fr. *ad-* + *nasci* to be born — more at NATION] **1 :** a relative whose kinship is traceable exclusively through males **2 :** a paternal kinsman
[2]**agnate** *adj* **1 :** related through male descent or on the father's side **2 :** ALLIED, AKIN — **ag·nat·ic** \ag-ˈnat-ik\ *adj* — **ag·nat·i·cal·ly** \-i-k(ə-)lē\ *adv* — **ag·na·tion** \-ˈnā-shən\ *n*
Ag·ne·an \ˈäg-nē-ən\ *n* [*Agni*, ancient kingdom in Turkestan] **:** TOCHARIAN A
ag·nize \ag-ˈnīz\ *vt* [L *agnoscere* to acknowledge (fr. *ad-* + *noscere* to know) + E *-ize* (as in *recognize*) — more at KNOW] *archaic* **:** RECOGNIZE, ACKNOWLEDGE
ag·no·men \ag-ˈnō-mən\ *n*, *pl* **ag·nom·i·na** \-ˈnäm-ə-nə\ *or* **agnomens** [L, irreg. fr. *ad-* + *nomen* name — more at NAME] **:** an additional cognomen given to a person by the ancient Romans (as in honor of some achievement)
ag·nos·tic \ag-ˈnäs-tik, əg-\ *adj* [Gk *agnōstos* unknown, unknowable, fr. *a-* + *gnōstos* known, fr. *gignōskein* to know — more at KNOW] **1 :** of or relating to the belief that the existence of any ultimate reality (as God) is unknown and prob. unknowable **2 :** NONCOMMITTAL, UNDOGMATIC **syn** see ATHEIST — **agnostic** *n* — **ag·nos·ti·cism** \-tə-ˌsiz-əm\ *n*
Ag·nus Dei \ˌäg-ˌnu̇s-ˈdā(-ˌē), ˌän-ˌyüs-; ˌag-nəs-ˈdē-ˌī\ *n* [ME, fr. LL, lamb of God, fr. its opening words] **1 :** a liturgical prayer said or sung to Christ as Savior **2 :** an image of a lamb often with a halo and a banner and cross as a symbol of Christ
ago \ə-ˈgō\ *adj* (*or adv*) [ME *agon*, *ago*, fr. pp. of *agon* to pass away, fr. OE *āgān*, fr. *ā-*, perfective prefix + *gān* to go — more at ABIDE, GO] **:** earlier than the present time
agog \ə-ˈgäg\ *adj* [MF *en gogues* in mirth] **:** full of intense interest or excitement **:** EAGER
a-go-go \ä-ˈgō-ˌgō\ *adj* [*Whisky à Gogo*, café and discotheque in Paris, France, fr. F *à gogo* galore, fr. MF] **:** GO-GO
-a·gogue \ə-ˌgäg\ *n comb form* [F & NL; F, fr. LL *-agogus* promoting the expulsion of, fr. Gk *-agōgos*, fr. *agein* to lead; NL *-agogon*, fr. Gk, neut. of *-agōgos* — more at AGENT] **:** substance that promotes the secretion or expulsion of ⟨emmen*agogue*⟩
agon \ˈäg-ˌän, ä-ˈgōn\ *n*, *pl* **agons** *also* **ago·nes** \ä-ˈgō-ˌnes, ə-ˈgō-(ˌ)nēz\ [Gk *agōn*] **:** CONTEST, CONFLICT; *specif* **:** the dramatic conflict between the chief characters in a literary work
ag·o·nal \ˈag-ən-ᵊl\ *adj* **:** of, relating to, or associated with agony and esp. the death agony
agone \ə-ˈgȯn *also* -ˈgän\ *adj* (*or adv*), *archaic* **:** AGO
agon·ic \(ˈ)ā-ˈgän-ik, ə-\ *adj* [Gk *agōnos* without angle, fr. *a-* + *gōnia* angle — more at -GON] **1 :** not forming an angle **2 :** being an imaginary line passing through points where there is no magnetic declination and where a freely suspended magnetic needle indicates true north
ag·o·nist \ˈag-ə-nəst\ *n* [LL *agonista* competitor, fr. Gk *agōnistēs*, fr. *agōnizesthai* to contend, fr. *agōn*] **1 :** one that is engaged in a struggle **2** [back-formation fr. *antagonist*] **:** a muscle that is checked and controlled by the opposing simultaneous contraction of another muscle
ag·o·nis·tic \ˌag-ə-ˈnis-tik\ *adj* **1 :** of or relating to the athletic contests of ancient Greece **2 :** ARGUMENTATIVE **3 :** striving for effect **:** STRAINED — **ag·o·nis·ti·cal** \-ti-kəl\ *adj* — **ag·o·nis·ti·cal·ly** \-k(ə-)lē\ *adv*
ag·o·nize \ˈag-ə-ˌnīz\ *vt* **:** to cause to suffer agony **:** TORTURE ~ *vi* **1 :** to suffer agony, torture, or anguish **2 :** STRUGGLE
ag·o·nized *adj* **:** characterized by, suffering, or expressing agony
ag·o·niz·ing *adj* **:** causing agony **:** PAINFUL
ag·o·ny \ˈag-ə-nē\ *n* [ME *agonie*, fr. LL *agonia*, fr. Gk *agōnia* struggle, anguish, fr. *agōn* gathering, contest for a prize, fr. *agein* to lead, celebrate — more at AGENT] **1 a :** intense pain of mind or body **:** ANGUISH, TORTURE **b :** death struggle **2 :** violent struggle or contest **3 :** a strong sudden display (as of joy or delight) **:** OUTBURST **syn** see DISTRESS
agony column *n* **:** a newspaper column of personal advertisements relating esp. to missing relatives or friends
[1]**ag·o·ra** \ˈag-ə-rə\ *n*, *pl* **agoras** *or* **ag·o·rae** \-ˌrē, -ˌrī\ [Gk — more at GREGARIOUS] **:** a gathering place or assembly; *esp* **:** the marketplace in ancient Greece
[2]**ago·ra** \ˌäg-ə-ˈrä\ *n*, *pl* **ago·rot** \-ˈrōt\ [NHeb *ʼăgōrāh*, fr. Heb, a small coin] — see *pound* at MONEY table
ag·o·ra·pho·bia \ˌag-ə-rə-ˈfō-bē-ə\ *n* [NL, fr. Gk *agora* + NL *phobia*] **:** abnormal fear of crossing or of being in open spaces — **ag·o·ra·pho·bic** \-ˈfō-bik, -ˈfäb-ik\ *adj*
agou·ti \ə-ˈgüt-ē\ *n* [F, fr. Sp *agutí*, fr. Guarani] **1 :** a tropical American rodent (genus *Dasyprocta* or *Myoprocta*) about the size of a rabbit **2 :** a grizzled color of fur resulting from the barring of each hair in several alternate dark and light bands
agrafe *or* **agraffe** \ə-ˈgraf\ *n* [F *agrafe*] **:** a hook-and-loop fastening; *esp* **:** an ornamental clasp used on armor or costumes
agran·u·lo·cyte \(ˈ)ā-ˈgran-yə-lō-ˌsīt\ *n* **:** a leukocyte without cytoplasmic granules
agran·u·lo·cy·to·sis \ˌā-ˌgran-yə-lō-ˌsī-ˈtō-səs\ *n* **:** a destructive condition marked by severe decrease in blood granulocytes and often associated with the use of certain drugs
ag·ra·pha \ˈag-rə-fə\ *n pl* [Gk, neut. pl. of *agraphos* unwritten, fr. *a-* + *graphein* to write] **:** sayings of Jesus not in the canonical gospels but found in other New Testament or early Christian writings
[1]**agrar·i·an** \ə-ˈgrer-ē-ən, -ˈgrar-\ *adj* [L *agrarius*, fr. *agr-*, *ager* field] **1 :** of or relating to fields or lands or their tenure **2 :** of, relating to, or characteristic of the farmer or his interests
[2]**agrarian** *n* **:** a member of an agrarian party or movement
agrar·i·an·ism \-ē-ə-ˌniz-əm\ *n* **:** a social or political movement designed to bring about land reforms or to improve the economic status of the farmer
agree \ə-ˈgrē\ *vb* [ME *agreen*, fr. MF *agreer*, fr. *a-* (fr. L *ad-*) + *gre* will, pleasure, fr. L *gratum*, neut. of *gratus* pleasing, agreeable — more at GRACE] *vt* **1 :** ADMIT, CONCEDE **2 :** to settle upon by common consent **:** ARRANGE ~ *vi* **1 :** to give assent **:** ACCEDE **2 a :** to achieve or be in harmony **:** CONCUR **b :** to get along together **c :** to come to terms **3 a :** to be similar **:** CORRESPOND ⟨both copies

~⟩ **b** : to be consistent ⟨story ~*s* with the facts⟩ **4** : to be fitting, pleasing, or healthful : SUIT ⟨climate ~*s* with him⟩ **5** : to have an inflectional form denoting identity or a regular correspondence other than identity in a grammatical category (as gender, number, case, or person)

syn AGREE, CONCUR, COINCIDE mean to come into or be in harmony regarding a matter of opinion. AGREE implies unison or complete accord often after discussion or adjustment of differences; CONCUR implies arriving at a specific or definite agreement, as through a vote, that may provide a basis for common effort toward a goal; COINCIDE applies chiefly to opinions or judgments that are in agreement rather than to persons

syn SQUARE, CONFORM, ACCORD, COMPORT, HARMONIZE, CORRESPOND: AGREE implies being in a relation that reveals no discrepancies, significant differences, inequalities, untoward effects; SQUARE suggests showing a precise or a mathematically exact agreement; CONFORM stresses agreement in essentials; ACCORD stresses a general compatibility; COMPORT suggests the absence of any incongruity; HARMONIZE and CORRESPOND may apply to the relation of dissimilar things, but HARMONIZE stresses their blending to produce an agreeable effect, and CORRESPOND stresses their matching, complementing, or answering to each other **syn** see in addition ASSENT

agree·abil·i·ty \ə-ˌgrē-ə-ˈbil-ət-ē\ *n* : AGREEABLENESS

agree·able \ə-ˈgrē-ə-bəl\ *adj* **1** : pleasing to the mind or senses : PLEASANT **2** : ready or willing to agree or consent **3** : being in harmony : CONSONANT **syn** see PLEASANT — **agree·able·ness** *n* — **agree·ably** \-blē\ *adv*

agree·ment \ə-ˈgrē-mənt\ *n* **1 a** : the act or fact of agreeing **b** : harmony of opinion, action, or character : CONCORD **2 a** : an arrangement as to a course of action **b** : COMPACT, TREATY **3 a** : a contract duly executed and legally binding **b** : the language or instrument embodying such a contract

agres·tic \ə-ˈgres-tik\ *adj* [L *agrestis*, fr. *ager*] : RUSTIC, RURAL

ag·ri·cul·tur·al \ˌag-ri-ˈkəlch-(ə-)rəl\ *adj* : of, relating to, used in, or concerned with agriculture — **ag·ri·cul·tur·al·ly** \-ē\ *adv*

ag·ri·cul·ture \ˈag-ri-ˌkəl-chər\ *n* [F, fr. L *agricultura*, fr. *ager* field + *cultura* cultivation — more at ACRE, CULTURE] : the science or art of cultivating the soil, producing crops, and raising livestock : FARMING — **ag·ri·cul·tur·ist** \ˌag-ri-ˈkəlch-(ə-)rəst\ *or* **ag·ri·cul·tur·al·ist** \-(ə-)rə-ləst\ *n*

ag·ri·mo·ny \ˈag-rə-ˌmō-nē\ *n* [ME, fr. MF & L; MF *aigremoine*, fr. L *agrimonia*, MS var. of *argemonia*, fr. Gk *argemōnē*] : a common yellow-flowered herb (genus *Agrimonia*) of the rose family having toothed leaves and fruits like burrs; *also* : any of several similar or related plants

ag·ri·ol·o·gy \ˌag-rē-ˈäl-ə-jē\ *n* [Gk *agrios* wild, fr. *agros* field, country] : the comparative study of the customs of nonliterate peoples

ag·ro·bi·o·log·ic \ˌag-ˌrō-ˌbī-ə-ˈläj-ik\ *adj* : of or relating to agrobiology — **ag·ro·bi·o·log·i·cal** \-i-kəl\ *adj* — **ag·ro·bi·o·log·i·cal·ly** \-k(ə-)lē\ *adv*

ag·ro·bi·ol·o·gy \ˌag-(ˌ)rō-(ˌ)bī-ˈäl-ə-jē\ *n* [Gk *agros*] : the study of plant nutrition and growth and crop production in relation to soil management

ag·ro·log·ic \ˌag-rə-ˈläj-ik\ *adj* : of or relating to agrology — **ag·ro·log·i·cal** \-i-kəl\ *adj* — **ag·ro·log·i·cal·ly** \-k(ə-)lē\ *adv*

agrol·o·gist \ə-ˈgräl-ə-jəst\ *n* : a specialist in agrology

agrol·o·gy \-jē\ *n* [ISV, fr. Gk *agros* field — more at ACRE] : a branch of agriculture dealing with soils esp. in relation to crops

ag·ro·nom·ic \ˌag-rə-ˈnäm-ik\ *adj* : of or relating to agronomy — **ag·ro·nom·i·cal** \-i-kəl\ *adj*

agron·o·mist \ə-ˈgrän-ə-məst\ *n* : a specialist in agronomy

agron·o·my \-mē\ *n* [prob. fr. F *agronomie*, fr. Gk *agros* field + *-nomie* -nomy] : a branch of agriculture dealing with field-crop production and soil management

aground \ə-ˈgrau̇nd\ *adv* (*or adj*) **1** : on or onto the shore or the bottom of a body of water : STRANDED **2** : on the ground

ague \ˈā-(ˌ)gyü\ *n* [ME, fr. MF *aguë*, fr. ML (*febris*) *acuta*, lit., sharp fever, fr. L, fem. of *acutus* sharp — more at ACUTE] **1** : a fever (as malaria) marked by paroxysms of chills, fever, and sweating that recur at regular intervals **2** : a fit of shivering : CHILL — **agu·ish** \ˈā-ˌgyü-ish\ *adj* — **agu·ish·ly** *adv*

ah \ˈä\ *interj* [ME] — used to express delight, relief, regret, or contempt

aha \ä-ˈhä\ *interj* [ME] — used to express surprise, triumph, or derision

Ahab \ˈā-ˌhab\ *n* [Heb *Aḥ'ābh*] : a king of Israel in the 9th century B.C.

ahead \ə-ˈhed\ *adv* **1 a** : in a forward direction or position : FORWARD **b** : in front **2** : in, into, or for the future **3** : in or toward a more advantageous position **4** : at or to an earlier time : in advance — **ahead** *adj*

ahead of *prep* **1** : in front or advance of **2** : in excess of : ABOVE

ahim·sa \ə-ˈhim-ˌsä\ *n* [Skt *ahiṁsā* noninjury] : the Hindu and Buddhist doctrine of refraining from harming any living being

A–horizon *n* : the outer dark-colored layer of a soil profile consisting largely of partly disintegrated organic debris

ahoy \ə-ˈhȯi\ *interj* [*a-* (as in *aha*) + *hoy*] — used in hailing ⟨ship ~⟩

ai \ˈī\ *n* [Pg *ai* or Sp *aí*, fr. Tupi *ai*] : a sloth (genus *Bradypus*) with three claws on each front foot

ai·blins \ˈā-blənz\ *adv* [*able* + *-lings*, *-lins* -lings] *chiefly Scot* : PERHAPS

¹**aid** \ˈād\ *vb* [ME *eyden*, fr. MF *aider*, fr. L *adjutare*, fr. *adjutus*, pp. of *adjuvare*, fr. *ad-* + *juvare* to help] *vt* : to provide with what is useful or necessary in achieving an end : ASSIST ~ *vi* : to give assistance **syn** see HELP — **aid·er** *n*

²**aid** *n* **1** : a subsidy granted to the king by the English parliament until the 18th century for an extraordinary purpose **2** : the act of helping or the help given : ASSISTANCE **3 a** : an assisting person or group — compare AIDE **b** : an auxiliary or instrumental device **4** : a tribute paid by a vassal to his lord

aide \ˈād\ *n* [short for *aide-de-camp*] : a person who acts as an assistant; *specif* : a military officer acting as assistant to a superior

aide–de–camp \ˌād-di-ˈkamp, -ˈkäⁿ\ *n, pl* **aides–de–camp** \ˌādz-di-\ [F *aide de camp*, lit., camp assistant] : AIDE

aid·man \ˈād-ˌman\ *n* : an army medical corpsman attached to a field unit

ai·glet \ˈā-glət\ *var of* AGLET

ai·grette \ā-ˈgret, ˈā-ˌ\ *n* [F] **1** : an ornamental spray of feathers (as of the egret) **2** : a spray of gems often worn on a hat or in hair

ai·guille \ā-ˈgwē(ə)l, -ˈgwē\ *n* [F, lit., needle — more at AGLET] **1** : a sharp-pointed pinnacle of rock **2** : an instrument for boring holes in stone or other masonry materials

ai·guil·lette \ˌā-gwə-ˈlet\ *n* [F — more at OGLET] : AGLET; *specif* : a shoulder cord worn by a high military aide

ail \ˈā(ə)l\ *vb* [ME *eilen*, fr. OE *eglan*; akin to MLG *egelen* to annoy] *vt* : to give physical or emotional pain, discomfort, or trouble to ~ *vi* : to have something the matter; *esp* : to suffer ill health

ai·lan·thus \ā-ˈlan(t)-thəs\ *n* [NL, genus name, fr. Amboinese *ai lantho*, lit., tree (of) heaven] : any of a small Asiatic genus (*Ailanthus* of the family Simaroubaceae, the ailanthus family) of chiefly tropical trees and shrubs with bitter bark, pinnate leaves, and terminal panicles of ill-scented greenish flowers

ai·le·ron \ˈā-lə-ˌrän\ *n* [F, fr. dim. of *aile* wing] : a movable part of an airplane wing or a movable airfoil external to the wing for imparting a rolling motion and thus providing lateral control

ail·ment \ˈā(ə)l-mənt\ *n* **1** : a bodily disorder or chronic disease **2** : UNREST, UNEASINESS

¹**aim** \ˈām\ *vb* [ME *aimen*, fr. MF *aesmer* & *esmer*; MF *aesmer*, fr. OF, fr. *a-* (fr. L *ad-*) + *esmer* to estimate, fr. L *aestimare* — more at ESTEEM] *vi* **1** : to direct a course : point a weapon **2** : ASPIRE ~ *vt* **1** *obs* : GUESS, CONJECTURE **2 a** : POINT **b** : to direct to or toward a specified object or goal **c** : INTEND

²**aim** *n* **1** *obs* : MARK, TARGET **2** : the pointing of a weapon at a mark; *also* : the weapon's accuracy or effectiveness **3** *obs* **a** : CONJECTURE, GUESS **b** : the purposive directing of effort **4** : OBJECT, PURPOSE **syn** see INTENTION

aim·less \ˈām-ləs\ *adj* : lacking aim or purpose — **aim·less·ly** *adv* — **aim·less·ness** *n*

¹**ain** \ˈān\ *adj or n* [ME *an*, fr. OE *ān*] *chiefly Scot* : ONE

²**ain** *adj or n* [prob. fr. ON *eiginn*] *dial Brit* : OWN

ain't \ˈānt\ [prob. contr. of *are not*] **1 a** : are not **b** : is not **c** : am not — though disapproved by many and more common in less educated speech, used orally in most parts of the U.S. by many educated speakers esp. in the phrase *ain't I* **2** *substand* **a** : have not **b** : has not

Ai·nu \ˈī-(ˌ)nü\ *n, pl* **Ainu** *or* **Ainus** [Ainu, lit., man] **1** : a member of an indigenous Caucasoid people of Japan **2** : the language of the Ainu people

¹**air** \ˈa(ə)r, ˈe(ə)r\ *n, often attrib* [ME, fr. OF, fr. L *aer*, fr. Gk *aēr*] **1 a** : the mixture of invisible odorless tasteless gases (as nitrogen and oxygen) that surrounds the earth **b** : a light breeze **c** : *archaic* : BREATH **2 a** : empty space **b** : NOWHERE **c** *slang* : a sudden severance of relations **3** : COMPRESSED AIR **4 a** (1) : AIRCRAFT ⟨go by ~⟩ ⟨~ attack⟩ (2) : AVIATION ⟨~ safety⟩ ⟨~ rights⟩ (3) : AIR FORCE ⟨~ headquarters⟩ **b** : the medium of transmission of radio waves; *also* : RADIO, TELEVISION ⟨went on the ~⟩ **5** : PUBLICITY **6 a** : the look, appearance, or bearing of a person esp. as expressive of some personal quality or emotion : DEMEANOR **b** : an artificial or affected manner : HAUGHTINESS ⟨to put on ~*s*⟩ **c** : outward appearance of a thing : MANNER **d** : a surrounding or pervading influence : ATMOSPHERE **7** [prob. trans. of It *aria*] **a** *Elizabethan & Jacobean music* : an accompanied song or melody in strophic form **b** : the chief voice part or melody in choral music **c** : TUNE, MELODY **syn** see POSE — **up in the air** : not yet settled

²**air** *vt* **1** : to expose to the air for drying, purifying, or refreshing : VENTILATE **2** : to expose to public view or bring to public notice ~ *vi* : to become exposed to the open air **syn** see EXPRESS

air base *n* : a base of operations for military aircraft

air bladder *n* : a sac containing gas and esp. air, occurring chiefly in fishes, and serving as a hydrostatic organ or assisting respiration

air·borne \-ˌbō(ə)rn, -ˌbȯ(ə)rn\ *adj* **1** : supported wholly by aerodynamic and aerostatic forces **2** : transported by air

air brake *n* **1** : a brake operated by a piston driven by compressed air **2** : a surface (as an aileron) that may be projected into the airstream for lowering the speed of an airplane

air·brush \-ˌbrəsh\ *n* : an atomizer for applying by compressed air a fine spray (as of paint or a protective coating) — **airbrush** *vt*

air·burst \-ˌbərst\ *n* : the burst of a shell or bomb in the air

air coach *n* : a passenger airliner offering service at less than first-class rates usu. with curtailed accommodations

air command *n* : a unit of the U.S. Air Force higher than an air force

air–con·di·tion \ˌa(ə)r-kən-ˈdish-ən, ˌe(ə)r-\ *vt* [back-formation fr. *air conditioning*] : to equip with an apparatus for washing air and controlling its humidity and temperature; *also* : to subject (air) to these processes — **air·con·di·tion·er** \-ˈdish-(ə-)nər\ *n*

air controlman *n* : a naval petty officer who controls and coordinates air traffic

air–cool \ˈa(ə)r-ˈkül, ˈe(ə)r-\ *vt* [back-formation fr. *air-cooled* & *air cooling*] : to cool the cylinders of (an internal-combustion engine) by air without the use of any intermediate medium

air·craft \ˈa(ə)r-ˌkraft, ˈe(ə)r-\ *n, pl* **aircraft** *often attrib* : a weight-carrying structure for navigation of the air that is supported either by its own buoyancy or by the dynamic action of the air against its surfaces

aircraft carrier *n* : a warship with a flight deck on which airplanes can be launched and landed

air·crew \ˈa(ə)r-ˌkrü, ˈe(ə)r-\ *n* : the crew manning an airplane

air division *n* : a unit of the U.S. Air Force higher than a wing and lower than an air force

air·drome \-ˌdrōm\ *n* [alter. of *aerodrome*] : AIRPORT

air·drop \-ˌdräp\ *n* : delivery of cargo or personnel by parachute from an airplane in flight — **air–drop** \-ˌdräp\ *vt*

air–dry \-ˈdrī\ *adj* : dry to such a degree that no further moisture is given up on exposure to air

Aire·dale \ˈa(ə)r-ˌdāl, ˈe(ə)r-\ *n* [*Airedale*, valley of the Aire river, England] : any of a breed of large terriers with a hard wiry coat that is dark on back and sides and tan elsewhere

air express *n* [fr. *Air Express*, a service mark] : package transport by airlines; *also* : the packages so shipped

air·field \ˈa(ə)r-ˌfēld, ˈe(ə)r-\ *n* **1** : the landing field of an airport **2** : AIRPORT

air·flow \-ˌflō\ *n* **:** the motion of air relative to the surface of a body immersed in it

air·foil \-ˌfȯil\ *n* **:** a body (as an airplane wing or propeller blade) designed to provide a desired reaction force when in motion relative to the surrounding air

air force *n* **1 :** the military organization of a nation for air warfare **2 :** a unit of the U.S. Air Force higher than an air division and lower than an air command

air·frame \-ˌfrām\ *n* [*aircraft* + *frame*] **:** the structure of an airplane or rocket without the power plant

air·freight \-ˈfrāt\ *n* **:** freight forwarding service by air in volume; *also* **:** the charge for this service

air·glow \-ˌglō\ *n* **:** light from the nighttime sky that originates in the high atmosphere and is associated with photochemical reactions of gases caused by solar radiation

air gun *n* **1 :** a rifle from which a projectile is propelled by compressed air **2 :** a pistol-shaped hand tool that works by compressed air **3 :** AIRBRUSH

air·head \-ˌhed\ *n* [¹*air* + *-head* (as in *beachhead*)] **:** an area in hostile territory secured usu. by airborne troops for further use in bringing in troops and materiel by air

air hole *n* **1 a :** a hole to admit or discharge air **b :** a spot not frozen over in ice **2 :** a condition of the atmosphere (as a local down current) that causes an airplane to drop suddenly

air·i·ly \ˈar-ə-lē, ˈer-\ *adv* **:** in an airy manner **:** LIGHTLY

air·i·ness \ˈar-ē-nəs, ˈer-\ *n* **:** the quality or state of being airy

air lane *n* **:** a path customarily followed by airplanes; *esp* **:** one made easy for navigation by steady winds

air letter *n* **1 :** an airmail letter **2 :** a letter sheet esp. for airmail

air·lift \ˈa(ə)r-ˌlift, ˈe(ə)r-\ *n* **1 :** a supply line operated by airplanes **2 :** improvised air transportation — **airlift** *vt*

air line *n* **1 :** a straight line through the air between two points **:** BEELINE **2 air·line** \-ˌlīn\ **:** an established system of aerial transportation, its equipment, or the organization owning or operating it

air·lin·er \-ˌlī-nər\ *n* **:** an airplane operating over an airline

air lock *n* **1 :** an intermediate chamber between the outer air and the working chamber of a pneumatic caisson; *also* **:** a similar intermediate chamber **2 :** a stoppage of flow caused by air being in a part where liquid ought to circulate

air·mail \ˈa(ə)r-ˈmā(ə)l, ˈe(ə)r-, -ˌmāl\ *n* **:** the system of transporting mail by airplanes; *also* **:** the mail transported — **airmail** *vt*

air·man \ˈa(ə)r-mən, ˈe(ə)r-\ *n* **1 :** an enlisted man or woman in the air force; *specif* **:** one of any of four ranks below a staff sergeant **2 :** a civilian or military pilot or aviator

airman basic *n* **:** an enlisted man of the lowest rank in the air force

air·man·ship \ˈa(ə)r-mən-ˌship, ˈe(ə)r-\ *n* **:** skill in piloting or navigating airplanes

air mass *n* **:** a body of air extending hundreds or thousands of miles horizontally and sometimes as high as the stratosphere and maintaining as it travels nearly uniform conditions of temperature and humidity at any given level

Air Medal *n* **:** a U. S. military decoration awarded for meritorious achievement while participating in an aerial flight

air mile *n* **:** a mile in air navigation; *specif* **:** a unit equal to 6076.1154 feet

air–mind·ed \ˈa(ə)r-ˈmīn-dəd, ˈe(ə)r-\ *adj* **:** interested in aviation or in air travel — **air–mind·ed·ness** *n*

air·plane \ˈa(ə)r-ˌplān, ˈe(ə)r-\ *n* [alter. of *aeroplane*, prob. fr. LGk *aeroplanos* wandering in air, fr. Gk *aer-* + *planos* wandering, fr. *planasthai* to wander — more at PLANET] **:** a fixed-wing aircraft heavier than air that is driven by a screw propeller or by a high-velocity jet and supported by the dynamic reaction of the air against its wings

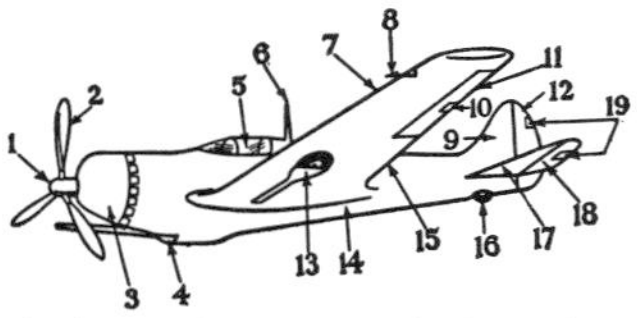

airplane, single-seat, single-engine: *1* spinner, *2* propeller, *3* cowling, *4* air scoop, *5* cockpit, *6* radio antenna mast, *7* leading edge of wing, *8* Pitot-static tube, *9* fin, *10* tab, *11* aileron, *12* rudder, *13* retractable landing gear, *14* fuselage, *15* trailing edge of wing, *16* retractable tail wheel, *17* stabilizer, *18* elevator, *19* tabs

air plant *n* **1 :** EPIPHYTE **2 :** a plant (genus *Kalanchoe*) that propagates new plants from the leaves

air pocket *n* **:** AIR HOLE 2

air police *n* **:** the military police of an air force

air·port \ˈa(ə)r-ˌpō(ə)rt, ˈe(ə)r-, -ˌpȯ(ə)rt\ *n* **:** a tract of land or water that is maintained for the landing and takeoff of airplanes and for receiving and discharging passengers and cargo and that usu. has facilities for the shelter, supply, and repair of planes

air·post \-ˈpōst\ *n* **:** AIRMAIL

air pump *n* **:** a pump for exhausting air from a closed space or for compressing air or forcing it through other apparatus

air raid *n* **:** an attack by armed airplanes on a surface target

air sac *n* **1 :** one of the air-filled spaces in the body of a bird connected with the air passages of the lungs **2 :** AIR BLADDER

air·screw \ˈa(ə)r-ˌskrü, ˈe(ə)r-\ *n* **1 :** a screw or screw propeller designed to operate in air **2** *Brit* **:** an airplane propeller

air·ship \-ˌship\ *n* **:** a lighter-than-air aircraft having propulsion and steering systems

air·sick \-ˌsik\ *adj* **:** affected with motion sickness associated with flying — **air·sick·ness** *n*

air sleeve *n* **:** WIND SOCK — called also *air sock*

air·space \ˈa(ə)r-ˌspās, ˈe(ə)r-\ *n* **:** the space lying above the earth or above a certain area of land or water; *esp* **:** the space lying above a nation and coming under its jurisdiction

air·speed \-ˌspēd\ *n* **:** the speed of an airplane with relation to the air as distinguished from its speed relative to the earth

air·stream \-ˌstrēm\ *n* **:** AIRFLOW

air·strip \-ˌstrip\ *n* **:** a runway without normal air base or airport facilities

¹**airt** \ˈart, ˈert\ *n* [ME *art*, fr. ScGael *ȧird*] *chiefly Scot* **:** compass point **:** DIRECTION

²**airt** *vt*, *chiefly Scot* **:** DIRECT, GUIDE **~** *vi*, *chiefly Scot* **:** to make one's way

air·tight \ˈa(ə)r-ˈtīt, ˈe(ə)r-\ *adj* **1 :** impermeable to air or nearly so **2 :** impenetrable esp. by an opponent; *also* **:** permitting no opportunity for an opponent to score — **air·tight·ness** *n*

air–to–air \ˌa(ə)rt-ə-ˈ(w)a(ə)r, ˌe(ə)rt-ə-ˈ(w)e(ə)r\ *adv* (*or adj*) **:** from one airplane in flight to another ⟨~ rockets⟩

air·wave \ˈa(ə)r-ˌwāv, ˈe(ə)r-\ *n* **1 :** the medium of radio and television transmission — usu. used in pl. **2 :** AIRWAY 4

air·way \-ˌwā\ *n* **1 :** a passage for a current of air (as in a mine or to the lungs) **2 :** a designated route along which airplanes fly from airport to airport; *esp* **:** such a route equipped with navigational aids **3 :** AIR LINE 2 **4 :** a channel of a designated radio frequency for broadcasting or other radio communication

air·wor·thi·ness \-ˌwər-t͟hē-nəs\ *n* **:** the quality or state of being airworthy

air·wor·thy \-ˌwər-t͟hē\ *adj* **:** fit for operation in the air

airy \ˈa(ə)r-ē, ˈe(ə)r-\ *adj* **1 a :** of or relating to air **:** ATMOSPHERIC **b :** high in the air **:** LOFTY **c :** performed in air **:** AERIAL **2 :** lacking reality **:** EMPTY **3 a :** SPRIGHTLY, VIVACIOUS **b :** ETHEREAL **4 :** open to the free circulation of air **:** BREEZY **5 :** AFFECTED, PROUD

aisle \ˈī(ə)l\ *n* [ME *ile*, fr. MF *aile* wing, fr. L *ala;* akin to OE *eaxl* shoulder, L *axilla* armpit — more at AXIS] **1 :** the side of a church nave separated by piers from the nave proper **2 :** a passage between sections of seats

ait \ˈāt\ *n* [ME, alter. of OE *īgeoth*, fr. *īg* island — more at ISLAND] *dial chiefly Brit* **:** a little island

aitch \ˈāch\ *n* [F *hache*, fr. (assumed) VL *hacca*] **:** the letter *h*

aitch·bone \ˈāch-ˌbōn\ *n* [ME *hachbon*, alter. (resulting from incorrect division of *a nachebon*) of (assumed) ME *nachebon*, fr. ME *nache* buttock (fr. MF, fr. LL *natica*, fr. L *natis*) + *bon* bone — more at NATES] **1 :** the hipbone esp. of cattle **2 :** the cut of beef containing the aitchbone

¹**ajar** \ə-ˈjär\ *adv* (*or adj*) [earlier *on char*, fr. *on* + *char* turn — more at CHARE] **:** slightly open

²**ajar** *adj* [¹*a-* + *jar*] **:** DISCORDANT

Ajax \ˈā-ˌjaks\ *n* [L, fr. Gk *Aias*] **1 :** a Greek hero in the Trojan War who kills himself because the armor of Achilles is awarded to Odysseus **2 :** a fleet-footed Greek hero in the Trojan War — called also *Ajax the Less*

Akan \ˈäk-ˌän\ *n*, *pl* **Akan** *or* **Akans 1 :** a language spoken over a wide area in Ghana and extending into the Ivory Coast **2 :** the Akan-speaking peoples

akim·bo \ə-ˈkim-(ˌ)bō\ *adv* (*or adj*) [ME *in kenebowe*] **:** with the hand on the hip and the elbow turned outward

akin \ə-ˈkin\ *adj* **1 :** related by blood **:** descended from a common ancestor or prototype **2 :** essentially similar, related, or compatible **syn** see SIMILAR

Ak·ka·di·an \ə-ˈkād-ē-ən\ *n* **1 :** a Semitic inhabitant of central Mesopotamia before 2000 B.C. **2 :** an ancient Semitic language of Mesopotamia used from about the 28th to the 1st century B.C. — **Akkadian** *adj*

ak·va·vit \ˈäk-wə-ˌvēt, ˈäk-vä-\ *var of* AQUAVIT

al- — see AD-

¹**-al** \əl, ᵊl\ *adj suffix* [ME, fr. OF & L; OF, fr. L *-alis*] **:** of, relating to, or characterized by ⟨direction*al*⟩ ⟨fiction*al*⟩

²**-al** *n suffix* [ME *-aille*, fr. OF, fr. L *-alia*, neut. pl. of *-alis*] **:** action **:** process ⟨rehears*al*⟩

³**-al** \ˌal, ˌȯl, əl, ᵊl\ *n suffix* [F, fr. *alcool* alcohol, fr. ML *alcohol*] **1 :** aldehyde ⟨butan*al*⟩ **2 :** acetal ⟨butyr*al*⟩

a la *or* **à la** \ˌal-ə, ˌäl-ə, ˌäl-(ˌ)ä\ [F *à la*] **:** in the manner of

ala \ˈā-lə\ *n*, *pl* **alae** \-ˌlē\ [L] **:** a wing or a winglike anatomic process or part — **alar** \ˈā-lər\ *adj* — **ala·ry** \-lə-rē\ *adj*

al·a·bas·ter \ˈal-ə-ˌbas-tər\ *n* [ME *alabastre*, fr. MF, fr. L *alabaster* vase of alabaster, fr. Gk *alabastros*] **1 :** a compact fine-textured gypsum usu. white and translucent **2 :** a hard compact calcite or aragonite that is translucent and sometimes banded — **alabaster** *or* **al·a·bas·trine** \ˌal-ə-ˈbas-trən\ *adj*

a la carte \ˌal-ə-ˈkärt, ˌäl-\ *adv* (*or adj*) [F *à la carte* by the bill of fare] **:** with a separate price for each item on the menu

alack \ə-ˈlak\ *interj* [ME] *archaic* — used to express sorrow, regret, or reproach

alac·ri·tous \ə-ˈlak-rət-əs\ *adj* **:** characterized by alacrity

alac·ri·ty \ə-ˈlak-rət-ē\ *n* [L *alacritas*, fr. *alacr-*, *alacer* lively, eager; akin to OE & OHG *ellen* zeal] **:** a cheerful promptness or readiness **:** BRISKNESS **syn** see CELERITY

Alad·din \ə-ˈlad-ᵊn\ *n* **:** a youth in the *Arabian Nights' Entertainments* who comes into possession of a magic lamp and ring

al·a·me·da \ˌal-ə-ˈmēd-ə, -ˈmād-\ *n* [Sp, fr. *álamo* poplar] **:** a public promenade bordered with trees

a la mode \ˌal-ə-ˈmōd, ˌäl-\ *adj* [F *à la mode* according to the fashion] **1 :** FASHIONABLE, STYLISH **2 :** topped with ice cream

ala·mode \-ˈmōd\ *n* **:** a thin glossy silk fabric (as for hoods)

al·a·nine \ˈal-ə-ˌnēn\ *n* [G *alanin*, irreg. fr. *aldehyd* aldehyde] **:** a white crystalline amino acid $C_3H_7NO_2$ formed esp. by the hydrolysis of proteins

¹**alarm** \ə-ˈlärm\ *also* **alar·um** \ə-ˈlar-əm\ *n* [ME *alarme*, *alarom*, fr. MF *alarme*, fr. OIt *all' arme*, lit., to the weapon] **1** *usu alarum*, *obs* **:** a call to arms **2 a :** a signal warning of danger **b :** a device that signals a warning of danger **3 :** the terror caused by danger **4 :** a warning notice **syn** see FEAR

²**alarm** *also* **alarum** *vt* **1 :** to arouse to a sense of danger **2 :** to strike with fear **:** TERRIFY **3 :** DISTURB, EXCITE

alarm clock *n* **:** a clock that can be set to give an alarm

alarm·ism \ə-ˈlär-ˌmiz-əm\ *n* **:** the often needless raising of alarms — **alarm·ist** \-məst\ *n or adj*

alarm reaction *n* **:** the complex of reactions of an organism to stress (as by increased hormonal activity)

alas \ə-ˈlas\ *interj* [ME, fr. OF, fr. *a* ah + *las* weary, fr. L *lassus* — more at LET] — used to express unhappiness, pity, or concern

Alas·kan malamute \ə-ˌlas-kən-\ *n* **:** any of a breed of powerful heavy-coated deep-chested dogs of Alaskan origin with erect ears, heavily cushioned feet, and plumy tail

Alaska time *n* **:** the time of the 10th time zone west of Greenwich that includes central Alaska

alate \ˈā-ˌlāt\ *also* **alat·ed** \-ˌlāt-əd\ *adj* [L *alatus*, fr. *ala*] **:** having wings or a winglike part — **ala·tion** \ā-ˈlā-shən\ *n*

alb \ˈalb\ *n* [ME *albe*, fr. OE, fr. ML *alba*, fr. L, fem. of *albus* white] **:** a full-length white linen vestment with close sleeves and often a cincture worn at the Eucharist

al·ba·core \ˈal-bə-ˌkō(ə)r, -ˌkȯ(ə)r\ *n*, *pl* **albacore** *or* **albacores** [Pg *albacor*, fr. Ar *al-bakūrah* the albacore] **1 :** a large pelagic tuna (*Thunnus germo*) with long pectoral fins that is the source of

most canned tuna; *broadly* **:** any of various tunas (as a bonito) **2 :** any of several carangid fishes
Al·ba·nian \al-ˈbā-nē-ən, -nyən *also* ȯl-\ *n* **1 :** a native or inhabitant of Albania **2 :** the Indo-European language of the Albanian people — **Albanian** *adj*
al·ba·tross \ˈal-bə-ˌtrȯs, -ˌträs\ *n, pl* **albatross** *or* **albatrosses** [prob. alter. of *alcatras* (water bird), fr. Pg or Sp *alcatraz* pelican] **:** any of various large web-footed seabirds (family Diomedeidae) that are related to the petrels and include the largest seabirds

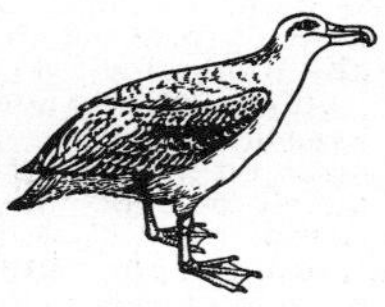

albatross

al·be·do \al-ˈbēd-(ˌ)ō\ *n* [LL, whiteness, fr. L *albus*] **:** reflective power; *specif* **:** the fraction of incident light or electromagnetic radiation that is reflected by a surface or body (as the moon or a cloud)
al·be·it \al-ˈbē-ət, ȯl-\ *conj* [ME, lit., all though it be] **:** even though **:** ALTHOUGH
Al·ber·ich \ˈäl-bə-rik\ *n* [G] **:** the king of the dwarfs and chief of the Nibelungs in Germanic legend
Al·bi·gen·ses \ˌal-bə-ˈjen-ˌsēz\ *n pl* [ML, pl. of *Albigensis*, lit., inhabitant of Albi, fr. *Albiga* (Albi), France] **:** members of a Catharistic sect of southern France between the 11th and 13th centuries — **Al·bi·gen·sian** \-ˈjen-chən, -ˈjen(t)-sē-ən\ *adj or n* — **Al·bi·gen·sian·ism** \-ˌiz-əm\ *n*
al·bin·ic \al-ˈbin-ik\ *adj* **:** of, relating to, or affected with albinism
al·bi·nism \ˈal-bə-ˌniz-əm, al-ˈbī-\ *n* **:** the condition of an albino
al·bi·no \al-ˈbī-(ˌ)nō\ *n, often attrib* [Pg, fr. Sp, fr. *albo* white, fr. L *albus*] **:** an organism exhibiting deficient pigmentation; *esp* **:** a human being or lower animal that is congenitally deficient in pigment and usu. has a milky or translucent skin, white or colorless hair, and eyes with pink or blue iris and deep-red pupil — **al·bi·not·ic** \ˌal-bə-ˈnät-ik, -ˌbī-\ *adj*
Al·bi·on \ˈal-bē-ən\ *n* [L] **:** England
al·bite \ˈal-ˌbīt\ *n* [Sw *albit*, fr. L *albus*] **:** a triclinic usu. white feldspar consisting of a sodium aluminum silicate $NaAlSi_3O_8$ — **al·bit·ic** \al-ˈbit-ik\ *adj*
al·bum \ˈal-bəm\ *n* [L, a white tablet, fr. neut. of *albus*] **1 a :** a book with blank pages for autographs, stamps, or photographs **b :** a container with envelopes for phonograph records **c :** one or more phonograph records or tape recordings carrying a major musical work or a group of related selections **2 :** a collection usu. in book form of literary selections, musical compositions, or pictures **:** ANTHOLOGY
al·bu·men \al-ˈbyü-mən\ *n* [L, fr. *albus*] **1 :** the white of an egg **2 :** ALBUMIN
al·bu·min \al-ˈbyü-mən\ *n* **:** any of numerous simple heat-coagulable water-soluble proteins that occur in blood plasma or serum, muscle, the whites of eggs, milk, and other animal substances and in many plant tissues and fluids
¹**al·bu·min·oid** \-mə-ˌnȯid\ *adj* **:** resembling albumin **:** PROTEIN
²**albuminoid** *n* **1 :** PROTEIN **2 :** SCLEROPROTEIN
al·bu·min·ous \al-ˈbyü-mə-nəs\ *adj* **:** relating to, containing, or having the properties of albumen or albumin
al·bu·min·uria \(ˌ)al-ˌbyü-mə-ˈn(y)u̇r-ē-ə\ *n* [NL] **:** the presence of albumin in the urine often symptomatic of kidney disease — **al·bu·min·uric** \-ˈn(y)u̇r-ik\ *adj*
al·bu·mose \ˈal-byə-ˌmōs, -ˌmōz\ *n* **:** any of various products of enzymatic protein hydrolysis
al·bur·num \al-ˈbər-nəm\ *n* [L, fr. *albus* white] **:** SAPWOOD
al·ca·ic \al-ˈkā-ik\ *adj, often cap* [LL *Alcaicus* of Alcaeus, fr. Gk *Alkaïkos*, fr. *Alkaios* Alcaeus, *fl ab* 600 B.C. Gk poet] **:** relating to or written in a verse or strophe marked by complicated variation of a dominant iambic pattern — **alcaic** *n*
al·cai·de *or* **al·cay·de** \al-ˈkīd-ē\ *n* [Sp *alcaide*, fr. Ar *al-qā'id* the captain] **:** a commander of a castle or fortress (as among Spaniards, Portuguese, or Moors)
al·cal·de \al-ˈkäl-dē\ *n* [Sp, fr. Ar *al-qāḍī* the judge] **:** the chief administrative and judicial officer of a Spanish town
al·ca·zar \al-ˈkaz-ər, ˌal-kə-ˈzär\ *n* [Sp *alcázar*, fr. Ar *al-qaṣr* the castle] **:** a Spanish fortress or palace
Al·ces·tis \al-ˈses-təs\ *n* [L, fr. Gk *Alkēstis*] **:** the wife of Admetus who saves her husband's life by dying in his place and who is brought back from Hades by Hercules
al·chem·ic \al-ˈkem-ik\ *adj* **:** of or relating to alchemy — **al·chem·i·cal** \-i-kəl\ *adj* — **al·chem·i·cal·ly** \-k(ə-)lē\ *adv*
al·che·mist \ˈal-kə-məst\ *n* **:** one who studies or practices alchemy — **al·che·mis·tic** \ˌal-kə-ˈmis-tik\ *or* **al·che·mis·ti·cal** \-ti-kəl\ *adj*
al·che·mize \ˈal-kə-ˌmīz\ *vt* **:** to change by alchemy **:** TRANSMUTE
al·che·my \ˈal-kə-mē\ *n* [ME *alkamie, alquemie*, fr. MF or ML; MF *alquemie*, fr. ML *alchymia*, fr. Ar *al-kīmiyā'*, fr. *al* the + *kīmiyā'* alchemy, fr. LGk *chēmeia*] **1 :** a medieval chemical science and speculative philosophy aiming to achieve the transmutation of the base metals into gold, the discovery of a universal cure for disease, and the discovery of a means of indefinitely prolonging life **2 :** a power or process of transforming something common into something precious
Alc·me·ne \alk-ˈmē-nē\ *n* [Gk *Alkmēnē*] **:** the mother of Hercules by Zeus
al·co·hol \ˈal-kə-ˌhȯl\ *n* [NL, fr. ML, powdered antimony, fr. OSp, fr. Ar *al-kuḥul* the powdered antimony] **1 :** a colorless volatile flammable liquid C_2H_5OH that is the intoxicating agent in fermented and distilled liquors — called also *ethyl alcohol* **2 :** any of various compounds that are analogous to ethyl alcohol in constitution and that are hydroxyl derivatives of hydrocarbons **3 :** liquor (as beer, wine, or whiskey) containing alcohol
¹**al·co·hol·ic** \ˌal-kə-ˈhȯl-ik, -ˈhäl-\ *adj* **1 a :** of, relating to, or caused by alcohol **b :** containing alcohol **2 :** addicted to the use of alcoholic drinks in excess — **al·co·hol·i·cal·ly** \-i-k(ə-)lē\ *adv*
²**alcoholic** *n* **:** one who is addicted to the excessive use of alcoholic drinks or suffers from alcoholism
al·co·hol·ism \ˈal-kə-ˌhȯ-ˌliz-əm\ *n* **1 :** continued excessive or compulsive use of alcoholic drinks **2 :** poisoning by alcohol; *esp* **:** a complex chronic psychological and nutritional disorder associated with excessive and usu. compulsive drinking
al·co·hol·ize \-ˌlīz\ *vt* **:** to treat or saturate with alcohol
al·co·hol·om·e·ter \ˌal-kə-ˌhȯ-ˈläm-ət-ər\ *n* [F *alcoolometre*, fr. *alcool* alcohol + *-o-* + *-metre* -meter] **:** a device for determining the alcoholic strength of liquids — **al·co·hol·om·e·try** \-ˈläm-ə-trē\ *n*
Al·co·ran \ˌal-kə-ˈran\ *n* [ME, fr. MF or ML; MF & ML, fr. Ar *al-qur'ān*, lit., the reading] *archaic* **:** KORAN
al·cove \ˈal-ˌkōv\ *n* [F *alcôve*, fr. Sp *alcoba*, fr. Ar *al-qubbah* the arch] **1 a :** a nook or small recess opening off a larger room **b :** a niche or arched opening (as in a wall) **2 :** SUMMERHOUSE
Al·cy·o·ne \al-ˈsī-ə-(ˌ)nē\ *n* [L, fr. Gk *Alkyonē*] **:** the brightest star in the Pleiades
Al·deb·a·ran \al-ˈdeb-ə-rən\ *n* [Ar *al-dabarān*, lit., the follower] **:** a red star of the first magnitude that is seen in the eye of Taurus and is the brightest star in the Hyades
al·de·hyde \ˈal-də-ˌhīd\ *n* [G *aldehyd*, fr. NL *al. dehyd.*, abbr. of *alcohol dehydrogenatum* dehydrogenated alcohol] **:** ACETALDEHYDE; *broadly* **:** any of various highly reactive compounds typified by acetaldehyde and characterized by the group —CHO — **al·de·hy·dic** \ˌal-də-ˈhīd-ik\ *adj*
al·der \ˈȯl-dər\ *n* [ME, fr. OE *alor;* akin to OHG *elira* alder, L *alnus*] **:** any of a genus (*Alnus*) of toothed-leaved trees or shrubs of the birch family growing in moist ground and having wood used by turners and bark used in dyeing and tanning
al·der·man \ˈȯl-dər-mən\ *n* [ME, fr. OE *ealdorman*, fr. *ealdor* parent (fr. *eald* old) + *man* — more at OLD] **1 :** a person governing a kingdom, district, or shire as viceroy for an Anglo-Saxon king **2** *in England & Ireland* **:** a magistrate ranking next below the mayor in cities and boroughs **3 :** a member of a city legislative body — **al·der·man·ic** \ˌȯl-dər-ˈman-ik\ *adj*
Al·dine \ˈȯl-ˌdīn, -ˌdēn\ *adj* [It *aldino*, fr. *Aldus* Manutius †1515] **:** printed or published by Aldus Manutius of Venice or his family in the late 15th and 16th centuries — **Aldine** *n*
al·dol \ˈal-ˌdȯl, -ˌdōl\ *n* [ISV, fr. *aldehyde*] **:** a colorless beta-hydroxy aldehyde $C_4H_8O_2$ used esp. in organic synthesis; *broadly* **:** any of various similar aldehydes — **al·dol·iza·tion** \ˌal-ˌdȯ-lə-ˈzā-shən, -ˌdō-\ *n*
al·dose \ˈal-ˌdōs, -ˌdōz\ *n* **:** a sugar containing one aldehyde group per molecule
ale \ˈā(ə)l\ *n* [ME, fr. OE *ealu;* akin to ON *öl* ale, L *alumen* alum] **1 :** a fermented liquor brewed esp. by rapid fermentation from an infusion of malt with the addition of hops **2 :** an English country festival at which ale is the principal beverage
ale·ato·ry \ˈā-lē-ə-ˌtōr-ē, -ˌtȯr-\ *adj* [L *aleatorius* of a gambler, fr. *aleator* gambler, fr. *alea* a dice game] **1 :** depending on an uncertain event or contingency as to both profit and loss ⟨an ~ contract⟩ **2 :** relating to good or esp. bad luck
alee \ə-ˈlē\ *adv (or adj)* **:** on or toward the lee
ale·house \ˈā(ə)l-ˌhau̇s\ *n* **:** a place where ale is sold to be drunk on the premises
Al·e·man·nic \ˌal-ə-ˈman-ik\ *n* [LL *alemanni*, of Gmc origin; akin to Goth *alamans* totality of people] **:** the group of dialects of German spoken in Alsace, Switzerland, and southwestern Germany
alem·bic \ə-ˈlem-bik\ *n* [ME, fr. MF & ML; MF *alambic* & ML *alembicum*, fr. Ar *al-anbīq*, fr. *al* the + *anbīq* still, fr. LGk *ambik-, ambix* alembic, fr. Gk, cap of a still] **1 :** an apparatus formerly used in distillation **2 :** something that refines or transmutes as if by distillation

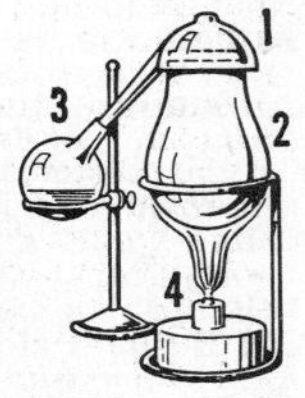

alembic: *1* head, *2* cucurbit, *3* receiver, *4* lamp

aleph \ˈäl-ˌef, ˈäl-əf\ *n* [Heb *āleph*, prob. fr. *eleph* ox] **:** the 1st letter of the Hebrew alphabet — symbol א
aleph-null \-ˈnəl\ *n* **:** the smallest transfinite cardinal number **:** the power of the aggregate of all the finite integers
¹**alert** \ə-ˈlərt\ *adj* [It *all'erta*, lit., on the ascent] **1 a :** watchful and prompt to meet danger **b :** quick to perceive and act **2 :** ACTIVE, BRISK **syn** see INTELLIGENT, WATCHFUL — **alert·ly** *adv* — **alert·ness** *n*
²**alert** *n* **1 :** an alarm or other signal of danger **2 :** the period during which an alert is in effect — **on the alert :** on the lookout for danger
³**alert** *vt* **:** to call to a state of readiness **:** WARN
-a·les \ˈā-(ˌ)lēz\ *n pl suffix* [NL, fr. L, pl. of *-alis* -al] **:** plants consisting of or related to — in the names of taxonomic orders
al·eu·rone \ˈal-yə-ˌrōn\ *n* [G *aleuron*, fr. Gk, flour; akin to Arm *alam* I grind] **:** protein matter in the form of minute granules or grains occurring in seeds in endosperm or in a special peripheral layer — **al·eu·ron·ic** \ˌal-yə-ˈrän-ik\ *adj*
Aleut \ə-ˈlüt\ *n* [Russ] **1 :** a member of a people of the Aleutian and Shumagin islands and the western part of Alaska peninsula **2 :** the language of the Aleuts
¹**ale·wife** \ˈā(ə)l-ˌwīf\ *n, pl* **alewives :** a woman who keeps an alehouse
²**alewife** *n, pl* **alewives :** a food fish (*Pomolobus pseudoharengus*) of the herring family (Clupeidae) very abundant on the Atlantic coast; *also* **:** any of several related fishes (as the menhaden)
al·ex·an·der \ˌal-ig-ˈzan-dər, ˌel-\ *n, often cap* **:** an iced cocktail made from crème de cacao, sweet cream, and gin or brandy
Al·ex·an·dri·an \ˌal-ig-ˈzan-drē-ən, ˌel-\ *adj* **:** HELLENISTIC
al·ex·an·drine \-ˈzan-drən\ *n, often cap* [MF *alexandrin*, adj., fr. *Alexandre* Alexander the Great †323 B.C. king of Macedonia; fr. its use in a poem on Alexander] **:** a verse of 12 syllables consisting regularly of 6 iambics with a caesura after the 3d iambic — **alexandrine** *adj*
al·ex·an·drite \-ˈzan-ˌdrīt\ *n* [G *alexandrit*, fr. *Alexander* I †1825 Russ emperor] **:** a grass-green chrysoberyl that shows a columbine-red color by transmitted or artificial light
alex·ia \ə-ˈlek-sē-ə\ *n* [NL, fr. *a-* + Gk *lexis* speech, fr. *legein* to speak] **:** aphasia characterized by loss of ability to read
Al·fa \ˈal-fə\ — a communications code word for the letter *a*
al·fal·fa \al-ˈfal-fə\ *n* [Sp, modif. of Ar dial. *al-faṣfaṣah* the alfalfa] **:** a deep-rooted European leguminous plant (*Medicago sativa*) widely grown for hay and forage
al·fil·a·ria \(ˌ)al-ˌfil-ə-ˈrē-ə\ *n* [AmerSp *alfilerillo*, fr. Sp, dim. of

alfiler pin, modif. of Ar *al-khilāl* the thorn] : a European weed (*Erodium cicutarium*) of the geranium family grown for forage in western America

al·for·ja \al-'fȯr-hə\ *n* [Sp, fr. Ar *al-khurj*] *West* : SADDLEBAG

al·fres·co \al-'fres-(,)kō\ *adv* (*or adj*) [It] : in the open air

alg- *or* **algo-** *comb form* [NL, fr. Gk *alg-*, fr. *algos*] : pain ⟨*algo*phobia⟩

al·ga \'al-gə\ *n, pl* **al·gae** \'al-(,)jē\ *also* **algas** [L, seaweed] : any of a group (Algae) of chiefly aquatic nonvascular plants (as seaweeds, pond scums, stoneworts) with chlorophyll often masked by a brown or red pigment — **al·gal** \-gəl\ *adj* — **al·goid** \-,gȯid\ *adj*

al·gar·ro·ba \,al-gə-'rō-bə\ *n* [Sp, fr. Ar *al-kharrūbah* the carob] **1** : CAROB **2** [MexSp, fr. Sp] : MESQUITE; *also* : its pods

al·ge·bra \'al-jə-brə\ *n* [ML, fr. Ar *al-jabr*, lit., the reduction] **1 a** : a generalization of arithmetic in which letters representing numbers are combined according to the rules of arithmetic **b** : a treatise on algebra **2** : a mathematical ring whose elements can be multiplied by elements of a specified field in accordance with special rules **3** : a logical or set calculus — compare BOOLEAN ALGEBRA — **al·ge·bra·ist** \'al-jə-,brā-əst\ *n*

al·ge·bra·ic \,al-jə-'brā-ik\ *adj* **1** : relating to, involving, or according to the laws of algebra **2** : involving only a finite number of algebraic operations ⟨~ equation⟩ — compare TRANSCENDENTAL — **al·ge·bra·i·cal·ly** \-'brā-ə-k(ə-)lē\ *adv*

algebraic number *n* : a root of an algebraic equation with rational coefficients

-al·gia \'al-j(ē-)ə\ *n comb form* [Gk, fr. *algos*] : pain ⟨neur*algia*⟩

al·gid \'al-jəd\ *adj* [L *algidus*, fr. *algēre* to feel cold; akin to Icel *elgur* slush] : CHILL, COLD — **al·gid·i·ty** \al-'jid-ət-ē\ *n*

al·gin \'al-jən\ *n* : any of various colloidal substances from marine brown algae including some used esp. as stabilizers or emulsifiers

Al·gol \'al-,gäl, -,gȯl\ *n* [Ar *al-ghūl*, lit., the ghoul] : a binary star in the constellation Perseus whose larger component revolves about and eclipses the smaller brighter star causing periodic variation in brightness

al·go·lag·nia \,al-gō-'lag-nē-ə\ *n* [NL, fr. *alg-* + Gk *lagneia* lust] : pleasure in inflicting or suffering pain — **al·go·lag·nic** \-nik\ *adj* — **al·go·lag·nist** \-nəst\ *n*

al·gol·o·gy \al-'gäl-ə-jē\ *n* : the study or science of algae

al·gom·e·ter \al-'gäm-ət-ər\ *n* : an instrument for measuring the smallest pressure that induces pain — **al·go·met·ric** \,al-gə-'me-trik\ *or* **al·go·met·ri·cal** \-tri-kəl\ *adj* — **al·gom·e·try** \al-'gäm-ə-trē\ *n*

1**Al·gon·ki·an** \al-'gäŋ-kē-ən\ *or* **Al·gon·kin** \-kən\ *or* **Al·gon·qui·an** \-'gän-kwē-ən, -'gäŋ-\ *or* **Al·gon·quin** \-'gän-kwən, -'gäŋ-\ *n* [CanF *Algonquin*] **1** : an Indian people of the Ottawa river valley **2** *usu Algonquin* : a dialect of Ojibwa **3** *usu Algonquian* : a stock of Indian languages spoken from Labrador to Carolina and westward to the Great Plains **4** *usu Algonquian* : any of the Indian peoples speaking Algonquian languages **5** *Algonkian* : the Algonkian era or system or group of systems

2**Algonkian** *adj* : PROTEROZOIC

al·go·pho·bia \,al-gə-'fō-bē-ə\ *n* [NL] : morbid fear of pain

al·go·rithm \'al-gə-,rith-əm\ *n* [alter. of ME *algorisme*, fr. OF & ML; OF, fr. ML *algorismus*, fr. Ar *al-khuwārizmi*, fr. *al-Khuwārizmi fl* 825 A.D. Arab mathematician] : a rule of procedure for solving a mathematical problem (as of finding the greatest common divisor) that frequently involves repetition of an operation

Al·ham·bra \al-'ham-brə\ *n* [Sp, fr. Ar *al-ḥamrā'* the red house] : the palace of the Moorish Kings at Granada, Spain

Al·ham·bresque \,al-,ham-'bresk\ *or* **Al·ham·bra·ic** \-'brā-ik\ *adj* : made or decorated after the fanciful style of the ornamentation in the Alhambra

ali- *comb form* [L, fr. *ala* — more at AISLE] : wing ⟨*ali*form⟩

1**alias** \'ā-lē-əs, 'āl-yəs\ *adv* [L, otherwise, fr. *alius* other — more at ELSE] : otherwise called : otherwise known as

2**alias** *n* : an assumed name

Ali Ba·ba \,al-ē-'bäb-ə\ *n* : a woodcutter in the *Arabian Nights' Entertainments* who enters the cave of the Forty Thieves by using the password *Sesame*

1**al·i·bi** \'al-ə-,bī\ *n* [L, elsewhere, fr. *alius*] **1** : the plea of having been at the time of the commission of an act elsewhere than at the place of commission; *also* : the fact or state of having been elsewhere at the time **2** : a plausible excuse esp. for failure or negligence **syn** see APOLOGY

2**alibi** *vb* **al·i·bied**; **al·i·bi·ing** *vi* : to offer an excuse ~ *vt* : to exonerate by an alibi

al·i·dade \'al-ə-,dād\ *n* [ME *allidatha*, fr. ML *alhidada*, fr. Ar *al-'idadah* the revolving radius of a circle] : a rule equipped with simple or telescopic sights and used for determination of direction: as **a** : a part of an astrolabe **b** : a part of a surveying instrument consisting of the telescope and its attachments

1**alien** \'ā-lē-ən, 'āl-yən\ *adj* [ME, fr. OF, fr. L *alienus*, fr. *alius*] **1 a** : belonging or relating to another person or place : STRANGE **b** : relating, belonging, or owing allegiance to another country or government : FOREIGN **2** : different in nature or character **syn** see EXTRINSIC

2**alien** *n* **1** : a person of another family, race, or nation **2** : a foreign-born resident who has not been naturalized and is still a subject or citizen of a foreign country; *broadly* : a foreign-born citizen

3**alien** *vt* **1** : ALIENATE, ESTRANGE **2** : to make over (as property)

alien·abil·i·ty \,āl-yə-nə-'bil-ət-ē, ,ā-lē-ə-nə-\ *n* : the capability of being transferred to other ownership

alien·able \'āl-yə-nə-bəl, 'ā-lē-ə-nə-\ *adj* : transferable to the ownership of another

alien·age \-nij\ *n* : the status of an alien

alien·ate \'ā-lē-ə-,nāt, 'āl-yə-\ *vt* **1** : to convey or transfer (as property) to another **2** : to make unfriendly, hostile, or indifferent where attachment formerly existed **3** : to cause to be withdrawn or diverted **syn** see ESTRANGE — **alien·ator** \-,nāt-ər\ *n*

alien·ation \,ā-lē-ə-'nā-shən, ,āl-yə-\ *n* **1** : a conveyance of property to another **2** : the estrangement of a person or of his affections **3** : mental derangement

alien·ee \-'nē\ *n* : one to whom property is transferred

alien·ism \'ā-lē-ə-,niz-əm, 'āl-yə-\ *n* : the status of an alien

alien·ist \-nəst\ *n* [F *aliéniste*, fr. *aliéné* insane, fr. L *alienatus*, pp. of *alienare* to estrange, fr. *alienus*] : one that treats diseases of the mind; *esp* : a specialist in legal aspects of psychiatry

alien·or \,ā-lē-ə-'nȯ(ə)r, ,āl-yə-\ *n* : one who alienates property

ali·form \'ā-lə-,fȯrm, 'al-ə-\ *adj* : having winglike extensions : wing-shaped

1**alight** \ə-'līt\ *vi* **alight·ed** *also* **alit** \ə-'lit\ **alight·ing** [ME *alighten*, fr. OE *ālīhtan*, fr. *ā-* (perfective prefix) + *līhtan* to alight — more at ABIDE, LIGHT] **1** : to get down : DISMOUNT **2** : to descend from the air and settle **3** *archaic* : to come by chance

2**alight** *adj* : lighted up : set on fire

align *also* **aline** \ə-'līn\ *vb* [F *aligner*, fr. OF, fr. *a-* (fr. L *ad-*) + *ligne* line, fr. L *linea*] *vt* **1** : to bring into line or alignment **2** : to array on the side of or against a party or cause ~ *vi* **1** : to get or fall into line **2** : to be in or come into precise adjustment or correct relative position **syn** see LINE — **align·er** *n*

align·ment *also* **aline·ment** \ə-'līn-mənt\ *n* **1** : the act of aligning or state of being aligned; *esp* : the proper positioning or state of adjustment of parts (as of a mechanical or electronic device) in relation to each other **2 a** : a forming in line **b** : the line thus formed **3** : the ground plan in distinction from the profile

1**alike** \ə-'līk\ *adj* [ME *ilik* (alter. of *ilich*) & *alik*, alter. of OE *onlīc*, fr. *on* + *līc* body] : LIKE **syn** see SIMILAR — **alike·ness** *n*

2**alike** *adv* : in the same manner, form, or degree : EQUALLY

1**al·i·ment** \'al-ə-mənt\ *n* [ME, fr. L *alimentum*, fr. *alere* to nourish — more at OLD] : FOOD, NUTRIMENT; *also* : SUSTENANCE — **al·i·men·tal** \,al-ə-'ment-ᵊl\ *adj* — **al·i·men·tal·ly** \-ᵊl-ē\ *adv*

2**al·i·ment** \'al-ə-,ment\ *vt* : to give aliment to

al·i·men·ta·ry \,al-ə-'ment-ə-rē, -'men-trē\ *adj* **1** : of or relating to nourishment or nutrition **2** : furnishing sustenance or maintenance

alimentary canal *n* : the tubular passage that extends from mouth to anus and functions in digestion and absorption of food and elimination of residual waste

al·i·men·ta·tion \,al-ə-mən-'tā-shən\ *n* : the act or process of affording nutriment; *also* : the state or mode of being nourished — **al·i·men·ta·tive** \,al-ə-'ment-ət-iv\ *adj*

al·i·mo·ny \'al-ə-,mō-nē\ *n* [L *alimonia* sustenance, fr. *alere*] **1** : the means of living : MAINTENANCE **2** : an allowance made to a woman for her support by a man pending or after her legal separation or divorce from him

Al·i·oth \'al-ē-,äth, -,ōth\ *n* : a star of the second magnitude in the handle of the Big Dipper

al·i·phat·ic \,al-ə-'fat-ik\ *adj* [ISV, fr. Gk *aleiphat-*, *aleiphar* oil, fr. *aleiphein* to smear; akin to Gk *lipos* fat — more at LEAVE] : of, relating to, or derived from fat; *specif* : belonging to a group of organic compounds having an open-chain structure and consisting of the paraffin, olefin, and acetylene hydrocarbons and their derivatives

al·i·quot \'al-ə-,kwät, -kwət\ *adj* [ML *aliquotus*, fr. L *aliquot* some, several, fr. *alius* other + *quot* how many — more at ELSE, QUOTA] **1** : contained an exact number of times in another **2** : FRACTIONAL — **aliquot** *n*

al·i·un·de \,al-ē-'ən-dē\ *adv* (*or adj*) [L, fr. *alius* other + *unde* whence; akin to *ubi* where — more at ELSE, UBIQUITY] : from another source : from elsewhere

alive \ə-'līv\ *adj* [ME, fr. OE *on life*, fr. *on* + *līf* life] **1 a** : having life : not dead or inanimate **b** : LIVING ⟨proudest boy ~⟩ **2** : still in existence, force, or operation : ACTIVE ⟨kept hope ~⟩ **3** : knowing or realizing the existence of : SENSITIVE ⟨~ to the danger⟩ **4** : marked by alertness, activity, or briskness **5** : marked by much life, animation, or activity : SWARMING **syn** see AWARE, LIVING — **alive·ness** *n*

aliz·a·rin \ə-'liz-ə-rən\ *n* [prob. fr. F *alizarine*] **1** : an orange or red crystalline compound $C_{14}H_8O_4$ formerly prepared from madder and now made synthetically and used esp. to dye Turkey reds and in making red pigments **2** : any of various acid, mordant, and solvent dyes derived like alizarin proper from anthraquinone

al·ka·hest \'al-kə-,hest\ *n* [NL *alchahest*] : the universal solvent supposed by the alchemists to exist — **al·ka·hes·tic** \,al-kə-'hes-tik\ *adj*

al·ka·les·cence \,al-kə-'les-ᵊn(t)s\ *also* **al·ka·les·cen·cy** \-ᵊn-sē\ *n* : somewhat alkaline property — **al·ka·les·cent** \-ᵊnt\ *adj*

al·ka·li \'al-kə-,lī\ *n, pl* **alkalies** *or* **alkalis** [ME, fr. ML, fr. Ar *al-qili* the ashes of the plant saltwort] **1** : a soluble salt obtained from the ashes of plants and consisting largely of potassium or sodium carbonate; *broadly* : a substance (as a hydroxide or carbonate of an alkali metal) having marked basic properties — compare BASE 7 **2** : ALKALI METAL **3** : a soluble salt or a mixture of soluble salts present in some soils of arid regions in quantity detrimental to agriculture

al·kal·i·fy \al-'kal-ə-,fī, 'al-kə-lə-\ *vt* : to convert or change into an alkali or make alkaline ~ *vi* : to become alkaline

alkali metal *n* : any of the univalent mostly basic metals of group I of the periodic table comprising lithium, sodium, potassium, rubidium, cesium, and francium

al·ka·lim·e·ter \,al-kə-'lim-ət-ər\ *n* [F *alcalimètre*, fr. *alcali* alkali + *-mètre* -meter] : an apparatus for measuring the strength or the amount of alkali in a mixture or solution — **al·ka·lim·e·try** \-'lim-ə-trē\ *n*

al·ka·line \'al-kə-lən, -,līn\ *adj* : of, relating to, or having the properties of an alkali; *esp* : having a pH of more than 7 — **al·ka·lin·i·ty** \,al-kə-'lin-ət-ē\ *n*

alkaline earth *n* : an oxide of any of several bivalent strongly basic metals comprising calcium, strontium, and barium and sometimes also magnesium, radium or less often beryllium

al·ka·lin·iza·tion \,al-kə-,lin-ə-'zā-shən, -lə-nə-'zā-\ *n* : the act or process of alkalinizing

al·ka·lin·ize \'al-kə-lə-,nīz\ *vt* : to make alkaline

al·ka·loid \'al-kə-,lȯid\ *n, often attrib* : any of numerous usu. colorless, complex, and bitter organic bases containing nitrogen and usu. oxygen that occur esp. in seed plants — **al·ka·loi·dal** \,al-kə-'lȯid-ᵊl\ *adj*

al·ka·lo·sis \,al-kə-'lō-səs\ *n* : a condition of increased alkalinity of the blood and tissues

al·ka·net \'al-kə-,net\ *n* [ME, fr. OSp *alcaneta*, dim. of *alcana* henna shrub, fr. ML *alchanna*, fr. Ar *Al-ḥinnā'* the henna] **1 a** : a European plant (*Alkanna tinctoria*) of the borage family; *also* : its root **b** : a red dyestuff prepared from the root **2** : BUGLOSS **3** : any of several American plants (genus *Lithospermum*) of the borage family

al·kyd \'al-kəd\ *n, often attrib* [blend of *alkyl* and *acid*] : any of numerous thermoplastic or thermosetting synthetic resins made by

heating polyhydroxy alcohols with polybasic acids or their anhydrides and used esp. for protective coatings

al·kyl \'al-kəl\ *n* [prob. fr. G, fr. *alkohol* alcohol, fr. ML *alcohol*] **1 a :** a univalent aliphatic radical C_nH_{2n+1} **b :** any univalent aliphatic, aromatic-aliphatic, or alicyclic hydrocarbon radical **2 :** a compound of alkyl radicals with a metal — **al·kyl·ic** \al-'kil-ik\ *adj*

[1]**all** \'ȯl\ *adj* [ME *all, al*, fr. OE *eall;* akin to OHG *al* all] **1 a :** the whole of ⟨sat up ~ night⟩ **b :** as much as possible **2 :** every member or individual component of ⟨~ men will go⟩ **3 :** the whole number or sum of ⟨~ the angles of a triangle are equal to two right angles⟩ **4 :** EVERY ⟨~ manner of hardship⟩ **5 :** any whatever ⟨beyond ~ doubt⟩ **6 :** nothing but **:** ONLY: **a :** completely taken up with, given to, or absorbed by ⟨became ~ attention⟩ **b :** having or seeming to have (some physical feature) in conspicuous excess or prominence ⟨~ legs⟩ **c :** paying full attention with ⟨~ ears⟩ **7** *dial* **:** used up **:** entirely consumed — used esp. of food and drink ⟨the beer was ~⟩ **8 :** being more than one person or thing **syn** see WHOLE — **all the :** as much of . . . as **:** as much of a . . . as ⟨*all the* home I ever had⟩

[2]**all** *adv* **1 :** WHOLLY, ALTOGETHER ⟨sat ~ alone⟩ — often used as an intensive ⟨~ across the country⟩ **2** *obs* **:** EXCLUSIVELY, ONLY **3** *archaic* **:** JUST **4 :** so much ⟨~ the better for it⟩ **5 :** for each side **:** APIECE ⟨the score is two ~⟩

[3]**all** *pron* **1 :** the whole number, quantity, or amount **:** TOTALITY ⟨~ that I have⟩ ⟨~ of us⟩ ⟨~ of the books⟩ **2 :** EVERYBODY, EVERYTHING ⟨sacrificed ~ for love⟩

all- *or* **allo-** *comb form* [Gk, fr. *allos* other — more at ELSE] **:** other **:** different **:** atypical ⟨*allo*gamous⟩ ⟨*allo*merism⟩

[1]**al·la breve** \ˌal-ə-'brev, ˌäl-ə-'brev-(ˌ)ā\ *adv (or adj)* [It, lit., according to the breve] **:** in duple or quadruple time with the beat represented by the half note

[2]**alla breve** *n* **:** the sign ₵ marking a piece or passage to be played alla breve; *also* **:** a passage so marked

Al·lah \'al-ə, ä-'lä\ *n* [Ar *allāh*] **:** the Supreme Being of the Muslims

all–Amer·i·can \ˌȯ-lə-'mer-ə-kən\ *adj* **1 :** composed wholly of American elements **2 :** representative of the U.S. as a whole; *esp* **:** selected as the best in the U.S. **3 :** of or relating to the American nations as a group

al·lan·to·ic \ˌal-ən-'tō-ik\ *adj* **:** of, relating to, or derived from the allantois

al·lan·to·is \ə-'lant-ə-wəs\ *n, pl* **al·lan·to·ides** \ˌal-ən-'tō-ə-ˌdēz\ [NL, deriv. of Gk *allant-, allas* sausage] **:** a vascular fetal membrane of reptiles, birds, or mammals formed as a pouch from the hindgut and in placental mammals intimately associated with the chorion in formation of the placenta

al·lar·gan·do \ˌäl-ˌär-'gän-(ˌ)dō\ *adj (or adv)* [It, widening, verbal of *allargare* to widen, fr. *al-* (fr. L *ad-*) + *largare* to widen] **:** becoming gradually broader with the same or greater volume — used as a direction in music

all–around \ˌȯ-lə-'raund\ *adj* **1 :** competent in many fields **2 :** having general utility **syn** see VERSATILE

al·lay \ə-'lā\ *vt* [ME *alayen*, fr. OE *ālecgan*, fr. *ā-* (perfective prefix) + *lecgan* to lay — more at ABIDE, LAY] **1 :** to subdue or reduce in intensity or severity **:** ALLEVIATE **2 :** to make quiet **:** CALM **syn** see RELIEVE

all but *adv* **:** very nearly **:** ALMOST

all clear *n* **:** a signal that a danger has passed

al·le·ga·tion \ˌal-i-'gā-shən\ *n* **1 :** the act of alleging **2 :** a positive assertion; *specif* **:** a statement by a party to a legal action of what he undertakes to prove **3 :** an assertion unsupported and by implication regarded as unsupportable

al·lege \ə-'lej\ *vt* [ME *alleggen*, fr. OF *alleguer*, fr. L *allegare* to dispatch, cite, fr. *ad-* + *legare* to depute — more at LEGATE] **1 a :** to declare as if under oath but without proof **b :** to assert without proof or before proving **2** *archaic* **:** to adduce or bring forward (as a source or authority) **3 :** to bring forward as a reason or excuse **syn** see ADDUCE

al·leged \ə-'lejd, -'lej-əd\ *adj* **1 :** ASSERTED, DECLARED ⟨an ~ miracle⟩ **2 :** SUPPOSED, SO-CALLED — **al·leg·ed·ly** \-'lej-əd-lē\ *adv*

Al·le·ghe·ny spurge \ˌal-ə-ˌgā-nē-\ *n* [*Allegheny* mts., U. S. A.] **:** a low herb or subshrub (*Pachysandra procumbens*) of the box family widely grown as a ground cover

al·le·giance \ə-'lē-jən(t)s\ *n* [ME *allegeaunce*, modif. of MF *ligeance*, fr. OF, fr. *lige* liege] **1 a :** the obligation of a feudal vassal to his liege lord **b** (1) **:** the fidelity owed by a subject or citizen to his sovereign or government (2) **:** the obligation of an alien to the government under which he resides **2 :** devotion or loyalty to a person, group, or cause **syn** see FIDELITY

al·le·giant \ə-'lē-jənt\ *adj* **:** giving allegiance **:** LOYAL

al·le·gor·i·cal \ˌal-ə-'gȯr-i-kəl, -'gär-\ *adj* **1 :** of or relating to allegory **2 :** having hidden spiritual meaning transcending the literal sense of a sacred text — **al·le·gor·i·cal·ly** \-k(ə-)lē\ *adv* — **al·le·gor·i·cal·ness** \-kəl-nəs\ *n*

al·le·go·rist \'al-ə-ˌgōr-əst, -ˌgȯr-\ *n* **:** a writer of allegory

al·le·go·ri·za·tion \ˌal-ə-ˌgōr-ə-'zā-shən, -ˌgȯr-, -ˌgär-, -gər-\ *n* **:** allegorical representation or interpretation

al·le·go·rize \'al-ə-ˌgōr-ˌīz, -ˌgȯr-, -gə-rīz\ *vt* **1 :** to make into allegory **2 :** to treat or explain as allegory **~** *vi* **1 :** to give allegorical explanations **2 :** to compose or use allegory — **al·le·go·riz·er** *n*

al·le·go·ry \'al-ə-ˌgōr-ē, -ˌgȯr-\ *n* [ME *allegorie*, fr. L *allegoria*, fr. Gk *allēgoria*, fr. *allēgorein* to speak figuratively, fr. *allos* other + *-agorein* to speak publicly, fr. *agora* assembly — more at ELSE, GREGARIOUS] **1 a :** the expression by means of symbolic fictional figures and actions of truths or generalizations about human conduct or experience **b :** an instance of such expression **2 :** a symbolic representation **:** EMBLEM

[1]**al·le·gret·to** \ˌal-ə-'gret-(ˌ)ō, äl-\ *adv (or adj)* [It, fr. *allegro*] **:** faster than andante but not so fast as allegro — used as a direction in music

[2]**allegretto** *n* **:** a piece or movement in allegretto tempo

[1]**al·le·gro** \ə-'leg-(ˌ)rō, -'lā-(ˌ)grō\ *adv (or adj)* [It, merry, fr. (assumed) VL *alecrus* lively, alter. of L *alacr-, alacer* — more at ALACRITY] **:** in a brisk lively manner — used as a direction in music

[2]**allegro** *n* **:** a piece or movement in allegro tempo

al·lele \ə-'lē(ə)l\ *n* [G *allel*, short for *allelomorph*] **1 :** either of a pair of alternative Mendelian characters **2 :** a gene that is the vehicle of an allele — **al·le·lic** \-'lē-lik, -'lel-ik\ *adj* — **al·lel·ism** \-'lē(ə)l-ˌiz-əm, -'lel-ˌiz-\ *n*

al·le·lo·morph \ə-'lel-ə-ˌmȯrf, -'lē-lə-\ *n* [Gk *allēlōn* of each other (fr. *allos . . . allos* one . . . the other, fr. *allos* other) + *morphē* form — more at ELSE] **:** ALLELE — **al·le·lo·mor·phic** \ə-ˌlel-ə-'mȯr-fik, -ˌlē-lə-\ *adj* — **al·le·lo·mor·phism** \ə-'lel-ə-ˌmȯr-ˌfiz-əm, -'lē-lə-\ *n*

al·le·lu·ia \ˌal-ə-'lü-yə\ *interj* [ME, fr. LL, fr. Gk *allēlouia*, fr. Heb *halălūyāh* praise ye Jehovah] **:** HALLELUJAH

al·le·mande \ˌal-ə-'mand; 'al-ə-ˌman(d), -mən\ *n, often cap* [F, fr. fem. of *allemand* German] **1 a :** a 17th and 18th century court dance developed in France from a German folk dance **b :** a step with arms interlaced **2 :** music for the allemande

al·ler·gen \'al-ər-jən\ *n* **:** a substance that induces allergy — **al·ler·gen·ic** \ˌal-ər-'jen-ik\ *adj*

al·ler·gic \ə-'lər-jik\ *adj* **1 :** of, relating to, or inducing allergy **2 :** disagreeably sensitive **:** ANTIPATHETIC

al·ler·gist \'al-ər-jəst\ *n* **:** a specialist in allergy

al·ler·gy \'al-ər-jē\ *n* [G *allergie*, fr. *all-* + Gk *ergon* work — more at WORK] **1 :** altered bodily reactivity (as to antigens) **2 :** exaggerated or pathological reaction (as by sneezing, respiratory embarrassment, itching, or skin rashes) to substances, situations, or physical states that are without comparable effect on the average individual **3 :** a feeling of antipathy or repugnance

al·le·thrin \'al-ə-thrən\ *n* [*allyl* + *pyrethrin*] **:** a light yellow viscous oily synthetic insecticide $C_{19}H_{26}O_3$ used esp. in household aerosols

al·le·vi·ate \ə-'lē-vē-ˌāt\ *vt* [LL *alleviatus*, pp. of *alleviare*, fr. L *ad-* + *levis* light — more at LIGHT] **1 :** to make easier to be endured **:** MODERATE **2 :** to remove or correct in part **:** LESSEN **syn** see RELIEVE — **al·le·vi·a·tion** \ə-ˌlē-vē-'ā-shən\ *n*

al·le·vi·a·tive \ə-'lē-vē-ˌāt-iv\ *or* **al·le·vi·a·to·ry** \-vē-ə-ˌtōr-ē, -ˌtȯr-\ *adj* **:** tending to alleviate **:** PALLIATIVE

[1]**al·ley** \'al-ē\ *n* [ME, fr. MF *alee*, fr. OF, fr. *aler* to go, modif. of L *ambulare* to walk] **1 :** a garden or park walk bordered by trees or bushes **2 a :** a grassed enclosure for bowling or skittles **b :** a hardwood lane for bowling **3 :** a narrow street; *esp* **:** a thoroughfare through the middle of a block giving access to the rear of buildings

[2]**alley** *n* [by shortening and alter. fr. *alabaster*] **:** a superior playing marble

al·ley·way \'al-ē-ˌwā\ *n* **:** a narrow passageway

All Fools' Day *n* **:** APRIL FOOLS' DAY

all fours *n pl* **1 :** all four legs of a quadruped or the two legs and two arms of a biped **2** *sing in constr* **:** any of various card games in which points are scored for winning high, low, jack, and the game

all hail *interj* — used to express greeting, welcome, or acclamation

All·hal·lows \ȯl-'hal-(ˌ)ōz, -əz\ *n, pl* **Allhallows** [short for *All Hallows' Day*] **:** ALL SAINTS' DAY

all·heal \'ȯl-ˌhēl\ *n* **:** any of several plants (as valerian or self-heal) used esp. in folk medicine

al·li·a·ceous \ˌal-ē-'ā-shəs\ *adj* [L *allium*] **:** resembling garlic or onion

al·li·ance \ə-'lī-ən(t)s\ *n* **1 a :** the state of being allied **:** the action of allying **b :** a bond or connection between families, states, parties, or individuals **2 :** an association to further the common interests of the members; *esp* **:** a confederation of nations by formal treaty **3 :** union by relationship in qualities **:** AFFINITY

al·lied \ə-'līd, 'al-ˌīd\ *adj* **1 :** JOINED, CONNECTED **2 a :** joined in alliance by compact or treaty **b** *cap* **:** of or relating to the nations united against the Central European powers in World War I or those united against the Axis powers in World War II **3 :** related esp. by common properties, characteristics, or ancestry

al·li·ga·tor \'al-ə-ˌgāt-ər\ *n* [Sp *el lagarto* the lizard, fr. *el* the (fr. L *ille* that) + *lagarto* lizard, fr. (assumed) VL *lacartus*, fr. L *lacertus, lacerta* — more at LARIAT, LIZARD] **1 a :** either of two crocodilians (genus *Alligator*) having broad heads not tapering to the snout and a special pocket in the upper jaw for reception of the enlarged lower fourth tooth **b :** CROCODILIAN **2 :** leather made from alligator's hide **3 :** a machine with a strong movable jaw like an alligator's **4 :** a devotee of current swing music

alligator pear *n* **:** AVOCADO

alligator snapper *n* **:** a voracious snapping turtle (*Macrochelys temminckii*) of the rivers of the Gulf states that may reach nearly 150 pounds in weight and 5 feet in length

al·lit·er·ate \ə-'lit-ə-ˌrāt\ *vb* [back-formation fr. *alliteration*] *vi* **1 :** to form an alliteration **2 :** to write or speak alliteratively **~** *vt* **:** to arrange or place so as to make alliteration

al·lit·er·a·tion \ə-ˌlit-ə-'rā-shən\ *n* [*ad-* + L *littera* letter] **:** the repetition of usu. initial consonant sounds in two or more neighboring words or syllables (as *w*ild and *w*oolly, *thr*eatening *thr*ongs) — called also *head rhyme, initial rhyme*

al·lit·er·a·tive \ə-'lit-ə-ˌrāt-iv, -rət-\ *adj* **:** of, related to, or marked by alliteration — **al·lit·er·a·tive·ly** *adv*

al·li·um \'al-ē-əm\ *n* [NL, genus name, fr. L, garlic] **:** any of a large genus (*Allium*) of bulbous herbs of the lily family including the onion, garlic, chive, leek, and shallot

al·lo \'al-(ˌ)ō\ *adj* [*all-*] **:** isomeric or closely related

[1]**allo-** — see ALL-

[2]**allo-** *comb form* [Gk *allos* other — more at ELSE] **:** being one of a group whose members together constitute a structural unit esp. of a language ⟨*allo*phone⟩ — compare -EME

al·lo·ca·ble \'al-ə-kə-bəl\ *or* **al·lo·cat·able** \'al-ə-ˌkāt-ə-bəl\ *adj* **:** capable of being allocated; *also* **:** assignable to a particular account or to a particular period of time

al·lo·cate \'al-ə-ˌkāt\ *vt* [ML *allocatus*, pp. of *allocare*, fr. L *ad-* + *locare* to place, fr. *locus* place — more at STALL] **1 :** to apportion for a specific purpose or to particular persons or things **:** DISTRIBUTE **2 :** ASSIGN, DESIGNATE **syn** see ALLOT — **al·lo·ca·tion** \ˌal-ə-'kā-shən\ *n*

al·lo·cu·tion \ˌal-ə-'kyü-shən\ *n* [L *allocution-, allocutio*, fr. *allocutus*, pp. of *alloqui* to speak to, fr. *ad-* + *loqui* to speak] **:** ADDRESS; *esp* **:** an authoritative or hortatory address

al·log·a·mous \ə-'läg-ə-məs\ *adj* **:** reproducing by cross-fertilization — **al·log·a·my** \-mē\ *n*

al·lo·graph \ˈal-ə-ˌgraf\ *n* **1 :** a letter of an alphabet in a particular shape (as A or a) **2 :** any letter or combination of letters that is one of several ways of representing one phoneme (as *pp* in *hopping* representing the phoneme p) — **al·lo·graph·ic** \ˌal-ə-ˈgraf-ik\ *adj*

al·lom·er·ism \ə-ˈläm-ə-ˌriz-əm\ *n* **:** variability in chemical constitution without variation in crystalline form — **al·lom·er·ous** \-rəs\ *adj*

al·lo·met·ric \ˌal-ə-ˈme-trik\ *adj* **:** of, relating to, or exhibiting allometry

al·lom·e·try \ə-ˈläm-ə-trē\ *n* **:** relative growth of a part in relation to an entire organism; *also* **:** the measure and study of such growth

1**al·lo·morph** \ˈal-ə-ˌmȯrf\ *n* [ISV] **1 :** any of two or more distinct crystalline forms of the same substance **2 :** a pseudomorph that has undergone change or substitution of material — **al·lo·mor·phic** \ˌal-ə-ˈmȯr-fik\ *adj* — **al·lo·mor·phism** \ˈal-ə-ˌmȯr-ˌfiz-əm\ *n*

2**allomorph** *n* [2*allo-* + *morph*eme] **:** one of two or more forms that a morpheme has at different points in the language ⟨the *-es* \əz\ of *dishes*, the *-s* \z\ of *dreams*, the *-s* \s\ of *traps*, the *-en* \ən\ of *oxen*, the vowel modification distinguishing *teeth* from *tooth*, and the zero suffix of *sheep* in *those sheep* are ~*s* of the same morpheme⟩ — **al·lo·mor·phic** \ˌal-ə-ˈmȯr-fik\ *adj* — **al·lo·mor·phism** \ˈal-ə-ˌmȯr-ˌfiz-əm\ *n*

al·lo·nym \ˈal-ə-ˌnim\ *n* [F *allonyme*, fr. *all-* + *-onyme* -onym] **:** the name of another person assumed by an author

al·lo·path \ˈal-ə-ˌpath\ *n* **:** one who practices allopathy — **al·lo·path·ic** \ˌal-ə-ˈpath-ik\ *adj* — **al·lo·path·i·cal·ly** \-i-k(ə-)lē\ *adv*

al·lop·a·thy \ə-ˈläp-ə-thē\ *n* [G *allopathie*, fr. *all-* + *-pathie* -pathy] **1 :** a system of medical practice that combats disease by remedies producing effects different from those produced by the disease treated **2 :** a system of medical practice making use of all measures proved of value in treatment of disease

al·lo·pat·ric \ˌal-ə-ˈpa-trik\ *adj* [*all-* + Gk *patra* fatherland, fr. *patēr* father — more at FATHER] **:** occurring in different areas or in isolation ⟨~ speciation⟩ — **al·lo·pat·ri·cal·ly** \-tri-k(ə-)lē\ *adv* — **al·lop·a·try** \ə-ˈläp-ə-trē\ *n*

al·lo·phane \ˈal-ə-ˌfān\ *n* [Gk *allophanēs* appearing otherwise, fr. *all-* + *phainesthai* to appear, pass. of *phainein* to show — more at FANCY] **:** an amorphous translucent mineral of various colors often in incrustations or stalactite forms consisting of a hydrous aluminum silicate

al·lo·phone \ˈal-ə-ˌfōn\ *n* [2*allo-* + *phone*] **:** one of two or more variants of the same phoneme ⟨the aspirated *p* of *pin* and the nonaspirated *p* of *spin* are ~*s* of the phoneme *p*⟩ — **al·lo·phon·ic** \ˌal-ə-ˈfän-ik\ *adj*

all–or–none \ˌȯ-lər-ˈnən\ *adj* **:** marked either by entire or complete operation or effect or by none at all

al·lot \ə-ˈlät\ *vt* **al·lot·ted; al·lot·ting** [ME *alotten*, fr. MF *aloter*, fr. *a-* (fr. L *ad-*) + *lot*, of Gmc origin; akin to OE *hlot* lot] **1 :** to assign as a share or portion **:** ALLOCATE **2 :** to distribute by lot or as if by lot

syn ASSIGN, APPORTION, ALLOCATE: ALLOT may imply haphazard or arbitrary distribution; ASSIGN stresses an authoritative and fixed allotting but carries no clear implication of an even division; APPORTION implies a dividing according to some principle; ALLOCATE suggests a fixed appropriation usu. of money to a person or group for a particular use

al·lot·ment \ə-ˈlät-mənt\ *n* **:** the act of allotting; *also* **:** something that is allotted

al·lo·trope \ˈal-ə-ˌtrōp\ *n* [ISV, back-formation fr. *allotropy*] **:** a form showing allotropy — **al·lo·trop·ic** \ˌal-ə-ˈträp-ik\ *adj* — **al·lo·trop·i·cal·ly** \-i-k(ə-)lē\ *adv*

al·lot·ro·py \ə-ˈlä-trə-pē\ *n* **:** the existence of a substance and esp. an element in two or more different forms usu. in the same phase

all' ot·ta·va \ˌal-ō-ˈtäv-ə, äl-\ *adv* (*or adj*) [It, at the octave] **:** OTTAVA

al·lot·tee \ə-ˌlät-ˈē\ *n* **:** one to whom an allotment is made

all out *adv* **:** with maximum effort

all–out \ˈȯ-ˈlau̇t\ *adj* **:** made with maximum effort **:** EXTREME

all over *adv* **:** EVERYWHERE

1**all·over** \ˈȯ-ˌlō-vər\ *adj* **:** covering the whole extent or surface

2**allover** *n* **1 :** an embroidered, printed, or lace fabric with a design covering most of the surface **2 :** a pattern or design repeated so as to cover the surface

al·low \ə-ˈlau̇\ *vb* [ME *allowen*, fr. MF *alouer* to place (fr. ML *allocare*) & *allouer* to approve, fr. L *adlaudare* to extol, fr. *ad-* + *laudare* to praise — more at ALLOCATE, LAUD] *vt* **1 a :** to assign as a share (as of time or money) **b :** to reckon as a deduction or an addition ⟨~ a gallon for leakage⟩ **2 :** ADMIT, CONCEDE **3 a :** PERMIT ⟨gaps ~ passage⟩ **b :** to neglect to restrain or prevent ⟨~ the meat to burn⟩ **4** *dial* **a :** to be of the opinion **:** THINK **b :** INTEND, PLAN ~ *vi* **1 :** to make a possibility **:** ADMIT — used with *of* **2 :** to make allowance — used with *for* **3** *dial* **:** SUPPOSE, CONSIDER **syn** see LET

al·low·able \ə-ˈlau̇-ə-bəl\ *adj* **:** PERMISSIBLE — **al·low·able·ness** *n* — **al·low·ably** \-blē\ *adv*

1**al·low·ance** \ə-ˈlau̇-ən(t)s\ *n* **1 a :** a share or portion allotted or granted **b :** a sum granted as a reimbursement or bounty or for expenses **2 :** HANDICAP **3 :** an allowed dimensional difference between mating parts of a machine **4 :** the act of allowing **:** PERMISSION **5 :** the taking into account of mitigating circumstances or contingencies

2**allowance** *vt* **1 :** to put upon a fixed allowance **2 :** to supply in a fixed or regular quantity

al·low·ed·ly \ə-ˈlau̇-əd-lē\ *adv* **:** by allowance **:** ADMITTEDLY

1**al·loy** \ˈal-ˌȯi, ə-ˈlȯi\ *n* [MF *aloi*, fr. *aloier* to combine, fr. L *alligare* to bind — more at ALLY] **1 :** the degree of mixture with base metals **:** FINENESS **2 :** a substance composed of two or more metals or of a metal and a nonmetal intimately united usu. by being fused together and dissolving in each other when molten; *also* **:** the state of union of the components **3** *archaic* **:** a metal mixed with a more valuable metal to give durability or some other desired quality **4 :** an admixture of something that debases

2**al·loy** \ə-ˈlȯi, ˈal-ˌȯi\ *vt* **1 :** to reduce the purity of by mixing with a less valuable metal **2 :** to mix so as to form an alloy **3 :** to debase by admixture

1**all right** *adv* **1 :** SATISFACTORILY **2 :** very well **:** YES **3 :** beyond doubt **:** CERTAINLY

2**all right** *adj* **1 :** SATISFACTORY, CORRECT **2 :** SAFE, WELL **3** *slang* **:** GOOD, HONEST

all–round \ˈȯl-ˈrau̇nd\ *var of* ALL-AROUND

All Saints' Day *n* **:** a Christian feast observed November 1 in honor of all the saints

all·seed \ˈȯl-ˌsēd\ *n* **:** any of several many-seeded plants (as knotgrass)

All Souls' Day *n* **:** a day of solemn supplication for the souls in purgatory observed November 2 in some Christian churches

all·spice \ˈȯl-ˌspīs\ *n* **:** the berry of a West Indian tree (*Pimenta dioica*) of the myrtle family or the mildly pungent and aromatic spice prepared from it; *also* **:** the allspice tree

all told *adv* **:** everything counted **:** in all

al·lude \ə-ˈlüd\ *vi* [L *alludere*, lit., to play with, fr. *ad-* + *ludere* to play] **:** to make indirect reference **syn** see REFER

1**al·lure** \ə-ˈlü(ə)r\ *vt* [ME *aluren*, fr. MF *alurer*, fr. OF, fr. *a-* (fr. L *ad-*) + *loire* lure — more at LURE] **:** to entice by charm or attraction **syn** see ATTRACT — **al·lure·ment** \-mənt\ *n*

2**allure** *n* **:** ATTRACTION, CHARM

al·lu·sion \ə-ˈlü-zhən\ *n* [LL *allusion-*, *allusio*, fr. L *allusus*, pp. of *alludere*] **1 :** the act of alluding or hinting at **2 :** an implied or indirect reference — **al·lu·sive** \ə-ˈlü-siv, -ziv\ *adj* — **al·lu·sive·ly** *adv* — **al·lu·sive·ness** *n*

1**al·lu·vi·al** \ə-ˈlü-vē-əl\ *adj* **:** relating to, composed of, or found in alluvium

2**alluvial** *n* **:** an alluvial deposit

alluvial fan *n* **:** the alluvial deposit of a stream where it issues from a gorge upon a plain or of a tributary stream at its junction with the main stream

al·lu·vi·on \ə-ˈlü-vē-ən\ *n* [L *alluvion-*, *alluvio*, fr. *alluere* to wash against, fr. *ad-* + *lavere* to wash — more at LYE] **1 :** the wash or flow of water against a shore **2 :** INUNDATION, FLOOD **3 :** ALLUVIUM **4 :** an accession to land by the gradual addition of matter (as by deposit of alluvium) that then belongs to the owner of the land to which it is added; *also* **:** the land so added

al·lu·vi·um \ə-ˈlü-vē-əm\ *n, pl* **alluviums** *or* **al·lu·via** \-vē-ə\ [LL, neut. of *alluvius* alluvial, fr. L *alluere*] **:** clay, silt, sand, gravel, or similar detrital material deposited by running water

1**al·ly** \ə-ˈlī, ˈal-ˌī\ *vb* [ME *allien*, fr. OF *alier*, fr. L *alligare* to bind to, fr. *ad-* + *ligare* to bind — more at LIGATURE] *vt* **1 :** to unite or form a connection between (as by marriage or by treaty) **:** ASSOCIATE **2 :** to connect or form a relation between (as by likeness or compatibility) ~ *vi* **:** to enter into an alliance

2**al·ly** \ˈal-ˌī, ə-ˈlī\ *n* **1 :** a plant or animal linked to another by genetic or evolutionary relationship **2 :** a sovereign or state associated with another by treaty or league **3 :** someone or something associated with another as a helper **:** AUXILIARY

-al·ly \(ə-)lē\ *adv suffix* [1*-al* + *-ly*] **:** 2-LY ⟨terrific*ally*⟩ — in adverbs formed from adjectives in *-ic* with no alternative form in *-ical*

al·lyl \ˈal-əl\ *n* [ISV, fr. L *allium* garlic] **:** an unsaturated univalent radical C_3H_5 compounds of which are found in the oils of garlic and mustard — **al·lyl·ic** \ə-ˈlil-ik\ *adj*

allyl resin *n* **:** any of various thermosetting transparent abrasion-resistant synthetic resins derived from allyl alcohol

al·ma·gest \ˈal-mə-ˌjest\ *n* [ME *almageste*, fr. MF & ML, fr. Ar *al-majusti* the almagest, fr. *al* the + Gk *megistē*, fem. of *megistos*, superl. of *megas* great — more at MUCH] **:** any of several early medieval treatises on a branch of knowledge

al·ma ma·ter \ˌal-mə-ˈmät-ər\ *n* [L, fostering mother] **1 :** a school (as a college) which one has attended **2 :** the song or hymn of a school or college

al·ma·nac \ˈȯl-mə-ˌnak, ˈal-\ *n* [ME *almenak*, fr. ML *almanach*, prob. fr. Ar *al-manākh* the almanac] **1 :** a publication containing astronomical and meteorological data arranged according to the days, weeks, and months of a given year and often including a miscellany of other information **2 :** a publication containing statistical, tabular, and general information

al·man·dine \ˈal-mən-ˌdēn\ *n* [ME *alabandine*, fr. ML *alabandina*, fr. *Alabanda* ancient city in Asia Minor] **1 :** ALMANDITE **2 :** a violet variety of the ruby spinel or sapphire **3 :** the purple Indian garnet

al·man·dite \ˈal-mən-ˌdīt\ *n* [alter. of *almandine*] **:** a deep red garnet consisting of an iron aluminum silicate $Fe_3Al_2(SiO_4)_3$

al·mighty \ȯl-ˈmīt-ē\ *adj* [ME, fr. OE *ealmihtig*, fr. *eall* all + *mihtig* mighty] **1** *often cap* **:** having absolute power over all ⟨*Almighty* God⟩ **2 :** relatively unlimited in power

Almighty *n* **:** 2GOD — used with *the*

al·mond \ˈäm-ənd, ˈam-, ˈal-mənd\ *n* [ME *almande*, fr. OF, fr. LL *amandula*, alter. of L *amygdala* fr. Gk *amygdalē*] **1 a :** a small tree (*Prunus amygdalus*) of the rose family resembling the peach in flowers **b :** the drupaceous fruit of this tree; *esp* **:** its ellipsoidal edible kernel **2 :** any of several similar fruits or the trees producing them

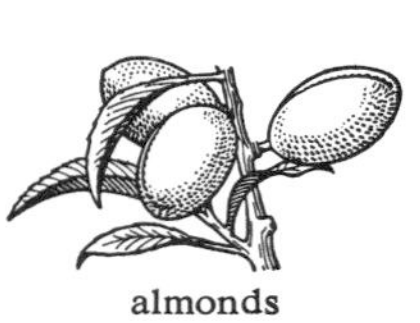

almonds

al·mond–eyed \ˌäm-ən-ˈdīd, ˌam-, ˌal-mən-\ *adj* **:** having narrow slant almond-shaped eyes

almond green *n* **:** a variable color averaging a moderate yellowish green

al·mo·ner \ˈal-mə-nər, ˈäm-ə-\ *n* [ME *almoiner*, fr. OF *almosnier*, fr. *almosne* alms, fr. LL *eleemosyna*] **:** an officer who distributes alms

al·most \ˈȯl-ˌmōst, ȯl-ˈ\ *adv* [ME, fr. OE *ealmǣst*, fr. *eall* + *mǣst* most] **:** only a little less than **:** NEARLY

alms \ˈämz, ˈälmz\ *n, pl* **alms** [ME *almesse*, *almes*, fr. OE *ælmesse*, *ælms*; akin to OHG *alamuosan* alms; both fr. a prehistoric WGmc word borrowed fr. LL *eleemosyna* alms, fr. Gk *eleēmosynē* pity, alms, fr. *eleēmōn* merciful, fr. *eleos* pity] **1** *archaic* **:** CHARITY **2 :** something given freely to relieve the poor — **alms·giv·er** \-ˌgiv-ər\ *n* — **alms·giv·ing** \-ˌgiv-iŋ\ *n*

alms·house \-ˌhau̇s\ *n* **1** *Brit* **:** a privately financed home for the poor **2** *archaic* **:** POORHOUSE

alms·man \-mən\ *n* **:** a recipient of alms

al·ni·co \ˈal-ni-ˌkō\ *n* [*al*uminum + *ni*ckel + *co*balt] **:** a powerful permanent-magnet alloy containing iron, nickel, aluminum, and one or more of the elements cobalt, copper, and titanium

al·oe \ˈal-(ˌ)ō\ *n* [ME, fr. LL, fr. L, dried juice of aloe leaves, fr. Gk *aloē* dried juice of aloe leaves] **1** *pl* **:** the fragrant wood of an East Indian tree (*Aquilaria agallocha*) of the mezereon family **2 a :** any of a large genus (*Aloe*) of succulent chiefly southern African plants of the lily family with basal leaves and spicate flowers **b :** the dried juice of the leaves of various aloes used as a purgative and tonic — usu. used in pl. but sing. in constr.

3 : any of a genus (*Furcraea*) of American plants of the amaryllis family somewhat like the African aloes
aloft \ə-'lȯft\ *adv (or adj)* [ME, fr. ON *ā lopt*, fr. *ā* on, in + *lopt* air] **1:** at or to a great height **2 :** in the air; *esp* **:** in flight **3 :** at, on, or to the masthead or the higher rigging
alo•ha \ə-'lō-ə, ä-'lō-,hä\ *interj* [Hawaiian, fr. *aloha* love] — used to express greeting or farewell
al•o•in \'al-ə-wən\ *n* **:** a bitter yellow crystalline cathartic obtained from the aloe
1alone \ə-'lōn\ *adj* [ME, fr. *al* all + *one* one] **1 :** separated from others **:** ISOLATED **2 :** exclusive of anyone or anything else **:** ONLY **3 :** INCOMPARABLE, UNIQUE
syn ALONE, SOLITARY, LONELY, LONESOME, FORLORN, DESOLATE mean being apart from others. ALONE stresses the objective fact of being entirely by oneself; SOLITARY implies the absence of any others of the same kind; LONELY adds to SOLITARY the suggestion of longing for companionship; LONESOME heightens the implication of dreariness; FORLORN and DESOLATE both emphasize dreariness and a sense of loss but DESOLATE implies a sharper and more poignant sense of loneliness
2alone *adv* **1 :** SOLELY, EXCLUSIVELY **2 :** without aid or support
1along \ə-'lȯŋ\ *prep* [ME, fr. OE *andlang*, fr. *and-* against + *lang* long — more at ANTE-] **1 :** in a line parallel with the length or direction of **2 :** in the course of **3 :** in accordance with **:** IN
2along *adv* **1 :** FORWARD, ON ⟨move ~⟩ **2 :** from one to another ⟨word was passed ~⟩ **3 :** as a companion or associate ⟨brought his wife ~⟩ ⟨work ~ with colleagues⟩ **4 a :** at or to an advanced point ⟨plans are far ~⟩ **b :** all the time ⟨knew all ~⟩ ⟨knew the truth all ~⟩ **5 :** at hand **:** as a necessary or useful item ⟨had his gun ~⟩
along of *prep* [ME *ilong on*, fr. OE *gelang on*, fr. *ge-*, associative prefix + *lang* — more at CO-] *dial* **:** because of
along•shore \ə-'lȯŋ-'shō(ə)r, -'shȯ(ə)r\ *adv (or adj)* **:** along the shore or coast
1along•side \ə-'lȯŋ-,sīd\ *adv* **1 :** along the side **:** PARALLEL **2 :** close at the side
2alongside *prep* **:** side by side with; *specif* **:** parallel to
alongside of *prep* **:** ALONGSIDE
1aloof \ə-'lüf\ *adv* [obs. *aloof* (to windward)] **:** at a distance **:** out of involvement
2aloof *adj* **:** removed or distant in interest or feeling **:** RESERVED **syn** see INDIFFERENT — **aloof•ly** *adv* — **aloof•ness** *n*
al•o•pe•cia \,al-ə-'pē-sh(ē-)ə\ *n* [ME *allopicia*, fr. L *alopecia*, fr. Gk *alōpekia*, fr. *alōpek-*, *alōpēx* fox — more at VULPINE] **:** loss of hair **:** BALDNESS — **al•o•pe•cic** \-'pē-sik\ *adj*
aloud \ə-'lau̇d\ *adv* [ME, fr. 1*a-* + *loud*] **1** *archaic* **:** LOUDLY **2 :** with the speaking voice
alow \ə-'lō\ *adv* [ME, fr. 1*a-* + *low*] **:** BELOW
alp \'alp\ *n* [back-formation fr. *Alps*, mountain system of Europe] **:** a high rugged mountain
al•paca \al-'pak-ə\ *n* [Sp, fr. Aymara *allpaca*] **1 :** a mammal with fine long woolly hair domesticated in Peru and prob. a variety of the guanaco **2 :** wool of the alpaca or a thin cloth made of or containing it; *also* **:** a rayon or cotton imitation of this cloth

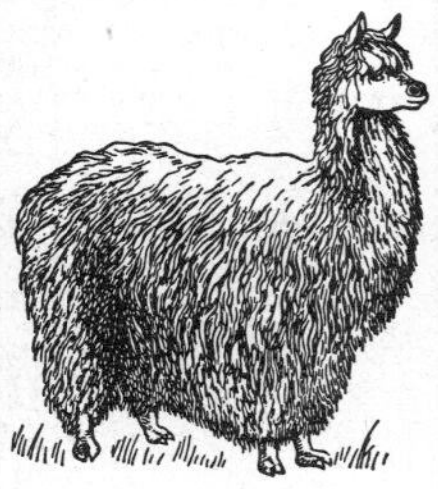
alpaca

al•pen•glow \'al-pən-,glō\ *n* [prob. part trans. of G *Alpenglühen*, fr. *Alpen* Alps + *glühen* glow] **:** a reddish glow seen near sunset or sunrise on the summits of mountains
al•pen•horn \'al-pən-,hȯ(ə)rn\ *or* **alp•horn** \'alp-,\ *n* [G, fr. *Alpen* + *horn*] **:** a straight wooden horn 7 to 15 feet in length that has an upturned bell and is used by Swiss herdsmen
al•pen•stock \'al-pən-,stäk\ *n* [G, fr. *Alpen* + *stock* staff] **:** a long iron-pointed staff used in mountain climbing
al•pes•trine \al-'pes-trən\ *adj* [ML *alpestris* mountainous, fr. L *Alpes* Alps] **:** growing at high elevations but not above the timber line **:** SUBALPINE
1al•pha \'al-fə\ *n* [ME, fr. L, fr. Gk, of Sem origin; akin to Heb *āleph* aleph] **1 :** the first letter of the Greek alphabet — symbol A or α **2 :** something that is first **:** BEGINNING **3 :** the chief or brightest star of a constellation
2alpha *or* α- *adj* **:** closest in the structure of an organic molecule to a particular group or atom ⟨α-substitution⟩ ⟨α-naphthol⟩
alpha and omega *n* [fr. the fact that alpha and omega are respectively the first and last letters of the Greek alphabet] **:** the beginning and ending
al•pha•bet \'al-fə-,bet, -bət\ *n* [ME *alphabete*, fr. LL *alphabetum*, fr. Gk *alphabētos*, fr. *alpha* + *bēta* beta] **1 a :** a set of letters or other characters with which one or more languages are written esp. if arranged in a customary order **b :** a system of signs or signals that serve as equivalents for letters **2 :** RUDIMENTS, ELEMENTS
al•pha•bet•ic \,al-fə-'bet-ik\ *adj* **1 :** of, relating to, or employing an alphabet **2 :** arranged in the order of the letters of the alphabet — **al•pha•bet•i•cal** \-i-kəl\ *adj* — **al•pha•bet•i•cal•ly** \-k(ə-)lē\ *adv*
al•pha•bet•iza•tion \,al-fə-,bet-ə-'zā-shən\ *n* **1 :** the act or process of alphabetizing **2 :** an alphabetically arranged series, list, or file
al•pha•bet•ize \'al-fə-bə-,tīz\ *vt* **1 :** to furnish with an alphabet **2 :** to arrange alphabetically — **al•pha•bet•iz•er** *n*
alpha iron *n* **:** the form of iron stable below 910°C
al•pha•mer•ic \,al-fə-'mer-ik\ *adj* [*alpha*bet + nu*meric*] **:** consisting of both letters and numbers; *specif* **:** capable of using both letters and numbers — **al•pha•mer•i•cal** \-i-kəl\ *adj*
al•pha•nu•mer•ic \,al-fə-n(y)ü-'mer-ik\ *adj* [*alpha*bet + *numeric*] **:** ALPHAMERIC
alpha particle *n* **:** a positively charged nuclear particle identical with the nucleus of a helium atom that consists of 2 protons and 2 neutrons and is ejected at high speed in certain radioactive transformations
alpha privative *n* **:** the English prefix *a-* expressing negation
alpha ray *n* **1 :** an alpha particle moving at high speed (as in radioactive emission) **2 :** a stream of alpha particles — called also *alpha radiation*
Al•phe•us \al-'fē-əs\ *n* [L, fr. Gk *Alpheios*] **:** a river-god in love with the nymph Arethusa
al•pine \'al-,pīn\ *n* **1 :** a plant native to alpine or boreal regions that is often grown for ornament **2** *cap* **:** a person possessing Alpine physical characteristics
Alpine *adj* **1** *often not cap* **:** relating to or resembling the Alps or any mountains **2** *often not cap* **:** of, relating to, or growing on elevated slopes above timberline **3 :** of or relating to a type of stocky broadheaded white men of medium height with brown hair or eyes often regarded as constituting a branch of the Caucasian race
al•pin•ism \'al-pə-,niz-əm\ *n, often cap* **:** mountain climbing in the Alps or other high mountains — **al•pin•ist** \-nəst\ *n*
al•ready \ȯl-'red-ē\ *adv* [ME *al redy*, fr. *al redy*, adj., wholly ready, fr. *al* all + *redy* ready] **1 :** prior to a specified or implied past, present, or future time **:** PREVIOUSLY **2 :** so soon
al•right \ȯl-'rīt\ *adv (or adj)* [ME, fr. *al* + *right*] **:** ALL RIGHT
Al•sa•tian \al-'sā-shən\ *n* [ML *Alsatia* Alsace] **:** GERMAN SHEPHERD
al•sike clover \,al-,sak-, -,sīk-\ *n* [*Alsike*, Sweden] **:** a European perennial clover (*Trifolium hybridum*) much used as a forage plant
al•so \'ȯl-(,)sō\ *adv* [ME, fr. OE *ealswā*, fr. *eall* all + *swā* so — more at SO] **1 :** LIKEWISE **2 :** in addition **:** TOO
al•so–ran \'ȯl-(,)sō-,ran\ *n* **1 :** a horse or dog that finishes out of the money in a race **2 :** a contestant that does not win
Al•ta•ic \al-'tā-ik\ *adj* **1 :** of or relating to the Altai mountains **2 :** of, relating to, or constituting a language family comprising the Turkic, Tungusic, and Mongolic subfamilies
Al•tair \al-'tī(ə)r, -'ta(ə)r, -'te(ə)r\ *n* [Ar *al-ṭā'ir*, lit., the flier] **:** the first magnitude star Alpha (α) Aquilae
al•tar \'ȯl-tər\ *n, often attrib* [ME *alter*, fr. OE *altar*, fr. L *altare*; akin to L *adolēre* to burn up] **1 :** a usu. raised structure or place on which sacrifices are offered or incense is burned in worship **2 :** a usu. enclosed table used in consecrating the eucharistic elements or as a center of worship or ritual
altar boy *n* **:** ACOLYTE 1
altar call *n* **:** an appeal by an evangelist to worshipers to come forward to signify their decision to commit their lives to Christ
altar of repose *often cap A&R* **:** REPOSITORY 2
al•tar•piece \'ȯl-tər-,pēs\ *n* **:** a work of art to decorate the space above and behind an altar
altar rail *n* **:** a railing in front of an altar separating the chancel from the body of the church
altar stone *n* **:** a stone slab with a compartment containing the relics of martyrs that forms an essential part of a Roman Catholic altar
alt•az•i•muth \(')al-'taz-(ə-)məth\ *n* [ISV *alt*itude + *azimuth*] **:** a telescope mounted so that it can swing horizontally and vertically; *also* **:** any of several other instruments similarly mounted
al•ter \'ȯl-tər\ *vb* **al•ter•ing** \-t(ə-)riŋ\ [ME *alteren*, fr. MF *alterer*, fr. ML *alterare*, fr. L *alter* other (of two); akin to L *alius* other — more at ELSE] *vt* **1 :** to make different without changing into something else **2 :** CASTRATE, SPAY ~ *vi* **:** to become different **syn** see CHANGE — **al•ter•abil•i•ty** \,ȯl-t(ə-)rə-'bil-ət-ē\ *n* — **al•ter•able** \'ȯl-t(ə-)rə-bəl\ *adj* — **al•ter•ably** \-blē\ *adv*
al•ter•ant \'ȯl-tə-rənt\ *n* **:** something that alters
al•ter•ation \,ȯl-tə-'rā-shən\ *n* **1 a :** the act or process of altering **b :** the state of being altered **2 :** the result of altering **:** MODIFICATION
1al•ter•ative \'ȯl-tə-,rāt-iv, -rət-\ *n* **:** a drug used empirically to alter favorably the course of an ailment
2alterative *adj* **:** causing alteration
al•ter•cate \'ȯl-tər-,kāt\ *vi* [L *altercatus*, pp. of *altercari*, fr. *alter*] **:** to dispute with zeal, heat, or anger **:** WRANGLE
al•ter•ca•tion \,ȯl-tər-'kā-shən\ *n* **:** a noisy or angry dispute **syn** see QUARREL
al•ter ego \,ȯl-tə-'rē-(,)gō *also* -'reg-(,)ō\ *n* [L, lit., second I] **:** a second self; *esp* **:** a trusted friend
al•tern \ȯl-'tərn, al-; 'ȯl-(,), 'al-(,)\ *adj* [L *alternus*] *archaic* **:** ALTERNATE
1al•ter•nate \'ȯl-tər-nət, 'al-\ *adj* [L *alternatus*, pp. of *alternare*, fr. *alternus* alternate, fr. *alter*] **1 a :** occurring or succeeding by turns **b :** RECIPROCATING **2 a :** arranged first on one side and then on the other at different levels or points along an axial line **b :** arranged one above or alongside the other **3 :** every other **:** every second **4 :** ALTERNATIVE, SUBSTITUTE **syn** see INTERMITTENT — **al•ter•nate•ly** *adv*
2al•ter•nate \-,nāt\ *vt* **1 :** to perform by turns or in succession **2 :** to cause to alternate ~ *vi* **:** to happen, succeed, or act by turns
3al•ter•nate \-nət\ *n* **1 :** ALTERNATIVE **2 :** one that takes the place of or alternates with another
alternating current *n* **:** an electric current that reverses its direction at regularly recurring intervals
al•ter•na•tion \,ȯl-tər-'nā-shən, ,al-\ *n* **1 a :** the act or process of alternating or causing to alternate **b :** alternating occurrence **:** SUCCESSION **2 :** DISJUNCTION 2a **3 :** the occurrence of different allomorphs or allophones
alternation of generations : the occurrence of two or more forms differently produced in the life cycle of a plant or animal usu. involving the regular alternation of a sexual with an asexual generation but not infrequently consisting of alternation of a dioecious generation with one or more parthenogenetic generations
1al•ter•na•tive \ȯl-'tər-nət-iv, al-\ *adj* **1 :** offering or expressing a choice ⟨~ plans⟩ **2 :** ALTERNATE — **al•ter•na•tive•ly** *adv* — **al•ter•na•tive•ness** *n*
2alternative *n* **1 a :** a proposition or situation offering a choice between two incompatible things **b :** an opportunity for deciding between two incompatible courses or propositions **2 :** one of two or more incompatible things, courses, or propositions to be chosen **syn** see CHOICE
al•ter•na•tor \'ȯl-tər-,nāt-ər, 'al-\ *n* **:** an electric generator for producing alternating current
al•thaea *or* **al•thea** \al-'thē-ə\ *n* [L *althaea* marsh mallow, fr. Gk *althaia*] **1 :** ROSE OF SHARON 2 **2 :** a hollyhock or related plant (genus *Althaea*)

ALPHABET TABLE

Showing the letters of five non-Roman alphabets and the transliterations used in the etymologies

HEBREW[1,4]

Letter	Name	Translit.
א	aleph	' [2]
ב	beth	b, bh
ג	gimel	g, gh
ד	daleth	d, dh
ה	he	h
ו	waw	w
ז	zayin	z
ח	heth	ḥ
ט	teth	ṭ
י	yod	y
כ ך	kaph	k, kh
ל	lamed	l
מ ם	mem	m
נ ן	nun	n
ס	samekh	s
ע	ayin	'
פ ף	pe	p, ph
צ ץ	sadhe	ṣ
ק	qoph	q
ר	resh	r
שׂ	sin	ś
שׁ	shin	sh
ת	taw	t, th

ARABIC[3,4]

Name	Translit.
alif	' [5]
bā	b
tā	t
thā	th
jīm	j
ḥā	ḥ
khā	kh
dāl	d
dhāl	dh
rā	r
zāy	z
sīn	s
shīn	sh
ṣād	ṣ
ḍād	ḍ
ṭā	ṭ
ẓā	ẓ
'ayn	'
ghayn	gh
fā	f
qāf	q
kāf	k
lām	l
mīm	m
nūn	n
hā	h [6]
wāw	w
yā	y

GREEK[7]

Letter	Name	Translit.
A α	alpha	a
B β	beta	b
Γ γ	gamma	g, n
Δ δ	delta	d
E ε	epsilon	e
Z ζ	zeta	z
H η	eta	ē
Θ θ	theta	th
I ι	iota	i
K κ	kappa	k
Λ λ	lambda	l
M μ	mu	m
N ν	nu	n
Ξ ξ	xi	x
O o	omicron	o
Π π	pi	p
P ρ	rho	r, rh
Σ σ ς	sigma	s
T τ	tau	t
Υ υ	upsilon	y, u
Φ φ	phi	ph
X χ	chi	ch
Ψ ψ	psi	ps
Ω ω	omega	ō

RUSSIAN[8]

Letter	Translit.
А а	a
Б б	b
В в	v
Г г	g
Д д	d
Е е	e
Ж ж	zh
З з	z
И и Й й	i, ĭ
К к	k
Л л	l
М м	m
Н н	n
О о	o
П п	p
Р р	r
С с	s
Т т	t
У у	u
Ф ф	f
Х х	kh
Ц ц	ts
Ч ч	ch
Ш ш	sh
Щ щ	shch
Ъ ъ[9]	"
Ы ы	y
Ь ь[10]	'
Э э	e
Ю ю	yu
Я я	ya

SANSKRIT[11]

Letter	Translit.		Letter	Translit.
अ	a		ञ	ñ
आ	ā		ट	ṭ
इ	i		ठ	ṭh
ई	ī		ड	ḍ
उ	u		ढ	ḍh
ऊ	ū		ण	ṇ
ऋ	r̥		त	t
ॠ	r̥̄		थ	th
लृ	l̥		द	d
लॄ	l̥̄		ध	dh
ए	e		न	n
ऐ	ai		प	p
ओ	o		फ	ph
औ	au		ब	b
ं	ṁ		भ	bh
ः	ḥ		म	m
क	k		य	y
ख	kh		र	r
ग	g		ल	l
घ	gh		व	v
ङ	ṅ		श	ś
च	c		ष	ṣ
छ	ch		स	s
ज	j		ह	h
झ	jh			

1 See ALEPH, BETH, etc., in the vocabulary. Where two forms of a letter are given, the one at the right is the form used at the end of a word. 2 Not represented in transliteration when initial. 3 The left column shows the form of each Arabic letter that is used when it stands alone, the second column its form when it is joined to the preceding letter, the third column its form when it is joined to both the preceding and the following letter, and the right column its form when it is joined to the following letter only. In the names of the Arabic letters, ā, ī, and ū respectively are pronounced like a in *father*, i in *machine*, u in *rude*. 4 Hebrew and Arabic are written from right to left. The Hebrew and Arabic letters are all primarily consonants; a few of them are also used secondarily to represent certain vowels, but full indication of vowels, when provided at all, is by means of a system of dots or strokes adjacent to the consonantal characters. 5 Alif represents no sound in itself, but is used principally as an indicator of the presence of a glottal stop (transliterated ' medially and finally; not represented in transliteration when initial) and as the sign of a long a. 6 When ة has two dots above it (ة), it is called *tā marbūta* and, if it immediately precedes a vowel, is transliterated t instead of h. 7 See ALPHA, BETA, GAMMA, etc., in the vocabulary. The letter gamma is transliterated n only before velars; the letter upsilon is transliterated u only as the final element in diphthongs. 8 See CYRILLIC in the vocabulary. 9 This sign indicates that the immediately preceding consonant is not palatalized even though immediately followed by a palatal vowel. 10 This sign indicates that the immediately preceding consonant is palatalized even though not immediately followed by a palatal vowel. 11 The alphabet shown here is the Devanagari. When vowels are combined with preceding consonants they are indicated by various strokes or hooks instead of by the signs here given, or, in the case of short a, not written at all. Thus the character क represents *ka*; the character का, *kā*; the character कि, *ki*; the character की, *kī*; the character कु, *ku*; the character कू, *kū*; the character कृ, *kr*; the character कॄ, *kr̄*; the character के, *ke*; the character कै, *kai*; the character को, *ko*; the character कौ, *kau*; and the character क्, *k* without any following vowel. There are also many compound characters representing combinations of two or more consonants.

alt·horn \'alt-,hȯ(ə)rn\ *n* [G, fr. *alt* alto + *horn* horn] **:** the alto member of the saxhorn family used most frequently in bands where it often replaces the French horn

al·though *also* **al·tho** \ȯl-'thō\ *conj* [ME *although,* fr. *al* all + *though*] **:** in spite of the fact that **:** even though **:** THOUGH

al·tim·e·ter \al-'tim-ət-ər, 'al-tə-,mēt-ər\ *n* [L *altus* + E *-meter*] **:** an instrument for measuring altitude; *specif* **:** an aneroid barometer designed to register changes in atmospheric pressure accompanying changes in altitude — **al·tim·e·try** \al-'tim-ə-trē\ *n*

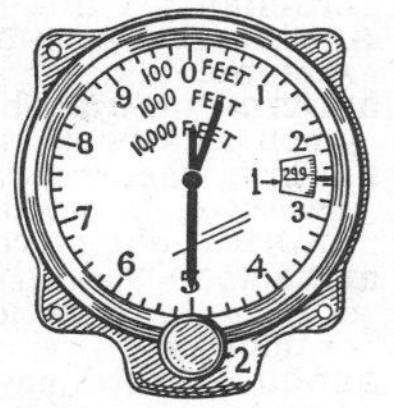

airplane altimeter, reading an indicated altitude of 500 feet: *1* barometer scale, reading 29.92 inches of mercury, *2* setting knob

al·ti·pla·no \,al-ti-'plän-(,)ō\ *n* [AmerSp, fr. L *altus* + *planum* plain] **:** a high plateau or plain **:** TABLELAND

al·ti·tude \'al-tə-,t(y)üd\ *n* [ME, fr. L *altitudo* height, depth, fr. *altus* high, deep — more at OLD] **1 a :** the angular elevation of a celestial object above the horizon **b :** the vertical elevation of an object above sea level **c :** the perpendicular distance from the base of a geometric figure to the vertex or to the side parallel to the base **2 :** the height or an extremity of some quality or degree of excellence **3 a :** vertical distance or extent **b :** position at a height **c :** an elevated region **:** EMINENCE — usu. used in pl. **syn** see HEIGHT — **al·ti·tu·di·nal** \,al-tə-'t(y)üd-nəl, -ᵊn-əl\ *adj*

altitude sickness *n* **:** the effects (as nosebleed or nausea) of oxygen deficiency in the blood and tissues developed in rarefied air at high altitudes

al·to \'al-(,)tō\ *n* [It, lit., high, fr. L *altus*] **1 a** (1) **:** COUNTERTENOR (2) **:** CONTRALTO **b :** the second highest of the four voice parts of the mixed chorus **2 :** the second highest member of a family of musical instruments; *specif* **:** ALTHORN

al·to·cu·mu·lus \,al-(,)tō-'kyü-myə-ləs\ *n* [NL, fr. L *altus* + NL *-o-* + *cumulus*] **:** a fleecy cloud formation consisting of large whitish globular cloudlets with shaded portions

¹**al·to·geth·er** \,ȯl-tə-'geth-ər\ *adv* [ME *altogedere,* fr. *al* all + *togedere* together] **1 :** WHOLLY, THOROUGHLY **2 :** on the whole

²**altogether** *n* **:** NUDE — used with *the*

al·to–re·lie·vo *or* **al·to–ri·lie·vo** \,al-(,)tō-ri-'lē-(,)vō, ,äl-(,)tō-rēl-'yä-(,)vō\ *n, pl* **alto–relievos** *or* **al·to–ri·lie·vi** \,äl-(,)tō-rēl-'yä-(,)vē\ [It *alto rilievo*] **1 :** HIGH RELIEF **2 :** a sculpture executed in high relief

al·to·stra·tus \,al-(,)tō-'strāt-əs, -'strat-\ *n* [NL, fr. L *altus* + NL *-o-* + *stratus*] **:** a cloud formation similar to cirrostratus but darker and at a lower level

al·tri·cial \al-'trish-əl\ *adj* [L *altric-, altrix* fem. of *altor* one who nourishes, fr. *altus* pp. of *alere* to nourish — more at OLD] **:** having the young hatched in a very immature and helpless condition so as to require care for some time — compare PRECOCIAL

al·tru·ism \'al-trü-,iz-əm\ *n* [F *altruisme,* fr. *autrui* other people, fr. OF, oblique case form of *autre* other, fr. L *alter*] **:** regard for or devotion to the interests of others — **al·tru·ist** \-trü-əst\ *n* — **al·tru·is·tic** \,al-trü-'is-tik\ *adj* — **al·tru·is·ti·cal·ly** \-ti-k(ə-)lē\ *adv*

al·u·la \'al-yə-lə\ *n, pl* **al·u·lae** \-,lē, -,lī\ [NL, fr. L, dim. of *ala* wing — more at AISLE] **:** BASTARD WING — **al·u·lar** \-lər\ *adj*

al·um \'al-əm\ *n* [ME, fr. MF *alum, alun,* fr. L *alumen* — more at ALE] **1 :** a potassium aluminum sulfate $KAl(SO_4)_2.12H_2O$ or an ammonium aluminum sulfate $NH_4Al(SO_4)_2.12H_2O$ used esp. as an emetic and as an astringent and styptic **2 :** any of various double salts isomorphous with potash alum **3 :** aluminum sulfate $Al_2(SO_4)_3$

alu·mi·na \ə-'lü-mə-nə\ *n* [NL, fr. L *alumin-, alumen* alum] **:** aluminum oxide Al_2O_3 occurring native as corundum and in hydrated forms (as in bauxite)

alu·mi·nate \-nət\ *n* **:** a compound of alumina with a metallic oxide

alu·mi·nif·er·ous \ə-,lü-mə-'nif-(ə-)rəs\ *adj* **:** containing alum or aluminum

al·u·min·i·um \,al-yə-'min-ē-əm\ *n* [NL, fr. *alumina*] *chiefly Brit* **:** ALUMINUM

alu·mi·nize \ə-'lü-mə-,nīz\ *vt* **:** to treat or coat with aluminum

alu·mi·no·sil·i·cate \ə-,lü-mə-nō-'sil-ə-,kāt, -'sil-i-kət\ *n* [L *alumin-, alumen* + *-o-* + ISV *silicate*] **:** a combined silicate and aluminate

alu·mi·nous \ə-'lü-mə-nəs\ *adj* **:** of, relating to, or containing alum or aluminum

alu·mi·num \ə-'lü-mə-nəm\ *n, often attrib* [NL, fr. *alumina*] **:** a bluish silver-white malleable ductile light trivalent metallic element with good electrical and thermal conductivity, high reflectivity, and resistance to oxidation that is the most abundant metal in the earth's crust occurring always in combination — see ELEMENT table

aluminum sulfate *n* **:** a colorless salt $Al_2(SO_4)_3$ usu. made by treating bauxite with sulfuric acid and used in making paper, water purification, and tanning

alum·na \ə-'ləm-nə\ *n, pl* **alum·nae** \-(,)nē\ [L, fem. of *alumnus*] **:** a girl or woman who has attended or has graduated from a particular school, college, or university

alum·nus \ə-'ləm-nəs\ *n, pl* **alum·ni** \-,nī\ [L, foster son, pupil, fr. *alere* to nourish — more at OLD] **:** one that has attended or graduated from a particular school, college, or university

al·um·root \'al-əm-,rüt, -,rụ̇t\ *n* **1 :** any of several No. American herbs (genus *Heuchera*) of the saxifrage family; *esp* **:** one (*H. americana*) with an astringent root **2 :** a geranium (*Geranium maculatum*)

al·u·nite \'al-(y)ə-,nīt\ *n* [F, fr. *alun* alum] **:** a mineral $K(AlO)_3(SO_4)_2.3H_2O$ consisting of a hydrous potassium aluminum sulfate and occurring massive or in rhombohedral crystals (hardness 3.5–4)

al·ve·o·lar \al-'vē-ə-lər\ *adj* **1 :** of, relating to, resembling, or having alveoli **2 :** of, relating to, or constituting the part of the jaws where the teeth arise, the air cells of the lungs, or glands with secretory cells about a central space **3 :** articulated with the tip of the tongue touching or near the teethridge — **al·ve·o·lar·ly** *adv*

al·ve·o·late \-lət\ *adj* **:** pitted like a honeycomb — **al·ve·o·la·tion** \al-,vē-ə-'lā-shən, ,al-(,)vē-\ *n*

al·ve·o·lus \al-'vē-ə-ləs\ *n, pl* **al·ve·o·li** \-,lī, -(,)lē\ [NL, fr. L, dim. of *alveus* cavity, hollow, fr. *alvus* belly; akin to ON hvan*njōli* stalk of angelica, Gk *aulos,* a reed instrument] **1 :** a small cavity or pit: as **a :** a socket for a tooth **b :** an air cell of the lungs **c :** an acinus of a compound gland **d :** a cell or compartment of a honeycomb **2 :** TEETHRIDGE

al·way \'ȯl-(,)wā\ *adv* [ME] *archaic* **:** ALWAYS

al·ways \'ȯl-wēz, -wəz, -(,)wāz\ *adv* [ME *alway, alwayes,* fr. OE *ealne weg,* lit., all the way, fr. *ealne* (acc. of *eall* all) + *weg* (acc.) way — more at WAY] **1 :** at all times **:** INVARIABLY **2 :** FOREVER, PERPETUALLY **3 :** without exception

Al·yce clover \,al-əs-\ *n* [prob. by folk etymology fr. NL *Alysicarpus,* genus name, fr. Gk *halysis* chain + *karpos* fruit] **:** a low spreading annual Old World legume (*Alysicarpus vaginalis*) used in southern U.S. as a cover crop and for hay and pasturage

alys·sum \ə-'lis-əm\ *n* [NL, fr. Gk *alysson,* plant believed to cure rabies, fr. neut. of *alyssos* curing rabies, fr. *a-* + *lyssa* rabies] **1 :** any of a genus (*Alyssum*) of Old World herbs of the mustard family with small yellow racemose flowers **2 :** SWEET ALYSSUM

am [ME, fr. OE *eom;* akin to ON *em* am, L *sum,* Gk *eimi,* OE *is* is] *pres 1st sing of* BE

amah \'äm-ə, 'am-(,)ä\ *n* [Pg *ama* wet nurse, fr. ML *amma*] **:** an Oriental female servant; *esp* **:** a Chinese nurse

amain \ə-'mān\ *adv* **1 :** with all one's might **2 a :** at full speed **b :** in great haste **3 :** GREATLY, EXCEEDINGLY

Ama·le·kite \'am-ə-,lek-,īt, ə-'mal-ə-,kīt\ *n* [Heb *'Ămālēqī,* pl. fr. *'Ămālēq* Amalek, grandson of Esau] **:** a member of an ancient nomadic people living south of Canaan

amal·gam \ə-'mal-gəm\ *n* [ME *amalgame,* fr. MF, fr. ML *amalgama*] **1 :** an alloy of mercury with another metal that is solid or liquid at room temperature according to the proportion of mercury present and used esp. in making tooth cements **2 :** a mixture of different elements

amal·ga·mate \ə-'mal-gə-,māt\ *vb* **:** to unite in or as if in an amalgam; *esp* **:** to merge into a single body **syn** see MIX — **amal·ga·ma·tor** \-,māt-ər\ *n*

amal·ga·ma·tion \ə-,mal-gə-'mā-shən\ *n* **1 a :** the act or process of amalgamating **:** UNITING **b :** the state of being amalgamated **2 :** the result of amalgamating **:** AMALGAM **3 :** MERGER ⟨~ of two corporations⟩ — **amal·ga·ma·tive** \-'mal-gə-,māt-iv\ *adj*

am·a·ni·ta \,am-ə-'nīt-ə, -'nēt-\ *n* [NL, genus name, fr. Gk *amanitai,* pl., a kind of fungus] **:** any of various mostly poisonous white-spored fungi (genus *Amanita*) with the volva separate from the cap

aman·ta·dine \ə-'mant-ə-,dēn\ *n* [*adamantanamine*] **:** an antiviral drug used esp. to prevent infection (as by an influenza virus) by interfering with virus penetration into host cells

aman·u·en·sis \ə-,man-yə-'wen(t)-səs\ *n, pl* **aman·u·en·ses** \-'wen(t)-(,)sēz\ [L, fr. (*servus*) *a manu* slave with secretarial duties] **:** one employed to write from dictation or to copy manuscript **:** SECRETARY

am·a·ranth \'am-ə-,ran(t)th\ *n* [L *amarantus,* a flower, fr. Gk *amaranton,* fr. neut. of *amarantos* unfading, fr. *a-* + *marainein* to waste away — more at SMART] **1 :** an imaginary flower that never fades **2 :** any of a large genus (*Amaranthus* of the family Amaranthaceae, the amaranth family) of coarse herbs including pigweeds and various forms cultivated for their showy flowers **3 :** a dark reddish purple

am·a·ran·thine \,am-ə-'ran(t)-thən, -'ran-,thīn\ *adj* **1 a :** of or relating to amaranth **b :** UNDYING **2 :** of the color amaranth

am·a·relle \,am-ə-'rel\ *n* [G, fr. ML *amarellum,* fr. L *amarus* bitter; akin to OE *ampre* sorrel, Gk *ōmos* raw] **:** any of several cultivated cherries derived from the sour cherry (*Prunus cerasus*) and distinguished from the morellos by their colorless juice

am·a·ryl·lis \,am-ə-'ril-əs\ *n* [NL, genus name, prob. fr. L, name of a shepherdess in Virgil's *Eclogues*] **:** any of a genus (*Amaryllis* of the family Amaryllidaceae, the amaryllis family) of bulbous African herbs with showy umbellate flowers; *also* **:** a plant of any of several genera (as *Hippeastrum* or *Sprebelia*)

amass \ə-'mas\ *vt* [MF *amasser,* fr. OF, fr. *a-* (fr. L *ad-*) + *masser* to gather into a mass, fr. *masse* mass] **1 :** to collect for oneself **:** ACCUMULATE **2 :** to collect into a mass **:** GATHER — **amass·er** *n* — **amass·ment** \-mənt\ *n*

am·a·teur \'am-ə-,tər, -ət-ər, -ə-,t(y)ụ̇(ə)r, -ə-,chụ̇(ə)r, -ə-chər\ *n* [F, fr. L *amator* lover, fr. *amatus,* pp. of *amare* to love] **1 :** DEVOTEE, ADMIRER **2 :** one who engages in a pursuit, study, science, or sport as a pastime rather than as a profession **3 :** one lacking in experience and competence in an art or science — **amateur** *adj* — **am·a·teur·ish** \,am-ə-'tər-ish, -'t(y)ụ̇(ə)r-\ *adj* — **am·a·teur·ish·ly** *adv* — **am·a·teur·ish·ness** *n* — **am·a·teur·ism** \'am-ə-,tər-,iz-əm, -ət-ə-,riz-, -ə-,t(y)ụ̇(ə)r-,iz-, -,chụ̇(ə)r-,iz-, -chə-,riz-\ *n*

syn DILETTANTE, DABBLER, TYRO: AMATEUR and DILETTANTE both imply a taste or liking for something rather than an expert knowledge of it; AMATEUR often applies to one practicing an art without mastery of its essentials but in sports it suggests not so clearly lack of skill but avoidance of direct remuneration; DILETTANTE often implies elegant trifling in the arts but may still apply simply to the lover of an art rather than its skilled practitioner; DABBLER suggests desultory habits of work and lack of persistence; TYRO implies inexperience often combined with audacity with resulting crudeness or blundering

Ama·ti \ä-'mät-ē, ə-\ *n* **:** a violin made by a member of the Amati family of Cremona

am·a·tive \'am-ət-iv\ *adj* [ML *amativus,* fr. L *amatus*] **:** disposed or disposing to love **:** AMOROUS — **am·a·tive·ly** *adv* — **am·a·tive·ness** *n*

am·a·tol \'am-ə-,tȯl, -,täl\ *n* [ISV *am*monium + connective *-a-* + trinitro*tol*uene] **:** an explosive consisting of ammonium nitrate and trinitrotoluene

am·a·to·ry \'am-ə-,tōr-ē, -,tȯr-\ *adj* **:** of, relating to, or expressing sexual love

am·au·ro·sis \,am-(,)ȯ-'rō-səs\ *n* [NL, fr. Gk *amaurōsis,* lit., dimming, fr. *amauroun* to dim, fr. *amauros* dim] **:** decay of sight occurring without perceptible external change — **am·au·rot·ic** \-'rät-ik\ *adj*

[1]amaze \ə-'māz\ vt [ME *amasen*, fr. OE *āmasian*, fr. *ā-* (perfective prefix) + (assumed) *masian* to confuse — more at ABIDE] 1 *obs* : BEWILDER, PERPLEX 2 : to fill with wonder : ASTOUND **syn** see SURPRISE — **amazed** *adj* — **amaz·ing** *adj* — **amaz·ing·ly** \-'mā-ziŋ-lē\ *adv*

[2]amaze *n* : AMAZEMENT

amaze·ment \ə-'māz-mənt\ *n* 1 *obs* : BEWILDERMENT, CONSTERNATION 2 : the quality or state of being amazed

am·a·zon \'am-ə-ˌzän, -ə-zən\ *n* [ME, fr. L, fr. Gk *Amazōn*] 1 *cap* : a member of a race of female warriors repeatedly warring with the ancient Greeks of mythology 2 : a tall strong masculine woman : VIRAGO

Am·a·zo·nian \ˌam-ə-'zō-nē-ən, -nyən\ *adj* 1 a : relating to, resembling, or befitting an Amazon b *of a woman, not cap* : MASCULINE, WARLIKE 2 : of or relating to the Amazon river or its valley

am·a·zon·ite \'am-ə-zə-ˌnīt\ *or* **am·a·zon·stone** \-zən-ˌstōn\ *n* [*Amazon* river] : an apple-green or verdigris-green microcline

am·bage \'am-bij\ *n* [back-formation fr. ME *ambages*, fr. MF or L; MF, fr. L, fr. *ambi-* + *agere* to drive — more at AGENT] 1 *archaic* : AMBIGUITY, CIRCUMLOCUTION — usu. used in pl. 2 *pl, archaic* : indirect ways or proceedings — **am·ba·gious** \am-'bā-jəs\ *adj*

am·bas·sa·dor \am-'bas-əd-ər, əm-, im-\ *n* [ME *ambassadour*, fr. MF *ambassadeur*, of Gmc origin; akin to OHG *ambaht* service] 1 : an official envoy; *esp* : a diplomatic agent of the highest rank accredited to a foreign sovereign or government as the resident representative of his own sovereign or government or appointed for a special and often temporary diplomatic assignment 2 a : an authorized representative or messenger b : an unofficial representative — **am·bas·sa·do·ri·al** \(ˌ)am-ˌbas-ə-'dōr-ē-əl, əm-, im-, -'dȯr-\ *adj* — **am·bas·sa·dor·ship** \am-'bas-əd-ər-ˌship, əm-, im-\ *n*

am·bas·sa·dress \am-'bas-ə-drəs, əm-, im-\ *n* 1 : a female ambassador 2 : the wife of an ambassador

[1]am·ber \'am-bər\ *n* [ME *ambre*, fr. MF, fr. ML *ambra*, fr. Ar *'anbar* ambergris] 1 : a hard yellowish to brownish translucent fossil resin that takes a fine polish and is used chiefly in making ornamental objects (as beads) 2 : a variable color averaging a dark orange yellow

[2]amber *adj* 1 : consisting of amber 2 : resembling amber; *esp* : having the color amber

am·ber·gris \-ˌgris, -ˌgrēs\ *n* [ME *ambregris*, fr. MF *ambre gris*, fr. *ambre* + *gris* gray — more at GRIZZLE] : a waxy substance found floating in or on the shores of tropical waters, believed to originate in the intestines of the sperm whale, and used in perfumery as a fixative

ambi- *prefix* [L *ambi-*, *amb-* both, around; akin to L *ambo* both, Gk *amphō* both, *amphi* around — more at BY] : both ⟨*ambi*valent⟩

am·bi·dex·trous \ˌam-bi-'dek-strəs\ *adj* [LL *ambidexter*, fr. L *ambi-* + *dexter*] 1 : using both hands with equal ease 2 : unusually skillful : VERSATILE 3 : characterized by duplicity : DOUBLE-DEALING — **am·bi·dex·trous·ly** *adv*

am·bi·ence *or* **am·bi·ance** \äⁿ-byäⁿs, 'am-bē-ən(t)s\ *n* : a surrounding or pervading atmosphere : ENVIRONMENT

am·bi·ent \'am-bē-ənt\ *adj* [L *ambient-*, *ambiens*, prp. of *ambire* to go around, fr. *ambi-* + *ire* to go — more at ISSUE] : surrounding on all sides : ENCOMPASSING

am·bi·gu·ity \ˌam-bə-'gyü-ət-ē\ *n* : the quality or state of being ambiguous in meaning; *also* : an ambiguous word or expression

am·big·u·ous \am-'big-yə-wəs\ *adj* [L *ambiguus*, fr. *ambigere* to wander about, fr. *ambi-* + *agere* to drive — more at AGENT] 1 : doubtful or uncertain esp. from obscurity or indistinctness; *also* : INEXPLICABLE 2 : capable of being understood in two or more possible senses : EQUIVOCAL **syn** see OBSCURE — **am·big·u·ous·ly** *adv* — **am·big·u·ous·ness** *n*

am·bit \'am-bət\ *n* [ME, fr. L *ambitus*, fr. *ambitus*, pp. of *ambire*] 1 : CIRCUIT, COMPASS 2 : PRECINCTS, BOUNDS

[1]am·bi·tion \am-'bish-ən\ *n* [ME, fr. MF or L; MF, fr. L *ambition-* *ambitio*, lit., going around, fr. *ambitus*, pp.] 1 a : an ardent desire for rank, fame, or power b : desire to achieve a particular end : ASPIRATION 2 : the object of ambition

syn AMBITION, ASPIRATION, PRETENSION mean strong desire for advancement. AMBITION applies to the desire for personal advancement or preferment and may suggest equally a praiseworthy or an inordinate desire; ASPIRATION implies a striving after something higher than oneself or one's present status which may be ennobling or uplifting or may be unwarranted and presumptuous; PRETENSION suggests ardent desire for recognition of accomplishment without actual possession of the necessary ability

[2]ambition *vt* : to have as one's ambition : DESIRE

am·bi·tious \am-'bish-əs\ *adj* 1 a : having or controlled by ambition b : having a desire to achieve a particular goal : ASPIRING 2 : resulting from, characterized by, or showing ambition — **am·bi·tious·ly** *adv*

am·biv·a·lence \am-'biv-ə-lən(t)s\ *n* [ISV] : simultaneous attraction toward and repulsion from an object, person, or action — **am·biv·a·lent** \-lənt\ *adj* — **am·biv·a·lent·ly** *adv*

am·bi·ver·sion \ˌam-bi-'vər-zhən, -shən\ *n* [*ambi-* + *-version* (as in *introversion*)] : the personality configuration of an ambivert — **am·bi·ver·sive** \-'vər-siv, -ziv\ *adj*

am·bi·vert \'am-bi-ˌvərt\ *n* [*ambi-* + *-vert* (as in *introvert*)] : a person having characteristics of both extrovert and introvert

[1]am·ble \'am-bəl\ *vi* **am·bling** \-b(ə-)liŋ\ [ME *amblen*, fr. MF *ambler*, fr. L *ambulare* to walk] : to go at or as if at an amble : SAUNTER

[2]amble *n* 1 a : an easy 4-beat equine gait with lateral motion b : [7]RACK b 2 : an easy gait 3 : a leisurely walk — **am·bler** \-b(ə-)lər\ *n*

am·blyg·o·nite \am-'blig-ə-ˌnīt\ *n* [G *amblygonit*, fr. Gk *amblygōnios* obtuse-angled, fr. *amblys* blunt + *gōnia* angle; akin to L *molere* to grind — more at MEAL, -GON] : a mineral (Li,Na) $AlPO_4(F,OH)$ consisting of basic lithium aluminum phosphate commonly containing sodium and fluorine and occurring in white cleavable masses

am·bly·o·pia \ˌam-blē-'ō-pē-ə\ *n* [NL, fr. Gk *amblyōpia*, fr. *amblys* + *-ōpia* -opia] : dimness of sight without apparent change in the eye structures associated esp. with toxic effects or dietary deficiencies — **am·bly·o·pic** \-'ō-pik, -'äp-ik\ *adj*

am·bo·cep·tor \'am-bō-ˌsep-tər\ *n* [ISV *ambi-* + *receptor*] : the lytic antibody used in complement-fixation tests

am·boy·na *or* **am·boi·na** \am-'bȯi-nə\ *n* [*Amboina*, Moluccas, Indonesia] : a mottled curly-grained wood of a leguminous tree (*Pterocarpus indicus*) of southeastern Asia

am·bro·sia \am-'brō-zh(ē-)ə\ *n* [L, fr. Gk, lit., immortality, fr. *ambrotos* immortal, fr. *a-* + *-mbrotos* (akin to *brotos* mortal) — more at MURDER] 1 a : the food of the Greek and Roman gods b : the ointment or perfume of the gods 2 : something extremely pleasing to taste or smell — **am·bro·sial** \-zh(ē-)əl\ *adj* — **am·bro·sial·ly** \-zh(ē-)ə-lē\ *adv*

Am·bro·sian \-zh(ē-)ən\ *adj* : of, relating to, or ascribed to St. Ambrose

am·bro·type \'am-brə-ˌtīp\ *n* [Gk *ambrotos* + E *type*] : a photograph made on glass by backing a thin negative with a black surface

am·bry \'am-brē; 'äm-rē, 'ȯm-\ *n* [ME *armarie*, fr. OF, fr. L *armarium*, fr. *arma* weapons — more at ARM] *dial chiefly Brit* : PANTRY; *also* : a cupboard or chest esp. for food

ambs·ace \'ām-ˌzās\ *n* [ME *ambes as*, fr. OF, fr. *ambes* both + *as* aces] *archaic* : the lowest throw at dice; *also* : something worthless or unlucky

am·bu·la·cral \ˌam-byə-'lak-rəl, -'lāk-\ *adj* : of or relating to an ambulacrum

am·bu·la·crum \-rəm\ *n, pl* **am·bu·la·cra** \-rə\ [NL, fr. L, alley, fr. *ambulare* to walk] : one of the radial areas of echinoderms along which run the principal nerves, blood vessels, and water tubes

am·bu·lance \'am-byə-lən(t)s\ *n* [F, field hospital, fr. *ambulant* itinerant, fr. L *ambulant-*, *ambulans*, prp. of *ambulare*] : a vehicle equipped for transporting wounded, injured, or sick persons or animals

ambulance chaser *n* : a lawyer or lawyer's agent who incites accident victims to bring suit for damages

am·bu·lant \'am-byə-lənt\ *adj* : moving about : AMBULATORY

am·bu·late \-ˌlāt\ *vi* [L *ambulatus*, pp. of *ambulare*] : to move from place to place : WALK — **am·bu·la·tion** \ˌam-byə-'lā-shən\ *n*

[1]am·bu·la·to·ry \'am-byə-lə-ˌtōr-ē, -ˌtȯr-\ *adj* 1 : of, relating to, or adapted to walking; *also* : occurring while walking 2 : moving from place to place : ITINERANT 3 : ALTERABLE 4 : able to walk about and not bedridden

[2]ambulatory *n* : a sheltered place to walk in (as in a cloister or church)

am·bus·cade \'am-bə-ˌskād\ *n* [MF *embuscade*, modif. of OIt *imboscata*, fr. *imboscare* to place in ambush, fr. *in* (fr. L) + *bosco* forest, perh. of Gmc origin; akin to OHG *busc* forest — more at IN, BUSH] : AMBUSH — **ambuscade** *vb* — **am·bus·cad·er** *n*

[1]am·bush \'am-ˌbu̇sh\ *vb* [ME *embushen*, fr. OF *embuschier*, fr. *en* in (fr. L *in*) + *busche* stick of firewood] *vt* 1 : to station in ambush 2 : to attack from an ambush : WAYLAY ~ *vi* : to lie in wait : LURK — **am·bush·ment** \-mənt\ *n*

[2]ambush *n* : a trap in which concealed persons lie in wait to attack by surprise; *also* : the persons lying in wait or their concealed position

ameba, ameban, amebic, ameboid *var of* AMOEBA, AMOEBAN, AMOEBIC, AMOEBOID

am·e·bi·a·sis \ˌam-i-'bī-ə-səs\ *n* : infection with or disease caused by amoebas

amebic dysentery *n* : acute intestinal amebiasis of man caused by an amoeba (*Endamoeba histolytica*) and marked by dysentery, griping pain, and erosion of the intestinal wall

amebocyte *var of* AMOEBOCYTE

âme dam·née \äm-dä-nā\ *n, pl* **âmes damnées** \äm-dä-nā(z)\ [F, lit., damned soul] : a willing tool of another person

ameer *var of* EMIR

ame·lio·rate \ə-'mēl-yə-ˌrāt, -'mē-lē-ə-\ *vb* [alter. of *meliorate*] *vt* : to make better or more tolerable ~ *vi* : to grow better **syn** see IMPROVE — **ame·lio·ra·tion** \-ˌmēl-yə-'rā-shən, -ˌmē-lē-ə-\ *n* — **ame·lio·ra·tive** \-'mēl-yə-ˌrāt-iv, -'mē-lē-ə-\ *adj* — **ame·lio·ra·tor** \-ˌrāt-ər\ *n* — **ame·lio·ra·to·ry** \-rə-ˌtōr-ē, -ˌtȯr-\ *adj*

amen \(')ā-'men, (')ä-\ *interj* [ME, fr. OE, fr. LL, fr. Gk *amēn*, fr. Heb *āmēn*] — used to express solemn ratification or hearty approval

ame·na·bil·i·ty \ə-ˌmē-nə-'bil-ət-ē, -ˌmen-ə-\ *n* : the quality or state of being amenable : TRACTABLENESS

ame·na·ble \ə-'mē-nə-bəl, -'men-ə-\ *adj* [prob. fr. (assumed) AF, fr. MF *amener* to lead up, fr. OF, fr. *a-* (fr. L ad-) + *mener* to lead, fr. L *minare* to drive, fr. *minari* to threaten — more at MOUNT] 1 : liable to be brought to account : ANSWERABLE 2 a : capable of submission to judgment or test b : readily brought to yield or submit : TRACTABLE **syn** see OBEDIENT, RESPONSIBLE — **ame·na·bly** \-blē\ *adv*

amen corner \ˌā-ˌmen-\ *n* : a conspicuous corner in a church occupied by fervent worshipers

amend \ə-'mend\ *vb* [ME *amenden*, fr. OF *amender*, modif. of L *emendare*, fr. *e*, *ex* out + *menda* fault; akin to L *mendax* lying, *mendicus* beggar, Skt *mindā* physical defect] *vt* 1 : to put right; *specif* : to make emendations in 2 a : to change or modify for the better : IMPROVE b : to alter esp. in phraseology; *specif* : to alter formally by modification, deletion, or addition ~ *vi* : to reform oneself **syn** see CORRECT — **amend·able** \-'men-də-bəl\ *adj* — **amend·er** *n*

amen·da·to·ry \ə-'men-də-ˌtōr-ē, -ˌtȯr-\ *adj* [*amend* + *-atory* (as in *emendatory*)] : CORRECTIVE

amend·ment \ə-'men(d)-mənt\ *n* 1 : the act of amending esp. for the better : CORRECTION 2 : a substance that aids plant growth indirectly by improving the condition of the soil 3 a : the process of amending by parliamentary or constitutional procedure b : an alteration proposed or effected by this process

amends \ə-'men(d)z\ *n pl but sing or pl in constr* [ME *amendes*, fr. OF, pl. of *amende* reparation, fr. *amender*] : compensation for a loss or injury : RECOMPENSE

ame·ni·ty \ə-'men-ət-ē, -'mē-nət-\ *n* [ME *amenite*, fr. L *amoenitat-*, *amoenitas*, fr. *amoenus* pleasant] 1 a : the quality of being pleasant or agreeable b (1) : the attractiveness and value of real estate or of a purely residential structure (2) : a feature conducive to such attractiveness and value 2 : something that conduces to material comfort or convenience 3 *usu pl* a : manner expressive of or conducive to pleasantness or smoothness of social intercourse b : an act or form conventionally observed esp. in social intercourse

amen·or·rhea \(ˌ)ā-ˌmen-ə-'rē-ə\ *n* [NL, fr. *a-* + Gk *mēn* month + NL *-o-* + *-rrhea* — more at MOON] : abnormal absence or sup-

pression of the menstrual discharge — **amen·or·rhe·ic** \-'rē-ik\ *adj*

ament \'am-ənt, 'ā-mənt\ *n* [NL *amentum*, fr. L, thong, strap] **:** an indeterminate spicate inflorescence bearing scaly bracts and apetalous unisexual flowers (as in the willow) — **amen·ta·ceous** \ˌam-ən-'tā-shəs, ˌā-mən-\ *adj* — **amen·tif·er·ous** \-'tif-(ə-)rəs\ *adj*

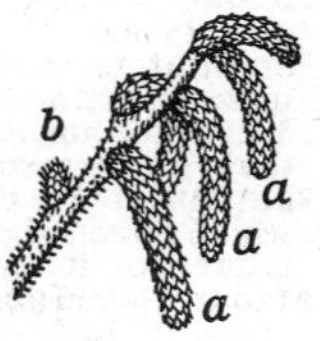

aments: *a, a, a,* staminate, *b* pistillate

amen·tia \(ˈ)ā-'men-ch(ē-)ə\ *n* [NL, fr. L, madness, fr. *ament-, amens* mad, fr. *a-* (fr. *ab-*) + *ment-, mens* mind — more at MIND] **:** mental deficiency; *specif* **:** a condition of lack of development of intellectual capacity

amerce \ə-'mərs\ *vt* [ME *amercien*, fr. AF *amercier*, fr. OF *a merci* at (one's) mercy] **:** to punish by a fine the amount of which is fixed by the court; *broadly* **:** PUNISH — **amerce·ment** \-'mər-smənt\ *n* — **amer·cia·ble** \-'mər-sē-ə-bəl, -'mər-shə-bəl\ *adj*

[1]**Amer·i·can** \ə-'mer-ə-kən\ *n* **1 :** an Indian of No. America or So. America **2 :** a native or inhabitant of No. America or So. America **3 :** a citizen of the U.S.

[2]**American** *adj* **1 :** of or relating to America **2 :** of or relating to the U.S. or its possessions or original territory **3 :** of or relating to the division of mankind that comprises the Indians of No. America and So. America

Amer·i·ca·na \ə-ˌmer-ə-'kan-ə, -'kän-, -'kā-nə\ *n pl* **:** materials concerning or characteristic of America, its civilization, or its culture; *also* **:** a collection of such materials

American chameleon *n* **:** a lizard (*Anolis carolinensis*) of the southeastern U.S.

American cheese *n* **1 :** cheddar cheese made in America **2 :** a process cheese made from American cheddar cheese

American English *n* **:** the native language of most inhabitants of the U.S. — used esp. with the implication that it is clearly distinguishable from British English yet not so divergent as to be a separate language

American Indian *n* **:** a member of any except usu. the Eskimos of the aboriginal peoples of the western hemisphere constituting one of the divisions of the Mongoloid stock

Amer·i·can·ism \ə-'mer-ə-kə-ˌniz-əm\ *n* **1 :** a characteristic feature of American English esp. as contrasted with British English **2 :** attachment or allegiance to the traditions, interests, or ideals of the U.S. **3 a :** a custom or trait peculiar to America **b :** the political principles and practices essential to American national culture

Amer·i·can·ist \-kə-nəst\ *n* **:** a specialist in the languages or cultures of the aboriginal inhabitants of America

American ivy *n* **:** VIRGINIA CREEPER

Amer·i·can·iza·tion \ə-ˌmer-ə-kə-nə-'zā-shən\ *n* **1 :** the act or process of americanizing **2 :** instruction of foreigners (as immigrants) in English and in U.S. history, government, and culture

amer·i·can·ize \ə-'mer-ə-kə-ˌnīz\ *vt, often cap* **:** to cause to acquire or conform to American characteristics **~** *vi, often cap* **:** to acquire or conform to American traits

American plan *n* **:** a hotel rate whereby guests are charged a fixed sum for room and meals combined

American sable *n* **:** a pine marten (*Martes americana*) or its fur

American saddle horse *n* **:** a 3-gaited or 5-gaited saddle horse of a breed developed chiefly in Kentucky from Thoroughbreds and native stock

American Standard Version *n* **:** an American revision of the Authorized Version of the Bible published in 1901 — called also *American Revised Version*

American trotter *n* **:** a Standardbred horse

am·er·i·ci·um \ˌam-ə-'ris(h)-ē-əm\ *n* **:** a radioactive metallic element produced by bombardment of uranium with high-energy helium nuclei — see ELEMENT table

Am·er·ind \'am-ə-ˌrind\ *n* [*American Indian*] **:** an American Indian or Eskimo — **Am·er·in·di·an** \ˌam-ə-'rin-dē-ən\ *adj* — **Am·er·in·dic** \-dik\ *adj*

amet·a·bol·ic \ˌā-ˌmet-ə-'bäl-ik\ *or* **ame·tab·o·lous** \-mə-'tab-ə-ləs\ *adj* [*a-* + Gk *metabolē* change — more at METABOLISM] **:** lacking metamorphosis — **ame·tab·o·lism** \-mə-'tab-ə-ˌliz-əm\ *n*

am·e·thyst \'am-ə-thəst, -(ˌ)thist\ *n* [ME *amatiste*, fr. OF & L; OF, fr. L *amethystus*, fr. Gk *amethystos*, lit., remedy against drunkenness, fr. *a-* + *methyein* to be drunk, fr. *methy* wine — more at MEAD] **1 a :** a clear purple or bluish violet variety of crystallized quartz much used as a jeweler's stone **b :** a deep purple variety of corundum **2 :** a variable color averaging a moderate purple — **am·e·thys·tine** \ˌam-ə-'this-tən\ *adj*

am·e·tro·pia \ˌam-ə-'trō-pē-ə\ *n* [NL, fr. Gk *ametros* without measure (fr. *a-* + *metron* measure) + NL *-opia* — more at MEASURE] **:** abnormal refractive condition of the eye in which images fail to focus upon the retina — **am·e·tro·pic** \-'trō-pik, -'träp-ik\ *adj*

Am·har·ic \am-'har-ik\ *n* **:** the Semitic language that is the official language of Ethiopia — **Amharic** *adj*

ami·a·bil·i·ty \ˌā-mē-ə-'bil-ət-ē\ *n* **:** the quality of being amiable

ami·a·ble \'ā-mē-ə-bəl\ *adj* [ME, fr. MF, fr. LL *amicabilis* friendly, fr. L *amicus* friend; akin to L *amare* to love] **1** *archaic* **:** PLEASING, ADMIRABLE **2 a** *obs* **:** AMOROUS **b :** generally agreeable **c :** having a friendly, sociable, and congenial disposition — **ami·a·ble·ness** *n* — **ami·a·bly** \-blē\ *adv*

syn GOOD-NATURED, OBLIGING, COMPLAISANT: AMIABLE implies having qualities that make one liked and easy to deal with or live with; GOOD-NATURED implies a cheerful desire to please or to be helpful and sometimes a willingness to be imposed upon; OBLIGING stresses a friendly readiness to be helpful; COMPLAISANT implies a courteous or amiable desire to please and sometimes suggests a weak lack of resistance

am·i·an·thus \ˌam-ē-'an(t)-thəs\ *or* **am·i·an·tus** \-'ant-əs\ *n* [L *amiantus*, fr. Gk *amiantos*, fr. *amiantos* unpolluted, fr. *a-* + *miainein* to pollute] **:** fine silky asbestos

am·i·ca·bil·i·ty \ˌam-i-kə-'bil-ət-ē\ *n* **:** the quality of being amicable

am·i·ca·ble \'am-i-kə-bəl\ *adj* [ME, fr. LL *amicabilis*] **:** characterized by friendship and goodwill **:** PEACEABLE — **am·i·ca·ble·ness** *n* — **am·i·ca·bly** \-blē\ *adv*

syn NEIGHBORLY, FRIENDLY: AMICABLE implies that the parties concerned are not disposed to quarrel and are at peace with each other; NEIGHBORLY implies a disposition to live on good terms with those nearby and to be helpful on principle; FRIENDLY positively implies cordiality and often warmth or intimacy of personal relations

am·ice \'am-əs\ *n* [ME *amis*, prob. fr. MF, pl. of *amit*, fr. ML *amictus*, fr. L, cloak, fr. *amicire* to wrap around, fr. *am-, amb-* around + *jacere* to throw — more at AMBI-, JET] **:** a liturgical vestment made of an oblong piece of cloth usu. of white linen and worn about the neck and shoulders and partly under the alb

ami·cro·nu·cle·ate \ˌā-ˌmī-krō-'n(y)ü-klē-ət\ *adj* **:** lacking a micronucleus

ami·cus cu·ri·ae \ə-ˌmē-kə-'sk(y)u̇r-ē-ˌī\ *n, pl* **ami·ci curiae** \-ˌmē-(ˌ)kē-'k(y)u̇r-\ [NL, lit., friend of the court] **:** a bystander that suggests or states some matter of law for the assistance of a court

amid \ə-'mid\ *or* **amidst** \-'midst, -'mitst\ *prep* [*amid* fr. ME *amidde*, fr. OE *onmiddan*, fr. *on* + *middan*, dat. of *midde* mid; *amidst* fr. ME *amiddes*, fr. *amidde* + *-es* -s] **1 :** in or into the middle of **:** AMONG **2 :** DURING

amid- *or* **amido-** *comb form* [ISV, fr. *amide*] **1 :** containing the group NH_2 characteristic of amides united to a radical of acid character ⟨*amido*sulfuric⟩ **2 :** AMIN- ⟨*amido*phenol⟩

am·ide \'am-ˌīd, -əd\ *n* [ISV, fr. NL *ammonia*] **:** a compound resulting from replacement of an atom of hydrogen in ammonia by an element or radical or of one or more atoms of hydrogen in ammonia by univalent acid radicals — compare IMIDE — **amid·ic** \ə-'mid-ik, a-\ *adj*

ami·do \ə-'mēd-(ˌ)ō, 'am-ə-ˌdō\ *adj* [*amid-*] **1 :** relating to or containing the group NH_2 or a substituted group NHR or NR_2 united to a radical of acid character — compare AMINO **2 :** AMINO

am·i·dol \'am-ə-ˌdȯl, -ˌdōl\ *n* [G, fr. *Amidol*, a trademark] **:** a colorless crystalline salt $C_6H_3(NH_2)_2OH.2HCl$ used chiefly as a photographic developer

amid·ships \ə-'mid-ˌships\ *adv* **:** in or toward the part of a ship midway between the bow and the stern

ami·go \ə-'mē-(ˌ)gō, ä-\ *n, pl* **amigos** [Sp, fr. L *amicus* — more at AMIABLE] **:** FRIEND

amin- *or* **amino-** *comb form* [ISV, fr. *amine*] **:** containing the group NH_2 united to a radical other than an acid radical ⟨*amino*benzoic acid⟩

amine \ə-'mēn, 'am-ən\ *n* [ISV, fr. NL *ammonia*] **:** any of various compounds derived from ammonia by replacement of hydrogen by one or more univalent hydrocarbon radicals — **ami·nic** \ə-'mē-nik, a-, -'min-ik\ *adj*

ami·no \ə-'mē-(ˌ)nō, 'am-ə-ˌnō\ *adj* [*amin-*] **:** relating to or containing the group NH_2 or a substituted group NHR or NR_2 united to a radical other than an acid radical — compare AMIDO

amino acid *n* **:** an amphoteric organic acid containing the amino group NH_2; *esp* **:** any of the alpha-amino acids that are the chief components of proteins

ami·no·ben·zo·ic acid \ə-ˌmē-(ˌ)nō-(ˌ)ben-ˌzō-ik-, ˌam-ə-(ˌ)nō-\ *n* [ISV] **:** any of three crystalline derivatives $C_7H_7NO_2$ of benzoic acid of which the yellowish para-substituted acid is a growth factor of the vitamin B complex and of folic acids

amino nitrogen *n* **:** nitrogen occurring as a constituent of the amino group

ami·no·py·rine \ə-ˌmē-nō-'pī(ə)r-ˌēn, ˌam-ə-nō-\ *n* [ISV, fr. *amin-* + anti*pyrine*] **:** a white crystalline powder $C_{13}H_{17}N_3O$ used to relieve fever and pain

amir *var of* EMIR

Amish \'äm-ish, 'am-\ *adj* **:** of or relating to a strict sect of Mennonite followers of the Swiss Mennonite bishop Amman that settled in America — **Amish** *n* — **Amish·man** \-mən\ *n*

[1]**amiss** \ə-'mis\ *adv* **1 a :** WRONGLY, FAULTILY **b :** ASTRAY **2 :** IMPROPERLY

[2]**amiss** *adj* **1 :** WRONG **2 :** FAULTY, IMPERFECT **3 :** IMPROPER — usu. used predicatively

ami·to·sis \ˌā-(ˌ)mī-'tō-səs\ *n* [NL] **:** cell division in which simple cleavage of the nucleus is followed by the division of the cytoplasm — **ami·tot·ic** \-'tät-ik\ *adj* — **ami·tot·i·cal·ly** \-i-k(ə-)lē\ *adv*

am·i·ty \'am-ət-ē\ *n* [ME *amite*, fr. MF *amité*, fr. ML *amicitas*, fr. L *amicus* friend — more at AMIABLE] **:** FRIENDSHIP; *esp* **:** friendly relations between nations

am·me·ter \'am-ˌēt-ər\ *n* [*am*pere + *-meter*] **:** an instrument for measuring electric current in amperes

am·mine \'am-ˌēn, -ən; ə-'mēn, a-\ *n* **1 :** a molecule of ammonia as it exists in a coordination complex ⟨hex-*ammine*-cobalt chloride $[Co(NH_3)_6]Cl_3$⟩ **2 :** an ammino compound

am·mi·no \'am-ə-ˌnō; ə-'mē-(ˌ)nō, a-\ *adj* [ISV *ammino-*, fr. *ammine*] **:** of, relating to, or being an ammine

am·mo \'am-(ˌ)ō\ *n* [by shortening & alter.] **:** AMMUNITION

am·mo·nia \ə-'mō-nyə\ *n* [NL, fr. L *sal ammoniacus* sal ammoniac, lit., salt of Ammon, fr. Gk *ammōniakos* of Ammon, fr. *Ammōn* Ammon, Amen, an Egyptian god near one of whose temples it was prepared] **1 :** a pungent colorless gaseous alkaline compound of nitrogen and hydrogen NH_3 that is very soluble in water and can easily be condensed by cold and pressure to a liquid **2 :** AMMONIA WATER

am·mo·ni·ac \ə-'mō-nē-ˌak\ *n* [ME & L; ME, fr. L *ammoniacum*, fr. Gk *ammōniakon*, fr. neut. of *ammōniakos* of Ammon] **:** the aromatic gum resin of a Persian herb (*Dorema ammoniacum*) of the carrot family used as an expectorant and stimulant and in plasters

am·mo·ni·a·cal \ˌam-ə-'nī-ə-kəl\ *or* **am·mo·ni·ac** \ə-'mō-nē-ˌak\ *adj* **:** of, relating to, containing, or having the properties of ammonia

am·mo·ni·ate \ə-'mō-nē-ˌāt\ *vt* **1 :** to combine or impregnate with ammonia or an ammonium compound **2 :** AMMONIFY — **am·mo·ni·a·tion** \ə-ˌmō-nē-'ā-shən\ *n*

ammonia water *n* **:** a water solution of ammonia

am·mo·ni·fi·ca·tion \ə-ˌmō-nə-fə-'kā-shən\ *n* **1 :** AMMONIATION **2 :** decomposition with production of ammonia or ammonium compounds esp. by the action of bacteria on nitrogenous organic matter — **am·mo·ni·fi·er** \ə-'mō-nə-ˌfī(-ə)r\ *n* — **am·mo·ni·fy** \-ˌfī\ *vb*

am·mo·nite \ˈam-ə-ˌnīt\ *n* [NL *ammonites,* fr. L *cornu Ammonis,* lit., horn of Ammon] **:** any of numerous flat spiral fossil shells of cephalopods (order Ammonoidea) esp. abundant in the Mesozoic age — **am·mo·nit·ic** \ˌam-ə-ˈnit-ik\ *adj*

Am·mon·ite \ˈam-ə-ˌnīt\ *n* [LL *Ammonites,* fr. Heb *ʽAmmōn,* Ammon (son of Lot), descendant of Ammon] **:** a member of a Semitic people who in Old Testament times lived east of the Jordan between the Jabbok and the Arnon — **Ammonite** *adj*

am·mo·nium \ə-ˈmō-nē-əm, -nyəm\ *n* **:** an ion NH_4^+ or radical NH_4 derived from ammonia by combination with a hydrogen ion or atom and known in compounds (as salts) that resemble in properties the compounds of the alkali metals and in organic compounds (as quaternary ammonium compounds)

ammonium chloride *n* **:** a white crystalline volatile salt NH_4Cl used in dry cells and as an expectorant — called also *sal ammoniac*

ammonium hydroxide *n* **:** a weakly basic compound NH_4OH that is formed when ammonia dissolves in water and that exists only in solution

ammonium nitrate *n* **:** a colorless crystalline salt NH_4NO_3 used in explosives and fertilizers

ammonium sulfate *n* **:** a colorless crystalline salt $(NH_4)_2SO_4$ used chiefly as a fertilizer

am·mo·noid \ˈam-ə-ˌnȯid\ *n* **:** AMMONITE

am·mu·ni·tion \ˌam-yə-ˈnish-ən\ *n* [obs. F *amunition,* fr. MF, alter. of *munition*] **1 a :** the projectiles with their fuzes, propelling charges, and primers fired from guns **b :** explosive military items (as grenades, bombs) **2 :** any material used in attack or defense

am·ne·sia \am-ˈnē-zhə\ *n* [NL, fr. Gk *amnēsia* forgetfulness, prob. alter. of *amnēstia*] **1 :** loss of memory due usu. to brain injury, shock, fatigue, repression, or illness **2 :** a gap in one's memory — **am·ne·si·ac** \-z(h)ē-ˌak\ *or* **am·ne·sic** \-zik, -sik\ *adj or n* — **am·nes·tic** \-ˈnes-tik\ *adj*

am·nes·ty \ˈam-nə-stē\ *n* [Gk *amnēstia* forgetfulness, fr. *amnēstos* forgotten, fr. *a-* + *mnasthai* to remember — more at MIND] **:** the act of an authority (as a government) by which pardon is granted to a large group of individuals — **amnesty** *vt*

am·ni·on \ˈam-nē-ˌän, -ən\ *n, pl* **amnions** *or* **am·nia** \-nē-ə\ [NL, fr. Gk, caul, prob. fr. dim. of *amnos* lamb — more at YEAN] **1 :** a thin membrane forming a closed sac about the embryos of reptiles, birds, and mammals and containing a serous fluid in which the embryo is immersed **2 :** an analogous membrane of various invertebrates — **am·ni·ote** \-nē-ˌōt\ *adj or n* — **am·ni·ot·ic** \ˌam-nē-ˈät-ik\ *adj*

amoe·ba \ə-ˈmē-bə\ *n, pl* **amoebas** *or* **amoe·bae** \-(ˌ)bē\ [NL, genus name, fr. Gk *amoibē* change, fr. *ameibein* to change — more at MIGRATE] **:** any of a large genus (*Amoeba*) of naked rhizopod protozoans with lobed and never anastomosing pseudopodia and without permanent organelles or supporting structures that are widely distributed in fresh and salt water and moist terrestrial situations; *broadly* **:** a naked rhizopod or other amoeboid protozoan — **amoe·bic** \-bik\ *also* **amoe·ban** \-bən\ *adj*

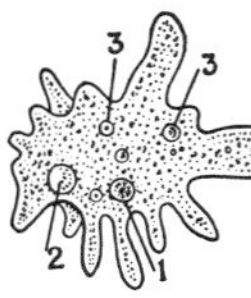

amoeba: *1* nucleus; *2* contractile vacuole; *3,3* food vacuole

amoebiasis *var of* AMEBIASIS

amoe·bo·cyte \ə-ˈmē-bə-ˌsīt\ *n* **:** a cell (as a phagocyte) having amoeboid form or movements

amoe·boid \-ˌbȯid\ *adj* **:** resembling an amoeba specif. in moving or changing in shape by means of protoplasmic flow

¹**amok** \ə-ˈmək, -ˈmäk\ *adv* [Malay *amok*] **:** in a murderously frenzied state or violently raging manner ⟨run ~⟩

²**amok** *adj* **:** possessed with a murderous or violently uncontrollable frenzy

³**amok** *n* **:** a murderous frenzy that occurs chiefly among Malays

amo·le \ə-ˈmō-lē\ *n* [Sp, fr. Nahuatl *amolli* soap] **:** a plant part (as a root) possessing detergent properties and serving as a substitute for soap; *also* **:** a plant so used

among \ə-ˈməŋ\ *also* **amongst** \-ˈməŋ(k)st\ *prep* [*among* fr. ME, fr. OE *on gemonge,* fr. *on* + *gemonge,* dat. of *gemong* crowd, fr. *ge-* (associative prefix) + *-mong* (akin to OE *mengan* to mix); *amongst* fr. ME *amonges,* fr. *among* + *-es* -s — more at CO-, MINGLE] **1 :** in or through the midst of **:** surrounded by **2 :** in company or association with ⟨living ~ artists⟩ **3 :** by or through the aggregate of ⟨discontent ~ the poor⟩ **4 :** in the number or class of ⟨wittiest ~ poets⟩ **5 :** in shares to each of ⟨divided ~ the heirs⟩ **6 a :** through the reciprocal acts of ⟨quarrel ~ themselves⟩ **b :** through the joint action of ⟨made a fortune ~ themselves⟩

amon·til·la·do \ə-ˌmän-tə-ˈläd-(ˌ)ō, -ti(l)-ˈyäth-(ˌ)ō\ *n* [Sp, fr. *a* to + *montilla* a sherry from Montilla, Spain] **:** a pale dry sherry

amor·al \(ˈ)ā-ˈmȯr-əl, (ˈ)a-, -ˈmär-\ *adj* **1 :** neither moral nor immoral; *specif* **:** outside the sphere to which moral judgments apply **2 :** lacking moral sensibility ⟨infants are ~⟩ — **amor·al·ism** \-ə-ˌliz-əm\ *n* — **amo·ral·i·ty** \ˌā-mə-ˈral-ət-ē, ˌa-, -(ˌ)mȯ-\ *n* — **amor·al·ly** \(ˈ)ā-ˈmȯr-ə-lē, (ˈ)a-, -ˈmär-\ *adv*

amo·ret·to \ˌam-ə-ˈret-(ˌ)ō, ˌäm-\ *n, pl* **amo·ret·ti** \-ˈret-(ˌ)ē\ *or* **amorettos** [It, dim. of *amore*] **:** CUPID, CHERUB 3

am·or·ist \ˈam-ə-rəst\ *n* **:** a devotee of love and esp. sexual love **:** GALLANT — **am·or·is·tic** \ˌam-ə-ˈris-tik\ *adj*

Am·o·rite \ˈam-ə-ˌrīt\ *n* [Heb *Ĕmōrī*] **:** a member of one of various Semitic peoples living in Mesopotamia, Syria, and Palestine during the 3d and 2d millenniums B.C. — **Amorite** *adj*

am·o·rous \ˈam-(ə-)rəs\ *adj* [ME, fr. MF, fr. ML *amorosus,* fr. L *amor* love, fr. *amare* to love] **1 :** inclined to love and esp. sexual love **2 :** being in love **:** ENAMORED **3 a :** indicative of love **b :** of or relating to love — **am·o·rous·ly** *adv* — **am·o·rous·ness** *n*

amor·phism \ə-ˈmȯr-ˌfiz-əm\ *n* **:** amorphous quality

amor·phous \-fəs\ *adj* [Gk *amorphos,* fr. *a-* + *morphē* form] **:** having no determinate form **:** SHAPELESS: as **a :** lacking complex bodily organization **b :** lacking division into parts **c :** UNCRYSTALLIZED — **amor·phous·ly** *adv* — **amor·phous·ness** *n*

amort \ə-ˈmȯ(ə)rt\ *adj* [short for *all-a-mort,* by folk etymology fr. MF *a la mort* to the death] *archaic* **:** at the point of death

amor·ti·za·tion \ˌam-ərt-ə-ˈzā-shən, ə-ˌmȯrt-\ *n* **1 :** the act or process of amortizing **2 :** the result of amortizing

am·or·tize \ˈam-ər-ˌtīz *also* ə-ˈmȯr-ˌtīz\ *vt* [ME *amortisen* to deaden, alienate in mortmain, modif. of MF *amortiss-,* stem of *amortir,* fr. (assumed) VL *admortire* to deaden, fr. L *ad-* + *mort-, mors* death — more at MURDER] **:** to provide for the gradual extinguishment of (as a mortgage) usu. by contribution to a sinking fund at the time of each periodic interest payment

Amos \ˈā-məs\ *n* [Heb *ʽĀmōs*] **:** a Hebrew prophet of the 8th century B.C.

¹**amount** \ə-ˈmau̇nt\ *vi* [ME *amounten,* fr. OF *amonter,* fr. *amont* upward, fr. *a-* (fr. L *ad-*) + *mont* mountain — more at MOUNT] **1 :** to add up ⟨bill ~*ed* to 10 dollars⟩ **2 :** to be equivalent ⟨acts that ~ to treason⟩

²**amount** *n* **1 :** the total number or quantity **:** AGGREGATE **2 :** the whole effect, significance, or import **3 :** a principal sum and the interest on it **syn** see SUM

amour \ə-ˈmu̇(ə)r, a-, ä-\ *n* [ME, love, affection, fr. OF, fr. OProv *amor,* fr. L, fr. *amare* to love] **:** a love affair esp. when illicit

amour pro·pre \ˌam-ˌu̇r-ˈprȯprᵊ, ˌäm-, -ˈprȯprᵊ\ *n* [F, lit., love of oneself] **:** SELF-ESTEEM

am·pe·lop·sis \ˌam-pə-ˈläp-səs\ *n* [NL, fr. Gk *ampelos* grapevine + *opsis* appearance — more at OPTIC] **:** any of a genus (*Parthenocissus*) of the grape family that includes the Virginia creeper

am·per·age \ˈam-p(ə-)rij, -ˌpi(ə)r-ij\ *n* **:** the strength of a current of electricity expressed in amperes

am·pere \ˈam-ˌpi(ə)r\ *n* [Andre M. *Ampère* †1836 F physicist] **:** the practical mks unit of electric current that is equivalent to a flow of one coulomb per second or to the steady current produced by one volt applied across a resistance of one ohm

ampere–hour *n* **:** a unit of electricity equal to the quantity carried past any point of a circuit in one hour by a steady current of one ampere

ampere–turn *n* **:** the mks unit of magnetomotive force equal to the magnetomotive force around a path that links with one turn of wire carrying an electric current of one ampere

am·per·sand \ˈam-pər-ˌsand\ *n* [alter. of *and* (&) *per se and,* lit., (the character) & by itself (is the word) *and*] **:** a character & standing for the word *and*

am·phet·amine \am-ˈfet-ə-ˌmēn, -mən\ *n* [ISV *alpha-methyl-phenethyl* + *amine*] **:** a compound $C_9H_{13}N$ used esp. as an inhalant and in solution as a spray in head colds and hay fever

amphi- *or* **amph-** *prefix* [L *amphi-* around, on both sides, fr. Gk *amphi-, amph-,* fr. *amphi* — more at AMBI-] **:** on both sides **:** of both kinds **:** both ⟨*amphi*biotic⟩ ⟨*amph*istylar⟩

am·phi·ar·thro·sis \ˌam(p)-fē-(ˌ)är-ˈthrō-səs\ *n* [NL] **:** articulation admitting slight motion and including symphysis and syndesmosis

am·phib·ia \am-ˈfib-ē-ə\ *n pl* **:** AMPHIBIANS

am·phib·i·an \-ē-ən\ *n* [deriv. of Gk *amphibion* amphibious being, fr. neut. of *amphibios*] **1 :** an amphibious organism; *esp* **:** any of a class (Amphibia) of cold-blooded vertebrates intermediate in many characters between fishes and reptiles with gilled aquatic larvae and air-breathing adults **2 :** an airplane designed to take off from and land on either land or water **3 :** a flat-bottomed vehicle that moves on tracks having finlike extensions by means of which it is propelled on land or water — **amphibian** *adj*

am·phi·bi·ot·ic \ˌam(p)-fi-(ˌ)bī-ˈät-ik\ *adj* [ISV] **:** terrestrial in one stage of existence and aquatic in another

am·phib·i·ous \am-ˈfib-ē-əs\ *adj* [Gk *amphibios,* lit., living a double life, fr. *amphi-* + *bios* mode of life — more at QUICK] **1 :** able to live both on land and in water ⟨~ plants⟩ **2 a :** relating to or adapted for both land and water **b :** executed by coordinated action of land, sea, and air forces organized for invasion; *also* **:** trained or organized for such action **3 :** combining two characteristics — **am·phib·i·ous·ly** *adv* — **am·phib·i·ous·ness** *n*

am·phi·bole \ˈam(p)-fə-ˌbōl\ *n* [F, fr. LL *amphibolus,* fr. Gk *amphibolos* ambiguous fr. *amphiballein* to throw round, doubt, fr. *amphi-* + *ballein* to throw — more at DEVIL] **1 :** HORNBLENDE **2 :** any of a group of minerals $A_2B_5(Si,Al)_8O_{22}(OH)_2$ with like crystal structures usu. containing three groups of metal ions

am·phib·o·lite \am-ˈfib-ə-ˌlīt\ *n* **:** a usu. metamorphic rock consisting essentially of amphibole — **am·phib·o·lit·ic** \(ˌ)am-ˌfib-ə-ˈlit-ik\ *adj*

am·phi·bol·o·gy \ˌam(p)-fə-ˈbäl-ə-jē\ *n* [ME *amphibologie,* fr. LL *amphibologia,* alter. of L *amphibolia,* fr. Gk *amphibolos*] **1 :** ambiguity in language **2 :** a phrase or sentence ambiguous because of its grammatical construction — called also *amphiboly*

am·phi·brach \ˈam(p)-fə-ˌbrak\ *n* [L *amphibrachys,* fr. Gk, lit., short at both ends, fr. *amphi-* + *brachys* short — more at BRIEF] **:** a metrical foot consisting of a long syllable between two short syllables in quantitative verse or of a stressed syllable between two unstressed syllables in accentual verse ⟨*romantic* is an accentual ~⟩ — **am·phi·brach·ic** \ˌam(p)-fə-ˈbrak-ik\ *adj*

am·phic·ty·on·ic \(ˌ)am-ˌfik-tē-ˈän-ik\ *adj* **:** relating to an amphictyony

am·phic·ty·o·ny \am-ˈfik-tē-ə-nē\ *n* [Gk *amphiktyonia*] **:** an association of neighboring states in ancient Greece to defend a common religious center; *broadly* **:** an association of neighboring states for their common interest

am·phi·dip·loid \ˌam(p)-fi-ˈdip-ˌlȯid\ *adj, of an interspecific hybrid* **:** having a complete diploid chromosome set from each parent strain — **amphidiploid** *n* — **am·phi·dip·loi·dy** \-ˌlȯid-ē\ *n*

am·phim·a·cer \am-ˈfim-ə-sər\ *n* [L *amphimacrus,* fr. Gk *amphimakros,* lit., long at both ends, fr. *amphi-* + *makros* long] **:** a metrical foot consisting of a short syllable between two long syllables in quantitative verse or of an unstressed syllable between two stressed syllables in accentual verse ⟨*runaway* is an accentual ~⟩

am·phi·mic·tic \ˌam(p)-fi-ˈmik-tik\ *adj* [ISV *amphi-* + Gk *miktos* blended, fr. *mignynai*] **:** capable of interbreeding freely and of producing fertile offspring — **am·phi·mic·ti·cal·ly** \-ti-k(ə-)lē\ *adv*

am·phi·mix·is \-ˈmik-səs\ *n* [NL, fr. *amphi-* + Gk *mixis* mingling, fr. *meignynai* to mix — more at MIX] **1 :** the union of germ cells in sexual reproduction **2 :** INTERBREEDING

Am·phi·on \am-ˈfī-ən\ *n* [L, fr. Gk *Amphiōn*] **:** a son of Zeus and Antiope noted for building the walls of Thebes by charming the stones into place with a lyre

am·phi·ox·us \ˌam(p)-fē-ˈäk-səs\ *n* [NL, fr. *amphi-* + Gk *oxys* sharp] **:** LANCELET; *esp* **:** any of a genus (*Branchiostoma*)

am·phi·ploid \ˈam(p)-fi-ˌplȯid\ *adj, of an interspecific hybrid* **:** having at least one complete diploid set of chromosomes derived from each ancestral species — **amphiploid** *n* — **am·phi·ploi·dy** \-ˌplȯid-ē\ *n*

am·phi·pod \-ˌpäd\ *n* [deriv. of Gk *amphi-* + *pod-, pous* foot — more at FOOT] **:** any of a large group (Amphipoda) of crustaceans comprising the sand fleas and related forms — **amphipod** *adj*

am·phi·pro·style \ˌam(p)-fi-ˈprō-ˌstīl\ *adj* [L *amphiprostylos,* fr.

Gk, fr. *amphi-* + *prostylos* having pillars in front, fr. *pro-* + *stylos* pillar] **:** having columns at each end only — **amphipro·style** *n*
am·phis·bae·na \ˌam(p)-fəs-ˈbē-nə\ *n* [L, fr. Gk *amphisbaina*, fr. *amphis* on both sides (fr. *amphi* around) + *bainein* to walk, go — more at BY, COME] **:** a serpent in classical mythology having a head at each end and capable of moving in either direction — **am·phis·bae·nic** \-nik\ *adj*
am·phi·sty·lar \ˌam(p)-fi-ˈstī-lər\ *adj* **:** having columns at both ends or on both sides
am·phi·the·ater \ˈam(p)-fə-ˌthē-ət-ər, -ˌthi-\ *n* [L *amphitheatrum*, fr. Gk *amphitheatron*, fr. *amphi-* + *theatron* theater] **1 :** an oval or circular building with rising tiers of seats about an open space **2 a :** a very large auditorium; *also* **:** ARENA **b :** a room with a gallery from which doctors and students may observe surgical operations **c :** a rising gallery in a modern theater **d :** a flat or gently sloping area surrounded by abrupt slopes — **am·phi·the·at·ric** \ˌam(p)-fə-thē-ˈa-trik\ *or* **am·phi·the·at·ri·cal** \-tri-kəl\ *adj* — **am·phi·the·at·ri·cal·ly** \-tri-k(ə-)lē\ *adv*
Am·phi·tri·te \ˌam(p)-fə-ˈtrīt-ē, ˈam(p)-fə-ˌ\ *n* [L, fr. Gk *Amphitritē*] **:** a Nereid and wife of Poseidon
am·phit·ro·pous \am-ˈfi-trə-pəs\ *adj* **:** having the ovule inverted but with the attachment near the middle of one side
Am·phi·try·on \am-ˈfi-trē-ən\ *n* [L, fr. Gk *Amphitryōn*] **:** the husband of Alcmene
am·pho·ra \ˈam(p)-fə-rə\ *n, pl* **am·pho·rae** \-ˌrē, -ˌrī\ *or* **am·phoras** [L, modif. of Gk *amphoreus*, *amphiphoreus*, fr. *amphi-* + *phoreus* bearer, fr. *pherein* to bear — more at BEAR] **:** an ancient Greek jar or vase with a large oval body, narrow cylindrical neck, and two handles that rise almost to the level of the mouth
am·pho·ter·ic \ˌam(p)-fə-ˈter-ik\ *adj* [ISV, fr. Gk *amphoteros* each of two, fr. *amphō* both — more at AMBI-] **:** partly one and partly the other; *specif* **:** capable of reacting chemically either as an acid or as a base
am·ple \ˈam-pəl\ *adj* [MF, fr. L *amplus*] **1 :** generous or more than adequate in size, scope, or capacity **:** COPIOUS **2 a :** enough to satisfy **:** ABUNDANT **b :** more than enough **syn** see PLENTIFUL — **am·ple·ness** *n* — **am·ply** \-plē\ *adv*
am·plex·i·caul \am-ˈplek-si-ˌkȯl\ *adj* [NL *amplexicaulis*, fr. L *amplexus* (pp. of *amplecti* to entwine, fr. *ambi-* + *plectere* to braid) + *-i-* + *caulis* stem — more at HOLE] *of a leaf* **:** sessile with the base or stipules surrounding the stem
am·pli·dyne \ˈam-plə-ˌdīn\ *n* [*ampli*fier + Gk *dyn*amis power — more at DYNAMIC] **:** a direct-current generator that by the use of compensating coils and a short circuit across two of its brushes precisely controls a large power output whenever a small power input is varied in the field winding of the generator
am·pli·fi·ca·tion \ˌam-plə-fə-ˈkā-shən\ *n* **1 :** an act, example, or product of amplifying **2 a :** matter by which a statement is expanded **b :** an expanded statement
am·pli·fi·er \ˈam-plə-ˌfī(-ə)r\ *n* **:** one that amplifies; *specif* **:** a device usu. employing vacuum tubes or transistors to obtain amplification of voltage, current, or power
am·pli·fy \-ˌfī\ *vb* [ME *amplifien*, fr. MF *amplifier*, fr. L *amplificare*, fr. *amplus*] *vt* **1 :** to expand (as a statement) by clarifying detail or illustration or by closer analysis **2 :** INCREASE, EXTEND **3 :** to utilize (an input of power) so as to obtain an output of greater magnitude through the relay action of a transducer ~ *vi* **:** to expand one's remarks or ideas **syn** see EXPAND
am·pli·tude \-ˌt(y)üd\ *n* **1 :** the quality or state of being ample **:** FULLNESS **2 :** the extent or range of a quality, property, process, or phenomenon: as **a :** the extent of a vibratory movement (as of a pendulum) measured from the mean position to an extreme **b :** the maximum departure of the value of an alternating current or wave from the average value **3 :** the arc of the horizon between the true east or west point and the foot of the vertical circle passing through any star or object
amplitude modulation *n* **:** modulation of the amplitude of a radio carrier wave in accordance with the strength of the audio or other signal; *also* **:** a broadcasting system using such modulation
am·pul *or* **am·poule** \ˈam-(ˌ)pyü(ə)l, -(ˌ)pül\ *n* [ME *ampulle* flask, fr. OE & OF; OE *ampulle* & OF *ampoule*, fr. L *ampulla*] **:** a small bulbous glass vessel hermetically sealed and used to hold a solution for hypodermic injection
am·pul·la \am-ˈpu̇l-ə, -ˈpəl-\ *n, pl* **am·pul·lae** \-(ˌ)ē, -ˌī\ [ME, fr. OE, fr. L, dim. of *amphora*] **1 :** a glass or earthenware flask with a globular body and two handles used esp. by the ancient Romans to hold ointment, perfume, or wine **2 :** a saccular anatomic swelling or pouch — **am·pul·lar** \-ər\ *adj*
am·pu·tate \ˈam-pyə-ˌtāt\ *vt* [L *amputatus*, pp. of *amputare*, fr. *am-*, *amb-* around + *putare* to cut, prune — more at AMBI-, PAVE] **:** to cut or lop off **:** PRUNE; *esp* **:** to cut (a limb or projecting part) from the body — **am·pu·ta·tion** \ˌam-pyə-ˈtā-shən\ *n* — **am·pu·ta·tor** \ˈam-pyə-ˌtāt-ər\ *n*
am·pu·tee \ˌam-pyə-ˈtē\ *n* **:** one that has had a limb amputated
am·trac *or* **am·track** \ˈam-ˌtrak\ *n* [*am*phibious + *trac*tor] **:** AMPHIBIAN
amuck \ə-ˈmək\ *var of* AMOK
am·u·let \ˈam-yə-lət\ *n* [L *amuletum*] **:** a charm (as an ornament) often inscribed with a magic incantation or symbol to protect the wearer against evil or to aid him **syn** see FETISH
amuse \ə-ˈmyüz\ *vb* [MF *amuser*, fr. OF, fr. *a-* (fr. L *ad-*) + *muser* to muse] *vt* **1 a** *archaic* **:** to divert the attention of **:** BEMUSE **b** *obs* **:** to occupy the attention of **:** ABSORB **2 a :** to entertain or occupy in a light, playful, or pleasant manner **:** DIVERT **b :** to appeal to the sense of humor of ~ *vi, obs* **:** MUSE — **amus·er** *n*
syn DIVERT, ENTERTAIN: AMUSE stresses engaging the attention so as to keep one interested or engrossed usu. lightly or frivolously; DIVERT implies the distracting of the attention from worry or routine occupation esp. by something causing laughter or gaiety; ENTERTAIN suggests the activity of supplying amusement or diversion by specially prepared or contrived methods
amuse·ment \-mənt\ *n* **1 :** a means of amusing or entertaining **2 :** the condition of being amused **3 :** pleasurable diversion **:** ENTERTAINMENT
amusement park *n* **:** a commercially operated park with various devices for entertainment
amus·ing \-ˈmyü-ziŋ\ *adj* **:** giving amusement **:** DIVERTING — **amus·ing·ly** \-ziŋ-lē\ *adv*
amu·sive \-ˈmyü-ziv, -siv\ *adj* **:** tending to amuse or to tickle the fancy or excite mirth **:** AMUSING
amyg·da·lin \ə-ˈmig-də-lən\ *n* [NL *Amygdalus*, genus name, fr. LL, almond tree, fr. Gk *amygdalos*; akin to Gk *amygdalē*] **:** a white crystalline cyanogenetic glucoside $C_{20}H_{27}NO_{11}$ found in the bitter almond (*Amygdalus communis amara*)
¹**amyg·da·loid** \-ˌlȯid\ *n* [Gk *amygdaloeidēs*, adj.] **:** an igneous and usu. volcanic rock orig. containing small cavities filled with deposits of different minerals (as chalcedony or calcite)
²**amygdaloid** *or* **amyg·da·loi·dal** \-ˌmig-də-ˈlȯid-ᵊl\ *adj* [Gk *amygdaloeidēs*, fr. *amygdalē* almond] **1 :** almond-shaped **2 :** having the characteristics of amygdaloid
am·yl \ˈam-əl\ *n* [blend of *amyl-* and *-yl*] **:** the normal pentyl radical $CH_3(CH_2)_3CH_2$—; *broadly* **:** PENTYL
amyl- *or* **amylo-** *comb form* [LL *amyl-*, fr. L *amylum*, fr. Gk *amylon*, fr. neut. of *amylos* not ground at the mill, fr. *a-* + *mylē* mill — more at MEAL] **:** starch ⟨*amyl*ase⟩
am·y·la·ceous \ˌam-ə-ˈlā-shəs\ *adj* **:** of, relating to, or having the characteristics of starch **:** STARCHY
amyl alcohol *n* **:** either of two commercially produced mixtures of alcohols $C_5H_{11}OH$ obtained from fusel oil or derived from pentanes and used esp. as solvents
am·y·lase \ˈam-ə-ˌlās, -ˌlāz\ *n* **:** any of the enzymes that accelerate the hydrolysis of starch and glycogen or their intermediate hydrolysis products
¹**am·y·loid** \-ˌlȯid\ *or* **am·y·loi·dal** \ˌam-ə-ˈlȯid-ᵊl\ *adj* **:** resembling or containing amylum
²**amyloid** *n* **:** a nonnitrogenous starchy food
am·y·lol·y·sis \ˌam-ə-ˈläl-ə-səs\ *n* [NL] **:** the conversion of starch into soluble products (as dextrins and sugars) esp. by enzymes — **am·y·lo·lyt·ic** \-lō-ˈlit-ik\ *adj*
am·y·lop·sin \-ˈläp-sən\ *n* [*amyl-* + *-psin* (as in *trypsin*)] **:** the amylase of the pancreatic juice
am·y·lose \ˈam-ə-ˌlōs, -ˌlōz\ *n* **1 :** any of various polysaccharides (as starch or cellulose) **2 :** any of various compounds $(C_6H_{10}O_5)_x$ obtained by the hydrolysis of starch
am·y·lum \-ləm\ *n* [L — more at AMYL-] **:** STARCH
amyo·to·nia \ˌā-ˌmī-ə-ˈtō-nē-ə\ *n* [NL] **:** deficiency of muscle tone
¹**an** \ən, (ˈ)an\ *indefinite article* [ME, fr. OE *ān* one — more at ONE] **:** ²A — in standard speech and writing used (1) invariably before words beginning with a vowel letter and sound ⟨*an* oak⟩; (2) invariably before *h*-initial words in which the *h* is silent ⟨*an* honor⟩; (3) frequently before *h*-initial words which have in an initial unstressed syllable an \h\ sound often lost after the *an* ⟨*an* historian⟩; (4) sometimes esp. in England before words like *union* and *European* whose initial letter is a vowel and whose initial sounds are \yü\ or \yu̇\
²**an** *or* **an'** *conj* **1** *see* AND\ *substand* **:** AND **2** \(ˈ)an\ *archaic* **:** IF
an- — see A-
¹**-an** *or* **-ian** *also* **-ean** *n suffix* [*-an* & *-ian* fr. ME *-an*, *-ian*, fr. OF & L; OF *-ien*, fr. L *-ianus*, fr. *-i-* + *-anus*, fr. *-anus*, adj. suffix; *-ean* fr. such words as *Mediterranean*, *European*] **1 :** one that is of or relating to ⟨Americ*an*⟩ ⟨Boston*ian*⟩ **2 :** one skilled in or specializing in ⟨phonetic*ian*⟩
²**-an** *or* **-ian** *also* **-ean** *adj suffix* **1 :** of or belonging to ⟨Americ*an*⟩ ⟨Florid*ian*⟩ **2 :** characteristic of **:** resembling ⟨Mozart*ean*⟩
³**-an** *n suffix* [ISV *-an*, *-ane*, alter. of *-ene*, *-ine*, & *-one*] **1 :** unsaturated carbon compound ⟨tol*an*⟩ **2 :** anhydride of a carbohydrate ⟨dextr*an*⟩
¹**ana** \ˈan-ə\ *adv* [ME, fr. ML, fr. Gk, at the rate of, lit., up] **:** of each an equal quantity — used in prescriptions
²**ana** \ˈan-ə, ˈän-\ *n, pl* **ana** *or* **anas** [*-ana*] **1 :** a collection of the memorable sayings or table talk of a person **2 :** a collection of anecdotes or interesting or curious information about a person or a place
ana- *or* **an-** *prefix* [L, fr. Gk, up, back, again fr. *ana* up — more at ON] **1 :** up **:** upward ⟨*ana*bolism⟩ **2 :** back **:** backward ⟨*ana*tropous⟩
-ana \ˈan-ə, ˈän-ə, ˈā-nə\ *or* **-i·ana** \ē-ˈ\ *n pl suffix* [NL, fr. L, neut. pl. of *-anus* -an & *-ianus* -ian] **:** collected items of information esp. anecdotal or bibliographical concerning ⟨Americ*ana*⟩ ⟨Johnson*iana*⟩
an'a \ə-ˈnȯ\ *Scot* **:** and all
ana·bap·tism \ˌan-ə-ˈbap-ˌtiz-əm\ *n* [NL *anabaptismus*, fr. LGk *anabaptismos* rebaptism, fr. *anabaptizein* to rebaptize, fr. *ana-* again + *baptizein* to baptize] **1** *cap* **a :** the doctrine or practices of the Anabaptists **b :** the Anabaptist movement **2 :** the baptism of adults previously baptized as infants
Ana·bap·tist \-ˈbap-təst\ *n* **:** a Protestant sectarian of a radical movement arising in Zurich in 1524 and advocating the baptism and church membership of adult believers only, the practice of holiness, simplicity, nonresistance, mutual help, and the separation of church and state — **Anabaptist** *adj*
anab·a·sis \ə-ˈnab-ə-səs\ *n, pl* **anab·a·ses** \-ˈnab-ə-ˌsēz\ [Gk, inland march, fr. *anabainein* to go up or inland, fr. *ana-* + *bainein* to go — more at COME] **1 :** a going or marching up **:** ADVANCE; *esp* **:** a military advance **2** [fr. the retreat of Gk mercenaries in Asia minor described in the *Anabasis* of Xenophon] **:** a difficult and dangerous military retreat
an·a·bat·ic \ˌan-ə-ˈbat-ik\ *adj* [Gk *anabatos*, verbal of *anabainein*] **:** upward-moving ⟨an ~ wind⟩
ana·bi·o·sis \ˌan-ə-(ˌ)bī-ˈō-səs\ *n* [NL, fr. Gk *anabiōsis* return to life, fr. *anabioun* to return to life, fr. *ana-* + *bios* life — more at QUICK] **:** a state of suspended animation induced in some organisms by desiccation — **ana·bi·ot·ic** \-ˈät-ik\ *adj*
an·a·bol·ic \ˌan-ə-ˈbäl-ik\ *adj* **:** of, relating to, or characterized by anabolism
anab·o·lism \ə-ˈnab-ə-ˌliz-əm\ *n* [ISV *ana-* + *-bolism* (as in *metabolism*)] **:** constructive metabolism
anab·o·lite \ə-ˈnab-ə-ˌlīt\ *n* **:** a product of an anabolic process — **anab·o·lit·ic** \ə-ˌnab-ə-ˈlit-ik\ *adj*
anach·ro·nism \ə-ˈnak-rə-ˌniz-əm\ *n* [prob. fr. MGk *anachronismos*, fr. *anachronizesthai* to be an anachronism, fr. LGk *anachronizein* to be late, fr. Gk *ana-* + *chronos* time] **1 :** an error in chronology; *esp* **:** a chronological misplacing of persons, events, objects, or customs in regard to each other **2 :** a person or a thing that is chronologically out of place — **anach·ro·nis·tic** \ə-ˌnak-rə-ˈnis-tik\ *also* **ana·chron·ic** \ˌan-ə-ˈkrän-ik\ *or* **anach·ro·nous**

\ə-ˈnak-rə-nəs\ *adj* — **anach·ro·nis·ti·cal·ly** \ə-ˌnak-rə-ˈnis-ti-k(ə-)lē\ *also* **anach·ro·nous·ly** *adv*

an·a·clit·ic \ˌan-ə-ˈklit-ik\ *adj* [Gk *anaklitos*, verbal of *anaklinein* to lean upon, fr. *ana-* + *klinein* to lean — more at LEAN] **:** characterized by dependence of libido on a nonsexual instinct

an·a·co·lu·thic \ˌan-ə-kə-ˈlü-thik\ *adj* **:** of or relating to anacoluthon — **an·a·co·lu·thi·cal·ly** \-thi-k(ə-)lē\ *adv*

an·a·co·lu·thon \ˌan-ə-kə-ˈlü-ˌthän\ *n, pl* **an·a·co·lu·tha** \-ˈlü-thə\ *or* **anacoluthons** [LL, fr. LGk *anakolouthon* inconsistency in logic, fr. Gk, neut. of *anakolouthos*, inconsistent, fr. *an-* + *akolouthos* following, fr. *ha-*, *a-* together + *keleuthos* path; akin to Gk *hama* together — more at SAME] **:** syntactical inconsistency or incoherence within a sentence; *esp* **:** the shift from one construction to another (as in "you really ought — well, do it your own way")

an·a·con·da \ˌan-ə-ˈkän-də\ *n* [prob. modif. of Sinhalese *henakandayā* a slender green snake] **:** a large arboreal snake (*Eunectes murinus*) of the boa family of tropical So. America that crushes its prey in its coils; *broadly* **:** any large constricting snake

anac·re·on·tic \ə-ˌnak-rē-ˈänt-ik\ *n* **:** a poem in the manner of Anacreon **:** a drinking song or light lyric

Anacreontic *adj* [L *anacreonticus*, fr. *Anacreont-*, *Anacreon* Anacreon, fr. Gk *Anakreont-*, *Anakreōn*] **1 :** of, relating to, or resembling the poetry of Anacreon **2 :** gay, convivial, or amatory in tone or theme

an·a·cru·sis \ˌan-ə-ˈkrü-səs\ *n* [NL, fr. Gk *anakrousis* beginning of a song, fr. *anakrouein* to begin a song, fr. *ana-* + *krouein* to strike, beat; akin to Lith *krušti* to stamp] **1 :** one or more syllables at the beginning of a line of poetry that are regarded as preliminary to and not a part of the metrical pattern **2 :** UPBEAT; *specif* **:** one or more notes or tones preceding the first downbeat of a musical phrase

ana·cul·ture \ˈan-ə-ˌkəl-chər\ *n* [ISV] **:** a mixed bacterial culture; *esp* **:** one used in the preparation of autogenous vaccines

an·a·dem \ˈan-ə-ˌdem\ *n* [L *anadema*, fr. Gk *anadēma*, fr. *anadein* to wreathe, fr. *ana-* + *dein* to bind — more at DIADEM] **:** GARLAND, CHAPLET

ana·di·plo·sis \ˌan-əd-ə-ˈplō-səs, ˌan-ə-(ˌ)dī-ˈplō-\ *n* [LL, fr. Gk *anadiplōsis*, lit., repetition, fr. *anadiploun* to double, fr. *ana-* + *diploun* to double — more at DIPLOMA] **:** repetition of a prominent word (as the last) in one phrase or clause at the beginning of the next (as "rely on his honor — honor such as his?")

anad·ro·mous \ə-ˈnad-rə-məs\ *adj* [Gk *anadromos* running upward, fr. *anadramein* to run upward, fr. *ana-* + *dramein* to run — more at DROMEDARY] **:** ascending rivers from the sea for breeding ⟨shad are ~⟩

anae·mia *var of* ANEMIA

an·aer·obe \ˈan-ə-ˌrōb; (ˈ)an-ˈa(-ə)r-ˌōb, -ˈe(-ə)r-\ *n* [ISV] **:** an anaerobic organism

an·aer·o·bic \ˌan-ə-ˈrō-bik; ˌan-ˌa-(ə-)ˈrō-, -ˌe-(ə-)ˈrō-\ *adj* **1 :** living or active in the absence of free oxygen **2 :** relating to or induced by anaerobes — **an·aer·o·bi·cal·ly** \-bi-k(ə-)lē\ *adv*

an·aes·the·sia, an·aes·thet·ic *var of* ANESTHESIA, ANESTHETIC

ana·glyph \ˈan-ə-ˌglif\ *n* [LL *anaglyphus* embossed, fr. Gk *anaglyphos*, fr. *anaglyphein* to emboss, fr. *ana-* + *glyphein* to carve — more at CLEAVE] **1 :** a sculptured, chased, or embossed ornament worked in low relief **2 :** a stereoscopic motion or still picture in which the right component of a composite image usu. red in color is superposed upon the left component in a contrasting color to produce a three-dimensional effect when viewed through correspondingly colored filters in the form of spectacles — **ana·glyph·ic** \ˌan-ə-ˈglif-ik\ *adj*

an·a·go·ge *or* **an·a·go·gy** \ˈan-ə-ˌgō-jē\ *n* [LL, fr. LGk *anagōgē*, fr. Gk, reference, fr. *anagein* to refer, fr. *ana-* + *agein* to lead — more at AGENT] **:** interpretation of a word, passage, or text (as of Scripture or poetry) that finds beyond the literal, allegorical, and moral senses a fourth and ultimate spiritual or mystical sense — **an·a·gog·ic** \ˌan-ə-ˈgäj-ik\ *or* **an·a·gog·i·cal** \-i-kəl\ *adj* — **an·a·gog·i·cal·ly** \-k(ə-)lē\ *adv*

[1]**ana·gram** \ˈan-ə-ˌgram\ *n* [prob. fr. MF *anagramme*, fr. NL *anagrammat-*, *anagramma*, modif. of Gk *anagrammatismos*, fr. *anagrammatizein* to transpose letters, fr. *ana-* + *grammat-*, *gramma* letter — more at GRAM] **1 :** a word or phrase made by transposing the letters of another word or phrase **2** *pl but sing in constr* **:** a game in which words are formed by rearranging the letters of other words or by arranging letters taken (as from a stock of cards or blocks) at random — **ana·gram·mat·ic** \ˌan-ə-grə-ˈmat-ik\ *or* **ana·gram·mat·i·cal** \-i-kəl\ *adj* — **ana·gram·mat·i·cal·ly** \-k(ə-)lē\ *adv*

[2]**anagram** *vt* **ana·grammed; ana·gram·ming 1 :** ANAGRAMMATIZE **2 :** to rearrange (the letters of a text) in order to discover a hidden message

ana·gram·ma·tize \ˌan-ə-ˈgram-ə-ˌtīz\ *vt* **:** to transpose (as letters in a word) so as to form an anagram

anal \ˈān-ᵊl\ *adj* **:** of, relating to, or situated near the anus — **anal·ly** \-ᵊl-ē\ *adv*

anal·cime \ə-ˈnal-ˌsēm\ *n* [F, fr. Gk *analkimos* weak, fr. *an-* + *alkimos* strong, fr. *alkē* strength] **:** a white or slightly colored zeolite occurring in various igneous rocks massive or in crystals

anal·cite \-ˌsīt\ *n* **:** ANALCIME

an·a·lects \ˈan-ᵊl-ˌek(t)s\ *n pl* [NL *analecta*, fr. Gk *analekta*, neut. pl. of *analektos*, verbal of *analegein* to collect, fr. *ana-* + *legein* to gather — more at LEGEND] **:** selected miscellaneous written passages

an·a·lem·ma \ˌan-ᵊl-ˈem-ə\ *n* [L, sundial on a pedestal, fr. Gk *analēmma*, lofty structure, sundial, fr. *analambanein* to take up, fr. *ana-* + *lambanein* to take — more at LATCH] **:** a graduated scale having the shape of a figure 8 and showing the sun's declination and the equation of time for each day of the year

an·a·lep·tic \ˌan-ᵊl-ˈep-tik\ *adj* [Gk *analēptikos*, fr. *analambanein* to take up, restore] **:** RESTORATIVE; *esp* **:** stimulant to the central nervous system — **analeptic** *n*

an·al·ge·sia \ˌan-ᵊl-ˈjē-zhə, -z(h)ē-ə\ *n* [NL, fr. Gk *analgēsia*, fr. *an-* + *algēsis* sense of pain, fr. *algein* to suffer pain, fr. *algos* pain] **:** insensibility to pain without loss of consciousness — **an·al·ge·sic** \-ˈjē-zik, -sik\ *adj or n* — **an·al·get·ic** \-ˈjet-ik\ *adj or n*

an·a·log *or* **an·a·logue** \ˈan-ᵊl-ˌȯg, -ˌäg\ *adj* **:** of or relating to an analog computer

analog computer *or* **analogue computer** *n* **:** a computer that operates with numbers represented by directly measurable quantities (as voltages, resistances, or rotations)

an·a·log·i·cal \ˌan-ᵊl-ˈäj-i-kəl\ *adj* **1 :** of, relating to, or based on analogy **2 :** expressing or implying analogy — **an·a·log·i·cal·ly** \-k(ə-)lē\ *adv*

anal·o·gist \ə-ˈnal-ə-jəst\ *n* **:** one who searches for or reasons from analogies

anal·o·gize \ə-ˈnal-ə-ˌjīz\ *vi* **:** to use or exhibit analogy ~ *vt* **:** to compare by analogy

anal·o·gous \ə-ˈnal-ə-gəs\ *adj* [L *analogus*, fr. Gk *analogos*, lit., proportionate, fr. *ana-* + *logos* reason, ratio, fr. *legein* to gather, speak — more at LEGEND] **1 :** showing an analogy or a likeness permitting one to draw an analogy **2 :** being or related to as an analogue **syn** see SIMILAR — **anal·o·gous·ly** *adv* — **anal·o·gous·ness** *n*

an·a·logue *or* **an·a·log** \ˈan-ᵊl-ˌȯg, -ˌäg\ *n* [F *analogue*, fr. *analogue* analogous, fr. Gk *analogos*] **1 :** something that is analogous or similar to something else **:** PARALLEL **2 :** an organ similar in function to an organ of another animal or plant but different in structure and origin

anal·o·gy \ə-ˈnal-ə-jē\ *n* **1 :** inference that if two or more things agree with one another in some respects they will prob. agree in others **2 :** resemblance in some particulars between things otherwise unlike **:** SIMILARITY **3 :** correspondence between the members of pairs or sets of linguistic forms that serves as a basis for the creation of another form **4 :** correspondence in function between anatomical parts of different structure and origin — compare HOMOLOGY **syn** see LIKENESS

an·al·pha·bet \(ˈ)an-ˈal-fə-ˌbet, -bət\ *n* [Gk *analphabētos* not knowing the alphabet, fr. *an-* + *alphabētos* alphabet] **:** ILLITERATE — **an·al·pha·bet·ic** \ˌan-ˌal-fə-ˈbet-ik\ *adj or n*

anal·y·sand \ə-ˈnal-ə-ˌsand\ *n* [*analyse* + *-and* (as in *multiplicand*)] **:** one who is undergoing psychoanalysis

anal·y·sis \ə-ˈnal-ə-səs\ *n, pl* **anal·y·ses** \-ˈnal-ə-ˌsēz\ [NL, fr. Gk, fr. *analyein* to break up, fr. *ana-* + *lyein* to loosen — more at LOSE] **1 :** separation of a whole into its component parts **2 a :** an examination of a complex, its elements, and their relations **b :** a statement of such an analysis **3 :** the use of function words instead of inflectional forms as a characteristic device of a language **4 a :** the identification or separation of ingredients of a substance **b :** a statement of the constituents of a mixture **5 a :** proof of a mathematical proposition by assuming the result and deducing a valid statement by a series of reversible steps **b** (1) **:** a branch of mathematics concerned mainly with functions and limits (2) **:** CALCULUS 3 b **6 a :** a method in philosophy of resolving complex expressions into simpler or more basic ones **b :** clarification of an expression by an elucidation of its use in discourse **7 :** PSYCHOANALYSIS

analysis si·tus \-ˈsīt-əs, -ˈsēt-; -ˈsī-ˌtüs, -ˈsē-\ *n* [NL, lit., analysis of situation] **:** TOPOLOGY 3

an·a·lyst \ˈan-ᵊl-əst\ *n* [prob. fr. *analyze*] **1 :** a person who analyzes or who is skilled in analysis **2 :** PSYCHOANALYST

an·a·lyt·ic \ˌan-ᵊl-ˈit-ik\ *adj* [LL *analyticus*, fr. Gk *analytikos*, fr. *analyein*] **1 :** of or relating to analysis or analytics; *esp* **:** separating something into component parts or constituent elements **2 :** skilled in or using analysis ⟨a keenly ~ man⟩ **3 :** not synthetic; *esp* **:** logically necessary **:** TAUTOLOGOUS ⟨~ truth⟩ **4 :** characterized by analysis rather than inflection **5 :** PSYCHOANALYTIC **6 :** treated or treatable by or using the methods of algebra and calculus rather than geometry — **an·a·lyt·i·cal** \-i-kəl\ *adj* — **an·a·lyt·i·cal·ly** \-k(ə-)lē\ *adv* — **an·a·ly·tic·i·ty** \ˌan-ᵊl-ə-ˈtis-ət-ē\ *n*

analytic geometry *n* **:** the study of geometric properties by means of algebraic operations upon symbols defined in terms of a coordinate system — called also *coordinate geometry*

an·a·lyt·ics \ˌan-ᵊl-ˈit-iks\ *n pl but sing or pl in constr* **:** the method of logical analysis

an·a·lyz·able \ˈan-ᵊl-ˌī-zə-bəl\ *adj* **:** capable of being analyzed

an·a·ly·za·tion \ˌan-ᵊl-ə-ˈzā-shən\ *n* **:** ANALYSIS

an·a·lyze *or chiefly Brit* **an·a·lyse** \ˈan-ᵊl-ˌīz\ *vt* [prob. irreg. fr. *analysis*] **1 :** to study or determine the nature and relationship of the parts of by analysis ⟨~ a traffic pattern⟩ **2 :** to subject to scientific or grammatical analysis **3 :** PSYCHOANALYZE — **an·a·lyz·er** *n*

syn RESOLVE, DISSECT, BREAK DOWN: ANALYZE suggests separating or distinguishing the component parts of something (as a substance, a process, a situation) so as to discover its true nature or inner relationships; RESOLVE does not commonly presuppose a personal agent and often suggests a permanent physical separation into parts with consequent alteration of the original whole; DISSECT suggests a searching analysis by laying bare parts or pieces for individual scrutiny; BREAK DOWN implies a reducing to simpler parts or divisions

an·am·ne·sis \ˌan-ˌam-ˈnē-səs\ *n, pl* **an·am·ne·ses** \-ˈnē-ˌsēz\ [NL, fr. Gk *anamnēsis*, fr. *anamimnēskesthai* to remember, fr. *ana-* + *mimnēskesthai* to remember — more at MIND] **1 :** a recalling to mind **:** REMINISCENCE **2 :** a preliminary case history of a medical or psychiatric patient — **an·am·nes·tic** \-ˈnes-tik\ *adj* — **an·am·nes·ti·cal·ly** \-ti-k(ə-)lē\ *adv*

ana·mor·phic \ˌan-ə-ˈmȯr-fik\ *adj* [NL *anamorphosis* distorted optical image] **:** producing or having different magnification of the image in each of two perpendicular directions — used of an optical device or its image

An·a·ni·as \ˌan-ə-ˈnī-əs\ *n* [Gk, prob. fr. Heb *Ḥănanyāh*] **1 :** an early Christian struck dead for lying **2 :** LIAR

an·a·pest \ˈan-ə-ˌpest\ *n* [L *anapaestus*, fr. Gk *anapaistos*, lit., struck back (a dactyl reversed), fr. (assumed) Gk *anapaiein* to strike back, fr. Gk *ana-* + *paiein* to strike] **1 :** a metrical foot consisting of two short syllables followed by one long syllable or of two unstressed syllables followed by one stressed syllable **2 :** a verse written in anapests — **an·a·pes·tic** \ˌan-ə-ˈpes-tik\ *adj or n*

ana·phase \ˈan-ə-ˌfāz\ *n* [ISV] **:** the stage of mitosis in which the chromosome halves move toward the poles of the spindle — **ana·pha·sic** \ˌan-ə-ˈfā-zik\ *adj*

anaph·o·ra \ə-ˈnaf-ə-rə\ *n* [LL, fr. LGk, fr. Gk, act of carrying back, reference fr. *anapherein* to carry back, refer, fr. *ana-* + *pherein* to carry — more at BEAR] **:** repetition at the beginning of two or more successive clauses or verses esp. for rhetorical or poetic effect

an·aph·ro·di·sia \ˌan-ˌaf-rə-ˈdizh-(ē-)ə\ *n* [NL, fr. *a-* + Gk *aphrodisios* sexual — more at APHRODISIAC] **:** absence or impairment of sexual desire — **an·aph·ro·dis·i·ac** \-ˈdiz-ē-ˌak\ *adj or n*

ana·phy·lac·tic \ˌan-ə-fə-ˈlak-tik\ *adj* **:** of, relating to, affected by,

or causing anaphylaxis — **ana·phy·lac·ti·cal·ly** \-ti-k(ə-)lē\ *adv*

ana·phy·lac·toid \-ˈlak-ˌtȯid\ *adj* **:** resembling anaphylaxis

ana·phy·lax·is \-ˈlak-səs\ *n* [NL, fr. *ana-* + *-phylaxis* (as in *prophylaxis*)] **:** hypersensitivity (as to foreign proteins or drugs) resulting from sensitization following prior contact with the causative

an·a·pla·sia \ˌan-ə-ˈplā-zh(ē-)ə\ *n* [NL] **:** reversion of cells to a more primitive or undifferentiated form — **an·a·plas·tic** \-ˈplas-tik\ *adj*

an·arch \ˈan-ˌärk\ *n* [back-formation fr. *anarchy*] **:** a leader or advocate of revolt or anarchy

an·ar·chic \a-ˈnär-kik\ *adj* **:** of, relating to, or tending toward anarchy **:** LAWLESS — **an·ar·chi·cal** \-ki-kəl\ *adj* — **an·ar·chi·cal·ly** \-k(ə-)lē\ *adv*

an·ar·chism \ˈan-ər-ˌkiz-əm\ *n* **1 :** a political theory holding all forms of governmental authority to be unnecessary and undesirable and advocating a society based on voluntary cooperation and free association of individuals and groups **2 :** the advocacy or practice of anarchistic principles

an·ar·chist \ˈan-ər-kəst\ *n* **1 :** one who rebels against any authority, established order, or ruling power **2 :** one who believes in, advocates, or promotes anarchism or anarchy; *esp* **:** one who uses violent means to overthrow the established order — **anarchist** *or* **an·ar·chis·tic** \ˌan-ər-ˈkis-tik\ *adj*

an·ar·cho–syn·di·cal·ism \a-ˌnär-kō-ˈsin-di-kə-ˌliz-əm, ˌan-ər-kō-\ *n* **:** SYNDICALISM — **an·ar·cho–syn·di·cal·ist** \-kə-ləst\ *n*

an·ar·chy \ˈan-ər-kē\ *n* [ML *anarchia*, fr. Gk, fr. *anarchos* rulerless, fr. *an-* + *archos* ruler — more at ARCH-] **1 a :** absence of government **b :** a state of lawlessness or political disorder due to the absence of governmental authority **c :** a utopian society having no government and made up of individuals who enjoy complete freedom **2 :** absence of order **:** DISORDER **3 :** ANARCHISM

an·ar·thria \a-ˈnär-thrē-ə\ *n* [NL, fr. Gk *anarthros* inarticulate, fr. *an-* + *arthron* joint — more at ARTHR-] **:** inability to articulate words as a result of brain lesion

an·a·sar·ca \ˌan-ə-ˈsär-kə\ *n* [NL, fr. *ana-* + Gk *sark-*, *sarx* flesh — more at SARCASM] **:** edema with accumulation of serum in the connective tissue — **ana·sar·cous** \-kəs\ *adj*

an·as·tig·mat \a-ˈnas-tig-ˌmat, ˌan-ə-ˈstig-\ *n* [G, back-formation fr. *anastigmatisch* anastigmatic] **:** an anastigmatic lens

an·astig·mat·ic \ˌan-ə-(ˌ)stig-ˈmat-ik, ˌan-ˌas-tig-\ *adj* [ISV] **:** not astigmatic — used esp. of lenses that are able to form approximately point images of object points

anas·to·mose \ə-ˈnas-tə-ˌmōz, -ˌmōs\ *vb* [prob. back-formation fr. *anastomosis*] *vt* **:** to connect or join by anastomosis ~ *vi* **:** to communicate by anastomosis

anas·to·mo·sis \ə-ˌnas-tə-ˈmō-səs\ *n, pl* **anas·to·mo·ses** \-ˈmō-ˌsēz\ [LL, fr. Gk *anastomōsis*, fr. *anastomoun* to provide with an outlet, fr. *ana-* + *stoma* mouth, opening — more at STOMACH] **1 :** the union of parts or branches (as of streams, blood vessels, or leaf veins) so as to intercommunicate **:** INOSCULATION **2 :** a product of anastomosis **:** NETWORK — **anas·to·mot·ic** \-ˈmät-ik\ *adj*

anas·tro·phe \ə-ˈnas-trə-(ˌ)fē\ *n* [ML, fr. Gk *anastrophē*, lit., turning back, fr. *anastrephein* to turn back, fr. *ana-* + *strephein* to turn — more at STROPHE] **:** inversion of the usual syntactical order of words for rhetorical effect

an·a·tase \ˈan-ə-ˌtās, -ˌtāz\ *n* [F, fr. Gk *anastasis* extension, fr. *anateinein* to extend, fr. *ana-* + *teinein* to stretch — more at THIN] **:** a tetragonal titanium dioxide used esp. as a white pigment

anath·e·ma \ə-ˈnath-ə-mə\ *n* [LL *anathemat-*, *anathema*, fr. Gk, thing devoted to evil, curse, fr. *anatithenai* to set up, dedicate, fr. *ana-* + *tithenai* to place, set — more at DO] **1 a :** a ban or curse solemnly pronounced by ecclesiastical authority and accompanied by excommunication **b :** the denunciation of anything as accursed **c :** a vigorous denunciation **:** CURSE **2 a :** one that is cursed by ecclesiastical authority **b :** one that is intensely disliked or loathed

anath·e·ma·tize \ə-ˈnath-ə-mə-ˌtīz\ *vt* **:** to pronounce an anathema upon **syn** see EXECRATE

An·a·to·lian \ˌan-ə-ˈtō-lē-ən, -ˈtōl-yən\ *n* **1 :** a native or inhabitant of Anatolia and specif. of the western plateau lands of Turkey in Asia **2 :** a group of extinct languages of ancient Anatolia sometimes considered a branch of the Indo-European language family — **Anatolian** *adj*

an·a·tom·ic \ˌan-ə-ˈtäm-ik\ *adj* **:** of or relating to anatomy — **an·a·tom·i·cal** \-i-kəl\ *adj* — **an·a·tom·i·cal·ly** \-k(ə-)lē\ *adv*

anat·o·mist \ə-ˈnat-ə-məst\ *n* **1 :** a student of anatomy; *esp* **:** one skilled in dissection **2 :** one who analyzes minutely and critically

anat·o·mize \ə-ˈnat-ə-ˌmīz\ *vt* **1 :** to cut in pieces in order to display or examine the structure and use of the parts **:** DISSECT **2 :** ANALYZE

anat·o·my \ə-ˈnat-ə-mē\ *n* [LL *anatomia* dissection, fr. Gk *anatomē*, fr. *anatemnein* to dissect, fr. *ana-* + *temnein* to cut — more at TOME] **1 :** a branch of morphology that deals with the structure of organisms **2 :** a treatise on anatomic science or art **3 :** the art of separating the parts of an animal or plant in order to ascertain their position, relations, structure, and function **:** DISSECTION **4** *obs* **:** a body dissected or to be dissected **5 :** structural makeup esp. of an organism or any of its parts **6 :** a separating or dividing into parts for detailed examination **:** ANALYSIS **7 a (1) :** SKELETON **(2) :** MUMMY **b :** the human body

anat·ro·pous \ə-ˈna-trə-pəs\ *adj* **:** having the ovule inverted so that the micropyle is bent down to the funiculus to which the body of the ovule is united

-ance \ən(t)s, ᵊn(t)s\ *n suffix* [ME, fr. OF, fr. L *-antia*, fr. *-ant-*, *-ans* -ant + *-ia* -y] **1 :** action or process ⟨further*ance*⟩ **:** instance of an action or process ⟨perform*ance*⟩ **2 :** quality or state **:** instance of a quality or state ⟨protuber*ance*⟩ **3 :** amount or degree ⟨conduct*ance*⟩

an·ces·tor \ˈan-ˌses-tər\ *n* [ME *ancestre*, fr. OF, fr. L *antecessor* one that goes before, fr. *antecessus*, pp. of *antecedere* to go before, fr. *ante-* + *cedere* to go — more at CEDE] **1 a :** one from whom a person is descended and who is usu. more remote in the line of descent than a grandparent **b :** FOREFATHER 2 **2 :** FORERUNNER, PROTOTYPE **3 :** a progenitor of a more recent or existing species or group — **an·ces·tress** \-trəs\ *n*

an·ces·tral \an-ˈses-trəl\ *adj* **:** of, relating to, or derived from an ancestor — **an·ces·tral·ly** \-trə-lē\ *adv*

an·ces·try \ˈan-ˌses-trē\ *n* **1 :** line of descent **:** LINEAGE; *specif* **:** honorable, noble, or aristocratic descent **2 :** persons initiating or comprising a line of descent **:** ANCESTORS

syn ANCESTRY, LINEAGE, PEDIGREE mean one's progenitors collectively or their quality or character. ANCESTRY stresses the image of a family tree branching and ramifying as it ascends ⟨only brothers and sisters have exactly the same *ancestry*⟩ LINEAGE stresses descent in line of generation, and may equal the broadest sense of *family* by designating all the descendants of a single progenitor; PEDIGREE implies known and recorded and usu. notable or distinguished ancestry

An·chi·ses \an-ˈkī-(ˌ)sēz, aŋ-\ *n* [L, fr. Gk *Anchisēs*] **:** the father of Aeneas

¹an·chor \ˈaŋ-kər\ *n, often attrib* [ME *ancre*, fr. OE *ancor*, fr. L *anchora*, fr. Gk *ankyra;* akin to L *uncus* hook — more at ANGLE] **1 :** a device usu. of metal attached to a ship or boat by a cable and cast overboard to hold the vessel in a particular place by means of a fluke that digs into the bottom **2 :** a reliable support **3 :** something that serves to hold an object firmly **4 :** an object shaped like a ship's anchor **5 :** one who competes or is placed last

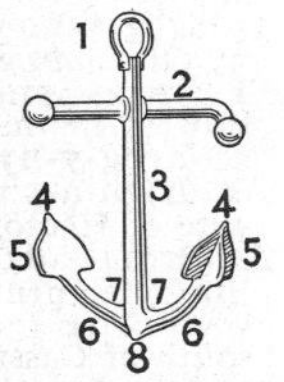

anchor 1: *1* ring, *2* stock, *3* shank, *4* bill, *5* fluke, *6* arm, *7* throat, *8* crown

²anchor *vb* **an·chor·ing** \-k(ə-)riŋ\ *vt* **1 :** to hold in place in the water by an anchor **2 :** to secure firmly **:** FIX ~ *vi* **1 :** to cast anchor **2 :** to become fixed

an·chor·age \ˈaŋ-k(ə-)rij\ *n* **1 a :** the act of anchoring **:** the condition of lying at anchor **b :** a place where vessels anchor **:** a place suitable for anchoring **2 :** a means of security **:** ground of trust **3 :** something that provides a secure hold

an·cho·ress \ˈaŋ-k(ə-)rəs\ *or* **an·cress** \-krəs\ *n* [ME *ankeresse*, fr. *anker* hermit, fr. OE *ancor*, fr. OIr *anchara*, fr. LL *anachoreta*] **:** a female anchorite

an·cho·rite \ˈaŋ-kə-ˌrīt\ *also* **an·cho·ret** \-ˌret\ *n* [ME, fr. ML *anchorita*, alter. of LL *anachoreta*, fr. LGk *anachōrētēs*, fr. Gk *anachōrein* to withdraw, fr. *ana-* + *chōrein* to make room, fr. *chōros* place; akin to Gk *chēros* left, bereaved — more at HEIR] **:** one who lives in seclusion usu. for religious reasons **:** RECLUSE — **an·cho·rit·ic** \ˌaŋ-kə-ˈrit-ik\ *adj*

anchor man *n* **:** a news broadcaster who coordinates the activities of other broadcasters (as at a political convention)

anchor ring *n* **:** TORUS 4

an·cho·vy \ˈan-ˌchō-vē, an-ˈ\ *n, pl* **anchovies** *or* **anchovy** [Sp *anchova*] **:** any of numerous small fishes (family Engraulidae) resembling herrings; *esp* **:** a common Mediterranean fish (*Engraulis encrasicholus*) used esp. for sauces and relishes

an·cien ré·gime \äⁿs-yaⁿ-rā-zhēm\ *n* [F, lit., old regime] **1 :** the political and social system of France before the Revolution of 1789 **2 :** a system or mode no longer prevailing

¹an·cient \ˈān-shənt, -chənt, ˈāŋ(k)-shənt\ *adj* [ME *ancien*, fr. MF, fr. (assumed) VL *anteanus*, fr. L *ante* before — more at ANTE-] **1 :** having had an existence of many years **2 :** of or relating to a remote period, to a time early in history, or to those living in such a period or time; *specif* **:** of or relating to the historical period beginning with the earliest known civilizations and extending to the fall of the western Roman Empire A.D.476 **3 :** having the qualities of age or long existence: **a :** VENERABLE **b :** OLD-FASHIONED, ANTIQUE **syn** see OLD — **an·cient·ly** *adv* — **an·cient·ness** *n*

²ancient *n* **1 :** an aged living being **2 :** one who lived in ancient times: **a** *pl* **:** the civilized peoples of antiquity; *esp* **:** those of the classical nations **b :** one of the classical authors

³ancient *n* [alter. of *ensign*] **1** *archaic* **:** ENSIGN, STANDARD, FLAG **2** *obs* **:** the bearer of an ensign

an·cient·ry \-rē\ *n* **:** ANCIENTNESS, ANTIQUITY

an·cil·la \an-ˈsil-ə\ *n, pl* **an·cil·lae** \-ˈsil-(ˌ)ē\ [L, female servant] **:** AID, HELPER

an·cil·lary \ˈan(t)-sə-ˌler-ē, an-ˈsil-ə-rē\ *adj* **1 :** SUBORDINATE, SUBSIDIARY **2 :** AUXILIARY, SUPPLEMENTARY

an·con \ˈaŋ-ˌkän\ *n, pl* **an·co·nes** \aŋ-ˈkō-nēz\ [L, fr. Gk *ankōn* elbow; akin to L *uncus* hook] **:** a bracket, elbow, or console used as an architectural support

-an·cy \ən-sē, ᵊn-\ *n suffix* [L *-antia*] **:** quality or state ⟨piqu*ancy*⟩

an·cy·lo·sto·mi·a·sis \ˌaŋ-ki-lō-stə-ˈmī-ə-səs, ˌan-sə-\ *n* [NL, fr. *Ancylostoma*, genus of hookworms, fr. Gk *ankylos* hooked + *stoma* mouth; akin to L *uncus* hook — more at ANGLE, STOMACH] **:** infestation with or disease caused by hookworms; *esp* **:** a lethargic anemic state in man due to blood loss through the feeding of hookworms in the small intestine

and \ən(d), (ˈ)an(d), *usu* ᵊn(d) *after* t, d, s *or* z, *often* ᵊm *after* p *or* b, *sometimes* ᵊŋ *after* k *or* g\ *conj* [ME, fr. OE; akin to OHG *unti* and] **1 —** used as a function word to indicate connection or addition esp. of items within the same class or type; used to join sentence elements of the same grammatical rank or function **2** *obs* **:** IF

an·da·lu·site \ˌan-də-ˈlü-ˌsīt\ *n* [F *andalousite*, fr. *Andalousie* Andalusia, region in Spain] **:** a mineral Al_2SiO_5 consisting of a silicate of aluminum usu. in thick nearly square orthorhombic prisms of various colors

¹an·dan·te \än-ˈdän-ˌtā, -ˈdänt-ē, an-ˈdant-ē\ *adj (or adv)* [It, lit., going, prp. of *andare* to go] **:** moderately slow — used as a direction in music

²andante *n* **:** a musical piece or movement in andante tempo

¹an·dan·ti·no \ˌän-ˌdän-ˈtē-(ˌ)nō\ *adj (or adv)* [It, dim. of *andante*] **:** rather quicker in tempo than andante — used as a direction in music

²andantino *n* **:** a musical piece or movement in andantino tempo

An·de·an \ˈan-(ˌ)dē-ən, an-ˈ\ *adj* **:** of, relating to, or characteristic of the Andes mountain system

an·des·ite \ˈan-(ˌ)dē-ˌzīt\ *n* [G *andesit*, fr. *Andes*] **:** an extrusive usu. dark grayish rock consisting essentially of oligoclase or feldspar

and·iron \ˈan-ˌdī(-ə)rn\ *n* [ME *aundiren*, modif. of OF *andier*] **:** one of a pair of metal supports for firewood used on a hearth and made of a horizontal bar mounted on short legs with usu. a vertical shaft surmounting the front end

and/or \ˈan-ˈdȯ(ə)r\ *conj* — used as a function word to indicate that words are to be taken together or individually

andr- *or* **andro-** *comb form* [MF, fr. L, fr. Gk, fr. *andr-*, *anēr* man (male); akin to Oscan *ner* man, Skt *nṛ*, OIr *nert* strength] **1 :** man ⟨*andro*phobia⟩ **2 :** male ⟨*andro*ecium⟩

an·dra·dite \an-ˈdräd-ˌīt\ *n* [José B. de *Andrada* e Silva †1838 Brazilian geologist] **:** a garnet $Ca_3Fe_2(SiO_4)_3$ of any of various colors ranging from yellow and green to brown and black

An·dro·cles \ˈan-drə-ˌklēz\ *n* [L, fr. Gk *Androklēs*] **:** a Roman slave held to have been spared in the arena by a lion from whose foot he had years before extracted a thorn

an·droe·ci·um \an-ˈdrē-s(h)ē-əm\ *n, pl* **an·droe·cia** \-s(h)ē-ə\ [NL, fr. *andr-* + Gk *oikion*, dim. of *oikos* house — more at VICINITY] **:** the aggregate of microsporophylls in the flower of a seed plant

an·dro·gen \ˈan-drə-jən\ *n* [ISV] **:** a substance (as a sex hormone) tending to stimulate the development of secondary sex characteristics in the male — **an·dro·gen·ic** \ˌan-drə-ˈjen-ik\ *adj*

an·drog·y·nous \an-ˈdräj-ə-nəs\ *adj* [L *androgynus* hermaphrodite, fr. Gk *androgynos*, fr. *andr-* + *gynē* woman — more at QUEEN] **1 :** HERMAPHRODITIC **2 :** bearing both staminate and pistillate flowers in the same cluster with the male flowers uppermost — **an·drog·y·ny** \-nē\ *n*

An·drom·a·che \an-ˈdräm-ə-(ˌ)kē\ *n* [L, fr. Gk *Andromachē*] **:** the wife of Hector

An·drom·e·da \an-ˈdräm-əd-ə\ *n* [L, fr. Gk *Andromedē*] **1 :** an Ethiopian princess rescued from a monster by Perseus and made his wife **2** [L (gen. *Andromedae*)] **:** a northern constellation directly south of Cassiopeia between Pegasus and Perseus

an·dros·ter·one \an-ˈdräs-tə-ˌrōn\ *n* [ISV *andr-* + *sterol* + *-one*] **:** an androgenic hormone that is a hydroxy ketone $C_{19}H_{30}O_2$ found esp. in human male urine

-an·drous \ˈan-drəs\ *adj comb form* [NL *-andrus*, fr. Gk *-andros* having (such or so many) men, fr. *andr-*, *anēr*] **:** having (such or so many) stamens ⟨mon*androus*⟩

An·dva·ri \ˈan-ˌdwär-ē\ *n* [ON] **:** a dwarf robbed of his treasure by Loki

ane \ˈān\ *adj or n or pron, chiefly Scot* **:** ONE

-ane \ˌān\ *n suffix* [ISV *-an*, *-ane*, alter. of *-ene*, *-ine*, & *-one*] **1 :** ³-AN 1 ⟨tol*ane*⟩ **2 :** saturated or completely hydrogenated carbon compound (as a hydrocarbon) ⟨meth*ane*⟩

an·ec·dot·age \ˈan-ik-ˌdōt-ij\ *n* **:** the telling of anecdotes; *also* **:** ANECDOTES

an·ec·dot·al \ˌan-ik-ˈdōt-ᵊl\ *adj* **:** relating to, characteristic of, or containing anecdotes — **an·ec·dot·al·ly** \-ᵊl-ē\ *adv*

an·ec·dote \ˈan-ik-ˌdōt\ *n* [F, fr. Gk *anekdota* unpublished items, fr. neut. pl. of *anekdotos* unpublished, fr. *a-* + *ekdidonai* to publish, fr. *ex* out + *didonai* to give — more at EX-, DATE] **:** a usu. short narrative of an interesting, amusing, or biographical incident — **an·ec·dot·ic** \ˌan-ik-ˈdät-ik\ *or* **an·ec·dot·i·cal** \-i-kəl\ *adj* — **an·ec·dot·i·cal·ly** \-k(ə-)lē\ *adv*

an·echo·ic \ˌan-i-ˈkō-ik\ *adj* **:** free from echoes and reverberations

anele \ə-ˈnē(ə)l\ *vt* [ME *anelen*, fr. *an* on + *elen* to anoint, fr. *ele* oil, fr. OE *æle*, fr. L *oleum* — more at ON, OIL] *archaic* **:** to anoint esp. in giving extreme unction

anem- *or* **anemo-** *comb form* [prob. fr. F *anémo-*, fr. Gk *anem-*, *anemo-*, fr. *anemos* — more at ANIMATE] **:** wind ⟨*anem*osis⟩ ⟨*anemo*meter⟩

ane·mia \ə-ˈnē-mē-ə\ *n* [NL, fr. Gk *anaimia* bloodlessness, fr. *a-* + *-aimia* -emia] **1 a :** a condition in which the blood is deficient in red blood cells, in hemoglobin, or in total volume **b :** ISCHEMIA **2 :** lack of vitality — **ane·mic** \ə-ˈnē-mik\ *adj* — **ane·mi·cal·ly** \-mi-k(ə-)lē\ *adv*

anemo·graph \ə-ˈnem-ə-ˌgraf\ *n* **:** a recording anemometer — **anemo·graph·ic** \ə-ˌnem-ə-ˈgraf-ik\ *adj*

an·e·mom·e·ter \ˌan-ə-ˈmäm-ət-ər\ *n* **:** an instrument for measuring and indicating the force or speed of the wind — **an·e·mo·met·ric** \ˌan-ə-mō-ˈme-trik\ *also* **an·e·mo·met·ri·cal** \-tri-kəl\ *adj*

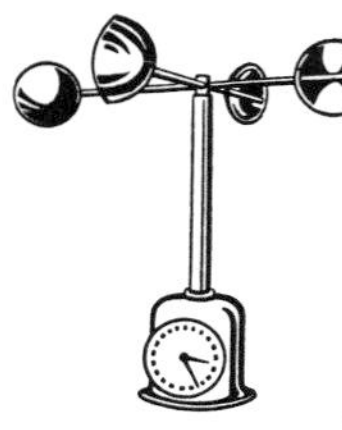

anemometer

an·e·mom·e·try \ˌan-ə-ˈmäm-ə-trē\ *n* **:** the act or process of ascertaining the force, speed, and direction of wind

anem·o·ne \ə-ˈnem-ə-nē\ *n* [L, fr. Gk *anemōnē*] **1 :** any of a large genus (*Anemone*) of the crowfoot family having lobed or divided leaves and showy flowers without petals but with conspicuous often colored sepals **2 :** SEA ANEMONE

an·e·moph·i·lous \ˌan-ə-ˈmäf-ə-ləs\ *adj* **:** normally wind-pollinated — **an·e·moph·i·ly** \-lē\ *n*

anent \ə-ˈnent\ *prep* [ME *onevent*, *anent*, fr. OE *on efen* alongside, fr. *on* + *efen* even] **:** ABOUT, CONCERNING

an·er·oid \ˈan-ə-ˌrȯid\ *adj* [F *anéroïde*, fr. Gk *a-* + LGk *nēron* water, fr. Gk, neut. of *nearos*, *nēros* fresh; akin to Gk *neos* new — more at NEW] **:** containing no liquid or actuated without the use of liquid

aneroid barometer *n* **:** a barometer in which the action of atmospheric pressure in bending a metallic surface is made to move a pointer

an·es·the·sia \ˌan-əs-ˈthē-zhə\ *n* [NL, fr. Gk *anaisthēsia* insensibility, fr. *a-* + *aisthēsis* perception, fr. *aisthanesthai* to perceive] **:** loss of sensation with or without loss of consciousness

an·es·the·si·ol·o·gist \ˌan-əs-ˌthē-zē-ˈäl-ə-jəst\ *n* **:** ANESTHETIST; *specif* **:** a physician specializing in anesthesiology

an·es·the·si·ol·o·gy \-jē\ *n* **:** a branch of medical science dealing with anesthesia and anesthetics

¹**an·es·thet·ic** \ˌan-əs-ˈthet-ik\ *adj* **1 :** of, relating to, or capable of producing anesthesia **2 :** lacking perceptive sensitiveness — **an·es·thet·i·cal·ly** \-i-k(ə-)lē\ *adv*

²**anesthetic** *n* **1 :** a substance that produces anesthesia **2 :** something that brings relief **:** PALLIATIVE

anes·the·tist \ə-ˈnes-thət-əst\ *n* **:** one who administers anesthetics

anes·the·tize \ə-ˈnes-thə-ˌtīz\ *vt* **:** to subject to anesthesia

an·es·trous \(ˈ)an-ˈes-trəs\ *adj* **1 :** not exhibiting estrus **2 :** of or relating to anestrus

an·es·trus \-trəs\ *n* [NL, fr. *a-* + *estrus*] **:** the period of sexual quiescence between two periods of sexual activity in cyclically breeding mammals

an·eu·rysm *also* **an·eu·rism** \ˈan-yə-ˌriz-əm\ *n* [Gk *aneurysma* fr. *aneurynein* to dilate, fr. *ana-* + *eurynein* to stretch, fr. *eurys* wide — more at EURY-] **:** a permanent abnormal blood-filled dilatation of a blood vessel resulting from disease of the vessel wall — **an·eu·rys·mal** \ˌan-yə-ˈriz-məl\ *adj*

anew \ə-ˈn(y)ü\ *adv* [ME *of newe*, fr. OE *of nīwe*, fr. *of* + *nīwe* new] **1 :** for an additional time **:** AFRESH **2 :** in a new form

an·frac·tu·os·i·ty \(ˌ)an-ˌfrak-chə-ˈwäs-ət-ē\ *n* **1 :** the quality or state of being anfractuous **2 :** a winding channel or course; *esp* **:** an intricate path or process (as of the mind)

an·frac·tu·ous \an-ˈfrak-chə-wəs\ *adj* [F *anfractueux*, fr. LL *anfractuosus*, fr. L *anfractus* coil, bend, fr. *anfractus* crooked, fr. *an-* (fr. *ambi-* around) + *fractus*, pp. of *frangere* to break — more at AMBI-, BREAK] **:** full of windings and intricate turnings **:** TORTUOUS

an·ga·ry \ˈaŋ-gə-rē\ *n* [LL *angaria* service to a lord, fr. Gk *angareia* compulsory public service, fr. *angaros* Persian courier] **:** the right in international law of a belligerent to seize, use, or destroy property of neutrals

an·gel \ˈān-jəl\ *n* [ME, fr. OF *angele*, fr. LL *angelus*, fr. Gk *angelos*, lit., messenger] **1 :** a spiritual being superior to man in power and intelligence; *specif* **:** one in the lowest rank **2 :** an attendant spirit or guardian **3 :** a white-robed winged figure of human form in fine art **4 :** MESSENGER, HARBINGER ⟨~ of death⟩ **5 :** a person felt to resemble an angel **6** *Christian Science* **:** a message originating from God in his aspects of Truth and Love **7** *slang* **:** one (as a backer of a theatrical venture) who supports with money or influence — **an·gel·ic** \an-ˈjel-ik\ *or* **an·gel·i·cal** \-i-kəl\ *adj* — **an·gel·i·cal·ly** \-k(ə-)lē\ *adv*

an·gel·fish \ˈān-jəl-ˌfish\ *n* **1 :** any of several compressed brightly colored teleost fishes (family Chaetodontidae) of warm seas **2 :** SCALARE

angel food cake *n* **:** a white sponge cake made of flour, sugar, and whites of eggs

an·gel·i·ca \an-ˈjel-i-kə\ *n* [NL, genus name, fr. ML, fr. LL, fem. of *angelicus* angelic, fr. LGk *angelikos*, fr. Gk, of a messenger, fr. *angelos*] **:** any of a genus (*Angelica*) of herbs of the carrot family; *esp* **:** a biennial (*A. archangelica*) whose roots and fruit furnish a flavoring oil

An·ge·lus \ˈan-jə-ləs\ *n* [ML, fr. LL, angel; fr. the first word of the opening versicle] **1 :** a Roman Catholic devotion that commemorates the Incarnation and is said morning, noon, and evenings **2 :** a bell announcing the time for the Angelus

¹**an·ger** \ˈaŋ-gər\ *n* [ME, affliction, anger, fr. ON *angr* grief; akin to OE *enge* narrow, L *angere* to strangle, Gk *anchein*] **:** a strong feeling of displeasure and usu. of antagonism

syn IRE, RAGE, FURY, INDIGNATION, WRATH: ANGER is the general term for the emotional reaction of extreme displeasure and suggests neither a definite degree of intensity nor a necessarily outward manifestation; IRE is now chiefly literary and suggests great intensity and its exhibition in acts or words; RAGE implies loss of self-control from violence of emotion; FURY suggests even more violence and connotes a degree of temporary madness; INDIGNATION stresses righteous anger at what one considers unfair, mean, or shameful; WRATH may imply either rage or indignation but suggests strongly a desire or intent to avenge or punish

²**anger** *vb* **an·ger·ing** \-g(ə-)riŋ\ *vt* **:** to make angry ~ *vi* **:** to become angry

An·ge·vin \ˈan-jə-vən\ *adj* [F, fr. OF, fr. ML *andegavinus*, fr. *Andegavia* Anjou] **:** of, relating to, or characteristic of Anjou or the Plantagenets — **Angevin** *n*

angi- *or* **angio-** *comb form* [NL, fr. Gk *angei-*, *angeio-*, fr. *angeion* vessel, blood vessel, dim. of *angos* vessel] **1 :** blood or lymph vessel ⟨*angi*oma⟩ **2 :** seed vessel ⟨*angio*carpous⟩

an·gi·na \an-ˈjī-nə\ *n* [L, quinsy, fr. *angere*] **:** a disease marked by spasmodic attacks of intense suffocative pain: as **a :** a severe inflammatory or ulcerated condition of the mouth or throat **b :** ANGINA PECTORIS — **an·gi·nal** \-ˈjīn-ᵊl\ *adj* — **an·gi·nose** \ˈan-jə-ˌnōs\ *adj*

angina pec·to·ris \an-ˌjī-nə-ˈpek-t(ə-)rəs\ *n* [NL, lit., angina of the chest] **:** a disease condition marked by brief paroxysmal attacks of chest pain precipitated by deficient oxygenation of the heart muscles

an·gio·car·pous \ˌan-jē-ō-ˈkär-pəs\ *or* **an·gio·car·pic** \-pik\ *adj* **:** having or being fruit enclosed within an external covering — **an·gio·car·py** \ˈan-jē-ō-ˌkär-pē\ *n*

an·gi·ol·o·gy \ˌan-jē-ˈäl-ə-jē\ *n* **:** the study of blood vessels and lymphatics

an·gi·o·ma \ˌan-jē-ˈō-mə\ *n* **:** a tumor composed chiefly of blood vessels or lymph vessels — **an·gi·o·ma·tous** \-ˈäm-ət-əs, -ˈō-mət-\ *adj*

an·gio·sperm \ˈan-jē-ə-ˌspərm\ *n* [deriv. of NL *angi-* + Gk *sperma* seed — more at SPERM] **:** any of a class (Angiospermae) of vascular plants having the seeds in a closed ovary — **an·gio·sper·mous** \ˌan-jē-ə-ˈspər-məs\ *adj*

¹**an·gle** \ˈaŋ-gəl\ *n* [ME, fr. MF, fr. L *angulus*; akin to OE *anclēow* ankle] **1 a** *archaic* **:** CORNER **b :** a projecting structure or fragment **2 a :** the figure formed by two lines extending from the same point or by two surfaces diverging from the same line **b :** a measure of the amount of turning necessary to bring one line or plane into coincidence with or parallel to another **3 a** (1) **:** POINT OF VIEW (2) **:** ASPECT **b :** a special approach, point of attack, or technique for accomplishing an objective **syn** see PHASE — **an·gled** \-gəld\ *adj*

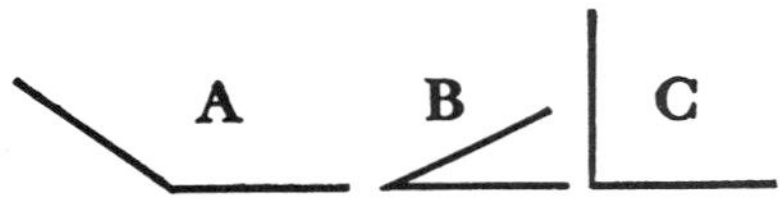

angles 2: obtuse, *A;* acute, *B;* right, *C*

²**angle** *vb* **an·gling** \-g(ə-)liŋ\ *vt* **1 :** to turn, move, or direct at an angle **2 :** to present (as a news story) from a particular or prejudiced point of view ~ *vi* **:** to turn or proceed at an angle

³**angle** *vi* **an·gling** \-g(ə-)liŋ\ [ME *angelen*, fr. *angel* fishhook, fr. OE, fr. *anga* hook; akin to OHG *ango* hook, L *uncus*, Gk *onkos* barbed hook, *ankos* glen] **1 :** to fish with a hook **2 :** to use artful means to attain an objective

An·gle \ˈaŋ-gəl\ *n* [L *Angli*, pl., of Gmc origin; akin to OE *Engle*, pl., Angles] **:** a member of a Germanic people conquering England with the Saxons and Jutes in the 5th century A.D. and merging with them to form the Anglo-Saxon peoples

An·gle·doz·er \ˈaŋ-gəl-ˌdō-zər\ *trademark* — used for a tractor-driven pusher and scraper with the blade at an angle for pushing material to one side

angle iron *n* **1 :** an iron cleat for joining parts of a structure at an angle **2 :** a piece of structural steel rolled with an L-shaped section

angle of attack : the acute angle between the direction of the relative wind and the chord of an airfoil

angle of incidence : the angle that a line (as a ray of light) falling on a surface makes with a perpendicular to the surface at the point of incidence

angle of reflection : the angle between a reflected ray and the normal drawn at the point of incidence to a reflecting surface

angle of refraction : the angle between a refracted ray and the normal drawn at the point of incidence to the interface at which refraction occurs

an·gler \ˈaŋ-glər\ *n* **1 :** one that angles **2 :** a marine fish (*Lophius piscatorius*) having a large flattened head and wide mouth with a lure on the head and fleshy mouth appendages used to attract smaller fishes as prey

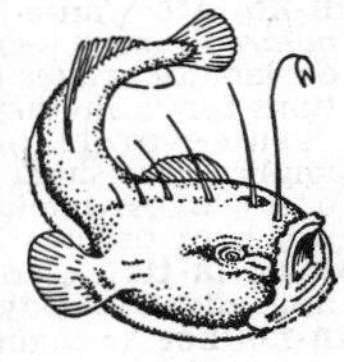

angler

an·gle·site \ˈaŋ-gəl-ˌsīt\ *n* [F *anglésite*, fr. *Anglesey* island, Wales] **:** a mineral $PbSO_4$ consisting of lead sulfate formed by the oxidation of galena

an·gle·worm \ˈaŋ-gəl-ˌwərm\ *n* **:** EARTHWORM

An·gli·an \ˈaŋ-glē-ən\ *n* **1 :** ANGLE **2 :** the Old English dialects of Mercia and Northumbria — **Anglian** *adj*

An·gli·can \ˈaŋ-gli-kən\ *adj* [ML *anglicanus*, fr. *anglicus* English, fr. LL *Angli* English people, fr. L, Angles] **1 :** of or relating to the established episcopal Church of England and churches of similar faith and order in communion with it **2 :** of or relating to England or the English nation — **Anglican** *n* — **An·gli·can·ism** \-kə-ˌniz-əm\ *n*

an·gli·cism \ˈaŋ-glə-ˌsiz-əm\ *n, often cap* [ML *anglicus* English] **1 :** a characteristic feature of English occurring in another language **2 :** adherence or attachment to English customs or ideas

An·gli·cist \ˈaŋ-glə-səst\ *n* **:** a specialist in English linguistics

an·gli·ci·za·tion \ˌaŋ-glə-sə-ˈzā-shən\ *n, often cap* **:** the process or the result of anglicizing or being anglicized

an·gli·cize \ˈaŋ-glə-ˌsīz\ *vt, often cap* **1 :** to make English in quality or characteristics **2 :** to adapt (a foreign word or phrase) to English usage; *esp* **:** to borrow into English without alteration of form or spelling and with or without change in pronunciation

an·gling *n* **:** the act of one who angles; *esp* **:** the act of fishing with hook and line usu. for sport

Anglo- *comb form* [NL, fr. LL *Angli*] **1 :** English ⟨*Anglo*-Norman⟩ **2 :** English and ⟨*Anglo*-Japanese⟩

An·glo–Cath·o·lic \ˌaŋ-(ˌ)glō-ˈkath-(ə-)lik\ *adj* **:** of or relating to a High Church movement in Anglicanism emphasizing its continuity with historic Catholicism and fostering Catholic dogmatic and liturgical traditions — **Anglo–Catholic** *n* — **An·glo–Ca·thol·i·cism** \-kə-ˈthäl-ə-ˌsiz-əm\ *n*

An·glo–French \ˌaŋ-(ˌ)glō-ˈfrench\ *n* **:** the French language used in medieval England

An·glo–Nor·man \-ˈnȯr-mən\ *n* **1 :** one of the Normans living in England after the Conquest **2 :** the form of Anglo-French used by Anglo-Normans

an·glo·phile \ˈaŋ-glə-ˌfīl\ *also* **an·glo·phil** \-ˌfil\ *n, often cap* [F, fr. *anglo-* + *-phile*] **:** one who greatly admires or favors England and things English

an·glo·phobe \ˈaŋ-glə-ˌfōb\ *n, often cap* [prob. fr. F, fr. *anglo-* + *-phobe*] **:** one who is averse to England and things English

an·glo·pho·bia \ˌaŋ-glə-ˈfō-bē-ə\ *n, often cap* [NL] **:** intense aversion to England or the English — **an·glo·pho·bic** \-ˈfō-bik, -ˈfäb-ik\ *adj, often cap*

An·glo–Sax·on \ˌaŋ-(ˌ)glō-ˈsak-sən\ *n* [NL *Anglo-Saxones*, pl., alter. of ML *Angli Saxones*, fr. L *Angli* Angles + LL *Saxones* Saxons] **1 :** a member of the Germanic peoples conquering England in the 5th century A.D. and forming the ruling class until the Norman conquest — compare ANGLE, JUTE, SAXON **2 :** ENGLISHMAN; *specif* **:** a person descended from the Anglo-Saxons **3 :** OLD ENGLISH 1 **4 :** direct plain English — **Anglo–Saxon** *adj*

an·go·ra \aŋ-ˈgōr-ə, an-, -ˈgȯr-\ *n* **1 :** the hair of the Angora rabbit or Angora goat **2 :** a yarn of Angora rabbit hair used esp. for knitting

Angora cat *n* [*Angora* (Ankara), Turkey] **:** a long-haired domestic cat

Angora goat *n* **:** any of a breed or variety of the domestic goat raised for its long silky hair which is the true mohair

Angora rabbit *n* **:** a long-haired usu. white rabbit with red eyes that is raised for fine wool

an·gos·tu·ra bark \ˌaŋ-gə-ˈst(y)u̇r-ə-\ *n* [*Angostura* (now Ciudad Bolívar), Venezuela] **:** an aromatic bitter bark used as a tonic and antipyretic and obtained from two So. American trees (*Galipea officinalis* and *Cusparia trifoliata*) of the rue family

an·gri·ly \ˈaŋ-grə-lē\ *adv* **:** in an angry manner

an·gri·ness \-grē-nəs\ *n* **:** the state of being angry

an·gry \ˈaŋ-grē\ *adj* **1 :** feeling or showing anger **:** WRATHFUL **2 a :** indicative of or proceeding from anger ⟨~ words⟩ **b :** seeming to show anger or to threaten angrily ⟨an ~ sky⟩ **3 :** painfully inflamed ⟨an ~ rash⟩

angst \ˈäŋ(k)st\ *n* [Dan & G; Dan, fr. G; akin to L *angustus*] **:** a feeling of anxiety **:** DREAD

ang·strom \ˈaŋ-strəm\ *n* [Anders J. *Ångström* †1874 Sw physicist] **:** either of two units of wavelength: **a :** one ten-billionth of a meter **b :** the wavelength of the red spectrum line of cadmium divided by 6438.4696

1**an·guish** \ˈaŋ-gwish\ *n* [ME *angwisshe*, fr. OF *angoisse*, fr. L *angustiae*, pl., straits, distress, fr. *angustus* narrow; akin to OE *enge* narrow — more at ANGER] **:** extreme pain or distress of either body or mind **syn** see SORROW

2**anguish** *vi* **:** to suffer intense pain or sorrow ~ *vt* **:** to cause to suffer anguish or distress

an·guished *adj* **:** produced, affected, or accompanied by anguish

an·gu·lar \ˈaŋ-gyə-lər\ *adj* [MF or L; MF *angulaire*, fr. L *angularis*, fr. *angulus* angle] **1 a :** having one or more angles **b :** forming an angle **:** sharp-cornered **2 :** measured by an angle ⟨~ distance⟩ **3 a :** stiff in character or manner **b :** having the bones prominent from lack of plumpness — **an·gu·lar·ly** *adv*

an·gu·lar·i·ty \ˌaŋ-gyə-ˈlar-ət-ē\ *n* **1 :** the quality of being angular **2** *pl* **:** angular outlines or characteristics

an·gu·late \ˈaŋ-gyə-lət, -ˌlāt\ *adj* **:** formed with corners **:** ANGLED ⟨~ leaves⟩ — **an·gu·late·ly** *adv*

an·gu·la·tion \ˌaŋ-gyə-ˈlā-shən\ *n* **1 :** the action of making angulate **2 :** an angular formation or shape

An·gus \ˈaŋ-gəs\ *n* [*Angus*, county in Scotland] **:** ABERDEEN ANGUS

an·gus·ti- \aŋ-ˌgəs-tə\ *comb form* [L, fr. *angustus*] **:** narrow ⟨*angusti*foliate⟩ ⟨*angusti*rostrate⟩

an·hy·dride \(ˈ)an-ˈhī-ˌdrīd\ *n* **:** a compound derived from another (as an acid) by removal of the elements of water

an·hy·drite \-ˈhī-ˌdrīt\ *n* [G *anhydrit*, fr. Gk *anydros*] **:** a mineral $CaSO_4$ consisting of an anhydrous calcium sulfate that is usu. massive and white or slightly colored

an·hy·drous \-ˈhī-drəs\ *adj* [Gk *anydros*, fr. *a-* + *hydōr* water — more at WATER] **:** free from water and esp. water of crystallization

ani \ä-ˈnē\ *n* [Sp *aní*, or Pg *ani*, fr. Tupi *ani*] **:** any of several black cuckoos (genus *Crotaphagus*) of the warmer parts of America

an·i·line \ˈan-ᵊl-ən\ *n* [G *anilin*, fr. *anil* indigo, fr. F, fr. Pg, fr. Ar *an-nīl* the indigo plant, fr. Skt *nīlī* indigo, fr. fem. of *nīla* dark blue] **:** an oily liquid poisonous amine $C_6H_5NH_2$ obtained esp. by the reduction of nitrobenzene and used chiefly in organic synthesis (as of dyes)

aniline dye *n* **:** a dye made by the use of aniline or one chemically related to such a dye; *broadly* **:** a synthetic organic dye

an·i·mad·ver·sion \ˌan-ə-ˌmad-ˈvər-zhən, -məd-, -ˈvər-shən\ *n* [L *animadversion-*, *animadversio*, fr. *animadversus*, pp. of *animadvertere*] **1 :** a critical and usu. censorious remark **2 :** adverse criticism

syn ANIMADVERSION, STRICTURE, ASPERSION, REFLECTION mean an adverse criticism. ANIMADVERSION implies criticism prompted by prejudice or ill will; STRICTURE implies censure that may be either ill-natured or judicious; ASPERSION imputes a slanderous character to the criticism; REFLECTION often indicates an implied rather than direct aspersion or criticism

an·i·mad·vert \-ˈvərt\ *vb* [L *animadvertere* to pay attention to, censure, fr. *animum advertere*, lit., to turn the mind to] *vt, archaic* **:** NOTICE, OBSERVE ~ *vi* **:** to make an animadversion

1**an·i·mal** \ˈan-ə-məl\ *n* [L, fr. *animale*, neut. of *animalis* animate, fr. *anima* soul] **1 :** any of a kingdom (Animalia) of living beings typically differing from plants in capacity for spontaneous movement and rapid motor response to stimulation **2 a :** one of the lower animals as distinguished from man **b :** MAMMAL **3 :** a human being considered chiefly with regard to his physical nature **4 :** ANIMALITY 2

2**animal** *adj* **1 :** of, relating to, or derived from animals **2 a :** of or relating to the physical or sentient as contrasted with the intellectual or rational **b :** SENSUAL, FLESHY **syn** see CARNAL — **an·i·mal·ly** \-mə-lē\ *adv*

an·i·mal·cu·lar \ˌan-ə-ˈmal-kyə-lər\ *adj* **:** of or relating to animalcules

an·i·mal·cule \-ˈmal-(ˌ)kyü(ə)l\ *or* **an·i·mal·cu·lum** \-ˈmal-kyə-ləm\ *n, pl* **animalcules** *or* **an·i·mal·cu·la** \-ˈmal-kyə-lə\ [NL *animalculum*, dim. of L *animal*] **:** a minute usu. microscopic organism

animal heat *n* **:** heat produced in the body of a living animal by functional chemical and physical activities

animal husbandry *n* **:** a branch of agriculture concerned with the production and care of domestic animals

an·i·mal·ism \ˈan-ə-mə-ˌliz-əm\ *n* **1 a** (1) **:** the qualities typical of animals; *esp* **:** buoyant health and uninhibited vitality (2) **:** the exercise of these qualities **b :** preoccupation with the satisfaction of physical drives or wants **2 :** a theory that human beings are nothing more than animals — **an·i·mal·ist** \-mə-ləst\ *n* — **an·i·mal·is·tic** \ˌan-ə-mə-ˈlis-tik\ *adj*

an·i·mal·i·ty \ˌan-ə-ˈmal-ət-ē\ *n* **1 :** ANIMALISM 1a(1) **2 a :** the state of being an animal **b :** animal nature **3 :** the animal world

an·i·mal·iza·tion \ˌan-ə-mə-lə-ˈzā-shən\ *n* **:** the act of animalizing **:** the state of being animalized

an·i·mal·ize \ˈan-ə-mə-ˌlīz\ *vt* **1 :** to represent in animal form **2 :** BRUTALIZE, SENSUALIZE

animal magnetism *n* **:** a force held to reside in some individuals by which a strong quasi-hypnotic influence can be exerted

animal spirits *n pl* **:** vivacity arising from physical health and energy

1**an·i·mate** \ˈan-ə-mət\ *adj* [ME, fr. L *animatus*, pp. of *animare* to give life to, fr. *anima* breath, soul; akin to OE *ōthian* to breathe, L *animus* spirit, mind, courage, Gk *anemos* wind] **1 :** possessing life **:** ALIVE **2 :** of or relating to animal life as opposed to plant life **3 :** full of life **:** ANIMATED **syn** see LIVING — **an·i·mate·ly** *adv* — **an·i·mate·ness** *n*

2**an·i·mate** \-ˌmāt\ *vt* **1 :** to give spirit and support to **:** ENCOURAGE **2 a :** to give life to **b :** to give vigor and zest to **3 :** to move to action **4 a :** to make or design in such a way that apparently spontaneous lifelike movement is effected **b :** to produce in the form of an animated cartoon **syn** see QUICKEN

an·i·mat·ed *adj* **1 a :** ALIVE, LIVING **b :** full of movement and activity **c :** full of vigor and spirit **:** VIVACIOUS **2 :** having the appearance of something alive **3 :** made in the form of an animated cartoon **syn** see LIVELY, LIVING — **an·i·mat·ed·ly** *adv*

animated cartoon *n* **:** a motion picture made from a series of drawings simulating motion by means of slight progressive changes

an·i·ma·tion \ˌan-ə-ˈmā-shən\ *n* **1 :** the act of animating or the state of being animate or animated **2 a :** ANIMATED CARTOON **b :** the preparation of animated cartoons

an·i·ma·to \ˌan-ə-ˈmät-(ˌ)ō\ *adv (or adj)* [It, fr. L *animatus*] **:** with animation — used as a direction in music

an·i·ma·tor \ˈan-ə-ˌmāt-ər\ *n* **:** one that contributes to the production of an animated cartoon

an·i·mism \ˈan-ə-ˌmiz-əm\ *n* [G *animismus*, fr. L *anima*] **1 :** a doctrine that the soul is the vital principle of organic development **2 :** attribution of conscious life to nature or natural objects **3 :** belief in the existence of spirits separable from bodies — **an·i·mist** \-məst\ *n* — **an·i·mis·tic** \ˌan-ə-ˈmis-tik\ *adj*

an·i·mos·i·ty \ˌan-ə-ˈmäs-ət-ē\ *n* [ME *animosite*, fr. MF or LL; MF *animosité*, fr. LL *animositat-*, *animositas*, fr. L *animosus* spirited, fr. *animus*] **:** ill will or resentment tending toward active hostility **syn** see ENMITY

an·i·mus \ˈan-ə-məs\ *n* [L, spirit, mind, courage, anger] **1 :** basic attitude or governing spirit **:** DISPOSITION, INTENTION **2 :** deep-seated hostility **:** ANTAGONISM **syn** see ENMITY

an·ion \ˈan-ˌī-ən, -ˌī-ˌän\ *n* [Gk, neut. of *aniōn*, prp. of *anienai* t

go up, fr. *ana-* + *ienai* to go — more at ISSUE] **:** the ion in an electrolyzed solution that migrates to the anode; *broadly* **:** a negatively charged ion

an·ion·ic \ˌan-(ˌ)ī-ˈän-ik\ *adj* **1 :** of or relating to anions **2 :** characterized by an active and esp. surface-active anion — **an·ion·i·cal·ly** \-i-k(ə-)lē\ *adv*

anis- *or* **aniso-** *comb form* [NL, fr. Gk, fr. *anisos*, fr. *a-* + *isos* equal] **:** unequal ⟨*anis*eikonia⟩ ⟨*aniso*dactylous⟩

an·ise \ˈan-əs\ *n* [ME *anis*, fr. OF, fr. L *anisum*, fr. Gk *annēson, anison*] **:** an herb (*Pimpinella anisum*) of the carrot family having carminative and aromatic seeds; *also* **:** ANISEED

ani·seed \ˈan-ə(s)-ˌsēd\ *n* [ME *anis seed*, fr. *anis* + *seed*] **:** the seed of anise often used as a flavoring in cordials and in cooking

an·is·ei·ko·nia \ˌan-ˌī-ˌsī-ˈkō-nē-ə\ *n* [NL, fr. *anis-* + Gk *eikōn* image — more at ICON] **:** a defect of binocular vision in which the two retinal images of an object differ in size — **an·is·ei·kon·ic** \-ˈkän-ik\ *adj*

an·is·ette \ˌan-ə-ˈset, -ˈzet\ *n* [F, fr. *anis*] **:** a usu. colorless sweet liqueur flavored with aniseed

an·isog·a·mous \ˌan-(ˌ)ī-ˈsäg-ə-məs\ *also* **an·iso·gam·ic** \-ˌī-sə-ˈgam-ik\ *adj* **:** characterized by fusion of unlike gametes or of individuals usu. differing chiefly in size ⟨~ reproduction⟩ — **an·isog·a·my** \-(ˌ)ī-ˈsäg-ə-mē\ *n*

an·iso·met·ric \ˌan-ˌī-sə-ˈme-trik\ *adj* [F *anisométrique*, fr. *a-* + *isométrique* isometric] **:** having unsymmetrical parts

an·iso·me·tro·pia \ˌan-ˌī-sə-mə-ˈtrō-pē-ə\ *n* [NL, fr. Gk *anisometros* of unequal measure (fr. *anis-* + *metron* measure) + NL *-opia* — more at MEASURE] **:** unequal refractive power in the two eyes — **an·iso·me·tro·pic** \-ˈträp-ik, -ˈtrō-pik\ *adj*

an·iso·trop·ic \ˌan-ˌī-sə-ˈträp-ik\ *adj* **1 :** exhibiting properties with different values when measured along axes in different directions ⟨an ~ crystal⟩ **2 :** assuming different positions in response to external stimuli — **an·iso·trop·i·cal·ly** \-i-k(ə-)lē\ *adv* — **an·isot·ro·py** \-(ˌ)ī-ˈsä-trə-pē\ *or* **an·isot·ro·pism** \-ˌpiz-əm\ *n*

an·ker·ite \ˈaŋ-kə-ˌrīt\ *n* [G *ankerit*, fr. M. J. *Anker* †1843 Austrian mineralogist] **:** a dolomitic iron-containing mineral $Ca(Fe,Mg,Mn)(CO_3)_2$

ankh \ˈaŋk\ *n* [Egypt *ʿnḫ*] **:** a cross having a loop for its upper vertical arm and serving esp. in ancient Egypt as an emblem of life

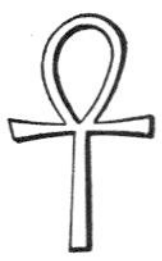

ankh

an·kle \ˈaŋ-kəl\ *n* [ME *ankel*, fr. OE *anclēow*; akin to OHG *anchlāo* ankle, L *angulus* angle] **1 :** the joint between the foot and the leg; *also* **:** the region of this joint **2 :** the joint between the cannon bone and pastern (as in the horse)

an·kle·bone \ˈaŋ-kəl-ˈbōn, -ˌbōn\ *n* **:** TALUS 1

an·klet \ˈaŋ-klət\ *n* **1 :** something (as an ornament) worn around the ankle **2 :** a short sock reaching slightly above the ankle **3 :** a woman's or child's low shoe having one or more ankle straps

an·ky·lose \ˈaŋ-ki-ˌlōs, -ˌlōz\ *vb* [back-formation fr. *ankylosis*] *vt* **:** to unite or stiffen by ankylosis ~ *vi* **:** to undergo ankylosis

an·ky·lo·sis \ˌaŋ-ki-ˈlō-səs\ *n* [NL, fr. Gk *ankylōsis*, fr. *ankyloun* to make crooked, fr. *ankylos* crooked; akin to L *uncus* hooked — more at ANGLE] **1 :** stiffness or fixation of a joint by disease or surgery **2 :** union of separate bones or hard parts to form a single bone or part — **an·ky·lot·ic** \-ˈlät-ik\ *adj*

an·la·ge \ˈän-ˌläg-ə\ *n, pl* **an·la·gen** \-ən\ *also* **anlages** [G, lit., act of laying on] **:** the foundation of a subsequent development **:** RUDIMENT; *specif* **:** the first recognizable commencement of a developing part or organ in an embryo

an·na \ˈän-ə\ *n* [Hindi *ānā*] **1 :** a former monetary unit of Burma, India, and Pakistan equal to 1⁄16 rupee **2 :** a coin representing one anna

an·nal·ist \ˈan-ᵊl-əst\ *n* **:** a writer of annals **:** HISTORIAN — **an·nal·is·tic** \ˌan-ᵊl-ˈis-tik\ *adj*

an·nals \ˈan-ᵊlz\ *n pl* [L *annales*, fr. pl. of *annalis* yearly — more at ANNUAL] **1 :** a record of events arranged in yearly sequence **2 :** historical records **:** CHRONICLES **3 :** records of the activities of an organization

An·nam·ese \ˌan-ə-ˈmēz, -ˈmēs\ *n, pl* **Annamese** **1 a :** a Mongolian people that occupies mainly Cochin China and the coast regions of Annam and Tonkin **b** *or* **An·nam·ite** \ˈan-ə-ˌmīt\ **:** a member of such people **2 :** the language of the Annamese people **:** VIETNAMESE — **Annamese** *adj*

an·nat·to \ə-ˈnät-(ˌ)ō\ *n* [of Cariban origin; akin to Galibi *annoto* tree producing annatto] **:** a yellowish red dyestuff made from the pulp around the seeds of a tropical tree (*Bixa orellana*, family Bixaceae)

an·neal \ə-ˈnē(ə)l\ *vt* [ME *anelen*, fr. OE *onǣlan*, fr. *on* + *ǣlan* to set on fire, burn, fr. *āl* fire; akin to OE *ād* funeral pyre — more at EDIFY] **1 :** to heat (as glass) in order to fix laid-on colors **2 :** to heat and then cool usu. for softening and rendering less brittle **3 :** STRENGTHEN, TOUGHEN ⟨was ~*ed* by hardship⟩

an·ne·lid \ˈan-ᵊl-əd\ *n* [deriv. of L *anellus* little ring — more at ANNULET] **:** any of a phylum (Annelida) of coelomate and usu. elongated segmented invertebrates including the earthworms, various marine worms, leeches, and related forms — **annelid** *adj* — **an·nel·i·dan** \ə-ˈnel-əd-ᵊn\ *adj or n*

¹an·nex \ə-ˈneks, ˈan-ˌeks\ *vt* [ME *annexen*, fr. MF *annexer*, fr. OF, fr. *annexe* joined, fr. L *annexus*, pp. of *annectere* to bind to, fr. *ad-* + *nectere* to bind] **1 :** to attach as a quality, consequence, or condition **2** *archaic* **:** to join together materially **:** UNITE **3 :** SUBJOIN, APPEND **4 :** to incorporate (a country or other territory) within the domain of a state **5 :** to obtain or take for oneself — **an·nex·a·tion** \ˌan-ˌek-ˈsā-shən\ *n* — **an·nex·a·tion·al** \-shnəl, -shən-ᵊl\ *adj* — **an·nex·a·tion·ist** \-sh(ə-)nəst\ *n*

²an·nex \ˈan-ˌeks, -iks\ *n* **:** something annexed or appended: as **a :** an added stipulation or statement **:** APPENDIX **b :** a subsidiary or supplementary structure **:** WING

an·ni·hi·late \ə-ˈnī-ə-ˌlāt\ *vt* [LL *annihilatus*, pp. of *annihilare* to reduce to nothing, fr. L *ad-* + *nihil* nothing — more at NIL] **1 a :** to cause to be of no effect **:** NULLIFY **b :** to destroy the substance or force of **2 :** to regard as of no consequence **3 :** to cause to cease to exist **4 a :** to destroy a considerable part of ⟨the army was *annihilated*⟩ **b :** to vanquish completely **:** ROUT **syn** see ABOLISH — **an·ni·hi·la·tion** \ə-ˌnī-ə-ˈlā-shən\ *n* — **an·ni·hi·la·tive** \ə-ˈnī-ə-ˌlāt-iv\ *adj* — **an·ni·hi·la·tor** \-ˌlāt-ər\ *n*

an·ni·ver·sa·ry \ˌan-ə-ˈvərs-(ə-)rē\ *n, often attrib* [ME *anniversarie*, fr. ML *anniversarium*, fr. L, neut. of *anniversarius* returning annually, fr. *annus* year + *versus*, pp. of *vertere* to turn — more at ANNUAL, WORTH] **1 :** the annual recurrence of a date marking a notable event **2 :** the celebration of an anniversary

an·no Do·mi·ni \ˌan-(ˌ)ō-ˈdäm-ə-nē, -ˈdō-mə-, -ˌnī\ *adv, often cap A* [ML, in the year of the Lord] — used to indicate that a time division falls within the Christian era

an·no he·gi·rae \-hi-ˈjī(ə)-(ˌ)rē, -ˈhej-ə-ˌrē\ *adv, often cap A&H* [NL, in the year of the Hegira] — used to indicate that a time division falls within the Muslim era

an·no·tate \ˈan-ə-ˌtāt\ *vb* [L *annotatus*, pp. of *annotare*, fr. *ad-* + *notare* to mark — more at NOTE] *vi* **:** to make or furnish critical or explanatory notes or comment ~ *vt* **:** to make or furnish annotations for (a literary work or subject) — **an·no·ta·tor** \-ˌtāt-ər\ *n*

syn ANNOTATE, GLOSS mean to add comment to a text. ANNOTATE implies furnishing a text with critical, historical, or explanatory notes; GLOSS implies supplying a text with definitions of difficult words or phrases

an·no·ta·tion \ˌan-ə-ˈtā-shən\ *n* **1 :** the act of annotating **2 :** a note added by way of comment or explanation

an·nounce \ə-ˈnaůn(t)s\ *vb* [ME *announcen*, fr. MF *annoncer*, fr. L *annuntiare*, fr. *ad-* + *nuntiare* to report, fr. *nuntius* messenger] *vt* **1 :** to make known publicly **:** PROCLAIM **2 a :** to give notice of the arrival, presence, or readiness of **b :** to indicate beforehand **:** FORETELL **3 :** to serve as an announcer of ~ *vi* **1 :** to serve as an announcer **2 :** to declare one's candidacy **:** give one's political support **syn** see DECLARE

an·nounce·ment \ə-ˈnaůn(t)-smənt\ *n* **1 :** the act of announcing or of being announced **2 :** a public notification or declaration **3 :** a piece of formal stationery designed for a social or business announcement

an·nounc·er \ə-ˈnaůn(t)-sər\ *n* **:** one that announces; *esp* **:** one that introduces television or radio programs, makes commercial announcements, reads news summaries, and gives station identification

an·noy \ə-ˈnȯi\ *vb* [ME *anoien*, fr. OF *enuier*, fr. LL *inodiare* to make loathsome, fr. L *in* + *odium* hatred — more at ODIUM] *vt* **1 :** to disturb or irritate esp. by repeated acts **:** VEX **2 :** HARASS, MOLEST ~ *vi* **:** to be a source of annoyance — **an·noy·er** *n*

syn VEX, IRK, BOTHER: ANNOY implies a wearing on the nerves by persistent petty unpleasantness; VEX implies greater provocation and stronger disturbance and usu. connotes anger but sometimes perplexity or anxiety; IRK stresses difficulty in enduring and resulting weariness or impatience of spirit; BOTHER may imply either a bewildering or upsetting but always suggests interference with comfort or peace of mind **syn** see in addition WORRY

an·noy·ance \ə-ˈnȯi-ən(t)s\ *n* **1 :** the act of annoying or of being annoyed **2 :** the state or feeling of being annoyed **:** VEXATION **3 :** a source of vexation or irritation **:** NUISANCE

an·noy·ing *adj* **:** IRRITATING, VEXING — **an·noy·ing·ly** \-iŋ-lē\ *adv*

¹an·nu·al \ˈan-yə(-wə)l\ *adj* [ME, fr. MF & LL; MF *annuel*, fr. LL *annualis*, blend of L *annuus* yearly (fr. *annus* year) and L *annalis* yearly (fr. *annus* year); akin to Goth *athnam* (dat. pl.) years, Skt *atati* he walks, goes] **1 :** covering the period of a year **2 :** occurring or performed once a year **:** YEARLY **3 :** completing the life cycle in one growing season — **an·nu·al·ly** \-ē\ *adv*

²annual *n* **1 :** a publication appearing yearly **2 :** an event that occurs yearly **3 :** something that lasts one year or season; *specif* **:** an annual plant

annual ring *n* **:** the layer of wood produced by a single year's growth of a woody plant

an·nu·itant \ə-ˈn(y)ü-ət-ənt\ *n* **:** a beneficiary of an annuity

an·nu·ity \ə-ˈn(y)ü-ət-ē\ *n* [ME *annuite*, fr. MF *annuité*, fr. ML *annuitat-, annuitas*, fr. L *annuus* yearly] **1 :** an amount payable yearly or at other regular intervals **2 :** the right to receive or the obligation to pay an annuity

an·nul \ə-ˈnəl\ *vt* **an·nulled; an·nul·ling** [ME *annullen*, fr. MF *annuller*, fr. LL *annullare*, fr. L *ad-* + *nullus* not any — more at NULL] **1 :** to reduce to nothing **:** OBLITERATE **2 :** to make ineffective or inoperative **:** NEUTRALIZE ⟨~ the drug's effect⟩ **3 :** to declare or make legally void **syn** see NULLIFY

an·nu·lar \ˈan-yə-lər\ *adj* [MF or L; MF *annulaire*, fr. L *annularis*, fr. *annulus*] **:** of, relating to, or forming a ring — **an·nu·lar·i·ty** \ˌan-yə-ˈlar-ət-ē\ *n* — **an·nu·lar·ly** *adv*

annular eclipse *n* **:** an eclipse in which a thin outer ring of the sun's disk is not covered by the apparently smaller dark disk of the moon

annular ligament *n* **:** a ringlike ligament or band of fibrous tissue encircling a part (as the wrist or ankle)

an·nu·late \ˈan-yə-lət, -ˌlāt\ *or* **an·nu·lat·ed** \-ˌlāt-əd\ *adj* **:** furnished with or composed of rings **:** RINGED

an·nu·la·tion \ˌan-yə-ˈlā-shən\ *n* **:** formation of rings; *also* **:** RING

an·nu·let \ˈan-yə-lət\ *n* [modif. of MF *annelet*, dim. of *anel*, fr. L *anellus*, dim. of *annulus*] **1 :** a little ring **2 :** a small architectural molding or ridge forming a ring

an·nul·ment \ə-ˈnəl-mənt\ *n* **:** the act of annulling or of being annulled; *specif* **:** a judicial pronouncement declaring the invalidity of a marriage

an·nu·lus \ˈan-yə-ləs\ *n, pl* **an·nu·li** \-ˌlī, -lē\ *also* **an·nu·lus·es** [L, dim. of *anus* ring, anus — more at ANUS] **:** RING; *esp* **:** a part, structure, or marking resembling a ring

an·nun·ci·ate \ə-ˈnən(t)-sē-ˌāt\ *vt* **:** ANNOUNCE

an·nun·ci·a·tion \ə-ˌnən(t)-sē-ˈā-shən\ *n* [ME *annunciacioun*, fr. MF *anunciation*, fr. LL *annuntiation-, annuntiatio*, fr. L *annuntiatus*, pp. of *annuntiare*—more at ANNOUNCE] **1 :** the act of announcing or of being announced **:** ANNOUNCEMENT **2** *cap* **:** the 25th of March on which many Christian churches commemorate the announcement of the Incarnation related in Luke 1:28–35

an·nun·ci·a·tor \ə-ˈnən(t)-sē-ˌāt-ər\ *n* **:** one that annunciates; *specif* **:** an electrically controlled signal board or indicator — **an·nun·ci·a·to·ry** \-sē-ə-ˌtōr-ē, -ˌtȯr-\ *adj*

an·ode \ˈan-ˌōd\ *n* [Gk *anodos* way up, fr. *ana-* + *hodos* way — more at CEDE] **1 :** the positive terminal of an electrolytic cell — compare CATHODE **2 :** the negative terminal of a primary cell or of a storage battery that is delivering current **3 :** the electron-collecting electrode of an electron tube — **an·od·ic** \a-ˈnäd-ik\ *adj* — **an·od·i·cal·ly** \-i-k(ə-)lē\ *adv*

an·od·ize \ˈan-ə-ˌdīz\ *vt* **:** to subject (a metal) to electrolytic action as the anode of a cell in order to coat with a protective or decorative film

¹an·o·dyne \ˈan-ə-ˌdīn\ *adj* [L *anodynos*, fr. Gk *anōdynos*, fr. *a-* + *odynē* pain; akin to OE *etan* to eat] **:** serving to assuage pain **:** SOOTHING

2anodyne *n* **1 :** a drug that allays pain **2 :** something that soothes, calms, or comforts — **an·o·dyn·ic** \ˌan-ə-ˈdin-ik\ *adj*

anoint \ə-ˈnȯint\ *vt* [ME *anointen,* fr. MF *enoint,* pp. of *enoindre,* fr. L *inunguere,* fr. *in-* + *unguere* to smear] **1 :** to rub over with oil or an oily substance **2 a :** to apply oil to as a sacred rite esp. for consecration **b :** to designate as if through the rite of anointment **:** CONSECRATE — **anoint·er** *n* — **anoint·ment** \-mənt\ *n*

anom·a·lis·tic \ə-ˌnäm-ə-ˈlis-tik\ *adj* **:** of or relating to the astronomical anomaly — **anom·a·lis·ti·cal** \-ti-kəl\ *adj*

anom·a·lous \ə-ˈnäm-ə-ləs\ *adj* [LL *anomalus,* fr. Gk *anōmalos,* lit., uneven, fr. *a-* + *homalos* even, fr. *homos* same — more at SAME] **1 :** deviating from a general rule, method, or analogy **:** ABNORMAL **2 :** being out of keeping with accepted notions of fitness or order; *also* **:** inconsistent with what would naturally be expected **syn** see IRREGULAR — **anom·a·lous·ly** *adv* — **anom·a·lous·ness** *n*

anom·a·ly \ə-ˈnäm-ə-lē\ *n* **1 :** the angular distance of a planet from its perihelion as seen from the sun **2 :** deviation from the common rule **:** IRREGULARITY **3 :** something anomalous; *esp* **:** something that deviates in excess of normal variation

an·o·mie \ˈan-ə-mē\ *n* [F *anomie,* fr. Gk *anomia* lawlessness, fr. *anomos* lawless, fr. *a-* + *nomos* law, fr. *nemein* to distribute] **:** a state of society in which normative standards of conduct and belief are weak or lacking; *also* **:** a similar condition in an individual commonly characterized by disorientation, anxiety, and isolation

anon \ə-ˈnän\ *adv* [ME, fr. OE *on ān,* fr. *on* in + *ān* one — more at ON, ONE] **1** *archaic* **:** at once **:** IMMEDIATELY **2 :** SOON, PRESENTLY; *also* **:** LATER ⟨more of that ~⟩ **3 :** at another time

an·o·nym *also* **an·o·nyme** \ˈan-ə-ˌnim\ *n* **1 :** one that retains anonymity or is of unknown name **2 :** PSEUDONYM

an·o·nym·i·ty \ˌan-ə-ˈnim-ət-ē\ *n* **1 :** the quality or state of being anonymous **2 :** one that is anonymous

anon·y·mous \ə-ˈnän-ə-məs\ *adj* [LL *anonymus,* fr. Gk *anōnymos,* fr. *a-* + *onyma* name — more at NAME] **1 :** having or giving no name ⟨~ author⟩ **2 :** of unknown or unnamed source or origin ⟨~ gifts⟩ **3 :** lacking marked individuality or personality ⟨brown ~ houses⟩ — **anon·y·mous·ly** *adv* — **anon·y·mous·ness** *n*

anoph·e·les \ə-ˈnäf-ə-ˌlēz\ *n* [NL, genus name, fr. Gk *anōphelēs* useless, fr. *a-* + *ophelos* advantage, help; akin to OE *ō-* behind, OHG *ā-,* Skt *ā-* toward and to Skt *phalam* fruit, profit] **:** any of a genus (*Anopheles*) of mosquitoes that includes all mosquitoes which transmit malaria to man — **anoph·e·line** \-ˌlīn\ *adj or n*

an·o·rak \ˈan-ə-ˌrak\ *n* [Greenland Esk *ánoráq*] **:** PARKA

an·orex·ia \ˌan-ə-ˈrek-sē-ə\ *n* [NL, fr. Gk, fr. *a-* + *orexis* appetite, fr. *oregein* to stretch out, reach after] **:** loss of appetite esp. when prolonged — **an·orexi·gen·ic** \ˌan-ə-ˌrek-sə-ˈjen-ik\ *adj*

an·or·thite \ə-ˈnȯr-ˌthīt\ *n* [F, fr. *a-* + Gk *orthos* straight] **:** a white, grayish, or reddish feldspar $CaAl_2Si_2O_8$ occurring in many igneous rocks — **an·or·thit·ic** \ˌan-(ˌ)ȯr-ˈthit-ik\ *adj*

an·or·tho·site \ə-ˈnȯr-thə-ˌsīt\ *n* [F *anorthose,* a feldspar, fr. *a-* + Gk *orthos*] **:** a granular plutonic igneous rock composed almost exclusively of a soda-lime feldspar (as labradorite)

an·os·mia \a-ˈnäz-mē-ə\ *n* [NL, fr. *a-* + Gk *osmē* smell] **:** loss or impairment of the sense of smell — **an·os·mic** \-mik\ *adj*

1an·oth·er \ə-ˈnəth-ər\ *adj* **1 :** different or distinct from the one considered **2 :** some other **:** LATER **3 :** being one more in addition to one or more of the same kind **:** NEW

2another *pron* **1 :** an additional one **:** one more **2 :** one that is different from the first or present one **3 :** one of a group of unspecified or indefinite things

anoth·er–guess \ə-ˈnəth-ər-ˌges\ *adj* [alter. of *anothergates,* fr. 1*another* + *gate*] *archaic* **:** of another sort

an·ovu·lant \a-ˈnäv-yə-lənt, -ˈnōv-\ *n* [2*a-* + *ovulate* + *-ant*] **:** a drug that suppresses ovulation — **anovulant** *adj*

an·ovu·la·tory \-lə-ˌtōr-ē, -ˌtȯr-\ *adj* [2*a-* + *ovulate* + *-ory*] **1 :** not involving or associated with ovulation ⟨~ bleeding⟩ **2 :** suppressing ovulation

an·ox·emia \ˌan-ˌäk-ˈsē-mē-ə\ *n* [NL] **a :** condition of subnormal oxygenation of the arterial blood — **an·ox·emic** \-mik\ *adj*

an·ox·ia \a-ˈnäk-sē-ə\ *n* [NL] **:** hypoxia esp. of such severity as to result in permanent damage — **an·ox·ic** \-sik\ *adj*

an·ser·ine \ˈan(t)-sə-ˌrīn\ *adj* [L *anserinus,* fr. *anser* goose — more at GOOSE] **:** of, relating to, or resembling a goose

1an·swer \ˈan(t)-sər\ *n* [ME, fr. OE *andswaru;* akin to ON *andsvar* answer; both fr. a prehistoric WGmc-NGmc compound whose first constituent is represented by OE *and-* against, and whose second constituent is akin to OE *swerian* to swear — more at ANTE-] **1 a :** something spoken or written in return to or satisfying a question **b :** a correct response **2 a :** a reply to a charge **:** DEFENSE **b :** a rejoinder made by the defendant in an equity case in reply to the charges made by the complainant in his bill **3 :** something done in response; *also* **:** responsive action **4 :** a solution of a problem

2answer *vb* **an·swer·ing** \ˈan(t)s-(ə-)riŋ\ *vi* **1 :** to speak or write in reply **2 a :** to be or make oneself responsible or accountable **b :** to make amends **:** ATONE **3 :** to be in conformity or correspondence ⟨~*ed* to the description⟩ **4 :** to act in response to an action performed elsewhere or by another **5 :** to be adequate **:** SERVE ~ *vt* **1 :** to speak or write in reply to; *also* **:** to say or write by way of reply **2 :** to reply in rebuttal, justification, or explanation **3 a :** to correspond to **b :** to be sufficient for **:** SERVE **4** *obs* **:** to atone for **5 :** to act in response to **6 :** to offer a solution for; *esp* **:** SOLVE — **an·swer·er** \ˈan(t)-sər-ər\ *n*

syn RESPOND, REPLY, REJOIN, RETORT: ANSWER implies either the logical or practical satisfying of a question, demand, call, or need; RESPOND implies reacting to any stimulus often spontaneously or without resistance or delay; REPLY implies making a return that covers the same ground as the question being answered; it may focus upon the act of answering ⟨he *answered* correctly; he *replied* vigorously⟩ REJOIN often implies answering an implied question or objection and may suggest sharpness or quickness in answering; RETORT suggests responding to an explicit charge or criticism by way of retaliation

an·swer·able \ˈan(t)s-(ə-)rə-bəl\ *adj* **1 :** liable to be called to account **:** RESPONSIBLE **2** *archaic* **:** SUITABLE, ADEQUATE **3** *archaic* **:** ACCORDANT, CORRESPONDING **4 :** capable of being refuted **syn** see RESPONSIBLE

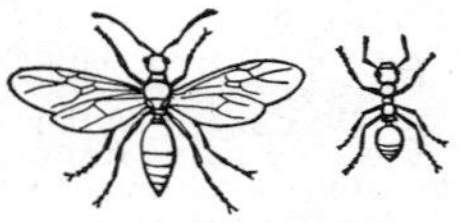

ants: winged male and worker

ant \ˈant\ *n* [ME *ante, emete,* fr. OE *æmette;* akin to OHG *āmeiza* ant] **:** any of a family (Formicidae) of colonial hymenopterous insects with complex social organization and various castes performing special duties

ant- — see ANTI-

1-ant \ənt, ᵊnt\ *n suffix* [ME, fr. OF, fr. *-ant,* prp. suffix, fr. L *-ant-, -ans,* prp. suffix of first conjugation, fr. *-a-* (stem vowel of first conjugation) + *-nt-, -ns,* prp. suffix; akin to OE *-nde,* prp. suffix, Gk *-nt-, -n,* pres., fut. & aor. part. suffix] **1 a :** one that performs (a specified action) **:** personal or impersonal agent ⟨claim*ant*⟩ ⟨cool*ant*⟩ **b :** thing that promotes (a specified action or process) ⟨expector*ant*⟩ **2 :** one connected with ⟨annuit*ant*⟩ **3 :** thing that is acted upon (in a specified manner) ⟨inhal*ant*⟩

2-ant *adj suffix* **1 :** performing (a specified action) or being (in a specified condition) ⟨somnambul*ant*⟩ **2 :** promoting (a specified action or process) ⟨expector*ant*⟩

an·ta \ˈan-tə\ *n, pl* **antas** *or* **an·tae** \ˈan-ˌtē, -ˌtī\ [L; akin to ON *önd* anteroom] **:** a pier produced by thickening a wall at its termination

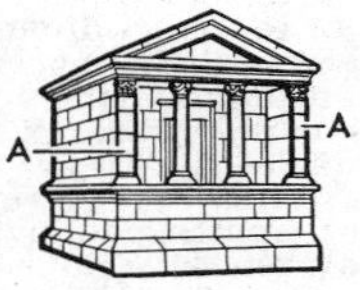

A,A, antas

ant·ac·id \(ˈ)ant-ˈas-əd\ *adj* **:** counteractive of acidity — **antacid** *n*

An·tae·an \an-ˈtē-ən\ *adj* **:** resembling Antaeus esp. in strength

An·tae·us \an-ˈtē-əs\ *n* [L, fr. Gk *Antaios*] **:** a mythical giant whom Hercules is able to overcome only by keeping him from touching his mother earth

an·tag·o·nism \an-ˈtag-ə-ˌniz-əm\ *n* **1 a :** actively expressed opposition, hostility, or antipathy **b :** opposition or contrariety of a conflicting force, tendency, or principle **2 :** opposition in physiological action; *esp* **:** interaction of two or more substances such that the action of any one of them on living cells or tissues is modified **syn** see ENMITY

an·tag·o·nist \an-ˈtag-ə-nəst\ *n* **1 :** one that opposes another esp. in combat **:** ADVERSARY **2 :** an agent of physiological antagonism: as **a :** a muscle that contracts with and limits the action of an agonist with which it is paired **b :** a drug that opposes the action of another **syn** see OPPONENT

an·tag·o·nis·tic \(ˌ)an-ˌtag-ə-ˈnis-tik\ *adj* **:** characterized by or resulting from antagonism **:** OPPOSING **syn** see ADVERSE — **an·tag·o·nis·ti·cal·ly** \-ti-k(ə-)lē\ *adv*

an·tag·o·nize \an-ˈtag-ə-ˌnīz\ *vt* [Gk *antagōnizesthai,* fr. *anti-* + *agōnizesthai* to struggle, fr. *agōn* contest — more at AGONY] **1 :** to act in opposition to **:** COUNTERACT **2 :** to incur or provoke the hostility of **syn** see OPPOSE

ant·arc·tic \(ˈ)ant-ˈärk-tik, -ˈärt-ik\ *adj, often cap* [ME *antartik,* fr. L *antarcticus,* fr. Gk *antarktikos,* fr. *anti-* + *arktikos* arctic] **:** relating to the south pole or to the region near it

antarctic circle *n, often cap A&C* **:** a small circle of the earth parallel to its equator approximately 23° 27′ from the south pole

An·tar·es \an-ˈta(ə)r-(ˌ)ēz, -ˈte(ə)r-\ *n* [Gk *Antarēs*] **:** a giant red star of very low density that is the brightest star in Scorpio

ant bear *n* **:** a large anteater (*Myrmecophaga jubata*) of So. America with shaggy gray fur, a black band across the breast, and a white stripe on the shoulder

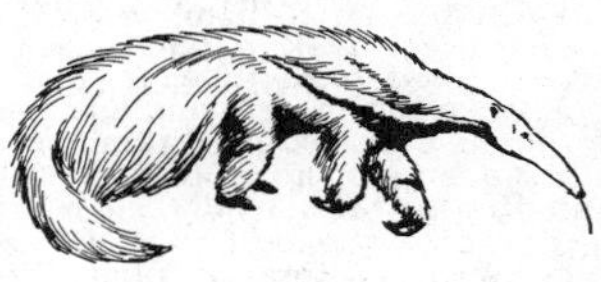

ant bear

ant cow *n* **:** an aphid from which ants obtain honeydew

1an·te \ˈant-ē\ *n* [*ante-*] **1 :** a poker stake usu. put up before the deal to build the pot **2 :** an amount paid **:** PRICE

2ante *vt* **an·ted; an·te·ing :** to put up (an ante); *also* **:** PAY, PRODUCE — often used with *up*

ante- *prefix* [ME, fr. L, fr. *ante* before, in front of; akin to OE *and-* against, Gk *anti* before, against — more at END] **1 a :** prior **:** earlier ⟨*ante*type⟩ **b :** anterior **:** forward ⟨*ante*room⟩ **2 a :** prior to **:** earlier than ⟨*ante*diluvian⟩ **b :** in front of ⟨*ante*choir⟩

ant·eat·er \ˈant-ˌēt-ər\ *n* **:** any of several mammals that feed largely or entirely on ants: as **a :** an edentate with a long narrow snout, a long tongue, and enormous salivary glands **b :** ECHIDNA **c :** AARDVARK

an·te·bel·lum \ˌant-i-ˈbel-əm\ *adj* [L *ante bellum* before the war] **:** existing before a war; *esp* **:** existing before the Civil War

an·te·cede \ˌant-ə-ˈsēd\ *vt* [L *antecedere,* fr. *ante-* + *cedere* to go — more at CEDE] **:** PRECEDE

an·te·ced·ence \ˌant-ə-ˈsēd-ᵊn(t)s\ *n* **:** PRIORITY, PRECEDENCE

1an·te·ced·ent \ˌant-ə-ˈsēd-ᵊnt\ *n* [ME, fr. ML & L; ML *antecedent-, antecedens,* fr. L, logical antecedent, lit., one that goes before, fr. neut. of *antecedent-, antecedens,* prp. of *antecedere*] **1 :** a substantive word, phrase, or clause referred to by a pronoun (as *John* in "I saw John and spoke to him"); *broadly* **:** a word or group of words replaced and referred to by a substitute **2 :** the conditional element in a proposition (as *if A* in "if A, then B") **3 :** the first term of a mathematical ratio **4 a :** a preceding event, condition, or cause **b** *pl* **:** the significant events, conditions, and traits of one's earlier life **5 a :** a predecessor in a series; *esp* **:** a model or stimulus for later developments **b** *pl* **:** ANCESTORS, PARENTS **syn** see CAUSE

2antecedent *adj* **1 :** prior in time or order **2 :** causally or logically prior **syn** see PRECEDING — **an·te·ced·ent·ly** *adv*

an·te·ces·sor \ˌant-i-ˈses-ər\ *n* [ME *antecessour,* fr. L *antecessor* — more at ANCESTOR] **:** one that goes before **:** PREDECESSOR

an·te·cham·ber \ˈant-i-ˌchām-bər\ *n* [F *antichambre,* fr. MF, fr. It *anti-* (fr. L *ante-*) + MF *chambre* room — more at CHAMBER] **:** an outer room leading to another usu. more important room

an·te·choir \ˈant-i-ˌkwī(ə)r\ *n* **:** a space enclosed or reserved for the clergy and choristers at the entrance to a choir

1an·te·date \ˈant-i-ˌdāt\ *n* **:** a date assigned to an event or document earlier than the actual date of the event or document

2antedate *vt* **1 a :** to date as of a time prior to that of execution **b :** to assign to a date prior to that of actual occurrence **2** *archaic* **:** ANTICIPATE **3 :** to precede in time

an·te·di·lu·vi·an \ˌant-i-də-ˈlü-vē-ən, -(ˌ)dī-\ *adj* [*ante-* + L *diluvium* flood — more at DELUGE] **1 :** of or relating to the period before the flood described in the Bible **2 :** made, evolved, or developed a long time ago **:** ANTIQUATED — **antediluvian** *n*

an·te·fix \'ant-i-ˌfiks\ *n* [L *antefixum*, fr. neut. of *antefixus*, pp. of *antefigere* to fasten before, fr. *ante-* + *figere* to fasten — more at DIKE] **1 :** an ornament at the eaves of a classical building concealing the ends of the joint tiles of the roof **2 :** an ornament of the molding of a classic cornice — **an·te·fix·al** \ˌant-i-'fik-səl\ *adj*

an·te·lope \'ant-ᵊl-ˌōp\ *n, pl* **antelope** *or* **antelopes** [ME, fabulous heraldic beast, prob. fr. MF *antelop* savage animal with sawlike horns, fr. ML *anthalopus*, fr. LGk *antholop-, antholops*] **1 a :** any of various Old World ruminant mammals (family Bovidae) that differ from the true oxen esp. in lighter racier build and horns directed upward and backward **b :** PRONGHORN **2 :** leather from antelope hide

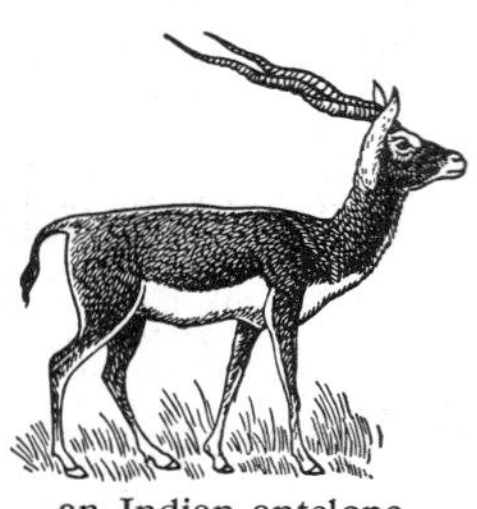
an Indian antelope (*Antilope cervicapra*)

an·te me·ri·di·em \ˌant-i-mə-'rid-ē-əm\ *adj* [L] **:** being before noon

an·te·mor·tem \-'mȯrt-əm\ *adj* [L *ante mortem*] **:** preceding death

an·te·na·tal \ˌant-i-'nāt-ᵊl\ *adj* **:** of or relating to an unborn child; *also* **:** occurring during pregnancy

an·ten·na \an-'ten-ə\ *n, pl* **an·ten·nae** \-'ten-(ˌ)ē\ *or* **antennas** [ML, fr. L, sail yard] **1 :** a movable segmented organ of sensation on the head of insects, myriapods, and crustaceans **2** *pl usu antennas* **:** a usu. metallic device (as a rod or wire) for radiating or receiving radio waves — **an·ten·nal** \-'ten-ᵊl\ *adj*

an·ten·nule \an-'ten-(ˌ)yü(ə)l\ *n* **:** a small antenna or similar appendage

an·te·pen·di·um \ˌant-i-'pen-dē-əm\ *n, pl* **antependiums** *or* **an·te·pen·dia** \-dē-ə\ [ML, fr. L *ante-* + *pendēre* to hang — more at PENDANT] **:** a hanging for the front of an altar, pulpit, or lectern

an·te·pe·nult \ˌant-i-'pē-ˌnəlt, -pi-'\ *also* **an·te·pen·ul·ti·ma** \-pi-'nəl-tə-mə\ *n* [LL *antepaenultima*, fem. of *antepaenultimus* preceding the next to last, fr. L *ante-* + *paenultimus* penultimate] **:** the 3d syllable of a word counting from the end (as *cu* in *accumulate*) — **an·te·pen·ul·ti·mate** \-pi-'nəl-tə-mət\ *adj or n*

an·te·ri·or \an-'tir-ē-ər\ *adj* [L, comp. of *ante* before — more at ANTE-] **1 a :** situated before or toward the front **b :** ABAXIAL **2 a :** coming before in time **:** ANTECEDENT **b :** logically prior **syn** see PRECEDING — **an·te·ri·or·ly** *adv*

an·te·room \'ant-i-ˌrüm, -ˌru̇m\ *n* **:** a room placed before or forming an entrance to another and often used as a waiting room

anth- — see ANTI-

an·the·lion \ant-'hēl-yən, an-'thēl-\ *n, pl* **an·the·lia** \-yə\ *or* **anthelions** [Gk *anthēlion*, fr. neut. of *anthēlios* opposite the sun, fr. *anti-* + *hēlios* sun — more at SOLAR] **:** a somewhat bright white spot appearing on the parhelic circle opposite the sun

an·thel·min·tic \ˌant-ˌhel-'mint-ik, ˌan-ˌthel-\ *adj* [*anti-* + Gk *helminth-, helmis* worm — more at HELMINTH] **:** expelling or destroying parasitic worms esp. of the intestine — **anthelmintic** *n*

an·them \'an(t)-thəm\ *n* [ME *antem*, fr. OE *antefn*, fr. LL *antiphona*, fr. LGk *antiphōna*, pl. of *antiphōnon*, fr. Gk, neut. of *antiphōnos* responsive, fr. *anti-* + *phōnē* sound — more at BAN] **1 a :** a psalm or hymn sung antiphonally or responsively **b :** a sacred vocal composition with words usu. from the Scriptures **2 :** a song or hymn of praise or gladness

an·the·mi·on \an-'thē-mē-ən\ *n, pl* **an·the·mia** \-mē-ə\ [Gk, fr. dim. of *anthemon* flower, fr. *anthos* — more at ANTHOLOGY] **:** an ornament of floral or foliated forms arranged in a radiating cluster but always flat (as in relief sculpture or in painting)

an·ther \'an(t)-thər\ *n* [NL *anthera*, fr. L, medicine made fr. flowers, fr. Gk *anthēra*, fr. fem. of *anthēros* flowery, fr. *anthos*] **:** the part of a stamen that develops and contains pollen and is usu. borne on a stalk — **an·ther·al** \-thə-rəl\ *adj*

an·ther·id·i·al \ˌan(t)-thə-'rid-ē-əl\ *adj* **:** of or relating to an antheridium

an·ther·id·i·um \-ē-əm\ *n, pl* **an·ther·id·ia** \-ē-ə\ [NL, fr. *anthera*] **:** the male reproductive organ of a cryptogamous plant

an·the·sis \an-'thē-səs\ *n* [NL, fr. Gk *anthēsis* bloom, fr. *anthein* to flower, fr. *anthos*] **:** the action or period of opening of a flower

ant·hill \'ant-ˌhil\ *n* **:** a mound thrown up by ants or termites in digging their nest

an·tho·cy·a·nin \ˌan(t)-thə-'sī-ə-nən\ *n* [Gk *anthos* + *kyanos* dark blue] **:** any of various soluble glucoside pigments producing blue to red coloring in flowers and plants

an·tho·di·um \an-'thōd-ē-əm\ *n, pl* **an·tho·dia** \-ē-ə\ [NL, fr. Gk *anthōdēs* flowerlike, fr. *anthos*] **:** the flower head of a composite plant; *also* **:** its involucre

an·thol·o·gist \an-'thäl-ə-jəst\ *n* **:** a maker of an anthology

an·thol·o·gize \-ˌjīz\ *vt* **:** to compile or publish in an anthology

an·thol·o·gy \an-'thäl-ə-jē\ *n* [NL *anthologia* collection of epigrams, fr. MGk, fr. Gk, flower gathering, fr. *anthos* flower + *logia* collecting, fr. *legein* to gather; akin to Skt *andha* herb — more at LEGEND] **:** a collection of selected literary pieces or passages

an·thoph·a·gous \an-'thäf-ə-gəs\ *adj* [Gk *anthos* + E *-phagous*] **:** feeding on flowers — **an·thoph·a·gy** \-ə-jē\ *n*

an·tho·phore \'an(t)-thə-ˌfō(ə)r, -ˌfȯ(ə)r\ *n* [Gk *anthophoros* flower-bearing, fr. *anthos* + *pherein* to bear — more at BEAR] **:** a prolongation of the receptacle that bears the pistil and corolla at its apex (as in the pinks)

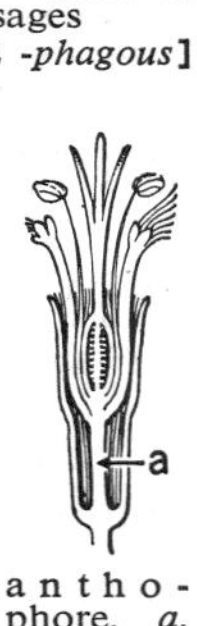

anthophore, *a*, in section of wild pink

an·tho·zo·an \ˌan(t)-thə-'zō-ən\ *n* [deriv. of Gk *anthos* + *zōion* animal; akin to Gk *zōē* life — more at QUICK] **:** any of a class (Anthozoa) of marine coelenterates (as the corals and sea anemones) having polyps with radial partitions — **anthozoan** *adj*

an·thra·cene \'an(t)-thrə-ˌsēn\ *n* **:** a crystalline cyclic hydrocarbon $C_{14}H_{10}$ obtained from coal-tar distillation

an·thra·cite \'an(t)-thrə-ˌsīt\ *n* [Gk *anthrakitis*, fr. *anthrak-*, *anthrax* coal] **:** a hard natural coal of high luster differing from bituminous coal in containing little volatile matter — **an·thra·cit·ic** \ˌan(t)-thrə-'sit-ik\ *adj*

an·thrac·nose \an-'thrak-ˌnōs\ *n* [F, fr. Gk *anthrak-*, *anthrax* + *nosos* disease] **:** any of numerous destructive plant diseases caused by imperfect fungi and characterized by often dark sunken lesions or blisters

an·thra·qui·none \ˌan(t)-thrə-kwin-'ōn, -'kwin-ˌōn\ *n* [prob. fr. F, fr. *anthracene* + *quinone*] **:** a yellow crystalline ketone $C_{14}H_8O_2$ derived from anthracene and used esp. in the manufacture of dyes

an·thrax \'an-ˌthraks\ *n* [ME *antrax* carbuncle, fr. L *anthrax*, fr. Gk, coal, carbuncle] **:** an infectious disease of warm-blooded animals (as cattle and sheep) caused by a spore-forming bacterium (*Bacillus anthracis*), found transmissible to man esp. by the handling of infected products (as hair), and characterized by external ulcerating nodules or by lesions in the lungs

anthrop- *or* **anthropo-** *comb form* [L *anthropo-*, fr. Gk *anthrōp-*, *anthrōpo-*, fr. *anthrōpos*] **:** human being ⟨*anthropo*genesis⟩

an·throp·ic \an-'thräp-ik\ *adj* [Gk *anthrōpikos*, fr. *anthrōpos*] **:** of or relating to mankind or the period of man's existence on earth — **an·throp·i·cal** \-i-kəl\ *adj*

an·thro·po·cen·tric \ˌan(t)-thrə-pə-'sen-trik\ *adj* **1 :** considering man to be the most significant entity of the universe **2 :** interpreting or regarding the world in terms of human values and experiences — **an·thro·po·cen·tri·cal·ly** \-tri-k(ə-)lē\ *adv* — **an·thro·po·cen·tric·i·ty** \-pō-(ˌ)sen-'tris-ət-ē\ *n*

an·thro·po·gen·e·sis \ˌan(t)-thrə-pə-'jen-ə-səs\ *n* [NL, fr. *anthrop-* + L *genesis*] **:** the study of the origin and development of man — **an·thro·po·ge·net·ic** \-pō-jə-'net-ik\ *adj*

an·thro·po·gen·ic \-pə-'jen-ik\ *adj* **1 :** of or relating to anthropogenesis **2 :** of, relating to, or involving the impact of man on nature

an·thro·pog·ra·phy \ˌan(t)-thrə-'päg-rə-fē\ *n* **:** a branch of anthropology dealing with the distribution of man as distinguished by physical character, language, institutions, and customs

[1]**an·thro·poid** \'an(t)-thrə-ˌpȯid\ *adj* [Gk *anthrōpoeidēs*, fr. *anthrōpos*] **1 :** resembling man **2 :** resembling an ape ⟨~ mobsters⟩

[2]**anthropoid** *n* **:** any of several large tailless semierect apes (family Pongidae) — **an·thro·poi·dal** \ˌan(t)-thrə-'pȯid-ᵊl\ *adj*

an·thro·po·log·i·cal \ˌan(t)-thrə-pə-'läj-i-kəl\ *adj* **:** of or relating to anthropology — **an·thro·po·log·i·cal·ly** \-i-k(ə-)lē\ *adv*

an·thro·pol·o·gist \ˌan(t)-thrə-'päl-ə-jəst\ *n* **:** a specialist in anthropology

an·thro·pol·o·gy \-jē\ *n* [NL *anthropologia*, fr. *anthrop-* + *-logia* -logy] **1 a :** the science of man; *esp* **:** the study of man in relation to distribution, origin, classification, and relationship of races, physical character, environmental and social relations, and culture **b :** a treatise on this science **2 :** teaching about the origin, nature, and destiny of man esp. from the perspective of his relation to God

an·thro·po·met·ric \ˌan(t)-thrə-pə-'me-trik\ *adj* **:** of or relating to anthropometry — **an·thro·po·met·ri·cal** \-tri-kəl\ *adj* — **an·thro·po·met·ri·cal·ly** \-k(ə-)lē\ *adv*

an·thro·pom·e·try \ˌan(t)-thrə-'päm-ə-trē\ *n* [F *anthropométrie*, fr. *anthrop-* + *-métrie* -metry] **:** the study of human body measurements esp. on a comparative basis

an·thro·po·mor·phic \ˌan(t)-thrə-pə-'mȯr-fik\ *adj* [LL *anthropomorphus* of human form, fr. Gk *anthrōpomorphos*, fr. *anthrōp-* + *-morphos* -morphous] **1 :** described or thought of as having a human form or with human attributes ⟨~ deities⟩ **2 :** ascribing human characteristics to nonhuman things ⟨~ supernaturalism⟩ — **an·thro·po·mor·phi·cal·ly** \-fi-k(ə-)lē\ *adv*

an·thro·po·mor·phism \-ˌfiz-əm\ *n* **:** an interpretation of what is not human or personal in terms of human or personal characteristics **:** HUMANIZATION — **an·thro·po·mor·phist** \-fəst\ *n*

an·thro·po·mor·phize \-ˌfīz\ *vt* **:** to attribute human form or personality to

an·thro·pop·a·thism \ˌan(t)-thrə-'päp-ə-ˌthiz-əm, -pō-'path-ˌiz-\ *n* [LGk *anthrōpopatheia* humanity, fr. Gk *anthrōpopathēs* having human feelings, fr. *anthrōp-* + *pathos* experience — more at PATHOS] **:** the ascription of human feelings to something not human

an·thro·poph·a·gous \ˌan(t)-thrə-'päf-ə-gəs\ *adj* **:** feeding on human flesh — **an·thro·poph·a·gy** \-'päf-ə-jē\ *n*

an·thro·poph·a·gus \-'päf-ə-gəs\ *n, pl* **an·thro·poph·a·gi** \-'päf-ə-ˌgī, -ˌjī, -ˌgē\ [L, fr. Gk *anthrōpophagos*, fr. *anthrōp-* + *-phagos* -phagous] **:** MAN-EATER, CANNIBAL

an·thro·pos·o·phy \ˌan(t)-thrə-'päs-ə-fē\ *n* **:** a 20th century spiritual and mystical doctrine growing out of theosophy

[1]**an·ti** \'an-ˌtī, 'ant-ē\ *n* [*anti-*] **:** one who is opposed

[2]**anti** *prep* **:** opposed to **:** AGAINST

[1]**anti-** *or* **ant-** *or* **anth-** *prefix* [*anti-* fr. ME, fr. OF & L; OF, fr. L, against, fr. Gk, fr. *anti*; *ant-* fr. ME, fr. L, against, fr. Gk, fr. *anti*; *anth-* fr. L, against, fr. Gk, fr. *anti* — more at ANTE-] **1 a :** of the same kind but situated opposite, exerting energy in the opposite direction, or pursuing an opposite policy ⟨*anti*clinal⟩ **b :** one that is opposite in kind to ⟨*anti*climax⟩ **2 a :** opposing or hostile to in opinion, sympathy, or practice ⟨*anti*-Semite⟩ **b :** opposing in effect or activity ⟨*ant*acid⟩ ⟨*anti*aircraft⟩ ⟨*anti*biotic⟩

[2]**an·ti-** \ˌant-i, 'ant-\ *prefix* [MF & ML, fr. L *ante-*] **:** ANTE- ⟨*anti*-masque⟩

[1]**an·ti·air·craft** \ˌant-ē-'a(ə)r-ˌkraft, -'e(ə)r-\ *adj* **:** designed for or concerned with defense against air attack

[2]**antiaircraft** *n* **:** an antiaircraft weapon

an·ti·bal·lis·tic missile \ˌant-i-bə-ˌlis-tik-, ˌan-ˌtī-\ *n* **:** a missile for intercepting and destroying ballistic missiles

an·ti·bi·o·sis \ˌant-i-(ˌ)bī-'ō-səs, ˌan-ˌtī-, -bē-\ *n* [NL] **:** antagonistic association between organisms to the detriment of one of them or between one organism and a metabolic product of another

[1]**an·ti·bi·ot·ic** \ˌant-i-(ˌ)bī-'ät-ik, ˌan-ˌtī-, -bē-\ *adj* **1 :** tending to prevent, inhibit, or destroy life **2 :** of or relating to antibiosis or antibiotics — **an·ti·bi·ot·i·cal·ly** \-i-k(ə-)lē\ *adv*

[2]**antibiotic** *n* **:** a substance produced by a microorganism and able in dilute solution to inhibit or kill another microorganism

an·ti·body \'ant-i-ˌbäd-ē\ *n* **:** any of the body globulins that combine specifically with antigens and neutralize toxins, agglutinate bacteria or cells, and precipitate soluble antigens

[1]**an·tic** \'ant-ik\ *n* **1 :** a grotesquely ludicrous act or action **:** CAPER **2** *archaic* **:** a performer of a grotesque or ludicrous part **:** BUFFOON

[2]**antic** *adj* [It *antico* ancient, fr. L *antiquus* — more at ANTIQUE] **1** *archaic* **:** GROTESQUE, BIZARRE **2 a :** characterized by clownish extravagance or absurdity **b :** whimsically gay **:** FROLICSOME

an·ti·cat·a·lyst \ˌant-i-'kat-ᵊl-əst, ˌan-ˌtī-\ *n* **1 :** an agent that retards a reaction **2 :** a catalytic poison

an·ti·cath·ode \-'kath-ˌōd\ *n* [ISV] **:** the target in an electron tube and esp. an X-ray tube

an·ti·cho·lin·er·gic \-ˌkō-lə-ˈnər-jik, -ˌkäl-ə-\ *adj* **:** opposing or annulling the physiologic action of acetylcholine — **anticholinergic** *n*
an·ti·cho·lin·es·ter·ase \-ˈnes-tə-ˌrās, -ˌrāz\ *n* **:** a substance that inhibits a cholinesterase by combination with it
an·ti·christ \ˈant-i-ˌkrīst\ *n* [ME *anticrist*, fr. OF & LL; OF, fr. LL *Antichristus*, fr. Gk *Antichristos*, fr. *anti-* + *Christos* Christ] **1 :** one who denies or opposes Christ; *specif, cap* **:** a great antagonist expected to fill the world with wickedness but to be conquered forever by Christ at his second coming **2 :** a false Christ
an·tic·i·pant \an-ˈtis-ə-pənt\ *adj* **:** ANTICIPATING, EXPECTANT — usu. used with *of* — **anticipant** *n*
an·tic·i·pate \an-ˈtis-ə-ˌpāt\ *vb* [L *anticipatus*, pp. of *anticipare*, fr. *ante-* + *-cipare* (fr. *capere* to take) — more at HEAVE] *vt* **1 :** to give advance thought, discussion, or treatment to **2 :** to meet (an obligation) before a due date **3 :** to foresee and deal with in advance **:** FORESTALL **4 :** to use or expend in advance of actual possession **5 :** to act before (another) often so as to check or counter **6 :** to look forward to as certain **:** EXPECT ~ *vi* **:** to speak or write in knowledge or expectation of later matter **syn** see FORESEE, PREVENT — **an·tic·i·pa·tor** \-ˌpāt-ər\ *n*
an·tic·i·pa·tion \(ˌ)an-ˌtis-ə-ˈpā-shən\ *n* **1 :** the use of money before it is available; *esp* **:** the taking or alienation of the income of a trust estate before it is due **2 a :** a prior action that takes into account or forestalls a later **b :** the act of looking forward **:** EXPECTATION; *specif* **:** pleasurable expectation **3 a :** visualization of a future event or state **b :** an object or form that anticipates a later type **4 :** the premature entry of one or more tones of a succeeding chord to form a temporary dissonance **syn** see PROSPECT
an·tic·i·pa·tive \an-ˈtis-ə-ˌpāt-iv, -pət-\ *adj* **:** given to or engaged in anticipation — **an·tic·i·pa·tive·ly** *adv*
an·tic·i·pa·to·ry \an-ˈtis-ə-pə-ˌtōr-ē, -ˌtȯr-\ *adj* **:** ANTICIPATING
an·ti·cli·mac·tic \ˌant-i-(ˌ)klī-ˈmak-tik\ *adj* **:** relating to or of the nature of an anticlimax — **an·ti·cli·mac·ti·cal** \-ti-kəl\ *adj* — **an·ti·cli·mac·ti·cal·ly** \-k(ə-)lē\ *adv*
an·ti·cli·max \ˌant-i-ˈklī-ˌmaks\ *n* **1 :** the usu. sudden transition in writing or speaking from a significant idea to a trivial or ludicrous idea; *also* **:** an instance of such transition **2 :** an event esp. closing a series that is strikingly less important than what has preceded it
an·ti·cli·nal \ˌant-i-ˈklīn-ᵊl\ *adj* [*anti-* + Gk *klinein* to lean — more at LEAN] **:** inclining in opposite directions; *specif* **:** of or relating to a geological anticline
an·ti·cline \ˈant-i-ˌklīn\ *n* [back-formation fr. *anticlinal*] **:** an arch of stratified rock in which the layers bend downward in opposite directions from the crest — compare SYNCLINE

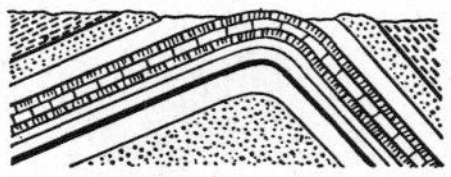
cross section of strata showing anticline

an·ti·co·ag·u·lant \ˌant-i-kō-ˈag-yə-lənt, ˌan-ˌtī-\ *n* **:** a substance that hinders clotting of blood
an·ti·cy·clone \ˌant-i-ˈsī-ˌklōn\ *n* **:** a system of winds that rotates about a center of high atmospheric pressure clockwise in the northern hemisphere and counterclockwise in the southern, that usu. advances at 20 to 30 miles per hour, and that usu. has a diameter of 1500 to 2500 miles — **an·ti·cy·clon·ic** \-(ˌ)sī-ˈklän-ik\ *adj*
an·ti·dot·al \ˌant-i-ˈdōt-ᵊl\ *adj* **:** of, relating to, or acting as an antidote — **an·ti·dot·al·ly** \-ᵊl-ē\ *adv*
an·ti·dote \ˈant-i-ˌdōt\ *n* [ME *antidot*, fr. L *antidotum*, fr. Gk *antidotos*, fr. fem. of *antidotos* given as an antidote, fr. *antididonai* to give as an antidote, fr. *anti-* + *didonai* to give — more at DATE] **1 :** a remedy to counteract the effects of poison **2 :** something that relieves, prevents, or counteracts
an·ti·en·zyme \ˌant-ē-ˈen-ˌzīm, ˌan-ˌtī-\ *n* **:** an inhibitor of enzyme action; *esp* **:** one produced by living cells
an·ti–fed·er·al·ist \ˌant-i-ˈfed-(ə-)rə-ləst, ˌan-ˌtī-\ *n, often cap A & F* **:** one opposing in 1787–88 the adoption of the U.S. Constitution
an·ti·foul·ing \-ˈfau̇-liŋ\ *adj* **:** intended to prevent fouling of underwater structures
an·ti·freeze \ˈant-i-ˌfrēz\ *n* **:** a substance added to a liquid to lower its freezing point
an·ti·gen \ˈant-i-jən\ *n* [ISV] **:** a usu. protein or carbohydrate substance (as a toxin or enzyme) that when introduced into the body stimulates the production of an antibody — **an·ti·gen·ic** \ˌant-i-ˈjen-ik\ *adj* — **an·ti·gen·i·cal·ly** \-i-k(ə-)lē\ *adv* — **an·ti·ge·nic·i·ty** \-jə-ˈnis-ət-ē\ *n*
An·tig·o·ne \an-ˈtig-ə-nē\ *n* [L, fr. Gk *Antigonē*] **:** a daughter of Oedipus and Jocasta who performs funeral rites over the body of her brother Polynices against the command of her uncle Creon
an·ti·he·lix \ˌant-i-ˈhē-liks, ˌan-ˌtī-\ *n* [NL] **:** the curved elevation of cartilage within or in front of the helix of the ear
an·ti·his·ta·mine \ˌant-i-ˈhis-tə-ˌmēn, -mən\ *n* **:** any of various compounds used for treating allergic reactions and cold symptoms presumably by inactivating histamine — **an·ti·his·ta·min·ic** \-ˌhis-tə-ˈmin-ik\ *adj or n*
an·ti·knock \ˌant-i-ˈnäk\ *n* **:** a substance used as a fuel or fuel additive to prevent knocking in an internal-combustion engine
an·ti·log·a·rithm \ˌant-i-ˈlȯg-ə-ˌrit͟h-əm, ˌan-ˌtī-, -ˈläg-\ *n* **:** the number corresponding to a given logarithm
an·ti·ma·cas·sar \ˌant-i-mə-ˈkas-ər\ *n* [*anti-* + *Macassar (oil)* (a hair dressing)] **:** a cover to protect the back or arms of furniture
an·ti·mag·net·ic \ˌant-i-(ˌ)mag-ˈnet-ik, ˌan-ˌtī-\ *adj, of a watch* **:** having a balance unit composed of alloys that will not remain magnetized
an·ti·ma·lar·i·al \-mə-ˈler-ē-əl\ *adj* **:** serving to prevent, check, or cure malaria — **antimalarial** *n*
an·ti·mat·ter \ˈant-i-ˌmat-ər\ *n* **:** matter composed of the counterparts of ordinary matter, antiprotons instead of protons, positrons instead of electrons, and antineutrons instead of neutrons
an·ti·mi·cro·bi·al \ˌant-i-(ˌ)mī-ˈkrō-bē-əl\ *adj* **:** inimical to microbes — **antimicrobial** *n*
antimissile missile *n* **:** a missile for intercepting another missile in flight
an·ti·mo·ni·al \ˌant-ə-ˈmō-nē-əl\ *adj* **:** of, relating to, or containing antimony — **antimonial** *n*
an·ti·mon·ic \-ˈmän-ik\ *adj* **:** of, relating to, or derived from antimony with a valence of five
an·ti·mo·ni·ous \-ˈmō-nē-əs\ *adj* **:** of, relating to, or derived from antimony with a valence of three
an·ti·mo·ny \ˈant-ə-ˌmō-nē\ *n* [ME *antimonie*, fr. ML *antimonium*] **1 :** STIBNITE **2 :** a trivalent and pentavalent metalloid commonly metallic silvery white, crystalline, and brittle element that is used esp. as a constituent of alloys and in medicine — see ELEMENT table
an·ti·neu·tri·no \ˌant-i-n(y)ü-ˈtrē-(ˌ)nō, ˌan-ˌtī-\ *n* **:** a hypothetical particle thought to be emitted during radioactive decay
an·ti·neu·tron \-ˈn(y)ü-ˌträn\ *n* **:** an uncharged particle of mass equal to that of the neutron but having a magnetic moment in the opposite direction
ant·ing \ˈant-iŋ\ *n* **:** the deliberate placing by some birds of living ants among the feathers
an·ti·node \ˈant-i-ˌnōd\ *n* [ISV] **:** a region of maximum amplitude situated between adjacent nodes in a vibrating body
an·ti·no·mi·an \ˌant-i-ˈnō-mē-ən\ *n* **:** one who holds that under the gospel dispensation the moral law is of no use or obligation because faith alone is necessary to salvation — **antinomian** *adj* — **an·ti·no·mi·an·ism** \-mē-ə-ˌniz-əm\ *n*
an·tin·o·my \an-ˈtin-ə-mē\ *n* [G *antinomie*, fr. L *antinomia* conflict of laws, fr. Gk, fr. *anti-* + *nomos* law — more at NIMBLE] **1 :** a contradiction between two apparently equally valid principles or between inferences correctly drawn from such principles **2 :** OPPOSITION, CONTRADICTION
an·ti·nu·cle·on \ˌant-i-ˈn(y)ü-klē-ˌän, ˌan-ˌtī-\ *n* **:** a particle of the same mass as a nucleon but differing from it in the sign of its electrical charge or the direction of its magnetic moment
an·ti·ox·i·dant \ˌant-ē-ˈäk-səd-ənt, ˌan-ˌtī-\ *n* **:** a substance that opposes oxidation or inhibits reactions promoted by oxygen or peroxides — **antioxidant** *adj*
an·ti·pas·to \ˌant-i-ˈpas-(ˌ)tō, -ˈpäs-\ *n* [It, fr. *anti-* (fr. L *ante-*) + *pasto* food, fr. L *pastus*, fr. *pastus*, pp. of *pascere* to feed — more at FOOD] **:** HORS D'OEUVRE
an·ti·pa·thet·ic \ˌant-i-pə-ˈthet-ik\ *adj* **1 :** having a constitutional aversion **2 :** arousing or manifesting antipathy — **an·ti·pa·thet·i·cal·ly** \-i-k(ə-)lē\ *adv*
an·tip·a·thy \an-ˈtip-ə-thē\ *n* [L *antipathia*, fr. Gk *antipatheia*, fr. *antipathēs* of opposite feelings, fr. *anti-* + *pathos* experience — more at PATHOS] **1** *obs* **:** opposition in feeling **:** INCOMPATIBILITY **2 :** settled aversion or dislike **:** DISTASTE **3 :** an object of aversion **syn** see ENMITY
an·ti·pe·ri·od·ic \ˌant-i-ˌpir-ē-ˈäd-ik, ˌan-ˌtī-\ *adj* [ISV] **:** preventive of periodic returns of disease — **antiperiodic** *n*
an·ti·per·son·nel \-ˌpərs-ᵊn-ˈel\ *adj* **:** designed for use against military personnel
an·ti·phlo·gis·tic \ˌant-i-flə-ˈjis-tik\ *adj* **:** counteracting inflammation — **antiphlogistic** *n*
an·ti·phon \ˈant-ə-fən, -ˌfän\ *n* [LL *antiphona* — more at ANTHEM] **1 :** a psalm, anthem, or verse sung antiphonally **2 :** a verse usu. from Scripture said or sung liturgically before and after a canticle, psalm, or psalm verse
¹**an·tiph·o·nal** \an-ˈtif-ən-ᵊl\ *n* **:** ANTIPHONARY
²**antiphonal** *adj* **:** of or relating to an antiphon or antiphony — **an·tiph·o·nal·ly** \-ᵊl-ē\ *adv*
an·tiph·o·nary \an-ˈtif-ə-ˌner-ē\ *n* **1 :** a book containing a collection of antiphons **2 :** a book containing the choral parts of the divine office
an·tiph·o·ny \an-ˈtif-ə-nē\ *n* **:** responsive alternation between two groups esp. of singers
an·tip·o·dal \an-ˈtip-əd-ᵊl\ *adj* **1 :** of or relating to the antipodes; *specif* **:** situated at the opposite side of the earth **2 :** diametrically opposite **3 :** OPPOSED
an·ti·pode \ˈant-ə-ˌpōd\ *n, pl* **an·tip·o·des** \an-ˈtip-ə-ˌdēz\ [ME *antipodes*, pl., persons dwelling at opposite points on the globe, fr. L, fr. Gk, fr. pl. of *antipod-*, *antipous* with feet opposite, fr. *anti-* + *pod-*, *pous* foot — more at FOOT] **1 :** the parts of the earth diametrically opposite — usu. used in pl. **2 :** the exact opposite or contrary — **an·tip·o·de·an** \(ˌ)an-ˌtip-ə-ˈdē-ən\ *adj*
an·ti·pope \ˈant-i-ˌpōp\ *n* [MF *antipape*, fr. ML *antipapa*, fr. *anti-* + *papa* pope] **:** one elected or claiming to be pope in opposition to the pope canonically chosen
an·ti·pro·ton \ˌant-i-ˈprō-ˌtän, -ˌan-ˌtī-\ *n* **:** a particle equal in mass but opposite in electrical charge to a proton
an·ti·py·ret·ic \ˌant-i-(ˌ)pī-ˈret-ik\ *n* **:** an agent that reduces fever
an·ti·py·rine \ˌant-i-ˈpī-ˌrēn\ *n* [fr. *Antipyrine*, a trademark] **:** a white crystalline compound $C_{11}H_{12}N_2O$ used to relieve fever, pain, or rheumatism
¹**an·ti·quar·i·an** \ˌant-ə-ˈkwer-ē-ən\ *n* **:** ANTIQUARY
²**antiquarian** *adj* **1 :** of or relating to antiquaries or antiquities **2 :** dealing in old or rare books — **an·ti·quar·i·an·ism** \-ē-ə-ˌniz-əm\ *n*
an·ti·quary \ˈant-ə-ˌkwer-ē\ *n* **:** one who collects or studies antiquities
an·ti·quate \ˈant-ə-ˌkwāt\ *vt* [LL *antiquatus*, pp. of *antiquare*, fr. L *antiquus*] **:** to make old or obsolete — **an·ti·qua·tion** \ˌant-ə-ˈkwā-shən\ *n*
an·ti·quat·ed *adj* **1 :** OBSOLETE **2 :** OLD-FASHIONED, OUTMODED **3 :** advanced in age **syn** see OLD
¹**an·tique** \an-ˈtēk\ *adj* [MF, fr. L *antiquus*, fr. *ante* before — more at ANTE-] **1 a :** belonging to antiquity **b :** among the oldest of its class **2 :** belonging to earlier periods **:** ANCIENT **3 :** in a former style or fashion **:** OLD-FASHIONED **4 :** imitating or suggesting the crafts or style of an earlier period **syn** see OLD — **an·tique·ly** *adv* — **an·tique·ness** *n*
²**antique** *n* **1 :** a relic or object of ancient times or of an earlier period **2 :** a work of art, piece of furniture, or decorative object made at an earlier period and according to U.S. customs laws at least 100 years ago
an·tiq·ui·ty \an-ˈtik-wət-ē\ *n* **1 :** ancient times; *esp* **:** those before the Middle Ages **2 :** the quality of being ancient **3** *pl* **a :** relics or monuments of ancient times **b :** matters relating to the life or culture of ancient times **4 :** the people of ancient times
an·tir·rhi·num \ˌant-ə-ˈrī-nəm\ *n* [NL, genus name, fr. L, snapdragon, fr. Gk *antirrhinon*, fr. *anti-* like (fr. *anti* against, equivalent to) + *rhin-*, *rhis* nose] **:** any of a large genus (*Antirrhinum*) of herbs of the figwort family with bright-colored irregular flowers

an·ti–Sem·ite \ˌant-i-ˈsem-ˌīt, ˌan-ˌtī-\ *n* **:** one who is hostile to or discriminates against Jews — **an·ti–Se·mit·ic** \-sə-ˈmit-ik\ *adj* — **an·ti–Sem·i·tism** \-ˈsem-ə-ˌtiz-əm\ *n*

an·ti·sep·sis \ˌant-ə-ˈsep-səs\ *n* **:** the inhibiting of the growth and multiplication of microorganisms by antiseptic means

[1]**an·ti·sep·tic** \ˌant-ə-ˈsep-tik\ *adj* [*anti-* + Gk *sēptikos* putrefying, septic] **1 a :** opposing sepsis, putrefaction, or decay; *esp* **:** preventing or arresting the growth of microorganisms (as on living tissue) **b :** acting or protecting like an antiseptic **2 :** relating to or characterized by the use of antiseptics **3 a :** scrupulously clean **:** ASEPTIC **b :** extremely neat or ordered; *esp* **:** neat to the point of being bare or uninteresting **c :** free from what is held to be contaminating **d :** IMPERSONAL, DETACHED; *esp* **:** coldly impersonal — **an·ti·sep·ti·cal·ly** \-ti-k(ə-)lē\ *adv*

[2]**antiseptic** *n* **:** a substance that checks the growth or action of microorganisms esp. in or on living tissue; *also* **:** GERMICIDE

an·ti·se·rum \ˈant-i-ˌsir-əm, ˈan-ˌtī-, -ˌser-\ *n* [ISV] **:** a serum containing antibodies

an·ti·slav·ery \ˌant-i-ˈslāv-(ə-)rē, ˌan-ˌtī-\ *n, often attrib* **:** opposition to slavery

an·ti·so·cial \-ˈsō-shəl\ *adj* **1 :** hostile to the well-being of society **2 :** averse to the society of others **:** MISANTHROPIC

an·ti·spas·mod·ic \-ˌspaz-ˈmäd-ik\ *adj* **:** capable of preventing or relieving spasms or convulsions — **antispasmodic** *n*

an·tis·tro·phe \an-ˈtis-trə-(ˌ)fē\ *n* [LL, fr. Gk *antistrophē*, fr. *anti-* + *strophē* strophe] **:** a returning movement in Greek choral dance exactly answering to a previous strophe; *specif* **:** the part of a choral song delivered during this movement — **an·ti·stroph·ic** \ˌant-ə-ˈsträf-ik\ *adj* — **an·ti·stroph·i·cal·ly** \-i-k(ə-)lē\ *adv*

an·ti·sub·ma·rine \ˌant-i-ˈsəb-mə-ˌrēn, ˌan-ˌtī-, -ˌsəb-mə-ˈ\ *adj* **:** designed or waged to destroy submarines

an·ti·tank \ˌant-i-ˈtaŋk\ *adj* **:** designed to destroy or check tanks

an·tith·e·sis \an-ˈtith-ə-səs\ *n, pl* **an·tith·e·ses** \-ˈtith-ə-ˌsēz\ [LL, fr. Gk, lit., opposition, fr. *antitithenai* to oppose, fr. *anti-* + *tithenai* to set — more at DO] **1 a** (1) **:** the rhetorical contrast of ideas by means of parallel arrangements of words, clauses, or sentences (2) **:** OPPOSITION, CONTRAST **b** (1) **:** the second of two opposing constituents of an antithesis (2) **:** the direct opposite **:** CONTRARY **2 :** the second stage of a dialectic process

an·ti·thet·i·cal \ˌant-ə-ˈthet-i-kəl\ *or* **an·ti·thet·ic** \-ˈthet-ik\ *adj* **:** constituting or marked by antithesis **syn** see OPPOSITE — **an·ti·thet·i·cal·ly** \-i-k(ə-)lē\ *adv*

an·ti·thy·roid \ˌant-i-ˈthī-ˌrȯid\ *adj* **:** able to counteract excessive thyroid activity

an·ti·tox·ic \ˌant-i-ˈtäk-sik\ *adj* **1 :** counteracting poison **2 :** of, relating to, or being an antitoxin

an·ti·tox·in \ˌant-i-ˈtäk-sən\ *n* [ISV] **:** an antibody formed in the body as a result of the introduction of a toxin and capable of neutralizing the specific toxin that stimulated its production and produced commercially in animals by injection of a toxin or toxoid (as of human disease) with the resulting serum being used to counteract the toxin in other individuals

an·ti·trades \ˈant-i-ˌtrādz\ *n pl* **1 :** the prevailing westerly winds of middle latitudes **2 :** the westerly winds above the trade winds

an·ti·trust \ˌant-i-ˈtrəst, ˌan-ˌtī-\ *adj* **:** of or relating to legislation or opposition to trusts or combinations; *specif* **:** consisting of laws to protect trade and commerce from unlawful restraints and monopolies or unfair business practices

an·ti·tus·sive \-ˈtəs-iv\ *adj* **:** tending or having the power to control or prevent cough

an·ti·type \ˈant-i-ˌtīp\ *n* [LL *antitypus*, fr. LGk *antitypon*, fr. Gk, neut. of *antitypos* corresponding, fr. *anti-* + *typtein* to strike] **:** something that corresponds to or is foreshadowed in a type — **an·ti·typ·i·cal** \ˌant-i-ˈtip-i-kəl\ *or* **an·ti·typ·ic** \-ˈtip-ik\ *adj*

an·ti·ven·in \ˌant-i-ˈven-ən, ˌan-ˌtī-\ *n* [ISV] **:** an antitoxin to a venom **:** an antiserum containing such antitoxin

an·ti·vi·ta·min \ˌant-i-ˈvīt-ə-mən\ *n* **:** a substance that renders a vitamin ineffective

ant·ler \ˈant-lər\ *n* [ME *aunteler*, fr. MF *antoillier*, fr. (assumed) VL *anteoculare*, fr. neut. of *anteocularis* located before the eye, fr. L *ante-* + *oculus* eye] **:** the solid deciduous horn of an animal of the deer family or a branch of such horn — **ant·lered** \-lərd\ *adj*

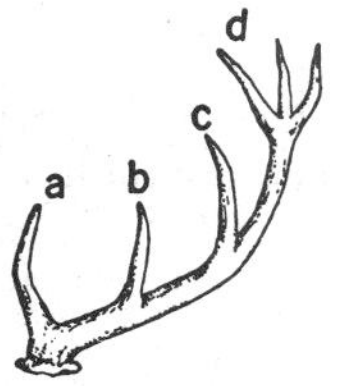

antlers: *a* brow antler, *b* bay antler, *c* royal antler, *d* surroyal

ant lion *n* **:** any of various neuropterous insects (as of the genus *Myrmeleon*) having a long-jawed larva that digs a conical pit in which it lies in wait to catch insects (as ants) on which it feeds

ant·onym \ˈan-tə-ˌnim, ˈant-ᵊn-ˌim\ *n* **:** a word of opposite meaning — **an·ton·y·mous** \an-ˈtän-ə-məs\ *adj* — **an·ton·y·my** \-mē\ *n*

an·tre \ˈant-ər\ *n* [F, fr. L *antrum*] **:** CAVE 1

an·trorse \ˈan-ˌtrȯ(ə)rs\ *adj* [NL *antrorsus*, irreg. fr. L *anterior* + *-orsus* (as in *dextrorsus* toward the right)] **:** directed forward or upward — **an·trorse·ly** *adv*

an·trum \ˈan-trəm\ *n, pl* **an·tra** \-trə\ [LL, fr. L, cave, fr. Gk *antron*] **:** the cavity of a hollow organ or a sinus

an·uran \ə-ˈn(y)u̇r-ən, a-\ *adj or n* [deriv. of *a-* + Gk *oura* tail — more at SQUIRREL] **:** SALIENTIAN

an·ure·sis \ˌan-yu̇-ˈrē-səs\ *n* [NL] **:** failure or inability to void urine — **an·uret·ic** \-ˈret-ik\ *adj*

an·uria \ə-ˈn(y)u̇r-ē-ə\ *n* [NL] **:** absence or defective excretion of urine — **an·uric** \-ˈn(y)u̇r-ik\ *adj*

an·urous \ə-ˈn(y)u̇r-əs, a-\ *adj* **:** having no tail

anus \ˈā-nəs\ *n* [L; akin to OIr *āinne* anus] **:** the posterior opening of the alimentary canal

an·vil \ˈan-vəl\ *n* [ME *anfilt*, fr. OE; akin to OHG *anafalz* anvil; both fr. a prehistoric WGmc compound whose first constituent is represented by OE *an* on, and whose second constituent is akin to Sw dial. *filta* to beat; akin to L *pellere* to beat — more at ON, FELT] **1 :** a heavy usu. steel-faced iron block on which metal is shaped **2 :** INCUS

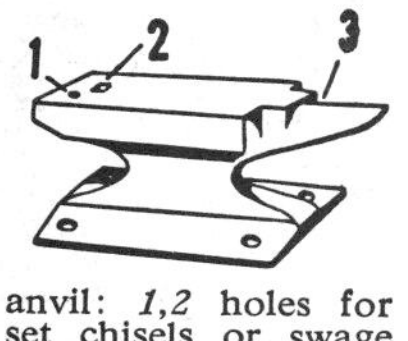

anvil: *1,2* holes for set chisels or swage blocks, *3* horn

anx·i·ety \aŋ-ˈzī-ət-ē\ *n* [L *anxietas*, fr. *anxius*] **1 a :** painful or apprehensive uneasiness of mind usu. over an impending or anticipated ill **b :** solicitous concern or interest **2 :** a cause of anxiety **syn** see CARE

anx·ious \ˈaŋ(k)-shəs\ *adj* [L *anxius*; akin to L *angere* to strangle, distress — more at ANGER] **1 :** characterized by extreme uneasiness of mind or brooding fear about some contingency **:** WORRIED **2 :** characterized by, resulting from, or causing anxiety **:** WORRYING **3 :** ardently or earnestly wishing **syn** see EAGER — **anx·ious·ly** *adv* — **anx·ious·ness** *n*

[1]**any** \ˈen-ē\ *adj* [ME, fr. OE *ǣnig*; akin to OHG *einag* any, OE *ān* one — more at ONE] **1 :** one or some indiscriminately of whatever kind: **a :** one or another taken at random ⟨ask ~ man you meet⟩ **b :** EVERY — used to indicate one selected without restriction ⟨~ child would know that⟩ **2 :** one, some, or all indiscriminately of whatever quantity: **a :** one or more — used to indicate an undetermined number or amount ⟨have you ~ money⟩ **b :** ALL — used to indicate a maximum or whole ⟨needs ~ help he can get⟩ **c :** a or some without reference to quantity or extent **3 a :** unmeasured or unlimited in amount, number, or extent ⟨~ quantity you desire⟩ **b :** appreciably large or extended ⟨could not endure it ~ length of time⟩

[2]**any** *pron, sing or pl in constr* **1 :** any person or persons **:** ANYBODY **2 a :** any thing or things **b :** any part, quantity, or number

[3]**any** *adv* **:** to any extent or degree **:** at all

any·body \ˈen-ē-ˌbäd-ē, -bəd-\ *pron* **:** any person **:** ANYONE

any·how \ˈen-ē-ˌhau̇\ *adv* **1 a :** in any manner whatever **b :** HAPHAZARDLY **2 a :** at any rate **b :** in any event

any·more \ˌen-ē-ˈmō(ə)r, -ˈmȯ(ə)r\ *adv* **:** at the present time **:** NOW — used in a negative context

any·one \ˈen-ē(ˌ)wən\ *pron* **:** any person at all **:** ANYBODY

any·place \ˈen-ē-ˌplās\ *adv* **:** in any place **:** ANYWHERE

[1]**any·thing** \ˈen-ē-ˌthiŋ\ *pron* **:** any thing whatever

[2]**anything** *adv* **:** at all

anything but *adv* **:** not at all

any·time \ˈen-ē-ˌtīm\ *adv* **:** at any time whatever

any·way \ˈen-ē-ˌwā\ *adv* **1 :** ANYWISE **2 :** in any case **:** ANYHOW

any·ways \ˈen-ē-ˌwāz\ *adv* **1** *archaic* **:** ANYWISE **2** *chiefly dial* **:** in any case

[1]**any·where** \ˈen-ē-ˌ(h)we(ə)r, -ˌ(h)wa(ə)r, -(h)wər\ *adv* **1 :** at, in, or to any place or point **2 :** at all **:** to any extent

[2]**anywhere** *n* **:** any place

any·wise \ˈen-ē-ˌwīz\ *adv* **:** in any way whatever **:** at all

An·zac \ˈan-ˌzak\ *n* [*A*ustralian and *N*ew *Z*ealand *A*rmy *C*orps] **:** a soldier from Australia or New Zealand

A1 \ˈā-ˈwən\ *adj* **1 :** having the highest possible classification — used of a ship **2 :** of the finest quality **:** FIRST-RATE

ao·rist \ˈā-ə-rəst, ˈe-ə-\ *n* [LL & Gk; LL *aoristos*, fr. Gk, fr. *aoristos* undefined, fr. *a-* + *horistos* definable, fr. *horizein* to define — more at HORIZON] **:** an inflectional form of a verb typically denoting simple occurrence of an action without reference to its completeness, duration, or repetition — **aorist** *or* **ao·ris·tic** \ˌā-ə-ˈris-tik, ˌe-ə-\ *adj* — **ao·ris·ti·cal·ly** \-ti-k(ə-)lē\ *adv*

aor·ta \ā-ˈȯrt-ə\ *n, pl* **aortas** *or* **aor·tae** \-ˈȯr-ˌtē\ [NL, fr. Gk *aortē*, fr. *aeirein* to lift] **:** the great trunk artery that carries blood from the heart to be distributed by branch arteries through the body — **aor·tal** \-ˈȯrt-ᵊl\ *adj* — **aor·tic** \-ˈȯrt-ik\ *adj*

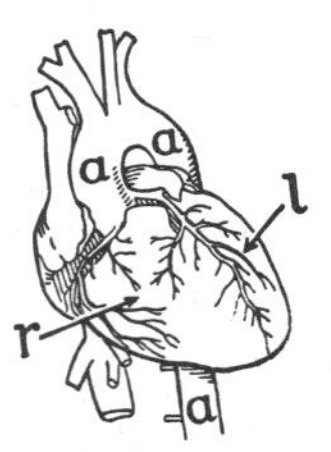

a,a,a aorta; *r* right ventricle; *l* left ventricle

aou·dad \ˈau̇-ˌdad\ *n* [F, fr. Berber *audad*] **:** a wild sheep (*Ammotragus lervia*) of No. Africa

à ou·trance \ˌä-ˌü-ˈträ^n s\ *adv* [F] **:** to the limit **:** UNSPARINGLY

[1]**ap-** — see AD-

[2]**ap-** — see APO-

apace \ə-ˈpās\ *adv* [ME, prob. fr. MF *à pas* on step] **:** at a quick pace **:** SWIFTLY

Apache \ə-ˈpach-ē, *in sense 3* ə-ˈpash\ *n* [Sp] **1 a :** an Athapaskan people of the American southwest **b :** a member of this people **2 :** any of the Athapaskan languages of the Apache people **3** *not cap* [F, fr. *Apache* Apache Indian] **a :** a member of a gang of criminals esp. in Paris **b :** RUFFIAN

ap·a·nage *var of* APPANAGE

ap·a·re·jo \ˌap-ə-ˈrā-(ˌ)(h)ō\ *n* [AmerSp] **:** a packsaddle of stuffed leather or canvas

[1]**apart** \ə-ˈpärt\ *adv* [ME, fr. MF *a part*, lit., to the side] **1 a :** at a little distance **b :** separately in space or time **2 :** as a separate unit **:** INDEPENDENTLY **3 :** ASIDE **4 :** into two or more parts **:** to pieces

[2]**apart** *adj* **1 :** SEPARATE, ISOLATED **2 :** DIVIDED — **apart·ness** *n*

apart from *prep* **:** other than **:** BESIDES

apart·heid \ə-ˈpär-ˌtāt, -ˌtīt; -ˈpärt-ˌhāt, -ˌhīt\ *n* [Afrik, lit., separateness] **:** racial segregation; *specif* **:** a policy of segregation and political and economic discrimination against non-European groups in the Union of So. Africa

apart·ment \ə-ˈpärt-mənt\ *n, often attrib* [F *appartement*, fr. It *appartamento*] **1 :** a room or set of rooms fitted esp. with housekeeping facilities and used as a dwelling **2 :** a building made up of individual dwelling units — **apart·men·tal** \ə-ˌpärt-ˈment-ᵊl\ *adj*

apartment building *n* **:** a building containing separate residential apartments — called also *apartment house*

ap·a·thet·ic \ˌap-ə-ˈthet-ik\ *adj* **1 :** having or showing little or no feeling or emotion **:** SPIRITLESS **2 :** having little or no interest or concern **:** INDIFFERENT **syn** see IMPASSIVE — **ap·a·thet·i·cal·ly** \-i-k(ə-)lē\ *adv*

ap·a·thy \ˈap-ə-thē\ *n* [Gk *apatheia*, fr. *apathēs* without feeling, fr. *a-* + *pathos* emotion] **1 :** lack of feeling or emotion **:** IMPASSIVENESS **2 :** lack of interest or concern **:** INDIFFERENCE

ap·a·tite \ˈap-ə-ˌtīt\ *n* [G *apatit*, fr. Gk *apatē* deceit] **:** any of a group of calcium phosphate minerals of the approximate general formula $Ca_5(F,Cl,OH,\frac{1}{2}CO_3)(PO_4)_3$ occurring variously as hexagonal crystals, as granular masses, or in fine-grained masses as the chief constituent of phosphate rock and of bones and teeth; *specif* **:** calcium phosphate fluoride $Ca_5F(PO_4)_3$

[1]**ape** \ˈāp\ *n* [ME, fr. OE *apa*; akin to OHG *affo* ape] **1 a :** MONKEY; *esp* **:** one of the larger tailless or short-tailed Old World forms **b :** any of a family (Pongidae) of large semierect primates (as the chimpanzee or gorilla) — called also *anthropoid ape* **2 a :** MIMIC **b :** a large uncouth person — **ape·like** \ˈā-ˌplīk\ *adj*

[2]**ape** *vt* **:** IMITATE, MIMIC **syn** see COPY — **ap·er** *n*

apeak \ə-ˈpēk\ *adv (or adj)* [alter. of earlier *apike*, prob. fr. *a-* + *pike*] **:** in a vertical position ⟨oars ~⟩

ape–man \'āp-'man, -,man\ *n* **:** a primate (as pithecanthropus) intermediate in character between Homo sapiens and the higher apes

aper·çu \à-per-sü̅, ,ap-ər-'sü\ *n, pl* **aperçus** \-sü̅(z), -'süz\ [F] **1 :** an immediate impression; *esp* **:** INSIGHT 2 **2 :** a brief survey or sketch **:** OUTLINE **syn** see COMPENDIUM

ape·ri·ent \ə-'pir-ē-ənt\ *adj* [L *aperient-, aperiens,* prp. of *aperire*] **:** gently moving the bowels **:** LAXATIVE — **aperient** *n*

ape·ri·od·ic \,ā-,pir-ē-'äd-ik\ *adj* **1 :** of irregular occurrence **2 :** not having periodic vibrations **:** not oscillatory — **ape·ri·od·i·cal·ly** \-i-k(ə-)lē\ *adv* — **ape·ri·o·dic·i·ty** \-ē-ə-'dis-ət-ē\ *n*

aper·i·tif \,äp-,er-ə-'tēf\ *n* [F *apéritif* aperient, aperitif, fr. MF *aperitif,* adj., aperient, fr. ML *aperitivus,* irreg. fr. L *aperire*] **:** an alcoholic drink taken before a meal as an appetizer

ap·er·ture \'ap-ə(r)-,chü(ə)r, -chər, -,t(y)ü(ə)r\ *n* [ME, fr. L *apertura,* fr. *apertus,* pp. of *aperire* to open — more at WEIR] **1 :** an opening or open space **:** HOLE **2 a :** the opening in a photographic lens that admits the light **b :** the diameter of the stop in an optical system that determines the diameter of the bundle of rays traversing the instrument

syn APERTURE, INTERSTICE, ORIFICE mean a passage through. APERTURE applies to any opening in an otherwise solid wall or surface; INTERSTICE applies to an unfilled gap or interval in a mass or a fabric; ORIFICE applies to an opening suggesting a mouth or a vent

apet·al·ous \(')ā-'pet-ᵊl-əs\ *adj* **:** having no petals — **apet·aly** \-ᵊl-ē\ *n*

apex \'ā-,peks\ *n, pl* **apex·es** *or* **api·ces** \'ā-pə-,sēz, 'ap-ə-\ [L] **1 a :** the uppermost point **:** VERTEX **b :** the narrowed or pointed end **:** TIP **2 :** the highest or culminating point **syn** see SUMMIT

aphaer·e·sis *or* **apher·e·sis** \ə-'fer-ə-səs\ *n* [LL, fr. Gk *aphairesis,* lit., taking off, fr. *aphairein* to take away, fr. *apo-* + *hairein* to take] **:** the loss of one or more sounds or letters at the beginning of a word (as in *round* for *around*) — **aph·ae·ret·ic** \,af-ə-'ret-ik\ *adj*

aph·a·nite \'af-ə-,nīt\ *n* [F, fr. Gk *aphanēs* invisible, fr. *a-* + *phainesthai* to appear — more at PHENOMENON] **:** a dark rock of such close texture that its separate grains are invisible to the naked eye — **aph·a·nit·ic** \,af-ə-'nit-ik\ *adj*

apha·sia \ə-'fā-zh(ē-)ə\ *n* [NL, fr. Gk, fr. *a-* + *-phasia*] **:** loss or impairment of the power to use words usu. resulting from a brain lesion — **apha·si·ac** \-zē-,ak\ *adj* — **apha·sic** \-zik\ *n or adj*

aph·elion \a-'fēl-yən\ *n, pl* **aph·elia** \-yə\ [NL, fr. *apo-* + Gk *hēlios* sun — more at SOLAR] **:** the point of a planet's or comet's orbit most distant from the sun

aph·e·sis \'af-ə-səs\ *n* [NL, fr. Gk, release, fr. *aphienai* to let go, fr. *apo-* + *hienai* to send — more at JET] **:** aphaeresis consisting of the loss of a short unaccented vowel (as in *lone* for *alone*) — **aphet·ic** \ə-'fet-ik\ *adj* — **aphet·i·cal·ly** \-i-k(ə-)lē\ *adv*

aphid \'ā-fəd, 'af-əd\ *n* **:** any of numerous small sluggish homopterous insects (superfamily Aphidoidea) that suck the juices of plants

aphis \'ā-fəs, 'af-əs\ *n, pl* **aphi·des** \'ā-fə-,dēz, 'af-ə-\ [NL *Aphid-, Aphis,* genus name] **:** an aphid of a common genus (*Aphis*); *broadly* **:** APHID

aphis lion *n* **:** any of several insect larvae (as a lacewing or ladybug larva) that feed on aphids

apho·nia \(')ā-'fō-nē-ə\ *n* [NL, fr. Gk *aphōnia,* fr. *aphōnos* voiceless, fr. *a-* + *phōnē* sound — more at BAN] **:** loss of voice and of all but whispered speech — **aphon·ic** \-'fän-ik\ *adj*

aph·o·rism \'af-ə-,riz-əm\ *n* [MF *aphorisme,* fr. LL *aphorismus,* fr. Gk *aphorismos* definition, aphorism, fr. *aphorizein* to define, fr. *apo-* + *horizein* to bound — more at HORIZON] **1 :** a concise statement of a principle **2 :** a terse formulation of a truth or sentiment **:** ADAGE, MAXIM — **aph·o·rist** \'af-ə-rəst\ *n* — **aph·o·ris·tic** \,af-ə-'ris-tik\ *adj* — **aph·o·ris·ti·cal·ly** \-ti-k(ə-)lē\ *adv*

aph·o·rize \'af-ə-,rīz\ *vi* **:** to write or speak in or as if in aphorisms

apho·tic \(')ā-'fōt-ik\ *adj* **:** lacking light

aph·ro·dis·i·ac \,af-rə-'diz-ē-,ak\ *adj* [Gk *aphrodisiakos* sexual, fr. *aphrodisia* sexual pleasures, fr. neut. pl. of *aphrodisios* of Aphrodite, fr. *Aphroditē*] **:** exciting sexual desire — **aphrodisiac** *n* — **aph·ro·di·si·a·cal** \,af-rəd-ə-'zī-ə-kəl, -'sī-\ *adj*

Aph·ro·di·te \,af-rə-'dīt-ē\ *n* [Gk *Aphroditē*] **1 :** the goddess of love and beauty in Greek mythology **2 :** a brown black-spotted butterfly (*Argynnis aphrodite*) of the U.S.

aphyl·lous \(')ā-'fil-əs\ *adj* [Gk *aphyllos,* fr. *a-* + *phyllon* leaf — more at BLADE] **:** not having foliage leaves — **aphyl·ly** \'ā-,fil-ē\ *n*

api·an \'ā-pē-ən\ *adj* [L *apianus,* fr. *apis*] **:** of or relating to bees

api·ar·i·an \,ā-pē-'er-ē-ən\ *adj* **:** of or relating to beekeeping or bees

api·a·rist \'ā-pē-ə-rəst, -pē-,er-əst\ *n* **:** BEEKEEPER

api·ary \'ā-pē-,er-ē\ *n* [L *apiarium,* fr. *apis* bee] **:** a place where bees are kept; *esp* **:** a collection of hives or colonies of bees kept for their honey

api·cal \'ap-i-kəl, 'ā-pi-\ *adj* [prob. fr. NL *apicalis,* fr. L *apic-, apex*] **:** of, relating to, or situated at an apex — **api·cal·ly** \-k(ə-)lē\ *adv*

apic·u·late \ə-'pik-yə-lət\ *adj* [NL *apiculus,* dim. of L *apic-, apex*] **:** ending abruptly in a small distinct point

api·cul·tur·al \,ā-pə-'kəlch-(ə-)rəl\ *adj* **:** of or relating to apiculture

api·cul·ture \'ā-pə-,kəl-chər\ *n* [prob. fr. F, fr. L *apis* bee + F *culture*] **:** beekeeping esp. on a large scale — **api·cul·tur·ist** \,ā-pə-'kəlch-(ə-)rəst\ *n*

apiece \ə-'pēs\ *adv* **:** for each one **:** INDIVIDUALLY

Apis \'ā-pəs\ *n* [L, fr. Gk, fr. Egypt *ḥp*] **:** a sacred bull worshiped by the ancient Egyptians

ap·ish \'ā-pish\ *adj* **:** resembling an ape: as **a :** given to slavish imitation **b :** extremely silly or affected — **ap·ish·ly** *adv* — **ap·ish·ness** *n*

apiv·o·rous \ā-'piv-ə-rəs\ *adj* [prob. fr. F *apivore,* fr. L *apis* + F *-vore* -vorous] **:** bee-eating

apla·cen·tal \,ā-plə-'sent-ᵊl\ *adj* **:** having or developing no placenta

ap·la·nat·ic \,ap-lə-'nat-ik\ *adj* [*a-* + Gk *planasthai* to wander — more at PLANET] **:** free from or corrected for spherical aberration

ap·lite \'ap-,līt\ *n* [prob. fr. G *aplit,* fr. Gk *haploos* simple — more at HAPL-] **:** a fine-grained light-colored granite consisting almost entirely of quartz and feldspar — **ap·lit·ic** \ap-'lit-ik\ *adj*

aplomb \ə-'pläm, -'pləm\ *n* [F, lit., perpendicularity, fr. MF, fr. *a plomb,* lit., according to the plummet] **:** complete composure or self-assurance **:** POISE **syn** see CONFIDENCE

ap·nea *or* **ap·noea** \'ap-nē-ə, ap-'\ *n* [NL] **1 :** transient cessation of respiration **2 :** ASPHYXIA — **ap·ne·ic** \ap-'nē-ik\ *adj*

apo- *or* **ap-** *or* **aph-** *prefix* [ME, fr. MF & L; MF, fr. L, fr. Gk, fr. *apo* — more at OF] **1 :** away from **:** off ⟨*aph*elion⟩ **2 :** detached **:** separate ⟨*apo*carpous⟩ **3 :** formed from **:** related to ⟨*apo*morphine⟩

apoc·a·lypse \ə-'päk-ə-,lips\ *n* [ME, revelation, Revelation, fr. LL *apocalypsis,* fr. Gk *apokalypsis,* fr. *apokalyptein* to uncover, fr. *apo-* + *kalyptein* to cover — more at HELL] **1 a :** one of the Jewish and Christian writings of 200 B.C. to A.D. 150 marked by pseudonymity, symbolic imagery, and the expectation of an imminent cosmic cataclysm in which God destroys the ruling powers of evil and raises the righteous to life in a messianic kingdom **b** *cap* **:** the biblical book of Revelation **2 :** something viewed as a prophetic revelation — **apoc·a·lyp·tic** \ə-,päk-ə-'lip-tik\ *or* **apoc·a·lyp·ti·cal** \-ti-kəl\ *adj* — **apoc·a·lyp·ti·cal·ly** \-k(ə-)lē\ *adv* — **apoc·a·lyp·ti·cism** \-tə-,siz-əm\ *n*

apoc·a·lyp·tist \-təst\ *n* **:** the writer of an apocalypse

apo·car·pous \,ap-ə-'kär-pəs\ *adj* **:** having the carpels of the gynoecium separate — **apo·car·py** \'ap-ə-,kär-pē\ *n*

apo·chro·mat·ic \,ap-ə-krō-'mat-ik\ *adj* [ISV] **:** free from chromatic and spherical aberration ⟨~ lens⟩

apoc·o·pe \ə-'päk-ə-(,)pē\ *n* [LL, fr. Gk *apokopē,* lit., cutting off, fr. *apokoptein* to cut off, fr. *apo-* + *koptein* to cut — more at CAPON] **:** the loss of one or more sounds or letters at the end of a word (as in *sing* from Old English *singan*)

apo·crine \'ap-ə-krən, -,krīn, -,krēn\ *adj* [ISV *apo-* + Gk *krinein* to separate — more at CERTAIN] **:** producing a secretion by separation of part of the cytoplasm of the secreting cells

apoc·ry·pha \ə-'päk-rə-fə\ *n pl but sing or pl in constr* [ML, fr. LL, neut. pl. of *apocryphus* secret, not canonical, fr. Gk *apokryphos* obscure, fr. *apokryptein* to hide away, fr. *apo-* + *kryptein* to hide — more at CRYPT] **1 :** writings or statements of dubious authenticity **2** *cap* **a :** books included in the Septuagint and Vulgate but excluded from the Jewish and Protestant canons of the Old Testament **b :** early Christian writings not included in the New Testament

apoc·ry·phal \-fəl\ *adj* **1** *often cap* **:** of or resembling the Apocrypha **2 :** not canonical **:** SPURIOUS **syn** see FICTITIOUS — **apoc·ry·phal·ly** \-fə-lē\ *adv* — **apoc·ry·phal·ness** *n*

apo·cyn·thi·on \,ap-ə-'sin(t)-thē-ən\ *n* [NL, fr. *apo-* + *Cynthia*] **:** APOLUNE

ap·o·dal \'ap-əd-ᵊl\ *or* **ap·o·dous** \-əd-əs\ *adj* [Gk *apod-, apous,* fr. *a-* + *pod-, pous* foot — more at FOOT] **:** having no feet or analogous appendages ⟨eels are ~⟩

apo·dic·tic \,ap-ə-'dik-tik\ *or* **apo·deic·tic** \-'dīk-tik\ *adj* [L *apodicticus,* fr. Gk *apodeiktikos,* fr. *apodeiknynai* to demonstrate, fr. *apo-* + *deiknynai* to show — more at DICTION] **:** expressing or of the nature of necessary truth or absolute certainty — **apo·dic·ti·cal·ly** \-ti-k(ə-)lē\ *adv*

apod·o·sis \ə-'päd-ə-səs\ *n* [NL, fr. Gk, fr. *apodidonai* to give back, deliver, fr. *apo-* + *didonai* to give — more at DATE] **:** the main clause of a conditional sentence

apo·en·zyme \,ap-ə-'wen-,zīm\ *n* [ISV] **:** a protein that forms an active enzyme system by combination with a coenzyme and determines the specificity of this system for a substrate

apo·gam·ic \,ap-ə-'gam-ik\ *or* **apog·a·mous** \ə-'päg-ə-məs\ *adj* **:** of or relating to apogamy — **apo·gam·i·cal·ly** \,ap-ə-'gam-i-k(ə-)lē\ *adv*

apog·a·my \ə-'päg-ə-mē\ *n* [ISV] **:** development of a sporophyte from a gametophyte without fertilization

apo·ge·an \,ap-ə-'jē-ən\ *adj* **:** of or connected with the apogee

apo·gee \'ap-ə-(,)jē\ *n* [F *apogée,* fr. NL *apogaeum,* fr. Gk *apogaion,* fr. neut. of *apogeios, apogaios* far from the earth, fr. *apo-* + *gē* earth] **1 :** the point in the orbit of a satellite of the earth at the greatest distance from the center of the earth — compare PERIGEE **2 :** the farthest or highest point **:** CULMINATION

apolit·i·cal \,ā-pə-'lit-i-kəl\ *adj* **1 :** having an aversion for or no interest or involvement in political affairs **2 :** having no political significance — **apolit·i·cal·ly** \-k(ə-)lē\ *adv*

Ap·ol·lin·i·an \,ap-ə-'lin-ē-ən\ *adj* **:** APOLLONIAN

Apol·lo \ə-'päl-(,)ō\ *n* [L *Apollin-, Apollo,* fr. Gk *Apollōn*] **:** the god of sunlight, prophecy, and music and poetry in Greek mythology

Ap·ol·lo·ni·an \,ap-ə-'lō-nē-ən\ *adj* **1 :** of, relating to, or resembling the god Apollo **2 :** harmonious, measured, ordered, or balanced in character

Apol·lyon \ə-'päl-yən, -'päl-ē-ən\ *n* [Gk *Apollyōn*] **:** the angel of hell

apol·o·get·ic \ə-,päl-ə-'jet-ik\ *adj* [Gk *apologētikos,* fr. *apologeisthai* to defend, fr. *apo-* + *logos* speech] **1 :** offered in defense or vindication **2 :** offered by way of excuse or apology — **apol·o·get·i·cal·ly** \-i-k(ə-)lē\ *adv*

apol·o·get·ics \-iks\ *n pl but sing or pl in constr* **:** systematic argumentative discourse in defense esp. of the divine origin and authority of Christianity

apo·lo·gia \,ap-ə-'lō-j(ē-)ə\ *n* [LL] **:** APOLOGY; *esp* **:** DEFENSE 3b **syn** see APOLOGY

apol·o·gist \ə-'päl-ə-jəst\ *n* **:** one who speaks or writes in defense of a faith, a cause, or an institution

apol·o·gize \-ə-,jīz\ *vi* **:** to make an apology — **apol·o·giz·er** *n*

apo·logue \'ap-ə-,lȯg, -,läg\ *n* [F, fr. L *apologus,* fr. Gk *apologos,* fr. *apo-* + *logos* speech, narrative] **:** an allegorical narrative usu. intended to convey a moral

apol·o·gy \ə-'päl-ə-jē\ *n* [MF or LL; MF *apologie,* fr. LL *apologia,* fr. Gk, fr. *apo-* + *logos* speech — more at LEGEND] **1 a :** a formal justification **:** DEFENSE **b :** EXCUSE 2a **2 :** an admission of error or discourtesy accompanied by an expression of regret **3 :** a poor substitute **:** MAKESHIFT

syn APOLOGIA, EXCUSE, PLEA, PRETEXT, ALIBI: APOLOGY now commonly applies to an expression of regret for a mistake or wrong with implied admission of guilt or fault; like APOLOGIA it may be used to imply not an admission of guilt or error but a desire to make clear the grounds for some belief or course of action; EXCUSE implies an intent to avoid or remove blame or censure; PLEA stresses an appeal for understanding or sympathy or mercy; PRETEXT suggests subterfuge, the offering of a pretended reason or motive in place of the real one usu. before the intended action; ALIBI applies to an explanation that is plausible rather than entirely truthful

apo·lune \'ap-ə-,lün\ *n* [*apo-* + L *luna* moon — more at LUNAR] **:** the point in the path of a body orbiting the moon that is farthest from the center of the moon

apo·mict \'ap-ə-ˌmikt\ *n* [prob. back-formation fr. ISV *apomictic*, fr. *apo-* + Gk *mignynai* to mix — more at MIX] **:** one produced or reproducing by apomixis — **apo·mic·tic** \ˌap-ə-'mik-tik\ *adj* — **apo·mic·ti·cal·ly** \-ti-k(ə-)lē\ *adv*
apo·mix·is \ˌap-ə-'mik-səs\ *n* [NL, fr. *apo-* + Gk *mixis* act of mixing, fr. *mignynai*] **:** reproduction (as apogamy) involving the specialized generative tissues but not dependent upon fertilization
apo·mor·phine \ˌap-ə-'mȯr-ˌfēn\ *n* [ISV] **:** an artificial crystalline alkaloid $C_{17}H_{17}NO_2$ from morphine with a powerful emetic action
apo·neu·ro·sis \ˌap-ə-n(y)u̇-'rō-səs\ *n* [NL, fr. Gk *aponeurōsis*, fr. *aponeurousthai* to pass into a tendon, fr. *apo-* + *neuron* sinew — more at NERVE] **:** any of the thicker and denser of the deep fasciae that cover, invest, and form the terminations and attachments of various muscles and differ from tendons in being flat and thin — **apo·neu·rot·ic** \-'rät-ik\ *adj*
apo·phyl·lite \ˌap-ə-'fil-ˌīt\ *n* [F, fr. *apo-* + Gk *phyllon* leaf] **:** a mineral $KCa_4Si_8O_{20}(F,OH).8H_2O$ composed of a hydrous potassium calcium silicate related to the zeolites and usu. found in transparent square prisms or white or grayish masses
apoph·y·se·al \ə-ˌpäf-ə-'sē-əl\ *adj* **:** of or relating to an apophysis
apoph·y·sis \ə-'päf-ə-səs\ *n, pl* **apoph·y·ses** \-'päf-ə-ˌsēz\ [NL, fr. Gk, fr. *apo-* + *phyein* to bring forth — more at BE] **:** an expanded or projecting part esp. of an organism
ap·o·plec·tic \ˌap-ə-'plek-tik\ *adj* [F or LL; F *apoplectique*, fr. LL *apoplecticus*, fr. Gk *apoplēktikos*, fr. *apoplēssein*] **1 :** of, relating to, or causing apoplexy **2 :** affected with, inclined to, or showing symptoms of apoplexy **3 :** of a kind to cause apoplexy ⟨an ~ partisanship⟩; *also* **:** highly excited **:** FRENETIC ⟨~ agitation⟩ ⟨an ~ rage⟩ — **ap·o·plec·ti·cal·ly** \-ti-k(ə-)lē\ *adv*
ap·o·plexy \'ap-ə-ˌplek-sē\ *n* [ME *apoplexie*, fr. MF & LL; MF, fr. LL *apoplexia*, fr. Gk *apoplēxia*, fr. *apoplēssein* to cripple by a stroke, fr. *apo-* + *plēssein* to strike — more at PLAINT] **:** sudden diminution or loss of consciousness, sensation, and voluntary motion caused by rupture or obstruction of an artery of the brain
aport \ə-'pō(ə)rt, -'pȯ(ə)rt\ *adv* (*or adj*) **:** on or toward the left side of a ship
apo·se·mat·ic \ˌap-ə-si-'mat-ik\ *adj* **:** being conspicuous and serving to warn — **apo·se·mat·i·cal·ly** \-i-k(ə-)lē\ *adv*
apo·si·o·pe·sis \ˌap-ə-ˌsī-ə-'pē-səs\ *n* [LL, fr. Gk *aposiōpēsis*, fr. *aposiōpan* to be quite silent, fr. *apo-* + *siōpan* to be silent, fr. *siōpē* silence] **:** the leaving of a thought incomplete usu. by a sudden breaking off — **apo·si·o·pet·ic** \-'pet-ik\ *adj*
apos·ta·sy \ə-'päs-tə-sē\ *n* [ME *apostasie*, fr. LL *apostasia*, fr. Gk, lit., revolt, fr. *aphistasthai* to revolt, fr. *apo-* + *histasthai* to stand] **1 :** renunciation of a religious faith **2 :** DEFECTION
apos·tate \ə-'päs-ˌtāt, -tət\ *n* **:** one who commits apostasy — **apos·tate** *adj*
apos·ta·tize \ə-'päs-tə-ˌtīz\ *vi* **:** to commit apostasy
a pos·te·ri·o·ri \ˌä-(ˌ)pō-ˌstir-ē-'ō(ə)r-ē, -ˌster-; ˌā-(ˌ)pä-ˌstir-ē-'ō(ə)r-ˌī, -(ˌ)pō-, -'ō(ə)r-ē; -'ȯ(ə)r-\ *adj* [L, lit., from the latter] **:** relating to or derived by reasoning from observed facts **:** SYNTHETIC; *specif* **:** INDUCTIVE — **a posteriori** *adv*
apos·tle \ə-'päs-əl\ *n* [ME, fr. OF & OE; OF *apostle* & OE *apostol*, fr. LL *apostolus*, fr. Gk *apostolos*, fr. *apostellein* to send away, fr. *apo-* + *stellein* to send — more at STALL] **1 :** one sent on a mission: as **a :** one of an authoritative New Testament group sent out to preach the gospel and made up esp. of Christ's 12 original disciples and Paul **b :** the first prominent Christian missionary to a region or group **2 :** one who initiates a great moral reform or first advocates any important belief or system **3 :** the highest ecclesiastical official in some church organizations **4 :** one of a Mormon administrative council of 12 men — **apos·tle·ship** \-əl-ˌship\ *n*
Apostles' Creed *n* **:** a Christian creed anciently ascribed to the Twelve Apostles that begins "I believe in God the Father Almighty"
apos·to·late \ə-'päs-tə-ˌlāt, -lət\ *n* [LL *apostolatus*, fr. *apostolus*] **:** the office or mission of an apostle
ap·os·tol·ic \ˌap-ə-'stäl-ik\ *adj* **1 a :** of or relating to an apostle **b :** of or relating to the New Testament apostles or conforming to their teachings **2 a :** of or relating to a succession of spiritual authority from the apostles held (as by Roman Catholics, Anglicans, Eastern Orthodox) to be perpetuated by successive ordinations of bishops and to be necessary for the validity of sacraments and orders **b :** PAPAL — **apos·to·lic·i·ty** \ə-ˌpäs-tə-'lis-ət-ē\ *n*
apostolic delegate *n* **:** an ecclesiastical representative of the Holy See in a country that has no formal diplomatic relations with it
Apostolic Father *n* **:** a church father of the 1st or 2d century A.D.
[1]**apos·tro·phe** \ə-'päs-trə-(ˌ)fē\ *n* [L, fr. Gk *apostrophē*, lit., act of turning away, fr. *apostrephein* to turn away, fr. *apo-* + *strephein* to turn] **:** the addressing of a usu. absent person or a usu. personified thing rhetorically — **ap·os·troph·ic** \ˌap-ə-'sträf-ik\ *adj*
[2]**apostrophe** *n* [MF & LL; MF, fr. LL *apostrophus*, fr. Gk *apostrophos*, fr. *apostrophos* turned away, fr. *apostrephein*] **:** a mark ' or ' used to indicate omission of letters or figures, the possessive case, or the plural of letters or figures — **apostrophic** *adj*
apos·tro·phize \ə-'päs-trə-ˌfīz\ *vt* **:** to address by or in apostrophe ~ *vi* **:** to make use of apostrophe
apothecaries' measure *n* **:** a measure of capacity — see MEASURE table
apothecaries' weight *n* — see MEASURE table
apoth·e·cary \ə-'päth-ə-ˌker-ē\ *n* [ME *apothecarie*, fr. ML *apothecarius*, fr. LL, shopkeeper, fr. L *apotheca* storehouse, fr. Gk *apothēkē*, fr. *apotithenai* to put away, fr. *apo-* + *tithenai* to put — more at DO] **1 :** one who prepares and sells drugs or compounds for medicinal purposes **2 :** PHARMACY
apo·the·cial \ˌap-ə-'thē-sh(ē-)əl\ *adj* **:** of or relating to an apothecium
apo·the·ci·um \-'thē-s(h)ē-əm\ *n, pl* **apo·the·cia** \-s(h)ē-ə\ [NL, fr. L *apotheca*] **:** a spore-bearing structure in many lichens and fungi consisting of a discoid or cupped body bearing asci on the exposed flat or concave surface
apo·thegm \'ap-ə-ˌthem\ *n* [Gk *apophthegmat-*, *apophthegma*, fr. *apophthengesthai* to speak out, fr. *apo-* + *phthengesthai* to utter] **:** a short, pithy, and instructive saying or formulation **:** APHORISM — **apo·theg·mat·ic** \ˌap-ə-(ˌ)theg-'mat-ik\ *or* **apo·theg·mat·i·cal** \-i-kəl\ *adj* — **apo·theg·mat·i·cal·ly** \-k(ə-)lē\ *adv*
ap·o·them \'ap-ə-ˌthem\ *n* [ISV *apo-* + *-them* (fr. Gk *thema* something laid down, theme)] **:** the perpendicular from the center of one of the sides of a regular polygon
apo·the·o·sis \ə-ˌpäth-ē-'ō-səs, ˌap-ə-'thē-ə-səs\ *n* [LL, fr. Gk *apotheōsis*, fr. *apotheoun* to deify, fr. *apo-* + *theos* god] **1 :** elevation to divine status **:** DEIFICATION **2 :** the perfect example — **apo·the·o·size** \ˌap-ə-'thē-ə-ˌsīz, ə-'päth-ē-ə-\ *vt*
Ap·pa·la·chian tea \ˌap-ə-ˌlā-chən-, -ˌlach-ən-\ *n* [*Appalachian* mountains, U.S.A.] **:** the leaves of either of two hollies (*Ilex glabra* and *I. vomitoria*) of the eastern U.S. used as a tea; *also* **:** either of the plants
ap·pall *also* **ap·pal** \ə-'pȯl\ *vb* **ap·palled; ap·pall·ing** [ME *appallen*, fr. MF *apalir*, fr. OF, fr. *a-* (fr. L *ad-*) + *palir* to grow pale, fr. L *pallescere*, incho. of *pallēre* to be pale] *vi, obs* **:** WEAKEN, FAIL ~ *vt* **:** to overcome with fear or dread **syn** see DISMAY
ap·pall·ing *adj* **:** inspiring horror or dismay **syn** see FEARFUL — **ap·pall·ing·ly** \-'pȯ-liŋ-lē\ *adv*
ap·pa·nage \'ap-ə-nij\ *n* [F *apanage*, fr. OF, fr. *apaner* to provide for a younger offspring, fr. OProv *apanar* to support, fr. *a-* (fr. L *ad-*) + *pan* bread, fr. L *panis* — more at FOOD] **1 a :** a grant (as of land or revenue) made by a sovereign or a legislative body to a dependent member of the royal family or a principal liege man **b :** a property or privilege appropriated by a person as his share **2 :** a rightful endowment or adjunct
ap·pa·ra·tus \ˌap-ə-'rat-əs, -'rāt-\ *n, pl* **apparatus** *or* **ap·pa·ra·tus·es** [L, fr. *apparatus*, pp. of *apparare* to prepare, fr. *ad-* + *parare* to prepare — more at PARE] **1 a :** a set of materials or equipment designed for a particular use **b :** an instrument or appliance designed for a specific operation **c :** a group of organs having a common function **2 :** the functional machinery by means of which a systematized activity is carried out; *esp* **:** the organization of a political party or an underground movement
[1]**ap·par·el** \ə-'par-əl\ *vt* **ap·par·eled** *or* **ap·par·elled; ap·par·el·ing** *or* **ap·par·el·ling** [ME *appareillen*, fr. OF *apareillier* to prepare, fr. (assumed) VL *appariculare*, irreg. fr. L *apparare*] **1 :** to put clothes on **:** DRESS **2 :** ADORN, EMBELLISH
[2]**apparel** *n* **1 :** the equipment of a ship (as sails, rigging) **2 :** personal attire **:** CLOTHING **3 :** something that clothes or adorns
ap·par·ent \ə-'par-ənt, -'per-\ *adj* [ME, fr. OF *aparent*, fr. L *apparent-*, *apparens*, prp. of *apparēre* to appear] **1 :** open to view **:** VISIBLE **2 :** clear or manifest to the understanding **:** EVIDENT **3 :** appearing as actual to the eye or mind **4 :** having an indefeasible right to succeed to a title or estate **5 :** having such an appearance of reality as to appear reasonably true under the circumstances — **ap·par·ent·ly** \-'par(-ə)nt-lē, -'per(-ə)nt-\ *adv* — **ap·par·ent·ness** \-'par-ənt-nəs, -'per-\ *n*
syn ILLUSORY, SEEMING, OSTENSIBLE: APPARENT suggests appearance to unaided senses that is not or may not be borne out by more rigorous examination or greater knowledge; ILLUSORY definitely implies a false impression based on deceptive resemblance or faulty observation, or influenced by emotions that prevent a clear view; SEEMING implies a character in the thing observed that gives it the appearance, sometimes through intent, of something else; OSTENSIBLE applies chiefly to reasons or motives and suggests a discrepancy between an openly declared or naturally implied aim or reason and the true one **syn** see in addition EVIDENT
ap·pa·ri·tion \ˌap-ə-'rish-ən\ *n* [ME *apparicioun*, fr. LL *apparition-*, *apparitio* appearance, fr. L *apparitus*, pp. of *apparēre*] **1 a :** an unusual or unexpected sight **:** PHENOMENON **b :** a ghostly figure **2 :** APPEARANCE — **ap·pa·ri·tion·al** \-'rish-nəl, -ən-ᵊl\ *adj*
ap·par·i·tor \ə-'par-ət-ər\ *n* [L, fr. *apparitus*] **:** an official formerly sent to carry out the orders of a magistrate, judge, or court
[1]**ap·peal** \ə-'pē(ə)l\ *n* **1 :** a legal proceeding by which a case is brought from a lower to a higher court for rehearing **2 :** a criminal accusation **3 a :** an application for corroboration or decision **b :** an earnest plea **:** ENTREATY **4 :** the power of arousing a sympathetic response **:** ATTRACTION
[2]**appeal** *vb* [ME *appelen* to accuse, appeal, fr. MF *apeler*, fr. L *appellare*, fr. *appellere* to drive to, fr. *ad-* + *pellere* to drive — more at FELT] *vt* **1 :** to charge with a crime **:** ACCUSE **2 :** to take proceedings to have (a case) reheard in a higher court ~ *vi* **1 :** to take a case to a higher court for rehearing **2 :** to call upon another for corroboration, vindication, or decision **3 :** to make an earnest request **4 :** to arouse a sympathetic response — **ap·peal·abil·i·ty** \ə-ˌpē-lə-'bil-ət-ē\ *n* — **ap·peal·able** \ə-'pē-lə-bəl\ *adj* — **ap·peal·er** *n* — **ap·peal·ing** *adj* — **ap·peal·ing·ly** \-'pē-liŋ-lē\ *adv*
ap·pear \ə-'pi(ə)r\ *vi* [ME *apperen*, fr. OE *aparoir*, fr. L *apparēre*, fr. *ad-* + *parēre* to show oneself; akin to Gk *peparein* to display] **1 :** to come into sight **2 :** to come formally before an authoritative body **3 :** to have an outward aspect **:** SEEM **4 :** to become evident **5 :** to come into public view **6 :** to come into existence
ap·pear·ance \ə-'pir-ən(t)s\ *n* **1 a :** the act, action, or process of appearing **b :** the coming into court of a party in an action or his attorney **2 a :** outward aspect **:** LOOK **b :** external show **:** SEMBLANCE **c** *pl* **:** outward indications **3 a :** a sense impression or aspect of a thing **b :** the world of sensible phenomena **4 a :** something that appears **:** PHENOMENON **b :** an instance of appearing
ap·peas·able \ə-'pē-zə-bəl\ *adj* **:** capable of being appeased
ap·pease \ə-'pēz\ *vt* [ME *appesen*, fr. OF *apaisier*, fr. *a-* (fr. L *ad-*) + *pais* peace — more at PEACE] **1 :** to bring to a state of peace or quiet **:** CALM **2 :** to cause to subside **:** ALLAY **3 :** PACIFY, CONCILIATE; *esp* **:** to buy off (a potential aggressor) by concessions usu. at the sacrifice of principles **syn** see PACIFY — **ap·pease·ment** \ə-'pēz-mənt\ *n* — **ap·peas·er** *n*
[1]**ap·pel·lant** \ə-'pel-ənt\ *adj* **:** APPEALING, APPELLATE
[2]**appellant** *n* **:** one that appeals; *specif* **:** one that appeals from a judicial decision or decree
ap·pel·late \ə-'pel-ət\ *adj* [L *appellatus*, pp. of *appellare*] **:** of, relating to, or taking cognizance of appeals; *specif* **:** having the power to review the judgment of another tribunal
ap·pel·la·tion \ˌap-ə-'lā-shən\ *n* **1** *archaic* **:** the act of calling by a name **2 :** an identifying name or title **:** DESIGNATION
ap·pel·la·tive \ə-'pel-ət-iv\ *adj* **1 :** of or relating to a common noun **2 :** of, relating to, or inclined to the giving of names — **ap·pel·la·tive** *n* — **ap·pel·la·tive·ly** *adv*
ap·pel·lee \ˌap-ə-'lē\ *n* **:** one against whom an appeal is taken
ap·pend \ə-'pend\ *vt* [F *appendre*, fr. LL *appendere*, fr. L, to weigh, fr. *ad-* + *pendere* to weigh — more at PENDANT] **1 :** ATTACH, AFFIX **2 :** to add as a supplement or appendix
ap·pend·age \ə-'pen-dij\ *n* **1 :** an adjunct to something larger or more important **:** APPURTENANCE **2 :** a dependent or subordinate person **3 :** a subordinate or derivative body part; *esp* **:** a limb or analogous part (as a seta) — **ap·pend·aged** \-dijd\ *adj*
ap·pen·dant \ə-'pen-dənt\ *adj* **1 :** associated as an attendant circumstance **2 :** belonging as a right **3 :** attached as an appendage — **appendant** *n*

ap·pen·dec·to·my \\,ap-ən-'dek-tə-mē\\ *n* [L *appendic-*, *appendix* + E *-ectomy*] **:** surgical removal of the vermiform appendix
ap·pen·di·ci·tis \\ə-,pen-də-'sīt-əs\\ *n* **:** inflammation of the vermiform appendix
ap·pen·dic·u·lar \\,ap-ən-'dik-yə-lər\\ *adj* **:** of or relating to an appendage and esp. a limb ⟨the ~ skeleton⟩
ap·pen·dix \\ə-'pen-diks\\ *n, pl* **ap·pen·dix·es** *or* **ap·pen·di·ces** \\-də-,sēz\\ [L *appendic-*, *appendix*, fr. *appendere*] **1 a :** APPENDAGE **b :** supplementary material usu. attached at the end of a piece of writing **2 :** a bodily outgrowth or process; *specif* **:** VERMIFORM APPENDIX
ap·per·ceive \\,ap-ər-'sēv\\ *vt* [ME *apperceiven*, fr. OF *aperceivre*, fr. *a-* (fr. L *ad-*) + *perceivre* to perceive] **:** PERCEIVE, APPREHEND
ap·per·cep·tion \\,ap-ər-'sep-shən\\ *n* [F *aperception*, fr. *apercevoir*] **1 :** introspective self-consciousness **2 :** the process of understanding something perceived in terms of previous experience — **ap·per·cep·tive** \\-'sep-tiv\\ *adj*
ap·per·tain \\,ap-ər-'tān\\ *vi* [ME *apperteinen*, fr. MF *apartenir*, fr. LL *appertinēre*, fr. L *ad-* + *pertinēre* to belong — more at PERTAIN] **:** to belong or be connected as a rightful part or attribute **:** PERTAIN
ap·pe·ten·cy \\'ap-ət-ən-sē\\ *or* **ap·pe·tence** \\-ən(t)s\\ *n* [L *appetentia*, fr. *appetent-*, *appetens*, prp. of *appetere*] **1 :** a fixed and strong desire **:** APPETITE **2 :** a natural affinity (as between chemicals) **3 :** an instinctive propensity in animals to perform particular actions (as sucking) — **ap·pe·tent** \\-ənt\\ *adj*
ap·pe·tite \\'ap-ə-,tīt\\ *n* [ME *apetit*, fr. MF, fr. L *appetitus*, fr. *appetitus*, pp. of *appetere* to strive after, fr. *ad-* + *petere* to go to — more at FEATHER] **1 :** one of the instinctive desires necessary to keep up organic life; *esp* **:** the desire to eat **2 a :** an inherent craving **b :** TASTE, PREFERENCE — **ap·pe·ti·tive** \\-,tīt-iv, a-'pet-ət-iv\\ *adj*
ap·pe·tiz·er \\'ap-ə-,tī-zər\\ *n* **:** a food or drink that stimulates the appetite and is usu. served before a meal
ap·pe·tiz·ing \\'ap-ə-,tī-ziŋ\\ *adj* **:** appealing to the appetite esp. in appearance or aroma — **ap·pe·tiz·ing·ly** \\-ziŋ-lē\\ *adv*
Ap·pi·an Way \\,ap-ē-ən-\\ *n* [*Appius* Claudius Caecus *fl*300 B.C. Roman statesman] **:** an ancient paved highway extending from Rome to Brundisium
ap·plaud \\ə-'plȯd\\ *vb* [MF or L; MF *applaudir*, fr. L *applaudere*, fr. *ad-* + *plaudere* to applaud] *vi* **:** to express approval esp. by clapping the hands ~ *vt* **1 :** PRAISE, APPROVE **2 :** to show approval of esp. by clapping the hands — **ap·plaud·able** \\-ə-bəl\\ *adj* — **ap·plaud·ably** \\-blē\\ *adv* — **ap·plaud·er** *n*
ap·plause \\ə-'plȯz\\ *n* [ML *applausus*, fr. L, clashing noise, fr. *applausus*, pp. of *applaudere*] **:** approval publicly expressed (as by clapping the hands) **:** ACCLAIM
ap·ple \\'ap-əl\\ *n, often attrib* [ME *appel*, fr. OE *æppel;* akin to OHG *apful* apple, OSlav *ablŭko*] **1 :** the fleshy usu. rounded and red or yellow edible pome fruit of a tree (genus *Malus*) of the rose family; *also* **:** an apple tree **2 :** a fruit or other vegetable production suggestive of an apple
ap·ple·jack \\'ap-əl-,jak\\ *n* **:** brandy distilled from cider; *also* **:** an alcoholic beverage consisting of the central unfrozen portion of a container of frozen hard cider
apple maggot *n* **:** the larva of a two-winged fly (*Rhagoletis pomonella*) that burrows in and feeds esp. on apples
ap·ple–pie \\,ap-əl-,pī\\ *adj* **:** EXCELLENT, PERFECT ⟨~ order⟩
Ap·ple·ton layer \\,ap-əl-tən-, əlt-ᵊn\\ *n* [Sir Edward *Appleton* *b*1892 E physicist] **:** F LAYER
ap·pli·ance \\ə-'plī-ən(t)s\\ *n* **1 :** an act of applying **2 a :** a piece of equipment for adapting a tool or machine to a special purpose **:** ATTACHMENT **b :** an instrument or device designed for a particular use **c :** a household or office mechanism (as a stove, fan, or refrigerator) operated by gas, electric current, or a small motor **3** *obs* **:** COMPLIANCE **syn** see IMPLEMENT
ap·pli·ca·bil·i·ty \\,ap-li-kə-'bil-ət-ē *also* ə-,plik-ə-\\ *n* **:** the quality or state of being applicable
ap·pli·ca·ble \\'ap-li-kə-bəl *also* ə-'plik-ə-\\ *adj* **:** capable of being applied **:** APPROPRIATE **syn** see RELEVANT
ap·pli·cant \\'ap-li-kənt\\ *n* **:** one who applies
ap·pli·ca·tion \\,ap-lə-'kā-shən\\ *n* [ME *applicacioun*, fr. L *application-*, *applicatio* inclination, fr. *applicatus*, pp. of *applicare*] **1 :** an act of applying: **a :** an act of putting to use **b :** an act of administering or superposing **c :** assiduous attention **2 :** REQUEST, PETITION **3 :** something applied or used in applying: as **a :** the practical inference to be derived from a principle or moral tale **b :** a medicated or protective layer or material ⟨an oily ~ for dry skin⟩ **c :** a form used in making a request **4 :** capacity for practical use
ap·pli·ca·tive \\'ap-lə-,kāt-iv *also* ə'plik-ət-\\ *adj* **1 :** APPLICABLE, PRACTICAL **2 :** APPLIED — **ap·pli·ca·tive·ly** *adv*
ap·pli·ca·tor \\'ap-lə-,kāt-ər\\ *n* **:** one that applies; *specif* **:** a device for applying a substance (as medicine or polish)
ap·pli·ca·to·ry \\'ap-li-kə-,tōr-ē, -,tȯr- *also* ə-'plik-ə-\\ *adj* **:** capable of being applied
ap·plied \\ə-'plīd\\ *adj* **:** put to practical use; *esp* **:** UTILITARIAN
ap·pli·er \\ə-'plī(-ə)r\\ *n* **:** one that applies
1**ap·pli·qué** \\,ap-lə-'kā\\ *n, often attrib* [F, pp. of *appliquer* to put on, fr. L *applicare*] **:** a cutout decoration fastened to a larger piece of material
2**appliqué** *vt* **ap·pli·quéd; ap·pli·qué·ing :** to apply (as a decoration or ornament) to a larger surface
ap·ply \\ə-'plī\\ *vb* [ME *applien*, fr. MF *aplier*, fr. L *applicare*, fr. *ad-* + *plicare* to fold — more at PLY] *vt* **1 a :** to put to use esp. for some practical purpose **b :** to lay or spread on **2 :** to employ diligently or with close attention ~ *vi* **1 :** to have relevance **2 :** to make an appeal or request esp. in the form of a written application
ap·pog·gia·tu·ra \\ə-,päj-ə-'tu̇r-ə\\ *n* [It, lit., support] **:** an embellishing note or tone preceding an essential melodic note or tone and usu. written as a note of smaller size

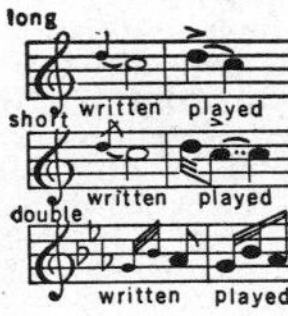

appoggiatura

ap·point \\ə-'pȯint\\ *vb* [ME *appointen*, fr. MF *apointier* to arrange, fr. *a-* (fr. L *ad-*) + *point*] *vt* **1 a :** to fix or set officially ⟨~ a trial date⟩ **b :** to name officially ⟨~ a committee⟩ **c** *archaic* **:** ARRANGE **d :** to determine the disposition of (an estate) to someone by virtue of a power of appointment **2 :** EQUIP ~ *vi* **1** *archaic* **:** to make an engagement **2 :** to exercise a power of appointment **syn** see FURNISH
ap·poin·tee \\ə-,pȯin-'tē, ,a-,pȯin-\\ *n* **1 :** one who is appointed **2 :** one to whom an estate is appointed
ap·point·ive \\ə-'pȯint-iv\\ *adj* **:** of, relating to, or subject to appointment
ap·point·ment \\ə-'pȯint-mənt\\ *n* **1 :** an act of appointing **:** DESIGNATION; *specif* **:** the designation by virtue of a vested power of a person to enjoy an estate **2 :** a nonelective office or position **3 :** an arrangement for a meeting **:** ENGAGEMENT **4 :** equipment or furnishings — usu. used in pl.
ap·por·tion \\ə-'pōr-shən, -'pȯr-\\ *vt* **ap·por·tion·ing** \\-sh(ə-)niŋ\\ [MF *apportionner*, fr. *a-* (fr. L *ad-*) + *portionner* to portion] **:** to make a proportionate division or distribution of **syn** see ALLOT
ap·por·tion·ment \\-shən-mənt\\ *n* **:** an act or result of apportioning; *esp* **:** the apportioning of representatives or taxes to the several states according to U.S. law
ap·pose \\a-'pōz\\ *vt* [MF *aposer*, fr. OF, fr. *a-* + *poser* to put — more at POSE] **1** *archaic* **:** to put before **:** apply (one thing) to another **2 :** to place in juxtaposition or proximity
ap·po·site \\'ap-ə-zət\\ *adj* [L *appositus*, fr. pp. of *apponere* to place near, fr. *ad-* + *ponere* to put — more at POSITION] **:** highly pertinent or appropriate **:** APT **syn** see RELEVANT — **ap·po·site·ly** *adv* — **ap·po·site·ness** *n*
ap·po·si·tion \\,ap-ə-'zish-ən\\ *n* **1 a :** a grammatical construction in which two typically adjacent nouns referring to the same person or thing stand in the same syntactical relation to the rest of a sentence (as *the poet* and *Burns* in "a biography of the poet Burns") **b :** the relation of one of such a pair of nouns or noun equivalents to the other **2 a :** an act or instance of apposing; *specif* **:** the deposition of successive layers upon those already present (as in cell walls) **b :** the state of being apposed — **ap·po·si·tion·al** \\-'zish-nəl, -ən-ᵊl\\ *adj* — **ap·po·si·tion·al·ly** \\-ē\\ *adv*
ap·pos·i·tive \\ə-'päz-ət-iv\\ *adj* **:** of, relating to, or standing in grammatical apposition — **appositive** *n* — **ap·pos·i·tive·ly** *adv*
ap·prais·al \\ə-'prā-zəl\\ *n* **:** an act or instance of appraising; *esp* **:** a valuation of property by the estimate of an authorized person
ap·praise \\ə-'prāz\\ *vt* [ME *appreisen*, fr. MF *aprisier* to apprize] **1 :** to set a value on **:** estimate the amount of **2 :** to evaluate the worth, significance or status of; *esp* **:** to give an expert judgment of the value or merit of **syn** see ESTIMATE — **ap·praise·ment** \\-mənt\\ *n* — **ap·prais·er** *n* — **ap·prais·ing** *adj* — **ap·prais·ing·ly** \\-'prā-ziŋ-lē\\ *adv*
ap·pre·cia·ble \\ə-'prē-shə-bəl\\ *adj* **:** capable of being perceived or measured **syn** see PERCEPTIBLE — **ap·pre·cia·bly** \\-blē\\ *adv*
ap·pre·ci·ate \\ə-'prē-shē-,āt\\ *vb* [LL *appretiatus*, pp. of *appretiare*, fr. L *ad-* + *pretium* price — more at PRICE] *vt* **1 a :** to evaluate the worth, quality, or significance of **b :** to admire greatly **c :** to judge with heightened perception or understanding **:** be fully aware of **d :** to recognize with gratitude **2 :** to increase the value of ~ *vi* **:** to increase in number or value — **ap·pre·ci·a·tor** \\-,āt-ər\\ *n* — **ap·pre·cia·to·ry** \\-shə-,tōr-ē, -,tȯr-\\ *adj*
syn APPRECIATE, VALUE, PRIZE, TREASURE, CHERISH mean to hold in high estimation. APPRECIATE often connotes sufficient understanding to enjoy or admire a thing's excellence but it may imply merely warm admiration and enjoyment; VALUE implies rating a thing highly for its essential or intrinsic worth; PRIZE implies taking a deep pride in or setting great store by; TREASURE emphasizes jealously guarding or keeping something as being precious and irreplaceable; CHERISH implies a special love and care for something and connotes a deep-seated, long-lasting, often irrational attachment **syn** see in addition UNDERSTAND
ap·pre·ci·a·tion \\ə-,prē-shē-'ā-shən\\ *n* **1 a :** sensitive awareness; *esp* **:** recognition of aesthetic values **b :** EVALUATION, JUDGMENT; *esp* **:** a favorable critical estimate **c :** an expression of admiration, approval, or gratitude **2 :** increase in value
ap·pre·cia·tive \\ə-'prē-shət-iv *also* -shē-,āt-\\ *adj* **:** having or showing appreciation — **ap·pre·cia·tive·ly** *adv* — **ap·pre·cia·tive·ness** *n*
ap·pre·hend \\,ap-ri-'hend\\ *vb* [ME *apprehenden*, fr. L *apprehendere*, lit., to seize, fr. *ad-* + *prehendere* to seize — more at PREHENSILE] *vt* **1 a** *obs* **:** to take hold of **b :** ARREST, SEIZE **2 a :** to become aware of **:** PERCEIVE **b :** to anticipate esp. with anxiety, dread, or fear **3 :** to grasp with the understanding **:** recognize the meaning of ~ *vi* **:** UNDERSTAND, GRASP **syn** see FORESEE
ap·pre·hen·si·ble \\,ap-ri-'hen(t)-sə-bəl\\ *adj* **:** capable of being apprehended — **ap·pre·hen·si·bly** \\-blē\\ *adv*
ap·pre·hen·sion \\,ap-ri-'hen-chən\\ *n* [ME, fr. LL *apprehension-*, *apprehensio*, fr. L *apprehensus*, pp. of *apprehendere*] **1 a :** the act or power of perceiving or comprehending **b :** the result of apprehending mentally **:** CONCEPTION **2 :** seizure by legal process **:** ARREST **3 :** suspicion or fear esp. of future evil **:** FOREBODING
ap·pre·hen·sive \\,ap-ri-'hen(t)-siv\\ *adj* **1 :** capable of apprehending or quick to do so **:** DISCERNING **2 :** having apprehension **:** COGNIZANT **3 :** viewing the future with anxiety or alarm **syn** see FEARFUL — **ap·pre·hen·sive·ly** *adv* — **ap·pre·hen·sive·ness** *n*
1**ap·pren·tice** \\ə-'prent-əs\\ *n, often attrib* [ME *aprentis*, fr. MF, fr. OF, fr. *aprendre* to learn, fr. L *apprendere*, *apprehendere*] **1 a :** one bound by indenture to serve another for a prescribed period with a view to learning an art or trade in consideration of instruction and formerly usu. of maintenance **b :** one who is learning by practical experience under skilled workers a trade, art, or calling **2 :** an inexperienced person **:** NOVICE — **ap·pren·tice·ship** \\-ə(sh)-,ship, -əs-,ship\\ *n*
2**apprentice** *vt* **:** to set at work as an apprentice; *esp* **:** to bind to an apprenticeship by contract or indenture
ap·pressed \\a-'prest\\ *adj* [L *appressus*, pp. of *apprimere* to press to, fr. *ad-* + *premere* to press — more at PRESS] **:** pressed close to or lying flat against something
ap·prise *also* **ap·prize** \\ə-'prīz\\ *vt* [F *appris*, pp. of *apprendre* to learn, fr. OF *aprendre*] **:** to give notice to **:** TELL **syn** see INFORM
ap·prize \\ə-'prīz\\ *vt* [ME *apprisen*, fr. MF *aprisier*, fr. OF, fr. *a-* (fr. L *ad-*) + *prisier* to appraise] **:** VALUE, APPRECIATE
1**ap·proach** \\ə-'prōch\\ *vb* [ME *approchen*, fr. OF *aprochier*, fr. LL *appropiare*, fr. L *ad-* + *prope* near; akin to L *pro* before — more at FOR] *vt* **1 a :** to draw closer to **:** NEAR **b :** APPROXIMATE **2 :** to take preliminary steps toward ~ *vi* **:** to draw nearer; *specif* **:** to hit a golf ball from the fairway toward the green
2**approach** *n* **1 a :** an act or instance of approaching **b :** APPROXIMATION **2 a :** a preliminary step **b :** manner of advance **3 :** a means of access **:** AVENUE

ap·proach·abil·i·ty \ə-ˌprō-chə-ˈbil-ət-ē\ *n* **:** the quality or state of being approachable

ap·proach·able \ə-ˈprō-chə-bəl\ *adj* **:** capable of being approached **:** ACCESSIBLE; *specif* **:** easy to meet or deal with

ap·pro·bate \ˈap-rə-ˌbāt\ *vt* [ME *approbaten*, fr. L *approbatus*, pp. of *approbare*] **:** APPROVE, SANCTION — **ap·pro·ba·to·ry** \ˈap-rə-bə-ˌtōr-ē, ə-ˈprō-bə-, -ˌtȯr-\ *adj*

ap·pro·ba·tion \ˌap-rə-ˈbā-shən\ *n* **1** *obs* **:** PROOF **2 a :** an act of approving formally or officially **b :** COMMENDATION, PRAISE

ap·pro·pri·a·ble \ə-ˈprō-prē-ə-bəl\ *adj* **:** capable of being appropriated

¹ap·pro·pri·ate \ə-ˈprō-prē-ˌāt\ *vt* [ME *appropriaten*, fr. LL *appropriatus*, pp. of *appropriare*, fr. L *ad-* + *proprius* own] **1 :** to take exclusive possession of **:** ANNEX **2 :** to set apart for or assign to a particular purpose or use **3 :** to take without permission — **ap·pro·pri·a·tor** \-ˌāt-ər\ *n*

syn APPROPRIATE, PREEMPT, ARROGATE, USURP, CONFISCATE mean to seize high-handedly. APPROPRIATE stresses making something one's own or converting to one's own use without authority or with questionable right; PREEMPT implies beforehandedness in taking something desired or needed by others; ARROGATE implies insolence, presumption, and exclusion of others in seizing rights, powers, or functions; USURP implies unlawful or unwarranted intrusion into the place of another and seizure of what is his by custom, right, or law; CONFISCATE always implies seizure through exercise of authority

²ap·pro·pri·ate \ə-ˈprō-prē-ət\ *adj* **:** especially suitable or compatible **:** FITTING **syn** see FIT — **ap·pro·pri·ate·ly** *adv* — **ap·pro·pri·ate·ness** *n*

ap·pro·pri·a·tion \ə-ˌprō-prē-ˈā-shən\ *n* **1 :** an act or instance of appropriating **2 :** something that has been appropriated; *specif* **:** money set aside by formal action for a specific use

ap·pro·pri·a·tive \ə-ˈprō-prē-ˌāt-iv\ *adj* **:** relating to appropriation

ap·prov·able \ə-ˈprü-və-bəl\ *adj* **:** capable of being approved — **ap·prov·ably** \-blē\ *adv*

ap·prov·al \ə-ˈprü-vəl\ *n* **:** an act or instance of approving **:** APPROBATION — **on approval :** subject to a prospective buyer's acceptance or refusal

ap·prove \ə-ˈprüv\ *vb* [ME *approven*, fr. OF *aprover*, fr. L *approbare*, fr. *ad-* + *probare* to prove — more at PROVE] *vt* **1** *obs* **:** PROVE, ATTEST **2 :** to have or express a favorable opinion of **3 a :** to accept as satisfactory **b :** to give formal or official sanction to **:** RATIFY ~ *vi* **:** to take a favorable view — **ap·prov·ing·ly** \-ˈprü-viŋ-lē\ *adv*

syn APPROVE, ENDORSE, SANCTION, ACCREDIT, CERTIFY mean to have or express a favorable opinion of. APPROVE often implies no more than this but may suggest esteem or admiration; ENDORSE adds to APPROVE the implication of backing as by an explicit statement; SANCTION implies both approval and authorization; ACCREDIT and CERTIFY usu. imply official endorsement attesting to conformity to set standards

¹ap·prox·i·mate \ə-ˈpräk-sə-mət\ *adj* [LL *approximatus*, pp. of *approximare* to come near, fr. L *ad-* + *proximare* to come near — more at PROXIMATE] **1 :** nearly correct or exact **2 :** located close together ⟨~ leaves⟩ — **ap·prox·i·mate·ly** *adv*

²ap·prox·i·mate \-ˌmāt\ *vt* **1 a :** to bring near or close **b :** to bring together **2 :** to come near to **:** APPROACH ~ *vi* **:** to come close

ap·prox·i·ma·tion \ə-ˌpräk-sə-ˈmā-shən\ *n* **1 :** the act or process of drawing together **2 :** the quality or state of being close esp. in value **3 :** something that is approximate; *esp* **:** a mathematical value that is nearly but not exactly correct — **ap·prox·i·ma·tive** \ə-ˈpräk-sə-ˌmāt-iv\ *adj* — **ap·prox·i·ma·tive·ly** *adv*

ap·pur·te·nance \ə-ˈpərt-nən(t)s, -ᵊn-ən(t)s\ *n* **1 :** an incidental right (as a right of way) attached to a principal property right and passing in possession with it **2 :** a subordinate adjunct **:** APPENDAGE **3** *pl* **:** accessory objects

ap·pur·te·nant \ə-ˈpərt-nənt, -ᵊn-ənt\ *adj* [ME *apertenant*, fr. MF, fr. OF, prp. of *apartenir* to belong] **1 :** constituting a legal accompaniment **2 :** AUXILIARY, ACCESSORY — **appurtenant** *n*

aprac·tic \ā-ˈprak-tik\ *or* **aprax·ic** \-ˈprak-sik\ *adj* [*apractic* fr. Gk *apraktos* inactive, fr. *a-* + *prassein; apraxic* fr. NL *apraxia*] **:** of, relating to, or marked by apraxia

aprax·ia \-ˈprak-sē-ə\ *n* [NL, fr. Gk, inaction, fr. *a-* + *praxis* action, fr. *prassein* to do — more at PRACTICAL] **:** loss or impairment of ability to execute complex coordinated movements

apri·cot \ˈap-rə-ˌkät, ˈā-prə-\ *n, often attrib* [alter. of earlier *abrecock*, deriv. of Ar *al-birqūq* the apricot] **1 a :** the oval orange-colored fruit of a temperate-zone tree (*Prunus armeniaca*) resembling the related peach and plum in flavor **b :** a tree that bears apricots **2 :** a variable color averaging a moderate orange

April \ˈā-prəl\ *n* [ME, fr. OF & L; OF *avrill*, fr. L *Aprilis*] **:** the 4th month of the Gregorian calendar

April fool *n* **:** the butt of a joke or trick played on April Fools' Day; *also* **:** such a joke or trick

April Fools' Day *n* **:** April 1 characteristically marked by the playing of practical jokes

a pri·o·ri \ˌä-prē-ˈō(ə)r-ē, ˌap-rē-; ˌā-(ˌ)prī-ˈō(ə)r-ˌī, ˌā-prē-ˈō(ə)r-ē; -ˈȯ(ə)r-\ *adj* [L, from the former] **1 a :** DEDUCTIVE **b :** relating to or derived by reasoning from self-evident propositions **:** ANALYTIC **c :** presupposed by experience **2 :** being without examination or analysis **:** PRESUMPTIVE — **a priori** *adv* — **apri·or·i·ty** \-ˈȯr-ət-ē\ *n*

apron \ˈā-prən, -pərn\ *n, often attrib* [ME, alter. (resulting fr. incorrect division of *a napron*) of *napron*, fr. MF *naperon*, dim. of *nape* cloth, modif. of L *mappa* napkin — more at MAP] **1 :** a garment usu. of cloth, plastic, or leather usu. tied onto the front of the body with strings around the waist and used to protect clothing or adorn a costume **2 :** something that suggests or resembles an apron in shape, position, or use: as **a :** the lower member under the sill of the interior casing of a window **b :** an upward or downward vertical extension of a sink or lavatory **c :** a piece of waterproof cloth spread out (as before the seat of a vehicle) as a protection from rain or mud **d :** a covering (as of sheet metal) for protecting parts of machinery **e :** an endless belt for carrying material **f :** an extensive fan-shaped deposit of detritus **g :** the part of the stage in front of the proscenium arch **h :** the area along the waterfront edge of a pier or wharf **i :** a shield (as of concrete, planking, or brushwood) along the bank of a river, along a sea wall, or below a dam **j :** the extensive paved part of an airport immediately adjacent to the terminal area or hangars

¹ap·ro·pos \ˌap-rə-ˈpō, ˈap-rə-ˌ\ *adv* [F *à propos*, lit., to the purpose] **1 :** at an opportune time **:** SEASONABLY **2 :** by the way

²apropos *adj* **:** being to the point **:** PERTINENT

³apropos *prep* **:** apropos of **syn** see RELEVANT

apropos of *prep* **:** with regard to **:** CONCERNING

apse \ˈaps\ *n* [ML & L; ML *apsis*, fr. L] **1 :** a projecting part of a building (as a church) usu. semicircular in plan and vaulted **2 :** APSIS 1

ap·si·dal \ˈap-səd-ᵊl\ *adj* **:** of or relating to an apse

ap·sis \ˈap-səs\ *n, pl* **ap·si·des** \-sə-ˌdēz\ [NL *apsid-, apsis*, fr. L, arch, orbit, fr. Gk *hapsid-, hapsis*, fr. *haptein* to fasten] **1 :** the point in an astronomical orbit at which the distance of the body from the center of attraction is either greatest or least **2 :** APSE 1

apt \ˈapt\ *adj* [ME, fr. L *aptus*, lit., fastened, fr. pp. of *apere* to fasten; akin to L *apisci* to reach, *apud* near, Skt *āpta* fit] **1 :** unusually fitted or qualified **:** READY, PREPARED **2 a :** having an habitual tendency or inclination **:** LIKELY **b :** ordinarily disposed **:** INCLINED **3 :** suited to its purpose; *specif* **:** being to the point **4 :** keenly intelligent **:** QUICK-WITTED **syn** see FIT, QUICK — **apt·ly** \ˈap-(t)lē\ *adv* — **apt·ness** \ˈap(t)-nəs\ *n*

ap·ter·ous \ˈap-tə-rəs\ *adj* [Gk *apteros*, fr. *a-* + *pteron* wing — more at FEATHER] **1 :** lacking wings **2 :** lacking winglike expansions

ap·ter·yx \ˈap-tə-riks\ *n* [NL, fr. *a-* + Gk *pteryx* wing; akin to Gk *pteron*] **:** KIWI

ap·ti·tude \ˈap-tə-ˌt(y)üd\ *n* **1 :** capacity for learning **:** APTNESS **2 a :** INCLINATION, TENDENCY **b :** a natural ability **:** TALENT **3 :** general suitability **syn** see GIFT — **ap·ti·tu·di·nal** \ˌap-tə-ˈt(y)üd-nəl, -ᵊn-əl\ *adj* — **ap·ti·tu·di·nal·ly** \-ē\ *adv*

aq·ua \ˈak-wə, ˈäk-\ *n, pl* **aq·uae** \ˈak-(ˌ)wē, ˈäk-ˌwī\ *or* **aquas** [L] **:** WATER; *esp* **:** an aqueous solution

aq·ua·cade \ˈak-wə-ˌkād, ˈäk-\ *n* [*Aquacade*, a water entertainment spectacle orig. at Cleveland, O. (1937)] **:** a water spectacle that consists usu. of exhibitions of swimming and diving with musical accompaniment

Aq·ua·dag \-ˌdag\ *trademark* — used for a colloidal suspension of fine particles of graphite in water for use as a lubricant

aq·ua·for·tis \ˌak-wə-ˈfȯrt-əs, ˌäk-\ *n* [NL *aqua fortis*, lit., strong water] **:** NITRIC ACID

aq·ua·lung·er \ˈak-wə-ˌləŋ-ər, ˈäk-\ *n* [fr. *Aqualung*, a trademark] **:** a scuba diver

aq·ua·ma·rine \ˌak-wə-mə-ˈrēn, ˌäk-\ *n* [NL *aqua marina*, fr. L, sea water] **1 :** a transparent beryl that is blue, blue-green, or green in color **2 :** a pale blue to light greenish blue

aq·ua·naut \ˈak-wə-ˌnȯt, ˈäk-\ *n* [L *aqua* + E *-naut* (as in *aeronaut*)] **:** a scuba diver that lives and operates both inside and outside an underwater shelter for an extended period

aq·ua·plane \ˈak-wə-ˌplān, ˈäk-\ *n* **:** a board towed behind a speeding motorboat and ridden by a person standing on it — **aquaplane** *vi* — **aq·ua·plan·er** *n*

aq·ua pu·ra \ˌak-wə-ˈpyu̇r-ə, ˌäk-\ *n* [L] **:** pure water

aqua re·gia \-ˈrē-j(ē-)ə\ *n* [NL, lit., royal water] **:** a mixture of nitric and hydrochloric acids that dissolves gold or platinum

aq·ua·relle \ˌak-wə-ˈrel, ˌäk-\ *n* [F, fr. obs. It *acquarella* (now *acquerello*), fr. *acqua* water, fr. L *aqua*] **:** a drawing in water color and esp. transparent water color — **aq·ua·rell·ist** \-ˈrel-əst\ *n*

aquar·ist \ə-ˈkwar-əst, -ˈkwer-\ *n* **:** one who keeps an aquarium

aquar·i·um \ə-ˈkwar-ē-əm, -ˈkwer-\ *n, pl* **aquariums** *or* **aquar·ia** \-ē-ə\ [L, watering place for cattle, fr. neut. of *aquarius* of water, fr. *aqua*] **1 :** a container (as a glass tank) or an artificial pond in which living aquatic animals or plants are kept **2 :** an establishment where such aquatic collections are kept and exhibited

Aquar·i·us \ə-ˈkwar-ē-əs, -ˈkwer-\ *n* [L (gen. *Aquarii*), lit., water carrier] **1 :** a constellation south of Pegasus pictured as a man pouring water **2 :** the 11th sign of the zodiac

¹aquat·ic \ə-ˈkwät-ik, -ˈkwat-\ *adj* **1 :** growing or living in or frequenting water **2 :** performed in or on water — **aquat·i·cal·ly** \-i-k(ə-)lē\ *adv*

²aquatic *n* **1 :** an aquatic animal or plant **2** *pl but sing or pl in constr* **:** water sports

aq·ua·tint \ˈak-wə-ˌtint, ˈäk-\ *n* [It *acqua tinta* dyed water] **:** etching with aquafortis so that the resulting print resembles a watercolor made with flat washes of different strengths; *also* **:** an engraving so made — **aquatint** *vt*

aq·ua·vit \ˈäk-wə-ˌvēt\ *n* [Sw, Dan & Norw *akvavit*, fr. ML *aqua vitae*] **:** a clear Scandinavian liquor flavored with caraway seeds

aq·ua vi·tae \ˌak-wə-ˈvīt-ē, ˌäk-\ *n* [ME, fr. ML, lit., water of life] **1 :** ALCOHOL **2 :** a strong liquor

aq·ue·duct \ˈak-wə-ˌdəkt\ *n* [L *aquaeductus*, fr. *aquae* (gen. of *aqua*) + *ductus* act of leading — more at DUCT] **1 a :** a conduit for water; *esp* **:** one for carrying a large quantity of flowing water **b :** a structure for conveying a canal over a river or hollow **2 :** a canal or passage in a part or organ

aque·ous \ˈā-kwē-əs, ˈak-wē-\ *adj* [ML *aqueus*, fr. L *aqua*] **1 a :** of, relating to, or resembling water **b :** made from, with, or by water **2 :** of or relating to the aqueous humor — **aque·ous·ly** *adv*

aqueous humor *n* **:** a limpid fluid occupying the space between the crystalline lens and the cornea of the eye

aq·ui·cul·tur·al \ˌak-wi-ˈkəlch-(ə-)rəl, ˌäk-\ *adj* **:** of or relating to aquiculture

aq·ui·cul·ture \ˈak-wi-ˌkəl-chər, ˈäk-\ *n* [L *aqua* + E *-culture* (as in *agriculture*)] **1 :** the cultivation of the natural produce of water **2 :** HYDROPONICS

aq·ui·fer \ˈak-wə-fər, ˈäk-\ *n* [NL, fr. L *aqua* + *-fer*] **:** a water-bearing stratum of permeable rock, sand, or gravel — **aquif·er·ous** \a-ˈkwif-(ə-)rəs, ä-\ *adj*

Aq·ui·la \ˈak-wə-lə\ *n* [L (gen. *Aquilae*), lit., eagle] **:** a northern constellation in the Milky Way southerly from Lyra and Cygnus

aq·ui·le·gia \ˌak-wə-ˈlē-j(ē-)ə\ *n* [NL] **:** COLUMBINE

aq·ui·line \ˈak-wə-ˌlīn, -lən\ *adj* [L *aquilinus*, fr. *aquila* eagle] **1 :** of, relating to, or resembling an eagle **2 :** curving like an eagle's beak — **aq·ui·lin·i·ty** \ˌak-wə-ˈlin-ət-ē\ *n*

ar \ˈär\ *n* [ME] **:** the letter *r*

-ar \ər\ *adj suffix* [ME, fr. L *-aris*, alter. of *-alis* -al] **:** of or relating to ⟨molecular⟩ **:** being ⟨spectacular⟩ **:** resembling ⟨orbicular⟩

Ar·ab \ˈar-əb, *in sense 2 often* ˈā-ˌrab\ *n* [ME, fr. L *Arabus, Arabs*, fr. Gk *Arab-, Araps*, fr. Ar *ʻArab*] **1 a :** a member of the Semitic people of the Arabian peninsula **b :** a member of an Arabic-speaking people **2** *not cap* **:** STREET ARAB **3 :** a horse of the stock used by the natives of Arabia and adjacent regions; *specif* **:** a

horse of a breed noted for its graceful build, speed, intelligence, and spirit — **Arab** *adj*

1ar·a·besque \ˌar-ə-ˈbesk\ *adj* [F, fr. It *arabesco* Arabian in fashion, fr. *Arabo* Arab, fr. L *Arabus*] **:** relating to or being in the style of arabesque

2arabesque *n* **1 :** an ornament or style that employs flower, foliage, or fruit and sometimes animal and figural outlines to produce an intricate pattern of interlaced sometimes angular and sometimes curved lines **2 :** a posture in ballet in which the body is bent forward from the hip on one leg with the corresponding arm extended forward and the other arm and leg backward

Ara·bi·an coffee \ə-ˌrā-bē-ən-\ *n* **:** an African large evergreen shrub or small tree (*Coffea arabica*) widely cultivated in warm regions for its seeds which form most of the coffee of commerce

1Ar·a·bic \ˈar-ə-bik\ *adj* **1 :** of, relating to, or characteristic of Arabia or the Arabs **2 :** of, relating to, or constituting Arabic

2Arabic *n* **:** a Semitic language orig. of the Arabs of the Hejaz and Nejd that is now the prevailing speech of Arabia, Jordan, Lebanon, Syria, Iraq, Egypt, and parts of northern Africa

arab·i·ca coffee \ə-ˌrab-i-kə-\ *n, often cap A* [NL *Coffea arabica* Arabian coffee] **:** a drink produced from Arabian coffee

arabic numeral *n, often cap A* **:** one of the number symbols 0, 1, 2, 3, 4, 5, 6, 7, 8, 9 — see NUMBER table

ar·a·bil·i·ty \ˌar-ə-ˈbil-ət-ē\ *n* **:** the state of being arable

Ar·ab·ist \ˈar-ə-bəst\ *n* **:** a specialist in the Arabic language or culture

1ar·a·ble \ˈar-ə-bəl\ *adj* [MF or L; MF, fr. L *arabilis*, fr. *arare* to plow — more at EAR] **:** fit for or cultivated by plowing or tillage

2arable *n* **:** land that is tilled or tillable

Ar·a·by \ˈar-ə-bē\ *n* **:** Arabia

Arach·ne \ə-ˈrak-nē\ *n* [L, fr. Gk *Arachnē*] **:** a Lydian girl transformed into a spider for challenging Athena to a contest in weaving

arach·nid \ə-ˈrak-nəd\ *n* [deriv. of Gk *arachnē* spider] **:** any of a class (Arachnida) of arthropods comprising mostly air-breathing invertebrates, including the spiders and scorpions, mites, and ticks, and having a segmented body divided into two regions of which the anterior bears four pairs of legs but no antennae — **arachnid** *adj* — **arach·ni·dan** \-nəd-ən\ *adj or n*

1arach·noid \ə-ˈrak-ˌnȯid\ *n* [NL *arachnoides*, fr. Gk *arachnoeidēs*, like a cobweb, fr. *arachnē* spider, spider's web] **:** a thin membrane of the brain and spinal cord that lies between the dura mater and the pia mater

2arachnoid *adj* **1 :** of or relating to the arachnoid membrane **2 :** covered with or composed of soft loose hairs or fibers

3arachnoid *adj* [deriv. of Gk *arachnē*] **:** resembling or related to the arachnids

ara·go·nite \ə-ˈrag-ə-ˌnīt, ˈar-ə-gə-\ *n* [G *aragonit*, fr. *Aragon*, Spain] **:** a mineral $CaCO_3$ consisting like calcite of calcium carbonate but differing from calcite in its orthorhombic crystallization, greater density, and less distinct cleavage

Ar·a·mae·an \ˌar-ə-ˈmē-ən\ *n* [L *Aramaeus*, fr. Gk *Aramaios*, fr. Heb *ʼĂrām* Aram, ancient name for Syria] **1 :** a member of a Semitic people of the 2d millennium B.C. in Syria and Upper Mesopotamia **2 :** ARAMAIC — **Aramaean** *adj*

Ar·a·ma·ic \ˌar-ə-ˈmā-ik\ *n* **:** a Semitic language known since the 9th century B.C. as the speech of the Aramaeans and later used extensively in southwest Asia as a commercial and governmental language and adopted as their customary speech by various non-Aramaean peoples including the Jews after the Babylonian exile

ara·ne·id \ə-ˈrā-nē-əd\ *n* [deriv. of L *aranea* spider] **:** SPIDER 1 — **ar·a·ne·idal** \ˌar-ə-ˈnē-əd-ᵊl\ *adj* — **ar·a·ne·idan** \-əd-ᵊn\ *adj or n*

Arap·a·ho *or* **Arap·a·hoe** \ə-ˈrap-ə-ˌhō\ *n, pl* **Arapaho** *or* **Arapahos** *or* **Arapahoe** *or* **Arapahoes** [perh. fr. Crow *aa-raxpé-ahu*, lit., tattoo] **1 :** an Algonquian people of the plains region from southern Saskatchewan and Manitoba to New Mexico and Texas **2 :** a member of the Arapaho people

ar·a·pai·ma \ˌar-ə-ˈpī-mə\ *n* [Pg & Sp, of Tupian origin; akin to Mura *uarapâinu* pirarucu] **:** PIRARUCU

ar·a·ro·ba \ˌar-ə-ˈrō-bə\ *n* [Pg, of Tupian origin; akin to Tupi *araribá*, a Brazilian tree] **:** GOA POWDER

Arau·ca·ni·an \ə-ˌrau̇-ˈkān-ē-ən\ *also* **Arau·can** \ə-ˈrau̇-kən\ *n* [Sp *araucano*, fr. *Arauco*, province in Chile] **1 :** a member of a group of Indian peoples of south central Chile and adjacent regions of Argentina **2 :** the language of the Araucanian people that constitutes an independent language family — **Araucanian** *adj*

ar·au·car·ia \ˌar-ˌȯ-ˈkar-ē-ə\ *n* [NL, genus name, fr. *Arauco*] **:** any of a genus (*Araucaria*) of So. American or Australian trees of the pine family

Ar·a·wak \ˈar-ə-ˌwäk\ *n* **1 a :** an Indian people of the Arawakan group now living chiefly along the coast of British Guiana **b :** a member of this people **2 :** the language of the Arawak people

Ar·a·wak·an \ˌar-ə-ˈwäk-ən\ *n* **1 a :** a group of Indian peoples of Bolivia, Brazil, Colombia, Guiana, Paraguay, Peru, Venezuela, and formerly the West Indies **b :** a member of any of these peoples **2 :** the language family of the Arawakan peoples — **Arawakan** *adj*

ar·ba·lest *or* **ar·ba·list** \ˈär-bə-ləst\ *n* [ME *arblast*, fr. OE, fr. OF *arbaleste*, fr. LL *arcuballista*, fr. L *arcus* bow + *ballista* — more at ARROW] **:** CROSSBOW; *esp* **:** a medieval military weapon with a steel bow used to throw balls, stones, and quarrels — **ar·ba·lest·er** \-ˌles-tər\ *n*

ar·bi·ter \ˈär-bət-ər\ *n* [ME *arbitre*, fr. MF, fr. L *arbitr-*, *arbiter*] **1 :** a person with power to decide a dispute **:** JUDGE **2 :** a person or agency having absolute power of judging and determining

ar·bi·tra·ble \ˈär-bə-trə-bəl\ *adj* **:** subject to decision by arbitration

ar·bi·trage \ˈär-bə-ˌträzh\ *n* [ME, arbitration, fr. MF, fr. OF, fr. *arbitrer* to render judgment, fr. L *arbitrari*, fr. *arbitr-*, *arbiter*] **:** simultaneous purchase and sale of the same or equivalent security in order to profit from price discrepancies

ar·bi·tral \ˈär-bə-trəl\ *adj* **:** of or concerning arbiters or arbitration

ar·bit·ra·ment \är-ˈbi-trə-mənt\ *n* [ME, fr. MF *arbitrement*, fr. *arbitrer*] **1** *archaic* **:** the right or power of deciding **2 :** the act of deciding as an arbiter **3 :** the judgment given by an arbitrator

ar·bi·trar·i·ly \ˌär-bə-ˈtrer-ə-lē\ *adv* **:** in an arbitrary manner

ar·bi·trar·i·ness \ˈär-bə-ˌtrer-ē-nəs\ *n* **:** the quality or state of being arbitrary

ar·bi·trary \ˈär-bə-ˌtrer-ē\ *adj* **1 :** depending on choice or discretion; *specif* **:** determinable by decision of a judge or tribunal **2 a :** arising from will or caprice **b :** selected at random and without reason **3 :** DESPOTIC, TYRANNICAL

ar·bi·trate \ˈär-bə-ˌtrāt\ *vi* **:** to act as arbitrator ~ *vt* **1 :** to act as arbiter upon **2 :** to submit or refer for decision to an arbiter **3** *archaic* **:** DECIDE, DETERMINE — **ar·bi·tra·tive** \-ˌtrāt-iv\ *adj*

ar·bi·tra·tion \ˌär-bə-ˈtrā-shən\ *n* **:** the act of arbitrating; *esp* **:** the hearing and determination of a case in controversy by a person chosen by the parties or appointed under statutory authority — **ar·bi·tra·tion·al** \-shnəl, -shən-ᵊl\ *adj*

ar·bi·tra·tor \ˈär-bə-ˌtrāt-ər\ *n* **1 :** a person chosen to settle differences between two parties in controversy **2 :** ARBITER

1ar·bor *or chiefly Brit* **ar·bour** \ˈär-bər\ *n* [ME *erber* plot of grass, arbor, fr. OF *herbier* plot of grass, fr. *herbe* herb, grass] **:** a bower of vines or branches or of latticework covered with climbing shrubs or vines

2arbor *n* [L, tree, shaft] **1 a :** a main shaft or beam **b :** a spindle or axle of a wheel **c :** a shaft on which a revolving cutting tool is mounted **d :** a spindle on a cutting machine that holds the work to be cut **2** *pl* **ar·bo·res** \ˈär-bə-ˌrēz\ **:** a tree as distinguished from a shrub

ar·bo·ra·ceous \ˌär-bə-ˈrā-shəs\ *adj* **:** ARBOREAL

Arbor Day *n* **:** a day designated for planting trees

ar·bo·re·al \är-ˈbōr-ē-əl, -ˈbȯr-\ *adj* [L *arboreus* of a tree, fr. *arbor*] **1 :** of, relating to, or like a tree **2 :** inhabiting or frequenting trees — **ar·bo·re·al·ly** \-ə-lē\ *adv*

ar·bo·re·ous \-ē-əs\ *adj* **1 :** WOODED **2 :** ARBORESCENT **3 :** ARBOREAL 2

ar·bo·res·cence \ˌär-bə-ˈres-ᵊn(t)s\ *n* **:** the condition of being arborescent

ar·bo·res·cent \-ᵊnt\ *adj* **:** resembling a tree in properties, growth, structure, or appearance — **ar·bo·res·cent·ly** *adv*

ar·bo·re·tum \ˌär-bə-ˈrēt-əm\ *n, pl* **arboretums** *or* **ar·bo·re·ta** \-ˈrēt-ə\ [NL, fr. L, place grown with trees, fr. *arbor*] **:** a place where trees, shrubs, and herbaceous plants are cultivated for scientific and educational purposes

ar·bo·ri·cul·ture \ˈär-bə-rə-ˌkəl-chər; är-ˈbōr-ə-, -ˈbȯr-\ *n* [*2arbor* + *-i-* + *culture*] **:** the cultivation of trees and shrubs esp. for ornament — **ar·bo·ri·cul·tur·ist** \ˌär-bə-rə-ˈkəlch-(ə-)rəst; är-ˌbōr-ə-, -ˌbȯr-\ *n*

ar·bo·ri·za·tion \ˌär-bə-rə-ˈzā-shən\ *n* **:** formation of or into an arborescent figure or arrangement; *also* **:** such a figure or arrangement

ar·bo·rize \ˈär-bə-ˌrīz\ *vi* **:** to branch freely and repeatedly

ar·bor·vi·tae \ˌär-bər-ˈvīt-ē\ *n* [NL *arbor vitae*, lit., tree of life] **:** any of various evergreen trees (esp. genus *Thuja*) of the pine family usu. with closely overlapping or compressed scale leaves that are often grown for ornament and hedges

ar·bu·tus \är-ˈbyüt-əs\ *n* [NL, genus name, fr. L, strawberry tree] **:** any of a genus (*Arbutus*) of shrubs and trees of the heath family with white or pink flowers and scarlet berries; *also* **:** a related trailing plant (*Epigaea repens*) of eastern No. America with fragrant pinkish flowers borne in early spring

1arc \ˈärk\ *n* [ME *ark*, fr. MF *arc* bow, fr. L *arcus* bow, arch, arc — more at ARROW] **1 :** the apparent path described above and below the horizon by the sun or other celestial body **2 :** something arched or curved; *esp* **:** a sustained luminous discharge of electricity across a gap in a circuit or between electrodes **3 :** a continuous portion of a circle or other curve

2arc *vi* **1 :** to form an electric arc **2 :** to follow an arc-shaped course

3arc *adj* [*arc sine* arc or angle (corresponding to the) sine (of so many degrees)] **:** INVERSE 2 ⟨~ sine⟩

ar·cade \är-ˈkād\ *n* **1 :** a long arched building or gallery **2 :** an arched covered passageway or avenue (as between shops) **3 :** a series of arches with their columns or piers

ar·cad·ed \-ˈkād-əd\ *adj* **:** formed in or furnished or decorated with arches or arcades

ar·ca·dia \är-ˈkād-ē-ə\ *n, often cap* [*Arcadia*, region of ancient Greece frequently chosen as background for pastoral poetry] **:** a region or scene of simple pleasure and quiet

Ar·ca·di·an \är-ˈkād-ē-ən\ *n* **1** *often not cap* **:** a person who lives a simple quiet life **2 :** a native or inhabitant of Arcadia **3 :** the dialect of ancient Greek used in Arcadia — **arcadian** *adj, often cap*

Ar·ca·dy \ˈär-kəd-ē\ *n* **:** ARCADIA

ar·cane \är-ˈkān\ *adj* [L *arcanus*] **:** SECRET, MYSTERIOUS

ar·ca·num \är-ˈkā-nəm\ *n, pl* **ar·ca·na** \-nə\ [L, fr. neut. of *arcanus* secret, fr. *arca* chest — more at ARK] **1 :** mysterious knowledge known only to the initiate **2 :** ELIXIR

arc–bou·tant \ˌär-bü-ˈtäⁿ\ *n, pl* **arcs–bou·tants** \-ˈtäⁿ(z)\ [F, lit., thrusting arch] **:** FLYING BUTTRESS

1arch \ˈärch\ *n* [ME *arche*, fr. OF, fr. (assumed) VL *arca*, fr. L *arcus* — more at ARROW] **1 :** a typically curved structural member spanning an opening and serving as a support (as for the wall or other weight above the opening) **2 a :** something resembling an arch in form or function; *esp* **:** either of two vaulted portions of the bony structure of the foot that impart elasticity to it **b :** a curvature having the form of an arch **3 :** ARCHWAY

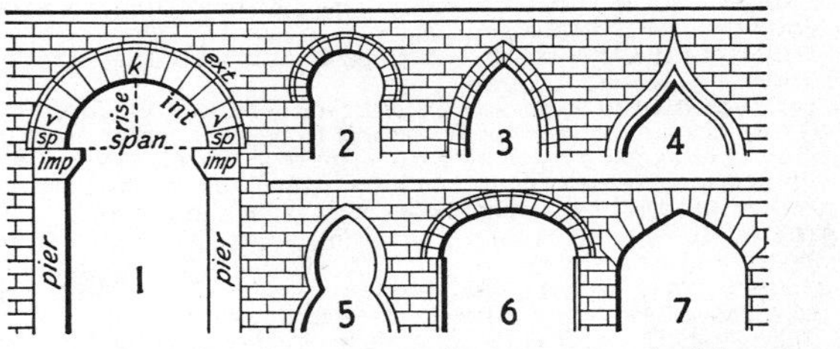

arches 1: *1* round: *imp* impost, *sp* springer, *v* voussoir, *k* keystone, *ext* extrados, *int* intrados; *2* horseshoe; *3* lancet; *4* ogee; *5* trefoil; *6* basket-handle; *7* Tudor

2arch *vt* **1 :** to cover or provide with an arch **2 :** to form or bend

into an arch ~ *vi* **1 :** to form an arch **2 :** to take an arch-shaped course

[3]**arch** *adj* [*arch-*] **1 :** PRINCIPAL, CHIEF ⟨an *arch*-villain⟩ **2** [*arch-* (as in *archrogue*)] **a :** cleverly sly and alert **b :** playfully saucy

arch- *prefix* [ME *arche-, arch-*, fr. OE & OF; OE *arce-*, fr. LL *arch-* & L *archi-*; OF *arch-*, fr. LL *arch-* & L *archi-*, fr. Gk *arch-, archi-*, fr. *archein* to begin, rule; akin to Gk *archē* beginning, rule, *archos* ruler] **1 :** chief **:** principal ⟨*arch*enemy⟩ **2 :** extreme **:** most fully embodying the qualities of his or its kind ⟨*arch*rogue⟩

[1]**-arch** \ˌärk, *in a few words also* ərk\ *n comb form* [ME *-arche*, fr. OF & LL & L; OF *-arche*, fr. LL *-archa*, fr. L *-arches, -archus*, fr. Gk *-archēs, -archos*, fr. *archein*] **:** ruler **:** leader ⟨matri*arch*⟩

[2]**-arch** \ˌärk\ *adj comb form* [prob. fr. G, fr. Gk *archē* beginning] **:** having (such) a point or (so many) points of origin ⟨end*arch*⟩

archae- *or* **archaeo-** *also* **archeo-** *comb form* [Gk *archaio-*, fr. *archaios* ancient, fr. *archē* beginning] **:** ancient **:** primitive ⟨*Archae*opteryx⟩ ⟨*Archeo*zoic⟩

ar·chae·o·log·i·cal *or* **ar·che·o·log·i·cal** \ˌär-kē-ə-ˈläj-i-kəl\ *adj* **:** of or relating to archaeology — **ar·chae·o·log·i·cal·ly** \-i-k(ə-)lē\ *adv*

ar·chae·ol·o·gist *or* **ar·che·ol·o·gist** \ˌär-kē-ˈäl-ə-jəst\ *n* **:** a specialist in archaeology

ar·chae·ol·o·gy *or* **ar·che·ol·o·gy** \-jē\ *n* [F *archéologie*, fr. LL *archaeologia* antiquarian lore, fr. Gk *archaiologia*, fr. *archaio-* + *-logia* -logy] **1 :** the scientific study of material remains (as fossil relics, artifacts, monuments) of past human life and activities **2 :** remains of the culture of a people **:** ANTIQUITIES

ar·chae·op·ter·yx \ˌär-kē-ˈäp-tə-riks\ *n* [NL, genus name, fr. *archae-* + Gk *pteryx* wing; akin to Gk *pteron* wing — more at FEATHER] **:** a primitive bird (genus *Archaeopteryx*) of the Upper Jurassic period of Europe with reptilian characteristics

ar·chae·or·nis \ˌär-kē-ˈȯr-nəs\ *n* [NL, genus name, fr. *archae-* + Gk *ornis* bird — more at ERNE] **:** any of a genus (*Archaeornis*) of Upper Jurassic toothed birds

ar·cha·ic \är-ˈkā-ik\ *adj* [F or Gk; F *archaïque*, fr. Gk *archaïkos*, fr. *archaios*] **1 :** of, relating to, or characteristic of an earlier or more primitive time **:** ANTIQUATED **2 :** having the characteristics of the language of the past and surviving chiefly in specialized uses **3 :** surviving from an earlier period; *specif* **:** typical of a previously dominant evolutionary stage **syn** see OLD — **ar·cha·ical·ly** \-i-k(ə-)lē\ *adv*

archaic smile *n* **:** an expression that resembles a smile and is characteristic of ancient Greek sculpture

ar·cha·ism \ˈär-kē-ˌiz-əm, -(ˌ)kā-ˌiz-\ *n* [NL *archaïsmus*, fr. Gk *archaïsmos*, fr. *archaios*] **1 :** the use of archaic diction or style **2 :** an instance of archaic usage **3 :** something archaic — **ar·cha·ist** \-əst\ *n* — **ar·cha·is·tic** \ˌär-kē-ˈis-tik, -(ˌ)kā-\ *adj* — **ar·cha·ize** \ˈär-kē-ˌīz, -(ˌ)kā-\ *vb*

arch·an·gel \ˈär-ˌkān-jəl\ *n* [ME, fr. OF or LL; OF *archangele*, fr. LL *archangelus*, fr. Gk *archangelos*, fr. *arch-* + *angelos* angel] **:** an angel of high rank — **arch·an·gel·ic** \ˌär-ˌkan-ˈjel-ik\ *adj*

arch·an·thro·pine \är-ˈkan(t)-thrə-ˌpīn\ *n* [deriv. of Gk *archi-* + *anthrōpos*] **:** a primitive man (as pithecanthropus)

arch·bish·op \(ˈ)ärch-ˈbish-əp\ *n* [ME, fr. OE *arcebiscop*, fr. LL *archiepiscopus*, fr. LGk *archiepiskopos*, fr. *archi-* + *episkopos* bishop] **:** a bishop at the head of an ecclesiastical province or one of equivalent honorary rank — **arch·bish·op·ric** \-ə-(ˌ)prik\ *n*

arch·dea·con \(ˈ)ärch-ˈdē-kən\ *n* [ME *archedeken*, fr. OE *arcediacon*, fr. LL *archidiaconus*, fr. LGk *archidiakonos*, fr. Gk *archi-* + *diakonos* deacon] **1 :** an ecclesiastical dignitary usu. ranking below a bishop **2 :** an Anglican priest who supervises a part of a diocese or the missionary work of a diocese — **arch·dea·con·ate** \-kə-nət\ *n* — **arch·dea·con·ry** \-kən-rē\ *n*

arch·di·oc·e·san \ˌärch-(ˌ)dī-ˈäs-ə-sən\ *adj* **:** of or relating to an archdiocese

arch·di·o·cese \(ˈ)ärch-ˈdī-ə-səs, -ˌsēz, -ˌsēs\ *n* **:** the diocese of an archbishop

arch·du·cal \(ˈ)ärch-ˈd(y)ü-kəl\ *adj* [F *archiducal*, fr. *archiduc*] **:** of or relating to an archduke or archduchy

arch·duch·ess \(ˈ)ärch-ˈdəch-əs\ *n* [F *archiduchesse*, fem. of *archiduc* archduke, fr. MF *archeduc*] **1 :** the wife or widow of an archduke **2 :** a woman having in her own right a rank equal to that of an archduke

arch·duchy \-ˈdəch-ē\ *n* [F *archiduché*, fr. MF *archeduché*, fr. *arche-* arch- + *duché* duchy] **:** the territory of an archduke or archduchess

arch·duke \(ˈ)ärch-ˈd(y)ük\ *n* [MF *archeduc*, fr. *arche-* arch- + *duc* duke] **:** a sovereign prince; *specif* **:** a prince of the imperial family of Austria — **arch·duke·dom** \-dəm\ *n*

Ar·che·an *or* **Ar·chae·an** \är-ˈkē-ən\ *adj* [Gk *archaios*] **:** of, relating to, or being the earlier part of the Precambrian era or the oldest known group of rocks; *also* **:** PRECAMBRIAN — **Archean** *n*

arched \ˈärcht\ *adj* **:** made with or formed in an arch

ar·che·go·ni·al \ˌär-ki-ˈgō-nē-əl\ *adj* **:** of or relating to an archegonium; *also* **:** ARCHEGONIATE

ar·che·go·ni·ate \-nē-ət\ *adj* **:** bearing archegonia — **archegoniate** *n*

ar·che·go·ni·um \-nē-əm\ *n, pl* **ar·che·go·nia** \-nē-ə\ [NL, fr. Gk *archegonos* originator, fr. *archein* to begin + *gonos* procreation; akin to Gk *gignesthai* to be born — more at ARCH-, KIN] **:** the flask-shaped female sex organ of mosses, ferns, and some gymnosperms

arch·en·e·my \(ˈ)ärˈchen-ə-mē\ *n* **:** a principal enemy

arch·en·ter·on \är-ˈkent-ə-ˌrän, -rən\ *n* [NL] **:** the cavity of the gastrula of an embryo

Ar·cheo·zo·ic *also* **Ar·chaeo·zo·ic** \ˌär-kē-ə-ˈzō-ik\ *adj* **:** of, relating to, or being the earliest era of geological history; *also* **:** relating to the system of rocks formed in this era — **Archeozoic** *n*

arch·er \ˈär-chər\ *n* [ME, fr. OF, fr. LL *arcarius*, alter. of *arcuarius*, fr. *arcuarius* of a bow, fr. L *arcus* bow — more at ARROW] **:** one who uses a bow and arrow — called also *bowman*

arch·ery \ˈärch-(ə-)rē\ *n* **1 :** the art, practice, or skill of shooting with bow and arrow **2 :** an archer's weapons **3 :** a body of archers

ar·che·spore \ˈär-ki-ˌspō(ə)r, -ˌspȯ(ə)r\ *or* **ar·che·spo·ri·um** \ˌär-ki-ˈspōr-ē-əm, -ˈspȯr-\ *n, pl* **archespores** *or* **ar·che·spo·ria** \-ē-ə\ [NL *archesporium*, fr. *arche-* (as in *archegonium*) + *-sporium* (fr. *spora* spore)] **:** the cell or group of cells from which spore mother cells develop — **ar·che·spo·ri·al** \ˌär-ki-ˈspōr-ē-əl, -ˈspȯr-\ *adj*

ar·che·typ·al \ˌär-ki-ˈtī-pəl\ *or* **ar·che·typ·i·cal** \-ˈtip-i-kəl\ *adj* **:** of, relating to, or constituting an archetype — **ar·che·typ·al·ly** \-ˈtī-pə-lē\ *or* **ar·che·typ·i·cal·ly** \-ˈtip-i-k(ə-)lē\ *adv*

ar·che·type \ˈär-ki-ˌtīp\ *n* [L *archetypum*, fr. Gk *archetypon*, fr. neut. of *archetypos* archetypal, fr. *archein* + *typos* type] **1 :** the original pattern or model of which all things of the same type are representations or copies **:** PROTOTYPE **2 :** IDEA 1a

arch·fiend \(ˈ)ärch-ˈfēnd\ *n* **:** a chief fiend; *esp* **:** SATAN

archi- *or* **arch-** *prefix* [F or L; F, fr. L, fr. Gk — more at ARCH-] **1 :** chief **:** principal ⟨*archi*blast⟩ **2 :** primitive **:** original **:** primary ⟨*arch*enteron⟩ ⟨*archi*carp⟩

ar·chi·carp \ˈär-ki-ˌkärp\ *n* **:** the female sex organ in ascomycetous fungi consisting usu. of a filamentous trichogyne and a basal fertile ascogonium

ar·chi·di·ac·o·nal \ˌär-ki-(ˌ)dī-ˈak-ən-ᵊl\ *adj* [LL *archidiaconus* archdeacon] **:** of or relating to an archdeacon — **ar·chi·di·ac·o·nate** \-ˈak-ə-nət\ *n*

ar·chi·epis·co·pal \ˌär-kē-ə-ˈpis-kə-pəl\ *adj* [ML *archiepiscopalis*, fr. LL *archiepiscopus* archbishop — more at ARCHBISHOP] **:** of or relating to an archbishop — **ar·chi·epis·co·pal·ly** \-pə-lē\ *adv* — **ar·chi·epis·co·pate** \-pət, -ˌpāt\ *n*

archiepiscopal cross *n* — see CROSS illustration

ar·chil \ˈär-chəl\ *n* [ME *orchell*] **1 :** a violet dye obtained from lichens (genera *Roccella* and *Lecanora*) **2 :** a plant that yields archil

ar·chi·man·drite \ˌär-kə-ˈman-ˌdrīt\ *n* [LL *archimandrites*, fr. LGk, fr. Gk *archi-* + LGk *mandra* monastery, fr. Gk, fold, pen] **:** a dignitary in an Eastern church ranking below a bishop; *specif* **:** the superior of a large monastery or group of monasteries

Ar·chi·me·de·an \ˌär-kə-ˈmēd-ē-ən, -mi-ˈdē-ən\ *adj* **:** of, relating to, or invented by Archimedes

Ar·chi·me·des' screw \ˌär-kə-ˈmēd-ēz-\ *n* [*Archimedes* †212 B.C. Gk mathematician and inventor] **:** a device made of a tube bent spirally around an axis or of a broad-threaded screw encased by a cylinder and used to raise water

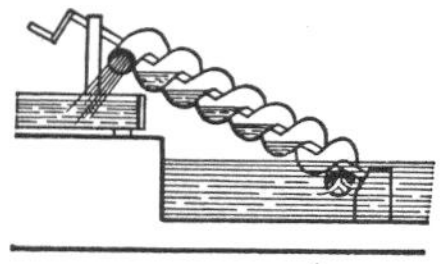

Archimedes' screw

ar·chi·pe·lag·ic \ˌär-kə-pə-ˈlaj-ik, ˌär-chə-\ *adj* **:** of, relating to, or located in an archipelago

ar·chi·pel·a·go \ˌär-kə-ˈpel-ə-ˌgō, ˌär-chə-\ *n, pl* **archipelagoes** *or* **archipelagos** [*Archipelago* Aegean sea, fr. It *Arcipelago*, lit., chief sea, fr. *arci-* (fr. L *archi-*) + Gk *pelagos* sea] **1 :** an expanse of water with many scattered islands **2 :** a group of islands

ar·chi·tect \ˈär-kə-ˌtekt\ *n* [MF *architecte*, fr. L *architectus*, fr. Gk *architektōn* master builder, fr. *archi-* + *tektōn* builder, carpenter] **1 :** one who designs buildings and superintends their construction **2 :** one who plans and achieves a difficult objective

ar·chi·tec·ton·ic \ˌär-kə-ˌtek-ˈtän-ik\ *adj* [L *architectonicus*, fr. Gk *architektonikos*, fr. *architektōn*] **1 :** of, relating to, or according with the principles of architecture **:** ARCHITECTURAL **2 :** resembling architecture in structure or organization — **ar·chi·tec·ton·i·cal·ly** \-i-k(ə-)lē\ *adv*

ar·chi·tec·ton·ics \-ˈtän-iks\ *n pl but sing or pl in constr, also* **ar·chi·tec·ton·ic** \-ik\ **1 :** the science of architecture **2 a :** the structural design of an entity **b :** system of structure

ar·chi·tec·tur·al \ˌär-kə-ˈtek-chə-rəl, -ˈtek-shrəl\ *adj* **:** of, relating to, or conforming to the rules of architecture — **ar·chi·tec·tur·al·ly** \-ē\ *adv*

ar·chi·tec·ture \ˈär-kə-ˌtek-chər\ *n* **1 :** the art or science of building; *specif* **:** the art or practice of designing and building structures and esp. habitable ones **2 :** formation or construction as or as if as the result of conscious act **3 :** architectural product or work **4 :** a method or style of building

ar·chi·trave \ˈär-kə-ˌtrāv\ *n* [MF, fr. OIt, fr. *archi-* + *trave* beam, fr. L *trabs*] **1 :** the lowest division of an entablature resting in classical architecture immediately on the capital of the column **2 :** the molding around a door or other rectangular opening

ar·chi·val \är-ˈkī-vəl\ *adj* **:** relating to, contained in, or constituting archives

ar·chive \ˈär-ˌkīv\ *n* [F & L; F, fr. L *archivum*, fr. Gk *archeion* government house (in pl., official documents), fr. *archē* rule, government] **:** a place in which public records or historical documents are preserved; *also* **:** the material preserved — usu. used in pl.

ar·chi·vist \ˈär-kə-vəst, -ˌkī-\ *n* **:** a person in charge of archives

ar·chi·volt \ˈär-kə-ˌvōlt\ *n* [It *archivolto*, fr. ML *archivoltum*] **:** an ornamental molding around an arch corresponding to an architrave

arch·ly *adv* **:** in an arch manner

arch·ness *n* **:** the quality of being arch

ar·chon \ˈär-ˌkän, -kən\ *n* [L, fr. Gk *archōn*, fr. prp. of *archein*] **1 :** a chief magistrate in ancient Athens **2 :** a presiding officer

arch·way \ˈärch-ˌwā\ *n* **:** a way or passage under an arch; *also* **:** an arch over a passage

-ar·chy \ˌär-kē, *in a few words also* ər-kē\ *n comb form* [ME *-archie*, fr. MF, fr. L *-archia*, fr. Gk, fr. *archein* to rule — more at ARCH-] **:** rule **:** government ⟨squire*archy*⟩

ar·ci·form \ˈär-sə-ˌfȯrm\ *adj* [L *arcus* bow + E *-i-* + *-form*] **:** having the form of an arch **:** CURVED

arc lamp *n* **:** an electric lamp that produces light by an arc made when a current passes between two incandescent electrodes surrounded by gas — called also *arc light*

[1]**arc·tic** \ˈärk-tik, ˈärt-ik\ *adj* [ME *artik*, fr. L *arcticus*, fr. Gk *arktikos*, fr. *arktos* bear, Ursa Major, north; akin to L *ursus* bear] **1** *often cap* **:** of, characteristic of, or relating to the region around the north pole to approximately 65° N **2 a :** bitter cold **:** FRIGID **b :** cold in temper or mood — **arc·ti·cal·ly** \-(ə-)lē\ *adv*

[2]**arc·tic** \ˈärt-ik, ˈärk-tik\ *n* **:** a rubber overshoe reaching to the ankle or above

arctic circle *n, often cap A&C* **:** a small circle of the earth parallel to its equator approximately 23° 27′ from the north pole and circumscribing the frigid zone

Arc·tu·rus \ärk-ˈt(y)u̇r-əs\ *n* [L, fr. Gk *Arktouros*, lit., bear watcher] **:** a giant fixed star of the first magnitude in Boötes

ar·cu·ate \ˈär-kyə-wət, -ˌwāt\ *adj* [L *arcuatus*, pp. of *arcuare* to bend like a bow, fr. *arcus* bow] **:** curved like a bow — **ar·cu·ate·ly** *adv*

-ard \ərd\ *also* **-art** \ərt\ *n suffix* [ME, fr. OF, of Gmc origin; akin to OHG *-hart* (in personal names such as *Gērhart* Gerard), OE *heard* hard] **:** one that is characterized by performing some action, possessing some quality, or being associated with some thing esp.

conspicuously or excessively ⟨braggart⟩ ⟨dullard⟩ ⟨pollard⟩ : large one of its kind ⟨staggard⟩
ar·deb \'är-ˌdeb\ *n* [Ar *ardabb*, *irdabb*] : any of numerous Egyptian units of capacity; *esp* : the customs unit equal to 5.44 imperial or 5.619 U.S. bushels
ar·den·cy \'ärd-ᵊn-sē\ *n* : the quality or state of being ardent
ar·dent \'ärd-ᵊnt\ *adj* [ME, fr. MF, fr. L *ardent-*, *ardens* prp. of *ardēre*] **1 a** : characterized by warmth of feeling : PASSIONATE **b** : ZEALOUS, DEVOTED **2** : FIERY, HOT **3** : GLOWING, SHINING **syn** see IMPASSIONED — **ar·dent·ly** *adv*
ardent spirits *n pl* : strong distilled liquors
ar·dor *or chiefly Brit* **ar·dour** \'ärd-ər\ *n* [ME *ardour*, fr. MF & L; MF, fr. L *ardor*, fr. *ardēre* to burn; akin to OHG *essa* forge, L *aridus* dry] **1 a** : warmth of feeling or sentiment : PASSION **b** : extreme vigor or energy : INTENSITY **c** : ZEAL, LOYALTY **2** : strong or burning heat **syn** see PASSION
ar·du·ous \'ärj-(ə-)wəs\ *adj* [L *arduus* high, steep, difficult; akin to ON *örthigr* high, steep, Gk *orthos* straight] **1 a** : hard to accomplish or achieve : DIFFICULT **b** : marked by great labor or effort : STRENUOUS **2** : hard to climb : STEEP **syn** see HARD — **ar·du·ous·ly** *adv* — **ar·du·ous·ness** *n*
1**are** [ME, fr. OE *earun;* akin to ON *eru*, *erum* are, OE *is* is] *pres 2d sing or pres pl of* BE
2**are** \'a(ə)r, 'e(ə)r, 'är\ *n* [F, fr. L *area*] — see METRIC SYSTEM table
ar·ea \'ar-ē-ə, 'er-\ *n* [L, piece of level ground, threshing floor, fr. *arēre* to be dry; akin to L *ardor*] **1** : a level piece of ground **2** : the surface included within a set of lines; *specif* : the number of unit squares equal in measure to the surface — see MEASURE table, METRIC SYSTEM table **3** : AREAWAY **4** : a particular extent of space or surface or one serving a special function **5** : the scope of a concept, operation, or activity : FIELD **6** : a part of the cerebral cortex having a particular function — **ar·e·al** \-ē-əl\ *adj* — **ar·e·al·ly** \-ə-lē\ *adv*
area code *n* : a 3-digit number that identifies each telephone service area in a country (as the U.S. or Canada)
area·way \-ē-ə-ˌwā\ *n* : a sunken space affording access, air, and light to a basement
are·ca \ə-'rē-kə, 'ar-i-kə\ *n* [NL, genus name, fr. Pg, fr. Malayalam *aṭekka*] : any of several tropical Asian palms (*Areca* or related genera); *esp* : BETEL PALM
are·na \ə-'rē-nə\ *n* [L *harena*, *arena* sand, sandy place] **1** : an area in a Roman amphitheater for gladiatorial combats **2 a** : an enclosed area used for public entertainment **b** : a building containing an arena **3** : a sphere of interest or activity
ar·e·na·ceous \ˌar-ə-'nā-shəs\ *adj* [L *arenaceus*, fr. *arena*] **1** : resembling, made of, or containing sand or sandy particles **2** : growing in sandy places
arena theater *n* : a theater having the acting area in the center of the auditorium with the audience seated on all sides of the stage
ar·e·nic·o·lous \ˌar-ə-'nik-ə-ləs\ *adj* [L *arena* + E *-i-* + *-colous*] : living, burrowing, or growing in sand
aren't \(')ärnt, 'är-ənt\ **1** : are not **2** : am not — used in questions
are·o·la \ə-'rē-ə-lə\ *n, pl* **are·o·lae** \-ˌlē\ *or* **areolas** [NL, fr. L, small open space, dim. of *area*] : a small area between things or about something; *esp* : a colored ring (as about the nipple, a vesicle, or a pustule) — **are·o·lar** \-lər\ *adj* — **are·o·late** \-lət\ *adj* — **are·o·la·tion** \ə-ˌrē-ə-'lā-shən, ˌar-ē-ə-\ *n*
ar·e·ole \'ar-ē-ˌōl\ *n* : AREOLA
Ar·e·op·a·gite \ˌar-ē-'äp-ə-ˌjīt, -ˌgīt\ *n* : a member of the Areopagus — **Ar·e·op·a·git·ic** \-ˌäp-ə-'jit-ik\ *adj*
Ar·e·op·a·gus \-'äp-ə-gəs\ *n* [L, fr. Gk *Areios pagos*, fr. *Areios pagos* (lit., hill of Ares), a hill in Athens where the tribunal met] : the supreme tribunal of Athens
Ares \'a(ə)r-(ˌ)ēz, 'e(ə)r-; 'ā-ˌrēz\ *n* [L, fr. Gk *Arēs*] : the god of war in Greek mythology
arête \ə-'rāt\ *n* [F, lit., fish bone, fr. LL *arista*, fr. L, beard of grain] : a sharp-crested ridge in rugged mountains
ar·e·thu·sa \ˌar-ə-'th(y)ü-zə\ *n* [L, fr. Gk *Arethousa*] **1** *cap* : a wood nymph transformed by Artemis into a stream running under the sea and emerging in Sicily as a fountain **2** : any of a genus (*Arethusa*) of bog orchids with a single linear leaf and solitary purple flower
ar·ga·li \'är-gə-lē\ *n* [Mongolian] : a large Asiatic wild sheep (*Ovis ammon*) noted for its large horns; *also* : any of several large wild sheep (as the bighorn)
ar·gent \'är-jənt\ *n* [ME, fr. MF & L; MF, fr. L *argentum;* akin to L *arguere* to make clear, Gk *argyros* silver, *argos* white] *archaic* : the metal silver; *also* : WHITENESS — **argent** *adj*
ar·gen·tic \är-'jent-ik\ *adj* : of, relating to, or containing silver esp. when bivalent
ar·gen·tif·er·ous \ˌär-jən-'tif-(ə-)rəs\ *adj* : producing or containing silver
1**ar·gen·tine** \'är-jən-ˌtīn, -ˌtēn\ *adj* : SILVER, SILVERY
2**argentine** *n* : SILVER; *also* : any of various materials resembling it
ar·gen·tite \'är-jən-ˌtīt\ *n* : native silver sulfide Ag_2S having a metallic luster and dark lead-gray color and constituting a valuable ore of silver
ar·gen·tous \är-'jent-əs\ *adj* : of, relating to, or containing silver esp. when univalent
ar·gil \'är-jəl\ *n* [ME, fr. L *argilla*, fr. Gk *argillos;* akin to Gk *argos* white] : CLAY; *esp* : potter's clay
ar·gil·la·ceous \ˌär-jə-'lā-shəs\ *adj* : of, relating to, or containing clay or clay minerals : CLAYEY
ar·gil·lite \'är-jə-ˌlīt\ *n* : a compact argillaceous rock differing from shale in being cemented by silica and from slate in having no slaty cleavage
ar·gi·nine \'är-jə-ˌnēn\ *n* [G *arginin*] : a crystalline basic amino acid $C_5H_{13}N_4COOH$ derived from guanidine
Ar·give \'är-ˌjīv, -ˌgīv\ *adj* [L *Argivus*, fr. Gk *Argeios*, lit., of Argos, fr. *Argos* city-state of ancient Greece] : of or relating to the Greeks or Greece and esp. the Achaean city of Argos or the surrounding territory of Argolis — **Argive** *n*
Ar·go \'är-(ˌ)gō\ *n* [L (gen. *Argus*), fr. Gk *Argō*] : a large constellation in the southern hemisphere lying principally between Canis Major and the Southern Cross
ar·gol \'är-gəl\ *n* [ME *argoile*] : crude tartar
ar·gon \'är-ˌgän\ *n* [Gk, neut. of *argos* idle, lazy, fr. *a-* + *ergon* work — more at WORK] : a colorless odorless inert gaseous element found in the air and in volcanic gases and used esp. as a filler for electric bulbs and electron tubes — see ELEMENT table
ar·go·naut \'är-gə-ˌnȯt, -ˌnät\ *n* [L *Argonautes*, fr. Gk *Argonautēs*, fr. *Argō*, ship in which the Argonauts sailed + *nautēs* sailor — more at NAUTICAL] **1 a** *cap* : one of a band of heroes sailing with Jason in quest of the Golden Fleece **b** : an adventurer engaged in a quest **2** : NAUTILUS 2
ar·go·sy \'är-gə-sē\ *n* [modif. of It *ragusea* Ragusan vessel, fr. *Ragusa*, Dalmatia (now Dubrovnik, Yugoslavia)] **1** : a large ship; *esp* : a large merchant ship **2** : a fleet of ships **3** : a rich supply
ar·got \'är-gət, -(ˌ)gō\ *n* [F] **1** : a special vocabulary and idiom used by a particular underworld group esp. as a means of private communication **2** : the language of a particular social group or class **syn** see DIALECT
ar·gu·able \'är-gyə-wə-bəl\ *adj* : open to argument, dispute, or question — **ar·gu·ably** \-blē\ *adv*
ar·gue \'är-(ˌ)gyü, -gyə-w\ *vb* [ME *arguen*, fr. MF *arguer* to accuse, reason & L *arguere* to make clear; MF *arguer*, fr. L *argutare* to prate, fr. *argutus* clear, noisy, fr. pp. of *arguere*] *vi* **1** : to give reasons for or against something : REASON **2** : to contend or disagree in words : DISPUTE ~ *vt* **1** : to give evidence of : INDICATE **2** : DEBATE **3** : MAINTAIN, CONTEND **4** : to persuade by giving reasons : INDUCE **syn** see DISCUSS — **ar·gu·er** \-gyə-wər\ *n*
ar·gu·fy \'är-gyə-ˌfī\ *vt* : DISPUTE, DEBATE ~ *vi* : WRANGLE
ar·gu·ment \'är-gyə-mənt\ *n* [ME, fr. MF, fr. L *argumentum*, fr. *arguere*] **1** *obs* : an outward sign : INDICATION **2** : a reason given in proof or rebuttal **3 a** : the act or process of arguing : ARGUMENTATION **b** : a coherent series of reasons offered **c** : DISAGREEMENT, QUARREL **4** : an abstract or summary esp. of a literary work **5** : the subject matter esp. of a literary work **6** : one of the independent variables upon whose value that of a function depends
ar·gu·men·ta·tion \ˌär-gyə-mən-'tā-shən, -ˌmen-\ *n* **1** : the act or process of forming reasons and of drawing conclusions and applying them to a case in discussion **2** : DEBATE, DISCUSSION
ar·gu·men·ta·tive \ˌär-gyə-'ment-ət-iv\ *or* **ar·gu·men·tive** \-'ment-iv\ *adj* **1** : characterized by argument : CONTROVERSIAL **2** : given to argument : DISPUTATIOUS — **ar·gu·men·ta·tive·ly** *adv*
ar·gu·men·tum \ˌär-gyə-'ment-əm\ *n, pl* **ar·gu·men·ta** \-'ment-ə\ [L] : ARGUMENT 3b
Ar·gus \'är-gəs\ *n* [L, fr. Gk *Argos*] **1** : a hundred-eyed monster of Greek legend **2** : a watchful guardian
Ar·gus–eyed \ˌär-gə-'sīd\ *adj* : vigilantly observant
ar·gyle *also* **ar·gyll** \'är-ˌgīl\ *n, often cap* [*Argyle*, *Argyll*, branch of the Scottish clan of Campbell, fr. whose tartan the design was adapted] : a geometric knitting pattern of varicolored diamonds in solid and outline shapes on a single background color; *also* : a sock knit in such a pattern
ar·gyr·o·dite \är-'jir-ə-ˌdīt\ *n* [ISV, fr. Gk *argyrōdēs* rich in silver, fr. *argyros* silver — more at ARGENT] : a steel-gray mineral Ag_8GeS_6 consisting of silver, germanium, and sulfur
ar·hat \'är-(ˌ)hət\ *n* [Skt, fr. prp. of *arhati* he deserves; akin to Gk *alphein* to gain] : a Buddhist monk who has attained nirvana — **ar·hat·ship** \-ˌship\ *n*
aria \'är-ē-ə\ *n* [It, lit., atmospheric air, modif. of L *aer*] : AIR, MELODY, TUNE; *specif* : an accompanied elaborate melody sung (as in an opera) by a single voice
Ar·i·ad·ne \ˌar-ē-'ad-nē\ *n* [L, fr. Gk *Ariadnē*] : a daughter of Minos who gives Theseus the thread whereby he escapes from the labyrinth
Ar·i·an \'ar-ē-ən, 'er-\ *adj* : of or relating to Arius or his doctrines esp. that the Son is not of the same substance as the Father but was created as an agent for creating the world — **Arian** *n* — **Ar·i·an·ism** \-ə-ˌniz-əm\ *n*
-ar·i·an \'er-ē-ən, 'ar-\ *n suffix* [L *-arius* -ary] **1** : believer ⟨necessitarian⟩ : advocate ⟨latitudinarian⟩ **2** : producer ⟨disciplinarian⟩
ari·bo·fla·vin·osis \ˌā-ˌrī-bə-ˌflā-və-'nō-səs\ *n* [NL] : a deficiency disease due to inadequate intake of riboflavin
ar·id \'ar-əd\ *adj* [F or L; F *aride*, fr. L *aridus* — more at ARDOR] **1** : excessively dry; *specif* : having insufficient rainfall to support agriculture **2** : lacking in interest and life : JEJUNE **syn** see DRY — **arid·i·ty** \ə-'rid-ət-ē, a-\ *n*
Ar·i·el \'ar-ē-əl, 'er-\ *n* **1** : an airy prankish spirit in Shakespeare's *The Tempest* **2** : the inner satellite of Uranus
Ar·i·es \'ar-ē-ˌēz, 'er-\ *n* [L (gen. *Arietis*), lit., ram; akin to Gk *eriphos* kid, OIr *heirp* doe] **1** : a constellation between Pisces and Taurus pictured as a ram **2** : the 1st sign of the zodiac
ari·et·ta \ˌär-ē-'et-ə, ˌar-\ *n* [It, dim. of *aria*] : a short aria
aright \ə-'rīt\ *adv* [ME, fr. OE *ariht*, fr. 1*a-* + *riht* right] : RIGHTLY, CORRECTLY
ar·il \'ar-əl\ *n* [prob. fr. NL *arillus*, fr. ML, raisin, grape seed] : an exterior covering or appendage of some seeds that develops after fertilization as an outgrowth from the ovule stalk — **ar·iled** \'ar-əld\ *adj* — **ar·il·late** \'ar-ə-ˌlāt\ *adj*
ar·il·lode \'ar-ə-ˌlōd\ *n* [NL *arillodium*, fr. *arillus* + *-odium* (fr. Gk *-ōdēs* -like)] : a false aril originating from the orifice instead of from the stalk of an ovule
ari·o·so \ˌär-ē-'ō-(ˌ)sō, -(ˌ)zō\ *adv* [It, fr. *aria*] : in the style of an aria — used as a direction in music — **arioso** *n*
arise \ə-'rīz\ *vi* **arose** \-'rōz\ **aris·en** \-'riz-ᵊn\ **aris·ing** \-'rī-ziŋ\ [ME *arisen*, fr. OE *ārīsan*, fr. *ā-*, perfective prefix + *rīsan* to rise] **1** : to get up : RISE **2 a** : to originate from a source **b** : to come into being or to attention **3** : ASCEND **syn** see SPRING
aris·ta \ə-'ris-tə\ *n, pl* **aris·tae** \-(ˌ)tē, -ˌtī\ *or* **aristas** [NL, fr. L, beard of grain] : a bristlelike structure or appendage — **aris·tate** \-ˌtāt\ *adj*
ar·is·toc·ra·cy \ˌar-ə-'stäk-rə-sē\ *n* [MF & LL; MF *aristocratie*, fr. LL *aristocratia*, fr. Gk *aristokratia*, fr. *aristos* best + *-kratia* -cracy] **1** : government by the best individuals or a small privileged class **2 a** : a government in which power is vested in a minority consisting of those felt to be best qualified **b** : a state with such a government **3** : a governing body or upper class usu. made up of an hereditary nobility **4** : the aggregate of those felt to be superior
aris·to·crat \ə-'ris-tə-ˌkrat, a-; 'ar-ə-stə-\ *n* **1** : a member of an aristocracy; *esp* : NOBLE **2** : one who has the bearing and viewpoint typical of the aristocracy; *also* : one who favors aristocracy

aris·to·crat·ic \ə-ˌris-tə-ˈkrat-ik, (ˌ)a-ˌris-tə-, ˌar-ə-stə-\ *adj* [MF *aristocratique*, fr. ML *aristocraticus*, fr. Gk *aristokratikos*, fr. *aristos* + *-kratikos* -cratic] **1 :** belonging to, having the qualities of, or favoring aristocracy **2 :** socially exclusive; *also* **:** SNOBBISH — **aris·to·crat·i·cal·ly** \-i-k(ə-)lē\ *adv*

Ar·is·to·te·lian *or* **Ar·is·to·te·lean** \ˌar-ə-stə-ˈtēl-yən, -ˈtē-lē-ən\ *adj* [L *Aristoteles* Aristotle, fr. Gk *Aristotelēs*] **:** of or relating to the Greek philosopher Aristotle or his philosophy — **Aristotelian** *n* — **Ar·is·to·te·lian·ism** \-ˌiz-əm\ *n*

arith·me·tic \ə-ˈrith-mə-ˌtik\ *n* [ME *arsmetrik*, fr. OF *arismetique*, fr. L *arithmetica*, fr. Gk *arithmētikē*, fr. fem. of *arithmētikos* arithmetical, fr. *arithmein* to count, fr. *arithmos* number; akin to Gk *arariskein* to fit] **1 a :** a branch of mathematics that deals with real numbers and computations with them **b :** a treatise on arithmetic **2 :** COMPUTATION, CALCULATION — **ar·ith·met·ic** \ˌar-ith-ˈmet-ik\ *or* **ar·ith·met·i·cal** \-i-kəl\ *adj* — **ar·ith·met·i·cal·ly** \-k(ə-)lē\ *adv* — **arith·me·ti·cian** \ə-ˌrith-mə-ˈtish-ən\ *n*

arithmetic mean *n* **:** a value that is computed by dividing the sum of a set of terms by the number of terms

arithmetic progression *n* **:** a progression (as 3, 5, 7, 9) in which the difference between any term and its predecessor is constant

-ar·i·um \ˈar-ē-əm, ˈer-\ *n suffix, pl* **-ariums** *or* **-ar·ia** \-ē-ə\ [L, fr. neut. of *-arius* -ary] **:** thing or place relating to or connected with ⟨planet*arium*⟩

ark \ˈärk\ *n* [ME, fr. OE *arc*; akin to OHG *arahha* ark; both fr. a prehistoric Gmc word borrowed fr. L *arca* chest; akin to L *arcēre* to hold off, defend, Gk *arkein*] **1 a :** a boat or ship held to resemble that in which Noah and his family were preserved from the Deluge **b :** something that affords protection and safety **2 a :** the sacred chest in which the ancient Hebrews kept the two tablets of the Law **b :** a repository traditionally in or against the wall of a synagogue for the scrolls of the Torah

Ar·kan·saw·yer \ˈär-kən-ˌsȯ-yər\ *n* [earlier *Arkansaw* Arkansas + *-yer*] **:** a native or resident of Arkansas — used as a nickname

Ar·kie \ˈär-kē\ *n* [*Ark*ansas + *-ie*] **:** an itinerant agricultural worker esp. from Arkansas — compare OKIE

¹**arm** \ˈärm\ *n* [ME, fr. OE *earm*; akin to L *armus* shoulder, Gk *harmos* joint, L *arma* weapons, *ars* skill, Gk *arariskein* to fit] **1 :** a human upper limb; *esp* **:** the part between the shoulder and the wrist **2 :** something like or corresponding to an arm: as **a :** the forelimb of a vertebrate **b :** a limb of an invertebrate animal **c :** a branch or lateral shoot of a plant **d :** a slender part of a structure, machine, or an instrument projecting from a main part, axis, or fulcrum **e :** the end of a ship's yard; *also* **:** the part of an anchor from the crown to the fluke **3 :** an inlet of water (as from the sea) **4 :** POWER, MIGHT **5 :** a support (as on a chair) for the elbow and forearm **6 :** SLEEVE **7 :** a functional division of a group or activity — **armed** \ˈärmd\ *adj* — **arm·less** \ˈärm-ləs\ *adj* — **arm·like** \-ˌlīk\ *adj*

²**arm** *vb* [ME *armen*, fr. OF *armer*, fr. L *armare*, fr. *arma* weapons, tools] *vt* **1 :** to furnish or equip with weapons **2 :** to furnish with something that strengthens or protects **3 :** to fortify morally **4 :** to equip or ready for action or operation ⟨~ a bomb⟩ **~** *vi* **:** to prepare oneself for struggle or resistance **syn** see FURNISH

³**arm** *n* [ME *armes* (pl.) weapons, fr. OF, fr. L *arma*] **1 a :** a means of offense or defense **:** WEAPON; *esp* **:** FIREARM **b :** a combat branch (as of an army) **c :** an organized branch of national defense (as the navy) **2** *pl* **a :** the hereditary heraldic devices of a family **b :** heraldic devices adopted by a government **3 a** *pl* **:** active hostilities **:** WARFARE **b** *pl* **:** military service

ar·ma·da \är-ˈmäd-ə, -ˈmād-\ *n* [Sp, fr. ML *armata* army, fleet, fr. L, fem. of *armatus*, pp. of *armare*] **1 :** a fleet of warships **2 :** a large force of moving things (as vehicles)

ar·ma·dil·lo \ˌär-mə-ˈdil-(ˌ)ō\ *n, pl* **armadillos** [Sp, fr. dim. of *armado* armed one, fr. L *armatus*] **:** any of several burrowing chiefly nocturnal edentate mammals (family Dasypodidae) of warm parts of the Americas having body and head encased in an armor of small bony plates in which many of them can curl up into a ball when attacked

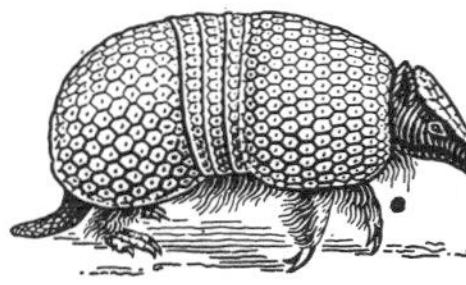

armadillo

Ar·ma·ged·don \ˌär-mə-ˈged-ᵊn\ *n* [Gk *Armageddōn*, *Harmagedōn*, scene of the battle foretold in Rev 16:14–16] **1 a :** a final and conclusive battle between the forces of good and evil **b :** the site or time of Armageddon **2 :** a vast decisive conflict

ar·ma·ment \ˈär-mə-mənt\ *n* [F *armement*, fr. L *armamenta* (pl.) utensils, military or naval equipment, fr. *armare* to arm, equip] **1 :** a military or naval force **2 a :** the aggregate of a nation's military strength **b :** arms and equipment of a combat unit **c :** means of protection or defense **:** ARMOR **3 :** the process of preparing for war

ar·ma·men·tar·i·um \ˌär-mə-ˌmen-ˈter-ē-əm, -mən-\ *n, pl* **ar·ma·men·tar·ia** \-ē-ə\ [L, armory, fr. *armamenta*] **1 :** the equipment and methods used esp. in medicine **2 :** matter available or utilized for an undertaking or field of activity

ar·ma·ture \ˈär-mə-ˌchu̇(ə)r, -chər, -ˌt(y)u̇(ə)r\ *n* [L *armatura* armor, equipment, fr. *armatus*] **1 :** an organ or structure (as teeth, thorns) for offense or defense **2 a :** a piece of soft iron or steel that connects the poles of a magnet or of adjacent magnets **b :** the movable part of a dynamo or motor consisting essentially of coils of wire around an iron core **c :** the movable part of an electromagnetic device

¹**arm·chair** \ˈärm-ˌche(ə)r, -ˌcha(ə)r, ˈärm-ˈ\ *n* **:** a chair with arm rests

²**armchair** *adj* **1 :** remote from direct dealing with problems ⟨~ strategist⟩ **2 :** sharing vicariously in another's experiences

armed forces *n pl* **:** the combined military, naval, and air forces of a nation

Ar·me·nian \är-ˈmē-nē-ən, -nyən\ *n* **1 :** a member of a people dwelling chiefly in Armenia **2 :** the Indo-European language of the Armenians — **Armenian** *adj*

arm·ful \ˈärm-ˌfu̇l\ *n, pl* **armfuls** \-ˌfu̇lz\ *or* **arms·ful** \ˈärmz-ˌfu̇l\ **:** as much as the arm can hold

arm·hole \ˈärm-ˌhōl\ *n* **:** an opening for the arm in a garment

ar·mi·ger \ˈär-mi-jər\ *n* [ML, fr. L, armor-bearer, fr. *armiger* bearing arms, fr. *arma* arms + *-ger* -gerous] **1 :** SQUIRE **2 :** one entitled to armorial bearings — **ar·mig·er·al** \är-ˈmij-ə-rəl\ *adj*

ar·mil·la·ry sphere \ˌär-mə-ˌler-ē-, är-ˌmil-ə-rē-\ *n* [F *sphère armillaire*, fr. ML *armilla*, fr. L, bracelet, iron ring, fr. *armus* arm, shoulder; akin to OE *earm* arm] **:** an old astronomical instrument composed of rings representing the positions of important circles of the celestial sphere

Ar·min·i·an \är-ˈmin-ē-ən\ *adj* **:** of or relating to Arminius or his doctrines opposing the absolute predestination of strict Calvinism and maintaining the possibility of salvation for all — **Arminian** *n* — **Ar·min·i·an·ism** \-ē-ə-ˌniz-əm\ *n*

ar·mi·stice \ˈär-mə-stəs\ *n* [F or NL; F, fr. NL *armistitium*, fr. L *arma* + *-stitium* (as in *solstitium* solstice)] **:** temporary suspension of hostilities by agreement between the two sides **:** TRUCE

Armistice Day *n* **:** VETERANS DAY — used before the official adoption of *Veterans Day* in 1954

arm·let \ˈärm-lət\ *n* **1 :** a band of cloth, metal, or other material worn around the upper arm **2 :** a small arm (as of the sea)

ar·moire \ˈär-mər\ *n* [MF, fr. OF *armaire*, fr. L *armarium*, fr. *arma*] **:** a usu. large and ornate cupboard, wardrobe, or clothespress

ar·mor *or chiefly Brit* **ar·mour** \ˈär-mər\ *n* [ME *armure*, fr. OF, fr. L *armatura* — more at ARMATURE] **1 :** defensive covering for the body; *esp* **:** covering (as of metal) used in combat **2 :** a quality or circumstance that affords protection **3 a :** a usu. metallic protective covering (as for a ship, fort, airplane, or automobile) **b :** a protective covering (as a diver's suit, the covering of a plant or animal, or a sheathing for wire, cordage, or hose) **4 :** armored forces and vehicles — **armor** *vt* — **ar·mored** \-mərd\ *adj*

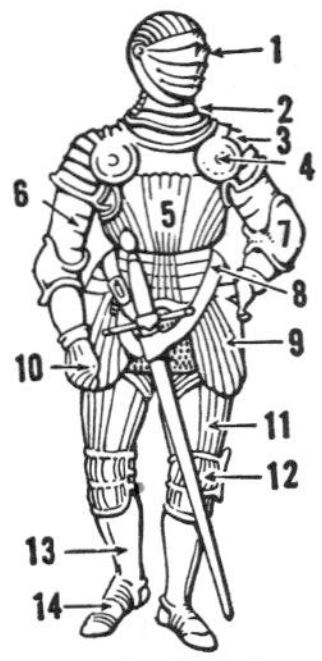

armor 1: *1* helmet, *2* gorget, *3* shoulder piece, *4* pallette, *5* breastplate, *6* brassard, *7* elbow piece, *8* skirt of tasses, *9* tuille, *10* gauntlet, *11* cuisse, *12* knee piece, *13* jambeau, *14* solleret

¹**ar·mor–clad** \ˈär-mər-ˌklad\ *adj* **:** sheathed in armor

²**armor–clad** *n* **:** an armor-clad warship

armored scale *n* **:** any of numerous scales constituting a family (Diaspididae) and having a firm covering of wax best developed in the female

ar·mor·er \ˈär-mər-ər\ *n* **1 :** one that makes armor or arms **2 :** one that repairs, assembles, and tests firearms

ar·mo·ri·al \är-ˈmōr-ē-əl, -ˈmȯr-\ *adj* [*armory* (heraldry)] **:** of, relating to, or bearing heraldic arms — **ar·mo·ri·al·ly** \-ē-ə-lē\ *adv*

Ar·mor·i·can \är-ˈmȯr-i-kən, -ˈmär-\ *or* **Ar·mor·ic** \-ik\ *n* **:** a native or inhabitant of Armorica; *esp* **:** BRETON — **Armorican** *or* **Armoric** *adj*

ar·mo·ry \ˈärm-(ə-)rē\ *n* **1 a :** a supply of arms for defense or attack **b :** a collection of available resources **2 :** a place where arms and military equipment are stored; *esp* **:** one used for training of military reserve personnel **3 :** a place where arms are manufactured

arm·pit \ˈärm-ˌpit\ *n* **:** the hollow beneath the junction of the arm and shoulder

arm·rest \ˈärm-ˌrest\ *n* **:** a support for the arm

ar·my \ˈär-mē\ *n* [ME *armee*, fr. MF, fr. ML *armata* — more at ARMADA] **1 a :** a large organized body of men armed and trained for war esp. on land **b :** a unit capable of independent action and consisting usu. of a headquarters, two or more corps, and auxiliary troops **c** *often cap* **:** the complete military organization of a nation for land warfare **2 :** a great multitude **3 :** a body of persons organized to advance a cause

army ant *n* **:** any of various nomadic social ants

ar·my·worm \ˈär-mē-ˌwərm\ *n* **:** any of numerous larval moths that travel in multitudes from field to field destroying grass, grain, and other crops; *esp* **:** the common armyworm (*Pseudaletia unipuncta*) of the northern U.S.

ar·ni·ca \ˈär-ni-kə\ *n* [NL, genus name] **1 :** any of many composite herbs (genus *Arnica*) including some with bright yellow ray flowers **2 :** the dried flower heads of an arnica (esp. *Arnica montana*) used esp. in the form of a tincture as a liniment (as for sprains or bruises); *also* **:** this tincture

ar·oid \ˈa(ə)r-ˌȯid, ˈe(ə)r-\ *adj* [NL *Arum*] **:** of or relating to the arum family — **aroid** *n*

aroint \ə-ˈrȯint\ *v imper* [origin unknown] **:** BEGONE ⟨~ thee⟩

aro·ma \ə-ˈrō-mə\ *n* [ME *aromat* spice, fr. OF, fr. L *aromat-*, *aroma*, fr. Gk *arōmat-*, *arōma*] **1 a (1) :** a distinctive pleasing odor **:** FRAGRANCE **(2) :** the bouquet of a wine **b :** any smell or odor **2 :** a distinctive quality **:** FLAVOR **syn** see SMELL

¹**ar·o·mat·ic** \ˌar-ə-ˈmat-ik\ *adj* **1 :** of, relating to, or having aroma: **a :** FRAGRANT **b :** having a strong smell **c :** having a distinctive quality **2 :** of, relating to, or characterized by the presence of at least one benzene ring — used of cyclic hydrocarbons and their derivatives — **ar·o·mat·i·cal·ly** \-i-k(ə-)lē\ *adv* — **ar·o·ma·tic·i·ty** \ˌar-ə-mə-ˈtis-ət-ē, ə-ˌrō-mə-\ *n* — **ar·o·mat·ic·ness** *n*

²**aromatic** *n* **1 :** an aromatic plant, drug, or medicine **2 :** an aromatic organic compound

aro·ma·ti·za·tion \ə-ˌrō-mət-ə-ˈzā-shən\ *n* **:** the act or process of aromatizing **:** the condition of being aromatic

aro·ma·tize \ə-ˈrō-mə-ˌtīz\ *vt* **1 :** to make aromatic **:** FLAVOR **2 :** to convert into one or more aromatic compounds

arose *past of* ARISE

¹**around** \ə-ˈrau̇nd\ *adv* [ME, fr. ¹*a-* + *round*] **1 a :** in circumference **b :** in, along, or through a circuit **2 a :** on all or various sides **b :** in close from all sides so as to surround **c :** NEARBY **3 a :** here and there in various places **b :** to a particular place **4 a :** in rotation or succession **b :** from beginning to end **:** THROUGH ⟨mild the year ~⟩ **c :** to a customary or improved condition **5 :** in or to an opposite direction or position **6 :** APPROXIMATELY

²**around** *prep* **1 a :** on all sides of **b :** so as to encircle or enclose **c :** on or to another side of **d :** NEAR **2 :** in all directions outward from **3 :** here and there in or throughout **4 :** so as to have a center or basis in

³**around** *adj* **1 :** ABOUT 1 **2 :** being in existence, evidence, or circulation

arouse \ə-ˈrau̇z\ *vb* [*a-* (as in *arise*) + *rouse*] *vt* **1 :** to awaken from sleep **2 :** to rouse to action **:** EXCITE **~** *vi* **:** to awake from sleep **:** STIR

ar·peg·gio \är-ˈpej-ē-ˌō, -ˈpej-(ˌ)ō\ *n* [It, fr. *arpeggiare* to play on

the harp, fr. *arpa* harp, of Gmc origin; akin to OHG *harpha* harp] **1 :** production of the tones of a chord in succession and not simultaneously **2 :** a chord played in arpeggio

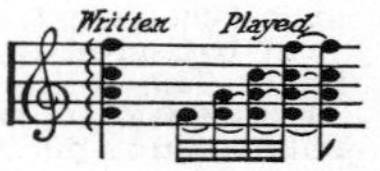

arpeggio

ar·pent \är-'pä^{n}\ *n, pl* **arpents** \-'pä^{n}(z)\ [MF] **1 :** any of various old French units of land area; *esp* **:** one still used in French sections of Canada and the U. S. equal to about 0.85 acre **2 :** a unit of length equal to one side of a square arpent

ar·que·bus \'är-\ *var of* HARQUEBUS

ar·rack \'ar-ək, ə-'rak\ *n* [Ar *'araq* sweet juice, liquor] **:** an alcoholic beverage of the Far East or Near East; *esp* **:** one distilled from the juice of the coconut palm or a mash of rice and molasses

ar·raign \ə-'rān\ *vt* [ME *arreinen*, fr. MF *araisner*, fr. OF, fr. *a-* (fr. L *ad-*) + *raisnier* to speak, fr. (assumed) VL *rationare*, fr. L *ration-, ratio* reason — more at REASON] **1 :** to call (a prisoner) before a court to answer to an indictment **:** CHARGE **2 :** to accuse of wrong, inadequacy, or imperfection — **ar·raign·ment** \-mənt\ *n*

ar·range \ə-'rānj\ *vb* [ME *arangen*, fr. MF *arangier*, fr. OF, fr. *a-* + *rengier* to set in a row, fr. *reng* row — more at RANK] *vt* **1 :** to put in proper order **:** DISPOSE **2 :** to make preparations for **:** PLAN **3 :** to come to an agreement or understanding about **:** SETTLE **4 a :** to adapt (a musical composition) by scoring for voices or instruments other than those for which orig. written **b :** ORCHESTRATE ~ *vi* **1 :** to come to an agreement or understanding **2 :** to make preparations **:** PLAN **syn** see ORDER — **ar·rang·er** *n*

ar·range·ment \ə-'rānj-mənt\ *n* **1 :** the act, manner, or result of arranging **:** the state of being arranged **2 a :** a preliminary measure **:** PREPARATION **b :** a preparatory agreement or settlement **3 :** something made by arranging parts or things together

ar·rant \'ar-ənt\ *adj* [alter. of *errant*] **1 :** THOROUGHGOING, CONFIRMED **2 :** notoriously or outstandingly bad — **ar·rant·ly** *adv*

ar·ras \'ar-əs\ *n, pl* **arras** [ME, fr. *Arras*, France] **1 :** a tapestry of Flemish origin used esp. for wall hangings and curtains **2 :** a wall hanging or screen of tapestry

¹ar·ray \ə-'rā\ *vt* [ME *arrayen*, fr. OF *arayer*, fr. (assumed) VL *arredare*, fr. L *ad-* + a base of Gmc origin; akin to Goth *garaiths* arranged — more at READY] **1 a :** to set or place in order **:** draw up **:** MARSHAL **b :** to set or set forth in order (as a jury) for the trial of a cause **2 :** to clothe or dress esp. in splendid or impressive attire **:** ADORN **syn** see LINE — **ar·ray·er** *n*

²array *n* **1 a :** a regular and imposing grouping or arrangement **:** ORDER **b :** military order **c :** an orderly listing of jurors impaneled **d :** a group of individuals or kinds that has a definite modal point forming a center of variations **2 a :** CLOTHING, ATTIRE **b :** rich or beautiful apparel **:** FINERY **3 :** a body of soldiers **:** MILITIA **4 :** an imposing group **:** large number **5 a :** a number of mathematical elements arranged in rows and columns **b :** a series of statistical data arranged in classes in order of magnitude

ar·rear \ə-'ri(ə)r\ *n* [ME *arrere* behind, backward, fr. MF, fr. (assumed) VL *ad retro* backward, fr. L *ad* to + *retro* backward, behind] **1 :** the state of being behind in the discharge of obligations — usu. used in pl. **2 a :** an unfinished duty — usu. used in pl. **b :** an unpaid and overdue debt — usu. used in pl.

ar·rear·age \-ij\ *n* **1 :** the condition of being in arrears **2 :** something that is in arrears; *esp* **:** something unpaid and overdue

¹ar·rest \ə-'rest\ *vt* [ME *aresten*, fr. MF *arester* to rest, arrest, fr. (assumed) VL *arrestare*, fr. L *ad-* + *restare* to remain, rest] **1 a :** to bring to a stop **b :** CHECK, SLOW **c :** to make inactive **2 :** SEIZE, CAPTURE; *specif* **:** to take or keep in custody by authority of law **3 :** to catch suddenly and hold for a while — **ar·rest·er** *or* **ar·res·tor** \-'res-tər\ *n* — **ar·rest·ment** \-'res(t)-mənt\ *n*

²arrest *n* **1 a :** the act of stopping **:** CHECK **b :** the condition of being stopped **2 a :** SEIZURE **b :** the taking or detaining in custody by authority of law **3 :** a device for arresting motion

ar·rest·ing *adj* **:** STRIKING, IMPRESSIVE

ar·rhyth·mia \ā-'rith-mē-ə\ *n* [NL, fr. Gk, lack of rhythm, fr. *arrhythmos* unrhythmical, fr. *a-* + *rhythmos* rhythm] **:** an alteration in rhythm of the heartbeat either in time or force

ar·rhyth·mic \a-'rith-mik\ *adj* [Gk *arrhythmos*] **:** lacking rhythm or regularity — **ar·rhyth·mi·cal** \-mi-kəl\ *adj* — **ar·rhyth·mi·cal·ly** \-k(ə-)lē\ *adv*

ar·ri·ère–ban \,ar-ē-,e(ə)r-'bän, -'ban\ *n* [F] **:** a proclamation of a king (as of France) calling his vassals to arms; *also* **:** the body of vassals summoned

ar·ri·ère–pen·sée \-(,)pä^{n}-'sā\ *n* [F, fr. *arrière* in back + *pensée* thought] **:** mental reservation

ar·ris \'ar-əs\ *n, pl* **arris** *or* **ar·ris·es** [prob. modif. of MF *areste*, lit., fishbone, fr. LL *arista* — more at ARÊTE] **:** the sharp edge or salient angle formed by the meeting of two surfaces esp. in moldings

ar·riv·al \ə-'rī-vəl\ *n* **1 :** the act of arriving **2 :** the attainment of an end or state **3 :** one that is arriving or has arrived

syn ADVENT: ARRIVAL implies reaching or appearing at a destination after precedent movement; ADVENT applies to a momentous or conspicuous arrival or to an appearance upon a scene, esp. a first appearance or beginning

¹ar·rive \ə-'rīv\ *vi* [ME *ariven*, fr. OF *ariver*, fr. (assumed) VL *arripare* to come to shore, fr. L *ad-* + *ripa* shore — more at RIVE] **1 a :** to reach a destination **b :** to make an appearance **2 a :** to achieve an end **b :** to reach a state or stage **3 a** *archaic* **:** HAPPEN **b :** to be near in time **:** COME **4 :** to be successful — **ar·riv·er** *n*

²ar·ri·vé \,ar-i-'vā\ *n* [F, fr. pp. of *arriver* to arrive, fr. OF *ariver*] **:** one who has risen rapidly to success, power, or fame

ar·ri·viste \-'vēst\ *n* [F, fr. *arriver*] **:** PARVENU, UPSTART

ar·ro·ba \ə-'rō-bə\ *n* [Sp & Pg, fr. Ar *ar-rub'*, lit., the quarter] **1 :** an old Spanish unit of weight equal to about 25 pounds used in some Spanish-American countries **2 :** an old Portuguese unit of weight equal to about 32 pounds used in Brazil

ar·ro·gance \'ar-ə-gən(t)s\ *n* **:** a feeling of superiority manifested in an overbearing manner or presumptuous claims

ar·ro·gant \'ar-ə-gənt\ *adj* [ME, fr. L *arrogant-, arrogans*, prp. of *arrogare*] **1 :** exaggerating or disposed to exaggerate one's own worth or importance in an overbearing manner **2 :** proceeding from or characterized by arrogance **syn** see PROUD — **ar·ro·gant·ly** *adv*

ar·ro·gate \'ar-ə-,gāt\ *vt* [L *arrogatus*, pp. of *arrogare*, fr. *ad-* + *rogare* to ask — more at RIGHT] **1 a :** to claim or seize without justification as one's right **b :** to make undue claims to having **:** ASSUME **2 :** to claim on behalf of another **:** ASCRIBE **syn** see APPROPRIATE — **ar·ro·ga·tion** \,ar-ə-'gā-shən\ *n*

ar·ron·disse·ment \ə-'rän-də-smənt, ə-,rän-di-'smä^{n}\ *n* [F] **1 :** the largest division of a French department **2 :** an administrative district of some large French cities

ar·row \'ar-(,)ō, -ə(-w)\ *n* [ME *arwe*, fr. OE; akin to Goth *arhwazna* arrow, L *arcus* bow, arch, arc] **1 :** a missile weapon shot from a bow and usu. having a slender shaft, a pointed head, and feathers at the butt **2 :** a mark (as on a map or signboard) to indicate direction

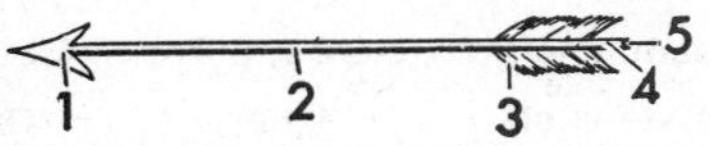

arrow: *1* head, *2* shaft, *3* feather, *4* butt, *5* nock

ar·row·head \'ar-ō-,hed, 'ar-ə-\ *n* **1 :** the usu. separate wedge-shaped striking end of an arrow **2 :** something resembling an arrowhead; *specif* **:** a wedge-shaped mark on a drawing to limit a dimension line **3 :** any of a genus (*Sagittaria*) of plants of the water-plantain family with leaves shaped like arrowheads

ar·row·root \-,rüt, -,rút\ *n* **1 :** any of a genus (*Maranta* of the family Marantaceae, the arrowroot family) of tropical American plants with tuberous roots; *esp* **:** one (*M. arundinacea*) whose roots yield a nutritive starch **2 :** starch yielded by the common arrowroot; *also* **:** a similar starch from other plants

ar·row·wood \-,wúd\ *n* **:** any of several shrubs (as several viburnums) having tough pliant shoots formerly used to make arrows

ar·rowy \'ar-ə-wē\ *adj* **1 :** consisting of arrows **2 :** resembling an arrow; *esp* **:** SWIFT, DARTING

ar·royo \ə-'rói-ə, -'rói-(,)ō\ *n* [Sp] **1 :** a watercourse (as a creek or stream) in an arid region **2 :** a water-carved gully or channel

ar·se·nal \'ärs-nəl, -ᵊn-əl\ *n* [It *arsenale*, modif. of Ar *dār ṣinā'ah* house of manufacture] **1 a :** an establishment for the manufacture or storage of arms and military equipment **b :** a collection of weapons **2 :** STORE, STOREHOUSE, REPERTORY

ar·se·nate \'ärs-nət, -ᵊn-ət, -ᵊn-,āt\ *n* **:** a salt or ester of an arsenic acid

¹ar·se·nic \'ärs-nik, -ᵊn-ik\ *n* [ME, fr. MF & L; MF, fr. L *arsenicum*, fr. Gk *arsenikon, arrhenikon* yellow orpiment, fr. Syr *zarnīg*, of Iranian origin; akin to Av *zaranya* gold, Skt *hari* yellowish — more at YELLOW] **1 :** a trivalent and pentavalent solid poisonous element commonly metallic steel-gray, crystalline, and brittle — see ELEMENT table **2 :** a poisonous trioxide As_2O_3 or As_4O_6 of arsenic used esp. as an insecticide or weed killer — called also *arsenic trioxide*

²ar·sen·ic \är-'sen-ik\ *adj* **:** of, relating to, or containing arsenic esp. with a valence of five

ar·sen·i·cal \-i-kəl\ *adj* **:** of, relating to, or containing arsenic — **arsenical** *n*

ar·se·nide \'ärs-ᵊn-,īd\ *n* **:** a binary compound of arsenic with a more positive element

ar·se·ni·ous \är-'sē-nē-əs\ *adj* **:** of, relating to, or containing arsenic esp. when trivalent

ar·se·nite \'ärs-ᵊn-,īt\ *n* **:** a salt or ester of an arsenious acid

ar·se·no·py·rite \,ärs-ᵊn-ō-'pī(ə)-,rīt\ *n* **:** a mineral FeAsS consisting of a hard tin-white or grayish iron sulfarsenide occurring in prismatic orthorhombic crystals or in masses or grains

ar·sine \är-'sēn, 'är-,\ *n* [ISV, fr. *arsenic*] **:** a colorless flammable extremely poisonous gas AsH_3 with an odor like garlic; *also* **:** a derivative of arsine

ar·sis \'är-səs\ *n, pl* **ar·ses** \-,sēz\ [LL & Gk; LL, raising of the voice, accented part of foot, fr. Gk, upbeat, less important part of foot, lit., act of lifting, fr. *aeirein, airein* to lift] **1 a :** the lighter or shorter part of a poetic foot esp. in quantitative verse **b :** the accented or longer part of a poetic foot esp. in accentual verse **2 :** the unaccented part of a musical measure

ar·son \'ärs-ᵊn\ *n* [obs. F, fr. OF, fr. *ars*, pp. of *ardre* to burn, fr. L *ardēre* — more at ARDOR] **:** the malicious burning of or attempt to burn property (as a building) — **ar·son·ist** \'ärs-nəst, -ᵊn-əst\ *n*

ars·phen·a·mine \ärs-'fen-ə-,mēn\ *n* [ISV *arsenic* + *phenamine*] **:** a light-yellow toxic hygroscopic powder $C_{12}H_{12}As_2N_2O_2 \cdot 2HCl \cdot 2H_2O$ formerly used in the treatment of spirochetal diseases

¹art \(')ärt, ərt\ [ME, fr. OE *eart;* akin to ON *est, ert* (thou) art, OE *is* is] *archaic pres 2d sing of* BE

²art \'ärt\ *n* [ME, fr. OF, fr. L *art-, ars* — more at ARM] **1 a :** skill in performance acquired by experience, study, or observation **:** KNACK **b :** human ingenuity in adapting natural things to man's use **2 a :** a branch of learning: (1) **:** one of the humanities (2) *pl* **:** the liberal arts **b** *archaic* **:** LEARNING, SCHOLARSHIP **3 a :** an occupation requiring knowledge or skill **:** TRADE **b :** a system of rules or methods of performing particular actions **c :** systematic application of knowledge or skill in effecting a desired result **4 a :** the conscious use of skill, taste, and creative imagination in the production of aesthetic objects; *also* **:** works so produced **b :** the craft of the artist **c** (1) **:** FINE ARTS (2) **:** one of the fine arts (3) **:** a graphic art **5 a** *archaic* **:** a skillful plan **b :** ARTFULNESS

syn ART, SKILL, CUNNING, ARTIFICE, CRAFT mean the faculty of performing what is devised. ART may be used interchangeably with all the other terms but in its most distinct sense it contrasts with them in implying a personal, unanalyzable creative power; SKILL stresses technical knowledge and proficiency; CUNNING suggests ingenuity and subtlety in devising, inventing, or executing; ARTIFICE suggests mechanical skill esp. in imitating things in nature; CRAFT may imply expertness in workmanship or suggest trickery and guile in attaining one's ends

-art — see -ARD

Ar·te·mis \'ärt-ə-məs\ *n* [L, fr. Gk] **:** the goddess of the moon, wild animals, and hunting in Greek mythology

ar·te·mi·sia \,ärt-ə-'mizh-(ē-)ə, -'miz-ē-ə\ *n* [NL, genus name, fr. L, artemisia, fr. Gk] **:** any of a genus (*Artemisia*) of composite herbs and shrubs with strong-smelling foliage

arteri- *or* **arterio-** *comb form* [MF, fr. LL, fr. Gk *artēri-, artērio-* fr. *artēria* artery] **1 :** artery ⟨*arterio*logy⟩ **2 :** arterial and ⟨*arterio*venous⟩

¹ar·te·ri·al \är-'tir-ē-əl\ *adj* **1 a :** of or relating to an artery **b :** relating to or being the bright red blood present in most arteries that has been oxygenated in lungs or gills **2 :** of, relating to, or

constituting through-traffic facilities — **ar·te·ri·al·ly** \-ə-lē\ *adv*

²arterial *n* **:** a through street or arterial highway

ar·te·ri·al·iza·tion \är-ˌtir-ē-ə-lə-ˈzā-shən\ *n* **:** the process of arterializing

ar·te·ri·al·ize \är-ˈtir-ē-ə-ˌlīz\ *vt* **:** to transform (venous blood) into arterial blood by oxygenation

ar·te·ri·og·ra·phy \(ˌ)är-ˌtir-ē-ˈäg-rə-fē\ *n* [ISV] **:** the roentgenographic visualization of an artery after injection of a special substance

ar·te·ri·o·lar \-ē-ˈō-lər, är-ˈtir-ē-ə-lər\ *adj* **:** of or relating to an arteriole

ar·te·ri·ole \är-ˈtir-ē-ˌōl\ *n* [F or NL; F *artériole,* prob. fr. NL *arteriola,* dim. of L *arteria*] **:** one of the small terminal twigs of an artery that ends in capillaries

ar·te·rio·scle·ro·sis \är-ˌtir-ē-ō-sklə-ˈrō-səs\ *n* [NL] **:** a chronic disease characterized by abnormal thickening and hardening of the arterial walls — **ar·te·rio·scle·rot·ic** \-ˈrät-ik\ *adj or n*

ar·te·rio·ve·nous \är-ˌtir-ē-(ˌ)ō-ˈvē-nəs\ *adj* [ISV] **:** of, relating to, or connecting the arteries and veins

ar·te·ri·tis \ˌärt-ə-ˈrīt-əs\ *n* [NL] **:** arterial inflammation

ar·te·ry \ˈärt-ə-rē\ *n* [ME *arterie,* fr. L *arteria,* fr. Gk *artēria;* akin to Gk *aortē* aorta] **1 :** one of the tubular branching muscular- and elastic-walled vessels that carry blood from the heart through the body **2 :** a channel (as a river or highway) of communication

ar·te·sian well \är-ˌtē-zhən-\ *n* [F *artésien,* lit., of Artois, fr. OF, fr. *Arteis* Artois, France] **1 :** a well made by boring into the earth until water is reached which from internal pressure flows up like a fountain **2 :** a deep-bored well

art·ful \ˈärt-fəl\ *adj* **1 :** performed with or showing art or skill **2 :** ARTIFICIAL **3 :** skillful in gaining an end; *also* **:** CRAFTY, WILY **syn** see SLY — **art·ful·ly** \-fə-lē\ *adv* — **art·ful·ness** *n*

arthr- *or* **arthro-** *comb form* [L, fr. Gk, fr. *arthron;* akin to Gk *arariskein* to fit — more at ARM] **:** joint ⟨*arthr*algia⟩ ⟨*arthro*pathy⟩

ar·thral·gia \är-ˈthral-j(ē-)ə\ *n* [NL] **:** neuralgic pain in one or more joints — **ar·thral·gic** \-jik\ *adj*

ar·thrit·ic \är-ˈthrit-ik\ *adj* **:** of, relating to, or affected with arthritis — **arthritic** *n* — **ar·thrit·i·cal·ly** \-i-k(ə-)lē\ *adv*

ar·thri·tis \är-ˈthrīt-əs\ *n* [L, fr. Gk, fr. *arthron*] **:** inflammation of joints due to infectious, metabolic, or constitutional causes

ar·thro·mere \ˈär-thrə-ˌmi(ə)r\ *n* **:** one of the body segments of a jointed animal — **ar·thro·mer·ic** \ˌär-thrə-ˈmer-ik, -ˈmi(ə)r-\ *adj*

ar·throp·a·thy \är-ˈthräp-ə-thē\ *n* [ISV] **:** a disease of a joint

ar·thro·pod \ˈär-thrə-ˌpäd\ *n* [NL *Arthropoda,* fr. *arthr-* + *-poda*] **:** any of a phylum (Arthropoda) of invertebrate animals with articulate body and limbs (as insects, arachnids, and crustaceans) — **arthropod** *adj* — **ar·throp·o·dal** \är-ˈthräp-əd-ᵊl\ *or* **ar·throp·o·dan** \-əd-ən\ *or* **ar·throp·o·dous** \-əd-əs\ *adj*

ar·thro·sis \är-ˈthrō-səs\ *n* [NL, fr. Gk *arthrōsis* jointing, articulation, fr. *arthroun* to articulate, fr. *arthron*] **:** an articulation or line of juncture between bones

ar·thro·spore \ˈär-thrə-ˌspō(ə)r, -ˌspȯ(ə)r\ *n* **:** a thick-walled vegetative resting cell formed by blue-green algae (as of the genus *Nostoc*); *also* **:** a similar body (as in fungi) — **ar·thro·spor·ic** \ˌär-thrə-ˈspōr-ik, -ˈspȯr-\ *or* **ar·thro·spo·rous** \-əs; är-ˈthräs-pə-rəs\ *adj*

Ar·thur \ˈär-thər\ *n* **:** a semilegendary 6th century king of the Britons — **Ar·thu·ri·an** \är-ˈth(y)u̇r-ē-ən\ *adj*

ar·ti·choke \ˈärt-ə-ˌchōk\ *n* [It dial. *articiocco,* fr. Ar *al-khurshūf* the artichoke] **1 :** a tall composite herb (*Cynara scolymus*) like a thistle with coarse pinnately incised leaves; *also* **:** its edible flower head which is cooked as a vegetable **2 :** JERUSALEM ARTICHOKE

¹ar·ti·cle \ˈärt-i-kəl\ *n* [ME, fr. OF, fr. L *articulus* joint, division, dim. of *artus* joint; akin to Gk *arariskein* to fit — more at ARM] **1 a :** a distinct often numbered section of a writing **b :** a separate clause **c :** a stipulation in a contract or a creed **d :** a nonfictional prose composition usu. forming an independent portion of a publication **2 :** an item of business **:** MATTER **3 :** any of a small set of words or affixes (as *a, an, the*) used with nouns to limit or give definiteness to their application **4 :** a member of a class of things; *esp* **:** a piece of goods **:** COMMODITY

²article *vt* **ar·ti·cling** \-k(ə-)liŋ\ **:** to bind by articles (as of apprenticeship)

ar·tic·u·lar \är-ˈtik-yə-lər\ *adj* [ME *articuler,* fr. L *articularis,* fr. *articulus*] **:** of or relating to a joint

¹ar·tic·u·late \är-ˈtik-yə-lət\ *adj* [NL *articulatus,* fr. L *articulus*] **1 a :** divided into syllables or words meaningfully arranged **:** INTELLIGIBLE **b :** able to speak **c :** expressing or expressed readily, clearly, or effectively **2 a :** consisting of segments united by joints **:** JOINTED ⟨~ animals⟩ **b :** marked into distinct parts — **ar·tic·u·late·ly** *adv* — **ar·tic·u·late·ness** *n*

²ar·tic·u·late \-ˌlāt\ *vb* [L *articulatus,* pp. of *articulare,* fr. *articulus*] *vt* **1 a :** to pronounce distinctly **b :** to give clear and effective utterance to **2 a :** to unite by means of a joint **:** JOINT **b :** to form or fit into a systematic whole ~ *vi* **1 :** to utter articulate sounds **2 :** to become united or connected by or as if by a joint — **ar·tic·u·la·tive** \-lət-iv, -ˌlāt-\ *adj* — **ar·tic·u·la·tor** \-ˌlāt-ər\ *n*

ar·tic·u·la·tion \(ˌ)är-ˌtik-yə-ˈlā-shən\ *n* **1 a :** the action or manner of jointing or interrelating **b :** the state of being jointed or interrelated **2 a** (1) **:** a joint or juncture between bones or cartilages in the skeleton of a vertebrate (2) **:** a movable joint between rigid parts of any animal **b** (1) **:** a joint between two separable plant parts (as the base of a leafstalk) (2) **:** a plant stem node or internode **3 a :** the act or manner of articulating sounds **b :** an articulated utterance or sound; *specif* **:** CONSONANT

ar·tic·u·la·to·ry \är-ˈtik-yə-lə-ˌtōr-ē, -ˌtȯr-\ *adj* **:** of or relating to articulation

ar·ti·fact *or* **ar·te·fact** \ˈärt-ə-ˌfakt\ *n* [L *arte* by skill (abl. of *art-, ars* skill) + *factum,* neut. of *factus,* pp. of *facere* to do — more at ARM, DO] **1 :** a usu. simple object (as a tool or ornament) showing human workmanship or modification **2 :** a product of artificial character due to extraneous (as human) agency — **ar·ti·fac·tu·al** \ˌärt-ə-ˈfak-chə-(wə)l, -ˈfaksh-wəl\ *adj*

ar·ti·fice \ˈärt-ə-fəs\ *n* [MF, fr. L *artificium,* fr. *artific-, artifex* artificer, fr. L *art-, ars* + *facere*] **1 a :** an artful stratagem **:** TRICK **b :** GUILE, TRICKERY **2 a :** an ingenious device or expedient **b :** INGENUITY, INVENTIVENESS **syn** see ART, TRICK

ar·ti·fi·cer \är-ˈtif-ə-sər, ˈärt-ə-fə-sər\ *n* **1 :** a skilled or artistic worker or craftsman **2 :** one that makes or contrives **:** DEVISER

ar·ti·fi·cial \ˌärt-ə-ˈfish-əl\ *adj* **1 a :** contrived by art rather than nature **b :** produced or effected by man to imitate nature **:** SIMULATED **2 :** having existence in legal, economic, or political theory **3** *obs* **:** ARTFUL, CUNNING **4 a :** FEIGNED, ASSUMED **b :** AFFECTED, STILTED **c :** IMITATION, SHAM **5 :** based on differential morphological characters not necessarily indicative of natural relationships — **ar·ti·fi·ci·al·i·ty** \ˌärt-ə-ˌfish-(ē-)ˈal-ət-ē\ *n* — **ar·ti·fi·cial·ly** \ˌärt-ə-ˈfish-(ə-)lē\ *adv* — **ar·ti·fi·cial·ness** \-ˈfish-əl-nəs\ *n*

syn ARTIFICIAL, FACTITIOUS, SYNTHETIC mean brought into being not by nature but by art or effort. ARTIFICIAL is applicable to anything that is not the result of natural process or conditions ⟨the state is an *artificial* society⟩ but esp. to something that has a counterpart in nature; FACTITIOUS applies chiefly to emotions or states of mind not naturally caused or spontaneously aroused; SYNTHETIC applies esp. to a manufactured substance or to a natural substance so treated that it acquires the appearance or qualities of another and may substitute for it; all three terms may suggest a lack of the natural and spontaneous in social or personal matters

artificial horizon *n* **1 :** HORIZON 1c **2 :** an aeronautical instrument based upon a gyroscope and designed to furnish a surface constantly perpendicular to the vertical and therefore parallel to the horizon

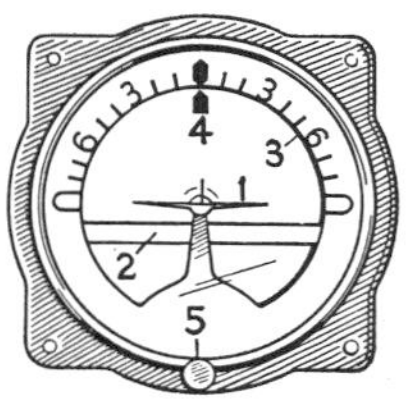

artificial horizon: *1* miniature airplane; *2* horizon bar; *3* degree of bank scale in 10's of degrees; *4* pointer; *5* inactivating knob

artificial respiration *n* **:** the rhythmic forcing of air into and out of the lungs of a person whose breathing has stopped

ar·til·ler·ist \är-ˈtil-(ə-)rəst\ *n* **:** GUNNER, ARTILLERYMAN

ar·til·lery \är-ˈtil-(ə-)rē\ *n* [ME *artillerie,* fr. MF] **1 :** weapons (as bows, slings, catapults) for discharging missiles **2 a :** large caliber crew-served mounted firearms (as guns, howitzers, rockets) **:** ORDNANCE **b** *slang* **:** SMALL ARMS **3 :** a branch of an army armed with artillery — **ar·til·lery·man** \-(ə-)rē-mən\ *n*

art·i·ly \ˈärt-ᵊl-ē\ *adv* **:** in an arty manner

art·i·ness \ˈärt-ē-nəs\ *n* **:** the quality or state of being arty

ar·tio·dac·tyl \ˌärt-ē-ō-ˈdak-tᵊl\ *n* [deriv. of Gk *artios* fitting, even-numbered + *daktylos* finger, toe; akin to Gk *arariskein* to fit — more at ARM] **:** any of an order (Artiodactyla) of hoofed mammals (as the camel or ox) with an even number of functional toes on each foot — **artiodactyl** *or* **ar·tio·dac·ty·lous** \-tə-ləs\ *adj*

ar·ti·san \ˈärt-ə-zən, -sən, *chiefly Brit* ˌärt-ə-ˈzan\ *n* [MF, fr. OIt *artigiano,* fr. *arte* art, fr. L *art-, ars*] **:** one trained to manual dexterity or skill in a trade

art·ist \ˈärt-əst\ *n* **1 a :** one who professes and practices an art in which conception and execution are governed by imagination and taste **b :** a person skilled in one of the fine arts **2 :** ARTISTE **3 a** *obs* **:** one skilled or versed in learned arts **b** *archaic* **:** ARTISAN **4 :** one who is adept at deception

ar·tiste \är-ˈtēst\ *n* [F] **:** a skilled adept performer; *specif* **:** a musical or theatrical entertainer

ar·tis·tic \är-ˈtis-tik\ *adj* **1 :** relating to or characteristic of art or artists **2 :** showing taste in arrangement or execution — **ar·tis·ti·cal·ly** \-ti-k(ə-)lē\ *adv*

syn AESTHETIC: ARTISTIC stresses the point of view of one who produces art and thinks in terms of creating beauty or form; AESTHETIC stresses the point of view of one who analyzes and reflects upon the effect a work of art has upon him; either term may suggest a contrast with the practical, functional, or moral aspects of something

art·ist·ry \ˈärt-ə-strē\ *n* **1 :** artistic quality of effect or workmanship **2 :** artistic ability

art·less \ˈärt-ləs\ *adj* **1 :** lacking art, knowledge, or skill **:** UNCULTURED **2 a :** made without skill **:** RUDE **b :** free from artificiality **:** NATURAL ⟨~ grace⟩ **3 :** free from guile or craft **:** sincerely simple **syn** see NATURAL — **art·less·ly** *adv* — **art·less·ness** *n*

art nou·veau \ˌär(t)-ˌnü-ˈvō\ *n, often cap A & N* [F, lit., new art] **:** a decorative style of late 19th century origin characterized esp. by sinuous lines and foliate forms

arty \ˈärt-ē\ *adj* **1 :** showily imitative of art **2 :** aspiring to be artistic **:** DILETTANTE

ar·um \ˈar-əm, ˈer-\ *n* [NL, genus name, fr. L, arum, fr. Gk *aron*] **:** any of a genus (*Arum* of the family Araceae, the arum family) of Old World plants with flowers in a fleshy spathe subtended by a leafy bract; *broadly* **:** a plant of the arum family

arun·di·na·ceous \ə-ˌrən-də-ˈnā-shəs\ *adj* [L *arundinaceus,* fr. *arundin-, arundo* reed + *-aceus* -aceous] **:** of, relating to, or resembling a reed

¹-ary *US usu* ˌer-ē *when an unstressed syllable precedes,* ə-rē *or* rē *when a stressed syllable precedes; Brit usu* ə-rē *or* rē *in all cases*\ *n suffix* [ME *-arie,* fr. OF & L; OF *-aire, -arie,* fr. L *-arius, -aria, -arium,* fr. *-arius,* adj. suffix] **1 :** thing belonging to or connected with; *esp* **:** place of ⟨ov*ary*⟩ **2 :** person belonging to, connected with, or engaged in ⟨function*ary*⟩

²-ary *adj suffix* [ME *-arie,* fr. MF & L; MF *-aire,* fr. L *-arius*] **:** of, relating to, or connected with ⟨budget*ary*⟩

¹Ary·an \ˈar-ē-ən, ˈer-\ *adj* [Skt *ārya* noble, belonging to the people speaking an Indo-European dialect who migrated into northern India] **1 :** of or relating to the Indo-European family of languages or to their hypothetical prototype **2 :** of or relating to speakers of Indo-European languages **3 a :** of or relating to a hypothetical ethnic type illustrated by or descended from early speakers of Indo-European languages **b :** NORDIC **4 :** of or relating to Indo-Iranian or its speakers

²Aryan *n* **1 :** a member of the Indo-European-speaking people early occupying the Iranian plateau or entering India and conquering and amalgamating with the earlier non-Indo-European inhabitants **2 a :** a member of the people speaking the language from which the Indo-European languages are derived **b :** an individual of any of those peoples speaking these languages since prehistoric times **:** INDO-EUROPEAN **c :** NORDIC **d :** GENTILE

ar·y·te·noid \ˌar-ə-ˈtē-ˌnȯid, ə-ˈrit-ᵊn-ˌȯid\ *adj* [NL *arytaenoides,* fr. Gk *arytainoeidēs,* lit., ladle-shaped, fr. *arytaina* ladle] **1 :** relating to or being either of two small laryngeal cartilages to which the vocal cords are attached **2 :** relating to or being either of a pair of small muscles or an unpaired muscle of the larynx — **arytenoid** *n*

¹as \əz, (ˌ)az\ *conj* [ME, fr. OE *eallswā* just as, likewise — more at ALSO] **1 :** as if ⟨looks ~ he had seen a ghost —S.T.Coleridge⟩ **2 :** in or to the same degree in which ⟨deaf ~ a post⟩ **3 :** in the way or manner that ⟨do ~ I do⟩ **4 :** in accordance with what or

the way in which ⟨quite good ~ boys go⟩ **5 :** WHILE, WHEN ⟨spilled the milk ~ she got up⟩ **6 :** regardless of the degree to which **:** THOUGH ⟨improbable ~ it seems, it's true⟩ **7 :** for the reason that ⟨stayed home ~ she had no car⟩ **8 :** that the result is **:** THAT ⟨so clearly guilty ~ to leave no doubt⟩

2**as** *adv* **1 :** to the same degree or amount **:** EQUALLY ⟨~ deaf as a post⟩ **2 :** for instance ⟨various trees, ~ oak or pine⟩ **3 :** when considered in a specified form or relation ⟨my opinion ~ distinguished from his⟩

3**as** *pron* **1 :** THAT, WHO, WHICH — used after *same* or *such* ⟨in the same building ~ my brother⟩ ⟨tears such ~ angels weep —John Milton⟩ and chiefly dial. after a substantive not modified by *same* or *such* ⟨that kind of fruit ~ maids call medlars —Shak.⟩ **2 :** a fact that ⟨is a foreigner, ~ is evident from his accent⟩

4**as** *prep* **1 a :** LIKE 2 ⟨all rose ~ one man⟩ **b :** LIKE 1a ⟨his face was ~ a mask —Max Beerbohm⟩ **2 :** in the capacity, character, condition, or role of ⟨works ~ an editor⟩

5**as** \'as\ *n, pl* **as·ses** \'as-,ēz, 'as-əz\ [L] **1 :** LIBRA 2a **2 a :** a bronze coin of the ancient Roman republic **b :** a unit of value equivalent to an as coin

as- — see AD-

asa·fet·i·da *or* **asa·foe·ti·da** \,as-ə-'fit-əd-ē, -'fet-əd-ə\ *n* [ME *asafetida*, fr. ML *asafoetida*, fr. Per *azā* mastic + L *foetida*, fem. of *foetidus* fetid] **:** the fetid gum resin of various oriental plants (genus *Ferula*) of the carrot family formerly used in medicine

as·bes·tos *also* **as·bes·tus** \as-'bes-təs, az-\ *n* [ME *albestron* mineral supposed to be inextinguishable when set on fire, prob. fr. MF, fr. ML *asbeston*, alter. of L *asbestos*, fr. Gk, unslaked lime, fr. *asbestos* inextinguishable, fr. *a-* + *sbennynai* to quench; akin to Lith *gesti* to be extinguished] **:** a mineral (as amphibole) that readily separates into long flexible fibers suitable for use as an incombustible, nonconducting, or chemically resistant material

as·bes·to·sis \,as-,bes-'tō-səs, ,az-\ *n* **:** a pneumoconiosis due to asbestos particles

asc- *or* **asco-** *comb form* [NL, fr. *ascus*] **:** bladder ⟨*ascocarp*⟩

as·ca·ri·a·sis \,as-kə-'rī-ə-səs\ *n* **:** infestation with or disease caused by ascarids

as·ca·rid \'as-kə-rəd\ *n* [deriv. of LL *ascarid-*, *ascaris* intestinal worm, fr. Gk *askarid-*, *askaris;* akin to Gk *skairein* to gambol] **:** a nematode worm of a family (Ascaridae) including the common roundworm (*Ascaris lumbricoides*) parasitic in the human intestine

as·ca·ris \'as-kə-rəs\ *n, pl* **as·car·i·des** \a-'skar-ə-,dēz\ [LL] **:** ASCARID

as·cend \ə-'send\ *vb* [ME *ascenden*, fr. L *ascendere*, fr. *ad-* + *scandere* to climb — more at SCAN] *vi* **1 a :** to move gradually upward **b :** to slope upward **2 a :** to rise from a lower level or degree **b :** to go back in time or in order of genealogical succession ~ *vt* **1 :** to go or move up **:** MOUNT **2 :** to succeed to **:** OCCUPY — **as·cend·able** *or* **as·cend·ible** \ə-'sen-də-bəl\ *adj*

syn ASCEND, MOUNT, CLIMB, SCALE mean to move upward or toward the top. ASCEND implies little more than progressive upward movement; MOUNT implies reaching the top or attaining impressive or dangerous heights; CLIMB suggests effort and the use of hands and feet; SCALE suggests an essentially vertical ascending requiring the use of ladder or rope

as·cen·dance *or* **as·cen·dence** \ə-'sen-dən(t)s\ *n* **:** ASCENDANCY

as·cen·dan·cy *or* **as·cen·den·cy** \ə-'sen-dən-sē\ *n* **:** governing or controlling influence **:** DOMINATION **syn** see SUPREMACY

1**as·cen·dant** *also* **as·cen·dent** \ə-'sen-dənt\ *n* [ME *ascendent*, fr. ML *ascendent-*, *ascendens*, fr. L, prp. of *ascendere*] **1 :** the point of the ecliptic or degree of the zodiac that rises above the eastern horizon at any moment **2 :** a state or position of dominant power **3 :** a lineal or collateral relative in the ascending line

2**ascendant** *also* **ascendent** *adj* **1 a :** moving upward **:** RISING **b :** directed upward ⟨an ~ stem⟩ **2 a :** SUPERIOR **b :** DOMINANT

as·cend·er \ə-'sen-dər, 'a-,\ *n* **:** the part of a lowercase letter that exceeds x height; *also* **:** a letter that has such a part

as·cend·ing *adj* **1 :** mounting or sloping upward **2 :** rising upward usu. from a more or less prostrate base or point of attachment

as·cen·sion \ə-'sen-chən\ *n* [ME, fr. L *ascension-*, *ascensio*, fr. *ascensus*, pp. of *ascendere*] **:** the act or process of ascending

as·cen·sion·al \ə-'sench-nəl, -ən-əl\ *adj* **:** of or relating to ascension or ascent

Ascension Day *n* **:** the Thursday 40 days after Easter on which is commemorated Christ's ascension into Heaven

as·cen·sive \ə-'sen(t)-siv\ *adj* **:** rising or tending to rise

as·cent \ə-'sent\ *n* [irreg. fr. *ascend*] **1 a :** the act of rising or mounting upward **:** CLIMB **b :** an upward slope or rising grade **:** ACCLIVITY **c :** INCLINATION, GRADIENT **2 :** an advance in social status or reputation **:** PROGRESS **3 :** a going back in time or upward in order of genealogical succession

as·cer·tain \,as-ər-'tān\ *vt* [ME *acertainen*, fr. MF *acertainer*, fr. *a-* (fr. L *ad-*) + *certain*] **1** *archaic* **:** to make certain, exact, or precise **2 :** to find out or learn with certainty **syn** see DISCOVER — **as·cer·tain·able** \-'tā-nə-bəl\ *adj* — **as·cer·tain·ment** \-'tān-mənt\ *n*

as·ce·sis \ə-'sē-səs\ *or* **as·ke·sis** \-'skē-\ *n* [LL or Gk; LL, fr. Gk *askēsis*, lit., exercise, fr. *askein*] **:** SELF-DISCIPLINE, ASCETICISM

as·cet·ic \ə-'set-ik\ *adj* [Gk *askētikos*, lit., laborious, fr. *askētēs* one that exercises, hermit, fr. *askein* to work, exercise] **:** practicing strict self-denial as a means of religious discipline; *also* **:** AUSTERE **syn** see SEVERE — **ascetic** *n* — **as·cet·i·cal** \-i-kəl\ *adj* — **as·cet·i·cal·ly** \-k(ə-)lē\ *adv* — **as·cet·i·cism** \ə-'set-ə-,siz-əm\ *n*

as·cid·i·an \ə-'sid-ē-ən\ *n* **:** any of an order (Ascidiacea) of simple or compound tunicates; *broadly* **:** TUNICATE

as·cid·i·um \ə-'sid-ē-əm\ *n, pl* **as·cid·ia** \-ē-ə\ [NL, fr. Gk *askidion*, dim. of *askos* wineskin, bladder] **:** a pitcher-shaped or flask-shaped organ or appendage of a plant

as·ci·tes \ə-'sīt-ēz\ *n* [ME *aschytes*, fr. LL *ascites*, fr. Gk *askitēs*, fr. *askos*] **:** accumulation of serous fluid in the abdomen — **as·cit·ic** \-'sit-ik\ *adj*

as·cle·pi·ad \ə-'sklē-pē-əd, a-, -,ad\ *n* [deriv. of Gk *asklēpiad-*, *asklēpias* swallowwort] **:** MILKWEED

As·cle·pi·us \-'sklē-pē-əs\ *n* [Gk *Asklēpios*] **:** the god of medicine in Greek mythology

as·co·carp \'as-kə-,kärp\ *n* **:** the mature fruiting body of an ascomycetous fungus; *broadly* **:** such a body with its enclosed asci, spores, and paraphyses — **as·co·car·pous** \,as-kə-'kär-pəs\ *adj*

as·co·go·ni·um \,as-kə-'gō-nē-əm\ *n, pl* **as·co·go·nia** \-nē-ə\ [NL, fr. *asc-* + Gk *gonos* procreation — more at GON-] **:** the fertile basal often one-celled portion of an archicarp; *broadly* **:** ARCHICARP

as·co·my·cete \,as-kō-'mī-,sēt, -,mī-'sēt\ *n* [deriv. of Gk *askos* + *mykēt-*, *mykēs* fungus; akin to L *mucus*] **:** any of a class (Ascomycetes) of higher fungi (as yeasts, molds) with septate hyphae and spores formed in asci — **as·co·my·ce·tous** \-,mī-'sēt-əs\ *adj*

ascor·bic acid \ə-,skȯr-bik-\ *n* [*a-* + NL *scorbutus* scurvy — more at SCORBUTIC] **:** VITAMIN C

as·co·spore \'as-kə-,spō(ə)r, -,spȯ(ə)r\ *n* **:** one of the spores contained in an ascus — **as·co·spor·ic** \,as-kə-'spōr-ik, -'spȯr-\ *or* **as·co·spo·rous** \-'spōr-əs, -'spȯr-; a-'skäs-pə-rəs\ *adj*

as·cot \'as-kət, -,kät\ *n* [*Ascot* Heath, racetrack near Ascot, England] **:** a broad neck scarf that is looped under the chin and sometimes pinned

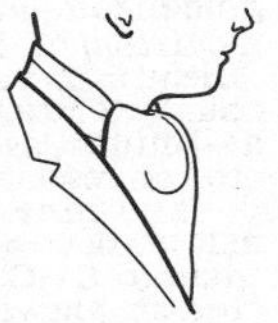

ascot

as·crib·able \ə-'skrī-bə-bəl\ *adj* **:** capable of being ascribed **:** ATTRIBUTABLE

as·cribe \ə-'skrīb\ *vt* [ME *ascriven*, fr. MF *ascrivre*, fr. L *ascribere*, fr. *ad-* + *scribere* to write — more at SCRIBE] **:** to refer to a supposed cause, source, or author **:** ATTRIBUTE

syn ATTRIBUTE, ASSIGN, IMPUTE, REFER, CREDIT: ASCRIBE suggests an inferring or conjecturing of cause, quality, authorship; ATTRIBUTE suggests less tentativeness than ASCRIBE, less definiteness than ASSIGN; ASSIGN implies ascribing with certainty or after deliberation; IMPUTE suggests ascribing something that brings discredit by way of accusation or blame; REFER suggests assigning a thing to a class or to an origin or cause; CREDIT implies ascribing a thing or esp. an action to a person or other thing as its agent, source, or explanation

as·crip·tion \ə-'skrip-shən\ *n* [LL *ascription-*, *ascriptio*, fr. L, written addition, fr. *ascriptus*, pp. of *ascribere*] **:** the act of ascribing **:** ATTRIBUTION

as·cus \'as-kəs\ *n, pl* **as·ci** \'as-,(k)ī, -,kē\ [NL, fr. Gk *askos* wineskin, bladder] **:** the membranous oval or tubular spore sac of an ascomycete

as·dic \'az-(,)dik\ *n* [*A*nti-*S*ubmarine *D*etection *I*nvestigation *C*ommittee] **:** SONAR

-ase \,ās, -,āz\ *n suffix* [F, fr. *diastase*] **:** enzyme ⟨prote*ase*⟩

asep·sis \(')ā-'sep-səs, ə-\ *n* [NL] **:** the condition of being aseptic **:** the methods of making or keeping aseptic

asep·tic \-'sep-tik\ *adj* [ISV] **1 :** preventing infection; *also* **:** free or freed from pathogenic microorganisms **2 a :** lacking vitality, emotion, or warmth **b :** DETACHED, OBJECTIVE **c :** CLEANSING, PURIFYING — **asep·ti·cal·ly** \-ti-k(ə-)lē\ *adv*

asex·u·al \(')ā-'seksh-(ə-)wəl, -'sek-shəl\ *adj* **1 :** lacking sex or functional sexual organs **2 :** produced without sexual action or differentiation — **asex·u·al·ly** \-ē\ *adv*

asexual generation *n* **:** the generation of an organism with alternation of generations that reproduce asexually

asexual reproduction *n* **:** reproduction without union of individuals or germ cells

as for *prep* **:** with regard to **:** CONCERNING ⟨*as for* me⟩

As·gard \'as-,gärd, 'az-\ *n* [ON *āsgarthr*] **:** the home of the gods in Norse mythology

as good as *adv* **:** in effect **:** PRACTICALLY ⟨*as good as* new⟩

1**ash** \'ash\ *n* [ME *asshe*, fr. OE *æsc;* akin to OHG *ask* ash, L *ornus* wild mountain ash] **1 :** any of a genus (*Fraxinus*) of trees of the olive family with pinnate leaves, thin furrowed bark, and gray branchlets **2 :** the tough elastic wood of an ash

2**ash** *n, often attrib* [ME *asshe*, fr. OE *asce;* akin to OHG *asca* ash, L *aridus* dry — more at ARDOR] **1 a:** the solid residue left when combustible material is thoroughly burned or is oxidized by chemical means **b :** fine particles of mineral matter from a volcanic vent **2** *pl* **:** RUINS **3** *pl* **:** the remains of the dead human body after cremation or disintegration **4 :** something that symbolizes grief, repentance, or humiliation **5** *pl* **:** deathly pallor

3**ash** *vt* **:** to convert into ash

ashamed \ə-'shāmd\ *adj* [ME, fr. OE *āscamod*, pp. of *ascamian* to shame, fr. *ā-* (perfective prefix) + *scamian* to shame — more at ABIDE, SHAME] **1 a :** feeling shame, guilt, or disgrace **b :** feeling inferior or unworthy **2 :** restrained by anticipation of shame — **asham·ed·ly** \-'shā-məd-lē\ *adv*

Ashan·ti \ə-'shant-ē, -'shänt-\ *n, pl* **Ashanti** *or* **Ashantis** [Ashanti *A*1*san*3*te*1] **1 :** a West African people of Ghana **2 :** the dialect of Akan spoken by the Ashanti people

ash can *n* **1 :** a metal receptacle for refuse **2** *slang* **:** DEPTH CHARGE

ash·can \'ash-,kan\ *adj, often cap* **:** depicting city life realistically ⟨~ school of artists⟩

1**ash·en** \'ash-ən\ *adj* **:** of, relating to, or made from the wood of the ash tree

2**ashen** *adj* **1 :** consisting of or resembling ashes **2 :** of the color of ashes **3 :** deadly pale **:** BLANCHED

Ash·er \'ash-ər\ *n* [Heb *Āshēr*] **:** a son of Jacob and ancestor of one of the tribes of Israel

ashe·rah \ə-'shir-ə\ *n, pl* **ashe·rim** \-əm\ *or* **asherahs** *often cap* [Heb *ăshērāh*] **:** a tree or pole found beside the altar in a Canaanite high place and held to be sacred to the goddess Asherah

Ash·ke·nazi \,äsh-kə-'näz-ē\ *n, pl* **Ash·ke·naz·im** \-'naz-əm\ [Heb *Ashkĕnāzī*] **:** a member of one of the two great divisions of Jews comprising the eastern European Yiddish-speaking Jews — **Ash·ke·naz·ic** \-'naz-ik\ *adj*

ash·lar \'ash-lər\ *n* [ME *asheler*, fr. MF *aisselier* a traverse beam, fr. OF, fr. *ais* board, fr. L *axis*, alter. of *assis*] **1 :** hewn or squared stone; *also* **:** masonry of such stone **2 :** a thin squared and dressed stone for facing

ashore \ə-'shō(ə)r, -'shȯ(ə)r\ *adv* (*or adj*) **:** on or to the shore

ash·ram \'äsh-rəm\ *n* [Skt *āśrama*, fr. *ā* toward + *śrama* religious exercise] **1 :** a secluded dwelling of a Hindu sage or the group of disciples he instructs there **2 :** a religious retreat

Ash·to·reth \'ash-tə-,reth\ *n* [Heb *'Ashtōreth*] **:** ASTARTE

Ashur \'ä-,shu̇(ə)r\ *n* [Assyrian *Ashūr*] **:** the chief deity of the Assyrian pantheon

Ash Wednesday *n* **:** the first day of Lent

ashy \'ash-ē\ *adj* **1 :** of or relating to ashes **2 :** deadly pale

Asian \'ā-zhən, -shən\ *adj* **:** of, relating to, or characteristic of the continent of Asia or its people — **Asian** *n*
Asian influenza *n* **:** influenza caused by a mutant strain of the influenza virus
Asi·at·ic \,ā-zhē-'at-ik\ *adj* **:** ASIAN — often taken to be offensive — **Asiatic** *n*
Asiatic cholera *n* **:** a destructive cholera of Asiatic origin caused by a bacterium (*Vibrio comma*)
[1]**aside** \ə-'sīd\ *adv* **1 :** to or toward the side ⟨stepped ~⟩ **2 :** out of the way **:** AWAY **3 :** out of consideration ⟨jesting ~⟩
[2]**aside** *prep, obs* **:** BEYOND, PAST
[3]**aside** *n* **1 :** words meant to be inaudible to someone; *esp* **:** an actor's words heard by the audience but supposedly not by other characters on stage **2 :** a straying from the theme **:** DIGRESSION
aside from *prep* **1 :** in addition to **:** BESIDES **2 :** except for
as if *conj* **1 :** as it would be if ⟨it was *as if* he had lost his last friend⟩ **2 :** as one would do if ⟨he ran *as if* ghosts were chasing him⟩ **3 :** THAT ⟨it seemed *as if* the day would never end⟩
as·i·nine \'as-ᵊn-,īn\ *adj* [L *asininus*, fr. *asinus* ass] **1 :** of, relating to, or resembling an ass **2 :** STUPID, OBSTINATE **syn** see SIMPLE — **as·i·nine·ly** *adv* — **as·i·nin·i·ty** \,as-ᵊn-'in-ət-ē\ *n*
ask \'ask\ *vb* **asked** \'as(k)t\ **ask·ing** [ME *asken*, fr. OE *āscian;* akin to OHG *eiscōn* to ask, L *aeruscare* to beg] *vt* **1 a :** to call on for an answer **b :** to put a question about **c :** SPEAK, UTTER ⟨~ a question⟩ **2 a :** to make a request of **:** BEG **b :** to make a request for ⟨she ~*ed* help from her teacher⟩ **3 :** to call for **:** REQUIRE **4 :** to set as a price **5 :** INVITE ~ *vi* **1 :** to seek information **2 :** to make a request ⟨~*ed* for food⟩ **3 :** LOOK — often used in the phrase *ask for trouble* — **ask·er** *n*
syn QUESTION, INTERROGATE, QUERY, INQUIRE: ASK implies no more than the putting of a question; QUESTION suggests the asking of series of questions; it may imply a challenging of truth or correctness; INTERROGATE suggests formal or official systematic questioning; QUERY implies a desire for authoritative information or confirmation or for the resolution of a doubt; INQUIRE implies a searching for facts or for truth often specifically by asking questions
syn ASK, REQUEST, SOLICIT mean to seek to obtain by making one's wants known. ASK implies merely the statement of the desire; REQUEST implies greater formality and courtesy and the expectation of an affirmative response; SOLICIT suggests a calling attention to one's wants or desires in the hope of having them satisfied
askance \ə-'skan(t)s\ *or* **askant** \-'skant\ *adv* [origin unknown] **1 :** with a side glance **:** OBLIQUELY **2 :** with disapproval or distrust
askew \ə-'skyü\ *adv (or adj)* [prob. fr. *a-* + *skew*] **:** AWRY, AMISS
[1]**aslant** \ə-'slant\ *adv* **:** in a slanting direction **:** OBLIQUELY
[2]**aslant** *prep* **:** over or across in a slanting direction
[1]**asleep** \ə-'slēp\ *adj* **1 :** SLEEPING **2 :** DEAD **3 :** lacking sensation **:** NUMB **4 :** INACTIVE, SLUGGISH
[2]**asleep** *adv* **1 :** into a state of sleep **2 :** into the sleep of death **3 :** into inactivity or sluggishness
as long as *conj* **1 :** provided that ⟨can do as they like *as long as* they have a B average⟩ **2 :** inasmuch as **:** SINCE ⟨*as long as* you're going, I'll go too⟩
[1]**aslope** \ə-'slōp\ *adj* **:** SLOPING, SLANTING
[2]**aslope** *adv* **:** in a sloping or slanting direction
As·mo·de·us \,az-mə-'dē-əs\ *n* [LL *Asmodaeus*, fr. Gk *Asmodaios*, fr. Heb *Ashmadhai*] **:** an evil spirit in Jewish demonology
aso·cial \(')ā-'sō-shəl\ *adj* **1 :** inconsiderate of others **:** SELFISH **2 :** SOLITARY, WITHDRAWN
as of *prep* **:** ON, AT, DURING, FROM ⟨takes effect *as of* July 1⟩
[1]**asp** \'asp\ *n* [ME] **:** ASPEN
[2]**asp** *n* [ME *aspis*, fr. L, fr. Gk] **:** a small venomous snake of Egypt variously identified as the cerastes or a small African cobra (*Naja haje*)
as·par·a·gine \ə-'spar-ə-,jēn\ *n* [F, fr. L *asparagus*] **:** a white crystalline amino acid $C_4H_8N_2O_3$ found in most plants
as·par·a·gus \ə-'spar-ə-gəs\ *n* [NL, genus name, fr. L, asparagus plant, fr. Gk *asparagos;* akin to Gk *spargan* to swell — more at SPARK] **:** any of a genus (*Asparagus*) of Old World perennial plants of the lily family having much-branched stems, minute scalelike leaves, and linear cladophylls; *esp* **:** one (*A. officinalis*) widely cultivated for its edible young shoots
as·par·tic acid \ə-,spärt-ik-\ *n* [ISV, irreg. fr. L *asparagus*] **:** a crystalline amino acid $C_4H_7NO_4$ found esp. in plants
as·pect \'as-,pekt\ *n* [ME, fr. L *aspectus*, fr. *aspectus*, pp. of *aspicere* to look at, fr. *ad-* + *specere* to look — more at SPY] **1 a :** the position of planets or stars with respect to one another held by astrologers to influence human affairs **b :** a position facing a particular direction **:** EXPOSURE **c :** the manner of presentation of a plane to a fluid through which it is moving or to a current **2 a :** a particular status or phase in which something appears or may be regarded ⟨studied every ~ of the question⟩ **b :** MIEN, AIR **3** *archaic* **:** an act of looking **:** GAZE **4 a :** the nature of the action of a verb as to its beginning, duration, completion, or repetition and without reference to its position in time **b :** a set of inflected verb forms that indicate aspect **syn** see PHASE — **as·pec·tu·al** \a-'spek-chə(-wə)l, -'speksh-wəl\ *adj*
aspect ratio *n* **:** the ratio of the width of a television image to its height
as·pen \'as-pən\ *n* [alter of ME *asp*, fr. OE *æspe;* akin to OHG *aspa* aspen, Latvian *apsa*] **:** any of several poplars (esp. *Populus tremula* of Europe and *P. tremuloides* and *P. grandidentata* of No. America) with leaves that flutter in the lightest wind on account of their flattened petioles — **aspen** *adj*
as·per·ges \ə-'spər-(,)jēz\ *n* [L, thou wilt sprinkle, fr. *aspergere*] **:** a ceremony of sprinkling altar, clergy, and people with holy water
as·per·gil·lo·sis \,as-pər-(,)jil-'ō-səs\ *n* **:** infection with or disease caused (as in poultry) by molds (genus *Aspergillus*)
as·per·gil·lum \,as-pər-'jil-əm\ *n, pl* **as·per·gil·la** \-'jil-ə\ *or* **aspergillums** [NL, fr. L *aspergere*] **:** a brush or perforated globe used for sprinkling holy water
as·per·gil·lus \-'jil-əs\ *n, pl* **as·per·gil·li** \-'jil-,ī\ [NL, genus name, fr. *aspergillum*] **:** any of a genus (*Aspergillus*) of ascomycetous fungi with branched radiate sporophores including many common molds
as·per·i·ty \a-'sper-ət-ē, ə-\ *n* [ME *asprete*, fr. OF *aspreté*, fr. *aspre* rough, fr. L *asper*] **1 :** RIGOR, SEVERITY **2 a :** roughness of surface **:** UNEVENNESS **b** *obs* **:** SOURNESS **c :** roughness of sound **3 :** roughness of manner or of temper **:** HARSHNESS **syn** see ACRIMONY
as·perse \ə-'spərs, a-\ *vt* [L *aspersus*, pp. of *aspergere*, fr. *ad-* + *spargere* to scatter] **1 :** SPRINKLE; *esp* **:** to sprinkle with holy water **2 :** to vilify with injurious charges **syn** see MALIGN
as·per·sion \ə-'spər-zhən, -shən\ *n* **1 :** a sprinkling with water esp. in religious ceremonies **2 a :** the act of calumniating **:** DEFAMATION **b :** a calumnious expression **syn** see ANIMADVERSION
as·phalt \'as-,fȯlt\ *or* **as·phal·tum** \as-'fȯl-təm\ *n* [ME *aspalt*, fr. LL *aspaltus*, fr. Gk *asphaltos*] **1 :** a brown to black bituminous substance that is found in natural beds and is also obtained as a residue in petroleum or coal-tar refining and consists chiefly of hydrocarbons **2 :** an asphaltic composition used for pavements and as a waterproof cement — **as·phal·tic** \as-'fȯl-tik\ *adj*
as·phal·tite \'as-,fȯl-,tīt\ *n* **:** a native asphalt occurring in vein deposits below the surface of the ground
aspher·ic \(')ā-'sfi(ə)r-ik, -'sfer-\ *adj* **:** departing slightly from the spherical form ⟨~ optical surface⟩ — **aspher·i·cal** \-'sfir-i-kəl, -'sfer-\ *adj*
as·pho·del \'as-fə-,del\ *n* [L *asphodelus*, fr. Gk *asphodelos*] **:** any of various Old World usu. perennial herbs (esp. genera *Asphodelus* and *Asphodeline*) of the lily family that bear their flowers in long erect racemes
as·phyx·ia \as-'fik-sē-ə\ *n* [NL, fr. Gk, stopping of the pulse, fr. *a-* + *sphyzein* to throb] **:** a lack of oxygen or excess of carbon dioxide in the body usu. caused by interruption of breathing and causing unconsciousness
as·phyx·i·ate \-sē-,āt\ *vt* **:** to cause asphyxia in; *also* **:** to kill or make unconscious through want of adequate oxygen, presence of noxious agents, or other obstruction to normal breathing ~ *vi* **:** to become asphyxiated — **as·phyx·i·a·tion** \(,)as-,fik-sē-'ā-shən\ *n* — **as·phyx·i·a·tor** \as-'fik-sē-,āt-ər\ *n*
[1]**as·pic** \'as-pik\ *n* [MF, alter. of *aspe*, fr. L *aspis*] *obs* **:** [2]ASP
[2]**aspic** *n* [F, lit., asp] **:** a savory jelly of fish or meat stock used cold to garnish meat or fish or to make a mold of meat, fish, or vegetables
as·pi·dis·tra \,as-pə-'dis-trə\ *n* [NL, irreg. fr. Gk *aspid-, aspis* shield] **:** an Asiatic plant (*Aspidistra lurida*) of the lily family with large basal leaves that is often grown as a foliage plant
[1]**as·pi·rant** \'as-p(ə-)rənt, ə-'spī-rənt\ *n* **:** one who aspires
[2]**aspirant** *adj* **:** ASPIRING
[1]**as·pi·rate** \'as-pə-,rāt\ *vt* [L *aspiratus*, pp. of *aspirare*] **1 :** to pronounce (a vowel or word) with an initial *h*-sound **2 a :** to draw by suction **b :** to remove (as blood) by aspiration
[2]**as·pi·rate** \'as-p(ə-)rət\ *n* **1 :** an independent sound \h\ or a character (as the letter *h*) representing it **2 :** a consonant having as its final element aspiration in the same syllable **3 :** material removed by aspiration
as·pi·ra·tion \,as-pə-'rā-shən, -(,)pir-'ā-\ *n* **1 :** the pronunciation or addition of an aspirate; *also* **:** the aspirate or its symbol **2 :** a drawing of something in, out, up, or through by or as if by suction: as **a :** the withdrawal of fluid from the body **b :** the taking of foreign matter into the lungs with the respiratory current **3 a :** a strong desire to achieve something high or great **b :** an object of such desire **syn** see AMBITION
as·pi·ra·tor \'as-pə-,rāt-ər\ *n* **:** an apparatus for producing suction or moving or collecting materials by suction; *esp* **:** a hollow tubular instrument connected with a partial vacuum and used to remove fluid or tissue or foreign bodies from the body
as·pire \ə-'spī(ə)r\ *vi* [ME *aspiren*, fr. MF or L; MF *aspirer*, fr. L *aspirare*, lit., to breathe upon, fr. *ad-* + *spirare* to breathe] **1 :** to desire a lofty object **2 :** ASCEND, SOAR — **as·pir·er** *n*
as·pi·rin \'as-p(ə-)rən\ *n, pl* **aspirin** *or* **aspirins** [ISV, fr. *acetyl* + *spiraeic acid* (former name of salicylic acid), fr. NL *Spiraea*, genus of shrubs — more at SPIREA] **1 :** a white crystalline derivative $C_9H_8O_4$ of salicylic acid used for relief of pain and fever **2 :** a tablet of aspirin
as regards *or* **as respects** *prep* **:** in regard to **:** with respect to
ass \'as\ *n* [ME, fr. OE *assa*, perh. fr. OIr *asan*, fr. L *asinus*] **1 :** any of several hardy gregarious mammals (genus *Equus*) that are smaller than the horse, have long ears, and include one domesticated form (*E. asinus*) used as a beast of burden **2 :** a stupid, obstinate, or perverse person
as·sa·fet·i·da *or* **as·sa·foe·ti·da** *var of* ASAFETIDA
as·sai \ä-'sī\ *adv* [It, fr. (assumed) VL *ad satis* enough — more at ASSET] **:** VERY — used with tempo direction in music ⟨allegro ~⟩
as·sail \ə-'sā(ə)l\ *vt* [ME *assailen*, fr. OF *asaillir*, fr. (assumed) VL *assalire*, alter. of L *assilire* to leap upon, fr. *ad-* + *salire* to leap] **:** to attack violently with blows or words **syn** see ATTACK — **as·sail·able** \-'sā-lə-bəl\ *adj* — **as·sail·ant** \-lənt\ *n*
As·sam·ese \,as-ə-'mēz, -'mēs\ *n, pl* **Assamese** **1 :** a native or inhabitant of Assam, India **2 :** the Indic language of Assam
as·sas·sin \ə-'sas-ᵊn\ *n* [ML *assassinus*, fr. Ar *ḥashshāshīn*, pl. of *ḥashshāsh* one addicted to hashish] **1** *cap* **:** one of a secret order of Muslims that at the time of the Crusades terrorized Christians and other enemies by secret murder committed under the influence of hashish **2 :** MURDERER; *esp* **:** one that murders either for hire or from fanatical motives
as·sas·si·nate \ə-'sas-ᵊn-,āt\ *vt* **1 :** to murder by sudden or secret attack **2 :** to injure or destroy unexpectedly and treacherously **syn** see KILL — **as·sas·si·na·tion** \ə-,sas-ᵊn-'ā-shən\ *n*
assassin bug *n* **:** a predaceous bug (family Reduviidae) living mostly on other insects though a few suck blood **:** CONENOSE
[1]**as·sault** \ə-'sȯlt\ *n* [ME *assaut*, fr. OF, fr. (assumed) VL *assaltus*, fr. *assaltus*, pp. of *assalire*] **1 :** a violent physical or verbal attack **2 a :** an apparently violent attempt or a willful offer with force or violence to do hurt to another without the actual doing of the hurt threatened (as by lifting the fist in a threatening manner) — compare BATTERY 1b **b :** RAPE
[2]**assault** *vt* **1 :** to make an assault upon **2 :** RAPE ~ *vi* **:** to make an assault **syn** see ATTACK
assault boat *n* **:** a small portable boat that is used in an amphibious military attack or in land warfare for crossing rivers or lakes
[1]**as·say** \'as-,ā, a-'sā\ *n* [ME, fr. OF *essai*, *assai* test, effort — more at ESSAY] **1** *archaic* **:** TRIAL, ATTEMPT **2 :** examination and determination as to characteristics (as weight, measure, quality) **3 :** analysis (as of an ore or drug) to determine the presence, absence, or quantity of one or more components **4 :** a substance to be assayed; *also* **:** the tabulated result of assaying
[2]**as·say** \a-'sā, 'as-,ā\ *vt* **1 :** TRY, ATTEMPT **2 a :** to analyze (as an ore) for one or more valuable components **b :** ESTIMATE ~ *vi* **:** to prove up in an assay — **as·say·er** *n*
as·se·gai *or* **as·sa·gai** \'as-i-,gī\ *n* [deriv. of Ar *az-zaghāya* the

assegai, fr. *al-* the + *zaghāya* assegai] : a slender hardwood spear or light javelin usu. tipped with iron and used in southern Africa

as·sem·blage \ə-'sem-blij, *for 3 also* ,a-,säm-'bläzh\ *n* **1** : a collection of persons or things : GATHERING **2** : the act of assembling : the state of being assembled **3 a** : an artistic composition made from scraps, junk, and odds and ends (as of paper, cloth, wood, stone, or metal) **b** : the art of making assemblages

as·sem·ble \ə-'sem-bəl\ *vb* **as·sem·bling** \-b(ə-)liŋ\ [ME *assemblen*, fr. OF *assembler*, fr. (assumed) VL *assimulare*, fr. L *ad-* + *simul* together — more at SAME] *vt* **1** : to collect into one place or group : CONVOKE **2** : to fit together the parts of ~ *vi* : to meet together : CONVENE **syn** see GATHER — **as·sem·bler** \-b(ə-)lər\ *n*

as·sem·bly \ə-'sem-blē\ *n* [ME *assemblee*, fr. MF, fr. OF, fr. *assembler*] **1** : a company of persons gathered for deliberation and legislation, worship, or entertainment **2** *cap* : a legislative body; *specif* : the lower house of a legislature **3** : ASSEMBLAGE **4** : a signal given by drum, bugle, trumpet, or all field music for troops to assemble or fall in **5 a** : the fitting together of manufactured parts into a complete machine, structure, or unit of a machine **b** : a collection of parts so assembled

assembly line *n* : an arrangement of machines, equipment, and workers in which work passes from operation to operation in direct line until the product is assembled

as·sem·bly·man \ə-'sem-blē-mən\ *n* : a member of an assembly

1**as·sent** \ə-'sent\ *vi* [ME *assenten*, fr. OF *assenter*, fr. L *assentari*, fr. *assentire*, fr. *ad-* + *sentire* to feel] : AGREE, CONCUR

syn ASSENT, CONSENT, ACCEDE, ACQUIESCE, AGREE, SUBSCRIBE mean to concur with what someone else has proposed. ASSENT implies an act involving the understanding or judgment and applies to propositions or opinions; CONSENT involves the will or feelings and indicates compliance with what is requested or desired; ACCEDE implies a yielding, often under pressure, of assent or consent; ACQUIESCE implies tacit acceptance or forbearance of opposition; AGREE usu. implies previous difference of opinion or precedent attempts at persuasion; SUBSCRIBE implies not only consent or assent but hearty approval and active support

2**assent** *n* : an act of assenting : ACQUIESCENCE, AGREEMENT

as·sen·ta·tion \,as-ᵊn-'tā-shən, ,as-,en-\ *n* : ready assent esp. when insincere or obsequious

as·sert \ə-'sərt\ *vt* [L *assertus*, pp. of *asserere*, fr. *ad-* + *serere* to join — more at SERIES] **1** : to state or declare positively **2 a** : MAINTAIN, VINDICATE **b** : POSIT, POSTULATE

syn DECLARE, AFFIRM, PROTEST, AVOW: ASSERT implies stating confidently without need for proof or regard for evidence; DECLARE adds to ASSERT an implication of open or public statement; AFFIRM implies conviction of truth and willingness to stand by one's statement because of evidence, experience, or faith; PROTEST emphasizes affirming in the face of denial or doubt; AVOW stresses frank declaration and acknowledgment of personal responsibility for the statement being made **syn** see in addition MAINTAIN — **assert oneself** : to compel recognition esp. of one's rights

as·ser·tion \ə-'sər-shən\ *n* : the act of asserting; *also* : AFFIRMATION, DECLARATION

as·sert·ive \ə-'sərt-iv\ *adj* : disposed to bold or confident assertion **syn** see AGGRESSIVE — **as·sert·ive·ly** *adv* — **as·sert·ive·ness** *n*

asses *pl of* AS

as·sess \ə-'ses\ *vt* [ME *assessen*, prob. fr. ML *assessus*, pp. of *assidēre*, fr. L, to sit beside, assist in the office of a judge — more at ASSIZE] **1** : to determine the rate or amount of (as a tax) **2 a** : to impose (as a tax) according to an established rate **b** : to subject to a tax, charge, or levy **3** : to make an official valuation of (property) for the purposes of taxation **4** : to determine the importance, size, or value of **syn** see ESTIMATE — **as·sess·able** \-'ses-ə-bəl\ *adj*

as·sess·ment \ə-'ses-mənt\ *n* **1** : the act of assessing : APPRAISAL **2** : the amount assessed

as·ses·sor \ə-'ses-ər\ *n* **1** : ASSISTANT, COADJUTOR **2** : an official who assesses property for taxation

as·set \'as-,et\ *n* [back-formation fr. *assets*, sing., sufficient property to pay debts and legacies, fr. AF *asetz*, fr. OF *assez* enough, fr. (assumed) VL *ad satis*, fr. L *ad* to + *satis* enough — more at AT, SAD] **1** *pl* **a** : the property of a deceased person subject by law to the payment of his debts and legacies **b** : the entire property of all sorts of a person, association, corporation, or estate applicable or subject to the payment of his or its debts **2** : ADVANTAGE, RESOURCE **3** *pl* : the items on a balance sheet showing the book value of property owned

as·sev·er·ate \ə-'sev-ə-,rāt\ *vt* [L *asseveratus*, pp. of *asseverare*, fr. *ad-* + *severus* severe] : to affirm or aver positively or earnestly — **as·sev·er·a·tion** \ə-,sev-ə-'rā-shən\ *n*

as·si·du·ity \,as-ə-'d(y)ü-ət-ē\ *n* : the quality or state of being assiduous : DILIGENCE

as·sid·u·ous \ə-'sij-(ə-)wəs\ *adj* [L *assiduus*, fr. *assidēre*] : steadily attentive : DILIGENT **syn** see BUSY — **as·sid·u·ous·ly** *adv* — **as·sid·u·ous·ness** *n*

1**as·sign** \ə-'sīn\ *vt* [ME *assignen*, fr. OF *assigner*, fr. L *assignare*, fr. *ad-* + *signare* to mark, fr. *signum* mark, sign] **1** : to transfer (property) to another esp. in trust or for the benefit of creditors **2 a** : to appoint to a post or duty **b** : PRESCRIBE ⟨~ the lesson⟩ **3** : to fix authoritatively : SPECIFY ⟨~ a limit⟩ **4** : to ascribe as motive or reason **syn** see ALLOT, ASCRIBE

2**assign** *n* : ASSIGNEE

as·sign·abil·i·ty \ə-,sī-nə-'bil-ət-ē\ *n* : the quality or state of being assignable

as·sign·able \ə-'sī-nə-bəl\ *adj* : capable of being assigned — **as·sign·ably** \-blē\ *adv*

as·si·gnat \,as-,ēn-'yä, 'as-ig-,nat\ *n* [F, fr. L *assignatus*, pp. of *assignare*] : a bill issued as currency by the French Revolutionary government (1790–95) on the security of expropriated lands

as·sig·na·tion \,as-ig-'nā-shən\ *n* **1** : the act of assigning or the assignment made; *esp* : ALLOTMENT **2** : TRYST

as·sign·ee \ə-,sī-'nē, ,as-,ī-; ,as-ə-'nē\ *n* **1** : a person to whom an assignment is made **2** : a person appointed to act for another **3** : a person to whom a right or property is legally transferred

as·sign·er \ə-'sī-nər\ *or* **as·sign·or** \ə-'sī-nər; ə-,sī-'nȯ(ə)r, ,as-,ī-; ,as-ə-'nȯ(ə)r\ *n* : one that assigns or makes an assignment

as·sign·ment \ə-'sīn-mənt\ *n* **1** : the act of assigning **2** : a post or duty to which one is assigned : APPOINTMENT **3** : the transfer of property; *esp* : the transfer of property to be held in trust or to be used for the benefit of creditors **syn** see TASK

as·sim·i·la·bil·i·ty \ə-,sim-ə-lə-'bil-ət-ē\ *n* : the quality or state of being assimilable

as·sim·i·la·ble \ə-'sim-ə-lə-bəl\ *adj* : capable of being assimilated

1**as·sim·i·late** \ə-'sim-ə-,lāt\ *vb* [ML *assimilatus*, pp. of *assimilare*, fr. L *assimulare* to make similar, fr. *ad-* + *simulare* to make similar, simulate] *vt* **1 a** : to take in and appropriate as nourishment : absorb into the system **b** : to take into the mind and thoroughly comprehend **2 a** : to make similar **b** : to alter by assimilation **c** : to absorb into the cultural tradition of a population or group **3** : COMPARE, LIKEN ~ *vi* : to become assimilated **syn** see ABSORB — **as·sim·i·la·tor** \-,lāt-ər\ *n*

2**as·sim·i·late** \-lət, -,lāt\ *n* : something that is assimilated

as·sim·i·la·tion \ə-,sim-ə-'lā-shən\ *n* **1 a** : an act, process, or instance of assimilating **b** : the state of being assimilated **2** : the incorporation or conversion of nutrients into protoplasm that in animals follows digestion and absorption and in higher plants involves both photosynthesis and root absorption **3** : adaptation of a sound to an adjacent sound ⟨in the word *cupboard* the \p\ sound of the word *cup* has undergone complete ~⟩

as·sim·i·la·tive \ə-'sim-ə-,lāt-iv\ *adj* : of, relating to, or causing assimilation

as·sim·i·la·to·ry \ə-'sim-(ə-)lə-,tōr-ē, -,tȯr-\ *adj* : ASSIMILATIVE

1**as·sist** \ə-'sist\ *vb* [MF or L; MF *assister* to help, stand by, fr. L *assistere*, fr. *ad-* + *sistere* to cause to stand; akin to L *stare* to stand — more at STAND] *vi* **1** : to give support or aid **2** : to be present as a spectator ~ *vt* : to give support or aid to : HELP **syn** see HELP

2**assist** *n* **1** : an act of assistance : AID **2** : the act of a player who by handling the ball (as in baseball) or passing the puck (as in hockey) enables a teammate to make a putout or score a goal

as·sis·tance \ə-'sis-tən(t)s\ *n* : the act of assisting or the aid supplied : SUPPORT

as·sis·tant \ə-'sis-tənt\ *n* : one who assists : HELPER; *also* : an auxiliary device or substance — **assistant** *adj*

as·size \ə-'sīz\ *n* [ME *assise*, fr. OF, session, settlement, fr. *asseoir* to seat, fr. (assumed) VL *assedēre*, fr. L *assidēre* to sit beside, assist in the office of a judge, fr. *ad-* + *sedēre* to sit — more at SIT] **1** : an enactment made by a legislative assembly : ORDINANCE **2 a** : a statute regulating weights and measures of articles sold in the market **b** : the regulation of the price of bread or ale by the price of grain **3** : a fixed or customary standard **4 a** : a judicial inquest **b** : an action to be decided by such an inquest, the writ for instituting it, or the verdict or finding rendered by the jury **5** *usu pl* **a** : the periodical sessions of the superior courts in English counties for trial of civil and criminal cases **b** : the time or place of holding such a court, the court itself, or a session of it

as·so·cia·ble \ə-'sō-sh(ē-)ə-bəl, -sē-ə-\ *adj* : capable of being associated, joined, or connected in thought

1**as·so·ci·ate** \ə-'sō-s(h)ē-,āt\ *vb* [ME *associat* associated, fr. L *associatus*, pp. of *associare* to unite, fr. *ad-* + *sociare* to join, fr. *socius* companion — more at SOCIAL] *vt* **1** : to join as a partner, friend, or companion **2** *obs* : to keep company with : ATTEND **3** : to join or connect together : COMBINE **4** : to bring together in any of various ways (as in memory or imagination) ~ *vi* **1** : to come together as partners, friends, or companions **2** : to combine or join with other parts : UNITE **syn** see JOIN

2**as·so·ciate** \ə-'sō-s(h)ē-ət, -shət, -s(h)ē-,āt\ *n* **1** : a fellow worker : PARTNER, COLLEAGUE **2** : COMPANION, COMRADE — **associate** *adj*

as·so·ci·a·tion \ə-,sō-sē-'ā-shən, -shē-\ *n* **1** : the act of associating : the state of being associated **2** : an organization of persons having a common interest : SOCIETY **3** : something linked in memory or imagination with a thing or person **4** : the process of forming mental connections or bonds between sensations, ideas, or memories **5** : the formation of polymers by linkage through hydrogen bonds **6** : a major unit in ecological community organization characterized by essential uniformity and usu. by two or more dominant species — **as·so·ci·a·tion·al** \-shnəl, -shən-ᵊl\ *adj*

association football *n* : SOCCER

as·so·cia·tive \ə-'sō-s(h)ē-,āt-iv, -shət-iv\ *adj* **1** : of or relating to association esp. of ideas or images **2** : dependent on or acquired by association or learning **3** : combining elements in such a manner that the result is independent of the grouping ⟨addition is an ~ operation⟩ — **as·so·cia·tive·ly** *adv*

as·soil \ə-'sȯi(ə)l\ *vt* [ME *assoilen*, fr. OF *assoldre*, fr. L *absolvere* to absolve] **1** *archaic* : ABSOLVE, PARDON **2** *archaic* : ACQUIT, CLEAR **3** *archaic* : EXPIATE — **as·soil·ment** \-mənt\ *n*, *archaic*

as·so·nance \'as-ə-nən(t)s\ *n* [F, fr. L *assonare* to answer with the same sound, fr. *ad-* + *sonare* to sound — more at SOUND] **1** : resemblance of sound in words or syllables **2 a** : relatively close juxtaposition of similar sounds esp. of vowels **b** : repetition of vowels without repetition of consonants (as in *stony* and *holy*) used as an alternative to rhyme in verse — **as·so·nant** \-nənt\ *adj or n*

as soon as *conj* : immediately at or just after the time that

as·sort \ə-'sȯ(ə)rt\ *vb* [MF *assortir*, fr. *a-* (fr. L *ad-*) + *sorte* sort] *vt* **1** : to distribute into groups of a like kind : CLASSIFY **2** : to supply with an assortment or variety (as of goods) ~ *vi* **1** : to agree in kind : HARMONIZE **2** : to keep company : ASSOCIATE — **as·sort·a·tive** \ə-'sȯrt-ət-iv\ *adj* — **as·sort·er** *n*

as·sort·ed \ə-'sȯrt-əd\ *adj* **1** : consisting of various kinds **2** : MATCHED, SUITED ⟨an ill-*assorted* pair⟩

as·sort·ment \-'sȯ(ə)rt-mənt\ *n* **1** : the act of assorting : the state of being assorted **2** : a collection of assorted things or persons

as·suage \ə-'swāj\ *vt* [ME *aswagen*, fr. OF *assouagier*, fr. (assumed) VL *assuaviare*, fr. L *ad-* + *suavis* sweet — more at SWEET] **1** : to lessen the intensity of (pain) : EASE **2** : PACIFY, QUIET **3** : APPEASE, QUENCH **syn** see RELIEVE — **as·suage·ment** \-mənt\ *n*

as·sua·sive \ə-'swā-siv, -ziv\ *adj* : CALMING, SOOTHING

as·sume \ə-'süm\ *vt* [ME *assumen*, fr. L *assumere*, fr. *ad-* + *sumere* to take — more at CONSUME] **1 a** : to take up or in : RECEIVE **b** : to take into partnership, employment, or use **2 a** : to take to or upon oneself : UNDERTAKE **b** : to put on (clothing) : DON **3** : SEIZE, USURP **4** : to take in appearance only **5** : to take as granted or true : SUPPOSE **6** : to take over (the debts of another) as one's own

syn ASSUME, AFFECT, PRETEND, SIMULATE, FEIGN, COUNTERFEIT, SHAM mean to put on a false or deceptive appearance. ASSUME often implies a justifiable motive rather than an intent to deceive; AFFECT implies making a false show of possessing, using, or feeling; PRETEND

implies overt and sustained profession of what is known to be false or not genuinely believed or felt; SIMULATE suggests assuming the appearance of something (as an emotion) by imitating the signs of it; FEIGN implies more artful invention than PRETEND, less specific mimicry than SIMULATE; COUNTERFEIT implies achieving the highest degree of verisimilitude of any of these words; SHAM implies an obvious falseness that fools only the gullible

as·sum·ing *adj* **:** PRETENTIOUS, PRESUMPTUOUS

as·sump·sit \ə-'səm(p)-sət\ *n* [NL, he undertook, fr. *assumere* to undertake, fr. L] **1 a :** a common-law action alleging damage from a breach of agreement **b :** an action to recover damages for breach of contract or promise **2 :** a promise or contract not under seal on which an action of assumpsit may be brought

as·sump·tion \ə-'səm(p)-shən\ *n* [ME, fr. LL *assumption-, assumptio,* fr. L, taking up, fr. *assumptus,* pp. of *assumere*] **1 a :** the taking up of a person into heaven **b** *cap* **:** the church feast commemorating the Assumption of the Virgin Mary that is observed on August 15 **2 :** a taking to or upon oneself **3 :** the act of laying claim to or taking possession of **4 :** ARROGANCE, PRETENSION **5 a :** the supposition that something is true **b :** a fact or statement taken for granted **6 :** the taking over of debts of another

as·sump·tive \ə-'səm(p)-tiv\ *adj* **:** ASSUMED, ASSUMING; *also* **:** ARROGANT

as·sur·ance \ə-'shu̇r-ən(t)s\ *n* **1 :** the act of assuring **:** PLEDGE **2 :** the state of being sure or certain **3 :** SECURITY, SAFETY **4 :** the act of conveying or the instrument or other legal evidence of the conveyance of real property **5** *chiefly Brit* **:** INSURANCE **6 :** SELF-CONFIDENCE, SELF-RELIANCE **7 :** AUDACITY, PRESUMPTION **syn** see CERTAINTY, CONFIDENCE

as·sure \ə-'shu̇(ə)r\ *vt* [ME *assuren,* fr. MF *assurer,* fr. ML *assecurare,* fr. L *ad-* + *securus* secure] **1 :** to make safe (as from risks or against overthrow) **:** INSURE **2 :** to give confidence to **:** REASSURE **3 :** to make sure or certain **:** CONVINCE **4 :** to inform positively **5 :** to make certain the coming or attainment of **:** GUARANTEE **syn** see ENSURE

[1]**as·sured** \ə-'shu̇(ə)rd\ *adj* **1 a :** SAFE, SURE **b :** UNQUESTIONABLE, CERTAIN **c :** GUARANTEED **2 a :** CONFIDENT, SELF-POSSESSED **b :** COMPLACENT **3 :** CONVINCED — **as·sured·ly** \-'shu̇r-əd-lē, -'shu̇(ə)rd-\ *adv* — **as·sured·ness** \-'shu̇r-əd-nəs, -'shu̇(ə)rd-\ *n*

[2]**assured** *n, pl* **assured** *or* **assureds 1 :** the person in whose favor an insurance policy stands **2 :** a person who is insured

as·sur·er *or* **as·sur·or** \ə-'shu̇r-ər\ *n* **:** one that assures **:** INSURER

as·sur·gent \ə-'sər-jənt\ *adj* [L *assurgent-, assurgens,* prp. of *assurgere* to rise, fr. *ad-* + *surgere* to rise — more at SURGE] **:** ASCENDING, RISING; *esp* **:** ASCENDANT 1b

As·syr·i·an \ə-'sir-ē-ən\ *n* **1 :** a member of an ancient Semitic race forming the Assyrian nation **2 :** the Semitic language of the Assyrians — **Assyrian** *adj*

As·syr·i·ol·o·gist \ə-ˌsir-ē-'äl-ə-jəst\ *n* **:** a specialist in Assyriology

As·syr·i·ol·o·gy \-jē\ *n* **:** the science or study of the history, language, and antiquities of ancient Assyria

-ast \ˌast, əst\ *n suffix* [ME, fr. L *-astes,* fr. Gk *-astēs,* fr. verbs in *-azein*] **:** one connected with ⟨ecdysiast⟩

astar·board \ə-'stär-bərd\ *adv* **:** toward or on the starboard side

As·tar·te \ə-'stärt-ē\ *n* [L, fr. Gk *Astartē*] **:** the Phoenician goddess of fertility and of sexual love

astat·ic \(')ā-'stat-ik\ *adj* **1 :** not static **:** not stable or steady **2 :** having little or no tendency to take a fixed or definite position or direction — **astat·i·cal·ly** \-i-k(ə-)lē\ *adv* — **astat·i·cism** \-'stat-ə-ˌsiz-əm\ *n*

as·ta·tine \'as-tə-ˌtēn\ *n* [Gk *astatos* unsteady, fr. *a-* + *statos* standing, fr. *histanai* to cause to stand — more at STAND] **:** a radioactive halogen element discovered by bombarding bismuth with helium nuclei and also formed by radioactive decay — see ELEMENT table

as·ter \'as-tər\ *n* **1** [NL, genus name, fr. L, aster, fr. Gk *aster-, astēr* star, aster — more at STAR] **:** any of various chiefly fall-blooming leafy-stemmed composite herbs (*Aster* and closely related genera) with often showy heads containing tubular flowers or both tubular and ray flowers **2** [NL, fr. Gk *aster-, astēr*] **:** a system of gelated cytoplasmic rays typically arranged radially about a centrosome at either end of the mitotic spindle and sometimes persisting between mitoses

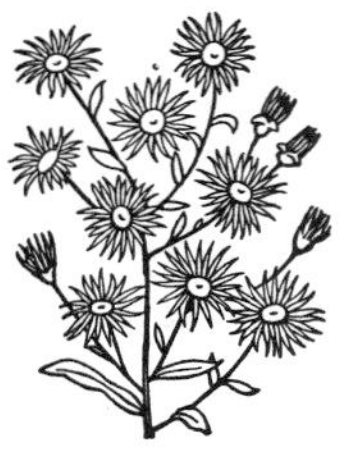
aster

[1]**-as·ter** \ˌas-tər, 'as-\ *n suffix* [ME, fr. L, suffix denoting partial resemblance] **:** one that is inferior, worthless, or not genuine ⟨critic*aster*⟩

[2]**-aster** *n comb form* [NL, fr. Gk *astēr*] **:** star ⟨di*aster*⟩

as·te·ria \a-'stir-ē-ə\ *n* [L, a precious stone, fr. Gk, fem. of *asterios* starry, fr. *aster-, astēr*] **:** a gem stone cut to show asterism

as·te·ri·at·ed \-ē-ˌāt-əd\ *adj* [Gk *asterios*] **:** exhibiting asterism (sense 2)

[1]**as·ter·isk** \'as-tə-ˌrisk\ *n* [LL *asteriscus,* fr. Gk *asteriskos,* lit., little star, dim. of *aster-, astēr*] **:** the character * used in printing or writing as a reference mark or an indication of the omission of letters or words

[2]**asterisk** *vt* **:** to mark with an asterisk **:** STAR

as·ter·ism \'as-tə-ˌriz-əm\ *n* [Gk *asterismos,* fr. *asterizein* to arrange in constellations, fr. *aster-, astēr*] **1 a :** CONSTELLATION **b :** a small group of stars **2 :** the optical phenomenon of a star-shaped figure exhibited by some crystals by reflected light (as in a star sapphire) or by transmitted light (as in some mica) **3 :** three asterisks arranged in the form of a pyramid (as * * * or * * *) esp. in order to direct attention to a following passage

astern \ə-'stərn\ *adv* **1 :** behind a ship or aircraft **:** in the rear **2 :** at or toward the stern of a ship or aircraft **3 :** stern foremost **:** BACKWARD

aster·nal \(')ā-'stərn-ᵊl\ *adj* **1 :** not attached to the sternum **2 :** having no sternum

[1]**as·ter·oid** \'as-tə-ˌrȯid\ *n* [Gk *asteroeidēs* starlike, fr. *aster-, astēr*] **1 :** one of thousands of small planets between Mars and Jupiter with diameters from a fraction of a mile to nearly 500 miles **2 :** STARFISH

[2]**asteroid** *adj* **1 :** resembling a star **2 :** of or resembling a starfish

as·the·nia \as-'thē-nē-ə\ *n* [NL, fr. Gk *astheneia,* fr. *asthenēs* weak, fr. *a-* + *sthenos* strength] **:** lack or loss of strength **:** DEBILITY

as·then·ic \-'then-ik\ *adj* **1 :** of, relating to, or exhibiting asthenia **:** WEAK **2 :** characterized by slender build and slight muscular development **:** ECTOMORPHIC

asth·ma \'az-mə\ *n* [ME *asma,* fr. ML, modif. of Gk *asthma*] **:** a condition of continuous or paroxysmal labored breathing accompanied by wheezing, a sense of constriction in the chest, and often attacks of coughing or gasping — **asth·mat·ic** \az-'mat-ik\ *adj or n* — **asth·mat·i·cal·ly** \-i-k(ə-)lē\ *adv*

as though *conj* **:** as if

as·tig·mat·ic \ˌas-tig-'mat-ik\ *adj* [*a-* + Gk *stigmat-, stigma* mark — more at STIGMA] **1 :** affected with, relating to, or correcting astigmatism **2 :** showing incapacity for observation or discrimination — **as·tig·mat·i·cal·ly** \-i-k(ə-)lē\ *adv*

astig·ma·tism \ə-'stig-mə-ˌtiz-əm\ *n* **1 :** a defect of an optical system (as a lens) in consequence of which rays from a point fail to meet in a focal point resulting in a blurred and imperfect image **2 :** a defect of vision due to astigmatism of the refractive system of the eye and esp. to corneal irregularity **3 :** distorted understanding suggestive of the blurred vision of an astigmatic person

astir \ə-'stər\ *adj* **1 :** exhibiting activity **2 :** being out of bed **:** UP

as to *prep* **1 :** with regard or reference to **:** as for **:** ABOUT ⟨at a loss *as to* how to explain the mistake⟩ **2 :** according to **:** BY ⟨graded *as to* size and color⟩

asto·ma·tal \(')ā-'stäm-ət-ᵊl, -'stō-mət-\ *adj* **:** lacking stomata

asto·ma·tous \-'stäm-ət-əs, -'stō-mət-\ *adj* **:** lacking a stoma

as·ton·ied \ə-'stän-ēd\ *adj* [ME, fr. pp. of *astonien*] *archaic* **:** DAZED, DISMAYED

as·ton·ish \ə-'stän-ish\ *vt* [prob. fr. earlier *astony* (fr. ME *astonen, astonien,* fr. OF *estoner,* fr. — assumed — VL *extonare,* fr. L *ex-* + *tonare* to thunder) + *-ish* (as in *abolish*)] **1** *obs* **:** to strike with sudden fear **2 :** to strike with sudden wonder **syn** see SURPRISE

as·ton·ish·ment \-mənt\ *n* **1 :** the state of being astonished; *also* **:** CONSTERNATION **2 :** a cause of amazement or wonder

[1]**as·tound** \ə-'stau̇nd\ *adj* [ME *astoned,* fr. pp. of *astonen*] *archaic* **:** ASTOUNDED

[2]**astound** *vb* **:** to fill with bewildered wonder **syn** see SURPRISE

astr- *or* **astro-** *comb form* [ME *astro-,* fr. OF, fr. L *astr-, astro-,* fr. Gk, fr. *astron* — more at STAR] **1 :** star **:** heavens **:** astronomical ⟨*astro*physics⟩ **2 :** aster of a cell ⟨*astro*sphere⟩

[1]**astrad·dle** \ə-'strad-ᵊl\ *adv* **:** on or above and extending onto both sides **:** ASTRIDE

[2]**astraddle** *prep* **:** with one leg on each side of **:** ASTRIDE

As·traea \a-'strē-ə\ *n* [L, fr. Gk *Astraia*] **:** the goddess of justice in Greek mythology

as·tra·gal \'as-tri-gəl\ *n* [L *astragalus,* fr. Gk *astragalos* anklebone, molding] **:** a narrow half-round molding — **as·trag·a·lar** \ə-'strag-ə-lər\ *adj*

as·trag·a·lus \ə-'strag-ə-ləs\ *n, pl* **as·trag·a·li** \-ˌlī, -ˌlē\ [NL, fr. Gk *astragalos*] **1 :** one of the proximal bones of the tarsus of the higher vertebrates — compare TALUS 1 **2 :** ASTRAGAL

as·tra·khan *or* **as·tra·chan** \'as-trə-kən, -ˌkan\ *n, often cap* [*Astrakhan,* U.S.S.R.] **1 :** karakul of Russian origin **2 :** a cloth with a usu. wool, curled, and looped pile resembling karakul

as·tral \'as-trəl\ *adj* [LL *astralis,* fr. L *astrum* star, fr. Gk *astron*] **1 a :** of or relating to the stars **b :** consisting of stars **:** STARRY **2 :** of or relating to a mitotic aster **3 :** of or consisting of a super-sensible substance held in theosophy to be next above the tangible world in refinement **4 :** VISIONARY; *also* **:** EXALTED — **as·tral·ly** \-trə-lē\ *adv*

astray \ə-'strā\ *adv* (*or adj*) [ME, fr. MF *estraié* wandering, fr. *estraier* to stray — more at STRAY] **1 :** off the right path or route **:** STRAYING **2 :** into error **:** MISTAKEN

[1]**astride** \ə-'strīd\ *adv* **1 :** with one leg on each side **2 :** with the legs stretched wide apart

[2]**astride** *prep* **1 :** on or above and with one leg on each side of **2 :** placed or lying on both sides of **3 :** SPANNING, BRIDGING

as·trin·gen·cy \ə-'strin-jən-sē\ *n* **:** the quality or state of being astringent

[1]**as·trin·gent** \ə-'strin-jənt\ *adj* [prob. fr. MF, fr. L *astringent-, astringens,* prp. of *astringere* to bind fast, fr. *ad-* + *stringere* to bind tight — more at STRAIN] **1 :** able to draw together the soft organic tissues **:** STYPTIC, PUCKERY ⟨~ lotions⟩ ⟨an ~ fruit⟩ **2 :** suggestive of an astringent effect upon tissue **:** AUSTERE; *also* **:** TONIC — **as·trin·gent·ly** *adv*

[2]**astringent** *n* **:** an astringent agent or substance

as·tro·cyte \'as-trə-ˌsīt\ *n* [ISV] **:** a star-shaped cell (as of the neuroglia) — **as·tro·cyt·ic** \ˌas-trə-'sit-ik\ *adj*

as·tro·dome \'as-trə-ˌdōm\ *n* [ISV] **:** a transparent dome in the upper surface of an airplane from within which the navigator makes celestial observations

as·tro·gate \'as-trə-ˌgāt\ *vb* [*astr-* + *-gate* (as in *navigate*)] **:** to navigate in interplanetary space — **as·tro·ga·tion** \ˌas-trə-'gā-shən\ *n* — **as·tro·ga·tor** \'as-trə-ˌgāt-ər\ *n*

as·tro·labe \'as-trə-ˌlāb\ *n* [ME, fr. MF & ML; MF, fr. ML *astrolabium,* fr. LGk *astrolabion,* dim. of Gk *astrolabos,* fr. *astr-* + *lambanein* to take] **:** a compact instrument used to observe the positions of celestial bodies before the invention of the sextant

as·trol·o·ger \ə-'sträl-ə-jər\ *n* **:** one who practices astrology

as·tro·log·i·cal \ˌas-trə-'läj-i-kəl\ *adj* **:** of or relating to astrology — **as·tro·log·i·cal·ly** \-k(ə-)lē\ *adv*

as·trol·o·gy \ə-'sträl-ə-jē\ *n* [ME *astrologie,* fr. MF, fr. L *astrologia,* fr. Gk, fr. *astr-* + *-logia* -logy] **1** *obs* **:** ASTRONOMY **2 :** the divination of the supposed influences of the stars upon human affairs and terrestrial events by their positions and aspects

as·tro·naut \'as-trə-ˌnȯt, -ˌnät\ *n* [*astr-* + *-naut* (as in *aeronaut*)] **:** a traveler in interplanetary space — **as·tro·nau·ti·cal** \ˌas-trə-'nȯt-i-kəl, -'nät-\ *adj* — **as·tro·nau·ti·cal·ly** \-k(ə-)lē\ *adv*

as·tro·nau·tics \-'nȯt-iks, -'nät-\ *n pl but sing or pl in constr* **1 :** the science of the construction and operation of vehicles for travel in interplanetary or interstellar space **2 :** ASTROGATION

as·tro·nav·i·ga·tion \ˌas-(ˌ)trō-ˌnav-ə-'gā-shən\ *n* **:** CELESTIAL NAVIGATION

as·tron·o·mer \ə-'strän-ə-mər\ *n* **:** one who is skilled in astronomy or who makes observations of celestial phenomena

as·tro·nom·i·cal \ˌas-trə-'näm-i-kəl\ *or* **as·tro·nom·ic** \-ik\ *adj* **1 :** of or relating to astronomy **2 :** enormously or inconceivably large ⟨~ figures⟩ — **as·tro·nom·i·cal·ly** \-i-k(ə-)lē\ *adv*

astronomical unit *n* **:** a unit of length used in astronomy equal to the mean distance of the earth from the sun or about 93 million miles

as·tron·o·my \ə-'strän-ə-mē\ *n* [ME *astronomie,* fr. OF, fr. L

astronomia, fr. Gk, fr. *astr-* + *-nomia* -nomy] **1 :** the science of the celestial bodies and of their magnitudes, motions, and constitution **2 :** a treatise on astronomy

as·tro·pho·tog·ra·phy \ˌas-(ˌ)trō-fə-ˈtäg-rə-fē\ *n* [ISV] **:** the application of photography to astronomical investigations

as·tro·phys·i·cal \ˌas-trə-ˈfiz-i-kəl\ *adj* **:** of or relating to astrophysics

as·tro·phys·i·cist \-ˈfiz-ə-səst\ *n* **:** a specialist in astrophysics

as·tro·phys·ics \-ˈfiz-iks\ *n pl but sing or pl in constr* [ISV] **:** a branch of astronomy dealing with the physical and chemical constitution of the celestial bodies

as·tro·sphere \ˈas-trə-ˌsfi(ə)r\ *n* [ISV] **1 :** CENTROSPHERE **2 :** an aster exclusive of the centrosome

as·tute \ə-ˈst(y)üt, a-\ *adj* [L *astutus*, fr. *astus* craft] **:** SAGACIOUS; *also* **:** WILY **syn** see SHREWD — **as·tute·ly** *adv* — **as·tute·ness** *n*

As·ty·a·nax \ə-ˈstī-ə-ˌnaks\ *n* [Gk] **:** a son of Hector and Andromache hurled by the Greeks from the walls of Troy

asty·lar \(ˈ)ā-ˈstī-lər\ *adj* [*a-* + Gk *stylos* pillar — more at STEER] **:** having no columns or pilasters

asun·der \ə-ˈsən-dər\ *adv (or adj)* **1 :** into parts ⟨torn ~⟩ **2 :** apart from each other in position ⟨wide ~⟩

as well as *prep* **:** in addition to **:** BESIDES

as yet *adv* **:** up to the present time **:** YET

asy·lum \ə-ˈsī-ləm\ *n* [ME, fr. L, fr. Gk *asylon*, neut. of *asylos* inviolable, fr. *a-* + *sylon* right of seizure] **1 :** an inviolable place of refuge and protection giving shelter to criminals and debtors **:** SANCTUARY **2 :** a place of retreat and security **:** SHELTER **3 a :** the protection or inviolability afforded by an asylum **:** REFUGE **b :** protection from arrest and extradition given esp. to political refugees by a nation or by an embassy or other agency enjoying diplomatic immunity **4 :** an institution for the relief or care of the destitute or afflicted and esp. the insane

asym·met·ric \ˌā-sə-ˈme-trik\ *adj* [Gk *asymmetria* lack of proportion, fr. *asymmetros* ill-proportioned, fr. *a-* + *symmetros* symmetrical — more at SYMMETRY] **:** not symmetrical — **asym·met·ri·cal** \-tri-kəl\ *adj* — **asym·met·ri·cal·ly** \-k(ə-)lē\ *adv* — **asym·me·try** \(ˈ)ā-ˈsim-ə-trē\ *n*

asymp·tom·at·ic \ˌā-ˌsim(p)-tə-ˈmat-ik\ *adj* **:** presenting no subjective evidence of disease — **asymp·tom·at·i·cal·ly** \-i-k(ə-)lē\ *adv*

as·ymp·tote \ˈas-əm(p)-ˌtōt\ *n* [prob. fr. (assumed) NL *asymptotus*, fr. Gk *asymptōtos*, fr. *asymptōtos* not meeting, fr. *a-* + *sympiptein* to meet — more at SYMPTOM] **:** a line that is the limiting position of a tangent to a curve as its point of contact recedes indefinitely along an infinite branch of the curve — **as·ymp·tot·ic** \ˌas-əm(p)-ˈtät-ik\ *adj* — **as·ymp·tot·i·cal·ly** \-i-k(ə-)lē\ *adv*

asyn·chro·nism \(ˈ)ā-ˈsiŋ-krə-ˌniz-əm, -ˈsin-\ *or* **asyn·chro·ny** \-krə-nē\ *n* **:** the quality or state of being asynchronous

asyn·chro·nous \-krə-nəs\ *adj* **:** not synchronous — **asyn·chro·nous·ly** *adv*

as·yn·det·ic \ˌas-ᵊn-ˈdet-ik\ *adj* **:** marked by asyndeton — **as·yn·det·i·cal·ly** \-i-k(ə-)lē\ *adv*

asyn·de·ton \ə-ˈsin-də-ˌtän\ *n, pl* **asyndetons** *or* **asyn·de·ta** \-dət-ə\ [LL, fr. Gk, fr. neut. of *asyndetos* unconnected, fr. *a-* + *syndetos* bound together, fr. *syndein* to bind together, fr. *syn-* + *dein* to bind] **:** omission of the conjunctions that ordinarily join coordinate words or clauses (as in *I came, I saw, I conquered*)

1**at** \ət, (ˈ)at\ *prep* [ME, fr. OE *æt;* akin to OHG *az* at, L *ad*] **1** — used as a function word to indicate presence or occurrence in, on, or near ⟨staying ~ a hotel⟩ ⟨~ a party⟩ ⟨sick ~ heart⟩ **2** — used as a function word to indicate the goal of an indicated or implied action or motion ⟨aim ~ the target⟩ ⟨laugh ~ him⟩ ⟨creditors are ~ him again⟩ **3** — used as a function word to indicate that with which one is occupied or employed ⟨~ work⟩ ⟨~ the controls⟩ ⟨an expert ~ chess⟩ **4** — used as a function word to indicate situation in an active or passive state or condition ⟨a criminal ~ liberty⟩ ⟨~ rest⟩ **5** — used as a function word to indicate the means, cause, or manner ⟨sold ~ auction⟩ ⟨laughed ~ his joke⟩ ⟨act ~ your own discretion⟩ **6 a** — used as a function word to indicate the rate, degree, or position in a scale or series ⟨the temperature ~ 90⟩ ⟨~ first⟩ **b** — used as a function word to indicate age or position in time ⟨will retire ~ 65⟩ ⟨awoke ~ midnight⟩

2**at** \ˈät\ *n, pl* **at** [Siamese] — see *kip* at MONEY table

at- — see AD-

At·a·brine \ˈat-ə-brən, -ˌbrēn\ *trademark* — used for quinacrine

At·a·lan·ta \ˌat-ᵊl-ˈant-ə\ *n* [L, fr. Gk *Atalantē*] **:** a beautiful and fleet-footed heroine of Greek legend who challenges her suitors to a race and who is defeated when she stops to pick up three golden apples dropped by one of the suitors

at all \ə-ˈtȯl, ət-ˈȯl\ *adv* **1 :** in all ways **:** INDISCRIMINATELY ⟨will go anywhere *at all*⟩ **2 :** in any way or respect **:** to the least extent or degree **:** under any circumstances ⟨not *at all* likely⟩

at·a·man \ˌat-ə-ˈman\ *n* [Russ] **:** HETMAN

at·a·mas·co lily \ˌat-ə-ˈmas-(ˌ)kō-\ *n* [*attamusco*, lit., it is red (in some Algonquian language of Virginia)] **:** any of a genus (*Zephyranthes*) of American bulbous herbs of the amaryllis family with pink, white, or yellowish flowers

at·a·rac·tic \ˌat-ə-ˈrak-tik\ *or* **at·a·rax·ic** \-ˈrak-sik\ *n* [*ataractic* fr. Gk *ataraktos* calm, fr. *a-* + *tarassein; ataraxic* fr. Gk *ataraxia* calmness, fr. *a-* + *tarassein* to disturb — more at DREG] **:** a tranquilizer drug — **ataractic** *adj*

at·a·vism \ˈat-ə-ˌviz-əm\ *n* [F *atavisme*, fr. L *atavus* ancestor] **1 :** recurrence in an organism or in any of its parts of a form typical of ancestors more remote than the parents usu. due to recombination of ancestral genes **2 :** an individual or character manifesting atavism **:** THROWBACK — **at·a·vist** \-vəst\ *n* — **at·a·vis·tic** \ˌat-ə-ˈvis-tik\ *adj* — **at·a·vis·ti·cal·ly** \-ˈvis-ti-k(ə-)lē\ *adv*

atax·ia \ə-ˈtak-sē-ə\ *n* [Gk, fr. *a-* + *tassein* to put in order — more at TACTICS] **1 :** lack of order **:** CONFUSION **2 :** an inability to coordinate voluntary muscular movements symptomatic of some nervous disorders — **atax·ic** \-sik\ *adj*

1**ate** *past of* EAT

2**ate** \ˈāt-ē, ˈāt-; ˈä-ˌtā, ˈā-ˌtā, ˈā-ˌtē\ *n* [Gk *Atē*] **1** *cap* **:** a Greek goddess held to lead gods and men to rash actions **2 :** blind impulse, reckless ambition, or excessive folly that drives men to ruin

1**-ate** \ət, ˌāt\ *n suffix* [ME *-at*, fr. OF, fr. L *-atus*, *-atum*, masc. & neut. of *-atus*, pp. ending] **1 :** one acted upon (in a specified way) ⟨distill*ate*⟩ **2** [NL *-atum*, fr. L] **:** chemical compound or complex anion derived from a (specified) compound or element ⟨phenol*ate*⟩ ⟨ferr*ate*⟩; *esp* **:** salt or ester of an acid with a name ending in *-ic* and not beginning with *hydro-* ⟨bor*ate*⟩

2**-ate** *n suffix* [ME *-at*, fr. OF, fr. L *-atus*, fr. *-atus*, pp. ending] **:** office **:** function **:** rank **:** group of persons holding a (specified) office or rank or having a (specified) function ⟨vicar*ate*⟩

3**-ate** *adj suffix* [ME *-at*, fr. L *-atus*, fr. pp. ending of 1st conj. verbs, fr. *-a-*, stem vowel of 1st conj. + *-tus*, pp. suffix — more at -ED] **1 :** acted on (in a specified way) **:** brought into or being in a (specified) state ⟨temper*ate*⟩ **2 :** marked by having ⟨crani*ate*⟩

4**-ate** \ˌāt\ *vb suffix* [ME *-aten*, fr. L *-atus*, pp. ending] **:** act on (in a specified way) ⟨insul*ate*⟩ **:** cause to be modified or affected by ⟨camphor*ate*⟩ **:** cause to become ⟨activ*ate*⟩ **:** furnish with ⟨capacit*ate*⟩

At·e·brin \ˈat-ə-brən\ *trademark* — used for quinacrine

-at·ed \ˌāt-əd\ *adj suffix* **:** 3-ATE ⟨locul*ated*⟩

ate·lier \ˌat-ᵊl-ˈyā\ *n* [F] **1 :** an artist's or designer's studio or workroom **2 :** WORKSHOP

a tem·po \ä-ˈtem-(ˌ)pō\ *adv (or adj)* [It] **:** in time — used as a direction in music to return to the original rate of speed

Ate·ri·an \ə-ˈtir-ē-ən\ *adj* [F *atérien*, fr. Bir el-*Ater* (Constantine), Algeria] **:** of or relating to a Paleolithic culture of northern Africa characterized by Mousterian features, tanged arrow points, and leaf-shaped spearheads

Ath·a·na·sian \ˌath-ə-ˈnā-zhən, -ˈnā-shən\ *adj* **:** of or relating to Athanasius (†373) the bishop of Alexandria or his advocation of the homoousian doctrine against Arianism

Athanasian Creed *n* **:** a Christian creed originating in Europe about A.D. 400 and relating esp. to the Trinity and Incarnation

Ath·a·pas·kan *or* **Ath·a·pas·can** \ˌath-ə-ˈpas-kən\ *or* **Ath·a·bas·can** *or* **Ath·a·bas·kan** \-ˈbas-\ *n* [Cree *Athap-askaw*, an Athapaskan people, lit., grass or reeds here and there] **1 :** a language stock of the Na-dene group in No. America **2 :** a member of a people speaking an Athapaskan language

athe·ism \ˈā-thē-ˌiz-əm\ *n* [MF *athéisme*, fr. *athée* atheist, fr. Gk *atheos* godless, fr. *a-* + *theos* god] **1 a :** disbelief in the existence of deity **b :** the doctrine that there is no deity **2 :** UNGODLINESS, WICKEDNESS

athe·ist \ˈā-thē-əst\ *n* **:** one who denies the existence of God — **athe·is·tic** \ˌā-thē-ˈis-tik\ *adj* — **athe·is·ti·cal·ly** \-ˈis-ti-k(ə-)lē\ *adv*

syn AGNOSTIC, DEIST, FREETHINKER, UNBELIEVER, INFIDEL: an ATHEIST is one who denies the existence of God and rejects all religious faith and practice; an AGNOSTIC withholds belief because he is unwilling to accept the evidence of revelation and spiritual experience; DEIST rejects the conception of God as an active ruler and guide known through revelation while believing in a supreme being as creator of the universe; FREETHINKER suggests loss of faith and a belief only in the rational and credible; UNBELIEVER implies loss or lack of religious faith without suggesting a substitute for it; INFIDEL usu. applies to one belonging to a faith (as the Muhammadan) other than Christian or Jewish and commonly connotes an enemy of the true faith

ath·e·ling \ˈath-ə-liŋ, ˈath-\ *n* [ME, fr. OE *ætheling*, fr. *æthelu* nobility, akin to OHG *adal* nobility] **:** an Anglo-Saxon prince or nobleman; *esp* **:** the heir apparent or a prince of the royal family

Athe·na \ə-ˈthē-nə\ *or* **Athe·ne** \-(ˌ)nē\ *n* [Gk *Athēnē*] **:** the goddess of wisdom and of women's crafts in Greek mythology

ath·e·nae·um *or* **ath·e·ne·um** \ˌath-ə-ˈnē-əm\ *n* [L *Athenaeum*, a school in ancient Rome for the study of arts, fr. Gk *Athēnaion*, a temple of Athena, fr. *Athēnē*] **1 :** a literary or scientific association **2 :** a building or room in which books, periodicals, and newspapers are kept for use

ath·er·o·ma \ˌath-ə-ˈrō-mə\ *n* [NL *atheromat-*, *atheroma*, fr. L, a tumor containing gruellike matter, fr. Gk *athērōma*, fr. *athēra* gruel] **:** fatty degeneration of the inner coat of the arteries — **ath·er·o·ma·to·sis** \-ˌrō-mə-ˈtō-səs\ *n* — **ath·er·o·ma·tous** \ˌath-ə-ˈräm-ət-əs, -ˈrōm-\ *adj*

ath·ero·scle·ro·sis \ˌath-ə-rō-sklə-ˈrō-səs\ *n* [NL, fr. *atheroma* + *sclerosis*] **:** an arteriosclerosis characterized by the deposition of fatty substances in and fibrosis of the inner layer of the arteries — **ath·ero·scle·rot·ic** \-sklə-ˈrät-ik\ *adj*

athirst \ə-ˈthərst\ *adj* [ME, fr. OE *ofthyrst*, pp. of *ofthyrstan* to suffer from thirst, fr. *of* off, from + *thyrstan* to thirst — more at OF] **1 :** THIRSTY **2 :** EAGER, LONGING **syn** see EAGER

ath·lete \ˈath-ˌlēt\ *n* [ME, fr. L *athleta*, fr. Gk *athlētēs*, fr. *athlein* to contend for a prize, fr. *athlon* prize, contest] **:** one who is trained to compete in exercises, sports, or games requiring physical strength, agility, or stamina

athlete's foot *n* **:** ringworm of the feet

ath·let·ic \ath-ˈlet-ik\ *adj* **1 :** of or relating to athletes or athletics **2 :** characteristic of an athlete; *esp* **:** VIGOROUS, ACTIVE **3 :** characterized by heavy frame, large chest, and powerful muscular development **:** MESOMORPHIC **4 :** used by athletes — **ath·let·i·cal·ly** \-ˈlet-i-k(ə-)lē\ *adv* — **ath·let·i·cism** \-ˈlet-ə-ˌsiz-əm\ *n*

ath·let·ics \ath-ˈlet-iks\ *n pl but sing or pl in constr* **1 :** exercises, sports, or games engaged in by athletes **2 :** the practice or principles of athletic activities

ath·o·dyd \ˈath-ə-ˌdid\ *n* [*a*ero-*th*erm*odyn*amic *d*uct] **:** a jet engine (as a ramjet engine) consisting essentially of a continuous duct of varying diameter which admits air at the forward end, adds heat to it by the combustion of fuel, and discharges it from the after end

at home \ət-ˈhōm\ *n* **:** a reception given at one's home

ath·ro·cyte \ˈath-rə-ˌsīt\ *n* [Gk *athroos* together, collected + ISV *-cyte*] **:** a cell capable of picking up foreign material and storing it in granular form in its cytoplasm — **ath·ro·cy·to·sis** \ˌath-rə-ˌsī-ˈtō-səs\ *n*

1**athwart** \ə-ˈthwȯ(ə)rt, *naut often* -ˈthȯ(ə)rt\ *adv* **1 :** across esp. obliquely **2 :** so as to thwart

2**athwart** *prep* **1 :** ACROSS **2 :** in opposition to

atilt \ə-ˈtilt\ *adj (or adv)* **1 :** TILTED **2 :** with lance in hand

-a·tion \ˈā-shən\ *n suffix* [ME *-acioun*, fr. OF *-ation*, fr. L *-ation-*, *-atio*, fr. *-atus* -ate + *-ion-*, *-io* -ion] **:** action or process ⟨flirt*ation*⟩

: something connected with an action or process ⟨discolor*ation*⟩
-a·tive \ˌāt-iv, ət-\ *adj suffix* [ME, fr. MF *-atif*, fr. L *-ativus*, fr. *-atus* + *-ivus* -ive] **:** of, relating to, or connected with ⟨authori*tative*⟩ **:** tending to ⟨talk*ative*⟩
At·ka mackerel \ˌat-kə-, ˌät-\ *n* [*Atka* Island, Alaska] **:** a greenling (*Pleurogrammus monopterygius*) of Alaska and adjacent regions valued as a food fish
¹At·lan·te·an \ˌat-ˌlan-'tē-ən, ət-'lant-ē-\ *adj* **:** of, relating to, or resembling Atlas **:** STRONG
²Atlantean *adj* **:** of or relating to Atlantis
At·lan·tic time \ət-'lant-ik-\ *n* [*Atlantic* ocean] **:** the time of the 4th time zone west of Greenwich that includes the Canadian Maritime provinces
At·lan·tis \ət-'lant-əs\ *n* [L, fr. Gk] **:** an island sunk according to the ancients beneath the ocean west of the Strait of Gibraltar
at·las \'at-ləs\ *n* [L *Atlant-*, *Atlas*, fr. Gk] **1** *cap* **a :** a Titan forced to bear the heavens on his shoulders **b :** one who bears a heavy burden **2 a :** a bound collection of maps **b :** a bound collection of tables, charts, or plates **3 :** the first vertebra of the neck **4** *pl usu* **at·lan·tes** \ət-'lant-(ˌ)ēz\ **:** a figure or half figure of a man used as a column to support an entablature
At·li \'ät-lē\ *n* [ON] **:** a king in Norse mythology who marries Gudrun after Sigurd's death and who is slain by her to avenge his treachery to her brothers
at·man \'ät-mən\ *n, often cap* [Skt *ātman*, lit., breath, soul; akin to OHG *ātum* breath] **1** *Hinduism* **:** the innermost essence of each individual **2 :** the supreme universal self
at·mom·e·ter \at-'mäm-ət-ər\ *n* [Gk *atmos* + E *-meter*] **:** an instrument for measuring the evaporating capacity of the air
at·mo·sphere \'at-mə-ˌsfi(ə)r\ *n* [NL *atmosphaera*, fr. Gk *atmos* vapor + L *sphaera* sphere; akin to Gk *aēnai* to blow — more at WIND] **1 a :** a gaseous mass enveloping a heavenly body (as a planet) **b :** the whole mass of air surrounding the earth **2 :** the air of a locality **3 :** a surrounding influence or environment **4 :** a unit of pressure equal to the pressure of the air at sea level or approximately 14.7 pounds to the square inch **5 a :** the overall aesthetic effect of a work of art **b :** a dominant effect or appeal
at·mo·spher·ic \ˌat-mə-'sfi(ə)r-ik, -'sfer-\ *adj* **1 a :** of or relating to the atmosphere **b :** resembling the atmosphere **:** AIRY **c :** occurring in or actuated by the atmosphere **2 :** having, marked by, or contributing aesthetic or emotional atmosphere — **at·mo·spher·i·cal·ly** \-i-k(ə-)lē\ *adv*
at·mo·spher·ics \-iks\ *n pl* **:** disturbances produced in radio receiving apparatus by atmospheric electrical phenomena; *also* **:** the electrical phenomena causing such disturbances
atoll \'a-ˌtȯl, -ˌtäl, -ˌtōl, 'ā-\ *n* [Maldivian *atolu*] **:** a coral island consisting of a reef surrounding a lagoon

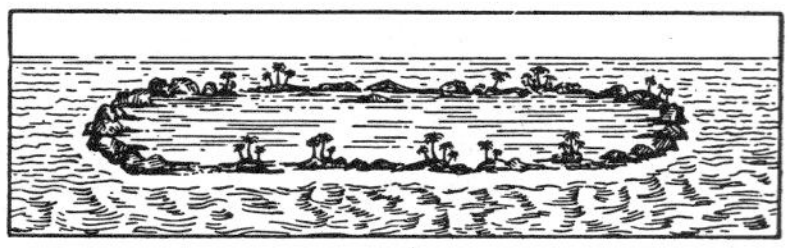
atoll

at·om \'at-əm\ *n* [ME, fr. L *atomus*, fr. Gk *atomos*, fr. *atomos* indivisible, fr. *a-* + *temnein* to cut — more at TOME] **1 :** one of the minute indivisible particles of which according to ancient materialism the universe is composed **2 :** a tiny particle **:** BIT **3 a :** the smallest particle of an element that can exist either alone or in combination **b :** a group of such particles constituting the smallest quantity of a radical **4 :** the atom considered as a source of vast potential energy
atom bomb *or* **atomic bomb** *n* **1 :** a bomb whose violent explosive power is due to the sudden release of atomic energy resulting from the splitting of nuclei of a heavy chemical element (as plutonium or uranium) by neutrons in a very rapid chain reaction — called also *fission bomb* **2 :** any bomb whose explosive power is due to the release of atomic energy — **at·om–bomb** \ˌat-əm-'bäm\ *vt*
atom·ic \ə-'täm-ik\ *adj* **1 :** of, relating to, or concerned with atoms, atomic energy, or atomic bombs **2 :** MINUTE **3** *of a chemical element* **:** existing in the state of separate atoms — **atom·i·cal·ly** \-i-k(ə-)lē\ *adv*
atomic clock *n* **:** a precision clock that depends for its operation on an electrical oscillator regulated by the natural vibration frequencies of an atomic system (as a beam of cesium atoms)
atomic cocktail *n* **:** a radioactive substance (as sodium iodide) administered orally in water to patients with cancer
atomic energy *n* **:** energy that can be liberated by changes in the nucleus of an atom (as by fission of a heavy nucleus or fusion of light nuclei into heavier ones with accompanying loss of mass)
at·o·mic·i·ty \ˌat-ə-'mis-ət-ē\ *n* **1 a :** VALENCE **b :** the number of atoms in the molecule of an element **c :** the number of replaceable atoms or groups in the molecule of a compound **2 :** the state of consisting of atoms
atomic mass *n* **:** the mass of any species of atom usu. expressed in atomic mass units
atomic mass unit *n* **:** a unit of mass for expressing masses of atoms, molecules, or nuclear particles equal to $1/12$ of the atomic mass of the most abundant carbon isotope $_6C^{12}$
atomic number *n* **:** an experimentally determined number characteristic of a chemical element that represents the number of protons in the nucleus which in a neutral atom equals the number of electrons outside of the nucleus and that determines the place of the element in the periodic table — see ELEMENT table
atomic pile *n* **:** REACTOR
atom·ics \ə-'täm-iks\ *n pl but sing in constr* **:** the science of atoms esp. when involving atomic energy
atomic theory *n* **1 :** a theory of the nature of matter: all material substances are composed of minute particles or atoms of a comparatively small number of kinds and all the atoms of the same kind are uniform in size, weight, and other properties — called also *atomic hypothesis* **2 :** any of several theories of the structure of the atom; *esp* **:** one based on experimentation and theoretical considerations holding that the atom is composed essentially of a small positively charged comparatively heavy nucleus surrounded by a comparatively large arrangement of electrons
atomic weight *n* **:** the average relative weight of an element referred to some element taken as a standard with hydrogen sometimes being assigned an atomic weight of 1 but oxygen with an atomic weight of 16 or carbon with an atomic weight of 12 usu. being taken as a basis — see ELEMENT table

at·om·ism \'at-ə-ˌmiz-əm\ *n* **:** a doctrine that the universe is composed of simple indivisible minute particles — **at·om·ist** \-məst\ *n*
at·om·is·tic \ˌat-ə-'mis-tik\ *adj* **1 :** of or relating to atoms or atomism **2 :** composed of many simple elements; *also* **:** divided into unconnected or antagonistic fragments ⟨an ~ society⟩ — **at·om·is·ti·cal·ly** \-ti-k(ə-)lē\ *adv*
at·om·is·tics \ˌat-ə-'mis-tiks\ *n pl but sing in constr* **:** a science dealing with the atom or with the use of atomic energy
at·om·iza·tion \-mə-'zā-shən\ *n* **:** the act or process of atomizing
at·om·ize \'at-ə-ˌmīz\ *vt* **1 :** to reduce to minute particles or to a fine spray **2 :** to treat as made up of many discrete units **3 :** to subject to atomic bombing
at·om·iz·er \-ˌmī-zər\ *n* **:** an instrument for atomizing esp. a perfume or disinfectant
atom smasher *n* **:** ACCELERATOR d
at·o·my \'at-ə-mē\ *n* [irreg. fr. L *atomi*, pl. of *atomus* atom] **:** ATOM, MITE
aton·al \(')ā-'tōn-ᵊl, (')a-\ *adj* **:** marked by avoidance of traditional musical tonality; *esp* **:** organized without reference to key or tonal center and using the tones of the chromatic scale impartially — **aton·al·ism** \-ᵊl-ˌiz-əm\ *n* — **aton·al·ist** \-ᵊl-əst\ *n* — **aton·al·is·tic** \ˌā-ˌtōn-ᵊl-'is-tik\ *adj* — **ato·nal·i·ty** \ˌā-tō-'nal-ət-ē\ *n* — **aton·al·ly** \(')ā-'tōn-ᵊl-ē\ *adv*
atone \ə-'tōn\ *vb* [ME *atonen* to become reconciled, fr. *at on* in harmony, fr. *at* + *on* one] *vt* **1** *obs* **:** RECONCILE **2 :** to supply satisfaction for **:** EXPIATE ~ *vi* **:** to make amends
atone·ment \-mənt\ *n* **1** *obs* **:** RECONCILIATION **2 :** the reconciliation of God and man through the death of Jesus Christ **3 :** reparation for an offense or injury **:** SATISFACTION **4** *Christian Science* **:** the exemplifying of man's oneness with God
aton·ic \(')ā-'tän-ik\ *adj* **1 :** characterized by atony **2 :** uttered without accent or stress — **ato·nic·i·ty** \ˌā-tō-'nis-ət-ē\ *n*
at·o·ny \'at-ᵊn-ē\ *n* [LL *atonia*, fr. Gk, fr. *atonos* without tone, fr. *a-* + *tonos* tone] **:** lack of physiological tone esp. of a contractile organ
¹atop \ə-'täp\ *prep* **:** on top of
²atop *adv (or adj)*, *archaic* **:** on, to, or at the top
-a·tor *n suffix* [ME *-atour*, fr. OF & L; OF, fr. L *-ator*, fr. *-atus* -ate + *-or*] **:** one that does ⟨totaliz*ator*⟩
at·ra·bil·ious \ˌa-trə-'bil-yəs\ *adj* [L *atra bilis* black bile] **1 :** given to or marked by melancholy **:** GLOOMY **2 :** ILL-NATURED, PEEVISH
Atreus \'ā-ˌtrüs, 'ā-trē-əs\ *n* [L, fr. Gk] **:** a king of Mycenae and father of Agamemnon and Menelaus
atri·al \'ā-trē-əl\ *adj* **:** of or relating to an atrium
atrio·ven·tric·u·lar \ˌā-trē-(ˌ)ō-(ˌ)ven-'trik-yə-lər\ *adj* [NL *atrium* + E *ventricular*] **:** of, relating to, or located between an atrium and ventricle of the heart
atrip \ə-'trip\ *adj, of an anchor* **:** hove just clear of the ground
atri·um \'ā-trē-əm\ *n, pl* **atria** \-trē-ə\ *also* **atri·ums** [L] **1 :** the central hall of a Roman house **2** [NL, fr. L] **:** an anatomical cavity or passage; *esp* **:** the main chamber of an auricle of the heart or the entire auricle
atro·cious \ə-'trō-shəs\ *adj* [L *atroc-*, *atrox* gloomy, atrocious, fr. *atr-*, *ater* black + *-oc-*, *-ox* (akin to Gk *ōps* eye) — more at EYE] **1 :** extremely wicked, brutal, or cruel **2 :** BARBARIC **3 :** savagely fierce **:** MURDEROUS **4 :** APPALLING, TERRIBLE, HORRIFYING ⟨an ~ act⟩ **5 :** very bad **:** ABOMINABLE ⟨~ handwriting⟩ **syn** see OUTRAGEOUS — **atro·cious·ly** *adv* — **atro·cious·ness** *n*
atroc·i·ty \ə-'träs-ət-ē\ *n* **1 :** the quality or state of being atrocious **2 :** an atrocious act, object, or situation
atroph·ic \ə-'träf-ik, a-\ *adj* **:** relating to or marked by atrophy
¹at·ro·phy \'a-trə-fē\ *n* [LL *atrophia*, fr. Gk, fr. *atrophos* ill fed, fr. *a-* + *trephein* to nourish; akin to Gk *thrombos* clot, curd] **:** decrease in size or wasting away of a body part or tissue; *also* **:** arrested development or loss of a part or organ incidental to the normal development or life of an animal or plant
²atrophy *vi* **:** to undergo atrophy ~ *vt* **:** to cause to undergo atrophy
at·ro·pine \'a-trə-ˌpēn, -pən\ *n* [G *atropin*, fr. NL *Atropa*, genus name of belladonna, fr. Gk *Atropos*] **:** a poisonous white crystalline alkaloid $C_{17}H_{23}NO_3$ from belladonna and related plants used esp. to relieve spasms and to dilate the pupil of the eye
At·ro·pos \'a-trə-ˌpäs, -pəs\ *n* [Gk] **:** the one of the three Fates in classical mythology who cuts off the thread of life
at·tach \ə-'tach\ *vb* [ME *attachen*, fr. MF *attacher*, fr. OF *estachier*, fr. *estache* stake, of Gmc origin; akin to OE *staca* stake] *vt* **1 :** to take by legal authority esp. under a writ **2 :** to bring (oneself) into an association **3 :** to bind by personal ties **4 :** CONNECT, TIE **5 :** ASCRIBE, ATTRIBUTE ~ *vi* **:** to become attached **:** ADHERE **syn** see FASTEN — **at·tach·able** \-'tach-ə-bəl\ *adj*
at·ta·ché \ˌat-ə-'shā, ˌa-ˌta-\ *n* [F, pp. of *attacher*] **:** a technical expert on the diplomatic staff of his country at a foreign capital
at·ta·ché case \ə-'tash-ē-, -'tash-ˌā-; ˌat-ə-'shā-, ˌa-ˌta-'shā-\ *n* **:** a small suitcase used esp. for carrying papers and documents
at·tached *adj* **:** permanently fixed when adult
at·tach·ment \ə-'tach-mənt\ *n* **1 :** a seizure by legal process; *also* **:** the writ or precept commanding such seizure **2 a :** the state of being personally attached **:** FIDELITY **b :** REGARD **3 :** a device attached to a machine or implement **4 :** the physical connection by which one thing is attached to another **5 :** the process of physically attaching
¹at·tack \ə-'tak, *substand* -'takt\ *vb* **at·tacked** \-'takt, *substand* -'tak-təd\ **at·tack·ing** \-'tak-iŋ, *substand* -'tak-tiŋ\ [MF *attaquer*, fr. (assumed) OIt *estaccare* to attach, fr. *stacca* stake, of Gmc origin; akin to OE *staca*] *vt* **1 :** to set upon forcefully **2 :** to threaten (a piece in chess) with immediate capture **3 :** to assail with unfriendly or bitter words **4 :** to begin to affect or to act upon injuriously **5 :** to set to work upon ~ *vi* **:** to make an attack
syn ATTACK, ASSAIL, ASSAULT, BOMBARD, STORM mean to make an onslaught upon. ATTACK implies taking the initiative in a struggle; ASSAIL implies attempting to break down resistance by repeated blows or shots; ASSAULT suggests a direct attempt to overpower by suddenness and violence of onslaught; BOMBARD implies attacking with bombs or shells; in extended use it suggests continuous pestering; STORM implies attempting to break into a defended position by the irresistible weight of rapidly advancing numbers
²attack *n* **1 :** the act of attacking **:** ASSAULT **2 :** an offensive or antagonistic action **3 :** the beginning of destructive action (as by a chemical agent) **4 :** the setting to work upon some undertaking **5 :** the act or manner of beginning a musical tone or phrase **6 :** a

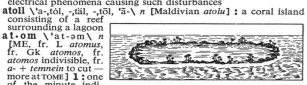

fit of sickness; *esp* : an active episode of a chronic or recurrent disease

at·tain \ə-ˈtān\ *vb* [ME *atteynen*, fr. OF *ataindre*, fr. (assumed) VL *attangere*, fr. L *attingere*, fr. *ad-* + *tangere* to touch — more at TANGENT] *vt* **1** : ACHIEVE, ACCOMPLISH **2** : to come into possession of : OBTAIN **3** : to arrive at ~ *vi* : to come or arrive by motion, growth, or effort **syn** see REACH — **at·tain·abil·i·ty** \ə-ˌtā-nə-ˈbil-ət-ē\ *n* — **at·tain·able** \-ˈtā-nə-bəl\ *adj* — **at·tain·able·ness** *n*

at·tain·der \ə-ˈtān-dər\ *n* [ME *attaynder*, fr. MF *ataindre* to accuse, attain] **1** : extinction of the civil rights and capacities of a person upon sentence of death or outlawry **2** : DISHONOR

at·tain·ment \ə-ˈtān-mənt\ *n* **1** : the act of attaining : the condition of being attained **2** : something attained : ACCOMPLISHMENT **syn** see ACQUIREMENT

1**at·taint** \ə-ˈtānt\ *vt* [ME *attaynten*, fr. MF *ataint*, pp. of *ataindre*] **1** : to affect by attainder **2 a** *obs* : INFECT, CORRUPT **b** *archaic* : TAINT, SULLY **3** *archaic* : ACCUSE

2**attaint** *n, obs* : a stain upon honor or purity : DISGRACE

at·tar \ˈat-ər, ˈa-ˌtär\ *n* [Per *ʿatir* perfumed, fr. *ʿiṭr* perfume, fr. Ar] : a fragrant essential oil (as from rose petals); *also* : FRAGRANCE

1**at·tempt** \ə-ˈtem(p)t\ *vt* [L *attemptare*, fr. *ad-* + *temptare* to touch, try — more at TEMPT] **1** : to make an effort toward : TRY — often used with an infinitive **2** *archaic* : TEMPT **3** *archaic* : to try to subdue : ATTACK — **at·tempt·able** \-ˈtem(p)-tə-bəl\ *adj*

syn ATTEMPT, TRY, ENDEAVOR, ESSAY, STRIVE mean to make an effort to accomplish an end. ATTEMPT implies making an essentially single effort and usu. suggests failure; TRY stresses effort or experiment made in the hope of testing or proving something; ENDEAVOR heightens the implications of exertion and difficulty; ESSAY implies difficulty but also suggests tentative trying or experimenting; STRIVE implies great exertion against great difficulty and specifically suggests persistent effort

2**attempt** *n* **1** : the act or an instance of attempting; *esp* : an unsuccessful effort **2** *archaic* : ATTACK, ASSAULT

at·tend \ə-ˈtend\ *vb* [ME *attenden*, fr. OF *atendre*, fr. L *attendere*, lit., to stretch to, fr. *ad-* + *tendere* to stretch — more at THIN] *vt* **1** *archaic* : to give heed to **2** : to look after or take charge of **3** *archaic* **a** : to wait for **b** : to be in store for **4 a** : to go or stay with as a companion, nurse, or servant **b** : to visit professionally as a physician **5** : to be present with : ACCOMPANY **6** : to be present at ~ *vi* **1** : to apply oneself **2** : to apply the mind or pay attention **3** : to be ready for service **4** *obs* : WAIT, STAY **5** : to take charge : SEE ⟨I'll ~ to that⟩ **syn** see ACCOMPANY

at·ten·dance \ə-ˈten-dən(t)s\ *n* **1** : the act or fact of attending **2 a** : the persons or number of persons attending **b** : the number of times a person attends

1**at·ten·dant** \ə-ˈten-dənt\ *adj* : accompanying or following as a consequence

2**attendant** *n* **1** : one who attends another to render a service; *esp* : an employee who waits on customers **2** : something that accompanies : CONCOMITANT **3** : one who is present

at·ten·tion \ə-ˈten-chən\ *n* [ME *attencioun*, fr. L *attention-*, *attentio*, fr. *attentus*, pp. of *attendere*] **1 a** : the act or state of attending esp. through applying the mind to an object of sense or thought **b** : a condition of readiness for such attention involving esp. a selective narrowing or focusing of consciousness and receptivity **2** : OBSERVATION, NOTICE; *esp* : consideration with a view to action **3 a** : an act of civility or courtesy esp. in courtship **b** : ATTENTIVENESS **4** : a position assumed by a soldier with heels together, body erect, arms at the sides, and eyes to the front — often used as a command — **at·ten·tion·al** \-ˈtench-nəl, -ˈten-chən-ᵊl\ *adj*

at·ten·tive \ə-ˈtent-iv\ *adj* **1** : HEEDFUL, OBSERVANT **2** : heedful of the comfort of others : COURTEOUS **3** : paying attentions **syn** see THOUGHTFUL — **at·ten·tive·ly** *adv* — **at·ten·tive·ness** *n*

1**at·ten·u·ate** \ə-ˈten-yə-ˌwāt\ *vb* [L *attenuatus*, pp. of *attenuare* to make thin, fr. *ad-* + *tenuis* thin — more at THIN] *vt* **1** : to make thin or slender **2** : to lessen the amount, force, or value of : WEAKEN **3** : to reduce the severity, virulence, or vitality of **4** : to make thin in consistency : RAREFY ~ *vi* : to become thin, fine, or less — **at·ten·u·a·tion** \ə-ˌten-yə-ˈwā-shən\ *n*

2**at·ten·u·ate** \ə-ˈten-yə-wət\ *adj* **1** : ATTENUATED **2** : tapering gradually usu. to a long slender point ⟨~ leaves⟩

at·test \ə-ˈtest\ *vb* [MF *attester*, fr. L *attestari*, fr. *ad-* + *testis* witness — more at TESTAMENT] *vt* **1 a** : to affirm to be true or genuine; *specif* : to authenticate by signing as a witness **b** : to authenticate officially **2** : to establish or verify the usage of **3** : to be proof of : MANIFEST **4** : to put on oath ~ *vi* : to bear witness : TESTIFY — **at·tes·ta·tion** \ˌa-ˌtes-ˈtā-shən, ˌat-ə-ˈstā-\ *n* — **at·test·er** *n*

at·tic \ˈat-ik\ *n* [F *attique*, fr. *attique* of Attica, fr. L *Atticus*] **1** : a low story or wall above the main order of a facade in the classical styles **2** : a room behind an attic **3** : the part of a building immediately below the roof

1**At·tic** \ˈat-ik\ *adj* [L *Atticus*, fr. Gk *Attikos*, fr. *Attikē* Attica, Greece] **1** : Athenian **2** : marked by simplicity, purity, and refinement

2**Attic** *n* : a dialect of ancient Greek orig. used in Attica and later the literary language of the Greek-speaking world

at·ti·cism \ˈat-ə-ˌsiz-əm\ *n, often cap* : a characteristic feature of Attic Greek language or literature

1**at·tire** \ə-ˈtī(ə)r\ *vt* [ME *attiren*, fr. OF *atirier*, fr. *a-* (fr. L *ad-*) + *tire* order, rank, of Gmc origin; akin to OE *tīr* glory; akin to L *deus* god] **1** : DRESS, ARRAY **2** : to clothe in rich garments

2**attire** *n* **1** : DRESS, CLOTHES; *esp* : splendid or decorative clothing **2** : the antlers or antlers and scalp of a stag or buck

at·ti·tude \ˈat-ə-ˌt(y)üd\ *n* [F, fr. It *attitudine*, fr. *attitudine* aptitude, fr. LL *aptitudin-*, *aptitudo* fitness — more at APTITUDE] **1** : the arrangement of the parts of a body or figure : POSTURE **2 a** : a mental position with regard to a fact or state **b** : a feeling or emotion toward a fact or state **3** : the position of something in relation to a frame of reference

at·ti·tu·di·nize \ˌat-ə-ˈt(y)üd-ᵊn-ˌīz\ *vi* : to assume an affected mental attitude : POSE

at·torn \ə-ˈtərn\ *vi* [ME *attournen*, fr. MF *atorner*, fr. OF, fr. *a-* (fr. L *ad-*) + *torner* to turn] : to agree to become tenant to a new owner or landlord of the same property — **at·torn·ment** \-mənt\ *n*

at·tor·ney \ə-ˈtər-nē\ *n* [ME *attourney*, fr. MF *atorné*, pp. of *atorner*] : one who is legally appointed by another to transact business for him; *specif* : a legal agent qualified to act for suitors and defendants in legal proceedings **syn** see LAWYER — **at·tor·ney·ship** \-ˌship\ *n*

attorney general *n, pl* **attorneys general** *or* **attorney generals** : the chief law officer of a nation or state who represents the government in litigation and serves as its principal legal advisor

at·tract \ə-ˈtrakt\ *vb* [ME *attracten*, fr. L *attractus*, pp. of *attrahere*, fr. *ad-* + *trahere* to draw — more at DRAW] *vt* : to cause to approach or adhere: as **a** : to pull to or toward oneself or itself **b** : to draw by appeal to natural or excited interest, emotion, or aesthetic sense : ENTICE ~ *vi* : to exercise attraction — **at·tract·able** \-ˈtrak-tə-bəl\ *adj* — **at·trac·tor** \-ˈtrak-tər\ *n*

syn ALLURE, CHARM, CAPTIVATE, FASCINATE, ENCHANT: ATTRACT is the broadest of these in application, stressing only the fact of having or exerting power to draw; ALLURE implies an enticing by what is fair, pleasing, or seductive; CHARM implies the power of casting a spell over the person or thing affected and so compelling a response, but it may, like CAPTIVATE, suggest no more than evoking delight or admiration; FASCINATE suggests a magical influence and tends to stress the ineffectiveness of attempts to resist; ENCHANT is perhaps the strongest of these terms in stressing the appeal of the agent and the degree of delight evoked in the subject

at·trac·tion \ə-ˈtrak-shən\ *n* **1** : the act, process, or power of attracting; *specif* : personal charm **2** : an attractive quality, object, or feature **3** : a force acting mutually between particles of matter, tending to draw them together, and resisting their separation

syn ATTRACTION, AFFINITY, SYMPATHY mean the relationship existing between things or persons that are naturally or involuntarily drawn together. ATTRACTION implies the possession by one thing of a quality that pulls another to it; AFFINITY implies a susceptibility or predisposition on the part of the thing or person that is drawn; SYMPATHY implies a reciprocal or natural relation between two things that are both susceptible to the same influences

at·trac·tive \ə-ˈtrak-tiv\ *adj* : having the power to attract; *specif* : CHARMING — **at·trac·tive·ly** *adv* — **at·trac·tive·ness** *n*

at·trib·ut·able \ə-ˈtrib-yət-ə-bəl\ *adj* : capable of being attributed

1**at·tri·bute** \ˈa-trə-ˌbyüt\ *n* [ME, fr. L *attributus*, pp. of *attribuere* to attribute, fr. *ad-* + *tribuere* to bestow — more at TRIBUTE] **1** : an inherent characteristic; *also* : an accidental quality **2** : an object closely associated with or belonging to a specific person, thing, or office; *esp* : such an object used for identification in painting or sculpture **3** : a word ascribing a quality; *esp* : ADJECTIVE **syn** see QUALITY

2**at·trib·ute** \ə-ˈtrib-yət\ *vt* **1** : to explain by way of cause **2 a** : to regard as a characteristic of a person or thing **b** : to reckon as made or originated in an indicated fashion **c** : CLASSIFY, DESIGNATE **syn** see ASCRIBE — **at·trib·ut·er** *n*

at·tri·bu·tion \ˌa-trə-ˈbyü-shən\ *n* : the act of attributing; *also* : an ascribed quality, character, or right

at·trib·u·tive \ə-ˈtrib-yət-iv\ *adj* : relating to or of the nature of an attribute : ATTRIBUTING; *specif* : joined directly to a modified noun without a linking verb ⟨*red* in *red hair* is an ~ adjective⟩ — compare PREDICATE — **attributive** *n* — **at·trib·u·tive·ly** *adv*

at·trit·ed \ə-ˈtrīt-əd\ *adj* : worn by attrition

at·tri·tion \ə-ˈtrish-ən\ *n* [L *attrition-*, *attritio*, fr. *attritus*, pp. of *atterere* to rub against, fr. *ad-* + *terere* to rub — more at THROW] **1** [ME *attricioun*, fr. (assumed) ML *attrition-*, *attritio*, fr. L] : sorrow for one's sins that arises from a motive other than that of the love of God **2** : the act of rubbing together : FRICTION; *also* : the act of wearing or grinding down by friction **3** : the act of weakening or exhausting by constant harassment or abuse **4** : a reduction (as in personnel) chiefly as a result of resignation, retirement, or death — **at·tri·tion·al** \-ˈtrish-nəl, -ˈtrish-ən-ᵊl\ *adj*

at·tune \ə-ˈt(y)ün\ *vt* : to bring into harmony : TUNE — **at·tune·ment** \-mənt\ *n*

atyp·i·cal \(ˈ)ā-ˈtip-i-kəl\ *adj* : not typical : IRREGULAR — **atyp·i·cal·ly** \-k(ə-)lē\ *adv*

au·bade \ō-ˈbäd\ *n* [F, fr. (assumed) OProv *aubada*, fr. OProv *alba*, *auba* dawn, fr. (assumed) VL *alba*, fr. L, fem. of *albus* white] **1** : a song or poem greeting the dawn **2 a** : a morning love song **b** : a song or poem of lovers parting at dawn **3** : morning music

1**au·burn** \ˈȯ-bərn\ *adj* [ME *auborne* blond, fr. MF, fr. ML *alburnus* whitish, fr. L *albus*] **1** : of the color auburn **2** : of a reddish brown color

2**auburn** *n* : a moderate brown

Au·bus·son \ˈō-bə-ˌsōⁿ\ *n* [*Aubusson*, France] **1** : a figured scenic tapestry used for wall hangings and upholstery **2** : a rug woven to resemble the tapestry Aubusson

au cou·rant \ō-kü-räⁿ\ *adj* [F, lit., in the current] : fully informed : UP-TO-DATE

1**auc·tion** \ˈȯk-shən\ *n* [L *auction-*, *auctio*, lit., increase, fr. *auctus*, pp. of *augēre* to increase] **1** : a public sale of property to the highest bidder **2** : the act or process of bidding in some card games

2**auction** *vt* **auc·tion·ing** \-sh(ə-)niŋ\ : to sell at auction ⟨~*ed* off his library⟩

auction bridge *n* : a bridge game differing from contract bridge in that tricks made in excess of the contract are scored toward game

auc·tion·eer \ˌȯk-shə-ˈni(ə)r\ *n* : an agent who sells goods at auction — **auctioneer** *vt*

auc·to·ri·al \ȯk-ˈtōr-ē-əl, -ˈtȯr-\ *adj* [L *auctor* author — more at AUTHOR] : of or relating to an author

au·da·cious \ȯ-ˈdā-shəs\ *adj* [MF *audacieux*, fr. *audace* boldness, fr. L *audacia*, fr. *audac-*, *audax* bold, fr. *audēre* to dare, fr. *avidus* eager — more at AVID] **1 a** : intrepidly daring : ADVENTUROUS **b** : recklessly bold : RASH **2** : contemptuous of law, religion, or decorum : INSOLENT **3** : marked by originality and verve — **au·da·cious·ly** *adv* — **au·da·cious·ness** *n*

au·dac·i·ty \ȯ-ˈdas-ət-ē\ *n* [ME *audacite*, fr. L *audac-*, *audax*] **1** : the quality or state of being audacious: **a** : BOLDNESS **b** : IMPUDENCE **2** : an audacious act **syn** see TEMERITY

au·di·bil·i·ty \ˌȯd-ə-ˈbil-ət-ē\ *n* : audible quality or state

au·di·ble \ˈȯd-ə-bəl\ *adj* [LL *audibilis*, fr. L *audire* to hear; akin to Gk *aisthanesthai* to perceive, Skt *āvis* evidently] : heard or capable of being heard — **au·di·bly** \-blē\ *adv*

au·di·ence \ˈȯd-ē-ən(t)s, ˈäd-\ *n* [ME, fr. MF, fr. L *audientia*, fr. *audient-*, *audiens*, prp. of *audire*] **1** : the act or state of hearing **2 a** : a formal hearing or interview **b** : an opportunity of being heard **3 a** : a group of listeners or spectators **b** : the reading public **4** : FOLLOWING

au·dile \'ȯ-ˌdīl\ *n* [L *audire* to hear] **:** a person whose mental imagery is auditory rather than visual or motor — **audile** *adj*

1**au·dio** \'ȯd-ē-ˌō\ *adj* [*audio-*] **1 :** of or relating to acoustic, mechanical, or electrical frequencies corresponding to normally audible sound waves which are of frequencies approximately from 15 to 20,000 cycles per second **2 a :** of or relating to sound or its reproduction and esp. high-fidelity reproduction **b :** relating to or used in the transmission or reception of sound

2**audio** *n* **1 :** the transmission, reception, or reproduction of sound **2 :** the section of television equipment that deals with sound

audio- *comb form* [L *audire* to hear] **1 :** hearing ⟨*audio*meter⟩ **2 :** sound ⟨*audio*phile⟩ **3 :** auditory and ⟨*audio*-visual⟩

au·di·om·e·ter \ˌȯd-ē-'äm-ət-ər\ *n* **:** an instrument used in measuring the acuity of hearing — **au·dio·met·ric** \ˌȯd-ē-ə-'me-trik\ *adj* — **au·di·om·e·try** \ˌȯd-ē-'äm-ə-trē\ *n*

au·dio·phile \'ȯd-ē-ə-ˌfīl\ *n* **:** one who is enthusiastic about sound reproduction and esp. music from high-fidelity broadcasts or recordings

au·dio·vi·su·al \ˌȯd-ē-(ˌ)ō-'vizh-(ə-)wəl, -'vizh-əl\ *adj* **1 :** of or relating to both hearing and sight **2 :** making use of both hearing and sight in teaching

1**au·dit** \'ȯd-ət\ *n* [ME, fr. L *auditus* act of hearing, fr. *auditus*, pp.] **1 a :** a formal or official examination and verification of an account book **b :** a methodical examination and review **2 :** the final report of an examination of books of account by auditors

2**audit** *vt* **1 :** to examine with intent to verify **2 :** to attend (a course) without working for a grade or receiving formal credit

1**au·di·tion** \ȯ-'dish-ən\ *n* [MF or L; MF, fr. L *audition-*, *auditio*, fr. *auditus*, pp. of *audire*] **1 :** the power or sense of hearing **2 :** the act of hearing; *esp* **:** a critical hearing **3 :** a trial performance to appraise an entertainer's merits

2**audition** *vb* **au·di·tion·ing** \-'dish-(ə-)niŋ\ *vt* **:** to test in an audition ~ *vi* **:** to give a trial performance

au·di·tive \'ȯd-ət-iv\ *adj* **:** AUDITORY

au·di·tor \'ȯd-ət-ər\ *n* **1 :** one that hears or listens **2 :** one authorized to examine and verify accounts **3 :** one that audits a course of study

au·di·to·ri·um \ˌȯd-ə-'tōr-ē-əm, -'tȯr-\ *n* **1 :** the part of a public building where an audience sits **2 :** a room, hall, or building used for public gatherings

au·di·to·ry \'ȯd-ə-ˌtōr-ē, -ˌtȯr-\ *adj* **:** of, relating to, or experienced through hearing

auditory nerve *n* **:** either of the 8th pair of cranial nerves connecting the inner ear with the brain and transmitting impulses concerned with hearing and balance

au fait \ō-'fā\ *adj* [F, lit., to the point] **1 :** fully competent **:** CAPABLE **2 :** fully informed **:** FAMILIAR **3 :** socially correct

Auf·klä·rung \'au̇f-ˌklā-rəŋ, -ˌkler-əŋ\ *n* [G] **:** ENLIGHTENMENT 2

au fond \ō-'fōⁿ\ *adv* [F] **:** at bottom **:** FUNDAMENTALLY

auf Wie·der·seh·en \au̇f-'vēd-ər-ˌzā(-ə)n\ *interj* [G, lit., till seeing again] — used to express farewell

Au·ge·an \ȯ-'jē-ən\ *adj* [L *Augeas*, king of Elis, fr. Gk *Augeias*; fr. the legend that his stable, left neglected for thirty years, was finally cleaned by Hercules] **:** extremely filthy or corrupt

au·gend \'ȯ-ˌjend\ *n* [L *augendus*, gerundive of *augēre* to increase — more at EKE] **:** a quantity to which an addend is added

au·ger \'ȯ-gər\ *n* [ME, alter. (resulting from incorrect division of *a nauger*) of *nauger*, fr. OE *nafogār*; akin to OHG *nabugēr* auger; both fr. a prehistoric WGmc-NGmc compound whose constituents are represented by OE *nafu* nave and *gār* spear — more at GORE] **1 :** a tool for boring holes in wood consisting of a shank with a crosswise handle for turning, a central tapered feed screw, and a pair of cutting lips **2 :** any of various instruments or devices made like an auger and used for boring (as in soil) or forcing through (as a meat grinder)

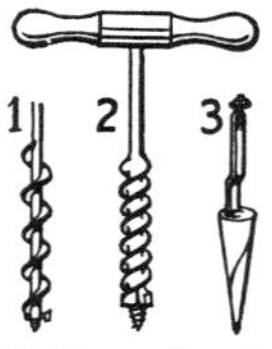

augers: *1*, *2*, screw, *3* tapering pod

1**aught** \'ȯt, 'ät\ *pron* [ME, fr. OE *āwiht*, fr. *ā* ever + *wiht* creature, thing — more at AYE, WIGHT] **1** *archaic* **:** ANYTHING **2 :** ALL ⟨for ~ I care⟩

2**aught** *adv*, *archaic* **:** at all

3**aught** *n* [alter. (resulting from incorrect division of *a naught*) of *naught*] **1 :** ZERO, CIPHER **2** *archaic* **:** NONENTITY, NOTHING

au·gite \'ȯ-ˌjīt\ *n* [L *augites*, a precious stone, fr. Gk *augitēs*] **1 :** a mineral consisting of an aluminous usu. black or dark green pyroxene in igneous rocks **2 :** PYROXENE — **au·git·ic** \ȯ-'jit-ik\ *adj*

1**aug·ment** \ȯg-'ment\ *vb* [ME *augmenten*, fr. MF *augmenter*, fr. LL *augmentare*, fr. L *augmentum* increase, fr. *augēre* to increase — more at EKE] *vi* **:** to become augmented **:** INCREASE ~ *vt* **1 :** to enlarge or increase esp. in size, amount, or degree **2 :** to add an augment to **syn** see INCREASE — **aug·ment·able** \-ə-bəl\ *adj* — **aug·ment·er** *n*

2**aug·ment** \'ȯg-ˌment\ *n* **:** a vowel prefixed or a lengthening of the initial vowel to mark past time esp. in Greek and Sanskrit verbs

aug·men·ta·tion \ˌȯg-mən-'tā-shən, -ˌmen-\ *n* **1 :** the act or process of augmenting **2 :** the state of being augmented **3 :** something that augments

1**aug·men·ta·tive** \ȯg-'ment-ət-iv\ *adj* **1 :** able to augment **2 :** indicating large size and sometimes awkwardness or unattractiveness — used of words and affixes; compare DIMINUTIVE

2**augmentative** *n* **:** an augmentative word or affix

aug·ment·ed \ȯg-'ment-əd\ *adj*, *of a musical interval* **:** made greater by one half step than a major or perfect interval

au gra·tin \ō-'grät-ᵊn, ȯ-, -'grat-\ *adj* [F, lit., with the burnt scrapings from the pan] **:** covered with bread crumbs, butter, and cheese and browned

1**au·gur** \'ȯ-gər\ *n* [L; prob. akin to L *augēre*] **1 :** an official diviner of ancient Rome **2 :** SOOTHSAYER, DIVINER

2**augur** *vt* **1 :** to foretell esp. from omens **2 :** to give promise of **:** PRESAGE ~ *vi* **:** to predict the future esp. from omens

au·gu·ry \'ȯ-gyə-rē, -gə-\ *n* **1 :** divination from omens or portents or from chance events (as the fall of lots) **2 :** OMEN, PORTENT

au·gust \ȯ-'gəst\ *adj* [L *augustus*; akin to L *augēre* to increase] **:** marked by majestic dignity or grandeur — **au·gust·ly** *adv* — **au·gust·ness** *n*

Au·gust \'ȯ-gəst\ *n* [ME, fr. OE, fr. L *Augustus*, fr. *Augustus* Caesar †14 A.D. Roman emperor] **:** the 8th month of the Gregorian calendar

Au·gus·tan \ȯ-'gəs-tən\ *adj* **1 :** of, relating to, or characteristic of Augustus Caesar or his age **2 :** of, relating to, or characteristic of the neoclassical period in England — **Augustan** *n*

1**Au·gus·tin·i·an** \ˌȯ-gə-'stin-ē-ən\ *adj* **1 :** of or relating to St. Augustine or his doctrines **2 :** of or relating to any of several orders under a rule ascribed to St. Augustine — **Au·gus·tin·i·an·ism** \-ē-ə-ˌniz-əm\ *n*

2**Augustinian** *n* **1 :** a follower of St. Augustine **2 :** a member of an Augustinian order; *specif* **:** a friar of the Hermits of St. Augustine founded in 1256 and devoted to educational, missionary, and parish work

au jus \ō-'zhü(s), -'jüs; ō-zhǖ\ *adj* [F, lit., with juice] **:** served in the juice obtained from roasting

auk \'ȯk\ *n* [Norw or Icel *alk*, *alka*, fr. ON *ālka*; akin to L *olor* swan] **:** any of several black and white short-necked diving seabirds (family Alcidae) that breed in colder parts of the northern hemisphere

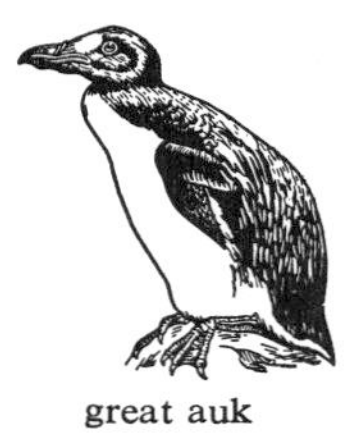
great auk

auk·let \'ȯ-klət\ *n* **:** any of several small auks of the No. Pacific coasts

au lait \ō-'lā\ *adj* [F] **:** containing milk

auld \'ȯl(d), 'äl(d)\ *adj*, *chiefly Scot* **:** OLD

auld lang syne \ˌōl-ˌ(d)aŋ-'zīn, ˌōl-ˌ(d)laŋ-, ˌȯl-, -'sīn\ *n* [Sc, lit., old long ago] **:** the good old times

au na·tu·rel \ˌō-ˌnat-ə-'rel\ *adj* [F] **1 a :** being in natural style or condition **b :** NUDE **2 :** cooked plainly

aunt \'ant, 'ånt\ *n* [ME, fr. OF *ante*, fr. L *amita*; akin to OHG *amma* mother, nurse, Gk *amma* nurse] **1 :** the sister of one's father or mother **2 :** the wife of one's uncle

aur- *or* **auri-** *comb form* [L, fr. *auris* — more at EAR] **1 :** ear ⟨*aur*al⟩ ⟨*auri*scope⟩ **2 :** aural and ⟨*auri*nasal⟩

au·ra \'ȯr-ə\ *n* [ME, fr. L, air, breeze, fr. Gk; akin to Gk *aēr* air] **1 a :** a subtle sensory stimulus **b :** a distinctive atmosphere surrounding a given source **2 :** a luminous radiation **:** NIMBUS **3 :** a subjective sensation (as of lights) experienced before an attack of some nervous disorders

au·ral \'ȯr-əl\ *adj* **:** of or relating to the ear or sense of hearing — **au·ral·ly** \-ə-lē\ *adv*

aurar *pl of* EYRIR

au·re·ate \'ȯr-ē-ət\ *adj* [ME *aureat*, fr. ML *aureatus* decorated with gold, fr. L *aureus* golden — more at ORIOLE] **1 :** of a golden color or brilliance **2 :** marked by grandiloquent and rhetorical style

au·re·ole \'ȯr-ē-ˌōl\ *or* **au·re·o·la** \ȯ-'rē-ə-lə\ *n* [ME *aureole* heavenly crown worn by saints, fr. ML *aureola*, fr. L, fem. of *aureolus* golden — more at ORIOLE] **1 :** a radiant light around the head or body of a representation of a sacred personage **2 :** RADIANCE, AURA **3 :** the luminous area surrounding the sun or other bright light when seen through thin cloud or mist **:** CORONA

au re·voir \ˌōr-əv-'wär, ˌȯr-\ *n* [F, lit., till seeing again] **:** GOOD-BYE

au·ric \'ȯr-ik\ *adj* [L *aurum* gold — more at ORIOLE] **:** of, relating to, or derived from gold esp. when trivalent

au·ri·cle \'ȯr-i-kəl\ *n* [L *auricula*, fr. dim. of *auris* ear] **1 a :** PINNA 2b **b :** the chamber or either of the chambers of the heart that receives blood from the veins and forces it into the ventricle or ventricles **2 :** an angular or ear-shaped anatomic lobe or process

au·ric·u·la \ȯ-'rik-yə-lə\ *n* [NL, fr. L, external ear] **1 :** a yellow-flowered Alpine primrose (*Primula auricula*) **2 :** AURICLE

au·ric·u·lar \ȯ-'rik-yə-lər\ *adj* **1 :** of, relating to, or using the ear or the sense of hearing **2 :** told privately **3 :** known by the sense of hearing **4 :** of or relating to an auricle or auricula

au·ric·u·late \ȯ-'rik-yə-lət\ *adj* **:** having ears or auricles

au·ric·u·lo·ven·tric·u·lar \ȯ-ˌrik-yə-ˌlō-(ˌ)ven-'trik-yə-lər\ *adj* **:** ATRIOVENTRICULAR

au·rif·er·ous \ȯ-'rif-(ə-)rəs\ *adj* [L *aurifer*, fr. *aurum* + *-fer* -ferous] **:** gold-bearing

Au·ri·ga \ȯ-'rī-gə\ *n* [L (gen. *Aurigae*), lit., charioteer] **:** a constellation between Perseus and Gemini

Au·ri·gna·cian \ˌȯr-ēn-'yā-shən\ *adj* [F *aurignacien*, fr. *Aurignac*, France] **:** of or relating to an Upper Paleolithic culture marked by finely made artifacts of stone and bone, paintings, and engravings

au·rochs \'au̇(ə)-ˌräks, 'ȯ(ə)-\ *n*, *pl* **aurochs** *also* **au·rochs·es** [G, fr. OHG *ūrohso*, fr. *ūro* aurochs + *ohso* ox; akin to OE *ūr* aurochs — more at OX] **1 :** URUS **2 :** WISENT

au·ro·ra \ə-'rōr-ə, ȯ-, -'rȯr-\ *n*, *pl* **auroras** *or* **au·ro·rae** \-(ˌ)ē\ [L — more at EAST] **1 :** DAWN **2 a :** AURORA BOREALIS **b :** AURORA AUSTRALIS — **au·ro·ral** \-əl\ *adj* — **au·ro·re·an** \-ē-ən\ *adj*

aurora aus·tra·lis \-ˌrōr-ə-(ˌ)ȯ-'strā-ləs, -ˌrȯr-\ *n* [NL, lit., southern aurora] **:** a phenomenon in the southern hemisphere corresponding to the aurora borealis in the northern

aurora bo·re·al·is \-ˌbōr-ē-'al-əs, -ˌbȯr-\ *n* [NL, lit., northern dawn] **:** a luminous phenomenon that consists of streamers or arches of light in the sky at night, is held to be of electrical origin, and appears to best advantage in the arctic regions

au·rous \'ȯr-əs\ *adj* [ISV, fr. L *aurum* gold — more at ORIOLE] **:** of, relating to, or containing gold esp. when univalent

aus·cul·tate \'ȯ-skəl-ˌtāt\ *vt* [back-formation fr. *auscultation*] **:** to examine by auscultation — **aus·cul·ta·to·ry** \ȯ-'skəl-tə-ˌtōr-ē -ˌtȯr-\ *adj*

aus·cul·ta·tion \ˌȯ-skəl-'tā-shən\ *n* [L *auscultation-*, *auscultatio* act of listening, fr. *auscultatus*, pp. of *auscultare* to listen; akin to L *auris* ear — more at EAR] **:** the act of listening to sounds arising within organs as an aid to diagnosis and treatment

aus·pi·cate \'ȯ-spə-ˌkāt\ *vt* [L *auspicatus*, pp. of *auspicari* to take auspices, fr. *auspic-*, *auspex*] **:** to initiate or enter upon esp. in a manner calculated to ensure good luck

aus·pice \'ȯ-spəs\ *n*, *pl* **aus·pic·es** \-spə-səz, -ˌsēz\ [L *auspicium*, fr. *auspic-* *auspex* diviner by birds, fr. *avis* bird + *specere* to look, look at — more at AVIARY, SPY] **1 :** observation in augury esp. of the flight and feeding of birds **2 :** a prophetic sign; *esp* **:** a favorable sign **3** *pl* **:** kindly patronage and guidance **:** PROTECTION

aus·pi·cious \ȯ-'spish-əs\ *adj* **1 :** affording a favorable auspice **2 :** attended by good auspices **:** PROSPEROUS **syn** see FAVORABLE — **aus·pi·cious·ly** *adv* — **aus·pi·cious·ness** *n*

aus·ten·ite \'ȯs-tə-ˌnīt, 'äs-\ *n* [F, fr. Sir W. C. Roberts-*Austen* †1902 E metallurgist] **:** a solid solution in iron of carbon and sometimes other solutes that occurs as a constituent of steel under certain conditions — **aus·ten·it·ic** \ˌȯs-tə-'nit-ik, ˌäs-\ *adj*

aus·tere \ȯ-'sti(ə)r\ adj [ME, fr. MF, fr. L austerus, fr. Gk austēros harsh, severe; akin to Gk hauos dry — more at SERE] **1 a :** stern and forbidding in appearance and manner **b :** SOMBER, GRAVE **2 :** rigidly abstemious **:** ASCETIC **3 :** UNADORNED, SIMPLE syn see SEVERE — **aus·tere·ly** adv — **aus·tere·ness** n

aus·ter·i·ty \ȯ-'ster-ət-ē\ n **1 :** the quality or state of being austere **2 a :** an austere act, manner, or attitude **b :** an ascetic practice **3 :** enforced or extreme economy

Aus·tin \'ȯs-tən, 'äs-\ adj [ME Austyn n., Augustinian, fr. LL Augustinus St. Augustine] chiefly Brit **:** AUGUSTINIAN

¹Austr- or **Austro-** comb form [ME austr-, fr. L, fr. Austr-, Auster south wind; akin to L aurora dawn — more at EAST] **1 :** south **:** southern ⟨Austroasiatic⟩ **2 :** Australian and ⟨Austro-Malayan⟩

²Austr- or **Austro-** comb form [prob. fr. NL, fr. Austria] **:** Austrian and ⟨Austro-Hungarian⟩

aus·tral \'ȯs-trəl, 'äs-\ adj **1 :** SOUTHERN **2** cap **:** Australian

Aus·tra·lia Day \ȯ-'strāl-yə-, ä-\ n **:** a national holiday in Australia observed in commemoration of the landing of the British at Sydney Cove in 1788 and observed on Jan. 26 if a Monday and otherwise on the next Monday

Aus·tra·lian ballot \-strāl-yən-\ n **:** an official ballot printed at public expense on which the names of all the nominated candidates and proposals appear and which is distributed only at the polling place and marked in secret

Australian terrier n **:** a small rather short-legged usu. grayish wirehaired terrier of Australian origin

Aus·tra·loid \'ȯs-trə-.lȯid, 'äs-\ adj [Australia + E -oid] **:** of or relating to an ethnic group including the Australian aborigines and other peoples of southern Asia and Pacific islands sometimes including the Ainu — **Australoid** n

aus·tra·lo·pith·e·cine \ȯ-.strā-lō-'pith-ə-.sīn, ä-\ adj [deriv. of L australis southern (fr. Austr-, Auster) + Gk pithēkos ape] **:** of or relating to extinct southern African apes (esp. genus Australopithecus) with near-human dentition — **australopithecine** n

Aus·tral·orp \'ȯs-trə-.lȯ(r)p, 'äs-\ n [Australian + Orpington] **:** a usu. black domestic fowl developed in Australia and valued for egg production

Aus·tro·asi·at·ic \.ȯs-(.)trō-.ā-zhē-'at-ik, .äs-\ adj **:** of, relating to, or constituting a family of languages once widespread over northeastern India and Indo-China

Aus·tro·ne·sian \.ȯs-trə-'nē-zhən, .äs-, -shən\ adj [Austronesia, islands of the southern Pacific] **:** of, relating to, or constituting a family of agglutinative languages spoken in the area extending from Madagascar eastward through the Malay peninsula and archipelago to Hawaii and Easter Island and including practically all the native languages of the Pacific islands with exception of the Australian, Papuan, and Negrito languages

aut- or **auto-** comb form [Gk, fr. autos same, -self, self] **1 :** self **:** same one ⟨autism⟩ ⟨autobiography⟩ **2 :** automatic **:** self-acting **:** self-regulating ⟨autodyne⟩

au·ta·coid \'ȯt-ə-.kȯid\ n [aut- + Gk akos remedy; akin to OIr hīcc healing] **:** a specific organic substance (as a hormone) forming in one part of the body, moving in the body fluid or the sap, and modifying the activity of the cells of another part — **au·ta·coi·dal** \.ȯt-ə-'kȯid-°l\ adj

au·tar·chic \ȯ-'tär-kik\ adj **:** AUTARKIC — **au·tar·chi·cal** \-ki-kəl\ adj

¹au·tar·chy \'ȯ-.tär-kē\ n [Gk autarchia, fr. aut- + -archia -archy] **1 :** absolute sovereignty **2 :** absolute or autocratic rule

²autarchy n [by alter.] **:** AUTARKY

au·tar·kic \ȯ-'tär-kik\ adj **:** of, relating to, or marked by autarky — **au·tar·ki·cal** \-ki-kəl\ adj

au·tar·ky \'ȯ-.tär-kē\ n [G autarkie, fr. Gk autarkeia, fr. autarkēs self-sufficient, fr. aut- + arkein to defend, suffice — more at ARK] **1 :** SELF-SUFFICIENCY, INDEPENDENCE; specif **:** national economic self-sufficiency and independence **2 :** a policy of establishing a self-sufficient and independent national economy

aut·ecol·o·gy \.ȯt-i-'käl-ə-jē\ n [ISV] **:** ecology dealing with individual organisms or individual kinds of organisms

au·then·tic \ə-'thent-ik, ȯ-\ adj [ME autentik, fr. MF autentique, fr. LL authenticus, fr. Gk authentikos, fr. authentēs perpetrator, master, fr. aut- + -hentēs (akin to Gk anyein to accomplish, Skt sanoti he gains)] **1 obs :** AUTHORITATIVE **2 :** worthy of acceptance or belief **:** TRUSTWORTHY **3 :** not imaginary, false, or imitation **:** GENUINE — **au·then·ti·cal·ly** \-i-k(ə-)lē\ adv — **au·then·tic·i·ty** \.ȯ-.then-'tis-ət-ē, -thən-\ n

syn AUTHENTIC, GENUINE, VERITABLE, BONA FIDE mean being actually and exactly what the thing in question is said to be. AUTHENTIC implies being fully trustworthy as according with fact or actuality ⟨authentic record⟩ GENUINE implies accordance with an original or a type without counterfeiting, admixture, or adulteration ⟨genuine maple syrup⟩ VERITABLE may stress true existence or actual identity ⟨veritable offspring⟩ but more commonly merely stresses the suitability of a metaphor ⟨veritable hail of questions⟩ BONA FIDE applies when sincerity of intention is in question ⟨bona fide sale of securities⟩

au·then·ti·cate \ə-'thent-i-.kāt, ȯ-\ vt **:** to prove or serve to prove the authenticity of syn see CONFIRM — **au·then·ti·ca·tion** \ə-.thent-i-'kā-shən, (.)ȯ-\ n — **au·then·ti·ca·tor** \ə-'thent-i-.kāt-ər, ȯ-\ n

au·thor \'ȯ-thər\ n [ME auctour, fr. ONF, fr. L auctor promoter, originator, author, fr. auctus, pp. of augēre to increase — more at EKE] **1 :** one that writes or composes a book or other literary work **2 :** one that originates or makes **:** CREATOR; esp **:** GOD — **author** vt — **au·thor·ing** \-th(ə-)riŋ\ n — **au·thor·ess** \'ȯ-th(ə-)rəs\ n — **au·tho·ri·al** \ȯ-'thōr-ē-əl, -'thȯr-\ adj

au·thor·i·tar·i·an \ə-.thär-ə-'ter-ē-ən, ə-, -.thȯr-\ adj **1 :** relating to or favoring blind submission to authority **2 :** relating to or favoring a concentration of power in a leader or an elite not constitutionally responsible to the people — **authoritarian** n — **au·thor·i·tar·i·an·ism** \-ē-ə-.niz-əm\ n

au·thor·i·ta·tive \ə-'thär-ə-.tāt-iv, ȯ-, -.thȯr-\ adj **1 a :** having or proceeding from authority **b :** entitled to obedience, credit, or acceptance **2 :** DICTATORIAL, PEREMPTORY — **au·thor·i·ta·tive·ly** adv — **au·thor·i·ta·tive·ness** n

au·thor·i·ty \ə-'thär-ət-ē, ȯ-, -'thȯr-\ n [ME auctorite, fr. OF auctorité, fr. L auctoritat-, auctoritas opinion, decision, power, fr. auctor] **1 a :** a citation used in defense or support; also **:** the source

from which the citation is drawn **b (1) :** a conclusive statement or set of statements; also **:** a decision taken as a precedent **(2) :** TESTIMONY **c :** an individual cited or appealed to as an expert **2 a :** power to influence or command thought, opinion, or behavior **b :** freedom granted **:** RIGHT **3 a :** persons in command; specif **:** GOVERNMENT **b :** a governmental agency or corporation to administer a revenue-producing public enterprise **4 a :** GROUNDS, WARRANT **b :** convincing force syn see INFLUENCE, POWER

au·tho·ri·za·tion \.ȯ-th(ə-)rə-'zā-shən\ n **:** the act of authorizing **:** an instrument that authorizes **:** SANCTION

au·tho·rize \'ȯ-thə-.rīz\ vt **1 :** to invest with esp. legal authority **:** EMPOWER **2 :** to establish by authority (as precedent) **:** SANCTION **3 :** to furnish a ground for **:** JUSTIFY — **au·tho·riz·er** n

Authorized Version n **:** a revision of the English Bible carried out under James I, published in 1611, and widely used by Protestants

au·thor·ship \'ȯ-thər-.ship\ n **1 :** the profession of writing **2 a :** the origin of a literary production **b :** the state or act of creating or causing

au·tism \'ȯ-.tiz-əm\ n **:** absorption in fantasy as escape from reality — **au·tis·tic** \ȯ-'tis-tik\ adj

au·to \'ȯt-(.)ō, 'ät-\ n **:** AUTOMOBILE

auto- comb form [¹automobile] **:** self-propelling **:** automotive ⟨autotruck⟩

au·to·an·ti·body \.ȯt-(.)ō-'ant-i-.bäd-ē\ n **:** an antibody against one of the constituents of the tissues of the individual that produces it

au·to·bahn \'ȯt-ō-.bän, 'aut-\ n [G, fr. auto + bahn road] **:** a German expressway

au·to·bi·og·ra·pher \.ȯt-ə-(.)bī-'äg-rə-fər, -bē-\ n **:** one who writes his biography

au·to·bio·graph·i·cal \.ȯt-ə-.bī-ə-'graf-i-kəl\ or **au·to·bio·graph·ic** \-ik\ adj **:** of, relating to, or of the nature of an autobiography — **au·to·bio·graph·i·cal·ly** \-i-k(ə-)lē\ adv

au·to·bi·og·ra·phy \.ȯt-ə-(.)bī-'äg-rə-fē, -bē-\ n **:** the biography of a person narrated by himself

au·to·bus \'ȯt-ō-.bəs\ n [auto + bus] **:** OMNIBUS 1

au·to·cat·a·ly·sis \.ȯt-ō-kə-'tal-ə-səs\ n [NL] **:** catalysis of a reaction by one of its products — **au·to·cat·a·lyt·ic** \-.kat-°l-'it-ik\ adj

au·toch·thon \ȯ-'täk-thən\ n, pl autochthons or **au·toch·tho·nes** \-thə-.nēz\ [Gk autochthōn, fr. aut- + chthōn earth — more at HUMBLE] **1 a :** one supposedly sprung from the ground he inhabits **b :** ABORIGINE, NATIVE **2 :** something that is autochthonous; esp **:** an indigenous plant or animal — **au·toch·tho·nism** \-thə-.niz-əm\ n

au·toch·tho·nous \ȯ-'täk-thə-nəs\ adj **:** INDIGENOUS, NATIVE — **au·toch·tho·nous·ly** adv — **au·toch·tho·ny** \-nē\ n

¹au·to·clave \'ȯt-ō-.klāv\ n [F, fr. aut- + L clavis key — more at CLAVICLE] **:** an apparatus using superheated steam under pressure

²autoclave vt **:** to subject to the action of an autoclave

au·toc·ra·cy \ȯ-'täk-rə-sē\ n **1 :** government in which one person possesses unlimited power **2 :** the authority or rule of an autocrat **3 :** a community or state governed by autocracy

au·to·crat \'ȯt-ə-.krat\ n [F autocrate, fr. Gk autokratēs ruling by oneself, absolute, fr. aut- + -kratēs ruling — more at -CRAT] **:** a monarch or other person ruling with unlimited authority

au·to·crat·ic \.ȯt-ə-'krat-ik\ adj **1 :** of, relating to, or being autocracy or an autocrat **:** ABSOLUTE **2 :** characteristic of or resembling an autocrat **:** DESPOTIC — **au·to·crat·i·cal** \-i-kəl\ adj — **au·to·crat·i·cal·ly** \-k(ə-)lē\ adv

au·to·da·fé \.aut-ō-də-'fā, .ȯt-\ n, pl **au·tos·da·fé** \-ōz-də-\ [Pg auto da fé, lit., act of the faith] **:** the ceremony accompanying the pronouncement of judgment by the Inquisition and followed by the execution of sentence by the secular authorities; broadly **:** the burning of a heretic

au·to·di·dact \.ȯt-ō-'dī-.dakt\ n [Gk autodidaktos self-taught, fr. aut- + didaktos taught, fr. didaskein to teach — more at DOCILE] **:** a self-taught person — **au·to·di·dac·tic** \-(.)dī-'dak-tik\ adj

au·to·dyne \'ȯt-ə-.dīn\ n [ISV aut- + heterodyne] **:** a heterodyne in which the auxiliary current is generated in the device used for rectification

au·toe·cious \ȯ-'tē-shəs\ adj [aut- + Gk oikia house — more at VICINITY] **:** passing through all life stages on the same host ⟨~ rusts⟩ — **au·toe·cious·ly** adv — **au·toe·cism** \-'tē-.siz-əm\ n

au·to·erot·ic \.ȯt-ō-i-'rät-ik\ adj **:** of, relating to, or marked by autoerotism — **au·to·erot·i·cal·ly** \-i-k(ə-)lē\ adv

au·to·er·o·tism \-'er-ə-.tiz-əm\ or **au·to·erot·i·cism** \-i-'rät-ə-.siz-əm\ n **1 :** sexual gratification obtained solely through one's own organism **2 :** sexual feeling arising without known external stimulation

au·tog·a·mous \ȯ-'täg-ə-məs\ adj **:** of, relating to, or reproducing by autogamy

au·tog·a·my \ȯ-'täg-ə-mē\ n [ISV] **:** SELF-FERTILIZATION: as **a :** pollination of a flower by its own pollen **b :** conjugation of two sister cells or sister nuclei of protozoans or fungi

au·to·gen·e·sis \.ȯt-ō-'jen-ə-səs\ n [NL] **:** ABIOGENESIS — **au·to·ge·net·ic** \-jə-'net-ik\ adj — **au·to·ge·net·i·cal·ly** \-i-k(ə-)lē\ adv

au·tog·e·nous \ȯ-'täj-ə-nəs\ or **au·to·gen·ic** \.ȯt-ə-'jen-ik\ adj [Gk autogenēs, fr. aut- + -genēs born, produced — more at -GEN] **1 :** produced independently of external influence or aid **:** ENDOGENOUS **2 :** originating within or derived from the same individual ⟨an ~ graft⟩ — **au·tog·e·nous·ly** adv

au·to·gi·ro also **au·to·gy·ro** \.ȯt-ō-'jī(ə)r-(.)ō\ n [fr. Autogiro, a trademark] **:** a rotary-wing aircraft that employs a propeller for forward motion and a freely rotating rotor for lift

¹au·to·graph \'ȯt-ə-.graf\ n [LL autographum, fr. L, neut. of autographus written with one's own hand, fr. Gk autographos, fr. aut- + -graphos written — more at -GRAPH] **1 :** something written with one's own hand: **a :** an original manuscript **b :** a person's handwritten signature **2 :** a representation or trace of an object produced in a photographic emulsion by the mechanical, electrical, chemical, or radiation effects of the object itself — **au·tog·ra·phy** \ȯ-'täg-rə-fē\ n

²autograph vt **1 :** to write with one's own hand **2 :** to write one's signature in or on

au·to·graph·ic \ˌȯt-ə-ˈgraf-ik\ *adj* **1 :** of, relating to, or constituting an autograph **2 a** *of an instrument* **:** SELF-RECORDING **b** *of a record* **:** recorded by a self-recording instrument — **au·to·graph·i·cal·ly** \-i-k(ə-)lē\ *adv*

au·to·hyp·no·sis \ˌȯt-ō-hip-ˈnō-səs\ *n* [NL] **:** self-induced and usu. automatic hypnosis

au·to·in·fec·tion \-in-ˈfek-shən\ *n* [ISV] **:** reinfection with larvae produced by parasitic worms already in the body

au·to·in·oc·u·la·tion \ˌȯt-(ˌ)ō-in-ˌäk-yə-ˈlā-shən\ *n* [ISV] **1 :** inoculation with vaccine prepared from material from one's own body **2 :** spread of infection from one part to other parts of the same body

au·to·in·tox·i·ca·tion \-in-ˌtäk-sə-ˈkā-shən\ *n* [ISV] **:** a state of being poisoned by toxic substances produced within the body

au·to·load·ing \ˌȯt-ō-ˈlōd-iŋ\ *adj* **:** SEMIAUTOMATIC b

au·tol·o·gous \ȯ-ˈtäl-ə-gəs\ *adj* [*aut-* + *-ologous* (as in *homologous*)] **:** derived from the same individual

au·tol·y·sate \ȯ-ˈtäl-ə-ˌsāt, -ˌzāt\ *n* **:** a product of autolysis

au·tol·y·sin \ȯ-ˈtäl-ə-sən\ *n* **:** a substance that produces autolysis

au·tol·y·sis \ȯ-ˈtäl-ə-səs\ *n* [NL] **:** self-digestion occurring in plant and animal tissues esp. when these are not in normal continuity with the organism — **au·to·lyt·ic** \ˌȯt-ᵊl-ˈit-ik\ *adj*

au·to·mat \ˈȯt-ə-ˌmat\ *n* [fr. *Automat*, a trademark] **:** a cafeteria in which food is delivered from coin-operated compartments

au·to·mate \ˈȯt-ə-ˌmāt\ *vt* [back-formation fr. *automation*] **1 :** to operate by automation **2 :** to convert to largely automatic operation **:** AUTOMATIZE

1**au·to·mat·ic** \ˌȯt-ə-ˈmat-ik\ *adj* [Gk *automatos* self-acting, fr. *aut-* + *-matos* (akin to L *ment-*, *mens* mind) — more at MIND] **1 a :** largely or wholly involuntary; *esp* **:** REFLEX 5 **b :** acting or done spontaneously or unconsciously; *also* **:** resembling an automaton **:** MECHANICAL **2 :** having a self-acting or self-regulating mechanism **3** *of a firearm* **:** using either gas pressure or force of recoil and mechanical spring action for repeatedly ejecting the empty cartridge shell, introducing a new cartridge, and firing it **syn** see SPONTANEOUS —**au·to·mat·i·cal·ly** \-i-k(ə-)lē\ *adv*

2**automatic** *n* **:** a machine or apparatus that operates automatically; *esp* **:** an automatic firearm

au·to·ma·tic·i·ty \ˌȯt-ə-mə-ˈtis-ət-ē\ *n* **:** the quality or state of being automatic

automatic pilot *n* **:** a device for automatically steering ships and aircraft — called also *auto pilot*

au·to·ma·tion \ˌȯt-ə-ˈmā-shən\ *n* [1*automatic*] **1 :** the technique of making an apparatus, a process, or a system operate automatically **2 :** the state of being operated automatically **3 :** automatically controlled operation of an apparatus, process, or system by mechanical or electronic devices that take the place of human organs of observation, effort, and decision

au·tom·a·tism \ȯ-ˈtäm-ə-ˌtiz-əm\ *n* [F *automatisme*, fr. *automate* automaton, fr. L *automaton*] **1 a :** the quality or state of being automatic **b :** an automatic action **2 :** a theory that views the body as a machine and consciousness as a noncontrolling adjunct of the body **3 :** the power or fact of moving independently of external stimuli or under the influence of external stimuli but independent of conscious control **4 :** suspension of the conscious mind to release subconscious images — **au·tom·a·tist** \-ˈtäm-ət-əst\ *n*

au·tom·a·ti·za·tion \ȯ-ˌtäm-ət-ə-ˈzā-shən\ *n* **:** AUTOMATION

au·tom·a·tize \ȯ-ˈtäm-ə-ˌtīz\ *vt* [1*automatic*] **:** to make automatic

au·tom·a·ton \ȯ-ˈtäm-ət-ən, -ə-ˌtän\ *n, pl* **automatons** *or* **au·tom·a·ta** \-ət-ə\ [L, fr. Gk, neut. of *automatos*] **1 :** a mechanism that is relatively self-operating; *esp* **:** ROBOT **2 :** a machine or control mechanism designed to follow automatically a predetermined sequence of operations or respond to encoded instructions **3 :** a creature who acts in a mechanical fashion

1**au·to·mo·bile** \ˌȯt-ə-mō-ˈbē(ə)l, ˈȯt-ə-mō-ˌbēl, ˌȯt-ə-ˈmō-ˌbēl\ *adj* [F, fr. *aut-* + *mobile*] **:** AUTOMOTIVE

2**automobile** *n* **:** a usu. 4-wheeled automotive vehicle designed for passenger transportation and commonly propelled by an internal-combustion engine using a volatile fuel — **automobile** *vi* — **au·to·mo·bil·ist** \-ˈbē-ləst, -ˌbē-\ *n*

au·to·mo·tive \ˌȯt-ə-ˈmōt-iv\ *adj* **1 :** SELF-PROPELLED **2 :** of, relating to, or concerned with automotive vehicles or machines

au·to·nom·ic \ˌȯt-ə-ˈnäm-ik\ *adj* **1 a :** acting independently of volition ⟨~ reflexes⟩ **b :** relating to, affecting, or controlled by the autonomic nervous system **2 :** due to internal causes or influences **:** SPONTANEOUS — **au·to·nom·i·cal·ly** \-i-k(ə-)lē\ *adv*

autonomic nervous system *n* **:** a part of the vertebrate nervous system that innervates smooth and cardiac muscle and glandular tissues and governs involuntary actions

au·ton·o·mist \ȯ-ˈtän-ə-məst\ *n* **:** one who advocates autonomy

au·ton·o·mous \ȯ-ˈtän-ə-məs\ *adj* [Gk *autonomos* independent, fr. *aut-* + *nomos* law — more at NIMBLE] **1 :** of, relating to, or marked by autonomy **2 a :** having the right or power of self-government **b :** undertaken or carried on without outside control **:** SELF-CONTAINED **3 a :** existing or capable of existing independently ⟨~ zooid⟩ **b :** responding, reacting, or developing independently of the whole ⟨an ~ growth⟩ **4 :** controlled by the autonomic nervous system **syn** see FREE — **au·ton·o·mous·ly** *adv*

au·ton·o·my \-mē\ *n* **1 :** the quality or state of being self-governing; *esp* **:** the right of self-government **2 :** a self-governing state

au·to·phyte \ˈȯt-ə-ˌfīt\ *n* **:** a plant capable of synthesizing its own food from simple inorganic substances — **au·to·phyt·ic** \ˌȯt-ə-ˈfit-ik\ *adj* — **au·to·phyt·i·cal·ly** \-i-k(ə-)lē\ *adv*

au·to·plas·tic \ˌȯt-ō-ˈplas-tik\ *adj* **:** of, relating to, or involving repair of lesions with tissue from the same body — **au·to·plas·ti·cal·ly** \-ti-k(ə-)lē\ *adv* — **au·to·plas·ty** \ˈȯt-ō-ˌplas-tē\ *n*

au·top·sy \ˈȯ-ˌtäp-sē, ˈȯt-əp-\ *n* [Gk *autopsia* act of seeing with one's own eyes, fr. *aut-* + *opsis* sight, fr. *opsesthai* to be going to see] **:** POSTMORTEM EXAMINATION — **autopsy** *vt*

au·to·ra·dio·graph \ˌȯt-ō-ˈrād-ē-ə-ˌgraf\ *or* **au·to·ra·dio·gram** \-ˌgram\ *n* [ISV] **:** an image produced on a photographic film or plate by the radiations from a radioactive substance in an object which is in close contact with the emulsion — **au·to·ra·dio·graph·ic** \-ˌrād-ē-ə-ˈgraf-ik\ *adj* — **au·to·ra·di·og·ra·phy** \-ˌrād-ē-ˈäg-rə-fē\ *n*

au·to·sex·ing \ˈȯt-ō-ˌsek-siŋ\ *adj* **:** showing characters that are differential for sex at birth or hatching

au·to·so·mal \ˌȯt-ə-ˈsō-məl\ *adj* **:** of or relating to an autosome

au·to·some \ˈȯt-ə-ˌsōm\ *n* **:** a chromosome other than a sex chromosome

au·to·sug·ges·tion \ˌȯt-ō-sə(g)-ˈjes(h)-chən\ *n* [ISV] **:** an influencing of one's own attitudes, behavior, or physical condition by mental processes other than conscious thought **:** SELF-HYPNOSIS

au·to·tel·ic \ˌȯt-ō-ˈtel-ik\ *adj* [Gk *autotelēs*, fr. *aut-* + *telos* end] **:** having a purpose in itself — **au·to·tel·ism** \-ˈtel-ˌiz-əm\ *n*

au·to·tom·ic \ˌȯt-ə-ˈtäm-ik\ *or* **au·tot·o·mous** \ȯ-ˈtät-ə-məs\ *adj* **:** of, relating to, or characterized by autotomy

au·tot·o·mize \ȯ-ˈtät-ə-ˌmīz\ *vt* **:** to effect autotomy of **~** *vi* **:** to undergo autotomy

au·tot·o·my \-mē\ *n* [ISV] **:** reflex separation of a part from the body **:** division of the body into two or more pieces

au·to·trans·form·er \ˌȯt-ō-(ˌ)tran(t)s-ˈfȯr-mər\ *n* **:** a transformer in which the primary and secondary coils have part or all of their turns in common

au·to·troph \ˈȯt-ə-ˌträf\ *n* [G, fr. *autotroph*, adj.] **:** an autotrophic organism — **au·tot·ro·phy** \ȯ-ˈtä-trə-fē\ *n*

au·to·tro·phic \ˌȯt-ə-ˈträf-ik, -ˈtrō-fik\ *adj* [prob. fr. G *autotroph*, fr. Gk *autotrophos* supplying one's own food, fr. *aut-* + *trephein* to nourish — more at ATROPHY] **1 :** needing only carbon dioxide or carbonates as a source of carbon and a simple inorganic nitrogen compound for metabolic synthesis **2 :** not requiring a specified exogenous factor for normal metabolism — **au·to·tro·phi·cal·ly** \-i-k(ə-)lē, -fi-\ *adv*

au·to·truck \ˈȯt-ō-ˌtrək\ *n* **:** a motor-driven truck

au·to·type \ˈȯt-ə-ˌtīp\ *n* **1 :** FACSIMILE **2 a :** CARBON PROCESS **b :** a picture made by the carbon process — **au·to·typ·ic** \ˌȯt-ə-ˈtip-ik\ *adj* — **au·to·typy** \ˈȯt-ə-ˌtī-pē\ *n*

au·tumn \ˈȯt-əm\ *n* [ME *autumpne*, fr. L *autumnus*] **1 :** the season between summer and winter comprising in the northern hemisphere usu. the months of September, October, and November or as reckoned astronomically extending from the September equinox to the December solstice — called also *fall* **2 :** a time of maturity or decline — **au·tum·nal** \ȯ-ˈtəm-nəl\ *adj* — **au·tum·nal·ly** \-nə-lē\ *adv*

autumn crocus *n* **:** an autumn-blooming colchicum

au·tun·ite \ō-ˈtən-ˌīt\ *n* [*Autun*, France] **:** a radioactive lemon-yellow mineral $Ca(UO_2)_2(PO_4)_2.10\text{–}12H_2O$ occurring in tabular crystals with basal cleavage and in scales resembling those of mica

aux·e·sis \ȯg-ˈzē-səs, ȯk-ˈsē-\ *n* [NL, fr. Gk *auxēsis* increase, growth, fr. *auxein* to increase — more at EKE] **:** GROWTH; *specif* **:** increase of cell size without cell division — **aux·et·ic** \-ˈzet-ik, -ˈset-\ *adj* — **aux·et·i·cal·ly** \-i-k(ə-)lē\ *adv*

1**aux·il·ia·ry** \ȯg-ˈzil-yə-rē, -ˈzil-(ə-)rē\ *adj* [L *auxiliaris*, fr. *auxilium* help; akin to Gk *auxein* to increase] **1 a :** offering or providing help **b :** functioning in a subsidiary capacity **2** *of a verb* **:** accompanying another verb and typically expressing person, number, mood, or tense **3 a :** SUPPLEMENTARY **b :** RESERVE **4 :** equipped with sails and a supplementary inboard engine

2**auxiliary** *n* **1 a :** an auxiliary person, group, or device; *specif* **:** a member of a foreign force serving a nation at war **b :** a Roman Catholic titular bishop assisting a diocesan bishop and not having the right of succession **2 :** an auxiliary boat or ship **3 :** an auxiliary verb

aux·in \ˈȯk-sən\ *n* [ISV, fr. Gk *auxein*] **:** an organic substance able in low concentrations to promote elongation of plant shoots and usu. to produce other specific growth effects; *broadly* **:** PLANT HORMONE — **aux·in·ic** \ȯk-ˈsin-ik\ *adj* — **aux·in·i·cal·ly** \-i-k(ə-)lē\ *adv*

ava *or* **ava'** \ə-ˈvȯ, -ˈvȧ\ *adv* [Sc *av* (alter. of E *of*) + *a* all] *Scot* **:** of all **:** at all

1**avail** \ə-ˈvā(ə)l\ *vb* [ME *availen*, prob. fr. *a-* (as in *abaten* to abate) + *vailen* to avail] *vi* **:** to be of use or advantage **:** SERVE **~** *vt* **:** to be of use or advantage to **:** PROFIT — **avail of :** to make use of

2**avail** *n* **1 :** advantage toward attainment of a goal or purpose **:** USE ⟨effort was of little ~⟩ **2** *pl, archaic* **:** profits or proceeds esp. from a business or from the sale of property

avail·abil·i·ty \ə-ˌvā-lə-ˈbil-ət-ē\ *n* **1 :** the quality or state of being available **2 :** an available person or thing

avail·able \ə-ˈvā-lə-bəl\ *adj* **1 a** *obs* **:** capable of availing **b** *archaic* **:** having a beneficial effect **2 :** VALID — used of a legal plea or charge **3 :** such as may be availed of **:** USABLE **4 :** ACCESSIBLE, OBTAINABLE **5 a :** having the requisite political associations and circumstantial qualifications for winning election to office **b :** willing to accept nomination or election **6 :** present in such chemical or physical form as to be usable (as by a plant) ⟨~ nitrogen⟩ ⟨~ water⟩ — **avail·able·ness** *n* — **avail·ably** \-blē\ *adv*

1**av·a·lanche** \ˈav-ə-ˌlanch\ *n* [F, fr. F dial. *lavantse*, *avalantse*] **1 :** a large mass of snow, ice, earth, rock, or other material in swift motion down a mountainside or over a precipice **2 :** a sudden great or overwhelming rush of something

2**avalanche** *vi* **:** to descend in or as if in an avalanche **~** *vt* **:** OVERWHELM, FLOOD

Av·a·lon \ˈav-ə-ˌlän\ *n* [F] **:** an island in the western seas held esp. in Arthurian legend to be an earthly paradise — called also *Avilion*

avant–garde \ˌäv-ˌän(t)-ˈgärd, -äⁿ-\ *n, often attrib* [F, vanguard] **:** those esp. in the arts who create, produce, or apply new, original, or experimental ideas, designs, and techniques; *esp* **:** a group that is extremist or bizarre — **avant–gard·ism** \-ˈgärd-ˌiz-əm\ *n* — **avant–gard·ist** \-ˈgärd-əst\ *n*

av·a·rice \ˈav-(ə-)rəs\ *n* [ME, fr. OF, fr. L *avaritia*, fr. *avarus* avaricious, fr. *avēre* to covet — more at AVID] **:** excessive or insatiable desire for wealth or gain **:** GREEDINESS, CUPIDITY

av·a·ri·cious \ˌav-ə-ˈrish-əs\ *adj* **:** greedy of gain **syn** see COVETOUS — **av·a·ri·cious·ly** *adv* — **av·a·ri·cious·ness** *n*

avast \ə-ˈvast\ *v imper* [perh. fr. D *houd vast* hold fast] — a nautical command to stop or cease

av·a·tar \ˈav-ə-ˌtär\ *n* [Skt *avatāra* descent, fr. *avatarati* he descends, fr. *ava-* away + *tarati* he crosses over] **1 :** the incarnation of a Hindu deity (as Vishnu) **2 a :** an incarnation of another person **b :** an embodiment usu. in a person (as of a concept or philosophy) **3 :** a variant phase or version of a continuing basic entity

avaunt \ə-ˈvȯnt, ə-ˈvänt\ *adv* [ME, fr. MF *avant*, fr. L *abante* forward, before, fr. *ab* from + *ante* before] *archaic* **:** AWAY, HENCE

ave \ˈäv-(ˌ)ā\ *n* [ME, fr. L, hail] **1 :** an expression of greeting or of leave-taking **:** HAIL, FAREWELL **2** *often cap* **:** AVE MARIA

avel·lan \ə-ˈvel-ən\ *or* **avel·lane** \ə-ˈvel-ˌān, ˈav-ə-ˌlān\ *adj* [L *abellana*, *avellana* filbert, fr. fem. of *Abellanus* of Abella, fr. *Abella*, ancient town in Italy] *of a heraldic cross* **:** having the four arms shaped like conventionalized filberts — see CROSS illustration

Ave Ma•ria \ˌäv-(ˌ)ā-mə-ˈrē-ə\ *n* [ME, fr. ML, hail, Mary] **:** a salutation to the Virgin Mary combined as now used in the Roman Catholic Church with a prayer to her as mother of God

avenge \ə-ˈvenj\ *vt* [ME *avengen*, prob. fr. *a-* (as in *abaten* to abate) + *vengen* to avenge, fr. OF *vengier* — more at VENGEANCE] **1 :** to take vengeance for or on behalf of **2 :** to exact satisfaction for (a wrong) by punishing the wrongdoer — **aveng•er** *n*

syn AVENGE, REVENGE mean to punish one who has wronged oneself or another. AVENGE implies inflicting just or merited punishment esp. on one who has injured someone other than oneself; REVENGE implies getting even or paying back in kind or degree

av•ens \ˈav-ənz\ *n, pl* **avens** [ME *avence*, fr. OF] **:** any of a genus (*Geum*) of perennial herbs of the rose family with white, purple, or yellow flowers

av•en•tail \ˈav-ən-ˌtāl\ *n* [ME, modif. of OF *ventaille*] **:** VENTAIL

aven•tu•rine \ə-ˈven-chə-ˌrēn, -rən\ *n* [F, fr. *aventure* chance — more at ADVENTURE] **1 :** glass containing opaque sparkling particles of foreign material usu. copper or chromic oxide **2 :** a translucent quartz spangled throughout with scales of mica or other mineral

av•e•nue \ˈav-ə-ˌn(y)ü\ *n* [MF, fr. fem. of *avenu*, pp. of *avenir* to come to, fr. L *advenire* — more at ADVENTURE] **1 :** an opening or passageway to a place **2 :** a way or means to an esp. intangible end **3 a** *chiefly Brit* **:** the principal walk or driveway to a house situated off a main road **b :** a broad passageway bordered by trees **4 :** a street esp. when broad and attractive

aver \ə-ˈvər\ *vt* **averred; aver•ring** [ME *averren*, fr. MF *averer*, fr. ML *adverare* to confirm as authentic, fr. L *ad-* + *verus* true — more at VERY] **1 a :** to verify or prove to be true in pleading a cause **b :** to allege or assert in pleading **2 :** to declare positively

[1]**av•er•age** \ˈav-(ə-)rij\ *n* [modif. of MF *avarie* damage to ship or cargo, fr. OIt *avaria*, fr. Ar *ʽawārīyah* damaged merchandise] **1 :** sundry petty charges regularly defrayed by the master of a ship and usu. included in the freight **2 a :** a less than total loss sustained by a ship or cargo **b :** a charge arising from damage caused by sea perils customarily distributed equitably and proportionately among all chargeable with it **3 a :** a single value (as a mean, mode, median) that summarizes or represents the general significance of a set of unequal values **b :** MEAN 1b(1) **4 a :** an estimation of or approximation to an arithmetic mean **b :** something typical of a group, class, or series **5 :** a ratio (usu. a rate per thousand) of successful tries to total tries ⟨batting ~ of .303⟩

syn MEAN, MEDIAN, NORM: AVERAGE is exactly or approximately the quotient obtained by dividing the sum total of a set of figures by the number of figures; MEAN may be the simple average or it may represent value midway between two extremes ⟨a high of 70° and a low of 50° give a *mean* of 60°⟩ MEDIAN applies to the value that represents the point at which there are as many instances above as there are below ⟨*average* of a group of persons earning 3, 4, 5, 8, and 10 dollars a day is 6 dollars, whereas the *median* is 5 dollars⟩ NORM means the computed or estimated average of performance of a significantly large group, class, or grade ⟨scores about the *norm* for 5th grade arithmetic⟩

[2]**average** *adj* **1 :** equaling an arithmetic mean **2 a :** approximating or resembling an arithmetic mean in being about midway between extremes **b :** not out of the ordinary **:** COMMON **c** *of a color* **:** medial in value — **av•er•age•ly** *adv* — **av•er•age•ness** *n*

[3]**average** *vi* **1 :** to be or come to an average ⟨the gain *averaged* out to 20 percent⟩ **2 :** to buy or sell additional shares or commodities to obtain a more favorable average price ~ *vt* **1 :** to do, get, or have on the average or as an average sum or quantity **2 :** to find the arithmetic mean of (a series of unequal quantities) **3 a :** to bring toward the average **b :** to divide among a number proportionately

aver•ment \ə-ˈvər-mənt\ *n* **:** the act of averring **:** that which is averred **:** AFFIRMATION

Aver•nus \ə-ˈvər-nəs\ *n* [L] **:** the infernal regions

averse \ə-ˈvərs\ *adj* [L *aversus*, pp. of *avertere*] **1 :** having an active feeling of repugnance or distaste ⟨~ to strenuous exercise⟩ **2 :** turned away from the stem or axis — compare ADVERSE **syn** see DISINCLINED — **averse•ly** *adv* — **averse•ness** *n*

aver•sion \ə-ˈvər-zhən, -shən\ *n* **1** *obs* **:** the act of turning away **2 a :** a feeling of repugnance towards something with a desire to avoid or turn from it **b :** a settled dislike **:** ANTIPATHY **3** *archaic* **:** a person or thing that is the object of aversion

avert \ə-ˈvərt\ *vt* [ME *averten*, fr. MF *avertir*, fr. L *avertere*, fr. *ab-* + *vertere* to turn — more at WORTH] **1 :** to turn away or aside (as the eyes) **2 :** to see coming and ward off **:** AVOID **syn** see PREVENT

Av•er•tin \ˈav-ərt-ən, ə-ˈvərt-ᵊn\ *trademark* — used for tribromoethanol

Aves•ta \ə-ˈves-tə\ *n* [MPer *Avastāk*, lit., original text] **:** the sacred books of Zoroastrianism

Aves•tan \-tən\ *n* **:** one of the two ancient languages of Old Iranian and of the sacred books of Zoroastrianism — **Avestan** *adj*

av•gas \ˈav-ˌgas\ *n* [aviation gasoline] **:** gasoline for airplanes

avi•an \ˈā-vē-ən\ *adj* [L *avis*] **:** of, relating to, or derived from birds

avi•an•ize \-vē-ə-ˌnīz\ *vt* **:** to modify or attenuate (as a virus) by repeated culture in the developing chick embryo

avi•a•rist \ˈā-vē-ə-rəst, -vē-ˌer-əst\ *n* **:** one who keeps an aviary

avi•ary \ˈā-vē-ˌer-ē\ *n* [L *aviarium*, fr. *avis* bird; akin to Gk *aetos* eagle] **:** a place for keeping birds confined

avi•ate \ˈā-vē-ˌāt, ˈav-ē-\ *vi* [back-formation fr. *aviation*] **:** to navigate the air (as in an airplane)

avi•a•tion \ˌā-vē-ˈā-shən, ˌav-ē-\ *n, often attrib* [F, fr. L *avis*] **1 :** the operation of heavier-than-air aircraft **2 :** military airplanes **3 :** airplane manufacture, development, and design

avi•a•tor \ˈā-vē-ˌāt-ər, ˈav-ē-\ *n* **:** the operator or pilot of an airplane

avi•a•trix \ˌā-vē-ˈā-triks, ˌav-ē-\ *n* **:** a woman aviator — called also *aviatress*

avi•cul•ture \ˈā-və-ˌkəl-chər, ˈav-ə-\ *n* [L *avis* + E *culture*] **:** the raising and care of birds and esp. of wild birds in captivity — **avi•cul•tur•ist** \ˌā-və-ˈkəlch-(ə-)rəst, ˌav-ə-\ *n*

av•id \ˈav-əd\ *adj* [F or L; F *avide*, fr. L *avidus*, fr. *avēre* to covet; akin to Goth *awiliuth* thanks, Gk *enēēs* gentle] **1 :** craving eagerly **:** GREEDY **2 :** characterized by enthusiasm and vigorous pursuit **syn** see EAGER — **av•id•ly** *adv* — **av•id•ness** *n*

av•i•din \ˈav-əd-ən\ *n* [fr. its avidity for biotin] **:** a protein found in white of egg that combines with biotin and makes it inactive

avid•ity \ə-ˈvid-ət-ē, a-\ *n* **1 :** the quality or state of being avid **2 :** an intense desire for gain **3 a :** the strength of an acid or base dependent on its degree of dissociation **b :** AFFINITY 2b

avi•fau•na \ˌā-və-ˈfȯ-nə, ˌav-ə-\ *n* [NL, fr. L *avis* + NL *fauna*] **:** the birds or the kinds of birds of a region, period, or environment — **avi•fau•nal** \-ˈfȯn-ᵊl\ *adj* — **avi•fau•nal•ly** \-ᵊl ē\ *adv* — **avi•fau•nis•tic** \-(ˌ)fȯ-ˈnis-tik\ *adj*

av•i•ga•tion \ˌav-ə-ˈgā-shən\ *n* [L *avis* + E *-gation* (as in *navigation*)] **:** navigation of airplanes

avi•on•ic \ˌā-vē-ˈän-ik, ˌav-ē-\ *adj* **:** of, for, or relating to the field of avionics

avi•on•ics \-iks\ *n pl* [*avi*ation electr*onics*] **:** the development and production of electrical and electronic devices for use in aviation, missilery, and astronautics; *also* **:** the devices and systems so developed

avir•u•lent \(ˈ)ā-ˈvir-(y)ə-lənt\ *adj* [ISV] **:** not virulent — compare NONPATHOGENIC

avi•ta•min•osis \ˌā-ˌvīt-ə-mə-ˈnō-səs\ *n* [NL] **:** disease resulting from a deficiency of one or more vitamins — **avi•ta•min•ot•ic** \-mə-ˈnät-ik\ *adj*

av•o•ca•do \ˌav-ə-ˈkäd-(ˌ)ō, ˌäv-\ *n, pl* **avocados** *also* **avocadoes** [modif. of Sp *aguacate*, fr. Nahuatl *ahuscatl*] **1 :** the pulpy green or purple edible fruit of various tropical American trees (genus *Persea*) of the laurel family **2 :** a tree bearing avocados

av•o•ca•tion \ˌav-ə-ˈkā-shən, ˈav-ə-ˌ\ *n* [L *avocation-*, *avocatio*, fr. *avocatus*, pp. of *avocare* to call away, fr. *ab-* + *vocare* to call, fr. *voc-*, *vox* voice — more at VOICE] **1** *archaic* **:** DIVERSION, DISTRACTION **2 :** a subordinate occupation pursued in addition to one's vocation esp. for enjoyment **:** HOBBY **3 :** customary employment **:** VOCATION — **av•o•ca•tion•al** \-shnəl, -shən-ᵊl\ *adj*

av•o•cet \ˈav-ə-ˌset\ *n* [F & It; F *avocette*, fr. It *avocetta*] **:** any of several rather large long-legged shorebirds (genus *Recurvirostra*) with webbed feet and slender upward-curving bill

avoid \ə-ˈvȯid\ *vt* [ME *avoiden*, fr. OF *esvuidier*, fr. *es-* (fr. L *ex-*) + *vuidier* to empty — more at VOID] **1** *obs* **:** VOID, EXPEL **2** *archaic* **:** to depart or withdraw from **:** LEAVE **3 :** to make legally void **:** ANNUL ⟨~ a plea⟩ **4 a :** to keep away from **:** SHUN **b :** to prevent the occurrence or effectiveness of **c :** to refrain from **syn** see ESCAPE — **avoid•able** \-ə-bəl\ *adj* — **avoid•ably** \-blē\ *adv*

avoid•ance \-ˈvȯid-ᵊn(t)s\ *n* **1** *obs* **a :** an action of emptying, vacating, or clearing away **b :** OUTLET **2 :** ANNULMENT **3 :** an act or practice of avoiding something undesirable or unwelcome

av•oir•du•pois \ˌav-ərd-ə-ˈpȯiz, ˈav-ərd-ə-ˌ\ *n* [ME *avoir de pois* goods sold by weight, fr. OF, lit., goods of weight] **1 :** AVOIRDUPOIS WEIGHT **2 :** WEIGHT, HEAVINESS; *esp* **:** personal weight

avoirdupois weight *n* **:** the series of units of weight based on the pound of 16 ounces and the ounce of 16 drams — see MEASURE table

avouch \ə-ˈvau̇ch\ *vt* [ME *avouchen* to cite as authority, fr. MF *avochier* to summon, fr. L *advocare* — more at ADVOCATE] **1 :** to declare as a matter of fact or as a thing that can be proved **:** AFFIRM **2 :** to vouch for **:** GUARANTEE **3 :** to acknowledge esp. as one's own **:** ADMIT — **avouch•ment** \-mənt\ *n*

avow \ə-ˈvau̇\ *vt* [ME *avowen*, fr. OF *avouer*, fr. L *advocare*] **1 :** to declare as a fact **:** CLAIM **2 :** to declare openly, bluntly, and without shame **syn** see ACKNOWLEDGE, ASSERT — **avow•er** \-ˈvau̇(-ə)r\ *n*

avow•al \-ˈvau̇(-ə)l\ *n* **:** an open declaration or acknowledgment

avowed \-ˈvau̇d\ *adj* **:** openly acknowledged or declared **:** ADMITTED — **avowed•ly** \-ˈvau̇(-ə)d-lē\ *adv*

avulse \ə-ˈvəls\ *vt* [L *avulsus*, pp. of *avellere* to tear off, fr. *ab-* + *vellere* to pluck — more at VULNERABLE] **:** to separate by avulsion

avul•sion \-ˈvəl-shən\ *n* **:** a forcible separation or detachment: as **a :** a tearing away of a body part accidentally or surgically **b :** a sudden cutting off of land by flood, currents, or change in course of a body of water; *esp* **:** one separating land from one person's property and joining it to another's

avun•cu•lar \ə-ˈvəŋ-kyə-lər\ *adj* [L *avunculus* maternal uncle — more at UNCLE] **:** of, relating to, or resembling an uncle

await \ə-ˈwāt\ *vb* [ME *awaiten*, fr. ONF *awaitier*, fr. *a-* (fr. L *ad-*) + *waitier* to watch — more at WAIT] *vt* **1** *obs* **:** to watch for **2 :** to wait for **3 :** to be in store for ~ *vi* **1** *obs* **:** ATTEND **2 :** to stay or be in waiting **:** WAIT **3 :** to be in store

[1]**awake** \ə-ˈwāk\ *vb* **awoke** \-ˈwōk\ *also* **awaked** \-ˈwākt\ **awaked** *also* **awoke** *or* **awo•ken** \-ˈwō-kən\ **awak•ing** *vi* **1 :** to cease sleeping **2 :** to become active again **3 :** to become conscious or aware of something ⟨*awoke* to their danger⟩ ~ *vt* **1 :** to arouse from sleep or a sleeplike state **2 :** to make active **:** stir up

[2]**awake** *adj* **:** roused from sleep **:** ALERT **syn** see AWARE

awak•en \ə-ˈwā-kən\ *vb* **awak•en•ing** \-ˈwāk-(ə-)niŋ\ [ME *awakenen*, fr. OE *awæcnian*, fr. *a-* + *wæcnian* to waken] **:** AWAKE — **awak•en•er** \-ˈwāk-(ə-)nər\ *n*

[1]**award** \ə-ˈwȯ(ə)rd\ *vt* [ME *awarden* to decide, fr. ONF *eswarder*, fr. *es-* (fr. L *ex-*) + *warder* to guard, of Gmc origin; akin to OHG *wartēn* to watch — more at WARD] **1 :** to give by judicial decree **2 :** to confer or bestow as an award **:** GIVE **syn** see GRANT — **award•able** \-ˈwȯrd-ə-bəl\ *adj* — **award•er** *n*

[2]**award** *n* **1 a :** a judgment or final decision; *esp* **:** the decision of arbitrators in a case submitted to them **b :** the document containing the decision of arbitrators **2 :** something that is conferred or bestowed **:** PRIZE

aware \ə-ˈwa(ə)r, -ˈwe(ə)r\ *adj* [ME *iwar*, fr. OE *gewær*, fr. *ge-* (associative prefix) + *wær* wary — more at CO-, WARY] **1** *archaic* **:** WATCHFUL **2 :** having or showing realization, perception, or knowledge — **aware•ness** *n*

syn COGNIZANT, CONSCIOUS, SENSIBLE, ALIVE, AWAKE: AWARE implies vigilance in observing or alertness in drawing inferences from what one sees or hears or learns; COGNIZANT implies having special or certain knowledge as from firsthand sources; CONSCIOUS implies having an awareness of the present existence of something; it may suggest a dominating realization or even preoccupation; SENSIBLE implies direct or intuitive perceiving esp. of intangibles or of emotional states or qualities; ALIVE adds to SENSIBLE the implication of acute sensitiveness to something; AWAKE implies that one has become alive to something and is on the alert

awash \ə-ˈwȯsh, -ˈwäsh\ *adv* (*or adj*) **1 :** washed by waves or tide **2 :** washing about **:** AFLOAT **3 :** overflowed by water

ə abut; ᵊ kitten; ər further; a back; ā bake; ä cot, cart; au̇ out; ch chin; e less; ē easy; g gift; i trip; ī life
j joke; ŋ sing; ō flow; ȯ flaw; ȯi coin; th thin; t͟h this; ü loot; u̇ foot; y yet; yü few; yu̇ furious; zh vision

1**away** \ə-ˈwā\ *adv* **1 :** on the way **:** ALONG ⟨get ~ early⟩ **2 :** from this or that place **:** HENCE, THENCE ⟨go ~⟩ **3 a :** in another place **b :** in another direction **4 :** out of existence **:** to an end ⟨echoes dying ~⟩ **5 :** from one's possession ⟨gave ~ a fortune⟩ **6 a :** UNINTERRUPTEDLY, ON ⟨clocks ticking ~⟩ **b :** without hesitation or delay **7 :** by a long distance or interval **:** FAR ⟨~ back in 1910⟩

2**away** *adj* **1 :** absent from a place **:** GONE **2 :** DISTANT ⟨a lake 10 miles ~⟩ **3 a :** played on an opponent's grounds ⟨home and ~ games⟩ **b** *of a golf ball* **:** lying farthest from the cup and to be played first **c** *baseball* **:** OUT ⟨two ~ in the 9th⟩ — **away·ness** *n*

1**awe** \ˈȯ\ *n* [ME, fr. ON *agi;* akin to OE *ege* awe, Gk *achos* pain] **1** *obs* **:** DREAD, TERROR **2** *archaic* **:** the power to inspire dread **3 a :** profound and reverent fear inspired by deity **b :** abashed fear inspired by authority or power **c :** fearful veneration inspired by something sacred or mysterious **d :** reverent wonder tinged with fear inspired by the sublime

2**awe** *vt* **1 :** to inspire with awe **2 :** to control or check by inspiring with awe

awea·ry \ə-ˈwi(ə)r-ē\ *adj* **:** WEARIED

aweath·er \ə-ˈwet͟h-ər\ *adv* **:** on or toward the weather or windward side

aweigh \ə-ˈwā\ *adj, of an anchor* **:** just clear of the ground and hanging perpendicularly

awe·less *or* **aw·less** \ˈȯ-ləs\ *adj* **1 :** feeling no awe **2** *obs* **:** inspiring no awe

awe·some \ˈȯ-səm\ *adj* **1 :** expressive of awe **2 :** inspiring awe — **awe·some·ly** *adv* — **awe·some·ness** *n*

awe·strick·en \ˈȯ-ˌstrik-ən\ *or* **awe·struck** \-ˌstrək\ *adj* **:** filled with awe

1**aw·ful** \ˈȯ-fəl\ *adj* **1 :** inspiring awe **2 :** filled with awe: as **a** *obs* **:** TERRIFIED, AFRAID **b :** deeply respectful or reverential **3 :** extremely disagreeable or objectionable **4 :** exceedingly great — used as an intensive ⟨~ chance⟩ **syn** see FEARFUL

2**awful** *adv* **:** AWFULLY, VERY, EXTREMELY

aw·ful·ly *usu* ˈȯ-fə-lē *in senses 1 & 2,* ˈȯ-flē *in senses 3 & 4*\ *adv* **1 :** in a manner to inspire awe **2** *archaic* **:** with a feeling of awe **3 :** in a disagreeable or objectionable manner **4 :** EXCEEDINGLY, EXTREMELY ⟨an ~ hard rain⟩

aw·ful·ness \ˈȯ-fəl-nəs\ *n* **:** the quality or state of being awful

awhile \ə-ˈhwī(ə)l, ə-ˈwī(ə)l\ *adv* **:** for a while

awhirl \ə-ˈhwər(-ə)l, ə-ˈwər(-ə)l\ *adv (or adj)* **:** in a whirl **:** WHIRLING

awk·ward \ˈȯ-kwərd\ *adj* [ME *awkeward* in the wrong direction, fr. *awke* turned the wrong way, fr. ON *öfugr;* akin to OHG *abuh* turned the wrong way, L *opacus* obscure] **1** *obs* **a :** PERVERSE **b :** ADVERSE **2 :** lacking or showing lack of dexterity or skill esp. in the use of the hands or of instruments **:** CLUMSY **3 a :** lacking ease or grace (as of movement or expression) **b :** appearing ill-proportioned, outsize, or poorly fitted together **:** UNGAINLY **4 a :** lacking social grace and assurance **b :** causing embarrassment **5 :** poorly adapted for use or handling **6 :** requiring caution — **awk·ward·ly** *adv* — **awk·ward·ness** *n*

syn CLUMSY, MALADROIT, INEPT, GAUCHE: AWKWARD is widely applicable and may suggest unhandiness, inconvenience, lack of muscular control, embarrassment, lack of tact; CLUMSY implies stiffness and heaviness and so may connote inflexibility, unwieldiness, or lack of ordinary skill; MALADROIT, INEPT, and GAUCHE imply lack of mental or social dexterity; MALADROIT suggests a tendency to create awkward situations; INEPT suggests a lack of aptness leading to futile or absurd situations or prompting inane remarks and often implies complete failure or inadequacy; GAUCHE implies the effects of shyness, inexperience, or ill breeding

awl \ˈȯl\ *n* [ME *al,* fr. ON *alr;* akin to OHG *āla* awl, Skt *ārā*] **:** a pointed instrument for marking surfaces or piercing small holes (as in leather or wood)

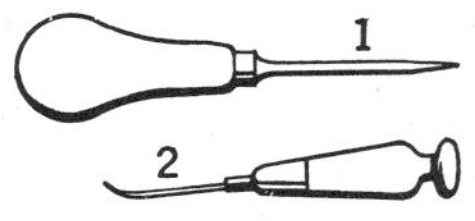

awls: *1* ordinary, *2* sewing

awl–shaped \ˈȯl-ˌshāpt\ *adj* **:** shaped like an awl; *specif* **:** being linear and tapering to a fine point

aw·mous \ˈȧ-məs, ˈȯ-\ *n* [ME (northern dial.) *almouse,* fr. ON *almusa,* fr. OS *almōsa* or OHG *alamuosan*] *Scot* **:** ALMS

awn \ˈȯn\ *n* [ME, fr. OE *agen,* fr. ON *ögn;* akin to OHG *agana* awn, OE *ecg* edge — more at EDGE] **:** one of the slender bristles that terminate the glumes of the spikelet in some cereal and other grasses; *broadly* **:** a small pointed process — **awned** \ˈȯnd\ *adj*

aw·ning \ˈȯ-niŋ, ˈän-iŋ\ *n* [origin unknown] **1 :** a rooflike cover extended over or before a place (as over the deck of a ship or before a window) as a shelter **2 :** a shelter resembling an awning — **aw·ninged** \-niŋd, -iŋd\ *adj*

awn·less \ˈȯn-ləs\ *adj* **:** lacking awns

AWOL \ˈā-ˌwȯl, ˌā-ˌdəb-əl-yü-ˌō-ˈel\ *n, often not cap* [*a*bsent *w*ith*o*ut *l*eave] **:** one who is absent without leave — **AWOL** *adv (or adj), often not cap*

awry \ə-ˈrī\ *adv (or adj)* **1 :** turned or twisted toward one side **:** ASKEW **2 :** out of the right, expected, or hoped-for course **:** AMISS

1**ax** *or* **axe** \ˈaks\ *n* [ME, fr. OE *æcx;* akin to OHG *ackus* ax, L *ascia,* Gk *axinē*] **1 :** a cutting tool that consists of a heavy edged head fixed to a handle with the edge parallel to the handle and that is used esp. for felling trees and chopping and splitting wood **2 :** a hammer with a sharp edge for dressing or spalling stone **3 :** removal from office or employment **:** DISMISSAL ⟨got the ~⟩

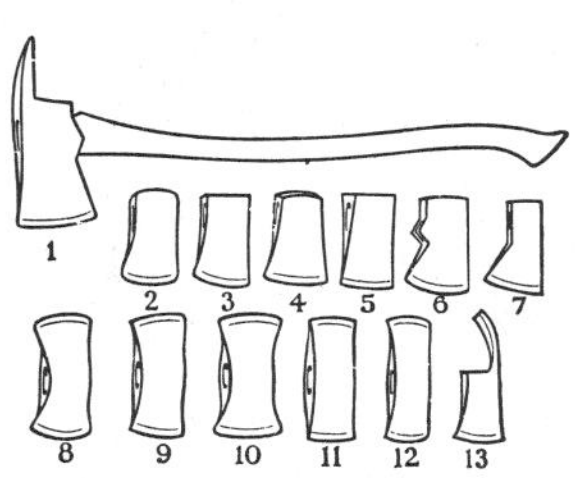

ax: *1* fireman's ax; *2-7* single-bit patterns: *2* Michigan, *3* Yankee, *4* Connecticut, *5* wedge, *6* rockaway, *7* Hudson Bay; *8-13* double-bit patterns: *8* crown, *9* Western, *10* peeling, *11* wedge, *12* Puget Sound falling, *13* forester's

2**ax** *or* **axe** *vt* **1 a :** to shape, dress, or trim with an ax **b :** to chop, split, or sever with an ax **2 :** to remove, kill, or curtail as if with an ax

axe·nic \(ˈ)ā-ˈzen-ik, -ˈzē-nik\ *adj* [*a-* + Gk *xenos* strange] **:** free from other living organisms

ax·i·al \ˈak-sē-əl\ *or* **ax·al** \-səl\ *adj* **1 :** of, relating to, or having the characteristics of an axis **2 :** situated around, in the direction of, on, or along an axis — **ax·i·al·i·ty** \ˌak-sē-ˈal-ət-ē\ *n* — **ax·i·al·ly** \ˈak-sē-ə-lē\ *adv*

axial skeleton *n* **:** the skeleton of the trunk and head

ax·il \ˈak-səl, -ˌsil\ *n* [NL *axilla,* fr. L] **:** the angle between a branch or leaf and the axis from which it arises

ax·ile \-ˌsīl\ *adj* **:** relating to or situated in an axis

ax·il·la \ak-ˈsil-ə\ *n, pl* **ax·il·lae** \-ˈsil-(ˌ)ē, -ˌī\ *or* **axillas** [L] **:** ARMPIT

ax·il·lar \ak-ˈsil-ər, ˈak-sə-lər\ *n* **:** an axillary part (as a vein, nerve, or feather)

1**ax·il·lary** \ˈak-sə-ˌler-ē\ *adj* **1 :** of, relating to, or located near the axilla **2 :** situated in or growing from an axil

2**axillary** *n* **:** AXILLAR; *esp* **:** one of the feathers arising from the axilla and closing the space between the flight feathers and body of a flying bird

ax·i·o·log·i·cal \ˌak-sē-ə-ˈläj-i-kəl\ *adj* **:** of or relating to axiology — **ax·i·o·log·i·cal·ly** \-i-k(ə-)lē\ *adv*

ax·i·ol·o·gy \ˌak-sē-ˈäl-ə-jē\ *n* [Gk *axios* + ISV *-logy*] **:** the study of the nature, types, and criteria of values and of value judgments esp. in ethics

ax·i·om \ˈak-sē-əm\ *n* [L *axioma,* fr. Gk *axiōma,* lit., honor, fr. *axioun* to think worthy, fr. *axios* worth, worthy; akin to Gk *agein* to drive] **1 :** a maxim widely accepted on its intrinsic merit **2 a :** a proposition regarded as a self-evident truth **b :** POSTULATE 1

ax·i·om·at·ic \ˌak-sē-ə-ˈmat-ik\ *adj* [MGk *axiōmatikos,* fr. Gk, honorable, fr. *axiōmat-, axiōma*] **:** of, relating to, or having the nature of an axiom — **ax·i·om·at·i·cal·ly** \-i-k(ə-)lē\ *adv*

ax·is \ˈak-səs\ *n, pl* **ax·es** \-ˌsēz\ [L, axis, axle; akin to OE *eax* axis, axle, Gk *axōn,* L *axilla* armpit, *agere* to drive — more at AGENT] **1 a :** a straight line about which a body or a geometric figure rotates or may be supposed to rotate **b :** a straight line with respect to which a body or figure is symmetrical **c :** a straight line that bisects at right angles a system of parallel chords of a curve and divides the curve into two symmetrical portions **d :** one of the reference lines of a coordinate system **2 a :** the second vertebra of the neck that serves as a pivot for the head to turn on **b :** any of various central, fundamental, or axial parts **3 :** a plant stem **4 :** one of several imaginary lines assumed in describing the positions of the planes by which a crystal is bounded, the positions of atoms in the structure of the crystal, and the directions associated with vectorial and tensorial physical properties **5 :** a main line of direction, motion, growth, or extension **6 a :** an implied line in painting or sculpture through a composition to which elements in the composition are referred **b :** a line actually drawn and used as the basis of measurements in an architectural or other working drawing **7 :** any of three fixed lines of reference in an airplane which are usu. centroidal and mutually perpendicular and of which the first is the principal longitudinal line in the plane of symmetry, the second is perpendicular to the first in the plane of symmetry, and the third is perpendicular to the other two — called also respectively *longitudinal axis, normal axis, lateral axis* **8 :** PARTNERSHIP, ALLIANCE

ax·ite \-ˌsīt\ *n* **:** AXON; *also* **:** one of its terminal branches

ax·le \ˈak-səl\ *n* [ME *axel-* (as in *axeltre*)] **1** *archaic* **:** AXIS **2 a :** a pin or shaft on or with which a wheel or pair of wheels revolves **b** (1) **:** the spindle of an axletree (2) **:** AXLETREE

axle·tree \-(ˌ)trē\ *n* [ME *axeltre,* fr. ON *öxultrē,* fr. *öxull* axle + *trē* tree] **:** a fixed bar or beam with bearings at its ends on which wheels (as of a cart) revolve

Ax·min·ster \ˈak-ˌsmin(t)-stər\ *n* [*Axminster,* England] **:** a machine-woven carpet with pile tufts inserted mechanically in a variety of textures and patterns

ax·o·lotl \ˈak-sə-ˌlät-ᵊl\ *n* [Nahuatl, lit., water doll] **:** any of several salamanders (genus *Ambystoma*) of mountain lakes of Mexico and the western U. S. that ordinarily live and breed without metamorphosing

ax·on \ˈak-ˌsän\ *also* **ax·one** \-ˌsōn\ *n* [NL *axon,* fr. Gk *axōn*] **:** a usu. long and single nerve-cell process that as a rule conducts impulses away from the cell body — **ax·o·nal** \ˈak-sən-ᵊl\ *or* **ax·on·ic** \ak-ˈsän-ik\ *adj*

ax·o·no·met·ric projection \ˌak-sə-nō-ˌme-trik-\ *n* **:** a drawing projection by lines perpendicular to the drawing surface in which a rectangular solid appears as inclined and shows three faces

ax·seed \ˈak(s)-ˌsēd\ *n* **:** a European herb (*Coronilla varia*) that is naturalized in the eastern U.S. and has umbels of pink-and-white flowers and sharp-angled pods

ay \ˈī\ *interj* [MF *aymi* ay me] — used usu. with following *me* to express sorrow or regret

ayah \ˈī-ə, ˈä-yə\ *n* [Hindi *āyā,* fr. Pg *aia,* fr. L *avia* grandmother] **:** a native nurse or maid in India

1**aye** *also* **ay** \ˈā\ *adv* [ME, fr. ON *ei;* akin to OE *ā* always, L *aevum* age, lifetime, Gk *aiōn* age] **:** EVER, ALWAYS, CONTINUALLY

2**aye** *also* **ay** \ˈī\ *adv* [perh. fr. ME *ye, yie* — more at YEA] **:** YES

3**aye** *also* **ay** \ˈī\ *n, pl* **ayes :** an affirmative vote or voter

aye–aye \ˈī-ˌī\ *n* [F, fr. Malagasy *aiay*] **:** a nocturnal lemur (*Daubentonia madagascariensis*) of Madagascar

ayin \ˈī-ən\ *n* [Heb *ʽayin,* lit., eye] **:** the 16th letter of the Hebrew alphabet — symbol ע

Ay·ma·ra \ˌī-mə-ˈrä\ *n, pl* **Aymara** *or* **Aymaras** [Sp *aymará*] **1 a :** an Indian people of Bolivia and Peru **b :** a member of this people **2 a :** the language of the Aymara people **b :** a language family of the Kechumaran stock comprising Aymara

Ayr·shire \ˈa(ə)r-ˌshi(ə)r, -shər, ˈe(ə)r-; ˈash-ˌī(ə)r\ *n* [*Ayrshire,* Scotland] **:** any of a breed of hardy dairy cattle originated in Ayr that vary in color from white to red or brown

az- *or* **azo-** *comb form* [ISV, fr. *azote*] **:** containing nitrogen esp. as the bivalent group —N=N— ⟨*azine*⟩

aza·lea \ə-ˈzāl-yə\ *n* [NL, genus name, fr. Gk, fem. of *azaleos* dry; akin to L *aridus* dry — more at ARDOR] **:** any of a genus or subgenus (*Azalea*) of rhododendrons with funnel-shaped corollas and usu. deciduous leaves including many species and hybrid forms cultivated as ornamentals

Aza·zel \ə-ˈzā-zəl, ˈaz-ə-ˌzel\ *n* [Heb *ʽăzāzēl*] **:** an evil spirit of the wilderness given a scapegoat by the ancient Hebrews in a ritual of atonement

azide \ˈaz-ˌīd, ˈā-ˌzīd\ *n* **:** a compound containing the group N_3 combined with an element or radical — **az·i·do** \ˈaz-ə-ˌdō\ *adj*

az·i·muth \ˈaz-(ə-)məth\ *n* [ME, fr. (assumed) ML, fr. Ar *as-sumūt* the azimuth, pl. of *as-samt* the way] **1 :** an arc of the horizon measured between a fixed point (as true north) and the vertical circle passing through the center of an object usu. in astronomy

and navigation clockwise from the north point through 360 degrees **2** : horizontal direction expressed as the angular distance between the direction of a fixed point (as the observer's heading) and the direction of the object — **az·i·muth·al** \,az-ə-'məth-əl\ *adj* — **az·i·muth·al·ly** \-'məth-ə-lē\ *adv*
azimuthal equidistant projection *n* : a map projection of the

azimuthal equidistant projection, centered on Washington, D.C.: *1* London, *2* Algiers, *3* Moscow, *4* Buenos Aires, *5* Tokyo, *6* Auckland

surface of the earth so centered at any given point that a straight line radiating from the center to any other point represents the shortest distance and can be measured to scale
azine \'az-,ēn, 'ā-,zēn\ *n* **1** : any of numerous organic compounds with a nitrogenous 6-membered ring **2** : a compound of the general formula $RCH=NN=CHR$ or $R_2C=NN=CR_2$ formed by

the action of hydrazine on aldehydes or ketones
azo \'az-(,)ō\ *adj* [*az-*] : relating to or containing the group $-N=N-$ united at both ends to carbon
azo dye *n* : any of numerous versatile dyes containing azo groups
azo·ic \(')ā-'zō-ik, ə-\ *adj* [*a-* + Gk *zōē* life — more at QUICK] : having no life; *specif* : of or relating to the part of geologic time that antedates life
azole \'az-,ōl, 'ā-,zōl\ *n* : any of numerous compounds characterized by a 5-membered ring containing at least one atom of nitrogen
azon·al \(')ā-'zōn-°l\ *adj* : of, relating to, or being a soil or a major soil group marked by soils lacking well-developed horizons often because of immaturity — compare INTRAZONAL, ZONAL
azote \'az-,ōt, ə-'zōt\ *n* [F, irreg. fr. *a-* + Gk *zōē*] : NITROGEN
az·o·te·mia \,az-ə-'tē-mē-ə\ *n* [ISV *azote* + NL *-emia*] : an excess of nitrogenous bodies in the blood as a result of kidney insufficiency — **az·o·te·mic** \-'tē-mik\ *adj*
az·oth \'az-,ōth\ *n* [Ar *az-zā'ūq* the mercury] **1** : mercury regarded by alchemists as the first principle of metals **2** : the universal remedy of Paracelsus
azo·tic \a-'zōt-ik, ə-, -'zät-\ *adj* : of or relating to azote
azo·to·bac·ter \a-'zōt-ə-,bak-tər, ə-'zōt-\ *n* [NL, genus name, fr. ISV *azote* + NL *bacterium*] : any of a genus (*Azotobacter*) of large rod-shaped or spherical bacteria occurring in soil and sewage and fixing atmospheric nitrogen
az·o·tu·ria \,az-ə-'t(y)ur-ē-ə\ *n* [ISV *azote* + NL *-uria*] : an excess of urea or other nitrogenous substances in the urine
Az·ra·el \'az-rā-,el\ *n* [Ar '*Azrā'īl* & Heb '*Azar'ēl*] : the angel of death in Jewish and Islamic belief
Az·tec \'az-,tek\ *n* [Sp *azteca*, fr. Nahuatl, pl. of *aztecatl*] **1 a** : a member of a Nahuatl people that founded the Mexican empire conquered by Cortes in 1519 **b** : a member of any people under Aztec influence **2 a** : the language of the Aztec people **b** : NAHUATL — **Az·tec·an** \-ən\ *adj*
azure \'azh-ər\ *n* [ME *asur*, fr. OF *azur*, prob. fr. OSp, modif. of Ar *lāzaward*, fr. Per *lāzhuward*] **1** *archaic* : LAPIS LAZULI **2** : the blue color of the clear sky **3** : the unclouded sky — **azure** *adj*
azur·ite \'azh-ə-,rīt\ *n* [F, fr. *azur* azure] **1** : a mineral $Cu_3(OH)_2(CO_3)_2$ consisting of blue basic carbonate of copper, occurring in monoclinic crystals, in mass, and in earthy form, and constituting an ore of copper **2** : a semiprecious stone derived from azurite
azygo- *comb form* [ISV, fr. Gk *azygos*] : azygous
az·y·gous or **az·y·gos** \'az-i-gəs\ *adj* [NL *azygos*, fr. Gk, fr. *a-* + *zygon* yoke] : not being one of a pair : SINGLE — **azy·gous** *n*

b \'bē\ *n*, *often cap, often attrib* **1 a** : the second letter of the English alphabet **b** : a graphic representation of this letter **c** : a speech counterpart of orthographic *b* **2** : the tone B **3** : a graphic device for reproducing the letter *b* **4** : one designated *b* esp. as the second in order or class **5 a** : a grade rating a student's work as good but short of excellent **b** : one graded or rated with a B **6** : something shaped like the letter B
baa \'bä, 'ba, 'bä\ *n* [imit.] : the bleat of a sheep — **baa** *vi*
baal \'bā-(-ə)l\ *n*, *pl* **baals** or **baa·lim** \'bā-(ə)ləm, 'bā-ə-,lim\ *often cap* [Heb *ba'al* lord] : any of numerous Canaanite and Phoenician local deities — **baal·ism** \'bā-(ə-),liz-əm\ *n*, *often cap*
ba·bas·su \,bäb-ə-'sü\ *n* [Pg *babaçú*] : a tall pinnate-leaved palm (*Orbignya speciosa* or *O. martiana*) of northeastern Brazil with hard-shelled nuts yielding a valuable oil
¹bab·bitt \'bab-ət\ *n* : a babbitt-metal lining for a bearing
²babbitt *vt* : to line or furnish with babbitt metal
Bab·bitt \'bab-ət\ *n* [George F. *Babbitt*, character in the novel *Babbitt* (1922) by Sinclair Lewis] : a business or professional man who conforms unthinkingly to prevailing middle-class standards — **Bab·bitt·ry** \-ə-trē\ *n*
babbitt metal *n* [Isaac *Babbitt* †1862 Am inventor] : an alloy used for lining bearings; *esp* : one containing tin, copper, and antimony
bab·ble \'bab-əl\ *vb* **bab·bling** \'bab-(ə-)liŋ\ [ME *babelen*, prob. of imit. origin] *vi* **1 a** : to utter meaningless sounds **b** : to talk foolishly : PRATTLE **c** : to talk excessively : CHATTER **2** : to make sounds as though babbling ~ *vt* **1** : to utter in an incoherently or meaninglessly repetitious manner **2** : to reveal by talk that is too free — **babble** *n* — **bab·ble·ment** \-əl-mənt\ *n* — **bab·bler** \'bab-(ə-)lər\ *n*
Bab·cock test \,bab-,käk-\ *n* [Stephen M. *Babcock* †1931 Am agricultural chemist] : a test for determining the fat content of milk and milk products
babe \'bāb\ *n* [ME, prob. of imit. origin] **1 a** : INFANT, BABY **b** *slang* : GIRL, WOMAN **2** : a naïve inexperienced person
Ba·bel \'bā-bəl, 'bab-əl\ *n* [Heb *Bābhel*, fr. Assyr-Bab *bāb-ilu* gate of god] **1** : a city in Shinar where the building of a tower is held in the Book of Genesis to have been interrupted by the confusion of tongues **2** *often not cap* **a** : a confusion of sounds or voices **b** : a scene of noise or confusion
ba·boon \ba-'bün, *chiefly Brit* bə-\ *n* [ME *babewin*, fr. MF *babouin*, fr. *baboue* grimace] : any of several large African and Asiatic apes (*Papio* and related genera) having doglike muzzles and short tails — **ba·boon·ish** \-'bü-nish\ *adj*
ba·bu \'bäb-(,)ü\ *n* [Hindi *bābū*, lit., father] **1** : a Hindu gentleman — a form of address corresponding to *Mr.* **2 a** : an Indian clerk who writes English **b** : an Indian having some education in English — often used disparagingly
ba·bul \bə-'bül\ *n* [Per *babūl*] : an acacia tree (*Acacia arabica*) widespread in northern Africa and across Asia that yields gum arabic and tannins as well as fodder and timber

ba·bush·ka \bə-'bùsh-kə\ *n* [Russ, grandmother, dim. of *baba* old woman] **1** : a usu. triangularly folded kerchief for the head **2** : a head covering resembling a babushka
¹ba·by \'bā-bē\ *n* [ME, fr. *babe*] **1 a** (1) : an extremely young child; *esp* : INFANT (2) : an extremely young animal **b** : the youngest of a group **2** : an infantile person **3 a** *slang* : GIRL, WOMAN **b** *slang* : PERSON, THING — **ba·by·hood** \-,hùd\ *n* — **ba·by·ish** \-ish\ *adj*
²baby *vt* **1** : to tend solicitously : GRATIFY **2** : to operate or treat with care **syn** see INDULGE
baby blue–eyes \,bā-bē-'blü-,īz\ *n pl but sing or pl in constr* : NEMOPHILA
baby farm *n* : a place where care of babies is provided for a fee — **baby farming** *n*
Bab·y·lon \'bab-ə-lən, -,län\ *n* [*Babylon*, ancient city of Babylonia] : a large city full of luxury and wickedness
¹Bab·y·lo·nian \,bab-ə-'lō-nyən, -nē-ən\ *n* **1** : a native or inhabitant of ancient Babylonia or Babylon **2** : the form of the Akkadian language used in ancient Babylonia
²Babylonian *adj* **1** : of, relating to, or characteristic of Babylonia or Babylon, the Babylonians, or Babylonian **2** : LUXURIOUS
baby's breath *n* **1** : GYPSOPHILA **2** : any of several plants (as a grape hyacinth) with delicate scented flowers
ba·by–sit \'bā-bē-,sit\ *vi* [back-formation fr. *baby-sitter*] : to care for children usu. during a short absence of the parents — **ba·by–sit·ter** *n*
bac·ca \'bak-ə\ *n, pl* **bac·cae** \'bak-,sē, 'bak-,ī\ [NL, fr. L *baca, bacca* berry] : BERRY 1c — **bac·cif·er·ous** \bak-'sif-(ə-)rəs\ *adj*
bac·ca·lau·re·ate \,bak-ə-'lòr-ē-ət, -'lär-\ *n* [ML *baccalaureatus*, fr. *baccalaureus* bachelor, alter. of *baccalarius*] **1** : the degree of bachelor conferred by universities and colleges **2 a** : a sermon to a graduating class **b** : the service at which such a sermon is delivered
bac·ca·rat \,bäk-ə-'rä, ,bak-\ *n* [F *baccara*] : a card game played in European casinos
bac·cate \'bak-,āt\ *adj* [L *bacca* berry] **1** : pulpy throughout like a berry **2** : bearing berries
Bac·chae \'bak-,ē, -,ī\ *n pl* [L, fr. Gk *Bakchai*, fr. *Bakchos*] **1** : the female attendants or priestesses of Bacchus **2** : the women participating in the Bacchanalia
¹bac·cha·nal \'bak-ən-°l\ *adj* [L *bacchanalis* of Bacchus] : BACCHANALIAN
²bac·cha·nal \'bak-ən-°l, ,bak-ə-'nal, -'näl\ *n* **1 a** : a devotee of Bacchus; *esp* : one who celebrates the Bacchanalia **b** : REVELER **2** : drunken revelry or carousal : BACCHANALIA
bac·cha·na·lia \,bak-ə-'nāl-yə\ *n, pl* **bacchanalia** [L, pl., fr. neut. pl. of *bacchanalis*] **1** *pl, cap* : a Roman festival of Bacchus celebrated with dancing, song, and revelry **2** : a drunken feast : ORGY — **bac·cha·na·lian** \-'nāl-yən\ *adj or n*
bac·chant \bə-'kant, -'känt; 'bak-ənt\ *n, pl* **bacchants** or **bacchantes** \bə-'kants, -'känts, -'kant-ēz, -'känt-ēz\ [L *bacchant-, bacchans*, prp. of *bacchari* to take part in the orgies of Bacchus] : BACCHANAL — **bacchant** *adj* — **bac·chan·tic** \bə-'kant-ik, -'känt-\ *adj*
bac·chante \bə-'kant-(ē), -'känt-(ē)\ *n* [F, fr. L *bacchant-, bac-*

chans] **:** a priestess or female follower of Bacchus **:** MAENAD
bac·chic \'bak-ik\ *adj* **1 :** of or relating to Bacchus **2 :** BACCHANALIAN
Bac·chus \'bak-əs\ *n* [L, fr. Gk *Bakchos*] **:** the god of wine in classical mythology
bach \'bach\ *vi, slang* **:** to live as a bachelor — **bach** *n, slang*
bach·e·lor \'bach-(ə-)lər\ *n* [ME *bacheler*, fr. OF, fr. ML *baccalarius* tenant farmer, squire, advanced student, of Celtic origin; akin to IrGael *bachlach* shepherd, peasant, fr. OIr *bachall* staff, fr. L *baculum*] **1 :** a young knight who follows the banner of another **:** KNIGHT BACHELOR **2 :** a person who has received the lowest degree conferred by a college, university, or professional school ⟨~ of arts⟩ **3 a :** an unmarried man **b :** a male animal (as a fur seal) without a mate during breeding time — **bach·e·lor·hood** \-,hu̇d\ *n*
bachelor's button *n* **:** any of numerous plants (as a daisy) with flowers or flower heads that suggest buttons; *esp* **:** CORNFLOWER 2
ba·cil·la·ry \'bas-ə-,ler-ē, bə-'sil-ə-rē\ *or* **ba·cil·lar** \bə-'sil-ər, 'bas-ə-lər\ *adj* [ML & NL *bacillus*] **1 :** shaped like a rod; *also* **:** consisting of small rods **2 :** of, relating to, or produced by bacilli
ba·cil·lus \bə-'sil-əs\ *n, pl* **ba·cil·li** \-,ī, -ē\ [NL, fr. ML, small staff, rod, dim. of L *baculus* staff, alter. of *baculum* — more at BACTERIUM] **1 :** any of a genus (*Bacillus*) of aerobic rod-shaped bacteria producing endospores that do not thicken the rod and including many saprophytes and some parasites (as *B. anthracis* of anthrax); *broadly* **:** a straight rod-shaped bacterium **2 :** BACTERIUM; *esp* **:** a disease-producing bacterium
bac·i·tra·cin \,bas-ə-'trās-ᵊn\ *n* [NL *Bacillus subtilis* (species of bacillus producing the toxin) + Margaret *Tracy b ab* 1936 Am child in whose tissues it was found] **:** a toxic antibiotic isolated from a bacillus (*Bacillus subtilis*) and usu. used topically against cocci
1back \'bak\ *n* [ME, fr. OE *bæc;* akin to OHG *bah* back] **1 a :** the rear part of the human body esp. from the neck to the end of the spine **b :** the corresponding part of a quadruped or other lower animal **c :** SPINAL COLUMN **d :** BACKBONE 4 **2 a :** the hinder part **:** REAR; *also* **:** the farther or reverse side **b :** something at or on the back for support ⟨~ of a chair⟩ **3 :** a position in some games behind the front line of players; *also* **:** a player in this position — **backed** \'bakt\ *adj* — **back·less** \'bak-ləs\ *adj*
2back *adv* **1 a :** to, toward, or at the rear **b :** in or into the past **:** AGO **c :** in or into a reclining position **d** (1) **:** under restraint (2) **:** in a delayed or retarded condition **2 a :** to, toward, or in a place from which a person or thing came **b :** to or toward a former state **c :** in return or reply
3back *adj* **1 a :** being at or in the back ⟨~ door⟩ **b :** distant from a central or main area **:** REMOTE **c :** articulated at or toward the back of the oral passage **2 :** being in arrears **:** OVERDUE **3 :** moving or operating backward **4 :** not current ⟨~ number of a magazine⟩
4back *vt* **1 a :** to support by material or moral assistance **:** UPHOLD **b :** SUBSTANTIATE **c :** COUNTERSIGN, ENDORSE; *also* **:** to assume financial responsibility for **2 :** to cause to go back or in reverse **3 a :** to furnish with a back **b :** to be at the back of ~ *vi* **1 :** to move backward **2** *of the wind* **:** to shift counterclockwise **3 :** to have the back in the direction of something **syn** see RECEDE, SUPPORT — **back and fill 1 :** to manage the sails of a ship to keep it clear of obstructions as it floats down with the current of a river or channel **2 :** to take opposite positions alternately **:** SHILLY-SHALLY
5back *n* [D *bak*] **:** a shallow vat or tub used esp. by brewers or dyers
back·ache \'bak-,āk\ *n* **:** a pain in the lower back
back–bench·er \-'ben-chər\ *n* **:** a rank-and-file member of a British legislature
back·bite \-,bīt\ *vt* **:** to say mean or spiteful things about (one absent) **:** SLANDER ~ *vi* **:** to backbite a person — **back·bit·er** *n*
back·board \-,bō(ə)rd, -,bȯ(ə)rd\ *n* **:** a board or other construction placed at or serving as the back
back·bone \-'bōn, -,bōn\ *n* **1 :** SPINAL COLUMN, SPINE **2 a :** a chief mountain ridge, range, or system **b :** the foundation or most substantial or sturdiest part of something **3 :** firm and resolute character **4 :** the back of a book usu. lettered with the title and the author's and publisher's names **syn** see FORTITUDE
back·cross \'bak-,krȯs\ *vt* [2*back*] **:** to cross (a first-generation hybrid) with or as if with one parent — **backcross** *n*
back·drop \'bak-,dräp\ *n* **1 :** a painted cloth hung across the rear of a stage **2 :** BACKGROUND
back·er \'bak-ər\ *n* **1 :** one that supports **2 :** a worker who works with backs or backing
back·field \-,fēld\ *n* **:** the football players whose positions are behind the line of scrimmage; *also* **:** the positions themselves
1back·fire \-,fī(ə)r\ *n* **1 :** a fire started to check an advancing fire by clearing an area **2 :** an improperly timed explosion of fuel mixture in the cylinder of an internal-combustion engine
2backfire *vi* **1 :** to make or undergo a backfire **2 :** to have the reverse of the desired or expected effect
back–formation *n* **1 :** a word formed by subtraction of a real or supposed affix from an already existing longer word (as *pea* from *pease*) **2 :** the formation of a back-formation
back·gam·mon \'bak-,gam-ən\ *n* [perh. fr. 3*back* + ME *gamen, game* game] **:** a game played with pieces on a double board in which the cast of dice determines the moves

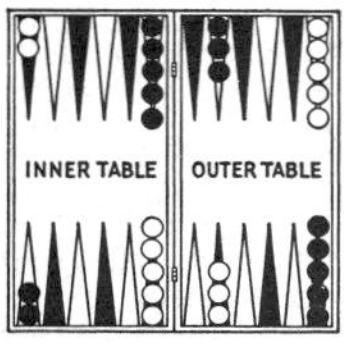
INNER TABLE
OUTER TABLE
backgammon board with men arranged as at beginning of a game

back·ground \-,grau̇nd\ *n* **1 a :** the scenery or ground behind something seen or represented **b :** the part of a painting representing what lies behind objects in the foreground **2 :** an inconspicuous position **3 a :** the natural conditions that form the setting within which something is experienced **b** (1) **:** the circumstances or events antecedent to a phenomenon or development (2) **:** information essential to understanding of a problem or situation **c :** the total of a person's experience, knowledge, and education **4 :** intrusive sound that interferes with received electronic signals
background music *n* **:** music to accompany the dialogue or action of a motion picture or radio or television drama
1back·hand \'bak-,hand\ *n* **1 :** a stroke made with the back of the hand turned in the direction of movement **2 :** handwriting whose strokes slant downward from left to right
2backhand *or* **back·hand·ed** \-,han-dəd\ *adv* **:** with a backhand
3backhand *vt* **:** to do, hit, or catch with a backhand
back·hand·ed \-,han-dəd\ *adj* **1 :** using or made with a backhand **2 :** HESITANT, DIFFIDENT **3 :** INDIRECT, DEVIOUS; *esp* **:** SARCASTIC
back·hoe \-,hō\ *n* **:** an excavating machine whose bucket is rigidly attached to a hinged stick on the boom and is drawn toward the machine in operation
back·ing \-iŋ\ *n* **1 :** something forming a back **2 a :** SUPPORT, AID **b :** endorsement esp. of a warrant by a magistrate
back·lash \-,lash\ *n* **1 :** a sudden violent backward movement or reaction **2 :** a snarl in that part of a fishing line wound on the reel **3 :** a strong adverse reaction (as to a recent political or social development) — **back·lash·er** *n*
1back·log \-,lȯg, -,läg\ *n* **1 :** a large log at the back of a hearth fire **2 :** a reserve that promises continuing work and profit **3 :** an accumulation of tasks unperformed or materials not processed
2backlog *vb* **:** to accumulate as a backlog
back matter *n* **:** matter following the main text of a book
back of *prep* **:** BEHIND
back·rest \'bak-,rest\ *n* **:** a rest at or for the back
back·saw \'bak-,sȯ\ *n* **:** a saw with a metal rib along its back
back·scat·ter \-,skat-ər\ *or* **back·scat·ter·ing** \-,skat-ə-riŋ\ *n* **:** the scattering of radiation (as X rays) in a direction opposite to that of the incident radiation due to reflection from particles of the medium traversed; *also* **:** the radiation so reversed
back·set \-,set\ *n* **:** SETBACK
back·side \-'sīd\ *n* **:** BUTTOCKS — often used in pl.
back·slap \-,slap\ *vt* **:** to display excessive or effusive goodwill for ~ *vi* **:** to display excessive cordiality or good-fellowship — **back·slap·per** *n* — **back·slap·ping** *adj or n*
back·slide \-,slīd\ *vi* **back·slid** \-,slid\ **backslid** *or* **back·slid·den** \-,slid-ᵊn\ **back·slid·ing** \-,slīd-iŋ\ **:** to lapse morally or in the practice of religion — **back·slid·er** \-,slīd-ər\ *n*
back·spin \-,spin\ *n* **:** a backward rotary motion of a ball
1back·stage \'bak-'stāj\ *adv* **1 :** in or to a backstage area **2 :** SECRETLY, PRIVATELY
2back·stage \-,stāj\ *adj* **1 :** relating to or occurring in the area behind the proscenium and esp. in the dressing rooms **2 :** of or relating to the private lives of theater people **3 :** of or relating to the inner workings or operations (as of an organization)
back·stairs \-,sta(ə)rz, -,ste(ə)rz\ *adj* **:** SECRET, FURTIVE; *also* **:** SORDID, SCANDALOUS
back·stay \-,stā\ *n* **1 :** a stay extending from the mastheads to the side of a ship and slanting aft **2 :** a strengthening or supporting device at the back
back·stitch \-,stich\ *n* **:** a hand stitch made by inserting the needle a stitch length to the right and bringing it up an equal distance to the left — **backstitch** *vb*
1back·stop \-,stäp\ *n* **:** something at the back serving as a stop: as **a :** a screen or fence for keeping a ball from leaving the field of play **b :** a player (as the catcher) whose position is behind the batter **c :** a stop (as a pawl) that prevents a backward movement
2backstop *vt* **1 :** to serve as a backstop to **2 :** SUPPORT, BOLSTER
back·stretch \-,strech, -'strech\ *n* **:** the side opposite the homestretch on a racecourse
back·stroke \-,strōk\ *n* **:** a swimming stroke executed on the back
back·swept \-,swept\ *adj* **:** swept or slanting backward
back swimmer *n* **:** a water bug (family Notonectidae) that swims on its back
back·sword \'bak-,sō(ə)rd, -,sȯ(ə)rd\ *n* **1 :** a single-edged sword **2 :** SINGLESTICK — **back·sword·man** \-mən\ *n*
back talk *n* **:** an impudent, insolent, or argumentative reply
back·track \-,trak\ *vi* **1 :** to retrace one's course **2 :** to reverse a position or stand
1back·ward \-wərd\ *or* **back·wards** \-wərdz\ *adv* **1 a :** toward the back **b :** with the back foremost **2 a :** in a reverse or contrary direction or way **b :** toward the past **c :** toward a worse state
2backward *adj* **1 a :** directed or turned backward **b :** done or executed backward **2** *archaic* **:** situated toward the back **3 :** DIFFIDENT, SHY **4 :** retarded in development — **back·ward·ly** *adv* — **back·ward·ness** *n*
3backward *n* **:** the part behind or past
back·wash \-,wȯsh, -,wäsh\ *n* **1 :** backward movement (as of water or air) produced by motion of oars or other propelling force **2 :** a consequence or by-product of an event **:** AFTERMATH
back·wa·ter \-,wȯt-ər, -,wät-\ *n* **1 a :** water turned back in its course by an obstruction, an opposing current, or the tide **b :** a body of water turned back **2 :** an isolated backward place
back·woods \-'wu̇dz, -,wu̇dz\ *n pl but sing or pl in constr* **1 :** wooded or partly cleared areas on the frontier **2 :** a remote culturally backward area — **back·woods·man** \-mən\ *n*
ba·con \'bā-kən\ *n* [ME, fr. MF, of Gmc origin; akin to OHG *bahho* side of bacon, *bah* back] **:** a side of a pig cured and smoked
Ba·co·ni·an \bā-'kō-nē-ən\ *adj* **1 :** of, relating to, or characteristic of Francis Bacon or his doctrines **2 :** of or relating to those who believe that Francis Bacon wrote the works usu. attributed to Shakespeare — **Baconian** *n*
bac·ter·emia \,bak-tə-'rē-mē-ə\ *n* [NL, alter. of *bacteriemia*, fr. *bacteri-* + *-emia*] **:** the usu. transient presence of bacteria or other microorganisms in the blood — **bac·ter·emic** \-mik\ *adj*
bacteri- *or* **bacterio-** *comb form* [NL *bacterium*] **:** bacteria ⟨*bacterial*⟩ ⟨*bacteriolysis*⟩
bacteria *pl of* BACTERIUM
bac·te·ri·al \bak-'tir-ē-əl\ *adj* **:** of, relating to, or caused by bacteria ⟨~ ooze⟩ — **bac·te·ri·al·ly** \-ə-lē\ *adv*
bac·te·ri·ci·dal \bak-,tir-ə-'sīd-ᵊl\ *adj* **:** destroying bacteria — **bac·te·ri·ci·dal·ly** \-ᵊl-ē\ *adv* — **bac·te·ri·cide** \-'tir-ə-,sīd\ *n*
bac·ter·in \'bak-tə-rən\ *n* **:** a suspension of killed or attenuated bacteria for use as an antigen
bac·te·ri·o·log·ic \bak-,tir-ē-ə-'läj-ik\ *adj* **:** of or relating to bacteriology — **bac·te·ri·o·log·i·cal** \-i-kəl\ *adj* — **bac·te·ri·o·log·i·cal·ly** \-i-k(ə-)lē\ *adv*
bac·te·ri·ol·o·gist \(,)bak-,tir-ē-'äl-ə-jəst\ *n* **:** a specialist in bacteriology
bac·te·ri·ol·o·gy \-jē\ *n* [ISV] **1 :** a science that deals with bacteria and their relations to medicine, industry, and agriculture **2 :** bacterial life and phenomena
bac·te·ri·ol·y·sis \-'äl-ə-səs\ *n* [NL] **:** destruction or dissolution of bacterial cells — **bac·te·ri·o·lyt·ic** \(,)bak-,tir-ē-ə-'lit-ik\ *adj*
bac·te·rio·phage \bak-'tir-ē-ə-,fāj, -,fäzh\ *n* [ISV] **:** any of various specific bacteriolytic viruses normally present in sewage and in body

products — **bac·te·rio·phag·ic** \-ˌtir-ē-ə-ˈfaj-ik\ *or* **bac·te·ri·oph·a·gous** \(ˌ)bak-ˌtir-ē-ˈäf-ə-gəs\ *adj* — **bac·te·ri·oph·a·gy** \(ˌ)bak-ˌtir-ē-ˈäf-ə-jē\ *n*
bac·te·rio·sta·sis \bak-ˌtir-ē-ō-ˈstā-səs\ *n* [NL] **:** inhibition of the growth of bacteria without destruction — **bac·te·rio·stat** \-ˈtir-ē-ō-ˌstat\ *n* — **bac·te·rio·stat·ic** \-ˌtir-ē-ō-ˈstat-ik\ *adj* — **bac·te·rio·stat·i·cal·ly** \-i-k(ə-)lē\ *adv*
bac·te·ri·um \bak-ˈtir-ē-əm\ *n, pl* **bac·te·ria** \-ē-ə\ [NL, fr. Gk *baktērion* staff; akin to L *baculum* staff] **:** any of a class (Schizomycetes) of microscopic plants having round, rodlike, spiral, or filamentous single-celled or noncellular bodies often aggregated into colonies or motile by means of flagella, living in soil, water, organic matter, or the bodies of plants and animals, and being autotrophic, saprophytic, or parasitic in nutrition and important to man because of their chemical effects and as pathogens
bac·te·ri·za·tion \ˌbak-tə-rə-ˈzā-shən\ *n* **:** the act of bacterizing **:** the state of being bacterized
bac·te·rize \ˈbak-tə-ˌrīz\ *vt* **:** to subject to bacterial action
1**bac·te·roid** \-ˌrȯid\ *or* **bac·te·roi·dal** \ˌbak-tə-ˈrȯid-ᵊl\ *adj* [ISV, fr. NL *bacterium*] **:** resembling bacteria
2**bacteroid** *n* **:** an enlarged branched bacterium
ba·cu·li·form \ˈbak-yə-lə-ˌfȯrm, ba-ˈkyü-lə-\ *adj* [L *baculum* staff] **:** shaped like a rod ⟨~ chromosomes⟩
1**bad** \ˈbad\ *archaic past of* BID
2**bad** \ˈbad\ *adj* **worse** \ˈwərs\ **worst** \ˈwərst\ [ME] **1 a :** below standard **:** POOR **b :** UNFAVORABLE ⟨~ impression⟩ **c :** DECAYED, SPOILED **2 a :** morally evil **b :** MISCHIEVOUS, DISOBEDIENT **3 :** INADEQUATE ⟨~ lighting⟩ **4 :** DISAGREEABLE, UNPLEASANT ⟨~ news⟩ **5 a :** INJURIOUS, HARMFUL **b :** SEVERE ⟨~ cold⟩ **6 :** INCORRECT, FAULTY ⟨~ grammar⟩ **7 :** ILL, SICK ⟨feel ~⟩ **8 :** SORROWFUL, SORRY **9 :** INVALID, VOID — **bad** *adv* — **bad·ly** *adv* — **bad·ness** *n*
syn EVIL, ILL, WICKED, NAUGHTY: BAD may apply to anything or anyone reprehensible for whatever reason and to whatever degree; EVIL is a stronger term than BAD and usu. carries a baleful or sinister connotation; ILL is a less emphatic synonym of EVIL and may imply malevolence or vice; WICKED implies violation of moral law and connotes malice and malevolence; NAUGHTY applies to trivial misbehavior chiefly of children
3**bad** *n* **1 :** something that is bad **2 :** an evil or unhappy state
bad blood *n* **:** ill feeling **:** BITTERNESS
bad·der·locks \ˈbad-ər-ˌläks\ *n pl but sing in constr* [origin unknown] **:** a large blackish seaweed (*Alaria esculenta*) often eaten as a vegetable in Europe
bade *past of* BID
badge \ˈbaj\ *n* [ME *bage, bagge*] **1 :** a device or token esp. of membership in a society or group **2 :** a characteristic mark **3 :** an emblem awarded for a particular accomplishment — **badge** *vt*
1**bad·ger** \ˈbaj-ər\ *n* [prob. fr. *badge;* fr. the white mark on its forehead] **1 a :** any of several sturdy burrowing mammals (genera *Meles* and *Taxidea* of the family Mustelidae) widely distributed in the northern hemisphere **b :** the pelt or fur of a badger **2** *Austral* **a :** WOMBAT **b :** BANDICOOT **3** *cap* **:** a native or resident of Wisconsin — used as a nickname
2**badger** *vt* **bad·ger·ing** \-(ə-)riŋ\ [fr. the sport of baiting badgers] **:** to harass or annoy persistently **syn** see BAIT
bad·i·nage \ˌbad-ᵊn-ˈäzh\ *n* [F] **:** playful repartee **:** BANTER
bad·land \ˈbad-ˌland\ *n* **:** a region marked by intricate erosional sculpturing, scanty vegetation, and fantastically formed hills—usu. used in pl.
bad·min·ton \-ˌmint-ᵊn\ *n* [*Badminton*, residence of the Duke of Beaufort, England] **:** a court game played with light long-handled rackets and a shuttlecock volleyed over a net
Bae·de·ker \ˈbād-i-kər\ *n* [Karl *Baedeker* †1859 G publisher of guidebooks] **:** GUIDEBOOK
1**baf·fle** \ˈbaf-əl\ *vt* **baf·fling** \-(ə-)liŋ\ [prob. alter. of ME (Sc) *bawchillen* to denounce, discredit publicly] **1 :** to defeat or check by confusing **:** PERPLEX **2 a :** to check or break the force or flow of by or as if by a baffle **b :** to prevent (sound waves) from interfering with each other (as by a baffle) **syn** see FRUSTRATE — **baf·fle·ment** \-əl-mənt\ *n* — **baf·fler** \-(ə-)lər\ *n*
2**baffle** *n* **1 :** a plate, wall, screen, or other device to deflect, check, or regulate flow **2 :** a partition or cabinet to impede the exchange of sound waves between front and back of a loudspeaker
1**bag** \ˈbag\ *n* [ME *bagge*, fr. ON *baggi*] **1 :** a flexible usu. closed container for holding, storing, or carrying something: as **a :** PURSE; *esp* **:** HANDBAG **b :** a bag for game **c :** SUITCASE **2 :** something resembling a bag: as **a :** a pouched or pendulous bodily part or organ; *esp* **:** UDDER **b :** a puffed-out sag or bulge in cloth **c :** a square white canvas container to mark a base in baseball **3 :** the amount contained in a bag **4 a** (1) **:** a quantity of game taken (2) **:** the maximum quantity of game permitted by law **b :** SPOILS **c :** a group of persons or things **5** *slang* **:** a slovenly unattractive woman — **in the bag :** SURE, CERTAIN
2**bag** *vb* **bagged; bag·ging** *vi* **1 :** to swell out **:** BULGE **2 :** to hang loosely ~ *vt* **1 :** to cause to swell **2 :** to put into a bag **3 a :** to take (animals) as game **b :** to get possession of **c :** CAPTURE, SEIZE; *also* **:** to shoot down **:** DESTROY **syn** see CATCH
ba·gasse \bə-ˈgas\ *n* [F] **:** plant residue (as of sugar cane) left after a product (as juice) has been extracted
bag·a·telle \ˌbag-ə-ˈtel\ *n* [F, fr. It *bagattella*] **1 :** TRIFLE **2 :** a game played with a cue and balls on an oblong table having cups or cups and arches at one end
ba·gel \ˈbā-gəl\ *n* [Yiddish *beygel*, deriv. of OHG *boug* ring; akin to OE *bēog* ring — more at BEE] **:** a hard glazed doughnut-shaped roll
bag·ful \ˈbag-ˌfu̇l\ *n, pl* **bagfuls** \-ˌfu̇lz\ *also* **bags·ful** \ˈbagz-ˌfu̇l\ **:** the quantity held by a bag; *esp* **:** a large quantity
bag·gage \ˈbag-ij\ *n* [ME *bagage*, fr. MF, fr. *bague* bundle] **1 :** a group of traveling bags and personal belongings of travelers **:** LUGGAGE **2 :** transportable equipment esp. of a military force **3 a :** superfluous or intrusive things and circumstances **b :** outmoded theories or practices **4** [prob. modif. of MF *bagassse*, fr. OProv *bagassa*] **a :** a worthless or vile woman; *esp* **:** PROSTITUTE **b :** a young woman or girl
bag·gi·ly \ˈbag-ə-lē\ *adv* **:** in a baggy way
bag·gi·ness \ˈbag-ē-nəs\ *n* **:** the quality or state of being baggy
bag·ging \ˈbag-iŋ\ *n* **:** material (as cloth) for bags
bag·gy \ˈbag-ē\ *adj* **:** loose, puffed out, or hanging like a bag
bag·man \ˈbag-mən\ *n* **1** *chiefly Brit* **:** TRAVELING SALESMAN **2 :** a person who collects or distributes illicit money on behalf of another
ba·gnio \ˈban-(ˌ)yō\ *n* [It *bagno*, lit., public baths (fr. the use of Roman baths at Constantinople for imprisonment of Christian prisoners by the Turks), fr. L *balneum*, fr. Gk *balaneion;* akin to OHG *quellan* to gush — more at DEVIL] **1** *obs* **:** PRISON **2 :** BROTHEL
bag·pipe \ˈbag-ˌpīp\ *n* **:** a musical wind instrument consisting of a leather bag, a valve-stopped tube, and three or four sounding pipes — often used in pl. — **bag·pip·er** \-ˌpī-pər\ *n*

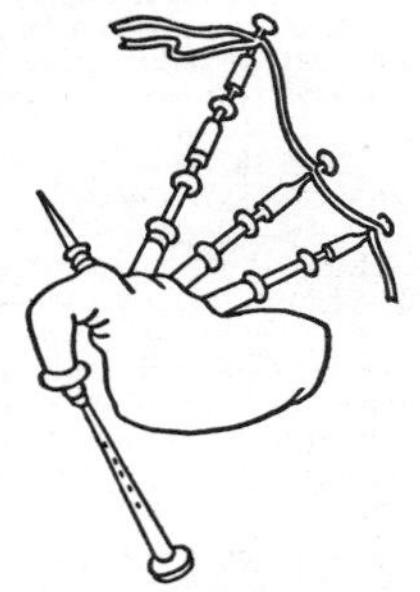
bagpipe

ba·guette \ba-ˈget\ *n* [F, lit., rod] **1 :** a small molding like but smaller than the astragal **:** BEAD **2 :** a gem having the shape of a long narrow rectangle; *also* **:** the shape itself
bag·wig \ˈbag-ˌwig\ *n* **:** an 18th century wig with the back hair enclosed in a small silk bag
bag·worm \-ˌwərm\ *n* **:** a larval moth (family Psychidae) living in a silk case covered with plant debris and feeding on foliage
bah \ˈbä, ˈba\ *interj* — used to express disdain or contempt
Ba·hai \bä-ˈhä-ˌē, -ˈhī\ *n* [Per *bahā'ī*, lit., of glory, fr. *bahā* glory] **:** an adherent of a religious movement originating among Shia Muslims in Iran in the 19th century and emphasizing the spiritual unity of mankind — **Bahai** *adj* — **Ba·ha·ism** \-ˈhä-ˌiz-əm, -ˈhī-ˌiz-\ *n*
baht \ˈbät\ *n, pl* **bahts** *or* **baht** [Thai *bāt*] — see MONEY table
1**bail** \ˈbā(ə)l\ *n* [ME, custody, security for appearance, fr. MF, custody, fr. *baillier* to have in charge, deliver fr. ML *bajulare* to control, fr. L, to carry a load, fr. *bajulus* porter] **1 :** security given for the due appearance of a prisoner in order to obtain his release from imprisonment **2 :** the temporary release of a prisoner upon security **3 :** one who provides bail
2**bail** *vt* [In sense 1, fr. AF *baillier*, fr. F, to deliver; in other senses, fr. 1*bail*] **1 :** to deliver (property) in trust to another for a special purpose and for a limited period **2 :** to release under bail **3 :** to procure the release of by giving bail **4 :** to help from a predicament usu. by financial aid
3**bail** *n* [ME *baille* bailey, fr. OF] *chiefly Brit* **:** a device for confining or separating animals
4**bail** *n* [ME *baille*, fr. MF, bucket, fr. ML *bajula* water vessel, fr. fem. of L *bajulus*] **:** a container used to remove water from a boat
5**bail** *vt* **1 :** to clear (water) from a boat by dipping and throwing over the side — usu. used with *out* **2 :** to clear water from by dipping and throwing — usu. used with *out* ~ *vi* **:** to parachute from an airplane — usu. used with *out* — **bail·er** \ˈbā-lər\ *n*
6**bail** *n* [ME *beil, baile*, prob. of Scand origin; akin to Sw *bygel* bow, hoop; akin to OE *būgan* to bend — more at BOW] **1 a :** a supporting half hoop **b :** a hinged bar for holding paper against the platen of a typewriter **2 :** the arched handle of a kettle or pail
bail·able \ˈbā-lə-bəl\ *adj* **1 :** entitled to bail **2 :** admitting of bail
bail·ee \bā-ˈlē\ *n* **:** the person to whom goods are bailed
bai·ley \ˈbā-lē\ *n* [ME *bailli*, fr. OF *baille, balie* palisade, bailey] **1 :** the outer wall of a castle or any of several walls surrounding the keep **2 :** the space immediately within the external wall or between two outer walls of a castle
Bai·ley bridge \ˌbā-lē-\ *n* [Sir Donald *Bailey* *b*1901 E engineer] **:** a bridge designed for rapid construction from interchangeable latticed steel panels that are coupled with steel pins
bai·lie \ˈbā-lē\ *n* [ME] **1** *chiefly dial* **:** BAILIFF **2 :** a Scottish municipal magistrate corresponding to an English alderman
bai·liff \ˈbā-ləf\ *n* [ME *baillif, bailie*, fr. OF *baillif*, fr. *bail* custody, jurisdiction] **1 a :** an official employed by a British sheriff to serve writs and make arrests and executions **b :** a minor officer of some U.S. courts usu. serving as a messenger or usher **2** *chiefly Brit* **:** one who manages an estate or farm — **bai·liff·ship** \-ˌship\ *n*
bai·li·wick \ˈbā-li-ˌwik\ *n* [ME *baillifwik*, fr. *baillif* + *wik* dwelling place, village, fr. OE *wīc;* akin to OHG *wīch* dwelling place, town] **1 :** the office or jurisdiction of a bailiff **2 :** one's special domain
bail·ment \ˈbā(ə)l-mənt\ *n* **:** the action of bailing a person, goods, or money
bail·or \bā-ˈlȯ(ə)r, ˈbā-lər\ *or* **bail·er** \ˈbā-lər\ *n* **:** one who delivers goods or money to another in trust
bails·man \ˈbā(ə)lz-mən\ *n* **:** one who gives bail for another
bairn \ˈba(ə)rn, ˈbe(ə)rn\ *n* [ME *bern, barn*, fr. OE *bearn* & ON *barn;* akin to OHG *barn* child] *chiefly Scot* **:** CHILD
1**bait** \ˈbāt\ *vt* [ME *baiten*, fr. ON *beita;* akin to OE *bǣtan* to bait, *bītan* to bite] **1 a :** to persecute or exasperate with wanton, malicious, or persistent attacks **b :** NAG, TEASE **2 a :** to harass with dogs usu. for sport **b :** to attack by biting and tearing **3 a :** to furnish with bait **b :** ENTICE, LURE **4 :** to give food and drink to (an animal) esp. on the road ~ *vi, archaic* **:** to stop for food and rest when traveling — **bait·er** *n*
syn BAIT, BADGER, HECKLE, HECTOR, CHIVY, HOUND mean to harass by efforts to break down. BAIT implies wanton cruelty or delight in persecuting a helpless victim; BADGER implies pestering so as to drive a person to confusion or frenzy; HECKLE implies persistent interruptive questioning of a speaker in order to confuse or discomfit him; HECTOR carries an implication of bullying and domineering that breaks the spirit; CHIVY suggests persecution by teasing or nagging; HOUND implies unrelenting pursuit and harassing
2**bait** *n* [ON *beit* pasturage & *beita* food; akin to OE *bītan* to bite] **1 :** something used in luring esp. to a hook or trap; *also* **:** a poisonous material distributed as food to kill pests **2 :** LURE, TEMPTATION
baize \ˈbāz\ *n* [MF *baies*, pl. of *baie* baize, fr. fem. of *bai* bay-colored] **:** a coarse woolen or cotton fabric napped to imitate felt
1**bake** \ˈbāk\ *vb* [ME *baken*, fr. OE *bacan;* akin to OHG *bahhan* to bake, Gk *phōgein* to roast] *vt* **1 :** to prepare (as food) by dry heat esp. in an oven **2 :** to dry or harden by subjecting to heat **3** *obs* **:** to make hard or solid ~ *vi* **1 :** to prepare food by baking it **2 :** to become baked — **bak·er** *n*
2**bake** *n* **1 :** the act or process of baking **2 :** a social gathering at which a baked food is served

Ba·ke·lite \'bā-kə-ˌlīt, -ˌklīt\ *trademark* — used for any of various synthetic resins and plastics
bake·meat \'bāk-ˌmēt\ *or* **baked meat** *n, obs* **:** cooked, usu. baked food; *specif* **:** a meat pie
Ba·ker \'bā-kər\ — a communications code word for the letter *b*
baker's dozen *n* **:** THIRTEEN
bakers' yeast *n* **:** a yeast (as *Saccharomyces cerevisiae*) used or suitable for use as leaven
bak·ery \'bā-k(ə-)rē\ *n* **:** a place for baking or selling baked goods
bake·shop \'bāk-ˌshäp\ *n* **:** BAKERY
baking powder *n* **:** a powder used as a leavening agent in making baked goods (as quick breads) that consists of a carbonate, an acid substance, and starch or flour
baking soda *n* **:** SODIUM BICARBONATE
bak·sheesh \'bak-ˌshēsh, bak-'\ *n, pl* **baksheesh** [Per *bakhshīsh*, fr. *bakhshīdan* to give; akin to Gk *phagein* to eat, Skt *bhajati* he allots] **:** TIP, GRATUITY; *also* **:** ALMS
BAL \'bal\ *n* [British *A*nti-*L*ewisite] **:** a compound $C_3H_8OS_2$ developed as an antidote against lewisite and used against other arsenicals and against mercurials
Ba·laam \'bā-ləm\ *n* [Gk, fr. Heb *Bil 'ām*] **:** an Old Testament prophet rebuked by the ass he is riding
bal·a·lai·ka \ˌbal-ə-'lī-kə\ *n* [Russ] **:** a triangular wooden instrument of the guitar kind used esp. in the U.S.S.R.
[1]**bal·ance** \'bal-ən(t)s\ *n* [ME, fr. OF, fr. (assumed) VL *bilancia*, fr. LL *bilanc-, bilanx* having two scalepans, fr. L *bi-* + *lanc-, lanx* plate; akin to OE *eln* ell — more at ELL] **1 :** an instrument for weighing; *esp* **:** a beam that is supported freely in the center and has two pans of equal weight suspended from its ends **2 :** a means of judging or deciding **3 :** a counterbalancing weight, force, or influence **4 :** a vibrating wheel operating with a hairspring to regulate the movement of a timepiece **5 a :** stability produced by even distribution of weight on each side of the vertical axis **b :** equipoise between two contrasting or opposing elements **c :** equality between the totals of the two sides of an account **6 a :** an aesthetically pleasing integration of elements **:** HARMONY **b :** the juxtaposition in writing of syntactically parallel constructions containing similar or contrasting ideas **7 :** physical equilibrium **8 a :** weight or force of one side in excess of another **b :** something left over **:** REMAINDER **c :** an amount in excess esp. on the credit side of an account **9 :** mental and emotional steadiness **10 :** the point on an object at which forces balance
[2]**balance** *vt* **1 a** (1) **:** to compute the difference between the debits and credits of (an account) (2) **:** to pay the amount due on **:** SETTLE **b :** to arrange so that one set of elements exactly equals another ⟨~ equations⟩ **2 a :** COUNTERBALANCE, OFFSET **b :** to equal or equalize in weight, number, or proportion **3 :** to compare the weight of in or as if in a balance **4 a :** to bring to a state or position of equipoise **b :** to poise in or as if in balance **c :** to bring into harmony or proportion ~ *vi* **1 :** to become balanced or established in balance **2 :** to be an equal counterpoise **3 :** FLUCTUATE, WAVER **4 :** to move with a swaying or swinging motion **syn** see COMPENSATE
balance of power : an equilibrium of power between two or more nations sufficient to prevent any one from becoming strong enough to make war or otherwise attempt to impose its will upon another
balance of trade : the difference in value over a period of time between a country's imports and exports
bal·anc·er \'bal-ən-sər\ *n* **:** one that balances: as **a :** [3]HALTER **b :** an electronic appliance used with a direction finder to improve the sharpness of the direction indication
balance sheet *n* **:** a statement of financial condition at a given date
balance wheel *n* **:** a wheel that regulates or stabilizes motion
bal·as \'bal-əs\ *n* [ME, fr. MF *balais*, fr. Ar *balakhsh*, fr. *Balakhshān*, ancient region of Afghanistan] **:** a ruby spinel of a pale rose-red or orange
ba·la·ta \bə-'lät-ə\ *n* [Sp, of Cariban origin; akin to Galibi *balata*] **:** a substance like gutta-percha that is the dried juice of tropical American trees (esp. *Manilkara bidentata*) of the sapodilla family and is used esp. in belting and golf balls; *also* **:** a tree yielding balata
bal·boa \bal-'bō-ə\ *n* [Sp, fr. Vasco Núñez de *Balboa* †1517 Sp explorer] — see MONEY table
bal·brig·gan \bal-'brig-ən\ *n* [*Balbriggan*, Ireland] **:** a knitted cotton fabric used esp. for underwear or hosiery
bal·co·ny \'bal-kə-nē\ *n* [It *balcone*, fr. OIt, scaffold, of Gmc origin; akin to OHG *balko* beam — more at BALK] **1 :** a platform that projects from the wall of a building and is enclosed by a parapet or railing **2 :** an interior projecting gallery in a public building
[1]**bald** \'bȯld\ *adj* [ME *balled;* akin to OE *bǣl* fire, pyre, Dan *baeldet* bald, L *fulica* coot, Gk *phalios* having a white spot] **1 :** lacking a natural or usual covering (as of hair) **2 :** UNADORNED **3 :** UNDISGUISED, PALPABLE **4 :** marked with white **syn** see BARE — **bald·ly** \'bȯl-(d)lē\ *adv* — **bald·ness** \'bȯl(d)-nəs\ *n*
[2]**bald** *vi* **:** to become bald
bal·da·chin \'bȯl-də-kən, 'bal-\ *or* **bal·da·chi·no** \ˌbal-də-'kē-(ˌ)nō\ *n* [It *baldacchino*, fr. *Baldacco* Baghdad, Iraq] **1 :** a rich embroidered fabric of silk and gold **2 :** a cloth canopy fixed or carried over an important person or a sacred object **3 :** an ornamental structure resembling a canopy used esp. over an altar
bald eagle *n* **:** the common eagle (*Haliaeetus leucocephalus*) of No. America that is wholly dark when young but has white head and neck feathers when mature and also a white tail when old
Bal·der \'bȯl-dər\ *n* [ON *Baldr*] **:** the son of Odin and Frigga and god of light and peace in Norse mythology
bal·der·dash \'bȯl-dər-ˌdash\ *n* [origin unknown] **:** NONSENSE
bald·head \'bȯld-ˌhed\ *n* **1 :** a bald-headed person **2 :** BALDPATE 2
bald·pate \'bȯl(d)-ˌpāt\ *n* **1 :** BALDHEAD 1 **2 :** a white-crowned No. American widgeon (*Mareca americana*)
bal·dric \'bȯl-drik\ *n* [ME *baudry, baudrik*] **:** an often ornamented belt worn over one shoulder to support a sword or bugle
[1]**bale** \'bā(ə)l\ *n* [ME, fr. OE *bealu;* akin to OHG *balo* evil, OSlav *bolŭ* sick man] **1 :** great evil **2 :** WOE, SORROW
[2]**bale** *n* [ME, fr. OF, of Gmc origin; akin to OHG *balla* ball] **:** a large bundle of goods; *specif* **:** a large closely pressed package of merchandise bound and usu. wrapped
[3]**bale** *vt* **:** to make up into a bale — **bal·er** *n*
ba·leen \bə-'lēn\ *n* [ME *baleine* whale, baleen, fr. L *balaena* whale, fr. Gk *phallaina;* akin to Gk *phallos* penis] **:** WHALEBONE
bale·fire \'bā(ə)l-ˌfī(ə)r\ *n* [ME, fr. OE *bǣlfȳr* funeral fire, fr. *bǣl* pyre + *fȳr* fire] **:** an outdoor fire often used as a signal fire
bale·ful \-fəl\ *adj* **1 :** deadly or pernicious in influence **2 :** foreboding evil **:** OMINOUS **syn** see SINISTER — **bale·ful·ly** \-fə-lē\ *adv* — **bale·ful·ness** \-fəl-nəs\ *n*
[1]**balk** \'bȯk\ *n* [ME *balke*, fr. OE *balca;* akin to OHG *balko* beam, L *fulcire* to prop, Gk *phalanx* log, phalanx] **1 :** a ridge of land left unplowed as a dividing line or through carelessness **2 :** BEAM, RAFTER **3 :** HINDRANCE, CHECK **4 a :** the space behind the balkline on a billiard table **b :** any of the outside divisions made by the balklines **5 :** failure of a player to complete a motion begun; *esp* **:** an illegal motion of the pitcher in baseball while in position
[2]**balk** *vt* **1** *archaic* **:** to pass over or by **2 :** to check or stop by or as if by an obstacle **:** BLOCK ~ *vi* **1 :** to stop short and refuse to go **2 :** to refuse abruptly — used with *at* **3 :** to commit a balk in sports **syn** see FRUSTRATE — **balk·er** *n*
bal·kan·iza·tion \ˌbȯl-kə-nə-'zā-shən\ *n, often cap* **:** the process of balkanizing or the state of being balkanized
bal·kan·ize \'bȯl-kə-ˌnīz\ *vt, often cap* [*Balkan* peninsula] **:** to break up (as a region) into smaller and often hostile units
balk·line \'bȯ-ˌklīn\ *n* **1 :** a line across a billiard table near one end behind which the cue balls are placed in making opening shots **2 a :** one of four lines parallel to the cushions of a billiard table dividing it into nine compartments **b :** a carom billiards game that sets restrictions determined by these lines
balky \'bȯ-kē\ *adj* **:** likely to balk **:** BALKING **syn** see CONTRARY
[1]**ball** \'bȯl\ *n* [ME *bal*, fr. ON *böllr;* akin to OE *bealluc* testis, OHG *balla* ball, OE *bula* bull] **1 :** a round or roundish body or mass: as **a :** a spherical or ovoid body used in a game or sport **b :** EARTH, GLOBE **c :** a spherical or conical projectile; *also* **:** projectiles used in firearms **d :** a roundish protuberant anatomic structure; *esp* **:** the rounded eminence at the base of the thumb or great toe **2 :** a game in which a ball is thrown, kicked, or struck; *esp* **:** BASEBALL **3 a :** the delivery of the ball ⟨curve ~⟩ **b :** a pitched baseball not struck at by the batter that fails to pass through the strike zone
[2]**ball** *vb* **:** to form or gather into a ball — **ball·er** *n*
[3]**ball** *n* [F *bal*, fr. OF, fr. *baller* to dance, fr. LL *ballare*, fr. Gk *ballizein;* akin to Skt *balbalīti* he whirls] **1 :** a large formal gathering for social dancing **2 :** a good time **:** PICNIC
bal·lad \'bal-əd\ *n* [ME *balade* song sung while dancing, song, fr. MF, fr. OProv *balada* dance, song sung while dancing, fr. *balar* to dance, fr. LL *ballare*] **1 :** a simple song **:** AIR **2 a :** a narrative composition in verse of strongly marked rhythm suitable for singing **b :** an art song accompanying a traditional or other ballad **3 :** a popular song; *esp* **:** a slow romantic or sentimental dance song
bal·lade \bə-'läd\ *n* [ME *balade*, fr. MF, ballad, ballade] **1 :** a fixed verse form consisting of usu. three stanzas with recurrent rhymes, an envoi, and an identical refrain for each part **2 a :** an elaborate musical setting of a ballad **b :** a musical composition usu. for piano suggesting the epic ballad
bal·lad·ry \'bal-ə-drē\ *n* **:** BALLADS
ball-and-socket joint *n* **:** a joint in which a ball moves within a socket so as to allow rotary motion in every direction within certain limits

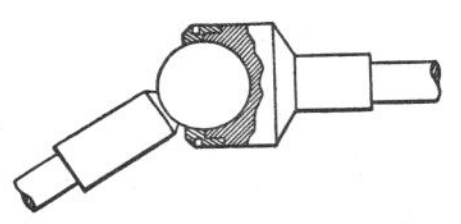
ball-and-socket joint

[1]**bal·last** \'bal-əst\ *n* [prob. fr. LG, of Scand origin; akin to Dan & Sw *barlast* ballast; akin to OE *baer* bare & to OE *blǣst* load — more at LAST] **1 :** a heavy substance used in a ship or balloon to improve its stability **2 :** something that gives stability esp in character or conduct **3 :** gravel or broken stone laid in a railroad bed or used in making concrete
[2]**ballast** *vt* **1 :** to steady or equip with or as if with ballast **2 :** to fill in (as a railroad bed) with ballast
ball bearing *n* **:** a bearing in which the journal turns upon loose hardened steel balls that roll easily in a race; *also* **:** one of the balls in such a bearing
ball cock *n* **:** an automatic valve whose opening and closing are controlled by a spherical float at the end of a lever
bal·le·ri·na \ˌbal-ə-'rē-nə\ *n* [It, fr. *ballare* to dance, fr. LL] **:** a female ballet dancer **:** DANSEUSE
bal·let \'ba-ˌlā, ba-'\ *n* [F, fr. It *balletto*, dim. of *ballo* dance, fr. *ballare*] **1 a :** dancing in which conventional poses and steps are combined with light flowing figures and movements **b :** a theatrical art form using ballet dancing to convey a story, theme, or atmosphere **2 :** music for a ballet **3 :** a group that performs ballets — **bal·let·ic** \ba-'let-ik\ *adj*
bal·let·o·mane \ba-'let-ə-ˌmān\ *n* [*ballet* + *-o-* + *-mane* (fr. *mania*)] **:** a devotee of ballet — **bal·let·o·ma·nia** \ba-ˌlet-ə-'mā-nē-ə, -nyə\ *n*
ball-flow·er \'bȯl-ˌflau̇(-ə)r\ *n* **:** an architectural ornament consisting of a ball placed in the hollow of a circular flower

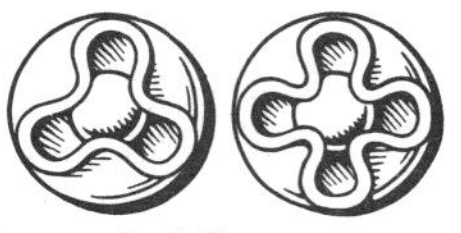
ball-flowers

bal·lis·ta \bə-'lis-tə\ *n, pl* **bal·lis·tae** \-ˌtē\ [L, fr. (assumed) Gk *ballistēs*, fr. *ballein* to throw — more at DEVIL] **:** an ancient military engine often in the form of a crossbow for hurling large missiles
bal·lis·tic \bə-'lis-tik\ *adj* [L *ballista*] **:** of or relating to ballistics or to a body in motion according to the laws of ballistics — **bal·lis·ti·cal·ly** \-ti-k(ə-)lē\ *adv*
ballistic missile *n* **:** a self-propelled missile guided in the ascent of a high-arch trajectory and freely falling in the descent
bal·lis·tics \bə-'lis-tiks\ *n pl but sing or pl in constr* **1 a :** the science of the motion of projectiles in flight **b :** the flight characteristics of a projectile **2 a :** the study of the processes within a firearm as it is fired **b :** the firing characteristics of a firearm or cartridge
bal·lo·net \ˌbal-ə-'nā\ *n* [F *ballonnet*, dim. of *ballon*] **:** a compartment of variable volume within the interior of a balloon or airship used to control ascent and descent
[1]**bal·loon** \bə-'lün\ *n* [F *ballon* large football, balloon, fr. It dial. *ballone* large football, aug. of *balla* ball, of Gmc origin] **1 :** a nonporous bag of tough light material filled with heated air or a gas lighter than air so as to rise and float in the atmosphere **2 :** a toy consisting of an inflatable rubber bag **3 :** the outline enclosing words represented as coming from the mouth of a pictured figure esp. in a cartoon — **bal·loon·ist** \-'lü-nəst\ *n*

2balloon *vt* : INFLATE, DISTEND ~ *vi* **1** : to ascend or travel in a balloon **2** : to swell or puff out **3** : to increase rapidly

balloon sail *n* : a large light sail set in addition to or in place of an ordinary light sail

balloon tire *n* : a pneumatic tire with a flexible carcass and large cross section designed to provide cushioning through low pressure

balloon vine *n* : a tropical American vine (*Cardiospermum halicacabum*) of the soapberry family bearing large ornamental pods

1bal·lot \'bal-ət\ *n* [It *ballotta*, fr. It dial., dim. of *balla* ball] **1 a** : a small ball used in secret voting **b** : a sheet of paper used to cast a vote **2 a** : the action or system of voting **b** : the right to vote **c** : 1VOTE 1a **3** : the number of votes cast

2ballot *vi* : to vote or decide by ballot — **bal·lot·er** *n*

bal·lotte·ment \bə-'lät-mənt\ *n* [F, lit., act of tossing, shaking, fr. *ballotter* to toss, fr. MF *baloter*, fr. *balotte* little ball, fr. It dial. *ballotta*] : a sharp upward pushing against the uterine wall with a finger for diagnosing pregnancy by feeling the return impact of the displaced fetus; *also* : a similar procedure for detecting a floating kidney

ball–point pen *n* : a pen having as the writing point a small rotating steel ball that inks itself by contact with an inner magazine

ball·room \'bȯl-ˌrüm, -ˌru̇m\ *n* : a large room for dances

ball valve *n* : a valve in which a ball regulates the aperture by its rise and fall due to fluid pressure, a spring, or its own weight

bal·ly·hoo \'bal-ē-ˌhü\ *n* [origin unknown] **1** : a noisy attention-getting demonstration or talk **2** : flamboyant, exaggerated, or sensational advertising or propaganda — **ballyhoo** *vt*

bal·ly·rag \-ˌrag\ *var of* BULLYRAG

balm \'bäm, 'bälm\ *n* [ME *basme, baume*, fr. OF, fr. L *balsamum* balsam, fr. Gk *balsamon*] **1** : a balsamic resin; *esp* : one from small tropical evergreen trees (genus *Commiphora* of the family Burseraceae) **2** : an aromatic preparation (as a healing ointment) **3** : any of various aromatic plants (as of the genera *Melissa* or *Monarda*) **4** : a spicy aromatic odor **5** : a soothing restorative agency

balm·i·ly \'bäm-ə-lē, 'bäl-mə-\ *adv* : in a balmy manner

balm·i·ness \-ē-nəs\ *n* : the quality or state of being balmy

balm of Gil·e·ad \-'gil-ē-əd\ [*Giliad*, region of ancient Palestine known for its balm (Jer 8:22)] **1** : a small evergreen African and Asian tree (*Commiphora meccanensis* of the family Burseraceae) with aromatic leaves; *also* : a fragrant oleoresin from this tree **2** : an agency that soothes, relieves, or heals **3** : any of several plants (as the fir *Abies balsamea* that yields Canada balsam)

bal·mor·al \bal-'mȯr-əl, -'mär-\ *n* [*Balmoral* Castle, Scotland] **1** : a laced boot or shoe; *esp* : an oxford shoe with quarters meeting over a separate tongue **2** *often cap* : a round flat cap with a top projecting all around

balmy \'bäm-ē, 'bäl-mē\ *adj* **1 a** : having the qualities of balm : SOOTHING **b** : MILD **2** : FOOLISH, INSANE

bal·ne·ol·o·gy \ˌbal-nē-'äl-ə-jē\ *n* [ISV, fr. L *balneum* bath — more at BAGNIO] : the science of the therapeutic use of baths

1ba·lo·ney \bə-'lō-nē\ *var of* BOLOGNA

2baloney *n* [*bologna*] *slang* : pretentious nonsense : BUNKUM — often a generalized expression of disagreement

bal·sa \'bȯl-sə\ *n* [Sp] **1** : a tropical American tree (*Ochroma lagopus*) of the silk-cotton family with extremely light strong wood used esp. for floats; *also* : its wood **2** : RAFT; *specif* : one made of two cylinders of metal or wood joined by a framework and used for landing through surf

bal·sam \'bȯl-səm\ *n* [L *balsamum*] **1 a** : an aromatic and usu. oily and resinous substance flowing from various plants; *esp* : any of several resinous substances containing benzoic or cinnamic acid and used esp. in medicine **b** : a preparation containing resinous substances and having a balsamic odor **2 a** : a balsam-yielding tree **b** : IMPATIENS; *esp* : a common garden ornamental (*Impatiens balsamina*) **3** : BALM 5 — **bal·sam·ic** \bȯl-'sam-ik\ *adj*

balsam of Pe·ru \-pə-'rü\ : a leguminous balsam from a tropical American tree (*Myroxylon pereirae*) used in perfumery and medicine

balsam of To·lu \-tə-'lü\ [Santiago de *Tolú*, Colombia] : a balsam from a tropical American leguminous tree (*Myroxylon balsamum*) used esp. in cough syrups and perfumes

Bal·tic \'bȯl-tik\ *adj* [ML (*mare*) *balticum* Baltic sea] **1** : of or relating to the Baltic sea or to the states of Lithuania, Latvia, and Estonia **2** : of or relating to a branch of the Indo-European languages containing Latvian, Lithuanian, and Old Prussian

Bal·to–Slav·ic \ˌbȯl-(ˌ)tō-'slav-ik, -'släv-\ *n* : a subfamily of Indo-European languages consisting of the Baltic and the Slavic branches

Ba·lu·chi \bə-'lü-chē\ *n, pl* **Baluchi** *or* **Baluchis** [Per *Balūchī*] **1 a** : an Indo-Iranian people of Baluchistan **b** : a member of this people **2** : the Iranian language of the Baluchi people

bal·us·ter \'bal-ə-stər\ *n* [F *balustre*, fr. It *balaustro*, fr. *balaustra* wild pomegranate flower, fr. L *balaustium*, fr. Gk *balaustion*; fr. its shape] : an upright often vase-shaped support for a rail

bal·us·trade \-ə-ˌstrād\ *n* [F, fr. It *balaustrata*, fr. *balaustro*] : a row of balusters topped by a rail

bam·bi·no \bam-'bē-(ˌ)nō, bäm-\ *n, pl* **bambinos** *or* **bam·bi·ni** \-(ˌ)nē\ [It, dim. of *bambo* child] **1** : CHILD, BABY **2** *pl usu bambini* : a representation of the infant Christ

bam·boo \bam-'bü\ *n* [Malay *bambu*] : any of various chiefly tropical woody or arborescent grasses (as of the genera *Bambusa*, *Arundinaria*, and *Dendrocalamus*) including some with hollow stems used for building, furniture, or utensils and young shoots used for food — **bamboo** *adj*

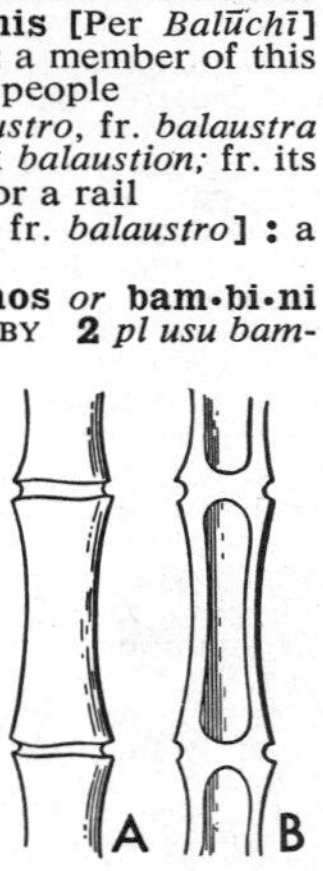

bamboo: *A* portion of stem; *B* longitudinal section of stem

bamboo curtain *n, often cap B&C* : a political, military, and ideological barrier in the Orient

bam·boo·zle \bam-'bü-zəl\ *vt* **bam·boo·zling** \-'büz-(ə-)liŋ\ [origin unknown] : to conceal one's true motives from esp. by elaborately feigning good intentions so as to gain an end : HOODWINK — **bam·boo·zle·ment** \-'bü-zəl-mənt\ *n*

1ban \'ban\ *vb* **banned; ban·ning** [ME *bannen* to summon, curse, fr. OE *bannan* to summon; akin to OHG *bannan* to command, L *fari* to speak, Gk *phanai* to say, *phōnē* sound, voice] *vt* **1** *archaic* : CURSE **2** : to prohibit esp. by legal means or social pressure ~ *vi* : to utter curses or maledictions

2ban *n* [ME, partly fr. *bannen* & partly fr. OF *ban*, of Gmc origin; akin to OHG *bannan* to command] **1** : the summoning in feudal times of the king's vassals for military service **2** : ANATHEMA, EXCOMMUNICATION **3** : MALEDICTION, CURSE **4** : legal prohibition **5** : censure or condemnation esp. through public opinion

3ban \'bän\ *n, pl* **ba·ni** \-(ˌ)ē\ [Romanian] — see *leu* at MONEY table

ba·nal \bə-'näl; bə-'nal, ba-', bā-'; 'bān-ᵊl\ *adj* [F, fr. MF, of compulsory feudal service, possessed in common, commonplace, fr. *ban*] **1** : wanting originality, freshness, or novelty : TRITE **2** : COMMON, ORDINARY **syn** see INSIPID — **ba·nal·i·ty** \bā-'nal-ət-ē, bə-, ba-\ *n* — **ba·nal·ly** \bə-'näl-lē; bə-'nal-lē, ba-, bā-; 'bān-ᵊl-(l)ē\ *adv*

ba·nana \bə-'nan-ə\ *n, often attrib* [Sp or Pg; Sp, fr. Pg, of African origin; akin to Wolof *banäna* banana] **1** : an elongated usu. tapering tropical fruit with soft pulpy flesh enclosed in a soft usu. yellow rind **2** : a widely cultivated perennial herb (genus *Musa* of the family Musaceae, the banana family) bearing fruits that are bananas in compact pendent bunches

banana oil *n* **1** : a colorless liquid acetate $C_7H_{14}O_2$ of amyl alcohol that has a pleasant fruity odor and is used as a solvent and in the manufacture of artificial fruit essences **2** : a lacquer containing amyl acetate

1band \'band\ *n* [in senses 1 & 2, fr. ME *band, bond* something that constricts, fr. ON *band*; akin to OE *bindan* to bind; in other senses, fr. ME *bande* strip, fr. MF, fr. (assumed) VL *binda*, of Gmc origin; akin to OHG *binta* fillet; akin to OE *bindan*] **1** : something that confines or constricts while allowing a degree of movement **2** : something that binds or restrains legally, morally, or spiritually: as **a** : a restraining obligation or tie affecting one's relations to others or to a tradition **b** *archaic* : a formal promise or guarantee **c** *archaic* : a pledge given : SECURITY **3** : a strip serving to join or hold things together: as **a** : BELT 2 **b** : a cord or strip across the backbone of a book to which the sections are sewn **4** : a thin flat encircling strip esp. for binding: as **a** : a close-fitting strip that confines material at the waist, neck, or cuff of clothing **b** : a strip of cloth used to protect a newborn baby's navel — called also *bellyband* **c** : a ring of elastic **5** : an elongated surface or section with parallel or roughly parallel sides; *specif* : a more or less well-defined range of wavelengths, frequencies, or energies of optical, electric, or acoustic radiation **6** : a narrow strip serving chiefly as decoration: as **a** : a narrow strip of material applied as trimming to an article of dress **b** *pl* : a pair of strips hanging at the front of the neck as part of a clerical, legal, or academic dress **c** : a ring without raised portions **7** : a strip of grooves on a phonograph record containing a single piece or a section of a long piece — **band·ed** \'ban-dəd\ *adj*

2band *vt* **1** : to affix a band to or tie up with a band **2** : to finish with a band **3 a** : to attach (oneself) to a group **b** : to gather together or summon for a purpose **c** : to unite in a company or confederacy ~ *vi* : to unite for a common purpose — **band·er** *n*

3band *n* [MF *bande* troop] : a group of persons, animals, or things; *esp* : a group of musicians organized for playing together

1ban·dage \'ban-dij\ *n* [MF, fr. *bande*] : a strip of fabric used esp. to dress and bind up wounds; *also* : a similarly used strip or band

2bandage *vt* : to bind, dress, or cover with a bandage — **ban·dag·er** *n*

ban·dan·na *or* **ban·dana** \ban-'dan-ə\ *n* [Hindi *bādhnū* a dyeing process involving the tying of cloth in knots, cloth so dyed, fr. *bādhnā* to tie, fr. Skt *badhnāti* he ties; akin to OE *bindan*] : a large figured handkerchief

band·box \'ban(d)-ˌbäks\ *n* **1** : a usu. cylindrical box of pasteboard or thin wood for holding light articles of attire **2** : a relatively small structure resembling a bandbox

ban·deau \ban-'dō\ *n, pl* **ban·deaux** \-'dōz\ [F, dim. of *bande*] **1** : a fillet or band esp. for the hair **2** : BRASSIERE

ban·de·role *or* **ban·de·rol** \'ban-də-ˌrōl\ *n* [F *banderole*, fr. It *banderuola*, dim. of *bandiera* banner, of Gmc origin; akin to Goth *bandwo* sign] : a long narrow forked flag, streamer, or scroll

ban·di·coot \'ban-di-ˌküt\ *n* [Telugu *pandikokku*] **1** : any of several very large rats (*Nesokia* and related genera) of India and Ceylon destructive to rice fields and gardens **2** : any of various small insectivorous and herbivorous marsupial mammals (family Peramelidae) of Australia, Tasmania, and New Guinea

ban·dit \'ban-dət\ *n* [It *bandito*, fr. pp. of *bandire* to banish, of Gmc origin; akin to OHG *bannan* to command — more at BAN] **1** *pl also* **ban·dit·ti** \ban-'dit-ē\ : OUTLAW, BRIGAND **2** : one who steals, profiteers, or kills : GANGSTER — **ban·dit·ry** \'ban-də-trē\ *n*

band·mas·ter \'ban(d)-ˌmas-tər\ *n* : a conductor of a musical band

ban·dog \'ban-ˌdȯg\ *n* [ME *bandogge*, fr. *band* + *dogge* dog] : a dog formerly kept tied as a watchdog or because ferocious

ban·do·lier *or* **ban·do·leer** \ˌban-də-'li(ə)r\ *n* [MF *bandouliere*, deriv. of OSp *bando* band, of Gmc origin; akin to Goth *bandwo*] : a belt worn over the shoulder and across the breast often for the suspending or supporting of some article (as cartridges) or as a part of an official or ceremonial dress

ban·dore \'ban-ˌdō(ə)r, -ˌdȯ(ə)r\ *or* **ban·do·ra** \ban-'dōr-ə, -'dȯr-\ *n* [Sp *bandurria* or Pg *bandurra*, fr. LL *pandura* 3-stringed lute, fr. Gk *pandoura*] : a bass stringed instrument resembling a guitar

band saw *n* : a saw in the form of an endless steel belt running over pulleys; *also* : a power sawing machine using this device

band shell *n* : a bandstand having at the rear a sounding board shaped like a huge concave seashell

bands·man \'ban(d)z-mən\ *n* : a member of a musical band

band·stand \'ban(d)-ˌstand\ *n* : a usu. roofed stand or raised platform on which a band or orchestra performs

band·wag·on \'ban-ˌdwag-ən\ *n* **1** : a usu. ornate and high wagon for a band of musicians esp. in a circus parade **2** : a party, faction, or cause that attracts adherents or amasses power by its timeliness, showmanship, or momentum

1ban·dy \'ban-dē\ *vb* [prob. fr. MF *bander* to be tight, to bandy, fr. *bande* strip — more at BAND] *vt* **1** : to bat (as a tennis ball) to and fro **2 a** : to toss from side to side or pass about from one to another **b** : EXCHANGE; *esp* : to exchange (words) argumentatively **c** : to discuss lightly or banteringly **d** : to use in a glib or offhand manner **3** *archaic* : to band together ~ *vi* **1** *obs* : CONTEND **2** *archaic* : UNITE

2bandy *n* [perh. fr. MF *bandé*, pp. of *bander*] **:** a game similar to hockey and believed to be its prototype

3bandy *adj* [prob. fr. *bandy* (hockey stick)] **1** *of legs* **:** BOWED **2 :** BOWLEGGED — **ban·dy–legged** \ˌban-dē-ˈleg(-ə)d, -ˈlāg(-ə)d\ *adj*

1bane \ˈbān\ *n* [ME, fr. OE *bana;* akin to OHG *bano* death, Av *banta* ill] **1 a** *obs* **:** MURDERER, SLAYER **b :** POISON **c :** DEATH, DESTRUCTION **d :** WOE **2 :** a source of harm or ruin **:** CURSE

2bane *vt, obs* **:** to kill esp. with poison

3bane *n* [ME (northern dial.) *ban*, fr. OE *bān*] *chiefly Scot* **:** BONE

bane·ber·ry \ˈbān-ˌber-ē\ *n* **:** the acrid poisonous berry of a plant (genus *Actaea*) of the crowfoot family; *also* **:** the plant itself

bane·ful \ˈbān-fəl\ *adj* **1** *archaic* **:** POISONOUS, NOXIOUS **2 :** creating destruction or woe **:** RUINOUS **syn** see PERNICIOUS — **bane·ful·ly** \-fə-lē\ *adv*

1bang \ˈbaŋ\ *vb* [prob. of Scand origin; akin to Icel *banga* to hammer] *vt* **1 :** to strike against **:** BUMP **2 :** to knock, beat, or thrust vigorously often with a sharp noise **∼** *vi* **1 :** to strike with a sharp noise or thump **2 :** to produce a sharp often metallic explosive or percussive noise or series of such noises

2bang *n* **1 :** a resounding blow **2 :** a sudden loud noise **3 a :** a sudden striking effect **b :** a quick burst of energy **c :** THRILL

3bang *adv* **:** RIGHT, DIRECTLY

4bang *n* [prob. short for *bangtail* (short tail)] **:** a fringe of banged hair

5bang *vt* **:** to cut short and squarely across (as front hair)

ban·ga·lore torpedo \ˌbaŋ-gə-ˌlō(ə)r-, -ˌlȯ(ə)r-\ *n* [*Bangalore*, India] **:** a metal tube that contains explosives and a firing mechanism and is used to cut barbed wire and detonate buried mines

bang·kok \ˈbaŋ-ˌkäk, baŋ-ˈ\ *n* [earlier *bangkok*, a fine straw, fr. *Bangkok*, Thailand] **:** a hat woven of fine palm fiber in the Philippines

ban·gle \ˈbaŋ-gəl\ *n* [Hindi *baṅglī*] **1 :** a stiff usu. ornamental bracelet or anklet slipped or clasped on **2 :** an ornamental disk

Bang's disease \ˈbaŋz-\ *n* [Bernhard L. F. *Bang* †1932 Dan veterinarian] **:** BRUCELLOSIS; *specif* **:** contagious abortion of cattle

bang·tail \ˈbaŋ-ˌtāl\ *n* [*bangtail* (short tail)] **1 :** RACEHORSE **2 :** a wild horse

bani *pl of* BAN

ban·ish \ˈban-ish\ *vt* [ME *banishen*, fr. MF *baniss-*, stem of *banir*, of Gmc origin; akin to OHG *bannan* to command — more at BAN] **1 :** to require by authority to leave a country **2 :** to drive out or remove from a home or place of usual resort or continuance **:** EXPEL — **ban·ish·er** *n* — **ban·ish·ment** \-ish-mənt\ *n*

syn BANISH, EXILE, DEPORT, TRANSPORT mean to remove by authority from a state or country. BANISH implies compulsory removal from a country not necessarily one's own; EXILE may imply compulsory removal or an enforced or voluntary absence from one's own country; DEPORT implies sending out of the country an alien who has illegally entered or whose presence is judged inimical to the public welfare; TRANSPORT implies sending a convicted criminal to an overseas penal colony

ban·is·ter *also* **ban·nis·ter** \ˈban-ə-stər\ *n* [alter. of *baluster*] **1 :** one of the upright supports of a handrail alongside a staircase **2 a :** a handrail with its supporting posts **b :** HANDRAIL

ban·jo \ˈban-(ˌ)jō\ *n, pl* **banjos** *also* **banjoes** [prob. of African origin; akin to Kimbundu *mbanza*, a similar instrument] **:** a musical instrument of the guitar class with a long narrow fretted neck and small drum-shaped body — **ban·jo·ist** \ˈban-ˌjō-əst\ *n*

1bank \ˈbaŋk\ *n* [ME, prob. of Scand origin; akin to ON *bakki* bank; akin to OE *benc* bench — more at BENCH] **1 :** a mound, pile, or ridge raised above the surrounding level: as **a :** a piled up mass of cloud or fog **b :** an undersea elevation rising esp. from the continental shelf **2 :** the rising ground bordering a lake, river, or sea or forming the edge of a cut or other hollow **3 a :** a steep acclivity **b :** the lateral inward tilt of a surface along a curve or of a vehicle when taking a curve **4 :** a protective or cushioning rim or piece

2bank *vt* **1 a :** to raise a bank about **b :** to cover (as a fire) with fresh fuel and adjust the draft of air so as to keep in an inactive state **c :** to build (a curve) with the roadbed or track inclined laterally upward from the inside edge **2 :** to heap or pile in a bank **3 :** to drive (a ball in billiards) into a cushion **4 :** to form or group in a tier **∼** *vi* **1 :** to rise in or form a bank **2 a :** to incline an airplane laterally **b** *of an airplane* **:** to incline laterally

3bank *n* [ME, fr. OF *banc* bench, of Gmc origin; akin to OE *benc*] **1 :** a bench for the rowers of a galley **2 :** a group or series of objects arranged near together in a row or a tier: as **a :** a row of keys on a typewriter **b :** a set of two or more elevators **3 :** one of the horizontal and usu. secondary or lower divisions of a headline

4bank *n* [ME, fr. MF or OIt; MF *banque*, fr. OIt *banca*, lit., bench, of Gmc origin; akin to OE *benc*] **1 a** *obs* **:** the table, counter, or place of business of a money changer **b :** an establishment for the custody, loan, exchange, or issue of money, for the extension of credit, and for facilitating the transmission of funds **2 :** a person conducting a gambling house or game; *specif* **:** DEALER **3 :** a supply of something held in reserve: as **a :** the fund of the banker or dealer in a gambling game **b :** a fund of pieces belonging to a game (as dominoes) from which the players draw **4 :** a place where something is held available

5bank *vi* **1 :** to keep a bank **2 :** to deposit money or have an account in a bank **∼** *vt* **:** to deposit in a bank — **bank on** *or* **bank upon :** to depend upon

bank·able \ˈbaŋ-kə-bəl\ *adj* **:** acceptable to or at a bank

bank acceptance *n* **:** a draft drawn on and accepted by a bank

bank annuities *n pl* **:** CONSOLS

bank·book \ˈbaŋk-ˌbu̇k\ *n* **:** the depositor's book in which a bank enters his deposits and withdrawals — called also *passbook*

bank discount *n* **:** the interest discounted in advance on a note and computed on the face value of the note

1bank·er \ˈbaŋ-kər\ *n* **1 :** one that engages in the business of banking **2 :** the player who keeps the bank in a gambling game

2banker *n* **:** a man or boat employed in the cod fishery on the Newfoundland banks

3banker *n* **:** a sculptor's or mason's workbench

banker's bill *n* **:** a bill of exchange drawn by a bank on a foreign bank

bank holiday *n* **1** *Brit* **:** LEGAL HOLIDAY **2 :** a period when banks in general are closed often by government fiat

bank·ing *n* **:** the business of a bank or a banker

bank money *n* **:** a medium of exchange consisting chiefly of checks and drafts

bank note *n* **:** a promissory note issued by a bank payable to bearer on demand without interest and acceptable as money

bank paper *n* **1 :** circulating bank notes **2 :** bankable commercial paper (as drafts or bills)

bank rate *n* **:** the discount rate fixed by a central bank

bank·roll \ˈbaŋ-ˌkrōl\ *n* **:** supply of money **:** FUNDS

1bank·rupt \ˈbaŋ-(ˌ)krəpt\ *n* [modif. of MF & OIt; MF *banqueroute*, fr. OIt *bancarotta*, fr. *banca* bank + *rotta* broken, fr. L *rupta*, fem. of *ruptus*, pp. of *rumpere* to break — more at BANK, REAVE] **1 a :** a person who has done any of the acts that by law entitle his creditors to have his estate administered for their benefit **b :** a person judicially declared subject to having his estate administered under the bankrupt laws for the benefit of his creditors **c :** a person who becomes insolvent **2 :** one who is destitute of a particular thing

2bankrupt *vt* **:** to reduce to bankruptcy **syn** see DEPLETE

3bankrupt *adj* **1 a :** reduced to a state of financial ruin **:** IMPOVERISHED; *specif* **:** legally declared a bankrupt **b :** of or relating to bankrupts or bankruptcy ⟨∼ laws⟩ **2 a :** BROKEN, RUINED ⟨a ∼ professional career⟩ **b :** DEPLETED, STERILE **c :** DESTITUTE

bank·rupt·cy \ˈbaŋ-(ˌ)krəp-(t)sē\ *n* **1 :** the quality or state of being bankrupt **2 :** utter failure or impoverishment

bank·sia \ˈbaŋ(k)-sē-ə\ *n* [NL, genus name, fr. Sir Joseph *Banks* †1820 E naturalist] **:** an Australian evergreen tree or shrub (genus *Banksia*) of the protea family with alternate leathery leaves and yellowish flowers in dense cylindrical heads

Bank·side \ˈbaŋk-ˌsīd\ *n* **:** the bank of the Thames at Southwark

1ban·ner \ˈban-ər\ *n* [ME *banere*, fr. OF, of Gmc origin; akin to Goth *bandwo* sign; akin to ON *benda* to give a sign] **1 a :** a piece of cloth attached by one edge to a staff and used by a monarch, feudal lord, or other commander as his standard and as a rallying point in battle **b :** FLAG 1 **c :** an ensign displaying a distinctive or symbolic device or legend **2 :** a headline in large type running across a newspaper page **3 :** a strip of cloth on which a sign is painted

2banner *adj* **:** distinguished from all others esp. in excellence

1ban·ner·et \ˈban-ə-rət, ˌban-ə-ˈret\ *n, often cap* [ME *baneret*, fr. OF, fr. *banere*] **:** a knight leading his vassals into the field under his own banner and therefore ranking above a knight bachelor

2banneret *also* **ban·ner·ette** *n* **:** a small banner

ban·ne·rol *also* **ban·ner roll** \ˈban-ə-ˌrōl\ *n* **:** BANDEROLE

ban·nock \ˈban-ək\ *n* [ME *bannok*] **1 :** an often unleavened bread of oat or barley flour baked in flat loaves **2** *NewEng* **:** CORN BREAD; *esp* **:** a thin cake baked on a griddle

banns \ˈbanz\ *n pl* [pl. of *bann*, fr. ME *bane*, *ban* proclamation, ban] **:** public announcement esp. in church of a proposed marriage

1ban·quet \ˈbaŋ-kwət, ˈban- *also* -ˌkwet\ *n* [MF, fr. OIt *banchetto*, fr. dim. of *banca* bench, bank] **:** an elaborate and often ceremonious meal for numerous people often honoring a person

2banquet *vt* **:** to treat with a banquet **:** FEAST **∼** *vi* **:** to partake of a banquet — **ban·quet·er** *n*

ban·quette \baŋ-ˈket, ban-\ *n* [F, fr. Prov *banqueta*, dim. of *banc* bench, of Gmc origin; akin to OE *benc* bench] **1 a :** a raised way along the inside of a parapet or trench for gunners or guns **b** *South* **:** SIDEWALK **2 a :** a long upholstered seat **b :** a sofa having one roll-over arm **c :** a built-in upholstered bench along a wall

Ban·quo \ˈbaŋ-(ˌ)kwō, ˈban-\ *n* **:** a Scottish thane in Shakespeare's *Macbeth* whose ghost appears to Macbeth after his murder

ban·shee \ˈban-(ˌ)shē\ *n* [ScGael *bean-sìth*, fr. or akin to OIr *ben síde* woman of fairyland] **:** a female spirit in Gaelic folklore whose wailing warns a family of the approaching death of a member

1ban·tam \ˈbant-əm\ *n* [*Bantam*, former residency in Java] **1 :** any of numerous small domestic fowls that are often miniatures of members of the standard breeds **2 :** a person of diminutive stature and often combative disposition **3 :** JEEP

2bantam *adj* **1 :** SMALL, DIMINUTIVE **2 :** pertly combative **:** SAUCY

ban·tam·weight \-ˌwāt\ *n* **:** a boxer of the class whose maximum weight is 118 pounds

1ban·ter \ˈbant-ər\ *vb* [origin unknown] *vt* **1 :** to speak to or address in a witty and teasing manner **:** RALLY **2** *archaic* **:** DELUDE **3** *chiefly South & Midland* **:** CHALLENGE **∼** *vi* **:** to speak or act playfully or wittily — **ban·ter·er** \-ər-ər\ *n* — **ban·ter·ing·ly** \ˈbant-ə-riŋ-lē\ *adv*

2banter *n* **:** good-natured and usu. witty and playful teasing

bant·ling \ˈbant-liŋ\ *n* [perh. modif. of G *bänkling* bastard, fr. *bank* bench, fr. OHG — more at BENCH] **:** a very young child

Ban·tu \ˈban-(ˌ)tü, ˈbän-\ *n, pl* **Bantu** *or* **Bantus** **1 a :** a family of Negroid peoples who occupy equatorial and southern Africa **b :** a member of this people **2 :** a group of African languages spoken generally south of a line from Cameroons to Kenya

ban·yan \ˈban-yən\ *n* [earlier *banyan* Hindu merchant, fr. Hindi *baniyā;* fr. a banyan pagoda erected under a tree of the species in Iran] **:** an East Indian tree (*Ficus bengalensis*) of the mulberry family with branches that send out shoots which grow down to the soil and root to form secondary trunks

ban·zai \(ˈ)bän-ˈzī\ *n* [Jap] **:** a Japanese cheer or cry of triumph

banzai attack \ˌbän-ˌzī-\ *n* **:** a reckless desperate mass attack originated by Japanese soldiers

bao·bab \ˈbau̇-ˌbab, ˈbā-ə-\ *n* [prob. native name in Africa] **:** a broad-trunked Old World tropical tree (*Adansonia digitata*) of the silk-cotton family with an edible acid fruit resembling a gourd

bap·ti·sia \bap-ˈtizh-(ē-)ə\ *n* [NL, genus name, fr. Gk *baptisis* a dipping, fr. *baptein*] **:** any of a genus (*Baptisia*) of No. American leguminous plants with showy pealike flowers

bap·tism \ˈbap-ˌtiz-əm\ *n* **1 a :** a Christian sacrament signifying spiritual rebirth and admitting the recipient to the Christian community through the ritual use of water **b :** a rite using water for ritual purification **c** *Christian Science* **:** purification by or submergence in Spirit **2 :** an act, experience, or ordeal by which one is purified, sanctified, initiated, or named ⟨∼ of fire⟩ — **bap·tis·mal** \bap-ˈtiz-məl\ *adj* — **bap·tis·mal·ly** \-mə-lē\ *adv*

bap·tist \ˈbap-təst\ *n* **1 :** one that baptizes ⟨John the *Baptist*⟩ **2** *cap* **:** a member or adherent of an evangelical Protestant denomination marked by congregational polity and baptism by immersion of believers only — **Baptist** *adj*

bap·tis·tery *or* **bap·tis·try** \ˈbap-tə-strē\ *n* **:** a part of a church or formerly a separate building used for baptism

bap·tize \bap-ˈtīz, ˈbap-ˌ\ *vb* [ME *baptizen*, fr. OF *baptiser*, fr LL

baptizare, fr. Gk *baptizein* to dip, baptize, fr. *baptos* dipped, fr. *baptein* to dip; akin to ON *kafa* to dive] *vt* **1 :** to administer baptism to **2 a :** to purify or cleanse spiritually esp. by a purging experience or ordeal **b :** INITIATE **3 :** to give a name to (as at baptism) **:** CHRISTEN ~ *vi* **:** to administer baptism — **bap·tiz·er** *n*

¹bar \'bär\ *n, often attrib* [ME *barre*, fr. OF] **1 a :** a straight piece (as of wood or metal) that is longer than it is wide and has any of various uses (as for a lever, support, barrier, or fastening) **b :** a solid piece or block of material usu. rectangular and considerably longer than it is wide **2 :** something that obstructs or prevents passage, progress, or action **:** IMPEDIMENT: as **a :** the complete and permanent destruction of an action or claim in law; *also* **:** a plea or objection that effects such destruction **b :** any intangible or nonphysical impediment **c :** a submerged or partly submerged bank (as of sand) along a shore or in a river often obstructing navigation **3 a** (1) **:** the railing in a courtroom that encloses the place about the judge where prisoners are stationed or where the business of the court is transacted in civil cases (2) **:** COURT, TRIBUNAL (3) **:** a particular system of courts (4) **:** any authority or tribunal that renders judgment **b** (1) **:** the barrier in the English Inns of Court that formerly separated the seats of the benchers or readers from the body of the hall occupied by the students (2) **:** the whole body of barristers or lawyers qualified to practice in any jurisdiction (3) **:** the profession of barrister or lawyer **4 :** a straight stripe, band, or line much longer than it is wide: as **a :** one of two or more horizontal stripes on a heraldic shield **b :** a metal or embroidered strip worn on a military uniform esp. to indicate rank or service **5 a :** a counter at which food or esp. alcoholic beverages are served **b :** BARROOM **6 a :** a vertical line across the musical staff before the initial measure accent **b :** MEASURE **7 :** a lace and embroidery joining covered with buttonhole stitch for connecting various parts of the pattern in needlepoint lace and cutwork

²bar *vt* **barred; bar·ring 1 a :** to fasten with a bar **b :** to place bars across to prevent ingress or egress **2 :** to mark with bars **:** STRIPE **3 a :** to confine or shut in by or as if by bars **b :** to set aside **:** rule out **c :** to keep out **:** EXCLUDE **4 a :** to interpose legal objection to or to the claim of **b :** PREVENT, FORBID

³bar *prep* **:** EXCEPT

⁴bar *n* [G, fr. Gk *baros*] **1 :** a unit of pressure equal to one million dynes per square centimeter **2 :** the absolute cgs unit of pressure equal to one dyne per square centimeter

bar- *or* **baro-** *comb form* [Gk *baros*; akin to Gk *barys* heavy — more at GRIEVE] **:** weight ⟨*barometer*⟩

Ba·rab·bas \bə-'rab-əs\ *n* [Gk, fr. Aram *Bar-abba*] **:** a prisoner released in preference to Christ at the demand of the multitude

¹barb \'bärb\ *n* [ME *barbe* barb, beard, fr. MF, fr. L *barba*] **1 a :** a sharp projection extending backward (as from the point of an arrow or fishhook) and preventing easy extraction **b :** a biting or pointedly critical remark or comment **2 :** a medieval cloth headdress passing over or under the chin and covering the neck **3 :** BARBEL 2 **4 :** one of the side branches of the shaft of a feather **5 :** a plant hair or bristle ending in a hook — **barbed** \'bärbd\ *adj*

²barb *vt* **:** to furnish with a barb

³barb *n* [F *barbe*, fr. It *barbero*, fr. *barbero* of Barbary, fr. *Barberia* Barbary, coastal region in Africa] **1 :** a horse of a breed related to the Arabs and introduced into Spain by the Moors **2 :** a pigeon of a domestic breed related to the carrier pigeons

bar·bar·ian \bär-'ber-ē-ən, -'bar-\ *adj* [L *barbarus*] **1 :** of or relating to a land, culture, or people alien and usu. believed to be inferior to one's own **2 :** lacking refinement, learning, or artistic or literary culture — **barbarian** *n* — **bar·bar·i·an·ism** \-ə-,niz-əm\ *n*

syn BARBARIAN, BARBAROUS, BARBARIC, SAVAGE mean characteristic of uncivilized man. BARBARIAN often implies a state somewhere between tribal savagery and full civilization; BARBAROUS tends to stress the harsher or more brutal side of uncivilized life; BARBARIC suggests crudeness of taste and fondness for gorgeous display; SAVAGE suggests more primitive culture than BARBARIAN and greater harshness or fierceness than BARBAROUS

bar·bar·ic \bär-'bar-ik\ *adj* **1 :** of, relating to, or characteristic of barbarians **2 a :** marked by a lack of restraint **:** WILD **b :** having a bizarre, primitive, or unsophisticated quality **syn** see BARBARIAN

bar·ba·rism \'bär-bə-,riz-əm\ *n* **1 :** a word or expression that in form or use offends against contemporary standards of correctness or purity **2 a :** a barbarian or barbarous social or intellectual condition **:** BACKWARDNESS **b :** the practice or display of barbarian acts, attitudes, or ideas

bar·bar·i·ty \bär-'bar-ət-ē\ *n* **1 :** BARBARISM **2 a :** barbarous cruelty **:** INHUMANITY **b :** an act or instance of barbarous cruelty

bar·ba·ri·za·tion \,bär-b(ə-)rə-'zā-shən\ *n* **:** the act or process of barbarizing **:** the state of being barbarized

bar·ba·rize \'bär-bə-,rīz\ *vi* **:** to become barbarous ~ *vt* **:** to make barbarian or barbarous

bar·ba·rous \'bär-b(ə-)rəs\ *adj* [L *barbarus*, fr. Gk *barbaros* foreign, ignorant] **1 :** characterized by the use of barbarisms in speech or writing **2 a :** UNCIVILIZED **b :** lacking culture or refinement **:** PHILISTINE **3 :** mercilessly harsh or cruel **syn** see BARBARIAN, FIERCE — **bar·ba·rous·ly** *adv* — **bar·ba·rous·ness** *n*

Bar·ba·ry ape \,bär-b(ə-)rē-\ *n* [*Barbary*, coastal region in Africa] **:** a tailless monkey (*Macaca sylvana*) of No. Africa and Gibraltar

bar·bate \'bär-,bāt\ *adj* [L *barbatus*, fr. *barba*] **:** bearded esp. with long stiff hairs

barbe \'bärb\ *n* [ME, fr. MF, lit., beard] **:** ¹BARB 2

¹bar·be·cue \'bär-bi-,kyü\ *n, often attrib* [AmerSp *barbacoa*, prob. fr. Taino] **1 :** a large animal (as a hog or steer) roasted or broiled whole or split over an open fire or barbecue pit **2 :** a social gathering esp. in the open air at which barbecued food is eaten

²barbecue *vt* **1 :** to roast or broil on a rack over hot coals or on a revolving spit before or over a source of cooking heat **2 :** to cook in a highly seasoned vinegar sauce

barbed wire \'bä(r)b-'(d)wī(ə)r\ *n* **:** twisted wires armed with barbs or sharp points — called also *barbwire*

bar·bel \'bär-bəl\ *n* [ME, fr. MF, fr. (assumed) VL *barbellus*, dim. of L *barbus* barbel, fr. *barba* beard — more at BEARD] **1 :** a European freshwater fish (*Barbus fluviatilis*) of the carp family with four barbels on its upper jaw; *also* **:** any of various other fishes of this genus **2 :** a slender tactile process on the lips of a fish

bar·bell \'bär-,bel\ *n* **:** a bar with adjustable weighted disks attached to each end used for exercise and in weight lifting

bar·bel·late \'bär-bə-,lāt, bär-'bel-ət\ *adj* [NL *barbella* short stiff hair, dim. of L *barbula*, dim. of *barba*] **:** having short stiff hooked bristles or hairs ⟨a ~ fruit⟩

¹bar·ber \'bär-bər\ *n* [ME, fr. MF *barbeor*, fr. *barbe* beard — more at BARB] **:** one whose business is cutting and dressing hair, shaving and trimming beards, and performing related services

²barber *vb* **bar·ber·ing** \-b(ə-)riŋ\ *vt* **:** to render the services of a barber to ~ *vi* **:** to perform the services of a barber

bar·ber·ry \'bär-,ber-ē\ *n* [ME *barbere*, fr. MF *barbarin*, fr. Ar *barbārīs*] **:** any of a genus (*Berberis* of the family Berberidaceae, the barberry family) of shrubs having spines, yellow flowers, and oblong red berries

barber's itch *n* **:** ringworm of the face and neck

bar·bet \'bär-bət\ *n* [prob. fr. ¹*barb*] **:** any of numerous nonpasserine tropical birds (family Capitonidae) having a stout bill

bar·bette \bär-'bet\ *n* [F, dim. of *barbe* headdress] **1 :** a mound of earth or a protected platform from which guns fire over a parapet **2 :** a cylinder of armor protecting a gun turret on a warship

bar·bi·can \'bär-bi-kən\ *n* [ME, fr. OF *barbacane*, fr. ML *barbacana*] **:** an outer defensive work; *esp* **:** a tower at a gate or bridge

bar·bi·cel \'bär-bə-,sel\ *n* [NL *barbicella*, dim. of L *barba*] **:** one of the small hook-bearing processes on a barbule of a feather

bar·bi·tal \'bär-bə-,tȯl\ *n* [*barbi*turic + *-al* (as in *Veronal*)] **:** a white crystalline addictive hypnotic $C_8H_{12}N_2O_3$ often administered in the form of its soluble sodium salt

bar·bi·tu·rate \bär-'bich-ə-rət, -,rāt; ,bär-bə-'t(y)u̇r-ət, -'t(y)u̇(ə)r-,āt\ *n* **1 :** a salt or ester of barbituric acid **2 :** any of various derivatives of barbituric acid used esp. as sedatives or hypnotics

bar·bi·tu·ric acid \,bär-bə-,t(y)u̇r-ik-\ *n* [part trans. of G *barbitursäure*, irreg. fr. the name *Barbara* + ISV *uric* + G *säure* acid] **:** a crystalline acid $C_4H_4N_2O_3$ derived from pyrimidine

bar·bule \'bär-(,)byü(ə)l\ *n* **:** a minute barb; *esp* **:** one of the processes that fringe the barbs of a feather

bar·ca·role *or* **bar·ca·rolle** \'bär-kə-,rōl\ *n* [F *barcarolle*, fr. It *barcarola*, fr. *barcarolo* gondolier, fr. *barca* bark, fr. LL] **1 :** a Venetian boat song characterized by the alternation of a strong and a weak beat suggesting a rowing rhythm **2 :** a piece of music imitating a barcarole

bar chart *n* **:** a graphic means of comparing numbers by rectangles with lengths proportional to the numbers represented — called also *bar graph*

¹bard \'bärd\ *n* [ME, fr. ScGael & MIr] **1 a :** a tribal poet-singer gifted in composing and reciting verses on heroes and their deeds **b :** a composer, singer, or declaimer of epic or heroic verse **2 :** POET — **bard·ic** \'bärd-ik\ *adj*

²bard *or* **barde** \'bärd\ *n* [MF *barde*, fr. OSp *barda*, fr. Ar *barda'ah*] **:** a piece of armor or ornament for a horse's neck, breast, or flank

³bard *vt* **:** to accouter with bards

bar·dol·a·ter \bär-'däl-ət-ər\ *n* [*Bard* (*of Avon*), epithet of Shakespeare + ido*later*] **:** one who idolizes Shakespeare — **bar·dol·a·try** \-ə-trē\ *n*

¹bare \'ba(ə)r, 'be(ə)r\ *adj* [ME, fr. OE *bær*; akin to OHG *bar* naked, Lith *basas* barefoot] **1 a :** lacking its natural, usual, or appropriate covering **b** (1) **:** lacking clothing (2) *obs* **:** BAREHEADED **c :** UNARMED **2 :** open to view **:** EXPOSED **3 a :** unfurnished or scantily supplied **b :** DESTITUTE ⟨~ of all safeguards⟩ **4 a :** having nothing left over or added **:** MERE **b :** devoid of amplification or adornment **5** *obs* **:** WORTHLESS — **bare·ly** *adv* — **bare·ness** *n*

syn BARE, NAKED, NUDE, BALD, BARREN mean deprived of naturally or conventionally appropriate covering. BARE implies the removal of what is additional, superfluous, ornamental, or dispensable; NAKED suggests absence of protective or ornamental covering but may imply a state of nature, of destitution, of defenselessness, of simple beauty; NUDE applies to the unclothed human figure and commonly lacks special connotation; BALD implies actual or seeming absence of natural covering and may suggest a conspicuous bareness; BARREN implies an absence of natural covering esp. of trees and may suggest aridity or impoverishment or sterility

²bare *vt* **:** to make or lay bare **:** UNCOVER, REVEAL

³bare *archaic past of* BEAR

bare·back \-,bak\ *or* **bare·backed** \-'bakt\ *adv* (*or adj*) **:** on the bare back of a horse **:** without a saddle

bare·faced \'ba(ə)r-'fāst, 'be(ə)r-\ *adj* **1 :** having the face uncovered: **a :** BEARDLESS **b :** wearing no mask **2 a :** UNCONCEALED, OPEN **b :** lacking scruples — **bare·faced·ly** \-'fā-səd-lē, -'fāst-lē\ *adv* — **bare·faced·ness** \-'fā-səd-nəs, -'fās(t)-nəs\ *n*

bare·foot \-,fu̇t\ *or* **bare·foot·ed** \-'fu̇t-əd\ *adv* (*or adj*) **:** with the feet bare **:** UNSHOD

ba·rege \bə-'rezh\ *n* [F *barège*, fr. *Barèges*, town in the Pyrenees, France] **:** a sheer fabric of open weave for women's clothing usu. made of wool in combination with silk or cotton

bare-hand·ed \'ba(ə)r-'han-dəd, 'be(ə)r-\ *adv* (*or adj*) **1 :** without gloves **2 :** without tools or weapons

bare·head·ed \-'hed-əd\ *adv* (*or adj*) **:** without a hat or other covering for the head — **bare·head·ed·ness** *n*

bar·fly \'bär-,flī\ *n* **:** a drinker who frequents bars

¹bar·gain \'bär-gən\ *n, often attrib* **1 :** an agreement between parties settling what each gives or receives in a transaction between them or what course of action or policy each pursues in respect to the other **2 :** something acquired by or as if by bargaining; *esp* **:** an advantageous purchase **3 :** a transaction, situation, or event with important good or bad results

²bargain *vb* [ME *bargainen*, fr. MF *bargaignier*, of Gmc origin; akin to OE *borgian* to borrow — more at BURY] *vi* **1 :** to negotiate over the terms of a purchase, agreement, or contract **:** HAGGLE **2 :** to come to terms **:** AGREE ~ *vt* **:** to sell or dispose of by bargaining **:** BARTER — **bar·gain·er** *n* — **bargain for :** to count on in advance

¹barge \'bärj\ *n* [ME, fr. OF, fr. LL *barca*] **:** any of various boats: as **a :** a roomy usu. flat-bottomed boat used chiefly for the transport of goods on inland waterways **b :** a large motorboat supplied to the flag officer of a flagship **c :** a roomy pleasure boat; *esp* **:** a boat of state elegantly furnished and decorated

²barge *vt* **:** to carry by barge ~ *vi* **:** to move or thrust oneself heedlessly or unceremoniously

barge·board \-,bō(ə)rd, -,bȯ(ə)rd\ *n* [origin unknown] **:** a board often ornamented that conceals roof timbers projecting over gables

barg·ee \bär-ˈjē\ *n, Brit* **:** BARGEMAN
barge·man \ˈbärj-mən\ *n* **:** the master or a deckhand of a barge
bar·ghest \ˈbär-gəst\ *n* [perh. fr. E dial. *bar* ridge (fr. ME *bergh* mound) + *ghest,* alter. of E *ghost*] *dial Eng* **:** a ghost or goblin portending misfortune
bar·ic \ˈbar-ik\ *adj* **:** of or relating to barium
ba·ri·lla \bə-ˈrēl-yə, -ˈrē-(y)ə\ *n* [Sp *barrilla*] **1 :** either of two European saltworts (*Salsola kali* and *S. soda*) or a related Algerian plant (*Halogeton souda*) **2 :** an impure sodium carbonate made from barilla ashes formerly used esp. in making soap and glass
bar·ite \ˈba(ə)r-ˌīt, ˈbe(ə)r-\ *n* [Gk *barytēs* weight, fr. *barys*] **:** barium sulfate $BaSO_4$ occurring as a mineral
bari·tone \ˈbar-ə-ˌtōn\ *n* [F *baryton* or It *baritono,* fr. Gk *barytonos* deep sounding, fr. *barys* heavy + *tonos* tone — more at GRIEVE] **1 a :** a male singing voice of medium compass between bass and tenor **b :** one having such a voice **2 :** the saxhorn intermediate in size between althorn and tuba
bar·i·um \ˈbar-ē-əm, ˈber-\ *n* [NL] **:** a silver-white malleable toxic bivalent metallic element of the alkaline-earth group that occurs only in combination — see ELEMENT table
barium sulfate *n* **:** a colorless crystalline insoluble compound $BaSO_4$ that occurs in nature as barite, is obtained artificially by precipitation, and is used as a pigment and extender, as a filler, and as a substance opaque to X rays
1**bark** \ˈbärk\ *vb* [ME *berken,* fr. OE *beorcan;* akin to ON *berkja* to bark, Lith *burgėti* to growl] *vi* **1 a :** to make the characteristic short loud cry of a dog **b :** to make a noise resembling a bark **2 :** to speak in a curt loud and usu. angry tone **:** SNAP ~ *vt* **1 :** to utter in a curt loud usu. angry tone **2 :** to advertise by persistent outcry
2**bark** *n* **1 a :** the sound made by a barking dog **b :** a similar sound **2 :** a short sharp peremptory tone of speech or utterance
3**bark** *n* [ME, fr. ON *bark-, börkr;* akin to MD & MLG *borke* bark] **1 :** the tough exterior covering of a woody root or stem **2 a :** TANBARK **b :** cinchona bark
4**bark** *vt* **1 :** to treat with an infusion of tanbark **2 a :** to strip the bark from; *specif* **:** GIRDLE 3 **b :** to rub off or abrade the skin of
5**bark** *n* [ME, fr. MF *barque,* fr. OProv *barca,* fr. LL] **1 a :** a small sailing ship **b :** a 3-masted ship with foremast and mainmast square-rigged and mizzenmast fore-and-aft rigged **2 :** a craft propelled by sails or oars

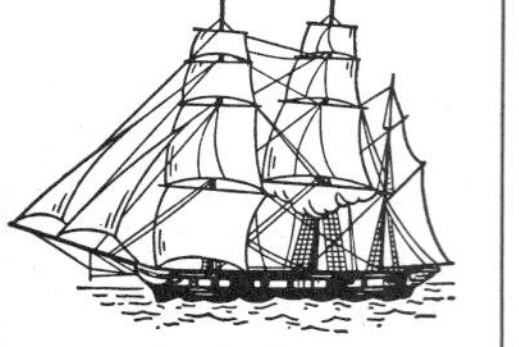
bark 1b

bark beetle *n* **:** a beetle (family Scolytidae) that bores under bark of trees both as larva and adult
bar·keep·er \ˈbär-ˌkē-pər\ *or* **bar·keep** \-ˌkēp\ *n* **:** one that keeps or tends a bar for the sale of liquors
bar·ken·tine \ˈbär-kən-ˌtēn\ *n* [5*bark* + *-entine,* alter. of *-antine* (as in *brigantine*)] **:** a 3-masted ship having the foremast square-rigged and the mainmast and mizzenmast fore-and-aft rigged
1**bark·er** \ˈbär-kər\ *n* **:** one that barks; *esp* **:** a person who barks at an entrance to a show
2**barker** *n* **:** one that removes or prepares bark
barky \ˈbär-kē\ *adj* **:** covered with or resembling bark
bar·ley \ˈbär-lē\ *n* [ME *barly,* fr. OE *bærlic* of barley; akin to OE *bere* barley, L *far* spelt] **:** a cereal grass (genus *Hordeum,* esp. *H. vulgare*) having the flowers in dense spikes with long awns and three spikelets at each joint of the rachis; *also* **:** its seed used in malt beverages and in breakfast foods and stock feeds
bar·ley·corn \-ˌkȯ(ə)rn\ *n* **1 :** a grain of barley **2 :** an old unit of length equal to the third part of an inch
barm \ˈbärm\ *n* [ME *berme,* fr. OE *beorma;* akin to L *fermentum* yeast, *fervēre* to boil] **:** yeast formed on fermenting malt liquors
bar·maid \ˈbär-ˌmād\ *n, chiefly Brit* **:** a female bartender
bar·man \-mən\ *n* **:** BARTENDER
Bar·me·ci·dal \ˌbär-mə-ˈsīd-ᵊl\ *or* **Bar·me·cide** \ˈbär-mə-ˌsīd\ *adj* [*Barmecide,* a wealthy Persian, who, in a tale of *The Arabian Nights,* invited a beggar to a feast of imaginary food] **:** providing only the illusion of plenty or abundance ⟨a ~ feast⟩
bar mitz·vah \bär-ˈmits-və\ *n, often cap B&M* [Heb *bar miṣwāh,* lit., son of the (divine) law] **1 :** a Jewish boy who reaches his 13th birthday and attains the age of religious duty and responsibility **2 :** the initiatory ceremony recognizing a boy as a bar mitzvah
barmy \ˈbär-mē\ *adj* **1 :** full of froth or ferment **2 :** BALMY 2
barn \ˈbärn\ *n* [ME *bern,* fr. OE *bereærn,* fr. *bere* barley + *ærn* place] **1 :** a usu. large building for the storage of farm products, for feed, and usu. for the housing of farm animals or farm equipment **2 :** a large building for the housing of a fleet of vehicles
Bar·na·bas \ˈbär-nə-bəs\ *n* [Gk, fr. Aram *Barnebhū'āh*] **:** a companion of the apostle Paul on his first missionary journey
bar·na·cle \ˈbär-ni-kəl\ *n* [ME *barnakille,* alter. of *bernake,* of Celt origin; akin to Corn *brennyk* limpet] **1 :** a European goose (*Branta leucopsis*) that breeds in the arctic and is larger than the related brant — called also *barnacle goose* **2 :** any of numerous marine crustaceans (order Cirripedia) with feathery appendages for gathering food that are free-swimming as larvae but fixed to rocks or floating logs as adults — **bar·na·cled** \-kəld\ *adj*
barn·storm \ˈbärn-ˌstȯrm\ *vi* **1 :** to tour through rural districts staging theatrical performances usu. in one-night stands **2 :** to travel from place to place making brief stops; *specif* **:** to pilot one's airplane in sightseeing flights with passengers or in exhibition stunts in an unscheduled itinerant course esp. in rural districts ~ *vt* **:** to travel across while barnstorming — **barn·storm·er** *n*
barn·yard \-ˌyärd\ *n* **:** a usu. fenced area adjoining a barn
baro- — see BAR-
baro·gram \ˈbar-ə-ˌgram\ *n* [ISV] **:** a barographic tracing
baro·graph \-ˌgraf\ *n* [ISV] **:** a self-registering barometer — **baro·graph·ic** \ˌbar-ə-ˈgraf-ik\ *adj*
ba·rom·e·ter \bə-ˈräm-ət-ər\ *n* **1 :** an instrument for determining the pressure of the atmosphere and hence for assisting in judgment as to probable weather changes and for determining the height of an ascent **2 :** something that serves to register fluctuations (as in public opinion) — **baro·met·ric** \ˌbar-ə-ˈme-trik\ *or* **baro·met·ri·cal** \-tri-kəl\ *adj* — **baro·met·ri·cal·ly** \-tri-k(ə-)lē\ *adv* — **ba·rom·e·try** \bə-ˈräm-ə-trē\ *n*
barometric gradient *n* **:** the rate of fall in atmospheric pressure between two stations **:** the slope of an isobaric surface
barometric pressure *n* **:** the pressure of the atmosphere usu. expressed in terms of the height of a column of mercury
bar·on \ˈbar-ən\ *n* [ME, fr. OF, of Gmc origin; akin to OHG *baro* freeman] **1 a :** one of a class of tenants holding chiefly by military or other honorable service directly from a feudal superior (as a king) **b :** a lord of the realm **:** NOBLE, PEER **2 a :** a member of the lowest grade of the peerage in Great Britain **b :** a nobleman on the continent of Europe of varying rank **c :** a member of the lowest order of nobility in Japan **3 :** a man of great or overweening power or influence in some field of activity
bar·on·age \-ə-nij\ *n* **:** the whole body of barons or peers **:** NOBILITY
bar·on·ess \-ə-nəs\ *n* **1 :** the wife or widow of a baron **2 :** a woman who holds a baronial title in her own right
bar·on·et \ˈbar-ə-nət, *US also* ˌbar-ə-ˈnet\ *n* **:** the holder of a rank of honor below a baron and above a knight
bar·on·et·age \-ij\ *n* **1 :** BARONETCY **2 :** the whole body of baronets
bar·on·et·cy \-sē\ *n* **:** the rank of a baronet
ba·rong \bə-ˈrȯŋ, -ˈräŋ\ *n* [native name in the Philippines] **:** a thick-backed thin-edged knife or sword used by Moros
ba·ro·nial \bə-ˈrō-nē-əl, -nyəl\ *adj* **1 :** of or relating to a baron or the baronage **2 :** STATELY, AMPLE
bar·ony \ˈbar-ə-nē\ *n* **1 :** the domain, rank, or dignity of a baron **2 :** a vast private landholding
ba·roque \bə-ˈrōk, ba-, -ˈräk\ *adj* [F, fr. It *barocco*] **:** of, relating to, or having the characteristics of a style of artistic expression prevalent esp. in the 17th century that is marked generally by elaborate and sometimes grotesque ornamentation and specifically also in architecture by dynamic opposition and the use of curved and plastic figures, in music by improvisation, contrasting effects, and powerful tensions, and in literature by complexity of form and bizarre, ingenious, and often ambiguous imagery — **baroque** *n*
ba·rouche \bə-ˈrüsh\ *n* [G *barutsche,* fr. It *biroccio,* deriv. of LL *birotus* two-wheeled, fr. L *bi-* + *rota* wheel — more at ROLL] **:** a four-wheeled carriage with a driver's seat high in front, two double seats inside facing each other, and a folding top over the back seat
barque \ˈbärk\, **bar·quen·tine** \ˈbär-kən-ˌtēn\ *var of* BARK, BARKENTINE
1**bar·rack** \ˈbar-ək, -ik\ *n* [F *baraque* hut, fr. Catal *barraca*] **1** *usu pl* **:** a building or set of buildings used esp. for lodging soldiers in garrison **2** *usu pl* **a :** a structure resembling a shed or barn that provides temporary housing **b :** housing characterized by extreme plainness or dreary uniformity
2**barrack** *vt* **:** to lodge in barracks
3**barrack** *vb* [origin unknown] *vi* **1** *chiefly Austral* **:** JEER, HECKLE **2** *chiefly Austral* **:** ROOT, CHEER ~ *vt, chiefly Austral* **:** to shout at derisively or sarcastically — **bar·rack·er** *n*
bar·ra·coon \ˌbar-ə-ˈkün\ *n* [Sp *barracón,* aug. of *barraca* hut, fr. Catal] **:** an enclosure or barracks formerly used for temporary confinement of slaves or convicts
bar·ra·cou·ta \ˌbar-ə-ˈküt-ə\ *n* [modif. of AmerSp *barracuda*] **1 :** a large marine food fish (*Thyrsites atun*) **2 :** BARRACUDA
bar·ra·cu·da \ˌbar-ə-ˈküd-ə\ *n, pl* **barracuda** *or* **barracudas** [AmerSp] **:** any of several large voracious marine fishes (genus *Sphyraena*) of warm seas related to the gray mullets and including excellent food fishes as well as forms regarded as toxic
1**bar·rage** \ˈbär-ij\ *n* [F, fr. *barrer* to bar, fr. *barre* bar] **:** an artificial dam placed in a watercourse to increase the depth of water or to divert it into a channel for navigation or irrigation
2**bar·rage** \bə-ˈräzh, -ˈräj\ *n* [F (*tir de*) *barrage* barrier fire] **1 :** a barrier of fire esp. of artillery laid on a line close to friendly troops to screen and protect them **2 :** a rapid-fire massive or concentrated delivery or outpouring (as of speech or writing)
3**bar·rage** \bə-ˈräzh, -ˈräj\ *vt* **:** to deliver a barrage against
barrage balloon *n* **:** a small captive balloon used to support wires or nets as protection against air attacks
bar·ra·mun·da \ˌbar-ə-ˈmən-də\ *or* **bar·ra·mun·di** \-dē\ *n* [native name in Australia] **:** any of several Australian fishes; *esp* **:** a large red-fleshed lungfish (*Neoceratodus forsteri*) of Australian rivers esteemed as food
bar·ran·ca \bə-ˈraŋ-kə\ *or* **bar·ran·co** \-(ˌ)kō\ *n* [Sp] **1 :** a deep gulley or arroyo with steep sides **2 :** a steep bank or bluff
bar·ra·tor *also* **bar·ra·ter** \ˈbar-ət-ər\ *n* **:** one who engages in barratry
bar·ra·try \-ə-trē\ *n* [ME *barratrie,* fr. MF *baraterie* deception, fr. *barater* to deceive, exchange] **1 :** the purchase or sale of office or preferment in church or state **2 :** a fraudulent breach of duty on the part of a master of a ship or of the mariners to the injury of the owner of the ship or cargo **3 :** the persistent incitement of litigation
barred \ˈbärd\ *adj* **:** marked by or divided off by bars; *specif* **:** having alternate bands of different color
1**bar·rel** \ˈbar-əl\ *n* [ME *barel,* fr. MF *baril*] **1 :** a round bulging vessel of greater length than breadth that is usu. made of staves bound with hoops and has flat ends of equal diameter **2 a :** the amount contained in a barrel; *esp* **:** the amount fixed for a certain commodity (as 5 bushels of corn) used as a unit of measure or weight **b :** a great quantity **3 :** a drum or cylinder or a round part similar to one of these: as **a :** the discharging tube of a gun **b :** the cylindrical metal box enclosing the mainspring of a timepiece **c :** the part of a fountain pen or of a pencil containing the ink or lead **d :** a cylindrical or tapering housing containing the optical components of a photographic-lens system and the iris diaphragm **e :** TUMBLING BARREL **f :** the fuel outlet from the carburetor on a gasoline engine **4 :** the trunk of a quadruped — **bar·reled** *adj*
2**barrel** *vb* **bar·reled** *or* **bar·relled; bar·rel·ing** *or* **bar·rel·ling** *vt* **:** to put or pack in a barrel ~ *vi* **:** to travel at a high speed
barrel chair *n* **:** an upholstered chair with a high solid rounded back
bar·rel·ful \ˈbar-əl-ˌfu̇l\ *n, pl* **barrelfuls** \-ˌfu̇lz\ *or* **bar·rels·ful** \-əlz-ˌfu̇l\ **:** BARREL 2a
bar·rel·house \-əl-ˌhau̇s\ *n* **1 :** a cheap drinking and usu. dancing establishment **2 :** a style of jazz characterized by a very heavy beat and simultaneous improvisation by each player
barrel organ *n* **:** an instrument for producing music by the action of a revolving cylinder studded with pegs upon a series of valves that admit air from a bellows to a set of pipes
barrel roll *n* **:** an aerial maneuver in which a complete revolution about the longitudinal axis is made
1**bar·ren** \ˈbar-ən\ *adj* [ME *bareine,* fr. OF *baraine*] **1 :** not

reproducing: as **a :** incapable of producing offspring — used esp. of females or matings **b :** not yet or not recently pregnant **c :** habitually failing to fruit **2 :** not productive: as **a :** producing inferior or scanty vegetation ⟨~ soils⟩ **b :** unproductive of results or gain **:** FRUITLESS ⟨a ~ scheme⟩ **3 :** DEVOID, LACKING **4 :** lacking interest, information, or charm **5 :** DULL, UNRESPONSIVE **syn** see BARE, STERILE — **bar·ren·ly** *adv* — **bar·ren·ness** \-ən-nəs\ *n*

2**barren** *n* **1 :** a tract of barren land **2** *pl* **:** an extent of usu. level land having an inferior growth of trees or little vegetation

bar·rette \bä-'ret, bə-\ *n* [F, dim. of *barre* bar] **:** a clip or bar for holding a woman's hair in place

1**bar·ri·cade** \'bar-ə-,kād, ,bar-ə-'\ *vt* **1 :** to block off or stop up with a barricade **2 :** to prevent access to by means of a barricade

2**barricade** *n* [F, fr. MF, fr. *barriquer* to barricade, fr. *barrique* barrel] **1 :** an obstruction or rampart thrown up across a way or passage to check the advance of the enemy **2 :** BARRIER, OBSTACLE

bar·ri·ca·do \,bar-ə-'kād-(,)ō\ *n, pl* **barricadoes** [modif. of F *barricade*] *archaic* **:** BARRICADE — **barricado** *vt, archaic*

bar·ri·er \'bar-ē-ər\ *n* [ME *barrere*, fr. MF *barriere*, fr. *barre*] **1 a :** a material object or set of objects that separates, demarcates, or serves as a barricade **b :** an extension of the antarctic continental ice sheet into the sea resting partly on the bottom **2** *pl, often cap* **:** a medieval war game in which combatants fight on foot with a fence or railing between them **3 :** the movable gate or device at the starting line in a racetrack **4 :** something immaterial that impedes or separates **5 :** a factor that tends to restrict the free movement and mingling of individuals or populations

barrier reef *n* **:** a coral reef roughly parallel to a shore and separated from it by a lagoon

bar·ring \'bär-iŋ\ *prep* **:** excluding by exception **:** EXCEPTING

bar·ris·ter \'bar-ə-stər\ *n* [1*bar* + *-i-* + *-ster*] **:** a lawyer who is permitted to plead cases in any English court — compare SOLICITOR **syn** see LAWYER

bar·room \'bär-,rüm, -,rům\ *n* **:** a room or establishment whose main feature is a bar for the sale of liquor

1**bar·row** \'bar-(,)ō, -ə(-w)\ *n* [ME *bergh*, fr. OE *beorg;* akin to OHG *berg* mountain, Skt *bṛhant* high] **1 :** MOUNTAIN, MOUND — used only in the names of hills in England **2 :** a large mound of earth or stones over the remains of the dead **:** TUMULUS

2**barrow** *n* [ME *barow*, fr. OE *bearg;* akin to OHG *barug* barrow, OE *borian* to bore] **:** a male hog castrated before sexual maturity

3**barrow** *n* [ME *barew*, fr. OE *bearwe;* akin to OE *beran* to carry — more at BEAR] **1 a :** HANDBARROW **b :** WHEELBARROW **2:** a cart with a shallow box body, two wheels, and shafts for pushing it

bar sinister *n* **1 :** a supposed heraldic charge held to be a mark of bastardy **2 :** the fact or condition of being of illegitimate birth

bar·tend·er \'bär-,ten-dər\ *n* **:** one that serves liquor at a bar

1**bar·ter** \'bärt-ər\ *vb* [ME *bartren*, fr. MF *barater*] *vi* **:** to trade by exchanging one commodity for another ~ *vt* **:** to trade or exchange by or as if by bartering — **bar·ter·er** \-ər-ər\ *n*

2**barter** *n* **1 :** the act or practice of carrying on trade by bartering **2 :** the thing given in exchange in bartering

Barth·ian \'bärt-ē-ən\ *adj* **:** of or relating to Barth or his theology

bar·ti·zan \'bärt-ə-zən, ,bärt-ə-'zan\ *n* [ME *bretasinge*, fr. *bretasce* parapet — more at BRATTICE] **:** a small structure (as a turret) projecting from a building and serving esp. for lookout or defense

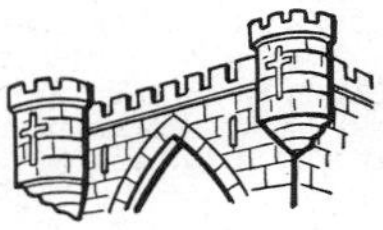

bartizans

ba·ry·ta \bə-'rīt-ə\ *n* [NL, modif. of Gk *barytēs* weight — more at BARITE] **:** any of several compounds of barium; *esp* **:** barium monoxide — **ba·ryt·ic** \-'rit-ik\ *adj*

bar·yte \'ba(ə)r-,īt, 'be(ə)r-\ *or* **ba·ry·tes** \bə-'rīt-ēz\ *var of* BARITE

bary·tone \'bar-ə-,tōn\ *var of* BARITONE

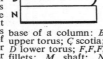

bas·al \'bā-səl, -zəl\ *adj* **1 a :** relating to, situated at, or forming the base **b :** arising from the base of a stem ⟨~ leaves⟩ **2 a :** of or relating to the foundation, base, or essence **:** FUNDAMENTAL **b :** of, relating to, or essential for maintaining the fundamental vital activities of an organism **:** MINIMAL — **ba·sal·ly** \-ē\ *adv*

basal metabolic rate *n* **:** the rate at which heat is given off by an organism at complete rest

basal metabolism *n* **:** the turnover of energy in a fasting and resting organism using energy solely to maintain vital cellular activity, respiration, and circulation as measured by the basal metabolic rate

ba·salt \bə-'sölt, 'bā-,\ *n* [L *basaltes*, MS var. of *basanites* touchstone, fr. Gk *basanitēs* (*lithos*), fr. *basanos* touchstone, fr. Egypt *bḫnw*] **:** a dark gray to black dense to fine-grained igneous rock that consists of basic plagioclase, augite, and usu. magnetite — **ba·sal·tic** \bə-'söl-tik\ *adj*

bas bleu \bä-blœ\ *n* [F *bas-bleu*] **:** BLUESTOCKING

bas·cule \'bas-(,)kyü(ə)l\ *n* [F, seesaw] **:** an apparatus or structure in which one end is counterbalanced by the other on the principle of the seesaw or by weights

1**base** \'bās\ *n, pl* **bas·es** \'bā-səz\ [ME, fr. MF, fr. L *basis*, fr. Gk, step, base, fr. *bainein* to go — more at COME] **1 a :** the bottom of something considered as its support **:** FOUNDATION **b** (1) **:** the lower part of a wall, pier, or column considered as a separate architectural feature (2) **:** the lower part of a complete architectural design **c :** that part of a bodily organ by which it is attached to another more central structure of the organism **2 a :** a main ingredient **b :** a supporting or carrying ingredient (as of a medicine) **3 :** the fundamental part of something **:** GROUNDWORK **4 :** the lower part of a heraldic field **5 a :** the point or line from which a start is made in an action or undertaking **b :** a line in a survey which serves as the origin for computations **c :** the locality or the installations on which a military force relies for supplies or from which it initiates operations **d :** the number with reference to which a set of numbers or a mathematical table is constructed **e :** ROOT 6 **6 a :** the starting place or goal in various games **b :** any one of the four stations a runner in baseball must touch in order to score **7 :** any of various typically water-soluble and acrid or brackish tasting compounds capable of reacting with an acid to form a salt that are molecules or ions able to take up a proton from an acid or substances able to give up an unshared pair of electrons to an acid **syn** BASIS, FOUNDATION, GROUND, GROUNDWORK: BASE implies a broad and solid bottom by which something is held up or stabilized; BASIS carries the same meaning but applies to immaterial things ⟨*basis* of belief⟩; FOUNDATION implies something laid down or constructed to serve as a base or basis; GROUND applies to a material, a substance, a surface upon which something is built or against which it is displayed; GROUNDWORK equals FOUNDATION but applies chiefly to immaterial things ⟨lay a *groundwork* for negotiations⟩ — **based** \'bāst\ *adj* — **off base 1 :** completely or absurdly mistaken **2 :** UNAWARES

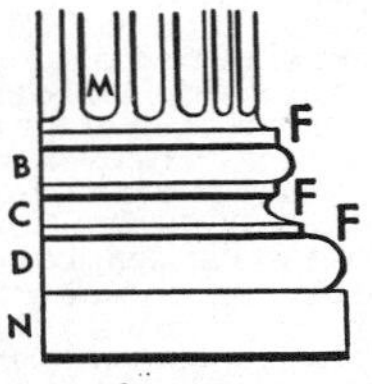

base of a column: *B* upper torus; *C* scotia; *D* lower torus; *F,F,F,* fillets: *M* shaft; *N* plinth

2**base** *vt* **1 :** to make, form, or serve as a base for **2 :** to find a base or basis for **:** ESTABLISH — usu. used with *on* or *upon*

3**base** *adj* **:** constituting or serving as a base

4**base** *adj* [ME *bas*, fr. MF, fr. ML *bassus* short, low] **1** *archaic* **:** of little height **2** *obs* **:** low in place or position **3** *obs* **:** BASS **4** *archaic* **:** BASEBORN **5 a :** resembling a villein **:** SERVILE ⟨a ~ tenant⟩ **b :** held by villenage ⟨~ tenure⟩ **6 a :** being of comparatively low value and having inferior properties ⟨a ~ metal⟩ **b :** containing a larger than usual proportion of base metals ⟨~ silver denarii⟩ **7 :** CONTEMPTIBLE, IGNOBLE **8 :** lacking higher values **9 :** of relatively little value — **base·ly** *adv* — **base·ness** *n* **syn** LOW, VILE: BASE stresses the ignoble and may suggest greed, grossness, cowardice, cruelty, treachery; LOW implies falling below ordinary human standards of dignity, taste, fairness, morality; VILE suggests filth or extreme depravity

5**base** *obs var of* 3BASS

base·ball \'bās-,böl\ *n, often attrib* **:** a game played with a bat and ball between two teams of nine players each on a large field centering upon four bases that mark the course a runner must take to score; *also* **:** the ball used in this game

base·board \-,bō(ə)rd, -,bö(ə)rd\ *n* **:** a board situated at or forming the base of something; *specif* **:** a molding covering the joint of a wall and the adjoining floor

base·born \-'bö(ə)rn\ *adj* **1 a :** of humble birth **:** LOWLY **b :** of illegitimate birth **:** BASTARD **2 :** MEAN, IGNOBLE

base burner *n* **:** a stove in which the fuel is fed from a hopper as the lower layer is consumed

base hit *n* **:** a hit in baseball that enables the batter to reach base safely with no error made and no base runner forced out

base·less \'bā-sləs\ *adj* **:** having no base or basis

base·lev·el \'bā-,slev-əl\ *n* **:** the level below which a land surface cannot be reduced by running water

base line *n* **1 :** a main line taken as or representing a base **2 :** the area within which a baseball player must keep when running between bases **3 :** the back line at each end of a tennis court

base·man \'bā-smən\ *n* **:** a man stationed at a base

base·ment \'bā-smənt\ *n, often attrib* [prob. fr. 1*base*] **1 :** the ground floor facade or interior in Renaissance architecture **2 :** the part of a building that is wholly or partly below ground level **3 :** the lowest or fundamental part of anything

ba·sen·ji \bə-'sen-jē\ *n* [of Bantu origin; akin to Lingala *basenji*, pl. of *mosenji* native] **:** any of an African breed of small compact curly-tailed chestnut-brown dogs that rarely bark

base on balls : an advance to first base given to a baseball player who receives four balls

base pay *n* **:** a rate or amount of pay for a standard work period, job, or position exclusive of additional payments or allowances

base runner *n* **:** a baseball player of the team at bat who is on base or is attempting to reach a base — **base·run·ning** \'bās-,rən-iŋ\ *n*

1**bash** \'bash\ *vb* [origin unknown] *vt* **:** HIT, SMASH ~ *vi* **:** CRASH

2**bash** *n, chiefly Brit* **:** a forceful blow

ba·shaw \bə-'shö\ *var of* PASHA

bash·ful \'bash-fəl\ *adj* [obs. *bash* (to be abashed)] **1 :** inclined to shrink from public attention **:** SHY, DIFFIDENT **2 :** characterized by, showing, or resulting from extreme sensitiveness, self-consciousness, or shyness **syn** see SHY — **bash·ful·ly** \-fə-lē\ *adv* — **bash·ful·ness** \-fəl-nəs\ *n*

bashi-ba·zouk \,bash-ē-bə-'zük\ *n* [Turk *başi bozuk* irregular soldier] **1 :** a member of an irregular ill-disciplined auxiliary of the Ottoman Empire **2 :** a turbulent ill-disciplined person

1**ba·sic** \'bā-sik\ *adj* **1 :** of, relating to, or forming the base or essence **:** FUNDAMENTAL **2 :** constituting or serving as the basis or starting point **3 a :** of, relating to, containing, or having the character of a base **b :** having an alkaline reaction **4** *of rocks* **:** containing relatively little silica **5 :** relating to or made by a basic process — **ba·si·cal·ly** \-si-k(ə-)lē\ *adv*

2**basic** *n* **:** something that is basic **:** FUNDAMENTAL

Basic English *n* **:** a copyrighted system of simplified English consisting of 850 words and a short list of grammatical rules

ba·sic·i·ty \bā-'sis-ət-ē\ *n* **:** the quality or degree of being a base

basic process *n* **:** a process carried on in a furnace lined with basic material and under a slag that is dominantly basic

basic slag *n* **:** a slag low in silica and high in base-forming oxides that is used in the basic process of steelmaking and that is then useful as a fertilizer

ba·sid·i·al \bə-'sid-ē-əl\ *adj* **:** of, relating to, or having a basidium

ba·sid·io·my·cete \bə-,sid-ē-ō-'mī-,sēt, -,mī-'sēt\ *n* [deriv. of NL *basidium* + Gk *mykēt-*, *mykēs* fungus] **:** any of a large class (Basidiomycetes) of higher fungi having septate hyphae, bearing spores on a basidium, and including rusts, smuts, mushrooms, and puffballs — **ba·sid·io·my·ce·tous** \-ē-ō-,mī-'sēt-əs\ *adj*

ba·sid·io·spore \bə-'sid-ē-ə-,spō(ə)r, -,spö(ə)r\ *n* [NL *basidium* + E *-o-* + *spore*] **:** a spore produced by a basidium — **ba·sid·io·spo·rous** \-,sid-ē-ə-'spōr-əs, -'spör-; -ē-'äs-pə-rəs\ *adj*

ba·sid·i·um \bə-'sid-ē-əm\ *n, pl* **ba·sid·ia** \-ē-ə\ [NL, fr. L *basis*] **:** a structure on a basidiomycete in which nuclear fusion occurs followed by meiosis and on which usu. four basidiospores are borne

ba·si·fixed \'bā-si-,fikst\ *adj* [*basis* + *fixed*] **:** attached at or near the base

ba·si·fy \-sə-,fī\ *vt* **:** to convert into a base or make alkaline

ba·sil \'baz-əl, 'bās-, 'bas-, 'bāz-\ *n* [MF *basile*, fr. LL *basilicum*, fr. Gk *basilikon*, fr. neut. of *basilikos*] **:** any of several plants of the mint family; *esp* **:** either of two plants (*Ocimum basilicum* and *O. suave*) with leaves used in cookery

bas·i·lar \'bas-ə-lər\ *also* **bas·i·lary** \-ˌler-ē\ *adj* [irreg. fr. *basis*] **:** of, relating to, or situated at the base

Ba·sil·i·an \bə-'zil-ē-ən, -'sil-\ *adj* **:** of or relating to St. Basil or a community under his monastic rule — **Basilian** *n*

ba·sil·i·ca \bə-'sil-i-kə, -'zil-\ *n* [L, fr. Gk *basilikē*, fr. fem. of *basilikos* royal, fr. *basileus* king] **1 :** an oblong building ending in a semicircular apse used in ancient Rome esp. for a court of justice and place of public assembly **2 :** an early Christian church building consisting of nave and aisles with clerestory and a large high transept from which an apse projects **3 :** a Roman Catholic church or cathedral given ceremonial privileges — **ba·sil·i·can** \-kən\ *adj*

bas·i·lisk \'bas-ə-ˌlisk, 'baz-\ *n* [ME, fr. L *basiliscus*, fr. Gk *basiliskos*, fr. dim. of *basileus*] **1 :** a legendary reptile with fatal breath and glance **2 :** any of several crested tropical American lizards (genus *Basiliscus*) related to the iguanas and noted for their ability to run upon their hind legs — **basilisk** *adj*

ba·sin \'bās-ᵊn\ *n* [ME, fr. OF *bacin*, fr. LL *bacchinon*] **1 a :** an open usu. circular vessel with sloping or curving sides used typically for holding water for washing **b :** the quantity contained in a basin **2 a :** a dock built in a tidal river or harbor **b :** a water area enclosed or partly enclosed **3 a :** a large or small depression in the surface of the land or in the ocean floor **b :** the entire tract of country drained by a river and its tributaries **c :** a great depression in the surface of the lithosphere occupied by an ocean **4 :** a broad area of the earth beneath which the strata dip usu. from the sides toward the center — **ba·sined** \-ᵊnd\ *adj*

bas·i·net \ˌbas-ə-'net\ *n* [ME *bacinet*, fr. OF, dim. of *bacin*] **:** a light often pointed steel helmet

ba·sip·e·tal \bā-'sip-ət-ᵊl\ *adj* [L *basis* + *petere* to go toward — more at FEATHER] **:** proceeding from the apex toward the base or from above downward — **ba·sip·e·tal·ly** \-ᵊl-ē\ *adv*

ba·sis \'bā-səs\ *n, pl* **ba·ses** \-ˌsēz\ [L] **1 :** FOUNDATION **2 :** the principal component of anything **3 :** something on which anything is constructed or established **4 :** the basic principle **syn** see BASE

bask \'bask\ *vb* [ME *basken*, fr. ON *bathask*, refl. of *batha* to bathe; akin to OE *bæth* bath] *vi* **1 :** to lie in or expose oneself to a pleasant warmth or atmosphere **2 :** to take pleasure or derive enjoyment ~ *vt, obs* **:** to warm by continued exposure to heat

bas·ket \'bas-kət\ *n* [ME, prob. fr. (assumed) ONF *baskot;* akin to OF *baschoue* wooden vessel; both fr. L *bascauda* dishpan, of Celt origin; akin to MIr *basc* necklace — more at FASCIA] **1 a :** a receptacle made of interwoven material (as osiers) **b :** any of various lightweight usu. wood containers **c :** the quantity contained in a basket **2 :** something that resembles a basket esp. in shape or use **3 a :** a net open at the bottom and suspended from a metal ring that constitutes the goal in basketball **b :** a field goal in basketball — **bas·ket·work** \-ˌwərk\ *n*

bas·ket·ball \-ˌbȯl\ *n, often attrib* **:** a usu. indoor court game in which each of two teams tries to toss an inflated ball through a raised goal; *also* **:** the ball used in this game

basket fern *n* **1 :** MALE FERN **2 :** a tropical American sword fern (*Nephrolepis pectinata*)

basket–handle arch *n* — see ARCH illustration

basket hilt *n* **:** a hilt with a basket-shaped guard to protect the hand — **bas·ket–hilt·ed** \'bas-kət-'hil-təd\ *adj*

Basket Maker *n* **1 :** any of three stages of an ancient culture of the plateau area of southwestern U. S. that preceded and formed one cultural development with the Pueblo **2 :** a member of the people who produced the Basket Maker culture

basket–of–gold *n* **:** a European perennial herb (*Alyssum saxatile*) widely cultivated for its grayish foliage and yellow flowers

bas·ket·ry \'bas-kə-trē\ *n* **1 :** the art or craft of making baskets or objects woven like baskets **2 :** objects produced by basketry

basket star *n* **:** an echinoderm (order Euryalida) resembling a starfish with slender complexly branched interlacing arms

basket weave *n* **:** a textile weave resembling the checkered pattern of a plaited basket

bas mitz·vah \bä-'smits-və\ *n, often cap B&M* [Heb *bath miṣwāh*, lit., daughter of the (divine) law] **1 :** a Jewish girl who at about 13 years of age assumes religious responsibilities **2 :** the synagogue ceremony recognizing a girl as a bas mitzvah

ba·so·phil \'bā-sə-ˌfil\ *or* **ba·so·phile** \-ˌfīl\ *n* **:** a basophilic substance or structure; *esp* **:** a white blood cell with basophilic granules

ba·so·phil·ic \ˌbā-sə-'fil-ik\ *adj* [ISV *base* + *-o-* + *-philic*] **:** staining readily with basic stains

Basque \'bask\ *n* [F, fr. L *Vasco*] **1 :** one of a people of obscure origin inhabiting the western Pyrenees on the Bay of Biscay **2 :** the language of the Basques of unknown relationship **3** *not cap* **:** a tight-fitting bodice for women — **Basque** *adj*

bas–re·lief \ˌbär-i-'lēf\ *n* [F, fr. *bas* low + *relief* raised work] **1 :** sculptural relief in which the projection from the surrounding surface is slight and no part of the modeled form is undercut **2 :** sculpture executed in bas-relief

1**bass** \'bas\ *n, pl* **bass** *or* **bass·es** [ME *base*, alter. of OE *bærs;* akin to OE *byrst* bristle] **:** any of numerous edible spiny-finned fishes (esp. families Centrarchidae and Serranidae)

2**bass** \'bās\ *adj* [ME *bas* base] **1 :** deep or grave in tone **2 :** of low pitch

3**bass** \'bās\ *n* **1 :** a deep or grave tone **:** low-pitched sound **2 a** (1) **:** the lowest part in polyphonic or harmonic music (2) **:** the lower half of the whole vocal or instrumental tonal range **b** (1) **:** the lowest male singing voice (2) **:** a person having such a voice **c :** the lowest member in range of a family of instruments

4**bass** \'bas\ *n* [alter. of *bast*] **1 :** a coarse tough fiber from palms **2 :** BASSWOOD 1

bass clef *n* **1 :** a clef placing the F below middle C on the fourth line of the staff **2 :** the bass staff

bass drum *n* **:** a large drum having two heads and giving a booming sound of low indefinite pitch

1**bas·set** \'bas-ət\ *n* [F, fr. MF, fr. *basset* short, fr. *bas* low — more at BASE] **:** any of an old French breed of short-legged slow-moving hunting dogs with very long ears and crooked front legs

2**basset** *n* [perh. fr. obs. F, low stool, fr. *basset* short] **:** the outcropping edge of a geological stratum

3**basset** *vi* **:** to appear at the surface

bas·set horn \'bas-ət-\ *n* [prob. fr. G *bassetthorn*, fr. It *bassetto* (dim. of *basso* bass) + G *horn*, fr. OHG] **:** a tenor clarinet in F

bass fiddle *n* **:** the double bass esp. as used in jazz orchestras

bass horn *n* **:** TUBA

bas·si·net \ˌbas-ə-'net\ *n* [prob. modif. of F *barcelonnette*, dim. of *berceau* cradle] **1 :** an infant's bed made of wickerwork, plastic, or other material and often having a hood over one end **2 :** a perambulator that resembles a bassinet

bass·ist \'bā-səst\ *n* **:** a double bass player

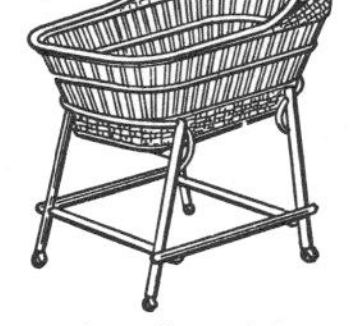

bassinet 1

bas·so \'bas-(ˌ)ō, 'bäs-\ *n* [It, fr. ML *bassus*, fr. *bassus* short, low] **:** a bass singer; *esp* **:** an operatic bass

bas·soon \bə-'sün, ba-\ *n* [F *basson*, fr. It *bassone*, fr. *basso*] **:** a tenor or bass double-reed woodwind instrument having a long doubled conical wooden body connected to the mouthpiece by a thin metal tube — **bas·soon·ist** \-'sü-nəst\ *n*

bas·so pro·fun·do \ˌbas(ˌ)ō-prə-'fən-(ˌ)dō, ˌbäs-, -'fün-\ *n, pl* **basso profundos** [It *basso profondo*, lit., deep bass] **1 :** a deep heavy bass voice with a compass extending to about C below the bass staff **2 :** a person having a basso profundo voice

bas·so–re·lie·vo *also* **bas·so–ri·lie·vo** \ˌbas-(ˌ)ō-ri-'lē-(ˌ)vō, ˌbäs-(ˌ)ō-rēl-'yā-(ˌ)vō\ *n* [It *bassorilievo*, fr. *basso* low + *rilievo* relief] **:** BAS-RELIEF

bass viol *n* **1 :** VIOLA DA GAMBA **2 :** DOUBLE BASS

bass·wood \'bas-ˌwu̇d\ *n* **1 :** any of a genus (*Tilia*, esp. *T. americana*) of trees of the linden family; *also* **:** its straight-grained white wood **2 a :** a tulip tree (*Liriodendron tulipifera*) **b :** TULIPWOOD 1

bast \'bast\ *n* [ME, fr. OE *bæst;* akin to OHG & ON *bast*] **1 :** PHLOEM **2 :** a strong woody fiber obtained chiefly from the phloem of plants and used esp. in cordage, matting, and fabrics

1**bas·tard** \'bas-tərd\ *n* [ME, fr. OF] **1 :** an illegitimate child **2 :** something that is spurious, irregular, inferior, or of questionable origin **3 :** an offensive or disagreeable person — used as a generalized term of abuse — **bas·tard·ly** \-lē\ *adj*

2**bastard** *adj* **1 :** ILLEGITIMATE **2 :** of inferior breed or stock **:** MONGREL **3 :** of abnormal shape or irregular size **4 :** of a kind similar to but inferior to or less typical than some standard ⟨~ measles⟩ **5 :** lacking genuineness or authority **:** SPURIOUS

bas·tard·iza·tion \ˌbas-tərd-ə-'zā-shən\ *n* **:** the act or process of bastardizing

bas·tard·ize \'bas-tər-ˌdīz\ *vt* **1 :** to declare or prove to be a bastard **2 :** to reduce from a higher to a lower state or condition

bastard wing *n* **:** the process of a bird's wing corresponding to the thumb and bearing a few short quills

bas·tardy \'bas-tərd-ē\ *n* **1 :** the quality or state of being a bastard **:** ILLEGITIMACY **2 :** the begetting of an illegitimate child

1**baste** \'bāst\ *vt* [ME *basten*, fr. MF *bastir*, of Gmc origin; akin to OHG *besten* to patch; akin to OE *bæst* bast] **:** to sew with long loose stitches in order to hold in place temporarily — **bast·er** *n*

2**baste** *vt* [origin unknown] **:** to moisten (as meat) at intervals with a liquid (as melted butter, fat, or pan drippings) esp. during the cooking process — **bast·er** *n*

3**baste** *vt* [prob. fr. ON *beysta;* akin to OE *bēatan* to beat] **1 :** to beat severely or soundly **:** THRASH **2 :** to scold vigorously **:** BERATE

bas·tille *or* **bas·tile** \ba-'stē(ə)l\ *n* [F *bastille*, fr. the *Bastille*, tower in Paris used as a prison] **:** PRISON, JAIL

Bastille Day *n* **:** July 14 observed in France as a national holiday in commemoration of the fall of the Bastille in 1789

1**bas·ti·na·do** \ˌbas-tə-'nād-(ˌ)ō, -'näd-\ *or* **bas·ti·nade** \ˌbas-tə-'nād, -'näd\ *n, pl* **bastinadoes** *or* **bastinades** [Sp *bastonada*, fr. *bastón* stick, fr. LL *bastum*] **1 :** a blow with a stick or cudgel **2 a :** a beating esp. with a stick **b :** a punishment consisting of beating the soles of the feet with a stick **3 :** STICK, CUDGEL

2**bastinado** *vt* **:** to subject to repeated blows

1**bast·ing** \'bā-stiŋ\ *n* **1 :** the action of a sewer who bastes **2 a :** the thread used by a baster **b :** the stitching made by a baster

2**basting** *n* **1 :** the action of one that bastes food **2 :** the liquid used by a baster

3**basting** *n* **:** a severe beating

bas·tion \'bas-chən, 'bas-tē-ən\ *n* [MF, fr. *bastille* fortress, modif. of OProv *bastida*, fr. *bastir* to build, of Gmc origin; akin to OHG *besten* to patch] **1 :** a projecting part of a fortification **2 :** a fortified area or position **3 :** something that is considered a stronghold **:** BULWARK — **bas·tioned** \-chənd, -tē-ənd\ *adj*

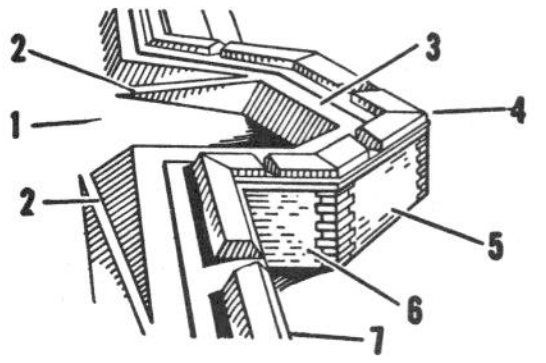

bastion: *1* gorge, *2* ramp, *3* banquette, *4* salient angle, *5* face, *6* flank, *7* curtain

Ba·su·to \bə-'süt-(ˌ)ō\ *n, pl* **Basuto** *or* **Basutos :** one of the Bantu-speaking people of Basutoland

1**bat** \'bat\ *n* [ME, fr. OE *batt*, prob. of Celt origin; akin to Gaulish anda*bata*, a gladiator] **1 :** a stout solid stick **:** CLUB **2 :** a sharp blow **:** STROKE **3 a :** a wooden implement used for hitting the ball in various games **b :** a racket used in various games (as squash) **c :** the short whip used by a jockey **4 a :** BATSMAN **b :** a turn at batting — usu. used with *at* **5 :** BATTING 2 — usu. used in pl. **6** *Brit* **:** GAIT **7 :** BINGE

2**bat** *vb* **bat·ted; bat·ting** *vt* **1 :** to strike or hit with or as if with a bat **2 a :** to advance (a base runner) by batting **b :** to have a batting average of **3 :** to compose esp. in a casual, careless, or hurried manner — usu. used with *out* **4 :** to discuss at length or consider in detail ~ *vi* **1 a :** to strike or hit a ball with a bat **b :** to take one's turn at bat **2 :** to wander aimlessly

3**bat** *n* [alter. of ME *bakke*, prob. of Scand origin, akin to OSw natt*bakka* bat] **:** any of an order (Chiroptera) of nocturnal placental flying mammals with forelimbs modified to form wings

4**bat** *vt* **bat·ted; bat·ting** [prob. alter. of 2*bate*] **:** to wink esp. in surprise or emotion ⟨never *batted* an eye⟩

1**batch** \'bach\ *n* [ME *bache;* akin to OE *bacan* to bake] **1 :** the quantity baked at one time **:** BAKING **2 a :** the quantity of material prepared or required for one operation; *specif* **:** a mixture of raw materials ready for fusion into glass **b :** the quantity produced at one operation **3 :** a group of persons or things **:** LOT

2**batch** *var of* BACH

1**bate** \'bāt\ *vb* [ME *baten*, short for *abaten* to abate] *vt* **1 :** to reduce the force or intensity of **:** MODERATE ⟨he *bated* his breath⟩

2 : to take away : DEDUCT 3 *archaic* : to lower esp. in amount or estimation 4 *archaic* : BLUNT ~ *vi, obs* : DIMINISH, DECREASE

2**bate** *vi* [ME *baten*, fr. MF *batre* to beat — more at DEBATE] *of a falcon* : to beat the wings impatiently

ba·teau *also* **bat·teau** \ba-'tō\ *n, pl* **ba·teaux** \-'tō(z)\ [CanF, fr. F, fr. OF *batel*, fr. OE *bāt* boat] : any of various small craft; *esp* : a flat-bottomed boat with raked bow and stern and flaring sides

bat·fish \'bat-,fish\ *n* : any of several fishes with winglike processes: as **a** : any of several flattened pediculate fishes (as a common West Indian form *Ogcocephalus vespertilio*) **b** : a flying gurnard (*Dactylopterus volitans*) of the Atlantic **c** : a California stingray (*Aetobatus californicus*)

bat·fowl \'bat-,faůl\ *vi* : to catch birds at night by blinding them with a light and knocking them down with a stick or netting them

1**bath** \'bath, 'båth\ *n, pl* **baths** \'ba*th*z, 'baths, 'bå*th*z, 'båths\ [ME, fr. OE *bæth;* akin to OHG *bad* bath, OE *bacan* to bake] **1** : a washing or soaking (as in water or steam) of all or part of the body **2 a** : water used for bathing **b** (1) : a contained liquid for a special purpose (2) : a receptacle holding the liquid **c** (1) : a medium for regulating the temperature of something placed in or on it (2) : a vessel containing such medium **3 a** : BATHROOM **b** : a building containing an apartment or a series of rooms designed for bathing **c** : SPA — usu. used in pl. **4** : the quality or state of being covered with a liquid **5** : BATHTUB

2**bath** *vt, Brit* : to give a bath to ~ *vi, Brit* : to take a bath

3**bath** *n* [Heb] : an ancient Hebrew liquid measure corresponding to the ephah of dry measure

bath- *or* **batho-** *comb form* [ISV, fr. Gk *bathos*, fr. *bathys* deep — more at BATHY-] : depth ⟨*batho*meter⟩

Bath brick \'bath-, 'båth-\ *n* [*Bath*, England] : an unfired brick of siliceous material used as a scourer and polisher of metals

bath chair *n, often cap B* : a hooded and sometimes glassed wheeled chair used esp. by invalids; *broadly* : WHEELCHAIR

1**bathe** \'bā*th*\ *vb* [ME *bathen*, fr. OE *bathian;* akin to OE *bæth* bath] *vt* **1** : to wash in water or another liquid **2** : MOISTEN, WET **3** : to apply water or a liquid medicament to **4** : to flow along the edge of : LAVE **5** : to suffuse with or as if with light ~ *vi* **1** : to take a bath **2** : to go swimming **3** : to become immersed or absorbed — **bath·er** \'bā-*th*ər\ *n* — **bath·ing** \-*th*iŋ\ *n*

2**bathe** *n* **1** *Brit* : 1BATH **2** *Brit* : SWIM, DIP

ba·thet·ic \bə-'thet-ik\ *adj* [*bathos* + *-etic* (as in *pathetic*)] : characterized by bathos — **ba·thet·i·cal·ly** \-i-k(ə-)lē\ *adv*

bath·house \'bath-,haůs, 'båth-\ *n* **1** : a building equipped for bathing **2** : a building containing dressing rooms for bathers

Bath·i·nette \,bath-ə-'net, ,båth-\ *trademark* — used for a portable bathtub for babies

batho·lith \'bath-ə-,lith\ *n* [ISV] : a great mass of intruded igneous rock that for the most part stopped in its rise a considerable distance below the surface — **batho·lith·ic** \,bath-ə-'lith-ik\ *adj*

ba·thom·e·ter \bə-'thäm-ət-ər\ *n* : an instrument for measuring depths in water

ba·thos \'bā-,thäs\ *n* [Gk] **1 a** : the sudden appearance of the commonplace in otherwise elevated matter or style **b** : ANTICLIMAX, LETDOWN **2** : FLATNESS, TRITENESS **3** : insincere or overdone pathos : SENTIMENTALISM

bath·room \'bath-,rüm, 'båth-, -,rům\ *n* : a room containing a bathtub or shower and usu. a washbowl and toilet

bath·tub \-,təb\ *n* : a usu. fixed tub for bathing

bathy- *comb form* [ISV, fr. Gk, fr. *bathys* deep; akin to Skt *gāhate* he dives into] **1** : deep : depth ⟨*bathy*al⟩ **2** : deep-sea ⟨*bathy*sphere⟩

bathy·al \'bath-ē-əl\ *adj* : DEEP-SEA

bathy·met·ric \,bath-i-'me-trik\ *adj* : of or relating to bathymetry — **bathy·met·ri·cal** \-tri-kəl\ *adj* — **bathy·met·ri·cal·ly** \-tri-k(ə-)lē\ *adv*

ba·thym·e·try \bə-'thim-ə-trē\ *n* [ISV] : the measurement of depths of water in oceans, seas, and lakes

bathy·scaphe \'bath-i-,skaf, -,skāf\ *n* [ISV *bathy-* + Gk *skaphē* light boat] : a navigable submersible ship for deep-sea exploration having a spherical watertight cabin attached to its underside

bathy·sphere \'bath-i-,sfi(ə)r\ *n* : a strongly built steel diving sphere for deep-sea observation

ba·tik \bə-'tēk, 'bat-ik\ *n* [Malay] **1 a** : an Indonesian method of hand-printing textiles by coating with wax the parts not to be dyed **b** : a design so executed **2** : a fabric printed by batik

bat·ing \'bāt-iŋ\ *prep* : with the exception of : EXCEPTING

ba·tiste \bə-'tēst, ba-\ *n* [F] : a fine soft sheer fabric of plain weave made of various fibers

bat·man \'bat-mən\ *n* : an orderly of a British military officer

ba·ton \bə-'tän, ba-, -'tōⁿ\ *n* [F *bâton*, fr. OF *baston*, fr. L *bastum* stick] **1** : CUDGEL, TRUNCHEON **2** : a staff borne as a symbol of office **3** : a narrow heraldic bend **4** : a stick or wand with which a leader directs a band or orchestra **5** : a hollow cylinder carried by each member of a relay team and passed to the succeeding runner **6** : a smooth staff with a ball at one end carried by a drum major or baton twirler

ba·tra·chi·an \bə-'trā-kē-ən\ *n* [deriv. of Gk *batrachos* frog] : FROG, TOAD, SALIENTIAN; *broadly* : a vertebrate amphibian — **batrachian** *adj*

bats·man \'bat-smən\ *n* : a batter esp. in cricket

batt *var of* BAT

bat·tai·lous \'bat-ᵊl-əs\ *adj* [ME *bataillous*, fr. MF *bataillos*, fr. *bataille* battle] *archaic* : ready for battle : WARLIKE

bat·ta·lia \bə-'tāl-yə\ *n* [It *battaglia*] **1** *obs* : a large body of men in battle array **2** *archaic* : order of battle

bat·tal·ion \bə-'tal-yən\ *n* [MF *bataillon*, fr. OIt *battaglione*, aug. of *battaglia* company of soldiers, battle, fr. LL *battalia* combat — more at BATTLE] **1** : a considerable body of troops organized to act together : ARMY **2** : a military unit composed of a headquarters and two or more companies, batteries, or similar units

1**bat·ten** \'bat-ᵊn\ *vb* **bat·ten·ing** \'bat-niŋ, -ᵊn-iŋ\ [prob. fr. ON *batna* to improve] *vi* **1 a** : to grow fat **b** : to feed gluttonously **2** : to grow prosperous ~ *vt* : FATTEN

2**batten** *n* [F *bâton*] **1 a** *Brit* : a piece of lumber used esp. for flooring **b** : a thin narrow strip of lumber used esp. to seal or reinforce a joint **2** : any of various strips, bars, or supports resembling or used similarly to battens

3**batten** *vt* : to furnish or fasten with battens

1**bat·ter** \'bat-ər\ *vb* [ME *bateren*, prob. freq. of *batten* to bat, fr. *bat*] *vt* **1 a** : to beat with successive blows so as to bruise, shatter, or demolish **b** : BOMBARD **2** : to subject to strong, overwhelming, or repeated attack **3** : to wear or damage by blows or hard usage ~ *vi* : to strike heavily and repeatedly : BEAT

2**batter** *n* [ME *bater*, prob. fr. *bateren*] **1** : a mixture that consists of flour, liquid, and other ingredients and is thin enough to pour or drop from a spoon **2** : a damaged area on a printing surface

3**batter** *vt* [origin unknown] : to give a receding upward slope to

4**batter** *n* : a receding upward slope of the outer face of a wall or other structure

5**batter** *n* : one that bats; *esp* : the player whose turn it is to bat

battering ram *n* **1** : a military siege engine consisting of a large wooden beam with a head of iron used in ancient times to beat down the walls of a besieged place **2** : a heavy metal bar with handles used to batter down doors and walls

bat·tery \'bat-ə-rē, 'ba-trē\ *n* **1 a** : the act of battering or beating **b** : the unlawful beating or use of force upon a person without his consent — compare ASSAULT 2a **2 a** : a grouping of artillery pieces for tactical purposes **b** : the guns of a warship **3** : an artillery unit in the army equivalent to a company **4 a** : a combination of apparatus for producing a single electrical effect **b** : a group of two or more cells connected together to furnish electric current; *also* : a single cell that furnishes electric current **5 a** : a number of similar articles, items, or devices arranged, connected, or used together : SET, SERIES **b** : an impressive or imposing group : ARRAY **6** : the position of readiness of a gun for firing **7** : the pitcher and catcher of a baseball team

bat·ting \'bat-iŋ\ *n* **1 a** : the act of one who bats **b** : the use of or ability with a bat **2** : layers or sheets of raw cotton or wool used for lining quilts or for stuffing or packaging

1**bat·tle** \'bat-ᵊl\ *n, often attrib* [ME *batel*, fr. OF *bataille* battle, fortifying tower, battalion, fr. LL *battalia* combat, alter. of *battualia* fencing exercises, fr. L *battuere* to beat, of Celt origin; akin to Gaulish anda*bata*, a gladiator; akin to L *fatuus* foolish, Russ *bat* cudgel] **1** : a general encounter between armies, ships of war, or airplanes **2** : a combat between two persons **3** *archaic* : BATTALION **4** : an extended contest, struggle, or controversy

syn BATTLE, ENGAGEMENT, ACTION mean a hostile meeting between opposing forces. BATTLE implies a general and prolonged combat; ENGAGEMENT stresses the actual encountering of forces in combat rather than strategic aspects; ACTION suggests combat at a particular place, time, or phase of an operation

2**battle** *vb* **bat·tling** \'bat-liŋ, -ᵊl-iŋ\ *vi* **1** : to engage in battle : FIGHT **2** : to contend with full strength, vigor, craft, or resources : STRUGGLE ~ *vt* : to fight against

3**battle** *vt* [ME *batailen*, fr. MF *bataillier* to fortify, fr. OF, fr. *bataille*] *archaic* : to fortify with battlements

bat·tle-ax *or* **bat·tle-axe** \'bat-ᵊl-,aks\ *n* **1** : a broadax formerly used as a weapon of war **2** *slang* : a quarrelsome domineering woman

battle cruiser *n* : a warship of battleship size and of the highest speed and heaviest battery but without the heavy armor protection of the battleship

bat·tle·dore \'bat-ᵊl-,dō(ə)r, -,dȯ(ə)r\ *n* [ME *batyldore* bat used in washing clothes, prob. fr. OProv *batedor* beating instrument, fr. *batre* to beat, fr. L *battuere*] : a light flat bat or racket used in striking a shuttlecock

bat·tle·field \-,fēld\ *n* : a place where a battle is fought — called also *battleground*

battle group *n* : a military unit normally made up of five companies

bat·tle·ment \'bat-ᵊl-mənt\ *n* [ME *batelment*, fr. MF *bataille*] : a parapet with open spaces that surmounts a wall and is used for defense or decoration — **bat·tle·ment·ed** \-,ment-əd\ *adj*

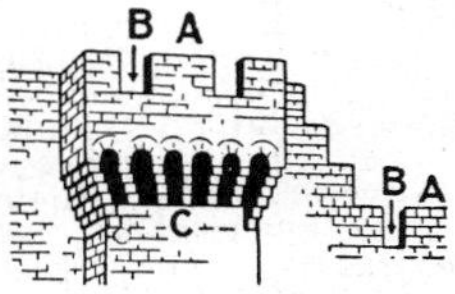

battlements: *A, A* merlons; *B, B* crenels; *C* machicolations

bat·tle·plane \-,plān\ *n* : WARPLANE

battle royal *n, pl* **battles royal** *or* **battle royals** **1 a** : a fight participated in by more than two combatants; *esp* : such a contest in which the last man in the ring or on his feet is declared the winner **b** : a violent struggle **2** : a heated dispute

bat·tle·ship \'bat-ᵊl-,ship\ *n* [short for *line-of-battle ship*] : a warship of the largest and most heavily armed and armored class

bat·tle·wag·on \-,wag-ən\ *n* : BATTLESHIP

bat·tue \ba-'t(y)ü, *F* bå-tᵫ\ *n* [F, fr. *battre* to beat, fr. OF *batre* — more at DEBATE] : the beating of woods and bushes to flush game; *also* : a hunt in which this procedure is used

bat·ty \'bat-ē\ *adj* **1** : of, relating to, or resembling a bat **2** *slang* : mentally unstable : CRAZY

bat·wing \'bat-,wiŋ\ *adj* : shaped like the wing of a bat

bau·ble \'bȯ-bəl, 'bäb-əl\ *n* [ME *babel*, fr. MF] **1** : TRINKET **2** : a fool's scepter **3** : TRIFLE

bau·drons \'bȯd-rənz, 'bȯ*th*-\ *n* [ME] *chiefly Scot* : CAT, KITTY

baulk *chiefly Brit var of* BALK

Bau·mé \bō-'mā\ *adj* [Antoine *Baumé* †1804 F chemist] : being, calibrated in accordance with, or according to either of two arbitrary hydrometer scales for liquids lighter than water or for liquids heavier than water that indicate specific gravity in degrees

baux·ite \'bȯk-,sīt, 'bäk-\ *n* [F *bauxite*, fr. Les *Baux*, near Arles, France] : an impure mixture of earthy hydrous aluminum oxides and hydroxides that commonly contains similar compounds of iron and occas. of manganese, usu. has a concretionary or oolitic structure, and is the principal source of aluminum — **baux·it·ic** \bȯk-'sit-ik, bäk-\ *adj*

Ba·var·i·an \bə-'ver-ē-ən, -'var-\ *n* **1** : a native or inhabitant of Bavaria **2** : the High German dialect of Bavaria and Austria — **Bavarian** *adj*

baw·bee *or* **bau·bee** \'bȯ-(,)bē\ *n* [prob. fr. Alexander Orrok, laird of Sille*bawbe* *fl* 1538 Sc mintmaster] **1 a** : any of various Scottish coins of small value **b** : an English halfpenny **2** : TRIFLE

baw·cock \'bȯ-,käk\ *n* [F *beau coq*, fr. *beau* fine + *coq* fellow, cock] : a fine fellow

bawd \ˈbȯd\ *n* [ME *bawde*] **1** *obs* **:** PANDER **2 a :** one who keeps a house of prostitution **:** MADAM **b :** PROSTITUTE

bawd·i·ness \ˈbȯd-ē-nəs\ *n* **:** the quality or state of being bawdy

bawd·ry \ˈbȯ-drē\ *n* [ME *bawderie*, fr. *bawde*] **1** *obs* **:** UNCHASTITY **2 :** offensively suggestive, coarse, or obscene language **:** BAWDINESS

[1]**bawdy** \ˈbȯd-ē\ *adj* **:** of, relating to, or having the characteristics of a bawd **:** OBSCENE, LEWD

[2]**bawdy** *n* [prob. fr. [1]*bawdy*] **:** BAWDRY 2

[1]**bawl** \ˈbȯl\ *vb* [ME *baulen*, prob. of Scand origin; akin to Icel *baula* to low] *vi* **1 :** to cry out loudly and unrestrainedly **:** YELL **2 :** to cry loudly or lustily **:** WAIL ~ *vt* **1 :** to cry out at the top of one's voice **2 :** to reprimand loudly or severely — **bawl·er** *n*

[2]**bawl** *n* **:** a loud prolonged cry **:** OUTCRY

[1]**bay** \ˈbā\ *adj* [ME, fr. MF *bai*, fr. L *badius;* akin to OIr *buide* yellow] **:** reddish brown ⟨a ~ mare⟩

[2]**bay** *n* **1 :** a bay-colored animal; *specif* **:** a horse with a bay-colored body and black mane, tail, and points **2 :** a moderate brown

[3]**bay** *n* [ME, berry, fr. MF *baie*, fr. L *baca*] **1 a :** LAUREL 1 **b :** any of several shrubs or trees (as of the genera *Magnolia*, *Myrica*, and *Gordonia*) resembling the laurel **2 a :** a garland or crown esp. of laurel given as a prize for victory or excellence **b :** HONOR, FAME — usu. used in pl.

[4]**bay** *n* [ME, fr. MF *baee* opening, fr. OF, fr. fem. of *baé*, pp. of *baer* to gape, yawn — more at ABEYANCE] **1 :** a principal compartment of the walls, roof, or other part of a building or of the whole building **2 :** a main division of any structure: as **a :** a compartment in a barn **b :** BAY WINDOW **c :** the forward part of a ship on each side between decks often used as a ship's hospital **d** (1) **:** a longitudinal part of an elongated aircraft structure lying between two adjacent transverse members or walls (2) **:** any of several compartments in the fuselage of an airplane **3 :** a vertical support on which various pieces of electronic apparatus are mounted

[5]**bay** *vb* [ME *baien*, *abaien*, fr. OF *abaiier*, of imit. origin] *vi* **:** to bark with prolonged tones ~ *vt* **1 :** to bark at **2 :** to bring to bay **3 :** to pursue with barking **4 :** to utter in deep prolonged tones

[6]**bay** *n* **1 :** the position of one unable to retreat and forced to face danger **2 :** the position of one checked **3 :** a baying of dogs

[7]**bay** *n, often attrib* [ME *baye*, fr. MF *baie*] **1 :** an inlet of the sea or other body of water usu. smaller than a gulf **2 :** a small body of water set off from the main body **3 :** any of various terrestrial formations resembling a bay of the sea

ba·ya·dere \ˈbī-ə-ˌdi(ə)r, -ˌde(ə)r\ *n* [F *bayadère* Hindu dancing girl] **:** a fabric with horizontal stripes in strongly contrasted colors

bay antler \ˈbā-\ *n* [earlier *bes antler*, fr. ME *bes-* secondary (fr. MF, fr. L *bis-* twice) + E *antler*] — see ANTLER illustration

bay·ber·ry \ˈbā-ˌber-ē\ *n* **1 :** a West Indian tree (*Pimenta racemosa*) of the myrtle family yielding a yellow aromatic oil **2 a :** WAX MYRTLE; *esp* **:** a hardy shrub (*Myrica pensylvanica*) of coastal eastern No. America **b :** the fruit of a wax myrtle

Bay·eux tapestry \ˌbī-ˌü-, ˌbā-ˌ(y)ü-, bä-ˈyə(r)-\ *n* [*Bayeux*, village in France] **:** a long narrow strip of embroidered linen that depicts events in the Norman invasion of England and is held to date from the 11th or 12th century

bay leaf *n* **:** the dried leaf of the European laurel used in cooking

[1]**bay·o·net** \ˈbā-ə-nət, -ˌnet, ˌbā-ə-ˈnet\ *n, often attrib* [F *baïonette*, fr. *Bayonne*, France] **:** a steel blade made to be attached at the muzzle end of a shoulder arm and used in hand-to-hand combat

[2]**bayonet** *vb* **bay·o·net·ed** *also* **bay·o·net·ted; bay·o·net·ing** *also* **bay·o·net·ting** *vt* **1 :** to stab with a bayonet **2 :** to compel or drive by or as if by the bayonet ~ *vi* **:** to use a bayonet

bay·ou \ˈbī-(ˌ)(y)ō, -(ˌ)(y)ü, -(y)ə\ *n* [LaF, fr. Choctaw *bayuk*] **1 :** a creek, secondary watercourse, or minor river that is tributary to another river or other body of water **2 :** any of various usu. marshy or sluggish bodies of water

bay rum *n* **:** a fragrant cosmetic and medicinal liquid distilled from the leaves of the West Indian bayberry or usu. prepared from essential oils, alcohol, and water

Bay Stat·er \ˈbā-ˌstāt-ər\ *n* **:** a native or resident of Massachusetts — used as a nickname

bay window *n* **:** a window or series of windows forming a bay or recess in a room and projecting outward from the wall

ba·zaar \bə-ˈzär\ *n* [Per *bāzār*] **1 :** an Oriental market consisting of rows of shops or stalls selling miscellaneous goods **2 a :** a place for the sale of goods **b :** DEPARTMENT STORE **3 :** a fair for the sale of articles esp. for charitable purposes

ba·zoo·ka \bə-ˈzü-kə\ *n* [*bazooka* (a crude musical instrument made of pipes and a funnel)] **:** a light portable shoulder weapon consisting of an open-breech smoothbore firing tube that launches armor-piercing rockets

B battery *n* **:** an electric battery connected in the plate circuit of an electron tube to cause flow of electron current in the tube

BCG vaccine \ˌbē-(ˌ)sē-ˈjē-\ *n* [*b*acillus *C*almette-*G*uérin] **:** a vaccine prepared from a living attenuated strain of tubercle bacilli and used to vaccinate human beings against tuberculosis

B complex *n* **:** VITAMIN B COMPLEX

BC soil \ˈbē-ˈsē-\ *n* **:** a soil whose profile has only B-horizons and C-horizons

bdel·li·um \ˈdel-ē-əm\ *n* [ME, fr. L, fr. Gk *bdellion*] **:** a gum resin similar to myrrh obtained from various trees (genus *Commiphora*)

be \(ˈ)bē\ *vb, past 1st & 3d sing* **was** \(ˈ)wəz, ˈwäz\ *2d sing* **were** \(ˈ)wər\ *pl* **were;** *past subjunctive* **were;** *past part* **been** \(ˈ)bin, *chiefly Brit* (ˈ)bēn\ *pres part* **be·ing** \ˈbē-iŋ\ *pres 1st sing* **am** \əm, (ˈ)am\ *2d sing* **are** \ər, (ˈ)är\ *3d sing* **is** \(ˈ)iz, əz\ *pl* **are;** *pres subjunctive* **be** [ME *been*, fr. OE *bēon;* akin to OHG *bim* am, L *fui* I have been, *futurus* about to be, *fieri* to become, be done, Gk *phynai* to be born, be by nature, *phyein* to bring forth] *vi* **1 a :** to equal in meaning **:** have the same connotation as ⟨God *is* love⟩ ⟨January *is* the first month⟩ ⟨let *x* ~ 10⟩ **:** represent symbolically **b :** to have identity with ⟨the first person I met *was* my brother⟩ **c :** to constitute the same class as **d :** to have a specified qualification or characterization ⟨the leaves *are* green⟩ **e :** to belong to the class of ⟨the fish *is* a trout⟩ — used regularly in senses 1a through 1e as the copula of simple predication **2 a :** to have an objective existence **:** have reality or actuality **:** LIVE ⟨I think, therefore I *am*⟩ ⟨once upon a time there *was* a knight⟩ **b :** to have, maintain, or occupy a place, situation, or position ⟨the book *is* on the table⟩ **c :** to remain unmolested, undisturbed, or uninterrupted — used only in infinitive form ⟨let him ~⟩ **d :** OCCUR **:** take place ⟨the concert *was* last night⟩ **e** *archaic* **:** BELONG, BEFALL ~ *verbal auxiliary* **1** — used with the past participle of transitive verbs as a passive-voice auxiliary ⟨the money *was* found⟩ ⟨the house is *being* built⟩ **2** — used as the auxiliary of the present participle in progressive tenses expressing continuous action ⟨he *is* reading⟩ ⟨I have *been* sleeping⟩ **3** — used with the past participle of some intransitive verbs as an auxiliary forming archaic perfect tenses ⟨Christ *is* risen from the dead —1 Cor 15:20 (DV)⟩ ⟨the minstrel boy to the war *is* gone —Thomas Moore⟩ **4** — used with the infinitive with *to* to express futurity, arrangement in advance, or obligation ⟨I *am* to interview him today⟩ ⟨he *was* to become famous⟩

be- *prefix* [ME, fr. OE *bi-*, *be-*; akin to OE *bī* by, near — more at BY] **1 :** on **:** around **:** over ⟨*be*daub⟩ ⟨*be*smear⟩ **2 :** to a great or greater degree **:** thoroughly ⟨*be*fuddle⟩ ⟨*be*rate⟩ **3 :** excessively **:** ostentatiously — in intensive verbs formed from simple verbs ⟨*be*deck⟩ and in adjectives based on adjectives ending in *-ed* ⟨*be*ribboned⟩ **4 :** about **:** to **:** at **:** upon **:** against **:** across ⟨*be*stride⟩ ⟨*be*speak⟩ **5 :** make **:** cause to be **:** treat as ⟨*be*little⟩ ⟨*be*fool⟩ ⟨*be*friend⟩ **6 :** call or dub esp. excessively ⟨*be*doctor⟩ **7 :** affect, afflict, treat, provide, or cover with esp. excessively ⟨*be*devil⟩ ⟨*be*fog⟩

[1]**beach** \ˈbēch\ *n* [origin unknown] **1 :** shore pebbles **:** SHINGLE **2 a :** a shore of an ocean, sea, or lake or the bank of a river covered by sand, gravel, or larger rock fragments **b :** a seashore area

[2]**beach** *vt* **:** to run or drive ashore

beach·comb·er \ˈbēch-ˌkō-mər\ *n* **:** a drifter or loafer usu. along the seacoast; *esp* **:** a white man living as a loafer in the So. Pacific

beach flea *n* **:** any of numerous amphipod crustaceans (family Orchestiidae) living on ocean beaches and leaping like fleas

beach grass *n* **:** any of several tough strongly rooted grasses that grow on exposed sandy shores; *esp* **:** a rhizomatous perennial (genus *Ammophila*) widely planted to bind sandy slopes

beach·head \ˈbēch-ˌhed\ *n* **1 :** an area on a hostile shore occupied to secure further landing of troops and supplies **2 :** FOOTHOLD

beach wagon *n* **:** STATION WAGON

beachy \ˈbē-chē\ *adj* **:** covered with pebbles or shingle

[1]**bea·con** \ˈbē-kən\ *n* [ME *beken*, fr. OE *bēacen* sign; akin to OHG *bouhhan* sign] **1 :** a signal fire commonly on a hill, tower, or pole **2 a :** a lighthouse or other signal for guidance **b :** a radio transmitter emitting signals for guidance of airplanes

[2]**beacon** *vt* **:** to furnish with a beacon ~ *vi* **:** to shine as a beacon

[1]**bead** \ˈbēd\ *n* [ME *bede* prayer, prayer bead, fr. OE *bed*, *gebed* prayer; akin to OE *biddan* to entreat, pray] **1 a** *obs* **:** PRAYER — usu. used in pl. **b** *pl* **:** a series of prayers and meditations made with a rosary **2 :** a small piece of material pierced for threading on a string or wire (as in a rosary) **3 :** a small ball-shaped body: as **a :** a drop of sweat or blood **b :** a bubble formed in or on a beverage **c :** a small metal knob on a firearm used as a front sight **d :** a blob or a line of weld metal **e :** a glassy drop of flux (as borax) used as a solvent and color test for several metallic oxides and salts **4 :** a projecting rim, band, or molding

[2]**bead** *vt* **1 :** to furnish, adorn, or cover with beads or beading **2 :** to string together like beads ~ *vi* **:** to form into a bead

bead·ing *n* **1 :** material or a part or a piece consisting of a bead **2 :** a beaded molding **3 :** an openwork trimming **4 :** BEADWORK

bea·dle \ˈbēd-ᵊl\ *n* [ME *bedel*, fr. OE *bydel;* akin to OHG *butil* bailiff] **:** a minor parish official whose duties include ushering and preserving order at services and sometimes civil functions

bead·roll \ˈbē-ˌdrōl\ *n* [fr. the reading in church of a list of names of persons for whom prayers are to be said] **1 :** a list of names **:** CATALOG **2 :** ROSARY

beads·man \ˈbēdz-mən\ *n, archaic* **:** one who prays for another

bead·work \ˈbē-ˌdwərk\ *n* **1 :** ornamental work in beads **2 :** joinery beading

beady \ˈbēd-ē\ *adj* **1 :** resembling beads; *esp* **:** small, round, and shiny with interest or greed ⟨~ eyes⟩ **2 :** marked by beads

bea·gle \ˈbē-gəl\ *n* [ME *begle*] **:** a small short-legged smooth-coated hound

beak \ˈbēk\ *n* [ME *bec*, fr. OF, fr. L *beccus*, of Gaulish origin] **1 a :** the bill of a bird; *esp* **:** the bill of a bird of prey adapted for striking and tearing **b** (1) **:** any of various rigid projecting mouth structures (as of a turtle) (2) **:** the elongated sucking mouth of some insects **c :** the human nose **2 :** a pointed structure or formation **a :** a metal-pointed beam projecting from the bow of an ancient galley for piercing an enemy ship **b :** the spout of a vessel **c :** a continuous slight architectural projection ending in an arris **d :** a process suggesting the beak of a bird — **beaked** \ˈbēkt\ *adj*

bea·ker \ˈbē-kər\ *n* [ME *biker*, fr. ON *bikarr*, prob. fr. OS *bikeri;* akin to OHG *behhari* beaker; both fr. a prehistoric WGmc word borrowed fr. ML *bicarius* beaker, fr. Gk *bikos* earthen jug] **1 :** a large drinking cup with a wide mouth and sometimes supported on a standard **2 :** a deep openmouthed and often projecting-lipped thin vessel used esp. by chemists and pharmacists

[1]**beam** \ˈbēm\ *n* [ME *beem*, fr. OE *bēam* tree, beam; akin to OHG *boum* tree] **1 a :** a long piece of heavy often squared timber suitable for use in construction **b :** a wood or metal cylinder in a loom on which the warp is wound **c :** the part of a plow to which handles, standard, and colter are attached **d :** the bar of a balance from which scales hang **e :** a horizontal supporting structural member; *also* **:** BOOM, SPAR **f :** the extreme width of a ship at the widest part **g :** an oscillating lever on a central axis receiving motion at one end from an engine piston rod and transmitting it at the other **2 a :** a ray or shaft of light **b :** a collection of nearly parallel rays (as X rays) or particles (as electrons) **c :** a constant directional radio signal transmitted for the guidance of pilots; *also* **:** the course indicated by a radio beam **3 :** the main stem of a deer's antler **4 :** the width of the buttocks — **on the beam :** on a true course

[2]**beam** *vt* **1 :** to emit in beams or as a beam **2 :** to support with beams **3 a :** to aim (a broadcast) by directional antennas **b :** to direct to a particular audience ~ *vi* **1 :** to send out beams of light **2 :** to smile with joy

beam–ends \ˈbē-ˈmen(d)z\ *n pl* **:** the ends of a ship's beams — **on her beam–ends :** inclined so much on one side that the beams approach a vertical position

beamy \ˈbē-mē\ *adj* **1 :** emitting beams of light **:** RADIANT **2 :** broad in the beam

bean \ˈbēn\ *n* [ME *bene*, fr. OE *bēan;* akin to OHG *bōna* bean] **1 a :** BROAD BEAN **b :** the seed of any of various other erect or climbing leguminous plants (esp. genera *Phaseolus*, *Dolichos*, and *Vigna*) **c :** a plant bearing beans **d :** a bean pod used when immature as a vegetable **2 a :** a valueless item **b** *pl* **:** a small amount **3 a :** any of various seeds or fruits that resemble beans

or bean pods **b :** a plant producing these **4 :** a protuberance on the upper mandible of waterfowl **5 :** HEAD, BRAIN

bean caper *n* **:** any of several perennial plants (genus *Zygophyllum* of the family Zygophyllaceae, the bean-caper family) having usu. ill-smelling foliage and flower buds used as capers

bean·ie \ˈbē-nē\ *n* **:** a small round tight-fitting skullcap worn esp. by schoolboys and collegians

beano \ˈbē-(ˌ)nō\ *n* [by alter.] **:** BINGO

bean tree *n* **:** any of several trees having fruits resembling a bean pod: as **a :** a yellow-flowered Australian leguminous tree (*Castanospermum australe*) with large pods containing seeds like chestnuts **b :** CATALPA

[1]**bear** \ˈba(ə)r, ˈbe(ə)r\ *n, pl* **bears** *often attrib* [ME *bere*, fr. OE *bera;* akin to OE *brūn* brown] **1** *or pl* **bear :** any of a family (Ursidae of the order Carnivora) of large heavy mammals having long shaggy hair, rudimentary tail, and plantigrade feet and feeding largely on fruit and insects as well as on flesh **2 :** a surly, uncouth, or shambling person **3** [prob. fr. the proverb about *selling the bearskin before catching the bear*] **:** one that sells securities or commodities in expectation of a price decline — compare BULL

[2]**bear** *vb* **bore** \ˈbō(ə)r, ˈbȯ(ə)r\ **borne** \ˈbō(ə)rn, ˈbȯ(ə)rn\ *also* **born** \ˈbȯ(ə)rn\ **bear·ing** [ME *beren*, fr. OE *beran;* akin to OHG *beran* to carry, L *ferre*, Gk *pherein*] *vt* **1 a :** to support and move **:** CARRY **b :** to be equipped or furnished with **c :** to hold in the mind **d :** DISSEMINATE **e :** BEHAVE, CONDUCT ⟨~*ing* himself well⟩ **f :** to have as a feature or characteristic **g :** to adduce in testifying ⟨~ false witness⟩ **h :** to have as an identification **i :** LEAD, ESCORT **j :** RENDER, GIVE **2 a :** to give birth to **b :** to produce as yield **c** (1) **:** to permit growth of (2) **:** CONTAIN ⟨oil-*bearing* shale⟩ **3 a :** to support the weight of **:** SUSTAIN **b :** TOLERATE, ENDURE **c :** ASSUME, ACCEPT **d :** to hold above, on top, or aloft **e :** to admit of **:** ALLOW **4 :** THRUST, PRESS **~** *vi* **1 a :** to force one's way **b :** to be situated **:** LIE **c :** to extend in a direction indicated or implied **d :** to become directed **e :** to go or incline in an indicated direction ⟨road ~*s* to the right⟩ **2 a :** APPLY, PERTAIN **b :** to exert influence or force **3 :** to support a weight or strain — often used with *up* **4 :** to produce fruit **:** YIELD

syn BEAR, SUFFER, ENDURE, ABIDE, TOLERATE, STAND mean to sustain something trying or painful. BEAR usu. implies the power to sustain without flinching or breaking; SUFFER suggests acceptance or passivity rather than courage or patience in bearing; ENDURE implies continuing firm or resolute through trials and difficulties; ABIDE suggests acceptance without resistance or protest; TOLERATE suggests overcoming or successfully controlling an impulse to resist, avoid, or resent something injurious or distasteful; STAND emphasizes even more strongly the ability to bear without discomposure or flinching **syn** see in addition CARRY

bear·able \ˈbar-ə-bəl, ˈber-\ *adj* **:** capable of being borne **:** TOLERABLE — **bear·ably** \-blē\ *adv*

bear·bait·ing \ˈba(ə)r-ˌbāt-iŋ, ˈbe(ə)r-\ *n* **:** the former practice of setting dogs on a chained bear

bear·ber·ry \-ˌber-ē\ *n* **1 :** a trailing evergreen plant (*Arctostaphylos uva-ursi*) of the heath family with astringent foliage and red berries **2 :** the large cranberry (*Oxycoccus macrocarpus*) **3 :** a deciduous holly (*Ilex decidua*) of the southern U. S. **4 :** CASCARA BUCKTHORN

[1]**beard** \ˈbi(ə)rd\ *n* [ME *berd*, fr. OE *beard;* akin to OHG *bart* beard, L *barba*] **1 :** the hair that grows on a man's face often excluding the moustache **2 :** a hairy or bristly appendage or tuft **3 :** BEVEL 1c; *also* **:** the bevel plus the shoulder — **beard·ed** \-əd\ *adj* — **beard·less** \-ləs\ *adj*

[2]**beard** *vt* **1 :** to furnish with a beard **2 :** to confront and oppose with boldness, resolution, and often effrontery **:** DEFY

beard·tongue \ˈbi(ə)rd-ˌtəŋ\ *n* **:** PENTSTEMON

bear·er \ˈbar-ər, ˈber-\ *n* **:** one that bears: as **a :** PORTER **b :** a plant yielding fruit **c :** one holding a check, draft, or other order for payment esp. if marked payable to bearer

bear garden *n* **1 :** an establishment for bearbaiting or similar practices **2 :** a scene of unruly rowdy disturbance

bear grass *n* **1 :** any of several plants of the lily family (as a yucca) chiefly of the southern and western U. S. with foliage resembling coarse blades of grass **2 :** any of several grasses

bear·ing *n* **1 :** the manner in which one bears or comports oneself **:** CARRIAGE, BEHAVIOR **2 a :** the act, power, or time of bringing forth offspring or fruit **b :** a product of bearing **:** CROP **3 :** PRESSURE, THRUST **4 a :** an object, surface, or point that supports **b :** a machine part in which a journal, pin, or other part turns **5 :** a charge in a coat of arms **6 a :** the situation or direction of one point with respect to another or to the compass **b :** a determination of position **c** *pl* **:** comprehension of one's position, environment, or situation **d :** RELATION, CONNECTION; *also* **:** PURPORT **7 :** the part of a structural member that rests upon its supports

syn BEARING, DEPORTMENT, DEMEANOR, MIEN, MANNER, CARRIAGE mean the way in which a person outwardly manifests his personality or attitude. BEARING is the most general of these words but now usu. implies characteristic posture; DEPORTMENT suggests actions or behavior as formed by breeding or training; DEMEANOR suggests one's attitude toward others as expressed in outward behavior; MIEN is a literary term referring both to bearing and demeanor; MANNER implies characteristic or customary way of moving and gesturing and addressing others; CARRIAGE applies chiefly to habitual posture in standing or walking

bearing rein *n* **:** CHECKREIN 1

bear·ish \ˈba(ə)r-ish, ˈbe(ə)r-\ *adj* **1 :** resembling a bear in roughness, gruffness, or surliness **2 :** marked by, tending to, or expecting a decline in stock prices — **bear·ish·ly** *adv* — **bear·ish·ness** *n*

bear·skin \ˈba(ə)r-ˌskin, ˈbe(ə)r-\ *n* **:** an article made of the skin of a bear; *esp* **:** a military hat made of the skin of a bear

beast \ˈbēst\ *n* [ME *beste*, fr. OF, fr. L *bestia*] **1 a :** an animal as distinguished from a plant **b :** a lower animal as distinguished from man **c :** a 4-footed mammal as distinguished from man, lower vertebrates, and invertebrates **d :** an animal under human control **2 :** a contemptible person

beas·tings \ˈbē-stiŋz\ *n pl but sing or pl in constr* [ME *bestynge*, fr. OE *bȳsting*, fr. *bēost* beastings] **:** the colostrum esp. of a cow

beast·li·ness \ˈbēst-lē-nəs\ *n* **:** the quality or state of being beastly

[1]**beast·ly** \ˈbēst-lē\ *adj* **1 :** of, relating to, or resembling a beast **2 :** BESTIAL **3 :** ABOMINABLE, DISGUSTING

[2]**beastly** *adv* **:** VERY

[1]**beat** \ˈbēt\ *vb* **beat; beat·en** \ˈbēt-ᵊn\ *or* **beat; beat·ing** [ME *beten*, fr. OE *bēatan;* akin to OHG *bōzan* to beat, L *-futare* to beat, *fustis* club] *vt* **1 :** to strike repeatedly: **a :** to hit repeatedly so as to inflict pain **b :** to walk on **:** TREAD **c :** to dash against **d :** to flap or thrash at vigorously **e :** to strike at to rouse game; *also* **:** to range over in or as if in quest of game **f :** to mix by stirring **:** WHIP **g :** to strike repeatedly to produce music or a signal ⟨~ a drum⟩ **2 a :** to drive or force by beating **b :** to pound into a powder, paste, or pulp **c :** to make by repeated treading or driving over **d :** to lodge or dislodge by repeated hitting **e :** to shape by beating ⟨~ swords into plowshares⟩; *esp* **:** to flatten thin by blows **f :** to sound or express by drum beat or sound **3 :** to cause to strike or flap repeatedly **4 a :** OVERCOME, DEFEAT; *also* **:** SURPASS **b :** to prevail despite ⟨~ the odds⟩ **c :** BEWILDER, BAFFLE **d** (1) **:** FATIGUE, EXHAUST (2) **:** to leave dispirited, irresolute, or hopeless **e :** CHEAT **5 a** (1) **:** to act ahead of usu. so as to forestall (2) **:** to report a news item in advance of **b :** to come or arrive before **c :** CIRCUMVENT ⟨~ the system⟩ **6 :** to indicate by beating ⟨~ the tempo⟩ **~** *vi* **1 a :** to become forcefully impelled **:** DASH **b :** to glare or strike with oppressive intensity **c :** to sustain distracting activity **d :** to beat a drum **2 a** (1) **:** PULSATE, THROB (2) **:** TICK **b :** to sound upon being struck **3 a :** to strike repeated blows **b :** to strike the air **:** FLAP **c :** to strike cover to rouse game; *also* **:** to range or scour for or as if for game **4 :** to progress with much tacking or with difficulty **syn** see CONQUER

[2]**beat** *n* **1 a :** a single stroke or blow esp. in a series; *also* **:** PULSATION, TICK **b :** a sound produced by or as if by beating **c :** a driving impact or force **2 :** one swing of the pendulum or balance of a timepiece **3 :** each of the pulsations of amplitude produced by the union of sound or radio waves or electric currents having different frequencies **4 a :** a metrical or rhythmic stress in poetry or music or the rhythmic effect of these stresses **b :** the tempo indicated to a musical performer **5 :** a regularly traversed round **6 a :** something that excels **b :** the reporting of a news story ahead of competitors **7 :** DEADBEAT **8 a :** an act of beating to windward **b :** one of the reaches so traversed **:** TACK

[3]**beat** *adj* [ME *beten, bete*, fr. pp. of *beten*] **1 a :** EXHAUSTED **b :** sapped of resolution or morale **2 :** of or relating to beatniks

[4]**beat** *n* **:** BEATNIK

beat·er \ˈbēt-ər\ *n* **1 :** a person or thing that beats **2 :** one that beats up game in hunting

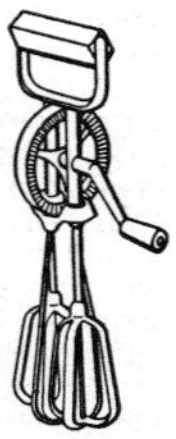
egg beater

be·atif·ic \ˌbē-ə-ˈtif-ik\ *adj* [L *beatificus* making happy, fr. *beatus* happy, fr. pp. of *beare* to bless; akin to L *bonus* good — more at BOUNTY] **1 :** of, possessing, or imparting beatitude **2 :** having a blissful or benign appearance — **be·atif·i·cal·ly** \-i-k(ə-)lē\ *adv*

be·at·i·fi·ca·tion \bē-ˌat-ə-fə-ˈkā-shən\ *n* **:** the act of beatifying **:** the state of being beatified

be·at·i·fy \bē-ˈat-ə-ˌfī\ *vt* [MF *beatifier*, fr. LL *beatificare*, fr. L *beatus*] **1 :** to make supremely happy **2 :** to declare to have attained the blessedness of heaven and authorize the title "Blessed" and limited public religious honor for

be·at·i·tude \bē-ˈat-ə-ˌt(y)üd\ *n* [L *beatitudo*, fr. *beatus*] **1 :** a state of utmost bliss — used as a title for a primate of an Eastern church **2 :** any of the declarations made in the Sermon on the Mount (Mt 5:3–12) beginning "Blessed are"

beat·nik \ˈbēt-nik\ *n* [[3]*beat* + Yiddish *-nik*, suffix denoting a person, fr. Russ & Pol] **:** a person having a predilection for unconventional behavior and dress and often a preoccupation with exotic philosophizing and self-expression

Be·atrice *n* [It] **1** \ˌbā-ə-ˈtrē-(ˌ)chā, ˈbē-ə-trəs\ **:** a Florentine woman immortalized in Dante's *Vita Nuova* and *Divina Commedia* **2** \ˈbē-ə-trəs\ **:** the witty heroine in Shakespeare's *Much Ado about Nothing*

beau \ˈbō\ *n, pl* **beaux** \ˈbōz\ *or* **beaus** [F, fr. *beau* beautiful, fr. L *bellus* pretty] **1 :** DANDY **2 :** a man who is a frequent or steady escort of a woman **:** LOVER

Beau Brum·mell \bō-ˈbrəm-əl\ *n* [nickname of G. B. *Brummell* †1840 E dandy] **:** DANDY

Beau·fort scale \ˌbō-fərt-\ *n* [Sir Francis *Beaufort* †1857 E

BEAUFORT SCALE

BEAUFORT NUMBER	NAME	MILES PER HOUR	DESCRIPTION
0	Calm	Less than 1	Calm; smoke rises vertically
1	Light air	1–3	Direction of wind shown by smoke but not by wind vanes
2	Light breeze	4–7	Wind felt on face; leaves rustle; ordinary vane moved by wind
3	Gentle breeze	8–12	Leaves and small twigs in constant motion; wind extends light flag
4	Moderate breeze	13–18	Raises dust and loose paper; small branches are moved
5	Fresh breeze	19–24	Small trees in leaf begin to sway; crested wavelets form on inland waters
6	Strong breeze	25–31	Large branches in motion; telegraph wires whistle; umbrellas used with difficulty
7	Moderate gale	32–38	Whole trees in motion; inconvenience in walking against wind
8	Fresh gale	39–46	Breaks twigs off trees; generally impedes progress
9	Strong gale	47–54	Slight structural damage occurs; chimney pots and slates removed
10	Whole gale	55–63	Trees uprooted; con-

			siderable structural damage occurs
11	Storm	64–72	Very rarely experienced; accompanied by widespread damage
12–17	Hurricane	73–136	Devastation occurs

naval officer & hydrographer] : a scale in which the force of the wind is indicated by numbers from 0 to 17 or orig. from 0 to 12

beau geste \bō-'zhest\ *n, pl* **beaux gestes** *or* **beau gestes** \bō-'zhest\ [F, lit., beautiful gesture] **1 :** a graceful or magnanimous gesture **2 :** an insubstantial conciliatory gesture

beau ide·al \ˌbō-ˌī-'dē(-ə)l\ *n, pl* **beau ideals** [F *beau idéal* ideal beauty] : the perfect type or model

Beau·mé *var of* BAUMÉ

beau monde \bō-'mänd, -mō^{n}d\ *n, pl* **beau mondes** \-'män(d)z\ *or* **beaux mondes** \-mō^{n}d\ [F, lit., fine world] : the world of high society and fashion

beau·te·ous \'byüt-ē-əs\ *adj* [ME, fr. *beaute*] **:** BEAUTIFUL — **beau·te·ous·ly** *adv* — **beau·te·ous·ness** *n*

beau·ti·cian \byü-'tish-ən\ *n* [*beauty* + *-ician*] **:** COSMETOLOGIST

beau·ti·fi·ca·tion \ˌbyüt-ə-fə-'kā-shən\ *n* **:** the act or process of beautifying

beau·ti·fi·er \'byüt-ə-ˌfī(-ə)r\ *n* **:** one that beautifies

beau·ti·ful \'byüt-i-fəl\ *adj* **:** having qualities of beauty or that excite sensuous or aesthetic pleasure — **beau·ti·ful·ly** \-f(ə-)lē\ *adv* — **beau·ti·ful·ness** \-fəl-nəs\ *n*

syn LOVELY, HANDSOME, PRETTY, COMELY, FAIR: BEAUTIFUL applies to whatever excites the keenest of pleasure to the senses and stirs emotion through the senses; LOVELY is close to BEAUTIFUL but applies to a narrower range of emotional excitation in suggesting the graceful, delicate, or exquisite; HANDSOME suggests essentially an approval of what conforms to a standard in regularity, symmetry, fitness of proportion, quality of workmanship; PRETTY applies to what gives an immediate but often superficial or insubstantial impression of attractiveness; COMELY is like HANDSOME in suggesting what is coolly approved rather than emotionally responded to; FAIR suggests beauty because of purity, flawlessness, or freshness

beau·ti·fy \'byüt-ə-ˌfī\ *vt* **:** to make beautiful or add beauty to **:** EMBELLISH ~ *vi* **:** to grow beautiful **syn** see ADORN

beau·ty \'byüt-ē\ *n* [ME *beaute*, fr. OF *biauté*, fr. *bel, biau* beautiful, fr. L *bellus* pretty; akin to L *bonus* good] **1 :** the quality or aggregate of qualities in a person or thing that gives pleasure to the senses or pleasurably exalts the mind or spirit **:** LOVELINESS **2 :** a beautiful person or thing; *esp* **:** a beautiful woman **3 :** a graceful, ornamental, or excellent quality that contributes to beauty

beauty bush *n* **:** a Chinese shrub (*Kolkwitzia amabilis*) of the honeysuckle family with pinkish flowers and bristly fruit

beauty shop *n* **:** an establishment or department where hairdressing, facials, and manicures are done — called also *beauty parlor*

beauty spot *n* **1 :** [1]PATCH 2 **2 a :** NEVUS **b :** a minor blemish

beaux arts \bō-'zär\ *n pl* [F] **:** FINE ARTS

beaux esprits *pl of* BEL ESPRIT

[1]**bea·ver** \'bē-vər\ *n, pl* **beavers** [ME *bever*, fr. OE *beofor;* akin to OHG *bibar* beaver, OE *brūn* brown] **1** *or pl* **beaver a :** either of two large semiaquatic rodents (genus *Castor*) with webbed hind feet and a broad flat tail that construct dams and underwater lodges and yield valuable fur and castor **b :** the fur or pelt of the beaver **2 a :** a hat made of beaver fur or a fabric imitation **b :** SILK HAT **3 :** a heavy fabric of felted wool or of cotton napped on both sides

[2]**beaver** *n* [ME *baviere*, fr. MF] **1 :** a piece of armor protecting the lower part of the face **2 :** a helmet visor

be·bop \'bē-ˌbäp\ *n* [imit.] **:** BOP — **be·bop·per** *n*

be·calm \bi-'käm, -'kälm\ *vt* **1 :** to keep motionless by lack of wind **2 :** to make calm **:** SOOTHE

be·cause \bi-'kȯz, -(')kəz\ *conj* [ME *because that, because,* fr. *by cause that*] **1 :** for the reason that **:** SINCE **2 :** the fact that **:** THAT

because of *prep* **:** by reason of **:** on account of

bec·ca·fi·co \ˌbek-ə-'fē-(ˌ)kō\ *n, pl* **beccaficos** *or* **beccaficoes** [It, fr. *beccare* to peck + *fico* fig, fr. L *ficus*] **:** any of various European songbirds esteemed as a table delicacy

bé·cha·mel \ˌbā-shə-'mel\ *n* [F *sauce béchamelle,* fr. Louis de *Béchamel* †1703 F courtier] **:** a white sauce sometimes enriched with cream

be·chance \bi-'chan(t)s\ *vb, archaic* **:** BEFALL

bêche–de–mer \ˌbāsh-də-'me(ə)r\ *n* [F, lit., sea grub] **1** *pl* **bêche–de–mer** *or* **bêches–de–mer** \ˌbāsh-(əz-)də-\ **:** TREPANG **2** *cap B&M* **:** a lingua franca based on English and used esp. in New Guinea, the Bismarck archipelago, and the Solomon islands

[1]**beck** \'bek\ *n* [ME *bek*, fr. ON *bekkr;* akin to OE *bæc* brook, OHG *bah,* MIr *būal* flowing water] *Brit* **:** BROOK

[2]**beck** *vt* [ME *becken*, alter. of *beknen*] *archaic* **:** BECKON

[3]**beck** *n* **1** *chiefly Scot* **:** BOW, CURTSY **2 a :** a beckoning gesture **b :** BIDDING, SUMMONS

beck·et \'bek-ət\ *n* [origin unknown] **:** a device for holding something in place; *esp* **:** a grommet or a loop of rope with a knot at one end to catch in an eye at the other

becket bend *n* **:** SHEET BEND

beck·on \'bek-ən\ *vb* **beck·on·ing** \'bek-(ə-)niŋ\ [ME *beknen*, fr. OE *bīecnan*, fr. *bēacen* sign — more at BEACON] *vi* **1 :** to summon or signal typically with a wave, nod, or other gesture **2 :** to appear inviting **:** ATTRACT ~ *vt* **:** to beckon to — **beckon** *n*

be·cloud \bi-'klau̇d\ *vt* **:** to obscure with or as if with a cloud

be·come \bi-'kəm\ *vb* **be·came** \-'kām\ **become; becom·ing** [ME *becomen* to come to, become, fr. OE *becuman,* fr. *be-* + *cuman* to come] *vi* **1 a :** to come into existence **b :** to come to be ⟨~ sick⟩ **:** HAPPEN **2 :** to undergo change or development ~ *vt* **:** to suit or be suitable to ⟨her clothes ~ her⟩

be·com·ing \-'kəm-iŋ\ *adj* **1 :** marked by fitness or propriety **2 :** having an attractive effect — **be·com·ing·ly** \-lē\ *adv*

Bec·que·rel ray \be-'krel-, ˌbek-ə-ˌrel-\ *n* [Antoine H. *Becquerel* †1908 F physicist] **:** a ray emitted by a radioactive substance

[1]**bed** \'bed\ *n* [ME, fr. OE *bedd;* akin to OHG *betti* bed, L *fodere* to dig] **1 a :** a piece of furniture on or in which one may lie and sleep **b** (1) **:** a place of marital sex relations (2) **:** marital relationship **c :** a place for sleeping **d :** SLEEP; *also* **:** a time for sleeping **e** (1) **:** a mattress filled with soft material (2) **:** BEDSTEAD **f :** the equipment and services needed to care for one hospitalized patient or hotel guest **2 :** a flat or level surface: as **a :** a plot of ground prepared for plants **b :** the bottom of a body of water; *esp* **:** an area of sea bottom supporting a heavy growth of a particular organism **3 :** a supporting surface or structure **:** FOUNDATION; *esp* **:** the earthwork that supports the ballast and track of a railroad **4 :** LAYER, STRATUM **5 a :** the place or material in which a block or brick is laid **b :** the lower surface of a brick, slate, or tile

[2]**bed** *vb* **bed·ded; bed·ding** *vt* **1 a :** to furnish with a bed or bedding **b :** to put or take to bed **2 a :** EMBED **b :** to plant or arrange in beds **c :** BASE, ESTABLISH **3 a :** to lay flat or in a layer **b :** to make a bed in or of ~ *vi* **1 a :** to find or make sleeping accommodations **b :** to go to bed **2 :** to form a layer **3 :** to lie flat or flush

be·daub \bi-'dȯb, -'däb\ *vt* **1 :** to daub over **:** BESMEAR **2 :** to ornament with vulgar excess

be·daz·zle \bi-'daz-əl\ *vt* **1 :** to confuse by a strong light **:** DAZZLE **2 :** to impress forcefully **:** ENCHANT — **be·daz·zle·ment** \-mənt\ *n*

bed·bug \'bed-ˌbəg\ *n* **:** a wingless bloodsucking bug (*Cimex lectularius*) sometimes infesting houses and esp. beds and feeding on human blood

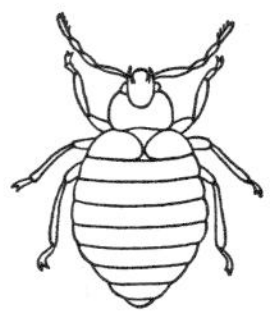

common bedbug

bed·clothes \'bed-ˌklō(th)z\ *n pl* **:** the covering (as sheets and blankets) used on a bed

bed·der \'bed-ər\ *n* **1 :** one that makes up beds **2 :** a bedding plant

[1]**bed·ding** \'bed-iŋ\ *n* [ME, fr. OE, fr. *bedd*] **1 :** BEDCLOTHES **2 :** a bottom layer **:** FOUNDATION **3 :** material to provide a bed for livestock

[2]**bedding** *adj* [fr. gerund of [2]*bed*] **:** appropriate or adapted for culture in open-air beds

be·deck \bi-'dek\ *vt* **:** to deck out **:** ADORN

be·dev·il \bi-'dev-əl\ *vt* **1 :** to possess with or as if with a devil **:** BEWITCH **2 :** to change for the worse **:** SPOIL **3 :** to drive frantic **:** HARASS **4 :** to confuse utterly **:** MUDDLE — **be·dev·il·ment** \-əl-mənt\ *n*

be·dew \bi-'d(y)ü\ *vt* **:** to wet with or as if with dew

bed·fast \'bed-ˌfast\ *adj* **:** BEDRIDDEN

Bed·ford cord \ˌbed-fərd-\ *n* [perh. fr. New *Bedford,* Massachusetts] **:** a clothing fabric with lengthwise ribs

be·dight \bi-'dīt\ *vt* **be·dight·ed** *or* **bedight; be·dight·ing** *archaic* **:** EQUIP, ARRAY

be·dim \bi-'dim\ *vt* **:** to make dim or obscure

Bed·i·vere \'bed-ə-ˌvi(ə)r\ *n* **:** a knight of the Round Table who is present at the departure of the dying Arthur for Avalon

be·di·zen \bi-'dīz-ᵊn, -'diz-\ *vt* **:** to dress or adorn with gaudy vulgarity — **be·di·zen·ment** \-mənt\ *n*

bed·lam \'bed-ləm\ *n* [*Bedlam,* popular name for the Hospital of St. Mary of Bethlehem, London, an insane asylum, fr. ME *Bedlem* Bethlehem] **1** *obs* **:** MADMAN, LUNATIC **2** *archaic* **:** a lunatic asylum **3 :** a place or scene of uproar and confusion — **bedlam** *adj*

bed·lam·ite \'bed-lə-ˌmīt\ *n* **:** MADMAN, LUNATIC — **bedlamite** *adj*

Bed·ling·ton terrier \ˌbed-liŋ-tən-\ *n* [*Bedlington,* England] **:** a swift rough-coated terrier of light build

bed molding *n* **:** the molding of a cornice below the corona and above the frieze; *also* **:** a molding below a deep projection

bed·ou·in \'bed-ə-wən\ *n, pl* **bedouin** *or* **bedouins** *often cap* [F *bédouin*, fr. Ar *badāwi, bidwān*, pl. of *badawi* desert dweller] **:** a nomadic Arab of the Arabian, Syrian, or No. African deserts

bed·pan \'bed-ˌpan\ *n* **:** a shallow vessel used by a person in bed for urination or defecation

bed·plate \'bed-ˌplāt\ *n* **:** a plate or framing used as a support

be·drag·gle \bi-'drag-əl\ *vt* **:** to wet thoroughly

be·drag·gled \bi-'drag-əld\ *adj* **1 :** soiled and stained by or as if trailing in mud **2 :** DILAPIDATED

bed·rid·den \'bed-ˌrid-ᵊn\ *or* **bed·rid** \-ˌrid\ *adj* [alter. of ME *bedrede, bedreden,* fr. OE *bedreda,* fr. *bedreda* one confined to bed, fr. *bedd* bed + *-rida, -reda* rider, fr. *rīdan* to ride] **:** confined to bed

bed·rock \'bed-'räk, -ˌräk\ *n* **1 :** the solid rock underlying other surface materials (as soil) **2 a :** lowest point **:** NADIR **b :** BASIS

bedrock valley *n* **:** a valley eroded in bedrock

bed·roll \'bed-ˌrōl\ *n* **:** bedding rolled up for carrying

bed·room \-ˌrüm, -ˌru̇m\ *n* **:** a room furnished with a bed and intended primarily for sleeping

bed·side \-ˌsīd\ *n* **:** the side of a bed esp. of a sick or dying person

bed·sore \-ˌsō(ə)r, -ˌsȯ(ə)r\ *n* **:** an ulceration of tissue deprived of nutrition by prolonged pressure

bed·spread \-ˌspred\ *n* **:** a usu. ornamental cloth cover for a bed

bed·spring \-ˌspriŋ\ *n* **:** a spring supporting a mattress

bed·stead \-ˌsted, -ˌstid\ *n* **:** the framework of a bed

bed·straw \-ˌstrȯ\ *n* [fr. its use for mattresses] **:** an herb (genus *Galium*) of the madder family having angled stems, opposite or whorled leaves, and small flowers

bed·time \-ˌtīm\ *n* **:** time to go to bed

bed·ward \'bed-wərd\ *or* **bed·wards** \-wərdz\ *adv* **:** toward bed

[1]**bee** \'bē\ *n* [ME, fr. OE *bēo;* akin to OHG *bīa* bee, Lith *bitis*] **1 :** a social colonial hymenopterous insect (*Apis mellifera*) often kept in a state of domestication for the honey that it produces; *broadly* **:** any of numerous insects (superfamily Apoidea) that differ from the related wasps esp. in the heavier hairier body and in having sucking as well as chewing mouthparts, that feed on pollen and nectar, and that store both and often also honey **2 :** an eccentric notion **:** FANCY **3** [perh. fr. E dial. *been* help given by neighbors, fr. ME *bene* prayer, boon, fr. OE *bēn* prayer — more at BOON] **:** a gathering of people for a specific purpose ⟨spelling ~⟩

[2]**bee** *n* [ME *beghe* metal ring, fr. OE *bēag;* akin to OE *būgan* to bend — more at BOW] **:** a piece of hard wood at the side of a bowsprit to reeve fore-topmast stays through

[3]**bee** *n* **:** the letter *b*

bee balm *n* **:** any of several mints (as monarda) attractive to bees

bee·bread \'bē-ˌbred\ *n* **:** bitter yellowish brown pollen stored up in honeycomb cells and used mixed with honey by bees as food

beech \'bēch\ *n, pl* **beech·es** *or* **beech** [ME *beche,* fr. OE *bēce;* akin to OE *bōc* beech, OHG *buohha,* L *fagus,* Gk *phēgos* oak] **:** any of a genus (*Fagus* of the family Fagaceae, the beech family) of hardwood trees with smooth gray bark and small edible nuts; *also* **:** its wood — **beech·en** \'bē-chən\ *adj*

beech·drops \'bēch-ˌdräps\ *n pl but sing or pl in constr* **1 :** a low wiry plant (*Epifagus virginiana*) of the broomrape family parasitic on the roots of beeches **2 :** SQUAWROOT

bee eater *n* **:** any of a family (Meropidae) of brightly colored slender-billed insectivorous chiefly tropical Old World birds

¹beef \'bēf\ *n, pl* **beefs** \'bēfs\ *or* **beeves** \'bēvz\ [ME, fr. OF *buef* ox, beef, fr. L *bov-, bos* head of cattle — more at COW] **1 :** the flesh of an adult domestic bovine **2 a :** an ox, cow, or bull in a full-grown or nearly full-grown state; *esp* **:** a steer or cow fattened for food **b :** a dressed carcass of a beef animal **c :** beef animals **3 :** muscular flesh **:** BRAWN **4** *pl beefs, slang* **:** COMPLAINT

²beef *vt* **:** to add strength or power to **~** *vi* **:** COMPLAIN

beef cattle *n pl* **:** cattle developed primarily for the efficient production of meat and marked by capacity for rapid growth, heavy well-fleshed body, and stocky build

beef·eat·er \'bē-,fēt-ər\ *n* **:** a yeoman of the guard of an English monarch

bee fly *n* **:** any of numerous two-winged flies (family Bombyliidae) many of which resemble bees

beef·steak \'bēf-,stāk\ *n* **:** a steak of beef usu. from the hindquarter

beefsteak fungus *n* **:** a bright red edible pore fungus (*Fistulina hepatica*) growing on dead trees

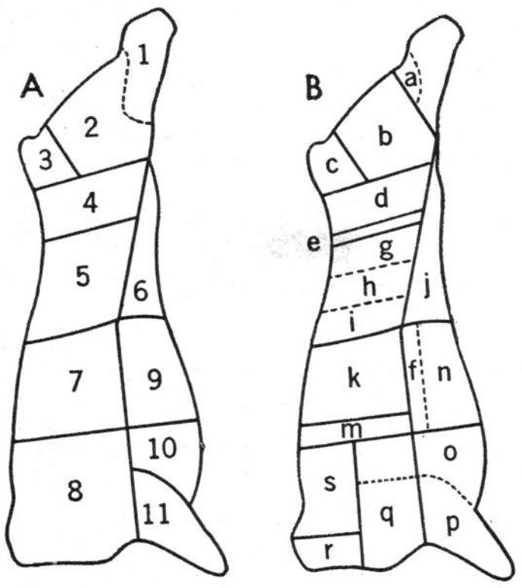

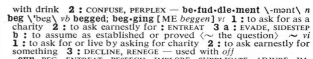

beef 1: *A* wholesale cuts: *1* shank, *2* round with rump and shank cut off, *3* rump, *4* sirloin, *5* short loin, *6* flank, *7* rib, *8* chuck, *9* plate, *10* brisket, *11* shank; *B* retail cuts: *a* heel pot roast, *b* round steak, *c* rump roast, *d* sirloin steak, *e* pinbone steak, *f* short ribs, *g* porterhouse steak, *h* T-bone steak, *i* club steak, *j* flank steak, *k* rib roast, *m* blade rib roast, *n* plate, *o* brisket, *p* crosscut shank, *q* arm pot roast, *r* boneless neck, *s* blade roast

beef·wood \'bēf-,wu̇d\ *n* **:** any of several hard heavy reddish chiefly tropical woods used esp. for cabinetwork; *also* **:** a tree (as a bully tree) yielding beefwood

beefy \'bē-fē\ *adj* **:** BRAWNY, THICKSET

bee·hive \'bē-,hīv\ *n* **1 :** a hive for bees **2 :** something resembling a hive for bees — **beehive** *adj*

bee·keep·er \-,kē-pər\ *n* **:** one who raises bees — **bee·keep·ing** *n*

bee·line \'bē-,līn\ *n* [fr. the belief that nectar-laden bees return to their hives in a direct line] **:** a straight direct course

Beel·ze·bub \bē-'el-zi-,bəb, 'bēl-zi-, 'bel-\ *n* [*Beelzebub*, prince of devils, fr. L, fr. Gk *Beelzeboub*, fr. Heb *Ba'al zĕbhūbh*, a Philistine god, lit., lord of flies] **1 :** DEVIL **2 :** a fallen angel in Milton's *Paradise Lost* ranking next to Satan

been *past part of* BE

bee plant *n* **:** a plant much frequented by bees for nectar: as **a :** a heavy-scented herb (*Cleome serrulata*) of the caper family with pink flowers **b :** any of various figworts (genus *Scrophularia*)

beer \'bi(ə)r\ *n* [ME *ber*, fr. OE *bēor;* akin to OHG *bior* beer] **1 :** a malted and hopped somewhat bitter alcoholic beverage; *specif* **:** such a beverage brewed by slow fermentation **2 :** a carbonated nonalcoholic or a fermented slightly alcoholic beverage with flavoring from roots or other plant parts ⟨birch ~⟩

beery \'bi(ə)r-ē\ *adj* **1 :** affected or caused by beer ⟨~ voices⟩ ⟨~ sentimentality⟩ **2 :** smelling or tasting of beer ⟨~ tavern⟩

bees·tings *var of* BEASTINGS

bees·wax \'bēz-,waks\ *n* **:** WAX 1

beet \'bēt\ *n* [ME *bete*, fr. OE *bēte*, fr. L *beta*] **:** a biennial garden plant (genus *Beta*) of the goosefoot family with thick long-stalked edible leaves and swollen root used as a vegetable, a source of sugar, or for forage; *also* **:** its root

¹bee·tle \'bēt-ᵊl\ *n* [ME *betylle*, fr. OE *bitula*, fr. *bītan* to bite] **1 :** any of an order (Coleoptera) of insects having four wings of which the outer pair are modified into stiff elytra which protect the inner pair when at rest **2 :** any of various insects resembling a beetle

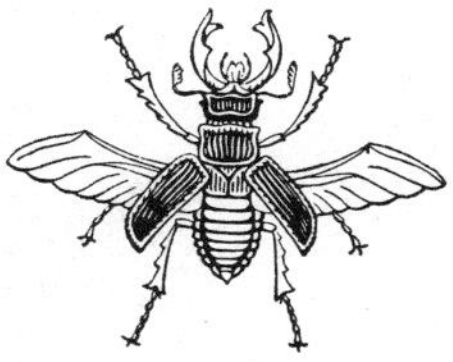

beetle

²beetle *n* [ME *betel*, fr. OE *bīetel;* akin to OE *bēatan* to beat] **1 :** a heavy wooden hammering or ramming instrument **2 :** a wooden pestle or bat for domestic tasks **3 :** a machine for giving fabrics a lustrous finish — **beetle** *vt*

³beetle *adj* [ME *bitel-browed* having overhanging brows, prob. fr. *betylle, bitel* beetle] **:** being prominent and overhanging

⁴beetle *vi* **bee·tling** \'bēt-liŋ, -ᵊl-iŋ\ **:** PROJECT, JUT

beet leafhopper *n* **:** a leafhopper (*Eutettix tenellus*) that transmits a virus disease to sugar beets and other plants in the western U.S.

bee tree *n* **1 :** a hollow tree in which honeybees nest **2 :** BASSWOOD 1

be·fall \bi-'fȯl\ *vi* **:** to happen esp. as if by fate **~** *vt* **:** to happen to

be·fit \bi-'fit\ *vt* **:** to be proper or becoming to — **be·fit·ting** *adj*

be·fog \bi-'fȯg, -'fäg\ *vt* **1 :** to make foggy **:** OBSCURE **2 :** CONFUSE

be·fool \bi-'fül\ *vt* **1 :** to make a fool of **2 :** DELUDE, DECEIVE

¹be·fore \bi-'fō(ə)r, -'fȯ(ə)r\ *adv* [ME, adv. & prep., fr. OE *beforan*, fr. *be-* + *foran* before, fr. *fore*] **1 :** in advance **:** AHEAD **2 :** EARLIER, PREVIOUSLY

²before *prep* **1 a** (1) **:** in front of (2) **:** in the presence of ⟨stood ~ the judge⟩ **b :** under the jurisdiction or consideration of ⟨the case ~ the court⟩ **c** (1) **:** at the disposal of (2) **:** in store for **:** in the future of **2 :** preceding in time ⟨come ~ six o'clock⟩ **3 :** in a higher or more important position than ⟨put quantity ~ quality⟩

³before *conj* **1 :** earlier than the time when **2 :** sooner than

be·fore·hand \bi-'fō(ə)r-,hand, -'fȯ(ə)r-\ *adv (or adj)* **1 a :** in anticipation **b :** in advance **2 :** at a previous time **:** EARLY — **be·fore·hand·ed·ness** \-,han-dəd-nəs, -'han-\ *n*

be·fore·time \-,tīm\ *adv* **:** FORMERLY

be·foul \bi-'fau̇(ə)l\ *vt* **:** to make foul with or as if with dirt or filth

be·friend \bi-'frend\ *vt* **:** to act as a friend to

be·fud·dle \bi-'fəd-ᵊl\ *vt* **1 :** to muddle or stupefy with or as if with drink **2 :** CONFUSE, PERPLEX — **be·fud·dle·ment** \-mənt\ *n*

beg \'beg\ *vb* **begged; beg·ging** [ME *beggen*] *vt* **1 :** to ask for as a charity **2 :** to ask earnestly for **:** ENTREAT **3 a :** EVADE, SIDESTEP **b :** to assume as established or proved ⟨~ the question⟩ **~** *vi* **1 :** to ask for or live by asking for charity **2 :** to ask earnestly for something **3 :** DECLINE, RENEGE — used with *off*

syn BEG, ENTREAT, BESEECH, IMPLORE, SUPPLICATE, ADJURE, IMPORTUNE mean to ask urgently. BEG suggests earnestness or insistence in asking for something to which one has no claim or right; ENTREAT implies an effort to overcome resistance or deflect from resolute purpose; BESEECH implies great eagerness or anxiety; IMPLORE adds to BESEECH a suggestion of greater urgency or anguished appeal; SUPPLICATE suggests a posture of humility; ADJURE implies enjoining as well as pleading and suggests the involving of something sacred; IMPORTUNE suggests an annoying persistence in trying to break down resistance to a request

be·gat \bi-'gat\ *archaic past of* BEGET

be·get \bi-'get\ *vt* **be·got** \-'gät\ **be·got·ten** \-'gät-ᵊn\ *or* **begot; be·get·ting** [ME *begeten*, alter. of *beyeten*, fr. OE *bigietan*] **1 :** to procreate as the father **:** SIRE **2 :** CAUSE — **be·get·ter** *n*

¹beg·gar \'beg-ər\ *n* [ME *beggere, beggare*, fr. *beggen* to beg + *-ere, -are* -er] **1 :** one that begs; *esp* **:** one that lives by asking for gifts **2 :** PAUPER **3 :** FELLOW

²beggar *vt* **beg·gar·ing** \'beg-(ə-)riŋ\ **1 :** to reduce to beggary **2 :** to exceed the resources or abilities of ⟨~*s* description⟩

beg·gar·li·ness \-lē-nəs\ *n* **:** the quality or state of being beggarly

beg·gar·ly \'beg-ər-lē\ *adj* **1 :** befitting or resembling a beggar; *esp* **:** marked by unrelieved poverty **2 :** MEAN **syn** see CONTEMPTIBLE

beg·gar's-lice \'beg-ərz-,līs\ *or* **beg·gar-lice** \-ər-,līs\ *n pl but sing or pl in constr* **:** any of several plants (as of the genera *Lappula, Desmodium*, and *Galium*) with prickly or adhesive fruits; *also* **:** one of these fruits

beg·gar-ticks *or* **beg·gar's-ticks** \-,tiks\ *n pl but sing or pl in constr* **1 :** BUR MARIGOLD; *also* **:** its prickly achenes **2 :** BEGGAR'S-LICE

beg·gar·weed \'beg-ər-,wēd\ *n* **1 :** any of various plants (as a knotgrass, spurry, or dodder) that grow in waste ground **2 :** any of several tick trefoils (genus *Desmodium*); *esp* **:** a West Indian forage plant (*D. tortuosum*) cultivated in the southern U.S.

beg·gary \'beg-ə-rē\ *n* **1 :** POVERTY, PENURY **2 :** the class or occupation of beggars **3 :** the act of begging **:** MENDICANCY

be·gin \bi-'gin\ *vb* **be·gan** \-'gan\ **be·gun** \-'gən\ **be·gin·ning** [ME *beginnen*, fr. OE *beginnan;* akin to OHG *biginnan* to begin, OE *onginnan*] *vi* **1 a :** to do the first part of an action **b :** to undergo initial steps **:** COMMENCE **2 a :** to come into existence **:** ARISE **b :** to have a starting point **3 :** to do or succeed in the least degree **~** *vt* **1 :** to set about the activity of **2 a :** to call into being **:** FOUND **b :** ORIGINATE, INVENT **3 :** to come first in — **be·gin·ner** *n*

syn COMMENCE, START, INITIATE, INAUGURATE: BEGIN and COMMENCE are practically identical in meaning but COMMENCE suggests slightly greater formality; START, opposed to *stop*, suggests a getting or setting into motion or setting out on a journey and implies a definitely marked change from a state of rest or waiting to movement; INITIATE implies the taking of a first step of a process or series that is to continue; INAUGURATE adds to INITIATE a stronger implication of both a ceremonious beginning and an expectation of long continuance

be·gin·ning \bi-'gin-iŋ\ *n* **1 :** the point at which something begins **2 :** the first part **3 :** ORIGIN, SOURCE **4 a :** a rudimentary stage or early period **b :** something undeveloped or incomplete

be·gird \bi-'gərd\ *vt* **1 :** GIRD 1a **2 :** SURROUND, ENCOMPASS

be·gone \bi-'gȯn *also* -'gän\ *vi* [ME, fr. *be gone* (imper.)] **:** to go away **:** DEPART — used esp. in the imperative

be·go·nia \bi-'gōn-yə\ *n* [NL, genus name, fr. Michel *Bégon* †1710 F governor of Santo Domingo] **:** any of a large genus (*Begonia* of the family Begoniaceae, the begonia family) of tropical herbs with asymmetrical leaves widely cultivated as ornamentals

be·grime \bi-'grīm\ *vt* **:** to make dirty with grime

be·grudge \bi-'grəj\ *vt* **1 :** to give or concede reluctantly **2 a :** to look upon with reluctance or disapproval **b :** to take little pleasure in **3 :** to envy the pleasure or enjoyment of

be·guile \bi-'gī(ə)l\ *vt* **1 :** to lead by deception **2 a :** DECEIVE, HOODWINK **b :** to deprive by guile **:** CHEAT **3 :** to while away **4 :** to please or persuade by the use of wiles **:** CHARM **syn** see DECEIVE, WHILE — **be·guile·ment** \-mənt\ *n* — **be·guil·er** *n*

be·guine \bi-'gēn\ *n* [AmerF *béguine*, fr. F *béguin* flirtation] **:** a vigorous popular dance of the islands of Saint Lucia and Martinique somewhat like the rumba

Be·guine \'bā-,gēn\ *n* [MF] **:** a member of one of various ascetic and philanthropic communities of women not under vows founded chiefly in the Netherlands in the 13th century

be·gum \'bē-gəm\ *n* [Hindi *begam*] **:** a Muslim lady of high rank

be·half \bi-'haf, -'håf\ *n* [ME, fr. *by* + *half* half, side] **:** INTEREST, BENEFIT; *also* **:** SUPPORT, DEFENSE — used esp. in the phrase *in behalf of* or *on behalf of*

be·have \bi-'hāv\ *vb* [ME *behaven*, fr. *be-* + *haven* to have, hold] *vt* **1 :** to bear or comport (oneself) in a particular way **2 :** to conduct (oneself) in a proper manner **~** *vi* **1 :** to act, function, or react in a particular way **2 :** to conduct oneself properly

syn BEHAVE, CONDUCT, DEPORT, COMPORT, ACQUIT mean when used with a reflexive to act or to cause oneself to do something in a certain way. BEHAVE implies meeting a standard usu. of what is proper or decorous; CONDUCT implies action or behavior that shows the extent of one's power to control or direct oneself; DEPORT implies behaving so as to show how far one conforms to conventional rules of discipline or propriety; COMPORT suggests conduct measured by what is expected or required of one in a certain class or position; ACQUIT applies to action under stress that deserves praise or meets expectations

be·hav·ior *or chiefly Brit* **be·hav·iour** \bi-'hā-vyər\ *n* [alter. of ME *behavour*, fr. *behaven*] **1 :** the manner of conducting oneself **2 :** the way in which something behaves — **be·hav·ior·al** \-vyə-rəl\ *adj* — **be·hav·ior·al·ly** \-rə-lē\ *adv*

be·hav·ior·ism \bi-'hā-vyə-,riz-əm\ *n* **:** a doctrine that the data of psychology consist of the observable evidences of organismic activity to the exclusion of introspective data or references to consciousness and mind — **be·hav·ior·ist** \-vyə-rəst\ *adj or n* —

be·hav·ior·is·tic \bi-ˌhā-vyə-'ris-tik\ *adj*

be·head \bi-'hed\ *vt* **:** to sever the head from **:** DECAPITATE

be·he·moth \bi-'hē-məth, 'bē-ə-ˌmȯth\ *n* [ME, fr. L, fr. Heb *bĕhēmōth*] **1** *often cap* **:** an animal that is prob. the hippopotamus described in Job 40:15–24 **2 :** something of oppressive or monstrous size or power

be·hest \bi-'hest\ *n* [ME, promise, command, fr. OE *behǣs* promise, fr. *behātan* to promise, fr. *be-* + *hātan* to command, promise] **1 :** COMMAND, DEMAND **2 :** urgent prompting

¹be·hind \bi-'hīnd\ *adv* [ME *behinde*, fr. OE *behindan*, fr. *be-* + *hindan* from behind; akin to OE *hinder* behind — more at HIND] **1 a :** in the place, situation, or time that is being or has been departed from ⟨stay ~⟩ **b :** in, to, or toward the back ⟨look ~⟩ **2 a :** in a secondary or inferior position **b :** in arrears **c :** SLOW **3** *archaic* **:** still to come

²behind *prep* **1 a :** in the place, situation, or time left by ⟨the staff stayed ~ the troops⟩ **b** (1) **:** in, to, or toward the back of ⟨look ~ you⟩ (2) **:** beyond in past time **2 :** inferior to **3 :** later than **:** AFTER **4 a** (1) **:** in a hidden or obscure causal relation to ⟨the conditions ~ the strike⟩ (2) **:** in the background of **b :** in a supporting position at the back of ⟨an argument with experience ~ it⟩

³behind *n* **1 :** the back side **2 :** BUTTOCKS

be·hind·hand \bi-'hīnd-ˌhand\ *adv (or adj)* **1 :** in arrears **2 a :** behind the times **b :** in an inferior position **c :** behind schedule

be·hold \bi-'hōld\ *vb* [ME *beholden* to keep, behold, fr. OE *behealdan*, fr. *be-* + *healdan* to hold] *vt* **1 :** to perceive through sight or apprehension **:** SEE **2 :** to gaze upon **:** OBSERVE ~ *vi* — used in the imperative esp. to call attention — **be·hold·er** *n*

be·hold·en \bi-'hōl-dən\ *adj* [ME, fr. pp. of *beholden*] **:** under obligation for a favor or gift **:** INDEBTED

be·hoof \bi-'hüf\ *n* [ME *behof*, fr. OE *behōf;* akin to OE *hebban* to raise — more at HEAVE] **:** ADVANTAGE, PROFIT

be·hoove \bi-'hüv\ *or* **be·hove** \-'hōv\ *vb* [ME *behoven*, fr. OE *behōfian*, fr. *behōf*] *vt* **:** to be necessary, proper, or advantageous for ⟨it ~*s* us to fight⟩ ~ *vi* **:** to be necessary, fit, or proper

beige \'bāzh\ *n* [F] **1 :** cloth made of natural undyed wool **2 a :** a variable color averaging light grayish yellowish brown **b :** a pale to grayish yellow — **beige** *adj*

be·ing \'bē-iŋ\ *n* **1 a :** the quality or state of having existence **b** (1) **:** something conceivable as existing (2) **:** something that actually exists (3) **:** the totality of existing things **c :** conscious existence **:** LIFE **2 :** the qualities that constitute an existent thing **:** ESSENCE; *esp* **:** PERSONALITY **3 :** a living thing; *esp* **:** PERSON

Be·ja \'bā-jə\ *n, pl* **Beja** **1 a :** a nomadic pastoral people living between the Nile and the Red sea **b :** a member of this people **2 :** the Cushitic language of the Beja people

bel \'bel\ *n* [Alexander Graham *Bell* †1922 Scottish-Am inventor of the telephone] **:** ten decibels

be·la·bor *or chiefly Brit* **be·la·bour** \bi-'lā-bər\ *vt* **1 :** to work on or at to absurd lengths ⟨~ the obvious⟩ **2 a :** to beat soundly **b :** ASSAIL, ATTACK

be·lat·ed \bi-'lāt-əd\ *adj* [pp. of *belate* (to make late)] **1 :** delayed beyond the usual time **2 :** existing or appearing past the normal time — **be·lat·ed·ly** *adv* — **be·lat·ed·ness** *n*

¹be·lay \bi-'lā\ *vb* [ME *beleggen* to beset, fr. OE *belecgan*, fr. *be-* + *lecgan* to lay] *vt* **1 a :** to secure (as a rope) by turns around a cleat, pin, or bitt **b :** to make fast **2 :** STOP **3 a :** to secure (a person) at the end of a rope **b :** to secure (a rope) to a person or object ~ *vi* **1 :** to be made fast **2 :** STOP, QUIT **3 :** to make fast by belaying

²belay *n* **1 :** the obtaining of a hold (as for a rope) during mountain climbing; *also* **:** a method of obtaining such a hold **2 :** something to which a mountain climber's rope is anchored

bel can·to \bel-'kän-(ˌ)tō\ *n* [It, lit., beautiful singing] **:** operatic singing originating in 17th century and 18th century Italy and stressing ease, purity, and evenness of tone production and an agile and precise vocal technique

belch \'belch\ *vb* [ME *belchen*, fr. OE *bealcian*] *vi* **1 :** to expel gas suddenly from the stomach through the mouth **2 :** to erupt, explode, or detonate violently **3 :** to issue forth spasmodically **:** GUSH ~ *vt* **1 :** to eject or emit violently **2 :** to expel (gas) from the stomach suddenly **:** ERUCT — **belch** *n*

bel·dam *or* **bel·dame** \'bel-dəm\ *n* [ME *beldam* grandmother, fr. MF *bel* beautiful + ME *dam*] **:** an old woman; *esp* **:** HAG

be·lea·guer \bi-'lē-gər\ *vt* **be·lea·guer·ing** \-g(ə-)riŋ\ [D *belegeren*, fr. *be-* (akin to OE *be-*) + *leger* camp; akin to OHG *legar* bed — more at LAIR] **1 :** to surround with an army so as to prevent escape **:** BESIEGE **2 :** BESET, HARASS

bel·em·nite \'bel-əm-ˌnīt\ *n* [F *bélemnite*, fr. Gk *belemnon* dart; akin to Gk *ballein* to throw — more at DEVIL] **:** a conical fossil shell of an extinct cephalopod (family Belemnitidae) — **bel·em·nit·ic** \ˌbel-əm-'nit-ik\ *adj*

bel es·prit \ˌbel-ə-'sprē\ *n, pl* **beaux es·prits** \ˌbō-ˌzes-'prē\ [F, lit., fine mind] **:** a person with a fine and gifted mind

bel·fry \'bel-frē\ *n* [ME *belfry*, alter. of *berfrey*, fr. MF *berfrei*, deriv. of Gk *pyrgos phorētos* movable war tower] **1 :** a bell tower; *esp* **:** one surmounting or attached to another structure **2 :** a room in which a bell is hung in a tower **3 :** a cupola, turret, or framework to enclose a bell

bel·ga \'bel-gə\ *n* [F, fr. L *Belga* Belgian] **:** a former Belgian unit of value for use in foreign exchange equal to 5 francs

Bel·gae \-ˌgī, -ˌjē\ *n pl* [L, pl. of *Belga*] **:** a people occupying northern France and Belgium in Caesar's time — **Bel·gic** \-jik\ *adj*

Bel·gian \'bel-jən\ *n* **1 :** a native or inhabitant of Belgium **2 :** any of a Belgian breed of heavy usu. roan or chestnut draft horses — **Belgian** *adj*

Belgian hare *n* **:** any of a breed of slender dark red domestic rabbits

Belgian sheepdog *n* **:** any of a breed of hardy black or gray dogs developed in Belgium esp. for herding sheep

Be·li·al \'bē-lē-əl, 'bēl-yəl\ *n* [Gk, fr. Heb *bĕlīya'al* worthlessness] **1 :** SATAN **2 :** one of the fallen angels in Milton's *Paradise Lost*

be·lie \bi-'lī\ *vt* **1** *archaic* **:** to tell lies about **2 a :** to give a false impression of **b :** to present a contrasting appearance to **3 a :** to prove false **b :** to run counter to — **be·li·er** \-'lī(-ə)r\ *n*

be·lief \bə-'lēf\ *n* [ME *beleave*, prob. alter. of OE *gelēafa*, fr. *ge-*, associative prefix + *lēafa;* akin to OE *lȳfan*] **1 :** a state or habit of mind in which trust or confidence is placed in some person or thing **2 :** something believed; *specif* **:** a tenet or body of tenets held by a group **3 :** conviction of the truth of some statement or reality of a fact esp. when well grounded

syn BELIEF, FAITH, CREDENCE, CREDIT mean the assent to the truth of something offered for acceptance. BELIEF and FAITH are often used interchangeably but BELIEF may or may not imply certitude in the believer whereas FAITH always does even where there is no evidence or proof; FAITH may also suggest credulity; CREDENCE suggests the fact of intellectual assent without implying anything about grounds for assent; CREDIT implies assent on grounds other than direct proof, usu. the known trustworthiness of the source of what is proposed for acceptance **syn** see in addition OPINION

be·liev·able \bə-'lē-və-bəl\ *adj* **:** capable of being believed — **be·liev·ably** \-blē\ *adv*

be·lieve \bə-'lēv\ *vb* [ME *beleven*, fr. OE *belēfan*, fr. *be-* + *lȳfan*, *lēfan* to allow, believe; akin to OHG *gilouben* to believe, OE *lēof* dear — more at LOVE] *vi* **1 :** to have a firm religious faith **2 :** to have a firm conviction as to the reality or goodness of something **3 :** THINK, SUPPOSE ~ *vt* **1 :** to take as true or honest ⟨~ the reports⟩ **2 :** to hold as an opinion **:** SUPPOSE — **be·liev·er** *n*

be·like \bi-'līk\ *adv, archaic* **:** most likely **:** PROBABLY

be·lit·tle \bi-'lit-ᵊl\ *vt* **be·lit·tling** \-'lit-liŋ, -ᵊl-iŋ\ **1 :** to make seem little or less **2 :** DISPARAGE **3** **syn** see DECRY — **be·lit·tle·ment** \-'lit-ᵊl-mənt\ *n* — **be·lit·tler** \-'lit-lər, -ᵊl-ər\ *n*

be·live \bi-'līv\ *adv* [ME *bilive*, fr. *by* + *live*, dat. of *lif* life] *Scot* **:** in due time **:** by and by

¹bell \'bel\ *n* [ME *belle*, fr. OE; akin to OE *bellan* to roar — more at BELLOW] **1 :** a hollow metallic device that vibrates and gives forth a ringing sound when struck **2 :** the sounding of a bell as a signal **3 a :** a bell rung to tell the hour **b :** a stroke of such a bell esp. on shipboard **c :** the time so indicated **d :** a half hour **4 :** something having the form of a bell: as **a :** the corolla of a flower **b :** a flaring mouth of a wind instrument **5 a :** a percussion instrument consisting of metal bars or tubes that when struck give out tones resembling bells — usu. used in pl. **b :** GLOCKENSPIEL

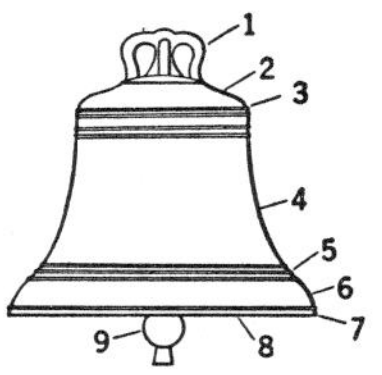

bell 1: *1* crown, *2* head, *3* shoulder, *4* waist, *5* bead lines, *6* sound bow, *7* lip, *8* mouth, *9* clapper

²bell *vt* **1 :** to provide with a bell **2 :** to make bell-mouthed ~ *vi* **:** to take the form of a bell **:** FLARE — **bell the cat :** to do a daring or risky deed

³bell *vi* [ME *bellen*, fr. OE *bellan*] **:** to make a resonant bellowing or baying sound

SHIP'S BELLS

NO. OF BELLS	HOUR (A.M. OR P.M.)		
1	12:30	4:30	8:30
2	1:00	5:00	9:00
3	1:30	5:30	9:30
4	2:00	6:00	10:00
5	2:30	6:30	10:30
6	3:00	7:00	11:00
7	3:30	7:30	11:30
8	4:00	8:00	12:00

⁴bell *n* **:** BELLOW, ROAR

bel·la·don·na \ˌbel-ə-'dän-ə\ *n* [It, lit., beautiful lady] **1 :** a European poisonous plant (*Atropa belladonna*) of the nightshade family having reddish bell-shaped flowers, shining black berries, and root and leaves that yield atropine — called also *deadly nightshade* **2 :** a medicinal extract from the belladonna plant

belladonna lily *n* **:** an amaryllis (*Amaryllis belladonna*) often cultivated for its fragrant usu. white or rose flowers

bell·bird \'bel-ˌbərd\ *n* **:** any of several birds whose notes are likened to the sound of a bell

bell·boy \'bel-ˌbȯi\ *n* **:** a hotel or club employee who escorts guests to rooms, assists them with luggage, and runs errands

belle \'bel\ *n* [F, fr. fem. of *beau* beautiful — more at BEAU] **:** a popular attractive girl or woman

Bel·ler·o·phon \bə-'ler-ə-ˌfän\ *n* [L, fr. Gk *Bellerophōn*] **:** a hero in Greek legend noted for killing the Chimera

belles let·tres \bel-letrᵊ\ *n pl but sing in constr* [F, lit., fine letters] **:** literature that is an end in itself and not practical or purely informative

bel·le·trist \bel-'le-trəst\ *n* [*belles lettres*] **:** a writer of belles lettres — **bel·le·tris·tic** \ˌbel-ə-'tris-tik\ *adj*

bell·flow·er \'bel-ˌflau̇(-ə)r\ *n* **:** any of a genus (*Campanula* of the family Campanulaceae, the bellflower family) having an acrid juice, alternate leaves, and usu. showy bell-shaped flowers

bell·hop \-ˌhäp\ *n* [short for *bell-hopper*] **:** BELLBOY

bel·li·cose \'bel-i-ˌkōs\ *adj* [ME, fr. L *bellicosus*, fr. *bellicus* of war, fr. *bellum* war] **:** favoring or inclined to start quarrels or warfare **:** WARLIKE **syn** see BELLIGERENT — **bel·li·cose·ly** *adv* — **bel·li·cose·ness** *n* — **bel·li·cos·i·ty** \ˌbel-i-'käs-ət-ē\ *n*

bel·lig·er·ence \bə-'lij-(ə-)rən(t)s\ *n* **:** an aggressive or truculent attitude, atmosphere, or disposition

bel·lig·er·en·cy \-(ə-)rən-sē\ *n* **:** the state of being at war or in conflict; *specif* **:** the status of a legally recognized belligerent

bel·lig·er·ent \bə-'lij-(ə-)rənt\ *adj* [modif. of L *belligerant-*, *belligerans*, prp. of *belligerare* to wage war, fr. *belliger* waging war, fr. *bellum* + *gerere* to wage — more at CAST] **1 :** waging war; *specif* **:** belonging to or recognized as a military power protected by and subject to the laws of war **2 :** inclined to or exhibiting assertiveness or combativeness — **belligerent** *n* — **bel·lig·er·ent·ly** *adv*

syn BELLICOSE, PUGNACIOUS, QUARRELSOME, CONTENTIOUS: BELLIGERENT implies being actually at war or in an actively hostile mood; BELLICOSE suggests a disposition to fight or to start a fight; PUGNACIOUS suggests a disposition that takes pleasure in personal combat; QUARRELSOME stresses an ill-natured readiness to fight without good cause; CONTENTIOUS implies perverse and irritating fondness for arguing and quarreling

bell jar *n* **:** a bell-shaped usu. glass vessel designed to cover objects or to contain gases or a vacuum

bell·man \'bel-mən\ *n* **:** a man (as a town crier) who rings a bell

bell metal *n* **:** bronze that consists usu. of three to four parts of copper to one of tin and is used for making bells

Bel·lo·na \bə-'lō-nə\ *n* [L] **:** the Roman goddess of war

bel·low \'bel-(ˌ)ō, -ə(-w)\ *vb* [ME *belwen*, fr. OE *bylgian*; akin to OE & OHG *bellan* to roar, Skt *bhāṣate* he talks] *vi* **1 :** to make the loud deep hollow sound characteristic of a bull **2 :** to shout in a deep voice ~ *vt* **:** BAWL — **bellow** *n*

bel·lows \'bel-(ˌ)ōz, -əz\ *n pl but sing or pl in constr* [ME *bely, below, belwes* — more at BELLY] **1 :** an instrument or machine that by expansion and contraction draws in air through a valve or orifice and expels it through a tube; *also* **:** any of various other blowers **2 :** LUNGS **3 :** the expansible part in a camera

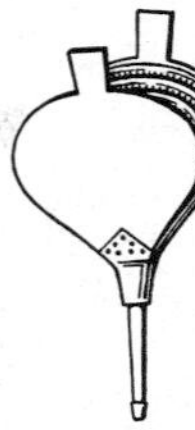

hand bellows

bell·pull \'bel-ˌpu̇l\ *n* **:** a handle or knob attached to a cord or wire by which one rings a bell; *also* **:** the cord itself

bell·weth·er \'bel-'weth-ər, -ˌweth-\ *n* [ME, leading sheep of a flock, leader, fr. *belle* bell + *wether;* fr. the practice of belling the leader of a flock] **:** one that takes the lead or initiative **:** LEADER

bell·wort \'bel-ˌwərt, -ˌwȯ(ə)rt\ *n* **1 :** BELLFLOWER **2 :** any of a small genus (*Uvularia*) of herbs of the lily family with yellow drooping bell-shaped flowers

¹bel·ly \'bel-ē\ *n* [ME *bely* bellows, belly, fr. OE *belg* bag, skin; akin to OHG *balg* bag, skin, OE *blāwan* to blow] **1 a :** ABDOMEN 1 **b :** the undersurface of an animal's body; *also* **:** hide from this part **c :** WOMB, UTERUS **d :** the stomach and its adjuncts; *also* **:** appetite for food **2 :** the internal cavity **:** INTERIOR **3 :** a surface or object curved or rounded like a human belly **4 a :** the part of a sail that swells out when filled with wind **b :** the enlarged fleshy body of a muscle

²belly *vb* **:** to swell or bulge out

¹bel·ly·ache \'bel-ē-ˌāk\ *n* **:** pain in the abdomen and esp. in the bowels **:** COLIC

²bellyache *vi* **:** to complain and find fault whiningly or peevishly

bel·ly·band \'bel-ē-ˌband\ *n* **:** a band around or across the belly: as **a :** GIRTH **b :** BAND 4b

belly button *n* **:** NAVEL 1

bel·ly–land \'bel-ē-ˌland\ *vi* **:** to land an airplane without use of landing gear — **belly landing** *n*

be·long \bi-'lȯŋ\ *vi* [ME *belongen,* fr. *be-* + *longen* to be suitable — more at LONG] **1 a :** to be suitable, appropriate, or advantageous **b :** to be in a proper situation **2 a :** to be the property of a person or thing — used with *to* **b :** to become attached or bound by birth, allegiance, or dependency **3 :** to be an attribute, part, adjunct, or function of a person or thing **4 :** to be properly classified

be·long·ing *n* **1 :** POSSESSION — usu. used in pl. **2 :** close or intimate relationship

Be·lo·rus·sian \ˌbel-ō-'rəsh-ən\ *n* **1 :** a native or inhabitant of Belorussia, U.S.S.R. **2 :** the Slavic language of the Belorussians — **Belorussian** *adj*

be·loved \bi-'ləv(-ə)d\ *adj* [ME, fr. pp. of *beloven* to love, fr. *be-* + *loven* to love] **:** dearly loved — **beloved** *n*

¹be·low \bi-'lō\ *adv* [*be-* + *low*, adj.] **1 :** in or to a lower place **2 a :** on earth **b :** in or to Hades or hell **3 :** on or to a lower floor or deck **4 :** in or to a lower rank or number **5 :** lower on the same page or on a following page

²below *prep* **1 :** in or to a lower place than **:** UNDER **2 :** inferior to (as in rank) **3 :** not suitable to the rank of **:** BENEATH

³below *n* **:** something that is below

⁴below *adj* **:** written or discussed lower on the same page or on a following page

Bel·shaz·zar \bel-'shaz-ər\ *n* [Heb *Bēlshaṣṣar*] **:** a son of Nebuchadnezzar and king of Babylon

¹belt \'belt\ *n* [ME, fr. OE; akin to OHG *balz* belt; both fr. a prehistoric WGmc-NGmc word borrowed fr. L *balteus* belt] **1 a :** a strip of flexible material worn around the waist **b :** a similar article worn as a corset or for protection or safety **2 :** a continuous band of tough flexible material for transmitting motion and power or conveying materials **3 :** a natural area characterized by some distinctive feature (as of habitation, geology, or life forms); *esp* **:** one suited to a particular crop ⟨the corn ~⟩ — **belt·ed** \'bel-təd\ *adj* — **below the belt :** UNFAIRLY

²belt *vt* **1 a :** to encircle or fasten with a belt **b :** to gird on **2 a :** to beat with or as if with a belt **:** THRASH **b :** STRIKE, HIT **3 :** to mark with a band **4 :** to sing in a forceful manner or style **~** *vi* **:** to move or act in a vigorous or violent manner

³belt *n* **:** a jarring blow **:** WHACK

Bel·tane \'bel-tən\ *n* [ME, fr. ScGael *bealltainn*] **1 :** the first day of May in the old Scottish calendar **2 :** the Celtic May Day festival

belt highway *n* **:** a highway skirting an urban area

belt·ing *n* **1 :** BELTS **2 :** material for belts

Belts·ville Small White \'belts-ˌvil-\ *n* [*Beltsville*, Md.] **:** a small white domestic turkey of a variety developed by the U.S. Department of Agriculture

belt·way \'belt-ˌwā\ *n* **:** BELT HIGHWAY

be·lu·ga \bə-'lü-gə\ *n* [Russ, fr. *belyĭ* white; akin to Gk *phainein* to show — more at FANCY] **1 :** a white sturgeon (*Acipenser huso*) of the Black sea, Caspian sea, and their tributaries **2** [Russ *belukha*, fr. *belyĭ*] **:** a cetacean (*Delphinapterus leucas*) of the dolphin family becoming about 10 feet long and white when adult

bel·ve·dere \'bel-və-ˌdi(ə)r\ *n* [It, lit., beautiful view] **:** a structure (as a summerhouse) designed to command a view

be·ma \'bē-mə\ *n* [LL & LGk; LL, fr. LGk *bēma*, fr. Gk, step, tribunal, fr. *bainein* to go — more at COME] **:** the part of an Eastern church containing the altar **:** SANCTUARY

be·mire \bi-'mī(ə)r\ *vt* **:** to cover or soil with, drag through, or sink in mire

be·moan \bi-'mōn\ *vt* **1 :** to express grief over **:** LAMENT **2 :** to look upon with regret, displeasure, or disapproval **syn** see DEPLORE

be·mock \bi-'mäk, -'mȯk\ *vt* **:** MOCK

be·muse \bi-'myüz\ *vt* **1 :** to make confused **:** BEWILDER **2 :** to cause to muse

¹ben \'ben\ *adv* [ME, fr. OE *binnan*, fr. *be-* + *innan* within, from within, fr. *in*] *Scot* **:** WITHIN

²ben \(')ben\ *prep, Scot* **:** WITHIN

³ben \'ben\ *n, Scot* **:** the inner room or parlor of a 2-room cottage

¹bench \'bench\ *n* [ME, fr. OE *benc;* akin to OHG *bank* bench] **1 a :** a long seat for two or more persons **b :** a thwart in a boat **c :** a seat on which the members of an athletic team await a turn or opportunity to play **2 a :** the seat where a judge sits in court **b :** the office or dignity of a judge **c :** the place where justice is administered **:** COURT **d :** the persons who sit as judges **3 a :** a seat for an official **b :** the office or dignity of such an official **c :** the officials occupying such a bench **4 a :** a long worktable **b :** a table forming part of a machine **5 :** TERRACE, SHELF; *esp* **:** a former shore of a sea or lake or floodplain of a river **6 a :** a platform on which a dog is placed at a dog show **b :** a dog show

²bench *vt* **1 :** to furnish with benches **2 a :** to seat on a bench **b :** to remove from or keep out of a game **3 :** to exhibit (dogs) on a bench **~** *vi* **:** to form a bench by natural processes

bench·er \'ben-chər\ *n* **:** one that sits on or presides at a bench

bench mark *n* **1 :** a mark on a permanent object indicating elevation and serving as a reference in topographical surveys and tidal observations **2** *usu* **bench·mark :** a point of reference from which measurements of any sort may be made

bench show *n* **:** an exhibition of small animals in competition for prizes on the basis of points of physical conformation and condition

bench warrant *n* **:** a warrant issued by a presiding judge or by a court against a person guilty of contempt or indicted for a crime

¹bend \'bend\ *n* [ME, fr. MF *bende*, of Gmc origin; akin to OHG *binta, bant* band — more at BAND] **1** *heraldry* **:** a diagonal band **2 :** the half of a butt or a hide trimmed of the thinner parts **3** [ME, band, fr. OE *bend* fetter — more at BAND] **:** a knot by which one rope is fastened to another or to some object

²bend *vb* **bent** \'bent\ **bend·ing** [ME *benden*, fr. OE *bendan;* akin to OE *bend* fetter] *vt* **1 :** to constrain or strain to tension ⟨~ a bow⟩ **2 a :** to turn or force from straight or even to curved or angular **b :** to force back to an original straight or even condition **c :** to force from a proper shape **3 :** FASTEN ⟨~ a sail to its yard⟩ **4 :** to make submissive **:** SUBDUE **5 :** DETERMINE, RESOLVE ⟨*bent* on self-destruction⟩ **6 a :** to cause to turn from a straight course **:** DEFLECT **b :** GUIDE, DIRECT **c :** INCLINE, DISPOSE **7 :** to direct strenuously or with interest **:** APPLY **~** *vi* **1 :** to curve out of a straight line or position; *specif* **:** to incline the body in token of submission **2** *archaic* **:** to direct oneself **3 :** INCLINE, TEND **4 :** to work vigorously **syn** see CURVE

³bend *n* **1 :** the act or process of bending **:** the state of being bent **2 :** something that is bent: as **a :** a curved part of a stream **b :** WALES — usu. used in pl. **3** *pl but sing or pl in constr* **:** CAISSON DISEASE ⟨a case of the ~*s*⟩

ben·day \'ben-'dā\ *adj, often cap* [*Ben*jamin *Day* †1916 Am printer] **:** involving a process for adding shaded or tinted areas made up of dots for reproduction by line engraving — **benday** *vt*

bend·er \'ben-dər\ *n* **1 :** one that bends **2 :** SPREE

bend sinister *n, heraldry* **:** a bend drawn from sinister chief to dexter base

¹be·neath \bi-'nēth\ *adv* [ME *benethe*, fr. OE *beneothan*, fr. *be-* + *neothan* below; akin to OE *nithera* nether] **1 :** in or to a lower position **:** BELOW **2 :** directly under **:** UNDERNEATH

²beneath *prep* **1 a :** in or to a lower position than **:** BELOW **b :** directly under **c :** at the foot of **2 :** not suitable to the rank of **:** lowering to **3 :** under the control, pressure, or influence of

be·ne·di·ci·te \ˌben-ə-'dis-ət-ē\ *interj* [ME, fr. LL, bless, pl. imper. of *benedicere*] *obs* — used to express a wish

Ben·e·dick \'ben-ə-ˌdik\ *n* **:** a young lord and confirmed bachelor who marries Beatrice in Shakespeare's *Much Ado about Nothing*

ben·e·dict \'ben-ə-ˌdikt\ *n* [alter. of *Benedick*] **:** a newly married man who has long been a bachelor

Ben·e·dic·tine \ˌben-ə-'dik-tən, -ˌtēn\ *n* **:** a monk or a nun of one of the congregations following the rule of St. Benedict and devoted esp. to scholarship and liturgical worship — **Benedictine** *adj*

bene·dic·tion \ˌben-ə-'dik-shən\ *n* [ME *benediccioun*, fr. LL *benediction-, benedictio*, fr. *benedictus*, pp. of *benedicere* to bless, fr. L, to speak well of, fr. *bene* well + *dicere* to say] **1 :** the invocation of a blessing; *esp* **:** the short blessing with which public worship is concluded **2** *often cap* **:** a Roman Catholic or Anglo-Catholic devotion including the exposition of the eucharistic Host in the monstrance and the blessing of the people with it

bene·dic·to·ry \-'dik-t(ə-)rē\ *adj* **:** of or expressing benediction

Bene·dic·tus \-'dik-təs\ *n* [LL, blessed, fr. pp. of *benedicere;* fr. its first word] **1 :** a canticle from Mt 21:9 beginning "Blessed is he that cometh in the name of the Lord" **2 :** a canticle from Lk 1:68 beginning "Blessed be the Lord God of Israel"

bene·fac·tion \ˌben-ə-'fak-shən, 'ben-ə-ˌ\ *n* [LL *benefaction-, benefactio*, fr. L *bene factus*, pp. of *bene facere* to do good to, fr. *bene* + *facere* to do — more at DO] **1 :** the act of benefiting **2 :** a benefit conferred; *esp* **:** a charitable donation

bene·fac·tor \'ben-ə-ˌfak-tər\ *n* **:** one that confers a benefit; *specif* **:** one that makes a gift or bequest

bene·fac·tress \-trəs\ *n* **:** a female benefactor

be·nef·ic \bə-'nef-ik\ *adj* [L *beneficus*, fr. *bene* + *facere*] **:** BENEFICENT

ben·e·fice \'ben-ə-fəs\ *n* [ME, fr. MF, fr. ML *beneficium*, fr. L, favor, promotion, fr. *beneficus*] **1 :** an ecclesiastical office (as a rectory) to which the revenue from an endowment is attached **2 :** a feudal estate in lands **:** FIEF — **benefice** *vt*

be·nef·i·cence \bə-'nef-ə-sən(t)s\ *n* [L *beneficentia*, fr. *beneficus*] **1 :** the quality or state of being beneficent **2 :** BENEFACTION

be·nef·i·cent \-sənt\ *adj* [back-formation fr. *beneficence*] **1 :** doing or producing good; *specif* **:** performing acts of kindness and charity **2 :** productive of benefit — **be·nef·i·cent·ly** *adv*

ben·e·fi·cial \ˌben-ə-'fish-əl\ *adj* [L *beneficium* favor, benefit] **1 :** conferring benefits **:** ADVANTAGEOUS **2 :** receiving or entitling one to receive for one's own benefit — **ben·e·fi·cial·ly** \-'fish-ə-lē\ *adv* — **ben·e·fi·cial·ness** *n*

syn ADVANTAGEOUS, PROFITABLE: BENEFICIAL implies esp. promoting health or well-being; ADVANTAGEOUS stresses a choice or preference that brings superiority or greater success in attaining an end; PROFITABLE implies the yielding of useful or lucrative returns

ben·e·fi·ciary \-'fish-ē-ˌer-ē, -'fish-(ə-)rē\ *n* **:** one who receives something: as **a :** the person designated to receive the income of a trust estate **b :** the person named (as in an insurance policy) to receive proceeds or benefits accruing — **beneficiary** *adj*

¹ben·e·fit \'ben-ə-ˌfit\ *n* [ME, fr. AF *benfet*, fr. L *bene factum*, fr. neut. of *bene factus*] **1** *archaic* **:** an act of kindness **:** BENEFACTION **2 a :** something that promotes well-being **:** ADVANTAGE **b :** useful aid **:** HELP **3 a :** financial help in time of sickness, old age, or unemployment **b :** a payment or service provided for under an annuity, pension plan, or insurance policy **4 :** an entertainment or

social event to raise funds for a person or cause

²**benefit** *vb* **ben·e·fit·ed** *or* **ben·e·fit·ted; ben·e·fit·ing** *or* **ben·e·fit·ting** *vt* **:** to be useful or profitable to ⟨medicines that ~ mankind⟩ ~ *vi* **:** to receive benefit ⟨~ from experience⟩

benefit of clergy **1 :** clerical exemption from trial in a civil court **2 :** the ministration or sanction of the church

be·nev·o·lence \bə-'nev-(ə-)lən(t)s\ *n* **1 :** disposition to do good **2 a :** an act of kindness **b :** a generous gift **3 :** a compulsory levy by certain English kings on the asserted claim of prerogative

be·nev·o·lent \-(ə-)lənt\ *adj* [ME, fr. L *benevolent-, benevolens,* fr. *bene* + *volent-, volens,* prp. of *velle* to wish — more at WILL] **1 :** marked by or disposed to benevolence **2 :** marked by or suggestive of benign feelings **3 :** arising from benevolence — **be·nev·o·lent·ly** *adv* — **be·nev·o·lent·ness** *n*

Ben·gali \ben-'gȯ-lē, beŋ-\ *n* [Hindi *baṅgālī,* fr. *Baṅgāl* Bengal] **1 :** a native or resident of Bengal **2 :** the modern Indic language of Bengal — **Bengali** *adj*

ben·ga·line \'beŋ-gə-,lēn\ *n* [F, fr. *Bengal*] **:** a fabric with a crosswise rib made from the major textile fibers or a combination of these

Ben·gal light \,ben-,gȯl, ,beŋ-\ *n* **1 :** a blue light used formerly for signaling and illumination (as in theaters) **2 :** any of various colored lights or flares

be·night·ed \bi-'nīt-əd\ *adj* **1 :** overtaken by darkness or night **2 :** existing in a state of intellectual, moral, or social darkness **:** UNENLIGHTENED — **be·night·ed·ness** *n*

be·nign \bi-'nīn\ *adj* [ME *benigne,* fr. MF, fr. L *benignus,* fr. *bene* well + *gigni* to be born, pass. of *gignere* to beget] **1 :** of a gentle disposition **:** GRACIOUS **2 a :** manifesting kindness and gentleness **b :** FAVORABLE **3 :** of a mild character ⟨~ tumor⟩ **syn** see KIND — **be·nig·ni·ty** \-'nig-nət-ē\ *n* — **be·nign·ly** \-'nīn-lē\ *adv*

be·nig·nan·cy \bi-'nig-nən-sē\ *n* **:** benignant quality

be·nig·nant \-nənt\ *adj* [*benign* + *-ant* (as in *malignant*)] **1 :** KINDLY, GENTLE **2 :** FAVORABLE, BENEFICIAL **syn** see KIND — **be·nig·nant·ly** *adv*

ben·i·son \'ben-ə-sən, -zən\ *n* [ME *beneson,* fr. OF *beneiçon,* fr. LL *benediction-, benedictio*] **:** BLESSING, BENEDICTION

ben·ja·min \'ben-jə-mən\ *n* [by folk etymology fr. MF *benjoin*] **1 :** BENZOIN 1 **2 :** any of several wake-robins **3 :** BALSAM 2b

Benjamin *n* [Heb *Binyāmīn*] **:** a son of Jacob and ancestor of one of the tribes of Israel

ben·ne *or* **ben·ni** \'ben-ē\ *n* [of African origin; akin to Mandingo *bĕne* sesame] **:** SESAME 1

ben·net \'ben-ət\ *n* [short for *herb bennet,* fr. ME *herbe beneit,* fr. MF *herbe beneite,* fr. ML *herba benedicta,* lit., blessed herb] **:** either of two American avens (*Geum virginianum* and *G. canadense*)

¹**bent** \'bent\ *n* [ME, grassy place, bent grass, fr. OE *beonot-;* akin to OHG *binuz* rush] **1 :** unenclosed grassland **2 a** (1) **:** a reedy grass (2) **:** a stalk of stiff coarse grass **b :** any of a genus (*Agrostis*) including important chiefly perennial and rhizomatous pasture and lawn grasses with fine velvety or wiry herbage

²**bent** *adj* [ME, fr. pp. of *benden* to bend] **1 :** changed by bending out of an original straight or even condition **2 :** strongly inclined

³**bent** *n* [irreg. fr. ²*bend*] **1 a :** strong inclination or interest **:** BIAS **b :** a special inclination or capacity **2 :** capacity of endurance **3 :** a transverse framework to carry lateral as well as vertical loads **syn** see GIFT

Ben·tham·ism \'ben(t)-thə-,miz-əm\ *n* [Jeremy *Bentham* †1832 E philosopher] **:** the utilitarian philosophy of Bentham and his followers — **Ben·tham·ite** \-,mīt\ *n*

ben·thic \'ben(t)-thik\ *or* **ben·thal** \-thəl\ *adj* [*benthos*] **1 :** of, relating to, or occurring at the bottom of a body of water **2 :** of, relating to, or occurring in the depths of the ocean

ben·thon·ic \ben-'thän-ik\ *adj* [irreg. fr. *benthos*] **:** BENTHIC

ben·thos \'ben-,thäs\ *n* [Gk; akin to Gk *bathys* deep] **1 :** the bottom of the sea esp. in the deep parts of the oceans **2 :** organisms that live on or in the bottom of bodies of water

ben·ton·ite \'bent-ᵊn-,īt\ *n* [Fort *Benton,* Montana] **:** an absorptive and colloidal clay mineral used esp. as a filler (as in paper) or carrier (as of drugs) — **ben·ton·it·ic** \,bent-ᵊn-'it-ik\ *adj*

ben tro·va·to \,ben-trə-'vät-(,)ō\ *adj* [It, lit., well found] **:** characteristic or appropriate but not true

be·numb \bi-'nəm\ *vt* [ME *benomen,* fr. *benomen, benome,* pp. of *benimen* to deprive, fr. OE *beniman,* fr. *be-* + *niman* to take] **1 :** to make inactive **:** DEADEN **2 :** to make numb esp. by cold

benz- *or* **benzo-** *comb form* [ISV, fr. *benzoic acid*] **:** related to benzene or benzoic acid ⟨*benzo*phenone⟩ ⟨*benz*yl⟩

benz·al·de·hyde \ben-'zal-də-,hīd\ *n* [G *benzaldehyd,* fr. *benz-* + *aldehyd* aldehyde] **:** a colorless nontoxic aromatic liquid C_6H_5CHO found in essential oils (as of peach kernels)

Ben·ze·drine \'ben-zə-,drēn\ *trademark* — used for amphetamine

ben·zene \'ben-,zēn, ben-'\ *n* [ISV *benz* + *-ene*] **:** a colorless volatile flammable toxic liquid aromatic hydrocarbon C_6H_6 used in organic synthesis, as a solvent, and as a motor fuel — called also *benzol* — **ben·ze·noid** \'ben-zə-,nȯid\ *adj*

benzene ring *n* **:** a structural arrangement of atoms held to exist in benzene and other aromatic compounds and marked by six carbon atoms linked by alternate single and double bonds in a planar symmetrical hexagon with each carbon attached to hydrogen in benzene itself or to other atoms or groups in substituted benzenes — called also *benzene nucleus;* compare META- 4b, ORTH- 3b, PARA- 2b

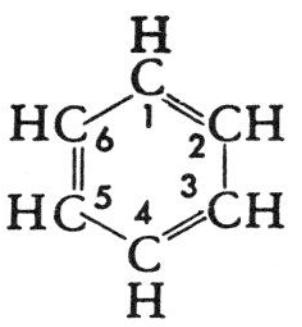

formula for benzene ring

ben·zi·dine \'ben-zə-,dēn\ *n* [prob. fr. G *benzidin,* fr. *benzin* + *-idin* -idine] **:** a crystalline base $C_{12}H_{12}N_2$ prepared from nitrobenzene and used esp. in making dyes

ben·zine \'ben-,zēn, ben-'\ *n* [G *benzin,* fr. *benz-*] **1 :** BENZENE **2 :** any of various volatile flammable petroleum distillates used esp. as solvents or as motor fuels

ben·zo·ate \'ben-zə-,wāt\ *n* **:** a salt or ester of benzoic acid

benzoate of soda **:** SODIUM BENZOATE

ben·zo·caine \'ben-zə-,kān\ *n* [ISV] **:** a white crystalline ester $C_9H_{11}NO_2$ used as a local anesthetic

ben·zo·ic acid \,ben-,zō-ik-\ *n* [ISV, fr. *benzoin*] **:** a white crystalline acid C_6H_5COOH found naturally (as in benzoin or in cranberries) or made synthetically (as by oxidation of toluene) and used esp. as a preservative in medicine and in organic synthesis

ben·zo·in \'ben-zə-wən, -,wēn, -,zōin\ *n* [MF *benjoin,* fr. OCatal *benjuí,* fr. Ar *lubān jāwī,* lit., frankincense of Java] **1 :** a hard fragrant yellowish balsamic resin from trees (genus *Styrax*) of southeastern Asia used esp. in medicine, as a fixative in perfumes, and as incense **2 :** a white crystalline hydroxy ketone $C_{14}H_{12}O_2$ made from benzaldehyde **3 a :** a tree yielding benzoin **b :** SPICEBUSH 1

ben·zol \'ben-,zȯl, -,zōl\ *n* [G, fr. *benz-* + *-ol*] **:** BENZENE; *also* **:** a mixture of benzene and other aromatic hydrocarbons

ben·zo·phe·none \,ben-(,)zō-fi-'nōn, -'fē-,nōn\ *n* [ISV] **:** a colorless crystalline ketone $C_{13}H_{10}O$ used chiefly in perfumery

ben·zo·yl \'ben-zə-,wil\ *n* [G, fr. *benzoësäure* benzoic acid + Gk *hylē* matter, lit., wood] **:** the radical C_6H_5CO- of benzoic acid

ben·zyl \'ben-,zēl, -zəl\ *n* [ISV *benz-* + *-yl*] **:** a univalent radical $C_6H_5CH_2$ derived from toluene by removal of one hydrogen atom from the side chain — **ben·zyl·ic** \ben-'zil-ik\ *adj*

Be·o·wulf \'bā-ə-,wu̇lf\ *n* **:** a Geatish warrior and hero of the Old English poem *Beowulf*

be·paint \bi-'pānt\ *vt, archaic* **:** TINGE

be·queath \bi-'kwēth, -'kwē*th*\ *vt* [ME *bequethen,* fr. OE *becwethan,* fr. *be-* + *cwethan* to say] **1 :** to give or leave by will — used esp. of personalty **2 :** to hand down — **be·queath·al** \-əl\ *n*

be·quest \bi-'kwest\ *n* [ME, irreg. fr. *bequethen*] **1 :** the action of bequeathing **2 :** something bequeathed **:** LEGACY

be·rate \bi-'rāt\ *vt* **:** to chide vehemently **syn** see SCOLD

Ber·ber \'bər-bər\ *n* [Ar *Barbar*] **1 :** a member of a Caucasoid people of northern Africa west of Tripoli **2 a :** a branch of the Afro-Asiatic language family comprising languages spoken by minorities in northern Africa **b :** any one of these languages

ber·ceuse \be(ə)r-'sə(r)z\ *n, pl* **ber·ceuses** \-'sə(r)z(-əz)\ [F] **1 :** LULLABY **2 :** a musical composition of a tranquil nature

be·reave \bi-'rēv\ *vt* **be·reaved** *or* **be·reft** \-'reft\ **be·reav·ing** [ME *bereven,* fr. OE *berēafian,* fr. *be-* + *rēafian* to rob — more at REAVE] **1 :** to deprive esp. by death **:** STRIP, DISPOSSESS ⟨*bereft* of hope⟩ **2** *obs* **:** to take away — **be·reave·ment** \-'rēv-mənt\ *n*

Ber·e·ni·ce's Hair \,ber-ə-,nī-sēz-\ *n* **:** COMA BERENICES

be·ret \bə-'rā\ *n* [F *berret,* fr. Prov] **:** a soft flat visorless wool cap

berg \'bərg\ *n* **:** ICEBERG

ber·ga·mot \'bər-gə-,mät\ *n* [F *bergamote,* fr. It *bergamotta,* of Turkic origin] **1 :** a pear-shaped orange (*Citrus bergamia*) whose rind yields an essential oil used in perfumery **2 :** any of several mints (esp. genera *Mentha* and *Monarda*)

beri·beri \,ber-ē-'ber-ē\ *n* [Sinhalese *bæribæri*] **:** a deficiency disease marked by inflammatory or degenerative changes of the nerves, digestive system, and heart and caused by a lack of or inability to assimilate thiamine

Be·ring time \'bi(ə)r-iŋ-, 'be(ə)r-\ *n* [*Bering* sea] **:** the time of the 11th time zone west of Greenwich that includes western Alaska and the Aleutian islands

Berke·le·ian *or* **Berke·ley·an** \'bär-klē-ən, 'bər-; bär-', ,bər-'\ *adj* **:** of or relating to Bishop Berkeley or his system of philosophical idealism — **Berkeleian** *n* — **Berke·le·ian·ism** \-ə-,niz-əm\ *n*

berke·li·um \'bər-klē-əm, ,bər-'kē-lē-əm\ *n* [NL, fr. *Berkeley,* Calif.] **:** a radioactive metallic element produced by bombarding americium 241 with helium ions — see ELEMENT table

Berk·shire \'bərk-,shi(ə)r, -shər\ *n* [*Berkshire,* England] **:** any of a breed of medium-sized black swine with white markings

ber·lin \(,)bər-'lin\ *n* [F *berline,* fr. *Berlin,* Germany] **:** a 4-wheeled 2-seated covered carriage with a hooded rear seat

berm *or* **berme** \'bərm\ *n* [F *berme,* fr. D *berm* strip of ground along a dike; akin to ME *brimme* brim] **:** a narrow shelf, path, or ledge

Ber·mu·da grass \bər-'myüd-ə-, *esp South* -'müd-\ *n* [*Bermuda* islands, No. Atlantic] **:** a trailing stoloniferous southern European grass (*Cynodon dactylon*)

Bermuda rig *n* **:** a fore-and-aft rig marked by a triangular sail and a mast with an extreme rake

Bermuda shorts *n pl* **:** knee-length walking shorts

Ber·nese mountain dog \,bər-,nēz-, -,nēs-\ *n* [*Bern,* Switzerland] **:** any of a Swiss breed of large powerful long-coated black dogs with brown and white markings formerly used for draft

ber·ried \'ber-ēd\ *adj* **1 :** furnished with berries **:** BACCATE **2 :** bearing eggs ⟨a ~ lobster⟩

¹**ber·ry** \'ber-ē, *esp in compounds in which a stressed syllable immediately precedes Brit often & US sometimes* b(ə-)rē\ *n* [ME *berye,* fr. OE *berie;* akin to OHG *beri* berry] **1 a :** a pulpy and usu. edible fruit (as a strawberry, raspberry, or checkerberry) of small size irrespective of its structure **b :** a simple fruit (as a currant, grape, tomato, or banana) with a pulpy or fleshy pericarp **c :** the dry seed of some plants (as coffee) **2 :** an egg of a fish or lobster

²**ber·ry** \'ber-ē\ *vi* **1 :** to bear or produce berries ⟨~*ing* wheat⟩ **2 :** to gather or seek berries

ber·ry·like \-,līk\ *adj* **1 :** resembling a berry esp. in size or structure **2 :** being small and rounded **:** COCCOID

ber·seem \(,)bər-'sēm\ *n* [Ar *barsīm,* fr. Copt *bersīm*] **:** a succulent clover (*Trifolium alexandrinum*) cultivated as a forage plant and green-manure crop esp. in the alkaline soils of the Nile valley and in the southwestern U.S. — called also *Egyptian clover*

¹**ber·serk** \bə(r)-'sərk, ,bər-, -'zərk; 'bər-,\ *or* **ber·serk·er** \-ər\ *n* [ON *berserkr,* fr. *björn* bear + *serkr* shirt] **:** an ancient Scandinavian warrior frenzied in battle and held to be invulnerable

²**berserk** *adj* **:** FRENZIED, CRAZED — **berserk** *adv*

¹**berth** \'bərth\ *n* [prob. fr. ²*bear* + *-th*] **1 :** sufficient distance for maneuvering a ship **2 :** the place where a ship lies when at anchor or at a wharf **3 :** a place to sit or sleep esp. on a ship or vehicle **:** ACCOMMODATION **4 a :** a billet on a ship **b :** JOB, POSITION

²**berth** *vt* **1 :** to bring into a berth **2 :** to allot a berth to ~ *vi* **:** to come into a berth

ber·tha \'bər-thə\ *n* [F *berthe,* fr. *Berthe* (Bertha) †783 queen of the Franks] **:** a wide round collar covering the shoulders

Ber·til·lon system \'bərt-ᵊl-,än-, 'bert-ē-,(y)ōⁿ-\ *n* [Alphonse *Bertillon* †1914 F criminologist] **:** a system of identification of persons by a description based on anthropometric measurements, standardized photographs, notation of markings, color, thumb line impressions, and other data

ber·yl \'ber-əl\ *n* [ME, fr. OF *beril,* fr. L *beryllus,* fr. Gk *bēryllos,* of Indic origin; akin to Skt *vaiḍūrya* cat's-eye] **:** a mineral $Be_3Al_2Si_6O_{18}$ consisting of a silicate of beryllium and aluminum of great hardness and occurring in green, bluish green, yellow, pink, or white hexagonal prisms

be·ryl·li·um \bə-'ril-ē-əm\ *n* [NL, fr. Gk *bēryllion,* dim. of *bēryllos*] **:** a steel-gray light strong brittle toxic bivalent metallic element — see ELEMENT table

be·seech \bi-'sēch\ *vb* **be·sought** \-'sȯt\ *or* **be·seeched; be·seech·ing** [ME *besechen*, fr. *be-* + *sechen* to seek] *vt* **1 :** to ask earnestly for **:** BEG **2 :** to request earnestly **:** IMPLORE ~ *vi* **:** to make supplication **syn** see BEG

be·seem \bi-'sēm\ *vi, archaic* **:** to be fitting or becoming ~ *vt, archaic* **:** to be suitable to **:** BEFIT

be·set \bi-'set\ *vt* **1 :** to set or stud with or as if with ornaments **2 :** TROUBLE, HARASS **3 a :** to set upon **:** ASSAIL **b :** to hem in **:** SURROUND — **be·set·ment** \-mənt\ *n*

be·set·ting *adj* **:** constantly present or attacking **:** OBSESSIVE

be·show \bi-'shō\ *n* [Makah *bishowk*] **:** SABLEFISH

be·shrew \bi-'shrü, *esp South* -'srü\ *vt, archaic* **:** CURSE

¹be·side \bi-'sīd\ *adv* [ME, adv. & prep., fr. OE *be sīdan* at or to the side, fr. *be* at (fr. *bī*) + *sīdan*, dat. & acc. of *sīde* side — more at BY] **1** *archaic* **:** NEARBY **2** *archaic* **:** BESIDES

²beside *prep* **1 a :** by the side of **b :** in comparison with **c :** on a par with **2 :** BESIDES **3 :** wide of ⟨~ the point⟩ — **beside oneself :** in a state of extreme excitement

¹be·sides \bi-'sīdz\ *prep* **1 :** other than **:** EXCEPT **2 :** in addition to

²besides *adv* **1 :** in addition **:** ALSO **2 :** MOREOVER, FURTHERMORE

³besides *adj* **:** ELSE

be·siege \bi-'sēj\ *vt* **1 :** to surround with armed forces **2 a :** to press with requests **:** IMPORTUNE **b :** BESET — **be·sieg·er** *n*

be·smear \bi-'smi(ə)r\ *vt* **:** SMEAR

be·smirch \bi-'smərch\ *vt* **:** SULLY, SOIL

be·som \'bē-zəm\ *n* [ME *beseme*, fr. OE *besma;* akin to OHG *besmo* broom] **1 :** BROOM 2; *esp* **:** one made of twigs **2 :** BROOM 1a

be·sot \bi-'sät\ *vt* **be·sot·ted; be·sot·ting** [*be-* + *sot* (to stultify)] **:** to make dull or stupid **:** STUPEFY; *esp* **:** to muddle with drunkenness or infatuation — **be·sot·ted** \-'sät-əd\ *adj*

be·spat·ter \bi-'spat-ər\ *vt* **:** SPATTER

be·speak \bi-'spēk\ *vt* **1 :** to hire, engage, or claim beforehand **2 :** to speak to esp. with formality **:** ADDRESS **3 :** REQUEST **4 a :** INDICATE, SIGNIFY **b :** to show beforehand **:** FORETELL

be·spoke \bi-'spōk\ *or* **be·spo·ken** \-'spō-kən\ *adj* [pp. of *bespeak*] **1** *Brit* **a :** CUSTOM-MADE **b :** dealing in or producing custom-made articles **2** *dial* **:** ENGAGED

be·sprent \bi-'sprent\ *adj* [ME *bespreynt*, fr. pp. of *besprengen* to besprinkle, fr. OE *besprengan*] *archaic* **:** sprinkled over

be·sprin·kle \bi-'spriŋ-kəl\ *vt* [ME *besprengeln*, freq. of *besprengen*] **:** SPRINKLE

Bes·se·mer converter \,bes-ə-mər-\ *n* [Sir Henry *Bessemer* †1898 E engineer] **:** the furnace used in the Bessemer process

Bessemer process *n* **:** a process of making steel from pig iron by burning out carbon and other impurities by means of a blast of air forced through the molten metal

¹best \'best\ *adj, superlative of* GOOD [ME, fr. OE *betst;* akin to OE *bōt* remedy] **1 :** excelling all others **2 :** most productive of good or of advantage, utility, or satisfaction **3 :** LARGEST, MOST

²best *adv, superlative of* WELL **1 :** in the best way **2 :** MOST

³best *n* **1 :** the best state or part **2 :** one that is best ⟨the ~ falls short⟩ **3 :** one's maximum effort ⟨do your ~⟩ **4 :** best clothes

⁴best *vt* **:** to get the better of **:** OUTDO

¹be·stead *also* **be·sted** \bi-'sted\ *adj* [ME *bested*, fr. *be-* + *sted*, pp. of *steden* to place] **1** *archaic* **:** PLACED, SITUATED **2** *archaic* **:** BESET

²bestead *vt* **be·stead·ed; bestead; be·stead·ing** [*be-* + *stead*] **1** *archaic* **:** HELP **2** *archaic* **:** to be useful to **:** AVAIL

bes·tial \'bes(h)-chəl, 'bēs(h)-\ *adj* [ME, fr. MF, fr. L *bestialis*, fr. *bestia* beast] **1 a :** of or relating to beasts **b :** resembling a beast **2 a :** lacking intelligence or reason **b :** marked by base or inhuman instincts or desires **:** BRUTAL — **bes·tial·ize** \-chə-,līz\ *vt* — **bes·tial·ly** \-chə-lē\ *adv*

bes·ti·al·i·ty \,bes(h)-chē-'al-ət-ē, ,bēs(h)-\ *n* **1 :** the condition or status of a lower animal **2 :** display or gratification of bestial traits or impulses **3 :** sexual relations between a human being and a lower animal

bes·ti·ary \'bes(h)-chē-,er-ē, 'bēs(h)-\ *n* [ML *bestiarium*, fr. L, neut. of *bestiarius* of beasts, fr. *bestia*] **:** a medieval allegorical or moralizing work on the appearance and habits of animals

be·stir \bi-'stər\ *vt* **:** to stir up **:** rouse to action

best man *n* **:** the principal groomsman at a wedding

be·stow \bi-'stō\ *vt* [ME *bestowen*, fr. *be-* + *stowe* place — more at STOW] **1 :** USE, APPLY **2 a :** PUT, PLACE **b :** DEPOSIT, STOW **3 :** QUARTER, LODGE **4 :** to present as a gift **:** CONFER — usu. used with *on* or *upon* **syn** see GIVE — **be·stow·al** \-'stō(-ə)l\ *n*

be·strew \bi-'strü\ *vt* **1 :** STREW **2 :** to lie scattered over

be·stride \bi-'strīd\ *vt* **1 :** to ride, sit, or stand astride **:** STRADDLE **2 :** to tower over **:** DOMINATE **3** *archaic* **:** to stride across

best seller *n* **:** an article (as a book) whose sales are among the highest of its class

¹bet \'bet\ *n* [origin unknown] **1 a :** something that is laid, staked, or pledged typically between two parties on the outcome of a contest or any contingent issue **:** WAGER **b :** the act of giving such a pledge **2 :** something to wager on

²bet *vb* **bet** *or* **bet·ted; bet·ting** *vt* **1 :** to stake on the outcome of an issue **2 a :** to maintain with or as if with a bet **b :** to make a bet with ~ *vi* **:** to lay a bet

¹be·ta \'bāt-ə, 'bēt-\ *n* [Gk *bēta*, of Sem origin; akin to Heb *bēth*- beth] **1 :** the second letter of the Greek alphabet — symbol Β or β **2 :** the second brightest star of a constellation **3 a :** BETA PARTICLE **b :** BETA RAY

²beta *or* **β-** *adj* **:** second in position in the structure of an organic molecule from a particular group or atom ⟨~ substitution⟩

be·ta·ine \'bēt-ə-,ēn\ *n* [ISV, fr. L *beta* beet] **:** a sweet crystalline quaternary ammonium salt $C_5H_{12}NO_3$ occurring esp. in beet juice; *also* **:** its hydrate $C_5H_{13}NO_3$ or the chloride of this

be·take \bi-'tāk\ *vt* **1** *archaic* **:** COMMIT **2 :** to cause (oneself) to go

beta particle *n* **:** an electron or positron ejected from the nucleus of an atom during radioactive decay

beta ray *n* **1 :** BETA PARTICLE **2 :** a stream of beta particles

be·ta·tron \'bāt-ə-,trän, 'bēt-\ *n* [ISV] **:** an accelerator in which electrons are propelled by the inductive action of a rapidly varying magnetic field

be·tel \'bēt-ᵊl\ *n* [Pg, fr. Tamil *verrilai*] **:** a climbing pepper (*Piper betle*) whose dried leaves are chewed together with betel nut and lime as a stimulant masticatory esp. by southeastern Asians

Be·tel·geuse \'bet-ᵊl-,jüz, 'bēt-, -,jə(r)z\ *n* [F *Bételgeuse*, fr. Ar *bayt al-jawzā'* Gemini, lit., the house of the twins (confused with Orion & Betelgeuse)] **:** a variable red giant star of the first magnitude near one shoulder of Orion

betel nut *n* **:** the astringent seed of the betel palm

betel palm *n* **:** an Asiatic pinnate-leaved palm (*Areca catechu*) with an orange-colored drupe with an outer fibrous husk

bête noire \,bāt-nə-'wär, bāt-'nwär\ *n, pl* **bêtes noires** \-'wär(z), -'nwär(z)\ [F, lit., black beast] **:** a person or thing strongly detested or avoided **:** BUGBEAR

beth \'bāt(h), 'bās\ *n* [Heb *bēth*, fr. *bayith* house] **:** the 2d letter of the Hebrew alphabet — symbol ב

beth·el \'beth-əl\ *n* [Heb *bēth' ēl* house of God] **1 :** a hallowed spot **2 :** a chapel for Nonconformists or seamen

be·think \bi-'thiŋk\ *vt* **1 a :** REMEMBER, RECALL **b :** to cause (oneself) to be reminded **2 :** to cause (oneself) to consider

be·tide \bi-'tīd\ *vt* **:** to happen to **:** BEFALL ~ *vi* **:** BEFALL, HAPPEN

be·times \bi-'tīmz\ *adv* **1 :** in good time **:** EARLY **2** *archaic* **:** in a short time **:** SPEEDILY

bê·tise \bā-'tēz\ *n, pl* **bê·tises** \-'tēz\ [F] **1 :** FOLLY, STUPIDITY **2 :** an act of foolishness or stupidity

be·to·ken \bi-'tō-kən\ *vt* **be·to·ken·ing** \-'tōk-(ə-)niŋ\ **1 :** to give evidence of **:** SHOW **2 :** FORESHOW, PRESAGE

bet·o·ny \'bet-ᵊn-ē\ *n* [ME *betone*, fr. OF *betoine*, fr. L *vettonica*, *betonica*, fr. *Vettones*, an ancient people inhabiting the Iberian peninsula] **1 :** any of several woundworts (genus *Stachys*) **2 :** any of several germanders (genus *Teucrium*)

be·tray \bi-'trā\ *vb* [ME *betrayen*, fr. *be-* + *trayen* to betray, fr. OF *traïr*, fr. L *tradere*] *vt* **1 :** to lead astray; *esp* **:** SEDUCE **2 :** to deliver to an enemy by treachery **3 :** to fail or desert esp. in time of need **4 a :** to reveal unintentionally **b :** SHOW, INDICATE **c :** to disclose in violation of confidence ~ *vi* **:** to prove false **syn** see REVEAL — **be·tray·al** \-'trā(-ə)l\ *n* — **be·tray·er** \-'trā-ər\ *n*

be·troth \bi-'träth, -'trȯth, -'trōth\ *vt* [ME *betrouthen*, fr. *be-* + *trouthe* truth, troth] **:** to promise to marry or give in marriage

be·troth·al \-əl\ *n* **1 :** the act of betrothing or fact of being betrothed **2 :** a mutual promise or contract for a future marriage

be·trothed *n* **:** the person to whom one is betrothed

bet·ta \'bet-ə\ *n* [NL] **:** any of a genus (*Betta*) of small brilliantly colored long-finned freshwater fishes of southeastern Asia

¹bet·ter \'bet-ər\ *adj, comparative of* GOOD [ME *bettre*, fr. OE *betera;* akin to OE *bōt* remedy, Skt *bhadra* fortunate] **1 :** more than half **2 :** improved in health **3 :** of high quality ⟨ladies' ~ dresses⟩

²better *adv, comparative of* WELL **1 :** in a more excellent manner **2 a :** to a higher or greater degree **b :** MORE

³better *n* **1 a :** something better **b :** a superior esp. in merit or rank **2 :** ADVANTAGE, VICTORY ⟨get the ~ of him⟩

⁴better *vt* **1 :** to make better: as **a :** AMELIORATE **b :** to improve the condition of **2 :** to surpass in excellence **:** EXCEL ~ *vi* **:** to become better **syn** see IMPROVE

bet·ter·ment \-mənt\ *n* **1 :** a making or becoming better **2 :** an improvement that adds to the value of a property or facility

bet·tor *or* **bet·ter** \'bet-ər\ *n* **:** one that bets

¹be·tween \bi-'twēn\ *prep* [ME *betwene*, prep. & adv., fr. OE *betwēonum*, fr. *be-* + *-twēonum* (dat. pl.) (akin to Goth *tweihnai* two each); akin to OE *twā* two] **1 :** by the common action of **:** in common to ⟨ate six ~ them⟩ **2 :** in the time, space, or interval that separates **3 :** in point of comparison of ⟨not much to choose ~ the two coats⟩ **4 :** from one to the other or another of ⟨the bond ~ the two men⟩

²between *adv* **:** in an intermediate space or interval

be·tween·brain \-,brān\ *n* **:** DIENCEPHALON

be·tween·times \-,tīmz\ *adv* **:** at or during intervals

be·tween·whiles \bi-'twēn-,hwīlz, -,wīlz\ *adv* **:** BETWEENTIMES

be·twixt \bi-'twikst\ *adv or prep* [ME, fr. OE *betwux*, fr. *be-* + *-twux* (akin to Goth *tweihnai*)] *archaic* **:** BETWEEN

Beu·lah \'byü-lə\ *n* **:** a land of rest and quiet near the end of life's journey in Bunyan's *Pilgrim's Progress*

¹bev·el \'bev-əl\ *adj* **:** OBLIQUE, BEVELED

²bevel *n* [(assumed) MF, fr. OF *baïf* with open mouth, fr. *baer* to yawn — more at ABEYANCE] **1 a :** the angle that one surface or line makes with another when they are not at right angles **b :** the slant or inclination of such a surface or line **c :** the part of printing type extending from face to shoulder **2 :** an instrument consisting of two rules or arms jointed together and opening to any angle for drawing angles or adjusting surfaces to be given a bevel

³bevel *vb* **bev·eled** *or* **bev·elled; bev·el·ing** *or* **bev·el·ling** \'bev-(ə-)liŋ\ *vt* **:** to cut or shape to a bevel ~ *vi* **:** INCLINE, SLANT

bevel gear *n* **:** one of a pair of toothed wheels whose working surfaces are inclined to nonparallel axes

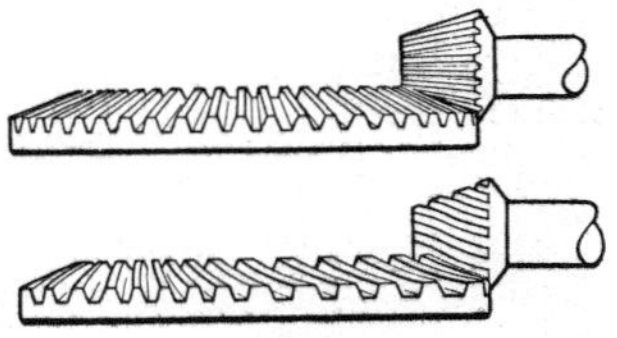

bevel gears

bev·er·age \'bev-(ə-)rij\ *n* [ME, fr. MF *bevrage*, fr. *beivre* to drink, fr. L *bibere* — more at POTABLE] **:** liquid for drinking; *esp* **:** such liquid other than water

bevy \'bev-ē\ *n* [ME *bevey*] **1 :** a large group or collection **2 :** a group of animals and esp. quail together

be·wail \bi-'wā(ə)l\ *vt* **1 :** to wail over **2 :** to express deep regret for **syn** see DEPLORE

be·ware \bi-'wa(ə)r, -'we(ə)r\ *vb* [ME *been war*, fr. *been* to be + *war* careful — more at BE, WARE] *vi* **:** to be on one's guard ⟨~ of the dog⟩ ~ *vt* **1 :** to take care of **2 :** to be wary of

be·wil·der \bi-'wil-dər\ *vt* **be·wil·der·ing** \-d(ə-)riŋ\ **1 :** to cause to lose one's bearings **2 :** to perplex or confuse esp. by a complexity, variety, or multitude of objects or considerations **syn** see PUZZLE — **be·wil·der·ment** \-dər-mənt\ *n*

be·witch \bi-'wich\ *vt* **1 a :** to influence or affect esp. injuriously by witchcraft **b :** to cast a spell over **2 :** CHARM, FASCINATE ~ *vi* **:** to act in a way that bewitches — **be·witch·ery** \-(ə-)rē\ *n*

be·witch·ment \-'wich-mənt\ *n* **1 a :** the act or power of bewitching **b :** a spell that bewitches **2 :** the state of being bewitched

be·wray \bi-'rā\ *vt* [ME *bewreyen*, fr. *be-* + *wreyen* to accuse, fr. OE *wrēgan*] *archaic* **:** DIVULGE, BETRAY

bey \'bā\ *n* [Turk, gentleman, chief] **1 a :** a provincial governor in the Ottoman Empire **b :** the former native ruler of Tunis or Tunisia **2** — formerly used as a courtesy title in Turkey and Egypt

¹be·yond \bē-'änd\ *adv* [ME, prep. & adv., fr. OE *begeondan*, fr. *be-* + *geondan* beyond, fr. *geond* yond — more at YOND] **1 :** on or to the farther side **:** FARTHER **2 :** in addition **:** BESIDES

²beyond *prep* **1 :** on or to the farther side of **2 :** out of the reach or sphere of **3 :** in addition to **:** BESIDES

³beyond *n* **1 :** something that lies beyond **2 :** something that lies outside the scope of ordinary experience; *specif* **:** ²HEREAFTER

bez·ant \'bez-ᵊnt, bə-'zant\ *n* [ME *besant*, fr. MF, fr. ML *Byzantius* Byzantine, fr. *Byzantium*, ancient name of Istanbul] **1 :** SOLIDUS 1 **2 :** a flat disk used in architectural ornament

bez·el \'bez-əl\ *n* [prob. F dial., alter. of F *biseau*] **1 :** a sloping edge or face esp. on a cutting tool **2 a :** the top part of a ring **b :** the oblique side or face of a cut gem; *specif* **:** the upper faceted portion of a brilliant projecting from the setting

be·zique \bə-'zēk\ *n* [F *bésique*] **:** a card game similar to pinochle that is played with a pack of 64 cards

be·zoar \'bē-,zō(ə)r, -,zȯ(ə)r\ *n* [F *bézoard*, fr. Sp *bezoar*, fr. Ar *bāzahr*, fr. Per *pād-zahr*, fr. *pād* protecting (against) + *zahr* poison] **:** any of various concretions found chiefly in the alimentary organs of ruminants and formerly believed to possess magical properties

bhak·ti \'bək-tē\ *n* [Skt, lit., portion] **:** devotion to a deity constituting a way to salvation in Hinduism

bhang \'baŋ\ *n* [Hindi *bhāg*] **1 a :** HEMP 1 **b :** the leaves and flowering tips of hemp **:** CANNABIS **2 :** any of several narcotic and intoxicant products obtained from bhang

B–horizon *n* **:** a soil layer immediately beneath the A-horizon from which it obtains organic matter chiefly by illuviation and is usu. distinguished by less weathering

¹bi- *prefix* [ME, fr. L; akin to OE *twi-*] **1 a :** two ⟨*bi*parous⟩ **b :** coming or occurring every two ⟨*bi*monthly⟩ ⟨*bi*weekly⟩ **c :** into two parts ⟨*bi*sect⟩ **2 a :** twice **:** doubly **:** on both sides ⟨*bi*convex⟩ ⟨*bi*serrate⟩ **b :** coming or occurring two times ⟨*bi*weekly⟩ — often disapproved in this sense because of the likelihood of confusion with sense 1b; compare SEMI- **3 :** between, involving, or affecting two (specified) symmetrical parts ⟨*bi*aural⟩ **4 a :** containing one (specified) constituent in double the proportion of the other constituent or in double the ordinary proportion ⟨*bi*carbonate⟩ **b :** DI- 2 ⟨*bi*phenyl⟩

²bi- *or* **bio-** *comb form* [Gk, fr. *bios* mode of life — more at QUICK] **:** life **:** living organisms or tissue ⟨*bio*ecology⟩ ⟨*bio*luminescence⟩

bi·an·nu·al \(')bī-'an-yə(-wə)l\ *adj* **:** occurring twice a year — **bi·an·nu·al·ly** \-ē\ *adv*

¹bi·as \'bī-əs\ *n* [MF *biais*] **1 :** a line diagonal to the grain of a fabric; *esp* **:** a line at a 45° angle to the selvage often utilized in the cutting of garments for smoother fit **2 a :** an inclination of temperament or outlook; *esp* **:** PREJUDICE **b :** BENT, TENDENCY **c :** a tendency of a statistical estimate to deviate in one direction from a true value **3 a :** a peculiarity in the shape of a bowl that causes it to swerve when rolled on the green **b :** the tendency of a bowl to swerve or the impulse causing this tendency; *also* **:** the swerve of the bowl **4 :** an unvarying component of the electric potential difference between a given element of an electron tube and the cathode **syn** see PREDILECTION

²bias *adj* **:** DIAGONAL, SLANTING — used chiefly of fabrics and their cut — **bi·as·ness** *n*

³bias *adv* **1 :** DIAGONALLY ⟨cut cloth ~⟩ **2** *obs* **:** AWRY

⁴bias *vt* **bi·ased** *or* **bi·assed; bi·as·ing** *or* **bi·as·sing 1 :** to give a bias to **:** PREJUDICE **2 :** to apply a slight negative or positive voltage to **syn** see INCLINE

bi·au·ral \(')bī-'ȯr-əl\ *var of* BINAURAL

bi·au·ric·u·late \,bī-ȯ-'rik-yə-lət\ *adj* **:** having two auricles

bi·ax·i·al \(')bī-'ak-sē-əl\ *adj* **:** having two axes — **bi·ax·i·al·ly** \-ə-lē\ *adv*

¹bib \'bib\ *vb* **bibbed; bib·bing** [ME *bibben*] *archaic* **:** DRINK

²bib *n* **1 :** a cloth or plastic shield tied under a child's chin to protect the clothes **2 :** the part of an apron or of overalls extending above the waist in front — **bibbed** \'bibd\ *adj* — **bib·less** \'bib-ləs\ *adj*

bib and tucker *n* **:** an outfit of clothing

bibb \'bib\ *n* [alter. of ²*bib*] **:** a side piece of timber bolted to the hounds of a ship's mast to support the trestletrees

bib·ber \'bib-ər\ *n* **:** TIPPLER — **bib·bery** \'bib-ə-rē\ *n*

bib·cock \'bib-,käk\ *also* **bibb cock** *n* **:** a stopcock or faucet having a bent-down nozzle

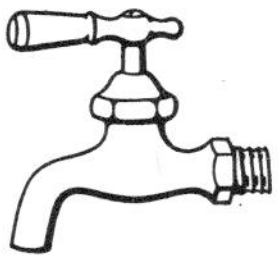

bibcock

bi·be·lot \,bib-(ə-)'lō, ,bēb-\ *n, pl* **bibelots** \-'lō(z)\ [F] **1 :** a small household ornament or decorative object **:** TRINKET **2 :** a miniature book esp. of elegant design or format

bi·ble \'bī-bəl\ *n, often attrib* [ME, fr. OF, fr. ML *biblia*, fr. Gk, pl. of *biblion* book, dim. of *byblos* papyrus, book, fr. *Byblos*, ancient Phoenician city from which papyrus was exported] **1** *cap* **:** the sacred scriptures of Christians comprising the Old Testament and the New Testament **2** *cap* **:** the sacred scriptures of Judaism or of some other religion **3** *obs* **:** BOOK **4** *cap* **:** a copy or an edition of the Bible **5 :** a publication that is preeminent esp. in authoritativeness **6 :** something suggesting a book: as **a :** a small holystone **b :** OMASUM

THE BOOKS OF THE OLD TESTAMENT

DOUAY VERSION	AUTHORIZED VERSION	DOUAY VERSION	AUTHORIZED VERSION
Genesis	Genesis	Wisdom	
Exodus	Exodus	Ecclesiasticus	
Leviticus	Leviticus	Isaias	Isaiah
Numbers	Numbers	Jeremias	Jeremiah
Deuteronomy	Deuteronomy	Lamentations	Lamentations
Josue	Joshua	Baruch	
Judges	Judges	Ezechiel	Ezekiel
Ruth	Ruth	Daniel	Daniel
1 & 2 Kings	1 & 2 Samuel	Osee	Hosea
3 & 4 Kings	1 & 2 Kings	Joel	Joel
1 & 2 Paralipomenon	1 & 2 Chronicles	Amos	Amos
		Abdias	Obadiah
1 Esdras	Ezra	Jonas	Jonah
2 Esdras	Nehemiah	Micheas	Micah
Tobias		Nahum	Nahum
Judith		Habacuc	Habakkuk
Esther	Esther	Sophonias	Zephaniah
Job	Job	Aggeus	Haggai
Psalms	Psalms	Zacharias	Zechariah
Proverbs	Proverbs	Malachias	Malachi
Ecclesiastes	Ecclesiastes	1 & 2 Machabees	
Canticle of Canticles	Song of Solomon		

JEWISH SCRIPTURES

Law	*Prophets:*	Jeremiah	Ruth
Genesis	*Former Prophets*	Ezekiel	Lamentations
Exodus	Joshua	The Twelve	Ecclesiastes
Leviticus	Judges	*Hagiographa*	Esther
Numbers	1 & 2 Samuel	Psalms	Daniel
Deuteronomy	1 & 2 Kings	Proverbs	Ezra
	Latter Prophets	Job	Nehemiah
	Isaiah	Song of Songs	1 & 2 Chronicles

PROTESTANT APOCRYPHA

1 & 2 Esdras[1]	Ecclesiasticus or the Wisdom of Jesus Son of Sirach	Prayer of Azariah and the Song of the Three Holy Children[3]	Bel and the Dragon[5]
Tobit	Baruch	Susanna[4]	The Prayer of Manasses[1]
Judith			1 & 2 Maccabees
part of Esther[2]			
Wisdom of Solomon			

[1]Not in *DV* [2]Ch. 11–16 in *DV* [3]Part of Ch. 3 of Daniel in *DV* [4]Ch. 13 of Daniel in *DV* [5]Ch. 14 of Daniel in *DV*

THE BOOKS OF THE NEW TESTAMENT

Matthew	Romans	Colossians	Hebrews
Mark	1 & 2 Corinthians	1 & 2 Thessalonians	James
Luke	Galatians	1 & 2 Timothy	1 & 2 Peter
John	Ephesians	Titus	1, 2, 3 John
Acts of the Apostles	Philippians	Philemon	Jude
			Revelation (*DV:* Apocalypse)

bib·li·cal \'bib-li-kəl\ *adj* [ML *biblicus*, fr. *biblia*] **1 :** of, relating to, or in accord with the Bible **2 :** suggestive of the Bible or Bible times — **bib·li·cal·ly** \-k(ə-)lē\ *adv*

bib·li·cism \'bib-lə-,siz-əm\ *n, often cap* **:** adherence to the letter of the Bible — **bib·li·cist** \-lə-səst\ *n, often cap*

biblio- *comb form* [MF, fr. L, fr. Gk, fr. *biblion*] **:** book ⟨*biblio*film⟩

bib·lio·film \'bib-lē-ō-,film\ *n* **:** a microfilm used esp. for photographing pages of books

bib·li·og·ra·pher \,bib-lē-'äg-rə-fər\ *n* **1 :** an expert in bibliography **2 :** a compiler of bibliography

bib·li·o·graph·ic \,bib-lē-ə-'graf-ik\ *adj* **:** of or relating to bibliography — **bib·li·o·graph·i·cal** \-i-kəl\ *adj* — **bib·li·o·graph·i·cal·ly** \-k(ə-)lē\ *adv*

bib·li·og·ra·phy \,bib-lē-'äg-rə-fē\ *n* [prob. fr. NL *bibliographia*, fr. Gk, the copying of books, fr. *biblio-* + *-graphia* -graphy] **1 :** the history, identification, or description of writings or publications **2 :** a list often with descriptive or critical notes of writings relating to a particular subject, period, or author; *also* **:** a list of works written by an author or printed by a publishing house **3 :** the works or a list of the works referred to in a text or consulted by the author in its production

bib·li·ol·a·ter \,bib-lē-'äl-ət-ər\ *n* **1 :** one overly devoted to books **2 :** one excessively venerating the Bible literally interpreted — **bib·li·ol·a·trous** \-'äl-ə-trəs\ *adj* — **bib·li·ol·a·try** \-trē\ *n*

bib·lio·ma·nia \,bib-lē-ə-'mā-nē-ə, -nyə\ *n* [F *bibliomanie*, fr. *biblio-* + *manie* mania, fr. LL *mania*] **:** extreme preoccupation with books esp. as possessions — **bib·lio·ma·ni·ac** \-nē-,ak\ *n or adj* — **bib·lio·ma·ni·a·cal** \-lē-ō-mə-'nī-ə-kəl\ *adj*

bib·li·op·e·gy \,bib-lē-'äp-ə-jē\ *n* [deriv. of Gk *biblio-* + *pēgnynai* to fasten together — more at PACT] **:** the art of binding books

bib·lio·phile \'bib-lē-ə-,fīl\ *n* [F, fr. *biblio-* + *-phile*] **:** a lover of books esp. for qualities of format; *also* **:** a book collector — **bib·lio·phil·ic** \,bib-lē-ə-'fil-ik\ *adj* — **bib·li·oph·i·lism** \-'äf-ə-,liz-əm\ *n* — **bib·li·oph·i·list** \-ləst\ *n* — **bib·li·oph·i·ly** \-lē\ *n*

bib·li·o·pole \'bib-lē-ə-,pōl\ *or* **bib·li·op·o·list** \,bib-lē-'äp-ə-ləst\ *n* [L *bibliopola* bookseller, fr. Gk *bibliopōlēs*, fr. *biblio-* + *pōlein* to sell] **:** a dealer esp. in rare or curious books — **bib·li·o·pol·ic** \,bib-lē-ə-'päl-ik\ *adj*

bib·lio·the·ca \,bib-lē-ə-'thē-kə\ *n* [L, fr. Gk *bibliothēkē*, fr. *biblio-* + *thēkē* case; akin to Gk *tithenai* to put, place] **1 :** a collection of books **2 :** a list of books — **bib·lio·the·cal** \-'thē-kəl\ *adj*

bib·li·ot·ic \,bib-lē-'ät-ik\ *adj* **:** of or relating to bibliotics

bib·li·ot·ics \-iks\ *n pl but sing or pl in constr* [*biblio-* + connective *-t-* + *-ics*] **:** the study of handwriting, documents, and writing materials esp. for determining genuineness or authorship — **bib·li·o·tist** \'bib-lē-ə-təst\ *n*

bib·u·lous \'bib-yə-ləs\ *adj* [L *bibulus*, fr. *bibere* to drink] **1 :** highly absorbent **2 a :** inclined to drink **b :** of or relating to drink or drinking — **bib·u·lous·ly** *adv* — **bib·u·lous·ness** *n*

bi·cam·er·al \(')bī-'kam-(ə-)rəl\ *adj* **:** having, consisting of, or based upon two legislative chambers ⟨~ legislature⟩ — **bi·cam·er·al·ism** \-(ə-)rə-,liz-əm\ *n*

bi·cap·su·lar \(')bī-'kap-sə-lər\ *adj* [prob. fr. F *bicapsulaire*, fr. *bi-* + *capsulaire* capsular] **:** having two capsules or a two-celled capsule

bi·car·bon·ate \(')bī-'kär-bə-,nāt, -nət\ *n* [ISV] **:** an acid carbonate

bicarbonate of soda : SODIUM BICARBONATE

bi·cen·te·na·ry \,bī-(,)sen-'ten-ə-rē, (')bī-'sent-ᵊn-,er-ē\ *adj* **:** BICENTENNIAL — **bicentenary** *n*

bi·cen·ten·ni·al \,bī-(,)sen-'ten-ē-əl\ *adj* **:** relating to a 200th anniversary — **bicentennial** *n*

bi·cen·tric \(')bī-'sen-trik\ *adj* **:** having or involving two centers — **bi·cen·tric·i·ty** \,bī-(,)sen-'tris-ət-ē\ *n*

bi·ceps \'bī-,seps\ *n* [NL *bicipit-*, *biceps*, fr. L, two-headed, fr. *bi-* + *capit-*, *caput* head — more at HEAD] **:** a muscle having two heads: as **a :** the large flexor muscle of the front of the upper arm **b :** the large flexor muscle of the back of the upper leg

bi·chlo·ride \(')bī-'klō(ə)r-,īd, -'klȯ(ə)r-\ *n* [ISV] **:** DICHLORIDE; *esp* **:** mercuric chloride

bi·chro·mate \(')bī-'krō-,māt\ *n* **:** DICHROMATE; *esp* **:** one of sodium or potassium — **bi·chro·mat·ed** \-,māt-əd, 'bī-krō-\ *adj*

bi·chrome \'bī-,krōm\ *adj* **:** two-colored

bi·cip·i·tal \bī-'sip-ət-ᵊl\ *adj* **:** of, relating to, or being a biceps

¹**bick·er** \'bik-ər\ *n* [ME *biker*] **1 a :** petulant quarreling **:** ALTERCATION **b :** a sound of or as if of bickering **2** *Scot* **:** BRAWL, FRACAS
²**bicker** *vi* **bick·er·ing** \-(ə-)riŋ\ **1 :** to contend in petulant or petty altercation **2 a :** to move quickly and unsteadily with a rapidly repeated noise **b :** QUIVER, FLICKER — **bick·er·er** \-ər-ər\ *n*
bi·col·or *or chiefly Brit* **bi·col·our** \'bī-ˌkəl-ər\ *adj* [L *bicolor*, fr. *bi-* + *color*] **:** two-colored — **bicolor** *n* — **bi·col·ored** \-'kəl-ərd\ *adj*
bicolor lespedeza *n* **:** an Asiatic leguminous shrub (*Lespedeza bicolor*) with purple flowers in axillary racemes widely used as an ornamental, as a source of wild-bird food, and in erosion control
bi·con·cave \ˌbī-(ˌ)kän-'kāv, (')bī-'kän-ˌ\ *adj* [ISV] **:** concave on both sides — **bi·con·cav·i·ty** \ˌbī-(ˌ)kän-'kav-ət-ē\ *n*
bi·con·vex \ˌbī-(ˌ)kän-'veks, (')bī-'kän-ˌ\ *adj* [ISV] **:** convex on both sides — **bi·con·vex·i·ty** \ˌbī-(ˌ)kän-'vek-sət-ē\ *n*
bi·corn \'bī-ˌkȯ(ə)rn\ *or* **bi·corned** \-ˌkȯ(ə)rnd\ *adj* [L *bicornis*, fr. *bi-* + *cornu* horn] **:** two-horned **:** resembling a crescent
bi·cor·nu·ate \(')bī-'kȯr-nyə-wət\ *adj* [*bi-* + L *cornu*] **:** having two horns or horn-shaped processes
¹**bi·cus·pid** \(')bī-'kəs-pəd\ *also* **bi·cus·pi·date** \-pə-ˌdāt\ *adj* [NL *bicuspid-*, *bicuspis*, fr. *bi-* + L *cuspid-*, *cuspis* point] **:** having or ending in two points
²**bicuspid** *n* **:** a human premolar tooth
¹**bi·cy·cle** \'bī-ˌsik-əl\ *n* [F, fr. *bi-* + *-cycle* (as in *tricycle*)] **:** a vehicle with two wheels tandem, a steering handle, a saddle seat, and pedals by which it is propelled
²**bicycle** *vi* **bi·cy·cling** \'bī-ˌsik-(ə-)liŋ\ **:** to ride a bicycle — **bi·cy·cler** \-ˌsik-(ə-)lər\ *n* — **bi·cy·clist** \'bī-ˌsik-(ə-)ləst\ *n*

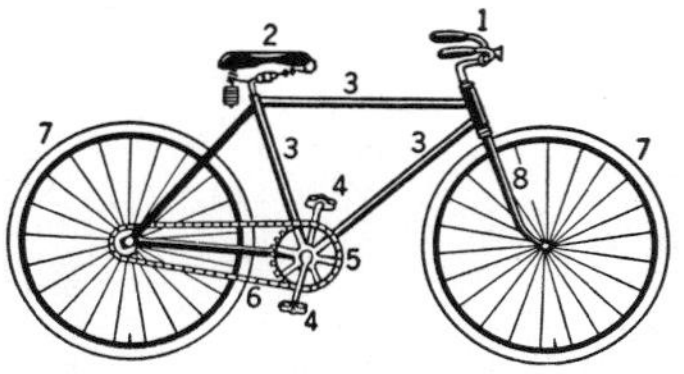

bicycle: *1* handlebar, *2* saddle, *3* frame, *4* pedal, *5* sprocket wheel, *6* chain, *7* tire, *8* fork

bi·cy·clic \(')bī-'sī-klik, -'sik-lik\ *adj* [ISV] **1 :** consisting of or arranged in two cycles **2 :** containing two usu. fused rings in the structure of the molecule
bi·cy·lin·dri·cal \ˌbī-sə-'lin-dri-kəl\ *adj* **:** having two cylindrical surfaces usu. with their axes parallel
¹**bid** \'bid\ *vb* **bade** \'bad, 'bād\ *or* **bid**; **bid·den** \'bid-ᵊn\ *or* **bid** *also* **bade**; **bid·ding** [partly fr. ME *bidden*, fr. OE *biddan*; akin to OHG *bitten* to entreat, Skt *bādhate* he harasses; partly fr. ME *beden* to offer, command, fr. OE *bēodan*; akin to OHG *biotan* to offer, Gk *pynthanesthai* to learn by inquiry] *vt* **1 a** *archaic* **:** BESEECH, ENTREAT **b :** to issue an order to **:** TELL **c :** to request to come **:** INVITE **2 :** to give expression to ⟨*bade* me a tearful farewell⟩ **3 a :** OFFER — usu. used in the phrase *to bid defiance* **b** *past* **bid** (1) **:** to offer (a price) whether for payment or acceptance (2) **:** to make a bid of or in (a suit at cards) ~ *vi* **:** to make a bid **syn** see COMMAND — **bid·der** *n* — **bid fair :** to seem likely
²**bid** *n* **1 a :** the act of one who bids **b :** a statement of what one will give or take for something; *esp* **:** an offer of a price **c :** something offered as a bid **2 :** an opportunity to bid **3 :** INVITATION **4 a :** an announcement of what a card player proposes to undertake **b :** the amount of such a bid **c :** a biddable bridge hand **5 :** an attempt or effort to win, achieve, or attract
bid·da·bil·i·ty \ˌbid-ə-'bil-ət-ē\ *n* **:** the quality or state of being biddable
bid·da·ble \'bid-ə-bəl\ *adj* **1 :** OBEDIENT, DOCILE **2 :** capable of being bid — **bid·da·bly** \-blē\ *adv*
¹**bid·dy** \'bid-ē\ *n* [perh. imit.] **:** HEN 1a; *also* **:** a young chicken
²**biddy** *n* [dim. of the name *Bridget*] **1 :** a hired girl or cleaning woman **2 :** WOMAN — usu. used disparagingly
bide \'bīd\ *vb* **bode** \'bōd\ *or* **bid·ed**; **bided**; **bid·ing** [ME *biden*, fr. OE *bīdan*; akin to OHG *bītan* to wait, L *fidere* to trust, Gk *peithesthai* to believe] *vi* **1 :** to continue in a state or condition **2 :** WAIT, TARRY **3 :** ABIDE, SOJOURN ~ *vt* **1** *past usu* **bided :** to wait for ⟨~ one's time⟩ **2** *archaic* **:** to encounter and resist **:** WITHSTAND **3** *chiefly dial* **:** to put up with **:** TOLERATE — **bid·er** *n*
bi·den·tate \(')bī-'den-ˌtāt\ *adj* [(assumed) NL *bidentatus*, fr. NL *bi-* + *dentatus* dentate] **:** having two teeth
bield \'bē(ə)ld\ *vt or n* [ME *belden* to encourage, protect, fr. OE *bieldan* to encourage; akin to OE *beald* bold] *chiefly Scot* **:** SHELTER
bi·en·ni·al \(')bī-'en-ē-əl\ *adj* **1 :** occurring every two years **2 :** continuing or lasting for two years; *specif* **:** growing vegetatively during the first year and fruiting and dying during the second — **biennial** *n* — **bi·en·ni·al·ly** \-ə-lē\ *adv*
bi·en·ni·um \bī-'en-ē-əm\ *n, pl* **bienniums** *or* **bi·en·nia** \-ē-ə\ [L, fr. *bi-* + *annus* year — more at ANNUAL] **:** a period of two years
bier \'bi(ə)r\ *n* [ME *bere*, fr. OE *bǣr*; akin to OE *beran* to carry] **1** *archaic* **:** a framework for carrying **2 :** a stand on which a corpse or coffin is placed; *also* **:** a coffin together with its stand
bi·fa·cial \(')bī-'fā-shəl\ *adj* **1 :** having opposite surfaces alike ⟨~ leaves⟩ **2 :** having two fronts or faces
biff \'bif\ *n* [prob. imit.] *slang* **:** WHACK, BLOW — **biff** *vt, slang*
bi·fid \'bī-ˌfid, -fəd\ *adj* [L *bifidus*, fr. *bi-* + *-fidus* -fid] **:** divided into two equal lobes or parts by a median cleft ⟨a ~ leaf⟩ — **bi·fid·i·ty** \bī-'fid-ət-ē\ *n* — **bi·fid·ly** *adv*
bi·fi·lar \(')bī-'fī-lər\ *adj* [ISV *bi-* + L *filum* thread — more at FILE] **1 :** involving two threads or wires **2 :** involving a single thread or wire doubled back upon itself — **bi·fi·lar·ly** *adv*
bi·flag·el·late \(')bī-'flaj-ə-lət, -ˌlāt\ *adj* **:** having two flagella
¹**bi·fo·cal** \(')bī-'fō-kəl\ *adj* [ISV] **:** having two focal lengths
²**bifocal** *n* **1 :** a bifocal glass or lens **2** *pl* **:** eyeglasses with bifocal lenses
bi·fo·li·ate \(')bī-'fō-lē-ət\ *adj* [(assumed) NL *bifoliatus*, fr. NL *bi-* + L *foliatus* leaved] **1 :** two-leaved **2 :** BIFOLIOLATE
bi·fo·li·o·late \(')bī-'fō-lē-ə-ˌlāt\ *adj* [(assumed) NL *bifoliolatus*, fr. L *bi-* + LL *foliolum*, dim. of L *folium* leaf — more at BLADE] **:** having two leaflets ⟨~ leaves⟩
bi·form \'bī-ˌfȯrm\ *adj* [L *biformis*, fr. *bi-* + *forma* form] **:** combining the qualities or forms of two distinct kinds of individuals
Bif·rost \'bē-ˌfrōst\ *n* [ON *bifrǫst*] **:** the rainbow bridge connecting heaven and earth in Norse mythology
bi·fur·cate \'bī-(ˌ)fər-ˌkāt, bī-'fər-\ *vb* [ML *bifurcatus*, pp. of *bifurcare*, fr. L *bifurcus* two-pronged, fr. *bi-* + *furca* fork] **:** to divide into two branches or parts — **bi·fur·cate** \(')bī-'fər-kət, -ˌkāt; 'bī-(ˌ)fər-ˌkāt\ *adj* — **bi·fur·cate·ly** *adv*
bi·fur·ca·tion \ˌbī-(ˌ)fər-'kā-shən\ *n* **1 :** the act of bifurcating **:** the state of being bifurcated **2 a :** the point at which bifurcating occurs **b :** BRANCH
¹**big** \'big\ *adj* **big·ger**; **big·gest** [ME, prob. of Scand origin; akin to Norw dial. *bugge* important man; akin to OE *bȳl* boil, Skt *bhūri* abundant] **1 a** *obs* **:** of great strength **b :** of great force ⟨a ~ storm⟩ **2 a :** large in dimensions, bulk, or extent ⟨~ house⟩; *also* **:** large in quantity, number, or amount ⟨a ~ fleet⟩ **b :** conducted on a large scale ⟨~ government⟩ **3 a :** PREGNANT; *esp* **:** nearly ready to give birth **b :** full to bursting **:** SWELLING **c** *of the voice* **:** full and resonant **4 a :** CHIEF, PREEMINENT **b :** OUTSTANDING, PROMINENT; *esp* **:** outstandingly worthy or able ⟨a truly ~ man⟩ **c :** of great importance or significance ⟨the ~ moment⟩ **d :** IMPOSING, PRETENTIOUS; *also* **:** BOASTFUL ⟨~ talk⟩ **e :** MAGNANIMOUS, GENEROUS **syn** see LARGE — **big·ly** *adv* — **big·ness** *n*
²**big** *adv* **1 :** to a large amount or extent **2 a :** in an outstanding manner **b :** POMPOUSLY, PRETENTIOUSLY **c :** MAGNANIMOUSLY
big·a·mist \'big-ə-məst\ *n* **:** one who practices bigamy
big·a·mous \'big-ə-məs\ *adj* **1 :** guilty of bigamy **2 :** involving bigamy — **big·a·mous·ly** *adv*
big·a·my \'big-ə-mē\ *n* [ME *bigamie*, fr. ML *bigamia*, fr. L *bi-* + LL *-gamia* -gamy, fr. Gk, fr. *gamos* marriage; akin to L *gener* son-in-law] **:** the act of entering into a ceremonial marriage with one person while still legally married to another that when willfully done constitutes a statutory offense
Big·ar·reau \ˌbig-ə-'rō\ *n* [F] **:** any of several cultivated sweet cherries with rather firm often light-colored globular fruits
Big Ben \-'ben\ *n* **:** a large bell in the clock tower of the Houses of Parliament in London
big brother *n* **1 :** an older brother **2 :** a man who befriends a delinquent or friendless boy **3** *often cap both Bs* **:** the leader of an authoritarian state or movement
bi·gem·i·nal \(')bī-'jem-ən-ᵊl\ *adj* [LL *bigeminus* doubled, fr. L *bi-* + *geminus* twin — more at GEMINATE] **:** DOUBLE, PAIRED ⟨a ~ pulse⟩ — **bi·gem·i·ny** \-'jem-ə-nē\ *n*
bi·ge·ner·ic \ˌbī-jə-'ner-ik\ *adj* **:** of, relating to, or involving two genera ⟨a ~ hybrid⟩
big·eye \'big-ˌī\ *n* **:** either of two small widely distributed reddish to silvery percoid fishes (*Priacanthus cruentatus* and *P. arenatus*) of tropical seas
big game *n* **1 :** large animals sought or taken by hunting or fishing for sport **2 :** an important objective esp. when involving risk
¹**big·gin** *or* **big·ging** \'big-ən\ *n* [ME *bigging*, fr. *biggen* to dwell, fr. ON *byggja*; akin to OE *bēon* to be] *dial Brit* **:** BUILDING
²**biggin** *n* [MF *beguin*] *dial Brit* **:** CAP: **a :** a child's cap **b :** NIGHTCAP
big·gish \'big-ish\ *adj* **:** somewhat big **:** comparatively big
big·head \'big-ˌhed\ *n* **1 :** any of several diseases of animals marked by swelling about the head **2 :** an exaggerated opinion of one's importance **:** CONCEIT — **big·head·ed** \-'hed-əd\ *adj*
big·heart·ed \'big-'härt-əd\ *adj* **:** being generous and kindly — **big·heart·ed·ly** *adv*
big·horn \'big-ˌhȯ(ə)rn\ *n, pl* **bighorn** *or* **bighorns :** a usu. grayish brown wild sheep (*Ovis canadensis*) of mountainous western No. America

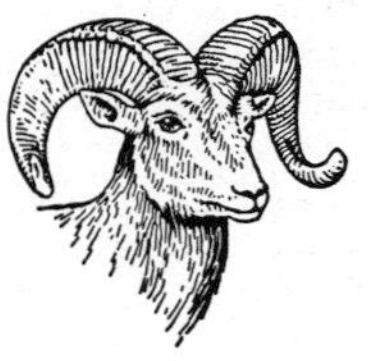
bighorn

¹**bight** \'bīt\ *n* [ME, fr. OE *byht*; akin to OE *būgan* to bend — more at BOW] **1** *obs* **:** a corner, bend, or angle esp. of a body part **2 a :** the middle part of a slack rope **b :** a loop esp. in a rope **3 a :** a bend esp. in a river or a mountain chain **b :** a bend in a coast forming an open bay; *also* **:** a bay formed by such a bend
²**bight** *vt* **1 :** to lay or fasten (a rope) in bights **2 :** to fasten with a bight
big league *n* **:** MAJOR LEAGUE — **big leagu·er** \-'lē-gər\ *n*
big·mouthed \'big-'mau̇t͟hd, -'mau̇tht\ *adj* **1 :** having a large mouth **2 :** LOUDMOUTHED
big·no·nia \big-'nō-nē-ə\ *n* [NL, genus name, fr. J. P. *Bignon* †1743 F royal librarian] **:** any of a genus (*Bignonia*) of American and Japanese woody vines of the trumpet-creeper family with compound leaves and tubular flowers
big·ot \'big-ət\ *n* [MF, hypocrite, bigot] **:** one obstinately or intolerantly devoted to his own church, party, belief, or opinion
big·ot·ed \'big-ət-əd\ *adj* **:** so obstinately attached to a creed, opinion, or practice as to be illiberal or intolerant — **big·ot·ed·ly** *adv*
big·ot·ry \'big-ə-trē\ *n* **:** the state of mind of a bigot; *also* **:** behavior or beliefs ensuing from such a state of mind
big shot \'big-ˌshät\ *n* **:** a person of consequence or prominence
big–tick·et \'big-'tik-ət\ *adj* **:** high-priced
big time \'big-ˌtīm\ *n* **1 :** a high-paying vaudeville circuit requiring only two performances a day **2 :** the top rank
big top \-ˌtäp\ *n* **1 :** the main tent of a circus **2 :** CIRCUS 2
big tree \-ˌtrē\ *n* **:** a California evergreen (*Sequoiadendron giganteum*) of the pine family that often exceeds 300 feet in height
big·wig \'big-ˌwig\ *n* **:** a person of consequence
Bi·ha·ri \bi-'här-ē\ *n* **:** a group of Indic dialects spoken by the inhabitants of Bihar
bi·jou \'bē-ˌzhü\ *n, pl* **bi·joux** \-ˌzhü(z)\ [F, fr. Bret *bizou* ring, fr. *biz* finger; akin to W *bys* finger] **:** a small dainty usu. ornamental piece of delicate workmanship **:** JEWEL — **bijou** *adj*
bi·jou·te·rie \bi-'zhüt-ə-ˌrē\ *n* [F, fr. *bijou*] **:** a collection of trinkets or ornaments **:** JEWELS
bi·ju·gate \'bī-jə-ˌgāt, (')bī-'jü-gət\ *also* **bi·ju·gous** \-gəs\ *adj* [*bi-* + L *jugum* yoke — more at YOKE] **:** having two pairs of leaflets — used of a pinnate leaf
¹**bike** \'bīk\ *n* [ME] **1** *chiefly Scot* **:** a nest of wild bees, wasps, or hornets **2** *chiefly Scot* **:** a crowd or swarm of people
²**bike** *n or vi* [by shortening & alter.] **:** BICYCLE — **bik·er** *n*
bi·ki·ni \bə-'kē-nē\ *n* [F, fr. *Bikini*, atoll of the Marshall islands] **:** a woman's abbreviated two-piece bathing suit

1bi·la·bi·al \(')bī-'lā-bē-əl\ *adj* [ISV] **1** *of a consonant* **:** produced with both lips **2 :** of or relating to both lips
2bilabial *n* **:** a bilabial consonant
bi·la·bi·ate \-bē-ət\ *adj* **:** having two lips ⟨a ~ corolla of a mint⟩
bi·lan·der \'bil-ən-dər, 'bī-lən-\ *n* [obs. D *billander*, fr. *bin* inside + D *land*] **:** a small 2-masted merchant ship
bi·lat·er·al \(')bī-'lat-ə-rəl, -'la-trəl\ *adj* **1 :** having two sides **2 :** affecting reciprocally two sides or parties ⟨~ treaty⟩ **3 :** bilaterally symmetrical — **bi·lat·er·al·ism** \-,iz-əm\ *n* — **bi·lat·er·al·ly** \-ē\ *adv* — **bi·lat·er·al·ness** *n*
bil·ber·ry \'bil-,ber-ē\ *n* [*bil-* (prob. of Scand origin; akin to Dan *bølle* whortleberry) + *berry*] **:** any of several plants (genus *Vaccinium*) that differ from the typical blueberries in having their flowers arise solitary or in very small clusters from axillary buds; *also* **:** its sweet edible bluish fruit
1bil·bo *or* **bil·boa** \'bil-(,)bō\ *n* [*Bilboa, Bilbao*, Spain] **:** a finely tempered sword
2bilbo *n* [perh. fr. *Bilboa*, Spain] **:** a long bar of iron with sliding shackles used to confine the feet
bile \'bī(ə)l\ *n* [F, fr. L *bilis;* akin to W *bustl* bile] **1 a :** a yellow or greenish viscid alkaline fluid secreted by the liver and passed into the duodenum where it aids esp. in the digestion and absorption of fats **b :** either of two humors associated in old physiology with irascibility and melancholy **2 :** proneness to anger **:** SPLEEN
bile acid *n* **:** a steroid acid of or derived from bile
1bilge \'bilj\ *n* [prob. modif. of MF *boulge, bouge* leather bag, curved part — more at BUDGET] **1 :** the bulging part of a cask or barrel **2 a :** the part of the underwater body of a ship between the flat of the bottom and the vertical topsides **b :** the lowest point of a ship's inner hull **3 :** stale or worthless remarks or ideas
2bilge *vi* **1 :** to undergo a fracture or other damage in the bilge **2 :** to rest on the bilge
bilge keel *n* **:** a longitudinal projection like a fin secured for a distance along a ship near the turn of the bilge on either side to check rolling
bilge water *n* **:** water that collects by seepage or leakage in the bilge of a ship or other vessel
bilgy \'bil-jē\ *adj* **:** resembling bilge water esp. in smell
bil·har·zia \bil-'här-zē-ə\ *n* [NL, fr. Theodor *Bilharz* †1862 G zoologist] **1 :** SCHISTOSOME **2 :** SCHISTOSOMIASIS
bil·ia·ry \'bil-ē-,er-ē, 'bil-yə-rē\ *adj* [F *biliare*, fr. L *bilis*] **:** of, relating to, or conveying bile; *also* **:** affecting the bile-conveying structures ⟨~ disorders⟩
bi·lin·ear \(')bī-'lin-ē-ər\ *adj* **:** linear with respect to each of two variables
bi·lin·gual \(')bī-'liŋ-gwəl\ *adj* [L *bilinguis*, fr. *bi-* + *lingua* tongue — more at TONGUE] **1 :** of, containing, or expressed in two languages **2 :** using or able to use two languages esp. with the fluency characteristic of a native speaker — **bilingual** *n* — **bi·lin·gual·ism** \-gwə-,liz-əm\ *also* **bi·lin·gual·i·ty** \,bī-(,)liŋ-'gwal-ət-ē\ *n* — **bi·lin·gual·ly** \(')bī-'liŋ-gwə-lē\ *adv*
bil·ious \'bil-yəs\ *adj* [MF *bilieux*, fr. L *biliosus*, fr. *bilis*] **1 a :** of or relating to bile **b :** marked by or suffering from disordered liver function and esp. excessive secretion of bile **c :** appearing as though affected by a bilious disorder **2 :** of a peevish ill-natured disposition **:** CHOLERIC — **bil·ious·ly** *adv* — **bil·ious·ness** *n*
bi·li·ru·bin \,bil-ə-'rü-bən, ,bī-lə-\ *n* [L *bilis* + *ruber* red — more at RED] **:** a reddish yellow pigment $C_{33}H_{36}N_4O_6$ occurring in bile, blood, urine, and gallstones
bi·li·ver·din \-'vərd-ᵊn\ *n* [Sw, fr. L *bilis* + obs. F *verd* green] **:** a green pigment $C_{33}H_{34}N_4O_6$ occurring in bile
1bilk \'bilk\ *vt* [perh. alter. of 2*balk*] **1 :** BALK, FRUSTRATE **2 :** to cheat out of what is due; *also* **:** to evade payment of **3 :** to slip away from **:** ELUDE — **bilk·er** *n*
2bilk *n* **:** an untrustworthy tricky individual **:** CHEAT
1bill \'bil\ *n* [ME *bile*, fr. OE; akin to OE *bill*] **1 :** the jaws of a

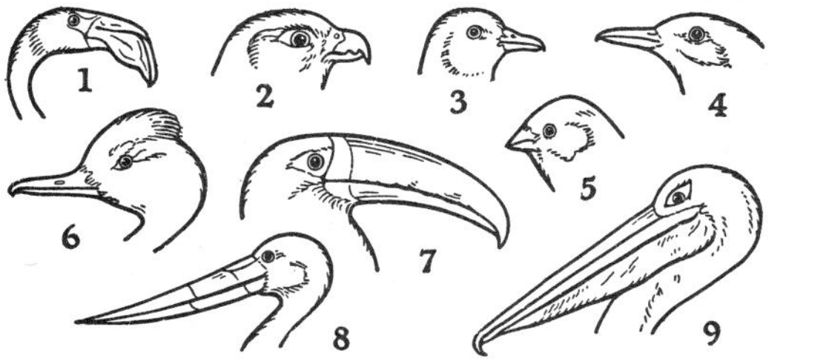

bills of birds: *1* flamingo, *2* hawk, *3* pigeon, *4* thrush, *5* finch, *6* duck (merganser), *7* toucan, *8* saddle-bill, *9* pelican

bird together with their horny covering **2 :** a beak (as of a turtle) or other mouthpart felt to resemble a bird's bill **3 :** a projection of land like a beak **4 :** the end of an anchor fluke or of a yard
2bill *vi* **1 :** to touch and rub bill to bill **2 :** to caress affectionately
3bill *n* [ME *bil*, fr. OE *bill;* akin to OHG *bill* pickax, Gk *phitros* log] **1 :** a weapon used up to the 18th century that consists of a long staff terminating in a hook-shaped blade **2 :** BILLHOOK
4bill *n* [ME, fr. ML *billa*, alter. of *bulla*, fr. L, bubble, boss] **1 a :** a written document **b :** MEMORANDUM **c :** LETTER **2** *obs* **:** a formal petition **3 :** a draft of a law presented to a legislature for enactment **4 :** a declaration in writing stating a wrong a complainant has suffered from a defendant or stating a breach of law by some person ⟨a ~ of complaint⟩ **5 :** a paper carrying a statement of particulars (as a list of men and their duties as part of a ship's crew) **6 a :** an itemized account of the separate cost of goods sold, services rendered, or work done **:** INVOICE **b :** a statement in gross of a creditor's claim **c :** a statement of charges for food or drink **:** CHECK **7 a :** a written or printed advertisement posted or otherwise distributed to announce an event of interest to the public; *esp* **:** an announcement of a theatrical entertainment **b :** a programmed presentation **:** the entertainment presented on a given program **8 a :** a piece of paper money **b :** an individual or commercial note
5bill *vt* **1 a :** to enter in a book of accounts **:** prepare a bill of (charges) **b :** to submit a bill of charges to **c :** to enter (as freight) in a waybill **d :** to issue a bill of lading to or for **2 a :** to advertise esp. by posters or placards **b :** to arrange for the presentation of
bil·la·bong \'bil-ə-,bȯŋ, -,bäŋ\ *n* [native name in Australia] *Austral* **1 a :** a blind channel leading out from a river **b :** a stream bed usu. dry but filled seasonally **2 :** a backwater forming a stagnant pool
1bill·board \'bil-,bō(ə)rd, -,bȯ(ə)rd\ *n* **:** a projection or ledge fixed on the bow of a vessel for the anchor to rest on
2billboard *n* [4*bill* + *board*] **:** a flat surface (as of a panel, wall, or fence) on which bills are posted; *specif* **:** a large panel designed to carry outdoor advertising
bill·bug \'bil-,bəg\ *n* [1*bill* + *bug*] **:** a weevil (esp. genus *Calendra*) having larvae that eat the roots of cereal and other grasses
billed \'bild\ *adj* **:** having a bill
bill·er \'bil-ər\ *n* **:** one that bills: as **a :** a clerk who makes out bills **b :** a machine for making out bills
1bil·let \'bil-ət\ *n* [ME *bylet*, fr. MF *billette*, dim. of *bulle* document, fr. ML *bulla*] **1** *archaic* **:** a brief letter **:** NOTE **2 a :** an official order directing that a member of a military force be provided with board and lodging (as in a private home) **b :** quarters assigned by or as if by a billet **3 :** POSITION, JOB, POST ⟨a soft ~⟩
2billet *vt* **1 :** to assign lodging to (as soldiers) by a billet **:** QUARTER **2 :** to serve with a billet ⟨~ a householder⟩ **~** *vi* **:** to have quarters
3billet *n* [ME *bylet*, fr. MF *billete*, dim. of *bille* log, of Celt origin; akin to OIr *bile* sacred tree] **1 a :** a chunky piece of wood (as for firewood) **:** BOLT 5 **b** *obs* **:** CUDGEL **2 a :** a bar of metal **b :** a piece of semifinished iron or steel nearly square in section made by rolling an ingot or bloom **c :** a section of nonferrous metal ingot hot-worked by forging, rolling, or extrusion **:** a nonferrous casting suitable for rolling or extrusion **3 :** an ornament in Norman moldings that resembles a billet of wood
bil·let–doux \,bil-(,)ā-'dü\ *n, pl* **billets–doux** \-(,)ā-'dü(z)\ [F *billet doux*, lit., sweet letter] **:** a love letter
bill·fish \'bil-,fish\ *n* **:** a fish with long slender jaws (as a gar)
bill·fold \-,fōld\ *n* [short for earlier *billfolder*] **1 :** a folding pocketbook for paper money **2 :** WALLET 2b
bill·head \-,hed\ *n* **:** a printed form usu. headed with a business address and used for billing charges
bill·hook \-,hu̇k\ *n* **:** a cutting tool consisting of a blade with a hooked point fitted with a handle and used esp. in pruning
bil·liard \'bil-yərd\ *n* [back-formation fr. *billiards*] **1 :** CAROM 1 **2** — used as an attributive form of *billiards* ⟨~ ball⟩
bil·liards \-yərdz\ *n pl but sing or pl in constr* [MF *billard* billiard cue, billiards, fr. *bille*] **:** any of several games played on an oblong table by driving small balls against one another or into pockets with a cue; *specif* **:** a game in which one scores by causing a cue ball to hit in succession two object balls
bil·lings·gate \'bil-iŋz-,gāt, *Brit usu* -git\ *n* [*Billingsgate*, old gate and fish market, London, England] **:** coarsely abusive language **syn** see ABUSE
bil·lion \'bil-yən\ *n* [F, fr. *bi-* + *-illion* (as in *million*)] **1** — see NUMBER table **2 :** a very large number — **billion** *adj* — **billionth** \-yən(t)th\ *adj* — **billionth** *n, pl* **billionths** \-yən(t)s, -yən(t)ths\
bil·lion·aire \,bil-yə-'na(ə)r, -'ne(ə)r, 'bil-yə-,\ *n* [*billion* + *-aire* (as in *millionaire*)] **:** one whose wealth is a billion or more
bill of exchange : an unconditional written order from one person to another to pay to a person designated a sum of money named
bill of fare 1 : MENU **2 :** PROGRAM
bill of goods : a consignment of merchandise
bill of health : a certificate of the state of health of a ship's company and of a port with regard to infectious diseases given to the ship's master at the time of leaving
bill of lading : a receipt listing goods shipped signed by the agent of the owner of a ship or issued by a common carrier
bill of rights *often cap B&R* **:** a summary of fundamental rights and privileges guaranteed to a people against violation by the state — used esp. of the first 10 amendments to the U.S. Constitution
bill of sale : a formal instrument for the conveyance or transfer of title to goods and chattels
bil·lon \'bil-ən\ *n* [F, fr. MF, fr. *bille* log] **1 :** an alloy of silver with more than its weight of copper, tin, or other base metal **2 :** gold or silver heavily alloyed with a less valuable metal
1bil·low \'bil-(,)ō, -ə(-w)\ *n* [prob. fr. ON *bylgja;* akin to OHG *balg* bag — more at BELLY] **1 :** WAVE; *esp* **:** a great wave or surge of water **2 :** a rolling mass (as of flame or smoke) like a high wave
2billow *vi* **1 :** to rise or roll in waves or surges **2 :** to bulge or swell out (as through action of the wind) **~** *vt* **:** to cause to billow
bil·lowy \'bil-ə-wē\ *adj* **:** characterized by billows
bill·post·er \'bil-,pō-stər\ *n* **:** one that posts advertising bills — called also *billsticker* — **bill·post·ing** \-stiŋ\ *n*
1bil·ly \'bil-ē\ *n* [prob. fr. the name *Billy*] **:** a heavy usu. wooden club; *esp* **:** a policeman's club
2billy *n* [prob. short for *billycan* (billy)] *chiefly Austral* **:** a can of metal or enamelware made with a lid and a wire bail and used for outdoor cooking or for carrying food or liquid
bil·ly·cock \'bil-ē-,käk\ *n* [origin unknown] *Brit* **:** a stiff felt hat
billy goat \'bil-ē-\ *n* [fr. the name *Billy*] **:** a male goat
bi·lo·bate \(')bī-'lō-,bāt\ *also* **bi·lo·bat·ed** \-,bāt-əd\ *adj* **:** divided into two lobes
bi·lobed \'bī-'lōbd\ *adj* **:** BILOBATE
bi·loc·u·lar \(')bī-'läk-yə-lər\ *or* **bi·loc·u·late** \-lət\ *adj* [*bi-* + NL *loculus*] **:** divided into two cells or compartments
bil·tong \'bil-,tȯŋ, -,täŋ\ *n* [Afrik, fr. *bil* buttock + *tong* tongue] *Africa* **:** jerked meat
bi·man·u·al \(')bī-'man-yə(-wə)l\ *adj* **:** done with or requiring the use of both hands — **bi·man·u·al·ly** \-ē\ *adv*
bi·mes·ter \(')bī-'mes-tər, 'bī-,\ *n* [*bi-* + *-mester* (as in *semester*)] **:** a period of two months
bi·mes·tri·al \bī-'mes-trē-əl\ *adj* [L *bimestris*, fr. *bi-* + *mensis* month — more at MOON] **:** continuing two months **:** BIMONTHLY
bi·met·al \'bī-,met-ᵊl\ *adj* **:** BIMETALLIC — **bimetal** *n*
bi·me·tal·lic \,bī-mə-'tal-ik\ *adj* **1 :** relating to, based on, or using bimetallism **2 :** composed of two different metals — often used of devices having a part in which two metals that expand differently are bonded together — **bimetallic** *n*
bi·met·al·lism \(')bī-'met-ᵊl-,iz-əm\ *n* [F *bimétallisme*, fr. *bi-* + *métal* metal] **:** the use of two metals (as gold and silver) jointly as a monetary standard with both constituting legal tender at a predetermined ratio — **bi·met·al·list** \-ᵊl-əst\ *n* — **bi·met·al·lis·tic** \,bī-,met-ᵊl-'is-tik\ *adj*

bi·mil·le·na·ry \(ˈ)bī-ˈmil-ə-ˌner-ē, ˌbī-mə-ˈlen-ə-rē\ *or* **bi·mil·len·i·al** \ˌbī-mə-ˈlen-ē-əl\ *n* **1 :** a period of 2000 years **2 :** a 2000th anniversary — **bimillenary** *adj*

bi·mod·al \(ˈ)bī-ˈmōd-ᵊl\ *adj* **:** possessing two statistical modes — **bi·mo·dal·i·ty** \ˌbī-mō-ˈdal-ət-ē\ *n*

bi·mo·lec·u·lar \ˌbī-mə-ˈlek-yə-lər\ *adj* [ISV] **:** relating to or formed from two molecules — **bi·mo·lec·u·lar·ly** *adv*

1bi·month·ly \(ˈ)bī-ˈmən(t)th-lē\ *adj* **1 :** occurring every two months **2 :** occurring twice a month **:** SEMIMONTHLY

2bimonthly *n* **:** a bimonthly publication

3bimonthly *adv* **1 :** once every two months **2 :** twice a month

bi·mor·phe·mic \ˌbī-(ˌ)mȯr-ˈfē-mik\ *adj* **:** consisting of two morphemes

bi·mo·tored \(ˈ)bī-ˈmōt-ərd\ *adj* **:** equipped with two motors

1bin \ˈbin\ *n* [ME *binn*, fr. OE] **:** a box, frame, crib, or enclosed place used for storage

2bin *vt* **binned; bin·ning :** to put into a bin

bin- *comb form* [ME, fr. LL, fr. L *bini* two by two; akin to OE *twīn* twine] **:** 1BI- ⟨*bin*aural⟩

1bi·na·ry \ˈbī-nə-rē\ *adj* [LL *binarius*, fr. L *bini*] **1 :** compounded or consisting of or marked by two things or parts **2 :** composed of two chemical elements, an element and a radical that acts as an element, or two such radicals **3 :** relating to, being, or belonging to a system of numbers having two as its base ⟨~ digit⟩ **4 :** relating two logical elements **5 a :** having two musical subjects or two complementary sections **b :** DUPLE — used of measure or rhythm

2binary *n* **:** something constituted of two things or parts

binary star *n* **:** a system of two stars that revolve around each other under their mutual gravitation

bi·nate \ˈbī-ˌnāt\ *adj* **:** growing in pairs — **bi·nate·ly** *adv*

bin·au·ral \(ˈ)bī-ˈnȯr-əl\ *adj* [ISV] **1 :** of, relating to, or used with two or both ears **2 :** of, relating to, or characterized by the placement of sound sources (as in sound transmission and recording) to achieve in sound reproduction an effect of hearing the sound sources in their original positions — **bin·au·ral·ly** \-ə-lē\ *adv*

1bind \ˈbīnd\ *vb* **bound** \ˈbau̇nd\ **bind·ing** [ME *binden*, fr. OE *bindan*; akin to OHG *bintan* to bind, Gk *peisma* cable] *vt* **1 a :** to make secure by tying **b :** to confine, restrain, or restrict as if with bonds **c :** to put under an obligation **d :** to constrain with legal authority **2 a :** to wrap around with something so as to enclose or cover **b :** BANDAGE **3 :** to fasten round about **4 :** to tie together **5 a :** to cause to stick together **b :** to take up and hold (as by chemical forces) **6 :** CONSTIPATE **7 :** to make firm or sure **:** SETTLE **8 :** to protect, strengthen, or decorate by a band or binding **9 :** to apply the parts of the cover to (a book) **10 :** INDENTURE, APPRENTICE **11 :** to cause to be attached (as by gratitude) **12 :** to fasten together **13 :** to effect (an insurance policy) by an oral commitment or a written instrument ~ *vi* **1 :** to form a cohesive mass **2 :** to hamper free movement or natural action **3 :** to become hindered from free operation **4 :** to exert a restraining or compelling effect

2bind *n* **1 a :** something that binds **b :** the act of binding **:** the state of being bound **c :** a place where binding occurs **2 a :** TIE 3 **b :** SLUR 1a **3 :** a position that restricts freedom of action

bind·er \ˈbīn-dər\ *n* **1 :** a person that binds something (as books) **2 a :** something used in binding **b :** a detachable cover or other device for holding together sheets of paper or similar material **c :** the sheet of tobacco that binds the filler in a cigar **3 :** something that produces or promotes cohesion in loosely assembled substances **4 :** a receipt for money paid to secure the right to purchase real estate upon agreed terms; *also* **:** the money itself

bind·ery \ˈbīn-d(ə-)rē\ *n* **:** a place where books are bound

1bind·ing \ˈbīn-diŋ\ *n* **1 :** the action of one that binds **2 :** a material or device used to bind: as **a :** the cover and fastenings of a book **b :** a narrow fabric used to finish raw edges **c :** a set of ski fastenings for holding the toe of the boot firm on the ski

2binding *adj* **1 :** that binds **2 :** imposing an obligation — **bind·ing·ly** \-diŋ-lē\ *adv* — **bind·ing·ness** *n*

binding energy *n* **:** the energy required to break up a molecule, atom, or atomic nucleus completely into its constituent particles

bind over *vt* **:** to put under bonds to do something

bind·weed \ˈbīn-ˌdwēd\ *n* **:** any of various twining plants (esp. genus *Convolvulus* of the morning-glory family) that mat or interlace with plants among which they grow

bine \ˈbīn\ *n* [alter. of *2bind*] **:** a twining stem or flexible shoot (as of the hop); *also* **:** a plant (as woodbine) whose shoots are bines

Bi·net–Si·mon scale \bi-ˌnā-sē-ˈmōⁿ-\ *n* [Alfred *Binet* †1911 and Théodore *Simon* †1961 F psychologists] **:** an intelligence test consisting orig. of tasks graded from the level of the average 3-year-old to that of the average 12-year-old but later extended in range

binge \ˈbinj\ *n* [E dial. *binge* (to drink heavily)] **1 a :** CAROUSAL, SPREE **b :** a riotous indulgence **2 :** a social gathering **:** PARTY

bin·go \ˈbiŋ-(ˌ)gō\ *n* [earlier *bingo* (interj. used to announce an unexpected event)] **:** a game like lotto played usu. by many players at once for prizes

bin·na·cle \ˈbin-i-kəl\ *n* [alter. of ME *bitakle*, fr. OPg or OSp; OPg *bitácola* & OSp *bitácula*, fr. L *habitaculum* dwelling place, fr. *habitare* to inhabit — more at HABITATION] **:** a case, box, or stand containing a ship's compass and a lamp

1bin·oc·u·lar \bī-ˈnäk-yə-lər, bə-\ *adj* **:** of, relating to, using, or adapted to the use of both eyes ⟨~ vision⟩ — **bin·oc·u·lar·i·ty** \(ˌ)bī-ˌnäk-yə-ˈlar-ət-ē, bə-\ *n* — **bin·oc·u·lar·ly** *adv*

2bin·oc·u·lar \bə-ˈnäk-yə-lər, bī-\ *n* **1 :** a binocular optical instrument **2 :** FIELD GLASS — usu. used in pl.

bi·no·mi·al \bī-ˈnō-mē-əl\ *n* [NL *binomium*, fr. ML, neut. of *binomius* having two names, alter. of L *binominis*, fr. *bi-* + *nomin-*, *nomen* name — more at NAME] **1 :** a mathematical expression consisting of two terms connected by a plus sign or minus sign **2 :** a biological species name consisting of two terms — **binomial** *adj* — **bi·no·mi·al·ly** \-mē-ə-lē\ *adv*

binomial distribution *n* **:** a frequency distribution of the probability that an attribute that occurs with a given probability among the members of a population will occur a certain number of times in a succession of samples of the population

binomial nomenclature *n* **:** a system of nomenclature in which each species of animal or plant receives a name of two terms of which the first identifies the genus to which it belongs and the second the species itself

binomial theorem *n* **:** a theorem by means of which a binomial may be raised to any power without performing the multiplications

bi·nu·cle·ar \(ˈ)bī-ˈn(y)ü-klē-ər\ *or* **bi·nu·cle·ate** \-klē-ət\ *or* **bi·nu·cle·at·ed** \-klē-ˌāt-əd\ *adj* **:** having two nuclei

bio- — see BI-

1bio·as·say \ˌbī-(ˌ)ō-ˈas-ˌā, -a-ˈsā\ *n* [*bio*logical *assay*] **:** determination of the relative strength of a substance (as a drug) by comparing its effect on a test organism with that of a standard preparation

2bio·as·say \-a-ˈsā, -ˈas-ˌā\ *vt* **:** to perform a bioassay on

bio·cat·a·lyst \ˌbī-(ˌ)ō-ˈkat-ᵊl-əst\ *n* **:** a substance (as an enzyme or a trace element) that activates or accelerates biological processes — **bio·cat·a·lyt·ic** \-ˌkat-ᵊl-ˈit-ik\ *adj*

bio·ce·nol·o·gy \-si-ˈnäl-ə-jē\ *n* **:** a branch of biology concerned with natural communities and the interaction of their members

bio·chem·i·cal \ˌbī-(ˌ)ō-ˈkem-i-kəl\ *adj* [ISV] **1 :** of or relating to biochemistry **2 :** characterized by, produced by, or involving chemical reactions in living organisms — **biochemical** *n* — **bio·chem·i·cal·ly** \-k(ə-)lē\ *adv*

bio·chem·ist \ˌbī-ō-ˈkem-əst\ *n* **:** a specialist in biochemistry

bio·chem·is·try \-ə-strē\ *n* [ISV] **:** chemistry that deals with the chemical compounds and processes occurring in organisms

bio·cide \ˈbī-ə-ˌsīd\ *n* **:** PESTICIDE

bio·cli·mat·ic \ˌbī-(ˌ)ō-klī-ˈmat-ik\ *adj* **:** of or relating to the relations of climate and living matter

bio·ecol·o·gy \ˌbī-(ˌ)ō-i-ˈkäl-ə-jē\ *n* **:** ecology dealing with the interrelation of plants and animals with their common environment

bio·fla·vo·noid \ˌbī-ō-ˈflā-və-ˌnȯid\ *n* **:** a biologically active flavonoid — called also *vitamin P*

bio·gen·e·sis \ˌbī-ō-ˈjen-ə-səs\ *n* [NL] **1 :** the development of life from preexisting life **2 :** a supposed tendency for stages in the evolutionary history of a race to briefly recur during the development and differentiation of an individual of that race — **bio·ge·net·ic** \-jə-ˈnet-ik\ *adj* — **bio·ge·net·i·cal·ly** \-i-k(ə-)lē\ *adv*

bio·gen·ic \ˌbī-ō-ˈjen-ik\ *adj* **:** produced by living organisms

bio·geo·graph·ic \-ˌjē-ə-ˈgraf-ik\ *adj* **:** of or relating to biogeography — **bio·geo·graph·ic·al** \-i-kəl\ *adj*

bio·ge·og·ra·phy \ˌbī-ō-jē-ˈäg-rə-fē\ *n* [ISV] **:** a branch of biology that deals with the geographical distribution of animals and plants

bi·og·ra·pher \bī-ˈäg-rə-fər, bē-\ *n* **:** a writer of a biography

bio·graph·i·cal \ˌbī-ə-ˈgraf-i-kəl\ *or* **bio·graph·ic** \-ik\ *adj* **1 :** of, relating to, or constituting biography **2 :** consisting of biographies **3 :** briefly identifying persons ⟨~ names⟩ — **bio·graph·i·cal·ly** \-i-k(ə-)lē\ *adv*

bi·og·ra·phy \bī-ˈäg-rə-fē, bē-\ *n* [LGk *biographia*, fr. Gk *bi-* + *-graphia* -graphy] **1 :** a usu. written history of a person's life **2 :** biographical writings in general **3 :** a life history (as of a coin)

1bi·o·log·ic \ˌbī-ə-ˈläj-ik\ *adj* **1 :** of or relating to biology or to life and living processes **2 :** used in or produced by applied biology — **bi·o·log·i·cal** \-i-kəl\ *adj* — **bi·o·log·i·cal·ly** \-k(ə-)lē\ *adv*

2biologic *n* **:** a biological product used in medicine — **biological** *n*

biological control *n* **:** attack upon noxious organisms by interference with their ecological adjustment

biological warfare *n* **:** warfare involving the use of living organisms (as disease germs) esp. against men, animals, or plants

bi·ol·o·gism \bī-ˈäl-ə-ˌjiz-əm\ *n* **:** preoccupation with biological explanations in the analysis of social situations

bi·ol·o·gist \bī-ˈäl-ə-jəst\ *n* **:** a specialist in biology

bi·ol·o·gis·tic \(ˌ)bī-ˌäl-ə-ˈjis-tik\ *adj* **:** of or relating to biologism

bi·ol·o·gy \bī-ˈäl-ə-jē\ *n, often attrib* [G *biologie*, fr. *bi-* + *-logie* -logy] **1 a :** a branch of knowledge that deals with living organisms and vital processes **b :** ECOLOGY **2 a :** the plant and animal life of a region or environment **b :** the laws and phenomena relating to an organism or group

bio·lu·mi·nes·cence \ˌbī-(ˌ)ō-ˌlü-mə-ˈnes-ᵊn(t)s\ *n* [ISV] **:** the emission of light from living organisms; *also* **:** the light so produced — **bio·lu·mi·nes·cent** \-ᵊnt\ *adj*

bio·mass \ˈbī-ō-ˌmas\ *n* **:** the amount of living matter (as in a unit area or volume of habitat)

bio·met·rics \ˌbī-ō-ˈme-triks\ *n pl but sing or pl in constr* **:** the statistical study of biological observations and phenomena

bi·o·nom·ic \ˌbī-ə-ˈnäm-ik\ *adj* [prob. fr. F *bionomique*, fr. *bionomie* ecology, fr. *bi-* + *-nomie* -nomy] **:** ECOLOGICAL — **bi·o·nom·i·cal** \-i-kəl\ *adj* — **bi·o·nom·i·cal·ly** \-k(ə-)lē\ *adv*

bi·o·nom·ics \-ˈnäm-iks\ *n pl but sing or pl in constr* **:** ECOLOGY

bi·ont \ˈbī-ˌänt\ *n* **:** a discrete unit of living matter **:** ORGANISM — **bi·on·tic** \bī-ˈänt-ik\ *adj*

bio·phys·ics \ˈbī-ō-ˌfiz-iks\ *n* **:** a branch of knowledge concerned with the application of physical principles and methods to biological problems

bi·op·sy \ˈbī-ˌäp-sē\ *n* [ISV *bi-* + Gk *opsis* appearance] **:** the removal and examination of tissue, cells, or fluids from the living body

bi·o·scope \ˈbī-ə-ˌskōp\ *n* **:** a motion-picture projector

-bi·o·sis \(ˌ)bī-ˈō-səs, bē-\ *n comb form, pl* **-bi·o·ses** \-ˌsēz\ [NL, fr. Gk *biōsis*, fr. *bioun* to live, fr. *bios*] **:** mode of life ⟨para*biosis*⟩

bio·sphere \ˈbī-ə-ˌsfi(ə)r\ *n* **1 :** the part of the world in which life can exist **2 :** living beings together with their environment

bio·syn·the·sis \ˌbī-ō-ˈsin(t)-thə-səs\ *n* [NL] **:** the production of a chemical compound by a living organism — **bio·syn·thet·ic** \-sin-ˈthet-ik\ *adj* — **bio·syn·thet·i·cal·ly** \-i-k(ə-)lē\ *adv*

bio·sys·te·mat·ic \ˌbī-ō-ˌsis-tə-ˈmat-ik\ *adj* **:** of or relating to experimental taxonomy esp. as based on cytogenetics — **bio·sys·tem·a·ty** \-ˈsis-ˈtem-ət-ē\ *n*

bi·o·ta \bī-ˈōt-ə\ *n* [NL, fr. Gk *biotē* life; akin to Gk *bios*] **:** the flora and fauna of a region

bio·tech·nol·o·gy \ˌbī-(ˌ)ō-tek-ˈnäl-ə-jē\ *n* **:** the aspect of technology concerned with the application of biological and engineering data to problems relating to man and the machine

bi·ot·ic \bī-ˈät-ik\ *adj* [Gk *biōtikos*, fr. *bioun*] **:** of or relating to life; *esp* **:** caused by living beings

-bi·ot·ic \(ˌ)bī-ˈät-ik, bē-\ *adj comb form* [prob. fr. NL *-bioticus*, fr. Gk *biōtikos*] **:** having a (specified) mode of life ⟨endo*biotic*⟩

biotic potential *n* **:** the inherent capacity of an organism or species to reproduce and survive

bi·o·tin \ˈbī-ə-tən\ *n* [ISV, fr. Gk *biotos* life, sustenance; akin to Gk *bios*] **:** a colorless crystalline growth vitamin $C_{10}H_{16}N_2O_3S$ of

the vitamin B complex found esp. in yeast, liver, and egg yolk

bi·o·tite \'bī-ə-,tīt\ *n* [G *biotit*, fr. Jean B. *Biot* †1862 F mathematician] : a generally black or dark green form of mica $K_2(Mg,Fe,Al)_6(Si,Al)_8O_{20}(OH)_4$ forming a constituent of crystalline rocks and consisting of a silicate of iron, magnesium, potassium, and aluminum (hardness 2.5–3) — **bi·o·tit·ic** \,bī-ə-'tit-ik\ *adj*

bio·tope \'bī-ə-,tōp\ *n* [[2]*bi-* + Gk *topos* place — more at TOPIC] : a region uniform in environmental conditions and in its populations of animals and plants for which it is the habitat

bio·type \'bī-ə-,tīp\ *n* [ISV] : the organisms sharing a specified genotype; *also* : the genotype shared or its distinguishing peculiarity — **bio·typ·ic** \,bī-ə-'tip-ik\ *adj*

bi·ovu·lar \(')bī-'ō-vyə-lər\ *adj, of fraternal twins* : derived from two ova

bi·pack \'bī-,pak\ *n* : a pair of films each sensitive to a different color used by simultaneous exposure one through the other

bip·a·rous \'bip-ə-rəs\ *adj* **1** : bringing forth two young at a birth **2** : branching dichotomously

bi·par·ti·san *also* **bi·par·ti·zan** \(')bī-'pärt-ə-zən, -sən\ *adj* : representing or composed of members of two parties — **bi·par·ti·san·ism** \-zə-,niz-əm, -sə-\ *n* — **bi·par·ti·san·ship** \-zən-,ship, -sən-\ *n*

bi·par·tite \(')bī-'pär-,tīt\ *adj* [L *bipartitus*, pp. of *bipartire* to divide in two, fr. *bi-* + *partire* to divide, fr. *part-, pars* part] **1 a** : being in two parts **b** : having two correspondent parts one for each party ⟨~ contract⟩ **c** : shared by two ⟨~ treaty⟩ **2** : divided into two parts almost to the base ⟨~ leaf⟩ — **bi·par·tite·ly** *adv* — **bi·par·ti·tion** \,bī-,pär-'tish-ən\ *n*

bi·ped \'bī-,ped\ *n* [L *biped-, bipes*, fr. *bi-* + *ped-, pes* foot] : a two-footed animal — **biped** *or* **bi·ped·al** \(')bī-'ped-ᵊl\ *adj*

bi·phe·nyl \(')bī-'fen-ᵊl, -'fēn-\ *n* [ISV] : a white crystalline hydrocarbon $C_6H_5.C_6H_5$ used esp. as a heat-transfer medium

bi·pin·nate \-'pin-,āt\ *adj* : twice pinnate — **bi·pin·nate·ly** *adv*

bi·plane \'bī-,plān\ *n* : an airplane with two main supporting surfaces usu. placed one above the other

bi·pod \'bī-,päd\ *n* [*bi-* + *-pod* (as in *tripod*)] : a two-legged stand

bi·po·lar \(')bī-'pō-lər\ *adj* **1** : having or involving the use of two poles **2** : relating to or associated with the polar regions **3** : having or marked by two mutually repellent forces or diametrically opposed natures or views — **bi·po·lar·i·ty** \,bī-pō-'lar-ət-ē\ *n*

bi·pro·pel·lant \,bī-prə-'pel-ənt\ *n* : a rocket propellant consisting of separate fuel and oxidizer that come together only in a combustion chamber

bi·quad·rat·ic \,bī-(,)kwä-'drat-ik\ *n* : a fourth power or equation involving a fourth power in mathematics — **biquadratic** *adj*

bi·ra·cial \(')bī-'rā-shəl\ *adj* : of, relating to, or involving members of two races — **bi·ra·cial·ism** \-shə-,liz-əm\ *n*

bi·ra·di·al \(')bī-'rād-ē-əl\ *adj* : having both bilateral and radial symmetry

bi·ra·mous \(')bī-'rā-məs\ *adj* : having two branches

[1]**birch** \'bərch\ *n* [ME, fr. OE *beorc;* akin to OHG *birka* birch, L *fraxinus* ash tree, OE *beorht* bright — more at BRIGHT] **1** : any of a genus (*Betula* of the family Betulaceae, the birch family) of monoecious deciduous usu. short-lived trees or shrubs having simple petioled leaves and typically a layered membranous outer bark that peels readily **2** : the hard pale close-grained wood of a birch **3** : a birch rod or bundle of twigs for flogging — **birch** *or* **birch·en** \'bər-chən\ *adj*

[2]**birch** *vt* : to beat with or as if with a birch : WHIP

birch·bark \'bərch-,bärk\ *n* : a canoe made of birch bark

[1]**bird** \'bərd\ *n* [ME, fr. OE *bridd*] **1** *archaic* : the young of a feathered vertebrate **2** : any of a class (Aves) of warm-blooded vertebrates distinguished by having the body more or less completely covered with feathers and the forelimbs modified as wings **3** : a game bird **4** : CLAY PIGEON **5** *slang* : FELLOW; *esp* : a peculiar person **6** : SHUTTLECOCK 1 **7** : a hissing or jeering expressive of disapproval; *also* : dismissal from employment **8** : GUIDED MISSILE

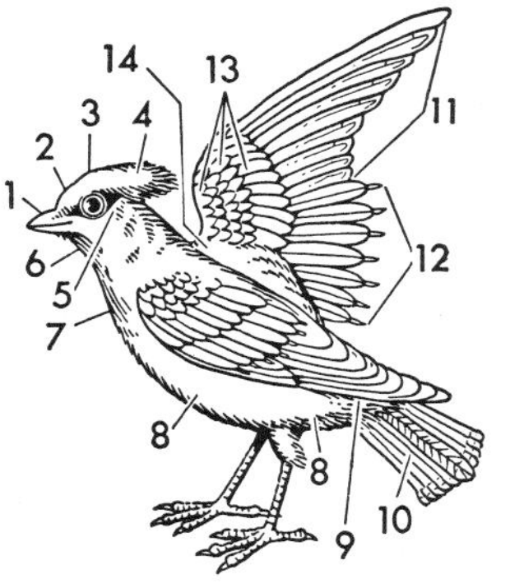

bird (waxwing): *1* bill, *2* forehead, *3* crown, *4* crest, *5* auricular region, *6* throat, *7* breast, *8* abdomen, *9* undertail coverts, *10* tail, *11* primaries, *12* secondaries, *13* upper wing coverts, *14* scapulars

[2]**bird** *vi* : to observe or identify wild birds in their natural environment

bird·bath \-,bath, -,bȧth\ *n* : a usu. ornamental basin set up for birds to bathe in

bird·brain \-,brān\ *n* : a stupid or a flighty thoughtless person

bird·call \-,kȯl\ *n* **1** : the note or cry of a bird or a sound imitative of it **2** : a device for imitating a birdcall

bird colonel *n, slang* : COLONEL 1a

bird dog *n* **1** : a gundog trained to hunt or retrieve birds **2 a** : one (as a canvasser or talent scout) who seeks out something for another **b** : one who steals another's date

bird·er \'bərd-ər\ *n* **1** : a catcher or hunter of birds esp. for market **2** : one that birds

bird·house \'bərd-,hau̇s\ *n* : an artificial nesting site for birds; *also* : AVIARY

[1]**bird·ie** \'bərd-ē\ *n* **1** : a little bird **2** : a golf score of one stroke less than par on a hole

[2]**birdie** *vt* : to shoot in one stroke under par

bird·lime \'bərd-,līm\ *n* **1** : a sticky substance usu. made from the bark of a holly (*Ilex aquifolium*) that is smeared on twigs to snare small birds **2** : something that ensnares — **birdlime** *vt*

bird louse *n* : any of numerous wingless insects (order Mallophaga) that are mostly parasitic on birds

bird·man \'bərd-mən\ *n* **1** : one who deals with birds **2** : AVIATOR

bird of paradise : any of numerous brilliantly colored plumed oscine birds (family Paradiseidae) of the New Guinea area

bird of passage : a migratory bird or person

bird of prey : a carnivorous bird that feeds wholly or chiefly on meat taken by hunting

bird pepper *n* : a capsicum (*Capsicum frutescens*) having very small oblong extremely pungent red fruits

bird·seed \'bərd-,sēd\ *n* : a mixture of small seeds (as of hemp or millet) used chiefly for feeding cage birds

[1]**bird's–eye** \'bərd-,zī\ *n* **1** : any of numerous plants with small bright-colored flowers **2 a** : an allover pattern for textiles consisting of a small diamond with a center dot **b** : a fabric woven with this pattern **3** : a small spot in wood surrounded with an ellipse of concentric fibers

[2]**bird's–eye** *adj* **1 a** : seen from above as if by a flying bird ⟨~ view⟩ **b** : CURSORY **2** : marked with spots resembling birds' eyes **3** : of or relating to wood (as maple) containing bird's-eyes

bird's–foot \'bərdz-,fu̇t\ *n, pl* **bird's–foots** : any of numerous plants with leaves or flowers resembling the foot of a bird; *esp* : any of several legumes (as of the genera *Ornithopus, Lotus,* and *Trigonella*) with bent and jointed pods

bird's–foot trefoil *n* : a European legume (*Lotus corniculatus*) having claw-shaped pods and widely used esp. in the U.S. as a forage and fodder plant

bi·re·frin·gence \,bī-ri-'frin-jən(t)s\ *n* [ISV] : the refraction of light in two slightly different directions to form two rays — **bi·re·frin·gent** \-jənt\ *adj*

bi·reme \'bī-,rēm\ *n* [L *biremis*, fr. *bi-* + *remus* oar] : a galley with two banks of oars common in the early classical period

bi·ret·ta \bə-'ret-ə\ *n* [It *berretta*, fr. OProv *berret* cap, irreg. fr. LL *birrus* cloak with a hood, of Celt origin; akin to MIr *berr* short] : a square cap with three ridges on top worn by clergymen esp. of the Roman Catholic Church

birk \'bi(ə)rk\ *n* [ME *birch, birk*] *chiefly Scot* : BIRCH

birk·ie \'bi(ə)r-kē, 'bər-\ *n* [origin unknown] **1** *Scot* : a lively smart assertive person **2** *Scot* : FELLOW, BOY

birl \'bər(-ə)l, *Scot also* 'bir(ə)l\ *vb* [ME *birlen*, fr. OE *byrelian;* akin to OE *beran* to carry — more at BEAR] *vt* **1** *also* **birle** *chiefly Scot* **a** : POUR **b** : to ply with drink **2 a** : to cause (a floating log) to rotate by treading **b** : SPIN ~ *vi* **1** *chiefly Scot* : CAROUSE **2** : to progress by whirling — **birl·er** \'bər-lər, 'bi(ə)r-lər\ *n*

[1]**birr** \'bər, 'bi(ə)r\ *n* [ME, strong wind, attack, fr. OE *byre* strong wind & ON *byrr* favoring wind; both akin to OE *beran*] **1** : force or onward rush (as of the wind); *also* : VIGOR **2** : a whirring sound

[2]**birr** *vi, chiefly Scot* : to make a whirring sound

birse \'bi(ə)rs, 'bərs\ *n* [(assumed) ME *birst*, fr. OE *byrst*] **1** *chiefly Scot* : a bristle or tuft of bristles **2** *chiefly Scot* : ANGER

[1]**birth** \'bərth\ *n, often attrib* [ME, fr. ON *byrth;* akin to OE *beran*] **1 a** : the emergence of a new individual from the body of its parent **b** : the act or process of bringing forth young from the womb **2 a** : LINEAGE, EXTRACTION **b** : high or noble birth **3 a** *archaic* : one that is born **b** : BEGINNING, START ⟨~ of an idea⟩

[2]**birth** *vt* **1** *chiefly dial* : to bring forth **2** : to give rise to : ORIGINATE ~ *vi, dial* : to bring forth a child or young

birth certificate *n* : a copy of an official record of a person's date and place of birth and parentage

birth control *n* : control of the number of children born esp. by preventing or lessening the frequency of impregnation

birth·day \'bərth-,dā\ *n* **1 a** : the day of a person's birth **b** : a day of origin **2 a** : an anniversary of one's birth **b** : a year of life

birth·mark \-,märk\ *n* : an unusual mark or blemish on the skin at birth : NEVUS — **birthmark** *vt*

birth·place \-,plās\ *n* : place of birth or origin

birth·rate \'bər-,thrāt\ *n* : the ratio between births and individuals in a specified population and time often expressed as number of live births per hundred or per thousand population

birth·right \-,thrīt\ *n* : a right, privilege, or possession to which a person is entitled by birth **syn** see HERITAGE

birth·root \-,thrüt, -,thru̇t\ *n* : any of several trilliums with astringent roots used in folk medicine

birth·stone \'bərth-,stōn\ *n* : a precious stone associated symbolically with the month of one's birth

birth·wort \-,wərt, -,wȯ(ə)rt\ *n* **1** : any of several plants (genus *Aristolochia* of the family Aristolochiaceae, the birthwort family) of herbs or woody vines with aromatic roots used in folk medicine to aid childbirth **2** : BIRTHROOT

bis \'bis\ *adv* [L, fr. OL *dvis;* akin to OHG *zwiro* twice, L *duo* two] : TWICE — used as a direction to repeat or as a mark of repetition

Bi·sa·yan \bə-'sī-ən\ *n* [Bisayan *Bisayâ*] **1** : a member of any of several peoples in the Visayan islands, Philippines **2** : the Austronesian language of the Bisayans

bis·cuit \'bis-kət\ *n, pl* **biscuits** *also* **biscuit** [ME *bisquite*, fr. MF *bescuit*, fr. (*pain*) *bescuit* twice-cooked bread] **1** : any of various hard or crisp dry baked products; *esp, Brit* : CRACKER 4 **2** : earthenware or porcelain after the first firing and before glazing : BISQUE **3** : a small quick bread made from dough that has been rolled and cut or dropped from a spoon

bise \'bēz\ *n* [ME, fr. OF, of Gmc origin] : a cold dry north wind of southern France, Switzerland, and Italy

bi·sect \'bī-,sekt, bī-'\ *vt* : to divide into two usu. equal parts ~ *vi* : SEPARATE; *also* : CROSS, INTERSECT — **bi·sec·tion** \'bī-,sek-shən, bī-'\ *n* — **bi·sec·tion·al** \-shnəl, -shən-ᵊl\ *adj* — **bi·sec·tion·al·ly** \-ē\ *adv*

bi·sec·tor \'bī-,sek-tər, bī-'\ *n* : one that bisects; *esp* : a straight line that bisects an angle or a line segment

bi·ser·rate \(')bī-'se(ə)r-,āt\ *adj* **1** : doubly serrate : having the serrations serrate **2** : serrate on both sides

bi·sex·u·al \(')bī-'seksh-(ə-)wəl, -'sek-shəl\ *adj* **1** : HERMAPHRODITIC; *broadly* : possessing characters of or sexually oriented toward both sexes **2** : of, relating to, or involving two sexes — **bisexual** *n* — **bi·sex·u·al·i·ty** \,bī-,sek-shə-'wal-ət-ē\ *n* — **bi·sex·u·al·ly** *adv*

bish·op \'bish-əp\ *n* [ME *bisshop*, fr. OE *bisceop*, fr. LL *episcopus* fr. Gk *episkopos*, lit., overseer, fr. *epi-* + *skeptesthai* to look — more at SPY] **1** : one having spiritual or ecclesiastical supervision: as **a** : an Eastern, Roman Catholic, Anglican, or Episcopal clergyman ranking above a priest, having authority to ordain and confirm, and typically governing a diocese **b** : any of various Protestant clerical officials who superintend other clergy **c** : a Mormon high priest presiding over a ward or over all other bishops

and over the Aaronic priesthood **2 :** a chess piece that can move diagonally across any number of unoccupied squares **3 :** a mulled beverage of port wine flavored with roasted orange and cloves

bish·op·ric \'bish-ə-(,)prik\ *n* [ME *bisshopriche*, fr. OE *bisceoprīce*, fr. *bisceop* + *rīce* kingdom — more at RICH] **1 :** DIOCESE **2 :** the office of bishop **3 :** a bishop's seat or residence **4 :** the administrative body of a Mormon ward consisting of a bishop and two high priests as counselors

bis·muth \'biz-məth\ *n* [obs. G *bismut* (now *wismut*), modif. of *wismut*, fr. *wise* meadow + *mut* claim to a mine] **:** a heavy brittle grayish white chiefly trivalent metallic element chemically like arsenic and antimony — see ELEMENT table — **bis·muth·al** \-mə-thəl\ *adj* — **bis·mu·thic** \biz-'məth-ik, -'myü-thik\ *adj*

bi·son \'bīs-ᵊn, 'bīz-\ *n, pl* **bison** [L *bisont-*, *bison*, of Gmc origin; akin to OHG *wisant* aurochs; akin to OPruss *wis*sambrs aurochs] **:** any of several large shaggy-maned usu. gregarious recent or extinct bovine mammals (genus *Bison*) having a large head with short horns and heavy forequarters surmounted by a large fleshy hump: as **a :** WISENT **b :** BUFFALO b — **bi·son·tine** \-ᵊn-,tīn\ *adj*

[1]**bisque** \'bisk\ *n* [F] **:** odds allowed an inferior player: as **a :** a point taken when desired in a set of tennis **b :** an extra turn in croquet **c :** one or more strokes off a golf score

[2]**bisque** *n* [F] **1 :** a thick cream soup made of shellfish or of the flesh of birds or rabbits; *also* **:** a cream soup of pureed vegetables **2 :** ice cream containing powdered nuts or macaroons

[3]**bisque** *n* [by shortening & alter.] **:** BISCUIT 2; *esp* **:** unglazed ceramic ware that is not to be glazed but is hard-fired and vitreous

bis·ter *or* **bis·tre** \'bis-tər\ *n* [F *bistre*] **1 :** a yellowish brown to dark brown pigment used in art **2 :** a grayish to yellowish brown — **bis·tered** \-tərd\ *adj*

bis·tort \'bis-,tȯ(ə)rt\ *n* [MF *bistorte*, fr. (assumed) ML *bistorta*, fr. L *bis-* + *torta*, fem. of *tortus*, pp. of *torquēre* to twist — more at TORTURE] **:** any of several polygonums; *esp* **:** a European herb (*Polygonum bistorta*) or a related American plant (*P. bistordoides*) with twisted roots used as astringents

bis·tro \'bis-(,)trō, 'bēs-\ *n* [F] **1 :** a small or unpretentious European wineshop or restaurant **2 a :** a small bar or tavern **b :** NIGHTCLUB — **bis·tro·ic** \bis-'trō-ik, bēs-\ *adj*

bi·sul·cate \(')bī-'səl-,kāt\ *adj* **:** CLOVEN ⟨~ hoof⟩

bi·sul·fate \(')bī-'səl-,fāt\ *n* [ISV] **:** an acid sulfate

bi·sul·fide \-,fīd\ *n* [ISV] **:** DISULFIDE

bi·sul·fite \-,fīt\ *n* [F, fr. *bi-* + *sulfite*] **:** an acid sulfite

[1]**bit** \'bit\ *n* [ME *bitt*, fr. OE *bite* act of biting; akin to OE *bītan*] **1 :** something bitten or held with the teeth: **a :** the usu. steel part of a bridle inserted in the mouth of a horse **b :** the rimmed mouth end on the stem of a pipe or cigar holder **2 a :** the biting or cutting edge or part of a tool; *also* **:** a replaceable part of a compound tool that actually performs the function (as drilling or boring) for which the whole tool is designed **b** *pl* **:** the jaws or nippers of tongs or pincers **3 :** something that curbs or restrains **4 :** the part of a key that enters the lock and acts on the bolt and tumblers

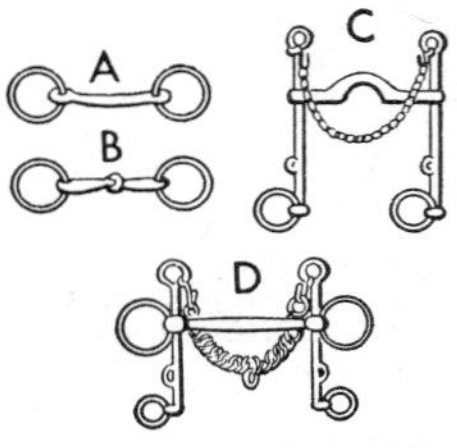

bits 1a: *A* bar bit, *B* snaffle, *C* curb, *D* Pelham

[2]**bit** *vt* **bit·ted; bit·ting 1 a :** to put a bit in the mouth of (a horse) **b :** to control as if with a bit **:** CURB **2 :** to form a bit on (a key)

[3]**bit** *n* [ME, fr. OE *bita*; akin to OE *bītan*] **1 :** a small quantity of food **:** MORSEL; *esp* **:** a small delicacy **2 a :** a small piece or quantity of some material thing **b** (1) **:** a small coin (2) **:** a unit of value equal to ⅛ of a dollar ⟨four ~*s*⟩ **3 :** something small or unimportant of its kind: as **a :** a brief period **:** WHILE **b :** SOMEWHAT **:** some degree or extent **c :** the smallest or an insignificant amount or degree **d :** a small part usu. with spoken lines in a theatrical performance

[4]**bit** *n* [*bi*nary digi*t*] **1 :** a unit of information equivalent to the result of a choice between two equally probable alternatives **2 :** a unit of computer memory corresponding to the ability to store the result of a choice between two alternatives

bi·tar·trate \(')bī-'tär-,trāt\ *n* [ISV] **:** an acid tartrate

[1]**bitch** \'bich\ *n* [ME *bicche*, fr. OE *bicce*; akin to OE *bæc* back] **1 :** the female of the dog or some other carnivorous mammals **2 a :** a lewd or immoral woman **b :** a malicious, spiteful, and domineering woman **3** *slang* **:** COMPLAINT

[2]**bitch** *vt* **1** *slang* **:** SPOIL, BOTCH **2** *slang* **:** to complain of or about **3** *slang* **:** CHEAT, DOUBLECROSS **~** *vi, slang* **:** COMPLAIN

[1]**bite** \'bīt\ *vb* **bit** \'bit\ **bit·ten** \'bit-ᵊn\ *also* **bit; bit·ing** \'bīt-iŋ\ [ME *biten*, fr. OE *bītan*; akin to OHG *bīzan* to bite, L *findere* to split] *vt* **1 :** to seize with teeth, jaws, or an analogous organ so as to enter, grip, or wound; *also* **:** to wound, pierce, or sting with a fang, a proboscis, or similar organ **2 :** to cut or pierce as if with an edged weapon **3 :** to cause sharp pain or stinging discomfort to **4 a :** to take hold of **b :** to affect profoundly **:** IMPRESS **5 :** to eat into **:** CORRODE **6 a :** to take in **:** CHEAT **b :** to catch as if with teeth by a sudden turn of events **~** *vi* **1 :** to bite something or have the habit of biting **2** *of a weapon or tool* **:** to cut, pierce, or take hold **3 :** to cause irritation or smarting **4 :** CORRODE **5 a** *of fish* **:** to take a bait **b :** to respond so as to be caught by something used as bait **6 :** to take or maintain a firm hold — **bit·er** \'bīt-ər\ *n*

[2]**bite** *n* **1 :** the act or manner of biting **2 :** FOOD: **a :** the amount of food taken at a bite **:** MORSEL **b :** a small amount of food **:** SNACK **c :** a meal esp. if impromptu **3** *archaic* **:** CHEAT, TRICK; *also* **:** SHARPER **4 :** a wound made by biting **5 :** the hold or grip by which friction is created or purchase obtained **6 :** a surface that creates friction or is brought into contact with another for the purpose of obtaining a hold **7 :** a keen incisive quality or sharp penetrating effect **8 :** the corroding of an etcher's plate by acid **9 :** an amount taken usu. in one operation for one purpose **:** CUT

bite·wing \'bīt-,wiŋ\ *n* **:** a dental X-ray film designed to show the crowns of the upper and lower teeth simultaneously

bit·ing \'bīt-iŋ\ *adj* **:** that causes sharp pain **syn** see INCISIVE

biting midge *n* **:** any of a family (Ceratopogonidae) of midges

bit·stock \'bit-,stäk\ *n* **:** a device for turning a bit by hand **:** BRACE

[1]**bitt** \'bit\ *n* [perh. fr. ON *biti* beam; akin to OE *bōt* boat] **1 :** a single or double post of metal or wood fixed on the deck of a ship for securing mooring or other lines **2 :** BOLLARD 1

[2]**bitt** *vt* **:** to make (a cable) fast about a bitt

[1]**bit·ter** \'bit-ər\ *adj* [ME, fr. OE *biter*; akin to OHG *bittar* bitter, OE *bītan*] **1 a :** having or being a peculiarly acrid, astringent, or disagreeable taste suggestive of an infusion of hops that is one of the four basic taste sensations **b :** distasteful or distressing to the mind **:** GALLING **2 :** marked by intensity or severity: **a :** accompanied by severe pain or suffering **b :** VEHEMENT, RELENTLESS ⟨~ partisan⟩; *also* **:** exhibiting intense animosity **c** (1) **:** harshly reproachful **:** sharp and resentful (2) **:** marked by cynicism and rancor **d :** intensely unpleasant esp. in coldness or rawness **3 :** expressive of severe pain, grief, or regret — **bit·ter·ish** \'bit-ə-rish\ *adj* — **bit·ter·ly** *adv* — **bit·ter·ness** *n*

[2]**bitter** *adv* **:** BITTERLY

[3]**bitter** *n* **1 :** bitter quality **2 a** *pl* **:** a usu. alcoholic solution of bitter and often aromatic plant products used esp. in preparing mixed drinks or as a mild tonic **b** *Brit* **:** a very dry heavily hopped ale

[4]**bitter** *vt* **:** to make bitter ⟨~*ed* ale⟩

[1]**bitter end** *n* **:** the inboard end of a ship's anchoring cable

[2]**bitter end** *n* [prob. fr. [1]*bitter end*] **:** the last extremity however painful or calamitous — **bit·ter–end·er** \,bit-ə-'ren-dər\ *n*

[1]**bit·tern** \'bit-ərn\ *n* [ME *bitoure*, fr. MF *butor*] **:** any of various small or medium-sized nocturnal herons (*Botaurus* and related genera) with a characteristic booming cry

[2]**bittern** *n* [irreg. fr. [1]*bitter*] **:** the bitter mother liquor that remains in saltworks after the salt has crystallized out

bitter principle *n* **:** any of various neutral substances of strong bitter taste (as aloin) extracted from plants

bit·ter·root \'bit-ə(r)-,rüt, -,ru̇t\ *n* **:** a succulent Rocky mountain herb (*Lewisia rediviva*) of the purslane family with fleshy farinaceous roots and pink flowers

[1]**bit·ter·sweet** \'bit-ər-,swēt\ *n* **1 :** something that is bittersweet; *esp* **:** pleasure alloyed with pain **2 a :** a sprawling poisonous weedy nightshade (*Solanum dulcamara*) with purple flowers and oval reddish orange berries **b :** a No. American vining staff tree (*Celastrus scandens*) having clusters of small greenish flowers succeeded by yellow capsules that open when ripe disclosing the scarlet aril

[2]**bittersweet** *adj* **1 :** being at once bitter and sweet **2 :** of or relating to a prepared chocolate containing little sugar

bit·ter·weed \'bit-ər-,wēd\ *n* **:** any of several American plants containing a bitter principle: as **a :** RAGWEED 2 **b :** HORSEWEED **c :** a sneezeweed (genus *Helenium*)

bit·tock \'bit-ək\ *n, chiefly Scot* **:** a little bit

[1]**bit·ty** *or* **bit·tie** \'bit-ē\ *adj* **:** made up of or containing bits

[2]**bitty** *or* **bittie** *adj, dial* **:** SMALL, TINY ⟨a little ~ dog⟩

bi·tu·men \bə-'t(y)ü-mən, bī-\ *n* [ME *bithumen* mineral pitch, fr. L *bitumin-*, *bitumen*] **1 :** an asphalt of Asia Minor used in ancient times as a cement and mortar **2 :** any of various mixtures of hydrocarbons (as tar) often together with their nonmetallic derivatives — **bi·tu·mi·ni·za·tion** \-,t(y)ü-mə-nə-'zā-shən\ *n* — **bi·tu·mi·nize** \-'t(y)ü-mə-,nīz\ *vt* — **bi·tu·mi·noid** \-,nȯid\ *adj*

bi·tu·mi·nous \bə-'t(y)ü-mə-nəs, bī-\ *adj* **1 :** resembling, containing, or impregnated with bitumen **2 :** of or relating to bituminous coal

bituminous coal *n* **:** a coal that yields when heated considerable volatile bituminous matter — called also *soft coal*

bi·va·lence \(')bī-'vā-lən(t)s\ *or* **bi·va·len·cy** \-lən-sē\ *n* **:** the quality or state of being bivalent

[1]**bi·va·lent** \-lənt\ *adj* **1 :** having a valence of two **2 :** associated in pairs in synapsis

[2]**bivalent** *n* **:** a pair of synaptic chromosomes

[1]**bi·valve** \'bī-,valv\ *also* **bi·valved** \-,valvd\ *adj* **1 :** having a shell composed of two valves **2 :** having or consisting of two corresponding movable pieces

[2]**bivalve** *n* **:** an animal (as a clam) with a 2-valved shell

bi·var·i·ate \(')bī-'ver-ē-ət, -'var-\ *adj* **:** of, relating to, or involving two variables

biv·ouac \'biv-,wak, -ə-,wak\ *n* [F, fr. LG *biwake*, fr. *bi* at + *wake* guard] **1 :** an encampment under little or no shelter usu. for a short time **2 :** a camping out for a night; *also* **:** a temporary shelter or settlement — **bivouac** *vi* **biv·ouacked; biv·ouack·ing**

[1]**bi·week·ly** \(')bī-'wē-klē\ *adj* **1 :** occurring every two weeks **:** FORTNIGHTLY **2 :** occurring twice a week — **biweekly** *adv*

[2]**biweekly** *n* **:** a biweekly publication

bi·year·ly \(')bī-'yi(ə)r-lē\ *adj* **1 :** BIENNIAL **2 :** BIANNUAL

[1]**bi·zarre** \bə-'zär\ *adj* [F, fr. It *bizzarro*] **:** strikingly out of the ordinary: as **a :** odd, extravagant, or eccentric in style or mode **b :** involving sensational contrasts or incongruities **c :** ATYPICAL **syn** see FANTASTIC — **bi·zarre·ly** *adv* — **bi·zarre·ness** *n*

[2]**bizarre** *n* **:** a flower with atypical striped marking

bi·zon·al \(')bī-'zōn-ᵊl\ *adj* **:** of or relating to the combined affairs of two administrative areas — **bi·zone** \'bī-,zōn\ *n*

[1]**blab** \'blab\ *n* [ME *blabbe*; akin to ME *blaberen*] **1 :** TATTLETALE **2 :** idle or excessive talk **:** CHATTER — **blab·by** \'blab-ē\ *adj*

[2]**blab** *vb* **blabbed; blab·bing** *vt* **:** to reveal esp. by talking without reserve or discretion **~** *vi* **1 :** to reveal a secret esp. by indiscreet chatter **2 :** PRATTLE

[1]**blab·ber** \'blab-ər\ *vb* **blab·ber·ing** \'blab-(ə-)riŋ\ [ME *blaberen*] **:** BABBLE, CHATTER

[2]**blabber** *n* **:** idle talk **:** BABBLE

[3]**blab·ber** \'blab-ər\ *n* [[2]*blab*] **:** one that blabs

blab·ber·mouth \'blab-ər-,mau̇th\ *n* **:** one who talks too much; *esp* **:** TATTLETALE

[1]**black** \'blak\ *adj* [ME *blak*, fr. OE *blæc*; akin to OHG *blah* black, L *flagrare* to burn, Gk *phlegein*, OE *bǣl* fire — more at BALD] **1 a :** of the color black **b :** very dark **2 a :** having dark skin, hair, and eyes **:** SWARTHY **b :** of or relating to a group or race characterized by dark pigmentation; *esp* **:** NEGROID **3 :** dressed in black **4 :** SOILED, DIRTY **5 a :** characterized by the absence of light ⟨a ~ night⟩ **b :** reflecting or transmitting little or no light ⟨~ water⟩ **6 a :** thoroughly evil **:** WICKED ⟨a ~ deed⟩ **b :** expressive of condemnation or discredit **7 :** invoking the supernatural and esp. the devil **8 a :** GLOOMY, CALAMITOUS; *specif* **:** marked by the occurrence of disaster **b :** SULLEN, HOSTILE **9 :** COMPLETE, UTTER

— **black·ish** \-ish\ *adj* — **black·ly** *adv* — **black·ness** *n*
²black *n* **1 :** a black pigment or dye; *esp* **:** one consisting largely of carbon **2 :** the achromatic object color of least lightness characteristically perceived to belong to objects that neither reflect nor transmit light **3 :** something that is black; *esp* **:** black clothing **4 :** a person belonging to a dark-skinned race; *also* **:** one stemming in part from such a race **5 :** total or nearly total absence of light **6 :** the condition of making a profit ⟨in the ~⟩
³black *vb* **:** BLACKEN
black·a·moor \'blak-ə-,mu̇(ə)r\ *n* [irreg. fr. *black* + *Moor*] **:** a dark-skinned person; *esp* **:** NEGRO
black-and-blue \,blak-ən-'blü\ *adj* **:** darkly discolored from blood effused by bruising
Black and Tan *n* **:** a recruit enlisted in England in 1920–21 for service in the Royal Irish Constabulary against Irish independence
black and white *n* **1 :** WRITING, PRINT **2 :** drawing or printing in black and white or in monochrome; *also* **:** a work so executed
black art *n* **:** magic practiced by conjurers and witches
black-a-vised *also* **black-a-viced** \'blak-ə-,vīst\ *adj* [*black* + F *à vis* as to face] **:** dark-complexioned
¹black·ball \'blak-,bȯl\ *n* **1 :** a small black ball for use as a negative vote in a ballot box **2 :** an adverse vote esp. against admitting someone to membership in an organization
²blackball *vt* **1 :** to vote against; *esp* **:** to exclude from membership by casting a negative vote **2 :** BOYCOTT, OSTRACIZE
black bass *n* **:** any of several highly prized freshwater sunfishes (genus *Micropterus*) native to eastern and central No. America
black·ber·ry \'blak-,ber-ē\ *n* **1 :** the usu. black or dark purple juicy but seedy edible fruit of various brambles (genus *Rubus*) of the rose family **2 :** a plant that bears blackberries
black bile *n* **:** a humor of medieval physiology believed to be secreted by the kidneys or spleen and to cause melancholy
black·bird \'blak-,bərd\ *n* **:** any of various birds of which the males are largely or entirely black: as **a :** a common and familiar British thrush (*Turdus merula*) that is black with orange bill and eye rim **b :** any of several American birds (family Icteridae)
black·board \'blak-,bō(ə)rd, -,bȯ(ə)rd\ *n, often attrib* **:** a hard smooth usu. dark surface used esp. in a classroom for writing or drawing on with chalk or crayons
black·body \'blak-'bäd-ē\ *n* **:** an ideal body or surface that completely absorbs all radiant energy falling upon it with no reflection
black book *n* **:** a book containing a blacklist
black calla *n* **:** an ornamental aroid (*Arum palaestinum*) with a dark purple or blackish spathe suggesting that of the calla
black·cap \'blak-,kap\ *n* **1 :** a black-fruited raspberry (*Rubus occidentalis*) native to eastern No. America and cultivated in varieties — called also *black raspberry* **2 :** any of several birds with black heads or crowns: as **a :** a small European warbler (*Sylvia atricapilla*) with a black crown **b :** CHICKADEE
black-capped \'blak-'kapt\ *adj, of a bird* **:** having the top of the head black
black·cock \-,käk\ *n* **:** BLACK GROUSE; *specif* **:** the male black grouse
black crappie *n* **:** a silvery black-mottled sunfish (*Pomoxis nigromaculatus*) of the Mississippi drainage and eastern U.S.
black·damp \'blak-'damp\ *n* **:** a carbon dioxide mixture occurring as a mine gas and incapable of supporting life or flame
black death *n* **:** a form of plague epidemic in Europe and Asia in the 14th century
black diamond *n* **1** *pl* **:** COAL 3a **2 :** ³CARBONADO **3 :** dense black hematite
black·en \'blak-ən\ *vb* **black·en·ing** \'blak-(ə-)niŋ\ *vi* **:** to become dark or black ~ *vt* **1 :** to make black **2 :** DEFAME, SULLY — **black·en·er** \'blak-(ə-)nər\ *n*
black-eyed pea \,blak-,īd-\ *n* **:** COWPEA
black-eyed Su·san \-'süz-ᵊn\ *n* **:** either of two No. American coneflowers (*Rudbeckia hirta* and *R. serotina*) having flower heads with deep yellow to orange rays and dark conical disks
black·face \'blak-,fās\ *n, often attrib* **1 :** makeup for a Negro role and esp. a comic one in a minstrel show **2 :** BOLDFACE
black·fin \'blak-,fin\ *n* **:** a whitefish (*Leucichthys nigripinnis*) of the Great Lakes valued as a food fish
black·fish \'blak-,fish\ *n* **1 :** any of numerous dark-colored fishes; *esp* **:** a small food fish (*Dallia pectoralis*) of Alaska and Siberia that is remarkable for its ability to revive after being frozen for a long time **2 :** any of several small toothed whales (genus *Globicephala*) related to the dolphins and found in warmer seas
black flag *n* **:** a pirate's flag usu. bearing a skull and crossbones
black·fly \'blak-,flī\ *n* **:** any of several small dark-colored insects; *esp* **:** a two-winged biting fly (*Simulium* or related genera) whose larvae live in flowing usu. clear streams
Black·foot \'blak-,fu̇t\ *n, pl* **Blackfeet** *or* **Blackfoot 1 a :** an Indian confederacy of Montana, Alberta, and Saskatchewan **b :** a member of a people belonging to this confederacy **2 :** the Algonquian language of the Blackfeet
black grouse *n* **:** a large grouse (*Lyrurus tetrix*) of western Asia and Europe of which the male is black with white wing patches and the female is barred and mottled
¹black·guard \'blag-ərd, -,ärd; 'blak-,gärd\ *n* **1** *obs* **:** the kitchen servants of a large household **2 a :** a rude or unscrupulous person **:** SCOUNDREL **b :** one who uses foul or abusive language — **blackguard·ism** \-,iz-əm\ *n* — **black·guard·ly** \-lē\ *adj or adv*
²blackguard *vi, archaic* **:** to behave in a ruffianly manner ~ *vt* **:** to talk about or address in abusive terms **:** DENOUNCE
black gum *n* **:** either of two tupelos (*Nyssa sylvatica* and *N. biflora*) with light and soft but tough wood
black hand *n, often cap B&H* **:** a Sicilian or Italian-American secret society engaged in crime — **black·hand·er** \'blak-,han-dər\ *n*
black·head \'blak-,hed\ *n* **1 :** any of various birds with black about the head **2 :** a small plug of sebum blocking the duct of a sebaceous gland esp. on the face **3 :** a destructive disease of turkeys and related birds caused by a protozoan (*Histomonas meleagridis*) that invades the intestinal ceca and liver **4 :** a larval clam or mussel attached to the skin or gills of a freshwater fish
black·heart \'blak-,härt\ *n* **1 :** a dark-fruited cherry **2 :** a plant disease in which the central tissues blacken
black·ing *n* **:** a substance that is applied to an object to make it black
¹black·jack \'blak-,jak\ *n* **1** [*black* + *jack* (vessel)] **:** a tankard for beer or ale usu. of tar-coated leather **2 :** SPHALERITE **3 :** a hand weapon typically consisting of a piece of leather-enclosed metal with a strap or springy shaft for a handle **4 :** a common often scrubby oak (*Quercus marilandica*) of the southeastern and southern U.S. with black bark **5 :** TWENTY-ONE 2
²blackjack *vt* **:** to strike with or as if with a blackjack
black knot *n* **:** a destructive disease of plum and cherry trees characterized by black excrescences on the branches and caused by a fungus (*Dibotryon morbosa*)
black lead *n* **:** GRAPHITE
black·leg \'blak-,leg, -,lāg\ *n* **1 :** an enzootic usu. fatal toxemia esp. of young cattle **2 :** a professional gambler **3** *chiefly Brit* **:** SCAB
black letter *n* **:** a style of type or lettering with a heavy face and angular outlines used by the earliest European printers and sometimes for printing German
black light *n* **:** invisible ultraviolet or infrared light
black·list \'blak-,list\ *n* **:** a list of persons who are disapproved of or are to be punished or boycotted — **blacklist** *vt*
black lung *n* **:** a disease of the lungs caused by habitual inhalation of coal dust
black magic *n* **:** WITCHCRAFT
black·mail \'blak-,māl\ *n* [*black* + ¹*mail*] **1 :** a tribute anciently exacted on the Scottish border by freebooting chiefs for immunity from pillage **2 a :** extortion by threats esp. of public exposure **b :** the payment extorted — **blackmail** *vt* — **black·mail·er** *n*
Black Ma·ria \,blak-mə-'rī-ə\ *n* **:** PATROL WAGON
black market *n* **:** illicit trade in goods in violation of official regulations; *also* **:** a place where such trade is carried on
black-mar·ket \'blak-'mär-kət\ *vb* **:** to buy or sell in a black market — **black marketer** *or* **black marketeer** *n*
Black Muslim *n* **:** a member of a Negro segregationist group following Muslim religious practices
black out *vi* **1 :** to become enveloped in darkness **2 :** to undergo a temporary loss of vision, consciousness, or memory **3 :** to extinguish or screen all lights for protection esp. against air attack ~ *vt* **1 :** to cause to black out **2 :** to suppress by censorship
black·out \'blak-,au̇t\ *n* **1 a :** a turning off of the stage lighting to separate scenes in a play **b :** a period of darkness enforced as a precaution against air raids **2 a :** a transient dulling or loss of vision or consciousness **b :** SUPPRESSION
black perch *n* **:** any of various dark-colored fishes (as a bass)
black·poll \'blak-,pōl\ *n* **:** a No. American warbler (*Dendroica striata*) having the top of the head of the male bird black when in full plumage
black power *n* **:** the mobilization of the political and economic power of American Negroes esp. to further racial equality
Black Rod *n* **:** the principal usher of the House of Lords and of various other legislative bodies in the British Commonwealth
black rot *n* **:** a bacterial or fungous rot of plants marked by dark brown discoloration
black sheep *n* **:** a discreditable member of a respectable group
Black·shirt \'blak-,shərt\ *n* **:** a member of a fascist organization having a black shirt as a distinctive part of its uniform
black·smith \'blak-,smith\ *n* [fr. his working with iron, known as black metal] **:** a smith who forges iron — **black·smith·ing** *n*
black·snake \'blak-,snāk\ *n* **1 :** any of several snakes largely black or very dark in color; *esp* **:** either of two harmless snakes (*Coluber constrictor* and *Elaphe obsoleta*) of the U.S. **2 :** a long tapering braided whip of rawhide or leather
black·thorn \'blak-,thȯ(ə)rn\ *n* **1 :** a European spiny plum (*Prunus spinosa*) with hard wood and small white flowers **2 :** any of several American hawthorns
black tie *n* **:** semiformal evening dress for men
black·top \'blak-,täp\ *n, often attrib* **:** a bituminous material used esp. for surfacing roads — **blacktop** *vt*
black vomit *n* **1 :** vomitus consisting of dark-colored matter **2 :** a condition characterized by black vomit; *esp* **:** YELLOW FEVER
Black·wall hitch \,blak-,wȯl-\ *n* [*Blackwall*, shipyard in London, England] **:** a hitch for securing a rope to a hook — see KNOT illustration
black walnut *n* **:** a walnut (*Juglans nigra*) of eastern No. America with hard strong heavy dark brown wood and oily edible nuts; *also* **:** its wood or nut
black·wa·ter \'blak-,wȯt-ər, -,wät-\ *n* **:** any of several diseases of lower animals or man characterized by dark-colored urine
black widow *n* **:** a venomous New World spider (*Latrodectus mactans*) having the female black with an hourglass-shaped red mark on the underside of the abdomen
blad·der \'blad-ər\ *n* [ME, fr. OE *blǣdre;* akin to OHG *blātara* bladder, OE *blāwan* to blow] **1 a :** a membranous sac in animals that serves as the receptacle of a liquid or contains gas; *esp* **:** the urinary bladder **b :** VESICLE **2 :** something resembling a bladder
bladder kelp *n* **:** any of various brown algae with prominent floats; *esp* **:** BLADDER WRACK
blad·der·like \-,līk\ *adj* **:** similar to or inflated like a bladder
blad·der·nut \-,nət\ *n* **:** an ornamental shrub or small tree (genus *Staphylea* of the family Staphyleaceae, the bladdernut family) with panicles of small white flowers followed by inflated capsules; *also* **:** one of the capsules
bladder worm *n* **:** a bladderlike larval tapeworm (as a cysticercus)
blad·der·wort \-,wərt, -,wȯ(ə)rt\ *n* **:** any of a genus (*Utricularia* of the family Lentibulariaceae, the bladderwort family) of chiefly aquatic plants with vesicular floats or insect traps
bladder wrack *n* **:** a common black rockweed (*Fucus vesiculosus*) used in preparing kelp and as a manure
blad·dery \'blad-ə-rē\ *adj* **:** having bladders; *also* **:** BLADDERLIKE
blade \'blād\ *n* [ME, fr. OE *blæd;* akin to OHG *blat* leaf, L *folium*, Gk *phyllon*, OE *blōwan* to blossom — more at BLOW] **1 a :** LEAF 1a(1); *esp* **:** the leaf of an herb or more narrowly of a grass **b :** the flat expanded part of a leaf as distinguished from the petiole **2 :** something resembling the blade of a leaf: as **a :** the broad flattened part of an oar or paddle **b :** an arm of a screw propeller, centrifugal fan, or steam turbine **c :** a broad flat body part; *specif* **:** SCAPULA — used chiefly in naming cuts of meat **d :** the flat portion of the tongue immediately behind the tip; *also* **:** this portion together with the tip **3 a :** the cutting part of an implement **b** (1) **:** SWORD (2) **:** SWORDSMAN (3) **:** a jaunty rakish fellow ⟨gay ~⟩ **c :** the runner of an ice skate — **blad·ed** \'blād-əd\ *adj*
blae \'blā\ *adj* [ME *bla, blo*, fr. ON *blār;* akin to OHG *blāo* blue — more at BLUE] *chiefly Scot* **:** dark blue or bluish gray
blain \'blān\ *n* [ME, fr. OE *blegen;* akin to MLG *bleine* blain, OE

blāwan to blow] **:** an inflammatory swelling or sore

blam·able *also* **blame·able** \'blā-mə-bəl\ *adj* **:** deserving of blame **:** REPREHENSIBLE — **blam·ably** \-blē\ *adv*

¹**blame** \'blām\ *vt* [ME *blamen*, fr. OF *blamer*, fr. LL *blasphemare* to blaspheme, fr. Gk *blasphēmein*] **1 :** to find fault with **:** CENSURE **2 a :** to hold responsible ⟨~ him for everything⟩ **b :** to place responsibility for ⟨~*s* it on me⟩ **syn** see CRITICIZE — **blam·er** *n*

²**blame** *n* **1 :** REPROOF, CENSURE **2 a :** a state of being blameworthy **:** CULPABILITY **b** *archaic* **:** FAULT, SIN **3 :** responsibility for something deserving censure

blame·ful \'blām-fəl\ *adj* **:** deserving of blame — **blame·ful·ly** \-fə-lē\ *adv*

blame·less \'blām-ləs\ *adj* **:** free from blame or fault **:** IRREPROACHABLE — **blame·less·ly** *adv* — **blame·less·ness** *n*

blame·wor·thi·ness \'blām-,wər-t͟hē-nəs\ *n* **:** the quality or state of being blameworthy

blame·wor·thy \-t͟hē\ *adj* **:** deserving blame **:** CENSURABLE
syn GUILTY, CULPABLE: BLAMEWORTHY is likely to be chosen in deliberate avoidance of the stronger connotation of the other words and is very wide in applicability; GUILTY implies responsibility for or consciousness of crime, sin, or at least unquestioned error or misdoing; CULPABLE usu. suggests less stringent blame than GUILTY and connotes malfeasance or errors of omission, negligence, or ignorance

blanc fixe \'blaŋk-'fiks\ *n* [F, lit., fixed white] **:** barium sulfate $BaSO_4$ prepared as a heavy white powder and used esp. as a filler in paper, rubber, and linoleum or as a pigment

blanch \'blanch\ *vb* [ME *blaunchen*, fr. MF *blanchir*, fr. OF *blanche*, fem. of *blanc*, adj., white] *vt* **1 :** to take the color out of: **a :** to bleach by excluding light ⟨~ celery⟩ **b :** to scald or parboil in water or steam in order to remove the skin from or whiten ⟨~ almonds⟩ ⟨~ kidney⟩ **c :** to clean (a coin blank) in an acid solution **d :** to cover (sheet iron or steel) with a coating of tin **2 :** to make ashen or pale ~ *vi* **:** to become white or pale **syn** see WHITEN — **blanch·er** *n*

blanc·mange \blə-'mänj\ *n* [ME *blancmanger*, fr. MF *blanc manger*, lit., white food] **:** a dessert made from gelatinous or starchy substances and milk usu. sweetened, flavored, and shaped in a mold

bland \'bland\ *adj* [L *blandus*] **1 :** characterized by smoothness or tranquillity **:** UNPERTURBED **2 a :** having a soothing effect ⟨a ~ climate⟩ **b :** DULL, INSIPID **syn** see SOFT, SUAVE — **bland·ly** \'blan-(d)lē\ *adv* — **bland·ness** \'blan(d)-nəs\ *n*

blan·dish \'blan-dish\ *vb* [ME *blandishen*, fr. MF *blandiss-*, stem of *blandir*, fr. L *blandiri*, fr. *blandus* mild, flattering] *vt* **:** to coax with flattery **:** CAJOLE ~ *vi* **:** to use flattery — **blan·dish·er** *n* — **blan·dish·ment** \-mənt\ *n*

¹**blank** \'blaŋk\ *adj* [ME, fr. MF *blanc*, of Gmc origin; akin to OHG *blanch* white; akin to L *flagrare* to burn — more at BLACK] **1** *archaic* **:** COLORLESS **2 a :** appearing or causing to appear dazed, confounded, or nonplussed ⟨~ dismay⟩ **b :** EXPRESSIONLESS ⟨a ~ stare⟩ **3 a :** lacking interest, variety, or change ⟨~ hours⟩ **b :** EMPTY; *esp* **:** free from writing or marks ⟨~ paper⟩ **c :** having spaces to be filled in **d :** MISSING, VOID ⟨a ~ suit at cards⟩ **4 :** ABSOLUTE, UNQUALIFIED ⟨a ~ refusal⟩ **5 :** UNFINISHED; *esp* **:** having a plain or unbroken surface where an opening is usual ⟨~ key⟩ ⟨~ arch⟩ **syn** see EMPTY — **blank·ly** *adv* — **blank·ness** *n*

²**blank** *n* **1 a :** an empty space (as on a paper) **b :** a paper with spaces for the entry of data **2 a :** an empty or featureless place or space **b :** a vacant or uneventful period **3 :** BULL'S-EYE 4 **4 :** a dash substituting for an omitted word **5 a :** a piece of material prepared to be made into something (as a key) by a further operation **b :** a cartridge loaded with powder but no bullet **6 :** VOID 4

³**blank** *vt* **1 a :** OBSCURE, OBLITERATE ⟨~ out a line⟩ **b :** to stop access to **:** SEAL ⟨~ off a tunnel⟩ **2 :** to keep from scoring ⟨~*ed* for eight innings⟩ **3 :** to cut with a die from a piece of stock

blank check *n* **1 :** a signed check with the amount unspecified **2 :** complete freedom of action

blank endorsement *n* **:** endorsement of commercial paper without a qualifying phrase making the paper payable to the bearer

¹**blan·ket** \'blaŋ-kət\ *n* [ME, fr. OF *blankete*, fr. *blanc*] **1 a :** a large usu. oblong piece of woven fabric used as a bed covering **b :** a similar piece of fabric used as a body covering **2 :** something that resembles a blanket; *esp* **:** a covering layer

²**blanket** *vt* **1 :** to cover with a blanket: **a :** to cover so as to obscure, interrupt, suppress, or extinguish **b :** to apply or cause to apply to uniformly despite wide separation or diversity among the elements included **2** *archaic* **:** to toss in a blanket

³**blanket** *adj* **1 :** covering a group or class **2 :** applicable in all instances

blan·ket·flow·er \'blaŋ-kət-,flau̇(-ə)r\ *n* **:** GAILLARDIA

blanket stitch *n* **:** a buttonhole stitch with spaces of variable width used on materials too thick to hem — **blanket-stitch** *vt*

blank verse *n* **:** unrhymed verse; *specif* **:** unrhymed iambic pentameter verse

¹**blare** \'bla(ə)r, 'ble(ə)r\ *vb* [ME *bleren*; akin to OE *blǣtan* to bleat] *vi* **:** to sound loud and strident ~ *vt* **1 :** to utter raucously **2 :** to proclaim flamboyantly

²**blare** *n* **1 :** a loud strident noise **2 :** FLAMBOYANCE

blar·ney \'blär-nē\ *n* [*Blarney* stone] **:** skillful flattery **:** BLANDISHMENT — **blarney** *vb*

Blarney stone *n* **:** a stone in Blarney Castle near Cork, Ireland, held to make those who kiss it skilled in flattery

bla·sé \blä-'zā\ *adj* [F] **:** apathetic to pleasure or excitement as a result of excessive indulgence or enjoyment **:** SOPHISTICATED

blas·pheme \blas-'fēm, 'blas-,\ *vb* [ME *blasfemen*, fr. LL *blasphemare*] *vt* **1 :** to speak of or address with irreverence **2 :** REVILE, ABUSE ~ *vi* **:** to utter blasphemy — **blas·phem·er** *n*

blas·phe·mous \'blas-fə-məs\ *adj* **:** impiously irreverent **:** PROFANE — **blas·phe·mous·ly** *adv* — **blas·phe·mous·ness** *n*

blas·phe·my \'blas-fə-mē\ *n* **1 a :** the act of insulting or showing contempt or lack of reverence for God **b :** the act of claiming the attributes of deity **2 :** irreverence toward something considered sacred or inviolable

¹**blast** \'blast\ *n* [ME, fr. OE *blǣst*; akin to OHG *blāst* blast, OE *blāwan* to blow] **1 a :** a violent gust of wind **b :** the effect or accompaniment of such a gust **2 :** the sound produced by an impulsion of air through a wind instrument or whistle **3 a :** a stream forced through a hole **b :** a violent outburst **c :** the continuous blowing to which a charge of ore or metal is subjected in a furnace **4 a :** a sudden pernicious influence or effect **b :** a disease that suggests the effect of a noxious wind; *esp* **:** one of plants that causes the foliage or flowers to wither **5 a :** an explosion or violent detonation **b :** the charge used esp. for shattering rock **c :** the violent effect produced in the vicinity of an explosion that consists of a wave of increased atmospheric pressure followed by a wave of decreased atmospheric pressure **6 :** SPEED, CAPACITY

²**blast** *vi* **1 :** to produce a strident sound **2 a :** to use an explosive **b :** SHOOT **3 :** to make a vigorous attack **4 :** SHRIVEL, WITHER ~ *vt* **1 a :** to injure by or as if by the action of wind **b :** to affect with a blighting influence **2 :** to shatter by or as if by an explosive **:** DEMOLISH **3 a :** to apply a forced draft to **b :** to strike with explosive force — **blast·er** *n* — **blast·ing** *n or adj*

blast- *or* **blasto-** *comb form* [G, fr. Gk, fr. *blastos*] **:** bud **:** budding **:** germ ⟨*blasto*disc⟩ ⟨*blast*ula⟩

-blast \,blast\ *n comb form* [NL *-blastus*, fr. Gk *blastos* bud, shoot; akin to OE *molda* top of the head, Skt *mūrdhan* head] **:** formative unit esp. of living matter **:** germ **:** cell **:** cell layer ⟨epi*blast*⟩

blast·ed *adj* **1 a :** BLIGHTED, WITHERED **b :** damaged by violence **:** BATTERED **2 :** CONFOUNDED, DETESTABLE

blas·te·ma \bla-'stē-mə\ *n, pl* **blastemas** *or* **blas·te·ma·ta** \-mət-ə\ [NL, fr. Gk *blastēma* offshoot, fr. *blastos*] **:** a mass of living substance capable of growth and differentiation — **blas·te·mat·ic** \,blas-tə-'mat-ik\ *or* **blas·te·mic** \bla-'stē-mik\ *adj*

blast furnace *n* **:** a furnace in which combustion is forced by a current of air under pressure; *esp* **:** one for the reduction of iron ore

-blas·tic \'blas-tik\ *adj comb form* [ISV, fr. *-blast*] **:** having (such or so many) buds, germs, cells, or cell layers ⟨diplo*blastic*⟩

blast·ie \'blas-tē\ *n* [Sc *blast* to wither, fr. ²*blast*] *Scot* **:** an ugly little creature

blast·ment \'blas(t)-mənt\ *n, archaic* **:** a blighting influence

blas·to·coel *or* **blas·to·coele** \'blas-tə-,sēl\ *n* [ISV] **:** the cavity of a blastula — **blas·to·coe·lic** \,blas-tə-'sē-lik\ *adj*

blas·to·cyst \'blas-tə-,sist\ *n* **:** the modified blastula of a placental mammal

blas·to·derm \-,dərm\ *n* [G, fr. *blast-* + *-derm*] **:** a blastodisc after completion of cleavage and formation of the blastocoel — **blas·to·der·mat·ic** \,blas-tə-,dər-'mat-ik\ *or* **blas·to·der·mic** \-'dər-mik\ *adj*

blas·to·disc \'blas-tə-,disk\ *n* **:** the embryo-forming portion of an egg with discoidal cleavage usu. appearing as a small disc on the upper surface of the yolk mass

blast off *vi* **:** to take off

blast-off \'blas-,tȯf\ *n* **:** a blasting off (as of a rocket)

blas·to·gen·e·sis \,blas-tə-'jen-ə-səs\ *n* [NL] **1 :** reproduction by budding **2 :** the transmission of inherited characters through the germ plasm — **blas·to·ge·net·ic** \-tō-jə-'net-ik\ *adj*

blas·to·mere \'blas-tə-,mi(ə)r\ *n* [ISV] **:** a cell produced during cleavage of an egg — **blas·to·mer·ic** \,blas-tə-'mi(ə)r-ik, -'mer-\ *adj*

blas·to·my·cete \,blas-tə-'mī-,sēt, -(,)mī-'sēt\ *n* [deriv. of *blast-* + Gk *mykēt-*, *mykēs* fungus — more at MYC-] **:** any of a group (Blastomycetes) of pathogenic fungi growing typically like yeasts

blas·to·my·co·sis \-(,)mī-'kō-səs\ *n* **:** a disease caused by a blastomycete — **blas·to·my·cot·ic** \-'kät-ik\ *adj*

blas·to·por·al \,blas-tə-'pōr-əl, -'pȯr-\ *or* **blas·to·por·ic** \-ik\ *adj* **:** of, relating to, or involving a blastopore

blas·to·pore \'blas-tə-,pō(ə)r, -,pȯ(ə)r\ *n* **:** the opening of the archenteron

blas·to·sphere \'blas-tə-,sfi(ə)r\ *n* **:** BLASTULA — **blas·to·spher·ic** \,blas-tə-'sfi(ə)r-ik, -'sfer-\ *adj*

blas·tu·la \'blas-chə-lə\ *n, pl* **blastulas** *or* **blas·tu·lae** \-,lē\ [NL, fr. Gk *blastos*] **:** an early metazoan embryo typically having the form of a hollow fluid-filled rounded cavity bounded by a single layer of cells — compare GASTRULA, MORULA — **blas·tu·lar** \-lər\ *adj* — **blas·tu·la·tion** \,blas-chə-'lā-shən\ *n*

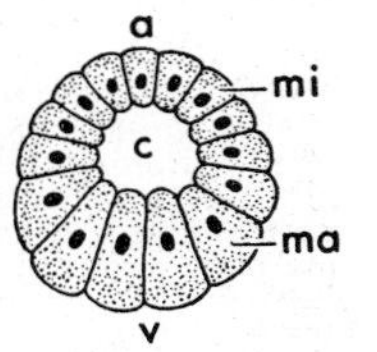

section of blastula: *c* blastocoel, *ma* macromere, *mi* micromere, *a* animal pole, *v* vegetal pole

blat \'blat\ *vb* **blat·ted**; **blat·ting** [imit.] *vi* **1 :** to cry esp. like a calf or sheep **2 a :** to make a raucous noise **b :** BLAB ~ *vt* **:** to utter loudly or foolishly **:** BLURT — **blat** *n*

bla·tan·cy \'blāt-ᵊn-sē\ *n* **1 :** the quality or state of being blatant **2 :** something that is blatant

bla·tant \'blāt-ᵊnt\ *adj* [perh. fr. L *blatire* to chatter] **1 :** noisy esp. in a vulgar or offensive manner **:** CLAMOROUS **2 :** OBTRUSIVE, BRAZEN **syn** see VOCIFEROUS — **bla·tant·ly** *adv*

blate \'blāt\ *adj* [ME] *chiefly Scot* **:** TIMID, SHEEPISH; *also* **:** SLOW

¹**blath·er** \'blat͟h-ər\ *vi* **blath·er·ing** \-(ə-)riŋ\ [ON *blathra*; akin to MHG *blōdern* to chatter] **:** to talk foolishly — **blath·er·er** \-ər-ər\ *n*

²**blather** *n* **1 :** voluble or nonsensical talk **2 :** STIR, COMMOTION

blath·er·skite \'blat͟h-ər-,skīt\ *n* [*blather* + Sc dial. *skate* a contemptible person] **:** a blustering talkative fellow

blaw \'blȯ\ *vb* **blawed**; **blawn** \'blȯn\ [ME (northern dial.) *blawen*, fr. OE *blāwan*] *chiefly Scot* **:** BLOW

¹**blaze** \'blāz\ *n* [ME *blase*, fr. OE *blæse* torch; akin to OE *bǣl* fire] **1 a :** an intensely burning fire **b :** intense direct light often accompanied by heat **c :** an active burning; *esp* **:** a sudden outburst of flame **2 :** something that resembles the blaze of a fire: as **a :** a dazzling display **b :** a sudden outburst **c :** BRILLIANCE
syn FLAME, FLARE, GLARE, GLOW: BLAZE implies great rapidity in kindling of material and the radiation of intense heat and light; FLAME suggests a tongue or sheet of glowing vapor in wavering or flickering motion; FLARE implies a sudden and rapid burst of fire or flame against a dark background; GLARE implies the reflection or diffusion of very bright steady light; GLOW stresses luminosity without flame and may suggest warmth and suffused radiance in contrast to blazing heat or blinding glare

²**blaze** *vi* **1 a :** to burn brightly **:** FLAME **b :** to flare up **2 :** to be conspicuously brilliant **3 :** to shoot rapidly and repeatedly ⟨~ away⟩ — **blaz·ing** *adj* — **blaz·ing·ly** \'blā-ziŋ-lē\ *adv*

3blaze *vt* [ME *blasen*, fr. MD *blāsen* to blow; akin to OHG *blāst* blast] **:** to make public or conspicuous **:** PROCLAIM
4blaze *n* [G *blas*, fr. OHG *plas;* akin to OE *blæse*] **1 a :** a white mark on the face of an animal **b :** a white or gray streak in the hair of the head **2 :** a trail marker; *esp* **:** a mark made on a tree by chipping off a piece of the bark
5blaze *vt* **1 :** to mark (as a trail) with blazes **2 :** PIONEER
blaz·er \'blā-zər\ *n* **1 :** one that blazes **2 :** a single-breasted sports jacket in bright stripes or solid color
blazing star *n* **1** *archaic* **:** COMET **2** *archaic* **:** a center of attraction **:** CYNOSURE **3 :** any of several plants having conspicuous flower clusters: as **a :** a plant (*Chamaelirium luteum*) of the bunchflower family **b :** BUTTON SNAKEROOT 1
1bla·zon \'blāz-ᵊn\ *n* [ME *blason*, fr. MF] **1 a :** COAT OF ARMS **b :** the proper description or representation of heraldic or armorial bearings **2 :** DESCRIPTION, SHOW; *esp* **:** ostentatious display
2blazon *vt* **bla·zon·ing** \'blāz-niŋ, -ᵊn-iŋ\ **1 :** to publish far and wide; *esp* **:** to boast of **2 a :** to describe (heraldic or armorial bearings) in technical terms **b :** to represent (armorial bearings) in drawing or engraving **3 a :** to depict or inscribe in colors **b :** DECK, ADORN — **bla·zon·er** \-nər, -ᵊn-ər\ *n* — **bla·zon·ing** *n*
bla·zon·ry \'blāz-ᵊn-rē\ *n* **1 a :** BLAZON 1b **b :** BLAZON 1a **2 :** dazzling display
1bleach \'blēch\ *vb* [ME *blechen*, fr. OE *blǣcean;* akin to OE *blāc* pale, *bǣl* fire] *vt* **1 :** to remove color or stains from **2 :** to make whiter or lighter **~** *vi* **:** to grow white or lose color **syn** see WHITEN
2bleach *n* **1 :** the act or process of bleaching **2 :** a preparation used in bleaching **3 :** the degree of whiteness obtained by bleaching
bleach·er \'blē-chər\ *n* **1 :** one that bleaches or is used in bleaching **2** *usu pl but sing or pl in constr* **:** a usu. uncovered stand of tiered planks providing seating space for spectators
bleaching powder *n* **:** a powder for bleaching; *esp* **:** a mixture of calcium hydroxide, chloride, and hypochlorite used as a bleach, disinfectant, or deodorant
1bleak \'blēk\ *adj* [ME *bleke* pale; prob. akin to OE *blāc*] **1 :** exposed and barren and often windswept **2 :** COLD, RAW **3 a :** lacking in warmth or kindliness **b :** not likely to be favorably concluded **c :** severely simple — **bleak·ly** *adv* — **bleak·ness** *n*
2bleak *n* [ME *bleke*] **:** a small European cyprinid river fish (*Alburnus lucidus*) with silvery scale pigment used in making artificial pearls
1blear \'bli(ə)r\ *vt* [ME *bleren*] **1 a :** to make (the eyes) sore or watery **b :** DIM, BLUR ⟨~*ed* sight⟩ **2** *archaic* **:** DECEIVE
2blear *adj* **1 :** dim with water or tears **2 :** DULL, DIM — **blear-eyed** \-'īd\ *adj*
bleary \'bli(ə)r-ē\ *adj* **1** *of the eyes or vision* **:** dull or dimmed esp. from fatigue or sleep **2 :** poorly outlined or defined **:** DIM **3 :** tired to the point of exhaustion
1bleat \'blēt\ *vb* [ME *bleten*, fr. OE *blǣtan;* akin to L *flēre* to weep, OE *bellan* to roar — more at BELLOW] *vi* **1 a :** to utter the natural cry of a sheep or goat **b :** to make a sound resembling this cry; *broadly* **:** WHIMPER **2 a :** to talk complainingly or with a whine **b :** BLATHER **~** *vt* **:** to utter in a bleating manner — **bleat·er** *n*
2bleat *n* **1 a :** the cry of a sheep or goat **b :** a sound resembling this cry **2 :** whining or foolish talk **:** BLATHER
bleb \'bleb\ *n* [perh. alter. of *blob*] **1 :** a small blister **2 :** BUBBLE — **bleb·by** \-ē\ *adj*
1bleed \'blēd\ *vb* **bled** \'bled\ **bleed·ing** [ME *bleden*, fr. OE *blēdan*, fr. *blōd* blood] *vi* **1 a :** to emit or lose blood **b :** to sacrifice one's blood esp. in battle **2 :** to feel anguish, pain, or sympathy ⟨his heart ~*s* for you⟩ **3 :** to escape by or as if by oozing or flowing from a wound **4 :** to give up some constituent (as sap or dye) by exuding or diffusing it **5 a :** to pay out or give money **b :** to have money extorted **6 :** to be printed so as to run off one or more edges of a printed page or sheet after trimming — often used with *off* **~** *vt* **1 :** to remove or draw blood from **2 :** to get or extort money from **3 :** to draw sap from (a tree) **4 a :** to extract or let out some or all of a contained substance from ⟨~ a tire⟩ **b :** to extract or cause to escape from a container **5 :** to cause (as a printed illustration) to bleed; *also* **:** to trim (as a page) so that some of the printing bleeds
2bleed *n* **:** an illustration or a page that bleeds or is bled; *also* **:** the part trimmed off in bleeding or the corresponding area of the printing plate
bleed·er \'blēd-ər\ *n* **:** one that bleeds; *esp* **:** HEMOPHILIAC
bleeding heart *n* **:** a garden plant (*Dicentra spectabilis*) of the poppy family with racemes of deep pink drooping heart-shaped flowers; *broadly* **:** any of several plants (genus *Dicentra*)
blel·lum \'blel-əm\ *n* [perh. blend of Sc *bleber* to babble and *skellum* rascal] *Scot* **:** a lazy talkative person
1blem·ish \'blem-ish\ *vt* [ME *blemisshen*, fr. MF *blesmiss-*, stem of *blesmir* to make pale, wound, of Gmc origin; akin to G *blass* pale; akin to OE *blæse* torch — more at BLAZE] **:** to spoil by a flaw **:** SULLY
2blemish *n* **:** a noticeable imperfection; *esp* **:** one that impairs appearance but not utility
syn BLEMISH, DEFECT, FLAW mean an imperfection. BLEMISH suggests something that affects only the surface or appearance; DEFECT implies a lack or want that is often hidden and is essential to completeness or perfect functioning; FLAW suggests a small defect in continuity or cohesion that is likely to cause failure under stress
1blench \'blench\ *vi* [ME *blenchen* to deceive, blench, fr. OE *blencan* to deceive; akin to ON *blekkja* to impose on] **:** to draw back or turn aside from lack of courage **:** FLINCH **syn** see RECOIL
2blench *vb* [alter. of *blanch*] **:** BLEACH, WHITEN
1blend \'blend\ *vb* **blend·ed** *also* **blent** \'blent\ **blend·ing** [ME *blenden*, modif. of ON *blanda;* akin to OE *blandan* to mix, Lith *blandus* thick (of soup)] *vt* **1 :** MIX; *esp* **:** to combine or associate so that the separate constituents or the line of demarcation cannot be distinguished **2 :** to prepare by thoroughly intermingling different varieties or grades **3 :** to darken the tips of (a fur) with dye **~** *vi* **1 a :** to mingle intimately **b :** to combine into an integrated whole **2 :** to produce a harmonious effect **:** HARMONIZE **syn** see MIX — **blend·er** *n*
2blend *n* **:** something produced by blending: as **a :** a product (as a whiskey) prepared by blending **b :** a word produced by combining other words or parts of words in an unusual way
blende \'blend\ *n* [G, fr. *blenden* to blind, fr. OHG *blenten;* akin to OE *blind*] **1 :** SPHALERITE **2 :** any of several minerals (as metallic sulfides) with somewhat bright but nonmetallic luster
blended whiskey *n* **:** whiskey consisting of either a blend of two or more straight whiskeys or a blend of whiskey and neutral spirits
blending inheritance *n* **:** inheritance by the progeny of characters intermediate between those of the parents
blen·ny \'blen-ē\ *n* [L *blennius*, a sea fish, fr. Gk *blennos*] **:** any of numerous usu. small and elongated and often scaleless fishes (Blenniidae and related families) living about rocky shores

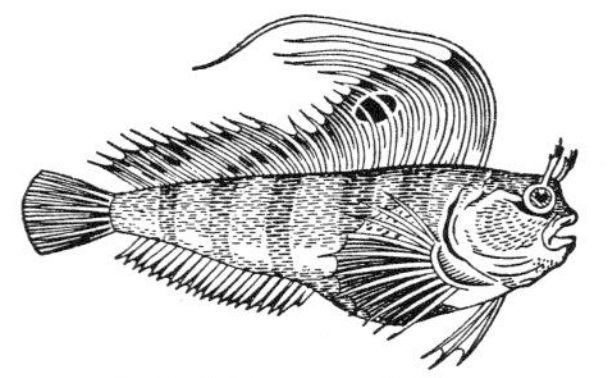

ocellated blenny of Europe

blephar- *or* **blepharo-** *comb form* [NL, fr. Gk, fr. *blepharon*] **1 :** eyelid ⟨*blepharo*spasm⟩ **2 :** cilium **:** flagellum ⟨*blepharo*plast⟩
bles·bok \'bles-,bäk\ *n* [Afrik, fr. *bles* blaze + *bok* male antelope] **:** a So. African antelope (*Damaliscus albifrons*) having a large white spot on the face
bless \'bles\ *vt* **blessed** \'blest\ *also* **blest** \'blest\ **bless·ing** [ME *blessen*, fr. OE *blētsian*, fr. *blōd* blood; fr. the use of blood in consecration] **1 :** to hallow or consecrate by religious rite or word **2 :** to make the sign of the cross upon or over **3 :** to invoke divine care for **4 :** PRAISE, GLORIFY **5 :** to confer prosperity or happiness upon **6 :** PROTECT, PRESERVE
bless·ed \'bles-əd\ *or* **blest** \'blest\ *adj* **1 :** HOLY ⟨The ~ Trinity⟩ **2 :** of or enjoying happiness; *specif* **:** enjoying the bliss of heaven — used as a title for a beatified person **3 :** bringing pleasure or contentment **:** DELIGHTFUL **4 :** CURSED, DAMNED — used as an intensive ⟨not a ~ drop⟩ — **bless·ed·ly** *adv* — **bless·ed·ness** *n*
Bless·ed Sacrament \,bles-əd-\ *n* **:** the consecrated Host
bless·ing *n* **1 a :** the act of one that blesses **b :** APPROVAL **2 :** a thing conducive to happiness or welfare **3 :** grace said at a meal
bleth·er \'bleth-ər\ *var of* BLATHER
blew *past of* BLOW
1blight \'blīt\ *n* [origin unknown] **1 a :** any disease or injury of plants resulting in withering, cessation of growth, and death of parts without rotting **b :** an organism that causes blight **2 :** something that frustrates one's plans or withers one's hopes **3 :** something that impairs or destroys **4 :** an impaired condition
2blight *vt* **1 :** to affect with blight **2 :** to cause to deteriorate **:** RUIN **~** *vi* **:** to suffer from or become affected with blight
blimp \'blimp\ *n* **1** [perh. fr. (*type*) *B* + *limp*] **:** a nonrigid airship **2** [Col. *Blimp*, cartoon character created by David Low] *often cap* **:** a person of ultraconservative nationalistic outlook and complacent stupidity — **blimp·ish** \'blim-pish\ *adj*
blin \'blin\ *n, pl* **blini** \-ē\ *or* **blin·is** \-ēz\ [Russ] **:** BLINTZE
1blind \'blīnd\ *adj* [ME, fr. OE; akin to OHG *blint* blind, OE *blandan* to mix — more at BLEND] **1 a** (1) **:** SIGHTLESS (2) **:** having less than 1/10 of normal vision in the more efficient eye when refractive defects are fully corrected by lenses **b :** of or relating to sightless persons **2 a :** unable or unwilling to discern or judge **b :** unsupported by evidence or plausibility ⟨~ faith⟩ **3 a :** having no regard to rational discrimination, guidance, or restriction ⟨~ choice⟩ **b :** lacking any directing or controlling consciousness ⟨~ chance⟩ **c :** marked by complete insensibility; *also* **:** DRUNK **4 :** made or done without sight of certain objects or knowledge of certain facts that could serve for guidance ⟨~ purchase⟩; *esp* **:** performed solely by the aid of instruments within an airplane ⟨a ~ landing⟩ **5 :** DEFECTIVE; *esp* **:** lacking a growing point or producing leaves instead of flowers **6 :** difficult to discern, make out, or discover: as **a :** ILLEGIBLE; *also* **:** lacking a complete or legible address ⟨~ mail⟩ **b :** hidden from sight **:** COVERED ⟨~ seam⟩ **7 :** having but one opening or outlet ⟨~ alley⟩ **8 :** having no opening for light or passage **:** BLANK ⟨~ wall⟩ — **blind·ly** \'blīn-(d)lē\ *adv* — **blind·ness** \'blīn(d)-nəs\ *n*
2blind *vt* **1 a :** to make blind **b :** DAZZLE **2 a :** to withhold light from **:** DARKEN **b :** HIDE, CONCEAL **c :** to make dim by comparison
3blind *n* **1 :** something to hinder sight or keep out light: as **a :** a window shutter **b :** a roller window shade **c :** VENETIAN BLIND **d :** 3BLINDER **2 :** a place of concealment **:** AMBUSH **3 a :** something put forward for the purpose of misleading **:** SUBTERFUGE **b** (1) **:** a person serving as an agent for another who keeps under cover (2) **:** one who acts as a decoy or distraction
4blind *adv* **:** BLINDLY; *esp* **:** to the point of insensibility
blind date *n* **1 :** a date between two persons of opposite sex who have not previously met **2 :** either participant in a blind date
blind·er \'blīn-dər\ *n* **:** either of two flaps on a horse's bridle to prevent sight of objects at his sides
blind·fish \'blīn(d)-,fish\ *n* **:** any of several small fishes with vestigial functionless eyes found usu. in the waters of caves
1blind·fold \'blīn(d)-,fōld\ *vt* [ME *blindfellen, blindfelden* to strike blind, blindfold, fr. *blind* + *fellen* to fell] **1 :** to cover the eyes of with or as if with a bandage **2 :** to hinder from seeing; *esp* **:** to keep from comprehension — **blindfold** *adj*
2blindfold *n* **1 :** a bandage for covering the eyes **2 :** something that obscures mental or physical vision
blind gut *n* **:** CECUM
blind·man's buff \,blīn(d)-,manz-\ *n* **:** a group game in which a blindfolded player tries to catch and identify another player
blind spot *n* **1 a :** the point in the retina not sensitive to light where the optic nerve enters **b :** a portion of a field that cannot be seen or inspected with available equipment **2 :** an area in which one fails to exercise judgment or discrimination **3 :** a locality in which radio reception is markedly poorer than in the surrounding area
blind tiger *n, slang* **:** a place that sells intoxicants illegally
blind·worm \'blīn-,dwərm\ *n* **:** a small burrowing limbless lizard with minute eyes; *esp* **:** a European lizard (*Anguis fragilis*) popularly believed to be blind — called also *slowworm*
1blink \'bliŋk\ *vb* [ME *blinken* to open one's eyes] *vi* **1 a** *obs* **:** to look glancingly **:** PEEP **b :** to look with half-shut winking eyes **c :** to wink esp. involuntarily **2 :** to shine dimly or intermittently **3 a :** to look with too little concern **b :** to look with surprise or dismay **~** *vt* **1 a :** to cause to blink **b :** to remove (as tears) from the eye by blinking **2 :** to deny recognition to **syn** see WINK
2blink *n* **1** *chiefly Scot* **:** GLIMPSE, GLANCE **2 :** GLIMMER, SPARKLE **3 :** an esp. involuntary shutting and opening of the eye **4 a :** a whiteness about the horizon caused by the reflection of light from ice at sea **b :** a dark appearance of the sky about the horizon caused by the absence of reflected light due to open water — **on the blink :** in or into a disabled or useless condition

[1]**blink·er** \ˈbliŋ-kər\ *n* **1 :** one that blinks; *esp* **:** a light that can be flashed on and off in a sequence of coded intervals for signaling a message **2 a :** BLINDER **b :** a cloth hood with shades projecting at the sides of the eye openings used on skittish racehorses — usu. used in pl.

[2]**blinker** *vt* **:** to put blinders or blinkers on

blin·tze \ˈblin(t)-sə\ *or* **blintz** \ˈblin(t)s\ *n* [Yiddish *blintse,* fr. Russ *blinets,* dim. of *blin* pancake] **:** a thin rolled pancake with a filling usu. of cream cheese

blip \ˈblip\ *n* [prob. fr. *blip* (a short crisp sound)] **:** an image on a screen esp. in radar

bliss \ˈblis\ *n* [ME *blisse,* fr. OE *bliss;* akin to OE *blīthe* blithe] **1 :** complete happiness **2 :** PARADISE, HEAVEN

bliss·ful \ˈblis-fəl\ *adj* **:** full of, marked by, or causing bliss — **bliss·ful·ly** \-fə-lē\ *adv* — **bliss·ful·ness** *n*

[1]**blis·ter** \ˈblis-tər\ *n* [ME, modif. of OF or MD; OF *blostre* boil, fr. MD *bluyster* blister; akin to OE *blǣst* blast] **1 :** an elevation of the epidermis containing watery liquid **2 :** an enclosed raised spot (as in paint) resembling a blister **3 :** an agent that causes blistering **4 :** a disease of plants marked by large swollen patches on the leaves **5 :** any of various structures that bulge out (as a gunner's compartment on an airplane) — **blis·tery** \-t(ə-)rē\ *adj*

[2]**blister** *vb* **blis·ter·ing** \-t(ə-)riŋ\ *vi* **:** to become affected with a blister ~ *vt* **1 :** to raise a blister on **2 a :** to administer severe physical punishment to esp. by whipping **b :** to scorch with words

blister beetle *n* **:** a beetle (as the Spanish fly) used medicinally dried and powdered to raise blisters on the skin; *broadly* **:** any of numerous soft-bodied beetles (family Meloidae)

blister copper *n* **:** metallic copper of a black blistered surface that is the product of converting copper matte and is about 98.5 to 99.5 percent pure

blister rust *n* **:** any of several diseases of pines that are caused by rust fungi (genus *Cronartium*) in the aecial stage and that affect the sapwood and inner bark and produce blisters externally

blithe \ˈblīth, ˈblīth\ *adj* [ME, fr. OE *blīthe;* akin to OHG *blīdi* joyous, OE *bǣl* fire] **1 :** of a happy lighthearted character or disposition **2 :** CASUAL, HEEDLESS **syn** see MERRY — **blithe·ly** *adv*

blith·er \ˈblith-ər\ *vi* **:** BLATHER ⟨~*ing* idiot⟩

blithe·some \ˈblīth-səm, ˈblīth-\ *adj* **:** GAY, MERRY — **blithe·some·ly** *adv*

blitz \ˈblits\ *n, often attrib* **1 a :** BLITZKRIEG 1 **b :** an intensive aerial campaign; *also* **:** AIR RAID **2 a :** an intensive nonmilitary campaign **b :** a rush on the passer in football — **blitz** *vb*

blitz·krieg \ˈblit-ˌskrēg\ *n* [G, lit., lightning war, fr. *blitz* lightning + *krieg* war] **1 :** war conducted with great speed and force; *specif* **:** a violent surprise offensive by massed air forces and mechanized ground forces in close coordination **2 :** a sudden overpowering bombardment — **blitzkrieg** *vt*

bliz·zard \ˈbliz-ərd\ *n* [origin unknown] **1 :** a long severe snowstorm **2 :** an intensely strong cold wind filled with fine snow

[1]**bloat** \ˈblōt\ *adj* [alter. of ME *blout*] **:** BLOATED, PUFFY

[2]**bloat** *vt* **1 :** to make turgid or swollen **2 a :** to fill to capacity or overflowing **:** INFLATE **b :** to make vain ~ *vi* **:** SWELL

[3]**bloat** *n* **1 a :** one that is bloated **b** *slang* **:** DRUNKARD **2 :** a flatulent digestive disturbance of domestic animals (esp. cattle) marked by abdominal bloating

[1]**bloat·er** \ˈblōt-ər\ *n* [obs. *bloat* (to cure)] **:** a large fat herring or mackerel lightly salted and briefly smoked

[2]**bloater** *n* [[2]*bloat*] **:** a small but common cisco (*Leucichthys hoyi*) of the Great Lakes

[1]**blob** \ˈbläb\ *n* [ME] **1 a :** a small drop or lump of something viscid or thick **b :** a spot of color **2 :** something ill-defined or amorphous

[2]**blob** *vt* **blobbed; blob·bing :** to mark with blobs **:** SPLOTCH

bloc \ˈbläk\ *n, often attrib* [F, lit., block] **1 a :** a temporary combination of parties in a legislative assembly **b :** a group of legislators in a U.S. legislative assembly who act together for some common purpose irrespective of party lines **2 a :** a combination of persons, groups, or nations forming a unit with a common interest or purpose **b :** a group of nations united by treaty or agreement for mutual support or joint action

[1]**block** \ˈbläk\ *n, often attrib* [ME *blok,* fr. MF *bloc,* fr. MD *blok;* akin to OHG *bloh* block, MIr *blog* fragment] **1 :** a compact usu. solid piece of substantial material esp. when worked or altered from its natural state to serve a particular purpose: as **a :** the piece of wood on which a person condemned to be beheaded lays his neck for execution **b :** a mold or form upon which articles are shaped or displayed **c :** a hollow rectangular building unit usu. of artificial material **d :** a lightweight usu. cubical and solid wooden or plastic toy that is usu. provided in sets permitting building activities **e :** the casting that contains the cylinders of an internal-combustion engine **2 a :** BLOCKHEAD **b** *slang* **:** [1]HEAD 1 **3 a :** OBSTACLE **b :** an obstruction of an opponent's play in sports; *esp* **:** a checking in football by use of the checker's body **c :** interruption of normal physiological function of a tissue or organ; *esp* **:** HEART BLOCK **d :** an instance or the result of psychological blockage or blocking **4 :** a wooden or metal case enclosing one or more pulleys and having a hook, eye, or strap by which it may be attached **5 :** a platform from which property is sold at auction; *broadly* **:** sale at auction **6 a :** a quantity, number, or section of things dealt with as a unit **b** (1) **:** a large building divided into separate functional units (2) **:** a line of row houses (3) **:** a part of a building or integrated group of buildings distinctive in some respect **c** (1) **:** a usu. rectangular space (as in a city) enclosed by streets and occupied by or intended for buildings (2) **:** the distance along one of the sides of such a block **d :** a length of railroad track of defined limits the use of which is governed by block signals **7 :** a piece of material having on its surface a hand-cut design from which impressions are to be printed

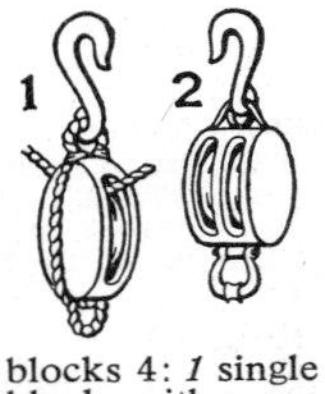

blocks 4: *1* single block with rope passed through the swallow and over the sheave; *2* double block

[2]**block** *vt* **1 a :** to make unsuitable for passage or progress by obstruction **b** *archaic* **:** BLOCKADE **c :** to hinder the passage, progress, or accomplishment of **d :** to interfere usu. legitimately with (as an opponent) in various games or sports **e :** to prevent normal functioning of **f :** to prohibit conversion of (foreign-held funds) into foreign exchange; *also* **:** to limit the use to be made of (such funds) within the country **2 :** to mark or indicate the outline or chief lines of **3 :** to shape on, with, or as if with a block **4 :** to make (two or more lines of writing or type) flush at the left or at both left and right **5 :** to secure, support, or provide with a block ~ *vi* **:** to block an opponent in sports **syn** see HINDER — **block·er** *n*

[1]**block·ade** \blä-ˈkād\ *n, often attrib* **1 :** a measure of war consisting of the isolation by a belligerent of a particular area vital to the interests of an enemy through deployment of armed forces so as to effectively hamper ingress and egress; *broadly* **:** any restrictive measure designed to obstruct the commerce and communications of an unfriendly nation **2 :** something that constitutes an obstacle

[2]**blockade** *vt* **:** to subject to a blockade — **block·ad·er** *n*

block·ade-run·ner \-ˌrən-ər\ *n* **:** a ship or person that runs through a blockade — **block·ade-run·ning** \-ˌrən-iŋ\ *n*

block·age \ˈbläk-ij\ *n* **:** an act or instance of obstructing **:** the state of being blocked

block and tackle *n* **:** pulley blocks with associated rope or cable for hoisting or hauling

block·bust·er \ˈbläk-ˌbəs-tər\ *n* **1 :** a huge high-explosive demolition bomb **2 :** something or someone notably effective or violent

block·head \ˈbläk-ˌhed\ *n* **:** a stupid person

block·house \-ˌhau̇s\ *n* **1 a :** a structure of heavy timbers formerly used for military defense with sides loopholed and pierced for gunfire and often a projecting upper story **b :** a small defensible building for protection from enemy fire **2 :** a building usu. of reinforced concrete serving as an observation point for an operation likely to be accompanied by heat, blast, or radiation hazard

block·ish \-ish\ *adj* **:** resembling a block — **block·ish·ly** *adv*

block letter *n* **:** a letter or lettering in sans serif

block plane *n* **:** a small plane made with the blade set at a lower pitch than other planes and used chiefly on end grains of wood

block signal *n* **:** a fixed signal at the entrance of a block to govern railroad trains entering and using that block

block system *n* **:** a system by which a railroad track is divided into short sections and trains are run by guidance signals

blocky \ˈbläk-ē\ *adj* **1 :** resembling a block in form or massiveness **:** CHUNKY **2 :** filled with or made up of blocks or patches

bloke \ˈblōk\ *n* [origin unknown] *chiefly Brit* **:** MAN, FELLOW

[1]**blond** *or* **blonde** \ˈbländ\ *adj* [F *blond,* masc., *blonde,* fem.] **1 a** *of human hair* **:** of a flaxen, golden, light auburn, or pale yellowish brown color **b** *of human skin* **:** of a pale white or rosy white color **c** *of a person* **:** having blond hair and skin and usu. blue or gray eyes **2 a :** of a light color **b :** of the color blond **c :** made light-colored by bleaching — **blond·ness** \ˈblän(d)-nəs\ *n*

[2]**blond** *or* **blonde** *n* **1 :** a blond person **2 :** a light yellowish brown to dark grayish yellow

[1]**blood** \ˈbləd\ *n, often attrib* [ME, fr. OE *blōd;* akin to OHG *bluot* blood] **1 a :** the fluid that circulates in the heart, arteries, capillaries, and veins of a vertebrate animal carrying nourishment and oxygen to and bringing away waste products from all parts of the body **b :** a comparable fluid of an invertebrate **c :** a fluid resembling blood **2 a :** LIFEBLOOD; *broadly* **:** LIFE **b :** human stock or lineage; *esp* **:** royal lineage ⟨a prince of the ~⟩ **c :** relationship by descent from a common ancestor **:** KINSHIP **d :** persons related through common descent **:** KINDRED **e** (1) **:** honorable or high birth or descent (2) **:** descent from parents of recognized breed or pedigree **3 :** the shedding of blood; *also* **:** the taking of life **4 a :** blood regarded as the seat of the emotions **:** TEMPER **b** *obs* **:** LUST **c :** a gay showy foppish man **:** RAKE **5 :** PERSONNEL

[2]**blood** *vt* **1 :** to stain or wet with blood **2 a :** to expose (a hunting dog) to sight, scent, or taste of the blood of its prey **b :** to give experience to

blood bank *n* **:** a place for storage of or an institution storing blood or plasma; *also* **:** blood so stored

blood·bath \-ˌbath, -ˌbȧth\ *n* **:** a great slaughter **:** MASSACRE

blood brother *n* **1 :** a brother by birth **2 :** one that is bound in ceremonial blood brotherhood

blood brotherhood *n* **:** a solemn friendship established between usu. unrelated men by a ceremonial use of each other's blood

blood cell *n* **:** a cell normally present in blood

blood count *n* **:** the determination of the blood cells in a definite volume of blood; *also* **:** the number of cells so determined

blood·cur·dling \ˈbləd-ˌkərd-liŋ, -ᵊl-iŋ\ *adj* **:** seeming to have the effect of congealing the blood through fear or horror ⟨~ screams⟩

blood·ed \ˈbləd-əd\ *adj* **1 :** entirely or largely of pure blood **2 :** having blood of a specified kind ⟨warm-*blooded*⟩

blood feud *n* **:** a feud between different clans or families

blood·fin \ˈbləd-ˌfin\ *n* **:** a small silvery So. American fish (*Aphyocharax rubripinnis*) with deep-red fins

blood group *n* **:** one of the classes into which human beings can be separated on the basis of the presence or absence in their blood of specific antigens — called also *blood type*

blood·guilt \-ˌgilt\ *n* **:** guilt resulting from the shedding of blood — **blood·guilt·i·ness** \-ˌgil-tē-nəs\ *n* — **blood·guilty** \-tē\ *adj*

blood heat *n* **:** a temperature approximating that of the human body

blood·hound \ˈbləd-ˌhau̇nd\ *n* **:** a large powerful hound of a breed of European origin remarkable for acuteness of smell

blood·i·ly \ˈbləd-ᵊl-ē\ *adv* **:** in a bloody manner

blood·i·ness \ˈbləd-ē-nəs\ *n* **:** the quality or state of being bloody

blood·less \ˈbləd-ləs\ *adj* **1 :** deficient in or free from blood **2 :** not accompanied by loss or shedding of blood **3 :** lacking in spirit or vitality **4 :** lacking in human feeling — **blood·less·ly** *adv* — **blood·less·ness** *n*

blood·let·ting \-ˌlet-iŋ\ *n* **1 :** PHLEBOTOMY **2 :** BLOODSHED

blood·line \-ˌlīn\ *n* **:** a sequence of direct ancestors esp. in a pedigree; *also* **:** FAMILY, STRAIN

blood·mo·bile \-mō-ˌbēl\ *n* [*blood* + *automobile*] **:** an automobile staffed and equipped for collecting blood from donors

blood money *n* **1 :** money obtained at the cost of another's life **2 :** money paid by a manslayer or members of his family, clan, or tribe to the next of kin of a person killed by him

blood platelet *n* **:** one of the minute protoplasmic disks of vertebrate blood that assist in blood clotting

blood poisoning *n* **:** SEPTICEMIA

blood pressure *n* **:** pressure exerted by the blood upon the walls of

the blood vessels and esp. arteries varying with the muscular efficiency of the heart, the blood volume and viscosity, the age and health of the individual, and the state of the vascular wall

blood·red \'bləd-'red\ *adj* **:** having the color of blood

blood·root \'bləd-,rüt, -,rüt\ *n* **:** a plant (*Sanguinaria canadensis*) of the poppy family having a red root and sap and bearing a solitary lobed leaf and white flower in early spring

blood sausage *n* **:** sausage containing a large proportion of blood so that it is very dark in color — called also *blood pudding*

blood serum *n* **:** blood plasma from which the fibrin has been removed

blood·shed \'bləd-,shed\ *n* **1 :** the shedding of blood **2 :** the taking of life **:** SLAUGHTER

blood·shot \-,shät\ *adj, of an eye* **:** inflamed to redness

blood·stain \-,stān\ *n* **:** a discoloration caused by blood — **blood·stained** \-,stānd\ *adj*

blood·stone \-,stōn\ *n* **:** a green chalcedony sprinkled with red spots resembling blood

blood·stream \-,strēm\ *n* **:** the flowing blood in a circulatory system

blood·suck·er \-,sək-ər\ *n* **1 :** an animal that sucks blood; *esp* **:** LEECH **2 :** a person who sponges or preys on another — **blood·suck·ing** \-iŋ\ *adj*

blood test *n* **:** a test of the blood; *esp* **:** a serologic test for syphilis

blood·thirst·i·ly \'bləd-,thər-stə-lē\ *adv* **:** in a bloodthirsty manner

blood·thirst·i·ness \-,thər-stē-nəs\ *n* **:** the quality or state of being bloodthirsty

blood·thirsty \-stē\ *adj* **:** eager for the shedding of blood

blood–type \'bləd-,tīp\ *vt* **:** to determine the blood group of

blood vessel *n* **:** a vessel in which blood circulates in an animal

blood·worm \-,wərm\ *n* **1 :** any of various reddish annelid worms often used as bait **2 :** the red aquatic larva of some midges

blood·wort \-,wərt, -,wȯ(ə)rt\ *n* **:** any of a family (Haemodoraceae, the bloodwort family) of perennial herbs with a deep red coloring matter in the roots

1**bloody** \'bləd-ē\ *adj* **1 a :** containing or made up of blood **b :** of or contained in the blood **2 :** smeared or stained with blood **3 :** accompanied by or involving bloodshed; *esp* **:** marked by great slaughter **4 a :** MURDEROUS **b :** MERCILESS, CRUEL **5 :** BLOODRED **6** *Brit* — used as an intensive; often considered vulgar — **bloody** *vt*

2**bloody** *adv, Brit* — used as an intensive; often considered vulgar

bloody mary *n* [prob. fr. *Bloody Mary*, appellation of Mary I †1558 queen of England] **:** a beverage made of vodka and tomato juice

bloody shirt *n* **:** a means employed to stir up or revive party or sectional animosity

1**bloom** \'blüm\ *n* [ME *blome* lump of metal, fr. OE *blōma*] **1 :** a mass of wrought iron from the forge or puddling furnace **2 :** a bar of iron or steel hammered or rolled from an ingot

2**bloom** *n* [ME *blome*, fr. ON *blōm*; akin to OE *blōwan* to blossom — more at BLOW] **1 a** (1) **:** FLOWER (2) **:** flowers or amount of flowers (as of a plant) **b :** the flowering state ⟨the roses in ~⟩ **c :** a period of flowering ⟨the spring ~⟩ **2 :** a state or time of beauty, freshness, and vigor **3 :** a surface coating or appearance: as **a :** a delicate powdery coating on some fruits and leaves **b :** a rosy appearance of the cheeks; *broadly* **:** an outward evidence of freshness or healthy vigor **c :** the grainy or powdery surface of a newly minted coin **d :** glare caused by an object reflecting too much light into a television camera **4 :** BOUQUET 3a

3**bloom** *vi* **1 :** to produce or yield flowers **2 a :** to flourish esp. in youthful beauty, freshness, or excellence **b :** to shine out **:** GLOW **3 :** to appear or occur unexpectedly or in surprising quantity or degree ~ *vt* **1** *obs* **:** to cause to bloom **2 :** to give bloom to

1**bloom·er** \'blü-mər\ *n* **1 :** a plant that blooms; *also* **:** a person who reaches full competence, skill, or maturity **2 :** a stupid blunder

2**bloo·mer** \'blü-mər\ *n* [Amelia *Bloomer* †1894 Am pioneer in feminism] **1 :** a costume for women consisting of a short skirt and long loose trousers gathered closely about the ankles **2** *pl* **a :** full loose trousers gathered at the knee formerly worn by women for athletics **b :** underpants of similar design worn chiefly by girls

bloom·ing \'blü-miŋ, *in sense 3 usu* -mən\ *adj* **1 :** FLOWERING **2 :** thriving in health, beauty, and vigor **3** [prob. euphemism for *bloody*] *slang* — used as a generalized intensive ⟨~ fool⟩ — **bloom·ing·ly** \-miŋ-lē\ *adv*

bloomy \'blü-mē\ *adj* **1 :** full of bloom **2 :** covered with bloom

bloop·er \'blü-pər\ *n* [*bloop* (an unpleasing sound)] **1 :** an embarrassing public blunder **2 a :** a high baseball pitch lobbed to the batter **b :** a fly ball hit barely beyond a baseball infield

1**blos·som** \'bläs-əm\ *n* [ME *blosme*, fr. OE *blōstm*; akin to OE *blōwan*] **1 a :** the flower of a seed plant ⟨apple ~s⟩ **b :** BLOOM 1a(2),1b **2 :** a period or stage of development analogous to the unfolding of a flower — **blos·somy** \-ə-mē\ *adj*

2**blossom** *vi* **1 :** BLOOM **2 :** to unfold like a blossom: as **a :** to flourish and prosper **b :** DEVELOP, EXPAND **c :** to come into being

1**blot** \'blät\ *n* [ME] **1 :** SPOT, STAIN **2 :** DISGRACE, BLEMISH

2**blot** *vb* **blot·ted; blot·ting** *vt* **1 :** to spot, stain, or spatter with some discoloring substance **2 :** to make obscure **:** ECLIPSE **3** *obs* **:** MAR; *esp* **:** to stain with infamy **4 a :** to dry with blotting paper or other absorbing agent **b :** to remove by blotting the surface ~ *vi* **1 :** to make a blot **2 :** to become marked with a blot

3**blot** *n* [origin unknown] **1 :** a backgammon man exposed to capture **2** *archaic* **:** a weak or exposed point

blotch \'bläch\ *n* [prob. alter. of *botch*] **1 :** IMPERFECTION, BLEMISH **2 :** a spot or mark (as of color or ink) esp. when large or irregular — **blotch** *vt* — **blotched** *adj* — **blotchy** \'bläch-ē\ *adj*

blot out *vt* **1 :** to make insignificant or inconsequential **2 :** to make obscure or invisible **:** HIDE **3 :** DESTROY, KILL **syn** see ERASE

blot·ter \'blät-ər\ *n* **1 :** a piece of blotting paper **2 :** a book in which entries are made temporarily pending their transfer to permanent record books

blotting paper *n* **:** a soft spongy unsized paper used to absorb ink

blouse \'blaus, 'blauz; *some say* 'blaus *but* 'blau-zəz\ *n* [F] **1 :** a loose overgarment like a shirt or smock varying from hip-length to calf-length **2 :** the dress and undress uniform coat of the U.S. Army; *also* **:** the upper outer garment of a uniform **3 :** a usu. loose-fitting garment covering the body from the neck to the waist

1**blow** \'blō\ *vb* **blew** \'blü\ **blown** \'blōn\ **blow·ing** [ME *blowen*, fr. OE *blāwan*; akin to OHG *blāen* to blow, L *flare*, Gk *phallos* penis] *vi* **1** *of air* **:** to move with speed or force **2 :** to send forth a current of air or other gas **3 a :** to make a sound by or as if by blowing **b** *of a wind instrument* **:** SOUND **4 a :** BOAST **b :** STORM, BLUSTER **5 a :** PANT, GASP **b** *of a cetacean* **:** to eject moisture-laden air from the lungs through the blowhole **6 :** to move or be carried by or as if by wind **7** *of an electrical fuse* **:** to melt when overloaded **8** *of a tire* **:** to release the contained air through a spontaneous rupture ~ *vt* **1 a :** to set (gas or vapor) in motion **b :** to act upon with a current of gas or vapor **2 :** to play or sound on (a wind instrument) **3 a :** to spread by report **b :** DAMN, DISREGARD ⟨~ the expense⟩ **4 a :** to drive with a current of gas or vapor **b :** to clear of contents by forcible passage of a current of air **5 a :** to distend with or as if with gas **b :** to produce or shape by the action of blown or injected air ⟨~*ing* bubbles⟩ ⟨~*ing* glass⟩ **6** *of insects* **:** to deposit eggs or larvae on or in **7 :** to shatter, burst, or destroy by explosion **8 a :** to put out of breath with exertion **b :** to let (as a horse) pause to catch the breath **9 a :** to spend (money) recklessly **b :** to treat with unusual expenditure ⟨I'll ~ you to a steak⟩ **10 :** to cause (a fuse) to blow **11 :** to rupture by too much pressure ⟨*blew* a gasket⟩ **12** *slang* **:** MISPLAY, MUFF **13 :** to leave esp. hurriedly ⟨*blew* town⟩ — **blow hot and cold :** to be favorable at one moment and adverse the next

2**blow** *n* **1 :** a blowing of wind esp. when strong or violent **:** GALE **2 a :** BOASTING, BRAG **b** *slang* **:** BOASTER **3 :** an act or instance of blowing from the mouth or nose or through or from an instrument **4 a :** the time during which air is forced through molten metal to refine it **b :** the quantity of metal refined during that time

3**blow** *vi* **blew** \'blü\ **blown** \'blōn\ **blow·ing** [ME *blowen*, fr. OE *blōwan*; akin to OHG *bluoen* to bloom, L *florēre* to bloom, *flor-, flos* flower] **:** FLOWER, BLOOM

4**blow** *n* **1 :** a display of flowers **2 :** 2BLOOM 1b

5**blow** *n* [ME (northern dial.) *blaw*] **1 :** a forcible stroke delivered with a part of the body or with an instrument **2 :** a hostile act or state **:** COMBAT ⟨come to ~*s*⟩ **3 :** a forcible or sudden act or effort **:** ASSAULT **4 :** a severe and usu. sudden calamity

blow–by–blow \-bī-, -bə-\ *adj* **:** minutely detailed ⟨~ account⟩

blow·er \'blō(-ə)r\ *n* **1 :** one that blows **2 :** BRAGGART **3 :** a device for producing a current of air or gas

blow·fish \'blō-,fish\ *n* **1 :** PUFFER 2 **2** *South* **:** WALLEYED PIKE

blow·fly \-,flī\ *n* **:** any of various two-winged flies (family Calliphoridae) that deposit their eggs or maggots esp. on meat or in wounds; *esp* **:** a widely distributed bluebottle (*Calliphora vicina*)

blow·gun \-,gən\ *n* **:** a tube through which a projectile may be impelled by the force of the breath

blow·hard \-,härd\ *n* **:** BRAGGART

blow·hole \-,hōl\ *n* **1 :** a nostril in the top of the head of a whale or other cetacean **2 :** a hole in the ice to which aquatic mammals (as seals) come to breathe

blow in *vi, slang* **:** to arrive casually or unexpectedly

blown \'blōn\ *adj* [ME *blowen*, fr. pp. of *blowen* to blow] **1 :** SWOLLEN; *esp* **:** afflicted with bloat **2 :** FLYBLOWN **3 :** out of breath

blow out *vi* **:** to become extinguished by a gust ~ *vt* **1 :** to extinguish by a gust **2 :** to dissipate (itself) by blowing — used of storms

blow·out \'blō-,aut\ *n* **1** *slang* **:** a big social affair **2 a :** a bursting of a container (as a tire) by pressure of the contents on a weak spot **b :** a hole made in a container by such bursting

blow over *vi* **:** to pass away without effect

blow·pipe \'blō-,pīp\ *n* **1 :** a small tubular instrument for directing a jet of air or other gas into a flame so as to concentrate and increase the heat **2 :** a tubular instrument used for revealing or cleaning a bodily cavity by blowing into it **3 :** BLOWGUN **4 :** a long metal tube on the end of which a glassmaker gathers a quantity of molten glass and through which he blows to expand and shape it

blow·sy *also* **blow·zy** \'blau-zē\ *adj* [E dial. *blowse, blowze* (wench)] **1 :** being coarse and ruddy of complexion **2 :** DISHEVELED, FROWZY

blow·torch \'blō-,tȯ(ə)rch\ *n* **:** a small lamp or torch with a device to intensify combustion by means of a blast

blow·tube \-,t(y)üb\ *n* **1 :** BLOWGUN **2 :** BLOWPIPE 4

blow up *vt* **1 :** to inflate or expand to unreasonable proportions **2 :** to bring into existence by blowing of wind **3 :** to make an enlargement of ~ *vi* **1 a :** EXPLODE **b :** to be disrupted or destroyed by or as if by explosion **c :** to lose self-control; *esp* **:** to become violently angry **2 a :** to become filled with or as if with air **b :** to become expanded to unreasonable proportions **3 :** to become or come into being by or as if by blowing of wind

blow·up \'blō-,əp\ *n* **:** a blowing up: as **a :** EXPLOSION **b :** an outburst of temper **c :** a photographic enlargement

blowy \'blō-ē\ *adj* **1 :** WINDY **2 :** readily blown about

1**blub·ber** \'bləb-ər\ *n* [ME *bluber* bubble, foam, prob. of imit. origin] **1 a :** the fat of whales and other large marine mammals **b :** excessive fat on the body **2 :** the action of blubbering

2**blubber** *vb* **blub·ber·ing** \'bləb-(ə-)riŋ\ [ME *blubren* to make a bubbling sound, fr. *bluber*] *vi* **:** to weep noisily ~ *vt* **1 :** to swell, distort, or wet with weeping **2 :** to utter while weeping

3**blubber** *adj* **:** puffed out **:** THICK ⟨~ lips⟩

1**blub·bery** \'bləb-(ə-)rē\ *adj* **:** 3BLUBBER

2**blubbery** *adj* **:** having or characterized by blubber

blu·cher \'blü-chər *also* -kər\ *n* [G. L. von *Blücher* †1819 Prussian field marshal] **:** a shoe having the tongue and vamp cut in one piece and the quarters lapped over the vamp and laced together for closing

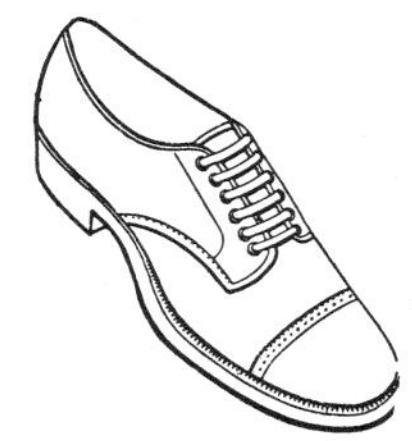

blucher

1**blud·geon** \'bləj-ən\ *n* [origin unknown] **:** a short stick used as a weapon usu. having one thick or loaded end

2**bludgeon** *vt* **1 :** to hit with or as if with a bludgeon **2 :** COERCE

1**blue** \'blü\ *adj* [ME, fr. OF *blou*, of Gmc origin; akin to OHG *blāo* blue; akin to L *flavus* yellow, OE *bǣl* fire — more at BALD] **1 :** of the color blue **2 a :** BLUISH **b :** LIVID ⟨~ with cold⟩ **c :** bluish gray ⟨~ cat⟩ **3 a :** low in spirits **:** MELANCHOLY **b :** productive of low spirits **:** DEPRESSING ⟨things looked ~⟩ **4 :** wearing blue **5** *of a woman* **:** LEARNED, INTELLECTUAL **6 :** PURITANICAL **7 :** PROFANE, INDECENT — **blue·ly** *adv* — **blue·ness** *n* — **blu·ish** *or* **blue·ish** \-ish\ *adj*

2**blue** *n* **1 :** a color whose hue is that of the clear sky or that of the portion of the color spectrum lying between green and violet **2 a :** a pigment or dye that colors blue **b :** BLUING **3 a :** blue clothing or cloth **b :** one belonging to an organization whose uniform or badge is blue **4 a** (1) **:** SKY (2) **:** the far distance **b :** SEA **5 :** a blue object **6 :** BLUESTOCKING

3**blue** *vb* **blued; blue·ing** *or* **blu·ing** *vt* **:** to make blue ~ *vi* **:** to turn blue

blue baby *n* **:** an infant with a bluish tint usu. from a congenital defect of the heart in which mingling of venous and arterial blood occurs

blue·beard \'blü-ˌbi(ə)rd\ *n* [*Bluebeard*, a fairy-tale character] **:** a man who marries and kills one wife after another

blue·bell \-ˌbel\ *n* **1 :** any of various bellflowers; *esp* **:** HAREBELL 1 **2 :** any of various plants bearing blue bell-shaped flowers: as **a :** the European wood hyacinth or grape hyacinth **b :** a low tufted New Zealand plant (*Wahlenbergia gracilis*) of the bellflower family **3 :** a blue-flowered columbine

blue·ber·ry \'blü-ˌber-ē, -b(ə-)rē\ *n* **:** the edible blue or blackish berry of any of several plants (genus *Vaccinium*) of the heath family; *also* **:** a low or tall shrub producing these berries

blue·bird \-ˌbərd\ *n* **:** any of several small No. American songbirds (genus *Sialia*) related to the robin but more or less blue above

blue blood *n* **1** \'blü-'bləd\ **:** membership in a noble or socially prominent family **2** \-ˌbləd\ **:** a member of a noble or socially prominent family — **blue-blood·ed** \-'bləd-əd\ *adj*

blue·bon·net \-ˌbän-ət\ *n* **1 a :** a wide flat round cap of blue wool formerly worn in Scotland **b :** one that wears such a cap; *specif* **:** SCOT **2 a :** CORNFLOWER 2 **b :** a low-growing annual lupine of Texas with silky foliage and blue flowers usu. held to constitute a single variable species (*Lupinus subcarnosus*)

blue book *n* **1** *often cap both Bs* **:** a government publication providing information on some topic **2 :** a directory or register esp. of persons of social prominence **3 :** a blank blue-covered booklet used in colleges for writing examinations

blue·bot·tle \'blü-ˌbät-ᵊl\ *n* **1 a :** CORNFLOWER 2; *broadly* **:** CENTAUREA **b :** GRAPE HYACINTH **2 :** any of several blowflies that have the abdomen or the whole body iridescent blue in color and make a loud buzzing noise in flight

blue cat *n* **:** a large bluish catfish (*Ictalurus furcatus*) of the Mississippi valley that may exceed 100 pounds in weight

blue cheese *n* **:** cheese marked with veins of greenish blue mold

blue chip *n* **1 :** a blue-colored poker chip usu. of high value **2 :** a stock issue that commands a high price as a result of public confidence in its stability

blue·coat \'blü-ˌkōt\ *n* **:** one that wears a blue coat: as **a :** a Union soldier during the Civil War **b :** POLICEMAN

blue-col·lar \'blü-'käl-ər\ *adj* **:** of, relating to, or constituting the wage-earning class

blue crab *n* **:** any of several largely blue swimming crabs; *esp* **:** an edible crab (*C. sapidus*) of the Atlantic and Gulf coasts

blue curls *n pl but sing or pl in constr* **1 :** a mint (genus *Trichostema*) with irregular blue flowers **2 :** SELF-HEAL

blue devils *n pl* **:** low spirits **:** DESPONDENCY

blue-eyed grass \ˌblü-ˌīd-\ *n* **:** a plant (genus *Sisyrinchium*) of the iris family with grasslike foliage and delicate blue flowers

blue·fin \'blü-ˌfin\ *n* **:** a very large tuna (*Thunnus thynnus*)

blue·fish \-ˌfish\ *n* **1 :** an active voracious fish (*Pomatomus saltatrix*) related to the pompanos that is bluish above and silvery below **2 :** any of various dark or bluish fishes (as the pollack)

blue flag *n* **:** a blue-flowered iris; *esp* **:** a common iris (*Iris versicolor*) of the eastern U.S. with a root formerly used medicinally

blue·gill \'blü-ˌgil\ *n* **:** a common sunfish (*Lepomis machrochirus*) of the eastern and central U.S. sought for food and sport

blue·grass \-ˌgras\ *n* **:** any of several grasses (genus *Poa*) having bluish green culms; *esp* **:** a valuable pasture and lawn grass (*P. pratensis*) — called also *Kentucky bluegrass*

blue-green alga \ˌblü-ˌgrēn-\ *n* **:** any of a class (Myxophyceae) of algae having the chlorophyll masked by bluish green pigments

blue gum *n* **:** any of several Australian timber trees (genus *Eucalyptus*)

blue·jack \'blü-ˌjak\ *n* [*blue* + *jack* (as in *blackjack*)] **:** an oak (*Quercus cinerea*) of the southern U.S. with entire leaves and small acorns

blue·jack·et \-ˌjak-ət\ *n* **:** an enlisted man in the navy **:** SAILOR

blue jay \-ˌjā\ *n* **:** JAY 1b

blue jeans *n pl* **:** work pants or overalls usu. made of blue denim

blue law *n* **1 :** one of numerous extremely rigorous laws designed to regulate morals and conduct in colonial New England **2 :** a statute regulating work, commerce, and amusements on Sundays

blue mold *n* **:** a fungus (genus *Penicillium*) that produces blue or blue-green surface growths

blue moon *n* **:** a very long period of time ⟨once in a *blue moon*⟩

blue·nose \'blü-ˌnōz\ *n* **:** one who advocates a rigorous moral code

blue note *n* **:** a minor interval occurring in a melody or harmony where a major would be expected

blue-pen·cil \'blü-'pen(t)-səl\ *vt* **:** to edit, delete, or revise

blue pe·ter \-'pēt-ər\ *n* **:** a blue signal flag with a white square in the center used to indicate that a merchant vessel is ready to sail

blue pike *n* **1 :** PIKE PERCH; *esp* **:** WALLEYE **2 :** MUSKELLUNGE

blue·point \'blü-ˌpȯint\ *n* [*Blue Point*, Long Island] **:** a small oyster typically from the south shore of Long Island

blue point *n* **:** a Siamese cat having a bluish cream body and dark gray points

blue·print \-ˌprint\ *n* **1 :** a photographic print in white on a bright blue ground used esp. for copying maps, mechanical drawings, and architects' plans **2 :** a program of action — **blueprint** *vt*

blue racer *n* **:** a blacksnake of a bluish green subspecies (*Coluber constrictor flaviventris*) occurring from Ohio to Texas

blue ribbon *n* **1 :** a blue ribbon awarded the first-place winner in a competition **2 :** an honor or award gained for preeminence

blue-ribbon jury *n* **:** SPECIAL JURY

blues \'blüz\ *n pl but sing or pl in constr* **1 :** low spirits **:** MELANCHOLY **2 :** a song sung or composed in a style originating among the American Negroes, expressing melancholy, and exhibiting continual occurrence of blue notes in melody and harmony **3 :** the blue uniform of the U.S. Navy

blue-sky \'blü-'skī\ *adj* **:** having little or no value ⟨~ stock⟩

blue-sky law *n* **:** a law providing for the regulation of the sale of stocks or other securities

blue·stem \'blü-ˌstem\ *n* **:** either of two important hay and forage grasses (*Andropogon furcatus* and *A. scaparius*) of the western U.S. with smooth bluish leaf sheaths

blue·stock·ing \-ˌstäk-iŋ\ *n* [*Bluestocking* society, 18th cent. literary clubs] **:** a woman having intellectual or literary interests

blue·stone \-ˌstōn\ *n* **:** a building or paving stone of bluish gray color; *specif* **:** a sandstone quarried near the Hudson river

blue streak *n* **1 :** something that moves very fast **2 :** a constant stream of words ⟨talked a *blue streak*⟩

blu·et \'blü-ət\ *n* [prob. fr. 1*blue*] **:** an American plant (*Houstonia caerulea*) of the madder family with bluish flowers and tufted stems

blue vitriol *n* **:** a hydrated copper sulfate $CuSo_4.5H_2O$

blue·weed \'blü-ˌwēd\ *n* **:** a coarse prickly blue-flowered European weed (*Echium vulgare*) of the borage family naturalized in the U.S.

1**bluff** \'bləf\ *adj* [obs. D *blaf* flat; akin to MLG *blaff* smooth] **1 a :** having a broad flattened front **b :** rising steeply with a broad front either flat or rounded **2 :** good-naturedly frank and outspoken — **bluff·ly** *adv* — **bluff·ness** *n*

syn BLUFF, BLUNT, BRUSQUE, CURT, CRUSTY, GRUFF mean abrupt and unceremonious in speech and manner. BLUFF connotes good-natured outspokenness and unconventionality; BLUNT suggests directness of expression in disregard of others' feelings; BRUSQUE applies to a sharpness or ungraciousness that may be intentional or merely incidental to loss of emotional control; CURT stresses shortness and may or may not imply discourtesy; CRUSTY suggests a harsh or surly manner sometimes concealing an inner kindliness; GRUFF suggests a hoarse or husky speech which may imply bad temper but more often implies embarrassment or shyness

2**bluff** *n* **:** a high steep bank **:** CLIFF

3**bluff** *vb* [prob. fr. D *bluffen* to boast, play a kind of card game] *vt* **1 :** to deceive (an opponent) in cards by a bold bet on an inferior hand with the result that the opponent withdraws a winning hand **2 a :** to deter or frighten by pretense or a mere show of strength **b :** DECEIVE **c :** FEIGN ~ *vi* **:** to bluff or try to bluff someone — **bluff·er** *n*

4**bluff** *n* **1 a :** an act or instance of bluffing **b :** the practice of bluffing **2 :** one who bluffs

blu·ing *or* **blue·ing** \'blü-iŋ\ *n* **:** a preparation used in laundering to counteract yellowing of white fabrics

1**blun·der** \'blən-dər\ *vb* **blun·der·ing** \-d(ə-)riŋ\ [ME *blundren*] *vi* **1 :** to move unsteadily or confusedly **2 :** to make a mistake through stupidity, ignorance, confusion, or carelessness ~ *vt* **1 :** to utter stupidly, confusedly, or thoughtlessly **2 :** to make a stupid, careless, or thoughtless mistake in — **blun·der·er** \-dər-ər\ *n*

2**blunder** *n* **:** a gross error or mistake resulting from stupidity, ignorance, confusion, or carelessness **syn** see ERROR

blun·der·buss \'blən-dər-ˌbəs\ *n* [by folk etymology fr. obs. D *donderbus*, fr. D *donder* thunder + obs. D *bus* gun] **1 :** an obsolete short firearm having a large bore and usu. a flaring muzzle so as to be effective at close quarters when loaded with a number of balls **2 :** a blundering person

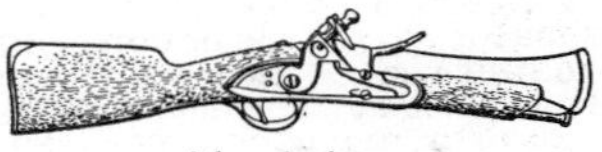
blunderbuss

1**blunt** \'blənt\ *adj* [ME] **1 a :** slow or deficient in feeling **:** INSENSITIVE **b :** obtuse in understanding or discernment **:** DULL **2 :** having an edge or point that is not sharp **3 :** lacking refinement or tact **syn** see BLUFF, DULL — **blunt·ly** *adv* — **blunt·ness** *n*

2**blunt** *vt* **:** to make blunt ~ *vi* **:** to become blunt

1**blur** \'blər\ *n* [perh. akin to ME *bleren* to blear] **1 :** a smear or stain that obscures but does not efface **2 :** something seen or perceived as vague or lacking definite outline — **blur·ry** \-ē\ *adj*

2**blur** *vb* **blurred; blur·ring** *vt* **1 :** to obscure or blemish by smearing **2 :** SULLY **3 :** to make dim, indistinct, or vague in outline or character **4 :** to make cloudy or confused ~ *vi* **1 :** to make blurs **2 :** to become vague, indistinct, or indefinite

blurb \'blərb\ *n* [coined by Gelett Burgess] **:** a short highly commendatory publicity notice

blurt \'blərt\ *vt* [prob. imit.] **:** to utter abruptly and impulsively — usu. used with *out* — **blurt** *n*

1**blush** \'bləsh\ *vi* [ME *blusshen*, fr. OE *blyscan* to redden, fr. *blȳsa* flame; akin to OHG *bluhhen* to burn brightly] **1 :** to become red in the face esp. from shame, modesty, or confusion **2 :** to feel shame or embarrassment **3 :** to have a rosy or fresh color **:** BLOOM — **blush·er** *n*

2**blush** *n* [ME, prob. fr. *blusshen*] **1 :** APPEARANCE, VIEW ⟨at first ~⟩ **2 :** a reddening of the face esp. from shame, modesty, or confusion **3 :** a red or rosy tint — **blush·ful** \-fəl\ *adj*

1**blus·ter** \'bləs-tər\ *vb* **blus·ter·ing** \'bləs-t(ə-)riŋ\ [ME *blustren*, prob. fr. MLG *blüsteren*] *vi* **1 a :** to blow in stormy noisy gusts **b :** to be windy and boisterous **2 :** to talk and act with noisy swaggering threats ~ *vt* **1 :** to utter with noisy self-assertiveness **2 :** to drive or force by blustering — **blus·ter·er** \-tər-ər\ *n*

2**bluster** *n* **1 :** a violent boisterous blowing **2 :** violent commotion **3 :** boastful empty speech — **blus·ter·ous** \-t(ə-)rəs\ *adj* — **blus·tery** \-t(ə-)rē\ *adj*

boa \'bō-ə\ *n* [L, a water snake] **1 :** a large snake (as the boa constrictor, anaconda, or python) that crushes its prey **2 :** a long fluffy scarf of fur, feathers, or delicate fabric

boa constrictor *n* **:** a tropical American boa (*Constrictor constrictor*) that is light brown barred or mottled with darker brown and reaches a length of 10 feet or more; *broadly* **:** BOA 1

boar \'bō(ə)r, 'bȯ(ə)r\ *n* [ME *bor*, fr. OE *bār*; akin to OHG & OS *bēr* boar] **1 a :** an uncastrated male swine **b :** the male of any of several mammals (as a guinea pig or coon) **2 :** the Old World wild hog (*Sus scrofa*) from which most domestic swine derive

1**board** \'bō(ə)rd, 'bȯ(ə)rd\ *n* [ME *bord* piece of sawed lumber, border, ship's side, fr. OE; akin to OHG *bort* ship's side, Skt *bardhaka* carpenter] **1** *obs* **:** BORDER, EDGE **2 a :** the side of a ship **b :** the stretch that a ship makes on one tack in beating to windward **3 a :** a piece of sawed lumber of little thickness and a length greatly exceeding its width **b** *pl* **:** STAGE 2a(2) **4 a** *archaic* **:** TABLE 3a **b :** a table spread with a meal **c :** daily meals esp. when furnished for pay **d :** a table at which a council or magistrates sit **e :** a group of persons having managerial, supervisory, or investigatory powers ⟨~ of directors⟩ ⟨school ~⟩ ⟨~ of examiners⟩ **f :** LEAGUE, ASSOCIATION **g** (1) **:** the exposed hands of all the players in a stud poker game (2) **:** an exposed dummy hand in bridge **5 a :** a flat

usu. rectangular piece of material designed for a special purpose **b :** a surface, frame, or device for posting notices or listing market quotations **6 a :** any of various wood pulps or composition materials formed into flat rectangular sheets **b :** the stiff foundation piece for the side of a book cover **7 :** an organized securities or commodities exchange — **on board :** ABOARD

2**board** *vt* **1** *archaic* **:** to come up against or alongside (a ship) usu. to attack **2 :** ACCOST, ADDRESS **3 :** to go aboard (as a ship or train) **4 :** to cover with boards ⟨~ up a window⟩ **5 :** to provide with regular meals and often also lodging usu. for compensation ~ *vi* **:** to take one's meals usu. as a paying customer — **board•er** *n*

board foot *n* **:** a unit of quantity for lumber equal to the volume of a board 12 x 12 x 1 inches

board•ing•house \'bōrd-iŋ-,hau̇s, 'bȯrd-\ *n* **:** a house at which persons are boarded

boarding school *n* **:** a school in which pupils are boarded and lodged as well as taught

board•like \'bō(ə)rd-,līk, 'bȯ(ə)rd-\ *adj* **:** resembling a board; *specif* **:** RIGID ⟨a ~ abdomen⟩

board measure *n* **:** measurement in board feet

board of trade 1 *cap B&T* **:** a British governmental department concerned with commerce and industry **2 :** an organization of businessmen for the protection and promotion of business interests **3 :** a commodities exchange

board rule *n* **:** a measuring stick with a scale for computing board feet

board•walk \'bō(ə)rd-,wȯk, 'bȯ(ə)rd-\ *n* **1 :** a walk constructed of planking **2 :** a promenade orig. of planking along a beach

boar•ish \'bō(ə)r-ish, 'bȯ(ə)r-\ *adj* **:** resembling a boar

boart \'bō(ə)rt, 'bȯ(ə)rt\ *var of* BORT

1**boast** \'bōst\ *n* [ME *boost*] **1 :** the act of boasting **:** BRAG **2 :** a cause for pride — **boast•ful** \'bōst-fəl\ *adj* — **boast•ful•ly** \-fə-lē\ *adv* — **boast•ful•ness** *n*

2**boast** *vi* **1 :** to vaunt oneself **:** BRAG **2** *archaic* **:** GLORY, EXULT ~ *vt* **1 :** to speak of or assert with excessive pride **2 :** to possess or display proudly — **boast•er** *n*

syn BOAST, BRAG, VAUNT, CROW mean to give expression to one's pride in oneself or one's accomplishment. BOAST implies ostentatiousness and usu. exaggeration; BRAG suggests a crude and artless glorifying of oneself; VAUNT is more literary than the others and usu. connotes more pomp and bombast than BOAST and less crudity than BRAG; CROW implies an exulting esp. over a defeated opponent

3**boast** *vt* [origin unknown] **:** to shape (stone) roughly with a broad chisel in sculpture and stonecutting as a preliminary to finer work

1**boat** \'bōt\ *n* [ME *boot*, fr. OE *bāt;* akin to ON *beit* boat] **1 :** a small vessel propelled by oars or paddles or by sail or power **2 :** SHIP **3 :** a boat-shaped utensil or device ⟨gravy ~⟩

2**boat** *vt* **:** to place in or bring into a boat ~ *vi* **:** to go by boat

boat•er \-ər\ *n* **1 :** one that boats **2** *chiefly Brit* **:** a stiff straw hat

boat hook *n* **:** a pole-handled hook with a point or knob on the back used esp. to pull or push a boat, raft, or log into place

boat•man \'bōt-mən\ *n* **:** a man who manages, works on, or deals in boats — **boat•man•ship** \-mən-,ship\ *n*

boat•swain \'bōs-ᵊn\ *n* [ME *bootswein*, fr. *boot* boat + *swein* boy, servant] **1 :** a petty officer on a merchant ship having charge of hull maintenance and related work **2 :** a naval warrant officer in charge of the hull and all related equipment

boat train *n* **:** a train scheduled to connect with a boat

1**bob** \'bäb\ *vb* **bobbed; bob•bing** [ME *boben*] *vt* **1 :** to strike with a quick light blow **:** RAP **2 :** to move up and down in a short quick movement ⟨~ the head⟩ **3 :** to polish with a bob **:** BUFF ~ *vi* **1 a :** to move up and down briefly or repeatedly ⟨a cork *bobbing* in the water⟩ **b :** to emerge, arise, or appear suddenly or unexpectedly ⟨~ up again⟩ **2 :** to nod or curtsy briefly **3 :** to try to seize something with the teeth ⟨~ for apples⟩

2**bob** *n* **1 a :** a short quick down-and-up motion **b** *Scot* **:** any of several dances **2** *obs* **:** a blow or tap esp. with the fist **3 a :** a modification of the order in change ringing **b :** a method of change ringing using a bob **4 :** a small polishing wheel of solid felt or leather with rounded edges

3**bob** *vt* **bobbed; bob•bing** [ME *bobben*, fr. MF *bober*] **1** *obs* **:** DECEIVE, CHEAT **2** *obs* **:** to take by fraud **:** FILCH

4**bob** *n* [ME *bobbe*] **1 a :** BUNCH, CLUSTER: as (1) *Scot* **:** NOSEGAY (2) **:** a bunch or tuft used for bait in angling; *also* **:** FLOAT 2a **b :** a knob, knot, twist, or curl esp. of ribbons, yarn, or hair **c :** a short haircut on a woman or child **2 :** a hanging ball or weight (as on a plumb line or on the tail of a kite) **3** *archaic* **:** the refrain of a song; *specif* **:** a short and abrupt refrain often of two syllables **4 :** a small insignificant piece **:** TRIFLE

5**bob** *vi* **bobbed; bob•bing :** to angle with a bob esp. through ice

6**bob** *vt* **bobbed; bob•bing 1 :** to cut shorter **:** CROP **2 :** to cut (hair) in the style of a bob

7**bob** *n, pl* **bob** [perh. fr. the name *Bob*] *slang* **:** SHILLING

8**bob** *n* **:** BOBSLED

bob•ber \'bäb-ər\ *n* **:** one that bobs

bob•bery \'bäb-(ə-)rē\ *n* [Hindi *bāp re*, lit., oh father!] **:** HUBBUB

bob•bin \'bäb-ən\ *n* [origin unknown] **1 a :** any of various small round devices on which threads are wound for working handmade lace **b :** a cylinder or spindle on which yarn or thread is wound **c :** a coil of insulated wire or the reel it is wound on **2 :** a narrow cotton cord formerly used by dressmakers for piping

bob•bi•net \,bäb-ə-'net\ *n* [blend of *bobbin* and *net*] **:** a machine-made net of cotton, silk, or nylon usu. with hexagonal mesh

bob•ble \'bäb-əl\ *vb* **bob•bling** \'bäb-(ə-)liŋ\ [freq. of 1*bob*] **1 :** 1BOB **2 :** FUMBLE — **bobble** *n*

bob•by \'bäb-ē\ *n* [*Bobby*, nickname for *Robert*, after Sir *Robert* Peel, who organized the London police force] *Brit* **:** POLICEMAN

bobby pin *n* [4*bob*] **:** a flat wire hairpin with prongs that press close together used esp. for bobbed hair

bobby socks *or* **bobby sox** *n pl* [fr. the name *Bobby*] **:** girls' socks reaching above the ankle

bob•by–sox•er \'bäb-ē-,säk-sər\ *or* **bob•by–sock•er** \-,säk-ər\ *n* **:** an adolescent girl

bob•cat \'bäb-,kat\ *n* [4*bob;* fr. the stubby tail] **:** a common No. American lynx (*Lynx rufus*) typically rusty or reddish in base color

bob•o•link \'bäb-ə-,liŋk\ *n* [imit.] **:** an American migratory songbird (*Dolichonyx oryzivorus*)

bob•sled \'bäb-,sled\ *n* [perh. fr. 4*bob*] **1 :** a short sled usu. used as one of a pair joined by a coupling **2 :** a compound sled formed of two bobsleds and a coupling — **bobsled** *vi*

bob•stay \'bäb-,stā\ *n* [prob. fr. 2*bob*] **:** a stay to hold a ship's bowsprit down

bob•tail \'bäb-,tāl\ *n* [4*bob*] **1 :** a bobbed tail or a horse or dog with one; *esp* **:** OLD ENGLISH SHEEPDOG **2 :** something curtailed or abbreviated — **bobtail** *or* **bob•tailed** \-,tāld\ *adj*

bob veal \'bäb-\ *n* [E dial. *bob* young calf] **:** the veal of a very young or unborn calf

bob•white \(')bäb-'(h)wīt\ *n* [imit.] **:** any quail of a genus (*Colinis*) of which the best-known species (*C. virginianus*) includes a favorite game bird of the eastern and central U.S. — called also *partridge*

bo•cac•cio \bə-'käch-(ē-)(,)ō\ *n* [perh. deriv. of Sp *bocacha*, aug. of *boca* mouth] **:** a large rockfish (*Sebastodes paucispinis*) of the Pacific coast locally important as a market fish

boc•cie *or* **boc•ci** *or* **boc•ce** \'bäch-ē\ *n pl but sing in constr* [It *bocce*, pl. of *boccia* ball, fr. (assumed) VL *bottia* boss] **:** Italian lawn bowling played in a long narrow court

bock \'bäk\ *n* [G, short for *bockbier*, by shortening & alter. fr. *Einbecker bier*, lit., beer from Einbeck, fr. *Einbeck*, Germany] **:** a heavy dark rich beer usu. sold in the early spring

1**bode** \'bōd\ *vt* [ME *boden*, fr. OE *bodian;* akin to OE *bēodan* to proclaim] **1** *archaic* **:** to announce beforehand **:** FORETELL **2 :** to indicate by signs **:** PRESAGE — **bode•ment** \-mənt\ *n*

2**bode** *past of* BIDE

bo•dhi•satt•va *or* **bod•dhi•satt•va** \,bōd-i-'sət-və\ *n* [Skt *bodhisattva* one whose essence is enlightenment, fr. *bodhi* enlightenment + *sattva* being] **:** a being that compassionately refrains from entering nirvana in order to save others and is worshiped as a deity in Mahayana Buddhism

bod•ice \'bäd-əs\ *n* [alter. of. *bodies*, pl. of 1*body*] **1** *archaic* **:** CORSET, STAYS **2 :** the waist of a woman's dress

bod•ied \'bäd-ēd\ *adj* **:** having a body or such a body ⟨long-*bodied*⟩

bod•i•less \'bäd-ē-ləs, -ᵊl-əs\ *adj* **:** having no body **:** INCORPOREAL

1**bod•i•ly** \'bäd-ᵊl-ē\ *adj* **1 :** having a body **:** PHYSICAL **2 :** of or relating to the body ⟨~ comfort⟩ ⟨~ organs⟩

syn BODILY, PHYSICAL, CORPOREAL, CORPORAL, SOMATIC mean of or relating to the human body. BODILY suggests contrast with *mental* or *spiritual;* PHYSICAL suggests more vaguely or less explicitly an organic structure; CORPOREAL suggests the substance of which the body is composed ⟨*corporeal* existence⟩ CORPORAL applies chiefly to things that affect or involve the body; SOMATIC implies contrast with PHYSICAL and is useful as being free of theological and poetic connotations

2**bodily** *adv* **1 :** in the flesh **2 :** as a whole **:** ALTOGETHER

bod•ing \'bōd-iŋ\ *n* **:** FOREBODING

bod•kin \'bäd-kən\ *n* [ME] **1 a :** DAGGER, STILETTO **b :** a sharp slender instrument for making holes in cloth **c :** an ornamental hairpin shaped like a stiletto **2 :** a blunt needle with a large eye for drawing tape or ribbon through a loop or hem

Bo•do•ni \bə-'dō-nē\ *n* [Giambattista *Bodoni* †1813 It printer] **:** a printing type based on original designs by Bodoni

1**body** \'bäd-ē\ *n* [ME, fr. OE *bodig;* akin to OHG *botah* body] **1 a :** the organized physical substance of an animal or plant either living or dead: as (1) **:** the material part or nature of man (2) **:** the dead organism **:** CORPSE (3) **:** the person of a human being before the law **b :** a human being **:** PERSON **2 a :** the main part of a plant or animal body esp. as distinguished from limbs and head **:** TRUNK **b :** the main, central, or principal part: as (1) **:** the nave of a church (2) **:** the bed or box of a vehicle on or in which the load is placed **3 a :** the part of a garment covering the body or trunk **b :** the main part of a document as distinguished from the title, preface, or appendixes **c :** the sound box or pipe of a musical instrument **d :** printed text **:** ordinary reading matter **4 a :** a mass of matter distinct from other masses **b :** one of the seven planets of the old astronomy **c :** something that embodies or gives concrete reality to a thing; *specif* **:** a sensible object in physical space **5 :** a group of persons or things: as **a :** a fighting unit **:** FORCE **b :** a group of individuals organized for some purpose **:** CORPORATION ⟨a legislative ~⟩ **6 a :** VISCOSITY, CONSISTENCY — used esp. of oils and grease **b :** resonance of musical tone **c :** richness of flavor — used of a beverage **7 :** the part of a printing type extending from foot to shoulder and underlying the bevel

2**body** *vt* **:** to give form or shape to **:** EMBODY

body corporate *n* **:** CORPORATION

body•guard \'bäd-ē-,gärd\ *n* **:** a guard to protect or defend the person; *also* **:** RETINUE

body politic *n* **1** *archaic* **:** CORPORATION 2 **2 :** a group of persons politically organized under a single governmental authority

body snatcher *n* **:** one that without authority takes corpses from graves usu. for dissection

boehm•ite \'bām-,īt, 'bə(r)m-\ *n* [G *böhmit*, fr. J. *Böhm* (*Boehm*), 20th cent. G scientist] **:** a mineral consisting of an orthorhombic form of aluminum oxide and hydroxide AlO(OH) found in bauxite

Boer \'bō(ə)r, 'bȯ(ə)r, 'bu̇(ə)r\ *n* [D, lit., farmer — more at BOOR] **:** a South African of Dutch or Huguenot descent

Bo•fors gun \,bō-,fȯrz-, ,bü-\ *n* [*Bofors*, munition works in Sweden] **:** a double-barreled automatic antiaircraft gun

1**bog** \'bäg, 'bȯg\ *n* [of Celt origin; akin to OIr *bocc* soft; akin to OE *būgan* to bend — more at BOW] **:** wet spongy ground; *esp* **:** a poorly drained usu. acid area rich in plant residues, frequently surrounding a body of open water, and having a characteristic flora (as of sedges, heaths, and sphagnum) — **bog•gy** \'bäg-ē, 'bȯg-\ *adj*

2**bog** *vb* **bogged; bog•ging :** to sink into or as if into a bog **:** MIRE

bog asphodel *n* **:** either of two bog herbs (*Narthecium ossifragum* of Europe and *N. americanum* of the U.S.) of the bunchflower family resembling the true asphodel

1**bo•gey** *or* **bo•gy** *or* **bo•gie** *n* [prob. alter. of *bogle*] **1** \'bu̇g-ē, 'bō-gē, 'bü-gē, 'bu̇g-ər\ **:** SPECTER, PHANTOM **2** \'bō-gē *also* 'bu̇g-ē *or* 'bü-gē\ **:** a source of annoyance, perplexity, or harassment **3** \'bō-gē\ **a** *chiefly Brit* **:** an average golfer's score used as a standard for a particular hole or course **b :** one stroke over par on a hole **4** \'bō-gē\ **:** a numerical standard of performance set up as a mark to be aimed at in competition

2**bo•gey** \'bō-gē\ *vt* **:** to shoot (a hole in golf) in one over par

bo•gey•man \'bu̇g-ē-,man, 'bō-gē-, 'bü-gē-, 'bu̇g-ər-\ *n* **:** a monstrous imaginary figure used in threatening children; *broadly* **:** a terrifying person or thing

bog•gle \'bäg-əl\ *vi* **bog•gling** \'bäg-(ə-)liŋ\ [perh. fr. *bogle*] **1 :** to start with fright or amazement **2 :** to hesitate because of doubt, fear, or scruples **3 :** BUNGLE — **boggle** *n*

bo·gie *also* **bo·gey** *or* **bo·gy** \'bō-gē\ *n* [origin unknown] **1 :** a low strongly built cart **2 a** *chiefly Brit* **:** a swiveling railway truck **b :** the driving-wheel assembly consisting of the rear four wheels of a 6-wheel truck **3 :** one of the weight-carrying wheels on the inside perimeter of the tread of a tank serving to keep the treads in line

bo·gle \'bō-gəl\ *also* **bog·gle** \'bäg-əl\ *n* [E dial. (Sc & northern), terrifying apparition; akin to ME *bugge* scarecrow] *dial Brit* **:** GOBLIN, SPECTER; *also* **:** any object of fear or loathing **:** BOGEY

bo·gus \'bō-gəs\ *adj* [*bogus* (a machine for making counterfeit money)] **:** SPURIOUS, SHAM

bog·wood \'bäg-,wu̇d, 'bȯg-\ *n* **:** the wood of trees preserved in peat bogs and used esp. for ornamental purposes

bo·hea \bō-'hē\ *n, often cap* [Chin (Pek) *wu*[3]*-i*[2], hills in China where it was grown] **:** BLACK TEA

bo·he·mia \bō-'hē-mē-ə\ *n, often cap* [trans. of F *bohème*] **:** a community of bohemians **:** the world of bohemians

Bo·he·mi·an \bō-'hē-mē-ən\ *n* **1 a :** a native or inhabitant of Bohemia **b :** the group of Czech dialects used in Bohemia **2** *often not cap* **a :** VAGABOND, WANDERER; *esp* **:** GYPSY **b :** a writer or artist living an unconventional life — **bohemian** *adj, often cap* — **bo·he·mi·an·ism** \-mē-ə-,niz-əm\ *n, often cap*

Bohemian Brethren *n pl* **:** a Christian body originating in Bohemia in 1467 and forming a parent body of the Moravian Brethren

Bohr theory \'bō(ə)r-, 'bȯ(ə)r-\ *n* [Neils H. D. *Bohr* †1962 Dan physicist] **:** a theory in physical chemistry: an atom consists of a positively charged nucleus about which revolves one or more electrons

[1]**boil** \'bȯi(ə)l\ *n* [alter. of ME *bile*, fr. OE *bȳl*] **:** a localized swelling and inflammation of the skin resulting from infection in a skin gland, having a hard central core, and forming pus

[2]**boil** *vb* [ME *boilen*, fr. OF *boillir*, fr. L *bullire* to bubble, fr. *bulla* bubble] *vi* **1 a :** to generate bubbles of vapor when heated — used of a liquid **b :** to come to the boiling point **2 :** to become agitated like boiling water **:** SEETHE **3 :** to be moved, excited, or stirred up **4 a :** to rush headlong **b :** to burst forth **:** ERUPT **5 :** to undergo the action of a boiling liquid ~ *vt* **1 :** to subject to the action of a boiling liquid **2 :** to heat to the boiling point **3 :** to form or separate (as sugar or salt) by boiling

[3]**boil** *n* **:** the act or state of boiling

boiled oil *n* **:** any fatty oil (as linseed oil) whose drying properties have been improved by heating usu. with driers

boil·er \'bȯi-lər\ *n* **1 :** one that boils **2 a :** a vessel used for boiling **b :** the part of a steam generator in which water is converted into steam and which consists usu. of metal shells and tubes **c :** a tank in which water is heated or hot water is stored

boil·er·mak·er \'bȯi-lər-,mā-kər\ *n* **1 :** a workman who makes, assembles, or repairs boilers **2 :** whiskey with a beer chaser

boiling point *n* **:** the temperature at which a liquid boils

bois·ter·ous \'bȯi-st(ə-)rəs\ *adj* [ME *boistous* rough] **1** *obs* **a :** DURABLE, STRONG **b :** COARSE **c :** MASSIVE **2 a :** noisily turbulent **:** ROWDY **b :** marked by exuberance and high spirits **3 :** STORMY, TUMULTUOUS **syn** see VOCIFEROUS — **bois·ter·ous·ly** *adv* — **bois·ter·ous·ness** *n*

bo·la \'bō-lə\ *or* **bo·las** \-ləs\ *n, pl* **bolas** \-ləz\ *also* **bo·las·es** [AmerSp *bolas*, fr. Sp *bola* ball] **:** a weapon consisting of two or more stone or iron balls attached to the ends of a cord for hurling at and entangling an animal

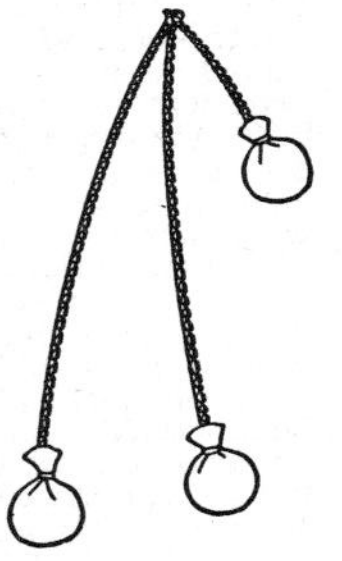
bola

bold \'bōld\ *adj* [ME, fr. OE *beald;* akin to OHG *bald* bold] **1 a :** fearless before danger **:** INTREPID **b :** showing or reflecting a courageous daring spirit and contempt of danger ⟨a ~ plan⟩ **2 :** IMPUDENT, PRESUMPTUOUS **3** *obs* **:** ASSURED, CONFIDENT **4 :** SHEER, STEEP ⟨~ cliffs⟩ **5 :** ADVENTUROUS, DARING ⟨a ~ thinker⟩ **6 :** standing out prominently **:** CONSPICUOUS **7 :** BOLD-FACED 2 — **bold·ly** \'bōl-(d)lē\ *adv* — **bold·ness** \'bōl(d)-nəs\ *n*

bold·face \'bōl(d)-,fās\ *n* **:** a heavy-faced type; *also* **:** printing in boldface

bold–faced \'bōl(d)-'fāst\ *adj* **1 :** bold in manner or conduct **2 :** set in boldface

bole \'bōl\ *n* [ME, fr. ON *bolr*] **:** the trunk of a tree

bo·le·ro \bə-'le(ə)r-(,)ō\ *n* [Sp] **1 :** a Spanish dance in ¾ time; *also* **:** the music for it **2 :** a loose waist-length jacket open at the front

bo·le·tus \bə-'lēt-əs\ *n, pl* **bo·le·tus·es** *or* **bo·le·ti** \-'lē-,tī\ [NL, genus name, fr. L, a fungus, fr. Gk *bōlitēs*] **:** any of a genus (*Boletus*) of soft pore fungi some of which are poisonous and others edible

bo·li·var \bə-'lē-,vär, 'bäl-ə-vər\ *n, pl* **bolivars** *or* **bo·li·va·res** \,bäl-ə-'vär-,ās, ,bō-li-\ [AmerSp *bolívar*, fr. Simón *Bolívar* †1830 So. American liberator] — see MONEY table

bo·li·vi·a·no \bə-,liv-ē-'än-(,)ō\ *n* [Sp] **:** a former monetary unit of Bolivia replaced in 1963 by the peso boliviano

boll \'bōl\ *n* [ME] **:** the pod or capsule of a plant (as cotton)

bol·lard \'bäl-ərd\ *n* [perh. irreg. fr. *bole*] **1 :** a post of metal or wood on a wharf around which to fasten mooring lines **2 :** BITT 1

bol·lix \'bäl-iks\ *vt* [alter. of *ballocks*, pl. of *ballock* testis, fr. ME, fr. OE *beallucl*] **:** to throw into disorder; *also* **:** BUNGLE — **bollix** *n*

boll weevil *n* **:** a grayish weevil (*Anthonomus grandis*) about ¼ inch long that infests the cotton plant puncturing and laying its eggs in the squares and bolls

boll·worm \'bōl-,wərm\ *n* **:** CORN EARWORM; *also* **:** any of several other moth larvae that feed on cotton bolls

bo·lo \'bō-(,)lō\ *n* [Sp] **:** a long heavy Philippine single-edged knife

bo·lo·gna \bə-'lō-nē *also* -n(y)ə\ *n* [short for *Bologna sausage*, fr. *Bologna*, Italy] **:** a large smoked sausage of beef, veal, and pork

bo·lo·graph \'bō-lə-,graf\ *n* [Gk *bolē* stroke, beam of light (fr. *ballein* to throw) + E *-o-* + *-graph* — more at DEVIL] **:** the record made by a bolometer — **bo·lo·graph·ic** \,bō-lə-'graf-ik\ *adj*

bo·lom·e·ter \bə-'läm-ət-ər\ *n* [Gk *bolē* + E *-o-* + *-meter*] **:** a very sensitive resistance thermometer used in the detection and measurement of feeble thermal radiation and esp. adapted to the study of infrared spectra — **bo·lo·met·ric** \,bō-lə-'me-trik\ *adj* — **bo·lo·met·ri·cal·ly** \-tri-k(ə-)lē\ *adv*

bo·lo·ney *var of* BALONEY

Bol·she·vik \'bōl-shə-,vik, 'bȯl-, 'bäl-, -,vēk\ *n, pl* **Bolsheviks** *also* **Bol·she·vi·ki** \,bōl-shə-'vik-ē, ,bȯl-, ,bäl-, -'vē-kē\ [Russ *bol'shevik*, fr. *bol'she* larger] **1 :** a member of the extremist wing of the Russian Social Democratic party in Russia that seized supreme power in the Revolution (1917–20) **2 :** COMMUNIST 3 — **Bolshevik** *adj*

bol·she·vism \'bōl-shə-,viz-əm, 'bȯl-, 'bäl-\ *n, often cap* **1 :** the doctrine or program of the Bolsheviks advocating violent overthrow of capitalism **2 :** Russian communism

Bol·she·vist \-shə-vəst\ *n or adj* **:** BOLSHEVIK

bol·she·vize \-shə-,vīz\ *vt* **:** to make Bolshevist

[1]**bol·ster** \'bōl-stər\ *n* [ME, fr. OE; akin to OE *belg* bag — more at BELLY] **1 :** a long pillow or cushion extending the full width of a bed **2 :** a structural part designed to eliminate friction or provide support or bearing; *esp* **:** the horizontal connection between the volutes of an Ionic capital

[2]**bolster** *vt* **bol·ster·ing** \-st(ə-)riŋ\ **:** to support with or as if with a bolster; *also* **:** REINFORCE — **bol·ster·er** \-stər-ər\ *n*

[1]**bolt** \'bōlt\ *n* [ME, fr. OE; akin to OHG *bolz* crossbow bolt, Lith *beldėti* to beat] **1 a :** a shaft or missile designed to be shot from a crossbow or catapult; *esp* **:** a short stout usu. blunt-headed arrow **b :** a lightning stroke **:** THUNDERBOLT **2 a :** a wood or metal bar or rod used to fasten a door **b :** the part of a lock that is shot or withdrawn by the key **3 a :** a roll of cloth of specified length **b :** a roll of wallpaper of specified length **4 :** a metal rod or pin for fastening objects together that usu. has a head at one end and a screw thread at the other and is secured by a nut **5 a :** a block of timber to be sawed or cut (as into shingles or staves) **b :** a short round section of a log **6 :** the breech closure of a breech-loading rifle

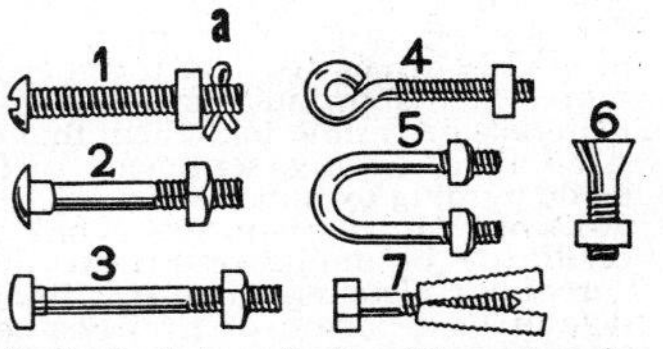

bolts 4: *1* stove bolt, with cotter pin, *a;* *2* carriage bolt; *3* machine bolt; *4* eyebolt; *5* U bolt; *6* plow bolt; *7* expansion bolt

[2]**bolt** *vi* **1 :** to move suddenly or nervously **:** START **2 :** to move rapidly **:** DASH **3 a :** to dart off or away **:** FLEE **b :** to break away from control or off a set course **4 :** to break away from or oppose one's political party ~ *vt* **1 a** *archaic* **:** SHOOT, DISCHARGE **b :** FLUSH, START ⟨~ rabbits⟩ **2 :** to say impulsively **:** BLURT **3 :** to secure with a bolt **4 :** to attach or fasten with bolts **5 :** to swallow hastily or without chewing **6 :** to break away from

[3]**bolt** *adv* **1 :** in the manner of a bolt **:** RIGIDLY ⟨sat ~ upright⟩ **2** *archaic* **:** DIRECTLY, STRAIGHT

[4]**bolt** *n* **:** an act of bolting

[5]**bolt** *vt* [ME *bultan*, fr. OF *buleter*, of Gmc origin; akin to MHG *biuteln* to sift, fr. *biutel* bag, fr. OHG *būtil*] **1 :** to sift (as flour) usu. through fine-meshed cloth **2** *archaic* **:** SIFT 2

[1]**bolt·er** \'bōl-tər\ *n* **:** a machine for bolting flour; *also* **:** the operator of such a machine

[2]**bolter** *n* **1 :** a horse given to running away **2 :** a voter who bolts

bolt·rope \'bōlt-,rōp\ *n* **:** a strong rope stitched to the edges of a sail to strengthen it

bo·lus \'bō-ləs\ *n* [LL, fr. Gk *bōlos* lump] **:** a rounded mass: as **a :** a large pill **b :** a soft mass of chewed food

[1]**bomb** \'bäm\ *n* [F *bombe*, fr. It *bomba*, prob. fr. L *bombus* deep hollow sound, fr. Gk *bombos*, of imit. origin] **1 :** an explosive device fused to detonate under specified conditions **2 :** a vessel for compressed gases **3 :** a rounded mass of lava exploded from a volcano **4 :** a lead-lined container for radioactive material **5 :** a long pass in football

[2]**bomb** *vt* **:** to attack with bombs

[1]**bom·bard** \'bäm-,bärd\ *n* [ME *bombarde*, fr. MF, prob. fr. L *bombus*] **:** a late medieval cannon

[2]**bom·bard** \bäm-'bärd, bəm-\ *vt* **1 :** to attack with artillery or bombers **2 :** to assail vigorously or persistently (as with questions) **3 :** to subject to the impact of rapidly moving particles (as electrons or alpha rays) **syn** see ATTACK — **bom·bard·ment** \-mənt\ *n*

bom·bar·dier \,bäm-bə(r)-'di(ə)r\ *n* **1 a** *archaic* **:** ARTILLERYMAN **b :** a noncommissioned officer in the British artillery **2 :** a bomber-crew member who uses the bombsight and releases the bombs

bom·bar·don \'bäm-'bärd-ᵊn, 'bäm-bər-dən\ *n* [F, fr. It *bombardone*] **1 :** the bass member of the shawm family **2 :** a bass tuba

bom·bast \'bäm-,bast\ *n* [MF *bombace*, fr. ML *bombac-*, *bombax* cotton, alter. of L *bombyc-*, *bombyx* silkworm, silk, fr. Gk *bombyk-*, *bombyx*] **1** *obs* **:** cotton or any soft fibrous material used as padding **2 :** pretentious inflated speech or writing — **bombast** *adj* — **bom·bast·er** \-,bas-tər\ *n* — **bom·bas·tic** \bäm-'bas-tik\ *adj*

syn RHAPSODY, RANT, FUSTIAN: BOMBAST implies verbose grandiosity or inflation of style disproportionate to the thought; RHAPSODY applies to an ecstatic or effusive utterance governed by the feelings rather than by logical thought; RANT suggests a sustained violence and extravagance of expression; FUSTIAN suggests a padding out with sonorous or grandiloquent inanities or banalities

bom·ba·zine \,bäm-bə-'zēn\ *n* [MF *bombasin*, fr. ML *bombacinum*, *bombycinum* silken texture, fr. L, neut. of *bombycinus* of silk, fr. *bombyc-*, *bombyx*] **1 :** a silk fabric in twill weave dyed black **2 :** a twilled fabric with silk warp and worsted filling

bomb bay *n* **:** a bomb-carrying compartment on the underside of a combat airplane

bombe \'bäm, 'bōⁿb\ *n* [F, lit., bomb] **:** a frozen dessert made by lining a round or melon-shaped mold with one mixture and filling it with another

bomb·er \'bäm-ər\ *n* **:** one that bombs; *specif* **:** an airplane designed for bombing

bom·bi·nate \'bäm-bə-,nāt\ *vi* [NL *bombinatus*, pp. of *bombinare*, alter. of L *bombilare*, fr. *bombus*] **:** BUZZ, DRONE — **bom·bi·na·tion** \,bäm-bə-'nā-shən\ *n*

bomb·proof \'bäm-'prüf\ *adj* **:** safe from the force of bombs

bomb·shell \'bäm-,shel\ *n* **1 :** BOMB 1 **2 :** a devastating surprise

bomb·sight \'bäm-,sīt\ *n* **:** a sighting device for aiming bombs

bo·na·ci \,bō-nə-'sē\ *n* [Sp *bonasí*] **:** a black grouper (*Mycteroperca bonaci*); *also* **:** any of several related marine food fishes

bona fide \'bō-nə-,fīd, 'bän-ə-; ,bō-nə-'fīd-ē, -'fīd-ə\ *adj* [L, in good faith] **1 :** made in good faith without fraud or deceit

2 : made with earnest intent : SINCERE 3 : GENUINE **syn** see AUTHENTIC

bo·nan·za \bə-'nan-zə\ *n* [Sp, lit., calm, fr. ML *bonacia*, alter. of L *malacia* calm at sea, fr. Gk *malakia*, lit., softness, fr. *malakos* soft] **1 :** an exceptionally large and rich ore shoot or pocket in veins carrying gold and silver **2 :** something that yields a large profit

Bo·na·part·ism \'bō-nə-,pärt-,iz-əm\ *n* **1 :** support of the French emperors Napoleon I, Napoleon III, or their dynasty **2 :** a political movement associated chiefly with authoritarian rule by a usu. military leader ostensibly supported by a popular mandate — **Bo·na·part·ist** \-,pärt-əst\ *n or adj*

bon·bon \'bän-,bän\ *n* [F, (baby talk), redupl. of *bon* good, fr. L *bonus* — more at BOUNTY] **:** a candy with chocolate or fondant coating and fondant center with fruits and nuts sometimes added

¹bond *n* [ME, fr. OE *bōnda* householder, fr. ON *bōndi*, alter. of *būandi*, fr. prp. of *būa* to dwell; akin to OE *būr* dwelling — more at BOWER] *obs* **:** BONDMAN — **bond** *adj*

²bond \'bänd\ *n* [ME *band*, *bond* — more at BAND] **1 :** something that binds or restrains **:** FETTER **2 :** a binding agreement **:** COVENANT **3 a :** a band or cord used to tie something **b :** a material or device for binding **c :** a mechanism by means of which atoms, ions, or groups of atoms are held together in a molecule or crystal — usu. represented in formulas by a line or dot **d :** an adhesive, cementing material, or fusible ingredient that combines, unites, or strengthens **4 :** a tie of loyalty, sentiment, or friendship **5 a :** an obligation made binding by a money forfeit; *also* **:** the amount of the money guarantee **b :** one who acts as bail or surety **c :** an interest-bearing certificate of public or private indebtedness **d :** an insurance agreement pledging surety for financial loss caused by the act or default of a person or by some contingency **6 :** the systematic lapping of brick in a wall **7 :** the state of goods manufactured, stored, or transported under the care of bonded agencies until the duties or taxes on them are paid

³bond *vt* **1 :** to lap (as brick) for solidity of construction **2 a :** to secure payment of duties and taxes on (goods) by giving a bond **b :** to convert into a debt secured by bonds **c :** to provide a bond (sense 5d) for or cause to provide such a bond **3 a :** to cause to adhere firmly **b :** to embed in a matrix ~ *vi* **:** to hold together or solidify by or as if by means of a bond or binder **:** COHERE — **bond·able** \'bän-də-bəl\ *adj* — **bond·er** *n*

bond·age \'bän-dij\ *n* **1 :** villein tenure or service **2 :** SERFDOM, SLAVERY **3 :** subjection to compulsion **syn** see SERVITUDE

bond·er·ize \'bän-də-,rīz\ *vt* [back-formation fr. *Bonderized*, a trademark] **:** to coat (steel) with a patented phosphate solution for protection against corrosion

bond·hold·er \'bänd-,hōl-dər\ *n* **:** a lender holding a bond

bond·maid \'bän(d)-,mād\ *n* **:** a female slave or bond servant

bond·man \'bän(d)-mən\ *n* **:** SLAVE, SERF — **bond·wom·an** \'bän-,dwu̇m-ən\ *n*

bond paper *n* **:** a strong durable paper used esp. for documents

bond servant *n* **:** one bound to service without wages; *also* **:** SLAVE

¹bonds·man \'bän(d)z-mən\ *n* **:** BONDMAN

²bondsman *n* **:** SURETY

bond·stone \'bän(d)-,stōn\ *n* **:** a stone long enough to extend through the full thickness of a wall to bind it together

¹bone \'bōn\ *n, often attrib* [ME *bon*, fr. OE *bān*; akin to OHG & ON *bein* bone] **1 a :** one of the hard parts of the skeleton of a vertebrate **b :** any of various hard animal substances or structures akin to or resembling bone **c :** the hard largely calcareous tissue of which the adult skeleton of most vertebrates is chiefly composed **2** *pl* **:** SKELETON; *also* **:** BODY 1 **3 a** *pl* **:** CLAPPERS **b :** a strip of whalebone or steel used to stiffen a corset or dress **c** *pl* **:** DICE **4** *pl but sing or pl in constr, often cap* **:** an end man in a minstrel show who may perform on the bones — **bone·less** \-ləs\ *adj*

²bone *vt* **1 :** to remove the bones from ⟨~ a fish⟩ **2 :** to provide (a garment) with stays ~ *vi* **:** to study hard **:** GRIND; *also* **:** CRAM

bone ash *n* **:** the white porous residue chiefly of tribasic calcium phosphate from bones calcined in air used esp. in ceramics; *also* **:** tribasic calcium phosphate

bone black *n* **:** the black residue chiefly of tribasic calcium phosphate and carbon from bones calcined in closed vessels used esp. as a pigment or adsorbent — called also *bone char*

bone china *n* **:** translucent white china made with bone ash or calcium phosphate

bone·fish \'bōn-,fish\ *n* **1 :** any of several slender silvery small-scaled fishes (family Albulidae); *esp* **:** a notable sport and food fish (*Albula vulpes*) of warm seas **2 :** TENPOUNDER

bone·head \'bōn-,hed\ *n* **:** a stupid person **:** NUMSKULL

bone meal *n* **:** fertilizer or feed made of crushed or ground bone

bon·er \'bō-nər\ *n* **1 :** one that bones **2 :** BLUNDER, HOWLER

bone·set \'bōn-,set\ *n* **:** any of several composite herbs (genus *Eupatorium*); *esp* **:** a perennial (*E. perfoliatum*) with opposite leaves and white-rayed flower heads used in folk medicine

bon·fire \'bän-,fī(ə)r\ *n* [ME *bonefire* a fire of bones, fr. *bon* bone + *fire*] **:** a large fire built in the open air

¹bong \'bäŋ, 'bȯŋ\ *n* [imit.] **:** the deep resonant sound esp. of a bell

²bong *vb* **:** RING

bon·go \'bäŋ-(,)gō\ *n, pl* **bongos** *also* **bongoes** [AmerSp *bongó*] **:** one of a pair of small tuned drums played with the hands

bon·ho·mie *also* **bon·hom·mie** \,bän-ə-'mē, ,bō-nə-\ *n* [F *bonhomie*, fr. *bonhomme* good-natured man, fr. *bon* good + *homme* man] **:** good-natured easy friendliness **:** GENIALITY

bon·i·face \'bän-ə-fəs, -,fās\ *n* [*Boniface*, innkeeper in *The Beaux' Stratagem* by George Farquhar] **:** the proprietor of a hotel, nightclub, or restaurant

bo·ni·to \bə-'nēt-(,)ō\ *n, pl* **bonitos** *or* **bonito** [Sp, fr. *bonito* pretty, fr. L *bonus* good] **:** any of various medium-sized tunas intermediate between the smaller mackerels and the larger tunas; *also* **:** any of various fishes somewhat resembling these

bon mot \bōⁿ-'mō\ *n, pl* **bons mots** \bōⁿ-'mō(z)\ *or* **bon mots** \-'mō(z)\ [F, lit., good word] **:** a clever remark **:** WITTICISM

bonne \'bȯn\ *n* [F, fr. fem. of *bon*] **:** a French nursemaid or maidservant

¹bon·net \'bän-ət\ *n* [ME *bonet*, fr. MF, fr. ML *abonnis*] **1 a** (1) *chiefly Scot* **:** a man's or boy's cap (2) **:** a brimless Scotch cap of seamless woolen fabric **b :** a woman's cloth or straw hat tied under the chin **2 a :** an additional piece of canvas laced to the foot of a jib or foresail **b** *Brit* **:** an automobile hood **c :** a cover for an open fireplace or a cowl or hood to increase the draft of a chimney **d :** a metal covering for valve chambers, hydrants, or ventilators

²bonnet *vt* **:** to provide with or dress in a bonnet

bon·ni·ly \'bän-ᵊl-ē\ *adv* **:** in a bonny manner

bon·ny *also* **bon·nie** \'bän-ē\ *adj* [ME *bonie*, fr. OF *bon* good, fr. L *bonus*] *chiefly Brit* **:** HANDSOME, ATTRACTIVE, FINE

bon·ny·clab·ber \'bän-ē-,klab-ər\ *n* [IrGael *bainne clabair*, fr. *bainne* milk + *clabair*, gen. of *clabar* sour thick milk] *North & Midland* **:** ¹CLABBER

bon·sai \bän-'sī\ *n, pl* **bonsai** [Jap] **:** a potted plant (as a tree) dwarfed by special methods of culture

bon·spiel \'bän-,spēl\ *n* [perh. fr. D *bond* league + *spel* game] **:** a match or tournament between curling clubs

bon ton \(')bän-'tän\ *n, pl* **bons tons** \(')bän-'tänz\ [F, lit., good tone] **1 :** fashionable manner or style **2 :** polite society

bo·nus \'bō-nəs\ *n* [L, good — more at BOUNTY] **1 :** something given in addition to what is usual or strictly due **2 a** *Brit* **:** DIVIDEND 1b **b :** money or an equivalent given in addition to an employee's usual compensation **c :** a premium given by a corporation to a purchaser of its securities, to a promoter, or to an employee **d** (1) **:** a government subsidy to an industry (2) **:** a government payment to war veterans **3 :** a sum of money in addition to interest or royalties charged for the granting of a loan or privilege to a company, or for the lease or transfer of property

bon vi·vant \,bän-vē-'vänt, ,bōⁿ-vē-'väⁿ\ *n, pl* **bons vivants** \,bän-vē-'vänts, ,bōⁿ-vē-'väⁿ(z)\ *or* **bon vivants** *same*\ [F, lit., good liver] **:** a person having cultivated or refined tastes esp. in food and drink **syn** see EPICURE

bon voy·age \,bōⁿv-,wī-'äzh, -,wä-'yäzh; ,bōⁿ-,vȯi-'äzh, ,bän-\ *n* [F] **:** a good trip **:** FAREWELL — often used interjectionally

bony *or* **bon·ey** \'bō-nē\ *adj* **bon·i·er; bon·i·est 1 a :** consisting of bone **b :** resembling bone **2 a :** full of bones **b :** having prominent bones; *also* **:** SKINNY, SCRAWNY **3 :** BARREN, LEAN

bony labyrinth *n* **:** the cavity in the temporal bone that contains the membranous labyrinth of the ear

bonze \'bänz\ *n* [F, fr. Pg *bonzo*, fr. Jap *bonsō*] **:** a Buddhist monk

¹boo \'bü\ *interj* [ME *bo*] — used to express contempt or disapproval or to startle or frighten

²boo *n* **:** a shout of disapproval or contempt — **boo** *vb*

boob \'büb\ *n* [short for *booby*] **:** SIMPLETON; *also* **:** BOOR

boob·oi·sie \,büb-,wä-'zē\ *n* [*boob* + *-oisie* (as in *bourgeoisie*)] **:** a class of the general public that is composed of boobs

boo–boo \'bü-(,)bü\ *n* [prob. baby-talk alter. of *boohoo*, imitation of the sound of weeping] **1** *dial* **:** BRUISE, SORE **2** *slang* **:** BLUNDER

boo·by \'bü-bē\ *n* [modif. of Sp *bobo*, fr. L *balbus* stammering, prob. of imit. origin] **1 :** an awkward foolish person **:** DOPE **2 a :** any of several small gannets (genus *Sula*) of tropical seas **b :** any of several American ducks **3 :** the poorest performer or lowest scorer in a group

booby hatch *n* **:** an insane asylum

booby trap *n* **:** a trap for the unwary or unsuspecting; *esp* **:** a concealed explosive device contrived to go off when some harmless-looking object is touched — **boo·by–trap** \'bü-bē-,trap\ *vt*

boo·dle \'büd-ᵊl\ *n* [D *boedel* estate, lot, fr. MD; akin to ON *būth* booth] **1 :** a collection or lot of persons **2 :** bribe money

boo·gie–woo·gie \,bu̇g-ē-'wu̇g-ē, ,bü-gē-'wü-gē\ *n* [origin unknown] **:** a percussive style of playing blues on the piano characterized by a persistent rhythmic bass and florid figurations of a simple melody

¹book \'bu̇k\ *n* [ME, fr. OE *bōc*; akin to OHG *buoh* book, OE *bōc* beech; prob. fr. the early Germanic practice of carving runic characters on beech wood tablets — more at BEECH] **1 a :** a set of written sheets of skin or paper or tablets of wood or ivory **b :** a set of written, printed, or blank sheets bound together into a volume **c :** a long written or printed literary composition **d :** a major division of a treatise or literary work **e :** a volume of business records of any of various kinds **2** *cap* **:** BIBLE **3 :** something felt to be a source of enlightenment or instruction **4 a :** the total available knowledge and experience that can be brought to bear on a task or problem **b :** the standards or authority relevant in a situation **c :** JUDGMENT, OPINION **5 a :** all the charges that can be made against an accused person ⟨threw the ~ at him⟩ **b :** RESPONSIBILITY, ACCOUNT **6 a :** LIBRETTO **b :** the script of a play **7 :** a packet of commodities bound together ⟨a ~ of matches⟩ **8 a :** BOOKMAKER **b :** the bets registered by a bookmaker **9 :** the tricks a card player must win before scoring — **book·bind·er** \-,bīn-dər\ *n* — **one for the book :** an act or occurrence worth noting

²book *vt* **1 a :** to enter, write, or register so as to engage transportation or reserve lodgings **b :** to schedule engagements for **c :** to set aside time for **2 :** to enter charges against in a police register ~ *vi* **1 :** to reserve something in advance **2 :** *chiefly Brit* **:** to register in a hotel — **book·er** *n*

³book *adj* **1 :** bookish or derived from books **2 :** shown by books of account

book·bind·ing \-,bīn-diŋ\ *n* **1 :** the binding of a book **2 :** the art or trade of binding books

book·end \'bu̇k-,end\ *n* **:** a support for the end of a row of books

book·ie \'bu̇k-ē\ *n* [by shortening & alter.] **:** BOOKMAKER 2

book·ish \'bu̇k-ish\ *adj* **1 a :** of or relating to books **b :** fond of books and reading **2 :** inclined to rely on book knowledge rather than practical experience — **book·ish·ly** *adv* — **book·ish·ness** *n*

book·keep·er \'bu̇k-,kē-pər\ *n* **:** one who records the accounts or transactions of a business — **book·keep·ing** \-piŋ\ *n*

book·let \'bu̇k-lət\ *n* **:** a little book; *esp* **:** PAMPHLET

book louse *n* **:** a minute wingless insect (order Corrodentia); *esp* **:** an insect (as *Liposcelis divinatorius*) injurious esp. to books

book·mak·er \'bu̇k-,mā-kər\ *n* **1 a :** a printer, binder, or designer of books **b :** one who compiles books from the writings of others **2 :** one who determines odds and receives and pays off bets — **book·mak·ing** \-kiŋ\ *n*

book·man \-mən\ *n* **1 :** LITTERATEUR **2 :** one who sells books

book·mark \-,märk\ *n* **:** a marker for finding a place in a book

book–match \-,mach\ *vt* **:** to match the grains of (as two sheets of veneer) so that one sheet seems to be the mirrored image of the other

book·mo·bile \'bu̇k-mō-,bēl\ *n* [*book* + auto*mobile*] **:** a truck that serves as a traveling library

book of account 1 : LEDGER **2 :** a book or record essential to a system of accounts

Book of Common Prayer : the service book of the Anglican Communion

book·plate \'bu̇k-,plāt\ *n* **:** a book owner's identification label that is usu. pasted to the inside front cover of a book

book review *n* : a critical estimate of a book
book·sell·er \ˈbu̇k-ˌsel-ər\ *n* : the proprietor of a bookstore
book·shelf \-ˌshelf\ *n* **1 :** an open shelf for holding books **2 :** a small collection of books
book value *n* : the value of something as shown by the books of account of the business owning it; *specif* **:** the value of capital stock as indicated by the excess of assets over liabilities
book·worm \-ˌwərm\ *n* **1 :** any of various insect larvae that feed on the binding and paste of books **2 :** a person unusually devoted to reading or study
Bool·ean algebra \ˌbü-lē-ən-\ *n* [George *Boole* †1864 E mathematician] **:** a logical calculus esp. of classes arranged as a system of theorems deduced from a set of undefined symbols and axioms concerning them
[1]**boom** \ˈbüm\ *n* [D, tree, beam; akin to OHG *boum* tree — more at BEAM] **1 :** a long spar used variously to extend the foot of a sail or facilitate handling of cargo or mooring **2 a :** a long beam projecting from the mast of a derrick to support or guide an object to be lifted or swung **b :** a long movable arm used to manipulate a microphone **3 :** a line of connected floating timbers across a river or enclosing an area of water to keep sawlogs together; *also* **:** the enclosed logs **4 :** a chain cable or line of spars extended across a river or the mouth of a harbor to defend it by obstructing navigation **5 :** a spar or outrigger connecting the tail surfaces and the main supporting structure of an airplane
[2]**boom** *vb* [imit.] *vi* **1 :** to make a deep hollow sound **2 a :** to increase in esteem or importance **b :** to experience a sudden rapid growth and expansion usu. with an increase in prices **c :** to develop rapidly in population and importance ~ *vt* **1 :** to cause to resound **2 :** to cause a rapid growth or increase of **:** BOOST
[3]**boom** *n* **1 :** a booming sound or cry **2 :** a rapid expansion or increase: as **a :** a general movement in support of a candidate for office **b :** rapid settlement and development of a town or district **c :** a rapid widespread expansion of economic activity
boo·mer·ang \ˈbü-mə-ˌraŋ\ *n* [native name in Australia] **1 :** a bent or angular throwing club which can be thrown so as to return near the starting point **2 :** an act or utterance that reacts to the damage of its originator — **boomerang** *vi*

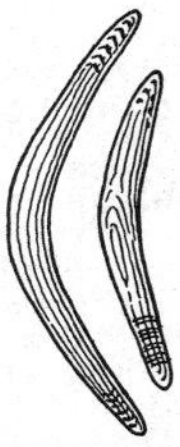
boomerangs

boom·let \ˈbüm-lət\ *n* : a small boom
[1]**boon** \ˈbün\ *n* [ME, fr. ON *bōn* petition; akin to OE *bēn* prayer, *bannan* to summon — more at BAN] **1 :** BENEFIT, FAVOR; *esp* **:** one that is given in answer to a request **2 :** a timely benefit **:** BLESSING
[2]**boon** *adj* [ME *bon,* fr. MF, good — more at BONNY] **1 :** BOUNTEOUS, BENIGN **2 :** MERRY, CONVIVIAL
boon·dog·gle \ˈbün-ˌdȯg-əl, -ˌdäg-\ *n* [coined by Robert H. Link] **1 :** a handicraft article of leather or wicker **2 :** a trivial, useless, or wasteful activity — **boondoggle** *vi* **boon·dog·gling** \-(ə-)liŋ\ — **boon·dog·gler** \-(ə-)lər\ *n*
boor \ˈbu̇(ə)r\ *n* [D *boer;* akin to OE *būan* to dwell] **1 :** PEASANT **2 :** BOER **3 a :** YOKEL **b :** a rude or insensitive person
boor·ish \ˈbu̇(ə)r-ish\ *adj* **:** resembling a boor **:** RUDE — **boor·ish·ly** *adv* — **boor·ish·ness** *n*
syn BOORISH, CHURLISH, LOUTISH, CLOWNISH mean uncouth in manners or appearance. BOORISH implies rudeness of manner due to insensitiveness to others' feelings and unwillingness to be agreeable; CHURLISH suggests surliness, unresponsiveness, and ungraciousness; LOUTISH implies bodily awkwardness together with stupidity or abjectness; CLOWNISH suggests ill-bred awkwardness, ignorance or stupidity, ungainliness, and often a propensity for absurd antics
[1]**boost** \ˈbüst\ *vt* [origin unknown] **1 :** to push or shove up from below **2 a :** INCREASE, RAISE **b :** ASSIST, PROMOTE ⟨~ morale⟩ **3 :** to promote the cause or interests of **:** PLUG **4 :** to increase in force, pressure, or amount; *esp* **:** to raise the voltage of or across (an electric circuit) **syn** see LIFT
[2]**boost** *n* **1 :** a push upwards **2 :** an increase in amount **3 :** an act that brings help or encouragement
boost·er \ˈbü-stər\ *n* **1 :** one that boosts **2 :** an enthusiastic supporter **3 :** an auxiliary device for increasing force, power, or pressure **4 :** a radio-frequency amplifier for a radio or television receiving set **5 :** the first stage of a multistage rocket providing thrust for the launching and the initial part of the flight **6 :** a substance that increases the effectiveness of a medicament; *esp* **:** a supplementary dose of an immunizing agent to increase immunity
[1]**boot** \ˈbüt\ *n* [ME, fr. OE *bōt* remedy; akin to OE *betera* better] **1** *archaic* **:** DELIVERANCE **2** *chiefly dial* **:** something to equalize a trade **3** *obs* **:** AVAIL — **to boot :** BESIDES
[2]**boot** *vb, archaic* **:** AVAIL, PROFIT
[3]**boot** *n* [ME, fr. MF *bote*] **1 :** a covering of leather or rubber for the foot and leg **2 :** an instrument of torture used to crush the leg and foot **3 :** a sheath or casing resembling a boot that provides a protective covering for the foot or leg or for an object or part resembling a leg **4 :** a sheath enclosing the inflorescence **5** *Brit* **:** an automobile trunk **6 :** a blow delivered by or as if by a booted foot **:** KICK; *also* **:** a rude discharge or dismissal **7 :** a navy or marine recruit undergoing basic training
[4]**boot** *vt* **1 :** to put boots on **2 a :** KICK **b :** to eject or discharge summarily **3 :** to make an error on (a grounder in baseball)
[5]**boot** *n* [[1]*boot*] *archaic* **:** BOOTY, PLUNDER
boot·black \ˈbüt-ˌblak\ *n* : one who shines shoes
boot camp *n* : a navy or marine camp for basic training
boot·ed \ˈbüt-əd\ *adj* **1 :** wearing boots **2 a :** having a continuous horny covering — used of the tarsus of a bird **b :** having the shanks and toes feathered — used esp. of domesticated birds
boo·tee *or* **boo·tie** \bü-ˈtē, *of infants' footwear* ˈbüt-ē\ *n* **:** a boot with a short leg; *esp* **:** an infant's knitted or crocheted sock
Bo·ö·tes \bō-ˈōt-ēz\ *n* [L (gen. *Boötis*), fr. Gk *Boōtēs,* lit., plowman, fr. *bous* head of cattle — more at COW] **:** a northern constellation containing the bright star Arcturus
booth \ˈbüth\ *n, pl* **booths** \ˈbü*th*z, ˈbüths\ [ME *bothe,* of Scand origin; akin to ON *būth* booth; akin to OE *būan* to dwell] **1 :** a temporary shelter for livestock or field workers **2 a :** a stall or stand for the sale or exhibition of goods **b :** a small enclosure affording privacy or isolation for one person at a time **c :** a restaurant accommodation consisting of a table between two backed benches
boot·jack \ˈbüt-ˌjak\ *n* : a metal or wood device shaped like the letter V and used in pulling off boots
boot·lace \-ˌlās\ *n, Brit* **:** SHOELACE
[1]**boot·leg** \-ˌleg, -ˌlāg\ *n* **1 :** the upper part of a boot **2 :** something bootlegged; *specif* **:** MOONSHINE — **bootleg** *adj*
[2]**bootleg** *vt* **1 a :** to carry (alcoholic liquor) on one's person illegally **b :** to manufacture, sell, or transport for sale (alcoholic liquor) contrary to law **2 a :** to produce or sell illicitly **b :** SMUGGLE ~ *vi* **:** to engage in bootlegging — **boot·leg·ger** \-ər\ *n*
boot·less \ˈbüt-ləs\ *adj* **:** USELESS, UNPROFITABLE — **boot·less·ly** *adv* — **boot·less·ness** *n*
boot·lick \-ˌlik\ *vt* **:** to fawn on obsequiously ~ *vi* **:** FAWN — **bootlick** *n* — **boot·lick·er** \-ər\ *n*
boots \ˈbüts\ *n pl but sing or pl in constr* [fr. pl. of [3]*boot*] *Brit* **:** a servant esp. in a hotel who shines shoes
boo·ty \ˈbüt-ē\ *n* [modif. of MF *butin,* fr. MLG *būte* exchange] **1 :** SPOILS; *esp* **:** loot taken in war **2 :** a rich gain or prize **syn** see SPOIL
[1]**booze** \ˈbüz\ *vi* [ME *bousen,* fr. MD or MFlem *būsen;* akin to MHG *būs* swelling] **:** to drink intoxicating liquor to excess — **booz·er** \ˈbü-zər\ *n* — **boozy** \-zē\ *adj*
[2]**booze** *n* **1 :** intoxicating drink; *esp* **:** hard liquor **2 :** SPREE
[1]**bop** \ˈbäp\ *vt* **bopped; bop·ping** [imit.] **:** HIT, SOCK
[2]**bop** *n* **:** BLOW
[3]**bop** *n, often attrib* [short for *bebop*] **:** jazz characterized by rhythmic harmonic complexity and innovation, lengthened melodic line, and usu. by loud bravura execution — **bop·per** *n*
bo·ra \ˈbōr-ə, ˈbȯr-\ *n* [It. dial., fr. L *boreas*] **:** a violent cold northerly wind of the Adriatic
bo·rac·ic \bə-ˈras-ik\ *adj* [ML *borac-, borax*] **:** BORIC
bor·age \ˈbȯr-ij, ˈbär-\ *n* [ME, fr. MF *bourage*] **:** a rough-hairy blue-flowered European herb (*Borago officinalis* of the family Boraginaceae, the borage family) used medicinally and in salads
bo·rane \ˈbō(ə)r-ˌān, ˈbȯ(ə)r-\ *n* [ISV, fr. *boron*] **:** a compound of boron and hydrogen or a derivative of such a compound
bo·rate \-ˌāt\ *n* **:** a salt or ester of a boric acid
bo·rat·ed \-ˌāt-əd\ *adj* **:** mixed or impregnated with borax or boric acid
bo·rax \ˈbō(ə)r-ˌaks, ˈbȯ(ə)r-, -əks\ *n* [ME *boras,* fr. MF, fr. ML *borac-, borax,* fr. Ar *būraq,* fr. Per *būrah*] **:** a hydrated sodium borate $Na_2B_4O_7 \cdot 10H_2O$ used esp. as a flux, cleansing agent, and water softener and as a preservative
bo·ra·zon \ˈbōr-ə-ˌzän, ˈbȯr-\ *n* [*boron* + *az-* + *-on*] **:** a boron nitride BN of cubical crystallization as hard as diamond but more resistant to high temperature
Bor·deaux \bȯr-ˈdō\ *n, pl* **Bor·deaux** \-ˈdōz\ **:** any of various white or red wines of the Bordeaux region of France
bordeaux mixture *n, often cap B* **:** a fungicide made by reaction of copper sulfate, lime, and water
bor·del \ˈbȯrd-ᵊl\ *n* [ME, fr. MF, fr. OF, fr. *borde* hut, of Gmc origin; akin to OE *bord* board] *archaic* **:** BROTHEL
bor·del·lo \bȯr-ˈdel-(ˌ)ō\ *n* [It, fr. OF *bordel*] **:** BROTHEL
[1]**bor·der** \ˈbȯrd-ər\ *n* [ME *bordure,* fr. MF, fr. OF, fr. *border* to border, fr. *bort* border, of Gmc origin; akin to OE *bord*] **1 :** an outer part or edge **2 :** BOUNDARY, FRONTIER **3 :** a narrow bed of planted ground along the edge of a garden or walk **4 :** an ornamental design at the edge of a fabric or rug **5 :** a plain or decorative margin around printed matter — **bor·dered** \-ərd\ *adj*
syn MARGIN, VERGE, EDGE, RIM, BRIM, BRINK: BORDER denotes the part of a surface that marks its boundary line; MARGIN denotes a border of definite width or distinguishing character; VERGE applies to the line marking an extreme limit or termination of something; EDGE denotes the terminating line made by two converging surfaces as of a blade or a box; RIM applies to an edge of something circular or curving; BRIM applies to the upper inner rim of something hollow; BRINK denotes the abrupt edge of something that falls away steeply
[2]**border** *vt* **bor·der·ing** \ˈbȯrd-(ə-)riŋ\ **1 :** to put a border on **2 :** to touch at the edge or boundary **:** BOUND ~ *vi* **1 :** to lie on the border **2 :** to approach the nature of a specified thing **:** VERGE ⟨~*s* on the ridiculous⟩ — **bor·der·er** \-ər-ər\ *n*
bor·de·reau \ˌbȯrd-ə-ˈrō\ *n, pl* **bor·de·reaux** \-ˈrō(z)\ [F] **:** a detailed note or memorandum of account; *esp* **:** one containing an enumeration of documents
bor·der·land \ˈbȯrd-ər-ˌland\ *n* **1 a :** territory at or near a border **:** FRONTIER **b :** an outlying region **:** FRINGE **2 :** a vague intermediate state or region **:** a twilight zone
border line *n* **:** a line of demarcation **:** a boundary line
bor·der·line \ˈbȯrd-ər-ˌlīn\ *adj* **1 :** situated at or near a border line **2 a :** INTERMEDIATE **b :** not quite average, standard, or normal **c :** not quite meeting accepted patterns; *esp* **:** verging on the indecent **d :** having only marginal certainty or validity
Border terrier *n* **:** a small terrier of British origin with a harsh dense coat and close undercoat
bor·dure \ˈbȯr-jər\ *n* [ME] **:** a border surrounding a heraldic shield
[1]**bore** \ˈbō(ə)r, ˈbȯ(ə)r\ *vb* [ME *boren,* fr. OE *borian;* akin to OHG *borōn* to bore, L *forare* to bore, *ferire* to strike] *vt* **1 :** to pierce with or as if with a rotary tool **2 :** to form or construct by boring ~ *vi* **1 a :** to make a hole by boring **b :** to sink a mine shaft or well **2 a :** to make one's way laboriously **b :** to move ahead steadily
[2]**bore** *n* **1 :** a hole made by or as if by boring **2 a :** an interior lengthwise cylindrical cavity **b :** the interior tube of a gun **3 a :** the size of a hole **b :** the interior diameter of a tube **:** CALIBER, GAUGE **c :** the diameter of an engine cylinder
[3]**bore** *past of* BEAR
[4]**bore** *n* [(assumed) ME *bore* wave, fr. ON *bāra*] **:** a tidal flood with a high abrupt front
[5]**bore** *n* [origin unknown] **:** one that causes boredom
[6]**bore** *vt* **:** to weary with ennui or tedium
bo·re·al \ˈbōr-ē-əl, ˈbȯr-\ *adj* [ME *boriall,* fr. LL *borealis,* fr. L *boreas* north wind, north, fr. Gk, fr. *Boreas*] **1 :** of, relating to, or located in northern regions **2** *cap* **:** of, relating to, or growing in northern and mountainous parts of the northern hemisphere
Bo·re·as \-ē-əs\ *n* [L, fr. Gk] **1 :** the god of the north wind in Greek mythology **2 :** the north wind personified
bore·dom \ˈbō(ə)rd-əm, ˈbȯ(ə)rd-\ *n* **:** the state of being bored
bor·er \ˈbōr-ər, ˈbȯr-\ *n* **:** one that bores: as **a :** a worker who bores

holes **b :** a tool used for boring **c** (1) **:** SHIPWORM (2) **:** an insect that as larva or adult bores in the woody parts of plants
bo·ric \'bōr-ik, 'bȯr-\ *adj* **:** of or containing boron
boric acid *n* **:** an acid derived from boron trioxide B_2O_3; *esp* **:** a white crystalline compound H_3BO_3 used esp. as a weak antiseptic
born \'bȯ(ə)rn\ *adj* [ME, fr. OE *boren*, pp. of *beran* to carry — more at BEAR] **1 a :** brought into existence by or as if by birth **b :** NATIVE ⟨American-*born*⟩ **2 a :** having from birth specified qualities ⟨a ~ leader⟩ **b :** being in specified circumstances from birth
borne *past part of* BEAR
bor·ne·ol \'bȯr-nē-,ȯl, -,ōl\ *n* [ISV, fr. *Borneo*, island in the Malay archipelago] **:** a crystalline cyclic alcohol $C_{10}H_{17}OH$ known in three optically different forms found in essential oils
born·ite \'bȯ(ə)r-,nīt\ *n* [G *bornit*, fr. Ignaz von *Born* †1791 Austrian mineralogist] **:** a brittle metallic-looking mineral Cu_5FeS_4 consisting of a sulfide of copper and iron and constituting a valuable ore of copper
bo·ron \'bō(ə)r-,än, 'bȯ(ə)r-\ *n* [*borax* + *-on* (as in *carbon*)] **:** a trivalent metalloid element found in nature only in combination and used in metallurgy and in nucleonics — see ELEMENT table — **bo·ron·ic** \bōr-'än-ik, bȯ-'rän-\ *adj*
bo·ro·sil·i·cate \,bōr-ō-'sil-i-kət, ,bȯr-, -ə-,kāt\ *n* [ISV *boron* + *silicate*] **:** a silicate containing boron in the anion and occurring naturally
bor·ough \'bər-(,)ō, 'bə-(,)rō, -ə(-w), -rə(-w)\ *n* [ME *burgh*, fr. OE *burg* fortified town; akin to OHG *burg* fortified place, OE *beorg* mountain — more at BARROW] **1 a :** a medieval fortified group of houses forming a town with special duties and privileges **b :** a town or urban constituency in Great Britain that sends a member or members to Parliament **c :** an urban area in Great Britain incorporated for purposes of self-government **2 a :** a municipal corporation proper in some states (as New Jersey and Minnesota) corresponding to the incorporated town or village of the other states **b :** one of the five constituent political divisions of New York City
borough English *n* **:** a custom formerly existing in parts of England by which the lands of a tenant intestate descend to the youngest son
bor·row \'bär-(,)ō, 'bȯr-, -ə(-w)\ *vb* [ME *borwen*, fr. OE *borgian*; akin to OE *beorgan* to preserve] *vt* **1 :** to receive with the implied or expressed intention of returning the same or an equivalent ⟨~ a book⟩ **2 a :** to appropriate for one's own use ⟨~ a metaphor⟩ **b :** DERIVE, ADOPT **3 :** to take (one) from a figure of the minuend in arithmetical subtraction in order to add as 10 to the next lower denomination **4 :** to introduce into one language from another **5 :** to dig from a borrow pit **6** *dial* **:** LEND ~ *vi* **:** to borrow something — **bor·row·er** \-ə-wər\ *n*
borrow pit *n* **:** an excavated area where material has been borrowed for use as fill at another location
Bors \'bȯ(ə)rz\ *n* **:** a knight of the Round Table and nephew of Lancelot
borscht *or* **borsch** \'bȯ(ə)rsh(t)\ *n* [Russ *borshch*] **:** a soup made primarily of beets and served hot or cold often with sour cream
borscht circuit *or* **borsch circuit** *n* **:** the theaters and nightclubs associated with the Jewish summer resorts in the Catskills
bort \'bȯ(ə)rt\ *n* [prob. fr. D *boort*] **:** imperfectly crystallized diamond or diamond fragments used as an abrasive
bor·zoi \'bȯr-,zȯi\ *n* [Russ *borzoĭ*, fr. *borzoĭ* swift; akin to L *festinare* to hasten] **:** any of a breed of large long-haired dogs of greyhound type developed in Russia esp. for pursuing wolves
bos·cage *also* **bosk·age** \'bäs-kij\ *n* [ME *boskage*, fr. MF *boscage*, fr. OF, fr. *bois, bosc* forest, perh. of Gmc origin; akin to ME *bush*] **:** a growth of trees or shrubs **:** THICKET
bosh \'bäsh\ *n* [Turk *boş* empty] **1 :** foolish talk or activity **:** NONSENSE **2 :** something worthless or trifling
bosk *or* **bosque** \'bäsk\ *n* [prob. back-formation fr. *bosky*] **:** a small wooded area
bosk·et *or* **bos·quet** \'bäs-kət\ *n* [F *bosquet*, fr. It *boschetto*, dim. of *bosco* forest, perh. of Gmc origin; akin to ME *bush*] **:** THICKET
Bos·kop man \,bäs-,käp-\ *n* [*Boskop*, locality in the Transvaal] **:** a late Pleistocene southern African man prob. ancestral to modern Bushmen and Hottentots — **bos·kop·oid** \'bäs-kə-,pȯid\ *adj*
bosky \'bäs-kē\ *adj* [E dial. *bosk* bush, fr. ME *bush, bosk*] **1:** having abundant trees or shrubs **2 :** of or relating to a woods
bo·s'n *or* **bo'·s'n** *or* **bo·sun** *or* **bo'·sun** \'bōs-ᵊn\ *var of* BOATSWAIN
1**bo·som** \'bu̇z-əm, 'büz-\ *n* [ME, fr. OE *bōsm*; akin to OHG *buosam* bosom, Skt *bhūri* abundant — more at BIG] **1 :** the front of the human chest; *esp* **:** the female breasts **2 a :** the anatomical center of secret thoughts and emotions **b :** close relationship **:** EMBRACE ⟨lived in the ~ of her family⟩ **3 a :** a broad surface **b :** an inmost recess **4 a :** the part of a garment covering the breast **b :** the space between the breast and the garment covering it
2**bosom** *vt* **1 :** to enclose or carry in the bosom **2 :** EMBRACE
3**bosom** *adj* **:** CLOSE, INTIMATE ⟨~ friends⟩
bo·somed \-əmd\ *adj* **:** having (such) a bosom ⟨flat-*bosomed*⟩
bo·somy \-ə-mē\ *adj* **1 :** swelling upward or outward ⟨~ hills⟩ **2 :** having prominent well-developed breasts
1**boss** \'bäs, 'bȯs\ *n* [ME *boce*, fr. OF, fr. (assumed) VL *bottia*] **1 a :** a protuberant part or body **b :** a raised ornamentation **:** STUD **c :** an ornamental projecting block used in architecture **2 :** a soft pad used in ceramics and glassmaking **3 :** the enlarged part of a shaft
2**boss** *vt* **1 :** to ornament with bosses **:** EMBOSS **2 :** to treat (as the surface of porcelain) with a boss
3**boss** \'bȯs\ *n* [D *baas* master; akin to Fris *baes* master] **1 :** one who exercises control or authority; *specif* **:** one who directs or supervises workers **2 a :** a politician who controls votes in a party organization or dictates appointments or legislative measures **b :** an official with dictatorial authority over an organization— **boss·dom** \-dəm\ *n*— **boss·ism** \-,iz-əm\ *n*

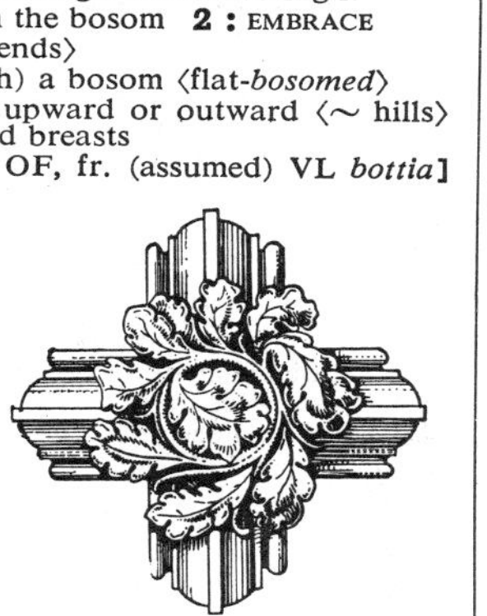

boss 1c

4**boss** \'bȯs\ *adj* **1 :** PRINCIPAL, MASTER **2** *slang* **:** EXCELLENT
5**boss** \'bȯs\ *vt* **1 :** DIRECT, SUPERVISE **2 :** ORDER
6**boss** \'bȯs\ *n* [E dial., young cow] **:** COW, CALF
bos·sa no·va \,bō-sə-'nō-və\ *n* [Pg, lit., new trend] **:** music resembling the samba with jazz interpolations
boss·i·ness \'bȯ-sē-nəs\ *n* **:** the quality or state of being bossy
1**bossy** \'bäs-ē, 'bȯ-sē\ *adj* **1 :** marked by a swelling or roundness **2 :** marked by bosses **:** STUDDED
2**bossy** \'bȯ-sē\ *n* **:** COW, CALF
3**bossy** \'bȯ-sē\ *adj* **:** inclined to domineer **:** DICTATORIAL
Bos·ton \'bȯ-stən\ *n* [F, fr. *Boston*, Massachusetts] **1 :** a card game for four players with two decks of cards **2 :** a dance somewhat like a waltz
Boston bag *n* **:** a handbag that is held together at the top opening by two handles
Boston cream pie *n* **:** a round cake that is split and filled with a custard or cream filling
Boston fern *n* **:** a luxuriant fern (*Nephrolepis exaltata bostoniensis*) often with drooping much-divided fronds
Boston ivy *n* **:** a woody Asiatic vine (*Parthenocissus tricuspidata*) of the grape family with 3-lobed leaves
Boston terrier *n* **:** any of a breed of small smooth-coated terriers originating as a cross of the bulldog and bullterrier and being brindle or black with white markings — called also *Boston bull*
Bos·well \'bäz-,wel, -wəl\ *n* [James *Boswell* †1795 Sc lawyer and biographer] **:** one who records in detail the conversation and activities of a usu. famous contemporary
bot *also* **bott** \'bät\ *n* [perh. modif. of ScGael *boiteag* maggot] **:** the larva of a botfly; *esp* **:** one infesting the horse
1**bo·tan·i·cal** \bə-'tan-i-kəl\ *adj* [F *botanique*, fr. Gk *botanikos* of herbs, fr. *botanē* pasture, herb, fr. *boskein* to feed; akin to Lith *gauja* herd] **1 :** of or relating to plants or botany **2 :** derived from plants **3 :** SPECIES — **bo·tan·i·cal·ly** \-k(ə-)lē\ *adv*
2**botanical** *n* **:** a vegetable drug esp. in the crude state
bot·a·nist \'bät-ᵊn-əst, 'bät-nəst\ *n* **:** a specialist in botany or in a branch of botany **b :** a professional student of plants
bot·a·nize \-ᵊn-,īz\ *vi* **:** to collect plants for botanical investigation; *also* **:** to study plants esp. on a field trip ~ *vt* **:** to explore for botanical purposes
bot·a·ny \'bät-ᵊn-ē, 'bät-nē\ *n* [back-formation fr. *botanical*] **1 :** a branch of biology dealing with plant life **2 a :** plant life **b :** the properties and life phenomena exhibited by a plant, plant type, or plant group **3 :** a botanical treatise or study; *esp* **:** a particular system of botany
1**botch** \'bäch\ *n* [ME *boche*, fr. ONF, fr. (assumed) VL *bottia* boss] **:** an inflammatory sore
2**botch** *vt* [ME *bocchen*] **1 :** to repair or patch ineptly **2 :** BUNGLE **3 :** to assemble or construct in a makeshift way — **botch·er** *n*
3**botch** *n* **1 :** something that is botched **:** MESS **2 :** PATCHWORK, HODGEPODGE — **botchy** \-ē\ *adj*
bot·fly \'bät-,flī\ *n* **:** any of various stout two-winged flies (group Oestroidea) with segmented larvae parasitic in cavities or tissues of various mammals including man
1**both** \'bōth\ *adj* [ME *bothe*, fr. ON *bāthir*; akin to OHG *beide* both] **:** being the two **:** affecting or involving the one and the other ⟨~ feet⟩
2**both** *pron* **:** the one as well as the other ⟨~ of us⟩ ⟨we are ~ well⟩
3**both** *conj* — used as a function word to indicate and stress the inclusion of each of two or more things specified by coordinated words, phrases, or clauses ⟨~ New York and London⟩
1**both·er** \'bät͟h-ər\ *vb* **both·er·ing** \-(ə-)riŋ\ [perh. fr. IrGael *bodhar* bothered] *vt* **1 a :** to cause to be nervous **:** FLUSTER **b :** PUZZLE, MYSTIFY **2 a :** to annoy esp. by petty provocation **:** IRK **b :** to intrude upon **:** PESTER **c :** to cause to be anxious or concerned **:** TROUBLE ~ *vi* **1 :** to feel mild concern or anxiety **2 :** to take pains **3 :** to stir up petty trouble **syn** see ANNOY
2**bother** *n* **1 a :** a state of petty discomfort, annoyance, or worry **b :** something that causes petty annoyance or worry **2 :** FUSS
both·er·ation \,bät͟h-ə-'rā-shən\ *n* **1 :** the act of bothering or the state of being bothered **2 :** something that bothers
both·er·some \'bät͟h-ər-səm\ *adj* **:** causing bother **:** VEXING
bot·o·née *or* **bot·on·née** \,bät-ᵊn-'ā\ *adj* [MF *botonné*] *of a heraldic cross* **:** having a cluster of three balls or knobs at the end of each arm — see CROSS illustration
bo tree \'bō-\ *n* [Sinhalese *bō*, fr. Skt *bodhi*] **:** PIPAL
bot·ry·oi·dal \,bä-trē-'ȯid-ᵊl\ *also* **bot·ry·oid** \'bä-trē-,ȯid\ *adj* [Gk *botryoeidēs*, fr. *botrys* bunch of grapes] **:** having the form of a bunch of grapes
1**bot·tle** \'bät-ᵊl\ *n, often attrib* [ME *botel*, fr. MF *bouteille*, fr. ML *butticula*, dim. of LL *buttis* cask] **1 a :** a rigid or semirigid container typically of glass or plastic having a comparatively narrow neck or mouth and no handle **b :** a bag made of skin **c :** the quantity held by a bottle **2 a :** intoxicating drink ⟨hit the ~⟩ **b :** bottled milk used in place of mother's milk — **bot·tle·ful** \-,fu̇l\ *n, pl* **bottlefuls** \-,fu̇lz\ *or* **bot·tles·ful** \-ᵊlz,-fu̇l\
2**bottle** *vt* **bot·tling** \'bät-liŋ, -ᵊl-iŋ\ **1 :** to put into a bottle **2 :** to confine as if in a bottle — usu. used with *up* — **bot·tler** \-lər, -ᵊl-ər\ *n*

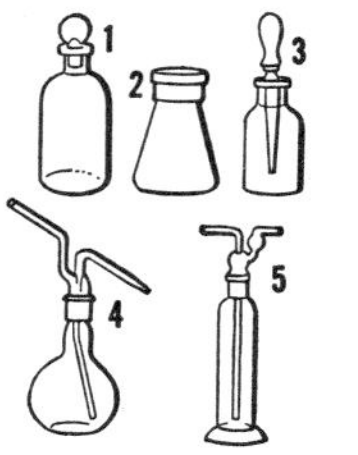

bottles 1a: chemical bottle: *1* reagent, *2* weighing, *3* dropping, *4* and *5* washing, *4* for precipitates, *5* for gases

bottle club *n* **:** an establishment that serves alcoholic drinks after legal closing hours
bottled gas *n* **:** gas under pressure in portable cylinders
1**bot·tle·neck** \'bät-ᵊl-,nek\ *n* **1 a :** a narrow route **b :** a point of traffic congestion **2 a :** OBSTRUCTION **b :** IMPASSE
2**bottleneck** *vt* **:** to slow or halt by causing a bottleneck
3**bottleneck** *adj* **:** NARROW ⟨~ harbor⟩
bot·tle–nosed dolphin \,bät-ᵊl-,nōz-\ *n* **:** any of various moderately large stout-bodied toothed whales (genus *Tursiops* and esp. *T. truncatus*) with a prominent beak and falcate dorsal fin
1**bot·tom** \'bät-əm\ *n* [ME *botme*, fr. OE *botm*; akin to OHG *bodam* bottom, L *fundus*, Gk *pythmēn*] **1 a :** the under surface of something **:** UNDERSIDE **b :** a surface designed to support something resting on it **c :** BUTTOCKS, RUMP **2 :** the surface on which a body of water lies **3 a :** the part of a ship's hull lying below the water **b :** BOAT, SHIP **4 a :** the lowest part or place **b :** the remotest or inmost point **c :** LAST ⟨~ dollar⟩ **d :** the trousers of pajamas — usu. used in pl. **e :** the last half of an inning of baseball **5 :** low-lying grassland along a watercourse — usu. used in pl. **6 :** BASIS, SOURCE **7 :** capacity (as of a horse) to endure strain **8 :** the main plowing mechanism of a plow **9 :** a color applied to textile fibers before dyeing — **at bottom :** BASICALLY, REALLY

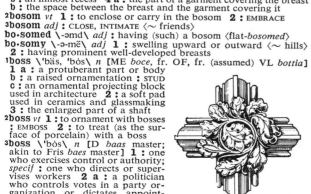

2**bottom** *vt* **1 :** to furnish with a bottom **2 :** to provide a foundation for **3 :** to bring to the bottom **4 :** to get to the bottom of ~ *vi* **1 :** to become based **2 :** to reach the bottom — **bot·tom·er** *n*

bot·tom·less \-əm-ləs\ *adj* **1 :** having no bottom ⟨a ~ chair⟩ **2 a :** extremely deep **b :** UNFATHOMABLE ⟨a ~ mystery⟩ **c :** BOUNDLESS, UNLIMITED — **bot·tom·less·ly** *adv* — **bot·tom·less·ness** *n*

bot·tom·most \-əm-ˌmōst\ *adj* **1 a :** LOWEST **b :** LAST **c :** DEEPEST **2 :** most basic

bottom round *n* **:** meat (as steak) from the outer part of a round of beef

bot·tom·ry \'bät-əm-rē\ *n* [modif. of D *bodemerij*, fr. *bodem* bottom, ship; akin to OHG *bodam*] **:** a contract by which a ship is hypothecated as security for repayment of a loan at the end of a successful voyage

bot·u·lin \'bäch-ə-lən\ *n* [prob. fr. NL *botulinus*] **:** a toxin that is formed by the botulinus and is the direct cause of botulism

bot·u·li·nal \ˌbäch-ə-'līn-ᵊl\ *adj* **:** of, relating to, or produced by the botulinus

bot·u·li·nus \-'lī-nəs\ *n* [NL, fr. L *botulus* sausage] **:** a spore-forming bacterium (*Clostridium botulinum*) that secretes botulin

bot·u·lism \'bäch-ə-ˌliz-əm\ *n* **:** acute food poisoning caused by botulin in food

bou·clé *or* **bou·cle** \bü-'klā\ *n* [F *bouclé* curly, fr. pp. of *boucler* to curl, fr. *bocle* buckle, curl] **1 :** an uneven yarn of three plies one of which forms loops at intervals **2 :** a textile fabric of bouclé yarn

bou·doir \'büd-ˌwär, 'bu̇d-, -ˌwȯ(ə)r\ *n* [F, fr. *bouder* to pout] **:** a woman's dressing room, bedroom, or private sitting room

bouf·fant \bü-'fänt, -'fäⁿ\ *adj* [F, fr. MF, fr. prp. of *bouffer* to puff] **:** puffed out ⟨~ hairdos⟩

bouffe \'büf\ *n* **:** OPÉRA BOUFFE

bou·gain·vil·lea *or* **bou·gain·vil·laea** \ˌbü-gən-'vil-yə, ˌbō-, -'vē-(y)ə\ *n* [NL, fr. Louis Antoine de *Bougainville* †1811 F navigator] **:** any of a genus (*Bougainvillaea*) of the four-o'clock family of ornamental tropical American woody vines with brilliant purple red floral bracts

bough \'bau̇\ *n* [ME, shoulder, bough, fr. OE *bōg*; akin to OHG *buog* shoulder, Gk *pēchys* forearm] **:** a branch of a tree; *esp* **:** a main branch **syn** see SHOOT — **boughed** \'bau̇d\ *adj*

bought \'bȯt\ *adj* [pp. of *buy*] **:** READY-MADE ⟨~ clothes⟩

bought·en \-ᵊn\ *adj* [*bought* + *-en* (as in *forgotten*)] *chiefly dial* **:** BOUGHT

bou·gie \'bü-ˌzhē, -ˌjē\ *n* [F, fr. *Bougie*, seaport in Algeria] **1 :** a wax candle **2 a :** a tapering cylindrical instrument for introduction into a tubular passage of the body **b :** SUPPOSITORY

bouil·la·baisse \ˌbü-yə-'bās\ *n* [F] **:** a highly seasoned fish stew made of at least two kinds of fish

bouil·lon \'bü-ˌyän; 'bu̇l-ˌyän, -yən\ *n* [F, fr. OF *boillon*, fr. *boillir* to boil] **:** a clear seasoned soup made usu. from lean beef

bouillon cube *n* **:** a cube of evaporated seasoned meat extract

boul·der \'bōl-dər\ *n* [short for *boulder stone*, fr. ME *bulder ston*, part trans. of a word of Scand origin; akin to Sw dial. *bullersten* large stone in a stream, fr. *buller* noise + *sten* stone] **:** a detached and rounded or much-worn mass of rock — **boul·dered** \-dərd\ *adj* — **boul·dery** \-d(ə-)rē\ *adj*

1**bou·le** \'bü-(ˌ)lē, bü-'lā\ *n* [Gk *boulē*, lit., will, fr. *boulesthai* to wish] **:** a legislative council of ancient Greece consisting first of an aristocratic advisory body but later of a representative senate

2**boule** \'bül\ *n* [F, ball — more at BOWL] **:** a pear-shaped mass (as of sapphire) formed synthetically in a special furnace with the atomic structure of a single crystal but with axes generally in a random position with respect to its length

bou·le·vard \'bu̇l-ə-ˌvärd, 'bül-\ *n* [F, modif. of MD *bolwerc* bulwark] **:** a broad often landscaped thoroughfare

bou·le·var·dier \ˌbül-(ə-)ˌvärd-'yā; ˌbu̇l-ə-ˌvär-'di(ə)r, ˌbül-\ *n* **:** a frequenter of the Parisian boulevards; *broadly* **:** MAN-ABOUT-TOWN

boule·ver·se·ment \bül-ver-sə-mäⁿ\ *n* [F] **1 :** REVERSAL **2 :** CONVULSION, DISORDER

boulle \'bül, 'byü(ə)l\ *n* [André Charles *Boulle* †1732 F cabinetmaker] **:** inlaid decoration of tortoiseshell, yellow metal, and white metal in cabinetwork

1**bounce** \'bau̇n(t)s\ *vb* [ME *bounsen*] *vt* **1** *obs* **:** BEAT, BUMP **2 :** to cause to rebound ⟨~ a ball⟩ **3 a :** DISMISS, FIRE **b :** to expel precipitately from a place ~ *vi* **1 :** to strike and rebound **2 :** to recover from a blow or a defeat quickly — usu. used with *back* **3 :** to be returned by a bank as no good ⟨his checks ~⟩ **4 a :** to leap suddenly **:** BOUND **b :** to walk with springing steps

2**bounce** *n* **1 a :** a sudden leap or bound **b :** REBOUND **2 :** BLUSTER **3 :** LIVELINESS, VERVE **4** *slang* **:** a peremptory dismissal

bounc·er \'bau̇n(t)-sər\ *n* **:** one that bounces; *specif* **:** one employed to restrain or eject disorderly persons

bounc·i·ly \-sə-lē\ *adv* **:** with verve **:** JAUNTILY, SPRINGILY

bounc·ing \-siŋ\ *adj* **:** HEALTHY, ROBUST — **bounc·ing·ly** \-lē\ *adv*

bouncing bet \ˌbau̇n(t)-siŋ-'bet\ *n*, *often cap 2d B* [fr. *Bet*, nickname for *Elizabeth*] **:** SOAPWORT — called also *bouncing bess*

bouncy \'bau̇n(t)-sē\ *adj* **1 :** BUOYANT, EXUBERANT **2 :** RESILIENT **3 :** marked by or producing bounces

1**bound** \'bau̇nd\ *adj* [ME *boun*, fr. ON *būinn*, pp. of *būa* to dwell, prepare; akin to OHG *būan* to dwell — more at BOWER] **1** *archaic* **:** READY **2 :** intending to go **:** GOING ⟨~ for home⟩

2**bound** *n* [ME, fr. OF *bodne*, fr. ML *bodina*] **1 a :** a limiting line **:** BOUNDARY — usu. used in pl. **b :** something that limits or restrains **2** *usu pl* **a :** BORDERLAND **b :** the land within certain bounds

3**bound** *vt* **1 :** to set limits to **:** CONFINE **2 :** to form the boundary of **:** ENCLOSE **3 :** to name the boundaries of

4**bound** *adj* [ME *bounden*, fr. pp. of *binden* to bind] **1 a :** fastened by or as if by a band **:** CONFINED ⟨desk-*bound*⟩ **b :** CERTAIN, SURE ⟨~ to rain soon⟩ **2 :** placed under legal or moral restraint or obligation **:** OBLIGED ⟨duty-*bound*⟩ **3 :** CONSTIPATED, COSTIVE **4** *of a book* **a :** secured to its covers by cords or tapes **b :** cased in **5 :** RESOLVED, DETERMINED **6 :** held in chemical or physical combination **7 :** always occurring in combination with another linguistic form (as *un-* in *unknown*, *-er* in *speaker*) — compare FREE

5**bound** *n* [MF *bond*, fr. *bondir* to leap, fr. (assumed) VL *bombitire* to hum, fr. L *bombus* deep hollow sound — more at BOMB] **1 :** LEAP, JUMP **2 :** BOUNCE, REBOUND

6**bound** *vi* **1 :** to move by leaping **2 :** REBOUND, BOUNCE

bound·a·ry \'bau̇n-d(ə-)rē\ *n* **:** something that indicates or fixes a limit or extent; *specif* **:** a bounding or separating line

boundary layer *n* **:** a region of retarded fluid near the surface of a body which moves through a fluid or past which a fluid moves

bound·en \'bau̇n-dən\ *adj* [ME] **1** *archaic* **:** being under obligation **:** BEHOLDEN **2 :** made obligatory **:** BINDING ⟨our ~ duty⟩

bound·er \-dər\ *n* **1 :** one that bounds **2** *chiefly Brit* **:** a man of objectionable social behavior **:** CAD — **bound·er·ish** \-də-rish\ *adj*

bound·less \'bau̇n-(d)ləs\ *adj* **:** having no boundaries **:** VAST — **bound·less·ly** *adv* — **bound·less·ness** *n*

bound up *adj* **:** entirely devoted **:** inseparable from

boun·te·ous \'bau̇nt-ē-əs\ *adj* [ME *bountevous*, fr. MF *bontif* kind, fr. OF, fr. *bonté*] **1 :** giving or disposed to give freely **2 :** liberally bestowed — **boun·te·ous·ly** *adv* — **boun·te·ous·ness** *n*

boun·tied \'bau̇nt-ēd\ *adj* **1 :** having the benefit of a bounty **2 :** rewarded or rewardable by a bounty

boun·ti·ful \'bau̇nt-i-fəl\ *adj* **1 :** full of bounty **:** GRACIOUS **2 :** ABUNDANT, PLENTIFUL **syn** see LIBERAL — **boun·ti·ful·ly** \-f(ə-)lē\ *adv* — **boun·ti·ful·ness** \-fəl-nəs\ *n*

boun·ty \'bau̇nt-ē\ *n* [ME *bounte* goodness, fr. OF *bonté*, fr. L *bonitat-*, *bonitas*, fr. *bonus* good, fr. OL *duenos*; akin to MHG *zwīden* to grant, L *bene* well] **1 :** liberality in giving **:** GENEROSITY **2 :** something that is given generously **3 :** yield esp. of a crop **4 :** a reward, premium, or subsidy esp. when offered or given by a government: as **a :** a grant to encourage an industry **b :** a payment to encourage the destruction of noxious animals

bounty hunter *n* **:** one that hunts for the reward offered

bou·quet \bō-'kā, bü-\ *n* [F, fr. MF, thicket, fr. ONF *bosquet*, fr. OF *bosc* forest — more at BOSCAGE] **1 a :** flowers picked and fastened together in a bunch **:** NOSEGAY **b :** a large flight of fireworks **2 :** COMPLIMENT **3 a :** the distinctive fragrance of a wine **b :** a subtle aroma or quality **syn** see FRAGRANCE

bour·bon \'bu̇(ə)r-bən, 'bō(ə)r-, 'bȯ(ə)r-; *usu* 'bər- *in sense 4*\ *n*, *often attrib* [*Bourbon*, seigniory in France] **1** *cap* **:** a member of a French family founded in 1272 to which belong the rulers of France from 1589 to 1793 and from 1814 to 1830, of Spain from 1700 to 1808, from 1814 to 1868, and from 1875 to 1931, of Naples from 1735 to 1805, and of the Two Sicilies from 1815 to 1860 **2** *often cap* **:** a person who clings obstinately to the social and political ideas of the old order of things; *specif* **:** an extremely conservative member of the U.S. Democratic party usu. from the South **3** [*Bourbon* (now Réunion), French island in the Indian ocean] **:** a rose (*Rosa borboniana*) of compact upright growth with shining leaves, prickly branches, and clustered flowers **4** [*Bourbon* county, Kentucky] **:** a whiskey distilled from corn mash; *specif* **:** a whiskey distilled from a mash of corn, malt, and rye and aged in new charred oak containers — **bour·bon·ism** \-bə-ˌniz-əm\ *n*, *often cap*

bour·don \'bu̇(ə)rd-ᵊn\ *n* [ME *burdoun*, fr. MF *bourdon* bass pipe, of imit. origin] **1 :** a drone bass (as in a bagpipe) **2 :** an organ stop of a droning quality sounding an octave below written pitch

bourg \'bu̇(ə)r(g)\ *n* [ME, fr. MF, fr. OF *borc*, fr. L *burgus* fortified place, of Gmc origin; akin to OHG *burg* fortified place] **:** TOWN, VILLAGE: as **a :** one neighboring a castle **b :** a market town

1**bour·geois** \'bu̇(ə)rzh-ˌwä, bu̇rzh-'\ *n*, *pl* **bourgeois** \-ˌwä(z), -'wä(z)\ [MF, fr. OF *borjois*, fr. *borc*] **1 a :** BURGHER **b :** a middle-class person; *esp* **:** BUSINESSMAN **2 :** one with social behavior and political views held to be influenced by private-property interest **:** CAPITALIST **3** *pl* **:** BOURGEOISIE

2**bourgeois** *adj* **1 :** of, relating to, or characteristic of the townsman or of the social middle class **2 :** marked by a concern for material interests and respectability and a tendency toward mediocrity **3 :** dominated by commercial and industrial interests **:** CAPITALISTIC

bour·geoise \-ˌwäz, -'wäz\ *n* [F, fem. of *bourgeois*] **1 :** a woman of the middle class **2 :** BOURGEOIS

bour·geoi·sie \ˌbu̇rzh-ˌwä-'zē\ *n*, *pl* **bourgeoisie** [F, fr. *bourgeois*] **1 :** BOURGEOIS **2 :** a social order dominated by bourgeois

bour·geon \'bər-jən\ *var of* BURGEON

1**bourn** *or* **bourne** \'bō(ə)rn, 'bȯ(ə)rn, 'bu̇(ə)rn\ *n* [ME *burn*, *bourne* — more at BURN] **:** STREAM, BROOK

2**bourn** *or* **bourne** *n* [MF *bourne*, fr. OF *bodne* — more at BOUND] **1** *archaic* **:** BOUNDARY, LIMIT **2** *archaic* **:** GOAL, DESTINATION

bour·rée \bu̇-'rā, 'bü-ˌ\ *n* [F] **:** a 17th century French dance usu. in duple time with an upbeat; *also* **:** a musical composition with the rhythm of such a dance

bourse \'bu̇(ə)rs\ *n* [F, lit., purse, fr. ML *bursa* — more at PURSE] **:** EXCHANGE 5a; *specif* **:** a European stock exchange

bour·tree \'bu̇(ə)r-(ˌ)trē\ *n* [ME *bourtre*] *Brit* **:** the common large black-fruited elder (*Sambucus nigra*) of Europe and Asia

bouse \'bau̇z\ *vb* [origin unknown] *vt* **:** to haul by means of a tackle ~ *vi* **:** to bouse something

bou·stro·phe·don \ˌbü-strə-'fēd-ˌän, -ᵊn\ *adj* [Gk *boustrophēdon*, adv., lit., turning like oxen in plowing, fr. *bous* ox, cow + *strephein* to turn — more at COW, STROPHE] **:** of or relating to the writing of alternate lines in opposite directions

bout \'bau̇t\ *n* [E dial., a trip going and returning in plowing, fr. ME *bought* bend] **:** a spell of activity: as **a :** an athletic match (as of boxing) **b :** OUTBREAK, ATTACK **c :** SESSION

bou·tique \bü-'tēk\ *n* [F] **:** a small retail store; *esp* **:** a fashionable specialty shop or department for women

bou·ton·niere \ˌbüt-ᵊn-'i(ə)r, ˌbü-tən-'ye(ə)r\ *n* [F *boutonnière* buttonhole, fr. MF, fr. *bouton* button] **:** a flower or bouquet worn in a buttonhole

Bou·vi·er des Flan·dres \ˌbü-vē-ˌād-ə-'flan-dərz, -'fläⁿdrᵊ\ *n* [F, lit., cowherd of Flanders] **:** any of a breed of large powerfully built rough-coated dogs originating in Belgium and used esp. for herding and in guard work

1**bo·vine** \'bō-ˌvīn, -ˌvēn\ *adj* [LL *bovinus*, fr. L *bov-*, *bos* ox, cow] **1 :** of, relating to, or resembling the ox or cow **2 :** having qualities (as sluggishness or patience) characteristic of oxen or cows — **bo·vine·ly** *adv* — **bo·vin·i·ty** \bō-'vin-ət-ē\ *n*

2**bovine** *n* **:** an ox (genus *Bos*) or a closely related animal

1**bow** \'bau̇\ *vb* [ME *bowen*, fr. OE *būgan*; akin to OHG *biogan* to bend, Skt *bhujati* he bends] *vi* **1 :** SUBMIT, YIELD **2 :** to bend the head, body, or knee in reverence, submission, or shame **3 :** to incline the head or body in salutation or assent or to acknowledge applause ~ *vt* **1 :** to cause to incline **2 :** to incline (as the head)

esp. in respect or submission **3 :** to crush with or as if with a heavy burden **4 a :** to express by bowing **b :** to usher in or out with a bow

[2]**bow** *n* **:** a bending of the head or body in respect, submission, assent, or salutation

[3]**bow** \'bō\ *n* [ME *bowe,* fr. OE *boga;* akin to OE *būgan*] **1 a :** something bent into a simple curve **:** BEND, ARCH **b :** RAINBOW **2 :** a weapon made of a strip of flexible material (as wood) with a cord connecting the two ends and holding the strip bent and used to propel an arrow **3 :** BOWMAN, ARCHER **4 a :** a metal ring or loop forming a handle (as of a key) **b :** a knot formed by doubling a ribbon or string into two or more loops **c :** BOW TIE **d :** a frame for the lenses of eyeglasses; *also* **:** the curved sidepiece of the frame passing over the ear **5 a :** a resilient wooden rod with horsehairs stretched from end to end used in playing an instrument of the viol or violin family **b :** a stroke of such a bow

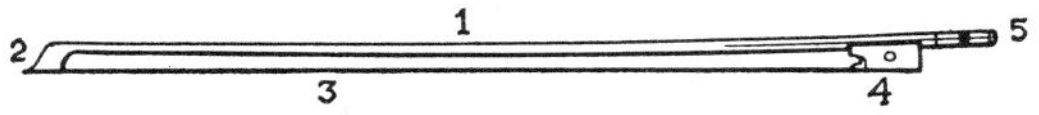

violin bow: *1* stick, *2* head, *3* hair, *4* frog, *5* screw

[4]**bow** \'bō\ *vi* **1 :** to bend into a curve **2 :** to play a stringed musical instrument with a bow ~ *vt* **1 :** to bend into a curve **2 :** to play (a stringed instrument) with a bow

[5]**bow** \'baů\ *n* [prob. fr. Dan *bov* shoulder, bow, fr. ON *bōgr;* akin to OE *bōg* bough] **1 :** the forward part of a ship **2 :** [2]BOWMAN

Bow bells \'bō-,\ *n pl* **:** the bells of the Church of St. Mary-le-Bow in London

bowd·ler·iza·tion \,bōd-lə-rə-'zā-shən, ,baůd-\ *n* **:** the act or result of bowdlerizing

bowd·ler·ize \'bōd-lə-,rīz, 'baůd-\ *vt* [Thomas *Bowdler* †1825 E editor] **:** to expurgate (as a book) by omitting or modifying parts considered indelicate

bow·el \'baů(-ə)l\ *n* [ME, fr. OF *boel,* fr. ML *botellus,* fr. L, dim. of *botulus* sausage] **1 :** INTESTINE **:** one of the divisions of the intestines **:** GUT — usu. used in pl. **2** *archaic* **:** the seat of pity, tenderness, or courage — usu. used in pl. **3** *pl* **:** the interior parts; *esp* **:** the deep or remote parts ⟨~*s* of the earth⟩ — **bow·el·less** \'baů(-ə)l-ləs\ *adj*

[1]**bow·er** \'baů(-ə)r\ *n* [ME *bour* dwelling, fr. OE *būr;* akin to OE & OHG *būan* to dwell, OE *bēon* to be] **1 :** an attractive dwelling or retreat **2 :** a lady's private apartment in a medieval hall or castle **3 :** a shelter (as in a garden) made with tree boughs or vines twined together **:** ARBOR — **bow·ery** \-ē\ *adj*

[2]**bower** *vt* **:** EMBOWER, ENCLOSE

[3]**bower** *n* **:** an anchor carried at the bow of a ship

bow·er·bird \'baů(-ə)r-,bərd\ *n* **:** any of various passerine birds (family Paradisaeidae) of the Australian region that build chambers or passages arched over with twigs and grasses, often adorned with bright-colored objects, and used esp. to attract the females

bow·ery \'baů-(-ə)r-ē\ *n* [D *bouwerij,* fr. *bouwer* farmer, fr. *bouwen* to till; akin to OHG *būan* to dwell] **1 :** a colonial Dutch plantation or farm **2** [*Bowery,* street in New York City] **:** a city street or district notorious for cheap saloons and homeless derelicts

bow·fin \'bō-,fin\ *n* **:** a voracious dull-green iridescent American freshwater ganoid fish (*Amia calva*) of little value for food or sport

bow·front \-,frənt\ *adj* **1 :** having an outward curving front ⟨~ furniture⟩ **2 :** having a bow window in front

bow·head \-,hed\ *n* **:** the whalebone whale (*Balaena mysticetus*) of the Arctic — called also *Greenland whale*

bow·ie knife \'bü-ē-, 'bō-\ *n* [James *Bowie* †1836 Am soldier] **:** a stout single-edged hunting knife with part of the back edge curved concavely to a point and sharpened

bow·ing \'bō-iŋ\ *n* **:** the technique of managing the bow in playing a stringed musical instrument

bow·knot \'bō-,nät, -'nät\ *n* **:** a knot with decorative loops

[1]**bowl** \'bōl\ *n* [ME *bolle,* fr. OE *bolla;* akin to OHG *bolla* blister, OE *blāwan* to blow] **1 :** a concave usu. hemispherical vessel used esp. for holding liquids; *specif* **:** a drinking vessel (as for wine) **2 :** the contents of a bowl **3 :** a bowl-shaped or concave part: as **a :** the hollow of a spoon or tobacco pipe **b :** the receptacle of a toilet **4 a :** a natural formation or geographical region shaped like a bowl **b :** a bowl-shaped structure; *esp* **:** an athletic stadium — **bowled** \'bōld\

[2]**bowl** *n* [ME *boule,* fr. MF, fr. L *bulla* bubble] **1 a :** a ball (as of lignum vitae) weighted or shaped to give it a bias when rolled in lawn bowling **b** *pl but sing in constr* **:** LAWN BOWLING **2 :** a cast of the ball in bowling **3 :** a cylindrical roller or drum

[3]**bowl** *vi* **1 :** to participate in a game of bowling **2 :** to roll a ball in bowling **3 :** to travel in a vehicle smoothly and rapidly ~ *vt* **1 a :** to roll (a ball) in bowling **b** (1) **:** to complete by bowling ⟨~ a string⟩ (2) **:** to score by bowling ⟨~*s* 150⟩ **2 a :** to strike with a swiftly moving object **b :** to overwhelm with surprise

bowlder *var of* BOULDER

bow·leg \'bō-,leg, -,lāg, 'bō-'\ *n* **:** a leg bowed outward at or below the knee — **bow·legged** \'bō-'leg(-ə)d, -'lāg(-ə)d\ *adj*

[1]**bowl·er** \'bō-lər\ *n* **:** one that bowls

[2]**bow·ler** \'bō-lər\ *n* [*Bowler,* 19th cent. family of E hatmakers] **:** DERBY 3

bow·line \'bō-lən, -,līn\ *n* [ME *bouline,* perh. fr. *bowe* bow + *line*] **1 :** a rope used to keep the weather edge of a square sail taut forward **2 :** a knot used to form a loop that neither slips nor jams

bowl·ing \'bō-liŋ\ *n* **:** any of several games in which balls are rolled on a green or down an alley at an object or group of objects

[1]**bow·man** \'bō-mən\ *n* **:** ARCHER

[2]**bow·man** \'baů-mən\ *n* **:** a boatman, oarsman, or paddler stationed in the front of a boat

bow out \(')baů-\ *vi* **:** RETIRE, WITHDRAW

bow saw \'bō-\ *n* **:** a saw having a narrow blade held under tension by a light bow-shaped frame

bowse \'baůz\ *var of* BOUSE

bow·sprit \'baů-,sprit, 'bō-\ *n* [ME *bouspret,* prob. fr. MLG *bōchsprēt,* fr. *bōch* bow + *sprēt* pole] **:** a large spar projecting forward from the stem of a ship

bow·string \'bō-,striŋ\ *n* **:** a waxed or sized cord joining the ends of a shooting bow

bowstring hemp *n* **:** any of various Asiatic and African sansevieras; *also* **:** its soft tough leaf fiber used esp. in cordage

bow tie \'bō-\ *n* **:** a short necktie tied in a bowknot

bow window \'bō-\ *n* **:** a usu. curved bay window

bow·wow \'baů-,waů, baů-'\ *n* [imit.] **1 :** the bark of a dog; *also* **:** DOG **2 :** noisy clamor or protest **3 :** arrogant dogmatic manner

bow·yer \'bō-yər\ *n* **:** one that makes shooting bows

[1]**box** \'bäks\ *n, pl* **box** *or* **box·es** [ME, fr. OE, fr. L *buxus,* fr. Gk *pyxos*] **:** an evergreen shrub or small tree (genus *Buxus* of the family Buxaceae, the box family); *esp* **:** a widely cultivated shrub (*B. sempervirens*) used for hedges, borders, and topiary figures

[2]**box** *n* [ME, fr. OE, fr. LL *buxis,* fr. Gk *pyxis,* fr. *pyxos*] **1 a :** a rigid typically rectangular receptacle often with a cover **b :** something having a flat bottom and four upright sides **c :** the contents of a box as a measure of quantity **d :** the driver's seat on a carriage or coach **2** *Brit* **:** a gift in a box **3 :** a small compartment (as for a group of spectators in a theater) **4 a :** a boxlike receptacle (as for a bearing) **b :** a signaling apparatus with its enclosing case **5 :** a square or oblong division or compartment **6 :** a square or oblong hollow space or recess **7 :** a small simple sheltering or enclosing structure **8 :** printed matter enclosed by rules or white space **9 :** any of six spaces on a baseball diamond where the batter, coaches, pitcher, and catcher stand **10 :** PREDICAMENT, FIX

[3]**box** *vt* **1 :** to furnish (as a wheel hub) with a box **2 :** to enclose in or as if in a box **3 :** BOXHAUL **4 :** to enclose with boarding or lathing so as to bring to a required form **5 :** to mix (paint) by pouring back and forth between two containers — **box the compass 1 :** to name the 32 points of the compass in their order **2 :** to make a complete reversal

[4]**box** *n* [ME] **:** a punch or slap esp. on the ear

[5]**box** *vt* **1 :** to hit (as the ears) with the hand **2 :** to engage in boxing with ~ *vi* **:** to fight with the fists **:** engage in boxing

box calf *n* **:** calfskin that is tanned with chromium salts and has square markings on the grain

box camera *n* **:** a camera of simple box shape with a simple lens and rotary shutter

box·car \'bäk-,skär\ *n* **:** a roofed freight car usu. with sliding doors in the sides

box coat *n* **1 :** a heavy overcoat formerly worn for driving **2 :** a loose coat usu. fitted at the shoulders

box elder *n* **:** a No. American maple (*Acer negundo*) with compound leaves

[1]**box·er** \'bäk-sər\ *n* **:** one that engages in the sport of boxing

[2]**boxer** *n* **:** one that makes boxes or packs things in boxes

[3]**boxer** *n* [G, fr. E [1]*boxer*] **:** a compact medium-sized short-haired usu. fawn or brindle dog of a breed originating in Germany

Box·er \'bäk-sər\ *n* [approx. trans. of Chin (Pek.) *i*[4] *hê*[2] *ch'üan*[2], lit., righteous harmonious fist] **:** a member of a Chinese secret society that in 1900 attempted by violence to drive foreigners out of China and to force native converts to renounce Christianity

box·haul \'bäks-,hól\ *vt* **:** to put (a square-rigged ship) on the other tack by luffing and then veering short round on the heel

box·i·ness \'bäk-sē-nəs\ *n* **:** the quality or state of being boxy

[1]**box·ing** \'bäk-siŋ\ *n* **1 :** an act of enclosing in a box **2 :** a boxlike enclosure **:** CASING **3 :** material used for boxes and casings

[2]**boxing** *n* **:** the art of attack and defense with the fists practiced as a sport

Boxing Day *n* **:** the first weekday after Christmas observed as a legal holiday in parts of the British Commonwealth and marked by the giving of Christmas boxes to postmen and other employees

boxing glove *n* **:** one of a pair of leather mittens heavily padded on the back and worn in boxing

box kite *n* **:** a tailless kite consisting of two or more open-ended connected boxes

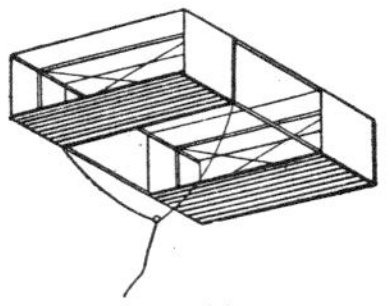

box kite

box·like \'bäk-,slīk\ *adj* **:** resembling a box esp. in shape

box office *n* **1 :** an office (as in a theater) where tickets of admission are sold **2 :** success (as of a show) in attracting ticket buyers; *also* **:** something that enhances such success

box score *n* [fr. its arrangement in a newspaper box] **:** a summary and score of a game (as baseball) in tabular form; *broadly* **:** total count **:** SUMMARY

box seat *n* **1 :** the driver's seat on a coach **2 a :** a seat in a theater or grandstand box **b :** a position favorable for viewing something

box spring *n* **:** a bedspring that consists of spiral springs attached to a foundation and enclosed in a cloth-covered frame

box stall *n* **:** an individual enclosure for an animal

box·thorn \'bäks-,thó(ə)rn\ *n* **:** MATRIMONY VINE

box·wood \'bäk-,swůd\ *n* **1 :** the very close-grained heavy tough hard wood of the box (*Buxus*); *also* **:** a wood of similar properties **2 :** a plant producing boxwood

boxy \'bäk-sē\ *adj* **:** resembling a box

boy \'bói\ *n, often attrib* [ME; akin to Fris *boi* boy] **1 a :** a male child from birth to puberty **b :** SON **c :** a male person not felt to be mature **:** YOUTH **d :** SWEETHEART, BEAU **2 a :** one native to a given place ⟨local ~⟩ **b :** FELLOW, PERSON **3 a :** a male servant **b :** a man of a race felt to be inferior — **boy·hood** \-,hůd\ *n* — **boy·ish** \-ish\ *adj* — **boy·ish·ly** *adv* — **boy·ish·ness** *n*

bo·yar *also* **bo·yard** \bō-'yär\ *n* [Russ *boyarin,* fr. OSlav *boljarinŭ*] **:** a member of a Russian aristocratic order next in rank below the ruling princes until its abolition by Peter the Great

[1]**boy·cott** \'bói-,kät\ *vt* [Charles C. *Boycott* †1897 E land agent in Ireland who was ostracized for refusing to reduce rents] **:** to engage in a concerted refusal to have anything to do with usu. as an expression of disapproval or to force acceptance of certain conditions

[2]**boycott** *n* **:** the process or an instance of boycotting

boy·friend \'bói-,frend\ *n* **1 :** a male friend **2 :** a frequent or regular male companion of a girl or woman **3 :** a male paramour

Boyg \'bóig\ *n* [Norw *bøig* bugbear] **:** a formless or pervasive obstacle, problem, or enemy

boyo \'bói-(,)ō\ *n* [*boy* + *-o*] *Irish* **:** BOY, LAD

boy scout *n* **:** a member of the Boy Scouts of America

boy·sen·ber·ry \'bóiz-ᵊn-,ber-ē, 'bóis-\ *n* [Rudolph *Boysen* *fl*1923 Am horticulturist + E *berry*] **:** a very large bramble fruit with a raspberry flavor; *also* **:** the trailing hybrid bramble of this fruit developed by crossing several blackberries and raspberries

bo·zo \'bō-(,)zō\ *n* [origin unknown] *slang* **:** FELLOW, GUY

bra \'brä\ *n* **:** BRASSIERE

brab·ble \'brab-əl\ *vi* **brab·bling** \-(ə-)liŋ\ [MD *brabbelen,* of imit. origin] **:** SQUABBLE — **brabble** *n*

[1]**brace** \'brās\ *n, pl* **brac·es** [ME, pair, clasp, fr. MF, two arms, fr. L *bracchia,* pl. of *bracchium* arm, fr. Gk *brachiōn,* fr. compar. of *brachys* short — more at BRIEF] **1** *or pl* **brace :** two of a kind ⟨several ~ of quail⟩ **2 :** something (as a clasp) that connects or fastens **3 :** a crank-shaped instrument for turning a bit **4 :** something that transmits, directs, resists, or supports weight or pressure: as **a :** a piece of structural material that serves as a tie or strut to bear transverse strains and prevent distortion **b :** a rope rove through a block at the end of a ship's yard to swing it horizontally **c** *pl* **:** SUSPENDERS **d :** an appliance for supporting a body part **e :** a dental appliance worn on the teeth to correct irregularities of growth and position **5 a :** a mark { or } or ⏟ used to connect words or items to be considered together **b :** this mark connecting two or more musical staffs the parts on which are to be performed simultaneously; *also* **:** the staffs so connected **c :** BRACKET 3a **6 :** an exaggerated position of rigidly erect bearing **7 :** something that arouses energy or strengthens morale

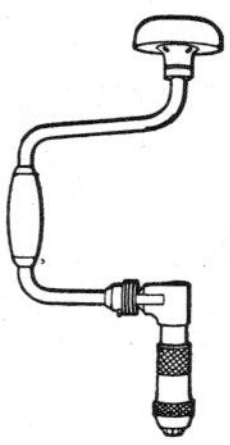
brace 3

[2]**brace** *vt* **1** *archaic* **:** to fasten tightly **:** BIND **2 a :** to prepare for use by making taut **b :** PREPARE, STEEL **c :** INVIGORATE, FRESHEN **3 :** to turn (a sail yard) by means of a brace **4 a :** to furnish or support with a brace **b :** STRENGTHEN, REINFORCE **5 :** to put or plant firmly ~ *vi* **1 :** to take heart — used with *up* **2 :** to get ready

brace·let \'brā-slət\ *n* [ME, fr. MF, dim. of *bras* arm, fr. L *bracchium*] **1 :** an ornamental band or chain worn around the wrist **2 :** something (as handcuffs) resembling a bracelet

[1]**bra·cer** \'brā-sər\ *n* **:** an arm or wrist protector

[2]**brac·er** \'brā-sər\ *n* **:** one that braces, binds, or makes firm

bra·ce·ro \brə-'se(ə)r-(,)ō\ *n* [Sp, laborer, fr. *brazo* arm, fr. L *brachium*] **:** a Mexican laborer admitted to the U.S. esp. for seasonal contract labor in agriculture — compare WETBACK

bra·chi·al \'brak-ē-əl, 'brā-kē-\ *adj* **:** of or relating to the arm or a comparable process

[1]**bra·chi·ate** \'brak-ē-,āt, 'brā-kē-, -ē-ət\ *adj* [L *bracchiatus,* fr. *bracchium*] **:** having widely spreading branches arranged in alternate pairs

[2]**bra·chi·ate** \-,āt\ *vi* [L *bracchium*] **:** to progress by swinging from one hold to another by the arms ⟨*brachiating* gibbon⟩ — **bra·chi·a·tion** \,brak-ē-'ā-shən, ,brā-kē-\ *n*

brach·io·pod \'brak-ē-ə-,päd\ *n* [deriv. of L *bracchium* + Gk *pod-, pous* foot — more at FOOT] **:** any of a phylum (Brachiopoda) of marine invertebrates with bivalve shells within which is a pair of arms bearing tentacles by which a current of water is made to bring microscopic food to the mouth — **brachiopod** *adj*

bra·chi·um \'brak-ē-əm, 'brā-kē-\ *n, pl* **bra·chia** \-ē-ə, -kē-ə\ [L *bracchium, brachium*] **1 :** the upper part of the arm or forelimb from shoulder to elbow **2 :** a process of an invertebrate comparable to an arm

brachy- *comb form* [Gk, fr. *brachys*] **:** short ⟨*brachy*dactylous⟩

brachy·ce·phal·ic \,brak-i-sə-'fal-ik\ *adj* [NL *brachycephalus,* fr. Gk *brachy-* + *kephalē* head] **:** short-headed or broad-headed with a cephalic index of over 80 — **brachy·ceph·a·ly** \-i-'sef-ə-lē\ *n*

brachy·cra·ni·al \,brak-i-'krā-nē-əl\ *also* **brachy·cra·nic** \-nik\ *adj* **:** short-skulled or broad-skulled with a cranial index of 80 and above — **brachy·cra·ny** \'brak-i-,krā-nē\ *n*

brachy·dac·ty·lous \,brak-i-'dak-tə-ləs\ *adj* **:** having abnormally short digits — **brachy·dac·ty·ly** \-lē\ *n*

bra·chyp·ter·ous \bra-'kip-tə-rəs\ *adj* [Gk *brachypteros,* fr. *brachy-* + *pteron* wing — more at FEATHER] **:** having rudimentary or abnormally small wings ⟨~ insects⟩

brachy·uran \,brak-ē-'yür-ən\ *n* [deriv. of Gk *brachy-* + *oura* tail — more at SQUIRREL] **:** any of a tribe or suborder (Brachyura) of crustaceans having the abdomen greatly reduced and including the typical crabs — **brachyuran** *adj* — **brachy·urous** \-'yür-əs\ *adj*

brack·en \'brak-ən\ *n* [ME *braken,* prob. of Scand origin; akin to OSw *brækne* fern] **:** a large coarse fern (as the common brake, *Pteridium aquilinum*); *also* **:** a growth of brakes

[1]**brack·et** \'brak-ət\ *n* [MF *braguette* codpiece, fr. dim. of *brague* breeches, fr. OProv *braga,* fr. L *braca,* fr. Gaulish *brāca,* of Gmc origin; akin to OHG *bruoh* breeches — more at BREECH] **1 :** an overhanging member that projects from a structure (as a wall) and is usu. designed to support a vertical load or to strengthen an angle **2 a :** a short wall shelf **b :** a fixture projecting from a wall or column (as for holding a lamp) **3 a :** one of a pair of marks [ ] used in writing and printing to enclose matter or in mathematics and logic as signs of aggregation — called also *square bracket* **b :** one of the pair of marks ⟨ ⟩ used to enclose matter — called also *angle bracket* **c :** PARENTHESIS 3 **d :** BRACE 5b **4 :** a pair of shots fired to determine the exact distance from gun to target **5 :** a section of a continuously numbered or graded series; *esp* **:** one of a graded series of income groups

[2]**bracket** *vt* **1 a :** to place within or as if within brackets **b :** SEPARATE **2 :** to furnish or fasten with brackets **3 a :** ASSOCIATE **b :** CLASSIFY, GROUP **4 :** to fire a bracket on (as a target)

bracket fungus *n* **:** a basidiomycete that forms shelflike sporophores

brack·ish \'brak-ish\ *adj* [D *brac* salty; akin to MLG *brac* salty] **1 :** somewhat salty **2 :** DISTASTEFUL — **brack·ish·ness** *n*

bract \'brakt\ *n* [NL *bractea,* fr. L, thin metal plate] **1 :** a leaf from the axil of which a flower or floral axis arises **2 :** a leaf borne on a floral axis; *esp* **:** one subtending a flower or flower cluster — **brac·te·al** \'brak-tē-əl\ *adj* — **brac·te·ate** \-tē-ət, -,āt\ *adj* — **bract·ed** \-təd\ *adj*

brac·te·o·late \brak-'tē-ə-lət, 'brak-tē-ə-,lāt\ *adj* **:** furnished with bracteoles

brac·te·ole \'brak-tē-,ōl\ *n* [NL *bracteola,* fr. L, dim. of *bractea*] **:** a small bract esp. on a floral axis — called also *bractlet*

[1]**brad** \'brad\ *n* [ME, fr. ON *broddr* spike] **1 :** a thin nail of the same thickness throughout but tapering in width and slightly headed **2 :** a slender wire nail with a small deep round head

[2]**brad** *vt* **brad·ded; brad·ding :** to fasten with brads

brad·awl \'brad-,ȯl\ *n* **:** an awl with chisel edge used to make holes for brads or screws

brady·car·dia \,brad-i-'kärd-ē-ə\ *n* [NL, fr. Gk *bradys* slow + NL *-cardia*] **:** a slow heart rate

brae \'brā\ *n* [ME *bra,* fr. ON *brā* eyelash; akin to OE *bregdan* to move quickly] *chiefly Scot* **:** a hillside esp. along a river

[1]**brag** \'brag\ *adj* **brag·ger; brag·gest** [ME] **:** FIRST-RATE

[2]**brag** *n* **1 :** a pompous or boastful statement **2 :** arrogant talk or manner **:** COCKINESS **3 :** BRAGGART

[3]**brag** *vb* **bragged; brag·ging** *vi* **:** to talk boastfully ~ *vt* **:** to assert boastfully **syn** see BOAST — **brag·ger** \'brag-ər\ *n* — **brag·gy** \-ē\ *adj*

brag·ga·do·cio \,brag-ə-'dō-s(h)ē-,ō, -(,)shō\ *n* [*Braggadocchio,* personification of boasting in *Faerie Queene* by Edmund Spenser] **1 :** BRAGGART, BOASTER **2 a :** empty boasting **b :** COCKINESS

brag·gart \'brag-ərt\ *n* **:** a loud arrogant boaster — **braggart** *adj*

Bra·gi \'bräg-ē, 'brag-\ *n* [ON] **:** one of the Aesir

brah·ma \'brä-mə, 'bräm-ə, 'bram-\ *n* [*Brahmaputra* river, India] **:** any of an Asian breed of large domestic fowls with feathered legs

[1]**Brah·ma** \'bräm-ə\ *n* [Skt *Brahman,* masc., God] **1 :** the ultimate ground of all being in Hinduism **2 :** the creator god of the Hindu sacred triad

[2]**Brah·ma** \'brā-mə, 'bräm-ə, 'bram-\ *n* **:** BRAHMAN 2

Brah·man *or* **Brah·min** \'bräm-ən; *2 is* 'brā-mən, 'bräm-ən, 'bram-ən\ *n, often attrib* [Skt *brāhmaṇa,* lit., having to do with prayer, fr. *brahman,* neut., prayer] **1 a :** a Hindu of the highest caste traditionally assigned to the priesthood **b :** [1]BRAHMA 1 **2 :** any of an Indian breed of humped cattle **:** ZEBU; *esp* **:** a large vigorous heat-resistant and tick-resistant usu. silvery gray animal evolved in the southern U.S. by interbreeding Indian cattle and used chiefly for crossbreeding — **Brah·man·ic** \brä-'man-ik\ *adj*

Brah·man·ism \'bräm-ə-,niz-əm\ *n* **:** orthodox Hinduism adhering to the pantheism of the Vedas and to the ancient sacrifices and family ceremonies

Brah·min \'bräm-ən\ *n* **:** an intellectually and socially cultivated person regarded as aloof; *esp* **:** such a person from one of the older New England families — **Brah·min·i·cal** \brä-'min-i-kəl\ *adj* — **Brah·min·ism** \'bräm-ə-,niz-əm\ *n*

[1]**braid** \'brād\ *vt* [ME *breyden,* lit., to move suddenly, fr. OE *bregdan;* akin to OHG *brettan* to draw (a sword), Gk *phorkon* something white or wrinkled] **1 a :** to form (three or more strands) into a braid **b :** to make by braiding **2 :** to do up (the hair) by interweaving three or more strands **3 :** INTERMINGLE, MIX **4 :** to ornament esp. with ribbon or braid — **braid·er** *n*

[2]**braid** *n* **1 a :** a cord or ribbon having usu. three or more component strands forming a regular diagonal pattern down its length; *esp* **:** a narrow fabric of intertwined threads used esp. for trimming **b :** a length of braided hair **2 :** high-ranking naval officers

braid·ing \'brād-iŋ\ *n* **:** something made of braided material

[1]**brail** \'brā(ə)l\ *n* [ME *brayle,* fr. AF *braiel,* fr. OF, strap] **1 :** a rope fastened to the leech of a sail and run through a block for hauling the sail up or in **2 :** a dip net with which fish are hauled aboard a boat from a purse seine or trap

[2]**brail** *vt* **1 :** to take in (a sail) by the brails **2 :** to hoist (fish) by means of a brail

braille \'brā(ə)l\ *n, often cap* [Louis *Braille* †1852 F teacher of the blind] **:** a system of writing for the blind that uses characters made up of raised dots — **braille** *vt*

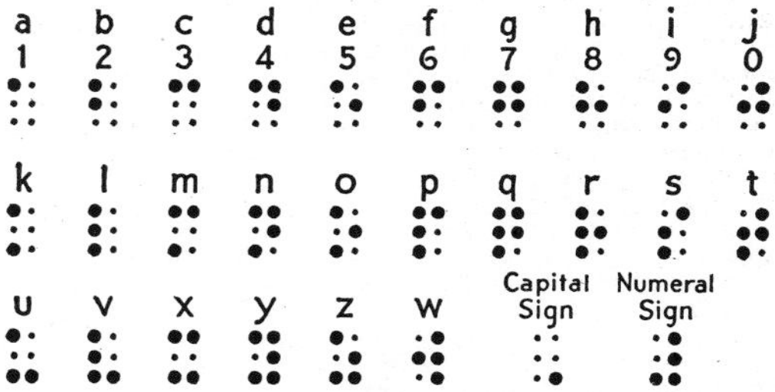
a b c d e f g h i j
1 2 3 4 5 6 7 8 9 0
k l m n o p q r s t
u v x y z w
Capital Sign
Numeral Sign
braille alphabet: the first ten letters serve also as numerals and each letter serves also, when standing alone, as a common word

braille·writ·er \-,rīt-ər\ *n, often cap* **:** a machine for writing braille

[1]**brain** \'brān\ *n* [ME, fr. OE *brægen;* akin to MLG *bregen* brain, Gk *brechmos* front part of the head] **1 a :** the portion of the vertebrate central nervous system that constitutes the organ of thought and neural coordination, includes all the higher nervous centers receiving stimuli from the sense organs and interpreting and correlating them to formulate the motor impulses, is made up of neurons and supporting and nutritive structures, is enclosed within the skull, and is continuous with the spinal cord through the foramen magnum **b :** a nervous center in invertebrates comparable in position and function to the vertebrate brain **2 a :** INTELLECT, INTELLIGENCE — often used in pl. **b** (1) **:** a very intelligent or intellectual person (2) **:** the chief planner of an organization or enterprise — usu. used in pl.

[2]**brain** *vt* **1 :** to kill by smashing the skull **2 :** to hit on the head

brain·case \-,kās\ *n* **:** the cranium enclosing the brain

brain·child \-,chīld\ *n* **:** a product of one's creative imagination

brain·i·ness \'brā-nē-nəs\ *n* **:** the quality or state of being brainy

brain·ish \'brā-nish\ *adj* **:** HOTHEADED, IMPETUOUS

brain·less \'brān-ləs\ *adj* **:** UNINTELLIGENT, STUPID, SILLY — **brain·less·ly** *adv* — **brain·less·ness** *n*

brain·pan \'brān-,pan\ *n* **:** BRAINCASE

brain·pow·er \-,paù(-ə)r\ *n* **1 :** intellectual ability **2 :** people with developed intellectual ability

brain·sick \-,sik\ *adj* **1 :** mentally disordered **2 :** arising from mental disorder — **brain·sick·ly** *adv*

brain·storm \-,stȯrm\ *n* **1 :** a violent transient fit of insanity **2 a :** a sudden bright idea **b :** a harebrained idea

brain trust *n* **:** expert advisers concerned esp. with planning and strategy and often lacking official or acknowledged status — **brain trust·er** \-,trəs-tər\ *n*

brain·wash \'brān-,wȯsh, -,wäsh\ *vt* [back-formation fr. *brainwashing*] **:** to subject to brainwashing — **brainwash** *n*

brain·wash·ing *n* [trans. of Chin (Pek) *hsi*[3] *nao*[3]] **1 :** a forcible indoctrination to induce someone to give up basic political, social, or religious beliefs and attitudes and to accept contrasting regimented ideas **2 :** persuasion by propaganda or salesmanship

brain wave *n* **1 :** rhythmic fluctuations of voltage between parts of the brain resulting in the flow of an electric current; *also* **:** the current produced **2 :** BRAINSTORM 2a

brainy \'brā-nē\ *adj* **:** INTELLIGENT, INTELLECTUAL

braise \'brāz\ *vt* [F *braiser*] **:** to cook slowly in fat and little moisture in a closed pot

[1]**brake** \'brāk\ *archaic past of* BREAK

[2]**brake** \'brāk\ *n* [ME, fern] **:** any of a genus (*Pteridium*) of tall ferns with ternately compound fronds

[3]**brake** *n* [ME, fr. MLG; akin to OE *brecan* to break] **1 :** a toothed instrument or machine for separating out the fiber of flax or hemp by breaking up the woody parts **2 :** a machine for bending, flanging, folding, and forming sheet metal

[4]**brake** *n* [ME] **1 :** a device for arresting the motion of a mechanism usu. employing friction **2 :** something used to slow down or stop movement or activity — **brake·less** \'brā-kləs\ *adj*

[5]**brake** *vt* **:** to retard or stop by or as if by a brake ~ *vi* **1 :** to operate or manage a brake; *esp* **:** to apply the brake on a vehicle **2 :** to become checked by a brake

[6]**brake** *n* [ME *-brake*] **:** rough or marshy land overgrown usu. with one kind of plant — **braky** \'brā-kē\ *adj*

brake·man \'brāk-mən\ *n* **:** a freight or passenger train crew member whose duties include inspection of the train and assistance of the conductor

bram·ble \'bram-bəl\ *n* [ME *brembel*, fr. OE *brēmel;* akin to OE *brōm* broom] **:** any of a genus (*Rubus*) of usu. prickly shrubs of the rose family including the raspberries and blackberries; *broadly* **:** a rough prickly shrub or vine — **bram·bly** \-b(ə-)lē\ *adj*

bran \'bran\ *n* [ME, fr. OF] **:** the broken coat of the seed of cereal grain separated from the flour or meal by sifting or bolting

[1]**branch** \'branch\ *n, often attrib* [ME, fr. OF *branche*, fr. LL *branca* paw] **1 :** a natural subdivision of a plant stem; *esp* **:** a secondary shoot or stem (as a bough) arising from a main axis (as of a tree) **2 :** something that extends from or enters into a main body or source: as **a** (1) **:** a stream that flows into another usu. larger stream **:** TRIBUTARY (2) *South & Midland* **:** CREEK 2 **b :** a side road or way **c :** a slender projection (as the tine of an antler) **d :** a part of a curve separated from others **3 :** a part of a complex body: as **a :** a division of a family descending from a particular ancestor **b :** an area of knowledge apart from related areas **c** (1) **:** a division of an organization (2) **:** a separate but dependent part of a central organization **d :** a language group less inclusive than a family **syn** see SHOOT — **branched** \'brancht\ *adj* — **branch·less** \'branch-ləs\ *adj* — **branchy** \'bran-chē\ *adj*

[2]**branch** *vi* **1 :** to put forth branches **:** RAMIFY **2 :** to spring out (as from a main stem) **:** DIVERGE **3 :** to be an outgrowth — used with *from* **4 :** to extend activities — usu. used with *out* ~ *vt* **1 :** to ornament with designs of branches **2 :** to divide up **:** SECTION

bran·chia \'braŋ-kē-ə\ *n, pl* **bran·chi·ae** \-kē-,ē, -,ī\ [L, sing., fr. Gk, pl. of *branchion* gill; akin to Gk *bronchos* trachea] **:** [2]GILL — **bran·chi·al** \-kē-əl\ *adj* — **bran·chi·ate** \-kē-ət, -,āt\ *adj*

bran·chio·pod \'braŋ-kē-ə-,päd\ *n* [deriv. of Gk *branchia* gills + *pod-, pous* foot — more at FOOT] **:** any of a group (Branchiopoda) of aquatic crustaceans typically having a long body, a carapace, and many pairs of leaflike appendages — **branchiopod** *adj* — **bran·chi·op·o·dan** \,braŋ-kē-'äp-əd-ən\ *adj* — **bran·chi·op·o·dous** \-əd-əs\ *adj*

branch·let \'branch-lət\ *n* **:** a small usu. terminal branch

[1]**brand** \'brand\ *n* [ME, torch, sword, fr. OE; akin to OE *bærnan* to burn] **1 a :** a charred or burning piece of wood **b :** something resembling a burning brand **2 :** SWORD **3 a** (1) **:** a mark made by burning with a hot iron to attest manufacture or quality or to designate ownership (2) **:** a mark made with a stamp or stencil for similar purposes **:** TRADEMARK **b** (1) **:** a mark put on criminals with a hot iron (2) **:** a mark of disgrace **:** STIGMA **4 a** (1) **:** a class of goods identified as the product of a single firm or manufacturer **:** MAKE (2) **:** MANUFACTURER **b :** a characteristic or distinctive kind **:** VARIETY **5 :** a tool used to produce a brand

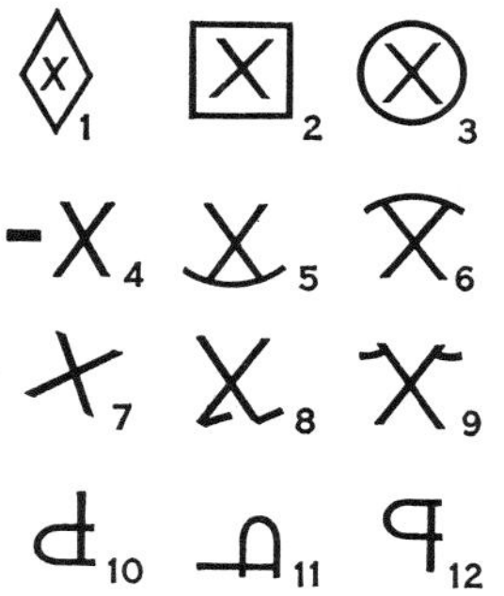

brands 3a(1): *1* diamond X, *2* box X, *3* circle X, *4* bar X, *5* rocking X, *6* swinging X, *7* tumbling X, *8* walking X, *9* flying X, *10* crazy P, *11* lazy P, *12* reverse P

[2]**brand** *vt* **1 :** to mark with a brand **2 :** to mark or expose as infamous **:** STIGMATIZE **3 :** to impress indelibly — **brand·er** *n*

[1]**bran·dish** \'bran-dish\ *vt* [ME *braundisshen*, fr. MF *brandiss-*, stem of *brandir*, fr. OF, fr. *brand* sword, of Gmc origin; akin to OE *brand*] **1 :** to shake or wave (as a weapon) menacingly **2 :** to exhibit in an ostentatious or aggressive manner **syn** see SWING

[2]**brandish** *n* **:** an act or instance of brandishing

brand·ling \'bran-(d)liŋ\ *n* **:** a small yellowish earthworm (*Eisenia foetida*) with brownish purple rings found in dunghills

brand–new \'bran-'n(y)ü\ *adj* **:** conspicuously new and unused

[1]**bran·dy** \'bran-dē\ *n* [short for *brandywine*, fr. D *brandewijn*, fr. MD *brantwijn*, fr. *brant* distilled + *wijn* wine] **:** an alcoholic liquor distilled from wine or fermented fruit juice (as of peaches)

[2]**brandy** *vt* **:** to flavor, blend, or preserve with brandy

brank \'braŋk\ *n* [origin unknown] **:** an instrument made of an iron frame surrounding the head and a sharp metal bit entering the mouth and formerly used to punish scolds — usu. used in pl.

bran·ni·gan \'bran-i-gən\ *n* **1 :** SPREE **2 :** SQUABBLE

brant \'brant\ *n, pl* **brant** *or* **brants** [origin unknown] **:** a wild goose; *esp* **:** any of several small dark geese (genus *Branta*) that breed in the Arctic and migrate southward

[1]**brash** \'brash\ *n* [obs. E *brash* to breach a wall] **:** a mass of fragments (as of ice)

[2]**brash** *adj* [origin unknown] **1 :** BRITTLE ⟨~ wood⟩ **2 a :** tending to act in headlong fashion **:** IMPETUOUS **b :** done in haste without regard for consequences **:** RASH **3 :** uninhibitedly energetic or demonstrative **:** BUMPTIOUS **4 a :** lacking restraint and discernment **:** TACTLESS **b :** aggressively self-assertive **:** IMPUDENT **5 :** piercingly sharp **:** HARSH — **brash·ly** *adv* — **brash·ness** *n*

brass \'bras\ *n* [ME *bras*, fr. OE *bræs;* akin to MLG *bras* metal] **1 :** an alloy consisting essentially of copper and zinc in variable proportions **2 a :** brass musical instruments — often used in pl. **b :** a usu. brass memorial tablet **c :** bright metal fittings or utensils **d :** a brass, bronze, or gunmetal lining for a bearing **e :** empty fired cartridge shells **3 :** brazen self-assurance **:** GALL **4 :** BRASS HATS — **brass** *adj*

bras·sard \brə-'särd, 'bras-,ärd\ *also* **bras·sart** \-'sär(t), -,är(t)\ *n* [F *brassard*, fr. MF *brassal*, fr. OIt *bracciale*, fr. *braccio* arm, fr. L *bracchium*] **1 :** armor to protect the arm **2 :** a cloth band worn around the upper arm usu. bearing an identifying mark

brass·bound \'bras-,baund,-'baund\ *adj* **1 :** having trim made of brass or a metal resembling brass **2 a** (1) **:** tradition-bound and opinionated (2) **:** UNCOMPROMISING, INFLEXIBLE **b :** BRAZEN

brass hat *n* **1 :** a high-ranking military officer **2 :** a person in a high position in civilian life

bras·si·ca \'bras-i-kə\ *n* [NL, genus name, fr. L, cabbage] **:** any of a large genus (*Brassica*) of Old World temperate zone herbs (as cabbages) with beaked cylindrical pods

brass·ie \'bras-ē\ *n* **:** a wooden golf club with more loft than a driver — called also *number two wood*

bras·siere \brə-'zi(ə)r *also* ,bras-ē-'e(ə)r\ *n* [obs. F *brassière* bodice, fr. OF *braciere* arm protector, fr. *bras* arm] **:** a woman's close-fitting undergarment having cups for bust support

brass·i·ly \'bras-ə-lē\ *adv* **:** in a brassy manner

brass·i·ness \'bras-ē-nəs\ *n* **:** the quality or state of being brassy

brass knuckles *n pl but sing or pl in constr* **:** KNUCKLE 4

brass tacks *n pl* **:** details of immediate practical importance

brassy \'bras-ē\ *adj* **1 :** BRAZEN, OBSTREPEROUS **2 :** resembling brass esp. in color **3 :** resembling the sound of a brass instrument

brat \'brat\ *n* [perh. fr. E dial. *brat* (ragamuffin)] **:** CHILD; *specif* **:** an ill-mannered annoying child — **brat·tish** \'brat-ish\ *adj* — **brat·ty** \-ē\ *adj*

brat·tice \'brat-əs, -ish\ *n* [ME *bretais* parapet, fr. OF *bretesche*, fr. ML *breteschia*] **:** an often temporary partition of planks or cloth used esp. in a mine to control ventilation — **brattice** *vt*

[1]**brat·tle** \'brat-ᵊl\ *n* [prob. imit.] *chiefly Scot* **:** CLATTER, SCAMPER

[2]**brattle** *vi, chiefly Scot* **:** to make a clattering or rattling sound

bra·va \'bräv-(,)ä, brä-'vä\ *n* [It, fem. of *bravo*] **:** BRAVO — used interjectionally in applauding a woman

bra·va·do \brə-'väd-(,)ō\ *n, pl* **bravadoes** *or* **bravados** [MF *bravade* & OSp *bravata*, fr. OIt *bravata*, fr. *bravare* to challenge, show off, fr. *bravo*] **1 a :** blustering swaggering conduct **b :** a pretense of bravery **2 :** FOOLHARDINESS

[1]**brave** \'brāv\ *adj* [MF, fr. OIt & OSp *bravo* courageous, wild, fr. L *barbarus* barbarous] **1 :** COURAGEOUS **2 :** making a fine show **:** COLORFUL **3 :** EXCELLENT, SPLENDID — **brave·ly** *adv*

[2]**brave** *vt* **1 :** to face or endure with courage **2** *obs* **:** to make showy ~ *vi, archaic* **:** to make a brave show — **brav·er** *n*

[3]**brave** *n* **1** *archaic* **:** BRAVADO **2 :** one who is brave; *specif* **:** a No. American Indian warrior **3** *archaic* **:** BULLY, ASSASSIN

brav·ery \'brāv-(ə-)rē\ *n* **1 a :** fine clothes **b :** showy display **2 :** the quality or state of being brave **:** COURAGE

[1]**bra·vo** \'bräv-(,)ō\ *n, pl* **bravos** *or* **bravoes** [It, fr. *bravo*, adj.] **:** VILLAIN, DESPERADO; *esp* **:** a hired assassin

[2]**bra·vo** \'bräv-(,)ō, brä-'vō\ *n, pl* **bravos :** a shout of approval — often used interjectionally in applauding a performance

[3]**bravo** *like* [2]BRAVO\ *vt* **:** to applaud by shouts of *bravo*

Bra·vo \'bräv-(,)ō\ — a communications code word for the letter *b*

bra·vu·ra \brə-'v(y)u̇r-ə\ *n, often attrib* [It, lit., bravery, fr. *bravare*] **1 :** a florid brilliant musical style **2 :** virtuosic self-assured performance

braw \'brȯ\ *adj* [modif. of MF *brave*] **1** *chiefly Scot* **:** GOOD, FINE **2** *chiefly Scot* **:** well dressed — **braw·ly** \'brȯ-lē\ *adv, chiefly Scot*

[1]**brawl** \'brȯl\ *vi* [ME *brawlen*] **1 :** to quarrel noisily **:** WRANGLE **2 :** to make a loud confused noise — **brawl·er** *n*

[2]**brawl** *n* **1 :** a noisy quarrel or fight **2 :** a loud tumultuous noise

brawn \'brȯn\ *n* [ME, fr. MF *braon* muscle, of Gmc origin; akin to OE *brǣd* flesh] **1 a :** full strong muscles esp. of the arm or leg **b :** muscular strength **2 a** *Brit* **:** the flesh of a boar **b :** HEADCHEESE

brawn·i·ness \'brȯ-nē-nəs\ *n* **:** the quality or state of being brawny

brawny \'brȯ-nē\ *adj* **1 :** MUSCULAR, STRONG **2 :** being swollen and hard ⟨a ~ infection⟩

[1]**bray** \'brā\ *vb* [ME *brayen*, fr. OF *braire* to cry, fr. (assumed) VL *bragere*, of Celt origin; akin to MIr *braigid* he breaks wind; akin to L *frangere* to break — more at BREAK] *vi* **:** to utter the characteristic loud harsh cry of a donkey ~ *vt* **:** to utter or play loudly, harshly, or discordantly — **bray** *n*

[2]**bray** *vt* [ME *brayen*, fr. MF *broiier*, of Gmc origin; akin to OHG *brehhan* to break] **1 :** to crush or grind fine **2 :** to spread thin

bray·er \'brā-ər\ *n* **:** a printer's hand inking roller

[1]**braze** \'brāz\ *vb* [irreg. fr. *brass*] *obs* **:** HARDEN

[2]**braze** *vb* [prob. fr. F *braser*, fr. OF, to burn, fr. *brese* live coals] **:** to solder with a relatively infusible alloy — **braz·er** *n*

[1]**bra·zen** \'brāz-ᵊn\ *adj* [ME *brasen*, fr. OE *bræsen*, fr. *bræs* brass] **1 :** made of brass **2 a :** sounding harsh and loud like struck brass **b :** of the color of polished brass **3 :** IMPUDENT, SHAMELESS — **bra·zen–faced** \,brāz-ᵊn-'fāst\ *adj* — **bra·zen·ly** *adv* — **bra·zen·ness** \'brāz-ᵊn-(n)əs\ *n*

[2]**brazen** *vt* **bra·zen·ing** \'brāz-niŋ, -ᵊn-iŋ\ **:** to face with defiance or impudence

[1]**bra·zier** \'brā-zhər\ *n* [ME *brasier*, fr. *bras* brass] **:** one that works in brass

[2]**brazier** *n* [F *brasier*, fr. OF, fire of hot coals, fr. *brese*] **1 :** a pan for holding burning coals **2 :** a utensil in which food is exposed to heat through a wire grill

bra·zil·ein \brə-'zil-ē-ən\ *n* [ISV *brazilin*] **:** a red crystalline dye $C_{16}H_{12}O_5$ related to hematein

bra·zi·lin \'braz-ə-lən, brə-'zil-ən\ *n* [F *brésiline*, fr. *brésil* brazilwood, prob. fr. Sp *brasil*] **:** a phenolic compound $C_{16}H_{14}O_5$ from brazilwood that oxidizes readily to brazilein

Bra·zil nut \brə-ˌzil-\ *n* [*Brazil*, country in So. America] **:** a tall So. American tree (*Bertholletia excelsa* of the family Lecythidaceae) that bears large globular capsules each containing several closely packed roughly triangular oily edible nuts; *also* **:** its nut

bra·zil·wood \brə-ˈzil-ˌwu̇d\ *n* [Sp *brasil*, fr. *brasa* live coals; fr. its color] **:** the heavy wood of any of various tropical leguminous trees (esp. genus *Caesalpinia*) used as red and purple dyewoods and in cabinetwork

1breach \ˈbrēch\ *n* [ME *breche*, fr. OE *bryce;* akin to OE *brecan* to break] **1 :** infraction or violation of a law, obligation, tie, or standard **2 a :** a broken, ruptured, or torn condition or area **b :** a gap (as in a wall) made by battering **3 a :** a break in accustomed friendly relations **b :** a temporary gap in continuity **:** HIATUS **4 :** the leap of a whale out of water

2breach *vt* **1 :** to make a breach in **2 :** BREAK, VIOLATE **~** *vi* **:** to leap out of water ⟨a whale *~ing*⟩

breach of promise : violation of a promise esp. to marry

1bread \ˈbred\ *n* [ME *breed*, fr. OE *brēad;* akin to OHG *brōt* bread OE *brēowan* to brew] **1 :** a usually baked and leavened food made of a mixture whose basic constituent is flour or meal **2 :** a portion of bread **3 :** FOOD, SUSTENANCE

2bread *vt* **:** to cover with bread crumbs

bread and butter *n* **:** a means of sustenance or livelihood

bread–and–butter *adj* **1 a :** of or relating to a means of livelihood or everyday activities **b :** dependable as a steady source of income **2 :** sent or given as thanks for hospitality ⟨~ letter⟩

bread·bas·ket \ˈbred-ˌbas-kət\ *n* **1** *slang* **:** STOMACH **2 :** a major cereal-producing region

bread·fruit \-ˌfrüt\ *n* **:** a round usu. seedless fruit that resembles bread in color and texture when baked; *also* **:** a tall tropical tree (*Artocarpus altilis*) of the mulberry family that bears it

bread·root \-ˌrüt, -ˌru̇t\ *n* **:** the nutritious root of a western U. S. hairy leguminous plant (*Psoralea esculenta*)

bread·stuff \ˈbred-ˌstəf\ *n* **1 :** GRAIN, FLOUR **2 :** BREAD

breadth \ˈbredth, ˈbretth\ *n* [obs. E *brede* breadth (fr. ME, fr. OE *brǣdu*, fr. *brād* broad) + *-th* (as in *length*)] **1 :** distance from side to side **:** WIDTH **2 a :** something of full width **b :** a wide expanse **3 a :** COMPREHENSIVENESS **b :** liberality of views or taste

breadth·ways \-ˌwāz\ *or* **breadth·wise** \-ˌwīz\ *adv* (*or adj*) **:** in the direction of the breadth

bread·win·ner \ˈbred-ˌwin-ər\ *n* **:** a member of a family whose wages supply its livelihood; *also* **:** a means of livelihood — **bread·win·ning** \-ˌwin-iŋ\ *n*

1break \ˈbrāk\ *vb* **broke** \ˈbrōk\ **bro·ken** \ˈbrō-kən\ **break·ing** [ME *breken*, fr. OE *brecan;* akin to OHG *brehhan* to break, L *frangere*] *vt* **1 a :** to separate into parts with suddenness or violence **b :** MAIM, MUTILATE **c :** RUPTURE **d :** to cut into and turn over the surface of **:** PLOW **2 a :** VIOLATE, TRANSGRESS **b :** to invalidate (a will) by action at law **3 a :** to force entry into **b :** to burst and force a way through **c :** to escape by force from **d :** to make or effect by cutting, forcing, or pressing through **e :** PENETRATE, PIERCE **4 :** to make ineffective as a binding force **:** SUNDER **5 a :** to disrupt the order or compactness of ⟨~ ranks⟩ **b :** to end, close, or destroy by dispersing ⟨~ up the gang⟩ **6 a :** to defeat utterly and end as an effective force **:** SMASH, DESTROY **b :** to crush the spirit of **c :** to make tractable or submissive: as (1) **:** to train (an animal) to adjust to the service or convenience of man (2) **:** INURE, ACCUSTOM **d :** to exhaust in health, strength, or capacity **7 a :** to ruin financially **b :** to reduce in rank **8 a :** to turn aside the force or intensity of **b :** to cause failure and discontinuance of (a strike) by measures outside bargaining processes **9 :** EXCEED, SURPASS ⟨~ a speed record⟩ **10 :** to ruin the prospects of **11 :** to demonstrate the falsity of ⟨~ an alibi⟩ **12 :** to reduce the price of sharply **13 a :** to stop or bring to an end suddenly **:** HALT ⟨~ a deadlock⟩ **b :** INTERRUPT, SUSPEND **c :** to open and bring about suspension of operation ⟨~ an electric circuit⟩ **d :** to destroy unity or completeness of **e :** to change the appearance of uniformity of **f :** to split the surface of ⟨fish *~ing* water⟩ **g :** to cause to discontinue a habit **14 :** to make known **15 a :** to find an explanation or solution for **:** SOLVE **b :** to discover the essentials of (a code or cipher system) **16 :** to alter sharply the direction or course of **17 :** to open the action of (a gun) **~** *vi* **1 a :** to escape with sudden forceful effort **b :** to develop or emerge with suddenness and force **c :** to come into being by or as if by bursting forth ⟨day was *~ing*⟩ **d :** to act or change with abruptness ⟨*~ing* into laughter⟩ **e :** to emerge from the surface of the water **f :** to make a sudden dash **g :** to separate after a clinch in boxing **2 a :** to come apart or split into pieces **:** BURST, SHATTER **b :** to open spontaneously or by pressure from within **c** *of a wave* **:** to curl over and fall apart in surf or foam **3 :** to become fair **:** CLEAR ⟨when the weather *~s*⟩ **4 :** to give way in disorderly retreat **5 a :** to fail in health, strength, vitality, or control ⟨*broke* under questioning⟩ **b :** to become crushed by grief, disappointment, or anguish **c :** to become inoperative because of damage, wear, or strain **6 :** to undergo a sudden marked decrease in price or value **7 :** to end a relationship, connection, accord, or agreement **8 a :** to swerve suddenly **b :** to curve, drop, or rise sharply **9 a :** to alter sharply in tone, pitch, or intensity **b :** to shift abruptly from one register to another **10 :** to fail to keep a prescribed gait **11 :** to interrupt one's activity or occupation for a brief period **12 :** to make the opening shot of a game of pool **13 a :** to divide into classes, categories, or types ⟨our cases ~ up into three types⟩ **b :** to fold, bend, lift, or come apart at a seam, groove, or joint **c** *of cream* **:** to separate during churning into liquid and fat **d** *of an emulsion* **:** to separate permanently usu. into oily and aqueous layers **14 :** HAPPEN, DEVELOP — **break even :** to emerge (as from a transaction) with balancing gains and losses; *esp* **:** to operate a business or enterprise without either loss or profit — **break the ice 1 :** to make a beginning **2 :** to get through the first difficulties in starting a conversation or discussion — **break wind :** to expel gas from the intestine

2break *n* **1 a :** an act or action of breaking **b :** the opening shot in a game of pool or billiards **c :** the act of opening a gap in an electrical circuit **2 a :** a condition produced by breaking **b :** a gap in an otherwise continuous electric circuit **3 :** the action or act of breaking in, out, or forth **4 :** DASH, RUSH ⟨a base runner making a ~ for home⟩; *esp* **:** a quick offensive thrust toward the basket in basketball **5 a :** the start of a race **b :** the act of separating after a clinch in boxing **6 :** an interruption in continuity ⟨waiting for a ~ in the bad weather⟩: as **a :** a notable change of subject matter, attitude, or treatment **b** (1) **:** an abrupt, significant, or noteworthy change or interruption in a continuous process, trend, or surface (2) **:** an interruption from work or duty for rest or relaxation (3) **:** a planned interruption in a radio or television program ⟨a ~ for the commercial⟩ **c** *pl* **:** a line of cliffs and associated spurs and small ravines (as at the edge of a mesa or a canyon) **d :** deviation of a pitched baseball from a straight line **e :** DISLOCATION, FAULT **f :** failure of a horse to maintain the prescribed gait **g :** an abrupt change in the quality or pitch of musical tone **h :** a notable variation in pitch, intensity, or tone in the voice **7 :** a rupture in previously friendly relations **:** disagreement causing separation **8 :** a sequence of successful shots in billiards **:** RUN **9 :** a place or situation at which a break occurs: **a :** the point where one musical register changes to another **b :** a short ornamental passage interpolated between phrases in jazz **c :** the place at which a word is divided (as at the end of a line) **d :** a pause or interruption (as a caesura or diaeresis) within or at the end of a verse **e :** a failure to make a strike or a spare on a frame in bowling **10 :** a sudden and abrupt decline of prices or values **11 :** an awkward social blunder **12 :** a stroke of luck and esp. of good luck ⟨a winning team gets the *~s*⟩ ⟨a succession of bad *~s*⟩

break·able \ˈbrā-kə-bəl\ *adj* **:** capable of being broken — **breakable** *n*

break·age \ˈbrā-kij\ *n* **1 a :** the action of breaking **b :** a quantity broken **2 :** allowance for things broken

break·away \ˈbrā-kə-ˌwā\ *n* **1 :** an act or instance of breaking away (as from a group or tradition) **2 :** an object made to shatter or collapse under pressure or impact — **breakaway** *adj*

break·bone fever \ˌbrāk-ˌbōn-\ *n* **:** DENGUE

break down *vt* **1 a :** to cause to fall or collapse by breaking or shattering **b :** to make ineffective **2 a :** to separate (as a chemical compound) into simpler substances **:** DECOMPOSE **b :** to take apart esp. for storage or shipment and for later reassembling **~** *vi* **1 a :** to become inoperative through breakage or wear **b :** to become inapplicable or ineffective **2 a :** to be susceptible to analysis or subdivision **b :** to undergo decomposition **syn** see ANALYZE

break·down \ˈbrāk-ˌdau̇n\ *n* **:** the action or result of breaking down: as **a :** a failure to function **b :** a physical, mental, or nervous collapse **c :** failure to progress or have effect **:** DISINTEGRATION **d :** DECOMPOSITION **e :** division into categories **:** CLASSIFICATION; *also* **:** an account analyzed into categories

1break·er \ˈbrā-kər\ *n* **1 a :** one that breaks **b :** a device or instrument that breaks; *specif* **:** a machine or plant for breaking rocks or crushing anthracite **2 :** a wave breaking into foam against the shore, a sandbank, or a rock **3 :** a strip of fabric under the tread of a tire for extra protection of the carcass

2brea·ker \ˈbrā-kər\ *n* [by folk etymology fr. Sp *barrica*] **:** a small water cask

break–even \brā-ˈkē-vən\ *adj* **:** having equal loss and profit

break·fast \ˈbrek-fəst\ *n* **:** the first meal of the day — **breakfast** *vb*

break·front \ˈbrāk-ˌfrənt\ *n* **:** a large cabinet or bookcase whose center section projects beyond the flanking end sections

break in *vi* **1 :** to enter a house or building by force **2 :** to interrupt in a conversation **3 :** to start in an activity or enterprise **~** *vt* **1 :** to accustom to a certain activity or occurrence **2 :** to overcome the stiffness of (a new article)

break·neck \ˈbrāk-ˌnek\ *adj* **:** extremely dangerous ⟨~ speed⟩

break out *vi* **:** to become affected with a skin eruption **~** *vt* **1 a :** to take from stowage preparatory to using **b :** to make ready for action or use **2 a :** to dislodge from the bottom and start pulling up (an anchor) **b :** to display flying and unfurled **c :** DISLODGE

break·out \ˈbrā-ˌkau̇t\ *n* **:** a violent or forceful break from restraint; *esp* **:** a military attack to break from encirclement

break·through \ˈbrāk-ˌthrü\ *n* **1 :** an act or point of breaking through an obstruction **2 :** an offensive thrust that penetrates and carries beyond a defensive line in warfare **3 :** a sudden advance in knowledge or technique

break up *vt* **1 :** to disrupt the continuity or flow of **2 :** to bring to an end **3 :** to break into pieces in scrapping or salvaging **:** SCRAP **~** *vi* **1 :** to cease to exist as a unified whole **2 :** to lose morale, composure, or resolution — **break·up** \ˈbrā-ˌkəp\ *n*

break·wa·ter \ˈbrā-ˌkwȯt-ər, -ˌkwät-\ *n* **:** a structure to protect a harbor or beach from the force of waves

1bream \ˈbrim, ˈbrēm\ *n, pl* **bream** *or* **breams** [ME *breme*, fr. MF, of Gmc origin; akin to OHG *brahsima* bream, *brettan* to draw (a sword) — more at BRAID] **1 :** a European freshwater cyprinid fish (*Abramis brama*); *broadly* **:** any of various related fishes **2 a :** porgy or related fish (family Sparidae) **b :** any of various freshwater sunfishes (*Lepomis* and related genera); *esp* **:** BLUEGILL

2bream \ˈbrēm\ *vt* [prob. fr. D *brem* furze] **:** to clean (a ship's bottom) by heating and scraping

1breast \ˈbrest\ *n* [ME *brest*, fr. OE *brēost;* akin to OHG *brust* breast, Russ *bryukho* belly] **1 :** either of two protuberant milk-producing glandular organs situated on the front of the chest in the human female and some other mammals; *broadly* **:** a discrete mammary gland **2 :** the fore or ventral part of the body between the neck and the abdomen **3 :** the seat of emotion and thought **:** BOSOM **4 a :** something resembling a breast **b :** FACE 6

2breast *vt* **1 :** CONFRONT **2 :** to contend with resolutely

breast·bone \ˈbres(t)-ˈbōn, -ˌbōn\ *n* **:** STERNUM

breast drill *n* **:** a portable drill with a plate that is pressed by the breast in forcing the drill against the work

breast·plate \ˈbres(t)-ˌplāt\ *n* **1 :** a metal plate worn as defensive armor for the breast **2 :** a vestment worn in ancient times by a Jewish high priest and set with 12 gems bearing the names of the tribes of Israel **3 :** a piece against which the workman presses his breast in operating a breast drill or similar tool **4 :** PLASTRON 2

breast·stroke \ˈbres(t)-ˌstrōk\ *n* **:** a swimming stroke executed by extending the arms in front of the head while drawing the knees forward and outward and then sweeping the arms back with palms out while kicking backward and outward

breast·work \ˈbres-ˌtwərk\ *n* **:** a temporary fortification

breath \ˈbreth\ *n* [ME *breth*, fr. OE *brǣth;* akin to OHG *brādam* breath, OE *beorma* yeast] **1 a :** air charged with a fragrance or odor **b :** a slight indication **:** SUGGESTION **2 a :** the faculty of breathing **b :** an act of breathing **c :** opportunity or time to

breathe : RESPITE **3** : a slight breeze **4 a** : air inhaled and exhaled in breathing **b** : something (as moisture on a cold surface) produced by breath or breathing **5** : a spoken sound : UTTERANCE **6** : SPIRIT, ANIMATION **7** : expiration of air with the glottis wide open (as in the formation of \f\ and \s\ sounds)

breathe \'brēth\ *vb* [ME *brethen*, fr. *breth*] *vi* **1 a** *obs* : to emit a fragrance or aura **b** : to become manifest **2 a** : to draw air into and expel it from the lungs : RESPIRE; *broadly* : to take in oxygen and give out carbon dioxide through natural processes **b** : to inhale and exhale freely **3** : LIVE **4** : to pause and rest before continuing **5** : to blow softly **6** : to use air to support combustion ~ *vt* **1 a** : to send out by exhaling **b** : to instill by or as if by breathing ⟨~ new life into the movement⟩ **2 a** : UTTER, EXPRESS **b** : MANIFEST, EVINCE **3** : to give rest from exertion to **4** : to take in in breathing

breathed \'breтht\ *adj* : VOICELESS 2

breath·er \'brē-thər\ *n* **1** : one that breathes **2** : a break in activity for rest **3** : a small vent in an airtight enclosure

breath·ing \'brē-thiŋ\ *n* **1** : BREATHER 2 **2** : either of the marks ʽ and ʼ used in writing Greek to indicate aspiration or its absence

breath·less \'breth-ləs\ *adj* **1 a** : not breathing **b** : DEAD **2 a** : panting or gasping for breath **b** : leaving one breathless **c** : holding one's breath from emotion **3** : STALE, STUFFY — **breath·less·ly** *adv*

breath·tak·ing \'breth-,tā-kiŋ\ *adj* **1** : making one out of breath **2** : EXCITING, THRILLING — **breath·tak·ing·ly** \-kiŋ-lē\ *adv*

breathy \'breth-ē\ *adj* : characterized by or accompanied with the audible passage of breath

brec·cia \'brech-(ē-)ə\ *n* [It] : a rock consisting of sharp fragments embedded in a fine-grained matrix

brec·ci·ate \'brech-ē-,āt\ *vt* : to form (rock) into breccia — **brec·ci·a·tion** \,brech-ē-'ā-shən\ *n*

brede \'brēd\ *n* [alter. of *braid*] **1** *archaic* : EMBROIDERY **2** *archaic* : BRAIDING; *esp* : interweaving of colors

bree \'brē\ *n* [ME *bre*] *chiefly Scot* : BROTH, LIQUOR

breech \'brēch; *"breeches" (garment) is usu* 'brich-əz\ *n* [ME, breches, fr. OE *brēc*, pl. of *brōc* leg covering; akin to OHG *bruoh* breeches, OE *brecan* to break] **1** *pl* **a** : short trousers covering the hips and thighs and fitting snugly at the lower edges at or just below the knee **b** : PANTS **2** : BUTTOCKS **3 a** : the part of a firearm at the rear of the bore **b** : the bottom of a pulley block

breech·block \'brēch-,bläk\ *n* : the block in breech-loading firearms that closes the rear of the bore against the force of the charge

breech·clout \-,klau̇t\ *or* **breech·cloth** \-,klȯth\ *n* : LOINCLOTH

breech·es buoy \'brē-chəz- *also* 'brich-əz-\ *n* : a canvas seat in the form of breeches hung from a life buoy running on a hawser and used to haul persons from one ship to another or from ship to shore

breech·ing \'brē-chiŋ, 'brich-iŋ\ *n* : the part of a harness that passes around the breech of a draft animal

breech·load·er \'brēch-'lōd-ər\ *n* : a firearm receiving its ammunition at the breech — **breech-load·ing** \-'lōd-iŋ\ *adj*

[1]**breed** \'brēd\ *vb* **bred** \'bred\; **breed·ing** [ME *breden*, fr. OE *brēdan*; akin to OE *brōd* brood] *vt* **1** : to produce (offspring) by hatching or gestation **2 a** : BEGET 1 **b** : PRODUCE, ENGENDER **3** : to propagate sexually: **a** : to propagate (plants) by artificial pollination **b** : to improve (a stock) by controlled propagation **c** : to develop (desired qualities) by breeding **4 a** : to bring up : NURTURE **b** : to inculcate by training **5 a** : to mate with : MATE, INSEMINATE **b** : IMPREGNATE **6** : to produce (a fissionable element) by bombarding a nonfissionable element with neutrons from a radioactive element ~ *vi* **1** : to produce offspring by sexual union **2** : to propagate animals or plants — **breed·er** *n*

[2]**breed** *n* **1** : a group of animals or plants presumably related by descent from common ancestors and visibly similar in most characters; *esp* : such a group differentiated from the wild type under the influence of man **2** : a number of persons of the same stock **3** : CLASS, KIND

breed·ing *n* **1** : the action or process of bearing or generating **2** : ANCESTRY **3 a** : EDUCATION **b** : training in or observance of the proprieties **4** : the propagation of plants or animals

breeks \'brēks\ *n pl* [ME (northern dial.) *breke*, fr. OE *brēc*] *chiefly Scot* : BREECHES

[1]**breeze** \'brēz\ *n* [ME *brise*] **1 a** : a light gentle wind **b** : a wind of from 4 to 31 miles an hour **2** : something easily done : CINCH

[2]**breeze** *vi* : to proceed quickly and easily ⟨*breezed* through the book⟩

[3]**breeze** *n* [prob. modif. of F *braise* cinders] : residue from the making of coke or charcoal

breeze·way \-,wā\ *n* : a roofed open passage connecting two buildings (as a house and garage) or halves of a building

breez·i·ly \'brē-zə-lē\ *adv* : in a breezy manner

breez·i·ness \'brē-zē-nəs\ *n* : a breezy quality or manner

breezy \'brē-zē\ *adj* **1** : swept by breezes **2** : BRISK, LIVELY

breg·ma \'breg-mə\ *n, pl* **breg·ma·ta** \-mət-ə\ [NL *bregmat-, bregma*, fr. LL, front part of the head, fr. Gk; akin to Gk *brechmos* front part of the head] : the point of junction of the coronal and sagittal sutures of the skull — **breg·mat·ic** \breg-'mat-ik\ *adj*

brems·strah·lung \'brem(psh)-,shträl-əŋ\ *n* [G, lit., decelerated radiation] : the electromagnetic radiation produced by the sudden retardation of an electrical particle in an intense electric field

brent \'brent\ *var of* BRANT

brethren *pl of* BROTHER — used chiefly in formal or solemn address

Breth·ren \'breth-(ə-)rən, -ərn\ *n pl* : members of various sects originating chiefly in 18th century German Pietism; *esp* : DUNKERS

Bret·on \'bret-ᵊn\ *n* [F, fr. ML *Briton-, Brito*, fr. L, Briton] **1** : a native or inhabitant of Brittany **2 a** : the Celtic language of the Breton people **b** : the Brythonic division of Celtic — **Breton** *adj*

breve \'brēv, 'brev\ *n* [ME — more at BRIEF] **1** : a curved mark ˘ used to indicate a short vowel or a short or unstressed syllable **2** : a note equivalent to four half notes

[1]**bre·vet** \brə-'vet, *chiefly Brit* 'brev-it\ *n* [ME, an official message, fr. MF, fr. OF, dim. of *brief* letter] : a commission giving a military officer higher nominal rank than that for which he receives pay

[2]**brevet** *vt* **bre·vet·ted** *or* **brev·et·ed**; **bre·vet·ting** *or* **brev·et·ing** : to confer rank upon by brevet

bre·via·ry \'brē-v(y)ə-rē, -vē-,er-ē\ *n* [L *breviarium*, fr. *brevis* — more at BRIEF] **1** : a brief summary : ABRIDGMENT **2** *often cap* [ML *breviarium*, fr. L] **a** : a book containing the prayers, hymns, psalms, and readings for the canonical hours **b** : DIVINE OFFICE

brev·i·ty \'brev-ət-ē\ *n* [L *brevitas*, fr. *brevis*] **1** : shortness of duration **2** : expression in few words : CONCISENESS

[1]**brew** \'brü\ *vb* [ME *brewen*, fr. OE *brēowan*; akin to L *fervēre* to boil] **1** : to prepare by steeping, boiling, and fermentation or by infusion and fermentation **2 a** : to bring about (trouble) as if by brewing magical potions **b** : CONTRIVE, PLOT ~ *vi* **1** : to brew beer or ale **2** : to be forming — **brew·er** \'brü-ər, 'bru̇(-ə)r\ *n*

[2]**brew** *n* **1 a** : a brewed beverage **b** : a product of brewing **2** : the process of brewing

brew·age \'brü-ij\ *n* : BREW

brewer's yeast *n* : a yeast used or suitable for use in brewing; *specif* : the dried pulverized cells of a yeast (*Saccharomyces cerevisiae*) used esp. as a source of B-complex vitamins

brew·ery \'brü-ə-rē, 'bru̇(-ə)r-ē\ *n* : a plant where malt liquors are manufactured

brewis \'brüz, 'brü-əs\ *n* [ME *brewes*, fr. OF *broez*, nom. sing. accus. pl. of *broet*, dim. of *breu* broth, of Gmc origin] *dial* : BROTH

[1]**bri·ar** \'brī(-ə)r\ *var of* BRIER

[2]**briar** *n* : a tobacco pipe made from the root of a brier

bri·ard \brē-'är(d)\ *n* [F, fr. *Brie*, district in France] : any of an old French breed of large strong usu. black dogs

brib·able \'brī-bə-bəl\ *adj* : capable of being bribed

[1]**bribe** \'brīb\ *vt* : to induce or influence by or as if by bribery ~ *vi* : to practice bribery — **brib·er** *n*

[2]**bribe** *n* [ME, something stolen, fr. MF, bread given to a beggar] **1** : money or favor bestowed on or promised to a person in a position of trust to pervert his judgment or corrupt his conduct **2** : something that serves to induce or influence

brib·ery \'brī-b(ə-)rē\ *n* : the act or practice of bribing

bric-a-brac \'brik-ə-,brak\ *n* [F *bric-à-brac*] : a miscellaneous collection of often antique articles of virtu : CURIOS

[1]**brick** \'brik\ *n* [ME *bryke*, fr. MF *brique*, fr. MD *bricke*; akin to OE *brecan* to break] **1** *pl* **bricks** *or* **brick** : a handy-sized unit of building or paving material typically of moist clay hardened by heat **2** *slang* : a good fellow **3** : a rectangular compressed mass

[2]**brick** *vt* : to close, face, or pave with bricks

brick·bat \'brik-,bat\ *n* **1** : a fragment of a hard material (as a brick) esp. when used as a missile **2** : an uncomplimentary remark

brick·lay·er \'brik-,lā-ər, -,le(-ə)r\ *n* : one who lays brick

brick·le \'brik-əl\ *adj* [ME *brekyl*] *dial* : BRITTLE

brick red *n* : a variable color averaging a moderate reddish brown

brick·work \'brik-,wərk\ *n* : work of or with brick

brick·yard \-,yärd\ *n* : a place where bricks are made

[1]**brid·al** \'brīd-ᵊl\ *n* [ME *bridale*, fr. OE *brȳdealu*, fr. *brȳd* + *ealu* ale — more at ALE] : a nuptial festival or ceremony : MARRIAGE

[2]**bridal** *adj* : of or relating to a bride or a wedding : NUPTIAL

bridal wreath *n* : a spirea (*Spiraea prunifolia*) widely grown for its umbels of small white flowers borne in spring

bride \'brīd\ *n* [ME, fr. OE *brȳd*; akin to OHG *brūt* bride] : a woman newly married or about to be married

bride·groom \'brīd-,grüm, -,gru̇m\ *n* [ME *bridegome*, fr. OE *brȳdguma*; akin to OHG *brūtigomo* bridegroom; both fr. a prehistoric NGmc-WGmc compound whose constituents are represented by OE *brȳd* and by OE *guma* man] : a man newly married or about to be married

brides·maid \'brīdz-,mād\ *n* : a woman attendant of a bride

bride·well \'brī-,dwel, -dwəl\ *n* [*Bridewell*, London jail] : PRISON

[1]**bridge** \'brij\ *n* [ME *brigge*, fr. OE *brycg*; akin to OHG *brucka*

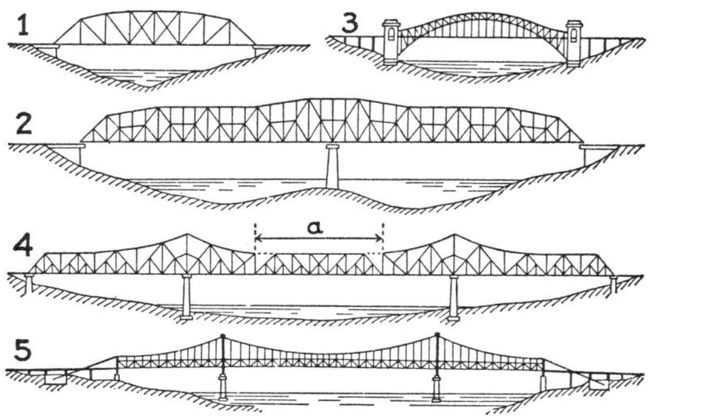

bridges 1a: *1* simple truss; *2* continuous truss; *3* steel arch; *4* cantilever, *a* suspended span; *5* suspension

bridge, OSlav *brŭvŭno* beam] **1 a** : a structure carrying a roadway over a depression or obstacle **b** : a time, place, or means of connection or transition **2** : something resembling a bridge in form or function: as **a** : the upper bony part of the nose; *also* : the part of a pair of glasses that rests upon it **b** : an arch serving to raise the strings of a musical instrument **c** : a raised transverse platform on a ship from which it is conned **d** : GANTRY 2b **3** : something (as a partial denture anchored to adjacent teeth) that fills a gap **4** : an electrical instrument or network for measuring or comparing resistances, inductances, capacitances, or impedances by comparing the ratio of two opposing voltages to a known ratio

[2]**bridge** *vt* **1** : to make a bridge over or across; *also* : to traverse by a bridge **2** : to provide with a bridge — **bridge·able** \-ə-bəl\ *adj*

[3]**bridge** *n* [origin unknown] : any of various card games for four players developed from whist; *esp* : CONTRACT BRIDGE

bridge·board \'brij-,bō(ə)rd, -,bȯ(ə)rd\ *n* : STRING 7a

bridge·head \-,hed\ *n* **1 a** : a defensive work protecting the end of a bridge nearest an enemy **b** : a locality fortified to protect a bridge site, ford, or defile from attack from the other side **c** : an area around the end of a bridge **2** : an advanced position seized in hostile territory as a foothold for further advance

bridge·work \'brij-,wərk\ *n* : a dental bridge

[1]**bri·dle** \'brīd-ᵊl\ *n* [ME *bridel*, fr. OE *brīdel*; akin to OE *bregdan* to move quickly] **1 a** : the headgear with which a horse is governed consisting of a headstall, a bit, and reins **b** : a strip of metal joining two parts of a machine esp. for limiting or restraining motion **2** : something resembling a bridle in shape or function: as **a** : a length of secured cable with a second cable attached to the bight to which force is applied **b** : CURB, RESTRAINT **c** : FRENUM

2**bridle** *vb* **bri·dling** \'brīd-liŋ, -ᵊl-iŋ\ *vt* **1 :** to put a bridle upon **2 :** to restrain with a bridle ~ *vi* **:** to show hostility or resentment esp. by drawing back the head and chin **syn** see RESTRAIN

bridle path *n* **:** a trail passable to or designed for horses

Brie \'brē\ *n* [F, fr. *Brie,* district in France] **:** a soft perishable cheese ripened by mold

1**brief** \'brēf\ *adj* [ME *bref, breve,* fr. MF *brief,* fr. L *brevis;* akin to OHG *murg* short, Gk *brachys*] **1 :** short in duration or extent **2 a :** CONCISE **b :** CURT, ABRUPT — **brief·ly** *adv* — **brief·ness** *n*
syn BRIEF, SHORT mean lacking length. BRIEF applies primarily to duration and may imply condensation, conciseness, or occas. intensity; SHORT may imply sudden stoppage or incompleteness

2**brief** *n* [ME *bref,* fr. MF, fr. ML *brevis,* fr. LL, summary, fr. L *brevis,* adj.] **1 :** an official letter or mandate; *esp* **:** a papal letter less formal than a bull **2 :** a brief written item or document: as **a :** a concise article **b :** SYNOPSIS, SUMMARY **c :** a concise statement of a client's case made out for the instruction of counsel in a trial at law **3 :** an outline of an argument; *esp* **:** a formal outline esp. in law that sets forth the main contentions with supporting statements or evidence **4 :** short snug underpants — usu. used in pl.

3**brief** *vt* **1 :** to make an abstract or abridgment of **2** *Brit* **:** to retain as legal counsel **3 a :** to give final precise instructions to **b :** to coach thoroughly in advance **c :** to give essential information to

brief·case \-,kās\ *n* **:** a flat leather case to carry papers

brief·less \'brē-fləs\ *adj* **:** having no legal clients

1**bri·er** \'brī(-ə)r\ *n* [ME *brere,* fr. OE *brēr*] **:** a plant (as of the genera *Rosa, Rubus,* and *Smilax*) with a woody thorny or prickly stem; *also* **:** a mass or twig of these — **bri·ery** \'brī-(ə-)rē\ *adj*

2**brier** *n* [F *bruyère* heath, fr. (assumed) VL *brucaria,* fr. LL *brucus* heather, of Celt origin] **:** a heath (*Erica arborea*) of southern Europe the root of which is used for making pipes

bri·er·root \'brī(-ə)r-,rüt, -,ru̇t\ *n* **:** a root (as of the brier *Erica arborea*) used for tobacco pipes

1**brig** \'brig\ *n* [short for *brigantine*] **:** a 2-masted square-rigged ship — compare HERMAPHRODITE BRIG

2**brig** *n* [prob. fr. 1*brig*] **:** a place (as on a ship) for temporary confinement of offenders in the U.S. Navy **:** GUARDHOUSE, PRISON

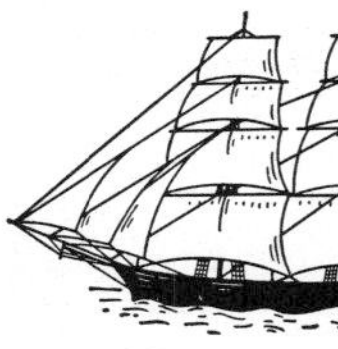
brig

3**brig** *chiefly Scot var of* BRIDGE

1**bri·gade** \brig-'ād\ *n* [F, fr. It *brigata,* fr. *brigare*] **1 a :** a large body of troops **b :** a tactical and administrative unit composed of a headquarters, one or more units of infantry or armor, and supporting units **2 :** a group of people organized for special activity

2**brigade** *vt* **:** to form or unite into a brigade

brig·a·dier \,brig-ə-'di(ə)r\ *n* [F, fr. *brigade*] **1 :** BRIGADIER GENERAL **2 :** an officer in the British army commanding a brigade

brigadier general *n* **:** a commissioned officer in the army, air force, or marine corps ranking above a colonel and below a major general

brig·and \'brig-ənd\ *n* [ME *brigaunt,* fr. MF *brigand,* fr. OIt *brigante,* fr. *brigare* to fight, fr. *briga* strife, of Celt origin] **:** one who lives by plunder usu. as a member of a band **:** BANDIT — **brig·and·age** \-ən-dij\ *n* — **brig·and·ism** \-ən-,diz-əm\ *n*

brig·an·dine \'brig-ən-,dēn\ *n* [ME, fr. MF, fr. *brigand*] **:** medieval body armor of scales or plates

brig·an·tine \'brig-ən-,tēn\ *n* [MF *brigantin,* fr. OIt *brigantino,* fr. *brigante*] **1 :** a 2-masted square-rigged ship differing from a brig in not carrying a square mainsail **2 :** HERMAPHRODITE BRIG

bright \'brīt\ *adj* [ME, fr. OE *beorht;* akin to OHG *beraht* bright Skt *bhrājate* it shines] **1 a :** radiating or reflecting light **:** SHINING **b :** radiant with happiness or good fortune **2 :** ILLUSTRIOUS, GLORIOUS **3 :** resplendent with charms **4 :** of high saturation or brilliance ⟨~ colors⟩ **5 :** INTELLIGENT, CLEVER; *also* **:** LIVELY, CHEERFUL — **bright** *adv* — **bright·ly** *adv* — **bright·ness** *n*
syn BRILLIANT, RADIANT, LUMINOUS, LUSTROUS: BRIGHT implies emitting or reflecting a high degree of light; BRILLIANT implies intense often sparkling brightness; RADIANT stresses sending forth light but often means no more than BRIGHT; LUMINOUS implies emission of steady, suffused, glowing light by reflection or in surrounding darkness; LUSTROUS stresses an even, rich light from a surface that reflects brightly without sparkling or glittering

bright·en \'brīt-ᵊn\ *vt* **bright·en·ing** \'brīt-niŋ, ᵊn-iŋ\ **:** to make bright or brighter ~ *vi* **:** to become bright or brighter

Bright's disease \'brīts-\ *n* [Richard *Bright* †1858 E physician] **:** any of several kidney diseases attended with albumin in the urine

bright·work \'brīt-,wərk\ *n* **:** polished or plated metalwork

brill \'bril\ *n, pl* **brill** [perh. fr. Corn *brȳthel* mackerel] **:** a European flatfish (*Bothus rhombus*) related to the turbot; *broadly* **:** TURBOT

bril·liance \'bril-yən(t)s\ *n* **:** the quality or state of being brilliant

bril·lian·cy \-yən-sē\ *n* **1 :** BRILLIANCE **2 :** an instance of brilliance

1**bril·liant** \'bril-yənt\ *adj* [F *brillant,* prp. of *briller* to shine, fr. It *brillare,* fr. *brillo* beryl, fr. L *beryllus*] **1 :** very bright **:** GLITTERING ⟨a ~ light⟩ **2 a :** STRIKING, DISTINGUISHED **b :** distinguished by unusual mental keenness or alertness **syn** see BRIGHT — **brilliant·ly** *adv* — **bril·liant·ness** *n*

2**brilliant** *n* **:** a diamond or other gem cut in a particular form with numerous facets so as to have especial brilliancy

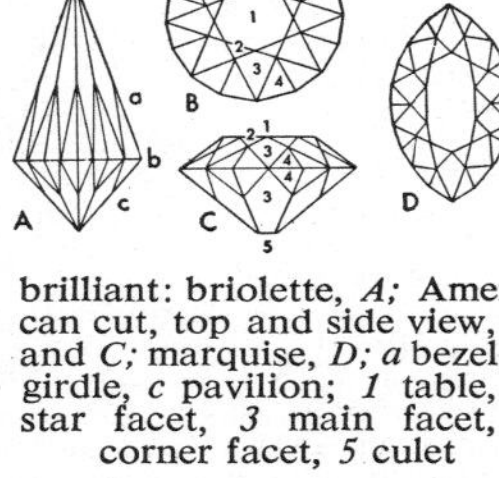
brilliant: briolette, *A;* American cut, top and side view, *B* and *C;* marquise, *D; a* bezel, *b* girdle, *c* pavilion; *1* table, *2* star facet, *3* main facet, *4* corner facet, *5* culet

bril·lian·tine \'bril-yən-,tēn\ *n* **1 :** a preparation for making hair glossy **2 :** a light lustrous fabric similar to alpaca usu. of cotton and mohair or worsted

Brill's disease \'brilz-\ *n* [Nathan E. *Brill* †1925 Am physician] **:** an acute infectious disease held to be a mild form of typhus

1**brim** \'brim\ *n* [ME *brimme;* akin to MHG *brem* edge] **1 a :** the edge or rim esp. of a cup, bowl, or depression ⟨the ~ of the crater⟩ **b :** BRINK, VERGE **2 :** the projecting rim of a hat **syn** see BORDER — **brim·ful** \-'fu̇l\ *adj*

2**brim** *vb* **brimmed; brim·ming** *vt* **:** to fill to the brim ~ *vi* **1 :** to become full to the brim **2 :** to reach or overflow a brim

brim·mer \'brim-ər\ *n* **:** a cup or glass brimful

brim·stone \'brim-,stōn, *chiefly Brit* 'brim(p)-stən\ *n* [ME *brinston,* prob. fr. *birnen* to burn + *ston* stone] **:** SULFUR

brind·ed \'brin-dəd\ *adj* [ME *brended*] *archaic* **:** BRINDLED

brin·dle \'brin-dᵊl\ *n* [*brindle,* adj.] **:** a brindled color or animal

brin·dled \-dᵊld\ *or* **brin·dle** \-dᵊl\ *adj* [alter. of *brinded*] **:** having obscure dark streaks or flecks on a gray or tawny ground

1**brine** \'brīn\ *n* [ME, fr. OE *brȳne;* akin to MD *brīne* brine, L *fricare* to rub — more at FRICTION] **1 a :** water saturated or strongly impregnated with common salt **b :** a strong saline solution (as of calcium chloride) **2 :** the water of a sea or salt lake

2**brine** *vt* **:** to treat (as by steeping) with brine — **brin·er** *n*

Bri·nell hardness \brə-,nel-\ *n* [Johann A. *Brinell* †1925 Sw engineer] **:** the hardness of a metal or alloy measured by hydraulically pressing a hard ball under a standard load into the specimen

Brinell number *n* **:** a number expressing Brinell hardness and denoting the load applied in testing in kilograms divided by the spherical area of indentation produced in the specimen in square millimeters

brine shrimp *n* **:** a branchiopod crustacean (genus *Artemia*)

bring \'briŋ\ *vb* **brought** \'bro̊t\ **bring·ing** \'briŋ-iŋ\ [ME *bringen,* fr. OE *bringan;* akin to OHG *bringan* to bring, W *hebrwng* to accompany] *vt* **1 a :** to convey, lead, carry, or cause to come along with one toward the place from which the action is being regarded **b :** to cause to be, act, or move in a special way: as (1) **:** ATTRACT (2) **:** PERSUADE, INDUCE (3) **:** FORCE, COMPEL (4) **:** to cause to come into a particular state or condition **c** *dial* **:** ESCORT, ACCOMPANY **2 :** to cause to exist or occur: as **a :** PRODUCE ⟨winter will ~ snow and ice⟩ **b :** to result in **:** EFFECT **c :** INSTITUTE ⟨~ legal action⟩ **d :** ADDUCE ⟨~ an argument⟩ **3 :** PREFER ⟨~ a charge⟩ **4 :** to procure in exchange **:** sell for ~ *vi, chiefly Midland* **:** YIELD, PRODUCE

bring about *vt* **:** to cause to take place **:** EFFECT

bring down *vt* **1 :** to cause to fall esp. by shooting **2 :** to carry (a total) forward

bring forth *vt* **:** to bear (as fruit) or give birth to **:** PRODUCE

bring forward *vt* **1 :** to produce to view **:** INTRODUCE **2 :** to carry (a total) forward

bring in *vt* **1 :** to produce as profit or return **2 :** to enable (a man on base) to reach home plate by a hit **3 :** to report to a court ⟨jury *brought in* a verdict⟩ **4 a :** to cause (as an oil well) to be productive **b :** to win tricks with the long cards of (a suit) in bridge

bring off *vt* **1 :** to cause to escape **:** RESCUE **2 :** to achieve or carry to a successful issue

bring on *vt* **:** to cause to come into action or existence

bring out *vt* **1 :** to make more noticeable **2 a :** to present to the public **b :** to introduce formally to society **3 :** UTTER

bring to *vt* **1 :** to cause (a boat) to lie to or come to a standstill **2 :** to restore to consciousness

bring up *vt* **1 :** REAR, EDUCATE **2 :** to cause to stop suddenly **3 :** to bring to attention **:** INTRODUCE **4 :** VOMIT ~ *vi* **:** to stop suddenly

brin·i·ness \'brī-nē-nəs\ *n* **:** the quality or state of being briny

brink \'briŋk\ *n* [ME, prob. of Scand origin; akin to ON *brekka* slope; akin to L *front-, frons* forehead] **1 :** EDGE, BORDER; *esp* **:** the very edge at the top of a steep place **2 :** a bank esp. of a river **3 :** the point of onset **:** VERGE ⟨~ of war⟩ **syn** see BORDER

brink·man·ship \'briŋk-mən-,ship\ *n* [*brink* + *-manship* (as in *horsemanship*)] **:** the practice of pushing a dangerous situation to the limit of safety before stopping

briny \'brī-nē\ *adj* **:** of or resembling brine or the sea **:** SALTY

brio \'brē-(,)ō\ *n* [It] **:** VIVACITY, SPIRIT

bri·oche \brē-'ōsh, -'o̊sh\ *n* [F, fr. MF dial., fr. *brier* to knead, of Gmc origin; akin to OHG *brehhan* to break — more at BREAK] **:** a roll baked from light yeast dough rich with eggs and butter

bri·o·lette \,brē-ə-'let\ *n* [F] **:** an oval or pear-shaped diamond cut in triangular facets

bri·quette *or* **bri·quet** \brik-'et\ *n* [F *briquette,* dim. of *brique* brick] **:** a compacted often brick-shaped mass of usu. fine material

bri·sance \bri-'zän(t)s, -'zäⁿs\ *n* [F, fr. *brisant,* prp. of *briser* to break, fr. OF *brisier,* of Celt origin; akin to OIr *brissim* I break; akin to L *fricare* to rub — more at FRICTION] **:** the shattering or crushing effect of an explosive — **bri·sant** \-'zänt, -'zäⁿ\ *adj*

Bri·se·is \brī-'sē-əs\ *n* [L, fr. Gk *Briseis*] **:** a woman captive of Achilles taken away from him by Agamemnon

1**brisk** \'brisk\ *adj* [prob. modif. of MF *brusque*] **1 :** keenly alert **:** LIVELY **2 a :** pleasingly tangy ⟨~ tea⟩ **b :** INVIGORATING, FRESH ⟨~ weather⟩ **3 :** sharp in tone or manner **4 :** ENERGETIC, QUICK ⟨a ~ pace⟩ **syn** see AGILE — **brisk·ly** *adv* — **brisk·ness** *n*

2**brisk** *vt* **:** to make brisk ~ *vi* **:** to become brisk ⟨the market ~*ed* up⟩

bris·ket \'bris-kət\ *n* [ME *brusket;* akin to OE *brēost* breast] **:** the breast or lower chest of a quadruped animal

bris·ling *or* **bris·tling** \'briz-liŋ, 'bris-\ *n* [Norw *brisling,* fr. LG *bretling,* fr. *bret* broad; akin to OE *brād* broad] **:** a small herring (*Clupea sprattus*) that resembles and is processed like a sardine

1**bris·tle** \'bris-əl\ *n* [ME *bristil,* fr. *brust* bristle, fr. OE *byrst;* akin to OHG *burst* bristle, L *fastigium* top] **:** a short stiff coarse hair or filament — **bris·tle·like** \'bris-ə(l)-,līk\ *adj* — **bris·tly** \'bris-(ə-)lē\ *adj*

2**bristle** *vb* **bris·tling** \'bris-(ə-)liŋ\ *vi* **1 a :** to rise and stand stiffly erect ⟨quills *bristling* in all directions⟩ **b :** to raise the bristles (as in anger) **2 :** to take on an aggressive attitude or appearance **3 :** to appear as if covered with bristles ⟨~ with difficulties⟩ ~ *vt* **1 :** to furnish with bristles **2 :** to make bristly **:** RUFFLE

bris·tle·tail \'bris-əl-,tāl\ *n* **:** any of various wingless insects (orders Thysanura and Entotrophi) with two slender caudal bristles

bris·tol \'brist-ᵊl\ *n* [*Bristol,* England] **:** cardboard with a smooth surface suitable for writing or printing

brit *or* **britt** \'brit\ *n* [Corn *brȳthel* mackerel] **1 :** young or small herring or other small schooling fishes **2 :** minute marine animals largely crustaceans and pteropods

bri·tan·nia metal \bri-,tan-yə-, -,tan-ē-ə-\ *n* [*Britannia,* poetic

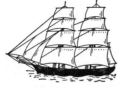

name for Great Britain, fr. L] **:** a silver-white alloy largely of tin, antimony, and copper similar to pewter

Bri·tan·nic \bri-'tan-ik\ *adj* **:** BRITISH

britch·es \'brich-əz\ *n pl* [alter. of *breeches*] **:** BREECHES, PANTS

Brit·i·cism \'brit-ə-,siz-əm\ *n* [*Brit*ish + *-icism* (as in *gallicism*)] **:** a characteristic feature of British English

Brit·ish \'brit-ish\ *n* [ME *Bruttische* of Britain, fr. OE *Brettisc*, of Celt origin; akin to W *Brython* Briton] **1 a :** the Celtic language of the ancient Britons **b :** BRITISH ENGLISH **2 :** the people of Great Britain or the British Commonwealth — **British** *adj*

British English *n* **:** the native language of most inhabitants of England; *esp* **:** English characteristic of England and clearly distinguishable from that used in the U.S., Australia, and elsewhere

Brit·ish·er \'brit-i-shər\ *n* **:** BRITON 2

British thermal unit *n* **:** the quantity of heat required to raise the temperature of one pound of water one degree Fahrenheit at or near 39.2°F

Brit·on \'brit-ᵊn\ *n* [ME *Breton*, fr. MF & L; MF, fr. L *Briton-*, *Brito*, of Celt origin; akin to W *Brython*] **1 :** a member of one of the peoples inhabiting Britain previous to the Anglo-Saxon invasions **2 :** a native or subject of Great Britain; *esp* **:** ENGLISHMAN

brits·ka *or* **britz·ska** \'brich-kə, 'brit-skə\ *n* [G *britschka*] **:** a long open carriage with a folding top over the rear seat and a front seat facing the rear

Brit·ta·ny spaniel \,brit-ᵊn-ē-\ *n* [*Brittany*, region in France] **:** a large active spaniel of a French breed developed by interbreeding pointers with spaniels of Brittany

1**brit·tle** \'brit-ᵊl\ *adj* [ME *britil;* akin to OE *brēotan* to break, Skt *bhrūṇa* embryo] **1 a :** easily broken, cracked, or snapped ⟨~ clay⟩ ⟨~ glass⟩ **b :** easily disrupted, overthrown, or damaged **:** FRAIL **c :** requiring careful handling **:** DIFFICULT ⟨~ personality⟩ **d :** SHARP, TENSE ⟨~ staccato of snare drums⟩ **2 a :** PERISHABLE, MORTAL **b :** TRANSITORY, EVANESCENT **3 :** lacking warmth, depth, or generosity of spirit **:** COLD **syn** see FRAGILE — **brit·tle·ness** *n*

2**brittle** *n* **:** candy made by boiling sugar until it caramelizes, adding nuts, and cooling in thin sheets

Brit·ton·ic \bri-'tän-ik\ *adj* [L *Britton-*, *Britto* Briton] **:** BRYTHONIC 2

Brix scale \'brik(s)-'skā(ə)l\ *n* [Adolf F. *Brix* †1870 G scientist] **:** a hydrometer scale for sugar solutions so graduated that its readings at a specified temperature represent percentages by weight of sugar in the solution

1**broach** \'brōch\ *n* [ME *broche*, fr. MF, fr. (assumed) VL *brocca*, fr. L, fem. of *broccus* projecting] **1 :** any of various pointed or tapered tools, implements, or parts: as **a :** a spit for roasting meat **b :** a tool for tapping casks **2 :** BROOCH

2**broach** *vt* **1 a :** to pierce (as a cask) in order to draw the contents **:** TAP **b :** to open up or break into (as a mine or stores) **2 :** to shape or enlarge (a hole) with a boring tool **3 a :** to make known for the first time **b :** to open up (a subject) for discussion ~ *vi* **:** to break the surface from below **syn** see EXPRESS — **broach·er** *n*

3**broach** *vb* [perh. fr. 2*broach*] *vi* **:** to veer or yaw dangerously esp. in a following sea so as to lie beam on to the waves — used chiefly with *to* ~ *vt* **:** to cause (a boat) to broach

1**broad** \'brȯd\ *adj* [ME *brood*, fr. OE *brād;* akin to OHG *breit* broad] **1 :** extended in breadth **:** WIDE **2 :** extending far and wide **:** SPACIOUS **3 a :** OPEN, FULL **b :** PLAIN, OBVIOUS **4 :** marked by lack of restraint, delicacy, or subtlety: **a** *obs* **:** OUTSPOKEN **b :** COARSE, INDELICATE ⟨~ stories⟩ **5 a :** LIBERAL, CATHOLIC ⟨~ views⟩ **b :** widely applicable or applied **:** GENERAL **6 :** relating to the main or essential points ⟨~ outlines⟩ **7 :** dialectal esp. in pronunciation **8** *of a vowel* **:** OPEN — used specif. of *a* pronounced as in *father* — **broad·ly** *adv* — **broad·ness** *n*

syn BROAD, WIDE, DEEP mean having horizontal extent. BROAD and WIDE apply to a surface measured or viewed from side to side ⟨*broad* pathway⟩ WIDE is more common when units of measurement are mentioned ⟨rugs eight feet *wide*⟩ or applied to unfilled space between limits ⟨*wide* doorway⟩ BROAD is preferred when full horizontal extent is considered ⟨*broad* shoulders⟩ DEEP may indicate horizontal extent away from the observer or from a front or peripheral point ⟨a *deep* lot⟩ ⟨*deep* woods⟩

2**broad** *adv* **:** BROADLY, WIDELY ⟨~ awake⟩

3**broad** *n* **1 :** the broad part (as of the hand) **2** *Brit* **:** an expansion of a river — often used in pl. **3** *slang* **:** WOMAN

broad arrow *n* **1 :** an arrow with a flat barbed head **2** *Brit* **:** a broad arrow mark identifying government property including convicts' clothing

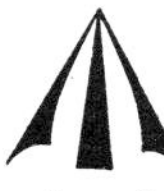

broad arrow 2

broad·ax *or* **broad·axe** \'brȯ-,daks\ *n* **:** a large ax with a broad blade

broad bean *n* **:** the large flat edible seed of an Old World upright vetch (*Vicia faba*); *also* **:** this plant widely grown for its seeds and as fodder

1**broad·cast** \'brȯd-,kast\ *adj* **1 :** cast or scattered in all directions **2 :** made public by means of radio or television — **broadcast** *adv*

2**broadcast** *n* **1 :** the act of transmitting sound or images by radio or television **2 :** a single radio or television program

3**broadcast** *vb* **broadcast** *also* **broad·cast·ed; broad·cast·ing** *vt* **1 :** to scatter or sow (seed) broadcast **2 :** to make widely known **3 :** to transmit as a broadcast ~ *vi* **1 :** to transmit a broadcast **2 :** to speak or perform on a broadcast program — **broad·cast·er** *n*

Broad Church *adj* **:** of or relating to a liberal party in the Anglican communion esp. in the later 19th century — **Broad Churchman** *n*

broad·cloth \'brȯd-,klȯth\ *n* **1 :** a twilled napped woolen or worsted fabric with smooth lustrous face and dense texture **2 :** a fabric usu. of cotton, silk, or rayon made in plain and rib weaves with soft semigloss finish

broad·en \'brȯd-ᵊn\ *vb* **broad·en·ing** \'brȯd-niŋ, -ᵊn-iŋ\ *vi* **:** to become broad ~ *vt* **:** to make broader

broad gauge *n* **:** a railroad gauge wider than standard gauge — **broad–gauged** \'brȯd-'gājd\ *adj*

broad hatchet *n* **:** a short-handled hatchet with a broad cutting blade and rectangular hammering face opposite

broad jump *n* **:** a jump for distance in track-and-field athletics — **broad jumper** *n*

broad·leaf \'brȯd-,lēf\ *adj* **:** BROAD-LEAVED

broad–leaved \-'lēvd\ *or* **broad–leafed** \-'lēft\ *adj* **:** having broad leaves; *specif* **:** having leaves that are not needles ⟨~ evergreens⟩

broad·loom \-,lüm\ *adj* **:** woven on a wide loom; *also* **:** so woven in solid color ⟨~ carpeting⟩ — **broadloom** *n*

broad–mind·ed \-'mīn-dəd\ *adj* **1 :** tolerant of varied views **:** CATHOLIC **2 :** inclined to condone minor departures from orthodox behavior — **broad–mind·ed·ly** *adv* — **broad–mind·ed·ness** *n*

1**broad·side** \'brȯd-,sīd\ *n* **1 :** the side of a ship above the waterline **2 :** a broad or unbroken surface **3 a** *archaic* **:** a sheet of paper printed on one side **b :** a sheet printed on one or both sides and folded **4 :** something (as a ballad) printed on a broadside **5 a :** all the guns on one side of a ship; *also* **:** their simultaneous discharge **b :** a volley of abuse or denunciation

2**broadside** *adv* **1 :** with the broadside toward a given object or point **2 :** in one volley **3 :** at random — **broadside** *adj*

broad–spectrum *adj* **:** effective against various microorganisms

broad·sword \'brȯd-,sō(ə)rd, -,sȯ(ə)rd\ *n* **:** a sword with a broad blade for cutting rather than thrusting

broad·tail \-,tāl\ *n* **1 a :** KARAKUL 1 **b :** a fat-tailed sheep **2 :** the fur or skin of a very young or premature karakul lamb having a flat and wavy appearance resembling moiré silk

broad·wife \-,wīf\ *n* [*abroad* + *wife*] **:** the wife of a slave belonging to another master in the slaveholding states of the U.S.

Brob·ding·nag·ian \,bräb-diŋ-'nag-ē-ən, -dig-'nag-\ *n* **:** an inhabitant of a country in Swift's *Gulliver's Travels* where everything is on a giant scale — **Brobdingnagian** *adj*

bro·cade \brō-'kād\ *n* [Sp *brocado*, fr. Catal *brocat*, fr. It *broccato*, fr. *broccare* to spur, brocade, fr. *brocco* small nail, fr. L *broccus* projecting] **1 :** a rich oriental silk fabric with raised patterns in gold and silver **2 :** a fabric characterized by raised designs — **brocade** *vt* — **bro·cad·ed** \-'kād-əd\ *adj*

broc·a·telle \,bräk-ə-'tel\ *n* [F, fr. It *broccatello*, dim. of *broccato*] **:** a stiff decorating fabric with patterns in high relief

broc·co·li *or* **broc·o·li** \'bräk-(ə-)lē\ *n* [It, pl. of *broccolo* flowering top of a cabbage, dim. of *brocco* small nail, sprout] **:** a large hardy cauliflower; *esp* **:** a branching cauliflower with a head of functional florets at the end of each branch — called also *sprouting broccoli*

bro·chette \brō-'shet\ *n* [F, fr. OF *brochete*, fr. *broche* pointed tool — more at BROACH] **:** a small spit **:** SKEWER

bro·chure \brō-'shü(ə)r\ *n* [F, fr. *brocher* to sew, fr. MF, to prick, fr. OF *brochier*, fr. *broche*] **:** PAMPHLET, BOOKLET

brock \'bräk\ *n* [ME, fr. OE *broc*, of Celt origin] **:** BADGER

brock·et \'bräk-ət\ *n* [ME *broket*] **1 :** a male red deer two years old — compare PRICKET **2 :** any of several small So. American deer (genus *Mazama*) with unbranched horns

bro·gan \'brō-gən, brō-'gan\ *n* [IrGael *brōgan*, dim. of *brōg*] **:** a heavy shoe; *esp* **:** a coarse work shoe reaching to the ankle

1**brogue** \'brōg\ *n* [IrGael & ScGael *brōg*, fr. MIr *brōc*, fr. ON *brōk* leg covering; akin to OE *brōc* leg covering — more at BREECH] **1 :** a stout coarse shoe worn formerly in Ireland and the Scottish Highlands **2 :** a heavy shoe often with a hobnailed sole **:** BROGAN **3 :** a stout oxford shoe with perforations and usu. a wing tip

2**brogue** *n* [perh. fr. IrGael *barrōg* wrestling hold; fr. the idea that unfamiliar features of pronunciation must be the result of a physical impediment of the tongue] **:** a dialect or regional pronunciation; *esp* **:** an Irish accent

broi·der \'brȯid-ər\ *vt* [ME *broideren*, modif. of MF *broder* — more at EMBROIDER] **:** EMBROIDER — **broi·dery** \'brȯid-(ə-)rē\ *n*

1**broil** \'brȯi(ə)l\ *vb* [ME *broilen*, fr. MF *bruler* to burn, modif. of L *ustulare* to singe, fr. *ustus*, pp. of *urere* to burn] *vt* **:** to cook by direct exposure to radiant heat **:** GRILL ~ *vi* **:** to become broiled

2**broil** *n* **1 :** the act or state of broiling **2 :** something broiled **:** GRILL

3**broil** *vb* [ME *broilen*, fr. MF *brouiller* to mix, broil, fr. OF *brooilier*, fr. *breu* broth — more at BREWIS] *vt* **:** EMBROIL ~ *vi* **:** BRAWL

4**broil** *n* **:** a noisy disturbance **:** TUMULT; *esp* **:** QUARREL

broil·er \'brȯi-lər\ *n* **1 :** one that broils **2 :** a bird fit for broiling; *esp* **:** a young chicken of up to 2½ pounds dressed

1**broke** \'brōk\ *adj* [ME, alter. of *broken*] **:** PENNILESS

2**broke** *past of* BREAK

bro·ken \'brō-kən\ *adj* [ME, fr. OE *brocen*, fr. pp. of *brecan* to break] **1 :** violently separated into parts **:** SHATTERED **2 :** damaged or altered by or as if by breaking: as **a :** FRACTURED ⟨a ~ leg⟩ **b** *of land surfaces* **:** being irregular, interrupted, or full of obstacles **c :** violated by transgression ⟨a ~ promise⟩ **d :** INTERRUPTED, DISCONTINUOUS **e :** disrupted by change ⟨~ home⟩ **f** *of a flower* **:** having an irregular, streaked, or blotched pattern esp. from virus infection **3 a :** made weak or infirm **b :** SUBDUED, CRUSHED ⟨a ~ spirit⟩ **c :** BANKRUPT **d :** reduced in rank **4 a :** cut off **:** DISCONNECTED **b :** imperfectly spoken or written ⟨~ English⟩ **5 :** not complete or full — **bro·ken·ly** *adv* — **bro·ken·ness** \-kən-nəs\ *n*

bro·ken·heart·ed \,brō-kən-'härt-əd\ *adj* **:** crushed by grief or despair

broken wind *n* **:** HEAVES — **bro·ken–wind·ed** \,brō-kən-'win-dəd\ *adj*

bro·ker \'brō-kər\ *n* [ME, negotiator, fr. (assumed) AF *brocour;* akin to OF *broche* pointed tool, tap of a cask] **1 a :** an agent who arranges marriages **b :** an agent who negotiates contracts of purchase and sale **2** *Brit* **:** a dealer in secondhand goods

bro·ker·age \'brō-k(ə-)rij\ *n* **1 :** the business of a broker **2 :** the fee or commission for transacting business as a broker

brom- *or* **bromo-** *comb form* [prob. fr. F *brome*, fr. Gk *brōmos* bad smell] **:** bromine ⟨*brom*ide⟩

1**bro·mate** \'brō-,māt\ *n* **:** a salt of bromic acid

2**bromate** *vt* **:** to treat with a bromate; *broadly* **:** BROMINATE

brome·grass \'brōm-,gras\ *n* [NL *Bromus*, genus name, fr. L *bromos* oats, fr. Gk] **:** any of a large genus (*Bromus*) of tall grasses often having drooping spikelets

bro·me·li·ad \brō-'mē-lē-,ad\ *n* [NL *Bromelia*, genus of tropical American plants, fr. Olaf *Bromelius* †1705 Sw botanist] **:** any of a family (Bromeliaceae) of chiefly tropical American and epiphytic herbaceous plants including the pineapple and various ornamentals

bro·mic \'brō-mik\ *adj* **:** of, relating to, or containing bromine esp. with a valence of five

bromic acid *n* **:** an unstable strongly oxidizing acid $HBrO_3$ known only in solution or in the form of its salts

bro·mide \'brō-,mīd\ *n* **1 :** a binary compound of bromine with another element or a radical including some (as potassium bromide) used as sedatives **2 a :** a commonplace or tiresome person **:** BORE **b :** a commonplace or hackneyed statement or notion

bro·mid·ic \brō-'mid-ik\ *adj* **:** DULL, TIRESOME, UNINTERESTING

bro·mi·nate \'brō-mə-,nāt\ *vt* **:** to treat or cause to combine with bromine or a compound of bromine — **bro·mi·na·tion** \,brō-mə-'nā-shən\ *n*

bro·mine \'brō-,mēn\ *n* [F *brome* bromine + E *-ine*] **:** a nonmetallic halogen element normally a deep red corrosive toxic liquid giving off an irritating reddish brown vapor of disagreeable odor — see ELEMENT table

bro·mism \'brō-,miz-əm\ *n* **:** an abnormal state due to excessive or prolonged use of bromides

bro·mo \'brō-(,)mō\ *n* [*brom-*] **:** a proprietary effervescent mixture usu. containing a bromide and used as a headache remedy, sedative, and alkalinizing agent

bronc \'bräŋk\ *n* **:** BRONCO

bronch- *or* **broncho-** *comb form* [prob. fr. F, throat, fr. LL, fr. Gk, fr. *bronchos*] **:** bronchial tube **:** bronchial ⟨*bronchi*tis⟩

bron·chi·al \'bräŋ-kē-əl\ *adj* **:** of or relating to the bronchi or their ramifications in the lungs — **bron·chi·al·ly** \-ə-lē\ *adv*

bronchial asthma *n* **:** asthma resulting from spasmodic contraction of bronchial muscles

bronchial tube *n* **:** a primary bronchus or any of its branches

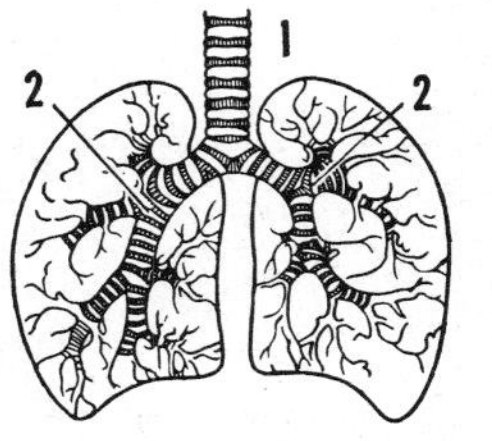

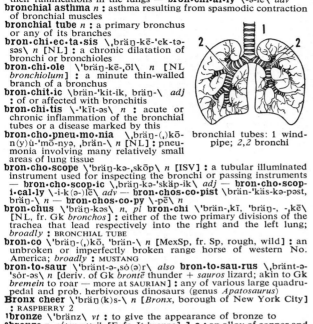

bronchial tubes: 1 windpipe; *2,2* bronchi

bron·chi·ec·ta·sis \,bräŋ-kē-'ek-tə-səs\ *n* [NL] **:** a chronic dilatation of bronchi or bronchioles

bron·chi·ole \'bräŋ-kē-,ōl\ *n* [NL *bronchiolum*] **:** a minute thin-walled branch of a bronchus

bron·chit·ic \brän-'kit-ik, bräŋ-\ *adj* **:** of or affected with bronchitis

bron·chi·tis \-'kīt-əs\ *n* **:** acute or chronic inflammation of the bronchial tubes or a disease marked by this

bron·cho·pneu·mo·nia \,bräŋ-(,)kō-n(y)ü-'mō-nyə, ,brän-\ *n* [NL] **:** pneumonia involving many relatively small areas of lung tissue

bron·cho·scope \'bräŋ-kə-,skōp\ *n* [ISV] **:** a tubular illuminated instrument used for inspecting the bronchi or passing instruments — **bron·cho·scop·ic** \,bräŋ-kə-'skäp-ik\ *adj* — **bron·cho·scop·i·cal·ly** \-i-k(ə-)lē\ *adv* — **bron·chos·co·pist** \brän-'käs-kə-pəst, bräŋ-\ *n* — **bron·chos·co·py** \-pē\ *n*

bron·chus \'bräŋ-kəs\ *n, pl* **bron·chi** \'brän-,kī, 'bräŋ-, -,kē\ [NL, fr. Gk *bronchos*] **:** either of the two primary divisions of the trachea that lead respectively into the right and the left lung; *broadly* **:** BRONCHIAL TUBE

bron·co \'bräŋ-(,)kō, 'brän-\ *n* [MexSp, fr. Sp, rough, wild] **:** an unbroken or imperfectly broken range horse of western No. America; *broadly* **:** MUSTANG

bron·to·saur \'bränt-ə-,sȯ(ə)r\ *also* **bron·to·sau·rus** \,bränt-ə-'sȯr-əs\ *n* [deriv. of Gk *brontē* thunder + *sauros* lizard; akin to Gk *bremein* to roar — more at SAURIAN] **:** any of various large quadrupedal and prob. herbivorous dinosaurs (genus *Apatosaurus*)

Bronx cheer \'bräŋ(k)s-\ *n* [*Bronx*, borough of New York City] **:** RASPBERRY 2

[1]**bronze** \'bränz\ *vt* **:** to give the appearance of bronze to

[2]**bronze** *n, often attrib* [F, fr. It *bronzo*] **1 a :** an alloy of copper and tin and sometimes other elements **b :** any of various copper-base alloys with little or no tin **2 :** a sculpture or artifact of bronze **3 :** a moderate yellowish brown — **bronzy** \'brän-zē\ *adj*

Bronze Age *n* **:** the period of human culture characterized by use of bronze tools and held to begin in Europe about 3500 B.C. and in western Asia and Egypt somewhat earlier

Bronze Star Medal *n* **:** a U.S. military decoration awarded for heroic or meritorious service except for aerial flights

bronz·ing *n* **:** a bronze coloring or discoloration (as of leaves)

brooch \'brōch, 'brüch\ *n* [ME *broche* pointed tool, brooch — more at BROACH] **:** an ornamental fastening device usu. with a clasp

[1]**brood** \'brüd\ *n* [ME, fr. OE *brōd*; akin to OE *beorma* yeast — more at BARM] **1 :** the young of an animal or a family of young; *esp* **:** the young (as of a bird or insect) hatched or cared for at one time **2 :** a group of similar nature or origin

[2]**brood** *vt* **1 a :** to sit on or incubate (eggs) **b :** to produce by or as if by incubation **:** HATCH **2** *of a bird* **:** to cover (young) with the wings **3 :** to think anxiously or moodily upon **:** PONDER ~ *vi* **1 a** *of a bird* **:** to brood eggs or young **b :** to sit quietly and thoughtfully **2 :** HOVER, LOOM **3 a :** to dwell moodily on a subject **b :** to be in a state of depression — **brood·ing·ly** \-iŋ-lē\ *adv*

[3]**brood** *adj* **:** kept for breeding ⟨~ mare⟩ ⟨~ flock⟩

brood·er \'brüd-ər\ *n* **1 :** a person or animal that broods **2 :** a heated structure used for raising young fowl

brood·i·ness \'brüd-ē-nəs\ *n* **:** the quality or state of being broody

broody \'brüd-ē\ *adj* **1 a :** physiologically ready to brood **b :** suitable for producing offspring **2 :** CONTEMPLATIVE, MOODY

[1]**brook** \'bru̇k\ *vt* [ME *brouken* to use, enjoy, fr. OE *brūcan*; akin to OHG *brūhhan* to use, L *frui* to enjoy] **:** ENDURE, TOLERATE

[2]**brook** *n* [ME, fr. OE *brōc*; akin to OHG *bruoh* marshy ground] **:** CREEK 2

brook·ite \'bru̇k-,īt\ *n* [Henry J. *Brooke* †1857 E mineralogist] **:** titanium dioxide TiO_2 occurring as a mineral in orthorhombic crystals commonly translucent brown or opaque brown to black

brook·let \-lət\ *n* **:** a small brook

brook trout *n* **:** the common speckled cold-water char (*Salvelinus fontinalis*) of eastern No. America

[1]**broom** \'brüm, 'bru̇m\ *n* [ME, fr. OE *brōm*; akin to OHG *brāmo* bramble, MF *brimme* brim] **1 a :** any of various leguminous shrubs (esp. genera *Cytisus* and *Genista*) with long slender branches, small leaves, and usu. showy yellow flowers **b :** HEATHER **2 :** a bundle of firm stiff twigs or fibers bound together on a long handle for sweeping and brushing

[2]**broom** *vt* **:** to sweep with or as if with a broom

broom·corn \-,kȯ(ə)rn\ *n* **:** any of several tall cultivated sorghums whose stiff-branched panicle is used in brooms and brushes

broom·rape \-,rāp\ *n* **1 :** any of various leafless herbs (family Orobanchaceae, the broomrape family) growing as parasites on the roots of other plants **2 :** INDIAN PIPE

broom·stick \-,stik\ *n* **:** the long thin handle of a broom

brose \'brōz\ *n* [perh. alter. of Sc *bruis* broth, fr. ME *brewes*] **:** a chiefly Scottish dish made with a boiling liquid and meal

broth \'brȯth\ *n, pl* **broths** \'brȯths, 'brȯthz\ [ME, fr. OE; akin to OHG *brod* broth, L *fervēre* to boil] **:** liquid in which meat, fish, cereal grains, or vegetables have been cooked **:** STOCK

broth·el \'bräth-əl, 'brȯth-\ *n* [ME, worthless fellow, prostitute, fr. *brothen*, pp. of *brethen* to waste away, go to ruin, fr. OE *brēothan* to waste away] **:** an establishment in which prostitutes are available

broth·er \'brəth-ər\ *n, pl* **brothers** *or* **breth·ren** \'breth-(ə-)rən, 'breth-ərn\ [ME, fr. OE *brōthor*; akin to OHG *bruodor* brother, L *frater*, Gk *phratēr* member of the same clan] **1 :** a male who has the same parents as another or has one parent in common with another **2 :** KINSMAN **3 :** a fellow member — used as a title for ministers in some evangelical denominations **4 :** one related to another by common ties or interests **5 a** *cap* **:** a member of a congregation of men not in holy orders and usu. in hospital or school work **b :** a member of a men's religious order who is not preparing for or ready for holy orders ⟨a lay ~⟩

broth·er·hood \-,hu̇d\ *n* [ME *brotherhede, brotherhod*, alter. of *brotherrede*, fr. OE *brōthorrǣden*, fr. *brōthor* + *rǣden* condition] **1 :** the quality or state of being brothers or a brother **2 :** an association (as a labor union) for a particular purpose **3 :** the whole body of persons engaged in a business or profession

broth·er–in–law \'brəth-(ə-)rən-,lȯ, 'brəth-ərn-,lȯ\ *n, pl* **broth·ers–in–law** \'brəth-ər-zən-\ **1 :** the brother of one's spouse — compare AFFINITY **2 :** the husband of one's sister; *broadly* **:** the husband of one's spouse's sister

broth·er·li·ness \'brəth-ər-lē-nəs\ *n* **:** the quality or state of being brotherly

broth·er·ly \'brəth-ər-lē\ *adj* **1 :** of or relating to brothers **2 :** natural or becoming to brothers **:** AFFECTIONATE ⟨~ love⟩

brougham \'brü(-ə)m, 'brō-əm\ *n* [Henry Peter *Brougham*, Baron Brougham and Vaux †1868 Sc jurist] **1 :** a light closed carriage with seats inside for two or four **2 :** a 2-door sedan

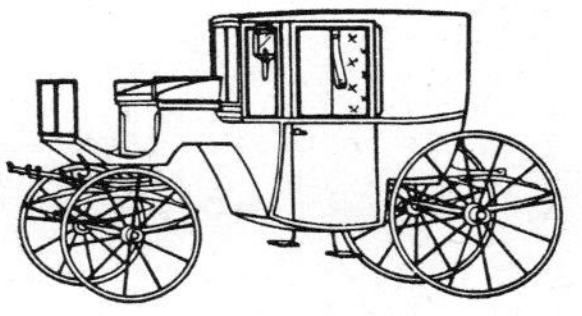
brougham 1

brought *past of* BRING

brou·ha·ha \brü-'hä-(,)hä, ,brü-,hä-'hä\ *n* [F] **:** HUBBUB, FURORE

brow \'brau̇\ *n* [ME, fr. OE *brū*; akin to ON *brūn* eyebrow, Gk *ophrys*] **1 a :** EYEBROW **b :** the ridge on which the eyebrow grows **c :** FOREHEAD **2 :** the projecting upper part or margin of a steep place **3 :** EXPRESSION, MIEN

brow antler *n* — see ANTLER illustration

brow·beat \'brau̇-,bēt\ *vt* **:** to depress or abash with stern manner or arrogant speech **:** BULLY

[1]**brown** \'brau̇n\ *adj* [ME *broun*, fr. OE *brūn*; akin to OHG *brūn* brown, Gk *phrynē* toad] **:** of the color brown; *esp* **:** of dark or tanned complexion

[2]**brown** *n* **:** any of a group of colors between red and yellow in hue, of medium to low lightness, and of moderate to low saturation

[3]**brown** *vi* **:** to become brown ~ *vt* **:** to make brown

brown alga *n* **:** any of a division (Phaeophyta) of variable mostly marine algae with their chlorophyll masked by brown pigment

brown Bet·ty \-'bet-ē\ *n* **:** a baked pudding of apples, bread crumbs, and spices

brown bread *n* **1 :** bread made of whole wheat flour **2 :** a dark brown steamed bread made usu. of cornmeal, white or whole wheat flours, molasses, soda, and milk or water

brown coal *n* **:** LIGNITE

brown–eyed Su·san \,brau̇-,nīd-'süz-ᵊn\ *n* [*brown-eyed* + *Susan* (as in black-eyed *Susan*)] **1 :** any of various dark-centered coneflowers (genus *Rudbeckia*) **2 :** a gaillardia (*Gaillardia aristata*) of the Rocky mountain area with brownish purple flowers

Brown·ian movement \,brau̇-nē-ən-\ *n* [Robert *Brown* †1858 Sc botanist] **:** a random movement of microscopic particles suspended in liquids or gases resulting from the impact of molecules of the fluid surrounding the particles — called also *Brownian motion*

brown·ie \'brau̇-nē\ *n* [[1]*brown*] **1 :** a good-natured goblin who performs helpful services at night **2 :** a member of the Girl Scouts from 7 through 9 years **3 :** a small square or rectangle of rich usu. chocolate cake containing nuts

brown·ish \'brau̇-nish\ *adj* **:** somewhat brown

brown·out \'brau̇-,nau̇t\ *n* [*brown* + *-out* (as in *blackout*)] **:** a curtailment of the use of electric power esp. in display lighting

brown·shirt \'brau̇n-,shərt\ *n, often cap* **:** NAZI; *esp* **:** STORM TROOPER

brown·stone \'brau̇n-,stōn\ *n* **1 :** a reddish brown sandstone used for building **2 :** a dwelling faced with brownstone

brown study *n* **:** a state of serious absorption or abstraction

brown sugar *n* **:** soft sugar whose crystals are covered by a film of refined dark syrup

Brown Swiss *n* **:** any of a breed of large hardy brown dairy cattle originating in Switzerland

brown–tail moth *n* **:** a tussock moth (*Nygmia phaeorrhoea*) whose larvae feed on foliage and are irritating to the skin

brown trout *n* **:** a speckled European trout (*Salmo trutta*) widely introduced as a game fish

[1]**browse** \'brau̇z\ *n* [prob. modif. of MF *brouts*, pl. of *brout* sprout, fr. OF *brost*, of Gmc origin; akin to OS *brustian* to sprout; akin to OE *brēost* breast] **1 :** tender shoots, twigs, and leaves of trees and shrubs fit for food for cattle **2 :** an act or instance of browsing

[2]**browse** *vt* **1 a :** to consume as browse **b :** GRAZE **2 :** to look over casually **:** SKIM ~ *vi* **1 a :** to feed on or as if on browse **b :** GRAZE **2 a :** to skim a book reading random passages **b :** to look over books esp. in order to select one to read **c :** to casually inspect goods offered for sale — **brows·er** *n*

bru·cel·lo·sis \,brü-sə-'lō-səs\ *n* [NL, fr. *Brucella*, genus name, fr. Sir David *Bruce* †1931 Brit bacteriologist] **:** infection with or disease caused by bacteria (genus *Brucella*) esp. in humans or cattle

bru·cine \'brü-,sēn\ *n* [prob. fr. F, fr. NL *Brucea* (genus name of *Brucea antidysenterica*, a shrub)] **:** a poisonous alkaloid $C_{23}H_{26}N_2O_4$ found with strychnine esp. in nux vomica

bru·in \'brü-ən\ *n* [D, name of the bear in *Reynard the Fox*] **:** BEAR

[1]**bruise** \'brüz\ *vb* [ME *brusen, brisen*, fr. MF & OE; MF *bruisier* to break, of Celt origin; akin to OIr *brūu* I shatter; OE *brȳsan* to bruise akin to OIr *brūu*, L *frustum* piece] *vt* **1 a** *archaic* **:** DISABLE **b :** BATTER, DENT **2 :** to inflict a bruise on **:** CONTUSE **3 :** CRUSH

4 : WOUND, INJURE; *esp* : to inflict psychological hurt on ~ *vi* 1 : to inflict a bruise 2 : to show the effects of bruising

2**bruise** *n* 1 a : an injury that does not break the skin but causes rupture of small underlying blood vessels with resulting discoloration of tissues : CONTUSION b : a similar injury to plant tissue 2 : ABRASION, SCRATCH 3 : an injury esp. to the feelings

bruis·er \'brü-zər\ *n* 1 *slang* : PUGILIST 2 : a big husky man

1**bruit** \'brüt\ *n* [ME, fr. MF, fr. OF, noise] *archaic* : a report esp. when favorable : RUMOR

2**bruit** *vt* : to noise abroad : REPORT

bru·mal \'brü-məl\ *adj, archaic* : indicative of or occurring in the winter

brume \'brüm\ *n* [F, mist, winter, fr. OProv *bruma*, fr. L, winter, fr. *brevis* short] : MIST, FOG — **bru·mous** \'brü-məs\ *adj*

1**brum·ma·gem** \'brəm-i-jəm\ *adj* [alter. of *Birmingham*, England, the source in the 17th cent. of counterfeit groats] : showy and cheap

2**brummagem** *n* : something cheap or inferior : TINSEL

brunch \'brənch\ *n* [*br*eakfast + l*unch*] : a late breakfast, an early lunch, or a combination of the two

bru·net *or* **bru·nette** \brü-'net\ *adj* [F *brunet*, masc. & *brunette*, fem., brownish, fr. OF, fr. *brun* brown, fr. ML *brunus*, of Gmc origin; akin to OHG *brūn* brown] : of dark or relatively dark pigmentation: a *of hair and eyes* : BROWN, BLACK b *of skin* : BROWN, OLIVE — **brunet** *n*

Brun·hild \'brün-,hilt\ *n* [G *Brunhilde*] : a queen in Germanic legend won by Siegfried for Gunther

bru·ni·zem \,brü-nə-'zem\ *n* [origin unknown] : any of a zonal group of deep dark prairie soils developed from loess

brunt \'brənt\ *n* [ME] 1 *obs* : ONSET, ATTACK 2 : the principal force, shock, or stress esp. of an attack

1**brush** \'brəsh\ *n* [ME *brusch*, fr. MF *broce*] 1 : BRUSHWOOD 2 a : scrub vegetation b : land covered with scrub vegetation

2**brush** *n* [ME *brusshe*, fr. MF *broisse*, fr. OF *broce*] 1 : a device composed of bristles set into a handle and used esp. for sweeping, scrubbing, or painting 2 : something resembling a brush: as a : a bushy tail b : a feather tuft worn on a hat 3 a : an electrical conductor made of copper strips or a block of carbon that makes sliding contact between a stationary and a moving part of a generator or a motor b : BRUSH DISCHARGE 4 a : an act of brushing b : a quick light touch or momentary contact

3**brush** *vt* 1 a : to apply a brush to b : to apply with a brush 2 a : to remove with or as if with a brush b : to dispose of in an offhand way : DISMISS ⟨~*ed* him off⟩ 3 : to pass lightly over or across : touch gently against in passing ~ *vi* : to move heedlessly past someone — **brush·er** *n*

4**brush** *vi* [ME *bruschen* to rush, fr. MF *brosser* to dash through underbrush, fr. *broce*] : to move so lightly as to be scarcely perceptible

5**brush** *n* [ME *brusche* rush, hostile collision, fr. *bruschen*] : a brief encounter or skirmish **syn** see ENCOUNTER

brush discharge *n* : a faintly luminous relatively slow electrical discharge having no spark

brushed *adj* : finished with a nap ⟨a ~ fabric⟩

brush–off \'brəsh-,ȯf\ *n* : a quietly curt or disdainful dismissal

brush up *vt* 1 : to polish up by eliminating small imperfections 2 : to renew one's skill in ~ *vi* : to refresh one's memory : renew one's skill ⟨*brush up* on his math⟩ — **brush·up** \'brəsh-,əp\ *n*

brush·wood \'brəsh-,wu̇d\ *n* 1 : wood of small branches esp. when cut or broken 2 : a thicket of shrubs and small trees

1**brushy** \'brəsh-ē\ *adj* : SHAGGY, ROUGH

2**brushy** *adj* : covered with or abounding in brush or brushwood

brusque *also* **brusk** \'brəsk\ *adj* [F *brusque*, fr. It *brusco*, fr. ML *bruscus* butcher's-broom] : markedly short and abrupt : sharp and often harsh **syn** see BLUFF — **brusque·ly** *adv* — **brusque·ness** *n*

brus·que·rie \,brəs-kə-'rē\ *n* [F, fr. *brusque*] : BRUSQUENESS

Brus·sels carpet \,brəs-əlz-\ *n* [*Brussels*, Belgium] : a carpet made of colored worsted yarns first fixed in a foundation web of strong linen thread and then drawn up in loops to form the pattern

Brussels lace *n* 1 : any of various fine needlepoint or bobbin laces with floral designs made orig. in or near Brussels 2 : a machine-made net of hexagonal mesh

brussels sprout *n, often cap B* 1 : any of the edible small green heads borne on the stem of a plant (*Brassica oleracea gemmifera*) 2 : the plant that bears brussels sprouts

brut \'brüt, 'brᵫt\ *adj* [F, lit., rough] *of champagne* : very dry : usu. containing less than 1.5 percent sugar by volume

bru·tal \'brüt-ᵊl\ *adj* 1 *archaic* : of, relating to, or typical of beasts : ANIMAL 2 : befitting or resembling a brute: as a : grossly ruthless : BRUTISH ⟨a ~ attack⟩ b : CRUEL, COLD-BLOODED ⟨~ treatment⟩ c : HARSH, SEVERE ⟨~ weather⟩ d : unpleasantly accurate and incisive ⟨the ~ truth⟩ — **bru·tal·ly** \-ᵊl-ē\ *adv*

bru·tal·i·ty \brü-'tal-ət-ē\ *n* 1 : the quality or state of being brutal 2 : a brutal act or course of action

bru·tal·iza·tion \,brüt-ᵊl-ə-'zā-shən\ *n* : the act or process of brutalizing : the state of being brutalized

bru·tal·ize \'brüt-ᵊl-,īz\ *vt* 1 : to make brutal, unfeeling, or inhuman 2 : to treat brutally

1**brute** \'brüt\ *adj* [ME, fr. MF *brut* rough, fr. L *brutus* stupid, lit., heavy; akin to L *gravis* heavy] 1 : of, relating to, or typical of beasts 2 : having neither life nor soul 3 : resembling an animal in quality, action, or instinct: as a : CRUEL, SAVAGE b : grossly sensual c : UNREASONING 4 : purely physical 5 : CRUDE

2**brute** *n* 1 : BEAST 2 : a brutal person

brut·ish \'brüt-ish\ *adj* 1 : of, relating to, or typical of beasts 2 a : strongly and grossly sensual : INSENSITIVE b : UNREASONING, IRRATIONAL c : stupidly cruel — **brut·ish·ly** *adv* — **brut·ish·ness** *n*

Bryn·hild \'brin-,hild\ *n* [ON *Brynhildr*] : a Valkyrie waked from an enchanted sleep by Sigurd who later forgets her and is killed through her agency

bry·ol·o·gy \brī-'äl-ə-jē\ *n* [Gk *bryon* moss + ISV *-logy*] : a branch of botany that deals with the bryophytes 2 : moss life or biology

bry·o·ny \'brī-ə-nē\ *n* [L *bryonia*, fr. Gk *bryōnia*; akin to Gk *bryon*] : any of a genus (*Bryonia*) of tendril-bearing vines of the gourd family with large leaves and red or black fruit

bryo·phyte \'brī-ə-,fīt\ *n* [deriv. of Gk *bryon* + *phyton* plant; akin to Gk *phyein* to bring forth — more at BE] : any of a division (Bryophyta) of nonflowering plants comprising the mosses and liverworts — **bryo·phyt·ic** \,brī-ə-'fit-ik\ *adj*

bryo·zo·an \,brī-ə-'zō-ən\ *n* [NL *Bryozoa*, class name, fr. Gk *bryon* + NL *-zoa*] : any of a phylum or class (Bryozoa) of aquatic mostly marine invertebrate animals that reproduce by budding and usu. form permanently attached branched or mossy colonies — **bryozoan** *adj*

Bryth·on \'brith-,än, -ən; 'brəth-ən\ *n* [W] 1 : a member of the British branch of Celts 2 : a speaker of a Brythonic language

1**Bry·thon·ic** \brith-'än-ik\ *adj* 1 : of, relating to, or characteristic of the Brythons 2 : of, relating to, or characteristic of the division of the Celtic languages that includes Welsh, Cornish, and Breton

2**Brythonic** *n* : the Brythonic branch of the Celtic languages

1**bub·ble** \'bəb-əl\ *vb* **bub·bling** \'bəb-(ə-)liŋ\ [ME *bublen*] *vi* 1 : to form or produce bubbles 2 : to flow out with a gurgling sound suggesting the forming and rising of bubbles 3 : to seem to give off bubbles : EFFERVESCE ~ *vt* 1 : to utter (as words) effervescently 2 a : to cause to bubble b : BURP

2**bubble** *n, often attrib* 1 : a small globule typically hollow and light: as a : a small body of gas within a liquid b : a thin film of liquid inflated with air or gas c : a globule in a transparent solid 2 a : something that lacks firmness, solidity, or reality b : a delusive scheme 3 : a sound like that of bubbling

bubble and squeak *n* : potatoes and cabbage fried together

bubble chamber *n* : a chamber of heated liquid in which the path of an ionizing particle is made visible by a string of vapor bubbles

bubble gum *n* : a chewing gum that can be blown into large bubbles

bub·bler \'bəb-(ə-)lər\ *n* : a drinking fountain from which a stream of water bubbles upward

1**bub·bly** \'bəb-(ə-)lē\ *adj* 1 : full of bubbles : EFFERVESCENT 2 : resembling a bubble

2**bubbly** *n* : CHAMPAGNE

bu·bo \'b(y)ü-(,)bō\ *n, pl* **buboes** [ML *bubon-*, *bubo*, fr. Gk *boubōn*] : an inflammatory swelling of a lymph gland esp. in the groin — **bu·bon·ic** \b(y)ü-'bän-ik\ *adj*

bubonic plague *n* : plague in which the formation of buboes is a prominent feature

buc·cal \'bək-əl\ *adj* [L *bucca* cheek — more at POCK] : of, relating to, or involving the cheeks or the cavity of the mouth

buc·ca·neer \,bək-ə-'ni(ə)r\ *n* [F *boucanier*] 1 : one of the freebooters preying upon Spanish ships and settlements esp. in the West Indies in the 17th century; *broadly* : PIRATE 2 : an unscrupulous adventurer esp. in politics or business — **buccaneer** *vi*

Bu·ceph·a·lus \byü-'sef-(ə-)ləs\ *n* [L, fr. Gk *Boukephalos*] : the war horse of Alexander the Great

1**buck** \'bək\ *n, pl* **bucks** [ME, fr. OE *bucca* stag, he-goat; akin to OHG *boc* he-goat, MIr *bocc*] 1 *or pl* **buck** : a male animal; *esp* : a male deer or antelope 2 a : a male human being : MAN b : a dashing fellow : DANDY 3 *or pl* **buck** : ANTELOPE 4 a : BUCKSKIN; *also* : an article made of buckskin b *slang* : DOLLAR 3b 5 [short for *sawbuck*] : SAWHORSE 6 a : a supporting rack or frame b : a short thick leather-covered block for gymnastic vaulting

2**buck** *vi* 1 *of a horse or mule* : to spring with a quick plunging leap 2 : to charge against something as if butting 3 a : to move or react jerkily b : BALK 4 : to strive for advancement sometimes without regard to ethical behavior ~ *vt* 1 : to throw (as a rider) by bucking 2 a *archaic* : 1BUTT b : OPPOSE, RESIST 3 : to charge into (the opponents' line in football) 4 : to pass esp. from one person to another — **buck·er** *n*

3**buck** *adj* [prob. fr. 1*buck*] : of the lowest grade within a military category ⟨~ private⟩

4**buck** *n* [short for earlier *buckhorn knife*] : an object formerly used in poker to mark the next player to deal; *broadly* : a token used as a mark or reminder

5**buck** *adv* [origin unknown] *South & Midland* : STARK ⟨~ naked⟩

buck–and–wing \,bək-ən-'wiŋ\ *n* : a solo tap dance with sharp foot accents, springs, leg flings, and heel clicks

buck·a·roo *or* **buck·er·oo** \,bək-ə-'rü\ *n* [by folk etymology fr. Sp *vaquero*, fr. *vaca* cow, fr. L *vacca*] 1 : COWBOY 2 : BRONCOBUSTER

buck·bean \'bək-,bēn\ *n* : a plant (*Menyanthes trifoliata* of the family Menyanthaceae) growing in bogs and having racemes of white or purplish flowers

buck·board \'bək-,bō(ə)rd, -,bȯ(ə)rd\ *n* [obs E *buck* body of a wagon + E *board*] : a four-wheeled vehicle with a springy platform carrying the seat

buckboard

1**buck·et** \'bək-ət\ *n* [ME, fr. AF *buket*, fr. OE *būc* pitcher, belly; akin to OHG *būh* belly, Skt *bhūri* abundant] 1 : a typically round vessel for catching, holding, or carrying liquids or solids 2 : something resembling a bucket: as a : the scoop of an excavating machine b : one of the receptacles on the rim of a water-wheel c : one of the cups of an endless-belt conveyor d : one of the vanes of a turbine rotor 3 : a large quantity

2**bucket** *vt* 1 : to draw or lift in or as if in buckets 2 *Brit* a : to ride (a horse) hard b : to drive hurriedly or roughly 3 : to deal with in or as if in a bucket shop ~ *vi* 1 : HUSTLE, HURRY 2 a : to move about haphazardly or irresponsibly b : to move roughly or jerkily

bucket brigade *n* : a chain of persons acting to put out a fire by passing buckets of water from hand to hand

bucket seat *n* : a low separate seat for one person used chiefly in automobiles and airplanes

bucket shop *n* [*bucket shop* (low gin mill); fr. the small speculations that took place there] 1 : a dishonest brokerage house that does not execute orders placed on margin by customers and anticipates a profit from market fluctuations adverse to the customer's interests 2 : a gambling establishment in which wagers are made on the changes in market quotations

buck·eye \'bək-,ī\ *n* 1 : a shrub or tree (genus *Aesculus*) of the horse-chestnut family; *also* : its large nutlike seed 2 *cap* : a native or resident of Ohio — used as a nickname

buck fever *n* : nervous excitement of an inexperienced hunter at the sight of game

buck·hound \'bək-,hau̇nd\ *n* : a dog used for coursing deer

1**buck·le** \'bək-əl\ *n* [ME *bocle*, fr. MF, boss of a shield, buckle, fr. L *buccula*, dim. of *bucca* cheek] 1 : a fastening for two loose ends that is attached to one and holds the other by a catch 2 : an ornamental device that suggests a buckle 3 *archaic* : a crisp curl

2**buckle** *vb* **buck·ling** \ˈbək-(ə-)liŋ\ *vt* **1 :** to fasten with a buckle **2 :** to prepare with vigor for action **3 :** to cause to bend, give way, or crumple ~ *vi* **1 :** to apply oneself with vigor **:** STRIVE ⟨~*s* down to the job⟩ **2 :** to bend, heave, warp, or kink usu. under the influence of some external agency **3 :** to become distorted by buckling; *broadly* **:** COLLAPSE **4 :** to give way **:** YIELD
3**buckle** *n* **:** a product of buckling
1**buck·ler** \ˈbək-lər\ *n* [ME *bocler*, fr. OF, shield with a boss, fr. *bocle*] **1 a :** a small round shield held by a handle at arm's length and used to ward off blows **b :** a shield worn on the left arm to protect the front of the body **2 :** one that shields and protects
2**buckler** *vt* **:** to shield or defend with or as if with a buckler
bucko \ˈbək-(ˌ)ō\ *n* **1 :** one who is domineering and bullying **:** SWAGGERER **2** *chiefly Irish* **:** young fellow **:** LAD
buck passer *n* **:** a person that habitually evades responsibility — **buck–pass·ing** \ˈbək-ˌpas-iŋ\ *n*
buck·ra \ˈbək-rə\ *n* [Ibibio & Efik *m*[1]*ba*[1]*ka*[2]*ra*[2], lit., master] **1** *chiefly South* **:** a white man — used chiefly by Negroes and often disparagingly **2** *chiefly South* **:** BOSS, MASTER
1**buck·ram** \ˈbək-rəm\ *n* [ME *bukeram*, fr. OF *boquerant*, fr. OProv *bocaran*, fr. *Bokhara*, city of central Asia] **1 :** a stiff-finished heavily sized fabric of cotton or linen used for interlinings in garments, stiffening in millinery, and in bookbinding **2** *archaic* **:** STIFFNESS, RIGIDITY
2**buckram** *adj* **:** suggesting buckram esp. in stiffness or formality
3**buckram** *vt* **1 :** to strengthen with or as if with buckram **2** *archaic* **:** to make pretentious
buck·saw \ˈbək-ˌsȯ\ *n* **:** a saw set in a usu. H-shaped frame that is used for sawing wood on a sawbuck
buck·shee \ˈbək-(ˌ)shē\ *n* [Hindi *bakhsis*] **1** *Brit* **:** something extra obtained free; *esp* **:** extra rations **2** *Brit* **:** WINDFALL, GRATUITY
buck·shot \ˈbək-ˌshät\ *n* **:** a coarse lead shot
buck·skin \ˈbək-ˌskin\ *n, often attrib* **1 a :** the skin of a buck **b :** a soft pliable usu. suede-finished leather **2 a** *pl* **:** buckskin breeches **b** *archaic* **:** a person dressed in buckskin; *esp* **:** an early American backwoodsman **3 :** a horse of a light yellowish dun color usu. with dark mane and tail
buck·tail \ˈbək-ˌtāl\ *n* **:** an angler's lure made of hairs from the tail of a deer or a similar material
buck·thorn \ˈbək-ˌthȯ(ə)rn\ *n* **1 :** any of a genus (*Rhamnus* of the family Rhamnaceae, the buckthorn family) of often thorny trees or shrubs some of which yield purgatives or pigments **2 :** a tree (*Bumelia lycioides* of the sapodilla family) of the southern U.S.
buck·tooth \ˈbək-ˈtüth\ *n* **:** a large projecting front tooth — **buck-toothed** \-ˈtütht\ *adj*
buck up *vb* [2*buck*] *vi* **:** to become encouraged ~ *vt* **1 :** IMPROVE, SMARTEN **2 :** to raise the morale of
buck·wheat \ˈbək-ˌ(h)wēt\ *n* [D *boekweit*, fr. MD *boecweit*, fr. *boec-* (akin to OHG *buohha* beech tree) + *weit* wheat] **1 :** any of a genus (*Fagopyrum* of the family Polygonaceae, the buckwheat family) of herbs with alternate leaves and clusters of apetalous flowers; *esp* **:** either of two plants (*F. esculeutum* and *F. tartaricum*) long cultivated for their edible seeds **2 :** the triangular seed of a buckwheat used as a cereal grain
1**bu·col·ic** \byü-ˈkäl-ik\ *adj* [L *bucolicus*, fr. Gk *boukolikos*, fr. *boukolos* cowherd, fr. *bous* head of cattle + *-kolos* (akin to L *colere* to cultivate)] **1 :** of or relating to shepherds or herdsmen **:** PASTORAL **2 :** RUSTIC **syn** see RURAL — **bu·col·i·cal·ly** \-i-k(ə-)lē\ *adv*
2**bucolic** *n* **:** a pastoral poem **:** ECLOGUE
1**bud** \ˈbəd\ *n* [ME *budde*; akin to OE *budda* beetle, Skt *bhūri* abundant — more at BIG] **1 :** a small lateral or terminal protuberance on the stem of a plant that is an undeveloped shoot **2 :** something not yet mature or at full development: as **a :** an incompletely opened flower **b :** YOUTH **c :** an outgrowth of an organism that differentiates into a new individual **:** GEMMA; *also* **:** PRIMORDIUM
2**bud** *vb* **bud·ded; bud·ding** *vi* **1** *of a plant* **a :** to set buds **b :** to commence growth from buds **2 :** to be or develop like a bud **3 :** to reproduce asexually esp. by the pinching off of a small part of the parent ~ *vt* **1 :** to produce or develop from or as if from buds **2 :** to cause (as a plant) to bud **3 :** to insert a bud from a plant of one kind into an opening in the bark of (a plant of another kind) usu. in order to propagate a desired variety — **bud·der** *n*
Bud·dha \ˈbüd-ə, ˈbu̇d-\ *n* [Skt, enlightened] **1 :** a person who has attained Buddhahood **2 :** a representation of Gautama Buddha
Bud·dha·hood \-ˌhu̇d\ *n* **:** a state of perfect spiritual fulfillment sought in Buddhism
Bud·dhism \ˈbü-ˌdiz-əm, ˈbu̇d-ˌiz-\ *n* **:** a religion of eastern and central Asia growing out of the teaching of Gautama Buddha that suffering is inherent in life and that one can be liberated from it by mental and moral self-purification — **Bud·dhist** \ˈbüd-əst, ˈbu̇d-\ *n or adj* — **Bud·dhis·tic** \bü-ˈdis-tik, bu̇-\ *adj*
bud·dle \ˈbəd-ᵊl\ *n* [origin unknown] **:** an apparatus on which crushed ore is washed
bud·dle·ia \ˈbəd-lē-ə, ˌbəd-ˈlē-\ *n* [NL, genus name, fr. Adam *Buddle* †1715 E botanist] **:** any of a genus (*Buddleia* of the family Loganiaceae) of shrubs or trees of warm regions with showy terminal clusters of usu. yellow or violet flowers
bud·dy \ˈbəd-ē\ *n* [prob. baby talk alter. of *brother*] **:** COMPANION, PARTNER; *esp* **:** fellow soldier
1**budge** \ˈbəj\ *n* [ME *bugee*, fr. AF *bogee*] **:** a fur formerly prepared from lambskin dressed with the wool outward
2**budge** *vb* [MF *bouger*, fr. (assumed) VL *bullicare*, fr. L *bullire* to boil] *vi* **:** MOVE, SHIFT; *esp* **:** YIELD ~ *vt* **:** to start or cause to move
3**budge** *adj* [origin unknown] *archaic* **:** POMPOUS, SOLEMN
bud·ger·i·gar \ˈbəj-(ə-)rē-ˌgär\ *n* [native name in Australia] **:** a small Australian parrot (*Melopsittacus undulatus*) usu. light green with black and yellow markings in the wild but bred under domestication in many colors
1**bud·get** \ˈbəj-ət\ *n* [ME *bowgette*, fr. MF *bougette*, dim. of *bouge* leather bag, fr. L *bulga*, of Gaulish origin; akin to MIr *bolg* bag; akin to OE *bælg* bag — more at BELLY] **1** *chiefly dial* **:** a usu. leather pouch, wallet, or pack; *also* **:** its contents **2 :** STOCK, SUPPLY **3 a :** a statement of the financial position of a sovereign body for a definite period of time based on estimates of expenditures during the period and proposals for financing them **b :** a plan for the coordination of resources and expenditures **c :** the amount of money that is available for, required for, or assigned to a particular purpose — **bud·get·ary** \ˈbəj-ə-ˌter-ē\ *adj*
2**budget** *vt* **1 a :** to put or allow for in a budget **b :** to put on a budget **2 a :** to plan expenditures for in a budget **b :** to plan or provide for the use of in detail ~ *vi* **:** to draw up a budget
bud·ge·teer \ˌbəj-ə-ˈti(ə)r\ *or* **bud·get·er** \ˈbəj-ət-ər\ *n* **:** a person who prepares or uses a budget
bud·gie \ˈbəj-ē\ *n* [by shortening and alter.] **:** BUDGERIGAR
bud scale *n* **:** one of the leaves resembling scales that form the sheath of a plant bud
bud sport *n* **:** a mutation arising in a plant bud
1**buff** \ˈbəf\ *n* [MF *buffle* wild ox, fr. OIt *bufalo*] **1 :** a garment (as a uniform) made of buff leather **2 :** the bare skin **3 a :** a moderate orange yellow **b :** a light to moderate yellow **4 :** a device (as a stick or block) having a soft absorbent surface (as of cloth) by which polishing material is applied **5** [earlier *buff* (an enthusiast about going to fires); fr. the buff overcoats worn by volunteer firemen in New York City *ab*1820] **:** FAN, ENTHUSIAST
2**buff** *adj* **:** of the color buff
3**buff** *vt* **1 :** to polish with or as if with a buff **2 :** to give a buff or velvety surface to (leather)
1**buf·fa·lo** \ˈbəf-ə-ˌlō\ *n, pl* **buffalo** *or* **buffaloes** [It *bufalo* & Sp *búfalo*, fr. LL *bufalus*, alter. of L *bubalus*, fr. Gk *boubalos* African gazelle, irreg. fr. *bous* head of cattle] **:** any of several wild oxen: as **a :** WATER BUFFALO **b :** any of a genus (*Bison*); *esp* **:** a large shaggy-maned No. American wild ox (*B. bison*) with short horns and heavy forequarters with a large muscular hump
2**buffalo** *vt* **:** BEWILDER, BAFFLE, OVERAWE
buffalo berry *n* **:** either of two silvery-foliaged western U.S. shrubs (*Shepherdia argentea* and *S. canadensis*) of the oleaster family; *also* **:** their edible scarlet berry
buffalo bug *n* **:** CARPET BEETLE
buffalo fish *n* **:** any of several large suckers (family Catostomidae) mostly of the Mississippi valley
buffalo grass *n* **:** a low-growing grass (*Buchloë dactyloides*) of former feeding grounds of the American buffalo; *also* **:** GRAMA
buffalo robe *n* **:** the hide of an American buffalo lined on the skin side with fabric and used as a coverlet or rug
1**buff·er** \ˈbəf-ər\ *n* **:** one that buffs
2**buffer** *n, often attrib* [*buff* (to react like a soft body when struck)] **1 :** any of various devices or pieces of material for reducing shock due to contact **2 :** a means or device used as a cushion against the shock of fluctuations in business or financial activity **3 :** something that serves to separate two items: as **a :** BUFFER STATE **b :** a person who shields another esp. from annoying routine matters **4 :** a substance or mixture capable in solution of neutralizing both acids and bases and thereby maintaining the original hydrogen-ion concentration of the solution; *also* **:** such a solution
3**buffer** *vt* **:** to treat or prepare (a solution) with a buffer
buffer state *n* **:** a small neutral state lying between two larger potentially rival powers
1**buf·fet** \ˈbəf-ət\ *n* [ME, fr. MF, fr. OF, dim. of *buffe*] **1 :** a blow esp. with the hand **2 :** something that affects like a blow
2**buffet** *vt* **1 :** to strike with or as if with the hand **2 a :** to strike repeatedly **:** BATTER **b :** to contend against ~ *vi* **1 :** STRIVE, CONTEND **2 :** to make one's way esp. under difficult conditions
3**buf·fet** \(ˌ)bə-ˈfā, bü-\ *n* [F] **1 :** a sideboard often without a mirror **2 :** a cupboard or set of shelves for the display of tableware **3 a :** a counter for refreshments **b** *chiefly Brit* **:** a restaurant operated as a public convenience (as in a railway station) **c :** a meal set out on a buffet or table to be eaten without formal service
buffing wheel *n* **:** a wheel covered with material for polishing
buff leather *n* **:** a strong supple oil-tanned leather produced chiefly from cattle hides
buf·fle·head \ˈbəf-əl-ˌhed\ *n* [archaic E *buffle* buffalo + E *head*] **:** a small No. American diving duck (*Bucephala albeola*)
buf·fo \ˈbü-(ˌ)fō\ *n* [It, fr. *buffone*] **:** CLOWN, BUFFOON; *specif* **:** a male singer of comic roles in opera
buf·foon \(ˌ)bə-ˈfün\ *n* [MF *bouffon*, fr. OIt *buffone*, fr. ML *bufon-*, *bufo*, fr. L, toad] **:** CLOWN — **buf·foon·ery** \-ˈfün-(ə-)rē\ *n* — **buf·foon·ish** \-ˈfü-nish\ *adj*
1**bug** \ˈbəg\ *n* [ME *bugge* scarecrow; akin to Norw dial. *bugge* important man — more at BIG] **1** *obs* **:** BOGEY, BUGBEAR **2 a :** an insect or other creeping or crawling invertebrate **b :** any of several insects commonly considered esp. obnoxious: as (1) **:** BEDBUG (2) **:** COCKROACH (3) **:** HEAD LOUSE **c :** any of an order (Hemiptera and esp. its suborder Heteroptera) of insects with sucking mouthparts, fore wings thickened at the base, and incomplete metamorphosis including many economic pests — called also *true bug* **3 :** an unexpected defect, fault, flaw, or imperfection **4 :** a disease-producing germ or a disease caused by it **5 a :** FAD, ENTHUSIASM **b :** ENTHUSIAST, HOBBYIST **c :** a crazy person **6 a** *archaic* **:** a self-important person **b :** a prominent person
2**bug** *vt* **bugged; bug·ging :** to plant a concealed microphone in
bug·a·boo \ˈbəg-ə-ˌbü\ *n* [origin unknown] **1 :** an imaginary object of fear **:** BUGBEAR, BOGEY **2 :** a source of concern
bug·bane \ˈbəg-ˌbān\ *n* **:** a perennial herb (*Cimicifuga racemosa*) of the crowfoot family with flowers believed to repel insects
bug·bear \ˈbəg-ˌba(ə)r, -ˌbe(ə)r\ *n* **1 :** an imaginary goblin or specter used to excite fear **2 :** an object or source of dread
bug·ger \ˈbüg-ər, ˈbəg-\ *n* [ME *bougre* heretic, sodomite, fr. MF, fr. ML *Bulgarus*, lit., Bulgarian] **1 :** SODOMITE **2 a :** a worthless person **:** RASCAL — often used affectionately **b :** FELLOW, CHAP
bug·gery \ˈbüg-ə-rē, ˈbəg-\ *n* **:** SODOMY
1**bug·gy** \ˈbəg-ē\ *adj* **:** infested with bugs
2**buggy** *n* [origin unknown] **1 :** a light one-horse carriage made with two wheels in England and with four wheels in the U.S. **2 :** a small cart or truck for short transportations of heavy materials

American buggy

1**bug·house** \ˈbəg-ˌhau̇s\ *n, slang* **:** an insane asylum
2**bughouse** *adj, slang* **:** mentally deranged **:** CRAZY
1**bu·gle** \ˈbyü-gəl\ *n* [ME, fr. OF, fr. LL *bugula*] **:** any of a genus (*Ajuga*) of plants of the mint family; *esp* **:** a

European annual (*A. reptans*) with spikes of blue flowers naturalized in the U.S.
²bugle *n* [ME, buffalo, instrument made fr. a buffalo horn, bugle, fr. OF, fr. L *buculus*, dim. of *bos* head of cattle — more at COW] : a brass instrument with a cupped mouthpiece like the trumpet but having a shorter and more conical tube
³bugle *vb* **bu·gling** \-g(ə-)liŋ\ *vt* : to sound or summon by or as if by a bugle call ~ *vi* : to sound a bugle — **bu·gler** \-glər\ *n*
⁴bugle *n* [perh. fr. ²*bugle*] : a small cylindrical bead of glass or plastic used for trimming esp. on women's clothing — **bugle** *adj*
bu·gle·weed \'byü-gəl-,wēd\ *n* : any of a genus (*Lycopus*) of mints; *esp* : one (*L. virginicus*) that is mildly narcotic and astringent
bu·gloss \'byü-,gläs, -,glȯs\ *n* [MF *buglosse*, fr. L *buglossa*, irreg. fr. Gk *bouglōssos*, fr. *bous* head of cattle + *glōssa* tongue] : any of a genus (*Anchusa*, esp. *A. officinalis*) of rough-hairy plants of the borage family; *also* : any of several rough-hairy herbs
bug·seed \'bəg-,sēd\ *n* : a fleshy annual herb (*Corispermum hyssopifolium*) of the goosefoot family with flat oval seeds
buhl \'bül, 'byü(ə)l\ *var of* BOULLE
buhr \'bər\ *n* : BUHRSTONE 2
buhr·stone \'bər-,stōn\ *n* [prob. fr. *burr* + *stone*] **1** : a siliceous rock used for millstones **2** : a millstone cut from buhrstone
¹build \'bild\ *vb* **built** \'bilt\ **build·ing** [ME *bilden*, fr. OE *byldan*; akin to OE *būan* to dwell — more at BOWER] *vt* **1** : to form by ordering and uniting materials by gradual means into a composite whole : CONSTRUCT **2** : to cause to be constructed **3** : to develop according to a systematic plan, by a definite process, or on a particular base **4 a** : INCREASE, ENLARGE **b** : to improve the status of : ENHANCE ⟨~ up a candidate⟩ ~ *vi* **1** : to engage in building **2** : to progress toward a peak ⟨tension ~*ing* up⟩
²build *n* : form or mode of structure : MAKE; *esp* : PHYSIQUE
build·ed *archaic past of* BUILD
build·er \'bil-dər\ *n* **1** : one that builds; *esp* : one that contracts to build and supervises building operations **2** : a substance added to or used with detergents to increase their cleansing action
builder's knot *n* : CLOVE HITCH
build in *vt* : to construct as an integral part of something
build·ing \'bil-diŋ\ *n* **1** : a usu. roofed and walled structure built for permanent use (as for a dwelling) **2** : the art or business of assembling materials into a structure
build·up \'bil-,dəp\ *n* **1** : the act of building up **2** : something produced by building up
built-in \'bil-'tin\ *adj* **1** : forming an integral part of a structure; *esp* : constructed as or in a recess in a wall **2** : INHERENT
built-up \'bil-'təp\ *adj* **1** : made of several sections or layers fastened together **2** : covered with buildings
buird·ly \'bü(ə)r(d)-lē\ *adj* [prob. alter. of *burly*] *Scot* : HUSKY
bulb \'bəlb\ *n* [L *bulbus*, fr. Gk *bolbos* bulbous plant; akin to Arm *bolk* radish] **1 a** : a mass of overlapping membranous or fleshy leaves on a short stem base enclosing one or more buds able to develop into new plants and constituting the resting stage of many plants (as lily, onion, hyacinth, tulip) **b** : a fleshy structure (as a tuber or corm) resembling a bulb in appearance **c** : a plant having or developing from a bulb **2** : a bulb-shaped part; *specif* : a rounded glass envelope enclosing the light source of an electric lamp or such an envelope together with the light source it encloses **3** : a rounded or swollen anatomical structure **4** : a camera setting that indicates that the shutter can be opened by pressing on the release and closed by ending the pressure — **bul·ba·ceous** \,bəl-'bā-shəs\ *adj* — **bulbed** \'bəlbd\ *adj*
bul·bar \'bəl-bər, -,bär\ *adj* : of or relating to a bulb; *specif* : involving the medulla oblongata
bul·bil \'bəl-bəl, -,bil\ *n* [F *bulbille*, dim. of *bulbe* bulb, fr. L *bulbus*] : a small or secondary bulb; *esp* : an aerial deciduous bud produced in a leaf axil or replacing the flowers
bul·bous \'bəl-bəs\ *adj* **1** : having a bulb : growing from or bearing bulbs **2** : resembling a bulb — **bul·bous·ly** *adv*
bul·bul \'bu̇l-,bu̇l\ *n* [Per, fr. Ar] **1** : a Persian songbird frequently mentioned in poetry that is prob. a nightingale (*Luscinia golzii*) **2** : any of a group of gregarious passerine birds (family Pycnonotidae) of Asia and Africa
Bul·gar \'bəl-,gär, 'bu̇l-\ *n* [ML *Bulgarus*] : BULGARIAN
Bul·gar·i·an \,bəl-'gar-ē-ən, bu̇l-, -'ger-\ *n* **1** : a native or inhabitant of Bulgaria **2** : the Slavic language of the Bulgarians — **Bulgarian** *adj*
¹bulge \'bəlj\ *n* [MF *boulge*, *bouge* leather bag, curved part] **1** : BILGE 1, 2 **2** : a swelling or protuberant part **3** : ADVANTAGE, UPPER HAND **4** : sudden expansion **syn** see PROJECTION
²bulge *vt* : to cause to bulge ~ *vi* **1** *archaic* : BILGE 1 **2 a** : to jut out : SWELL **b** : to bend outward **c** : to become protuberant
bulgy \'bəl-jē\ *adj* : BULGED, BULGING; *esp* : PROTUBERANT
bu·lim·ia \byü-'lim-ē-ə\ *n* [NL, fr. Gk *boulimia* great hunger, fr. *bous* head of cattle + *limos* hunger — more at COW, LESS] : an abnormal and constant craving for food
¹bulk \'bəlk\ *n* [ME, heap, bulk, fr. ON *bulki* cargo] **1 a** : MAGNITUDE, VOLUME **b** : bulky material felt to promote intestinal motility **2 a** : BODY 1a; *esp* : a large or corpulent human body **b** : a large mass **3** : the main or greater part
syn BULK, MASS, VOLUME mean the aggregate that forms a body or unit with reference to size or amount. BULK implies an aggregate that is impressively large, heavy, or numerous; MASS suggests an aggregate made by piling together things of the same kind; VOLUME applies to an aggregate without shape or outline and capable of flowing or fluctuating
— **in bulk** : not divided into parts or packaged in separate units
²bulk *vt* **1** : to cause to swell or bulge : STUFF **2** : to gather into a mass or aggregate **3** : to have a bulk of ~ *vi* **1** : SWELL, EXPAND **2 a** : to have a bulky appearance : LOOM **b** : to be weighty or impressive **3** : to form into a cohesive mass
bulk·head \'bəlk-,hed, 'bəl-,ked\ *n* [*bulk* (structure projecting from a building) + *head*] **1** : an upright partition separating compartments **2** : a structure or partition to resist pressure or to shut off water, fire, or gas **3** : a projecting framework with a sloping door giving access to a cellar stairway or a shaft
bulk·i·ly \'bəl-kə-lē\ *adv* : in a bulky manner
bulk·i·ness \-kē-nəs\ *n* : the quality or state of being bulky
bulky \'bəl-kē\ *adj* : having bulk: as **a** : large of its kind; *esp* : CORPULENT **b** : having great volume in proportion to weight
bulky color *n* : any partly or wholly transparent color perceived as filling a space in three dimensions
¹bull \'bu̇l\ *n* [ME *bule*, fr. OE *bula*; akin to OE *blāwan* to blow] **1 a** : an adult male bovine animal; *also* : a usu. adult male of various large animals **b** : ELEPHANT **c** : a draft ox **2** : one who buys securities or commodities in expectation of a price rise or who acts to effect such a rise — compare BEAR 3 **3** : one that resembles a bull **4** : BULLDOG **5** *slang* : POLICEMAN, DETECTIVE **6** *cap* : TAURUS
²bull *adj* **1 a** : MALE **b** : of, relating to, or resembling a bull **2** : large of its kind **3** : RISING ⟨a ~ market⟩
³bull *vi* : to behave like a bull; *esp* : to advance forcefully ~ *vt* **1** : to try to raise the price of (as stocks) or in (a market) **2** : to act on with the violence of a bull : FORCE
⁴bull *n* [ME *bulle*, fr. ML *bulla*, fr. L, bubble, amulet] **1** : a solemn papal letter sealed with a bulla or with a red-ink imprint of the device on the bulla **2** : EDICT, DECREE
⁵bull *n* [perh. fr. obs. *bull* to mock] **1** : a grotesque blunder in language **2** *slang* **a** : empty boastful talk **b** : NONSENSE
⁶bull *vi*, *slang* : to engage in idle often boastful talk ~ *vt*, *slang* : to fool esp. by fast boastful talk
bul·la \'bu̇l-ə\ *n*, *pl* **bul·lae** \'bu̇l-,ē, -,ī\ **1** [ML] : the round usu. lead seal attached to a papal bull **2** [NL, fr. L] : a hollow thin-walled rounded bony prominence **3** : a large vesicle or blister — **bul·late** \'bu̇l-,āt\ *adj*
bul·lace \'bu̇l-əs\ *n* [ME *bolace*, fr. MF *beloce*, fr. ML *bolluca*] : a European plum (*Prunus domestica insititia*) with small ovoid fruit in clusters
bull·bat \'bu̇l-,bat\ *n* : NIGHTHAWK 1a
¹bull·dog \'bu̇l-,dȯg\ *n* **1** : a compact muscular short-haired dog of an English breed marked by vigor and sagacity with forelegs set widely apart and an undershot lower jaw **2** : a revolver of large caliber and short barrel **3** : a proctor's attendant at an English university
²bulldog *adj* : resembling a bulldog
³bulldog *vt* : to throw (a steer) by seizing the horns and twisting the neck
bull·doze \'bu̇l-,dōz\ *vt* [perh. fr. ¹*bull* + alter. of *dose*] **1** : BULLY **2** : to move, clear, gouge out, or level off by pushing with a bulldozer **3** : to force as if by using a bulldozer
bull·doz·er \-,dō-zər\ *n* **1** : one that bulldozes **2** : a tractor-driven machine having a broad blunt horizontal blade or ram for clearing land, road building, or comparable activities
bul·let \'bu̇l-ət\ *n* [MF *boulette* small ball & *boulet* missile, dims. of *boule* ball] **1** *archaic* : a small round mass **2** : a round or elongated missile (as of lead) designed to be fired from a firearm; *broadly* : CARTRIDGE 1a **3** : something suggesting a bullet esp. in form or vigor of action — **bul·let·proof** \,bu̇l-ət-'prüf\ *adj*
¹bul·le·tin \'bu̇l-ət-ᵊn\ *n* [F, fr. It *bullettino*, dim. of *bulla* papal edict, fr. ML] **1** : a brief public notice issuing usu. from an authoritative source **2** : PERIODICAL; *esp* : the organ of an institution or association
²bulletin *vt* : to make public by bulletin
bull fiddle *n* : DOUBLE BASS — **bull fiddler** *n*
bull·fight \'bu̇l-,fīt\ *n* : a spectacle in which men ceremonially excite, fight with, and usu. kill bulls in an arena for public amusement — **bull·fight·er** *n*
bull·finch \'bu̇l-,finch\ *n* : a European finch (*Pyrrhula pyrrhula*) having in the male rosy red underparts, blue-gray back, and black cap, chin, tail, and wings; *also* : any of several other finches
bull·frog \'bu̇l-,frȯg, -,fräg\ *n* : FROG; *esp* : a heavy-bodied deep-voiced frog (as of the genus *Rana*)
bull·head \'bu̇l-,hed\ *n* : any of various large-headed fishes (as a miller's-thumb or sculpin) *esp* : any of several common freshwater catfishes (genus *Ameiurus*) of the U.S.
bull·head·ed \'bu̇l-'hed-əd\ *adj* : stupidly stubborn : HEADSTRONG — **bull·head·ed·ly** *adv* — **bull·head·ed·ness** *n*
bul·lion \'bu̇l-yən\ *n* [ME, fr. AF, mint] **1** : gold or silver considered as so much metal; *specif* : uncoined gold or silver in bars or ingots **2** : lace, braid, or fringe of gold or silver threads
bull·ish \'bu̇l-ish\ *adj* **1** : of, relating to, or suggestive of a bull **2 a** : marked by, tending to cause, or hopeful of rising prices (as in a stock market) **b** : OPTIMISTIC — **bull·ish·ly** *adv*
bull mastiff *n* : a large powerful dog of a breed developed by crossing bulldogs with mastiffs
Bull Moose *n* [*bull moose*, emblem of the Progressive party of 1912] : a follower of Theodore Roosevelt in the U.S. presidential campaign of 1912
bull neck *n* : a thick short powerful neck — **bull·necked** \'bu̇l-'nekt\ *adj*
bul·lock \'bu̇l-ək\ *n* **1** : a young bull **2** : a castrated bull : STEER — **bul·locky** \-ə-kē\ *adj*
bull·pen \'bu̇l-,pen\ *n* **1** : a large detention cell where prisoners are held until brought into court **2** : a place on a baseball field where relief pitchers warm up during a game
bull·pout \'bu̇l-,pau̇t\ *n* [*bull*head + *pout*] : BULLHEAD; *esp* : the common dark bullhead (*Ameiurus nebulosus*)
bull·ring \'bu̇l-,riŋ\ *n* : an arena for bullfights
bull-roar·er \'bu̇l-'rōr-ər, -'rȯr-\ *n* : a slat of wood tied to the end of a thong that makes an intermittent roaring sound when whirled
bull session *n* [⁵*bull*] : an informal discursive group discussion
bull's-eye \'bu̇l-,zī\ *n*, *pl* **bull's-eyes** **1** : a small circular or oval wooden block without sheaves having a groove around it and a hole through it **2** : a small thick disk of glass inserted (as in a deck) to let in light **3** : a very hard globular candy **4 a** : the center of a target; *also* : something central or crucial **b** : a shot that hits the bull's-eye; *broadly* : something that precisely attains a desired end **5** : a simple lens of short focal distance or a lantern with such a lens **6** : a circular opening for air or light
bull snake *n* : any of several large harmless No. American snakes (genus *Pituophis*) feeding chiefly on rodents
bull·ter·ri·er \'bu̇l-'ter-ē-ər\ *n* [*bull*dog + *terrier*] : a short-haired terrier of a breed originated in England by crossing the bulldog with terriers
bull tongue *n* : a wide blade attached to a cultivator or plow to stir the soil, kill weeds, or mark furrows
bull·whip \'bu̇l-,hwip, -,wip\ *n* : a rawhide whip with plaited lash 15 to 25 feet long
¹bul·ly \'bu̇l-ē\ *n* [prob. modif. of D *boel* lover, fr. MHG *buole*] **1** *archaic* **a** : SWEETHEART **b** : a fine chap **2 a** : a blustering browbeating fellow; *esp* : one habitually cruel to others weaker

than himself **b :** the protector of a prostitute **:** PIMP **3 a :** a hired ruffian **b** *dial Brit* **:** a fellow workman
2bully *adj* **1 :** EXCELLENT, FIRST-RATE — often used interjectionally **2 :** resembling or characteristic of a bully
3bully *vt* **:** to act the part of a bully toward **:** DOMINEER ~ *vi* **:** to act as a bully **:** BLUSTER
4bully *adv* **:** VERY, OUTSTANDINGLY
5bully *n* [prob. modif. of F (*bœuf*) *boulli* boiled beef] **:** pickled or canned usu. corned beef
bul·ly·rag \ˈbu̇l-ē-ˌrag\ *vt* [origin unknown] **1 :** to intimidate by bullying **2 :** to vex by teasing **:** BADGER
bully tree *n* [by folk etymology fr. AmerSp *balata*] **:** any of several tropical American trees of the sapodilla family; *esp* **:** one (*Manilkara bidentata*) that yields balata gum and a heavy red timber
bul·rush \ˈbu̇l-ˌrəsh\ *n* [ME *bulrysche*] **:** any of several large sedges growing in wet land or water: as **a :** a sedge (genus *Scirpus*, esp. *S. lacustris*) **b** *Brit* **:** either of two cattails (*Typha latifolia* and *T. angustifolia*) **c :** a common American rush (*Juncus effusus*) **d :** PAPYRUS
1bul·wark \ˈbu̇l-(ˌ)wərk, -ˌwȯrk; ˈbəl-(ˌ)wərk\ *n* [ME *bulwerke*, fr. MD *bolwerc*, fr. MHG, fr. *bole* plank + *werc* work] **1 a :** a solid wall-like structure raised for defense **:** RAMPART **b :** BREAKWATER, SEAWALL **2 :** a strong support or protection in danger **3 :** the side of a ship above the upper deck — usu. used in pl.
2bulwark *vt* **:** to fortify or safeguard with a bulwark **:** PROTECT
1bum \ˈbəm\ *n* [ME *bom*] *chiefly Brit* **:** BUTTOCKS
2bum *vi* **bummed; bum·ming** [ME *bumben*, of imit. origin] *dial chiefly Brit* **:** to make a droning or murmuring sound **:** HUM
3bum *vb* **bummed; bumming** [prob. back-formation fr. *bummer*, prob. modif. of G *bummler* loafer] *vi* **:** to go around in the manner of a bum: **a :** LOAF **b :** to wander esp. like a tramp ~ *vt* **:** to obtain by begging **:** CADGE — **bum·mer** *n*
4bum *n* [prob. short for *bummer*] **1 :** one inclined to sponge off others and avoid work **2 :** HOBO, TRAMP
5bum *adj* **1 :** INFERIOR, WORTHLESS **2 :** DISABLED ⟨a ~ knee⟩
6bum *n* [prob. fr. 3*bum*] **:** a drinking spree **:** BENDER
1bum·ble \ˈbəm-bəl\ *vi* **bum·bling** \-b(ə-)liŋ\ [ME *bomblen* to boom, of imit. origin] **1 :** BUZZ **2 :** DRONE, RUMBLE
2bumble *vb* [prob. alter. of *bungle*] *vi* **1 :** BLUNDER; *specif* **:** to speak ineptly in a stuttering and faltering manner **2 :** to proceed unsteadily **:** STUMBLE ~ *vt* **:** BUNGLE — **bum·bler** \-b(ə-)lər\ *n*
bum·ble·bee \ˈbəm-bəl-ˌbē\ *n* **:** any of numerous large robust hairy social bees (genus *Bombus*)
bum·boat \ˈbəm-ˌbōt\ *n* [prob. fr. LG *bumboot*, fr. *bum* tree + *boot* boat] **:** a boat that brings provisions and commodities for sale to larger ships in port or offshore
1bump \ˈbəmp\ *vb* [imit.] *vt* **1 :** to strike or knock with force or violence **2 :** to collide with **3 a :** to knock out of place **b :** to oust usu. by virtue of seniority right **4 :** to apply pressure to (as sheet metal) so as to make or remove a concavity or convexity ~ *vi* **1 :** to knock against something with a forceful jolt **2 :** to proceed in a series of bumps — **bump into :** to encounter esp. by chance
2bump *n* **1 a :** a sudden forceful blow, impact, or jolt **b :** DEMOTION **2 :** a relatively abrupt convexity or protuberance on a surface: as **a :** a swelling of tissue **b :** a cranial protuberance
1bump·er \ˈbəm-pər\ *n* [prob. fr. *bump* (to bulge)] **1 :** a brimming cup or glass **2 :** something unusually large — **bumper** *adj*
2bumper *n* **1 :** one that bumps **2 :** a device for absorbing shock or preventing damage (as in collision); *specif* **:** a metal bar at either end of an automobile
bump·i·ly \ˈbəm-pə-lē\ *adv* **:** in a bumpy manner
bump·i·ness \-pē-nəs\ *n* **:** the quality or state of being bumpy
1bump·kin \ˈbəm(p)-kən\ *n* [perh. fr. Flem *bommekijn* small cask, fr. MD, fr. *bomme* cask] **:** an awkward and unsophisticated rustic — **bump·kin·ly** *adj*
2bump·kin *or* **bum·kin** \ˈbəm(p)-kən\ *n* [prob. fr. Flem *boomken*, dim. of *boom* tree] **:** a projecting boom of a ship
bump·tious \ˈbəm(p)-shəs\ *adj* [1*bump* + *-tious* (as in *fractious*)] **:** presumptuously, obtusely, and often noisily self-assertive **:** OBTRUSIVE — **bump·tious·ly** *adv* — **bump·tious·ness** *n*
bumpy \ˈbəm-pē\ *adj* **1 :** having or covered with bumps **2 :** causing bumps or jolts
1bun \ˈbən\ *n* [ME *bunne*] **1 :** any of various sweet or plain small breads; *esp* **:** a round roll **2 :** a knot of hair shaped like a bun
2bun *n* [perh. alter. of E dial. *bung* (intoxicated)] **:** LOAD 4
Bu·na \ˈb(y)ü-nə\ *trademark* — used for any of several rubbers made by polymerization or copolymerization of butadiene
1bunch \ˈbənch\ *n* [ME *bunche*] **1 :** PROTUBERANCE, SWELLING **2 a :** a number of things of the same kind **:** CLUSTER ⟨a ~ of grapes⟩ **b :** a homogeneous group — **bunch·i·ly** \ˈbən-chə-lē\ *adv* — **bunchy** \-chē\ *adj*
2bunch *vi* **1 :** SWELL, PROTRUDE **2 :** to form a group or cluster ~ *vt* **:** to form into a bunch
bunch·flow·er \ˈbənch-ˌflau̇(-ə)r\ *n* **:** a tall summer-blooming herb (*Melanthium virginicum* of the family Melanthaceae, the bunch-flower family) of the eastern and southern U.S. bearing a panicle of small greenish flowers; *broadly* **:** a plant of this genus
bun·co *or* **bun·ko** \ˈbəŋ-(ˌ)kō\ *n* [perh. alter. of Sp *banca* bench, bank, fr. It] **:** a swindling game or scheme — **bunco** *vt*
1bund \ˈbənd\ *n* [Hindi *band*, fr. Per] **1 :** an embankment used esp. in India to control the flow of water **2 :** an embanked thoroughfare along a river or the sea esp. in the Far East
2bund \ˈbu̇nd, ˈbənd\ *n, often cap* [G, fr. MHG *bunt*] **:** a political association; *specif* **:** a pro-Nazi German-American organization of the 1930s — **bund·ist** \-əst\ *n, often cap*
1bun·dle \ˈbən-dᵊl\ *n* [ME *bundel*, fr. MD; akin to OE *byndel* bundle, *bindan* to bind] **1 a :** a group of things fastened together for convenient handling **b :** PACKAGE, PARCEL **c :** a considerable accumulation **d** *slang* **:** a sizable sum of money **2 a :** a small band of mostly parallel fibers (as of nerve) **b :** VASCULAR BUNDLE
2bundle *vb* **bun·dling** \ˈbən-(d)liŋ, -dᵊl-iŋ\ *vt* **1 :** to make into a bundle **:** WRAP **2 :** to hustle unceremoniously ~ *vi* **1 :** HUSTLE, HURRY **2 :** to practice bundling — **bun·dler** \-dlər, -dᵊl-ər\ *n*
bundle up *vb* **:** to dress warmly
bundling *n* **:** a former custom of an unmarried couple's occupying the same bed without undressing esp. during courtship
1bung \ˈbəŋ\ *n* [ME, fr. MD *bonne, bonghe*, fr. LL *puncta* puncture, fr. L, fem. of *punctus*, pp. of *pungere* to prick — more at PUNGENT] **1 :** the stopper in the bunghole of a cask; *also* **:** BUNGHOLE **2 :** the cecum or anus esp. of a slaughter animal
2bung *vt* **1 :** to plug with or as if with a bung **2 :** HEAVE, TOSS **3 a :** BATTER, BRUISE ⟨badly ~*ed* up⟩ **b :** to cause to bulge or swell
bun·ga·low \ˈbəŋ-gə-ˌlō\ *n* [Hindi *baṅglā*, lit., (house) in the Bengal style] **:** a usu. one-storied house of a type first developed in India and characterized by low sweeping lines and a wide veranda
bung·hole \ˈbəŋ-ˌhōl\ *n* **:** a hole for emptying or filling a cask
bun·gle \ˈbəŋ-gəl\ *vb* **bun·gling** \-g(ə-)liŋ\ [perh. of Scand origin; akin to Icel *banga* to hammer] *vi* **:** to act or work clumsily and awkwardly ~ *vt* **:** MISHANDLE, BOTCH — **bun·gler** \-g(ə-)lər\ *n* — **bun·gling** \-g(ə-)liŋ\ *adj or n* — **bun·gling·ly** \-g(ə-)liŋ-lē\ *adv*
bun·ion \ˈbən-yən\ *n* [prob. irreg. fr. *bunny* (swelling)] **:** an enlargement from chronic inflammation of the small sac on the first joint of the great toe
1bunk \ˈbəŋk\ *n* [prob. short for *bunker*] **1 a :** a built-in bed (as on a ship) that is often one of a tier of berths **b :** a sleeping place **2 :** a feeding trough for cattle
2bunk *vi* **:** to occupy a bunk ~ *vt* **:** to provide with a bunk
3bunk *n* **:** BUNKUM, NONSENSE
1bun·ker \ˈbəŋ-kər\ *n* [Sc *bonker* chest or box] **1 :** a bin or compartment for storage **2 a :** a protective embankment or dugout; *esp* **:** a fortified chamber mostly below ground often built of reinforced concrete and provided with embrasures **b :** a sand trap or embankment constituting a hazard on a golf course
2bunker *vb* **bun·ker·ing** \-k(ə-)riŋ\ *vi* **:** to fill a ship's bunker with coal or oil ~ *vt* **1 :** to store in a bunker **2 :** to hit (a golf ball) into a bunker
bunk·house \ˈbəŋk-ˌhau̇s\ *n* **:** a rough simple building providing sleeping quarters
bun·kum *or* **bun·combe** \ˈbəŋ-kəm\ *n* [*Buncombe* County, N.C.; fr. the defense of a seemingly irrelevant speech made by its congressional representative that he was speaking to Buncombe] **:** insincere or foolish talk **:** NONSENSE
bun·ny \ˈbən-ē\ *n* [E dial. *bun* (rabbit)] **:** RABBIT
Bun·sen burner \ˌbən(t)-sən-\ *n* [Robert W. *Bunsen* †1899 G chemist] **:** a gas burner consisting typically of a straight tube with small holes at the bottom where air enters and mixes with the gas and produces a blue intensely hot flame
1bunt \ˈbənt\ *n* [perh. fr. LG, bundle, fr. MLG; akin to OE *byndel* bundle] **1 a :** the middle part of a square sail **b :** the part of a furled sail gathered up in a bunch at the center of the yard **2 :** the bagging portion of a fishing net
2bunt *n* [origin unknown] **:** a destructive covered smut of wheat caused by a fungus (*Tilletia foetida* or *T. caries*)
3bunt *vb* [alter. of *butt*] *vt* **1 :** to strike or push with or as if with the head **:** BUTT **2 :** to push or tap (a baseball) lightly without swinging the bat ~ *vi* **:** to bunt a baseball — **bunt·er** *n*
4bunt *n* **1 :** an act or instance of bunting **2 :** a bunted ball
1bun·ting \ˈbənt-iŋ\ *n* [ME] **:** any of various stout-billed birds (*Emberiza* and related genera) usu. included in the finch family
2bunting *n* [perh. fr. E dial. *bunt* (to sift)] **1 :** a lightweight loosely woven fabric used chiefly for flags and festive decorations **2 a :** FLAGS **b :** decorations esp. in the colors of the national flag
bunt·line \ˈbənt-ˌlīn, -lən\ *n* **:** one of the ropes attached to the foot of a square sail to haul the sail up to the yard for furling
1buoy \ˈbü-ē, ˈbȯi\ *n* [ME *boye*, fr. (assumed) MF *boie*, of Gmc origin; akin to OE *bēacen* sign — more at BEACON] **1 :** FLOAT 2; *esp* **:** a floating object moored to the bottom to mark a channel or something (as a shoal) lying under the water **2 :** LIFE BUOY
2buoy *vt* **1 :** to mark by or as if by a buoy **2 a :** to keep afloat **b :** SUPPORT, SUSTAIN ⟨hope ~*s* him up⟩ ~ *vi* **:** FLOAT

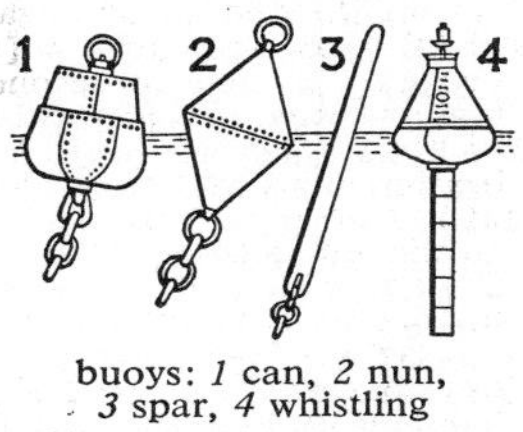

buoys: *1* can, *2* nun, *3* spar, *4* whistling

buoy·an·cy \ˈbȯi-ən-sē, ˈbü-yən-\ *n* **1 a :** the tendency of a body to float or to rise when submerged in a fluid **b :** the power of a fluid to exert an upward force on a body placed in it **2 :** RESILIENCE, VIVACITY
buoy·ant \ˈbȯi-ənt, ˈbü-yənt\ *adj* **:** having buoyancy: as **a :** capable of floating **b :** CHEERFUL, GAY — **buoy·ant·ly** *adv*
buq·sha \ˈbu̇k-shə\ *n* [Ar] — see *riyal* at MONEY table
bur *var of* BURR
Bur·ber·ry \ˈbər-bə-rē, ˈbər-ˌber-ē\ *trademark* — used for various usu. wool fabrics used esp. for coats for outdoor wear
1bur·ble \ˈbər-bəl\ *vi* **bur·bling** \-b(ə-)liŋ\ [ME *burblen*] **1 :** BUBBLE **2 :** BABBLE, PRATTLE — **bur·bler** \-b(ə-)lər\ *n*
2burble *n* **1 :** PRATTLE **2 :** the breaking up of the streamline flow of air about a body (as an airplane wing) — **bur·bly** \-b(ə)lē\ *adj*
bur·bot \ˈbər-bət\ *n, pl* **burbot** *also* **burbots** [ME *borbot*, fr. MF *bourbotte*, fr. *bourbeter* to burrow in the mud] **:** a freshwater fish (*Lota lota*) of the cod family having barbels on the nose and chin and existing in the northern parts of the Old World and the New
1bur·den \ˈbərd-ᵊn\ *n* [ME, fr. OE *byrthen;* akin to OE *beran* to carry] **1 a :** something that is carried **:** LOAD **b :** DUTY, RESPONSIBILITY **2 :** something oppressive or worrisome **:** ENCUMBRANCE **3 a :** CARGO, LADING ⟨beast of ~⟩ **b :** capacity for carrying cargo
2burden *vt* **bur·den·ing** \ˈbərd-niŋ, -ᵊn-iŋ\ **:** LOAD, OPPRESS
3burden *n* [alter. of *bourdon*] **1** *archaic* **:** a bass or accompanying part **2 a :** CHORUS **b :** a recurring or emphasized idea or theme
burden of proof : the duty of proving a disputed assertion or charge
bur·den·some \ˈbərd-ᵊn-səm\ *adj* **:** difficult or distressing to bear **syn** see ONEROUS — **bur·den·some·ly** *adv* — **bur·den·some·ness** *n*
bur·dock \ˈbər-ˌdäk\ *n* **:** any of a genus (*Arctium*) of coarse composite herbs with globular flower heads bearing prickly bracts
bu·reau \ˈbyu̇(ə)r-(ˌ)ō\ *n, pl* **bureaus** *also* **bu·reaux** \-(ˌ)ōz\ [F, desk, cloth covering for desks, fr. OF *burel* woolen cloth, fr. (assumed) OF *bure*, fr. LL *burra* shaggy cloth] **1 a** *Brit* **:** WRITING DESK; *esp* **:** one having drawers and a slant top **b :** a low chest of drawers with a mirror for use in a bedroom **2 a :** a specialized

administrative unit; *esp* **:** a subdivision of an executive department of a government **b :** a business establishment for exchanging information, making contacts, or coordinating activities

bu·reau·cra·cy \byu̇-'räk-rə-sē\ *n* [F *bureaucratie*, fr. *bureau* + *-cratie* -cracy] **1 a :** a body of nonelective government officials **b :** an administrative policy-making group **2 :** government characterized by specialization of functions, adherence to fixed rules, and a hierarchy of authority **3 :** a system of administration marked by officialism, red tape, and proliferation

bu·reau·crat \'byu̇r-ə-,krat\ *n* **:** a member of a bureaucracy; *esp* **:** a government official following a narrow rigid formal routine — **bu·reau·crat·ic** \,byu̇r-ə-'krat-ik\ *adj* — **bu·reau·crat·i·cal·ly** \-i-k(ə-)lē\ *adv*

bu·rette *or* **bu·ret** \byu̇-'ret\ *n* [F *burette*, fr. MF, cruet, fr. *buire* pitcher, alter. of OF *buie*, of Gmc origin] **:** a graduated glass tube with a small aperture and stopcock for delivering measured quantities of liquid or for measuring the liquid or gas received or discharged

burg \'bərg\ *n* [OE — more at BOROUGH] **1 :** an ancient or medieval fortress or walled town **2 :** CITY, TOWN

bur·gage \'bər-gij\ *n* [ME, property held by burgage tenure, fr. MF *bourgage*, lit., burgage, fr. OF, fr. *bourg*, *borc* town] **:** a tenure by which real property in England and Scotland was held of the king or other lord for a yearly rent or for watching and warding

bur·gee \,bər-'jē, 'bər-,\ *n* [perh. fr. F dial. *bourgeais* shipowner] **:** a swallow-tailed flag used esp. by ships for signals or identification

bur·geon \'bər-jən\ *vi* [ME *burjonen*, fr. *burjon* bud, fr. OF, fr. (assumed) VL *burrion-*, *burrio*, fr. LL *burra* shaggy cloth] **1 a :** to send forth buds, branches, or other new growth **:** SPROUT **b :** BLOSSOM, BLOOM **2 :** EXPAND, FLOURISH

burg·er \'bər-gər\ *n* [*hamburger*] **:** a fried or grilled patty of meat or meat substitute usu. served in a sandwich

bur·gess \'bər-jəs\ *n* [ME *burgeis*, fr. OF *borjois*, fr. *borc*] **1 a :** a citizen of a British borough **b :** a representative of a borough, corporate town, or university in the British Parliament **2 :** a representative in the popular branch of the legislatures of colonial Maryland and Virginia

burgh \'bər-(,)ō, 'bə-(,)rō, -ə(-w), -rə(-w)\ *n* [ME — more at BOROUGH] **:** BOROUGH; *specif* **:** an incorporated town in Scotland having local jurisdiction of certain services

bur·gher \'bər-gər\ *n* **:** an inhabitant of a borough or a town

bur·glar \'bər-glər\ *n* [AF *burgler*, fr. ML *burglator*, prob. alter. of *burgator*, fr. *burgatus*, pp. of *burgare* to commit burglary, fr. L *burgus* fortified place] **:** one who commits burglary **:** THIEF

bur·glar·i·ous \,bər-'glar-ē-əs, -'gler-\ *adj* **:** of, relating to, or resembling burglary — **bur·glar·i·ous·ly** *adv*

bur·glar·ize \'bər-glə-,rīz\ *vt* **:** to rifle by burglary

bur·gla·ry \'bər-glə-rē\ *n* **:** the act of breaking into a building esp. with intent to steal; *specif* **:** the act of breaking into and entering the dwelling house of another at night with felonious intent

bur·gle \'bər-gəl\ *vt* **bur·gling** \-g(ə-)liŋ\ [back-formation fr. *burglar*] **:** BURGLARIZE

bur·go·mas·ter \'bər-gə-,mas-tər\ *n* [part modif., part trans. of D *burgemeester*, fr. *burg* town + *meester* master] **:** the chief magistrate of a town in certain European countries **:** MAYOR

bur·go·net \'bər-gə-nət, ,bər-gə-'net\ *n* [modif. of MF *bourguignotte*] **:** either of two 16th century helmets

bur·goo \'bər-,gü, (,)bər-'\ *n* [origin unknown] **1 :** oatmeal gruel **2 :** hardtack and molasses cooked together **3 a :** a stew or thick soup of meat and vegetables orig. served at outdoor gatherings (as a political rally or barbecue) **b :** a picnic at which burgoo is served

Bur·gun·dy \'bər-gən-dē\ *n* [*Burgundy*, region in France] **:** a red or white table wine from the vineyards of Côte d'Or, Yonne, and Saône-et-Loire, France; *also* **:** a similar wine made elsewhere

buri·al \'ber-ē-əl\ *n, often attrib* [ME *beriel*, *berial*, back-formation fr. *beriels* (taken as a plural), fr. OE *byrgels;* akin to OS *burgisli* tomb] **1 :** GRAVE, TOMB **2 :** the act or process of burying

bur·i·er \'ber-ē-ər\ *n* **:** one that buries

bu·rin \'byu̇r-ən, 'bər-\ *n* [F] **1 :** a steel cutting tool with the blade ground obliquely to a sharp point **2 :** a prehistoric flint tool with a beveled point

burke \'bərk\ *vt* [William *Burke* †1829 Ir criminal executed for this crime] **1 :** to suffocate or strangle in order to obtain a body to be sold for dissection **2 a :** to suppress quietly or indirectly ⟨~ an inquiry⟩ **b :** BYPASS, AVOID ⟨~ an issue⟩

1burl \'bər(-ə)l\ *n* [ME *burle*, fr. (assumed) MF *bourle* tuft of wool, fr. (assumed) VL *burrula*, dim. of LL *burra* shaggy cloth] **1 :** a knot or lump in thread or cloth **2 a :** a hard woody often flattened hemispherical outgrowth on a tree **b :** veneer made from burls

2burl *vt* **burl·ing** \'bər-liŋ\ **:** to finish (cloth) esp. by repairing loose threads and knots — **burl·er** \'bər-lər\ *n*

bur·lap \'bər-,lap\ *n* [alter. of earlier *borelapp*] **:** a coarse heavy plain-woven fabric usu. of jute or hemp used for bagging and wrapping and in furniture and linoleum manufacture

burled \'bər(-ə)ld\ *adj* **:** having a distorted grain due to burls

1bur·lesque \(,)bər-'lesk\ *adj* [F, comic, fr. It *burlesco*, fr. *burla* joke, fr. Sp] **:** of, relating to, or having the characteristics of burlesque — **bur·lesque·ly** *adv*

2burlesque *n* **1 a :** mockery usu. by caricature **b :** a witty or derisive usu. literary imitation **2 :** theatrical entertainment of a broadly humorous often earthy character consisting of short turns, comic skits, and sometimes striptease acts **syn** see CARICATURE

3burlesque *vt* **:** to imitate in a humorous or derisive manner **:** MOCK **~** *vi* **:** to employ burlesque — **bur·lesqu·er** *n*

bur·ley \'bər-lē\ *n, often cap* [prob. fr. the name *Burley*] **:** a thin-bodied air-cured tobacco grown mainly in Kentucky

bur·li·ly \'bər-lə-lē\ *adv* **:** in a burly manner

bur·li·ness \'bər-lē-nəs\ *n* **:** the quality or state of being burly

bur·ly \'bər-lē\ *adj* [ME] **1 :** strongly and heavily built **:** HUSKY **2 :** BLUFF, HEARTY

bur marigold *n* **:** any of a genus (*Bidens*) of coarse composite herbs with prickly adherent fruits

Bur·mese \,bər-'mēz, -'mēs\ *n, pl* **Burmese 1 :** a native or inhabitant of Burma **2 :** the Tibeto-Burman language of the Burmese people — **Burmese** *adj*

Burmese cat *n* **:** any of a breed of cats resembling the Siamese cat but of solid and darker color and with orange eyes

1burn \'bərn\ *n* [ME, fr. OE; akin to OHG *brunno* spring of water, L *fervēre* to boil] *Brit* **:** BROOK, RIVULET

2burn \'bərn\ *vb* **burned** \'bərnd\ *or* **burnt** \'bərnt\ **burn·ing** [ME *birnen*, fr. OE *byrnan*, v.i., *bærnan*, v.t.; akin to OHG *brinnan* to burn, L *fervēre* to boil] *vi* **1 a :** BLAZE **b :** to undergo combustion **c :** to contain a fire ⟨the stove is ~*ing*⟩ **2 :** to produce or undergo an effect suggestive of fire: as **a :** to feel hot **b :** to become altered by or as if by the action of fire or heat; *esp* **:** SCORCH ⟨crops ~ under a torrid sun⟩ **c :** to die in the electric chair **d :** to appear as if on fire **:** GLOW **~** *vt* **1 a :** to cause to undergo combustion; *esp* **:** to destroy by fire ⟨~ trash⟩ **b :** to use as fuel ⟨this furnace ~*s* gas⟩ **c :** to produce by the action of fires or heat ⟨~ a hole⟩ **2 a :** to injure or alter by or as if by fire or heat **b :** EXHAUST, DISSIPATE **c :** to subject to excessive speed or use **3** *slang* **a :** IRRITATE, ANNOY **b :** CHEAT — **burn·able** \'bər-nə-bəl\ *adj* — **burn·ing** \-niŋ\ *adj* — **burn·ing·ly** \-niŋ-lē\ *adv*

3burn *n* **1 :** an injury, damage, or effect produced by or as if by burning **2 :** the act, process, or result of burning **3 :** the firing of a spacecraft rocket engine in flight

burn·er \'bər-nər\ *n* **:** one that burns; *esp* **:** the part of a fuel-burning device (as a stove or furnace) where the flame is produced

bur·net \(,)bər-'net, 'bər-nət\ *n* [ME, fr. OF *burnete*, fr. *brun* brown] **:** any of a genus (*Sanguisorba*) of herbs of the rose family with odd-pinnate stipulate leaves and spikes of apetalous flowers

burning bush *n* **:** any of several plants associated with fire (as by redness): as **a :** 2WAHOO a **b :** FRAXINELLA **c :** SUMMER CYPRESS

burning ghat *n* **:** a level space at the head of a ghat for cremation

1bur·nish \'bər-nish\ *vt* [ME *burnischen*, fr. MF *bruniss-*, stem of *brunir*, lit., to make brown, fr. *brun*] **:** to make shiny or lustrous esp. by rubbing **:** POLISH — **bur·nish·er** *n* — **bur·nish·ing** *adj or n*

2burnish *n* **:** LUSTER, GLOSS

bur·noose *or* **bur·nous** \(,)bər-'nüs\ *n* [F *burnous*, fr. Ar *burnus*] **:** a hooded cloak worn by Arabs and Moors

burn·out \'bərn-,au̇t\ *n* **:** the cessation of operation of a jet or rocket engine; *also* **:** the point at which burnout occurs

burn·sides \'bərn-,sīdz\ *n pl* [Ambrose E. *Burnside* †1881 Am general] **:** SIDE-WHISKERS; *esp* **:** full muttonchop whiskers

1burp \'bərp\ *n* [imit.] **:** BELCH

2burp *vi* **:** BELCH **~** *vt* **:** to help (a baby) expel gas from the stomach esp. by patting or rubbing the back

burp gun *n* **:** a small submachine gun

1burr \'bər\ *n* [ME *burre;* akin to OE *byrst* bristle — more at BRISTLE] **1** *usu* **bur a :** a rough or prickly envelope of a fruit **b :** a weed that bears burs **2 a :** something that resembles a bur **b** (1) **:** a small rotary cutting tool (2) *usu* **bur :** a bit used on a dental drill **3** [ME *burwhe* circle] **:** a small washer put on the end of a rivet before swaging it down **4 :** an irregular rounded mass; *esp* **:** a tree burl **5 :** a thin ridge or area of roughness produced in cutting or shaping **6 a :** a trilled uvular *r* as used by some speakers of English esp. in northern England and in Scotland **b :** a tongue-point trill that is the usual Scottish *r* **7 :** a rough humming sound **:** WHIR — **burred** \'bərd\ *adj*

2burr *vi* **1 :** to speak with a burr **2 :** to make a whirring sound **~** *vt* **1 :** to pronounce with a burr **2 a :** to form into a projecting edge **b :** to remove burrs from — **burr·er** \'bər-ər\ *n*

3burr *n* [perh. fr. 1*burr*] **:** BUHRSTONE

bur reed *n* **:** any of a genus (*Sparganium*, family Sparganiaceae) of plants with globose fruits resembling burs

bur·ro \'bər-(,)ō, 'bu̇r-, -ə(-w); 'bə-(,)rō, -rə(-w)\ *n* [Sp, irreg. fr. *borrico*, fr. LL *burricus* small horse] **:** DONKEY; *esp* **:** a small one

1bur·row \'bər-(,)ō, 'bə-(,)rō, -ə(-w), -rə(-w)\ *n* [ME *borow*] **1 :** a hole in the ground made by an animal (as a rabbit) for shelter and habitation **2 :** PASSAGE, GALLERY

2burrow *vt* **1** *archaic* **:** to hide in or as if in a burrow **2 a :** to construct by tunneling **b :** to penetrate by means of a burrow **~** *vi* **1 :** to conceal oneself in or as if in a burrow **2 a :** to make a burrow **b :** to progress by or as if by digging — **bur·row·er** *n*

burrstone *var of* BUHRSTONE

bur·ry \'bər-ē\ *adj* **1 :** containing burs **2 :** resembling a bur **:** PRICKLY **3** *of speech* **:** characterized by a burr

bur·sa \'bər-sə\ *n, pl* **bur·sas** \-səz\ *or* **bur·sae** \-,sē, -,sī\ [NL, fr. ML, bag, purse] **:** a bodily pouch or sac; *esp* **:** a small serous sac between a tendon and a bone — **bur·sal** \-səl\ *adj*

bur·sar \'bər-sər, -,sär\ *n* [ML *bursarius*, fr. *bursa*] **:** an officer (as of a monastery or college) in charge of funds **:** TREASURER

bur·sa·ry \-s(ə-)rē\ *n* [ML *bursaria*, fr. *bursa*] **1 :** the treasury of a college or monastery **2 :** a monetary grant to a needy student

burse \'bərs\ *n* [MF *bourse*, fr. ML *bursa*] **1** *obs* **:** EXCHANGE, BOURSE **2 a :** PURSE **b :** a square cloth case used to carry the corporal in a Communion service

bur·seed \'bər-,sēd\ *n* **:** STICKSEED

bur·si·form \'bər-sə-,fȯrm\ *adj* [ML *bursa* + E *-iform*] **:** shaped like a pouch

bur·si·tis \(,)bər-'sīt-əs\ *n* [NL, fr. *bursa*] **:** inflammation of a bursa esp. of the shoulder or elbow

1burst \'bərst\ *vb* **burst** *or* **burst·ed** \'bər-stəd\ **burst·ing** [ME *bersten*, fr. OE *berstan;* akin to OHG *brestan* to burst, MIr *brosc* noise] *vi* **1 :** to break open, apart, or into pieces usu. from impact or from pressure from within **2 a :** to give way from an excess of emotion ⟨his heart will ~ with grief⟩ **b :** to give vent suddenly to a repressed emotion ⟨~ into tears⟩ **3 a :** to emerge or spring suddenly ⟨~ out of a house⟩ **b :** LAUNCH, PLUNGE ⟨~ into song⟩ **4 :** to be filled to the breaking point **~** *vt* **1 :** to cause to burst **2 :** to produce by or as if by bursting — **burst·er** *n*

2burst *n* **1 a :** a sudden outbreak; *esp* **:** a vehement outburst (as of emotion) **b :** EXPLOSION, ERUPTION **c :** a sudden intense effort **d :** a volley of shots **2 :** an act of bursting **3 :** a result of bursting; *specif* **:** a visible puff accompanying the explosion of a shell

bur·then \'bər-thən\ *var of* BURDEN

bur·ton \'bərt-ᵊn\ *n* [origin unknown] **:** any of several arrangements of hoisting tackle; *esp* **:** one with a single and a double block

bur·weed \'bər-,wēd\ *n* **:** any of various plants (as a cocklebur or burdock) having burry fruit

bury \'ber-ē\ *vt* [ME *burien*, fr. OE *byrgan;* akin to OHG *bergan* to shelter, Russ *berech'* to save] **1 :** to dispose of by depositing in or as if in the earth; *esp* **:** to inter with funeral ceremonies **2 :** CONCEAL, HIDE ⟨*buried* her face in her hands⟩ **3 a :** to consign to oblivion **:** ABANDON **b :** SUBMERGE, ENGROSS **syn** see HIDE

1bus \'bəs\ *n, pl* **bus·es** *or* **bus·ses** *often attrib* [short for *omnibus*] **1 a :** a large motor-driven passenger vehicle **b :** AUTOMOBILE **2 :** a small hand truck **3 :** a usu. uninsulated bar or tube used as an electrical conductor at a circuit junction

2bus *vb* **bussed; bus·sing** *vi* **1 :** to travel by bus **2 :** to work as a busboy ~ *vt* **:** to transport by bus

bus·boy \'bəs-,bȯi\ *n* [*omnibus* (busboy)] **:** a waiter's assistant; *specif* **:** one who removes dirty dishes and resets tables in a restaurant

bus·by \'bəz-bē\ *n* [prob. fr. the name *Busby*] **1 :** a military full-dress fur hat with a pendent bag on one side usu. of the color of regimental facings **2 :** the bearskin worn by British guardsmen

busby

1bush \'bu̇sh\ *n, often attrib* [ME; akin to OHG *busc* forest] **1 a :** SHRUB; *esp* **:** a low densely branched shrub **b :** a thicket of shrubs suggesting a single plant **2 :** a large uncleared or sparsely settled area (as in Australia) usu. scrub-covered or forested **:** WILDERNESS **3 a** (1) *archaic* **:** a bunch of ivy formerly hung outside a tavern to indicate wine for sale (2) *obs* **:** TAVERN **b :** ADVERTISING ⟨good wine needs no ~ —Shak.⟩ **4 :** a bushy tuft or mass; *esp* **:** BRUSH 2a

2bush *vt* **:** to support, mark, or protect with bushes ~ *vi* **:** to extend like or resemble a bush

3bush *n* [D *bus* bushing, box, fr. MD *busse* box, fr. LL *buxis* — more at BOX] **1 :** BUSHING **2 :** a threaded socket

4bush *vt* **:** to furnish with a bushing

bush baby *n* **:** any of several small African lemurs (genus *Galago*)

bush bean *n* **:** any of various low-growing compact bushy cultivated beans that form a variety of the kidney bean

bushed \'bu̇sht\ *adj* **1 :** covered with or as if with a bushy growth **2** *chiefly Austral* **:** LOST, BEWILDERED **3 :** TIRED, EXHAUSTED

1bush·el \'bu̇sh-əl\ *n* [ME *busshel*, fr. OF *boissel*, fr. (assumed) OF *boisse* one sixth of a bushel, of Celt origin; akin to MIr *boss* palm of the hand] **1 :** any of various units of dry capacity — see MEASURE table **2 :** a container holding a bushel **3 :** a large quantity **:** LOTS — **bush·el·age** \-ə-lij\ *n*

2bushel *vb* **bush·eled; bush·el·ing** \-(ə-)liŋ\ [prob. fr. G *bosseln* to do poor work, to patch; akin to OE *bēatan* to beat] **:** REPAIR, RENOVATE — **bush·el·man** \-əl-mən\ *n*

Bu·shi·do \,bü-shē-'dō\ *n* [Jap *bushidō*] **:** a feudal-military Japanese code of chivalry valuing honor above life

bush·i·ly \'bu̇sh-ə-lē\ *adv* **:** in a bushy manner

bush·i·ness \'bu̇sh-ē-nəs\ *n* **:** the quality or state of being bushy

bush·ing \'bu̇sh-iŋ\ *n* **1 :** a usu. removable cylindrical lining for an opening (as of a mechanical part) used to limit the size of the opening, resist abrasion, or serve as a guide **2 :** an electrically insulating lining for a hole to protect a through conductor

bush·man \'bu̇sh-mən\ *n* **1** [modif. of obs. Afrik *boschjesman*, fr. *boschje* (dim. of *bosch* forest) + Afrik *man*] *cap* **:** one of a race of nomadic hunters of southern Africa **2 a :** WOODSMAN **b** *chiefly Austral* **:** one that lives in the bush; *specif* **:** HICK

bush·mas·ter \-,mas-tər\ *n* **:** a tropical American pit viper (*Lachesis mutus*) that is the largest New World venomous snake

bush·rang·er \-,rān-jər\ *n* **1 :** FRONTIERSMAN, WOODSMAN **2** *Austral* **:** an outlaw living in the bush

bush·tit \-,tit\ *n* **:** any of several titmice (genus *Psaltriparus*) of western No. America

bush·whack \'bu̇sh-,hwak, -,wak\ *vb* [back-formation fr. *bushwhacker*] *vi* **1 a :** to clear a path through thick woods esp. by chopping down bushes and low branches **b :** to propel a boat by pulling on bushes along the bank **2 a :** to live or hide out in the woods **b :** to fight in or attack from the bush ~ *vt* **:** AMBUSH — **bush·whack·er** *n* — **bush·whack·ing** *n*

bushy \'bu̇sh-ē\ *adj* **1 :** full of or overgrown with bushes **2 :** resembling a bush; *esp* **:** thick and spreading

busi·ly \'biz-(ə-)lē\ *adv* **:** in a busy manner

busi·ness \'biz-nəs, -nəz\ *n, often attrib* **1** *archaic* **:** BUSYNESS **2 a :** OCCUPATION, CALLING **b :** an immediate task or objective **:** MISSION **3 a :** a commercial or industrial enterprise **b :** TRADE, COMMERCE; *esp* **:** PATRONAGE **4 :** AFFAIR, MATTER ⟨a strange ~⟩ **5 :** movement or action (as lighting a cigarette) by an actor intended esp. to establish atmosphere, reveal character, or explain a situation **6 :** a rightful interest **:** personal concern ⟨none of your ~⟩ **7 a :** a maximum effort; *esp* **:** a damaging assault **b :** DOUBLE CROSS

syn BUSINESS, COMMERCE, TRADE, INDUSTRY, TRAFFIC mean activity in supplying commodities. BUSINESS may be an inclusive term but specifically designates the activities of those engaged in the purchase or sale of commodities or in related financial transactions; COMMERCE and TRADE imply the exchange and transportation of commodities; INDUSTRY applies to the producing of commodities, esp. by manufacturing or processing, on so large a scale that capital and labor are significantly involved; TRAFFIC applies to the operation and functioning of public carriers of goods and persons **syn** see in addition WORK

business cycle *n* **:** a recurring succession of fluctuations in economic activity

busi·ness·like \'biz-nə-,slīk, -nəz-,līk\ *adj* **1 :** exhibiting qualities felt to be advantageous in business **2 :** SERIOUS, PURPOSEFUL

busi·ness·man \'biz-nə-,sman\ *n* **:** a man who transacts business; *esp* **:** a business executive

busk \'bəsk\ *vb* [ME *busken*, fr. ON *būask* to prepare oneself, refl. of *būa* to prepare, dwell] *dial Brit* **:** PREPARE

bus·kin \'bəs-kən\ *n* [perh. modif. of Sp *borceguí*] **1 :** a laced boot reaching halfway or more to the knee **2 a :** COTHURNUS **b :** TRAGEDY; *esp* **:** tragedy resembling that of ancient Greek drama

bus·man's holiday \,bəs-mənz-\ *n* **:** a holiday spent in following or observing the practice of one's usual occupation

buss \'bəs\ *n* [prob. imit.] **:** KISS — **buss** *vt*

1bust \'bəst\ *n* [F *buste*, fr. It *busto*, fr. L *bustum* tomb] **1 :** a sculptured representation of the upper part of the human figure including the head and neck and usu. part of the shoulders and breast **2 :** the upper portion of the human torso between neck and waist; *esp* **:** the breasts of a woman

2bust *vb* **bust·ed** *also* **bust; bust·ing** [alter. of *burst*] *vt* **1 :** HIT, PUNCH **2 a :** BURST, BREAK **b :** to ruin financially **3 :** DEMOTE **4 :** TAME ~ *vi* **1 a :** BURST **b :** to break down **2 :** to go broke

3bust *n* **1** *slang* **:** PUNCH, SOCK **2 a :** a complete failure **:** FLOP **b :** a business depression **3 :** SPREE

bus·tard \'bəs-tərd\ *n* [ME, modif. of MF *bistarde*, fr. OIt *bistarda*, fr. L *avis tarda*, lit., slow bird] **:** any of a family (Otididae) of Old World and Australian game birds

bust·er \'bəs-tər\ *n* **1 a :** an unusually sturdy child **b** *often cap* **:** FELLOW **2 :** one that breaks or breaks up: as **a :** PLOW **b** [short for *broncobuster*] **:** one who breaks horses **3** *Austral* **:** a sudden violent wind often coming from the south **4 :** something having unusual destructive force: as **a :** a jarring fall **b :** BLOCKBUSTER

1bus·tle \'bəs-əl\ *vi* **bus·tling** \'bəs-(ə-)liŋ\ [prob. alter. of obs. *buskle* to prepare, freq. of *busk*] **1 :** to move briskly and often ostentatiously **2 :** to be busily astir — **bus·tling** \-(ə-)liŋ\ *adj* — **bus·tling·ly** \-(ə-)liŋ-lē\ *adv*

2bustle *n* **:** noisy or energetic activity **syn** see STIR

3bustle *n* [origin unknown] **:** a pad or framework expanding and supporting the fullness and drapery of the back of a woman's skirt

1busy \'biz-ē\ *adj* [ME *bisy*, fr. OE *bisig*; akin to MD & MLG *besich* busy] **1 a :** engaged in action **:** OCCUPIED **b :** being in use ⟨~ telephone⟩ **2 :** full of activity **:** BUSTLING **3 :** OFFICIOUS, MEDDLING **4 :** full of distracting detail ⟨a ~ design⟩

syn INDUSTRIOUS, DILIGENT, ASSIDUOUS, SEDULOUS: BUSY chiefly stresses activity as opposed to idleness or leisure; it may connote purposive activity; INDUSTRIOUS implies characteristic or habitual devotion to work; DILIGENT suggests earnest application to some specific object or pursuit; ASSIDUOUS stresses careful and unremitting application; SEDULOUS implies painstaking and persevering application

2busy *vt* **:** to make busy **:** OCCUPY ~ *vi* **:** BUSTLE

busy·body \'biz-ē-,bäd-ē\ *n* **:** an officious or inquisitive person

busy·ness \'biz-ē-nəs\ *n* **:** the quality or state of being busy

1but \(')bət\ *conj* [ME, fr. OE *būtan*, prep. & conj., outside, without, except, except that; akin to OHG *būzan* without, except] **1 a :** except for the fact ⟨would have protested ~ that he was afraid⟩ **b :** THAT ⟨there is no doubt ~ he won⟩ **c :** without the concomitant that ⟨it never rains ~ it pours⟩ **d :** if not **:** UNLESS **e** *substand* **:** THAN ⟨no sooner started ~ it stopped⟩ **2 a :** on the contrary ⟨not peace ~ a sword⟩ **b :** YET ⟨poor ~ proud⟩ **c :** with the exception of ⟨none ~ the brave deserve the fair —John Dryden⟩ — **but what** **:** that . . . not ⟨I don't know *but what* I will go⟩

2but *prep* **1** *Scot* **a :** WITHOUT, LACKING **b :** OUTSIDE **2 a :** with the exception of **:** BARRING ⟨no one there ~ me⟩ **b :** other than

3but *adv* **1 :** ONLY, MERELY ⟨he is ~ a child⟩ **2** *Scot* **:** OUTSIDE **3 :** to the contrary ⟨who knows ~ that he may succeed⟩ **4 :** DEFINITELY, POSITIVELY ⟨get there ~ fast⟩

4but *pron* **:** that not **:** who not ⟨nobody ~ has his fault —Shak.⟩

5but \'bət\ *n* [Sc *but*, adj. (outer)] *Scot* **:** the kitchen or living quarters of a 2-room cottage

but- *or* **buto-** *comb form* [ISV, fr. *butyric*] **:** containing a group of four carbon atoms ⟨*butane*⟩

bu·ta·di·ene \,byüt-ə-'dī-,ēn, -,dī-'\ *n* **:** a flammable gaseous hydrocarbon C_4H_6 used in making synthetic rubbers

bu·tane \'byü-,tān\ *n* **:** either of two isomeric flammable gaseous paraffin hydrocarbons C_4H_{10} obtained usu. from petroleum or natural gas

bu·ta·nol \'byüt-ᵊn-,ȯl, -,ōl\ *n* **:** a butyl alcohol derived from normal butane

1butch·er \'bu̇ch-ər\ *n* [ME *bocher*, fr. OF *bouchier*, fr. *bouc* he-goat, prob. of Celt origin; akin to MIr *bocc* he-goat — more at BUCK] **1 a :** one who slaughters animals or dresses their flesh **b :** a dealer in meat **2 :** one that kills ruthlessly or brutally **3 :** BOTCHER **4 :** a vendor esp. on trains or in theaters

2butcher *vt* **butch·er·ing** \-(ə-)riŋ\ **1 :** to slaughter and dress for market ⟨~ hogs⟩ **2 :** to kill in a barbarous manner **3 :** BOTCH — **butch·er·er** \-ər-ər\ *n*

butch·er–bird \'bu̇ch-ər-,bərd\ *n* **:** any of various shrikes

butch·er·ly \'bu̇ch-ər-lē\ *adj* **:** resembling a butcher **:** SAVAGE

butch·er's–broom \'bu̇ch-ərz-,brüm, -,bru̇m\ *n* **:** a European leafless plant (*Ruscus aculeatus*) of the lily family with stiff-pointed leaflike twigs used for brooms

butch·ery \'bu̇ch-(ə-)rē\ *n* **1** *chiefly Brit* **:** SLAUGHTERHOUSE **2 :** the preparation of meat for sale **3 :** CARNAGE **4 :** BOTCH

bu·tene \'byü-,tēn\ *n* **:** a normal butylene

bu·teo \'byüt-ē-,ō\ *n* [NL, genus name, fr. L, a hawk] **:** any of a genus (*Buteo*) of hawks with broad rounded wings and soaring flight; *broadly* **:** a hawk of similar appearance or habit of flight — **bu·te·o·nine** \byü-'tē-ə-,nīn\ *adj or n*

but·ler \'bət-lər\ *n* [ME *buteler*, fr. OF *bouteillier* bottle bearer, fr. *bouteille* bottle — more at BOTTLE] **1 :** a manservant having charge of the wines and liquors **2 :** the chief male servant of a household

butler's pantry *n* **:** a service room between kitchen and dining room

1butt \'bət\ *vb* [ME *butten*, fr. OF *boter*, of Gmc origin; akin to OHG *bōzan* to beat] *vi* **:** to thrust or push head foremost **:** strike with the head or horns ~ *vt* **:** to strike with the head or horns

2butt *n* **:** a blow or thrust usu. with the head or horns

3butt *n* [ME, partly fr. MF *but* target, end, of Gmc origin; akin to ON *būtr* log, LG *butt* blunt; partly fr. MF *bute* backstop, fr. *but* target] **1 a :** a mound, bank, or other backstop for catching missiles shot at a target **b :** TARGET **c** *pl* **:** RANGE 5b **d :** a blind for shooting birds **2 a** *obs* **:** LIMIT, BOUND **b** *archaic* **:** GOAL **3 :** an object of abuse or ridicule **:** VICTIM

4butt *vb* [partly fr. ³*butt*, partly fr. ⁵*butt*] *vi* **:** ABUT ~ *vt* **1 a :** to place end to end without overlapping **b :** to join along the edges **2 :** to trim or square off at the end

5butt *n* [ME; prob. akin to ME *buttok* buttock, LG *butt* blunt, OHG *bōzan* to beat] **1 a :** the large or thicker end of something **b :** the base of a plant from which the roots spring **c :** the thicker or handle end of a tool or weapon **2 :** an unused remainder

6butt *n* [ME, fr. MF *botte*, fr. OProv *bota*, fr. LL *buttis*] **1 :** a large cask esp. for wine, beer, or water **2 :** any of various units of liquid capacity; *esp* **:** a measure equal to 108 imperial gallons **3 :** the part of a hide or skin corresponding to the animal's back and sides

butte \'byüt\ *n* [F, knoll, fr. MF *bute* mound of earth serving as a backstop] **:** an isolated hill or small mountain with steep or precipitous sides usu. having a smaller summit area than a mesa

1but·ter \'bət-ər\ *n* [ME, fr. OE *butere*; akin to OHG *butera* butter; both fr. a prehistoric WGmc word borrowed fr. L *butyrum* butter, fr. Gk *boutyron*, fr. *bous* cow + *tyros* cheese; akin to Av *tūiri-* whey — more at COW] **1 :** a solid emulsion of fat globules, air, and water made by churning milk or cream and used as food **2 :** a buttery substance: as **a :** any of various fatty oils remaining nearly solid at ordinary temperatures **b :** a food spread made

from fruit, nuts, or other food ⟨peanut ~⟩ **3 :** BLANDISHMENT
[2]**butter** *vt* **1 :** to spread with or as if with butter **2 :** BLANDISH
but·ter–and–eggs \ˌbət-ə-rə-ˈnegz, -ˈnāgz\ *n pl but sing or pl in constr* **:** any of several plants (as toadflax) having flowers of two shades of yellow
but·ter·ball \ˈbət-ər-ˌbȯl\ *n* **1 :** a chubby person **2 :** BUFFLEHEAD
butter bean *n* **1 :** WAX BEAN **2 :** LIMA BEAN: as **a** *chiefly South & Midland* **:** a large dried lima bean **b :** SIEVA BEAN **3 :** a green shell bean esp. as opposed to a snap bean
butter clam *n* **:** either of two large delicately flavored clams (*Saxidomus nuttallii* and *S. giganteus*) of the Pacific coast of No. America
but·ter·cup \ˈbət-ər-ˌkəp\ *n* **:** a yellow-flowered crowfoot (genus *Ranunculus*)
but·ter·fat \ˈbət-ər-ˌfat\ *n* **:** the natural fat of milk and chief constituent of butter consisting essentially of a mixture of glycerides and chiefly of butyrin, olein, and palmitin
but·ter·fin·gered \ˈbət-ər-ˌfiŋ-gərd\ *adj* **:** apt to let things fall or slip through the fingers **:** CARELESS — **but·ter·fin·gers** \ˈbət-ər-ˌfiŋ-gərz\ *n pl but sing or pl in constr*
but·ter·fish \-ˌfish\ *n* **:** any of numerous mostly percoid fishes with a slippery coating of mucus
but·ter·fly \ˈbət-ər-ˌflī\ *n, often attrib* **1 :** any of numerous slender-bodied diurnal insects (order Lepidoptera) with large broad usu. brightly colored wings **2 :** something that resembles a butterfly; *esp* **:** a person chiefly occupied with the pursuit of pleasure
butterfly bush *n* **:** BUDDLEIA
butterfly fish *n* **:** any of various fishes having variegated colors, broad expanded fins, or both: as **a :** a European blenny (*Blennius ocellaris*) **b :** FLYING GURNARD **c :** any of a family (Chaetodontidae) of small brilliantly colored spiny-finned fishes of tropical seas with a narrow deep body and fins partly covered with scales
butterfly valve *n* **1 :** a double clack valve **2 :** a damper or throttle valve in a pipe consisting of a disk turning on a diametral axis
butterfly weed *n* **:** an orange-flowered showy milkweed (*Asclepias tuberosa*) of eastern No. America
but·ter·milk \ˈbət-ər-ˌmilk\ *n* **1 :** the liquid left after butter has been churned from milk or cream **2 :** cultured milk made by the addition of certain organisms to sweet milk
but·ter·nut \-ˌnət\ *n* **1 a :** the edible nut of an American tree (*Juglans cinerea*) of the walnut family **b :** the tree itself **2 a** *pl* **:** homespun overalls dyed brown with a butternut extract **b** *slang* **:** a soldier or partisan of the Confederacy during the Civil War
but·ter·scotch \ˈbət-ər-ˌskäch\ *n, often attrib* **:** a candy made from brown sugar, corn syrup, and water; *also* **:** the flavor of such candy
butter tree *n* **:** any of various trees (as the shea tree) whose seeds yield a substance similar to butter
but·ter·weed \ˈbət-ər-ˌwēd\ *n* **:** any of several plants having yellow flowers or smooth soft foliage: as **a :** HORSEWEED 1 **b :** an American wild lettuce (*Lactuca canadensis*) **c :** an American ragwort (*Senecio glabellus*)
but·ter·wort \-ˌwərt, -ˌwȯ(ə)rt\ *n* **:** any of a genus (*Pinguicula*) of herbs of the bladderwort family with fleshy greasy leaves
[1]**but·tery** \ˈbət-ə-rē, ˈbə-trē\ *n* [ME *boterie*, fr. MF, fr. *botte* cask, butt — more at BUTT] **1 :** a storeroom for liquors **2 a** *chiefly dial* **:** PANTRY **b :** a room (as in an English college) stocking provisions for sale to students
[2]**but·tery** \ˈbət-ə-rē\ *adj* **1 a :** having the qualities, consistency, or appearance of butter **b :** containing or spread with butter **2 :** FLATTERING
butt hinge *n* **:** a hinge usu. mortised flush into the edge of a door
butt joint *n* **:** a joint made by fastening the parts together end-to-end without overlap and often with reinforcement
but·tock \ˈbət-ək\ *n* [ME *buttok* — more at BUTT] **1 :** either rounded half of the lower part of the back together forming the part on which a person sits **2** *pl* **a :** the seat of the body **b :** RUMP
[1]**but·ton** \ˈbət-ᵊn\ *n, often attrib* [ME *boton*, fr. MF, fr. OF, fr. *boter* to thrust] **1 :** a small knob or disk secured to an article and used as a fastener by passing it through a buttonhole or loop **2 :** something that resembles a button: as **a :** any of various parts of a plant or of an animal **b :** a small globule of metal remaining after fusion **c :** a guard on the tip of a fencing foil **3** *slang* **a :** the point of the chin **b** *pl* **:** WITS
[2]**but·ton** \ˈbət-ᵊn\ *vb* **but·ton·ing** \ˈbət-niŋ, -ᵊn-iŋ\ *vt* **1 :** to furnish or decorate with buttons **2 :** to close or fasten with buttons ~ *vi* **:** to have buttons for fastening — **but·ton·er** \-nər, -ᵊn-ər\ *n*
but·ton·ball \ˈbət-ᵊn-ˌbȯl\ *n* **1 :** [2]PLANE **2 :** BUTTONBUSH
but·ton·bush \-ˌbu̇sh\ *n* **:** a No. American shrub (*Cephalanthus occidentalis*) of the madder family with globular flower heads
[1]**but·ton·hole** \-ˌhōl\ *n* **:** a slit or loop for fastening a button
[2]**buttonhole** *vt* **1 :** to furnish with buttonholes **2 :** to work with buttonhole stitch — **but·ton·hol·er** *n*
[3]**buttonhole** *vt* [alter. of *buttonhold*] **:** to detain in conversation by or as if by holding on to the outer garments of
buttonhole stitch *n* **:** a closely worked loop stitch used to make a firm edge (as on a buttonhole)
but·ton·hook \ˈbət-ᵊn-ˌhu̇k\ *n* **:** a hook for drawing small buttons through buttonholes
button quail *n* **:** any of various small terrestrial Old World birds (family Turnicidae) that resemble quails but lack a hind toe and are related to the cranes and bustards
button snakeroot *n* **1 :** any of a genus (*Liatris*) of composite plants with spikes of rosy-purple rayless flower heads **2 :** any of several usu. prickly herbs (genus *Eryngium*) of the carrot family
but·ton·wood \ˈbət-ᵊn-ˌwu̇d\ *n* **:** [2]PLANE
but·tony \ˈbət-ᵊn-ē, ˈbət-nē\ *adj* **1 :** ornamented with buttons **2 :** resembling a button
[1]**but·tress** \ˈbə-trəs\ *n* [ME *butres*, fr. MF *bouterez*, fr. OF *boterez*, fr. *boter*] **1 :** a projecting structure of masonry or wood for supporting or giving stability to a wall or building **2 :** something that resembles a buttress: as **a :** a projecting part of a mountain or hill **b :** a horny protuberance on a horse's hoof at the heel **c :** the broadened base of a tree trunk or a thickened vertical part of it — **but·tressed** \-trəst\ *adj*
[2]**buttress** *vt* **:** to furnish or shore up with a buttress
butt shaft *n* **:** a target arrow
butt·stock \ˈbət-ˌstäk\ *n* **:** the stock of a firearm in the rear of the breech mechanism
butt weld *n* **:** a butt joint made by welding — **butt–weld** \ˈbət-ˈweld\ *vt* — **butt welding** *n*
bu·tyl \ˈbyüt-ᵊl\ *n* **:** any of four isomeric univalent radicals C_4H_9 derived from butanes
Butyl *trademark* — used for any of various synthetic rubbers made by polymerizing isobutylene
butyl alcohol *n* **:** any of four flammable alcohols C_4H_9OH derived from butanes and used in organic synthesis and as solvents
bu·tyl·ate \ˈbyüt-ᵊl-ˌāt\ *vt* **:** to introduce the butyl group into (a compound) — **bu·tyl·ation** \ˌbyüt-ᵊl-ˈā-shən\ *n*
bu·tyl·ene \ˈbyüt-ᵊl-ˌēn\ *n* **:** any of three isomeric hydrocarbons C_4H_8 of the ethylene series obtained usu. by cracking petroleum
butyr- *or* **butyro-** *comb form* [ISV, fr. *butyric*] **:** butyric ⟨*butyr*al⟩
bu·ty·ra·ceous \ˌbyüt-ə-ˈrā-shəs\ *adj* [L *butyrum* butter — more at BUTTER] **1 :** resembling or having the qualities of butter **2 :** yielding a buttery substance
bu·ty·ral \ˈbyüt-ə-ˌral\ *n* **:** an acetal of butyraldehyde
bu·tyr·al·de·hyde \ˌbyüt-ə-ˈral-də-ˌhīd\ *n* [ISV] **:** either of two aldehydes C_3H_7CHO used esp. in making polyvinyl butyral resins
bu·ty·rate \ˈbyüt-ə-ˌrāt\ *n* **:** a salt or ester of butyric acid
bu·tyr·ic \byü-ˈtir-ik\ *adj* [F *butyrique*, fr. L *butyrum*] **:** being or producing butyric acid ⟨~ fermentation⟩
butyric acid *n* **:** either of two isomeric fatty acids C_3H_7COOH; *esp* **:** a normal acid $C_4H_8O_2$ found in butter in the form of glycerides
bu·ty·rin \ˈbyüt-ə-rən\ *n* **:** any of the three liquid glycerides of butyric acid
bux·om \ˈbək-səm\ *adj* [ME *buxsum*, fr. (assumed) OE *būhsum*, fr. OE *būgan* to bend — more at BOW] **1** *obs* **:** OBEDIENT, TRACTABLE **2** *archaic* **:** full of gaiety **:** BLITHE **3 :** vigorously or healthily plump; *specif* **:** full-bosomed — **bux·om·ly** *adv* — **bux·om·ness** *n*
[1]**buy** \ˈbī\ *vb* **bought** \ˈbȯt\ **buy·ing** [ME *byen*, fr. OE *bycgan*; akin to Goth *bugjan* to buy] *vt* **1 :** to acquire by payment **:** PURCHASE **2 a :** to obtain in exchange for something **b :** REDEEM 6 **3 :** BRIBE, HIRE **4 :** to be the purchasing equivalent of **5** *slang* **:** ACCEPT, BELIEVE ⟨I don't ~ that hooey⟩ ~ *vi* **:** to make a purchase
[2]**buy** *n* **1 :** PURCHASE **2 :** something of value at a favorable price
buy·er \ˈbī(-ə)r\ *n* **:** one that buys; *esp* **:** a department head of a retail store
buy off *vt* **1 :** to induce to refrain (as from prosecution) by a payment or other consideration **2 :** to free by payment
buy out *vt* **:** to purchase the share or interest of
[1]**buzz** \ˈbəz\ *vb* [ME *bussen*, of imit. origin] *vi* **1 :** to make a low continuous humming sound like that of a bee **2 a :** MURMUR, WHISPER **b :** to be filled with a confused murmur ⟨the room ~*ed* with excitement⟩ **3 :** to make a signal with a buzzer ~ *vt* **1 :** to utter covertly by or as if by whispering **2 :** to cause to buzz **3 :** to fly low and fast over ⟨planes ~ the crowd⟩ **4 :** to summon or signal with a buzzer **5** *dial Eng* **:** to drink to the last drop
[2]**buzz** *n* **1 :** a persistent vibratory sound **2 a :** a confused murmur or flurry of activity **b :** RUMOR, GOSSIP **3 :** a signal conveyed by buzzer; *specif, slang* **:** a call on the telephone
buz·zard \ˈbəz-ərd\ *n* [ME *busard*, fr. OF, alter. of *buison*, fr. L *buteon-*, *buteo*] **1** *chiefly Brit* **:** BUTEO **2 :** any of various usu. large birds of prey **3 :** a contemptible or rapacious person
buzz bomb *n* **:** ROBOT BOMB
buzz·er \ˈbəz-ər\ *n* **:** one that buzzes; *specif* **:** an electric signaling device that makes a buzzing sound
buzz saw *n* **:** a circular saw having teeth on its periphery and revolving upon a spindle
[1]**by** \(ˈ)bī, *esp before consonants* bə\ *prep* [ME, prep. & adv., fr. OE, prep., *be*, *bī*; akin to OHG *bī* by, near, L *ambi-* on both sides, around, Gk *amphi*] **1 :** in proximity to **:** NEAR **2 a :** through or through the medium of **:** VIA ⟨enter ~ the door⟩ **b :** in the direction of **:** TOWARD ⟨north ~ east⟩ **c :** into the vicinity of and beyond **:** PAST ⟨went right ~ him⟩ **3 a :** during the course of ⟨studied ~ night⟩ **b :** not later than ⟨~ 2 p.m.⟩ **4 a :** through the agency or instrumentality of ⟨~ force⟩ **b :** sired by **5 :** with the witness or sanction of ⟨swear ~ all that is holy⟩ **6 :** in conformity with ⟨~ the rules⟩ **:** according to **7 :** with respect to **8 a :** in or to the amount or extent of ⟨win ~ a nose⟩ **b** *chiefly Scot* **:** in comparison with **:** BESIDE **9 :** in successive units of ⟨walk two ~ two⟩ **10** — used as a function word in multiplication and in measurements ⟨2 ~ 4⟩
[2]**by** \ˈbī\ *adv* **1 a :** close at hand **:** NEAR **b :** at or to another's home ⟨stop ~ for a chat⟩ **2 :** PAST ⟨saw him go ~⟩ **3 :** ASIDE, AWAY
[3]**by** *or* **bye** \ˈbī\ *adj* **1 :** off the main route **:** SIDE **2 :** INCIDENTAL
[4]**by** *or* **bye** \ˈbī\ *n, pl* **byes** \ˈbīz\ **:** something of secondary importance **:** a side issue — **by the by :** by the way **:** INCIDENTALLY
by and by \ˌbī-ən-ˈbī\ *adv* **:** before long **:** SOON
by–and–by \ˌbī-ən-ˈbī\ *n* **:** a future time or occasion
by and large \ˌbī-ən-ˈlärj\ *adv* **:** on the whole **:** in general
by–blow \ˈbī-ˌblō\ *n* **1 :** an indirect blow **2 :** an illegitimate child
bye \ˈbī\ *n* [alter. of [2]*by*] **:** the position of a participant in a tournament who has no opponent after pairs are drawn and advances to the next round without playing
by–elec·tion *also* **bye–election** \ˈbī-ə-ˌlek-shən\ *n* **:** a special election held between regular elections in order to fill a vacancy
by·gone \ˈbī-ˌgȯn *also* -ˌgän\ *adj* **:** gone by **:** PAST; *esp* **:** OUTMODED — **bygone** *n*
by·law *or* **bye·law** \ˈbī-ˌlȯ\ *n* [ME *bilawe*, prob. fr. (assumed) ON *bȳlög*, fr. ON *bȳr* town + *lög* law] **:** a rule adopted by an organization chiefly for the government of its members and the regulation of its affairs
by–line \ˈbī-ˌlīn\ *n* **1 :** a secondary line **:** SIDELINE **2 :** a line at the head of a newspaper or magazine article giving the writer's name
by·name \ˈbī-ˌnām\ *n* **1 :** a secondary name **2 :** NICKNAME
[1]**by·pass** \ˈbī-ˌpas\ *n* **1 :** a passage to one side; *esp* **:** a deflected route usu. around a town **2 a :** a channel carrying a fluid around a part and back to the main stream **b :** [2]SHUNT b
[2]**bypass** *vt* **1 a :** to avoid by means of a bypass **b :** to cause to follow a bypass **2 a :** to neglect or ignore usu. intentionally **b :** CIRCUMVENT
by·past \ˈbī-ˌpast\ *adj* **:** BYGONE
by·path \ˈbī-ˌpath, -ˌpȧth\ *n* **:** BYWAY
by·play \-ˌplā\ *n* **:** action engaged in on the side while the main action proceeds; *specif* **:** incidental stage business
by–prod·uct \ˈbī-ˌpräd-(ˌ)əkt\ *n* **1 :** something produced (as in manufacturing) in addition to the principal product **2 :** a secondary and sometimes unexpected or unintended result
byre \ˈbī(ə)r\ *n* [ME, fr. OE *bȳre*; akin to OE *būr* dwelling — more at BOWER] *chiefly Brit* **:** a cow barn

by·road \'bī-ˌrōd\ *n* : BYWAY

By·ron·ic \bī-'rän-ik\ *adj* : of, relating to, or having the characteristics of the poet Byron or his writings — **By·ron·i·cal·ly** \-i-k(ə-)lē\ *adv* — **By·ron·ism** \'bī-rə-ˌniz-əm\ *n*

bys·sus \'bis-əs\ *n* [L, fr. Gk *byssos* flax, of Sem origin; akin to Heb *būṣ* linen cloth] **1** : a fine prob. linen cloth of ancient times **2** [NL, fr. L] : a tuft of long tough filaments by which some bivalve mollusks (as mussels) make themselves fast

by·stand·er \'bī-ˌstan-dər\ *n* : a nonparticipant observer

by·street \'bī-ˌstrēt\ *n* : a street off a main thoroughfare : side street

byte \'bīt\ *n* [perh. alter. of 2*bite*] : a group of adjacent binary digits often shorter than a word that a computer processes as a unit ⟨an 8-bit ~⟩

by the way *adv* : in passing : INCIDENTALLY

by·way \'bī-ˌwā\ *n* **1** : a side road esp. little traveled **2** : a secondary or little known aspect or field

by·word \'bī-ˌwərd\ *n* **1** : a proverbial saying : PROVERB **2 a** : one that personifies a type **b** : one that is noteworthy or notorious **3** : EPITHET **4** : a frequently used word or phrase

1**By·zan·tine** \'biz-ᵊn-ˌtēn, bə-'zan-, 'bī-zᵊn-; 'biz-ᵊn-ˌtīn; bə-'zant-ᵊn\ *n* : a native or inhabitant of Byzantium

2**Byzantine** *adj* **1** : of, relating to, or characteristic of the ancient city of Byzantium **2** : of, relating to, or having the characteristics of a style of architecture developed in the Byzantine Empire esp. in the 5th and 6th centuries featuring the dome carried on pendentives over a square and incrustation with marble veneering and with colored mosaics on grounds of gold **3** : of or relating to the Eastern Orthodox Church or the rite characteristic of it

C D

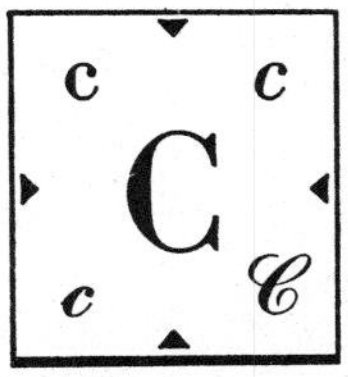

c \'sē\ *n, often cap, often attrib* **1 a** : the third letter of the English alphabet **b** : a graphic representation of this letter **c** : a speech counterpart of orthographic *c* **2 a** : one hundred **b** *slang* : a sum of $100 **3** : the tone C **4** : a graphic device for reproducing the letter *c* **5** : one designated *c* esp. as the third in order or class **6 a** : a grade rating a student's work as fair or mediocre in quality **b** : one graded or rated with a C **7** : something shaped like the letter C

ca' \'kȯ, 'kȧ\ *Scot var of* CALL

1**cab** \'kab\ *n* [Heb *qabh*] : an ancient Hebrew unit of capacity equal to about two quarts

2**cab** \'kab\ *n* [short for *cabriolet*] **1 a** : CABRIOLET : a similar light closed carriage (as a hansom) **b** : a carriage for hire **2** : TAXICAB **3** [short for *cabin*] **a** : the part of a locomotive that houses the engineer and operating controls **b** : a comparable shelter on a truck, tractor, or crane

1**ca·bal** \kə-'bal\ *n* [F *cabale*, cabala, intrigue, cabal, fr. ML *cabbala* cabala, fr. LHeb *qabbālāh*, lit., received (lore)] **1** : a number of persons secretly united to bring about an overturn or usurpation esp. in public affairs **2** : the artifices and intrigues of such a group **syn** see PLOT

2**cabal** *vi* **ca·balled**; **ca·bal·ling** : to unite in or form a cabal

ca·ba·la *or* **cab·ba·la** *or* **cab·ba·lah** \'kab-ə-lə, kə-'bäl-ə\ *n, often cap* [ML *cabbala*] **1** : a medieval and modern system of Jewish theosophy, mysticism, and thaumaturgy marked by belief in creation through emanation and a cipher method of interpreting Scripture **2 a** : a traditional, esoteric, occult, or secret matter **b** : esoteric doctrine or mysterious art — **cab·a·lism** \'kab-ə-ˌliz-əm\ *n* — **cab·a·list** \-ləst\ *n* — **cab·a·lis·tic** \ˌkab-ə-'lis-tik\ *adj*

ca·bal·le·ro \ˌkab-ə-'le(ə)r-(ˌ)ō, -ə(l)-'ye(ə)r-\ *n, pl* **caballeros** [Sp, fr. LL *caballarius* hostler — more at CAVALIER] **1** : KNIGHT, CAVALIER **2** *chiefly Southwest* : HORSEMAN

ca·bana \kə-'ban-(y)ə\ *n* [Sp *cabaña*, lit., hut, fr. ML *capanna*] **1** : a beach shelter resembling a cabin usu. with an open side facing the sea **2** : a lightweight structure with living facilities

cab·a·ret \ˌkab-ə-'rā\ *n* [F, fr. ONF] **1** *archaic* : a shop selling wines and liquors **2** : a restaurant serving liquor and providing entertainment (as by singers or dancers); *also* : the show provided

1**cab·bage** \'kab-ij\ *n, often attrib* [ME *caboche*, fr. ONF, head] **1** : a leafy garden plant (*Brassica oleracea capitata*) of European origin having a short stem and a dense globular head of usu. green leaves that is used as a vegetable **2** : a terminal bud of a palm tree that resembles a head of cabbage and is eaten as a vegetable **3** *slang* : paper money or bank notes

2**cabbage** *n* [perh. by folk etymology fr. MF *cabas* cheating, theft] *Brit* : pieces of cloth left in cutting out garments and traditionally said to be kept by tailors as perquisites

3**cabbage** *vb* : to take surreptitiously : STEAL, FILCH

cabbage butterfly *n* : any of several largely white butterflies (family Pieridae) the green larvae of which are cabbageworms

cabbage palm *n* : a palm with terminal buds eaten as a vegetable

cabbage palmetto *n* : a fan-leaved cabbage palm (*Sabal palmetto*) native to coastal southern U.S.

cab·bage·worm \'kab-ij-ˌwərm\ *n* : an insect larva that feeds on cabbages; *esp* : the toxic green larva of the cabbage butterflies

cab·by *or* **cab·bie** \'kab-ē\ *n* : CABDRIVER

cab·driv·er \'kab-ˌdrī-vər\ *n* : a driver of a cab

ca·ber \'käb-ər, 'kā-bər\ *n* [ScGael *cabar*] : POLE; *esp* : a young tree trunk used for tossing as a trial of strength in a Scottish sport

1**cab·in** \'kab-ən\ *n* [ME *cabane*, fr. MF, fr. OProv *cabana* hut, fr. ML *capanna*] **1 a** : a private room on a ship for one or a few persons — compare CABIN CLASS **b** : a compartment below deck on a small boat for passengers or crew **c** : an airplane or airship compartment for cargo, crew, or passengers **2** : a small one-story dwelling usu. of simple construction **3 a** *chiefly Brit* : CAB 3 **b** : the part of a passenger trailer used for living quarters

2**cabin** *vi* : to live in or as if in a cabin ~ *vt* : CONFINE

cabin boy *n* : a boy acting as servant on a ship

cabin class *n* : a class of accommodations on a passenger ship superior to tourist class and inferior to first class

1**cab·i·net** \'kab-(ə-)nət\ *n* [MF, small room, dim. of ONF *cabine* gambling house] **1 a** : a case or cupboard usu. having doors and shelves **b** : a collection of mineralogical specimens **c** : an upright case housing a radio or television receiver : CONSOLE **d** : a chamber having temperature and humidity controls and used esp. for incubating biological samples **2 a** *archaic* : a small room providing seclusion **b** : a small exhibition room in a museum **3 a** *archaic* (1) : the private room serving as council chamber of the chief councillors or ministers of a sovereign (2) : the consultations and actions of these councillors **b** (1) *often cap* : a body of advisers of a sovereign or other head of a state (2) : a similar advisory council of a governor of a state or a mayor **c** *Brit* : a meeting of a cabinet

2**cabinet** *adj* **1** : suitable by reason of size for a small room or by reason of attractiveness or perfection for preservation and display in a cabinet **2** : belonging to a governmental cabinet **3 a** : used or adapted for cabinetmaking **b** : done or used by a cabinetmaker

cab·i·net·mak·er \-ˌmā-kər\ *n* : a skilled woodworker who makes fine furniture — **cab·i·net·mak·ing** \-ˌmā-kiŋ\ *n*

cab·i·net·work \'kab-(ə-)nət-ˌwərk\ *n* : finished woodwork made by a cabinetmaker

1**ca·ble** \'kā-bəl\ *n, often attrib* [ME, fr. ONF, fr. ML *capulum* lasso, fr. L *capere* to take — more at HEAVE] **1 a** : a strong rope esp. of 10 or more inches in circumference **b** : a cable-laid rope **c** : a wire rope or metal chain of great tensile strength **d** : a wire or wire rope by which force is exerted to control or operate a mechanism **2** : CABLE LENGTH **3 a** : an assembly of electrical conductors insulated from each other but laid up together usu. by being twisted around a central core **b** : CABLEGRAM **4** : something resembling or fashioned like a cable

cable

2**cable** *vb* **ca·bling** \'kā-b(ə-)liŋ\ *vt* **1** : to fasten with or as if with a cable **2** : to provide with cables **3** : to telegraph by submarine cable **4** : to make into a cable or into a form resembling a cable ~ *vi* : to communicate by a submarine cable

cable car *n* : a car made to be moved on a railway by an endless cable operated by a stationary motor or along an overhead cable

ca·ble·gram \'kā-bəl-ˌgram\ *n* : a message sent by a submarine telegraph cable

ca·ble–laid \ˌkā-bəl-'lād\ *adj* : composed of three ropes laid together left-handed with each containing three strands twisted together ⟨~ rope⟩

cable length *n* : a maritime unit of length variously reckoned as 100 fathoms, 120 fathoms, or 608 feet

ca·blet \'kā-blət\ *n* : a small cable; *specif* : a cable-laid rope less than 10 inches in circumference

ca·ble·way \'kā-bəl-ˌwā\ *n* : a suspended cable used as a track along which carriers can be pulled

cab·man \'kab-mən\ *n* : CABDRIVER

cab·o·chon \'kab-ə-ˌshän\ *n* [MF, aug. of ONF *caboche* head] : a gem or bead cut in convex form and highly polished but not faceted; *also* : this style of cutting — **cabochon** *adv*

ca·boo·dle \kə-'büd-ᵊl\ *n* [prob. fr. *ca-* (intensive prefix, prob. of imit. origin) + *boodle*] : COLLECTION, LOT

ca·boose \kə-'büs\ *n* [prob. fr. D *kabuis*, fr. MLG *kabūse*] **1 a** : a deckhouse for cooking **b** : an open-air cooking oven **2** : a freight-train car attached usu. to the rear mainly for the use of the train crew and railroad workmen

cab·o·tage \'kab-ə-ˌtäzh\ *n* [F, fr. *caboter* to sail along the coast] **1** : trade or transport in coastal waters or between two points within a country **2** : the right to engage in cabotage

ca·bret·ta \kə-'bret-ə\ *n* [modif. of Pg and Sp *cabra* goat] : a light soft leather from hair sheepskins

ca·bri·lla \kə-'brē-(y)ə, -'bril-ə\ *n* [Sp, fr. dim. of *cabra* goat, fr. L *capra* she-goat, fem. of *caper* he-goat — more at CAPRIOLE] : any of various sea basses of the Mediterranean, the California coast, and the warmer parts of the western Atlantic

cab·ri·ole \'kab-rē-ˌōl\ *n* [F, caper] **1** : a curved furniture leg ending in an ornamental foot **2** : a ballet leap in which one leg is extended in mid-air and the other struck against it

cab·ri·o·let \ˌkab-rē-ə-'lā\ *n* [F, fr. dim. of *cabriole* caper, alter. of MF *capriole*] **1** : a light 2-wheeled one-horse carriage with a folding leather hood, a large apron, and upward-curving shafts **2** : a convertible coupe

cab·stand \'kab-ˌstand\ *n* : a place where cabs await hire

cac- *or* **caco-** *comb form* [NL, fr. Gk *kak-*, *kako-*, fr. *kakos* bad] : bad ⟨cacogenics⟩

ca' can·ny \kȯ-'kan-ē\ *n, Brit* : SLOWDOWN — **ca' canny** *vi, Brit*

ca·cao \kə-'kaù, kə-'kā-(ˌ)ō\ *n* [Sp, fr. Nahuatl *cacahuatl* cacao beans] **1** : any of several trees (genus *Theobroma*) of the chocolate family; *esp* : CHOCOLATE TREE **2** : the dried partly fermented fatty seeds of the chocolate tree used in making cocoa and chocolate

cacao butter *var of* COCOA BUTTER

cach·a·lot \'kash-ə-ˌlät, -ˌlō\ *n* [F] : SPERM WHALE

1**cache** \'kash\ *n* [F, fr. *cacher* to press, hide, fr. (assumed) VL *coacticare* to press together, fr. L *coactare* to compel, fr. *coactus*, pp. of *cogere* to compel — more at COGENT] **1 a** : a hiding place esp. for concealing and preserving provisions or implements **b** : a secure place of storage **2** : something hidden or stored in a cache

2**cache** *vt* : to place, hide, or store in a cache

ca·chec·tic \ka-'kek-tik\ *adj* [F *cachectique*, fr. L *cachecticus*, fr. Gk *kachektikos*, fr. *kak-* + *echein*] : affected by cachexia

ca·chet \ka-'shā\ *n* [MF, fr. *cacher* to press, hide] **1 a** : a seal used esp. as a mark of official approval **b** : an indication of

approval carrying great prestige **2 a :** a characteristic feature or quality conferring prestige **b :** PRESTIGE **3 :** a flour-paste case in which an unpleasant medicine is swallowed **4 a :** a design or inscription on an envelope to commemorate a postal or philatelic event **b :** an advertisement forming part of a postal meter impression **c :** a motto or slogan included in a postal cancellation

ca·chex·ia \ka-'kek-sē-ə\ *also* **ca·chexy** \'kak-,ek-sē, ka-'kek-\ *n* [LL *cachexia*, fr. Gk *kachexia* bad condition, fr. *kak-* cac- + *hexis* condition, fr. *echein* to have, be disposed] **:** general physical wasting and malnutrition usu. associated with chronic disease

cach·in·nate \'kak-ə-,nāt\ *vi* [L *cachinnatus*, pp. of *cachinnare*, of imit. origin] **:** to laugh loudly or immoderately — **cach·in·na·tion** \,kak-ə-'nā-shən\ *n*

ca·chou \ka-'shü, 'kash-(,)ü\ *n* [F, fr. Pg *cachu*, fr. Malayalam *kāccu*] **1 :** CATECHU **2 :** a pill or pastille used to sweeten the breath

ca·chu·cha \kə-'chü-chə\ *n* [Sp, small boat, cachucha] **:** a gay Andalusian solo dance in triple time done with castanets

ca·cique \kə-'sēk\ *n* [Sp, of Arawakan origin; akin to Taino *cacique* chief] **1 a :** a native Indian chief in areas dominated primarily by a Spanish culture **b :** a local political boss in Spain and Latin America [AmerSp, fr. Sp] **2 :** any of numerous tropical American orioles (as of the genus *Cacicus*) having the base of the bill expanded into a frontal shield — **ca·ciqu·ism** \-'sē-,kiz-əm\ *n*

cack·le \'kak-əl\ *vi* **cack·ling** \-(ə-)liŋ\ [ME *cakelen*, of imit. origin] **1 :** to make the sharp broken noise or cry characteristic of a hen esp. after laying **2 :** to laugh in a way suggestive of a hen's cackle **3 :** CHATTER — **cackle** *n* — **cack·ler** \-(ə-)lər\ *n*

caco·de·mon \,kak-ə-'dē-mən\ *n* [Gk *kakodaimōn*, fr. *kak-* cac- + *daimōn* spirit] **:** DEMON — **caco·de·mon·ic** \-di-'män-ik\ *adj*

cac·o·dyl \'kak-ə-,dil\ *n* [ISV, fr. Gk *kakōdēs* ill smelling, fr. *kak-* + *-ōdēs* (akin to Gk *ozein* to smell)] **1 :** an arsenical radical As-(CH₃)₂ whose compounds are noted for their vile smell and poisonous properties **2 :** a colorless liquid As₂(CH₃)₄ consisting of two cacodyl radicals — **cac·o·dyl·ic** \,kak-ə-'dil-ik\ *adj*

caco·ë·thes \,kak-ə-'wē-(,)thēz\ *n* [L, fr. Gk *kakoēthes* wickedness, fr. neut. of *kakoēthēs* malignant, fr. *kak-* cac- + *ēthos* character — more at ETHICAL] **:** an insatiable desire **:** MANIA

caco·gen·e·sis \-'jen-ə-səs\ *n* [NL] **:** racial deterioration esp. when due to the retention of inferior breeding stock — **caco·gen·ic** \-'jen-ik\ *adj*

caco·gen·ics \-'jen-iks\ *n pl but sing or pl in constr* [*cac-* + *-genics* (as in *eugenics*)] **1 :** DYSGENICS **2 :** CACOGENESIS

ca·cog·ra·phy \ka-'käg-rə-fē\ *n* **1 :** bad handwriting — compare CALLIGRAPHY **2 :** bad spelling — compare ORTHOGRAPHY

cac·o·mis·tle \'kak-ə-,mis-əl\ *n* [MexSp, fr. Nahuatl *tlacomiztli*, fr. *tlaco* half + *miztli* mountain lion] **:** a carnivore (*Bassariscus astutus*) related to and resembling the raccoon; *also* **:** its fur or pelt

ca·coph·o·nous \ka-'käf-ə-nəs\ *adj* [Gk *kakophōnos*, fr. *kak-* + *phōnē* voice, sound] **:** harsh-sounding — **ca·coph·o·nous·ly** *adv*

ca·coph·o·ny \-nē\ *n* **:** harsh or discordant sound **:** DISSONANCE; *specif* **:** harshness in the sound of words or phrases

cac·tus \'kak-təs\ *n, pl* **cac·ti** \-,tī, -(,)tē\ *or* **cac·tus·es** [NL, genus name, fr. L, cardoon, fr. Gk *kaktos*] **:** any of a family (Cactaceae, the cactus family) of plants with fleshy stems and branches with scales or spines instead of leaves

ca·cu·mi·nal \ka-'kyü-mən-əl\ *adj* [ISV, fr. L *cacumin-, cacumen* top, point] **:** RETROFLEX

cad \'kad\ *n* [E dial., unskilled assistant, short for Sc *caddie*] **1** *obs* **:** an omnibus conductor **2 :** a person without gentlemanly instincts

ca·das·tral \kə-'das-trəl\ *adj* **1 :** of or relating to a cadastre **2 :** showing or recording property boundaries, subdivision lines, buildings, and related details — **ca·das·tral·ly** \-trə-lē\ *adv*

ca·das·tre \kə-'das-tər\ *n* [F, fr. It *catastro*, fr. OIt *catastico*, fr. LGk *katastichon* notebook, fr. Gk *kata* by + *stichos* row, line — more at CATA-, DISTICH] **:** an official register of the quantity, value, and ownership of real estate used in apportioning taxes

ca·dav·er \kə-'dav-ər\ *n* [L, fr. *cadere* to fall] **:** a dead body usu. intended for dissection — **ca·dav·er·ic** \-'dav-(ə-)rik\ *adj*

ca·dav·er·ine \kə-'dav-ə-,rēn\ *n* **:** a syrupy colorless fuming ptomaine C₅H₁₄N₂ formed by decarboxylation of lysine esp. in putrefaction of flesh

ca·dav·er·ous \kə-'dav-(ə-)rəs\ *adj* **1 a :** of or relating to a corpse **b :** suggestive of corpses or tombs **2 a :** PALLID, LIVID **b :** GAUNT, EMACIATED — **ca·dav·er·ous·ly** *adv*

cad·die *or* **cad·dy** \'kad-ē\ *n* [F *cadet* military cadet] **1** *Scot* **:** one that waits about for odd jobs **2 :** one that assists a golfer esp. by carrying his clubs **b :** a small wheeled device for conveying things inconvenient to carry by hand — **caddie** *or* **caddy** *vi*

¹cad·dis *or* **cad·dice** \'kad-əs\ *n* [ME *cadas* cotton wool, prob. fr. MF *cadaz*, fr. OProv *cadarz*] **:** worsted yarn; *specif* **:** a worsted ribbon or binding often used for garters

²caddis *or* **caddice** *n* **:** CADDISWORM

caddis fly *n* **:** any of an order (Trichoptera) of 4-winged insects with aquatic larvae — compare CADDISWORM

cad·dish \'kad-ish\ *adj* **:** resembling a cad — **cad·dish·ly** *adv* — **cad·dish·ness** *n*

cad·dis·worm \'kad-ə-,swərm\ *n* [prob. alter. of *codworm;* fr. the case or tube in which it lives] **:** the larva of a caddis fly that lives in and carries around a silken case covered with bits of debris

cad·dy \'kad-ē\ *n* [Malay *kati*] **:** a small box, can, or chest; *esp* **:** one to keep tea in

¹cade \'kād\ *adj* [E dial. *cade* pet lamb, fr. ME *cad*] **:** left by its mother and reared by hand **:** PET ⟨a ~ lamb⟩ ⟨a ~ colt⟩

²cade *n* [MF, fr. OProv, fr. ML *catanus*] **:** a European juniper (*Juniperus oxycedrus*) whose wood yields by distillation a dark tarry liquid used locally in treating skin diseases

-cade \,kād, 'kād\ *n comb form* [*cavalcade*] **:** procession ⟨motorcade⟩

ca·delle \kə-'del\ *n* [F, fr. Prov *cadello*, fr. L *catella*, fem. of *catellus* little dog, dim. of *catulus* young animal] **:** a small cosmopolitan black beetle (*Tenebroides mauritanicus*) destructive to stored grain

ca·dence \'kād-ᵊn(t)s\ *n* [ME, fr. OIt *cadenza*, fr. *cadere* to fall, fr. L] **1 a :** a rhythmic sequence or flow of sounds in language **b :** the beat, time, or measure of rhythmical motion or activity **2 a :** a falling inflection of the voice **b :** a concluding and usu. falling strain; *specif* **:** a musical chord sequence moving to a harmonic close or point of rest **3 :** the modulated and rhythmic recurrence of a sound esp. in nature — **ca·denced** \-ᵊn(t)st\ *adj*

ca·den·cy \'kād-ᵊn-sē\ *n* **:** CADENCE

ca·dent \'kād-ᵊnt\ *adj* [L *cadent-, cadens*, prp. of *cadere*] **1** *archaic* **:** FALLING **2 :** having rhythmic fall

ca·den·za \kə-'den-zə\ *n* [It, cadence, cadenza] **1 :** a parenthetic flourish in an aria or other solo piece commonly just before a final or other important cadence **2 :** a technically brilliant sometimes improvised solo passage toward the close of a concerto

ca·det \kə-'det\ *n, often attrib* [F, fr. F dial. *capdet* chief, fr. LL *capitellum*, dim. of L *capit-, caput* head — more at HEAD] **1 a :** a younger brother or son **b :** youngest son **c :** a younger branch of a family or a member of it **2 :** one in training for a military or naval commission; *esp* **:** a student in a service academy **3 :** a junior in a business or occupation who is engaged principally in learning **4** *slang* **:** PIMP — **ca·det·ship** \-,ship\ *n*

cadge \'kaj\ *vb* [back-formation fr. Sc *cadger* carrier, huckster, fr. ME *caggear*, fr. *caggen* to tie] **:** BEG, SPONGE — **cadg·er** *n*

cad·mi·um \'kad-mē-əm\ *n* [NL, fr. L *cadmia* calamine; fr. the occurrence of its ores together with calamine — more at CALAMINE] **:** a tin-white malleable ductile toxic bivalent metallic element used esp. in protective platings and in bearing metals — see ELEMENT table

Cad·mus \'kad-məs\ *n* [L, fr. Gk *Kadmos*] **:** a Phoenician prince held in Greek legend to have killed a dragon and sown its teeth from which sprang armed men who fought together

cad·re \'kad-rē\ *n* [F, fr. It *quadro*, fr. L *quadrum* square — more at QUARREL] **1 :** FRAME, FRAMEWORK **2 :** a nucleus esp. of trained personnel capable of assuming control and of training others

ca·du·ce·an \kə-'d(y)ü-sē-ən\ *adj* **:** of or relating to a caduceus

ca·du·ce·us \kə-'d(y)ü-sē-əs\ *n, pl* **ca·du·cei** \-sē-,ī\ [L, modif. of Gk *karykeion*, fr. *karyx, kēryx* herald; akin to OE *hrēth* glory] **1 :** the symbolic staff of a herald; *specif* **:** a representation of a staff with two entwined snakes and two wings at the top **2 :** an insignia bearing a caduceus and symbolizing a physician

caduceus 2

ca·du·ci·ty \kə-'d(y)ü-sət-ē\ *n* [F *caducité*, fr. *caduc* transitory, fr. L *caducus*] **1 :** the quality of being transitory or perishable **2 :** SENILITY

ca·du·cous \kə-'d(y)ü-kəs\ *adj* [L *caducus* tending to fall, transitory, fr. *cadere* to fall] **:** falling off easily or before the usual time — used esp. of floral organs

cae·cal, cae·cum *var of* CECAL, CECUM

cae·cil·ian \si-'sil-yən, -'sēl-, -'sē-ən\ *n* [deriv. of L *caecilia*, a lizard, fr. *caecus* blind] **:** any of an order (Gymnophiona) of chiefly tropical burrowing amphibians resembling worms — **caecilian** *n*

caen- *or* **caeno-** — see CEN-

Cae·sar \'sē-zər\ *n* [Gaius Julius *Caesar* †44 B.C. Roman general and statesman] **1 :** any of the Roman emperors succeeding Augustus Caesar — used as a title **2 a** *often not cap* **:** a powerful ruler: (1) **:** EMPEROR (2) **:** AUTOCRAT, DICTATOR **b** [fr. the reference in Mt 22:21] **:** the civil power **:** temporal ruler — **Cae·sar·e·an** *or* **Cae·sar·i·an** \si-'zar-ē-ən, -'zer-\ *adj*

Cae·sar·ism \'sē-zə-,riz-əm\ *n* **:** imperial authority or system **:** political absolutism **:** DICTATORSHIP — **Cae·sar·ist** \-zə-rəst\ *n*

cae·si·um *var of* CESIUM

caes·pi·tose \'ses-pə-,tōs\ *adj* [NL *caespitosus*, fr. L *caespit-, caespes* turf] **1 :** forming a dense turf or sod **2 :** growing in clusters or tufts

cae·su·ra \si-'z(h)ur-ə\ *n, pl* **caesuras** *or* **cae·su·rae** \-'z(h)ù(ə)r-(,)ē\ [LL, fr. L, act of cutting, fr. *caedere* to cut] **1** *in Greek and Latin prosody* **:** a break in the flow of sound in a verse caused by the ending of a word within a foot **2** *in modern prosody* **:** a usu. rhetorical break in the flow of sound in the middle of a line of verse **3 :** BREAK, INTERRUPTION **4 :** a pause marking a rhythmic point of division in a melody — **cae·su·ral** \-'z(h)ùr-əl\ *adj*

ca·fé *also* **ca·fe** \ka-'fā, kə-\ *n, often attrib* [F *café* coffee, café, fr. Turk *kahve* — more at COFFEE] **1 :** COFFEE **2 :** RESTAURANT **3 :** BARROOM **4 :** CABARET, NIGHTCLUB

ca·fé au lait \(,)ka-,fā-ō-'lā\ *n* [F, coffee with milk] **:** coffee with usu. hot milk in about equal parts

ca·fé noir \-,fän-(ə-)'wär\ *n* [F, black coffee] **:** coffee without milk or cream; *also* **:** DEMITASSE

caf·e·te·ria \,kaf-ə-'tir-ē-ə\ *n* [AmerSp *cafetería* retail coffee store, fr. Sp *café* coffee] **:** a self-service restaurant or lunchroom

caf·feine \ka-'fēn, 'kaf-,ēn\ *n* [G *kaffein*, fr. *kaffee* coffee, fr. F *café*] **:** a bitter compound C₈H₁₀N₄O₂ found esp. in coffee, tea, and kola nuts and used medicinally as a stimulant and diuretic — **caf·fein·ic** \ka-'fē-nik, ,kaf-ē-'in-ik\ *adj*

caf·tan \kaf-'tan, 'kaf-,tan\ *n* [Russ *kaftan*, fr. Turk, fr. Per *qaftān*] **:** a usu. cotton or silk often striped ankle-length garment with very long sleeves and a sash fastening that is common throughout the Levant

¹cage \'kāj\ *n* [ME, fr. OF, fr. L *cavea* cavity, cage, fr. *cavus* hollow — more at CAVE] **1 :** a box or enclosure having some openwork for confining or carrying birds or animals **2 a :** a barred cell for confining prisoners **b :** a fenced area for prisoners of war **3 :** a framework serving as support **4 :** an enclosure like a cage in form or purpose **5 a :** a screen placed behind home plate to stop baseballs during batting practice **b :** a goal structure consisting of posts or a frame with a net attached (as in ice hockey) **c :** a basketball basket **6 :** a large building with unobstructed area for practicing outdoor sports and often adapted for indoor events

²cage *vt* **1 :** to confine or keep in or as if in a cage **2 :** to put (as a puck) into a cage and score a goal

cage·ling \'kāj-liŋ\ *n* **:** a caged bird

ca·gey *also* **ca·gy** \'kā-jē\ *adj* **ca·gi·er; ca·gi·est** [origin unknown] **1 :** hesitant about committing oneself **2 :** wary of being trapped or deceived **:** SHREWD, CAUTIOUS — **ca·gey·ness** *or* **ca·gi·ness** \-jē-nəs\ *n* — **ca·gi·ly** \-jə-lē\ *adv*

ca·hier \kä-'yā\ *n* [F, fr. MF *quaer, caier* quire] **1 :** a report or memorial concerning policy esp. of a parliamentary body **2 :** a number of sheets of paper put together for binding or bound loosely

ca·hoot \kə-'hüt\ *n* [perh. fr. F *cahute* cabin, hut] **:** PARTNERSHIP, LEAGUE — usu. used in pl. ⟨in ~s with the devil⟩

cai·man \kā-'man, kī-; 'kā-mən\ *n* [Sp *caimán*, prob. fr. Carib *caymán*] **:** any of several Central and So. American crocodilians similar to alligators but often superficially resembling crocodiles

Cain \'kān\ *n* [Heb *Qayin*] **:** the brother and murderer of Abel

-caine \,kān, 'kān\ *n comb form* [G *-kain*, fr. *kokain* cocaine] **:** synthetic alkaloid anesthetic ⟨*procaine*⟩

ca·ïque \kä-'ēk\ *n* [Turk *kayιk*] **1 :** a light skiff used on the Bosporus **2 :** a Levantine sailing vessel

caird \'kārd\ *n* [ScGael *ceard;* akin to Gk *kerdos* profit] *Scot* **:** a traveling tinker; *also* **:** TRAMP, GYPSY

cairn \'ka(ə)rn, 'ke(ə)rn\ *n* [ME *carne,* fr. ScGael *carn;* akin to OIr & W *carn* cairn] **:** a heap of stones piled up as a memorial or as a landmark — **cairned** \'ka(ə)rnd, 'ke(ə)rnd\ *adj*

cairn·gorm \'ka(ə)rn-,gò(ə)rm, 'ke(ə)rn-\ *n* [*Cairngorm,* mountain in Scotland] **:** a yellow or smoky-brown crystalline quartz

cairn terrier *n* [fr. its use in hunting among cairns] **:** a small compactly built hard-coated terrier of Scottish origin

cais·son \'kā-,sän, 'kās-ᵊn\ *n* [F, aug. of *caisse* box, fr. OProv *caisa,* fr. L *capsa* chest, case — more at CASE] **1 a :** a chest to hold ammunition **b :** a 2-wheeled vehicle for artillery ammunition attachable to a horse-drawn limber **2 a :** a watertight chamber used in construction work under water or as a foundation **b :** a float for raising a sunken vessel **c :** a hollow floating box or a boat used as a floodgate for a dock or basin **3 :** COFFER 4

caisson disease *n* **:** a sometimes fatal disorder marked by neuralgic pains and paralysis and caused by too rapid decrease in air pressure after a stay in compressed atmosphere — called also *bends*

cai·tiff \'kāt-əf\ *adj* [ME *caitif,* fr. ONF, captive, vile, fr. L *captivus* captive] **:** being base, cowardly, or despicable — **caitiff** *n*

caj·e·put \'kaj-ə-pət, -,pùt\ *n* [Malay *kayu puteh,* fr. *kayu* wood, tree + *puteh* white] **1** *or* **caj·a·put** *or* **caj·u·put** \'kaj-ə-\ **:** an East Indian tree (*Melaleuca leucadendron*) of the myrtle family that yields a pungent medicinal oil **2 :** CALIFORNIA LAUREL

ca·jole \kə-'jōl\ *vt* [F *cajoler* to chatter like a jay in a cage, cajole, alter. of MF *gaioler,* fr. ONF *gaiole* birdcage, fr. LL *caveola,* dim. of L *cavea* cage] **1 :** to persuade with deliberate flattery esp. in the face of reluctance **2 :** to deceive with soothing words or false promises — **ca·jole·ment** \-mənt\ *n* — **ca·jol·er** *n* — **ca·jol·ery** \-'jōl-(ə-)rē\ *n*

Ca·jun *also* **Ca·jan** \'kā-jən\ *n* [by alter. of *Acadian*] **1 :** a Louisianan descended from French-speaking immigrants from Acadia **2 :** one of a people of mixed white, Indian, and Negro ancestry in southwest Alabama and southeast Mississippi

1**cake** \'kāk\ *n* [ME, fr. ON *kaka;* akin to OHG *kuocho* cake] **1 a :** fried or baked bread usu. small in size and round and flat in shape **b :** fancy sweetened baked bread usu. prepared as a batter and often coated with an icing **c :** a flattened usu. round mass of food baked or fried **2 a :** a block of compacted or congealed matter ⟨~ of ice⟩ **b :** a hard or brittle layer or deposit

2**cake** *vt* **1 :** ENCRUST **2 :** to fill (a space) with a packed mass ~ *vi* **:** to form or harden into a mass

cake·walk \'kā-,kwòk\ *n* **1 :** an American Negro entertainment having a cake as prize for the most accomplished steps and figures in walking **2 :** a stage dance developed from walking steps and figures typically involving a high prance with backward tilt — **cakewalk** *vi* — **cake·walk·er** *n*

Cal·a·bar bean \,kal-ə-,bär-\ *n* [*Calabar,* Nigeria] **:** the dark brown highly poisonous seed of a tropical African woody vine (*Physostigma venenosum*) used as a source of physostigmine and as an ordeal poison in native witchcraft trials

cal·a·bash \'kal-ə-,bash\ *n, often attrib* [F & Sp; F *calebasse* gourd, fr. Sp *calabaza,* prob. fr. Ar *qar'ah yābisah* dry gourd] **1 :** GOURD; *esp* **:** the common bottle gourd **2 :** a tropical American tree (*Crescentia cujete*) of the trumpet-creeper family; *also* **:** its hard globose fruit **3 :** a utensil made from the shell of a calabash

cal·a·boose \'kal-ə-,büs\ *n* [Sp *calabozo* dungeon] *dial* **:** JAIL

ca·la·di·um \kə-'lād-ē-əm\ *n* [NL, genus name, fr. Malay *kĕladi,* an aroid plant] **:** any of a genus (*Caladium,* esp. *C. bicolor*) of tropical American ornamental plants of the arum family with showy variously colored leaves

cal·a·man·der \'kal-ə-,man-dər\ *n* [prob. fr. D *kalamanderhout* calamander wood] **:** the hazel-brown black-striped wood of an East Indian tree (genus *Diospyros,* esp. *D. quaesita*) related to ebony

cal·a·mary \'kal-ə-,mer-ē\ *or* **cal·a·mar** \-,mär\ *n* [L *calamarius* of a pen, fr. *calamus* reed; fr. the shape of its inner shell] **:** SQUID

cal·a·mine \'kal-ə-,mīn, -mən\ *n* [F, ore of zinc, fr. ML *calamina,* alter. of L *cadmia,* fr. Gk *kadmeia,* lit., Theban (earth), fr. fem. of *kadmeios* Theban, fr. *Kadmos* Cadmus, founder of Thebes] **:** a mixture of zinc oxide with a small amount of ferric oxide used in lotions, liniments, and ointments in skin treatment

cal·a·mint \'kal-ə-,mint\ *n* [ME *calament,* fr. OF, fr. ML *calamentum,* fr. Gk *kalaminthē*] **:** any of a genus (*Satureja,* esp. *S. calamintha*) of mints — called also *basil thyme*

cal·a·mite \'kal-ə-,mīt\ *n* [NL *Calamites,* genus of fossil plants, fr. L *calamus*] **:** a Paleozoic fossil plant (esp. genus *Calamites*) resembling a giant horsetail

ca·lam·i·tous \kə-'lam-ət-əs\ *adj* **:** producing or attended with calamity — **ca·lam·i·tous·ly** *adv* — **ca·lam·i·tous·ness** *n*

ca·lam·i·ty \kə-'lam-ət-ē\ *n* [MF *calamité,* fr. L *calamitat-, calamitas;* akin to L *clades* destruction — more at HALT] **1 :** a state of deep distress or misery caused by major misfortune or loss **2 :** an extraordinarily grave event marked by great loss and lasting distress and affliction **syn** see DISASTER

cal·a·mon·din \,kal-ə-'män-dən\ *n* [Tag *kalamunding*] **:** a small spiny citrus tree (*Citrus mitis*) of the Philippines; *also* **:** its fruit

cal·a·mus \'kal-ə-məs\ *n, pl* **cal·a·mi** \-,mī, -,mē\ [L, reed, reed pen, fr. Gk *kalamos* — more at HAULM] **1 :** the sweet flag (*Acorus calamus*) or its aromatic root **2 :** the barrel of a feather **:** QUILL

ca·lan·do \kä-'län-(,)dō\ *adj (or adv)* [It, fr. L *calandum,* gerund of *calare* to slacken, fr. Gk *chalan*] **:** diminishing in rapidity and loudness **:** dying away — used as a direction in music

ca·lash \kə-'lash\ *n* [F *calèche,* fr. G *kalesche,* fr. Czech *kolesa* wheels, carriage; akin to Gk *kyklos* wheel — more at WHEEL] **1 a :** a light small-wheeled 4-passenger carriage with a folding top **b :** CALÈCHE 2 **2 a :** a large hood worn by women in the 18th century **b :** a folding carriage top

cal·a·thos \'kal-ə-,thäs\ *or* **cal·a·thus** \-thəs\ *n, pl* **cal·a·thi** \-,thī, -,thē\ [Gk *kalathos* basket] **:** a flared fruit basket borne on the head as a symbol in Greek and Egyptian art of fruitfulness

calc- *or* **calci-** *or* **calco-** *comb form* [L *calc-, calx* lime — more at CHALK] **:** calcium **:** calcium salt ⟨*calcic*⟩ ⟨*calcify*⟩

cal·ca·ne·al \kal-'kā-nē-əl\ *adj* **:** relating to the heel or calcaneus

cal·ca·ne·um \-nē-əm\ *n, pl* **cal·ca·nea** \-nē-ə\ [L, heel — more at CALK] **1 :** CALCANEUS **2 :** a process of the tarsometatarsus of a bird analogous to the calcaneus

cal·ca·ne·us \-nē-əs\ *n, pl* **cal·ca·nei** \-nē-,ī\ [LL, heel, alter. of L *calcaneum*] **:** a tarsal bone that in man is the great bone of the heel

cal·car \'kal-,kär\ *n, pl* **cal·car·ia** \kal-'kar-ē-ə, -'ker-\ [L, fr. *calc-, calx* heel — more at CALK] **:** a spurred prominence

cal·car·e·ous \kal-'kar-ē-əs, -'ker-\ *adj* [L *calcarius* of lime, fr. *calc-, calx* lime] **1 a :** resembling calcite or calcium carbonate esp in hardness **b :** consisting of or containing calcium carbonate; *also* **:** containing calcium **2 :** growing on limestone or in soil impregnated with lime — **cal·car·e·ous·ly** *adv* — **cal·car·e·ous·ness** *n*

cal·ce·iform \'kal-sē-ə-,fòrm\ *adj* [L *calceus* shoe] **:** shaped like a slipper ⟨the ~ lip of certain orchids⟩

cal·ce·o·lar·ia \,kal-sē-ə-'lar-ē-ə, -'ler-\ *n* [NL, genus name, fr. L *calceolus* small shoe, dim. of *calceus* shoe, fr. *calc-, calx* heel] **:** any of a genus (*Calceolaria*) of tropical American plants of the figwort family with showy pouch-shaped flowers

cal·ce·o·late \'kal-sē-ə-,lāt\ *adj* [L *calceolus*] **:** CALCEIFORM — **cal·ce·o·late·ly** *adv*

calces *pl of* CALX

Cal·chas \'kal-kəs\ *n* [L, fr. Gk *Kalchas*] **:** a priest of Apollo in the Greek army at Troy

cal·cic \'kal-sik\ *adj* **:** derived from or containing calcium or lime

cal·ci·cole \'kal-sə-,kōl\ *n* [F, calcicolous, fr. *calc-* + *-cole* -colous] **:** a plant normally growing on calcareous soils — **cal·cic·o·lous** \kal-'sik-ə-ləs\ *adj*

cal·cif·er·ol \kal-'sif-ə-,ròl, -,rōl\ *n* [blend of *calciferous* + *ergosterol*] **:** VITAMIN D_2

cal·cif·er·ous \kal-'sif-(ə-)rəs\ *adj* **:** producing or containing calcium carbonate esp. calcite

cal·cif·ic \kal-'sif-ik\ *adj* [*calcify*] **:** involving or caused by calcification

cal·ci·fi·ca·tion \,kal-sə-fə-'kā-shən\ *n* **1 :** the process of calcifying; *specif* **:** deposition of insoluble lime salts (as in tissue) **2 :** a calcified structure

cal·ci·fuge \'kal-sə-,fyüj\ *n* [F, calcifugous, fr. *calc-* + L *fugere* to flee — more at FUGITIVE] **:** a plant not normally growing on calcareous soils — **cal·cif·u·gous** \kal-'sif-yə-gəs\ *adj*

cal·ci·fy \'kal-sə-,fī\ *vt* **:** to make calcareous by deposit of calcium salts ~ *vi* **:** to become calcareous

cal·ci·mine \'kal-sə-,mīn\ *n* [alter. of *kalsomine,* of unknown origin] **:** a white or tinted wash of glue, whiting or zinc white, and water used esp. on plastered surfaces — **calcimine** *vt*

cal·ci·na·tion \,kal-sə-'nā-shən\ *n* **:** the act or process of calcining **:** the state of being calcined

cal·cine \kal-'sīn\ *vb* [ME *calcenen,* fr. MF *calciner,* fr. L *calc-, calx* lime — more at CHALK] *vt* **:** to heat (as inorganic materials) to a high temperature but without fusing in order to effect useful changes (as oxidation or pulverizing) ~ *vi* **:** to undergo calcination

cal·cite \'kal-,sīt\ *n* **:** a mineral $CaCO_3$ consisting of calcium carbonate crystallized in hexagonal form and including common limestone chalk and marble — **cal·cit·ic** \kal-'sit-ik\ *adj*

cal·ci·um \'kal-sē-əm\ *n, often attrib* [NL, fr. L *calc-, calx* lime] **:** a silver-white bivalent metallic element of the alkaline-earth group occurring only in combination — see ELEMENT table

calcium carbide *n* **:** a usu. dark gray crystalline compound CaC_2 used for the generation of acetylene

calcium carbonate *n* **:** a salt $CaCO_3$ found in nature as calcite and aragonite and in plant ashes, bones, and shells and used in making lime and portland cement

calcium chloride *n* **:** a deliquescent salt $CaCl_2$ used in its anhydrous state as a white porous solid as a drying and dehumidifying agent and in a hydrated state to lay dust

calcium cyanamide *n* **:** a compound $CaCN_2$ obtained in impure form by passing dry nitrogen over calcium carbide at a high temperature and used as a fertilizer and a weed killer and as a source of other nitrogen compounds

calcium light *n* **:** LIMELIGHT 1a, 1b

calcium phosphate *n* **:** any of various phosphates of calcium: as **a :** the phosphate $CaH_4(PO_4)_2$ used as a fertilizer and in baking powder **b :** the phosphate $CaHPO_4$ used in pharmaceutical preparations and animal feeds **c :** the phosphate $Ca_3(PO_4)_2$ used as a fertilizer **d :** a naturally occurring phosphate of calcium $Ca_5(F,Cl,OH,\frac{1}{2}CO_3)(PO_4)_3$ containing other elements or radicals (as fluorine) and occurring as the chief constituent of phosphate rock, bones, and teeth

calc–sin·ter \'kalk-,sint-ər\ *n* [G *kalksinter,* fr. *kalk* lime + *sinter*] **:** calcareous sinter **:** TRAVERTINE

calc·spar \'kalk-,spär\ *n* [part trans. of Sw *kalkspat,* fr. *kalk* lime + *spat* spar] **:** CALCITE

calc–tu·fa \-,t(y)ü-fə\ *or* **calc–tuff** \-,təf\ *n* [G *kalk* + E *tufa* or *tuff*] **:** calcareous tufa

cal·cu·la·bil·i·ty \,kal-kyə-lə-'bil-ət-ē\ *n* **:** the quality of being calculable

cal·cu·la·ble \'kal-kyə-lə-bəl\ *adj* **1 :** subject to or ascertainable by calculation **2 :** that may be counted on **:** DEPENDABLE — **cal·cu·la·ble·ness** *n* — **cal·cu·la·bly** \-blē\ *adv*

cal·cu·late \'kal-kyə-,lāt\ *vb* [L *calculatus,* pp. of *calculare,* fr. *calculus* pebble (used in reckoning), dim. of *calc-, calx* stone used in gaming, lime — more at CHALK] *vt* **1 a :** to determine by mathematical processes **b :** to reckon by exercise of practical judgment **:** ESTIMATE **c :** to solve or probe the meaning of **:** figure out **2 :** to design or adapt for a purpose **3** *chiefly North* **a :** to judge to be true or probable **b :** INTEND ~ *vi* **1 a :** to make a calculation **b :** to forecast consequences **2 :** COUNT, RELY

syn CALCULATE, COMPUTE, ESTIMATE, RECKON mean to determine something mathematically. CALCULATE is usu. preferred in reference to highly intricate process and problematical rather than exact or definite result; COMPUTE is the simpler term for reaching an exact result by simpler arithmetic process; ESTIMATE applies chiefly to the forecasting of costs or trends and suggests a seeking of usable but tentative and approximate results; RECKON usu. suggests the simpler arithmetical processes or rough-and-ready methods

cal·cu·lat·ed \-,lāt-əd\ *adj* **1 a :** worked out by mathematical calculation **b :** engaged in, undertaken, or displayed after reckoning or estimating the statistical probability of success or failure **2 :** planned or contrived to accomplish a purpose **3 :** brought

about by deliberate intent **4 :** APT, LIKELY — **cal·cu·lat·ed·ly** *adv*

cal·cu·lat·ing \-ˌlāt-iŋ\ *adj* **1 :** making calculations ⟨~ machine⟩ **2 :** marked by prudent and deliberate analysis or by shrewd consideration of self-interest **:** SCHEMING

cal·cu·la·tion \ˌkal-kyə-'lā-shən\ *n* **1 a :** the process or an act of calculating **b :** the result of an act of calculating **2 a :** studied care in analyzing or planning **b :** cold heartless planning to promote self-interest — **cal·cu·lat·ive** \'kal-kyə-ˌlāt-iv\ *adj*

cal·cu·la·tor \'kal-kyə-ˌlāt-ər\ *n* **1 :** one that calculates: as **a :** a machine for performing mathematical operations mechanically **b :** a person who operates such a machine **2 :** a set or book of tables for facilitating computations

cal·cu·lous \'kal-kyə-ləs\ *adj* **:** caused or characterized by a calculus or calculi

cal·cu·lus \-ləs\ *n, pl* **cal·cu·li** \-ˌlī, -ˌlē\ *also* **cal·cu·lus·es** [L, pebble, stone in the bladder or kidney, stone used in reckoning] **1 :** a concretion usu. of mineral salts around organic material found esp. in hollow organs or ducts **2** *archaic* **:** CALCULATION **3 a :** a method of computation or calculation in a special symbolic notation **b :** the mathematical methods comprising differential and integral calculus

calculus of variations : a branch of mathematics dealing with maxima and minima of integrals of functions of curves as the curves vary in a specified way

cal·de·ra \kal-'der-ə, -'dir-\ *n* [Sp, lit., caldron, fr. LL *caldaria*] **:** a crater with a diameter many times that of the volcanic vent formed by collapse of the central part of a volcano or by explosions of extraordinary violence

cal·dron \'kȯl-drən\ *n* [ME, alter. of *cauderon*, fr. ONF, dim. of *caudiere*, fr. LL *caldaria*, fr. L, warm bath, fr. fem. of *caldarius* suitable for warming, fr. *calidus* warm, fr. *calēre* to be warm] **1 :** a large kettle or boiler **2 :** something resembling a boiling caldron

ca·lèche *or* **ca·leche** \kə-'lesh\ *n* [F *calèche* — more at CALASH] **1 :** CALASH 1a **2 :** a 2-wheeled horse-drawn vehicle with a driver's seat on the splashboard used in Quebec **3 :** CALASH 2a

cal·e·fac·to·ry \ˌkal-ə-'fak-t(ə-)rē\ *n* [ML *calefactorium*, fr. L *calefactus*, pp. of *calefacere* to warm] **:** a monastery sitting room

[1]**cal·en·dar** \'kal-ən-dər\ *n* [ME *calender*, fr. AF or ML; AF *calender*, fr. ML *kalendarium*, fr. L, moneylender's account book, fr. *kalendae* calends] **1 :** a system for fixing the beginning, length, and divisions of the civil year and arranging days and longer divisions of time (as weeks and months) in a definite order **2 :** a tabular register of days according to a system usu. covering one year and referring the days of each month to the days of the week **3 :** an orderly list: as **a :** a list of cases to be tried in court **b :** a list of bills or other items reported out of committee for consideration by a legislative assembly **c :** a list of events or activities giving dates and details **4** *Brit* **:** a university catalog

MONTHS OF THE PRINCIPAL CALENDARS

GREGORIAN[1] name	days	JEWISH name	days	MUHAMMADAN name	days
January begins 10 days after winter solstice	31	Tishri begins first new moon after autumnal equinox	30	Muharram[4] in A.H. 1378 began July 18, 1948	30
February	28	Heshvan	29	Safar	29
in leap years	29		or 30	Rabi I	30
March	31	Kislev	29	Rabi II	29
April	30		or 30	Jumada I	30
May	31	Tebet	29	Jumada II	29
June	30	Shebat	30	Rajab	30
July	31	Adar[2]	29	Sha'ban	29
August	31		or 30	Ramadan	30
September	30	Nisan[3]	30	Shawwal	29
October	31	Iyar	29	Dhu'l-Qa'dah	30
November	30	Sivan	30	Dhu'l-Hijja	29
December	31	Tammuz	29	in leap years	30
		Ab	30		
		Elul	29		

[1]The equinoxes occur on March 21 and September 23, the solstices on June 22 and December 22. [2]In leap years Adar is followed by Veadar or Adar Sheni, an intercalary month of 29 days. [3]Anciently called Abib; the first month of the postexilic calendar; sometimes called the first month of the ecclesiastical year. [4]Retrogresses through the seasons; the Muhammadan year is lunar and each month begins at the approximate new moon; the year 1 A.H. began on Friday, July 16, A.D. 622.

[2]**calendar** *vt* **cal·en·dar·ing** \-d(ə-)riŋ\ **:** to enter in a calendar

[1]**cal·en·der** \'kal-ən-dər\ *vt* **cal·en·der·ing** \-d(ə-)riŋ\ [MF *calandrer*, fr. *calandre* machine for calendering, modif. of Gk *kylindros* cylinder] **:** to press between rollers or plates in order to smooth and glaze or thin into sheets — **cal·en·der·er** \-dər-ər\ *n*

[2]**calender** *n* **:** a machine for calendering something

[3]**calender** *n* [Per *qalandar*, fr. Ar, fr. Per *kalandar* uncouth man] **:** one of a Sufic order of wandering mendicant dervishes

ca·len·dri·cal \kə-'len-dri-kəl\ *also* **ca·len·dric** \-drik\ *adj* **:** of, relating to, characteristic of, or used in a calendar

cal·ends \'kal-ən(d)z\ *n pl but sing or pl in constr* [ME *kalendes*, fr. L *kalendae, calendae*] **:** the first day of the ancient Roman month from which days were counted backward to the ides

ca·len·du·la \kə-'len-jə-lə\ *n* [NL, genus name, fr. ML, fr. L *calendae* calends] **:** any of a small genus (*Calendula*) of yellow-rayed composite herbs of temperate regions

cal·en·ture \'kal-ən-ˌchu̇(ə)r\ *n* [Sp *calentura*, fr. *calentar* to heat, fr. L *calent-, calens*, prp. of *calēre* to be warm — more at LEE] **:** a tropical fever caused by exposure to heat

[1]**calf** \'kaf, 'kȧf\ *n, pl* **calves** \'kavz, 'kȧvz\ *also* **calfs** *often attrib* [ME, fr. OE *cealf;* akin to OHG *kalb* calf, ON *kalfi* calf of the leg, L *galla* gallnut] **1 a :** the young of the domestic cow or of some closely related mammals **b :** the young of various other large animals **2** *pl* **calfs :** the hide of the domestic calf; *esp* **:** CALFSKIN **3 :** an awkward or silly boy or youth **4 :** a small mass of ice set free from a coast glacier or from an iceberg or floe

[2]**calf** *n, pl* **calves** \'kavz, 'kȧvz\ [ME, fr. ON *kalfi*] **:** the fleshy hinder part of the leg below the knee

calf love *n* **:** transitory affection felt by a boy or a girl for one of the opposite sex — called also *puppy love*

calf's–foot jelly \ˌkavz-ˌfu̇t-, ˌkafs-, ˌkȧvz-, ˌkȧfs-\ *n* **:** jelly made from gelatin obtained by boiling calves' feet

calf·skin \'kaf-ˌskin, 'kȧf-\ *n* **:** leather made of the skin of a calf

Cal·gon \'kal-ˌgän\ *trademark* — used for a complex sodium phosphate glass used esp. in water softening

Cal·i·ban \'kal-ə-ˌban\ *n* **:** a savage and deformed slave in Shakespeare's *The Tempest*

cal·i·ber *or* **cal·i·bre** \'kal-ə-bər\ *n* [MF *calibre*, fr. OIt *calibro*, fr. Ar *qālib* shoemaker's last] **1 a :** the diameter of a bullet or other projectile **b :** the diameter of a bore (as of a cannon or other firearm) **2 :** the diameter of a round body; *esp* **:** the internal diameter of a hollow cylinder **3 a :** degree of mental capacity or moral quality **b :** degree of excellence or importance **:** QUALITY

cal·i·brate \'kal-ə-ˌbrāt\ *vt* **1 :** to ascertain the caliber of (as a thermometer tube) **2 :** to determine, rectify, or mark the graduations of — **cal·i·bra·tion** \ˌkal-ə-'brā-shən\ *n* — **cal·i·bra·tor** \'kal-ə-ˌbrāt-ər\ *n*

ca·li·che \kə-'lē-chē\ *n* [AmerSp, fr. Sp, flake of lime, fr. *cal* lime, fr. L *calx* — more at CHALK] **1 :** the nitrate-bearing gravel or rock of the sodium-nitrate deposits of Chile and Peru **2 :** a crust of calcium carbonate that forms on the stony soil of arid regions

cal·i·co \'kal-i-ˌkō\ *n, pl* **calicoes** *or* **calicos** [*Calicut*, India] **1 a :** cotton cloth imported from India **b** *Brit* **:** a plain white cotton fabric that is heavier than muslin **c :** any of various cheap cotton fabrics with figured patterns **2 :** a blotched or spotted animal (as a piebald horse) — **calico** *adj*

calico bass *n* **1 :** BLACK CRAPPIE **2 :** a mottled California sea bass (*Paralabrus clathratus*) esteemed as a sport fish

calico bush *n* **:** MOUNTAIN LAUREL

calico printing *n* **:** the process of making fast-color designs on cotton fabrics (as calico)

Cal·i·for·nia laurel \ˌkal-ə-ˌfȯr-nyə-, -nē-ə-\ *n* [*California*, state of western U.S.] **:** a Pacific coast tree (*Umbellularia californica*) of the laurel family with evergreen foliage and small umbellate flowers

California poppy *n* **:** any of a genus (*Eschscholtzia*) of herbs of the poppy family; *esp* **:** one (*E. californica*) widely cultivated for its pale yellow to red flowers

California rosebay *n* **:** a usu. pink-flowered rhododendron (*Rhododendron macrophyllum*) of the Pacific coast

cal·i·for·ni·um \ˌkal-ə-'fȯr-nē-əm\ *n* [NL, fr. *California*, state of western U.S.] **:** a radioactive element discovered by bombarding curium 242 with alpha particles — see ELEMENT table

ca·lig·i·nous \kə-'lij-ə-nəs\ *adj* [MF or L; MF *caligineux*, fr. L *caliginosus*, fr. *caligin-, caligo* darkness] **:** MISTY, DARK, OBSCURE

cal·i·pash \'kal-ə-ˌpash, ˌkal-ə-'\ *n* **:** a fatty gelatinous dull greenish edible substance next to the upper shell of a turtle

cal·i·pee \'kal-ə-ˌpē, ˌkal-ə-'\ *n* **:** a fatty gelatinous light yellow edible substance attached to the lower shell of a turtle

[1]**cal·i·per** *or* **cal·li·per** \'kal-ə-pər\ *n* [alter. of *caliber*] **1 a :** a measuring instrument with two legs or jaws that can be adjusted to determine thickness, diameter, and distance between surfaces ⟨a pair of ~*s*⟩ **b :** an instrument for measuring diameters (as of logs or trees) consisting of a graduated beam and at right angles to it a fixed arm and a movable arm **2 :** thickness esp. of paper, paperboard, or a tree

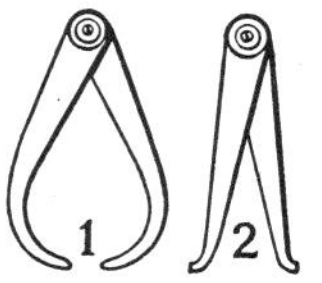

calipers 1: *1* outside, *2* inside

[2]**caliper** *or* **calliper** *vt* **cal·i·per·ing** *or* **cal·li·per·ing** \-p(ə-)riŋ\ **:** to measure by or as if by calipers

ca·liph *or* **ca·lif** \'kā-ləf, 'kal-əf\ *n* [ME *caliphe*, fr. MF *calife*, fr. Ar *khalīfah* successor] **:** a successor of Muhammad as temporal and spiritual head of Islam — used as a title

ca·liph·ate \-ˌāt, -ət\ *n* **:** the office or dominion of a caliph

cal·is·then·ic \ˌkal-əs-'then-ik\ *adj* **:** of or relating to calisthenics

cal·is·then·ics \-iks\ *n pl but sing or pl in constr* [Gk *kalos* beautiful + *sthenos* strength — more at CALLIGRAPHY] **1 :** systematic bodily exercises without apparatus or with light hand apparatus **2** *usu sing in constr* **:** the art or practice of calisthenics

ca·lix \'kā-liks, 'kal-iks\ *n, pl* **ca·li·ces** \'kā-lə-ˌsēz, 'kal-ə-\ [L *calic-, calix* — more at CHALICE] **:** CUP; *esp* **:** an ecclesiastical chalice

[1]**calk** \'kȯk\ **calk·er** \'kȯ-kər\ *var of* CAULK, CAULKER

[2]**calk** \'kȯk\ *n* [prob. alter. of *calkin*, fr. ME *kakun*, fr. MD or ONF; MD *calcoen* horse's hoof, fr. ONF *calcain* heel, fr. L *calcaneum*, fr. *calc-, calx* heel; akin to Gk *kōlon* limb, *skelos* leg] **:** a tapered piece projecting downward on the shoe of a horse to prevent slipping; *also* **:** a similar device worn on the sole of a shoe

[3]**calk** *vt* **1 :** to furnish with calks **2 :** to wound with a calk

[1]**call** \'kȯl\ *vb* [ME *callen*, prob. fr. ON *kalla;* akin to OE *hildecalla* battle herald, OHG *kallōn* to talk loudly, OSlav *glasŭ* voice] *vi* **1 a :** to speak in a loud distinct voice so as to be heard at a distance **:** SHOUT **b :** to make a request or demand ⟨~ for an investigation⟩ **c** *of an animal* **:** to utter a characteristic note or cry **d :** to get or try to get into communication by telephone — often used with *up* **e :** to make a demand in card games (as for a particular card or for a show of hands) **f :** to give the calls for a square dance **2** *Scot* **:** DRIVE **3 :** to make a brief visit ~ *vt* **1 a** (1) **:** to utter in a loud distinct voice — often used with *out* (2) **:** to announce or read out loudly or authoritatively **b** (1) **:** to command or request to come or be present **:** SUMMON ⟨~*ed* to testify⟩ (2) **:** to cause to come **:** BRING ⟨~*s* to mind an old saying⟩ **c :** to summon to a particular activity, employment, or office **d :** to invite or command to meet **:** CONVOKE ⟨~ a meeting⟩ **e :** to rouse from sleep or summon to get up **f :** to give the order for **:** bring into action ⟨~ a strike⟩ **g** (1) **:** to make a demand in bridge for (a card or suit) (2) **:** to require (a player) to show the hand in poker by making an equal bet (3) **:** to challenge to make good on a statement (4) **:** to charge with or censure for an offense ⟨deserves to be ~*ed* on that⟩ **h :** to attract (as game) by imitating the characteristic cry **i :** to halt (as a baseball game) because of unsuitable conditions **j :** to rule on the status of ⟨~ a base runner safe⟩ **k :** to give the calls for (a square dance) — often used with *off* **l** (1) **:** to get or try to get in communication with by telephone (2) **:** to deliver (a message) by telephone (3) **:** to make a signal to in order to transmit a message **m :** SUSPEND ⟨time was ~*ed* while the field was cleared⟩ **n** (1) **:** to demand payment of esp. by formal notice ⟨~ a loan⟩ (2) **:** to demand presentation of (a bond issue) for redemption **2 a :** to speak of or address by a specified name ⟨~ her Kitty⟩ **:** give a name to **b** (1) **:** to regard or characterize as of a certain kind **:** CONSIDER (2) **:** to estimate or consider for purposes of an estimate or for convenience **c** (1) **:** to describe correctly in advance of or without knowledge of the event **:** PREDICT (2) **:** to name in advance **syn** see SUMMON

[2]**call** *n* **1 a :** an act of calling with the voice **:** SHOUT **b :** an imitation of the cry of a bird or other animal made to attract it **c :** an instrument used for calling ⟨a duck ~⟩ **d :** the cry of a bird or other animal **2 a :** a request or command to come or assemble **b :** a summons or signal on a drum, bugle, or pipe **c :** admission to the bar as a barrister **d :** an invitation to become the minister of a church or to accept a professional appointment **e :** a divine vocation or strong inner prompting to a particular course of action **f :** a summoning of actors to rehearsal **g :** the attraction or appeal of a particular activity, condition, or place **h :** an order specifying the number of men to be inducted into the armed services during a specified period **3 a :** DEMAND, CLAIM **b :** NEED, JUSTIFICATION **c :** a demand for payment of money **d :** an option to buy a certain amount of stock, grain, or other commodity at a fixed price or within a certain time **e :** an instance of asking for something **:** REQUEST ⟨many ~*s* for Christmas stories⟩ **4 :** ROLL CALL **5 :** a short usu. formal visit **6 :** the name or thing called ⟨the ~ was heads⟩ **7 :** the act of calling in a card game **8 :** the act of calling on the telephone **9 :** the score at any given time in a tennis game **10 :** a direction or a succession of directions for a square dance rhythmically called to the dancers **11 :** a decision or ruling made by an official of a sports contest

cal·la \ˈkal-ə\ *n* [NL, genus name, modif. of Gk *kallaia* rooster's wattles] **:** a familiar house or greenhouse plant (*Zantedeschia aethiopica*) of the arum family with a white showy spathe and yellow spadix; *also* **:** a plant resembling this

call·able \ˈkȯ-lə-bəl\ *adj* **:** capable of being called; *specif* **:** subject to a demand for presentation for payment ⟨~ bond⟩

cal·lant \ˈkal-ənt\ *or* **cal·lan** \-ən\ *n* [D or ONF; D *kalant* customer, fellow, fr. ONF *calland* customer, fr. L *calent-, calens,* prp. of *calēre* to be warm — more at LEE] *chiefly Scot* **:** BOY, LAD

call–board \ˈkȯl-ˌbō(ə)rd, -ˌbȯ(ə)rd\ *n* **:** a bulletin board

call·boy \-ˌbȯi\ *n* **1 :** BELLBOY, PAGE **2 :** a boy who summons actors to go on stage

call down *vt* **1 :** to cause or entreat to descend **2 :** REPRIMAND

[1]**cal·ler** \ˈkal-ər\ *adj* [ME *callour*] **1** *Scot* **:** FRESH **2** *Scot* **:** COOL

[2]**call·er** \ˈkȯ-lər\ *n* **:** one that calls

cal·let \ˈkal-ət\ *n* [perh. fr. MF *caillette* frivolous person, fr. *Caillette fl* 1500 F court fool] *chiefly Scot* **:** TRULL, PROSTITUTE

call girl *n* **:** a prostitute who may be procured by telephone

call house *n* **:** a house or apartment where call girls may be procured

cal·lig·ra·pher \kə-ˈlig-rə-fər\ *n* **1 :** one that writes a beautiful hand **2 :** PENMAN ⟨a fair ~⟩ **3 :** a professional copyist or engrosser

cal·li·graph·ic \ˌkal-ə-ˈgraf-ik\ *adj* **:** of or relating to calligraphy — **cal·li·graph·i·cal·ly** \-i-k(ə-)lē\ *adv*

cal·lig·ra·phist \kə-ˈlig-rə-fəst\ *n* **:** CALLIGRAPHER

cal·lig·ra·phy \-fē\ *n* [F or Gk; F *calligraphie,* fr. Gk *kalligraphia,* fr. *kalli-* beautiful (fr. *kallos* beauty) + *-graphia* -graphy; akin to Gk *kalos* beautiful, Skt *kalya* healthy] **1 :** fair or elegant handwriting or the art of producing such writing **2 :** PENMANSHIP

call·ing \ˈkȯ-liŋ\ *n* **1 :** a strong inner impulse toward a particular course of action esp. when accompanied by conviction of divine influence **2 :** the vocation or profession in which one customarily engages **3 :** sexual heat esp. of the female cat **syn** see WORK

calling card *n* **:** VISITING CARD

cal·li·ope \kə-ˈlī-ə-(ˌ)pē, *in sense 2 also* ˈkal-ē-ˌōp\ *n* [L, fr. Gk *Kalliopē*] **1** *cap* **:** the Greek Muse of eloquence and heroic poetry **2 :** a musical instrument consisting of a series of whistles played by keys arranged as in an organ

cal·li·op·sis \ˌkal-ē-ˈäp-səs\ *n* [NL, fr. Gk *kalli-* + *opsis* appearance — more at OPTIC] **:** COREOPSIS — used esp. of annual forms

Cal·lis·to \kə-ˈlis-(ˌ)tō\ *n* [*Callisto,* Gk nymph] **:** the so-called 4th but really 5th satellite of Jupiter

cal·li·thump \ˈkal-ə-ˌthəmp\ *n* [back-formation fr. *callithumpian,* adj., alter. of E dial. *gallithumpian* disturber of order at elections in 18th cent.] **:** a noisy boisterous parade — **cal·li·thump·ian** \ˌkal-ə-ˈthəm-pē-ən\ *adj*

call loan *n* **:** a loan payable on demand of either party

call market *n* **:** the market for call loans

call money *n* **:** money loaned or ready to be loaned on call

call number *n* **:** a combination of characters assigned to a library book to indicate its place on a shelf

call off *vt* **1 :** to draw away **:** DIVERT **2 :** to give up **:** CANCEL

cal·lose \ˈkal-ˌōs, -ˌōz\ *n* [L *callosus* callous] **:** a carbohydrate component of plant cell walls

cal·los·i·ty \ka-ˈläs-ət-ē, kə-\ *n* **1 :** the quality or state of being callous: as **a :** marked or abnormal hardness and thickness **b :** lack of feeling or capacity for emotion **2 :** CALLUS 1

[1]**cal·lous** \ˈkal-əs\ *adj* [MF *calleux,* fr. L *callosus,* fr. *callum, callus* callous skin; akin to Skt *kiṇa* callosity] **1 a :** hardened and thickened **b :** having calluses **2 a :** feeling no emotion **b :** feeling no sympathy for others — **cal·lous·ly** *adv* — **cal·lous·ness** *n*

[2]**callous** *vt* **:** to make callous

call out *vt* **1 :** to summon into action ⟨*call out* troops⟩ **2 :** to challenge to a duel **3 :** to order on strike

cal·low \ˈkal-(ˌ)ō, -ə(-w)\ *adj* [ME *calu* bald, fr. OE; akin to OHG *kalo* bald] **1** *of a bird* **:** not yet having enough feathers to fly **2 :** lacking adult sophistication **:** IMMATURE ⟨~ youth⟩ **syn** see RUDE — **cal·low·ness** \ˈkal-ō-nəs, -ə-nəs\ *n*

call rate *n* **:** the interest rate charged on call loans

call to quarters : a bugle call usu. shortly before taps that summons soldiers to their quarters

call up *vt* **1 :** to bring to mind **:** EVOKE **2 :** to summon before an authority **3 :** to summon together **4 :** to summon for active military duty **5 :** to bring forward for consideration or action

call–up \ˈkȯ-ˌləp\ *n* **:** an order to report for military service

[1]**cal·lus** \ˈkal-əs\ *n* [L] **1 :** a thickening of or a hard thickened area on skin or bark **2 :** a substance exuded around the fragments of a broken bone that is converted into bone and repairs the break **3 :** soft tissue that forms over a wounded or cut plant surface

[2]**callus** *vi* **:** to form callus ~ *vt* **:** to cause callus to form on

[1]**calm** \ˈkäm, ˈkälm\ *n* [ME *calme,* fr. MF, fr. OIt *calma,* fr. LL *cauma* heat, fr. Gk *kauma,* fr. *kaiein* to burn — more at CAUSTIC] **1 a :** a period or condition of freedom from storms, high winds, or rough activity of water **b :** complete absence of wind or presence of wind having a speed no greater than one mile per hour **2 :** a state of repose and freedom from turmoil or agitation

[2]**calm** *adj* **1 :** marked by calm **:** STILL **2 :** free from agitation, excitement, or disturbance — **calm·ly** *adv* — **calm·ness** *n*
syn TRANQUIL, SERENE, PLACID, PEACEFUL: CALM implies freedom from agitation of any sort often in the face of danger or provocation; TRANQUIL suggests a more settled or deeper quietude or composure and lacks the implication of previous agitation or activity; SERENE implies a lofty and unclouded tranquillity; PLACID implies an undisturbed appearance and often suggests a degree of complacency; PEACEFUL implies repose or attainment of tranquillity often in contrast with or following strife or turmoil or bustle

[3]**calm** *vi* **:** to become calm ~ *vt* **:** to make calm

calm·ative \ˈkäm-ət-iv, ˈkäl-mət-\ *n or adj* [[3]*calm* + *-ative* (as in *sedative*)] **:** SEDATIVE

cal·o·mel \ˈkal-ə-məl, -ˌmel\ *n* [prob. fr. (assumed) NL *calomelas,* fr. Gk *kalos* beautiful + *melas* black] **:** mercurous chloride Hg_2Cl_2 used in medicine esp. as a purgative and fungicide

[1]**ca·lo·ric** \kə-ˈlȯr-ik, -ˈlōr-, -ˈlär-; ˈkal-ə-rik\ *n* [F *calorique,* fr. L *calor*] **1 :** a supposed form of matter formerly held responsible for the phenomena of heat and combustion **2** *archaic* **:** HEAT

[2]**caloric** *adj* **1 :** of or relating to heat **2 :** of or relating to calories — **ca·lo·ri·cal·ly** \kə-ˈlȯr-i-k(ə-)lē, -ˈlōr-, -ˈlär-\ *adv*

cal·o·rie *also* **cal·o·ry** \ˈkal-(ə-)rē\ *n* [F *calorie,* fr. L *calor* heat, fr. *calēre* to be warm — more at LEE] **1 a :** the amount of heat required at a pressure of one atmosphere to raise the temperature of one gram of water one degree centigrade — called also *gram calorie, small calorie* **b :** the amount of heat required to raise the temperature of one kilogram of water one degree centigrade **:** 1000 gram calories or 3.968 Btu — called also *kilogram calorie, large calorie* **2 a :** a unit equivalent to the large calorie expressing heat-producing or energy-producing value in food when oxidized in the body **b :** an amount of food having an energy-producing value of one large calorie

cal·o·rif·ic \ˌkal-ə-ˈrif-ik\ *adj* [F or L; F *calorifique,* fr. L *calorificus,* fr. *calor*] **1 :** CALORIC **2 :** productive of heat

cal·o·rim·e·ter \ˌkal-ə-ˈrim-ət-ər\ *n* [ISV, fr. L *calor*] **:** any of several apparatuses for measuring quantities of absorbed or evolved heat or for determining specific heats — **ca·lori·met·ric** \ˌkal-ə-rə-ˈme-trik, kə-ˌlȯr-ə-, -ˌlär-\ *adj* — **ca·lori·met·ri·cal·ly** \-tri-k(ə-)lē\ *adv* — **cal·o·rim·e·try** \ˌkal-ə-ˈrim-ə-trē\ *n*

ca·lotte \kə-ˈlät\ *n* [F] **:** SKULLCAP; *esp* **:** ZUCCHETTO

ca·loy·er \kə-ˈlȯi-(ə)r, ˈkal-ə-yər\ *n* [It & F; F *caloyer,* fr. obs. It *caloiero,* fr. MGk *kalogēros* venerable, fr. *kalos* beautiful + *gēras* old age] **:** a monk of the Eastern Church

cal·pac *or* **cal·pack** \ˈkal-ˌpak, kal-ˈ\ *n* [Turk *kalpak*] **:** a high-crowned cap worn in Turkey, Iran, and neighboring countries

cal·trop \ˈkal-trəp, ˈkȯl-\ *also* **cal·throp** \-thrəp\ *n* [ME *calketrappe* star thistle, fr. OE *calcatrippe,* fr. ML *calcatrippa*] **1 :** any of several plants with spined fruits or flower heads: as **a :** STAR THISTLE **b :** any of various herbs (genera *Tribulus* and *Kallstroemia*) of the bean-caper family **c :** WATER CHESTNUT 1 **2 :** a device with four metal points so arranged that when any three are on the ground the fourth projects upward as a hazard to the hoofs of horses or to pneumatic tires

caltrop 2

cal·u·met \ˈkal-yə-ˌmet, -mət; ˌkal-yə-ˈmet\ *n* [AmerF, fr. F dial., straw, fr. LL *calamellus,* dim. of L *calamus* reed] **:** a highly ornamented ceremonial Amerindian pipe

ca·lum·ni·ate \kə-ˈləm-nē-ˌāt\ *vt* **1 :** to utter maliciously false statements, charges, or imputations about **2 :** to injure the reputation of by calumny **syn** see MALIGN — **ca·lum·ni·a·tion** \kə-ˌləm-nē-ˈā-shən\ *n* — **ca·lum·ni·a·tor** \kə-ˈləm-nē-ˌāt-ər\ *n*

ca·lum·ni·ous \kə-ˈləm-nē-əs\ *adj* **:** constituting or marked by calumny **:** SLANDEROUS — **ca·lum·ni·ous·ly** *adv*

cal·um·ny \ˈkal-(y)əm-nē\ *n* [MF & L; MF *calomnie,* fr. L *calumnia,* fr. *calvi* to deceive; akin to OE *hōl* calumny, Gk *kēlein* to beguile] **1 :** the malicious uttering of false charges or misrepresentations calculated to damage another's reputation **2 :** a misrepresentation intended to blacken another's reputation

cal·va·dos \ˌkal-və-ˈdȯs, -ˈdōs, -ˈdäs\ *n, often cap* [F, fr. *Calvados,* Normandy, France] **:** a dry brown apple brandy

cal·var·i·um \kal-ˈvar-ē-əm, -ˈver-\ *n, pl* **cal·var·ia** \-ē-ə\ [NL, fr. L *calvaria* skull, fr. *calvus* bald; akin to Skt ati*kulva* completely bald] **:** a skull lacking the lower jaw or lower jaw and facial portion

cal·va·ry \ˈkalv-(ə-)rē\ *n* [*Calvary,* the hill near Jerusalem where Jesus was crucified] **1 :** an open-air representation of the crucifixion of Christ **2 :** an experience of intense usu. mental suffering

Calvary cross *n* — see CROSS illustration

calve \ˈkav, ˈkȧv\ *vb* [ME *calven,* fr. OE *cealfian,* fr. *cealf* calf] *vi* **1 :** to give birth to a calf; *also* **:** to produce offspring **2** *of an ice mass* **:** to separate or break so that a part becomes detached ~ *vt* **1 :** to produce by birth **2** *of an ice mass* **:** to let become detached

calves *pl of* CALF

Cal·vin·ism \ˈkal-və-ˌniz-əm\ *n* [John *Calvin* †1564 F theologian] **:** the theological system of Calvin and his followers emphasizing the sovereignty of God and including the doctrines of predestination, limited atonement, total depravity, irresistibility of grace, and the perseverance of saints — **Cal·vin·ist** \-və-nəst\ *n or adj* — **Cal·vin·is·tic** \ˌkal-və-ˈnis-tik\ *adj* — **Cal·vin·is·ti·cal·ly** \-ti-k(ə-)lē\ *adv*

calx \ˈkalks\ *n, pl* **calx·es** *or* **cal·ces** \ˈkal-ˌsēz\ [ME *cals,* fr. L *calx* lime — more at CHALK] **:** the friable residue left when a metal or other mineral has been subjected to calcination or combustion

ca·ly·ce·al \ˌkā-lə-ˈsē-əl, ˌkal-ə-\ *adj* **:** of or relating to a calyx

ca·ly·cine \ˈkā-lə-ˌsīn, ˈkal-ə-\ *adj* **:** relating to or resembling a calyx

ca·ly·cle \ˈkā-li-kəl, ˈkal-i-\ *n* [L *calyculus,* dim. of *calyc-, calyx* calyx] **:** EPICALYX

ca·lyc·u·late \kə-ˈlik-yə-ˌlāt, -lət\ *adj* **1 :** having a calyculus **2 :** having pitted surfaces

ca·lyc·u·lus \-yə-ləs\ *n, pl* **ca·lyc·u·li** \-ˌlī, -ˌlē\ [NL, modif. of E *calicle*] **:** a small cup-shaped structure (as a taste bud)

[1]**ca·lyp·so** \kə-ˈlip-(ˌ)sō\ *n* [L, fr. Gk *Kalypsō*] **1** *cap* **:** a sea nymph held in the *Odyssey* to have kept Odysseus seven years on the island of Ogygia **2** [NL, genus name, prob. fr. L] **:** a bulbous bog orchid (genus *Cytherea*) of northern regions bearing a single white flower variegated with purple, pink, and yellow

²**ca·lyp·so** *n* [prob. fr. *Calypso*] **:** an improvised ballad usu. satirizing current events in a style originating in the West Indies — **ca·lyp·so·ni·an** \kə-ˌlip-ˈsō-nē-ən, ˌkal-(ˌ)ip-\ *n or adj*
ca·lyp·tra \kə-ˈlip-trə\ *n* [NL, fr. Gk *kalyptra* veil, fr. *kalyptein* to cover — more at HELL] **1 :** the archegonium of a liverwort or moss; *esp* **:** one forming a membranous hood over the capsule in a moss **2 :** a covering of a flower or fruit suggestive of a cap or hood **3 :** ROOT CAP — **ca·lyp·trate** \kə-ˈlip-ˌtrāt, ˈkal-əp-\ *adj*
ca·lyx \ˈkā-liks, ˈkal-iks\ *n, pl* **ca·lyx·es** *or* **ca·ly·ces** \ˈkā-lə-ˌsēz, ˈkal-ə-\ [L *calyc-, calyx*, fr. Gk *kalyx* — more at CHALICE] **1 :** the external usu. green or leafy part of a flower consisting of sepals **2 :** a cuplike animal structure
cam \ˈkam\ *n* [perh. fr. F *came*, fr. G *kamm*, lit., comb, fr. OHG *kamb*] **:** a rotating or sliding piece that imparts motion to a roller moving against its edge or to a pin free to move in a groove on its face or that receives motion from such a roller or pin
ca·ma·ra·de·rie \ˌkam-(ə-)ˈrad-ə-rē, ˌkäm-(ə-)ˈräd-\ *n* [F, fr. *camarade* comrade] **:** friendly good-fellowship among comrades
cam·a·ril·la \ˌkam-ə-ˈril-ə, -ˈrē-(y)ə\ *n* [Sp, lit., small room] **:** a group of unofficial often secret and scheming advisers **:** CABAL
cam·as *or* **cam·ass** \ˈkam-əs\ *n* [Chinook Jargon *kamass*] **:** any of a genus (*Camassia*) of plants of the lily family of the western U.S. with edible bulbs — compare DEATH CAMAS
¹**cam·ber** \ˈkam-bər\ *vb* **cam·ber·ing** \-b(ə-)riŋ\ [F *cambrer*, fr. MF *cambre* curved, fr. L *camur*] *vi* **:** to curve upward in the middle ~ *vt* **1 :** to arch slightly **2 :** to impart camber to
²**camber** *n* **1 :** a slight convexity, arching, or curvature (as of a beam, deck, road) **2 :** the convexity of the curve of an airfoil from its chord **3 :** a setting of the wheels of an automotive vehicle closer together at the bottom than at the top
cam·bi·al \ˈkam-bē-əl\ *adj* **:** of, relating to, or being cambium
cam·bi·um \-bē-əm\ *n, pl* **cambiums** *or* **cam·bia** \-bē-ə\ [NL, fr. ML, exchange, fr. L *cambiare* to exchange] **:** a thin formative layer between the xylem and phloem of most vascular plants that gives rise to new cells and is responsible for secondary growth
Cam·bo·di·an \kam-ˈbōd-ē-ən\ *n* **1 :** a native or inhabitant of Cambodia **2 :** KHMER 2 — **Cambodian** *adj*
Cam·bri·an \ˈkam-brē-ən\ *adj* [ML *Cambria* Wales, fr. W *Cymry* Welshmen] **1 :** WELSH **2 :** of, relating to, or being the earliest geologic period of the Paleozoic era or the corresponding system of rocks marked by fossils of every great animal type except the vertebrate and scarcely recognizable plant fossils — **Cambrian** *n*
cam·bric \ˈkām-brik\ *n* [obs. Flem *Kameryk* Cambrai, city of France] **1 :** a fine thin white linen fabric **2 :** a cotton fabric that resembles cambric
cambric tea *n* **:** a hot drink of water, milk, sugar, and often tea
¹**came** *past of* COME
²**came** \ˈkām\ *n* [origin unknown] **:** a slender grooved lead rod used to hold together panes of glass esp. in a stained-glass window
cam·el \ˈkam-əl\ *n* [ME, fr. OE & ONF, fr. L *camelus*, fr. Gk *kamēlos*, of Sem origin; akin to Heb & Phoenician *gāmāl* camel] **1 :** either of two large ruminant mammals used as draft and saddle animals in desert regions esp. of Africa and Asia: **a :** the Arabian camel (*Camelus dromedarius*) with a single large hump on the back **b :** the Bactrian camel (*C. bactrianus*) with two humps **2 :** a watertight structure used esp. to lift submerged ships
cam·el·back \-ˌbak\ *n* **1 :** a steam locomotive with the cab astride the boiler **2 :** an uncured compound chiefly of reclaimed or synthetic rubber used for retreading or recapping pneumatic tires
cam·el·eer \ˌkam-ə-ˈli(ə)r\ *n* **:** a camel driver
ca·mel·lia *also* **ca·me·lia** \kə-ˈmēl-yə\ *n* [NL *Camellia*, genus name, fr. *Camellus* (Georg Josef Kamel †1706 Moravian Jesuit missionary)] **:** any of several shrubs or trees (genus *Camellia*) of the tea family; *esp* **:** an ornamental greenhouse shrub (*C. japonica*) with glossy evergreen leaves and showy roselike flowers
ca·mel·o·pard \kə-ˈmel-ə-ˌpärd\ *n* [LL *camelopardus*, alter. of L *camelopardalis*, fr. Gk *kamēlopardalis*, fr. *kamēlos* + *pardalis* leopard] **1 :** GIRAFFE **2** *cap* **:** a northern constellation between Cassiopeia and Ursa Major
Cam·e·lot \ˈkam-ə-ˌlät\ *n* **:** the site of King Arthur's palace and court in Arthurian legend
camel's hair *n* **1 :** the hair of the camel or a substitute for it (as hair from squirrels' tails) **2 :** cloth made of camel's hair or a mixture of camel's hair and wool usu. light tan and of soft silky texture
Cam·em·bert \ˈkam-əm-ˌbe(ə)r\ *n* [F, fr. *Camembert*, Normandy, France] **:** a soft unpressed cheese with an odor and flavor produced by a blue mold (*Penicillium camemberti*)
cam·eo \ˈkam-ē-ˌō\ *n* [It] **1 a :** a gem carved in relief; *esp* **:** a small piece of sculpture on a stone or shell cut in relief in one layer with another contrasting layer serving as background **b :** a small medallion with a profiled head in relief **2 :** a carving or sculpture made in the manner of a cameo **3 :** a small vivid theatrical role often limited to a single scene
cam·era \ˈkam-(ə-)rə\ *n* [LL, room — more at CHAMBER] **1** *pl also* **cam·er·ae** \ˈkam-ə-ˌrē, -ˌrī\ **:** CHAMBER; *esp* **:** a judge's chamber **2 :** the treasury department of the papal curia **3 a :** CAMERA OBSCURA **b :** a lightproof box fitted with a lens through the aperture of which the image of an object is recorded on a light-sensitive material **c :** the part of a television transmitting apparatus in which the image to be televised is formed for conversion into electrical impulses — **cam·era·man** \-ˌman, -mən\ *n* — **in camera :** PRIVATELY, SECRETLY
cam·er·al \ˈkam-(ə-)rəl\ *adj* **:** of or relating to a legislative or judicial chamber
cam·er·a·lism \-(ə-)rə-ˌliz-əm\ *n* [G *kameralismus*, fr. ML *cameralis* of the royal treasury, fr. *camera* royal treasury, fr. LL, chamber] **:** the mercantilism of a group of 18th century German public administrators emphasizing economic policies designed to strengthen the power of the ruler — **cam·er·a·list** \-ləst\ *n*
camera lu·ci·da \ˌkam-(ə-)rə-ˈlü-səd-ə\ *n* [NL, lit., light chamber] **:** an instrument that by means of a prism or mirrors and often a microscope causes a virtual image of an object to appear as if projected upon a plane surface so that an outline may be traced
camera ob·scu·ra \ˌkam-(ə-)rə-əb-ˈskyu̇r-ə\ *n* [NL, lit., dark chamber] **:** a darkened enclosure having an aperture usu. provided with a lens through which light from external objects enters to form an image of the objects on the opposite surface
cam·er·len·go \ˌkam-ər-ˈleŋ-(ˌ)gō\ *n* [It *camarlingo*] **:** a cardinal who heads the Apostolic Camera
ca·mion \kȧ-myōⁿ\ *n* [F] **:** MOTORTRUCK; *also* **:** BUS
cam·i·sa·do \ˌkam-ə-ˈsäd-(ˌ)ō, -ˈsäd-\ *n* [prob. fr. obs. Sp *camisada*] *archaic* **:** an attack by night
ca·mise \kə-ˈmēz, -ˈmēs\ *n* [Ar *qamīṣ*, fr. LL *camisia*] **:** a light shirt, gown, or tunic
cam·i·sole \ˈkam-ə-ˌsōl\ *n* [F, prob. fr. OProv *camisolla*, dim. of *camisa* shirt, fr. LL *camisia*] **1 :** a short negligee jacket for women **2 :** a short sleeveless undergarment for women
cam·let \ˈkam-lət\ *n* [ME *cameloit*, fr. MF *camelot*, fr. Ar *ḥamlat* woolen plush] **1 a :** a medieval Asiatic fabric of camel's hair or Angora wool **b :** a European fabric of silk and wool **c :** a fine lustrous woolen **2 :** a garment made of camlet
camomile *var of* CHAMOMILE
ca·mor·ra \kə-ˈmȯr-ə, -ˈmär-\ *n* [It] **:** a group of persons united for dishonest or dishonorable ends; *esp* **:** a secret organization formed about 1820 at Naples, Italy — **ca·mor·ris·ta** \ˌkä-ˌmȯ-ˈrē-stə\ *n*
cam·ou·flage \ˈkam-ə-ˌfläzh, -ˌfläj\ *n, often attrib* [F, fr. *camoufler* to disguise, fr. It *camuffare*] **1 a :** the disguising of equipment or an installation with paint, nets, or foliage **b :** the disguise so applied **2 a :** concealment by means of disguise **b :** behavior or an expedient designed to deceive or hide — **camouflage** *vt*
¹**camp** \ˈkamp\ *n, often attrib* [MF, prob. fr. ONF or OProv, fr. L *campus* plain, field; akin to OHG *hamf* crippled, Gk *kampē* bend] **1 a :** ground on which tents or buildings are erected for usu. temporary shelter (as for troops) **b :** the group of tents or buildings erected on such ground **c :** a tent, cabin, or other shelter **d :** an open-air location where one or more persons camp **e :** a town newly sprung up in a lumbering or mining region **2 a :** a body of persons encamped **b** (1) **:** a group or body of persons; *esp* **:** a group engaged in promoting or defending a theory or doctrine (2) **:** an ideological position **3 :** military service or life
²**camp** *vi* **1 :** to pitch or occupy a camp **2 :** to live in a camp or outdoors ~ *vt* **:** to put into a camp; *also* **:** ACCOMMODATE
³**camp** *n* [origin unknown] **1 :** HOMOSEXUAL **2 :** something so outrageous, inappropriate, or in such bad taste as to be considered amusing — **camp** *adj* — **campy** *adj*
cam·paign \kam-ˈpān\ *n* [F *campagne*, prob. fr. It *campagna* level country, campaign, fr. LL *campania* level country, fr. L, the level country around Naples] **1 :** a connected series of military operations forming a distinct phase of a war **2 :** a connected series of operations designed to bring about a particular result ⟨election ~⟩ — **campaign** *vi* — **cam·paign·er** *n*
campaign ribbon *n* **:** a narrow ribbon-covered bar or strip of ribbon whose distinctive coloring indicates a military campaign in which the wearer has taken part
cam·pa·ni·le \ˌkam-pə-ˈnē-lē\ *n, pl* **campaniles** \-lēz\ *or* **cam·pa·ni·li** \-(ˌ)lē\ [It, fr. *campana* bell, fr. LL] **:** a usu. freestanding bell tower
cam·pa·nol·o·gist \ˌkam-pə-ˈnäl-ə-jəst\ *n* **:** one that practices or is skilled in campanology
cam·pa·nol·o·gy \-jē\ *n* [NL *campanologia*, fr. LL *campana* + NL *-o-* + *-logia* -logy] **:** the art of bell ringing
cam·pan·u·la \kam-ˈpan-yə-lə\ *n* [NL, dim. of LL *campana*] **:** BELLFLOWER
cam·pan·u·late \-lət, -ˌlāt\ *adj* [NL *campanula* bell-shaped part, dim. of LL *campana*] **:** shaped like a bell
Camp·bell·ite \ˈkam-(b)ə-ˌlīt\ *n, often attrib* [Alexander *Campbell* †1866 Am preacher] **:** DISCIPLE 2 — often taken to be offensive
camp·er \ˈkam-pər\ *n* **1 :** one that camps **2 :** a portable dwelling for use during casual travel and camping
cam·pes·tral \kam-ˈpes-trəl\ *adj* [L *campestr-, campester*, fr. *campus*] **:** of or relating to fields or open country **:** RURAL
camp fire girl *n* [fr. *Camp Fire Girls*, Inc.] **:** a member of a national organization for girls from 7 to 18
camp follower *n* **1 :** a civilian who follows a military unit to attend or exploit military personnel; *specif* **:** PROSTITUTE **2 :** a disciple or follower who is not of the main body of members or adherents
cam·phene \ˈkam-ˌfēn\ *n* **:** any of several terpenes related to camphor; *esp* **:** a colorless crystalline terpene $C_{10}H_{16}$ used in insecticides
cam·phine *or* **cam·phene** \ˈkam-ˌfēn\ *n* [ISV, fr. *camphor*] **:** an explosive mixture of turpentine and alcohol
cam·phire \ˈkam-ˌfī(ə)r\ *n* [ME *caumfre*] **:** HENNA
cam·phor \ˈkam(p)-fər\ *n* [ME *caumfre*, fr. AF, fr. ML *camphora*, fr. Ar *kāfūr*, fr. Malay *kāpūr*] **1 :** a tough gummy volatile fragrant crystalline compound $C_{10}H_{16}O$ obtained esp. from the wood and bark of the camphor tree and used as a carminative and stimulant in medicine, as a plasticizer, and as an insect repellent **2 :** any of several similar compounds — **cam·pho·ra·ceous** \ˌkam(p)-fə-ˈrā-shəs\ *adj* — **cam·phor·ic** \kam-ˈfȯr-ik, -ˈfär-\ *adj*
cam·phor·ate \ˈkam(p)-fə-ˌrāt\ *vt* **:** to impregnate or treat with camphor
camphor ice *n* **:** a cerate made chiefly of camphor, white wax, spermaceti, and castor oil
camphor tree *n* **:** a large evergreen tree (*Cinnamomum camphora*) of the laurel family grown in most warm countries
cam·pi·on \ˈkam-pē-ən\ *n* [prob. fr. obs. *campion* (champion)] **:** any of various plants (genera *Lychnis* and *Silene*) of the pink family: as **a :** a European crimson-flowered plant (*L. coronaria*) **b :** an herb (*S. cucubalus*) with white flowers
camp meeting *n* **:** a series of evangelistic meetings held outdoors or in a tent and attended by families who often camp nearby
cam·po \ˈkam-(ˌ)pō, ˈkäm-\ *n* [AmerSp, fr. Sp, field, fr. L *campus*] **:** a grassland plain in So. America with scattered perennial herbs
campong *var of* KAMPONG
cam·po·ree \ˌkam-pə-ˈrē\ *n* [*camp* + jamb*oree*] **:** a gathering of boy or girl scouts from a given geographic area
camp·stool \ˈkamp-ˌstül\ *n* **:** a folding stool
cam·pus \ˈkam-pəs\ *n, often attrib* [L, plain — more at CAMP] **:** the grounds and buildings of a university, college, or school; *also* **:** the grassy area in the central part of the grounds
cam·py·lot·ro·pous \ˌkam-pi-ˈlä-trə-pəs\ *adj* [Gk *kampylos* bent + ISV *-tropous*; akin to Gk *kampē* bend] **:** having the ovule curved
cam·shaft \ˈkam-ˌshaft\ *n* **:** a shaft to which a cam is fastened or of which a cam forms an integral part
cam wheel *n* **:** a wheel set or shaped to act as a cam
¹**can** \kən, (ˈ)kan *sometimes* kᵊŋ\ *vb, past* **could** \kəd, (ˈ)ku̇d\ *pres sing & pl* **can** [ME (1st & 3d sing. pres. indic.), fr. OE; akin to OHG *kan* (1st & 3d sing. pres. indic.) know, am able, OE *cnāwan* to know — more at KNOW] *vt* **1** *obs* **:** KNOW, UNDERSTAND **2 :** to be able to

do, make, or accomplish ~ *vi, archaic* **:** to have knowledge or skill ~ *verbal auxiliary* **1 a :** know how to ⟨he ~ read⟩ **b :** be physically or mentally able to ⟨he ~ lift 200 pounds⟩ **c :** may perhaps ⟨do you think he ~ still be living⟩ **d :** be permitted by conscience or feeling to ⟨~ hardly blame him⟩ **e :** be inherently able or designed to ⟨everything that money ~ buy⟩ **f :** be logically or axiologically able to ⟨2 + 2 ~ also be written 3 + 1⟩ **g :** be enabled by law, agreement, or custom to **2 :** have permission to — used interchangeably with *may* ⟨you ~ go now if you like⟩

[2]**can** \ˈkan\ *n* [ME *canne*, fr. OE; akin to OHG *channa*] **1 :** a usu. cylindrical receptacle: **a :** a vessel for holding liquids; *specif* **:** a drinking vessel **b :** a cylindrical metal receptacle usu. with an open top, often with a removable cover, and sometimes with a spout or side handles (as for holding milk, oil, coffee, tobacco, ashes, or garbage) **c :** a tinplate container in which perishable foods or other products are hermetically sealed for preservation until use — called also *tin* **d :** a jar for packing or preserving fruit or vegetables **2** *slang* **:** JAIL **3 :** DEPTH CHARGE **4 :** DESTROYER 2

[3]**can** \ˈkan\ *vt* **canned; can·ning 1 a :** to put in a can **:** preserve by sealing in airtight cans or jars **b :** to hit (a golf ball) into the cup **2** *slang* **:** to expel from school **:** discharge from employment **3** *slang* **:** to put a stop or end to **4 :** to record on discs or tape ⟨*canned* music⟩ — **can·ner** *n*

Ca·naan·ite \ˈkā-nə-ˌnīt\ *n* [Gk *Kananitēs*, fr. *Kanaan* Canaan] **:** a member of a Semitic people inhabiting ancient Palestine and Phoenicia from about 3000 B.C. — **Canaanite** *adj*

Can·a·da balsam \ˌkan-əd-ə-\ *n* [Canada, country in No. America] **:** a viscid yellowish to greenish oleoresin exuded by the balsam fir (*Abies balsamea*) that solidifies to a transparent mass and is used as a transparent cement esp. in microscopy

Canada thistle *n* **:** a European thistle (*Cirsium arvense*) naturalized in No. America where it is a pernicious weed

Canadian French \kə-ˌnād-ē-ən-\ *n* **:** the language of the French Canadians

ca·naille \kə-ˈnā(ə)l, -ˈnī\ *n* [F, fr. It *canaglia*, fr. *cane* dog, fr. L *canis* — more at HOUND] **:** RABBLE, RIFFRAFF

[1]**ca·nal** \kə-ˈnal\ *n* [ME, fr. L *canalis* pipe, channel, fr. *canna* reed — more at CANE] **1 :** CHANNEL, WATERCOURSE **2 :** a tubular anatomical passage or channel **:** DUCT **3 :** an artificial waterway for navigation or for draining or irrigating land **4 :** any of various faint narrow markings on the planet Mars

[2]**canal** *vt* **ca·nalled** *or* **ca·naled; ca·nal·ling** *or* **ca·nal·ing :** to construct a canal through or across

ca·nal·boat \-ˌbōt\ *n* **:** a boat for use on a canal

can·a·lic·u·late \ˌkan-ᵊl-ˈik-yə-lət, -ˌlāt\ *adj* **:** grooved or channeled longitudinally ⟨a ~ leafstalk⟩

can·a·lic·u·lus \-yə-ləs\ *n, pl* **can·a·lic·u·li** \-yə-ˌlī, -ˌlē\ [L, dim. of *canalis*] **:** a minute canal in a bodily structure

ca·nal·iza·tion \kə-ˌnal-ə-ˈzā-shən, ˌkan-ᵊl-ə-\ *n* **1 :** an act or instance of canalizing **2 :** a system of channels

ca·nal·ize \kə-ˈnal-ˌīz, ˈkan-ᵊl-\ *vt* **1 a :** to provide with a canal or other channel **b :** to make into or like a canal **2 :** to provide with an outlet; *esp* **:** to direct into preferred channels ~ *vi* **1 :** to flow in or into a channel **2 :** to establish new channels

can·a·pé \ˈkan-ə-pē, -ˌpā\ *n* [F, lit., sofa, fr. ML *canopeum*, *canapeum* mosquito net — more at CANOPY] **:** an appetizer consisting of a piece of bread or toast or a cracker topped with caviar, anchovy, or other savory food

ca·nard \kə-ˈnärd\ *n* [F, lit., duck, fr. MF *vendre des canards à moitié* to cheat, lit., to half-sell ducks] **:** a false or unfounded report or story; *esp* **:** a fabricated report

ca·nary \kə-ˈne(ə)r-ē\ *n* [MF *canarie*, fr. OSp *canario*, fr. *Islas Canarias* Canary islands] **1 :** a lively 16th century court dance **2 :** a Canary islands usu. sweet wine similar to Madeira **3 a :** a small finch (*Serinus canarius*) native to the Canary islands and usu. greenish to yellow that is kept as a cage bird and singer **b :** any of various small birds largely yellow in color **4** *slang* **:** INFORMER 2

canary seed *n* **1 :** seed of a Canary islands grass (*Phalaris canariensis*) used as food for cage birds **2 :** seed of a common plantain (*Plantago major*)

canary yellow *n* **:** a light to a moderate or vivid yellow

ca·nas·ta \kə-ˈnas-tə\ *n* [Sp, lit., basket] **1 :** rummy using two full decks plus four jokers which are all wild along with the eight deuces and having the object of melding groups of seven of the same rank **2 :** a combination of seven cards of the same rank in canasta

can·can \ˈkan-ˌkan\ *n* [F] **:** a woman's dance of French origin characterized by high kicking

[1]**can·cel** \ˈkan(t)-səl\ *vb* **can·celed** *or* **can·celled; can·cel·ing** *or* **can·cel·ling** \-s(ə-)liŋ\ [ME *cancellen*, fr. MF *canceller*, fr. LL *cancellare*, fr. L, to make like a lattice, fr. *cancelli* (pl.), dim. of *cancer* lattice, alter. of *carcer* prison] *vt* **1 a :** to mark or strike out for deletion **b :** OMIT, DELETE **2 a :** to destroy the force, effectiveness, or validity of **:** ANNUL **b :** to bring to nothingness **:** DESTROY **c :** to match in force or effect **:** OFFSET **3 a :** to remove (a common divisor) from numerator and denominator **b :** to remove (equivalents) on opposite sides of an equation or account **4 :** to deface (a postage or revenue stamp) esp. with a set of parallel lines so as to invalidate for reuse ~ *vi* **:** to neutralize each other's strength or effect **:** COUNTERBALANCE **syn** see ERASE — **can·cel·er** *or* **can·cel·ler** \-s(ə-)lər\ *n* — **can·cel·la·tion** \ˌkan(t)-sə-ˈlā-shən\ *n*

[2]**cancel** *n* **1 :** CANCELLATION **2 a :** a deleted part or passage **b :** a passage or page from which something has been deleted **c** (1) **:** a leaf containing deleted matter (2) **:** a new leaf or slip substituted for matter already printed

can·cel·late \ˈkan(t)-sə-ˌlāt, -lət\ *adj* [L *cancellatus*, pp. of *cancellare*] **:** RETICULATE, CHAMBERED ⟨~ leaves⟩; *specif* **:** CANCELLOUS

can·cel·lous \ˈkan(t)-s(ə-)ləs, kan-ˈsel-əs\ *adj* [NL *cancelli* intersecting osseous plates and bars in cancellous bone, fr. L, lattice] *of bone* **:** having a porous structure

can·cer \ˈkan(t)-sər\ *n* [ME, fr. L (gen. *Cancri*), lit., crab; akin to Gk *karkinos* crab, cancer] **1** *cap* **a :** a northern zodiacal constellation between Gemini and Leo **b :** the 4th sign of the zodiac **2** [L, crab, cancer] **a :** a malignant tumor characterized by potentially unlimited growth with local expansion by invasion and systemic by metastasis **b :** an abnormal state marked by such tumors **3 :** a source of evil **4 a :** an enlarged tumorlike growth **b :** a disease marked by such growths — **can·cer·ous** \ˈkan(t)s-(ə-)rəs\ *adj*

can·croid \ˈkaŋ-ˌkrȯid\ *adj* [L *cancr-*, *cancer* crab, cancer] **1 :** resembling a crab **2 :** resembling a cancer

can·de·la·bra \ˌkan-də-ˈläb-rə, -ˈlab-, -ˈlāb-\ *n* **:** CANDELABRUM

can·de·la·brum \-rəm\ *n, pl* **can·de·la·bra** \-rə\ *also* **candelabrums** [L, fr. *candela*] **:** a branched candlestick or lamp with several lights

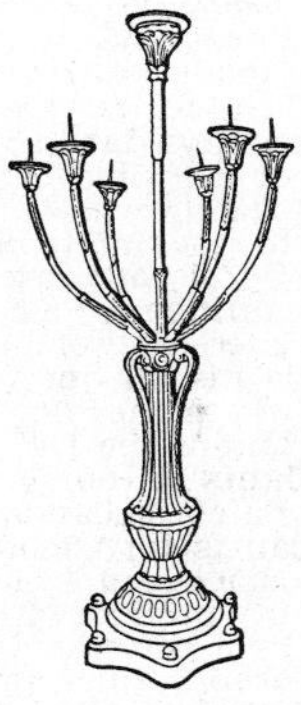
candelabrum

can·dent \ˈkan-dənt\ *adj* [L *candent-*, *candens*, prp. of *candēre*] **:** heated to whiteness **:** GLOWING

can·des·cence \kan-ˈdes-ᵊn(t)s\ *n* **:** a candescent state **:** glowing whiteness

can·des·cent \-ᵊnt\ *adj* [L *candescent-*, *candescens*, prp. of *candescere*, incho. of *candēre*] **:** glowing or dazzling esp. from great heat

can·did \ˈkan-dəd\ *adj* [F & L; F *candide*, fr. L *candidus* bright, white, fr. *candēre* to shine, glow; akin to shine, glow; akin to LGk *kandaros* ember] **1 :** WHITE **2 :** free from bias, prejudice, or malice **:** FAIR **3 a :** marked by honest sincere expression **b :** indicating or suggesting sincere honesty and absence of deception **c :** disposed to criticize severely **:** BLUNT **4 :** relating to photography of subjects acting naturally or spontaneously without being posed ⟨~ picture⟩ **syn** see FRANK — **can·did·ly** *adv* — **can·did·ness** *n*

can·di·da·cy \ˈkan-(d)əd-ə-sē\ *n* **:** the state of being a candidate

can·di·date \ˈkan-(d)ə-ˌdāt, -(d)əd-ət\ *n* [L *candidatus*, fr. *candidatus* clothed in white, fr. *candidus* white; fr. the white toga worn by candidates for office in ancient Rome] **:** one who offers himself or is offered by others for an office, membership, or honor

can·di·da·ture \ˈkan-(d)əd-ə-ˌchu̇(ə)r, -chər\ *n, chiefly Brit* **:** CANDIDACY

candid camera *n* **1 :** a usu. small camera equipped with a fast lens and used for taking informal photographs of unposed subjects often without their knowledge **2 :** a miniature camera

can·died \ˈkan-dēd\ *adj* **1 :** encrusted or coated with sugar **2 :** baked with sugar or syrup until translucent

[1]**can·dle** \ˈkan-dᵊl\ *n* [ME *candel*, fr. OE, fr. L *candela*, fr. *candēre*] **1 :** a long slender cylindrical mass of tallow or wax containing a loosely twisted linen or cotton wick that is burned to give light **2 :** something resembling a candle in shape or use ⟨a sulfur ~ for fumigating⟩ **3 a :** an international unit of luminous intensity equal to the luminous intensity of five square millimeters of platinum at its solidification temperature — called also *international candle* **b :** a similar unit equal to one sixtieth of the luminous intensity of one square centimeter of a blackbody surface at the solidification temperature of platinum — called also *candela*, *new candle*

[2]**candle** *vt* **can·dling** \ˈkan-(d)liŋ, -dᵊl-iŋ\ **:** to examine by holding between the eye and a light — **can·dler** \ˈkan-(d)lər, -dᵊl-ər\ *n*

can·dle·ber·ry \ˈkan-dᵊl-ˌber-ē\ *n* **1 a :** CANDLENUT **b :** WAX MYRTLE **2 :** the fruit of a candleberry

can·dle·fish \-ˌfish\ *n* **1 :** a marine food fish (*Thaleichthys pacificus*) of the north Pacific coast related to the smelt **2 :** SABLEFISH

can·dle–foot \-ˈfu̇t\ *n* **:** FOOTCANDLE

can·dle·light \-dᵊl-ˌ(l)īt\ *n, often attrib* **1 a :** the light of a candle **b :** a soft artificial light **2 :** the time for lighting up **:** TWILIGHT

Can·dle·mas \-məs\ *n* [ME *candelmasse*, fr. OE *candelmæsse*, fr. *candel* + *mæsse* mass, feast; fr. the candles blessed and carried in celebration of the feast] **:** the church feast celebrated on February 2 in commemoration of the presentation of Christ in the temple and the purification of the Virgin Mary

can·dle·nut \-ˌnət\ *n* **1 :** the oily seed of a tropical tree (*Aleurites moluccana*) of the spurge family used locally to make candles and commercially as a source of oil; *also* **:** this tree

can·dle·pin \-ˌpin\ *n* **1 :** a slender bowling pin tapering toward top and bottom **2** *pl but sing in constr* **:** a bowling game using candlepins and a smaller ball than that used in tenpins

can·dle·pow·er \-ˌpau̇(-ə)r\ *n* **:** luminous intensity expressed in candles

can·dle·stick \-ˌstik\ *n* **:** a holder with a socket for a candle

can·dle·wick \-ˌwik\ *n* **1 :** the wick of a candle **2 a :** a soft cotton embroidery yarn **b :** embroidery made with this yarn usu. in tufts

can·dle·wood \-ˌwu̇d\ *n* **1 :** any of several trees or shrubs (as ocotillo) chiefly of resinous character **2 :** slivers of resinous wood

can·dor *or chiefly Brit* **can·dour** \ˈkan-dər\ *n* [F & L; F *candeur*, fr. L *candor*, fr. *candēre* — more at CANDID] **1 a :** WHITENESS, BRILLIANCE **b** *obs* **:** unstained purity **2 :** freedom from prejudice or malice **:** FAIRNESS **3** *archaic* **:** KINDLINESS **4 :** FORTHRIGHTNESS

[1]**can·dy** \ˈkan-dē\ *n* [ME *sugre candy*, part trans. of MF *sucre candi*, part trans. of OIt *zucchero candi*, fr. *zucchero* sugar + Ar *qandī* candied, fr. *qand* cane sugar] **1 :** crystallized sugar formed by boiling down sugar syrup **2 a :** a confection made of sugar often with flavoring and filling **b :** a piece of such confection

[2]**candy** *vt* **1 :** to encrust in or coat with sugar often by cooking to a thicker consistency in a heavy syrup **2 :** to make seem attractive **:** SWEETEN **3 :** to crystallize into sugar ~ *vi* **:** to become coated or encrusted with sugar crystals **:** become crystallized into sugar

can·dy·tuft \ˈkan-dē-ˌtəft\ *n* [*Candy* (now *Candia*) Crete, Greek island + E *tuft*] **:** any of a genus (*Iberis*) of plants of the mustard family cultivated for their white, pink, or purple flowers

[1]**cane** \ˈkān\ *n* [ME, fr. MF, fr. OProv *cana*, fr. L *canna*, fr. Gk *kanna*, of Sem origin; akin to Ar *qanāh* hollow stick, reed] **1 a** (1) **:** a hollow or pithy and usu. slender and flexible jointed stem (as of a reed) (2) **:** any of various slender woody stems; *esp* **:** an elongated flowering or fruiting stem (as of a rose) usu. arising directly from the ground **b :** any of various tall woody grasses or reeds: as (1) **:** any of a genus (*Arundinaria*) of coarse grasses (2) **:** SUGARCANE (3) **:** SORGHUM **2 :** cane dressed for use: as **a :** a cane walking stick; *broadly* **:** WALKING STICK **b :** a cane or rod for flogging **c :** RATTAN; *esp* **:** split rattan for wickerwork or basketry

[2]**cane** *vt* **1 :** to beat with a cane **2 :** to weave or furnish with cane

cane·brake \-ˌbrāk\ *n* **:** a thicket of cane

can·er \ˈkā-nər\ *n* **:** one that weaves cane seats and backs of chairs

ca·nes·cent \kə-ˈnes-ᵊnt\ *adj* [L *canescent-*, *canescens*, prp. of

canescere, incho. of *canēre* to be gray, be white, fr. *canus* white, hoary — more at HARE] **:** growing white, whitish, or hoary; *esp* **:** having a fine grayish white pubescence ⟨~ leaves⟩

cane sugar *n* **:** sucrose from sugarcane

ca·nic·o·la fever \kə-ˌnik-ə-lə-\ *n* [NL *canicola* (specific epithet of *Leptospira canicola*) fr. L *canis* dog + *-cola* inhabitant] **:** an acute disease in man and dogs characterized by gastroenteritis and mild jaundice and caused by a spirochete (*Leptospira canicola*)

Ca·nic·u·la \kə-ˈnik-yə-lə\ *n* [L, dim. of *canis*] **:** SIRIUS

ca·nic·u·lar \kə-ˈnik-yə-lər\ *adj* **1 :** of or relating to the Dog Star or its rising **2 :** of or relating to the dog days

1ca·nine \ˈkā-ˌnīn\ *adj* [L *caninus*, fr. *canis* dog] **1 :** of or relating to dogs or to the family (Canidae) including the dogs, wolves, jackals, and foxes **2 :** of, relating to, or resembling a dog

2canine *n* **1 :** a conical pointed tooth; *esp* **:** one situated between the lateral incisor and the first premolar **2 :** DOG

Ca·nis Ma·jor \ˌkā-nə-ˈsmā-jər, ˌkan-ə-\ *n* [L (gen. *Canis Majoris*), lit., greater dog] **:** a constellation to the southeast of Orion containing the Dog Star

Canis Mi·nor \-ˈsmī-nər\ *n* [L, (gen. *Canis Minoris*), lit., lesser dog] **:** a constellation to the east of Orion containing Procyon

can·is·ter \ˈkan-ə-stər\ *n* [L *canistrum* basket, fr. Gk *kanastron*, fr. *kanna* reed — more at CANE] **1 :** a small box or can for holding a dry product **2 :** encased shot for close-range artillery fire **3 :** a light perforated metal box for gas masks that contains material to absorb, filter, or detoxify poisons and irritants in the air

1can·ker \ˈkaŋ-kər\ *n* [ME, fr. ONF *cancre*, fr. L *cancer* crab, cancer] **1 a** (1) **:** an erosive or spreading sore (2) *obs* **:** GANGRENE 1 (3) **:** an area of necrosis in a plant **b :** any of various disorders of plants or animals marked by chronic inflammatory changes **2** *archaic* **:** a caterpillar destructive to plants **3** *chiefly dial* **a :** RUST **b :** VERDIGRIS 2 **4 :** a source of corruption or debasement **5** *chiefly dial* **:** a common European wild rose (*Rosa canina*) — **can·ker·ous** \ˈkaŋ-k(ə-)rəs\ *adj*

2canker *vb* **can·ker·ing** \ˈkaŋ-k(ə-)riŋ\ *vt* **1** *obs* **:** to infect with a spreading sore **2 :** to corrupt with a malignancy of mind or spirit ~ *vi* **1 :** to become infested with canker **2 :** to undergo corruption

canker sore *n* **:** a small painful ulcer esp. of the mouth

can·ker·worm \ˈkaŋ-kər-ˌwərm\ *n* **:** any of various insect larvae that injure plants esp. by feeding on buds and foliage

can·na \ˈkan-ə\ *n* [NL, genus name, fr. L, reed] **:** any of a genus (*Canna* of the family Cannaceae) of tropical herbs with simple stems, large leaves, and a terminal raceme of irregular flowers

can·na·bin \ˈkan-ə-bən\ *n* [L *cannabis*] **:** a dark resin from pistillate hemp plants

can·na·bis \-bəs\ *n* [L, hemp, fr. Gk *kannabis*, fr. the source of OE *hænep* hemp] **:** the dried flowering spikes of the pistillate plants of the hemp

canned \ˈkand\ *adj* **1 :** sealed in a can or jar **2 :** transcribed for radio or television reproduction **3 a :** SYNDICATED **b :** HACKNEYED, STEREOTYPED **4** *slang* **:** DRUNK

can·nel coal \ˌkan-ᵊl-\ *n* [prob. fr. E dial. *cannel* candle, fr. ME *candel*] **:** a bituminous coal containing much volatile matter that burns brightly

can·nery \ˈkan-(ə-)rē\ *n* **:** a factory for the canning of foods

can·ni·bal \ˈkan-ə-bəl\ *n* [NL *Canibalis* Carib, fr. Sp *Caníbal*, fr. Arawakan *Caniba*, *Carib*, of Cariban origin; akin to Carib *Galibi* Caribs, lit., strong men] **1 :** a human being who eats human flesh **2 :** an animal that devours its own kind — **cannibal** *adj* — **can·ni·bal·ic** \ˌkan-ə-ˈbal-ik\ *adj* — **can·ni·bal·ism** \ˈkan-ə-bə-ˌliz-əm\ *n* — **can·ni·bal·is·tic** \ˌkan-ə-bə-ˈlis-tik\ *adj*

can·ni·bal·ize \ˈkan-ə-bə-ˌlīz\ *vt* **1 :** to dismantle (a machine) for parts to be used as replacements in other machines **2 :** to deprive of parts or men in order to repair or strengthen another unit ~ *vi* **1 :** to practice cannibalism **2 :** to cannibalize one unit for the sake of another of the same kind

can·ni·kin \ˈkan-i-kən\ *n* [prob. fr. obs. D *kanneken*, fr. MD *canneken*, dim. of *canne* can; akin to OE *canne* can] **1 :** a small can or drinking vessel **2** *NewEng* **:** a wooden bucket

can·ni·ly \ˈkan-ᵊl-ē\ *adv* **:** in a canny manner

can·ni·ness \ˈkan-ē-nəs\ *n* **:** the state of being canny

1can·non \ˈkan-ən\ *n, pl* **cannons** *or* **cannon** [MF *canon*, fr. It *cannone*, lit., large tube, aug. of *canna* reed, tube, fr. L, cane, reed — more at CANE] **1** *pl usu* *cannon* **a :** an artillery piece **:** big gun **b :** a heavy-caliber automatic aircraft gun firing explosive shells **2 :** a smooth round horse bit **3** *or* **can·on :** the projecting part of a bell by which it is hung **:** EAR **4** [alter. of *carom*] *Brit* **:** a carom in billiards and bagatelle **5 :** the part of the leg in which the cannon bone is found

2cannon *vi* **1 :** to discharge cannon **2** *Brit* **:** to carom in billiards ~ *vt* **1 :** CANNONADE **2** *Brit* **:** to carom into

1can·non·ade \ˌkan-ə-ˈnād\ *n* **:** a heavy fire of artillery

2cannonade *vt* **:** to attack with artillery ~ *vi* **1 :** to deliver artillery fire **2 :** 2CANNON 2

1can·non·ball \ˈkan-ən-ˌbȯl\ *n* **1 a :** a round solid missile made for firing from a cannon **b :** a missile of a solid or hollow shape made for cannon **2 :** a hard flat tennis service **3 :** a fast train

2cannonball *vi* **:** to travel with great speed

cannon bone *n* [F *canon*, lit., cannon] **:** a bone in hoofed mammals that supports the leg from the hock joint to the fetlock

can·non·eer \ˌkan-ə-ˈni(ə)r\ *n* **:** an artillery gunner

can·non·ry \ˈkan-ən-rē\ *n* **1 :** CANNONADING **2 :** ARTILLERY

can·not \ˈkan-(ˌ)ät; kə-ˈnät, ka-ˈ\ **:** can not — **cannot but :** to be bound to **:** MUST

can·nu·la \ˈkan-yə-lə\ *n, pl* **cannulas** *or* **can·nu·lae** \-ˌlē\ [NL, fr. L, dim. of *canna* reed — more at CANE] **:** a small tube for insertion into a body cavity or into a duct or vessel

can·nu·lar \-lər\ *adj* **:** TUBULAR

1can·ny \ˈkan-ē\ *adj* [1*can*] **1 a :** FORESIGHTED, KNOWING **b :** PRUDENT, WARY **c :** CLEVER, SLY **d :** FRUGAL, THRIFTY **e :** shrewd in worldly affairs **:** sharp-witted **2** *Scot* **a :** FORTUNATE, LUCKY **b :** free from unnatural powers or ill-omened aspects **c :** skilled in the supernatural or occult **3 a** *Scot* **:** CAREFUL, STEADY **b** *Scot* **:** QUIET, SNUG **c** *dial Brit* **:** agreeable to the eyes **:** PLEASANT

2canny *adv, Scot* **:** in a canny manner

ca·noe \kə-ˈnü\ *n* [F, fr. NL *canoa*, fr. Sp, fr. Arawakan, of Cariban origin; akin to Galibi *canaoua*] **:** a long light narrow boat with both ends sharp and sides curved that is usu. paddled by hand — **canoe** *vb* — **ca·noe·ist** \-ˈnü-əst\ *n*

1can·on \ˈkan-ən\ *n* [ME, fr. OE, fr. LL, fr. L, ruler, rule, model, standard, fr. Gk *kanōn*; akin to Gk *kanna* reed — more at CANE] **1 a :** a regulation or dogma decreed by a church council **b :** a provision of canon law **2** [ME, prob. fr. OF, fr. LL, fr. L, model] **:** the most solemn and unvarying part of the Mass including the act of consecration **3** [ME, fr. LL, fr. L, standard] **a :** an authoritative list of books accepted as Holy Scripture **b :** the authentic works of a writer **4 a :** an accepted principle or rule **b :** a criterion or standard of judgment **c :** a body of principles, rules, standards, or norms **5** [LGk *kanōn*, fr. Gk, model] **:** a contrapuntal musical composition in two or more voice parts in which the melody is imitated exactly and completely by the successive voices **syn** see LAW

2canon *n* [ME *canoun*, fr. AF *canunie*, fr. LL *canonicus* one living under a rule, fr. L according to rule, fr. Gk *kanonikos*, fr. *kanōn*] **1 :** one of the clergy of a medieval cathedral or large church living in community under a rule **2 :** a clergyman belonging to the chapter or the staff of a cathedral or collegiate church **3 :** CANON REGULAR

3ca·ñon \ˈkan-yən\ *var of* CANYON

can·on·ess \ˈkan-ə-nəs\ *n* **1 :** a woman living in community under a religious rule but not under a perpetual vow **2 :** a member of a Roman Catholic congregation of women corresponding to canons regular

ca·non·ic \kə-ˈnän-ik\ *adj* **1 :** CANONICAL **2 :** of or relating to musical canon

ca·non·i·cal \-i-kəl\ *adj* **1 :** of or relating to a canon **2 :** conforming to a general rule **:** ORTHODOX **3 :** accepted as forming the canon of scripture **4 :** of or relating to a clergyman who is a canon **5 :** reduced to the simplest or clearest schema possible — **ca·non·i·cal·ly** \-i-k(ə-)lē\ *adv*

canonical hour *n* **1 :** a time of day canonically appointed for an office of devotion **2 :** one of the daily offices of devotion that compose the Divine Office and include matins with lauds, prime, terce, sext, none, vespers, and compline

ca·non·i·cals \kə-ˈnän-i-kəlz\ *n pl* **:** the vestments prescribed by canon for a clergyman when officiating

can·on·ic·i·ty \ˌkan-ə-ˈnis-ət-ē\ *n* **:** the quality or state of being canonical

can·on·ist \ˈkan-ə-nəst\ *n* **:** a specialist in canon law

can·on·iza·tion \ˌkan-ə-nə-ˈzā-shən\ *n* **:** the act of canonizing **:** the state of being canonized

can·on·ize \ˈkan-ə-ˌnīz\ *vt* [ME *canonizen*, fr. ML *canonizare*, fr. LL *canon* catalog of saints, fr. L, standard] **1 :** to declare (a deceased person) an officially recognized saint **2 :** to make canonical **3 :** to sanction by ecclesiastical authority **4 :** to accord sacrosanct or authoritative standing to

canon law *n* **:** the ecclesiastical law governing a Christian church

canon regular *n, pl* **canons regular :** a member of one of several Roman Catholic religious institutes of regular priests living in community under a usu. Augustinian rule

can·on·ry \ˈkan-ən-rē\ *n* **1 :** the prebend or office of a canon **2 :** a body of canons

ca·no·pic jar \kə-ˌnō-pik-, -ˌnäp-ik-\ *n, often cap C* [*Canopus*, city in ancient Egypt] **:** a jar used by the ancient Egyptians for preserving the viscera of a deceased person usu. for burial with the mummy

Ca·no·pus \kə-ˈnō-pəs\ *n* [L, fr. Gk *Kanōpos*] **:** a star of the first magnitude in the constellation Argo not visible north of 37° latitude

1can·o·py \ˈkan-ə-pē\ *n* [ME *canope*, fr. ML *canopeum* mosquito net, fr. L *conopeum*, fr. Gk *kōnōpion*, fr. *kōnōps* mosquito] **1 a :** a cloth covering suspended over a bed **b :** a cover (as of cloth) suspended above an exalted personage or sacred object **:** BALDACHIN **c :** the uppermost spreading branchy layer of a forest **d :** AWNING, MARQUEE **2 :** an ornamental rooflike structure **3 a :** the transparent enclosure over an airplane cockpit **b :** the lifting or supporting surface of a parachute

2canopy *vt* **:** to cover with or as if with a canopy

ca·no·rous \kə-ˈnōr-əs, -ˈnȯr-; ˈkan-ə-rəs\ *adj* [L *canorus*, fr. *canor* melody, fr. *canere* to sing — more at CHANT] **:** sounding pleasantly **:** MELODIOUS — **ca·no·rous·ly** *adv* — **ca·no·rous·ness** *n*

canst \kən(t)st, (ˈ)kan(t)st\ *archaic pres 2d sing of* CAN

1cant \ˈkant\ *adj* [ME, prob. fr. (assumed) MLG *kant*] *dial Eng* **:** LIVELY, LUSTY

2cant *n* [ME, prob. fr. MD or ONF; MD, edge, corner fr. ONF, fr. L *canthus*, *cantus* iron tire, perh. of Celt origin; akin to W *cant* rim; akin to Gk *kanthos* corner of the eye] **1** *obs* **:** CORNER, NICHE **2 :** an external angle (as of a building) **3 a :** a sudden thrust producing a bias **b :** the bias so caused **4 :** an oblique or slanting surface **5 :** an inclination from a given line **:** SLOPE

3cant *vt* **1 :** to give a cant or oblique edge to **:** BEVEL **2 :** to set at an angle **:** tip or tilt up or over **3 :** to turn or throw off or out by tilting or rotating ⟨~ a rifle⟩ **4** *chiefly Brit* **:** to give a sudden turn or new direction to ~ *vi* **1 :** to pitch to one side **:** LEAN **2 :** SLOPE

4cant *adj* **1 :** having canted corners or sides **2 :** slanting with respect to a particular straight line

5cant *vi* [prob. fr. ONF *canter* to tell, lit., to sing, fr. L *cantare* — more at CHANT] **1 :** BEG **2 :** to speak in cant or technical terms **3 :** to talk hypocritically

6cant *n, often attrib* **1 :** affected singsong speech **2 a :** ARGOT 1 **b** *obs* **:** the phraseology peculiar to a religious class or sect **c :** JARGON 2 **3 :** a set or stock phrase **4 :** the expression or repetition of conventional, trite, or unconsidered opinions or sentiments; *esp* **:** the insincere use of pious phraseology **syn** see DIALECT

can't \(ˈ)kant, (ˈ)kȧnt, *esp South* ˈkānt\ **:** can not

can·ta·bi·le \kän-ˈtäb-ə-ˌlā, kan-ˈtab-ə-lē\ *adv* (*or adj*) [It, fr. LL *cantabilis* worthy to be sung, fr. L *cantare*] **:** in a singing manner — often used as a direction in music

Can·ta·bri·gian \ˌkant-ə-ˈbrij-(ē-)ən\ *n* [ML *Cantabrigia* Cambridge] **1 :** a student or graduate of Cambridge University **2 :** a native or resident of Cambridge, Mass. — **Cantabrigian** *adj*

can·ta·la \kan-ˈtäl-ə\ *n* [origin unknown] **:** a hard fiber produced from the leaves of an agave (*Agave cantala*)

can·ta·loupe \ˈkant-ᵊl-ˌōp\ *n* [*Cantalupo*, former papal villa near Rome, Italy] **1 :** a muskmelon (*Cucumis melo cantalupensis*) with a hard ridged or warty rind and reddish orange flesh **2 :** any of several muskmelons resembling the cantaloupe; *broadly* **:** MUSKMELON

can·tan·ker·ous \kan-ˈtaŋ-k(ə-)rəs, kən-\ *adj* [perh. irreg. fr. obs. *contack* (contention)] **:** ILL-NATURED, QUARRELSOME — **can·tan·ker·ous·ly** *adv* — **can·tan·ker·ous·ness** *n*

can·ta·ta \kən-ˈtät-ə\ *n* [It, fr. L, sung mass, ecclesiastical chant, fr.

fem. of *cantatus,* pp. of *cantare*] **:** a choral composition comprising choruses, solos, recitatives, and interludes usu. accompanied by organ, piano, or orchestra

can·ta·trice \ˌkänt-ə-ˈtrē-chē, ˌkäⁿ-tə-ˈtrēs\ *n, pl* **can·ta·trices** \-ˈtrē-chēz, -ˈtrēs(-əz)\ *or* **can·ta·tri·ci** \-ˈtrē-chē\ [It & F; F, fr. It, fr. LL *cantatric-, cantatrix,* fem. of L *cantator* singer, fr. *cantatus,* pp.] **:** a woman singer; *esp* **:** an opera singer

cant dog *n* [2*cant*] **:** PEAVEY

can·teen \kan-ˈtēn\ *n* [F *cantine* bottle case, sutler's shop, fr. It *cantina* wine cellar, fr. *canto* corner, fr. L *canthus* iron tire] **1 :** POST EXCHANGE **2 :** a recreation room maintained by civilians for servicemen **3 :** a temporary or mobile restaurant **4 a :** a partitioned chest or box for holding cutlery **b :** a soldier's mess kit **5 :** a usu. cloth-jacketed flask for carrying water or other liquids

1**cant·er** \ˈkant-ər\ *n* **:** one that talks cant: as **a :** BEGGAR, VAGABOND **b :** a user of professional or religious cant

2**can·ter** \ˈkant-ər\ *vb* [short for obs. *canterbury,* fr. *canterbury,* n. (canter), fr. *Canterbury,* England; fr. the supposed gait of pilgrims to Canterbury] *vi* **1 :** to move at or as if at a canter **:** LOPE **2 :** to ride or go on a cantering horse ~ *vt* **:** to cause to go at a canter

3**can·ter** *n* **1 :** a 3-beat gait resembling but smoother and slower than the gallop **2 :** a ride at such a gait

Can·ter·bury bell \ˌkant-ə(r)-ˌber-ē-\ *n* [*Canterbury,* England] **:** any of several bellflowers (as *Campanula medium*) cultivated for their showy flowers

can·tha·ris \ˈkan(t)-thə-rəs\ *n, pl* **can·thar·i·des** \kan-ˈthar-ə-ˌdēz\ [ME & L; ME *cantharide,* fr. L *cantharid-, cantharis,* fr. Gk *kantharid-, kantharis*] **1 :** SPANISH FLY 1 **2** *pl but sing or pl in constr* **:** a preparation of dried beetles (as Spanish flies) used as a counterirritant and formerly as an aphrodisiac

cant hook *n* [2*cant*] **:** a stout wooden lever used esp. in handling logs that has a blunt usu. metal-clad end and a movable spiked metal arm

can·thus \ˈkan(t)-thəs\ *n, pl* **can·thi** \ˈkan-ˌthī-, ˌthē\ [LL, fr. Gk *kanthos* — more at CANT] **:** either of the angles formed by the meeting of the upper and lower eyelids

can·ti·cle \ˈkant-i-kəl\ *n* [ME, fr. L *canticulum,* dim. of *canticum* song, fr. *cantus,* pp. of *canere* to sing] **:** SONG; *specif* **:** one of several liturgical songs (as the Magnificat) taken from the Bible

can·ti·le·ver \ˈkant-ᵊl-ˌē-vər, -ˌev-ər\ *n* [perh. fr. 2*cant* + *-i-* + *lever*] **:** a projecting beam or member supported at only one end: as **a :** a bracket-shaped member supporting a balcony or a cornice **b :** either of the two beams or trusses that project from piers toward each other and that when joined directly or by a suspended connecting member form a span of a cantilever bridge

can·til·late \ˈkant-ᵊl-ˌāt\ *vt* [L *cantillatus,* pp. of *cantillare* to sing low, fr. *cantare* to sing — more at CHANT] **:** to recite with musical usu. improvised tones — **can·til·la·tion** \ˌkant-ᵊl-ˈā-shən\ *n*

can·ti·na \kan-ˈtē-nə\ *n* [AmerSp, fr. Sp, canteen, fr. It, wine cellar — more at CANTEEN] *Southwest* **1 :** a pouch or bag at the pommel of a saddle **2 :** a small barroom **:** SALOON

can·tle \ˈkant-ᵊl\ *n* [ME *cantel,* fr. ONF, dim. of *cant* edge, corner] **1 :** SLICE, PORTION **2 :** the upward projecting rear part of a saddle

can·to \ˈkan-(ˌ)tō\ *n* [It, fr. L *cantus* song, fr. *cantus,* pp. of *canere* to sing] **:** one of the major divisions of a long poem

1**can·ton** \ˈkant-ᵊn, ˈkan-ˌtän\ *n* [MF, fr. OProv, fr. *cant* edge, corner fr. L *canthus* iron tire — more at CANT] **1** *obs* **:** DIVISION, SECTION **2** [MF, fr. It *cantone,* fr. *canto* corner, fr. L *canthus*] **:** a small territorial division of a country: as **a :** one of the states of the Swiss confederation **b :** a division of a French arrondissement **3 :** the top inner quarter of a flag **4 :** the dexter chief region of a heraldic field — **can·ton·al** \ˈkant-ᵊn-əl, kan-ˈtän-ᵊl\ *adj*

2**can·ton** \ˈkant-ᵊn, ˈkan-ˌtän, *in sense 2 usu* kan-ˈtōn *or* -ˈtän\ *vt* **1 :** to divide into parts; *specif* **:** to divide into cantons **2 :** QUARTER

can·ton crepe \ˌkan-ˌtän-\ *n, often cap 1st C* [*Canton,* China] **:** a soft thick dress crepe made in plain weave with fine crosswise ribs

Can·ton·ese \ˌkant-ᵊn-ˈēz, -ˈēs\ *n, pl* **Cantonese 1 :** a native or inhabitant of Canton, China **2 :** the dialect of Chinese spoken in and around Canton — **Cantonese** *adj*

can·ton flannel \ˌkan-ˌtän-\ *n, often cap C* [*Canton,* China] **:** FLANNEL 1b

can·ton·ment \kan-ˈtōn-mənt, -ˈtän-\ *n* **1 :** the quartering of troops **2 a :** a group of more or less temporary structures for housing troops **b** *India* **:** a permanent military station

can·tor \ˈkant-ər\ *n* [L, singer, fr. *cantus* pp. of *canere* to sing] **1 :** a choir leader **:** PRECENTOR **2 :** a synagogue official who sings or chants liturgical music and leads the congregation in prayer

can·trip \ˈkan-trəp\ *n* [prob. alter. of *caltrop*] *chiefly Scot* **:** SPELL

can·tus \ˈkant-əs\ *n, pl* **can·tus** \ˈkant-əs, ˈkan-ˌtüs\ **1 :** CANTUS FIRMUS **2 :** the principal melody or voice

can·tus fir·mus \ˌkant-əs-ˈfi(ə)r-məs, -ˈfər-\ *n* [ML, lit., fixed song] **1 :** the plainchant or simple Gregorian melody orig. sung in unison and prescribed as to form and use by ecclesiastical tradition **2 :** a melodic theme or subject; *esp* **:** one for contrapuntal treatment

canty \ˈkant-ē\ *adj* [1*cant*] *dial Brit* **:** CHEERFUL, SPRIGHTLY

Ca·nuck \kə-ˈnək\ *n* [prob. alter. of *Canadian*] **1 :** CANADIAN **2** *chiefly Canad* **:** FRENCH CANADIAN **3 :** CANADIAN FRENCH — usu. used disparagingly

can·vas *also* **can·vass** \ˈkan-vəs\ *n, often attrib* [ME *canevas,* fr. ONF, fr. (assumed) VL *cannabaceus* hempen, fr. L *cannabis* hemp — more at CANNABIS] **1 :** a firm closely woven cloth usu. of linen, hemp, or cotton used for clothing and sails **2 :** a set of sails **:** SAIL **3 :** a piece of canvas used for a particular purpose **4 :** a military or camping tent or a group of tents **5 :** a cloth surface prepared to receive an oil painting; *also* **:** the painting on such a surface **6 :** a coarse cloth so woven as to form regular meshes for working with the needle **7 :** the floor of a boxing or wrestling ring

can·vas·back \-ˌbak\ *n* **:** a No. American wild duck (*Aythya valisineria*) esteemed for sport and food

can·vass *also* **can·vas** \ˈkan-vəs\ *vt* **1** *obs* **:** to toss in a canvas sheet in sport or punishment **2 a** *obs* **:** BEAT, TROUNCE **b** *archaic* **:** CASTIGATE **3 a :** to examine in detail; *specif* **:** to examine (votes) officially for authenticity **b :** DISCUSS, DEBATE **4 :** to go through (a district) or go to (persons) to solicit orders or political support or to determine opinions or sentiments ~ *vi* **:** to seek orders or votes **:** SOLICIT — **canvass** *n* — **can·vass·er** *n*

can·yon \ˈkan-yən\ *n* [AmerSp *cañón,* prob. alter. of obs. Sp *callón,* aug. of *calle* street, fr. L *callis* footpath] **:** a deep narrow valley with precipitous sides often with a stream flowing through it

can·zo·ne \kan-ˈzō-nē, känt-ˈsō-(ˌ)nā\ *n, pl* **can·zo·nes** \-nēz, -(ˌ)nāz\ *or* **can·zo·ni** \-nē\ [It, fr. L *cantion-, cantio* song, fr. *cantus,* pp. of *canere* to sing — more at CHANT] **1 :** a medieval Italian or Provençal lyric poem **2 :** the melody of a canzone

can·zo·net \ˌkan-zə-ˈnet\ *n* [It *canzonetta,* dim. of *canzone*] **1 :** a part-song resembling but less elaborate than a madrigal **2 :** a light and graceful song

caou·tchouc \kaù-ˈchük, -ˈchùk\ *n* [F, fr. obs. Sp *cauchuc* (now *caucho*), fr. Quechua] **:** 1RUBBER 2a

1**cap** \ˈkap\ *n, often attrib* [ME *cappe,* fr. OE *cæppe,* fr. LL *cappa* head covering, cloak] **1 :** a usu. tight-fitting covering for the head; *esp* **:** one for men and boys usu. with a visor and without a brim **2 :** a natural cover or top: as **a :** an overlying rock layer usu. hard to penetrate **b** (1) **:** PILEUS (2) **:** CALYPTRA **c :** the top of a bird's head or a patch of distinctively colored feathers in this area **3 a :** something that serves as a cover or protection esp. for a tip, knob, or end **b :** a fitting for closing the end of a tube **c :** a layer of new rubber fused onto the worn surface of a pneumatic tire **4 a :** a cardinal's biretta **b :** MORTARBOARD **5 :** an overlaying or covering structure **6 :** a paper or metal container holding an explosive charge

2**cap** *vt* **capped; cap·ping 1 a :** to provide or protect with or as if with a cap **b :** to give a cap to as a symbol of honor or rank **2 :** to form a cap over **:** CROWN **3 a :** to follow with something more noticeable or more significant **:** OUTDO **b :** MATCH **c :** CLIMAX

ca·pa·bil·i·ty \ˌkā-pə-ˈbil-ət-ē\ *n* **1 :** the quality or state of being capable **2 :** a feature or faculty capable of development **:** POTENTIALITY **3 :** the capacity for an indicated use or development

ca·pa·ble \ˈkā-pə-bəl\ *adj* [MF or LL; MF *capable,* fr. LL *capabilis,* irreg. fr. L *capere* to take] **1 :** SUSCEPTIBLE **2** *obs* **:** COMPREHENSIVE **3 :** having sufficient physical or mental ability **4 :** having traits conducive to or admitting of **5 :** having general efficiency and ability **6** *obs* **:** having legal right to own, enjoy, or perform **syn** see ABLE — **ca·pa·ble·ness** *n* — **ca·pa·bly** \-blē\ *adv*

ca·pa·cious \kə-ˈpā-shəs\ *adj* [L *capac-, capax* capacious, capable, fr. L *capere*] **:** able to contain a great deal — **ca·pa·cious·ly** *adv* — **ca·pa·cious·ness** *n*

ca·pac·i·tance \kə-ˈpas-ət-ən(t)s\ *n* [*capacity*] **1 a :** the property of an electric nonconductor that permits the storage of energy as a result of electric displacement when opposite surfaces of the nonconductor are maintained at a difference of potential **b :** the measure of this property equal to the ratio of the charge on either surface to the potential difference between the surfaces **2 :** a part of a circuit or network that possesses capacitance — **ca·pac·i·tive** \-ˈpas-ət-iv\ *adj* — **ca·pac·i·tive·ly** *adv*

ca·pac·i·tate \kə-ˈpas-ə-ˌtāt\ *vt* **:** to make capable **:** QUALIFY

ca·pac·i·tor \-ˈpas-ət-ər\ *n* **:** a device giving capacitance usu. consisting of conducting plates or foils separated by thin layers of dielectric with the plates on opposite sides of the dielectric layers oppositely charged by a source of voltage and the electrical energy of the charged system stored in the polarized dielectric

ca·pac·i·ty \kə-ˈpas-ət-ē, -ˈpas-tē\ *n* [ME *capacite,* fr. MF *capacité,* fr. L *capacitat-, capacitas,* fr. *capac-, capax*] **1 a :** the ability to hold, receive, store, or accommodate **b :** a measure of content **:** the measured ability to contain **:** VOLUME — see MEASURE table, METRIC SYSTEM table **c :** maximum production or output **d** (1) **:** CAPACITANCE (2) **:** the quantity of electricity that a battery can deliver under specified conditions **2 :** legal qualification, competency, power, or fitness **3 a :** ABILITY, CALIBER **b :** power to grasp and analyze ideas and cope with problems **c :** POTENTIALITY **4 :** a position or character assigned or assumed

cap-a-pie *or* **cap-à-pie** \ˌkap-ə-ˈpē\ *adv* [MF (*de*) *cap a pé* from head to foot] **:** from head to foot **:** at all points

ca·par·i·son \kə-ˈpar-ə-sən\ *n* [MF *caparaçon,* fr. OSp *caparazón*] **1 a :** an ornamental covering for a horse **b :** decorative trappings and harness **2 :** rich clothing **:** ADORNMENT — **caparison** *vt*

1**cape** \ˈkāp\ *n, often attrib* [ME *cap,* fr. MF, fr. OProv, fr. L *caput* head — more at HEAD] **:** a point or extension of land jutting out into water as a peninsula or as a projecting point

2**cape** *n* [prob. fr. Sp *capa* cloak, fr. LL *cappa* head covering, cloak] **1 :** a sleeveless outer garment or part of a garment that fits closely at the neck and hangs loosely from the shoulders **2 :** the short feathers covering the shoulders of a fowl below the hackle

Cape Cod cottage \(ˌ)kāp-ˌkäd-\ *n* [*Cape Cod, Mass.*] **:** a compact rectangular dwelling of one or one-and-a-half stories usu. with a central chimney and a steep gable roof

Cape crawfish *n* [*Cape* of Good Hope] **:** the common edible spiny lobster (*Jasus lalandii*) of southern Africa

cap·e·lin \ˈkap-(ə-)lən\ *n* [CanF *capelan,* fr. F, codfish, fr. OProv, chaplain, codfish, fr. ML *cappellanus* chaplain — more at CHAPLAIN] **:** a small northern sea fish (*Mallotus villosus*) related to the smelts

Ca·pel·la \kə-ˈpel-ə\ *n* [L, lit., she-goat, fr. *caper* he-goat — more at CAPRIOLE] **:** a star of the first magnitude in Auriga

1**ca·per** \ˈkā-pər\ *n* [back-formation fr. earlier *capers* (taken as a plural), fr. ME *caperis,* fr. L *capparis,* fr. Gk *kapparis*] **1 :** any of a genus (*Capparis* of the family Capparidaceae, the caper family) of low prickly shrubs of the Mediterranean region; *esp* **:** one (*C. spinosa*) cultivated for its buds **2 :** one of the greenish flower buds or young berries of the caper pickled for use as a relish

2**caper** *vi* **ca·per·ing** \-p(ə-)riŋ\ [prob. by shortening & alter. fr. *capriole*] **:** to leap about in a gay frolicsome way **:** PRANCE

3**caper** *n* **1 :** a gay bounding leap **2 :** a capricious escapade

cap·er·cail·lie \ˌkap-ər-ˈkāl-(y)ē\ *or* **cap·er·cail·zie** \-ˈkāl-zē\ *n* [ScGael *capalcoille,* lit., horse of the woods] **:** the largest Old World grouse (*Tetrao urogallus*)

cape·skin \ˈkāp-ˌskin\ *n, often attrib* [*Cape* of Good Hope] **:** a light flexible leather made from sheepskins with the natural grain retained and used esp. for gloves and garments

Ca·pe·tian \kə-ˈpē-shən\ *adj* **:** of or relating to the French dynasty founded by Hugh Capet and reigning 987–1328 — **Capetian** *n*

ca·pi·as \ˈkā-pē-əs\ *n* [ME, fr. L, you should seize, fr. *capere* to take — more at HEAVE] **:** a legal writ or process commanding the officer to arrest the person named in it

cap·il·lar·i·ty \ˌkap-ə-ˈlar-ət-ē\ *n* **1 :** the quality or state of being

capillary **2 :** the action by which the surface of a liquid where it is in contact with a solid is elevated or depressed depending upon the relative attraction of the molecules of the liquid for each other and for those of the solid

[1]cap·il·lary \'kap-ə-,ler-ē, *Brit usu* kə-'pil-ə-rē\ *adj* [F or L; F *capillaire*, fr. L *capillaris*, fr. *capillus* hair] **1 :** resembling a hair esp. in slender elongated form; *esp* **:** having a very small bore ⟨a ~ tube⟩ **2 :** involving, held by, or resulting from surface tension (as in the soil) **3 :** of or relating to capillaries or capillarity

[2]capillary *n* **:** a capillary tube; *esp* **:** any of the smallest vessels of the blood-vascular system connecting arterioles with venules and forming networks throughout the body

capillary attraction *n* **:** the force of adhesion between a solid and a liquid in capillarity

[1]cap·i·tal \'kap-ət-ᵊl, 'kap-tᵊl\ *adj* [ME, fr. L *capitalis*, fr. *capit-*, *caput* head] **1 a :** punishable by death ⟨a ~ crime⟩ **b :** involving execution ⟨~ punishment⟩ **c :** most serious ⟨a ~ error⟩ **2** *of a letter* **:** of or conforming to the series A, B, C, etc. rather than a, b, c, etc. **3 a :** chief in importance or influence **b :** being the seat of government **4 :** of or relating to capital **5 :** EXCELLENT

[2]capital *n* [F or It; F, fr. It *capitale*, fr. *capitale*, adj. chief, principal, fr. L *capitalis*] **1 a :** a stock of accumulated goods esp. at a specified time and in contrast to income received during a specified period **b :** the value of these accumulated goods **c :** accumulated goods devoted to the production of other goods **d :** net worth **e :** CAPITAL STOCK **f :** accumulated possessions calculated to bring in income **g :** persons holding capital **h :** ADVANTAGE, GAIN **2** [[1]*capital*] **a :** a capital letter; *esp* **:** an initial capital letter **b :** a letter belonging to a style of alphabet modeled upon the style customarily used in inscriptions **3** [[1]*capital*] **a :** a city serving as a seat of government **b :** a city preeminent in some special activity

[3]capital *n* [ME *capitale*, modif. of ONF *capitel*, fr. LL *capitellum* small head, top of column, dim. of L *capit-*, *caput*] **:** the uppermost member of a column or pilaster crowning the shaft and taking the weight of the entablature

capital account *n* **1 a :** an account representing ownership in a business **b :** a corporation account classified as part of net worth **c :** [2]CAPITAL 1a **2 :** a capital assets account

capital assets *n pl* **:** long-term assets either tangible or intangible

capital expenditure *n* **:** an expenditure for long-term additions or betterments properly chargeable to a capital assets account

cap·i·tal·ism \'kap-ət-ᵊl-,iz-əm, 'kap-tᵊl-\ *n* **:** an economic system characterized by private or corporation ownership of capital goods, by investments that are determined by private decision rather than by state control, and by prices, production, and the distribution of goods that are determined mainly in a free market

[1]cap·i·tal·ist \-əst\ *n* **:** a person who has capital esp. invested in business; *broadly* **:** a person of wealth **:** PLUTOCRAT

[2]capitalist *or* **cap·i·tal·is·tic** \,kap-ət-ᵊl-'is-tik, ,kap-tᵊl-\ *adj* **1 :** owning capital **2 a :** practicing or advocating capitalism **b :** marked by capitalism — **cap·i·tal·is·ti·cal·ly** \-ti-k(ə-)lē\ *adv*

cap·i·tal·iza·tion \,kap-ət-ᵊl-ə-'zā-shən, ,kap-tᵊl-\ *n* **1 a :** the act or process of capitalizing **b :** a sum resulting from a process of capitalizing **c :** the total liabilities of a business including both ownership capital and borrowed capital **d :** the total value of such liabilities **2 :** the use of a capital letter in writing or printing

cap·i·tal·ize \'kap-ət-ᵊl-,īz, 'kap-tᵊl-\ *vt* **1 :** to write or print with an initial capital or in capitals **2 :** to convert into capital **3 a :** to compute the present value of (an income extended over a period of time) **b :** to convert (a periodic payment) into an equivalent capital sum **4 :** to supply capital for ~ *vi* **:** to gain by turning something to advantage **:** PROFIT ⟨~ on an opponent's mistake⟩

capital levy *n* **:** a levy on personal or industrial capital in addition to income tax and other taxes **:** a general property tax

cap·i·tal·ly \'kap-ət-ᵊl-ē, 'kap-tᵊl-\ *adv* **1 :** in a manner involving the death sentence **2 :** EXCELLENTLY, ADMIRABLY

capital ship *n* **:** a warship of the first rank in size and armament

capital stock *n* **1 :** the outstanding shares of a joint-stock company considered as an aggregate **2 :** CAPITALIZATION 1d **3 :** the ownership element of a corporation divided into shares and represented by certificates

cap·i·tate \'kap-ə-,tāt\ *adj* [L *capitatus* headed, fr. *capit-*, *caput* head] **1 :** forming a head **2 :** abruptly enlarged and globose

cap·i·ta·tion \,kap-ə-'tā-shən\ *n, often attrib* [LL *capitation-*, *capitatio* poll tax, fr. L *capit-*, *caput*] **1 :** a direct uniform tax imposed upon each head or person **:** POLL TAX **2 :** a uniform per capita payment or fee

cap·i·tol \'kap-ət-ᵊl, 'kap-tᵊl\ *n* [L *Capitolium*, temple of Jupiter at Rome on the Capitoline hill] **1 :** a building in which a state legislative body meets **2** *cap* **:** the building in which the U. S. Congress meets at Washington

Cap·i·to·line \'kap-ət-ᵊl-,īn, *Brit usu* kə-'pit-ə-,līn\ *adj* [L *Capitolinus*, fr. *Capitolium*] **:** of or relating to the smallest of the seven hills of ancient Rome, the temple on it, or the gods worshiped there

ca·pit·u·lar \kə-'pich-ə-lər\ *adj* [ML *capitularis*, fr. *capitulum* chapter] **:** of or relating to an ecclesiastical chapter

ca·pit·u·lary \-,ler-ē\ *n* [ML *capitulare*, lit., document divided into sections, fr. LL *capitulum* section, chapter — more at CHAPTER] **:** a civil or ecclesiastical ordinance; *also* **:** a collection of ordinances

ca·pit·u·late \kə-'pich-ə-,lāt\ *vi* [ML *capitulatus*, pp. of *capitulare* to distinguish by heads or chapters, fr. LL *capitulum*] **1** *archaic* **:** PARLEY, NEGOTIATE **2 a :** to surrender esp. upon terms **b :** to cease resisting **:** ACQUIESCE **syn** see YIELD

ca·pit·u·la·tion \kə-,pich-ə-'lā-shən\ *n* **1 :** a set of terms or articles constituting an agreement between governments **2 :** the act or agreement of one that surrenders upon stipulated terms

ca·pit·u·lum \kə-'pich-ə-ləm\ *n, pl* **ca·pit·u·la** \-lə\ [NL, fr. L, small head] **1 :** a rounded protuberance of an anatomical part (as a bone) **2 :** a racemose inflorescence with the axis shortened and dilated to form a rounded or flattened cluster of sessile flowers

ca·pon \'kā-,pän, -pən\ *n* [ME, fr. OE *capūn*, prob. fr. ONF *capon*, fr. L *capon-*, *capo*; akin to Gk *koptein* to cut] **:** a castrated male chicken — **ca·pon·ize** \'kā-pə-,nīz\ *vt*

cap·o·ral \'kap-(ə-)rəl, ,kap-ə-'ral\ *n* [F, lit., corporal — more at CORPORAL] **:** a coarse tobacco

ca·pote \kə-'pōt\ *n* [F, fr. *cape* cloak, fr. LL *cappa*] **:** a usu. long and hooded cloak or overcoat

cap·per \'kap-ər\ *n* **1 :** one that caps; *esp* **:** an operator or a machine that applies the closure or cap **2 :** DECOY 3, SHILL

cap·ping \'kap-iŋ\ *n* **:** something that caps

cap·ric acid \,kap-rik-\ *n* [ISV, fr. L *capr-*, *caper* goat; fr. its odor] **:** a fatty acid $C_{10}H_{20}O_2$ found in fats and oils

ca·pric·cio \kə-'prē-(,)chō, -chē-,ō\ *n* [It] **1 :** WHIMSY, FANCY **2 :** CAPER, PRANK **3 :** an instrumental piece in free form usu. lively in tempo and brilliant in style

ca·price \kə-'prēs\ *n* [F, fr. It *capriccio*, lit., head with hair standing on end, shudder, fr. *capo* head (fr. L *caput*) + *riccio* hedgehog, fr. L *ericius*] **1 :** a sudden unpredictable turn or change; *esp* **:** WHIM **2 :** a disposition to change one's mind impulsively **3 :** CAPRICCIO 3
syn CAPRICE, FREAK, WHIM, VAGARY, CROTCHET mean an irrational or fanciful notion. CAPRICE emphasizes lack of evident motivation and suggests willfulness; FREAK suggests an impulsive, causeless change of mind; WHIM stresses the unaccountability or quaintness of a notion or desire; VAGARY suggests the erratic, extravagant, or irresponsible character of a notion or impulse; CROTCHET implies a perversely heretical or eccentric preference esp. on a trivial matter

ca·pri·cious \kə-'prish-əs, -'prē-shəs\ *adj* **:** governed or characterized by caprice **:** apt to change suddenly or unpredictably **syn** see INCONSTANT — **ca·pri·cious·ly** *adv* — **ca·pri·cious·ness** *n*

Cap·ri·corn \'kap-ri-,kȯ(ə)rn\ *n* [ME *Capricorne*, fr. L *Capricornus* (gen. *Capricorni*), fr. *caper* goat + *cornu* horn — more at HORN] **1 :** a southern zodiacal constellation between Sagittarius and Aquarius **2 :** the 10th sign of the zodiac

cap·ri·fi·ca·tion \,kap-rə-fə-'kā-shən\ *n* [L *caprification-*, *caprificatio*, fr. *caprificatus*, pp. of *caprificare* to pollinate by caprification, fr. *caprificus*] **:** artificial pollination of figs by hanging in the trees flowering branches of the caprifig to facilitate pollen transfer by a wasp to the edible figs

cap·ri·fig \'kap-rə-,fig\ *n* [ME *caprifige*, part trans. of L *caprificus*, fr. *capr-*, *caper* goat + *ficus* fig — more at FIG] **:** a wild fig (*Ficus carica sylvestris*) of southern Europe and Asia Minor used for caprification of the edible fig; *also* **:** its fruit

cap·rine \'kap-,rīn\ *adj* [L *caprinus*, fr. *capr-*, *caper*] **:** of, relating to, or being a goat

cap·ri·ole \'kap-rē-,ōl\ *n* [MF or OIt; MF *capriole*, fr. OIt *capriola*, fr. *capriolo* roebuck, fr. L *capreolus* goat, roebuck, fr. *capr-*, *caper* he-goat; akin to OE *hæfer* goat, Gk *kapros* wild boar] **1 :** CAPER **2** *of a trained horse* **:** a vertical leap with a backward kick of the hind legs at the height of the leap — **capriole** *vi*

ca·pro·ic acid \kə-,prō-ik-\ *n* [ISV, fr. L *capr-*, *caper*] **:** a liquid fatty acid $C_6H_{12}O_2$ that is found as a glycerol ester in fats and oils or made synthetically and used in pharmaceuticals and flavors

ca·pryl·ic acid \kə-,pril-ik-\ *n* [ISV *capryl*, a radical contained in it] **:** a fatty acid $C_{14}H_{16}O_2$ of rancid odor occurring in fats and oils

cap·sa·icin \kap-'sā-ə-sən\ *n* [irreg. fr. NL *Capsicum*] **:** a colorless irritant phenolic amide $C_{18}H_{27}NO_3$ from various capsicums

Cap·si·an \'kap-sē-ən\ *adj* [F *capsien*, fr. L *Capsa* Gafsa, Tunisia] **:** of or relating to a Paleolithic culture of northern Africa and southern Europe

cap·si·cum \'kap-si-kəm\ *n* [NL, genus name] **1 :** any of a genus (*Capsicum*) of tropical herbs and shrubs of the nightshade family widely cultivated for their many-seeded usu. fleshy-walled berries — called also *pepper* **2 :** the dried ripe fruit of some capsicums (as *C. frutescens*) used as a gastric and intestinal stimulant

cap·size \'kap-,sīz, kap-'\ *vb* [origin unknown] *vt* **:** to cause to overturn ~ *vi* **:** to turn over **:** UPSET

cap·stan \'kap-stən\ *n* [ME] **:** a machine for moving or raising heavy weights by winding cable around a vertical spindle-mounted drum that is rotated manually or driven by steam or electric power

capstan

cap·stone \'kap-,stōn\ *n* [[1]*cap*] **1 :** a coping stone **:** COPING **2 :** the crowning point **:** ACME

cap·su·lar \'kap-sə-lər\ *adj* **1 :** of, relating to, or resembling a capsule **2 :** CAPSULATE

cap·su·late \-,lāt, -lət\ *or* **cap·su·lat·ed** \-,lāt-əd\ *adj* **:** enclosed in a capsule

[1]cap·sule \'kap-səl, -(,)sül\ *n* [F, fr. L *capsula*, dim. of *capsa* box — more at CASE] **1 a :** a membrane or sac enclosing a body part **b :** either of two layers of white matter in the cerebrum **2 :** a closed receptacle containing spores or seeds: as **a :** a dry dehiscent usu. many-seeded fruit composed of two or more carpels **b :** the spore sac of a moss **3 :** a gelatin shell enclosing medicine **4 :** an often polysaccharide envelope surrounding a microorganism **5 :** an extremely brief condensation **6 :** a compact usu. detachable receptacle **7 :** a small pressurized compartment for an aviator or astronaut for flight or emergency escape

[2]capsule *adj* **1 :** extremely brief **2 :** small and very compact

[1]cap·tain \'kap-tən\ *n* [ME *capitane*, fr. MF *capitain*, fr. LL *capitaneus*, adj. & n., chief, fr. L *capit-*, *caput* head — more at HEAD] **1 a :** the commander of a body of troops or of a military establishment **b :** a commander under a sovereign or general **c** (1) **:** an officer in charge of a ship (2) **:** a commissioned officer in the navy ranking above a commander and below a commodore or a rear admiral **d :** a commissioned officer in the army, air force, or marine corps ranking above a first lieutenant and below a major **e :** a distinguished military leader **f :** a leader of a side or team **2 :** a dominant figure — **cap·tain·cy** \-sē\ *n* — **cap·tain·ship** \-,ship\ *n*

[2]captain *vt* **:** to be captain of **:** LEAD

[1]cap·tion \'kap-shən\ *n* [ME *capcioun*, fr. L *caption-*, *captio*, fr. *captus*, pp. of *capere* to take — more at HEAVE] **1 :** the part of a legal instrument that shows where, when, and by what authority it was taken, found, or executed **2 a :** the heading esp. of an article or document **:** TITLE **b :** the explanatory comment or designation accompanying a pictorial illustration **c :** a motion-picture subtitle

[2]caption *vt* **cap·tion·ing** \'kap-sh(ə-)niŋ\ **:** to furnish with a caption **:** ENTITLE

cap·tious \'kap-shəs\ *adj* [ME *capcious*, fr. MF or L; MF *captieux* fr. L *captiosus*, fr. *captio* act of taking, deception] **1 :** calculated to confuse, entrap, or entangle in argument **2 :** marked by an inclination to stress faults and raise objections **syn** see CRITICAL — **cap·tious·ly** *adv* — **cap·tious·ness** *n*

cap·ti·vate \'kap-tə-,vāt\ *vt* **1** *archaic* **:** SEIZE, CAPTURE **2 :** to influence and dominate by some special charm, art, or trait and with an irresistible appeal **syn** see ATTRACT — **cap·ti·va·tion** \,kap-tə-'vā-shən\ *n* — **cap·ti·va·tor** \'kap-tə-,vāt-ər\ *n*

cap·tive \'kap-tiv\ *adj* [ME, fr. L *captivus*, fr. *captus*, pp. of *capere*] **1 a :** taken and held as prisoner esp. by an enemy in war **b :** kept within bounds **:** CONFINED **c** (1) **:** held under control (2) **:** owned or controlled by another concern and operated for its needs rather

than for an open market ⟨a ~ mine⟩ **2** : of or relating to captivity **3** : CAPTIVATED, CHARMED — **captive** n

cap·tiv·i·ty \kap-'tiv-ət-ē\ n **1** : the state of being captive **2** archaic : a group of captives

cap·tor \'kap-tər, -,tȯ(ə)r\ n [LL, fr. L captus] : one that has captured a person or thing

¹cap·ture \'kap-chər\ n [MF, fr. L captura, fr. captus,. pp. of capere] **1** : the act of catching or gaining control by force, stratagem, or guile **2** : one that has been taken; esp : a prize ship **3** : the act of moving so as to take an opponent's chessman or checker **4** : the coalescence of an atomic nucleus with an elementary particle that may result in an emission from or fission of the nucleus

²capture vt **cap·tur·ing** \'kap-chə-riŋ, 'kap-shriŋ\ **1 a** : to take captive : WIN, GAIN ⟨~ a city⟩ **b** : to preserve in a relatively permanent form **2** : to take according to rules of a game **3** : to bring about the capture of (an elementary particle) **syn** see CATCH

ca·puche \kə-'püch, -'püsh\ n [It cappuccio, fr. cappa cloak, fr. LL] : HOOD; esp : the cowl of a Capuchin friar

ca·pu·chin \'kap-yə-shən, -chən; kə-'p(y)ü-\ n [MF, fr. OIt cappuccino, fr. cappuccio; fr. his cowl] **1** cap : a member of the Order of Friars Minor Capuchin forming since 1529 an austere branch of the first order of St. Francis of Assisi engaged in missionary work and preaching **2** : a hooded cloak for women **3** : any of a genus (Cebus) of So. American monkeys; esp : one (C. capucinus) with the hair on its crown resembling a monk's cowl

Cap·u·let \'kap-yə-lət\ n : the family of Juliet in Shakespeare's Romeo and Juliet

cap·y·bara \,kap-i-'bar-ə, -'bär-\ n [Pg capibara, fr. Tupi] : a tailless largely aquatic So. American rodent (Hydrochoerus capybara) often exceeding four feet in length

car \'kär\ n [ME carre, fr. AF, fr. L carra, pl. of carrum, alter. of carrus, of Celt origin; akin to OIr & MW carr vehicle; akin to L currere to run] **1** : a vehicle moving on wheels: **a** archaic : CARRIAGE, CART, WAGON **b** : a chariot of war or of triumph **c** : a vehicle adapted to the rails of a railroad or street railway **d** : AUTOMOBILE **2** : the cage of an elevator **3** : the portion of an airship or balloon that carries the power plant, personnel, and cargo

ca·ra·bao \,kar-ə-'baú, ,kär-\ n [Phil Sp, fr. Eastern Bisayan karabáw] : WATER BUFFALO

car·a·bi·neer or **car·a·bi·nier** \,kar-ə-bə-'ni(ə)r\ n [F carabinier, fr. carabine carbine] : a soldier armed with a carbine

car·a·bi·ner \,kar-ə-'bē-nər\ n [G karabiner] : an oblong ring that snaps to the eye or link of a piton to hold a freely running rope

cara·cara \,kar-ə-'kar-ə, -ə-kə-'rä\ n [Sp caracara & Pg caracará, fr. Tupi caracará, of imit. origin] : any of various large long-legged mostly So. American hawks like vultures in habits

car·a·cole \'kar-ə-,kōl\ n [F, fr. Sp caracol snail, spiral stair, caracole] **1** : a half turn to right or left executed by a mounted horse **2** : a turning or capering movement — **caracole** vb

car·a·cul \'kar-ə-kəl\ n [alter. of karakul] : the pelt of a karakul lamb after the curl begins to loosen

ca·rafe \kə-'raf\ n [F, fr. It caraffa, fr. Ar gharrāfah] : a bottle with a flaring lip used to hold water or beverages

car·a·ga·na \,kar-ə-'gän-ə\ n [NL, genus name, of Turkic origin; akin to Kirghiz karaghan Siberian pea tree] : any of a genus (Caragana) of Asiatic leguminous shrubs or small trees extensively used in dry areas for hedges and in shelterbelts

car·a·geen var of CARRAGEEN

car·a·mel \'kar-ə-məl, 'kär-məl\ n [F, fr. Sp caramelo, fr. Pg, icicle, caramel, fr. LL calamellus small reed — more at SHAWM] **1** : an amorphous brittle brown and somewhat bitter substance obtained by heating sugar and used as a coloring and flavoring agent **2** : a firm chewy candy usu. cut in small blocks

car·a·mel·ize \-mə-,līz\ vb : to turn into caramel

ca·ran·gid \kə-'ran-jəd, -'raŋ-gəd\ adj [deriv. of F carangue shad, horse mackerel, fr. Sp caranga] : of or relating to a large family (Carangidae) of marine spiny-finned fishes including important food fishes — **carangid** n

car·a·pace \'kar-ə-,pās\ n [F, fr. Sp carapacho] **1** : a bony or chitinous case or shield covering the back or part of the back of an animal (as a turtle) **2** : a hard protective outer covering

¹carat var of KARAT

²car·at \'kar-ət\ n [prob. fr. ML carratus, fr. Ar qīrāṭ bean pod, a small weight, fr. Gk keration carob bean, a small weight, fr. dim. of kerat-, keras horn] : a unit of weight for precious stones equal to 200 milligrams

car·a·van \'kar-ə-,van, -vən\ n [It caravana, fr. Per kārwān] **1 a** : a company of travelers on a journey through desert or hostile regions; also : a train of pack animals **b** : a group of vehicles traveling together in a file **2** : a covered vehicle: as **a** : a vehicle equipped as traveling living quarters **b** Brit : TRAILER 3b

car·a·van·sa·ry \,kar-ə-'van(t)-sə-rē\ or **car·a·van·se·rai** \-sə-,rī\ n [Per kārwānsarāī, fr. kārwān caravan + sarāī palace, inn] **1** : an inn in eastern countries where caravans rest at night that is usu. a large bare building surrounding a court **2** : HOTEL, INN

car·a·vel \'kar-ə-,vel, -vəl\ n [MF caravelle, fr. OPg caravela] : any of several sailing ships; specif : a small 15th and 16th century ship with broad bows, high narrow poop, and lateen sails

car·a·way \'kar-ə-,wā\ n [ME, prob. fr. ML carvi, fr. Ar karawyā, fr. Gk karon] : a biennial usu. white-flowered aromatic herb (Carum carvi) of the carrot family with pungent fruits

carb- or **carbo-** comb form [F, fr. carbone] : carbon : carbonic : carbonyl : carboxyl ⟨carbohydrate⟩

car·ba·mate \'kär-bə-,māt, kär-'bam-,āt\ n : a salt or ester of carbamic acid

car·bam·ic acid \(,)kär-,bam-ik-\ n [ISV carb- + amide] : an acid CH_3NO_2 known in the form of salts and esters that is a half amide of carbonic acid

carb·an·ion \kär-'ban-,ī-ən, -,ī-,än\ n : an organic ion carrying a negative charge at a carbon location

car·ba·zole \'kär-bə-,zōl\ n [ISV] : a crystalline feebly basic cyclic compound $C_{12}H_9N$ found in anthracene that is the parent of various dyes

car·bide \'kär-,bīd\ n [ISV] : a binary compound of carbon with a more electropositive element; esp : CALCIUM CARBIDE

car·bine \'kär-,bīn, -,bēn\ n [F carabine, fr. MF carabin carabineer] **1** : a short-barreled lightweight shoulder firearm **2** : a light automatic or semiautomatic military rifle

car·bi·nol \'kär-bə-,nȯl, -,nōl\ n [ISV, fr. obs. G karbin methyl, fr. G karb- carb-] : METHANOL; also : an alcohol derived from it

car·bo·cy·clic \,kär-bō-'sī-klik, -'sik-lik\ adj [ISV] : being or having an organic ring composed of carbon atoms

car·bo·hy·drate \,kär-bō-'hī-,drāt, -drət\ n : any of various neutral compounds of carbon, hydrogen, and oxygen (as sugars, starches, celluloses) most of which are formed by green plants and which constitute a major class of animal foods

car·bo·lat·ed \'kär-bə-,lāt-əd\ adj : impregnated with carbolic acid

car·bol·ic acid \(,)kär-,bäl-ik-\ n [ISV carb- + L oleum oil — more at OIL] : PHENOL 1

car·bon \'kär-bən\ n, often attrib [F carbone, fr. L carbon-, carbo ember, charcoal] **1** : a nonmetallic chiefly tetravalent element found native (as in the diamond and graphite) or as a constituent of coal, petroleum, and asphalt, of limestone and other carbonates, and of organic compounds or obtained artificially in varying degrees of purity esp. as carbon black, lampblack, activated carbon, charcoal, and coke — see ELEMENT table **2 a** : a sheet of carbon paper **b** : CARBON COPY **3 a** : a carbon rod used in an arc lamp **b** : a piece of carbon used as an element in a voltaic cell

car·bo·na·ceous \,kär-bə-'nā-shəs\ adj **1** : rich in carbon **2** : relating to, containing, or composed of carbon **3** : CARBONOUS 2

¹car·bo·na·do \,kär-bə-'nād-(,)ō, -'näd-\ n, pl **carbonados** or **carbonadoes** [Sp carbonada] archaic : a broiled or grilled piece of meat scored before cooking

²carbonado vt **1** archaic : to make a carbonado of **2** archaic : CUT

³carbonado n, pl **carbonados** [Pg, lit., carbonated] : an impure opaque dark-colored fine-grained aggregate of diamond particles valuable for its superior toughness

¹car·bon·ate \'kär-bə-,nāt, -nət\ n : a salt or ester of carbonic acid

²car·bon·ate \-,nāt\ vt **1** : to convert into a carbonate **2** : to impregnate with carbon dioxide ⟨carbonated beverage⟩ — **car·bon·ation** \,kär-bə-'nā-shən\ n

carbon black n : any of various colloidal black substances consisting wholly or principally of carbon used esp. as pigments

carbon copy n **1** : a copy made by carbon paper **2** : DUPLICATE

carbon cycle n **1** : a cycle of thermonuclear reactions in which four hydrogen atoms synthesize into a helium atom with the release of nuclear energy and which is held to be the source of most of the energy radiated by the sun and stars **2** : the cycle of carbon in living beings in which carbon dioxide is fixed by photosynthesis to form organic nutrients and ultimately restored to the inorganic state by respiration and protoplasmic decay

carbon dioxide n : a heavy colorless gas CO_2 that does not support combustion, dissolves in water to form carbonic acid, is formed esp. by the combustion and decomposition of organic substances, is absorbed from the air by plants in photosynthesis, and is used in the carbonation of beverages

carbon disulfide n : a colorless flammable poisonous liquid CS_2 used as a solvent for rubber and as an insect fumigant — called also carbon bisulfide

carbon 14 n : a heavy radioactive isotope of carbon of mass number 14 used esp. in tracer studies and in dating archaeological and geological materials

car·bon·ic \kär-'bän-ik\ adj : of, relating to, or derived from carbon, carbonic acid, or carbon dioxide

carbonic acid n : a weak dibasic acid H_2CO_3 known only in solution that reacts with bases to form carbonates

carbonic acid gas n : CARBON DIOXIDE

car·bon·if·er·ous \,kär-bə-'nif-(ə-)rəs\ adj **1** : producing or containing carbon or coal **2** cap : of, relating to, or being the period of the Paleozoic era between the Devonian and the Permian or the corresponding system of rocks — **Carboniferous** n

car·bo·ni·um \kär-'bō-nē-əm\ n [carb- + -onium] : an organic ion carrying a positive charge at a carbon location

car·bon·iza·tion \,kär-bə-nə-'zā-shən\ n : the process of carbonizing; esp : destructive distillation (as of coal)

car·bon·ize \'kär-bə-,nīz\ vt **1** : to convert into carbon or a carbonic residue **2** : CARBURIZE 1 ~ vi : to become carbonized

carbon monoxide n : a colorless odorless very toxic gas CO that burns to carbon dioxide with a blue flame and is formed as a product of the incomplete combustion of carbon

car·bon·ous \'kär-bə-nəs\ adj **1** : derived from, containing, or resembling carbon **2** : brittle and dark in color

carbon paper n **1** : a thin paper faced with a waxy pigmented coating so that when placed between two sheets of paper the pressure of writing or typing on the top sheet causes transfer of pigment to the bottom sheet **2** : gelatin-coated paper used in the carbon process

carbon process n : a photographic printing process utilizing a sheet of paper coated with bichromated gelatin mixed with a pigment

carbon tetrachloride n : a colorless nonflammable toxic liquid CCl_4 that has an odor resembling that of chloroform and is used as a solvent and a fire extinguisher

car·bon·yl \'kär-bə-,nil, -,nēl\ n **1** : a bivalent radical CO occurring in aldehydes, ketones, carboxylic acids, esters, acid halides, and amides **2** : a compound of the carbonyl radical with a metal — **car·bon·yl·ic** \,kär-bə-'nil-ik\ adj

Car·bo·run·dum \,kär-bə-'rən-dəm\ trademark — used for various abrasives

car·box·yl \'kär-'bäk-səl\ n [ISV] : a univalent radical —COOH typical of organic acids — **car·box·yl·ic** \,kär-(,)bäk-'sil-ik\ adj

car·box·yl·ase \kär-'bäk-sə-,lās, -,lāz\ n [ISV] : an enzyme that catalyzes decarboxylation or carboxylation

¹car·box·yl·ate \-,lāt, -lət\ n : a salt or ester of a carboxylic acid

²car·box·yl·ate \-,lāt\ vt : to introduce carboxyl or carbon dioxide into (a compound) with formation of a carboxylic acid — **car·box·yl·ation** \(,)kär-,bäk-sə-'lā-shən\ n

car·boy \'kär-,bȯi\ n [Per qarāba, fr. Ar qarrābah demijohn] : a large cylindrical container for liquids made of glass, plastic, or metal and cushioned in a special container

car·bun·cle \'kär-,bəŋ-kəl\ n [ME, fr. MF, fr. L carbunculus small coal, carbuncle, dim. of carbon-, carbo charcoal, ember — more at CARBON] **1 a** obs : any of several red precious stones **b** : the garnet cut cabochon **2** : a painful local purulent inflammation of the skin and deeper tissues with multiple openings for the discharge of pus and usu. necrosis and sloughing of dead tissue — **car·bun·cled**

\-kəld\ *adj* — **car·bun·cu·lar** \kär-ˈbəŋ-kyə-lər\ *adj*

car·bu·ret \ˈkär-b(y)ə-ˌrāt, *esp by chemists* -ˌret\ *vt* **car·bu·ret·ed** *also* **car·bu·ret·ted; car·bu·ret·ing** *also* **car·bu·ret·ting** [obs. *carburet* (carbide)] **1 :** to combine chemically with carbon **2 :** to enrich by mixing with volatile carbon compounds — **car·bu·re·tion** \ˌkär-b(y)ə-ˈrā-shən\ *n*

car·bu·ret·or \ˈkär-b(y)ə-ˌrāt-ər\ *n* **:** an apparatus for supplying an internal-combustion engine with vaporized fuel mixed with air

car·bu·ri·za·tion \ˌkär-byə-rə-ˈzā-shən\ *n* **:** the process of carburizing

car·bu·rize \ˈkär-byə-ˌrīz\ *vt* [obs. *carburet* (carbide)] **1 :** to combine or impregnate (as metal) with carbon **2 :** CARBURET 2

car·ca·jou \ˈkär-kə-ˌjü, -ˌzhü\ *n* [CanF, fr. Algonquian Montagnais *karkajou*] **:** WOLVERINE

car·ca·net \ˈkär-kə-nət\ *n* [MF *carcan*] *archaic* **:** an ornamental necklace or headband

car·case \ˈkär-kəs\ *Brit var of* CARCASS

car·cass \ˈkär-kəs\ *n* [MF *carcasse*, fr. OF *carcois*] **1 :** a dead body **:** CORPSE; *esp* **:** the dressed body of a meat animal **2 :** the living, material, or physical body **3 :** the decaying or worthless remains of a structure **4 :** the foundation structure of something (as a tire)

carcin- *or* **carcino-** *comb form* [Gk *karkin-*, *karkino-*, fr. *karkinos*] **1 :** crab ⟨*carcino*logy⟩ **2 :** tumor **:** cancer ⟨*carcino*genic⟩

car·cin·o·gen \kär-ˈsin-ə-jən, ˈkärs-ᵊn-ə-ˌjen\ *n* **:** a substance or agent producing or inciting cancer — **car·ci·no·gen·e·sis** \ˌkärs-ᵊn-ō-ˈjen-ə-səs\ *n* — **car·ci·no·gen·ic** \-ˈjen-ik\ *adj* — **car·ci·no·ge·nic·i·ty** \-jə-ˈnis-ət-ē\ *n*

car·ci·no·ma \ˌkärs-ᵊn-ˈō-mə\ *n, pl* **carcinomas** *or* **car·ci·no·ma·ta** \-mət-ə\ [L, fr. Gk *karkinōma* cancer, fr. *karkinos*] **:** a malignant tumor of epithelial origin — **car·ci·no·ma·tous** \ˌkärs-ᵊn-ˈäm-ət-əs, -ˈō-mət-\ *adj*

car·ci·no·ma·to·sis \-ˌō-mə-ˈtō-səs\ *n* [NL, fr. L *carcinomat-*, *carcinoma*] **:** a condition in which multiple carcinomas are developing simultaneously usu. after dissemination from a primary source

1**card** \ˈkärd\ *vt* **:** to cleanse, disentangle, and collect together (as fibers) by the use of a card preparatory to spinning — **card·er** *n*

2**card** *n* [ME *carde*, fr. MF, fr. LL *cardus* thistle, fr. L *carduus*] **1 :** an implement for raising a nap on cloth **2 :** an instrument or machine for carding fibers consisting usu. of bent wire teeth set closely in rows in a thick piece of leather fastened to a back

3**card** *n* [ME *carde*, modif. of MF *carte*, prob. fr. OIt *carta*, lit., leaf of paper, fr. L *charta* leaf of papyrus, fr. Gk *chartēs*] **1 :** PLAYING CARD **2** *pl but sing or pl in constr* **a :** a game played with cards **b :** card playing **3 :** something compared to a valuable playing card in one's hand **4 :** a usu. clownishly amusing person **:** WAG **5 :** COMPASS CARD **6 a :** a flat stiff usu. small and rectangular piece of paper or thin paperboard as (1) **:** POSTCARD (2) **:** VISITING CARD **b :** PROGRAM; *esp* **:** a sports program **c** (1) **:** a wine list (2) **:** MENU

4**card** *vt* **1 :** to place or fasten on or by means of a card **2 :** to provide with a card **3 :** to list or record on a card **4 :** SCORE

car·da·mom \ˈkärd-ə-məm, -ˌmäm\ *n* [L *cardamomum*, fr. Gk *kardamōmon*, blend of *kardamon* peppergrass & *amōmon*, an Indian spice plant] **:** the aromatic capsular fruit of an East Indian herb (*Elettaria cardamomum*) of the ginger family with seeds used as a condiment and in medicine; *also* **:** this plant

1**card·board** \ˈkärd-ˌbō(ə)rd, -ˌbȯ(ə)rd\ *n* **:** a stiff moderately thick paperboard

2**cardboard** *adj* **:** made of or as if of cardboard

cardi- *or* **cardio-** *comb form* [Gk *kardi-*, *kardio-*, fr. *kardia* — more at HEART] **:** heart ⟨*cardio*gram⟩

-car·dia \ˈkärd-ē-ə\ *n comb form* [NL, fr. Gk *kardia*] **:** heart action or location (of a specified type) ⟨dextro*cardia*⟩ ⟨tachy*cardia*⟩

1**car·di·ac** \ˈkärd-ē-ˌak\ *adj* [L *cardiacus*, fr. Gk *kardiakos*, fr. *kardia*] **1 a :** of, relating to, situated near, or acting on the heart **b :** of or relating to the part of the stomach into which the esophagus opens or to the stomach exclusive of the pyloric end **2 :** of or relating to heart disease

2**cardiac** *n* **:** a person with heart disease

car·di·al·gia \ˌkärd-ē-ˈal-j(ē-)ə\ *n* [NL, fr. Gk *kardialgia*, fr. *kardia* + *-algia*] **1 :** HEARTBURN **2 :** pain in the heart

car·di·gan \ˈkärd-i-gən\ *n* [James Thomas Brudenell, 7th Earl of *Cardigan* †1868 E soldier] **:** a usu. collarless sweater or jacket that opens the full length of the center front

Cardigan *n* [*Cardigan* county, Wales] **:** a Welsh corgi with rounded ears, slightly bowed forelegs, and long tail

1**car·di·nal** \ˈkärd-nəl, -ᵊn-əl\ *adj* [ME, fr. OF, fr. LL *cardinalis*, fr. L, of a hinge, fr. *cardin-*, *cardo* hinge; akin to OE *hratian* to rush, Gk *skairein* to gambol] **:** of basic importance **:** MAIN, CHIEF, PRIMARY **syn** see ESSENTIAL — **car·di·nal·ly** \-ē\ *adv*

2**cardinal** *n* **1 :** a high ecclesiastical official of the Roman Catholic Church who ranks next below the pope and is appointed by him to assist him as a member of the college of cardinals **2 :** CARDINAL NUMBER — usu. used in pl. **3 :** a woman's short hooded cloak orig. of scarlet cloth **4** [fr. its color, resembling that of the cardinal's robes] **:** any of several American finches (genus *Richmondena*) of the southern and middle U.S. of which the male is bright red with a black face and pointed crest — **car·di·nal·ship** \-ˌship\ *n*

car·di·nal·ate \-ət, -ˌāt\ *n* **1 :** the office, rank, or dignity of a cardinal **2 :** CARDINALS

cardinal flower *n* **:** the brilliant red flower of a No. American lobelia (*Lobelia cardinalis*); *also* **:** this plant

car·di·nal·i·ty \ˌkärd-ᵊn-ˈal-ət-ē\ *n* [2*cardinal* + *-ity*] **:** the number of elements in a given mathematical set

cardinal number *n* **1 :** a number (as 1, 5, 15) that is used in simple counting and that indicates how many elements there are in an assemblage — see NUMBER table **2 :** the property that a mathematical set has in common with all sets that can be put in one-to-one correspondence with it

cardinal point *n* **:** one of the four principal compass points north, south, east, and west

cardinal virtue *n* **:** one of the four natural virtues prudence, justice, temperance, or fortitude; *also* **:** one of the three theological virtues faith, hope, and charity

car·dio·gram \ˈkärd-ē-ə-ˌgram\ *n* [ISV] **:** the curve or tracing made by a cardiograph

car·dio·graph \-ˌgraf\ *n* [ISV] **:** an instrument that registers graphically movements of the heart — **car·di·og·ra·pher** \ˌkärd-ē-ˈäg-rə-fər\ *n* — **car·dio·graph·ic** \ˌkärd-ē-ə-ˈgraf-ik\ *adj* — **car·di·og·ra·phy** \ˌkärd-ē-ˈäg-rə-fē\ *n*

car·di·oid \ˈkärd-ē-ˌȯid\ *n* **:** a heart-shaped curve traced by a point on the circumference of a circle rolling completely around an equal fixed circle

car·di·ol·o·gist \ˌkärd-ē-ˈäl-ə-jəst\ *n* **:** a specialist in cardiology

car·di·ol·o·gy \-jē\ *n* [ISV] **:** the study of the heart and its action and diseases

car·dio·re·spi·ra·to·ry \ˌkärd-ē-(ˌ)ō-ˈres-p(ə-)rə-ˌtōr-ē, -ri-ˈspī-rə-, -ˌtȯr-\ *adj* **:** of or relating to the heart and lungs

car·dio·vas·cu·lar \-ˈvas-kyə-lər\ *adj* [ISV] **:** of, relating to, or involving the heart and blood vessels

car·doon \kär-ˈdün\ *n* [F *cardon*, fr. LL *cardon-*, *cardo* thistle, fr. *cardus*, fr. L *carduus* thistle, artichoke — more at CHARD] **:** a large perennial plant (*Cynara cardunculus*) related to the artichoke

card·sharp·er \ˈkärd-ˌshär-pər\ *or* **card·sharp** \-ˌshärp\ *n* **:** one who habitually cheats at cards

1**care** \ˈke(ə)r, ˈka(ə)r\ *n* [ME, fr. OE *caru*; akin to OHG *kara* lament, L *garrire* to chatter] **1 :** suffering of mind **:** GRIEF **2 a :** a burdensome sense of responsibility **:** ANXIETY **b :** a cause for such anxiety **3 :** painstaking or watchful attention **4 :** regard coming from desire or esteem **5 :** CHARGE, SUPERVISION **6 :** a person or thing that is an object of attention, anxiety, or solicitude

syn CONCERN, SOLICITUDE, ANXIETY, WORRY: CARE implies oppression of the mind weighed down by responsibility or disquieted by apprehension; CONCERN implies a troubled state of mind because of personal interest, relation, or affection; SOLICITUDE implies great concern and connotes either thoughtful or hovering attentiveness to one in pain, illness, or distress; ANXIETY stresses anguished uncertainty or fear of misfortune or failure; WORRY suggests fretting over matters that may or may not be real cause for anxiety

2**care** *vi* **1 a :** to feel trouble or anxiety **b :** to feel interest or concern ⟨~ about freedom⟩ **2 :** to give care ⟨~ for the sick⟩ **3 a :** to have a liking, fondness, or taste ⟨don't ~ for her⟩ **b :** to have an inclination ⟨would you ~ for some pie⟩ ~ *vt* **1 :** to be concerned about or to the extent of **2 :** WISH — **car·er** *n*

1**ca·reen** \kə-ˈrēn\ *n* [MF *carène* keel, fr. OIt *carena*, fr. L *carina* keel, lit., nutshell; akin to Gk *karyon* nut] *archaic* **:** the act or process of careening **:** the state of being careened

2**careen** *vt* **1 a :** to cause (a boat) to lean over on one side **b :** to clean, caulk, or repair (a boat) in this position **2 :** to cause to heel over ~ *vi* **1 a :** to careen a boat **b :** to undergo this process **2 :** to heel over **3 :** to sway from side to side **:** LURCH

1**ca·reer** \kə-ˈri(ə)r\ *n* [MF *carrière*, fr. OProv *carriera* street, fr. ML *carraria* road for vehicles, fr. L *carrus* car] **1 a :** COURSE, PASSAGE **b :** full speed or exercise of activity **2 :** ENCOUNTER, CHARGE **3 :** a course of continued progress **4 :** a profession for which one trains and which is undertaken as a permanent calling

2**career** *vi* **:** to go at top speed esp. in a headlong manner

ca·reer·ism \-ˌiz-əm\ *n* **:** the policy or practice of advancing one's career often at the cost of one's integrity — **ca·reer·ist** \-əst\ *n*

care·free \ˈke(ə)r-ˌfrē, ˈka(ə)r-\ *adj* **:** free from care

care·ful \-fəl\ *adj* **1** *archaic* **a :** SOLICITOUS, ANXIOUS **b :** filling with care or solicitude **2 :** exercising or taking care **3 a :** marked by attentive concern and solicitude **b :** marked by wary caution or prudence **c :** marked by painstaking effort — **care·ful·ly** \-f(ə-)lē\ *adv* — **care·ful·ness** \-fəl-nəs\ *n*

syn CAREFUL, METICULOUS, SCRUPULOUS, PUNCTILIOUS mean showing close attention to details of behavior or performance. CAREFUL implies attentiveness and cautiousness in avoiding mistakes; METICULOUS may imply either commendable extreme carefulness or hampering finical caution over minutiae; SCRUPULOUS applies to painstaking attention to what is proper or fitting or ethical; PUNCTILIOUS implies minute often excessive attention to fine points

care·less \-ləs\ *adj* **1 a :** free from care **:** UNTROUBLED ⟨~ days⟩ **b :** UNCONCERNED, INDIFFERENT ⟨~ of the consequences⟩ **2 :** not taking care **3 :** not showing or receiving care: **a :** NEGLIGENT, SLOVENLY **b :** UNSTUDIED, SPONTANEOUS ⟨~ grace⟩ **c** *obs* **:** UNVALUED, DISREGARDED — **care·less·ly** *adv* — **care·less·ness** *n*

1**ca·ress** \kə-ˈres\ *n* [F *caresse*, fr. It *carezza*, fr. *caro* dear, fr. L *carus* — more at CHARITY] **1 :** an act or expression of kindness or affection **:** ENDEARMENT **2 a :** a light stroking, rubbing, or patting **b :** KISS — **ca·res·sive** \-ˈres-iv\ *adj* — **ca·res·sive·ly** *adv*

2**caress** *vt* **1 :** to treat with tokens of fondness, affection, or kindness **:** CHERISH **2 :** to touch or stroke lightly in a loving or endearing manner — **ca·ress·er** *n*

syn FONDLE, PET, CUDDLE: CARESS implies expressing affection by light stroking or patting; FONDLE suggests handling or caressing in a doting manner; PET applies to caressing or fondling children or animals but may suggest an indulging or pampering; CUDDLE suggests closely but gently embracing so as to soothe or comfort

car·et \ˈkar-ət\ *n* [L, there is lacking, fr. *carēre* to lack, be without — more at CASTE] **:** a mark ∧ made on written or printed matter to indicate the place where something is to be inserted

care·tak·er \ˈke(ə)r-ˌtā-kər, ˈka(ə)r-\ *n* **1 :** one that takes care (usu. as occupant) of the house or land of an owner who may be absent **2 :** one temporarily fulfilling the functions of office

care·worn \-ˌwō(ə)rn, -ˌwȯ(ə)rn\ *adj* **:** showing the effect of grief or anxiety

car·fare \ˈkär-ˌfa(ə)r, -ˌfe(ə)r\ *n* **:** passenger fare (as on a bus)

car·go \ˈkär-(ˌ)gō\ *n, pl* **cargoes** *or* **cargos** [Sp, load, charge, fr. *cargar* to load, fr. LL *carricare* — more at CHARGE] **:** the goods or merchandise conveyed in a ship, airplane, or vehicle **:** FREIGHT

car·hop \ˈkär-ˌhäp\ *n* [*car* + *-hop* (as in *bellhop*)] **:** one who serves customers at a drive-in restaurant

Car·ib \ˈkar-əb\ *n* [NL *Caribes* (pl.), fr. Sp *Caribe*, fr. Arawakan *Carib*] **1 :** a member of an Indian people of northern So. America and the Lesser Antilles **2 :** the language of the Caribs

Ca·ri·ban \ˈkar-ə-bən, kə-ˈrē-bən\ *n* **1 :** a member of a group of Amerindian peoples of northern So. America, the Lesser Antilles, and the Caribbean coast of Honduras, Guatemala, and British Honduras **2 :** the language family comprising the languages of the Cariban peoples

Ca·rib·be·an \ˌkar-ə-ˈbē-ən, kə-ˈrib-ē-\ *adj* [NL *Caribbaeus*, fr. *Caribes*] **:** of or relating to the Caribs, the eastern and southern West Indies, or the Caribbean sea

ca·ri·be \kə-ˈrē-bē\ *n* [AmerSp, fr. Sp, Carib, cannibal] **:** a small voracious So. American characin fish (genus *Serrasalmo*)

car·i·bou \ˈkar-ə-ˌbü\ *n, pl* **caribou** *or* **caribous** [CanF, of Algonquian origin] **:** any of several large palmate-antlered deer (genus *Rangifer*) of northern No. America that are related to the reindeer

car·i·ca·ture \'kar-i-kə-,chu̇(ə)r, -,t(y)u̇(ə)r\ *n* [It *caricatura,* lit., act of loading, fr. *caricare* to load, fr. LL *carricare*] **1 :** exaggeration by means of often ludicrous distortion of parts or characteristics **2 :** a representation esp. in literature or art that has the qualities of caricature **3 :** a distortion so gross as to seem like caricature — **caricature** *vt* — **car·i·ca·tur·ist** \-əst\ *n*

syn CARICATURE, BURLESQUE, PARODY, TRAVESTY mean a comic or grotesque imitation. CARICATURE implies ludicrous exaggeration of the characteristic features of a subject; BURLESQUE implies mockery either through treating a trivial subject in a mock-heroic style or through giving a serious or lofty subject a frivolous treatment; PARODY applies esp. to treatment of a trivial or ludicrous subject in the exactly imitated style of a well-known author or work; TRAVESTY implies that the subject remains unchanged but that the style and effect is extravagant or absurd

car·ies \'kar-ēz, 'ker-\ *n, pl* **caries** [L, decay; akin to Gk *kēr* death] **:** a progressive destruction of bone or tooth; *esp* **:** tooth decay

car·il·lon \'kar-ə-,län, kə-'ril-yən\ *n* [F, alter. of OF *quarregnon,* fr. LL *quaternion-, quaternio* set of four] **1 a :** a set of fixed bells sounded by hammers controlled by a keyboard **b :** a stop in a pipe organ imitating a carillon **c :** an electronic instrument imitating a carillon **2 :** a composition for the carillon

car·il·lon·neur \,kar-ə-(,)lä-'nər, kə-,ril-yə-'nər\ *n* [F, fr. *carillon*] **:** a carillon player

ca·ri·na \kə-'rī-nə, -'rē-\ *n, pl* **carinas** *or* **ca·ri·nae** \-'rī-,nē, -'rē-,nī\ [NL, fr. L, keel] **:** a keel-shaped anatomical part, ridge, or process; *esp* **:** the part of a papilionaceous flower that encloses the stamens and pistil — **ca·ri·nal** \kə-'rīn-ᵊl\ *adj*

car·i·nate \'kar-ə-,nāt, -nət\ *also* **car·i·nat·ed** \-,nāt-əd\ *adj* **:** KEELED, RIDGED ⟨a ~ sepal⟩

car·i·o·ca \,kar-ē-'ō-kə\ *n* [Pg, fr. Tupi] **1** *cap* **:** a native or resident of Rio de Janeiro **2 a :** the samba adapted to ballroom dancing **b :** the music for such a dance

car·i·ole \'kar-ē-,ōl\ *n* [F *carriole,* fr. OProv *carriola,* deriv. of L *carrus* car] **1 :** a light one-horse carriage **2 :** a dog-drawn toboggan

car·i·ous \'kar-ē-əs, 'ker-\ *adj* [L *cariosus,* fr. *caries*] **:** affected with caries

[1]**cark** \'kärk\ *vb* [ME *carken,* lit., to load, burden, fr. ONF *carquier,* fr. LL *carricare*] *vt* **:** WORRY ~ *vi* **:** to be anxious

[2]**cark** *n* **:** TROUBLE, DISTRESS

carl *or* **carle** \'kär(ə)l\ *n* [ME, fr. OE *-carl,* fr. ON *karl* man, carl] **1 :** a man of the common people **2** *chiefly dial* **:** CHURL, BOOR

car·line *or* **car·lin** \'kär-lən\ *n* [ME *kerling,* fr. ON, fr. *karl* man] *chiefly Scot* **:** WOMAN; *esp* **:** an old woman

car·ling \'kär-liŋ, -lən\ *n* [F *carlingue,* fr. ONF *calingue,* fr. ON *kerling,* lit., old woman] **:** a fore-and-aft member supporting a deck of a ship or framing a deck opening

Car·list \'kär-ləst\ *n* [Sp *carlista,* fr. Don *Carlos* claimant to the Spanish throne under the Salic law] **:** a supporter of Don Carlos or his successors as having rightful title to the Spanish throne

car·load \'kär-'lōd\ *n* **1 :** a load that fills a car **2 :** the minimum number of tons required for shipping at carload rates

carload rate \,kär-,lōd-\ *n* **:** a rate for large shipments lower than that quoted for less-than-carload lots of the same class

Car·lo·vin·gian \,kär-lə-'vin-j(ē-)ən\ *adj* [F *carlovingien,* prob. fr. ML *Carlus* Charles + F *-ovingien* (as in *mérovingien* Merovingian)] **:** CAROLINGIAN

car·ma·gnole \'kär-mən-,yōl\ *n* [F] **1 :** a lively song popular at the time of the first French Revolution **2 :** a street dance in a meandering course to the tune of the carmagnole

Car·mel·ite \'kär-mə-,līt\ *n, often attrib* [ME, fr. ML *carmelita,* fr. *Carmel* Mount Carmel, Palestine] **:** a member of the Roman Catholic mendicant Order of Our Lady of Mount Carmel founded in the 12th century

car·mi·na·tive \kär-'min-ət-iv, 'kär-mə-,nāt-\ *adj* [F *carminatif,* fr. L *carminatus,* pp. of *carminare* to card, fr. *carmin-, carmen* card, fr. *carrere* to card — more at CHARD] **:** expelling gas from the alimentary canal so as to relieve colic or griping — **carminative** *n*

car·mine \'kär-mən, -,mīn\ *n* [F *carmin,* fr. ML *carminium,* irreg. fr. Ar *qirmiz* kermes + L *minium* — more at MINIUM] **1 :** a rich crimson or scarlet lake made from cochineal **2 :** a vivid red

car·nage \'kär-nij\ *n* [MF, fr. ML *carnaticum* tribute consisting of animals or meat, fr. L *carn-, caro*] **1 :** the flesh of slain animals or men **2 :** great destruction of life

car·nal \'kärn-ᵊl\ *adj* [ME, fr. ONF or LL; ONF, fr. LL *carnalis,* fr. L *carn-, caro* flesh; akin to Gk *keirein* to cut] **1 :** BODILY, CORPOREAL **2 a :** marked by sexuality **b :** relating to or given to crude bodily pleasures **3 a :** TEMPORAL **b :** WORLDLY — **car·nal·i·ty** \kär-'nal-ət-ē\ *n* — **car·nal·ly** \'kärn-ᵊl-ē\ *adv*

syn CARNAL, FLESHLY, SENSUAL, ANIMAL mean having a relation to the body. CARNAL may mean only this but more often connotes derogatorily an action or manifestation of man's lower nature; FLESHLY is somewhat less condemnatory than CARNAL; SENSUAL may apply to any gratification of a bodily desire or pleasure but commonly implies sexual appetite with absence of the spiritual or intellectual; ANIMAL stresses a relation to man's physical as distinguished from his rational nature usu. without definitely derogatory suggestion

car·nall·ite \'kärn-ᵊl-,īt\ *n* [G *carnallit,* fr. Rudolf von *Carnall* †1874 G mining engineer] **:** a hydrous potassium-magnesium chloride $KMgCl_3.6H_2O$ important as a source of potassium

car·nas·si·al \kär-'nas-ē-əl\ *adj* [F *carnassier* carnivorous, deriv. of L *carn-, caro*] **:** of, relating to, or being teeth of a carnivore larger and longer than adjacent teeth and adapted for cutting rather than tearing — **carnassial** *n*

car·na·tion \kär-'nā-shən\ *n* [MF, fr. OIt *carnagione,* fr. *carne* flesh, fr. L *carn-, caro*] **1 a** (1) **:** the variable color of human flesh (2) **:** a pale to grayish yellow **b :** a moderate red **2 :** any of the numerous cultivated usu. double-flowered pinks derived from the common gillyflower

car·nau·ba \kär-'nȯ-bə, ,kär-nə-'ü-bə\ *n* [Pg] **:** a fan-leaved palm (*Copernicia cerifera*) of Brazil with an edible root and leaves yielding a useful fiber and a brittle yellowish wax used esp. in polishes

carnauba wax *n* **:** a hard brittle high-melting wax from the leaves of the carnauba palm used chiefly in polishes

Car·ne·gie unit \,kär-nə-gē-, (,)kär-,neg-ē-\ *n* [fr. its having been first defined by the Carnegie Foundation for the Advancement of Teaching] **:** the credit given for the successful completion of a year's study of one subject in a secondary school

car·ne·lian \kär-'nēl-yən\ *n* [alter. of *cornelian* fr. ME *corneline,* fr. MF, perh. fr. *cornelle* cornel] **:** a hard tough chalcedony that has a red or reddish color and is much used for seals

car·ni·val \'kär-nə-vəl\ *n, often attrib* [It *carnevale,* alter. of earlier *carnelevare,* lit., removal of meat, fr. *carne* flesh (fr. L *carn-, caro*) + *levare* to remove fr. L, to raise] **1 :** a season or festival of merrymaking before Lent **2 :** a merrymaking, feasting, or masquerading **3 a :** a traveling enterprise offering amusements **b :** an organized program of entertainment or exhibition

car·ni·vore \'kär-nə-,vō(ə)r, -,vȯ(ə)r\ *n* [deriv. of L *carnivorus*] **1 :** a flesh-eating animal; *esp* **:** any of an order (Carnivora) of flesh-eating mammals **2 :** an insectivorous plant

car·niv·o·rous \kär-'niv-(ə-)rəs\ *adj* [L *carnivorus,* fr. *carn-, caro* flesh + *-vorus* -vorous — more at CARNAL] **1 :** subsisting or feeding on animal tissues **2** *of a plant* **:** subsisting on nutrients obtained from the breakdown of animal protoplasm **3 :** of or relating to the carnivores — **car·niv·o·rous·ly** *adv* — **car·niv·o·rous·ness** *n*

car·no·tite \'kär-nə-,tīt\ *n* [F, fr. M. A. *Carnot* †1920 F inspector general of mines] **:** a mineral $K_2(UO_2)_2(VO_4)_2.3H_2O$ consisting of a hydrous radioactive vanadate of uranium and potassium

car·ny *or* **car·ney** *or* **car·nie** \'kär-nē\ *n* **1 :** CARNIVAL 3a **2 :** one who works with a carnival

car·ob \'kar-əb\ *n* [MF *carobe,* fr. ML *carrubium,* fr. Ar *kharrūbah*] **1 :** a Mediterranean evergreen leguminous tree (*Ceratonia siliqua*) with racemose red flowers **2 :** a carob pod or its sweet pulp

ca·roche \kə-'rōch, -'rōsh\ *n* [MF *carroche,* fr. OIt *carroccio,* aug. of *carro* car, fr. L *carrus*] **:** a luxurious or stately carriage for persons

[1]**car·ol** \'kar-əl\ *n* [ME *carole,* fr. OF, modif. of LL *choraula* choral song, fr. L, choral accompanist, fr. Gk *choraulēs,* fr. *choros* chorus + *aulein* to play a reed instrument, fr. *aulos,* a reed instrument] **1 :** an old round dance with singing **2 :** a song of joy or mirth **3 :** a popular song or ballad of religious joy

[2]**carol** *vb* **car·oled** *or* **car·olled; car·ol·ing** *or* **car·ol·ling** *vi* **1 :** to sing esp. in a joyful manner **2 :** to sing carols; *specif* **:** to go about outdoors in a group singing Christmas carols ~ *vt* **1 :** to praise in or as if in song **2 :** to sing esp. in a cheerful manner **:** WARBLE

Car·o·line \'kar-ə-,līn, -lən\ *or* **Car·o·le·an** \,kar-ə-'lē-ən\ *adj* [NL *carolinus,* fr. ML *Carolus* Charles] **:** of or relating to Charles — used esp. with ref. to Charles I and Charles II of England

Car·o·lin·gian \,kar-ə-'lin-j(ē-)ən\ *adj* [F *carolingien,* fr. ML *karolingi* French people, prob. fr. (assumed) OHG *karling* Frenchman, fr. *Karl* Charles] **:** of or relating to a Frankish dynasty dating from about A.D. 613 and including among its members the rulers of France from 751 to 987, of Germany from 752 to 911, and of Italy from 774 to 961 — **Carolingian** *n*

Car·o·lin·ian \,kar-ə-'lin-yən, -'lin-ē-ən\ *adj* **:** of, relating to, or characteristic of No. Carolina or So. Carolina or both or their people — **Carolinian** *n*

[1]**car·om** \'kar-əm\ *n* [by shortening & alter. fr. obs. *carambole,* fr. Sp *carambola*] **1 :** a shot in billiards in which the cue ball strikes each of two object balls **2 :** a rebounding esp. at an angle

[2]**carom** *vi* **1 :** to make a carom **2 :** to strike and rebound **:** GLANCE

car·o·tene \'kar-ə-,tēn\ *n* [ISV, fr. LL *carota* carrot] **:** any of several orange or red crystalline hydrocarbon pigments (as $C_{40}H_{56}$) occurring in the chromoplasts of plants and in the fatty tissues of plant-eating animals and convertible to vitamin A

ca·rot·enoid \kə-'rät-ᵊn-,ȯid\ *n* **:** any of various unsaturated usu. yellow to red pigments (as carotenes) found widely in plants and animals and characterized chemically by a long aliphatic polyene chain composed of isoprene units — **carotenoid** *adj*

ca·rot·id \kə-'rät-əd\ *adj* [F or Gk; F *carotide,* fr. Gk *karōtides* carotid arteries, fr. *karoun* to stupefy; akin to Gk *kara* head] **:** of, relating to, or being the chief artery or pair of arteries that pass up the neck and supply the head — **carotid** *n*

ca·rous·al \kə-'rau̇-zəl\ *n* **:** CAROUSE 2

[1]**ca·rouse** \kə-'rau̇z\ *n* [MF *carrousse,* fr. *carous,* adv., all out (in *boire carous* to empty the cup), fr. G *garaus*] **1** *archaic* **:** a large cup of liquor drunk up **2 :** a drunken revel

[2]**carouse** *vi* **1 :** to drink deeply or freely **2 :** to take part in a carouse ~ *vt, obs* **:** to drink up **:** QUAFF — **ca·rous·er** *n*

car·ou·sel *var of* CARROUSEL

[1]**carp** \'kärp\ *vi* [ME *carpen,* of Scand origin; akin to Icel *karpa* to dispute] **:** to find fault or complain querulously — **carp·er** *n*

[2]**carp** *n, pl* **carp** *or* **carps** [ME *carpe,* fr. MF, fr. LL *carpa,* prob. of Gmc origin; akin to OHG *karpfo* carp] **:** a large variable Old World soft-finned freshwater fish (*Cyprinus carpio*) of sluggish waters often reared for food; *also* **:** any of various related fishes (family Cyprinidae) or similar fishes (as the European sea bream)

carp- *or* **carpo-** *comb form* [F & NL, fr. Gk *karp-, karpo-,* fr. *karpos* — more at HARVEST] **:** fruit ⟨*carpel*⟩ ⟨*carpology*⟩

-carp \,kärp\ *n comb form* [NL *-carpium,* fr. Gk *-karpion,* fr. *karpos*] **:** part of a fruit ⟨meso*carp*⟩ **:** fruit ⟨schizo*carp*⟩

[1]**car·pal** \'kär-pəl\ *adj* [NL *carpalis,* fr. *carpus*] **:** relating to the carpus

[2]**carpal** *n* **:** a carpal element **:** CARPALE

car·pa·le \kär-'pal-(,)ē, -'pāl-, -'päl-\ *n, pl* **car·pa·lia** \-ē-ə\ [NL, neut. of *carpalis*] **:** a carpal bone

car·pel \'kär-pəl\ *n* [NL *carpellum,* fr. Gk *karpos* fruit] **:** one of the structures in a seed plant comprising the innermost whorl of a flower, functioning as megasporophylls, and collectively constituting the gynoecium — **car·pel·lary** \-pə-,ler-ē\ *adj* — **car·pel·late** \-,lāt, -lət\ *adj*

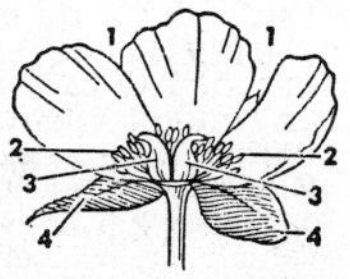

carpels: flower cut away: *1,1,* petals; *2,2,* stamens; *3,3,* carpels; *4,4,* sepals

car·pen·ter \'kär-pən-tər, 'kärp-ᵊm-tər\ *n* [ME, fr. ONF *carpentier,* fr. L *carpentarius* carriage maker, fr. *carpentum* carriage, of Celt origin; akin to OIr *carr* vehicle — more at CAR] **:** a workman who builds or repairs wooden structures or their structural parts — **carpenter** *vb* **car·pen·ter·ing** \-t(ə-)riŋ\ — **car·pen·try** \-trē\ *n*

carpenter bee *n* **:** any of various solitary bees (*Xylocopa* and related genera) that gnaw galleries in sound timber

car·pet \'kär-pət\ *n* [ME, fr. MF *carpite*, fr. OIt *carpita*, fr. *carpire* to pluck, modif. of L *carpere* to pluck] **:** a heavy woven or felted fabric used as a floor covering; *esp* **:** a fabric made in breadths to be sewed together and tacked to the floor — **carpet** *vt*

1car·pet·bag \-,bag\ *n* **:** a traveling bag made orig. of carpet and widely used in the U.S. in the 19th century

2carpetbag *adj* **:** of, relating to, or characteristic of carpetbaggers

car·pet·bag·ger \-,bag-ər\ *n* [fr. their carrying all their belongings in carpetbags] **1 :** a Northerner in the South after the American Civil War esp. seeking private gain under the reconstruction governments **2 :** a nonresident who meddles in politics — **car·pet·bag·gery** \-,bag-(ə-)rē\ *n*

carpet beetle *n* **:** a small beetle (*Bothynus gibbosus*) whose larva damages woolen goods; *broadly* **:** any beetle of similar habits

car·pet·ing \'kär-pət-iŋ\ *n* **:** material for carpets; *also* **:** CARPETS

carpet knight *n* [fr. the carpet's having been a symbol of luxury] **:** a knight devoted to idleness and luxury

car·pet·weed \'kär-pət-,wēd\ *n* **:** a No. American mat-forming weed (*Mollugo verticillata* of the family Aizoaceae, the carpetweed family)

-car·pic \'kär-pik\ *adj comb form* [prob. fr. NL *-carpicus*, fr. Gk *karpos* fruit] **:** -CARPOUS ⟨poly*carpic*⟩

carp·ing \'kär-piŋ\ *adj* **:** likely to carp **:** FAULTFINDING **syn** see CRITICAL — **carp·ing·ly** \-piŋ-lē\ *adv*

car·po·go·ni·um \,kär-pə-'gō-nē-əm\ *n, pl* **car·po·go·nia** \-nē-ə\ [NL] **1 :** the flask-shaped egg-bearing portion of the female reproductive branch in some thallophytes **2 :** ASCOGONIUM

car·pol·o·gy \kär-'päl-ə-jē\ *n* [ISV] **:** a branch of plant morphology dealing with fruit and seeds

car·poph·a·gous \kär-'päf-ə-gəs\ *adj* [Gk *karpophagos*, fr. *karp-* carp- + *-phagos* -phagous] **:** feeding on fruits

car·po·phore \'kär-pə-,fō(ə)r, -,fȯ(ə)r\ *n* [prob. fr. NL *carpophorum*, fr. *carp-* + *-phorum* -phore] **1 :** the stalk of a fungal fruiting body or the entire fruiting body **2 :** a slender prolongation of a floral axis from which the carpels are suspended

car·port \'kär-,pō(ə)rt, -,pȯ(ə)rt\ *n* **:** an open-sided automobile shelter usu. formed by extension of a roof from the side of a building

car·po·spore \'kär-pə-,spō(ə)r, -,spȯ(ə)r\ *n* **:** a diploid spore of a red alga — **car·po·spor·ic** \,kär-pə-'spōr-ik, -'spȯr-\ *adj*

-car·pous \'kär-pəs\ *adj comb form* [NL *-carpus*, fr. Gk *-karpos*, fr. *karpos* fruit — more at HARVEST] **:** having (such) fruit or (so many) fruits ⟨poly*carpous*⟩ — **-car·py** \,kär-pē\ *n comb form*

car·pus \'kär-pəs\ *n* [NL, fr. Gk *karpos* — more at WHARF] **1 :** WRIST **2 :** the bones of the wrist

car·rack \'kar-ək\ *n* [ME *carrake*, fr. MF *caraque*, fr. OSp *carraca*, fr. Ar *qarāqīr*, pl. of *qurqūr* merchant ship] **:** a large galleon

car·ra·geen *or* **car·ra·gheen** \'kar-ə-,gēn\ *n* [*Carragheen*, near Waterford, Ireland] **:** a dark purple branching cartilaginous seaweed (*Chondrus crispus*) found on the coasts of northern Europe and No. America

car·re·four \,kar-ə-'fu̇(ə)r\ *n* [MF, fr. LL *quadrifurcum*, neut. of *quadrifurcus* having four forks, fr. L *quadri-* + *furca* fork] **1 :** CROSSROADS **2 :** SQUARE, PLAZA

car·rel \'kar-əl\ *n* [alter. of ME *carole* round dance, ring] **:** a table with bookshelves that is often partitioned or enclosed and is used for individual study in a library

car·riage \'kar-ij\ *n* [ME *cariage*, fr. ONF, fr. *carier* to transport in a vehicle] **1 :** the act of carrying **2 a** *archaic* **:** DEPORTMENT **b :** manner of bearing the body **:** POSTURE **3** *archaic* **:** MANAGEMENT **4 :** the price or expense of carrying **5** *obs* **:** BURDEN, LOAD **6** *obs* **:** IMPORT, SENSE **7 a :** a wheeled vehicle; *esp* **:** a horse-drawn vehicle designed for private use and comfort **b** *Brit* **:** a railway passenger coach **8 :** a wheeled support carrying a burden **9 :** a movable part of a machine for supporting some other movable object or part **10** *obs* **:** a hanger for a sword **syn** see BEARING

carriage trade *n* **:** trade from well-to-do or upper-class people

car·rick bend \,kar-ik-\ *n* [prob. fr. obs. E *carrick* carrack, fr. ME *carrake*, *carryk*] **:** a knot used to join the ends of two large ropes

carrick bitts *n pl* **:** the bitts supporting a ship's windlass

car·ri·er \'kar-ē-ər\ *n* **1 :** BEARER, MESSENGER **2 a :** an individual or organization engaged in transporting passengers or goods for hire **b :** a transportation line carrying mail between post offices **c :** a postal employee who delivers or collects mail **d :** one that delivers newspapers **3 a :** a container for carrying **b :** a device or machine that carries **:** CONVEYER **4 :** AIRCRAFT CARRIER **5 :** one that harbors and disseminates the causative agent of disease infectious to its kind to which it is immune **6 a :** a usu. inactive accessory substance **b :** a substance (as a catalyst) by whose agency some element or group is transferred from one compound to another **7 :** an electric wave or alternating current whose modulations are used as signals in radio, telephonic, or telegraphic transmission

carrier pigeon *n* **1 :** a pigeon used to carry messages; *esp* **:** HOMING PIGEON **2 :** any of a breed of large long-bodied show pigeons

car·ri·ole *var of* CARIOLE

car·ri·on \'kar-ē-ən\ *n* [ME *caroine*, fr. AF, fr. (assumed) VL *caronia*, irreg. fr. L *carn-*, *caro* flesh — more at CARNAL] **:** dead and putrefying flesh; *also* **:** flesh unfit for food

car·ron·ade \,kar-ə-'nād\ *n* [*Carron*, Scotland] **:** an obsolete short light iron cannon

car·rot \'kar-ət\ *n* [MF *carotte*, fr. LL *carota*, fr. Gk *karōton*] **1 :** a biennial herb (*Daucus carota* of the family Umbelliferae, the carrot family) with a usu. orange spindle-shaped edible root; *also* **:** its root **2 :** a promised often illusory reward or advantage

car·roty \-ət-ē\ *adj* **1 :** resembling carrots in color **2 :** having hair the color of carrots

car·rou·sel \,kar-ə-'sel, -'zel\ *n* [F *carrousel*, fr. It *carosello*] **1 :** a tournament or exhibition in which horsemen execute evolutions **2 :** MERRY-GO-ROUND

1car·ry \'kar-ē\ *vb* [ME *carien*, fr. ONF *carier* to transport in a vehicle, fr. *car* vehicle, fr. L *carrus* — more at CAR] *vt* **1 :** to move while supporting (as a package) **:** TRANSPORT **2 :** CONVEY, TAKE **3** *chiefly dial* **:** CONDUCT, ESCORT **4 :** to influence by mental or emotional appeal **:** SWAY **5 :** to get possession or control of **:** CAPTURE **6 :** to transfer from one place to another ⟨~ a number in adding⟩ **7 :** to contain and direct the course of ⟨the drain *carries* sewage⟩ **8 a :** to wear or have upon one's person **b :** to bear upon or within one **9 a :** to have as a mark, attribute, or property ⟨~ a scar⟩ **b :** IMPLY, INVOLVE ⟨the crime *carried* a heavy penalty⟩ **10 :** to hold or comport (as one's person) in a specified manner **11 :** to sustain the weight or burden of ⟨pillars ~ an arch⟩ **12 :** to bear as a crop **13 :** to sing with reasonable correctness of pitch **14 a :** to keep in stock for sale; *also* **:** to provide sustenance for ⟨land ~*ing* 10 head of cattle⟩ **b :** to have or maintain on a list or record ⟨~ a person on a payroll⟩ **15 :** to maintain and cause to continue through financial support or personal effort **16 :** to prolong in space, time, or degree **17 a :** to gain victory for; *esp* **:** to secure the adoption or passage of **b** (1) **:** to succeed in (an election) (2) **:** to win a majority of votes in (as a legislative body or a state) **18 :** PUBLISH **19 a :** to bear the charges of holding or having (as stocks or merchandise) from one time to another **b :** to keep on one's books as a debtor **20 :** to hold to and follow after (as a scent) **21 :** to hoist and maintain (a sail) in use **22 :** to cover (a distance) or pass (an object) at a single stroke in golf **23 :** to allow (an opponent) to make a good showing by lessening one's opposition ~ *vi* **1 :** to act as a bearer **2 a :** to reach or penetrate to a distance ⟨voices ~ well⟩ **b :** to convey itself to a reader or audience **3 :** to undergo or admit of carriage in a specified way **4** *of a hunting dog* **:** to keep and follow the scent **5 :** to win adoption

syn CARRY, BEAR, CONVEY, TRANSPORT mean to move something from one place to another. CARRY tends to emphasize the means by which something is moved or the fact of supporting off the ground while moving; BEAR stresses the effort of sustaining or the importance of what is carried ⟨*bear* the banner aloft⟩ CONVEY suggests the continuous movement of something in the mass; TRANSPORT implies the moving of something to its destination

2carry *n* **1 :** the range of a gun or projectile or of a struck or thrown ball **2 a :** the act or method of carrying **b :** PORTAGE **3 :** the position assumed by a bearer with color staff or guidon in position for marching

car·ry·all \'kar-ē-,ȯl\ *n* **1** [by folk etymology fr. F *carriole*] **a :** a light covered carriage for four or more persons **b :** a passenger automobile similar to a station wagon but with a higher body often on a truck chassis **2** [1*carry* + *all*] **:** a capacious bag or case **3 :** a self-loading carrier esp. for hauling earth and crushed rock

carrying capacity *n* **:** the population (as of deer) that an area will support without undergoing deterioration

carrying charge *n* **1 :** expense incident to ownership or use of property **2 :** a charge added to the price of merchandise sold on the installment plan

carry off *vt* **1 :** to cause the death of **2 :** to perform easily or successfully **3 :** to brave out

carry on *vt* **:** CONDUCT, MANAGE ~ *vi* **1 :** to behave in a foolish, excited, or improper manner **2 :** to continue one's course or activity in spite of hindrance or discouragement

carry out *vt* **1 :** to put into execution **2 :** to bring to a successful issue **3 :** to continue to an end or stopping point

carry over *vt* **1 a :** to hold over (as goods) for another season **b :** to transfer (an amount) to the succeeding column, page, or book relating to the same account **2 :** to deduct (a loss or an unused credit) from taxable income of a subsequent period ~ *vi* **:** to persist from one stage or sphere of activity to another

car·ry–over \'kar-ē-,ō-vər\ *n* **1 :** the act or process of carrying over **2 :** something carried over

car·sick \'kär-,sik\ *adj* **:** affected with motion sickness esp. in an automobile — **car sickness** *n*

1cart \'kärt\ *n* [ME, prob. fr. ON *kartr;* akin to OE *cræt* cart, OE *cradol* cradle] **1 :** a heavy usu. horse-drawn 2-wheeled vehicle used for farming or transporting freight **2 :** a lightweight 2-wheeled vehicle drawn by a horse, pony, or dog **3 :** a small wheeled vehicle

2cart *vt* **:** to carry or convey in or as if in a cart — **cart·er** *n*

cart·age \'kärt-ij\ *n* **:** the act of or rate charged for carting

carte blanche \'kärt-'blänsh, -'blänch\ *n, pl* **cartes blanches** \'kärt-'blänsh(-əz), -'blänch(-əz)\ [F] **:** full discretionary power

car·tel \kär-'tel\ *n* [MF, letter of defiance, fr. OIt *cartello*, lit., placard, fr. *carta* leaf of paper] **1 :** a written agreement between belligerent nations **2 :** a combination of independent commercial enterprises designed to limit competition **3 :** a combination of political groups for common action **syn** see MONOPOLY

Car·te·sian \kär-'tē-zhən\ *adj* [NL *cartesianus*, fr. *Cartesius* Descartes] **:** of or relating to René Descartes or his philosophy — **Cartesian** *n* — **Car·te·sian·ism** \-zhə-,niz-əm\ *n*

Cartesian coordinate *n* **1 :** the distance of a point from either of two intersecting straight-line axes measured parallel to the other axis **2 :** the distance from any of three intersecting coordinate planes measured parallel to that one of three straight-line axes that is the intersection of the other two planes

Car·thu·sian \kär-'th(y)ü-zhən\ *n* [ML *cartusiensis*, irreg. fr. OF *Chartrouse*, motherhouse of the Carthusian order, near Grenoble, France] **:** a member of an austere contemplative religious order founded by St. Bruno in 1084 — **Carthusian** *adj*

car·ti·lage \'kärt-ᵊl-ij, 'kärt-lij\ *n* [L *cartilagin-*, *cartilago;* akin to L *cratis* wickerwork] **1 :** a translucent elastic tissue that composes most of the skeleton of the embryos and very young of vertebrates and becomes for the most part converted into bone in the higher vertebrates **2 :** a part or structure composed of cartilage

car·ti·lag·i·nous \,kärt-ᵊl-'aj-ə-nəs\ *adj* **1 :** of, relating to, or resembling cartilage **2 :** having a skeleton mostly of cartilage

car·to·gram \'kärt-ə-,gram\ *n* [F *cartogramme*, fr. *carte* + *-gramme* -gram] **:** a map showing statistics geographically

car·tog·ra·pher \kär-'täg-rə-fər\ *n* **:** one that makes maps

car·to·graph·ic \,kärt-ə-'graf-ik\ *adj* **:** of or relating to cartography — **car·to·graph·i·cal** \-i-kəl\ *adj*

car·tog·ra·phy \kär-'täg-rə-fē\ *n* [F *cartographie*, fr. *carte* card, map + *-graphie* -graphy] **:** the science or art of making maps

car·ton \'kärt-ᵊn\ *n* [F, fr. It *cartone* pasteboard] **:** a cardboard box or container

car·toon \kär-'tün\ *n* [It *cartone* pasteboard, cartoon, aug. of *carta* leaf of paper — more at CARD] **1 :** a preparatory design, drawing, or painting **2 a :** a satirical drawing commenting on public and usu. political matters **b :** COMIC STRIP **3 :** ANIMATED CARTOON — **cartoon** *vb* — **car·toon·ist** \-'tü-nəst\ *n*

car·touche *or* **car·touch** \kär-'tüsh\ *n* [F, fr. It *cartoccio*, fr. *carta*] **1 :** a gun cartridge with a paper case **2 :** an ornate or ornamental frame **3 :** an oval or oblong figure (as on ancient Egyptian monuments) enclosing a sovereign's name

car·tridge \'kär-trij, *dial or archaic* 'ka-trij\ *n* [alter. of earlier *cartage*, modif. of MF *cartouche*] **1 a :** a tube of metal, paper, or both containing a complete charge for a firearm and usu. a cap or other initiating device **b :** a case containing an explosive charge

for blasting **2 :** an often cylindrical container of material for insertion into a larger mechanism or apparatus **3 :** a small case in a phonograph pickup containing the needle and the mechanism for translating stylus motion into electrical voltage

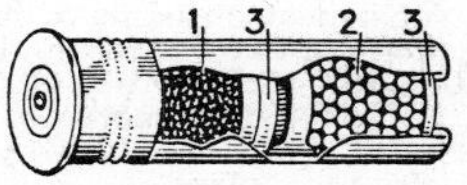

cartridge for shotgun, cut away: *1* powder, *2* shot, *3,3* wads

car·tu·lary \'kär-chə-,ler-ē\ *n* [ML *chartularium,* fr. *chartula* charter — more at CHARTER] **:** a collection of charters; *esp* **:** a book containing duplicates of the charters and title deeds of an estate

cart·wheel \'kärt-,hwēl, -,wēl\ *n* **1 :** a large coin (as a silver dollar) **2 :** a lateral handspring with arms and legs extended

car·un·cle \'kar-,əŋ-kəl, kə-'rəŋ-\ *n* [obs. F *caruncule,* fr. L *caruncula* little piece of flesh, dim. of *caro* flesh] **1 :** a naked fleshy outgrowth (as a bird's wattle) **2 :** an outgrowth on a seed adjacent to the micropyle — **ca·run·cu·lar** \kə-'rəŋ-kyə-lər\ *adj* — **ca·run·cu·late** \-lət, -,lāt\ *or* **ca·run·cu·lat·ed** \-,lāt-əd\ *adj*

car·va·crol \'kär-və-,krōl, -,krōl\ *n* [ISV, fr. NL *carvi* (specific epithet of *Carum carvi* caraway) + L *acr-, acer* sharp] **:** a liquid phenol $C_{10}H_{14}O$ of various mints used as an antiseptic

carve \'kärv\ *vb* [ME *kerven,* fr. OE *ceorfan;* akin to MHG *kerben* to notch, Gk *graphein* to scratch, write] *vt* **1 :** to cut with care or precision ⟨*carved* fretwork⟩ **2 :** to make or get by cutting **3 :** to cut into pieces or slices ~ *vi* **1 :** to cut up and serve meat **2 :** to work as a sculptor or engraver — **carv·er** *n*

car·vel \'kär-vəl, -,vel\ *n* [ME *carvile,* fr. MF *caravelle, carvelle*] **:** CARAVEL

car·vel–built \-,bilt\ *adj* [prob. fr. D *karveel-,* fr. *karveel* caravel, fr. MF *carvelle*] **:** built with the planks meeting flush at the seams

carv·en \'kär-vən\ *adj* **:** CARVED

carv·ing \'kär-viŋ\ *n* **1 :** the act or art of one who carves **2 :** a carved object, design, or figure

cary- *or* **caryo-** — see KARY-

cary·at·id \,kar-ē-'at-əd\ *n, pl* **caryatids** *or* **cary·at·i·des** \-ə-,dēz\ [L *caryatides,* pl., fr. Gk *karyatides* priestesses of Artemis at Caryae, caryatids, fr. *Karyai* Caryae in Laconia] **:** a draped female figure supporting an entablature

cary·op·sis \,kar-ē-'äp-səs\ *n, pl* **cary·op·ses** \-'äp-,sēz\ *or* **cary·op·si·des** \-'äp-sə-,dēz\ [NL] **:** a small one-seeded dry indehiscent fruit in which the fruit and seed fuse in a single grain

ca·sa \'käs-ə\ *n* [Sp & It, fr. L, cabin] *Southwest* **:** DWELLING

ca·sa·ba \kə-'säb-ə\ *n* [*Kasaba* (now Turgutlu), Turkey] **:** any of several winter melons with yellow rind and sweet flesh

Cas·bah \'kaz-,bä, 'käz-\ *n* [F, fr. Ar dial. *qaṣbah*] **1 :** a No. African castle or fortress **2 :** the native section of a No. African city

cas·ca·bel \'kas-kə-,bel\ *n* [Sp, lit., small bell like a sleigh bell] **1 :** a projection behind the breech of a muzzle-loading cannon **2 :** a small hollow perforated spherical bell enclosing a loose pellet

¹cas·cade \ka-'skād\ *n* [F, fr. It *cascata,* fr. *cascare* to fall, fr. (assumed) VL *casicare,* fr. L *casus* pp. of *cadere* to fall] **1 :** a steep usu. small fall of water; *esp* **:** one of a series **2 a :** something arranged in a series **b :** a fall of material (as lace) that hangs in a zigzag line **3 :** something falling or rushing forth in quantity

²cascade *vi* **:** to fall in a cascade ~ *vt* **1 :** to cause to fall like a cascade **2 :** to connect in a cascade arrangement

cas·cara \ka-'skar-ə\ *n* [Sp *cáscara* bark, fr. *cascar* to crack, break, fr. (assumed) VL *quassicare* to shake, break, fr. L *quassare* — more at QUASH] **1 :** CASCARA BUCKTHORN **2 :** CASCARA SAGRADA

cascara buckthorn *n* **:** a buckthorn (*Rhamnus purshiana*) of the Pacific coast of the U.S. yielding cascara sagrada

cascara sa·gra·da \-sə-'gräd-ə\ *n* [AmerSp *cáscara sagrada,* lit., sacred bark] **:** the dried bark of cascara buckthorn used as a mild laxative

cas·ca·ril·la \,kas-kə-'ril-ə\ *n* [Sp, dim. of *cáscara*] **:** the aromatic bark of a West Indian shrub (*Croton eluteria*) of the spurge family used for making incense and as a tonic; *also* **:** this shrub

¹case \'kās\ *n* [ME *cas,* fr. OF, fr. L *casus* fall, chance, fr. *casus,* pp. of *cadere* to fall — more at CHANCE] **1 a :** a set of circumstances or conditions **b** (1) **:** a situation requiring investigation or action by the police or other agency (2) **:** the object of investigation or consideration **2 :** CONDITION; *specif* **:** condition of body or mind **3** [ME *cas,* fr. MF, fr. L *casus,* trans. of Gk *ptōsis,* lit., fall] **a :** an inflectional form of a noun, pronoun, or adjective indicating its grammatical relation to other words **b :** such a relation whether indicated by inflection or not **4 :** what actually exists or happens **:** FACT **5 a :** a suit or action in law or equity **b** (1) **:** the evidence supporting a conclusion or judgment (2) **:** ARGUMENT; *esp* **:** a convincing argument **6 a :** an instance of disease or injury; *also* **:** PATIENT **b :** INSTANCE, EXAMPLE **c :** a peculiar person **:** CHARACTER **syn** see INSTANCE — **in case 1 :** IF **2 :** as a precaution **3 :** as a precaution against the event that

²case *n* [ME *cas,* fr. ONF *casse,* fr. L *capsa* chest, case, fr. *capere* to take — more at HEAVE] **1 a :** a box or receptacle to contain something **b :** a box together with its contents **c :** SET; *specif* **:** PAIR **2 :** an outer covering or housing **3 :** a shallow divided tray for holding printing type **4 :** the frame of a door or window **:** CASING

³case *vt* **1 :** to enclose in or cover with a case **:** ENCASE **2 :** to line (as a well) with supporting material **3** *slang* **:** to inspect or study esp. with intent to rob

ca·se·ate \'kā-sē-,āt\ *vi* [L *caseus* cheese] **:** to undergo caseation

ca·se·ation \,kā-sē-'ā-shən\ *n* **:** necrosis with conversion of damaged tissue into a soft cheesy substance

case hard·en \'kās-,härd-ᵊn\ *vt* **1 :** to harden (a ferrous alloy) so that the surface layer is harder than the interior **2 :** to make callous — **case–hard·ened** *adj*

case history *n* **:** a record of history, environment, and other relevant details (as of an individual) esp. for use in analysis or illustration

ca·sein \kā-'sēn, 'kā-sē-ən\ *n* [prob. fr. F *caséine,* fr. L *caseus*] **:** a phosphoprotein of milk: as **a :** one that is precipitated from milk by heating with an acid or by lactic acid in souring and that is used in making paints and adhesives **b :** one that is produced when milk is curdled by rennet, that is one of the chief constituents of cheese, and that is used in making plastics

case knife *n* **1 :** SHEATH KNIFE **2 :** a table knife

case law *n* **:** law established by judicial decision in cases

case·mate \'kā-,smāt\ *n* [MF, fr. OIt *casamatta*] **:** a fortified position or chamber or an armored enclosure on a warship from which guns are fired through embrasures

case·ment \'kā-smənt\ *n* [ME, hollow molding, prob. fr. ONF *encassement* frame, fr. *encasser* to enchase, frame, fr. *en-* + *casse*] **:** a window sash that opens on hinges on the sides; *also* **:** a window with such a sash

ca·se·ous \'kā-sē-əs\ *adj* [L *caseus* cheese] **:** marked by caseation; *also* **:** CHEESY

ca·sern *or* **ca·serne** \kə-'zərn\ *n* [F *caserne*] **:** a military barracks in a garrison town

case shot *n* **:** an artillery projectile consisting of a number of balls or metal fragments enclosed in a case

case system *n* **:** a system of teaching law in which instruction is chiefly on the basis of leading or selected cases as primary authorities instead of from textbooks

case·work \'kā-,swərk\ *n* **:** intensive sociological study of the history and environment of a maladjusted individual or family for diagnosis and treatment — **case·work·er** *n*

case·worm \'kā-,swərm\ *n* **:** an insect larva that makes a case for its body

¹cash \'kash\ *n* [MF or OIt; MF *casse* money box, fr. OIt *cassa,* fr. L *capsa* chest — more at CASE] **1 :** ready money **2 :** money or its equivalent paid promptly after purchasing

²cash *vt* **:** to pay or obtain cash for ⟨~ a check⟩

³cash *n, pl* **cash** [Pg *caixa,* fr. Tamil *kācu,* a small copper coin, fr. Skt *karṣa,* a weight of gold or silver; akin to OPer *karsha-,* a weight] **1 :** any of various coins of small value in China and southern India; *esp* **:** a Chinese coin usu. of copper alloy that has a square hole in the center **2 :** a unit of value equivalent to one cash

cash·book \-,bu̇k\ *n* **:** a book in which record is kept of all cash receipts and disbursements

ca·shew \'kash-(,)ü, kə-'shü\ *n* [Pg *acajú, cajú,* fr. Tupi *acajú*] **:** a tropical American tree (*Anacardium occidentale*) of the sumac family grown for its edible kidney-shaped nut and receptacle and the gum it yields; *also* **:** its nut

¹cash·ier \ka-'shi(ə)r, kə-\ *vt* [D *casseren,* fr. MF *casser* to discharge, annul — more at QUASH] **1 :** to dismiss from service; *esp* **:** to dismiss ignominiously **2 :** REJECT, DISCARD

²cash·ier \ka-'shi(ə)r\ *n* [D or MF; D *kassier,* fr. MF *cassier,* fr. *casse* money box] **:** one that has charge of money: as **a :** a high officer in a bank or trust company responsible for moneys received and expended **b :** one who collects and records payments

cashier's check *n* **:** a check drawn by a bank upon its own funds and signed by the cashier

cash·mere \'kazh-,mi(ə)r, 'kash-\ *n* [*Cashmere* (Kashmir)] **1 :** fine wool from the undercoat of the Kashmir goat or a yarn of this wool **2 :** a soft twilled fabric made orig. from cashmere

cash register *n* **:** a business machine that records the amount of money received, that usu. has a money drawer, and that exhibits the amount of each sale

cas·ing \'kā-siŋ\ *n* **:** something that encases **:** material for encasing: as **a :** an enclosing frame esp. around a door or window opening **b :** a metal pipe used to case a well **c :** TIRE 2b **d :** a membranous case for processed meat

ca·si·no \kə-'sē-(,)nō\ *n* [It, fr. *casa* house, fr. L, cabin] **1 :** a building or room used for social amusements; *specif* **:** one used for gambling **2 :** SUMMERHOUSE **3** *or* **cas·si·no :** a card game

cask \'kask\ *n* [MF *casque* helmet, fr. Sp *casco* potsherd, skull, helmet, fr. *cascar* to break — more at CASCARA] **1 :** a barrel-shaped vessel of staves, headings, and hoops usu. for liquids **2 :** a cask and its contents; *also* **:** the quantity contained in a cask

cas·ket \'kas-kət\ *n* [ME, modif. of MF *cassette*] **1 :** a small chest or box (as for jewels) **2 :** a usu. ornamented and lined rectangular box or chest for a corpse to be buried in — **casket** *vt*

casque \'kask\ *n* [MF — more at CASK] **1 :** a piece of armor for the head **:** HELMET **2 :** an anatomic structure suggestive of a helmet

cas·sa·ba *var of* CASABA

Cas·san·dra \kə-'san-drə\ *n* [L, fr. Gk *Kassandra*] **1 :** a daughter of Priam endowed with the gift of prophecy but fated never to be believed **2 :** one who prophesies misfortune or disaster

cas·sa·va \kə-'säv-ə\ *n* [Sp *cazabe* cassava bread, fr. Taino *caçábi*] **:** any of several plants (genus *Manihot*) of the spurge family grown in the tropics for their fleshy edible rootstocks which yield a nutritious starch; *also* **:** the rootstock or its starch

cas·se·role \'kas-ə-,rōl, 'kaz-\ *n* [F, saucepan, fr. MF, irreg. fr. *casse* ladle, dripping pan, deriv. of Gk *kyathos* ladle] **1 :** a deep round usu. porcelain dish with a handle used for heating substances in the laboratory **2 :** a dish in which food may be baked and served **3 :** the food cooked and served in a casserole

cas·sette \kə-'set\ *n* [F, fr. MF, dim. of ONF *casse* case] **:** a lighttight magazine for holding film or plates for use in a camera

cas·sia \'kash-ə\ *n* [ME, fr. OE, fr. L, fr. Gk *kassia,* of Sem origin; akin to Heb *qĕṣī'āh* cassia] **1 :** a coarse cinnamon bark (as from *Cinnamomum cassia*) **2 :** any of a genus (*Cassia*) of leguminous herbs, shrubs, and trees of warm regions

cas·si·mere \'kaz-ə-,mi(ə)r, 'kas-\ *n* [obs. *Cassimere* (Kashmir)] **:** a smooth twilled usu. wool fabric

Cas·si·o·pe·ia \,kas-ē-ə-'pē-(y)ə\ *n* [L, fr. Gk *Kassiopeia*] **1 :** the mother of Andromeda **2** [L (gen. *Cassiopeiae*), fr. Gk *Kassiopeia*] **:** a northern constellation between Andromeda and Cepheus

Cassiopeia's Chair *n* **:** a group of stars in the constellation Cassiopeia resembling a chair

cas·sit·er·ite \kə-'sit-ə-,rīt\ *n* [F *cassitérite,* fr. Gk *kassiteros* tin] **:** a brown or black mineral that consists of tin dioxide SnO_2 and is the chief source of metallic tin

cas·sock \'kas-ək\ *n* [MF *casaque,* fr. Per *kazhāghand* padded jacket, fr. *kazh* raw silk + *āghand* stuffed] **:** an ankle-length garment with close-fitting sleeves worn esp. in Roman Catholic and Anglican churches by the clergy and by laymen assisting in divine services

cas·so·wary \'kas-ə-,wer-ē\ *n* [Malay *kĕsuari*] **:** any of several large ratite birds (genus *Casuarius*) esp. of New Guinea and Australia closely related to the emu

¹cast \'kast\ *vb* **cast; cast·ing** [ME *casten,* fr. ON *kasta;* akin to ON *kǫs* heap and perh. to L *gerere* to carry, wage] *vt* **1 a :** to cause to move by throwing ⟨~ a fishing lure⟩ **b :** DIRECT ⟨~ a glance⟩

c (1) : to put forth ⟨the fire ~s a warm glow⟩ (2) : to place as if by throwing ⟨~ doubt upon their reliability⟩ d : to deposit (a ballot) formally e (1) : to throw off or away ⟨the horse ~ a shoe⟩ (2) : to get rid of : DISCARD ⟨~ off all restraint⟩ (3) : SHED, MOLT (4) : to bring forth; *esp* : to give birth to prematurely f : to throw to the ground esp. in wrestling g : to build by throwing up earth 2 a (1) : to perform arithmetical operations on : ADD (2) : to calculate by means of astrology b *archaic* : DECIDE, INTEND 3 a : to dispose or arrange into parts or into a suitable form or order b (1) : to assign the parts of to actors (2) : to assign to a role or part 4 a : to give a shape to (a substance) by pouring in liquid or plastic form into a mold and letting harden without pressure ⟨~ steel⟩ b : to form by this process ⟨~ machine parts⟩ c : to make a stereotype or other printing plate from (letterpress matter) : PLATE 5 : TURN ⟨~ the scale slightly⟩ 6 : to make (a knot or stitch) by looping or catching up 7 : TWIST, WARP ⟨a beam ~ by age⟩ ~ *vi* 1 : to throw something; *specif* : to throw out a lure with a fishing rod 2 *dial Brit* : VOMIT 3 *dial Eng* : to bear fruit : YIELD 4 a : to perform addition b *obs* : ESTIMATE, CONJECTURE 5 : WARP 6 : to make a cast — used of hunting dogs or trackers 7 a : VEER b : to wear ship 8 : to take form in a mold **syn** see DISCARD, THROW — **cast lots** : to draw lots to determine a matter by chance

[2]**cast** *n* 1 a : an act of casting b : something that happens as a result of chance c : a throw of dice d : a throw of a line (as a fishing line) or net 2 a : the form in which a thing is constructed b : the set of characters in a play or narrative c : the arrangement of draperies in a painting 3 : the distance to which a thing can be thrown; *specif* : the distance a bow can shoot 4 a : a turning of the eye in a particular direction; *also* : EXPRESSION b : a slight strabismus 5 : something that is thrown or the quantity thrown: as a : the number of hawks released by a falconer at one time b *Brit* : the leader of a fishing line c : the quantity of metal cast at a single operation 6 a : something that is formed by casting in a mold or form: as (1) : a reproduction (as of a statue) in metal or plaster : CASTING (2) : a fossil reproduction of the details of a natural object by mineral infiltration b : an impression taken from an object with a liquid or plastic substance : MOLD c : a rigid dressing of gauze impregnated with plaster of paris for immobilizing a diseased or broken part 7 : FORECAST, CONJECTURE 8 a : an overspread of a color : SHADE b : TINGE, SUGGESTION 9 a : a ride on one's way in a vehicle : LIFT b *Scot* : HELP, ASSISTANCE 10 a : SHAPE, APPEARANCE b : characteristic quality 11 : something that is thrown out or off, shed, or ejected: as a : the excrement of an earthworm b : a mass of plastic matter formed in cavities of diseased organs and discharged from the body c : the skin of an insect 12 : the ranging in search of a trail by a dog, hunting pack, or tracker

cas·ta·net \ˌkas-tə-ˈnet\ *n* [Sp *castañeta*, fr. *castaña* chestnut, fr. L *castanea* — more at CHESTNUT] : a rhythm instrument used esp. by dancers that consists of two small shells of ivory, hard wood, or plastic fastened to the thumb and clicked together by the other fingers — usu. used in pl.

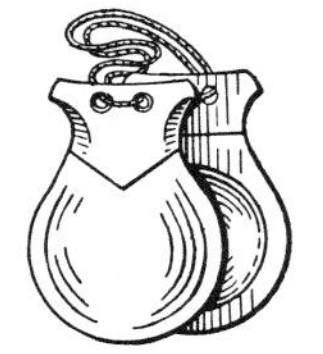
castanets

cast·away \ˈkas-tə-ˌwā\ *adj* 1 : thrown away : REJECTED 2 : cast adrift or ashore as a survivor of a shipwreck — **castaway** *n*

caste \ˈkast\ *n* [Pg *casta*, lit., race, lineage, fr. fem. of *casto* pure, chaste, fr. L *castus*; akin to L *carēre* to be without, Gk *keazein* to split, Skt *śasati* he cuts to pieces] 1 : one of the hereditary social classes in Hinduism that restrict the occupation of their members and their intercourse with the members of other castes 2 a : a division of society based upon differences of wealth, inherited rank or privilege, profession, or occupation b : the position conferred by caste standing : PRESTIGE 3 : a system of rigid social stratification characterized by hereditary status, endogamy, and social barriers sanctioned by custom, law, or religion 4 : a polymorphic social insect (as the bee) that carries out a particular function in the colony

cas·tel·lan \ˈkas-tə-lən, ka-ˈstel-ən\ *n* [ME *castelleyn*, fr. ONF *castelain*, fr. L *castellanus* occupant of a castle, fr. *castellanus* of a castle, fr. *castellum* castle] : a governor or warden of a castle or fort

cas·tel·lat·ed \ˈkas-tə-ˌlāt-əd\ *adj* [ML *castellatus*, pp. of *castellare* to fortify, fr. L *castellum*] 1 : having battlements like a castle 2 : having or supporting a castle

cast·er \ˈkas-tər\ *n* 1 : one that casts (as a machine that casts type) 2 *or* **cas·tor** \-tər\ a : a cruet, sifter, or other small container for condiments b : a stand for holding casters 3 *or* **castor** : a wheel or set of wheels mounted in a swivel frame used for supporting furniture, trucks, and portable machines

cas·ti·gate \ˈkas-tə-ˌgāt\ *vt* [L *castigatus*, pp. of *castigare*] : to punish, reprove, or criticize severely — **syn** see PUNISH — **cas·ti·ga·tion** \ˌkas-tə-ˈgā-shən\ *n* — **cas·ti·ga·tor** \ˈkas-tə-ˌgāt-ər\ *n*

cas·tile soap \(ˌ)ka-ˌstēl-\ *n*, *often cap C* [*Castile*, region of Spain] : a fine hard bland soap made from olive oil and sodium hydroxide; *also* : any of various similar soaps

Cas·til·ian \ka-ˈstil-yən\ *n* 1 : a native or inhabitant of Castile; *broadly* : SPANIARD 2 a : the dialect of Castile b : the official and literary language of Spain based on this dialect — **Castilian** *adj*

cast·ing *n* 1 : the act of one that casts 2 : something cast in a mold 3 : something that is cast out or off

casting vote *n* : a deciding vote cast by a presiding officer

cast iron *n* : a commercial alloy of iron, carbon, and silicon that is cast in a mold and is hard, brittle, nonmalleable, and incapable of being hammer-welded but more easily fusible than steel

[1]**cas·tle** \ˈkas-əl\ *n* [ME *castel*, fr. OE, fr. ONF, fr. L *castellum* fortress, castle, dim. of *castrum* fortified place; akin to L *castrare* to castrate] 1 a : a large fortified building or set of buildings b : a massive or imposing house 2 : a retreat safe against intrusion or invasion 3 : [3]ROOK

[2]**castle** *vb* **cas·tled**; **cas·tling** \ˈkas-(ə-)liŋ\ *vt* 1 : to establish in a castle 2 : to move (the king in chess) in castling ~ *vi* 1 : to move the king two squares toward a rook and in the same move the rook to the square next past the king 2 *of the king* : to move in castling

cas·tled \ˈkas-əld\ *adj* : CASTELLATED

castle in the air : a visionary project — called also *castle in Spain*

cast–off \ˈkas-ˌtȯf\ *adj* : thrown away or aside — **cast·off** *n*

cast on *vt* : to place (stitches) on a knitting needle for beginning or enlarging knitted work

cas·tor \ˈkas-tər\ *n* [ME, fr. L, fr. Gk *kastōr*, fr. *Kastōr* Castor] 1 : BEAVER 1a 2 : a bitter strong-smelling creamy orange-brown substance consisting of the dried perineal glands of the beaver and their secretion used esp. by perfumers 3 : a beaver or other hat

Cas·tor \ˈkas-tər\ *n* [L, fr. Gk *Kastōr*] 1 : the mortal twin of Pollux 2 : the more northern of the two bright stars in Gemini

castor bean *n* : the very poisonous seed of the castor-oil plant; *also* : this plant

castor oil *n* [prob. fr. its former use as a substitute for castor in medicine] : a pale viscous fatty oil from castor beans used esp. as a cathartic or lubricant

castor–oil plant *n* : a tropical Old World herb (*Ricinus communis*) widely grown as an ornamental or for its oil-rich castor beans

cas·trate \ˈkas-ˌtrāt\ *vt* [L *castratus*, pp. of *castrare*; akin to Skt *śasati* he cuts to pieces] 1 a : to deprive of the testes : GELD b : to deprive of the ovaries : SPAY 2 : to deprive of vitality or effect : EMASCULATE — **castrate** *n* — **cas·tra·tion** \ka-ˈstrā-shən\ *n*

[1]**ca·su·al** \ˈkazh-(ə-)wəl, ˈkazh-əl\ *adj* [ME, fr. MF & LL; MF *casuel*, fr. LL *casualis*, fr. L *casus* fall, chance] 1 : subject to, resulting from, or occurring by chance 2 a : occurring without regularity : OCCASIONAL b : employed for irregular periods 3 a : feeling or showing little concern : NONCHALANT b (1) : INFORMAL, NATURAL (2) : designed for informal use **syn** see ACCIDENTAL, RANDOM — **ca·su·al·ly** \-ē\ *adv* — **ca·su·al·ness** *n*

[2]**casual** *n* 1 : a casual or migratory worker 2 : an officer or enlisted man awaiting assignment or transportation to his unit

ca·su·al·ty \ˈkazh-əl-tē, ˈkazh-(ə-)wəl-\ *n* 1 : serious or fatal accident : DISASTER 2 a : a military person lost through death, wounds, injury, sickness, internment, or capture or through being missing in action b : a person or thing injured, lost, or destroyed

ca·su·ist \ˈkazh-(ə-)wəst\ *n* [prob. fr. Sp *casuista*, fr. L *casus* fall, chance — more at CASE] : one skilled in or given to casuistry — **ca·su·is·tic** \ˌkazh-ə-ˈwis-tik\ *or* **ca·su·is·ti·cal** \-ti-kəl\ *adj*

ca·su·ist·ry \ˈkazh-(ə-)wə-strē\ *n* 1 : a method or doctrine dealing with cases of conscience and the resolution of questions of right or wrong in conduct 2 : sophistical, equivocal, or specious reasoning

ca·sus bel·li \ˌkäs-əs-ˈbel-ˌē, ˌkā-səs-ˈbel-ˌī\ *n* [NL, occasion of war] : an event or action that justifies or allegedly justifies war

[1]**cat** \ˈkat\ *n*, *often attrib* [ME, fr. OE *catt*; akin to OHG *kazza* cat; both fr. a prehistoric NGmc-WGmc word prob. borrowed fr. LL *cattus*, *catta* cat] 1 a : a carnivorous mammal (*Felis catus*) long domesticated and kept by man as a pet or for catching rats and mice b : any of a family (Felidae) including the domestic cat, lion, tiger, leopard, jaguar, cougar, wildcat, lynx, and cheetah c : the fur or pelt of the domestic cat 2 : one resembling a cat 3 : a strong tackle used to hoist an anchor to the cathead of a ship 4 : CATBOAT 5 : CAT-O'-NINE-TAILS 6 : CATFISH 7 *slang* a : a player or devotee of hot jazz b : GUY

[2]**cat** *vt* **cat·ted**; **cat·ting** : to bring (an anchor) up to the cathead

Cat *trademark* — used for a Caterpillar tractor

cata- *or* **cat-** *or* **cath-** *prefix* [Gk *kata-*, *kat-*, *kath-*, fr. *kata* down, in accordance with, by; akin to L *com-* with] : down ⟨*cata*clinal⟩

cat·a·bol·ic \ˌkat-ə-ˈbäl-ik\ *adj* : of or relating to catabolism — **cat·a·bol·i·cal·ly** \-i-k(ə-)lē\ *adv*

ca·tab·o·lism \kə-ˈtab-ə-ˌliz-əm\ *n* [Gk *katabolē* throwing down, fr. *kataballein* to throw down, fr. *kata-* + *ballein* to throw — more at DEVIL] : destructive metabolism

ca·tab·o·lize \-ˌlīz\ *vt* : to subject to catabolism ~ *vi* : to undergo catabolism

cat·a·chre·sis \ˌkat-ə-ˈkrē-səs\ *n*, *pl* **cat·a·chre·ses** \-ˈkrē-ˌsēz\ [L, fr. Gk *katachrēsis* misuse, fr. *katachrēsthai* to use up, misuse, fr. *kata-* + *chrēsthai* to use] 1 : use of the wrong word for the context 2 : use of a forced and esp. paradoxical figure of speech (as *blind mouths*) — **cat·a·chres·tic** \-ˈkres-tik\ *or* **cat·a·chres·ti·cal** \-ti-kəl\ *adj* — **cat·a·chres·ti·cal·ly** \-ti-k(ə-)lē\ *adv*

cat·a·clysm \ˈkat-ə-ˌkliz-əm\ *n* [F *cataclysme*, fr. L *cataclysmos*, fr. Gk *kataklysmos*, fr. *kataklyzein* to inundate, fr. *kata-* + *klyzein* to wash — more at CLYSTER] 1 : FLOOD, DELUGE 2 : a violent geologic change 3 : a momentous and violent event marked by overwhelming upheaval and demolition **syn** see DISASTER — **cat·a·clys·mal** \ˌkat-ə-ˈkliz-məl\ *adj* — **cat·a·clys·mic** \-mik\ *adj*

cat·a·comb \ˈkat-ə-ˌkōm\ *n* [MF *catacombe*, prob. fr. OIt *catacomba*, fr. LL *catacumbae*, pl.] : a subterranean cemetery of galleries with recesses for tombs — usu. used in pl.

ca·tad·ro·mous \kə-ˈtad-rə-məs\ *adj* [prob. fr. NL *catadromus*, fr. *cata-* + *-dromus* -dromous] : living in fresh water and going to the sea to spawn

cat·a·falque \ˈkat-ə-ˌfalk, -ˌfȯ(l)k\ *n* [It *catafalco*, fr. (assumed) VL *catafalicum* scaffold, fr. *cata-* + L *fala* siege tower] 1 : an ornamental structure sometimes used in solemn funerals for the lying in state of the body 2 : a pall-covered coffin-shaped structure used at requiem masses celebrated after burial

Cat·a·lan \ˈkat-ᵊl-ən, -ˌan\ *n* [Sp *Catalán*] 1 : a native or inhabitant of Catalonia 2 : the Romance language of Catalonia, Valencia, and the Balearic islands — **Catalan** *adj*

cat·a·lase \ˈkat-ᵊl-ˌās, -ˌāz\ *n* [*catalysis*] : an enzyme that catalyzes the decomposition of hydrogen peroxide into water and oxygen and the oxidation by hydrogen peroxide of alcohols to aldehydes — **cat·a·lat·ic** \ˌkat-ᵊl-ˈat-ik\ *adj*

cat·a·lec·tic \ˌkat-ᵊl-ˈek-tik\ *adj* [LL *catalecticus*, fr. Gk *katalēktikos*, fr. *katalēgein* to leave off, fr. *kata-* + *lēgein* to stop] : lacking a syllable at the end or ending in an imperfect foot — **catalectic** *n*

cat·a·lep·sy \ˈkat-ᵊl-ˌep-sē\ *n* [ME *catalempsi* fr. ML *catalepsia*, fr. LL *catalepsis*, fr. Gk *katalēpsis*, lit., act of seizing, fr. *katalambanein* to seize, fr. *kata-* + *lambanein* to take — more at LATCH] : a condition of suspended animation and loss of voluntary motion in which the limbs hold any position they are placed in — **cat·a·lep·tic** \ˌkat-ᵊl-ˈep-tik\ *adj or n*

cat·a·lex·is \ˌkat-ᵊl-ˈek-səs\ *n*, *pl* **cat·a·lex·es** \-ˈek-ˌsēz\ [NL, fr. Gk *katalēxis* close, cadence, fr. *katalēgein*] : omission or incompleteness in the last foot of a line or other unit in metrical verse

[1]**cat·a·log** *or* **cat·a·logue** \ˈkat-ᵊl-ˌȯg, -ˌäg\ *n* [ME *cateloge*, fr. MF *catalogue*, fr. LL *catalogus*, fr. Gk *katalogos*, fr. *katalegein* to list, enumerate, fr. *kata-* + *legein* to gather, speak] 1 : LIST, REGISTER 2 a : a complete enumeration of items arranged systematically with descriptive details b : a pamphlet or book that contains such a list c : material in such a list

[2]**catalog** *or* **catalogue** *vt* 1 : to make a catalog of 2 : to enter in a catalog; *esp* : to classify (books or other library material) descriptively — **cat·a·log·er** *or* **cat·a·logu·er** *n*

catalogue rai·son·né \-ˌrāz-ᵊn-ˈā\ *n* [F, lit., reasoned catalog] **:** a systematic annotated catalog; *esp* **:** a critical bibliography

ca·tal·pa \kə-ˈtal-pə, -ˈtȯl-\ *n* [Creek *kutuhlpa*, lit., head with wings] **:** any of a small genus (*Catalpa*) of American and Asiatic trees of the trumpet-creeper family with cordate leaves and pale showy flowers in terminal racemes

ca·tal·y·sis \kə-ˈtal-ə-səs\ *n* [Gk *katalysis* dissolution, fr. *katalyein* to dissolve, fr. *kata-* cata- + *lyein* to dissolve, release] **:** modification and esp. increase in the rate of a chemical reaction induced by material unchanged chemically at the end of the reaction; *also* **:** any reaction brought about by a separate agent — **cat·a·lyt·ic** \ˌkat-ᵊl-ˈit-ik\ *adj* — **cat·a·lyt·i·cal·ly** \-i-k(ə-)lē\ *adv*

cat·a·lyst \ˈkat-ᵊl-əst\ *n* **1 :** a substance or agent inducing catalysis **2 :** a substance that initiates a chemical reaction and enables it to proceed under milder conditions than otherwise possible

catalytic cracker *n* **:** the unit in a petroleum refinery in which cracking is carried out in the presence of a catalyst

cat·a·lyze \ˈkat-ᵊl-ˌīz\ *vt* **:** to subject to or produce or alter by catalysis — **cat·a·lyz·er** *n*

cat·a·ma·ran \ˌkat-ə-mə-ˈran\ *n* [Tamil *kaṭṭumaram*, fr. *kaṭṭu* to tie + *maram* tree] **1 :** a raft consisting of logs or pieces of wood lashed together and propelled by paddles or sails **2 :** a boat with twin hulls or planing surfaces side by side

cata·me·nia \ˌkat-ə-ˈmē-nē-ə\ *n pl but sing or pl in constr* [NL, fr. Gk *katamēnia*, fr. neut. pl. of *katamēnios* monthly, fr. *kata* by + *mēn* month] **:** MENSES — **cata·me·ni·al** \-nē-əl\ *adj*

cat·a·mite \ˈkat-ə-ˌmīt\ *n* [L *catamitus*, fr. *Catamitus* Ganymede, fr. Etruscan *Catmite*, fr. Gk *Ganymēdēs*] **:** a boy kept for purposes of sexual perversion

cat·a·mount \ˈkat-ə-ˌmau̇nt\ *n* [short for *cat-a-mountain*] **:** any of various wild cats: as **a :** COUGAR **b :** LYNX

cat–a–moun·tain \ˌkat-ə-ˈmau̇nt-ᵊn\ *n* [ME *cat of the mountaine*] **:** any of various wild cats: as **a :** the European wildcat **b :** LEOPARD

cat·a·pho·re·sis \ˌkat-ə-fə-ˈrē-səs\ *n* [NL] **:** ELECTROPHORESIS — **cat·a·pho·ret·ic** \-ˈret-ik\ *adj* — **cat·a·pho·ret·i·cal·ly** \-i-k(ə-)lē\ *adv*

cat·a·pla·sia \ˌkat-ə-ˈplā-zh(ē-)ə\ *n* [NL] **:** reversion of cells or tissues to more primitive character — **cat·a·plas·tic** \-ˈplas-tik\ *adj*

cat·a·plasm \ˈkat-ə-ˌplaz-əm\ *n* [MF *cataplasme*, fr. L *cataplasma*, fr. Gk *kataplasma*, fr. *kataplassein* to plaster over] **:** POULTICE

cat·a·plexy \ˈkat-ə-ˌplek-sē\ *n* [G *kataplexie*, fr. Gk *kataplēxis*, fr. *kataplēssein* to strike down, terrify, fr. *kata-* + *plēssein* to strike — more at PLAINT] **:** sudden loss of muscle power following a strong emotional stimulus

¹cat·a·pult \ˈkat-ə-ˌpəlt, -ˌpu̇lt\ *n* [MF or L; MF *catapulte*, fr. L *catapulta*, fr. Gk *katapaltēs*, fr. *kata-* + *pallein* to hurl — more at POLEMIC] **1 :** an ancient military device for hurling missiles **2 :** a device for launching an airplane at flying speed

²catapult *vt* **:** to throw or launch by or as if by a catapult ~ *vi* **:** to become catapulted

cat·a·ract \ˈkat-ə-ˌrakt\ *n* [L *cataracta* waterfall, portcullis, fr. Gk *katarraktēs*, fr. *katarassein* to dash down, fr. *kata-* cata- + *arassein* to strike, dash] **1** [MF or ML; MF *cataracte*, fr. ML *cataracta*, fr. L, portcullis] **:** a clouding of the lens of the eye or of its capsule obstructing the passage of light **2 a** *obs* **:** WATERSPOUT **b :** WATERFALL; *esp* **:** a large one over a precipice **c :** steep rapids in a river **d :** DOWNPOUR, FLOOD — **cat·a·rac·tal** \ˌkat-ə-ˈrak-tᵊl\ *adj*

ca·tarrh \kə-ˈtär\ *n* [MF or LL; MF *catarrhe*, fr. LL *catarrhus*, fr. Gk *katarrhous*, fr. *katarrhein* to flow down + *kata-* + *rhein* to flow — more at STREAM] **:** inflammation of a mucous membrane; *esp* **:** one chronically affecting the human nose and air passages — **ca·tarrh·al** \-əl\ *adj* — **ca·tarrh·al·ly** \-ə-lē\ *adv*

ca·tas·ta·sis \kə-ˈtas-tə-səs\ *n, pl* **ca·tas·ta·ses** \-tə-ˌsēz\ [Gk *katastasis* settlement, fr. *kathistanai* to set in order, fr. *kata-* + *histanai* to cause to stand — more at STAND] **:** the complication immediately prior to the climax of a play; *also* **:** the climax of a play

ca·tas·tro·phe \kə-ˈtas-trə-(ˌ)fē\ *n* [Gk *katastrophē*, fr. *katastrephein* to overturn, fr. *kata-* + *strephein* to turn] **1 :** the final event of the dramatic action esp. of a tragedy **2 :** a momentous tragic event ranging from extreme misfortune to utter overthrow or ruin **3 :** a violent and sudden change in a feature of the earth **4 :** utter failure **:** FIASCO **syn** see DISASTER — **cat·a·stroph·ic** \ˌkat-ə-ˈsträf-ik\ *adj* — **cat·a·stroph·i·cal·ly** \-i-k(ə-)lē\ *adv*

cata·to·nia \ˌkat-ə-ˈtō-nē-ə\ *n* [NL, fr. G *katatonie*, fr. *kata-* cata- + NL *tonus*] **1 :** CATALEPSY **2 :** a disorder marked by catalepsy — **cata·ton·ic** \-ˈtän-ik\ *adj or n*

cat·bird \ˈkat-ˌbərd\ *n* **:** an American songbird (*Dumetella carolinensis*) dark gray in color with black cap and reddish under tail coverts

cat·boat \-ˌbōt\ *n* **:** a sailboat having a cat rig and usu. a centerboard and being of light draft and broad beam

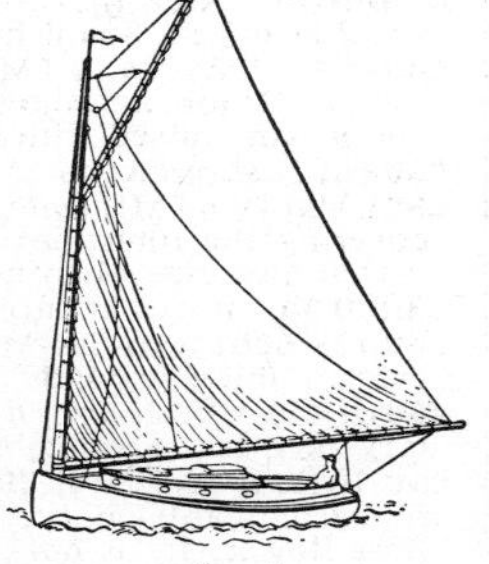
catboat

cat·bri·er \-ˌbrī(-ə)r\ *n* **:** any of several prickly climbers (genus *Smilax*) of the lily family

cat·call \-ˌkȯl\ *n* **:** a sound like the cry of a cat or a noise made to express disapproval (as at a sports event) — **catcall** *vb*

¹catch \ˈkach, ˈkech\ *vb* **caught** \ˈkȯt\ **catch·ing** [ME *cacchen*, fr. ONF *cachier* to hunt, fr. (assumed) VL *captiare*, alter. of L *captare* to chase, fr. *captus*, pp. of *capere* to take — more at HEAVE] *vt* **1 a :** to capture or seize esp. after pursuit **b :** TRAP, ENSNARE **c :** DECEIVE **d :** to discover unexpectedly **:** FIND ⟨*caught* in the act⟩ **e :** to check suddenly or momentarily **f :** to become suddenly aware of **2 a :** to take hold of **:** SEIZE **b :** to affect suddenly **c :** SNATCH, INTERCEPT **d :** to avail oneself of **:** TAKE **e :** to obtain through effort **:** GET **f :** to get entangled ⟨~ a sleeve on a nail⟩ **3 a :** to become affected by ⟨~ fire⟩ ⟨~ pneumonia⟩ **b :** to be struck by **4 a :** to seize and hold firmly **b :** FASTEN **5 :** to take or get usu. momentarily or quickly ⟨~ a glimpse of a friend⟩ **6 a :** OVERTAKE **b :** to get aboard in time ⟨~ the bus⟩ **7 :** ATTRACT, ARREST **8 :** to make contact with **9 :** to grasp by the senses or the mind **:** APPREHEND ~ *vi* **1 :** to grasp hastily or try to grasp **2 :** to become caught **3** *of a crop* **:** to come up and become established **4 :** to play the position of catcher on a baseball team
syn CAPTURE, TRAP, SNARE, ENTRAP, ENSNARE, BAG: CATCH implies the seizing of something in motion or in flight or in hiding; CAPTURE suggests taking by overcoming resistance or difficulty; TRAP, SNARE, ENTRAP, ENSNARE imply seizing by some device that holds the one caught at the mercy of his captor; TRAP and SNARE apply more commonly to physical seizing, ENTRAP and ENSNARE more often to figurative; BAG implies getting possession of by shooting down a fleeing or distant quarry **syn** see in addition INCUR

²catch *n* **1 :** something caught; *esp* **:** the total quantity caught at one time **2 a :** the act, action, or fact of catching **b :** a game in which a ball is thrown and caught **3 :** something that checks or holds immovable **4 :** one worth catching esp. as a spouse **5 :** a round for three or more unaccompanied voices written out as one continuous melody with each succeeding singer taking up a part in turn **6 :** FRAGMENT, SNATCH **7 :** a concealed difficulty **8 :** the catching of a field crop

catch·all \-ˌȯl\ *n* **:** something to hold a variety of odds and ends

catch·er \ˈkach-ər, ˈkech-\ *n* **:** one that catches; *specif* **:** a baseball player stationed behind home plate

catch·fly \-ˌflī\ *n* **:** any of various plants (as of the genera *Lychnis* and *Silene*) with viscid stems to which small insects adhere

catch·ing *adj* **1 :** INFECTIOUS, CONTAGIOUS **2 :** ALLURING, CATCHY

catch·ment \ˈkach-mənt, ˈkech-\ *n* **1 :** the action of catching water **2 :** something that catches water; *also* **:** the amount of water caught

catch on *vi* **1 :** UNDERSTAND, TUMBLE **2 :** to become popular

catch·pen·ny \ˈkach-ˌpen-ē, ˈkech-\ *adj* **:** designed esp. to get small sums of money from the ignorant

catch·pole *or* **catch·poll** \-ˌpōl\ *n* [ME *cacchepol*, fr. OE *cæcepol*, fr. (assumed) ONF *cachepol*, lit., chicken chaser, fr. ONF *cachier* + *pol* chicken, fr. L *pullus* — more at CATCH, PULLET] **:** a sheriff's deputy; *esp* **:** one who makes arrests for debt

catch up *vi* **:** to travel or work fast enough to overtake or complete

catch·up \ˈkech-əp, ˈkach-; ˈkat-səp\ *var of* CATSUP

catch·word \ˈkach-ˌwərd, ˈkech-\ *n* **1 a :** a word under the right-hand side of the last line on a book page that repeats the first word on the following page **b :** either of the terms to right and left of the head of a page of an alphabetical reference work (as a dictionary) indicating the alphabetically first and last entries on the page **2 :** a word or expression repeated until it becomes representative of a party, school, or a point of view

catchy \ˈkach-ē, ˈkech-\ *adj* **1 :** apt or tending to catch the interest or attention **2 :** TRICKY **3 :** FITFUL, IRREGULAR

cat distemper *n* **:** PANLEUCOPENIA

cate \ˈkāt\ *n* [ME, article of purchased food, short for *acate*, fr. ONF *acat* purchase, fr. *acater* to buy, fr. (assumed) VL *accaptare*, fr. L *acceptare* to accept] **:** a dainty or choice food

cat·e·che·sis \ˌkat-ə-ˈkē-səs\ *n, pl* **cat·e·che·ses** \-ˈkē-ˌsēz\ [LL, fr. Gk *katēchēsis*, fr. *katēchein* to teach] **:** oral instruction of catechumens — **cat·e·chet·i·cal** \ˌkat-ə-ˈket-i-kəl\ *adj*

cat·e·chism \ˈkat-ə-ˌkiz-əm\ *n* **1 :** oral instruction **2 :** a manual for catechizing; *specif* **:** a summary of religious doctrine often in the form of questions and answers **3 :** a set of formal questions put as a test — **cat·e·chis·mal** \ˌkat-ə-ˈkiz-məl\ *adj* — **cat·e·chis·tic** \-ˈkis-tik\ *adj*

cat·e·chist \ˈkat-ə-ˌkist, ˈkat-i-kəst\ *n* **:** one that catechizes

cat·e·chi·za·tion \ˌkat-i-kə-ˈzā-shən\ *n* **:** the act of catechizing or being catechized

cat·e·chize \ˈkat-ə-ˌkīz\ *vt* [LL *catechizare*, fr. Gk *katēchein* to teach, lit., to din into, fr. *kata-* cata- + *ēchein* to resound, fr. *ēchē* sound — more at ECHO] **1 :** to instruct systematically esp. by questions, answers, and explanations and corrections; *specif* **:** to give religious instruction in such a manner **2 :** to question systematically or searchingly — **cat·e·chiz·er** *n*

cat·e·chu \ˈkat-ə-ˌchü\ *n* [prob. fr. Malay *kachu*, of Dravidian origin; akin to Tamil & Kannada *kācu* catechu] **:** any of several dry, earthy, or resinous astringent substances obtained from tropical Asiatic plants: as **a :** an extract of the heartwood of an East Indian acacia (*Acacia catechu*) **b :** GAMBIER

cat·e·chu·men \ˌkat-ə-ˈkyü-mən\ *n* [ME *cathecumyn*, fr. MF *cathecumine*, fr. LL *catechumenus*, fr. Gk *katēchoumenos*, pres. pass. part. of *katēchein*] **1 :** a convert to Christianity receiving training in doctrine and discipline before baptism **2 :** one receiving instruction in the basic doctrines of Christianity before admission to communicant membership in a church

cat·e·gor·i·cal \ˌkat-ə-ˈgȯr-i-kəl, -ˈgär-\ *also* **cat·e·gor·ic** \-ik\ *adj* [LL *categoricus*, fr. Gk *katēgorikos*, fr. *katēgoria* affirmation, category] **1 a :** ABSOLUTE, UNQUALIFIED **b :** having no qualification or reservation **2 :** of, relating to, or constituting a category — **cat·e·gor·i·cal·ly** \-i-k(ə-)lē\ *adv*

categorical imperative *n* **:** a moral obligation or command that is unconditionally and universally binding

cat·e·go·ri·za·tion \ˌkat-i-gə-rə-ˈzā-shən\ *n* **:** the act of categorizing **:** the state of being categorized **:** CLASSIFICATION

cat·e·go·rize \ˈkat-i-gə-ˌrīz\ *vt* **:** to put into a category **:** CLASSIFY

cat·e·go·ry \ˈkat-ə-ˌgōr-ē, -ˌgȯr-\ *n* [LL *categoria*, fr. Gk *katēgoria* predication, category, fr. *katēgorein* to accuse, affirm, predicate, fr. *kata-* + *agora* public assembly — more at GREGARIOUS] **1 a :** a general class to which a logical predicate or that which it predicates belongs **b :** one of the underlying forms to which any fact known by experience must conform **2 :** CLASS, GROUP, CLASSIFICATION

ca·te·na \kə-ˈtē-nə\ *n, pl* **ca·te·nae** \-(ˌ)nē\ *or* **catenas** [ML, fr. L, chain — more at CHAIN] **:** a connected series of related things

cat·e·nary \ˈkat-ə-ˌner-ē, *esp Brit* kə-ˈtē-nə-rē\ *n* [NL *catenaria*, fr. L, fem. of *catenarius* of a chain, fr. *catena*] **1 :** the curve assumed by a perfectly flexible inextensible cord of uniform density and cross section hanging freely from two fixed points **2 :** something in the form of a catenary — **catenary** *adj*

cat·e·nate \ˈkat-ə-ˌnāt\ *vt* [L *catenatus*, pp. of *catenare*, fr. *catena*] **:** to connect in a series **:** LINK — **cat·e·na·tion** \ˌkat-ə-ˈnā-shən\ *n*

ca·ten·u·late \kə-ˈten-yə-lət\ *adj* [ISV, fr. LL *catenula*, dim. of L *catena*] **:** shaped like a chain

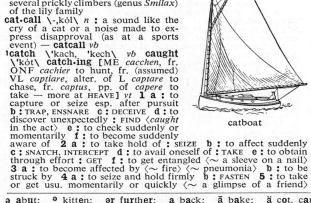

ca·ter \'kāt-ər\ *vi* [obs. *cater* (buyer of provisions), fr. ME *catour,* short for *acatour,* fr. AF, fr. ONF *acater* to buy] **1 :** to provide a supply of food **2 :** to supply what is required or desired

cat·er·an \'kat-ə-rən\ *n* [ME *ketharan,* prob. fr. ScGael *ceathairneach* freebooter, robber] **:** a former military irregular or brigand of the Scottish Highlands

cat·er·cor·ner \ˌkat-ē-'kȯ(r)-nər, ˌkat-ə-, ˌkit-ē-\ *or* **cat·er–cor·nered** \-nərd\ *adv (or adj)* [obs. *cater* (four-spot) + E *corner*] **:** in a diagonal or oblique position**:** on a diagonal or oblique line

ca·ter–cous·in \'kāt-ər-ˌkəz-ᵊn\ *n* **:** an intimate friend

ca·ter·er \'kāt-ər-ər\ *n* **:** one that caters; *esp* **:** one who provides food and service for a social affair — **ca·ter·ess** \'kāt-ə-rəs\ *n*

cat·er·pil·lar \'kat-ə(r)-ˌpil-ər\ *n, often attrib* [ME *catyrpel,* fr. ONF *catepelose,* lit., hairy cat] **:** the elongated wormlike larva of a butterfly or moth; *also* **:** any of various similar larvae

Caterpillar *trademark* — used for a tractor made for use on rough or soft ground and moved on two endless metal belts

cat·er·waul \'kat-ər-ˌwȯl\ *vi* [ME *caterwawen*] **:** to make the characteristic harsh cry of a rutting cat — **caterwaul** *n*

cat·fac·ing \'kat-ˌfā-siŋ\ *n* **:** a disfigurement or malformation of fruit suggesting a cat's face in appearance

cat·fish \'kat-ˌfish\ *n* **:** any of numerous usu. stout-bodied large-headed voracious fishes (order Ostariophysi) with long tactile barbels

cat·gut \-ˌgət\ *n* **:** a tough cord made usu. from sheep intestines

cath- — see CATA-

Cath·ar \'kath-ˌär\ *n, pl* **Cath·a·ri** \'kath-ə-ˌrī, -ˌrē\ [LL *cathari* (pl.), fr. LGk *katharoi,* fr. Gk, pl. of *katharos,* adj.] **:** a member of one of various ascetic and dualistic Christian sects of the later Middle Ages — **Cath·a·rism** \'kath-ə-ˌriz-əm\ *n* — **Cath·a·rist** \-ə-rəst\ *or* **Cath·a·ris·tic** \ˌkath-ə-'ris-tik\ *adj*

ca·thar·sis \kə-'thär-səs\ *n, pl* **ca·thar·ses** \-'thär-ˌsēz\ [NL, fr. Gk *katharsis,* fr. *kathairein* to cleanse, purge, fr. *katharos* pure] **1 :** PURGATION **2 a :** purification or purgation of the emotions (as pity and fear) primarily through art **b :** a purification or purgation that brings about spiritual renewal or release from tension **3 :** elimination of a complex by bringing it to consciousness and affording it expression

[1]**ca·thar·tic** \kə-'thärt-ik\ *adj* [LL or Gk; LL *catharticus,* fr. Gk *kathartikos,* fr. *kathairein*] **:** of, relating to, or producing catharsis

[2]**cathartic** *n* **:** a cathartic medicine **:** PURGATIVE

cat·head \'kat-ˌhed\ *n* **:** a projecting piece of timber or iron near the bow of a ship to which the anchor is hoisted and secured

ca·thect \kə-'thekt\ *vt* [back-formation fr. *cathectic*] **:** to invest with libidinal energy

ca·thec·tic \kə-'thek-tik\ *adj* [NL *cathexis*] **:** of, relating to, or invested with libidinal energy

ca·the·dra \kə-'thē-drə\ *n* [L, chair] **:** a bishop's official throne

[1]**ca·the·dral** \kə-'thē-drəl\ *adj* **1 :** of, relating to, or containing a cathedra **2 :** emanating from a chair of authority **3 :** suggestive of a cathedral

[2]**cathedral** *n* **:** a church that contains a cathedra and is the principal church of a diocese

cath·er·ine wheel \ˌkath-(ə-)rən-\ *n, often cap C* [St. *Catherine* of Alexandria †*ab*307 Christian martyr] **1 :** a wheel with spikes projecting from the rim **2 :** PINWHEEL 2 **3 :** CARTWHEEL 2

cath·e·ter \'kath-ət-ər\ *n* [LL, fr. Gk *kathetēr,* fr. *kathienai* to send down, fr. *kata-* cata- + *hienai* to send — more at JET] **:** a tubular medical device for insertion into canals, vessels, passageways, or body cavities usu. to permit injection or withdrawal of fluids or to keep a passage open

cath·e·ter·iza·tion \ˌkath-ət-ə-rə-'zā-shən, ˌkath-tə-rə-\ *n* **:** the act or an instance of catheterizing

cath·e·ter·ize \'kath-ət-ə-ˌrīz, 'kath-tə-\ *vt* **:** to introduce a catheter into

ca·thex·is \kə-'thek-səs\ *n* [NL (intended as trans. of G *besetzung*), fr. Gk *kathexis* holding, fr. *katechein* to hold fast, occupy, fr. *kata-* + *echein* to have, hold — more at SCHEME] **:** investment of libidinal energy in a person, object, or idea

cath·ode \'kath-ˌōd\ *n* [Gk *kathodos* way down, fr. *kata-* + *hodos* way — more at CEDE] **1 :** the negative terminal of an electrolytic cell — compare ANODE **2 :** the positive terminal of a primary cell or of a storage battery that is delivering current **3 :** the electron-emitting electrode of an electron tube — **ca·thod·ic** \ka-'thäd-ik\ *adj* — **ca·thod·i·cal·ly** \-i-k(ə-)lē\ *adv*

cathode ray *n* **1 :** one of the high-speed electrons projected in a stream from the heated cathode of a vacuum tube under the propulsion of a strong electric field **2 :** a stream of cathode-ray electrons

cathode–ray tube *n* **:** a vacuum tube in which cathode rays usu. in the form of a slender beam are projected upon a fluorescent screen and produce a luminous spot

cath·o·lic \'kath-(ə-)lik\ *adj* [MF & LL; MF *catholique,* fr. LL *catholicus,* fr. Gk *katholikos* universal, general, fr. *katholou* in general, fr. *kata* by + *holos* whole — more at CATA-, SAFE] **1 :** COMPREHENSIVE, UNIVERSAL; *esp* **:** broad in sympathies, tastes, or interests **2** *cap* **a :** of, relating to, or forming the church universal **b :** of, relating to, or forming the ancient undivided Christian church or a church claiming historical continuity from it; *specif* **:** Roman Catholic — **ca·thol·i·cal·ly** \kə-'thäl-i-k(ə-)lē\ *adv* — **ca·thol·i·cize** \kə-'thäl-ə-ˌsīz\ *vb*

Cath·o·lic \'kath-(ə-)lik\ *n* **1 :** a person who belongs to the universal Christian church **2 :** a member of a Catholic church; *specif* **:** ROMAN CATHOLIC

ca·thol·i·cate \kə-'thäl-ə-ˌkāt, -i-kət\ *n* **:** the see of a catholicos

Ca·thol·i·cism \kə-'thäl-ə-ˌsiz-əm\ *n* **1 :** the faith, practice, or system of Catholic Christianity **2 :** ROMAN CATHOLICISM

cath·o·lic·i·ty \ˌkath-ə-'lis-ət-ē\ *n* **1** *cap* **:** the character of being in conformity with a Catholic church **2 a :** liberality of sentiments or views **b :** UNIVERSALITY **c :** comprehensive range

ca·thol·i·con \kə-'thäl-ə-ˌkän\ *n* [F or ML; F, fr. ML, fr. Gk *katholikon,* neut. of *katholikos*] **:** CURE-ALL, PANACEA

ca·thol·i·cos \kə-'thäl-i-kəs\ *n, pl* **ca·thol·i·cos·es** \-kə-səz\ *or* **ca·thol·i·coi** \-'thäl-ə-ˌkȯi\ *often cap* [LGk *katholikos,* fr. Gk, general] **:** the patriarch of the separated Armenian or Nestorian Church

cat·ion \'kat-ˌī-ən\ *n* [Gk *kation,* neut. of *katiōn,* prp. of *katienai* to go down, fr. *kata-* cata- + *ienai* to go — more at ISSUE] **:** the ion in an electrolyzed solution that migrates to the cathode; *broadly* **:** a positively charged ion

cat·ion·ic \ˌkat-(ˌ)ī-'än-ik\ *adj* **:** characterized by an active and esp. surface-active cation — **cat·ion·i·cal·ly** \-i-k(ə-)lē\ *adv*

cat·kin \'kat-kən\ *n* [fr. its resemblance to a cat's tail] **:** a usu. long ament densely crowded with bracts — **cat·kin·ate** \-ˌāt\ *adj*

cat·like \'kat-ˌlīk\ *adj* **:** resembling a cat **:** STEALTHY

cat·nap \-ˌnap\ *n* **:** a very short light nap — **catnap** *vi*

cat·nip \-ˌnip\ *n* [[1]*cat* + obs. *nep* (catnip), fr. ME, fr. OE *nepte,* fr. L *nepeta*] **:** a strong-scented mint (*Nepeta cataria*) with whorls of small pale flowers in terminal spikes

cat–o'–nine–tails \ˌkat-ə-'nīn-ˌtālz\ *n, pl* **cat–o'–nine–tails** [fr. the resemblance of its scars to the scratches of a cat] **:** a whip made of usu. nine knotted lines or cords fastened to a handle

ca·top·tric \kə-'täp-trik\ *adj* [Gk *katoptrikos,* fr. *katoptron* mirror, fr. *katopsesthai* to be going to observe, fr. *kata-* cata- + *opsesthai* to be going to see] **:** of or relating to a mirror or reflected light; *also* **:** produced by reflection — **ca·top·tri·cal·ly** \-tri-k(ə-)lē\ *adv*

cat rig *n* **:** a rig consisting of a single mast far forward carrying a single large sail extended by a boom — **cat–rigged** \'kat-'rigd\ *adj*

cat's cradle *n* **:** a game in which a string looped in a pattern like a cradle on the fingers of one person's hands is transferred to the hands of another so as to form a different figure

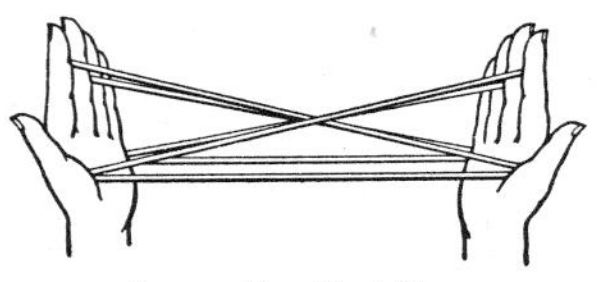

cat's cradle, first figure

cat's–eye \'kat-ˌsī\ *n* **1 :** any of various gems (as a chrysoberyl or a chalcedony) exhibiting opalescent reflections from within **2 :** a small reflector placed to reflect beams from automobile headlights

cat's–foot \'kats-ˌfu̇t\ *n* **1 :** GROUND IVY **2 :** any of several composite plants (genus *Antennaria,* esp. *A. neodioica*)

cat's–paw \'kat-ˌspȯ\ *n* **1 :** a light air that ruffles the surface of the water in irregular patches during a calm **2** [fr. the fable of the monkey that used a cat's paw to draw chestnuts from the fire] **:** one used by another as a tool **:** DUPE **3 :** a hitch in the bight of a rope so made as to form two eyes into which a tackle may be hooked

cat·sup \'kech-əp, 'kach-; 'kat-səp\ *n* [Malay *kĕchap* spiced fish sauce] **:** a seasoned sauce of puree consistency usu. of tomatoes

cat·tail \'kat-ˌtāl\ *n* **:** any of a genus (*Typha* of the family Typhaceae, the cattail family) of tall reedy marsh plants; *esp* **:** a plant (*Typha latifolia*) with long flat leaves

cat·ta·lo \'kat-ᵊl-ˌō\ *n, pl* **cattaloes** *or* **cattalos** [blend of *cattle* and *buffalo*] **:** a hybrid between the American buffalo and domestic cattle that is hardier than the latter

cat·ti·ly \'kat-ᵊl-ē\ *adv* **:** in a catty manner

cat·ti·ness \'kat-ē-nəs\ *n* **:** the quality or state of being catty

cat·tle \'kat-ᵊl\ *n, pl* **cattle** [ME *catel,* fr. ONF, personal property, fr. ML *capitale,* fr. L, neut. of *capitalis* of the head — more at CAPITAL] **1 :** domesticated quadrupeds held as property or raised for use; *specif* **:** bovine animals kept on a farm or ranch **2 :** a class of contemptible persons

cat·tle·man \-mən, -ˌman\ *n* **:** a man who tends or raises cattle

cat·tleya \'kat-lē-ə, kat-'lā-ə\ *n* [NL, fr. Wm. *Cattley* †1832 E patron of botany] **:** any of a genus (*Cattleya*) of tropical American epiphytic orchids with showy hooded flowers

[1]**cat·ty** \'kat-ē\ *n* [Malay *kati*] **:** any of various units of weight of China and southeast Asia varying around 1⅓ pounds; *also* **:** a standard Chinese unit equal to 1.1023 pounds

[2]**cat·ty** *adj* **1 :** resembling a cat**:** as **a :** STEALTHY **b :** AGILE **c :** slyly spiteful **:** MALICIOUS **2 :** of or relating to a cat

cat·ty–cor·ner *or* **cat·ty–cor·nered** *var of* CATERCORNER

cat·walk \'kat-ˌwȯk\ *n* **:** a narrow walkway (as along a bridge)

Cau·ca·sian \kȯ-'kā-zhən, -'kazh-ən\ *adj* **1 :** of or relating to the Caucasus or its inhabitants **2 a :** of or relating to the white race of mankind as classified according to physical features **b :** of or relating to the white race as defined by law specif. as composed of persons of European, No. African, or southwest Asian ancestry — **Caucasian** *n* — **Cau·ca·soid** \'kȯ-kə-ˌsȯid\ *adj or n*

[1]**cau·cus** \'kȯ-kəs\ *n* [prob. of Algonquian origin] **:** a closed meeting of a group of persons belonging to the same political party or faction usu. to select candidates or to decide on policy

[2]**caucus** *vi* **:** to hold or meet in a caucus

cau·dad \'kȯ-ˌdad\ *adv* [L *cauda*] **:** toward the tail or posterior end

cau·dal \'kȯd-ᵊl\ *adj* [NL *caudalis,* fr. L *cauda* tail — more at COWARD] **1 :** of, relating to, or being a tail **2 :** situated in or directed toward the hind part of the body — **cau·dal·ly** \-ᵊl-ē\ *adv*

cau·date \'kȯ-ˌdāt\ *also* **cau·dat·ed** \-əd\ *adj* **:** having a tail or a taillike appendage **:** TAILED — **cau·da·tion** \kȯ-'dā-shən\ *n*

cau·dex \'kȯ-ˌdeks\ *n, pl* **cau·di·ces** \'kȯd-ə-ˌsēz\ *or* **cau·dex·es** [L, tree trunk or stem — more at CODE] **1 :** the stem of a palm or tree fern **2 :** the woody base of a perennial plant

cau·dil·lo \kau̇-'thē-(ˌ)(y)ō, -'thēl-(ˌ)yō\ *n* [Sp, fr. LL *capitellum* small head] **:** a Spanish or Latin-American military strong man

cau·dle \'kȯd-ᵊl\ *n* [ME *caudel,* fr. ONF, fr. *caut* warm, fr. L *calidus* — more at CALDRON] **:** a drink (as for invalids) usu. of warm ale or wine mixed with bread or gruel, eggs, sugar, and spices

caught *past of* CATCH

caul \'kȯl\ *n* [ME *calle,* fr. MF *cale*] **1 :** the large fatty omentum covering the intestines **2 :** the inner fetal membrane of higher vertebrates esp. when not ruptured or covering the head at birth

cauldron *var of* CALDRON

cau·les·cent \kȯ-'les-ᵊnt\ *adj* [ISV, fr. L *caulis*] **:** having a stem evident above ground

cau·li·cle \'kȯ-li-kəl\ *n* [L *cauliculus,* dim. of *caulis*] **:** a rudimentary stem (as of an embryo or seedling)

cau·li·flow·er \'kȯ-li-ˌflau̇(-ə)r, 'käl-i-\ *n, often attrib* [It *cavolfiore,* fr. *cavolo* cabbage (fr. LL *caulus,* fr. L *caulis* stem, cabbage) + *fiore* flower, fr. L *flor-, flos*] **:** a garden plant (*Brassica oleracea capitata*) related to the cabbage and grown for its compact edible head of usu. white undeveloped flowers; *also* **:** the flower cluster

cauliflower ear *n* **:** an ear deformed from injury and excessive growth of reparative tissue

cau·line \'kȯ-ˌlīn\ *adj* [prob. fr. NL *caulinus,* fr. L *caulis*] **:** of, relating to, or growing on a stem; *specif* **:** growing on the upper portion of a stem

[1]**caulk** \'kȯk\ *vt* [ME *caulken,* fr. ONF *cauquer* to trample, fr. L *calcare,* fr. *calc-, calx* heel] **1 :** to stop up and make watertight the seams of by filling with a waterproofing compound or material **2 :** to stop up and make tight against leakage — **caulk·er** *n*

2**caulk** *var of* CALK
caus·al \'kȯ-zəl\ *adj* **1 :** expressing or indicating cause **:** CAUSATIVE **2 :** of, relating to, or constituting a cause **3 :** involving causation or a cause **4 :** arising from a cause — **caus·al·ly** \-zə-lē\ *adv*
cau·sal·i·ty \kȯ-'zal-ət-ē\ *n* **1 :** a causal quality or agency **2 :** the relation between a cause and its effect or between regularly correlated events or phenomena
cau·sa·tion \kȯ-'zā-shən\ *n* **1 a :** the act or process of causing **b :** the act or agency by which an effect is produced **2 :** CAUSALITY
caus·ative \'kȯ-zət-iv\ *adj* **1 :** effective or operating as a cause or agent **2 :** expressing causation — **causative** *n* — **caus·ative·ly** *adv*
1**cause** \'kȯz\ *n* [ME, fr. OF, fr. L *causa*] **1 a :** something that occasions or effects a result **b :** a person or thing that is the occasion of an action or state; *esp* **:** an agent that brings something about **c :** REASON, MOTIVE **2 a :** a ground of legal action **b :** CASE **3 :** a matter or question to be decided **4 :** a principle or movement militantly defended or supported — **cause·less** \-ləs\ *adj*
syn CAUSE, DETERMINANT, ANTECEDENT, REASON, OCCASION mean something that produces an effect. CAUSE applies to any event, circumstance, or condition or any combination of these that brings about or helps bring about a result; DETERMINANT applies to a cause that fixes the nature of what results as a product or an outcome; ANTECEDENT applies to that which has preceded and may therefore be in some degree responsible for what follows or derives or descends from it; REASON applies to a traceable or explainable cause of a known effect; OCCASION applies to a particular time or situation at which underlying causes become effective
2**cause** *vt* **1 :** to serve as cause or occasion of **2 :** to effect by command, authority, or force — **caus·er** *n*
cause cé·lè·bre \,kōz-sā-'lebrᵊ, ,kȯz-\ *n, pl* **causes cé·lè·bres** *same*\ [F, lit., celebrated case] **1 :** a legal case that excites widespread interest **2 :** a notorious incident or episode
cau·se·rie \,kōz-(ə-)'rē\ *n* [F, fr. *causer* to chat, fr. L *causari* to plead, discuss, fr. *causa*] **1 :** an informal conversation **:** CHAT **2 :** a short informal composition
cause·way \'kȯz-,wā\ *n* [ME *cauciwey*, fr. *cauci* causey + *wey* way] **1 :** a raised way across wet ground **2 :** HIGHWAY; *esp* **:** one of ancient Roman construction in Britain — **causeway** *vt*
cau·sey \'kȯ-zē\ *n* [ME *cauci*, fr. ONF *caucie*, fr. ML *calciata* paved highway, fr. fem. of *calciatus* paved with limestone, fr. L *calc-*, *calx* limestone] **1 :** CAUSEWAY 1 **2** *obs* **:** CAUSEWAY 2
caus·tic \'kȯ-stik\ *adj* [L *causticus*, fr. Gk *kaustikos*, fr. *kaiein* to burn; akin to Lith *kulė* smut of plants] **1 :** capable of destroying or eating away by chemical action **:** CORROSIVE **2 :** INCISIVE, BITING ⟨~ wit⟩ **3 :** relating to or being the envelope of rays emanating from a point and reflected or refracted by a curved surface — **caustic** *n* — **caus·ti·cal·ly** \-sti-k(ə-)lē\ *adv* — **caus·tic·i·ty** \kȯ-'stis-ət-ē\ *n*
caustic potash *n* **:** POTASSIUM HYDROXIDE
caustic soda *n* **:** SODIUM HYDROXIDE
cau·ter·i·za·tion \,kȯt-ə-rə-'zā-shən\ *n* **:** the act or effect of cauterizing
cau·ter·ize \'kȯt-ə-,rīz\ *vt* **:** to sear with a cautery or caustic
cau·tery \'kȯt-ə-rē\ *n* [L *cauterium*, fr. Gk *kautērion* branding iron, fr. *kaiein*] **1 :** CAUTERIZATION **2 :** a hot iron, caustic, or other agent used to burn, sear, or destroy tissue
1**cau·tion** \'kȯ-shən\ *n* [L *caution-*, *cautio* precaution, fr. *cautus*, pp. of *cavēre* to be on one's guard] **1 :** WARNING, ADMONISHMENT **2 :** PRECAUTION **3 :** prudent forethought to minimize risk **4 :** one that arouses astonishment or commands attention
2**caution** *vt* **cau·tion·ing** \'kȯ-sh(ə-)niŋ\ **:** to advise caution to **syn** see WARN
cau·tion·ary \'kȯ-shə-,ner-ē\ *adj* **:** serving as or offering a caution
cau·tious \'kȯ-shəs\ *adj* **:** marked by or given to caution — **cau·tious·ly** *adv* — **cau·tious·ness** *n*
syn CIRCUMSPECT, WARY, CHARY: CAUTIOUS implies the exercise of forethought usu. prompted by fear of probable or even of merely possible danger; CIRCUMSPECT suggests less fear and stresses the surveying of all possible consequences before acting or deciding; WARY emphasizes suspiciousness and alertness in watching for danger and cunning in escaping it; CHARY implies a cautious reluctance to give, act, or speak freely
cav·al·cade \,kav-əl-'kād, 'kav-əl-,\ *n* [MF, ride on horseback, fr. OIt *cavalcata*, fr. *cavalcare* to go on horseback, fr. LL *caballicare*, fr. L *caballus* horse; akin to Gk dial. *kaballeion* horse-drawn vehicle] **1 a :** a procession of riders or carriages **b :** a procession of vehicles or ships **2 :** a dramatic sequence or procession **:** PARADE
1**cav·a·lier** \,kav-ə-'li(ə)r\ *n* [MF, fr. OIt *cavaliere*, fr. OProv *cavalier*, fr. LL *caballarius* horseman, fr. L *caballus*] **1 :** a gentleman trained in arms and manege **2 :** a mounted soldier **:** KNIGHT **3** *cap* **:** an adherent of Charles I of England **4 :** GALLANT
2**cavalier** *adj* **1 :** DEBONAIR **2 :** given to offhand dismissal of important matters **:** DISDAINFUL **3 a** *cap* **:** of or relating to the party of Charles I of England in his struggles with the Puritans and Parliament **b :** ARISTOCRATIC **c** *cap* **:** of or relating to the English Cavalier poets of the mid-17th century — **cav·a·lier·ly** *adv*
ca·val·la \kə-'val-ə\ *n, pl* **cavalla** *or* **cavallas** [Sp *caballa*, a fish, fr. LL, mare, fem. of L *caballus*] **1 :** CERO **2** *also* **ca·val·ly** \-'val-ē\ **:** any of various carangid fishes (esp. genus *Caranx*)
cav·al·ry \'kav-əl-rē\ *n* [It *cavalleria* cavalry, chivalry, fr. *cavaliere*] **1 :** HORSEMEN **2 :** an army component mounted on horseback or moving in motor vehicles and assigned to combat missions that require great mobility — **cav·al·ry·man** \-mən, -,man\ *n*
cav·a·ti·na \,kav-ə-'tē-nə\ *n* [It, fr. *cavata* production of sound from an instrument, fr. *cavare* to dig out, fr. L, to make hollow, fr. *cavus*] **1 :** an operatic solo simpler and briefer than an aria **2 :** a sustained melody
1**cave** \'kāv\ *n* [ME, fr. OF, fr. L *cava*, fr. *cavus* hollow; akin to ON *hūnn* cub, Gk *kyein* to be pregnant, *koilos* hollow, Skt *śvayati* he swells] **1 :** a natural underground chamber open to the surface **2** *Brit* **:** a secession or a group of seceders from a political party
2**cave** *vt* **:** to form a cave in or under **:** HOLLOW, UNDERMINE
3**cave** \'kāv\ *vb* [prob. alter. of *calve*] *vi* **1 :** to fall in or down esp. from being undermined **2 :** to cease to resist **:** SUBMIT — usu. used with *in* ~ *vt* **:** to cause to fall or collapse — usu. used with *in*
ca·ve·at \'kā-vē-,at, 'kav-ē-, -ət; 'käv-ē-,ät, -ət\ *n* [L, let him beware, fr. *cavēre* — more at HEAR] **1 a :** a warning enjoining from certain acts or practices **b :** an explanation to prevent misinterpretation **2 :** a legal warning to a judicial officer to suspend a proceeding until the opposition has a hearing
caveat emp·tor \-'em(p)-tər, -,tȯ(ə)r\ *n* [NL, let the buyer beware] **:** a principle in commerce: without a warranty the buyer takes the risk of quality upon himself
cave dweller *n* **:** one (as a prehistoric man) that dwells in a cave
cave–in \'kā-,vin\ *n* **1 :** the action of caving in **2 :** a place where earth has caved in
cave·man \'kāv-,man\ *n* **1 :** a cave dweller esp. of the Stone Age **2 :** a man who acts with rough violent directness
1**cav·ern** \'kav-ərn\ *n* [ME *caverne*, fr. MF, fr. L *caverna*, fr. *cavus*] **:** an underground chamber often of large or indefinite extent **:** CAVE
2**cavern** *vt* **1 :** to place in or as if in a cavern **2 :** to form a cavern of **:** HOLLOW — used with *out*
cav·ern·ous \-ər-nəs\ *adj* **1 :** having caverns or cavities **2 :** constituting or suggesting a cavern **3** *of animal tissue* **:** composed largely of vascular sinuses and capable of dilating with blood to bring about the erection of a body part — **cav·ern·ous·ly** *adv*
ca·vet·to \kə-'vet-(,)ō\ *n, pl* **ca·vet·ti** \-ē\ [It, fr. *cavo* hollow, fr. L *cavus*] **:** a concave molding having a curve that roughly approximates a quarter circle
cav·i·ar *or* **cav·i·are** \'kav-ē-,är\ *n* [earlier *cavery, caviarie*, fr. obs. It *caviari*, pl. of *caviaro*, fr. Turk *havyar*] **:** processed salted roe of the sturgeon or other large fish prepared as an appetizer
cav·il \'kav-əl\ *vb* **cav·iled** *or* **cav·illed**; **cav·il·ing** *or* **cav·il·ling** \-(ə-)liŋ\ [L *cavillari* to jest, cavil, fr. *cavilla* raillery] *vi* **:** to raise trivial and frivolous objection ~ *vt* **:** to raise trivial objections to — **cavil** *n* — **cav·il·er** *or* **cav·il·ler** \-(ə-)lər\ *n*
cav·i·ta·tion \,kav-ə-'tā-shən\ *n* [*cavity* + *-ation*] **1 :** the formation of partial vacuums in a liquid by a swiftly moving solid body (as a propeller) or by high-frequency sound waves; *also* **:** a cavity so formed **2 :** the formation of cavities in an organ or tissue
cav·i·ty \'kav-ət-ē\ *n* [MF *cavité*, fr. LL *cavitas*, fr. L *cavus* hollow] **:** an unfilled space within a mass; *esp* **:** a space hollowed out
ca·vort \kə-'vȯ(ə)rt\ *vi* [perh. alter. of *curvet*] **:** PRANCE, FRISK
ca·vy \'kā-vē\ *n* [NL *Cavia*, genus name, fr. obs. Pg *çavia* (now *savia*), fr. Tupi *sawiya* rat] **1 :** any of several short-tailed rough-haired So. American rodents (family Caviidae); *esp* **:** GUINEA PIG **2 :** any of several rodents related to the cavies
caw \'kȯ\ *vi* [imit.] **:** to utter the harsh raucous natural call of the crow or a similar cry — **caw** *n*
cay \'kē, 'kā\ *n* [Sp *cayo*] **:** a low island or reef of sand or coral
cay·enne pepper \(,)kī-,en-, (,)kā-\ *n* [by folk etymology fr. earlier *cayan*, modif. of Tupi *kyinha*] **1 :** a pungent condiment consisting of the ground dried fruits or seeds of hot peppers **2 :** HOT PEPPER 2; *esp* **:** a cultivated pepper with very long twisted pungent red fruits **3 :** the fruit of a cayenne pepper
cay·man *var of* CAIMAN
Ca·yu·ga \kē-'ü-gə, 'kyü-, kā-'(y)ü-\ *n, pl* **Cayuga** *or* **Cayugas** **1 a :** an Iroquois people of New York state **b :** a member of this people **2 :** the language of the Cayuga people
Cay·use \'kī-,(y)üs, kī-'\ *n, pl* **Cayuse** *or* **Cay·us·es** **1 a :** an Indian people of Washington and Oregon **b :** a member of this people **2** *pl cayuses, not cap, West* **:** a native range horse
C battery *n* **:** a battery used to maintain the potential of a grid-controlled electron tube at a desired value constant except for signals superposed upon it
C clef *n* **:** a movable clef indicating middle C by its placement on one of the lines of the staff
1**cease** \'sēs\ *vb* [ME *cesen*, fr. OF *cesser*, fr. L *cessare* to delay, fr. *cessus*, pp. of *cedere*] *vt* **:** to bring to an end **:** TERMINATE ~ *vi* **1 a :** to come to an end **b :** to bring an activity or action to an end **:** DISCONTINUE **2** *obs* **:** to die out **:** become extinct **syn** see STOP
2**cease** *n* **:** CESSATION — usu. used with *without*
cease–fire \'sēs-'fī(ə)r\ *n* **1 :** a military order to cease firing **2 :** a suspension of active hostilities
cease·less \'sē-sləs\ *adj* **:** CONSTANT, CONTINUAL — **cease·less·ly** *adv* — **cease·less·ness** *n*
ce·cal \'sē-kəl\ *adj* **:** of or relating to a cecum — **ce·cal·ly** \-ē\ *adv*
ce·cro·pia moth \si-,krō-pē-ə-\ *n* [NL *cecropia*, fr. L, fem. of *Cecropius* Athenian, fr. Gk *Kekropios*, fr. *Kekrops* Cecrops, legendary king of Athens] **:** a large silkworm moth (*Samia cecropia*)
ce·cum \'sē-kəm\ *n, pl* **ce·ca** \-kə\ [NL, fr. L *intestinum caecum*, lit., blind intestine] **:** a cavity open at one end (as the blind end of a duct); *esp* **:** the blind pouch in which the large intestine begins and into which the ileum opens from one side
ce·dar \'sēd-ər\ *n* [ME *cedre*, fr. OF, fr. L *cedrus*, fr. Gk *kedros;* akin to Lith *kadagys* juniper] **1 a :** any of a genus (*Cedrus*) of usu. tall coniferous trees (as the cedar of Lebanon, *C. libani*, or the deodar) of the pine family noted for their fragrant durable wood **b :** any of numerous coniferous trees (as of the genera *Juniperus*, *Chamaecyparis*, or *Thuja*) felt to resemble the true cedars esp. in the fragrance and durability of their wood **2 :** the wood of a cedar
ce·darn \'sēd-ərn\ *adj, archaic* **:** made or suggestive of cedar
cede \'sēd\ *vt* [F or L; F *céder*, fr. L *cedere* to go, withdraw, yield; prob. akin to L *cis* on this side] **1 :** to yield or grant typically by treaty **2 :** ASSIGN, TRANSFER — **ced·er** *n*
ce·di \'sād-ē\ *n* [Akan *sedie* cowry] — see MONEY table
ce·dil·la \si-'dil-ə\ *n* [obs. Sp *cedilla*, dim. of *ceda* zee, fr. LL *zeta;* fr. the use of a small *z* placed after or under a *c* to indicate a sibilant pronunciation] **:** a mark placed under the letter *c* (as ç) to show that the *c* is to be pronounced like *s*
cee \'sē\ *n* **:** the letter *c*
cei·ba \'sā-bə\ *n* [Sp] **1 :** a massive tropical tree (*Ceiba pentandra*) of the silk-cotton family with large pods filled with seeds invested with a silky floss that yields the fiber kapok **2 :** KAPOK
ceil \'sē(ə)l\ *vt* [ME *celen*, prob. fr. (assumed) MF *celer*, fr. L *caelare* to carve, fr. *caelum* chisel, fr. *caedere* to cut] **1 :** to furnish (as a wooden ship) with a lining **2 :** to furnish with a ceiling
ceil·ing \'sē-liŋ\ *n* **1 a :** the overhead inside lining of a room **b :** material used to ceil a wall or roof of a room **2 :** something thought of as an overhanging shelter **3 a :** the height above the ground from which prominent objects on the ground can be seen and identified **b :** the height above the ground of the base of the lowest layer of clouds when over half of the sky is obscured **4 a :** ABSOLUTE CEILING **b :** SERVICE CEILING **5 :** an upper usu.

prescribed limit — **ceil·inged** \-liŋd\ *adj*

ceil·om·e·ter \sē-ˈläm-ət-ər\ *n* [*ceil*ing + *-o-* + *-meter*] **:** a photoelectric instrument for determining by triangulation the height of the cloud ceiling above the earth

cel·an·dine \ˈsel-ən-ˌdīn, -ˌdēn\ *n* [ME *celidoine*, fr. MF, fr. L *chelidonia*, fr. fem. of *chelidonius* of the swallow, fr. Gk *chelidonios*, fr. *cheilidon-*, *chelidōn* swallow] **1 :** a yellow-flowered biennial herb (*Chelidonium majus*) of the poppy family **2 :** a yellow-flowered perennial crowfoot (*Ranunculus ficaria*) — called also *lesser celandine*

-cele \ˌsēl\ *n comb form* [MF, fr. L, fr. Gk *kēlē*; akin to OE *hēala* hernia, OSlav *kyla*] **:** tumor **:** hernia ⟨varicocele⟩

cel·e·brant \ˈsel-ə-brənt\ *n* **:** one who celebrates; *specif* **:** the priest officiating at the Eucharist

cel·e·brate \ˈsel-ə-ˌbrāt\ *vb* [L *celebratus*, pp. of *celebrare* to frequent, celebrate, fr. *celebr-*, *celeber* much frequented, famous; akin to L *celer*] *vt* **1 :** to perform (a sacrament or solemn ceremony) publicly and with appropriate rites ⟨~ the mass⟩ **2 a :** to honor (as a holy day or feast day) by solemn ceremonies or by refraining from ordinary business **b :** to demonstrate satisfaction in by festivities or other deviation from routine **3 :** to hold up for public acclaim **:** EXTOL ~ *vi* **1 :** to observe a holiday, perform a religious ceremony, or take part in a festival **2 :** to observe a notable occasion with festivities **syn** see KEEP — **cel·e·bra·tion** \ˌsel-ə-ˈbrā-shən\ *n* — **cel·e·bra·tor** \ˈsel-ə-ˌbrāt-ər\ *n*

cel·e·brat·ed *adj* **:** widely known and often referred to **:** RENOWNED **syn** see FAMOUS — **cel·e·brat·ed·ness** *n*

ce·leb·ri·ty \sə-ˈleb-rət-ē\ *n* **1 :** the state of being celebrated **2 :** a celebrated person

ce·le·ri·ac \sə-ˈler-ē-ˌak, -ˈlir-\ *n* [irreg. fr. *celery*] **:** a celery grown for its thickened edible root

ce·ler·i·ty \sə-ˈler-ət-ē\ *n* [ME *celerite*, fr. MF *célérité*, fr. L *celeritat-*, *celeritas*, fr. *celer* swift] **:** rapidity of motion **:** SWIFTNESS

syn CELERITY, ALACRITY, LEGERITY mean quickness in movement or action. CELERITY implies speed in accomplishing work; ALACRITY stresses promptness in response to suggestion or command; LEGERITY implies lightness and ease as well as swiftness of movement

cel·ery \ˈsel-(ə-)rē\ *n* [prob. fr. It dial. *seleri*, pl. of *selero*, modif. of LL *selinon*, fr. Gk] **:** a European herb (*Apium graveolens*) of the carrot family; *specif* **:** one of a cultivated variety (*A. graveolens dulce*) with leafstalks eaten raw or cooked

ce·les·ta \sə-ˈles-tə\ *n* [F *célesta*, alter. of *céleste*, lit., heavenly, fr. L *caelestis*] **:** a keyboard instrument with hammers that strike steel plates producing a tone similar to that of a glockenspiel

[1]**ce·les·tial** \sə-ˈles(h)-chəl\ *adj* [ME, fr. MF, fr. L *caelestis* celestial, fr. *caelum* sky; akin to Skt *citra* bright] **1 :** of, relating to, or suggesting heaven **2 :** of or relating to the sky or visible heavens ⟨a ~ body⟩ **3 a :** ETHEREAL, OTHERWORLDLY **b :** OLYMPIAN, SUPREME **4** [*Celestial* Empire, old name for China] *cap* **:** of or relating to China or the Chinese — **ce·les·tial·ly** \-chə-lē\ *adv*

[2]**celestial** *n* **1 :** a heavenly or mythical being **2** *cap* **:** CHINESE 1

celestial equator *n* **:** the great circle on the celestial sphere midway between the celestial poles

celestial globe *n* **:** a globe depicting the celestial bodies

celestial marriage *n* **:** marriage solemnized in a Mormon temple for eternity

celestial navigation *n* **:** navigation by observation of the positions of celestial bodies

celestial pole *n* **:** one of the two points on the celestial sphere around which the diurnal rotation of the stars appears to take place

celestial sphere *n* **:** an imaginary sphere of infinite radius against which the celestial bodies appear to be projected and of which the apparent dome of the visible sky forms half

ce·les·tite \ˈsel-ə-ˌstīt, sə-ˈles-ˌtīt\ *n* [G *zölestin*, fr. L *caelestis*] **:** a usu. white mineral $SrSO_4$ consisting of strontium sulfate

ce·li·ac disease \ˈsē-lē-ˌak-\ *n* **:** a chronic nutritional disturbance in young children characterized by defective digestion and utilization of fats and by abdominal distention, diarrhea, and fatty stools

cel·i·ba·cy \ˈsel-ə-bə-sē\ *n* **1 :** the state of not being married **2 a :** abstention from sexual intercourse **b :** abstention by vow from marriage

cel·i·bate \ˈsel-ə-bət\ *n* [L *caelibatus*, fr. *caelib-*, *caelebs* unmarried; akin to Skt *kevala* alone and to OE *libban* to live] **:** one who lives in celibacy — **celibate** *adj*

cell \ˈsel\ *n* [ME, fr. OE, religious house and OF *celle* hermit's cell, fr. L *cella* small room; akin to L *celare* to conceal — more at HELL] **1 :** a small religious house dependent on a monastery or convent **2 a :** a one-room dwelling occupied by a solitary person (as a hermit) **b :** a single room usu. for one person (as in a convent or prison) **3 :** a small compartment (as in a honeycomb), receptacle (as the calyculus of a polyp), cavity (as in a plant ovary), or bounded space (as in an insect wing) **4 :** a small usu. microscopic mass of protoplasm bounded externally by a semipermeable membrane, usu. including one or more nuclei and various nonliving products, capable alone or interacting with other cells of performing all the fundamental functions of life, and forming the least structural aggregate of living matter capable of functioning as an independent unit **5 :** a receptacle (as a cup or jar) containing electrodes and an electrolyte either for generating electricity by chemical action or for use in electrolysis **6 :** a set of points in one-to-one correspondence with a set in a euclidean space of any number of dimensions **7 :** the basic and usu. smallest unit of an organization or movement; *esp* **:** the primary unit of a Communist organization **8 :** a portion of the atmosphere that behaves as a unit **9 :** a single unit in a device for converting radiant energy into electrical energy or for varying the intensity of an electrical current in accordance with radiation — **celled** \ˈseld\ *adj*

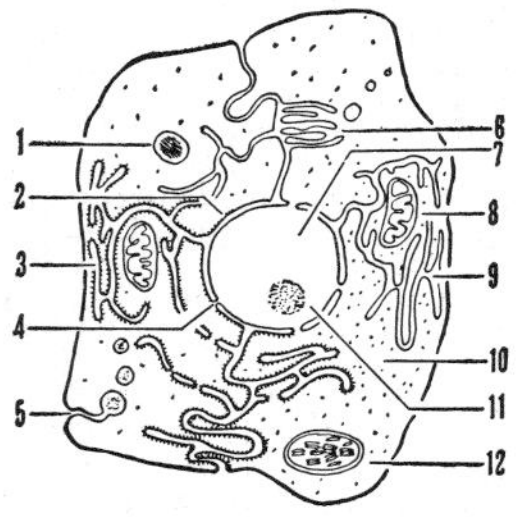

a schematic cell: *1* lysosome, *2* nuclear membrane, *3* endoplasmic reticulum with associated ribosomes, *4* nuclear pore, *5* intrusion of cell membrane, *6* Golgi apparatus, *7* nucleus, *8* mitochondrion, *9* endoplasmic reticulum, *10* cytoplasm and ribosomes, *11* nucleolus, *12* chloroplast

cel·lar \ˈsel-ər\ *n* [ME *celer*, fr. AF, fr. L *cellarium* storeroom, fr. *cella*] **1 a :** BASEMENT **b :** the lowest rank **2 :** a stock of wines

cel·lar·age \ˈsel-ə-rij\ *n* **1 :** a cellar esp. for storage **2 :** charge for storage in a cellar

cel·lar·er \ˈsel-ər-ər\ *n* [ME *celerer*, fr. OF, fr. LL *cellariarius*, fr. L *cellarium*] **:** an official (as in a monastery) in charge of provisions

cel·lar·ette *or* **cel·lar·et** \ˌsel-ə-ˈret\ *n* **:** a case or sideboard for a few bottles of wine or liquor

cel·list \ˈchel-əst\ *n* **:** one that plays the cello

cell membrane *n* **1 :** PLASMA MEMBRANE **2 :** a cell wall

cel·lo \ˈchel-(ˌ)ō\ *n* [short for *violoncello*] **:** the bass member of the violin family tuned an octave below the viola

cel·loi·din \se-ˈlȯid-ᵊn\ *n* [*cell*ulose + *-oid* + *-in*] **:** a purified pyroxylin used chiefly in microscopy

cel·lo·phane \ˈsel-ə-ˌfān\ *n* [F, fr. *cellulose* + *-phane* (as in *diaphane* diaphanous, fr. ML *diaphanus*)] **:** a transparent tissue of regenerated cellulose used chiefly for packaging

cel·lu·lar \ˈsel-yə-lər\ *adj* [NL *cellularis*, fr. *cellula* living cell, fr. L, dim. of *cella* small room] **1 :** of, relating to, or consisting of cells **2 :** containing cavities **:** having a porous texture — **cel·lu·lar·i·ty** \ˌsel-yə-ˈlar-ət-ē\ *n* — **cel·lu·lar·ly** \ˈsel-yə-lər-lē\ *adv*

cel·lu·lase \ˈsel-yə-ˌlās, -ˌlāz\ *n* [ISV *cellul*ose + *-ase*] **:** an enzyme that hydrolyzes cellulose

cel·lule \ˈsel-(ˌ)yü(ə)l\ *n* [L *cellula*] **:** a small cell

cel·lu·li·tis \ˌsel-yə-ˈlīt-əs\ *n* [NL, fr. *cellula*] **:** diffuse and esp. subcutaneous inflammation of connective tissue

cel·lu·loid \ˈsel-(y)ə-ˌlȯid\ *n* [fr. *Celluloid*, a trademark] **:** motion-picture film — **celluloid** *adj*

Celluloid *trademark* — used for a tough flammable thermoplastic composed essentially of cellulose nitrate and camphor

cel·lu·lose \ˈsel-yə-ˌlōs, -ˌlōz\ *n* [F, fr. *cellule* living cell, fr. NL *cellula*] **:** a complex polymeric carbohydrate $(C_6H_{10}O_5)_x$ yielding only glucose on complete hydrolysis, constituting the chief part of the cell walls of plants, and yielding many fibrous products

cellulose acetate *n* **:** any of several compounds insoluble in water formed esp. by the action of acetic acid, anhydride of acetic acid, and sulfuric acid on cellulose and used for making textile fibers, packaging sheets, photographic films, and varnishes

cellulose nitrate *n* **:** any of several esters of nitric acid formed by the action of nitric acid on cellulose (as paper, linen, or cotton) and used for making explosives, plastics, rayon, and varnishes

[1]**cel·lu·los·ic** \ˌsel-yə-ˈlō-sik, -zik\ *adj* **:** of, relating to, or made from cellulose ⟨~ fibers⟩

[2]**cellulosic** *n* **:** a substance made or derived from cellulose

Cel·si·us \ˈsel-sē-əs, -shəs\ *adj* [Anders *Celsius* †1744 Sw astronomer] **:** CENTIGRADE ⟨10° ~⟩

celt \ˈselt\ *n* [LL *celtis* chisel] **:** a prehistoric stone or metal implement shaped like a chisel or ax head

Celt \ˈselt, ˈkelt\ *n* [F *Celte*, sing. of *Celtes*, fr. L *Celtae*] **1 :** a member of a division of the early Indo-European peoples distributed from the British Isles and Spain to Asia Minor **2 :** a modern Gael, Highland Scot, Irishman, Welshman, Cornishman, or Breton

[1]**Celt·ic** \ˈsel-tik, ˈkel-\ *adj* **:** of, relating to, or characteristic of the Celts or their languages

[2]**Celtic** *n* **:** a group of languages closely related to the Italic, usu. subdivided into Brythonic and Goidelic, and confined to Brittany, Wales, western Ireland, and the Scottish Highlands

Celtic cross *n* — see CROSS illustration

Celt·i·cist \ˈsel-tə-səst, ˈkel-\ *n* **:** a specialist in Celtic languages or cultures

cem·ba·lo \ˈchem-bə-ˌlō\ *n* [It] **:** HARPSICHORD

[1]**ce·ment** \si-ˈment\ *n* [ME *sement*, fr. OF *ciment*, fr. L *caementum* stone chips used in making mortar, fr. *caedere* to cut — more at CONCISE] **1 :** a powder of alumina, silica, lime, iron oxide, and magnesia burned together in a kiln and finely pulverized and used as an ingredient of mortar and concrete **2 :** a binding element or agency: as **a :** a substance to make objects adhere to each other **b :** a notion or feeling serving to unite firmly **3 :** CEMENTUM **4 :** a plastic composition usu. made of zinc, copper, or silica for filling dental cavities **5 :** the fine-grained groundmass or glass of a porphyry

[2]**cement** *vt* **1 :** to unite by or as if by cement **2 :** to overlay with concrete ~ *vi* **:** to become cemented — **cement·er** *n*

ce·men·ta·tion \ˌsē-ˌmen-ˈtā-shən\ *n* **1 a :** the act or process of cementing **b :** the state of being cemented **2 :** a process of surrounding a solid with a powder and heating the whole so that the solid is changed by chemical combination with the powder

ce·ment·ite \si-ˈment-ˌīt\ *n* [[1]*cement*] **:** a hard brittle iron carbide Fe_3C in steel, cast iron, and iron-carbon alloys

ce·men·ti·tious \ˌsē-ˌmen-ˈtish-əs\ *adj* **:** having the properties of cement

ce·men·tum \si-ˈment-əm\ *n* [NL, fr. L *caementum*] **:** a specialized external bony layer of the part of a tooth normally within the gum

cem·e·tery \ˈsem-ə-ˌter-ē\ *n* [ME *cimitery*, fr. MF *cimitere*, fr. LL *coemeterium*, fr. Gk *koimētērion* sleeping chamber, burial place, fr. *koiman* to put to sleep; akin to L *cunae* cradle] **:** a burial ground

cen- *or* **ceno-** *or* **caen-** *or* **caeno-** *comb form* [Gk *kain-*, *kaino-*, fr. *kainos* — more at RECENT] **:** new **:** recent ⟨*Cenozoic*⟩

-cene \ˌsēn\ *adj comb form* [Gk *kainos*] **:** recent — in names of geologic periods ⟨*Eocene*⟩

cen·o·bite \ˈsen-ə-ˌbīt\ *n* [LL *coenobita*, fr. *coenobium* monastery, fr. LGk *koinobion*, deriv. of Gk *koin-* coen- + *bios* life — more at QUICK] **:** a member of a religious group living in common — **cen·o·bit·ic** \ˌsen-ə-ˈbit-ik\ *or* **cen·o·bit·i·cal** \-i-kəl\ *adj*

ce·no·gen·e·sis \ˌsē-nə-ˈjen-ə-səs, ˌsen-ə-\ *n* [G *zänogenesis*, fr. *zän-* cen- + L *genesis*] **:** introduction during development of adaptive characters absent from the earlier phylogeny of a strain — **ce·no·ge·net·ic** \-jə-ˈnet-ik\ *adj* — **ce·no·ge·net·i·cal·ly** \-i-k(ə-)lē\ *adv*

ce·no·spe·cies \ˌsē-nə-ˈspē-(ˌ)shēz, -(ˌ)sēz\ *n* **1 :** the sum of the possible expressions of a complex genotype **2 :** a group of biological units capable by reason of closely related genotypes of essentially free gene interchange

ceno·taph \ˈsen-ə-ˌtaf\ *n* [F *cénotaphe*, fr. L *cenotaphium*, fr. Gk *kenotaphion*, fr. *kenos* empty + *taphos* tomb; akin to Arm *sin* empty — more at EPITAPH] **:** a tomb or a monument erected in honor of a person whose body is elsewhere

ce·no·te \si-ˈnōt-ē\ *n* [Sp, fr. Maya *tzonot*] **:** a deep sinkhole in limestone having a pool at the bottom found esp. in Yucatán

Ce·no·zo·ic \ˌsē-nə-ˈzō-ik, ˌsen-ə-\ *adj* **:** of, relating to, or being an era of geological history that extends from the beginning of the Tertiary period to the present time and is marked by a rapid evolution of mammals and birds and of grasses, shrubs, and higher flowering plants and by little change in the invertebrates; *also* **:** relating to the system of rocks formed in this era — **Cenozoic** *n*

cense \ˈsen(t)s\ *vt* [ME *censen*, prob. short for *encensen* to incense, fr. MF *encenser*, fr. LL *incensare*, fr. *incensum* incense] **:** to perfume esp. with a censer

cen·ser \ˈsen(t)-sər\ *n* **:** a vessel for burning incense; *esp* **:** a covered incense burner swung on chains in a religious ritual

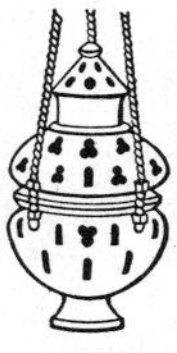
censer

¹**cen·sor** \ˈsen(t)-sər\ *n* [L, fr. *censēre* to assess, tax; akin to Skt *śaṁsati* he recites] **1 :** one of two magistrates of early Rome acting as census takers, assessors, and inspectors of morals and conduct **2 a :** an official who examines publications for objectionable matter **b :** an official who reads communications and deletes forbidden material **3** *archaic* **:** a faultfinding critic **4 :** the psychic agency that represses unacceptable notions before they reach consciousness — **cen·so·ri·al** \sen-ˈsōr-ē-əl, -ˈsȯr-\ *adj*

²**censor** *vt* **cen·sor·ing** \ˈsen(t)s-(ə-)riŋ\ **:** to subject to censorship

cen·so·ri·ous \sen-ˈsōr-ē-əs, -ˈsȯr-\ *adj* [L *censorius* of a censor, fr. *censor*] **:** marked by or given to censure **syn** see CRITICAL — **cen·so·ri·ous·ly** *adv* — **cen·so·ri·ous·ness** *n*

cen·sor·ship \ˈsen(t)-sər-ˌship\ *n* **1 :** the institution, system, or practice of censoring or censors **2 :** the office, power, or term of a Roman censor **3 :** exclusion from consciousness by the psychic censor

cen·sur·able \ˈsench-(ə-)rə-bəl\ *adj* **:** deserving or open to censure

¹**cen·sure** \ˈsen-chər\ *n* [L *censura*, fr. *censēre*] **1 :** a judgment involving condemnation **2** *archaic* **:** OPINION, JUDGMENT **3 :** the act of blaming or condemning sternly **4 :** an official reprimand

²**censure** *vt* **cen·sur·ing** \ˈsench-(ə-)riŋ\ **1** *obs* **:** ESTIMATE, JUDGE **2 :** to find fault with and criticize as blameworthy **syn** see CRITICIZE — **cen·sur·er** \ˈsen-chər-ər\ *n*

cen·sus \ˈsen(t)-səs\ *n* [L, fr. *censēre*] **1 :** a count of the population and a property evaluation in early Rome **2 :** a periodic governmental enumeration of population **3 :** COUNT, TALLY — **census** *vt*

cent \ˈsent\ *n* [MF, hundred, fr. L *centum* — more at HUNDRED] **1 :** a unit of value equal to 1/100 part of a basic monetary unit (as in the U.S. and Canada 1/100 dollar) — see MONEY table **2 :** a coin, token, or note representing one cent

cen·tal \ˈsent-ᵊl\ *n* [L *centum* + E *-al* (as in *quintal*)] *chiefly Brit* **:** a short hundredweight

cent·are \ˈsen-ˌta(ə)r, -ˌte(ə)r, -ˌtär\ *or* **cen·ti·are** \ˈsent-ē-ˌa(ə)r, -ˌe(ə)r, -ˌär\ *n* [F *centiare*, fr. *centi-* hundred + *are*] — see METRIC SYSTEM table

cen·taur \ˈsen-ˌtȯ(ə)r\ *n* [ME, fr. L *Centaurus*, fr. Gk *Kentauros*] **1 :** one of a race fabled to be half man and half horse and to dwell in the mountains of Thessaly **2** *cap* **:** CENTAURUS

cen·tau·rea \sen-ˈtȯr-ē-ə\ *n* [NL, genus name, fr. ML] **:** any of a large genus (*Centaurea*) of composite herbs including several cultivated for their showy heads of tubular florets

Cen·tau·rus \-ˈtȯr-əs\ *n* [L (gen. *Centauri*)] **:** a southern constellation between the Southern Cross and Hydra

cen·tau·ry \ˈsen-ˌtȯr-ē\ *n* [ME *centaure*, fr. MF *centaurée*, fr. ML *centaurea*, fr. L *centaureum*, fr. Gk *kentaureion*, fr. *Kentauros*] **1 a :** any of a genus (*Centaurium*) of low herbs of the gentian family; *esp* **:** an Old World herb (*C. umbellatum*) formerly used as a tonic **b :** a related American plant (genus *Sabatia*) **2 :** KNAPWEED

¹**cen·ta·vo** \sen-ˈtäv-(ˌ)ō\ *n* [Sp] **1 :** a unit of value equal to 1/100 part of a basic monetary unit (as in the Mexican peso) — see MONEY table **2 :** a coin representing one centavo

²**cen·ta·vo** \-ˈtäv-(ˌ)ü, -(ˌ)ō\ *n* [Pg, fr. Sp] — see *cruzeiro*, *escudo* at MONEY table

cen·te·nar·i·an \ˌsent-ᵊn-ˈer-ē-ən\ *n* **:** one that is 100 years old or older — **centenarian** *adj*

cen·te·na·ry \sen-ˈten-ə-rē, ˈsent-ᵊn-ˌer-ē\ *adj or n* [LL *centenarium*, fr. L *centenarius* of a hundred, fr. *centeni* one hundred each, fr. *centum* hundred — more at HUNDRED] **:** CENTENNIAL

cen·ten·ni·al \sen-ˈten-ē-əl\ *n* [L *centum* + E *-ennial* (as in *biennial*)] **:** a 100th anniversary or its celebration — **centennial** *adj* — **cen·ten·ni·al·ly** \-ə-lē\ *adv*

¹**cen·ter** *or chiefly Brit* **cen·tre** \ˈsent-ər\ *n* [ME *centre*, fr. MF, fr. L *centrum*, fr. Gk *kentron* sharp point, center of a circle, fr. *kentein* to prick; akin to OHG *hantag* pointed, Latvian *sīts* hunting spear] **1 :** the point equidistant or at the average distance from the exterior points of a circle, sphere, or other geometric figure **2 a :** a place in or around which an activity concentrates or from which something originates ⟨propaganda ~⟩ **b :** a group of nerve cells having a common function ⟨respiratory ~⟩ **c :** a region of concentrated population **3 a :** a middle part (as of an army or stage) **b** *often cap* (1) **:** political figures holding moderate views esp. between those of conservatives and liberals (2) **:** the views of such politicians (3) **:** adherents of such views **4 :** a player occupying a middle position on a team **5 a :** one of two tapered rods which support work in a lathe or grinding machine and about or with which the work revolves **b :** a conical recess in the end of work (as a shaft) for receiving such a center

²**center** *or chiefly Brit* **centre** *vt* **cen·ter·ing** \ˈsent-ə-riŋ, ˈsen-triŋ\ **1 :** to place or fix at or around a center or central area or position **2 :** to gather to a center **:** CONCENTRATE **3 :** to adjust (as lenses) so that the axes coincide ~ *vi* **:** to have a center

center bit *n* **:** a bit with a sharp center point for guidance, a scorer for marking the outline of the hole, and a lip for cutting away the wood inside the hole

cen·ter·board \ˈsent-ər-ˌbō(ə)rd, -ˌbȯ(ə)rd\ *n* **:** a retractable keel used esp. in sailboats

center field *n* **1 :** the part of the baseball outfield between right and left field **2 :** the position of the player for defending center field — **center fielder** *n*

center of gravity **1 :** CENTER OF MASS **2 :** the single point in a body toward which every particle of matter external to the body is gravitationally attracted **3 :** CENTER 2a

center of mass : the point that represents the mean position of the matter in a body — called also *center of inertia*

cen·ter·piece \ˈsent-ər-ˌpēs\ *n* **:** an object occupying a central position; *specif* **:** an adornment in the center of a table

center punch *n* **:** a hand punch consisting of a short steel bar with a hardened conical point at one end used for marking the centers of holes to be drilled

cen·tes·i·mal \sen-ˈtes-ə-məl\ *adj* [L *centesimus* hundredth, fr. *centum*] **:** marked by or relating to division into hundredths

¹**cen·tes·i·mo** \chen-ˈtez-ə-ˌmō\ *n, pl* **cen·tes·i·mi** \-(ˌ)mē\ [It] — see *lira* at MONEY table

²**cen·tes·i·mo** \sen-ˈtes-ə-ˌmō\ *n* [Sp *centésimo*] — see *balboa*, *escudo*, *peso* at MONEY table

centi- *comb form* [F&L; F, hundredth, fr. L, hundred, fr. *centum* — more at HUNDRED] **1 :** hundred ⟨*centi*pede⟩ **2 :** hundredth part ⟨*centi*meter⟩

cen·ti·grade \ˈsent-ə-ˌgrād, ˈsänt-\ *adj* [F, fr. L *centi-* hundred + F *grade*] **:** relating, conforming to, or having a thermometric scale on which the interval between the freezing point and the boiling point of water is divided into 100 degrees with 0° representing the freezing point and 100° the boiling point ⟨10° ~⟩

cen·ti·gram \-ˌgram\ *n* — see METRIC SYSTEM table

cen·ti·li·ter \-ˌlēt-ər\ *n* — see METRIC SYSTEM table

cen·til·lion \sen-ˈtil-yən\ *n, often attrib* [L *centum* + E *-illion* (as in *million*)] — see NUMBER table

cen·time \ˈsän-ˌtēm, ˈsen-\ *n* [F, fr. *cent* hundred, fr. L *centum*] — see *franc*, *gourde* at MONEY table

cen·ti·me·ter \ˈsent-ə-ˌmēt-ər, ˈsänt-\ *n* — see METRIC SYSTEM table

centimeter–gram–second *adj* **:** of, relating to, or being a system of units based upon the centimeter as the unit of length, the gram as the unit of mass, and the mean solar second as the unit of time

cen·ti·mo \ˈsent-ə-ˌmō\ *n* [Sp] — see *bolivar*, *colon*, *guarani*, *peseta* at MONEY table

cen·ti·pede \ˈsent-ə-ˌpēd\ *n* [L *centipeda*, fr. *centi-* + *ped-*, *pes* foot — more at FOOT] **:** any of a class (Chilopoda) of long flattened many-segmented predaceous arthropods with each segment bearing one pair of legs of which the foremost pair is modified into poison fangs

cent·ner \ˈsent-nər\ *n* [prob. fr. LG] **:** any of various units of weight used in Germany and Scandinavia corresponding to the hundredweight ⟨a ~ of 110.23 pounds⟩

cen·to \ˈsen-(ˌ)tō\ *n, pl* **cen·to·nes** \sen-ˈtō-(ˌ)nēz\ [LL, fr. L, patchwork garment; akin to OHG *hadara* rag, Skt *kanthā* patched garment] **:** a literary work made up of parts from other works

centr- *or* **centri-** *or* **centro-** *comb form* [Gk *kentr-*, *kentro-*, fr. *kentron* center — more at CENTER] **:** center ⟨*centri*fugal⟩ ⟨*centr*oid⟩

¹**cen·tral** \ˈsen-trəl\ *adj* [L *centralis*, fr. *centrum* center — more at CENTER] **1 :** containing or constituting a center **2 :** ESSENTIAL, PRINCIPAL **3 :** situated at, in, or near the center **4 a :** centrally placed and superseding separate scattered units ⟨~ heating⟩ **b :** controlling or directing local or branch activities **5 :** holding to a middle between extremes **:** MODERATE **6 :** of, relating to, or comprising the brain and spinal cord; *also* **:** originating within the central nervous system ⟨~ deafness⟩ — **cen·tral·ly** \-trə-lē\ *adv*

²**central** *n* **:** a telephone exchange or operator

cen·tral·ism \ˈsen-trə-ˌliz-əm\ *n* **:** the concentration of power and control in the central authority of a political system or other organization — compare FEDERALISM — **cen·tral·ist** \-ləst\ *n or adj* — **cen·tral·is·tic** \ˌsen-trə-ˈlis-tik\ *adj*

cen·tral·i·ty \sen-ˈtral-ət-ē\ *n* **1 :** the quality or state of being central **2 :** central situation **3 :** tendency to remain in the center

cen·tral·iza·tion \ˌsen-trə-lə-ˈzā-shən\ *n* **:** the act or process of centralizing

cen·tral·ize \ˈsen-trə-ˌlīz\ *vt* **:** to concentrate by placing power and authority in a center or central organization — **cen·tral·iz·er** *n*

central time *n, often cap C* **:** the time of the 6th time zone west of Greenwich that includes the central U.S.

cen·tric \ˈsen-trik\ *adj* [Gk *kentrikos* of the center, fr. *kentron*] **1 :** located in or at a center **:** CENTRAL **2 :** concentrated about or directed to a center **3 :** of or relating to a nerve center — **cen·tri·cal·ly** \-tri-k(ə-)lē\ *adv* — **cen·tric·i·ty** \sen-ˈtris-ət-ē\ *n*

-cen·tric \ˈsen-trik\ *adj comb form* [ML *-centricus*, fr. L *centrum* center] **:** having (such) a center or (such or so many) centers ⟨poly*centric*⟩ **:** having (something specified) as its center ⟨helio*centric*⟩

¹**cen·trif·u·gal** \sen-ˈtrif-yə-gəl, -ˈtrif-i-gəl\ *adj* [NL *centrifugus*, fr. *centr-* + L *fugere* to flee] **1 :** proceeding or acting in a direction away from a center or axis **2 :** using or acting by centrifugal force **3 :** EFFERENT — **cen·trif·u·gal·ly** \-gə-lē\ *adv*

²**centrifugal** *n* **:** a centrifugal machine or a drum in such a machine

centrifugal force *n* **:** the force that tends to impel a thing or parts of a thing outward from a center of rotation

cen·trif·u·ga·tion \(ˌ)sen-ˌtrif-(y)ə-ˈgā-shən, (ˌ)sän-\ *n* **:** the process of centrifuging

¹**cen·tri·fuge** \ˈsen-trə-ˌfyüj, ˈsän-\ *n* [F, fr. *centrifuge* centrifugal, fr. NL *centrifugus*] **:** a machine using centrifugal force for separating substances of different densities, for removing moisture, or for simulating gravitational effects

²**centrifuge** *vt* **:** to subject to centrifugal action esp. in a centrifuge

cen·tri·ole \ˈsen-trē-ˌōl\ *n* [G *zentriol*, fr. *zentrum* center] **1 :** a minute body forming the center of a centrosome **2 :** CENTROSOME 1

cen·trip·e·tal \sen-ˈtrip-ət-ᵊl\ *adj* [NL *centripetus*, fr. *centr-* + L *petere* to go to, seek] **1 :** proceeding or acting in a direction toward a center or axis **2 :** AFFERENT — **cen·trip·e·tal·ly** \-ᵊl-ē\ *adv*

centripetal force *n* **:** the force that tends to impel a thing or parts of a thing inward toward a center of rotation

cen·trist \ˈsen-trəst\ *n* **1** *often cap* **:** a member of a center party **2 :** one who holds moderate views

cen·troid \ˈsen-ˌtrȯid\ *n* **:** CENTER OF MASS — **cen·troi·dal** \sen-ˈtrȯid-ᵊl\ *adj*

cen·tro·mere \ˈsen-trə-ˌmi(ə)r\ *n* [ISV] **:** the point on a chromosome by which it appears to attach to the spindle in mitosis — **cen·tro·mer·ic** \ˌsen-trə-ˈmer-ik, -ˈmir-\ *adj*

cen·tro·some \ˈsen-trə-ˌsōm\ *n* [G *zentrosom*, fr. *zentr-* centr- + *-som* -some] **1 :** a minute protoplasmic body sometimes held to be the dynamic center of mitotic activity **2 :** CENTRIOLE 1 — **cen-**

tro·so·mic \ˌsen-trə-ˈsō-mik\ *adj*

cen·tro·sphere \ˈsen-trə-ˌsfi(ə)r\ *n* [ISV] **1 :** the differentiated layer of cytoplasm surrounding the centriole within the centrosome **2 :** the central part of the earth

cen·trum \ˈsen-trəm\ *n, pl* **centrums** *or* **cen·tra** \-trə\ [L — more at CENTER] **1 :** CENTER **2 :** the body of a vertebra

cen·tum \ˈkent-əm, ˈken-ˌtu̇m\ *adj* [L, hundred; fr. the fact that its initial sound (a velar stop) is the representative of an IE palatal stop] **:** of, relating to, or constituting that part of the Indo-European language family in which the palatal stops did not in prehistoric times become palatal or alveolar fricatives

cen·tu·ri·on \sen-ˈt(y)u̇r-ē-ən\ *n* [ME, fr. MF & L; MF, fr. L *centurion-, centurio,* fr. *centuria*] **:** an officer commanding a Roman century

cen·tu·ry \ˈsench-(ə-)rē\ *n* [L *centuria,* irreg. fr. *centum* hundred] **1 :** a subdivision of the Roman legion **2 :** a group, sequence, or series of 100 like things **3 :** a period of 100 years esp. of the Christian era or of the preceding period

century plant *n* **:** a Mexican agave (*Agave americana*) maturing and flowering only once in many years and then dying

ceorl \ˈchā-ˌȯr(ə)l\ *n* [OE — more at CHURL] **:** a freeman of the lowest rank in Anglo-Saxon England

cephal- *or* **cephalo-** *comb form* [L, fr. Gk *kephal-, kephalo-,* fr. *kephalē*] **:** head ⟨*cephal*ad⟩ ⟨*Cephalo*poda⟩

ceph·a·lad \ˈsef-ə-ˌlad\ *adv* **:** toward the head or anterior end of the body

ce·phal·ic \sə-ˈfal-ik\ *adj* [MF *céphalique,* fr. L *cephalicus,* fr. Gk *kephalikos,* fr. *kephalē* head; akin to OHG *gebal* skull, ON *gafl* gable, Toch A *śpāl-* head] **1 :** of or relating to the head **2 :** directed toward or situated on or in or near the head — **ce·phal·i·cal·ly** \-i-k(ə-)lē\ *adv*

cephalic index *n* **:** the ratio multiplied by 100 of the maximum breadth of the head to its maximum length

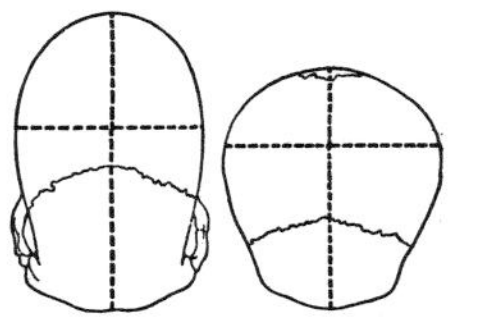

cephalic index: dotted lines in the brachycephalic (right) and dolichocephalic (left) skulls above indicate measurements taken

ceph·a·lin \ˈsef-ə-lən\ *n* [ISV] **:** any of various acidic phosphatides of living tissues (as of the brain) with marked thromboplastic activity

ceph·a·li·za·tion \ˌsef-ə-lə-ˈzā-shən\ *n* **:** an evolutionary tendency to specialization of the body with concentration of sensory and neural organs in an anterior head

ceph·a·lom·e·try \ˌsef-ə-ˈläm-ə-trē\ *n* [ISV] **:** the science of measuring the head

ceph·a·lo·pod \ˈsef-ə-lə-ˌpäd\ *n* [deriv. of *cephal-* + Gk *pod-, pous* foot — more at FOOT] **:** any of a class (Cephalopoda) of mollusks including the squids, cuttlefishes, and octopuses, having a tubular siphon under the head, around the front of the head a group of muscular arms usu. furnished with suckers, highly developed eyes, and usu. a bag of inky fluid which they can eject from their siphons — **cephalopod** *adj* — **ceph·a·lop·o·dan** \ˌsef-ə-ˈläp-əd-ən\ *adj or n*

ceph·a·lo·tho·rax \ˌsef-ə-lō-ˈthō(ə)r-ˌaks, -ˈthȯ(ə)r-\ *n* [ISV] **:** the united head and thorax of an arachnid or higher crustacean

Ce·phe·id \ˈsē-fē-əd, ˈsef-ē-\ *n* **:** one of a class of pulsating stars whose intrinsic light variations are very regular

Ce·pheus \ˈsē-ˌfyüs, -fē-əs\ *n* [L (gen. *Cephei*), fr. Gk *Kēpheus*] **:** a constellation between Cygnus and the north pole

ce·ra·ceous \sə-ˈrā-shəs\ *adj* [L *cera* wax] **:** resembling wax

ce·ram·al \sə-ˈram-əl\ *n* [*ceram*ic + *al*loy] **:** CERMET

1**ce·ram·ic** \sə-ˈram-ik\ *adj* [Gk *keramikos,* fr. *keramos* potter's clay, pottery] **:** of or relating to the manufacture of any product (as earthenware, porcelain, brick, glass, vitreous enamels) made essentially from a nonmetallic mineral by firing at high temperatures; *also* **:** of or relating to such a product

2**ceramic** *n* **1** *pl but sing in constr* **:** the art of making articles from clay by shaping and firing at high temperatures **2 :** a product of ceramic manufacture

ce·ra·mist \sə-ˈram-əst, ˈser-ə-məst\ *or* **ce·ram·i·cist** \sə-ˈram-ə-səst\ *n* **:** one who engages in ceramics

ce·ras·tes \sə-ˈras-(ˌ)tēz\ *n* [ME, fr. L, fr. Gk *kerastēs,* lit., horned, fr. *keras*] **:** a venomous viper (*Cerastes cornutus*) of the Near East having a horny process over each eye — called also *horned viper*

cerat- *or* **cerato-** *or* **kerat-** *or* **kerato-** *comb form* [NL, fr. Gk *kerat-, kerato-,* fr. *keras*] **:** horn **:** horny ⟨*Cerat*odus⟩ ⟨*kerat*in⟩

ce·rate \ˈsi(ə)r-ˌāt\ *n* [L *ceratum* wax salve, fr. *cera* wax] **:** an unctuous preparation for external use consisting of wax or resin or spermaceti mixed with oil, lard, and medicinal ingredients

ce·rat·odus \sə-ˈrat-əd-əs\ *n* [NL, genus name, fr. *cerat-* + Gk *odous* tooth — more at TOOTH] **:** any of various recent or fossil dipnoan fishes (as of the genus *Ceratodus*); *esp* **:** BARRAMUNDA

Cer·be·re·an \(ˌ)sər-ˈbir-ē-ən, ˌsər-bə-ˈrē-ən\ *adj* **:** of, relating to, or resembling Cerberus

Cer·ber·us \ˈsər-b(ə-)rəs\ *n* [L, fr. Gk *Kerberos*] **:** a 3-headed dog held in classical mythology to guard the entrance to Hades

-cer·cal \ˈsər-kəl\ *adj comb form* [F *-cerque,* fr. Gk *kerkos* tail] **:** -tailed ⟨homo*cercal*⟩

cer·car·ia \(ˌ)sər-ˈkar-ē-ə, -ˈker-\ *n, pl* **cer·car·i·ae** \-ē-ˌē\ *also* **cer·car·i·as** [NL, fr. Gk *kerkos* tail] **:** a usu. tadpole-shaped larval trematode worm produced in a molluscan host by a redia — **cer·car·i·al** \-ē-əl\ *adj*

cer·cis \ˈsər-səs\ *n* [NL, genus name, fr. Gk *kerkis* Judas tree] **:** any of a small genus (*Cercis*) of leguminous shrubs or low trees

1**cere** \ˈsi(ə)r\ *vt* [ME *ceren* to wax, fr. MF *cirer,* fr. L *cerare,* fr. *cera*] **:** to wrap in or as if in a cerecloth

2**cere** *n* [ME *sere,* fr. MF *cere,* fr. ML *cera,* fr. L, wax] **:** a usu. waxy protuberance or tumid area at the base of the bill of a bird

1**ce·re·al** \ˈsir-ē-əl\ *adj* [F or L; F *céréale,* fr. L *cerealis* of Ceres, of grain, fr. *Ceres*] **:** relating to grain or to the plants that produce it; *also* **:** made of grain

2**cereal** *n* **1 :** a plant (as a grass) yielding farinaceous grain suitable for food; *also* **:** its grain **2 :** a prepared foodstuff of grain

cer·e·bel·lar \ˌser-ə-ˈbel-ər\ *adj* **:** of or relating to the cerebellum

cer·e·bel·lum \ˌser-ə-ˈbel-əm\ *n, pl* **cerebellums** *or* **cer·e·bel·la** \-ˈbel-ə\ [ML, fr. L, dim. of *cerebrum*] **:** a large dorsally projecting part of the brain esp. concerned with the coordination of muscles and the maintenance of bodily equilibrium, situated anterior to and above the medulla which it partly overlaps, and formed in man of two lateral lobes and a median lobe

cerebr- *or* **cerebro-** *comb form* [*cerebrum*] **1 :** brain **:** cerebrum ⟨*cerebr*ation⟩ **2 :** cerebral and ⟨*cerebro*spinal⟩

ce·re·bral \sə-ˈrē-brəl, ˈser-ə-\ *adj* [F *cérébral,* fr. L *cerebrum* brain; akin to Gk *kara* head, *keras* horn — more at HORN] **1 a :** of or relating to the brain or the intellect **b :** of, relating to, or being the cerebrum **2 :** appealing to intellectual appreciation — **ce·re·bral·ly** \-brə-lē\ *adv*

cerebral accident *n* **:** a sudden damaging occurrence (as of hemorrhage) within the cerebrum — compare APOPLEXY

cerebral hemisphere *n* **:** either of the two hollow convoluted lateral halves of the cerebrum

cerebral palsy *n* **:** a disability resulting from damage to the brain before or during birth and outwardly manifested by muscular incoordination and speech disturbances

cer·e·brate \ˈser-ə-ˌbrāt\ *vi* [back-formation fr. *cerebration,* fr. *cerebrum*] **:** THINK — **cer·e·bra·tion** \ˌser-ə-ˈbrā-shən\ *n*

cer·e·bro·side \ˈser-ə-brō-ˌsīd\ *n* [*cerebrose* (galactose)] **:** any of various lipides found esp. in nerve tissue

ce·re·bro·spi·nal \sə-ˌrē-brō-ˈspīn-ᵊl, ˌser-ə-brō-\ *adj* **:** of or relating to the brain and spinal cord or to these together with the cranial and spinal nerves that innervate voluntary muscles

cerebrospinal fluid *n* **:** a liquid comparable to serum secreted from the blood into the lateral ventricles of the brain

cerebrospinal meningitis *n* **:** inflammation of the meninges of both brain and spinal cord; *specif* **:** an infectious epidemic often fatal meningitis caused by the meningococcus

ce·re·brum \sə-ˈrē-brəm, ˈser-ə-brəm\ *n, pl* **cerebrums** *or* **ce·re·bra** \-brə\ [L] **1 :** BRAIN 1a **2 :** an enlarged anterior or upper part of the brain: **a :** the forebrain and midbrain with their derivatives **b :** FOREBRAIN 2a **c :** the expanded anterior portion of the brain that in higher mammals overlies the rest of the brain, consists of cerebral hemispheres and connecting structures, and is held to be the seat of conscious mental processes **:** TELENCEPHALON

cere·cloth \ˈsi(ə)r-ˌklȯth\ *n* [alter. of earlier *cered cloth* (waxed cloth)] **:** cloth treated with melted wax or gummy matter and formerly used esp. for wrapping a dead body

cere·ment \ˈser-ə-mənt, ˈsi(ə)r-mənt\ *n* **:** a usu. waxed winding-sheet — usu. used in pl.

1**cer·e·mo·ni·al** \ˌser-ə-ˈmō-nē-əl\ *adj* **:** of, relating to, or forming a ceremony — **cer·e·mo·ni·al·ism** \-ə-ˌliz-əm\ *n* — **cer·e·mo·ni·al·ist** \-ə-ləst\ *n* — **cer·e·mo·ni·al·ly** \-ə-lē\ *adv*

syn CEREMONIOUS, FORMAL, CONVENTIONAL: CEREMONIAL and CEREMONIOUS both imply strict attention to what is prescribed by custom or by state or church ritual, but CEREMONIAL applies to things that are themselves ceremonies or an essential part of them ⟨a *ceremonial* offering⟩, CEREMONIOUS to persons addicted to ceremony or to acts attended by ceremony ⟨a *ceremonious* old man⟩ FORMAL applies both to things prescribed and to persons obedient to custom and may suggest stiff, restrained, or old-fashioned behavior; CONVENTIONAL implies accord with general custom and usage and may suggest a stodgy lack of originality or independence

2**ceremonial** *n* **:** a ceremonial act, action, or system

cer·e·mo·ni·ous \ˌser-ə-ˈmō-nē-əs\ *adj* **1 :** of, relating to, or constituting a ceremony **2 :** devoted to forms and ceremony **:** PUNCTILIOUS **3 :** according to formal usage or prescribed procedures **4 :** marked by ceremony **syn** see CEREMONIAL — **cer·e·mo·ni·ous·ly** *adv* — **cer·e·mo·ni·ous·ness** *n*

cer·e·mo·ny \ˈser-ə-ˌmō-nē\ *n* [ME *ceremonie,* fr. MF *cérémonie,* fr. L *caerimonia*] **1 :** a formal act or series of acts prescribed by ritual, protocol, or convention **2 a :** a conventional act of politeness or etiquette **b :** an action performed only formally with no deep significance **c :** a routine action performed with elaborate pomp **3 a :** prescribed procedures **:** USAGES **b :** observance of an established code of civility or politeness

Ce·res \ˈsi(ə)r-(ˌ)ēz\ *n* [L] **1 :** the goddess of agriculture in Roman mythology **2 :** the largest asteroid and the one first discovered

ce·re·us \ˈsir-ē-əs\ *n* [NL, genus name, fr. L, wax candle, fr. *cera* wax — more at CERUMEN] **:** any of various cacti (as of the genus *Cereus*) of the western U.S. and tropical America

ce·ric \ˈsi(ə)r-ik, ˈser-\ *adj* **:** of, relating to, or containing cerium

ce·rise \sə-ˈrēs, -ˈrēz\ *n* [F, lit., cherry, fr. LL *ceresia* — more at CHERRY] **:** a moderate red

ce·ri·um \ˈsir-ē-əm\ *n* [NL, fr. *Ceres*] **:** a malleable ductile metallic element that is the most abundant of the rare-earth group — see ELEMENT table

cerium metal *n* **:** any of a group of related rare-earth metals comprising cerium, lanthanum, praseodymium, neodymium, promethium, samarium, and sometimes europium

cer·met \ˈsər-ˌmet\ *n* [*cer*amic + *met*al] **:** a strong alloy of a heat-resistant compound (as titanium carbide) and a metal (as nickel) used esp. for turbine blades — called also *ceramal*

cer·nu·ous \ˈsər-nyə-wəs\ *adj* [L *cernuus* with the face turned earthward; akin to L *cerebrum*] **:** NODDING, PENDULOUS

cero \ˈse(ə)r-(ˌ)ō\ *n, pl* **cero** *or* **ceros** [modif. of Sp *sierra* saw, cero] **:** either of two large food and sport fishes (*Scomberomorus cavalia* and *S. regalis*) of the warmer parts of the western Atlantic ocean

ce·ro·tic acid \sə-ˌrōt-ik-, -ˌrät-\ *n* [L *cerotum,* a pomade, fr. Gk *kērōton,* fr. *kēros* wax — more at CERUMEN] **:** a solid fatty acid $C_{26}H_{52}O_2$ occurring in waxes (as beeswax) and some fats

ce·rous \ˈsir-əs\ *adj* **:** of, relating to, or containing cerium esp. in the trivalent state

1**cer·tain** \ˈsərt-ᵊn\ *adj* [ME, fr. OF, fr. (assumed) VL *certanus,* fr. L *certus,* fr. pp. of *cernere* to sift, discern, decide; akin to Gk *krinein* to separate, decide, judge, *keirein* to cut — more at SHEAR] **1 a :** FIXED, SETTLED **b :** proved to be true **2 :** of a specific but unspecified character **:** PARTICULAR **3 a :** DEPENDABLE, RELIABLE **b :** INDISPUTABLE **4 a :** INEVITABLE **b :** incapable of failing **:** DESTINED **5 :** assured in mind or action **syn** see SURE — **cer·tain·ly** \-lē\ *adv*

2**certain** *pron, pl in constr* **:** certain ones

cer·tain·ty \-tē\ *n* **1 :** something that is certain **2 :** the quality or state of being certain

syn CERTAINTY, CERTITUDE, ASSURANCE, CONVICTION mean a state of being free from doubt. CERTAINTY and CERTITUDE are very close, but CERTAINTY may stress the existence of objective unquestionable proofs, CERTITUDE may emphasize a faith strong enough to resist all attack; ASSURANCE implies confidence rather than intellectual certainty; CONVICTION applies esp. to belief strongly held by an in-

dividual and usu. concerned with moral or spiritual rather than factual matters
cer·tes \'sərt-ēz, 'sərts\ *adv* [ME, fr. OF, fr. *cert* certain, fr. L *certus*] *archaic* : CERTAINLY
cer·ti·fi·able \'sərt-ə-,fī-ə-bəl\ *adj* : capable of being certified — **cer·ti·fi·ably** \-blē\ *adv*
1**cer·tif·i·cate** \(,)sər-'tif-i-kət\ *n* [ME *certificat*, fr. MF, fr. ML *certificatum*, fr. LL, neut. of *certificatus*, pp. of *certificare* to certify] **1** : a document containing a certified statement esp. as to the truth; *specif* : a document certifying that one has fulfilled the requirements of and may practice in a field **2** : something serving the end of a certificate **3** : a document evidencing ownership or debt
2**cer·tif·i·cate** \-'tif-ə-,kāt\ *vt* : to testify to, furnish with, or authorize by a certificate — **cer·tif·i·ca·to·ry** \(,)sər-'tif-i-kə-,tōr-ē, -,tȯr-\ *adj*
cer·ti·fi·ca·tion \,sərt-ə-fə-'kā-shən\ *n* **1** : the act of certifying : the state of being certified **2** : a certified statement
certified check *n* : a check certified to be good by the bank upon which it is drawn
certified mail *n* : first class mail for which proof of delivery is secured but no indemnity value is claimed
certified milk *n* : milk produced in dairies that operate under the rules and regulations of an authorized medical milk commission
certified public accountant *n* : an accountant who has met the requirements of a state law and has been granted a state certificate
cer·ti·fi·er \'sərt-ə-,fī(-ə)r\ *n* : one that certifies
cer·ti·fy \'sərt-ə-,fī\ *vt* [ME *certifien*, fr. MF *certifier*, fr. LL *certificare*, fr. L *certus* certain] **1** : to attest authoritatively: as **a** : CONFIRM **b** : to present in formal communication **c** : to attest as being true or as represented or as meeting a standard **d** : to attest officially to the insanity of **2** : to inform with certainty **3** : to guarantee (a personal check) as to signature and amount by so indicating on the face **4** : CERTIFICATE, LICENSE **syn** see APPROVE
cer·tio·ra·ri \,sər-sh(ē-)ə-'re(ə)r-ē, -'rär-ē\ *n* [ME, fr. L, to be informed; fr. the use of the word in the writ] : a writ of a superior court to call up the records of an inferior court or a body acting in a quasi-judicial capacity
cer·ti·tude \'sərt-ə-,t(y)üd\ *n* [ME, fr. LL *certitudo*, fr. L *certus*] **1** : the state of being or feeling certain **2** : unfailingness of act or event **syn** see CERTAINTY
ce·ru·le·an \sə-'rü-lē-ən\ *adj* [L *caeruleus* dark blue] : somewhat resembling the blue of the sky
ce·ru·men \sə-'rü-mən\ *n* [NL, irreg. fr. L *cera* wax, prob. fr. Gk *kēros*; akin to Lith *korys* honeycomb] : the yellow waxy secretion from the glands of the external ear — called also *earwax* — **ce·ru·mi·nous** \-mə-nəs\ *adj*
ce·ruse \sə-'rüs, 'si(ə)r-,üs\ *n* [ME, fr. MF *céruse*, fr. L *cerussa*] **1** : white lead as a pigment **2** : a cosmetic containing white lead
ce·rus·site \sə-'rəs-,īt\ *n* [G *zerussit*, fr. L *cerussa*] : a mineral $PbCO_3$ consisting of lead carbonate occurring in colorless transparent crystals and also massive
cer·ve·lat \'sər-və-,lat, -,lä\ *n* [obs. F, (now *cervelas*)] : smoked sausage made of varying proportions of pork and beef
cer·vi·cal \'sər-vi-kəl\ *adj* : of or relating to a neck or cervix
cer·vi·ci·tis \,sər-və-'sīt-əs\ *n* : inflammation of the uterine cervix
cer·vine \'sər-,vīn\ *adj* [L *cervinus* of a deer, fr. *cervus* stag, deer — more at HART] : of, relating to, or resembling deer
cer·vix \'sər-viks\ *n, pl* **cer·vi·ces** \'sər-və-,sēz, (,)sər-'vī-(,)sēz\ *or* **cer·vix·es** [L *cervic-*, *cervix*] **1** : NECK; *esp* : the back part of the neck **2** : a constricted portion of an organ or part; *esp* : the narrow outer end of the uterus
ce·sar·e·an *or* **ce·sar·i·an** \si-'zar-ē-ən, -'zer-\ *n* [fr. the belief that Julius Caesar was born this way] : surgical incision of the walls of the abdomen and uterus for delivery of offspring — **cesarean** *or* **cesarian** *adj*
ce·si·um \'sē-zē-əm\ *n* [NL, fr. L *caesius* bluish gray] : a silver-white soft ductile element of the alkali metal group that is the most electropositive element known — see ELEMENT table
1**cess** \'ses\ *n* [ME *cessen* to tax, short for *assessen*] : LEVY, TAX
2**cess** *n* [prob. short for *success*] : LUCK ⟨bad ~ to you⟩
ces·sa·tion \se-'sā-shən\ *n* [ME *cessacioun*, fr. MF *cessation*, fr. L *cessation-*, *cessatio* delay, idleness, fr. *cessatus*, pp. of *cessare* to delay, be idle] : a temporary or final ceasing (as of action) : STOP
ces·sion \'sesh-ən\ *n* [ME, fr. MF, fr. L *cession-*, *cessio*, fr. *cessus*, pp. of *cedere* to withdraw] : a yielding to another : CONCESSION
cess·pit \'ses-,pit\ *n* [*cesspool* + *pit*] : a pit for the disposal of sewage and other refuse
cess·pool \-,pül\ *n* [by folk etymology fr. ME *suspiral* vent, cesspool, fr. MF *souspirail* ventilator, fr. *soupirer* to sigh, fr. L *suspirare*, lit., to draw a long breath — more at SUSPIRE] : an underground catch basin for household sewage or other liquid waste
ces·tode \'ses-,tōd\ *n* [deriv. of Gk *kestos* girdle] : any of a subclass (Cestoda) of internally parasitic flatworms comprising the tapeworms — **cestode** *adj*
1**ces·tus** \'ses-təs\ *n* [L, girdle, belt, fr. Gk *kestos*, fr. *kestos* stitched; akin to Gk *kentron* sharp point — more at CENTER] : a woman's belt; *esp* : a symbolic one worn by a bride
2**cestus** *n* [L *caestus*, fr. *caedere* to strike — more at CONCISE] : a boxer's hand covering in ancient Rome of leather bands often loaded with lead or iron
cesura *var of* CAESURA
ce·ta·cean \si-'tā-shən\ *n* [deriv. of L *cetus* whale, fr. Gk *kētos*] : any of an order (Cetacea) of aquatic mostly marine mammals including the whales, dolphins, porpoises, and related forms with large head, fishlike nearly hairless body, and paddle-shaped forelimbs — **cetacean** *adj* — **ce·ta·ceous** \-shəs\ *adj*
ce·tane \'sē-,tān\ *n* [fr. *cetyl* (the radical $C_{16}H_{33}$)] : a colorless oily hydrocarbon $C_{16}H_{34}$ found in petroleum and used as a standard of comparison in testing the ignition value of diesel fuels
ce·te·ris pa·ri·bus \,kāt-ə-rə-'spar-ə-bəs\ *adv* [NL, other things being equal] : if all other relevant things, factors, or elements remain unaltered
Ce·tus \'sēt-əs\ *n* [L (gen. *Ceti*), lit., whale] : an equatorial constellation south of Pisces and Aries
ce·vi·tam·ic acid \,sē-(,)vī-,tam-ik-\ *n* [*cee* + *vitamin*] : VITAMIN C
Cha·blis \'shab-,lē, sha-'blē\ *n, pl* **Cha·blis** \-,lēz, -'blēz\ [F, fr. *Chablis*, France] : a dry white Burgundy table wine
cha–cha \'chä-,chä\ *n* [AmerSp *cha-cha-cha*] : a fast rhythmic ballroom dance originating in Latin America
chac·ma \'chak-mə\ *n* [Hottentot] : a large dusky southern African baboon (*Papio comatus*)
Chad \'chad\ *n* : a branch of the Afro-Asiatic language family comprising numerous languages of northern Nigeria and Cameroons
chae·ta \'kēt-ə\ *n, pl* **chae·tae** \'kē-,tē\ [NL, fr. Gk *chaitē* long flowing hair] : BRISTLE, SETA — **chae·tal** \'kēt-ᵊl\ *adj*
chae·to·gnath \'kēt-,äg-,nath, -ə(g)-\ *n* [deriv. of Gk *chaitē* + *gnathos* jaw — more at GNATH-] : any of a class (Chaetognatha) of small free-swimming marine worms with movable curved chaetae on either side of the mouth — **chaetognath** *adj* — **chae·tog·na·than** \kē-'täg-nə-thən\ *adj or n*
1**chafe** \'chāf\ *vb* [ME *chaufen* to warm, fr. MF *chaufer*, fr. (assumed) VL *calfare*, alter. of L *calefacere*, fr. *calēre* to be warm + *facere* to make — more at LEE, DO] *vt* **1** : IRRITATE, VEX **2** : to warm by rubbing esp. with the hands **3 a** : to rub so as to wear away : ABRADE **b** : to make sore by or as if by rubbing ~ *vi* **1** : to feel irritation or discontent : FRET **2** : RUB, WEAR
2**chafe** *n* **1** : a state of vexation : RAGE **2** : injury or wear caused by friction; *also* : RUBBING, FRICTION
cha·fer \'chā-fər\ *n* [ME *cheaffer*, fr. OE *ceafor*; akin to OE *ceafl* jowl] : any of various large beetles (esp. family Scarabaeidae)
1**chaff** \'chaf\ *n* [ME *chaf*, fr. OE *ceaf*; akin to OHG *cheva* husk] **1** : the seed coverings and other debris separated from the seed in threshing grain **2** : something light and worthless **3** : the scales borne on the receptacle among the florets in the heads of many composite plants — **chaffy** \-ē\ *adj*
2**chaff** *n* [prob. fr. 1*chaff*] : light jesting talk : BANTER
3**chaff** *vb* : to tease good-naturedly : BANTER
1**chaf·fer** \'chaf-ər\ *n* [ME *chaffare*, fr. *chep* trade + *fare* journey] **1** *obs* : TRADE **2** *archaic* : a haggling about price : BARGAINING
2**chaffer** *vb* **chaf·fer·ing** \'chaf-(ə-)riŋ\ *vi* **1** *obs* : to engage in buying and selling : TRADE **2** : HAGGLE **3** *Brit* : to exchange small talk ~ *vt* **1** *obs* **a** : to engage in buying or selling **b** : EXCHANGE, BARTER **2** : to bargain for — **chaf·fer·er** \-ər-ər\ *n*
chaf·finch \'chaf-(,)inch\ *n* [ME, fr. OE *ceaffinc*, fr. *ceaf* + *finc* finch] : a European finch (*Fringilla coelebs*) of which the male has a reddish breast plumage and a cheerful song
chaf·ing dish \'chā-fiŋ-\ *n* [ME *chafing*, prp. of *chafen*] : a utensil for cooking food at the table
Cha·gas' disease \'shäg-əs-(əz-)\ *n* [Carlos *Chagas* †1934 Braz physician] : a tropical American trypanosomiasis
1**cha·grin** \shə-'grin\ *n* [F, fr. *chagrin* sad] : disquietude or distress of mind caused by humiliation, disappointment, or failure
2**chagrin** *vt* **cha·grined** \-'grind\ **cha·grin·ing** \-'grin-iŋ\ : to vex acutely by disappointing or humiliating : MORTIFY
1**chain** \'chān\ *n* [ME *cheyne*, fr. OF *chaeine*, fr. L *catena*; akin to L *cassis* net] **1 a** : a series of usu. metal links or rings connected to or fitted into one another and used for various purposes (as support, restraint, or transmission of mechanical power) **b** : a series of links used or worn as an ornament or insignia **c** (1) : a measuring instrument of 100 links used in surveying (2) : a unit of length equal to 66 feet **2** : something that confines, restrains, or secures **3 a** : a series of things linked, connected, or associated together **b** : a number of atoms united like links in a chain
2**chain** *vt* : to fasten, bind, or connect with a chain; *also* : FETTER
chain gang *n* : a gang of convicts chained together
chain letter *n* **1** : a social letter sent to a series of persons in succession and often added to by each **2** : a letter sent to several persons with a request that each send copies to an equal number
chain mail *n* : flexible armor of interlinked metal rings
chain·omat·ic \,chā-nə-'mat-ik\ *adj* [fr. *Chainomatic*, a trademark] *of a balance or scale* : having suspended from the beam an adjustable fine chain the length of which is measured to determine minute weights
chain–re·act \,chān-rē-'akt\ *vi* [back-formation fr. *chain reaction*] : to take part in or undergo chain reaction
chain–reacting pile *n* : REACTOR 3b
chain reaction *n* **1** : a series of events so related to each other that each one initiates the succeeding one **2** : a chemical or nuclear reaction yielding energy or products that cause further reactions of the same kind and so becoming self-sustaining
chain saw *n* : a portable power saw that has teeth linked together to form an endless chain
chain stitch *n* **1** : an ornamental stitch like the links of a chain **2** : a machine stitch forming a chain on the underside of the work
chain store *n* : a retail store that is a unit of a chain
1**chair** \'che(ə)r, 'cha(ə)r\ *n* [ME *chaiere*, fr. OF, fr. L *cathedra*, fr. Gk *kathedra*, fr. *kata-* cata- + *hedra* seat — more at SIT] **1 a** : a seat with four legs and a back for one person **b** : ELECTRIC CHAIR **2 a** : an official seat or a seat of authority, state, or dignity **b** : an office or position of authority or dignity **c** : CHAIRMAN **3** : a sedan chair **4** : any of various devices that hold up or support
2**chair** *vt* **1 a** : to place in a chair **b** : to install in office **2** *chiefly Brit* : to carry shoulder-high in acclaim **3** : to preside as chairman of
chair car *n* **1** : a railroad car having pairs of chairs with individually adjustable backs on each side of the aisle **2** : PARLOR CAR
1**chair·man** \-mən\ *n* **1** : the presiding officer of a meeting or an organization or committee **2** : a carrier of a sedan chair — **chair·man·ship** \-,ship\ *n* — **chair·wom·an** \-,wu̇m-ən\ *n*
2**chairman** *vt* **chair·maned** *or* **chair·manned**; **chair·man·ing** *or* **chair·man·ning** : to act as chairman of
chaise \'shāz\ *n* [F, chair, chaise, alter. of OF *chaiere*] **1 a** : a 2-wheeled carriage for one or two persons with a calash top and the body hung on leather straps and usu. drawn by one horse **b** : a similar 4-wheeled pleasure carriage **c** : POST CHAISE **2** : a light carriage or pleasure cart

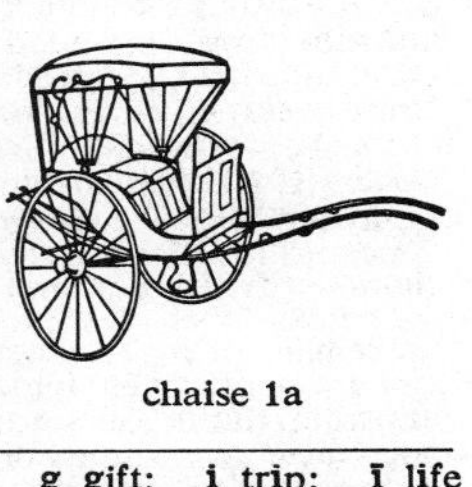
chaise 1a

chaise longue \'shāz-'lȯŋ\ *n, pl* **chaise longues** *also* **chaises longues** \'shāz-'lȯŋz\ [F *chaise longue*, lit., long chair] : a long reclining chair — called also *chaise lounge* \-'lau̇nj\

cha·la·za \kə-'lā-zə\ *n, pl* **cha·la·zae** \-,zē\ *or* **chalazas** [NL, fr. Gk, hailstone; akin to Per *zhāla* hail] **1 :** either of a pair of spiral bands in the white of a bird's egg that extend from the yolk and attach to opposite ends of the lining membrane **2 :** the point at the base of a plant ovule where the seed stalk is attached — **cha·la·zal** \-zəl\ *adj*

Chal·ce·do·ni·an \,kal-sə-'dō-nē-ən\ *adj* **:** of or relating to Chalcedon or the ecumenical council held there in A.D. 451 declaring Monophysitism heretical — **Chalcedonian** *n*

chal·ced·o·ny \kal-'sed-ᵊn-ē\ *n* [ME *calcedonie*, a precious stone, fr. LL *chalcedonius*, fr. Gk *Chalkēdōn* Chalcedon] **:** a translucent quartz commonly pale blue or gray with nearly waxlike luster

chal·cid \'kal-səd\ *n* [deriv. of Gk *chalkos* copper] **:** any of a very large superfamily (Chalcidoidea) of mostly minute hymenopterous insects parasitic in the larval state on the larvae or pupae of other insects — **chalcid** *adj*

chal·co·py·rite \,kal-kə-'pī(ə)r-,īt\ *n* [NL *chalcopyrites*, fr. Gk *chalkos* + L *pyrites*] **:** a yellow mineral $CuFeS_2$ consisting of copper-iron sulfide and constituting an important ore of copper

Chal·da·ic \kal-'dā-ik\ *adj or n* **:** CHALDEAN

Chal·de·an \kal-'dē-ən\ *n* [L *Chaldaeus* Chaldean, astrologer, fr. Gk *Chaldaios*, fr. *Chaldaia* Chaldea, region of ancient Babylonia] **1 a :** one of an ancient Semitic people that became dominant in Babylonia **b :** the Semitic language of the Chaldeans **2 :** a person versed in the occult arts — **Chaldean** *adj*

Chal·dee \'kal-,dē\ *n* [ME *Caldey*, prob. fr. MF *chaldée*, fr. L *Chaldaeus*] **:** the Aramaic vernacular used as the original language of some parts of the Bible

chal·dron \'chòl-drən\ *n* [MF *chauderon*, fr. *chaudere* pot, fr. LL *caldaria*] **:** any of various old units of measure varying from 32 to 72 imperial bushels

cha·let \sha-'lā\ *n* [F] **1 :** a remote herdsman's hut in the Alps **2 a :** a Swiss dwelling with unconcealed structural members and a wide overhang at the front and sides **b :** a cottage or house in chalet style

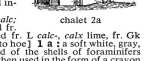

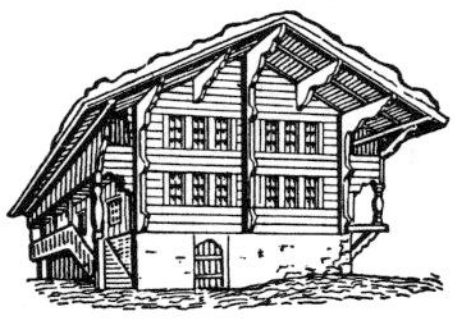
chalet 2a

chal·ice \'chal-əs\ *n* [ME, fr. AF, fr. L *calic-, calix;* akin to Gk *kalyx* calyx] **1 :** a drinking cup **:** GOBLET; *esp* **:** the eucharistic cup **2 :** the cup-shaped interior of a flower

1chalk \'chòk\ *n* [ME, fr. OE *cealc;* akin to OHG & MLG *kalk* lime; all fr. a prehistoric WGmc word borrowed fr. L *calc-, calx* lime, fr. Gk *chalix* pebble; akin to Gk *skallein* to hoe] **1 a :** a soft white, gray, or buff limestone chiefly composed of the shells of foraminifers **b :** chalk or a chalky material esp. when used in the form of a crayon **2 a :** a mark made with chalk **b** *Brit* **:** a point scored in a game — **chalky** \'chò-kē\ *adj*

2chalk *vt* **1 :** to rub or mark with chalk **2 :** to write or draw with chalk **3 a :** to delineate roughly **:** SKETCH **b :** to set down or add up **:** TOT ~ *vi* **:** to become chalky

chalk·stone \'chòk-,stōn\ *n* **:** TOPHUS

chalk up *vt* **1 :** ASCRIBE, CREDIT **2 :** ATTAIN, ACHIEVE

1chal·lenge \'chal-ənj\ *vb* [ME *chalengen* to accuse, fr. OF *chalengier*, fr. L *calumniari* to accuse falsely, fr. *calumnia* calumny] *vt* **1 :** to demand as of right **:** REQUIRE **2** *of a sentry* **:** HALT **3 :** to take exception to **:** DISPUTE **4 :** to question the legality or legal qualifications of **5 a :** DARE, DEFY **b :** to call out to duel or combat **c :** to invite into competition ~ *vi* **1 :** to make or present a challenge **2 :** to take legal exception — **chal·leng·er** *n*

2challenge *n* **1 a :** a calling to account or into question **:** PROTEST **b :** an exception taken to a juror before he is sworn **c :** a sentry's command to halt and prove identity **d :** a questioning of the right or validity of a vote or voter **2 a :** a summons often threatening, provocative, stimulating, or inciting; *specif* **:** a summons to a duel to answer an affront **b :** an invitation to compete in a sport **3 :** a test of immunity by exposure to virulent infective material after specific immunization

chal·lis \'shal-ē\ *n, pl* **chal·lises** \-ēz\ [prob. fr. the name *Challis*] **:** a lightweight soft clothing fabric esp. of cotton or wool

chal·one \'kal-,ōn\ *n* [Gk *chalōn*, prp. of *chalan* to slacken] **:** an internal secretion that depresses activity — compare HORMONE

1cha·ly·be·ate \kə-'lib-ē-ət, -'lē-bē-\ *adj* [prob. fr. NL *chalybeatus*, irreg. fr. L *chalybs* steel, fr. Gk *chalyb-, chalyps*, fr. *Chalybes*, ancient people in Asia Minor] **:** impregnated with salts of iron; *also* **:** having a taste due to iron ⟨~ springs⟩

2chalybeate *n* **:** a chalybeate liquid or medicine

cham \'kam\ *var of* KHAN

cham·ae·phyte \'kam-i-,fīt\ *n* [Gk *chamai* on the ground + E *-phyte* — more at HUMBLE] **:** a perennial plant that bears its overwintering buds above the surface of but near the soil

1cham·ber \'chām-bər\ *n* [ME *chambre*, fr. OF, fr. LL *camera*, fr. L, arched roof, fr. Gk *kamara* vault; akin to L *camur* curved] **1 :** ROOM; *esp* **:** BEDROOM **2 :** a natural or artificial enclosed space or cavity **3 a :** a hall for the meetings of a deliberative, legislative, or judicial body **b :** a room where a judge transacts business **c :** the reception room of a person of rank or authority **4 a :** a legislative or judicial body; *esp* **:** either of the houses of a bicameral legislature **b :** a voluntary board or council **5 a :** the part of the bore of a gun that holds the charge **b :** a compartment in the cartridge cylinder of a revolver — **cham·bered** \-bərd\ *adj*

2chamber *vt* **cham·ber·ing** \-b(ə-)riŋ\ **1 :** to place in or as if in a chamber **:** HOUSE **2 :** to furnish with a chamber ⟨~*ed* corridors⟩ **3 :** to serve as a chamber for; *esp* **:** to accommodate in the chamber

3chamber *adj* **:** intended for performance by a few musicians for a small audience ⟨~ music⟩

1chamberer *n, obs* **:** CHAMBERMAID

2cham·ber·er \'chām-bər-ər\ *n* [ME, chamberlain, fr. MF *chamberier*, fr. LL *camerarius*, fr. *camera*] *archaic* **:** GALLANT, LOVER

cham·ber·lain \'chām-bər-lən\ *n* [ME, fr. OF *chamberlayn*, of Gmc origin; akin to OHG *chamarling* chamberlain, fr. *chamara* chamber, fr. LL *camera*] **1 :** an attendant on a sovereign or lord in his bedchamber **2 a :** a chief officer in the household of a king or nobleman **b :** TREASURER **3 :** an often honorary papal attendant; *specif* **:** a priest having a rank of honor below domestic prelate

cham·ber·maid \'chām-bər-,mād\ *n* **:** a maid who makes beds and does general cleaning of bedrooms

chamber of commerce : an association of businessmen to promote commercial and industrial interests

chamber pot *n* **:** a bedroom vessel for urine or other waste

cham·bray \'sham-,brā, -brē\ *n* [irreg. fr. *Cambrai*, France] **:** a lightweight clothing fabric with colored warp and white filling yarns

cha·me·leon \kə-'mēl-yən, -'mē-lē-ən\ *n* [ME *camelion*, fr. MF, fr. L *chamaeleon*, fr. Gk *chamaileōn*, fr. *chamai* on the ground + *leōn* lion — more at HUMBLE] **1 :** any of a group (Rhiptoglossa) of Old World lizards with granular skin, prehensile tail, independently movable eyeballs, and unusual ability to change the color of the skin **2 :** a fickle or changeable person **3 :** any of various American lizards (as of the genus *Anolis*) capable of changing their color

1cham·fer \'cham(p)-fər, 'cham-pər\ *n* [MF *chanfreint*, fr. pp. of *chanfraindre* to bevel, fr. *chant* edge (fr. L *canthus* iron tire) + *fraindre* to break, fr. L *frangere*] **:** a beveled edge

2chamfer *vt* **cham·fer·ing** \-f(ə-)riŋ, -p(ə-)riŋ\ **1 :** to cut a furrow in (as a column) **:** GROOVE **2 :** to make a chamfer on **:** BEVEL

cham·fron \'cham(p)-frən\ *n* [ME *shamfron*, fr. MF *chanfrein*] **:** the headpiece of a horse's bard

cham·ois \'sham-ē, *in sense 1 also* sham-'wä\ *n, pl* **cham·ois** *also* **cham·oix** *in sense 1* 'sham-ē(z) *or* sham-'wä(z), *in sense 2* 'sham-ēz\ [MF, fr. LL *camox*] **1 :** a small goatlike antelope (*Rupicapra rupicapra*) of Europe and the Caucasus **2** *also* **cham·my** \'sham-ē\ **:** a soft pliant leather prepared from the skin of the chamois or from sheepskin

cham·o·mile \'kam-ə-,mīl, -,mēl\ *n* [ME *camemille*, fr. ML *camomilla*, modif. of L *chamaemelon*, fr. Gk *chamaimēlon*, fr. *chamai* + *mēlon* apple] **:** any of a genus (*Anthemis*, esp. the common European *A. nobilis*) of composite herbs with strong-scented foliage and flower heads that contain a bitter medicinal principle; *also* **:** a similar plant of a related genus (*Matricaria*)

1champ \'champ, 'chämp\ *vb* [perh. imit.] *vt* **1 :** to chew or bite on noisily **2 :** MASH, TRAMPLE ~ *vi* **1 :** to make biting or gnashing movements **2 :** to show impatience of delay or restraint

2champ \'champ\ *n* **:** CHAMPION

cham·pac *or* **cham·pak** \'cham-,pak, 'chəm-(,)pək\ *n* [Hindi & Skt; Hindi *campak*, fr. Skt *campaka*] **:** an East Indian tree (*Michelia champaca*) of the magnolia family with yellow flowers

cham·pagne \sham-'pān\ *n* [F, fr. *Champagne*, region in France] **:** a white sparkling wine made in the old province of Champagne, France; *broadly* **:** a wine of the champagne type

cham·paign \sham-'pān\ *n* [ME *champaine*, fr. MF *champagne*, fr. LL *campania* — more at CAMPAIGN] **1 :** an expanse of level open country **:** PLAIN **2** *archaic* **:** BATTLEFIELD — **champaign** *adj*

cham·per·tous \'cham-pərt-əs\ *adj* **:** of or relating to champerty

cham·per·ty \-pərt-ē\ *n* [ME *champartie*, fr. MF *champart* field rent, fr. *champ* field (fr. L *campus*) + *part* portion — more at CAMP, PART] **:** a proceeding by which a person not a party in a suit bargains to aid in or carry on its prosecution or defense in consideration of a share of the matter in suit

cham·pi·gnon \sham-'pin-yən, cham-\ *n* [MF, fr. *champagne*] **:** an edible fungus; *esp* **:** the common meadow mushroom (*Agaricus campestris*)

1cham·pi·on \'cham-pē-ən\ *n* [ME, fr. OF, fr. ML *campion-, campio*, of WGmc origin] **1 :** WARRIOR, FIGHTER **2 :** a militant advocate or defender **3 :** one that fights for another's rights or honor **4 :** a winner of first prize or place in competition

2champion *vt* **1** *archaic* **:** CHALLENGE, DEFY **2 :** to protect or fight for as a champion **syn** see SUPPORT

cham·pi·on·ship \-,ship\ *n* **1 :** the position or title of a champion **2 :** DEFENSE **3 :** a contest held to determine a champion

champ·le·vé \,shäⁿ-lə-'vā\ *adj* [F] **:** having the metal ground engraved, cut out, or depressed and the resultant spaces filled in with enamel pastes and fired — used of enamel work — **champlevé** *n*

1chance \'chan(t)s\ *n* [ME, fr. OF, fr. (assumed) VL *cadentia* fall, fr. L *cadent-, cadens*, prp. of *cadere* to fall; akin to Skt *śad* to fall] **1 a :** something that happens unpredictably without discernible human intention or observable cause **b :** the assumed impersonal purposeless determiner of unaccountable happenings **:** LUCK **c :** the fortuitous or incalculable element in existence **:** CONTINGENCY **2 :** a situation favoring some purpose **3 :** a fielding opportunity in baseball **4 a :** the possibility of an indicated or a favorable outcome in an uncertain situation **b :** the degree of likelihood of such an outcome **5 a :** RISK **b :** a ticket in a raffle — **chance** *adj*

2chance *vi* **1 a :** to take place or come about by chance **:** HAPPEN **b :** to be found by chance **c :** to have the good or bad luck **2 :** to come or light by chance ~ *vt* **1 :** to leave the outcome of to chance **2 :** to accept the hazard of **:** RISK **syn** see HAPPEN

chance·ful \-fəl\ *adj* **1** *archaic* **:** CASUAL **2 :** EVENTFUL

chan·cel \'chan(t)-səl\ *n* [ME, fr. MF, fr. LL *cancellus* lattice, fr. L *cancelli;* fr. the latticework enclosing it] **:** the part of a church lying east of the nave and including choir and sanctuary

chan·cel·lery *or* **chan·cel·lory** \'chan(t)-s(ə-)lə-rē, -səl-rē\ *n* **1 a :** the position, court, or department of a chancellor **b :** the building or room where a chancellor has his office **2 :** the office of secretary of the court of a person high in authority **3 :** the office or staff of an embassy or consulate

chan·cel·lor \'chan(t)-s(ə-)lər\ *n* [ME *chanceler*, fr. OF *chancelier*, fr. LL *cancellarius* doorkeeper, secretary, fr. *cancellus*] **1 a :** the secretary of a nobleman, prince, or king **b :** the lord chancellor of Great Britain **c** *Brit* **:** the chief secretary of an embassy **d :** a Roman Catholic priest heading the office in which diocesan business is transacted and recorded **2 a :** the titular head of a British university **b :** a university president **3 a :** a lay legal officer or advisor of an Anglican diocese **b :** a judge in a court of chancery or equity in various states of the U.S. **4 :** the chief minister of state in some European countries — **chan·cel·lor·ship** \-,ship\ *n*

chancellor of the exchequer *often cap C&E* **:** a member of the British cabinet in charge of the public income and expenditure

chance–med·ley \'chan(t)-'smed-lē\ *n* [AF *chance medlée* mingled chance] **1 :** accidental homicide not entirely without fault of the killer but without evil intent **2 :** HAPHAZARDNESS

chan·cery \'chan(t)s-(ə-)rē\ *n* [ME *chancerie*, alter. of *chancellerie* chancellery, fr. OF, fr. *chancelier*] **1 a** *cap* **:** a high court of equity in England and Wales with common-law functions and jurisdiction over causes in equity **b :** a court of equity in the American judicial system **c :** the principles and practice of judicial equity **2 :** a record office for public archives or those of ecclesiastical, legal, or diplomatic proceedings **3 a :** a chancellor's court or office or the building in which he has his office **b :** the office of an embassy **:** CHANCELLERY 3 **4 :** a wrestling hold that imprisons the head or encircles the neck **:** STRANGLEHOLD — **in chancery 1 :** in litigation

in a court of chancery; *also* **:** under the superintendence of the lord chancellor ⟨a ward *in chancery*⟩ **2 :** in a hopeless predicament

chan·cre \'shaŋ-kər\ *n* [F, fr. L *cancer*] **:** a primary sore or ulcer at the site of entry of a pathogen (as in tularemia); *specif* **:** the initial lesion of syphilis — **chan·crous** \-k(ə-)rəs\ *adj*

chan·croid \'shaŋ-ˌkrȯid\ *n* **:** a venereal sore resembling a chancre but differing in being the starting point of a local process and never a systemic disease and in being caused by a different microorganism (*Hemophilus ducreyi*) — **chan·croi·dal** \shaŋ-'krȯid-ᵊl\ *adj*

chancy \'chan(t)-sē\ *adj* **1** *Scot* **:** bringing good luck **:** AUSPICIOUS **2 :** uncertain in outcome or prospect **:** RISKY

chan·de·lier \ˌshan-də-'li(ə)r\ *n* [F, lit., candlestick, modif. of L *candelabrum*] **:** a branched often ornate lighting fixture suspended from a ceiling

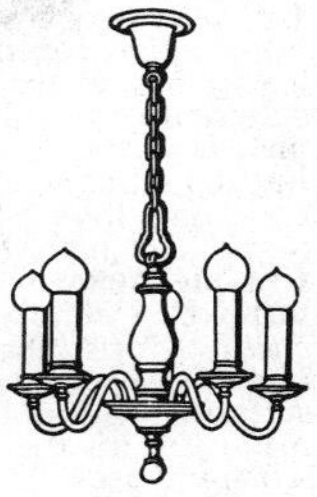

chandelier

chan·delle \shan-'del, shäⁿ-\ *n* [F, lit., candle] **:** an abrupt climbing turn of an airplane in which the momentum of the plane is used to attain a higher rate of climb — **chandelle** *vi*

chan·dler \'chan-(d)lər\ *n* [ME *chandeler*, fr. MF *chandelier*, fr. OF, fr. *chandelle* candle, fr. L *candela*] **1 :** a maker or seller of tallow or wax candles and usu. soap **2 :** a retail dealer in provisions and supplies or equipment of a specified kind ⟨yacht ~⟩

chan·dlery \-(d)lə-rē\ *n* **1 :** a place where candles are kept **2 :** the business of a chandler **3 :** the commodities sold by a chandler

1**change** \'chānj\ *vb* [ME *changen*, fr. OF *changier*, fr. L *cambiare* to exchange, of Celt origin; akin to OIr *camm* crooked; akin to Gk *skambos* crooked] *vt* **1 a :** to make different in some particular **:** MODIFY **b :** to make radically different **:** TRANSFORM **c :** to give a different position, course, or direction to **d :** REVERSE ⟨~ one's vote⟩ **2 a :** to replace with another **b :** to move to another; *also* **:** SWITCH **c :** to exchange for an equivalent sum or comparable item **d :** to undergo a loss or modification of ⟨foliage *changing* color⟩ **e :** to put fresh clothes or covering on ⟨~ a bed⟩ ~ *vi* **1 :** to become different **:** ALTER **2** *of the moon* **:** to pass from one phase to another **3 :** to shift one's means of conveyance **:** TRANSFER **4** *of the voice* **:** to shift to lower register **:** BREAK **5 :** to undergo transformation, transition, or substitution **6 :** to put on different clothes **7 :** to accept something else in return **:** EXCHANGE

syn ALTER, VARY, MODIFY: CHANGE implies making either an essential difference often amounting to a loss of original identity or a substitution of one thing for another; ALTER implies a difference in some particular respect without suggesting loss of identity; VARY stresses a breaking away from sameness, duplication, or exact repetition; MODIFY suggests a difference that limits, restricts, or adapts to a new purpose

—change hands : to pass from the possession of one person to that of another

2**change** *n* **1 :** the act, process, or result of changing: as **a :** ALTERATION **b :** TRANSFORMATION **c :** SUBSTITUTION **d :** the passage of the moon from one monthly revolution to another; *also* **:** the passage of the moon from one phase to another **2 :** a fresh set of clothes **3** *Brit* **:** EXCHANGE **4 a :** money in small denominations received in exchange for an equivalent sum in larger denominations **b :** money returned when a payment exceeds the amount due **c :** coins of low denominations ⟨a pocketful of ~⟩ **5 :** an order in which a set of bells is struck in change ringing

syn MUTATION, PERMUTATION, VICISSITUDE: CHANGE may imply any variation whatever whether affecting a thing essentially or superficially; MUTATION stresses lack of permanence and stability and presents change as inevitable; PERMUTATION implies transposition within a group of otherwise unchanged items; VICISSITUDE implies a change great enough to constitute a reversal of what has been

change·abil·i·ty \ˌchān-jə-'bil-ət-ē\ *n* **:** CHANGEABLENESS

change·able \'chān-jə-bəl\ *adj* **:** capable of change: as **a :** VARIABLE **b :** ALTERABLE **c :** FICKLE **d :** IRIDESCENT — **change·able·ness** *n* — **change·ably** \-blē\ *adv*

change·ful \'chānj-fəl\ *adj* **:** notably variable **:** UNCERTAIN — **change·ful·ly** \-fə-lē\ *adv* — **change·ful·ness** *n*

change·less \'chānj-ləs\ *adj* **:** UNCHANGING, CONSTANT — **change·less·ly** *adv* — **change·less·ness** *n*

change·ling \'chānj-liŋ\ *n* **1** *archaic* **:** TURNCOAT **2 :** a child secretly exchanged for another in infancy **3** *archaic* **:** IMBECILE — **changeling** *adj*

change off *vi* **1 :** to alternate with another at doing an act **2 :** to alternate between acts or instruments or between action and rest

change of life : MENOPAUSE

chang·er \'chān-jər\ *n* **1 :** one that changes **2** *obs* **:** MONEY CHANGER

change ringing *n* **:** the art or practice of ringing a set of tuned bells in continually varying order

1**chan·nel** \'chan-ᵊl\ *n* [ME *chanel*, fr. OF, fr. L *canalis* channel — more at CANAL] **1 a :** the bed where a natural stream of water runs **b :** the deeper part of a river, harbor, or strait **c :** a strait or narrow sea between two close land masses **d :** a means of communication or expression **e :** a way or course of thought or action **f :** a band of frequencies of sufficient width for a single radio or television communication **2 :** a usu. tubular enclosed passage **:** CONDUIT **3 :** a long gutter, groove, or furrow **4 :** a metal bar of flattened U-shaped section

2**channel** *vt* **chan·neled** *or* **chan·nelled**; **chan·nel·ing** *or* **chan·nel·ling 1 a :** to form, cut, or wear a channel in **b :** GROOVE ⟨~ a chair leg⟩ **2 :** to convey into or through a channel

3**channel** *n* [alter. of *chainwale*, fr. *chain* + *wale*] **:** one of the flat ledges of heavy plank or metal bolted edgewise to the outside of a ship to increase the spread of the shrouds

chan·nel·iza·tion \ˌchan-ᵊl-ə-'zā-shən\ *n* **:** the act or process of channeling

chan·nel·ize \'chan-ᵊl-ˌīz\ *vt* **:** CHANNEL

chan·son \shäⁿ-sōⁿ\ *n, pl* **chan·sons** \-sōⁿ(z)\ [F, fr. L *cantion-*, *cantio*, fr. *cantus*, pp.] **:** SONG; *specif* **:** a music-hall or cabaret song

chan·son de geste \-sōⁿd-ə-zhest, -sōⁿ-jest\ *n, pl* **chansons de geste** *same, or* -sōⁿz-də-zhest\ [F, lit., song of heroic deeds] **:** any of several Old French epic poems of the 11th to the 13th centuries

1**chant** \'chant\ *vb* [ME *chanten*, fr. MF *chanter*, fr. L *cantare*, fr. *cantus*, pp. of *canere*; akin to OE *hana* rooster, Gk *kanachē* ringing sound] *vi* **1 :** to make melodic sounds with the voice **:** SING; *esp* **:** to sing a chant **2 :** to recite in a monotonous repetitive tone ~ *vt* **1 :** to utter as in chanting **2 :** to celebrate or praise in song

2**chant** *n* **1 :** SONG **2 a :** a repetitive liturgical melody in which as many syllables are assigned to each tone as required **b :** a rhythmic monotonous utterance or song **c :** a composition for chanting

chant·er \-ər\ *n* **1 :** one that chants: **a :** CHORISTER **b :** CANTOR **2 :** the chief singer in a chantry **3 :** the reed pipe of a bagpipe with finger holes on which the melody is played — **chant·ress** \'chan-trəs\ *n*

chan·te·relle \ˌshant-ə-'rel, ˌshänt-\ *n* [F] **:** an edible mushroom (*Cantharellus cibarius*) of rich yellow color and pleasant aroma

chan·teuse \shäⁿ-'tə(r)z, shan-'tüz\ *n, pl* **chan·teuses** \-'tə(r)z(-əz), -'tüz(-əz)\ [F, fem. of *chanteur* singer, fr. *chanter*] **:** a female concert or nightclub singer

chan·tey *or* **chan·ty** \'shant-ē, 'chant-\ *n* [modif. of F *chanter*] **:** a song sung by sailors in rhythm with their work

chan·ti·cleer \ˌchant-ə-'kli(ə)r, ˌshant-\ *n* [ME *Chantecleer*, rooster in verse narratives, fr. OF *Chantecler*, rooster in the *Roman de Renart*] **:** 1COCK 1

chan·try \'chan-trē\ *n* [ME *chanterie*, fr. MF, singing, fr. *chanter*] **1 :** an endowment for the chanting of masses commonly for the founder **2 :** a chapel endowed by a chantry

Cha·nu·kah *like* HANUKKAH\ *var of* HANUKKAH

cha·os \'kā-ˌäs\ *n* [L, fr. Gk — more at GUM] **1** *obs* **:** CHASM, ABYSS **2 a** *often cap* **:** a state of things in which chance is supreme; *esp* **:** the confused unorganized state of primordial matter before the creation of distinct forms **b :** a state of utter confusion **c :** a confused mass or heterogeneous agglomeration — **cha·ot·ic** \kā-'ät-ik\ *adj* — **cha·ot·i·cal·ly** \-i-k(ə-)lē\ *adv*

1**chap** \'chap\ *n* [short for *chapman*] **1** *dial chiefly Eng* **:** BUYER **2 :** FELLOW

2**chap** *vb* **chapped; chap·ping** [ME *chappen*; akin to MD *cappen* to cut down] **:** to open in slits or chinks **:** CRACK

3**chap** *n* **:** a crack or a sore roughening of the skin from exposure

4**chap** \'chäp, 'chap\ *n* [2*chap*] **:** JAW **:** the fleshy covering of a jaw; *also* **:** the forepart of the face — usu. used in pl.

chap·a·ra·jos *or* **chap·a·re·jos** \ˌshap-ə-'rā-ˌōs, -əs\ *n pl* [MexSp *chaparreras*] **:** CHAPS

chap·ar·ral \ˌshap-ə-'ral, -'rel\ *n* [Sp, fr. *chaparro* dwarf evergreen oak, fr. Basque *txapar*] **:** a thicket of dwarf evergreen oaks; *broadly* **:** a dense impenetrable thicket of shrubs or dwarf trees

chaparral bird *n* **:** ROADRUNNER — called also *chaparral cock*

chaparral pea *n* **:** a thorny California leguminous shrub (*Pickeringia montana*) forming dense thickets

chap·book \'chap-ˌbu̇k\ *n* [*chap*man + *book*] **:** a small book containing ballads, tales, or tracts

chape \'chāp, 'chap\ *n* [ME, scabbard, fr. MF, cape, fr. LL *cappa*] **:** the metal mounting or trimming of a scabbard or sheath

cha·peau \sha-'pō\ *n, pl* **cha·peaus** \-'pōz\ *or* **cha·peaux** \-'pō(z)\ [MF, fr. OF *chapel* — more at CHAPLET] **:** HAT

chap·el \'chap-əl\ *n* [ME, fr. OF *chapele*, fr. ML *cappella*, fr. dim. of LL *cappa* cloak; fr. the cloak of St. Martin of Tours preserved as a sacred relic in a chapel built for that purpose] **1 :** a subordinate or private place of worship: as **a :** a place of worship in a residence or institution **b :** a room or recess in a church for meditation and prayer or small religious services **2 :** a choir of singers belonging to a chapel (as of a prince) **3 :** a chapel service or assembly at a school or college **4 :** an association of the employees in a printing office **5 :** a place of worship used by a Christian group other than an established church ⟨a nonconformist ~⟩ **6 a :** FUNERAL HOME **b :** a room for funeral services in a funeral home

1**chap·er·on** *or* **chap·er·one** \'shap-ə-ˌrōn\ *n* [F, lit., hood, fr. MF, head covering, fr. *chape*] **1 :** a person (as a matron) who accompanies one or more young unmarried women in public or in mixed company for propriety **2 :** an older person who accompanies young people at a social gathering to ensure proper behavior

2**chaperon** *or* **chaperone** *vt* **1 :** ESCORT **2 :** to act as chaperon to or for ~ *vi* **:** to act as a chaperon — **chap·er·on·age** \-ˌrō-nij\ *n*

chap·fall·en \'chap-ˌfȯ-lən, 'chäp-\ *adj* **1 :** having the lower jaw hanging loosely **2 :** DEJECTED, DEPRESSED

chap·i·ter \'chap-ət-ər\ *n* [ME *chapitre*, fr. MF, alter. of OF *chapitle*, fr. L *capitulum*, lit., little head] **:** the capital of a column

chap·lain \'chap-lən\ *n* [ME *chapelain*, fr. OF, fr. ML *cappellanus*, fr. *cappella*] **1 :** a clergyman in charge of a chapel **2 :** a clergyman officially attached to the army or navy, to a public institution, or to a family or court **3 :** a person chosen to conduct religious exercises — **chap·lain·cy** \-sē\ *n* — **chap·lain·ship** \-ˌship\ *n*

chap·let \'chap-lət\ *n* [ME *chapelet*, fr. MF, fr. OF, dim. of *chapel* hat, garland, fr. ML *cappellus* head covering, fr. LL *cappa*] **1 :** a wreath to be worn on the head **2 a :** a string of beads **b :** a part of a rosary comprising five decades **3 :** a small molding carved with small decorative forms — **chap·let·ed** \-əd\ *adj*

chap·man \'chap-mən\ *n* [ME, fr. OE *cēapman*, fr. *cēap* trade + *man*] **1** *archaic* **:** MERCHANT, TRADER **2** *Brit* **:** an itinerant dealer

chaps \'shaps\ *n pl* [modif. of MexSp *chaparreras*] **:** leather leggings resembling trousers without a seat that are worn esp. by western ranch hands

chap·ter \'chap-tər\ *n* [ME *chapitre* division of a book, meeting of canons, fr. OF, fr. LL *capitulum* division of a book & ML, meeting place of canons, fr. L, dim. of *capit-*, *caput* head — more at HEAD] **1 :** a main division of a book **2 a :** a regular meeting of the canons of a cathedral or collegiate church or of the members of a religious house **b :** the body of canons of a cathedral or collegiate church **3 :** a local branch of a society or fraternity

chapter house *n* **:** the building or rooms where a chapter meets

1**char** \'chär\ *n, pl* **char** *or* **chars** [origin unknown] **:** any of a genus (*Salvelinus*) of small-scaled trouts

2**char** *vb* **charred; char·ring** [back-formation fr. *charcoal*] **1 :** to burn to charcoal **:** BURN **2 :** to burn slightly or partly **:** SCORCH

3**char** *n* **:** a charred substance **:** CHARCOAL

4**char** *vi* **charred; char·ring** [back-formation fr. *charwoman*] **:** to work as a charwoman

5**char** *n* [short for *charwoman*] *Brit* **:** CHARWOMAN

char·a·banc \'shar-ə-,baŋ\ *n* [F *char à bancs*, lit., wagon with benches] *Brit* **:** a sightseeing motor coach

char·a·cin \'kar-ə-sən\ *n* [deriv. of Gk *charak-*, *charax* pointed stake, a fish] **:** any of a family (Characidae) of usu. small brightly colored tropical fishes — **characin** *adj*

[1]**char·ac·ter** \'kar-ik-tər\ *n* [ME *caracter*, fr. MF *caractère*, fr. L *character* mark, distinctive quality, fr. Gk *charaktēr*, fr. *charassein* to scratch, engrave; akin to Lith *žerti* to scratch] **1 a :** a conventionalized graphic device placed on an object as an indication of ownership, origin, or relationship **b :** a graphic symbol (as a hieroglyph, alphabet letter) used in writing or printing **c :** a magical or astrological emblem **d :** ALPHABET **e** (1) **:** WRITING, PRINTING (2) **:** style of writing or printing (3) **:** CIPHER **2 a :** one of the attributes or features that make up and distinguish the individual **b** (1) **:** a feature used to separate distinguishable things (as organisms) into categories (2) **:** the detectable expression of the action of a gene or group of genes **c :** the complex of mental and ethical traits marking a person, group, or nation **3 :** POSITION, RANK **4 :** a short literary sketch of the qualities of a social type **5 :** REFERENCE 4b **6 a :** a person marked by notable or conspicuous traits **:** PERSONAGE **b :** one of the persons of a drama or novel **c :** the personality or part which an actor re-creates **7 :** REPUTATION **8 :** moral excellence and firmness **syn** see DISPOSITION, QUALITY, TYPE — **char·ac·ter·less** \-ləs\ *adj*

[2]**character** *vt* **1** *archaic* **:** ENGRAVE, INSCRIBE **2 a** *archaic* **:** REPRESENT, PORTRAY **b :** CHARACTERIZE

[1]**char·ac·ter·is·tic** \,kar(-i)k-tə-'ris-tik\ *adj* **:** serving to mark the individual character — **char·ac·ter·is·ti·cal·ly** \-ti-k(ə-)lē\ *adv*

syn CHARACTERISTIC, INDIVIDUAL, PECULIAR, DISTINCTIVE mean indicating a special quality or identity. CHARACTERISTIC applies to something that distinguishes or identifies a person or thing or class; INDIVIDUAL stresses qualities that distinguish one from all other members of the same kind or class; PECULIAR applies to qualities possessed only by a particular individual or class or kind and stresses rarity or uniqueness; DISTINCTIVE indicates qualities distinguishing and uncommon and often superior or praiseworthy

[2]**characteristic** *n* **1 :** a distinguishing trait, quality, or property **2 :** the integral part of a common logarithm

char·ac·ter·iza·tion \,kar-ik-t(ə-)rə-'zā-shən\ *n* **:** the act of characterizing; *esp* **:** the representation of human character or motives through the arts

char·ac·ter·ize \'kar-ik-tə-,rīz\ *vt* **1 :** to describe the character or quality of **:** DELINEATE **2 :** to be a characteristic of **:** DISTINGUISH

char·ac·tery \'kar-ik-t(ə-)rē, kə-'rak-\ *n* **:** written letters or symbols

cha·rade \shə-'rād\ *n* [F] **:** a word represented in riddling verse or by picture, tableau, or dramatic action

char·coal \'chär-,kōl\ *n* [ME *charcole*] **1 :** a dark or black porous carbon prepared from vegetable or animal substances **2 a :** a piece or pencil of fine charcoal used in drawing **b :** a charcoal drawing

chard \'chärd\ *n* [F *carde*, fr. OProv *cardo* edible cardoon, fr. L *carduus* thistle, artichoke; akin to MLG *harst* rake, L *carrere* to card] **:** a beet (*Beta vulgaris cicla*) with large leaves and succulent stalks often cooked as a vegetable — called also *Swiss chard*

chare \'cha(ə)r, 'che(ə)r\ *or* **char** \'chär\ *n* [ME *char* turn, piece of work, fr. OE *cierr;* akin to OE *cierran* to turn] **:** CHORE

[1]**charge** \'chärj\ *vb* [ME *chargen*, fr. OF *chargier*, fr. LL *carricare*, fr. L *carrus* wheeled vehicle — more at CAR] *vt* **1 a** *archaic* **:** to lay or put a load on or in **:** LOAD **b** (1) **:** to place a charge (as of powder) in (2) **:** to load or fill to capacity **c** (1) **:** to restore the active materials in (a storage battery) by the passage of a direct current through in the opposite direction to that of discharge (2) **:** to give an electric charge to **d** (1) **:** to assume as a heraldic bearing (2) **:** to place a heraldic bearing on **e :** to fill full **2 a :** to impose a task or responsibility on **b :** to command, instruct, or exhort with right or authority **c** *of a judge* **:** to give a charge to (a jury) **3 a :** ACCUSE, BLAME **b :** to impute blame or guilt for **4 a :** to bring (a weapon) into position for attack **:** LEVEL ⟨~ a lance⟩ **b :** to rush against or bear down upon **:** ATTACK **5 a** (1) **:** to impose a pecuniary burden on ⟨~ his estate with debts incurred⟩ (2) **:** to impose or record as a pecuniary obligation ⟨~ debts to an estate⟩ **b** (1) **:** to fix or ask as fee or payment (2) **:** to ask payment of (a person) ⟨~ a student $50 for meals⟩ ~ *vi* **1 :** to rush forward in assault **:** ATTACK **2 :** to ask or set a price **syn** see COMMAND

[2]**charge** *n* **1 a** *obs* **:** a material load or weight **b :** a figure borne on a heraldic field **2 a :** the quantity that an apparatus is intended to receive and fitted to hold **b :** a store or accumulation of force **c :** a definite quantity of electricity **d** *slang* **:** THRILL, KICK **3 a :** OBLIGATION, REQUIREMENT **b :** MANAGEMENT, SUPERVISION **c :** the ecclesiastical jurisdiction (as a parish) committed to a clergyman **d :** a person or thing committed to the care of another **4 a :** INSTRUCTION, COMMAND **b :** instruction in points of law given by a court to a jury **5 a :** EXPENSE, COST **b :** PRICE **c :** a debit to an account **6 a :** ACCUSATION, INDICTMENT **b :** a complaint of error, failure, or wrong **7 :** ATTACK, ASSAULT

charge·able \'chär-jə-bəl\ *adj* **1** *obs* **:** financially burdensome **:** EXPENSIVE **2 a :** liable to be accused or held responsible **b :** suitable to be charged to a particular account **c :** qualified to be made a charge on the county or parish — **charge·able·ness** *n*

charge-a-plate \'chär-jə-,plāt\ *or* **charge plate** *n* [fr. *Charga-plate*, a trademark] **:** an embossed address plate used by a customer when buying on credit

char·gé d'af·faires \(,)shär-,zhād-ə-'fa(ə)r, -'fe(ə)r\ *n, pl* **char·gés d'af·faires** \-,zhād-ə-, -,zhāz-də-\ [F, lit., one charged with affairs] **1 :** a subordinate diplomat who substitutes for an ambassador or minister in his absence **2 :** a diplomat inferior in rank to an ambassador or minister and accredited by one government to the foreign minister of another

charge of quarters : an enlisted man designated to maintain order after duty hours in the area of his unit

[1]**char·ger** \'chär-jər\ *n* [ME *chargeour;* akin to ME *chargen* to charge] *archaic* **:** a large flat platter for carrying meat

[2]**charg·er** *n* **1 :** one that charges: as **a :** an appliance for holding or inserting a charge of powder or shot in a gun **b :** a cartridge clip **2 :** a cavalry horse

char·i·ly \'char-ə-lē, 'cher-\ *adv* **:** in a chary manner **:** CAREFULLY

char·i·ness \'char-ē-nəs, 'cher-\ *n* **1 :** the quality or state of being chary **:** CAUTION **2 :** carefully preserved state **:** INTEGRITY

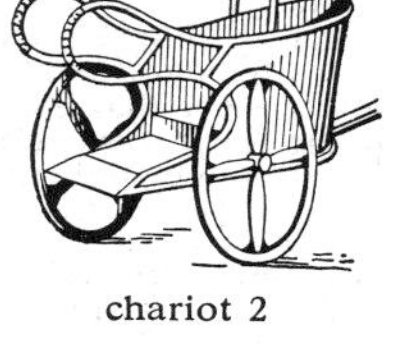

chariot 2

[1]**char·i·ot** \'char-ē-ət\ *n* [ME, fr. MF, fr. OF, fr. *char* wheeled vehicle, fr. L *carrus*] **1 :** a light 4-wheeled pleasure or state carriage **2 :** a 2-wheeled horse-drawn battle car of antiquity used also in processions and races

[2]**chariot** *vt* **:** to carry in or as if in a chariot ~ *vi* **:** to drive or ride in or as if in a chariot

char·i·o·teer \,char-ē-ə-'ti(ə)r\ *n* **1 :** one who drives a chariot **2** *cap* **:** the constellation Auriga

cha·ris·ma \kə-'riz-mə\ *or* **char·ism** \'kar-,iz-əm\ *n, pl* **cha·ris·ma·ta** \kə-'riz-mət-ə\ *or* **char·isms** [Gk *charisma* favor, gift, fr. *charizesthai* to favor, fr. *charis* grace; akin to Gk *chairein* to rejoice] **1 :** an extraordinary power (as of healing) given a Christian by the Holy Spirit for the good of the church **2 :** a personal magic of leadership arousing special popular loyalty or enthusiasm for a statesman or military commander — **char·is·mat·ic** \,kar-əz-'mat-ik\ *adj*

char·i·ta·ble \'char-ət-ə-bəl\ *adj* **1 :** exhibiting the virtue of Christian love **:** BENEVOLENT **2 :** liberal in benefactions to the poor **3 :** merciful or kind in judging others **:** LENIENT — **char·i·ta·ble·ness** *n* — **char·i·ta·bly** \-blē\ *adv*

char·i·ty \'char-ət-ē\ *n* [ME *charite*, fr. OF *charité*, fr. LL *caritat-*, *caritas* Christian love, fr. L, dearness, fr. *carus* dear; akin to Skt *kāma* love] **1 :** LOVE 3a(1) **2 a :** kindness or help for the needy or suffering **b :** an institution engaged in relief of the poor **c :** public provision for the relief of the needy **3 a :** a gift for public benevolent purposes **b :** an institution (as a hospital) founded by such a gift **4 :** lenient judgment of others **syn** see MERCY

cha·ri·va·ri \,shiv-ə-'rē, 'shiv-ə-,\ *n* [F, fr. LL *caribaria* headache, fr. Gk *karēbaria*, fr. *kara*, *karē* head + *barys* heavy] **:** SHIVAREE

char·ka *or* **char·kha** \'chər-kə, 'chär-\ *n* [Hindi *carkha*] **:** a domestic spinning wheel used in India chiefly for cotton

char·la·tan \'shär-lə-tən\ *n* [It *ciarlatano*, alter. of *cerretano*, lit., inhabitant of Cerreto, fr. *Cerreto*, village in Italy] **:** a pretender to medical knowledge **:** QUACK; *also* **:** FAKER, FRAUD — **char·la·tan·ism** \-tə-,niz-əm\ *n* — **char·la·tan·ry** \-tən-rē\ *n*

Charles's Wain \,chärl-zəz-'wān, 'chärlz-'wān\ *n* [*Charlemagne* †814 king of the Franks] **:** the Big Dipper

Charles·ton \'chärl-stən\ *n* [*Charleston*, S. C.] **:** a ballroom dance in which the knees are twisted in and out and the heels are swung sharply outward on each step

char·ley horse \'chär-lē-,hȯrs\ *n* [fr. *Charley*, nickname for *Charles*] **:** pain and stiffness from muscular strain in an arm or leg

Char·lie \'chär-lē\ [fr. the name *Charlie*] — a communications code word for the letter *c*

char·lock \'chär-,läk, -lək\ *n* [ME *cherlok*, fr. OE *cerlic*] **:** a wild mustard (*Brassica kaber*) often troublesome in grainfields

char·lotte \'shär-lət\ *n* [F] **:** a dessert consisting of a filling of fruit, whipped cream, or custard placed over strips of bread, cake, or ladyfingers

char·lotte russe \,shär-lət-'rüs\ *n* [F, lit., Russian charlotte] **:** a charlotte made with sponge cake or ladyfingers and a whipped-cream or custard-gelatin filling

[1]**charm** \'chärm\ *n* [ME *charme*, fr. OF, fr. L *carmen* song, fr. *canere* to sing — more at CHANT] **1 a :** the chanting or reciting of a magic spell **:** INCANTATION **b :** an act or expression believed to have magic power **2 :** something worn about the person to ward off evil or ensure good fortune **:** AMULET **3 a :** a trait that fascinates, allures, or delights **b :** a physical grace or attraction **4 :** a small ornament worn on a bracelet or chain **syn** see FETISH

[2]**charm** *vt* **1 :** to affect by or as if by magic **:** COMPEL; *also* **:** DELIGHT **2 :** to endow with supernatural powers by means of charms; *also* **:** to protect by spells, charms, or supernatural influences **3 :** to control (an animal) typically by charms ~ *vi* **1 :** to practice magic and enchantment **2 :** to have the effect of a charm **:** FASCINATE **syn** see ATTRACT

charm·er \'chär-mər\ *n* **1 :** ENCHANTER, MAGICIAN **2 :** one that pleases or fascinates; *esp* **:** an attractive woman

char·nel \'chärn-ᵊl\ *n* [ME, fr. MF, fr. ML *carnale*, fr. LL, neut. of *carnalis* of the flesh] **1** *obs* **:** CEMETERY **2 :** a building or chamber in which bodies or bones are deposited — **charnel** *adj*

Char·on \'kar-ən, 'ker-ən\ *n* [L, fr. Gk *Charōn*] **:** a son of Erebus held in Greek myth to ferry the souls of the dead over the Styx

char·poy \'chär-,pȯi\ *n* [Hindi *cārpāī*] **:** a bed consisting of a frame strung with tapes or light rope used esp. in India

char·qui \'chär-kē, 'shär-\ *n* [Sp, fr. Quechua *ch'arki* dried meat] **:** jerked beef

charr \'chär\ *var of* CHAR

[1]**chart** \'chärt\ *n* [MF *charte*, fr. L *charta* piece of papyrus, document — more at CARD] **1 :** MAP: as **a :** an outline map exhibiting something (as climatic or magnetic variations) in its geographical aspects **b :** a map for the use of navigators **2 a :** a sheet giving information in tabular form **b :** GRAPH **c :** DIAGRAM **d :** a sheet of paper ruled and graduated for use in a recording instrument

[2]**chart** *vt* **1 :** to make a map or chart of **2 :** to lay out a plan for

char·ta·ceous \kär-'tā-shəs\ *adj* **:** resembling or made of paper

[1]**char·ter** \'chärt-ər\ *n* [ME *chartre*, fr. OF, fr. ML *chartula*, fr. L, dim. of *charta*] **1 :** a written instrument or contract (as a deed) executed in due form **2 a :** a grant or guarantee of rights, franchises, or privileges from the sovereign power of a state or country **b :** CONSTITUTION **3 :** an instrument in writing from the authorities of a society creating a lodge or branch **4 :** a special privilege, immunity, or exemption **5 :** a mercantile lease of a ship or some principal part of it

[2]**charter** *vt* **1 a :** to establish, enable, or convey by charter **b** *Brit* **:** CERTIFY ⟨~*ed* mechanical engineer⟩ **2 :** to hire, rent, or lease for temporary use **syn** see HIRE — **char·ter·er** \-ər-ər\ *n*

chartered accountant *n, Brit* **:** a member of a chartered institute of accountants

Char·tism \'chärt-,iz-əm\ *n* [ML *charta* charter, fr. L, document] **:** the principles and practices of a body of 19th century English political reformers advocating better social and industrial conditions for the working classes

chart·ist \'chärt-əst\ *n* **1 :** CARTOGRAPHER **2 :** a stock-market analyst who relies on charts and graphs for his predictions

Char·tist \'chärt-əst\ *n* **:** an advocate of Chartism

char·treuse \shär-'trüz, -'trüs\ *n* [F, fr. La Grande *Chartreuse*, chief monastery of the Carthusian order] **1 :** a usu. green or yellow liqueur **2 :** a variable color averaging a brilliant yellow green

char·tu·lary \'kär-chə-,ler-ē\ *n* [ML *chartularium*] **:** CARTULARY

char·wom·an \'chär-,wu̇m-ən\ *n* [*chare* + *woman*] **1** *Brit* **:** a woman hired to char **2 :** a cleaning woman usu. in a large building

chary \'cha(ə)r-ē, 'che(ə)r-\ *adj* [ME, sorrowful, dear, fr. OE *cearig* sorrowful, fr. *caru* sorrow] **1** *archaic* **:** TREASURED, DEAR **2 a :** CAUTIOUS, SPARING **b :** WATCHFUL **syn** see CAUTIOUS

Cha·ryb·dis \kə-'rib-dəs\ *n* [L, fr. Gk] **:** a whirlpool off the Sicilian coast personified by the ancients as a female monster

[1]**chase** \'chās\ *vb* [ME *chasen*, fr. MF *chasser*, fr. (assumed) VL *captiare* — more at CATCH] *vt* **1 a :** to follow rapidly **:** PURSUE **b :** HUNT **c :** to follow regularly or persistently with the intention of attracting or alluring **2** *obs* **:** HARASS **3 :** to seek out **4 a :** to cause to depart or flee **:** DRIVE **b** *slang* **:** to take (oneself) off ~ *vi* **1 :** to chase an animal, person, or thing **2 :** RUSH, HASTEN

syn PURSUE, FOLLOW, TRAIL: CHASE implies going swiftly after and trying to overtake something fleeing or running; PURSUE suggests a continuing effort to overtake, reach, attain; FOLLOW puts less emphasis upon speed or intent to overtake and may not imply an awareness on the part of the leader that he is pursued; TRAIL may stress a following of tracks or traces rather than a visible object

[2]**chase** *n* **1 a :** the act of chasing **:** PURSUIT **b :** HUNTING — used with *the* **c :** an earnest or frenzied seeking after something desired **2 :** something pursued **3 a :** a franchise to hunt within certain limits of land **b :** a tract of unenclosed land used as a game preserve

[3]**chase** *vt* [ME *chassen*, modif. of MF *enchasser* to set] **1 a :** to ornament (metal) by indenting with a hammer and tools without a cutting edge **b :** to make by such indentation **c :** to set with gems **2 a :** GROOVE, INDENT **b :** to cut (a thread) with a chaser

[4]**chase** *n* [F *chas* eye of a needle, fr. LL *capsus* enclosed space, fr. L, pen, alter. of *capsa* box — more at CASE] **1 :** GROOVE, FURROW **2 :** the bore of a cannon **3 a :** TRENCH **b :** a channel (as in a wall) for something to lie in or pass through

[5]**chase** *n* [prob. fr. F *châsse* frame, fr. L *capsa*] **:** a rectangular steel or iron frame into which letterpress matter is locked for printing or plating — compare FORM

[1]**chas·er** \'chā-sər\ *n* **1 :** one that chases **2 :** a mild drink (as water or beer) taken after hard liquor

[2]**chaser** *n* **:** a skilled worker who produces ornamental chasing

[3]**chaser** *n* **:** a tool for cutting screw threads

Cha·sid \'has-əd, 'kä̱s-\ *n, pl* **Cha·si·dim** \'has-əd-əm, kə̱-'sēd-\ *var of* HASID

chasm \'kaz-əm\ *n* [L *chasma*, fr. Gk; akin to L *hiare* to yawn] **1 :** a deep cleft in the earth **:** GORGE **2 :** GULF

[1]**chas·sé** \sha-'sā\ *vi* **chas·séd; chas·sé·ing** [F, n., fr. pp. of *chasser* to chase] **1 :** to make a chassé **2 :** SASHAY

[2]**chassé** *n* **:** a sliding dance step resembling the galop

chasse·pot \'shas-(,)pō\ *n* [F, fr. Antoine A. *Chassepot* †1905 F inventor] **:** a bolt-action rifle firing a paper cartridge

chas·seur \sha-'sər\ *n* [F, fr. MF *chasser*] **1 :** HUNTER, HUNTSMAN **2 :** one of a body of light cavalry or infantry trained for rapid maneuvering **3 :** a liveried attendant **:** FOOTMAN

chas·sis \'shas-ē, 'chas-\ *n, pl* **chas·sis** \-ēz\ [F *châssis*, fr. (assumed) VL *capsicum*, fr. L *capsa* box — more at CASE] **1 :** the frame upon which is mounted the body (as of an automobile or airplane), the working parts (as of a radio), the barrel and other recoiling parts (of a cannon), or the roof, walls, floors, and facing (as of a building) **2 :** the frame and working parts as opposed to the body (as of an automobile) or cabinet (as of a radio or television set)

chaste \'chāst\ *adj* [ME, fr. OF, fr. L *castus* pure — more at CASTE] **1 :** innocent of unlawful sexual intercourse **2 :** CELIBATE **3 :** pure in thought and act **:** MODEST **4 :** pure or severe in design and expression — **chaste·ly** *adv* — **chaste·ness** \'chās(t)-nəs\ *n*

syn PURE, MODEST, DECENT: CHASTE primarily implies a refraining from acts or even thoughts or desires that are not virginal or not sanctioned by marriage vows; it may imply avoidance of anything that cheapens or debases; PURE differs from CHASTE in implying innocence and absence of temptation rather than control of one's impulses and actions; MODEST and DECENT apply esp. to deportment and dress as outward signs of inward chastity or purity

chas·ten \'chās-ᵊn\ *vt* **chas·ten·ing** \'chās-niŋ, -ᵊn-iŋ\ [alter. of obs. E *chaste* to chasten, fr. ME *chasten*, fr. OF *chastier*, fr. L *castigare*, fr. *castus* + *-igare* (fr. *agere* to drive) — more at ACT] **1 :** to correct by punishment or suffering **:** DISCIPLINE; *also* **:** PURIFY **2 :** to prune of excess, pretense, or falsity **:** REFINE **syn** see PUNISH — **chas·ten·er** \'chās-nər, -ᵊn-ər\ *n*

chas·tise \cha-'stīz\ *vt* [ME *chastisen*, alter. of *chasten*] **1 :** to inflict punishment on (as by whipping) **2 :** to censure severely **:** CASTIGATE **3** *archaic* **:** CHASTEN 2 **syn** see PUNISH — **chas·tise·ment** \cha-'stīz-mənt, 'chas-təz-\ *n* — **chas·tis·er** \cha-'stī-zər\ *n*

chas·ti·ty \'chas-tət-ē\ *n* **1 :** the quality or state of being chaste: as **a :** abstention from unlawful sexual intercourse **b :** abstention from all sexual intercourse **c :** purity in conduct and intention **d :** restraint and simplicity in design or expression **2 :** personal integrity

cha·su·ble \'chaz(h)-ə-bəl, 'chas-ə-\ *n* [F, fr. LL *casubla* hooded garment] **:** the outer vestment of the celebrant at the Eucharist

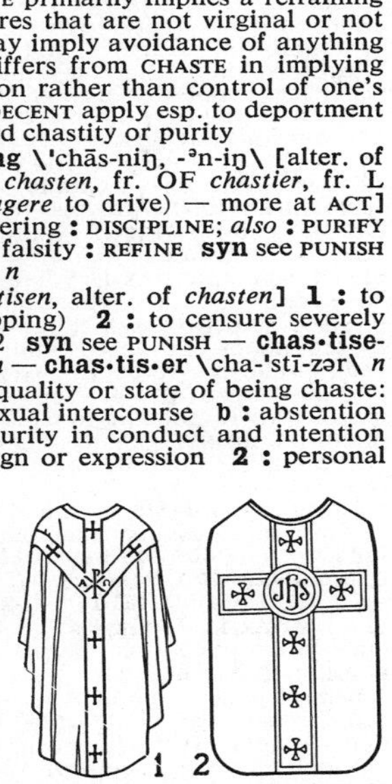

1 2

chasubles: *1* Gothic, *2* fiddle-back

[1]**chat** \'chat\ *vi* **chat·ted; chat·ting** [ME *chatten*, short for *chatteren*] **1 :** CHATTER, PRATTLE **2 :** to talk in a light, informal, or familiar manner

[2]**chat** *n* **1** *archaic* **:** idle small talk **:** CHATTER **2 :** light familiar talk; *esp* **:** CONVERSATION **3** [imit.] **:** any of several songbirds (as of the genera *Saxicola* or *Icteria*)

châ·teau \sha-'tō\ *n, pl* **châ·teaus** \-'tōz\ *or* **châ·teaux** \-'tō(z)\ [F, fr. L *castellum* castle] **1 :** a feudal castle in France **2 :** a large country house **3 :** a French vineyard estate

chat·e·lain \'shat-ᵊl-,ān\ *n* [MF *châtelain*, fr. L *castellanus* occupant of a castle] **:** CASTELLAN

chat·e·laine \'shat-ᵊl-,ān\ *n* [F *châtelaine*, fem. of *châtelain*] **1 a :** the wife of a castellan **b :** the mistress of a château **2 :** a clasp or hook for a watch, purse, or bunch of keys

cha·toy·ance \shə-'tȯi-ən(t)s, ,sha-,twä-'yä^{n}s\ *or* **cha·toy·an·cy** \shə-'tȯi-ən-sē\ *n* **:** the quality or state of being chatoyant

[1]**cha·toy·ant** \shə-'tȯi-ənt, ,sha-,twä-'yä^{n}\ *adj* [F, fr. prp. of *chatoyer* to shine like a cat's eyes] **:** having a changeable luster or color with an undulating narrow band of white light

[2]**chatoyant** *n* **:** a chatoyant gem

chat·tel \'chat-ᵊl\ *n* [ME *chatel* property, fr. OF, fr. ML *capitale* — more at CATTLE] **1 :** an item of tangible movable or immovable property except real estate, freehold, and the things which are parcel of it **2 :** SLAVE, BONDSMAN

chat·ter \'chat-ər\ *vb* [ME *chatteren*, of imit. origin] *vi* **1 :** to utter rapidly succeeding sounds somewhat like language but inarticulate and indistinct ⟨squirrels ~*ed* angrily⟩ ⟨a ~*ing* stream⟩ **2 :** to talk idly, incessantly, or fast **:** JABBER **3 a :** to click repeatedly or uncontrollably ⟨~*ing* teeth⟩ **b** *of a tool* **:** to vibrate rapidly in cutting ~ *vt* **1 :** to utter rapidly, idly, or indistinctly **2** *dial Eng* **:** TEAR, SHATTER **3 :** to cut unevenly with a chattering tool — **chatter** *n*

chat·ter·box \-,bäks\ *n* **:** one who talks much and idly

chat·ter·er \'chat-ər-ər\ *n* **1 :** one that chatters **2 :** any of various passerine birds (as a waxwing)

chatter mark *n* **1 :** a fine undulation formed on the surface of work by a chattering tool **2 :** one of a series of short curved cracks on a glaciated rock surface transverse to the glacial striae

chat·ti·ly \'chat-ᵊl-ē\ *adv* **:** in a chatty manner

chat·ti·ness \'chat-ē-nəs\ *n* **:** the quality or state of being chatty

chat·ty \'chat-ē\ *adj* **1 :** given to informal friendly talk **2 :** of or relating to chat ⟨a ~ letter⟩

[1]**chauf·feur** \'shō-fər, shō-'\ *n* [F, lit., stoker, fr. *chauffer* to heat, fr. MF *chaufer*] **:** a person employed to drive a motor vehicle

[2]**chauffeur** *vb* **chauf·feur·ing** \'shō-f(ə-)riŋ, shō-'fər-iŋ\ *vi* **:** to do the work of a chauffeur ~ *vt* **1 :** to transport in the manner of a chauffeur **2 :** to operate as chauffeur

chaul·moo·gra \chȯl-'mü-grə\ *n* [Beng *cāulmugrā*] **:** any of several East Indian trees (family Flacourtiaceae) that yield an acrid oil used in treating leprosy and skin diseases

chaunt \'chȯnt, 'chänt\ **chaunter** *archaic var of* CHANT, CHANTER

chaus·sure \shō-sue̅r\ *n, pl* **chaussures** *same*\ [ME *chaucer*, fr. MF *chaussure*] **1 :** FOOTGEAR **2** *pl* **:** SHOES

chau·tau·qua \shə-'tȯ-kwə\ *n* [*Chautauqua* lake, western New York] **:** a popular lyceum and amusement enterprise of the late 19th and early 20th centuries

chau·vin·ism \'shō-və-,niz-əm\ *n* [F *chauvinisme*, fr. Nicolas *Chauvin fl* 1815 F soldier of excessive patriotism and devotion to Napoleon] **:** excessive or blind patriotism — compare JINGOISM — **chau·vin·ist** \-və-nəst\ *n* — **chau·vin·is·tic** \,shō-və-'nis-tik\ *adj* — **chau·vin·is·ti·cal·ly** \-ti-k(ə-)lē\ *adv*

[1]**chaw** \'chȯ\ *vb* [by alter.] *dial* **:** CHEW

[2]**chaw** *n, dial* **:** a chew esp. of tobacco

[1]**cheap** \'chēp\ *n* [ME *chep*, fr. OE *cēap* trade; akin to OHG *kouf* trade; both fr. a prehistoric Gmc stem borrowed fr. L *caupo* tradesman] *obs* **:** BARGAIN

[2]**cheap** *adj* **1 a :** purchasable below the going price or the real value **b :** charging a low price **c :** depreciated in value (as by currency inflation) ⟨~ dollars⟩ **2 :** costing little trouble to obtain ⟨a ~ victory⟩ **3 a :** SHODDY, MERETRICIOUS **b :** worthy of scorn **4 a :** yielding small satisfaction **b :** paying or able to pay less than going prices **5** *of money* **:** obtainable at a low rate of interest **6** *Brit* **:** specially reduced in price **syn** see CONTEMPTIBLE — **cheap** *adv* — **cheap·ly** *adv* — **cheap·ness** *n*

cheap·en \'chē-pən\ *vb* **cheap·en·ing** \'chēp-(ə-)niŋ\ *vt* **1** [obs. E *cheap* (to price, bid for)] *archaic* **a :** to ask the price of **b :** to bid or bargain for **2 a :** to make cheap in price or value **b :** to lower in general esteem **c :** to make tawdry, vulgar, or inferior ~ *vi* **:** to become cheap

cheap–jack \'chēp-,jak\ *n, often attrib* [*cheap* + the name *Jack*] **1 :** a chaffering huckster **2 :** a dealer in cheap merchandise

cheap·skate \-,skāt\ *n* **:** a shabby or miserly person

[1]**cheat** \'chēt\ *n* [earlier *cheat* forfeited property, fr. ME *chet* escheat, short for *eschete* — more at ESCHEAT] **1 :** the act of fraudulently deceiving **:** DECEPTION, FRAUD **2 :** one that cheats **:** PRETENDER, DECEIVER **3 :** any of several grasses; *esp* **:** the common chess (*Bromus secalinus*) **4 :** the obtaining of property from another by an intentional active distortion of the truth

[2]**cheat** *vt* **1 :** to deprive of something valuable by the use of deceit or fraud **2 :** to influence or lead by deceit, trick, or artifice **3 :** to defeat in an expectation or purpose by deceit and trickery ~ *vi* **1 a :** to practice fraud or trickery **b :** to violate rules dishonestly (as at cards) **2 :** to be sexually unfaithful — **cheat·er** *n*

syn CHEAT, COZEN, DEFRAUD, SWINDLE, OVERREACH mean to get something from another by dishonesty or deception. CHEAT suggests using trickery that escapes observation; COZEN implies artful persuading or flattering to attain a thing or a purpose; DEFRAUD stresses depriving one of his rights and usu. connotes deliberate perversion of the truth; SWINDLE implies large-scale cheating by means of misrepresentation or mean abuse of confidence; OVERREACH implies getting the better of in dealing or bargaining

[1]**check** \'chek\ *n* [ME *chek*, fr. OF *eschec*, fr. Ar *shāh*, fr. Per, lit., king; akin to Gk *ktasthai* to acquire] **1 :** exposure of a chess king to an attack from which he must be moved to safety **2 a :** a sudden stoppage of a forward course or progress **:** ARREST **b :** [2]STOP 9 **c :** a checking of an opposing player in ice hockey **3 :** a sudden pause or break in a progression **4** *archaic* **:** REPRIMAND, REBUKE **5 :** something or someone that arrests, limits, or restrains **:** RESTRAINT **6 a :** a standard for testing and evaluation **:** CRITERION **b :** EXAMINATION **c :** INSPECTION, INVESTIGATION **d :** the act of testing or verifying; *also* **:** the sample or unit used for testing or verifying **7 :** a written order directing a bank to pay money as instructed **8 a :** a ticket or token showing ownership or identity or indicating payment made **b :** a counter in various games **c :** a slip indicating the amount due **:** BILL **9** [ME *chek*, short for *cheker* checker] **a :** a pattern in squares that resembles a checkerboard **b :** a fabric woven or printed with such a design **10 :** a mark typically √ placed beside an item to show it has been noted, examined, or verified **11 :** CRACK, BREAK **12 :** a rabbet-shaped cutting **:** RABBET — **in check :** under restraint or control

[2]**check** *vt* **1 :** to place (a chess king) in check **2** *chiefly dial* **:** REBUKE, REPRIMAND **3 a :** to slow or bring to a stop **:** BRAKE **b :** to block the progress of (a hockey player) **4 a :** to restrain or diminish the action or force of **:** CONTROL **b :** to slack or ease

off and then belay again (as a purchase or rope) **5 a :** to compare with a source, original, or authority **:** VERIFY **b :** to inspect for satisfactory condition, accuracy, safety, or performance **c :** to mark with a check as examined, verified, or satisfactory **6 a :** to consign for shipment for the holder of a passenger ticket **b :** to ship or accept for shipment under such a consignment **7 :** to mark into squares **:** CHECKER **8 :** to leave or accept for safekeeping in a checkroom **9 :** to make checks or chinks in ~ *vi* **1 a** *of a dog* **:** to stop in a chase esp. when scent is lost **b :** to halt through caution, uncertainty, or fear **:** STOP **2 a :** to investigate conditions **b :** to correspond point for point **:** TALLY **3 :** to draw a check on a bank **4 :** to waive the right to initiate the betting in a round of poker **5 :** CRACK, SPLIT **syn** see RESTRAIN

check·book \-,bu̇k\ *n* **:** a book containing blank checks on a bank

¹**check·er** \'chek-ər\ *n* [ME *cheker*, fr. OF *eschequier*, fr. *eschec*] **1** *archaic* **:** CHESSBOARD **2 :** a square or spot resembling checkerboard markings **3 a :** either of two Old World service trees (*Sorbus domestica* and *S. torminalis*) **b :** the fruit of a checker **4** [back-formation fr. *checkers*] **:** a man in checkers

²**checker** *vt* **check·er·ing** \'chek-(ə-)riŋ\ **1 a :** to variegate with different colors or shades **b :** to vary with contrasting elements or situations **2 :** to mark into squares

³**checker** *n* **:** one that checks

check·er·ber·ry \'chek-ə(r)-,ber-ē\ *n* [*checker* (wild service tree) + *berry*] **1 :** any of several reddish berries; *esp* **:** the spicy red berrylike fruit of a wintergreen (*Gaultheria procumbens*) **2 :** a plant producing checkerberries

check·er·bloom \-ər-,blüm\ *n* [prob. fr. ¹*checker* + *bloom*] **:** a purple-flowered mallow (*Sidalcea malvaeflora*) of the western U.S.

check·er·board \-ə(r)-,bō(ə)rd, -,bȯ(ə)rd\ *n* **:** a board used in checkers and other games with usu. 64 squares in 2 alternating colors

check·ers \'chek-ərz\ *n pl but sing in constr* **:** a checkerboard game for 2 players each with 12 men

checking account *n* **:** a demand deposit account in a bank against which the depositor can draw checks

¹**check·mate** \'chek-,māt\ *vt* [ME *chekmaten*, fr. *chekmate*, interj. used to announce checkmate, fr. MF *eschec mat*, fr. Ar *shāh māt*, fr. Per, lit., the king is left unable to escape] **1 :** to arrest, thwart, or counter completely **2 :** to check (a chess opponent's king) so that escape is impossible

²**checkmate** *n* **1 a :** the act of checkmating **b :** the situation of a checkmated king **2 :** a complete check

check·point \-,pȯint\ *n* **:** a point at which vehicular traffic is halted for inspection or clearance

check·rein \-,rān\ *n* **1 :** a short rein looped over a hook on the saddle of a harness to prevent a horse from lowering his head **2 :** a branch rein connecting the driving rein of one horse of a span or pair with the bit of the other

check·room \-,rüm, -,ru̇m\ *n* **:** a room at which baggage, parcels, or clothing is checked

check·row \'chek-,rō\ *vt* **:** to plant (as corn) at the points of intersection of right-angled rows to permit two-way cultivation

check·up \'chek-,əp\ *n* **:** EXAMINATION; *esp* **:** a general physical examination

ched·dar \'ched-ər\ *n, often cap* [*Cheddar*, England] **:** a hard pressed standard factory cheese of smooth texture

che·der \'k̲ād-ər, 'ked-\ *var of* HEDER

¹**cheek** \'chēk\ *n* [ME *cheke*, fr. OE *cēace*; akin to MLG *kāke* jawbone] **1 :** the fleshy side of the face below the eye and above and to the side of the mouth; *broadly* **:** the lateral aspect of the head **2 :** something suggestive of the human cheek in position or form; *broadly* **:** SIDE **3 :** EFFRONTERY, IMPUDENCE **syn** see TEMERITY — **cheek by jowl :** in close proximity

²**cheek** *vt* **:** to address rudely or impudently

cheek·bone \-'bōn, -,bōn\ *n* **:** the prominence below the eye that is formed by the zygomatic bone; *also* **:** ZYGOMATIC BONE

cheek·i·ly \'chē-kə-lē\ *adv* **:** IMPUDENTLY, BOLDLY

cheek·i·ness \'chē-kē-nəs\ *n* **:** EFFRONTERY, INSOLENCE

cheeky \'chē-kē\ *adj* **1 :** having or showing cheek **:** IMPUDENT **2 :** having well-developed cheeks — used esp. of a bulldog

cheep \'chēp\ *vb* [imit.] *vi* **1 :** to utter faint shrill sounds **:** PEEP **2 :** to make a small sound ~ *vt* **:** CHIRP — **cheep** *n*

¹**cheer** \'chi(ə)r\ *n* [ME *chere* face, cheer, fr. OF, face] **1 a** *obs* **:** FACE **b** *archaic* **:** facial expression **2 :** state of mind or heart **:** SPIRIT **3 :** ANIMATION, GAIETY **4 :** hospitable entertainment **:** WELCOME **5 :** food and drink for a feast **:** FARE **6 :** something that gladdens **7 :** a shout of applause or encouragement

²**cheer** *vt* **1 a :** to arouse to hope or courage when dejected **:** COMFORT **b :** to make glad or happy **2 :** to urge on or encourage esp. by shouts **3 :** to applaud with shouts ~ *vi* **1** *obs* **:** to be mentally or emotionally disposed **2 :** to grow or be cheerful **:** REJOICE — usu. used with *up* **3 :** to utter a shout of applause or triumph

cheer·ful \'chir-fəl\ *adj* **1 a :** full of good spirits **:** MERRY **b :** UNGRUDGING ⟨~ obedience⟩ **2 :** conducive to cheer **:** likely to dispel gloom or worry ⟨sunny ~ room⟩ **syn** see GLAD — **cheer·ful·ly** \-f(ə-)lē\ *adv* — **cheer·ful·ness** \-fəl-nəs\ *n*

cheer·i·ly \'chir-ə-lē\ *adv* **:** in a cheery manner **:** CHEERFULLY

cheer·i·ness \'chir-ē-nəs\ *n* **:** the quality or state of being cheery

cheer·io \,chi(ə)r-ē-'ō\ *interj* [*cheery* + *-o*] *chiefly Brit* — usu. used as a farewell and sometimes as a greeting or toast

cheer·less \'chi(ə)r-ləs\ *adj* **:** BLEAK, DISPIRITING — **cheer·less·ly** *adv* — **cheer·less·ness** *n*

cheer·ly \'chi(ə)r-lē\ *adv* **:** CHEERILY, HEARTILY

cheery \'chi(ə)r-ē\ *adj* **:** BRIGHT, GAY

¹**cheese** \'chēz\ *n, often attrib* [ME *chese*, fr. OE *cēse*; akin to OHG *kāsi* cheese; both fr. a prehistoric WGmc word borrowed fr. L *caseus* cheese; akin to OE *hwatherian* to foam, Skt *kvathati* he boils] **1 a :** curd separated from whey, consolidated by molding or pressure, and ripened for use as a food **b :** an often cylindrical cake of this food **2 :** something like cheese in shape or consistency

²**cheese** *n* [perh. fr. Urdu *chīz* thing] **1** *slang* **:** something first-rate **2** *slang* **:** someone important **:** BOSS

cheese·burg·er \-,bər-gər\ *n* [*cheese* + ham*burger*] **:** a hamburger with a slice of toasted cheese

cheese·cake \-,kāk\ *n* **1 :** a cake made by baking a mixture of cottage cheese, eggs, and sugar or a filling of similar texture in a pastry shell or a mold lined with sweet crumbs **2 :** publicity photographs featuring the curves of female legs or buttocks

cheese·cloth \-,klȯth\ *n* [fr. its use in cheesemaking] **:** a very lightweight unsized cotton gauze

cheese·par·ing \-,par-iŋ, -,per-\ *n* **1 :** a worthless bit **2 :** miserly or petty economizing **:** STINGINESS — **cheeseparing** *adj*

cheesy \'chē-zē\ *adj* **1 :** resembling or suggesting cheese esp. in consistency or odor **2** *slang* **:** SHABBY, CHEAP ⟨~ comedy⟩

chee·tah \'chēt-ə\ *n* [Hindi *cītā*, fr. Skt *citrakāya* tiger, fr. *citra* bright + *kāya* body; akin to Skt *cinoti* he heaps up] **:** a long-legged spotted swift-moving African and formerly Asiatic cat (*Acinonyx jubatus*) about the size of a small leopard that has blunt nonretractile claws and is often trained to run down game

chef \'shef\ *n* [F, short for *chef de cuisine* head of the kitchen] **1 :** a skilled male cook who manages a kitchen **2 :** COOK

chef d'oeu·vre \shā-dœvrᵊ\ *n, pl* **chefs d'oeuvre** *same*\ [F, lit., leading work] **:** a masterpiece esp. in art or literature

che·la \'kē-lə\ *n, pl* **che·lae** \-(,)lē\ [NL, fr. Gk *chēlē* claw] **:** a pincerlike organ or claw borne by a limb of a crustacean or arachnid

¹**che·late** \'kē-,lāt\ *adj* **1 :** resembling or having chelae **2** [Gk *chēlē* claw, hoof] **:** of, relating to, or having a cyclic structure usu. containing five or six atoms in a ring in which a central metallic ion is held in a coordination complex — **chelate** *n*

²**chelate** *vt* **:** to combine with (a metal) so as to form a chelate ring ~ *vi* **:** to react so as to form a chelate ring — **che·la·tion** \kē-'lā-shən\ *n*

che·lic·era \ki-'lis-ə-rə\ *n, pl* **che·lic·er·ae** \-,rē\ [NL, fr. F *chélicère*, fr. Gk *chēlē* + *keras* horn — more at HORN] **:** one of the anterior pair of appendages of an arachnid often specialized as fangs — **che·lic·er·al** \-ə-rəl\ *adj*

Chel·le·an *or* **Chel·li·an** \'shel-ē-ən\ *adj* [F *chelléen*, fr. *Chelles*, France] **:** ABBEVILLIAN

che·lo·ni·an \ki-'lō-nē-ən\ *adj* [Gk *chelōnē* tortoise] **:** of, relating to, or being a tortoise or turtle — **chelonian** *n*

chem- *or* **chemo-** *also* **chemi-** *comb form* [NL, fr. LGk *chēmeia* alchemy — more at ALCHEMY] **1 :** chemical **:** chemistry ⟨*chemo*smosis⟩ ⟨*chemo*taxis⟩ **2 :** chemically ⟨*chemi*sorb⟩

chem·ic \'kem-ik\ *adj* [NL *chimicus* alchemist, fr. ML *alchimicus*, fr. *alchymia* alchemy] **1** *archaic* **:** ALCHEMIC **2 :** CHEMICAL

¹**chem·i·cal** \'kem-i-kəl\ *adj* **1 :** of, relating to, used in, or produced by chemistry **2 :** acting or operated or produced by chemicals — **chem·i·cal·ly** \-i-k(ə-)lē\ *adv*

²**chemical** *n* **:** a substance obtained by a chemical process or used for producing a chemical effect

chemical engineering *n* **:** engineering dealing with the industrial application of chemistry

chemical warfare *n* **:** tactical warfare using incendiary mixtures, smokes, or irritant, burning, or asphyxiating gases

chemi·lu·mi·nes·cence \,kem-ē-,lü-mə-'nes-ᵊn(t)s\ *n* [ISV] **:** luminescence due to chemical reaction usu. at low temperatures; *esp* **:** BIOLUMINESCENCE — **chemi·lu·mi·nes·cent** \-'nes-ᵊnt\ *adj*

che·min de fer \shə-,man-də-'fe(ə)r\ *n, pl* **che·mins de fer** \-,man-də-\ [F, lit., railroad] **:** a card game resembling baccarat

che·mise \shə-'mēz\ *n* [ME, fr. OF, shirt, fr. LL *camisia*] **1 :** a woman's one-piece undergarment **2 :** a loose straight-hanging dress

chem·i·sette \,shem-ē-'zet\ *n* [F, dim. of *chemise*] **:** a woman's garment; *esp* **:** one (as of lace) to fill the open front of a dress

chem·ism \'kem-,iz-əm\ *n* **:** operation in obedience to chemical laws

chemi·sorb \'kem-i-,sȯrb\ *or* **chemo·sorb** \'kem-ə-\ *vt* [*chem-* + *-sorb* (as in *adsorb*)] **:** to take up and hold usu. irreversibly by chemical forces — **chemi·sorp·tion** \,kem-i-'sȯrp-shən\ *n*

chem·ist \'kem-əst\ *n* [NL *chimista*, short for ML *alchimista*] **1 a** *obs* **:** ALCHEMIST **b :** one trained in chemistry **2** *Brit* **:** PHARMACIST

chem·is·try \'kem-ə-strē\ *n* **1 :** a science that deals with the composition, structure, and properties of substances and of the transformations that they undergo **2 a :** the composition and chemical properties of a substance ⟨the ~ of iron⟩ **b :** chemical processes and phenomena (as of an organism) ⟨blood ~⟩

che·mo·au·to·tro·phic \,kem-ō-,ȯt-ə-'träf-ik, ,kē-mō-, -'trō-fik\ *adj* **:** being autotrophic and oxidizing some inorganic compound as a source of energy — **chemo·au·to·tro·phi·cal·ly** \-(ə-)lē\ *adv* — **chemo·au·tot·ro·phy** \-ō-'tä-trə-fē\ *n*

che·mo·pro·phy·lac·tic \-,prō-fə-'lak-tik\ *adj* **:** of or relating to chemoprophylaxis

che·mo·pro·phy·lax·is \-'lak-səs\ *n* **:** the prevention of infectious disease by the use of chemical agents

che·mo·re·cep·tion \-ri-'sep-shən\ *n* [ISV] **:** the physiological reception of chemical stimuli — **che·mo·re·cep·tive** \-'sep-tiv\ *adj* — **che·mo·re·cep·tiv·i·ty** \-(,)rē-,sep-'tiv-ət-ē\ *n*

che·mo·re·cep·tor \-ri-'sep-tər\ *n* [ISV] **:** any sense organ as a taste bud) responding to chemical stimuli

chem·os·mo·sis \,kem-äs-'mō-səs, -äz-'mō-səs\ *n* [NL] **:** chemical action taking place through an intervening membrane — **chem·os·mot·ic** \-'mät-ik\ *adj*

che·mo·syn·the·sis \,kem-ō-'sin(t)-thə-səs, ,kē-mō-\ *n* [ISV] **:** synthesis of organic compounds by energy derived from chemical reactions — **che·mo·syn·thet·ic** \(,)sin-'thet-ik\ *adj*

che·mo·tac·tic \-'tak-tik\ *adj* **:** involving or exhibiting chemotaxis — **che·mo·tac·ti·cal·ly** \-ti-k(ə-)lē\ *adv*

che·mo·tax·is \-'tak-səs\ *n* [NL] **:** orientation or movement in relation to chemical agents

che·mo·ther·a·peu·tic \-,ther-ə-'pyüt-ik\ *adj* **:** of or relating to chemotherapy — **chemotherapeutic** *n* — **che·mo·ther·a·peu·ti·cal** \-i-kəl\ *adj* — **che·mo·ther·a·peu·ti·cal·ly** \-i-k(ə-)lē\ *adv*

che·mo·ther·a·py \-'ther-ə-pē\ *n* [ISV] **:** the use of chemical agents in the treatment or control of disease

che·mot·ro·pism \ke-'mä-trə-,piz-əm\ *n* [ISV] **:** orientation of cells or organisms in relation to chemical stimuli

chem·ur·gic \ke-'mər-jik, kə-\ *adj* **:** of, relating to, or produced by chemurgy — **chem·ur·gi·cal·ly** \-ji-k(ə-)lē\ *adv*

chem·ur·gy \'kem-(,)ər-jē, kə-'mər-\ *n* **:** a branch of applied chemistry that deals with industrial utilization of organic raw materials esp. from farm products

che·nille \shə-'nē(ə)l\ *n* [F, lit., caterpillar, fr. L *canicula*, dim. of *canis* dog; fr. its hairy appearance] **1 :** a wool, cotton, silk, or rayon yarn with protruding pile; *also* **:** a pile-face fabric with a filling of this yarn **2 :** an imitation of chenille yarn or fabric

che·no·pod \'kē-nə-,päd, 'ken-ə-\ *n* [deriv. of Gk *chēn* goose + *podion*, dim. of *pod-*, *pous* foot] **:** a plant of the goosefoot family

cheque \'chek\ *chiefly Brit var of* CHECK 7

cher·ish \'cher-ish\ *vt* [ME *cherisshen*, fr. MF *cheriss-*, stem of *cherir* to cherish, fr. OF, fr. *chier* dear, fr. L *carus* — more at CHARITY] **1 a :** to hold dear **:** feel or show affection for **b :** to keep or cultivate with care and affection **:** NURTURE **2 :** to entertain or harbor in the mind deeply and resolutely **syn** see APPRECIATE

cher·no·zem \,cher-nə-'zhȯm\ *n* [Russ, lit., black earth] **:** a dark-colored zonal soil with a deep rich humus horizon found in temperate to cool climates of rather low humidity

Cher·o·kee \'cher-ə-,kē, ,cher-ə-'\ *n, pl* **Cherokee** *or* **Cherokees** [prob. fr. Creek *tciloki* people of a different speech] **1 a :** an Iroquoian people orig. of the Appalachian mountains of Tennessee and No. Carolina **b :** a member of this people **2 :** the language of the Cherokee people

Cherokee rose *n* **:** a Chinese climbing rose (*Rosa laevigata*) with a fragrant white blossom

che·root \shə-'rüt, chə-\ *n* [Tamil *curuṭṭu*, lit., roll] **:** a cigar cut square at both ends

cher·ry \'cher-ē\ *n* [ME *chery*, fr. ONF *cherise* (taken as a plural), fr. LL *ceresia*, fr. L *cerasus* cherry tree, fr. Gk *kerasos* — more at CORNEL] **1 a :** any of numerous trees and shrubs (genus *Prunus*) of the rose family that have pale yellow to deep red or blackish smooth-skinned nearly globular rather small fruits which are drupes enclosing a smooth seed and that include various improved forms cultivated for their fruits or ornamental flowers **b :** the fruit or wood of a cherry **2 :** a variable color averaging a moderate red

cherry laurel *n* **1 :** a European evergreen shrub (*Prunus laurocerasus*) common in cultivation **2 :** an evergreen shrub (*Prunus caroliniana*) of the southern U.S.

cherry plum *n* **:** an Asiatic plum (*Prunus cerasifera*) used extensively in Europe as a stock on which to bud domestic varieties

cher·ry·stone \'cher-ē-,stōn\ *n* **:** a small quahog

cher·so·nese \'kər-sə-,nēz, -,nēs\ *n* [L *chersonesus*, fr. Gk *chersonēsos*, fr. *chersos* dry land + *nēsos* island] **:** PENINSULA

chert \'chərt, 'chat\ *n* [origin unknown] **:** a rock resembling flint and consisting essentially of cryptocrystalline quartz or fibrous chalcedony — **cherty** \-ē\ *adj*

cher·ub \'cher-əb\ *n, pl* **cherubs** *or* **cher·u·bim** \'cher-(y)ə-,bim, 'ker-\ [L, fr. Gk *cheroub*, fr. Heb *kĕrūbh*] **1 :** a biblical figure often represented as a being with large wings, a human head, and an animal body and regarded as a guardian of a sacred place **2 :** an angel of the second highest rank **3** *pl* **cherubs a :** a beautiful usu. winged child **b :** an innocent-looking esp. chubby and rosy person — **che·ru·bic** \chə-'rü-bik, -'rəb-ik; 'cher-ə-bik\ *adj*

cher·vil \'chər-vəl\ *n* [ME *cherville*, fr. OE *cerfille*; akin to OHG *kervila*] **:** an aromatic herb (*Anthriscus cerefolium*) of the carrot family with divided leaves often used in soups and salads; *also* **:** any of several related plants

Ches·a·peake Bay retriever \,ches-(ə-),pēk-,bā-\ *n* **:** a large powerful sporting dog developed in Maryland by crossing Newfoundlands with native retrievers

Chesh·ire cat \,chesh-ər-\ *n* [*Cheshire*, England] **:** a cat with a broad grin in Lewis Carroll's *Alice's Adventures in Wonderland*

Cheshire cheese *n* **:** a cheese similar to cheddar made chiefly in Cheshire, England

¹chess \'ches\ *n* [ME *ches*, fr. OF *esches*, acc. pl. of *eschec* check at chess — more at CHECK] **:** a game for 2 players each of whom moves his 16 pieces according to fixed rules across a checkerboard and tries to checkmate his opponent's king — **chess·board** \-,bō(ə)rd, -,bȯ(ə)rd\ *n* — **chess·man** \-,man, -mən\ *n*

²chess *n* [origin unknown] **:** a weedy annual bromegrass (*Bromus secalinus*) widely distributed as a weed esp. in grain; *broadly* **:** any weedy bromegrass

chest \'chest\ *n* [ME, fr. OE *cest*; akin to OHG & ON *kista* chest] **1 :** a container for storage or shipping; *esp* **:** a box with a lid esp. for safekeeping of belongings **2 :** the place where money of a public institution is kept **:** TREASURY; *also* **:** the fund so kept **3 :** the part of the body enclosed by the ribs and breastbone — **chest·ed** \'ches-təd\ *adj*

ches·ter·field \'ches-tər-,fēld\ *n* [fr. a 19th cent. Earl of *Chesterfield*] **1 :** a single-breasted or double-breasted semifitted overcoat with velvet collar **2 :** a davenport usu. with upright armrests

Ches·ter White \,ches-tər-\ *n* [*Chester* County, Pa.] **:** any of a breed of large white swine

¹chest·nut \'ches-(,)nət\ *n* [ME *chasteine*, *chesten* chestnut tree, fr. MF *chastaigne*, fr. L *castanea*, fr. Gk *kastanea*] **1 :** the edible nut of a tree or shrub (genus *Castanea*) of the beech family; *also* **:** a plant bearing chestnuts or its wood **2 :** a grayish brown **3 :** HORSE CHESTNUT **4 :** a horse having a body color of any shade of pure or reddish brown with mane, tail, and points of the same or a lighter shade — compare ²BAY 1, ¹SORREL **5 :** a callosity on the inner side of the leg of the horse **6 a :** an old joke or story **b :** something repeated to the point of staleness

²chestnut *adj* **1 :** of, relating to, or resembling a chestnut **2 :** of the color chestnut

chestnut blight *n* **:** a destructive fungous disease of the American chestnut marked by cankers of bark and cambium

che·val-de-frise \shə-,val-də-'frēz\ *n, pl* **che·vaux-de-frise** \shə-,vōd-ə-\ [F, lit., horse from Friesland] **1 :** a defense consisting of a timber or an iron barrel covered with projecting spikes and often strung with barbed wire **2 :** a protecting line (as of spikes) on top of a wall — usu. used in pl.

che·val glass \shə-'val-\ *n* [F *cheval* horse, support] **:** a full-length mirror that may be tilted in a frame

che·va·lier \,shev-ə-'li(ə)r, *esp for 1b & 2 also* shə-'val-,yā\ *n* [ME, fr. MF, fr. LL *caballarius* horseman] **1 a :** CAVALIER 2 **b :** a member of any of various orders of knighthood or of merit (as the Legion of Honor) **2 a :** a member of the lowest rank of French nobility **b :** a cadet of the French nobility **3 :** a chivalrous man

che·ve·lure \shəv-'lu̇r\ *n* [F, fr. L *capillatura*, fr. *capillatus* having hair, fr. *capillus* hair] **:** a head of hair

chev·i·ot \'shev-ē-ət, *esp Brit* 'chev-\ *n, often cap* [*Cheviot* hills, England and Scotland] **1 :** any of a breed of hardy hornless medium-wooled meat-type sheep originating in the Cheviot hills **2 a :** a fabric of cheviot wool **b :** a heavy rough napped plain or twill fabric of coarse wool or worsted **c :** a sturdy soft-finished plain or twill cotton shirting

chev·ron \'shev-rən\ *n* [ME, fr. MF, rafter, chevron, fr. (assumed) VL *caprion-*, *caprio* rafter; akin to L *caper* goat] **1** *or* **chev·er·on** \-(ə-)rən\ **:** a heraldic charge consisting of two diagonal stripes meeting at an angle usu. with the point up **2 :** a sleeve badge usu. indicating the wearer's rank and service (as in the armed forces)

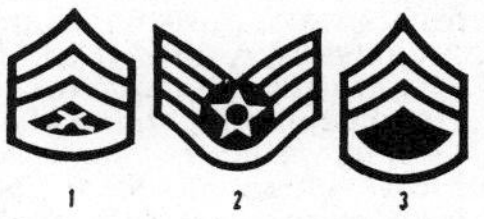

1 2 3

chevrons 2: *1* marine staff sergeant, *2* air force staff sergeant, *3* army staff sergeant

chev·ro·tain \'shev-rə-,tān\ *n* [F, dim. of *chevrot* kid, fawn, fr. MF, dim. of *chèvre* goat, fr. L *capra* she-goat, fem. of *capr-*, *caper* he-goat] **:** any of several very small hornless ruminants (family Tragulidae) of tropical Asia and West Africa

¹chew \'chü\ *vb* [ME *chewen*, fr. OE *cēowan*; akin to OHG *kiuwan* to chew, OSlav *žīvati*] *vt* **:** to crush or grind (as food) with the teeth **:** MASTICATE ~ *vi* **:** to chew something; *specif* **:** to chew tobacco — **chew·able** \-ə-bəl\ *adj* — **chew·er** *n* — **chewy** \'chü-ē\ *adj*

²chew *n* **1 :** the act of chewing **2 :** something for chewing

chewing gum *n* **:** a preparation of chicle and sometimes other plastic insoluble substances sweetened and flavored for chewing

che·wink \chi-'wiŋk\ *n* [imit.] **:** TOWHEE

Chey·enne \shī-'an, -'en\ *n, pl* **Cheyenne** *or* **Cheyennes** [Can F, fr. Dakota *Shaiyena*, fr. *shaia* to speak unintelligibly] **1 a :** an Indian people of the western plains **b :** a member of this people **2 :** the Algonquian language of the Cheyenne people

chi \'kī\ *n* [Gk *chei*] **:** the 22d letter of the Greek alphabet — symbol X or χ

Chi·an·ti \kē-'änt-ē, -'ant-\ *n* [It, fr. the *Chianti* mt. area, Italy] **:** a still dry usu. red table wine

chiao \'tyau̇\ *n, pl* **chiao** [Chin (Pek) *chiao³*] — see *yuan* at MONEY table

chiar·oscu·rist \kē-,är-ə-'sk(y)u̇r-əst, kē-,ar-\ *n* **:** an artist in chiaroscuro

chiar·oscu·ro \-'sk(y)u̇(ə)r-(,)ō\ *n* [It, fr. *chiaro* clear, light + *oscuro* obscure, dark] **1 :** pictorial representation in terms of light and shade without regard to color **2 :** the arrangement or treatment of light and dark parts in a pictorial work of art

chi·as·ma \kī-'az-mə\ *n, pl* **chi·as·ma·ta** \-mət-ə\ *or* **chiasmas** [NL, fr. Gk, crosspiece, fr. *chiazein* to mark with a chi, fr. *chi* (x)] **1 :** an anatomical intersection ⟨the optic ~⟩ **2 :** a fusion and exchange of segments of chromatids between members of a bivalent during meiosis — **chi·as·mal** \-məl\ *adj* — **chi·as·mat·ic** \,kī-əz-'mat-ik\ *adj* — **chi·as·mic** \kī-'az-mik\ *adj*

chi·as·ma·ty·py \kī-'az-mə-,tī-pē\ *n* [NL *chiasma* + ISV *type*] **:** the spiral twisting of homologous chromosomes during zygotene that results in chiasma formation and provides the mechanism for crossing over

chiaus \'chau̇s(h)\ *n* [Turk *çavuş*, fr. *çav* voice, news] **:** a Turkish messenger or sergeant

Chib·cha \'chib-(,)chä\ *n, pl* **Chibcha** *or* **Chibchas** [Sp, of Amer Ind origin] **1 a :** a Chibchan people of central Colombia **b :** a member of this people **2 :** the extinct language of the Chibcha people

Chib·chan \-chən\ *adj* **:** of, relating to, or constituting a language stock of Colombia and Central America

chi·bouk *or* **chi·bouque** \chə-'bük, shə-\ *n* [F *chibouque*, fr. Turk *çıbuk*] **:** a long-stemmed Turkish tobacco pipe with a clay bowl

¹chic \'shēk\ *n* [F] **:** easy elegance and sophistication of dress or manner **:** STYLE

²chic *adj* **1 :** cleverly stylish **:** SMART **2 :** currently fashionable

Chi·ca·go \shə-'käg-(,)ō, -'kȯg-\ *n* [*Chicago*, Ill.] **:** a method of playing contract bridge in sets of four deals

chi·ca·lo·te \,chē-kə-'lōt-ē\ *n* [Sp, fr. Nahuatl *chicalotl*] **:** a white-flowered prickly poppy (*Argemone platyceras*) of Mexico and the southwestern U.S.

¹chi·cane \shik-'ān, chik-\ *vb* [F *chicaner*, fr. MF, to quibble, prevent justice] *vi* **:** to use chicanery ~ *vt* **:** TRICK, CHEAT

²chicane *n* **1 :** CHICANERY **2 :** an obstacle on a racecourse **3 :** the absence of trumps in a hand of cards

chi·ca·nery \-'ān-(ə-)rē\ *n* **1 :** deception by artful subterfuge or sophistry **2 :** a piece of sharp practice **:** TRICK — usu. used in pl.

chi·chi \'shē-(,)shē, 'chē-(,)chē\ *adj* [F] **1 :** elaborately ornamented **:** SHOWY **2 :** ARTY, PRECIOUS **3 :** FASHIONABLE, CHIC — **chichi** *n*

chi·chi·pa·te \,chē-chə-'pät-ē\ *n* [AmerSp, fr. Nahuatl *chichipatli*, lit., bitter medicine] **:** a tropical American leguminous timber tree (*Sweetia panamensis*)

chick \'chik\ *n* **1 a :** CHICKEN; *esp* **:** one newly hatched **b :** the young of any bird **2 :** CHILD **3** *slang* **:** a young woman

chick·a·dee \'chik-ə-(,)dē\ *n* [imit.] **:** any of several crestless American titmice (genus *Penthestes* or *Parus*) usu. with the crown of the head sharply demarked and darker than the body

chick·a·ree \'chik-ə-,rē\ *n* [imit.] **:** an American red squirrel (*Sciurus hudsonicus*) or a related squirrel

Chick·a·saw \'chik-ə-,sȯ\ *n, pl* **Chickasaw** *or* **Chickasaws** **1 a :** a Muskogean people of northern Mississippi and Alabama **b :** a member of this people **2 :** a dialect of Choctaw spoken by the Chickasaw

¹chick·en \'chik-ən\ *n* [ME *chiken*, fr. OE *cicen* young chicken; akin to OE *cocc* cock] **1 a :** the common domestic fowl (*Gallus gallus*) esp. when young; *also* **:** its flesh used as food **b :** any of various birds or their young **2 a** *slang* **:** a young woman **b :** COWARD **3** *slang* **:** petty esp. military detail strictly enforced

²chicken *adj* **1** *slang* **:** CHICKENHEARTED, CHICKEN-LIVERED **2** *slang* **:** insistent on petty esp. military discipline

³chicken *vi* **chick·en·ing** \'chik-(ə-)niŋ\ *slang* **:** to lose one's nerve ⟨~*ed* out before the robbery⟩

chicken colonel *n* [fr. the eagle worn on the shoulders] *slang* **:** COLONEL 1a

chicken feed *n, slang* **:** a trifling sum

chicken hawk *n* **:** a hawk that preys or is believed to prey on chickens

chick·en·heart·ed \,chik-ən-'härt-əd\ *adj* **:** TIMID, COWARDLY

chick·en-liv·ered \-'liv-ərd\ *adj* **:** FAINTHEARTED, COWARDLY

chicken pox *n* **:** an acute contagious virus disease esp. of children

marked by low-grade fever and formation of vesicles
chicken snake *n* : any of various large harmless No. American colubrid snakes (genus *Elaphe*) — called also *rat snake*
chick–pea \'chik-,pē\ *n* [by folk etymology fr. ME *chiche*, fr. MF, fr. L *cicer*] : an Asiatic leguminous herb (*Cicer arietinum*) cultivated for its short pods with one or two seeds; *also* : its seed
chick•weed \'chik-,wēd\ *n* : any of various low-growing small-leaved weedy plants of the pink family (esp. genera *Arenaria*, *Cerastium*, and *Stellaria*) several of which are relished by birds or used as potherbs
chic•le \'chik-əl, -lē\ *n* [Sp, fr. Nahuatl *chictli*] : a gum from the latex of the sapodilla used as the chief ingredient of chewing gum
chi•co \'chē-(,)kō\ *n* [modif. of Sp *chicalote*] : a greasewood (*Sarcobatus vermiculatus*)
chic•o•ry \'chik-(ə-)rē\ *n* [ME *cicoree*, fr. MF *cichorée*, *chicorée*, fr. L *cichoreum*, fr. Gk *kichoreia*] **1** : a thick-rooted usu. blue-flowered European perennial composite herb (*Cichorium intybus*) widely grown for its roots and as a salad plant **2** : the dried ground roasted root of chicory used to flavor or adulterate coffee
chide \'chīd\ *vb* **chid** \'chid\ *or* **chid•ed** \'chīd-əd\ **chid** *or* **chid•den** \'chid-ᵊn\ *or* **chided**; **chid•ing** \'chīd-iŋ\ [ME *chiden*, fr. OE *cīdan* to quarrel, chide, fr. *cīd* strife] *vi* : to speak out in angry or displeased rebuke ~ *vt* : to voice disapproval to : SCOLD **syn** see REPROVE
1**chief** \'chēf\ *n* [ME, fr. OF, head, chief, fr. L *caput* head — more at HEAD] **1** : the upper part of an heraldic field **2** : the head of a body or organization : LEADER **3** : the principal or most valuable part
2**chief** *adj* **1** : accorded highest rank or office **2** : of greatest importance, significance, or influence — **chief•ly** *adv or adj*
3**chief** *adv, archaic* : CHIEFLY
chief justice *n* : the presiding or principal judge of a court of justice
chief master sergeant *n* : a noncommissioned officer of the highest enlisted rank in the air force
chief of staff 1 : the ranking officer of a staff in the armed forces serving as principal adviser to a commander **2** : the ranking office of the army or air force
chief of state : the formal head of a national state as distinguished from the head of the government
chief petty officer *n* : an enlisted man in the navy ranking above a petty officer and below a senior chief petty officer
chief•tain \'chēf-tən\ *n* [ME *chieftaine*, fr. MF *chevetain*, fr. LL *capitaneus* chief — more at CAPTAIN] : a chief esp. of a band, tribe, or clan — **chief•tain•cy** \-sē\ *n* — **chief•tain•ship** \-,ship\ *n*
chief warrant officer *n* : a warrant officer of senior rank in the armed forces
chiel \'chē(ə)l\ *or* **chield** \'chē(ə)ld\ *n* [ME (Sc) *cheld*, alter. of ME *child* child] *chiefly Scot* : FELLOW, LAD
chiff•chaff \'chif-,chaf\ *n* [imit.] : a small grayish European warbler (*Phylloscopus collybita*)
1**chif•fon** \shif-'än, 'shif-,\ *n* [F, lit., rag, fr. *chiffe* old rag, alter. of MF *chipe*, fr. ME *chip* chip] **1** : an ornamental addition (as a knot of ribbons) to a woman's dress **2** : a sheer fabric esp. of silk
2**chiffon** *adj* **1** : resembling chiffon in sheerness or softness **2** : having a light delicate texture achieved usu. by adding whipped egg whites or whipped gelatin ⟨lemon ~ pie⟩
chif•fo•nier \,shif-ə-'ni(ə)r\ *n* [F *chiffonnier*, fr. *chiffon*] : a high narrow chest of drawers

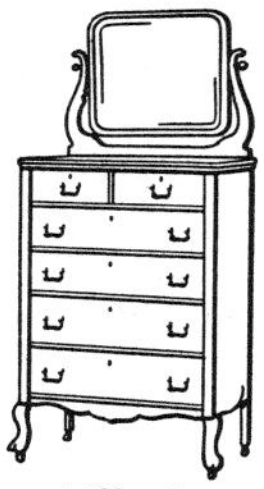
chiffonier

chig•ger \'chig-ər, 'jig-\ *n* **1** : CHIGOE 1 **2** [of African origin; akin to Wolof *jiga* insect] : a 6-legged larval mite (family Trombiculidae) that sucks the blood of vertebrates and causes intense irritation
chi•gnon \'shēn-,yän\ *n* [F, fr. MF *chaignon* chain, collar, nape] : a knot of hair worn at the back of the head
chi•goe \'chig-(,)ō, 'chē-(,)gō\ *n* [of Cariban origin; akin to Galibi *chico* chigoe] **1** : a tropical flea (*Tunga penetrans*) of which the fertile female burrows under the skin causing great discomfort — called also *chigger* **2** : CHIGGER 2
Chi•hua•hua \chə-'wä-(,)wä, shə-, -wə\ *n* [MexSp, fr. *Chihuahua*, Mexico] : a very small round-headed large-eared short-coated dog held to antedate Aztec civilization
chil•blain \'chil-,blān\ *n* [3*chill*] : an inflammatory swelling or sore caused by exposure (as of the feet or hands) to cold
child \'chī(ə)ld\ *n, pl* **chil•dren** \'chil-drən, -dərn *also* 'chùl-\ [ME, fr. OE *cild*; akin to Goth *kilthei* womb, Skt *jathara* belly] **1 a** : an unborn or recently born person **b** *dial* : a female infant **2 a** : a young person of either sex esp. between infancy and youth **b** : a childlike or childish person **c** : a person not yet of age **3** *usu* **childe** \'chī(ə)ld\ *archaic* : a youth of noble birth **4 a** : a son or daughter of human parents **b** : DESCENDANT **5** : one strongly influenced by another or by a place or state of affairs **6** : PRODUCT, RESULT — **child•less** \'chī(ə)l-(d)ləs\ *adj* — **child•less•ness** *n* — **with child** : PREGNANT
child•bear•ing \'chīl(d)-,bar-iŋ, -,ber-\ *n* : the act of bringing forth children : PARTURITION — **childbearing** *adj*
child•bed \-,bed\ *n* : the condition of a woman in childbirth
childbed fever *n* : puerperal fever
child•birth \'chīl(d)-,bərth\ *n* : PARTURITION
child•hood \'chīld-,hùd\ *n* : the state or time of being a child
child•ish \'chīl-dish\ *adj* **1** : of, relating to, or characteristic of a child **2** : SIMPLEMINDED, PUERILE **syn** see CHILDLIKE — **child•ish•ly** *adv* — **child•ish•ness** *n*
child•like \'chī(ə)l-,(d)līk\ *adj* : of, relating to, or resembling a child or childhood; *esp* : marked by innocence, trust, and ingenuousness — **child•like•ness** *n*
syn CHILDISH: CHILDLIKE suggests attractive and admirable qualities of childhood such as innocence, straightforwardness, trust; CHILDISH implies having qualities (as fretful impatience or undeveloped taste and mentality) that are appropriate to children but deplorable in adults; both terms may apply to any age
child•ly \'chī(ə)l-(d)lē\ *adj* : CHILDLIKE
Chile saltpeter \'chil-ē-\ *n* [*Chile*, country in So. America] : sodium nitrate esp. occurring naturally — called also *Chile niter*
chili *or* **chile** *or* **chil•li** \'chil-ē\ *n, pl* **chil•ies** *or* **chil•es** *or* **chil•lies** [Sp *chile*, fr. Nahuatl *chilli*] **1 a** : HOT PEPPER 1 **b** *usu chilli, chiefly Brit* : a pepper whether hot or sweet **2** : HOT PEPPER 2 **3 a** : a thick sauce of meat and chilies **b** : CHILI CON CARNE
chil•i•ad \'kil-ē-,ad, -əd\ *n* [LL *chiliad-*, *chilias*, fr. Gk, fr. *chilioi* thousand] **1** : a group of 1000 **2** : a period of 1000 years
chil•i•asm \'kil-ē-,az-əm\ *n* [NL *chiliasmus*, fr. LL *chiliastes* one that believes in chiliasm, fr. *chilias*] : MILLENARIANISM — **chil•i•ast** \-ē-,ast -ē-əst\ *n* — **chil•i•as•tic** \,kil-ē-'as-tik\ *adj*
chili con car•ne \,chil-ē-,kän-'kär-nē, -kən-\ *n* [Sp *chile con carne* chili with meat] : a spiced stew of ground beef and minced chilies or chili powder usu. with beans
chili sauce *n* : a spiced tomato sauce orig. made with chilies
1**chill** \'chil\ *vb* [ME *chillen*, fr. *chile* cold, frost, fr. OE *cele*; akin to OE *ceald* cold] *vi* **1 a** : to become cold **b** : to shiver or quake with or as if with cold **2** : to become taken with a chill **3** *of a metal* : to become surface-hardened by sudden cooling ~ *vt* **1 a** : to make cold or chilly **b** : to make cool esp. without freezing **2** : CHECK, DAMPEN **3** : to surface-harden (metal) by sudden cooling — **chill•er** *n* — **chill•ing•ly** \'chil-iŋ-lē\ *adv*
2**chill** *adj* **1 a** : moderately cold **b** : COLD, RAW **2** : affected by cold **3** : DISTANT, FORMAL **4** : DEPRESSING, DISPIRITING — **chill•ness** *n*
3**chill** *n* **1 a** : a sensation of cold attended with shivering **b** : a disagreeable sensation of coldness **2** : a moderate but disagreeable degree of cold **3** : a check to enthusiasm or warmth of feeling
chill•i•ly \'chil-ə-lē\ *adv* : in a chilly manner
chill•i•ness \'chil-ē-nəs\ *n* : the quality or state of being chilly
chilly \'chil-ē\ *adj* **1** : noticeably cold : CHILLING **2** : unpleasantly affected by cold **3** : lacking warmth of feeling **4** : tending to arouse fear or apprehension
chi•mae•ra \kī-'mir-ə, kə-\ *n* [NL, genus name, fr. L, chimera] : any of a family (Chimaeridae) of marine elasmobranch fishes with a tapering or threadlike tail and usu. no anal fin
1**chime** \'chīm\ *n* [ME, cymbal, fr. OF *chimbe*, fr. L *cymbalum* cymbal] **1** : an apparatus for chiming a bell or set of bells **2** : a musically tuned set of bells **3 a** : the sound of a set of bells — usu. used in pl. **b** : a musical sound suggesting that of bells **4** : ACCORD, HARMONY
2**chime** *vi* **1 a** : to make a musical esp. harmonious sound **b** : to make the sounds of a chime **2** : to be or act in accord ~ *vt* **1** : to cause to sound musically by striking **2** : to produce by chiming **3** : to call or indicate by chiming ⟨clock *chiming* midnight⟩ **4** : to utter repetitively : DIN 2 — **chim•er** *n*
3**chime** \'chīm\ *or* **chine** \'chīn\ *n* [ME *chimbe*, fr. OE *cimb-*; akin to OE *camb* comb] : the edge or rim of a cask
chime in *vi* : to break into a conversation or discussion ~ *vt* : to remark while chiming in
chi•me•ra *or* **chi•mae•ra** \kī-'mir-ə, kə-\ *n* [L *chimaera*, fr. Gk *chimaira* she-goat, chimera; akin to Gk *cheimōn* winter] **1 a** *cap* : a she-monster in Greek mythology usu. with a lion's head vomiting flames, a goat's body, and a serpent's tail **b** : an imaginary monster compounded of incongruous parts **2** : an illusion or fabrication of the mind; *esp* : an unrealizable dream **3** : an individual, organ, or part consisting of tissues of diverse genetic constitution and occurring esp. in plants and most frequently at a graft union
chi•mere \shə-'mi(ə)r, chə-\ *n* [ME *chimmer*, *chemeyr*] : a loose sleeveless robe often with balloon sleeves of lawn attached worn by some bishops of the Anglican Communion
chi•me•ri•cal \kī-'mer-i-kəl, kə-, -'mir-\ *or* **chi•me•ric** \-ik\ *adj* [*chimera*] **1** : existing only as the product of unrestrained imagination : UNREAL **2** : inclined to fantastic schemes or projects **syn** see IMAGINARY — **chi•me•ri•cal•ly** \-i-k(ə-)lē\ *adv*
chim•ney \'chim-nē\ *n* [ME, fr. MF *cheminée*, fr. LL *caminata*, fr. L *caminus* furnace, fireplace, fr. Gk *kaminos*; akin to Gk *kamara* vault] **1** *dial* : FIREPLACE, HEARTH **2** : a vertical structure incorporated into a building and enclosing a flue or flues that carry off smoke; *esp* : the part of such a structure extending above a roof **3** : SMOKESTACK **4** : a tube usu. of glass placed around a flame (as of a lamp) **5** : something resembling a chimney
chimney piece *n* : a decorative construction over a fireplace
chimney pot *n* : a usu. earthenware pipe placed at the top of a chimney
chimney sweep *n* : a person who cleans soot from chimneys
chimp \'chimp, 'shimp\ *n* : CHIMPANZEE
chim•pan•zee \,chim-,pan-'zē, ,shim-, -pən-; chim-'pan-zē, shim-\ *n* [Kongo dial. *chimpenzi*] : an anthropoid ape (*Pan troglodytes*) of equatorial Africa that is smaller, more arboreal, and less fierce than the gorilla
1**chin** \'chin\ *n* [ME, fr. OE *cinn*; akin to OHG *kinni* chin, L *gena* cheek, Gk *genys* jaw, cheek] **1** : the lower portion of the face lying below the lower lip and including the prominence of the lower jaw **2** : the surface beneath or between the branches of the lower jaw
2**chin** *vb* **chinned**; **chin•ning** *vt* **1** : to bring to or hold with the chin **2** : to raise (oneself) while hanging by the hands until the chin is level with the support ~ *vi, slang* : to talk idly : CHATTER
chi•na \'chī-nə\ *n* [Per *chīnī* Chinese porcelain] **1** : a vitrified ceramic ware of clay, feldspar, and flint differing from porcelain in being made in two firings **2** : PORCELAIN; *also* : EARTHENWARE
China aster *n* [*China*, country of Asia] : a Chinese annual aster (*Callistephus chinensis*) occurring in many showy forms
chi•na•ber•ry \'chī-nə-,ber-ē\ *n* **1** : a soapberry (*Sapindus saponaria*) of the southern U.S. and Mexico **2** : a small Asiatic tree (*Melia azedarach* of the mahogany family) naturalized in the southern U.S. where it is widely planted for shade or ornament
Chi•na•man \'chī-nə-mən\ *n* : a native of China : CHINESE — often taken to be offensive
China rose *n* **1** : any of numerous garden roses derived from a shrubby Chinese rose (*Rosa chinensis*) **2** : a large showy-flowered Asiatic hibiscus (*Hibiscus rosa-sinensis*)
Chi•na•town \'chī-nə-,taùn\ *n* : the Chinese quarter of a city
China tree *n* : CHINABERRY
chi•na•ware \'chī-nə-,wa(ə)r, -,we(ə)r\ *n* : CHINA
chin•bone \'chin-'bōn, -,bōn\ *n* : MANDIBLE; *esp* : the median anterior part of the human mandible
chinch \'chinch\ *n* [Sp *chinche*, fr. L *cimic-*, *cimex*] : BEDBUG
chinch bug *n* : a small black-and-white bug (*Blissus leucopterus*) very destructive to cereal grasses
chin•che•rin•chee \,chiŋ-kə-ri(n)-'chē\ *n, pl* **chincherinchee** *or* **chincherinchees** [origin unknown] : a southern African perennial bulbous herb (*Ornithogalum thyrsoides*) with long-lasting spikes of starry white blossoms
chin•chil•la \chin-'chil-ə\ *n* [Sp] **1** : a small rodent (*Chinchilla laniger*) the size of a large squirrel with very soft fur of a pearly

gray color that is native to the mountains of Peru and Chile but extensively bred in captivity; *also* **:** its fur **2 :** a heavy twilled woolen coating

1**chine** \'chīn\ *n* [ME, fr. MF *eschine*, of Gmc origin; akin to OHG *scina* shinbone, needle — more at SHIN] **1 :** BACKBONE, SPINE; *also* **:** a cut of meat or fish including the backbone or part of it and the surrounding flesh **2 :** RIDGE, CREST

2**chine** *vt* **:** to cut through the backbone of (as in butchering)

Chi·nese \chī-'nēz, -'nēs\ *n, pl* **Chinese 1 :** a native or inhabitant of China or one of his descendants **2 :** a group of related languages used by the people of China that are often mutually unintelligible in their spoken form but share a single system of writing and that constitute a branch of the Sino-Tibetan language family; *specif* **:** MANDARIN — **Chinese** *adj*

Chinese cabbage *n* **:** either of two Asiatic brassicas (*Brassica pekinensis* and *B. chinensis*) widely used as greens

Chinese chestnut *n* **:** an Asiatic chestnut (*Castanea mollissima*) of importance chiefly for its resistance to chestnut blight

Chinese date *n* **:** an Asiatic tree (*Ziziphus jujuba*) of the buckthorn family; *also* **:** its edible fruit — called also *jujube*

Chinese lantern *n* **:** a collapsible lantern of thin colored paper

Chinese puzzle *n* **1 :** an intricate or ingenious puzzle **2 :** something intricate and obscure

Chinese wall *n* [*Chinese Wall*, a defensive wall built in the 3d cent. B.C. between China and Mongolia] **:** a strong barrier; *esp* **:** a serious obstacle to intercourse or understanding

Chinese white *n* **:** zinc white esp. in a dense form

Ching *or* **Ch'ing** \'chiŋ\ *n* [Chin (Pek) *ch'ing*¹] **:** a Manchu dynasty in China dated 1644–1912 and the last imperial dynasty

1**chink** \'chiŋk\ *n* [prob. alter. of ME *chin* crack, fissure, fr. OE *cine;* akin to OE *cīnan* to gape, OHG *chīnan* to split open] **1 :** a small cleft, rent, or fissure **2 :** a means of evasion or escape

2**chink** *vt* **:** to fill the chinks of (as by caulking) **:** stop up

3**chink** *n* [imit.] **1 :** a short sharp sound **2** *slang* **:** COIN, MONEY

4**chink** *vi* **:** to make a slight sharp metallic sound **∼** *vt* **:** to cause to make a chink

chi·no \'chē-(,)nō, 'shē-\ *n* [AmerSp] **1 :** a usu. khaki cotton twill of the type used for military uniforms **2 :** an article of clothing made of chino — usu. used in pl.

Chi·no- \,chī-,nō\ *comb form* **:** Chinese and ⟨*Chino*-Japanese⟩

chi·noi·se·rie \,shēn-,wäz-(ə-)'rē, shēn-'wäz-(ə-)rē\ *n* [F, fr. *chinois* Chinese, fr. *Chine* China] **:** a style in art (as in decoration) reflecting Chinese qualities or motifs; *also* **:** an object or decoration in this style

Chi·nook \shə-'nu̇k, chə-\ *n, pl* **Chinook** *or* **Chinooks** [Chehalis *Tsinúk*] **1 a :** an Indian people of the north shore of the Columbia river at its mouth **b :** a member of this people **2 :** a Chinookan language of the Chinook and other nearby peoples **3** *not cap* **a :** a warm moist southwest wind of the coast from Oregon northward **b :** a warm dry wind that descends the eastern slopes of the Rocky mountains

Chi·nook·an \-ən\ *n* **:** a language family of Washington and Oregon — **Chinookan** *adj*

Chinook Jargon *n* **:** a pidgin language based on Chinook and other Indian languages, French, and English and formerly used as a lingua franca in the northwestern U.S. and on the Pacific coast of Canada and Alaska

chin·qua·pin \'chiŋ-ki-,pin\ *n* [alter. of earlier *chincomen*, of Algonquian origin] **1 :** any of several trees (genera *Castanea* or *Castanopsis*); *esp* **:** a dwarf chestnut (*Castanea pumila*) of the U.S. **2 :** the edible nut of a chinquapin

chintz \'chin(t)s\ *n* [earlier *chints*, pl. of *chint*, fr. Hindi *chīṭ*] **1 :** a printed calico from India **2 :** a usu. glazed printed cotton fabric

chintzy \'chin(t)-sē\ *adj* **1 :** decorated with or as if with chintz **2 :** GAUDY, CHEAP

1**chip** \'chip\ *n* [ME] **1 a :** a small usu. thin and flat piece (as of wood or stone) cut, struck, or flaked off **b** (1) **:** a small thin slice of food (as a potato chip) (2) **:** FRENCH FRY **2 :** something small, worthless, or trivial **3 a :** one of the counters used as a token for money in poker and other games **b** *pl, slang* **:** MONEY **c** *pl* **:** something hazarded **4 :** a piece of dried dung — usu. used in combination ⟨cow ∼⟩ **5 :** a flaw left after a chip is removed — **chip off the old block :** a child that resembles his parent — **chip on one's shoulder :** a challenging or bellicose attitude

2**chip** *vb* **chipped; chip·ping** *vt* **1 a :** to cut or hew with an ax, chisel, or other edged tool **b** (1) **:** to cut or break (a small piece) from something (2) **:** to cut or break a fragment from **2** *slang Brit* **:** CHAFF, BANTER **∼** *vi* **1 :** to break off in small pieces **2 :** to play a chip shot

chip in *vb* **:** CONTRIBUTE

chip·munk \'chip-,məŋk\ *n* [alter. of earlier *chitmunk*, of Algonquian origin; akin to Ojibwa *atchitamō* squirrel] **:** any of numerous small striped semiterrestrial American squirrels (genera *Tamias* and *Eutamias*) — called also *ground squirrel*

chipped beef \'chip(t)-\ *n* **:** smoked dried beef sliced thin

Chip·pen·dale \'chip-ən-,dāl\ *adj* [Thomas *Chippendale* †1779 E cabinetmaker] **:** of or relating to an 18th century English furniture style characterized by graceful outline and often ornate rococo ornamentation

1**chip·per** \'chip-ər\ *n* **:** one that chips

2**chipper** *adj* [perh. alter. of E dial. *kipper* (lively)] **:** GAY, SPRIGHTLY

Chip·pe·wa \'chip-ə-,wȯ, -,wä, -,wā, -(ə-)wə\ *n, pl* **Chippewa** *or* **Chippewas :** OJIBWA

chip shot *n* **:** a short usu. low approach shot in golf that lofts the ball to the green and allows it to roll

chir- *or* **chiro-** *comb form* [L, fr. Gk *cheir-*, *cheiro-*, fr. *cheir;* akin to Hitt *kesar* hand] **:** hand ⟨*chiro*practic⟩

chirk \'chərk\ *vb* [ME *charken*, *chirken* to creak, chirp, fr. OE *cearcian* to creak; akin to OE *cracian* to crack] **:** CHEER ⟨∼ up⟩

chi·rog·ra·pher \kī-'räg-rə-fər\ *n* **:** one who studies or practices chirography

chi·ro·graph·ic \,kī-rə-'graf-ik\ *adj* **:** of, relating to, or in handwriting — **chi·ro·graph·i·cal** \-i-kəl\ *adj*

chi·rog·ra·phy \kī-'räg-rə-fē\ *n* **1 :** HANDWRITING, PENMANSHIP **2 :** CALLIGRAPHY **1**

chi·ro·man·cer \'kī-rə-,man(t)-sər\ *n* **:** one who practices chiromancy

chi·ro·man·cy \-sē\ *n* [prob. fr. MF *chiromancie*, fr. ML *chiromantia*, fr. Gk *cheir-* chir- + *-manteia* -mancy — more at -MANCY] **:** divination by examination of the hand **:** PALMISTRY

chi·rop·o·dist \kə-'räp-əd-əst, shə-\ *n* [*chir-* + *pod-*; fr. his originally treating both hands and feet] **:** a practitioner of chiropody

chi·rop·o·dy \-'räp-əd-ē\ *n* **:** the care and treatment of the human foot in health and disease — called also *podiatry*

chi·ro·prac·tic \'kī-rə-,prak-tik\ *n* [*chir-* + Gk *praktikos* practical, operative — more at PRACTICAL] **:** a system of healing holding that disease results from a lack of normal nerve function and employing manipulation and specific adjustment of body structures (as the spinal column) — **chi·ro·prac·tor** \-tər\ *n*

chi·rop·ter \kī-'räp-tər\ *n* [deriv. of Gk *cheir* hand + *pteron* wing — more at FEATHER] **:** 3BAT — **chi·rop·ter·an** \-tə-rən\ *adj or n*

chirp \'chərp\ *n* [imit.] **:** the characteristic short sharp sound of a small bird or cricket — **chirp** *vb*

chirr \'chər\ *n* [imit.] **:** the short vibrant or trilled sound characteristic of an insect (as a grasshopper or cicada) — **chirr** *vi*

chir·rup \'chər-əp, 'chir-\ *n* [imit.] **:** CHIRP — **chirrup** *vb*

chi·rur·geon \kī-'rər-jən\ *n* [ME *cirurgian*, fr. OF *cirurgien*, fr. *cirurgie* surgery] *archaic* **:** SURGEON

1**chis·el** \'chiz-əl\ *n* [ME, fr. ONF, prob. alter. of *chisoir* gold-

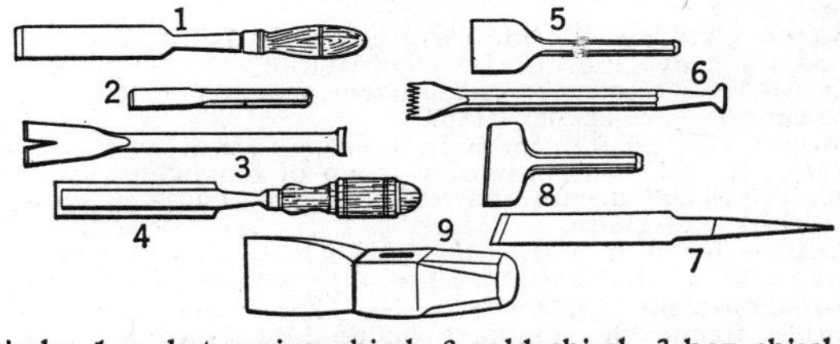

chisels: *1* socket paring chisel, *2* cold chisel, *3* box chisel, *4* beveled firmer chisel, *5* floor chisel, *6* stonecutter's chisel, *7* turning chisel, *8* bricklayer's chisel, *9* blacksmith's chisel

smith's chisel, fr. (assumed) VL *caesorium* cutting instrument, fr. L *caesus*, pp. of *caedere* to cut — more at CONCISE] **:** a metal tool with a cutting edge at the end of a blade used in dressing, shaping, or working a solid material (as wood, stone, or metal)

2**chisel** *vb* **chis·eled** *or* **chis·elled; chis·el·ing** *or* **chis·el·ling** \'chiz-(ə-)liŋ\ *vt* **1 :** to cut or work with or as if with a chisel **2 :** CHEAT **∼** *vi* **1 :** to work with a chisel **2 a :** to employ shrewd sometimes unfair practices **b :** INTRUDE ⟨∼ in on the racket⟩ — **chis·el·er** \'chiz-(ə-)lər\ *n*

chis·eled *or* **chis·elled** \'chiz-əld\ *adj* **1 :** cut or wrought with a chisel **2 :** appearing as if chiseled **:** CLEAR-CUT ⟨sharply ∼ profile⟩

chi–square \'kī-'skwa(ə)r, -'skwe(ə)r\ *n* **:** the sum of the quotients obtained by dividing the square of the difference between the observed and theoretical values of a quantity by the theoretical value

1**chit** \'chit\ *n* [ME *chitte* kitten, cub] **1 :** CHILD **2 :** a pert young woman

2**chit** *n* [Hindi *ciṭṭhī*] **:** a short letter or note; *esp* **:** a signed voucher of a small debt (as for food)

chit·chat \'chit-,chat\ *n* [redupl. of *chat*] **:** SMALL TALK, GOSSIP — **chitchat** *vi*

chi·tin \'kīt-ᵊn\ *n* [F *chitine*, fr. Gk *chitōn* chiton, tunic] **:** an amorphous horny polysaccharide that forms part of the hard outer integument of insects, crustaceans, and some other invertebrates — **chi·tin·ous** \'kīt-ᵊn-əs, 'kīt-nəs\ *adj*

chi·ton \'kīt-ᵊn, 'kī-,tän\ *n* [NL, genus name, fr. Gk *chitōn* tunic; of Sem origin; akin to Heb *kuttōneth* tunic] **1 :** any of an order (Polyplacophora) of elongated bilaterally symmetrical marine mollusks with a dorsal shell of calcareous plates **2** [Gk *chitōn*] **:** the basic garment of ancient Greece worn usu. knee-length by men and full-length by women

chit·ter \'chit-ər\ *vi* [ME *chiteren*, prob. of imit. origin] **:** TWITTER, CHIRP; *also* **:** CHATTER

chit·ter·lings *or* **chit·lings** *or* **chit·lins** \'chit-lənz\ *n pl* [ME *chiterling*] **:** the intestines of hogs esp. prepared as food

chi·val·ric \shə-'val-rik\ *adj* **:** relating to chivalry **:** CHIVALROUS

chiv·al·rous \'shiv-əl-rəs\ *adj* **1 :** VALIANT **2 :** of, relating to, or characteristic of chivalry and knight-errantry **3 a :** marked by honor, generosity, and courtesy **b :** marked by especial courtesy and consideration to women **syn** see CIVIL — **chiv·al·rous·ly** *adv* — **chiv·al·rous·ness** *n*

chiv·al·ry \'shiv-əl-rē\ *n* [ME *chivalrie*, fr. OF *chevalerie*, fr. *chevalier*] **1 :** mounted men-at-arms **2** *archaic* **a :** martial valor **b :** knightly skill **3 :** gallant or distinguished gentlemen **4 :** the dignity or system of knighthood **5 :** the qualifications or character of the ideal knight

chive \'chīv\ *n* [ME, fr. ONF, fr. L *cepa* onion] **:** a perennial plant (*Allium schoenoprasum*) related to the onion

chivy *or* **chiv·vy** \'chiv-ē\ *vt* **1 :** CHASE, PURSUE **2 a :** HARASS, ANNOY, TEASE **b :** MANEUVER, MANIPULATE **syn** see BAIT

chla·mydo·spore \klə-'mid-ə-,spō(ə)r, -,spȯ(ə)r\ *n* [L *chlamyd-*, *chlamys* + ISV *spore*] **:** a thick-walled usu. resting spore — **chla·mydo·spor·ic** \klə-,mid-ə-'spōr-ik, -'spȯr-\ *adj*

chla·mys \'klam-əs, 'klā-məs\ *n* [L *chlamyd-*, *chlamys*, fr. Gk] **:** a short oblong mantle worn by young men of ancient Greece

Chloë \'klō-ē\ *n* [L, fr. Gk *Chloē*] **:** a shepherdess of pastoral poetry

chlor- *or* **chloro-** *comb form* [NL, fr. Gk, fr. *chlōros* greenish yellow — more at YELLOW] **1 :** green ⟨*chlor*ine⟩ ⟨*chlor*osis⟩ **2 :** chlorine **:** containing chlorine ⟨*chlor*ic⟩ ⟨*chloro*prene⟩

chlo·ral \'klōr-əl, 'klȯr-\ *n* [F, fr. *chlor-* + *al*cool alcohol] **1 :** a pungent colorless oily aldehyde CCl_3CHO obtained by the action of chlorine on ethyl alcohol and used in making DDT and chloral hydrate **2 :** a bitter crystalline hydrate $CCl_3CH(OH)_2$ of chloral used as a hypnotic — called also *chloral hydrate*

chlo·ral·ose \-ə-,lōs, -,lōz\ *n* **:** a bitter crystalline compound $C_8H_{11}Cl_3O_6$ formed by heating chloral with dextrose and used as a hypnotic — **chlo·ral·osed** \-,lōst, -,lōzd\ *adj*

chlo·ra·mine \'klōr-ə-ˌmēn, 'klȯr-\ *n* [ISV] **:** any of various compounds containing nitrogen and chlorine

chlor·am·phen·i·col \ˌklōr-ˌam-'fen-i-ˌkȯl, 'klȯr-, -ˌkōl\ *n* [*chlor-* + *am*id- + *phen-* + *ni*tr- + gly*col*] **:** a broad-spectrum antibiotic $C_{11}H_{12}Cl_2N_2O_5$ isolated from cultures of a soil microorganism (*Streptomyces venezuelae*) or prepared synthetically

chlo·rate \'klō(ə)r-ˌāt, 'klȯ(ə)r-\ *n* **:** a salt of chloric acid

chlor·dane \'klȯ(ə)r-ˌdān\ *or* **chlor·dan** \-ˌdan\ *n* [*chlor-* + *indane*, *indan* (C_9H_{10})] **:** a highly chlorinated viscous volatile liquid insecticide $C_{10}H_6Cl_8$

chlo·rel·la \klə-'rel-ə\ *n* [NL, genus name, fr. Gk *chlōros*] **:** any of a genus (*Chlorella*) of unicellular green algae potentially a cheap source of high-grade protein and B-complex vitamins

chlo·ric \'klōr-ik, 'klȯr-\ *adj* **:** relating to or obtained from chlorine

chloric acid *n* **:** a strong acid $HClO_3$ like nitric acid in oxidizing properties but far less stable

chlo·ride \'klō(ə)r-ˌīd, 'klȯ(ə)r-\ *n* [G *chlorid*, fr. *chlor-* + *-id* -ide] **:** a compound of chlorine with another element or radical; *esp* **:** a salt or ester of hydrochloric acid

chloride of lime : BLEACHING POWDER

chlo·ri·nate \'klōr-ə-ˌnāt, 'klȯr-\ *vt* **:** to treat or cause to combine with chlorine or a chlorine compound — **chlo·ri·na·tion** \ˌklōr-ə-'nā-shən, ˌklȯr-\ *n* — **chlo·ri·na·tor** \'klōr-ə-ˌnāt-ər, 'klȯr-\ *n*

chlo·rine \'klō(ə)r-ˌēn, 'klȯ(ə)r-, -ən\ *n* **:** a halogen element isolated as a heavy greenish yellow irritating gas of pungent odor used esp. as a bleach, oxidizing agent, and disinfectant in water purification — see ELEMENT table

¹**chlo·rite** \-ˌīt\ *n* [G *chlorit*, fr. L *chloritis*, a green stone, fr. Gk *chlōritis*, fr. *chlōros*] **:** any of a group of monoclinic usu. green minerals associated with and resembling the micas — **chlo·rit·ic** \klə-'rit-ik, klȯ-\ *adj*

²**chlorite** *n* [prob. fr. F, fr. *chlor-*] **:** a salt of chlorous acid

chlo·ro \'klōr-(ˌ)ō, 'klȯr-\ *adj* [*chlor-*] **:** containing chlorine

chlo·ro·ben·zene \ˌklōr-ō-'ben-ˌzēn, ˌklȯr-, -ˌben-'\ *n* [ISV] **:** a colorless flammable volatile toxic liquid C_6H_5Cl made usu. by chlorination of benzene and used in organic synthesis and as a solvent

¹**chlo·ro·form** \'klōr-ə-ˌfȯrm, 'klȯr-\ *n* [F *chloroforme*, fr. *chlor-* + *formyle* formyl; fr. its having been regarded as a trichloride of this radical] **:** a colorless volatile heavy toxic liquid $CHCl_3$ of ethereal odor and sweetish taste used esp. as a solvent or as a general anesthetic or a carminative and anodyne

²**chloroform** *vt* **:** to treat with chloroform esp. so as to produce anesthesia or death

chlo·ro·hy·drin \ˌklōr-ō-'hī-drən, ˌklȯr-\ *n* [ISV, fr. *chlor-* + *hydr-*] **:** any of various organic compounds derived from glycols or polyhydroxy alcohols by substitution of chlorine for part of the hydroxyl groups

Chlo·ro·my·ce·tin \ˌklōr-ō-ˌmī-'sēt-ᵊn, ˌklȯr-\ *trademark* — used for chloramphenicol

chlo·ro·phyll *also* **chlo·ro·phyl** \'klōr-ə-ˌfil, 'klȯr-, -fəl\ *n* [F *chlorophylle*, fr. *chlor-* + Gk *phyllon* leaf — more at BLADE] **1 :** the green photosynthetic coloring matter of plants found in chloroplasts and made up chiefly of a blue-black ester $C_{55}H_{72}MgN_4O_5$ and a dark green ester $C_{55}H_{70}MgN_4O_6$ — called also respectively *chlorophyll a*, *chlorophyll b* **2 :** a waxy green chlorophyll-containing substance extracted from green plants and used as a coloring agent or for its claimed deodorant properties — **chlo·ro·phyl·lose** \ˌklōr-ə-'fil-ˌōs, ˌklȯr-\ *adj* — **chlo·ro·phyl·lous** \-əs\ *adj*

chlo·ro·pic·rin \ˌklōr-ə-'pik-rən, ˌklȯr-\ *n* [G *chlorpikrin*, fr. *chlor-* + Gk *pikros* bitter] **:** a heavy colorless liquid CCl_3NO_2 that causes tears and vomiting and is used esp. as a soil fumigant

chlo·ro·plast \'klōr-ə-ˌplast, 'klȯr-\ *n* [ISV] **:** a plastid containing chlorophyll and being the seat of photosynthesis and starch formation

chlo·ro·prene \'klōr-ə-ˌprēn, 'klȯr-\ *n* [*chlor-* + iso*prene*] **:** a colorless liquid C_4H_5Cl made from acetylene and hydrochloric acid and used esp. in making neoprene by polymerization

chlo·ro·sis \klə-'rō-səs\ *n* **1 :** an iron-deficiency anemia in young girls characterized by a greenish color of the skin — called also *greensickness* **2 :** a diseased condition in green plants marked by yellowing or blanching — **chlo·rot·ic** \-'rät-ik\ *adj* — **chlo·rot·i·cal·ly** \-i-k(ə-)lē\ *adv*

chlo·rous acid \ˌklōr-əs-, ˌklȯr-\ *n* [F *acide chloreux*, fr. *chlor-*] **:** a strongly oxidizing acid $HClO_2$ known only in solution and in the form of its salts

chlor·prom·a·zine \klōr-'präm-ə-ˌzēn, klȯr-\ *n* [*chlor-* + *prom*ethazine ($C_{17}H_{20}N_2S$)] **:** a phenothiazine derivative $C_{17}H_{19}ClN_2S$ used as a tranquilizer in the form of its hydrochloride

chlor·tet·ra·cy·cline \ˌklōr-ˌte-trə-'sī-ˌklēn, ˌklȯr-\ *n* **:** a yellow crystalline antibiotic $C_{22}H_{23}ClN_2O_8$ produced by a soil actinomycete (*Streptomyces aureofaciens*), used in the treatment of diseases, and added to animal feeds for stimulating growth

¹**chock** \'chäk\ *n* [origin unknown] **1 :** a wedge or block for steadying a body (as a cask) and holding it motionless, for filling in an unwanted space, or for blocking the movement of a wheel **2 :** a heavy metal casting with two short horn-shaped arms curving inward between which ropes or hawsers may pass for mooring or towing

²**chock** *vt* **:** to provide, stop, or make fast with or as if with chocks

³**chock** *adv* **:** as close or as completely as possible

chock·a·block \'chäk-ə-ˌbläk\ *adj* **1 :** brought close together **2 :** very full **:** CROWDED

chock–full \'chək-'fu̇l, 'chäk-\ *adj* [ME *chokkefull*, prob. fr. *choken* to choke + *full*] **:** full to the limit **:** CRAMMED

choc·o·late \'chäk-(ə-)lət, 'chȯk-\ *n* [Sp, fr. Nahuatl *xocoatl*] **1 :** a food prepared from ground roasted cacao beans **2 :** a beverage of chocolate in water or milk **3 :** a small candy with a center (as a fondant) and a chocolate coating **4 :** a variable color averaging a brownish gray — **chocolate** *adj*

chocolate tree *n* **:** a cacao (*Theobroma cacao* of the family Sterculiaceae, the chocolate family) cultivated esp. in tropical America

Choc·taw \'chäk-(ˌ)tȯ\ *n*, *pl* **Choctaw** *or* **Choctaws** [Choctaw *Chahta*] **1 a :** a Muskogean people of Mississippi, Alabama, and Louisiana **b :** a member of this people **2 :** the language of the Choctaw and Chickasaw people

¹**choice** \'chȯis\ *n* [ME *chois*, fr. OF, fr. *choisir* to choose, of Gmc origin; akin to OHG *kiosan* to choose] **1 :** the act of choosing **:** SELECTION **2 :** power of choosing **:** OPTION **3 a :** a person or thing chosen **b :** the best part **:** CREAM **4 :** a sufficient number and variety to choose among **5 :** care in selecting

syn OPTION, ALTERNATIVE, PREFERENCE, SELECTION, ELECTION: CHOICE suggests the opportunity or privilege of choosing freely; OPTION implies a power to choose that is specifically granted or guaranteed; ALTERNATIVE implies a necessity to choose one and reject another or other possibilities; PREFERENCE suggests the guidance of choice by one's judgment or predilections; SELECTION implies a wide range of choice; ELECTION implies an end or purpose which requires exercise of judgment

²**choice** *adj* **1 :** worthy of being chosen **:** SELECT **2 :** selected with care **:** well chosen **3 a :** of high quality **b** *of meat* **:** of a grade between prime and good — **choice·ly** *adv* — **choice·ness** *n*

syn EXQUISITE, ELEGANT, RARE, DAINTY, DELICATE: CHOICE stresses preeminence in quality or kind; EXQUISITE implies a perfection in workmanship or design that appeals only to very sensitive taste; ELEGANT applies to what is rich and luxurious but restrained by good taste; RARE suggests an uncommon excellence; DAINTY and DELICATE both imply exquisiteness, subtlety, fragility, but DAINTY usu. carries an additional suggestion of the effeminate or mincing

¹**choir** \'kwī(-ə)r\ *n* [ME *quer*, fr. OF *cuer*, fr. ML *chorus*, fr. L, chorus] **1 :** an organized company of singers esp. in church service **2 :** a group of instruments of the same class **3 :** an organized group of persons or things **4 :** a division of angels **5 :** the part of a church occupied by the singers or by the clergy; *specif* **:** the part of the chancel between sanctuary and nave **6 :** a group organized for ensemble speaking

²**choir** *vb* **:** to sing or sound in chorus or concert

³**choir** *adj* **:** of the class in a religious order bound to recite the Divine Office and devoted chiefly to the order's special work

choir·boy \-ˌbȯi\ *n* **:** a boy member of a church choir

choir loft *n* **:** a gallery occupied by a church choir

choir·mas·ter \-ˌmas-tər\ *n* **:** the director of a choir (as in a church)

¹**choke** \'chōk\ *vb* [ME *choken*, alter. of *achoken*, fr. OE *acēocian*] *vt* **1 :** to check normal breathing of by compressing or obstructing the windpipe or by poisoning or adulterating available air **2 :** to check or suppress expression of or by **:** SILENCE **3 a :** to check the growth, development, or activity of **b :** to obstruct by filling up or clogging; *also* **:** to fill completely **:** JAM **4 :** to enrich the fuel mixture of (a motor) by partially shutting off the air intake of the carburetor **5 :** to grip (as a baseball bat) some distance from the end of the handle ~ *vi* **1 :** to become choked in breathing **2 :** to become obstructed or checked **3 :** to shorten one's grip esp. on the handle of a bat

²**choke** *n* **1 :** the act of choking **:** SUFFOCATION **2 :** something that chokes: as **a :** a valve for choking a gasoline engine **b :** a narrowing toward the muzzle in the bore of a gun

choke·ber·ry \-ˌber-ē\ *n* **:** a small berrylike astringent fruit; *also* **:** a shrub (genus *Aronia*) of the rose family bearing chokeberries

choke·cher·ry \-ˌcher-ē, -'cher-\ *n* **:** any of several American wild cherries with bitter or astringent fruit; *also* **:** this fruit

choke coil *n* **:** REACTOR 2

choke·damp \'chōk-ˌdamp\ *n* **:** BLACKDAMP

chok·er \'chō-kər\ *n* **1 :** one that chokes **2 :** something worn closely about the throat or neck: as **a :** a wide neckcloth; *esp* **:** STOCK **b :** a high stiff collar **c :** a short necklace

choky \'chō-kē\ *adj* **:** tending to cause choking or become choked

chol- *or* **chole-** *or* **cholo-** *comb form* [Gk *chol-*, *cholē-*, *cholo-*, fr. *cholē*, *cholos* — more at GALL] **:** bile **:** gall ⟨*chol*ate⟩ ⟨*chole*lith⟩

cho·late \'kō-ˌlāt\ *n* **:** a salt or ester of cholic acid

cho·le·cys·tec·to·my \ˌkō-lə-ˌsis-'tek-tə-mē, ˌkäl-ə-\ *n* [NL *cholecystis* gallbladder (fr. *chol-* + Gk *kystis* bladder) + ISV *-ectomy* — more at CYST] **:** surgical excision of the gallbladder

cho·le·cys·ti·tis \-'tīt-əs\ *n* [NL, fr. *cholecystis*] **:** inflammation of the gallbladder

cho·ler \'käl-ər, 'kō-lər\ *n* [ME *coler*, fr. MF *colere*, fr. L *cholera* bilious disease, fr. Gk, fr. *cholē*] **1 a** *archaic* **:** YELLOW BILE **b** *obs* **:** BILE 1a **2** *obs* **:** BILIOUSNESS **3 :** IRASCIBILITY

chol·era \'käl-ə-rə\ *n*, *often attrib* [ME *colera* bile, fr. L *cholera*] **:** any of several diseases of man and domestic animals usu. marked by severe gastrointestinal symptoms; *esp* **:** ASIATIC CHOLERA — **chol·e·ra·ic** \ˌkäl-ə-'rā-ik\ *adj*

cho·ler·ic \'käl-ə-rik, kə-'ler-ik\ *adj* **1 :** easily moved to anger **:** hot-tempered **2 :** ANGRY, IRATE **syn** see IRASCIBLE

cho·les·ter·ol \kə-'les-tə-ˌrȯl, -ˌrōl\ *n* [F *cholésterine*, fr. *chol-* + Gk *stereos* solid] **:** a steroid alcohol $C_{27}H_{45}OH$ present in animal cells and body fluids, important in physiological processes, and implicated experimentally as a factor in arteriosclerosis

cho·lic acid \ˌkō-lik-, ˌkäl-ik-\ *n* [Gk *cholikos*, fr. *cholē*] **:** a crystalline bile acid $C_{24}H_{40}O_5$

cho·line \'kō-ˌlēn, 'käl-ˌēn\ *n* [ISV] **:** a base $C_5H_{15}NO_2$ that is widely distributed esp. in animal and plant products and is a vitamin of the B complex essential to the liver function

cho·lin·er·gic \ˌkō-lə-'nər-jik, ˌkäl-ə-\ *adj* [ISV acetyl*choline* + Gk *ergon* work — more at WORK] **1** *of autonomic nerve fibers* **:** liberating or activated by acetylcholine **2 :** resembling acetylcholine esp. in physiologic action

cho·lin·es·ter·ase \ˌkō-lə-'nes-tə-ˌrās, ˌkäl-ə-, -ˌrāz\ *n* **:** an enzyme that hydrolyzes choline esters

chon \chän\ *n*, *pl* **chon** [Korean] — see *hwan* at MONEY table

chondr- *or* **chondri-** *or* **chondro-** *comb form* [NL, fr. Gk *chondr-*, *chondro-*, fr. *chondros* grain, cartilage] **:** cartilage ⟨*chondro*cranium⟩

chon·drio·some \'kän-drē-ə-ˌsōm\ *n* [Gk *chondrion*, dim. of *chondros*, + ISV *-some*] **:** any of the minute apparently self-perpetuating lipoprotein complexes in cytoplasm that are held to function in cellular metabolism and secretion

chon·drite \'kän-ˌdrīt\ *n* [ISV, fr. Gk *chondros* grain] **:** a meteoric stone characterized by the presence of chondrules — **chon·drit·ic** \kän-'drit-ik\ *adj*

chon·dro·cra·ni·um \ˌkän-drō-'krā-nē-əm\ *n* **:** the embryonic cartilaginous cranium; *also* **:** the part of the adult skull derived therefrom

chon·drule \'kän-(ˌ)drül\ *n* [Gk *chondros* grain] **:** a rounded granule of cosmic origin often found embedded in meteoric stones

choose \'chüz\ *vb* **chose** \'chōz\ **cho·sen** \'chōz-ᵊn\ **choos·ing** \'chü-ziŋ\ [ME *chosen*, fr. OE *cēosan*; akin to OHG *kiosan* to choose, L *gustare* to taste] *vt* **1 :** to select esp. freely and after consideration **2 a :** to have a preference for **b** (1) **:** DECIDE ⟨*chose* to go by train⟩ (2) **:** PREFER ~ *vi* **1 :** to make a selection **2 :** to

take an alternative **3 :** to see fit **:** INCLINE — **choos·er** *n*

choosy *or* **choos·ey** \'chü-zē\ *adj* **choos·i·er; choos·i·est :** fastidiously selective **:** PARTICULAR

1**chop** \'chäp\ *vb* **chopped; chop·ping** [ME *chappen, choppen* — more at CHAP] *vt* **1 a :** to sever by usu. repeated blows of a sharp instrument **b :** to cut into pieces **:** MINCE **2 :** to strike (a ball) with a short quick downward stroke ~ *vi* **1 :** to make a quick stroke or repeated strokes with or as if with a sharp instrument (as an ax) **2** *archaic* **:** to move or act suddenly or violently

2**chop** *n* **1 a :** a forceful usu. slanting blow with or as if with an ax or cleaver **b :** a sharp downward blow or stroke **2 :** a small cut of meat often including a part of a rib **3 :** a mark made by or as if by chopping **4 :** material that has been chopped up **5 a :** a short abrupt motion **b :** a stretch of choppy sea

3**chop** *vi* **chopped; chop·ping** [ME *chappen, choppen* to barter, fr. OE *cēapian* — more at CHEAP] **1 :** to change direction **2 :** to veer with or as if with the wind — **chop logic :** to argue with sophistical reasoning and minute distinctions

4**chop** *n* [Hindi *chāp* stamp] **1 a :** a seal or official stamp or its impression **b :** a license validated by a seal **2 a :** a mark on goods or coins to indicate nature or quality **b :** a kind, brand, or lot of goods bearing the same chop **c :** QUALITY, GRADE

chop·fall·en \'chäp-,fȯ-lən\ *var of* CHAPFALLEN

chop·house \'chäp-,hau̇s\ *n* **:** RESTAURANT

cho·pine \chō-'pēn, 'chäp-ən\ *n* [MF *chapin,* fr. OSp] **:** a woman's shoe of the 16th and 17th centuries with a very high sole

chop mark *n* **:** an indentation made on a coin to attest weight, silver content, or legality — **chop–marked** \'chäp-,märkt\ *adj*

chop·per \'chäp-ər\ *n* **1 :** one that chops **2** *slang* **:** HELICOPTER

chop·pi·ness \'chäp-ē-nəs\ *n* **:** the quality or state of being choppy

1**chop·py** \'chäp-ē\ *adj* [*chop* (crack)] **:** CHAPPED

2**choppy** *adj, of the wind* **:** CHANGEABLE, VARIABLE

3**choppy** *adj* **1 :** rough with small waves **2 :** JERKY, DISCONNECTED

chops \'chäps\ *n pl* [alter. of 4*chap*] **1 :** JAW **2 a :** MOUTH **b :** the fleshy covering of the jaws

chop·stick \'chäp-,stik\ *n* [pidgin E, fr. *chop* fast (of Chinese origin; akin to Cant *kap*) + E *stick*] **:** one of a pair of slender sticks held between thumb and fingers and used chiefly in oriental countries to lift food to the mouth

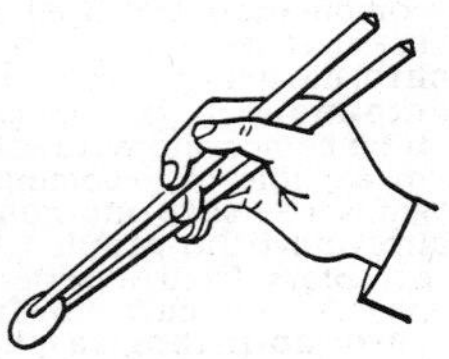

chopsticks

chop su·ey \chäp-'sü-ē\ *n* [Chin (Cant) *shap sui* odds and ends, fr. *shap* miscellaneous + *sui* bits] **:** a dish prepared chiefly from bean sprouts, bamboo shoots, water chestnuts, onions, mushrooms, and meat or fish and served with rice and soy sauce

cho·rag·ic \kə-'raj-ik\ *adj* **:** of or relating to a choragus

cho·ra·gus \kə-'rā-gəs\ *or* **cho·re·gus** \-'rē-\ *n* [L & Gk; L *choragus,* fr. Gk *chorāgos, chorēgos,* fr. *choros* chorus + *agein* to lead — more at AGENT] **1 :** the leader of a chorus or choir **2 :** a leader of a dramatic chorus in ancient Greece

cho·ral \'kōr-əl, 'kȯr-\ *adj* [F or ML; F *choral,* fr. ML *choralis,* fr. L *chorus*] **:** of, relating to, or performed by a chorus or choir **:** performed in chorus — **cho·ral·ly** \-ə-lē\ *adv*

cho·rale *also* **cho·ral** \kə-'ral, -'räl\ *n* [G *choral,* short for *choralgesang* choral song] **1 :** a hymn or psalm sung to a traditional or composed melody in church; *also* **:** a hymn tune or a harmonization of a traditional melody ⟨a Bach ~⟩ **2 :** CHORUS, CHOIR

chorale prelude *n* **:** a composition usu. for organ based upon a chorale

choral speaking *n* **:** ensemble speaking of poetry or prose by a group often using various voice combinations and contrasts

1**chord** \'kȯ(ə)rd\ *n* [alter. of ME *cord,* short for *accord*] **:** a combination of tones that blend harmoniously when sounded together

2**chord** *vi* **1 :** ACCORD **2 :** to play chords on a stringed instrument ~ *vt* **1 :** to make chords on **2 :** HARMONIZE

3**chord** *n* [alter. of 1*cord*] **1 :** CORD 3a **2 :** a straight line joining two points on a curve; *specif* **:** the segment of a secant between its intersections with a curve **3 :** an individual emotion or disposition **4 :** either of the two outside members of a truss connected and braced by the web members **5 :** the straight line joining the leading and trailing edges of an airfoil

chord·al \'kȯrd-ᵊl\ *adj* **1 :** of or relating to a chord **2 :** relating to music characterized more by harmony than by counterpoint

chor·da·meso·derm \,kȯrd-ə-'mez-ə-,dərm, -'mes-\ *n* [NL *chorda* cord + E *mesoderm*] **:** the portion of the embryonic mesoderm that forms notochord and related structures and serves as an inductor of neural structures — **chor·da·meso·der·mal** \-,mez-ə-'dər-məl, -,mes-\ *adj*

chor·date \'kȯrd-ət, 'kȯ(ə)r-,dāt\ *n* [deriv. of L *chorda* cord] **:** any of a phylum or subkingdom (Chordata) of animals having at least at some stage of development a notochord, dorsally situated central nervous system, and gill clefts and including the vertebrates, lancelets, and tunicates — **chordate** *adj*

chore \'chō(ə)r, 'chȯ(ə)r\ *n* [alter. of *chare*] **1** *pl* **:** the regular or daily light work of a household or farm **2 :** a routine task or job **3 :** a difficult or disagreeable task **syn** see TASK

-chore \,kō(ə)r, ,kȯ(ə)r\ *n comb form* [Gk *chōrein* to withdraw, go; akin to Gk *chēros* bereaved — more at HEIR] **:** plant distributed by (such) an agency ⟨zoochore⟩ — **-cho·rous** \'kōr-əs, 'kȯr-\ *adj comb form* — **-cho·ry** \,kōr-ē, ,kȯr-\ *n comb form*

cho·rea \kə-'rē-ə\ *n* [NL, fr. L, dance, fr. Gk *choreia,* fr. *choros* chorus] **:** a nervous disorder (as of man or dogs) marked by spasmodic movements and incoordination

cho·reo·graph \'kōr-ē-ə-,graf, 'kȯr-\ *vt* **:** to compose the choreography of ~ *vi* **:** to engage in choreography — **cho·re·og·ra·pher** \,kōr-ē-'äg-rə-fər, ,kȯr-\ *n*

cho·reo·graph·ic \,kōr-ē-ə-'graf-ik, ,kȯr-\ *adj* **:** of or relating to choreography — **cho·reo·graph·i·cal·ly** \-i-k(ə-)lē\ *adv*

cho·re·og·ra·phy \,kōr-ē-'äg-rə-fē, ,kȯr-\ *n* [F *chorégraphie,* fr. Gk *choreia* + F *-graphie* -graphy] **1 :** the art of symbolically representing dancing **2 :** DANCING; *esp* **:** stage dancing as distinguished from social or ballroom dancing **3 :** composition and arrangement of dances esp. for ballet

chor·iamb \'kōr-ē-,am(b), 'kȯr-\ *n, pl* **choriambs** \-,amz\ [LL *choriambus,* fr. Gk *choriambos,* fr. *choreios* of a chorus, (fr. *choros*) + *iambos* iambus] **:** a prosodic foot consisting of a trochee followed by an iamb — **chor·iam·bic** \,kōr-ē-'am-bik, ,kȯr-\ *adj*

cho·ric \'kōr-ik, 'kȯr-, 'kär-\ *adj* **:** of, relating to, or in the style of a chorus and esp. a Greek chorus

cho·rio·al·lan·to·ic \,kōr-ē-(,)ō-,al-ən-'tō-ik, ,kȯr-\ *adj* **:** of, relating to, or produced by chorioallantois

cho·rio·al·lan·to·is \-ə-'lant-ə-wəs\ *n* [NL, fr. Gk *chorion* + NL *allantois*] **:** a vascular fetal membrane composed of the fused chorion and adjacent wall of the allantois that in the hen's egg is used as a living culture medium for viruses and for tissues

cho·ri·on \'kōr-ē-,än, 'kȯr-\ *n* [NL, fr. Gk] **:** the highly vascular outer embryonic membrane of higher vertebrates that in placental mammals is associated with the allantois in the formation of the placenta — **cho·ri·on·ic** \,kōr-ē-'än-ik, ,kȯr-\ *adj*

cho·ri·pet·al·ous \,kōr-i-'pet-ᵊl-əs, ,kȯr-\ *adj* [deriv. of Gk *chōris* apart + *petalon* leaf; akin to Gk *chēros* bereaved] **:** POLYPETALOUS

cho·ris·ter \'kōr-ə-stər, 'kȯr-, 'kär-\ *n* [ME *querister,* fr. AF *cueristre,* fr. ML *chorista,* fr. L *chorus*] **:** a singer in a choir; *specif* **:** CHOIRBOY

C–horizon *n* **:** the layer of a soil profile lying beneath the B-horizon and consisting essentially of more or less weathered parent rock

cho·ro·graph·ic \,kōr-ə-'graf-ik, ,kȯr-\ *adj* **:** of or relating to chorography

cho·rog·ra·phy \kə-'räg-rə-fē\ *n* [L *chorographia,* fr. Gk *chōrographia,* fr. *chōros* place + *-graphia* -graphy; akin to Gk *chēros*] **1 :** the art of describing or mapping a region or district **2 :** a description or map of a region; *also* **:** the physical conformation and features of such a region

cho·roid coat \,kōr-,ȯid-, ,kȯr-\ *or* **cho·ri·oid coat** \-ē-,ȯid-\ *n* [NL *choroides,* fr. Gk *chorioeidēs,* fr. *chorion*] **:** a vascular membrane containing large branched pigment cells that lies between the retina and the sclerotic coat of the vertebrate eye

chor·tle \'chȯrt-ᵊl\ *vi* **chor·tling** \'chȯrt-liŋ, -ᵊl-iŋ\ [blend of *chuckle* and *snort*] **1 :** to sing or chant exultantly **2 :** to laugh or chuckle esp. in satisfaction or exultation — **chortle** *n* — **chor·tler** \'chȯrt-lər, -ᵊl-ər\ *n*

1**cho·rus** \'kōr-əs, 'kȯr-\ *n* [L, ring dance, chorus, fr. Gk *choros*] **1 a :** a company of singers and dancers in Athenian drama participating in or commenting on the action; *also* **:** a similar company in later plays **b :** a character in Elizabethan drama who speaks the prologue and epilogue and comments on the action **c :** an organized company of singers who sing in concert **:** CHOIR; *specif* **:** a body of singers who sing the choral parts of a work (as in opera) **d :** a group of dancers and singers supporting the featured players in a musical comedy or revue **2 a :** a part of a song or hymn recurring at intervals **b :** the part of a drama sung or spoken by the chorus **c :** a composition to be sung by a number of voices in concert **d :** the main part of a popular song **3 :** something performed, sung, or uttered simultaneously by a number of persons or animals; *also* **:** sounds so uttered **4 :** a unanimous utterance by the members of a group — **in chorus :** in unison

2**chorus** *vb* **:** to sing or utter in chorus

chorus girl *n* **:** a young woman who sings or dances in a chorus (as of a musical comedy) — called also *cho·rine* \'kō(ə)r-,ēn, 'kȯ(ə)r-\

1**chose** *past of* CHOOSE

2**chose** \'shōz\ *n* [F, fr. L *causa* cause, reason] **:** a piece of personal property **:** THING

cho·sen \'chōz-ᵊn\ *adj* [ME, fr. pp. of *chosen* to choose] **1 :** selected or marked for favor or special privilege **2 :** ELECT

chott \'shät\ *n* [F *chott,* fr. Ar *shaṭṭ*] **:** a shallow saline lake of northern Africa; *also* **:** the dried bed of such a lake

Chou \'jō\ *n* [Chin (Pek) *Chou*[1]] **:** a Chinese dynasty traditionally dated 1122 to about 256 B.C. and marked by the development of the philosophical schools of Confucius, Mencius, Lao-tzu, and Mo Ti

chough \'chəf\ *n* [ME] **:** a bird of an Old World genus (*Pyrrhocorax*) related to the crows with red legs and glossy black plumage

1**chouse** \'chau̇s\ *vt* [Turk *çavuş* doorkeeper, messenger] **:** CHEAT, TRICK

2**chouse** *vt* [origin unknown] *West* **:** to drive or herd roughly

chow \'chau̇\ *n* [perh. fr. Chin (Pek) *chiao*[3] meat dumpling] *slang* **:** FOOD, VICTUALS

chow·chow \'chau̇-,chau̇\ *n* [pidgin E] **1 :** a Chinese preserve of ginger, fruits, and peels in heavy syrup **2 :** chopped mixed pickles in mustard sauce

chow chow \'chau̇-,chau̇\ *n, often cap both Cs* [fr. a Chin dial. word akin to Cant *kaú* dog] **:** a heavy-coated blocky dog with a broad head and muzzle, a very full ruff of long hair, and a distinctive blue-black tongue and black-lined mouth — called also *chow*

chow·der \'chau̇d-ər\ *n* [F *chaudière* kettle, contents of a kettle, fr. LL *caldaria* — more at CALDRON] **1 :** a thick soup or stew of seafood (as clams) usu. made with milk, salt pork or bacon, onions, and potatoes or other vegetables **2 :** a thick soup resembling chowder

chow mein \'chau̇-'mān\ *n* [Chin (Pek) *ch'ao*[3] *mien*[4], fr. *ch'ao*[3] to fry + *mien*[4] dough] **1 :** fried noodles **2 :** a thick stew of shredded or diced meat, mushrooms, vegetables, and seasonings that is served with fried noodles

chres·tom·a·thy \kre-'stäm-ə-thē\ *n* [NL *chrestomathia,* fr. Gk *chrēstomatheia,* fr. *chrēstos* useful + *manthanein* to learn; akin to Skt *hrasva* small] **1 :** a selection of passages compiled to aid in learning a language **2 :** a volume of selections from an author

chrism \'kriz-əm\ *n* [ME *crisme,* fr. OE *crisma,* fr. LL *chrisma,* fr. Gk, ointment, fr. *chriein* to anoint; akin to OE *grēot* grit, sand] **:** consecrated oil used in Roman Catholic and some other liturgical churches esp. in baptism, confirmation, and ordination

chris·om \'kriz-əm\ *n* [ME *crisom,* short for *crisom cloth,* fr. *crisom* chrism + *cloth*] **:** a white cloth or robe put upon a person at baptism as a symbol of innocence

chrisom child *n* **:** a child that dies in its first month

Christ \'krīst\ *n* [ME *Crist,* fr. OE, fr. L *Christus,* fr. Gk *Christos,* lit., anointed, fr. *chriein* to anoint] **1 :** MESSIAH **2 :** JESUS **3 :** an ideal type of humanity **4** *Christian Science* **:** the ideal truth that comes as a divine manifestation of God to destroy incarnate error

chris·ten \'kris-ᵊn\ *vt* **chris·ten·ing** \'kris-niŋ, -ᵊn-iŋ\ [ME *cristnen,* fr. OE *cristnian,* fr. *cristen* Christian, fr. L *christianus*] **1 a :** BAPTIZE **b :** to name at baptism **2 :** to name or dedicate (as

a ship) by a ceremony suggestive of baptism **3 :** DENOMINATE **4 :** to use for the first time

Chris·ten·dom \'kris-ᵊn-dəm\ *n* [ME *cristendom*, fr. OE *cristendōm*, fr. *cristen*] **1 :** CHRISTIANITY **2 :** the portion of the world in which Christianity prevails

chris·ten·ing *n* **:** the ceremony of baptizing and naming a child

1Chris·tian \'kris(h)-chən\ *n* [L *christianus*, adj. & n., fr. Gk *christianos*, fr. *Christos*] **1 a :** an adherent of Christianity **b :** (1) **:** DISCIPLE 2 (2) **:** a member of one of the Churches of Christ separating from the Disciples of Christ in 1906 and seeking a united New Testament Christianity (3) **:** a member of one of the churches in the union of Congregational Christian Churches **2 :** the hero in Bunyan's *Pilgrim's Progress*

2Christian *adj* **1 :** of, relating to, or professing Christianity **2 a :** of or relating to Jesus Christ **b :** of, based on, or conforming with Christianity **c :** of or relating to a Christian **d :** representing Christianity ⟨his most ~ majesty, the king⟩ — **Chris·tian·ly** *adv*

Christian Brother *n* **:** a member of the Roman Catholic institute of Brothers of the Christian Schools founded in France in 1680 and devoted to primary and secondary education

Christian era *n* **:** the era used in Christian countries for numbering the years since the birth of Christ

chris·ti·a·nia \,kris(h)-chē-'an-ē-ə, ,kris-tē-, -'än-\ *n, often cap* [*Christiania* (now Oslo), Norway] **:** a skiing turn used for altering direction of descent or for checking or stopping and executed usu. at high speed by shifting body weight forward and skidding into a turn with parallel skis — called also *chris·tie, chris·ty* \'kris-tē\

Chris·tian·i·ty \,kris(h)-chē-'an-ət-ē, kris(h)-'chan-\ *n* **1 :** the whole body of Christian believers **2 :** the religion derived from Jesus Christ, based on the Bible as sacred scripture, and professed by Eastern, Roman Catholic, and Protestant bodies **3 :** conformity to the Christian religion

Chris·tian·iza·tion \,kris(h)-chə-nə-'zā-shən\ *n* **:** the act or process of Christianizing or state of being Christianized

Chris·tian·ize \'kris(h)-chə-,nīz\ *vt* **:** to make Christian — **Chris·tian·iz·er** *n*

christian name *n, often cap C* **:** the name given at birth or christening as distinct from the family name

Christian Reformed *adj* **:** of or relating to a church formed in the Netherlands in 1834 by dissenters from the Netherlands Reformed Church or one formed in the U.S. in 1857 by dissenters from the Reformed Church in America

Christian Science *n* **:** a religion discovered by Mary Baker Eddy in 1866 that was organized under the official name of the Church of Christ, Scientist, that derives its teachings from the Scriptures as understood by its adherents, and that includes a practice of spiritual healing based upon the teaching that cause and effect are mental and that sin, sickness, and death will be destroyed by a full understanding of the divine principle of Jesus's teaching and healing — **Christian Scientist** *n*

Christ·like \'krīst-,līk\ *adj* **:** resembling Christ in character, spirit, or action — **Christ·like·ness** *n*

Christ·ly \'krīst-lē\ *adj* **:** of, relating to, or resembling Christ

Christ·mas \'kris-məs\ *n* [ME *Christemasse*, fr. OE *Cristes mæsse*, lit., Christ's mass] **1 :** a Christian feast on December 25 or among the Armenians on January 6 that commemorates the birth of Christ and is usu. observed as a legal holiday **2 :** CHRISTMASTIDE

Christ·mas·tide \'kris-mə-,stīd\ *n* **:** the festival season from Christmas eve till after New Year's Day or esp. in England till Epiphany

Christmas tree *n* **:** a usu. evergreen tree decorated at Christmas

chris·to·log·i·cal \,kris-tə-'läj-i-kəl\ *adj, often cap* **:** of or relating to Christology

Chris·tol·o·gy \kris-'täl-ə-jē\ *n* [Gk *Christos* Christ + E *-logy*] **:** theological interpretation of the person and work of Christ

Christ's–thorn \'krīs(ts)-'thȯ(ə)rn\ *n* **:** any of several prickly or thorny shrubs of Palestine (esp. the shrub *Paliurus spina-christi* or the jujube *Ziziphus jujuba*)

chrom- *or* **chromo-** *comb form* [F, fr. Gk *chrōma* color] **1 :** chromium ⟨*chrom*ize⟩ **2 a :** color **:** colored ⟨*chromo*sphere⟩ **b :** pigment ⟨*chromo*gen⟩

chro·ma \'krō-mə\ *n* [Gk *chrōma*] **1 :** SATURATION 4a **2 :** a quality of color combining hue and saturation **syn** see COLOR

chromat- *or* **chromato-** *comb form* [Gk *chrōmat-*, *chrōma*] **1 :** color ⟨*chromat*id⟩ **2 :** chromatin ⟨*chromato*lysis⟩

chro·mate \'krō-,māt\ *n* [F, fr. Gk *chrōma*] **:** a salt or ester of chromic acid

1chro·mat·ic \krō-'mat-ik\ *adj* [Gk *chrōmatikos*, fr. *chrōmat-*, *chrōma* skin, color, modified tone; akin to OE *grēot* sand — more at GRIT] **1 a :** of or relating to color or color phenomena or sensations **b :** highly colored **2 :** of or relating to chroma **3 a :** of, relating to, or giving all the tones of the chromatic scale **b :** characterized by frequent use of nonharmonic tones or of harmonies based on nonharmonic tones — **chro·mat·i·cal·ly** \-i-k(ə-)lē\ *adv* — **chro·mat·i·cism** \-'mat-ə-,siz-əm\ *n*

2chromatic *n* **:** ACCIDENTAL 2

chromatic aberration *n* **:** aberration caused by the differences in refraction of the colored rays of the spectrum

chro·ma·tic·i·ty \,krō-mə-'tis-ət-ē\ *n* **1 :** the quality or state of being chromatic **2 :** the quality of color characterized by its dominant or complementary wavelength and purity taken together

chro·mat·ics \krō-'mat-iks\ *n pl but sing in constr* **:** the branch of colorimetry that deals with hue and saturation

chromatic scale *n* **:** a musical scale consisting entirely of half steps

chro·ma·tid \'krō-mə-təd\ *n* **:** one of the paired complex constituent strands of a chromosome

chro·ma·tin \'krō-mə-tən\ *n* **:** the part of a cell nucleus that stains intensely with basic dyes; *specif* **:** a complex of a polymerized nucleic acid with basic proteins of protamine or histone type present in chromomeres and held to be the physical carrier of genes — **chro·ma·tin·ic** \,krō-mə-'tin-ik\ *adj*

chro·ma·to·graph·ic \krō-,mat-ə-'graf-ik, ,krō-mət-ə-\ *adj* **:** of or relating to chromatography — **chro·ma·to·graph·i·cal·ly** \-i-k(ə-)lē\ *adv*

chro·ma·tog·ra·phy \,krō-mə-'täg-rə-fē\ *n* **:** a separating esp. of closely related compounds by allowing a solution or mixture of them to seep through an adsorbent (as clay or paper) so that each compound becomes adsorbed in a separate often colored layer

chro·ma·tol·y·sis \-'täl-ə-səs\ *n* [NL] **:** the dissolution and breaking up of chromophil material (as chromatin) of a cell — **chro·ma·to·lyt·ic** \krō-,mat-ᵊl-'it-ik, ,krō-mət-\ *adj*

chro·mato·phore \krō-'mat-ə-,fō(ə)r, -,fȯ(ə)r\ *n* [ISV] **1 :** a pigment-bearing cell; *esp* **:** one of the integumental cells of an animal capable of causing skin color changes by expanding or contracting **2 :** CHROMOPLAST, CHLOROPLAST — **chro·ma·to·phor·ic** \krō-,mat-ə-'fȯr-ik, ,krō-mət-ə-, -'fär-\ *adj* — **chro·ma·toph·o·rous** \,krō-mə-'täf-(ə-)rəs\ *adj*

1chrome \'krōm\ *n* [F, fr. Gk *chrōma*] **1 a :** CHROMIUM **b :** a chromium pigment **2 :** something plated with an alloy of chromium

2chrome *vt* **:** to treat with a compound of chromium (as in dyeing)

-chrome \,krōm\ *n comb form or adj comb form* [ML *-chromat-*, *-chroma* colored thing, fr. Gk *chrōmat-*, *chrōma*] **1 :** colored thing ⟨helio*chrome*⟩ **:** colored ⟨hetero*chrome*⟩ **2 :** coloring matter ⟨uro*chrome*⟩

chrome alum *n* **:** an alum in which chromium is the trivalent metal; *esp* **:** a dark violet salt $KCr(SO_4)_2.12H_2O$ used in tanning and as a mordant in dyeing

chrome green *n* **:** any of various brilliant green pigments containing or consisting of chromium compounds

chrome red *n* **:** a pigment consisting of basic lead chromate Pb_2OCrO_4

chrome yellow *n* **:** a pigment consisting essentially of neutral lead chromate $PbCrO_4$

chro·mic \'krō-mik\ *adj* **:** of, relating to, or derived from chromium esp. when trivalent

chromic acid *n* **:** an acid H_2CrO_4 analogous to sulfuric acid but known only in solution and esp. in the form of its salts

chro·mide \'krō-,mīd\ *n* [deriv. of Gk *chromis*, a sea fish] **:** any of several small brightly colored African fishes (family Cichlidae)

chro·mi·nance \'krō-mə-nən(t)s\ *n* [*chrom-* + lum*inance*] **:** the difference between a color and a chosen reference color of the same luminous intensity in color television

chro·mite \'krō-,mīt\ *n* [G *chromit*, fr. *chrom-*] **:** a mineral $FeCr_2O_4$ that consists of an oxide of iron and chromium

chro·mi·um \'krō-mē-əm\ *n, often attrib* [NL, fr. F *chrome*] **:** a blue-white multivalent metallic element found naturally only in combination and used esp. in alloys and in electroplating — see ELEMENT table

chro·mo \'krō-(,)mō\ *n* **:** CHROMOLITHOGRAPH

chro·mo·gen \'krō-mə-jən\ *n* [ISV] **1 a :** a precursor of a pigment **b :** a compound not itself a dye but containing a chromophore and so capable of becoming one **2 :** a pigment-producing microorganism — **chro·mo·gen·ic** \,krō-mə-'jen-ik\ *adj*

chro·mo·litho·graph \,krō-mə-'lith-ə-,graf\ *n* **:** a picture printed in colors from a series of stones prepared by the lithographic process — **chro·mo·litho·graph·ic** \-,lith-ə-'graf-ik\ *adj* — **chro·mo·li·thog·ra·phy** \-lith-'äg-rə-fē\ *n*

chro·mo·mere \'krō-mə-,mi(ə)r\ *n* [ISV] **:** one of the enlargements of the chromonema at which nucleoproteins appear to be concentrated — **chro·mo·mer·ic** \,krō-mə-'mer-ik, -'mir-\ *adj*

chro·mo·ne·ma \,krō-mə-'nē-mə\ *n, pl* **chro·mo·ne·ma·ta** \-'nē-mət-ə\ [NL, fr. *chrom-* + Gk *nēma* thread — more at NEEDLE] **:** the coiled filamentous core of a chromatid held to be the actual carrier of the genes — **chro·mo·ne·mal** \-'nē-məl\ *or* **chro·mo·ne·mat·ic** \-ni-'mat-ik\ *or* **chro·mo·ne·mic** \-'nē-mik\ *adj*

chro·mo·phil \'krō-mə-,fil\ *or* **chro·mat·o·phil** \krō-'mat-ə-,fil\ *adj* [ISV] **:** staining readily with dyes

chro·mo·phore \'krō-mə-,fō(ə)r, -,fȯ(ə)r\ *n* [ISV] **:** a group that gives rise to color in a molecule — **chro·mo·phor·ic** \,krō-mə-'fȯr-ik, -'fär-\ *adj*

chro·mo·plast \'krō-mə-,plast\ *n* [ISV] **:** a colored plastid usu. containing red or yellow pigment

chro·mo·pro·tein \,kro-mə-'prō-,tēn, -'prōt-ē-ən\ *n* **:** a compound of a protein with a metal-containing pigment or a carotenoid

chro·mo·som·al \,krō-mə-'sō-məl\ *adj* **:** of or relating to chromosomes — **chro·mo·som·al·ly** \-mə-lē\ *adv*

chro·mo·some \'krō-mə-,sōm\ *n* [ISV] **:** one of the usu. elongated chromatin-containing basophilic bodies of the cell nucleus made up of chromatids and usu. constant in number in the cells of any one kind of plant or animal — **chro·mo·so·mic** \,krō-mə-'sō-mik\ *adj*

chro·mo·sphere \'krō-mə-,sfi(ə)r\ *n* **:** the lower part of the atmosphere of the sun thousands of miles thick and composed chiefly of hydrogen gas; *also* **:** a similar portion of the atmosphere of any star — **chro·mo·sphe·ric** \,krō-mə-'sfi(ə)r-ik, -'sfer-\ *adj*

chro·mous \'krō-məs\ *adj* **:** of, relating to, or derived from chromium esp. when bivalent

chron- *or* **chrono-** *comb form* [Gk, fr. *chronos*] **:** time ⟨*chrono*gram⟩

chro·nax·ie \'krō-,nak-sē\ *n* [F, fr. *chron-* + Gk *axia* value, fr. *axios* worthy] **:** the minimum time required for excitation of a structure by a constant electric current of twice the threshold voltage

chron·ic \'krän-ik\ *adj* [F *chronique*, fr. Gk *chronikos* of time, fr. *chronos*] **1 a :** marked by long duration or frequent recurrence **:** not acute **b :** suffering from a chronic disease **2 a :** always present or encountered; *esp* **:** constantly vexing, weakening, or troubling ⟨~ petty warfare⟩ **b :** HABITUAL, ACCUSTOMED **syn** see INVETERATE — **chronic** *n* — **chron·i·cal** \-i-kəl\ *adj* — **chron·i·cal·ly** \-k(ə-)lē\ *adv* — **chro·nic·i·ty** \krä-'nis-ət-ē\ *n*

chron·i·cle \'krän-i-kəl\ *n* [ME *cronicle*, fr. AF, alter. of OF *chronique*, fr. L *chronica*, fr. Gk *chronika*, fr. neut. pl. of *chronikos*] **1 :** a usu. continuous and detailed historical account of events arranged in order of time without analysis or interpretation **2 :** HISTORY, NARRATIVE — **chronicle** *vt* **chron·i·cling** \-k(ə-)liŋ\ — **chron·i·cler** \-k(ə-)lər\ *n*

chro·no·gram \'krän-ə-,gram, 'krō-nə-\ *n* **1 :** an inscription, sentence, or phrase in which certain letters express a date or epoch **2 :** the record made by a chronograph — **chro·no·gram·mat·ic** \,krän-ə-grə-'mat-ik, ,krō-nə-\ *or* **chro·no·gram·mat·i·cal** \-i-kəl\ *adj*

chro·no·graph \'krän-ə-,graf, 'krō-nə-\ *n* **:** an instrument for measuring and recording time intervals: as **a :** an instrument having a revolving drum on which a stylus makes marks **b :** a watch with a sweep-second hand **c :** an instrument for measuring the time of flight of projectiles — **chro·no·graph·ic** \,krän-ə-'graf-ik, ,krō-nə-\ *adj* — **chro·nog·ra·phy** \krə-'näg-rə-fē\ *n*

chro·nol·o·ger \krə-'näl-ə-jər\ *n* **:** CHRONOLOGIST

chro·no·log·ic \,krän-ᵊl-'äj-ik, ,krōn-\ *adj* **:** of, relating to, or arranged in chronology — **chro·no·log·i·cal** \-i-kəl\ *adj* — **chro·no·log·i·cal·ly** \-i-k(ə-)lē\ *adv*

chro·nol·o·gist \krə-'näl-ə-jəst\ *n* **:** an expert in chronology

chro·nol·o·gy \-jē\ *n* [NL *chronologia*, fr. *chron-* + *-logia* -logy] **1 :** the science that deals with measuring time by regular divisions

and that assigns to events their proper dates **2 :** a chronological table or list **3 :** an arrangement in order of occurrence

chro·nom·e·ter \krə-ˈnäm-ət-ər\ *n* **:** an instrument for measuring time **:** TIMEPIECE; *esp* **:** one intended to keep time with great accuracy — **chro·no·met·ric** \ˌkrän-ə-ˈme-trik, ˌkrō-nə-\ *or* **chro·no·met·ri·cal** \-tri-kəl\ *adj* — **chro·no·met·ri·cal·ly** \-k(ə-)lē\ *adv*

chro·nom·e·try \krə-ˈnäm-ə-trē\ *n* **1 :** the science of measuring time **2 :** the measuring of time by periods or divisions

chro·no·scope \ˈkrän-ə-ˌskōp, ˈkrō-nə-\ *n* **:** an instrument for precise measurement of small time intervals

chrys- *or* **chryso-** *comb form* [Gk, fr. *chrysos*] **:** gold **:** yellow ⟨*chrys*arobin⟩

chrys·a·lid \ˈkris-ə-ləd\ *n* **:** CHRYSALIS — **chrysalid** *adj*

chrys·a·lis \ˈkris-ə-ləs\ *n, pl* **chry·sal·i·des** \krə-ˈsal-ə-ˌdēz\ *or* **chrys·a·lis·es** \ˈkris-ə-lə-səz\ [L *chrysallid-*, *chrysallis* gold-colored pupa of butterflies, fr. Gk, fr. *chrysos* gold, of Sem origin] **:** the pupa of insects (as butterflies) that pass the pupal stage in a quiescent condition enclosed in a firm case

chry·san·the·mum \kris-ˈan(t)-thə-məm\ *n* [L, fr. Gk *chrysanthemon*, fr. *chrys-* + *anthemon* flower, fr. *anthos*] **1 :** any of various composite plants (genus *Chrysanthemum*) including weeds, ornamentals grown for their brightly colored often double flower heads, and others important as sources of medicinals and insecticides **2 :** a flower head of an ornamental chrysanthemum

chrys·a·ro·bin \ˌkris-ə-ˈrō-bən\ *n* [*chrys-* + *araroba*] **:** a powder obtained from Goa powder and used to treat skin diseases

Chry·se·is \krī-ˈsē-əs\ *n* [L, fr. Gk *Chryseïs*] **:** a daughter of a priest of Apollo captured by the Greeks at Troy and given to Agamemnon but later restored to her father

chryso·ber·yl \ˈkris-ə-ˌber-əl\ *n* [L *chrysoberyllus*, fr. Gk *chrysobēryllos*, fr. *chrys-* + *bēryllos* beryl] **1** *obs* **:** a yellowish beryl **2 :** a usu. yellow or pale green mineral $BeAl_2O_4$ consisting of beryllium aluminum oxide with a little iron sometimes used as a gem

chrys·o·lite \ˈkris-ə-ˌlīt\ *n* [ME *crisolite*, fr. OF, fr. L *chrysolithos*, fr. Gk, fr. *chrys-* + *-lithos* -lite] **:** OLIVINE

chryso·phyte \ˈkris-ə-ˌfīt\ *n* [deriv. of Gk *chrysos* + *phyton* plant — more at PHYT-] **:** any of a major group (Chrysophyta) of algae (as diatoms) with yellowish green to golden brown pigments

chrys·o·prase \ˈkris-ə-ˌprāz\ *n* [ME *crisopace*, fr. OF, fr. L *chrysoprasus*, fr. Gk *chrysoprasos*, fr. *chrys-* + *prason* leek; akin to L *porrum* leek] **:** an apple-green chalcedony valued as a gem

chthon·ic \ˈthän-ik\ *or* **chtho·ni·an** \ˈthō-nē-ən\ *adj* [Gk *chthon-*, *chthōn* earth] **:** INFERNAL ⟨~ deities⟩

chub \ˈchəb\ *n, pl* **chub** *or* **chubs** [ME *chubbe*] **1 :** a common European freshwater cyprinid fish (*Leuciscus cephalus*); *also* **:** any of various related fishes (as the fallfish) **2 :** any of several marine or freshwater fishes not closely related to the true chub

chub·bi·ness \ˈchəb-ē-nəs\ *n* **:** PLUMPNESS

chub·by \ˈchəb-ē\ *adj* [*chub*] **:** PLUMP ⟨a ~ boy⟩

[1]**chuck** \ˈchək\ *vb* [ME *chukken*] **:** CLUCK

[2]**chuck** *n* — used as a term of endearment

[3]**chuck** *vt* [origin unknown] **1 :** PAT, TAP **2 a :** TOSS **b :** DISCARD; *also* **:** EJECT, OUST **3 :** to have done with ⟨~*ed* up his job⟩

[4]**chuck** *n* **1 :** a pat or nudge under the chin **2 :** TOSS, JERK

[5]**chuck** *n* [E dial. *chuck* (lump)] **1 a :** a portion of a side of dressed beef including most of the neck, the parts about the shoulder blade, and those about the first three ribs **b :** a similar cut of dressed veal or lamb **2** *chiefly West* **:** FOOD **3 :** an attachment for holding a workpiece or tool in a machine (as a drill press or lathe)

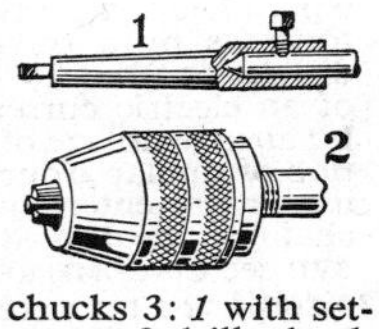

chucks 3: *1* with set-screw, *2* drill chuck

chuck·hole \ˈchək-ˌhōl, ˈchəg-\ *n* [[3]*chuck* + *hole*] **:** a hole or rut in a road

chuck·le \ˈchək-əl\ *vi* **chuck·ling** \ˈchək-(ə-)liŋ\ [prob. freq. of [1]*chuck*] **:** to laugh inwardly or quietly — **chuckle** *n*

chuck·le·head \ˈchək-əl-ˌhed\ *n* [*chuckle* (lumpish) + *head*] **:** BLOCKHEAD — **chuck·le·head·ed** \ˌchək-əl-ˈhed-əd\ *adj*

chuck wagon *n* [[5]*chuck*] **:** a wagon equipped with a stove and provisions for cooking

chuck-will's-wid·ow \ˌchək-ˌwilz-ˈwid-(ˌ)ō, -ə(-w)\ *n* [imit.] **:** a goatsucker (*Caprimulgus carolinensis*) of the southern U.S.

chuff \ˈchəf\ *n* [ME *chuffe*] **:** BOOR, CHURL

chuffy \ˈchəf-ē\ *adj* [perh. fr. E dial. *chuff* chubby] **:** FAT, CHUBBY

chug \ˈchəg\ *n* [imit.] **:** a dull explosive sound made by or as if by a laboring engine — **chug** *vi* **chugged; chug·ging**

chu·kar \chə-ˈkär\ *n, pl* **chukar** *or* **chukars** [Hindi *cakor*] **:** a largely gray and black Indian partridge (*Alectoris graeca chukar*) introduced into dry parts of the western U.S.

chuk·ka \ˈchək-ə\ *n* [*chukka*, alter. of chukker; fr. a similar polo player's boot] **:** a 2-eyelet usu. ankle-length leather boot

chuk·ker *or* **chuk·kar** \ˈchək-ər\ *or* **chuk·ka** \ˈchək-ə\ *n* [Hindi *cakkar* circular course, fr. Skt *cakra* wheel, circle — more at WHEEL] **:** a playing period of a polo game

[1]**chum** \ˈchəm\ *n* [perh. by shortening & alter. fr. *chamber fellow* (roommate)] **:** an intimate friend

[2]**chum** *vi* **chummed; chum·ming 1 :** to room together **2 :** to be an intimate friend

[3]**chum** *n* [origin unknown] **:** chopped fish or other matter thrown overboard to attract fish

chum·mi·ly \ˈchəm-ə-lē\ *adv* **:** in a chummy manner

chum·mi·ness \ˈchəm-ē-nəs\ *n* **:** the quality or state of being chummy

chum·my \ˈchəm-ē\ *adj* **:** INTIMATE, SOCIABLE

chump \ˈchəmp\ *n* [perh. blend of *chunk* and *lump*] **:** FOOL, DUPE

chunk \ˈchəŋk\ *n* [perh. alter. of *chuck* (short piece of wood)] **1 :** a short thick piece **:** LUMP **2 :** a large noteworthy quantity **3 :** a strong thickset horse usu. smaller than a draft horse

chunky \ˈchəŋ-kē\ *adj* **:** STOCKY

[1]**church** \ˈchərch\ *n* [ME *chirche*, fr. OE *cirice;* akin to OHG *kirihha* church; both fr. a prehistoric WGmc word derived fr. LGk *kyriakon*, fr. Gk, neut. of *kyriakos* of the lord, fr. *kyrios* lord, master, fr. *kyros* power; akin to L *cavus* hollow — more at CAVE] **1 :** a building for public esp. Christian worship **2 :** the clergy or officialdom of a religious body **3 :** a body or organization of religious believers as: **a :** the whole body of Christians **b :** DENOMINATION **c :** CONGREGATION **4 :** public divine worship

[2]**church** *vt* **:** to bring to church to receive one of its rites

[3]**church** *adj* **1 :** of or relating to a church ⟨~ government⟩ **2** *chiefly Brit* **:** of or relating to the established church

church·go·er \-ˌgō(-ə)r\ *n* **:** one that goes to church esp. habitually — **church·go·ing** \-ˌgō-iŋ\ *adj or n*

church·less \ˈchərch-ləs\ *adj* **:** not affiliated with a church

church·li·ness \-lē-nəs\ *n* **:** the quality or state of being churchly

church·ly \ˈchərch-lē\ *adj* **1 :** of or relating to a church **2 :** suitable to or suggestive of a church **3 :** adhering to a church

church·man \-mən\ *n* **1 :** CLERGYMAN **2 :** a member of a church

Church of England : the established episcopal church of England

Church Slavic *n* **:** OLD CHURCH SLAVONIC

church·war·den \ˈchərch-ˌwȯrd-ᵊn\ *n* **:** one of two lay parish officers in the Church of England with responsibility esp. for parish property and alms

church·wom·an \-ˌwu̇m-ən\ *n* **:** a woman adherent of a church

church·yard \-ˌyärd\ *n* **:** a yard that belongs to a church and is often used as a burial ground

churl \ˈchər(-ə)l\ *n* [ME, fr. OE *ceorl* man, ceorl; akin to Gk *gēras* old age] **1 :** CEORL **2 :** a medieval peasant **3 :** RUSTIC, COUNTRYMAN **4 a :** a rude ill-bred person **b :** a stingy morose person

churl·ish \ˈchər-lish\ *adj* **1 :** of or resembling a churl **:** VULGAR **2 :** characteristic of or befitting a churl **:** RUDE **3 :** difficult to work with or deal with **:** INTRACTABLE ⟨~ soil⟩ **syn** see BOORISH — **churl·ish·ly** *adv* — **churl·ish·ness** *n*

[1]**churn** \ˈchərn\ *n* [ME *chyrne*, fr. OE *cyrin;* akin to OE *corn* grain; fr. the granular appearance of cream as it is churned — more at CORN] **:** a vessel in which milk or cream is agitated to separate the oily globules from the other parts and thus to obtain butter

[2]**churn** *vt* **1 :** to agitate (milk or cream) in a churn in order to make butter **2 a :** to stir or agitate violently **b :** to make (as foam) by so doing ~ *vi* **1 :** to work a churn **2 a :** to produce or be in violent agitation **b :** to proceed by means of rotating members

churr \ˈchər\ *vi* [imit.] **:** to make a vibrant or whirring noise like that of a partridge — **churr** *n*

chur·ri·gue·resque \ˌchu̇r-i-gə-ˈresk\ *adj* [Sp *churrigueresco*, fr. José *Churriguera* †1723 Sp architect] **:** of or relating to a Spanish baroque architectural style characterized by elaborate surface decoration or its Latin-American adaptation

chute \ˈshüt\ *n* [F, fr. OF, fr. *cheoir* to fall, fr. L *cadere* — more at CHANCE] **1 a :** FALL 6b **b :** a quick descent (as in a river) **:** RAPID **2 :** an inclined plane, sloping channel, or passage down or through which things may pass **:** SLIDE **3 :** PARACHUTE

chut·ney \ˈchət-nē\ *n* [Hindi *caṭnī*] **:** a condiment of acid fruits with raisins, dates, and onions seasoned with spices

chy·la·ceous \kī-ˈlā-shəs\ *adj* **:** of, resembling, or being chyle

chyle \ˈkī(ə)l\ *n* [LL *chylus*, fr. Gk *chylos* juice, chyle, fr. *chein* to pour] **:** lymph that is milky from emulsified fats, characteristically present in the lacteals, and most apparent during intestinal absorption of fats which pass to the blood largely by way of the lacteals and thoracic duct — **chy·lous** \ˈkī-ləs\ *adj*

chyme \ˈkīm\ *n* [NL *chymus*, fr. LL, chyle, fr. Gk *chymos* juice, fr. *chein*] **:** the semifluid mass of partly digested food expelled by the stomach into the duodenum — **chy·mous** \ˈkī-məs\ *adj*

chy·mo·tryp·sin \ˌkī-mə-ˈtrip-sən\ *n* [*chyme* + *-o-* + *trypsin*] **:** a pancreatic proteinase secreted as a zymogen and able when activated to break internal peptide bonds

ci·bo·ri·um \sə-ˈbōr-ē-əm, -ˈbȯr-\ *n, pl* **ci·bo·ria** \-ē-ə\ [ML, fr. L, cup, fr. Gk *kibōrion*] **1 :** a goblet-shaped vessel for holding eucharistic bread **2 :** BALDACHIN; *specif* **:** a freestanding vaulted canopy supported by four columns over a high altar

ci·ca·da \sə-ˈkād-ə, -ˈkäd-\ *n* [NL, genus name, fr. L, cicada] **:** any of a family (Cicadidae) of homopterous insects with a stout body, wide blunt head, and large transparent wings

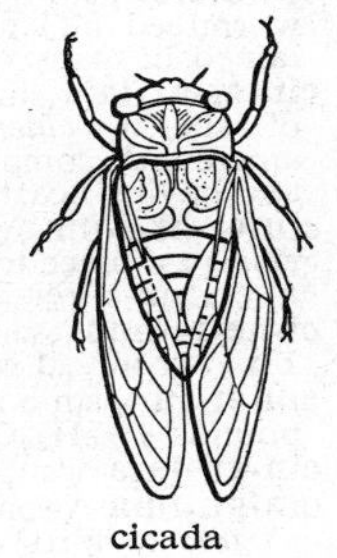
cicada

ci·ca·la \sə-ˈkäl-ə\ *n* [It, fr. ML, alter. of L *cicada*] **:** CICADA

cic·a·tri·cial \ˌsik-ə-ˈtrish-əl\ *adj* **:** of or relating to a cicatrix

cic·a·tri·cle \ˈsik-ə-ˌtrik-əl\ *n* [L *cicatricula*] **1 :** CICATRIX 2a **2 :** BLASTODISC

ci·ca·trix \ˈsik-ə-ˌtriks, sə-ˈkā-triks\ *n, pl* **ci·ca·tri·ces** \ˌsik-ə-ˈtrī-(ˌ)sēz, sə-ˈkā-trə-ˌsēz\ [L *cicatric-*, *cicatrix*] **1 :** a scar resulting from formation and contraction of fibrous tissue in a flesh wound **2 :** a mark resembling a scar esp. when caused by the previous attachment of a part or organ: as **a :** a mark left on a stem after the fall of a leaf or bract **b :** HILUM 1a

cic·a·trize \ˈsik-ə-ˌtrīz\ *vt* **1 :** to induce the formation of a scar in **2 :** SCAR ~ *vi* **:** to heal by forming a scar

cic·e·ly \ˈsis-(ə-)lē\ *n* [by folk etymology fr. L *seselis*, fr. Gk] **:** any of several herbs of the carrot family (as of the genus *Myrrhis*); *esp* **:** one (*M. odorata*) with white flowers and aromatic root

ci·ce·ro·ne \ˌsis-ə-ˈrō-nē, ˌchich-ə-\ *n, pl* **ci·ce·ro·ni** \-(ˌ)nē\ [It, fr. *Cicerone* Cicero] **:** a guide who conducts sightseers

Cic·er·o·ni·an \ˌsis-ə-ˈrō-nē-ən\ *adj* [L *Ciceronianus*, fr. Marcus Tullius *Cicero* †43 B.C. Roman orator] **:** of, relating to, or characteristic of Cicero or his writings ⟨~ eloquence⟩

cich·lid \ˈsik-ləd\ *n* [deriv. of Gk *kichlē* thrush, a kind of wrasse; akin to Gk *chelidōn* swallow — more at CELANDINE] **:** any of a family (Cichlidae) of mostly tropical spiny-finned freshwater fishes including several kept in the tropical aquarium — **cichlid** *adj*

ci·cis·beo \ˌchē-chəz-ˈbā-(ˌ)ō\ *n* [It] **:** LOVER, GALLANT

-ci·dal \ˈsīd-ᵊl\ *adj comb form* [LL *-cidalis*, fr. L *-cida*] **:** killing **:** having power to kill ⟨filaricidal⟩

-cide \ˌsīd\ *n comb form* [MF, fr. L *-cida*, fr. *caedere* to cut, kill — more at CONCISE] **1 :** killer ⟨insecti*cide*⟩ **2** [MF, fr. L *-cidium*, fr. *caedere*] **:** killing ⟨sui*cide*⟩

ci·der \ˈsīd-ər\ *n* [ME *sidre*, fr. OF, fr. LL *sicera* strong drink, fr. Gk *sikera*, fr. Heb *shēkhār*] **:** the expressed juice of fruit (as apples) used as a beverage or for making other products (as vinegar)

ci-de·vant \ˌsēd-ə-ˈväⁿ\ *adj* [F, lit., formerly] **:** FORMER

ə abut; ᵊ kitten; ər further; a back; ā bake; ä cot, cart; au̇ out; ch chin; e less; ē easy; g gift; i trip; ī life
j joke; ŋ sing; ō flow; ȯ flaw; ȯi coin; th thin; t͟h this; ü loot; u̇ foot; y yet; yü few; yu̇ furious; zh vision

ci·gar \sig-'är\ *n* [Sp *cigarro*] **:** a small roll of tobacco leaf for smoking

cig·a·rette *also* **cig·a·ret** \ˌsig-ə-'ret, 'sig-ə-ˌ\ *n* [F *cigarette*, dim. of *cigare* cigar, fr. Sp *cigarro*] **:** a narrow short tube of cut tobacco enclosed in paper and designed for smoking

cil·i·ary \'sil-ē-ˌer-ē\ *adj* **1 :** of or relating to cilia **2 :** of, relating to, or being the annular suspension of the lens of the eye

¹**cil·i·ate** \'sil-ē-ət, -ˌāt\ *or* **cil·i·at·ed** \-ˌāt-əd\ *adj* **:** provided with cilia — **cil·i·ate·ly** *adv*

²**ciliate** *n* **:** any of a subphylum (Ciliophora) of ciliate protozoans

cil·i·o·late \'sil-ē-ə-ˌlāt\ *adj* [NL *ciliolum*] **:** minutely ciliate

cil·i·um \'sil-ē-əm\ *n, pl* **cil·ia** \-ē-ə\ [NL, fr. L, eyelid] **1 :** EYELASH **2 :** a minute hairlike process often forming a fringe; *esp* **:** a hairlike process of many cells that is capable of lashing movement and serves esp. in free unicellular organisms to produce locomotion or in higher forms a current of fluid

ci·mex \'sī-ˌmeks\ *n, pl* **cim·i·ces** \'sim-ə-ˌsēz\ [L *cimic-, cimex* — more at CHINCH] **:** BEDBUG

¹**Cim·me·ri·an** \sə-'mir-ē-ən\ *adj* **:** very dark or gloomy **:** STYGIAN

²**Cimmerian** *n* [L *Cimmerii*, a mythical people, fr. Gk *Kimmerioi*] **:** one of a mythical people described by Homer as dwelling in a remote realm of mist and gloom

¹**cinch** \'sinch\ *n* [Sp *cincha*, fr. L *cingula* girdle, girth, fr. *cingere*] **1 :** a strong girth for a pack or saddle **2 :** a tight grip **3 a :** a thing done with ease **b :** a certainty to happen

²**cinch** *vt* **1 :** to put a cinch on **2 :** to make certain **:** ASSURE

cin·cho·na \siŋ-'kō-nə, sin-'chō-\ *n* [NL, genus name, fr. the countess of *Chinchón* †1641 wife of the Peruvian viceroy] **1 :** any of a genus (*Cinchona*) of So. American trees and shrubs of the madder family **2 :** the dried bark of a cinchona (as *C. ledgeriana*) containing alkaloids (as quinine) and used as a specific in malaria

cin·cho·nine \'siŋ-kə-ˌnēn\ *n* **:** a bitter white crystalline alkaloid $C_{19}H_{22}N_2O$ found esp. in cinchona bark and used like quinine

cin·cho·nism \'siŋ-kə-ˌniz-əm\ *n* **:** a disorder due to excessive or prolonged use of cinchona or its alkaloids and marked by temporary deafness, ringing in the ears, headache, dizziness, and rash

cinc·ture \'siŋ(k)-chər\ *n* [L *cinctura* girdle, fr. *cinctus*, pp. of *cingere* to gird; akin to Skt *kāñcī* girdle] **1 :** the act of encircling **2 a :** an encircling area **b :** GIRDLE, BELT

cin·der \'sin-dər\ *n* [ME *sinder*, fr. OE; akin to OHG *sintar* dross, slag, OSlav *sędra* stalactite] **1 :** the slag from a metal furnace **:** DROSS **2** *pl* **:** ASHES **3 a :** a partly burned combustible in which fire is extinct **b :** a hot coal without flame **c :** a partly burned coal capable of further burning without flame **4 :** a fragment of lava from an erupting volcano — **cin·dery** \-d(ə-)rē\ *adj*

Cin·der·el·la \ˌsin-də-'rel-ə\ *n* **:** the heroine of a fairy tale who is mistreated by her stepmother but elevated to happiness and affluence through the intervention of a fairy godmother

cine \'sin-ē\ *n* [short for *cinema*] **:** MOTION PICTURE

cin·e·ma \'sin-ə-mə\ *n* [short for *cinematograph*] **1** *chiefly Brit* **a :** MOTION PICTURE **b :** a motion-picture theater **2 a :** MOVIES; *esp* **:** the motion-picture industry **b :** the art or technique of making motion pictures — **cin·e·mat·ic** \ˌsin-ə-'mat-ik\ *adj* — **cin·e·mat·i·cal·ly** \-i-k(ə-)lē\ *adv*

cin·e·mat·o·graph \ˌsin-ə-'mat-ə-ˌgraf\ *n* [F *cinématographe*, fr. Gk *kinemat-, kinēma* movement (fr. *kinein* to move) + *-o-* + *-graphe* -graph — more at HIGHT] **1** *chiefly Brit* **:** a motion-picture camera, projector, theater, or show **2** *chiefly Brit* **:** CINEMA 2b

cin·e·ma·tog·ra·pher \ˌsin-ə-mə-'täg-rə-fər\ *n* **1 :** a motion-picture cameraman **2 :** a motion-picture projectionist

cin·e·mat·o·graph·ic \ˌsin-ə-ˌmat-ə-'graf-ik\ *adj* **:** of or relating to cinematography — **cin·e·mat·o·graph·i·cal** \-i-kəl\ *adj* — **cin·e·mat·o·graph·i·cal·ly** \-i-k(ə-)lē\ *adv*

cin·e·ma·tog·ra·phy \ˌsin-ə-mə-'täg-rə-fē\ *n* **:** the art or science of motion-picture photography

cin·e·ole \'sin-ē-ˌōl\ *n* [ISV, by transposition fr. NL *oleum cinae* wormseed oil] **:** a liquid $C_{10}H_{18}O$ of camphoraceous odor contained in many essential oils and used esp. as an expectorant

cin·er·ar·ia \ˌsin-ə-'rer-ē-ə, -'rar-\ *n* [NL, fr. L, fem. of *cinerarius* of ashes, fr. *ciner-, cinis*] **:** any of several pot plants deriving from a perennial composite herb (*Senecio cruentus*) of the Canary islands and having heart-shaped leaves and clusters of bright flower heads

cin·er·ar·i·um \-ē-əm\ *n, pl* **cin·er·ar·ia** \-ē-ə\ [L, fr. *ciner-, cinis*] **:** a place to receive the ashes of the cremated dead — **cin·er·ary** \'sin-ə-ˌrer-ē\ *adj*

ci·ne·re·ous \sə-'nir-ē-əs\ *adj* [L *cinereus*, fr. *ciner-, cinis* ashes] **1 :** gray tinged with black **2 :** resembling or consisting of ashes

cin·er·in \'sin-ə-rən\ *n* [L *ciner-, cinis* ashes] **:** either of two compounds $C_{20}H_{28}O_3$ and $C_{21}H_{28}O_5$ of high insecticidal properties

cin·gu·late \'siŋ-gyə-lət\ *adj* **:** having a cingulum

cin·gu·lum \-ləm\ *n, pl* **cin·gu·la** \-lə\ [NL, fr. L, girdle, fr. *cingere* to gird] **:** a differentiated band or girdle (as of color)

cin·na·bar \'sin-ə-ˌbär\ *n* [ME *cynabare*, fr. MF & L; MF *cenobre*, fr. L *cinnabaris*, fr. Gk *kinnabari* of non-IE origin; akin to Ar *zinjafr* cinnabar] **1 :** native red mercuric sulfide HgS that is the only important ore of mercury **2 :** artificial red mercuric sulfide used esp. as a pigment — **cin·na·bar·ine** \-ˌbär-ˌīn, -ˌēn\ *adj*

cin·nam·ic \sə-'nam-ik\ *adj* [F *cinnamique*, fr. *cinname* cinnamon, fr. L *cinnamon*] **:** of, relating to, or obtained from cinnamon

cin·na·mon \'sin-ə-mən\ *n, often attrib* [ME *cynamone*, fr. L *cinnamomum, cinnamon*, fr. Gk *kinnamōmon, kinnamon*, of non-IE origin; akin to Heb *qinnāmōn* cinnamon] **1 a :** the highly aromatic bark of any of several trees (genus *Cinnamomum*) of the laurel family used as a spice **b :** a tree that yields cinnamon **2 :** a light yellowish brown

cinnamon stone *n* **:** ESSONITE

cin·quain \siŋ-'kān\ *n* [F, fr. *cinq*] **:** a five-line stanza

cinque \'siŋk, 'saŋk\ *n* [ME *cink*, fr. MF *cinq*, fr. L *quinque* — more at FIVE] **:** FIVE; *esp* **:** the number five in dice or cards

cin·que·cen·tist \ˌchiŋ-kwi-'chent-əst\ *n* **:** an Italian of the cinquecento; *esp* **:** a poet or artist of this period

cin·que·cen·to \ˌchiŋ-kwi-'chen-(ˌ)tō\ *n* [It, lit., five hundred, fr. *cinque* five (fr. L *quinque*) + *cento* hundred, fr. L *centum* — more at HUNDRED] **:** the 16th century esp. in Italian art

cinque·foil \'siŋk-ˌfȯil, 'saŋk-\ *n* [ME *sink foil*, fr. MF *cincfoille*, fr. L *quinquefolium*, fr. *quinque* five + *folium* leaf — more at BLADE] **1 :** any of a genus (*Potentilla*) of plants of the rose family with 5-lobed leaves **2 :** a design enclosed by five joined foils

ci·on *var of* SCION

¹**ci·pher** \'sī-fər\ *n, often attrib* [ME, fr. MF *cifre*, fr. ML *cifra*, fr. Ar *ṣifr* empty, cipher, zero] **1 a :** the symbol 0 denoting the absence of all magnitude or quantity **:** ZERO **b :** an insignificant individual **:** NONENTITY **2 a :** a method of transforming a text in order to conceal its meaning — compare CODE 3 **b :** a message in code **3 :** an arabic numeral **4 :** a combination of symbolic letters; *esp* **:** the interwoven initials of a name

²**cipher** *vb* **ci·pher·ing** \-f(ə-)riŋ\ *vi* **:** to use figures in a mathematical process ~ *vt* **1 :** ENCIPHER **2 :** to compute arithmetically

cir·ca \'sər-kə, 'ki(ə)r-(ˌ)kä\ *prep* [L, fr. *circum* around] **:** at, in, or of approximately

Cir·cas·sian \(ˌ)sər-'kash-ən\ *n* [*Circassia*, region in Russia] **1 :** a member of a group of peoples of the Caucasus of Caucasian race but not of Indo-European speech **2 :** the North Caucasic language of the Circassian peoples — **Circassian** *adj*

Circassian walnut *n* **:** the light brown irregularly black-veined wood of the English walnut much used for veneer and cabinetwork

Cir·ce \'sər-(ˌ)sē\ *n* [L, fr. Gk *Kirkē*] **:** an island sorceress in the *Odyssey* who turns her victims into beasts — **Cir·ce·an** \'sər-sē-ən, ˌsər-'\ *adj*

cir·ci·nate \'sərs-ᵊn-ˌāt\ *adj* [L *circinatus*, pp. of *circinare* to round, fr. *circinus* pair of compasses, fr. *circus*] **:** COILED, ROUNDED; *esp* **:** rolled up on the axis with the apex as a center — **cir·ci·nate·ly** *adv*

¹**cir·cle** \'sər-kəl\ *n, often attrib* [ME *cercle*, fr. OF, fr. L *circulus*, dim. of *circus* circle, circus, fr. or akin to Gk *krikos, kirkos* ring] **1 a :** RING, HALO **b :** a closed plane curve every point of which is equidistant from a fixed point within the curve **c :** the plane surface bounded by such a curve **2 :** the orbit or period of revolution of a heavenly body **3 :** something in the form of a circle or section of a circle: as **a :** CIRCLET, DIADEM **b :** an instrument of astronomical observation the graduated limb of which consists of an entire circle **c :** a balcony or tier of seats in a theater **d :** a circle formed on the surface of a sphere by the intersection of a plane that passes through it ⟨~ of latitude⟩ **e :** ROTARY **4 :** an area of action or influence **:** REALM **5 a :** CYCLE, ROUND **b :** fallacious reasoning in which something to be demonstrated is covertly assumed **6 :** a group bound by a common tie; *specif* **:** COTERIE **7 :** a territorial or administrative division or district

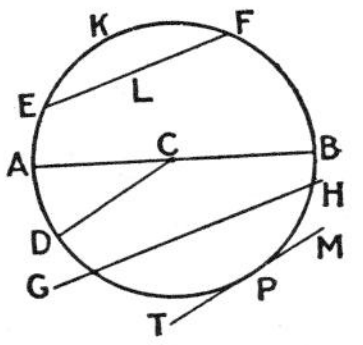

circle 1b: *AB* diameter; *C* center; *CD, CA, CB*, radii; *EKF* arc on chord *EF; EKFL* (area) segment on chord *EF; ACD* (area) sector; *GH* secant; *TPM* tangent at point *P; EKFBPDA* circumference

²**circle** *vb* **cir·cling** \-k(ə-)liŋ\ *vt* **1 :** to enclose in or as if in a circle **2 :** to move or revolve around ~ *vi* **1 a :** to move in or as if in a circle **b :** CIRCULATE **2 :** to describe or extend in a circle — **cir·cler** \-k(ə-)lər\ *n*

cir·clet \'sər-klət\ *n* **:** a little circle; *esp* **:** a circular ornament

¹**cir·cuit** \'sər-kət\ *n, often attrib* [ME, fr. MF *circuite*, fr. L *circuitus*, fr. pp. of *circumire, circuire* to go around, fr. *circum-* + *ire* to go — more at ISSUE] **1 a :** a usu. circular line encompassing an area **b :** the space enclosed within such a line **2 a :** a course around a periphery **b :** a circuitous or indirect route **3 a :** an accustomed tour (as by a traveling judge or preacher) around an assigned district or territory **b :** the route traveled **4 a :** the complete path of an electric current including usu. the source of electric energy **b :** an assemblage of electronic elements **:** HOOKUP **5 a :** an association of similar groups **:** LEAGUE **b :** a group of establishments offering similar entertainment or presenting a series of contests; *esp* **:** a chain of theaters at which productions are successively presented **syn** see CIRCUMFERENCE — **cir·cuit·al** \-kət-ᵊl\ *adj*

²**circuit** *vt* **:** to make a circuit about ~ *vi* **:** to make a circuit

circuit breaker *n* **:** a switch that automatically interrupts an electric circuit under an infrequent abnormal condition

cir·cu·itous \(ˌ)sər-'kyü-ət-əs\ *adj* **1 :** marked by a circular or winding course ⟨a ~ route⟩ **2 :** marked by roundabout or indirect procedure — **cir·cu·itous·ly** *adv* — **cir·cu·itous·ness** *n*

cir·cuit·ry \'sər-kə-trē\ *n* **1 :** the detailed plan of an electric circuit **2 :** the components of an electric circuit

cir·cu·ity \(ˌ)sər-'kyü-ət-ē\ *n* [irreg. fr. *circuit*] **:** INDIRECTION

¹**cir·cu·lar** \'sər-kyə-lər\ *adj* [ME *circuler*, fr. MF, fr. LL *circularis*, fr. L *circulus* circle] **1 :** having the form of a circle **:** ROUND **2 :** moving in or describing a circle or spiral **3 :** CIRCUITOUS, INDIRECT **4 :** marked by or moving in a cycle **5 :** intended for circulation — **cir·cu·lar·i·ty** \ˌsər-kyə-'lar-ət-ē\ *n* — **cir·cu·lar·ly** *adv* — **cir·cu·lar·ness** *n*

²**circular** *n* **:** a paper (as a leaflet) intended for wide distribution

cir·cu·lar·iza·tion \ˌsər-kyə-lə-rə-'zā-shən\ *n* **:** an act or instance of circularizing

cir·cu·lar·ize \'sər-kyə-lə-ˌrīz\ *vt* **1 a :** to send circulars to **b :** to poll by questionnaire **2 :** PUBLICIZE

circular measure *n* **:** the measure of an angle in radians

cir·cu·late \'sər-kyə-ˌlāt\ *vb* [L *circulatus*, pp. of *circulare*, fr. *circulus* circle] *vi* **1 :** to move in a circle, circuit, or orbit; *esp* **:** to follow a course that returns to the starting point ⟨blood ~*s* through the body⟩ **2 :** to pass from person to person or place to place: as **a :** to flow without obstruction **b :** to become well known or widespread **c :** to go from group to group at a social gathering **d :** to come into the hands of readers; *specif* **:** to become sold or distributed ~ *vt* **:** to cause to circulate — **cir·cu·la·tor** \-ˌlāt-ər\ *n*

circulating decimal *n* **:** REPEATING DECIMAL

cir·cu·la·tion \ˌsər-kyə-'lā-shən\ *n* **1 :** FLOW **2 :** orderly movement through a circuit; *esp* **:** the movement of blood through the vessels of the body induced by the pumping action of the heart **3 a :** passage or transmission from person to person or place to place; *esp* **:** the interchange of currency ⟨coins in ~⟩ **b :** the extent of dissemination: as (1) **:** the average number of copies of a publication sold over a given period (2) **:** the total number of items taken by borrowers from a library — **cir·cu·la·tive** \'sər-kyə-ˌlāt-iv\ *adj* — **cir·cu·la·to·ry** \-lə-ˌtōr-ē, -ˌtȯr-\ *adj*

circum- *prefix* [OF or L; OF, fr. L, fr. *circum*, fr. *circus* circle — more at CIRCLE] **:** around **:** about ⟨*circum*polar⟩

cir·cum·am·bi·ent \ˌsər-kə-'mam-bē-ənt\ *adj* [LL *circumambient-, circumambiens*, prp. of *circumambire* to surround in a circle, fr. L *circum-* + *ambire* to go around] **:** SURROUNDING, ENCOMPASSING

cir·cum·am·bu·late \-byə-ˌlāt\ *vb* [LL *circumambulatus*, pp. of

circumambulare, fr. L *circum* + *ambulare* to walk — more at CIRCUM-] **:** to circle on foot esp. ritualistically

cir·cum·cise \ˈsər-kəm-ˌsīz\ *vt* [ME *circumcisen*, fr. L *circumcisus*, pp. of *circumcidere*, fr. *circum-* + *caedere* to cut] **:** to cut off the prepuce of (a male) or the clitoris of (a female)

cir·cum·ci·sion \ˌsər-kəm-ˈsizh-ən\ *n* **1 :** the act of circumcising or being circumcised; *specif* **:** a Jewish rite performed on male infants as a sign of inclusion in the covenant between God and Abraham **2** *cap* **:** a feast on January 1 commemorating the circumcision of Jesus

cir·cum·fer·ence \sə(r)-ˈkəm(p)-fərn(t)s, -f(ə-)rən(t)s\ *n* [ME, fr. MF, fr. L *circumferentia*, fr. *circumferre* to carry around, fr. *circum-* + *ferre* to carry — more at BEAR] **1 :** the perimeter of a circle **2 :** the external boundary or surface of a figure or object **:** PERIPHERY — **cir·cum·fer·en·tial** \-ˌkəm(p)-fə-ˈren-chəl\ *adj*

syn CIRCUMFERENCE, PERIMETER, PERIPHERY, CIRCUIT, COMPASS mean a continuous line enclosing an area. CIRCUMFERENCE and PERIMETER apply to the line enclosing a circle or ellipse and therefore also to the closed curve marking the section of a sphere or cylinder; PERIMETER applies additionally to the bounding line of any area or the bounding surface of a solid; PERIPHERY applies to the circular area lying near the actual bordering line of an area regarded as approximately round; CIRCUIT applies to a journey or route around a periphery or, broadly, to any path that returns to its starting point; COMPASS applies to the range or extent of the area enclosed by a circle or figuratively to the field or aggregate embraced by any general principle

1**cir·cum·flex** \ˈsər-kəm-ˌfleks\ *adj* [L *circumflexus*, pp. of *circumflectere* to bend around, mark with a circumflex, fr. *circum-* + *flectere* to bend] **1 a :** characterized by the pitch, quantity, or quality indicated by a circumflex **b :** marked with a circumflex **2 :** bending around ⟨a ~ artery⟩

2**circumflex** *n* **:** a mark ^, ⌒, or ˜ orig. used in Greek over long vowels to indicate a rising-falling tone and in other languages to mark length, contraction, or a particular vowel quality

cir·cum·flu·ent \(ˌ)sər-ˈkəm-flə-wənt\ *adj* [fr. L *circumfluent-*, *circumfluens*, prp. of *circumfluere* to flow around, fr. *circum-* + *fluere* to flow] **:** flowing round or surrounding in the manner of a fluid — **cir·cum·flu·ous** \-wəs\ *adj*

cir·cum·fuse \ˌsər-kəm-ˈfyüz\ *vt* [L *circumfusus*, pp. of *circumfundere* to pour around, fr. *circum-* + *fundere* to pour — more at FOUND] **:** SURROUND, ENVELOP — **cir·cum·fu·sion** \-ˈfyü-zhən\ *n*

cir·cum·lo·cu·tion \ˌsər-kəm-lō-ˈkyü-shən\ *n* [L *circumlocution-*, *circumlocutio*, fr. *circum-* + *locutio* speech, fr. *locutus*, pp. of *loqui* to speak] **1 :** the use of an unnecessarily large number of words to express an idea **2 :** evasion in speech — **cir·cum·loc·u·to·ry** \-ˈläk-yə-ˌtōr-ē, -ˌtȯr-\ *adj*

cir·cum·lu·nar \ˌsər-kəm-ˈlü-nər\ *adj* **:** revolving about or surrounding the moon

cir·cum·nav·i·gate \-ˈnav-ə-ˌgāt\ *vt* [L *circumnavigatus*, pp. of *circumnavigare* to sail around, fr. *circum-* + *navigare* to navigate] **:** to go completely around (as the earth) esp. by water — **cir·cum·nav·i·ga·tion** \-ˌnav-ə-ˈgā-shən\ *n* — **cir·cum·nav·i·ga·tor** \-ˈnav-ə-ˌgāt-ər\ *n*

cir·cum·po·lar \ˌsər-kəm-ˈpō-lər\ *adj* **1 :** continually visible above the horizon ⟨a ~ star⟩ **2 :** surrounding or found in the vicinity of a terrestrial pole

cir·cum·scis·sile \-ˈsis-əl\ *adj* [L *circumscissus*, pp. of *circumscindere* to tear around, fr. *circum-* + *scindere* to cut, split] **:** dehiscing by fissure around the circumference of the pyxidium

cir·cum·scribe \ˈsər-kəm-ˌskrīb\ *vt* [L *circumscribere*, fr. *circum-* + *scribere* to write, draw] **1 a :** to draw a line around **b :** to surround by a boundary **2 a :** to constrict the range or activity of **b :** to define or mark off carefully **3 :** to encircle (a geometrical figure) so as to touch at as many points as possible **syn** see LIMIT

cir·cum·scrip·tion \ˌsər-kəm-ˈskrip-shən\ *n* [L *circumscription-*, *circumscriptio*, fr. *circumscriptus*, pp. of *circumscribere*] **1 :** something that circumscribes: as **a :** LIMIT, BOUNDARY **b :** RESTRICTION **c :** an outline or inscription around something **2 :** the act of circumscribing **:** the state of being circumscribed: as **a :** DELIMITATION, DEFINITION **b :** LIMITATION **3 :** a circumscribed area or district

cir·cum·spect \ˈsər-kəm-ˌspekt\ *adj* [ME, fr. MF or L; MF *circonspect*, fr. L *circumspectus*, fr. pp. of *circumspicere* to look around, be cautious, fr. *circum-* + *specere* to look — more at SPY] **:** careful to consider all circumstances and possible consequences **:** PRUDENT **syn** see CAUTIOUS — **cir·cum·spec·tion** \ˌsər-kəm-ˈspek-shən\ *n* — **cir·cum·spect·ly** \ˈsər-kəm-ˌspek-tlē\ *adv*

cir·cum·stance \ˈsər-kəm-ˌstan(t)s, -stən(t)s\ *n* [ME, fr. MF, fr. L *circumstantia*, fr. *circumstant-*, *circumstans*, prp. of *circumstare* to stand around, fr. *circum-* + *stare* to stand] **1 a :** a condition, fact, or event accompanying, conditioning, or determining another **b :** an accessory condition **2** *pl* **:** the sum of essential and environmental factors; *esp* **:** situation with regard to wealth **3 :** CEREMONY **4 a :** accompanying incident **:** DETAIL **b :** HAPPENING, FACT **5 :** CHANCE, FATE **syn** see OCCURRENCE

cir·cum·stanced \-ˌstan(t)st, -stən(t)st\ *adj* **:** placed in particular circumstances esp. in regard to property or income

cir·cum·stan·tial \ˌsər-kəm-ˈstan-chəl\ *adj* **1 :** belonging to, consisting in, or dependent on circumstances **2 :** pertinent but not essential **:** INCIDENTAL **3 :** abounding in factual detail ⟨~ account⟩ **4 :** CEREMONIAL — **cir·cum·stan·tial·ly** \-ˈstanch-(ə-)lē\ *adv*

syn MINUTE, PARTICULAR, DETAILED: CIRCUMSTANTIAL suggests treatment that fixes in time and place with precise mention of concrete items and happenings; MINUTE implies searching, close attention to the smallest details; PARTICULAR implies zealous attention to every feature or item; DETAILED stresses abundance or completeness of detail

circumstantial evidence *n* **:** evidence that tends to prove a fact by proving other events or circumstances which afford a basis for a reasonable inference of the occurrence of the fact in issue

cir·cum·stan·ti·al·i·ty \ˌsər-kəm-ˌstan-chē-ˈal-ət-ē\ *n* **:** the quality or state of being circumstantial; *esp* **:** minuteness of detail

cir·cum·stan·ti·ate \-ˈstan-chē-ˌāt\ *vt* **:** to supply with circumstantial evidence or support

1**cir·cum·val·late** \ˌsər-kəm-ˈval-ˌāt, -ˈval-ət\ *adj* **:** surrounded by or as if by a rampart; *esp* **:** enclosed by a ridge of tissue ⟨~ papilla⟩

2**cir·cum·val·late** \-ˈval-ˌāt\ *vt* [L *circumvallatus*, pp. of *circumvallare*, fr. *circum-* + *vallum* rampart] **:** to surround by or as if by a rampart — **cir·cum·val·la·tion** \-ˌval-ˈā-shən\ *n*

cir·cum·vent \ˌsər-kəm-ˈvent\ *vt* [L *circumventus*, pp. of *circumvenire*, fr. *circum-* + *venire* to come] **1 a :** to hem in **b :** to make a circuit around **2 :** to check or defeat esp. by ingenuity or stratagem **syn** see FRUSTRATE — **cir·cum·ven·tion** \-ˈven-chən\ *n*

cir·cum·vo·lu·tion \(ˌ)sər-ˌkəm-və-ˈlü-shən, ˌsər-kəm-vō-\ *n* [ME *circumvolucioun*, fr. ML *circumvolution-*, *circumvolutio*, fr. L *circumvolutus*, pp. of *circumvolvere* to revolve, fr. *circum-* + *volvere* to roll] **:** an act or instance of turning around an axis

cir·cus \ˈsər-kəs\ *n, often attrib* [L, circle, circus — more at CIRCLE] **1 a :** a large arena enclosed by tiers of seats on three or all four sides and used for athletic contests, exhibitions of horsemanship or in ancient times chariot racing and other spectacles **b :** a public spectacle **2 a :** an arena often covered by a tent and used for variety shows usu. including feats of physical skill and daring, wild animal acts, and performances by jugglers and clowns **b :** a circus performance **c :** the physical plant, livestock, and personnel of such a circus **3 a** *obs* **:** CIRCLE, RING **b** *Brit* **:** a usu. circular area at an intersection of streets

cirque \ˈsərk\ *n* [F, fr. L *circus*] **1** *archaic* **:** CIRCUS **2 :** CIRCLE, CIRCLET **3 :** a deep steep-walled basin on a mountain shaped like half a bowl

cirr- *or* **cirri-** *or* **cirro-** *comb form* [NL *cirrus*] **:** cirrus ⟨*Cirri*pedia⟩ ⟨*cirr*ose⟩ ⟨*cirro*stratus⟩

cir·rate \ˈsi(ə)r-ˌāt\ *adj* [L *cirratus* having ringlets, fr. *cirrus*] **1 :** bearing a cirrus **2 :** curled like a cirrus ⟨a ~ leaf⟩

cir·rho·sis \sə-ˈrō-səs\ *n* [NL, fr. Gk *kirrhos* orange-colored] **:** fibrosis esp. of the liver with hardening caused by excessive formation of connective tissue followed by contraction — **cir·rhot·ic** \-ˈrät-ik\ *adj or n*

cir·ri·ped \ˈsir-ə-ˌped\ *or* **cir·ri·pede** \-ˌpēd\ *n* [deriv. of NL *cirr-* + L *ped-*, *pes* foot] **:** any of a subclass (Cirripedia) of specialized marine crustaceans (as barnacles) free-swimming as larvae but permanently attached or parasitic as adults — **cirriped** *adj*

cir·ro·cu·mu·lus \ˌsir-(ˌ)ō-ˈkyü-myə-ləs\ *n* [NL] **:** a cloud form of small white rounded masses at a high altitude usu. in regular groupings forming a mackerel sky

cir·rose *or* **cir·rhose** \ˈsi(ə)r-ˌōs\ *adj* [NL *cirrosus*, fr. *cirr-* + L *-osus* -ose] **:** CIRRATE

cir·ro·stra·tus \ˌsir-(ˌ)ō-ˈstrāt-əs, -ˈstrat-\ *n* [NL] **:** a fairly uniform layer of high stratus darker than cirrus

cir·rous \ˈsir-əs\ *adj* **1 :** CIRRATE **2 :** resembling cirrus clouds

cir·rus \ˈsir-əs\ *n, pl* **cir·ri** \ˈsir-ˌī\ [NL, fr. L, curl] **1 :** TENDRIL **2 :** a slender usu. flexible animal appendage: as **a :** an arm of a barnacle **b :** a filament of a crinoid **c :** a tactile barbel (as of a fish) **d :** a tuft of hair on the legs or antennae of many insects **e :** a fused group of cilia functioning like a limb on some protozoans **f :** the male copulatory organ of various invertebrate animals **3 :** a wispy white cloud usu. of minute ice crystals formed at altitudes of 20,000 to 40,000 feet

cis- *prefix* [L, fr. *cis* — more at HE] **:** on this side ⟨*cis*-Alleghany⟩

cis·co \ˈsis-(ˌ)kō\ *n* [short for CanF *ciscoette*] **:** any of various whitefishes (genus *Leucichthys*) including important food fishes of the Great Lakes region (esp. *L. artedi*)

cis·lu·nar \(ˈ)sis-ˈlü-nər\ *adj* **:** lying between the earth and the moon or the moon's orbit

Cis·ter·cian \sis-ˈtər-shən\ *n* [ML *Cistercium* Cîteaux] **:** a member of a monastic order founded at Cîteaux, France, in 1098 under an austere Benedictine rule — **Cistercian** *adj*

cis·tern \ˈsis-tərn\ *n* [ME, fr. OF *cisterne*, fr. L *cisterna*, fr. *cista* box, chest — more at CHEST] **1 :** an artificial reservoir for storing liquids, esp. water; *specif* **:** an often underground tank for storing rainwater **2 :** a fluid-containing sac or cavity in an organism

cis·ter·na \sis-ˈtər-nə\ *n, pl* **cis·ter·nae** \-ˌnē\ [NL, fr. L, reservoir] **:** CISTERN 2; *esp* **:** one of the large spaces under the arachnoid membrane — **cis·ter·nal** \sis-ˈtərn-ᵊl\ *adj*

cit·able \ˈsīt-ə-bəl\ *adj* **:** capable of being cited

cit·a·del \ˈsit-əd-ᵊl, -ə-ˌdel\ *n* [MF *citadelle*, fr. OIt *cittadella*, dim. of *cittade* city, fr. ML *civitat-*, *civitas* — more at CITY] **1 a :** a fortress that commands a city **b :** STRONGHOLD **2** *archaic* **:** the protected central structure in a heavily armored warship

ci·ta·tion \sī-ˈtā-shən\ *n* **1 :** an official summons to appear (as before a court) **2 a :** an act of quoting; *esp* **:** the citing of a previously settled case at law **b :** EXCERPT, QUOTE **3 :** MENTION: as **a :** a formal statement of the achievements of a person receiving an academic honor **b :** specific reference in a military dispatch to meritorious performance of duty **syn** see ENCOMIUM

cite \ˈsīt\ *vt* [MF *citer* to cite, summon, fr. L *citare* to put in motion, rouse, summon, fr. *citus*, pp. of *ciēre* to stir, move — more at HIGHT] **1 :** to summon to appear before a court **2 :** to quote by way of example, authority, or proof **3 a :** to refer to; *esp* **:** to mention formally in commendation or praise **b :** to name in a citation **syn** see ADDUCE, SUMMON

cith·a·ra \ˈsith-ə-rə, ˈkith-\ *n* [L] **:** an ancient Greek stringed instrument of the lyre class with a wooden sounding board

cith·er \ˈsith-ər, ˈsith-\ *n* [F *cithare*, fr. L *cithara*] **:** CITTERN

cit·ied \ˈsit-ēd\ *adj* **:** occupied by cities

cit·i·fy \ˈsit-i-ˌfī\ *vt* **:** to stamp with or accustom to urban ways

cit·i·zen \ˈsit-ə-zən\ *n* [ME *citizein*, fr. AF *citezein*, alter. of OF *citeien*, fr. *cité* city] **1 :** an inhabitant of a city or town; *esp* **:** one entitled to the rights and privileges of a freeman **2 a :** a member of a state **b :** a native or naturalized person who owes allegiance to a government and is entitled to reciprocal protection from it **3 :** a civilian as distinguished from a specialized servant of the state — **cit·i·zen·ess** \-zə-nəs\ *n* — **cit·i·zen·ly** \-zən-lē\ *adj*

syn CITIZEN, SUBJECT, NATIONAL mean a person owing allegiance to and entitled to the protection of a sovereign state. CITIZEN is preferred for one owing allegiance to a state in which sovereign power is retained by the people and sharing in the political rights of those people; SUBJECT implies allegiance to a personal sovereign such as a monarch; NATIONAL designates one who may claim the protection of a state whether or not he is an actual citizen or subject and applies esp. to one living or traveling outside that state

cit·i·zen·ry \-zən-rē\ *n* **:** the whole body of citizens

cit·i·zen·ship \-ˌship\ *n* **1 :** the status of being a citizen **2 :** the

quality of an individual's response to membership in a community
citr- *or* **citri-** *or* **citro-** *comb form* [NL, fr. *Citrus,* genus name] **1 :** citrus ⟨*citri*culture⟩ **2 :** citric acid ⟨*citr*ate⟩
cit·ral \'si-ˌtral\ *n* [ISV] **:** an unsaturated liquid aldehyde $C_9H_{15}CHO$ of many essential oils that has a strong lemon and verbena odor and is used esp. in perfumery
ci·trate \'si-ˌtrāt *also* 'sī-\ *n* [ISV] **:** a salt or ester of citric acid
cit·ric acid \ˌsi-trik-\ *n* [ISV] **:** a tricarboxylic acid $C_6H_8O_7$ of pleasant taste obtained esp. from lemon and lime juices or by fermentation of sugars and used as a flavoring
cit·ri·cul·ture \'si-trə-ˌkəl-chər\ *n* **:** the cultivation of citrus fruits — **cit·ri·cul·tur·ist** \ˌsi-trə-'kəlch-(ə-)rəst\ *n*
[1]**cit·rine** \'si-ˌtrīn\ *adj* [ME, fr. MF *citrin,* fr. ML *citrinus,* fr. L *citrus* citron tree] **:** resembling a citron or lemon esp. in color
[2]**ci·trine** \-ˌtrēn\ *n* **:** a black quartz changed in color by heating into a semiprecious yellow stone resembling topaz
cit·ron \'si-trən\ *n* [ME, fr. MF, fr. OProv, modif. of L *citrus* citron tree] **1 a :** the fruit of a tree (*Citrus medica*) like the lemon in appearance and structure but larger; *also* **:** this tree **b :** the preserved rind of the citron used esp. in fruitcake **2 :** a small hard-fleshed watermelon used esp. in pickles and preserves
cit·ro·nel·la \ˌsi-trə-'nel-ə\ *n* [NL, fr. F *citronnelle* lemon balm, fr. *citron*] **:** a fragrant grass (*Cymbopogon nardus*) of southern Asia that yields an oil used in perfumery and as an insectifuge
cit·ro·nel·lal \-'nel-ˌal\ *n* [ISV, fr. NL *citronella*] **:** a lemon-odored aldehyde $C_{10}H_{18}O$ found in many essential oils
cit·rus \'si-trəs\ *n, pl* **citrus** *or* **cit·rus·es** *often attrib* [NL, genus name, fr. L, citron tree] **:** any of a genus (*Citrus*) of often thorny trees and shrubs of the rue family grown in warm regions for their large fruit (as the orange) with firm usu. thick rind and pulpy flesh
cit·tern \'sit-ərn\ *or* **cith·ern** \'sith-ərn, 'sith-\ *or* **cith·ren** \'sith-rən\ *n* [blend of *cither* and *gittern*] **:** a guitar with a pear-shaped flat-backed body popular esp. in Renaissance England
city \'sit-ē\ *n, often attrib* [ME *citie* large or small town, fr. OF *cité* capital city, fr. ML *civitat-, civitas,* fr. L, citizenship, state, city of Rome, fr. *civis* citizen — more at HOME] **1 a :** an inhabited place of greater size, population, or importance than a town or village **b :** an incorporated British town usu. of major size or importance having the status of an episcopal see **c :** a usu. large or important municipality in the U.S. governed under a charter granted by the state **d :** an incorporated municipal unit of the highest class in Canada **2 :** CITY-STATE **3 :** the people of a city
city manager *n* **:** an official employed by an elected council to direct the administration of a city government
city slicker *n* **:** SLICKER 2
city–state \'sit-ē-'stāt, -ˌstāt\ *n* **:** an autonomous state consisting of a city and surrounding territory
civ·et \'siv-ət\ *n* [MF *civette,* fr. OIt *zibetto,* fr. Ar *zabād* civet perfume] **:** a thick yellowish musky-odored substance found in a pouch near the sexual organs of the civet cat and used in perfume
civet cat *n* **1 a :** any of several carnivorous mammals (family Viverridae); *esp* **:** a long-bodied short-legged African animal (*Civettictis civetta*) that produces most of the civet of commerce **b :** CACOMISTLE **c :** any of the small spotted skunks (genus *Spilogale*) of western No. America **2 :** the fur of a civet cat
civ·ic \'siv-ik\ *adj* [L *civicus,* fr. *civis* citizen] **:** of or relating to a citizen, a city, citizenship, or civil affairs — **civ·i·cal·ly** \'siv-i-k(ə-)lē\ *adv*
civ·ics \'siv-iks\ *n pl but sing or pl in constr* **:** a social science dealing with the rights and duties of citizens
civ·il \'siv-əl\ *adj* [ME, fr. MF, fr. L *civilis,* fr. *civis*] **1 a :** of or relating to citizens ⟨~ liberties⟩ **b :** of or relating to the state or its citizenry **2 a :** CIVILIZED ⟨~ society⟩ **b :** COURTEOUS, URBANE **3 a :** of, relating to, or based on civil law **b :** relating to private rights and to remedies sought by action or suit distinct from criminal proceedings **c :** established by law **4** *of time* **:** based on the mean sun and legally recognized for use in ordinary affairs **5 :** of or relating to civic as distinguished from military or religious affairs
syn POLITE, COURTEOUS, GALLANT, CHIVALROUS: CIVIL suggests no more than a bare minimum fulfillment of the requirements of good breeding and forbearance from roughness or unpleasantness; POLITE implies polished manners and thoughtfulness but often suggests lack of cordiality; COURTEOUS implies more actively considerate or dignified politeness; GALLANT and CHIVALROUS imply courteous attentiveness esp. to women but GALLANT suggests spirited and dashing behavior and ornate expressions of courtesy and CHIVALROUS high-minded and self-sacrificing behavior
civil death *n* **:** the status of a living person equivalent in its legal consequences to natural death; *specif* **:** extinction of civil rights
civil defense *n* **:** the complex of protective measures and emergency relief activities conducted by civilians in case of hostile attack or sabotage or natural disaster
civil engineer *n* **:** an engineer whose training or occupation is in the designing and construction of public works (as roads or harbors) and of various private works — **civil engineering** *n*
ci·vil·ian \sə-'vil-yən\ *n* **1 :** a specialist in Roman or modern civil law **2 :** one not on active duty in a military, police, or fire-fighting force — **civilian** *adj*
ci·vil·i·ty \sə-'vil-ət-ē\ *n* **1** *archaic* **:** training in the humanities **2 a :** POLITENESS, COURTESY **b :** a polite act or expression
civ·i·liz·able \'siv-ə-ˌlī-zə-bəl\ *adj* **:** capable of being civilized
civ·i·li·za·tion \ˌsiv-ə-lə-'zā-shən\ *n* **1 a :** a relatively high level of cultural and technological development; *specif* **:** the stage of cultural development at which writing and the keeping of written records is attained **b :** the culture characteristic of a particular time or place **2 :** the process of becoming civilized **3 a :** refinement of thought, manners, or taste **b :** a situation of urban comfort
civ·i·lize \'siv-ə-ˌlīz\ *vt* **1 :** to cause to develop out of a primitive state; *specif* **:** to bring to a technically advanced and rationally ordered stage of cultural development **2 a :** EDUCATE, REFINE **b :** to render social ~ *vi* **:** to acquire the customs and amenities of a civil community — **civ·i·lized** *adj*
civil law *n, often cap C&L* **1 :** Roman law esp. as set forth in the Justinian code **2 :** the body of private law developed from Roman law and used in Louisiana and in many countries outside the English-speaking world **3 :** the law established by a nation or state for its own jurisdiction **4 :** the law of civil or private rights
civ·il·ly \'siv-ə(l)-lē\ *adv* **1 :** in a civil manner **:** POLITELY **2 :** in terms of civil rights, matters, or law ⟨~ dead⟩
civil rights *n pl* **:** the nonpolitical rights of a citizen; *esp* **:** the rights of personal liberty guaranteed to U. S. citizens by the 13th and 14th amendments to the Constitution and by acts of Congress
civil servant *n* **:** a member of a civil service
civil service *n* **:** the administrative service of a government or international agency exclusive of the armed forces; *esp* **:** one in which appointments are determined by competitive examination
civil war *n* **:** a war between opposing groups of citizens of the same country or nation
[1]**clab·ber** \'klab-ər\ *n* [short for *bonnyclabber*] *chiefly dial* **:** sour milk that has thickened or curdled
[2]**clabber** *vb, chiefly Midland* **:** CURDLE
clach·an \'klak-ən\ *n* [ME, fr. ScGael] *Scot & Irish* **:** HAMLET
[1]**clack** \'klak\ *vb* [ME *clacken,* of imit. origin] *vi* **1 :** CHATTER, PRATTLE **2 :** to make an abrupt striking sound or series of sounds **3** *of fowl* **:** CACKLE, CLUCK ~ *vt* **1 :** to cause to make a clatter **2 :** to produce with a chattering sound; *specif* **:** BLAB — **clack·er** *n*
[2]**clack** *n* **1 a :** rapid continuous talk **:** CHATTER **b :** TONGUE **2** *archaic* **:** an object (as a clack valve) that produces clapping or rattling noises usu. in regular rapid sequence **3 :** a sound of clacking
clack valve *n* **:** a valve usu. hinged at one edge that permits flow of fluid in one direction only and that closes with a clacking sound
Clac·to·ni·an \klak-'tō-nē-ən\ *adj* [*Clacton*-on-Sea, England] **:** of or relating to a Lower Paleolithic culture characterized by stone flakes with a half cone at the point of striking
[1]**clad** \'klad\ *adj* **:** CLOTHED, COVERED
[2]**clad** *vt* **clad; clad·ding :** SHEATHE, FACE; *specif* **:** to cover (a metal) with another metal by bonding
clad·ding \'klad-iŋ\ *n* **:** metal coating bonded to a metal core
clad·ode \'klad-ˌōd\ *n* [NL *cladodium,* fr. Gk *klados*] **:** CLADOPHYLL — **cla·do·di·al** \kla-'dōd-ē-əl\ *adj*
clado·phyll \'klad-ə-ˌfil\ *n* [NL *cladophyllum,* fr. Gk *klados* branch + *phyllon* leaf — more at GLADIATOR, BLADE] **:** a branch assuming the form of and closely resembling an ordinary foliage leaf and often bearing leaves or flowers on its margins
[1]**claim** \'klām\ *vt* [ME *claimen,* fr. OF *clamer,* fr. L *clamare* to cry out, shout; akin to L *calare* to call — more at LOW] **1 a :** to ask for esp. as a right **b :** to call for **:** REQUIRE **2 :** to assert in the face of possible contradiction **:** MAINTAIN **syn** see DEMAND — **claim·able** \'klā-mə-bəl\ *adj* — **claim·ant** \-mənt\ *n* — **claim·er** *n*
[2]**claim** *n* **1 :** a demand for something due or believed to be due ⟨insurance ~⟩ **2 a :** a right to something; *specif* **:** a title to a debt, privilege, or other thing in the possession of another **b :** an assertion open to challenge ⟨a ~ of authenticity⟩ **3 :** something that is claimed; *esp* **:** a tract of land staked out
claiming race *n* **:** a race in which a claim to purchase at a stipulated price any of the horses running can be entered before the race usu. by another owner starting a horse at that meeting
clair·voy·ance \kla(ə)r-'vȯi-ən(t)s, kle(ə)r-\ *n* **1 :** the professed power of discerning objects not present to the senses **2 :** acuteness of perception **:** PENETRATION
[1]**clair·voy·ant** \-ənt\ *adj* [F, fr. *clair* clear (fr. L *clarus*) + *voyant,* prp. of *voir* to see, fr. L *vidēre*] **1 :** unusually perceptive **:** DISCERNING **2 :** of or relating to clairvoyance — **clair·voy·ant·ly** *adv*
[2]**clairvoyant** *n* **:** one held to have the power of clairvoyance
[1]**clam** \'klam\ *n* [ME, fr. OE *clamm* bond, fetter; akin to OHG *klamma* constriction, L *glomus* ball] **:** CLAMP, CLASP
[2]**clam** *n, often attrib* [[1]*clam;* fr. the clamping action of the shells] **1 a :** any of numerous usu. equivalve edible marine bivalve mollusks living in sand or mud **b :** a freshwater mussel **c :** the flesh of a clam used as food **2 :** a stolid or closemouthed person **3 :** CLAMSHELL

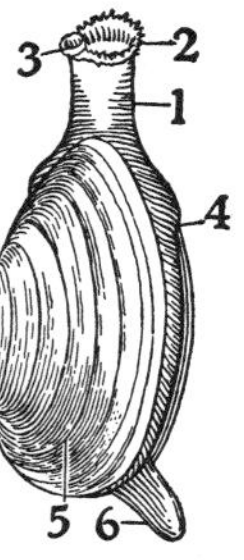

clam: *1* siphon, *2* incurrent orifice, *3* excurrent orifice, *4* mantle, *5* shell, *6* foot

[3]**clam** *vi* **clammed; clam·ming :** to gather clams esp. by digging
cla·mant \'klā-mənt, 'klam-ənt\ *adj* [L *clamant-, clamans,* prp. of *clamare* to cry out] **1 :** CLAMOROUS, BLATANT **2 :** demanding attention **:** URGENT — **cla·mant·ly** *adv*
clam·a·to·ri·al \ˌklam-ə-'tōr-ē-əl, -'tȯr-\ *adj* [deriv. of L *clamator* bawler, fr. *clamatus,* pp. of *clamare*] **:** of or relating to a large group (Clamatores) of passerine birds with little ability to sing
clam·bake \'klam-ˌbāk\ *n* **1 a :** an outdoor party; *esp* **:** a seashore outing where food is cooked on heated rocks covered by seaweed **b :** the food served at a clambake **2 :** a gathering characterized by noisy sociability; *esp* **:** a political rally
clam·ber \'klam-(b)ər\ *vb* **clam·ber·ing** \'klam-b(ə-)riŋ, 'klam-ə-riŋ\ [ME *clambren;* akin to OE *climban* to climb] **:** to climb awkwardly (as by scrambling) — **clam·ber·er** \-(b)ər-ər\ *n*
clam·mi·ly \'klam-ə-lē\ *adv* **:** in a clammy manner
clam·mi·ness \'klam-ē-nəs\ *n* **:** the quality or state of being clammy
clam·my \'klam-ē\ *adj* [ME, prob. fr. *clammen* to smear, stick, fr. OE *clǣman;* akin to OE *clǣg* clay] **1 :** damp, soft, sticky, and usu. cool **2 a :** causing clamminess ⟨~ fear⟩ **b :** ALOOF, REPELLENT
[1]**clam·or** *or chiefly Brit* **clam·our** \'klam-ər\ *n* [ME, fr. MF *clamour,* fr. L *clamor,* fr. *clamare* to cry out] **1 a :** noisy shouting **b :** a loud continuous noise **2 :** insistent public expression (as of support or protest)
[2]**clamor** *or chiefly Brit* **clamour** *vb* **clam·or·ing** \-(ə-)riŋ\ *vi* **1 :** to make a din **2 :** to become loudly insistent ~ *vt* **1 :** to utter or proclaim insistently and noisily **2 :** to influence by means of clamor
[3]**clamor** *or chiefly Brit* **clamour** *vt* [origin unknown] *obs* **:** SILENCE
clam·or·ous \'klam-(ə-)rəs\ *adj* **1 :** full of clamor **:** NOISY **2 :** noisily insistent **syn** see VOCIFEROUS — **clam·or·ous·ly** *adv* — **clam·or·ous·ness** *n*
[1]**clamp** \'klamp\ *n* [ME, prob. fr. (assumed) MD *klampe;* akin to OE *clamm* bond, fetter — more at CLAM] **1 :** a device designed to bind or constrict or to press two or more parts together so as to hold them firmly **2 :** any of various instruments or appliances having parts brought together for holding or compressing something
[2]**clamp** *vt* **1 :** to fasten with a clamp **2 a :** to place by decree **:** IMPOSE **b :** to hold tightly
clamp down *vi* **:** to impose restrictions **:** become repressive
clam·shell \'klam-ˌshel\ *n* **:** a bucket or grapple (as on a dredge) having two hinged jaws
clam up *vi, slang* **:** to become silent
clan \'klan\ *n* [ME, fr. ScGael *clann* offspring, clan, fr. OIr *cland*

plant, offspring, fr. L *planta* plant] **1 a :** a Celtic group esp. in the Scottish Highlands comprising a number of households the heads of which claim descent from a common ancestor **b :** SIB 3 **2 :** a group united by a common interest or common characteristics

clan·des·tine \klan-'des-tən\ *adj* [MF or L; MF *clandestin,* fr. L *clandestinus,* irreg. fr. *clam* secretly; akin to L *celare* to hide — more at HELL] **:** held in or conducted with secrecy **:** SURREPTITIOUS **syn** see SECRET — **clan·des·tine·ly** *adv* — **clan·des·tine·ness** *n*

1**clang** \'klaŋ\ *vb* [L *clangere;* akin to Gk *klazein* to scream, bark, OE *hlōwan* to low] *vi* **1 a :** to make a loud metallic ringing sound **b :** to go with a clang **2 :** to utter the characteristic harsh cry of a bird ~ *vt* **:** to cause to clang

2**clang** *n* **1 :** a loud ringing metallic sound **2 :** a harsh cry of a bird

1**clan·gor** *or chiefly Brit* **clan·gour** \'klaŋ-ər *also* -gər\ *n* [L *clangor* fr. *clangere*] **:** a resounding clang or medley of clangs — **clan·gor·ous** \-(g)ə-rəs\ *adj* — **clan·gor·ous·ly** *adv*

2**clangor** *or chiefly Brit* **clangour** *vi* **:** to make a clangor

1**clank** \'klaŋk\ *vb* [prob. imit.] *vi* **1 :** to make a clank or series of clanks **2 :** to go with a clank ~ *vt* **:** to cause to clank — **clank·ing·ly** \'klaŋ-kiŋ-lē\ *adv*

2**clank** *n* **:** a sharp brief metallic resonance

clan·nish \'klan-ish\ *adj* **1 :** of or relating to a clan **2 :** tending to associate only with a select group of similar background or status — **clan·nish·ly** *adv* — **clan·nish·ness** *n*

clans·man \'klanz-mən\ *n* **:** a member of a clan

1**clap** \'klap\ *vb* **clapped** *also* **clapt; clap·ping** [ME *clappen,* fr. OE *clæppan;* akin to OHG *klaphōn* to beat, L *glēba* clod — more at CLIP] *vt* **1 :** to strike together (as two flat hard surfaces) so as to produce a sharp percussive noise **2 a :** to strike (the hands) together repeatedly usu. in applause **b :** APPLAUD **3 :** to strike with the flat of the hand in a friendly way **4 :** to put or apply energetically **5 :** to improvise hastily ~ *vi* **1 :** to produce a percussive sound; *esp* **:** SLAM **2 :** to go abruptly or briskly **3 :** APPLAUD

2**clap** *n* **1 :** a device that makes a clapping noise **2** *obs* **:** a sudden stroke of fortune and esp. ill fortune **3 :** a loud percussive noise; *specif* **:** a sudden crash of thunder **4 a :** a sudden blow **b :** a friendly slap **5 :** the sound of clapping hands; *esp* **:** APPLAUSE

3**clap** *n* [MF *clapoir* bubo] **:** GONORRHEA

clap·board \'klab-ərd; 'kla(p)-,bō(ə)rd, -,bȯ(ə)rd\ *n* [part trans. of D *klaphout*] **1** *archaic* **:** a size of board for making staves and wainscoting **2 :** a narrow board usu. thicker at one edge than the other used for siding — **clapboard** *vt*

clap·per \'klap-ər\ *n* **:** one that makes a clapping sound: as **a :** the tongue of a bell **b** *slang* **:** the tongue of a talkative person **c :** one of a pair of flat sticks held between the fingers and used to produce musical rhythms **d :** a person who applauds

clap·per·claw \'klap-ər-,klȯ\ *vt* [perh. fr. *clapper* + *claw* (v.)] **1** *dial Eng* **:** to claw with the nails **2** *dial Eng* **:** SCOLD, REVILE

clap·trap \'klap-,trap\ *n* **:** pretentious nonsense **:** TRASH

claque \'klak\ *n* [F, fr. *claquer* to clap, of imit. origin] **1 :** a group hired to applaud at a performance **2 :** a group of sycophants

clar·ence \'klar-ən(t)s\ *n* [duke of *Clarence,* later William IV of England †1837] **:** a closed 4-wheeled 4-passenger carriage

clar·et \'klar-ət\ *n* [ME, fr. MF (*vin*) *claret* clear wine, fr. *claret* clear, fr. *cler* clear] **1 :** a dry red table wine; *specif* **:** one from the Bordeaux district of France **2 :** a dark purplish red — **claret** *adj*

Cla·re·tian \klə-'rē-shən, kla-\ *n* [St. Anthony *Claret* †1870 Sp priest & founder of the order] **:** a member of the Congregation of the Missionary Sons of the Immaculate Heart of Mary founded in Vich, Spain, in 1849 — **Claretian** *adj*

clar·i·fi·ca·tion \,klar-ə-fə-'kā-shən\ *n* **:** the act or process of clarifying

clar·i·fi·er \'klar-ə-,fī(-ə)r\ *n* **:** one that clarifies

clar·i·fy \'klar-ə-,fī\ *vb* [ME *clarifien,* fr. MF *clarifier,* fr. LL *clarificare,* fr. L *clarus* clear — more at CLEAR] *vt* **1 :** to make (as a liquid) clear, pure, or pellucid usu. by freeing from suspended matter **2 :** to free of confusion **3 :** to make understandable ~ *vi* **:** to become clear

clar·i·net \,klar-ə-'net, 'klar-ə-nət\ *also* **clar·i·o·net** \,klar-ē-ə-'net\ *n* [F *clarinette,* prob. deriv. of ML *clarion-, clario*] **:** a single-reed woodwind instrument having a cylindrical tube with moderately flaring end — **clar·i·net·ist** *or* **clar·i·net·tist** \,klar-ə-'net-əst\ *n*

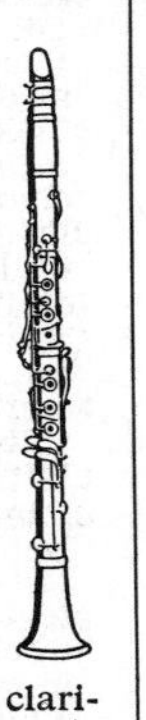

clarinet

1**clar·i·on** \'klar-ē-ən\ *n* [ME, fr. MF & ML; MF *clairon,* fr. ML *clarion-, clario,* fr. L *clarus* clear] **1 :** a medieval trumpet with clear shrill tones **2 :** the sound of or as if of a clarion

2**clarion** *adj* **:** brilliantly clear; *esp* **:** STENTORIAN

clar·i·ty \'klar-ət-ē\ *n* [ME *clarite,* fr. L *claritat-, claritas,* fr. *clarus*] **:** the quality or state of being clear **:** LUCIDITY

clark·ia \'klär-kē-ə\ *n* [NL, fr. William *Clark* †1838 Am explorer] **:** a showy annual herb (genus *Clarkia*) of the evening-primrose family of the Pacific slope of No. America

cla·ro \'klär-(,)ō\ *n* [Sp, fr. *claro* light, fr. L *clarus*] **:** a light-colored generally mild cigar

clary \'kla(ə)r-ē, 'kle(ə)r-\ *n* [ME *clarie,* fr. MF *sclaree,* fr. ML *sclareia*] **:** an aromatic mint (*Salvia sclarea*) of southern Europe grown as a potherb and ornamental

1**clash** \'klash\ *vb* [imit.] *vi* **1 :** to make a clash **2 :** to come into conflict ~ *vt* **:** to cause to clash — **clash·er** *n*

2**clash** *n* **1 :** a noisy usu. metallic sound of collision **2 a :** a hostile encounter **:** SKIRMISH **b :** a sharp conflict

clas·mat·o·cyte \klaz-'mat-ə-,sīt\ *n* [ISV, fr. Gk *klasmat-, klasma* fragment (fr. *klan* to break) + ISV *-cyte* — more at HALT] **:** HISTIOCYTE — **clas·mat·o·cyt·ic** \(,)klaz-,mat-ə-'sit-ik\ *adj*

1**clasp** \'klasp\ *n* [ME *claspe*] **1 a :** a device (as a hook) for holding objects or parts together **b :** a bar or other device attached to a military medal to indicate an additional award of the medal or the action or service for which it was awarded **2 :** EMBRACE, GRASP

2**clasp** *vt* **1 :** to fasten with or as if with a clasp **2 :** to enclose and hold with the arms; *specif* **:** EMBRACE **3 :** to seize with or as if with the hand **:** GRASP

clasp·er \'klas-pər\ *n* **:** a structure (as a fin) modified for use in copulation

clasp knife *n* **:** POCKETKNIFE; *esp* **:** a large one-bladed folding knife having a catch to hold the blade open

1**class** \'klas\ *n, often attrib* [F *classe,* fr. L *classis* group called to arms, class of citizens] **1 a :** a group sharing the same economic or social status **b :** social rank; *esp* **:** high social rank **c :** high quality **:** ELEGANCE **2 a :** a course of instruction **b :** a body of students meeting regularly to study the same subject **c :** the period during which such a body meets **d :** a body of students or alumni whose year of graduation is the same **3 a :** a group, set, or kind sharing common attributes; *esp* **:** a major category in biological taxonomy ranking above the order and below the phylum or division **b :** a division or rating based on grade or quality — **class·less** \-ləs\ *adj*

2**class** *vt* **:** CLASSIFY

class–con·scious \'klas-,kän-chəs\ *adj* **:** actively aware of one's common status with others in a particular economic or social level of society — **class consciousness** *n*

1**clas·sic** \'klas-ik\ *adj* [F or L; F *classique,* fr. L *classicus* of the highest class of Roman citizens, of the first rank, fr. *classis*] **1 a :** of recognized value **:** serving as a standard of excellence **b :** TRADITIONAL, ENDURING **c :** characterized by simple tailored lines in fashion year after year **2 :** of or relating to the ancient Greeks and Romans or their culture **:** CLASSICAL **3 a :** historically memorable **b :** noted because of special literary or historical associations **4 a :** AUTHENTIC, AUTHORITATIVE **b :** TYPICAL

2**classic** *n* **1 :** a literary work of ancient Greece or Rome **2 a :** a work of enduring excellence or its author **b :** an authoritative source **3 :** a typical example **4 :** a traditional event

clas·si·cal \'klas-i-kəl\ *adj* [L *classicus*] **1 :** STANDARD, CLASSIC **2 a :** of or relating to classicism **b :** versed in the classics **3 a :** AUTHORITATIVE, TRADITIONAL **b :** of or relating to a form or system felt to be of first significance before modern times **c :** conforming to a pattern of usage sanctioned by a body of literature rather than by everyday speech **4 :** concerned with or giving instruction in the humanities, the fine arts, and the broad aspects of science

clas·si·cal·ism \-,iz-əm\ *n* **:** CLASSICISM — **clas·si·cal·ist** \-əst\ *n*

clas·si·cal·i·ty \,klas-ə-'kal-ət-ē\ *n* **1 :** the quality or state of being classic **2 :** classical scholarship

clas·si·cal·ly \'klas-i-k(ə-)lē\ *adv* **:** in a classic or classical manner

clas·si·cism \'klas-ə-,siz-əm\ *n* **1 a :** the principles or style embodied in the literature, art, or architecture of ancient Greece and Rome **b :** classical scholarship **c :** a classical idiom or expression **2 :** adherence to traditional standards (as of simplicity, restraint, proportion) universally and enduringly valid

clas·si·cist \-səst\ *n* **1 :** an advocate or follower of classicism **2 :** a classical scholar — **clas·si·cis·tic** \,klas-ə-'sis-tik\ *adj*

clas·si·cize \'klas-ə-,sīz\ *vt* **:** to make classic or classical ~ *vi* **:** to follow classic style

clas·si·fi·able \'klas-ə-,fī-ə-bəl\ *adj* **:** capable of being classified

clas·si·fi·ca·tion \,klas-ə-fə-'kā-shən\ *n* **1 :** the act or process of classifying **2 a :** systematic arrangement in groups or categories according to established criteria; *specif* **:** TAXONOMY **b :** CLASS, CATEGORY — **clas·si·fi·ca·to·ri·ly** \,klas-(ə-)fə-kə-'tōr-ə-lē, kla-,sif-ə-, -'tȯr-\ *adv* — **clas·si·fi·ca·to·ry** \'klas-(ə-)fə-kə-,tōr-ē, kla-'sif-ə-, -,tȯr-; 'klas-(ə-)fə-,kāt-ə-rē\ *adj*

clas·si·fied \'klas-ə-,fīd\ *adj* **1 :** divided into classes or placed in a class **2 :** withheld from general circulation for reasons of national security

clas·si·fi·er \'klas-ə-,fī(-ə)r\ *n* **1 :** one that classifies; *specif* **:** a machine for sorting out the constituents of a substance (as ore) **2 :** a word or morpheme used with numerals or with nouns designating countable or measurable objects

clas·si·fy \'klas-ə-,fī\ *vt* **1 :** to arrange in classes **2 :** to assign (as a document) to a category

clas·sis \'klas-əs\ *n, pl* **clas·ses** \'klas-,ēz\ [NL, fr. L, class] **1 :** a governing body in some Reformed churches corresponding to a presbytery **2 :** the district governed by a classis

class·mate \'klas-,māt\ *n* **:** a member of the same class in a school or college

class·room \-,rüm, -,ru̇m\ *n* **:** a place where classes meet

classy \'klas-ē\ *adj, slang* **:** ELEGANT, STYLISH

clas·tic \'klas-tik\ *adj* [ISV, fr. Gk *klastos* broken, fr. *klan* to break — more at HALT] **:** made up of fragments of preexisting rocks

clath·rate \'klath-,rāt\ *adj* [L *clathratus,* fr. *clathri* (pl.) lattice, fr. Gk *klēithron* bar, fr. *kleiein* to close] **:** resembling a lattice

1**clat·ter** \'klat-ər\ *vb* [ME *clatren,* fr. (assumed) OE *clatrian;* of imit. origin] *vi* **1 :** to make a rattling sound **2 :** to move or go with a clatter **3 :** PRATTLE ~ *vt* **:** to cause to clatter — **clat·ter·er** \-ər-ər\ *n* — **clat·ter·ing·ly** \'klat-ə-riŋ-lē\ *adv*

2**clatter** *n* **1 :** a rattling sound (as of hard bodies striking together) **2 :** COMMOTION **3 :** noisy chatter — **clat·tery** \'klat-ə-rē\ *adj*

clau·di·ca·tion \,klȯd-ə-'kā-shən\ *n* [L *claudication-, claudicatio,* fr. *claudicatus,* pp. of *claudicare* to limp, fr. *claudus* lame; akin to L *claudere* to close — more at CLOSE] **:** LAMENESS, LIMPING

claus·al \'klȯ-zəl\ *adj* **:** relating to or of the nature of a clause

clause \'klȯz\ *n* [ME, fr. OF, clause, fr. ML *clausa* close of a rhetorical period, fr. L. fem. of *clausus,* pp. of *claudere* to close] **1 :** a separate section of a discourse or writing; *specif* **:** a distinct article in a formal document **2 :** a group of words containing a subject and predicate and functioning as a member of a complex or compound sentence

claus·tral \'klȯ-strəl\ *adj* [ME, fr. ML *claustralis,* fr. *claustrum* cloister — more at CLOISTER] **:** CLOISTRAL

claus·tro·pho·bia \,klȯ-strə-'fō-bē-ə\ *n* [NL, fr. L *claustrum* bar, bolt + NL *phobia* — more at CLOISTER] **:** abnormal dread of being in closed or narrow spaces — **claus·tro·pho·bic** \-bik\ *adj*

cla·vate \'klā-,vāt\ *adj* [NL *clavatus,* fr. L *clava* club, fr. *clavus* nail, knot in wood] **:** gradually thickening near the distal end **:** CLAVIFORM — **cla·vate·ly** *adv* — **cla·va·tion** \klā-'vā-shən\ *n*

clave *past of* CLEAVE

cla·ver \'klā-vər\ *vi* [prob. of Celt origin; akin to ScGael *clabaire* babbler] *chiefly Scot* **:** PRATE, GOSSIP — **claver** *n, chiefly Scot*

clav·i·chord \'klav-ə-,kȯ(ə)rd\ *n* [ML *clavichordium,* fr. L *clavis* key + *chorda* string — more at CORD] **:** an early keyboard instrument having strings pressed by tangents attached directly to the key ends — **clav·i·chord·ist** \-əst\ *n*

clav·i·cle \'klav-i-kəl\ *n* [F *clavicule,* fr. NL *clavicula,* fr. L, dim. of L *clavis* key; akin to Gk *kleid-, kleis* key, L *claudere* to close]

: a bone of the vertebrate shoulder girdle typically serving to link the scapula and sternum — **cla·vic·u·lar** \klə-'vik-yə-lər\ *adj*

clav·i·corn \'klav-ə-,kȯ(ə)rn\ *adj* [ISV, fr. L *clava* club + *cornu* horn — more at HORN] : having club-shaped antennae ⟨~ beetles⟩

cla·vier \klə-'vi(ə)r; 'klā-vē-ər, 'klav-\ *n* [F, fr. OF, key bearer, fr. L *clavis* key] **1** : the keyboard of a musical instrument **2** [G *klavier*, fr. F *clavier*] : an early keyboard instrument — **cla·vier·ist** \klə-'vir-əst; 'klā-vē-ə-rəst, 'klav-\ *n* — **cla·vier·is·tic** \klə-,vi(ə)r-'is-tik; ,klā-vē-ə-'ris-tik, ,klav-\ *adj*

clav·i·form \'klav-ə-,fȯrm\ *adj* [L *clava* club] : shaped like a club

[1]**claw** \'klȯ\ *n, often attrib* [ME *clawe*, fr. OE *clawu* hoof, claw; akin to ON *klō* claw, OE *cliewen* ball — more at CLEW] **1** : a sharp usu. slender and curved nail on the toe of an animal **2** : any of various similar sharp curved processes esp. if at the end of a limb (as of an insect); *also* : a limb ending in such a process **3** : one of the pincerlike organs terminating some limbs of arthropods (as a lobster or scorpion) **4** : something that resembles a claw; *specif* : the forked end of a tool (as a hammer) **5** : a wound from or as if from a claw — **clawed** \'klȯd\ *adj*

[2]**claw** *vb* : to rake, seize, or dig with or as if with claws

claw hammer *n* **1** : a hammer with one end of the head forked for pulling out nails **2** : TAILCOAT

claw hatchet *n* : a hatchet with one end of the head forked

clay \'klā\ *n, often attrib* [ME, fr. OE *clǣg*; akin to OHG *klīwa* bran, LL *glut-, glus* glue, MGk *glia*] **1 a** : an earthy material plastic when moist but hard when fired composed mainly of fine particles of hydrous aluminum silicates and other minerals and used for brick, tile, and earthenware; *specif* : soil composed chiefly of this material having particles less than a specified size **b** : EARTH, MUD **2 a** : a substance that resembles clay in plasticity and is used for modeling **b** : the human body as distinguished from the spirit — **clay·ey** \'klā-ē\ *adj* — **clay·ish** \'klā-ish\ *adj*

clay·bank \'klā-,baŋk\ *n* : a horse of yellowish color

clay loam *n* : a loam consisting of from 20 to 30 percent clay

clay·more \'klā-,mō(ə)r, -,mȯ(ə)r\ *n* [ScGael *claidheamh mōr*, lit., great sword] : a large 2-edged sword formerly used by Scottish Highlanders; *also* : their basket-hilted broadsword

clay·pan \-,pan\ *n* : hardpan consisting mainly of clay

clay pigeon *n* : a saucer-shaped target usu. made of baked clay and pitch and thrown from a trap in skeet and trapshooting

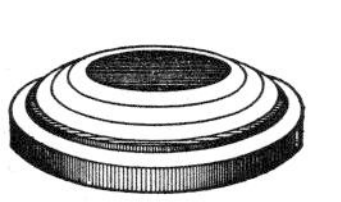

clay pigeon

[1]**clean** \'klēn\ *adj* [ME *clene*, fr. OE *clǣne*; akin to OHG *kleini* delicate, dainty, Gk *glainoi* ornaments] **1 a** : free from dirt or pollution; *specif* : not fouled ⟨ship with a ~ bottom⟩ **b** : free from contamination or disease **c** : relatively free from radioactive fallout **2 a** : free from admixture : PURE **b** *of a precious stone* : having no interior flaws visible **c** : free from growth that hinders tillage **3** : characterized by moral integrity : HONORABLE **4** : ceremonially or spiritually pure **5 a** : THOROUGH, COMPLETE **b** : deftly executed : SKILLFUL **6 a** : relatively free from error or blemish : CLEAR; *specif* : LEGIBLE ⟨~ copy⟩ **b** : UNENCUMBERED ⟨~ bill of sale⟩ **7 a** : characterized by clarity and precision : TRIM **b** : EVEN, SMOOTH ⟨a ~ edge⟩ **8 a** : having or carrying nothing : EMPTY **b** *slang* : carrying no concealed weapons **9** : habitually neat — **clean·ness** \'klēn-nəs\ *n*

[2]**clean** *adv* : in a clean manner

[3]**clean** *vt* **1** : to rid of dirt, impurities, or extraneous matter : PURGE **2 a** : STRIP, EMPTY **b** *slang* : to deprive of money or possessions ~ *vi* : to undergo or perform a process of cleaning ⟨~ up before dinner⟩ — **clean·able** \'klē-nə-bəl\ *adj* — **clean·er** *n*

clean–cut \'klēn-'kət\ *adj* **1** : cut so that the surface or edge is smooth and even **2** : sharply defined **3** : of wholesome appearance

clean·hand·ed \-'han-dəd\ *adj* : innocent of wrongdoing

clean–limbed \-'limd\ *adj* : well proportioned : TRIM

clean·li·ness \'klen-lē-nəs\ *n* : the quality or state of being cleanly

[1]**clean·ly** \'klen-lē\ *adj* **1** : careful to keep clean : FASTIDIOUS **2** : habitually kept clean

[2]**clean·ly** \'klēn-lē\ *adv* : in a clean manner

cleanse \'klenz\ *vb* [ME *clensen*, fr. OE *clǣnsian* to purify, fr. *clǣne* clean] : CLEAN — **cleans·er** *n*

clean·up \'klē-,nəp\ *n* **1** : an act or instance of cleaning **2** *slang* : an exceptionally large profit : KILLING

[1]**clear** \'kli(ə)r\ *adj* [ME *clere*, fr. OF *cler*, fr. L *clarus* clear, bright; akin to L *calare* to call — more at LOW] **1 a** : BRIGHT, LUMINOUS **b** : CLOUDLESS; *specif* : less than one-tenth covered ⟨a ~ sky⟩ **c** : free from mist, haze, or dust ⟨a ~ day⟩ **d** : UNTROUBLED, SERENE ⟨a ~ gaze⟩ **2** : CLEAN, PURE: as **a** : free from blemishes **b** : easily seen through : TRANSPARENT **c** : free from abnormal sounds on auscultation **3 a** : easily heard **b** : easily visible : PLAIN **c** : easily understood : UNMISTAKABLE **4 a** : capable of sharp discernment : KEEN **b** : free from doubt : SURE **5** : free from guile or guilt : INNOCENT **6** : unhampered by restriction or limitation: as **a** : unencumbered by debts or charges **b** : NET ⟨a ~ profit⟩ **c** : UNQUALIFIED, ABSOLUTE **d** : free from obstruction **e** : emptied of contents or cargo **f** : free from entanglement **g** : DENUDED, BARE — **clear·ly** *adv* — **clear·ness** *n*

syn CLEAR, TRANSPARENT, TRANSLUCENT, PELLUCID, LIMPID mean capable of being seen through. CLEAR implies absence of cloudiness, haziness, or muddiness; TRANSPARENT implies being so clear that objects can be seen distinctly; TRANSLUCENT implies the passage of light but not vision; PELLUCID suggests a shining clearness as of crystal; LIMPID implies the soft clearness of pure water

syn CLEAR, PERSPICUOUS, LUCID mean quickly and easily understood. CLEAR implies freedom from obscurity, ambiguity, or undue complexity; PERSPICUOUS applies to a style that is simple and elegant as well as clear; LUCID suggests a clear logical coherence and evident order of arrangement **syn** see in addition EVIDENT

[2]**clear** *adv* **1** : in a clear manner **2** : WHOLLY, ENTIRELY

[3]**clear** *vt* **1 a** : to make clear or translucent **b** : to free from pollution or cloudiness **2 a** : to free from accusation or blame : VINDICATE **b** : to certify as trustworthy **3 a** : to give insight to : ENLIGHTEN **b** : to make intelligible : EXPLAIN **4 a** : to free from obstruction: as (1) : OPEN (2) : DISENTANGLE (3) : to rid or make a rasping noise as if ridding (the throat) of phlegm **b** (1) : to submit for approval (2) : AUTHORIZE **5 a** : to free from obligation or encumbrance **b** : SETTLE, DISCHARGE ⟨~ an account⟩ **c** (1) : to free (a ship or shipment) by payment of duties or harbor fees (2) : to pass through (customs) **d** : to gain without deduction : NET ⟨~ a profit⟩ **e** : to put through a clearinghouse **6 a** : to get rid of : REMOVE **b** : TRANSMIT, DISPATCH **7 a** : to leap over or go by without touching **b** : PASS ⟨the bill ~*ed* the legislature⟩ ~ *vi* **1 a** : to become clear **b** : to go away : VANISH **c** : SELL **2 a** : to obtain permission to discharge cargo **b** : to conform to regulations or pay requisite fees prior to leaving port **3** : to pass through a clearinghouse **4** : to go to an authority (as for approval) before becoming effective — **clear·able** \'klir-ə-bəl\ *adj* — **clear·er** \'klir-ər\ *n*

[4]**clear** *n* : a clear space or part — **in the clear 1** : in inside measurement **2** : free from guilt or suspicion

clear·ance \'klir-ən(t)s\ *n* **1** : an act or process of clearing: as **a** : the act of clearing a ship at the customhouse; *also* : the papers showing that a ship has cleared **b** : the offsetting of checks and other claims among banks through a clearinghouse **c** : AUTHORIZATION **d** : a sale to clear out stock **2** : the distance by which one object clears another or the clear space between them

clear–cut \'kli(ə)r-'kət\ *adj* **1** : sharply outlined : DISTINCT **2** : DEFINITE, UNEQUIVOCAL **syn** see INCISIVE

clear–eyed \-'īd\ *adj* **1** : having clear eyes **2** : DISCERNING

clear·head·ed \-'hed-əd\ *adj* : having a clear understanding : PERCEPTIVE — **clear·head·ed·ly** *adv* — **clear·head·ed·ness** *n*

clear·ing \'kli(ə)r-iŋ\ *n* **1** : the act or process of making or becoming clear **2** : a tract of land cleared of wood and brush **3 a** : a method of exchanging and offsetting commercial papers or accounts with cash settlement only of the balances due after the clearing **b** *pl* : the gross amount of balances so adjusted

clear·ing·house \-,haùs\ *n* **1** : an establishment maintained by banks for settling mutual claims and accounts **2** : a central agency for collection, classification, and distribution esp. of information

clear–sight·ed \'kli(ə)r-'sīt-əd\ *adj* **1** : having clear vision **2** : DISCERNING — **clear–sight·ed·ly** *adv* — **clear–sight·ed·ness** *n*

clear·wing \'kli(ə)r-,wiŋ\ *n* : a moth (as of the families Aegeriidae or Sphingidae) having the wings largely transparent and devoid of scales

[1]**cleat** \'klēt\ *n* [ME *clete* wedge, fr. (assumed) OE *clēat*; akin to MHG *klōz* lump — more at CLOUT] **1 a** : a wedge-shaped piece fastened to or projecting from something and serving as a support or check **b** : a wooden or metal fitting usu. with two projecting horns around which a rope may be made fast **2 a** : a strip fastened across something to give strength or hold in position **b** : a projecting piece (as on the bottom of a shoe) that furnishes a grip

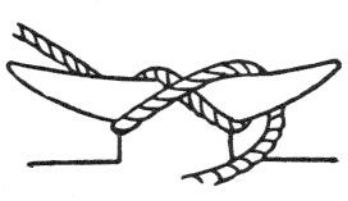

cleat 1b

[2]**cleat** *vt* **1** : to secure to or by a cleat **2** : to provide with a cleat

cleav·able \'klē-və-bəl\ *adj* : capable of being split

cleav·age \'klē-vij\ *n* **1 a** : the quality of a crystallized substance or rock of splitting along definite planes **b** : a fragment (as of a diamond) obtained by splitting **2** : the action of cleaving : the state of being cleft **3** : cell division; *esp* : the series of mitotic divisions of the egg that results in the formation of the blastomeres and changes the single-celled zygote into a multicellular embryo

[1]**cleave** \'klēv\ *vi* **cleaved** \'klēvd\ *or* **clove** \'klōv\ *also* **clave** \'klāv\ **cleav·ing** [ME *clevien*, fr. OE *clifian*] : ADHERE, CLING **syn** see STICK

[2]**cleave** *vb* **cleaved** \'klēvd\ *also* **cleft** \'kleft\ *or* **clove** \'klōv\ **cleaved** *also* **cleft** *or* **clo·ven** \'klō-vən\ **cleav·ing** [ME *cleven*, fr. OE *clēofan*; akin to ON *kljūfa* to split, L *glubere* to peel, Gk *glyphein* to carve] *vt* **1** : to divide by or as if by a cutting blow : SPLIT **2** : to separate into distinct parts and esp. into groups having divergent views ~ *vi* **1** : to split esp. along the grain **2** : to penetrate or pass through something by or as if by cutting **syn** see TEAR

cleav·er \'klē-vər\ *n* : one that cleaves; *esp* : a butcher's implement for cutting animal bodies into joints or pieces

cleav·ers \-vərz\ *n pl but sing or pl in constr* [ME *clivre*, alter. of OE *clife* burdock, cleavers; akin to OE *clifian* to cleave, adhere] : any of several plants (genus *Galium*, esp. *G. aparine*) of the madder family having the stems covered with curved prickles

cleek \'klēk\ *n* [ME (northern) *cleke*, fr. *cleken* to clutch] **1** *chiefly Scot* : a large hook (as for a pot over a fire) **2** : a wooden golf club with more loft than a spoon — called also *number four wood*

clef \'klef\ *n* [F, lit., key, fr. L *clavis*] : a sign placed at the beginning of a musical staff to determine the position of the notes

[1]**cleft** \'kleft\ *n* [ME *clift*, fr. OE *geclyft*; akin to OE *clēofan* to cleave] **1** : a space or opening made by splitting : FISSURE **2** : a usu. V-shaped indentation resembling a cleft

[2]**cleft** *adj* [ME, fr. pp. of *cleven*] : partially split or divided; *specif* : divided about halfway to the midrib ⟨a ~ leaf⟩

cleft palate *n* : congenital fissure of the roof of the mouth

cleis·tog·a·mous \klī-'stäg-ə-məs\ *or* **cleis·to·gam·ic** \,klī-stə-'gam-ik\ *adj* : of, relating to, or exhibiting cleistogamy — **cleis·tog·a·mous·ly** *adv*

cleis·tog·a·my \klī-'stäg-ə-mē\ *n* [Gk *kleistos* closed (fr. *kleiein* to close) + ISV *-gamy* — more at CLOSE] : the production (as in violets) of small inconspicuous closed self-pollinating flowers additional to and often more fruitful than the showier type

cle·ma·tis \'klem-ət-əs; kli-'mat-əs, -'māt-, -'mät-\ *n* [NL, genus name, fr. L, fr. Gk *klēmatis* brushwood, clematis, fr. *klēmat-, klēma* twig, fr. Gk *klan* to break — more at HALT] : a vine or herb (genera *Clematis, Atragene*, or *Viorna*) of the crowfoot family having three leaflets and usu. white or purple flowers

clem·en·cy \'klem-ən-sē\ *n* **1 a** : disposition to be merciful **b** : an act or instance of leniency **2** : MILDNESS **syn** see MERCY

clem·ent \'klem-ənt\ *adj* [ME, fr. L *clement-, clemens*] **1** : inclined to be merciful : LENIENT **2** : MILD — **clem·ent·ly** *adv*

[1]**clench** \'klench\ *vt* [ME *clenchen*, fr. OE *-clencan*; akin to OE *clingan* to cling] **1** : CLINCH 1 **2** : to hold fast : CLUTCH **3** : to set or close tightly

[2]**clench** *n* **1** : the end of a nail that is turned back in clinching **2** : an act or instance of clenching

clepe \'klēp\ *vt* **cleped** \'klēpt, 'klept\ **cleped** *or* **ycleped** \i-\ *or* **yclept** \i-'klept\ **clep·ing** [ME *clepen*, fr. OE *clipian* to speak, call; akin to OFris *kleppa* to ring, knock] *archaic* : NAME, CALL

clep·sy·dra \'klep-sə-drə\ *n, pl* **clepsydras** *or* **clep·sy·drae** \-,drē, -,drī\ [L, fr. Gk *klepsydra*, fr. *kleptein* to steal + *hydōr* water — more at KLEPT-, WATER] : WATER CLOCK

clere·sto·ry *or* **clear·sto·ry** \ˈkli(ə)r-ˌstōr-ē, -ˌstȯr-\ *n* [ME, fr. *clere* clear + *story*] **1 :** an outside wall of a room or building carried above an adjoining roof and pierced with windows **2 :** GALLERY **3 :** a ventilating section of a railroad car roof

cler·gy \ˈklər-jē\ *n* [ME *clergie*, fr. OF, knowledge, learning, fr. *clerc* clergyman] **1 :** the body of men ordained to the service of God in the Christian church **2 :** the official or sacerdotal class of a religion **3 :** CLERGYMEN

cler·gy·man \-ji-mən\ *n* **:** a member of the clergy

cler·ic \ˈkler-ik\ *n* [LL *clericus*] **:** a member of the clergy; *specif* **:** one in orders below the grade of priest

1**cler·i·cal** \ˈkler-i-kəl\ *adj* **1 :** of, relating to, or characteristic of the clergy, a clergyman, or a cleric **2 :** of or relating to a clerk or office worker — **cler·i·cal·ly** \-i-k(ə-)lē\ *adv*

2**clerical** *n* **1 :** CLERGYMAN **2 :** CLERICALIST

clerical collar *n* **:** a narrow stiffly upright white collar buttoned at the back of the neck and worn by clergymen

cler·i·cal·ism \ˈkler-i-kə-ˌliz-əm\ *n* **:** a policy of maintaining or increasing the power of a religious hierarchy — **cler·i·cal·ist** \-kə-ləst\ *n*

cler·i·hew \ˈkler-i-ˌhyü\ *n* [Edmund *Clerihew* Bentley †1956 E writer] **:** a light verse quatrain rhyming *aabb* and usu. dealing with a person named in the initial rhyme

cler·i·sy \ˈkler-ə-sē\ *n* [G *klerisei* clergy, fr. ML *clericia*, fr. LL *clericus* cleric] **:** INTELLIGENTSIA

1**clerk** \ˈklərk, *Brit usu rhymes with* "lark"\ *n* [ME, fr. OF *clerc* & OE *cleric, clerc*, both fr. LL *clericus*, fr. LGk *klērikos*, fr. Gk *klēros* lot, inheritance (in allusion to Deut 18:2); akin to Gk *klan* to break — more at HALT] **1 :** CLERIC **2** *archaic* **:** SCHOLAR **3 a :** an official responsible for correspondence, records, and accounts **b :** one employed to keep records or accounts or to perform general office work **c :** one who works at a sales or service counter

2**clerk** *vi* **:** to act or work as a clerk

clerk·ly \ˈklər-klē\ *adj* **1 :** of, relating to, or characteristic of a clerk **2** *archaic* **:** SCHOLARLY — **clerkly** *adv*

clerk regular *n* **:** a religious combining monastic vows with the ministry of a diocesan priest

clerk·ship \ˈklərk-ˌship\ *n* **:** the office or business of a clerk

clev·er \ˈklev-ər\ *adj* [ME *cliver*, prob. of Scand origin; akin to ON *kljūfa* to split] **1 :** showing skill or resourcefulness often with physical dexterity **2 :** marked by wit or ingenuity **3** *dial* **a :** GOOD **b :** easy to use or handle — **clev·er·ish** \-(ə-)rish\ *adj* — **clev·er·ly** \-ər-lē\ *adv* — **clev·er·ness** \-ər-nəs\ *n*

syn ADROIT, CUNNING, INGENIOUS: CLEVER stresses physical or mental quickness, deftness, or great aptitude; ADROIT often implies a skillful use of expedients to achieve one's purpose in spite of difficulties; CUNNING implies great skill in constructing or creating; INGENIOUS suggests the power of inventing or discovering a new way of accomplishing something **syn** see in addition INTELLIGENT

clev·is \ˈklev-əs\ *n* [earlier *clevi*, prob. of Scand origin; akin to ON *kljūfa* to split] **:** a usu. U-shaped metal shackle with the ends drilled to receive a pin or bolt used for attaching or suspending parts

1**clew** *or* **clue** \ˈklü\ *n* [ME *clewe*, fr. OE *cliewen;* akin to OHG *kliuwa* ball, Skt *glau* lump] **1 :** a ball of thread, yarn, or cord **2** *usu* **clue :** something that guides through an intricate procedure or maze of difficulties; *specif* **:** a piece of evidence tending to lead one toward the solution of a problem **3 a :** a metal loop attached to the lower corner of a sail **b** *pl* **:** a combination of lines by which a hammock is suspended

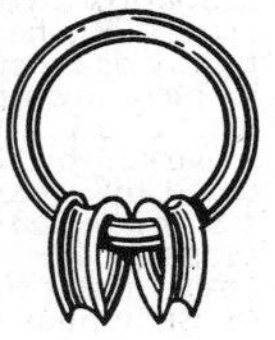

clews 3a

2**clew** *or* **clue** *vt* **clewed** *or* **clued; clew·ing** *or* **clue·ing** *or* **clu·ing 1 :** to roll into a ball **2** *usu* **clue :** to provide with a clue **3 :** to haul (a sail) up or down by ropes through the clews

cli·ché \klē-ˈshā\ *n* [F, lit., stereotype, fr. pp. of *clicher* to stereotype, of imit. origin] **1 :** a trite phrase or expression; *also* **:** the idea expressed by it **2 :** a hackneyed theme or situation — **cliché** *adj*

1**click** \ˈklik\ *n* [prob. imit.] **1 a :** a slight sharp noise **b :** a speech sound in some languages made by enclosing air between two stop articulations of the tongue, enlarging the enclosure to rarefy the air, and suddenly opening the enclosure **2 :** DETENT

2**click** *vt* **:** to strike, move, or produce with a click ~ *vi* **1 :** to make a click **2 a :** to fit or agree exactly **b :** to fit together **c :** to function smoothly **d :** SUCCEED

click beetle *n* **:** a beetle (family Elateridae) able to spring over with a click when inverted

cli·ent \ˈklī-ənt\ *n* [ME, fr. MF & L; MF *client*, fr. L *client-, cliens;* akin to L *clinare* to lean — more at LEAN] **1 :** a person under the protection of another **:** VASSAL, DEPENDENT **2 a :** a person who engages the professional services of another **b :** PATRON, CUSTOMER — **cli·ent·age** \-ən-tij\ *n* — **cli·en·tal** \klī-ˈent-ᵊl\ *adj*

cli·en·tele \ˌklī-ən-ˈtel, ˌklē-ˌän-\ *n* [F *clientèle*, fr. L *clientela*, fr. *client-, cliens*] **:** a body of clients

cliff \ˈklif\ *n* [ME *clif*, fr. OE; akin to OE *clifian* to adhere to] **:** a very steep or overhanging face of rock **:** PRECIPICE

cliff dweller *n* **1** *often cap C&D* **a :** one of the people of the American southwest who erected their dwellings on rock ledges or in the recesses of canyon walls and cliffs **b :** a member of any cliff-dwelling people **2 :** a person who lives in a large usu. metropolitan apartment building — **cliff dwelling** *n*

cliff–hang·er \-ˌhaŋ-ər\ *n* **1 :** an adventure serial or melodrama; *esp* **:** one presented in installments each ending in suspense **2 :** a contest whose outcome is in doubt up to the very end

1**cli·mac·ter·ic** \klī-ˈmak-tə-rik, ˌklī-ˌmak-ˈter-ik\ *adj* [L *climactericus*, fr. Gk *klimaktērikos*, fr. *klimaktēr* critical point, lit., rung of a ladder, fr. *klimak-, klimax*] **1 :** constituting or relating to a critical period (as of life) **2 :** CRITICAL, CRUCIAL

2**climacteric** *n* **1 :** a major turning point or critical stage **2 :** MENOPAUSE; *also* **:** a corresponding phenomenon of reduced sexual activity and competence in the male

cli·mac·tic \klī-ˈmak-tik\ *adj* **:** of, relating to, or constituting a climax — **cli·mac·ti·cal·ly** \-ti-k(ə-)lē\ *adv*

cli·mate \ˈklī-mət\ *n* [ME *climat*, fr. MF, fr. LL *climat-, clima*, fr. Gk *klimat-, klima* inclination, latitude, climate, fr. *klinein* to lean] **1 :** a region of the earth having specified climatic conditions **2 :** the average course or condition of the weather at a place over a period of years as exhibited by temperature, wind velocity, and precipitation **3 :** the prevailing temper or environmental conditions characterizing a group or period **:** MILIEU — **cli·mat·ic** \klī-ˈmat-ik\ *adj* — **cli·mat·i·cal·ly** \-i-k(ə-)lē\ *adv*

cli·ma·to·log·i·cal \ˌklī-mət-ᵊl-ˈäj-i-kəl\ *adj* **:** relating to climatology

cli·ma·tol·o·gist \ˌklī-mə-ˈtäl-ə-jəst\ *n* **:** a specialist in climatology

cli·ma·tol·o·gy \-jē\ *n* **:** the science that deals with climates and their phenomena

1**cli·max** \ˈklī-ˌmaks\ *n* [L, fr. Gk *klimax* ladder, fr. *klinein* to lean] **1 :** a figure of speech in which a series of phrases or sentences is arranged in ascending order of rhetorical forcefulness **2 a :** the highest point **:** CULMINATION **b :** the point of highest dramatic tension or a major turning point in the action (as of a play) **c :** ORGASM **d :** MENOPAUSE **3 :** a relatively stable stage or community achieved by a population of plants or animals through successful adjustment to an environment **syn** see SUMMIT

2**climax** *vi* **:** to come to a climax ~ *vt* **:** to bring to a climax

1**climb** \ˈklīm\ *vb* [ME *climben*, fr. OE *climban;* akin to OE *clamm* bond, fetter] *vi* **1 a :** to go upward with gradual or continuous progress **:** RISE **b :** to slope upward **2 a :** to go upward or raise oneself esp. by grasping or clutching with the hands **b** *of a plant* **:** to ascend in growth (as by twining) **3 :** to go about or down usu. by grasping or holding with the hands ~ *vt* **1 :** to go upwards upon or along, to the top of, or over **2 :** to draw or pull oneself up, over, or to the top of by using hands and feet **3 :** to grow up or over **syn** see ASCEND — **climb·able** \ˈklī-mə-bəl\ *adj*

2**climb** *n* **1 :** a place where climbing is necessary to progress **2 :** the act or an instance of climbing **:** ascent by climbing

climb·er \ˈklī-mər\ *n* **:** one that climbs or helps in climbing

climbing iron *n* **:** a steel framework with spikes attached that may be affixed to one's boots for climbing

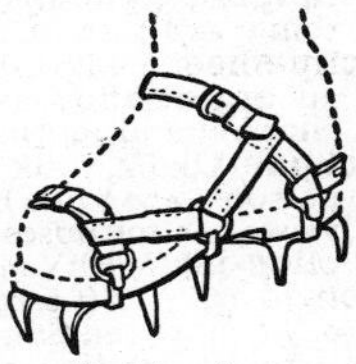

climbing iron

clime \ˈklīm\ *n* [L *clima*] **:** CLIMATE

clin- *or* **clino-** *comb form* [NL, fr. Gk *klinein* to lean] **:** lean **:** slant ⟨*clino*meter⟩

-cli·nal \ˈklīn-ᵊl\ *adj comb form* [ISV, fr. Gk *klinein*] **:** sloping ⟨mono*clinal*⟩

1**clinch** \ˈklinch\ *vb* [prob. alter. of 1*clench*] *vt* **1 a :** to turn over or flatten the protruding pointed end of (a driven nail); *also* **:** to treat (a screw, bolt, or rivet) in a similar way **b :** to fasten in this way **2 :** CLENCH 2 **3 :** to make final or irrefutable **:** SETTLE ~ *vi* **1 :** to hold an opponent (as in boxing) at close quarters with one or both arms **2 :** to hold fast or firmly

2**clinch** *n* **1 :** a fastening by means of a clinched nail, rivet, or bolt; *also* **:** the clinched part of a nail, bolt, or rivet **2** *archaic* **:** PUN **3 :** an act or instance of clinching in boxing

clinch·er \ˈklin-chər\ *n* **:** one that clinches: as **a :** a decisive fact, argument, act, or remark **b :** an automobile tire with flanged beads fitting into the wheel rim

cline \ˈklīn\ *n* [Gk *klinein* to lean] **:** a graded series of morphological or physiological differences exhibited by a group of related organisms usu. along a line of environmental or geographic transition

-cline \ˌklīn\ *n comb form* [back-formation fr. *-clinal*] **:** slope ⟨mono*cline*⟩

cling \ˈkliŋ\ *vi* **clung** \ˈkləŋ\ **cling·ing** [ME *clingen*, fr. OE *clingan;* akin to OHG *klunga* tangled ball of thread, MIr *glacc* hand] **1 a :** to hold together **b :** to adhere as if glued firmly **c :** to hold or hold on tightly or tenaciously **2 a :** to have a strong emotional attachment or dependence **b :** to linger near **syn** see STICK

cling·stone \ˈkliŋ-ˌstōn\ *n* **:** a fruit (as a peach) whose flesh adheres strongly to the pit

clin·ic \ˈklin-ik\ *n* [F *clinique*, fr. Gk *klinikē* medical practice at the sickbed, fr. fem. of *klinikos* of a bed, fr. *klinē* bed, fr. *klinein* to lean, recline] **1 :** a class of medical instruction in which patients are examined and discussed **2 :** a class meeting devoted to the analysis and treatment of cases in some special field **3 a :** a facility (as of a hospital) for diagnosis and treatment of outpatients **b :** a group practice in which several physicians work cooperatively

-clin·ic \ˈklin-ik\ *adj comb form* [ISV, fr. Gk *klinein*] **1 :** inclining **:** dipping ⟨iso*clinic*⟩ **2 :** having (so many) oblique intersections of the axes ⟨mono*clinic*⟩ ⟨tri*clinic*⟩

clin·i·cal \ˈklin-i-kəl\ *adj* **1 :** of, relating to, or conducted in or as if in a clinic: as **a :** involving direct observation of the patient **b :** apparent to or based on clinical observation **2 :** analytical, detached, or coolly dispassionate — **clin·i·cal·ly** \-k(ə-)lē\ *adv*

clinical thermometer *n* **:** a self-registering thermometer for measuring body temperature

cli·ni·cian \kli-ˈnish-ən\ *n* **:** one qualified in the clinical practice of medicine, psychiatry, or psychology as distinguished from one specializing in laboratory or research techniques

1**clink** \ˈkliŋk\ *vb* [ME *clinken*, of imit. origin] *vi* **:** to give out a slight sharp short metallic sound ~ *vt* **:** to cause to clink

2**clink** *n* **:** a clinking sound

3**clink** *n* [*Clink*, a prison in Southwark, London, England] *slang* **:** a prison cell **:** JAIL

1**clin·ker** \ˈkliŋ-kər\ *n* [alter. of earlier *klincard* (a hard yellowish Dutch brick)] **1 :** a brick that has been burned too much in the kiln **2 :** stony matter fused together **:** SLAG

2**clinker** *vb* **clin·ker·ing** \ˈkliŋ-k(ə-)riŋ\ *vt* **1 :** to cause to form clinker **2 :** to clear out the clinkers from ~ *vi* **:** to turn to clinker under heat

3**clink·er** \ˈkliŋ-kər\ *n* [1*clink*] **1** *Brit* **:** something first-rate **2** *slang* **a :** a wrong note; *also* **:** BONER **b :** an utter failure **:** FLOP

clin·ker-built \-ˌbilt\ *adj* [*clinker*, n. (clinch)] **:** having the external planks or plates overlapping like the clapboards on a house ⟨a ~ boat⟩

cli·nom·e·ter \klī-ˈnäm-ət-ər\ *n* **:** any of various instruments for measuring angles of elevation or inclination — **cli·no·met·ric** \ˌklī-nə-ˈme-trik\ *adj* — **cli·nom·e·try** \klī-ˈnäm-ə-trē\ *n*

-cli·nous \ˈklī-nəs\ *adj comb form* [prob. fr. NL *-clinus*, fr. Gk *klinē* bed — more at CLINIC] **:** having the androecium and gynoecium in a (single or different) flower or (two separate) flowers ⟨di*clinous*⟩

1**clin·quant** \ˈkliŋ-kənt, klaⁿ-ˈkäⁿ\ *adj* [MF, fr. prp. of *clinquer* to glitter, lit., to clink, of imit. origin] **:** glittering with gold or tinsel

2**clinquant** *n* [F, fr. *clinquant*, adj.] **:** imitation gold leaf **:** TINSEL

clin·to·nia \klin-'tō-nē-ə\ *n* [NL, genus name, fr. DeWitt *Clinton* †1828 Am statesman] **:** any of a genus (*Clintonia*) of herbs of the lily family with yellow or white flowers

Clio \'klī-(,)ō\ *n* [L, fr. Gk *Kleiō*] **:** the Greek Muse of history

¹**clip** \'klip\ *vt* **clipped; clip·ping** [ME *clippen*, fr. OE *clyppan;* akin to OHG *klāftra* fathom, L *gleba* clod, *globus* globe] **1 :** ENCOMPASS **2 a :** to hold in a tight grip **:** CLUTCH **b :** to clasp or fasten with a clip **3 :** to block (an opposing player other than the ball carrier) by hitting with the body from behind

²**clip** *n* **1 :** any of various devices that grip, clasp, or hook **2 :** a device to hold cartridges for charging the magazines of some rifles; *also* **:** a magazine from which ammunition is fed into the chamber of a firearm **3 :** a piece of jewelry held in position by a spring clip

³**clip** *vb* **clipped; clip·ping** [ME *clippen*, fr. ON *klippa*] *vt* **1 a :** to cut or cut off with shears **b :** to cut off the distal or outer part of **c** (1) **:** ³EXCISE (2) **:** to cut items out of **2 a :** CURTAIL, DIMINISH **b :** to abbreviate in speech or writing **3** *slang* **:** HIT, PUNCH **4 :** to take money from unfairly or dishonestly esp. by overcharging ~ *vi* **1 :** to clip something **2 :** to travel or pass rapidly

⁴**clip** *n* **1 a** *pl, Scot* **:** SHEARS **b :** a 2-bladed instrument for cutting esp. the nails **2 :** something that is clipped: as **a :** the product of a single shearing (as of sheep) **b :** a crop of wool of a sheep, a flock, or a region **c :** a section of filmed material **3 :** an act of clipping **4 :** a sharp blow **5 :** a rapid pace

clip·board \'klip-,bō(ə)rd, -,bȯ(ə)rd\ *n* **:** a small writing board with a spring clip at the top for holding papers

clip·per \'klip-ər\ *n* **1 :** one that clips something **2 :** an implement for clipping esp. hair, fingernails, or toenails — usu. used in pl. **3 a :** one that moves swiftly **b :** a fast sailing ship; *esp* **:** one with long slender lines, an overhanging bow, tall raking masts, and a large sail area

clip·ping \'klip-iŋ\ *n* **:** something that is clipped off or out of something; *esp* **:** an item clipped from a publication

clip·sheet \'klip-,shēt\ *n* **:** a sheet of newspaper material issued by an organization and usu. printed on only one side to facilitate clipping and reprinting

clique \'klēk, 'klik\ *n* [F] **:** a narrow exclusive circle or group of persons; *esp* **:** one held together by a presumed identity of interests, views, or purposes — **cliqu·ey** *or* **cliquy** \'klē-kē, 'klik-ē\ *adj* — **cliqu·ish** \-ish\ *adj* — **cliqu·ish·ly** *adv* — **cliqu·ish·ness** *n*

cli·to·ral \'klit-ə-rəl, 'klīt-\ *or* **cli·tor·ic** \klī-'tȯr-ik, klə-, -'tär-\ *adj* **:** of or relating to the clitoris

cli·to·ris \'klit-ə-rəs, 'klīt-\ *n* [NL, fr. Gk *kleitoris*] **:** a small organ at the anterior or ventral part of the vulva homologous to the penis

clo·aca \klō-'ā-kə\ *n, pl* **clo·acae** \-,kē, -,sē\ [L; akin to Gk *klyzein* to wash] **1 :** ³SEWER **2** [NL, fr. L] **:** the common chamber into which the intestinal, urinary, and generative canals discharge in birds, reptiles, amphibians, and many fishes; *also* **:** a comparable chamber of an invertebrate — **clo·acal** \-'ā-kəl\ *adj*

¹**cloak** \'klōk\ *n* [ME *cloke*, fr. ONF *cloque* bell, cloak, fr. ML *clocca* bell; fr. its shape] **1 :** a loose outer garment **2 :** something that conceals **:** PRETENSE, DISGUISE

²**cloak** *vt* **:** to cover or hide with a cloak **syn** see DISGUISE

cloak-and-dag·ger *adj* **:** dealing in or suggestive of melodramatic intrigue and action usu. involving secret agents and espionage

clob·ber \'kläb-ər\ *vt* **clob·ber·ing** \-(ə-)riŋ\ [origin unknown] **1** *slang* **:** to pound mercilessly **2** *slang* **:** to defeat overwhelmingly

cloche \'klōsh\ *n* [F, lit., bell, fr. ML *clocca*] **:** a woman's small helmetlike hat usu. with deep rounded crown and very narrow brim

¹**clock** \'kläk\ *n, often attrib* [ME *clok*, fr. MD *clocke* bell, clock, fr. ONF or ML; ONF *cloque* bell, fr. ML *clocca*, of Celt origin; akin to MIr *clocc* bell] **1 :** a device other than a watch for indicating or measuring time commonly by means of hands moving on a dial **2 :** a registering device with a dial and indicator attached to a mechanism to measure or gauge its functioning or to record its output; *specif* **:** SPEEDOMETER **3 :** TIME CLOCK

²**clock** *vt* **1 :** to time with a stopwatch or by an electric timing device **2 :** to register on a mechanical recording device — **clock·er** *n*

³**clock** *n* [prob. fr. *clock* (bell); fr. its original bell-like shape] **:** an ornamental figure on the ankle or side of a stocking or sock

clock·wise \-,wīz\ *adv* **:** in the direction in which the hands of a clock rotate as viewed from in front — **clockwise** *adj*

clock·work \-,wərk\ *n* **:** machinery containing a train of wheels of small size (as in a mechanical toy or a bomb-actuating device)

clod \'kläd\ *n* [ME, alter. of *clot*] **1 a :** a lump or mass esp. of earth or clay **b :** SOIL, EARTH **2 :** OAF, DOLT — **clod·dish** \-ish\ *adj* — **clod·dish·ness** *n* — **clod·dy** \'kläd-ē\ *adj*

clod·hop·per \'kläd-,häp-ər\ *n* **1 :** a clumsy and uncouth rustic **2 :** a large heavy shoe

clod·hop·ping \-iŋ\ *adj* **:** BOORISH, RUDE

clod·poll *or* **clod·pole** \-,pōl\ *n* **:** BLOCKHEAD 2

¹**clog** \'kläg\ *n* [ME *clogge* short thick piece of wood] **1 a :** a weight attached to a man or an animal to hinder motion **b :** something that shackles or impedes **:** ENCUMBRANCE 1 **2 :** a shoe, sandal, or overshoe having a thick typically wooden sole

²**clog** *vb* **clogged; clog·ging** *vt* **1 a :** ENCUMBER **b :** to impede with a clog **:** HINDER **2 :** to fill beyond capacity **:** OVERLOAD ~ *vi* **1 :** to become filled with extraneous matter **2 :** to unite in a mass **:** CLOT **3 :** to dance a clog dance **syn** see HAMPER

clog dance *n* **:** a dance in which the performer wears clogs and beats out a clattering rhythm upon the floor — **clog dancer** *n* — **clog dancing** *n*

¹**cloi·son·né** \,klȯiz-ᵊn-'ā\ *adj* [F, fr. pp. of *cloisonner* to partition] **:** consisting of, used in, or forming cloisonné

²**cloisonné** *n* **:** a multicolored decoration made of enamels poured into the divided areas in a design outlined with bent wire fillets or metal strips secured to a usu. metal ground

¹**clois·ter** \'klȯi-stər\ *n* [ME *cloistre*, fr. OF, fr. ML *claustrum*, fr. L, bar, bolt, fr. *claudere* to close] **1 a :** a monastic establishment **b :** monastic life **2 :** a covered passage on the side of a court usu. having one side walled and the other an open arcade or colonnade

syn CLOISTER, CONVENT, MONASTERY, NUNNERY, ABBEY, PRIORY mean a house of persons living under religious vows. CLOISTER and CONVENT are both general terms, though cloister connotes seclusion from the world and CONVENT stresses community of living; a MONASTERY is specifically a cloister for monks; a NUNNERY is a cloister for nuns and is now more commonly called a CONVENT; an ABBEY is a house for monks or for nuns governed by an abbot or by an abbess; a PRIORY is governed by a prior or prioress and may be subordinate to an abbey

²**cloister** *vt* **clois·ter·ing** \'klȯi-st(ə-)riŋ\ **1 :** to seclude from the world in or as if in a cloister **2 :** to surround with a cloister

clois·tral \'klȯi-strəl\ *adj* **:** of, relating to, or suggestive of a cloister

clois·tress \'klȯi-strəs\ *n, obs* **:** NUN

clon·al \'klōn-ᵊl\ *adj* **:** of, relating to, or occurring in or as a clone — **clon·al·ly** \-ᵊl-ē\ *adv*

clone \'klōn\ *n* [Gk *klōn* twig, slip; akin to Gk *klan* to break] **:** the aggregate of the asexually produced progeny of an individual

clo·nic \'klō-nik, 'klän-ik\ *adj* **:** exhibiting, relating to, or involving clonus — **clo·nic·i·ty** \klō-'nis-ət-ē, klä-\ *n*

clo·nus \'klō-nəs\ *n* [NL, fr. Gk *klonos* agitation; akin to L *celer* swift] **:** a forced series of alternating contractions and partial relaxations of a muscle occurring in some nervous diseases

cloot \'klüt\ *n* [prob. of Scand origin; akin to ON *klō* claw] **1** *Scot* **:** a cloven hoof **2** *cap, Scot* **:** DEVIL — usu. used in pl.

Cloot·ie \'klüt-ē\ *n* [dim. of *cloot*] *chiefly Scot* **:** DEVIL

clop \'kläp\ *n* [imit.] **:** a sound made by or as if by a hoof or wooden shoe against pavement

¹**close** \'klōz\ *vb* [ME *closen*, fr. OF *clos-*, stem of *clore*, fr. L *claudere*] *vt* **1 a :** to move so as to bar passage through something ⟨~ the gate⟩ **b :** to block against entry or passage ⟨~ a street⟩ **c :** to deny access to **d :** SCREEN, EXCLUDE ⟨~ a view⟩ **e :** to suspend or stop the operations of ⟨~ school⟩ **2** *archaic* **:** ENCLOSE, CONTAIN **3 :** to bring to an end or period **:** TERMINATE **4 a :** to bring or bind together the parts or edges of ⟨a *closed* fist⟩ **b :** to fill up (as an opening) ~ *vi* **1 a :** to contract, fold, swing, or slide so as to leave no opening **b :** to cease operation **2 a :** to draw near **b :** to engage in a struggle at close quarters **:** GRAPPLE ⟨~ with the enemy⟩ **3 :** to come together **:** MEET **4 :** to enter into or complete an agreement **5 :** to come to an end or period — **clos·er** *n*

syn END, CONCLUDE, FINISH, COMPLETE, TERMINATE: CLOSE suggests making no longer accessible to outside forces that cause change or development; END more strongly connotes finality and usu. implies an achievement of progress or sequence; CONCLUDE adds to CLOSE or to END a suggestion of formality; FINISH implies that what one has set out to do has been done; COMPLETE implies that what has been done has no deficiencies; TERMINATE implies setting a limit in time or space with or without completing or fulfilling

²**close** \'klōz\ *n* **1 a :** a coming or bringing to a conclusion **b :** a conclusion or end in time or existence **:** CESSATION **c :** the concluding passage (as of a speech or play) **2 :** the conclusion of a musical strain or period **:** CADENCE **3** *archaic* **:** a hostile encounter

³**close** \'klōs\ *n* [ME *clos*, lit., enclosure, fr. OF *clos*, fr. L *clausum*, fr. neuter of *clausus*, pp.] **1** *Brit* **:** an enclosed area; *esp* **:** the precinct of a cathedral **2** *chiefly Brit* **a :** a narrow passage leading from a street to a court and the houses within or to the common stairway of tenements **b :** a road closed at one end

⁴**close** \'klōs\ *adj* [ME *clos*, fr. MF, fr. L *clausus*, pp. of *claudere* to shut, close; akin to Gk *kleiein* to close, OHG *sliozan*] **1 :** having no openings **:** CLOSED **2 a :** confined or confining strictly **b** (1) *of a vowel* **:** HIGH 12 (2) **:** formed with the tongue in a higher position than for the other vowel of a pair **3 :** restricted to a privileged class **4 a :** SECLUDED, SECRET **b :** SECRETIVE **5 :** STRICT, RIGOROUS ⟨keep ~ watch⟩ **6 :** SULTRY, STUFFY **7 :** STINGY, TIGHTFISTED **8 :** having little space between items or units **9 a :** fitting tightly or exactly **b :** very short or near to the surface **c :** matching or blending without gap **10 :** being near in time, space, effect, or degree **11 :** INTIMATE, FAMILIAR **12 a :** ACCURATE, PRECISE **b :** marked by fidelity to an original **c :** TERSE, COMPACT **13 :** decided by a narrow margin **14 :** difficult to obtain ⟨money is ~⟩ **15** *of punctuation* **:** characterized by liberal use esp. of commas — **close·ly** *adv* — **close·ness** *n*

syn CLOSE, DENSE, COMPACT, THICK mean massed tightly together. CLOSE implies the least possible space or interval between elements without actual pressure or loss of individual identity; DENSE implies compression of parts or elements so great as to be almost impenetrable; COMPACT suggests a firm union or consolidation of parts within a small compass; THICK implies a concentrated abundance of parts or units **syn** see in addition STINGY

⁵**close** \'klōs\ *adv* **:** in a close position or manner **:** NEAR

close corporation \'klōs-\ *n* **:** a corporation whose stock is held by a few persons who are often those active in the management

closed \'klōzd\ *adj* **1 :** not open **:** ENCLOSED **2 a :** forming a self-contained unit ⟨~ association⟩ **b** (1) **:** traced by a moving point that returns to an arbitrary starting point ⟨~ curve⟩; *also* **:** so made that every plane section is a closed curve ⟨~ surface⟩ (2) **:** having elements subject to an operation that produces again elements of the set ⟨set ~ under division⟩ **3 a :** confined to a few ⟨~ membership⟩ **b :** rigidly excluding outside influence ⟨~ economy⟩ **4 :** ending in a consonant ⟨~ syllable⟩

closed chain *n* **:** RING 10

closed circuit *n* **:** a television installation in which the signal is transmitted by wire to a limited number of receivers

closed-end \'klōz-'dend\ *adj* **:** organized on a fixed basis: as **a :** issued to the full amount authorized **b :** having a fixed capitalization of shares traded on the open market instead of being redeemable daily on demand

closed shop *n* **:** an establishment in which the employer by agreement hires only union members in good standing

close·fist·ed \'klōs-'fis-təd\ *adj* **:** STINGY, TIGHTFISTED

close-grained \-'grānd\ *adj* **:** having a closely compacted smooth texture; *esp* **:** having narrow annual rings or small wood elements

close-hauled \-'hȯld\ *adj* **:** having the sails set for sailing as nearly against the wind as the ship will go

close·mouthed \-'mau̇thd, -'mau̇tht\ *adj* **:** cautious in speaking **:** UNCOMMUNICATIVE; *also* **:** SECRETIVE

close·stool \'klōz-,stül, 'klōs-\ *n* **:** a stool holding a chamber pot

¹**clos·et** \'kläz-ət, 'klȯ-zət\ *n* [ME, fr. MF, dim. of *clos* enclosure] **1 a :** an apartment or small room for privacy **b :** a monarch's or official's private chamber for counsel or devotions **2 :** a cabinet or recess for china, household utensils, or clothing **:** CUPBOARD **3 :** WATER CLOSET

²**closet** *adj* **1 :** closely private **2 :** working in or suited to the closet as the place of seclusion or study **:** THEORETICAL

³**closet** *vt* **1 :** to shut up in or as if in a closet **2 :** to take into a closet for a secret interview

closet drama *n* **:** drama suited primarily for reading

close-up \'klō-,səp\ *n* **1 :** a photograph or movie shot taken at close range **2 :** an intimate view or examination of something

clos·trid·i·al \klä-'strid-ē-əl\ *adj* **:** of or relating to clostridia

clos·trid·i·um \-ē-əm\ *n, pl* **clos·trid·ia** \-ē-ə\ [NL, genus name, fr. Gk *klōstēr* spindle, fr. *klōthein* to spin] **:** any of various spore-forming mostly anaerobic soil or intestinal bacteria (esp. genus *Clostridium*)

¹**clo·sure** \'klō-zhər\ *n* [ME, fr. MF, fr. L *clausura*, fr. *clausus*, pp. of *claudere* to close — more at CLOSE] **1** *archaic* **:** means of enclosing **:** ENCLOSURE **2 :** an act of closing **:** the condition of being closed **3 :** something that closes **4** [trans. of F *clôture*] **:** CLOTURE

²**closure** *vt* **clo·sur·ing** \'klōzh-(ə-)riŋ\ **:** CLOTURE

¹**clot** \'klät\ *n* [ME, fr. OE *clott;* akin to MHG *klōz* lump, ball — more at CLOUT] **1 :** a portion of a substance cleaving together in a thick nondescript mass (as of clay or gum) **2 a :** a roundish viscous lump formed by coagulation of a portion of liquid or by melting **b :** the coagulum produced by clotting of blood **3 :** CLUSTER

²**clot** *vb* **clot·ted; clot·ting** *vi* **1 :** to become a clot **:** form clots **2 :** to undergo a sequence of complex chemical and physical reactions that results in conversion of fluid blood into a coagulum **:** COAGULATE ~ *vt* **1 :** to cause to clot **2 :** to fill with clots

cloth \'klȯth\ *n, pl* **cloths** \'klȯthz, 'klȯths\ *often attrib* [ME, fr. OE *clāth;* akin to OE *clīthan* to adhere to, LL *glut-, glus* glue] **1 a :** a pliable fabric made usu. by weaving, felting, or knitting natural or synthetic fibers and filaments **b :** a similar material (as of glass) **2 :** a piece of cloth adapted for a particular purpose; *esp* **:** TABLECLOTH **3 a :** distinctive dress of a profession or calling **b :** the dress of the clergy; *also* **:** CLERGY

clothe \'klōth\ *vt* **clothed** *or* **clad** \'klad\ **cloth·ing** [ME *clothen*, fr. OE *clāthian*, fr. *clāth* cloth, garment] **1 a :** to cover with or as if with cloth or clothing **:** DRESS **b :** to provide with clothes **2 :** to express or enhance by suitably significant language **:** COUCH **3 :** to endow esp. with power or a quality

clothes \'klō(th)z\ *n pl, often attrib* [ME, fr. OE *clāthas*, pl. of *clāth* cloth, garment] **1 :** CLOTHING **2 :** BEDCLOTHES **3 :** all the cloth articles of personal and household use that can be washed

clothes·horse \-ˌhȯ(ə)rs\ *n* **1 :** a frame on which to hang clothes **2 :** a conspicuously dressy person

clothes moth *n* **:** any of several small yellowish moths whose larvae eat wool, fur, or feathers

clothes·pin \-ˌpin\ *n* **:** a forked piece of wood or plastic or a small spring clamp used for fastening clothes on a line

clothes·press \-ˌpres\ *n* **:** a receptacle for clothes

clothes tree *n* **:** an upright post-shaped stand with hooks or pegs around the top on which to hang clothes

cloth·ier \'klōth-yər, 'klō-thē-ər\ *n* [ME, alter. of *clother*, fr. *cloth*] **:** one who makes or sells cloth or clothing

cloth·ing \'klō-thiŋ\ *n* **:** garments in general; *also* **:** COVERING

Clo·tho \'klō-(ˌ)thō\ *n* [L, fr. Gk *Klōthō*, lit., the spinner, fr. *klōthein* to spin] **:** the one of the three Fates in classical mythology who spins the thread of life

cloth yard *n* **:** a yard esp. for measuring cloth; *specif* **:** a unit of 37 inches equal to the Scotch ell and used also as a length for arrows

clo·ture \'klō-chər\ *n* [F *clôture*, lit., closure, alter. of MF *closure*] **:** the closing or limitation of debate in a legislative body by calling for a vote or by other authorized methods — **cloture** *vt* **clo·tur·ing** \'klōch(ə-)riŋ\

¹**cloud** \'klau̇d\ *n, often attrib* [ME rock, cloud, fr. OE *clūd;* akin to Gk *gloutos* buttock] **1 a :** a visible mass of particles of water or ice in the form of fog, mist, or haze suspended usu. at a considerable height in the air **b :** a light filmy, puffy, or billowy mass seeming to float in the air **2 :** a usu. visible mass of minute particles suspended in the air or in a gas; *also* **:** one of the masses of obscuring matter in interstellar space **3 :** a great crowd or multitude **:** SWARM **4 :** something that has a dark, lowering, or threatening aspect **5 :** something that obscures or blemishes **6 :** a dark or opaque vein or spot (as in marble)

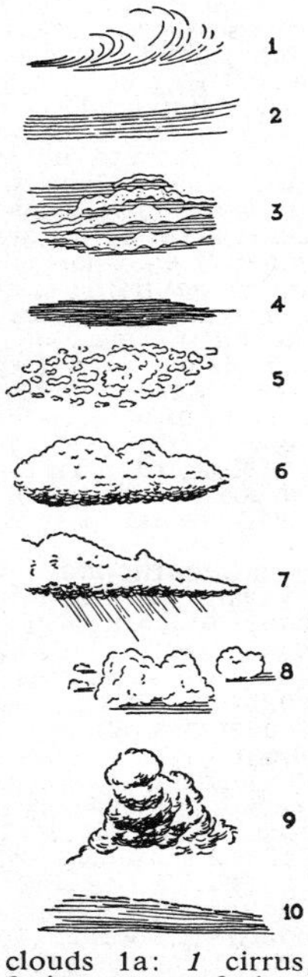

clouds 1a: *1* cirrus, *2* cirrostratus, *3* cirrocumulus, *4* altostratus, *5* altocumulus, *6* stratocumulus, *7* nimbostratus, *8* cumulus, *9* cumulonimbus, *10* stratus

²**cloud** *vi* **1 :** to grow cloudy **2 a** *of facial features* **:** to become troubled, apprehensive, or distressed in appearance **b :** to become blurry, dubious, or ominous **3 :** to billow up in the form of a cloud ~ *vt* **1 a :** to envelop or hide with a cloud or as if by a cloud **b :** to make opaque esp. by condensation of moisture **c :** to make murky esp. with smoke or mist **2 :** to make unclear or indistinct **3 :** TAINT, SULLY **4 :** to cast gloom over

cloud·ber·ry \-ˌber-ē\ *n* **:** a creeping herbaceous raspberry (*Rubus chamaemorus*) of north temperate regions; *also* **:** its pale edible fruit

cloud burst \-ˌbərst\ *n* **:** a sudden copious rainfall

cloud chamber *n* **:** a vessel containing saturated water vapor whose sudden expansion reveals the passage of an ionizing particle by a trail of visible droplets

cloud·i·ly \'klau̇d-ᵊl-ē\ *adv* **:** in a cloudy or clouded manner **:** INDISTINCTLY

cloud·i·ness \'klau̇d-ē-nəs, 'klau̇d-ᵊn-(n)əs\ *n* **:** the quality or state of being cloudy

cloud·land \-ˌland\ *n* **1 :** the region of the clouds **2 :** the realm of visionary speculation or poetic imagination

cloud·less \-ləs\ *adj* **:** free from any cloud **:** CLEAR — **cloud·less·ly** *adv* — **cloud·less·ness** *n*

cloud·let \'klau̇d-lət\ *n* **:** a small cloud

cloudy \'klau̇d-ē\ *adj* **1 :** of, relating to, or resembling cloud **2 :** darkened by gloom or anxiety **3 a :** overcast with clouds; *specif* **:** six tenths to nine tenths covered with clouds **b :** having a cloudy sky **4 :** obscure in meaning **5 :** dimmed or dulled as if by clouds **6 :** uneven in color or texture **:** MURKY

¹**clout** \'klau̇t\ *n* [ME, fr. OE *clūt;* akin to MHG *klōz* lump, Russ *gluda*] **1 a** *dial chiefly Brit* **:** a piece of cloth or leather **:** RAG **b :** a household cloth **c :** an article of clothing (as for infants) **2 :** a blow esp. with the hand; *also* **:** a hit in baseball **3 :** a white cloth on a stake or frame used as a target in archery

²**clout** *vt* **1 :** to cover or patch with a clout **2 :** to hit forcefully

¹**clove** \'klōv\ *n* [ME, fr. OE *clufu;* akin to OE *clēofan* to split] **:** one of the small bulbs developed in the axils of the scales of a large bulb

²**clove** *past of* CLEAVE

³**clove** \'klōv\ *n* [alter. of ME *clowe*, fr. OF *clou* (*de girofle*), lit., nail of clove, fr. L *clavus* nail] **:** the dried flower bud of a tropical tree (*Eugenia aromatica*) of the myrtle family; *also* **:** this tree

clove hitch \'klōv-\ *n* [ME *cloven, clove* divided, fr. pp. of *clevien* to cleave] **:** a knot securing a rope temporarily to an object (as a post or spar) and consisting of a turn around the object, over the standing part, around the object again, and under the last turn

clo·ven \'klō-vən\ *past part of* CLEAVE

cloven foot *n* **1 :** a foot (as of a sheep) divided into two parts at its distal extremity — called also *cloven hoof* **2** [fr. the traditional representation of Satan as cloven-footed] **:** the sign of devilish character — **clo·ven–foot·ed** \ˌklō-vən-'fu̇t-əd\ *adj*

clo·ver \'klō-vər\ *n* [ME, fr. OE *clāfre;* akin to OHG *klēo* clover] **:** any of a genus (*Trifolium*) of low leguminous herbs having trifoliolate leaves and flowers in dense heads and including many valuable forage and bee plants; *also* **:** any of various other leguminous plants (as of the genera *Melilotus, Lespedeza,* or *Medicago*)

clo·ver·leaf \-ˌlēf\ *n* **:** a road plan passing one highway over another and routing turning traffic onto connecting roadways which branch only to the right and lead around in a circle to enter the other highway from the right and thus merge traffic without left-hand turns or direct crossings

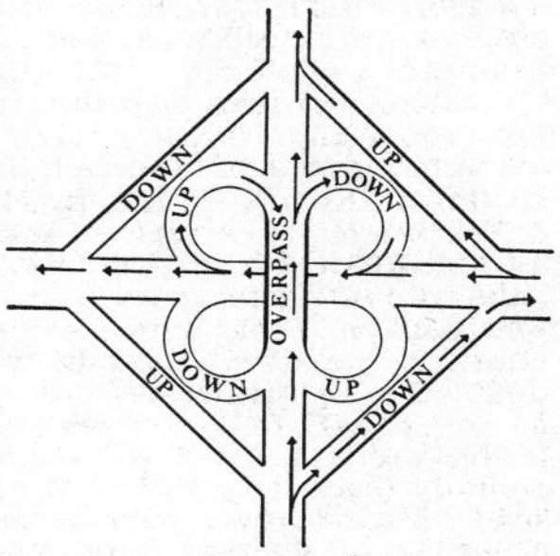

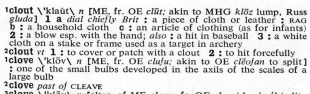

cloverleaf

¹**clown** \'klau̇n\ *n* [perh. fr. MF *coulon* settler, fr. L *colonus* colonist, farmer — more at COLONY] **1 :** FARMER, COUNTRYMAN **2 :** a rude ill-bred person **:** BOOR **3 a :** a fool, jester, or comedian in a play or other entertainment; *specif* **:** a grotesquely dressed comedy performer in a circus **b :** one who habitually plays the buffoon **:** JOKER

²**clown** *vi* **:** to act as a clown

clown·ish \'klau̇-nish\ *adj* **:** of or resembling a clown **:** RUDE **syn** see BOORISH — **clown·ish·ly** *adv* — **clown·ish·ness** *n*

cloy \'klȯi\ *vb* [ME *acloien* to lame, fr. MF *encloer* to drive in a nail, fr. ML *inclavare*, fr. L *in* + *clavus*, nail] *vt* **:** to surfeit with an excess usu. of something orig. pleasing ~ *vi* **:** to cause surfeit **syn** see SATIATE — **cloy·ing·ly** \-iŋ-lē\ *adv*

¹**club** \'kləb\ *n* [ME *clubbe*, fr. ON *klubba;* akin to OHG *kolbo* club, OE *clamm* bond] **1 a :** a heavy usu. tapering staff esp. of wood wielded as a weapon **b :** a stick or bat used to hit a ball with in any of various games **c :** a playing card of the suit having a figure like a clover leaf **d :** something resembling a club **e :** a light spar **f :** INDIAN CLUB **2 a :** an association of persons for some common object usu. jointly supported and meeting periodically **b :** the meeting place of a club **c :** an association of persons participating in a plan by which they agree to make regular payments or purchases in order to secure some advantage **d :** NIGHTCLUB

²**club** *vb* **clubbed; club·bing** *vt* **1 a :** to beat or strike with or as if with a club **b :** to gather into a club-shaped mass **c :** to hold like a club **2 a :** to unite or combine for a common cause **b :** to contribute to a common fund ~ *vi* **1 :** to form a club **:** COMBINE **2 :** to pay a share of a common expense **:** CONTRIBUTE

³**club** *adj* **1 :** of or relating to a club **2 :** consisting of foods in a fixed combination offered on a menu at a set price

club·ba·ble *or* **club·able** \'kləb-ə-bəl\ *adj* **:** SOCIABLE

club·by \'kləb-ē\ *adj* **:** characteristic of a club or club members: as **a :** SOCIABLE **b :** SELECT

club car *n* **:** LOUNGE CAR

club chair *n* **:** a deep low thickly upholstered easy chair often with rather low back and heavy sides and arms

club·foot \'kləb-'fu̇t\ *n* **:** a misshapen foot twisted out of position from birth; *also* **:** this deformity — **club·foot·ed** \-'fu̇t-əd\ *adj*

club·house \'kləb-ˌhau̇s\ *n* **1 :** a house occupied by a club or used for club activities **2 :** locker rooms used by an athletic team

club moss *n* **:** any of an order (Lycopodiales) of primitive vascular plants often with the sporangia borne in club-shaped strobiles

club steak *n* **:** a small steak cut from the end of the short loin

¹**cluck** \'klək\ *vb* [imit.] *vi* **1 :** to make a cluck **2 :** to make a clicking sound with the tongue ~ *vt* **:** to call with a cluck

²**cluck** *n* **1 :** the characteristic sound made by a hen esp. in calling her chicks **2 :** a broody fowl

clue *var of* CLEW

clum·ber spaniel \ˌkləm-bər-\ *n, often cap C & S* [*Clumber*, estate in Nottinghamshire, England] **:** a large massive heavyset spaniel with a dense silky largely white coat

¹**clump** \'kləmp\ *n* [prob. fr. LG *klump;* akin to OE *clamm*] **1 :** a group of things clustered together **2 :** a compact mass **3 :** a heavy tramping sound — **clumpy** \'kləm-pē\ *adj*

²**clump** *vi* **1 :** to tread clumsily and noisily **2 :** to form clumps ~ *vt* **:** to arrange in or cause to form clumps

clum·si·ly \'kləm-zə-lē\ *adv* **:** in a clumsy manner

clum·si·ness \-zē-nəs\ *n* **:** the quality of being clumsy

clum·sy \'kləm-zē\ *adj* [prob. fr. obs. E *clumse* (benumbed with cold)] **1 a :** lacking dexterity, nimbleness, or grace ⟨~ fingers⟩ **b :** lacking tact or subtlety ⟨a ~ joke⟩ **2 :** awkwardly or poorly made **:** UNWIELDY **syn** see AWKWARD

clung *past of* CLING

clu·pe·id \'klü-pē-əd\ *n* [deriv. of L *clupea*, a small river fish] **:** any of a large family (Clupeidae) of soft-finned teleost fishes

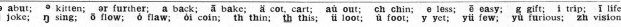

including the herrings and related forms — **clupeid** *adj*

1clus·ter \'kləs-tər\ *n* [ME, fr. OE *clyster;* akin to OE *clott* clot] **1 :** a number of similar things growing together or of things or persons collected or grouped closely together **:** BUNCH **2 :** two or more consecutive consonants or vowels in a segment of speech — **clus·tery** \-t(ə-)rē\ *adj*

2cluster *vb* **clus·ter·ing** \-t(ə-)riŋ\ *vt* **1 :** to collect into a cluster **2 :** to furnish with clusters ~ *vi* **:** to grow or assemble in a cluster

1clutch \'kləch\ *vb* [ME *clucchen,* fr. OE *clyccan;* akin to MIr *glacc* hand — more at CLING] *vt* **1 :** to grasp or hold with or as if with the hand or claws usu. strongly, tightly, or suddenly **2** *obs* **:** CLENCH ~ *vi* **:** to seek to grasp and hold **syn** see TAKE

2clutch *n* **1 a :** the claws or a hand in the act of grasping or seizing firmly **b :** CONTROL, POWER **c :** the act of grasping, holding, or restraining **2 :** a device for gripping an object (as at the end of a chain or tackle) **3 a :** a coupling used to connect and disconnect a driving and a driven part of a mechanism **b :** a lever operating such a clutch **4 :** a tight or critical situation **:** PINCH

3clutch *n* [alter. of dial. E *cletch* (hatching, brood)] **:** a nest of eggs or a brood of chicks

1clut·ter \'klət-ər\ *vb* [ME *clotteren* to clot, fr. *clot*] *vt* **:** to fill or cover with scattered or disordered things that impede movement or reduce effectiveness ~ *vi, chiefly dial* **:** to run in disorder

2clutter *n* **1 a :** a crowded or confused mass or collection **b :** LITTER, DISORDER **2** *chiefly dial* **:** DISTURBANCE, HUBBUB

Clydes·dale \'klīdz-,dāl\ *n* **:** a heavy feathered-legged draft horse of a breed orig. from Clydesdale, Scotland

Clydesdale terrier *n* **:** a small terrier of a breed distinguished by erect ears, long silky coat, and short legs

clyp·e·ate \'klip-ē-ət\ *or* **clyp·e·at·ed** \-ē-,āt-əd\ *adj* **1 :** SCUTATE **2 :** having a clypeus or peltate part

clyp·e·us \'klip-ē-əs\ *n, pl* **clyp·ei** \-ē-ī, -ē-,ē\ [NL] **:** a plate on the anterior median aspect of an insect's head

clys·ter \'klis-tər\ *n* [ME, fr. MF or L; MF *clistere,* fr. L *clyster,* fr. Gk *klystēr,* fr. *klyzein* to wash out] **:** ENEMA

Cly·tem·nes·tra \,klīt-əm-'nes-trə\ *n* [L, fr. Gk *Klytaimnēstra*] **:** the wife of Agamemnon

c–mitosis *n* [colchicine + *mitosis*] **:** an artificially induced abortive nuclear division in which the chromosome number is doubled — **c–mitotic** *adj*

co- *prefix* [ME, fr. L, fr. *com-;* akin to OE *ge-,* perfective and collective prefix, Gk *koinos* common] **1 :** with **:** together **:** joint **:** jointly ⟨*co*exist⟩ ⟨*co*heir⟩ **2 :** in or to the same degree ⟨*co*extensive⟩ **3 a :** fellow **:** partner ⟨*co*author⟩ ⟨*co*-worker⟩ **b :** having a usu. lesser share in duty or responsibility **:** alternate **:** deputy ⟨*co*pilot⟩ **4 :** of, relating to, or constituting the complement of an angle ⟨*co*sine⟩ ⟨*co*declination⟩

co·ac·er·vate \kō-'as-ər-,vāt\ *n* [L *coacervatus,* pp. of *coacervere* to heap up, fr. *co-* + *acervus* heap] **:** an aggregate of colloidal droplets held together by electrostatic attractive forces — **co·ac·er·va·tion** \(,)kō-,as-ər-'vā-shən\ *n*

1coach \'kōch\ *n, often attrib* [ME *coche,* fr. MF, fr. G *kutsche*] **1 a :** a large usu. closed four-wheeled carriage having doors in the sides and an elevated seat in front for the driver **b :** a railroad passenger car intended primarily for day travel **c :** BUS 1a **d :** a house trailer **e :** an automobile body esp. of a closed model **f :** a class of passenger air transportation at a lower fare than first class **2** [fr. the concept that the tutor conveys the student through his examinations] **a :** a private tutor **b :** one who instructs or trains a performer or a team of performers; *specif* **:** one who instructs players in the fundamentals of a competitive sport and directs team strategy

coach 1a

2coach *vt* **1 :** to train intensively by instruction, demonstration, and practice **2 :** to act as coach to **3 :** to direct the movements of (a player) ~ *vi* **1 :** to go in a coach **2 :** to instruct, direct, or prompt as a coach — **coach·er** *n*

coach dog *n* **:** DALMATIAN

coach·man \'kōch-mən\ *n* **1 :** a man whose business is to drive a coach or carriage **2 :** an artificial fly with white wings, peacock feather body, brown hackle, and gold tag

co·act \kō-'akt\ *vi* **:** to act or work together — **co·ac·tive** \-'ak-tiv\ *adj*

co·ac·tion \-'ak-shən\ *n* **1 :** joint action **2 :** the interaction between individuals or kinds (as species) in an ecological community

co·ad·ju·tor \,kō-ə-'jüt-ər, kō-'aj-ət-ər\ *n* [ME *coadjutour,* fr. MF *coadjuteur,* fr. L *coadjutor,* fr. *co-* + *adjutor* aid, fr. *adjutus,* pp. of *adjuvare* to help — more at AID] **1 :** one who works together with another **:** ASSISTANT **2 :** a bishop assisting a diocesan bishop and having the right of succession — **coadjutor** *adj*

co·ad·u·nate \kō-'aj-ə-nət, -,nāt\ *adj* [LL *coadunatus,* pp. of *coadunare* to combine, fr. L *co-* + *adunare* to unite, fr. *ad-* + *unus* one — more at ONE] **:** UNITED; *esp* **:** grown together **:** CONFLUENT — **co·ad·u·na·tion** \(,)kō-,aj-ə-'nā-shən\ *n*

co·ag·u·la·bil·i·ty \kō-,ag-yə-lə-'bil-ət-ē\ *n* **:** the quality or state of being coagulable

co·ag·u·la·ble \kō-'ag-yə-lə-bəl\ *adj* **:** capable of being coagulated

co·ag·u·lant \-yə-lənt\ *n* **:** something that produces coagulation

co·ag·u·lase \-,lās, -,lāz\ *n* **:** an enzyme that causes coagulation

1co·ag·u·late \kō-'ag-yə-lət, -,lāt\ *adj* **:** COAGULATED

2co·ag·u·late \-,lāt\ *vb* [L *coagulatus,* pp. of *coagulare* to curdle, fr. *coagulum* curdling agent, fr. *cogere* to drive together — more at COGENT] *vt* **:** to cause to become viscous or thickened into a coherent mass **:** CURDLE, CLOT ~ *vi* **:** to become coagulated — **co·ag·u·la·tion** \(,)kō-,ag-yə-'lā-shən\ *n*

co·ag·u·lum \kō-'ag-yə-ləm\ *n, pl* **co·ag·u·la** \-lə\ [L, coagulant] **:** a coagulated mass or substance **:** CLOT, CURD

1coal \'kōl\ *n, often attrib* [ME *col,* fr. OE; akin to OHG & ON *kol* burning ember, IrGael *gual* coal] **1 :** a piece of glowing carbon or charred wood **:** EMBER **2 :** CHARCOAL 1 **3 a :** a black or brownish black solid combustible substance formed by the partial decomposition of vegetable matter without free access of air and under the influence of moisture and often increased pressure and temperature that is widely used as a natural fuel **b** *pl, Brit* **:** pieces or a quantity of the fuel broken up for burning

2coal *vt* **1 :** to burn to charcoal **:** CHAR **2 :** to supply with coal ~ *vi* **:** to take in coal

coal·er \'kō-lər\ *n* **:** something employed in transporting or supplying coal

co·alesce \,kō-ə-'les\ *vi* [L *coalescere,* fr. *co-* + *alescere* to grow] **1 :** to grow together **2 :** to unite into a whole **:** FUSE **syn** see MIX — **co·ales·cence** \-'les-ᵊn(t)s\ *n* — **co·ales·cent** \-ᵊnt\ *adj*

coal·fish \'kōl-,fish\ *n* **:** any of several blackish or dark-backed fishes (as a pollack or sablefish)

coal gas *n* **:** gas made from coal: as **a :** the mixture of gases thrown off by burning coal **b :** gas made by carbonizing bituminous coal in retorts and used for heating and lighting

coaling station *n* **:** a port at which vessels may coal

co·ali·tion \,kō-ə-'lish-ən\ *n, often attrib* [MF, fr. L *coalitus,* pp. of *coalescere*] **1 a :** the act of coalescing **:** UNION **b :** a body formed by the coalescing of orig. distinct elements **:** COMBINATION **2 :** a temporary alliance of distinct parties, persons, or states for joint action — **co·ali·tion·ist** \-'lish-(ə-)nəst\ *n*

coal measures *n pl* **:** beds of coal with the associated rocks

coal oil *n* **1 :** petroleum or a refined oil prepared from it **2 :** KEROSINE

Coal·sack \'kōl-,sak\ *n* **:** either of two dark nebulae in the Milky Way located one near the Northern Cross and the other near the Southern Cross

coal tar *n* **:** tar obtained by distillation of bituminous coal

coal–tar dye *n* **:** a dye made from a coal-tar derivative; *broadly* **:** a synthetic organic dye

coam·ing \'kō-miŋ\ *n* [prob. irreg. fr. *comb*] **:** a raised frame (as around a hatchway in the deck of a ship) to keep out water

co·apt \kō-'apt\ *vt* [LL *coaptare,* fr. L *co-* + *aptus* fastened, fit] **:** to fit together and make fast — **co·ap·ta·tion** \(,)kō-,ap-'tā-shən\ *n*

co·arc·tate \kō-'ärk-,tāt\ *adj* [L *coarctatus,* pp. of *coartare* to press together, fr. *co-* + *artus* narrow, confined; akin to L *artus* joint] **:** CONSTRICTED; *specif* **:** enclosed in a rigid case — **co·arc·ta·tion** \(,)kō-,ärk-'tā-shən\ *n*

coarse \'kō(ə)rs, 'kȯ(ə)rs\ *adj* [ME *cors,* fr *course,* n.,] **1 :** of ordinary or inferior quality or value **:** COMMON, BASE **2 a** (1) **:** composed of relatively large parts or particles ⟨~ sand⟩ (2) **:** loose or rough in texture ⟨~ skin⟩ **b :** adjusted or designed for heavy, fast, or less delicate work **c :** not precise or detailed with respect to adjustment or discrimination **3 :** crude or unrefined in taste, manners, or language **4 :** harsh, raucous, or rough in tone — **coarse·ly** *adv* — **coarse·ness** *n*

syn VULGAR, GROSS, OBSCENE, RIBALD: COARSE implies roughness, rudeness, or crudeness of spirit, behavior, or language; VULGAR is more condemnatory and implies actual offensiveness to good taste; GROSS implies extreme coarseness and insensitiveness; OBSCENE applies to anything strongly repulsive to the physical senses or the sense of decency and propriety but esp. to flagrant violation of taboo in sexual matters; RIBALD applies to what is amusingly or picturesquely vulgar or irreverent or mildly indecent

coarse–grained \-'grānd\ *adj* **1 :** having a coarse grain **2 :** CRUDE

coars·en \'kōrs-ᵊn, 'kȯrs-\ *vb* **coars·en·ing** \'kōrs-niŋ, 'kȯrs-, -ᵊn-iŋ\ *vt* **:** to make coarse ~ *vi* **:** to become coarse

1coast \'kōst\ *n* [ME *cost,* fr. MF *coste,* fr. L *costa* rib, side; akin to OSlav *kosti* bone] **1** *obs* **:** BORDER, FRONTIER **2 :** land near the seashore **:** SEASHORE **3 :** a hill or slope suited to coasting; *also* **:** a slide down a slope (as on a sled) — **coast·al** \'kōst-ᵊl\ *adj*

2coast *vt* **1** *obs* **:** to move along or past the side of **:** SKIRT **2 :** to sail along the shore of ~ *vi* **1 a** *archaic* **:** to travel on land along a coast or along or past the side of something **b :** to sail along the shore **2 a :** to slide, run, or glide downhill by the force of gravity **b :** to move along without or as if without further application of propulsive power (as by momentum or gravity)

coast artillery *n* **:** artillery for defending a coast

coast·er \'kō-stər\ *n* **1 :** one that coasts: as **a :** a person engaged in coastal traffic or commerce **b :** a ship sailing along a coast or engaged in trade between ports of the same country **2 a :** a round tray usu. of silver and often on wheels that is used for circulating a decanter after a meal **b :** a shallow container or a plate or mat to protect a surface **c :** a small vehicle used in coasting

coaster brake *n* **:** a brake in the hub of the rear wheel of a bicycle operated by reverse pressure on the pedals

coast guard *n* **1 :** a military or naval force employed in guarding a coast or responsible for the safety, order, and operation of maritime traffic in neighboring waters **2 :** a member of a coast guard

coast·guards·man \'kōs(t)-,gärdz-mən\ *or* **coast·guard·man** \-,gärd-mən\ *n* **:** a member of a coast guard

coast·line \'kōst-,līn\ *n* **:** the outline or shape of a coast

coast·ward \'kōs-twərd\ *or* **coast·wards** \-twərdz\ *adv* **:** toward the coast — **coastward** *adj*

coast·wise \'kōs-,twīz\ *adv* **:** by way of or along the coast — **coastwise** *adj*

1coat \'kōt\ *n, often attrib* [ME *cote,* fr. OF, of Gmc origin; akin to OHG *kozza* coarse mantle] **1 a :** an outer garment varying in length and style according to fashion and use **b :** something resembling a coat **2 :** the external growth on an animal **3 :** a layer of one substance covering another — **coat·ed** \-əd\ *adj*

2coat *vt* **1 :** to cover with a coat **2 :** to cover or spread with a finishing, protecting, or enclosing layer

co·ati \kə-'wät-ē, ,kō-ə-'tē\ *n* [Pg *coatí,* fr. Tupi] **:** a tropical American mammal (genus *Nasua*) related to the raccoon but with a longer body and tail and a long flexible snout

coat·ing \'kōt-iŋ\ *n* **1 :** COAT, COVERING **2 :** cloth for coats

coat of arms [trans. of F *cotte d'armes*] **1 :** a tabard or surcoat embroidered with armorial bearings **2 a :** the particular heraldic bearings (as of a person) usu. depicted on an escutcheon **b :** a similar symbolic emblem

coat·tail \'kōt-,tāl\ *n* **1 :** the rear flap of a man's coat **2** *pl* **:** the skirts of a dress coat, cutaway, or frock coat

co·au·thor \(')kō-'ȯ-thər\ *n* **:** a joint or associate author

coax \'kōks\ *vt* [earlier *cokes,* fr. *cokes,* n. (simpleton)] **1** *obs* **:** FONDLE, PET **2 :** to influence or urge by gentle urging, caressing, or flattering **:** WHEEDLE **3 :** to draw, gain, or persuade by means of gentle urging or flattery — **coax·er** *n*

co·ax·i·al \(')kō-'ak-sē-əl\ *adj* **1 :** having coincident axes **2 :** mounted on concentric shafts — **co·ax·i·al·ly** \-ə-lē\ *adv*

coaxial cable *n* **:** a cable that consists of a tube of electrically conducting material surrounding a central conductor held in place by insulators and that is used to transmit telegraph, telephone, and television signals of high frequency
cob \'käb\ *n* [ME *cobbe* leader; akin to OE *cot* cottage — more at COT] **1 :** a male swan **2** *dial Eng* **:** a rounded mass, lump, or heap **3 :** a piece of eight **:** a Spanish-American dollar **4 :** CORNCOB 1 **5 :** a short-legged stocky horse usu. with an artificially high stylish action — **cob·by** \'käb-ē\ *adj*
co·balt \'kō-,bȯlt\ *n* [G *kobalt,* alter. of *kobold,* lit., goblin, fr. MHG *kobolt*] **:** a tough lustrous silver-white magnetic metallic element that is related to and occurs with iron and nickel — see ELEMENT table—**co·bal·tic** \kō-'bȯl-tik\ *adj*—**co·bal·tous** \-təs\ *adj*
cobalt blue *n* **:** a greenish blue pigment consisting essentially of cobalt oxide and alumina
co·balt·ite \'kō-,bȯl-,tīt\ *or* **co·balt·ine** \'kō-,bȯl-,tēn\ *n* [*cobaltite,* alter. of *cobaltine,* fr. F, fr. *cobalt*] **:** a mineral consisting of a grayish to silver-white cobalt sulfarsenide CoAsS used in making smalt
cobalt 60 *n* **:** a heavy radioactive isotope of cobalt of the mass number 60 produced in nuclear reactors and used as a source of gamma rays
cob·ber \'käb-ər\ *n* [origin unknown] *Austral* **:** BUDDY
[1]**cob·ble** \'käb-əl\ *vt* **cob·bling** \-(ə-)liŋ\ [ME *coblen,* perh. back-formation fr. *cobelere* cobbler] **1** *chiefly Brit* **:** to mend or patch coarsely **2 :** to make or put together roughly or hastily
[2]**cobble** *n* [back-formation fr. *cobblestone*] **1 :** a naturally rounded stone larger than a pebble and smaller than a boulder; *esp* **:** such a stone used in paving a street or in other construction **2** *pl, chiefly Brit* **:** lump coal about the size of small cobblestones
[3]**cobble** *vt* **cob·bling** \-(ə-)liŋ\ **:** to pave with cobblestones
cob·bler \'käb-lər\ *n* [ME *cobelere*] **1 :** a mender or maker of shoes and often of other leather goods **2** *archaic* **:** a clumsy workman **3 :** a tall iced drink consisting usu. of wine, rum, or whiskey and sugar garnished with mint or a slice of lemon or orange **4 :** a deep-dish fruit pie with a thick top crust
cob·ble·stone \'käb-əl-,stōn\ *n* [ME, fr. *cobble-* (prob. fr. *cob*) + *stone*] **:** [2]COBBLE 1
cob coal *n* **:** coal in large rounded lumps
co·bel·lig·er·ent \,kō-bə-'lij-(ə-)rənt\ *n* **:** a country fighting with another power against a common enemy — **cobelligerent** *adj*
co·bia \'kō-bē-ə\ *n* [origin unknown] **:** a large percoid fish (*Rachycentron canadus*) of warm seas outstanding as a food and sport fish
co·ble \'kō-bəl\ *n* [ME] *Scot* **:** a short flat-bottomed boat
cob·nut \'käb-,nət\ *n* **:** the fruit of a European hazel (*Corylus avellana grandis*); *also* **:** the plant bearing this fruit
co·bra \'kō-brə\ *n* [Pg *cobra* (*de capello*), lit., hooded snake, fr. L *colubra* snake] **:** any of several venomous Asiatic and African elapid snakes (genus *Naja*) that when excited expand the skin of the neck into a hood by movement of the anterior ribs; *also* **:** any of several related African snakes
cob·web \'käb-,web\ *n* [ME *coppeweb,* fr. *coppe* spider (fr. OE *ātorcoppe*) + *web;* akin to MD *coppe* spider] **1 :** the network spread by a spider **2 :** a single thread spun by a spider or insect larva **3 :** something resembling a spider web — **cob·webbed** \-,webd\ *adj* — **cob·web·by** \-,web-ē\ *adj*
co·ca \'kō-kə\ *n* [Sp, fr. Quechua *kúka*] **1 :** any of several So. American shrubs (genus *Erythroxylon,* family Erythroxylaceae); *esp* **:** one (*E. coca*) with leaves resembling tea **2 :** dried leaves of a coca (as *E. coca*) containing alkaloids including cocaine
co·caine \kō-'kān, 'kō-,\ *n* **:** a bitter crystalline alkaloid $C_{17}H_{21}NO_4$ obtained from coca leaves and used as a narcotic and local anesthetic
co·cain·ism \kō-'kā-,niz-əm\ *n* **:** addiction to cocaine
co·cain·ize \kō-'kā-,nīz\ *vt* **:** to treat or anesthetize with cocaine
coc·cal \'käk-əl\ *adj* **:** of or relating to a coccus
coc·cid \'käk-səd\ *n* [NL *Coccus,* genus of scales, fr. Gk *kokkos* grain, kermes berry] **:** SCALE INSECT, MEALYBUG
coc·cid·i·oi·do·my·co·sis \(,)käk-,sid-ē-,ȯid-ō-(,)mī-'kō-səs\ *n* [NL, fr. *Coccidioides,* genus of fungi, (fr. *coccidium*) + *mycosis*] **:** a disease of man and lower animals caused by a fungus (*Coccidioides immitis*) and marked esp. by fever and localized pulmonary symptoms
coc·cid·i·o·sis \(,)käk-,sid-ē-'ō-səs\ *n* **:** infestation with or disease caused by coccidia
coc·cid·i·um \käk-'sid-ē-əm\ *n, pl* **coc·cid·ia** \-ē-ə\ [NL, dim. of *coccus*] **:** any of an order (Coccidia) of protozoans usu. parasitic in the digestive epithelium of vertebrates
coc·coid \'käk-,ȯid\ *adj* **:** related to or resembling a coccus **:** GLOBOSE — **coccoid** *n*
coc·cus \'käk-əs\ *n, pl* **coc·ci** \'käk-,(s)ī, 'käk-(,)(s)ē\ [NL, fr. Gk *kokkos*] **1 :** one of the separable carpels of a schizocarp **2 :** a spherical bacterium
-coccus *n comb form, pl* **-cocci** [NL, fr. Gk *kokkos*] **:** berry-shaped organism ⟨Micro*coccus*⟩
coc·cyg·eal \käk-'sij-(ē-)əl\ *adj* [ML *coccygeus* of the coccyx, fr. Gk *kokkyk-, kokkyx*] **:** of or relating to the coccyx
coc·cyx \'käk-siks\ *n, pl* **coc·cy·ges** \'käk-sə-,jēz, käk-'sī-(,)jēz\ *also* **coc·cyx·es** \'käk-sik-səz\ [NL, fr. Gk *kokkyx* cuckoo, coccyx; fr. its resemblance to a cuckoo's beak] **:** the end of the vertebral column beyond the sacrum in man and tailless apes
Co·chin Chi·na \,kō-chən-'chī-nə, ,käch-ən-\ *n* **:** any of an Asian breed of large domestic fowls with thick plumage, small wings and tail, and densely feathered legs and feet
co·chi·neal \'käch-ə-,nēl, 'kō-chə-\ *n* [MF & Sp; MF *cochenille,* fr. OSp *cochinilla* wood louse, cochineal] **:** a red dyestuff consisting of the dried bodies of female cochineal insects used esp. as a biological stain and as an indicator
cochineal insect *n* **:** a small bright red insect (*Dactylopius coccus*) that is related to and resembles the mealybug and feeds on cactus
coch·lea \'käk-lē-ə\ *n, pl* **coch·le·ae** \-lē-,ē, -,ī\ *or* **coch·le·as** [NL, fr. L, snail, snail shell, fr. Gk *kochlias,* fr. *kochlos* land snail; akin to Gk *konchē* mussel] **:** a division of the labyrinth of the ear of higher vertebrates that is usu. coiled like a snail shell and is the seat of the hearing organ — **coch·le·ar** \-lē-ər\ *adj*
coch·le·ate \'käk-lē-ət,-,āt\ *or* **coch·le·at·ed** \-,āt-əd\ *adj* **:** having the form of a snail shell
[1]**cock** \'käk\ *n* [ME *cok,* fr. OE *cocc,* of imit. origin] **1 a :** the adult male of the domestic fowl (*Gallus gallus*) **b :** the male of birds other than the domestic fowl **c :** WOODCOCK **d** *archaic* **:** the crowing of a cock; *also* **:** COCKCROW **e :** WEATHERCOCK **2 :** a device (as a faucet or valve) for regulating the flow of a liquid **3 a :** a chief person **:** LEADER **b :** a person of spirit and often a certain swagger or arrogance **4 a :** the hammer in the lock of a firearm **b :** the cocked position of the hammer — **cock of the walk :** one who dominates a group or situation esp. overbearingly

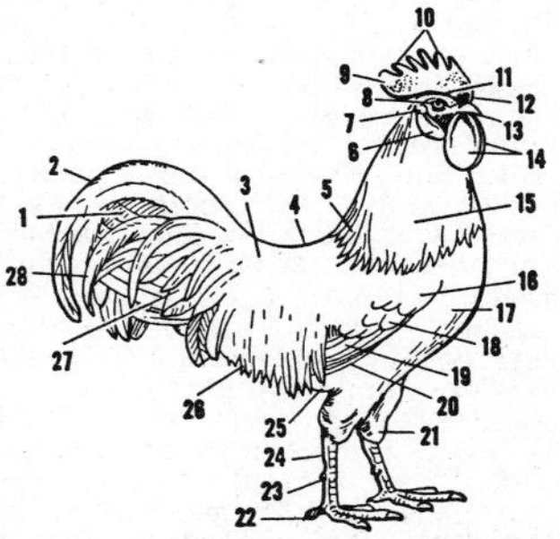

diagram of male fowl: *1* main tail, *2* sickles, *3* saddle, *4* back, *5* cape, *6* ear lobe, *7* ear, *8* eye, *9* blade, *10* points, *11* base, *12* comb, *13* beak, *14* wattles, *15* hackle, *16* wing bow, *17* breast, *18* wing bar, *19* secondaries, *20* primaries, *21* hock, *22* claw, *23* spur, *24* shank, *25* fluff, *26* saddle feathers, *27* tail coverts, *28* lesser sickles

[2]**cock** *vi* **1 :** STRUT, SWAGGER **2 :** to turn, tip, or stick up **3 :** to position the hammer of a firearm for firing ~ *vt* **1 a :** to draw the hammer of (a firearm) back and set for firing; *also* **:** to set (the trigger) for firing **b :** to draw or bend back in preparation to throw or hit **c :** to set a mechanism for tripping **2 a :** to set erect **b :** to turn, tip, or tilt usu. to one side **c :** to lift and place high **3 :** to turn up (as a hat brim)
[3]**cock** *n* **:** TILT, SLANT ⟨~ of the head⟩
[4]**cock** *n* [ME *cok,* of Scand origin] **:** a small pile (as of hay)
[5]**cock** *vt* **:** to put (as hay) into cocks
cock·ade \kä-'kād\ *n* [modif. of F *cocarde,* fr. fem. of *cocard* vain, fr. *coq* cock, fr. OF *coc,* of imit. origin] **:** a rosette or a similar ornament worn on the hat as a badge — **cock·ad·ed** \-əd\ *adj*
cock–a–hoop \,käk-ə-'hüp, -'hu̇p\ *adj* [fr. the phrase *to set cock a hoop* to be festive] **1 :** triumphantly boastful **:** EXULTING **2 :** AWRY
Cock·aigne \kä-'kān\ *n* [ME *cokaygne,* fr. MF (*pais de*) *cocaigne* land of plenty] **:** an imaginary land of extreme luxury and ease
cock–a–leek·ie \,käk-i-'lē-kē\ *n* [alter. of *cockie* (dim. of [1]*cock*) + *leekie,* dim. of *leek*] **:** a soup made of chicken boiled with leeks
cock·a·lo·rum \,käk-ə-'lōr-əm, -'lȯr-\ *n* [prob. modif. of obs. Flem *kockeloeren* to crow, of imit. origin] **1 :** a self-important little man **2 :** the game of leapfrog **3 :** boastful talk
cock–and–bull story \,käk-ən-'bu̇l-\ *n* **:** an extravagant incredible story told as true
cock·a·tiel \,käk-ə-'tē(ə)l\ *n* [D *kaketielje,* deriv. of Malay *kakatua*] **:** a small crested gray Australian parrot (*Nymphicus hollandicus*) with a yellow head
cock·a·too \'käk-ə-,tü\ *n* [D *kaketoe,* fr. Malay *kakatua,* fr. *kakak* elder sibling + *tua* old] **:** any of numerous large noisy usu. showy and crested chiefly Australasian parrots (esp. genus *Kakatoe*)
cock·a·trice \'käk-ə-trəs, -,trīs\ *n* [ME *cocatrice,* fr. MF *cocatris* ichneumon, cockatrice, fr. ML *cocatric-, cockatrix* ichneumon] **:** a legendary serpent with deadly glance hatched by a reptile from a cock's egg on a dunghill
cock·boat \'käk-,bōt\ *n* **:** a small boat; *esp* **:** one used as a tender to a larger boat
cock·cha·fer \'käk-,chā-fər\ *n* [[1]*cock* + *chafer*] **:** a large European beetle (*Melolontha melolontha*) destructive to vegetation both as larva and adult; *also* **:** any of various related beetles
cock·crow \'käk-,krō\ *n* **:** the time at which cocks first crow **:** early morning
cocked hat \'käkt-\ *n* **1 :** a hat with brim turned up to give a three-cornered appearance **2 :** a hat with brim turned up on two sides and worn either front to back or sideways
[1]**cock·er** \'käk-ər\ *vt* [ME *cokeren*] **:** INDULGE, PAMPER
[2]**cocker** *n* **:** a keeper or handler of fighting cocks
cock·er·el \'käk-(ə-)rəl\ *n* [ME *cokerelle,* fr. OF dial. *kokerel,* dim. of OF *coc*] **:** a young male domestic fowl
cock·er spaniel \,käk-ər-\ *n* [*cocking* (woodcock hunting)] **:** a small spaniel with long ears, square muzzle, and silky coat
cock·eye \'käk-'ī, -,ī\ *n* **:** a squinting eye
cock·eyed \'käk-'īd\ *adj* **1 :** having a cockeye **2 a :** ASKEW, AWRY **b :** slightly crazy **:** TOPSY-TURVY **c :** DRUNK
cock·fight \'käk-,fīt\ *n* **:** a contest of gamecocks usu. fitted with metal spurs — **cock·fight·ing** \-iŋ\ *adj or n*
cock·horse \'käk-,hȯ(ə)rs\ *n* [perh. fr. *cock,* adj., (male) + *horse*] **:** ROCKING HORSE
cock·i·ness \'käk-ē-nəs\ *n* **:** the quality or state of being cocky
[1]**cock·le** \'käk-əl\ *n* [ME, fr. OE *coccel*] **:** any of several grainfield weeds; *esp* **:** CORN COCKLE
[2]**cockle** *n* [ME *cokille,* fr. MF *coquille* shell, modif. of L *conchylia,* pl. of *conchylium,* fr. Gk *konchylion,* fr. *konchē* conch] **1 :** a bivalve mollusk (family Cardiidae) having a shell with convex radially ribbed valves; *esp* **:** a common edible European bivalve (*Cardium edule*) **2 :** COCKLESHELL
[3]**cockle** *n* [MF *coquille*] **:** PUCKER, WRINKLE — **cockle** *vb*
cock·le·bur \'käk-əl-,bər, 'kək-\ *n* **:** any of a genus (*Xanthium*) of prickly-fruited composite plants; *also* **:** one of its stiff-spined fruits
cock·le·shell \'käk-əl-,shel\ *n* **1 a :** the shell or one of the shell valves of a cockle **b :** a shell (as a scallop shell) suggesting this **2 :** a light flimsy boat
cock·les of the heart \,käk-əlz-\ [perh. fr. [2]*cockle*] **:** the core of one's being
cock·loft \'käk-,lȯft\ *n* [prob. fr. [1]*cock*] **:** a small garret
cock·ney \'käk-nē\ *n* [ME *cokeney,* lit., cock's egg, fr. *coken* (gen. pl. of *cok* cock) + *ey* egg, fr. OE *ǣg*] **1** *obs* **a :** a spoiled child **b :** a squeamish woman **2 a :** a native of London and esp. of the East End of London **b :** the dialect of London or of the East End of London — **cockney** *adj* — **cock·ney·ish** \-ish\ *adj* — **cock·ney·ism** \-,iz-əm\ *n*

cock·ney·fy \'käk-ni-,fī\ *vt* **:** to make cockney or like a cockney
cock·pit \'käk-,pit\ *n* **1 :** a pit for cockfights **2** *obs* **:** the pit of a theater **3 a :** an apartment of an old sailing warship used as quarters for junior officers and for treatment of the wounded in an engagement **b :** an open space aft of a decked area from which a small ship is steered **c :** a space in the fuselage of an airplane for the pilot or the pilot and passengers or in large passenger planes the pilot and crew **d :** a space resembling an airplane cockpit
cock·roach \'käk-,rōch\ *n* [by folk etymology fr. Sp *cucaracha* cockroach, irreg. fr. *cuca* caterpillar] **:** any of an order (Blattaria) of chiefly nocturnal insects including some that are domestic pests
cocks·comb \'käk-,skōm\ *n* **1 :** COXCOMB **2 :** a garden plant (genus *Celosia*) of the amaranth family grown for its flowers
cock·shut \'käk-,shət\ *n* [fr. the time poultry are shut in to rest] *dial Eng* **:** evening twilight
cock·shy \-,shī\ *n* [1*cock* + *shy*, n.] **:** a throw at an object set up as a mark; *also* **:** a mark or target so set up
cock·sure \'käk-'shu̇(ə)r\ *adj* [prob. fr. 1*cock* + *sure*] **1 :** perfectly sure **:** CERTAIN **2 :** marked by overconfidence or presumptuousness **:** COCKY **syn** see SURE — **cock·sure·ly** *adv* — **cock·sure·ness** *n*
1**cock·tail** \'käk-,tāl\ *n* [1*cock* + *tail*] **1 :** a horse with its tail docked **2 :** a horse not of pure breed
2**cocktail** *n* [prob. fr. 1*cock* + *tail*] **1 :** an iced drink of distilled liquor mixed with flavoring ingredients **2 :** an appetizer (as tomato juice) served as a first course at a meal
3**cocktail** *adj* **:** designed for semiformal wear ⟨~ dress⟩
cocky \'käk-ē\ *adj* **1 :** PERT, ARROGANT **2 :** JAUNTY
1**co·co** \'kō-(,)kō\ *n* [Sp & Pg; Sp, fr. Pg *côco*, lit., bogeyman] **:** the coconut palm or its fruit
2**coco** *adj* **:** made from the fibrous husk of the coconut
co·coa \'kō-(,)kō\ *n* [modif. of Sp *cacao*] **1 :** CACAO 1 **2 a :** chocolate deprived of a portion of its fat and pulverized **b :** a beverage prepared by cooking the resulting powder with water or milk
cocoa butter *n* **:** a pale low-melting fat from cacao beans
1**co·con·scious** \(')kō-'kän-chəs\ *adj* **:** conscious of the same things
2**coconscious** *or* **co·con·scious·ness** *n* **:** mental processes outside the main stream of consciousness but sometimes available to it
co·co·nut *also* **co·coa·nut** \'kō-kə-(,)nət\ *n* **:** the drupaceous fruit of the coconut palm whose outer fibrous husk yields coir and whose nut contains thick edible meat and coconut milk
coconut palm *n* **:** a tall pinnate-leaved tropical palm (*Cocos nucifera*) prob. of American origin
co·coon \kə-'kün\ *n* [F *cocon*, fr. Prov *coucoun*, fr. *coco* shell, fr. L *coccum* excrescence on a tree, fr. Gk *kokkos* grain seed, kermes berry] **1 a :** an envelope often largely of silk which an insect larva forms about itself and in which it passes the pupa stage **b :** any of various other protective coverings produced by animals **2 :** a covering suggesting a cocoon; *specif* **:** a protective covering placed or sprayed over military or naval equipment in storage
co·cotte \kȯ-kȯt\ *n, pl* **cocottes** \-kȯt(s)\ [F] **:** PROSTITUTE
coc·o·zel·le \,käk-ə-'zel-ē\ *n* [prob. deriv. of It *cocuzza* squash] **:** a summer squash resembling the zucchini
Co·cy·tus \kō-'sīt-əs\ *n* [L, fr. Gk *Kōkytos*] **:** a river tributary to the Acheron in Hades
cod \'käd\ *n, pl* **cod** *also* **cods** [ME] **1 a :** a soft-finned fish (*Gadus morrhua*) of the colder parts of the No. Atlantic that is a major food fish **b :** a fish of the cod family (Gadidae); *esp* **:** a Pacific fish (*Gadus macrocephalus*) closely related to the Atlantic cod **2 :** any of various spiny-finned fishes resembling the true cods
co·da \'kōd-ə\ *n* [It, lit., tail, fr. L *cauda*] **:** a concluding musical section that is formally distinct from the main structure
cod·dle \'käd-ᵊl\ *vt* **cod·dling** \'käd-liŋ, -ᵊl-iŋ\ [perh. fr. *caudle*] **1 :** to cook (as eggs) in liquid slowly and gently just below the boiling point **2 :** to treat with extreme care **:** PAMPER
1**code** \'kōd\ *n* [ME, fr. MF, fr. L *caudex*, *codex* trunk of a tree, tablet of wood covered with wax for writing on, book; akin to L *cudere* to beat] **1 :** a systematic statement of a body of law; *esp* **:** one given statutory force **2 :** a system of principles or rules **3 :** a system of signals for communication; *also* **:** a system of words or other symbols arbitrarily used to represent words
2**code** *vt* **:** to put in or into the form or symbols of a code — **cod·er** *n*
co·dec·li·na·tion \,kō-,dek-lə-'nā-shən\ *n* **:** the complement of the declination
co·de·fen·dant \,kō-di-'fen-dənt\ *n* **:** a joint defendant
co·deine \'kō-,dēn, 'kōd-ē-ən\ *n* [F *codéine*, fr. Gk *kōdeia* poppyhead, fr. *kōos* cavity; akin to Gk *koilos* hollow] **:** a crystalline alkaloid $C_{18}H_{21}NO_3.H_2O$ associated in opium with and similar to morphine but feebler in its action and used esp. in cough remedies
co·dex \'kō-,deks\ *n, pl* **co·di·ces** \'kōd-ə-,sēz, 'käd-\ [L] **1** *obs* **:** CODE 1, 2 **2 :** a manuscript book esp. of Scripture, classics, or ancient annals
cod·fish \'käd-,fish\ *n* **:** COD; *also* **:** its flesh used as food
cod·ger \'käj-ər\ *n* [prob. alter. of *cadger*] **:** a mildly eccentric or disreputable fellow
cod·i·cil \'käd-ə-səl, -,sil\ *n* [MF *codicille*, fr. L *codicillus*, dim. of *codic-*, *codex* book] **:** a legal instrument made subsequently to a will and modifying it — **cod·i·cil·la·ry** \,käd-ə-'sil-ə-rē\ *adj*
cod·i·fi·ca·tion \,käd-ə-fə-'kā-shən, ,kōd-\ *n* **:** the act of codifying **:** the state of being codified
cod·i·fy \'käd-ə-,fī, 'kōd-\ *vt* **1 :** to reduce to a code **2 a :** SYSTEMATIZE **b :** CLASSIFY
1**cod·ling** \'käd-liŋ\ *n* **1 :** a young cod **2 :** a hake (esp. genus *Urophycis*)
2**cod·ling** \'käd-liŋ\ *or* **cod·lin** \-lən\ *n* [alter. of ME *querdlyng*] **:** a small immature apple; *also* **:** any of several elongated greenish English cooking apples
codling moth *n* **:** a small moth (*Carpocapsa pomonella*) whose larva lives in apples, pears, quinces, and English walnuts
cod·piece \'käd-,pēs\ *n* [ME *codpese*, fr. *cod* bag, scrotum (fr. OE *codd*) + *pese* piece] **:** a flap or bag concealing an opening in the front of men's breeches esp. in the 15th and 16th centuries
1**co–ed** \'kō-,ed\ *n* [short for *coeducational student*] **:** a female student in a coeducational institution
2**co–ed** *adj* **1 :** COEDUCATIONAL **2 :** of, or relating to a co-ed
co·ed·u·ca·tion \(,)kō-,ej-ə-'kā-shən\ *n* **:** the education of students of both sexes at the same institution — **co·ed·u·ca·tion·al** \-'kā-shnəl, -shən-ᵊl\ *adj* — **co·ed·u·ca·tion·al·ly** \-ē\ *adv*
co·ef·fi·cient \,kō-ə-'fish-ənt\ *n* [NL *coefficient-*, *coefficiens*, fr. L *co-* + *efficient-*, *efficiens* efficient] **1 :** any of the factors of a product considered in relation to a specific factor **2 a :** a number that serves as a measure of some property or characteristic (as of a device or process) **b :** MEASURE, DEGREE
coe·la·canth \'sē-lə-,kan(t)th\ *n* [deriv. of Gk *koilos* hollow + NL *-acanthus* — more at CAVE] **:** a fish or fossil of a family (Coelacanthidae) of mostly extinct fishes — **coelacanth** *adj* — **coe·la·can·thine** \,sē-lə-'kan-,thīn, -'kan(t)-thən\ *adj* — **coe·la·can·thous** \-'kan(t)-thəs\ *adj*
-coele *or* **-coel** \,sēl\ *n comb form* [prob. fr. NL *-coela*, fr. neut. pl. of *-coelus* hollow, concave, fr. Gk *-koilos*, fr. *koilos*] **:** cavity **:** chamber **:** ventricle ⟨blasto*coel*⟩ ⟨entero*coele*⟩
coe·len·ter·ate \si-'lent-ə-,rāt, -rət\ *n* [deriv. of Gk *koilos* + *enteron* intestine — more at INTER-] **:** any of a phylum (Coelenterata) of basically radially symmetrical invertebrate animals including the corals, sea anemones, jellyfishes, and hydroids — **coelenterate** *adj*
coe·len·ter·on \-,rän, -rən\ *n, pl* **coe·len·tera** \-rə\ [NL, fr. Gk *koilos* + *enteron*] **:** the internal cavity of a coelenterate
coe·li·ac \'sē-lē-,ak\ *adj* [L *coeliacus*, fr. Gk *koiliakos*, fr. *koilia* cavity, fr. *koilos*] **:** of or relating to the abdominal cavity
coe·lom \'sē-ləm\ *n, pl* **coeloms** *or* **coe·lo·ma·ta** \si-'lō-mət-ə\ [G, fr. Gk *koilōma* cavity, fr. *koilos*] **:** the usu. epithelium-lined body cavity of metazoans above the lower worms — **coe·lo·mate** \'sē-lə-,māt\ *adj or n* — **coe·lo·mic** \si-'läm-ik, -'lō-mik\ *adj*
coen- *or* **coeno-** *comb form* [NL, fr. Gk *koin-*, *koino-*, fr. *koinos* — more at CO-] **:** common **:** general ⟨*coeno*cyte⟩
coe·no·bite \'sē-nə-,bīt\ *var of* CENOBITE
coe·no·cyte \'sē-nə-,sīt\ *n* [ISV] **1 a :** a multinucleate mass of protoplasm resulting from repeated nuclear division unaccompanied by cell fission **b :** an organism consisting of such a structure **2 :** SYNCYTIUM 1 — **coe·no·cyt·ic** \,sē-nə-'sit-ik\ *adj*
coe·nu·rus \si-'n(y)u̇r-əs\ *n, pl* **coe·nu·ri** \-'n(y)u̇(ə)r-,ī\ [NL, fr. *coen-* + Gk *oura* tail] **:** a complex tapeworm larva consisting of a sac from the inner wall of which numerous scolices develop
co·en·zyme \(')kō-'en-,zīm\ *n* **:** a thermostable nonprotein compound that forms the active portion of an enzyme system after combination with an apoenzyme
co·equal \(')kō-'ē-kwəl\ *adj* **:** equal with one another — **co·equal·i·ty** \,kō-ē-'kwäl-ət-ē\ *n* — **co·equal·ly** \(')kō-'ē-kwə-lē\ *adv*
co·erce \kō-'ərs\ *vt* [L *coercēre*, fr. *co-* + *arcēre* to shut up, enclose — more at ARK] **1 :** to restrain or dominate by nullifying individual will **2 :** to compel to an act or choice **3 :** to enforce by force or threat **syn** see FORCE — **co·erc·ible** \-'ər-sə-bəl\ *adj*
co·er·cion \kō-'ər-zhən, -shən\ *n* **:** the act, process, or power of coercing
co·er·cive \-'ər-siv\ *adj* **:** serving or intended to coerce — **co·er·cive·ly** *adv* — **co·er·cive·ness** *n*
co·eta·ne·ous \,kō-ə-'tā-nē-əs\ *adj* [L *coaetaneus*, fr. *co-* + *aetas* age — more at AGE] **:** COEVAL
co·eter·nal \,kō-i-'tərn-ᵊl\ *adj* **:** equally or jointly eternal — **co·eter·nal·ly** \-ᵊl-ē\ *adv* — **co·eter·ni·ty** \-'tər-nət-ē\ *n*
co·eval \kō-'ē-vəl\ *adj* [L *coaevus*, fr. *co-* + *aevum* age, lifetime] **:** of the same or equal age, antiquity, or duration **syn** see CONTEMPORARY — **coeval** *n* — **co·eval·i·ty** \,kō-(,)ē-'val-ət-ē\ *n*
co·ex·ist \,kō-ig-'zist\ *vi* **1 :** to exist together or at the same time **2 :** to live in peace with each other esp. as a matter of policy — **co·ex·is·tence** \-'zis-tən(t)s\ *n* — **co·ex·is·tent** \-tənt\ *adj*
co·ex·ten·sive \,kō-ik-'sten(t)-siv\ *adj* **:** having the same spatial or temporal scope or boundaries — **co·ex·ten·sive·ly** *adv*
cof·fee \'kȯ-fē, 'käf-ē\ *n, often attrib* [It & Turk; It *caffè*, fr. Turk *kahve*, fr. Ar *qahwah*] **1 :** a drink made by percolation, infusion, or decoction from the roasted and ground or pounded seeds of several trees or shrubs (genus *Coffea*) of the madder family; *also* **:** these seeds either green or roasted or a plant producing them **2 :** a cup of coffee ⟨two ~*s*⟩

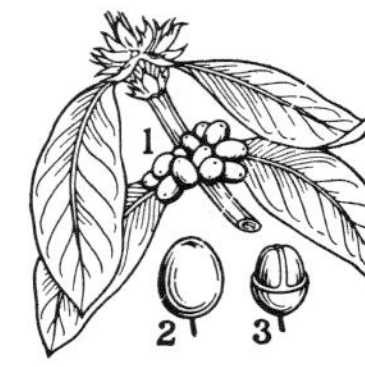

coffee: *1* flowering and fruiting branch with leaves, *2* fruit, *3* fruit with pericarp partly removed to show seeds

cof·fee·house \-,hau̇s\ *n* **:** a place where coffee and other refreshments are sold **:** CAFÉ
cof·fee·pot \-,pät\ *n* **:** a utensil for preparing or serving coffee
coffee shop *n* **:** a small restaurant esp. for light refreshments
coffee table *n* **:** a low table customarily placed in front of a sofa — called also *cocktail table*
coffee tree *n* **1 :** a tree (genus *Coffea*) yielding coffee beans **2 :** KENTUCKY COFFEE TREE
cof·fer \'kȯ-fər, 'käf-ər\ *n* [ME *coffre*, fr. OF, fr. L *cophinus* basket, fr. Gk *kophinos*] **1 :** CHEST, BOX; *esp* **:** a strongbox for valuables **2 :** TREASURY, EXCHEQUER — usu. used in pl. **3 a :** the chamber of a canal lock **b :** CAISSON **c :** COFFERDAM **4 :** a recessed panel in a vault, ceiling, or soffit
cof·fer·dam \-,dam\ *n* **1 :** a watertight enclosure from which water is pumped to expose the bottom of a body of water and permit construction (as of a pier) **2 :** a watertight structure for making repairs below the waterline of a ship
1**cof·fin** \'kȯ-fən\ *n* [ME, basket, receptacle, fr. MF *cofin*, fr. L *cophinus*] **1 :** a box or chest for a corpse to be buried in **2 :** the horny body forming the hoof of a horse's foot
2**coffin** *vt* **:** to enclose in or as if in a coffin
coffin bone *n* **:** the bone enclosed within the hoof of the horse
coffin corner *n* **:** one of the corners formed by a goal line and a sideline on a football field into which a punt is often aimed so that it may go out of bounds close to the defenders' goal line
cof·fle \'kȯ-fəl, 'käf-əl\ *n* [Ar *qāfilah* caravan] **:** a train of slaves or animals fastened together
1**cog** \'käg\ *n* [ME *cogge*, of Scand origin; akin to Norw *kug* cog; akin to OE *cycgel* cudgel] **1 :** a tooth on the rim of a wheel or gear **2 :** a subordinate person or part — **cogged** \'kägd\ *adj*
2**cog** *vb* **cogged; cog·ging** [*cog* (a trick)] *vi* **1** *obs* **:** to cheat in throwing dice **2** *obs* **:** DECEIVE **3** *obs* **:** to use venal flattery ~ *vt* **1 :** to direct the fall of (dice) fraudulently **2** *obs* **:** WHEEDLE
3**cog** *vb* **cogged; cog·ging** [prob. alter. of *cock* (cog)] **:** to connect by means of tenons
4**cog** *n* **:** a tenon on a beam or timber received into a mortise in another beam to secure the two together

co·gen·cy \'kō-jən-sē\ *n* **:** the quality or state of being cogent

co·gent \'kō-jənt\ *adj* [L *cogent-, cogens,* prp. of *cogere* to drive together, collect, fr. *co-* + *agere* to drive — more at AGENT] **:** having power to compel or constrain; *esp* **:** appealing forcibly to the mind or reason **:** CONVINCING **syn** see VALID — **co·gent·ly** *adv*

cog·i·ta·ble \'käj-ət-ə-bəl\ *adj* **:** THINKABLE

cog·i·tate \'käj-ə-,tāt\ *vb* [L *cogitatus,* pp. of *cogitare* to think, think about, fr. *co-* + *agitare* to drive, agitate — more at AGITATE] *vt* **1 :** to ponder or meditate on usu. with intentness and objectivity **2 :** PLAN, PLOT ~ *vi* **:** to think deeply **:** PONDER **syn** see THINK — **cog·i·ta·tion** \,käj-ə-'tā-shən\ *n*

cog·i·ta·tive \'käj-ə-,tāt-iv\ *adj* **1 :** of or relating to cogitation **2 :** capable of or given to cogitation

co·gnac \'kōn-,yak, 'kän-, 'kón-\ *n* [F, fr. *Cognac,* France] **1** *cap* **:** a brandy from the departments of Charente and Charente-Maritime distilled from white wine **2 :** a French brandy

¹cog·nate \'käg-,nāt\ *adj* [L *cognatus,* fr. *co-* + *gnatus, natus,* pp. of *nasci* to be born; akin to L *gignere* to beget — more at KIN] **1 a :** related by blood **b :** related on the mother's side **2 a :** related by descent from the same ancestral language **b** *of a word or morpheme* **:** related by derivation, borrowing, or descent **c** *of a substantive* **:** related usu. in derivation to the verb of which it is the object **3 :** of the same or similar nature — **cog·nate·ly** *adv*

²cognate *n* **:** one that is cognate with another

cog·na·tion \käg-'nā-shən\ *n* **:** cognate relationship

cog·ni·tion \käg-'nish-ən\ *n* [ME *cognicioun,* fr. L *cognition-, cognitio,* fr. *cognitus,* pp. of *cognoscere* to become acquainted with, know, fr. *co-* + *gnoscere* to come to know — more at KNOW] **:** the act or process of knowing including both awareness and judgment; *also* **:** a product of this act — **cog·ni·tion·al** \-'nish-nəl, -'nish-ən-ᵊl\ *adj* — **cog·ni·tive** \'käg-nət-iv\ *adj* — **cog·ni·tive·ly** *adv*

cog·ni·za·ble \'käg-nə-zə-bəl, käg-'nī-\ *adj* **1 :** capable of being known **2 :** capable of being judicially heard and determined — **cog·ni·za·bly** \-blē\ *adv*

cog·ni·zance \'käg-nə-zən(t)s\ *n* [ME *conisaunce,* fr. OF *conoissance,* fr. *conoistre* to know, fr. L *cognoscere*] **1 :** a distinguishing mark or emblem (as a heraldic bearing) **2 a :** SURVEILLANCE, CONTROL **b :** APPREHENSION, PERCEPTION **c :** range of apprehension **d :** NOTICE, OBSERVANCE **3 a :** the right and power to hear and decide controversies **b :** the judicial hearing of a matter

cog·ni·zant \-zənt\ *adj* **:** having cognizance **syn** see AWARE

cog·nize \käg-'nīz\ *vt* [back-formation fr. *cognizance*] **:** KNOW

cog·no·men \käg-'nō-mən\ *n, pl* **cognomens** *or* **cog·no·mi·na** \-'näm-ə-nə, -'nō-mə-\ [L, irreg. fr. *co-* + *nomen* name — more at NAME] **1 :** SURNAME; *esp* **:** the third of usu. three names of a person among the ancient Romans **2 :** NAME; *esp* **:** a distinguishing nickname or epithet — **cog·nom·i·nal** \-'näm-ən-ᵊl\ *adj*

co·gno·scen·te \,kän-yō-'shent-ē\ *n, pl* **co·gno·scen·ti** \-ē\ [obs. It (now *conoscente*), fr. *cognoscente,* adj., wise, fr. L *cognoscent-, cognoscens,* prp. of *cognoscere*] **:** CONNOISSEUR

cog·nos·ci·ble \käg-'näs-ə-bəl\ *adj* [LL *cognoscibilis,* fr. L *cognoscere*] **:** COGNIZABLE

co·gon \kō-'gōn\ *n* [Sp *cogón,* fr. Tag, Bisayan, Bikol *kugon*] **:** any of several coarse tall grasses (genus *Imperata*) used in the Philippines and adjacent lands for thatching

cog railway *n* **:** a steep mountain railroad that has a rail with cogs that engages a cogwheel on the locomotive to ensure traction

cogs·well chair \,kägz-,wel-, -wəl-\ *n, often cap 1st C* [fr. the name *Cogswell*] **:** an upholstered easy chair with inclined back, thin open arms, and cabriole legs

cog·wheel \'käg-,hwēl, -,wēl\ *n* **:** a wheel with cogs or teeth

co·hab·it \kō-'hab-ət\ *vi* [LL *cohabitare,* fr. L *co-* + *habitare* to inhabit, fr. *habitus,* pp. of *habēre* to have] **1 :** to live together as husband and wife **2 :** to live together — **co·hab·i·tant** \-ət-ənt\ *n* — **co·hab·i·ta·tion** \(,)kō-,hab-ə-'tā-shən\ *n*

co·heir \(')kō-'a(ə)r, -'e(ə)r\ *n* **:** a joint heir

co·here \kō-'hi(ə)r\ *vi* [L *cohaerēre,* fr. *co-* + *haerēre* to stick] **1 a :** to hold together firmly as parts of the same mass **b :** ADHERE **c :** to display cohesion **2 :** to consist of parts that cohere **3 a :** to become united in principles, relationships, or interests **b :** to be logically or aesthetically consistent **syn** see STICK

co·her·ence \kō-'hir-ən(t)s, -'her-\ *n* **:** the quality or state of cohering; *esp* **:** systematic connection esp. in logical discourse

co·her·en·cy \-ən-sē\ *n* **:** COHERENCE

co·her·ent \kō-'hir-ənt, -'her-\ *adj* [MF or L; MF *cohérent,* fr. L *cohaerent-, cohaerens,* prp. of *cohaerēre*] **1 :** having the quality of cohering **2 :** logically consistent **3 :** having waves in phase and of one wavelength ⟨~ light⟩ — **co·her·ent·ly** *adv*

co·her·er \kō-'hir-ər\ *n* **:** a radio detector in which an imperfectly conducting contact between pieces of metal or other conductors loosely resting against each other is materially improved in conductance by the passage of high-frequency current

co·he·sion \kō-'hē-zhən\ *n* [L *cohaesus,* pp. of *cohaerēre*] **1 :** the act or process of sticking together tightly **2 :** union between similar plant parts or organs **3 :** molecular attraction by which the particles of a body are united throughout the mass

co·he·sive \kō-'hē-siv, -ziv\ *adj* **:** exhibiting or producing cohesion or coherence — **co·he·sive·ly** *adv* — **co·he·sive·ness** *n*

co·hort \'kō-,hȯ(ə)rt\ *n* [MF & L; MF *cohorte,* fr. L *cohort-, cohors* — more at COURT] **1 a :** one of 10 divisions of an ancient Roman legion **b :** a group of warriors or soldiers **c :** BAND, GROUP **2 a :** COMPANION, ACCOMPLICE **b :** FOLLOWER, SUPPORTER

co·hosh \'kō-,häsh\ *n* [of Algonquian origin; akin to Natick *kôshki* it is rough] **:** any of several American medicinal or poisonous plants: as **a :** a bugbane (*Cimicifuga racemosa*) **b :** a perennial herb (*Caulophyllum thalictroides*) of the barberry family **c :** BANEBERRY

coif \'kȯif, *in sense 2 usu* 'kwäf\ *n* [ME *coife,* fr. MF, fr. LL *cofea*] **1 :** a close-fitting cap: as **a :** a hoodlike cap worn by nuns under a veil **b :** a soldier's defensive skullcap worn under a hood of mail **c :** a white cap formerly worn by English lawyers and esp. by serjeants-at-law; *also* **:** the order or rank of a serjeant-at-law **2 :** COIFFURE — **coif** \'kȯif, 'kwäf\ *or* **coiffe** \'kwäf\ *vt* **coiffed** *or* **coifed; coiff·ing** *or* **coif·ing**

coif·feur \kwä-'fər\ *n* [F, fr. *coiffer*] **:** a male hairdresser

¹coif·fure \kwä-'fyů(ə)r\ *n* [F, fr. *coiffer* to cover with a coif, arrange (hair), fr. *coife*] **:** a manner of arranging or styling the hair

²coiffure *vt* **:** to arrange in a coiffure

coign of van·tage \,kȯi-nə-'vant-ij\ **:** an advantageous position

¹coil \'kȯi(ə)l\ *n* [origin unknown] **1 :** TUMULT **2 :** TROUBLE

²coil *vb* [MF *coillir* to collect] *vt* **1 :** to wind into rings or spirals **2 :** to roll or twist into a shape resembling a coil ~ *vi* **1 :** to move in a circular, spiral, or winding course **2 :** to form or lie in a coil

³coil *n* **1 a :** a series of loops or a spiral **b :** a single loop of such a coil **2 :** a number of turns of wire esp. in spiral form usu. for electromagnetic effect or for providing electrical resistance **3 :** a series of connected pipes in rows, layers, or windings

¹coin \'kȯin\ *n* [ME, fr. MF, wedge, corner, fr. L *cuneus* wedge] **1** *archaic* **a :** CORNER, CORNERSTONE **b :** WEDGE **2 a :** a piece of metal issued by governmental authority as money **b :** metal money

²coin *vt* **1 a :** to make (a coin) esp. by stamping **:** MINT **b :** to convert (metal) into coins **2 :** CREATE ⟨~ a phrase⟩ — **coin·er** *n*

coin·age \'kȯi-nij\ *n* **1 :** the act or process of coining **2 a :** COINS **b :** something (as a word) made up or invented

co·in·cide \,kō-ən-'sīd, 'kō-ən-,\ *vi* [ML *coincidere,* fr. L *co-* + *incidere* to fall on, fr. *in-* + *cadere* to fall — more at CHANCE] **1 a :** to occupy the same place in space or time **b :** to occupy exactly corresponding or equivalent positions on a scale or in a series **2 :** to correspond in nature, character, or function **3 :** to be in accord or agreement **:** CONCUR **syn** see AGREE

co·in·ci·dence \kō-'in(t)-səd-ən(t)s, -sə-,den(t)s\ *n* **1 :** the condition or fact or an instance of coinciding **:** CORRESPONDENCE **2 :** a group of concurrent events or circumstances remarkable for lack of apparent causal connection

co·in·ci·dent \-səd-ənt, -sə-,dent\ *adj* [F *coincident,* fr. ML *coincident-, coincidens,* prp. of *coincidere*] **1 :** occupying the same space or time ⟨~ events⟩ **2 :** of similar nature **:** HARMONIOUS ⟨a theory ~ with the facts⟩ **syn** see CONTEMPORARY — **co·in·ci·dent·ly** *adv*

co·in·ci·den·tal \(,)kō-,in(t)-sə-'dent-ᵊl\ *adj* **1 :** resulting from a coincidence **2 :** occurring or existing at the same time — **co·in·ci·den·tal·ly** \-'dent-ᵊl-ē, -'dent-lē\ *adv*

co·in·sur·ance \,kō-ən-'shůr-ən(t)s\ *n* **:** joint assumption of risk (as by two underwriters) with another

co·in·sure \,kō-ən-'shů(ə)r\ *vb* **:** to insure jointly — **co·in·sur·er** *n*

coir \'kȯi(-ə)r\ *n* [Tamil *kayiṛu* rope] **:** a stiff coarse fiber from the outer husk of the coconut

cois·trel \'kȯi-strəl\ *n* [MF *coustillier* soldier carrying a short sword, fr. *coustille* short sword, fr. L *cultellus* knife — more at CUTLASS] *archaic* **:** a mean fellow **:** VARLET

co·ital \'kō-ət-ᵊl\ *adj* **:** of or relating to coitus

co·ition \kō-'ish-ən\ *n* [LL, fr. L *coition-, coitio* a coming together fr. *coitus,* pp. of *coire* to come together, fr. *co-* + *ire* to go — more at ISSUE] **:** COITUS — **co·ition·al** \-'ish-nəl, -ən-ᵊl\ *adj*

co·itus \'kō-ət-əs\ *n* [L, fr. *coitus,* pp.] **:** the natural conveying of semen to the female reproductive tract **:** SEXUAL INTERCOURSE

¹coke \'kōk\ *n* [ME; akin to Sw *kälk* pith, Gk *gelgis* bulb of garlic] **:** the residue of coal left after destructive distillation and used as fuel; *also* **:** a similar residue left by other materials (as petroleum) distilled to dryness

²coke *vt* **:** to change into coke ~ *vi* **:** to become coked

³coke *n* [by shortening & alter.] *slang* **:** COCAINE

col \'käl\ *n* [F, fr. MF, neck, fr. L *collum*] **1 :** a pass in a mountain range **2 :** a saddle-shaped depression in the crest of a ridge

¹col- — see COM-

²col- *or* **coli-** *or* **colo-** *comb form* [NL, fr. L *colon*] **1 :** colon ⟨*col*itis⟩ ⟨*colo*stomy⟩ **2 :** colon bacillus ⟨*coli*form⟩

¹cola *pl of* COLON

²co·la \'kō-lə\ *n* [fr. *Coca-Cola,* a trademark] **:** a carbonated soft drink flavored with extract from coca leaves, kola nut, sugar, caramel, and acid and aromatic substances

col·an·der \'kəl-ən-dər, 'käl-\ *n* [ME *colyndore,* prob. modif. of OProv *colador,* fr. ML *colatorium,* fr. L *colatus,* pp. of *colare* to sieve, fr. *colum* sieve] **:** a perforated utensil for draining food

co·lat·i·tude \(')kō-'lat-ə-,t(y)üd\ *n* **:** the complement of the latitude

col·can·non \käl-'kan-ən\ *n* [IrGael *cāl ceannan,* lit., white-headed cabbage] **:** potatoes and cabbage or other greens boiled and mashed

col·chi·cine \'käl-chə-,sēn, 'käl-kə-\ *n* **:** a poisonous alkaloid $C_{22}H_{25}NO_6$ extracted from the corms or seeds of the meadow saffron (*Colchicum autumnale*) and used on mitotic cells to induce polyploidy and in the treatment of gout

col·chi·cum \'käl-chi-kəm, 'käl-ki-\ *n* [NL, genus name, fr. L, a kind of plant with a poisonous root] **1 :** any of a genus (*Colchicum*) of Old World corm-producing herbs of the lily family with flowers like crocuses **2 :** the dried corm or dried ripe seeds of autumn crocus containing colchicine, possessing emetic, diuretic, and cathartic action, and used for gout and rheumatism

col·co·thar \'käl-kə-thər, -,thär\ *n* [ML, fr. MF or OSp; MF *colcotar,* fr. OSp *cólcotar,* fr. Ar dial. *qulquṭār*] **:** a reddish brown oxide of iron left as a residue when ferrous sulfate is heated and used as glass polish and as a pigment

¹cold \'kōld\ *adj* [ME, fr. OE *ceald, cald;* akin to OHG *kalt* cold, L *gelu* frost, *gelare* to freeze] **1 :** having a temperature notably below a norm **2 a :** marked by lack of warm feeling **:** UNEMOTIONAL **b :** done after deliberation or calculation and uncolored by personal feeling ⟨a ~ act of aggression⟩ **3 a :** DEPRESSING, CHEERLESS **b :** producing a sensation of cold **:** CHILLING ⟨~ blank walls⟩ **c :** COOL **4 a :** DEAD **b :** UNCONSCIOUS ⟨out ~⟩ **c :** CERTAIN, SURE **5 :** made uncomfortable by cold **6 a :** retaining only faint scents, traces, or clues ⟨~ trail⟩; *also* **:** far from discovering **b :** STALE, UNINTERESTING ⟨~ news⟩ **7 :** UNPREPARED — **cold·ly** \'kōl-(d)lē\ *adv* — **cold·ness** \'kōl(d)-nəs\ *n* — **in cold blood :** with premeditation **:** DELIBERATELY

²cold *n* **1 a :** a condition of low temperature **b :** cold weather **2 :** bodily sensation produced by loss or lack of heat **:** CHILL **3 :** a bodily disorder popularly associated with chilling; *specif* **:** COMMON COLD — **in the cold :** without heating — **out in the cold :** deprived of benefits given others **:** NEGLECTED

cold–blood·ed \'kōl(d)-'bləd-əd\ *adj* **1 a :** done or acting without consideration, compunction, or clemency ⟨~ murder⟩ **b :** MATTER-OF-FACT, EMOTIONLESS **2 :** having cold blood; *specif* **:** having a

body temperature not internally regulated but approximating that of the environment 3 *or* **cold·blood** \\-'bləd\\ **:** of mixed or inferior breeding 4 **:** noticeably sensitive to cold — **cold-blood·ed·ly** *adv* — **cold-blood·ed·ness** *n*
cold chisel *n* **:** a chisel made of tool steel of a strength, shape, and temper suitable for chipping or cutting cold metal
cold cream *n* **:** a soothing and cleansing cosmetic basically a perfumed emulsion of a bland vegetable oil or heavy mineral oil
cold cuts *n pl* **:** sliced assorted cold meats and cheeses
cold frame *n* **:** a usu. glass-covered frame without artificial heat used to protect plants and seedlings
cold front *n* **:** an advancing edge of a cold air mass
cold rubber *n* **:** a wear-resistant synthetic rubber made at a low temperature (as 41° F.) and used esp. for tire treads
cold shoulder *n* **:** intentionally cold or unsympathetic treatment — **cold-shoul·der** \\'kōl(d)-'shōl-dər\\ *vt*
cold sore *n* **:** the group of blisters appearing about or within the mouth in herpes simplex
cold sweat *n* **:** concurrent perspiration and chill usu. associated with fear, pain, or shock
cold war *n* **:** a conflict characterized by the use of means short of sustained overt military action
cold wave *n* **:** a period of unusually cold weather
cole \\'kōl\\ *n* [ME, fr. OE *cāl*, fr. L *caulis* stem, cabbage] **:** any of a genus (*Brassica*) of herbaceous plants; *esp* **:** RAPE
cole·man·ite \\'kōl-mə-,nīt\\ *n* [William T. *Coleman* †1893 Am businessman and mine owner] **:** a mineral $Ca_2B_6O_{11}.5H_2O$ consisting of a hydrous calcium borate occurring in brilliant colorless or white massive monoclinic crystals
co·le·op·ter·on \\,kō-lē-'äp-tə-,rän, käl-ē-\\ *n, pl* **co·le·op·tera** \\-tə-rə\\ [NL, deriv. of Gk *koleon* sheath + *pteron* wing — more at FEATHER] **:** 1BEETLE 1 — **co·le·op·ter·ous** \\-tə-rəs\\ *adj*
co·le·op·tile \\-'äp-tᵊl\\ *n* [NL *coleoptilum*, fr. Gk *koleon* + *ptilon* down; akin to Gk *pteron*] **:** the first leaf of a monocotyledon forming a protective sheath about the plumule
co·leo·rhi·za \\,kō-lē-ə-'rī-zə, ,käl-ē-\\ *n, pl* **co·leo·rhi·zae** \\-(,)zē\\ [NL, fr. Gk *koleon* + NL *-rhiza*] **:** the sheath investing the hypocotyl in some plants through which the roots burst
cole·slaw \\'kōl-,slȯ\\ *n* [D *koolsla*, fr. *kool* cabbage + *sla* salad] **:** a salad made of raw sliced or chopped cabbage
co·le·us \\'kō-lē-əs\\ *n* [NL, genus name, fr. Gk *koleos*, *koleon* sheath] **:** any of a large genus (*Coleus*) of herbs of the mint family
cole·wort \\'kōl-,wərt, -,wȯ(ə)rt\\ *n* **:** COLE; *esp* **:** one (as kale) that forms no head
1**col·ic** \\'käl-ik\\ *n* [ME, fr. MF *colique*, fr. L *colicus* colicky, fr. Gk *kōlikos*, fr. *kōlon*, alter. of *kolon* colon] **:** a paroxysm of acute abdominal pain localized in a hollow organ and caused by spasm, obstruction, or twisting — **col·icky** \\'käl-ə-kē\\ *or* **colic** *adj*
2**co·lic** \\'kō-lik, 'käl-ik\\ *adj* **:** of or relating to the colon
col·ic·root \\'käl-ik-,rüt, -,ru̇t\\ *n* **:** any of several plants having roots reputed to cure colic: as **a :** either of two bitter herbs (*Aletris farinosa* and *A. aurea*) of the lily family **b :** a wild yam (*Dioscorea paniculata*)
col·ic·weed \\'käl-ik-,wēd\\ *n* **:** SQUIRREL CORN
co·li·form \\'kō-lə-,fȯrm, 'käl-ə-\\ *adj* **:** relating to, resembling, or being the colon bacillus — **coliform** *n*
co·lin \\kə-'lēn\\ *n* [Sp *colín*, modif. of Nahuatl *çolin*] **:** the bobwhite or a related New World game bird
col·i·se·um \\,käl-ə-'sē-əm\\ *n* [ML *Colosseum*, *Colisseum*] **1** *cap* **:** COLOSSEUM 1 **2 :** a large structure for public entertainments
co·li·tis \\kō-'līt-əs\\ *n* **:** inflammation of the colon
coll- *or* **collo-** *comb form* [NL, fr. Gk *koll-*, *kollo-*, fr. *kolla* — more at PROTOCOL] **1 :** glue ⟨*coll*enchyma⟩ **2 :** colloid ⟨*collo*type⟩
col·lab·o·rate \\kə-'lab-ə-,rāt\\ *vi* [LL *collaboratus*, pp. of *collaborare* to labor together, fr. L *com-* + *laborare* to labor] **1 :** to work jointly with others esp. in an intellectual endeavor **2 :** to cooperate with or assist usu. willingly an enemy of one's country and esp. an occupying force **3 :** to cooperate with an agency or instrumentality with which one is not immediately connected — **col·lab·o·ra·tion** \\-,lab-ə-'rā-shən\\ *n* — **col·lab·o·ra·tive** \\-'lab-ə-,rāt-iv\\ *adj* — **col·lab·o·ra·tor** \\-,rāt-ər\\ *n*
col·lab·o·ra·tion·ism \\kə-,lab-ə-'rā-shə-,niz-əm\\ *n* **:** the advocacy or practice of collaboration with an enemy — **col·lab·o·ra·tion·ist** \\-sh(ə-)nəst\\ *adj or n*
col·lage \\kə-'läzh\\ *n* [F, gluing, fr. *coller* to glue, fr. *colle* glue, fr. (assumed) VL *colla*, fr. Gk *kolla*] **1 :** an artistic composition of fragments of printed matter and other materials pasted on a picture surface **2 :** the art of making collages **3 :** an assembly of diverse fragments
col·la·gen \\'käl-ə-jən\\ *n* [Gk *kolla* + ISV *-gen*] **:** an insoluble fibrous protein that occurs in vertebrates as the chief constituent of connective tissue fibrils and in bones and yields gelatin and glue on prolonged heating with water — **col·la·gen·ic** \\,käl-ə-'jen-ik\\ *adj* — **col·lag·e·nous** \\kə-'laj-ə-nəs\\ *adj*
1**col·lapse** \\kə-'laps\\ *vb* [L *collapsus*, pp. of *collabi*, fr. *com-* + *labi* to fall, slide — more at SLEEP] *vi* **1 :** to break down completely **:** DISINTEGRATE **2 :** to fall or shrink together abruptly and completely **3 :** to cave or fall in or give way **4 :** to suddenly lose force, significance, effectiveness, or worth **5 :** to break down in vital energy, stamina, or self-control through exhaustion or disease; *esp* **:** to fall helpless or unconscious **6 :** to fold down into a more compact shape ~ *vt* **:** to cause to collapse — **col·laps·ibil·i·ty** \\-,lap-sə-'bil-ət-ē\\ *n* — **col·laps·ible** \\-'lap-sə-bəl\\ *adj*
2**collapse** *n* **:** the act or an instance of collapsing **:** BREAKDOWN
1**col·lar** \\'käl-ər\\ *n* [ME *coler*, fr. OF, fr. L *collare*, fr. *collum* neck; akin to ON & OHG *hals* neck, OE *hwēol* wheel — more at WHEEL] **1 :** a band, strip, or chain worn around the neck: as **a :** a band that serves to finish or decorate the neckline of a garment **b :** a short necklace **c :** a band about the neck of an animal **d :** a part of the harness of draft animals fitted over the shoulders and taking strain when a load is drawn **2 :** something resembling a collar in shape or use (as a ring or round flange to restrain motion or hold something in place) **3 :** any of various animal structures or markings likened to a collar — **col·lar·less** \\-ər-ləs\\ *adj*
2**collar** *vt* **1 a :** to seize by the collar or neck **b :** CAPTURE, GRAB **c :** to get control of **:** PREEMPT **2 :** to put a collar on
col·lar·bone \\,käl-ər-'bōn, 'käl-ər-,\\ *n* **:** CLAVICLE
col·lard \\'käl-ərd\\ *n* [alter. of *colewort*] **:** a stalked smooth-leaved kale — usu. used in pl.
col·late \\kə-'lāt, 'käl-,āt\\ *vt* [back-formation fr. *collation*] **1 a :** to compare critically **b :** to collect, compare carefully in order to verify, and often to integrate or arrange in order **2** [L *collatus*, pp.] **:** to admit and institute (a cleric) to a benefice **3 a :** to verify the order of (printed sheets) **b :** GATHER 2e **syn** see COMPARE — **col·la·tor** \\kə-'lāt-ər, 'käl-,āt-\\ *n*
1**col·lat·er·al** \\kə-'lat-ə-rəl, -'la-trəl\\ *adj* [ME, prob. fr. MF, fr. ML *collateralis*, fr. L *com-* + *lateralis* lateral] **1 a :** accompanying as secondary or subordinate **:** CONCOMITANT **b :** INDIRECT **c :** serving to support or reinforce **:** ANCILLARY **2 :** belonging to the same ancestral stock but not in a direct line of descent **3 :** parallel, coordinate, or corresponding in position, order, time, or significance **4 a :** of, relating to, or being an obligation or security attached to another to secure its performance **b :** secured or guaranteed by additional security — **col·lat·er·al·i·ty** \\-,lat-ə-'ral-ət-ē\\ *n* — **col·lat·er·al·ly** \\-'lat-ə-rə-lē, -'la-trə-\\ *adv*
2**collateral** *n* **1 :** a collateral relative **2 :** something used as collateral security **3 :** a branch of a bodily part (as a vein)
col·la·tion \\kə-'lā-shən, kä-\\ *n* **1** [ME, fr. ML *collation-*, *collatio*, fr. LL, conference, fr. L, bringing together, comparison, fr. *collatus* (pp. of *conferre* to bring together, bestow upon), fr. *com-* + *latus*, pp. of *ferre* to carry] **a :** a light meal allowed on fast days in place of lunch or supper **b :** a light meal **2** [ME, fr. L *collation-*, *collatio*] **:** the act, process, or result of collating
col·league \\'käl-,ēg\\ *n* [MF *collegue*, fr. L *collega*, fr. *com-* + *legare* to appoint, depute — more at LEGATE] **:** an associate in a profession or a civil or ecclesiastical office
1**col·lect** \\'käl-ikt, -,ekt\\ *n* [ME *collecte*, fr. OF, fr. ML *collecta*, short for *oratio ad collectam* prayer upon assembly] **:** a short prayer comprising an invocation, petition, and conclusion; *specif, often cap* **:** one preceding the eucharistic Epistle and varying with the day
2**col·lect** \\kə-'lekt\\ *vb* [L *collectus*, pp. of *colligere* to collect, fr. *com-* + *legere* to gather] *vt* **1 a :** to bring together into one body or place **b :** to gather or exact from a number of persons or other sources ⟨~ taxes⟩ **2 :** INFER, DEDUCE **3 :** to gain or regain control of ⟨~ his thoughts⟩ **4 :** to claim as due and receive payment for ~ *vi* **1 :** ASSEMBLE; *also* **:** ACCUMULATE **2 a :** to collect objects **b :** to receive payment ⟨~*ing* on his insurance⟩ **syn** see GATHER — **col·lect·ible** *or* **col·lect·able** \\-'lek-tə-bəl\\ *adj*
3**col·lect** \\kə-'lekt\\ *adv* (*or adj*) **:** to be paid for by the receiver
col·lec·ta·nea \\,käl-,ek-'tā-nē-ə\\ *n pl* [L, neut. pl. of *collectaneus* collected, fr. *collectus*, pp.] **:** collected writings; *also* **:** literary items forming a collection
col·lect·ed \\kə-'lek-təd\\ *adj* **1 :** SELF-POSSESSED, CALM **2** *of a gait* **:** performed or performable by a horse from a state of collection **syn** see COOL — **col·lect·ed·ly** *adv* — **col·lect·ed·ness** *n*
col·lec·tion \\kə-'lek-shən\\ *n* **1 :** the act or process of collecting **2 :** something collected **:** ASSEMBLAGE; *esp* **:** an accumulation of objects gathered for study, comparison, or exhibition **3 :** a standard pose of a well-handled saddle horse in which it is brought well up to the bit with the center of gravity toward the rear quarters
1**col·lec·tive** \\kə-'lek-tiv\\ *adj* **1 :** denoting a number of persons or things considered as one group or whole ⟨*flock* is a ~ word⟩ **2 a :** formed by collecting **:** AGGREGATED **b** *of a fruit* **:** MULTIPLE **3 a :** of, relating to, or being a group of individuals **b :** involving all members of a group as distinct from its individuals **4 :** marked by similarity among or with the members of a group **5 :** collectivized or characterized by collectivism **6 :** shared or assumed by all members of the group ⟨~ leadership⟩ — **col·lec·tive·ly** *adv*
2**collective** *n* **1 :** a collective body **:** GROUP **2 :** a cooperative unit or organization; *specif* **:** COLLECTIVE FARM
collective bargaining *n* **:** negotiation between an employer and union representatives usu. on wages, hours, and working conditions
collective farm *n* **:** a farm esp. in a communist country formed from many small holdings collected into a single unit for joint operation under governmental supervision
collective security *n* **:** the maintenance by common action of the security of all members of an association of nations
col·lec·tiv·ism \\kə-'lek-ti-,viz-əm\\ *n* **:** a political or economic theory advocating collective control esp. over production and distribution or a system marked by such control — **col·lec·tiv·ist** \\-vəst\\ *adj or n* — **col·lec·tiv·is·tic** \\-,lek-ti-'vis-tik\\ *adj*
col·lec·tiv·i·ty \\,käl-,ek-'tiv-ət-ē, kə-,lek-\\ *n* **1 :** the quality or state of being collective **2 :** a collective whole; *specif* **:** the people as a body
col·lec·tiv·iza·tion \\kə-,lek-ti-və-'zā-shən\\ *n* **:** the act or process of collectivizing **:** the state of being collectivized
col·lec·tiv·ize \\kə-'lek-ti-,vīz\\ *vt* **:** to organize under collective control
col·lec·tor \\kə-'lek-tər\\ *n* **1 :** an official who collects funds or moneys **2 :** one that makes a collection ⟨stamp ~⟩ **3 :** an object or device that collects **4 :** a conductor maintaining contact between moving and stationary parts of an electric circuit — **col·lec·tor·ship** \\-,ship\\ *n*
col·leen \\'käl-,ēn, kä-'lēn\\ *n* [IrGael *cailīn*] **:** an Irish girl
col·lege \\'käl-ij\\ *n* [ME, fr. MF, fr. L *collegium* society, fr. *collega* colleague — more at COLLEAGUE] **1 :** a body of clergy living together on a foundation **2 :** a building used for an educational or religious purpose **3 a :** a self-governing constituent body of a university **b :** a preparatory or high school **c :** an independent institution of higher learning offering a course of general studies leading to a bachelor's degree **d :** a part of a university offering a specialized group of courses **e :** an institution offering instruction usu. in a professional, vocational, or technical field ⟨business ~⟩ ⟨barber ~⟩ **4 :** COMPANY, GROUP; *specif* **:** an organized body of persons engaged in a common pursuit or having common interests or duties **5 :** the faculty, students, or administration of a college
col·le·gial \\kə-'lē-j(ē-)əl\\ *adj* **1 :** COLLEGIATE **2 :** marked by power or authority vested equally in each of a number of colleagues
col·le·gian \\kə-'lē-j(ē-)ən\\ *n* **:** a student or recent graduate of a college
col·le·giate \\kə-'lē-j(ē-)ət\\ *adj* [ML *collegiatus*, fr. L *collegium*] **1 :** of or relating to a collegiate church **2 :** of, relating to, or comprising a college **3 :** COLLEGIAL 2 **4 :** designed for or characteristic of college students
collegiate church *n* **1 :** a church other than a cathedral that has a chapter of canons **2 :** a church or corporate group of churches under the joint pastorate of two or more ministers
col·le·gium \\kə-'lē-j(ē-)əm\\ *n* [modif. of Russ *kollegya*, fr. L

collegium] : a group in which each member has approximately equal power and authority; *specif* : one in a soviet organization
col·lem·bo·lan \kə-ˈlem-bə-lən\ *n* [deriv. of *coll-* + Gk *embolos* wedge, stopper — more at EMBOLUS] : SPRINGTAIL — **collembolan** *or* **col·lem·bo·lous** \-ləs\ *adj*
col·len·chy·ma \kə-ˈleŋ-kə-mə, -ˈlen-\ *n* [NL] : a plant tissue of living usu. elongated cells with walls variously thickened esp. at the angles but capable of further growth — compare SCLERENCHYMA — **col·len·chym·a·tous** \ˌkäl-ən-ˈkim-ət-əs\ *adj*
col·let \ˈkäl-ət\ *n* [MF, dim. of *col* collar, fr. L *collum* neck — more at COLLAR] : a metal band, collar, ferrule, or flange: as **a** : a small collar pierced to receive the inner end of a balance spring on a timepiece **b** : a circle or flange in which a precious stone is set
col·lide \kə-ˈlīd\ *vi* [L *collidere*, fr. *com-* + *laedere* to injure by striking] **1** : to come together with solid impact **2** : CLASH
col·lie \ˈkäl-ē\ *n* [prob. fr. E dial. *colly* (black)] : a large dog of a breed developed in Scotland with a rough thick coat or less often with a smooth coat and used in herding sheep
col·lier \ˈkäl-yər\ *n* [ME *colier*, fr. *col* coal] **1** : one that produces charcoal **2** : a coal miner **3** : a ship employed in transporting coal
col·liery \ˈkäl-yə-rē\ *n* : a coal mine and its connected buildings
col·lie·shang·ie \ˈkäl-ē-ˌshaŋ-ē\ *n* [perh. fr. *collie* + *shang* (kind of meal)] *Scot* : SQUABBLE, BRAWL
col·li·gate \ˈkäl-ə-ˌgāt\ *vt* [L *colligatus*, pp. of *colligare*, fr. *com-* + *ligare* to tie] **1** : to bind, unite, or group together **2** : to bring together (isolated facts) under a general concept or to elicit a general principle — **col·li·ga·tion** \ˌkäl-ə-ˈgā-shən\ *n*
col·li·mate \ˈkäl-ə-ˌmāt\ *vt* [L *collimatus*, pp. of *collimare*, MS var. of *collineare* to make straight, fr. *com-* + *linea* line] **1** : to make (as rays of light) parallel **2** : to adjust the line of sight of (a transit or level) — **col·li·ma·tion** \ˌkäl-ə-ˈmā-shən\ *n*
col·li·ma·tor \ˈkäl-ə-ˌmāt-ər\ *n* **1** : a device for producing a beam of parallel rays of light or other radiation or for forming an infinitely distant virtual image that can be viewed without parallax **2** : a device for obtaining a beam of molecules, atoms, or nuclear particles of limited cross section
col·lin·ear \kə-ˈlin-ē-ər, kä-\ *adj* [ISV] : lying on or passing through the same straight line
col·lins \ˈkäl-ənz\ *n* [prob. fr. the name *Collins*] : a tall iced drink with a base of distilled liquor (as gin)
col·lin·sia \kə-ˈlin-zē-ə\ *n* [NL, genus name, fr. Zaccheus *Collins* †1831 Am botanist] : any of a genus (*Collinsia*) of U.S. biennial or annual herbs of the figwort family
col·li·sion \kə-ˈlizh-ən\ *n* [ME, fr. L *collision-*, *collisio*, fr. *collisus*, pp. of *collidere*] : an act or instance of colliding
collo- — see COLL-
col·lo·cate \ˈkäl-ə-ˌkāt\ *vt* [L *collocatus*, pp. of *collocare*, fr. *com-* + *locare* to place, fr. *locus* place — more at STALL] : to set or arrange in a place or position; *esp* : to set side by side
col·lo·ca·tion \ˌkäl-ə-ˈkā-shən\ *n* : the act or result of placing or arranging together; *specif* : a noticeable arrangement or conjoining of linguistic elements (as words)
col·lo·di·on \kə-ˈlōd-ē-ən\ *n* [modif. of NL *collodium*, fr. Gk *kollōdēs* glutinous, fr. *kolla* glue] : a viscous solution of pyroxylin used esp. as a coating for wounds or for photographic films
col·logue \kə-ˈlōg\ *vi* [origin unknown] **1** *dial* : INTRIGUE, CONSPIRE **2** : to talk privately : CONFER
col·loid \ˈkäl-ˌȯid\ *n, often attrib* **1** : a substance that is in a state of division preventing passage through a semipermeable membrane, consists of particles too small for resolution with an ordinary light microscope, and in suspension or solution diffracts a beam of light and fails to settle out; *also* : a system consisting of such a substance together with the gaseous, liquid, or solid medium in which it is dispersed **2** : a gelatinous or mucinous substance found in tissues in disease or normally (as in the thyroid) — **col·loi·dal** \kə-ˈlȯid-ᵊl, kä-\ *adj* — **col·loi·dal·ly** \-ᵊl-ē\ *adv*
col·lop \ˈkäl-əp\ *n* [ME] **1** : a small piece or slice esp. of meat **2** : a fold of fat flesh
col·lo·qui·al \kə-ˈlō-kwē-əl\ *adj* **1** : of or relating to conversation : CONVERSATIONAL **2 a** : used in or characteristic of familiar and informal conversation **b** : using conversational style — **colloquial** *n* — **col·lo·qui·al·ly** \-ə-lē\ *adv*
col·lo·qui·al·ism \-ə-ˌliz-əm\ *n* **1 a** : a colloquial expression **b** : a local or regional dialect expression **2** : colloquial style
col·lo·quist \ˈkäl-ə-kwəst\ *n* : TALKER
col·lo·qui·um \kə-ˈlō-kwē-əm\ *n, pl* **colloquiums** *or* **col·lo·quia** \-kwē-ə\ [L, conversation] : CONFERENCE; *specif* : a seminar that several lecturers take turns in leading
col·lo·quy \ˈkäl-ə-kwē\ *n* [L *colloquium*, fr. *colloqui* to converse, fr. *com-* + *loqui* to speak] **1** : CONVERSATION **2** : CONFERENCE
col·lo·type \ˈkäl-ə-ˌtīp\ *n* [ISV] **1** : a photomechanical process for making prints directly from a hardened film of gelatin or other colloid that has ink-receptive and ink-repellent parts **2** : a print made by collotype
col·lude \kə-ˈlüd\ *vi* [L *colludere*, fr. *com-* + *ludere* to play, fr. *ludus* game — more at LUDICROUS] : CONSPIRE, PLOT
col·lu·sion \kə-ˈlü-zhən\ *n* [ME, fr. MF, fr. L *collusion-*, *collusio*, fr. *collusus*, pp. of *colludere*] : secret agreement or cooperation for a fraudulent or deceitful purpose — **col·lu·sive** \-ˈlü-siv, -ziv\ *adj* — **col·lu·sive·ly** *adv*
col·lu·vi·al \kə-ˈlü-vē-əl\ *adj* : of, relating to, or marked by colluvium
col·lu·vi·um \-vē-əm\ *n, pl* **col·lu·via** \-vē-ə\ *or* **colluviums** [NL, fr. ML, offscourings, alter. of L *colluvies*, fr. *colluere* to wash, fr. *com-* + *lavere* to wash — more at LYE] : rock detritus and soil accumulated at the foot of a slope
col·ly \ˈkäl-ē\ *vt* [alter. of ME *colwen*, fr. (assumed) OE *colgian*, fr. OE *col* coal] *dial chiefly Brit* : to blacken with or as if with soot
col·lyr·i·um \kə-ˈlir-ē-əm\ *n, pl* **col·lyr·ia** \-ē-ə\ *or* **collyriums** [L, fr. Gk *kollyrion* pessary, eye salve, fr. dim. of *kollyra* roll of bread] : an eye lotion : EYEWASH
col·ly·wob·bles \ˈkäl-ē-ˌwäb-əlz\ *n pl but sing or pl in constr* [prob. by folk etymology, fr. NL *cholera morbus*, lit., the disease cholera] : BELLYACHE
colo- — see COL-
col·o·cynth \ˈkäl-ə-ˌsin(t)th\ *n* [L *colocynthis*] : a Mediterranean and African herbaceous vine (*Citrullus colocynthis*) related to the watermelon; *also* : its spongy fruit from which a powerful cathartic is prepared
co·logne \kə-ˈlōn\ *n* [*Cologne*, Germany] : a perfumed toilet water
¹**co·lon** \ˈkō-lən\ *n, pl* **colons** *or* **co·la** \-lə\ [L, fr. Gk *kolon*] : the part of the large intestine that extends from the cecum to the rectum — **co·lon·ic** \kō-ˈlän-ik\ *adj*
²**colon** *n* [L, part of a poem, fr. Gk *kōlon* limb, part of a strophe — more at CALK] **1** *pl* **co·la** \-lə\ : a rhythmical unit of an utterance; *specif, in Greek or Latin verse* : a system or series of from two to not more than six feet having a principal accent and forming part of a line **2** *pl* **colons** : a punctuation mark : used chiefly to direct attention to matter that follows (as a list, explanation, or quotation)
³**co·lon** \kō-ˈlän, kə-ˈlōn\ *n* [L *colonus*] : a colonial farmer
⁴**co·lon** \kə-ˈlōn\ *n, pl* **co·lo·nes** \-ˈlō-ˌnās\ [Sp *colón*] — see MONEY table
col·o·nel \ˈkərn-ᵊl\ *n* [alter. of *coronel*, fr. MF, modif. of OIt *colonnello* column of soldiers, colonel, dim. of *colonna* column, fr. L *columna*] **1 a** : a commissioned officer in the army, air force, or marine corps ranking above a lieutenant colonel and below a brigadier general **b** : LIEUTENANT COLONEL **2** : a minor titular official of a state esp. in southern or midland U.S. — used as an honorific title — **col·o·nel·cy** \-ᵊl-sē\ *n*
Colonel Blimp \ˌkərn-ᵊl-ˈblimp\ *n* [*Colonel Blimp*, cartoon character created by David Low] : a reactionary pompous army officer or government official; *broadly* : an elderly pompous reactionary
¹**co·lo·nial** \kə-ˈlō-nyəl, -nē-əl\ *adj* **1** : of, relating to, or characteristic of a colony **2** *often cap* : of or relating to the original 13 colonies forming the United States **3** : possessing or composed of colonies — **co·lo·nial·ly** \-ē\ *adv* — **co·lo·nial·ness** *n*
²**colonial** *n* : a member or inhabitant of a colony
co·lo·nial·ism \-nyə-ˌliz-əm, -nē-ə-ˌliz-\ *n* **1** : colonial status **2** : something characteristic of a colony **3 a** : control by one power over a dependent area or people **b** : a policy advocating or based on such control — **co·lo·nial·ist** \-ləst\ *n or adj*
col·o·nist \ˈkäl-ə-nəst\ *n* **1** : a member or inhabitant of a colony **2** : one who colonizes or settles in a new country
col·o·ni·za·tion \ˌkäl-ə-nə-ˈzā-shən\ *n* : an act or instance of colonizing or of being colonized — **col·o·ni·za·tion·ist** \-sh(ə-)nəst\ *n*
col·o·nize \ˈkäl-ə-ˌnīz\ *vt* **1 a** : to establish a colony in or on **b** : to establish in a colony **2** : to send illegal or irregularly qualified voters into **3** : to infiltrate with usu. subversive militants for propaganda and strategy reasons ⟨~ industries⟩ ~ *vi* : to make or establish a colony : SETTLE — **col·o·niz·er** *n*
col·on·nade \ˌkäl-ə-ˈnād\ *n* [F, fr. It *colonnato*, fr. *colonna*] : a series of columns set at regular intervals and usu. supporting the base of the roof structure — **col·on·nad·ed** \-ˈnād-əd\ *adj*
col·o·ny \ˈkäl-ə-nē\ *n, often attrib* [ME *colonie*, fr. MF & L; MF, fr. L *colonia*, fr. *colonus* farmer, colonist, fr. *colere* to cultivate — more at WHEEL] **1 a** : a body of people living in a new territory but retaining ties with the parent state **b** : the territory inhabited by such a body **2** : a distinguishable localized population within a species ⟨~ of termites⟩ **3 a** : a circumscribed mass of microorganisms usu. growing in or on a solid medium **b** : the aggregation of zooids of a compound animal **4 a** : a group of individuals with common characteristics or interests situated in close association **b** : the section occupied by such a group
col·o·phon \ˈkäl-ə-fən, -ˌfän\ *n* [L, fr. Gk *kolophōn* summit, finishing touch] **1** : an inscription placed at the end of a book or manuscript usu. with facts relative to its production **2** : an identifying device used by a printer or a publisher
co·lo·pho·ny \ˈkäl-ə-ˌfō-nē, kə-ˈläf-ə-\ *n* [ME *colophonie*, deriv. of Gk *Kolophōn* Colophon, an Ionian city] : ROSIN
¹**col·or** *or chiefly Brit* **col·our** \ˈkəl-ər\ *n, often attrib* [ME *colour*, fr. OF, fr. L *color*; akin to L *celare* to conceal — more at HELL] **1 a** : a phenomenon of light (as red, brown, pink, gray) or visual perception that enables one to differentiate otherwise identical objects **b** : the aspect of objects and light sources that may be described in terms of hue, lightness, and saturation for objects and hue, brightness, and saturation for light sources — used in this sense as the psychological basis for definitions of color in this dictionary **c** : a hue as contrasted with black, white, or gray **2 a** : an outward often deceptive show : APPEARANCE **b** : a legal claim to or appearance of a right, authority, or office **c** : a pretense offered as justification : PRETEXT **d** : an appearance of authenticity : PLAUSIBILITY **3** : complexion tint: **a** : the tint characteristic of good health **b** : BLUSH **4 a** : vividness or variety of effects of language **b** : LOCAL COLOR **5 a** : a distinctively colored badge or device or distinctively colored clothing — usu. used in pl. **b** (1) *pl* : STAND, POINT OF VIEW (2) : CHARACTER, NATURE — usu. used in pl. **6** : the use or combination of colors **7 a** : an identifying flag, ensign, or pennant — usu. used in pl. **b** *pl* : a navy or nautical salute to a flag being hoisted or lowered **c** *pl* : ARMED FORCES **8** : VITALITY, INTEREST **9** : something used to give color : PIGMENT **10** : tonal quality in music **11 a** : skin pigmentation other than white characteristic of race **b** : the members of a race or group with such pigmentation; *esp* : NEGROES **12** : a small particle of gold in a gold miner's pan after washing
syn CHROMA, HUE, SHADE, TINT, TINGE: COLOR is the general term for any quality of light distinguishable by the visual sense, but it specifically applies to the property of things seen as red, yellow, blue, and so on as distinguished from black, gray, or white; CHROMA is a technical term for this specific sense; HUE usu. implies some modification of a finer discrimination of a primary color; SHADE usu. applies to a color modified toward black, TINT to one modified toward white, but COLOR, HUE, SHADE, and TINT are often interchangeable; TINGE suggests an interfusion or overlying stain of one color over another background color
²**color** *or chiefly Brit* **colour** *vb* **col·or·ing** \ˈkəl-(ə-)riŋ\ *vt* **1 a** : to give color to **b** : to change the color of : PAINT **2** : to change as if by dyeing or painting: as **a** : MISREPRESENT, DISTORT **b** : GLOSS, EXCUSE ⟨~ a lie⟩ **c** : INFLUENCE, AFFECT ~ *vi* : to take on color; *specif* : BLUSH — **col·or·er** \ˈkəl-ər-ər\ *n*
col·or·able *or chiefly Brit* **col·our·able** \ˈkəl-(ə-)rə-bəl\ *adj* **1** : seemingly valid or genuine **2** : FEIGNED, COUNTERFEIT **syn** see PLAUSIBLE — **col·or·ably** \-blē\ *adv*
col·or·ation *or chiefly Brit* **col·our·ation** \ˌkəl-ə-ˈrā-shən\ *n* **1 a** : the state of being colored **b** : use or choice of colors; *specif*

: arrangement of colors **2 :** characteristic quality **3 :** COLOR 10
col·or·a·tu·ra \ˌkəl-ə-rə-'t(y)u̇r-ə\ *n, often attrib* [obs. It, lit., coloring, fr. LL, fr. L *coloratus*, pp. of *colorare* to color, fr. *color*] **1 :** florid ornamentation in vocal music; *broadly* **:** music with ornate figuration **2 :** a soprano specializing in coloratura
color bar *n* **:** a barrier preventing colored persons from participating with whites in various activities — called also *color line*
col·or–blind \'kəl-ər-ˌblīnd\ *adj* **1 :** affected with partial or total inability to distinguish one or more chromatic colors **2 :** INSENSITIVE, OBLIVIOUS — **color blindness** *n*
col·or·breed \'kəl-ər-ˌbrēd\ *vt* **:** to breed selectively for the development of particular colors ⟨~*ing* canaries for red⟩
col·or·cast \-ˌkast\ *n* [*color* + tele*cast*] **:** a telecast in color — **colorcast** *vb*
1**col·ored** *or chiefly Brit* **col·oured** \'kəl-ərd\ *adj* **1 :** having color **2 a :** COLORFUL **b :** SLANTED, BIASED **3 a :** of a race other than the white; *esp* **:** NEGRO **b :** of mixed race **4 :** of or relating to colored persons
2**colored** *n, often cap* **1 :** colored people **2 :** a colored person
col·or·fast \'kəl-ər-ˌfast\ *adj* **:** having color that retains its original hue without fading or running — **col·or·fast·ness** \-ˌfas(t)-nəs\ *n*
col·or·ful *or chiefly Brit* **col·our·ful** \'kəl-ər-fəl\ *adj* **1 :** having striking colors **2 :** full of variety or interest — **col·or·ful·ly** \-f(ə-)lē\ *adv* — **col·or·ful·ness** \-fəl-nəs\ *n*
color guard *n* **:** a guard of honor for the colors of an organization
col·or·if·ic \ˌkəl-ə-'rif-ik\ *adj* **:** capable of communicating color
col·or·im·e·ter \-'rim-ət-ər\ *n* [ISV] **:** an instrument or device for determining and specifying colors; *specif* **:** one used for chemical analysis by comparison of a liquid's color with standard colors — **col·or·i·met·ric** \ˌkəl-ə-rə-'me-trik\ *adj* — **col·or·i·met·ri·cal·ly** \-tri-k(ə-)lē\ *adv* — **col·or·im·e·try** \ˌkəl-ə-'rim-ə-trē\ *n*
col·or·ing *or chiefly Brit* **col·our·ing** *n* **1 a :** the act of applying colors **b :** something that produces color **c** (1) **:** the effect produced by applying or combining colors (2) **:** natural color (3) **:** COMPLEXION, COLORATION **d :** change of appearance (as by adding color) **2 :** INFLUENCE, BIAS **3 :** COLOR 4 **4 :** TIMBRE, QUALITY
col·or·ist *or chiefly Brit* **col·our·ist** \'kəl-ə-rəst\ *n* **:** one that colors or deals with color — **col·or·is·tic** \ˌkəl-ə-'ris-tik\ *adj* — **col·or·is·ti·cal·ly** \-ti-k(ə-)lē\ *adv*
col·or·less *or chiefly Brit* **col·our·less** \'kəl-ər-ləs\ *adj* **1 :** lacking color **2 :** PALLID, BLANCHED **3 :** DULL, UNINTERESTING — **col·or·less·ly** *adv* — **col·or·less·ness** *n*
color phase *n* **1 a :** a genetic variant manifested by the occurrence of a skin or pelage color unlike the wild type of the animal group in which it appears **b :** an individual marked by such a variant **2 :** a seasonally variant pelage color
co·los·sal \kə-'läs-əl\ *adj* **1 :** of, relating to, or resembling a colossus **2 :** of a bulk, extent, power, or effect approaching or suggesting the stupendous or incredible **3 :** of an exceptional or astonishing degree **syn** see ENORMOUS — **co·los·sal·ly** \-ə-lē\ *adv*
col·os·se·um \ˌkäl-ə-'sē-əm\ *n* [ML, fr. L, neut. of *colosseus* colossal, fr. *colossus*] **1** *cap* **:** an amphitheater built in Rome in the first century A.D. **2 :** COLISEUM 2
co·los·sus \kə-'läs-əs\ *n, pl* **co·los·sus·es** \-'läs-ə-səz\ *or* **co·los·si** \-'läs-ˌī, -(ˌ)ē\ [L, fr. Gk *kolossos*] **1 :** a statue of gigantic size and proportions **2 :** one resembling a colossus in size or scope
co·los·to·my \kə-'läs-tə-mē\ *n* [ISV] **:** surgical formation of an artificial anus
co·los·trum \kə-'läs-trəm\ *n* [L, beastings] **:** milk secreted for a few days after parturition and characterized by high protein and immune body content
colour *chiefly Brit var of* COLOR
-c·o·lous \k-ə-ləs\ *adj comb form* [L *-cola* inhabitant; akin to L *colere* to inhabit] **:** living or growing in or on ⟨areni*colous*⟩
col·por·tage \'käl-ˌpōrt-ij, -ˌpȯrt-\ *n* **:** a colporteur's work
col·por·teur \-ˌpōrt-ər, -ˌpȯrt-\ *n* [F, alter. of MF *comporteur*, fr. *comporter* to bear, peddle] **:** a peddler of religious books
colt \'kōlt\ *n* [ME, fr. OE; akin to OE *cild* child] **1 a :** FOAL **b :** a young male horse either sexually immature or before attaining an arbitrarily designated age **2 :** a young untried person **:** NOVICE
col·ter \'kōl-tər\ *n* [ME, fr. OE *culter* & OF *coltre*, both fr. L *culter* plowshare] **:** a cutter on a plow to cut the turf
colt·ish \'kōl-tish\ *adj* **1 :** UNDISCIPLINED; *esp* **:** FRISKY, PLAYFUL **2 :** of, relating to, or resembling a colt — **colt·ish·ly** *adv*
colts·foot \'kōlts-ˌfu̇t\ *n, pl* **coltsfoots :** any of various plants with large rounded leaves resembling the foot of a colt; *esp* **:** a perennial composite herb (*Tussilago farfara*)
col·u·brid \'käl-(y)ə-brəd\ *n* [deriv. of L *colubra* snake] **:** any of a large cosmopolitan family (Colubridae) of nonvenomous snakes — **colubrid** *adj*
col·u·brine \-ˌbrīn\ *adj* **1 :** of, relating to, or resembling a snake **2 :** COLUBRID
co·lu·go \kə-'lü-(ˌ)gō\ *n* **:** FLYING LEMUR
col·um·bar·i·um \ˌkäl-əm-'bar-ē-əm, -'ber-\ *n, pl* **col·um·bar·ia** \-ē-ə\ [L, lit., dovecote, fr. *columba* dove] **1 :** a structure of vaults lined with recesses for cinerary urns **2 :** a recess in a columbarium
Co·lum·bia \kə-'ləm-bē-ə\ *n* [NL, fr. Christopher *Columbus* †1506 It explorer] **:** the United States
Co·lum·bi·an \-bē-ən\ *adj* **:** of or relating to the United States or Christopher Columbus
col·um·bine \'käl-əm-ˌbīn\ *n* [ME, fr. ML *columbina*, fr. L, fem. of *columbinus* dovelike, fr. *columba* dove; akin to OHG *holuntar* elder tree, Gk *kolymbos* a bird, *kelainos* black] **:** any of a genus (*Aquilegia*) of plants of the crowfoot family with showy flowers
Col·um·bine \-ˌbīn, -ˌbēn\ *n* [It *Colombina*] **:** the saucy sweetheart of Harlequin in comedy and pantomime
co·lum·bite \kə-'ləm-ˌbīt\ *n* [NL *columbium*] **:** a black mineral $(Fe,Mn)(Cb,Ta)_2O_6$ consisting essentially of iron and columbium
co·lum·bi·um \kə-'ləm-bē-əm\ *n* [NL, fr. *Columbia*] **:** NIOBIUM
Co·lum·bus Day \kə-'ləm-bəs-\ *n* **:** October 12 observed as a legal holiday in many states of the U.S. in commemoration of the landing of Columbus in the Bahamas in 1492 — called also *Discovery Day*
col·u·mel·la \ˌkäl-(y)ə-'mel-ə\ *n, pl* **col·u·mel·lae** \-'mel-(ˌ)ē, -ˌī\ [NL, fr. L, dim. of *columna*] **:** any of various plant or animal parts resembling a column — **col·u·mel·lar** \-'mel-ər\ *adj* — **col·u·mel·late** \-ət, -ˌāt\ *adj*

col·umn \'käl-əm\ *n* [ME *columne*, fr. MF *colomne*, fr. L *columna*, fr. *columen* top; akin to L *collis* hill — more at HILL] **1 a :** a vertical arrangement of items printed or written on a page **b :** one of two or more vertical sections of a printed page separated by a rule or blank space **c :** an accumulation arranged vertically **:** STACK **d :** a special department in a newspaper or periodical **2 :** a supporting pillar; *esp* **:** one consisting of a usu. round shaft, a capital, and a base **3 :** something resembling a column in form, position, or function ⟨a ~ of water⟩ **4 :** a long row (as of soldiers) — **co·lum·nar** \kə-'ləm-nər\ *adj* — **col·umned** \'käl-əmd\ *adj*

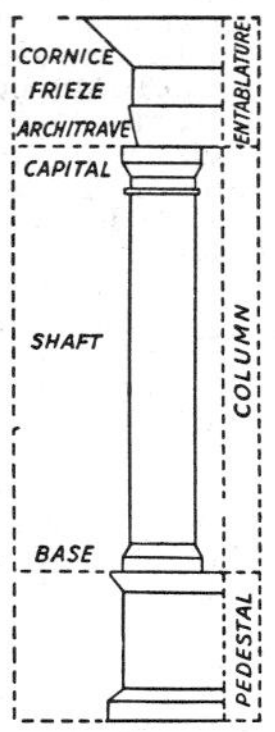

column 2 with pedestal and entablature

co·lum·ni·a·tion \kə-ˌləm-nē-'ā-shən\ *n* [modif. of L *columnation-, columnatio*, fr. *columna*] **:** the employment or the arrangement of columns in a structure
col·um·nist \'käl-əm-(n)əst *also* 'käl-yəm-\ *n* **:** one who writes a newspaper column
col·za \'käl-zə, 'kōl-\ *n* [F, fr. D *koolzaad*, fr. MD *coolsaet*, fr. *coole* cabbage + *saet* seed] **1 :** any of several coles; *esp* **:** one (as rape) producing seed used as a source of oil **2 :** RAPESEED
com- *or* **col-** *or* **con-** *prefix* [ME, fr. OF, fr. L, with, together, thoroughly] **:** with **:** together **:** jointly — usu. *com-* before *b, p,* or *m* ⟨*com*mingle⟩, *col-* before *l* ⟨*col*linear⟩, and *con-* before other sounds ⟨*con*centrate⟩
1**co·ma** \'kō-mə\ *n* [NL, fr. Gk *kōma* deep sleep] **1 :** a state of profound unconsciousness caused by disease, injury, or poison **2 :** a state of mental or physical sluggishness **:** TORPOR
2**coma** *n, pl* **co·mae** \-ˌmē, -ˌmī\ [L, hair, fr. Gk *komē*] **1 :** a tufted bunch (as of hairs) **2 :** the head of a comet usu. containing a nucleus **3 :** spherical aberration in which the image of a point source is a comet-shaped blur
Co·ma Ber·e·ni·ces \'kō-mə-ˌber-ə-'nī-(ˌ)sēz\ *n* [L (gen. *Comae Berenices*), lit., Berenice's hair] **:** a constellation north of Virgo and between Boötes and Leo
Co·man·che \kə-'man-chē\ *n, pl* **Comanche** *or* **Comanches** [Sp, of Shoshonean origin; perh. akin to Hopi *kománči* scalp lock] **1 :** a Shoshonean people ranging from Wyoming and Nebraska south into New Mexico and northwestern Texas **2 :** a member of the Comanche people
Co·man·che·an \-chē-ən\ *adj* [*Comanche*, Texas] **:** of, relating to, or being the period of the Mesozoic era between the Jurassic and the Cretaceous or the corresponding system of rocks — **Comanchean** *n*
1**co·mate** \(')kō-'māt, 'kō-ˌ\ *n* **:** COMPANION
2**co·mate** \'kō-ˌmāt\ *adj* **:** covered with hair or filaments **:** SHAGGY
co·ma·tose \'kō-mə-ˌtōs, 'käm-ə-\ *adj* [F *comateux*, fr. Gk *kōmat-, kōma*] **1 :** of, resembling, or affected with coma **2 :** LETHARGIC, TORPID
co·mat·u·la \kə-'mach-ə-lə\ *n, pl* **co·mat·u·lae** \-ə-ˌlē, -ˌlī\ [NL, former generic name, fr. LL, fem. of *comatulus* having hair neatly curled, fr. L *comatus* hairy, fr. *coma*] **:** COMATULID
co·mat·u·lid \-ə-ləd\ *n* **:** a free-swimming stalkless crinoid
1**comb** \'kōm\ *n* [ME, fr. OE *camb*; akin to OHG *kamb* comb, Gk *gomphos* tooth] **1 a :** a toothed instrument used esp. for adjusting, cleaning, or confining hair **b :** a structure resembling such a comb; *esp* **:** any of several toothed devices used in handling or ordering textile fibers **c :** CURRYCOMB **2 a :** a fleshy crest on the head of the domestic fowl and other gallinaceous birds **b :** something resembling the comb of a cock **3 :** HONEYCOMB — **combed** *adj*
2**comb** *vt* **1 :** to draw a comb through for the purpose of arranging or cleaning **2 :** SCRAPE, RAKE **3 a :** to remove with or as if with a comb **b :** to search or examine systematically **4 :** to use in the manner of a comb ~ *vi* **:** to roll over or break into foam ⟨waves ~⟩
1**com·bat** \kəm-'bat, 'käm-ˌ\ *vb* **com·bat·ed** *or* **com·bat·ted; com·bat·ing** *or* **com·bat·ting** [MF *combattre*, fr. (assumed) VL *combattere*, fr. L *com-* + *battuere* to beat — more at BATTLE] *vi* **:** STRUGGLE, FIGHT ~ *vt* **1 :** to fight with **:** BATTLE **2 :** to struggle against; *esp* **:** to strive to reduce or eliminate **syn** see OPPOSE
2**com·bat** \'käm-ˌbat\ *n, often attrib* **1 :** a fight or contest between individuals or groups **2 :** CONFLICT, CONTROVERSY **3 :** active fighting in a war **:** ACTION
com·ba·tant \kəm-'bat-ᵊnt, 'käm-bət-ənt\ *adj* **:** engaging in or ready to engage in combat — **combatant** *n*
combat fatigue *n* **:** a traumatic psychoneurotic reaction or an acute psychotic reaction occurring under conditions (as wartime combat) causing intense stress
com·bat·ive \kəm-'bat-iv\ *adj* **:** eager to fight **:** PUGNACIOUS — **com·bat·ive·ly** *adv* — **com·bat·ive·ness** *n*
combe \'küm, 'kōm\ *n* [of Celt origin] **1** *Brit* **:** a deep narrow valley **2** *Brit* **:** a valley or basin on the flank of a hill
comb·er \'kō-mər\ *n* **1 :** one that combs **2 :** a long curling wave of the sea
com·bin·abil·i·ty \kəm-ˌbī-nə-'bil-ət-ē\ *n* **:** ability to enter into combination — **com·bin·able** \-'bī-nə-bəl\ *adj*
com·bi·na·tion \ˌkäm-bə-'nā-shən\ *n, often attrib* **1 a :** a result or product of combining; *esp* **:** an alliance of individuals, corporations, or states united to achieve a social, political, or economic end **b :** two or more persons working as a team **2 :** an ordered sequence: as **a :** a sequence of letters or numbers chosen in setting a lock; *also* **:** the mechanism operating or moved by the sequence **b :** any of the different sets into which a number of individuals (as letters) may be grouped without regard to order within the group **3 :** any of various one-piece undergarments for the upper and lower parts of the body **4 :** an instrument designed to perform two or more tasks **5 a :** the act or process of combining; *esp* **:** that of uniting to form a chemical compound **b :** the quality or state of being combined — **com·bi·na·tion·al** \-'nā-shnəl, -shən-ᵊl\ *adj*
com·bi·na·tive \'käm-bə-ˌnāt-iv, kəm-'bī-nət-\ *adj* **1 :** tending or able to combine **2 :** resulting from combination
com·bi·na·to·ri·al \kəm-ˌbī-nə-'tōr-ē-əl, -'tȯr-\ *adj* **:** of, relating to, or involving combinations
com·bi·na·to·ry \kəm-'bī-nə-ˌtōr-ē, -ˌtȯr-\ *adj* **:** COMBINATIVE
1**com·bine** \kəm-'bīn\ *vb* [ME *combinen*, fr. MF *combiner*, fr. LL *combinare*, fr. L *com-* + *bini* two by two] *vt* **1 :** to bring into close relationship; *specif* **:** to cause to unite into a chemical compound **2 :** INTERMIX, BLEND **3 :** to possess in combination ~ *vi* **1 a :** to

become one **b :** to unite to form a chemical compound **2 :** to act together **syn** see JOIN — **com·bin·er** *n*

²**com·bine** \'käm-ˌbīn\ *n* **1 :** an act or result of combining **2 :** a combination to effect some object **3 :** a harvesting machine that heads, threshes, and cleans grain while moving over a field

³**com·bine** \'käm-ˌbīn\ *vt* **:** to harvest with a combine

comb·ings \'kō-miŋz\ *n pl* **:** loose hair removed by a comb

combing wool *n* **:** long-stapled strong-fibered wool found suitable for combing and used esp. in the manufacture of worsteds

combining form \kəm-'bī-niŋ-\ *n* **:** a linguistic form that occurs only in compounds or derivatives and can be distinguished descriptively from an affix by its ability to occur as one immediate constituent of a form whose only other immediate constituent is an affix (as *cephal-* in *cephalic*) or by its being an allomorph of a morpheme having another allomorph that may occur alone or can be distinguished historically from an affix by the fact that it is borrowed from another language in which it is descriptively a word or a combining form

com·bo \'käm-(ˌ)bō\ *n* [*comb*ination + *-o*] **1 :** COMBINATION **2 :** a usu. small jazz or dance band

com·bust \kəm-'bəst\ *vb* [L *combustus*, pp. of *comburere* to burn up, irreg. fr. *com-* + *urere* to burn — more at EMBER] **:** BURN

com·bus·ti·bil·i·ty \kəm-ˌbəs-tə-'bil-ət-ē\ *n* **:** the quality or state of being combustible

com·bus·ti·ble \kəm-'bəs-tə-bəl\ *adj* **1 :** capable of combustion **2 :** easily excited — **combustible** *n* — **com·bus·ti·bly** \-blē\ *adv*

com·bus·tion \kəm-'bəs-chən\ *n* **1 :** an act or instance of burning **2 a :** a chemical process (as an oxidation) accompanied by the evolution of light and heat **b :** a slower oxidation **3 :** violent agitation **:** TUMULT — **com·bus·tive** \-'bəs-tiv\ *adj*

com·bus·tor \-'bəs-tər\ *n* **:** the chamber in a gas turbine or a jet engine in which combustion occurs

come \'kəm, *sometimes without stress when a stress follows*\ *vb* **came** \'kām\ **come; com·ing** \'kəm-iŋ\ [ME *comen*, fr. OE *cuman;* akin to OHG *queman* to come, L *venire*, Gk *bainein* to walk, go] *vi* **1 a :** to move toward something **:** APPROACH ⟨~ here⟩ **b :** to move toward or enter a scene of action or into a field of interest — used with an implication of purpose ⟨he *came* to see us⟩ **c :** to reach a particular station in a series ⟨now we ~ to the section on health⟩ **d** (1) **:** to approach in kind or quality ⟨this ~*s* near perfection⟩ (2) **:** to result in ⟨his plans ~ to naught⟩ (3) **:** to reach a condition through change ⟨their fury *came* to a boil⟩ **e** (1) **:** to advance toward maturity or a culminating state ⟨the job is *coming* nicely⟩ (2) **:** to advance in a particular manner ⟨~ running when I call⟩ (3) **:** to advance, rise, or improve in rank or condition ⟨general had ~ up through the ranks⟩ **f :** to get along **:** FARE **g :** EXTEND ⟨her dress *came* to her ankles⟩ **2 a** (1) **:** to arrive at a particular place, end, result, or conclusion ⟨*came* to his senses⟩ ⟨~ untied⟩ (2) **:** AMOUNT ⟨taxes ~ to more than it's worth⟩ **b :** to appear to the mind ⟨the answer *came* to him⟩ **c :** HAPPEN, OCCUR ⟨no harm will ~ to you⟩ **d** (1) **:** ORIGINATE, ARISE ⟨wine ~*s* from grapes⟩ ⟨~ of sturdy stock⟩ (2) **:** to be or have been a native or resident ⟨he ~*s* from Toronto⟩ **e :** to enter or assume a condition, relation, use, or position ⟨artillery *came* into action⟩ **f :** to fall within a field of view or a range of application ⟨this ~*s* within the terms of the treaty⟩ **g :** to issue forth ⟨sob *came* from her throat⟩ **h :** to take form ⟨churn till the butter ~*s*⟩ **i :** to be available ⟨this model ~*s* in several sizes⟩ **:** EXIST ⟨as good as they ~⟩ **j :** to experience orgasm **3 :** to fall to a person in a division or inheritance of property **4 :** to become moved favorably **:** RELENT **5 :** to require a specified exertion or expenditure ⟨good clothes ~ high⟩ ⟨easy ~, easy go⟩ **6 :** BECOME ⟨portrait seemed to ~ alive⟩ ⟨things will ~ clear if we are patient⟩ ~ *vt* **1 :** to approach or be near (an age) ⟨child *coming* eight years old⟩ **2 :** to act or play the part of ⟨~ the stern parent⟩ — **come across :** to meet or find by chance — **come at :** to reach a mastery of **:** ATTAIN — **come by 1** *chiefly Midland* **:** VISIT **2 :** ACQUIRE — **come into :** to acquire as an inheritance — **come off :** to cease to utter pretentious or foolish talk ⟨*come off* it⟩ — **come through 1 :** SURVIVE **2 :** GIVE, PROVIDE — **come to pass :** HAPPEN — used with *it*

come about *vi* **1 :** to come to pass **:** HAPPEN **2 :** to change direction ⟨the wind has *come about* into the north⟩ **3 :** to shift to a new tack

come across *vi* **:** to supply or furnish something demanded; *esp* **:** to pay over money **:** CONTRIBUTE

come along *vi* **1 :** to make progress **:** SUCCEED **2 :** APPEAR

come around *vi* **:** to come round

come back *vi* **1 :** to return to life or vitality **2 :** to return to memory **3 :** REPLY, RETORT **4 :** to regain a former condition or position

come·back \'kəm-ˌbak\ *n* **1 a :** a sharp or witty reply **:** RETORT **b :** a cause for complaint **2 :** RECOVERY

co·me·di·an \kə-'mēd-ē-ən\ *n* **1 :** an actor who plays comedy **2 :** a comical individual; *esp* **:** a professional entertainer who uses any of various physical or verbal means to be amusing

co·me·dic \-'mēd-ik, -'med-\ *adj* **:** of or relating to comedy

co·me·di·enne \kə-ˌmēd-ē-'en\ *n* [F *comédienne*, fem. of *comédien* comedian, fr. *comedie*] **:** a female comedian

com·e·do \'käm-ə-ˌdō\ *n, pl* **com·e·do·nes** \ˌkäm-ə-'dō-(ˌ)nēz\ [NL, fr. L, glutton, fr. *comedere*] **:** BLACKHEAD 2

come down *vi* **1 :** to lose or fall in estate or condition **2 :** to fall sick

come·down \'kəm-ˌdau̇n\ *n* **:** a descent in rank or dignity

com·e·dy \'käm-əd-ē\ *n* [ME, fr. MF *comedie*, fr. L *comoedia*, fr. Gk *kōmōidia*, fr. *kōmos* revel + *aeidein* to sing — more at ODE] **1 a :** a theatrical, film, radio, or television drama of light and amusing character and typically with a happy ending **b :** the genre of dramatic literature dealing with the comic or with the serious in a light or satirical manner **2 a :** a medieval narrative that ends happily ⟨Dante's *Divine Comedy*⟩ **b :** a literary work written in a comic style or treating a comic theme **3 :** a ludicrous or farcical event or series of events **4 :** the comic element

come–hith·er \(ˌ)kəm-'hit͟h-ər, (ˌ)kə-'mit͟h-\ *adj* **:** SEDUCTIVE

come in *vi* **1 :** to place among those finishing ⟨*came in* second⟩ **2 a :** to become of use **b :** to make reply to a signal or call **3 :** to be the recipient **4 :** to attain maturity, fruitfulness, or production

come·li·ness \'kəm-lē-nəs\ *n* **:** the quality or state of being comely

come·ly \'kəm-lē\ *adj* [ME *comly*, alter. of OE *cȳmlic* glorious, fr. *cȳme* lively, fine; akin to OHG *kūmig* weak, Gk *goan* to lament] **1 :** attractive because of good looks **:** HANDSOME **2 :** generally pleasant and attractive-looking **:** SEEMLY **syn** see BEAUTIFUL

come off *vi* **1 :** to acquit oneself **2 :** SUCCEED **3 :** HAPPEN, OCCUR

come on *vi* **1 :** to begin by degrees **2 :** to make progress in growth or development **3 :** PLEASE — used in cajoling or pleading

come–on \'kəm-ˌȯn, -ˌän\ *n* **:** INDUCEMENT, LURE

come out *vi* **1 :** to come into view **:** EMERGE **2 :** to turn out **3 a :** to declare oneself **b :** UTTER — used with *with*

come–out·er \(ˌ)kə-'mau̇t-ər\ *n* **:** RADICAL, REFORMER

come over *vi* **1 a :** to change from one side (as of a controversy) to the other **b :** to visit casually **:** drop in **2** *Brit* **:** BECOME

com·er \'kəm-ər\ *n* **1 :** one that comes or arrives ⟨all ~*s*⟩ **2 :** one making rapid progress or showing promise

come round *vi* **1 :** to return to a former condition; *esp* **:** to come to **2 :** to change in direction or opinion; *also* **:** to come about

¹**co·mes·ti·ble** \kə-'mes-tə-bəl\ *adj* [MF, fr. ML *comestibilis*, fr. L *comestus*, pp. of *comedere* to eat, fr. *com-* + *edere* to eat] **:** EDIBLE

²**comestible** *n* **:** FOOD — usu. used in pl.

com·et \'käm-ət\ *n* [ME *comete*, fr. OE *cometa*, fr. L, fr. Gk *komētēs*, lit., long-haired, fr. *koman* to wear long hair, fr. *komē* hair] **:** a celestial body that consists of a fuzzy head usu. surrounding a bright nucleus, that often when in the part of its orbit near the sun develops a long tail which points away from the sun, and that has an orbit varying in eccentricity between nearly round and parabolic — **com·e·tary** \-ə-ˌter-ē\ *adj* — **co·met·ic** \kə-'met-ik, kä-\ *adj*

come to *vi* **1 :** to recover consciousness **2 a :** to bring a ship's head nearer the wind **:** LUFF **b :** to anchor or stop at a certain point

come up *vi* **1 :** to become mentioned **2** *Brit* **:** to enter a university **3** *of a sailing ship* **:** to come to a certain direction esp. as near as may be to the wind **4 :** to come before an authoritative person or group for decision **5 :** to be equal

come·up·pance \(ˌ)kə-'məp-ən(t)s\ *n* [*come up* + *-ance*] **:** a deserved rebuke or penalty **:** DESERTS

com·fit \'kəm(p)-fət, 'käm(p)-\ *n* [ME *confit*, fr. MF, fr. pp. of *confire* to prepare, fr. L *conficere*, fr. *com-* + *facere* to make — more at DO] **:** a confection consisting of a piece of fruit, a root, or a seed coated and preserved with sugar

¹**com·fort** \'kəm(p)-fərt\ *n* **1 :** strengthening aid: **a :** ASSISTANCE, SUPPORT **b :** consolation in trouble or worry **:** SOLACE **2 a :** state or feeling of relief or encouragement **b :** contented well-being **3 :** SATISFACTION, ENJOYMENT **4 :** one that gives or brings comfort — **com·fort·less** \-ləs\ *adj*

²**comfort** *vt* [ME *comforten*, fr. OF *conforter*, fr. LL *confortare* to strengthen greatly, fr. L *com-* + *fortis* strong] **1 :** to give strength and hope to **:** CHEER **2 :** to ease the grief or trouble of **:** CONSOLE

syn CONSOLE, SOLACE: COMFORT implies imparting cheer, strength, or encouragement as well as lessening pain; CONSOLE emphasizes the alleviating of grief or mitigating the sense of loss rather than distinct or full relief; SOLACE suggests a lifting of spirits often from loneliness or boredom as well as from pain or grief

com·fort·able \'kəm(p)(f)-tə-bəl, 'kəm(p)-fərt-ə-bəl\ *adj* **1 :** giving comfort; *esp* **:** providing physical comfort **2 :** more than adequate ⟨~ income⟩ **3 a :** physically at ease **b :** PLACID, UNDISTURBED — **com·fort·able·ness** *n* — **com·fort·ably** \-blē\ *adv*

syn COZY, SNUG, EASY, RESTFUL, REPOSEFUL: COMFORTABLE applies to anything that encourages serenity, well-being, or complacency as well as physical ease; COZY suggests warmth, shelter, assured ease, and friendliness; SNUG suggests having just enough space for comfort and safety but no more; EASY implies relief from or absence of anything likely to cause physical or mental discomfort or constraint; RESTFUL and REPOSEFUL apply to whatever induces or contributes to rest or relaxation

com·fort·er \'kəm(p)-fə(r)t-ər\ *n* **1 :** one that gives comfort **2 a :** a long narrow usu. knitted neck scarf **b :** QUILT, PUFF

comfort station *n* **:** REST ROOM

com·frey \'kəm(p)-frē\ *n* [ME *cumfirie*, fr. OF, fr. L *conferva*] **:** any of a genus (*Symphytum*) of plants of the borage family

com·fy \'kəm(p)-fē\ *adj* [by shortening & alter.] **:** COMFORTABLE

¹**com·ic** \'käm-ik\ *adj* [L *comicus*, fr. Gk *kōmikos*, fr. *kōmos* revel] **1 a :** of, relating to, or marked by comedy **b :** composing or acting in comedies **2 :** causing laughter or amusement **:** FUNNY **3 :** of or relating to comic strips **syn** see LAUGHABLE

²**comic** *n* **1 :** COMEDIAN **2 :** the comic element **3 a :** COMIC STRIP **b** (1) **:** a magazine composed of comic strips (2) *pl* **:** the part of a newspaper devoted to comic strips

com·i·cal \'käm-i-kəl\ *adj* **1** *archaic* **:** of or relating to comedy **2 :** amusingly whimsical **:** DROLL **syn** see LAUGHABLE — **com·i·cal·i·ty** \ˌkäm-i-'kal-ət-ē\ *n* — **com·i·cal·ly** \'käm-i-k(ə-)lē\ *adv*

comic strip *n* **:** a group of cartoons in narrative sequence

com·ing \'kəm-iŋ\ *adj* **1 :** APPROACHING, NEXT ⟨~ year⟩ **2 :** DUE, DESERVED **3 :** gaining importance

co·mi·tia \kə-'mish-(ē-)ə\ *n, pl* **comitia** [L, pl. of *comitium*, fr. *com-* + *itus*, pp. of *ire* to go — more at ISSUE] **:** one of several public assemblies of the people in ancient Rome for the exercise of legislative, judicial, and electoral functions — **co·mi·tial** \-'mish-əl\ *adj*

com·i·ty \'käm-ət-ē\ *n* [L *comitat-*, *comitas*, fr. *comis* courteous, fr. OL *cosmis*, fr. *com-* + *-smis* (akin to Skt *smayate* he smiles)] **1 a :** a courteous code of behavior **b :** COMITY OF NATIONS **c :** the informal and voluntary recognition by courts of one jurisdiction of the laws and judicial decision of another **2 :** avoidance of proselytizing members of another religious denomination

comity of nations 1 : the courtesy and friendship of nations marked esp. by mutual recognition of executive, legislative, and judicial acts **2 :** the group of nations practicing international comity

com·ma \'käm-ə\ *n* [LL, fr. L, part of a sentence, fr. Gk *komma* segment, clause, fr. *koptein* to cut] **1 :** a punctuation mark , used esp. as a mark of separation within the sentence **2 :** PAUSE, INTERVAL

comma bacillus *n* **:** a bacterium (*Vibrio comma*) that causes Asiatic cholera

comma fault *n* **:** the careless or unjustified use of a comma between coordinate main clauses not connected by a conjunction

¹**com·mand** \kə-'mand\ *vb* [ME *comanden*, fr. OF *comander*, fr. (assumed) VL *commandare*, alter. of L *commendare* to commit to one's charge — more at COMMEND] *vt* **1 :** to direct authoritatively **:** ORDER **2 :** to exercise a dominating influence over: as **a :** to have at one's immediate disposal **b :** to demand as one's due **:** EXACT ⟨~*s* a high fee⟩ **c :** to overlook or dominate from a strategic position **d :** to have military or naval command of as senior officer

2 *obs* : to order or request to be given ~ *vi* **1** : to have or to exercise direct authority : GOVERN **2** : to give orders **3** : to be commander **4** : to dominate from an elevated position

syn COMMAND, ORDER, BID, ENJOIN, DIRECT, INSTRUCT, CHARGE mean to issue orders. COMMAND and ORDER imply authority and usu. some degree of formality and impersonality; COMMAND stresses official exercise of authority, ORDER may suggest peremptory or arbitrary exercise; BID suggests giving orders peremptorily as to children or servants; ENJOIN implies giving an order or direction authoritatively and urgently and often with admonition or solicitude; DIRECT and INSTRUCT both connote expectation of obedience and usu. concern specific points of procedure or method, INSTRUCT sometimes implying greater explicitness or formality; CHARGE adds to ENJOIN an implication of imposing as a duty or responsibility

2**command** *n* **1** : the act of commanding **2** : an order given **3 a** : the ability to control : MASTERY **b** : the authority or right to command **c** (1) : the power to dominate (2) : scope of vision **d** : facility in use **4** : the personnel, area, or organization under a commander **5** : a position of highest authority **syn** see POWER

3**command** *adj* : done on command or request

com·man·dant \ˈkäm-ən-ˌdant, -ˌdänt\ *n* : COMMANDING OFFICER

com·man·deer \ˌkäm-ən-ˈdi(ə)r\ *vt* [Afrik *kommandeer*, fr. F *commander* to command, fr. OF *comander*] **1 a** : to compel to perform military service **b** : to seize for military purposes **2** : to take arbitrary or forcible possession of

com·mand·er \kə-ˈman-dər\ *n* **1** : one in an official position of command or control: as **a** : COMMANDING OFFICER **b** : the presiding officer of a society or organization **2** : a commissioned officer in the navy ranking above a lieutenant commander and below a captain — **com·mand·er·ship** \-ˌship\ *n*

commander in chief : one who holds the supreme command of an armed force

com·mand·ery \kə-ˈman-d(ə-)rē\ *n* **1** : a district under the control of a commander of an order of knights **2** : an assembly or lodge in a secret order

commanding officer *n* : an officer in command; *esp* : an officer in the armed forces in command of an organization or installation

com·mand·ment \kə-ˈman(d)-mənt\ *n* **1** : the act or power of commanding **2** : something that is commanded; *specif* : one of the biblical Ten Commandments

com·man·do \kə-ˈman-(ˌ)dō\ *n, pl* **commandos** *or* **commandoes** [Afrik *kommando*, fr. D *commando* command, fr. Sp *comando*, fr. *comandar* to command, fr. F *commander*] **1** *Africa* **a** : a military unit or command of the Boers **b** : a raiding expedition **2 a** : a military unit trained and organized as shock troops esp. for hit-and-run raids into enemy territory **b** : a member of a commando or other specialized raiding unit

com·me·dia dell'ar·te \kə-ˌmād-ē-ə-(ˌ)del-ˈärt-ē, -ˌmed-\ *n* [It, lit., comedy of art] : Italian comedy of the 16th to 18th centuries improvised from standardized situations and stock characters

comme il faut \ˌkəm-ˌēl-ˈfō\ *adj* [F, lit., as it should be] : conforming to accepted standards : PROPER

com·mem·o·rate \kə-ˈmem-ə-ˌrāt\ *vt* [L *commemoratus*, pp. of *commemorare*, fr. *com-* + *memorare* to remind of, fr. *memor* mindful — more at MEMORY] **1** : to call to remembrance **2** : to mark by some ceremony or observation : OBSERVE **3** : to be a memorial of **syn** see KEEP — **com·mem·o·ra·tor** \-ˌrāt-ər\ *n*

com·mem·o·ra·tion \kə-ˌmem-ə-ˈrā-shən\ *n* **1** : the act of commemorating **2** : something that commemorates

com·mem·o·ra·tive \kə-ˈmem-(ə-)rət-iv, -ˈmem-ə-ˌrāt-iv\ *adj* : intended as a commemoration : COMMEMORATING — **commemorative** *n* — **com·mem·o·ra·tive·ly** *adv*

com·mence \kə-ˈmen(t)s\ *vb* [ME *comencen*, fr. MF *comencer*, fr. (assumed) VL *cominitiare*, fr. L *com-* + LL *initiare* to begin, fr. L, to initiate] *vt* **1** : to enter upon : BEGIN **2** : to initiate formally by performing the first act of ~ *vi* **1** : to have a beginning : START **2** *chiefly Brit* : to begin to be or to act as **3** *chiefly Brit* : to take a degree at a university **syn** see BEGIN — **com·menc·er** *n*

com·mence·ment \-ˈmen(t)-smənt\ *n* **1** : an act, instance, or time of commencing **2 a** : the ceremonies or the day for conferring degrees or diplomas **b** : the period of activities at this time

com·mend \kə-ˈmend\ *vb* [ME *commenden*, fr. L *commendare*, fr. *com-* + *mandare* to entrust — more at MANDATE] *vt* **1** : to entrust for care or preservation **2** : to recommend as worthy of confidence or notice **3** : to mention with approbation : PRAISE ~ *vi* : to commend or serve as a commendation of something — **com·mend·able** \-ˈmen-də-bəl\ *adj* — **com·mend·ably** \-blē\ *adv*

com·men·da·tion \ˌkäm-ən-ˈdā-shən, -ˌen-\ *n* **1 a** : an act of commending **b** : something that commends **2** *archaic* : COMPLIMENT — **com·men·da·to·ry** \kə-ˈmen-də-ˌtōr-ē, -ˌtȯr-\ *adj*

com·men·sal \kə-ˈmen(t)-səl\ *adj* [ME, fr. ML *commensalis*, fr. L *com-* + LL *mensalis* of the table, fr. L *mensa* table] **1** : of or relating to those who habitually eat together **2** : living in a state of commensalism — **commensal** *n* — **com·men·sal·ly** \-sə-lē\ *adv*

com·men·sal·ism \-sə-ˌliz-əm\ *n* : a relation between two kinds of organisms in which one obtains food or other benefits from the other without damaging or benefiting it

com·men·su·ra·bil·i·ty \kə-ˌmen(t)s-(ə-)rə-ˈbil-ət-ē, -ˌmench-(ə-)rə-\ *n* : the quality or state of being commensurable

com·men·su·ra·ble \kə-ˈmen(t)s-(ə-)rə-bəl, -ˈmench-(ə-)rə-\ *adj* **1** : having a common measure; *specif* : divisible by a common unit an integral number of times **2** : COMMENSURATE 2 **syn** see PROPORTIONAL — **com·men·su·ra·bly** \-blē\ *adv*

com·men·su·rate \kə-ˈmen(t)s-(ə-)rət, -ˈmench-(ə-)rət\ *adj* [LL *commensuratus*, fr. L *com-* + LL *mensuratus*, pp. of *mensurare* to measure, fr. L *mensura* measure] **1** : equal in measure or extent : COEXTENSIVE **2** : PROPORTIONATE, CORRESPONDING **3** : COMMENSURABLE 1 **syn** see PROPORTIONAL — **com·men·su·rate·ly** *adv* — **com·men·su·ra·tion** \kə-ˌmen(t)-sə-ˈrā-shən, -ˌmen-chə-ˈrā-\ *n*

1**com·ment** \ˈkäm-ˌent\ *n* [ME, fr. LL *commentum*, fr. L, invention, fr. neut. of *commentus*, pp. of *comminisci* to invent, fr. *com-* + *-minisci* (akin to *ment-*, *mens* mind)] **1** : COMMENTARY **2** : a note explaining, illustrating, or criticizing the meaning of a writing **3 a** : REMARK, OBSERVATION **b** : expression of opinion

2**comment** *vi* : to make or write comment ~ *vt* : to make a comment on

com·men·tary \ˈkäm-ən-ˌter-ē\ *n* **1 a** : an explanatory treatise — usu. used in pl. **b** : a record of events usu. written by a participant — usu. used in pl. **2 a** : a systematic series of explanations or interpretations of a writing **b** : COMMENT 2 **c** : a descriptive or critical oral narration **3** : something that serves for explanation

com·men·tate \ˈkäm-ən-ˌtāt\ *vb* [back-formation fr. *commentator*] *vt* : to give a commentary on ~ *vi* : to act as a commentator

com·men·ta·tor \-ˌtāt-ər\ *n* : one who gives a commentary; *esp* : one who reports and discusses news on radio or television

1**com·merce** \ˈkäm-(ˌ)ərs\ *n* [MF, fr. L *commercium*, fr. *com-* + *merc-*, *merx* merchandise] **1** : social intercourse : interchange of ideas, opinions, or sentiments **2** : the exchange or buying and selling of commodities on a large scale involving transportation from place to place **3** : SEXUAL INTERCOURSE **syn** see BUSINESS

2**com·merce** \ˈkäm-(ˌ)ərs, kə-ˈmərs\ *vi, archaic* : COMMUNE

1**com·mer·cial** \kə-ˈmər-shəl\ *adj* **1 a** : of, relating to, characteristic of, or suitable for commerce **b** : of an average or inferior quality ⟨~ oxalic acid⟩ **2 a** : viewed with regard to profit **b** : designed for profit; *esp* : designed for mass appeal **3** : emphasizing skills and subjects useful in business **4** : paid for by advertisers ⟨~ TV⟩ — **com·mer·cial·ly** \-ˈmərsh-(ə-)lē\ *adv*

2**commercial** *n* : an advertisement broadcast on radio or television

commercial bank *n* : a bank including in its functions the acceptance of demand deposits subject to withdrawal by check

com·mer·cial·ism \-ˈmər-shə-ˌliz-əm\ *n* **1** : commercial spirit, institutions, or methods **2** : excessive emphasis on profit — **com·mer·cial·ist** \-ˈmər-shə-ləst, -ˈmərsh-ləst\ *n* — **com·mer·cial·is·tic** \-ˌmər-shə-ˈlis-tik\ *adj*

com·mer·cial·iza·tion \kə-ˌmərsh-(ə-)lə-ˈzā-shən\ *n* : the act of commercializing : the state of being commercialized

com·mer·cial·ize \kə-ˈmər-shə-ˌlīz\ *vt* **1 a** : to manage on a business basis for profit **b** : to develop commerce in **2** : to exploit for profit ⟨~ Christmas⟩ **3** : to debase in quality for more profit

commercial paper *n* : short-term negotiable instruments arising out of commercial transactions

commercial traveler *n* : TRAVELING SALESMAN

com·mie \ˈkäm-ē\ *n, often cap* [by shortening and alter.] : COMMUNIST

com·mi·na·tion \ˌkäm-ə-ˈnā-shən\ *n* [ME, fr. MF or L; MF, fr. L *commination-*, *comminatio*, fr. *comminatus*, pp. of *comminari* to threaten, fr. *com-* + *minari* to threaten] : DENUNCIATION — **com·mi·na·to·ry** \ˈkäm-ə-nə-ˌtōr-ē, -ˌtȯr-; kə-ˈmin-ə-, -ˈmīn-\ *adj*

com·min·gle \kə-ˈmiŋ-gəl, kä-\ *vb* : MINGLE, BLEND **syn** see MIX

com·mi·nute \ˈkäm-ə-ˌn(y)üt\ *vt* [L *comminutus*, pp. of *comminuere*, fr. *com-* + *minuere* to lessen] : to reduce to minute particles : PULVERIZE — **com·mi·nu·tion** \ˌkäm-ə-ˈn(y)ü-shən\ *n*

com·mis·er·ate \kə-ˈmiz-ə-ˌrāt\ *vb* [L *commiseratus*, pp. of *commiserari*, fr. *com-* + *miserari* to pity, fr. *miser* wretched] *vt* : to feel or express sorrow or compassion for ~ *vi* : CONDOLE, SYMPATHIZE — **com·mis·er·a·tive** \-ˈmiz-ə-ˌrāt-iv\ *adj*

com·mis·er·a·tion \-ˌmiz-ə-ˈrā-shən\ *n* : the act of commiserating **syn** see PITY

com·mis·sar \ˈkäm-ə-ˌsär\ *n* [Russ *komissar*, fr. G *kommissar*, fr. ML *commissarius*] **1 a** : a Communist party official assigned to a military unit to teach party principles and policies and to ensure party loyalty **b** : one resembling a political commissar in attempting to control public opinion or its expression **2** : the head of a government department in the U.S.S.R. until 1946

com·mis·sar·i·at \ˌkäm-ə-ˈser-ē-ət\ *n* [NL *commissariatus*, fr. ML *commissarius*] **1** : a system for supplying an army with food **2** : food supplies **3** [Russ *komissariat*, fr. G *kommissariat*, fr. NL *commissariatus*] : a government department in the U.S.S.R. until 1946

com·mis·sary \ˈkäm-ə-ˌser-ē\ *n* [ME *commissarie*, fr. ML *commissarius*, fr. L *commissus*, pp.] **1** : one delegated by a superior to execute a duty or an office **2 a** : a store for equipment and provisions; *specif* **c** : a supermarket operated for military personnel **b** : food supplies **c** : a lunchroom esp. in a motion-picture studio

1**com·mis·sion** \kə-ˈmish-ən\ *n* [ME, fr. MF, fr. L *commission-*, *commissio* act of bringing together, fr. *commissus*, pp. of *committere*] **1 a** : a formal written warrant granting the power to perform various acts or duties **b** : a certificate conferring military rank and authority; *also* : the rank and authority so conferred **2** : an authorization or command to act in a prescribed manner or to perform prescribed acts : CHARGE **3 a** : authority to act for, in behalf of, or in place of another **b** : a task or matter entrusted to one as an agent for another **4 a** : a group of persons directed to perform some duty **b** : a government agency having administrative, legislative, or judicial powers **c** : a city council having legislative and executive functions **5** : an act of committing (as a crime) **6** : a fee paid to an agent or employee for transacting a piece of business or performing a service; *esp* : a percentage of the money received in a transaction paid to the agent responsible for the business **7** : an act of entrusting or giving authority — **in commission** *or* **into commission 1** : under the authority of commissioners **2** *of a ship* : ready for active service **3** : in use or in condition for use — **on commission** : with commission serving as partial or full pay for work done — **out of commission 1** : out of active service or use **2** : out of working order

2**commission** *vt* **com·mis·sion·ing** \-ˈmish-(ə-)niŋ\ **1** : to furnish with a commission: as **a** : to confer a formal commission on **b** : to order to be made **2** : to put (a ship) in commission

com·mis·sion·aire \kə-ˌmish-ə-ˈna(ə)r, -ˈne(ə)r\ *n* [F *commissionnaire*, fr. *commission*] *chiefly Brit* : a uniformed attendant

commissioned officer *n* : an officer of the armed forces holding by a commission a rank of second lieutenant or ensign or above

com·mis·sion·er \kə-ˈmish-(ə-)nər\ *n* : a person with a commission: as **a** : a member of a commission **b** : the representative of the governmental authority in a district, province, or other unit often having both judicial and administrative powers **c** : the officer in charge of a department or bureau of the public service **d** : the administrative head of a professional sport

commission merchant *n* : one who buys or sells another's goods for a commission

commission plan *n* : a method of municipal government under which a small elective commission exercises both executive and legislative powers and each commissioner directly administers one or more municipal departments

com·mis·sur·al \ˌkäm-ə-ˈshu̇r-əl\ *adj* : of, relating to, or being commissure

com·mis·sure \ˈkäm-ə-ˌshu̇(ə)r\ *n* [ME, fr. MF or L; MF, fr. L *commissura* a joining, fr. *commissus*, pp.] **1** : the place where two bodies or parts unite : CLOSURE **2** : a connecting band of nerve tissue in the brain or spinal cord

com•mit \kə-'mit\ *vb* **com•mit•ted; com•mit•ting** [ME *committen*, fr. L *committere* to connect, entrust, fr. *com-* + *mittere* to send] *vt* **1 a :** to put into charge or trust : ENTRUST **b :** to place in a prison or mental institution **c :** to consign or record for preservation ⟨~ it to memory⟩ **d :** to put into a place for disposal or safekeeping **e :** to refer (as a legislative bill) to a committee for consideration and report **2 :** to bring about : PERFORM ⟨~ a crime⟩ **3 a :** OBLIGATE, BIND **b :** to pledge or assign to some particular course or use **c :** to reveal the views of ~ *vi, obs* **:** to perform an offense — **com•mit•ta•ble** \-'mit-ə-bəl\ *adj*

syn ENTRUST, CONFIDE, CONSIGN, RELEGATE: COMMIT may express the general idea of delivering into another's charge or the special sense of transferring to a superior power or to a special place of custody; ENTRUST implies committing with trust and confidence; CONFIDE implies entrusting with assurance or reliance; CONSIGN suggests transferring to remove from one's control with formality or finality; RELEGATE implies a consigning to a particular class or sphere often with a suggestion of getting rid of

com•mit•ment \kə-'mit-mənt\ *n* **1 a :** an act of committing to a charge or trust: as (1) **:** a consignment to a penal or mental institution (2) **:** an act of referring a matter to a legislative committee **b :** MITTIMUS **2 a :** an agreement or pledge to do something in the future; *esp* **:** an engagement to assume a financial obligation at a future date **b :** something pledged **c :** the state of being obligated

com•mit•tal \kə-'mit-ᵊl\ *n* **:** COMMITMENT, CONSIGNMENT

com•mit•tee \kə-'mit-ē, *sense 1 also* ,käm-ə-'tē\ *n* **1** *archaic* **:** a person to whom a charge or trust is committed **2 a :** a body of persons delegated to consider, investigate, take action on, or report on some matter; *specif* **:** a body of members chosen by a legislative body to give consideration to legislative matters **b :** a self-constituted organization for the promotion of some common object

com•mit•tee•man \kə-'mit-ē-mən, -,man\ *n* **1 :** a member of a committee **2 :** a party leader of a ward or precinct — **com•mit•tee•wom•an** \-,wu̇m-ən\ *n*

committee of the whole : the whole membership of a legislative house sitting as a committee and operating under informal rules

com•mix \kə-'miks, kä-\ *vb* [back-formation fr. ME *comixt* blended, fr. L *commixtus*, pp. of *commiscēre* to mix together, fr. *com-* + *miscēre* to mix — more at MIX] **:** MIX, BLEND

com•mix•ture \-chər\ *n* [L *commixtura*, fr. *commixtus*] **1 :** the act or process of mixing **:** the state of being mixed **2 :** COMPOUND, MIXTURE

com•mode \kə-'mōd\ *n* [F, fr. *commode*, adj., suitable, convenient, fr. L *commodus*, fr. *com-* + *modus* measure — more at METE] **1 :** a woman's ornate cap popular in the late 17th and early 18th centuries **2 a :** a low chest of drawers **b :** a movable washstand with a cupboard underneath **c :** a boxlike structure holding a chamber pot under an open seat; *also* **:** CHAMBER POT **d :** TOILET 3b

com•mo•di•ous \kə-'mōd-ē-əs\ *adj* [ME, useful, fr. MF *commodieux*, fr. ML *commodiosus*, irreg. fr. L *commodum* convenience, fr. neut. of *commodus*] **1 :** HANDY, SERVICEABLE **2 :** comfortably or conveniently spacious **:** ROOMY — **com•mo•di•ous•ly** *adv* — **com•mo•di•ous•ness** *n*

com•mod•i•ty \kə-'mäd-ət-ē\ *n* [ME *commoditee*, fr. MF *commodité*, fr. L *commoditat-, commoditas*, fr. *commodus*] **1 a :** CONVENIENCE, ADVANTAGE **b :** something useful or valuable **2 :** an economic good: as **a :** a product of agriculture or mining **b :** an article of commerce **3** *obs* **:** QUANTITY, LOT

com•mo•dore \'käm-ə-,dō(ə)r, -,dȯ(ə)r\ *n* [prob. modif. of D *commandeur* commander, fr. F, fr. OF *comandeor*, fr. *comander* to command] **1 :** a commissioned officer in the navy ranking above a captain and below a rear admiral **2 :** the ranking officer commanding a body of merchant ships **3 :** the chief officer of a yacht club or boating association

¹**com•mon** \'käm-ən\ *adj* [ME *commun*, fr. OF, fr. L *communis* — more at MEAN] **1 a :** of or relating to a community at large **:** PUBLIC **b :** known to the community ⟨~ nuisance⟩ **2 a :** belonging to or shared by two or more individuals or by all members of a group **b :** belonging equally to two or more quantities **c :** having two or more branches ⟨~ carotid artery⟩ **3 a :** occurring or appearing frequently **:** FAMILIAR **b :** of the best known kind ⟨~ salt⟩ **4 a :** WIDESPREAD, GENERAL ⟨~ knowledge⟩ **b :** characterized by a lack of privilege or special status ⟨~ people⟩ **c :** ELEMENTARY, SIMPLE ⟨~ decency⟩ **5 a :** falling below ordinary standards **:** SECOND-RATE **b :** lacking refinement **c :** completely unprincipled **6 a** *of gender* **:** either masculine or feminine **b** *of a substantive* **:** naming any of a class of beings or things **c** *of a grammatical case* **:** denoting relations by a single form that in a more highly inflected language might be denoted by two or more different case forms — **com•mon•ly** *adv* — **com•mon•ness** \-ən-nəs\ *n*

syn ORDINARY, FAMILIAR, POPULAR, VULGAR: COMMON implies usual everyday quality or frequency of occurrence and occasionally connotes inferiority; ORDINARY stresses accordance in quality or kind with the regular order of things rather than frequency; FAMILIAR stresses the fact of being generally known and easily recognized; POPULAR applies to what is accepted by or prevalent among people in general sometimes in contrast to upper classes or special groups; VULGAR may occasionally apply to popular esp. as opposed to the learned but nearly always now connotes crudeness of manners or taste **syn** see in addition RECIPROCAL

²**common** *n* **1** *pl* **:** the common people **2** *pl but sing in constr* **:** a dining hall **3** *pl but sing or pl in constr, often cap* **a :** the political group or estate comprising the commoners **b :** the parliamentary representatives of the commoners **c :** HOUSE OF COMMONS **4 :** the legal right of taking a profit in another's land in common with the owner **5 :** a piece of land subject to common use: as **a :** undivided land used esp. for pasture **b :** a public open area in a municipality **6 a :** a religious service suitable for any of various festivals **b :** the ordinary of the mass — **in common 1 :** shared together **2 :** in a community

com•mon•age \'käm-ə-nij\ *n* **1 :** community land **2 :** COMMONALTY 1a(2)

com•mon•al•i•ty \,käm-ə-'nal-ət-ē\ *n* [ME *communalitie*, alter. of *communalte*] **1 :** COMMONNESS **2 :** the common people

com•mon•al•ty \'käm-ən-ᵊl-tē\ *n* [ME *communalte*, fr. OF *comunalté*, fr. *comunal* communal] **1 a** (1) **:** the common people (2) **:** the political estate formed by the common people **b :** COMMONNESS **2 :** a general group or body

common carrier *n* **:** an individual or corporation undertaking to transport for compensation persons, goods, or messages

common cold *n* **:** an acute virus disease of the upper respiratory tract marked by inflammation of mucous membranes

common denominator *n* **1 :** a common multiple of the denominators of a number of fractions **2 :** a common trait or theme

common divisor *n* **:** a number or expression that divides two or more numbers or expressions without remainder — called also *common factor*

com•mon•er \'käm-ə-nər\ *n* **1 a :** one of the common people **b :** one who is not of noble rank **2 :** a student (as at Oxford) who pays for his own board

common fraction *n* **:** a fraction in which both numerator and denominator are expressed

common law *n* **:** the body of law developed in England primarily from judicial decisions based on custom and precedent, unwritten in statute or code, and constituting the basis of the English legal system and of the system in all of the U.S. except Louisiana

common–law marriage *n* **:** a marriage relationship created by agreement and usu. cohabitation between a man and a woman without ecclesiastical or civil ceremony

common logarithm *n* **:** a logarithm whose base is 10

common measure *n* **:** a meter consisting chiefly of iambic lines of 7 accents each arranged in rhymed pairs usu. printed in 4-line stanza — called also *common meter*

common multiple *n* **:** a multiple of each of two or more numbers or expressions

¹**com•mon•place** \'käm-ən-,plās\ *n* [trans. of L *locus communis* widely applicable argument, trans. of Gk *koinos topos*] **1** *archaic* **:** a striking passage entered in a commonplace book **2 a :** an obvious or trite observation **b :** something taken for granted

²**commonplace** *adj* **:** ORDINARY, UNREMARKABLE — **com•mon•place•ness** *n*

commonplace book *n* **:** a book of memorabilia

common pleas *n pl* **1 :** a former superior court of English common law having jurisdiction over ordinary civil suits **2 :** a court of intermediate rank in some American states usu. having civil and criminal jurisdiction

common room *n* **1 :** a lounge available to all members of a residential community **2 :** a room in a college for the use of the faculty

common school *n* **:** a free public school

common sense *n* **1 :** sound prudent judgment **2 :** the unreflective opinions of ordinary men **syn** see SENSE — **com•mon•sen•si•ble** \,käm-ən-'sen(t)-sə-bəl\ *adj* — **com•mon•sen•si•cal** \-'sen(t)-si-kəl\ *adj*

common stock *n* **:** capital stock other than preferred stock

common time *n* **:** four beats to a measure in music

common touch *n* **:** the gift of appealing to or arousing the sympathetic interest of the generality of men

com•mon•weal \'käm-ən-,wēl\ *n* **1 :** the general welfare **2** *archaic* **:** COMMONWEALTH

com•mon•wealth \-,welth\ *n* **1** *archaic* **:** COMMONWEAL 1 **2 :** a nation, state, or other political unit: as **a :** one founded on law and united by compact or tacit agreement of the people for the common good **b :** one in which supreme authority is vested in the people **c :** REPUBLIC **3** *cap* **a :** the English state from the death of Charles I in 1649 to the Restoration in 1660 **b :** PROTECTORATE 1b **4 :** a state of the U.S. — used officially of Kentucky, Massachusetts, Pennsylvania, and Virginia **5** *cap* **:** a federal union of constituent states — used officially of Australia **6** *often cap* **:** an association of self-governing autonomous states having a somewhat common political and cultural background and united by a common allegiance ⟨the British *Commonwealth*⟩ **7** *often cap* **:** a political unit having local autonomy but voluntarily united with the U.S. — used officially of Puerto Rico

Commonwealth Day *n* **:** May 24 observed in parts of the British Commonwealth as the anniversary of Queen Victoria's birthday

common year *n* **:** a calendar year containing no intercalary period

com•mo•tion \kə-'mō-shən\ *n* [ME, fr. MF, fr. L *commotion-, commotio*, fr. *commotus*, pp. of *commovēre*] **1 :** a condition of civil unrest or insurrection **2 :** steady or recurrent motion **3 :** mental excitement or confusion **4 a :** a flurried disturbance **:** TO-DO **b :** noisy confusion **:** AGITATION

com•move \kə-'müv, kä-\ *vt* [ME *commoeven*, fr. MF *commuev-*, pres. stem of *commovoir*, fr. L *commovēre*, fr. *com-* + *movēre* to move] **1 :** to move violently **:** AGITATE **2 :** EXCITE, IMPASSION

com•mu•nal \kə-'myün-ᵊl, 'käm-yən-ᵊl\ *adj* [F, fr. LL *communalis*, fr. L *communis*] **1 :** of or relating to one or more communes **2 :** of or relating to a community **3 a :** characterized by collective ownership and use of property **b :** participated in, shared, or used in common by members of a group or community **4 a :** of, relating to, or based upon racial or cultural groups

com•mu•nal•ism \-ᵊl-,iz-əm\ *n* **1 :** social organization on a communal basis **2 :** loyalty to a sociopolitical grouping based on religious affiliation — **com•mu•nal•ist** \-ᵊl-əst\ *n or adj*

com•mu•nal•i•ty \,käm-yu̇-'nal-ət-ē\ *n* **1 :** communal state or character **2 :** group unity

com•mu•nal•ize \kə-'myün-ᵊl-,īz, 'käm-yən-\ *vt* **:** to make communal

Com•mu•nard \,käm-yu̇-'närd\ *n* **:** one who supported or participated in the Commune of Paris in 1871

¹**com•mune** \kə-'myün\ *vi* [ME *communen* to converse, administer Communion, fr. MF *comunier* to converse, administer or receive Communion, fr. LL *communicare*, fr. L] **1 :** to receive Communion **2 :** to communicate intimately ⟨~ with nature⟩

²**com•mune** \'käm-,yün, kə-'myün\ *n* [F, alter. of MF *comugne*, fr. ML *communia*, fr. L, neut. pl. of *communis*] **1 :** the smallest administrative district of many countries esp. in Europe **2 :** COMMONALTY 1 **3 :** COMMUNITY: as **a :** a medieval usu. municipal corporation **b** (1) **:** MIR (2) **:** a usu. rural community organized on a communal basis

com•mu•ni•ca•bil•i•ty \kə-,myü-ni-kə-'bil-ət-ē\ *n* **:** the quality of being communicable

com•mu•ni•ca•ble \kə-'myü-ni-kə-bəl\ *adj* **1 :** capable of being communicated **:** TRANSMITTABLE **2 :** COMMUNICATIVE — **com•mu•ni•ca•ble•ness** *n* — **com•mu•ni•ca•bly** \-blē\ *adv*

com•mu•ni•cant \kə-'myü-ni-kənt\ *n* **1 :** a church member

entitled to receive Communion; *broadly* : a member of a group **2** : one who communicates; *specif* : INFORMANT — **communicant** *adj*

com·mu·ni·cate \kə-'myü-nə-,kāt\ *vb* [L *communicatus*, pp. of *communicare* to impart, participate, fr. *communis* common — more at MEAN] *vt* **1** *archaic* : SHARE **2 a** : to make known ⟨~ the news⟩ **b** : TRANSFER, TRANSMIT ⟨~ a disease⟩ ~ *vi* **1** : to receive Communion **2** : to have communication ⟨~ by mail⟩ **3** : JOIN, CONNECT ⟨the rooms ~⟩ — **com·mu·ni·ca·tor** \-,kāt-ər\ *n*

syn COMMUNICATE, IMPART mean to convey or transfer something intangible. COMMUNICATE implies making common to all what one presently possesses; IMPART suggests causing another or others to have what is primarily one's own

com·mu·ni·ca·tion \kə-,myü-nə-'kā-shən\ *n* **1** : an act or instance of transmitting **2 a** : information communicated **b** : a verbal or written message **3** : an exchange of information **4** *pl* **a** : a system (as of telephones) for communicating **b** : a system of routes for moving troops, supplies, and vehicles **c** : personnel engaged in communicating **5** : a process by which meanings are exchanged between individuals through a common system of symbols **6** *pl but sing or pl in constr* **a** : a technique for expressing ideas effectively (as in speech) **b** : the technology of the transmission of information

com·mu·ni·ca·tive \kə-'myü-nə-,kāt-iv, -ni-kət-iv\ *adj* **1** : tending to communicate : TALKATIVE **2** : of or relating to communication — **com·mu·ni·ca·tive·ly** *adv* — **com·mu·ni·ca·tive·ness** *n*

com·mu·nion \kə-'myü-nyən\ *n* [ME, fr. L *communion-, communio* mutual participation, fr. *communis*] **1** : an act or instance of sharing **2 a** *cap* : a Christian sacrament in which bread and wine are partaken of as a commemoration of the death of Christ **b** : the act of receiving the sacrament **c** *cap* : the part of the Mass in which the sacrament is received **3** : COMMUNICATION, INTERCOURSE **4** : a body of Christians having a common faith and discipline

com·mu·ni·qué \kə-'myü-nə-,kā, -,myü-nə-'\ *n* [F, fr. pp. of *communiquer* to communicate, fr. L *communicare*] : BULLETIN 1

com·mu·nism \'käm-yə-,niz-əm\ *n* [F *communisme*, fr. *commun* common] **1 a** : a theory advocating elimination of private property **b** : a system in which goods are owned in common and are available to all as needed **2** *cap* **a** : a doctrine based upon revolutionary Marxian socialism and Marxism-Leninism that is the official ideology of the U.S.S.R. **b** : a totalitarian system of government in which a single authoritarian party controls state-owned means of production with the professed aim of establishing a stateless society **c** : a final stage of society in Marxist theory in which the state has withered away and economic goods are distributed equally

com·mu·nist \'käm-yə-nəst\ *n* **1** : an adherent or advocate of communism **2** *cap* : COMMUNARD **3 a** *cap* : a member of a Communist party or movement **b** *often cap* : an adherent or advocate of a Communist government, party, or movement **4** *often cap* : one held to engage in left-wing, subversive, or revolutionary activities — **communist** *adj, often cap* — **com·mu·nis·tic** \,käm-yə-'nis-tik\ *adj, often cap* — **com·mu·nis·ti·cal·ly** \-ti-k(ə-)lē\ *adv*

com·mu·ni·tar·i·an \kə-,myü-nə-'ter-ē-ən\ *adj* : advocating, practicing, or based on social organization in small cooperative partially collectivist communities — **communitarian** *n* — **com·mu·ni·tar·i·an·ism** \-ē-ə-,niz-əm\ *n*

com·mu·ni·ty \kə-'myü-nət-ē\ *n* [ME *comunete*, fr. MF *comuneté*, fr. L *communitat-, communitas*, fr. *communis*] **1** : a unified body of individuals: as **a** : STATE, COMMONWEALTH **b** : the people with common interests living in a particular area; *broadly* : the area itself **c** : an interacting population of various kinds of individuals (as species) in a common location **d** : a group of people with a common characteristic or interest living together within a larger society **e** : a group linked by a common policy **f** : a body of persons or nations having a history or social, economic, and political interests in common **2** : society at large **3 a** : joint ownership or participation **b** : LIKENESS **c** : FELLOWSHIP **d** : a social state or condition

community center *n* : a building or group of buildings for a community's educational and recreational activities

community chest *n* : a general fund accumulated from individual subscriptions to defray demands on a community for charity and social welfare

community property *n* : property held jointly by husband and wife

com·mu·ni·za·tion \,käm-yə-nə-'zā-shən\ *n, often cap* : an act of communizing : the state of being communized

com·mu·nize \'käm-yə-,nīz\ *vt* [back-formation fr. *communization*] **1 a** : to make common **b** : to make into state-owned property **2** : to subject to Communist principles of organization

com·mut·able \kə-'myüt-ə-bəl\ *adj* : capable of being commuted

com·mu·tate \'käm-yə-,tāt\ *vt* [back-formation fr. *commutation*] : to reverse every other cycle of (an alternating current) to form a unidirectional current

com·mu·ta·tion \,käm-yə-'tā-shən\ *n* [ME, fr. MF, fr. L *commutation-, commutatio*, fr. *commutatus*, pp. of *commutare*] **1** : EXCHANGE, TRADE **2** : REPLACEMENT; *specif* : a substitution of one form of payment or charge for another **3** : a change of a legal penalty or punishment to a lesser one **4** : an act of commuting **5** : the action of commutating

commutation ticket *n* : a transportation ticket sold for a fixed number of trips over the same route during a limited period

com·mu·ta·tive \'käm-yə-,tāt-iv, kə-'myüt-ət-\ *adj* **1** : of, relating to, or showing commutation **2** : combining elements in such a manner that the result is independent of the order in which the elements are taken ⟨addition is ~⟩

com·mu·ta·tiv·i·ty \kə-,myüt-ə-'tiv-ət-ē, ,käm-yə-tə-\ *n* : the property of being commutative ⟨the ~ of a mathematical operation⟩

com·mu·ta·tor \'käm-yə-,tāt-ər\ *n* **1** : a switch for reversing the direction of an electric current **2** : a series of bars or segments so connected to armature coils of a dynamo that rotation of the armature will in conjunction with fixed brushes result in unidirectional current output in the case of a generator and in the reversal of the current into the coils in the case of a motor

com·mute \kə-'myüt\ *vb* [L *commutare* to change, exchange, fr. *com-* + *mutare* to change] *vt* **1 a** : to give in exchange for another : EXCHANGE **b** : CHANGE, ALTER **2** : to convert (as a payment) into another form **3** : to exchange (a penalty) for another less severe **4** : COMMUTATE ~ *vi* **1** : to make up for something **2** : to pay in gross **3** : to travel back and forth regularly — **com·mut·er** *n*

com·my \'käm-ē\ *var of* COMMIE

co·mose \'kō-,mōs\ *adj* [L *comosus* hairy, fr. *coma* hair — more at COMA] : bearing a tuft of soft hairs

1**com·pact** \kəm-'pakt, käm-', 'käm-,\ *adj* [ME, firmly put together, fr. L *compactus*, fr. pp. of *compingere* to put together, fr. *com-* + *pangere* to fasten] **1** : COMPOSED, MADE **2** : closely united, collected, or packed : SOLID, FIRM **3** : not gangling or lanky in appearance ⟨a ~ body⟩ **4** : concentrated in a limited area or small space **syn** see CLOSE — **com·pact·ly** *adv* — **com·pact·ness** *n*

2**compact** *vt* **1 a** : COMBINE, CONSOLIDATE **b** : COMPRESS **2** : to make up by connecting or combining : COMPOSE ~ *vi* : to become compacted — **com·pac·tor** *or* **com·pact·er** *n*

3**com·pact** \'käm-,pakt\ *n* **1** : a small cosmetic case **2** : a relatively small automobile

4**com·pact** \'käm-,pakt\ *n* [L *compactum*, fr. neut. of *compactus*, pp. of *compacisci* to make an agreement, fr. *com-* + *pacisci* to contract] : an agreement or covenant between two or more parties

com·pac·tion \kəm-'pak-shən\ *n* : the act or process of compacting : the state of being compacted

1**com·pan·ion** \kəm-'pan-yən\ *n* [ME *compainoun*, fr. OF *compagnon*, fr. LL *companion-, companio*, fr. L *com-* + *panis* bread, food] **1** : COMRADE **2** *obs* : RASCAL **3 a** : one of a pair of matching things **b** : one employed to live with and serve another

2**companion** *vt* : ACCOMPANY

3**companion** *n* [by folk etymology fr. D *kampanje* poop deck] **1** : a hood covering at the top of a companionway **2** : COMPANIONWAY

com·pan·ion·able \-yə-nə-bəl\ *adj* : marked by, conducive to, or suggestive of companionship : SOCIABLE — **com·pan·ion·able·ness** *n* — **com·pan·ion·ably** \-blē\ *adv*

com·pan·ion·ate \kəm-'pan-yə-nət\ *adj* : relating to or in the manner of companions

companionate marriage *n* : a proposed form of marriage in which legalized birth control would be practiced, the divorce of childless couples by mutual consent permitted, and neither party would have any claim on the other

com·pan·ion·ship \kəm-'pan-yən-,ship\ *n* : the fellowship existing among companions

com·pan·ion·way \-yən-,wā\ *n* [3*companion*] : a ship's stairway from one deck to another

1**com·pa·ny** \'kəmp-(ə-)nē\ *n* [ME *companie*, fr. OF *compagnie*, fr. *compain* companion, fr. LL *companio*] **1 a** : association with another : FELLOWSHIP **b** : COMPANIONS, ASSOCIATES **c** : VISITORS, GUESTS **2 a** : a group of persons or things **b** : a body of soldiers; *specif* : a unit (as of infantry) consisting usu. of a headquarters and two or more platoons **c** : an organization of musical or dramatic performers ⟨opera ~⟩ **d** : the officers and men of a ship **e** : a fire-fighting unit **f** : a local congregation of Jehovah's Witnesses **3 a** : a chartered commercial organization or medieval trade guild **b** : an association of persons for carrying on a commercial or industrial enterprise **c** : those members of a partnership firm whose names do not appear in the firm name ⟨John Doe and *Company*⟩

2**company** *vt* : ACCOMPANY ~ *vi* : ASSOCIATE

company union *n* : an unaffiliated labor union of the employees of a single firm

com·pa·ra·bil·i·ty \,käm-p(ə-)rə-'bil-ət-ē\ *n* : the quality or state of being comparable

com·pa·ra·ble \'käm-p(ə-)rə-bəl\ *adj* **1** : capable of or suitable for comparison — usu. used with *to* **2** : EQUIVALENT, SIMILAR — **com·pa·ra·ble·ness** *n* — **com·pa·ra·bly** \-blē\ *adv*

1**com·par·a·tive** \kəm-'par-ət-iv\ *adj* **1** : of, relating to, or constituting the degree of comparison in a language that denotes increase in the quality, quantity, or relation expressed by an adjective or adverb **2** : considered as if in comparison to something else as a standard not quite attained : RELATIVE ⟨~ stranger⟩ **3** : studied systematically by comparison of phenomena ⟨~ literature⟩ — **com·par·a·tive·ly** *adv* — **com·par·a·tive·ness** *n*

2**comparative** *n* **1** : one that compares with another esp. on equal footing : RIVAL; *specif* : one that makes witty or mocking comparisons **2** : the comparative degree or form in a language

com·pa·ra·tor \kəm-'par-ət-ər, 'käm-pə-,rāt-\ *n* : an instrument for comparing something with a like thing or with a standard measure

1**com·pare** \kəm-'pa(ə)r, -'pe(ə)r\ *vb* [ME *comparen*, fr. MF *comparer*, fr. L *comparare* to couple, compare, fr. *compar* like, fr. *com-* + *par* equal] *vt* **1** : to represent as similar : LIKEN **2** : to examine the character or qualities of esp. to discover resemblances or differences **3** : to inflect or modify (an adjective or adverb) according to the degrees of comparison ~ *vi* **1** : to bear being compared **2** : to make comparisons **3** : to be equal or alike

syn COMPARE, CONTRAST, COLLATE mean to set side by side in order to show differences and likenesses. COMPARE implies an aim of showing relative values or excellences by bringing out characteristic qualities whether similar or divergent; CONTRAST implies an emphasis on differences; COLLATE implies minute and critical inspection in order to note points of agreement or divergence

2**compare** *n* : COMPARISON ⟨beauty beyond ~⟩

com·par·i·son \kəm-'par-ə-sən\ *n* [ME, fr. MF *comparaison*, fr. L *comparation-, comparatio*, fr. *comparatus*, pp. of *comparare*] **1** : the act or process of comparing: **a** : LIKENING **b** : the juxtaposing of items to establish similarities and dissimilarities **2** : identity of features : SIMILARITY **3** : the modification of an adjective or adverb to denote different levels of quality, quantity, or relation

com·part \kəm-'pärt\ *vt* [It *compartire*, fr. LL *compartiri* to share out, fr. L *com-* + *partiri* to share, fr. *part-, pars* part, share] : to mark out into parts; *specif* : to lay out in parts according to a plan

com·part·ment \kəm-'pärt-mənt\ *n* [MF *compartiment*, fr. It *compartimento*, fr. *compartire*] **1** : one of the parts into which an enclosed space is divided **2** : a separate division or section — **com·part·men·tal** \kəm-,pärt-'ment-ᵊl\ *adj* — **com·part·ment·ed** \-'pärt-,ment-əd\ *adj*

com·part·men·tal·ize \kəm-,pärt-'ment-ᵊl-,īz\ *vt* : to separate into isolated compartments or categories

1**com·pass** \'kəm-pəs, 'käm-\ *vt* [ME *compassen*, fr. OF *compasser* to measure, fr. (assumed) VL *compassare* to pace off, fr. L *com-* + *passus* pace] **1** : CONTRIVE, PLOT **2 a** : ENCOMPASS **b** : to travel entirely around **3 a** : ACHIEVE, ACCOMPLISH; *also* : OBTAIN **b** : COMPREHEND **syn** see REACH — **com·pass·able** \-pə-sə-bəl\ *adj*

2**compass** *n* **1 a** : BOUNDARY, CIRCUMFERENCE **b** : a circumscribed space **c** : RANGE, SCOPE **2** : a curved or roundabout path **3 a** : a device for determining directions by means of a magnetic needle or group of needles turning freely on a pivot and pointing to the magnetic north **b** : any of various nonmagnetic devices that serve the same purpose as the magnetic compass **c** *usu pl* : an instrument for describing circles or transferring measurements consisting of two pointed branches joined at the top by a pivot — called also

pair of compasses **syn** see CIRCUMFERENCE
[3]**compass** *adj* **:** CURVED, CIRCULAR ⟨a ~ timber⟩; *specif* **:** SEMICIRCULAR
compass card *n* **:** the circular card attached to the needles of a mariner's compass on which are marked 32 points of the compass and the 360° of the circle

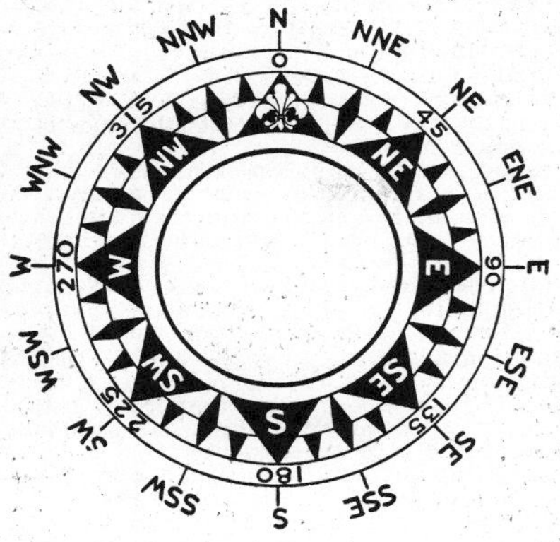

compass card

com·pas·sion \kəm-'pash-ən\ *n* [ME, fr. MF or LL; MF, fr. LL *compassion-, compassio,* fr *compassus,* pp. of *compati* to sympathize, fr. L *com-* + *pati* to bear, suffer] **:** sympathetic consciousness of others' distress together with a desire to alleviate it **syn** see PITY
[1]**com·pas·sion·ate** \kəm-'pash-(ə-)nət\ *adj* **:** marked by compassion — **com·pas·sion·ate·ly** *adv* — **com·pas·sion·ate·ness** *n*
[2]**com·pas·sion·ate** \-'pash-ə-,nāt\ *vt* **:** PITY
compass plant *n* **:** any of several plants whose leaves or branches grow on the axis so as to indicate the cardinal points of the compass
com·pat·i·bil·i·ty \kəm-,pat-ə-'bil-ət-ē\ *n* **:** the quality or state of being compatible
com·pat·i·ble \kəm-'pat-ə-bəl\ *adj* [MF, fr. ML *compatibilis,* lit., sympathetic, fr. LL *compati*] **1 :** capable of existing together in harmony **2 :** capable of cross-fertilizing freely or uniting vegetatively **3 :** being or relating to a system in which color television broadcasts may be received in black and white on receivers without special modification **4 :** capable of forming a homogeneous mixture that neither separates nor is altered by chemical interaction **syn** see CONSONANT — **com·pat·i·ble·ness** *n* — **com·pat·i·bly** \-blē\ *adv*
com·pa·tri·ot \kəm-'pā-trē-ət, -,ät, *chiefly Brit* -'pa-\ *n* [F *compatriote,* fr. LL *compatriota,* fr. L *com-* + LL *patriota* fellow countryman] **1 :** a fellow countryman **2 :** COMPEER, COLLEAGUE
[1]**com·peer** \'käm-,pi(ə)r, kəm-'\ *n* **1** [ME, fr. OF *compere,* lit., godfather, fr. ML *compater,* fr. L *com-* + *pater* father] **:** COMPANION **2** [modif. of L *compar,* fr. *compar,* adj., like] **:** EQUAL, PEER
[2]**compeer** *vt, obs* **:** EQUAL, MATCH
com·pel \kəm-'pel\ *vt* **com·pelled; com·pel·ling** [ME *compellen,* fr. MF *compellir,* fr. L *compellere,* fr. *com-* + *pellere* to drive — more at FELT] **1 :** to drive or urge with force **:** CONSTRAIN **2 :** EXACT, EXTORT **3** *archaic* **:** to drive together **syn** see FORCE — **com·pel·la·ble** \-ə-bəl\ *adj* — **com·pel·ler** *n*
com·pel·la·tion \,käm-pə-'lā-shən, -,pel-'ā-\ *n* [L *compellation-, compellatio,* fr. *compellatus,* pp. of *compellare* to address, fr. *com-* + *-pellare* (as in *appellare* to accost, appeal to)] **1 :** an act or action of addressing someone **2 :** APPELLATION 2
com·pend \'käm-,pend\ *n* [ML *compendium*] **:** COMPENDIUM
com·pen·di·ous \kəm-'pen-dē-əs\ *adj* **:** marked by brief expression of a comprehensive matter **syn** see CONCISE — **com·pen·di·ous·ly** *adv* — **com·pen·di·ous·ness** *n*
com·pen·di·um \kəm-'pen-dē-əm\ *n, pl* **compendiums** *or* **com·pen·dia** \-dē-ə\ [ML, fr. L, saving, shortcut, fr. *compendere* to weigh together, fr. *com-* + *pendere* to weigh] **:** a brief summary of a larger work or of a field of knowledge **:** ABSTRACT
syn SYLLABUS, DIGEST, SURVEY, SKETCH, PRÉCIS, APERÇU: a COMPENDIUM gathers together and presents in concise or in outline form all the essential facts and details of a subject; a SYLLABUS gives the material necessary for a comprehensive view of a whole subject often in the form of a series of heads or propositions; a DIGEST presents material gathered from many sources and arranged for ready reference; a SURVEY is a brief but comprehensive treatment presented often as a preliminary to further study or discussion; a SKETCH is a similar but slighter and more tentative treatment; a PRÉCIS is a concise statement of essential facts or points; an APERÇU ignores details and gives a quick impression of the whole
com·pen·sa·ble \kəm-'pen(t)-sə-bəl\ *adj* **:** that is to be or can be compensated
com·pen·sate \'käm-pən-,sāt, -,pen-\ *vb* [L *compensatus,* pp. of *compensare,* fr. *compensus,* pp. of *compendere*] *vt* **1 :** to be equivalent to **:** COUNTERBALANCE **2 :** to make proper payment to **3 a :** to provide with means of counteracting variation **b :** to neutralize the effect of (variations) ~ *vi* **1 :** to supply an equivalent — used with *for* **2 :** to offset an error, defect, or undesired effect — **com·pen·sa·tive** \'käm-pən-,sāt-iv, -,pen-; kəm-'pen(t)-sət-\ *adj* — **com·pen·sa·tor** \'käm-pən-,sāt-ər, -,pen-\ *n* — **com·pen·sa·to·ry** \kəm-'pen(t)-sə-,tōr-ē, -,tȯr-\ *adj*
syn COMPENSATE, COUNTERVAIL, BALANCE, OFFSET mean to make up for what is excessive or deficient, helpful or harmful in another. COMPENSATE implies making up a lack or making amends for loss or injury; COUNTERVAIL suggests counteracting a bad or harmful influence or the damage suffered through it; BALANCE implies the equalizing or adjusting of two or more things that are contrary or opposed so that no one outweighs the other or others in effect; OFFSET implies neutralizing one thing's good or evil effect by something that exerts a contrary effect **syn** see in addition PAY
com·pen·sa·tion \,käm-pən-'sā-shən, -,pen-\ *n* **1 a** (1) **:** correction of an organic inferiority or loss by hypertrophy or by increased functioning of another organ or unimpaired parts of the same organ (2) **:** a comparable psychic mechanism **b :** adjustment of the phase retardation of one light ray with respect to that of another **2 a :** something that constitutes an equivalent or recompense; *specif* **:** payment to an unemployed or injured worker or his dependents **b :** PAYMENT, WAGES — **com·pen·sa·tion·al** \-'sā-shnəl, -shən-ᵊl\ *adj*
com·pete \kəm-'pēt\ *vi* [LL *competere* to seek together, fr. L, to come together, agree, be suitable, fr. *com-* + *petere* to go to, seek — more at FEATHER] **:** to vie with another for or as if for a prize
com·pe·tence \'käm-pət-ən(t)s\ *n* **1 :** means sufficient for the necessities of life **2 :** the quality or state of being competent
com·pe·ten·cy \-ən-sē\ *n* **:** COMPETENCE
com·pe·tent \'käm-pət-ənt\ *adj* [ME, suitable, fr. MF & L; MF, fr. L *competent-, competens,* fr. prp. of *competere* to be suitable] **1 :** having requisite ability or qualities **:** FIT **2 :** rightfully belonging **:** PROPER **3 :** legally qualified or capable **syn** see ABLE, SUFFICIENT — **com·pe·tent·ly** *adv*
com·pe·ti·tion \,käm-pə-'tish-ən\ *n* [LL *competition-, competitio,* fr. L *competitus,* pp. of *competere*] **1 :** the act or process of competing **:** RIVALRY **2 :** a contest between rivals; *also* **:** the person competing ⟨first-rate ~⟩ **3 :** the effort of two or more parties to secure the business of a third party by the offer of the most favorable terms — **com·pet·i·to·ry** \kəm-'pet-ə-,tōr-ē, -,tȯr-\ *adj*
com·pet·i·tive \kəm-'pet-ət-iv\ *adj* **:** relating to, characterized by, or based on competition ⟨~ sports⟩ ⟨~ bidding⟩ — **com·pet·i·tive·ly** *adv* — **com·pet·i·tive·ness** *n*
com·pet·i·tor \kəm-'pet-ət-ər\ *n* **:** one that competes; *esp* **:** one selling or buying goods or services in the same market as another
com·pi·la·tion \,käm-pə-'lā-shən\ *n* **1 :** the act or process of compiling **2 :** something compiled; *esp* **:** a book composed of materials gathered from other books or documents
com·pile \kəm-'pī(ə)l\ *vt* [ME *compilen,* fr. MF *compiler,* fr. L *compilare* to plunder] **1 :** to collect into a volume **2 :** to compose out of materials from other documents — **com·pil·er** *n*
com·pla·cence \kəm-'plās-ᵊn(t)s\ *n* **1 :** calm or secure satisfaction with one's self or lot **:** SELF-SATISFACTION **2** *obs* **:** COMPLAISANCE
com·pla·cen·cy \-ᵊn-sē\ *n* **:** COMPLACENCE; *esp* **:** self-satisfaction accompanied by unawareness of actual dangers or deficiencies
com·pla·cent \kəm-'plās-ᵊnt\ *adj* [L *complacent-, complacens,* prp. of *complacēre* to please greatly, fr. *com-* + *placēre* to please — more at PLEASE] **1 :** SATISFIED; *esp* **:** SELF-SATISFIED **2 :** feeling or showing complaisance — **com·pla·cent·ly** *adv*
com·plain \kəm-'plān\ *vi* [ME *compleynen,* fr. MF *complaindre,* fr. (assumed) VL *complangere,* fr. L *com-* + *plangere* to lament — more at PLAINT] **1 :** to express grief, pain, or discontent **2 :** to make a formal accusation or charge — **com·plain·er** *n* — **com·plain·ing·ly** \-'plā-niŋ-lē\ *adv*
com·plain·ant \kəm-'plā-nənt\ *n* **:** the party who makes the complaint in a legal action or proceeding
com·plaint \kəm-'plānt\ *n* [ME *compleynte,* fr. MF *complainte,* fr. OF, fr. *complaindre*] **1 :** expression of grief, pain, or resentment **2 a :** that concerning which one complains **b :** a bodily ailment or disease **3 :** a formal allegation against a party
com·plai·sance \kəm-'plās-ᵊn(t)s, -'plāz-; 'käm-plā-,zan(t)s\ *n* **:** disposition to please or oblige **:** AFFABILITY
com·plai·sant \-ᵊnt, -,zant\ *adj* [F, fr. MF, fr. prp. of *complaire* to gratify, acquiesce, fr. L *complacēre* to please greatly] **1 :** marked by an inclination to please or oblige **2 :** tending to consent to others' wishes **syn** see AMIABLE — **com·plai·sant·ly** *adv*
com·plect·ed \kəm-'plek-təd\ *adj* [irreg. fr. *complexion*] **:** COMPLEXIONED ⟨dark-*complected*⟩
[1]**com·ple·ment** \'käm-plə-mənt\ *n* [ME, fr. L *complementum,* fr. *complēre*] **1 a :** something that fills up, completes, or makes perfect **b :** the quantity or number required to make a thing complete; *specif* **:** the whole force or personnel of a ship **c :** one of two mutually completing parts **:** COUNTERPART **2 :** the amount of angle or arc by which a given angle or arc falls short of 90 degrees **3 :** the interval in music required with a given interval to complete the octave **4 :** an added word or expression by which a predication is made complete (as *president* in "they elected him president") **5 :** the thermolabile substance in normal blood serum and plasma that in combination with antibodies causes the destruction of bacteria, foreign blood corpuscles, and other antigens

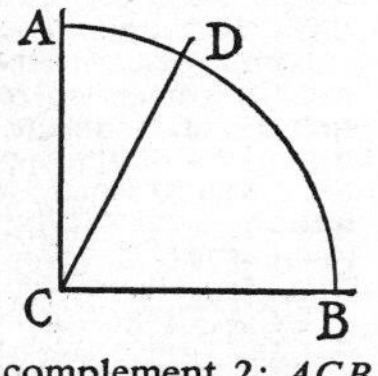

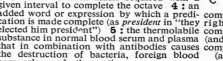

complement 2: *ACB* right angle; *ACD* complement of *DCB* (and vice versa); *AD* complement of *DB* (and vice versa)

[2]**com·ple·ment** \-,ment\ *vt* **1 :** to be complementary to **2** *obs* **:** COMPLIMENT ~ *vi, obs* **:** to exchange formal courtesies
com·ple·men·tal \,käm-plə-'ment-ᵊl\ *adj* **1 :** relating to or being a complement **2** *obs* **:** CEREMONIOUS, COMPLIMENTARY
com·ple·men·tar·i·ty \,käm-plə-(,)men-'tar-ət-ē, -mən-\ *n* **:** the quality or state of being complementary
com·ple·men·ta·ry \,käm-plə-'ment-ə-rē, -'men-trē\ *adj* **1 :** serving to fill out or complete **2 :** mutually supplying each other's lack **3 :** relating to or constituting one of a pair of contrasting colors that produce a neutral color when combined in suitable proportions — **complementary** *n*
complementary angles *n pl* **:** two angles whose sum is 90 degrees
complement fixation *n* **:** the absorption of complement to the product of the union of an antibody and the antigen for which it is specific when added to a mixture of such antibody and antigen
[1]**com·plete** \kəm-'plēt\ *adj* [ME *complet,* fr. MF, fr. L *completus* fr. pp. of *complēre* to fill up, complete, fr. *com-* + *plēre* to fill — more at FULL] **1 a :** possessing all necessary parts **:** ENTIRE **b :** having all four sets of floral organs **:** MONOCLINOUS **c** *of a subject or predicate* **:** including modifiers, complements, or objects **2 :** brought to an end **:** CONCLUDED **3 :** highly proficient **4 :** fully carried out **:** THOROUGH **syn** see FULL — **com·plete·ly** *adv* — **com·plete·ness** *n* — **com·ple·tive** \-'plēt-iv\ *adj*
[2]**complete** *vt* **1 :** to bring to an end **:** FINISH **2 :** to make whole or perfect; *esp* **:** to provide with all lacking parts **syn** see CLOSE
complete fertilizer *n* **:** a fertilizer that contains the three chief plant nutrients (nitrogen, phosphoric acid, and potash)
com·ple·tion \kəm-'plē-shən\ *n* **:** the act or process of completing **:** the state of being complete
[1]**com·plex** \käm-'pleks, kəm-', 'käm-,\ *adj* [L *complexus,* pp. of *complecti* to embrace, comprise (a multitude of objects), fr. *com-* + *plectere* to braid — more at PLY] **1 a :** composed of two or more parts **:** COMPOSITE **b** (1) *of a word* **:** having a bound form as one or both of its immediate constituents ⟨*unmanly* is a ~ word⟩ (2) *of a sentence* **:** consisting of a main clause and one or more

subordinate clauses **2 :** hard to separate, analyze, or solve — **com·plex·ly** *adv* — **com·plex·ness** *n*

syn COMPLEX, COMPLICATED, INTRICATE, INVOLVED, KNOTTY mean having confusingly interrelated parts. COMPLEX suggests the unavoidable result of a necessary combining or folding and does not imply a fault or failure; COMPLICATED applies to what offers great difficulty in understanding, solving, or explaining; INTRICATE suggests such interlacing of parts as to make it nearly impossible to follow or grasp them separately; INVOLVED implies extreme complication and often disorder; KNOTTY suggests complication and entanglement that make solution or understanding improbable

2com·plex \'käm-,pleks\ *n* **1 :** a whole made up of complicated or interrelated parts **2 a :** a group of culture traits relating to a single activity (as hunting), process (as use of flint), or culture unit **b** (1) **:** a system of repressed desires and memories that exerts a dominating influence upon the personality (2) **:** an exaggerated reaction to a subject or situation **c :** a group of obviously related units of which the degree and nature of the relationship is imperfectly known **3 :** a complex substance in which the constituents are more intimately associated than in a simple mixture

complex fraction *n* **:** a fraction with a fraction or mixed number in the numerator or denominator or both

com·plex·ion \kəm-'plek-shən\ *n* [ME, fr. MF, fr. ML *complexion-complexio*, fr. L, combination, fr. *complexus*, pp.] **1 :** the combination of the hot, cold, moist, and dry qualities held in medieval physiology to determine the quality of a body **2 a :** an individual complex of ways of thinking or feeling **b :** a complex of attitudes and inclinations **3 :** the hue or appearance of the skin and esp. of the face **4 :** general appearance or impression — **com·plex·ion·al** \-shnəl, -shən-ᵊl\ *adj* — **com·plex·ioned** \-shənd\ *adj*

com·plex·i·ty \kəm-'plek-sət-ē, käm-\ *n* **1 :** the quality or state of being complex **2 :** something complex

complex number *n* **:** a number of the form $a+b\sqrt{-1}$ where *a* and *b* are real numbers

com·pli·ance \kəm-'plī-ən(t)s\ *n* **1 :** the act or process of complying to a desire, demand, or proposal or to coercion **2 :** a disposition to yield to others

com·pli·an·cy \-ən-sē\ *n* **:** COMPLIANCE

com·pli·ant \-ənt\ *adj* **:** ready or disposed to comply **:** SUBMISSIVE — **com·pli·ant·ly** *adv*

com·pli·ca·cy \'käm-pli-kə-sē\ *n* [*2complicate*] **1 :** the quality or state of being complicated **2 :** something that is complicated

1com·pli·cate \'käm-plə-,kāt\ *vt* **1 :** to combine esp. in an involved or inextricable manner **2 :** to make complex or difficult ~ *vi* **:** to become complicated

2com·pli·cate \-pli-kət\ *adj* [L *complicatus*, pp. of *complicare* to fold together, fr. *com-* + *plicare* to fold — more at PLY] **1 :** COMPLEX, INTRICATE **2 a :** CONDUPLICATE **b :** folded longitudinally one or more times — used of insect wings

com·pli·cat·ed *adj* **1 :** consisting of parts intricately combined **2 :** difficult to analyze, understand, or explain — **syn** see COMPLEX — **com·pli·cat·ed·ly** *adv* — **com·pli·cat·ed·ness** *n*

com·pli·ca·tion \,käm-plə-'kā-shən\ *n* **1 a :** COMPLEXITY, INTRICACY; *specif* **:** a situation or a detail of character complicating the main thread of a plot **b :** a making difficult, involved, or intricate **c :** a complex or intricate feature or element **d :** a difficult factor or issue often appearing unexpectedly and changing existing plans, methods, or attitudes **2 :** the act or process of complicating **:** the state of being complicated **3 :** a secondary disease or condition developing in the course of a primary disease

com·plice \'käm-pləs, 'kəm-\ *n* [ME, fr. MF, fr. LL *complic-*, *complex*, fr. L *com-* + *plicare* to fold] *archaic* **:** ASSOCIATE

com·plic·i·ty \kəm-'plis-ət-ē\ *n* **:** association or participation in or as if in a wrongful act

com·pli·er \-'plī(-ə)r\ *n* **:** one that complies

1com·pli·ment \'käm-plə-mənt\ *n* [F, fr. It *complimento*, fr. Sp *cumplimiento*, fr. *cumplir* to be courteous — more at COMPLY] **1 a :** a formal expression of esteem, respect, affection, or admiration; *specif* **:** a flattering remark **b :** formal and respectful recognition **:** DEFERENCE **2** *pl* **:** best wishes **:** REGARDS

2com·pli·ment \-,ment\ *vt* **1 :** to pay a compliment to **2 :** to present with a token of esteem

com·pli·men·tar·i·ly \,käm-plə-(,)men-'ter-ə-lē, -mən-\ *adv* **:** in a complimentary manner

com·pli·men·ta·ry \,käm-plə-'ment-ə-rē, -'men-trē\ *adj* **1 :** expressing or containing a compliment **2 :** given free as a courtesy or favor ⟨~ ticket⟩

com·pline \'käm-plən, -,plīn\ *n, often cap* [ME *complie, compline*, fr. OF *complie*, modif. of LL *completa*, fr. L, fem. of *completus* complete] **:** the 7th and last of the canonical hours

com·plot \'käm-,plät\ *n* [MF *complot* crowd, plot] *archaic* **:** PLOT, CONSPIRACY — **com·plot** \käm-'plät, kəm-\ *vb, archaic*

com·ply \kəm-'plī\ *vi* [It *complire*, fr. Sp *cumplir* to complete, perform what is due, be courteous, fr. L *complēre* to complete] **1** *obs* **:** to be ceremoniously courteous **2 :** to conform or adapt one's actions to another's wishes, to a rule, or to necessity

com·po \'käm-(,)pō\ *n* [short for *composition*] **:** any of various composition materials

1com·po·nent \kəm-'pō-nənt, 'käm-,, käm-'\ *n* [L *component-*, *componens*, prp. of *componere* to put together — more at COMPOUND] **1 :** a constituent part **:** INGREDIENT **2 :** any one of the vector terms added to form a vector sum or resultant **syn** see ELEMENT — **com·po·nen·tial** \,käm-pə-'nen-chəl\ *adj*

2component *adj* **:** serving or helping to constitute **:** CONSTITUENT

1com·port \kəm-'pō(ə)rt, -'pȯ(ə)rt\ *vb* [MF *comporter* to bear, conduct, fr. L *comportare* to bring together, fr. *com-* + *portare* to carry — more at PORT] *vi* **:** ACCORD, SUIT ⟨acts that ~ with ideals⟩ ~ *vt* **:** CONDUCT ⟨~*s* himself blamelessly⟩ **syn** see AGREE, BEHAVE

2com·port \'käm-,pō(ə)rt, -,pȯ(ə)rt\ *n* **:** COMPOTE 2

com·port·ment \kəm-'pōrt-mənt, -'pȯrt-\ *n* **:** BEARING

com·pose \kəm-'pōz\ *vb* [MF *composer*, fr. L *componere* (perf. indic. *composui*) — more at COMPOUND] *vt* **1 a :** to form by putting together **:** FASHION **b :** to form the substance of **:** CONSTITUTE ⟨*composed* of many ingredients⟩ **c** (1) **:** ARRANGE, SET ⟨~ type⟩ (2) **:** to set type for (a work) **2 a :** to create by mental or artistic labor **b :** to compose music for **3 :** to reduce to a minimum ⟨~ their differences⟩ **4 :** to arrange in proper form **5 :** to free from agitation **:** CALM ~ *vi* **:** to practice composition **:** CREATE

com·posed \-'pōzd\ *adj* **:** free from agitation **:** CALM; *esp* **:** SELF-POSSESSED **syn** see COOL — **com·pos·ed·ly** \-'pō-zəd-lē\ *adv* — **com·pos·ed·ness** \-'pō-zəd-nəs\ *n*

com·pos·er \kəm-'pō-zər\ *n* **:** one that composes; *esp* **:** a person who writes music

composing stick *n* **:** a shallow tray usu. of metal with an adjustable slide that is held in one hand by a compositor as he sets type into it with the other hand

1com·pos·ite \käm-'päz-ət, kəm-\ *adj* [L *compositus*, pp. of *componere*] **:** made up of distinct parts: as **a** *cap* **:** relating to or being a modification of the Corinthian order combining angular Ionic volutes with the acanthus-circled bell of the Corinthian **b :** of or relating to a very large family (Compositae) of dicotyledonous herbs, shrubs, and trees often held to be the most highly evolved plants and characterized by florets arranged in dense heads that resemble single flowers **c :** made up of two or more integral or real rational prime factors — **com·pos·ite·ly** *adv*

2composite *n* **1 :** something composite **:** COMPOUND **2 :** a composite plant

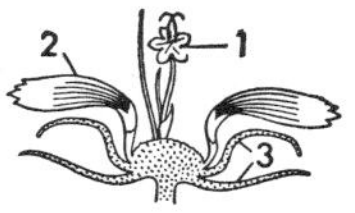

composite 2: section of a composite flower head: *1* disk flower, *2* ray flower, *3* bracts

com·po·si·tion \,käm-pə-'zish-ən\ *n* [ME *composicioun*, fr. MF *composition*, fr. L *composition-*, *compositio*, fr. *compositus*] **1 a :** the act or process of composing; *specif* **:** arrangement into proper proportion or relation and esp. into artistic form **b :** the work of a compositor **2 a :** the manner in which something is composed **b :** personal constitution **:** MAKEUP **c :** the qualitative and quantitative makeup of a chemical compound **3 :** mutual settlement or agreement **4 :** a product of mixing or combining various elements or ingredients **5 :** an intellectual creation: as **a :** a piece of writing; *esp* **:** a written exercise in school **b :** a written piece of music esp. of considerable size and complexity **c :** a work of art whose elements are combined artistically **6 :** the quality or state of being compound — **com·po·si·tion·al** \-'zish-nəl, -ən-ᵊl\ *adj*

com·pos·i·tor \kəm-'päz-ət-ər\ *n* **:** one who sets type

com·pos men·tis \,käm-pə-'sment-əs\ *adj* [L, lit., having mastery of one's mind] **:** of sound mind, memory, and understanding

1com·post \'käm-,pōst\ *n* [MF, fr. ML *compostum*, fr. L, neut. of *compositus*, *compostus*, pp. of *componere* to put together] **1 :** a mixture consisting usu. largely of decayed organic matter and used for fertilizing and conditioning land **2 :** MIXTURE, COMPOUND

2compost *vt* **:** to convert (as plant debris) to compost

com·po·sure \kəm-'pō-zhər\ *n* **:** calmness or repose esp. of mind, bearing, or appearance **:** SELF-POSSESSION **syn** see EQUANIMITY

com·po·ta·tor \'käm-pō-,tāt-ər\ *n* [LL, fr. L *com-* + *potator* drinker, fr. *potatus*, pp. of *potare* to drink] **:** a fellow drinker

com·pote \'käm-,pōt\ *n* [F, fr. OF *composte*, fr. L *composta*, fem. of *compostus*, pp.] **1 :** fruits cooked in syrup **2 :** a bowl of glass, porcelain, or metal usu. with a base and stem and sometimes a cover from which compotes, fruits, nuts, or sweets are served

1com·pound \käm-'paùnd, kəm-', 'käm-,\ *vb* [ME *compounen*, fr. MF *compondre*, fr. L *componere*, fr. *com-* + *ponere* to put — more at POSITION] *vt* **1 :** to put together (parts) to form a whole **:** COMBINE **2 :** to form by combining parts **3 :** to settle amicably **:** COMPROMISE **4 a :** to increase by geometric progression or by an increment that itself increases **b :** to add to **5 :** to agree for a consideration not to prosecute (an offense) ~ *vi* **1 :** to become joined in a compound **2 :** to come to terms of agreement — **com·pound·able** \-ə-bəl\ *adj* — **com·pound·er** *n*

2com·pound \'käm-,paùnd, käm-', kəm-'\ *adj* [ME *compouned*, pp. of *compounen*] **1 :** composed of or resulting from union of separate elements, ingredients, or parts; *specif* **:** composed of united similar elements esp. of a kind usu. independent **2 :** involving or used in a combination **3 a** *of a word* **:** constituting a compound **b** *of a sentence* **:** having two or more main clauses

3com·pound \'käm-,paùnd\ *n* **1 a :** a word consisting of components that are words (as *rowboat, high school, devil-may-care*) **b :** a word consisting of any of various combinations of words, combining forms, or affixes (as *anthropology, kilocycle, builder*) **2 :** something formed by a union of elements or parts; *specif* **:** a distinct substance formed by chemical union of two or more ingredients in definite proportion by weight

4com·pound \'käm-,paùnd\ *n* [by folk etymology fr. Malay *kampong* group of buildings, village] **1 :** an enclosure of European residences and commercial buildings esp. in the Orient **2 :** a large fenced or walled-in area

compound–complex *adj, of a sentence* **:** having two or more main clauses and one or more subordinate clauses

compound fracture *n* **:** a bone fracture associated with lacerated soft tissues through which bone fragments usu. protrude

compound interest *n* **:** interest computed on the sum of an original principal and accrued interest

compound leaf *n* **:** a leaf in which the blade is divided to the midrib forming two or more leaflets on a common axis

compound microscope *n* **:** a microscope consisting of an objective and an eyepiece mounted in a drawtube

compound number *n* **:** a number (as 2 ft. 5 in.) involving different denominations or more than one unit

com·pra·dor \,käm-prə-'dō(ə)r\ *or* **com·pra·dore** \-'dō(ə)r, -'dȯ(ə)r\ *n* [Pg *comprador*, lit., buyer] **:** a Chinese agent engaged by a foreign establishment in China to have charge of its Chinese employees and to act as an intermediary in business affairs

com·pre·hend \,käm-pri-'hend\ *vt* [ME *comprehenden*, fr. L *comprehendere*, fr. *com-* + *prehendere* to grasp] **1 :** to grasp the meaning of mentally **2 :** EMBRACE **syn** see INCLUDE, UNDERSTAND — **com·pre·hend·ible** \-'hen-də-bəl\ *adj*

com·pre·hen·si·bil·i·ty \-,hen(t)-sə-'bil-ət-ē\ *n* **:** the quality or state of being comprehensible

com·pre·hen·si·ble \-'hen(t)-sə-bəl\ *adj* **:** capable of being comprehended **:** INTELLIGIBLE — **com·pre·hen·si·ble·ness** *n* — **com·pre·hen·si·bly** \-blē\ *adv*

com·pre·hen·sion \,käm-pri-'hen-chən\ *n* [MF & L; MF, fr. L *comprehension-*, *comprehensio*, fr. *comprehensus*, pp. of *comprehendere* to understand, comprise] **1 a :** the act or process of comprising **b :** COMPREHENSIVENESS **2 a :** the act or action of grasping with the intellect **b :** knowledge gained by comprehending **c :** the capacity for understanding **3 :** CONNOTATION 3

com·pre·hen·sive \-'hen(t)-siv\ *adj* **1 :** covering completely

: INCLUSIVE **2** : having wide mental comprehension — **com·pre·hen·sive·ly** *adv* — **com·pre·hen·sive·ness** *n*

1com·press \kəm-ˈpres\ *vb* [ME *compressen*, fr. LL *compressare* to press hard, fr. L *compressus*, pp. of *comprimere* to compress, fr. *com-* + *premere* to press] *vt* : to press or squeeze together : CONDENSE ~ *vi* : to undergo compression **syn** see CONTRACT

2com·press \ˈkäm-ˌpres\ *n* [MF *compresse*, fr. *compresser* to compress, fr. LL *compressare*] **1** : a folded cloth or pad applied so as to press upon a body part **2** : a machine for compressing

com·pressed \kəm-ˈprest *also* ˈkäm-ˌ\ *adj* : flattened as though subjected to compression: **a** : flattened laterally ⟨petioles ~⟩ **b** : narrow from side to side and deep in a dorsoventral direction — **com·pressed·ly** \kəm-ˈprest-lē, -ˈpres-əd-lē\ *adv*

compressed air *n* : air under pressure greater than that of the atmosphere

com·press·ibil·i·ty \kəm-ˌpres-ə-ˈbil-ət-ē\ *n* : the quality or state of being compressible

com·press·ible \kəm-ˈpres-ə-bəl\ *adj* : capable of being compressed

com·pres·sion \kəm-ˈpresh-ən\ *n* **1** : the act or process of compressing : the state of being compressed **2** : the process of compressing the working substance in a heat engine — **com·pres·sion·al** \-ˈpresh-nəl, -ən-ᵊl\ *adj*

com·pres·sive \kəm-ˈpres-iv\ *adj* **1** : of or relating to compression **2** : tending to compress — **com·pres·sive·ly** *adv*

com·pres·sor \-ˈpres-ər\ *n* : one that compresses: as **a** : a muscle that compresses a part **b** : a machine that compresses gases

com·prise \kəm-ˈprīz\ *vt* [ME *comprisen*, fr. MF *compris*, pp. of *comprendre*, fr. L *comprehendere*] **1** : INCLUDE, CONTAIN **2** : to be made up of **3** : to make up : CONSTITUTE

1com·pro·mise \ˈkäm-prə-ˌmīz\ *n* [ME, mutual promise to abide by an arbiter's decision, fr. MF *compromis*, fr. L *compromissum*, fr. neut. of *compromissus*, pp. of *compromittere* to promise mutually, fr. *com-* + *promittere* to promise — more at PROMISE] **1 a** : the process or a result of settlement by arbitration or by consent reached by mutual concessions **b** : something blending the characteristics of two others **2** : a committal to something prejudicial : SURRENDER

2compromise *vt* **1** *obs* : to bind by mutual agreement **2** : to adjust or settle by mutual concessions **3** : to expose to discredit or mischief ~ *vi* **1** : to come to agreement by concession **2** : to make a shameful or disreputable concession — **com·pro·mis·er** *n*

compt \ˈkau̇nt, ˈkäm(p)t\ *archaic var of* COUNT

comp·trol·ler \kən-ˈtrō-lər, ˈkäm(p)-ˌ, ˌkäm(p)-ˈ\ *n* [ME, alter. of *conterroller* controller] **1** : a royal-household official who examines and supervises expenditures **2** : a public official who audits government accounts and sometimes certifies expenditures **3** : CONTROLLER 1c — **comp·trol·ler·ship** \-ˌship\ *n*

com·pul·sion \kəm-ˈpəl-shən\ *n* [ME, fr. MF or LL; MF, fr. LL *compulsion-*, *compulsio*, fr. L *compulsus*, pp. of *compellere* to compel] **1 a** : an act of compelling : the state of being compelled **b** : a force or agency that compels **2** : an irresistible impulse to perform an irrational act

com·pul·sive \-ˈpəl-siv\ *adj* **1** : having power to compel **2** : of, relating to, caused by, or suggestive of psychological compulsion or obsession — **com·pul·sive·ly** *adv* — **com·pul·sive·ness** *n*

com·pul·so·ry \kəm-ˈpəls-(ə-)rē\ *adj* **1** : ENFORCED, MANDATORY **2** : COERCIVE, COMPELLING

com·punc·tion \kəm-ˈpəŋ(k)-shən\ *n* [ME *compunccioun*, fr. MF *componction*, fr. LL *compunction-*, *compunctio*, fr. L *compunctus*, pp. of *compungere* to prick hard, sting, fr. *com-* + *pungere* to prick] **1** : anxiety arising from guilt : REMORSE **2** : an uneasy twinge **syn** see PENITENCE, QUALM — **com·punc·tious** \-shəs\ *adj*

com·pur·ga·tion \ˌkäm-(ˌ)pər-ˈgā-shən\ *n* [LL *compurgation-*, *compurgatio*, fr. L *compurgatus*, pp. of *compurgare* to clear completely, fr. *com-* + *purgare* to purge] : the clearing of an accused person by oaths of persons who swear to his veracity or innocence

com·pur·ga·tor \ˈkäm-(ˌ)pər-ˌgāt-ər\ *n* : one that under oath vouches for the character or conduct of an accused person

com·put·abil·i·ty \kəm-ˌpyüt-ə-ˈbil-ət-ē\ *n* : the quality or state of being computable

com·put·able \kəm-ˈpyüt-ə-bəl\ *adj* : capable of being computed

com·pu·ta·tion \ˌkäm-pyu̇-ˈtā-shən\ *n* **1** : the act or action of computing : CALCULATION **2** : a system of reckoning **3** : an amount computed — **com·pu·ta·tion·al** \-shnəl, -shən-ᵊl\ *adj*

1com·pute \kəm-ˈpyüt\ *n* : COMPUTATION ⟨numbers beyond ~⟩

2compute *vb* [L *computare*] *vt* : to determine esp. by mathematical means ~ *vi* : to make calculation : RECKON **syn** see CALCULATE

com·put·er \kəm-ˈpyüt-ər\ *n* : one that computes; *specif* : an automatic electronic machine for performing calculations

com·put·er·ize \-ˈpyüt-ə-ˌrīz\ *vt* **1** : to carry out or conduct by means of a computer **2** : to equip with computers

com·rade \ˈkäm-ˌrad, -rəd\ *n* [MF *camarade* group sleeping in one room, roommate, companion, fr. OSp *camarada*, fr. *cámara* room, fr. LL *camera*, *camara*] **1 a** : an intimate friend or associate : COMPANION **b** : a fellow soldier **2** [fr. its use as a form of address by communists] : COMMUNIST — **com·rade·ship** \-ˌship\ *n*

Comt·ian *or* **Comt·ean** \ˈkäm(p)-tē-ən, ˈkōⁿt-ē-\ *adj* : of or relating to Auguste Comte or his doctrines — **Comt·ism** \ˈkäm(p)-ˌtiz-əm, ˈkōⁿt-ˌiz-\ *n* — **Comt·ist** \ˈkäm(p)-təst, ˈkōⁿt-əst\ *adj or n*

1con \ˈkän\ *vt* **conned**; **con·ning** [ME *connen* to know, learn, study, alter. of *cunnen* to know, infin. of *can* — more at CAN] **1** : to study or examine closely : PERUSE **2** : to commit to memory

2con *var of* CONN

3con *adv* [ME, short for *contra*] : on the negative side : in opposition

4con *n* **1** : an argument or evidence in opposition **2** : the negative position or one holding it

5con *adj* : 2CONFIDENCE

6con *vt* **conned**; **con·ning** [5*con*] **1** : SWINDLE **2** : COAX, CAJOLE

7con *n* [short for *consumption*] *slang* : a destructive disease of the lungs; *esp* : TUBERCULOSIS

con- — see COM-

con amo·re \ˌkän-ə-ˈmōr-ē, ˌkō-nə-\ *adv* [It] **1** : with love, devotion, or zest **2** : TENDERLY — used as a direction in music

co·na·tion \kō-ˈnā-shən\ *n* [L *conation-*, *conatio* act of attempting, fr. *conatus*, pp. of *conari* to attempt — more at DEACON] : the power or an act of striving that may appear as conscious volition or desire or behavioral tendencies — **co·na·tion·al** \-shnəl, -shən-ᵊl\ *adj* — **co·na·tive** \ˈkō-nət-iv, -ˌnāt-; ˈkän-ət-\ *adj*

co·na·tus \kō-ˈnāt-əs, -ˈnät-\ *n*, *pl* **co·na·tus** \-əs; -ˈnā-ˌtüs, -ˈnä-\ [NL, fr. L, attempt, effort, fr. *conatus*, pp.] : a natural tendency, impulse, or striving

con brio \kän-ˈbrē-(ˌ)ō, kōn-\ *adv* [It, lit., with vigor] : VIGOROUSLY — used as a direction in music

1con·cat·e·nate \kän-ˈkat-ə-nət, kən-\ *adj* [ME, fr. LL *concatenatus*, pp. of *concatenare* to link together, fr. L *com-* + *catena* chain — more at CHAIN] : linked together

2con·cat·e·nate \-ə-ˌnāt\ *vt* : to link together in a series or chain — **con·cat·e·na·tion** \(ˌ)kän-ˌkat-ə-ˈnā-shən, kən-\ *n*

1con·cave \kän-ˈkāv, ˈkän-ˌ\ *adj* [MF, fr. L *concavus*, fr. *com-* + *cavus* hollow — more at CAVE] : hollowed or rounded inward like the inside of a bowl — **con·cave·ly** *adv* — **con·cave·ness** *n*

2con·cave \ˈkän-ˌkāv\ *n* : a concave line or surface

con·cav·i·ty \kän-ˈkav-ət-ē\ *n* **1** : a concave line, surface, or space : HOLLOW **2** : the quality or state of being concave

con·ca·vo–con·cave \kän-ˌkā-(ˌ)vō-\ *adj* : concave on both sides

concavo–convex *adj* **1** : concave on one side and convex on the other **2** : having the concave side curved more than the convex

con·ceal \kən-ˈsē(ə)l\ *vt* [ME *concelen*, fr. MF *conceler*, fr. L *concelare*, fr. *com-* + *celare* to hide] **1** : to prevent disclosure or recognition of **2** : to place out of sight **syn** see HIDE — **con·ceal·able** \-ˈsē-lə-bəl\ *adj* — **con·ceal·ment** \-ˈsē(ə)l-mənt\ *n*

con·cede \kən-ˈsēd\ *vb* [F or L; F *concéder*, fr. L *concedere*, fr. *com-* + *cedere* to yield — more at CEDE] *vt* **1** : to grant as a right or privilege **2 a** : ADMIT, ACKNOWLEDGE **b** : to acknowledge grudgingly ~ *vi* : to make concession : YIELD **syn** see GRANT — **con·ced·ed·ly** \-ˈsēd-əd-lē\ *adv* — **con·ced·er** *n*

1con·ceit \kən-ˈsēt\ *n* [ME, fr. *conceiven*] **1 a** (1) : a result of mental activity : THOUGHT (2) : individual opinion **b** : favorable opinion; *esp* : excessive appreciation of one's own worth or virtue **2 a** : a fanciful idea **b** : an elaborate or strained metaphor **c** : use or presence of such conceits in poetry **3** : a fancy article

2conceit *vt* **1** *obs* : CONCEIVE, UNDERSTAND **2** *dial* : IMAGINE **3** *dial Brit* : to take a fancy to

con·ceit·ed \-ˈsēt-əd\ *adj* [1*conceit*] **1** : ingeniously contrived : FANCIFUL **2** : having an excessively high opinion of oneself — **con·ceit·ed·ly** *adv* — **con·ceit·ed·ness** *n*

con·ceiv·abil·i·ty \kən-ˌsē-və-ˈbil-ət-ē\ *n* : the quality or state of being conceivable

con·ceiv·able \kən-ˈsē-və-bəl\ *adj* : capable of being conceived — **con·ceiv·able·ness** *n* — **con·ceiv·ably** \-blē\ *adv*

con·ceive \kən-ˈsēv\ *vb* [ME *conceiven*, fr. OF *conceivre*, fr. L *concipere* to take in, conceive, fr. *com-* + *capere* to take] *vt* **1** : to become pregnant with (young) **2 a** : to take into one's mind ⟨~ a prejudice against him⟩ **b** : to form a conception of : IMAGINE, IMAGE **3** *archaic* : to apprehend by reason or imagination : UNDERSTAND **4** : to be of the opinion ~ *vi* **1** : to become pregnant **2** : to have a conception **syn** see THINK — **con·ceiv·er** *n*

con·cent \kən-ˈsent\ *n* [L *concentus*, fr. *concentus*, pp. of *concinere* to sing together, fr. *com-* + *canere* to sing] *archaic* : HARMONY

con·cen·ter \kən-ˈsent-ər, kän-\ *vb* [MF *concentrer*, fr. *com-* + *centre* center] *vt* : to draw or direct to a common center : CONCENTRATE ~ *vi* : to come to a common center

1con·cen·trate \ˈkän(t)-sən-ˌtrāt, -ˌsen-\ *vb* [*com-* + L *centrum* center] *vt* **1 a** : to bring or direct toward a common center or objective **b** : to gather into one body, mass, or force **2 a** : to make less dilute ⟨~ syrup⟩ **b** : to express or exhibit in condensed form ~ *vi* **1** : to draw toward or meet in a common center **2** : GATHER, COLLECT **3** : to concentrate one's powers, efforts, or attentions ⟨~ on a problem⟩ — **con·cen·tra·tor** \-ˌtrāt-ər\ *n*

2concentrate *n* : something concentrated

con·cen·tra·tion \ˌkän(t)-sən-ˈtrā-shən, -ˌsen-\ *n* **1** : the act or process of concentrating : the state of being concentrated; *specif* : direction of attention on a single object **2** : a concentrated mass or thing **3** : the relative content of a component : STRENGTH

concentration camp *n* : a camp where persons (as prisoners of war, political prisoners, or refugees) are detained or confined

con·cen·tra·tive \ˈkän(t)-sən-ˌtrāt-iv, -ˌsen-\ *adj* : serving or tending to concentrate

con·cen·tric \kən-ˈsen-trik, (ˈ)kän-\ *adj* [ML *concentricus*, fr. L *com-* + *centrum* center] **1** : having a common center ⟨~ circles⟩ **2** : having a common axis : COAXIAL — **con·cen·tri·cal·ly** \-tri-k(ə-)lē\ *adv* — **con·cen·tric·i·ty** \ˌkän-ˌsen-ˈtris-ət-ē\ *n*

con·cept \ˈkän-ˌsept\ *n* [L *conceptum*, neut. of *conceptus*, pp. of *concipere* to conceive] **1** : something conceived in the mind : THOUGHT, NOTION **2** : an abstract idea generalized from particular instances **syn** see IDEA

con·cep·ta·cle \kən-ˈsep-ti-kəl\ *n* [NL *conceptaculum*, fr. L, receptacle, fr. *conceptus*, pp. of *concipere* to take in] : an external cavity containing reproductive cells in algae (as of the genus *Fucus*)

con·cep·tion \kən-ˈsep-shən\ *n* [ME *concepcioun*, fr. OF *conception*, fr. L *conception-*, *conceptio*, fr. *conceptus*, pp. of *concipere* to take in, conceive] **1 a** (1) : the act of becoming pregnant : the state of being conceived (2) : EMBRYO, FETUS **b** *archaic* : BEGINNING **2 a** : the function or process of forming or understanding ideas or abstractions or their symbols **b** : a general idea : CONCEPT **c** : a complex product of abstract or reflective thinking **d** : the sum of a person's ideas and beliefs concerning something **3** : the originating of something in the mind **syn** see IDEA — **con·cep·tion·al** \-shnəl, -shən-ᵊl\ *adj* — **con·cep·tive** \-ˈsep-tiv\ *adj*

con·cep·tu·al \kən-ˈsep-chə(-wə)l, kän-, -ˈsepsh-wəl\ *adj* [ML *conceptualis* of thought, fr. LL *conceptus* act of conceiving, thought, fr. L *conceptus*, pp.] : of, relating to, or consisting of concepts — **con·cep·tu·al·ly** \-ē\ *adv*

con·cep·tu·al·ism \-ˌiz-əm\ *n* : a theory intermediate between realism and nominalism that universals exist in the mind as subjects of discourse or as predicates that may be properly affirmed of reality — **con·cep·tu·al·ist** \-əst\ *n* — **con·cep·tu·al·is·tic** \-ˌsep-chə(-wə)l-ˈis-tik, -ˌsepsh-wəl-\ *adj*

con·cep·tu·al·iza·tion \-ˌsep-chə(-wə)l-ə-ˈzā-shən, -ˌsepsh-wəl-\ *n* : the act or process of conceptualizing

con·cep·tu·al·ize \-ˈsep-chə(-wə)l-ˌīz, -ˈsepsh-wəl-\ *vt* : to form a concept of; *esp* : to interpret conceptually

1con·cern \kən-ˈsərn\ *vb* [ME *concernen*, fr. MF & ML; MF *concerner*, fr. ML *concernere*, fr. LL, to sift together, mingle, fr. L *com-* + *cernere* to sift] *vt* **1 a** : to relate to : be about **b** : to bear

on **2 :** to have an influence on **:** INVOLVE; *also* **:** to be the business or affair of **3 :** to be a care, trouble, or distress to **4 :** ENGAGE, OCCUPY ~ *vi, obs* **:** to be of importance **:** MATTER

[2]**concern** *n* **1 :** something that relates or belongs to one **:** AFFAIR **2 :** matter for consideration **3 a :** marked interest or regard usu. arising through a personal tie or relationship **b :** a state of uncertainty and apprehension **4 :** an organization or establishment for business or manufacture **5 :** CONTRIVANCE, GADGET **syn** see CARE

con·cerned *adj* **:** DISTURBED, ANXIOUS ⟨~ for his health⟩

con·cern·ing \kən-'sər-niŋ\ *prep* **:** relating to **:** REGARDING

con·cern·ment \kən-'sərn-mənt\ *n* **1 :** something in which one is concerned **2 :** IMPORTANCE, CONSEQUENCE **3** *archaic* **:** INVOLVEMENT, PARTICIPATION **4 :** SOLICITUDE, ANXIETY

[1]**con·cert** \kən-'sərt\ *vb* [MF *concerter*, fr. OIt *concertare*, fr. LL, fr. L, to contend, fr. *com-* + *certare* to strive, fr. *certus* decided, determined] *vt* **1 a :** to plan together **b :** to settle by agreement **2 :** DEVISE, ARRANGE ~ *vi* **:** to act in harmony or conjunction

[2]**con·cert** \'kän(t)-sərt, 'kän-,sərt\ *n* [F, fr. It *concerto*, fr. *concertare*] **1 a :** agreement in design or plan **b :** a concerted action **2 :** musical harmony **:** CONCORD **3 a :** a musical performance of some length by several voices or instruments or both **b :** RECITAL 3a

con·cert·ed \kən-'sərt-əd\ *adj* **1 a :** mutually contrived or agreed on **b :** performed in unison **2 :** arranged in parts for several voices or instruments

con·cer·ti·na \,kän(t)-sər-'tē-nə\ *n* **1 :** a musical instrument of the accordion family **2 :** a coiled barbed wire for use as an obstacle

con·cer·ti·no \,kän-chər-'tē-(,)nō\ *n* [It, dim. of *concerto*] **1 :** the solo instruments in a concerto grosso **2 :** a short concerto

con·cert·mas·ter \'kän(t)-sərt-,mas-tər\ *or* **con·cert·meis·ter** \-,mī-stər\ *n* [G *konzertmeister*, fr. *konzert* concert + *meister* master] **:** the leader of the first violins and assistant conductor

con·cer·to \kən-'chert-(,)ō\ *n, pl* **con·cer·ti** \-(,)ē\ *or* **concertos** [It, fr. *concerto* concert] **:** a piece for one or more soloists and orchestra usu. in symphonic form with three contrasting movements

concerto gros·so \kən-,chert-ō-'grō-(,)sō\ *n, pl* **concerti gros·si** \-,chert-ē-'grō-(,)sē\ [It, lit., big concerto] **:** a baroque orchestral composition with a small group of solo instruments contrasting with the full orchestra

concert pitch *n* **1 a :** PHILHARMONIC PITCH 1 **b :** INTERNATIONAL PITCH **2 :** a high state of fitness, tension, or readiness

con·ces·sion \kən-'sesh-ən\ *n* [F or L; F, fr. L *concession-*, *concessio*, fr. *concessus*, pp. of *concedere* to concede] **1 a :** the act or an instance of conceding **b :** the admitting of a point claimed in argument **2 :** something conceded: **a :** ACKNOWLEDGMENT, ADMISSION **b :** GRANT **c** (1) **:** a grant of land or property esp. by a government in return for services or for a particular use (2) **:** a right to undertake and profit by a specified activity (3) **:** a lease of a portion of premises for a particular purpose; *also* **:** the portion leased or the activities carried on

con·ces·sion·aire \kən-,sesh-ə-'na(ə)r, -'ne(ə)r\ *n* [F *concessionnaire*, fr. *concession*] **:** the beneficiary of a concession; *esp* **:** one that operates a refreshment stand at a recreational center

con·ces·sion·er \kən-'sesh-(ə-)nər\ *n* **:** CONCESSIONAIRE

con·ces·sive \kən-'ses-iv\ *adj* **1 :** making for or being a concession **2 :** denoting concession ⟨a ~ clause⟩ — **con·ces·sive·ly** *adv*

conch \'käŋk, 'känch, 'kȯŋk\ *n, pl* **conchs** \'käŋks, 'kȯŋks\ *or* **conch·es** \'kän-chəz\ [L *concha* mussel, mussel shell, fr. Gk *konchē*; akin to Skt *śaṅkha* conch shell] **1 :** any of various large spiral-shelled marine gastropod mollusks (as of the genera *Strombus* and *Cassis*); *also* **:** its shell used esp. for cameos **2 :** CONCHA 2

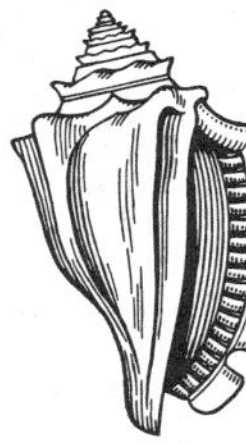

conch

conch- *or* **concho-** *comb form* [Gk *konch-*, *koncho-*, fr. *konchē*] **:** shell ⟨*concho*logy⟩ ⟨*conch*iolin⟩

con·cha \'käŋ-kə\ *n, pl* **con·chae** \-,kē, -,kī\ [It & L; It *conca* semidome, apse, fr. LL *concha*, fr. L, shell] **1 a :** the plain semidome of an apse **b :** APSE **2 :** something shaped like a shell; *esp* **:** the largest and deepest concavity of the external ear — **con·chal** \-kəl\ *adj*

conch·if·er·ous \käŋ-'kif-(ə-)rəs\ *adj* [ISV] **:** shell-bearing

con·chi·o·lin \käŋ-'kī-ə-lən\ *n* **:** a scleroprotein forming the organic basis of mollusk shells

con·choi·dal \käŋ-'kȯid-ᵊl, kän-\ *adj* [Gk *konchoeidēs* like a mussel, fr. *konchē*] **:** having elevations or depressions shaped like the inside surface of a bivalve shell — **con·choi·dal·ly** \-ᵊl-ē\ *adv*

con·chol·o·gy \käŋ-'käl-ə-jē\ *n* **1 :** a branch of zoology that deals with shells **2 :** a treatise on shells

con·cierge \kōⁿ-'syerzh\ *n, pl* **con·cierges** \-'syerzh(-əz)\ [F, modif. of L *conservus* fellow slave, fr. *com-* + *servus* slave] **:** an attendant at the entrance of a building esp. in France who oversees ingress and egress, handles mail, and acts as a janitor or porter

con·cil·i·ar \kən-'sil-ē-ər\ *adj* [L *concilium* council] **:** of, relating to, or issued by a council — **con·cil·i·ar·ly** *adv*

con·cil·i·ate \kən-'sil-ē-,āt\ *vt* [L *conciliatus*, pp. of *conciliare* to assemble, unite, win over, fr. *concilium* assembly, council — more at COUNCIL] **1 :** to gain (as goodwill) by pleasing acts **2 :** to make compatible **:** RECONCILE **3 :** to gain the goodwill or favor of **syn** see PACIFY — **con·cil·i·a·tion** \-,sil-ē-'ā-shən\ *n* — **con·cil·i·a·tive** \-'sil-ē-,āt-iv\ *adj* — **con·cil·i·a·tor** \-'sil-ē-,āt-ər\ *n* — **con·cil·ia·to·ry** \-'sil-yə-,tōr-ē, -'sil-ē-ə-, -,tȯr-\ *adj*

con·cin·ni·ty \kən-'sin-ət-ē\ *n* [L *concinnitas*, fr. *concinnus* skillfully put together] **:** harmony and often elegance of design esp. of literary style in adaptation of parts to a whole or to each other

con·cise \kən-'sīs\ *adj* [L *concisus*, fr. pp. of *concidere* to cut up, fr. *com-* + *caedere* to cut, strike; akin to MHG *heie* mallet, Arm *xait'* to prick] **1 :** marked by brevity of expression or statement **2 :** cut short **:** BRIEF — **con·cise·ly** *adv* — **con·cise·ness** *n*

syn CONCISE, TERSE, SUCCINCT, LACONIC, SUMMARY, PITHY, COMPENDIOUS mean very brief in statement or expression. CONCISE suggests the removal of all that is superfluous or elaborative; TERSE implies conciseness that is pointed and elegant; SUCCINCT implies compression into the smallest possible space; LACONIC implies brevity to the point of seeming rude, indifferent, or mysterious; SUMMARY suggests the statement of main points with no elaboration or explanation; PITHY adds to SUCCINCT or TERSE the implication of richness of meaning or substance; COMPENDIOUS applies to a treatment at once full in scope and brief and concise in treatment

con·ci·sion \kən-'sizh-ən\ *n* [ME, fr. L *concision-*, *concisio*, fr. *concisus*, pp.] **1** *archaic* **:** a cutting up or off **2 :** CONCISENESS

con·clave \'kän-,klāv\ *n* [ME, fr. MF or ML; MF, fr. ML, fr. L, room that can be locked up, fr. *com-* + *clavis* key — more at CLAVICLE] **1 :** a private meeting or secret assembly; *esp* **:** a meeting of Roman Catholic cardinals secluded continuously while choosing a pope **2 :** a gathering of a group or association **:** CONVENTION

con·clude \kən-'klüd\ *vb* [ME *concluden*, fr. L *concludere* to shut up, end, infer, fr. *com-* + *claudere* to shut] *vt* **1** *obs* **:** to shut up **:** ENCLOSE **2 :** to bring to an end **3 a :** to reach as an end of reasoning **b :** to bring to a close (as an argument) by inferring **4 :** JUDGE, DECIDE **5 :** to bring about as a result **:** COMPLETE ~ *vi* **1 :** END **2 a :** to form a final judgment **b :** to reach a decision or agreement **syn** see CLOSE, INFER — **con·clud·er** *n*

con·clu·sion \kən-'klü-zhən\ *n* [ME, fr. MF, fr. L *conclusion-*, *conclusio*, fr. *conclusus*, pp. of *concludere*] **1 a :** a reasoned judgment **:** INFERENCE **b :** the necessary consequence of two or more propositions taken as premises; *esp* **:** the inferred proposition of a syllogism **2 :** TERMINATION, END: as **a :** RESULT, OUTCOME **b** *pl* **:** trial of strength or skill — used in the phrase *try conclusions* **c :** a final summing up **d :** the final decision in a law case **e :** the final part of a pleading in law **3 :** an act or instance of concluding

con·clu·sive \-'klü-siv, -ziv\ *adj* **1 :** of or relating to a conclusion **2 :** DECISIVE, FINAL — **con·clu·sive·ly** *adv* — **con·clu·sive·ness** *n*

syn CONCLUSIVE, DECISIVE, DETERMINATIVE, DEFINITIVE mean bringing to an end. CONCLUSIVE applies to reasoning or logical proof that puts an end to debate or questioning; DECISIVE may apply to something that ends a controversy, a contest, or any uncertainty; DETERMINATIVE adds an implication of giving a fixed course or direction; DEFINITIVE applies to what is put forth as final and permanent

con·coct \kən-'käkt, kän-\ *vt* [L *concoctus*, pp. of *concoquere* to cook together, fr. *com-* + *coquere* to cook] **1 :** to prepare by combining crude materials **2 :** DEVISE, FABRICATE — **con·coct·er** *n* — **con·coc·tion** \-'käk-shən\ *n* — **con·coc·tive** \-'käk-tiv\ *adj*

con·com·i·tance \kən-'käm-ət-ən(t)s, kän-\ *n* **1 :** ACCOMPANIMENT; *esp* **:** regular conjunction with correlative variation of concomitants **2 :** CONCOMITANT

con·com·i·tant \-ət-ənt\ *adj* [L *concomitant-*, *concomitans*, prp. of *concomitari* to accompany, fr. *com-* + *comitari* to accompany, fr. *comit-*, *comes* companion] **:** accompanying esp. in a subordinate or incidental way — **concomitant** *n* — **con·com·i·tant·ly** *adv*

con·cord \'kän-,kȯ(ə)rd, 'käŋ-\ *n* [ME, fr. OF *concorde*, fr. L *concordia*, fr. *concord-*, *concors* agreeing, fr. *com-* + *cord-*, *cor* heart] **1 a :** a state of agreement **:** HARMONY **b :** a harmonious combination of tones simultaneously heard **2 :** agreement by stipulation, compact, or covenant **3 :** grammatical agreement

con·cor·dance \kən-'kȯrd-ᵊn(t)s, kän-\ *n* [ME, fr. MF, fr. ML *concordantia*, fr. L *concordant-*, *concordans*] **1 :** an alphabetical index of the principal words in a book or the works of an author with their immediate contexts **2 :** CONCORD, AGREEMENT

con·cor·dant \-ᵊnt\ *adj* [ME, fr. MF, fr. L *concordant-*, *concordans*, prp. of *concordare* to agree, fr. *concord-*, *concors*] **:** AGREEING, CONSONANT — **con·cor·dant·ly** *adv*

con·cor·dat \kən-'kȯr-,dat\ *n* [F, fr. ML *concordatum*, fr. L, neut. of *concordatus*, pp. of *concordare*] **:** COMPACT, COVENANT; *specif* **:** an agreement between a pope and a sovereign or government for the regulation of ecclesiastical matters

con·course \'kän-,kō(ə)rs, 'käŋ-, -,kȯ(ə)rs\ *n* [ME, fr. MF & L; MF *concours*, fr. L *concursus*, fr. *concursus*, pp. of *concurrere* to run together] **1 :** an act or process of coming together and merging **2 :** a meeting produced by voluntary or spontaneous coming together **3 a :** an open space where roads or paths meet **b :** an open space or hall (as in a railroad terminal) where crowds gather

con·cres·cence \kən-'kres-ᵊn(t)s, kän-\ *n* [L *concrescentia*, fr. *concrescent-*, *concrescens*, prp. of *concrescere*] **1 :** increase by the addition of particles **2 :** a growing together **:** COALESCENCE; *esp* **:** convergence and fusion of the lateral lips of the blastopore to form the primordium of an embryo — **con·cres·cent** \-ᵊnt\ *adj*

[1]**con·crete** \kän-'krēt, 'kän-,\ *adj* [ME, fr. L *concretus*, fr. pp. of *concrescere* to grow together, fr. *com-* + *crescere* to grow] **1 :** formed by coalition of particles into one solid mass **2 :** naming a real thing or class of things **3 a :** characterized by or belonging to immediate experience of actual things or events **b :** SPECIFIC, PARTICULAR **c :** REAL, TANGIBLE **4 :** relating to or made of concrete **syn** see SPECIAL — **con·crete·ly** *adv* — **con·crete·ness** *n*

[2]**con·crete** \'kän-,krēt, kän-'\ *n* **1 :** a mass formed by concretion or coalescence of separate particles of matter in one body **2 :** a hard strong building material made by mixing a cementing material and a mineral aggregate with sufficient water to cause the cement to set and bind the entire mass

[3]**con·crete** \'kän-,krēt, kän-'\ *vt* **1 a :** to form into a solid mass **:** SOLIDIFY **b :** COMBINE, BLEND **2 :** to cover with, form of, or set in concrete ~ *vi* **:** to become concreted

con·cre·tion \kän-'krē-shən, kən-\ *n* **1 :** the act or process of concreting **:** the state of being concreted ⟨~ of ideas in an hypothesis⟩ **2 :** something concreted: as **a :** a hard usu. inorganic mass (as a bezoar or tophus) formed in a living body **b :** a mass of mineral matter found generally in rock of a composition different from its own and produced by deposition from aqueous solution in the rock — **con·cre·tion·ary** \-shə-,ner-ē\ *adj*

con·cu·bi·nage \kän-'kyü-bə-nij, kən-\ *n* **1 :** cohabitation of persons not legally married **2 :** the state of being a concubine

con·cu·bine \'käŋ-kyə-,bīn, 'kän-\ *n* [ME, fr. OF, fr. L *concubina*, fr. *com-* + *cubare* to lie — more at HIP] **1 :** a woman living in a socially recognized state of concubinage **2 :** MISTRESS

con·cu·pis·cence \kän-'kyü-pə-sən(t)s\ *n* [ME, fr. MF, fr. LL *concupiscentia*, fr. L *concupiscent-*, *concupiscens*, prp. of *concupiscere* to desire ardently, fr. *com-* + *cupere* to desire] **:** ardent desire; *esp* **:** sexual desire — **con·cu·pis·cent** \-sənt\ *adj*

con·cu·pis·ci·ble \kän-'kyü-pə-sə-bəl\ *adj* [ME, fr. MF or LL; MF, fr. LL *concupiscibilis*, fr. L *concupiscere*] **:** moved by concupiscence

con·cur \kən-'kər, kän-\ *vi* **con·curred**; **con·cur·ring** [ME *concurren*, fr. L *concurrere*, fr. *com-* + *currere* to run] **1** *obs* **:** to come together **:** MEET **2 :** to happen together **:** COINCIDE **3 :** to act together to a common end or single effect **4 a :** APPROVE ⟨~ in a statement⟩ **b :** AGREE ⟨~ with an opinion⟩ **syn** see AGREE

con·cur·rence \kən-'kər-ən(t)s, kän-, -'kə-rən(t)s\ *n* **1 a :** agreement or union in action **:** COOPERATION **b** (1) **:** agreement in opinion or design (2) **:** CONSENT **2 :** a coming together **:** CONJUNCTION **3 :** a coincidence of equal powers in law

con·cur·rent \-'kər-ənt, -'kə-rənt\ *adj* [ME, fr. MF & L; MF, fr. L *concurrent-, concurrens*, prp. of *concurrere*] **1 a :** CONVERGING **b :** running parallel **2 :** operating at the same time **3 :** acting in conjunction **4 :** exercised over the same matter or area by two different authorities — **concurrent** *n* — **con·cur·rent·ly** *adv*

concurrent resolution *n* **:** a resolution passed by both houses of a legislative body that lacks the force of law

con·cuss \kən-'kəs\ *vt* [L *concussus*, pp.] **:** to affect with concussion

con·cus·sion \kən-'kəsh-ən\ *n* [MF or L; MF, fr. L *concussion-, concussio*, fr. *concussus*, pp. of *concutere* to shake violently, fr. *com-* + *quatere* to shake] **1 :** SHAKING, AGITATION **2 a :** a smart or hard blow or collision **b :** a stunning, damaging, or shattering effect from such a blow; *esp* **:** a jarring injury of the brain resulting in disturbance of cerebral function — **con·cus·sive** \-'kəs-iv\ *adj*

con·demn \kən-'dem\ *vt* [ME *condemnen*, fr. OF *condemner*, fr. L *condemnare*, fr. *com-* + *damnare* to condemn — more at DAMN] **1 :** to declare to be wrong **:** CENSURE **2 a :** to pronounce guilty **:** CONVICT **b :** SENTENCE, DOOM **3 :** to adjudge unfit for use or consumption **4 :** to declare convertible to public use under the right of eminent domain **syn** see CRITICIZE — **con·dem·nable** \-'dem-(n)ə-bəl\ *adj* — **con·demn·er** *or* **con·demn·or** \-'dem-ər\ *n*

con·dem·na·tion \ˌkän-ˌdem-'nā-shən, -dəm-\ *n* **1 :** CENSURE, BLAME **2 :** the act of judicially condemning **3 :** the state of being condemned **4 :** a reason for condemning — **con·dem·na·to·ry** \kən-'dem-nə-ˌtōr-ē, -ˌtȯr-\ *adj*

con·dens·able *also* **con·dens·ible** \kən-'den(t)-sə-bəl\ *adj* **:** capable of being condensed

con·den·sate \'kän-dən-ˌsāt, -ˌden-; kən-'den-\ *n* **:** a product of condensation

con·den·sa·tion \ˌkän-ˌden-'sā-shən, -dən-\ *n* **1 :** the act or process of condensing: as **a :** a chemical reaction involving union between atoms in the same or different molecules often with elimination of a simple molecule to form a new more complex compound of often greater molecular weight **b :** a reduction to a denser form (as from steam to water) **c :** compression of a written or spoken work into more concise form **2 :** the quality or state of being condensed **3 :** a product of condensing; *specif* **:** an abridgment of a literary work — **con·den·sa·tion·al** \-shnəl, -shən-ᵊl\ *adj*

con·dense \kən-'den(t)s\ *vb* [ME *condensen*, fr. MF *condenser*, fr. L *condensare*, fr. *com-* + *densare* to make dense, fr. *densus* dense] *vt* **:** to make denser or more compact; *esp* **:** to subject to condensation ~ *vi* **:** to undergo condensation **syn** see CONTRACT

con·densed *adj* **:** reduced to a more compact form; *specif* **:** having a face that is narrower than that of a typeface not so characterized

condensed milk *n* **:** evaporated milk with sugar added

con·dens·er \kən-'den(t)-sər\ *n* **1 :** one that condenses: as **a :** a lens or mirror used to concentrate light upon an object **b :** an apparatus in which gas or vapor is condensed **2 :** CAPACITOR

con·de·scend \ˌkän-di-'send\ *vi* [ME *condescenden*, fr. MF *condescendre*, fr. LL *condescendere*, fr. L *com-* + *descendere* to descend] **1 a :** to descend to a less formal or dignified level **:** STOOP **b :** to waive the privileges of rank **2 :** to assume an air of superiority **syn** see STOOP

con·de·scen·dence \-'sen-dən(t)s\ *n* **:** CONDESCENSION

con·de·scend·ing *adj* **:** showing or characterized by condescension **:** PATRONIZING — **con·de·scend·ing·ly** \-'sen-diŋ-lē\ *adv*

con·de·scen·sion \ˌkän-di-'sen-chən\ *n* [LL *condescension-, condescensio*, fr. *condescensus*, pp. of *condescendere*] **1 :** voluntary descent from one's rank or dignity in relations with an inferior **2 :** a patronizing attitude

con·dign \kən-'dīn, 'kän-ˌ\ *adj* [ME *condigne*, fr. MF, fr. L *condignus* very worthy, fr. *com-* + *dignus* worthy — more at DECENT] **:** DESERVED, APPROPRIATE ⟨~ punishment⟩ — **con·dign·ly** *adv*

con·di·ment \'kän-də-mənt\ *n* [ME, fr. MF, fr. L *condimentum*, fr. *condire* to pickle, fr. *condere* to build, store up, fr. *com-* + *-dere* to put — more at DO] **:** something used to enhance the flavor of food; *esp* **:** a pungent seasoning

¹con·di·tion \kən-'dish-ən\ *n* [ME *condicion*, fr. MF, fr. L *condicion-, condicio* terms of agreement, condition, fr. *condicere* to agree, fr. *com-* + *dicere* to say, determine — more at DICTION] **1 a :** a premise upon which the fulfillment of an agreement depends **:** STIPULATION **b** *obs* **:** COVENANT **c :** a provision making the effect of a legal instrument contingent upon an uncertain event; *also* **:** the event itself **2 :** something essential to the appearance or occurrence of something else **:** PREREQUISITE: as **a :** an environmental requirement **b :** the subordinate clause of a conditional sentence **3 a :** a restricting or modifying factor **:** QUALIFICATION **b :** an unsatisfactory academic grade that may be raised by doing additional work **4 a :** a state of being **b :** social status **:** RANK **c :** a state of health **d :** a state of physical fitness or readiness for use **e** *pl* **:** attendant circumstances **5 a** *obs* **:** temper of mind **b** *obs* **:** TRAIT **c** *pl, archaic* **:** MANNERS, WAYS **syn** see STATE

²condition *vb* **con·di·tion·ing** \-'dish-(ə-)niŋ\ *vi, archaic* **:** to make stipulations ~ *vt* **1 :** to agree by stipulating **2 :** to make conditional **3 a :** to put into a proper state for work or use **b :** AIR-CONDITION **4 :** to give a grade of condition to **5 a :** to adapt, modify, or mold to conform to an environing culture **b :** to modify so that an act or response previously associated with one stimulus becomes associated with another — **con·di·tion·er** \-'dish-(ə-)nər\ *n*

con·di·tion·al \kən-'dish-nəl, -ən-ᵊl\ *adj* **1 :** subject to, implying, or dependent upon a condition **2 :** expressing, containing, or implying a supposition **3 :** stating conditions ⟨~ equations⟩ **4** *of a reflex* **:** CONDITIONED — **conditional** *n* — **con·di·tion·al·i·ty** \-ˌdish-ə-'nal-ət-ē\ *n* — **con·di·tion·al·ly** \-'dish-nə-lē, -ən-ᵊl-ē\ *adv*

con·di·tioned *adj* **1 :** CONDITIONAL **2 :** brought or put into a specified state **3 :** determined or established by conditioning

con·dole \kən-'dōl\ *vb* [LL *condolēre*, fr. L *com-* + *dolēre* to feel pain; akin to Gk *daidalos* ingeniously formed] *vi* **1** *obs* **:** GRIEVE **2 :** to express sympathetic sorrow ~ *vt, archaic* **:** LAMENT, GRIEVE

con·do·lence \kən-'dō-lən(t)s, 'kän-də-\ *n* **1 :** sympathy with another in sorrow **2 :** an expression of sympathy **syn** see PITY

con·do·min·i·um \ˌkän-də-'min-ē-əm\ *n* [NL, fr. L *com-* + *dominium* domain] **1 a :** joint dominion; *esp* **:** joint sovereignty by two or more nations **b :** a government operating under joint rule **2 :** a politically dependent territory under condominium **3 :** individual ownership of a unit in a multi-unit structure (as an apartment building); *also* **:** a unit so owned

con·do·na·tion \ˌkän-dō-'nā-shən, -də-\ *n* **:** implied pardon of an offense by treating the offender as if it had not been committed

con·done \kən-'dōn\ *vt* [L *condonare* to forgive, fr. *com-* + *donare* to give — more at DONATE] **:** to pardon or overlook voluntarily **syn** see EXCUSE — **con·don·er** *n*

con·dor \'kän-dər, -ˌdȯ(ə)r\ *n* [Sp *cóndor*, fr. Quechua *kúntur*] **:** a very large American vulture (*Vultur gryphus*) of the high Andes having the head and neck bare and the plumage dull black with a downy white neck ruff and white patches on the wings

con·dot·tie·re \ˌkän-də-'tye(ə)r-ē, ˌkän-ˌdät-ē-'e(ə)r-\ *n, pl* **con·dot·tie·ri** \-ē\ [It *condottiere*] **1 :** a leader of a band of mercenaries common in Europe between the 14th and 16th centuries; *also* **:** a member of such a band **2 :** a mercenary soldier

con·duce \kən-'d(y)üs\ *vi* [ME *conducen* to conduct, fr. L *conducere* to conduct, conduce, fr. *com-* + *ducere* to lead — more at TOW] **:** to lead or tend to a desirable result **:** CONTRIBUTE

syn CONDUCE, CONTRIBUTE, REDOUND mean to lead to an end. CONDUCE implies having a predictable tendency to further an end; CONTRIBUTE suggests having an effective part in furthering an end; REDOUND implies leading to an unforeseen end or state by a flowing back of consequences

con·du·cive \-'d(y)ü-siv\ *adj* **:** tending to promote or assist **:** CONTRIBUTIVE — **con·du·cive·ness** *n*

¹con·duct \'kän-(ˌ)dəkt\ *n* [alter. of ME *conduit*, fr. OF, act of leading, escort, fr. ML *conductus*, fr. L *conductus*, pp. of *conducere*] **1** *obs* **:** ESCORT, GUIDE **2 :** the act, manner, or process of carrying on **:** MANAGEMENT **3 :** a mode or standard of personal behavior esp. as based on moral principles

²con·duct \kən-'dəkt\ *vt* **1 :** GUIDE, ESCORT **2 :** LEAD, DIRECT **3 a :** to convey in a channel **b :** to act as a medium for conveying **4 :** BEHAVE ~ *vi* **1** *of a road or passage* **:** to show the way **:** LEAD **2 a :** to act as leader or director **b :** to have the quality of transmitting light, heat, sound, or electricity — **con·duct·ibil·i·ty** \kən-ˌdək-tə-'bil-ət-ē\ *n* — **con·duct·ible** \-'dək-tə-bəl\ *adj*

syn MANAGE, CONTROL, DIRECT: CONDUCT implies taking responsibility for the acts and achievements of a group; MANAGE implies direct handling and manipulating or maneuvering toward a desired result; CONTROL implies a regulating or restraining in order to keep within bounds or on a course; DIRECT implies constant guiding and regulating so as to achieve smooth operation **syn** see in addition BEHAVE

con·duc·tance \kən-'dək-tən(t)s\ *n* **1 :** conducting power **2 a :** the readiness with which a conductor transmits an electric current **b :** the reciprocal of electrical resistance

con·duc·tion \kən-'dək-shən\ *n* **1 :** the act of conducting or conveying **2 :** transmission through or by means of a conductor; *also* **:** CONDUCTIVITY **3 :** the transmission of excitation through living and esp. nervous tissue

con·duc·tive \kən-'dək-tiv\ *adj* **:** having conductivity

con·duc·tiv·i·ty \ˌkän-ˌdək-'tiv-ət-ē, kən-\ *n* **:** the quality or power of conducting or transmitting: as **a :** the reciprocal of electrical resistivity **b :** the quality of living matter responsible for the transmission of and progressive reaction to stimuli

con·duc·tor \kən-'dək-tər\ *n* **:** one that conducts: as **a :** GUIDE **b :** a collector of fares in a public conveyance **c :** the leader of a musical ensemble **d :** a substance or body capable of transmitting electricity, heat, or sound — **con·duc·to·ri·al** \ˌkän-ˌdək-'tōr-ē-əl, kən-, -'tȯr-\ *adj* — **con·duc·tress** \kən-'dək-trəs\ *n*

con·duit \'kän-ˌd(y)ü-ət, -ˌdwit, -də-wət, -dət\ *n* [ME, fr. MF, lit., act of leading] **1 :** a natural or artificial channel through which water or other fluid is conveyed **2** *archaic* **:** FOUNTAIN **3 :** a pipe, tube, or tile for protecting electric wires or cables

con·du·pli·cate \(')kän-'d(y)ü-pli-kət\ *adj* [L *conduplicatus*, pp. of *conduplicare* to double, fr. *com-* + *duplic-, duplex* double — more at DUPLEX] **:** folded lengthwise — used of leaves or petals in the bud — **con·du·pli·ca·tion** \ˌkän-ˌd(y)ü-pli-'kā-shən\ *n*

con·dy·lar \'kän-də-lər\ *adj* **:** of or relating to a condyle

con·dyle \'kän-ˌdīl, -dᵊl\ *n* [F & L; F, fr. L *condylus* knuckle, fr. Gk *kondylos*] **:** an articular prominence on a bone; *esp* **:** one of a pair like knuckles — **con·dy·loid** \'kän-də-ˌlȯid\ *adj*

con·dy·lo·ma \ˌkän-də-'lō-mə\ *n* [NL, fr. Gk *kondylōma*, fr. *kondylos*] **:** a warty growth on the skin or adjoining mucous membrane usu. near the anus and genital organs — **con·dy·lo·ma·tous** \-'läm-ət-əs, -'lōm-\ *adj*

¹cone \'kōn\ *n* [MF or L; MF, fr. L *conus*, fr. Gk *kōnos* — more at HONE] **1 a :** a mass of ovule-bearing or pollen-bearing scales or bracts in trees of the pine family or in cycads arranged usu. on a somewhat elongated axis **b :** any of several flower or fruit clusters suggesting a cone **2 a :** a solid generated by rotating a right triangle about one of its legs — called also *right circular cone* **b :** a solid figure whose base is a circle or other closed plane figure and whose sides taper evenly up to a point — see VOLUME table **c :** any surface traced by a moving straight line passing through a fixed vertex **3 :** something that resembles a cone in shape: as **a :** one of the short sensory end

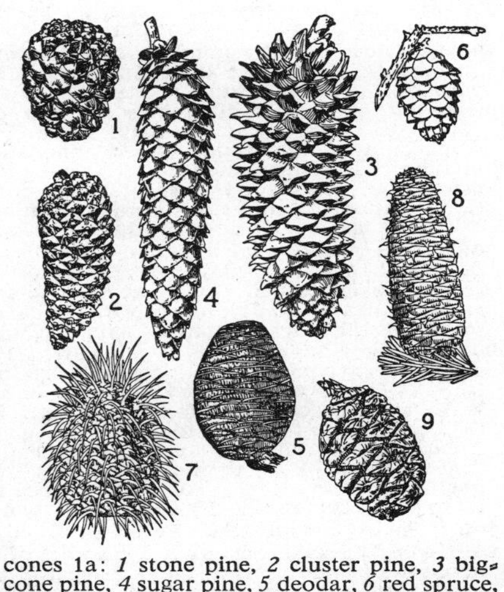

cones 1a: *1* stone pine, *2* cluster pine, *3* bigcone pine, *4* sugar pine, *5* deodar, *6* red spruce, *7* Santa Lucia fir, *8* Nordmann's fir, *9* giant sequoia

organs of the vertebrate retina usu. held to function in color vision **b :** any of numerous somewhat conical tropical gastropod mollusks (family Conidae) **c :** the apex of a volcano **d :** an ice-cream holder

2cone *vt* **1 :** to make cone-shaped **2 :** to bevel like the slanting surface of a cone ⟨~ a tire⟩

cone·flow·er \ˈkōn-ˌflau̇(-ə)r\ *n* **:** any of several composite plants having cone-shaped flower disks; *esp* **:** RUDBECKIA

con·el·rad \ˈkän-ᵊl-ˌrad\ *n* [*con*trol of *el*ectromagnetic *rad*iation] **:** a system for preventing the use of radio signals from an AM station as a guide for hostile aircraft or missiles by shifting all AM stations to the frequencies 640 or 1240 and having them broadcast in a group in random order for short intervals on only these frequencies

cone·nose \ˈkōn-ˌnōz\ *n* **:** any of various large bloodsucking bugs (esp. genus *Triatoma*) including some capable of inflicting painful bites — called also *assassin bug, big bedbug, kissing bug*

Con·es·to·ga \ˌkän-ə-ˈstō-gə\ *n* [*Conestoga*, Pa.] **:** a broad-wheeled covered wagon usu. drawn by six horses and used esp. for transporting freight across the prairies

co·ney \ˈkō-nē\ *n* [ME *conies*, pl., fr. OF *conis*, pl. of *conil*, fr. L *cuniculus*] **1 a** (1) **:** RABBIT; *esp* **:** the European rabbit (*Oryctolagus cuniculus*) (2) **:** PIKA **b :** HYRAX **c :** rabbit fur **2** *obs* **:** DUPE **3 :** any of several fishes; *esp* **:** a dusky black-spotted reddish-finned grouper (*Cephalopholis fulvus*) of the tropical Atlantic

con·fab \kən-ˈfab, ˈkän-ˌ\ *vi* **con·fabbed; con·fab·bing :** CONFABULATE — **con·fab** \ˈkän-ˌfab, kən-ˈ\ *n*

con·fab·u·late \kən-ˈfab-yə-ˌlāt\ *vi* [L *confabulatus*, pp. of *confabulari*, fr. *com-* + *fabulari* to talk, fr. *fabula* story — more at FABLE] **1 :** CHAT **2 :** POWWOW — **con·fab·u·la·tion** \kən-ˌfab-yə-ˈlā-shən, ˌkän-\ *n* — **con·fab·u·la·tor** \kən-ˈfab-yə-ˌlāt-ər\ *n* — **con·fab·u·la·to·ry** \-lə-ˌtōr-ē, -ˌtȯr-\ *adj*

con·fect \kən-ˈfekt\ *vt* [L *confectus*, pp. of *conficere* to prepare — more at COMFIT] **1 :** CONCOCT, COMPOUND **2 :** to make a confection of **:** PRESERVE — **con·fect** \ˈkän-ˌfekt\ *n*

con·fec·tion \kən-ˈfek-shən\ *n* **1 :** the act or process of confecting **2 :** something confected: as **a :** a fancy dish or sweetmeat **:** DELICACY; *esp* **:** a fruit or nut preserve **b :** a medicinal preparation usu. made with sugar, syrup, or honey **c :** a piece of fine craftsmanship — **confection** *vt, archaic*

con·fec·tion·ary \-shə-ˌner-ē\ *n* **1** *archaic* **:** CONFECTIONER **2 :** CONFECTIONERY 3 **3 :** SWEETS — **confectionary** *adj*

con·fec·tion·er \-sh(ə-)nər\ *n* **:** a manufacturer of or dealer in confections

con·fec·tion·ery \-shə-ˌner-ē\ *n* **1 :** sweet edibles (as candy) **2 :** the confectioner's art or business **3 :** a confectioner's shop

con·fed·er·a·cy \kən-ˈfed-(ə-)rə-sē\ *n* **1 :** a league or compact for mutual support or common action **:** ALLIANCE **2 :** a combination of persons for unlawful purposes **:** CONSPIRACY **3 :** the body formed by persons, states, or nations united by a league; *specif, cap* **:** the 11 southern states seceding from the U.S. in 1860 and 1861 — **con·fed·er·al** \-(ə-)rəl\ *adj* — **con·fed·er·al·ist** \-əst\ *n*

1con·fed·er·ate \kən-ˈfed-(ə-)rət\ *adj* [ME *confederat*, fr. LL *confoederatus*, pp. of *confoederare* to unite by a league, fr. L *com-* + *foeder-, foedus* compact] **1 :** united in a league **:** ALLIED **2** *cap* **:** of or relating to the Confederate States of America

2confederate *n* **1 :** ALLY, ACCOMPLICE **2** *cap* **:** an adherent of the Confederate States of America or their cause

3con·fed·er·ate \-ˈfed-ə-ˌrāt\ *vb* **:** to unite in a confederacy

Confederate Memorial Day *n* **:** any of several days appointed for the commemoration of servicemen of the Confederacy: **a :** April 26 in Alabama, Florida, Georgia, and Mississippi **b :** May 10 in No. and So. Carolina **c :** June 3 in Kentucky, Louisiana, and Texas **d :** May 30 in Virginia

confederate rose *n, often cap C* **:** a Chinese mallow (*Hibiscus mutabilis*) with white or pink flowers that become deep red at night

con·fed·er·a·tion \kən-ˌfed-ə-ˈrā-shən\ *n* **1 :** an act of confederating **:** a state of being confederated **:** ALLIANCE **2 :** LEAGUE

con·fed·er·a·tive \-ˈfed-(ə-)rət-iv, -ə-ˌrāt-\ *adj* **:** of, relating to, or characteristic of a confederation or confederates

con·fer \kən-ˈfər\ *vb* **con·ferred; con·fer·ring** [L *conferre* to bring together, fr. *com-* + *ferre* to carry — more at BEAR] *vt* **1** *obs* **:** COMPARE **2 :** GRANT, BESTOW ~ *vi* **:** to compare views **:** CONSULT **syn** see GIVE — **con·fer·ee** *or* **con·fer·ree** \ˌkän-fə-ˈrē\ *n* — **con·fer·ment** \kən-ˈfər-mənt\ *n* — **con·fer·ra·ble** \-ˈfər-ə-bəl\ *adj* — **con·fer·ral** \-ˈfər-əl\ *n* — **con·fer·rer** \-ˈfər-ər\ *n*

con·fer·ence \ˈkän-f(ə-)rən(t)s, -fərn(t)s\ *n* **1 a :** a usu. formal interchange of views **:** CONSULTATION **b :** a meeting for this purpose; *specif* **:** a meeting of members of the two branches of a legislature to adjust differences **2** *also* **con·fer·rence** \kən-ˈfər-ən(t)s\ **:** BESTOWAL **3 a :** the representative assembly or administrative organization of a denomination or of a territorial division of a denomination: as (1) **:** one of a gradated system of meetings of clergy and laymen (2) **:** an organization uniting the Congregational churches of several associations **b :** an association of athletic teams — **con·fer·en·tial** \ˌkän-fə-ˈren-chəl\ *adj*

con·fer·va \kən-ˈfər-və\ *n, pl* **con·fer·vae** \-(ˌ)vē, -ˌvī\ *also* **con·fervas** [L, a water plant, fr. *confervēre* to boil together, heal, fr. *com-* + *fervēre* to boil — more at BURN] **:** any of a genus (*Tribonema*) of algae; *broadly* **:** any of various filamentous algae forming scums on still water — **con·fer·void** \-ˌvȯid\ *adj or n*

con·fess \kən-ˈfes\ *vb* [ME *confessen*, fr. MF *confesser*, fr. OF, fr. *confes* having confessed, fr. L *confessus*, pp. of *confitēri* to confess, fr. *com-* + *fatēri* to confess; akin to L *fari* to speak — more at BAN] *vt* **1 :** to make acknowledgment of **:** ADMIT **2 :** to acknowledge to God or to a priest; *specif* **:** to receive the confession of (a penitent) **3 :** to declare faith in or adherence to **:** PROFESS **4 :** to give evidence of ~ *vi* **1 a :** to disclose one's faults; *specif* **:** to unburden one's sins or the state of one's conscience to God or to a priest **b :** to hear a confession **2 :** ADMIT, OWN **syn** see ACKNOWLEDGE

con·fessed·ly \-əd-lē, -ˈfest-lē\ *adv* **:** by confession **:** ADMITTEDLY

con·fes·sion \kən-ˈfesh-ən\ *n* **1 :** an act of confessing; *specif* **:** a disclosure of one's sins in the sacrament of penance **2 :** a statement of what is confessed: as **a :** a written acknowledgment of guilt by a party accused of an offense **b :** a formal statement of religious beliefs **:** CREED **3 :** an organized religious body having a common creed — **con·fes·sion·al** \-ˈfesh-nəl, -ən-ᵊl\ *adj*

confessional *n* **1 :** a place where a priest hears confessions **2 :** the practice of confessing to a priest

con·fes·sor \kən-ˈfes-ər\ *n* **1 :** one that confesses **2 :** one who gives heroic evidence of faith but does not suffer martyrdom **3 a :** a priest who hears confessions **b :** a priest who is one's regular spiritual guide

con·fet·ti \kən-ˈfet-ē\ *n pl but sing in constr* [It, pl. of *confetto* sweetmeat, fr. ML *confectum*, fr. L, neut. of *confectus*, pp. of *conficere* to prepare] **1 :** little candies **2 :** small bits or streamers of brightly colored paper made for throwing (as at weddings)

con·fi·dant \ˈkän-fə-ˌdant, -ˌdänt, ˌkän-fə-ˈ\ *n* [F *confident*, fr. It *confidente*, fr. *confidente* confident, trustworthy, fr. L *confident-, confidens*] **:** one to whom secrets are entrusted; *esp* **:** INTIMATE

con·fi·dante *like* CONFIDANT\ *n* [F *confidente*, fem. of *confident*] **:** a female confidant

con·fide \kən-ˈfīd\ *vb* [ME *confiden*, fr. MF or L; MF *confider*, fr. L *confidere*, fr. *com-* + *fidere* to trust] *vi* **1 :** to have confidence **:** TRUST **2 :** to show confidence by imparting secrets ~ *vt* **1 :** to tell confidentially **2 :** ENTRUST **syn** see COMMIT — **con·fid·er** *n*

1con·fi·dence \ˈkän-fəd-ən(t)s, -fə-ˌden(t)s\ *n* **1 :** FAITH, TRUST **2 a :** consciousness of feeling sure **:** SELF-RELIANCE **b :** bold certainty **:** COCKSURENESS **3 :** the quality or state of being certain **:** ASSURANCE **4 a :** a relation of trust or intimacy **b :** reliance on another's discretion **c :** legislative support ⟨vote of ~⟩ **5 :** a communication made in confidence **:** SECRET

syn ASSURANCE, SELF-POSSESSION, APLOMB: CONFIDENCE stresses faith in oneself and one's powers but does not usu. imply conceit; ASSURANCE carries a stronger implication of certainty and often of arrogance; SELF-POSSESSION implies the ease and coolness under stress that arise from command of one's powers; APLOMB suggests a conspicuously manifest self-possession in trying situations

2confidence *adj* **:** of or relating to swindling by false promises

con·fi·dent \ˈkän-fəd-ənt, -fə-ˌdent\ *adj* [L *confident-, confidens*, fr. prp. of *confidere*] **1** *obs* **:** TRUSTFUL, CONFIDING **2 :** characterized by assurance; *esp* **:** SELF-RELIANT **3 a :** full of conviction **:** CERTAIN **b :** COCKSURE — **con·fi·dent·ly** *adv*

con·fi·den·tial \ˌkän-fə-ˈden-chəl\ *adj* **1 :** PRIVATE, SECRET **2 :** showing or indicative of intimacy or willingness to confide ⟨a ~ tone⟩ **3 :** entrusted with confidences ⟨~ clerk⟩ — **con·fi·den·ti·al·i·ty** \-ˌden-chē-ˈal-ət-ē, -ˌden-ˈshal-\ *n* — **con·fi·den·tial·ly** \-ˈdench-(ə-)lē\ *adv* — **con·fi·den·tial·ness** \-ˈden-chəl-nəs\ *n*

con·fid·ing \kən-ˈfīd-iŋ\ *adj* **:** tending to confide **:** TRUSTFUL — **con·fid·ing·ly** \-iŋ-lē\ *adv* — **con·fid·ing·ness** *n*

con·fig·u·ra·tion \-ˌfig-(y)ə-ˈrā-shən, ˌkän-\ *n* [LL *configuration-, configuratio* similar formation, fr. L *configuratus*, pp. of *configurare* to form from or after, fr. *com-* + *figurare* to form, fr. *figura* figure] **1 a :** relative arrangement of parts **b :** the figure, contour, or pattern produced by such arrangement **c :** the structural makeup of a chemical compound esp. with reference to the space relations of the constituent atoms **2 :** GESTALT **syn** see FORM — **con·fig·u·ra·tion·al** \-shnəl, -shən-ᵊl\ *adj* — **con·fig·u·ra·tion·al·ly** \-shnə-lē, -shən-ᵊl-ē\ *adv* — **con·fig·u·ra·tive** \kən-ˈfig-(y)ə-ˌrāt-iv, -rət-\ *adj*

1con·fine \ˈkän-ˌfīn, *in sense 2a usu* kən-ˈfīn\ *n* [MF or L; MF *confines*, pl., fr. L *confine* border, fr. neut. of *confinis* adjacent, fr. *com-* + *finis* end] **1** *usu pl* **a :** BOUNDS, BORDERS **b :** outlying parts **:** LIMITS **c :** TERRITORY **2 a** *archaic* **:** RESTRICTION **b** *obs* **:** PRISON

2con·fine \kən-ˈfīn\ *vi, archaic* **:** BORDER ~ *vt* **1 :** to keep within limits **:** RESTRICT **2 a :** to shut up **:** IMPRISON **b :** to keep indoors **syn** see LIMIT — **con·fin·er** *n*

con·fined *adj* **:** restricted to quarters; *esp* **:** undergoing childbirth

con·fine·ment \kən-ˈfīn-mənt\ *n* **:** an act of confining **:** the state of being confined; *specif* **:** LYING-IN

con·firm \kən-ˈfərm\ *vt* [ME *confirmen*, fr. OF *confirmer*, fr. L *confirmare*, fr. *com-* + *firmare* to make firm, fr. *firmus* firm] **1 :** to make firm or firmer **:** STRENGTHEN **2 :** to give approval to **:** RATIFY **3 :** to administer the rite of confirmation to **4 :** to give new assurance of the validity of **5 :** ASSERT, MAINTAIN — **con·firm·abil·i·ty** \-ˌfər-mə-ˈbil-ət-ē\ *n* — **con·firm·able** \-ˈfər-mə-bəl\ *adj*

syn CONFIRM, CORROBORATE, SUBSTANTIATE, VERIFY, AUTHENTICATE, VALIDATE mean to attest to the truth or validity of something. CONFIRM implies the removing of doubts by an authoritative statement or indisputable fact; CORROBORATE suggests the strengthening of what is already partly established; SUBSTANTIATE implies the offering of evidence that sustains the contention; VERIFY implies the establishing of correspondence of actual facts or details with those proposed or guessed at; AUTHENTICATE implies establishing genuineness by adducing legal or official documents or expert opinion; VALIDATE implies establishing validity by authoritative affirmation or by factual proof

con·fir·ma·tion \ˌkän-fər-ˈmā-shən\ *n* **1 :** an act or process of confirming: as **a** (1) **:** a Christian rite admitting a baptized person to full church privileges (2) **:** a ceremony confirming Jewish youths in their ancestral faith **b :** the ratification of an executive act by a legislative body **2 a :** confirming proof **:** CORROBORATION **b :** the process of supporting a statement by evidence

con·fir·ma·to·ry \kən-ˈfər-mə-ˌtōr-ē, -ˌtȯr-\ *adj* **:** serving to confirm **:** CORROBORATIVE

con·firmed \kən-ˈfərmd\ *adj* **1 a :** made firm **:** STRENGTHENED **b :** deeply ingrained **c :** CHRONIC **2 :** having received the rite of confirmation **syn** see INVETERATE — **con·firm·ed·ly** \-ˈfər-məd-lē\ *adv* — **con·firmed·ness** \-ˈfər-məd-nəs, -ˈfərm(d)-nəs\ *n*

con·fis·ca·ble \kən-ˈfis-kə-bəl\ *also* **con·fis·cat·able** \ˈkän-fə-ˌskāt-ə-bəl\ *adj* **:** liable to confiscation

1con·fis·cate \ˈkän-fə-ˌskāt, kən-ˈfis-kət\ *adj* [L *confiscatus*, pp. of *confiscare* to confiscate, fr. *com-* + *fiscus* treasury — more at FISCAL] **1 :** appropriated by the government **:** FORFEITED **2 :** deprived of property by confiscation

2con·fis·cate \ˈkän-fə-ˌskāt\ *vt* **1 :** to seize as forfeited to the public treasury **2 :** to seize by authority **syn** see APPROPRIATE — **con·fis·ca·tion** \ˌkän-fə-ˈskā-shən\ *n* — **con·fis·ca·tor** \ˈkän-fə-ˌskāt-ər\ *n* — **con·fis·ca·to·ry** \kən-ˈfis-kə-ˌtōr-ē, -ˌtȯr-\ *adj*

con·fi·te·or \kən-ˈfēt-ē-ər\ *n* [ME, fr. L, I confess, fr. *confitēri* to confess — more at CONFESS] **:** a prayer in which sins are confessed

con·fi·ture \ˈkän-fə-ˌchu̇(ə)r\ *n* [F, fr. MF, fr. *confit* comfit] **:** preserved or candied fruit **:** JAM

con·fla·grant \kən-ˈflā-grənt\ *adj* [L *conflagrant-, conflagrans*, prp. of *conflagrare* to burn, fr. *com-* + *flagrare* to burn — more at BLACK] **:** BURNING, BLAZING

con·fla·gra·tion \ˌkän-flə-ˈgrā-shən\ *n* [L *conflagration-, conflagratio*, fr. *conflagratus*, pp. of *conflagrare*] **:** FIRE; *esp* **:** a large disastrous fire

con·fla·tion \kən-ˈflā-shən\ *n* [LL *conflation-, conflatio*, fr. L *conflatus*, pp. of *conflare* to blow together, fr. *com-* + *flare* to blow

— more at BLOW] : BLEND, FUSION; *esp* : a composite reading or text

¹con·flict \ˈkän-ˌflikt\ *n* [ME, fr. L *conflictus* act of striking together, fr. *conflictus*, pp. of *confligere* to strike together, fr. *com-* + *fligere* to strike] **1 a** : DISAGREEMENT **b** : emotional tension resulting from incompatible inner needs or drives **2** : WAR, BATTLE **3** : COLLISION **4** : the opposition of persons or forces that gives rise to the dramatic action in a drama or fiction **syn** see DISCORD

²con·flict \kən-ˈflikt, ˈkän-ˌ\ *vi* **1** *archaic* : to contend in warfare **2** : to show antagonism or irreconcilability — **con·flic·tion** \kən-ˈflik-shən\ *n* — **con·flic·tive** \kən-ˈflik-tiv, ˈkän-ˌ\ *adj*

con·flu·ence \ˈkän-ˌflü-ən(t)s\ *n* **1 a** : an act or instance of congregating **b** : CROWD **2 a** : the flowing together of two or more streams **b** : the place of meeting of two streams **c** : the combined stream formed by conjunction

¹con·flu·ent \ˈkän-ˌflü-ənt, kən-ˈ\ *adj* [L *confluent-*, *confluens*, prp. of *confluere* to flow together, fr. *com-* + *fluere* to flow — more at FLUID] **1** : flowing or coming together; *also* : run together ⟨~ pustules⟩ **2** : characterized by confluent lesions

²confluent *n* : a confluent stream; *broadly* : TRIBUTARY

con·flux \ˈkän-ˌfləks\ *n* [ML *confluxus*, fr. L *confluxus*, pp. of *confluere*] : CONFLUENCE

con·fo·cal \(ˈ)kän-ˈfō-kəl\ *adj* : having the same foci ⟨~ ellipses⟩

¹con·form \kən-ˈfȯ(ə)rm\ *vb* [ME *conformen*, fr. MF *conformer*, fr. L *conformare*, fr. *com-* + *formare* to form, fr. *forma* form] *vt* : to bring into harmony or agreement ~ *vi* **1** : to be similar or identical **2** : to be obedient or compliant; *esp* : to adapt oneself to prevailing standards or customs **syn** see ADAPT, AGREE — **con·form·er** *n* — **con·form·ism** \-ˈfȯr-ˌmiz-əm\ *n* — **con·form·ist** \-məst\ *n*

²conform *adj* : CONFORMABLE

con·form·able \kən-ˈfȯr-mə-bəl\ *adj* **1** : corresponding in form or character : SIMILAR — usu. used with *to* **2** : SUBMISSIVE, COMPLIANT **3** : following in unbroken sequence — used of geologic strata formed under uniform conditions — **con·form·ably** \-blē\ *adv*

con·for·mal \kən-ˈfȯr-məl, (ˈ)kän-\ *adj* [LL *conformalis* having the same shape, fr. L *com-* + *formalis* formal, fr. *forma*] **1** : leaving the size of the angle between corresponding curves unchanged **2** *of a map* : representing small areas in their true shape

con·for·mance \kən-ˈfȯr-mən(t)s\ *n* : CONFORMITY

con·for·ma·tion \ˌkän-(ˌ)fȯr-ˈmā-shən, -fər-\ *n* **1** : the act of conforming or producing conformity : ADAPTATION **2** : formation of anything by symmetrical arrangement of its parts **3 a** : correspondence esp. to a model or plan **b** : STRUCTURE **c** : the proportionate shape or contour esp. of an animal **syn** see FORM

con·for·mi·ty \kən-ˈfȯr-mət-ē\ *n* **1** : correspondence in form, manner, or character : AGREEMENT **2 a** : an act or instance of conforming **b** : a point of agreement **3** : action in accordance with some specified standard or authority : OBEDIENCE

con·found \kən-ˈfau̇nd, kän-\ *vt* [ME *confounden*, fr. OF *confondre*, fr. L *confundere* to pour together, confuse, fr. *com-* + *fundere* to pour] **1** *archaic* : to bring to ruin : DESTROY **2** *obs* : CONSUME, WASTE **3 a** : to put to shame : DISCOMFIT **b** : REFUTE **4** : DAMN **5** : BEWILDER, PERPLEX **6 a** : to mix up **b** : to increase the confusion of **syn** see PUZZLE — **con·found·er** *n*

con·found·ed \kən-ˈfau̇n-dəd, (ˈ)kän-ˈ, ˈkän-ˌ\ *adj* **1** : CONFUSED, PERPLEXED **2** : DAMNED — **con·found·ed·ly** *adv*

con·fra·ter·ni·ty \ˌkän-frə-ˈtər-nət-ē\ *n* [ME *confraternite*, fr. MF *confraternité*, fr. ML *confraternitat-*, *confraternitas*, fr. *confrater* fellow, brother, fr. L *com-* + *frater* brother] **1** : a society devoted to a religious or charitable cause **2** : fraternal union

con·frere \ˈkōⁿ-ˌfre(ə)r, ˈkän-, -ˌfra(ə)r, kōⁿ-ˈ, kän-ˈ\ *n* [ME, fr. MF, trans. of ML *confrater*] : COLLEAGUE, COMRADE

con·front \kən-ˈfrənt\ *vt* [MF *confronter* to border on, confront, fr. ML *confrontare* to bound, fr. L *com-* + *front-*, *frons* forehead, front — more at BRINK] **1** : to face esp. in challenge : OPPOSE **2 a** : to cause to meet : bring face to face **b** : ENCOUNTER — **con·fron·tal** \-ˈfrənt-ᵊl\ *or* **con·fron·ta·tion** \ˌkän-(ˌ)frən-ˈtā-shən\ *n*

Con·fu·cian \kən-ˈfyü-shən\ *adj* : of or relating to the Chinese philosopher Confucius or his teachings or followers — **Confucian** *n* — **Con·fu·cian·ism** \-shə-ˌniz-əm\ *n*

con·fuse \kən-ˈfyüz\ *vt* [back-formation fr. ME *confused* perplexed, fr. MF *confus*, fr. L *confusus*, pp. of *confundere*] **1** *archaic* : to bring to ruin **2** : PERPLEX, DISCONCERT **3 a** : to make indistinct : BLUR **b** : to mix indiscriminately : JUMBLE **c** : to mistake for another — **con·fused·ly** \-ˈfyüz(-ə)d-lē\ *adv* — **con·fused·ness** \-ˈfyü-zəd-nəs, -ˈfyüz(d)-nəs\ *n* — **con·fus·ing** \-ˈfyü-ziŋ\ *adj* — **con·fus·ing·ly** \-ziŋ-lē\ *adv*

con·fu·sion \kən-ˈfyü-zhən\ *n* **1** : an act or instance of confusing **2** : the quality or state of being confused — **con·fu·sion·al** \-ˈfyüzh-nəl, -ˈfyü-zhən-ᵊl\ *adj*

con·fu·ta·tion \ˌkän-fyu̇-ˈtā-shən\ *n* **1** : the act or process of confuting : REFUTATION **2** : something that confutes (as an argument) — **con·fu·ta·tive** \kən-ˈfyüt-ət-iv\ *adj*

con·fute \kən-ˈfyüt\ *vt* [L *confutare*, fr. *com-* + *-futare* to beat — more at BEAT] **1** : to overwhelm by argument : refute conclusively **2** *obs* : CONFOUND **syn** see DISPROVE — **con·fut·er** *n*

con·ga \ˈkäŋ-gə\ *n* [AmerSp, fr. Sp, fem. of *congo* of the Congo, fr. *Congo*, region in Africa] **1** : a Cuban dance of African origin involving three steps followed by a kick and performed by a group usu. in single file **2** : a tall narrow bass drum beaten with the hands

con·gé \kōⁿ-ˈzhā, ˈkän-ˌjā\ *n* [F, fr. L *commeatus* going back and forth, leave, fr. *commeatus*, pp. of *commeare* to go back and forth, fr. *com-* + *meare* to go — more at PERMEATE] **1 a** : a formal permission to depart **b** : DISMISSAL **2** : a ceremonious bow **3** : FAREWELL **4** : an architectural molding of concave profile

con·geal \kən-ˈjē(ə)l\ *vb* [ME *congelen*, fr. MF *congeler*, fr. L *congelare*, fr. *com-* + *gelare* to freeze] *vt* **1** : to change from a fluid to a solid state by or as if by cold **2** : to make viscid or curdled : COAGULATE **3** : to make rigid, inflexible, or immobile ~ *vi* : to become congealed — **con·geal·ment** \-mənt\ *n*

con·gee \ˈkän-(ˌ)jē\ *n* : CONGÉ — **congee** *vi* **congeed**; **congee·ing**

con·ge·la·tion \ˌkän-jə-ˈlā-shən\ *n* : the process or result of congealing

con·ge·ner \ˈkän-jə-nər, kən-ˈjē-\ *n* [L, of the same kind, fr. *com-* + *gener-*, *genus* kind] **1** : a member of the same taxonomic genus as another plant or animal **2** : a person or thing resembling another in nature or action — **con·ge·ner·ic** \ˌkän-jə-ˈner-ik\ *adj* — **con·ge·ner·ous** \kən-ˈje-nə-rəs, -ˈjen-ə-, (ˈ)kän-\ *adj*

con·ge·nial \kən-ˈjē-nyəl, -ˈjē-nē-əl\ *adj* [*com-* + *genius*] **1** : having the same nature, disposition, or tastes : KINDRED **2 a** : existing or associated together harmoniously **b** : PLEASANT; *esp* : agreeably suited to one's nature, tastes, or outlook **c** : SOCIABLE, GENIAL **syn** see CONSONANT — **con·ge·nial·i·ty** \-ˌjē-nē-ˈal-ət-ē, -ˌjēn-ˈyal-\ *n* — **con·ge·nial·ly** \-ˈjē-nyə-lē, -nē-ə-\ *adv*

con·gen·i·tal \kən-ˈjen-ə-tᵊl\ *adj* [L *congenitus*, fr. *com-* + *genitus* pp. of *gignere* to bring forth — more at KIN] **1 a** : existing at or dating from birth ⟨~ idiocy⟩ **b** : constituting an essential characteristic : INHERENT ⟨~ fear of snakes⟩ **c** : acquired during development in the uterus and not through heredity **2** : being such by nature ⟨~ liar⟩ **syn** see INNATE — **con·gen·i·tal·ly** \-tᵊl-ē\ *adv*

con·ger eel \ˌkäŋ-gər-\ *n* [ME *congre*, fr. OF, fr. L *congr-*, *conger*, fr. Gk *gongros*; akin to ON *kökkr* ball, L *gingiva* gum] : a large strictly marine scaleless eel (*Conger conger*) important as a food fish; *broadly* : any of various related eels (family Congridae)

con·ge·ries \ˈkän-jə-(ˌ)rēz; ˈkäŋ-gə-(ˌ)rēz, -grēz\ *n, pl* **congeries** *same*\ [L, fr. *congerere*] : AGGREGATION, COLLECTION

con·gest \kən-ˈjest\ *vb* [L *congestus*, pp. of *congerere* to bring together, fr. *com-* + *gerere* to bear] *vt* **1** : to cause an excessive fullness of the blood vessels of (as an organ) **2** : CLOG **3** : to concentrate in a small or narrow space ~ *vi* : to become congested — **con·ges·tion** \-ˈjes(h)-chən\ *n* — **con·ges·tive** \-ˈjes-tiv\ *adj*

con·gi·us \ˈkän-jē-əs, ˈkäŋ-gē-\ *n, pl* **con·gii** \-jē-ˌī\ [ME, Roman liquid measure, fr. L] : GALLON

con·glo·bate \ˈkän-glō-ˌbāt, kən-ˈ\ *vb* [L *conglobatus*, pp. of *conglobare*, fr. *com-* + *globus* globe] : to form in a round mass — **con·glo·bate** \kən-ˈglō-bət, -ˌbāt; ˈkän-glō-ˌbāt\ *adj* — **con·glo·ba·tion** \ˌkän-glō-ˈbā-shən, kən-ˌ\ *n*

con·globe \kən-ˈglōb\ *vb* : CONGLOBATE

¹con·glom·er·ate \kən-ˈgläm-(ə-)rət\ *adj* [L *conglomeratus*, pp. of *conglomerare* to roll together, fr. *com-* + *glomerare* to wind into a ball, fr. *glomer-*, *glomus* ball — more at CLAM] **1** : made up of parts from various sources or of various kinds **2** : densely and often irregularly clustered ⟨~ flowers⟩ ⟨~ eyes⟩

²con·glom·er·ate \-ə-ˌrāt\ *vb* : to collect or form into a mass or coherent whole

³con·glom·er·ate \-(ə-)rət\ *n* **1** : a composite mass or mixture; *specif* : rock composed of rounded fragments varying from small pebbles to large boulders in a cement (as of hardened clay) **2** : a widely diversified company — **con·glom·er·at·ic** \-ˌgläm-ə-ˈrat-ik\ *adj*

con·glom·er·a·tion \kən-ˌgläm-ə-ˈrā-shən, ˌkän-\ *n* **1** : COLLECTION **2** : a mixed coherent mass

con·glu·ti·nate \kən-ˈglüt-ᵊn-ˌāt\ *vb* [L *conglutinatus*, pp. of *conglutinare* to glue together, fr. *com-* + *glutin-*, *gluten* glue] *vt* : to unite by or as if by a glutinous substance ~ *vi* : to become conglutinated — **con·glu·ti·na·tion** \-ˌglüt-ᵊn-ˈā-shən\ *n*

Con·go dye \ˌkäŋ-(ˌ)gō-\ *n* [*Congo*, territory in Africa] : any of various direct azo dyes mostly derived from benzidine

Congo red *n* : an azo dye red in alkaline and blue in acid solution

congo snake *n* : an elongated bluish black amphibian (*Amphiuma means*) of the southeastern U.S. that has two pairs of very short limbs each with two or three toes — called also *congo eel*

con·gou \ˈkäŋ-(ˌ)gü, (ˌ)gō\ *n* [prob. fr. Chin (Amoy) *kong-hu* pains taken] : a black tea from China

con·grat·u·late \kən-ˈgrach-ə-ˌlāt\ *vt* [L *congratulatus*, pp. of *congratulari* to wish joy, fr. *com-* + *gratulari* to wish joy, fr. *gratus* pleasing] **1** : to express sympathetic pleasure to on account of success or good fortune **2** *archaic* : to express sympathetic pleasure at **3** *obs* : SALUTE, GREET **syn** see FELICITATE — **con·grat·u·la·tor** \-ˌlāt-ər\ *n* — **con·grat·u·la·to·ry** \-ˈgrach-(ə-)lə-ˌtōr-ē, -ˌtȯr-\ *adj*

con·grat·u·la·tion \kən-ˌgrach-ə-ˈlā-shən\ *n* **1** : the act of congratulating **2** : a congratulatory expression — usu. used in pl.

con·gre·gate \ˈkäŋ-gri-ˌgāt\ *vb* [ME *congregaten*, fr. L *congregatus*, pp. of *congregare*, fr. *com-* + *greg-*, *grex* flock — more at GREGARIOUS] : to collect into a group or crowd : ASSEMBLE **syn** see GATHER — **con·gre·ga·tor** \-ˌgāt-ər\ *n*

con·gre·ga·tion \ˌkäŋ-gri-ˈgā-shən\ *n* **1 a** : an assembly of persons : GATHERING; *esp* : an assembly of persons met for worship and religious instruction **b** : a religious community: as (1) : an organized body of believers in a particular locality (2) : a Roman Catholic religious institute with only simple vows (3) : a group of monasteries forming an independent subdivision of an order **2** : the act or an instance of congregating or bringing together : the state of being congregated **3** : a body of cardinals and officials forming an administrative division of the papal curia

con·gre·ga·tion·al \-shnəl, -shən-ᵊl\ *adj* **1** : of or relating to a congregation **2** *cap* : of or relating to a body of Protestant churches deriving from the English Independents of the 17th century and affirming the essential importance and the autonomy of the local congregation **3** : of or relating to church government placing final authority in the assembly of the local congregation — **con·gre·ga·tion·al·ism** \-shnə-ˌliz-əm, -shən-ᵊl-ˌiz-\ *n, often cap* — **con·gre·ga·tion·al·ist** \-shnə-ləst, -shən-ᵊl-əst\ *n, often cap*

Congregational Christian *adj* : of or relating to a denomination formed in the U.S. in 1931 by the union of the Congregational Church and the Christian Church

con·gress \ˈkäŋ-grəs\ *n* [L *congressus*, fr. *congressus*, pp. of *congredi* to come together, fr. *com-* + *gradi* to go — more at GRADE] **1 a** : the act or action of coming together and meeting **b** : COITION **2** : a formal meeting of delegates for discussion and usu. action on some question **3** : the supreme legislative body of a nation and esp. of a republic **4** : an association usu. made up of delegates from constituent organizations **5** : a single meeting or session of a group — **con·gres·sio·nal** \kən-ˈgresh-nəl, -ən-ᵊl\ *adj* — **con·gres·sio·nal·ly** \-ē\ *adv*

congress gaiter *n, often cap C* : an ankle-high shoe with elastic gussets in the sides — called also *congress shoe*

congressional district *n* : a territorial division of a state from which a member of the U.S. House of Representatives is elected

Congressional Medal *n* : MEDAL OF HONOR

con·gress·man \ˈkäŋ-grə-smən\ *n* : a member of a congress; *esp* : a member of the U.S. House of Representatives — **con·gress·wom·an** \-grə-ˌswu̇m-ən\ *n*

con·gru·ence \kən-ˈgrü-ən(t)s, ˈkäŋ-grə-wən(t)s\ *n* **1** : the quality

or state of according or coinciding **2 :** grammatical agreement **3 :** a statement that two numbers are congruent with respect to a modulus

con·gru·en·cy \-ən-sē, -wən-sē\ *n* **:** CONGRUENCE

con·gru·ent \-ənt, -wənt\ *adj* [L *congruent-, congruens,* prp. of *congruere*] **1 :** CONGRUOUS **2 :** superposable so as to be coincident throughout **3 :** having the difference divisible by a modulus ⟨12 is ~ to 2 (modulo 5) since 12−2=2·5⟩ — **con·gru·ent·ly** *adv*

con·gru·ity \kən-ˈgrü-ət-ē, kän-\ *n* **1 :** the quality or state of being congruent or congruous **2 :** a point of agreement

con·gru·ous \ˈkäŋ-grə-wəs\ *adj* [L *congruus,* fr. *congruere* to come together, agree, fr. *com-* + *-gruere* (akin to Gk *zachrēēs* attacking violently)] **1 a :** being in agreement, harmony, or correspondence **b :** SUITABLE, APPROPRIATE **2 :** marked by harmony among parts **syn** see CONSONANT — **con·gru·ous·ly** *adv* — **con·gru·ous·ness** *n*

con·ic \ˈkän-ik\ *adj* **1 :** CONICAL **2 :** of or relating to a cone

con·i·cal \-i-kəl\ *adj* **:** resembling a cone esp. in shape ⟨~ roots⟩ — **con·i·cal·ly** \-i-k(ə-)lē\ *adv* — **con·i·cal·ness** \-kəl-nəs\ *n*

conic section *n* **1 :** a plane section of a right circular conical surface **2 :** a curve generated by a point which always moves so that the ratio of its distance from a fixed point to its distance from a fixed line is constant

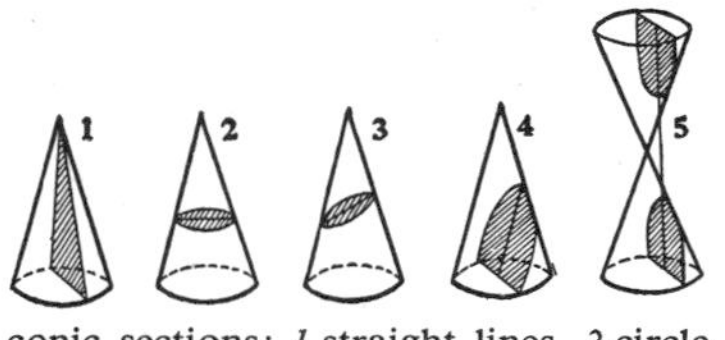

conic sections: *1* straight lines, *2* circle, *3* ellipse, *4* parabola, *5* hyperbola

co·nid·i·al \kə-ˈnid-ē-əl\ *adj* **:** of, relating to, or resembling conidia

co·nid·io·phore \kə-ˈnid-ē-ə-ˌfō(ə)r, -ˌfȯ(ə)r\ *n* [NL *conidium* + ISV *-phore*] **:** a structure that bears conidia; *specif* **:** a specialized hyphal branch that produces successive conidia usu. by abstriction — **co·nid·i·oph·o·rous** \kə-ˌnid-ē-ˈäf-(ə-)rəs\ *adj*

co·nid·i·um \kə-ˈnid-ē-əm\ *n, pl* **co·nid·ia** \-ē-ə\ [NL, fr. Gk *konis* dust] **:** an asexual spore produced on a conidiophore

co·ni·fer \ˈkän-ə-fər *also* ˈkō-nə-\ *n* [deriv. of L *conifer* cone-bearing, fr. *conus* cone + *-fer*] **:** any of an order (Coniferales) of mostly evergreen trees and shrubs including forms (as pines) with true cones and others (as yews) with an arillate fruit — **co·nif·er·ous** \kō-ˈnif-(ə-)rəs, kə-\ *adj*

co·ni·ine \ˈkō-nē-ˌēn\ *n* [G *koniin,* fr. L *conium*] **:** a poisonous alkaloid $C_8H_{17}N$ found in poison hemlock (*Conium maculatum*)

co·ni·um \kō-ˈnī-əm, ˈkō-nē-əm\ *n* [NL, genus name, fr. LL, hemlock, fr. Gk *kōneion*] **:** any of a genus (*Conium*) of poisonous herbs of the carrot family

con·jec·tur·al \kən-ˈjek-chə-rəl, -ˈjeksh-rəl\ *adj* **1 :** of the nature of or involving or based on conjecture **2 :** given to conjectures — **con·jec·tur·al·ly** \-ē\ *adv*

[1]**con·jec·ture** \kən-ˈjek-chər\ *n* [ME, fr. MF or L; MF, fr. L *conjectura,* fr. *conjectus,* pp. of *conicere,* lit., to throw together, fr. *com-* + *jacere* to throw] **1** *obs* **a :** interpretation of omens **b :** SUPPOSITION **2 a :** inference from defective or presumptive evidence **b :** a conclusion deduced by surmise or guesswork

[2]**conjecture** *vb* **con·jec·tur·ing** \-ˈjek-chə-riŋ, -ˈjek-shriŋ\ *vt* **1 :** to arrive at by conjecture **2 :** to make conjectures as to ~ *vi* **:** to form conjectures — **con·jec·tur·er** \-ˈjek-chər-ər\ *n*

syn CONJECTURE, SURMISE, GUESS mean to draw an inference from slight evidence. CONJECTURE implies forming an opinion or judgment upon evidence insufficient for definite knowledge; SURMISE implies even slighter evidence and suggests the influence of imagination or suspicion; GUESS stresses a hitting upon a conclusion either wholly at random or from very uncertain evidence

con·join \kən-ˈjȯin, kän-\ *vb* [ME *conjoinen,* fr. MF *conjoindre* fr. L *conjungere,* fr. *com-* + *jungere* to join — more at YOKE] **:** to join together for a common purpose

con·joint \-ˈjȯint\ *adj* [ME, fr. MF, pp. of *conjoindre*] **1 :** UNITED, CONJOINED **2 :** related to, made up of, or carried on by two or more in combination **:** JOINT — **con·joint·ly** *adv*

con·ju·gal \ˈkän-ji-gəl, kən-ˈjü-\ *adj* [MF or L; MF, fr. L *conjugalis,* fr. *conjug-, conjux* husband, wife, fr. *conjungere* to join, unite in marriage] **:** of or relating to marriage, the married state, or matrimonial relations **syn** see MATRIMONIAL — **con·ju·gal·i·ty** \ˌkän-ji-ˈgal-ət-ē, -jü-\ *n* — **con·ju·gal·ly** *adv*

con·ju·gant \ˈkän-ji-gənt\ *n* **:** either of a pair of conjugating gametes or organisms

[1]**con·ju·gate** \ˈkän-ji-gət, -jə-ˌgāt\ *adj* [ME *conjugat,* fr. L *conjugatus,* pp. of *conjugare* to unite, fr. *com-* + *jugare* to join, fr. *jugum* yoke] **1 a :** joined together esp. in pairs **:** COUPLED **b :** acting or operating as if joined **2 :** having features in common but opposite or inverse in some particular **3 :** BIJUGATE **4 :** having the same derivation and therefore usu. some likeness in meaning ⟨~ words⟩ — **con·ju·gate·ly** *adv* — **con·ju·gate·ness** *n*

[2]**con·ju·gate** \-jə-ˌgāt\ *vt* **1 :** to give in prescribed order the various inflectional forms of — used esp. of a verb **2 a :** to join together **b :** to unite chemically so that the product is easily broken down into the original compounds ~ *vi* **1 :** to join together **2 a :** to pair and fuse in conjugation **b :** to pair in synapsis

[3]**conjugate** *like* [1]CONJUGATE\ *n* **:** something conjugate **:** a product of conjugating

conjugated protein *n* **:** a compound of a protein with a nonprotein

con·ju·ga·tion \ˌkän-jə-ˈgā-shən\ *n* **1 :** the act of conjugating **:** the state of being conjugated **2 a :** a schematic arrangement of the inflectional forms of a verb **b :** verb inflection **c :** a class of verbs having the same type of inflectional forms ⟨the weak ~⟩ **3 a :** fusion of usu. similar gametes with ultimate union of their nuclei that among lower thallophytes replaces the typical fertilization of higher forms **b :** temporary cytoplasmic union with exchange of nuclear material that is the usual sexual process in ciliated protozoans — **con·ju·ga·tion·al** \-shnəl, -shən-ᵊl\ *adj* — **con·ju·ga·tion·al·ly** \-ē\ *adv* — **con·ju·ga·tive** \ˈkän-jə-ˌgāt-iv\ *adj*

[1]**con·junct** \kən-ˈjəŋ(k)t, kän-\ *adj* [ME, fr. L *conjunctus,* pp. of *conjungere*] **1 :** JOINED, UNITED **2 :** JOINT

[2]**con·junct** \ˈkän-ˌjəŋ(k)t\ *n* **:** something joined or associated with another; *specif* **:** one of the components of a conjunction

con·junc·tion \kən-ˈjəŋ(k)-shən\ *n* **1 :** the act or an instance of conjoining **:** the state of being conjoined **2 :** occurrence together in time or space **:** CONCURRENCE **3 a :** the apparent meeting or passing of two or more celestial bodies in the same degree of the zodiac **b :** a configuration in which two celestial bodies have their least apparent separation **4 :** an uninflected linguistic form that joins together sentences, clauses, phrases, or words **:** CONNECTIVE **5 :** a compound statement in logic true only if all its components are true — **con·junc·tion·al** \-shnəl, -shən-ᵊl\ *adj* — **con·junc·tion·al·ly** \-ē\ *adv*

con·junc·ti·va \ˌkän-ˌjəŋk-ˈtī-və, kən-, -ˈtē-\ *n, pl* **conjunctivas** *or* **con·junc·ti·vae** \-ˈtī-(ˌ)vē, -ˈtē-ˌvī\ [NL, fr. LL, fem. of *conjunctivus* conjoining, fr. L *conjunctus*] **:** the mucous membrane that lines the inner surface of the eyelids and is continued over the forepart of the eyeball — **con·junc·ti·val** \-vəl\ *adj*

con·junc·tive \kən-ˈjəŋ(k)-tiv\ *adj* **1 :** CONNECTIVE **2 :** CONJOINED, CONJUNCT **3 :** being or functioning like a conjunction **4 :** COPULATIVE 1a — **conjunctive** *n* — **con·junc·tive·ly** *adv*

con·junc·ti·vi·tis \kən-ˌjəŋ(k)-ti-ˈvīt-əs\ *n* **:** inflammation of the conjunctiva

con·junc·ture \kən-ˈjəŋ(k)-chər\ *n* **1 :** CONJUNCTION, UNION **2 :** a combination of circumstances or events esp. producing a crisis **:** JUNCTURE

con·ju·ra·tion \ˌkän-jə-ˈrā-shən ˌkən-\ *n* **1 :** the act or process of conjuring **:** INCANTATION **2 :** an expression or trick used in conjuring **3 :** a solemn appeal **:** ADJURATION

con·jure *in vt 2 & vi senses* ˈkän-jər *also* ˈkən-; *in vt 1 sense* kən-ˈjù(ə)r\ *vb* **con·jur·ing** \ˈkänj-(ə-)riŋ, ˈkənj-; kən-ˈjù(ə)r-iŋ\ [ME *conjuren,* fr. OF *conjurer,* fr. L *conjurare* to swear together, fr. *com-* + *jurare* to swear] *vt* **1 :** to charge or entreat earnestly or solemnly **2 a :** to summon by invocation or incantation **b** (1) **:** to affect or effect by or as if by magic (2) **:** IMAGINE, CONTRIVE ~ *vi* **1 a :** to summon a devil or spirit by invocation or incantation **b :** to practice magical arts **2 :** to use a conjurer's tricks

con·jur·er *or* **con·ju·ror** \ˈkän-jər-ər, ˈkən-\ *n* **1 :** one that practices magic arts **:** WIZARD **2 :** one that performs feats of legerdemain and illusion **:** MAGICIAN, JUGGLER

[1]**conk** \ˈkäŋk, ˈkȯŋk\ *n* [prob. alter. of *conch*] **:** the visible fruiting body of a tree fungus; *also* **:** decay caused by such a fungus — **conky** \-ē\ *adj*

[2]**conk** *vi* [prob. imit.] **1 :** to break down; *esp* **:** STALL ⟨the motor ~*ed* out suddenly⟩ **2 a :** FAINT **b :** to go to sleep

[1]**conn** \ˈkän\ *vt* [alter. of ME *condien* to conduct, fr. MF *conduire,* fr. L *conducere*] **:** to conduct or direct the steering of (as a ship)

[2]**conn** *n* **:** the control exercised by one who conns a ship

con·nate \kä-ˈnāt, ˈkän-ˌāt\ *adj* [LL *connatus,* pp. of *connasci* to be born together, fr. L *com-* + *nasci* to be born] **1 :** INNATE, INBORN **2 :** AKIN, CONGENIAL **3 :** born or originated together **4 :** congenitally or firmly united — **con·nate·ly** *adv*

con·nat·u·ral \kä-ˈnach-(ə-)rəl, kə-\ *adj* [ML *connaturalis,* fr. L *com-* + *naturalis* natural] **1 :** connected by nature **:** INBORN **2 :** of the same nature — **con·nat·u·ral·i·ty** \(ˌ)kä-ˌnach-ə-ˈral-ət-ē, kə-\ *n* — **con·nat·u·ral·ly** *adv*

con·nect \kə-ˈnekt\ *vb* [L *conectere, connectere,* fr. *com-* + *nectere* to bind] *vt* **1 :** to join or fasten together usu. by something intervening **2 :** to place or establish in relationship ~ *vi* **1 a :** JOIN, UNITE **b :** to have a relationship **2 :** to hit solidly or successfully ⟨~*ed* for a home run⟩ **syn** see JOIN — **con·nec·tor** *also* **con·nect·er** \-ˈnek-tər\ *n*

con·nect·ed·ly *adv* **:** in a connected manner **:** COHERENTLY

con·nect·ed·ness *n* **:** the quality or state of being connected

connecting rod *n* **:** a rod that transmits power from one rotating part of a machine to another in reciprocating motion

con·nec·tion *or chiefly Brit* **con·nex·ion** \kə-ˈnek-shən\ *n* [L *connexion-, connexio,* fr. *conexus,* pp. of *conectere*] **1 :** the act of connecting **:** the state of being connected: as **a :** causal or logical relation or sequence **b :** contextual relations or associations **c :** a relation of personal intimacy (as of family ties) **d :** COHERENCE, CONTINUITY **2 a :** something that connects **:** LINK **b :** a means of communication or transport **3 :** a person connected with others esp. by marriage or kinship **4 :** a social, professional, or commercial relationship: as **a :** POSITION, JOB **b :** an arrangement to execute orders or advance interests of another **c** *slang* **:** a source of contraband **5 :** a set of persons associated together: as **a :** DENOMINATION **b :** CLAN — **con·nec·tion·al** \-shnəl, -shən-ᵊl\ *adj*

[1]**con·nec·tive** \kə-ˈnek-tiv\ *adj* **:** tending to connect — **con·nec·tive·ly** *adv* — **con·nec·tiv·i·ty** \ˌkä-ˌnek-ˈtiv-ət-ē, kə-\ *n*

[2]**connective** *n* **:** something that connects: as **a :** the tissue connecting the pollen sacs of an anther **b :** a linguistic form that connects words or word groups

connective tissue *n* **:** a tissue of mesodermal origin rich in intercellular substance or interlacing processes with little tendency for the cells to come together in sheets or masses; *specif* **:** connective tissue of stellate or spindle-shaped cells with interlacing processes that pervades, supports, and binds together other tissues and forms ligaments, tendons, and aponeuroses

conning tower *n* **1 :** an armored pilothouse (as on a battleship) **2 :** a raised structure on the deck of a submarine used as an observation post and often as an entrance to the vessel

con·nip·tion \kə-ˈnip-shən\ *n* [origin unknown] **:** a fit of rage, hysteria, or alarm

con·niv·ance \kə-ˈnī-vən(t)s\ *n* **:** the act of conniving; *esp* **:** knowledge of and active or passive consent to wrongdoing

con·nive \kə-ˈnīv\ *vi* [F or L; F *conniver,* fr. L *conivēre, connivēre* to close the eyes, connive, fr. *com-* + *-nivēre* (akin to *nictare* to wink); akin to OE & OHG *hnīgan* to bow, L *nicere* to beckon] **1 :** to pretend ignorance of or fail to take action against something one ought in duty to oppose **2 a :** to be indulgent or in secret sympathy **:** WINK **b :** to cooperate secretly or have a secret understanding **3 :** CONSPIRE, INTRIGUE — **con·niv·er** *n*

con·ni·vent \-ˈnī-vənt\ *adj* [L *connivent-, conivens,* prp. of *conivēre*] **:** converging but not fused ⟨~ stamens⟩

con·nois·seur \ˌkän-ə-ˈsər *also* -ˈsù(ə)r\ *n* [obs. F (now *connaisseur*), fr. OF *connoisseor,* fr. *connoistre* to know, fr. L *cognoscere* — more at COGNITION] **:** EXPERT; *esp* **:** one who understands the details, technique, or principles of an art and is competent to act as a critical judge — **con·nois·seur·ship** \-ˌship\ *n*

con·no·ta·tion \ˌkän-ə-ˈtā-shən\ *n* **1 a :** the suggesting of a meaning by a word apart from the thing it explicitly names or describes **b :** something suggested by a word or thing **2 :** the meaning of a word **:** SIGNIFICATION **3 :** the property or properties connoted by a term in logic — compare DENOTATION — **con·no·ta·tion·al** \-shnəl, -shən-ᵊl\ *adj*

con·no·ta·tive \'kän-ə-,tāt-iv, kə-'nōt-ət-iv\ *adj* **1 :** connoting or tending to connote **2 :** relating to connotation — **con·no·ta·tive·ly** *adv*
con·note \kə-'nōt, kä-\ *vt* [ML *connotare*, fr. L *com-* + *notare* to note] **1 :** to have as a connotation **2 :** to be associated with or inseparable from as a consequence or concomitant **3 :** to indicate as an essential attribute of something denoted **syn** see DENOTE
con·nu·bi·al \kə-'n(y)ü-bē-əl\ *adj* [L *conubialis*, fr. *conubium, connubium* marriage, fr. *com-* + *nubere* to marry — more at NUPTIAL] **:** of or relating to marriage or the marriage state **:** CONJUGAL **syn** see MATRIMONIAL — **con·nu·bi·al·i·ty** \-,n(y)ü-bē-'al-ət-ē\ *n* — **con·nu·bi·al·ly** \-'n(y)ü-bē-ə-lē\ *adv*
co·noid \'kō-,nȯid\ *or* **co·noi·dal** \kō-'nȯid-ᵊl\ *adj* **:** shaped like or nearly like a cone — **conoid** *n*
con·quer \'käŋ-kər\ *vb* **con·quer·ing** \-k(ə-)riŋ\ [ME *conqueren* to acquire, conquer, fr. OF *conquerre*, fr. (assumed) VL *conquaerere* fr. L *conquirere* to search for, collect, fr. *com-* + *quaerere* to ask, search] *vt* **1 :** to gain or acquire by force of arms **:** SUBJUGATE **2 :** to overcome by force of arms **:** VANQUISH **3 :** to gain or win by overcoming obstacles or opposition **4 :** to overcome by mental or moral power **:** SURMOUNT ~ *vi* **:** to be victorious
syn CONQUER, VANQUISH, DEFEAT, BEAT, LICK, SUBDUE, REDUCE, OVERCOME, OVERTHROW, ROUT mean to get the better of by force or strategy. CONQUER implies gaining mastery of; VANQUISH implies a complete overpowering or discomfiture of someone; DEFEAT does not imply the finality or completeness of VANQUISH which it otherwise equals; BEAT is an informal equivalent for DEFEAT and sometimes for VANQUISH; LICK implies a humiliating beating; SUBDUE implies a defeating and suppression; REDUCE implies a forcing to capitulate or surrender; OVERCOME suggests getting the better of with difficulty or after hard struggle; OVERTHROW stresses the bringing down or destruction of enemy power; ROUT emphasizes complete scattering of enemy forces
con·quer·or \-kər-ər\ *n* **:** one that conquers **:** VICTOR
con·quest \'kän-,kwest, 'käŋ-; 'käŋ-kwəst\ *n* [ME, fr. OF, fr. (assumed) VL *conquaesitus*, alter. of L *conquisitus*, pp. of *conquirere*] **1 :** the act or process of conquering **2 a :** something conquered; *esp* **:** territory appropriated in war **b :** a person whose favor or hand has been won **syn** see VICTORY
con·qui·an \'käŋ-kē-ən\ *n* [MexSp *con quien*] **:** a card game for two played with 40 cards from which all games of rummy developed
con·quis·ta·dor \kȯŋ-'kēs-tə-,dȯ(ə)r, kän-'k(w)is-, kən-\ *n, pl* **con·quis·ta·do·res** \(,)kȯŋ-,kēs-tə-'dȯr-ēz, -'dȯr-,ās, -'dōr-, (,)kän-,k(w)is-, kən-\ *or* **con·quis·ta·dors** [Sp, deriv. of L *conquirere*] **:** CONQUEROR; *specif* **:** a leader in the Spanish conquest of America and esp. of Mexico and Peru in the 16th century
con·san·guine \kän-'saŋ-gwən, kən-\ *adj* **:** CONSANGUINEOUS
con·san·guin·e·ous \,kän-,san-'gwin-ē-əs, -,saŋ-\ *adj* [L *consanguineus*, fr. *com-* + *sanguin-*, *sanguis* blood — more at SANGUINE] **:** of the same blood or origin; *specif* **:** descended from the same ancestor — **con·san·guin·e·ous·ly** *adv*
con·san·guin·i·ty \-'gwin-ət-ē\ *n* **1 :** the quality or state of being consanguineous **2 :** a close relation or connection
con·science \'kän-chən(t)s\ *n* [ME, fr. OF, fr. L *conscientia*, fr. *conscient-*, *consciens*, prp. of *conscire* to be conscious, be conscious of guilt, fr. *com-* + *scire* to know — more at SCIENCE] **1 a :** the sense or consciousness of the moral goodness or blameworthiness of one's own conduct, intentions, or character together with a feeling of obligation to do right or be good **b :** a faculty, power, or principle enjoining good acts **c :** the part of the superego in psychoanalysis that transmits commands and admonitions to the ego **2** *obs* **:** CONSCIOUSNESS **3 :** conformity to the dictates of conscience **:** CONSCIENTIOUSNESS — **in all conscience** *or* **in conscience :** in all fairness
conscience money *n* **:** money paid to relieve the conscience by restoring what has been wrongfully acquired
con·sci·en·tious \,kän-chē-'en-chəs\ *adj* **1 :** governed by or conforming to the dictates of conscience **:** SCRUPULOUS **2 :** METICULOUS, CAREFUL **syn** see UPRIGHT — **con·sci·en·tious·ly** *adv* — **con·sci·en·tious·ness** *n*
conscientious objector *n* **:** one who refuses to serve in the armed forces or bear arms as contrary to his moral or religious principles
con·scio·na·ble \'känch-(ə-)nə-bəl\ *adj* [irreg. fr. *conscience*] *obs* **:** CONSCIENTIOUS
¹**con·scious** \'kän-chəs\ *adj* [L *conscius*, fr. *com-* + *scire* to know] **1** *archaic* **:** sharing another's knowledge or awareness of an inward state or outward fact **2 :** perceiving, apprehending, or noticing with a degree of controlled thought or observation **3 :** subjectively perceived ⟨~ guilt⟩ **4 :** capable of or marked by thought, will, design, or perception **5 :** SELF-CONSCIOUS **6 :** having mental faculties undulled by sleep, faint, or stupor **:** AWAKE **7 :** done or acting with critical awareness **syn** see AWARE — **con·scious·ly** *adv*
²**conscious** *n* **:** CONSCIOUSNESS 5
con·scious·ness \'kän-chə-snəs\ *n* **1 :** awareness esp. of something within oneself; *also* **:** the state or fact of being conscious of an external object, state, or fact **2 :** the state of being characterized by sensation, emotion, volition, and thought **:** MIND **3 :** the totality of conscious states of an individual **4 :** the normal state of conscious life **5 :** the upper level of mental life as contrasted with unconscious processes
¹**con·script** \'kän-,skript\ *adj* [MF, fr. L *conscriptus*, pp. of *conscribere* to enroll, fr. *com-* + *scribere* to write — more at SCRIBE] **1 :** CONSCRIPTED, DRAFTED **2 :** made up of conscripted persons
²**conscript** *n* **:** a conscripted person (as a military recruit)
³**con·script** \kən-'skript\ *vt* **:** to enroll into service by compulsion — **con·scrip·tion** \-'skrip-shən\ *n*
¹**con·se·crate** \'kän(t)-sə-,krāt\ *adj* **:** CONSECRATED, HALLOWED
²**consecrate** *vt* [ME *consecraten*, fr. L *consecratus*, pp. of *consecrare*, fr. *com-* + *sacrare* to consecrate — more at SACRED] **1 :** to induct (a person) into a permanent office with a religious rite; *specif* **:** to ordain to the office of bishop **2 a :** to make or declare sacred; *specif* **:** to devote irrevocably to the worship of God by a solemn ceremony **b :** to devote to a purpose with deep solemnity or dedication **3 :** to make inviolate or venerable ⟨rules *consecrated* by time⟩ **syn** see DEVOTE — **con·se·cra·tive** \-,krāt-iv\ *adj* — **con·se·cra·tor** *n* — **con·se·cra·to·ry** \'kän(t)-si-krə-,tōr-ē, -,tȯr-\ *adj*
con·se·cra·tion \,kän(t)-sə-'krā-shən\ *n* **1 :** the act or ceremony of consecrating **2 :** the state of being consecrated
con·se·cu·tion \,kän(t)-sə-'kyü-shən\ *n* [L *consecution-*, *consecutio*, fr. *consecutus*, pp. of *consequi* to follow along] **:** SEQUENCE
con·sec·u·tive \kən-'sek-(y)ət-iv\ *adj* **:** following one after the other in order without gaps **:** CONTINUOUS — **con·sec·u·tive·ly** *adv* — **con·sec·u·tive·ness** *n*
syn CONSECUTIVE, SUCCESSIVE mean following one after the other. CONSECUTIVE stresses immediacy in following and implies that no interruption or interval occurs ⟨four *consecutive* days⟩; SUCCESSIVE may apply to things of the same kind or class that follow each other regardless of length of interval between ⟨four *successive* weekends⟩
con·sen·su·al \kən-'sench-(ə-)wəl, -'sen-chəl\ *adj* [L *consensus* + E *-al*] **1 :** existing or made by mutual consent without an act of writing ⟨a ~ contract⟩ **2 :** involving or being involuntary action or movement accompanying or correlative with voluntary action or movement — **con·sen·su·al·ly** \-ē\ *adv*
con·sen·sus \kən-'sen(t)-səs\ *n* [L, fr. *consensus*, pp. of *consentire*] **1 :** group solidarity in sentiment and belief **2 a :** general agreement **:** UNANIMITY **b :** collective opinion
¹**con·sent** \kən-'sent\ *vi* [ME *consenten*, fr. L *consentire*, fr. *com-* + *sentire* to feel] **1** *archaic* **:** to be in concord in opinion or sentiment **2 :** to give assent or approval **:** AGREE **syn** see ASSENT
²**consent** *n* **1 :** compliance in or approval of what is done or proposed by another **:** ACQUIESCENCE **2 :** agreement as to action or opinion; *specif* **:** voluntary agreement by a people to organize a civil society and give authority to the government — **con·sent·er** *n*
con·sen·ta·ne·ous \,kän(t)-sən-'tā-nē-əs, ,kän-,sen-\ *adj* [L *consentaneus*, fr. *consentire* to agree] **1 :** AGREEING, SUITED **2 :** done or made by the consent of all — **con·sen·ta·ne·ous·ly** *adv*
con·se·quence \'kän(t)-sə-,kwen(t)s, -si-kwən(t)s\ *n* **1 :** something produced by a cause or necessarily following from a set of conditions **2 :** a conclusion that results from reason or argument **3 a :** importance with respect to power to produce an effect **:** MOMENT **b :** social importance **4 :** the appearance of importance; *esp* **:** SELF-IMPORTANCE **syn** see EFFECT, IMPORTANCE
¹**con·se·quent** \-kwənt, -,kwent\ *n* **1 a :** DEDUCTION 2 **b :** the conclusion of a conditional sentence **2 :** the second term of a ratio
²**consequent** *adj* [MF, fr. L *consequent-*, *consequens*, prp. of *consequi* to follow along, fr. *com-* + *sequi* to follow] **1 :** following as a result or effect **2 :** observing logical sequence **:** RATIONAL — **con·se·quent·ly** \-,kwent-lē, -kwənt-\ *adv*
con·se·quen·tial \,kän(t)-sə-'kwen-chəl\ *adj* **1 a :** following or being a physical or logical consequence **b :** CONSEQUENT 2 **2 :** RESULTANT **3 :** having significant consequences **:** IMPORTANT **4 :** SELF-IMPORTANT — **con·se·quen·ti·al·i·ty** \-,kwen-chē-'al-ət-ē\ *n* — **con·se·quen·tial·ly** \-'kwench-(ə-)lē\ *adv* — **con·se·quen·tial·ness** \-'kwen-chəl-nəs\ *n*
con·ser·van·cy \kən-'sər-vən-sē\ *n* [alter. of obs. *conservacy* conservation, fr. AF *conservacie*, fr. ML *conservatia*, fr. L *conservatus*, pp.] **1** *Brit* **:** a board regulating fisheries and navigation in a river or port **2 a :** CONSERVATION **b :** an organization or area designated to conserve and protect natural resources
con·ser·va·tion \,kän(t)-sər-'vā-shən\ *n* [ME, fr. MF, fr. L *conservation-*, *conservatio*, fr. *conservatus*, pp. of *conservare*] **:** a careful preservation and protection of something; *esp* **:** planned management of a natural resource to prevent exploitation, destruction, or neglect — **con·ser·va·tion·al** \-shnəl, -shən-ᵊl\ *adj*
con·ser·va·tion·ist \,kän(t)-sər-'vā-sh(ə-)nəst\ *n* **:** one who advocates conservation esp. of natural resources
conservation of energy : a principle in classical physics: the total energy of an isolated system remains constant irrespective of whatever internal changes may take place
conservation of mass : a principle in classical physics: the total mass of any material system is neither increased nor diminished by reactions between the parts — called also *conservation of matter*
con·ser·va·tism \kən-'sər-və-,tiz-əm\ *n* **1 a :** disposition in politics to preserve what is established **b :** a political philosophy based on tradition and social stability, stressing established institutions, and preferring gradual development to abrupt change **2** *cap* **a :** the principles and policies of the Conservative party in the United Kingdom **b :** the Conservative party **3 :** tendency to prefer an existing situation to change
¹**con·ser·va·tive** \-'sər-vət-iv\ *adj* **1 :** PRESERVATIVE **2 a :** of or relating to a philosophy of conservatism **b :** of or constituting a political party professing the principles of conservatism: as (1) *cap* **:** of or constituting a party of the United Kingdom advocating support of established institutions (2) *cap* **:** Progressive Conservative **3 a :** tending or disposed to maintain existing views, conditions, or institutions **:** TRADITIONAL **b :** MODERATE, CAUTIOUS **4** *cap* **:** of or relating to a movement in Judaism that holds sacred the Torah and the religious traditions but accepts some liturgical and ritual change — **con·ser·va·tive·ly** *adv* — **con·ser·va·tive·ness** *n*
²**conservative** *n* **1 a :** an adherent or advocate of political conservatism **b** *cap* **:** a member or supporter of a conservative political party **2 a :** one who adheres to traditional methods or views **b :** a cautious or discreet person
con·ser·va·toire \kən-'sər-və-,twär\ *n* [F, fr. It *conservatorio*] **:** CONSERVATORY
con·ser·va·tor \kən-'sər-vət-ər, -və-,tȯ(ə)r; 'kän(t)-sər-,vāt-ər\ *n* **1 :** one that preserves from injury or violation **:** PROTECTOR **2 :** a person, official, or institution designated to take over and protect the interests of an incompetent **3 :** an official charged with the protection of something affecting public welfare and interests
con·ser·va·to·ry \kən-'sər-və-,tōr-ē, -,tȯr-\ *n* **1 :** a greenhouse for growing or displaying plants **2** [It *conservatorio* home for foundlings, music school, fr. L *conservatus*, pp.] **:** a school specializing in one of the fine arts
¹**con·serve** \kən-'sərv\ *vt* [ME *conserven*, fr. MF *conserver*, fr. L *conservare*, fr. *com-* + *servare* to keep, guard, observe; akin to OE *searu* armor, Av *haurvaiti* he guards] **1 :** to keep in a safe or sound state **:** PRESERVE **2 :** to preserve with sugar — **con·serv·er** *n*
²**con·serve** \'kän-,sərv\ *n* **1 :** SWEETMEAT; *esp* **:** a candied fruit **2 :** PRESERVE; *specif* **:** one prepared from a mixture of fruits
con·sid·er \kən-'sid-ər\ *vb* **con·sid·er·ing** \-'sid-(ə-)riŋ\ [ME *consideren*, fr. MF *considerer*, fr. L *considerare*, lit., to observe the stars, fr. *com-* + *sider-*, *sidus* star] *vt* **1 :** to think about with care or caution **2 :** to regard or treat with attention or solicitude **3 :** to gaze on steadily or reflectively **4 :** to come to view ⟨~ thrift essential⟩ **5 :** ESTEEM **6 :** SUPPOSE ~ *vi* **:** REFLECT, DELIBERATE

syn STUDY, CONTEMPLATE, WEIGH, REVOLVE: CONSIDER often indicates no more than *think about* but may suggest a conscious direction of thought; STUDY implies sustained purposeful concentration and attention to details and minutiae; CONTEMPLATE stresses focusing one's thoughts on something but implies nothing as to purpose or result of such thinking; WEIGH implies attempting to reach the truth or arrive at a decision by balancing conflicting claims or evidence; REVOLVE suggests turning over a matter under consideration so that all sides are taken into account

1**con·sid·er·able** \kən-ˈsid-ər-(ə-)bəl, -ˈsid-rə-bəl\ *adj* **1 :** worth consideration **2 :** large in extent or degree — **con·sid·er·a·bly** *adv*

2**considerable** *n* **:** a considerable amount, degree, or extent

con·sid·er·ate \kən-ˈsid-(ə-)rət\ *adj* **1 :** marked by or given to careful consideration **:** CIRCUMSPECT **2 :** thoughtful of the rights and feelings of others **syn** see THOUGHTFUL — **con·sid·er·ate·ly** \-lē, -ˈsid-ərt-lē\ *adv* — **con·sid·er·ate·ness** \-nəs\ *n*

con·sid·er·ation \kən-ˌsid-ə-ˈrā-shən\ *n* **1 :** continuous and careful thought **2 a :** something considered as a ground **:** REASON **b :** a taking into account **3 :** thoughtful and sympathetic regard **4 :** an opinion obtained by reflection **5 a :** RECOMPENSE, PAYMENT **b :** the inducement to a contract or other legal transaction; *specif* **:** an act or forbearance or the promise thereof done or given by one party in return for the act or promise of another

con·sid·ered \kən-ˈsid-ərd\ *adj* **1 :** matured by extended deliberative thought **2 :** regarded with respect or esteem

con·sid·er·ing *prep* **:** in view of **:** taking into account

con·sign \kən-ˈsīn\ *vb* [MF *consigner*, fr. L *consignare*, fr. *com-* + *signum* sign, mark, seal] *vt* **1 :** to give over to another's care **:** ENTRUST **2 :** to give, transfer, or deliver formally **3 :** to send or address to an agent to be cared for or sold ~ *vi, obs* **:** AGREE, SUBMIT **syn** see COMMIT — **con·sign·able** \-ˈsī-nə-bəl\ *adj* — **con·sig·na·tion** \ˌkän-ˌsī-ˈnā-shən, ˌkän(t)-sig-\ *n* — **con·sign·or** \kən-ˈsī-nər; ˌkän-ˌsī-ˈnȯ(ə)r, ˌkän(t)-sə-\ *n*

con·sign·ee \ˌkän-ˌsī-ˈnē, kən-ˌsī-, ˌkän(t)-sə-\ *n* **:** one to whom something is consigned or shipped

con·sign·ment \kən-ˈsīn-mənt\ *n* **1 :** the act or process of consigning **2 :** something consigned esp. in a single shipment

con·sist \kən-ˈsist\ *vi* [MF & L; MF *consister*, fr. L *consistere*, lit., to stand together, fr. *com-* + *sistere* to take a stand; akin to L *stare* to stand] **1 :** LIE, RESIDE — used with *in* **2** *archaic* **a :** EXIST, BE **b :** to be capable of existing **3 :** to become made up — used with *of* **4 :** to be consistent ⟨it ~*s* with the facts⟩

con·sis·tence \kən-ˈsis-tən(t)s\ *n* **:** CONSISTENCY

con·sis·ten·cy \kən-ˈsis-tən-sē\ *n* **1 a :** condition of adhering together **:** FIRMNESS **b :** firmness of constitution or character **:** PERSISTENCY **2 :** degree of firmness, density, viscosity, or resistance to movement or separation of constituent particles **3 a :** agreement or harmony of parts or features to one another or a whole **:** CORRESPONDENCE; *specif* **:** ability to be asserted together without contradiction **b :** harmony of conduct or practice with profession

con·sis·tent \kən-ˈsis-tənt\ *adj* [L *consistent-*, *consistens*, prp. of *consistere*] **1 :** possessing firmness or coherence **2 a :** agreeing with itself or something else **:** COMPATIBLE **b :** uniform throughout **3 :** living or acting conformably to one's own belief, professions, or character **syn** see CONSONANT — **con·sis·tent·ly** *adv*

con·sis·to·ri·al \ˌkän-ˌsis-ˈtōr-ē-əl, -ˈtȯr-, kən-\ *adj* **:** of or relating to a consistory

con·sis·to·ry \kən-ˈsis-t(ə-)rē\ *n* [ME *consistorie*, fr. MF, fr. ML & LL; ML *consistorium* church tribunal, fr. LL, imperial council, fr. L *consistere* to stand together] **1 :** a solemn assembly **:** COUNCIL **2 :** a church tribunal or governing body: as **a :** a solemn meeting of Roman Catholic cardinals convoked and presided over by the pope **b :** a church session in some Reformed churches **3 :** the organization that confers the degrees of the Ancient and Accepted Scottish Rite of Freemasonry usu. from the 19th to the 32d inclusive; *also* **:** a meeting of such an organization

con·so·ci·ate \kən-ˈsō-s(h)ē-ˌāt\ *vb* [L *consociatus*, pp. of *consociare*, fr. *com-* + *socius* companion — more at SOCIAL] *vt* **:** to bring into association ~ *vi* **:** to associate esp. in fellowship or partnership

con·so·ci·a·tion \-ˌsō-sē-ˈā-shən, -shē-\ *n* **1 :** association in fellowship or alliance **2 :** an association of churches or religious societies **3 :** an ecological community with a single dominant — **con·so·ci·a·tion·al** \-shnəl, -shən-ᵊl\ *adj*

con·sol \kən-ˈsäl, ˈkän-ˌ\ *n* [short for *Consolidated Annuities*, British government securities] **:** an interest-bearing government bond having no maturity date but redeemable on call; *specif* **:** one first issued by the British government in 1751 — usu. used in pl.

con·so·la·tion \ˌkän(t)-sə-ˈlā-shən\ *n* **:** the act or an instance of consoling **:** the state of being consoled **:** COMFORT; *also* **:** something that consoles (as a contest held for those who have lost early in a tournament) — **con·so·la·to·ry** \kən-ˈsō-lə-ˌtōr-ē, -ˈsäl-ə-, -ˌtȯr-\ *adj*

1**con·sole** \kən-ˈsōl\ *vt* [F *consoler*, fr. L *consolari*, fr. *com-* + *solari* to console] **:** to alleviate the grief of **syn** see COMFORT

2**con·sole** \ˈkän-ˌsōl\ *n* [F, fr. MF, short for *consolateur* bracket in human shape, lit., consoler, fr. L *consolator*, fr. *consolatus*, pp. of *consolari*] **1 :** an architectural member projecting from a wall to form a bracket or from a keystone for ornament **2 a :** the desk from which an organ is played and which contains the keyboards, pedal board, and other controlling mechanisms **b :** a panel or cabinet on which are mounted dials, switches, and other apparatus used in centrally controlling electrical or mechanical devices **3 :** a cabinet (as for a radio or television set) designed to rest directly on the floor

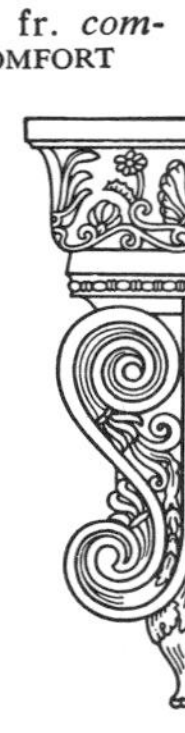

console supporting a cornice

console table *n* **:** a table fixed to a wall with its top supported by consoles; *broadly* **:** a table designed to fit against a wall

con·sol·i·date \kən-ˈsäl-ə-ˌdāt\ *vb* [L *consolidatus*, pp. of *consolidare* to make solid, fr. *com-* + *solidus* solid] *vt* **1 :** to join together into one whole **:** UNITE **2 :** to make firm or secure **:** STRENGTHEN ⟨~ the beachhead⟩ **3 :** to form into a compact mass ~ *vi* **:** to become consolidated; *specif* **:** MERGE

consolidated school *n* **:** a public usu. elementary school formed by merging other schools

con·sol·i·da·tion \kən-ˌsäl-ə-ˈdā-shən\ *n* **1 :** the act or process of consolidating **:** the state of being consolidated **2 :** the merger of two or more corporations **3 :** alteration of lung tissue from an aerated condition to one of solid consistency

con·som·mé \ˌkän(t)-sə-ˈmā\ *n* [F, fr. pp. of *consommer* to complete, boil down, fr. L *consummare* to complete — more at CONSUMMATE] **:** a clear soup usu. of beef, veal, and chicken

con·so·nance \ˈkän(t)-s(ə-)nən(t)s\ *n* **1 :** harmony or agreement among components **2 a :** correspondence or recurrence of sounds esp. in words; *specif* **:** recurrence or repetition of consonants esp. at the end of stressed syllables without the like correspondence of vowels **b :** an agreeable combination of musical tones **c :** SYMPATHETIC VIBRATION, RESONANCE

con·so·nan·cy \-s(ə-)nən-sē\ *n* **:** CONSONANCE 1

1**con·so·nant** \ˈkän(t)-s(ə-)nənt\ *n* [ME, fr. L *consonant-*, *consonans*, fr. prp. of *consonare*] **1 :** one of a class of speech sounds (as \p\, \g\, \n\, \l\, \s\, \r\) characterized by constriction or closure at one or more points in the breath channel **2 :** a letter representing a consonant; *esp* **:** any letter of the English alphabet except *a*, *e*, *i*, *o*, and *u*

2**consonant** *adj* [MF, fr. L *consonant-*, *consonans* prp. of *consonare* to sound together, agree, fr. *com-* + *sonare* to sound] **1 :** being in agreement or harmony **2 :** marked by musical consonances **3 :** having like sounds ⟨~ words⟩ **4 :** relating to or exhibiting consonance **:** RESONANT — **con·so·nant·ly** *adv*

syn CONSISTENT, COMPATIBLE, CONGRUOUS, CONGENIAL, SYMPATHETIC: CONSONANT implies the absence of elements making for discord or difficulty; CONSISTENT may also imply this or it may stress absence of contradiction between things or between details of the same thing; COMPATIBLE suggests having a capacity for existing or functioning together without disagreement, discord, or mutual interference; CONGRUOUS is more positive in suggesting a pleasing effect resulting from fitness or appropriateness of component elements; CONGENIAL implies a generally satisfying harmony between personalities or a fitness to one's personal taste; SYMPATHETIC suggests a more subtle or quieter kind of harmony than CONGENIAL

con·so·nan·tal \ˌkän(t)-sə-ˈnant-ᵊl\ *adj* **:** relating to, being, or marked by a consonant or group of consonants

consonant shift *n* **:** a set of regular changes in consonant articulation in the history of a language or dialect: **a :** such a set affecting the Indo-European stops and distinguishing the Germanic languages from the other Indo-European languages **b :** such a set affecting the Germanic stops and distinguishing High German from the other Germanic languages

1**con·sort** \ˈkän-ˌsȯ(ə)rt\ *n* [ME, fr. MF, fr. L *consort-*, *consors*, lit., one who shares a common lot, fr. *com-* + *sort-*, *sors* lot, share] **1 :** ASSOCIATE **2 :** a ship accompanying another **3 :** SPOUSE

2**consort** *n* [MF *consorte*, fr. *consort*] **1 :** CONJUNCTION, ASSOCIATION **2 a :** a group of musicians entertaining by voice or instrument **b :** a set of musical instruments of the same family

3**con·sort** \kən-ˈsȯ(ə)rt, kän-ˈ, ˈkän-ˌ\ *vt* **1 :** UNITE, ASSOCIATE **2** *obs* **:** ESCORT ~ *vi* **1 :** to keep company **2** *obs* **:** to make harmony **:** PLAY **3 :** ACCORD, HARMONIZE

con·sor·tium \kən-ˈsȯr-sh(ē-)əm, -ˈsȯrt-ē-əm\ *n, pl* **con·sor·tia** \-ˈsȯr-sh(ē-)ə, -ˈsȯrt-ē-ə\ [L, fellowship, fr. *consort-*, *consors*] **1 :** an international business or banking agreement or combination **2 :** ASSOCIATION, SOCIETY **3 :** the legal right of one spouse to the company, affection, and service of the other

con·spe·cif·ic \ˌkän(t)-spi-ˈsif-ik\ *adj* [NL *conspecies* congeneric species] **:** of the same species

con·spec·tus \kən-ˈspek-təs\ *n* [L, fr. *conspectus*, pp. of *conspicere*] **1 :** a usu. brief survey or summary often providing an overall view **2 :** OUTLINE, SYNOPSIS **syn** see ABRIDGMENT

con·spic·u·ous \kən-ˈspik-yə-wəs\ *adj* [L *conspicuus*, fr. *conspicere* to get sight of, fr. *com-* + *specere* to look] **1 :** obvious to the eye or mind **2 :** attracting attention **:** STRIKING **3 :** marked by a noticeable violation of good taste **syn** see NOTICEABLE — **con·spic·u·ous·ly** *adv* — **con·spic·u·ous·ness** *n*

con·spir·a·cy \kən-ˈspir-ə-sē\ *n* [ME *conspiracie*, fr. L *conspiratus*, pp. of *conspirare*] **1 :** the act of conspiring together **2 a :** an agreement among conspirators **b :** a group of conspirators **syn** see PLOT

con·spir·a·tor \kən-ˈspir-ət-ər\ *n* **:** one that conspires **:** PLOTTER

con·spir·a·to·ri·al \kən-ˌspir-ə-ˈtōr-ē-əl, -ˈtȯr-\ *adj* **:** of, relating to, or suggestive of a conspiracy — **con·spir·a·to·ri·al·ly** \-ē\ *adv*

con·spire \kən-ˈspī(ə)r\ *vb* [ME *conspiren*, fr. MF *conspirer*, fr. L *conspirare* to breathe together, agree, conspire, fr. *com-* + *spirare* to breathe — more at SPIRIT] *vt* **:** PLOT, CONTRIVE ~ *vi* **1 :** to join in a secret agreement to do an unlawful or wrongful act or to use such means to accomplish a lawful end **2 :** to act in harmony

con·sta·ble \ˈkän(t)-stə-bəl, ˈkən(t)-\ *n* [ME *conestable*, fr. OF, fr. LL *comes stabuli*, lit., officer of the stable] **1 :** a high officer of a medieval royal or noble household **2 :** the warden or governor of a royal castle or a fortified town **3 a :** a public officer responsible for keeping the peace and for minor judicial duties **b :** a British policeman of the lowest rank

1**con·stab·u·lary** \kən-ˈstab-yə-ˌler-ē\ *n* **1 :** the organized body of constables of a particular district or country **2 :** a military police force organized separately from the regular army

2**constabulary** *adj* **:** of or relating to a constable or constabulary

con·stan·cy \ˈkän(t)-stən-sē\ *n* **1 a :** steadfastness of mind under duress **:** FORTITUDE **b :** FIDELITY, LOYALTY **2 :** freedom from change

1**con·stant** \ˈkän(t)-stənt\ *adj* [ME, fr. MF, fr. L *constant-*, *constans*, fr. prp. of *constare* to stand firm, be consistent, fr. *com-* + *stare* to stand — more at STAND] **1 :** STEADFAST, RESOLUTE; *also* **:** FAITHFUL **2 :** INVARIABLE, UNIFORM **3 :** continually recurring **:** REGULAR **syn** see FAITHFUL, CONTINUAL — **con·stant·ly** *adv*

2**constant** *n* **:** something invariable or unchanging: as **a :** a number that has a fixed value in a given situation or universally or that is characteristic of some substance or instrument **b :** a number that is assumed not to change value in a given mathematical discussion **c :** a term in logic with a fixed designation

con·stel·late \ˈkän(t)-stə-ˌlāt\ *vt* **1 :** to unite in a cluster **2 :** to set or adorn with or as if with constellations ~ *vi* **:** CLUSTER

con·stel·la·tion \ˌkän(t)-stə-ˈlā-shən\ *n* [ME *constellacioun*, fr. MF *constellation*, fr. LL *constellation-*, *constellatio*, fr. *constellatus* studded with stars, fr. L *com-* + *stella* star — more at STAR] **1 a :** the configuration of stars esp. at one's birth **b** *obs* **:** character or constitution as determined by the stars **2 :** any of 88 arbitrary configurations of stars or an area of the celestial sphere covering one of these configurations **3 :** an assemblage, collection, or gathering of usu. related persons, qualities, or things — **con·stel·la·to·ry** \kən-ˈstel-ə-ˌtōr-ē, -ˌtȯr-\ *adj*

con·ster·nate \ˈkän(t)-stər-ˌnāt\ *vt* **:** to fill with consternation

con·ster·na·tion \ˌkän(t)-stər-ˈnā-shən\ *n* [F or L; F, fr. L *con-*

sternation-, consternatio, fr. *consternatus,* pp. of *consternare* to bewilder, alarm, fr. *com-* + *-sternare* (akin to OE *starian* to stare)] **:** amazement or dismay that hinders or throws into confusion

con·sti·pate \'kän(t)-stə-,pāt\ *vt* [ML *constipatus,* pp. of *constipare,* fr. L, to crowd together, fr. *com-* + *stipare* to press together — more at STIFF] **:** to make costive **:** cause constipation in

con·sti·pa·tion \,kän(t)-stə-'pā-shən\ *n* **:** abnormally delayed or infrequent passage of dry hardened feces

con·stit·u·en·cy \kən-'stich-(ə-)wən-sē\ *n* **1 :** a body of citizens entitled to elect a representative to a legislative or other public body **2 :** the residents in an electoral district **3 :** an electoral district

1**con·stit·u·ent** \kən-'stich-(ə-)wənt\ *n* [F *constituant,* fr. MF, fr. prp. of *constituer* to constitute, fr. L *constituere*] **1 :** one who authorizes another to act for him **:** PRINCIPAL **2 :** an essential part **:** COMPONENT, ELEMENT **3 :** one of two or more linguistic forms that enter into a construction or a compound and are either immediate (as *he* and *writes reviews* in the construction "he writes reviews") or ultimate (as *he, write, -s, review,* and *-s* in the same construction) **4 a :** one of a group who elects another to represent him in a public office **b :** a voter in a constituency **syn** see ELEMENT

2**constituent** *adj* [L *constituent-, constituens,* prp. of *constituere*] **1 :** serving to form, compose, or make up a unit or whole **:** COMPONENT **2 :** having the power to create a government or frame or amend a constitution ⟨a ~ assembly⟩ — **con·stit·u·ent·ly** *adv*

con·sti·tute \'kän(t)-stə-,t(y)üt\ *vt* [L *constitutus,* pp. of *constituere* to set up, constitute, fr. *com-* + *statuere* to set — more at STATUTE] **1 :** to appoint to an office, function, or dignity **2 :** to set up **:** ESTABLISH: as **a :** ENACT **b :** FOUND **c** (1) **:** to give due or lawful form to (2) **:** to legally process **3 :** FORM, COMPOSE

con·sti·tu·tion \,kän(t)-stə-'t(y)ü-shən\ *n* **1 :** an established law or custom **:** ORDINANCE **2 :** the act of establishing, making, or setting up **3 a :** the physical makeup of the individual comprising inherited qualities modified by environment **:** PHYSIQUE **b :** the structure, composition, physical makeup, or nature of something **4 :** the mode in which a state or society is organized; *esp* **:** the manner in which sovereign power is distributed **5 a :** the fundamental principles of a nation, state, or body politic that determine the powers and duties of the government and guarantee certain rights to the people and that together constitute the organic law of the land **b :** a written instrument embodying such rules

1**con·sti·tu·tion·al** \-shnəl, -shən-ᵊl\ *adj* **1 :** relating to, inherent in, or affecting the constitution of body or mind **2 :** of, relating to, or entering into the fundamental makeup of something **:** ESSENTIAL **3 :** in accordance with or authorized by the constitution of a state or society **4 :** regulated by or ruling according to a constitution ⟨~ monarchy⟩ **5 :** of or relating to a constitution **6 :** loyal to or supporting an established constitution or form of government

2**constitutional** *n* **:** a walk or other exercise taken for one's health

con·sti·tu·tion·al·ism \-,iz-əm\ *n* **:** adherence to or government according to constitutional principles; *also* **:** a constitutional system of government — **con·sti·tu·tion·al·ist** \-əst\ *n*

con·sti·tu·tion·al·i·ty \-,t(y)ü-shə-'nal-ət-ē\ *n* **:** the quality or state of being constitutional; *esp* **:** accordance with the provisions of a constitution

con·sti·tu·tion·al·ly \-'t(y)ü-shnə-lē, -shən-ᵊl-ē\ *adv* **1 a :** in accordance with one's constitution **b :** in structure, composition, or constitution **2 :** in accordance with political constitution

con·sti·tu·tive \'kän(t)-stə-,t(y)üt-iv, kən-'stich-ət-iv\ *adj* **1 :** having the power to enact or establish **:** CONSTRUCTIVE **2 :** CONSTITUENT, ESSENTIAL **3 :** relating to or dependent on constitution ⟨a ~ property⟩ — **con·sti·tu·tive·ly** *adv*

con·strain \kən-'strān\ *vt* [ME *constrainen,* fr. MF *constraindre,* fr. L *constringere* to constrict, constrain, fr. *com-* + *stringere* to draw tight — more at STRAIN] **1 :** COMPEL **2 :** to force or produce in an unnatural or strained manner ⟨a ~*ed* smile⟩ **3 :** to secure by or as if by bond **:** CONFINE **4 :** to bring into narrow compass; *also* **:** to clasp tightly **5 :** to hold back by force; **syn** see FORCE — **con·strained·ly** \-'strā-nəd-lē, -'strān-dlē\ *adv*

con·straint \kən-'strānt\ *n* [ME, fr. MF *constrainte,* fr. *constraindre*] **1 a :** the act of constraining **:** the state of being constrained **:** COMPULSION; *also* **:** RESTRAINT **b :** a constraining agency or force **:** CHECK **2 a :** repression of one's own feelings, behavior, or actions **b :** a sense of being constrained **:** EMBARRASSMENT

con·strict \kən-'strikt\ *vb* [L *constrictus,* pp. of *constringere*] *vt* **1 a :** to draw together **b :** COMPRESS, SQUEEZE **2 :** to cause to falter **:** STULTIFY ~ *vi* **:** to become constricted **syn** see CONTRACT — **con·stric·tive** \-'strik-tiv\ *adj*

con·stric·tion \kən-'strik-shən\ *n* **1 :** an act or product of constricting **2 :** the quality or state of being constricted **3 :** something that constricts

con·stric·tor \kən-'strik-tər\ *n* **1 :** one that constricts **2 :** a muscle that contracts a cavity or orifice or compresses an organ **3 :** a snake that kills prey by compression in its coils

con·stringe \kən-'strinj\ *vt* [L *constringere*] **1 :** CONSTRICT **2 :** to cause to shrink — **con·strin·gent** \-'strin-jənt\ *adj*

con·stru·able \kən-'strü-ə-bəl\ *adj* **:** that may be construed

1**con·struct** \kən-'strəkt\ *vt* [L *constructus,* pp. of *construere,* fr. *com-* + *struere* to build] **1 :** to make or form by combining parts **2 :** to set in logical order **3 :** to draw (a geometrical figure) with suitable instruments and under specified conditions — **con·struct·ible** \-'strək-tə-bəl\ *adj* — **con·struc·tor** \-tər\ *n*

2**con·struct** \'kän-,strəkt\ *n* **:** something constructed esp. by mental synthesis (as the concept of a physical object out of sense-data)

con·struc·tion \kən-'strək-shən\ *n* **1 :** the arrangement and connection of words or groups of words in a sentence **:** syntactical arrangement **2 :** the process, art, or manner of constructing; *also* **:** a thing constructed **3 :** the act or result of construing, interpreting, or explaining **4 :** a nonrepresentational sculptural creation composed of often disparate elements — **con·struc·tion·al** \-shnəl, -shən-ᵊl\ *adj* — **con·struc·tion·al·ly** \-ē\ *adv*

con·struc·tion·ist \kən-'strək-sh(ə-)nəst\ *n* **:** one who construes an instrument (as the U.S. Constitution) in a specific way ⟨a strict ~⟩

con·struc·tive \kən-'strək-tiv\ *adj* **1 :** declared such by judicial construction or interpretation ⟨~ fraud⟩ **2 :** of or relating to construction **3 :** promoting improvement or development ⟨~ criticism⟩ — **con·struc·tive·ly** *adv* — **con·struc·tive·ness** *n*

con·struc·tiv·ism \kən-'strək-ti-,viz-əm\ *n* **:** nonfigurative art concerned with formal organization of planes and expression of volume in terms of modern industrial materials (as glass and plastic) — **con·struc·tiv·ist** \-ti-vəst\ *adj or n*

con·strue \kən-'strü\ *vb* [ME *construen,* fr. LL *construere,* fr. L, to construct] *vt* **1 :** to analyze the arrangement and connection of words in (a sentence or sentence part) **2 :** to understand or explain the sense or intention of usu. in a particular way or with respect to a given set of circumstances ~ *vi* **:** to construe a sentence or sentence part esp. in connection with translating

con·sub·stan·tial \,kän(t)-səb-'stan-chəl\ *adj* [LL *consubstantialis,* fr. L *com-* + *substantia* substance] **:** of the same substance

con·sub·stan·ti·a·tion \,kän(t)-səb-,stan-chē-'ā-shən\ *n* **:** the actual substantial presence and combination of the body of Christ with the eucharistic bread and wine

con·sue·tude \'kän(t)-swi-,t(y)üd, kən-'sü-ə-\ *n* [ME, fr. L *consuetudo* — more at CUSTOM] **:** social usage **:** CUSTOM — **con·sue·tu·di·nary** \,kän(t)-swi-'t(y)üd-ᵊn-,er-ē, kən-,sü-ə-\ *adj*

con·sul \'kän(t)-səl\ *n* [ME, fr. L, fr. *consulere*] **1 a :** either of two joint annually elected chief magistrates of the Roman republic **b :** one of three chief magistrates of the French republic from 1799 to 1804 **2 :** an official appointed by a government to reside in a foreign country to represent the commercial interests of citizens of the appointing country — **con·sul·ar** \-s(ə-)lər\ *adj* — **con·sul·ship** \-səl-,ship\ *n*

con·sul·ate \'kän(t)-s(ə-)lət\ *n* **1 :** a government by consuls **2 :** the office, term of office, or jurisdiction of a consul **3 :** the residence of a consul

1**con·sult** \kən-'səlt\ *vb* [MF or L; MF *consulter,* fr. L *consultare,* fr. *consultus,* pp. of *consulere* to deliberate, counsel, consult] *vt* **1 a :** to ask the advice or opinion of ⟨~ a doctor⟩ **b :** to refer to **2 :** to have regard to **:** CONSIDER ~ *vi* **1 :** to consult a person **2 :** to deliberate together **:** CONFER — **con·sult·er** *n*

2**con·sult** \kən-'səlt, 'kän-,\ *n* **:** CONSULTATION

con·sul·tant \kən-'səlt-ᵊnt\ *n* **1 :** one who consults another **2 :** one who gives professional advice or services **:** EXPERT

con·sul·ta·tion \,kän(t)-səl-'tā-shən\ *n* **1 :** COUNCIL, CONFERENCE; *specif* **:** a deliberation between physicians on a case or its treatment **2 :** the act of consulting or conferring

con·sul·ta·tive \kən-'səl-tət-iv, 'kän(t)-səl-,tāt-iv\ *adj* **:** of, relating to, or intended for consultation **:** ADVISORY ⟨~ committee⟩

con·sul·tive \kən-'səl-tiv\ *adj* **:** CONSULTATIVE

con·sul·tor \kən-'səl-tər\ *n* **:** one that consults or advises; *esp* **:** a member of a Roman Catholic diocesan advisory council similar to a cathedral chapter

con·sum·able \kən-'sü-mə-bəl\ *adj* **:** capable of being consumed

con·sume \kən-'süm\ *vb* [ME *consumen,* fr. MF or L; MF *consumer,* fr. L *consumere,* fr. *com-* + *sumere* to take up, take, fr. *sub-* up + *emere* to take — more at SUB-, REDEEM] *vt* **1 :** to do away with completely **:** DESTROY **2 a :** to spend wastefully **:** SQUANDER **b :** to use up **:** EXPEND **3 :** to eat or drink esp. in great quantity **4 :** to engage fully **:** ENGROSS ~ *vi* **:** to waste or burn away **:** PERISH

con·sum·ed·ly \kən-'sü-məd-lē\ *adv* **:** EXCESSIVELY

con·sum·er \kən-'sü-mər\ *n* **:** one that consumes; *specif* **:** one that utilizes economic goods

consumer credit *n* **:** credit granted to an individual esp. to finance purchase of consumer goods or defray personal or family expenses

consumer goods *n pl* **:** goods that directly satisfy human wants

1**con·sum·mate** \kən-'səm-ət, 'kän(t)-sə-mət\ *adj* [ME, fr. L *consummatus,* pp. of *consummare* to sum up, finish, fr. *com-* + *summa* sum] **1 :** complete in every detail **:** PERFECT **2 :** extremely skilled and accomplished ⟨a ~ liar⟩ **3 :** of the highest excellence or greatest degree ⟨~ skill⟩ — **con·sum·mate·ly** *adv*

2**con·sum·mate** \'kän(t)-sə-,māt, *vt 1 & vi also* kən-'səm-ət, -,āt\ *vt* **1 a :** FINISH, COMPLETE **b :** to make perfect **:** ACHIEVE **2 :** to complete by sexual intercourse ⟨~ a marriage⟩ ~ *vi* **:** to become perfected — **con·sum·ma·tion** \,kän(t)-sə-'mā-shən\ *n* — **con·sum·ma·tive** \'kän(t)-sə-,māt-iv, kən-'səm-ət-iv\ *adj* — **con·sum·ma·tor** \'kän(t)-sə-,māt-ər, *also* kən-'səm-ət-ər, -,āt-\ *n* — **con·sum·ma·to·ry** \kən-'səm-ə-,tōr-ē, -,tȯr-\ *adv*

con·sump·tion \kən-'səm(p)-shən\ *n* [ME *consumpcioun,* fr. L *consumption-, consumptio,* fr. *consumptus,* pp. of *consumere*] **1 :** the act or process of consuming **2 :** the utilization of economic goods in the satisfaction of wants or in the process of production resulting chiefly in their destruction, deterioration, or transformation **3 a :** a progressive wasting away of the body esp. from pulmonary tuberculosis **b :** TUBERCULOSIS

1**con·sump·tive** \kən-'səm(p)-tiv\ *adj* **1 :** tending to consume **2 :** of, relating to, or affected with consumption — **con·sump·tive·ly** *adv*

2**consumptive** *n* **:** a person affected with consumption

1**con·tact** \'kän-,takt\ *n* [F or L; F, fr. L *contactus,* fr. *contactus,* pp. of *contingere* to have contact with] **1 a :** union or junction of surfaces **b** (1) **:** the junction of two electrical conductors through which a current passes (2) **:** a special part made for such a junction or connection **2 a :** ASSOCIATION, RELATIONSHIP **b :** CONNECTION, COMMUNICATION **c :** direct visual observation of the earth's surface made from an airplane esp. as an aid to navigation **d :** an establishing of communication with someone or an observing or receiving of a significant signal from a person or object **3 :** one serving as a carrier or source

2**con·tact** \'kän-,takt, kən-'takt\ *vt* **1 :** to bring into contact **2 a :** to enter or be in contact with **:** JOIN **b :** to get in communication with ⟨~ your local dealer⟩ ~ *vi* **:** to make contact

3**con·tact** \'kän-,takt\ *adj* **:** maintaining, involving, or caused by contact

4**con·tact** \'kän-,takt\ *adv* **:** by contact flying

contact flying *n* **:** navigation of an airplane by means of direct observation of landmarks

contact lens *n* **:** a thin lens designed to fit over the cornea

contact print *n* **:** a photographic print made with the negative in contact with the sensitized paper, plate, or film

con·ta·gion \kən-'tā-jən\ *n* [ME, fr. MF & L; MF, fr. L *contagion-contagio,* fr. *contingere* to have contact with, pollute] **1 a :** the transmission of a disease by direct or indirect contact **b :** a contagious disease **c :** a disease-producing agent (as a virus) **2 a :** POISON **b :** contagious influence, quality, or nature **c :** corrupting influence or contact **3 a :** rapid communication of an influence (as a doctrine or emotional state) **b :** an influence that spreads rapidly

ə abut; ᵊ kitten; ər further; a back; ā bake; ä cot, cart; aù out; ch chin; e less; ē easy; g gift; i trip; ī life
j joke; ŋ sing; ō flow; ȯ flaw; ȯi coin; th thin; th this; ü loot; ú foot; y yet; yü few; yú furious; zh vision

con·ta·gious \kən-'tā-jəs\ *adj* **1 :** communicable by contact **:** CATCHING **2 :** bearing contagion **3 :** used for contagious diseases — **con·ta·gious·ly** *adv* — **con·ta·gious·ness** *n*

contagious abortion *n* **:** a contagious or infectious disease (as a brucellosis) of domestic animals characterized by abortion

con·ta·gium \kən-'tā-j(ē-)əm\ *n, pl* **con·ta·gia** \-j(ē-)ə\ [L, contagion, fr. *contingere*] **:** a virus or living organism capable of causing a communicable disease

con·tain \kən-'tān\ *vb* [ME *conteinen*, fr. OF *contenir*, fr L *continēre* to hold together, hold in, contain, fr. *com-* + *tenēre* to hold — more at THIN] *vt* **1 :** to keep within limits **:** RESTRAIN; *specif* **:** to follow successfully a policy of containment toward **2 a :** to have within **:** HOLD **b :** COMPRISE, INCLUDE **3 a :** to be divisible by usu. without a remainder **b :** ENCLOSE, BOUND ~ *vi* **:** to restrain oneself — **con·tain·able** \-'tā-nə-bəl\ *adj*

syn HOLD, ACCOMMODATE: CONTAIN implies the actual presence of a specified substance or quantity within something; HOLD implies the capacity of containing or the usual or permanent function of containing or keeping; ACCOMMODATE stresses holding without crowding or inconvenience

con·tain·er \kən-'tā-nər\ *n* **:** one that contains; *esp* **:** a receptacle or a flexible covering for shipment of goods

con·tain·ment \kən-'tān-mənt\ *n* **1 :** the act or process of containing **2 :** the policy, process, or result of preventing the expansion of a hostile power or ideology

con·tam·i·nant \kən-'tam-ə-nənt\ *n* **:** something that contaminates

con·tam·i·nate \kən-'tam-ə-,nāt\ *vt* [L *contaminatus*, pp. of *contaminare;* akin to L *contagio* contagion] **1 :** to soil, stain, or infect by contact or association **2 :** to make unfit for use by introduction of unwholesome or undesirable elements — **con·tam·i·na·tive** \-,nāt-iv\ *adj* — **con·tam·i·na·tor** \-,nāt-ər\ *n*

syn CONTAMINATE, TAINT, POLLUTE, DEFILE mean to make impure or unclean. CONTAMINATE implies intrusion of or contact with an outside source as the cause; TAINT implies that corruption and decay have begun to take effect; POLLUTE stresses the loss of purity and cleanness through contamination; DEFILE implies befouling of what ought to be clean and pure and suggests violation or desecration

con·tam·i·na·tion \kən-,tam-ə-'nā-shən\ *n* **:** a contaminating or state of being contaminated; *also* **:** something that contaminates

conte \kōnt\ *n* [F] **:** a short tale esp. of adventure

con·temn \kən-'tem\ *vt* [ME *contempnen*, fr. MF *contempner*, fr. L *contemnere*, fr. *com-* + *temnere* to despise — more at STAMP] **:** to view or treat with contempt **:** DISDAIN, SCORN **syn** see DESPISE — **con·tem·ner** *also* **con·tem·nor** \-'tem-ər, -'tem-nər\ *n*

con·tem·plate \'känt-əm-,plāt, 'kän-,tem-\ *vt* [L *contemplatus*, pp. of *contemplari*, fr. *com-* + *templum* space marked out for observation of auguries — more at TEMPLE] **1 :** to view or consider with continued attention **:** meditate on **2 :** to have in view as contingent or probable or as an end or intention ~ *vi* **:** PONDER, MEDITATE **syn** see CONSIDER — **con·tem·pla·tor** \-,plāt-ər\ *n*

con·tem·pla·tion \,känt-əm-'plā-shən, ,kän-,tem-\ *n* **1 a :** concentration on spiritual things as a form of private devotion **b :** a state of mystical awareness of God's being **2 :** an act of considering with attention **:** STUDY **3 :** the act of regarding steadily **4 :** INTENTION, EXPECTATION

1**con·tem·pla·tive** \kən-'tem-plət-iv; 'känt-əm-,plāt-, 'kän-,tem-\ *adj* **:** marked by or given to contemplation; *specif* **:** of or relating to a religious order devoted to prayer and penance — **con·tem·pla·tive·ly** *adv* — **con·tem·pla·tive·ness** *n*

2**contemplative** *n* **:** one who practices contemplation

con·tem·po·ra·ne·ity \kən-,tem-p(ə-)rə-'nē-ət-ē, ,kän-\ *n* **:** the quality or state of being contemporaneous

con·tem·po·ra·ne·ous \-pə-'rā-nē-əs\ *adj* [L *contemporaneus*, fr. *com-* + *tempor-*, *tempus* time] **:** existing, occurring, or originating during the same time **syn** see CONTEMPORARY — **con·tem·po·ra·ne·ous·ly** *adv* — **con·tem·po·ra·ne·ous·ness** *n*

1**con·tem·po·rary** \kən-'tem-pə-,rer-ē\ *adj* [*com-* + L *tempor-*, *tempus*] **1 :** happening, existing, living, or coming into being during the same period of time **2 a :** SIMULTANEOUS **b :** marked by characteristics of the present period **:** MODERN

syn CONTEMPORARY, CONTEMPORANEOUS, COEVAL, SYNCHRONOUS, SIMULTANEOUS, COINCIDENT mean existing or occurring at the same time. CONTEMPORARY is likely to apply to people and what relates to them, CONTEMPORANEOUS to events; both suggest time spans measured in years; COEVAL refers usu. to periods, ages, eras, eons; SYNCHRONOUS implies exact correspondence in time and esp. in periodic intervals; SIMULTANEOUS implies correspondence in instant of time; COINCIDENT stresses simultaneousness of events and may be used in order to avoid implication of causal relationship

2**contemporary** *n* **1 :** one that is contemporary with another **2 :** one of the same or nearly the same age as another

con·tempt \kən-'tem(p)t\ *n* [ME, fr. L *contemptus*, fr. *contemptus*, pp. of *contemnere*] **1 a :** the act of despising or the state of mind of one who despises **:** DISDAIN **b :** lack of respect or reverence for something **2 :** the state of being despised **3 :** willful disobedience to or open disrespect of a court, judge, or legislative body

con·tempt·ible \kən-'tem(p)-tə-bəl\ *adj* **1 :** worthy of contempt **:** DESPICABLE **2** *obs* **:** SCORNFUL, CONTEMPTUOUS — **con·tempt·ible·ness** *n* — **con·tempt·ibly** \-blē\ *adv*

syn DESPICABLE, PITIABLE, SORRY, SCURVY, CHEAP, BEGGARLY mean arousing or deserving scorn. CONTEMPTIBLE may imply any quality provoking scorn or a low standing in any scale of values; DESPICABLE may imply utter worthlessness and usu. suggests arousing an attitude of moral indignation; PITIABLE applies to what inspires mixed contempt and pity; SORRY may stress pitiable inadequacy or may suggest wretchedness or sordidness; SCURVY adds to DESPICABLE an implication of arousing disgust; CHEAP and BEGGARLY imply the mean and paltry; CHEAP may also stress meretricious availability

con·temp·tu·ous \-'tem(p)-chə(-wə)s, -'tem(p)sh-wəs\ *adj* [L *contemptus* contempt] **:** manifesting, feeling, or expressing contempt — **con·temp·tu·ous·ly** *adv* — **con·temp·tu·ous·ness** *n*

con·tend \kən-'tend\ *vb* [MF or L; MF *contendre*, fr. L *contendere*, fr. *com-* + *tendere* to stretch] *vi* **1 :** to strive or vie in contest or rivalry or against difficulties **2 :** to strive in debate **:** ARGUE ~ *vt* **1 :** MAINTAIN, ASSERT **2 :** to struggle for — **con·tend·er** *n*

1**con·tent** \kən-'tent\ *adj* [ME, fr. MF, fr. L *contentus*, fr. pp. of *continēre* to hold in, contain] **:** SATISFIED, CONTENTED

2**content** *vt* **1 :** to appease the desires of **2 :** to limit (oneself) in requirements, desires, or actions **syn** see SATISFY

3**content** *n* **:** CONTENTMENT; *esp* **:** freedom from care or discomfort

4**con·tent** \'kän-,tent\ *n* [ME, fr. L *contentus*, pp. of *continēre* to contain] **1** *usu pl* **a :** something contained ⟨room's ~*s*⟩ **b :** the topics or matter treated in a written work **2 a :** SUBSTANCE, GIST **b :** essential meaning **:** SIGNIFICANCE **c :** the events, physical detail, and information in a work of art **3 a :** the matter dealt with in a field of study **b :** a part, element, or complex of parts **4 :** the amount of specified material contained **:** PROPORTION

con·tent·ed \kən-'tent-əd\ *adj* **:** satisfied or manifesting satisfaction with one's possessions, status, or situation ⟨a ~ smile⟩ — **con·tent·ed·ly** *adv* — **con·tent·ed·ness** *n*

con·ten·tion \kən-'ten-chən\ *n* [ME *contencioun*, fr. MF, fr. L *contention-*, *contentio*, fr. *contentus*, pp. of *contendere* to contend] **1 :** an act or instance of contending **:** STRIFE **2 :** a point advanced or maintained in a debate or argument **syn** see DISCORD

con·ten·tious \kən-'ten-chəs\ *adj* **1 :** ARGUMENTATIVE, QUARRELSOME **2 :** likely to cause contention ⟨a ~ argument⟩ **syn** see BELLIGERENT — **con·ten·tious·ly** *adv* — **con·ten·tious·ness** *n*

con·tent·ment \kən-'tent-mənt\ *n* **1 :** the quality or state of being contented **2 :** something that contents

con·ter·mi·nous \kən-'tər-mə-nəs, kän-\ *adj* [L *conterminus*, fr. *com-* + *terminus* boundary — more at TERM] **1 :** having a common boundary **2 :** COTERMINOUS **3 :** enclosed within one common boundary — **con·ter·mi·nous·ly** *adv*

1**con·test** \kən-'test, 'kän-,\ *vb* [MF *contester*, fr. L *contestari* (*litem*) to bring an action at law, fr. *contestari* to call to witness, fr. *com-* + *testis* witness] *vt* **:** to make the subject of dispute, contention, or litigation; *esp* **:** DISPUTE, CHALLENGE ~ *vi* **:** STRIVE, VIE — **con·test·able** \-ə-bəl\ *adj* — **con·test·er** *n*

2**con·test** \'kän-,test\ *n* **1 :** a struggle for superiority or victory **2 :** a competition in which each contestant performs without direct contact with or interference from his competitors

con·tes·tant \kən-'tes-tənt, *also* 'kän-,\ *n* **1 :** one that participates in a contest **2 :** one that contests an award or decision

con·tes·ta·tion \,kän-,tes-'tā-shən\ *n* **:** CONTROVERSY

con·text \'kän-,tekst\ *n* [ME, weaving together of words, fr. L *contextus* connection of words, coherence, fr. *contextus*, pp. of *contexere* to weave together, fr. *com-* + *texere* to weave] **1 :** the parts of a discourse that surround a word or passage and can throw light upon its meaning **2 :** MILIEU, ENVIRONMENT — **con·tex·tu·al** \kän-'teks-chə(-wə)l, kən-\ *adj* — **con·tex·tu·al·ly** \-ē\ *adv*

con·tex·ture \kən-'teks-chər, 'kän-,, kän-'\ *n* [F, fr. L *contextus*, pp.] **1 :** the act, process, or manner of weaving parts into a whole; *also* **:** a structure so formed ⟨a ~ of lies⟩ **2 :** CONTEXT

con·ti·gu·ity \,känt-ə-'gyü-ət-ē\ *n* **:** the quality or state of being contiguous **:** PROXIMITY

con·tig·u·ous \kən-'tig-yə-wəs\ *adj* [L *contiguus*, fr. *contingere* to have contact with] **1 :** being in actual contact **:** TOUCHING **2 :** ADJOINING **3 :** next or near in time or sequence **syn** see ADJACENT — **con·tig·u·ous·ly** *adv* — **con·tig·u·ous·ness** *n*

con·ti·nence \'känt-ən-ən(t)s\ *n* **1 :** SELF-RESTRAINT **2 :** ability to refrain from a bodily activity

1**con·ti·nent** \'känt-ən-ənt\ *adj* [ME, fr. MF, fr. L *continent-*, *continens*, fr. prp. of *continēre* to hold in] **1 :** exercising continence **2** *obs* **:** RESTRICTIVE — **con·ti·nent·ly** *adv*

2**con·ti·nent** \'känt-ən-ənt, 'känt-nənt\ *n* [in senses 1 & 2, fr. L *continent-*, *continens*, prp. of *continēre* to hold together, contain; in senses 3 & 4, fr. L *continent-*, *continens* continuous mass of land, mainland, fr. *continent-*, *continens*, prp.] **1** *archaic* **:** CONTAINER, RECEPTACLE **2** *archaic* **:** a summary example **:** EPITOME **3 :** MAINLAND **4 a :** one of the usu. seven great divisions of land on the globe **b** *cap* **:** the continent of Europe — used with *the*

1**con·ti·nen·tal** \,känt-ən-'ent-əl\ *adj* **1 :** of, relating to, or characteristic of a continent ⟨~ waters⟩; *specif* **:** of or relating to the continent of Europe as distinguished from the British Isles **2** *often cap* **:** of or relating to the colonies later forming the U.S. ⟨*Continental* Congress⟩ — **con·ti·nen·tal·ly** \-əl-ē\ *adv*

2**continental** *n* **1 a** *often cap* **:** an American soldier of the Revolution in the Continental army **b :** a piece of Continental paper currency **c :** an inhabitant of a continent and esp. the continent of Europe **2 :** the least bit ⟨not worth a ~⟩

continental code *n* **:** the international Morse code

continental divide *n* **:** a divide separating streams which flow to opposite sides of a continent

continental shelf *n* **:** a shallow submarine plain of varying width forming a border to a continent and typically ending in a steep slope to the oceanic abyss

con·tin·gence \kən-'tin-jən(t)s\ *n* **1 :** TANGENCY **2 :** CONTINGENCY

con·tin·gen·cy \kən-'tin-jən-sē\ *n* **1 :** the quality or state of being contingent **2 :** a contingent event or condition: as **a :** a possible or unforeseen occurrence **b :** something liable to happen as an adjunct to something else **syn** see JUNCTURE

1**con·tin·gent** \kən-'tin-jənt\ *adj* [ME, fr. MF, fr. L *contingent-*, *contingens*, prp. of *contingere* to have contact with, befall, fr. *com-* + *tangere* to touch] **1 :** likely but not certain to happen **:** POSSIBLE **2 a :** happening by chance or unforeseen causes **b :** intended for use in circumstances not completely foreseen **c :** UNPREDICTABLE **3 :** dependent on or conditioned by something else **4 :** not logically necessary; *esp* **:** EMPIRICAL, FACTUAL **5 :** not necessitated **:** FREE **syn** see ACCIDENTAL — **con·tin·gent·ly** *adv*

2**contingent** *n* **1 :** something contingent **:** CONTINGENCY **2 :** a quota or share esp. of persons (as troops or athletes) supplied from or representative of an area or group

con·tin·u·al \kən-'tin-yə(-wə)l\ *adj* [ME, fr. MF, fr. L *continuus* continuous] **1 :** continuing indefinitely in time without interruption ⟨~ fear⟩ **2 :** recurring in steady rapid succession **3 :** forming a continuous series — **con·tin·u·al·ly** \-ē\ *adv*

syn CONTINUOUS, CONSTANT, INCESSANT, PERPETUAL, PERENNIAL: CONTINUAL implies a close prolonged succession or recurrence; CONTINUOUS usu. implies an uninterrupted flow or spatial extension; CONSTANT implies uniform or persistent occurrence or recurrence; INCESSANT implies ceaseless or uninterrupted activity; PERPETUAL suggests unfailing repetition or lasting duration; PERENNIAL implies enduring existence often through constant renewal

con·tin·u·ance \kən-'tin-yə-wən(t)s\ *n* **1 a :** the act or process of continuing in a state, condition, or course of action **b :** PROLONGATION, DURATION **2 :** CONTINUITY **3 :** SEQUEL **4 :** adjournment of court proceedings to a future day **syn** see CONTINUATION

con·tin·u·ant \-yə-wənt\ *n* **:** something that continues or serves as a continuation (as a consonant that may be prolonged without alteration during one emission of breath) — **continuant** *adj*

con·tin·u·ate \-wət, -ˌwāt\ *adj, obs* **:** CONTINUOUS

con·tin·u·a·tion \kən-ˌtin-yə-'wā-shən\ *n* **1 :** continuance in or prolongation of a state or activity **2 :** resumption after an interruption **3 :** something that continues, increases, or adds
syn CONTINUANCE, CONTINUITY: CONTINUATION suggests prolongation or resumption; CONTINUANCE implies duration, perseverance, or persistent lingering; CONTINUITY stresses uninterrupted connection, sequence, or extent

con·tin·u·a·tive \kən-'tin-yə-ˌwāt-iv, -yə-wət-iv\ *adj* **:** relating to, causing, or in the process of continuation

con·tin·u·a·tor \kən-'tin-yə-ˌwāt-ər\ *n* **:** one that continues

con·tin·ue \kən-'tin-(ˌ)yü, -yə(-w)\ *vb* [ME *continuen*, fr. MF *continuer*, fr. L *continuare*, fr. *continuus*] *vi* **1 :** to maintain without interruption a condition, course, or action **2 :** to remain in existence **:** ENDURE **3 :** to remain in a place or condition **:** STAY **4 :** to resume an activity after interruption ~ *vt* **1 a :** to carry on or keep up **:** MAINTAIN ⟨*continued* walking⟩ **b :** PROLONG; *specif* **:** to resume after intermission **2 :** to cause to continue **3 :** to allow to remain in a place or condition **:** RETAIN **4 :** to postpone (a legal proceeding) by a continuance — **con·tin·u·er** \-yə-wər\ *n*
syn CONTINUE, LAST, ENDURE, ABIDE, PERSIST mean to exist indefinitely. CONTINUE applies to a process going on without ending; LAST stresses existing beyond what is normal or expected; ENDURE adds an implication of resisting destructive forces or agencies; ABIDE implies stable and constant existing esp. as opposed to mutability; PERSIST suggests outlasting the normal or appointed time and often connotes obstinacy or doggedness

con·tin·ued *adj* **1 :** lasting or extending without interruption **:** CONTINUOUS **2 :** resumed after interruption ⟨~ story⟩

continued fraction *n* **:** a fraction whose numerator is an integer and whose denominator is an integer plus a fraction whose numerator is an integer and whose denominator is an integer plus a fraction and so on

con·tin·u·ing \kən-'tin-yə-wiŋ\ *adj* **1 :** CONTINUOUS, CONSTANT **2 :** needing no renewal **:** LASTING

con·ti·nu·ity \ˌkänt-ᵊn-'(y)ü-ət-ē\ *n* **1 a :** uninterrupted connection, succession, or union **:** COHESION, COHERENCE **b :** persistence without essential change **c :** uninterrupted duration in time **2 :** something that has, exhibits, or provides continuity: as **a :** a script or scenario in the performing arts **b :** transitional spoken or musical matter esp. for a radio or television program **c :** the story and dialogue of a comic strip **syn** see CONTINUATION

con·tin·uo \kən-'tin-(y)ə-ˌwō\ *n* [It, fr. *continuo* continuous, fr. L *continuus*] **:** a bass part usu. for keyboard instrument used esp. in baroque ensemble music

con·tin·u·ous \kən-'tin-yə-wəs\ *adj* [L *continuus*, fr. *continēre* to hold together] **1 :** marked by uninterrupted extension in space, time, or sequence **2** *of a function* **:** having a numerical difference between a value at a point and a nearby point that can be made arbitrarily small as the second point nears the first **syn** see CONTINUAL — **con·tin·u·ous·ly** *adv* — **con·tin·u·ous·ness** *n*

con·tin·u·um \kən-'tin-yə-wəm\ *n, pl* **con·tin·ua** \-wə\ *also* **continuums** [L, neut. of *continuus*] **1 :** something absolutely continuous and homogeneous of which no distinction of content can be affirmed except by reference to something else (as duration) **2 a :** something in which a fundamental common character is discernible amid a series of insensible or indefinite variations **b :** an uninterrupted ordered sequence **c :** an identity of substance uniting discrete parts; *broadly* **:** CONTINUITY **3 :** a set with the same transfinite cardinal number as the set of real numbers

con·tort \kən-'tȯ(ə)rt\ *vb* [L *contortus*, pp. of *contorquēre*, fr. *com-* + *torquēre* to twist] *vt* **:** to twist in a violent manner ~ *vi* **:** to twist into a strained shape or expression **syn** see DEFORM — **con·tor·tion** \-'tȯr-shən\ *n* — **con·tor·tive** \-'tȯrt-iv\ *adj*

con·tort·ed \kən-'tȯrt-əd\ *adj* **:** CONVOLUTE ⟨~ leaves⟩

con·tor·tion·ist \kən-'tȯr-sh(ə-)nəst\ *n* **:** one who contorts; *specif* **:** an acrobat who specializes in unnatural body postures — **con·tor·tion·is·tic** \kən-ˌtȯr-shə-'nis-tik\ *adj*

[1]**con·tour** \'kän-ˌtu̇(ə)r\ *n* [F, fr. It *contorno* fr. *contornare* to round off, sketch in outline, fr. L *com-* + *tornare* to turn in a lathe, fr. *tornus* lathe] **:** the outline of an esp. curving or irregular figure; *also* **:** the line representing this outline **syn** see OUTLINE

[2]**contour** *vt* **1 a :** to shape the contour of **b :** to shape to fit contours **2 :** to construct (as a road) in conformity to a contour

[3]**contour** *adj* **1 :** following contour lines or forming furrows or ridges along them to retard erosion of sloping land by runoff rainwater ⟨~ plowing⟩ **2 :** made to fit the contour of something

contour feather *n* **:** one of the medium-sized feathers that form the general covering of a bird and determine the external contour

contour line *n* **:** a line (as on a map) connecting the points on a land surface that have the same elevation

contour map *n* **:** a map having contour lines

contra- *prefix* [ME, fr. L, fr. *contra* against, opposite — more at COUNTER] **1 :** against **:** contrary **:** contrasting ⟨*contra*distinction⟩ **2 :** pitched below normal bass ⟨*contra*octave⟩

con·tra·band \'kän-trə-ˌband\ *n* [It *contrabbando*, fr. ML *contrabannum*, fr. *contra-* + *bannus*, *bannum* decree, of Gmc origin] **1 :** illegal or prohibited traffic **2 :** goods or merchandise whose importation, exportation, or possession is forbidden; *also* **:** smuggled goods **3 :** a Negro slave who during the Civil War escaped to or was brought within the Union lines — **contraband** *adj*

con·tra·band·ist \-ˌban-dəst\ *n* **:** SMUGGLER

con·tra·bass \'kän-trə-ˌbās\ *n* [It *contrabbasso*, fr. *contra-* + *basso* bass] **:** DOUBLE BASS — **con·tra·bass·ist** \-ˌbā-səst\ *n*

con·tra·bas·soon \ˌkän-trə-bə-'sün, -(ˌ)ba-\ *n* **:** the largest member of the oboe family an octave lower in pitch than the bassoon

con·tra·cep·tion \ˌkän-trə-'sep-shən\ *n* [*contra-* + *conception*] **:** voluntary prevention of conception or impregnation — **con·tra·cep·tive** \-'sep-tiv\ *adj or n*

[1]**con·tract** \'kän-ˌtrakt\ *n* [ME, fr. L *contractus*, fr. *contractus*, pp. of *contrahere* to draw together, make a contract, reduce in size, fr. *com-* + *trahere* to draw] **1 a :** a binding agreement between two or more persons or parties **:** COVENANT **b :** BETROTHAL **2 :** a writing made by the parties to evidence the terms and conditions of a contract **3 :** the department or principles of law having to do with contracts **4 :** an undertaking to win a specified number of tricks or points in bridge **5** [[2]*contract*] **:** a word or form undergoing contraction or resulting from contraction

[2]**contract** *adj* **:** CONTRACTED ⟨a ~ noun⟩

[3]**con·tract** *vt 1a & vi 1 usu* 'kän-ˌtrakt, *others usu* kən-'trakt\ *vb* [partly fr. MF *contracter* to agree upon, fr. L *contractus* n.; partly fr. L *contractus*, pp. of *contrahere* to draw together] *vt* **1 a :** to establish or undertake by contract **b :** BETROTH **2 a :** CATCH ⟨~ a disease⟩ **b :** INCUR ⟨~ an obligation⟩ **3 a :** LIMIT, RESTRICT **b :** KNIT, WRINKLE ⟨frown ~*ed* his brow⟩ **c :** to draw together **:** CONCENTRATE **4 :** SHORTEN, SHRINK **5 :** to shorten (as a word) by omitting one or more sounds or letters ~ *vi* **1 :** to make a contract **2 a :** to diminish in size **b** *of muscle* **:** to draw to shorter and broader size — **con·tract·ibil·i·ty** \kən-ˌtrak-tə-'bil-ət-ē, ˌkän-\ *n* — **con·tract·ible** \kən-'trak-tə-bəl, 'kän-ˌ\ *adj*
syn CONTRACT, SHRINK, CONDENSE, COMPRESS, CONSTRICT, DEFLATE mean to decrease in bulk or volume. CONTRACT is a general antonym for *expand* and applies to any drawing together of bounding surfaces or component particles or to a reducing of area, compass, or length; SHRINK implies a contracting or a loss of material and stresses a falling short of original dimensions; CONDENSE implies a reducing of something homogeneous to greater compactness without significant loss of content; COMPRESS implies a pressing into a small compass and definite shape usu. against resistance; CONSTRICT implies a tightening that reduces diameter; DEFLATE implies a contracting by reducing the internal pressure of contained air or gas **syn** see in addition INCUR

contract bridge \ˌkän-ˌtrak(t)-\ *n* **:** a card game identical with auction bridge except that odd tricks do not count toward game or slam bonuses unless undertaken in the contract

con·trac·tile \kən-'trak-tᵊl\ *adj* **:** having the power or property of contracting — **con·trac·til·i·ty** \ˌkän-ˌtrak-'til-ət-ē\ *n*

con·trac·tion \kən-'trak-shən\ *n* **1 a :** the action or process of contracting **:** the state of being contracted **b :** the shortening and thickening of a functioning muscle or muscle fiber **c :** a reduction in business activity **2 :** a shortening of a word, syllable, or word group by omission of a sound or letter; *also* **:** a form produced by such shortening — **con·trac·tion·al** \-'trak-shnəl, -shən-ᵊl\ *adj* — **con·trac·tive** \-'trak-tiv\ *adj*

con·trac·tor \'kän-ˌtrak-tər, kən-'\ *n* **1 :** one that contracts or is party to a contract: as **a :** one that contracts to perform work or provide supplies on a large scale **b :** one that contracts to erect buildings **2 :** something (as a muscle) that contracts or shortens

con·trac·tu·al \kən-'trak-chə(-wə)l, kän-, -'traksh-wəl\ *adj* [L *contractus* contract] **:** of, relating to, or constituting a contract — **con·trac·tu·al·ly** \-ē\ *adv*

con·trac·ture \kən-'trak-chər\ *n* **:** a permanent shortening (as of muscle, tendon, or scar tissue) producing deformity or distortion

con·tra·dict \ˌkän-trə-'dikt\ *vt* [L *contradictus*, pp. of *contradicere*, fr. *contra-* + *dicere* to say, speak] **1 :** to resist or oppose in argument **2 a :** to assert the contrary of **:** GAINSAY **b :** to deny the truth of **3 a :** to be the contradictory of **b :** to go counter to **c :** to act in a manner contrary to **syn** see DENY — **con·tra·dict·able** \-'dik-tə-bəl\ *adj* — **con·tra·dic·tor** \-'dik-tər\ *n*

con·tra·dic·tion \ˌkän-trə-'dik-shən\ *n* **1 :** the act of contradicting **2 :** an expression or proposition containing contradictory parts **3 a :** logical incongruity **b :** opposition of inherent factors

con·tra·dic·tious \-shəs\ *adj* **1 :** CONTRADICTORY, OPPOSITE **2 :** given to or marked by contradiction **:** CONTRARY

con·tra·dic·to·ri·ly \-'dik-t(ə-)rə-lē\ *adv* **:** in a contradictory manner

con·tra·dic·to·ri·ness \-t(ə-)rē-nəs\ *n* **:** the quality or state of being contradictory

[1]**con·tra·dic·to·ry** \ˌkän-trə-'dik-t(ə-)rē\ *n* **1 a :** something that contradicts **b :** OPPOSITE, CONTRARY **2 :** a proposition so related to another that if either is true or false the other is false or true

[2]**contradictory** *adj* **1 :** CONTRADICTIOUS **2 :** involving, causing, or constituting a contradiction **syn** see OPPOSITE

con·tra·dis·tinc·tion \ˌkän-trə-dis-'tiŋ(k)-shən\ *n* **:** distinction by contrast ⟨painting in ~ to sculpture⟩ — **con·tra·dis·tinc·tive** \-'tiŋ(k)-tiv\ *adj* — **con·tra·dis·tinc·tive·ly** *adv*

con·tra·dis·tin·guish \-'tiŋ-gwish\ *vt* **:** to distinguish by contrast of qualities

con·trail \'kän-ˌtrāl\ *n* [*con*densation *trail*] **:** streaks of condensed water vapor created in the air by an airplane or rocket at high altitudes

con·tra·in·di·cate \ˌkän-trə-'in-də-ˌkāt\ *vt* **:** to make (a treatment or procedure) inadvisable — **con·tra·in·di·ca·tion** \-ˌin-də-'kā-shən\ *n* — **con·tra·in·dic·a·tive** \-in-'dik-ət-iv\ *adj*

con·tra·lat·er·al \-'lat-ə-rəl, -'la-trəl\ *adj* [ISV] **:** occurring on or acting in conjunction with similar parts on an opposite side

con·tral·to \kən-'tral-(ˌ)tō\ *n, often attrib* [It, fr. *contra-* + *alto*] **1 :** the lowest female singing voice **:** a singer with such a voice **2 :** the part sung by a contralto

con·tra·oc·tave \ˌkän-trə-'äk-tiv, -təv, -ˌtāv\ *n* **:** the musical octave that begins on the third C below middle C

con·tra·po·si·tion \-pə-'zish-ən\ *n* [LL *contraposition-*, *contrapositio*, fr. L *contrapositus*, pp. of *contraponere* to place opposite, fr. *contra-* + *ponere* to place] **:** OPPOSITION, ANTITHESIS

con·trap·tion \kən-'trap-shən\ *n* [perh. blend of *contrivance*, *trap*, and *invention*] **:** CONTRIVANCE, GADGET

con·tra·pun·tal \ˌkän-trə-'pənt-ᵊl\ *adj* [It *contrappunto* counterpoint, fr. ML *contrapunctus*] **1 :** of or relating to counterpoint **2 :** POLYPHONIC — **con·tra·pun·tal·ly** \-ᵊl-ē\ *adv*

con·tra·pun·tist \-'pənt-əst\ *n* **:** one who writes counterpoint

con·tra·ri·ety \ˌkän-trə-'rī-ət-ē\ *n* [ME *contrariete*, fr. MF *contrarieté*, fr. LL *contrarietat-*, *contrarietas*, fr. L *contrarius* contrary] **1 :** the quality or state of being contrary **2 :** something contrary

con·trar·i·ly \'kän-ˌtrer-ə-lē, kən-'\ *adv* **:** in a contrary way

con·trar·i·ness \-ē-nəs\ *n* **:** the quality or state of being contrary

con·trar·i·ous \kən-'trer-ē-əs, kän-\ *adj* **:** PERVERSE, ANTAGONISTIC

con·trari·wise \'kän-ˌtrer-ē-ˌwīz, kən-'\ *adv* **1 :** on the contrary **2 :** CONVERSELY, VICE VERSA **3 :** PERVERSELY, CONTRARILY

[1]**con·trary** \'kän-ˌtrer-ē\ *n* **1 :** a fact or condition incompatible with another **:** OPPOSITE **2 :** one of a pair of opposites **3 a :** a proposition so related to another that though both may be false they cannot both be true **b :** either of two terms (as black and white) that cannot both be affirmed of the same subject — **by contraries :** in a manner opposite to what is logical or expected

— **on the contrary** : just the opposite : NO — **to the contrary** : NOTWITHSTANDING

[2]**con·trary** \'kän-,trer-ē, *in sense 4 often* kən-'tre(ə)r-ē\ *adj* [ME *contrarie*, fr. MF *contraire*, fr. L *contrarius*, fr. *contra* opposite] **1 a** : diametrically different **b** : opposite in character : tending to an opposing course **c** : mutually opposed : ANTAGONISTIC **2** : opposite in position, direction, or nature **3** : UNFAVORABLE — used of wind or weather **4** : disposed to contradict or oppose
syn PERVERSE, RESTIVE, BALKY, FROWARD, WAYWARD: CONTRARY implies a temperamental unwillingness to accept dictation or advice; PERVERSE may imply wrongheaded, determined, or cranky opposition to what is reasonable or normal; RESTIVE suggests unwillingness or inability to submit to discipline or follow orders; BALKY suggests a refusing to proceed or acquiesce for no evident or explainable reason; FROWARD implies habitual and often defiant disobedience; WAYWARD suggests strong-willed capriciousness and irregularity in behavior **syn** see in addition OPPOSITE

[3]**con·trary** *like* [2]CONTRARY\ *adv* : CONTRARILY, CONTRARIWISE

[1]**con·trast** \'kän-,trast\ *n* **1** : the act or process of contrasting : the state of being contrasted **2** : a person or thing that exhibits differences when contrasted **3** : diversity of adjacent parts in color, emotion, and tone

[2]**con·trast** \kən-'trast, 'kän-,\ *vb* [F *contraster*, fr. MF, to oppose, resist, alter. of *contrester*, fr. (assumed) VL *contrastare*, fr. L *contra-* + *stare* to stand] *vi* : to exhibit contrast ~ *vt* : to put in contrast **syn** see COMPARE — **con·trast·able** \-ə-bəl\ *adj*

con·trasty \'kän-,tras-tē, kən-'\ *adj* : having or producing in photography great contrast between highlights and shadows

con·tra·vene \,kän-trə-'vēn\ *vt* [MF or LL; MF *contrevenir*, fr. LL *contravenire*, fr. L *contra-* + *venire* to come] **1** : to go or act contrary to ⟨~ a law⟩ **2** : to oppose in argument : CONTRADICT ⟨~ a proposition⟩ **syn** see DENY — **con·tra·ven·er** *n*

con·tra·ven·tion \,kän-trə-'ven-chən\ *n* [MF, fr. LL *contraventus*, pp. of *contravenire*] : the act of contravening : VIOLATION

con·tre·danse \'kän-trə-,dan(t)s, kō^{n}-trə-dä^{n}s\ *or* **con·tra dance** \'kän-trə-,dan(t)s\ *n* [F *contredanse*, by folk etymology fr. E *country-dance*] **1** : a folk dance in which couples face each other in two lines or in a square **2** : a piece of music for a contredanse

con·tre·temps \'kän-trə-,tä^{n}, kō^{n}-trə-tä^{n}\ *n, pl* **con·tre·temps** \-(,)tä^{n}(z)\ [F, fr. *contre-* counter- + *temps* time, fr. L *tempus*] : an inopportune embarrassing occurrence : MISHAP

con·trib·ute \kən-'trib-yət\ *vb* [L *contributus*, pp. of *contribuere*, fr. *com-* + *tribuere* to grant — more at TRIBUTE] *vt* **1** : to give or supply in common with others **2** : to supply (as an article) for a publication ~ *vi* **1 a** : to give a part to a common fund or store **b** : to share in a joint effort **2** : to submit articles to a publication **syn** see CONDUCE — **con·trib·u·tor** \-yət-ər\ *n*

con·tri·bu·tion \,kän-trə-'byü-shən\ *n* **1** : an esp. extraordinary levy or tax **2** : the act of contributing; *also* : the sum or thing contributed **3** : a writing for publication esp. in a periodical — **con·trib·u·tive** \kən-'trib-yət-iv\ *adj* — **con·trib·u·tive·ly** *adv*

con·trib·u·to·ry \kən-'trib-yə-,tōr-ē, -,tòr-\ *adj* **1 a** : contributing to a common fund or enterprise **b** : subject to a levy of supplies, money, or men **2** : of, relating to, or forming a contribution

con·trite \'kän-,trīt, kən-'\ *adj* [ME *contrit*, fr. MF, fr. ML, fr. L, pp. of *conterere* to grind, bruise, fr. *com-* + *terere* to rub] **1** : grieving and penitent for sin or shortcoming **2** : proceeding from contrition ⟨~ sighs⟩ — **con·trite·ly** *adv* — **con·trite·ness** *n*

con·tri·tion \kən-'trish-ən\ *n* : the state of being contrite : REPENTANCE **syn** see PENITENCE

con·triv·ance \kən-'trī-vən(t)s\ *n* **1** : the act or faculty of contriving : the state of being contrived **2** : a thing contrived; *esp* : a mechanical device

con·trive \kən-'trīv\ *vb* [ME *controven*, *contreven*, fr. MF *controver*, fr. LL *contropare* to compare] *vt* **1 a** : DEVISE, PLAN **b** : to fabricate as a work of art or ingenuity **2** : to bring about by stratagem or with difficulty ~ *vi* : to make schemes — **con·triv·er** *n*

con·trived *adj* : ARTIFICIAL, LABORED

[1]**con·trol** \kən-'trōl\ *vt* **con·trolled**; **con·trol·ling** [ME *controllen*, fr. MF *contreroller*, fr. *contrerolle* copy of an account, audit, fr. *contre-* counter- + *rolle* roll, account] **1** : to check, test, or verify by evidence or experiments **2 a** : to exercise restraining or directing influence over : REGULATE **b** : to have power over : RULE **syn** see CONDUCT — **con·trol·la·ble** \-'trō-lə-bəl\ *adj* — **con·trol·ment** \-'trōl-mənt\ *n*

[2]**control** *n* **1 a** : an act or instance of controlling **b** : skill in the use of a tool, instrument, technique, or artistic medium **c** : direction, regulation, and coordination of production, administration, and other business activities **2** : RESTRAINT, RESERVE **3** : a means or method of controlling : one that controls: as **a** : the subject of a control experiment **b** : a mechanism used to regulate or guide the operation of a machine, apparatus, or system **c** : a personality or spirit believed to actuate the utterances or performances of a spiritualist medium **syn** see POWER

control experiment *n* : an experiment to check the results of other experiments

con·trol·ler \kən-'trō-lər, 'kän-,\ *n* [ME *conterroller*, fr. MF *contrerolleur*, fr. *contrerolle*] **1 a** : COMPTROLLER 1 **b** : COMPTROLLER 2 **c** : the chief accounting officer of a business enterprise or an institution (as a college) **2** : one that controls or has power or authority to control — **con·trol·ler·ship** \-,ship\ *n*

con·tro·ver·sial \,kän-trə-'vər-shəl, -'vər-sē-əl\ *adj* **1** : subject to, relating to, or arousing controversy ⟨a ~ public figure⟩ **2** : given to controversy : DISPUTATIOUS — **con·tro·ver·sial·ism** \-,iz-əm\ *n* — **con·tro·ver·sial·ist** \-əst\ *n* — **con·tro·ver·sial·ly** \-ē\ *adv*

con·tro·ver·sy \'kän-trə-,vər-sē\ *n* [ME *controversie*, fr. L *controversia*, fr. *controversus* disputable, lit., turned opposite, fr. *contro-* (akin to *contra-*) + *versus*, pp. of *vertere* to turn — more at WORTH] **1** : a discussion marked esp. by expression of opposing views : DISPUTE **2** : QUARREL, STRIFE

con·tro·vert \'kän-trə-,vərt, ,kän-trə-'\ *vb* [*controversy*] *vt* : to dispute or oppose by reasoning : DENY, CONTRADICT ⟨~ a point in a discussion⟩ ~ *vi* : to engage in controversy **syn** see DISPROVE — **con·tro·vert·er** \-ər\ *n* — **con·tro·vert·ible** \-ə-bəl\ *adj*

con·tu·ma·cious \,kän-t(y)ə-'mā-shəs, ,kän-chə-\ *adj* : stubbornly disobedient : REBELLIOUS — **con·tu·ma·cious·ly** *adv*

con·tu·ma·cy \kən-'t(y)ü-mə-sē; 'kän-t(y)ə-, 'kän-chə-\ *n* [ME *contumacie*, fr. L *contumacia*, fr. *contumac-*, *contumax* insubordinate, fr. *com-* + *tumēre* to swell, be proud] : stubborn resistance to authority; *specif* : willful contempt of court

con·tu·me·li·ous \,kän-t(y)ə-'mē-lē-əs, ,kän-chə-\ *adj* : insolently abusive and humiliating — **con·tu·me·li·ous·ly** *adv*

con·tu·me·ly \kən-'t(y)ü-mə-lē; 'kän-t(y)ə-,mē-lē, 'kän-chə-; 'käntəm-lē\ *n* [ME *contumelie*, fr. MF, fr. L *contumelia*; perh. akin to L *contumacia*] : rude language or treatment arising from haughtiness and contempt; *also* : an instance of such language or treatment

con·tuse \kən-'t(y)üz\ *vt* [MF *contuser*, fr. L *contusus*, pp. of *contundere* to crush, bruise, fr. *com-* + *tundere* to beat — more at STINT] : to injure (tissue) usu. without laceration : BRUISE — **con·tu·sion** \-'t(y)ü-zhən\ *n*

co·nun·drum \kə-'nən-drəm\ *n* [origin unknown] **1** : a riddle whose answer is or involves a pun **2 a** : a question or problem having only a conjectural answer **b** : an intricate and difficult problem **syn** see MYSTERY

con·ur·ba·tion \,kän-(,)ər-'bā-shən\ *n* [*com-* + L *urb-*, *urbs* city] : an aggregation or continuous network of urban communities

con·va·lesce \,kän-və-'les\ *vi* [L *convalescere*, fr. *com-* + *valescere* to grow strong, fr. *valēre* to be strong, be well — more at WIELD] : to recover health and strength gradually after sickness or weakness

con·va·les·cence \,kän-və-'les-^{ə}n(t)s\ *n* : the process or period of convalescing — **con·va·les·cent** \-^{ə}nt\ *adj or n*

con·vect \kən-'vekt\ *vb* [back-formation fr. *convection*] *vi* : to transfer heat by convection ~ *vt* : to circulate (warm air) by convection

con·vec·tion \kən-'vek-shən\ *n* [LL *convection-*, *convectio*, fr. L *convectus*, pp. of *convehere* to bring together, fr. *com-* + *vehere* to carry] **1** : the action or process of conveying **2 a** : the circulatory motion that occurs in a fluid at a nonuniform temperature owing to the variation of its density and the action of gravity **b** : the transfer of heat by this automatic circulation of a fluid — **con·vec·tion·al** \-shnəl, -shən-^{ə}l\ *adj* — **con·vec·tive** \-'vek-tiv\ *adj*

con·vec·tor \-'vek-tər\ *n* : a heating unit in which air heated by contact with a heating device in a casing circulates by convection

con·vene \kən-'vēn\ *vb* [ME *convenen*, fr. MF *convenir* to come together] *vi* : to come together in a body ~ *vt* **1** : to summon before a tribunal **2** : to cause to assemble **syn** see SUMMON — **con·ven·er** *n*

con·ve·nience \kən-'vē-nyən(t)s\ *n* **1** : fitness or suitability for performing an action or fulfilling a requirement **2** : an appliance, device, or service conducive to comfort **3** : a suitable time : OPPORTUNITY **4** : freedom from discomfort : EASE

con·ve·nien·cy \-nyən-sē\ *n, archaic* : CONVENIENCE

con·ve·nient \kən-'vē-nyənt\ *adj* [ME, fr. L *convenient-*, *conveniens*, fr. prp. of *convenire* to come together, be suitable] **1** *obs* : SUITABLE, PROPER **2 a** : suited to personal comfort or to easy performance **b** : suited to a particular situation **3** : near at hand : HANDY — **con·ve·nient·ly** *adv*

[1]**con·vent** \'kän-vənt, -,vent\ *n* [ME *covent*, fr. OF, fr. ML *conventus*, fr. L, assembly, fr. *conventus*, pp. of *convenire*] : a local community or house of a religious order or congregation; *specif* : an establishment of nuns **syn** see CLOISTER

[2]**con·vent** \kən-'vent\ *vb* [L *conventus*, pp.] *obs* : CONVENE

con·ven·ti·cle \kən-'vent-i-kəl\ *n* [ME, fr. L *conventiculum*, dim. of *conventus* assembly] **1** : ASSEMBLY, MEETING **2** : an assembly of an irregular or unlawful character **3** : an assembly for religious worship; *esp* : a secret meeting for worship not sanctioned by law **4** : MEETINGHOUSE — **con·ven·ti·cler** \-i-k(ə-)lər\ *n*

con·ven·tion \kən-'ven-chən\ *n* [ME, fr. MF or L; MF, fr. L *convention-*, *conventio*, fr. *conventus*, pp. of *convenire* to come together, be suitable, fr. *com-* + *venire* to come] **1 a** : AGREEMENT, CONTRACT **b** : an agreement between states for regulation of matters affecting all of them **c** : a compact between opposing commanders esp. concerning prisoner exchange or armistice **d** : a general agreement about basic principles; *also* : a principle that is true by convention **2 a** : the summoning or convening of an assembly **b** : an assembly of persons met for a common purpose **c** : the usu. state or national organization of a religious denomination **3 a** : usage or custom esp. in social matters **b** : a rule of conduct or behavior **c** : a practice in bidding or playing that conveys information between partners in a card game (as bridge)

con·ven·tion·al \kən-'vench-nəl, -'ven-chən-^{ə}l\ *adj* **1** : formed by agreement or compact **2 a** : according with or based on convention **b** : TRITE, COMMONPLACE **3 a** : according with a mode of artistic representation that simplifies or provides symbols or substitutes for natural forms **b** : of traditional design **4** : of, resembling, or relating to a convention, assembly, or public meeting **syn** see CEREMONIAL — **con·ven·tion·al·ism** \-,iz-əm\ *n* — **con·ven·tion·al·ist** \-əst\ *n* — **con·ven·tion·al·ly** \-ē\ *adv*

con·ven·tion·al·i·ty \kən-,ven-chə-'nal-ət-ē\ *n* **1** : the quality or state of being conventional; *specif* : adherence to conventions **2** : a conventional usage, practice, or thing

con·ven·tion·al·iza·tion \kən-,vench-nə-lə-'zā-shən, -,ven-chən-^{ə}l-ə-'zā-\ *n* : the act, practice, or product of conventionalizing

con·ven·tion·al·ize \kən-'vench-nə-,līz, -'ven-chən-^{ə}l-,īz\ *vt* : to make conventional

con·ven·tion·eer \kən-,ven-chə-'ni(ə)r\ *n* : a person attending a convention

[1]**con·ven·tu·al** \kən-'vench-(ə-)wəl, kän-\ *adj* [ME, fr. MF or ML; MF, fr. ML *conventualis*, fr. *conventus* convent] **1** : of, relating to, or befitting a convent or monastic life : MONASTIC **2** *cap* : of or relating to the Conventuals — **con·ven·tu·al·ly** \-ē\ *adv*

[2]**conventual** \"\ *n* **1** : a member of a conventual community **2** *cap* : a member of the Order of Friars Minor Conventual forming a branch of the first order of St. Francis of Assisi under a mitigated rule

con·verge \kən-'vərj\ *vb* [ML *convergere*, fr. L *com-* + *vergere* to bend, incline] *vi* **1** : to tend or move toward one point or one another : come together : MEET **2** : to come together and unite in a common interest or focus **3** : to approach a limit as the number of terms increases without limit ~ *vt* : to cause to converge

con·ver·gence \kən-'vər-jən(t)s\ *n* **1** : the act of converging and esp. moving toward union or uniformity; *esp* : coordinated movement of the two eyes resulting in impingement of the image of a point on corresponding retinal areas **2** : the condition of converging; *esp* : independent development of similar characters (as of bodily structure or cultural traits) often associated with similarity of habits or environment — **con·ver·gent** \-jənt\ *adj*

con·ver·gen·cy \-jən-sē\ *n* : CONVERGENCE

con·vers·able \kən-'vər-sə-bəl\ *adj* **1** : pleasant and easy to converse with **2** *archaic* : relating to or suitable for social intercourse

con·ver·sance \kən-'vərs-^{ə}n(t)s *also* 'kän-vər-sən(t)s\ *or* **con-**

ver·san·cy \kən-ˈvərs-ᵊn-sē\ *n* **:** the quality or state of being conversant
con·ver·sant \kən-ˈvərs-ᵊnt *also* ˈkän-vər-sənt\ *adj* **1** *archaic* **:** OCCUPIED, CONCERNED **2** *archaic* **:** having frequent, customary, or familiar association **3 :** having knowledge or experience — **con·ver·sant·ly** *adv*
con·ver·sa·tion \ˌkän-vər-ˈsā-shən\ *n* [ME *conversacioun*, fr. MF *conversation*, fr. L *conversation-, conversatio*, fr. *conversatus*, pp. of *conversari* to live, keep company with] **1** *obs* **:** CONDUCT, BEHAVIOR **2 :** SEXUAL INTERCOURSE **3 a** (1) **:** oral exchange of sentiments, observations, opinions, ideas (2) **:** an instance of such exchange **:** TALK **b :** an informal discussion of an issue by representatives of governments, institutions, or groups — **con·ver·sa·tion·al** \-shnəl, -shən-ᵊl\ *adj* — **con·ver·sa·tion·al·ly** \-ē\ *adv*
con·ver·sa·tion·al·ist \-shnə-ləst, -shən-ᵊl-əst\ *n* **:** TALKER
conversation piece *n* **1 :** a painting of a group of persons in their customary surroundings **2 :** something novel or striking intended to stimulate conversation
con·ver·sa·zi·o·ne \ˌkän-vər-ˌsät-sē-ˈō-nē\ *n, pl* **con·ver·sa·zi·o·nes** \-nēz\ *or* **con·ver·sa·zi·o·ni** \-(ˌ)nē\ [It, lit. conversation, fr. L *conversation-, conversatio*] **:** a meeting for conversation esp. about art, literature, or science
¹con·verse \kən-ˈvərs\ *vi* [ME *conversen*, fr. MF *converser*, fr. L *conversari* to live, keep company with, fr. *conversus*, pp. of *convertere* to turn around] **1 a** *archaic* **:** to become occupied or engaged **b :** to have acquaintance or familiarity **2 :** to engage in conversation **:** TALK **syn** see SPEAK — **con·vers·er** *n*
²con·verse \ˈkän-ˌvərs\ *n* **1** *obs* **:** INTERCOURSE **2 :** CONVERSATION
³con·verse \kən-ˈvərs, ˈkän-ˌ\ *adj* [L *conversus*, pp. of *convertere*] **:** reversed in order, relation, or action — **con·verse·ly** *adv*
⁴con·verse \ˈkän-ˌvərs\ *n* **:** something converse to another; *esp* **:** a proposition in logic obtained by conversion
con·ver·sion \kən-ˈvər-zhən, -shən\ *n* [ME, fr. MF, fr. L *conversion-, conversio*, fr. *conversus*, pp. of *convertere*] **1 :** the act of converting **:** the process of being converted **2 :** an experience associated with a definite and decisive adoption of religion **3 a :** interchange of the terms of a logical proposition **b :** reduction of a mathematical expression by clearing of fractions **4 :** the making of a score on a try for point after touchdown in football or a free throw in basketball **5 :** something converted from one use to another — **con·ver·sion·al** \-ˈvərzh-nəl, -ˈvərsh-, -ən-ᵊl\ *adj*
¹con·vert \kən-ˈvərt\ *vb* [ME *converten*, fr. OF *convertir*, fr. L *convertere*, to turn around, transform, convert, fr. *com-* + *vertere* to turn — more at WORTH] *vt* **1 a :** to bring over from one belief, view, or party to another **b :** to bring about a religious conversion in **2 a :** to alter the physical or chemical nature or properties of esp. in manufacturing **b** (1) **:** to change from one form or function to another (2) **:** to alter for more effective utilization (3) **:** to appropriate without right **c :** to exchange for an equivalent **3** *obs* **:** TURN **4 :** to subject to logical conversion ~ *vi* **1 :** to undergo conversion **2 :** to make good on a try for point after touchdown or on a free throw **syn** see TRANSFORM
²con·vert \ˈkän-ˌvərt\ *n* **:** one that is converted; *esp* **:** one who has experienced conversion
syn CONVERT, PROSELYTE mean one who has changed from one creed, belief, or opinion to a different one. CONVERT implies a change toward the belief or opinion of the user of the word, PROSELYTE a change away from it; CONVERT therefore suggests sincere and voluntary change or acceptance, PROSELYTE suggests the effect of persuasion or special inducement
con·vert·er \kən-ˈvərt-ər\ *n* **:** one that converts: as **a :** the furnace used in the Bessemer process **b** *or* **con·ver·tor** \-ˈvərt-ər\ **:** a device employing mechanical rotation for changing electrical energy from one form to another; *also* **:** a radio device for converting one frequency to another **c :** a device for adapting a television receiver to receive channels for which it was not orig. designed
con·vert·ibil·i·ty \kən-ˌvərt-ə-ˈbil-ət-ē\ *n* **:** the quality of being convertible
¹con·vert·ible \kən-ˈvərt-ə-bəl\ *adj* **1 :** capable of being converted **2 :** having a top that may be lowered or removed ⟨~ coupe⟩ **3 :** capable of being exchanged without restriction for gold or currency of another kind — **con·vert·ible·ness** *n* — **con·vert·ibly** \-blē\ *adv*
²convertible *n* **:** something convertible; *esp* **:** a convertible automobile
con·verti·plane *or* **con·verta·plane** \kən-ˈvərt-ə-ˌplān\ *n* **:** an aircraft that takes off and lands like a helicopter and is convertible to a fixed-wing configuration for forward flight
con·vex \kän-ˈveks; ˈkän-ˌ, kən-ˈ\ *adj* [MF or L; MF *convexe*, fr. L *convexus* vaulted, concave, convex, fr. *com-* + *-vexus* (akin to OE *wōh* crooked, bent)] **:** curved or rounded like the exterior of a sphere or circle — **con·vex·ly** *adv* — **con·vex·ness** *n*
con·vex·i·ty \kən-ˈvek-sət-ē, kän-\ *n* **1 :** the quality or state of being convex **2 :** a convex surface or part
con·vexo–con·cave \-ˌvek-(ˌ)sō-\ *adj* **1 :** CONCAVO-CONVEX **2 :** having the convex side of greater curvature than the concave
con·vey \kən-ˈvā\ *vt* [ME *conveyen*, fr. OF *conveier* to accompany, escort, fr. (assumed) VL *conviare*, fr. L *com-* + *via* way — more at VIA] **1** *obs* **:** LEAD, CONDUCT **2 a :** to bear from one place to another **:** TRANSPORT **b :** to impart or communicate by statement, suggestion, gesture, or appearance **c** (1) *archaic* **:** STEAL (2) *obs* **:** to carry away secretly **d :** to transfer or deliver to another; *specif* **:** to transfer by a sealed writing **e :** to cause to pass from one place or person to another **:** TRANSMIT **syn** see CARRY
con·vey·ance \kən-ˈvā-ən(t)s\ *n* **1 :** the action of conveying **2 :** a means or way of conveying: as **a :** an instrument by which title to property is conveyed **b :** a means of transport **:** VEHICLE
con·vey·anc·er \-ən-sər\ *n* **:** one whose business is conveyancing
con·vey·anc·ing \-ən-siŋ\ *n* **:** the act or business of drawing deeds, leases, or other writings for transferring the title to property
con·vey·er *or* **con·vey·or** \kən-ˈvā-ər\ *n* **:** one that conveys: as **a :** a person who transfers property **b** *usu conveyor* **:** a mechanical apparatus for carrying packages or bulk material from place to place (as by an endless moving belt or a chain of receptacles)
¹con·vict \kən-ˈvikt\ *adj, archaic* **:** CONVICTED
²con·vict \ˈkän-ˌvikt\ *n* **1 :** a person convicted of and under sentence for a crime **2 :** a person serving a prison sentence usu. for a long term
³con·vict \kən-ˈvikt\ *vt* [ME *convicten*, fr. L *convictus*, pp. of *convincere* to refute, convict] **1 :** to find or prove to be guilty **2 :** to convince of error or sinfulness
con·vic·tion \kən-ˈvik-shən\ *n* **1 :** the act or process of convicting of a crime esp. in a court of law **2 a :** the act of convincing a person of error or of compelling the admission of a truth **b :** the state of being convinced of error or compelled to admit the truth **3 a :** a strong persuasion or belief **b :** the state of being convinced **syn** see CERTAINTY, OPINION
con·vince \kən-ˈvin(t)s\ *vt* [L *convincere* to refute, convict, prove, fr. *com-* + *vincere* to conquer] **1 a** *obs* **:** to overcome by argument **b** *obs* **:** OVERPOWER, OVERCOME **2** *obs* **:** DEMONSTRATE, PROVE **3 :** to bring by argument to assent or belief — **con·vinc·er** *n*
con·vinc·ing \kən-ˈvin(t)-siŋ\ *adj* **:** having power to convince of its truth, rightness, or reality **:** PLAUSIBLE **syn** see VALID — **con·vinc·ing·ly** \-siŋ-lē\ *adv* — **con·vinc·ing·ness** *n*
con·viv·ial \kən-ˈviv-yəl, -ˈviv-ē-əl\ *adj* [LL *convivialis*, fr. L *convivium* banquet, fr. *com-* + *vivere* to live] **:** relating to, occupied with, or fond of feasting, drinking, and good company — **con·viv·i·al·i·ty** \-ˌviv-ē-ˈal-ət-ē\ *n* — **con·viv·ial·ly** \kən-ˈviv-yə-lē, -ˈviv-ē-ə-lē\ *adv*
con·vo·ca·tion \ˌkän-və-ˈkā-shən\ *n* [ME, fr. MF, fr. L *convocation-, convocatio*, fr. *convocatus*, pp. of *convocare*] **1 a :** an assembly of persons convoked **b** (1) **:** an assembly of bishops and representative clergy of the Church of England (2) **:** a consultative assembly of clergy and lay delegates from one part of an Episcopal diocese; *also* **:** a territorial division of an Episcopal diocese **c :** a ceremonial assembly of members of a college or university **2 :** the act or process of convoking — **con·vo·ca·tion·al** \-shnəl, -shən-ᵊl\ *adj*
con·voke \kən-ˈvōk\ *vt* [MF *convoquer*, fr. L *convocare*, fr. *com-* + *vocare* to call] **:** to call together to a meeting **syn** see SUMMON
¹con·vo·lute \ˈkän-və-ˌlüt\ *vb* [L *convolutus*, pp. of *convolvere*] **:** TWIST, COIL
²convolute *adj* **:** rolled or wound together one part upon another **:** COILED ⟨a ~ shell⟩ — **con·vo·lute·ly** *adv*
con·vo·lut·ed *adj* **1 :** folded in curved or tortuous windings; *specif* **:** having convolutions **2 :** INVOLVED, INTRICATE
con·vo·lu·tion \ˌkän-və-ˈlü-shən\ *n* **1 :** one of the irregular ridges upon the surface of the brain and esp. of the cerebrum of higher mammals **2 :** a convoluted form or structure — **con·vo·lu·tion·al** \-shnəl, -shən-ᵊl\ *adj*
con·volve \kən-ˈvälv, -ˈvȯlv\ *vb* [L *convolvere*, fr. *com-* + *volvere* to roll — more at VOLUBLE] *vt* **:** to roll together **:** WRITHE ~ *vi* **:** to roll together or circulate involvedly
con·vol·vu·lus \kən-ˈväl-vyə-ləs, -ˈvȯl-\ *n, pl* **con·vol·vu·lus·es** *or* **con·vol·vu·li** \-ˌlī, -ˌlē\ [NL, fr. L *convolvere* to roll together, roll up] **:** any of a genus (*Convolvulus*) of erect, trailing, or twining herbs and shrubs of the morning-glory family
¹con·voy \ˈkän-ˌvȯi, kən-ˈ\ *vt* [ME *convoyen*, fr. MF *conveier*, *convoier*] **:** ACCOMPANY, GUIDE; *esp* **:** to escort for protection
²convoy \ˈkän-ˌvȯi\ *n* **1 :** one that convoys; *esp* **:** a protective escort (as for ships) **2 :** the act of convoying **3 :** a group convoyed or organized for convenience or protection in moving
con·vulse \kən-ˈvəls\ *vt* [L *convulsus*, pp. of *convellere* to pluck up, convulse, fr. *com-* + *vellere* to pluck] **:** to shake or agitate violently; *esp* **:** to shake with or as if with irregular spasms **syn** see SHAKE
con·vul·sion \kən-ˈvəl-shən\ *n* **1 :** an abnormal violent and involuntary contraction or series of contractions of the muscles **2 a :** a violent disturbance **b :** an uncontrolled fit **:** PAROXYSM — **con·vul·sion·ary** \-shə-ˌner-ē\ *adj*
con·vul·sive \kən-ˈvəl-siv\ *adj* **:** constituting or producing a convulsion; *also* **:** attended or affected with convulsions **syn** see FITFUL — **con·vul·sive·ly** *adv* — **con·vul·sive·ness** *n*
cony *var of* CONEY
coo \ˈkü\ *vi* [imit.] **1 :** to make the low soft cry of a dove or pigeon or a similar sound **2 :** to talk fondly or amorously — **coo** *n*
¹cook \ˈku̇k\ *n* [ME, fr. OE *cōc;* akin to OHG *koch;* both fr. a prehistoric WGmc word borrowed fr. L *coquus*, fr. *coquere* to cook; akin to OE *āfigen* fried, Gk *pessein* to cook] **1 :** one who prepares food for eating **2 :** a technical or industrial process comparable to cooking food; *also* **:** a substance so processed
²cook *vi* **1 :** to prepare food for eating **2 :** to undergo the action of being cooked **3 :** OCCUR, HAPPEN ~ *vt* **1 :** CONCOCT, IMPROVISE ⟨~*ed* up a scheme⟩ **2 :** to prepare for eating by a heating process **3 :** FALSIFY, DOCTOR **4 :** to subject to the action of heat or fire — **cook·er** *n* — **cook one's goose :** to ruin (one) irretrievably
cook·book \-ˌbu̇k\ *n* **:** a book of cooking directions and recipes
cook·ery \ˈku̇k-(ə-)rē\ *n* **1 :** the art or practice of cooking **2 :** an establishment for cooking
cook·ie *or* **cooky** \ˈku̇k-ē\ *n* [D *koekje*, dim. of *koek* cake] **:** any of various small sweet flat or slightly raised cakes
cook·out \ˈku̇k-ˌau̇t\ *n* **:** an outing at which a meal is cooked and served in the open; *also* **:** the meal cooked
¹cool \ˈkül\ *adj* [ME *col*, fr. OE *cōl*; akin to OHG *kuoli* cool, OE *ceald* cold] **1 :** moderately cold **:** lacking in warmth **2 a :** marked by steady calmness and self-control **b :** lacking ardor or friendliness **3 :** not scant or bare **4 :** UNABASHED, INSOLENT **5 a :** facilitating or suggesting relief from heat **b :** marked by restrained emotion or excitement ⟨~ jazz⟩ **c** *of a color* **:** producing an impression of coolness; *specif* **:** of a hue in the range violet through blue to green **6** *slang* **:** EXCELLENT — **cool·ish** \ˈkü-lish\ *adj* — **cool·ly** \ˈkül-(l)ē\ *adv* — **cool·ness** \ˈkül-nəs\ *n*
syn COOL, COMPOSED, COLLECTED, UNRUFFLED, IMPERTURBABLE, NONCHALANT mean actually or apparently free from agitation or excitement. COOL may imply calmness, deliberateness, or dispassionateness; COMPOSED implies freedom from agitation as a result of self-discipline or a sedate disposition; COLLECTED implies a concentration of mind that eliminates distractions esp. in moments of crisis; UNRUFFLED suggests apparent serenity and poise in the face of setbacks or in the midst of excitement; IMPERTURBABLE implies coolness or assurance even under severe provocation; NONCHALANT stresses outward casualness of manner that may or may not imply genuine unconcern or indifference
²cool *vb* **1 :** to make or become cool **2 :** MODERATE, CALM
³cool *n* **1 :** a cool time, place, or situation **2 :** COOLNESS **3 :** COMPOSURE
cool·ant \ˈkü-lənt\ *n* **:** a usu. fluid cooling agent
cool·er \ˈkü-lər\ *n* **1 :** one that cools: as **a :** a container for cooling

liquids **b** : REFRIGERATOR **2** : LOCKUP, JAIL; *esp* : a cell for violent prisoners **3** : an iced drink with an alcoholic beverage as base

coo·lie \'kü-lē\ *n* [Hindi *kulī*] : an unskilled laborer or porter usu. in or from the Far East

coon \'kün\ *n* : RACCOON

coon·can \'kün-ˌkan\ *n* [by folk etymology fr. MexSp *con quien* conquian, fr. Sp *¿con quién?* with whom?] : a game of rummy played with two packs including the two jokers

coon cat *n* **1** *chiefly NewEng* : ANGORA CAT **2** : CACOMISTLE **3** : COATI

coon·tie \'künt-ē\ *n* [Seminole *kunti* coontie flour] : any of several tropical American woody plants (genus *Zamia*) of the cycad family whose roots and stems yield arrowroot

[1]**coop** \'küp, 'ku̇p\ *n* [ME *cupe;* akin to OE *cȳpe* basket, *cot* cot] **1** : a cage or small enclosure (as for poultry); *also* : a small building for housing poultry **2 a** : a confined area **b** : JAIL

[2]**coop** *vt* **1** : to confine in a restricted often crowded area **2** : to place or keep in a coop : PEN

co-op \'kō-ˌäp, kō-'; 'küp\ *n* : COOPERATIVE

[1]**coo·per** \'kü-pər, 'ku̇p-ər\ *n* [ME *couper, cowper,* fr. MD *cūper* (fr. *cūpe* cask) or MLG *kūper,* fr. *kūpe* cask; MD *cūpe* & MLG *kūpe,* fr. L *cupa;* akin to Gk *kypellon* cup — more at HIVE] : one that makes or repairs wooden casks or tubs

[2]**cooper** *vb* **coo·per·ing** \'kü-p(ə-)riŋ, 'ku̇p-(ə-)riŋ\ *vt* : to work as a cooper on ~ *vi* : to work at or do coopering

coo·per·age \'kü-p(ə-)rij, 'ku̇p-(ə-)\ *n* **1** : a cooper's place of business **2** : a cooper's work or products

co·op·er·ate \kō-'äp-(ə-)ˌrāt\ *vi* [LL *cooperatus,* pp. of *cooperari,* fr. L *co-* + *operari* to work — more at OPERATE] **1** : to act or work with another or others **2** : to associate with another or others for mutual often economic benefit — **co·op·er·a·tor** \-ˌrāt-ər\ *n*

co·op·er·a·tion \(ˌ)kō-ˌäp-ə-'rā-shən\ *n* **1** : the act or process of cooperating **2** : association of persons for common benefit **3** : a dynamic ecological state of organisms living in aggregation characterized by sufficient mutual benefit to outweigh disadvantages associated with crowding — **co·op·er·a·tion·ist** \-sh(ə-)nəst\ *n*

[1]**co·op·er·a·tive** \kō-'äp-(ə-)rət-iv, -'äp-ə-ˌrāt-\ *adj* **1 a** : marked by cooperation ⟨~ efforts⟩ **b** : marked by a willingness and ability to work with others ⟨~ neighbors⟩ **2** : of, relating to, or organized as a cooperative **3** : relating to or comprising a program of combined usu. liberal arts and technical studies at different schools — **co·op·er·a·tive·ly** *adv* — **co·op·er·a·tive·ness** *n*

[2]**cooperative** *n* : an enterprise or organization owned by and operated for the benefit of those using its services

co-opt \kō-'äpt\ *vt* [L *cooptare,* fr. *co-* + *optare* to choose] **1** : to choose or elect as a fellow member or colleague **2** : to appoint or deputize summarily; *also* : PREEMPT — **co-op·ta·tion** \ˌkō-ˌäp-'tā-shən\ *n* — **co-op·ta·tive** \kō-'äp-tət-iv\ *adj* — **co-op·tion** \kō-'äp-shən\ *n* — **co-op·tive** \kō-'äp-tiv\ *adj*

[1]**co·or·di·nate** \kō-'ȯrd-nət, -ᵊn-ət, -ᵊn-ˌāt\ *adj* [back-formation fr. *coordination*] **1 a** : equal in rank, quality, or significance **b** (1) : being of equal rank in a sentence (2) : joining words or word groups of the same rank ⟨~ conjunction⟩ **2** : relating to or marked by coordination — **co·or·di·nate·ly** *adv* — **co·or·di·nate·ness** *n*

[2]**coordinate** *n* **1** : one who is of equal rank, authority, or importance with another **2 a** : any of a set of numbers used in specifying the location of a point on a line, or surface, or in space **b** : any one of a set of variables used in specifying the state of a substance or the motion of a particle or momentum

[3]**co·or·di·nate** \kō-'ȯrd-ᵊn-ˌāt\ *vb* [back-formation fr. *coordination*] *vt* **1** : to put in the same order or rank **2** : to bring into a common action, movement, or condition : HARMONIZE ~ *vi* : to be or become coordinate esp. so as to act together in a smooth concerted way — **co·or·di·na·tive** \kō-'ȯrd-nət-iv, -ᵊn-ət-, -ᵊn-ˌāt-\ *adj* — **co·or·di·na·tor** \-ᵊn-ˌāt-ər\ *n*

coordinate bond *n* : a covalent bond held to consist of a pair of electrons supplied by only one of the two atoms it joins

co·or·di·na·tion \(ˌ)kō-ˌȯrd-ᵊn-'ā-shən\ *n* [F or LL; F, fr. LL *coordination-, coordinatio,* fr. L *co-* + *ordination-, ordinatio* arrangement] **1** : the act of coordinating **2** : the state of being coordinate

coordination complex *n* : a compound or ion with a central usu. metallic atom or ion combined by coordinate bonds with a definite number of surrounding ions, groups, or molecules

coot \'küt\ *n* [ME *coote;* akin to D *koet* coot] **1** : any of various sluggish slow-flying slaty-black birds (genus *Fulica*) of the rail family that somewhat resemble ducks and have lobed toes and the upper mandible prolonged on the forehead as a horny frontal shield **2** : a No. American scoter; *also* : any of several other American ducks ⟨mud ~⟩ **3** : a harmless simple often old person

coo·tie \'küt-ē\ *n* [perh. modif. of Malay *kutu*] : a body louse

[1]**cop** \'käp\ *n* [ME, fr. OE *copp*] **1** *dial chiefly Eng* : TOP, CREST **2** : a cylindrical or conical mass of thread, yarn, or roving wound on a quill or tube; *also* : a tube or quill upon which it is wound

[2]**cop** *vt* **copped; cop·ping** [perh. fr. D *kapen* to steal, fr. Fris *kāpia* to take away; akin to OHG *kouf* trade — more at CHEAP] **1** *slang* : CATCH, CAPTURE **2** *slang* : STEAL, SWIPE

[3]**cop** *n* [short for [3]*copper*] : POLICEMAN

co·pa·cet·ic *or* **co·pe·set·ic** \ˌkō-pə-'set-ik\ *adj* [origin unknown] *slang* : very satisfactory

co·pai·ba \kō-'pī-bə, -'pā-; ˌkō-pə-'ē-bə\ *n* [Sp & Pg; Sp, fr. Pg *copaíba,* of Tupian origin; akin to Guarani *cupaiba* copaiba] : a stimulant oleoresin obtained from So. American leguminous trees (genus *Copaifera*); *also* : one of these trees

co·pal \'kō-pəl, -ˌpal; kō-'pal\ *n* [Sp, fr. Nahuatl *copalli* resin] : a recent or fossil resin from various tropical trees

co·par·ce·nary \kō-'pärs-ᵊn-ˌer-ē\ *n* **1** : joint heirship **2** : joint ownership

co·par·ce·ner \-'pärs-nər, -ᵊn-ər\ *n* : a joint heir

co·part·ner \(')kō-'pärt-nər\ *n* : PARTNER — **co·part·ner·ship** \-ˌship\ *n*

[1]**cope** \'kōp\ *n* [ME, fr. OE *-cāp,* fr. LL *cappa* head covering] **1** : a long enveloping ecclesiastical vestment **2 a** : something resembling a cope **b** : COPING

[2]**cope** *vt* : to cover or furnish with a cope or coping

[3]**cope** *vb* [ME *copen,* fr. MF *couper* to strike, cut, fr. OF, fr. *coup* blow, fr. LL *colpus,* alter. of L *colaphus,* fr. Gk *kolaphos* buffet] *vi* **1** *obs* : STRIKE, FIGHT **2 a** : to maintain a contest or combat usu. on even terms or with success **b** : to overcome problems and difficulties **3** *archaic* : MEET, ENCOUNTER ~ *vt* **1** *obs* : to meet in combat **2** *obs* : to come in contact with **3** *obs* : MATCH

[4]**cope** *vt* [prob. fr. F *couper* to cut] **1** : NOTCH **2** : to shape to fit a coping or conform to the shape of another member

copeck *var of* KOPECK

cope·mate \'kōp-ˌmāt\ *or* **copes·mate** \'kōp-ˌsmāt\ *n* [[3]*cope* + *mate*] **1** *obs* : ANTAGONIST **2** *obs* : PARTNER, COMRADE

co·pe·pod \'kō-pə-ˌpäd\ *n* [deriv. of Gk *kōpē* oar + *pod-, pous* foot] : any of a large subclass (Copepoda) of usu. minute freshwater and marine crustaceans — **copepod** *adj*

cop·er \'kō-pər\ *n* [[4]*cope*] *Brit* : a horse dealer esp. if dishonest

Co·per·ni·can \kō-'pər-ni-kən\ *adj* : of or relating to Copernicus or the belief that the earth rotates daily on its axis and the planets revolve in orbits round the sun — **Copernican** *n*

cope·stone \'kōp-ˌstōn\ *n* **1** : a stone forming a coping **2** : a finishing touch : CROWN

cop·i·er \'käp-ē-ər\ *n* : one that copies

co·pi·lot \'kō-ˌpī-lət\ *n* : a qualified airplane pilot who assists or relieves the pilot

cop·ing \'kō-piŋ\ *n* : the covering course of a wall usu. with a sloping top

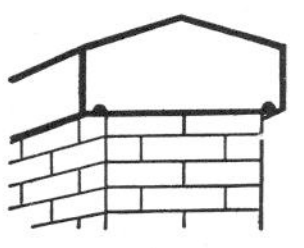

coping

coping saw *n* [fr. prp. of [4]*cope*] : a saw of ribbon shape under tension in a U-shaped frame used for cutting intricate patterns in wood

co·pi·ous \'kō-pē-əs\ *adj* [ME, fr. L *copiosus,* fr *copia* abundance, fr. *co-* + *ops* wealth — more at OPULENT] **1** : yielding an abundance : RICH **2 a** : full of thought, information, or matter **b** : profuse or exuberant in words, expression, or style **3** : LAVISH **syn** see PLENTIFUL — **co·pi·ous·ly** *adv* — **co·pi·ous·ness** *n*

co·pol·y·mer \(')kō-'päl-ə-mər\ *n* : a product of copolymerization — **co·pol·y·mer·ic** \ˌkō-ˌpäl-ə-'mer-ik\ *adj*

co·po·ly·mer·iza·tion \ˌkō-pə-ˌlim-ə-rə-'zā-shən, ˌkō-ˌpäl-ə-mə-rə-\ *n* : the act or process of copolymerizing

co·po·ly·mer·ize \ˌkō-pə-'lim-ə-ˌrīz, (')kō-'päl-ə-mə-\ *vb* : to polymerize together

[1]**cop·per** \'käp-ər\ *n, often attrib* [ME *coper,* fr. OE; akin to OHG *kupfar* copper; both fr. a prehistoric WGmc-NGmc word borrowed fr. LL *cuprum* copper, fr. L *(aes) Cyprium,* lit., Cyprian metal] **1** : a common reddish chiefly univalent and bivalent metallic element that is ductile and malleable and one of the best conductors of heat and electricity — see ELEMENT table **2** : a coin or token made of copper or bronze **3** *chiefly Brit* : a large boiler (as for cooking) **4** : any of various small butterflies (family Lycaenidae) with copper-colored wings — **cop·pery** \'käp-(ə-)rē\ *adj*

[2]**copper** *vt* **cop·per·ing** \'käp-(ə-)riŋ\ **1** : to coat or sheathe with or as if with copper **2 a** : to bet against (as in faro) **b** : HEDGE

[3]**copper** *n* [[2]*cop*] : POLICEMAN

cop·per·as \'käp-(ə-)rəs\ *n* [alter. of ME *coperose,* fr. MF, fr. (assumed) VL *cuprirosa,* fr. LL *cuprum* + L *rosa* rose] : a green hydrated ferrous sulfate $FeSO_4.7H_2O$

cop·per·head \'käp-ər-ˌhed\ *n* **1 a** : a common largely coppery brown pit viper (*Agkistrodon contortrix*) found esp. in uplands of the eastern U.S. **b** : a very venomous but sluggish Australian elapid snake (*Denisonia superba*) **2** : a person in the northern states who sympathized with the South during the Civil War

cop·per·plate \ˌkäp-ər-'plāt\ *n* : an intaglio printing process using engraved or etched copper plates; *also* : a print made by this process

copper pyrites *n* : CHALCOPYRITE

cop·per·smith \'käp-ər-ˌsmith\ *n* : a worker in copper

cop·pice \'käp-əs\ *n* [MF *copeiz,* fr. *couper* to cut — more at COPE] **1** : a thicket, grove, or growth of small trees **2** : forest originating mainly from sprouts or root suckers rather than seed

copr- *or* **copro-** *comb form* [NL, fr. Gk *kopr-, kopro-,* fr. *kopros* akin to Skt *śakṛt* dung] : dung : feces ⟨*copro*lite⟩

co·pra \'kō-prə *also* 'käp-rə\ *n* [Pg, fr. Malayalam *koppara*] : dried coconut meat yielding coconut oil

cop·ro·lite \'käp-rə-ˌlīt\ *n* : fossil excrement — **cop·ro·lit·ic** \ˌkäp-rə-'lit-ik\ *adj*

co·proph·a·gous \kä-'präf-ə-gəs\ *adj* [Gk *koprophagos,* fr. *kopr-* + *-phagos* -phagous] : feeding on dung — **co·proph·a·gy** \-ə-jē\ *n*

copse \'käps\ *n* [by alter.] : COPPICE 1

Copt \'käpt\ *n* [Ar *qubṭ* Copts, fr. Coptic *gyptios* Egyptian, fr. Gk *aigyptios*] : an Egyptian of the native race descended from the ancient Egyptians; *esp* : a member of the ancient Monophysite Christian church of Egypt

cop·ter \'käp-tər\ *n* : HELICOPTER

[1]**Cop·tic** \'käp-tik\ *adj* : of or relating to the Copts, their language, or their church

[2]**Coptic** *n* : an Afro-Asiatic language descended from ancient Egyptian and used as the liturgical language of the Coptic church

cop·u·la \'käp-yə-lə\ *n* [L, bond] : something that connects: as **a** : the connecting link between subject and predicate of a proposition **b** : a linguistic form that links a subject with its predicate and sometimes has some additional meaning of its own

cop·u·late \'käp-yə-ˌlāt\ *vi* [L *copulatus,* pp. of *copulare* to join, fr. *copula*] **1** : to engage in sexual intercourse **2** *of gametes* : to fuse permanently — **cop·u·la·tion** \ˌkäp-yə-'lā-shən\ *n* — **cop·u·la·to·ry** \'käp-yə-lə-ˌtōr-ē, -ˌtȯr-\ *adj*

[1]**cop·u·la·tive** \'käp-yə-ˌlāt-iv\ *adj* **1 a** : joining together coordinate words or word groups and expressing addition of their meanings ⟨~ conjunction⟩ **b** : functioning as a copula **2** : relating to or serving for copulation **3** : of or relating to coupling of chemical compounds or radicals — **cop·u·la·tive·ly** *adv*

[2]**copulative** *n* : a copulative word or word group

[1]**copy** \'käp-ē\ *n* [ME *copie,* fr. MF, fr. ML *copia,* fr. L, abundance — more at COPIOUS] **1** : an imitation, transcript, or reproduction of an original work **2** : one of the printed reproductions of an original text, engraving, or photograph **3** *archaic* : something to be imitated : MODEL **4** : matter to be set up for printing or photoengraving **syn** see REPRODUCTION

[2]**copy** *vt* **1** : to make a copy of **2** : to model oneself on ~ *vi* **1** : to make a copy **2** : to undergo copying

syn IMITATE, MIMIC, APE, MOCK: COPY implies duplicating an original as nearly as possible; IMITATE suggests following a model or pattern without precluding some variation; MIMIC implies a close copying esp. of voice or mannerisms for sport or for lifelike simulation or representation; APE may suggest presumptuous or servile or inept imitating of a superior original; MOCK adds to MIMIC the clear implication of derisive intent

copy·book \-ˌbu̇k\ *n* **1** : a book containing copies **2** : a book used in teaching penmanship and containing models for imitation

copy·boy \\-ˌbȯi\\ *n* **:** one who carries copy and runs errands

copy·cat \\-ˌkat\\ *n* **:** a sedulous imitator

copy·desk \\-ˌdesk\\ *n* **:** the desk at which newspaper copy is edited

copy·hold \\-ˌhōld\\ *n* **1 :** a former tenure of land in England and Ireland by right of being recorded in the court of the manor **2 :** an estate held by copyhold

copy·hold·er \\-ˌhōl-dər\\ *n* **1 :** a device for holding copy esp. for a typesetter **2 :** one who reads copy for a proofreader

copy·ist \\ˈkäp-ē-əst\\ *n* **1 :** one who makes copies **2 :** IMITATOR

copy·read·er \\-ˌrēd-ər\\ *n* **:** a publishing-house editor who reads and corrects manuscript copy; *also* **:** one who edits and headlines newspaper copy

¹**copy·right** \\-ˌrīt\\ *n* **:** the exclusive legal right to reproduce, publish, and sell the matter and form of a literary, musical, or artistic work — **copyright** *adj*

²**copyright** *vt* **:** to secure a copyright on

¹**co·quet** *n* [F, dim. of *coq* cock] **1** \\kō-ˈket, -ˈkā\\ *obs* **:** a man who indulges in coquetry **2** \\-ˈket\\ **:** COQUETTE

²**co·quet** \\kō-ˈket\\ *adj* **:** COQUETTISH

³**co·quet** *or* **co·quette** \\-ˈket\\ *vi* **co·quet·ted; co·quet·ting :** to play the coquette **:** FLIRT **syn** see TRIFLE

co·quet·ry \\ˈkō-kə-trē, kō-ˈket-ə-rē, -ˈke-trē\\ *n* **1 :** a flirtatious act or attitude **2 :** trifling attention or consideration

co·quette \\kō-ˈket\\ *n* [F, fem. of *coquet*] **:** a woman who endeavors without affection to capture men's amorous attention — **co·quett·ish** \\-ish\\ *adj* — **co·quett·ish·ly** *adv* — **co·quett·ish·ness** *n*

co·qui·lla nut \\kō-ˈkē-(y)ə-, -ˈkēl-yə-\\ *n* [Pg *coquilho*, dim of *côco* coconut] **:** the nut of a piassava palm (*Attalea funifera*) of Brazil having a hard brown shell much used by turners

co·qui·na \\kō-ˈkē-nə\\ *n* [Sp, prob. irreg. dim. of *concha* shell — more at CONCHA] **1 :** a small marine clam (genus *Donax*) used for broth or chowder **2 :** a soft whitish limestone formed of broken shells and corals cemented together and used for building

co·ra·cii·form \\kə-ˈras-ē-ə-ˌfȯrm; ˌkȯr-ə-ˈsī-ə-, ˌkär-\\ *adj* [deriv. of Gk *korak-*, *korax* raven + L *forma* form — more at RAVEN] **:** of or relating to an order (Coraciiformes) of arboreal nonpasserine birds including the rollers, kingfishers, and hornbills

cor·a·cle \\ˈkȯr-ə-kəl, ˈkär-\\ *n* [W *corwgl*] **1 :** a small boat made by covering a wicker frame with hide or leather and used by the ancient Britons **2 :** a boat made of broad hoops covered with horsehide or tarpaulin and used in parts of the British Isles

cor·a·coid \\ˈkȯr-ə-ˌkȯid, ˈkär-\\ *adj* [NL *coracoides*, fr. Gk *korakoeidēs*, lit., like a raven, fr. *korak-*, *korax*] **:** of, relating to, or being a process or cartilage bone of many vertebrates that extends from the scapula to or toward the sternum — **coracoid** *n*

cor·al \\ˈkȯr-əl, ˈkär-\\ *n* [ME, fr. MF, fr. L *corallium*, fr. Gk *korallion*] **1 a :** the calcareous or horny skeletal deposit produced by anthozoan or rarely hydrozoan polyps; *esp* **:** a richly red precious coral secreted by a gorgonian (*Corallium nobile*) **b :** a polyp or polyp colony together with its membranes and skeleton **2 :** a piece of coral and esp. of red coral **3 a :** a bright reddish ovary (as of a lobster or scallop) **b :** a variable color averaging a deep pink — **coral** *adj* — **cor·al·loid** \\-ə-ˌlȯid\\ *or* **cor·al·loi·dal** \\ˌkȯr-ə-ˈlȯid-ᵊl, ˌkär-\\ *adj*

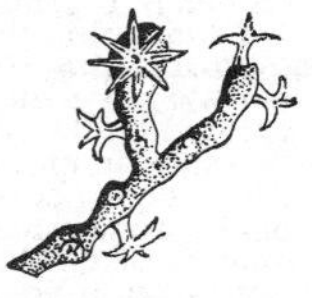

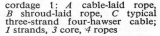

coral: portion of a colony of red coral with polyps expanded

cor·al·bells \\ˈkȯr-əl-ˌbelz, ˈkär-\\ *n pl but sing or pl in constr* **:** a perennial alumroot (*Heuchera sanguinea*) widely cultivated for its feathery spikes of tiny coral flowers

¹**cor·al·line** \\ˈkȯr-ə-ˌlīn, ˈkär-\\ *adj* [F *corallin*, fr. LL *corallinus*, fr. L *corallium*] **:** of, relating to, or resembling coral or a coralline

²**coralline** *n* **1 :** any of a family (Corallinaceae) of calcareous red algae **2 :** an animal that resembles a coral

coral pink *n* **:** a moderate yellowish pink

coral snake *n* **1 :** any of several venomous chiefly tropical New World elapid snakes (genus *Micrurus*) brilliantly banded in red, black, and yellow or white that include two (*M. fulvius* and *M. euryxanthus*) ranging northward into the southern U.S. **2 :** any of several harmless snakes resembling the coral snakes

co·ran·to \\kə-ˈrant-(ˌ)ō\\ *n, pl* **corantos** *or* **corantoes** [modif. of F *courante*] **:** COURANTE

cor·ban \\ˈkȯ(ə)r-ˌban\\ *n* [Heb *qorbān* offering] **:** a sacrifice or offering to God among the ancient Hebrews

cor·beil *or* **cor·beille** \\ˈkȯr-bəl, kȯr-ˈbā\\ *n* [F *corbeille*, lit., basket, fr. LL *corbicula*, dim. of *corbis* basket] **:** a sculptured basket of flowers or fruit as an architectural decoration

¹**cor·bel** \\ˈkȯr-bəl\\ *n* [ME, fr. MF, fr. dim. of *corp* raven, fr. L *corvus* — more at RAVEN] **:** an architectural member that projects from within a wall and supports a weight; *esp* **:** one that is stepped upward and outward from a vertical surface

²**corbel** *vt* **cor·beled** *or* **cor·belled; cor·bel·ing** *or* **cor·bel·ling :** to furnish with or make into a corbel

corbeling *or* **corbelling** *n* **1 :** corbel work **2 :** the construction of a corbel

cor·bie \\ˈkȯr-bē\\ *n* [ME, modif. of OF *corbin*, fr. L *corvinus* of a raven] *chiefly Scot* **:** a carrion crow; *also* **:** RAVEN

corbie gable *n* **:** a gable having corbiesteps

cor·bie·step \\ˈkȯr-bē-ˌstep\\ *n* **:** one of a series of steps terminating the upper part of a gable wall

cor·bi·na \\kȯr-ˈbē-nə\\ *n* [MexSp, fr. Sp, an acanthopterygian fish, fr. fem. of *corvino* of a raven, fr. L *corvinus*] **:** any of several American marine fishes; *esp* **:** a spotted whiting (*Menticirrhus undulatus*) favored by surf casters along the California coast

¹**cord** \\ˈkȯ(ə)rd\\ *n* [ME, fr. OF *corde*, fr. L *chorda* string, fr. Gk *chordē* — more at YARN] **1 a :** a string consisting of several strands woven or twisted together **b :** the hangman's rope **2 :** a moral, spiritual, or emotional bond **3 a :** an anatomical structure (as a nerve) resembling a cord **b :** a small flexible insulated electrical cable having a plug at one or both ends used to connect a lamp or other appliance with a receptacle **4 :** a unit of wood cut for fuel equal to a stack 4x4x8 feet or 128 cubic feet **5 a :** a rib like a cord on a textile **b (1) :** a fabric made with such ribs or a garment made of such a fabric **(2)** *pl* **:** trousers made of such fabric

²**cord** *vt* **1 :** to furnish, bind, or connect with a cord **2 :** to pile up (wood) in cords — **cord·er** *n*

cord·age \\ˈkȯrd-ij\\ *n* **1 :** ropes or cords; *esp* **:** the ropes in the rigging of a ship **2 :** the number of cords (as of wood) on a given area

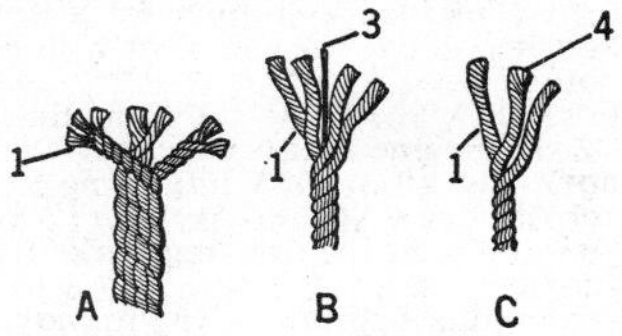

cordage 1: *A* cable-laid rope, *B* shroud-laid rope, *C* typical three-strand four-hawser cable; *1* strands, *3* core, *4* ropes

cor·date \\ˈkȯr-ˌdāt\\ *adj* [NL *cordatus*, fr. L *cord-*, *cor*] **:** shaped like a heart — **cor·date·ly** *adv*

cord·ed \\ˈkȯrd-əd\\ *adj* **1 a :** made of or provided with cords or ridges; *specif* **:** muscled in ridges **b** *of a muscle* **:** TENSE, TAUT **2 :** bound, fastened, or wound about with cords **3 :** striped or ribbed with or as if with cord **:** TWILLED

¹**cor·dial** \\ˈkȯr-jəl\\ *adj* [ME, fr. ML *cordialis*, fr. L *cord-*, *cor* heart — more at HEART] **1** *obs* **:** of or relating to the heart **:** VITAL **2 :** tending to revive, cheer, or invigorate **3 :** HEARTFELT, HEARTY **syn** see GRACIOUS — **cor·dial·ly** \\ˈkȯrj-(ə-)lē\\ *adv* — **cor·dial·ness** *n*

²**cordial** *n* **1 :** a stimulating medicine or drink **2 :** LIQUEUR

cor·dial·i·ty \\ˌkȯr-jē-ˈal-ət-ē, kȯr-ˈjal-ət-\\ *n* **:** HEARTINESS

cor·di·er·ite \\ˈkȯrd-ē-ə-ˌrīt\\ *n* [F, fr. Pierre L. A. *Cordier* †1861 F geologist] **:** a blue mineral $(Mg,Fe)_2Al_4Si_5O_{18}$ with vitreous luster and strong dichroism consisting of a silicate of aluminum, iron, and magnesium

cor·di·form \\ˈkȯrd-ə-ˌfȯrm\\ *adj* [F *cordiforme*, fr. L *cord-*, *cor* + F *-iforme* -iform] **:** shaped like a heart

cor·dil·le·ra \\ˌkȯrd-ᵊl-ˈ(y)er-ə, kȯr-ˈdil-ə-rə\\ *n* [Sp] **:** a system of mountain ranges often consisting of a number of more or less parallel chains — **cor·dil·le·ran** \\-ˈ(y)er-ən, -ə-rən\\ *adj*

cord·ite \\ˈkȯ(ə)r-ˌdīt\\ *n* **:** a smokeless powder composed of nitroglycerin, guncotton, and mineral jelly usu. gelatinized by addition of acetone and pressed into cords resembling brown twine

cor·do·ba \\ˈkȯrd-ə-bə, -ə-və\\ *n* [Sp *córdoba*, fr. Francisco Fernández de *Córdoba* †1526 Sp explorer] — see MONEY table

cor·don \\ˈkȯrd-ᵊn, ˈkȯ(ə)r-ˌdän\\ *n* [F, dim. of *corde* cord] **1 a :** an ornamental cord used esp. on costumes **b :** a cord or ribbon worn as a badge of honor or a decoration **c :** STRINGCOURSE **2 a :** a line of troops or of military posts enclosing an area **b :** a line of persons or objects around a person or place

¹**cor·do·van** \\ˈkȯrd-ə-vən\\ *adj* [OSp *cordovano*, fr. *Córdova* (now *Córdoba*), Spain] **1** *cap* **:** of or relating to Córdoba and esp. Córdoba, Spain **2 :** made of cordovan leather

²**cordovan** *n* **:** a soft fine-grained colored leather

¹**cor·du·roy** \\ˈkȯrd-ə-ˌrȯi\\ *n, often attrib* [perh. alter. of the name *Corderoy*] **1 a :** a durable usu. cotton pile fabric with vertical ribs or wales **b** *pl* **:** trousers of corduroy **2 :** a road built of logs laid side by side transversely

²**corduroy** *vt* **:** to build (a road) of logs laid side by side transversely

cord·wain \\ˈkȯ(ə)r-ˌdwān\\ *n* [ME *cordwane*, fr. MF *cordoan*, fr. OSp *cordovano*, *cordován*] *archaic* **:** cordovan leather

cord·wain·er \\-ˌdwā-nər\\ *n* **1** *archaic* **:** a worker in cordovan leather **2 :** SHOEMAKER — **cord·wain·ery** \\-ˌdwā-nə-rē\\ *n*

cord·wood \\ˈkȯ(ə)r-ˌdwu̇d\\ *n* **:** wood piled or sold in cords; *also* **:** standing timber suitable for use as fuel

¹**core** \\ˈkō(ə)r, ˈkȯ(ə)r\\ *n* [ME] **1 :** a central or foundational part: as **a :** the usu. inedible central part of some fruits (as a pineapple); *esp* **:** the papery or leathery carpels composing the ripened ovary in a pome fruit **b :** the portion of a foundry mold that shapes the interior of a hollow casting **c :** a part removed from the interior of a mass **d :** the central strand around which other strands twist in some ropes **e :** a mass of iron serving to concentrate and intensify the magnetic field resulting from a current in the coil **f :** the conducting wire with its insulation in an electric cable **g :** a layer of wood on which veneers are glued (as in making plywood) **h :** an arrangement of a course of studies that combines under certain basic topics material from subjects conventionally separated and aims to provide a common background for all students **2 a :** a basic, essential, or enduring part **b :** the essential meaning **:** GIST

²**core** *vt* **:** to remove the core from — **cor·er** *n*

³**core** *n* [ME *chore* chorus, company, fr. L *chorus*] *chiefly Scot* **:** COMPANY; *esp* **:** a company of players in a curling match

co·re·late \\ˌkō-ri-ˈlāt\\ *vt* [back-formation fr. *corelation*] *chiefly Brit* **:** CORRELATE — **co·re·la·tion** \\ˌkō-ri-ˈlā-shən\\ *n* — **co·rel·a·tive** \\kō-ˈrel-ət-iv, kə-\\ *adj* — **co·rel·a·tive·ly** *adv*

co·re·li·gion·ist \\ˌkō-ri-ˈlij-ə-nəst\\ *n* **:** one of the same religion

co·re·op·sis \\ˌkōr-ē-ˈäp-səs, ˌkȯr-\\ *n* [NL, genus name, fr. Gk *koris* bedbug + NL *-opsis*; akin to Gk *keirein* to cut — more at SHEAR] **:** any of a genus (*Coreopsis*) of composite herbs

co·re·spon·dent \\ˌkō-ri-ˈspän-dənt\\ *n* **:** a person named as guilty of adultery with the defendant in a divorce suit

corf \\ˈkȯ(ə)rf\\ *n, pl* **corves** \\ˈkȯ(ə)rvz\\ [ME, basket, fr. MD *corf* or MLG *korf*] *Brit* **:** a basket, tub, or truck used in a mine

co·ri·a·ceous \\ˌkōr-ē-ˈā-shəs, ˌkȯr-\\ *adj* [LL *coriaceus* — more at CUIRASS] **:** resembling leather

co·ri·an·der \\ˈkōr-ē-ˌan-dər, ˈkȯr-; ˌkōr-ē-ˈ, ˌkȯr-\\ *n* [ME *coriandre*, fr. OF, fr. L *coriandrum*, fr. Gk *koriandron*] **:** an Old World herb (*Coriandrum sativum*) of the carrot family with aromatic fruits

¹**Co·rin·thi·an** \\kə-ˈrin(t)-thē-ən\\ *n* **1 :** a native or resident of Corinth, Greece **2 a :** a gay profligate man **b :** a fashionable man-about-town; *esp* **:** SPORTSMAN **c :** an amateur yachtsman

²**Corinthian** *adj* **1 :** of, relating to, or characteristic of Corinth or Corinthians **2 :** of or relating to the lightest and most ornate of the three Greek orders of architecture characterized esp. by its bell-shaped capital enveloped with acanthuses

Co·ri·o·lis force \\ˌkōr-ē-ˌō-ləs-, ˌkȯr-\\ *n* [Gaspard G. *Coriolis* †1843 F civil engineer] **:** a deflecting force acting on a body in motion (as an airplane or projectile) due to the earth's rotation

co·ri·um \\ˈkōr-ē-əm, ˈkȯr-\\ *n, pl* **co·ria** \\-ē-ə\\ [NL, fr. L, leather — more at CUIRASS] **1 :** DERMIS **2 :** the layer of a mucous membrane corresponding to the dermis

¹**cork** \\ˈkȯ(ə)rk\\ *n* [ME, cork, bark, prob. fr. Ar *qurq*, fr. L *cortic-*, *cortex*] **1 a :** the elastic tough outer tissue of a European oak

(*Quercus suber*) used esp. for stoppers and insulation **b :** PHELLEM **2 :** a usu. cork stopper for a bottle or jug **3 :** an angling float

²**cork** *vt* **1 :** to furnish or fit with cork or a cork **2 :** to blacken with burnt cork

cork·er \'kȯr-kər\ *n* **1 :** one that corks bottles or other containers **2** *slang* **:** one that is excellent

cork·ing \'kȯr-kiŋ\ *adj, slang* **:** extremely fine

¹**cork·screw** \'kȯrk-,skrü\ *n* **:** a pointed spiral piece of metal with a handle used for drawing corks from bottles

²**corkscrew** *vt* **1 :** WIND **2 :** to draw out with difficulty **3 :** to twist into a spiral ~ *vi* **:** to move in a winding course

cork·wood \'kȯr-,kwu̇d\ *n* **:** any of several trees having light or corky wood; *esp* **:** a small or shrubby tree (*Leitneria floridana*) of the southeastern U.S. that has extremely light soft wood and is the sole member of its genus and family

corky \'kȯr-kē\ *adj* **:** resembling cork

corm \'kȯ(ə)rm\ *n* [NL *cormus*, fr. Gk *kormos* tree trunk, fr. *keirein* to cut] **:** a rounded thick modified underground stem base bearing membranous or scaly leaves and buds and acting as a vegetative reproductive structure — compare BULB, TUBER

cor·mel \'kȯr-məl\ *n* [dim. of *corm*] **:** a small or secondary corm produced by a larger corm

cor·mo·rant \'kȯrm-(ə-)rənt, 'kȯr-mə-,rant\ *n* [ME *cormeraunt*, fr. MF *cormorant*, fr. OF *cormareng*, fr. *corp* raven + *marenc* of the sea, fr. L *marinus*] **1 :** any of various dark-colored web-footed voracious seabirds (family Phalacrocoracidae) with a long neck, wedge-shaped tail, hooked bill, and a patch of bare often brightly colored distensible skin under the mouth that are used in eastern Asia for catching fish **2 :** a gluttonous, greedy, or rapacious person

¹**corn** \'kȯ(ə)rn\ *n, often attrib* [ME, fr. OE; akin to OHG & ON *korn* grain, L *granum*, Gk *gēras* old age] **1** *chiefly dial* **:** a small hard particle **:** GRAIN **2 :** a small hard seed **3 a :** the seeds of a cereal grass and esp. of the important cereal crop of a particular region (as in Britain wheat, in Scotland and Ireland oats, and in the New World and Australia Indian corn) **b :** the kernels of sweet corn served as a vegetable while still soft and milky **4 :** a plant that produces corn **5 :** something that is corny

²**corn** *vt* **1 :** to form into grains **:** GRANULATE **2 a :** to preserve or season with salt in grains **b :** to salt lightly in brine containing preservatives ⟨~ beef⟩ **3 :** to feed with corn ⟨~ horses⟩

³**corn** *n* [ME *corne*, fr. MF, horn, corner, fr. L *cornu* horn, point] **:** a local hardening and thickening of epidermis (as on a toe)

corn borer *n* **:** any of several insects that bore in maize; *esp* **:** the larva of an Old World moth (*Pyrausta nubilalis*) widespread in eastern No. America where it is a major pest esp. in the stems and crowns of Indian corn, dahlias, and potatoes

corn bread *n* **:** bread made with cornmeal

corn·cob \'kȯ(ə)rn-,käb\ *n* **1 :** the axis on which the kernels of Indian corn are arranged **2 :** an ear of Indian corn

corn cockle *n* **:** an annual hairy weed (*Agrostemma githago*) with purplish red flowers found in grainfields

corn·crake \'kȯ(ə)rn-,krāk\ *n* **:** a common Eurasian short-billed rail (*Crex crex*) that frequents grainfields — called also *land rail*

corn·crib \-,krib\ *n* **:** a crib for storing ears of Indian corn

corn dodger *n, chiefly South & Midland* **:** a cake of corn bread fried, baked, or boiled as a dumpling

cor·nea \'kȯr-nē-ə\ *n* [ML, fr. L, fem. of *corneus* horny, fr. *cornu*] **:** the transparent part of the coat of the eyeball that covers the iris and pupil and admits light to the interior — **cor·ne·al** \-əl\ *adj*

corn earworm *n* **:** a large striped yellow-headed larva of a moth (*Heliothis zea*) esp. destructive to the ear of Indian corn

cor·nel \'kȯrn-ᵊl, 'kȯr-,nel\ *n* [deriv. of L *cornus* cornel cherry tree; akin to Gk *kerasos* cherry tree] **:** any of various shrubs or trees (*Cornus* and related genera) with very hard wood and perfect flowers; *specif* **:** DOGWOOD

cor·ne·lian \kȯr-'nēl-yən\ *n* **:** CARNELIAN

cor·ne·ous \'kȯr-nē-əs\ *adj* [L *corneus*] **:** HORNY

¹**cor·ner** \'kȯ(r)-nər\ *n* [ME, fr. OF *cornere*, fr. *corne*] **1 a :** the point where converging lines, edges, or sides meet **:** ANGLE **b :** the place of intersection of two streets or roads **c :** a piece designed to form, mark, or protect a corner **2 a :** the space between meeting lines, walls, or borders close to the vertex of the angle **b :** a position from which escape or retreat is difficult or impossible **3 :** control or ownership of enough of the available supply of a commodity or security to permit manipulation of the price **syn** see MONOPOLY — **cor·nered** \-nərd\ *adj*

²**cor·ner** *vb* **cor·ner·ing** \'kȯ(r)n-(ə-)riŋ\ *vt* **1 :** to drive into a corner **2 :** to get a corner on ⟨~ wheat⟩ ~ *vi* **1 :** to meet or converge at a corner or angle **2 :** to turn a corner ⟨a car that ~s well⟩

³**corner** *adj* **1 :** situated at a corner **2 :** used or fitted for use in or on a corner

cor·ner·stone \'kȯ(r)-nər-,stōn\ *n* **1 :** a stone forming a part of a corner or angle in a wall; *specif* **:** such a stone laid at a formal ceremony **2 :** the most basic element **:** FOUNDATION

cor·ner·wise \-,wīz\ *or* **cor·ner·ways** \-,wāz\ *adv* **:** DIAGONALLY

cor·net \kȯr-'net\ *n* [ME, fr. MF, fr. dim. of *corn* horn, fr. L *cornu*] **1 :** a brass band instrument resembling the trumpet but having a shorter tube, greater agility, and less brilliant tone **2 :** something shaped like a cone: as **a :** a piece of paper twisted for use as a container **b :** a cone-shaped pastry shell that is often filled with whipped cream **c** *Brit* **:** an ice-cream cone

cor·net–à–pis·tons \kȯr-,net-(,)ä-'pis-tənz\ *n, pl* **cor·nets–à–pis·tons** \-,net-(,)(s)ä-\ [F, lit., cornet with valves] **:** CORNET 1

cor·net·ist *or* **cor·net·tist** \kȯr-'net-əst\ *n* **:** a cornet player

corn flour *n, Brit* **:** CORNSTARCH

corn·flow·er \'kȯ(ə)rn-,flau̇(-ə)r\ *n* **1 :** CORN COCKLE **2 :** a European plant (*Centaurea cyanus*) having flower heads with blue, pink, or white rays that is often cultivated in No. America

cornflower blue *n* **:** a variable color averaging a moderate purplish blue

corn·husk·ing \'kȯrn-,həs-kiŋ\ *n* **:** the husking of corn; *specif* **:** HUSKING

cor·nice \'kȯr-nəs\ *n* [MF, fr. It] **1 a :** the molded and projecting horizontal member that crowns an architectural composition **b :** a top course that crowns a wall **2 :** a decorative band of metal or wood used to conceal curtain fixtures — **cornice** *vt*

cor·niche \'kȯr-nish, kȯr-'nēsh\ *n* [F *cornice, corniche*, lit., cornice] **:** a road usu. along the face of a cliff

cor·nic·u·late \kȯr-'nik-yə-lət\ *adj* [L *corniculatus*, fr. *corniculum*, dim. of *cornu*] **:** having small horn-shaped processes

¹**Cor·nish** \'kȯr-nish\ *adj* [*Corn*wall, England] **:** of, relating to, or characteristic of Cornwall, Cornishmen, or Cornish

²**Cornish** *n* **1 :** a Celtic language of Cornwall extinct since the late 18th century **2 :** any of an English breed of domestic fowls much used in crossbreeding for meat production

Cor·nish·man \-mən\ *n* **:** a native or resident of Cornwall, England

Corn Law *n* **:** one of a series of laws in force in Great Britain before 1846 prohibiting or discouraging the importation of foreign grain

corn·meal \'kȯ(ə)rn-'mē(ə)l\ *n* **:** meal ground from corn

corn pone *n, South & Midland* **:** corn bread often made without milk or eggs and baked or fried

corn poppy *n* **:** an annual red-flowered poppy (*Papaver rhoeas*) common in European grainfields and cultivated in several varieties

corn snow *n* **:** granular snow formed by alternate thawing and freezing

corn·stalk \'kȯ(ə)rn-,stȯk\ *n* **:** a stalk of Indian corn

corn·starch \-,stärch\ *n* **:** starch made from corn and used in foods as a thickening agent, in making corn syrup and sugars, and in the manufacture of adhesives and sizes for paper and textiles

corn sugar *n* **:** DEXTROSE; *esp* **:** that made by hydrolysis of cornstarch

corn syrup *n* **:** a syrup containing dextrins, maltose, and dextrose that is obtained by partial hydrolysis of cornstarch

cor·nu \'kȯr-(,)n(y)ü\ *n, pl* **cor·nua** \-n(y)ə-wə\ [L] **:** HORN; *esp* **:** a horn-shaped anatomical structure — **cor·nu·al** \-nyə-wəl\ *adj*

cor·nu·co·pia \,kȯr-n(y)ə-'kō-pē-ə\ *n* [LL, fr. L *cornu copiae* horn of plenty] **1 :** a curved goat's horn overflowing with fruit and ears of grain that is used as a decorative motif emblematic of abundance **2 :** ABUNDANCE **3 :** a receptacle shaped like a horn or cone

cor·nut·ed \kȯr-'n(y)üt-əd\ *adj* [L *cornutus* horned, fr. *cornu* horn — more at HORN] **1 :** having horns **2 :** shaped like a horn

cor·nu·to \kȯr-'n(y)üt-(,)ō\ *n* [It, fr. L *cornutus*] **:** CUCKOLD

corn whiskey *n* **:** whiskey distilled from a mash made up of not less than 80 percent corn

¹**corny** \'kȯr-nē\ *adj* **1** *archaic* **:** tasting strongly of malt **2 :** of or relating to corn **3 :** characterized by threadbare moralizing, exaggerated theatricality, or stereotyped sentiments **:** TRITE

²**corny** *adj* **:** relating to or having corns on the feet

cor·o·dy \'kȯr-əd-ē, 'kär-\ *n* [ME *corrodie*, fr. ML *corrodium*] **:** an allowance of provisions for maintenance dispensed as a charity

co·rol·la \kə-'räl-ə\ *n* [NL, fr. L, dim. of *corona*] **:** the petals of a flower constituting the inner floral envelope surrounding the sporophylls — **co·rol·late** \kə-'räl-ət; 'kȯr-ə-,lāt, 'kär-\ *adj*

cor·ol·lary \'kȯr-ə-,ler-ē, 'kär-, *Brit* kə-'räl-ə-rē\ *n* [ME *corolarie*, fr. LL *corollarium*, fr. L, money paid for a garland, gratuity, fr. *corolla*] **1 :** an immediate inference from a proved proposition **2 :** something that naturally follows **:** RESULT — **corollary** *adj*

co·ro·na \kə-'rō-nə\ *n* [L, garland, crown, cornice — more at CROWN] **1 :** the projecting part of a classic cornice **2 a :** a usu. colored circle often seen around and close to a luminous body (as the sun or moon) caused by diffraction produced by suspended droplets or occas. particles of dust **b :** the tenuous outermost part of the atmosphere of the sun appearing as a gray halo around the moon's black disk during a total eclipse of the sun **c :** the upper portion of a body part (as a tooth or the skull) **d :** an appendage on the inner side of the corolla in some flowers (as the daffodil, jonquil, or milkweed) **e :** a faint glow adjacent to the surface of an electrical conductor at high voltage **3** [fr. *La Corona*, a trademark] **:** a long straight cigar roundly blunt at the sealed end

Corona Aus·tra·lis \kə-,rō-nə-(,)ȯ-'strā-ləs\ *n* [L (gen. *Coronae Australis*), lit., southern crown] **:** a southern constellation adjoining Sagittarius on the south

Corona Bo·re·al·is \-,bōr-ē-'al-əs, -,bȯr-\ *n* [L (gen. *Coronae Borealis*), lit., northern crown] **:** a northern constellation between Hercules and Boötes

cor·o·nach \'kȯr-ə-nək, 'kär-\ *n* [ScGael *corranach* & IrGael *corānach*] **:** a lamentation for the dead as sung or played on the bagpipes in Scotland and Ireland **:** DIRGE

co·ro·na·graph *or* **co·ro·no·graph** \kə-'rō-nə-,graf\ *n* **:** a telescope for observation of the sun's corona without a total solar eclipse

¹**cor·o·nal** *also* **cor·o·nel** \'kȯr-ən-ᵊl, 'kär-\ *n* [ME *coronal*, fr. AF, fr. L *coronalis* of a crown, fr. *corona*] **:** a circlet for the head

²**co·ro·nal** \'kȯr-ən-ᵊl, 'kär-; *with reference to a corona, also* kə-'rōn-\ *adj* **1 :** of or relating to a corona or crown **2 :** lying in the direction of the coronal suture

coronal suture *n* **:** a suture extending across the skull between the parietal and frontal bones

¹**cor·o·nary** \'kȯr-ə-,ner-ē, 'kär-\ *adj* **1 :** of, relating to, or being a crown or coronal **2 a :** resembling a crown or circlet esp. in encircling another body part **b :** relating to or being the coronary arteries or veins of the heart; *broadly* **:** of or relating to the heart

²**coronary** *n* **1 :** a coronary artery or vein **2 :** CORONARY THROMBOSIS

coronary thrombosis *n* **:** the blocking of a coronary artery of the heart by a thrombus — called also *coronary occlusion*

cor·o·na·tion \,kȯr-ə-'nā-shən, ,kär-\ *n* [ME *coronacion*, fr. MF *coronation*, fr. *coroner* to crown] **:** the act or ceremony of investing a sovereign or his consort with the royal crown

cor·o·ner \'kȯr-ə-nər, 'kär-\ *n* [ME, an officer of the crown, fr. AF, fr. OF *corone* crown, fr. L *corona*] **:** a public officer whose principal duty is to inquire by an inquest held in the presence of a jury into the cause of any death which there is reason to suppose is not due to natural causes

cor·o·net \,kȯr-ə-'net, ,kär-\ *n* [MF *coronette*, fr. OF *coronete*, fr. *corone*] **1 :** a small or lesser crown usu. signifying a rank below that of a sovereign **2 a :** an ornamental wreath or band for the head usu. for wear by women on formal occasions **b :** the lower part of a horse's pastern where the horn terminates in skin

¹**cor·po·ral** \'kȯr-p(ə-)rəl\ *n* [ME, fr. MF, fr. ML *corporale*, fr. L, neut. of *corporalis*; fr. the doctrine that the bread of the Eucharist becomes or represents the body of Christ] **:** a linen cloth on which the eucharistic elements are placed

²**corporal** *adj* [ME, fr. MF, fr. L *corporalis*, fr. *corpor-*, *corpus* body] **1 :** of or relating to the body ⟨~ punishment⟩ **2** *obs* **:** CORPOREAL, PHYSICAL **syn** see BODILY — **cor·po·ral·ly** \-p(ə-)rə-lē\ *adv*

³**corporal** *n* [MF, lowest noncommissioned officer, alter. of *caporal*, fr. OIt *caporale*, fr. *capo* head, fr. L *caput*] **:** an enlisted man of the lowest noncommissioned rank in the army or marine corps

cor·po·ral·i·ty \ˌkȯr-pə-ˈral-ət-ē\ *n* **:** the quality or state of being or having a body or a material or physical existence

corporal's guard *n* **1 :** the small detachment commanded by a corporal **2 :** a small group

cor·po·rate \ˈkȯr-p(ə-)rət\ *adj* [L *corporatus*, pp. of *corporare* to make into a body, fr. *corpor-*, *corpus*] **1 a :** formed into an association and endowed by law with the rights and liabilities of an individual **:** INCORPORATED **b :** of or relating to a corporation **2 :** of or relating to a whole composed of individuals **3 :** CORPORATIVE 2 — **cor·po·rate·ly** *adv*

cor·po·ra·tion \ˌkȯr-pə-ˈrā-shən\ *n* **1 a** *obs* **:** a group of merchants or traders united in a trade guild **b :** the municipal authorities of a town or city **2 :** a body formed and authorized by law to act as a single person although constituted by one or more persons and legally endowed with various rights and duties including the capacity of succession **3 :** an association of employers and employees in a basic industry or of members of a profession organized as an organ of political representation in a corporative state **4 :** POTBELLY

cor·po·rat·ism \ˈkȯr-p(ə-)rət-ˌiz-əm\ *or* **cor·po·ra·tiv·ism** \-pə-ˌrāt-i-ˌviz-, -p(ə-)rət-\ *n* **:** the organization of a society into corporations — **cor·po·rat·ist** \-p(ə-)rət-əst\ *adj*

cor·po·ra·tive \ˈkȯr-pə-ˌrāt-iv, -p(ə-)rət-\ *adj* **1 :** of or relating to a corporation **2 :** of or relating to corporatism

cor·po·ra·tor \ˈkȯr-pə-ˌrāt-ər\ *n* **:** a corporation organizer, member, or stockholder

cor·po·re·al \kȯr-ˈpōr-ē-əl, -ˈpȯr-\ *adj* [L *corporeus* of the body, fr. *corpor-*, *corpus*] **1 :** having, consisting of, or relating to a physical material body: as **a :** not spiritual **b :** not immaterial or intangible **:** SUBSTANTIAL **2** *archaic* **:** CORPORAL **syn** see BODILY, MATERIAL — **cor·po·re·al·ly** \-ē-ə-lē\ *adv* — **cor·po·re·al·ness** *n*

cor·po·re·al·i·ty \(ˌ)kȯr-ˌpōr-ē-ˈal-ət-ē, -ˌpȯr-\ *n* **:** corporeal existence

cor·po·re·ity \ˌkȯr-pə-ˈrē-ət-ē\ *n* **:** the quality or state of having or being a body **:** MATERIALITY

cor·po·sant \ˈkȯr-pə-ˌsant, -ˌzant\ *n* [Pg *corpo-santo*, lit., holy body] **:** SAINT ELMO'S FIRE

corps \ˈkō(ə)r, ˈkȯ(ə)r\ *n, pl* **corps** \ˈkō(ə)rz, ˈkȯ(ə)rz\ [F, fr. L *corpus* body] **1 a :** an organized subdivision of the military establishment ⟨Marine *Corps*⟩ **b :** a tactical unit usu. consisting of two or more divisions and auxiliary arms and services **2 a :** a group of persons associated together or acting under common direction **b :** an association of German university students

corps area *n* **:** a territorial division of the U.S. for purposes of military administration and training

corps de bal·let \ˌkōrd-ə-(ˌ)ba-ˈlā, ˌkȯrd-\ *n, pl* **corps de ballet** *same*\ [F] **:** the ensemble or chorus of a ballet company

corpse \ˈkȯ(ə)rps\ *n* [ME *corps*, fr. MF, fr. L *corpus*] **1** *obs* **:** a human or animal body whether living or dead **2 a :** a dead body esp. of a human being **b :** something discarded or defunct

corps·man \ˈkō(ə)r(z)-mən, ˈkȯ(ə)r(z)-\ *n* **:** a navy enlisted man trained to give first aid and apprentice medical treatment

cor·pu·lence \ˈkȯr-pyə-lən(t)s\ *n* **:** FLESHINESS, OBESITY

cor·pu·len·cy \-lən-sē\ *n* **:** CORPULENCE

cor·pu·lent \-lənt\ *adj* [ME, fr. L *corpulentus*, fr. *corpus*] **:** having a large bulky body **:** OBESE — **cor·pu·lent·ly** *adv*

cor·pus \ˈkȯr-pəs\ *n, pl* **cor·po·ra** \-p(ə-)rə\ [ME, fr. L] **1 :** the body of a man or animal esp. when dead **2 a :** the main part or body of a body structure or organ ⟨the ~ of the jaw⟩ **b :** the main body or corporeal substance of a thing; *specif* **:** the principal of a fund or estate as distinct from income or interest **3 :** all the writings of a particular kind or on a particular subject

cor·pus cal·lo·sum \ˌkȯr-pə-(ˌ)ska-ˈlō-səm\ *n, pl* **cor·po·ra cal·lo·sa** \ˌkȯr-p(ə-)rə-(ˌ)ka-ˈlō-sə\ [NL, lit., callous body] **:** the great band of commissural fibers uniting the cerebral hemispheres in man and in the higher mammals

Cor·pus Chris·ti \ˌkȯr-pə-ˈskris-tē\ *n* [ME, fr. ML, lit., body of Christ] **:** a Roman Catholic festival in honor of the Eucharist observed on the Thursday after Trinity Sunday

cor·pus·cle \ˈkȯr-ˌpəs-əl, -pə-səl\ *n* [L *corpusculum*, dim. of *corpus*] **1 :** a minute particle **2 a :** a living cell; *esp* **:** one (as a red or white blood cell or a cell in cartilage or bone) not aggregated into continuous tissues **b :** a small circumscribed multicellular body — **cor·pus·cu·lar** \kȯr-ˈpəs-kyə-lər\ *adj*

cor·pus de·lic·ti \ˌkȯr-pəs-di-ˈlik-ˌtī, -(ˌ)tē\ *n, pl* **cor·po·ra delicti** \ˌkȯr-p(ə-)rə-\ [NL, lit., body of the crime] **1 :** the substantial and fundamental fact necessary to prove the commission of a crime **2 :** the material substance (as the body of the victim of a murder) upon which a crime has been committed

cor·pus lu·te·um \ˌkȯr-pə-ˈslüt-ē-əm\ *n, pl* **cor·po·ra lu·tea** \ˌkȯr-p(ə-)rə-ˈlüt-ē-ə\ [NL, lit., yellowish body] **1 :** a reddish yellow mass of endocrine tissue that forms from a ruptured Graafian follicle in the mammalian ovary **2 :** a preparation of the corpus luteum of the hog or cow used to treat ovarian dysfunction

cor·rade \kə-ˈrād\ *vb* [L *corradere* to scrape together, fr. *com-* + *radere* to scrape — more at RAT] **:** to wear away by abrasion — **cor·ra·sion** \-ˈrā-zhən\ *n* — **cor·ra·sive** \-ˈrā-siv, -ziv\ *adj*

[1]**cor·ral** \kə-ˈral\ *n* [Sp, fr. (assumed) VL *currale* enclosure for vehicles, fr. L *currus* cart, fr. *currere* to run — more at CURRENT] **1 :** a pen or enclosure for confining or capturing livestock **2 :** an enclosure made with wagons for defense of an encampment

[2]**corral** *vt* **cor·ralled; cor·ral·ling 1 :** to enclose in a corral **2 :** to arrange so as to form a corral **3 :** COLLECT, GATHER **syn** see ENCLOSE

[1]**cor·rect** \kə-ˈrekt\ *vt* [ME *correcten*, fr. L *correctus*, pp. of *corrigere*, fr. *com-* + *regere* to lead straight — more at RIGHT] **1 a :** to make or set right **:** AMEND **b :** COUNTERACT, NEUTRALIZE **c :** to alter or adjust so as to bring to some standard or required condition **2 a :** REBUKE, PUNISH **b :** to point out for amendment the errors or faults of — **cor·rect·able** \-ˈrek-tə-bəl\ *adj*

syn CORRECT, RECTIFY, EMEND, REMEDY, REDRESS, AMEND, REFORM, REVISE mean to make right what is wrong. CORRECT implies taking action to remove errors, faults, deviations, defects; RECTIFY implies a more essential changing to make something right, just, or properly controlled or directed; EMEND specifically implies correction of a text or manuscript; REMEDY implies removing or making harmless a cause of trouble, harm, or evil; REDRESS implies making compensation or reparation for an unfairness, injustice, or imbalance; AMEND, REFORM, REVISE imply an improving by making corrective changes, AMEND usu. suggesting slight changes, REFORM implying drastic change, and REVISE suggesting a detailed search for imperfections **syn** see in addition PUNISH

[2]**correct** *adj* [ME, corrected, fr. L *correctus*, fr. pp. of *corrigere*] **1 :** conforming to an approved or conventional standard **2 :** conforming to or agreeing with fact, logic, or known truth **:** ACCURATE **3 :** conforming to a set figure (as an established price) — **cor·rect·ly** \kə-ˈrek-(t)lē\ *adv* — **cor·rect·ness** \-ˈrek(t)-nəs\ *n*

syn CORRECT, ACCURATE, EXACT, PRECISE, NICE, RIGHT mean conforming to fact, standard, or truth. CORRECT usu. implies freedom from fault or error as judged by some standard; ACCURATE implies fidelity to fact or truth attained by exercise of care; EXACT stresses a very strict agreement with fact, standard, or truth; PRECISE adds to EXACT an emphasis on sharpness of definition or delimitation; NICE stresses great precision and delicacy of adjustment or discrimination; RIGHT is close to CORRECT but has a stronger positive emphasis on conformity to fact or truth rather than mere absence of error or fault

cor·rec·tion \kə-ˈrek-shən\ *n* **1 :** the action or an instance of correcting: as **a :** AMENDMENT, RECTIFICATION **b :** REBUKE, PUNISHMENT **c :** a bringing into conformity with a standard **d :** COUNTERACTION, NEUTRALIZATION **2 :** a decline in market price or business activity following and counteracting a rise **3 a :** something substituted in place of what is wrong **b :** a quantity applied by way of correcting (as for adjustment or inaccuracy of an instrument) **4 :** the treatment of offenders through a program involving penal custody, parole, and probation — **cor·rec·tion·al** \-shnəl, -shən-ᵊl\ *adj*

cor·rec·ti·tude \kə-ˈrek-tə-ˌt(y)üd\ *n* [blend of *correct* and *rectitude*] **:** correctness or propriety of conduct

cor·rec·tive \kə-ˈrek-tiv\ *adj* **:** tending to correct — **corrective** *n* — **cor·rec·tive·ly** *adv* — **cor·rec·tive·ness** *n*

cor·rec·tor \-tər\ *n* **:** one that corrects

[1]**cor·re·late** \ˈkȯr-ə-ˌlāt, ˈkär-\ *n* [back-formation fr. *correlation*] **:** either of two things so related that one directly implies or is complementary to the other (as husband and wife) — **correlate** *adj*

[2]**correlate** *vi* **:** to bear reciprocal or mutual relations ~ *vt* **1 a :** to establish a mutual or reciprocal relation of **b :** to show a causal relationship between **2 :** to relate so that to each member of one set or series a corresponding member of another is assigned

cor·re·la·tion \ˌkȯr-ə-ˈlā-shən, ˌkär-\ *n* [ML *correlation-*, *correlatio*, fr. L *com-* + *relation-*, *relatio* relation] **1 :** the act of correlating **:** the state of being correlated; *specif* **:** a relation of invariable accompaniment **2 :** reciprocal relation in the occurrence of different structures, characteristics, or processes in organisms — **cor·re·la·tion·al** \-shnəl,-shən-ᵊl\ *adj*

cor·rel·a·tive \kə-ˈrel-ət-iv\ *adj* **1 :** naturally related **:** CORRESPONDING **2 :** reciprocally related **3** *of paired words or expressions* **:** regularly used together but typically not adjacent ⟨~ conjunctions⟩ — **correlative** *n* — **cor·rel·a·tive·ly** *adv*

cor·re·spond \ˌkȯr-ə-ˈspänd, ˌkär-\ *vi* [MF or ML; MF *correspondre*, fr. ML *correspondēre*, fr. L *com-* + *respondēre* to respond] **1 a :** to be in conformity or agreement **:** SUIT **b :** to compare closely **:** MATCH **c :** to be equivalent or parallel **2 :** to communicate with a person by exchange of letters **syn** see AGREE

cor·re·spon·dence \-ˈspän-dən(t)s\ *n* **1 a :** the agreement of things with one another **b :** a particular similarity **c :** association of members of one set with each member of a second and of members of the second with each member of the first **2 :** communication by letters; *also* **:** the letters exchanged

correspondence school *n* **:** a school that teaches nonresident students by mailing them lessons and exercises which upon completion are returned to the school for grading

cor·re·spon·den·cy \-dən-sē\ *n* **:** CORRESPONDENCE

[1]**cor·re·spon·dent** \ˌkȯr-ə-ˈspän-dənt, ˌkär-\ *adj* [ME, fr. MF or ML; MF, fr. ML *correspondent-*, *correspondens*, prp. of *correspondēre*] **1 :** SIMILAR **2 :** CONFORMING, FITTING

[2]**correspondent** *n* **1 :** something that corresponds **2 a :** one who communicates with another by letter **b :** one who has regular commercial relations with another **c :** one who contributes news or comment to a newspaper often from a distant place

cor·re·spon·sive \-ˈspän(t)-siv\ *adj* **:** mutually responsive

cor·ri·da \kȯ-ˈrē-t͟hə\ *n* [Sp *corrida*, lit., act of running] **:** BULLFIGHT

cor·ri·dor \ˈkȯr-əd-ər, ˈkär-, -ə-ˌdȯ(ə)r\ *n* [MF, fr. OIt *corridore*, fr. *correre* to run, fr. L *currere* — more at CURRENT] **1 :** a passageway into which compartments or rooms open (as in a hotel) **2 :** a narrow strip of land through foreign-held territory

cor·rie \ˈkȯr-ē, ˈkär-ē\ *n* [ScGael *coire*, lit., kettle] **:** CIRQUE 3

Cor·rie·dale \-ˌdāl\ *n* [*Corriedale*, ranch in New Zealand] **:** any of a dual-purpose breed of rather large usu. hornless sheep developed in New Zealand

cor·ri·gen·dum \ˌkȯr-ə-ˈjen-dəm, ˌkär-\ *n, pl* **cor·ri·gen·da** \-də\ [L, neut. of *corrigendus*, gerundive of *corrigere* to correct] **:** an error in a printed work discovered after printing and shown with its correction on a separate sheet bound with the original

cor·ri·gi·bil·i·ty \ˌkȯr-ə-jə-ˈbil-ət-ē, ˌkär-\ *n* **:** the quality or state of being corrigible

cor·ri·gi·ble \ˈkȯr-ə-jə-bəl, ˈkär-\ *adj* [ME, fr. MF, fr. ML *corrigibilis*, fr. L *corrigere*] **:** capable of being set right **:** REPARABLE ⟨a ~ defect⟩ — **cor·ri·gi·bly** \-blē\ *adv*

cor·ri·val \kə-ˈrī-vəl, kȯ-, kō-\ *n* [MF, fr. L *corrivalis*, fr. *com-* + *rivalis* rival] **:** RIVAL, COMPETITOR — **corrival** *adj*

cor·rob·o·rant \kə-ˈräb-(ə-)rənt\ *adj, archaic* **:** INVIGORATING

cor·rob·o·rate \kə-ˈräb-ə-ˌrāt\ *vt* [L *corroboratus*, pp. of *corroborare*, fr. *com-* + *robor-*, *robur* strength] **:** to support with evidence or authority **:** make more certain **syn** see CONFIRM — **cor·rob·o·ra·tion** \-ˌräb-ə-ˈrā-shən\ *n* — **cor·rob·o·ra·tive** \-ˈräb-ə-ˌrāt-iv, -ˈräb-(ə-)rət-\ *adj* — **cor·rob·o·ra·tor** \-ˈräb-ə-ˌrāt-ər\ *n* — **cor·rob·o·ra·to·ry** \-ˈräb-(ə-)rə-ˌtōr-ē, -ˌtȯr-\ *adj*

cor·rob·o·ree \kə-ˈräb-ə-rē\ *n* [fr. native name in New South Wales, Australia] **1 :** a nocturnal festivity with songs and symbolic dances by which the Australian aborigines celebrate events of importance **2** *Austral* **a :** a noisy festivity **b :** TUMULT

cor·rode \kə-ˈrōd\ *vb* [ME *corroden*, fr. L *corrodere* to gnaw to pieces, fr. *com-* + *rodere* to gnaw — more at RAT] *vt* **1 :** to eat away by degrees as if by gnawing; *esp* **:** to wear away gradually

usu. by chemical action **2 :** CONSUME, IMPAIR ~ *vi* **:** to undergo corrosion — **cor·rod·ible** \-'rōd-ə-bəl\ *adj*

cor·ro·dy *var of* CORODY

cor·ro·sion \kə-'rō-zhən\ *n* [ME, fr. LL *corrosion-, corrosio* act of gnawing, fr. L *corrosus,* pp. of *corrodere*] **1 :** the action, process, or effect of corroding **2 :** a product of corroding

[1]**cor·ro·sive** \-'rō-siv, -ziv\ *adj* **1 :** tending or having the power to corrode ⟨~ acids⟩ ⟨~ action⟩ **2 :** FRETTING, VEXING — **cor·ro·sive·ly** *adv* — **cor·ro·sive·ness** *n*

[2]**corrosive** *n* **:** something that corrodes

corrosive sublimate *n* **:** MERCURY CHLORIDE b

cor·ru·gate \'kȯr-ə-,gāt, 'kär-\ *vb* [L *corrugatus,* pp. of *corrugare,* fr. *com-* + *ruga* wrinkle] *vt* **:** to form or shape into wrinkles or folds or ridges and grooves **:** FURROW ~ *vi* **:** to become corrugated

corrugated iron *n* **:** usu. galvanized sheet iron or sheet steel shaped into straight parallel regular and equally curved ridges and hollows

cor·ru·ga·tion \,kȯr-ə-'gā-shən, ,kär-\ *n* **1 :** the act of corrugating **2 :** a ridge or groove of a corrugated surface

[1]**cor·rupt** \kə-'rəpt\ *vb* [ME *corrupten,* fr. L *corruptus,* pp. of *corrumpere,* fr. *com-* + *rumpere* to break — more at REAVE] *vt* **1 :** to change from good to bad in morals, manners, or actions; *specif* **:** BRIBE **2 :** ROT, SPOIL **3 :** to subject to corruption of blood **4 :** to alter from the original or correct form or version ~ *vi* **1 a :** to become tainted or rotten **b :** to become morally debased **2 :** to cause disintegration or ruin **syn** see DEBASE

[2]**corrupt** *adj* [ME, fr. MF or L; MF, fr. L *corruptus,* fr. pp. of *corrumpere*] **1 a :** morally perverted **:** DEPRAVED **b :** characterized by bribery, the selling of political favors, or other improper conduct **2** *archaic* **:** TAINTED, PUTRID **syn** see VICIOUS — **cor·rupt·ly** \-'rəp-(t)lē\ *adv* — **cor·rupt·ness** \-'rəp(t)-nəs\ *n*

cor·rupt·er *or* **cor·rup·tor** \kə-'rəp-tər\ *n* **:** one that corrupts

cor·rupt·ibil·i·ty \kə-,rəp-tə-'bil-ət-ē\ *n* **:** capability of being corrupted — **cor·rupt·ible** \-'rəp-tə-bəl\ *adj* — **cor·rupt·ibly** \-blē\ *adv*

cor·rup·tion \kə-'rəp-shən\ *n* **1 a :** impairment of integrity, virtue, or moral principle **:** DEPRAVITY **b :** DECAY, DECOMPOSITION **c :** inducement to wrong by bribery or other unlawful or improper means **d :** a departure from what is pure or correct **2** *archaic* **:** an agency or influence that corrupts **3** *chiefly dial* **:** PUS

cor·rup·tion·ist \-sh(ə-)nəst\ *n* **:** one who practices or defends corruption esp. in politics

corruption of blood : a legal taint resulting from a conviction by attainder and barring the attainted person from inheriting, retaining, or transmitting any estate, rank, or title

cor·rup·tive \kə-'rəp-tiv\ *adj* **:** producing corruption — **cor·rup·tive·ly** *adv*

cor·sage \kȯr-'säzh, -'säj, 'kȯr-,\ *n* [F, bust, bodice, fr. OF, bust, fr. *cors* body, fr. L *corpus*] **1 :** the waist or bodice of a woman's dress **2 :** an arrangement of flowers to be worn by a woman

cor·sair \'kȯr-,sa(ə)r, -,se(ə)r\ *n* [MF & OIt; MF *corsaire* pirate, fr. OProv *corsari,* fr. OIt *corsaro,* fr. ML *cursarius,* fr. L *cursus* course — more at COURSE] **1 :** a privateer of the Barbary coast **2 :** PIRATE

corse \'kȯ(ə)rs\ *n* [ME *cors,* fr. OF, body] *archaic* **:** CORPSE

corse·let *in sense 1* 'kȯr-slət, *in sense 2* ,kȯr-sə-'let\ *n* **1** *or* **cors·let** [MF, dim. of *cors* body, bodice] **a :** a piece of armor for the trunk **b :** a pikeman's armor including helmet **2** *or* **cor·se·lette** [fr. *Corselette,* a trademark] **:** a foundation garment combining girdle and brassiere

[1]**cor·set** \'kȯr-sət\ *n* [ME, fr. OF, dim. of *cors*] **1 :** a medieval jacket usu. close-fitting and often laced **2 :** a woman's close-fitting boned supporting undergarment often hooked and laced that extends from above or beneath the bust or from the waist to below the hips and has garters attached — sometimes used in pl.

[2]**corset** *vt* **:** to dress in or fit with a corset

corset cover *n* **:** a woman's undergarment worn over a corset

cor·se·tiere \,kȯr-sə-'ti(ə)r, -'tye(ə)r\ *n* [F *corsetière,* fem. of *corsetier,* fr. *corset*] **:** one who makes, fits, or sells corsets, girdles, or brassieres

cor·tege *also* **cor·tège** \'kȯr-,tezh, kȯr-'\ *n* [F *cortège,* fr. It *corteggio,* fr. *corteggiare* to court, fr. *corte* court, fr. L *cohort-, cohors* throng — more at COURT] **1 :** a train of attendants **:** RETINUE **2 :** PROCESSION; *esp* **:** a funeral procession

cor·tex \'kȯr-,teks\ *n, pl* **cor·ti·ces** \'kȯrt-ə-,sēz\ *or* **cor·tex·es** [L *cortic-, cortex* bark] **1 :** a plant bark or rind used medicinally **2 :** the outer or superficial part of an organ or body structure; *esp* **:** the outer layer of gray matter of the cerebrum and cerebellum **3 a :** the typically parenchymatous layer of tissue external to the vascular tissue and internal to the corky or epidermal tissues of a green plant; *broadly* **:** all tissues external to the xylem **b :** an outer or investing layer of various algae, lichens, or fungi

cor·ti·cal \'kȯrt-i-kəl\ *adj* **1 :** of, relating to, or consisting of cortex **2 :** involving or resulting from the action or condition of the cerebral cortex — **cor·ti·cal·ly** \-k(ə-)lē\ *adv*

cor·ti·cate \'kȯrt-ə-,kāt\ *adj* **:** having a cortex

cor·ti·coid \-,kȯid\ *n* **:** any of various adrenal-cortex steroids

cor·ti·co·ste·roid \,kȯrt-ə-'käs-tə-,rȯid, ,kȯrt-i-kō-'sti(ə)r-,ȯid\ *n* [L *cortic-, cortex* + ISV *steroid*] **:** CORTICOID

cor·ti·co·ste·rone \,kȯrt-ə-'käs-tə-,rōn, ,kȯrt-i-kō-'sti(ə)r-,ōn\ *n* **:** a colorless crystalline steroid hormone $C_{21}H_{30}O_4$ of the adrenal cortex

cor·tin \'kȯrt-ᵊn\ *n* **:** the active principle of the adrenal cortex

cor·ti·sone \'kȯrt-ə-,sōn, -,zōn\ *n* [alter. of *corticosterone*] **:** a steroid hormone $C_{21}H_{28}O_5$ of the adrenal cortex used esp. in the treatment of rheumatoid arthritis

co·run·dum \kə-'rən-dəm\ *n* [Tamil *kuruntam,* fr. Skt *kuruvinda* ruby] **:** a very hard mineral Al_2O_3 that consists of aluminum oxide occurring massive and as variously colored crystals which include the ruby and sapphire, that can be synthesized, and that is used as an abrasive (hardness 9, sp. gr. 3.95–4.10)

co·rus·cant \kə-'rəs-kənt\ *adj* **:** GLITTERING, CORUSCATING

cor·us·cate \'kȯr-ə-,skāt, 'kär-\ *vi* [L *coruscatus,* pp. of *coruscare*] **:** FLASH, SPARKLE

cor·us·ca·tion \,kȯr-ə-'skā-shən, ,kär-\ *n* **1 :** GLITTER, SPARKLE **2 :** a flash of wit

cor·vée \'kȯr-,vā, kȯr-'\ *n* [ME *corvee,* fr. MF, fr. ML *corrogata,* fr. L, fem. of *corrogatus,* pp. of *corrogare* to collect, requisition, fr. *com-* + *rogare* to ask] **1 :** unpaid labor esp. on roads due from a feudal vassal to his lord **2 :** labor exacted in lieu of taxes by public authorities esp. for highway construction or repair

corves *pl of* CORF

cor·vette \kȯr-'vet\ *n* [F] **1 :** a warship ranking in the old sailing navies next below a frigate **2 :** a highly maneuverable armed escort ship that is smaller than a destroyer

cor·vi·na \kȯr-'vē-nə\ *var of* CORBINA

cor·vine \'kȯr-,vīn\ *adj* [L *corvinus,* fr. *corvus* raven — more at RAVEN] **:** of or relating to the crows **:** resembling a crow

Cor·vus \'kȯr-vəs\ *n* [L (gen. *Corvi*), lit., raven] **:** a small constellation adjoining Virgo on the south

Cor·y·bant \'kȯr-ə-,bant, 'kär-\ *n, pl* **Cor·y·bants** \-,ban(t)s\ *or* **Cor·y·ban·tes** \,kȯr-ə-'ban-,tēz, ,kär-\ [F *Corybante,* fr. L *Corybas,* fr. Gk *Korybas*] **:** one of the attendants or priests of Cybele noted for orgiastic processions and rites — **Cor·y·ban·tic** \,kȯr-ə-'bant-ik, ,kär-\ *adj*

co·ryd·a·lis \kə-'rid-ᵊl-əs\ *n* [NL, genus name, fr. Gk *korydallis* crested lark; akin to L *cornu* horn — more at HORN] **:** any of a large genus (*Corydalis*) of herbs of the fumitory family with racemose irregular flowers

cor·ymb \'kȯr-,im(b), 'kär-, -əm(b)\ *n, pl* **corymbs** \-,imz, -əmz\ [F *corymbe,* fr. L *corymbus* cluster of fruit or flowers, fr. Gk *korymbos*] **:** a flat-topped inflorescence; *specif* **:** one in which the flower stalks arise at different levels on the main axis and reach about the same height and in which the outer flowers open first and the inflorescence is indeterminate — **cor·ym·bose** \-əm-,bōs\ *also* **co·rym·bous** \kə-'rim-bəs, kō-\ *adj* — **cor·ym·bose·ly** *adv*

corymb of cherry: *1* peduncle; *2, 2* pedicels; *3, 3* bracts

cor·y·phae·us \,kȯr-ə-'fē-əs, ,kär-\ *n, pl* **cor·y·phaei** \-'fē-,ī\ [L, leader, fr. Gk *koryphaios,* fr. *koryphē* summit; akin to L *cornu*] **1 :** the leader of a chorus **2 :** the leader of a party or school of thought

co·ry·phée \,kȯr-i-'fā\ *n* [F, fr. L *coryphaeus*] **:** a ballet dancer who dances in a small group instead of in the corps de ballet or as a soloist; *broadly* **:** a dancer in the chorus **:** CHORUS GIRL

co·ry·za \kə-'rī-zə\ *n* [LL, fr. Gk *koryza* nasal mucus; akin to OHG *hroz* nasal mucus, Skt *kardama* mud] **:** an acute inflammatory contagious disease involving the upper respiratory tract; *esp* **:** COMMON COLD — **co·ry·zal** \-zəl\ *adj*

co·se·cant \(')kō-'sē-,kant, -kənt\ *n* [NL *cosecant-, cosecans,* fr. *co-* + *secant-, secans* secant] **:** the trigonometric function that for an acute angle in a right triangle is the ratio between the hypotenuse and the side opposite the angle

cosh \'käsh\ *n* [perh. fr. Romany *kosh* stick] *slang Brit* **:** a weighted weapon similar to a blackjack; *also* **:** an attack with a cosh

co·sig·na·to·ry \(')kō-'sig-nə-,tōr-ē, -,tȯr-\ *n* **:** a joint signer

co·sine \'kō-,sīn\ *n* [NL *cosinus,* fr. *co-* + ML *sinus* sine] **:** the trigonometric function that for an acute angle in a right triangle is the ratio between the side adjacent to the angle and the hypotenuse

cos lettuce \'käs-, 'kōs-\ *n* [*Kos, Cos,* Gk island] **:** a lettuce (*Lactuca sativa longifolia*) with long crisp leaves and columnar heads

[1]**cos·met·ic** \käz-'met-ik\ *n* **:** a cosmetic preparation for external use

[2]**cosmetic** *adj* [Gk *kosmētikos* skilled in adornment, fr. *kosmein* to arrange, adorn, fr. *kosmos* order] **:** relating to or making for beauty esp. of the complexion **:** BEAUTIFYING ⟨~ salves⟩; *also* **:** correcting defects esp. of the face ⟨~ surgery⟩

cos·me·tol·o·gist \,käz-mə-'täl-ə-jəst\ *n* **:** one who gives beauty treatments (as to skin and hair) — called also *beautician*

cos·me·tol·o·gy \,käz-mə-'täl-ə-jē\ *n* [F *cosmétologie,* fr. *cosmétique* cosmetic (fr. E *cosmetic*) + *-logie* -logy] **:** the cosmetic treatment of the skin, hair, and nails

cos·mic \'käz-mik\ *adj* [Gk *kosmikos,* fr. *kosmos* order, universe] **1 :** of or relating to the cosmos **2 :** extremely vast; *also* **:** GRANDIOSE — **cos·mi·cal·ly** \-mi-k(ə-)lē\ *adv*

cosmic dust *n* **:** very fine particles of solid matter in any part of the universe

cosmic noise *n* **:** GALACTIC NOISE — called also *cosmic static*

cosmic ray *n* **:** a stream of atomic nuclei of heterogeneous extremely penetrating character that enter the earth's atmosphere from outer space at speeds approaching that of light and bombard atmospheric atoms to produce mesons as well as secondary particles possessing some of the original energy

cos·mo·gon·ic \,käz-mə-'gän-ik\ *adj* **:** of or relating to cosmogony — **cos·mo·gon·i·cal** \-i-kəl\ *adj*

cos·mog·o·nist \käz-'mäg-ə-nəst\ *n* **:** a specialist in cosmogony

cos·mog·o·ny \-ə-nē\ *n* [NL *cosmogonia,* fr. Gk *kosmogonia,* fr. *kosmos* + *gonos* offspring] **1 :** the creation or origination of the world or universe **2 :** a theory of the origin of the universe

cos·mog·ra·pher \käz-'mäg-rə-fər\ *n* **:** a specialist in cosmography

cos·mo·graph·ic \,käz-mə-'graf-ik\ *adj* **:** of or relating to cosmography — **cos·mo·graph·i·cal** \-i-kəl\ *adj* — **cos·mo·graph·i·cal·ly** \-i-k(ə-)lē\ *adv*

cos·mog·ra·phy \käz-'mäg-rə-fē\ *n* [ME *cosmographie,* fr. LL *cosmographia,* fr. Gk *kosmographia,* fr. *kosmos* + *-graphia* -graphy] **1 :** a general description of the world or of the universe **2 :** the science that deals with the constitution of the whole order of nature

cos·mo·line \'käz-mə-,lēn\ *vt* **:** to smear with Cosmoline grease (as for storage)

Cosmoline *trademark* — used for petrolatum

cos·mo·log·ic \,käz-mə-'läj-ik\ *adj* **:** of or relating to cosmology — **cos·mo·log·i·cal** \-i-kəl\ *adj* — **cos·mo·log·i·cal·ly** \-i-k(ə-)lē\ *adv*

cos·mol·o·gist \käz-'mäl-ə-jəst\ *n* **:** a specialist in cosmology

cos·mol·o·gy \käz-'mäl-ə-jē\ *n* [NL *cosmologia,* fr. Gk *kosmos* + NL *-logia* -logy] **1 :** a branch of metaphysics that deals with the universe as an orderly system **2 :** a branch of astronomy that deals with the origin, structure, and space-time relationships of the universe

cos·mo·naut \'käz-mə-,nȯt, -,nät\ *n* [part trans. of Russ *kosmonavt,* fr. Gk *kosmos* + Russ *-navt* (as in *aeronavt* aeronaut)] **:** a traveler beyond the earth's atmosphere **:** ASTRONAUT

cos·mop·o·lis \käz-'mäp-ə-ləs\ *n* [NL, back-formation fr. *cosmopolites*] **:** a cosmopolitan city

cos·mo·pol·i·tan \,käz-mə-'päl-ət-ᵊn\ *adj* **1 :** having worldwide rather than limited or provincial scope or bearing **2 :** having

wide international sophistication **3 :** composed of persons, constituents, or elements from all or many parts of the world **4 :** found in most parts of the world and under varied ecological conditions ⟨a ~ herb⟩ — **cosmopolitan** *n* — **cos·mo·pol·i·tan·ism** \-ᵊn-,iz-əm\ *n*

cos·mop·o·lite \käz-'mäp-ə-,līt\ *n* [NL *cosmopolites*, fr. Gk *kosmopolitēs*, fr. *kosmos* + *politēs* citizen] **:** a cosmopolitan person or organism — **cos·mop·o·lit·ism** \-,līt-,iz-əm\ *n*

cos·mos \'käz-məs, *1 & 2 also* -,mōs, -,mäs\ *n* [G *kosmos*, fr. Gk] **1 a :** an orderly harmonious systematic universe — compare CHAOS **b :** ORDER, HARMONY **2 :** a complex orderly self-inclusive system **3** *pl* **cosmos** *also* **cos·mos·es** [NL, genus name, fr. Gk *kosmos*] **:** any of a genus (*Cosmos*) of tropical American composite herbs; *esp* **:** a widely cultivated tall fall-blooming annual (*C. bipinnatus*) with yellow or red disks and showy ray flowers

cos·sack \'käs-,ak, -ək\ *n* [Russ *kazak* & Ukrainian *kozak*, fr. Turk *kazak* free person] **:** a member of a favored military caste of Russian frontiersmen and border guards in czarist Russia

1**cos·set** \'käs-ət\ *n* [origin unknown] **:** a pet lamb; *broadly* **:** PET

2**cosset** *vt* **:** to treat as a pet **:** FONDLE

1**cost** \'kȯst\ *n* **1 a :** the amount or equivalent paid or charged for something **:** PRICE **b :** the outlay or expenditure (as of effort or sacrifice) made to achieve an object **2 :** loss or penalty incurred in gaining something **3** *pl* **:** expenses incurred in litigation; *esp* **:** those given by the law or the court to the prevailing against the losing party

2**cost** *vb* **cost; cost·ing** [ME *costen*, fr. MF *coster*, fr. L *constare* to stand firm, to cost — more at CONSTANT] *vi* **1 :** to require a specified expenditure or payment **2 :** to require effort, suffering, or loss ~ *vt* **1 :** to have a price of **2 :** to cause to pay, suffer, or lose **3 :** to estimate or set the cost of

cos·ta \'käs-tə\ *n, pl* **cos·tae** \-(,)tē, -,tī\ [L — more at COAST] **1 :** 1RIB 1a **2 :** a part (as the midrib of a leaf or the anterior vein of an insect wing) likened to a rib — **cos·tal** \'käst-ᵊl\ *adj* — **cos·tate** \'käs-,tāt\ *adj*

cost accountant *n* **:** a specialist in cost accounting

cost accounting *n* **:** the systematic recording and analysis of the costs of material, labor, and overhead incident to production

cos·tard \'käs-tərd\ *n* [ME] **1 :** any of several large English cooking apples **2** *archaic* **:** NODDLE, PATE

cos·ter \'käs-tər\ *n*, *Brit* **:** COSTERMONGER

cos·ter·mon·ger \'käs-tər-,məŋ-gər, -,mäŋ-\ *n* [*costard, coster* + *monger*] *Brit* **:** a hawker of fruit or vegetables

cos·tive \'käs-tiv\ *adj* [ME, fr. MF *costivé*, pp. of *costiver* to constipate, fr. L *constipare*] **1 a :** CONSTIPATED **b :** causing constipation **2 :** slow in action or expression **3 :** NIGGARDLY — **cos·tive·ly** *adv* — **cos·tive·ness** *n*

cost·li·ness \'kȯs(t)-lē-nəs\ *n* **:** DEARNESS, EXPENSIVENESS

cost·ly \'kȯs(t)-lē\ *adj* **1 :** of great cost or value **2 :** GORGEOUS, SPLENDID **3 :** made at heavy expense or sacrifice

syn EXPENSIVE, DEAR, VALUABLE, PRECIOUS, INVALUABLE, PRICELESS: COSTLY implies high price and may suggest sumptuousness, luxury, or rarity; EXPENSIVE may further imply a price beyond the thing's value or the buyer's means; DEAR implies a relatively high or exorbitant price usu. due to factors other than the thing's intrinsic value; VALUABLE may suggest worth measured in usefulness as well as in market value; PRECIOUS applies to what is of great or even incalculable value because scarce or irreplaceable; INVALUABLE and PRICELESS imply such great worth as to make valuation nearly impossible, but INVALUABLE now often means little more than very useful, PRICELESS little more than amusingly odd or original

cost·mary \'kȯst-,mer-ē\ *n* [ME *costmarie*, fr. *coste* costmary (fr. OE *cost*, fr. L *costum*, fr. Gk *kostos*, a fragrant root) + *Marie* the Virgin Mary] **:** a tansy-scented composite herb (*Chrysanthemum majus*) used as a potherb and in flavoring

cost–plus \'kȯs(t)-'pləs\ *adj* **:** paid on the basis of a fixed fee or a percentage added to actual cost ⟨a ~ contract⟩

cos·trel \'käs-trəl\ *n* [ME, fr. MF *costerel*, fr. *costier* at the side, fr. *coste* rib, side] *dial Eng* **:** a leather, earthenware, or wooden container for liquids having ears by which it may be hung up

cos·tume \'käs-,t(y)üm, käs-'\ *n* [F, fr. It, custom, dress, fr. L *consuetudin-*, *consuetudo* custom] **1 :** the prevailing fashion in coiffure, jewelry, and apparel of a period, country, or class **2 :** a suit or dress characteristic of a period, country, or class **3 :** a person's ensemble of outer garments; *esp* **:** a woman's ensemble of dress with coat or jacket — **costume** *vt* — **costume** *adj*

cos·tum·er \'käs-,t(y)ü-mər, käs-'\ *n* **:** a maker or dealer in costumes

cos·tu·mi·er \käs-'t(y)ü-mē-ər\ *n* **:** COSTUMER

co·sy \'kō-zē\ *var of* COZY

1**cot** \'kät\ *n* [ME, fr. OE; akin to ON *kot* small hut, L *guttur* throat] **1 :** a small house **2 :** COVER, SHEATH; *esp* **:** STALL 4

2**cot** *n* [Hindi *khāt* bedstead, fr. Skt *khaṭvā*, of Dravidian origin] **:** a small often collapsible bed usu. of fabric stretched on a frame

co·tan·gent \(')kō-'tan-jənt\ *n* [NL *cotangent-*, *cotangens*, fr. *co-* + *tangent-*, *tangens* tangent] **:** the trigonometric function that for an acute angle in a right triangle is the ratio between the side adjacent to the angle and the side opposite

1**cote** \'kōt, 'kät\ *n* [ME, fr. OE] **1** *dial Eng* **:** 1COT 1 **2 :** a shed or coop for small domestic animals and esp. pigeons

2**cote** \'kōt\ *vt* [prob. fr. MF *cotoyer*] *obs* **:** to pass by

co·te·rie \'kōt-ə-(,)rē, ,kōt-ə-'\ *n, often attrib* [F, fr. MF, tenants, fr. (assumed) MF *cotier* cottager, fr. ML *cotarius*] **:** an intimate often exclusive group of persons with a common interest or purpose

co·ter·mi·nal \(')kō-'tərm-nəl, -ən-ᵊl\ *adj* **:** COTERMINOUS 1

co·ter·mi·nous \(')kō-'tər-mə-nəs\ *adj* [alter. of *conterminous*] **1 :** having the same or coincident boundaries **2 :** coextensive in scope or duration — **co·ter·mi·nous·ly** *adv*

co·thur·nus \kō-'thər-nəs\ *n, pl* **co·thur·ni** \-,nī, -(,)nē\ [L, fr. Gk *kothornos*] **1 :** a high thick-soled laced boot worn by actors in Greek and Roman tragic drama — called also *cothurn* **2 :** the dignified somewhat stylized spirit of ancient tragedy

co·tid·al \(')kō-'tīd-ᵊl\ *adj* **:** marking an equality in the tides or a coincidence in the time of high or low tide

co·til·lion \kō-'til-yən\ *also* **co·til·lon** \kō-'til-yən, kō-tē-(y)ōⁿ\ *n* [F *cotillon*, lit., petticoat, fr. OF, fr. *cote* coat] **1 :** a ballroom dance for couples that resembles the quadrille **2 :** an elaborate dance with frequent changing of partners executed under the leadership of one couple at formal balls **3 :** a formal ball

co·to·neas·ter \kə-'tō-nē-,as-tər, 'kät-ᵊn-,ēs-\ *n* [NL, genus name, fr. L *cydonia*, *cotoneum* quince + NL *-aster*] **:** any of a genus (*Cotoneaster*) of Old World flowering shrubs of the rose family

cot·quean \'kät-,kwēn\ *n* **1** *archaic* **:** a coarse masculine woman **2** *archaic* **:** a man who busies himself with affairs properly feminine

Cots·wold \'kät-,swōld\ *n* [*Cotswold* hills, Gloucestershire, England] **:** a sheep of an English breed of large long-wooled sheep

cot·ta \'kät-ə\ *n* [ML, of Gmc origin; akin to OHG *kozza* coarse mantle — more at COAT] **:** a waist-length surplice

cot·tage \'kät-ij\ *n* [ME *cotage*, fr. (assumed) AF, fr. ME *cot*] **1 :** the dwelling of a rural laborer or small farmer **2 :** a small usu. frame one-family house **3 :** a small detached dwelling unit at an institution **4 :** a small house for vacation use

cottage cheese *n* **:** a soft uncured cheese made from soured skim milk — called also *Dutch cheese, pot cheese, smearcase*

cottage pudding *n* **:** plain cake covered with a hot sweet sauce

cot·tag·er \'kät-ij-ər\ *n* **:** one who lives in a cottage (as at a vacation resort)

cottage tulip *n* **:** any of various tall-growing May-flowering tulips

1**cot·ter** *or* **cot·tar** \'kät-ər\ *n* [ME *cottar*, fr. ML *cotarius*, fr. ME *cot*] **:** a peasant or rural laborer occupying a cottage and sometimes a small holding of land usu. in return for services

2**cotter** *n* [origin unknown] **:** a wedge-shaped or tapered piece used to fasten together parts of a structure

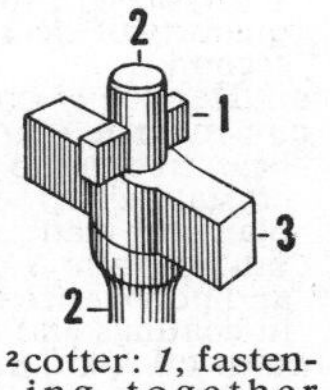

2cotter: *1*, fastening together parts *2* and *3*

cotter pin *n* **:** a half-round metal strip bent into a pin whose ends can be flared after insertion through a slot or hole

1**cot·ton** \'kät-ᵊn\ *n* [ME *coton*, fr. MF, fr. Ar *quṭn*] **1 a :** a soft usu. white fibrous substance composed of the hairs surrounding the seeds of various erect freely branching tropical plants (genus *Gossypium*) of the mallow family **b :** a plant producing cotton; *esp* **:** one grown for its cotton **c :** a crop of cotton **2 a :** fabric made of cotton **b :** yarn spun from cotton **3 :** a downy cottony substance produced by various plants (as the cottonwood)

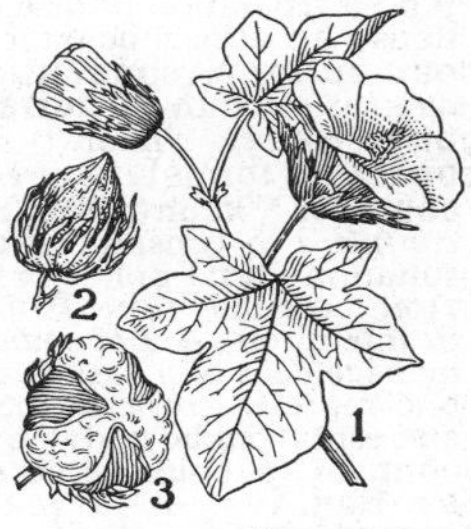

cotton: *1* flowering branch; *2* fruit, unopened; *3* fruit, partly open

2**cotton** *vi* **cot·ton·ing** \'kät-niŋ, -ᵊn-iŋ\ **:** to take a liking ⟨~s to people easily⟩

cotton candy *n* **:** a candy made by spinning sugar that has been boiled to a high temperature

cotton gin *n* **:** a machine that separates the seeds, hulls, and foreign material from cotton

cotton grass *n* **:** any of a genus (*Eriophorum*) of sedges with tufted spikes

cot·ton·mouth \'kät-ᵊn-,maùth\ *n* **:** WATER MOCCASIN

cot·ton·seed \-,sēd\ *n* **:** the seed of the cotton plant yielding a fixed semidrying oil used esp. in cooking and a protein-rich meal

cotton stainer *n* **:** any of several red and black or dark brown bugs (genus *Dysdercus*) that damage and stain the lint of developing cotton

cot·ton·tail \'kät-ᵊn-,tāl\ *n* **:** any of several rather small No. American rabbits (genus *Sylvilagus*) sandy brown in color with a white-tufted underside of the tail

cot·ton·weed \-,wēd\ *n* **:** any of various weedy plants (as cudweed) with hoary pubescence or cottony seeds

cot·ton·wood \-,wùd\ *n* **:** a poplar with a tuft of cottony hairs on the seed; *esp* **:** one (*Populus deltoides*) of the eastern and central U.S. often cultivated for its rapid growth and luxuriant foliage

cotton wool *n* **:** raw cotton; *esp* **:** cotton batting

cot·tony \'kät-nē, -ᵊn-ē\ *adj* **:** resembling cotton in appearance or character: as **a :** covered with hairs or pubescence **b :** SOFT

cotyl- *or* **cotyli-** *or* **cotylo-** *comb form* [Gk *kotyl-*, *kotylo-*, fr. *kotylē*] **:** cup **:** organ or part like a cup ⟨*cotyl*oid⟩ ⟨*cotyli*form⟩

-cot·yl \,kät-ᵊl\ *n comb form* [cotyledon] **:** cotyledon ⟨di*cotyl*⟩

cot·y·le·don \,kät-ᵊl-'ēd-ᵊn\ *n* [NL, fr. Gk *kotylēdōn* cup-shaped hollow, fr. *kotylē* cup] **1 :** a placental lobule **2 :** the first leaf or one of the first pair or whorl of leaves developed by the embryo of a seed plant — **cot·y·le·don·al** \-'ēd-nəl, -ᵊn-əl\ *adj* — **cot·y·le·don·ary** \-'ēd-ᵊn-,er-ē\ *or* **cot·y·le·don·ous** \-'ēd-ᵊn-əs\ *adj*

co·type \'kō-,tīp\ *n* **:** any of several secondary taxonomic types

1**couch** \'kaùch\ *vb* [ME *couchen*, fr. MF *coucher*, fr. L *collocare* to set in place] *vt* **1 :** to lay (oneself) down for rest or sleep **2 :** to embroider (a design) by laid threads fastened by small stitches at regular intervals **3 :** to place or hold level and pointed forward ready for use **4 :** to phrase in a specified manner **5 :** to treat (a cataract) by displacing the lens of the eye into the vitreous humor ~ *vi* **1 :** to lie down or recline for sleep or rest **2 :** to lie in ambush

2**couch** *n* **1 :** an article of furniture (as a bed) for sitting or reclining; *specif* **:** SOFA **2 :** the den of an animal (as an otter)

couch·ant \'kaù-chənt\ *adj* [ME, fr. MF, fr. prp. of *coucher*] **:** lying down esp. with the head up ⟨a heraldic lion ~⟩

couch grass \'kaùch-, 'küch-\ *n* [alter. of *quitch grass*] **:** a grass spreading vigorously by creeping rhizomes; *esp* **:** a European grass (*Agropyron repens*) naturalized in No. America as a weed

cou·gar \'kü-gər, -,gär\ *n, pl* **cougars** *also* **cougar** [F *couguar*, fr. NL *cuguacuarana*, modif. of Tupi *suasuarana*, lit., false deer, fr. *suasú* deer + *rana* false] **:** a large powerful tawny brown cat (*Felis concolor*) formerly widespread in the Americas but now extinct in many areas — called also *catamount, mountain lion, panther, puma*

1**cough** \'kȯf\ *vb* [ME *coughen*, fr. (assumed) OE *cohhian*; akin to MHG *kūchen* to breathe heavily] *vi* **1 :** to expel air from the lungs suddenly with an explosive noise **2 :** to make a noise like that of coughing ~ *vt* **:** to expel by coughing ⟨~ up mucus⟩

2**cough** *n* **1 :** a condition marked by repeated or frequent coughing **2 :** an act or sound of coughing

cough up *vt* : DELIVER, PAY ⟨*cough up* the money⟩
could \kəd, (ˈ)ku̇d\ [ME *couthe, coude*, fr. OE *cūthe;* akin to OHG *konda* could] *past of* CAN — used in auxiliary function in the past ⟨he found he ~ go⟩ ⟨he said he would go if he ~⟩ and as an alternative to *can* suggesting less force or certainty or as a polite form in the present ⟨~ you do this for me⟩ ⟨if you ~ come we would be pleased⟩
couldn't \ˈku̇d-ᵊnt\ : could not
cou·lee \ˈkü-lē\ *n* [CanF *coulée*, fr. F, flowing, flow of lava, fr. *couler* to flow, fr. L *colare* to strain, fr. *colum* sieve] **1** *chiefly West* **a** : a small stream **b** : a dry creek bed **c** : a steep-walled valley or ravine **2** : a thick sheet or stream of lava
cou·lisse \kü-ˈlēs\ *n* [F] **1 a** : a side scene of a theater stage or the space between the side scenes **b** : a backstage area **c** : HALLWAY **2** : a piece of timber having a groove in which something glides
cou·loir \kül-ˈwär\ *n* [F, lit., strainer, fr. LL *colatorium*, fr. L *colatus*, pp. of *colare*] : a mountainside gorge esp. in the Swiss Alps
cou·lomb \ˈkü-ˌläm, -ˌlōm, kü-ˈ\ *n* [Charles A. de *Coulomb* †1806 F physicist] : the practical mks unit of electric charge equal to the quantity of electricity transferred by a current of one ampere in one second
coulter *var of* COLTER
cou·ma·rin \ˈk(y)ü-mə-rən\ *n* [F *coumarine*, fr. *coumarou* tonka bean tree, fr. Sp or Pg; Sp *coumarú*, fr. Pg, fr. Tupi] : a toxic white crystalline lactone $C_9H_6O_2$ with an odor of new-mown hay found in plants or made synthetically and used esp. in perfumery
cou·ma·rone \-ˌrōn\ *n* : a compound C_8H_6O found in coal tar and polymerized with indene to form thermoplastic resins used esp. in coatings and printing inks
coun·cil \ˈkau̇n(t)-səl\ *n* [ME *counceil*, fr. OF *concile*, fr. L *concilium*, fr. *com-* + *calare* to call — more at LOW] **1** : an assembly or meeting for consultation, advice, or discussion **2** : a group elected or appointed as an advisory or legislative body **3 a** : a usu. administrative body **b** : an executive body whose members are equal in power and authority **c** : a governing body of delegates from local units of a federation **4** : deliberation in a council **5 a** : a federation of or a central body uniting a group of organizations **b** : a local chapter of an organization **c** : CLUB, SOCIETY
coun·cil·lor *or* **coun·cil·or** \ˈkau̇n(t)-s(ə-)lər\ *n* : a member of a council — **coun·cil·lor·ship** \-ˌship\ *n*
coun·cil·man \ˈkau̇n(t)-səl-mən\ *n* : a member of a council
council of ministers *often cap C&M* : CABINET 3b
1**coun·sel** \ˈkau̇n(t)-səl\ *n* [ME *conseil*, fr. OF, fr. L *consilium*, fr. *consulere* to consult] **1 a** : advice given esp. as a result of consultation **b** : a policy or plan of action or behavior **2** : DELIBERATION, CONSULTATION **3 a** *archaic* : PURPOSE **b** : guarded thoughts or intentions **4 a** *pl counsel* (1) : a lawyer engaged in the trial or management of a case in court (2) : a lawyer appointed to advise and represent in legal matters an individual client or a corporate and esp. a public body **b** : CONSULTANT 2 **syn** see ADVICE, LAWYER
2**counsel** *vb* **coun·seled** *or* **coun·selled; coun·sel·ing** *or* **coun·sel·ling** \-s(ə-)liŋ\ *vt* : ADVISE ~ *vi* : CONSULT
coun·sel·ing *n* : the use of psychological methods in testing the interests of and giving professional guidance to individuals
coun·sel·or *or* **coun·sel·lor** \ˈkau̇n(t)-s(ə-)lər\ *n* **1** : ADVISER **2** : LAWYER; *specif* : one that gives advice in law and manages cases for clients in court **3** : one who has supervisory duties at a summer camp **syn** see LAWYER — **coun·sel·or·ship** \-ˌship\ *n*
1**count** \ˈkau̇nt\ *vb* [ME *counten*, fr. MF *compter*, fr. L *computare*, fr. *com-* + *putare* to consider] *vt* **1 a** : to indicate or name by units or groups to find the total number of units involved : NUMBER **b** : to name the numbers in order up to and including ⟨~ ten⟩ **c** : to include in a tallying and reckoning ⟨about 100 present, ~*ing* children⟩ **2 a** : CONSIDER, ACCOUNT ⟨~ oneself lucky⟩ **b** : ESTIMATE, ESTEEM **c** : to record as of an opinion or persuasion ⟨~ me as uncommitted⟩ **3** : to include or exclude by or as if by counting ⟨~ me in⟩ ~ *vi* **1 a** : to recite or indicate the numbers in order by units or groups ⟨~ by fives⟩ **b** : to count the units in a group **2 a** : DEPEND ⟨a man you can ~ on⟩ **b** : to take something into consideration ⟨~*ed* on being present⟩ **3** : ADD, TOTAL **4** : to have value or significance **syn** see RELY — **count·able** \-ə-bəl\ *adj*
2**count** *n* **1** : the act or process of counting; *also* : a total obtained by counting : TALLY **2** *archaic* **a** : RECKONING, ACCOUNT **b** : CONSIDERATION, ESTIMATION **3 a** : ALLEGATION, CHARGE; *specif* : one separately stating the cause of action or prosecution in a legal declaration or indictment ⟨guilty on all ~*s*⟩ **b** : a specific point under consideration : ISSUE **4** : the total number of individual things in a given unit or sample ⟨blood ~⟩ **5** : the calling off of the seconds from one to ten when a boxer has been knocked down
3**count** *n* [MF *comte*, fr. LL *comit-*, *comes*, fr. L, companion, one of the imperial court, fr. *com-* + *ire* to go — more at ISSUE] : a European nobleman whose rank corresponds to that of an English earl
count·down \ˈkau̇nt-ˌdau̇n\ *n* : an audible backward counting in fixed units (as seconds) from an arbitrary starting number to mark the time remaining before an event; *also* : preparations carried on during such a count
1**coun·te·nance** \ˈkau̇nt-ᵊn-ən(t)s, ˈkau̇n-tə-nən(t)s, ˈkau̇nt-nən(t)s\ *n* [ME *contenance*, fr. MF, fr. ML *continentia*, fr. L, restraint, fr. *continent-*, *continens*, prp. of *continēre* to hold together] **1** *obs* : BEARING, DEMEANOR **2 a** : calm expression **b** : mental composure **c** : LOOK, EXPRESSION **3** *archaic* **a** : ASPECT, SEMBLANCE **b** : PRETENSE **4** : FACE, VISAGE; *esp* : the face as an indication of mood, emotion, or character **5** : appearance or expression seeming to approve or encourage **syn** see FACE, FAVOR
2**countenance** *vt* : to extend approval or toleration to : SANCTION — **coun·te·nanc·er** *n*
1**count·er** \ˈkau̇nt-ər\ *n* [ME *countour*, fr. MF *comptouer*, fr. ML *computatorium* computing place, fr. L *computatus*, pp. of *computare*] **1** : a piece (as of metal or ivory) used in reckoning or in games **2** : something of value in bargaining : ASSET **3** : a level surface (as a table) over which transactions are conducted or food is served or on which goods are displayed or work is conducted
2**count·er** *n* [ME, fr. MF *conteor*, fr. *compter* to count] : one that counts; *esp* : a device for indicating a number or amount
3**coun·ter** \ˈkau̇nt-ər\ *vb* [ME *countren*, fr. MF *contre*] *vt* **1 a** : to act in opposition to : OPPOSE **b** : OFFSET, NULLIFY **2** : to adduce in answer ~ *vi* : to meet attacks or arguments with defensive or retaliatory steps
4**coun·ter** *adv* [ME *contre*, fr. MF, fr. L *contra* against, opposite; akin to L *com-* with, together] **1** : in an opposite or wrong direction **2** : to or toward a different or opposite result or effect
5**coun·ter** *n* **1** : CONTRARY, OPPOSITE **2** : the after portion of a boat from the waterline to the extreme outward swell or stern overhang **3 a** : a circular parry in fencing in which the blade follows that of the opponent **b** : the act of giving a blow while receiving or parrying one (as in boxing); *also* : the blow given **c** : an agency or force that offsets : CHECK **4** : a stiffener to give permanent form to a boot or shoe upper around the heel **5** : any area in the face of a letter that is less than type-high and enclosed by the strokes
6**coun·ter** *adj* **1** : marked by or tending toward or in an opposite direction or effect : OPPOSED **2** : given to or marked by opposition or hostility **3** : situated or lying opposite **4** : COUNTERMANDING **syn** see ADVERSE
counter- *prefix* [ME *contre-*, fr. MF, fr. *contre*] **1 a** : contrary : opposite ⟨*counter*clockwise⟩ ⟨*counter*march⟩ **b** : opposing : retaliatory ⟨*counter*irritant⟩ ⟨*counter*offensive⟩ **2** : complementary : corresponding ⟨*counter*weight⟩ ⟨*counter*part⟩ **3** : duplicate : substitute ⟨*counter*foil⟩
coun·ter·act \ˌkau̇nt-ə-ˈrakt\ *vt* : to make ineffective or mitigate the ill effects of by opposite force : OFFSET — **coun·ter·ac·tion** \-ˈrak-shən\ *n*
coun·ter·ac·tive \-ˈrak-tiv\ *adj* : tending to counteract **syn** see ADVERSE
coun·ter·at·tack \ˈkau̇nt-ə-rə-ˌtak\ *n* : an attack made to counter an enemy's attack — **counterattack** *vb*
1**coun·ter·bal·ance** \ˈkau̇nt-ər-ˌbal-ən(t)s, ˌkau̇nt-ər-ˈ\ *n* **1** : a weight that balances another : COUNTERPOISE **2** : a force or influence that offsets or checks an opposing force
2**counterbalance** \ˌkau̇nt-ər-ˈ, ˈkau̇nt-ər-ˌ\ *vt* **1** : to oppose with an equal weight or force **2** : to equip with counterbalances
coun·ter·change \ˈkau̇nt-ər-ˌchānj\ *vt* : INTERCHANGE, EXCHANGE
1**coun·ter·check** \ˈkau̇nt-ər-ˌchek\ *n* : a check or restraint often operating against something that is itself a check
2**countercheck** *vt* **1** : CHECK, COUNTERACT **2** : to check a second time for verification
counter check *n* : a check obtainable at a bank esp. to be cashed only at the bank by the drawer
coun·ter·claim \ˈkau̇nt-ər-ˌklām\ *n* : an opposing claim esp. in law — **counterclaim** *vb*
coun·ter·clock·wise \ˌkau̇nt-ər-ˈkläk-ˌwīz\ *adv* : in a direction opposite to that in which the hands of a clock rotate — **counterclockwise** *adj*
coun·ter·es·pi·o·nage \ˌkau̇nt-ə-ˈres-pē-ə-ˌnäzh, -nij, -ˌnäj; -rə-ˈspē-ə-nij\ *n* : the attempt to discover and defeat enemy espionage
1**coun·ter·feit** \ˈkau̇nt-ər-ˌfit\ *vt* : to imitate or copy esp. with intent to deceive ~ *vi* **1** : PRETEND, FEIGN **2** : to engage in counterfeiting valuables **syn** see ASSUME — **coun·ter·feit·er** *n*
2**counterfeit** *adj* [ME *countrefet*, fr. MF *contrefait*, fr. pp. of *contrefaire* to imitate, fr. *contre-* + *faire* to make, fr. L *facere* — more at DO] **1** : made in imitation of something else with intent to deceive : FORGED **2 a** : FEIGNED **b** : SHAM, PRETENDED
3**counterfeit** *n* **1** : something counterfeit : FORGERY **2** : something likely to be confused with the genuine thing **syn** see IMPOSTURE
coun·ter·foil \ˈkau̇nt-ər-ˌfȯil\ *n* : a detachable stub usu. serving as a record or receipt (as on a check or ticket)
coun·ter·in·tel·li·gence \ˌkau̇nt-ə-rən-ˈtel-ə-jən(t)s\ *n* : organized activity of an intelligence service designed to block an enemy's sources of information, to deceive the enemy, to prevent sabotage, and to gather political and military information
coun·ter·ir·ri·tant \ˌkau̇nt-ə-ˈrir-ə-tənt\ *n* : an agent applied locally to produce superficial inflammation with the object of reducing inflammation in deeper adjacent structures — **counterirritant** *adj*
count·er·man \ˈkau̇nt-ər-ˌman, -mən\ *n* : one who tends a counter
coun·ter·mand \ˈkau̇nt-ər-ˌmand, ˌkau̇nt-ər-ˈ\ *vt* [ME *countermaunden*, fr. MF *contremander*, fr. *contre-* counter- + *mander* to command, fr. L *mandare*] **1** : to revoke (a former command) by a contrary order **2** : to recall or order back by a superseding contrary order — **countermand** *n*
coun·ter·march \ˈkau̇nt-ər-ˌmärch\ *n* : a marching back; *specif* : an evolution by which a unit of troops reverses direction while marching but keeps the same order — **countermarch** *vi*
coun·ter·mea·sure \-ˌmezh-ər, -ˌmā-zhər\ *n* : an action undertaken to counter another
coun·ter·mine \-ˌmīn\ *n* **1** : a tunnel for intercepting an enemy mine **2** : a stratagem for defeating an attack : COUNTERPLOT — **countermine** *vb*
coun·ter·of·fen·sive \ˈkau̇nt-ə-rə-ˌfen(t)-siv\ *n* : a large-scale military offensive undertaken by a force previously on the defensive
coun·ter·pane \ˈkau̇nt-ər-ˌpān\ *n* [alter. of ME *countrepointe*, modif. of MF *coute pointe*, lit., embroidered quilt] : BEDSPREAD
coun·ter·part \-ˌpärt\ *n* **1** : one of two corresponding copies of a legal instrument : DUPLICATE **2 a** : a thing that fits another perfectly **b** : something that completes : COMPLEMENT **3 a** : one remarkably similar to another **b** : one having the same function or characteristics as another : EQUIVALENT
1**coun·ter·plot** \-ˌplät\ *vt* : to intrigue against or foil with a plot
2**counterplot** *n* : a plot opposed to another
coun·ter·point \ˈkau̇nt-ər-ˌpȯint\ *n* [MF *contrepoint*, fr. ML *contrapunctus*, fr. L *contra-* counter- + ML *punctus* musical note, melody, fr. L, act of pricking, fr. *punctus*, pp. of *pungere* to prick — more at POINT] **1 a** : one or more independent melodies added above or below a given melody **b** : combination of two or more related independent melodies into a single harmonic texture in which each retains its linear character : POLYPHONY **2 a** : a complementing or contrasting item : OPPOSITE **b** : use of contrast or interplay of elements in a work of art (as a drama)
1**coun·ter·poise** \-ˌpȯiz\ *vt* [ME *countrepesen*, fr. MF *contrepeser*, fr. *contre-* + *peser* to weigh — more at POISE] : COUNTERBALANCE
2**counterpoise** *n* **1** : COUNTERBALANCE **2** : an equivalent power or force acting in opposition **3** : a state of balance
coun·ter·pose \ˌkau̇nt-ər-ˈpōz\ *vt* [*counter-* + *-pose* (as in *compose*)] : to place in opposition, contrast, or equilibrium
coun·ter·pro·pos·al \ˈkau̇nt-ər-prə-ˌpō-zəl\ *n* : a countering proposal
coun·ter·punch \-ˌpənch\ *n* : a counter in boxing; *also* : a countering blow or attack — **coun·ter·punch·er** \-ˌpən-chər\ *n*
coun·ter·ref·or·ma·tion \ˌkau̇nt-ə(r)-ˌref-ər-ˈmā-shən\ *n* **1** : an opposing reformation **2** *usu* **Counter-Reformation** : the reform movement in the Roman Catholic Church following the Reformation
coun·ter·rev·o·lu·tion \-ˌrev-ə-ˈlü-shən\ *n* : a revolution in

opposition to a current or earlier one — **coun·ter·rev·o·lu·tion·ary** \-shə-ˌner-ē\ *adj or n* — **coun·ter·rev·o·lu·tion·ist** \-sh(ə-)nəst\ *n*
coun·ter·shaft \ˈkau̇nt-ər-ˌshaft\ *n* **:** a shaft that receives motion from a main shaft and transmits it to a working part
1coun·ter·sign \-ˌsīn\ *n* **1 :** a signature attesting the authenticity of a document already signed by another **2 :** a sign used in reply to another; *specif* **:** a military secret signal that must be given by one wishing to pass a guard
2countersign *vt* **1 :** to add one's signature to after another's to attest authenticity **2 :** CONFIRM, CORROBORATE — **coun·ter·sig·na·ture** \ˌkau̇nt-ər-ˈsig-nə-ˌchu̇(ə)r, -chər, -ˌt(y)u̇(ə)r\ *n*
1coun·ter·sink \ˈkau̇nt-ər-ˌsiŋk\ *vt* **1 :** to make a countersink on **2 :** to set the head of (as a screw) at or below the surface
2countersink *n* **1 :** a funnel-shaped enlargement at the outer end of a drilled hole **2 :** a bit or drill for making such an enlargement
coun·ter·spy \-ˌspī\ *n* **:** a spy employed against enemy espionage
coun·ter·ten·or \-ˌten-ər\ *n* [ME *countretenour*, fr. MF *contreteneur*, fr. *contre-* + *teneur* tenor] **:** a tenor with an unusually high range and tessitura
coun·ter·vail \ˌkau̇nt-ər-ˈvā(ə)l\ *vb* [ME *countrevailen*, fr. MF *contrevaloir*, fr. *contre-* counter- + *valoir* to be worth, fr. L *valēre* — more at WIELD] *vt* **1 :** to compensate for **2** *archaic* **:** EQUAL, MATCH **3 :** to exert force against **:** COUNTERACT **~** *vi* **:** to exert force against an opposing side **syn** see COMPENSATE
coun·ter·view \ˈkau̇nt-ər-ˌvyü\ *n, archaic* **:** CONFRONTATION
coun·ter·weight \-ˌwāt\ *n* **:** an equivalent weight **:** COUNTERBALANCE — **counterweight** *vt*
count·ess \ˈkau̇nt-əs\ *n* **:** the wife or widow of an earl or count or a woman who holds in her own right the rank of earl or count
count·ing·house \ˈkau̇nt-iŋ-ˌhau̇s\ *n* **:** a building, room, or office used for keeping books and transacting business
counting room *n* **:** COUNTINGHOUSE
counting tube *n* **:** an ionization chamber designed to respond to passage through it of fast-moving ionizing particles and usu. connected to some device for counting the particles — called also *counter tube*
count·less \ˈkau̇nt-ləs\ *adj* **:** too numerous to be counted **:** MYRIAD
count noun *n* **:** a noun (as *bean* or *sheet*) that forms a plural and is used with a numeral, with words such as *many* or *few*, or with the indefinite article *a* or *an*
count palatine *n* **1 a :** a high judicial official in the Holy Roman Empire **b :** a count of the Holy Roman Empire having imperial powers in his own domain **2 :** the proprietor of a county palatine in England or Ireland
coun·tri·fied *also* **coun·try·fied** \ˈkən-tri-ˌfīd\ *adj* [*country* + *-fied* (as in *glorified*)] **:** RURAL, RUSTIC
1coun·try \ˈkən-trē\ *n* [ME *contree*, fr. OF *contrée*, fr. ML *contrata* fr. L *contra* against, on the opposite side] **1 :** an indefinite usu. extended expanse of land **:** REGION **2 a :** the land of a person's birth, residence, or citizenship **b :** a political state or nation or its territory **3 a :** the people of a state or district **:** POPULACE **b :** JURY **c :** ELECTORATE **4 :** rural as distinguished from urban areas
2country *adj* **1 :** of, relating to, or characteristic of the country **2 :** prepared or processed with farm supplies and procedures
country club *n* **:** a suburban club for social life and recreation
coun·try–dance \ˈkən-trē-ˌdan(t)s\ *n* **:** an English dance in which partners face each other esp. in rows
coun·try·man \ˈkən-trē-mən, *3 often* -ˌman\ *n* **1 :** an inhabitant or native of a specified country **2 :** COMPATRIOT **3 :** one living in the country or marked by country ways **:** RUSTIC — **coun·try·wom·an** \-ˌwu̇m-ən\ *n*
coun·try·seat \ˌkən-trē-ˈsēt\ *n* **:** a mansion or estate in the country
coun·try·side \ˈkən-trē-ˌsīd\ *n* **:** a rural area or its people
1coun·ty \ˈkau̇nt-ē\ *n* [ME *counte*, fr. OF *conté*, fr. ML *comitatus*, fr. LL, office of a count, fr. *comit-*, *comes* count — more at COUNT] **1 :** the domain of a count **2 a :** one of the territorial divisions of Great Britain and Ireland constituting the chief units for administrative, judicial, and political purposes **b** (1) **:** the people of a county (2) *Brit* **:** the gentry of a county **3 :** the largest territorial division for local government within a state of the U.S. **4 :** the largest local administrative unit in various countries
2county *n* [modif. of MF *comte*] *obs* **:** 3COUNT
county agent *n* **:** a consultant employed jointly by federal and state governments to advise about agriculture and home economics by means of lectures, demonstrations, and discussions in rural areas
county palatine *n* **:** the territory of a count palatine
county seat *n* **:** a town that is the seat of county administration
1coup \ˈkōp\ *vb* [ME *coupen* to strike, fr. MF *couper* — more at COPE] *chiefly Scot* **:** OVERTURN, UPSET
2coup \ˈkü\ *n, pl* **coups** \ˈküz\ [F, blow, stroke] **1 :** a brilliant, sudden, and usu. highly successful stroke **2 :** COUP D'ETAT
coup de grace \ˌküd-ə-ˈgräs\ *n, pl* **coups de grace** \ˌküd-ə-\ [F *coup de grâce*, lit., stroke of mercy] **1 :** a death blow or shot administered to end the suffering of one mortally wounded **2 :** a decisive finishing blow or event
coup de main \-ˈmaⁿ\ *n, pl* **coups de main** \ˌküd-ə-\ [F, lit., hand stroke] **:** a sudden attack in force
coup d'etat \ˌküd-ə-ˈtä, ˌküd-(ˌ)ā-\ *n, pl* **coups d'etat** \ˌküd-ə-ˈtä(z), ˌküd-(ˌ)ā-\ [F *coup d'état*, lit., stroke of state] **:** a sudden decisive exercise of force in politics; *esp* **:** the violent overthrow or alteration of an existing government by a small group
coup de the·atre \ˌküd-ə-tā-ˈätrᵊ\ *n, pl* **coups de theatre** \ˌküd-ə-\ [F *coup de théâtre*, lit., stroke of theater] **:** a sudden sensational turn in a play; *also* **:** a sudden dramatic turn of events
coup d'oeil \kü-ˈdə(r), -ˈdə(r)-yə, -ˈdəi\ *n, pl* **coups d'oeil** *same*\ [F, lit., stroke of the eye] **:** a brief survey **:** GLANCE
cou·pé *or* **coupe** \kü-ˈpā, *2 often* ˈküp\ *n* [F *coupé*] **1 :** a four-wheeled closed horse-drawn carriage for two persons inside with an outside seat for the driver in front **2** *usu* *coupe* **:** a closed 2-door automobile with one seat compartment and a separate luggage compartment

coupé 1

1cou·ple \ˈkəp-əl\ *vb* **cou·pling** \-(ə-)liŋ\ *vt* **1 :** to connect for consideration together **2 a :** to fasten together **:** LINK **b :** to bring (two electric circuits) into such close proximity as to permit mutual influence **3 :** to join in marriage or sexual union **~** *vi* **1 :** to unite in sexual union **2 :** JOIN
2couple *n* [ME, pair, bond, fr. OF *cople*, fr. L *copula* bond, fr. *co-* + *apere* to fasten] **1 a :** a man and woman married, engaged, or otherwise paired **b :** any two persons paired together **2 :** PAIR, BRACE **3 :** something that joins or links two things together: as **a :** two equal and opposite forces that act along parallel lines **b :** GALVANIC COUPLE **4 :** an indefinite small number **:** FEW
3couple *adj* **:** TWO — used with *a* ⟨a ~ more oaths⟩
cou·ple·ment \ˈkəp-əl-mənt\ *n* [MF, fr. *coupler* to join, fr. L *copulare*, fr. *copula*] *archaic* **:** the act or result of coupling
cou·pler \ˈkəp-(ə-)lər\ *n* **1 :** one that couples **2 :** a contrivance on a keyboard instrument by which keyboards or keys are connected to play together
cou·plet \ˈkəp-lət\ *n* [MF, dim. of *cople*] **1 :** two successive lines of verse forming a unit marked usu. by rhythmic correspondence, rhyme, or the inclusion of a self-contained utterance **2 :** COUPLE
cou·pling \ˈkəp-liŋ (*usual for 2*), -ə-liŋ\ *n* **1 :** the act of bringing or coming together **:** PAIRING; *specif* **:** sexual union **2 :** a device that serves to connect the ends of adjacent parts or objects **3 :** the joining of or the part of the body that joins the hindquarters to the forequarters of a quadruped **4 :** means of electric connection of two electric circuits by having a part common to both
cou·pon \ˈk(y)ü-ˌpän\ *n* [F, fr. OF, piece, fr. *couper* to cut — more at COPE] **1 :** a statement of due interest to be cut from a bearer bond when payable and presented for payment **2 :** a form surrendered in order to obtain an article, service, or accommodation: as **a :** one of a series of attached tickets or certificates often to be detached and presented as needed **b :** a ticket or form authorizing purchases of rationed commodities **c :** a certificate or similar evidence of a purchase redeemable in premiums **d :** a part of a printed advertisement to be cut off for use as an order blank or inquiry form
cour·age \ˈkər-ij, ˈkə-rij\ *n* [ME *corage*, fr. OF, fr. *cuer* heart, fr. L *cor* — more at HEART] **:** mental or moral strength to venture, persevere, and withstand danger, fear, or difficulty
syn METTLE, SPIRIT, RESOLUTION, TENACITY: COURAGE implies firmness of mind and will in the face of danger or extreme difficulty; METTLE suggests an ingrained capacity for meeting strain or difficulty with fortitude and resilience; SPIRIT also suggests a quality of temperament enabling one to hold one's own or keep up one's morale when opposed or threatened; RESOLUTION stresses firm determination to achieve one's ends; TENACITY adds to RESOLUTION implications of stubborn persistence and unwillingness to admit defeat
cou·ra·geous \kə-ˈrā-jəs\ *adj* **:** having or characterized by courage **:** BRAVE — **cou·ra·geous·ly** *adv* — **cou·ra·geous·ness** *n*
cou·rante \ku̇-ˈränt, -ˈrant\ *n* [MF, fr. *courir* to run, fr. L *currere*] **1 :** a dance of Italian origin marked by quick running steps **2 :** music for a courante
cou·reur de bois \ku̇-ˌrərd-əb-ˈwä\ *n, pl* **coureurs de bois** *same*\ [CanF, lit., woods runner] **:** a French or half-breed trapper of No. America and esp. of Canada
cou·ri·er \ˈku̇r-ē-ər, ˈkər-ē-, ˈkə-rē-\ *n, often attrib* [MF *courrier*, fr. OIt *corriere*, fr. *correre* to run, fr. L *currere*] **:** MESSENGER: as **a :** a member of a diplomatic service entrusted with bearing messages **b** (1) **:** an espionage agent transferring secret information (2) **:** a runner of contraband **c :** a member of the armed services whose duties include carrying mail, information, or supplies
cour·lan \ˈku̇(ə)r-lən, ku̇(ə)r-ˈläⁿ\ *n* [F, modif. of Galibi *kurliri*] **:** a long-billed bird (*Aramus guarana*) intermediate in some respects between the cranes and rails occurring in So. and Central America
1course \ˈkō(ə)rs, ˈkȯ(ə)rs\ *n* [ME, fr. OF, fr. L *cursus*, fr. *cursus*, pp. of *currere* to run — more at CURRENT] **1 a :** the act or action of moving in a path from point to point **b :** LIFE HISTORY, CAREER **2 :** the path over which something moves: as **a :** RACECOURSE **b** (1) **:** the direction of flight of an airplane usu. measured as a clockwise angle from north (2) **:** a point of the compass **c :** WATERCOURSE **d :** land laid out for golf **3 a :** accustomed procedure or normal action **b :** a chosen manner of conducting oneself **:** BEHAVIOR **c :** progression through a series of acts or events or a development or period **4 :** an ordered process or succession: as **a :** a series of lectures or other matter dealing with a subject or a series of such courses constituting a curriculum **b :** a series of doses or medicaments administered over a designated period **5 a :** a part of a meal served at one time **b :** ROW, LAYER; *esp* **:** a continuous level range of brick or masonry throughout a wall **c :** the lowest sail on a square-rigged mast — **of course 1 :** following the ordinary way or procedure **2 :** as might be expected
2course *vt* **1 a :** to hunt or pursue (game) with hounds **b :** to cause (dogs) to run (as after game) **2 :** to follow close upon **:** PURSUE **3 :** to run or move swiftly through or over **:** TRAVERSE **~** *vi* **:** to run or pass rapidly usu. along an indicated path
1cours·er \ˈkōr-sər, ˈkȯr-\ *n* [ME, fr. OF *coursier*, fr. *course* course, run] **:** a swift or spirited horse **:** CHARGER
2courser *n* **1 :** a dog for coursing **2 :** one that courses **:** HUNTSMAN **3 :** any of a group of birds of Africa and southern Asia related to the plovers and remarkable for their speed in running
cours·ing *n* **1 :** the act of one that courses **2 :** the pursuit of running game with dogs that follow by sight instead of by scent
1court \ˈkō(ə)rt, ˈkȯ(ə)rt\ *n, often attrib* [ME, fr. OF, fr. L *cohort-*, *cohors* enclosure, throng, cohort, fr. *co-* + *-hort-*, *-hors* (akin to *hortus* garden) — more at YARD] **1 a :** the residence or establishment of a sovereign or similar dignitary **b :** a sovereign's formal assembly of his councillors and officers **c :** the sovereign and his officers and advisers who are the governing power **d :** the family and retinue of a sovereign **e :** a reception held by a sovereign **2 a :** a manor house or large building surrounded by usu. enclosed grounds **b :** MOTEL **c :** an open space enclosed wholly or partly by buildings or circumscribed by a single building **d :** a quadrangular space walled or marked off for playing one of various games with a ball (as lawn tennis, racquets, handball, or basketball) or a division of such a court **e :** a wide alley with only one opening onto a street **3 a :** an official assembly for the transaction of judi-

cial business **b :** a session of such a court ⟨~ is now adjourned⟩ **c :** a chamber or other place for the administration of justice **d :** a judge or judges in session **e :** a faculty or agency of judgment or evaluation **4 a :** an assembly or board with legislative or administrative powers **b :** PARLIAMENT, LEGISLATURE **5 :** conduct or attention intended to win favor or dispel hostility

²court *vt* **1 a :** to seek to gain or achieve **b** (1) **:** ALLURE, TEMPT (2) **:** to act so as to invite or provoke **2 a :** to seek the affections of **b** *of an animal* **:** to perform actions to attract for mating **3 :** to seek to attract by attentions and flatteries **~** *vi* **1 :** to engage in social activities leading to engagement and marriage **2** *of an animal* **:** to engage in activity leading to mating **syn** see INVITE

cour·te·ous \'kərt-ē-əs\ *adj* [ME *corteis*, fr. OF, fr. *court*] **1 :** marked by polished manners, gallantry, or ceremonial usage of a court **2 :** marked by respect for and consideration of others **syn** see CIVIL — **cour·te·ous·ly** *adv* — **cour·te·ous·ness** *n*

cour·te·san \'kōrt-ə-zən, 'kȯrt-, 'kərt-, -sən, -ˌzan, -ˌsan\ *n* [MF *courtisane*, fr. OIt *cortigiana* woman courtier, fem. of *cortigiano* courtier, fr. *corte* court, fr. L *cohort-*, *cohors*] **:** a prostitute with a courtly, wealthy, or upper-class clientele

cour·te·sy \'kərt-ə-sē\ *n* [ME *corteisie*, fr. OF, fr. *corteis*] **1 a :** courteous behavior **b :** a courteous act or expression **2 a :** general allowance despite facts **:** INDULGENCE ⟨hills called mountains by ~ only⟩ **b :** consideration, cooperation, and generosity in providing; *also* **:** AGENCY, MEANS

court game *n* **:** an athletic game played on a court

court·house \'kō(ə)rt-ˌhau̇s, 'kȯ(ə)rt-\ *n* **1 a :** a building in which courts of law are regularly held **b :** the principal building in which county offices are housed **2 :** COUNTY SEAT

court·ier \'kōrt-ē-ər, 'kōrt-yər, 'kȯrt-; kōr-chər, 'kȯr-\ *n* **1 :** one in attendance at a royal court **2 :** one who practices flattery

court·li·ness \'kōrt-lē-nəs, 'kȯrt-\ *n* **:** the quality of being courtly

¹court·ly \'kō(ə)rt-lē, 'kȯ(ə)rt-\ *adj* **1 a :** of a quality befitting the court **:** ELEGANT **b :** insincerely flattering **2 :** favoring the policy or party of the court

²courtly *adv* **:** in a courtly manner **:** POLITELY

courtly love *n* **:** a late medieval conventionalized code prescribing conduct and emotions of ladies and their lovers

¹court–mar·tial \'kōrt-ˌmär-shəl, 'kȯrt-\ *n, pl* **courts–martial** *also* **court–martials** **1 :** a court consisting of commissioned officers and in some instances enlisted personnel for the trial of members of the armed forces or others within its jurisdiction **2 :** a trial by court-martial

²court–martial *vt* **court–mar·tialed** *also* **court–mar·tialled; court–mar·tial·ing** *also* **court–mar·tial·ling** \-ˌmärsh-liŋ, -ˌmär-shə-liŋ\ **:** to subject to trial by court-martial

Court of St. James \-(ˌ)sānt-'jāmz, -sənt-\ [fr. *St. James's* Palace, London, former seat of the British court] **:** the British court

court plaster *n* **:** an adhesive plaster esp. of silk coated with isinglass and glycerin

court·room \'kō(ə)rt-ˌrüm, 'kȯ(ə)rt-, -ˌru̇m\ *n* **:** a room in which a court of law is held

court·ship \-ˌship\ *n* **:** the act or process of courting

court tennis *n* **:** a game played with a ball and racket in an enclosed court

court·yard \'kō(ə)rt-ˌyärd, 'kȯ(ə)rt-\ *n* **:** a court or enclosure attached to a building (as a house or palace)

cous·in \'kəz-ᵊn\ *n* [ME *cosin*, fr. OF, fr. L *consobrinus*, fr. *com-* + *sobrinus* cousin on the mother's side, fr. *soror* sister] **1 a :** a child of one's uncle or aunt **b :** a relative descended from one's grandparent or more remote ancestor in a different line **c :** KINSMAN, RELATIVE **2 :** one associated with another **:** EQUIVALENT **3** — used as a title by a sovereign in addressing a nobleman **4 :** a person of a race or people ethnically or culturally related or similar

cous·in–ger·man \ˌkəz-ᵊn-'jər-mən\ *n, pl* **cous·ins–ger·man** \ˌkəz-ᵊnz-\ [ME *cosin germain*, fr. MF, fr. OF, fr. *cosin* + *germain* german] **:** COUSIN 1a

couth \'küth\ *adj* [back-formation fr. *uncouth*] **:** POLISHED, SOPHISTICATED

couth·ie \'kü-thē\ *adj* [ME *couth*] *chiefly Scot* **:** PLEASANT, KINDLY

cou·ture \kü-'tu̇(ə)r\ *n* [F, fr. OF *cousture* sewing, fr. (assumed) VL *consutura*, fr. L *consutus*, pp. of *consuere* to sew together, fr. *com-* + *suere* to sew — more at SEW] **:** the business of designing, making, and selling fashionable custom-made women's clothing; *also* **:** the designers and establishments engaged in this business

cou·tu·ri·er \kü-'tu̇r-ē-ər, -ē-ˌā\ *n* [F, dressmaker, fr. OF *cousturier* tailor's assistant, fr. *cousture*] **:** an establishment engaged in couture; *also* **:** the proprietor of or designer for such an establishment

cou·tu·ri·ere \kü-'tu̇r-ē-ər, -ē-ˌe(ə)r\ *n* [F *couturière*, fr. OF *cousturiere*, fem. of *cousturier*] **:** a female couturier

cou·vade \kü-'väd\ *n* [F, fr. MF, cowardly inactivity, fr. *cover* to sit on, brood over — more at COVEY] **:** a primitive custom in which when a child is born the father takes to bed as if bearing the child, cares for it, and submits himself to fasting, purification, or taboos

co·va·lence \(')kō-'vā-lən(t)s\ *or* **co·va·len·cy** \-lən-sē\ *n* **:** the number of pairs of electrons an atom can share with its neighbors — **co·va·lent** \-lənt\ *adj*

covalent bond *n* **:** a nonionic chemical bond formed by shared electrons

co·var·i·ant \(')kō-'ver-ē-ənt, -'var-\ *adj* [ISV] **:** varying with something else so as to preserve certain mathematical interrelations

¹cove \'kōv\ *n* [ME, den, fr. OE *cofa;* akin to OE *cot*] **1 :** a concavity or recessed place: as **a :** an architectural member with a concave cross section **b :** a trough for concealed lighting at the upper part of a wall **2 :** a small sheltered inlet or bay **3 a :** a deep recess or small valley in the side of a mountain **b :** a level area sheltered by hills or mountains

²cove *vt* **:** to make in a hollow concave form

³cove *n* [Romany *kova* thing, person] *slang Brit* **:** MAN, FELLOW

co·ven \'kəv-ən, 'kō-vən\ *n* [ME *covin* band, fr. MF, fr. ML *convenium* agreement, fr. L *convenire* to agree — more at CONVENTION] **:** an assembly or band of esp. 13 witches

¹cov·e·nant \'kəv-(ə-)nənt\ *n* [ME, fr. OF, fr. prp. of *covenir* to agree, fr. L *convenire*] **1 :** a usu. formal, solemn, and binding agreement **:** COMPACT **2 a :** a written agreement or promise usu. under seal between two or more parties esp. for the performance of some action **b :** the common-law action to recover damages for breach of such a contract — **cov·e·nan·tal** \ˌkəv-ə-'nant-ᵊl\ *adj*

²cov·e·nant \'kəv-(ə-)nənt, -ə-ˌnant\ *vt* **:** to promise by a covenant **:** PLEDGE **~** *vi* **:** to enter into a covenant **:** CONTRACT

cov·e·nan·tee \ˌkəv-ə-ˌnan-'tē\ *n* **:** the person to whom a promise in the form of a covenant is made

cov·e·nant·er \'kəv-ə-ˌnant-ər, 2 *also* ˌkəv-ə-'\ *n* **1 :** one that makes a covenant **2** *cap* **:** a signer or adherent of the Scottish National Covenant of 1638

cov·e·nan·tor \'kəv-ə-ˌnant-ər, ˌkəv-ə-ˌnan-'tȯ(ə)r\ *n* **:** the party to a covenant bound to perform the obligation expressed in it

Cov·en·try \'kəv-ən-trē, 'käv-\ *n* [*Coventry*, England] **:** a state of ostracism or exclusion ⟨sent to ~⟩

¹cov·er \'kəv-ər\ *vb* **cov·er·ing** \'kəv-(ə-)riŋ\ [ME *coveren*, fr. OF *covrir*, fr. L *cooperire*, fr. *co-* + *operire* to close, cover — more at WEIR] *vt* **1 a :** to guard from attack **b** (1) **:** to have within the range of one's guns **:** COMMAND (2) **:** to hold within range of an aimed firearm **c** (1) **:** to afford protection or security to **:** INSURE (2) **:** to afford protection against or compensation for **d** (1) **:** to guard (an opponent) in order to obstruct a play (2) **:** to be in position to receive a throw to (a base in baseball) **e** (1) **:** to make provision for (a demand or charge) by means of a reserve or deposit (2) **:** to maintain a check on esp. by patrolling (3) **:** to protect by contrivance or expedient **2 a :** to hide from sight or knowledge **:** CONCEAL ⟨~ up a scandal⟩ **b :** to lie over **:** ENVELOP **3 :** to lay or spread something over **:** OVERLAY **4 a :** to spread over **b :** to appear here and there on the surface of **5 :** to place or set a cover or covering over **6 a :** to copulate with (a female) ⟨a horse ~*s* a mare⟩ **b :** to sit on and incubate (eggs) **7 :** to invest with a large or excessive amount of something ⟨~*s* himself with glory⟩ **8 :** to play a higher-ranking card on (a previously played card) **9 :** to have sufficient scope to include or take into account **10 :** to deal with **:** TREAT **11 a :** to have as one's territory or field of activity **b :** to report news about **12 :** to pass over **:** TRAVERSE **13 :** to place one's stake in equal jeopardy with in a bet **14 :** to buy securities or commodities for delivery against (an earlier short sale) **~** *vi* **1 :** to conceal something illicit, blameworthy, or embarrassing from notice ⟨~ up for a friend⟩ **2 :** to act as a substitute or replacement during an absence — **cov·er·er** \'kəv-ər-ər\ *n*

²cover *n, often attrib* **1 :** something that protects, shelters, or guards: as **a :** natural shelter for an animal or the factors that provide such shelter **b** (1) **:** a position or situation affording protection from enemy fire (2) **:** the protection offered by airplanes in tactical support of a military operation **2 :** something that is placed over or about another thing: **a :** LID, TOP **b :** a binding or case for a book; *also* **:** the front or back of such a binding **c :** an overlay or outer layer esp. for protection **d :** a tablecloth and the other table fittings **e :** ROOF **f :** a cloth used on a bed **g :** something (as vegetation or snow) that covers the ground **h :** the extent to which clouds obscure the sky **3 :** something that conceals or obscures **:** SCREEN **4 :** an envelope or wrapper for mail

cov·er·age \'kəv-(ə-)rij\ *n* **1 :** the act or fact of covering or something that covers: as **a :** inclusion within the scope of an insurance policy or protective plan **:** INSURANCE **b :** the amount available to meet liabilities **c :** inclusion within the scope of discussion or reporting **2 :** the total group covered **:** SCOPE: as **a :** all the risks covered by the terms of an insurance contract **b :** the number or percentage of persons reached by a communications medium

cov·er·all \'kəv-ə-ˌrȯl\ *n* **:** a one-piece outer garment worn to protect other garments — usu. used in pl.

cover charge *n* **:** a charge made by a restaurant or nightclub in addition to the charge for food and drink

cover crop *n* **:** a crop planted to prevent soil erosion and to provide humus

covered smut *n* **:** a smut disease of grains in which the spore masses are held together by the persistent grain membrane and glumes

covered wagon *n* **:** a wagon with canvas top supported by bows

¹cov·er·ing \'kəv-(ə-)riŋ\ *n* **:** something that covers or conceals

²covering *adj* **:** containing explanation of or additional information about an accompanying communication ⟨~ letter⟩

cov·er·let \'kəv-ər-lət, -ˌlet, -ˌlid, -ləd\ *n* [ME, alter. of *coverlite*, fr. AF *coverelyth*, fr. OF *covrir* + *lit* bed, fr. L *lectus*] **:** BEDSPREAD

¹co·vert \'kəv-ərt; 'kō-(ˌ)vərt, kō-'\ *adj* [ME, fr. OF, pp. of *covrir* to cover, fr. L *cooperire*] **1 :** HIDDEN **2 :** covered over **:** SHELTERED **3 :** being married and under the authority or protection of her husband **syn** see SECRET — **co·vert·ly** *adv* — **co·vert·ness** *n*

²co·vert \'kəv-ərt, 'kō-vərt\ *n* **1 a :** hiding place **:** SHELTER **b :** a thicket affording cover for game **c :** a masking or concealing device **2 :** a feather covering the bases of the quills of the wings and tail of a bird **3 :** a firm durable twilled sometimes waterproofed cloth usu. of mixed-color yarns

cov·er·ture \'kəv-ər-ˌchu̇(ə)r, -chər, -ˌt(y)u̇(ə)r\ *n* **1 a :** COVERING **b :** SHELTER **2 :** the legal status of a woman during marriage

cov·et \'kəv-ət\ *vb* [ME *coveiten*, fr. OF *coveitier*, fr. *coveitié* desire, modif. of L *cupiditat-*, *cupiditas*, fr. *cupidus* desirous, fr. *cupere* to desire; akin to L *vapor* steam, vapor, Gk *kapnos* smoke] *vt* **1 :** to wish for enviously **2 :** to desire (what belongs to another) inordinately or culpably **~** *vi* **:** to feel inordinate desire for what belongs to another **syn** see DESIRE — **cov·et·able** \-ə-bəl\ *adj* — **cov·et·er** \-ər\ *n* — **cov·et·ing·ly** \-iŋ-lē\ *adv*

cov·et·ous \-əs\ *adj* **1 :** marked by inordinate desire for wealth or possessions or for another's possessions **2 :** having a craving for possession ⟨~ of fame⟩ — **cov·et·ous·ly** *adv* — **cov·et·ous·ness** *n*

syn GREEDY, ACQUISITIVE, GRASPING, AVARICIOUS: COVETOUS implies inordinateness of desire often for another's possessions; GREEDY stresses lack of restraint and often of discrimination in desire; ACQUISITIVE implies both eagerness to possess and ability to acquire and keep; GRASPING adds to COVETOUS and GREEDY an implication of selfishness and often suggests unfair or ruthless means; AVARICIOUS implies obsessive acquisitiveness esp. of money and strongly suggests stinginess

cov·ey \'kəv-ē\ *n* [ME, fr. MF *covee*, fr. OF, fr. *cover* to sit on, brood over, fr. L *cubare* to lie] **1 :** a mature bird or pair of birds with a brood of young; *also* **:** a small flock **2 :** COMPANY, BAND

¹cow \'kau̇\ *n* [ME *cou*, fr. OE *cū*; akin to OHG *kuo* cow, L *bos* head of cattle, Gk *bous*, Skt *go*] **1 :** the mature female of cattle (genus *Bos*) or of any animal the male of which is called *bull* (as the moose) **2 :** a domestic bovine animal regardless of sex or age — **cowy** \-ē\ *adj*

²cow *vt* [alter. of *coll* (to poll)] *chiefly Scot* **:** to cut short **:** POLL

[3]**cow** *vt* [prob. of Scand origin; akin to Dan *kue* to subdue] **:** to intimidate with threats or show of strength **:** DAUNT

cow·age *or* **cow·hage** \'kau̇-ij\ *n* [Hindi *kavāc*] **:** a tropical leguminous woody vine (*Mucuna pruritum*) with crooked pods covered with barbed hairs that cause severe itching; *also* **:** these hairs sometimes used as a vermifuge

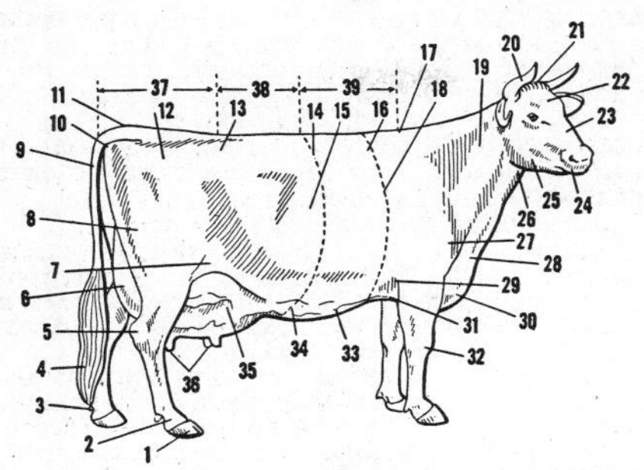

cow: *1* hoof, *2* pastern, *3* dewclaw, *4* switch, *5* hock, *6* rear udder, *7* flank, *8* thigh, *9* tail, *10* pinbone, *11* tail head, *12* thurl, *13* hip, *14* barrel, *15* ribs, *16* crops, *17* withers, *18* heart girth, *19* neck, *20* horn, *21* poll, *22* forehead, *23* bridge of nose, *24* muzzle, *25* jaw, *26* throat, *27* point of shoulder, *28* dewlap, *29* point of elbow, *30* brisket, *31* chest floor, *32* knee *33* milk well, *34* milk vein, *35* fore udder, *36* teats, *37* rump, *38* loin, *39* chine

cow·ard \'kau̇(-ə)rd\ *n* [ME, fr. OF *coart*, fr. *coe* tail, fr. L *cauda*] **:** one who shows ignoble fear or timidity — **coward** *adj*

cow·ard·ice \-əs\ *n* [ME *cowardise*, fr. OF *coardise*, fr. *coart*] **:** lack of courage or resolution

cow·ard·li·ness \'kau̇(-ə)rd-lē-nəs\ *n* **:** the quality or state of being cowardly

[1]**cow·ard·ly** \-lē\ *adv* **:** in a cowardly manner

[2]**cowardly** *adj* **:** resembling or befitting a coward
syn PUSILLANIMOUS, CRAVEN, DASTARDLY: COWARDLY implies a weak or ignoble lack of courage; PUSILLANIMOUS suggests a contemptible lack of courage; CRAVEN suggests a dishonoring abject yielding to fear; DASTARDLY implies behavior that is both cowardly and treacherous or skulking or outrageous

cow·bane \'kau̇-,bān\ *n* **:** any of several poisonous plants of the carrot family (as a water hemlock)

cow·bell \'kau̇-,bel\ *n* **:** a bell hung about the neck of a cow to make a sound by which it can be located

cow·ber·ry \-,ber-ē\ *n* **:** any of several pasture shrubs (as *Vaccinium vitis-idaea*) or their berries or fruits

cow·bird \-,bərd\ *n* **:** a small No. American blackbird (*Molothrus ater*) that lays its eggs in the nests of other birds

cow·boy \-,bȯi\ *n* **:** one who tends or drives cattle; *esp* **:** a usu. mounted cattle ranch hand — **cow·girl** \-,gər(-ə)l\ *n*

cow·catch·er \-,kach-ər, -,kech-\ *n* **:** PILOT 3

cow·er \'kau̇(-ə)r\ *vi* [ME *couren*, of Scand origin; akin to Norw *kura* to cower; akin to Gk *gyros* circle, OE *cot*] **1 :** to stand or crouch quivering in abject fear of something menacing or domineering **2 :** to shrink away from the cold **syn** see FAWN

cow·fish \'kau̇-,fish\ *n* **1 a :** any of various small cetaceans **b :** SIRENIAN **2 :** any of various small bright-colored fishes (family Ostraciontidae) with projections resembling horns over the eyes

cow·hand \'kau̇-,hand\ *n* **:** COWBOY

cow·herd \-,hərd\ *n* **:** one who tends cows

[1]**cow·hide** \-,hīd\ *n* **1 :** the hide of a cow or leather from it **2 :** a coarse whip of rawhide or braided leather

[2]**cowhide** *vt* **:** to flog with a cowhide whip

cowl \'kau̇(ə)l\ *n* [ME *cowle*, fr. OE *cugele*, fr. LL *cuculla* monk's hood, fr. L *cucullus* hood] **1 :** a hood or long hooded cloak esp. of a monk **2 a :** a chimney covering designed to improve the draft **b :** the top portion of the front part of an automobile body forward of the two front doors to which are attached the windshield and instrument board **c :** COWLING — **cowl** *vt*

cowled \'kau̇(ə)ld\ *adj* **:** shaped like a hood **:** HOODED ⟨a ~ flower⟩

cow·lick \'kau̇-,lik\ *n* **:** a tuft of hair growing in a different direction from the rest and usu. turned up or awry as if licked by a cow

cowl·ing \'kau̇-liŋ\ *n* **:** a removable metal covering that houses the engine and sometimes a portion of the fuselage or nacelle of an airplane; *also* **:** a metallic cover for any engine

cowl·staff \'kōl-,staf, 'kau̇(ə)l-\ *n* [ME *cuvelstaff*, fr. *cuvel* vessel (fr. OE *cȳfel*, fr. ONF *cuvele* small vat) + *staff*] *dial Eng* **:** a staff from which a vessel is suspended and carried between two persons

cow·man \'kau̇-mən, -,man\ *n* **1 :** COWHERD, COWBOY **2 :** a cattle owner or rancher

co–work·er \'kō-,wər-kər\ *n* **:** a fellow worker

cow·pea \'kau̇-,pē\ *n* **:** a sprawling leguminous herb (*Vigna sinensis*) related to the bean and widely cultivated in southern U.S. esp. for forage and green manure; *also* **:** its edible seed

Cow·per's gland \,kau̇-pərz-, ,kü-pərz-, ,ku̇p-ərz-\ *n* [William *Cowper* †1709 E surgeon] **:** either of two small glands discharging into the male urethra

cow·poke \'kau̇-,pōk\ *n* **:** COWBOY

cow pony *n* **:** a light saddle horse trained for herding cattle

cow·pox \'kau̇-,päks\ *n* **:** a mild eruptive disease of the cow that when communicated to man protects against smallpox

cow·punch·er \-,pən-chər\ *n* **:** COWBOY

cow·rie *or* **cow·ry** \'kau̇(ə)r-ē\ *n* [Hindi *kaurī*] **:** any of numerous marine gastropods (family Cypraeidae) widely distributed in warm seas with glossy often brightly colored shells

cow·slip \'kau̇-,slip\ *n* [ME *cowslyppe*, fr. OE *cūslyppe*, lit., cow dung, fr. *cū* cow + *slypa, slyppe* paste] **1 :** a common British primrose (*Primula veris*) with fragrant yellow or purplish flowers **2 :** MARSH MARIGOLD **3 :** SHOOTING STAR **4 :** VIRGINIA COWSLIP

cox \'käks\ *n* **:** COXSWAIN — **cox** *vb*

coxa \'käk-sə\ *n, pl* **cox·ae** \-,sē, -,sī\ [L; akin to OHG *hāhsina* hock, Skt *kakṣa* armpit] **:** the basal segment of an arthropod limb — **cox·al** \-səl\ *adj*

cox·comb \'käk-,skōm\ *n* [ME *cokkes comb*, lit., cock's comb] **1 a** *obs* **:** a jester's cap adorned with a strip of red **b** *archaic* **:** PATE, HEAD **2 a** *obs* **:** FOOL **b :** a conceited foolish person **:** FOP — **cox·comb·ical** \käk-'skō-mi-kəl, -'skäm-i-\ *adj*

Cox·sack·ie virus \(,)ku̇k-,säk-ē-, (,)käk-,sak-ē-\ *n* [*Coxsackie*, N.Y.] **:** any of several viruses apparently related to that of poliomyelitis and associated with human diseases

cox·swain \'käk-sən, -,swān\ *n* [ME *cokswayne*, fr. *cok* cockboat + *swain* servant] **1 :** a sailor who has charge of a ship's boat and its crew **2 :** a steersman of a racing shell

[1]**coy** \'kȯi\ *adj* [ME, quiet, shy, fr. MF *coi* calm, fr. L *quietus* quiet] **1 a :** BASHFUL, SHY **b :** archly affecting shy or demure reserve **2 :** showing reluctance to make a definite commitment **syn** see SHY — **coy·ly** *adv* — **coy·ness** *n*

[2]**coy** *vt, obs* **:** CARESS **~** *vi, archaic* **:** to act coyly

coy·ote \'kī-,ōt, kī-'ōt-ē\ *n, pl* **coyotes** *or* **coyote** [MexSp, fr. Nahuatl *coyotl*] **:** a small wolf (*Canis latrans*) native to western No. America

coy·o·til·lo \,kī-ə-'til-(,)ō, ,kȯi-ə-, -'tē-(,)(y)ō\ *n* [MexSp, dim. of *coyote*] **:** a low poisonous shrub (*Karwinskia humboldtiana*) of the buckthorn family of the southwestern U.S. and Mexico

coy·pu \'kȯi-(,)pü, kȯi-'\ *n* [AmerSp *coipú*, fr. Araucan *coypu*] **1 :** a So. American aquatic rodent (*Myocastor coypus*) with webbed feet and dorsal mammae **2 :** NUTRIA 2

coz \'kəz\ *n* [by shortening & alter.] **:** COUSIN

coz·en \'kəz-ᵊn\ *vb* **coz·en·ing** \'kəz-niŋ, -ᵊn-iŋ\ [obs. It *cozzonare*, fr. It *cozzone* horse trader, fr. L *cocion-, cocio* trader] *vt* **1 :** CHEAT, DEFRAUD **2 :** to beguile craftily **:** DECEIVE **~** *vi* **:** to act with artful deceit **syn** see CHEAT— **coz·en·er** \'kəz-nər, -ᵊn-ər\ *n*

coz·en·age \'kəz-nij, -ᵊn-ij\ *n* **1 :** the art or practice of cozening **:** FRAUD **2 :** an act of cozening or deception

co·zi·ly \'kō-zə-lē\ *adv* **:** in a cozy manner

co·zi·ness \'kō-zē-nəs\ *n* **:** the quality or state of being cozy

[1]**co·zy** \'kō-zē\ *adj* [prob. of Scand origin; akin to Norw *koselig* cozy] **1 :** enjoying or affording warmth and ease **:** SNUG **2 a :** marked by the intimacy of the family or close group **b :** suggesting close association or connivance ⟨~ cartel⟩ **3 :** marked by a discreet and cautious attitude or procedure **syn** see COMFORTABLE

[2]**cozy** *adv* **:** in a cautious manner

[3]**cozy** *n* **:** a padded covering esp. for a teapot to keep the contents hot

CQ \'sē-'kyü\ [abbr. for *call to quarters*] — communication code letters used at the beginning of radiograms of general information or safety notices or by shortwave amateurs as an invitation to talk to other shortwave amateurs

[1]**crab** \'krab\ *n, often attrib* [ME *crabbe*, fr. OE *crabba;* akin to OHG *krebiz* crab, OE *ceorfan* to carve] **1 :** any of numerous chiefly marine broadly built crustaceans: **a :** any of a tribe (Brachyura) with a short broad usu. flattened carapace, a small abdomen that curls forward beneath the body, short antennae, and the anterior pair of limbs modified as grasping pincers **b :** any of various other crustaceans resembling true crabs in the more or less reduced condition of the abdomen **2 :** any of various machines for raising or hauling heavy weights **3 :** failure to raise an oar clear of the water on recovery of a stroke or missing the water altogether when attempting a stroke ⟨catch a ~⟩ **4 :** apparent sideways motion of an airplane headed into a crosswind

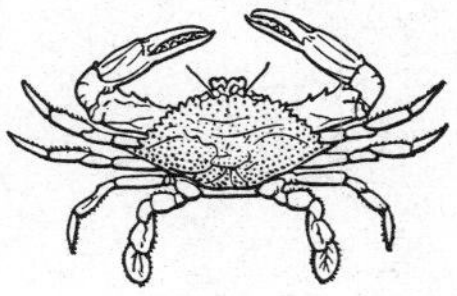

blue crab

[2]**crab** *vb* **crabbed; crab·bing** *vt* **1 :** to cause to move sideways or in an indirect or diagonal manner; *specif* **:** to head (an airplane) by means of the rudder into a crosswind to counteract drift **2 :** to subject to crabbing **~** *vi* **1 a** (1) **:** to move sideways indirectly or diagonally (2) **:** to crab an airplane **b :** to scuttle or scurry sideways like a crab **2 :** to fish for crabs — **crab·ber** *n*

[3]**crab** *n* [ME *crabbe*, perh. fr. *crabbe* [1]crab] **:** CRAB APPLE

[4]**crab** *vb* **crabbed; crab·bing** [ME *crabben*, prob. back-formation fr. *crabbed*] *vt* **1 :** to make sullen **:** SOUR **2 :** to complain about peevishly **3 :** SPOIL, RUIN **~** *vi* **:** CARP, GROUSE — **crab·ber** *n*

[5]**crab** *n* **:** a sour ill-tempered person **:** CROSSPATCH

crab apple *n* [[3]*crab*] **1 :** a small wild sour apple **2 :** a cultivated apple with small usu. highly colored acid fruit

crab·bed \'krab-əd\ *adj* [ME, partly fr. *crabbe* [1]crab, partly fr. *crabbe* [3]crab] **1 :** MOROSE, PEEVISH **2 :** difficult to read or understand **syn** see SULLEN — **crab·bed·ly** *adv* — **crab·bed·ness** *n*

crab·by \'krab-ē\ *adj* [[5]*crab*] **:** CROSS, ILL-NATURED

crab cactus *n* **:** a So. American cactus (*Zygocactus truncatus*)

crab·grass \'krab-,gras\ *n* **:** a grass (esp. *Digitaria sanguinalis*) with creeping or decumbent stems which root freely at the nodes

crab louse *n* **:** a louse (*Phthirus pubis*) infesting the human body in the pubic region

crab·stick \'krab-,stik\ *n* **1 :** a stick, cane, or cudgel of crab apple tree wood **2 :** a crabbed ill-natured person

[1]**crack** \'krak\ *vb* [ME *crakken*, fr. OE *cracian;* akin to Skt *jarate* it crackles — more at CRANE] *vi* **1 :** to make a very sharp explosive sound in or as if in breaking **2 :** to break without parting **3 :** FAIL: as **a :** to lose control or effectiveness under pressure **b :** to fail in tone ⟨voice ~*ed*⟩ **c :** to smash up a vehicle esp. by losing control ⟨~*ed* up on a curve⟩ **4 :** to go at good speed; *specif* **:** to proceed under full sail or steam **5 :** to break up into simpler compounds usu. as a result of heating **~** *vt* **1 a :** to break so that fissures appear on the surface **b :** to break with a sudden sharp sound ⟨~ nuts⟩ **2 a :** to utter esp. suddenly or strikingly ⟨~ a joke⟩ **b :** EXTOL, PRAISE ⟨wasn't all it was ~*ed* up to be⟩ **3 :** to strike with a sharp noise **:** RAP **4 :** to put on (as full speed) **5 a** (1) **:** to open (as a bottle) for drinking (2) **:** to open (a book) for studying **b :** to puzzle out and solve or reveal the mystery of ⟨~ a code⟩ **c :** to break into ⟨~ a safe⟩ **d :** to break through (as a barrier) so as to gain acceptance or recognition **6 a :** to impair seriously or irreparably **:** WRECK ⟨~ a car up⟩ **b :** to destroy the tone of (a voice) **c :** DISORDER, CRAZE **d :** to interrupt sharply or abruptly **7 :** to cause to make a sharp noise **8 a** (1) **:** to subject (hydrocarbons) to cracking (2) **:** to produce by cracking **b :** to break up (chemical compounds) into simpler compounds by means of heat

[2]**crack** *n* **1 :** a sudden sharp noise **2 a** *dial chiefly Brit* **:** TALK, GOSSIP **b :** a sharp witty remark **:** QUIP **3 a :** a narrow break **:** FISSURE **b :** a narrow opening **4 a :** a weakness or flaw caused by decay, age, or deficiency **:** UNSOUNDNESS **b :** a broken tone of the voice **c :** CRACKPOT **5 :** MOMENT, INSTANT **6 :** HOUSEBREAKING,

BURGLARY **7 :** a sharp resounding blow **8 :** ATTEMPT, TRY
3crack *adj* **:** of superior excellence or ability
crack·brain \'krak-,brān\ *n* **:** an erratic person **:** CRACKPOT — **crack·brained** \-'brānd\ *adj*
crack down *vi* **:** to take positive disciplinary action
crack·down \'krak-,dau̇n\ *n* **:** an act or instance of cracking down
crack·er \'krak-ər\ *n* **1** *chiefly dial* **:** a bragging liar **:** BOASTER **2 :** something that makes a cracking or snapping noise: as **a :** FIRECRACKER **b :** the snapping end of a whiplash **:** SNAPPER **c :** a paper holder for a party favor that pops when the ends are pulled sharply **3** *pl* **:** NUTCRACKER **4 :** a dry thin crisp bakery product made of flour and water **5 a** *South* **:** POOR WHITE — usu. used disparagingly **b** *cap* **:** a native or resident of Georgia or Florida — used as a nickname **6 :** the equipment in which cracking is carried out
crack·er·jack \'krak-ər-,jak\ *or* **crack·a·jack** \-ə-,jak\ *n* [1*crack* + *-er* + *jack*] **:** HUMDINGER — **crackerjack** *adj*
Cracker Jack *trademark* — used for a candied popcorn confection
crack·ers \'krak-ərz\ *adj* [prob. alter. of *cracked*] *slang Brit* **:** CRAZY
1crack·ing \'krak-iŋ\ *adj (or adv)* **:** GREAT, SMASHING
2cracking *n* **:** a process in which relatively heavy hydrocarbons are broken up by heat into lighter products
1crack·le \'krak-əl\ *vb* **crack·ling** \-(ə-)liŋ\ [freq. of 1*crack*] *vi* **1 a :** to make small sharp sudden repeated noises **b :** to show animation **:** SPARKLE **2 :** to develop a surface network of fine cracks ~ *vt* **:** to crush or crack with snapping noises
2crackle *n* **1 a :** the noise of repeated small cracks or reports **b :** SPARKLE, EFFERVESCENCE **2 :** a network of fine cracks on an otherwise smooth surface
crack·le·ware \'krak-əl-,wa(ə)r, -,we(ə)r\ *n* **:** glazed ceramic ware with a crazed finish
crack·ling *n* **1** \'krak-(ə-)liŋ\ **:** a series of small sharp cracks or reports **2** \'krak-lən, -liŋ\ **:** the crisp residue left after lard has been removed — usu. used in pl.
crack·ly \'krak-(ə-)lē\ *adj* **:** inclined to crackle **:** CRISP
crack·nel \'krak-nᵊl\ *n* [ME *krakenelle*] **1 :** a hard brittle biscuit **2 :** CRACKLING 2 — usu. used in pl.
crack·pot \'krak-,pät\ *n* **:** an eccentric person — **crack·pot** *adj*
cracks·man \'krak-smən\ *n* **:** BURGLAR; *also* **:** SAFECRACKER
crack-up \'krak-,əp\ *n* **1 :** BREAKDOWN **2 :** CRASH, WRECK
-c·ra·cy \k-rə-sē\ *n comb form* [MF & LL; MF *-cratie*, fr. LL *-cratia*, fr. Gk *-kratia*, fr. *kratos* strength, power — more at HARD] **1 :** form of government; *also* **:** state having such a form ⟨mono*cracy*⟩ **2 :** social or political class (as of powerful persons) ⟨mobo*cracy*⟩ **3 :** theory of social organization ⟨techno*cracy*⟩
1cra·dle \'krād-ᵊl\ *n* [ME *cradel*, fr. OE *cradol;* akin to OHG *kratto* basket, Skt *grantha* knot] **1 a :** a bed or cot for a baby usu. on rockers or pivots **b :** a place of origin **2 :** a framework or support suggestive of a baby's cradle: as **a** (1) **:** a framework of bars and rods (2) **:** the support for a telephone receiver or handset **b** (1) **:** an implement with rods like fingers attached to a scythe and used formerly for harvesting grain (2) **:** a low frame on casters on which mechanics lie while working under an automobile **c :** a frame to keep the bedclothes from contact with an injured part of the body **3 :** a rocking device used in panning for gold
2cradle *vb* **cra·dling** \'krād-liŋ, -ᵊl-iŋ\ *vt* **1 a :** to place or keep in or as if in a cradle **b:** SHELTER, REAR **c :** to support protectively or intimately **2 :** to cut (grain) with a cradle scythe **3 :** to place, raise, support, or transport on a cradle **4 :** to wash in a miner's cradle ~ *vi, obs* **:** to rest in or as if in a cradle
cra·dle·song \'krād-ᵊl-,sȯŋ\ *n* **:** LULLABY, BERCEUSE
craft \'kraft\ *n* [ME, strength, skill, fr. OE *cræft;* akin to OHG *kraft* strength] **1 :** DEXTERITY, SKILL **2 :** an occupation or trade requiring manual dexterity or artistic skill **3 :** skill in deceiving to gain an end **4 :** the members of a trade or trade association **5** *pl usu* **craft a :** a boat esp. of small size **b :** AIRCRAFT **syn** see ART
craft·i·ly \'kraf-tə-lē\ *adv* **:** in a crafty manner
craft·i·ness \'kraf-tē-nəs\ *n* **:** the quality or state of being crafty
crafts·man \'kraf(t)-smən\ *n* **1 :** a workman who practices a trade or handicraft **:** ARTISAN **2 :** a workman in any skilled occupation — **crafts·man·ship** \-,ship\ *n*
craft union *n* **:** a labor union with membership limited to workmen of the same craft — compare INDUSTRIAL UNION
crafty \'kraf-tē\ *adj* **1** *dial chiefly Brit* **:** SKILLFUL, INGENIOUS **2 :** GUILEFUL, WILY **syn** see SLY
1crag \'krag\ *n* [ME, of Celt origin] **1 :** a steep rugged rock or cliff **2** *archaic* **:** a sharp detached fragment of rock — **crag·ged** \-əd\ *adj* — **crag·gi·ness** \-ē-nəs\ *n* — **crag·gy** \-ē\ *adj*
2crag *n* [ME, fr. MD *crāghe*] *chiefly Scot* **:** NECK, THROAT
crags·man \'kragz-mən\ *n* **:** one expert in climbing crags or cliffs
crake \'krāk\ *n* [ME, prob. fr. ON *krāka* crow or *krākr* raven; akin to OE *crāwan* to crow] **1 :** any of various rails; *esp* **:** a short-billed rail (as the corncrake) **2 :** the corncrake's cry
1cram \'kram\ *vb* **crammed; cram·ming** [ME *crammen*, fr. OE *crammian;* akin to Gk *ageirein* to collect] *vt* **1 :** to pack tight **:** JAM **2 a :** to fill with food to satiety **:** STUFF **b :** to eat voraciously **:** BOLT **3 :** CROWD, FORCE **4 :** to prepare hastily for an examination ~ *vi* **1 :** to eat greedily or to satiety **:** STUFF **2 :** to study hastily at the last minute for an examination — **cram·mer** *n*
2cram *n* **1 :** CRUSH **2 :** last-minute study for an examination
cram·bo \'kram-(,)bō\ *n* [alter. of earlier *crambe*, fr. L, cabbage] **1 :** a game in which one player gives a word or line of verse to be matched in rhyme by other players **2 :** sloppy rhyme
cram·oi·sie *or* **cram·oi·sy** \'kram-,ȯi-zē, 'kram-ə-zē\ *n* [ME *crammassy*, fr. MF *cramoisi*, fr. *cramoisi* crimson] **:** crimson cloth
1cramp \'kramp\ *n* [ME *crampe*, fr. MF, of Gmc origin; akin to LG *krampe* hook] **1 :** a spasmodic painful involuntary contraction of a muscle **2 :** a temporary paralysis of muscles from overuse **3 :** sharp abdominal pain — used usu. in pl.
2cramp *n* [LG or obs. D *krampe* hook; akin to OE *cradol* cradle] **1 a :** a device usu. of iron bent at the ends used to hold timbers or blocks of stone together **b :** 1CLAMP **2 a :** something that confines **:** SHACKLE **b :** the state of being confined — **cramp** *adj*
3cramp *vt* **1 :** to affect with or as if with cramp **2 :** CONFINE, RESTRAIN **3 :** to turn (the front wheels of a vehicle) to right or left **4 :** to fasten or hold with a cramp ~ *vi* **:** to suffer from cramps
cramp·fish \'kramp-,fish\ *n* **:** ELECTRIC RAY
cram·pon \'kram-,pän\ *also* **cram·poon** \kram-'pün\ *n* [MF *crampon*, of Gmc origin; akin to LG *krampe*] **1 :** a hooked clutch or dog for raising heavy objects — used usu. in pl. **2 :** CLIMBING IRON — used usu. in pl.
cran·ber·ry \'kran-,ber-ē, -b(ə-)rē\ *n* [part trans. of LG *kraanbere*, fr. *kraan* crane + *bere* berry] **1 :** the bright red acid berry produced by some plants (as *Vaccinium oxycoccus* and *V. macrocarpon*) of the heath family; *also* **:** a plant producing these **2 :** any of various plants with fruit like cranberries
cranberry bush *n* **:** a shrub or tree (*Viburnum trilobum*) of No. America and Europe with prominently 3-lobed leaves and red fruit
cranch \'kränch\ *var of* CRAUNCH
1crane \'krān\ *n* [ME *cran*, fr. OE; akin to OHG *krano* crane, Gk *geranos*, L *grus*, Skt *jarate* it crackles] **1 :** any of a family (Gruidae of the order Gruiformes) of tall wading birds superficially resembling the herons but structurally more nearly related to the rails **2 :** any of several herons **3 :** a projection often horizontal swinging about a vertical axis: as **a :** a machine for raising, shifting, and lowering heavy weights by means of a projecting swinging arm or with the hoisting apparatus supported on an overhead track **b :** an iron arm in a fireplace for supporting kettles **c :** a boom for holding a motion-picture or television camera
2crane *vt* **1 :** to raise or lift by or as if by a crane **2 :** to stretch forward ~ *vi* **1 :** to stretch one's neck to see better **2 :** HESITATE
crane fly *n* **:** any of numerous long-legged slender two-winged flies (family Tipulidae) that resemble large mosquitoes but do not bite
cranes·bill \'krānz-,bil\ *n* **:** GERANIUM 1
crani- *or* **cranio-** *comb form* [ML *cranium*] **:** cranium ⟨crani*ate*⟩ **:** cranial and ⟨cranio*sacral*⟩
cra·ni·al \'krā-nē-əl\ *adj* **1 :** of or relating to the skull or cranium **2 :** CEPHALIC — **cra·ni·al·ly** \-ə-lē\ *adv*
cranial index *n* **:** the ratio of the maximum breadth of the skull to its maximum height multiplied by 100
cranial nerve *n* **:** any of the paired nerves that arise from the lower surface of the brain and pass through openings in the skull
cra·ni·ate \'krā-nē-ət, -,āt\ *adj* **:** having a cranium — **craniate** *n*
cra·ni·ol·o·gy \,krā-nē-'äl-ə-jē\ *n* [prob. fr. G *kraniologie*, fr. *kranio-* crani- + *-logie* -logy] **:** a science dealing with variations in size, shape, and proportions of skulls among the races of men
cra·ni·om·e·try \-'äm-ə-trē\ *n* [ISV] **:** a science dealing with cranial measurement
cra·nio·sa·cral \,krā-nē-ō-'sak-rəl, -'sā-krəl\ *adj* **1 :** of or relating to the cranium and the sacrum **2 :** PARASYMPATHETIC
cra·ni·um \'krā-nē-əm\ *n, pl* **craniums** \-əmz\ *or* **cra·nia** \-ə\ [ML, fr. Gk *kranion;* akin to Gk *kara* head] **:** SKULL; *specif* **:** the part that encloses the brain
1crank \'kraŋk\ *n* [ME *cranke*, fr. OE *cranc-* (as in *crancstaef*, a weaving instrument); akin to OE *cradol* cradle] **1 :** a bent part of an axle or shaft or an arm keyed at right angles to the end of a shaft by which circular motion is imparted to or received from it **2 a** *archaic* **:** BEND **b :** a twist or turn of speech **:** CONCEIT **c** (1) **:** CAPRICE, CROTCHET (2) **:** an eccentric person; *also* **:** ENTHUSIAST **d :** a bad-tempered person **:** GROUCH

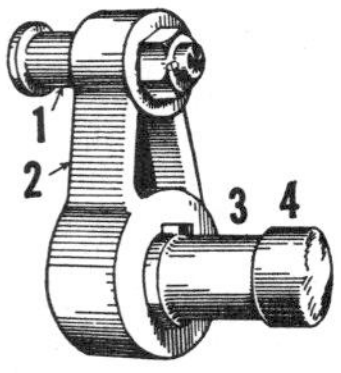

single overhung crank: *1* crankpin, *2* web, *3* journal, *4* crankshaft

2crank *vi* **1 :** to move with a winding course **:** ZIGZAG **2 :** to turn a crank ~ *vt* **1 :** to bend into the shape of a crank **2 :** to furnish or fasten with a crank **3 :** to move or operate by a crank; *specif* **:** to start by use of a crank
3crank *adj* [Sc, bent, distorted, prob. fr. 1*crank*] **:** out of kilter **:** LOOSE
4crank *adj* [ME *cranke*, of unknown origin] **1** *chiefly dial* **:** MERRY, HIGH-SPIRITED **2** *chiefly dial* **:** COCKY, CONFIDENT
5crank *adj* [short for *crank-sided* (easily tipped)] *of a boat* **:** easily tipped by an external force
crank·case \'kraŋk-,kās\ *n* **:** the housing of a crankshaft
crank·i·ly \'kraŋ-kə-lē\ *adv* **:** in a cranky manner
crank·i·ness \'kraŋ-kē-nəs\ *n* **:** the quality or state of being cranky
1cran·kle \'kraŋ-kəl\ *vb* [freq. of 2*crank*] *vt, obs* **:** to break into turns, bends, or angles **:** CRINKLE ~ *vi, archaic* **:** WIND, ZIGZAG
2crankle *n* **:** BEND, CRINKLE
crank·pin \'kraŋk-,pin\ *n* **:** the cylindrical piece which forms the handle of a crank or to which the connecting rod is attached
crank·shaft \'kraŋ(k)-,shaft\ *n* **:** a shaft driven by or driving a crank
1cranky \'kraŋ-kē\ *adj* [1*crank* & 3*crank*] **1** *dial* **:** IMBECILE, CRAZY **2 :** being out of order **3 :** CROTCHETY, IRRITABLE **4 :** full of twists and turns **:** TORTUOUS **syn** see IRASCIBLE
2cranky *adj* [5*crank*] *of a boat* **:** liable to heel or tip
cran·nog \'kran-,ȯg, -,äg\ *n* [ScGael *crannag* & IrGael *crannōg*] **:** an artificial fortified island constructed in a lake or marsh orig. in prehistoric Ireland and Scotland
cran·ny \'kran-ē\ *n* [ME *crany*, fr. MF *cren*, *cran* notch] **1 :** a small break or slit **:** CREVICE **2 :** an obscure nook or corner
cran·reuch \'kran-(,)rük\ *n* [prob. modif. of ScGael *crannreotha*] *Scot* **:** HOARFROST, RIME
1crap \'krap\ *n* [back-formation fr. *craps*] **:** a throw of 2, 3, or 12 in the game of craps losing the shooter his bet unless he has a point
2crap *vi* **crapped; crap·ping 1 :** to throw a crap **2 :** to throw a seven while trying to make a point — usu. used with *out*
1crape \'krāp\ *n* [alter. of F *crêpe*, fr. MF *crespe*, fr. *crespe* curly, fr. L *crispus* — more at CRISP] **1 :** CREPE **2 :** a band of crepe worn on a hat or sleeve as a sign of mourning
2crape *vt* **:** to cover or shroud with or as if with crape
3crape *vt* [F *crêper*, fr. L *crispare*, fr. *crispus*] **:** to make (the hair) curly
crape myrtle *n* **:** an East Indian shrub (*Lagerstroemia indica*) of the loosestrife family widely grown in warm regions for its flowers
craps \'kraps\ *n pl but sing or pl in constr* [LaF, fr. F *crabs*, *craps*, fr. E *crabs* lowest throw at hazard, fr. pl. of 1*crab*] **1 :** a gambling game played with two dice **2 :** CRAP
crap·shoot·er \'krap-,shüt-ər\ *n* **:** one who plays craps
crap·u·lous \'krap-yə-ləs\ *adj* [LL *crapulosus*, fr. L *crapula*, fr. Gk *kraipalē*] **1 :** intemperate in drinking or eating **2 :** sick from excessive indulgence in liquor
1crash \'krash\ *vb* [ME *crasschen*] *vt* **1 a :** to break violently and noisily **:** SMASH **b :** to damage (an airplane) in landing **2 a :** to cause to make a loud noise **b :** to force through with loud crashing

noises **3 :** to enter or attend without invitation or without paying ~ *vi* **1 a :** to break noisily **b :** to crash an airplane **2 a :** to make a smashing noise **b :** to move with or as if with a crashing noise **3 :** to force one's way with or as if with a crash — **crash·er** *n*

[2]**crash** *n* **1 :** a loud sound (as of things smashing) **2 :** a breaking to pieces by or as if by collision; *also* **:** an instance of crashing **3 :** a sudden decline or failure (as of a business)

[3]**crash** *adj* **:** effected hastily on an emergency basis ⟨a ~ program⟩

[4]**crash** *n* [prob. fr. Russ *krashenina* colored linen] **:** a coarse fabric used for draperies, toweling, and clothing

crash dive *n* **:** a dive made by a submarine in the least possible time — **crash-dive** \'krash-'dīv\ *vi* **crash-dived; crash-div·ing**

crash-land \'krash-'land\ *vt* **:** to land (an airplane) under emergency conditions usu. with damage to the craft ~ *vi* **:** to crash-land an airplane — **crash landing** *n*

cra·sis \'krā-səs\ *n, pl* **cra·ses** \'krā-,sēz\ [NL, fr. Gk *krasis* mixture, fr. *kerannynai* to mix] **:** CONSTITUTION, MAKEUP

crass \'kras\ *adj* [L *crassus* thick, gross] **:** GROSS, INSENSITIVE **syn** see STUPID — **cras·si·tude** \'kras-ə-,t(y)üd\ *n* — **crass·ly** *adv* — **crass·ness** *n*

-crat \,krat\ *n comb form* [F *-crate*, back-formation fr. *-cratie* -cracy] **1 :** advocate or partisan of a (specified) theory of government ⟨theo*crat*⟩ **2 :** member of a (specified) dominant class ⟨pluto*crat*⟩ — **-crat·ic** \'krat-ik\ *adj comb form*

cratch \'krach\ *n* [ME *cracche*, fr. OF *creche* manger] **1** *dial Brit* **:** a crib or rack esp. for fodder; *also* **:** FRAME **2** *archaic* **:** MANGER

[1]**crate** \'krāt\ [L *cratis* wickerwork — more at HURDLE] **1 :** an open box of wooden slats or a usu. wooden protective case or framework for shipping **2 :** JALOPY

[2]**crate** *vt* **:** to pack in a crate

cra·ter *n* [L, mixing bowl, crater, fr. Gk *kratēr*, fr. *kerannynai* to mix; akin to Skt *āśīrta* mixed] **1** \'krāt-ər\ **a :** the bowl-shaped depression around the orifice of a volcano **b :** a depression formed by the impact of a meteorite **c :** a hole in the ground made by the explosion of a bomb or shell **d :** an eroded lesion **2** \'krāt-ər, krā-'te(ə)r\ **:** KRATER

C ration *n* **:** an army canned field ration

craunch \'krönch, 'kränch\ *vb or n* [prob. imit.] **:** CRUNCH

cra·vat \krə-'vat\ *n* [F *cravate*, fr. *Cravate* Croatian] **1 :** an obsolete neck scarf **2 :** NECKTIE

crave \'krāv\ *vb* [ME *craven*, fr. OE *crafian;* akin to OHG *krāpfo* hook, OE *cradol* cradle] *vt* **1 :** to ask earnestly **:** BEG, DEMAND **2 a :** to want greatly **:** REQUIRE **b :** to yearn for ~ *vi* **:** to have a strong or inward desire **syn** see DESIRE — **crav·er** *n*

cra·ven \'krā-vən\ *adj* [ME *cravant*] **1 :** DEFEATED, VANQUISHED **2 :** lacking courage **syn** see COWARDLY — **craven** *n* — **cra·ven·ly** *adv* — **cra·ven·ness** \-vən-nəs\ *n*

craw \'krȯ\ *n* [ME *crawe*, fr. (assumed) OE *crawa;* akin to Gk *bronchos* trachea, throat, L *vorare* to devour] **1 :** the crop of a bird or insect **2 :** the stomach esp. of a lower animal

[1]**craw·fish** \'krȯ-,fish\ *n* [by folk etymology fr. ME *crevis, kraveys*] **1 :** CRAYFISH **2 :** SPINY LOBSTER

[2]**crawfish** *vi* **:** to retreat from a position

[1]**crawl** \'krȯl\ *vb* [ME *crawlen*, fr. ON *krafla;* akin to OE *crabba* crab] *vi* **1 :** to move slowly with the body close to the ground **:** CREEP **2 :** to drag along slowly or feebly **3 :** to advance by guile or servility **4 :** to spread by extending stems or tendrils **5 a :** to be alive or swarming with or as if with creeping things **b :** to have the sensation of insects creeping over one ~ *vt* **1 :** to move upon in or as if in a creeping manner **2** *slang* **:** to reprove harshly **syn** see CREEP — **crawl·er** *n*

[2]**crawl** *n* **1 a :** the act of crawling **b :** *chiefly Brit* **:** a progress from one pub to another **2 :** a prone speed swimming stroke consisting of a double overarm stroke combined with a flutter kick

[3]**crawl** *n* [Afrik *kraal* pen] **:** an enclosure in shallow waters

crawly \'krȯ-lē\ *adj* **:** CREEPY

cray·fish \'krā-,fish\ *n* [by folk etymology fr. ME *crevis*, fr. MF *crevice*, of Gmc origin; akin to OHG *krebiz* crab — more at CRAB] **1 :** any of numerous freshwater crustaceans (tribe Astacura) resembling the lobster but usu. much smaller **2 :** SPINY LOBSTER

[1]**cray·on** \'krā-,än, -ən; 'kran\ *n* [F, crayon, pencil, fr. dim. of *craie* chalk, fr. L *creta*] **1 :** a stick of white or colored chalk or of colored wax used for writing or drawing **2 :** a crayon drawing

[2]**crayon** *vt* **:** to draw with a crayon — **cray·on·ist** \'krā-ə-nəst\ *n*

[1]**craze** \'krāz\ *vb* [ME *crasen* to crush, craze, of Scand origin; akin to OSw *krasa* to crush] *vt* **1** *obs* **:** BREAK, SHATTER **2 :** to produce minute cracks on the surface or glaze of **3 :** to make insane or as if insane ~ *vi* **1** *archaic* **:** SHATTER, BREAK **2 :** to become insane **3 :** to develop a mesh of fine cracks

[2]**craze** *n* **1** *obs* **a :** BREAK, FLAW **b :** physical weakness **:** INFIRMITY **2 :** a transient infatuation **:** MANIA, FAD **3 :** a crack in glaze or enamel **syn** see FASHION

cra·zi·ly \'krā-zə-lē\ *adv* **:** in a crazy manner

cra·zi·ness \-zē-nəs\ *n* **:** the quality or state of being crazy

cra·zy \'krā-zē\ *adj* **1 :** full of cracks or flaws **:** UNSOUND; *also* **:** CROOKED, ASKEW **2 a :** MAD, INSANE **b** (1) **:** IMPRACTICAL (2) **:** ERRATIC **3 :** distracted with desire or excitement

crazy bone *n* **:** FUNNY BONE

crazy quilt *n* **:** a patchwork quilt without a design

cra·zy·weed \'krā-zē-,wēd\ *n* **:** LOCOWEED

[1]**creak** \'krēk\ *vi* [ME *creken* to croak, of imit. origin] **:** to make a prolonged grating or squeaking sound

[2]**creak** *n* **:** a rasping or grating noise — **creaky** \'krē-kē\ *adj*

[1]**cream** \'krēm\ *n, often attrib* [ME *creime, creme*, fr. MF *craime, cresme*, fr. LL *cramum*, of Celt origin; akin to W *cramen* scab] **1 :** the yellowish part of milk containing from 18 to about 40 percent butterfat **2 a :** a food prepared with cream **b :** something the consistency of cream **c :** a usu. emulsified medicinal or cosmetic preparation **3 :** the choicest part **4 :** CREAMER 2 **5 a :** a pale yellow **b :** a cream-colored animal — **creamy** \'krē-mē\ *adj*

[2]**cream** *vi* **1 :** to form cream or a surface layer like the cream on standing milk **2 :** to break into or cause something to break into a creamy froth; *also* **:** to move like froth ~ *vt* **1 a :** SKIM 1c **b** (1) **:** to take the choicest part of (2) **:** to take off (the choicest part) **2 :** to furnish, prepare, or treat with cream; *also* **:** to dress with a cream sauce **3 a :** to beat into a creamy froth **b :** to work or blend to the consistency of cream **c :** to drub thoroughly; *also* **:** WRECK **4 :** to cause to form a surface layer of or like cream

cream cheese *n* **:** an unripened cheese made from whole sweet milk enriched with cream; *also* **:** CHEDDAR

cream·cups \'krēm-,kəps\ *n pl but sing or pl in constr* **:** any of several California annuals (esp. *Platystemon californicus*) of the poppy family

cream·er \'krē-mər\ *n* **1 :** a device for separating cream from milk **2 :** a small vessel for serving cream

cream·ery \'krēm-(ə-)rē\ *n* **:** an establishment where butter and cheese are made or where milk and cream are sold or prepared

cream·i·ly \'krē-mə-lē\ *adv* **:** in a creamy manner

cream·i·ness \-mē-nəs\ *n* **:** the quality or state of being creamy

cream of tartar : a white crystalline salt $C_4H_5KO_6$ used esp. in baking powder and in certain treatments of metals

cream puff *n* **:** a round shell of light pastry filled with whipped cream or a cream filling

[1]**crease** \'krēs\ *n* [prob. alter. of earlier *creaste*, fr. ME *creste* crest] **1 :** a line or mark made by or as if by folding a pliable substance **2 :** a specially marked area in various sports (as hockey)

[2]**crease** *vt* **1 :** to make a crease in or on **:** WRINKLE **2 :** to wound slightly esp. by grazing ~ *vi* **:** to become creased — **creas·er** *n*

[1]**cre·ate** \krē-'āt, 'krē-,āt\ *adj, archaic* **:** CREATED

[2]**create** *vt* [ME *createn*, fr. L *creatus*, pp. of *creare*] **1 :** to bring into existence **2 a :** to invest with a new form, office, or rank **b :** to bring about by a course of action **3 :** CAUSE, MAKE **4 a :** to produce through imaginative skill **b :** DESIGN **syn** see INVENT

cre·atine \'krē-ə-,tēn\ *n* [ISV, fr. Gk *kreat-*, *kreas* flesh — more at RAW] **:** a white crystalline nitrogenous substance $C_4H_9N_3O_2$ found esp. in the muscles of vertebrates free or as phosphocreatine

cre·at·i·nine \krē-'at-ᵊn-,ēn\ *n* [G *kreatinin*, fr. *kreatin* creatine] **:** a white crystalline strongly basic compound $C_4H_7N_3O$ formed from creatine and found esp. in muscle, blood, and urine

cre·ation \krē-'ā-shən\ *n* **1 :** the act of creating; *esp* **:** the act of bringing the world into existence from nothing **2 :** the act of making, inventing, or producing: as **a :** the act of investing with a new rank or office **b :** the first representation of a dramatic role **3 :** something that is created: as **a :** WORLD **b :** creatures singly or in aggregate **c :** an original work of art

cre·ative \krē-'āt-iv\ *adj* **1 :** having the power or quality of creating **2 :** PRODUCTIVE **3 :** having the quality of something created rather than imitated — **cre·ative·ly** *adv* — **cre·ative·ness** *n*

creative evolution *n* **:** evolution that is a creative rather than a mechanically explicable process

cre·ativ·i·ty \,krē-(,)ā-'tiv-ət-ē, ,krē-ə-\ *n* **:** ability to create

cre·ator \krē-'āt-ər\ *n* **:** one that creates or produces **:** MAKER

crea·tur·al \'krēch-(ə-)rəl\ *adj* **:** of, relating to, or being a creature

crea·ture \'krē-chər\ *n* **1 :** something created **2 a :** a lower animal; *esp* **:** a farm animal **b :** a human being **:** PERSON **c :** a being of anomalous or uncertain aspect or nature **3 :** one who is the servile dependent or tool of another

creature comfort *n* **:** something that gives bodily comfort

crea·ture·ly \'krē-chər-lē\ *adj* **:** of, relating to, or befitting a finite or dependent being

crèche \'kresh, 'krāsh\ *n* [F, fr. OF *creche* manger, crib, of Gmc origin] **1 :** a day nursery **2 :** a foundling hospital **3 :** a representation of the Nativity scene in the stable at Bethlehem

cre·dence \'krēd-ᵊn(t)s\ *n* [ME, fr. MF or ML; MF, fr. ML *credentia*, fr. L *credent-*, *credens*, prp. of *credere* to believe, trust] **1 :** mental acceptance **:** BELIEF **2 :** CREDENTIALS — used in the phrase *letters of credence* **3** [MF, fr. OIt *credenza*] **:** a Renaissance sideboard used chiefly for valuable plate **4 :** a small table where the bread and wine rest before consecration **syn** see BELIEF

cre·dent \'krēd-ᵊnt\ *adj* [L *credent-*, *credens*, prp.] **1** *archaic* **:** giving credence **:** CONFIDING **2** *obs* **:** CREDIBLE

[1]**cre·den·tial** \kri-'den-chəl\ *adj* **:** warranting credit or confidence

[2]**credential** *n* **1 :** something that gives a title to credit or confidence **2** *pl* **:** testimonials showing that a person is entitled to credit or has a right to exercise official power **3 :** CERTIFICATE, DIPLOMA

cre·den·za \kri-'den-zə\ *n* [It, lit., belief, confidence, fr. ML *credentia*] **1 :** CREDENCE 3 **2 :** a sideboard, buffet, or bookcase patterned after a Renaissance credence; *esp* **:** one without legs

cred·i·bil·i·ty \,kred-ə-'bil-ət-ē\ *n* **:** the quality or state of being credible

cred·i·ble \'kred-ə-bəl\ *adj* [ME, fr. L *credibilis*, fr. *credere*] **:** capable of being believed **syn** see PLAUSIBLE — **cred·i·bly** \-blē\ *adv*

[1]**cred·it** \'kred-ət\ *n* [MF, fr. OIt *credito*, fr. L *creditum* something entrusted to another, loan, fr. neut. of *creditus*, pp. of *credere* to believe, entrust — more at CREED] **1 a :** the balance in a person's favor in an account **b :** an amount or sum placed at a person's disposal by a bank **c :** time given for payment for goods or services sold on trust **d** (1) **:** an entry on the right-hand side of an account constituting an addition to a revenue, net worth, or liability account (2) **:** a deduction from an expense or asset account **e :** any one of or the sum of the items entered on the right-hand side of an account **f :** a deduction from an amount otherwise due **2 :** reliance on the truth or reality of something **:** FAITH **3 a :** influence or power derived from enjoying the confidence of another or others **:** STANDING **b :** good name **:** ESTEEM; *also* **:** financial or commercial trustworthiness **4** *archaic* **:** CREDIBILITY **5 :** a source of honor **6 a :** something that gains or adds to reputation or esteem **:** HONOR **b :** RECOGNITION, ACKNOWLEDGMENT **7 :** recognition by a school or college that a student has fulfilled a requirement leading to a degree **syn** see BELIEF, INFLUENCE

[2]**credit** *vt* [partly fr. [1]*credit;* partly fr. L *creditus*, pp.] **1 :** to supply goods on credit to **2 :** to trust in the truth of **:** BELIEVE **3** *archaic* **:** to bring credit or honor upon **4 :** to enter upon the credit side of an account **5 a :** to give credit to **b :** to attribute to some person **syn** see ASCRIBE

cred·it·abil·i·ty \,kred-ət-ə-'bil-ət-ē\ *n* **:** the quality or state of being creditable

cred·it·able \'kred-ət-ə-bəl\ *adj* **1 :** worthy of belief **2 :** worthy of esteem or praise **3 :** worthy of commercial credit **4 :** ASSIGNABLE — **cred·it·able·ness** *n* — **cred·it·ably** \-blē\ *adv*

credit card *n* **:** a card authorizing credit purchases

credit line *n* **1 :** a line giving the name of a reporter, author, or producer **2 :** the top amount of a customer's credit

cred·i·tor \'kred-ət-ər\ *n* **:** one who gives credit in business matters
credit union *n* **:** a cooperative association that makes small loans to its members at low interest rates
cre·do \'krēd-(,)ō, 'krād-\ *n* [ME, fr. L, I believe] **:** CREED
cre·du·li·ty \kri-'d(y)ü-lət-ē\ *n* **:** undue readiness of belief
cred·u·lous \'krej-ə-ləs\ *adj* [L *credulus*, fr. *credere*] **1 :** ready to believe esp. on slight or uncertain evidence **2 :** proceeding from credulity — **cred·u·lous·ly** *adv* — **cred·u·lous·ness** *n*
Cree \'krē\ *n, pl* **Cree** *or* **Crees** [short for earlier *Christeno*, fr. CanF *Christino*, prob. modif. of Ojibwa *Kenistenoag*] **1 :** an Indian people ranging from Ontario to Saskatchewan and south into Montana **2 :** a member of the Cree people
creed \'krēd\ *n* [ME *crede*, fr. OE *crēda*, fr. L *credo* (first word of the Apostles' and Nicene Creeds), fr. *credere* to believe, trust, entrust; akin to OIr *cretim* I believe, Skt *śrad-dadhāti* he believes] **1 :** a brief authoritative formula of religious belief **2 :** a set of fundamental beliefs — **creed·al** *or* **cre·dal** \'krēd-ᵊl\ *adj*
creek \'krēk, 'krik\ *n* [ME *crike, creke*, fr. ON *-kriki* bend; akin to ON *krōkr* hook — more at CROOK] **1** *chiefly Brit* **:** a small inlet or bay narrower and extending farther inland than a cove **2 :** a natural stream of water normally smaller than and often tributary to a river **3** *dial chiefly Brit* **:** a narrow or winding passage
Creek \'krēk\ *n* **:** a member of a confederacy of peoples chiefly of Muskogean stock formerly occupying most of Alabama and Georgia and parts of Florida
creel \'krē(ə)l\ *n* [ME *creille, crele*, prob. fr. (assumed) MF *creille* grill, fr. L *craticula*] **1 :** a wickerwork receptacle (as for fish) **2 :** a bar with skewers for holding bobbins in a spinning machine
[1]**creep** \'krēp\ *vi* **crept** \'krept\ **creep·ing** [ME *crepen*, fr. OE *crēopan;* akin to Gk *grypos* curved, bent] **1 :** to move along with the body prone and close to the ground; *also* **:** to move slowly on hands and knees **2 :** to move or advance slowly, timidly, or stealthily **3** *of a plant* **:** to spread or grow over a surface rooting at intervals or clinging with tendrils, stems, or aerial roots **4 a :** to slip or gradually shift position **b :** to change shape permanently from prolonged stress or exposure to high temperatures
syn CREEP, CRAWL mean to move along a surface in a prone or crouching posture. CREEP is likely to suggest stealthy, noiseless progress; CRAWL is likely to suggest the movement of legless creatures or the slow laborious progress of a turtle or a badly maimed animal; CRAWL may also connote abjectness or submission
[2]**creep** *n* **1 :** a movement of or like creeping **2 :** a distressing sensation like that caused by the creeping of insects over one's flesh; *esp* **:** a feeling of apprehension or horror — usu. used in pl. **3 :** an enclosure that young animals can enter while adults are excluded **4 :** the slow change of dimensions of an object from prolonged exposure to high temperature or stress **5** *slang* **a :** a flophouse sneak thief **b :** an obnoxious or insignificant person
creep·age \'krē-pij\ *n* **:** gradual movement **:** CREEP
creep·er \'krē-pər\ *n* **1 :** one that creeps: as **a :** a creeping plant **b :** a bird (as of the family Certhiidae) that creeps about on trees or bushes searching for insects **c :** a creeping insect or reptile **2 :** any of various tools or implements: as **a :** a fixture with iron points worn on the shoe to prevent slipping **b :** CLIMBING IRON **c :** a strip (as of sealskin) attachable to the bottom of a ski to prevent sliding backward in uphill climbing **d :** GRAPNEL **3 :** a device for supplying or moving material in a steady flow
creep·i·ness \'krē-pē-nəs\ *n* **:** the quality or state of being creepy
creeping eruption *n* **:** a skin disorder marked by a spreading red line of eruption and caused esp. by larvae (as of hookworms not normally parasitic in man) burrowing beneath the human skin
creepy \'krē-pē\ *adj* **:** having or producing a nervous shivery fear
creese *var of* KRIS
creesh \'krēsh\ *n* [ME *cresche*, fr. MF *craisse*] *chiefly Scot* **:** GREASE
cre·mains \kri-'mānz\ *n pl* [blend of *cremated* and *remains*] **:** the ashes of a cremated human body
cre·mate \'krē-,māt, kri-'\ *vt* [L *crematus*, pp. of *cremare* to burn up, cremate] **:** to reduce (a dead body) to ashes by the action of fire — **cre·ma·tion** \kri-'mā-shən\ *n*
cre·ma·tor \'krē-,māt-ər, kri-'\ *n* **1 :** one that cremates corpses **2 :** CREMATORY
cre·ma·to·ri·um \,krē-mə-'tōr-ē-əm, ,krem-ə-, -'tȯr-\ *n, pl* **crematoriums** *or* **cre·ma·to·ria** \-ē-ə\ **:** CREMATORY
cre·ma·to·ry \'krē-mə-,tōr-ē, 'krem-ə-, -,tȯr-\ *n* **:** a furnace for cremation — **crematory** *adj*
crème \'krem, 'krēm\ *n, pl* **crèmes** \'krem(z), 'krēmz\ [F, fr. OF *cresme* — more at CREAM] **1 :** cream or cream sauce as used in cookery **2 :** a sweet liqueur **3 :** CREAM 2b, 2c
crème de ca·cao \,krēm-də-'kō-(,)kō; ,krēm-də-kə-'kaù, -də-kə-'kā-(,)ō\ *n* [F, lit., cream of cacao] **:** a sweet liqueur flavored with cacao beans and vanilla
crème de la crème \,krem-də-(,)lä-'krem\ *n* [F, lit., cream of the cream] **:** the very best
crème de menthe \,krēm-də-'mint, -'men(t)th; ,krem-də-'mänt\ *n* [F, lit., cream of mint] **:** a sweet green or white mint-flavored liqueur
cre·nate \'krē-,nāt, 'kren-,āt\ *or* **cre·nat·ed** \-əd\ *adj* [NL *crenatus*, fr. ML *crena* notch] **:** having the margin cut into rounded scallops ⟨a bi*crenate* leaf⟩ — **cre·nate·ly** *adv*
cre·na·tion \kri-'nā-shən, kre-\ *n* **1 a :** a crenate formation; *esp* **:** one of the rounded projections on an edge (as of a leaf or coin) **b :** the quality or state of being crenate **2 :** shrinkage of red blood cells in hypertonic solution resulting in crenate margins
[1]**cren·el** \'kren-ᵊl\ *or* **cre·nelle** \krə-'nel\ *n* [MF *crenel*, fr. OF, dim. of *cren* notch, fr. *crener* to notch; akin to ML *crena* notch] **:** one of the embrasures alternating with merlons in a battlement
[2]**cren·el** *vt* **cren·eled** *or* **cren·elled** \'kren-ᵊld\ **cren·el·ing** *or* **cren·el·ling** \'kren-ᵊl-iŋ\ **:** CRENELLATE
cren·el·late *or* **cren·el·ate** \'kren-ᵊl-,āt\ *vt* **:** to furnish with battlements — **cren·el·late** \-,āt, -ət\ *adj* — **cren·el·la·tion** \,kren-ᵊl-'ā-shən\ *n*
cren·el·lat·ed *or* **cren·el·at·ed** \'kren-ᵊl-,āt-əd\ *adj* **:** having battlements
cren·u·late \'kren-yə-lət, -,lāt\ *also* **cren·u·lat·ed** \-,lāt-əd\ *adj* [NL *crenulatus*, fr. *crenula*, dim. of ML *crena*] **:** minutely crenate
cren·u·la·tion \,kren-yə-'lā-shən\ *n* **1 :** a minute crenation **2 :** the state of being crenulate
cre·ole \'krē-,ōl\ *adj* **1** *cap* **:** of or relating to Creoles **2** *often cap* **:** of or relating to Creoles or their language **3** *of food* **:** prepared with rice, okra, tomatoes, peppers, and high seasoning
Cre·ole \'krē-,ōl\ *n* [F *créole*, fr. Sp *criollo*, fr. Pg *crioulo* white person born in the colonies] **1 :** a person of native birth but of European descent — used esp. in the West Indies and Spanish America **2 :** a white person descended from early French or Spanish settlers of the U.S. Gulf states and preserving their speech and culture **3 :** a person of mixed French or Spanish and Negro descent speaking a dialect of French or Spanish **4 a :** the French spoken by many Negroes in southern Louisiana **b :** HAITIAN
cre·o·sol \'krē-ə-,sȯl, -,sōl\ *n* [ISV *creos*ote + *-ol*] **:** a colorless aromatic phenol $C_8H_{10}O_2$ obtained from guaiacum resin and the tar made from beech
[1]**cre·o·sote** \'krē-ə-,sōt\ *n* [G *kreosot*, fr. Gk *kreas* flesh + *sōtēr* preserver, fr. *sōzein* to preserve, fr. *sōs* safe] **1 :** a clear or yellowish oily liquid mixture of phenolic compounds obtained by the distillation of wood tar esp. from beech wood **2 :** a brownish oily liquid consisting chiefly of aromatic hydrocarbons obtained by distillation of coal tar and used esp. as a wood preservative
[2]**creosote** *vt* **:** to impregnate with creosote
creosote bush *n* **:** a resinous desert shrub (*Covillea mexicana*) of the bean-caper family found in the southwestern U. S. and Mexico
crepe *or* **crêpe** \'krāp\ *n* [F *crêpe*] **1 :** a light crinkled fabric woven of any of various fibers **2 :** CRAPE 2 **3 :** a small very thin pancake — **crepe** *adj* — **crep·ey** *or* **crepy** \'krā-pē\ *adj*
crepe de chine \,krāp-də-'shēn\ *n, often cap 2d C* [F *crêpe de Chine*, lit., China crepe] **:** a soft fine clothing crepe
crepe myrtle *or* **crêpe myrtle** *var of* CRAPE MYRTLE
crepe paper *n* **:** paper with a crinkled or puckered texture
crepe rubber *n* **:** crude rubber in the form of nearly white to brown crinkled sheets used esp. for shoe soles
crepe su·zette \,krāp-sü-'zet\ *n, pl* **crepes suzette** \,krāp(s)-sü-\ *or* **crepe suzettes** \,krāp-sü-'zets\ [F *crêpe Suzette*, fr. *crêpe* pancake + *Suzette* Susy] **:** a thin pancake folded in quarters or rolled and heated in a sauce of butter, sugar, orange or lemon juice and grated rind, and a liqueur with added cognac, curaçao, or rum usu. set ablaze for serving
crep·i·tant \'krep-ət-ənt\ *adj* **:** having or making a crackling sound
crep·i·tate \'krep-ə-,tāt\ *vi* [L *crepitatus*, pp. of *crepitare* to crackle, fr. *crepitus*, pp. of *crepare* to rattle, crack] **:** to make a crackling sound **:** CRACKLE — **crep·i·ta·tion** \,krep-ə-'tā-shən\ *n*
crept *past of* CREEP
cre·pus·cu·lar \kri-'pəs-kyə-lər\ *adj* **1 :** of, relating to, or resembling twilight **:** DIM **2 :** active in the twilight ⟨~ insects⟩
cre·pus·cule \kri-'pəs-(,)kyü(ə)l\ *or* **cre·pus·cle** \-'pəs-əl\ *n* [L *crepusculum*, fr. *creper* dusky] **:** TWILIGHT
cre·scen·do \kri-'shen-(,)dō, -'sen-\ *n* [It, fr. *crescendo*, adj., increasing, verbal of *crescere* to grow, fr. L] **1 a :** a swelling in volume of sound esp. in music **b :** a passage so performed **2 :** a gradual increase — **crescendo** *adj* (*or adv*)
[1]**cres·cent** \'kres-ᵊnt\ *n* [ME *cressant*, fr. MF *creissant*, fr. prp. of *creistre* to grow, increase, fr. L *crescere;* akin to OHG *hirsi* millet, L *creare* to create, Gk *koros* boy] **1 a :** the moon at any stage between new moon and first quarter and between last quarter and the succeeding new moon when less than half of the illuminated hemisphere is visible **b :** the figure of the moon at such a stage defined by a convex and a concave edge **2 :** something shaped like a crescent — **cres·cen·tic** \kre-'sent-ik\ *adj*
[2]**crescent** *adj* [L *crescent-*, *crescens*, prp. of *crescere*] **:** INCREASING
cres·cive \'kres-iv\ *adj* [L *crescere* to grow] **:** INCREASING, GROWING — **cres·cive·ly** *adv*
cre·sol \'krē-,sȯl, -,sōl\ *n* [ISV, irreg. fr. *creosote*] **:** any of three poisonous colorless crystalline or liquid isomeric phenols C_7H_8O
cress \'kres\ *n* [ME *cresse*, fr. OE *cærse*, *cressa;* akin to OHG *kressa* cress] **:** any of numerous plants (esp. genera *Rorippa*, *Arabis*, and *Barbarea*) of the mustard family with moderately pungent leaves used in salads and garnishes
cres·set \'kres-ət\ *n* [ME, fr. MF, fr. OF *craisset*, fr. *craisse* grease] **:** an iron vessel or basket used for holding an illuminant (as burning oil) and mounted as a torch or suspended as a lantern
Cres·si·da \'kres-əd-ə\ *n* **:** a Trojan woman who in medieval legend is unfaithful to her lover Troilus
[1]**crest** \'krest\ *n* [ME *creste*, fr. MF, fr. L *crista;* akin to OE *hrisian* to shake, L *curvus* curved] **1 a :** a showy tuft or process on the head of a bird or other animal **b :** the plume or identifying emblem worn on a knight's helmet **c** (1) **:** a heraldic representation of the crest (2) **:** a heraldic device depicted above the escutcheon but not upon a helmet **2 :** something suggesting a crest esp. in being an upper prominence, edge, or limit: as **a :** PEAK; *esp* **:** the top line of a mountain or hill **b :** the ridge or top of a wave or roof **3 a :** a high point of an action or process **b :** CLIMAX, CULMINATION
[2]**crest** *vt* **1 :** to furnish with a crest **:** CROWN **2 :** to reach the crest of ~ *vi* **:** to rise to a crest
crest·ed \'kres-təd\ *adj* **:** having a crest ⟨fan-*crested*⟩
crest·fall·en \'kres(t)-,fȯ-lən\ *adj* **:** having a drooping crest or hanging head **:** DEJECTED; *also* **:** SHAMEFACED, HUMILIATED — **crest·fall·en·ly** *adv* — **crest·fall·en·ness** \-lən-nəs\ *n*
crest·less \'krest-ləs\ *adj* **:** lacking a crest; *specif* **:** LOWBORN
cre·syl·ic \krə-'sil-ik\ *adj* [ISV, fr. *cresyl* (the radical $CH_3C_6H_4$—)] **:** of or relating to cresol or creosote
cre·ta·ceous \kri-'tā-shəs\ *adj* [L *cretaceus*, fr. *creta* chalk] **1 :** having the characteristics of or abounding in chalk **2** *cap* **:** of, relating to, or being the last period of the Mesozoic era or the corresponding system of rocks — **cretaceous** *n* — **cre·ta·ceous·ly** *adv*
cre·tin \'krēt-ᵊn, *esp Brit* 'kre-tin\ *n* [F *crétin*, fr. F dial. *cretin* Christian, human being, kind of idiot found in the Alps, fr. L *christianus* Christian] **:** one afflicted with cretinism; *broadly* **:** a person with marked mental deficiency — **cre·tin·ous** \-əs\ *adj*
cre·tin·ism \-,iz-əm\ *n* **:** a usu. congenital abnormal condition marked by physical and mental stunting and caused by severe thyroid deficiency
cre·tonne \'krē-,tän, kri-'\ *n* [F, fr. *Creton*, Normandy] **:** a strong unglazed cotton or linen cloth used esp. for curtains and upholstery
cre·vasse \kri-'vas\ *n* [F, fr. OF *crevace*] **1 :** a deep crevice or fissure (as in a glacier or the earth) **2 :** a breach in a levee
crev·ice \'krev-əs\ *n* [ME, fr. MF *crevace*, fr. OF, fr. *crever* to break, fr. L *crepare* to crack — more at RAVEN] **:** a narrow opening resulting from a split or crack **:** FISSURE
[1]**crew** \'krü\ *chiefly Brit past of* CROW
[2]**crew** *n* [ME *crue*, lit., reinforcement, fr. MF *creue* increase, fr. *creistre* to grow] **1** *archaic* **:** a band or force of armed men **2 :** ASSEMBLAGE **3 a :** SET, GANG **b :** a company of men working on one

job or under one foreman or operating a machine **4 a :** the whole company belonging to a ship sometimes including the officers and master **b :** the persons who man an aircraft in flight **c :** the body of men manning a racing shell — **crew·man** \-mən\ *n*

crew cut *n* **:** a very short haircut with the hair resembling the bristle surface of a brush

crew·el \ˈkrü-əl\ *n* [ME *crule*] **:** slackly twisted worsted yarn used for embroidery — **crew·el·work** \-ˌwərk\ *n*

[1]**crib** \ˈkrib\ *n* [ME, fr. OE *cribb;* akin to OHG *krippa* manger, Gk *griphos* reed basket, OE *cradol* cradle] **1 :** a manger for feeding animals **2 :** an enclosure esp. of framework: as **a :** a stall for a stabled animal **b :** a small child's bedstead with high enclosing usu. slatted sides **c :** any of various devices resembling a crate or framework in structure **d :** a building for storage **:** BIN **3 :** a small narrow room or dwelling **:** HUT, SHACK **4 :** the cards discarded in cribbage for the dealer to use in scoring **5 a :** a small theft **b :** PLAGIARISM **c :** a literal translation; *esp* **:** PONY 3 **d :** a device used for cheating in an examination **6 :** CRÈCHE 3

[2]**crib** *vt* **cribbed; crib·bing 1 :** CONFINE, CRAMP **2 :** to provide with or put into a crib **3 :** PILFER, STEAL; *esp* **:** PLAGIARIZE ~ *vi* **1 a :** STEAL, PLAGIARIZE **b :** to use a crib **:** CHEAT **2 :** to have the vice of crib biting — **crib·ber** \ˈkrib-ər\ *n*

crib·bage \ˈkrib-ij\ *n* [[1]*crib*] **:** a card game in which the object is to form various counting combinations and in which each player is dealt six cards and discards one or two to make up the crib

crib biting *n* **:** a vice of horses in which they gnaw (as at the manger) while slobbering and salivating

crib·ri·form \ˈkrib-rə-ˌfȯrm\ *adj* [L *cribrum* sieve; akin to L *cernere* to sift — more at CERTAIN] **:** pierced with small holes

cri·ce·tid \krī-ˈsēt-əd, -ˈset-\ *n* [deriv. of NL *Cricetus*, genus name, of Slav origin; akin to Czech *křeček* hamster] **:** any of a family (Cricetidae) of small rodents (as the hamsters) — **cricetid** *adj*

crick \ˈkrik\ *n* [ME *cryk*] **:** a painful spasmodic condition of muscles (as of the neck or back) — **crick** *vt*

[1]**crick·et** \ˈkrik-ət\ *n* [ME *criket*, fr. MF *criquet*, of imit. origin] **1 :** a leaping orthopterous insect (family Gryllidae) noted for the chirping notes produced by the male by rubbing together specially modified parts of the fore wings **2 :** a low wooden footstool

[2]**cricket** *n* [MF *criquet* goal stake in a bowling game] **1 :** a game played with a ball and bat by two sides of usu. 11 players each on a large field centering upon two wickets each defended by a batsman **2 :** fair and honorable behavior

[3]**cricket** *vi* **:** to play cricket — **crick·et·er** *n*

cri·coid \ˈkrī-ˌkȯid\ *adj* [NL *cricoides*, fr. Gk *krikoeidēs* ring-shaped, fr. *krikos* ring] **:** of, relating to, or being a cartilage of the larynx with which the arytenoid cartilages articulate

cri·er \ˈkrī(-ə)r\ *n* **:** one that cries: **a :** an officer who proclaims the orders of a court **b :** TOWN CRIER

crime \ˈkrīm\ *n* [ME, fr. L *crimen* accusation, fault, crime] **1 :** an act or the commission of an act that is forbidden or the omission of a duty that is commanded by a public law and that makes the offender liable to punishment by that law; *esp* **:** a gross violation of law **2 :** a grave offense esp. against morality **3 :** criminal activity **syn** see OFFENSE

[1]**crim·i·nal** \ˈkrim-ən-ᵊl, ˈkrim-nəl\ *adj* [ME, fr. MF or LL; MF *criminel*, fr. LL *criminalis*, fr. L *crimin- crimen* crime] **1 :** involving or being a crime **2 :** relating to crime or its punishment **3 :** guilty of crime **4 :** DISGRACEFUL — **crim·i·nal·ly** \-ē\ *adv*

[2]**criminal** *n* **:** one that has committed a crime **:** MALEFACTOR

criminal conversation *n* **:** adultery considered as a tort

crim·i·nal·i·ty \ˌkrim-ə-ˈnal-ət-ē\ *n* **:** the quality or state of being criminal

criminal law *n* **:** the law of crimes and their punishments

crim·i·nate \ˈkrim-ə-ˌnāt\ *vt* [L *criminatus*, pp. of *criminari*, fr. *crimin-, crimen* accusation] **1 a :** to accuse of a crime **b :** INCRIMINATE **2 :** to represent as criminal **:** CONDEMN — **crim·i·na·tion** \ˌkrim-ə-ˈnā-shən\ *n*

crim·i·no·log·i·cal \ˌkrim-ən-ᵊl-ˈäj-i-kəl, ˌkrim-nəl-\ *adj* **:** of or relating to criminology — **crim·i·no·log·i·cal·ly** \-k(ə-)lē\ *adv*

crim·i·nol·o·gist \ˌkrim-ə-ˈnäl-ə-jəst\ *n* **:** a specialist in criminology

crim·i·nol·o·gy \-jē\ *n* [It *criminologia*, fr. L *crimin- crimen* + It *-o-* + *-logia* -logy] **:** the scientific study of crime as a social phenomenon, of criminals, and of penal treatment

crim·i·nous \ˈkrim-ə-nəs\ *adj* **:** CRIMINAL

[1]**crimp** \ˈkrimp\ *vt* [D or LG *krimpen* to shrivel; akin to LG *krampe* hook — more at CRAMP] **1 :** to cause to become wavy, bent, or warped: as **a :** to form (leather) into a desired shape **b :** to draw or pinch in or together in glass manufacturing **c :** to roll the edge of **2 :** GASH **3 :** to put a crimp in — **crimp·er** *n*

[2]**crimp** *n* **1 :** something produced by or as if by crimping: as **a :** a section of hair artificially waved or curled **b :** a succession of waves (as in wool fiber) **2 :** something that cramps or inhibits

[3]**crimp** *n* [perh. fr. [1]*crimp*] **:** a person who entraps or forces men into shipping as sailors or enlisting in an army or navy

[4]**crimp** *vt* **:** to trap into military service

crimpy \ˈkrim-pē\ *adj* **:** having a crimped appearance **:** FRIZZY

[1]**crim·son** \ˈkrim-zən\ *n* [ME *crimisin*, fr. OSp *cremesín*, fr. Ar *qirmizī*, fr. *qirmiz* kermes] **:** any of several deep purplish reds

[2]**crimson** *adj* **:** of the color crimson

[3]**crimson** *vt* **:** to make crimson ~ *vi* **:** to become crimson

[1]**cringe** \ˈkrinj\ *vi* [ME *crengen;* akin to OE *cringan* to yield, *cradol* cradle] **1 :** to draw in or contract one's muscles involuntarily **2 :** to shrink in fear or servility **3 :** to approach someone with fawning and self-abasement **syn** see FAWN — **cring·er** *n*

[2]**cringe** *n* **:** a cringing act; *specif* **:** a servile bow

crin·gle \ˈkriŋ-gəl\ *n* [LG *kringel*, dim. of *kring* ring] **:** a thimble, grommet, eyelet, or rope loop worked into or attached to the edge of a sail and used for making fast rope and lines

[1]**crin·kle** \ˈkriŋ-kəl\ *vb* **crin·kling** \ˈkriŋ-k(ə-)liŋ\ [ME *crynkelen;* akin to OE *cringan* to yield] *vi* **1 a :** to form many short bends or turns **b :** WRINKLE, RIPPLE **2 :** to give forth a thin crackling sound **:** RUSTLE ~ *vt* **:** to cause to crinkle

[2]**crinkle** *n* **1 :** WINDING, WRINKLE **2 :** any of several plant diseases marked by crinkling of leaves — **crin·kly** \-k(ə-)lē\ *adj*

cri·noid \ˈkrī-ˌnȯid\ *n* [deriv. of Gk *krinon* lily] **:** any of a large class (Crinoidea) of echinoderms having usu. a somewhat cup-shaped body with five or more feathery arms — **crinoid** *adj*

crin·o·line \ˈkrin-ᵊl-ən\ *n* [F, fr. It *crinolino*, fr. *crino* horsehair (fr. L *crinis* hair; akin to L *crista* crest) + *lino* flax, linen, fr. L *linum*] **1 :** an open-weave fabric of horsehair or cotton usu. stiffened and used esp. for interlinings and millinery **2 a :** HOOPSKIRT **b :** a full stiff skirt or underskirt — **crinoline** *adj*

cri·num \ˈkrī-nəm\ *n* [NL, genus name, fr. L, lily, fr. Gk *krinon*] **:** any of a large genus (*Crinum*) of chiefly tropical bulbous herbs of the amaryllis family (family Amaryllidaceae) grown for their umbels of often fragrant white red-marked flowers

cri·o·llo \krē-ˈō(l)-(ˌ)yō\ *n* [Sp] **1 a :** a person of pure Spanish descent born in Spanish America **b :** a person born and usu. raised in a Spanish-American country **2 :** a domestic animal of a breed or strain developed in Latin America — **criollo** *adj*

[1]**crip·ple** \ˈkrip-əl\ *n* [ME *cripel*, fr. OE *crypel;* akin to OE *crēopan* to creep — more at CREEP] **1 :** a lame or partly disabled person or animal **2 :** something flawed or imperfect

[2]**cripple** *adj* **:** being a cripple **:** LAME; *also* **:** worn out **:** INFERIOR

[3]**cripple** *vt* **crip·pling** \-(ə-)liŋ\ **1 :** to deprive of the use of a limb and esp. a leg **2 :** to deprive of strength, efficiency, wholeness, or capability for service **syn** see WEAKEN — **crip·pler** \-(ə-)lər\ *n*

cri·sis \ˈkrī-səs\ *n, pl* **cri·ses** \ˈkrī-ˌsēz\ [L, fr. Gk *krisis*, lit., decision, fr. *krinein* to decide — more at CERTAIN] **1 a :** the turning point for better or worse in an acute disease or fever **b :** a paroxysmal attack of pain, distress, or disordered function **c :** an emotionally significant event or radical change of status in a person's life **2 :** the decisive moment (as in a literary plot) **3 :** an unstable or crucial time or state of affairs; *specif* **:** the period of strain following the culmination of a period of business prosperity when forced liquidation occurs **syn** see JUNCTURE

[1]**crisp** \ˈkrisp\ *adj* [ME, fr. OE, fr. L *crispus;* akin to L *curvus* curved — more at CROWN] **1 a :** CURLY, WAVY; *also* **:** having close stiff or wiry curls or waves **b :** having the surface roughened into small folds or curling wrinkles **2 a :** easily crumbled **:** BRITTLE **b** *of pastry* **:** SHORT **c :** being firm and fresh ⟨~ lettuce⟩ **3 a :** being sharp, clean-cut, and clear ⟨a ~ illustration⟩ **b :** noticeably neat **c :** SPRIGHTLY, LIVELY **d :** FROSTY, SNAPPY; *also* **:** FRESH, INVIGORATING **syn** see FRAGILE, INCISIVE — **crisp·ly** *adv* — **crisp·ness** *n*

[2]**crisp** *vt* **1 :** CURL, CRIMP **2 :** to cause to ripple **:** WRINKLE **3 :** to make or keep crisp ~ *vi* **1 :** CURL **2 :** RIPPLE **3 :** to become crisp — **crisp·er** *n*

[3]**crisp** *n* **1 :** something crisp or brittle **2** *chiefly Brit* **:** POTATO CHIP

cris·pa·tion \kris-ˈpā-shən\ *n* **1 a :** the act or process of curling **b :** the state of being curled **2 :** a slight spasmodic contraction

crisp·i·ness \ˈkris-pē-nəs\ *n* **:** CRISPNESS, BRITTLENESS

crispy \ˈkris-pē\ *adj* **:** CRISP

[1]**criss·cross** \ˈkris-ˌkrȯs\ *n* [obs. *christcross, crisscross* (mark of a cross)] **1 :** a crisscross pattern **:** NETWORK **2 :** a confused state

[2]**crisscross** *vt* **1 :** to mark with intersecting lines **2 :** to pass back and forth through or over ~ *vi* **:** to go or pass back and forth

[3]**crisscross** *adj* **:** marked or characterized by crisscrossing

[4]**crisscross** *adv* **1 :** in a way to cross something else **2 :** AWRY

cris·tate \ˈkris-ˌtāt\ *also* **cris·tat·ed** \-ˌtāt-əd\ *adj* **:** CRESTED

cri·te·ri·on \krī-ˈtir-ē-ən\ *n, pl* **cri·te·ria** \-ē-ə\ *also* **criterions** [Gk *kritērion*, fr. *krinein* to judge, decide] **:** a standard on which a judgment or decision may be based **syn** see STANDARD

[1]**crit·ic** \ˈkrit-ik\ *n* [L *criticus*, fr. Gk *kritikos* able to discern or judge, fr. *krinein* to judge] **1 a :** one who expresses a reasoned opinion on any matter involving a judgment of its value, truth, or righteousness, an appreciation of its beauty or technique, or an interpretation **b :** one who engages often professionally in the analysis, evaluation, or appreciation of works of art **2 :** one given to harsh or captious judgment **:** CARPER

[2]**critic** *adj* **:** CRITICAL

[3]**critic** *n* [Gk *kritikē* art of the critic, fr. fem. of *kritikos* able to discern] **1** *archaic* **:** CRITICISM **2** *archaic* **:** CRITIQUE

crit·i·cal \ˈkrit-i-kəl\ *adj* **1 a :** inclined to criticize severely and unfavorably **b :** consisting of or involving criticism ⟨~ writings⟩ **c :** exercising or involving careful judgment or judicious evaluation **d :** including variant readings and scholarly emendations ⟨a ~ edition⟩ **2 a :** of, relating to, or being a turning point or specially important juncture ⟨~ phase⟩ **b :** relating to or being a state in which or a measurement or point at which some quality, property, or phenomenon suffers a definite change ⟨~ temperature⟩ **c :** CRUCIAL, DECISIVE ⟨~ test⟩ **d :** indispensable for the weathering, solution, or overcoming of a crisis **3 :** of doubtful issue **4 :** of sufficient size to sustain a chain reaction — used of a mass of fissionable material — **crit·i·cal·i·ty** \ˌkrit-ə-ˈkal-ət-ē\ *n* — **crit·i·cal·ly** \ˈkrit-i-k(ə-)lē\ *adv* — **crit·i·cal·ness** \-kəl-nəs\ *n*

syn HYPERCRITICAL, FAULTFINDING, CAPTIOUS, CARPING, CENSORIOUS: CRITICAL may imply an effort to see a thing clearly and truly in order to judge it fairly; often it implies harshness in judging; HYPERCRITICAL suggests a tendency to judge by unreasonably strict standards; FAULTFINDING implies a querulous or exacting temperament; CAPTIOUS suggests a readiness to detect trivial faults or raise objections on trivial grounds; CARPING implies an ill-natured or perverse picking of flaws; CENSORIOUS implies a disposition to be severely critical and condemnatory **syn** see in addition ACUTE

critical angle *n* **1 :** the least angle of incidence at which total reflection takes place **2 :** the angle of attack at which the flow about an airfoil changes abruptly with corresponding abrupt changes in the lift and drag

crit·ic·as·ter \ˈkrit-i-ˌkas-tər\ *n* **:** an inferior or contemptible critic

crit·i·cism \ˈkrit-ə-ˌsiz-əm\ *n* **1 a :** the act of criticizing usu. unfavorably **b :** a critical observation or remark **c :** CRITIQUE **2 :** the art of evaluating or analyzing with knowledge and propriety esp. works of art or literature **3 :** the scientific investigation of literary documents (as the Bible) in regard to such matters as origin, text, composition, character, or history

crit·i·ciz·able \ˈkrit-ə-ˌsī-zə-bəl\ *adj* **:** subject to criticism

crit·i·cize \ˈkrit-ə-ˌsīz\ *vi* **:** to act as a critic ~ *vt* **1 :** to consider the merits and demerits of and judge accordingly **:** EVALUATE **2 :** to stress the faults of **:** cavil at — **crit·i·ciz·er** *n*

syn REPREHEND, BLAME, CENSURE, REPROBATE, CONDEMN, DENOUNCE: CRITICIZE implies finding fault esp. with methods or policies or intentions; REPREHEND implies both criticism and severe rebuking; BLAME may imply simply the opposite of *praise* but more often suggests the placing of responsibility for something bad or unfortunate; CENSURE carries a stronger suggestion of authority

and of reprimanding than BLAME; REPROBATE implies strong disapproval or firm refusal to sanction; CONDEMN usu. suggests an unqualified and final unfavorable judgment; DENOUNCE adds to CONDEMN the implication of a public declaration

cri·tique \krə-'tēk, kri-\ *n* [alter. of 3*critic*] **:** an act of criticizing; *esp* **:** a critical estimate or discussion

crit·ter \'krit-ər\ *n* [by alter.] *dial* **:** CREATURE

1**croak** \'krōk\ *vb* [ME *croken*, of imit. origin] *vi* **1 a :** to make a deep harsh sound **b :** to speak in a hoarse throaty voice **2 :** to predict evil **:** GRUMBLE **3** *slang* **:** DIE ~ *vt* **1 :** to forebode or utter in a hoarse raucous voice **2** *slang* **:** KILL

2**croak** *n* **:** a hoarse harsh cry (as of a frog) — **croaky** \'krō-kē\ *adj*

croak·er \'krō-kər\ *n* **1 :** an animal that croaks **2 :** any of various fishes (esp. family Sciaenidae) that produce croaking or grunting noises **3 :** one that habitually forbodes evil **:** GRUMBLER

Croat \'krōt *also* 'krō-,at\ *n* [NL *Croata*, fr. Serbo-Croatian *Hrvat*] **:** CROATIAN

Cro·atian \krō-'ā-shən\ *n* **1 :** a native or inhabitant of Croatia **2 :** a south Slavic language spoken by the Croatian people and distinct from Serbian chiefly in its use of the Latin alphabet — **Croatian** *adj*

1**cro·chet** \krō-'shā\ *n* [F, hook, crochet, fr. MF, dim. of *croche* hook, of Scand origin; akin to ON *krōkr* hook — more at CROOK] **:** needlework consisting of the interlocking of looped stitches formed with a single thread and a hooked needle

2**crochet** *vt* **:** to make of crochet ⟨~*ed* a bedspread⟩ ~ *vi* **:** to work with crochet — **cro·chet·er** \-'shā-ər\ *n*

cro·cid·o·lite \krō-'sid-ᵊl-,īt\ *n* [G *krokydolith*, fr. Gk *krokyd-*, *krokys* nap on cloth + G *-lith* -lite] **:** a lavender-blue or leek-green mineral of the amphibole group that occurs in silky fibers and massively — compare TIGEREYE

1**crock** \'kräk\ *n* [ME, fr. OE *crocc;* akin to MHG *krūche* crock] **1 :** a thick earthenware pot or jar **2** [fr. its formation on cooking pots] *dial* **:** SOOT, SMUT **3 :** coloring matter that rubs off from cloth

2**crock** *vt, dial* **:** to soil with crock **:** SMUDGE ~ *vi* **:** to transfer color under rubbing

3**crock** *n* [ME *crok*, prob. of Scand origin; akin to Norw dial. *krokje* crock] **:** one that is broken down, disabled, or impaired

4**crock** *vt* **:** to cause to become disabled ~ *vi* **:** to break down

crock·ery \'kräk-(ə-)rē\ *n* **:** EARTHENWARE

crock·et \'kräk-ət\ *n* [ME *croket*, fr. ONF *croquet* crook, dim. of *croc* hook, of Scand origin; akin to ON *krōkr* hook] **:** an ornament usu. in the form of curved and bent foliage used on the edge of a gable or spire

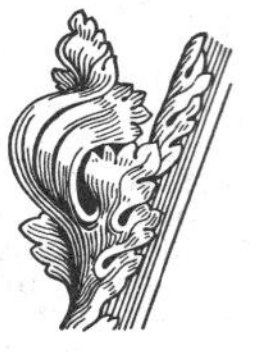

crocket

croc·o·dile \'kräk-ə-,dīl\ *n* [ME & L; ME *cocodrille*, fr. OF, fr. ML *cocodrillus*, alter. of L *crocodilus*, fr. Gk *krokodilos* lizard, crocodile, fr. *krokē* pebble + *drilos* worm; akin to Skt *śarkara* pebble — more at SUGAR] **1 a :** any of several large voracious thick-skinned long-bodied aquatic reptiles (as of the genus *Crocodylus*) of tropical and subtropical waters; *broadly* **:** CROCODILIAN **b :** the skin or hide of a crocodile **2** *archaic* **:** one who hypocritically affects sorrow

crocodile bird *n* **:** an African plover (*Pluvianus aegypticus*) that alights upon the crocodile and devours its insect parasites

crocodile tears *n pl* **:** false or affected tears **:** hypocritical sorrow

croc·o·dil·ian \,kräk-ə-'dil-ē-ən, -'dil-yən\ *n* **:** any of an order (Loricata) of reptiles including the crocodiles, alligators, and related extinct forms — **crocodilian** *adj*

croco·ite \'kräk-ə-,wīt\ *or* **croc·oi·site** \'kräk-wə-,zīt\ *n* [G *krokoisit, krokoit*, fr. F *crocoise*, fr. Gk *krokoeis* saffron-colored, fr. *krokos*] **:** a mineral $PbCrO_4$ consisting of lead chromate

cro·cus \'krō-kəs\ *n, pl* **cro·cus·es** [NL, genus name, fr. L, saffron, fr. Gk *krokos*, of Sem origin] **1** *pl also* **cro·ci** \-,kē, -,kī, -,sī\ **:** any of a large genus (*Crocus*) of herbs of the iris family having solitary long-tubed flowers and slender linear leaves **2 a :** a dark red ferric oxide used for polishing metals **b :** SAFFRON 2

croft \'krȯft\ *n* [ME, fr. OE; akin to OE *crēopan* to creep — more at CREEP] **1** *chiefly Brit* **:** a small enclosed field usu. adjoining a house **2** *chiefly Brit* **:** a small farm worked by a tenant — **croft·er** *n*

crois·sant \krə-,wä-'sän\ *n, pl* **croissants** \-'sän(z)\ [F, lit., crescent, fr. MF *creissant*] **:** a rich crescent-shaped roll

Croix de Guerre \krə-,wäd-ə-'ge(ə)r\ *n* [F, lit., war cross] **:** a French military decoration awarded for gallant action in war

Cro–Ma·gnon \krō-'mag-nən, -'man-yən\ *n* [*Cro-Magnon*, a cave near Les Eyzies, France] **:** a tall erect race of men known from skeletal remains found chiefly in southern France and held to be of the same species (*Homo sapiens*) as recent man

crom·lech \'kräm-,lek\ *n* [W, lit., bent stone] **1 :** DOLMEN **2 :** a circle of monoliths usu. enclosing a dolmen or mound

crone \'krōn\ *n* [ME, fr. ONF *carogne*, lit., carrion, fr. (assumed) VL *caronia* — more at CARRION] **:** a withered old woman

Cro·nus \'krō-nəs, 'krän-əs\ *n* [L, fr. Gk *Kronos*] **:** a Titan unthroned by his son Zeus

cro·ny \'krō-nē\ *n* [perh. fr. Gk *chronios* long-lasting, fr. *chronos* time] **:** an intimate companion

1**crook** \'krůk\ *n* [ME *crok*, fr. ON *krōkr* hook; akin to OE *cradol* cradle] **1 :** an implement having a bent or hooked form: as **a :** POTHOOK **b** (1) **:** a shepherd's staff (2) **:** CROSIER 1 **2 :** a person given to fraudulent practices **:** THIEF **3 :** BEND, CURVE **4 :** a portion of something that is hook-shaped, curved, or bent

2**crook** *vt* **1 :** BEND **2** *slang* **a :** CHEAT **b :** STEAL ~ *vi* **:** CURVE, WIND

crook·back \'krůk-,bak\ *n* **1** *obs* **:** a crooked back **2** *obs* **:** HUNCHBACK — **crook·backed** \-'bakt\ *adj*

crook·ed \'krůk-əd\ *adj* **1 :** having or marked by a crook or curve **:** BENT **2 :** DISHONEST — **crook·ed·ly** *adv* — **crook·ed·ness** *n*

syn CROOKED, DEVIOUS, OBLIQUE mean not straight or straightforward. CROOKED implies having curves, bends, or twists and suggests cheating or fraudulence; DEVIOUS implies a straying from the direct path and may suggest slippery evasiveness or a delaying or deceptive circuitousness; OBLIQUE implies departure from a perpendicular or horizontal direction and may suggest indirection or lack of perfect straightforwardness

Crookes tube \'krůks-\ *n* [Sir William *Crookes* †1919 E physicist] **:** a vacuum tube evacuated to a high degree for demonstrating the properties of cathode rays

crook·neck \'krůk-,nek\ *n* **:** a squash with a long recurved neck

croon \'krün\ *vb* [ME *croynen*, fr. MD *cronen;* akin to OE *cran* crane] *vi* **1** *chiefly Scot* **a :** BELLOW, BOOM **b :** WAIL **2 a :** to sing in a gentle murmuring manner **b :** to sing in half voice ~ *vt* **:** to sing in a crooning manner — **croon** *n* — **croon·er** *n*

1**crop** \'kräp\ *n* [ME, craw, head of a plant, yield of a field, fr. OE *cropp* craw, head of a plant; akin to OHG *kropf* goiter, craw, OE *crēopan* to creep — more at CREEP] **1 :** the stock or handle of a whip; *also* **:** a riding whip with a short straight stock and a loop **2 :** a pouched enlargement of the gullet of a bird or insect that serves as a receptacle for food and for its preliminary maceration **3** [2*crop*] **a :** an earmark on an animal; *esp* **:** one made by a straight cut squarely removing the upper part of the ear **b :** a close cut of the hair **4 a :** a plant or animal or plant or animal product that can be grown and harvested extensively for profit or subsistence **b :** the product or yield of something formed together **c :** BATCH, LOT **5 :** the total yearly production from a specified area

2**crop** *vb* **cropped; crop·ping** *vt* **1 a :** to remove the upper or outer parts of ⟨~ a hedge⟩ **b :** HARVEST ⟨~ trout⟩ **c :** to cut off short **:** CLIP **2 :** to cause (land) to bear produce; *also* **:** to grow as a crop ~ *vi* **1 :** to feed by cropping something **2 :** to yield or make a crop **3 :** to appear unexpectedly or casually ⟨problems ~ up daily⟩

crop–eared \'kräp-'i(ə)rd\ *adj* **1 :** having the ears cropped **2 :** having the hair cropped so that the ears are conspicuous

1**crop·per** \'kräp-ər\ *n* **1 :** one that crops **2 :** one that raises crops

2**cropper** *n* [prob. fr. E dial. *crop* neck, fr. 1*crop*] **1 :** a severe fall **2 :** a sudden or violent failure or collapse

cro·quet \krō-'kā\ *n* [F dial., hockey stick, fr. ONF, crook] **1 :** a game in which players drive wooden balls with mallets through a series of wickets set out on a lawn **2 :** the act of driving away an opponent's croquet ball by striking one's own ball placed against it — **croquet** *vb*

cro·quette \krō-'ket\ *n* [F, fr. *croquer* to crunch] **:** a small cone-shaped or rounded mass consisting usu. of minced fowl, meat, or vegetable coated with egg and bread crumbs and fried in deep fat

cro·qui·gnole \'krō-kən-,(y)ōl\ *n* [F, a kind of biscuit, fr. *croquer*] **:** a method used in waving the hair by winding it on curlers from the ends of the hair toward the scalp

cro·quis \krō-'kē\ *n, pl* **cro·quis** \-'kē(z)\ [F, fr. *croquer* to crunch, sketch] **:** a rough draft **:** SKETCH

crore \'krō(ə)r, 'krȯ(ə)r\ *n, pl* **crores** *also* **crore** [Hindi *karoṛ*] **:** ten million; *specif* **:** a unit of value equal to ten million rupees

cro·sier \'krō-zhər\ *n* [ME *croser* crosier bearer, fr. MF *crossier*, fr. *crosse* crosier, of Gmc origin; akin to OE *crycc* crutch — more at CRUTCH] **1 :** a staff with a pointed foot carried by bishops and abbots as a symbol of office **2 :** a plant structure with a coiled end

1**cross** \'krȯs\ *n* [ME, fr. OE, fr. ON or OIr; ON *kross*, fr. (assumed) OIr *cross*, fr. L *cruc-* *crux* — more at RIDGE] **1 a :** a structure consisting of an upright with a transverse beam used esp. by the ancient Romans for execution **b** *often cap* **:** the cross on which Jesus Christ was crucified **2 :** an affliction that tries one's virtue, steadfastness, or patience **3 :** a cruciform sign made to invoke the blessing of Christ esp. by touching the forehead, breast, and shoulders **4 a :** a device composed of an upright bar traversed by a horizontal one; *specif* **:** one used as a Christian emblem **b** *cap* **:** the Christian religion **5 :** a structure (as a monument) shaped like or surmounted by a cross **6 :** a figure or mark formed by two intersecting lines crossing at their midpoints; *specif* **:** such a mark used as a signature **7 :** a cruciform badge, emblem, or decoration **8 :** the intersection of two ways or lines **:** CROSSING **9 :** THWARTING, ANNOYANCE ⟨a ~ in love⟩ **10 a :** an act of crossing unlike individuals **b :** a crossbred individual or kind **c :** one that combines characteristics of two different types or individuals **11 a :** a fraudulent or dishonest contest **b :** dishonest or illegal practices — used esp. in the phrase *on the cross* **12 a :** a movement from one part of the stage of a theater to another **b :** a hook crossed over the opponent's lead in boxing **13** *cap* **a :** NORTHERN CROSS **b :** SOUTHERN CROSS

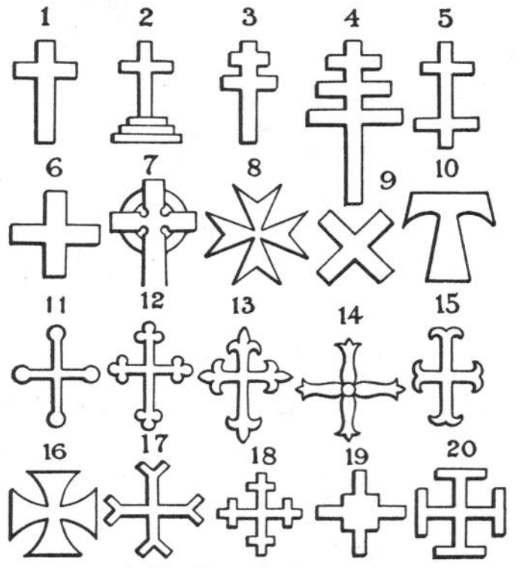

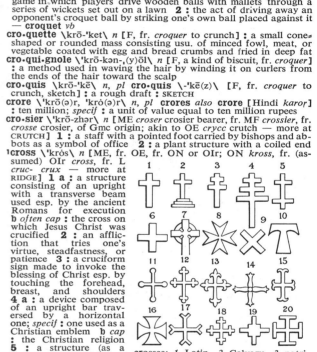

crosses: *1* Latin, *2* Calvary, *3* patriarchal or archiepiscopal, *4* papal, *5* Lorraine, *6* Greek, *7* Celtic, *8* Maltese, *9* Saint Andrew's, *10* tau, *11* pommée, *12* botonée, *13* fleury, *14* avellan, *15* moline, *16* formée, *17* fourchée, *18* crosslet, *19* quadrate, *20* potent

2**cross** *vt* **1 a :** to lie or be situated across **b :** INTERSECT **2 :** to make the sign of the cross upon or over **3 :** to cancel by marking a cross on or drawing a line through **:** strike out ⟨~ names off a list⟩ ⟨~ out portions of a text⟩ **4 :** to place or fold crosswise one over the other ⟨~ the arms⟩ **5 a** (1) **:** to run counter to **:** OPPOSE, THWART (2) **:** CONTRADICT **b :** to confront in a troublesome manner **:** OBSTRUCT **c** (1) **:** to spoil completely **:** DISRUPT — used with *up* ⟨his not appearing ~*ed* up the whole program⟩ (2) **:** to turn against **:** BETRAY **6 a :** to extend across **:** TRAVERSE **b** (1) **:** to go from one to the other side of ⟨~ a street⟩ (2) **:** to pass over on ⟨~ a bridge⟩ **7 a :** to draw a line across **b :** to mark or figure with lines **:** STREAK **8 :** to cause (an animal or plant) to interbreed with one of a different kind **:** HYBRIDIZE **9 :** to meet and pass on the way ⟨our letters must have ~*ed* each other⟩ **10 :** to carry or take across ~ *vi* **1 :** to move, pass, or extend across something; *specif* **:** to pass from one side of the theater stage to another — used with *over* **2 :** to lie or be athwart each other **3 :** to meet in passing esp. from opposite directions **4 :** INTERBREED, HYBRIDIZE

3**cross** *adj* **1 a :** lying across or athwart **b :** moving across ⟨~ traffic⟩ **2 a :** running counter **:** OPPOSING **b :** mutually opposed ⟨~ purposes⟩ **3 :** involving mutual interchange **:** RECIPROCAL **4 :** marked by bad temper **:** GRUMPY **5 :** extending over or treating several groups or classes ⟨a *cross*-cultural perspective⟩ **6 :** CROSSBRED, HYBRID **syn** see IRASCIBLE — **cross·ly** *adv* — **cross·ness** *n*

4**cross** *adv* **:** not parallel **:** CROSSWISE ⟨to *cross*-wind wire⟩

cross·able \'krȯ-sə-bəl\ *adj* **:** capable of being crossed

cross·bar \'krȯs-,bär\ *n* **:** a traverse bar or stripe

cross·bill \ˈkrȯs-ˌbil\ *n* **:** any of a genus (*Loxia*) of finches with mandibles strongly curved and crossing each other

cross·bones \-ˌbōnz\ *n pl* **:** two leg or arm bones placed or depicted crosswise

cross·bow \-ˌbō\ *n* **:** a weapon for discharging quarrels and stones that consists chiefly of a short bow mounted crosswise near the end of a wooden stock — **cross·bow·man** \-mən\ *n*

cross·bred \ˈkrȯs-ˈbred\ *adj* **:** HYBRID; *specif* **:** produced by interbreeding two pure but different breeds, strains, or varieties — **cross·bred** \-ˌbred\ *n*

1**cross·breed** \ˈkrȯs-ˌbrēd, -ˈbrēd\ *vt* **:** HYBRIDIZE, CROSS; *esp* **:** to interbreed two varieties or breeds of the same species ~ *vi* **:** to engage in or undergo crossbreeding

2**cross·breed** \-ˌbrēd\ *n* **:** HYBRID

1**cross–coun·try** \ˈkrȯ-ˈskən-trē\ *adj* **1 :** proceeding over countryside (as across fields and through woods) and not by roads **2 :** of or relating to cross-country sports — **cross–country** *adv*

2**cross–country** *n* **:** cross-country sports

cross·cur·rent \ˈkrȯ-ˈskər-ənt, -ˈskə-rənt\ *n* **1 :** a current traverse to the general forward direction **2 :** a conflicting tendency

1**cross·cut** \ˈkrȯ-ˌskət, -ˈskət\ *vt* **1 :** to cut with a crosscut saw **2 :** to cut, go, or move across or through **:** INTERSECT

2**crosscut** *adj* **1 :** made or used for cutting traversely ⟨a ~ saw⟩ **2 :** cut across or traversely ⟨a ~ incision⟩

3**cross·cut** \ˈkrȯ-ˌskət\ *n* **1 :** something that cuts across or through; *specif* **:** a mine working driven horizontally and at right angles to an adit, drift, or level **2 :** CROSS SECTION

crosse \ˈkrȯs\ *n* [F, lit., crosier] **:** the stick used in lacrosse

cross·er \ˈkrȯ-sər\ *n* **:** one that crosses

cross–ex·am·i·na·tion \ˌkrȯ-sig-ˌzam-ə-ˈnā-shən\ *n* **:** the act or process of cross-examining

cross–ex·am·ine \-ˈzam-ən\ *vt* **:** to examine by a series of questions designed to check or discredit the answers to previous questions — **cross–ex·am·in·er** \-ˈzam-(ə-)nər\ *n*

cross–eye \ˈkrȯ-ˌsī\ *n* **1 :** strabismus in which the eye turns inward toward the nose **2** *pl* **:** eyes affected with cross-eye — **cross–eyed** \-ˈsīd\ *adj*

cross–fer·tile \ˈkrȯs-ˈfərt-ᵊl\ *adj* **:** fertile in a cross or capable of cross-fertilization

cross–fer·til·iza·tion \ˈkrȯs-ˌfərt-ᵊl-ə-ˈzā-shən\ *n* **1 a :** fertilization between gametes produced by separate individuals or sometimes by individuals of different kinds **b :** CROSS-POLLINATION **2 :** INTERCHANGE, INTERACTION — **cross–fer·til·ize** \-ˈfərt-ᵊl-ˌīz\ *vb*

cross–file \-ˈfī(ə)l\ *vb* **:** to register as a candidate in the primary elections of more than one political party

cross fire *n* **1 :** firing (as in combat) from two or more points so that the lines of fire cross; *also* **:** a situation wherein the forces of opposing factions meet or cross **2 :** rapid or heated interchange

cross–grained \ˈkrȯs-ˈgrānd\ *adj* **1 :** having the grain or fibers running diagonally, transversely, or irregularly **2 :** difficult to deal with — **cross–grained·ness** \-ˈgrā-nəd-nəs, -ˈgrān(d)-nəs\ *n*

cross hair *n* **:** one of the fine wires or threads in the focus of the eyepiece of an optical instrument used as a reference line in the field or for marking the instrumental axis

cross·hatch \ˈkrȯs-ˌhach\ *vb* **:** to mark with a series of parallel lines that cross esp. obliquely — **crosshatch** *n* — **cross–hatch·ing** *n*

cross·head \ˈkrȯs-ˌhed\ *n* **:** a metal block to which one end of a piston rod is secured, which slides on parallel guides, and which has a pin for attachment of the connecting rod

cross·ing *n* **1 :** the act or action of crossing: as **a :** a traversing or traveling across **b :** an opposing, blocking, or thwarting esp. in an unfair or dishonest manner **c :** INTERBREEDING, HYBRIDIZING **2 :** a point of intersection **3 :** a place where a street or stream is crossed

cross·ing–over \ˌkrȯ-siŋ-ˈō-vər\ *n* **:** an interchange of genes or segments between associated parts of homologous chromosomes during synapsis

cross·let \ˈkrȯ-slət\ *n* **:** a small cross; *esp* **:** one used as a heraldic bearing — see CROSS illustration

cross–link \ˈkrȯ-ˌsliŋk\ *n* **:** a crosswise connecting part (as an atom or group that connects parallel chains in a complex chemical molecule) — **cross–link** *vb*

cross of Lor·raine \-lə-ˈrān, -lō-\ [*Lorraine*, region of western Europe] — see CROSS illustration

cross·over \ˈkrȯ-ˌsō-vər\ *n* **1 :** a crossing from one side, level, or track to another or the place where such crossing is made; *also* **:** a passageway for effecting such a crossing **2 :** an instance or product of genetic crossing-over

cross·patch \ˈkrȯ-ˌspach\ *n* [3*cross* + *patch* (fool)] **:** GROUCH 2

cross·piece \ˈkrȯ-ˌspēs\ *n* **:** a horizontal member (as of a structure)

cross–pol·li·nate \ˈkrȯ-ˈspäl-ə-ˌnāt\ *or* **cross–pol·li·nize** \-ə-ˌnīz\ *vt* **:** to subject to cross-pollination

cross–pol·li·na·tion \ˌkrȯ-ˌspäl-ə-ˈnā-shən\ *n* **:** the transfer of pollen from one flower to the stigma of another

cross–pur·pose \ˈkrȯ-ˈspər-pəs\ *n* **:** a purpose usu. unintentionally contrary to another purpose of oneself or of someone else

cross–ques·tion \ˈkrȯ-ˈskwes(h)-chən\ *n* **:** a question asked in cross-examination — **cross–question** *vt*

cross–re·fer \ˌkrȯs-ri-ˈfər\ *vb* **:** to refer by a notation or direction from one place to another (as in a book, list, or catalog) — **cross–ref·er·ence** \ˈkrȯs-ˈref-ərn(t)s, -ˈref-(ə-)rən(t)s\ *n or vb*

cross·road \ˈkrȯs-ˌrōd, -ˈrōd\ *n* **1 :** a road that crosses a main road or runs cross-country between main roads **2** *usu pl but sing or pl in constr* **a :** the place of intersection of two or more roads **b** (1) **:** a small community located at such a crossroads (2) a central meeting place **c :** a crucial point esp. where a decision must be made

cross·ruff \ˈkrȯs-ˌrəf, -ˈrəf\ *n* **:** a series of plays in a card game in which partners alternately trump different suits and lead to each other for that purpose — **crossruff** *vb*

cross section *n* **1 :** a cutting or piece of something cut off at right angles to an axis; *also* **:** a representation of such a cutting **2 :** a measure of the probability of an encounter between particles such as will result in a specified effect (as ionization or capture) **3 :** a composite representation typifying the constituents of a thing in their relations — **cross–sec·tion·al** \-ˈsek-shnəl, -shən-ᵊl\ *adj*

cross–ster·ile \ˈkrȯs-ˈster-əl\ *adj* **:** mutually sterile — **cross–ste·ril·i·ty** \ˌkrȯs-stə-ˈril-ət-ē\ *n*

cross–stitch \ˈkrȯs-ˌstich\ *n* **1 :** any needlework stitch that forms an X **2 :** work having cross-stitch — **cross–stitch** *vb*

cross talk *n* **:** unwanted sound reproduced by an electronic receiver resulting from the inductive effect produced by another transmission channel

cross·tree \ˈkrȯ-(ˌ)strē\ *n* **:** two horizontal crosspieces of timber or metal supported by trestletrees at a masthead that spread the upper shrouds in order to support the mast — usu. used in pl.

cross vault *n* **:** a vault formed by the intersection of two or more simple vaults — called also *cross vaulting*

cross·walk \ˈkrȯ-ˌswȯk\ *n* **:** a specially paved or marked path for pedestrians crossing a street or road

cross·way \ˈkrȯ-ˌswā\ *n* **:** CROSSROAD — often used in pl.

cross·wind \ˈkrȯ-ˌswind\ *n* **:** a wind blowing in a direction not parallel to a course

1**cross·wise** \ˈkrȯ-ˌswīz\ *also* **cross·ways** \-ˌswāz\ *adv* **1** *archaic* **:** in the form of a cross **2 :** so as to cross something **:** ACROSS

2**crosswise** *adj* **:** TRANSVERSE, CROSSING

cross·word puzzle \ˌkrȯ-ˌswərd-\ *n* **:** a puzzle in which words are filled into a pattern of numbered squares in answer to similarly numbered clues and in such a way that they read across and down

crotch \ˈkräch\ *n* [prob. alter. of 1*crutch*] **1 :** a pole with a forked end used esp. as a prop **2 :** an angle formed by the parting of two legs, branches, or members — **crotched** \ˈkrächt\ *adj*

crotch·et \ˈkräch-ət\ *n* [ME *crochet*, fr. MF] **1** *obs* **a :** a small hook or hooked instrument **b :** BROOCH **2 a :** PECULIARITY **b :** a peculiar trick, dodge, or device **3 :** QUARTER NOTE **syn** see CAPRICE

crotch·et·i·ness \-ē-nəs\ *n* **:** the quality or state of being crotchety

crotch·ety \ˈkräch-ət-ē\ *adj* **1 :** given to crotchets **2 :** full of or arising from crotchets

cro·ton \ˈkrōt-ᵊn\ *n* [NL, genus name, fr. Gk *krotōn* castor-oil plant] **1 :** any of a genus (*Croton*) of herbs and shrubs of the spurge family: as **a :** one (*C. eluteria*) of the Bahamas yielding cascarilla bark **b :** an East Indian plant (*C. tiglium*) yielding a viscid acrid fixed oil used as a drastic cathartic, a vesicant, or a pustulant **2 :** any of a genus (*Codiaeum*) of shrubs related to the crotons

Cro·ton bug \ˈkrōt-ᵊn-\ *n* [*Croton* river, N.Y., used as a water supply for New York City] **:** a small active winged cockroach (*Blatella germanica*) common where food and moisture are found

crouch \ˈkrau̇ch\ *vb* [ME *crouchen*] *vi* **1 :** to stoop with the limbs close to the body **2 :** to bend or bow servilely **:** CRINGE ~ *vt* **:** to bow esp. in humility or fear **:** BEND — **crouch** *n*

1**croup** \ˈkrüp\ *n* [ME *croupe*, fr. OF, of Gmc origin; akin to OHG *kropf* craw — more at CROP] **:** the rump of a quadruped

2**croup** *n* [E dial. *croup* to cry hoarsely, cough, prob. of imit. origin] **:** a spasmodic laryngitis esp. of infants marked by episodes of difficult breathing and hoarse metallic cough — **croup·ous** \ˈkrü-pəs\ *adj* — **croupy** \-pē\ *adj*

crou·pi·er \ˈkrü-pē-ər, -pē-ˌā\ *n* [F, lit. rider on the croup of a horse, fr. *croupe* croup] **:** an employee of a gambling casino who collects and pays bets

crouse \ˈkrüs\ *adj* [ME] *chiefly Scot & Irish* **:** COCKY; *also* **:** BRISK

crou·ton \ˈkrü-ˌtän, krü-ˈ\ *n* [F *croûton*, dim. of *croûte* crust, fr. MF *crouste*] **:** a small cube of bread toasted or fried crisp

1**crow** \ˈkrō\ *n* [ME *crowe*, fr. OE *crāwe*; akin to OHG *krāwa* crow, OE *crāwan* to crow] **1 :** any of various large usu. entirely glossy black oscine birds (family Corvidae and esp. genus *Corvus*) **2 :** CROWBAR **3** *cap* **a** (1) **:** a Siouan people inhabiting the region between the Platte and Yellowstone rivers (2) **:** a member of this people **b :** the language of the Crow people **4** *cap* **:** CORVUS — **as the crow flies :** in a straight line

2**crow** *vi* **crowed** \ˈkrōd\ *also in sense 1 chiefly Brit* **crew** \ˈkrü\ **crow·ing** [ME *crowen*, fr. OE *crāwan*] **1 :** to make the loud shrill sound characteristic of a cock **2 :** to utter a sound expressive of pleasure **3 a :** EXULT, GLOAT **b :** BRAG **syn** see BOAST

3**crow** *n* **1 :** the cry of the cock **2 :** a triumphant cry

crow·bar \ˈkrō-ˌbär\ *n* **:** an iron or steel bar usu. wedge-shaped at the working end for use as a pry or lever

crow·ber·ry \ˈkrō-ˌber-ē\ *n* **1 :** any of several heaths or related plants: **a :** an undershrub (*Empetrum nigrum*) of arctic and alpine regions with an insipid black berry **b :** BEARBERRY 1 **c :** WHORTLEBERRY 1 **2 :** the fruit of a crowberry

1**crowd** \ˈkrau̇d\ *vb* [ME *crouden*, fr. OE *crūdan*; akin to MHG *kroten* to crowd, OE *crod* multitude, MIr *gruth* curds] *vi* **1 a :** to press on **:** HURRY **b :** to press close **2 :** to collect in numbers ~ *vt* **1 a :** to fill by pressing or thronging together **b :** to press, force, or thrust into a small space **2 :** PUSH, FORCE **3 a :** to urge on **b :** to put on (sail) in excess of the usual for greater speed **4 :** to put pressure on **5 :** THRONG, JOSTLE **6 :** to press close to

2**crowd** *n* **1 :** a large number of persons esp. when collected into a somewhat compact body without order **:** THRONG **2 :** the great body of the people **:** POPULACE **3 :** a large number of things close together **4 :** a group of people having a common interest

syn THRONG, CRUSH, MOB, ROUT, HORDE: CROWD implies a massing together and often suggests a loss of individuality of the unit or member; THRONG carries a stronger implication of movement and pushing; CRUSH stresses compact concentration that causes discomfort; MOB may be a casual intensive for CROWD but specifically implies a disorderly crowd bent on destruction or violence; ROUT and HORDE apply to a rushing or tumultuous crowd

3**crowd** \ˈkrau̇d, ˈkrüd\ *n* [ME *crowde*, fr. (assumed) MW *crwth*] **1 :** an ancient Celtic stringed instrument played by plucking or with a short bow — called also *crwth* **2** *dial Eng* **:** FIDDLE

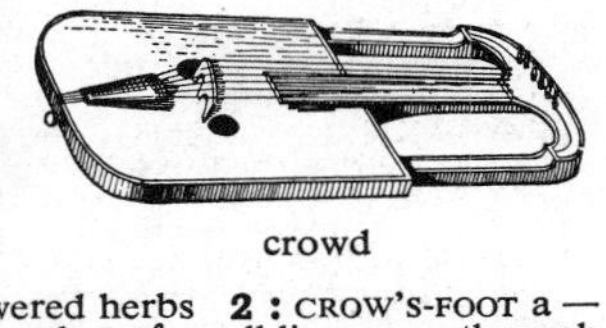

crowd

crow·foot \ˈkrō-ˌfu̇t\ *n, pl* **crow·feet** \-ˌfēt\ **1** *pl usu* **crowfoots :** any of numerous plants having leaves pedately lobed; *esp* **:** any of a genus (*Ranunculus* of the family Ranunculaceae, the crowfoot family) of mostly yellow-flowered herbs **2 :** CROW'S-FOOT a — usu. used in pl. **3** *on a boat* **:** a number of small lines rove through a long block

crow·keep·er \ˈkrō-ˌkē-pər\ *n, dial Eng* **:** a person employed to scare off crows

1**crown** \ˈkrau̇n\ *n* [ME *coroune*, *crowne*, fr. OF *corone*, fr. L *corona* wreath, crown, fr. Gk *korōnē*; akin to Gk *korōnos* curved, L

curvus, MIr *cruind* round] **1 :** a reward of victory or mark of honor; *esp* **:** the title representing the championship in a sport **2 :** a royal or imperial headdress or cap of sovereignty **:** DIADEM **3 :** the highest part: as **a :** the topmost part of the skull or head **b :** the summit of a mountain **c :** the head of foliage of a tree or shrub **d :** the part of a hat or other headgear covering the crown of the head **e :** the part of a tooth external to the gum or an artificial substitute for this **4 :** a wreath, band, or circular ornament for the head **5 :** something resembling a wreath or crown **6 a** (1) *often cap* **:** imperial or regal power **:** SOVEREIGNTY (2) *cap* **:** the government under a constitutional monarchy **b :** MONARCH **7 :** something that imparts splendor, honor, or finish **:** CULMINATION **8 a :** any of several old gold coins with a crown as part of the device **b :** an English silver coin worth five shillings **c :** a size of paper usu. 15 x 20 in. **9 a :** a unit of value equivalent to the value of a crown **b** (1) **:** KORUNA (2) **:** KRONA (3) **:** KRONE (4) **:** KROON **10 a :** the region of a seed plant at which stem and root merge **b :** the thick arching end of the shank of an anchor where the arms join it

2crown *vt* [ME *corounen,* fr. OF *coroner,* fr. L *coronare,* fr. *corona*] **1 a :** to place a crown or wreath upon the head of; *specif* **:** to invest with regal dignity and power **:** ENTHRONE **b :** to recognize officially as **2 :** to bestow something upon as a mark of honor or recompense **:** ADORN **3 :** SURMOUNT, TOP; *esp* **:** to top (a checker) with a checker to make a king **4 :** to bring to a successful conclusion **:** CLIMAX **5 :** to provide with something like a crown: as **a :** to fill so that the surface forms a crown **b :** to put an artificial crown upon (a tooth) **6 :** to hit on the head

crown canopy *n* **:** the cover formed by the top branches of trees in a forest

Crown Colony *n* **:** a colony of the British Commonwealth over which the Crown retains some control

crow·ner \'krü-nər, 'kraù-\ *n* [ME, alter. of *coroner*] *chiefly dial* **:** CORONER

crown·et \'kraù-nət\ *n, archaic* **:** CORONET

crown glass *n* **1 :** a glass blown and whirled into the form of a disk with a center lump left by the worker's rod **2 :** alkali-lime silicate optical glass having relatively low index of refraction and low dispersion value

crown land *n* **1 :** land belonging to the Crown and yielding revenues that the reigning sovereign is entitled to **2 :** public land in some British dominions or colonies

crown lens *n* **:** the crown glass component of an achromatic lens

crown prince *n* **:** the heir apparent to a crown or throne

crown princess *n* **1 :** the wife of a crown prince **2 :** a female heir apparent or heir presumptive to a crown or throne

crown saw *n* **:** a saw having teeth at the edge of a hollow cylinder

crow's–foot \'krōz-,fùt\ *n, pl* **crow's–feet** \-,fēt\ **:** something resembling a crow's foot: as **a :** any of the wrinkles around the outer corners of the eyes — usu. used in pl. **b :** CROWFOOT 1

crow's nest *n* **:** a partly enclosed platform high on a ship's mast for a lookout; *also* **:** a similar lookout on land

cro·zier *var of* CROSIER

cruces *pl of* CRUX

cru·cial \'krü-shəl\ *adj* [F, fr. L *cruc-, crux* cross — more at RIDGE] **1** *archaic* **:** CRUCIFORM **2 :** marked by final determination of a doubtful issue **:** DECISIVE; *broadly* **:** SEVERE, TRYING **syn** see ACUTE — **cru·cial·ly** \'krüsh-(ə-)lē\ *adv*

cru·ci·ate \'krü-shē-,āt\ *adj* [NL *cruciatus,* fr. L *cruc-, crux*] **:** cross-shaped: **a :** having leaves or petals in the form of a cross **b :** CROSSING ⟨~ wings of an insect⟩ — **cru·ci·ate·ly** *adv*

cru·ci·ble \'krü-sə-bəl\ *n* [ME *corusible,* fr. ML *crucibulum,* modif. of OF *croiseul*] **1 :** a pot of a very refractory material used for melting and calcining a substance that requires a high degree of heat **2 :** a severe test

crucible steel *n* **:** hard cast steel made in pots that are lifted from the furnace before the metal is poured into molds

cru·ci·fer \'krü-sə-fər\ *n* [deriv. of L *cruc-, crux* + *-fer*] **:** any plant of the mustard family — **cru·cif·er·ous** \krü-'sif-(ə-)rəs\ *adj*

cru·ci·fix \'krü-sə-,fiks\ *n* [ME, fr. LL *crucifixus* the crucified Christ, fr. *crucifixus,* pp. of *crucifigere* to crucify, fr. L *cruc-, crux* + *figere* to fasten] **:** a representation of Christ on the cross

cru·ci·fix·ion \,krü-sə-'fik-shən\ *n* **1 :** the act of crucifying **2 :** extreme and painful punishment, affliction, or suffering

cru·ci·form \'krü-sə-,fòrm\ *adj* [L *cruc-, crux* + E *-form*] **:** forming or arranged in a cross — **cruciform** *n* — **cru·ci·form·ly** *adv*

cru·ci·fy \'krü-sə-,fī\ *vt* [ME *crucifien,* fr. OF *crucifier,* fr. LL *crucifigere*] **1 :** to put to death by nailing or binding the hands and feet to a cross **2 :** to destroy the power of **:** MORTIFY ⟨~ the flesh⟩ **3 :** to treat cruelly **:** TORTURE, PERSECUTE

1crud \'krəd\ *n* [ME *curd, crudd*] **1** *dial* **:** 1CURD **2 :** a deposit or incrustation of filth, grease, or refuse **3 :** a usu. ill-defined or imperfectly identified bodily disorder — **crud·dy** \-ē\ *adj*

2crud *vb* **crud·ded; crud·ding** *dial* **:** 2CURD

1crude \'krüd\ *adj* [ME, fr. L *crudus* raw — more at RAW] **1 :** existing in a natural state and unaltered by cooking or processing **2** *obs* **:** UNRIPE, IMMATURE **3 :** marked by the primitive, gross, or elemental or by uncultivated simplicity or vulgarity **4 :** rough or inexpert in plan or execution **5 :** lacking a covering, glossing, or concealing **6 :** tabulated without being broken down into classes ⟨~ death rate⟩ **syn** see RUDE — **crude·ly** *adv* — **crude·ness** *n*

2crude *n* **:** a substance in its natural unprocessed state; *esp* **:** unrefined petroleum

cru·di·ty \'krüd-ət-ē\ *n* **1 :** the quality or state of being crude **2 :** something that is crude

cru·el \'krü(-ə)l, 'krù(-ə)l\ *adj* **cru·el·er** *or* **cru·el·ler; cru·el·est** *or* **cru·el·lest** [ME, fr. OF, fr. L *crudelis,* irreg. fr. *crudus*] **1 :** disposed to inflict pain **2 a :** causing or conducive to injury, grief, or pain **b :** unrelieved by leniency **syn** see FIERCE — **cru·el·ly** \'krü-ə-lē, 'krù-; 'krül-lē, 'krùl-lē\ *adv* — **cru·el·ness** *n*

cru·el·ty \'krü(-ə)l-tē, 'krù(-ə)l-\ *n* [ME *cruelte,* fr. OF *cruelté,* fr. L *crudelitat-, crudelitas,* fr. *crudelis*] **1 :** the quality or state of being cruel **2 :** a cruel action **:** inhuman treatment **3 :** marital conduct held (as in a divorce action) to endanger life or health or to cause mental suffering or fear

cru·et \'krü-ət\ *n* [ME, fr. AF, dim. of OF *crue,* of Gmc origin; akin to OE *crocc* crock] **1 :** a usu. glass bottle for condiments for the table **2 :** a vessel for wine or water for altar service

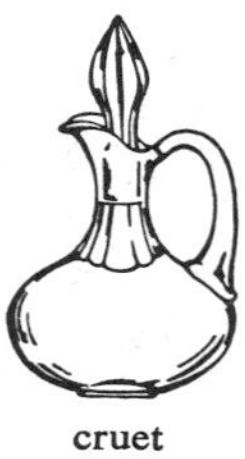

cruet

1cruise \'krüz\ *vb* [D *kruisen* to make a cross, cruise, fr. MD *crucen,* fr. *crūce* cross, fr. L *cruc-, crux* — more at RIDGE] *vi* **1 :** to sail about touching at a series of ports **2 :** to travel for the sake of traveling **3 :** to go about the streets at random **4 :** to travel at the most efficient operating speed ~ *vt* **1 :** to cruise over or about **2 :** to inspect (as land) with reference to possible lumber yield

2cruise *n* **:** an act or an instance of cruising

cruis·er \'krü-zər\ *n* **1 :** a boat or vehicle that cruises **2 :** a large fast moderately armored and gunned warship usu. of 6000 to 15,000 tons displacement **3 :** a motorboat with cabin, plumbing, and other arrangements necessary for living aboard — called also *cabin cruiser* **4 :** a person who cruises

crul·ler \'krəl-ər\ *n* [D *krulle,* a twisted cake, fr. *krul* curly, fr. MD *crul*] **1 :** a small sweet cake formed into twisted strips and fried in deep fat **2** *North & Midland* **:** an unraised doughnut

1crumb \'krəm\ *n* [ME *crumme,* fr. OE *cruma;* akin to MHG *krume* crumb] **1 :** a small fragment esp. of bread **2 :** BIT **3 :** the soft part of bread **4** *slang* **:** a worthless person

2crumb *vt* **1 :** to break into crumbs **2 :** to cover or thicken with crumbs **3 :** to remove crumbs from ⟨~ a table⟩

crum·ble \'krəm-bəl\ *vb* **crum·bling** \-b(ə-)liŋ\ [alter. of ME *kremelen,* freq. of OE *gecrymian* to crumble, fr. *cruma*] **:** to break into small pieces **:** DISINTEGRATE — **crumble** *n*

crum·bli·ness \'krəm-b(ə-)lē-nəs\ *n* **:** the quality or state of being crumbly

crum·blings \'krəm-b(ə-)liŋz\ *n pl* **:** crumbled particles **:** CRUMBS

crum·bly \-b(ə-)lē\ *adj* **:** easily crumbled **:** FRIABLE ⟨~ soil⟩

crum·mie *or* **crum·my** \'krəm-ē\ *n* [Sc *crumb* crooked, fr. ME, fr. OE] *chiefly Scot* **:** COW; *esp* **:** one with crumpled horns

crum·my *or* **crumby** \'krəm-ē\ *adj* [ME *crumme*] **1** *obs* **:** CRUMBLY **2** *slang* **a :** MISERABLE, FILTHY **b :** CHEAP, WORTHLESS

1crump \'krəmp\ *vi* [imit.] **1 :** CRUNCH **2 :** to explode heavily

2crump *n* **1 :** a crunching sound **2 :** SHELL, BOMB

3crump *adj* [perh. alter. of *crimp* (friable)] *chiefly Scot* **:** BRITTLE, FRIABLE, CRISP

crum·pet \'krəm-pət\ *n* [perh. fr. ME *crompid* (cake) wafer, lit., curled-up cake, fr. *crumped,* pp. of *crumpen* to curl up, fr. *crump, crumb* crooked] **:** a small round cake of unsweetened batter cooked on a griddle

1crum·ple \'krəm-pəl\ *vb* **crum·pling** \-p(ə-)liŋ\ [(assumed) ME *crumplen,* freq. of ME *crumpen*] *vt* **1 :** to press, bend, or crush out of shape **:** RUMPLE **2 :** to cause to collapse ~ *vi* **1 :** to become crumpled **2 :** COLLAPSE

2crumple *n* **:** a wrinkle or crease made by crumpling

1crunch \'krənch\ *vb* [alter. of *craunch*] **:** to chew, grind, or press with a crushing noise

2crunch *n* **1 :** an act of crunching **2 :** a sound made by crunching — **crunchy** \'krən-chē\ *adj*

crup·per \'krəp-ər, 'krùp-\ *n* [ME *cruper,* fr. OF *crupiere,* fr. *croupe* hindquarters] **1 :** a leather loop passing under a horse's tail and buckled to the saddle **2 :** CROUP; *broadly* **:** BUTTOCKS

cru·ral \'krù(ə)r-əl\ *adj* **:** of or relating to the thigh or leg; *specif* **:** FEMORAL

crus \'krüs, 'krəs\ *n, pl* **cru·ra** \'krù(ə)r-ə\ [L *crur-, crus;* akin to Arm *srunk* shinbones] **1 :** the part of the hind limb between the femur or thigh and the tarsus or ankle **:** SHANK **2 :** any of various parts likened to a leg or to a pair of legs

1cru·sade \krü-'sād\ *n* [blend of MF *croisade* & Sp *cruzada;* both derivs. of L *cruc-, crux* cross] **1** *cap* **:** any of the military expeditions undertaken by Christian powers in the 11th, 12th, and 13th centuries to recover the Holy Land from the Muslims **2 :** any remedial enterprise undertaken with zeal and enthusiasm

2crusade *vi* **:** to engage in a crusade — **cru·sad·er** *n*

cru·sa·do *also* **cru·za·do** \krü-'zäd-(,)ō, -(,)ü\ *n, pl* **crusadoes** *or* **crusados** [Pg *cruzado,* lit., marked with a cross] **:** an old gold or silver coin of Portugal having a cross on the reverse

cruse \'krüz, 'krüs\ *n* [ME; akin to OE *crūse* pitcher] **:** a small vessel (as a jar or pot) for holding a liquid (as water or oil)

1crush \'krəsh\ *vb* [ME *crusshen,* fr. MF *cruisir,* of Gmc origin; akin to MLG *krossen* to crush] *vt* **1 a :** to squeeze or force by pressure so as to alter or destroy structure **b :** to squeeze together into a mass **2 :** HUG, EMBRACE **3 :** to reduce to particles by pounding or grinding **4 a :** SUPPRESS, OVERWHELM **b :** to oppress or burden grievously **c :** to subdue completely **5 :** CROWD, PUSH **6** *archaic* **:** DRINK ~ *vi* **1** *obs* **:** CRASH **2 :** to become crushed **3 :** to advance with or as if with crushing — **crush·er** *n*

2crush *n* **1** *obs* **:** CRASH **2 :** an act of crushing **3 a :** a violent crowding (as of people) **b :** a large reception or party **4 :** INFATUATION; *also* **:** the object of infatuation **syn** see CROWD

crust \'krəst\ *n* [ME, fr. L *crusta;* akin to OE *hrūse* earth, Gk *kryos* icy cold] **1 a :** the hardened exterior or surface part of bread **b :** a piece of this or of bread grown dry or hard **2 :** the pastry cover of a pie **3 :** a hard or brittle external coat or covering: as **a :** a hard surface layer (as of soil or snow) **b :** the outer part of the earth composed essentially of crystalline rocks **c :** a deposit built up on the interior surface of a wine bottle during long aging **d :** an encrusting deposit of dried secretions or exudate; *esp* **:** SCAB **4** *slang* **:** IMPUDENCE, NERVE — **crust** *vb*

crus·ta·cean \,krə-'stā-shən\ *n* [deriv. of L *crusta* crust, shell] **:** any of a large class (Crustacea) of mostly aquatic arthropods having a chitinous or calcareous and chitinous exoskeleton and including the lobsters, shrimps, crabs, wood lice, water fleas, and barnacles — **crustacean** *adj*

crus·ta·ceous \-shəs\ *adj* **1 :** of, relating to, having, or forming a crust or shell ⟨a ~ lichen⟩ **2 :** CRUSTACEAN

crust·al \'krəst-ᵊl\ *adj* **:** relating to a crust esp. of the earth or the moon

crust·i·fi·ca·tion \,krəs-tə-fə-'kā-shən\ *n* **:** INCRUSTATION

crust·i·ly \'krəs-tə-lē\ *adv* **:** in a crusty or surly manner

crust·i·ness \-tē-nəs\ *n* **:** SURLINESS, IRRITABILITY

crusty \'krəs-tē\ *adj* **1 :** having or being a crust **2 :** SURLY, IRASCIBLE **syn** see BLUFF

1crutch \'krəch\ *n* [ME *crucche,* fr. OE *crycc;* akin to OHG *krucka* crutch, OE *cradol* cradle] **1 a :** a support typically fitting under the armpit for use by the disabled in walking **b :** PROP, STAY **2 :** a forked leg rest constituting the pommel of a sidesaddle **3 :** the crotch of a human being **4 :** a forked support

2crutch *vt* **:** to support on crutches **:** prop up

crux \'krəks, 'krùks\ *n, pl* **crux·es** *also* **cru·ces** \'krü-,sēz\ [L *cruc-, crux* cross, torture — more at RIDGE] **1 a :** a puzzling or

difficult problem : unsolved question **b** : a determinative point at issue **2** : a main or central feature

cru·zei·ro \krü-'zā-(,)rō, -(,)rü\ *n* [Pg] — see MONEY table

crwth \'krüth\ *n* [W] : 3CROWD 1

1**cry** \'krī\ *vb* **cried; cry·ing** [ME *crien*, fr. OF *crier*, fr. L *quiritare* to cry out for help (from a citizen), to scream, fr. *Quirit-*, *Quiris* Roman citizen] *vi* **1** : to call loudly : SHOUT **2** : WEEP, LAMENT **3** : to utter a characteristic sound or call ~ *vt* **1** : BEG, BESEECH **2** : to proclaim publicly : call out — **cry havoc** : to sound an alarm — **cry wolf** : to give alarm without occasion

2**cry** *n, pl* **cries 1** : an instance of crying: as **a** : an inarticulate utterance of distress, rage, or pain **b** *obs* : OUTCRY, CLAMOR **2 a** *obs* : PROCLAMATION **b** *pl, Scot* : BANNS **3** : ENTREATY, APPEAL **4** : a loud shout **5** : WATCHWORD, SLOGAN **6 a** : common report **b** : prevailing fashion **7** : the public voice **8** : a pack of hounds — **a far cry** : a long way — **in full cry** : in full pursuit

cry- *or* **cryo-** *comb form* [G *kryo-*, fr. Gk, fr. *kryos* — more at CRUST] : cold : freezing ⟨*cry*anesthesia⟩ ⟨*cryo*gen⟩

cry down *vt* : DISPARAGE, DEPRECIATE

cry·ing *adj* **1** : calling for notice **2** : NOTORIOUS, HEINOUS

cry·mo·ther·a·py \,krī-mō-'ther-ə-pē\ *or* **cryo·ther·a·py** \,krī-ō-\ *n* [Gk *krymos*, *kryos* icy cold + ISV *therapy*] : therapeutic use of cold

cry off *vt* : to call off ~ *vi, chiefly Brit* : to beg off

cryo·gen \'krī-ə-jən\ *n* : REFRIGERANT — **cry·o·gen·ic** \,krī-ə-'jen-ik\ *adj*

cryo·gen·ics \,krī-ə-'jen-iks\ *n pl but sing or pl in constr* : a branch of physics that relates to the production and effects of very low temperatures

cryo·lite \'krī-ə-,līt\ *n* [ISV] : a mineral Na_3AlF_6 consisting of sodium-aluminum fluoride found in Greenland usu. in white cleavable masses and used in making soda and aluminum

cryo·phil·ic \,krī-ə-'fil-ik\ *adj* : thriving at low temperatures

cryo·scop·ic \,krī-ə-'skäp-ik\ *adj* : of or relating to cryoscopy

cry·os·co·py \krī-'äs-kə-pē\ *n* [ISV] : the determination of the lowered freezing points produced in liquid by dissolved substances to determine molecular weights of solutes and various properties of solutions

cryo·stat \'krī-ə-,stat\ *n* [ISV] : an apparatus for maintaining a constant low temperature

crypt \'kript\ *n* [L *crypta*, fr. Gk *kryptē*, fr. fem. of *kryptos* hidden, fr. *kryptein* to hide; akin to ON *hreysar* heap of stones, Lith *krauti* to pile up] **1** : a chamber (as a vault) wholly or partly underground; *esp* : a vault under the main floor of a church **2** : a simple gland, glandular cavity, or tube : FOLLICLE — **crypt·al** \'krip-tᵊl\ *adj*

crypt- *or* **crypto-** *comb form* [NL, fr. Gk *kryptos*] : hidden : covered ⟨*crypto*genic⟩

crypt·anal·y·sis \,krip-tə-'nal-ə-səs\ *n* [*crypt*ogram + *analysis*] : the solving of cryptograms or cryptographic systems — **crypt·an·a·lyst** \krip-'tan-ᵊl-əst\ *n* — **crypt·an·a·lyt·ic** \,krip-,tan-ᵊl-'it-ik\ *adj* — **crypt·an·a·lyze** \krip-'tan-ᵊl-,īz\ *vt*

cryp·tic \'krip-tik\ *adj* [LL *crypticus*, fr. Gk *kryptikos*, fr. *kryptos*] **1** : SECRET, OCCULT **2** : ENIGMATIC, MYSTERIOUS **3** : serving to conceal **4** : UNRECOGNIZED **5** : employing cipher or code **syn** see OBSCURE — **cryp·ti·cal** \-ti-kəl\ *adj* — **cryp·ti·cal·ly** \-ti-k(ə-)lē\ *adv*

cryp·to \'krip-(,)tō\ *n* [*crypt-*] : one who adheres or belongs secretly to a party, sect, or other group

cryp·to·crys·tal·line \,krip-(,)tō-'kris-tə-lən\ *adj* [ISV] : having a crystalline structure so fine that no distinct particles are recognizable under the microscope

cryp·to·gam \'krip-tə-,gam\ *n* [deriv. of Gk *kryptos* + *-gamia* -gamy] : a plant (as a fern, moss, alga, or fungus) reproducing by spores and not producing flowers or seed — **cryp·to·gam·ic** \,krip-tə-'gam-ik\ *or* **cryp·tog·a·mous** \krip-'täg-ə-məs\ *adj*

cryp·to·gen·ic \,krip-tə-'jen-ik\ *adj* : of obscure or unknown origin ⟨a ~ disease⟩

cryp·to·gram \'krip-tə-,gram\ *n* [F *cryptogramme*, fr. *crypt-* + *-gramme* -gram] **1** : a writing in cipher or code **2** : a figure or representation having a hidden significance — **cryp·to·gram·mic** \,krip-tə-'gram-ik\ *adj*

1**cryp·to·graph** \'krip-tə-,graf\ *n* **1** : CRYPTOGRAM **2** : a device for enciphering and deciphering — **cryp·tog·ra·pher** \krip-'täg-rə-fər\ *n* — **cryp·to·graph·ic** \,krip-tə-'graf-ik\ *adj* — **cryp·to·graph·i·cal·ly** \-i-k(ə-)lē\ *adv* — **cryp·tog·ra·phist** \krip-'täg-rə-fəst\ *n*

2**cryptograph** *vt* : to convert into code or cipher

cryp·tog·ra·phy \krip-'täg-rə-fē\ *n* [NL *cryptographia*, fr. *crypt-* + *-graphia* -graphy] **1** : the enciphering and deciphering of messages in secret code **2** : CRYPTANALYSIS

cryp·to·me·ria \,krip-tə-'mir-ē-ə\ *n* [NL, genus name, fr. *crypt-* + Gk *meros* part] : an evergreen tree (*Cryptomeria japonica*) of the pine family that is a valuable timber tree of Japan

cryp·to·zo·ite \,krip-tə-'zō-,īt\ *n* [*crypt-* + *-zoite* (as in *sporozoite*)] : a malaria parasite that develops in tissue cells and gives rise to the forms that invade blood cells

1**crys·tal** \'krist-ᵊl\ *n* [ME *cristal*, fr. OF, fr. L *crystallum*, fr. Gk *krystallos*] **1** : quartz that is transparent or nearly so and that is either colorless or only slightly tinged **2** : something resembling crystal in transparency and colorlessness **3** : a body that is formed by the solidification of a chemical element, a compound, or a mixture and has a regularly repeating internal arrangement of its atoms and often external plane faces **4** : a clear colorless glass of superior quality **5** : the glass or transparent plastic cover over a watch or clock dial **6** : a crystalline material used in electronics as a frequency-determining element or for rectification

2**crystal** *adj* **1** : consisting of or resembling crystal : CLEAR, LUCID **2** : relating to or using a crystal ⟨a ~ radio receiver⟩

crystal detector *n* : a detector that depends for its operation on the rectifying action of the surface of contact between various crystals (as of galena) and a metallic electrode

crystal gazer *n* : one that practices divination by gazing into a glass or crystal ball — **crystal gazing** *n*

crys·tal·lif·er·ous \,kris-tə-'lif-(ə-)rəs\ *adj* [ISV] : producing or bearing crystals

crys·tal·line \'kris-tə-lən\ *adj* [ME *cristallin*, fr. MF & L; MF, fr. L *crystallinus*, fr. Gk *krystallinos*, fr. *krystallos*] **1** : made of crystal or composed of crystals **2** : resembling crystal: as **a** : TRANSPARENT **b** : CLEAR-CUT **3** : constituting or relating to a crystal

crystalline lens *n* : the lens of the eye in vertebrates

crys·tal·lite \'kris-tə-,līt\ *n* [G *kristallit*, fr. Gk *krystallos*] **1 a** : a minute mineral form like those common in glassy volcanic rocks usu. not referable to any mineral species but marking the first step in crystallization **b** : a single grain in a medium composed of many crystals **2** : MICELLE — **crys·tal·lit·ic** \,kris-tə-'lit-ik\ *adj*

crys·tal·liz·able \'kris-tə-,lī-zə-bəl\ *adj* : capable of forming or of being formed into crystals

crys·tal·li·za·tion \,kris-tə-lə-'zā-shən\ *n* : the process of crystallizing; *also* : a form resulting from this

crys·tal·lize *also* **crys·tal·ize** \'kris-tə-,līz\ *vt* **1** : to cause to form crystals or assume crystalline form **2** : to cause to take a definite form ⟨tried to ~ his thoughts⟩ **3** : to coat with crystals esp of sugar ~ *vi* : to become crystallized — **crys·tal·liz·er** *n*

crys·tal·log·ra·pher \,kris-tə-'läg-rə-fər\ *n* : a specialist in crystallography — **crys·tal·lo·graph·ic** \-lō-'graf-ik\ *adj* — **crys·tal·lo·graph·i·cal** \-i-kəl\ *adj*

crys·tal·log·ra·phy \-'läg-rə-fē\ *n* [F or NL; F *cristallographie*, fr. NL *crystallographia*, fr. *crystall-* + *-graphia* -graphy] : the science dealing with the system of forms among crystals, their structure, and their forms of aggregation

1**crys·tal·loid** \'kris-tə-,lȯid\ *adj* : having properties of crystal

2**crystalloid** *n* **1** : a substance that forms a true solution and is capable of being crystallized **2** : a crystalloid particle of protein found esp. in oily seeds — **crys·tal·loi·dal** \,kris-tə-'lȯid-ᵊl\ *adj*

crystal violet *n* : a triphenylmethane dye found in gentian violet

cry up *vt* : to enhance in value or repute by public praise : EXTOL

cte·noid \'ten-,ȯid, 'tē-,nȯid\ *adj* [ISV, fr. Gk *ktenoeidēs*, fr. *kten-*, *kteis* comb — more at PECTINATE] : having the margin toothed ⟨~ scale⟩; *also* : having or consisting of ctenoid scales ⟨~ fishes⟩

cte·noph·o·ran \ti-'näf-ə-rən\ *adj* : of or relating to a ctenophore — **ctenophoran** *n*

cteno·phore \'ten-ə-,fō(ə)r, -,fȯ(ə)r\ *n* [deriv. of Gk *kten-*, *kteis* + *pherein* to carry — more at BEAR] : any of a phylum (Ctenophora) of marine animals superficially resembling jellyfishes but having decided biradial symmetry and swimming by means of eight meridional bands of transverse ciliated plates

cub \'kəb\ *n* [origin unknown] **1 a** : a young fox or other carnivorous mammal **b** : a young shark **2** : a young person **3** : APPRENTICE; *esp* : an inexperienced newspaper reporter

Cu·ban heel \,kyü-bən-\ *n* [*Cuba*, island in the West Indies] : a broad medium-high heel with a moderately curved back

cu·ba·ture \'kyü-bə-,chu̇(ə)r, -chər\ *n* [*cube* + *-ature* (as in *quadrature*)] **1** : determination of cubic contents **2** : cubic content

cub·by \'kəb-ē\ *n* [obs. E *cub* pen, fr. D *kub* thatched roof; akin to OE *cofa* den — more at COVE] : a small room

cub·by·hole \-,hōl\ *n* **1** : a snug place **2** : PIGEONHOLE 2

1**cube** \'kyüb\ *n* [ME, fr. L *cubus*, fr. Gk *kybos* cube, vertebra] **1** : the regular solid of six equal square sides — see VOLUME table **2** : the product got by taking a number three times as a factor

2**cube** *vt* **1** : to raise to the third power **2** : to form into a cube **3** : to cut partly through (a steak) in a checkered pattern to increase tenderness by breaking the fibers — **cub·er** *n*

3**cube** *adj* : raised to the third power

4**cu·be** \'kyü-,bā, kyü-'\ *n* [AmerSp *cubé*] : any of several tropical American plants furnishing rotenone

cu·beb \'kyü-,beb\ *n* [MF *cubebe*, fr. OF, fr. ML *cubeba*, fr. Ar *kubābah*] : the dried unripe berry of a tropical shrub (*Piper cubeba*) of the pepper family that is crushed and smoked in cigarettes for catarrh

cube root *n* : a number whose cube is a given number

cu·bic \'kyü-bik\ *adj* **1** : having the form of a cube : CUBICAL **2 a** : relating to the cube considered as a crystal form **b** : ISOMETRIC b **3 a** : THREE-DIMENSIONAL **b** : being the volume of a cube whose edge is a specified unit ⟨~ inch⟩ **4** : CUBE — **cu·bic·ly** *adv*

cu·bi·cal \'kyü-bi-kəl\ *adj* **1** : CUBIC; *esp* : shaped like a cube **2** : relating to volume — **cu·bi·cal·ly** \-k(ə-)lē\ *adv*

cu·bi·cle \'kyü-bi-kəl\ *n* [L *cubiculum*, fr. *cubare* to lie, recline — more at HIP] **1** : a sleeping compartment partitioned off from a large room **2** : a small partitioned space; *esp* : CARREL

cubic measure *n* : a unit (as cubic inch or cubic centimeter) for measuring volume — see MEASURE table, METRIC SYSTEM table

cu·bi·form \'kyü-bə-,fȯrm\ *adj* [L *cubus* + E *-form*] : having the shape of a cube

cub·ism \'kyü-,biz-əm\ *n* : a phase of Postimpressionism that stresses abstract form at the expense of other pictorial elements largely by use of intersecting often transparent cubes and cones — **cub·ist** \-bəst\ *n* — **cubist** *or* **cu·bis·tic** \kyü-'bis-tik\ *adj*

cu·bit \'kyü-bət\ *n* [ME, fr. L *cubitus* elbow, cubit — more at HIP] : any of various ancient units of length based on the length of the forearm from the elbow to the tip of the middle finger and usu. equal to about 18 inches

cu·boid \'kyü-,bȯid\ *adj* : approximately cubic in shape; *specif* : being the outermost of the distal row of tarsal bones of many higher vertebrates

cu·boi·dal \kyü-'bȯid-ᵊl\ *adj* : somewhat cubical

cub scout *n* : a member of the scouting program of the Boy Scouts of America for boys of the age range 8–10

cuck·ing stool \'kək-iŋ-\ *n* [ME *cucking stol*, lit., defecating chair] : a chair formerly used for punishing offenders (as scolds or dishonest tradesmen) by public exposure or ducking in water

1**cuck·old** \'kək-əld, 'ku̇k-\ *n* [ME *cokewold*] : a man whose wife is unfaithful

2**cuckold** *vt* : to make a cuckold of

cuck·old·ry \-əl-drē\ *n* : the practice of making cuckolds

1**cuck·oo** \'kük-(,)ü, 'ku̇k-\ *n* [ME *cuccu*, of imit. origin] **1** : a largely grayish brown European bird (*Cuculus canorus*) noted for its habit of laying eggs in the nests of other birds for them to hatch; *broadly* : any of a large family (Cuculidae of the order Cuculiformes) to which this bird belongs **2** : the call of the cuckoo

2**cuckoo** *vb* : to repeat monotonously as a cuckoo does its call

3**cuckoo** *adj* **1** : of or resembling the cuckoo **2** : SILLY, CRAZY

cuckoo clock *n* **:** a wall or shelf clock that announces the hours by sounds resembling a cuckoo's call
cuck·oo·flow·er \'kük-(,)ü-,flau̇(-ə)r, 'ku̇k-\ *n* **1 :** a bitter cress (*Cardamine pratensis*) of Europe and America **2 :** RAGGED ROBIN **3 :** WOOD SORREL 1
cuck·oo·pint \-,pint\ *n* [ME *cuccupintel*, fr. *cuccu* + *pintel* pintle] **:** a European arum (*Arum maculatum*) with erect spathe and short purple spadix
cuckoo spit *n* **1 :** a frothy secretion exuded upon plants by the nymphs of spittle insects **2 :** SPITTLE INSECT
cu·cu·li·form \k(y)ə-'k(y)ü-lə-,fȯrm\ *adj* [L *cuculus* cuckoo (of imit. origin) + E *-form*] **:** of or relating to the cuckoos or the order (Cuculiformes) including the cuckoos; *also* **:** resembling a cuckoo
cu·cul·late \'kyü-kə-,lāt, kyü-'kəl-ət\ *also* **cu·cul·lat·ed** \'kyü-kə-,lāt-əd\ *adj* [ML *cucullatus*, fr. L *cucullus* hood] **:** hood-shaped ⟨a ~ leaf⟩ **:** HOODED
cu·cum·ber \'kyü-(,)kəm-bər\ *n* [ME, fr. MF *cocombre*, fr. L *cucumer-, cucumis*] **:** the fruit of a vine (*Cucumis sativus*) of the gourd family cultivated as a garden vegetable; *also* **:** this vine
cucumber tree *n* **:** any of several American magnolias (esp. *Magnolia acuminata*) having fruit like a small cucumber
cu·cur·bit \kyü-'kər-bət\ *n* [ME *cucurbite*, fr. MF, fr. L *cucurbita* gourd] **1 :** a vessel or flask for distillation used with or forming part of an alembic **2 :** a plant of the gourd family
cud \'kəd, 'ku̇d\ *n* [ME *cudde*, fr. OE *cwudu;* akin to OHG *kuti* glue Skt *jatu* gum] **1 :** food brought up into the mouth by a ruminating animal from its first stomach to be chewed again **2 :** QUID
cud·bear \'kəd-,ba(ə)r, -,be(ə)r\ *n* [irreg. fr. Dr. *Cuthbert* Gordon, 18th cent. Sc chemist] **:** a reddish coloring matter from lichens
1**cud·dle** \'kəd-ᵊl\ *vb* **cud·dling** \'kəd-liŋ, -ᵊl-iŋ\ [origin unknown] *vt* **:** to hold close for warmth or comfort or in affection ~ *vi* **:** to lie close or snug **:** NESTLE, SNUGGLE **syn** see CARESS
2**cuddle** *n* **:** a close embrace **:** the act of nestling
cud·dle·some \'kəd-ᵊl-səm\ *adj* **:** fit for or inviting cuddling
cud·dly \'kəd-lē, -ᵊl-ē\ *adj* **:** CUDDLESOME
1**cud·dy** \'kəd-ē\ *n* [origin unknown] **1 :** a small cabin; *also* **:** the galley or pantry of a small ship **2 :** a small room or cupboard
2**cud·dy** *or* **cud·die** \'ku̇d-ē, 'kəd-\ *n* [perh. fr. *Cuddy*, nickname for *Cuthbert*] **1** *dial Brit* **:** DONKEY **2** *dial Brit* **:** BLOCKHEAD
1**cud·gel** \'kəj-əl\ *n* [ME *kuggel*, fr. OE *cycgel;* akin to MHG *kugele* ball, OE *cot* den — more at COT] **:** a short heavy club
2**cudgel** *vt* **cud·geled** *or* **cud·gelled; cud·gel·ing** *or* **cud·gel·ling** \-(ə-)liŋ\ **:** to beat with or as if with a cudgel — **cudgel one's brains :** to think hard (as for a solution to a problem)
cud·weed \'kəd-,wēd, 'ku̇d-\ *n* **:** any of several composite plants (as of the genus *Gnaphalium*) with silky or woolly foliage
1**cue** \'kyü\ *n* [ME *cu*] **:** the letter *q*
2**cue** *n* [prob. fr. *qu*, abbr. (used as a direction in actors' copies of plays) of L *quando* when] **1 a :** a word, phrase, or bit of stage business in a play serving as a signal for a specific speech or action **b :** something serving a comparable purpose **:** HINT **2 :** a feature indicating the nature of something perceived **3 :** the part one has to perform in or as if in a play **4** *archaic* **:** MOOD, HUMOR
3**cue** *vt* **cu·ing** *or* **cue·ing 1 :** to give a cue to **:** PROMPT **2 :** to insert into a continuous performance ⟨~ in sound effects⟩
4**cue** *n* [F *queue*, lit., tail, fr. L *cauda*] **1 :** QUEUE 2 **2 :** a leather-tipped tapering rod for striking balls in billiards and other games
5**cue** *vb* **cu·ing** *or* **cue·ing 1 :** BRAID, TWIST **2 :** to strike with a cue
cue ball *n* **:** the ball a player strikes with his cue in billiards and pool
cues·ta \'kwes-tə\ *n* [Sp, fr. L *costa* side, rib] **:** a hill or ridge with a steep face on one side and gentle slope on the other
1**cuff** \'kəf\ *n* [ME] **1 :** something (as a part of a sleeve or glove) encircling the wrist **2 :** the turned-back hem of a trouser leg **3 :** HANDCUFF — usu. used in pl. — **on the cuff :** on credit
2**cuff** *vt* **1 :** to furnish with a cuff **2 :** HANDCUFF
3**cuff** *vb* [perh. fr. obs. E, glove, fr. ME] *vt* **:** to strike esp. with or as if with the palm of the hand **:** BUFFET ~ *vi* **:** FIGHT, SCUFFLE
4**cuff** *n* **:** a blow with the hand esp. when open **:** SLAP
cui bo·no \'kwē-'bō-(,)nō\ *n* [L, to whose advantage?] **1 :** a principle that probable responsibility for an act or event lies with one with something to gain **2 :** usefulness or utility as a principle in estimating the value of an act or policy
1**cui·rass** \kwi-'ras, kyu̇-\ *n* [ME *curas*, fr. MF *curasse*, fr. LL *coreacea*, fem. of *coreaceus* leathern, fr. L *corium* skin, leather; akin to OE *heortha* deerskin, L *cortex* bark, Gk *keirein* to cut — more at SHEAR] **1 :** a piece of armor covering the body from neck to girdle; *also* **:** the breastplate of such a piece **2 :** something (as bony plates covering an animal) resembling a cuirass
2**cuirass** *vt* **:** to cover or armor with a cuirass
cui·ras·sier \,kwir-ə-'si(ə)r, ,kyu̇r-\ *n* **:** a mounted soldier wearing a cuirass
cui·sine \kwi-'zēn\ *n* [F, lit., kitchen, fr. LL *coquina* — more at KITCHEN] **:** manner of preparing food
cuisse \'kwis\ *also* **cuish** \'kwish\ *n* [ME *cusseis*, pl., fr. MF *cuissaux*, pl. of *cuissel*, fr. *cuisse* thigh, fr. L *coxa* hip — more at COXA] **:** a piece of plate armor for the thigh esp. in front
cuit·tle \'küt-ᵊl, 'kət-\ *vt* [origin unknown] *Scot* **:** COAX, WHEEDLE
cul–de–sac \,kəl-di-'sak, ,ku̇l-\ *n, pl* **culs–de–sac** \,kəl(z)-, ,ku̇l(z)-\ *also* **cul–de–sacs** \,kəl-də-'saks, ,ku̇l-\ [F, lit., bottom of the bag] **1 :** a blind diverticulum or pouch **2 :** a street closed at one end
cu·let \'kyü-lət\ *n* [F, fr. dim. of *cul* backside, fr. L *culus;* akin to OE *hȳdan* to hide] **1 :** the small flat facet at the bottom of a brilliant parallel to the table **2 :** plate armor covering the buttocks
cu·lex \'kyü-,leks\ *n* [NL, genus name, fr. L, gnat; akin to OIr *cuil* gnat] **:** any of a large cosmopolitan genus (*Culex*) of mosquitoes that includes the common house mosquito (*C. pipiens*) of Europe and No. America — **cu·li·cine** \'kyü-lə-,sīn\ *adj or n*
cu·li·nary \'kəl-ə-,ner-ē, 'kyü-lə-\ *adj* [L *culinarius*, fr. *culina* kitchen — more at KILN] **:** of or relating to the kitchen or cookery
1**cull** \'kəl\ *vt* [ME *cullen*, fr. MF *cuillir*, fr. L *colligere* to bind together — more at COLLECT] **1 :** to select from a group **:** CHOOSE **2 :** to identify and remove the culls from — **cull·er** *n*
2**cull** *n* **:** something rejected for inferiority or worthlessness
cul·len·der *var of* COLANDER
cul·let \'kəl-ət\ *n* [perh. fr. F *cueillette* act of gathering, fr. L *collecta*, fr. fem. of *collectus*, pp. of *colligere*] **:** broken or refuse glass usu. added to new material to facilitate melting in making glass
cul·lion \'kəl-yən\ *n* [ME *coillon* testicle, fr. MF, fr. (assumed) VL *coleon-, coleo*, fr. L *coleus* scrotum] *archaic* **:** a mean or base fellow
cul·lis \'kəl-əs\ *n* [F *coulisse* groove] **:** a gutter in a roof
1**cul·ly** \'kəl-ē\ *n* [perh. alter. of *cullion*] *archaic* **:** DUPE, GULL
2**cully** *vt* **:** to impose on **:** TRICK, CHEAT, DECEIVE
1**culm** \'kəlm\ *n* [ME] **1 :** refuse coal screenings **:** SLACK **2 :** a Lower Carboniferous formation in which marine fossil-bearing beds alternate with those containing plant remains
2**culm** *n* [L *culmus* stalk] **:** a monocotyledonous stem
cul·mi·nant \'kəl-mə-nənt\ *adj* **1 :** being at greatest altitude or on the meridian **2 :** CULMINATING **:** fully developed
cul·mi·nate \'kəl-mə-,nāt\ *vb* [ML *culminatus*, pp. of *culminare*, fr. LL, to crown, fr. L *culmin-, culmen* top] *vi* **1** *of a celestial body* **:** to reach its highest altitude; *also* **:** to be directly overhead **2 a :** to rise to or form a summit **b :** to reach the highest or a climactic or decisive point ~ *vt* **:** to bring to a head or to the highest point
cul·mi·na·tion \,kəl-mə-'nā-shən\ *n* **1 :** the action of culminating **2 :** culminating position **:** SUMMIT, CLIMAX **syn** see SUMMIT
cu·lotte \k(y)ü-'lät\ *n* [F, breeches, fr. dim. of *cul* backside] **:** a divided skirt; *also* **:** a garment having a divided skirt — often used in pl.
cul·pa·bil·i·ty \,kəl-pə-'bil-ət-ē\ *n* **:** the state of being culpable
cul·pa·ble \'kəl-pə-bəl\ *adj* [ME *coupable*, fr. MF, fr. L *culpabilis*, fr. *culpare* to blame, fr. *culpa* guilt] **1** *obs* **:** GUILTY, CRIMINAL **2 :** meriting condemnation or blame ⟨~ negligence⟩ **syn** see BLAMEWORTHY — **cul·pa·ble·ness** *n* — **cul·pa·bly** \-blē\ *adv*
cul·prit \'kəl-prət, -,prit\ *n* [AF *cul.* (abbr. of *culpable* guilty) + *prest, prit* ready (i.e. to prove it), fr. L *praestus*] **1 :** one accused of or arraigned for a crime **2 :** one guilty of a crime or a fault
cult \'kəlt\ *n* [F & L; F *culte*, fr. L *cultus* care, adoration, fr. *cultus*, pp. of *colere* to cultivate — more at WHEEL] **1 :** formal religious veneration **:** WORSHIP **2 :** a system of religious beliefs and ritual; *also* **:** its body of adherents **3 :** a system for the cure of disease based on dogma set forth by its promulgator **4 :** great and esp. faddish devotion; *also* **:** its object or adherents — **cul·tic** \'kəl-tik\ *adj* — **cult·ism** \'kəl-,tiz-əm\ *n* — **cult·ist** \'kəl-təst\ *n*
cultch *or* **culch** \'kəlch\ *n* [perh. fr. a F dial. form of F *couche* couch] **:** material (as oyster shells) laid down on oyster grounds to furnish points of attachment for the spat
cul·ti·gen \'kəl-tə-jən\ *n* [*culti*vated + *-gen*] **1 :** a cultivated organism (as maize) of a variety or species for which a wild ancestor is unknown **2 :** CULTIVAR
cul·ti·va·bil·i·ty \,kəl-tə-və-'bil-ət-ē\ *n* **:** the quality or state of being cultivable
cul·ti·va·ble \'kəl-tə-və-bəl\ *adj* **:** capable of being cultivated
cul·ti·var \'kəl-tə-,vär, -,ve(ə)r, -,va(ə)r\ *n* [*culti*vated + *var*iety] **:** an organism of a kind originating and persistent under cultivation
cul·ti·vat·able \'kəl-tə-,vāt-ə-bəl\ *adj* **:** CULTIVABLE
cul·ti·vate \'kəl-tə-,vāt\ *vt* [ML *cultivatus*, pp. of *cultivare*, fr. *cultivus* cultivable, fr. L *cultus*, pp.] **1 :** to prepare or prepare and use for the raising of crops **:** TILL; *specif* **:** to loosen or break up the soil about (growing plants) **2 a :** to foster the growth of ⟨~ vegetables⟩ **b :** CULTURE 2a **c :** IMPROVE, REFINE ⟨writers ~ style⟩ **3 :** FURTHER, ENCOURAGE ⟨~ the arts⟩ **4 :** to seek the society of
cul·ti·vat·ed *adj* **:** REFINED, EDUCATED ⟨~ speech⟩
cul·ti·va·tion \,kəl-tə-'vā-shən\ *n* **1 :** the act or art of cultivating; *specif* **:** TILLAGE **2 :** CULTURE, REFINEMENT
cul·ti·va·tor \'kəl-tə-,vāt-ər\ *n* **:** one that cultivates; *esp* **:** an implement to loosen the soil while crops are growing

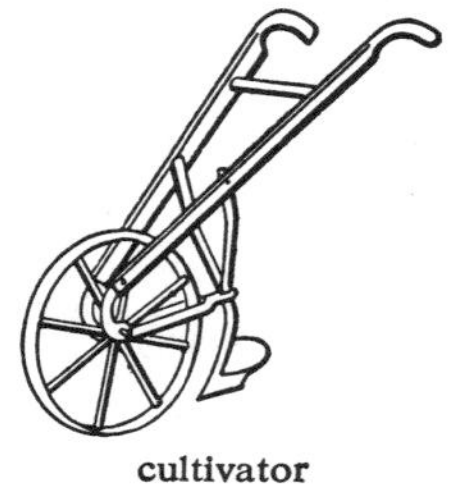
cultivator

cul·trate \'kəl-,trāt\ *also* **cul·trat·ed** \-əd\ *adj* [L *cultratus* knife-shaped, fr. *cultr-, culter* knife, plowshare — more at COLTER] **:** having a sharp edge and point **:** knife-shaped
cul·tur·al \'kəlch-(ə-)rəl\ *adj* **1 :** of or relating to culture or culturing **2 :** concerned with the fostering of plant or animal growth — **cul·tur·al·ly** \-ē\ *adv*
1**cul·ture** \'kəl-chər\ *n* [ME, fr. MF, fr. L *cultura*, fr. *cultus*, pp.] **1 :** CULTIVATION, TILLAGE **2 :** the act of developing the intellectual and moral faculties esp. by education **3 :** expert care and training ⟨beauty ~⟩ **4 :** enlightenment and excellence of taste acquired by intellectual and aesthetic training **5 a :** a particular stage of advancement in civilization **b :** the characteristic features of such a stage or state **c :** behavior typical of a group or class **6 :** cultivation of living material in prepared nutrient media; *also* **:** a product of such cultivation
2**culture** *vt* **cul·tur·ing** \'kəlch-(ə-)riŋ\ **1 :** CULTIVATE **2 a :** to grow in a prepared medium **b :** to start a culture from
cul·tured \'kəl-chərd\ *adj* **1 :** CULTIVATED **2 :** produced under artificial conditions ⟨~ viruses⟩ ⟨~ pearls⟩
cul·tus \'kəl-təs\ *n* [L, adoration] **:** CULT
cul·ver \'kəl-vər, 'ku̇l-\ *n* [ME, fr. OE *culfer*, fr. (assumed) VL *columbra*, fr. L *columbula*, dim. of L *columba* dove] **:** PIGEON
cul·ver·in \'kəl-və-rən\ *n* [ME, fr. MF *couleuvrine*, fr. *couleuvre* snake, fr. L *colubra*] **:** an early firearm: **a :** a rude musket **b :** a long cannon of the 16th and 17th centuries
cul·vert \'kəl-vərt\ *n* [origin unknown] **1 :** a transverse drain **2 :** a conduit for a culvert **3 :** a bridge over a culvert
1**cum** \(,)ku̇m, (,)kəm\ *prep* [L; akin to L *com-* — more at CO-] **:** WITH **:** combined with **:** along with ⟨served as an office-*cum*-den⟩
2**cum** \'ku̇m, 'kəm\ *adj (or adv)* [1*cum*] **:** including dividend ⟨the ~ price of a stock⟩
1**cum·ber** \'kəm-bər\ *vt* **cum·ber·ing** \-b(ə-)riŋ\ [ME *cumbren*] **1** *obs* **a :** DESTROY, DEFEAT **b :** TROUBLE, HARASS **2 :** to burden needlessly **:** clutter up
2**cumber** *n* **:** something that cumbers; *esp* **:** HINDRANCE
cum·ber·some \'kəm-bər-səm\ *adj* **1** *dial* **:** BURDENSOME, TROUBLESOME **2 :** CLUMSY, UNWIELDY **3 :** slow-moving **:** LUMBERING — **syn** see HEAVY — **cum·ber·some·ly** *adv* — **cum·ber·some·ness** *n*
cum·brous \'kəm-b(ə-)rəs\ *adj* **:** CUMBERSOME **syn** see HEAVY — **cum·brous·ly** *adv* — **cum·brous·ness** *n*
cum·in \'kəm-ən\ *n* [ME, fr. OE *cymen;* akin to OHG *kumīn* cumin; both fr. a prehistoric WGmc word borrowed fr. L *cuminum*, fr. Gk *kyminon*, of Sem origin] **:** a low plant (*Cuminum cyminum*) of the carrot family long cultivated for its aromatic seeds

cum lau·de \kům-'laůd-ə, -ē; ˌkəm-'lȯd-ē\ *adv (or adj)* [NL, with praise] **:** with academic distinction ⟨graduated *cum laude*⟩
cum·mer·bund \'kəm-ər-ˌbənd\ *n* [Hindi *kamarband,* fr. Per, fr. *kamar* waist + *band*] **:** a broad sash worn as a waistband
cumquat *var of* KUMQUAT
cum·shaw \'kəm-ˌshȯ\ *n* [Chin (Amoy) *kam sia* grateful thanks (a phrase used by beggars)] **:** PRESENT, GRATUITY, TIP
cumul- *or* **cumuli-** *or* **cumulo-** *comb form* [NL, fr. L *cumulus*] **:** cumulus and ⟨*cumulo*cirrus⟩
cu·mu·late \'kyü-myə-ˌlāt\ *vb* [L *cumulatus,* pp. of *cumulare,* fr. *cumulus* mass] **:** ACCUMULATE — **cu·mu·late** \-lət, -ˌlāt\ *adj* — **cu·mu·la·tion** \ˌkyü-myə-'lā-shən\ *n*
cu·mu·la·tive \'kyü-myə-lət-iv, -ˌlāt-\ *adj* **1 :** increasing by successive additions **2 a :** tending to prove the same point ⟨~ evidence⟩ **b :** additional rather than repeated ⟨~ legacy⟩ **3 a :** taking effect upon completion of another sentence ⟨~ sentence⟩ **b :** increasing in severity with repetition of the offense ⟨~ penalty⟩ **4 :** to be added if not paid when due to the next or a future payment ⟨~ dividends⟩ **5 :** formed by the addition of new material of the same kind ⟨~ book index⟩ — **cu·mu·la·tive·ly** *adv* — **cu·mu·la·tive·ness** *n*
cu·mu·lo·cir·rus \ˌkyü-myə-lō-'sir-əs\ *n* [NL] **:** a small cumulus cloud at a high altitude having the white delicacy of the cirrus
cu·mu·lo·nim·bus \-'nim-bəs\ *n* [NL] **:** a cumulus cloud often spread out in the shape of an anvil extending to great heights
cu·mu·lo·stra·tus \-'strāt-əs, -'strat-\ *n* [NL] **:** a cumulus whose base extends horizontally as a stratus cloud
cu·mu·lous \'kyü-myə-ləs\ *adj* **:** resembling cumulus
cu·mu·lus \-ləs\ *n, pl* **cu·mu·li** \-ˌlī, -ˌlē\ [L] **1 :** HEAP, ACCUMULATION **2** [NL, fr. L] **:** a massy cloud form having a flat base and rounded outlines often piled up like a mountain
cunc·ta·tion \ˌkəŋ(k)-'tā-shən\ *n* [L *cunctation-, cunctatio,* fr. *cunctatus,* pp. of *cunctari* to hesitate; akin to Skt *śaṅkate* he wavers] **:** DELAY — **cunc·ta·tive** \'kəŋ(k)-ˌtāt-iv, ˌkəŋ(k)-'; 'kəŋ(k)-tət-\ *adj*
cu·ne·ate \'kyü-nē-ˌāt, -ət\ *adj* [L *cuneatus,* fr. *cuneus* wedge; akin to Skt *śūla* spear] **:** narrowly triangular with the acute angle toward the base ⟨a ~ leaf⟩ — **cu·ne·ate·ly** *adv*
cu·ne·at·ic \ˌkyü-nē-'at-ik\ *adj* **:** CUNEIFORM
[1]**cu·ne·i·form** \kyù-'nē-ə-ˌfȯrm, 'kyü-n(ē-)ə-ˌ\ *adj* [prob. fr. F *cunéiforme,* fr. MF, fr. L *cuneus* + MF *-iforme* -iform] **1 :** having the shape of a wedge **2 :** composed of or written in wedge-shaped characters ⟨~ alphabet⟩
[2]**cuneiform** *n* **1 :** cuneiform writing **2 :** a cuneiform part; *specif* **:** a cuneiform bone or cartilage

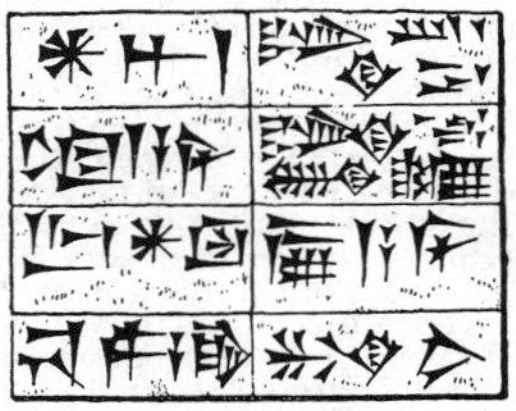
cuneiform 1

cun·ner \'kən-ər\ *n* [origin unknown] **:** either of two wrasses: **a :** an English wrasse (*Crenilabrus melops*) **b :** a wrasse (*Tautogolabrus adspersus*) abundant on the New England shore
cun·ni·lin·gus \ˌkən-i-'liŋ-gəs\ *or* **cun·ni·linc·tus** \-'liŋ(k)-təs\ *n* [*cunnilingus,* NL, fr. L, one who licks the vulva, fr. *cunnus* vulva + *lingere* to lick; *cunnilinctus,* NL, fr. L *cunnus* + *linctus,* act of licking, fr. *linctus,* pp. of *lingere*] **:** oral stimulation of the vulva or clitoris
[1]**cun·ning** \'kən-iŋ\ *adj* [ME, fr. prp. of *can* know] **1 :** exhibiting skill **2 :** CRAFTY, ARTFUL **3 :** prettily appealing **:** CUTE **syn** see CLEVER, SLY — **cun·ning·ly** \-iŋ-lē\ *adv* — **cun·ning·ness** *n*
[2]**cunning** *n* **1** *obs* **:** KNOWLEDGE, LEARNING; *esp* **:** magic art **2 :** SKILL, DEXTERITY **3 :** SLYNESS, CRAFT **syn** see ART
[1]**cup** \'kəp\ *n* [ME *cuppe,* fr. OE; akin to OHG *kopf* cup; both fr. a prehistoric WGmc word borrowed fr. LL *cuppa* cup, alter. of L *cupa* tub; akin to OE *hȳf* hive] **1 :** an open bowl-shaped drinking vessel **2 a :** the beverage or food contained in a cup **b :** the consecrated wine of the Communion **3 :** something that falls to one's lot **4 :** an ornamental cup offered as a prize **5 a :** something resembling a cup **b :** a cup-shaped plant organ **6 :** a usu. iced beverage resembling punch but served from a pitcher rather than a bowl **7 :** CUPFUL **8 :** a food served in a cup-shaped usu. footed vessel ⟨fruit ~⟩ — **cup·like** \'kəp-ˌlīk\ *adj* — **in one's cups :** DRUNK
[2]**cup** *vt* **cupped; cup·ping 1 :** to treat by cupping **2 a :** to curve into the shape of a cup **b :** to place in a cup — **cup·per** *n*
cup·bear·er \-ˌbar-ər, -ˌber-\ *n* **:** one who has the duty of filling and handing cups of wine
cup·board \'kəb-ərd\ *n* **:** a closet with shelves for cups, dishes, or food; *also* **:** any small closet
cup·cake \'kəp-ˌkāk\ *n* **:** a small cake baked in a cuplike mold
[1]**cu·pel** \kyü-'pel, 'kyü-pəl\ *n* [F *coupelle,* dim. of *coupe* cup, fr. LL *cuppa*] **:** a small shallow porous cup esp. of bone ash used in assaying to separate precious metals from lead
[2]**cupel** *vt* **cu·pelled** *or* **cu·peled; cu·pel·ling** *or* **cu·pel·ing :** to refine by means of a cupel — **cu·pel·ler** *or* **cu·pel·er** \kyü-'pel-ər, 'kyü-pə-lər\ *n*
cu·pel·la·tion \ˌkyü-pə-'lā-shən, -ˌpe-\ *n* **:** refinement (as of gold or silver) in a cupel by exposure to high temperature in a blast of air by which the lead, copper, tin, and other unwanted metals are oxidized and partly sink into the porous cupel
cup·ful \'kəp-ˌfůl\ *n, pl* **cup·fuls** \-ˌfůlz\ *or* **cups·ful** \'kəps-ˌfůl\ **1 :** as much as a cup will hold **2 :** a half pint **:** eight ounces
cup·hold·er \'kəp-ˌhōl-dər\ *n* **:** a sports contestant successful in the latest trial for a cup
Cu·pid \'kyü-pəd\ *n* [L *Cupido*] **1 :** the god of love in Roman mythology **2** *not cap* **:** a winged naked infantile figure representing Cupid often with a bow and arrow
cu·pid·i·ty \kyù-'pid-ət-ē\ *n* [ME *cupidite,* fr. MF *cupidité,* fr. L *cupiditat-, cupiditas* — more at COVET] **1** *archaic* **:** strong desire **:** LUST **2 :** inordinate desire for wealth **:** AVARICE, GREED
Cupid's bow *n* **:** the classical form of bow
cu·po·la \'kyü-pə-lə, -ˌlō\ *n* [It, fr. L *cupula,* dim. of *cupa* tub] **1 a :** a rounded vault resting on a circular or other base and forming a roof or a ceiling **b :** a small structure built on top of a roof **2 :** a vertical cylindrical furnace for melting iron in the foundry having tuyeres and tapping spouts near the bottom
cup·ping *n* **:** an operation of drawing blood to or from the surface of the body by use of a glass vessel evacuated by heat
cup·py \'kəp-ē\ *adj* **1 :** resembling a cup **2 :** full of small holes
cu·pre·ous \'k(y)ü-prē-əs\ *adj* [LL *cupreus,* fr. *cuprum*] **:** containing or resembling copper **:** COPPERY
cu·pric \-prik\ *adj* [LL *cuprum*] **:** of, relating to, or containing bivalent copper
cu·prite \-ˌprīt\ *n* [G *kuprit,* fr. LL *cuprum*] **:** a mineral Cu_2O consisting of copper oxide and constituting an ore of copper
cu·prous \-prəs\ *adj* [LL *cuprum*] **:** of, relating to, or containing univalent copper
cu·pu·late \'kyü-pyə-ˌlāt, -lət\ *also* **cu·pu·lar** \-lər\ *adj* **:** shaped like or having or bearing a cupule
cu·pule \'kyü-(ˌ)pyü(ə)l\ *n* [NL *cupula,* fr. LL, dim. of L *cupa* tub — more at CUP] **:** a cup-shaped involucre characteristic of the oak in which the bracts are indurated and coherent
cur \'kər\ *n* [ME, short for *curdogge,* fr. (assumed) ME *curren* to growl + ME *dogge* dog; akin to OE *cran* crane] **1 :** a mongrel or inferior dog **2 :** an objectionable often surly or cowardly fellow
cur·abil·i·ty \ˌkyůr-ə-'bil-ət-ē\ *n* **:** the quality or state of being curable
cur·able \'kyůr-ə-bəl\ *adj* **:** capable of being cured — **cur·able·ness** *n* — **cur·ably** \-blē\ *adv*
cu·ra·çao \ˌk(y)ůr-ə-'saů, -'sō\ *also* **cu·ra·çoa** \-'sō(-ə)\ *n* [D *curaçao,* fr. *Curaçao,* island in Netherlands Antilles] **:** a liqueur flavored with the dried peel of the sour orange
cu·ra·cy \'kyůr-ə-sē\ *n* **:** the office or term of office of a curate
cu·ra·re *or* **cu·ra·ri** \k(y)ù-'rär-ē\ *n* [Pg & Sp *curare,* fr. Carib *kurari*] **:** a dried aqueous extract esp. of a vine (as *Strychnos toxifera* of the family Loganiaceae) used in arrow poisons by So. American Indians and in medicine to produce muscular relaxation
cu·ra·rine \-'rär-ən, -ˌēn\ *n* **:** any of several alkaloids from curare
cu·ra·ri·za·tion \k(y)ù-ˌrär-ə-'zā-shən\ *n* **:** treatment with curare; *also* **:** the resulting state — **cu·ra·rize** \kyù-'rär-ˌīz\ *vt*
cu·ras·sow \'kyůr-ə-ˌsō\ *n* [alter. of *Curaçao*] **:** any of several large arboreal game birds (esp. genus *Crax*) of So. and Central America related to the domestic fowls
cu·rate \'kyůr-ət\ *n* [ME, fr. ML *curatus,* fr. *cura* cure of souls, fr. L, care] **1 :** a clergyman in charge of a parish **2 :** a clergyman who assists a rector or vicar
cu·ra·tive \'kyůr-ət-iv\ *adj* **:** relating to or used in the cure of diseases — **cu·ra·tive·ly** *adv*
cu·ra·tor \kyù-'rāt-ər, 'kyůr-ˌāt-, 'kyůr-ət-\ *n* **:** one that has the care and superintendence of something; *esp* **:** one in charge of a museum, zoo, or other place of exhibit — **cu·ra·to·ri·al** \ˌkyůr-ə-'tōr-ē-əl, -'tȯr-\ *adj* — **cu·ra·tor·ship** *n*
[1]**curb** \'kərb\ *n, often attrib* [MF *courbe* curve, curved piece of wood or iron, fr. *courbe* curved, fr. L *curvus*] **1 :** a chain or strap on the upper part of the branches of a bit used to restrain a horse **2 :** an enclosing frame, border, or edging **3 :** CHECK, RESTRAINT **4 :** a raised edge or margin to strengthen or confine **5 :** an edging built along a street to form part of a gutter **6** [fr. the fact that it orig. transacted its business on the street] **:** a market for trading in securities not listed on a stock exchange
[2]**curb** *vt* **:** to control or furnish with a curb **syn** see RESTRAIN
curb·ing \'kər-biŋ\ *n* **1 :** the material for a curb **2 :** CURB
curb roof *n* **:** a roof with a ridge at the center and a double slope on each of its two sides
curb·stone \'kərb-ˌstōn\ *n* **:** a stone set along a margin as a limit and protection
curch \'kərch\ *n* [ME] *Scot* **:** KERCHIEF 1
cur·cu·lio \(ˌ)kər-'kyü-lē-ˌō\ *n* [L, grain weevil] **:** any of various weevils; *esp* **:** one that injures fruit
cur·cu·ma \'kər-kyə-mə\ *n* [NL, genus name, fr. Ar *kurkum* saffron] **:** any of a genus (*Curcuma*) of Old World tropical herbs of the ginger family with tuberous roots that includes the turmeric
[1]**curd** \'kərd\ *n* [ME] **1 :** the thick casein-rich part of coagulated milk **2 :** something resembling the curd of milk
[2]**curd** *vb* **:** COAGULATE, CURDLE
cur·dle \'kərd-ᵊl\ *vb* **cur·dling** \'kərd-liŋ, -ᵊl-iŋ\ [freq. of [2]*curd*] *vt* **1 :** to cause curds to form in **2 :** SPOIL, SOUR ~ *vi* **1 :** to form curds **:** COAGULATE **2 :** to go bad or wrong **:** SPOIL
curdy \'kərd-ē\ *adj* **:** resembling or coagulating into curds
[1]**cure** \'kyů(ə)r\ *n* [ME, fr. OF, fr. ML & L; ML *cura,* cure of souls, fr. L, care] **1 a :** spiritual charge **:** CARE **b :** pastoral charge of a parish **2 a :** recovery or relief from a disease **b :** an agency that cures a disease **c :** a course or period of treatment **d :** SPA **3 :** a process or method of curing — **cure·less** \-ləs\ *adj*
[2]**cure** *vt* **1 a :** to restore to health, soundness, or normality **b :** to bring about recovery from **2 a :** RECTIFY, REMEDY **b :** to free from something objectionable or harmful **3 :** to prepare by chemical or physical processing for keeping or use ~ *vi* **1 :** to undergo a curing process **2 :** to effect a cure — **cur·er** \'kyůr-ər\ *n*
syn HEAL, REMEDY: CURE implies restoration to health after disease; HEAL may also apply to this but commonly suggests restoring to soundness after a wound or sore; REMEDY suggests correction or relief of a morbid or evil condition often without implying permanence or completeness of effect
[3]**cu·ré** \kyů-'rā, 'kyů(ə)r-ˌā\ *n* [F, fr. *cure* cure of souls — more at CURATE] **:** a parish priest
cure–all \'kyů(ə)r-ˌȯl\ *n* **:** a remedy for all ills **:** PANACEA
cu·ret·tage \kyů-'ret-ij, ˌkyůr-ə-'täzh\ *n* **:** surgical scraping or cleaning by means of a curette
[1]**cu·rette** *or* **cu·ret** \kyů-'ret\ *n* [F *curette,* fr. *curer* to cure, fr. L *curare,* fr. *cura*] **:** a scoop, loop, or ring used in performing curettage
[2]**curette** *or* **curet** *vt* **cu·rett·ed; cu·rett·ing :** to perform curettage on — **cu·rette·ment** \-mənt\ *n*
cur·few \'kər-(ˌ)fyü\ *n* [ME, fr. MF *covrefeu,* signal given to bank the hearth fire, curfew, fr. *covrir* to cover + *feu* fire, fr. L *focus* hearth] **1 :** a regulation enjoining withdrawal of usu. specified persons from the streets or the closing of business establishments or places of assembly at a stated hour **2 a :** the sounding of a bell or other signal to announce the beginning of a time of curfew **b :** the signal used **3 :** the hour at which a curfew becomes effective or the period during which it is in effect

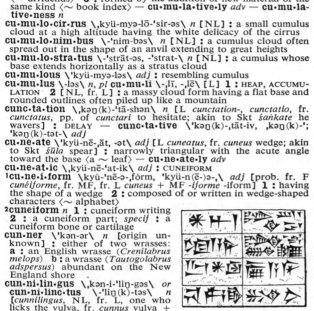

cu·ria \'k(y)u̇r-ē-ə\ *n, pl* **cu·ri·ae** \'kyu̇r-ē-,ē, 'ku̇r-ē-,ī\ [L, fr. *co-* + *vir* man — more at MAN] **1 :** a division of the ancient Roman people comprising several gentes of a tribe **2 a :** the court of a medieval king **b :** a court of justice **3** *often cap* **:** the body of congregations, tribunals, and offices through which the pope governs the Roman Catholic Church — **cu·ri·al** \'kyu̇r-ē-əl\ *adj*

cu·rie \'kyu̇(ə)r-(,)ē, kyu̇-'rē\ *n* [Mme. Marie *Curie* †1934 Pol-F chemist] **1 :** a unit quantity of any radioactive nuclide in which 3.7 × 10^{10} disintegrations occur per second **2 :** a unit of radioactivity equal to 3.7 × 10^{10} disintegrations per second

Cu·rie point \kyu̇-,rē-, ,kyu̇r-ē-\ *n* [Pierre *Curie* †1906 F chemist] **1 :** the temperature at which there is a transition between the ferromagnetic and paramagnetic phases **2 :** a temperature at which the anomalies that characterize a ferroelectric substance disappear

cu·rio \'kyu̇r-ē-,ō\ *n* [short for *curiosity*] **:** something arousing interest as being novel, rare, or bizarre **:** CURIOSITY

cu·ri·o·sa \,kyu̇r-ē-'ō-sə, -'ō-zə\ *n pl* [NL, fr. L, neut. pl. of *curiosus*] **:** CURIOSITIES, RARITIES; *esp* **:** strange or unusual books

cu·ri·os·i·ty \,kyu̇r-ē-'äs-ət-ē, -'äs-tē\ *n* **1 :** desire to know: **a** *archaic* **:** a blamable desire to seek knowledge (as of sacred matters) **b :** NOSINESS **c :** interest leading to inquiry **2** *archaic* **a :** careful workmanship **b :** undue nicety or fastidiousness **3 a :** one that arouses interest esp. for uncommon or exotic characteristics **b :** an unusual knickknack **c :** a curious trait or aspect

cu·ri·ous \'kyu̇r-ē-əs\ *adj* [ME, fr. MF *curios*, fr. L *curiosus* careful, inquisitive, fr. *cura* cure] **1 a** *archaic* **:** made carefully **b** *obs* **:** ABSTRUSE **c** *archaic* **:** precisely accurate **2 a :** marked by desire to investigate and learn **b :** marked by inquisitiveness about others' concerns **:** PRYING **3 :** exciting attention as strange or novel **:** ODD — **cu·ri·ous·ly** *adv* — **cu·ri·ous·ness** *n*

syn INQUISITIVE, PRYING: CURIOUS always implies an eager desire to learn and may or may not suggest objectionable intrusiveness or officiousness; INQUISITIVE implies habitual impertinent curiosity usu. about things secret or unrevealed; PRYING implies officious or busy meddling esp. in personal affairs

cu·rite \'kyu̇(ə)r-,īt\ *n* [F, fr. Pierre *Curie*] **:** a radioactive mineral $2PbO.5UO_3.4H_2O$ found in orange acicular crystals

cu·ri·um \'kyu̇r-ē-əm\ *n* [NL, fr. Marie & Pierre *Curie*] **:** a metallic radioactive trivalent element artificially produced — see ELEMENT table

[1]**curl** \'kər(-ə)l\ *vb* [ME *curlen*, fr. *crul* curly, prob. fr. MD; akin to OHG *krol* curly, OE *cradol* cradle] *vt* **1 :** to form into coils or ringlets **2 :** to form into a curved shape **:** TWIST **3 :** to furnish with curls ~ *vi* **1 a :** to grow in coils or spirals **b :** to form ripples or crinkles **2 :** to move or progress in curves or spirals **3 :** TWIST, CONTORT **4 :** to play the game of curling

[2]**curl** *n* **1 :** a lock of hair that coils **:** RINGLET **2 :** something having a spiral or winding form **:** COIL **3 :** the action of curling **:** the state of being curled **4 :** an abnormal rolling or curling of leaves **5 :** a curved or spiral marking in the grain of wood **6 :** TENDRIL

curl·er \'kər-lər\ *n* **1 :** one that curls **2 :** a player of curling

cur·lew \'kərl-(,)(y)ü\ *n, pl* **curlews** *or* **curlew** [ME, fr. MF *corlieu*, of imit. origin] **:** any of various largely brownish chiefly migratory birds (esp. genus *Numenius*) related to the woodcocks but distinguished by long legs and a long slender down-curved bill

[1]**curli·cue** *also* **curly·cue** \'kər-li-,kyü\ *n* [*curly* + *cue* (a braid of hair)] **:** a fancifully curved or spiral figure

[2]**curlicue** *vi* **:** to form curlicues ~ *vt* **:** to decorate with curlicues

curl·i·ness \'kər-lē-nəs\ *n* **:** the quality or state of being curly

curl·ing *n* **:** a game in which two teams of four men each slide curling stones over a stretch of ice toward a target circle

curling iron *n* **:** a rod-shaped usu. metal instrument which can be heated to curl or wave a lock of hair wound around it

curling stone *n* **:** an ellipsoid stone or occas. piece of iron with a gooseneck handle for delivery in the game of curling

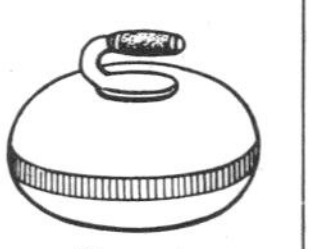
curling stone

curl·pa·per \'kər(-ə)l-,pā-pər\ *n* **:** a strip or piece of paper around which a lock of hair is wound for curling

curly \'kər-lē\ *adj* **1 :** tending to curl; *also* **:** having curls **2 :** having fibers that undulate without crossing ⟨~ maple⟩

curly–coat·ed retriever \,kər-lē-,kōt-əd-\ *n* **:** any of a breed of sporting dogs with a short curly coat

cur·mud·geon \(,)kər-'məj-ən\ *n* [origin unknown] **1** *archaic* **:** MISER **2 :** an irascible often old man — **cur·mud·geon·ly** *adj*

curn \'kərn\ *or* **cur·ran** \'kə-rən\ *n* [ME *curn;* akin to ME *corn*] **1** *Scot* **:** GRAIN **2** *Scot* **:** a small number **:** FEW

curr \'kər\ *vi* [imit.] **:** to make a murmuring sound (as of doves)

cur·ragh *or* **cur·rach** \'kə-rə(k)\ *n* [ScGael *curach* & IrGael *currach;* akin to MIr *curach* coracle] **1** *Irish* **:** marshy wasteland **2** *Irish & Scot* **:** CORACLE

cur·rant \'kər-ənt, 'kə-rənt\ *n, often attrib* [ME *raison of Coraunte*, lit., raisin of Corinth] **1 :** a small seedless raisin grown chiefly in the Levant **2 :** the acid edible fruit of several shrubs (genus *Ribes*) of the saxifrage family; *also* **:** a plant bearing currants

cur·ren·cy \'kər-ən-sē, 'kə-rən-\ *n, often attrib* **1 a :** circulation as a medium of exchange **b :** general use or acceptance **2 a :** something that is in circulation as a medium of exchange including coin, government notes, and bank notes **b :** paper money in circulation

[1]**cur·rent** \'kər-ənt, 'kə-rənt\ *adj* [ME *curraunt*, fr. OF *curant*, prp of *courre* to run, fr. L *currere*] **1 a** *archaic* **:** RUNNING, FLOWING **b (1) :** presently elapsing **(2) :** occurring in or belonging to the present time **(3) :** most recent ⟨~ issue⟩ **2 :** used as a medium of exchange **3 :** generally accepted, used, or practiced **syn** see PREVAILING — **cur·rent·ly** *adv* — **cur·rent·ness** *n*

[2]**current** *n* **1 a :** the part of a fluid body moving continuously in a certain direction **b :** the swiftest part of a stream **c :** a tidal or nontidal movement of lake or ocean water **d :** flow marked by force or strength **2 :** flux of forces **:** TREND **3 :** a movement of electricity analogous to the flow of a stream of water; *also* **:** the rate of such movement **syn** see TENDENCY

current assets *n pl* **:** assets of a short-term nature

cur·ri·cle \'kər-i-kəl, 'kə-ri-\ *n* [L *curriculum* running, chariot] **:** a 2-wheeled chaise usu. drawn by two horses

cur·ric·u·lar \kə-'rik-yə-lər\ *adj* **:** of or relating to a curriculum

cur·ric·u·lum \-ləm\ *n, pl* **cur·ric·u·la** \-lə\ *also* **curriculums** [NL, fr. L, running, fr. *currere*] **1 :** the courses offered by an educational institution or one of its branches **2 :** a set of courses

cur·ric·u·lum vi·tae \kə-,rik-ə-ləm-'wē-,tī, -yə-ləm-'vīt-ē\ *n* [L, course of (one's) life] **:** a short account of one's career and qualifications prepared typically by an applicant for a position

cur·ri·er \'kər-ē-ər, 'kə-rē-\ *n* [ME *corier*, fr. MF, fr. L *coriarius*, fr. *corium* leather — more at CUIRASS] **:** one that curries

cur·ri·ery \'kər-ē-ə-rē, 'kə-rē-\ *n* **1 :** the trade of a currier of leather **2 :** a place where currying is done

cur·rish \'kər-ish\ *adj* **:** resembling a cur **:** MONGREL; *also* **:** IGNOBLE

[1]**cur·ry** \'kər-ē, 'kə-rē\ *vt* [ME *curraye*, fr. OF *correer* to prepare, curry, fr. (assumed) VL *conredare*, fr. L *com-* + a base of Gmc origin] **1 :** to dress the coat of with a currycomb **2 :** to treat (tanned leather) esp. by incorporating oil or grease **3 :** BEAT, THRASH — **curry fa·vor** \-'fā-vər\ [ME *currayen favel* to curry a chestnut horse] **:** to seek to gain favor by flattery or attentions

[2]**cur·ry** *also* **cur·rie** \'kər-ē, 'kə-rē\ *n* [Tamil-Malayalam *kari*] **1 :** CURRY POWDER **2 :** a food seasoned with curry powder

[3]**curry** *vt* **:** to flavor or cook with curry

cur·ry·comb \-,kōm\ *n* **:** a comb made of rows of metallic teeth or serrated ridges and used esp. to curry horses — **currycomb** *vt*

curry powder *n* **:** a condiment consisting of ground spices

[1]**curse** \'kərs\ *n* [ME *curs*, fr. OE] **1 :** a prayer or invocation for harm or injury to come upon one **:** IMPRECATION **2 :** something that is cursed or accursed **3 :** evil that comes as if in response to imprecation or as retribution **4 :** the cause of great harm or misfortune **:** TORMENT

[2]**curse** *vt* **1 a :** to call upon divine or supernatural power to send injury upon **b :** EXECRATE **2 :** to use profanely insolent language against **:** BLASPHEME **3 :** to bring great evil upon **:** AFFLICT ~ *vi* **:** to utter imprecations **:** SWEAR **syn** see EXECRATE

cursed \'kər-səd, 'kərst\ *also* **curst** \'kərst\ *adj* **:** being under or deserving a curse — **cursed·ly** *adv* — **cursed·ness** *n*

[1]**cur·sive** \'kər-siv\ *adj* [F or ML; F, fr. ML *cursivus*, lit., running, fr. L *cursus*, pp. of *currere* to run] **:** RUNNING, COURSING: as **a** *of writing* **:** flowing often with the strokes of successive characters joined and the angles rounded **b :** having a flowing, easy, impromptu character — **cur·sive·ly** *adv* — **cur·sive·ness** *n*

[2]**cursive** *n* **1 :** a manuscript written in cursive writing **2 :** a style of printed letter imitating handwriting

cur·so·ri·al \,kər-'sōr-ē-əl, -'sȯr-\ *adj* **:** adapted to running

cur·so·ri·ly \'kərs-(ə-)rə-lē\ *adv* **:** in a cursory manner

cur·so·ri·ness \-(ə-)rē-nəs\ *n* **:** the quality of being cursory

cur·so·ry \'kərs-(ə-)rē\ *adj* [LL *cursorius* of running, fr. L *cursus* running, fr. *cursus*, pp.] **:** rapidly often superficially performed **:** HASTY **syn** see SUPERFICIAL

curt \'kərt\ *adj* [L *curtus* shortened] **1 a :** sparing of words **:** TERSE **b :** marked by rude or peremptory shortness **:** BRUSQUE **2** *archaic* **:** SHORTENED **syn** see BLUFF — **curt·ly** *adv* — **curt·ness** *n*

cur·tail \(,)kər-'tā(ə)l\ *vt* [alter. of *curtal* to make a curtal of, fr. *curtal*, n.] **:** to cut off the end or any part of **syn** see SHORTEN — **cur·tail·er** \-'tā-lər\ *n* — **cur·tail·ment** \-'tā(ə)l-mənt\ *n*

[1]**cur·tain** \'kərt-ᵊn\ *n* [ME *curtine*, fr. OF, fr. LL *cortina*, fr. L *cohort-*, *cohors* enclosure, court] **1 :** a hanging screen usu. capable of being drawn back or up; *esp* **:** window drapery **2 :** a device or agency that conceals or acts as a barrier **3 a :** the part of a bastioned front that connects two neighboring bastions **b (1) :** a similar stretch of plain wall **(2) :** a nonbearing exterior wall **4 a :** the screen separating the stage from the auditorium of a theater **b :** the ascent of the curtain at the beginning of a play or its descent at the end of a scene or act **c :** the final situation or line of an act or the closing scene of a play **d** *pl* **:** END; *esp* **:** DEATH

[2]**curtain** *vt* **cur·tain·ing** \'kərt-niŋ, -ᵊn-iŋ\ **1 :** to furnish with curtains **2 :** to veil or shut off with a curtain

curtain call *n* **:** an appearance by a performer (as at the final curtain of a play) in response to the applause of the audience

curtain lecture *n* **:** a private lecture by a wife to her husband

curtain raiser *n* **1 :** a short play usu. of one scene with few characters used to open a performance **2 :** a usu. short preliminary

[1]**cur·tal** \'kərt-ᵊl\ *n, archaic* **:** an animal with a docked tail

[2]**curtal** *adj* [MF *courtault*, fr. *court* short, fr. L *curtus*] **1** *obs* **:** having a docked tail **2** *obs* **:** CURTAILED. **3** *archaic* **:** wearing a short frock ⟨a ~ friar⟩

cur·tal ax *or* **cur·tle ax** \'kərt-ᵊl-\ *n* [modif. of MF *coutelas*] **:** CUTLASS

cur·ti·lage \'kərt-ᵊl-ij\ *n* [ME, fr. OF *cortillage*, fr. *cortil* courtyard, fr. *cort* court] **:** a yard within the fence surrounding a house

[1]**curt·sy** *or* **curt·sey** \'kərt-sē\ *n, pl* **curtsies** *or* **curtseys** [alter. of *courtesy*] **:** an act of civility, respect, or reverence made mainly by women and marked by a slight dropping of the body with bending of the knees

[2]**curtsy** *or* **curtsey** *vi* **curt·sied** *or* **curt·seyed; curt·sy·ing** *or* **curt·sey·ing :** to make a curtsy

cu·rule \'kyu̇(ə)r-,ül\ *adj* [L *currulis* of a chariot, fr. *currus* chariot, fr. *currere* to run] **1 :** of or relating to a seat reserved in ancient Rome for the use of the highest dignitaries and usu. made like a campstool with curved legs **2 :** privileged to sit in a curule chair

cur·va·ceous *also* **cur·va·cious** \,kər-'vā-shəs\ *adj* **:** having a well-proportioned feminine figure marked by pronounced curves

cur·va·ture \'kər-və-,chu̇(ə)r, -chər, -,t(y)u̇(ə)r\ *n* **1 :** the act of curving **:** the state of being curved **2 :** a measure or amount of curving; *specif* **:** the rate of change of the angle through which the tangent to a curve turns in moving along the curve **3 a :** an abnormal curving **b :** a curved surface of an organ

[1]**curve** \'kərv\ *adj* [L *curvus* curved] *archaic* **:** CURVED

[2]**curve** *vb* [L *curvare*, fr. *curvus*] *vi* **:** to have or take a turn, change, or deviation from a straight line without sharp breaks or angularity ~ *vt* **:** to cause to curve **:** BEND

syn CURVE, BEND, TURN, TWIST mean to swerve or cause to swerve from a straight line. CURVE implies following or producing a line suggesting the arc of a circle or ellipse; BEND suggests a yielding to force and usu. implies a distortion from normal or desirable straightness; TURN implies change of direction essentially by rotation and not usu. as a result of force; TWIST implies the influence of irresistible force having a spiral effect throughout the object or course involved

[3]**curve** *n* **1 :** a curving line or surface **:** BEND **2 :** something curved: as **a :** a curving line of the human body **b** *pl* **:** PARENTHESES **3 a :** a ball thrown so that it swerves from its normal course **b :** TRICK, DECEPTION **4 a :** a line representing graphically a variable affected by conditions **b :** a graphic indication of development or progress **5 a :** a line that may be precisely defined by an equa-

tion in such a way that the coordinates of its points are functions of a single independent variable or parameter **b** (1) **:** the intersection of two geometrical surfaces (2) **:** the path of a moving point

1**cur·vet** \(ˌ)kər-ˈvet\ *n* [It *corvetta*, fr. MF *courbette*, fr. *courber* to curve, fr. L *curvare*] **:** a prancing leap of a horse in which first the forelegs and then the hind are raised so that for an instant all the legs are in the air

2**curvet** *vi* **cur·vet·ted** *or* **cur·vet·ed**; **cur·vet·ting** *or* **cur·vet·ing** **:** to make a curvet; *also* **:** PRANCE, CAPER

cur·vi·lin·ear \ˌkər-və-ˈlin-ē-ər\ *or* **cur·vi·lin·eal** \-ē-əl\ *adj* [L *curvus* + *linea* line] **1 :** consisting of or bounded or represented by a curved line **2 :** marked by flowing tracery ⟨~ Gothic⟩ — **cur·vi·lin·ear·i·ty** \-ˌlin-ē-ˈar-ət-ē\ *n* — **cur·vi·lin·ear·ly** *adv*

cu·sec \ˈkyü-ˌsek\ *n* [*cu*bic foot per *sec*ond] **:** a volumetric unit of flow equal to a cubic foot per second

cush·at \ˈkəsh-ət, ˈku̇sh-\ *n* [ME *cowschote*, fr. OE *cūscote*] *chiefly Scot* **:** RINGDOVE 1

cu·shaw \ku̇-ˈshȯ, ˈkü-ˌ\ *n* [perh. of Algonquian origin] **:** WINTER CROOKNECK

cush·i·ly \ˈku̇sh-ə-lē\ *adv* **:** in a cushy manner

Cush·ing's disease \ˈku̇sh-iŋz-\ *n* [Harvey *Cushing* †1939 Am surgeon] **:** a disease characterized by obesity and muscular weakness associated with adrenal or pituitary dysfunction

1**cush·ion** \ˈku̇sh-ən\ *n, often attrib* [ME *cusshin*, fr. MF *coissin*, fr. (assumed) VL *coxinus*, fr. L *coxa* hip — more at COXA] **1 :** a soft pillow or pad to rest on or against **2 :** a bodily part resembling a pad **3 :** something resembling a cushion: as **a :** PILLOW 3 **b :** RAT 3 **c :** a pad of springy rubber along the inside of the rim of a billiard table **d :** the head of a drill brace **e :** a padded insert in a shoe **f :** a strip of soft resilient rubber between the breaker and carcass of a pneumatic tire **g :** an artificial pool provided to absorb the kinetic energy of falling water and so prevent erosion **h :** an elastic body for reducing shock **i :** a mat laid under a large rug to ease the effect of wear **4 :** something serving to mitigate the effects of disturbances or disorders: as **a :** a factor that lessens adverse developments in the economy **b :** a medical procedure or drug that eases a patient's discomfort

2**cushion** *vt* **cush·ion·ing** \-(ə-)niŋ\ **1 :** to seat or place on a cushion **2 :** to suppress by ignoring **3 :** to furnish with a cushion **4 a :** to mitigate the effects of **b :** to protect against force or shock **5 :** to check gradually so as to minimize shock of moving parts

Cush·it·ic \ˌkəsh-ˈit-ik, ku̇sh-\ *n* [*Cush* (Kush), ancient country in the Nile valley] **:** a subfamily of the Afro-Asiatic language family comprising various languages spoken in East Africa and esp. in Ethiopia and Somaliland — **Cushitic** *adj*

cushy \ˈku̇sh-ē\ *adj* [Hindi *khush* pleasant, fr. Per *khūsh*] **:** EASY

cusk \ˈkəsk\ *n, pl* **cusk** *or* **cusks** [prob. alter. of *tusk* (a kind of codfish)] **1 :** a large edible marine fish (*Brosme brosme*) related to the cod **2 :** the New World burbot

cusp \ˈkəsp\ *n* [L *cuspis* point] **:** POINT, APEX: as **a :** either horn of a crescent moon **b :** a fixed point on a mathematical curve at which a point tracing the curve would exactly reverse its direction of motion **c :** a pointed projection formed by or arising from the intersection of two arcs or foils **d** (1) **:** a point on the grinding surface of a tooth (2) **:** a fold or flap of a cardiac valve — **cus·pate** \ˈkəs-ˌpāt, -pət\ *also* **cus·pat·ed** \-ˌpāt-əd\ *adj*

cus·pid \ˈkəs-pəd\ *n* [back-formation fr. *bicuspid*] **:** a canine tooth

cus·pi·date \ˈkəs-pə-ˌdāt\ *or* **cus·pi·dat·ed** \-ˌdāt-əd\ *adj* [L *cuspidatus*, pp. of *cuspidare* to make pointed, fr. *cuspid-*, *cuspis* point] **:** having a cusp **:** terminating in a point ⟨a ~ leaf⟩

cus·pi·da·tion \ˌkəs-pə-ˈdā-shən\ *n* **:** decoration with cusps

cus·pi·dor \ˈkəs-pə-ˌdȯ(ə)r, -ˌdō(ə)r\ *n* [Pg *cuspidouro* place for spitting, fr. *cuspir* to spit, fr. L *conspuere*, fr. *com-* + *spuere* to spit — more at SPEW] **:** SPITTOON

1**cuss** \ˈkəs\ *n* [alter. of *curse*] **1 :** CURSE **2 :** FELLOW

2**cuss** *vb* **:** CURSE — **cuss·er** *n*

cuss·ed \ˈkəs-əd\ *adj* **:** CURSED — **cuss·ed·ly** *adv*

cuss·ed·ness \-nəs\ *n* **:** disposition to perversity **:** OBSTINACY

cus·tard \ˈkəs-tərd\ *n* [ME, a kind of pie] **:** a sweetened mixture of milk and eggs baked, boiled, or frozen

custard apple *n* **1 a :** any of several chiefly tropical American soft-fleshed edible fruits **b :** any of a genus (*Annona* of the family Annonaceae, the custard-apple family) of trees or shrubs bearing this fruit; *esp* **:** a small West Indian tree (*A. reticulata*) **2 :** PAPAW 2

cus·to·di·al \ˌkə-ˈstōd-ē-əl\ *adj* **:** relating to guardianship

cus·to·di·an \ˌkə-ˈstōd-ē-ən\ *n* **:** one that guards and protects or maintains; *esp* **:** one entrusted with guarding and keeping property or records or with custody or guardianship of prisoners or inmates — **cus·to·di·an·ship** \-ˌship\ *n*

cus·to·dy \ˈkəs-təd-ē\ *n* [ME *custodie*, fr. L *custodia* guarding, fr. *custod-*, *custos* guardian] **:** immediate charge and control exercised by a person or an authority (as over a ward)

1**cus·tom** \ˈkəs-təm\ *n* [ME *custume*, fr. OF, fr. L *consuetudin-*, *consuetudo*, fr. *consuetus*, pp. of *consuescere* to accustom, fr. *com-* + *suescere* to accustom; akin to *suus* one's own — more at SUICIDE] **1 a :** a usage or practice common to many or to a particular place or class or habitual with an individual **b :** long-established practice considered as unwritten law **c :** repeated practice **d :** the whole body of usages, practices, or conventions that regulate social life **2** *pl* **a :** duties, tolls, or imposts imposed by the sovereign law of a country on imports or exports **b** *usu sing in constr* **:** the agency, establishment, or procedure for collecting such customs **3 a :** business patronage **b :** CUSTOMERS **syn** see HABIT

2**custom** *adj* **1 :** made or performed according to personal order **2 :** specializing in custom work or operation

cus·tom·able \-tə-mə-bəl\ *adj, archaic* **:** subject to customs

cus·tom·ar·i·ly \ˌkəs-tə-ˈmer-ə-lē\ *adv* **:** by custom

cus·tom·ar·i·ness \ˈkəs-tə-ˌmer-ē-nəs\ *n* **:** the quality or state of being customary

cus·tom·ary \ˈkəs-tə-ˌmer-ē\ *adj* **1 :** based on or established by custom **2 :** commonly practiced, used, or observed **syn** see USUAL

cus·tom–built \ˌkəs-təm-ˈbilt\ *adj* **:** built to individual order

cus·tom·er \ˈkəs-tə-mər\ *n* [ME *custumer*, fr. *custume*] **1 a :** one that purchases a commodity or service usu. systematically or frequently **b :** one that patronizes or uses services (as of a restaurant) **2 :** an often strange or unusual individual ⟨a queer ~⟩

cus·tom·house \ˈkəs-təm-ˌhau̇s\ *also* **cus·toms·house** \-təmz-\ *n* **:** a building where customs and duties are paid or collected and where vessels are entered and cleared

cus·tom·ize \ˈkəs-tə-ˌmīz\ *vt* **:** to build, fit, or alter according to individual specifications

cus·tom–made \ˌkəs-təm-ˈmād\ *adj* **:** made to individual order

1**cut** \ˈkət\ *vb* **cut**; **cut·ting** [ME *cutten*] *vt* **1 a :** to penetrate with or as if with an edged instrument **b :** to hurt the feelings of **c :** to strike sharply with a cutting effect **d :** to strike (a ball) with a glancing blow imparting a reverse spin **e :** to experience the growth of (a tooth) through the gum **2 a :** TRIM, PARE **b :** to shorten by omissions **c :** DISSOLVE, DILUTE **d :** to reduce in amount **3 a :** MOW, REAP **b** (1) **:** to divide into parts with an edged tool (2) **:** FELL, HEW **c :** to separate from an organization **:** DETACH **d :** to change the direction of sharply **4 a :** to divide into segments **b :** INTERSECT, CROSS **c :** BREAK, INTERRUPT **d** (1) **:** to divide (a deck of cards) into two portions (2) **:** to draw (a card) from the deck **e :** to divide into shares **:** SPLIT **5 a :** STOP, CEASE **b :** to refuse to recognize (an acquaintance) **:** OSTRACIZE **c :** to absent oneself from (as a class) **d :** to stop (a motor) by opening a switch **e :** to terminate the photographing of (a motion-picture scene) **6 a :** to make by or as if by cutting: as (1) **:** CARVE (2) **:** to shape by grinding (3) **:** ENGRAVE (4) **:** to shear or hollow out **b :** to record sounds (as speech or music) on (a phonograph record) **c :** to type on a stencil **7 a :** EXECUTE, PERFORM **b :** to give the appearance or impression of ⟨~ a fine figure⟩ ~ *vi* **1 a :** to function as or as if as an edged tool **b :** to admit of being cut **c :** to perform the operation of dividing, severing, incising, or intersecting **d :** to pierce through incisively **e :** to make a stroke with a whip, sword, or other weapon **f :** to wound feelings or sensibilities **g :** to cause constriction or chafing **h :** to be of effect, influence, or significance **2 a** (1) **:** to divide a pack of cards esp. in order to decide the deal or settle a bet (2) **:** to draw a card from the pack **b :** to divide spoils **:** SPLIT **3 a :** to go across rather than around **b :** to move swiftly **c :** to describe an oblique or diagonal line **d :** to change sharply in direction **:** SWERVE **e :** to make an abrupt transition from one sound or image to another in motion pictures, radio, or television **4 :** to cease photographing motion pictures

2**cut** *n* **1 :** something that is cut or cut off: as **a :** a length of cloth varying from 40 to 100 yards in length **b :** the yield of products cut esp. during one harvest **c :** a customary segment of a meat carcass **d :** a group of animals selected from a herd **e :** SHARE **2 :** the effect produced by cutting: as **a :** a creek, channel, or inlet made by excavation or worn by natural action **b :** an opening made with an edged instrument **c :** a surface or outline left by cutting **d :** a passage cut as a roadway **e :** a grade or step esp. in a social scale **f :** a subset of a set that when subtracted from the set leaves the remainder disconnected **g :** a pictorial illustration **3 :** the act or an instance of cutting: as **a :** a gesture or expression that wounds the feelings **b :** a straight passage or course **c :** a stroke or blow with the edge of a knife or other edged tool **d :** the lash of a whip **e :** the act of reducing or removing a part **f :** a quick replacement of one foot by the other in dancing **g :** an act or turn of cutting cards; *also* **:** the result of cutting **4 :** a voluntary absence from a class **5 a :** a stroke that cuts a ball; *also* **:** the spin imparted by such a stroke **b :** a swing by a batter at a pitched baseball **c :** an exchange of captures in checkers **6 :** an abrupt transition from one sound or image to another in motion pictures, radio, or television **7 a :** the shape and style in which a thing is cut, formed, or made **b :** PATTERN, TYPE

cut–and–dried \ˌkət-ᵊn-ˈdrīd\ *also* **cut–and–dry** \-ˈdrī\ *adj* **:** according to a plan, set procedure, or formula **:** ROUTINE

cu·ta·ne·ous \kyu̇-ˈtā-nē-əs\ *adj* [NL *cutaneus*, fr. L *cutis* skin] **:** of, relating to, or affecting the skin — **cu·ta·ne·ous·ly** *adv*

1**cut·away** \ˈkət-ə-ˌwā\ *adj* **:** having or showing parts cut away

2**cutaway** *n* **1 :** a coat with skirts tapering from the front waistline to form tails at the back **2 :** a cutaway picture or representation

cut back *vt* **1 :** PRUNE **2 :** to return (a distillate) to a still **3 :** REDUCE, DECREASE ~ *vi* **:** to interrupt the sequence of a plot by introducing events prior to those last presented

cut·back \ˈkət-ˌbak\ *n* **1 :** something cut back **2 :** REDUCTION

cutch \ˈkəch\ *n* [modif. of Malay *kachu*] **:** CATECHU a

cut down *vt* **1 a :** to remodel by removing extras or unwanted furnishings and fittings **b :** to remake in a smaller size **2 :** to strike down and kill or incapacitate **3 :** REDUCE, CURTAIL ~ *vi* **:** to reduce or curtail volume or activity

cute \ˈkyüt\ *adj* [short for *acute*] **1 :** CLEVER, SHREWD **2 :** attractive or pretty esp. by reason of daintiness or delicacy **3 :** obviously straining for effect — **cute·ly** *adv* — **cute·ness** *n*

cut glass *n* **:** glass ornamented with patterns cut into its surface by an abrasive wheel and polished

cut–grass \ˈkət-ˌgras\ *n* **:** a grass (esp. genus *Leersia*) with minute hooked bristles along the edges of the leaf blade

cu·ti·cle \ˈkyüt-i-kəl\ *n* [L *cuticula*, dim. of *cutis* skin — more at HIDE] **1 :** SKIN, PELLICLE: as **a :** an external investment secreted usu. by epidermal cells **b :** the epidermis when the outermost layer **c :** a thin continuous fatty film on the external surface of many higher plants **2 :** dead or horny epidermis — **cu·tic·u·lar** \kyu̇-ˈtik-yə-lər\ *adj*

cut in *vi* **1 :** to thrust oneself into a position between others or belonging to another **2 :** to join in something suddenly **3 :** to interrupt a dancing couple and take one as one's partner **4 :** to become automatically connected or started in operation ~ *vt* **1 :** to mix with cutting motions **2 :** to introduce into a number, group, or sequence **3 :** to connect into an electrical circuit to a mechanical apparatus so as to permit operation **4 :** to include esp. among those benefiting or favored

cut–in \ˈkət-ˌin\ *n* **:** something cut in — **cut–in** *adj*

cu·tin \ˈkyüt-ᵊn\ *n* [ISV, fr. L *cutis*] **:** an insoluble mixture containing waxes, fatty acids, soaps, and resinous material that forms a continuous layer on the outer epidermal wall of a plant

cu·tis \ˈkyüt-əs\ *n, pl* **cu·tes** \ˈkyü-ˌtēz\ *or* **cu·tis·es** [L] **:** DERMIS

cut·lass *also* **cut·las** \ˈkət-ləs\ *n* [MF *coutelas*, aug. of *coutel* knife, fr. L *cultellus*, dim. of *culter* knife, plowshare] **1 :** a short curving sword formerly used by sailors on warships **2 :** MACHETE

cut·ler \ˈkət-lər\ *n* [ME, fr. MF *coutelier*, fr. LL *cultellarius*, fr. L *cultellus*] **:** one who makes, deals in, or repairs cutlery

cut·lery \ˈkət-lə-rē\ *n* **1 :** edged or cutting tools; *specif* **:** implements for cutting and eating food **2 :** the business of a cutler

cut·let \'kət-lət\ *n* [F *côtelette*, fr. OF *costelette*, dim. of *coste* rib, side, fr. L *costa*] **1 :** a small slice of meat broiled or fried **2 :** a food mixture shaped to resemble a cutlet
cut off *vt* **1 :** to strike off **:** SEVER **2 :** to cause the death of **3 :** to stop the passage of **4 :** to shut off **:** BAR **5 :** TERMINATE **6 :** SEPARATE, ISOLATE **7 :** DISINHERIT **8 :** to stop the operation of ~ *vi* **:** to cease operating
cut·off \'kət-,ȯf\ *n* **1 :** the action or act of cutting off **2 a :** the new and relatively short channel formed when a stream cuts through the neck of an oxbow **b :** SHORTCUT **c :** a channel made to straighten a stream **3 :** a device for cutting off **4 :** something cut off **5 :** the point, date, or period for a cutoff — **cutoff** *adj*
[1]**cut out** *vt* **1 :** to form by erosion **2 :** to form or shape by cutting **3 :** to determine or assign through necessity ⟨his work is *cut out* for him⟩ **4 :** to take the place of **:** SUPPLANT **5 a :** ELIMINATE **b :** to stop or desist from **6 a :** to remove from a series or circuit **:** DISCONNECT **b :** to make inoperative ~ *vi* **1 :** to depart in haste **2 :** to cease operating **3 :** to swerve out of a traffic line
[2]**cut out** *adj* **:** naturally fitted
cut·out \'kət-,au̇t\ *n* **1 :** something cut out or off from something else **2 :** one that cuts out — **cutout** *adj*
cut·over \,kət-,ō-vər\ *adj* **:** having most of its salable timber cut
cut·purse \'kət-,pərs\ *n* **1 :** a thief working by cutting purses worn at the waist **2 :** PICKPOCKET
cut-rate \'kət-'rāt\ *adj* **1 :** marked by, offering, or making use of a reduced rate or price **2 :** SECOND-RATE, CHEAP
cut·ter \'kət-ər\ *n, often attrib* **1 :** one that cuts: **a :** one whose work is cutting or involves cutting **b** (1) **:** an instrument, machine, machine part, or tool that cuts (2) **:** a device for vibrating a cutting stylus in disc recording (3) **:** the cutting stylus or its point **2 a :** a ship's boat for carrying stores or passengers **b :** a fore-and-aft rigged sailing boat with a jib, forestaysail, mainsail, and single mast **c :** a small armed boat in government service **3 :** a light sleigh
[1]**cut·throat** \'kət-,thrōt\ *n* **:** one likely to cut throats **:** MURDERER
[2]**cutthroat** *adj* **1 :** MURDEROUS, CRUEL **2 :** MERCILESS, RUTHLESS
cutthroat contract *n* **1 :** contract bridge in which partnerships are determined by the bidding **2 :** any of various three-hand forms of contract bridge
cut time *n* **:** ALLA BREVE
[1]**cut·ting** *n* **1 :** something cut or cut off or out: as **a :** a section of a plant capable of developing into a new plant **b :** HARVEST **2 :** something made by cutting; *esp* **:** RECORDING
[2]**cutting** *adj* **:** given to or designed for cutting: as **a :** EDGED, SHARP **b :** marked by sharp piercing cold **c :** SARCASTIC **d :** SHARP, INTENSE **syn** see INCISIVE — **cut·ting·ly** \-iŋ-lē\ *adv*
cut·tle·bone \'kət-ᵊl-,bōn\ *n* [ME *cotul* cuttlefish (fr. OE *cudele*) + E *bone;* akin to OE *codd* bag] **:** the shell of cuttlefishes used for polishing powder or for supplying cage birds with lime and salts
cut·tle·fish \-,fish\ *n* [ME *cotul* + E *fish*] **:** a 10-armed marine cephalopod mollusk (family Sepiidae) differing from the related squid in having a calcified internal shell
cut·ty sark \'kət-ē-,särk\ *n* [E dial. *cutty* (short) + *sark*] **1** *chiefly Scot* **:** a short garment **2** *chiefly Scot* **:** WOMAN, HUSSY
cutty stool *n* **1** *chiefly Scot* **:** a low stool **2 :** a seat in a Scottish church where offenders formerly sat for public rebuke
cut up *vt* **1 a :** to cut into parts or pieces **b :** to distress deeply **2 :** GASH, SLASH **3 :** to subject to carping hostile criticism ~ *vi* **1 :** to undergo being cut up **2 :** to behave in a comic, boisterous, or unruly manner
cut·up \'kət-,əp\ *n* **:** one that clowns or acts boisterously
cut·wa·ter \-,wȯt-ər, -,wät-\ *n* **:** the forepart of a ship's stem
cut·work \-,wərk\ *n* **:** embroidery in which a design is outlined in buttonhole stitch and the intervening material then cut away
cut·worm \-,wərm\ *n* **:** any of various smooth-bodied caterpillars (family Noctuidae) that hide by day and feed at night
cu·vette \kyü-'vet\ *n* [F, dim. of *cuve* tub, fr. L *cupa* — more at HIVE] **:** a small often transparent vessel (as a tube)
cwm \'küm\ *n* [W, valley] **:** CIRQUE 3
-cy \sē\ *n suffix* [ME *-cie*, fr. OF, fr. L *-tia*, partly fr. *-t-* (final stem consonant) + *-ia* -y, partly fr. Gk *-tia, -teia*, fr. *-t-* (final stem consonant) + *-ia, -eia* -y] **:** action **:** practice ⟨mendican*cy*⟩ **:** rank **:** office ⟨baronet*cy*⟩ ⟨chaplain*cy*⟩ **:** body **:** class ⟨magistra*cy*⟩ **:** state **:** quality ⟨accura*cy*⟩ ⟨bankrupt*cy*⟩ ⟨normal*cy*⟩ — often replacing a final *-t* or *-te* of the base word
cyan- *or* **cyano-** *comb form* [G, fr. Gk *kyan-, kyano-*, fr. *kyanos* dark blue enamel] **1 :** dark blue **:** blue ⟨*cyano*type⟩ **2 :** cyanogen ⟨*cyan*ide⟩ **3 :** cyanide ⟨*cyano*genetic⟩
cy·an·a·mide *also* **cy·an·a·mid** \sī-'an-ə-məd\ *n* [ISV] **1 :** an acidic compound $CNNH_2$ obtained by the action of ammonia gas on cyanogen chloride and by acidification of calcium cyanamide **2 :** a salt or ester of cyanamide
cy·a·nate \'sī-ə-,nāt, -nət\ *n* [ISV] **:** a salt or ester of cyanic acid
cy·an·ic \sī-'an-ik\ *adj* [ISV] **1 :** relating to or containing cyanogen **2 :** of a blue or bluish color
cyanic acid *n* **:** a strong acid HOCN obtained as a mobile volatile liquid by heating cyanuric acid
[1]**cy·a·nide** \'sī-ə-,nīd, -nəd\ *n* [ISV] **:** a compound of cyanogen usu. with a more electropositive element or radical
[2]**cy·a·nide** \-,nīd\ *vt* **:** to treat with a cyanide; *specif* **:** to treat (iron or steel) with molten cyanide to produce a hard surface
cyanide process *n* **:** a method of extracting gold and silver from ores by treatment with a sodium cyanide or calcium cyanide solution
cy·a·nine \'sī-ə-,nēn, -nən\ *n* [ISV] **:** any of various dyes that sensitize photographic film to light from the green, yellow, red, and infrared regions of the spectrum
cy·a·nite \'sī-ə-,nīt\ *var of* KYANITE
cy·a·no \'sī-ə-(,)nō\ *adj* [*cyan-*] **:** relating to or containing the cyanogen group
cy·a·no·co·bal·a·min \,sī-ə-(,)nō-kə-'bȯ-lə-mən\ *n* [*cyan-* + *cobalt* + *vitamin*] **:** VITAMIN B_{12}
cy·ano·gen \sī-'an-ə-jən\ *n* [F *cyanogène*, fr. *cyan-* + *gène* -gen] **1 :** a univalent radical —CN present in simple and complex cyanides **2 :** a colorless flammable poisonous gas $(CN)_2$
cy·a·no·ge·net·ic \,sī-ə-nō-jə-'net-ik, (,)sī-,an-ə-\ *also* **cy·a·no·gen·ic** \-'jen-ik\ *adj* **:** capable of producing cyanide
cy·a·no·hy·drin \,sī-ə-nō-'hī-drən\ *n* [ISV] **:** any of various compounds containing both cyano and alcoholic hydroxyl groups
cy·a·nosed \'sī-ə-,nōzd, -,nōst\ *adj* **:** affected with cyanosis
cy·a·no·sis \,sī-ə-'nō-səs\ *n* [NL, fr. Gk *kyanōsis* dark blue color, fr. *kyan-* cyan-] **:** a bluish or purplish discoloration (as of skin) due to deficient oxygenation of the blood — **cy·a·not·ic** \-'nät-ik\ *adj*
cy·an·urate \,sī-ə-'n(y)u̇(ə)r-,āt, -'n(y)u̇r-ət\ *n* **:** a salt or ester of cyanuric acid
cy·an·uric acid \,sī-ə-,n(y)u̇r-ik-\ *n* [*cyan-* + *urea*] **:** a crystalline weak acid $C_3N_3(OH)_3$ yielding cyanic acid when heated
Cyb·e·le \'sib-ə-lē\ *n* [L, fr. Gk *Kybelē*] **:** a nature goddess of the ancient peoples of Asia Minor
cy·ber·net·ic \,sī-bər-'net-ik\ *adj* **:** of, relating to, or involving cybernetics
cy·ber·net·ics \-iks\ *n pl but sing or pl in constr* [Gk *kybernētēs* pilot, governor (fr. *kybernan* to steer, govern) + E *-ics*] **:** comparative study of the automatic control system formed by the nervous system and brain and by mechanical-electrical communication systems
cy·cad \'sī-kəd\ *n* [NL *Cycad-, Cycas*] **:** any of a family (Cycadaceae) of tropical gymnospermous plants resembling palms but reproducing by means of spermatozoids — **cy·ca·de·an** \,sī-kə-'dē-ən, sī-'kad-ē-\ *adj* — **cy·cadi·form** \sī-'kad-ə-,fȯrm\ *adj*
cy·cas \'sī-kəs\ *n* [NL *Cycad-, Cycas* genus name] **:** any of a genus (*Cycas*) of cycads between tree ferns and palms in appearance
cycl- *or* **cyclo-** *comb form* [NL, fr. Gk *kykl-, kyklo-*, fr. *kyklos*] **1 :** circle ⟨*cyclo*meter⟩ **2 :** cyclic ⟨*cyclo*hexane⟩
cy·cla·mate \'sī-klə-,māt\ *n* [*cyclo*hexyl-sulf*amate*] **:** an artificially prepared salt of sodium or calcium used as a sweetener
cy·cla·men \'sī-klə-mən, 'sik-lə-\ *n* [NL, genus name, fr. Gk *kyklaminos*] **:** any of a genus (*Cyclamen*) of plants of the primrose family having showy nodding flowers
[1]**cy·cle** \'sī-kəl, *6 also* 'sik-əl\ *n, often attrib* [F or LL; F, fr. LL *cyclus*, fr. Gk *kyklos* circle, wheel, cycle — more at WHEEL] **1 :** an interval of time during which a sequence of a recurring succession of events or phenomena is completed **2 a :** a course or series of events or operations that recur regularly and usu. lead back to the starting point **b :** one complete performance of a vibration, electric oscillation, current alternation, or other periodic process **3 :** a circular or spiral arrangement: as **a :** an imaginary circle or orbit in the heavens **b :** WHORL **c :** RING 10 **4 :** a long period of time **:** AGE **5 a :** a group of poems, plays, novels, or songs treating the same theme **b :** a series of narratives dealing typically with the exploits of a legendary hero **6 a :** BICYCLE **b :** TRICYCLE **c :** MOTORCYCLE — **cy·clic** \'sī-klik, 'sik-lik\ *or* **cy·cli·cal** \'sī-kli-kəl, 'sik-li-\ *adj* — **cy·cli·cal·ly** \-k(ə-)lē\ *adv*
[2]**cy·cle** \'sī-kəl, *"ride" also* 'sik-əl\ *vb* **cy·cling** \'sī-k(ə-)liŋ, 'sik(-ə)-\ *vi* **1 a :** to pass through a cycle **b :** to recur in cycles **2 :** to ride a cycle; *specif* **:** BICYCLE ~ *vt* **:** to cause to go through a cycle — **cy·cler** \'sī-k(ə-)lər, 'sik(-ə)-\ *n*
cy·clist \'sī-k(ə-)ləst, 'sik(-ə)-\ *n* **:** one who rides a cycle
cy·clo·hex·ane \,sī-klō-'hek-,sān\ *n* [ISV] **:** a pungent saturated cyclic hydrocarbon C_6H_{12} found in petroleum or made synthetically and used chiefly as a solvent and in organic synthesis
[1]**cy·cloid** \'sī-,klȯid\ *n* [F *cycloïde*, fr. Gk *kykloeidēs* circular, fr. *kyklos*] **1 :** a curve generated by a point on the circumference of a circle rolling along a straight line **2 :** CYCLOTHYME — **cy·cloi·dal** \sī-'klȯid-ᵊl\ *adj*

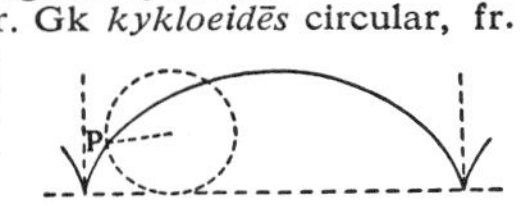

cycloid

[2]**cycloid** *adj* **1 :** CIRCULAR; *esp* **:** arranged or progressing in circles **2 :** smooth with concentric lines of growth ⟨~ scales⟩; *also* **:** having or consisting of cycloid scales **3 :** CYCLOTHYMIC
cy·clom·e·ter \sī-'kläm-ət-ər\ *n* **:** a device made for recording the revolutions of a wheel and often used for registering distance traversed by a wheeled vehicle
cy·clone \'sī-,klōn\ *n* [modif. of Gk *kyklōma* wheel, coil, fr. *kykloun* to go around, fr. *kyklos* circle] **1 :** a storm or system of winds that rotates about a center of low atmospheric pressure clockwise in the southern hemisphere and counterclockwise in the northern, advances at a speed of 20 to 30 miles an hour, and often brings abundant rain **2 :** TORNADO — **cy·clon·ic** \sī-'klän-ik\ *adj* — **cy·clon·i·cal·ly** \-i-k(ə-)lē\ *adv*
cy·clo·ole·fin \,sī-klō-'ō-lə-fən\ *n* [ISV] **:** a hydrocarbon (as of the formula C_nH_{2n-2}) containing an unsaturated ring
cy·clo·par·af·fin \-'par-ə-fən\ *n* **:** a saturated cyclic hydrocarbon of the formula C_nH_{2n}
cy·clo·pe·an \,sī-klə-'pē-ən, sī-'klō-pē-\ *adj* **1** *often cap* **:** of, relating to, or characteristic of a Cyclops **2 :** HUGE, MASSIVE **3 :** of or relating to a style of stone construction marked typically by the use of large irregular blocks without mortar
cy·clo·pe·dia *or* **cy·clo·pae·dia** \,sī-klə-'pēd-ē-ə\ *n* **:** ENCYCLOPEDIA — **cy·clo·pe·dic** \-'pēd-ik\ *adj*
cy·clo·pro·pane \,sī-klə-'prō-,pān\ *n* [ISV] **:** a saturated cyclic gaseous hydrocarbon C_3H_6 used esp. as an anesthetic
cy·clops \'sī-,kläps\ *n* [L, fr. Gk *Kyklōps*, fr. *kykl-* cycl- + *ōps* eye] **1** *pl* **cy·clo·pes** \sī-'klō-(,)pēz\ *cap* **:** one of a race of giants in Greek mythology with a single eye in the middle of the forehead **2** *pl* **cyclops** [NL, genus name, fr. L] **:** WATER FLEA
cy·clo·ra·ma \,sī-klə-'ram-ə, -'räm-\ *n* [*cycl-* + *-orama* (as in *panorama*)] **1 :** a large pictorial representation encircling the spectator and often having real objects as a foreground **2 :** a curved cloth or wall used as a background of a stage set to suggest unlimited space — **cy·clo·ram·ic** \-'ram-ik\ *adj*
cy·clo·sis \sī-'klō-səs\ *n* [NL, fr. Gk *kyklōsis* encirclement, fr. *kykloun* to go around] **:** the streaming of protoplasm within a cell
cy·clos·to·mate \sī-'kläs-tə-mət\ *also* **cy·clo·sto·ma·tous** \,sī-klə-'stäm-ət-əs, -'stōm-\ *adj* [*cycl-* + Gk *stomat-, stoma* mouth] **1 :** having a circular mouth **2 :** CYCLOSTOME
cy·clo·stome \'sī-klə-,stōm\ *n* [deriv. of Gk *kykl-* + *stoma* mouth] **:** any of a class (Cyclostomi or Cyclostomata) of lowly craniate vertebrates having a large sucking mouth with no jaws and comprising the hagfishes and lampreys — **cyclostome** *adj*
cy·clo·thyme \'sī-klə-,thīm\ *n* [back-formation fr. *cyclothymia*] **:** a cyclothymic individual
cy·clo·thy·mia \,sī-klə-'thī-mē-ə\ *n* [NL, fr. G *zyklothymie*, fr. *zykl-* cycl- + *-thymie* -thymia] **:** a temperament marked by alternate lively and depressed moods — **cy·clo·thy·mic** \-'thī-mik\ *adj*
cy·clo·tron \'sī-klə-,trän\ *n* [*cycl-* + *-tron;* fr. the circular movement of the particles] **:** an accelerator in which particles are propelled by an alternating electric field in a constant magnetic field
cy·der *Brit var of* CIDER

cyg·net \'sig-nət\ *n* [ME *sygnett*, fr. MF *cygne* swan, fr. L *cycnus*, *cygnus* fr. Gk *kyknos*] **:** a young swan

Cyg·nus \'sig-nəs\ *n* [L (gen. *Cygni*), lit., swan] **:** a northern constellation between Lyra and Pegasus in the Milky Way

cyl·in·der \'sil-ən-dər\ *n* [MF or L; MF *cylindre*, fr. L *cylindrus*, fr. Gk *kylindros*, fr. *kylindein* to roll] **1 a :** the surface traced by a straight line moving parallel to a fixed straight line and intersecting a fixed curve **b :** the space bounded by any such surface and two parallel planes cutting all the elements — see VOLUME table **2 :** a cylindrical body: as **a :** the turning chambered breech of a revolver **b** (1) **:** the piston chamber in an engine (2) **:** a chamber in a pump from which the piston expels the fluid **c :** any of various rotating members in printing presses; *esp* **:** one that impresses paper on an inked form **d :** a cylindrical clay object inscribed with cuneiform inscriptions — **cyl·in·dered** \-dərd\ *adj*

cylinder seal *n* **:** a cylinder (as of stone) engraved in intaglio and used esp. in ancient Mesopotamia to roll an impression on wet clay

cy·lin·dri·cal \sə-'lin-dri-kəl\ *or* **cy·lin·dric** \-drik\ *adj* **:** relating to or having the form or properties of a cylinder — **cy·lin·dri·cal·ly** \-'lin-dri-k(ə-)lē\ *adv*

cy·ma \'sī-mə\ *n* [Gk *kyma*, lit., wave] **1 :** a projecting molding whose profile is a double curve **2 :** a double curve formed by the union of a concave line and a convex line

cy·mar *var of* SIMAR

cy·ma·tium \sī-'mā-sh(ē-)əm\ *n, pl* **cy·ma·tia** \-sh(ē-)ə\ [L, fr. Gk *kymation*, dim. of *kymat-*, *kyma*] **:** a crowning molding in classic architecture; *esp* **:** CYMA

cym·bal \'sim-bəl\ *n* [ME, fr. OE *cymbal* & MF *cymbale*, fr. L *cymbalum*, fr. Gk *kymbalon*, fr. *kymbē* bowl] **:** a concave brass plate that produces a brilliant clashing tone and that is struck with a drumstick or is used in pairs struck glancingly together — **cym·bal·ist** \-bə-ləst\ *n*

cym·bid·i·um \sim-'bid-ē-əm\ *n* [NL, genus name, fr. L *cymba* boat, fr. Gk *kymbē* bowl, boat] **:** any of a genus (*Cymbidium*) of tropical Old World orchids with showy boat-shaped flowers

cyme \'sīm\ *n* [NL *cyma*, fr. L, cabbage sprout, fr. Gk *kyma* swell, wave, cabbage sprout, fr. *kyein* to be pregnant] **:** an inflorescence in which all floral axes terminate in a single flower; *esp* **:** a determinate inflorescence of this type containing several flowers with the first-opening central flower terminating the main axis and subsequent flowers developing from lateral buds

cy·mene \'sī-,mēn\ *n* [F *cymène*, fr. Gk *kyminon* cumin + F *-ène* -ene — more at CUMIN] **:** any of three liquid isomeric hydrocarbons $C_{10}H_{14}$ that are methyl isopropyl derivatives of benzene; *esp* **:** a colorless liquid of pleasant odor from essential oils

cy·mo·gene \'sī-mə-,jēn\ *n* [ISV *cymene* + *-o-* + *-gen*] **:** a flammable gaseous petroleum product consisting chiefly of butane

cy·mo·phane \-,fān\ *n* [F, fr. Gk *kyma* wave + F *-phane*] **:** CHRYSOBERYL; *esp* **:** an opalescent chrysoberyl

cy·mose \'sī-,mōs\ *also* **cy·mous** \-məs\ *adj* **:** of, relating to, being, or bearing a cyme — **cy·mose·ly** *adv*

[1]**Cym·ric** \'kəm-rik, 'kim-\ *adj* **:** of, relating to, or characteristic of the non-Gaelic Celtic people of Britain or their language; *specif* **:** WELSH

[2]**Cymric** *n* **:** BRYTHONIC; *specif* **:** the Welsh language

Cym·ry \-rē\ *n pl* [W] **:** the Brythonic Celts; *specif* **:** WELSH

cyn·ic \'sin-ik\ *n* [MF or L, MF *cynique*, fr. L *cynicus*, fr. Gk *kynikos*, lit., like a dog, fr. *kyn-*, *kyōn* dog] **1** *cap* **:** an adherent or advocate of the view that virtue is the only good and that its essence lies in self-control and independence **2 :** one who believes that human conduct is motivated wholly by self-interest — **cynic** *adj*

cyn·i·cal \'sin-i-kəl\ *adj* **1 :** CAPTIOUS, PEEVISH **2 :** having the attitude or temper of a cynic; *esp* **:** contemptuously distrustful of human nature and motives — **cyn·i·cal·ly** \-k(ə-)lē\ *adv*

syn CYNICAL, MISANTHROPIC, PESSIMISTIC, MISOGYNIC mean deeply distrustful. CYNICAL implies having a sneering disbelief in sincerity or nobility; MISANTHROPIC suggests a rooted distrust and dislike of human beings in general and discomfort in their society; PESSIMISTIC implies having a gloomy, distrustful view of life in general and of the future; MISOGYNIC applies to a man having a deep-seated distrust of and aversion to women

cyn·i·cism \'sin-ə-,siz-əm\ *n* **1** *cap* **:** the doctrine of the Cynics **2 a :** cynical character or quality **b :** an expression of such quality

cy·no·sure \'sī-nə-,shu̇(ə)r, 'sin-ə-\ *n* [MF & L; MF, Ursa Minor, guide, fr. L *cynosura* Ursa Minor, fr. Gk *kynosoura*, fr. *kynos oura* dog's tail] **1** *cap* **:** the northern constellation Ursa Minor; *also* **:** NORTH STAR **2 :** a center of attraction or attention

Cyn·thia \'sin(t)-thē-ə\ *n* [L, fr. fem. of *Cynthius* of Cynthus, fr, *Cynthus*, mountain on Delos where she was born] **1 :** ARTEMIS **2 :** MOON

cy·pher *chiefly Brit var of* CIPHER

[1]**cy pres** \(')sē-'prā\ *adv* **:** in accordance with the rule of cy pres

[2]**cy pres** *n* [AF so near, as near (as may be)] **:** a rule providing for the construction of instruments in equity as nearly as possible in conformity to the intention of the testator when literal construction is illegal, impracticable, or impossible

[1]**cy·press** \'sī-prəs\ *n* [ME, fr. OF *ciprès*, fr. L *cyparissus*, fr. Gk *kyparissos*] **1 a** (1) **:** any of a genus (*Cupressus*) of mostly evergreen trees of the pine family with symmetrical habit (2) **:** any of several related trees; *esp* **:** either of two large swamp trees (*Taxodium distichum* and *T. ascendens*) of the southern U.S. with hard red wood used for shingles **b :** the wood of a cypress tree **2 :** branches of cypress used as a symbol of mourning

[2]**cypress** \'sī-prəs\ *n* [ME *ciprus*, *cipres*, fr. *Cyprus*, Mediterranean island] **:** a silk or cotton usu. black gauze formerly used for mourning

cypress vine *n* **:** a tropical American vine (*Quamoclit pennata*) of the morning-glory family with red or white tubular flowers and finely dissected leaves

cyp·ri·an \'sip-rē-ən\ *n, often cap* [L *cyprius* of Cyprus, fr. Gk *kyprios*, fr. *Kypros* Cyprus, birthplace of Aphrodite] **:** PROSTITUTE

cyp·ri·nid \'sip-rə-nəd\ *n* [deriv. of L *cyprinus* carp, fr. Gk *kyprinos*] **:** any of a family (Cyprinidae) of soft-finned freshwater fishes including the carps and minnows — **cyprinid** *adj* — **cyp·ri·noid** \-,nȯid\ *adj or n*

cy·prin·odont \sə-'prin-ə-,dänt\ *n* [deriv. of L *cyprinus* + Gk *odont-*, *odous* tooth — more at TOOTH] **:** any of an order (Microcyprini) of soft-finned fishes including the topminnows and killifishes — **cyprinodont** *adj*

cyp·ri·pe·di·um \,sip-rə-'pēd-ē-əm\ *n* [NL, genus name, fr. LL *Cypris*, a name for Venus + Gk *pedilon* sandal] **:** any of a genus (*Cypripedium*) of leafy-stemmed terrestrial orchids having large usu. showy drooping flowers with the lip inflated or pouched

cyp·se·la \'sip-sə-lə\ *n, pl* **cyp·se·lae** \-,lē\ [NL, fr. Gk *kypselē* vessel, box] **:** an achene with two carpels and adherent calyx tube

Cy·re·na·ic \,sir-ə-'nā-ik, ,sī-rə-\ *n* [L *cyrenaicus*, fr. Gk *kyrēnaikos*, fr. *Kyrēnē* Cyrene, Africa, home of Aristippus, author of the doctrine] **:** an adherent or advocate of the doctrine that pleasure is the chief end of life — **Cyrenaic** *adj* — **Cy·re·na·icism** \-'nā-ə-,siz-əm\ *n*

Cy·ril·lic \sə-'ril-ik\ *adj* [St. *Cyril* †869, apostle of the Slavs, reputed inventor of the Cyrillic alphabet] **:** of, relating to, or constituting an alphabet used for writing Old Church Slavonic and for Russian and various other Slavic languages

cyst \'sist\ *n* [NL *cystis*, fr. Gk *kystis* bladder, pouch] **1 :** a closed sac having a distinct membrane and developing abnormally in a cavity or structure of the body **2 :** a body resembling a cyst: as **a :** a resting spore of many algae **b :** an air vesicle (as of a rockweed) **c :** a capsule formed about a minute organism going into a resting or spore stage; *also* **:** this capsule with its contents **d :** a resistant cover about a parasite produced by the parasite or the host

cyst- *or* **cysti-** *or* **cysto-** *comb form* [F, fr. Gk *kyst-*, *kysto-*, fr. *kystis*] **:** bladder ⟨*cyst*itis⟩ **:** sac ⟨*cysto*carp⟩

-cyst \,sist\ *n comb form* [NL *-cystis*, fr. Gk *kystis*] **:** bladder **:** sac ⟨blasto*cyst*⟩

cys·te·ine \'sis-,tē-ən\ *n* [ISV, fr. *cystine* + *-ein*] **:** a crystalline amino acid $C_3H_7NO_2S$ readily oxidizable to cystine

cys·tic \'sis-tik\ *adj* **1 :** relating to, composed of, or containing cysts **2 :** of or relating to the urinary bladder or the gall bladder **3 :** ENCYSTED

cys·ti·cer·coid \,sis-tə-'sər-,kȯid\ *n* **:** a larval tapeworm having an invaginated scolex and solid tailpiece

cys·ti·cer·cus \-'sər-kəs\ *n, pl* **cys·ti·cer·ci** \-'sər-,sī\ [NL, fr. *cyst-* + Gk *kerkos* tail] **:** a tapeworm larva consisting of a scolex invaginated in a fluid-filled sac in tissues of an intermediate host

cystic fibrosis *n* **:** an hereditary disease that appears usu. in early childhood, involves generalized disorder of exocrine glands, and is marked esp. by deficiency of pancreatic enzymes, respiratory symptoms, and excessive loss of salt in the sweat

cys·tine \'sis-,tēn\ *n* [fr. its discovery in bladder stones] **:** a crystalline amino acid $C_6H_{12}N_2O_4S_2$ widespread in proteins (as keratins) and a major metabolic sulfur source

cys·ti·tis \sis-'tīt-əs\ *n* [NL] **:** inflammation of the urinary bladder

cys·to·carp \'sis-tə-,kärp\ *n* [ISV] **:** the fruiting structure produced in the red algae after fertilization

[1]**cys·toid** \'sis-,tȯid\ *adj* [ISV] **:** resembling a bladder

[2]**cystoid** *n* **:** a cystoid structure; *specif* **:** a mass resembling a cyst but lacking a membrane

cys·to·lith \'sis-tə-,lith\ *n* [G *zystolith*, fr. *zyst-* cyst- + *-lith*] **1 :** a calcium carbonate concretion arising from the cellulose wall of cells of higher plants **2 :** a urinary calculus

cys·to·scope \'sis-tə-,skōp\ *n* [ISV] **:** an instrument for the visual examination of the bladder and the passage of instruments under visual control — **cys·to·scop·ic** \,sis-tə-'skäp-ik\ *adj*

cyt- *or* **cyto-** *comb form* [G *zyt-*, *zyto-*, fr. Gk *kytos* hollow vessel — more at HIDE] **1 :** cell ⟨*cyto*logy⟩ **2 :** cytoplasm ⟨*cyto*kinesis⟩

cyt·as·ter \'sīt-,as-tər\ *n* [ISV] **:** ASTER 2

-cyte \,sīt\ *n comb form* [NL *-cyta*, fr. Gk *kytos* hollow vessel] **:** cell ⟨leuko*cyte*⟩

Cyth·er·ea \,sith-ə-'rē-ə\ *n* [L, fr. Gk *Kythereia*] **:** APHRODITE — **Cyth·er·e·an** \-'rē-ən\ *adj*

cy·to·ar·chi·tec·ture \,sīt-ō-'är-kə-,tek-chər\ *n* **:** the cellular makeup of a bodily tissue or structure

cy·to·chem·is·try \-'kem-ə-strē\ *n* **1 :** microscopical biochemistry **2 :** the chemistry of cells

cy·to·chrome \'sīt-ə-,krōm\ *n* **:** any of several iron-containing respiratory pigments prominent in intracellular oxidations

cy·to·ge·net·ic \,sīt-ə-jə-'net-ik\ *adj* [ISV] **:** of or relating to cytogenetics — **cy·to·ge·net·i·cal** \-i-kəl\ *adj* — **cy·to·ge·net·i·cal·ly** \-i-k(ə-)lē\ *adv* — **cy·to·ge·net·i·cist** \-'net-ə-səst\ *n*

cy·to·ge·net·ics \-jə-'net-iks\ *n pl but sing or pl in constr* [ISV] **:** a branch of biology that deals with the study of heredity and variation by the methods of both cytology and genetics

cy·to·ki·ne·sis \,sīt-ə-kə-'nē-səs, -(,)kī-\ *n* [NL, fr. *cyt-* + Gk *kinēsis* motion] **1 :** cytoplasmic changes accompanying karyokinesis **2 :** cleavage of the cytoplasm into daughter cells following nuclear division — **cy·to·ki·net·ic** \-'net-ik\ *adj*

cy·to·log·i·cal \,sīt-ᵊl-'äj-i-kəl\ *or* **cy·to·log·ic** \-'äj-ik\ *adj* **:** of or relating to cytology — **cy·to·log·i·cal·ly** \-i-k(ə-)lē\ *adv*

cy·tol·o·gist \sī-'täl-ə-jəst\ *n* **:** a specialist in cytology

cy·tol·o·gy \-jē\ *n* [ISV] **1 :** a branch of biology dealing with the structure, function, multiplication, pathology, and life history of cells **2 :** the cytological aspects of a process or structure

cy·to·ly·sin \sī-'täl-ə-sən, ,sīt-ᵊl-'īs-ᵊn\ *n* [ISV] **:** a substance producing cytolysis

cy·tol·y·sis \sī-'täl-ə-səs\ *n* [NL] **:** the usu. pathologic dissolution or disintegration of cells — **cy·to·lyt·ic** \,sīt-ᵊl-'it-ik\ *adj*

cy·to·phag·ic \,sīt-ə-'faj-ik\ *also* **cy·toph·a·gous** \sī-'täf-ə-gəs\ *adj* [*cyt-* + *-phagic* (fr. *-phagy*) or *-phagous*] **:** of, relating to, or involving phagocytosis — **cy·toph·a·gy** \sī-'täf-ə-jē\ *n*

cy·to·plasm \'sīt-ə-,plaz-əm\ *n* [ISV] **:** the protoplasm of a protoplast external to the nuclear membrane — **cy·to·plas·mic** \,sīt-ə-'plaz-mik\ *adj* — **cy·to·plas·mi·cal·ly** \-mi-k(ə-)lē\ *adv*

cy·to·plast \'sīt-ə-,plast\ *n* **:** the cytoplasmic content of a cell — **cy·to·plas·tic** \,sīt-ə-'plas-tik\ *adj*

cy·to·tax·o·nom·ic \,sīt-ō-,tak-sə-'näm-ik\ *adj* **:** of or relating to cytotaxonomy — **cy·to·tax·o·nom·i·cal·ly** \-i-k(ə-)lē\ *adv*

cy·to·tax·on·o·my \,sīt-(,)ō-(,)tak-'sän-ə-mē\ *n* **1 :** study of the relationships and classification of organisms using both classical systematic techniques and comparative studies of chromosomes **2 :** the nuclear cytologic makeup of a kind of organism

cy·to·trop·ic \,sīt-ə-'träp-ik\ *adj* **:** attracted to cells ⟨a ~ virus⟩

czar \'zär\ *n* [obs. Pol *czar*, fr. Russ *tsar'*, fr. Goth *kaisar*, fr. Gk or L; Gk, fr. L *Caesar* — more at CAESAR] **1 :** EMPEROR; *specif* **:** the ruler of Russia until the 1917 revolution **2 :** one having great power or authority — **czar·dom** \'zärd-əm\ *n*
czar·das \'chär-ˌdash, -däsh\ *n, pl* **czardas** *same*\ [Hung *csárdás*] **:** a Hungarian dance that starts slowly and ends in a whirl
cza·ri·na \zä-'rē-nə\ *n* [prob. modif. of G *zarin*, fr. *zar* czar, fr. Russ *tsar'*] **:** the wife of a czar
czar·ism \'zär-ˌiz-əm\ *n* **1 :** the government of Russia under the czars **2 :** autocratic rule — **czar·ist** \'zär-əst\ *n or adj*
Czech \'chek\ *n* [Czech *Čech*] **1 :** a native or inhabitant of Czechoslovakia; *esp* **:** a native or inhabitant of Bohemia, Moravia, or Silesia provinces **2 :** the Slavic language of the Czechs — **Czech** *adj* — **Czech·ish** \-ish\ *adj*

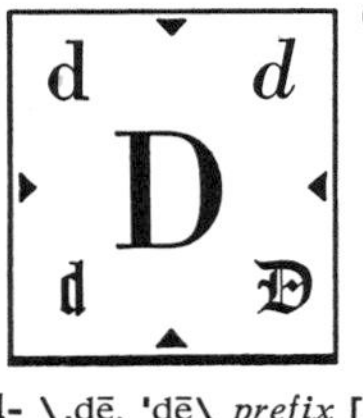

d \'dē\ *n, often cap, often attrib* **1 a :** the fourth letter of the English alphabet **b :** a graphic representation of this letter **c :** a speech counterpart of orthographic *d* **2 :** 500 **3 :** the tone D **4 :** a graphic device for reproducing the letter *d* **5 :** one designated *d* esp. as the fourth in order or class **6 a :** a grade rating a student's work as poor in quality **b :** one graded or rated with a D **7 :** something shaped like the letter D; *specif* **:** a semicircle on a pool table about 22 inches in diameter and for use esp. in snooker
d- \ˌdē, 'dē\ *prefix* [ISV, fr. *dextr-*] **1 :** dextrorotatory ⟨*d*-tartaric acid⟩ **2 :** having a similar configuration at a selected carbon atom to the configuration of dextrorotatory glyceraldehyde ⟨D-fructose⟩
'd \d, əd\ *vb* **1 :** HAD **2 :** WOULD **3 :** DID
¹dab \'dab\ *n* [ME *dabbe*] **1 :** a sudden blow or thrust **:** POKE **2 :** a gentle touch or stroke **:** PAT
²dab *vb* **dabbed; dab·bing** *vt* **1 :** to strike or touch lightly **:** PAT **2 :** to apply lightly or irregularly **:** DAUB **~** *vi* **:** to make a dab
³dab *n* **1 :** DAUB **2 :** a small amount
⁴dab *n* [AF *dabbe*] **:** FLATFISH; *esp* **:** any of several flounders (genus *Limanda*)
⁵dab *n* [perh. alter. of *adept*] *chiefly Brit* **:** a skillful person **:** EXPERT
dab·ber \'dab-ər\ *n* **1 :** one that dabs **2 :** a pad or ball used to ink type or engraving plates
dab·ble \'dab-əl\ *vb* **dab·bling** \'dab-(ə-)liŋ\ [perh. freq. of *dab*] *vt* **:** to wet by splashing or by little dips or strokes **:** SPATTER **~** *vi* **1 a :** to paddle, splash, or play in or as if in water **b :** to reach with the bill to the bottom of shallow water to obtain food **2 :** to work or concern oneself superficially ⟨~*s* in art⟩
dab·bler \'dab-(ə-)lər\ *n* **:** one that dabbles: as **a :** DILETTANTE **b :** a duck that feeds by dabbling **syn** see AMATEUR
dab·chick \'dab-ˌchik\ *n* [prob. irreg. fr. obs. E *dop* (to dive) + E *chick*] **:** any of several small grebes
da ca·po \dä-'käp-(ˌ)ō, də-\ *adv (or adj)* [It] **:** from the beginning — used as a direction in music to repeat
dace \'dās\ *n, pl* **dace** [ME, fr. MF *dars*, fr. ML *darsus*] **1 :** a small freshwater European cyprinid fish (*Leuciscus leuciscus*) **2 :** any of various small No. American freshwater cyprinid fishes
da·cha \'däch-ə\ *n* [Russ, lit., act of giving] **:** a Russian country house
dachs·hund \'däks-ˌhünt, 'däk-sənt\ *n, pl* **dachs·hunds** *or* **dachs·hun·de** \'däks-ˌhün-də\ [G, fr. *dachs* badger + *hund* dog] **:** a small dog of a breed of German origin with a long body, short legs, and long drooping ears
Da·cron \'dā-ˌkrän, 'dak-ˌrän\ *trademark* **1** — used for a synthetic textile fiber **2 :** a yarn or fabric made of Dacron fiber
dac·tyl \'dak-tᵊl\ *n* [ME *dactile*, fr. L *dactylus*, fr. Gk *daktylos*, lit., finger; fr. the fact that the three syllables have the first one longest like the joints of the finger] **:** a metrical foot consisting of one long and two short syllables or of one stressed and two unstressed syllables (as in *tenderly*) — **dac·tyl·ic** \dak-'til-ik\ *adj or n*
dactyl- *or* **dactylo-** *comb form* [Gk *daktyl-*, *daktylo-*, fr. *daktylos*] **:** finger **:** toe **:** digit ⟨*dactyl*itis⟩
-dac·ty·lous \'dak-tə-ləs\ *adj comb form* [Gk *-daktylos*, fr. *daktylos*] **:** having (such or so many) fingers or toes ⟨di*dactylous*⟩
dac·ty·lus \'dak-tə-ləs\ *n, pl* **dac·ty·li** \-ˌlī, -ˌlē\ [NL, fr. Gk *daktylos* finger, toe] **:** one or more joints of the tarsus of some insects following the enlarged and modified first joint
dad \'dad\ *n* [prob. baby talk] **:** FATHER
da·da \'däd-(ˌ)ä\ *n, often cap* [F] **:** an artistic movement based on deliberate irrationality and negation of the laws of beauty and organization — called also *dadaism* — **da·da·ist** \'dä-ˌdä-əst\ *n, often cap* — **da·da·is·tic** \ˌdä-(ˌ)dä-'is-tik\ *adj, often cap*
dad·dy \'dad-ē\ *n* **:** FATHER
dad·dy long·legs \ˌdad-ē-'lȯŋ-ˌlegz, -ˌlägz\ *n pl but sing or pl in constr* **:** any of various animals with long slender legs: as **a :** CRANE FLY **b :** HARVESTMAN
¹da·do \'dād-(ˌ)ō\ *n, pl* **da·does** [It, die, plinth] **1 a :** the part of a pedestal of a column between the base and the surbase **b :** the lower part of an interior wall when specially decorated or faced; *also* **:** the decoration adorning this part of a wall **2 :** a groove made by dadoing **3 :** a tool for dadoing

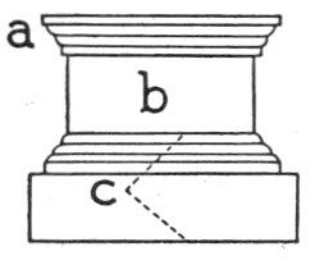

dado: *a* surbase, *b* dado, *c* base

²dado *vt* **1 :** to provide with a dado **2 a :** to set into a groove **b :** to cut a rectangular groove in
Dae·da·lian \di-'dāl-yən\ *or* **Dae·da·lean** \di-'dāl-yən, ˌded-ᵊl-'ē-ən\ *adj* **:** of, relating to, or suggesting Daedalus
Daed·a·lus \'ded-ᵊl-əs\ *n* [L, fr. Gk *Daidalos*] **:** the builder of the Cretan labyrinth according to Greek legend and inventor of wings whereby he and his son Icarus escape imprisonment
daemon *var of* DEMON
daff *vt* [alter. of *doff*] **1** *archaic* **:** to thrust aside **2** *obs* **:** DOFF
daf·fo·dil \'daf-ə-ˌdil\ *n* [prob. fr. D *de affodil* the asphodel, fr. *de* the (fr. MD) + *affodil* asphodel, fr. MF *afrodille*, fr. L *asphodelus*; akin to OHG *thaz* the — more at THAT, ASPHODEL] **:** any of various bulbous herbs (genus *Narcissus*); *esp* **:** a plant whose flowers have a large corona elongated into a trumpet
daf·fy \'daf-ē\ *adj* [obs. E *daff*, n. (fool)] *slang* **:** CRAZY, FOOLISH
daft \'daft\ *adj* [ME *dafte* gentle, stupid] **1 a :** SILLY, FOOLISH **b :** MAD, INSANE **2** *Scot* **:** frivolously gay — **daft·ly** \'daft-lē\ *adv* — **daft·ness** \'daf(t)-nəs\ *n*
dag \'dag\ *n* [ME *dagge*] **1 :** a hanging end or shred **2 :** matted or manure-coated wool
dag·ger \'dag-ər\ *n* [ME] **1 :** a short weapon for stabbing **2 a :** something that resembles a dagger **b :** a mark † used typically to designate a reference or a death date
da·guerre·o·type \də-'ger-(ē-)ə-ˌtīp\ *n* [F *daguerreotype*, fr. L. J. M. *Daguerre* †1851 F painter + F *-o-* + *type*] **:** an early photograph produced on a silver or a silver-covered copper plate; *also* **:** the process of producing such pictures — **daguerreotype** *vt* — **da·guerre·o·typy** \də-'ger-(ē-)ə-ˌtī-pē\ *n*
dah \'dä\ *n* [imit.] **:** a dash in radio or telegraphic code
dahl·ia \'dal-yə, 'däl-\ *n* [NL, genus name, fr. Anders *Dahl* †1789 Sw botanist] **:** any of a genus (*Dahlia*) of American tuberous-rooted composite herbs having opposite pinnate leaves and rayed flower heads and including many that are cultivated as ornamentals
dai·li·ness \'dā-lē-nəs\ *n* **:** the quality or state of being daily
¹dai·ly \'dā-lē\ *adj* **1 a :** occurring, made, or acted upon every day **b :** issued every day or every weekday **c :** of or providing for every day **2 a :** reckoned by the day ⟨average ~ wage⟩ **b :** covering the period of or based on a day ⟨~ statistics⟩
syn DIURNAL, QUOTIDIAN: DAILY is often used in contrast to *nightly* in referring to the ordinary concerns of the day or daytime; it may refer also to weekdays in contrast to holidays and Sundays; DIURNAL is used in contrast to *nocturnal* and is now chiefly in astronomical or poetic use; QUOTIDIAN emphasizes the quality of daily occurrence
²daily *adv* **:** every day **:** every weekday
³daily *n* **:** a newspaper published every weekday
daily double *n* **:** a system of betting on races in which the bettor must pick the winners of two stipulated races in order to win
dai·mon \'dī-ˌmōn\ *n, pl* **dai·mo·nes** \'dī-mə-ˌnēz\ *or* **dai·mons** [Gk *daimōn*] **:** DEMON 1, 3 — **dai·mon·ic** \dī-'män-ik\ *adj*
dai·myo *or* **dai·mio** \'dī-mē-ˌō\ *n* [Jap *daimyō*] **:** a Japanese feudal baron
dain·ti·ly \'dānt-ᵊl-ē\ *adv* **:** in a dainty manner
dain·ti·ness \'dānt-ē-nəs\ *n* **:** the quality or state of being dainty
¹dain·ty \'dānt-ē\ *n* [ME *deinte*, fr. OF *deintié*, fr. L *dignitat-*, *dignitas* dignity, worth] **1 a :** something delicious to the taste **b :** something choice or pleasing **2** *obs* **:** FASTIDIOUSNESS
²dainty *adj* **1 a :** tasting good **:** TASTY **b :** attractively prepared and served **2 :** marked by delicate beauty **3** *obs* **:** CHARY, RELUCTANT **4 a :** marked by fastidious discrimination or finical taste **b :** showing avoidance of anything rough **syn** see CHOICE, NICE
dai·qui·ri \'dī-kə-rē, 'dak-ə-\ *n* [*Daiquirí*, Cuba] **:** a cocktail made of rum, lime juice, and sugar
dairy \'de(ə)r-ē\ *n, often attrib* [ME *deyerie*, fr. *deye* dairymaid, fr. OE *dǣge* kneader of bread; akin to OE *dāg* dough — more at DOUGH] **1 :** a room, building, or establishment where milk is kept and butter or cheese is made **2 a :** the department of farming or of a farm that is concerned with the production of milk, butter, and cheese **b :** a farm devoted to such production **3 :** an establishment for the sale or distribution chiefly of milk and milk products
dairy breed *n* **:** a cattle breed developed chiefly for milk production
dairy cattle *n pl* **:** cattle of one of the dairy breeds
dairy·ing \'der-ē-iŋ\ *n* **:** the business of operating a dairy
dairy·maid \-ē-ˌmād\ *n* **:** a woman employed in a dairy
dairy·man \-ē-mən, -ˌman\ *n* **:** one who operates a dairy farm or works in a dairy
da·is \'dā-əs, 'dī-\ *n* [ME *deis*, fr. OF, fr. L *discus* dish, quoit — more at DISH] **:** a raised platform usu. above the floor of a hall or large room to give prominence to those occupying it
dai·sy \'dā-zē\ *n* [ME *dayeseye*, fr. OE *dægesēage*, fr. *dæg* day + *ēage* eye] **1 a :** a composite plant (as of the genera *Bellis* or *Chrysanthemum*) having a flower head with well-developed ray flowers usu. arranged in one or a few whorls; *esp* **:** a low European herb (*B. perennis*) with white or pink ray flowers **b :** the flower head of a daisy **2** *slang* **:** a first-rate person or thing
daisy ham *n* **:** a boned and smoked piece of pork from the shoulder
Da·ko·ta \də-'kōt-ə\ *n, pl* **Da·ko·tas** *also* **Dakota** **1 :** a member of a Siouan people of the northern Mississippi valley **2 :** the language of the Dakota people
Da·lai La·ma \ˌdäl-ˌī-'läm-ə\ *n* [Mongolian *dalai* ocean] **:** the spiritual head of Lamaism
dale \'dā(ə)l\ *n* [ME, fr. OE *dæl*; akin to OHG *tal* valley, Gk *tholos* rotunda] **:** VALE, VALLEY
dales·man \'dā(ə)lz-mən\ *n, Brit* **:** one living or born in a dale
da·leth \'däl-ˌeth, -ˌet\ *n* [Heb *dāleth*, fr. *deleth* door] **:** the fourth letter of the Hebrew alphabet — symbol ד
dal·li·ance \'dal-ē-ən(t)s\ *n* **:** an act of dallying: as **a :** PLAY; *esp* **:** amorous play **b :** frivolous action **:** TRIFLING
dal·li·er \'dal-ē-ər\ *n* **:** one that dallies
Dal·lis grass \'dal-əs-\ *n* [perh. alter. of *Dallas*, Texas] **:** a tall tufted tropical perennial grass (*Paspalum dilatatum*) introduced as a pasture and forage grass in the southern U. S.
Dall sheep \'dȯl-\ *or* **Dall's sheep** \'dȯlz-\ *n* [William H. *Dall* †1927 Am naturalist] **:** a large white wild sheep (*Ovis montana dalli* or *O. dalli*) of northwestern No. America
dal·ly \'dal-ē\ *vi* [ME *dalyen*, fr. AF *dalier*] **1 a :** to act playfully; *esp* **:** to play amorously **b :** to deal lightly **:** TOY **2 a :** to waste time **b :** LINGER, DAWDLE **syn** see DELAY, TRIFLE
dal·ma·tian \dal-'mā-shən\ *n, often cap* **:** a large dog of a breed

prob. originating in Dalmatia and having a white short-haired coat with black or brown spots
dal·mat·ic \-'mat-ik\ *n* [LL *dalmatica*, fr. L, fem. of *dalmaticus* Dalmatian, fr. *Dalmatia*] **1 :** an outer vestment worn by a deacon or prelate **2 :** a robe worn by a British sovereign at his coronation
dal se·gno \däl-'sān-(,)yō\ *adv* [It] — used as a direction in music to return to the sign that marks the beginning of a repeat
1**dam** \'dam\ *n* [ME *dam, dame* lady, dam — more at DAME] **:** a female parent — used esp. of a domestic animal
2**dam** *n* [ME] **1 a :** a barrier preventing the flow of water; *esp* **:** a barrier built across a watercourse **b :** a barrier to check the flow of liquid, gas, or air **2 :** a body of water confined by a dam
3**dam** *vt* **dammed; dam·ming 1 :** to provide or restrain with a dam **2 :** to stop up **:** BLOCK
1**dam·age** \'dam-ij\ *n* [ME, fr. OF, fr. *dam* damage, fr. L *damnum*] **1 :** loss or harm resulting from injury to person, property, or reputation **2** *pl* **:** compensation in money imposed by law for loss or injury **3 :** EXPENSE, COST
2**damage** *vt* **:** to cause damage to **syn** see INJURE
dam·ag·ing *adj* **:** causing or able to cause damage **:** INJURIOUS — **dam·ag·ing·ly** \'dam-i-jiŋ-lē\ *adv*
1**dam·a·scene** \'dam-ə-,sēn, ,dam-ə-'\ *n* **1** *cap* **:** a native or inhabitant of Damascus **2 :** DAMASK 2b
2**damascene** *adj* **1** *cap* **:** of, relating to, or characteristic of Damascus or the Damascenes **2 :** of or relating to damask or the art of damascening
3**damascene** *vt* [MF *damasquiner*, fr. *damasquin* of Damascus] **:** to ornament (as iron or steel) with wavy patterns like those of watered silk or with inlaid work of precious metals
Da·mas·cus steel \də-,mas-kə(s)-\ *n* **:** hard elastic steel ornamented with wavy patterns and used esp. for sword blades
1**dam·ask** \'dam-əsk\ *n* [ME *damaske*, fr. ML *damascus*, fr. *Damascus*] **1 :** a firm lustrous reversible figured fabric made of various fibers and used esp. for household linen **2 a :** DAMASCUS STEEL **b :** the characteristic markings of such steel **3 :** a grayish red
2**damask** *adj* **1 :** made of or resembling damask or Damascus steel **2 :** of the color damask
damask rose *n* [obs. *Damask* of Damascus, fr. obs. *Damask* Damascus] **:** a large hardy fragrant pink rose (*Rosa damascena*) that is cultivated in Asia Minor as a source of attar of roses and is a parent of many hybrid perpetual roses
dame \'dām\ *n* [ME, fr. OF, fr. L *domina*, fem. of *dominus* master; akin to L *domus* house — more at TIMBER] **1 :** a woman of rank, station, or authority: as **a** *archaic* **:** the mistress of a household **b :** the wife or daughter of a lord **c :** a female member of an order of knighthood — used as a title prefixed to the given name **2 a :** an elderly woman **b** *slang* **:** WOMAN
dame's violet *n* **:** a Eurasian perennial plant (*Hesperis matronalis*) widely cultivated for its spikes of showy, single or double, and fragrant white or purple flowers — called also *dame's rocket*
dam·mar *or* **dam·ar** *also* **dam·mer** \'dam-ər\ *n* [Malay *damar*] **1 :** any of various hard resins derived esp. from evergreen trees (genus *Agathis*) of the pine family **2 :** a clear to yellow resin obtained in Malaya from several timber trees (family Dipterocarpaceae) and used in varnishes and inks
1**damn** \'dam\ *vb* [ME *dampnen*, fr. OF *dampner*, fr. L *damnare*, fr. *damnum* damage, loss, fine] *vt* **1 :** to condemn to a punishment or fate; *specif* **:** to condemn to hell **2 a :** to condemn as invalid, illegal, or immoral **b :** to condemn as a failure by public criticism **3 :** to bring ruin on **4 :** to swear at **:** CURSE ~ *vi* **:** CURSE, SWEAR **syn** see EXECRATE — **damn·ing·ly** \'dam-iŋ-lē\ *adv*
2**damn** *n* **1 :** the utterance of the word *damn* as a curse **2 :** something of little value
3**damn** *adj (or adv)* **:** DAMNED
dam·na·ble \'dam-nə-bəl\ *adj* **1 :** liable to or deserving condemnation **2 :** very bad **:** EXECRABLE ⟨~ weather⟩ — **dam·na·ble·ness** *n* — **dam·na·bly** \-blē\ *adv*
dam·na·tion \dam-'nā-shən\ *n* **1 :** the act of damning **2 :** the state of being damned
dam·na·to·ry \'dam-nə-,tōr-ē, -,tȯr-\ *adj* **:** expressing, imposing or causing condemnation **:** CONDEMNATORY
1**damned** \'damd\ *adj* **damned·er** \'dam-dər\ **damned·est** *or* **damnd·est** \-dəst\ **1 :** DAMNABLE **2 :** COMPLETE, UTTER **3 :** EXTRAORDINARY — used in the superlative
2**damned** \'dam(d)\ *adv* **:** EXTREMELY, VERY
dam·ni·fy \'dam-nə-,fī\ *vt* **:** to cause loss or damage to
Dam·o·cles \'dam-ə-,klēz\ *n* [L, fr. Gk *Damoklēs*] **:** a courtier of ancient Syracuse held to have been seated at a banquet beneath a sword hung by a single hair
Da·mon \'dā-mən\ *n* [L, fr. Gk *Damōn*] **:** a Sicilian who pledges his life for his friend Pythias
1**damp** \'damp\ *n* [MD or MLG, vapor; akin to OHG *damph* vapor, OE *dim* dim] **1 :** a noxious gas esp. in a coal mine **2 :** MOISTURE: **a :** DAMPNESS, HUMIDITY **b** *archaic* **:** FOG, MIST **3 a :** DISCOURAGEMENT, CHECK **b** *archaic* **:** DEPRESSION, DEJECTION
2**damp** *vt* **1 a :** to affect with a noxious gas **:** CHOKE **b** (1) **:** DEPRESS, DEJECT (2) **:** RESTRAIN, CHECK **c :** to check the vibration or oscillation of **2 :** DAMPEN ~ *vi* **:** to diminish progressively in vibration or oscillation
3**damp** *adj* **1 a** *archaic* **:** DAZED, STUPEFIED **b :** DEJECTED, DEPRESSED **2 :** slightly or moderately wet **syn** see WET — **damp·ish** \'dam-pish\ *adj* — **damp·ly** *adv* — **damp·ness** *n*
damp·en \'dam-pən, 'damp-ᵊm\ *vb* **damp·en·ing** \'damp-(ə-)niŋ\ *vt* **1 :** to check or diminish the activity or vigor of **:** DEADEN **2 :** to make damp **3 :** DAMP 1c ~ *vi* **1 :** to become damp **2 :** to become deadened or depressed — **damp·en·er** \'damp-(ə-)nər\ *n*
damp·er \'dam-pər\ *n* **:** one that damps: as **a :** a valve or plate (as in the flue of a furnace) for regulating the draft **b :** a small felted block to stop the vibration of a piano string **c :** a device designed to bring a mechanism to rest with minimum oscillation
damp·ing–off \,dam-piŋ-'ȯf\ *n* **:** a diseased condition of seedlings or cuttings caused by fungi and marked by wilting and rotting
dam·sel \'dam-zəl\ *or* **dam·o·sel** *or* **dam·o·zel** \'dam-ə-,zel\ *n* [ME *damesel*, fr. OF *dameisele*, fr. (assumed) VL *domnicella* young noblewoman, dim. of L *domina* lady] **:** a young woman: **a** *archaic* **:** a young unmarried woman of high birth **b :** GIRL, MAIDEN
dam·sel·fly \-,flī\ *n* **:** any of numerous insects (suborder Zygoptera) distinguished from dragonflies by laterally projecting eyes and petiolate wings folded above the body when at rest
dam·son \'dam-zən\ *n* [ME, fr. L *prunum damascenum*, lit., plum of Damascus] **:** an Asiatic plum (*Prunus insititia* or *P. domestica insititia*) cultivated for its small acid purple fruit; *also* **:** its fruit
1**Dan** \'dan\ *n* [Heb *Dān*] **:** a son of Jacob and ancestor of one of the tribes of Israel
2**Dan** \,dan\ *n* [ME, title of members of religious orders, fr. MF, fr. ML *domnus*, fr. L *dominus* master] *archaic* **:** MASTER, SIR
Dan·aë \'dan-ə-,ē\ *n* [L, fr. Gk *Danaē*] **:** the mother of Perseus visited by Zeus as a shower of gold during her imprisonment
1**dance** \'dan(t)s\ *vb* [ME *dauncen*, fr. OF *dancier*] *vi* **1 :** to perform a rhythmic and patterned succession of bodily movements usu. to music **2 :** to move quickly up and down or about ~ *vt* **1 :** to perform or take part in as a dancer **2 :** to cause to dance **3 :** to bring into a specified condition by dancing — **danc·er** *n*
2**dance** *n, often attrib* **1 :** an act or instance of dancing **2 :** a social gathering for dancing **3 :** a piece of music by which dancing may be guided **4 :** the art of dancing
dan·de·li·on \'dan-dᵊl-,ī-ən\ *n* [MF *dent de lion*, lit., lion's tooth] **:** a yellow-flowered composite plant (genus *Taraxacum*); *esp* **:** an herb (*T. officinale*) sometimes grown as a potherb and nearly cosmopolitan as a weed
dan·der \'dan-dər\ *n* [alter. of *dandruff*] **1 :** minute scales from hair, feathers, or skin that may be allergenic **2 :** ANGER, TEMPER
dan·di·a·cal \dan-'dī-ə-kəl\ *adj* [1*dandy* + *-acal* (as in *demoniacal*)] **:** of, relating to, or suggestive of a dandy — **dan·di·a·cal·ly** \-ə-k(ə-)lē\ *adv*
Dan·die Din·mont \,dan-dē-'din-,mänt\ *n* [*Dandie Dinmont*, character owning 2 such dogs in the novel *Guy Mannering* by Sir Walter Scott] **:** a terrier of a breed characterized by short legs, a long body, pendulous ears, a rough coat, and a full silky topknot
dan·di·fy \'dan-di-,fī\ *vt* **:** to make characteristic of a dandy
dan·dle \'dan-dᵊl\ *vt* **dan·dling** \-(d)liŋ, -dᵊl-iŋ\ [origin unknown] **1 :** to move up and down in one's arms or on one's knee in affectionate play **2 :** PAMPER, PET
dan·druff \'dan-drəf\ *n* [prob. fr. *dand-* (origin unknown) + *-ruff*, of Scand origin; akin to ON *hrūfa* scab; akin to OHG *hruf* scurf, Lith *kraupus* rough] **:** a scurf that forms on the scalp and comes off in small white or grayish scales — **dan·druffy** \-ē\ *adj*
1**dan·dy** \'dan-dē\ *n* [prob. short for *jack-a-dandy*, fr. 1*jack* + *a* (of) + *dandy* (origin unknown)] **1 :** a man unduly attentive to dress **2 :** something excellent in its class **3 :** a small 2-masted sailboat with a modified ketch rig — **dan·dy·ish** \-dē-ish\ *adj*
2**dandy** *adj* **1 :** of, relating to, or suggestive of a dandy **:** FOPPISH **2 :** very good **:** FIRST-RATE
dan·dy·ism \'dan-dē-,iz-əm\ *n* **1 :** the style or conduct of a dandy **2 :** a literary and artistic style of the latter part of the 19th century marked by artificiality and preciosity
Dane \'dān\ *n* [ME *Dan*, fr. ON *Danr*] **1 :** a native or inhabitant of Denmark **2 :** a person of Danish descent
dane·geld \'dān-,geld\ *n, often cap* **:** an annual tax believed to have been imposed orig. to buy off Danish invaders in England or to maintain forces to oppose them but continued as a land tax
Dane·law \'dān-,lȯ\ *n* **1 :** the law in force in the part of England held by the Danes in pre-Conquest times **2 :** the part of England under the Danelaw
dan·ger \'dān-jər\ *n* [ME *daunger*, fr. OF *dangier*, alter. of *dongier*, fr. (assumed) VL *dominiarium*, fr. L *dominium* ownership] **1 a** *archaic* **:** JURISDICTION **b** *obs* **:** REACH, RANGE **2** *obs* **:** HARM, DAMAGE **3 :** exposure or liability to injury, pain, or loss **4 :** a case or cause of danger — **danger** *vt, archaic*
dan·ger·ous \'dānj-(ə-)rəs\ *adj* **1 :** exposing to or involving danger **2 :** able or likely to inflict injury — **dan·ger·ous·ly** *adv* — **dan·ger·ous·ness** *n*
syn HAZARDOUS, PRECARIOUS, PERILOUS, RISKY: DANGEROUS applies to something that may cause harm or loss unless dealt with carefully; HAZARDOUS implies great and continuous risk of harm or failure and small chance of successfully avoiding disaster; PRECARIOUS suggests both insecurity and uncertainty; PERILOUS strongly implies the immediacy of danger; RISKY often applies to a known and accepted danger
1**dan·gle** \'daŋ-gəl\ *vb* **dan·gling** \-g(ə-)liŋ\ [prob. of Scand origin; akin to Dan *dangle* to dangle] *vi* **1 :** to hang loosely esp. with a swinging motion **2 :** to be a hanger-on or dependent **3 :** to occur in a sentence without having a normally expected syntactic relation to the rest of the sentence ~ *vt* **1 :** to cause to dangle **:** SWING **2 :** to keep hanging uncertainly — **dan·gler** \-g(ə-)lər\ *n* — **dan·gling·ly** \-g(ə-)liŋ-lē\ *adv*
2**dangle** *n* **1 :** the action of dangling **2 :** something that dangles
Dan·iel \'dan-yəl\ *n* [Heb *Dānī'ēl*] **:** a Hebrew prophet captive in Babylon
da·nio \'dā-nē-,ō\ *n* [NL, genus name] **:** any of several small brightly colored Asiatic cyprinid fishes
1**Dan·ish** \'dā-nish\ *adj* **:** of, relating to, or characteristic of Denmark, the Danes, or the Danish language
2**Danish** *n* **:** the Germanic language of the Danes
Danish pastry *n* **:** a pastry made of yeast-raised dough
dank \'daŋk\ *adj* [ME *danke*] **:** unpleasantly moist or wet **syn** see WET — **dank·ly** *adv* — **dank·ness** *n*
dan·seuse \däⁿ-'sə(r)z, dän-'süz\ *n* [F] **:** a female ballet dancer
1**Dan·te·an** \'dant-ē-ən\ *adj* [*Dante* Alighieri †1321 It poet] **:** DANTESQUE
2**Dantean** *n* **:** a student or admirer of Dante
Dan·tesque \dan-'tesk\ *adj* **:** of, relating to, or characteristic of Dante or his writings
Daph·ne \'daf-nē\ *n* [L, fr. Gk *daphnē*] **1 :** a nymph transformed into a laurel tree to escape the pursuing Apollo **2** [NL, genus name, fr. L, laurel, fr. Gk *daphnē*] **:** any of a genus (*Daphne*) of Eurasian shrubs of the mezereon family with apetalous flowers whose colored calyx resembles a corolla
Daph·nis \'daf-nəs\ *n* [L, fr. Gk] **:** a Sicilian shepherd held in Greek legend to be the inventor of pastoral poetry

dap·per \'dap-ər\ *adj* [ME *dapyr,* fr. MD *dapper* quick, strong; akin to OHG *tapfar* heavy, OSlav *debelŭ* thick] **1 a :** NEAT, TRIM **b :** excessively spruce and stylish **2 :** alert and lively in movement and manners — **dap·per·ly** *adv* — **dap·per·ness** *n*

1dapple *n* **1 :** any of numerous usu. cloudy and rounded spots or patches of a color or shade different from their background **2 :** the quality or state of being dappled **3 :** a dappled animal

2dapple *vb* **dap·pling** \'dap-(ə-)liŋ\ *vt* **:** to mark with dapples ~ *vi* **:** to become marked with dapples

darb \'därb\ *n* [perh. alter. of 5*dab*] *slang* **:** something superlative

Dar·by and Joan \,där-bē-ən-'jō(-ə)n, -jō-'an\ *n* [prob. fr. *Darby & Joan,* couple in an 18th cent. song] **:** a happily married usu. elderly couple

Dard \'därd\ *n* **:** a complex of Indic languages spoken in the upper valley of the Indus — called also *Dardic*

Dar·dan \'därd-ᵊn\ *adj* [L *Dardanus,* fr. Gk *Dardanos*] *archaic* **:** TROJAN — **Dardan** *n* — **Dar·da·ni·an** \där-'dā-nē-ən\ *adj*

1dare \'da(ə)r, 'de(ə)r\ *vb* [ME *dar* (1st & 3d sing. pres. indic.), fr. OE *dear;* akin to OHG *gitar* (1st & 3d sing. pres. indic.) dare, L in*festus* hostile] *verbal auxiliary* **:** to be sufficiently courageous to ⟨no one *dared* say a word⟩ ~ *vi* **:** to have sufficient courage ~ *vt* **1 a :** to challenge to perform an action esp. as a proof of courage ⟨I ~ you⟩ **b :** to confront boldly **2 :** to have the courage to contend against, venture, or try — **dar·er** \'dar-ər, 'der-\ *n*

2dare *n* **1 :** an act or instance of daring **:** CHALLENGE **2 :** imaginative or vivacious boldness **:** DARING

1dare·dev·il \'da(ə)r-,dev-əl, 'de(ə)r-\ *n* **:** a recklessly bold person — **dare·dev·il·ry** \-əl-rē\ *n* — **dare·dev·il·try** \-əl-trē\ *n*

2daredevil *adj* **:** recklessly daring **syn** see ADVENTUROUS

dareful *adj, obs* **:** DARING

dare·say \da(ə)r-'sā, de(ə)r-\ *vt* **:** venture to say **:** BELIEVE — used in pres. 1st sing. ~ *vi* **:** SUPPOSE, AGREE — used in pres. 1st sing.

1dar·ing *adj* **:** venturesomely bold — **syn** see ADVENTUROUS — **dar·ing·ly** \-iŋ-lē\ *adv* — **dar·ing·ness** *n*

2daring *n* **:** venturesome boldness

Dar·jee·ling \där-'jē-liŋ\ *n* [*Darjeeling,* India] **:** a tea of high quality grown esp. in the mountainous districts of northern India

1dark \'därk\ *adj* [ME *derk,* fr. OE *deorc;* akin to OHG *tarchannen* to hide, Gk *thrassein* to trouble] **1 a :** devoid or partially devoid of light **:** not receiving, reflecting, transmitting, or radiating light **b :** transmitting only a portion of light **2 a :** wholly or partially black **b** *of a color* **:** of low or very low lightness **3 a :** arising from or showing evil traits or desires **:** EVIL **b :** GLOOMY, ANGRY **c :** lacking knowledge or culture **4 :** not clear to the understanding **5 :** not fair **:** SWARTHY **6 :** SECRET **7 :** possessing depth and richness — **dark·ish** \'där-kish\ *adj* — **dark·ly** *adv* — **dark·ness** *n*
syn DIM, DUSKY, MURKY, GLOOMY: DARK, the general term, implies utter or virtual lack of illumination; DIM suggests too weak a light for things to be seen clearly or distinctly; DUSKY suggests deep twilight and close approach to darkness; MURKY implies a heavy darkness such as that caused by smoke, fog, or dust in air or mud in water; GLOOMY implies the serious interference with the normal radiation of daylight caused by dense clouds and connotes cheerlessness and pessimism **syn** see in addition OBSCURE

2dark *n* **1 a :** absence of light **:** DARKNESS **b :** a place or time of little or no light **:** NIGHT, NIGHTFALL **2 :** a dark or deep color

3dark *vi, obs* **:** to grow dark ~ *vt* **:** to make dark

dark adaptation *n* **:** the phenomena including dilatation of the pupil, increase in retinal sensitivity, shift of the region of maximum luminosity toward the blue, and regeneration of visual purple by which the eye adapts to conditions of reduced illumination — **dark-adapt·ed** \,där-kə-'dap-təd\ *adj*

Dark Ages *n pl* **:** the period from about A.D. 476 to about 1000; *broadly* **:** MIDDLE AGES

dark·en \'där-kən\ *vb* **dark·en·ing** \'därk-(ə-)niŋ\ *vi* **:** to grow dark **:** become obscured ~ *vt* **1 :** to make dark **2 :** to make less clear **:** OBSCURE **3 :** TAINT, TARNISH **4 :** to cast a gloom over **5 :** to make of darker color — **dark·en·er** \'därk-(ə-)nər\ *n*

dark–field microscope *n* **:** ULTRAMICROSCOPE

dark horse *n* **:** a racehorse or other contestant whose ability is not known or whose chances of success are not good

dark lantern *n* **:** a lantern that can be closed to conceal the light

dar·kle \'där-kəl\ *vi* **dar·kling** \-k(ə-)liŋ\ [back-formation fr. *darkling*] **1 :** to become concealed in the dark **2 a :** to grow dark **b :** to become clouded or gloomy

1dark·ling \'där-kliŋ\ *adv* [ME *derkelyng,* fr. *derk* dark + *-lyng* -ling] **:** in the dark

2dark·ling *adj* **1 :** DARK **2 :** done or taking place in the dark

darkling beetle *n* **:** a usu. hard-bodied black sluggish terrestrial plant-eating beetle (family Tenebrionidae)

dark·room \'där-,krüm, -,krům\ *n* **:** a room with no light or with a safelight for handling and processing light-sensitive materials

dark·some \'därk-səm\ *adj* **:** gloomily somber **:** DARK

1dar·ling \'där-liŋ\ *n* [ME *derling,* fr. OE *dēorling,* fr. *dēore* dear] **1 :** a dearly loved person **2 :** FAVORITE

2darling *adj* **1 :** dearly loved **:** FAVORITE **2 :** very pleasing **:** CHARMING — **dar·ling·ly** \-liŋ-lē\ *adv* — **dar·ling·ness** *n*

1darn \'därn\ *vb* [prob. fr. F dial. *darner*] *vt* **1 :** to mend with interlacing stitches **2 :** to embroider by filling in with long running or interlacing stitches ~ *vi* **:** to do darning — **darn·er** *n*

2darn *n* **:** a place that has been darned

3darn *vb* [euphemism] **:** DAMN — **darned** *adj* (*or adv*)

4darn *adj* (*or adv*) **:** DAMNED

5darn *n* **:** 2DAMN 2

dar·nel \'därn-ᵊl\ *n* [ME] **:** any of several usu. weedy grasses (genus *Lolium*)

darning needle *n* **1 :** a long needle with a large eye for use in darning **2 :** DRAGONFLY, DAMSELFLY

1dart \'därt\ *n* [ME, fr. MF, of Gmc origin; akin to OHG *tart* dart] **1 a** *archaic* **:** a light spear **b** (1) **:** a small missile usu. with a shaft pointed at one end and feathered on the other (2) *pl but sing in constr* **:** a game in which darts are thrown at a target **2 a :** something projected with sudden speed; *esp* **:** a sharp glance **b :** something causing a sudden pain **3 :** something with a slender pointed shaft or outline; *specif* **:** a stitched tapering fold in a garment **4 :** a quick movement

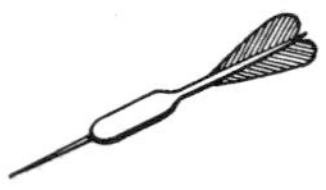

dart 1b(1)

2dart *vt* **1 :** to throw with a sudden movement **2 :** to thrust or move with sudden speed ~ *vi* **:** to move suddenly or rapidly

dart·er \'därt-ər\ *n* **1 :** SNAKEBIRD **2 :** any of numerous small American freshwater fishes closely related to the perches

Dar·win·ian \där-'win-ē-ən\ *adj* **:** of or relating to Charles Darwin, his theories, or his followers — **Darwinian** *n*

Dar·win·ism \'där-wə-,niz-əm\ *n* **:** a theory of the origin and perpetuation of new species of animals and plants by a process of natural selection that tends to perpetuate adaptive variations; *broadly* **:** biological evolutionism — **Dar·win·ist** \-wə-nəst\ *n* — **darwinist** *or* **dar·win·is·tic** \,där-wə-'nis-tik\ *adj, often cap*

1dash \'dash\ *vb* [ME *dasshen*] *vt* **1 :** to knock, hurl, or thrust violently **2 :** to break by striking or knocking **3 :** SPLASH, SPATTER **4 a :** DESTROY, RUIN **b :** DEPRESS, SADDEN **c :** to make ashamed **5 :** to affect by mixing in something different **6 :** to perform or finish hastily ~ *vi* **:** to move violently or rapidly **:** SMASH

2dash *n* **1 a** *archaic* **:** BLOW **b** (1) **:** a sudden burst or splash (2) **:** the sound produced by such a burst **2 a :** a stroke of a pen **b :** a punctuation mark — used esp. to indicate a break in the thought or structure of a sentence **3 :** a small usu. distinctive addition **4 :** conspicuous display **5 :** animation in style and action **6 a :** a sudden onset, rush, or attempt **b :** a short fast race **7 :** a long click or buzz forming a letter or part of a letter **8 :** DASHBOARD 2

dash·board \'dash-,bō(ə)rd, -,bȯ(ə)rd\ *n* **1 :** a screen on the front of a vehicle to intercept water, mud, or snow **2 :** a panel extending across an automobile or airplane below the windshield and usu. containing dials and controls

dash·er \'dash-ər\ *n* **1 :** a dashing person **2 :** one that dashes

dash·ing *adj* **1 :** marked by vigorous action **2 :** marked by smartness esp. in dress and manners — **dash·ing·ly** \-iŋ-lē\ *adv*

das·sie \'däs-ē\ *n* [Afrik] **:** a hyrax (genus *Procavia*) of southern Africa

das·tard \'das-tərd\ *n* [ME] **:** COWARD; *esp* **:** one who sneakingly commits malicious acts

das·tard·li·ness \-lē-nəs\ *n* **:** COWARDICE, TREACHERY

das·tard·ly \-lē\ *adj* **:** treacherously cowardly **syn** see COWARDLY

dasy·ure \'das-ē-,yů(ə)r\ *n* [deriv. of Gk *dasys* thick with hair + *oura* tail] **:** any of a genus (*Dasyurus*) of arboreal carnivorous marsupial mammals of Australia and Tasmania resembling martens

data *pl of* DATUM

dat·able *or* **date·able** \'dāt-ə-bəl\ *adj* **:** capable of being dated

data processing *n* **:** operations for converting (as by computers) crude information into usable or storable form — **data processor** *n*

1da·ta·ry \'dāt-ə-rē\ *n* [ML *datarius* official who added dates to papal letters, fr. LL *data* date of a letter] **:** the cardinal who is head of the datary

2datary *n* **:** an office of the Roman curia charged esp. with investigating the fitness of candidates for papal benefices

1date \'dāt\ *n* [ME, fr. OF, deriv. of L *dactylus,* fr. Gk *daktylos,* lit., finger] **1 :** the oblong edible fruit of a palm (*Phoenix dactylifera*) **2 :** the tall palm with pinnate leaves that yields the date

2date *n* [ME, fr. MF, fr. LL *data,* fr. *data* (as in *data Romae* given at Rome), fem. of L *datus,* pp. of *dare* to give; akin to Gk *didonai* to give] **1 a :** the time at which an event occurs **b :** a statement of the time of execution or making **2 :** DURATION **3 :** the period of time to which something belongs **4 a :** an appointment for a specified time; *esp* **:** a social engagement between two persons of opposite sex **b :** a person of the opposite sex with whom one has a social engagement — **to date :** up to the present moment

3date *vt* **1 :** to determine the date of **2 :** to record the date of **3 a :** to mark with characteristics typical of a particular period **b :** to show up plainly the age of **4 :** to make or have a date with ~ *vi* **1 :** to reckon chronologically **2 :** to become dated and written **3 a :** ORIGINATE **b :** EXTEND **4 :** to show qualities typical of a past period — **dat·er** \'dāt-ər\ *n*

date·less \'dāt-ləs\ *adj* **1 :** ENDLESS **2 :** having no date **3 :** too ancient to be dated **4 :** TIMELESS

date·line \'dāt-,līn\ *n* **1 :** a line in an article or other publication giving the date and place of composition or issue **2** *usu* **date line :** a hypothetical line approximately along the 180th meridian designated as the place where each calendar day begins — **dateline** *vt*

1da·tive \'dāt-iv\ *adj* [ME *datif,* fr. L *dativus,* fr. *datus*] **1 :** of, relating to, or being the grammatical case that marks typically the indirect object of a verb, the object of some prepositions, or a possessor **2 :** formed by contribution of a pair of electrons by one atom

2dative *n* **:** a dative case or form — **da·tive·ly** *adv*

da·tum \'dāt-əm, 'dat-, 'dät-\ *n* [L, fr. neut. of *datus*] **1** *pl* **da·ta** \-ə\ **:** something given or admitted esp. as a basis for reasoning or inference **2 da·ta** \-ə\ *pl but sing or pl in constr* **:** factual material used as a basis esp. for discussion or decision **:** INFORMATION **3** *pl* **datums :** something used as a basis for calculating or measuring

da·tu·ra \də-'t(y)ůr-ə\ *n* [NL, genus name, fr. Hindi *dhatūrā* jimsonweed] **:** any of a genus (*Datura*) of widely distributed strong-scented herbs, shrubs, or trees of the nightshade family

1daub \'dȯb, 'däb\ *vb* [ME *dauben,* fr. OF *dauber*] *vt* **1 :** to cover or coat with soft adhesive matter **:** PLASTER **2 :** to coat with a dirty substance **3 a :** to apply coloring material crudely to **b :** to apply crudely ~ *vi* **1** *archaic* **:** to put on a false exterior **2 :** to apply colors crudely — **daub·er** *n*

2daub *n* **1 :** material used to daub walls **2 :** an act or instance of daubing **3 :** something daubed on **:** SMEAR **4 :** a crude picture

1daugh·ter \'dȯt-ər\ *n* [ME *doughter,* fr. OE *dohtor;* akin to OHG *tohter* daughter, Gk *thygatēr*] **1 a** (1) **:** a human female having the relation of child to parent (2) **:** a female offspring of a lower animal **b :** a human female having a specified ancestor or belonging to a group of common ancestry **2 :** something derived from its origin as if feminine **3 :** an atomic species that is the immediate product of the radioactive decay of a given element

2daughter *adj* **1 :** having the characteristics or relationship of a daughter **2 :** being offspring of the first generation ⟨~ cell⟩

daugh·ter–in–law \-ə-rən-,lȯ, -ərn-,lȯ\ *n, pl* **daugh·ters–in–law** \-ər-zən-\ **:** the wife of one's son

daunt \'dȯnt, 'dänt\ *vt* [ME *daunten,* fr. OF *danter,* alter. of *donter,* fr. L *domitare* to tame, fr. *domitus,* pp. of *domare* — more at TAME] **:** to lessen the courage of **:** INTIMIDATE **syn** see DISMAY

daunt·less \'dȯnt-ləs, 'dänt-\ *adj* **:** FEARLESS, UNDAUNTED — **daunt·less·ly** *adv* — **daunt·less·ness** *n*

dau·phin \'dȯ-fən\ *n, often cap* [MF *dalfin,* fr. OF, title of lords of the Dauphiné, fr. *Dalfin,* a surname] **:** the eldest son of a king of France

dau·phine \dȯ-ˈfēn\ *n, often cap* [F] **:** the wife of the dauphin
dav·en·port \ˈdav-ən-ˌpō(ə)rt, ˈdav-ᵊm-, -ˌpȯ(ə)rt\ *n* [origin unknown] **:** a large upholstered sofa
Da·vid \ˈdā-vəd\ *n* [Heb *Dāwīdh*] **:** a son of Jesse of Bethlehem who kills Goliath, charms Saul with his harping, and reigns over Israel for about 40 years
da·vit \ˈdā-vət, ˈdav-ət\ *n* [prob. fr. the name *David*] **:** a crane that projects over the side of a ship or a hatchway and is used esp. for boats, anchors, or cargo
Da·vy Jones \ˌdā-vē-ˈjōnz\ *n* **:** the spirit of the sea
Da·vy Jones's locker \ˈdā-vē-ˌjōnz(-əz)-\ *n* **:** the bottom of the ocean
Da·vy lamp \ˌdā-vē-\ *n* [Sir Humphry *Davy* †1829 E chemist] **:** an early safety lamp having the flame enclosed by fine wire gauze

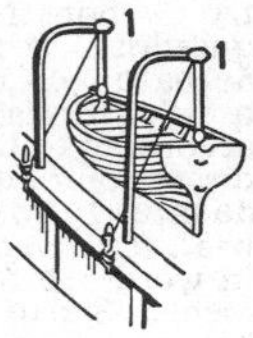

davits 1, 1

[1]**daw** \ˈdȯ, ˈdȯ\ *vi* [ME *dawen*, fr. OE *dagian;* akin to OHG *tagēn* to dawn, OE *dæg* day] *chiefly Scot* **:** DAWN
[2]**daw** \ˈdȯ\ *n* [ME *dawe;* akin to OHG *taha* jackdaw] **:** JACKDAW
daw·dle \ˈdȯd-ᵊl\ *vb* **daw·dling** \ˈdȯd-liŋ, -ᵊl-iŋ\ [origin unknown] *vi* **1 :** to spend time idly **2 :** to act sluggishly ~ *vt* **:** IDLE **syn** see DELAY — **daw·dler** \ˈdȯd-lər, ᵊl-ər\ *n*
[1]**dawn** \ˈdȯn, ˈdän\ *vi* [ME *dawnen*, prob. back-formation fr. *dawning* daybreak, alter. of *dawing*, fr. OE *dagung*, fr. *dagian*] **1 :** to begin to grow light as the sun rises **2 :** to begin to appear or develop **3 :** to begin to be perceived or understood
[2]**dawn** *n* **1 :** the first appearance of light in the morning **2 :** a first appearance **:** BEGINNING
day \ˈdā\ *n* [ME, fr. OE *dæg;* akin to OHG *tag* day] **1 a :** the time of light between one night and the next **b :** DAYLIGHT **2 a :** the period of the earth's rotation on its axis **b :** the time required by a celestial body to turn once on its axis **3 :** the mean solar day of 24 hours beginning at mean midnight **4 :** a specified day or date **5 :** a specified time or period **:** AGE **6 :** the conflict or contention of the day **7 :** the time established by usage or law for work
Day·ak \ˈdī-ˌak\ *n* [Malay, up-country] **1 :** a member of any of several Indonesian peoples of the interior of Borneo **2 :** the language of the Dayak peoples
day·bed \ˈdā-ˌbed\ *n* **1 :** a chaise longue of a type made 1680–1780 **2 :** a couch with low head and foot pieces
day·book \ˈdā-ˌbu̇k\ *n* **1 :** DIARY, JOURNAL **2 :** a book formerly used in accounting for recording the transactions of the day
day·break \ˈdā-ˌbrāk\ *n* **:** DAWN
[1]**day·dream** \ˈdā-ˌdrēm\ *n* **:** a dream experienced while awake; *esp* **:** a pleasant reverie usu. of wish fulfillment
[2]**daydream** *vi* **:** to have a daydream — **day·dream·er** \-ˌdrē-mər\ *n*
day laborer *n* **:** one who works for daily wages esp. as an unskilled laborer
day letter *n* **:** a telegram sent during the day that has a lower priority than a regular telegram
[1]**day·light** \ˈdā-ˌlīt\ *n* **1 :** the light of day **2 :** DAWN **3 a :** knowledge or understanding of something that has been obscure **b :** OPENNESS **4** *pl* **a :** CONSCIOUSNESS **b :** WITS
[2]**daylight** *vt* **:** to provide with daylight ~ *vi* **:** to supply daylight
daylight saving time *n* **:** time usu. one hour ahead of standard time
day lily *n* **1 :** any of various Eurasian plants (genus *Hemerocallis*) of the lily family with short-lived flowers resembling lilies that are widespread in cultivation and as escapes **2 :** PLANTAIN LILY
day neutral *adj* **:** developing and maturing regardless of relative length of alternating exposures to light and dark periods
day nursery *n* **:** a public center for the care and training of young children; *specif* **:** NURSERY SCHOOL
Day of Atonement : YOM KIPPUR
days \ˈdāz\ *adv* **:** in the daytime repeatedly **:** on any day
day school *n* **:** an elementary or secondary school held on weekdays; *specif* **:** a private school without boarding facilities
days of grace : the days allowed for payment of a note or insurance premium after it becomes due
day·star \ˈdā-ˌstär\ *n* **1 :** MORNING STAR **2 :** SUN 1a
day·time \ˈdā-ˌtīm\ *n* **:** the time during which there is daylight
daze \ˈdāz\ *vt* [ME *dasen*, fr. ON *dasa* (in *dasask* to become exhausted)] **1 :** to stupefy esp. by a blow **:** STUN **2 :** to dazzle with light — **daze** *n* — **daz·ed·ness** \-zəd-nəs\ *n*
daz·zle \ˈdaz-əl\ *vb* **daz·zling** \ˈdaz-(ə-)liŋ\ [freq. of [1]*daze*] *vi* **1 :** to lose clear vision esp. from looking at bright light **2 :** to shine brilliantly ~ *vt* **1 :** to overpower with light **2 :** to impress deeply, overpower, or confound with brilliance — **dazzle** *n* — **daz·zler** \-(ə-)lər\ *n* — **daz·zling·ly** \-(ə-)liŋ-lē\ *adv*
D day *n* [*D*, abbr. for *day*] **:** a day set for launching an operation
DDT \ˌdē-(ˌ)dē-ˈtē\ *n* [*d*ichloro-*d*iphenyl-*t*richloro-ethane] **:** a colorless odorless water-insoluble crystalline insecticide $C_{14}H_9Cl_5$
de- *prefix* [ME, fr. OF *de-, des-*, partly fr. L *de-* from, down, away (fr. *de*) and partly fr. L *dis-;* L *de* akin to OIr *di* from, OE *tō* to — more at TO, DIS-] **1 a :** do the opposite of ⟨*de*vitalize⟩ **b :** reverse of ⟨*de*-emphasis⟩ **2 :** remove (a specified thing) from ⟨*de*louse⟩ **:** remove from (a specified thing) ⟨*de*throne⟩ **3 :** reduce ⟨*de*value⟩ **4 :** something derived from (a specified thing) ⟨*de*compound⟩ **:** derived from something (of a specified nature) ⟨*de*nominative⟩ **5 :** get off of (a specified thing) ⟨*de*train⟩
dea·con \ˈdē-kən\ *n* [ME *dekene*, fr. OE *dēacon*, fr. LL *diaconus*, fr. Gk *diakonos*, lit., servant, fr. *dia-* + *-konos* (akin to en*konein* to be active)] **:** a subordinate officer in a Christian church: as **a** (1) **:** a Roman Catholic cleric in the second of the major orders (2) **:** an ordained Anglican candidate for the priesthood **b :** one of the laymen elected by a church with congregational polity to serve in worship, in pastoral care, and on administrative committees **c :** a Mormon in the lowest grade of the Aaronic priesthood
dea·con·ess \ˈdē-kə-nəs\ *n* **:** a woman chosen to assist in church work; *specif* **:** one in a Protestant order devoted to service
de·ac·ti·vate \(ˈ)dē-ˈak-tə-ˌvāt\ *vt* **:** to make inactive or ineffective — **de·ac·ti·va·tion** \(ˌ)dē-ˌak-tə-ˈvā-shən\ *n*
[1]**dead** \ˈded\ *adj* [ME *deed*, fr. OE *dēad;* akin to ON *dauthr* dead, *deyja* to die — more at DIE] **1 :** deprived of life **:** having died **2 a** (1) **:** having the appearance of death **:** DEATHLY ⟨in a ~ faint⟩ (2) **:** lacking power to move, feel, or respond **:** NUMB **b :** very tired **c** (1) **:** incapable of being stirred emotionally or intellectually **:** UNRESPONSIVE ⟨~ to pity⟩ (2) **:** grown cold **:** EXTINGUISHED ⟨~ coals⟩ **3 a :** INANIMATE, INERT ⟨~ matter⟩ **b :** BARREN, INFERTILE ⟨~ soil⟩ **c :** no longer producing or functioning **:** EXHAUSTED ⟨~ battery⟩ **4 a** (1) **:** lacking power or effect ⟨~ law⟩ (2) **:** no longer having interest, relevance, or significance ⟨~ issue⟩ **b :** no longer in use **:** OBSOLETE ⟨~ language⟩ **c :** no longer active **:** EXTINCT ⟨~ volcano⟩ **d :** lacking in gaiety or animation ⟨~ party⟩ **e** (1) **:** lacking in commercial activity **:** QUIET (2) **:** commercially idle or unproductive ⟨~ capital⟩ **f :** lacking elasticity ⟨~ tennis ball⟩ **g :** out of action or out of use; *specif* **:** free from any connection to a source of voltage and free from electric charges **h** (1) **:** out of play ⟨~ ball⟩ ⟨~ cards⟩ (2) *of a player* **:** temporarily forbidden to play or make a certain play **i :** being something that has been used or is not to be used in printing ⟨~ copy⟩ **5 a :** not running or circulating **:** STAGNANT ⟨~ air⟩ **b :** not turning **c :** lacking warmth, vigor, or taste **6 a :** absolutely uniform ⟨~ level⟩ **b** (1) **:** UNERRING (2) **:** EXACT ⟨~ center of the target⟩ (3) **:** DOOMED ⟨~ duck⟩ (4) **:** IRREVOCABLE **c :** ABRUPT **d :** COMPLETE, ABSOLUTE **7 :** DESERTED
syn DEAD, DEFUNCT, DECEASED, DEPARTED, LATE mean devoid of life. DEAD applies literally to what is deprived of vital force but is used figuratively of anything that has lost any attribute (as energy, activity, radiance) suggesting life; DEFUNCT stresses cessation of active existence or operation; DECEASED, DEPARTED, and LATE apply to persons who have died recently, DECEASED occurring chiefly in legal use, DEPARTED in religious use, and LATE with reference to a person in a specific relation or status ⟨his *late* wife⟩
[2]**dead** *n, pl* **dead 1 :** one that is dead — usu. used collectively **2 :** the time of greatest quiet
[3]**dead** *adv* **1 :** UTTERLY **2 :** suddenly and completely **3 :** DIRECTLY
dead–air space *n* **:** a sealed or unventilated air space
[1]**dead·beat** \ˈded-ˌbēt\ *adj* **1 :** making a beat without recoil **2 :** having a pointer that gives a reading with little or no oscillation
[2]**deadbeat** *n* **:** one who persistently fails to pay his debts or his way
dead center *n* **1 :** either of the two positions at the ends of a stroke in a crank and connecting rod when the crank and rod are in the same straight line — called also *dead point* **2 :** a center that does not revolve in a machine tool

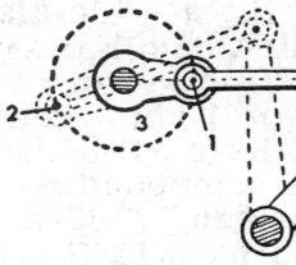

dead center: *1, 2*, dead centers, *3* crank, *4* lever

dead·en \ˈded-ᵊn\ *vb* **dead·en·ing** \ˈded-niŋ, -ᵊn-iŋ\ *vt* **1 :** to impair in vigor or sensation **:** BLUNT **2 a :** to deprive of brilliancy **b :** to make vapid or spiritless **c :** to make (as a wall) impervious to sound **3 :** to deprive of life **:** KILL ~ *vi* **:** to become dead **:** lose life or vigor
dead end *n* **:** an end (as of a street) without an exit
dead–end \ˈded-ˌend\ *adj* **1 :** leading nowhere **2 :** TOUGH
dead·en·ing *n* **:** material used to soundproof walls or floors
dead·eye \ˈded-ˌī\ *n* **:** a rounded wood block that is encircled by a rope or an iron band and pierced with holes to receive the lanyard and is used esp. to set up shrouds and stays
dead·fall \ˈded-ˌfȯl\ *n* **:** a trap so constructed that a weight falls on an animal and kills or disables it
dead hand *n* **1 :** MORTMAIN **2 :** the oppressive influence of the past
[1]**dead·head** \ˈded-ˌhed\ *n* **:** one who has not paid for a ticket
[2]**deadhead** *vi* **:** to make a return trip without a load
dead heat *n* **:** a race in which there is no single winner
dead letter *n* **1 :** something that has lost its force or authority without being formally abolished **2 :** a letter that is undeliverable and unreturnable by the post office
dead·light \ˈded-ˌlīt\ *n* **1 a :** a metal cover or shutter fitted to a port to keep out light and water **b :** a heavy glass set in a ship's deck or hull to admit light **2 :** a skylight made so as not to open
dead·line \ˈded-ˌlīn\ *n* **1 :** a line drawn within or around a prison that a prisoner passes at the risk of being shot **2 :** a date or time before which something must be done; *specif* **:** the time after which copy is not accepted for a particular issue of a publication
dead·li·ness \ˈded-lē-nəs\ *n* **:** the quality or state of being deadly
dead load *n* **:** a constant load that in structures (as a bridge, building, or machine) is due to the weight of the members, the supported structure, and permanent attachments or accessories
dead·lock \ˈded-ˌläk\ *n* **1 :** a state of inaction or neutralization resulting from the opposition of equally powerful persons or factions **2 :** a tie score — **deadlock** *vt*
[1]**dead·ly** \ˈded-lē\ *adj* **1 :** likely to cause or capable of producing death ⟨a ~ disease⟩ ⟨a ~ weapon⟩ **2 a :** aiming to kill or destroy **:** IMPLACABLE ⟨a ~ enemy⟩ **b :** highly effective ⟨~ exposé⟩ **c :** UNERRING ⟨a ~ marksman⟩ **d :** marked by determination or extreme seriousness **3 a :** tending to deprive of force or vitality ⟨a ~ habit⟩ **b :** suggestive of death **4 :** very great **:** EXTREME
syn DEADLY, MORTAL, FATAL, LETHAL mean causing or capable of causing death. DEADLY applies to anything certain or extremely likely to cause death; MORTAL usu. implies that death has already occurred or will soon ensue ⟨received a *mortal* wound⟩ FATAL stresses the inevitability of eventual death, destruction, or utter defeat; LETHAL applies to something having the power of killing as a significant attribute or often as the sole reason for existence
[2]**deadly** *adv* **1** *archaic* **:** in a manner to cause death **:** MORTALLY **2 :** suggesting death **3 :** EXTREMELY ⟨~ dull⟩
deadly sin *n* **:** one of seven sins of pride, covetousness, lust, anger, gluttony, envy, and sloth held to be fatal to spiritual progress
dead march *n* **:** a solemn march for a funeral
dead pan *n* **:** an expressionless immobile face — **deadpan** *adj or adv* — **deadpan** *vi*
dead reckoning *n* **1 :** the determination without the aid of celestial observations of the position of a ship or airplane from the record of the courses sailed or flown, the distance made, and the known or estimated drift **2 :** GUESSWORK
dead space *n* **:** the portion of the respiratory system which is external to the bronchioles and through which air must pass to reach the bronchioles and alveoli
dead·weight \ˈded-ˈwāt\ *n* **:** the unrelieved weight of an inert mass **2 :** DEAD LOAD
dead·wood \ˈded-ˌwu̇d\ *n* **1 :** wood dead on the tree **2 :** useless

personnel or material **3 :** solid timbers built in at the extreme bow and stern of a ship when too narrow to permit framing **4 :** bowling pins that have been knocked down but remain on the alley

deaf \'def\ *adj* [ME *deef*, fr. OE *dēaf;* akin to Gk *typhlos* blind, *typhein* to smoke, L *fumus* smoke — more at FUME] **1 :** lacking or deficient in the sense of hearing **2 :** unwilling to hear or listen — **deaf·ish** \'def-ish\ *adj* — **deaf·ly** *adv* — **deaf·ness** *n*

deaf·en \'def-ən\ *vb* **deaf·en·ing** \'def-(ə-)niŋ\ *vt* **1 :** to make deaf **2 :** to make soundproof ~ *vi* **:** to cause deafness or stun one with noise — **deaf·en·ing·ly** \-(ə-)niŋ-lē\ *adv*

deaf–mute \'def-ˌmyüt\ *n* **:** a deaf person who cannot speak — **deaf–mute** *adj*

1**deal** \'dē(ə)l\ *n* [ME *deel*, fr. OE *dǣl;* akin to OE *dāl* division, portion, OHG *teil* part] **1** *obs* **:** PART, PORTION **2 a :** an indefinite quantity or degree ⟨means a great ~⟩ **b :** a large quantity ⟨a ~ of money⟩ **3 a :** the act or right of distributing cards to players in a card game **b :** HAND 10 b **4 a :** an extensive governmental program — compare NEW DEAL **b :** the period of such a program

2**deal** *vb* **dealt** \'delt\ **deal·ing** \'dē-liŋ\ *vt* **1 :** to give as one's portion **2 :** ADMINISTER, BESTOW ⟨*dealt* him a blow⟩ ~ *vi* **1 :** to distribute the cards in a card game **2 :** to have to do **:** TREAT ⟨the book ~*s* with education⟩ **3 a :** to engage in bargaining **:** TRADE **b :** to sell or distribute something as a business ⟨~ in insurance⟩ **4 :** to take action with regard to someone or something ⟨~ with an offender⟩ **syn** see DISTRIBUTE — **deal·er** *n*

3**deal** *n* **1 :** an act of dealing **:** TRANSACTION **2 :** treatment received ⟨a dirty ~⟩ **3 :** an arrangement for mutual advantage

4**deal** *n* [MD or MLG *dele* plank; akin to OHG *dili* plank — more at THILL] **1 a** *Brit* **:** a board of fir or pine **b :** sawed yellow-pine lumber nine inches or wider and three, four, or five inches thick **2 :** pine or fir wood — **deal** *adj*

de·alate \(ˈ)dē-ˈā-ˌlāt\ *n* **:** a dealated insect

de·alat·ed \-ˌlāt-əd\ *adj* **:** divested of the wings — used of postnuptial adults of insects (as ants) that drop their wings after a nuptial flight — **de·ala·tion** \ˌdē-(ˌ)ā-'lā-shən\ *n*

deal·fish \'dē(ə)l-ˌfish\ *n* [4*deal*] **:** any of several long thin fishes (genus *Trachypterus*) inhabiting the deep sea

deal·ing *n* **1** *pl* **:** INTERCOURSE, TRAFFIC **2 :** manner of conduct

de·am·i·nate \(ˈ)dē-'am-ə-ˌnāt\ *vt* **:** to remove the amino group from (a compound) — **de·am·i·na·tion** \(ˌ)dē-ˌam-ə-'nā-shən\ *n*

de·am·i·nize \(ˈ)dē-'am-ə-ˌnīz\ *vt* **:** DEAMINATE

dean \'dēn\ *n* [ME *deen*, fr. MF *deien*, fr. LL *decanus*, lit., chief of ten, fr. L *decem* ten — more at TEN] **1 a :** the head of the chapter of a collegiate or cathedral church **b :** a priest usu. of one of the parishes who supervises one district of a diocese **2 a :** the head of a division, faculty, college, or school of a university **b :** a college or secondary school administrator in charge of counseling and disciplining students **3 :** DOYEN 1 — **dean·ship** \'dēn-ˌship\ *n*

dean·ery \'dēn-(ə-)rē\ *n* **:** the office, jurisdiction, or official residence of a clerical dean

1**dear** \'di(ə)r\ *adj* [ME *dere*, fr. OE *dēor*] **:** SEVERE, SORE

2**dear** *adj* [ME *dere*, fr. OE *dēore*] **1** *obs* **:** NOBLE **2 :** highly valued **:** PRECIOUS **3 :** AFFECTIONATE, FOND **4 :** high-priced **:** EXPENSIVE **5 :** HEARTFELT **syn** see COSTLY — **dear** *adv* — **dear·ly** *adv* — **dear·ness** *n*

3**dear** *n* **1 :** a loved one **:** SWEETHEART **2 :** a lovable person

dearth \'dərth\ *n* [ME *derthe*, fr. *dere* dear, costly] **1 :** scarcity that makes dear **:** FAMINE **2 :** inadequate supply

dea·sil \'dē-zəl\ *adv* [ScGael *deiseil;* akin to L *dexter*] **:** CLOCKWISE

death \'deth\ *n* [ME *deeth*, fr. OE *dēath;* akin to ON *dauthi* death, *deyja* to die — more at DIE] **1 :** a permanent cessation of all vital functions **:** the end of life **2 :** the cause or occasion of loss of life **3** *cap* **:** the destroyer of life represented usu. as a skeleton with a scythe **4 :** the state of being dead **5 :** DESTRUCTION, EXTINCTION **6 :** CIVIL DEATH **7 :** SLAUGHTER **8** *Christian Science* **:** the lie of life in matter **:** that which is unreal and untrue **:** ILLUSION

death·bed \'deth-'bed\ *n* **1 :** the bed in which a person dies **2 :** the last hours of life

death benefit *n* **:** money payable to the beneficiary of a deceased

death·blow \'deth-'blō\ *n* **:** a destructive or killing stroke or event

death camas *n* **:** any of several plants (genus *Zigadenus*) of the lily family that cause poisoning of livestock in the western U.S.

death cup *n* **:** a very poisonous mushroom (*Amanita phalloides*) ranging in color from pure white to olive or yellow and having a prominent volva at the base

death duty *n, chiefly Brit* **:** DEATH TAX

death·less \'deth-ləs\ *adj* **:** IMMORTAL, IMPERISHABLE ⟨~ fame⟩ — **death·less·ly** *adv* — **death·less·ness** *n*

death·ly \'deth-lē\ *adj* **1 :** FATAL **2 :** of, relating to, or suggestive of death ⟨a ~ pallor⟩ — **deathly** *adv*

death mask *n* **:** a cast taken from the face of a dead person

death point *n* **:** a limit (as of degree of heat or cold) beyond which an organism or living protoplasm cannot survive

death's–head \'deths-ˌhed\ *n* **:** a human skull emblematic of death

deaths·man \'deth-smən\ *n, archaic* **:** EXECUTIONER

death tax *n* **:** a tax arising on the transmission of property after the owner's death

death warrant *n* **1 :** a warrant for the execution of a death sentence **2 :** DEATHBLOW

1**death·watch** \'deth-ˌwäch\ *n* [*death* + *watch* (timepiece); fr. the superstition that its ticking presages death] **:** any of several small insects that make a ticking sound

2**deathwatch** *n* [*death* + *watch* (vigil)] **1 :** a vigil kept with the dead or dying **2 :** the guard set over a criminal before his execution

de·ba·cle \di-'bäk-əl, -'bak-\ *n* [F *débâcle*, fr. *débâcler* to unbar, fr. MF *desbacler*, fr. *des-* de- + *bacler* to bar, fr. OProv *baclar*, fr. (assumed) VL *bacculare*, fr. L *baculum* staff — more at BACTERIUM] **1 :** a tumultuous breakup of ice in a river **2 :** a violent disruption (as of an army) **:** ROUT **3 :** BREAKDOWN, COLLAPSE

de·bar \di-'bär\ *vt* [ME *debarren*, fr. MF *desbarrer* to unbar, fr. *des-* de- + *barrer* to bar] **:** to bar from having or doing something **:** PRECLUDE **syn** see EXCLUDE — **de·bar·ment** \-'bär-mənt\ *n*

de·bark \di-'bärk\ *vb* [MF *debarquer*, fr. *de-* + *barque* bark] **:** DISEMBARK — **de·bar·ka·tion** \ˌdē-ˌbär-'kā-shən\ *n*

de·base \di-'bās\ *vt* **1 :** to lower in status, esteem, quality, or character **2 :** to reduce the intrinsic value of by increasing the base-metal content **b :** to reduce the exchange value of — **de·base·ment** \-'bā-smənt\ *n* — **de·bas·er** \-'bā-sər\ *n*

syn VITIATE, DEPRAVE, CORRUPT, DEBAUCH, PERVERT: DEBASE implies a loss of position, worth, value, or dignity; VITIATE implies a destruction of purity, validity, or effectiveness by allowing entrance of a fault or defect; DEPRAVE implies moral deterioration by evil thoughts or influences; CORRUPT implies loss of soundness, purity, or integrity; DEBAUCH implies a debasing through sensual indulgence; PERVERT implies a twisting or distorting from what is natural or normal **syn** see in addition ABASE

de·bat·able \di-'bāt-ə-bəl\ *adj* **1 :** claimed by more than one country ⟨~ border territory⟩ **2 a :** open to dispute **:** DOUBTFUL ⟨a ~ question⟩ **b :** open to debate **3 :** capable of producing debate

1**de·bate** \di-'bāt\ *n* **:** a contention by words or arguments: as **a :** the formal discussion of a motion before a deliberative body according to the rules of parliamentary procedure **b :** a regulated discussion of a proposition between two matched sides

2**debate** *vb* [ME *debaten*, fr. MF *debatre*, fr. OF, fr. *de-* + *batre* to beat, fr. L *battuere*] *vi* **1** *obs* **:** FIGHT, CONTEND **2 a :** to contend in words **b :** to discuss a question by considering opposed arguments **3 :** to participate in a debate ~ *vt* **1 a :** to argue about **b :** to engage (an opponent) in debate **2 :** to turn over in one's mind **syn** see DISCUSS — **de·bate·ment** \-mənt\ *n* — **de·bat·er** *n*

1**de·bauch** \di-'bȯch, -'bäch\ *vt* [MF *debaucher*, fr. OF *desbauchier* to scatter, roughhew (timber), fr. *des-* de- + *bauch* beam, of Gmc origin] **1 a** *archaic* **:** to make disloyal **b :** to seduce from chastity **2 a :** to lead away from virtue or excellence **b :** to corrupt by intemperance or sensuality **syn** see DEBASE — **de·bauch·er** *n*

2**debauch** *n* **1 :** an act or occasion of debauchery **2 :** ORGY

de·bauch·ee \di-ˌbȯch-'ē, -ˌbäch-; ˌdeb-ə-'shē, -'shā\ *n* [F *débauché*, fr. pp. of *débaucher*] **:** one given to sensual excesses

de·bauch·ery \di-'bȯch-(ə-)rē, -'bäch-\ *n* **1 a :** extreme indulgence in sensuality **b** *pl* **:** ORGIES **2** *archaic* **:** corruption of fidelity

de·ben·ture \di-'ben-chər\ *n* [ME *debentur*, fr. L, they are due, 3d pl. pres. pass. of *debēre* to owe] **1 :** a writing or certificate signed by a public officer as evidence of a debt or of a right to demand a sum of money **2 a** *Brit* **:** a security issued by a company other than its shares **b :** a bond usu. secured by an indenture containing protective provisions but without a specific lien on any asset

de·bil·i·tate \di-'bil-ə-ˌtāt\ *vt* [L *debilitatus*, pp. of *debilitare* to weaken, fr. *debilis*] **:** to impair the strength of **:** ENFEEBLE **syn** see WEAKEN — **de·bil·i·ta·tion** \di-ˌbil-ə-'tā-shən\ *n*

de·bil·i·ty \di-'bil-ət-ē\ *n* [MF *debilité*, fr. L *debilitat-*, *debilitas*, fr. *debilis* weak] **:** WEAKNESS, INFIRMITY

1**deb·it** \'deb-ət\ *n* [L *debitum* debt] **1 :** a record of an indebtedness; *specif* **:** an entry on the left-hand side of an account constituting an addition to an expense or asset account or a deduction from a revenue, net worth, or liability account **2 :** the sum of the items so entered **3 :** a charge against a bank deposit account

2**debit** *vt* **:** to enter on the left-hand side of an account **:** CHARGE

deb·o·nair \ˌdeb-ə-'na(ə)r, -'ne(ə)r\ *adj* [ME *debonere*, fr. OF *debonaire*, fr. *de bonne aire* of good family or nature] **1** *archaic* **:** GENTLE, COURTEOUS **2 a :** gaily charming **:** URBANE **b :** LIGHTHEARTED, NONCHALANT — **deb·o·nair·ly** *adv* — **deb·o·nair·ness** *n*

Deb·o·rah \'deb-(ə-)rə\ *n* [Heb *Dĕbhōrāh*] **:** a Hebrew prophetess who helped free the Israelites from the Canaanites

de·bouch \di-'büsh, -'bau̇ch\ *vb* [F *déboucher*, fr. *dé-* de- + *bouche* mouth, fr. L *bucca* cheek] *vi* **1 :** to march out (as from a defile) into open ground **2 :** to pass out ~ *vt* **:** to cause to emerge

de·bouch·ment \-mənt\ *n* **1 :** the act or process of debouching **2 :** a mouth or outlet esp. of a river

de·bou·chure \di-ˌbü-'shu̇(ə)r\ *n* **:** DEBOUCHMENT 2

de·bride·ment \də-'brēd-ˌmäⁿ, -mənt\ *n* [F *débridement*, fr. *débrider* to remove unhealthy tissue, lit., to unbridle, fr. MF *desbrider*, fr. *des-* de- + *bride* bridle, fr. MHG *brīdel*] **:** the surgical removal of lacerated, devitalized, or contaminated tissue

de·brief \di-'brēf, 'dē-\ *vt* **1 :** to interrogate (as a pilot) in order to obtain useful information **2 :** to instruct not to reveal any classified information after release from a sensitive position

de·bris \də-'brē, 'dā-ˌbrē\ *n, pl* **de·bris** \-'brēz, -ˌbrēz\ [F *débris*, fr. MF, fr. *debriser* to break to pieces, fr. OF *debrisier*, fr. *de-* + *brisier* to break] **1 :** the remains of something broken down or destroyed **:** RUINS **2 :** an accumulation of fragments of rock

debt \'det\ *n* [ME *dette*, *debte*, fr. OF *dette* something owed, fr. (assumed) VL *debita*, fr. L, pl. of *debitum* debt, fr. neut. of *debitus*, pp. of *debēre* to owe, fr. *de-* + *habēre* to have] **1 :** SIN, TRESPASS **2 :** a state of owing **3 :** something owed **:** OBLIGATION **4 :** the common-law action for the recovery of money held to be due

debt·or \'det-ər\ *n* **1 :** one guilty of neglect or violation of duty **2 :** one in debt

de·bunk \(ˈ)dē-'bəŋk\ *vt* **:** to expose the sham or falseness in ⟨~ a hero legend⟩ — **de·bunk·er** *n*

de·but \'dā-ˌbyü, dā-'byü\ *n* [F *début*, fr. *débuter* to begin, fr. MF *desbuter* to play first, fr. *des-* de- + *but* starting point, goal] **1 :** a first public appearance **2 :** a formal entrance into society

deb·u·tant \'deb-yu̇-ˌtänt\ *n* [F *débutant*, fr. prp. of *débuter*] **:** one making a debut

deb·u·tante \'deb-yu̇-ˌtänt\ *n* [F *débutante*, fem. of *débutant*] **:** a young woman making her formal entrance into society

deca- *or* **dec-** *or* **deka-** *or* **dek-** *comb form* [ME, fr. L, fr. Gk *deka-*, *dek-*, fr. *deka* — more at TEN] **:** ten ⟨*deca*merous⟩

de·cade \'dek-ˌād, -əd; de-'kād\ *n* [ME, fr. MF *décade*, fr. LL *decad-*, *decas*, fr. Gk *dekad-*, *dekas*, fr. *deka*] **1 :** a group or set of 10 **2 :** a period of 10 years **3 :** a division of the rosary

de·ca·dence \'dek-əd-ən(t)s, di-'kād-ᵊn(t)s\ *n* [MF, fr. ML *decadentia*, fr. LL *decadent-*, *decadens*, prp. of *decadere* to fall, sink — more at DECAY] **1 :** the process of becoming or the quality or state of being decadent **2 :** a period of decline **syn** see DETERIORATION

1**de·ca·dent** \'dek-əd-ənt, di-'kād-ᵊnt\ *adj* [back-formation fr. *decadence*] **1 :** marked by decay or decline **2 :** of, relating to, or having the characteristics of the decadents — **de·ca·dent·ly** *adv*

2**decadent** *n* **1 :** one that is decadent **2 :** one of a group of late 19th century French and English writers tending toward artificial and abnormal subjects and subtilized style

deca·gon \'dek-ə-ˌgän\ *n* [NL *decagonum*, fr. Gk *dekagōnon*, fr. *deka-* deca- + *-gōnon* -gon] **:** a polygon of 10 angles and 10 sides

deca·gram \-ˌgram\ *n* [F *décagramme*, fr. *déca-* deca- + *gramme* gram] — see METRIC SYSTEM table

deca·he·dron \ˌdek-ə-'hē-drən\ *n* [ISV] **:** a polyhedron of 10 faces

de·cal \'dē-ˌkal, di-'kal, 'dek-əl\ *n* **:** DECALCOMANIA

de·cal·ci·fi·ca·tion \(ˌ)dē-ˌkal-sə-fə-'kā-shən\ *n* **:** the removal or loss of calcium or calcium compounds (as from bones or soil)

de·cal·ci·fy \(ˈ)dē-ˈkal-sə-ˌfī\ *vt* [ISV] **:** to remove calcium or calcium compounds from

de·cal·co·ma·nia \di-ˌkal-kə-ˈmā-nē-ə\ *n* [F *décalcomanie*, fr. *décalquer* to copy by tracing (fr. *dé-* de- + *calquer* to trace, fr. It *calcare*, lit., to trample, fr. L) + *manie* mania, fr. LL *mania* — more at CAULK] **1 :** the art or process of transferring pictures and designs from specially prepared paper (as to glass) **2 :** a picture or design prepared for transfer by decalcomania

de·ca·les·cence \ˌdē-kə-ˈles-ᵊn(t)s\ *n* [ISV *de-* + *-calescence* (as in *recalescence*)] **:** a decrease in temperature that occurs while heating metal through a range in which change in structure occurs

deca·li·ter \ˈdek-ə-ˌlēt-ər\ *n* [F *décalitre*, fr. *déca-* + *litre* liter] — see METRIC SYSTEM table

deca·logue \ˈdek-ə-ˌlȯg, -ˌläg\ *n* [ME *decaloge*, fr. LL *decalogus*, fr. Gk *dekalogos*, fr. *deka-* + *logos* word] **1** *often cap* **:** TEN COMMANDMENTS **2 :** a basic set of rules carrying binding authority

1**de·cam·e·ter** \de-ˈkam-ət-ər\ *n* [Gk *dekametron*, fr. *deka-* + *metron* measure, meter] **:** a poetic line of 10 feet

2**deca·me·ter** \ˈdek-ə-ˌmēt-ər\ *n* [F *décamètre*, fr. *déca-* + *mètre* meter] — see METRIC SYSTEM table

de·camp \di-ˈkamp\ *vi* [F *décamper*, fr. MF *descamper*, fr. *des-* de- + *camper* to camp] **1 :** to break up a camp **2 :** to depart suddenly **:** ABSCOND — **de·camp·ment** \-mənt\ *n*

dec·ane \ˈdek-ˌān\ *n* [ISV *deca-*] **:** any of several isomeric liquid hydrocarbons $C_{10}H_{22}$ of the methane series

dec·a·no·ic acid \ˌdek-ə-ˌnō-ik-\ *n* [ISV, fr. *decane*] **:** CAPRIC ACID

de·cant \di-ˈkant\ *vt* [NL *decantare*, fr. L *de-* + ML *cantus* side, fr. L, iron ring round a carriage wheel] **1 :** to pour from one vessel into another **2 :** to draw off without disturbing the sediment or the lower liquid layers — **de·can·ta·tion** \ˌdē-ˌkan-ˈtā-shən\ *n*

de·cant·er \di-ˈkant-ər\ *n* **:** a vessel used to decant or to receive decanted liquids

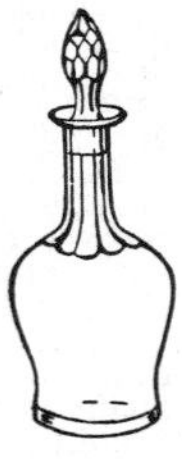
decanter

de·cap·i·tate \di-ˈkap-ə-ˌtāt\ *vt* [LL *decapitatus*, pp. of *decapitare*, fr. L *de-* + *capit-*, *caput* head — more at HEAD] **:** to cut off the head of **:** BEHEAD — **de·cap·i·ta·tion** \di-ˌkap-ə-ˈtā-shən, ˌdē-\ *n*

deca·pod \ˈdek-ə-ˌpäd\ *n* [NL *Decapoda*, order name] **1 :** any of an order (Decapoda) of highly organized crustaceans (as shrimps, lobsters, crabs) with five pairs of thoracic appendages one or more of which are modified into pincers, stalked eyes, and the head and thorax fused into a cephalothorax and covered by a carapace **2 :** any of an order (Decapoda) of cephalopod mollusks including the cuttlefishes, squids, and related forms that have 10 arms — **decapod** *adj* — **de·cap·o·dal** \di-ˈkap-əd-ᵊl\ *adj* — **de·cap·o·dan** \-əd-ən\ *adj or n* — **de·cap·o·dous** \-əd-əs\ *adj*

de·car·bon·ate \(ˈ)dē-ˈkär-bə-ˌnāt\ *vt* **:** to remove carbon dioxide or carbonic acid from — **de·car·bon·a·tion** \(ˌ)dē-ˌkär-bə-ˈnā-shən\ *n*

de·car·bon·ize \(ˈ)dē-ˈkär-bə-ˌnīz\ *vt* [ISV] **:** to remove carbon from

de·car·box·yl·ate \ˌdē-ˌkär-ˈbäk-sə-ˌlāt\ *vt* **:** to remove carboxyl from — **de·car·box·yl·a·tion** \ˌdē-ˌkär-ˌbäk-sə-ˈlā-shən\ *n*

de·car·bu·rize \(ˈ)dē-ˈkär-b(y)ə-ˌrīz\ *vt* **:** DECARBONIZE

dec·are \ˈdek-ˌa(ə)r, -ˌe(ə)r, -ˌär\ *n* [F *décare*, fr. *déca-* deca- + *are*] **:** a metric unit of area equal to 10 ares or 0.2471 acre

deca·stere \ˈdek-ə-ˌsti(ə)r, -ˌste(ə)r\ *n* [F *décastère*, fr. *déca-* + *stère* stere] — see METRIC SYSTEM table

1**deca·syl·lab·ic** \ˌdek-ə-sə-ˈlab-ik\ *adj* [prob. fr. F *décasyllabique*, fr. Gk *dekasyllabos* decasyllabic, fr. *deka-* deca- + *syllabē* syllable] **:** having verses of 10 syllables

2**decasyllabic** *n* **:** a line of 10 syllables

decasyllable *n* **:** a word or verse having 10 syllables

de·cath·lon \di-ˈkath-lən, -ˌlän\ *n* [F *décathlon*, fr. *déca-* deca- + Gk *athlon* contest — more at ATHLETE] **:** a 10-event composite athletic contest consisting of the 100-meter, 400-meter, and 1500-meter runs, the 110-meter high hurdles, the javelin and discus throws, shot put, pole vault, high jump, and broad jump

1**de·cay** \di-ˈkā\ *vb* [ME *decayen*, fr. ONF *decaïr*, fr. LL *decadere* to fall, sink, fr. L *de-* + *cadere* to fall] *vi* **1 :** to decline from a sound or prosperous condition **2 :** to decrease gradually in quantity, activity, or force **3 :** to fall into ruin **4 :** to decline in health, strength, or vigor **5 :** to undergo decomposition ~ *vt* **1** *obs* **:** to cause to decay **:** IMPAIR **2 :** to destroy by decomposition

syn DECAY, DECOMPOSE, ROT, PUTREFY, SPOIL mean to undergo destructive dissolution. DECAY implies a slow change from a state of soundness or perfection; DECOMPOSE stresses a breaking down by chemical change and when applied to organic matter a corruption; ROT is a close synonym of DECOMPOSE and often connotes foulness; PUTREFY implies the rotting of animal matter and offensiveness to sight and smell; SPOIL applies chiefly to the decomposition of foods

2**decay** *n* **1 :** gradual decline in strength, soundness, or prosperity or in degree of excellence or perfection **2 :** a wasting or wearing away **:** RUIN **3** *obs* **:** DESTRUCTION, DEATH **4 a :** ROT; *specif* **:** aerobic decomposition of proteins chiefly by bacteria **b :** the product of decay **5 :** a decline in health or vigor **6 :** decrease in quantity, activity, or force: as **a :** spontaneous decrease in the number of radioactive atoms in radioactive material **b :** spontaneous disintegration (as of an atom or a meson)

de·cease \di-ˈsēs\ *n* [ME *deces*, fr. MF, fr. L *decessus* departure, death, fr. *decessus*, pp. of *decedere* to depart, die, fr. *de-* + *cedere* to go — more at CEDE] **:** departure from life **:** DEATH — **decease** *vi*

de·ceased \-ˈsēst\ *n, pl* **deceased :** a dead person ⟨the will of the ~⟩

de·ce·dent \di-ˈsēd-ᵊnt\ *n* [L *decedent-*, *decedens*, prp. of *decedere*] **:** a deceased person

de·ceit \di-ˈsēt\ *n* [ME *deceite*, fr. OF, fr. L *decepta*, fem. of *deceptus*, pp. of *decipere*] **1 :** the act or practice of deceiving **:** DECEPTION **2 :** an attempt or device to deceive **:** TRICK **3 :** DECEITFULNESS

de·ceit·ful \-fəl\ *adj* **:** having a tendency or disposition to deceive: **a :** not honest ⟨lying, ~ child⟩ **b :** DECEPTIVE, MISLEADING **syn** see DISHONEST — **de·ceit·ful·ly** \-fə-lē\ *adv* — **de·ceit·ful·ness** *n*

de·ceiv·able \di-ˈsē-və-bəl\ *adj* **1** *archaic* **:** DECEITFUL, DECEPTIVE **2** *archaic* **:** capable of being deceived — **de·ceiv·able·ness** *n*

de·ceive \di-ˈsēv\ *vb* [ME *deceiven*, fr. OF *deceivre*, fr. L *decipere*, fr. *de-* + *capere* to take] *vt* **1** *archaic* **:** ENSNARE **2 a** *obs* **:** to be false to **b** *archaic* **:** to fail to fulfill **3** *obs* **:** CHEAT **4 :** to cause to believe an untruth **5** *archaic* **:** to while away ~ *vi* **:** to practice deceit — **de·ceiv·er** *n* — **de·ceiv·ing·ly** \-ˈsē-viŋ-lē\ *adv*

syn MISLEAD, DELUDE, BEGUILE: DECEIVE implies the imposing of a false idea or belief that causes bewilderment or helplessness or furthers the agent's purpose; MISLEAD stresses a leading astray from the truth usu. by deliberately deceiving; DELUDE and BEGUILE stress the action of the one deceived, DELUDE implying an inability to distinguish between the true and the false, BEGUILE a readiness to be charmed or persuaded by the deceiver

de·cel·er·ate \(ˈ)dē-ˈsel-ə-ˌrāt\ *vb* [*de-* + *accelerate*] *vt* **:** to cause to slow down ~ *vi* **:** to move at decreasing speed — **de·cel·er·a·tion** \(ˌ)dē-ˌsel-ə-ˈrā-shən\ *n* — **de·cel·er·a·tor** \(ˈ)dē-ˈsel-ə-ˌrāt-ər\ *n*

de·cel·er·on \dē-ˈsel-ə-ˌrän\ *n* [blend of *decelerate* and *aileron*] **:** a combination of aileron and air brakes on an airplane

De·cem·ber \di-ˈsem-bər\ *n* [ME *Decembre*, fr. OF, fr. L *December* (tenth month), fr. *decem* ten — more at TEN] **:** the 12th month of the Gregorian calendar

De·cem·brist \-brəst\ *n* **:** one taking part in the unsuccessful uprising against the Russian emperor Nicholas I in December 1825

de·cem·vir \di-ˈsem-vər\ *n* [L, back-formation fr. *decemviri*, pl., fr. *decem* + *viri*, pl. of *vir* man — more at VIRILE] **:** one of a ruling body of 10; *specif* **:** one of a body of 10 magistrates in ancient Rome — **de·cem·vi·ral** \-və-rəl\ *adj* — **de·cem·vi·rate** \-rət\ *n*

de·cen·cy \ˈdēs-ᵊn-sē\ *n* **1** *archaic* **a :** FITNESS **b :** ORDERLINESS **2 a :** the quality or state of being decent **:** PROPRIETY **b :** conformity to standards of taste, propriety, or quality **3 :** standard of propriety — usu. used in pl. **4 :** literary decorum **syn** see DECORUM

de·cen·ni·al \di-ˈsen-ē-əl\ *adj* **1 :** consisting of or lasting for 10 years **2 :** occurring or being done every 10 years — **decennial** *n* — **de·cen·ni·al·ly** \-ē-ə-lē\ *adv*

de·cen·ni·um \-ē-əm\ *n, pl* **de·cen·ni·ums** *or* **de·cen·nia** \-ē-ə\ [L, fr. *decem* + *annus* year] **:** a period of 10 years

de·cent \ˈdēs-ᵊnt\ *adj* [MF or L; MF, fr. L *decent-*, *decens*, prp. of *decēre* to be fitting; akin to L *decus* honor, *dignus* worthy, Gk *dokein* to seem, seem good] **1** *archaic* **a :** APPROPRIATE **b :** well-formed **:** HANDSOME **2 a :** conforming to standards of propriety, good taste, or morality **b :** modestly clothed **3 :** free from immodesty or obscenity **4 :** ADEQUATE ⟨~ housing⟩ **5 :** having praiseworthy qualities **syn** see CHASTE — **de·cent·ly** *adv*

de·cen·tral·iza·tion \(ˌ)dē-ˌsen-trə-lə-ˈzā-shən\ *n* **1 :** the dispersion or distribution of functions and powers from a central authority to regional and local authorities **2 :** the redistribution of population and industry from urban centers to outlying areas — **de·cen·tral·ize** \(ˈ)dē-ˈsen-trə-ˌlīz\ *vt*

de·cep·tion \di-ˈsep-shən\ *n* [ME *decepcioun*, fr. MF *deception*, fr. LL *deception-*, *deceptio*, fr. L *deceptus*, pp. of *decipere* to deceive] **1 a :** the act of deceiving **b :** the fact or condition of being deceived **2 :** something that deceives **:** TRICK

syn FRAUD, DOUBLE-DEALING, SUBTERFUGE, TRICKERY: DECEPTION may or may not imply blameworthiness, since it may suggest cheating or merely tactical resource; FRAUD always implies guilt and often criminality in act or practice; DOUBLE-DEALING suggests treachery or at least action contrary to a professed attitude; SUBTERFUGE suggests the adoption of a stratagem or the telling of a lie in order to escape guilt or to gain an end; TRICKERY implies ingenious acts intended to dupe or cheat

de·cep·tive \di-ˈsep-tiv\ *adj* **:** tending or having power to deceive — **de·cep·tive·ly** *adv* — **de·cep·tive·ness** *n*

de·cern \di-ˈsərn\ *vb* [ME *decernen*, fr. MF *decerner*, fr. L *decernere* to decide] **1** *archaic* **:** DECREE **2** *archaic* **:** DISCERN

deci- *comb form* [F *déci-*, fr. L *decimus* tenth, fr. *decem* ten — more at TEN] **:** tenth part ⟨*deci*normal⟩

deci·are \ˈdes-ē-ˌa(ə)r, -ˌe(ə)r, -ˌär\ *n* [F *déciare*, fr. *déci-* + *are*] **:** a metric unit of area equal to 10 square meters or 11.96 square yards

deci·bel \ˈdes-ə-ˌbel, -bəl\ *n* [ISV *deci-* + *bel*] **1 a :** a unit for expressing the ratio of two amounts of electric or acoustic signal power equal to 10 times the common logarithm of this ratio **b :** a unit for expressing the ratio of the magnitudes of two electric voltages or currents or analogous acoustic quantities equal to 20 times the common logarithm of the voltage or current ratio **2 :** a unit for measuring the relative loudness of sounds equal approximately to the smallest degree of difference of loudness ordinarily detectable by the human ear whose range includes about 130 decibels on a scale beginning with 1 for the faintest audible sound

de·cid·able \di-ˈsīd-ə-bəl\ *adj* **:** capable of being decided

de·cide \di-ˈsīd\ *vb* [ME *deciden*, fr. MF *decider*, fr. L *decidere*, lit., to cut off, fr. *de-* + *caedere* to cut] *vt* **1 :** to arrive at a solution that ends uncertainty or dispute about **2 :** to bring to a definitive end ⟨one blow *decided* the fight⟩ **3 :** to induce to come to a choice ~ *vi* **:** to make a choice or judgment — **de·cid·er** *n*

syn DETERMINE, SETTLE, RULE, RESOLVE: DECIDE implies the cutting off of debate, doubt, or wavering; DETERMINE adds the implication of fixing something definitely or unalterably ⟨*decide* to give a dinner; *determine* the guest list⟩ SETTLE implies a decision reached by someone with power to end all dispute or uncertainty; RULE implies a determination by judicial or administrative authority; RESOLVE implies a firm decision to act or refrain esp. after clearing up doubts or uncertainties or difficulties

de·cid·ed *adj* **1 :** UNQUESTIONABLE ⟨a ~ advantage⟩ **2 :** free from doubt or wavering — **de·cid·ed·ly** *adv* — **de·cid·ed·ness** *n*

de·cid·ua \di-ˈsij-ə-wə\ *n, pl* **de·cid·u·ae** \-ˌwē\ [NL, fr. L, fem. of *deciduus*] **1 :** the part of the mucous membrane lining the uterus that in higher placental mammals undergoes special modifications in preparation for and during pregnancy and is cast off at parturition **2 :** the part of the mucous membrane of the uterus cast off in the process of menstruation — **de·cid·u·al** \-wəl\ *adj*

de·cid·u·ate \-wət\ *adj* **:** having the fetal and maternal tissues firmly interlocked so that a layer of maternal tissue is torn away at parturition and forms a part of the afterbirth

de·cid·u·ous \di-ˈsij-ə-wəs\ *adj* [L *deciduus*, fr. *decidere* to fall off, fr. *de-* + *cadere* to fall] **1 :** falling off (as at the end of a growing period or stage of development) **2 :** having deciduous parts **3 :** EPHEMERAL — **de·cid·u·ous·ly** *adv* — **de·cid·u·ous·ness** *n*

deci·gram \ˈdes-ə-ˌgram\ *n* [F *décigramme*, fr. *déci-* + *gramme* gram] — see METRIC SYSTEM table

dec·ile \ˈdes-ˌīl, -əl\ *n* [L *decem* ten — more at TEN] **:** any one of nine numbers in a series dividing the distribution of the individuals in the series into 10 groups of equal frequency; *also* **:** any one of these 10 groups — **decile** *adj*

deci·li·ter \'des-ə-,lēt-ər\ *n* [F *décilitre*, fr. *déci-* + *litre* liter] — see METRIC SYSTEM table
de·cil·lion \di-'sil-yən\ *n, often attrib* [L *decem* + E *-illion* (as in *million*)] — see NUMBER table
1dec·i·mal \'des-ə-məl\ *adj* [(assumed) NL *decimalis*, fr. ML, of a tithe, fr. L *decima* tithe] **:** numbered or proceeding by tens: **a :** based on the number 10 **b :** subdivided into 10th or 100th units **c :** expressed in a decimal fraction — **dec·i·mal·ly** \-mə-lē\ *adv*
2decimal *n* **:** a proper fraction in which the denominator is a power of 10 usu. not expressed but signified by a point placed at the left of the numerator (as .2=2/10, .25=25/100, .025=25/1000)
dec·i·mal·ize \-mə-,līz\ *vt* **:** to reduce to a decimal system
decimal point *n* **:** the dot at the left of a decimal fraction
dec·i·mate \'des-ə-,māt\ *vt* [L *decimatus*, pp. of *decimare*, fr. *decimus* tenth, fr. *decem* ten] **1 :** to select by lot and kill every tenth man of **2 :** to take a tenth from **:** TITHE **3 :** to destroy a large part of — **dec·i·ma·tion** \,des-ə-'mā-shən\ *n*
deci·me·ter \'des-ə-,mēt-ər\ *n* [F *décimètre*, fr. *déci-* deci- + *mètre* meter] — see METRIC SYSTEM table
de·ci·pher \di-'sī-fər\ *vt* **1** *archaic* **:** REVEAL **2 a :** to convert into intelligible form **b :** DECODE **3** *obs* **:** DEPICT **4 :** to make out the meaning of despite indistinctness or obscurity — **de·ci·pher·able** \-f(ə-)rə-bəl\ *adj* — **de·ci·pher·ment** \-fər-mənt\ *n*
de·ci·sion \di-'sizh-ən\ *n* [MF, fr. L *decision-, decisio*, fr. *decisus*, pp. of *decidere* to decide] **1 a :** the act or process of deciding esp. by giving judgment **b :** DETERMINATION, CONCLUSION **2 :** a report of a conclusion **3 :** the quality of being decided **:** FIRMNESS
de·ci·sive \di-'sī-siv\ *adj* **1 :** having the power or quality of deciding **:** CONCLUSIVE **2 :** marked by decision **:** RESOLUTE **syn** see CONCLUSIVE — **de·ci·sive·ly** *adv* — **de·ci·sive·ness** *n*
deci·stere \'des-ə-,sti(ə)r, -,ste(ə)r\ *n* [F *décistère*, fr. *déci-* + *stère* stere] — see METRIC SYSTEM table
1deck \'dek\ *n* [prob. modif. of (assumed) LG *verdeck* (whence G *verdeck*), fr. (assumed) MLG *vordeck*, fr. MLG *vordecken* to cover, fr. *vor-* (akin to OHG *fur-* for-) + *decken* to cover; akin to OHG *decken* to cover — more at THATCH] **1 :** a platform in a ship serving usu. as a structural element and forming the floor for its compartments **2 :** something resembling the deck of a ship: as **a :** the roadway of a bridge **b :** a flat floored roofless area adjoining a house **3 :** a pack of playing cards — **on deck 1 :** ready for duty **2 :** next in line

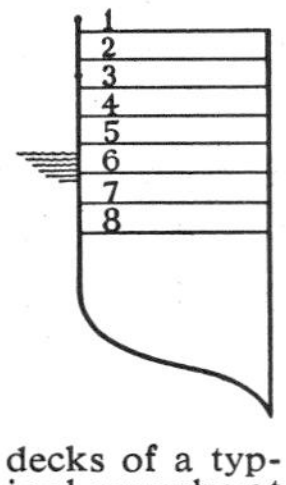

decks of a typical merchant ship, amidships: *1* bridge, *2* boat, *3* promenade, *4* shelter, weather, or superstructure, *5* upper or freeboard, *6* main or second, *7* lower or third, *8* orlop or fourth

2deck *vt* [D *dekken* to cover; akin to OHG *decken*] **1** *obs* **:** COVER **2 a :** to clothe elegantly **:** ARRAY **b :** DECORATE **3** [*1deck*] **:** to furnish with or as if with a deck **syn** see ADORN
deck chair *n* **:** a folding chair often having an adjustable leg rest
deck·er \'dek-ər\ *n* **:** something having a deck or a specified number of levels, floors, or layers
deck·hand \'dek-,hand\ *n* **:** a seaman who performs manual duties
deck·house \'dek-,haůs\ *n* **:** a superstructure on a ship's upper deck
deck·le \'dek-əl\ *n* [G *deckel*, lit., cover, fr. *decken* to cover, fr. OHG] **1 :** a detachable wooden frame around the outside edges of a hand mold used in making paper **2 :** either of the bands that run longitudinally upon the edges of the wire of a paper machine and determine the width of the web
deckle edge *n* **:** the rough untrimmed edge of paper left by a deckle or produced artificially — **deck·le-edged** \,dek-ə-'lejd\ *adj*
de·claim \di-'klām\ *vb* [ME *declamen*, fr. L *declamare*, fr. *de-* + *clamare* to cry out; akin to L *calare* to call] *vi* **1 :** to speak rhetorically; *specif* **:** to recite something as an exercise in elocution **2 :** HARANGUE ~ *vt* **:** to deliver rhetorically; *specif* **:** to recite in elocution — **de·claim·er** *n* — **dec·la·ma·tion** \,dek-lə-'mā-shən\ *n*
de·clam·a·to·ry \di-'klam-ə-,tōr-ē, -,tȯr-\ *adj* **:** of, relating to, or marked by declamation or rhetorical display
de·clar·able \di-'klar-ə-bəl, -'kler-\ *adj* **:** capable of being declared **:** that must be declared
de·clar·ant \-ənt\ *n* **:** one that makes a declaration; *specif* **:** an alien who has declared his intention of becoming a citizen of the U.S. by signing his first papers
dec·la·ra·tion \,dek-lə-'rā-shən\ *n* **1 :** the act of declaring **:** ANNOUNCEMENT **2 a :** the first pleading in a common-law action **b :** a statement made by a party to a legal transaction usu. not under oath **3 a :** something that is declared **b :** the document containing such a declaration **4 a :** MELD **b** (1) **:** the final bid in auction bridge (2) **:** the contract in contract bridge
de·clar·a·tive \di-'klar-ət-iv, -'kler-\ *adj* **:** making a declaration **:** DECLARATORY ⟨~ sentence⟩ — **de·clar·a·tive·ly** *adv*
de·clar·a·to·ry \-ə-,tōr-ē, -,tȯr-\ *adj* **1 :** serving to declare **2 a :** declaring what is the existing law ⟨~ statute⟩ **b :** declaring a legal right or interpretation ⟨a ~ judgment⟩
de·clare \di-'kla(ə)r, -'kle(ə)r\ *vb* [ME *declaren*, fr. MF *declarer*, fr. L *declarare*, fr. *de-* + *clarare* to make clear, fr. *clarus* clear] *vt* **1** *obs* **:** to make clear **2 :** to make known formally or explicitly **3 :** to make evident **:** SHOW **4 :** to state emphatically **:** AFFIRM ⟨~*s* his innocence⟩ **5 :** to make a full statement of (one's taxable or dutiable property) **6 a :** to announce (as a trump suit) in a card game **b :** MELD **7 :** to make payable ~ *vi* **1 :** to make a declaration **2 :** to avow one's support — **de·clar·er** *n*
syn DECLARE, ANNOUNCE, PUBLISH, PROCLAIM, PROMULGATE mean to make known publicly. DECLARE implies explicitness and usu. formality in making known; ANNOUNCE implies the declaration for the first time of something that is of interest or has created speculation; PUBLISH implies making public through print; PROCLAIM implies a publishing clearly, forcefully, and authoritatively; PROMULGATE implies the proclaiming of a dogma, doctrine, or law **syn** see in addition ASSERT
de·class \(')dē-'klas\ *vt* **:** to remove from a class
dé·clas·sé \,dā-,klas-'ā, -,kläs-\ *adj* [F, fr. pp. of *déclasser* to declass] **:** fallen or lowered in class, rank, or social position
de·clas·si·fy \(')dē-'klas-ə-,fī\ *vt* **:** to remove or reduce the security classification of ⟨~ a secret document⟩
de·clen·sion \di-'klen-chən\ *n* [prob. alter. of earlier *declenson*, modif. of MF *declinaison*, fr. LL *declination-, declinatio*, fr. L, grammatical inflection, turning aside, fr. *declinatus*, pp. of *declinare* to inflect, turn aside] **1 a :** noun, adjective, or pronoun inflection esp. in some prescribed order of the forms **b :** a class of nouns or adjectives having the same type of inflectional forms **2 :** a falling off or away **:** DETERIORATION **3 :** DESCENT, SLOPE — **de·clen·sion·al** \-'klench-nəl, -'klen-chən-ᵊl\ *adj*
de·clin·able \di-'klī-nə-bəl\ *adj* **:** capable of declension
dec·li·nate \'dek-lə-,nāt, -nət\ *adj* **:** bent or curved down or aside
dec·li·na·tion \,dek-lə-'nā-shən\ *n* [ME *declinacioun*, fr. MF *declination*, fr. L *declination-, declinatio* turning aside, altitude of the pole] **1 :** angular distance north or south from the celestial equator measured along a great circle passing through the celestial poles **2 :** a turning aside or swerving **3 :** a decline esp. from vigor **4 :** a bending downward **:** INCLINATION **5 :** a formal refusal **6 :** the angle formed between a magnetic needle and the geographical meridian — **dec·li·na·tion·al** \-'nā-shnəl, -shən-ᵊl\ *adj*
1de·cline \di-'klīn\ *vb* [ME *declinen*, fr. MF *decliner*, fr. L *declinare* to turn aside, inflect, fr. *de-* + *clinare* to incline] *vi* **1 :** to turn from a straight course **:** STRAY **2 a :** to slope downward **:** DESCEND **b :** to bend down **:** DROOP **c :** to stoop to what is unworthy **3 a** *of a celestial body* **:** to sink toward setting **b :** to draw toward a close **:** WANE **4 :** to withhold consent ~ *vt* **1 :** to give in prescribed order the grammatical forms of (a noun, pronoun, or adjective) **2** *obs* **a :** AVERT **b :** AVOID **3 :** to cause to bend or bow downward **4 a :** to refuse to undertake, engage in, or comply with **b :** to refuse to accept
syn DECLINE, REFUSE, REJECT, REPUDIATE, SPURN mean to turn away by not accepting, receiving, or considering. DECLINE implies courteous refusal esp. of offers or invitations; REFUSE suggests more positiveness or ungraciousness and often implies the denial of something asked for; REJECT implies a peremptory refusal by sending away or discarding; REPUDIATE implies a casting off or disowning as untrue, unauthorized, or unworthy of acceptance; SPURN stresses contempt or disdain in rejection or repudiation
2decline *n* **1 :** the process of declining: **a :** a gradual physical or mental sinking and wasting away **b :** a change to a lower state or level **2 :** the period during which something is approaching its end **3 :** a downward slope **:** DECLIVITY **4 :** a wasting disease; *esp* **:** pulmonary tuberculosis **syn** see DETERIORATION
de·cliv·i·tous \di-'kliv-ət-əs\ *adj* **:** moderately steep
de·cliv·i·ty \-ət-ē\ *n* [L *declivitat-, declivitas*, fr. *declivis* sloping down, fr. *de-* + *clivus* slope, hill; akin to L *clinare*] **1 :** downward inclination **2 :** a descending slope
de·coct \di-'käkt\ *vt* [L *decoctus*, pp. of *decoquere*, fr. *de-* + *coquere* to cook — more at COOK] **:** to extract the flavor of by boiling
de·coc·tion \-'käk-shən\ *n* **1 :** the act or process of decocting **2 :** an extract obtained by decocting
de·code \(')dē-'kōd\ *vt* **:** to convert (a message in code) from code into ordinary language — **de·cod·er** *n*
de·col·late \di-'käl-,āt\ *vt* [L *decollatus*, pp. of *decollare*, fr. *de-* + *collum* neck] **:** BEHEAD — **de·col·la·tion** \,dē-,kä-'lā-shən\ *n*
dé·col·le·tage \(,)dā-,käl-ə-'täzh, ,dek-lə-'täzh\ *n* [F, action of cutting or wearing a low neckline, fr. *décolleter*] **1 :** the low-cut neckline of a dress **2 :** a décolleté dress
dé·col·le·té \-'tā\ *adj* [F, fr. pp. of *décolleter* to give a low neckline to, fr. *dé-* de- + *collet* collar, fr. OF *colet*, fr. *col* collar, neck, fr. L *collum* neck] **1 :** wearing a strapless or low-necked dress **2 :** having a low-cut neckline
de·col·or·iza·tion \(,)dē-,kəl-(ə-)rə-'zā-shən\ *n* **:** the process of decolorizing
de·col·or·ize \(')dē-'kəl-ə-,rīz\ *vt* **:** to remove color from (as liquids by adsorption on activitated carbon) — **de·col·or·iz·er** *n*
de·com·pen·sate \(')dē-'käm-pən-,sāt, -,pen-\ *vi* [prob. back-formation fr. *decompensation*] **:** to undergo decompensation
de·com·pen·sa·tion \(,)dē-,käm-pən-'sā-shən, -,pen-\ *n* [ISV] **:** loss of compensation; *esp* **:** inability of the heart to maintain adequate circulation
de·com·pose \,dē-kəm-'pōz\ *vb* [F *décomposer*, fr. *dé-* de- + *composer* to compose] *vt* **1 :** to separate into constituent parts or elements or into simpler compounds **2 :** ROT ~ *vi* **:** to break up into constituent elements through chemical change **:** ROT **syn** see DECAY — **de·com·po·si·tion** \(,)dē-,käm-pə-'zish-ən\ *n*
1de·com·pound \(')dē-'käm-,paůnd\ *n* **:** a compound that has a compound as one of its parts
2de·com·pound \'dē-'käm-,paůnd; ,dē-,käm-', -kəm-\ *adj* **1 :** compounded again **2** *of a leaf* **:** having divisions that are themselves compound
de·com·press \,dē-kəm-'pres\ *vt* **:** to release from pressure or compression — **de·com·pres·sion** \-'presh-ən\ *n*
de·con·cen·trate \(')dē-'kän(t)-sən-,trāt, -,sen-\ *vt* **:** DECENTRALIZE
de·con·tam·i·nate \,dē-kən-'tam-ə-,nāt\ *vt* **:** to rid of contamination — **de·con·tam·i·na·tion** \-,tam-ə-'nā-shən\ *n*
de·con·trol \,dē-kən-'trōl\ *vt* **:** to end control of — **decontrol** *n*
de·cor *or* **dé·cor** \dā-'kȯ(ə)r, 'dā-,kȯ(ə)r\ *n* [F *décor*, fr. *décorer* to decorate, fr. L *decorare*] **1 :** DECORATION; *esp* **:** ornamental disposition of accessories in interior decoration **2 :** a stage setting
dec·o·rate \'dek-ə-,rāt\ *vt* [L *decoratus*, pp. of *decorare*, fr. *decor-*, *decus* ornament] **1 :** to add honor to **2 :** to furnish with something ornamental **3 :** to award a mark of honor to **syn** see ADORN
dec·o·ra·tion \,dek-ə-'rā-shən\ *n* **1 :** the act or process of decorating **2 :** ORNAMENT **3 :** a badge of honor (as a U.S. military award)
dec·o·ra·tive \'dek-(ə-)rət-iv, 'dek-ə-,rāt-\ *adj* **:** serving to decorate; *esp* **:** purely ornamental — **dec·o·ra·tive·ly** *adv* — **dec·o·ra·tive·ness** *n*
1dec·o·ra·tor \'dek-ə-,rāt-ər\ *n* **:** one that decorates; *esp* **:** one that designs or executes interiors and their furnishings
2decorator *adj* **:** suitable for interior decoration
de·co·rous \'dek-(ə-)rəs; di-'kōr-əs,' -'kȯr-\ *adj* [L *decorus*, fr. *decor* beauty, grace; akin to L *decēre* to be fitting — more at DECENT] **:** marked by propriety and good taste **:** CORRECT ⟨~ conduct⟩ — **de·co·rous·ly** *adv* — **de·co·rous·ness** *n*
de·cor·ti·cate \(')dē-'kȯrt-ə-,kāt\ *vt* [L *decorticatus*, pp. of *decorticare* to remove the bark from, fr. *de-* + *cortic-, cortex* bark] **:** to peel the outer covering from — **de·cor·ti·ca·tion** \(,)dē-,kȯrt-ə-'kā-shən\ *n* — **de·cor·ti·ca·tor** \(')dē-'kȯrt-ə-,kāt-ər\ *n*
de·co·rum \di-'kōr-əm, -'kȯr-\ *n* [L, fr. neut. of *decorus*] **1 :** literary and dramatic propriety **:** FITNESS **2 :** propriety and good taste in conduct or appearance **3 :** ORDERLINESS **4** *pl* **:** OBSERVANCE, CONVENTION

syn DECENCY, PROPRIETY, DIGNITY, ETIQUETTE: DECORUM suggests conduct according with good taste, often formally prescribed; DECENCY implies behavior according with normal self-respect or humane feeling for others, or with what is fitting to a particular profession or condition in life; PROPRIETY suggests an artificial standard of what is correct in conduct or speech; DIGNITY implies reserve or restraint in conduct prompted less by obedience to a code than by a sense of personal integrity or of social importance; ETIQUETTE is the usual term for the detailed rules governing manners and conduct and for the observance of these rules

1de·coy \di-ˈkȯi, ˈdē-ˌkȯi\ *n* [prob. fr. D *de kooi*, lit., the cage, fr. *de*, masc. def. art. (akin to OE *thæt*, neut. def. article) + *kooi* cage, fr. L *cavea* — more at THAT, CAGE] **1 :** a pond into which wild fowl are lured for capture **2 :** something intended to lure into a trap; *specif* **:** an artificial bird used to attract live birds within shot **3 :** a person used to lead another into a trap

2decoy *vt* **:** to lure by or as if by a decoy **:** ENTICE **syn** see LURE

1de·crease \di-ˈkrēs, ˈdē-ˌkrēs\ *vb* [ME *decreessen*, fr. (assumed) AF *decreistre*, fr. L *decrescere*, fr. *de-* + *crescere* to grow — more at CRESCENT] *vi* **:** to grow less ∼ *vt* **:** to cause to grow less

syn DECREASE, LESSEN, DIMINISH, REDUCE, ABATE, DWINDLE mean to grow or make less. DECREASE suggests a progressive decline in size, amount, numbers, or intensity; LESSEN suggests decline of any sort but is not used with stated numbers; DIMINISH emphasizes a perceptible loss and implies its subtraction from a total; REDUCE implies a bringing down or lowering; ABATE implies a reducing of something excessive or oppressive in force or amount; DWINDLE implies progressive lessening and is applied to things growing visibly smaller usu. to the point of insignificance or disappearance

2de·crease \ˈdē-ˌkrēs, di-ˈkrēs\ *n* **1 :** the process of decreasing **2 :** an amount of diminution

1de·cree \di-ˈkrē\ *n* [ME, fr. MF *decré*, fr. L *decretum*, fr. neut. of *decretus*, pp. of *decernere* to decide, fr. *de-* + *cernere* to sift, decide] **1 :** an order usu. having the force of law **2 a :** a religious ordinance enacted by council or titular head **b :** a foreordaining will **3 a :** a judicial decision of the Roman emperor **b (1) :** a decision or sentence given in a cause by a court **(2) :** JUDGMENT 2a

2decree *vb* **de·creed; de·cree·ing** *vt* **1 :** to command or enjoin by decree ⟨∼ an amnesty⟩ **2 :** to determine or order judicially ⟨∼ a punishment⟩ ∼ *vi* **:** ORDAIN — **de·cre·er** \di-ˈkrē-ər\ *n*

de·cree–law \di-ˈkrē-ˌlȯ\ *n* **:** a decree of a ruler or ministry having the force of a law enacted by the legislature

dec·re·ment \ˈdek-rə-mənt\ *n* [L *decrementum*, fr. *decrescere*] **1 :** gradual decrease **2 a :** the quantity lost by diminution or waste **b :** a negative mathematical increment

de·crep·it \di-ˈkrep-ət\ *adj* [ME, fr. MF, fr. L *decrepitus*] **1 :** wasted and weakened by or as if by the infirmities of old age **2 :** WORN-OUT **3 :** RUN-DOWN **syn** see WEAK — **de·crep·it·ly** *adv*

de·crep·i·tate \di-ˈkrep-ə-ˌtāt\ *vb* [prob. fr. (assumed) NL *decrepitatus*, pp. of *decrepitare*, fr. L *de-* + *crepitare* to crackle — more at CREPITATE] *vt* **:** to roast or calcine (as salt) so as to cause crackling or until crackling stops ∼ *vi* **:** to become decrepitated — **de·crep·i·ta·tion** \di-ˌkrep-ə-ˈtā-shən\ *n*

de·crep·i·tude \di-ˈkrep-ə-ˌt(y)üd\ *n* **:** the quality or state of being decrepit

1de·cre·scen·do \ˌdā-krə-ˈshen-(ˌ)dō\ *adj (or adv)* [It, lit., decreasing, fr. L *decrescendum*, gerund of *decrescere*] **:** diminishing in volume — used as a direction in music

2decrescendo *n* **1 :** a lessening in volume of sound **2 :** a decrescendo musical passage

de·cres·cent \di-ˈkres-ᵊnt\ *adj* [alter. of earlier *decressant*, prob. fr. AF, prp. of (assumed) AF *decreistre* to decrease] **:** DECREASING

de·cre·tal \di-ˈkrēt-ᵊl\ *n* [ME *decretale*, fr. MF, fr. LL *decretalis* of a decree, fr. L *decretum* decree] **:** DECREE; *esp* **:** a papal letter giving an authoritative decision on a point of canon law

de·cre·tive \-ˈkrēt-iv\ *adj* **:** having the force of a decree **:** DECRETORY

de·cre·to·ry \ˈdek-rə-ˌtōr-ē, -ˌtȯr-; di-ˈkrēt-ə-rē\ *adj* **:** relating to or fixed by a decree or decision

de·cri·er \di-ˈkrī(-ə)r\ *n* **:** one that decries

de·cry \di-ˈkrī\ *vt* [F *décrier*, fr. OF *descrier*, fr. *des-* de- + *crier* to cry] **1 :** to depreciate (as a coin) officially or publicly **2 :** to express strong disapproval of ⟨∼ the emphasis on sex⟩

syn DEPRECIATE, DISPARAGE, BELITTLE, MINIMIZE: DECRY implies open condemnation with intent to discredit; DEPRECIATE implies a representing as being of less value than commonly believed; DISPARAGE implies depreciation by indirect means such as slighting or invidious comparison; BELITTLE and MINIMIZE imply depreciation, BELITTLE suggesting usu. a contemptuous or envious attitude, MINIMIZE connoting less personal animus

de·cum·bent \di-ˈkəm-bənt\ *adj* [L *decumbent-*, *decumbens*, prp. of *decumbere* to lie down, fr. *de-* + *-cumbere* to lie down — more at SUCCUMB] **1 :** lying down **2** *of a plant* **:** reclining on the ground but with ascending apex or extremity

dec·u·ple \ˈdek-yə-pəl\ *adj* [F *décuple*, fr. MF, fr. LL *decuplus*, fr. L *decem* ten + *-plus* multiplied by — more at TEN, DOUBLE] **1 :** TENFOLD **2 :** taken in groups of 10

de·cu·ri·on \di-ˈkyu̇r-ē-ən\ *n* [ME *decurioun*, fr. L *decurion-*, *decurio*, fr. *decuria* division of ten, fr. *decem*] **1 :** a Roman cavalry officer in command of 10 men **2 :** a member of a Roman senate

de·curved \(ˈ)dē-ˈkərvd\ *adj* [part trans. of LL *decurvatus*, fr. L *de-* + *curvatus* curved] **:** curved downward **:** bent down

1de·cus·sate \ˈdek-ə-ˌsāt, di-ˈkəs-ˌāt\ *vb* [L *decussatus*, pp. of *decussare*, fr. *decussis* the number ten, numeral X, intersection, fr. *decem* + *ass-*, *as* unit — more at ACE] **:** INTERSECT

2de·cus·sate \ˈdek-ə-ˌsāt, di-ˈkəs-ət\ *adj* **1 :** shaped like an X **2 :** arranged in pairs each at right angles to the next pair above or below ⟨∼ leaves⟩ — **de·cus·sate·ly** *adv*

de·cus·sa·tion \ˌdek-ə-ˈsā-shən, ˌdē-ˌkə-\ *n* **1 :** an intersection in the form of an X **2 :** a band of nerve fibers that connects unlike centers of opposite sides of the central nervous system

de·dans \də-ˈdäⁿ\ *n, pl* **dedans** \-ˈdäⁿ(z)\ [F, lit., interior] **1 :** an open gallery at the service end of the court in court tennis **2 :** the spectators at a court-tennis match

1ded·i·cate \ˈded-i-kət\ *adj* [ME, fr. L *dedicatus*, pp. of *dedicare* to dedicate, fr. *de-* + *dicare* to proclaim, dedicate] **:** DEDICATED

2ded·i·cate \ˈded-i-ˌkāt\ *vt* **1 :** to devote to the worship of a divine being; *specif* **:** to set apart (a church) to sacred uses with solemn rites **2 :** to set apart to a definite use **3 :** to become committed to **4 :** to inscribe or address by way of compliment **5 :** to open to public use **syn** see DEVOTE — **ded·i·ca·tor** \-ˌkāt-ər\ *n*

ded·i·ca·tion \ˌded-i-ˈkā-shən\ *n* **1 :** an act or rite of dedicating to a divine being or to a sacred use **2 :** a setting aside for a particular purpose **3 :** a name and often a message prefixed to a literary, musical, or artistic production in tribute to a person or cause **4 :** self-sacrificing devotion — **ded·i·ca·tive** \ˈded-i-ˌkāt-iv, -kət-\ *adj* — **ded·i·ca·to·ry** \ˈded-i-kə-ˌtōr-ē, -ˌtȯr-\ *adj*

de·dif·fer·en·ti·a·tion \(ˈ)dē-ˌdif-ə-ˌren-chē-ˈā-shən\ *n* **:** reversion of specialized structures (as cells) to a more generalized or primitive condition often as a preliminary to major change

de·duce \di-ˈd(y)üs\ *vt* [L *deducere*, lit., to lead away, fr. *de-* + *ducere* to lead] **1 :** to trace the course of **2 a :** to draw (a conclusion) necessarily from given premises **b :** to infer from a general principle **syn** see INFER — **de·duc·ible** \-ˈd(y)ü-sə-bəl\ *adj*

de·duct \di-ˈdəkt\ *vt* [L *deductus*, pp. of *deducere*] **1 :** to take away (an amount) from a total **:** SUBTRACT **2 :** DEDUCE, INFER — **de·duct·ibil·i·ty** \di-ˌdək-tə-ˈbil-ət-ē\ *n*

de·duct·ible \di-ˈdək-tə-bəl\ *adj* **:** capable of being deducted

de·duc·tion \di-ˈdək-shən\ *n* **1 a :** an act of taking away **b :** the deriving of a conclusion by reasoning; *specif* **:** inference in which the conclusion follows necessarily from the premises **2 a :** a conclusion reached by mental deduction **b :** something that is or may be subtracted ⟨∼*s* from taxable income⟩ **:** ABATEMENT — **de·duc·tive** \-ˈdək-tiv\ *adj* — **de·duc·tive·ly** *adv*

dee \ˈdē\ *n* **:** the letter *d*

1deed \ˈdēd\ *n* [ME *dede*, fr. OE *dǣd*; akin to OE *dōn* to do] **1 :** something done **2 :** FEAT, EXPLOIT **3 :** PERFORMANCE **4 :** a signed and usu. sealed instrument containing some legal transfer, bargain, or contract **syn** see ACTION — **deed·less** \-ləs\ *adj*

2deed *vt* **:** to convey or transfer by deed

deem \ˈdēm\ *vb* [ME *demen*, fr. OE *dēman*; akin to OHG *tuomen* to judge, OE *dōm* doom] *vt* **:** to come to think or judge **:** HOLD ⟨∼*ed* it wise to go slow⟩ ∼ *vi* **:** to have an opinion **:** BELIEVE

1deep \ˈdēp\ *adj* [ME, fr. OE *dēop*; akin to OHG *tiof* deep, OE *dyppan* to dip — more at DIP] **1 :** extending far from some surface or area: as **a :** extending far downward ⟨∼ well⟩ **b (1) :** extending well inward from an outer surface ⟨∼ gash⟩ **(2) :** not located superficially within the body ⟨∼ pressure receptors in muscles⟩ **c :** extending well back from a front surface ⟨a ∼ closet⟩ **d :** extending far laterally from the center ⟨∼ border⟩ **e :** occurring or located near the outer limits of the playing area ⟨hit to ∼ right field⟩ **2 :** having a specified extension downward or backward ⟨shelf 20 inches ∼⟩ **3 a :** difficult to penetrate or comprehend **:** RECONDITE ⟨∼ problem⟩ **b :** MYSTERIOUS, OBSCURE ⟨∼ dark secret⟩ **c :** grave in nature or effect **:** GRIEVOUS ⟨∼*est* disgrace⟩ **d :** WISE ⟨∼ thinker⟩ **e :** ENGROSSED, INVOLVED **f :** very great **:** INTENSE ⟨∼ sleep⟩ **4 a** *of color* **:** high in saturation and low in lightness **b :** having a low musical pitch or pitch range **5 a :** situated well within the boundaries **b :** remote in time or space **c :** being below the level of the conscious **d :** covered, enclosed, or filled to a specified degree — **deep·ly** *adv* — **deep·ness** *n*

syn DEEP, PROFOUND, ABYSMAL mean having great extension downward or inward; applied to physical space they follow a climactic order, DEEP being the general and least emphatic term, PROFOUND adding the implication of great depth or extent, and ABYSMAL of immeasurable depth. DEEP implies the opposite of what is shallow, superficial, simple, or even straightforward; PROFOUND implies reaching to the roots and attaining to what is massive, enduring, unshakable; ABYSMAL applies to what is measureless in extent or degree often with a suggestion of being hopelessly beyond correction or redemption **syn** see in addition BROAD

2deep *adv* **1 :** to a great depth **:** DEEPLY **2 :** far on **:** LATE

3deep *n* **1 :** any of the fathom points on a sounding line that is not a mark **2 a :** a vast or immeasurable extent **:** ABYSS **b (1) :** the extent of surrounding space or time **(2) :** OCEAN **3 :** the most intense or characteristic part ⟨∼ of winter⟩ **4 :** one of the deep portions of any body of water; *specif* **:** a generally long and narrow area in the ocean where the depth exceeds 3000 fathoms

deep·en \ˈdē-pən, ˈdēp-ᵊm\ *vb* **deep·en·ing** \ˈdēp-(ə-)niŋ\ *vt* **:** to make deep or deeper ∼ *vi* **:** to become deeper or more profound

deep–root·ed \ˈdē-ˈprüt-əd, -ˈpru̇t-\ *adj* **:** deeply implanted or established ⟨a ∼ loyalty⟩ **syn** see INVETERATE

deep–sea \ˌdēp-ˌsē\ *adj* **:** of, relating to, occurring in, or for use in the deeper parts of the sea ⟨∼ fishing⟩

deep–seat·ed \ˈdēp-ˈsēt-əd\ *adj* **1 :** situated far below the surface **2 :** firmly established ⟨a ∼ tradition⟩ **syn** see INVETERATE

deep space *n* **:** space well beyond the limits of the earth's atmosphere including space outside the solar system

deer \ˈdi(ə)r\ *n, pl* **deer** [ME, deer, animal, fr. OE *dēor* beast; akin to OHG *tior* wild animal, Skt *dhvaṁsati* he perishes] **1** *obs* **:** ANIMAL **2 :** a ruminant mammal (family Cervidae, the deer family) having two large and two small hoofs on each foot and antlers borne by the males of nearly all and by the females of a few forms

deer·fly \ˈdi(ə)r-ˌflī\ *n* **:** any of numerous small horseflies (as of the genus *Chrysops*) that include important vectors of tularemia

deer·hound \ˈdi(ə)r-ˌhau̇nd\ *n* **:** a large tall slender dog of a breed developed in Scotland and formerly used in hunting deer

deer·skin \ˈdi(ə)r-ˌskin\ *n* **:** leather made from the skin of a deer; *also* **:** a garment of such leather

deer·yard \ˈdi(ə)r-ˌyärd\ *n* **:** a place where deer herd in winter

de–es·ca·late \(ˈ)dē-ˈes-kə-ˌlāt\ *vi* **:** to decrease in extent, volume, or scope ∼ *vt* **:** LIMIT 2 — **de–es·ca·la·tion** \(ˌ)dē-ˌes-kə-ˈlā-shən\ *n*

de·face \di-ˈfās\ *vt* [ME *defacen*, fr. MF *desfacier*, fr. OF, fr. *des-* de- + *face*] **1 :** to destroy or mar the face of **2 :** IMPAIR **3** *obs* **:** DESTROY — **de·face·ment** \-ˈfā-smənt\ *n* — **de·fac·er** *n*

syn DEFACE, DISFIGURE, DISFEATURE mean to mar the appearance of. DEFACE implies superficial injuries (as by scratching, scribbling, or the removal of detail); DISFIGURE suggests deeper and more permanent injuries; DISFEATURE suggests the marring (as by distortion) of something having beauty of outline or contour

1de fac·to \di-ˈfak-(ˌ)tō, dā-\ *adv* [NL] **:** ACTUALLY **:** in reality

2de facto *adj* **1 :** exercising power as if legally constituted ⟨a ∼ government⟩ **2 :** ACTUAL ⟨∼ state of war⟩ — compare DE JURE

de·fal·cate \di-ˈfal-ˌkāt, di-ˈfȯl-, ˈdef-əl-\ *vb* [ML *defalcatus*, pp. of *defalcare*, fr. L *de-* + *falc-*, *falx* sickle] *vt, archaic* **:** CURTAIL ∼ *vi* **:** to engage in embezzlement — **de·fal·ca·tor** \-ˌkāt-ər\ *n*

de·fal·ca·tion \ˌdē-ˌfal-'kā-shən, ˌdē-ˌfȯl-, ˌdef-əl-\ *n* **1** *archaic* **:** DEDUCTION **2 :** EMBEZZLEMENT **3 :** a falling away **:** DEFECTION

def·a·ma·tion \ˌdef-ə-'mā-shən\ *n* **:** the act of defaming another **:** CALUMNY — **de·fam·a·to·ry** \di-'fam-ə-ˌtōr-ē, -ˌtȯr-\ *adj*

de·fame \di-'fām\ *vt* [ME *diffamen, defamen,* fr. MF & L; ME *diffamen* fr. MF *diffamer,* fr. L *diffamare,* fr. *dis-* + *fama* fame; ME *defamen* fr. MF *defamer,* fr. ML *defamare,* fr. L *de-* + *fama*] **1** *archaic* **:** DISGRACE **2 :** to harm the reputation of by libel or slander **3** *archaic* **:** ACCUSE **syn** see MALIGN — **de·fam·er** *n*

1de·fault \di-'fȯlt\ *n* [ME *defaute, defaulte,* fr. OF *defaute,* fr. (assumed) VL *defallita,* fr. fem. of *defallitus,* pp. of *defallere* to be lacking, fail, fr. L *de-* + *fallere* to deceive] **1 :** failure to do something required by duty or law **:** NEGLECT **2** *archaic* **:** FAULT **3 :** a failure to pay financial debts **4 a :** failure to appear at the required time in a legal proceeding **b :** failure to compete in or to finish an appointed contest — **in default of :** in the absence of

2default *vi* **:** to fail to fulfill a contract, agreement, or duty: as **a :** to fail to meet a financial obligation **b :** to fail to appear in court **c :** to fail to compete in or to finish an appointed contest; *also* **:** to forfeit a contest by such failure ~ *vt* **1 :** to fail to perform, pay, or make good **2 :** FORFEIT — **de·fault·er** \-'fȯl-tər\ *n*

de·fea·sance \di-'fēz-ᵊn(t)s\ *n* [ME *defesance,* fr. AF, fr. OF *deffesant,* prp. of *deffaire*] **1 a :** a rendering null or void **b** (1) **:** the termination of a property interest in accordance with stipulated conditions (as in a deed) (2) **:** an instrument stating such conditions of limitation **2 :** DEFEAT, OVERTHROW

de·fea·si·ble \di-'fē-zə-bəl\ *adj* **:** capable of being annulled

1de·feat \di-'fēt\ *vt* [ME *deffeten,* fr. MF *deffait,* pp. of *deffaire* to destroy, fr. ML *disfacere,* fr. L *dis-* + *facere* to do — more at DO] **1** *archaic* **:** DESTROY **2 a :** NULLIFY ⟨~ an estate⟩ **b :** FRUSTRATE ⟨~ a hope⟩ **3 :** to win victory over **:** BEAT **syn** see CONQUER

2defeat *n* **1** *archaic* **:** DESTRUCTION **2 :** frustration by prevention of success **3 :** an overthrow esp. of an army **:** loss of a contest

de·feat·ism \di-'fēt-ˌiz-əm\ *n* **:** acceptance of or resignation to defeat — **de·feat·ist** \-'fēt-əst\ *n or adj*

1de·fea·ture \di-'fē-chər\ *n* [prob. fr. *de-* + *feature*] *archaic* **:** DISFIGUREMENT

2defeature *n* ['defeat] *archaic* **:** DEFEAT

def·e·cate \'def-i-ˌkāt\ *vb* [L *defaecatus,* pp. of *defaecare,* fr. *de-* + *faec-, faex* dregs, lees] *vt* **1 :** to free from impurity or corruption **:** REFINE **2 :** to discharge through the anus ~ *vi* **:** to discharge feces from the bowels — **def·e·ca·tion** \ˌdef-i-'kā-shən\ *n*

1de·fect \'dē-ˌfekt, di-'fekt\ *n* [ME *defaicte,* fr. MF *defect,* fr. L *defectus* lack, fr. *defectus,* pp. of *deficere* to desert, fail, fr. *de-* + *facere* to do] **1 :** SHORTCOMING, IMPERFECTION **2** [L *defectus*] **:** want of something necessary for completeness **syn** see BLEMISH

2de·fect \di-'fekt\ *vi* [L *defectus,* pp.] **:** to desert a cause or party esp. in order to espouse another — **de·fec·tor** \-'fek-tər\ *n*

de·fec·tion \di-'fek-shən\ *n* **:** conscious abandonment of allegiance or duty (as to a person, cause, or doctrine) **:** DESERTION

1de·fec·tive \di-'fek-tiv\ *adj* **1 :** wanting in something essential **:** FAULTY **2 :** lacking one or more of the usual forms of grammatical inflection ⟨a ~ verb⟩ **3 :** markedly subnormal mentally or physically — **de·fec·tive·ly** *adv* — **de·fec·tive·ness** *n*

2defective *n* **:** a person who is subnormal physically or mentally

defective year *n* **:** a common year of 353 days or a leap year of 383 days in the Jewish calendar

de·fend \di-'fend\ *vb* [ME *defenden,* fr. OF *defendre,* fr. L *defendere,* fr. *de-* + *-fendere* to strike; akin to OE *gūth* battle, war, Gk *theinein* to strike] *vt* **1** *archaic* **:** PREVENT **2 :** to drive danger or attack away from **3 :** to act as attorney for **4 :** to deny or oppose the right of a plaintiff in regard to (a suit or a wrong charged) ~ *vi* **:** to take action against attack or challenge — **de·fend·er** *n*

syn PROTECT, SHIELD, GUARD, SAFEGUARD: DEFEND implies warding off what immediately threatens or repelling what actually attacks; PROTECT is wider in application and less active in suggestion, implying a keeping safe by any means from injury or destruction; SHIELD suggests the interposition of a cover or barrier against imminent and specific danger; GUARD implies protecting with vigilance and force against expected danger; SAFEGUARD implies taking precautionary protective measures against merely possible danger **syn** see in addition MAINTAIN

de·fen·dant \di-'fen-dənt\ *n* **1** *obs* **:** DEFENDER **2 :** a person required to make answer in a legal action or suit — compare PLAINTIFF

de·fen·es·tra·tion \(ˌ)dē-ˌfen-ə-'strā-shən\ *n* [*de-* + L *fenestra* window] **:** a throwing of a person or thing out of a window

de·fense *or* **de·fence** \di-'fen(t)s, 'dē-ˌ\ *n* [ME, fr. OF, fr. (assumed) VL *defensa,* fr. L, fem. of *defensus,* pp. of *defendere*] **1 a :** the act of defending **b :** a defendant's denial, answer, or plea **2 :** capability of resisting attack **3 a :** means or method of defending **b :** an argument in support or justification **c :** a sequence of moves available in chess to the second player in the opening **4 :** defenders or the positions taken up by them — **de·fense·less** \-ləs\ *adj* — **de·fense·less·ly** *adv* — **de·fense·less·ness** *n*

defense mechanism *n* **1 :** a defensive reaction by an organism **2 :** an unconscious mental process (as repression) that enables the ego to reach compromise solutions to problems

de·fen·si·bil·i·ty \di-ˌfen(t)-sə-'bil-ət-ē\ *n* **:** the quality or state of being defensible

de·fen·si·ble \di-'fen(t)-sə-bəl\ *adj* **:** capable of being defended — **de·fen·si·bly** \-blē\ *adv*

1de·fen·sive \di-'fen(t)-siv, 'dē-ˌ\ *adj* **1 :** serving to defend **2 :** devoted to resisting or preventing aggression or attack **3 a :** valuable in defensive play **b :** designed to keep opponent from being the highest bidder — **de·fen·sive·ly** *adv* — **de·fen·sive·ness** *n*

2defensive *n* **:** a defensive position

1de·fer \di-'fər\ *vt* **de·ferred; de·fer·ring** [ME *deferren, differren,* fr. MF *differer,* fr. L *differre* to postpone, be different — more at DIFFER] **:** to put off **:** DELAY ⟨~s action on the bill⟩ — **de·fer·rer** *n*

syn DEFER, POSTPONE, INTERMIT, SUSPEND, STAY mean to delay an action or proceeding. DEFER implies a deliberate putting off to a later time; it may also imply a delay in fulfillment or attainment ⟨hopes long *deferred*⟩ POSTPONE implies an intentional deferring usu. to a definite time; INTERMIT implies a stopping for a short or set interval usu. with expectation of quick resumption; SUSPEND also implies temporary stoppage with an added suggestion of waiting until some condition is satisfied; STAY suggests the stopping or checking by an intervening agency or authority

2defer *vb* **deferred; deferring** [ME *deferren, differren,* fr. MF *deferer, defferer,* fr. LL *deferre,* fr. L, to bring down, bring, fr. *de-* + *ferre* to carry] *vt* **1 :** to refer for decision **2 :** PROFFER ~ *vi* **:** to submit or yield to another's wish or opinion **syn** see YIELD

def·er·ence \'def-(ə-)rən(t)s\ *n* **:** courteous, respectful, or ingratiating regard for another's wishes **syn** see HONOR

def·er·ent \'def-(ə-)rənt\ *adj* [L *deferent-, deferens,* prp. of *deferre*] **:** serving to carry down or out ⟨a ~ conduit⟩

def·er·en·tial \ˌdef-ə-'ren-chəl\ *adj* **:** showing or expressing deference ⟨~ attention⟩ — **def·er·en·tial·ly** \-'rench-(ə-)lē\ *adv*

de·fer·ment \di-'fər-mənt\ *n* **:** the act of delaying; *specif* **:** official postponement of military service

de·fer·ra·ble \di-'fər-ə-bəl\ *adj* **:** capable of or suitable or eligible for being deferred — **deferrable** *n*

de·ferred *adj* **1 :** put off **:** withheld for or until a stated time ⟨a ~ payment⟩ **2 :** charged in cases of delayed handling ⟨a ~ rate⟩

de·fer·ves·cence \ˌdē-(ˌ)fər-'ves-ᵊn(t)s, ˌdef-ər-\ *n* [G *deferveszenz,* fr. L *defervescent-, defervescens,* prp. of *defervescere* to stop boiling, fr. *de-* + *fervescere* to begin to boil] **:** the subsidence of a fever

de·fi·ance \di-'fī-ən(t)s\ *n* **1 :** the act or an instance of defying **:** CHALLENGE **2 :** disposition to resist **:** contempt of opposition

de·fi·ant \-ənt\ *adj* [F *défiant,* fr. OF, prp. of *defier* to defy] **:** full of defiance **:** BOLD, INSOLENT — **de·fi·ant·ly** *adv*

de·fi·cien·cy \di-'fish-ən-sē\ *n* **1 :** the quality or state of being deficient **2 :** INADEQUACY: as **a :** a shortage of substances necessary to health **b :** absence of one or more genes from a chromosome

deficiency disease *n* **:** a disease (as scurvy) caused by a lack of essential dietary elements and esp. a vitamin or mineral

1de·fi·cient \di-'fish-ənt\ *adj* [L *deficient-, deficiens,* prp. of *deficere* to be wanting — more at DEFECT] **1 :** lacking in some necessary quality or element ⟨~ in judgment⟩ **2 :** not up to a normal standard or complement **:** DEFECTIVE — **de·fi·cient·ly** *adv*

2deficient *n* **:** one that is deficient ⟨a mental ~⟩

def·i·cit \'def-ə-sət\ *n* [F *déficit,* fr. L *deficit* it is wanting, 3d sing. pres. indic. of *deficere*] **1 :** deficiency in amount **2 a :** an excess of debit over credit items **b :** a loss in business operations

deficit spending *n* **:** the spending of funds raised by borrowing

de·fi·er \di-'fī-(ə)r\ *n* **:** one that defies

1def·i·lade \'def-ə-ˌlād, -ˌläd\ *vt* [prob. fr. *de-* + *-filade* (as in *enfilade*)] **:** to arrange (fortifications) so as to protect the lines from frontal or enfilading fire and the interior of the works from plunging or reverse fire

2defilade *n* **:** the act or process of defilading

1de·file \di-'fī(ə)l\ *vt* [ME *defilen,* alter. of *defoulen* to trample, defile, fr. OF *defouler* to trample, fr. *de-* + *fouler* to trample, lit., to foul] **1 :** to make filthy **:** DIRTY **2 :** to corrupt the purity or perfection of **3 :** RAVISH, VIOLATE **4 :** to make ceremonially unclean **5 :** SULLY, DISHONOR **syn** see CONTAMINATE — **de·file·ment** \-'fī(ə)l-mənt\ *n* — **de·fil·er** *n*

2de·file \di-'fī(ə)l, 'dē-ˌfīl\ *vi* [F *défiler,* fr. *dé-* de- + *filer* to move in a column — more at FILE] **:** to march in line **:** file off

3de·file \di-'fī(ə)l, 'dē-ˌfīl\ *n* [F *défilé,* fr. pp. of *défiler*] **:** a narrow passage or gorge

de·fin·able \di-'fī-nə-bəl\ *adj* **:** capable of being defined

de·fine \di-'fīn\ *vb* [ME *definen,* fr. MF & L; MF *definer,* fr. L *definire,* fr. *de-* + *finire* to limit, end, fr. *finis* boundary, end] *vt* **1 a :** to fix or mark the limits of **b :** to make distinct in outline **2 a :** to determine the essential qualities or precise meaning of ⟨~ the concept of loyalty⟩ **b :** to discover and set forth the meaning of **3 :** CHARACTERIZE, DISTINGUISH ~ *vi* **:** to make a definition — **de·fine·ment** \-'fīn-mənt\ *n* — **de·fin·er** \-'fī-nər\ *n*

de·fin·i·en·dum \di-ˌfin-ē-'en-dəm\ *n, pl* **de·fin·i·en·da** \-də\ [L, neut. of *definiendus,* gerundive of *definire*] **:** an expression being defined

de·fin·i·ens \di-'fin-ē-ˌenz\ *n, pl* **de·fin·i·en·tia** \di-ˌfin-ē-'en-chē-ə\ [L, prp. of *definire*] **:** an expression that defines **:** DEFINITION

def·i·nite \'def-(ə-)nət\ *adj* [L *definitus,* pp. of *definire*] **1 :** having distinct or certain limits **2 :** clear and unmistakable **:** PRECISE ⟨a ~ answer, yes or no⟩ **3** *of a grammatical modifier* **:** designating an identified or immediately identifiable person or thing ⟨the ~ article *the*⟩ **4 a :** constant in number, usu. less than 20, and occurring in multiples of the petal number ⟨stamens ~⟩ **b :** CYMOSE **syn** see EXPLICIT — **def·i·nite·ly** *adv* — **def·i·nite·ness** *n*

definite integral *n* **:** a number whose value is the difference between the values of the indefinite integral of a given function at the ends of a specific interval

def·i·ni·tion \ˌdef-ə-'nish-ən\ *n* **1 :** an act of determining; *specif* **:** the formal proclamation of a Roman Catholic dogma **2 :** a word or phrase expressing the essential nature of a person or thing **3 a :** a statement of the meaning of a word or word group or a sign or symbol **b :** the action or process of stating such a meaning **4 a :** the action or the power of making definite and clear **b :** CLARITY — **def·i·ni·tion·al** \-'nish-nəl, -'nish-ən-ᵊl\ *adj*

de·fin·i·tive \di-'fin-ət-iv\ *adj* **1 :** serving to provide a final solution **:** CONCLUSIVE ⟨a ~ victory⟩ **2 :** authoritative and apparently exhaustive ⟨the ~ book on the subject⟩ **3 :** serving to define or specify precisely **4 :** fully differentiated or developed **syn** see CONCLUSIVE — **de·fin·i·tive·ly** *adv* — **de·fin·i·tive·ness** *n*

definitive host *n* **:** the host in which the sexual reproduction of a parasite takes place

de·fi·ni·tize \'def-(ə-)nə-ˌtīz, di-'fin-ə-\ *vt* **:** to make definite

de·fin·i·tude \di-'fin-ə-ˌt(y)üd\ *n* [irreg. fr. *definite*] **:** PRECISION

def·la·grate \'def-lə-ˌgrāt\ *vb* [L *deflagratus,* pp. of *deflagrare* to burn down, fr. *de-* + *flagrare* to burn] *vi* **:** to burn with sudden and sparkling combustion ~ *vt* **:** to cause to deflagrate — **def·la·gra·tion** \ˌdef-lə-'grā-shən\ *n*

de·flate \di-'flāt, 'dē-\ *vb* [*de-* + *-flate* (as in *inflate*)] *vt* **1 :** to release air or gas from **2 :** to reduce in size or importance **3 :** to reduce (a price level) or cause (a volume of credit) to contract ~ *vi* **:** COLLAPSE **syn** see CONTRACT — **de·fla·tor** \-'flāt-ər\ *n*

de·fla·tion \di-'flā-shən, 'dē-\ *n* **1 :** an act or instance of deflating **:** the state of being deflated **2 :** a contraction in the volume of available money or credit resulting in a decline of the general price level — **de·fla·tion·ary** \-shə-ˌner-ē\ *adj*

de·flect \di-'flekt\ *vb* [L *deflectere* to bend down, turn aside, fr. *de-* + *flectere* to bend] *vt* **:** to turn from a straight course or fixed direction **:** BEND ~ *vi* **:** to turn aside **:** DEVIATE — **de·flec·tive** \-'flek-tiv\ *adj* — **de·flec·tor** \-tər\ *n*

de·flec·tion \di-'flek-shən\ *n* **1 :** a turning aside or off course **:** DEVIATION **2 :** the departure of an indicator or pointer from the

zero reading on the scale of an instrument

de·flexed \di-'flekst, 'dē-\ *adj* [L *deflexus*, pp. of *deflectere*] **:** turned abruptly downward ⟨a ~ leaf⟩

def·lo·ra·tion \,def-lə-'rā-shən\ *n* [ME *defloracioun*, fr. LL *deflora-tion-, defloratio*, fr. *defloratus*, pp. of *deflorare*] **:** rupture of the hymen

de·flow·er \(')dē-'flaù(-ə)r\ *vt* [ME *deflouren*, fr. MF or LL; MF *deflorer*, fr. LL *deflorare*, fr. L *de-* + *flor-*, *flos* flower] **1 :** to deprive of virginity **:** RAVISH **2 :** to take away the prime beauty of

de·fo·li·ant \(')dē-'fō-lē-ənt\ *n* **:** a chemical spray or dust applied to plants to cause the leaves to drop off prematurely

de·fo·li·ate \(')dē-'fō-lē-,āt\ *vt* [LL *defoliatus*, pp. of *defoliare*, fr. L *de-* + *folium* leaf — more at BLADE] **:** to deprive of leaves esp. prematurely — **de·fo·li·ate** \-lē-ət\ *adj* — **de·fo·li·a·tion** \(,)dē-,fō-lē-'ā-shən\ *n* — **de·fo·li·a·tor** \(')dē-'fō-lē-,āt-ər\ *n*

de·force \(')dē-'fō(ə)rs, -'fò(ə)rs\ *vt* [ME *deforcen*, fr. OF *deforcier*, fr. *de-* + *forcier* to force] **1 :** to keep (as lands) by force from the rightful owner **2 :** to eject (a person) from possession by force — **de·force·ment** \-'fōr-smənt, -'fòr-\ *n*

de·for·ciant \(')dē-'fōr-shənt, -'fòr-\ *n* [AF, fr. OF, prp. of *deforcier*] **:** one who deforces the rightful owner

de·for·est \(')dē-'fòr-əst, -'fär-\ *vt* **:** to clear of forests — **de·for·es·ta·tion** \(,)dē-,fòr-ə-'stā-shən, -,fär-\ *n* — **de·for·est·er** \(')dē-'fòr-ə-stər, -'fär-\ *n*

de·form \di-'fò(ə)rm, 'dē-\ *vb* [ME *deformen*, fr. MF or L; MF *deformer*, fr. L *deformare*, fr. *de-* + *formare* to form, fr. *forma* form] *vt* **1 :** to spoil the form of **2 a :** to spoil the looks of **:** DISFIGURE **b :** to make hideous or monstrous **3 :** to alter the shape of by stress ~ *vi* **:** to become misshapen or changed in shape **syn** DISTORT, CONTORT, WARP, GNARL: DEFORM is the least specific of these and may imply a change of shape through stress, injury, or some accident of growth; DISTORT and CONTORT both imply a wrenching from the natural, normal, or justly proportioned, but CONTORT suggests a more involved twisting and a more grotesque and painful result; WARP indicates physically an uneven shrinking that bends or twists out of a flat plane and suggests a bias, a wrong slant, or an abnormal direction; GNARL suggests contortions produced by harsh weather, heavy work, old age

de·for·ma·tion \,dē-,fòr-'mā-shən, ,def-ər-\ *n* **1 :** the action of deforming **:** the state of being deformed **2 :** change for the worse **3 :** alteration of form or shape; *also* **:** the product of such alteration — **de·for·ma·tion·al** \-shnəl, -shən-ᵊl\ *adj*

deformed *adj* **:** distorted or unshapely in form **:** MISSHAPEN

de·for·mi·ty \di-'fòr-mət-ē\ *n* [ME *deformite*, fr. MF *deformité*, fr. L *deformitat-, deformitas*, fr. *deformis* deformed, fr. *de-* + *forma*] **1 :** the state of being deformed **2 :** a physical blemish or distortion **:** DISFIGUREMENT **3 :** a moral or esthetic flaw or defect

de·fraud \di-'fròd\ *vt* [ME *defrauden*, fr. MF *defrauder*, fr. L *defraudare*, fr. *de-* + *fraudare* to cheat, fr. *fraud-*, *fraus* fraud] **:** to deprive of something by deception or fraud **syn** see CHEAT — **de·frau·da·tion** \,dē-,frò-'dā-shən\ *n* — **de·fraud·er** \di-'fròd-ər\ *n*

de·fray \di-'frā\ *vt* [MF *deffrayer*, fr. *des-* de- + *frayer* to expend, fr. OF, fr. (assumed) OF *frai* expenditure, lit., damage by breaking, fr. L *fractum*, neut. of *fractus*, pp. of *frangere* to break] **1 :** to provide for the payment of **:** PAY **2** *archaic* **:** to bear the expenses of — **de·fray·able** \-'frā-ə-bəl\ *adj* — **de·fray·al** \-'frā(-ə)l\ *n*

de·frock \(')dē-'fräk\ *vt* **:** UNFROCK

de·frost \di-'fròst, 'dē-\ *vt* **1 :** to release from a frozen state ⟨~ meat⟩ **2 :** to free from ice ~ *vi* **:** to thaw out esp. from a deep-frozen state — **de·frost·er** *n*

deft \'deft\ *adj* [ME *defte*] **:** marked by facility and skill **syn** see DEXTEROUS — **deft·ly** *adv* — **deft·ness** \'def(t)-nəs\ *n*

de·funct \di-'fəŋ(k)t\ *adj* [L *defunctus*, fr. pp. of *defungi* to finish, die, fr. *de-* + *fungi* to perform — more at FUNCTION] **:** having finished the course of life or existence **syn** see DEAD

¹de·fy \di-'fī\ *vt* [ME *defyen* to renounce faith in, challenge, fr. OF *defier*, fr. *de-* + *fier* to entrust, fr. (assumed) VL *fidare*, alter. of L *fidere* to trust] **1** *archaic* **:** to challenge to combat **2 :** to goad into trying to perform something proposed as impossible **3 :** to confront with assured power of resistance ⟨~ public opinion⟩

²de·fy \di-'fī, 'dē-,fī\ *n* **:** CHALLENGE, DEFIANCE

dé·ga·gé \,dā-,gä-'zhā\ *adj* [F, fr. pp. of *dégager* to redeem a pledge, free, fr. OF *desgagier*, fr. *des-* de- + *gage* pledge] **1 :** free of constraint **:** NONCHALANT **2 :** free and easy ⟨clothes with a ~ look⟩ **3 :** extended with toe pointed in preparation for a ballet step

de·gas \(')dē-'gas\ *vt* **:** to free from gas

de Gaull·ism \di-'gō-,liz-əm\ *n* **:** GAULLISM — **de Gaullist** *n*

de·gauss \(')dē-'gaùs\ *vt* **:** to make (a steel ship) effectively nonmagnetic by means of electrical coils carrying currents that neutralize the magnetism of the ship

de·gen·er·a·cy \di-'jen-(ə-)rə-sē\ *n* **1 :** the state of being degenerate **2 :** the process of becoming degenerate **3 :** sexual perversion

¹de·gen·er·ate \-'jen-(ə-)rət\ *adj* [ME *degenerat*, fr. L *degeneratus*, pp. of *degenerare* to degenerate, fr. *de-* + *gener-*, *genus* race, kind — more at KIN] **1 :** having degenerated: **a** (1) **:** having declined markedly from one's ancestors, predecessors, or former self (2) **:** RETROGRADE **b :** having deteriorated from a former level **c :** DEGRADED **d :** DEBASED **2 :** marked by lowered standards **syn** see VICIOUS — **de·gen·er·ate·ly** *adv* — **de·gen·er·ate·ness** *n*

²degenerate *n* **:** one that is degenerate: as **a :** one degraded from the normal moral standard **b :** one debased by a psychopathic tendency **c :** a sexual pervert **d :** one showing signs of reversion to an earlier culture stage

³de·gen·er·ate \di-'jen-ə-,rāt\ *vi* **1 :** to pass from a higher to a lower type or condition **:** DETERIORATE ⟨~ from the ancestral stock⟩ **2 :** to undergo progressive deterioration **:** become of a lower biological type **3 :** to sink into a low intellectual or moral state **4 :** to decline in quality ~ *vt* **:** to cause to degenerate

de·gen·er·a·tion \di-,jen-ə-'rā-shən, ,dē-\ *n* **1 :** a lowering of effective power, vitality, or essential quality to an enfeebled and worsened kind or state **2 a :** intellectual or moral decline **b :** degenerate condition **3 a :** progressive deterioration of physical characters from a level representing the norm of earlier generations or forms **b :** deterioration of a tissue or an organ in which its vitality is diminished or its structure impaired **4 :** marked decline in excellence (as of workmanship or originality) **syn** see DETERIORATION

de·gen·er·a·tive \di-'jen-ə-,rāt-iv, -'jen-(ə-)rət-\ *adj* **:** of, relating to, or tending to cause degeneration ⟨a ~ disease⟩

de·glu·ti·tion \,dē-glü-'tish-ən, ,deg-lü-\ *n* [F *déglutition*, fr. L *deglutitus*, pp. of *deglutire* to swallow down, fr. *de-* + *glutire*, *gluttire* to swallow] **:** the act or process of swallowing

de·grad·able \di-'grād-ə-bəl\ *adj* **:** capable of being degraded

deg·ra·da·tion \,deg-rə-'dā-shən\ *n* **1 :** the act or process of degrading **2 a :** decline to a low, destitute, or demoralized state **b :** moral or intellectual decadence **:** DEGENERATION

de·grade \di-'grād, 'dē-\ *vb* [ME *degraden*, fr. MF *degrader*, fr. LL *degradare*, fr. L *de-* + *gradus* step, grade] *vt* **1 a :** to lower in grade, rank, or status **:** DEMOTE **b :** to strip of rank or honors **c :** to deprive of standing or true function **:** PERVERT **d :** to scale down in desirability or salability **2 :** to bring to low esteem or disrepute **3 :** to drag down in moral or intellectual character **:** CORRUPT **4 :** to impair in respect to some physical property **5 :** to wear down by erosion **6 :** to reduce the complexity of (a chemical compound) **:** DECOMPOSE ~ *vi* **:** to pass from a higher grade or class to a lower **syn** see ABASE — **de·grad·er** *n*

de·grad·ed *adj* **1 :** reduced far below ordinary standards of civilized life and conduct **2 :** characterized by degeneration of structure or function — **de·grad·ed·ly** *adv* — **de·grad·ed·ness** *n*

de·grad·ing *adj* **:** that degrades **:** DEBASING

de·gree \di-'grē\ *n* [ME, fr. OF *degré*, fr. (assumed) VL *degradus*, fr. L *de-* + *gradus*] **1 a** *obs* **:** STEP, STAIR **b** *archaic* **:** a member of a series arranged in steps **2 :** a step or stage in a process, course, or classificatory order **3 :** a measure of damage to tissue caused by disease or other force **4 a :** the extent, measure, or scope of an action, condition, or relation **b :** relative intensity **c :** one of the forms or sets of forms used in the comparison of an adjective or adverb **d :** a legal measure of guilt or negligence **5 a :** a rank or grade of official, ecclesiastical, or social position **b** *archaic* **:** a particular standing esp. as to dignity or worth **c :** the civil condition or status of a person **6 :** a step in a direct line of descent or in the line of ascent to a common ancestor **7 a :** a grade of membership attained in a ritualistic order or society **b :** the formal ceremonies observed in the conferral of such a distinction **c :** a title conferred upon students by a college, university, or professional school upon completion of a unified program of study **d :** an academic title conferred honorarily **8** *archaic* **:** a position or space on the earth or in the heavens as measured by degrees of latitude **9 :** one of the divisions or intervals marked on a scale of a measuring instrument **10 :** a 360th part of the circumference of a circle **11 a :** the sum of the exponents of the variable factors of a monomial **b :** the sum of the exponents of the variable factors of the term of highest degree in a polynomial **12 a :** a line or space of the musical staff **b :** a step, note, or tone of a musical scale — **to a degree 1 :** to a remarkable extent **2 :** in a small way

de·gree–day \di-'grē-'dā\ *n* **:** a unit that represents one degree of declination from a given point (as 65°) in the mean daily outdoor temperature and is used to measure heat requirements

degree of freedom : the number of unrestricted variables in a frequency distribution

de·gum \(')dē-'gəm\ *vt* **:** to free from gum or gummy substance

de·gust \di-'gəst\ *vt* [L *degustare*, fr. *de-* + *gustare* to taste — more at CHOOSE] **:** TASTE, SAVOR — **de·gus·ta·tion** \,dē-,gə-'stā-shən\ *n*

de·hisce \di-'his\ *vi* [L *dehiscere* to split open, fr. *de-* + *hiscere* to gape; akin to L *hiare* to yawn] **:** to split along a natural line or discharge contents by so splitting ⟨seedpods *dehiscing* at maturity⟩

de·his·cence \-'his-ᵊn(t)s\ *n* [NL *dehiscentia*, fr. L *dehiscent-*, *dehiscens*, prp. of *dehiscere*] **:** an act or instance of dehiscing ⟨pollen freed by ~ of the anther⟩ — **de·his·cent** \-ᵊnt\ *adj*

de·horn \(')dē-'hò(ə)rn\ *vt* **1 :** to deprive of horns **2 :** to prevent the growth of the horns of — **de·horn·er** *n*

de·hu·man·iza·tion \(,)dē-,hyü-mə-nə-'zā-shən, (,)dē-,yü-\ *n* **:** the act or process or an instance of dehumanizing

de·hu·man·ize \(')dē-'hyü-mə-,nīz, (')dē-'yü-\ *vt* **:** to divest of human qualities or personality

de·hu·mid·i·fy \,dē-hyü-'mid-ə-,fī, ,dē-yü-\ *vt* **:** to remove moisture from (as the air)

de·hy·drate \(')dē-'hī-,drāt\ *vt* **1 a :** to remove hydrogen and oxygen from in the proportion in which they form water **b :** to remove water from (foods) **2 :** to deprive of vitality or savor ~ *vi* **:** to lose water or body fluids — **de·hy·dra·tor** \-, drāt-ər\ *n*

de·hy·dra·tion \,dē-,hī-'drā-shən\ *n* **:** the process of dehydrating; *esp* **:** an abnormal depletion of body fluids

de·hy·dro·ge·nase \,dē-,hī-'dräj-ə-,nās, (')dē-'hī-drə-jə-, -,nāz\ *n* [ISV] **:** an enzyme that accelerates the removal of hydrogen from metabolites and its transfer to other substances ⟨succinic ~⟩

de·hy·dro·ge·nate \,dē-,hī-'dräj-ə-,nāt, (')dē-'hī-drə-jə-\ *vt* **:** to remove hydrogen from — **de·hy·dro·ge·na·tion** \,dē-,hī-,dräj-ə-'nā-shən, (,)dē-,hī-drə-jə-\ *n*

de·hyp·no·tize \(')dē-'hip-nə-,tīz\ *vt* **:** to remove from hypnosis

de·ice \(')dē-'īs\ *vt* **:** to keep free or rid of ice — **de·ic·er** \-'ī-sər\ *n*

deic·tic \'dīk-tik\ *adj* [Gk *deiktikos*, fr. *deiktos*, verbal of *deiknynai* to show] **:** showing or pointing out directly

de·ifi·ca·tion \,dē-ə-fə-'kā-shən\ *n* **1 :** the act or an instance of deifying **2 :** absorption of the soul into deity

de·ify \'dē-ə-,fī\ *vt* [ME *deifyen*, fr. MF *deifier*, fr. LL *deificare*, fr. L *deus* god] **1 a :** to make a god of **b :** to take as an object of worship **2 :** to glorify as of supreme worth

deign \'dān\ *vb* [ME *deignen*, fr. OF *deignier*, fr. L *dignare*, *dignari*, fr. *dignus* worthy] *vi* **:** to think it appropriate to one's dignity ~ *vt* **:** to condescend to give or offer **syn** see STOOP

deil \'dē(ə)l\ *n* [ME *devel*, *del*] *Scot* **:** DEVIL

de·ism \'dē-,iz-əm\ *n* **:** a movement or system of thought advocating natural religion based on human reason rather than revelation, emphasizing morality, and in the 18th century denying the interference of the Creator with the laws of the universe

de·ist \'dē-əst\ *n*, *often cap* **:** an adherent of deism **syn** see ATHEIST — **de·is·tic** \dē-'is-tik\ *adj* — **de·is·ti·cal** \-ti-kəl\ *adj* — **de·is·ti·cal·ly** \-ti-k(ə-)lē\ *adv*

de·ity \'dē-ət-ē\ *n* [ME *deitee*, fr. MF *deité*, fr. LL *deitat-*, *deitas*, fr. L *deus* god; akin to OE *Tīw*, god of war, L *divus* god, *dies* day] **1 a :** the rank or essential nature of a god or a supreme being **:** DIVINITY **b** *cap* **:** SUPREME BEING, ²GOD **2 :** a god or goddess **3 :** one exalted or revered as supremely good or powerful

dé·jà vu *or* **déjà vue** \dā-zhá-vᵫ\ *n* [F, adj., already seen] **:** PARAMNESIA b

ə abut; ᵊ kitten; ər further; a back; ā bake; ä cot, cart; aù out; ch chin; e less; ē easy; g gift; i trip; ī life
j joke; ŋ sing; ō flow; ò flaw; òi coin; th thin; t͟h this; ü loot; ù foot; y yet; yü few; yù furious; zh vision

1**de·ject** \di-ˈjekt\ *vt* [ME *dejecten* to throw down, fr. L *dejectus,* pp. of *deicere,* fr. *de-* + *jacere* to throw] **:** to make gloomy

2**deject** *adj, archaic* **:** DEJECTED

de·jec·ta \di-ˈjek-tə\ *n pl* [NL, fr. L, neut. pl. of *dejectus*] **:** EXCREMENTS

de·ject·ed *adj* **1 :** cast down in spirits **:** DEPRESSED **2 a** *obs, of the eyes* **:** DOWNCAST **b** *archaic* **:** thrown down **3** *obs* **:** lowered in rank or condition — **de·ject·ed·ly** *adv* — **de·ject·ed·ness** *n*

de·jec·tion \di-ˈjek-shən\ *n* **:** lowness of spirits **syn** see SADNESS

de ju·re \(ˌ)dē-ˈju̇(ə)r-ē, (ˌ)dā-ˈyu̇(ə)r-\ *adv (or adj)* [NL] **:** by right **:** of right **:** by a lawful title ⟨*de jure* recognition⟩

deka- *or* **dek-** — see DECA-

de·lam·i·nate \(ˌ)dē-ˈlam-ə-ˌnāt\ *vi* **:** to undergo delamination

de·lam·i·na·tion \(ˌ)dē-ˌlam-ə-ˈnā-shən\ *n* **1 :** separation into constituent layers **2 :** gastrulation in which the endoderm is split off as a layer from the inner surface of the blastoderm and the archenteron is represented by the space between this endoderm and the yolk mass

de·late \di-ˈlāt\ *vt* [L *delatus* (pp. of *deferre* to bring down, report, accuse), fr. *de-* + *latus,* pp. of *ferre* to bear] **1 a** *chiefly Scot* **:** ACCUSE **b** *archaic* **:** REPORT, RELATE **2** *archaic* **:** REFER — **de·la·tion** \-ˈlā-shən\ *n* — **de·la·tor** \-ˈlāt-ər\ *n*

Del·a·ware \ˈdel-ə-ˌwa(ə)r, -ˌwe(ə)r, -wər\ *n, pl* **Delaware** *or* **Delawares** [*Delaware* river] **1 :** a member of an Indian people of the Delaware valley **2 :** the Algonquian language of the Delaware

1**de·lay** \di-ˈlā\ *n* **1 :** the act of delaying **:** the state of being delayed **2 :** the time during which something is delayed

2**delay** *vb* [ME *delayen,* fr. OF *delaier,* fr. *de-* + *laier* to leave, alter. of *laissier,* fr. L *laxare* to slacken — more at RELAX] *vt* **1 :** to put off **:** POSTPONE **2 :** to stop, detain, or hinder for a time ~ *vi* **:** to move or act slowly — **de·lay·er** *n* — **de·lay·ing** *adj*

syn DELAY, RETARD, SLOW, SLACKEN, DETAIN, mean to cause to be late or behind in movement or progress. DELAY implies a holding back, usu. by interference, from completion or arrival; RETARD applies chiefly to motion and suggests reduction of speed without actual stopping; SLOW and SLACKEN both imply also a reduction of speed, SLOW often suggesting deliberate intention, SLACKEN an easing up or relaxing of power or effort; DETAIN implies a holding back beyond a reasonable or appointed time

syn DELAY, PROCRASTINATE, LAG, LOITER, DAWDLE, DALLY mean to move or act slowly so as to fall behind. DELAY usu. implies a putting off (as a beginning or departure); PROCRASTINATE implies blameworthy delay esp. through laziness or apathy; LAG implies failure to maintain a speed set by others; LOITER and DAWDLE imply delay while in progress, esp. in walking, but DAWDLE more clearly suggests an aimless wasting of time; DALLY suggests delay through trifling or vacillation when promptness is necessary

1**de·le** \ˈdē-(ˌ)lē\ *vt* **deled; deleing** [L, imper. sing. of *delēre*] **1 :** to remove (as a word) from typeset matter **:** ERASE **2 :** to mark with a dele

2**dele** *n* **:** a mark indicating that something is to be deled

de·lec·ta·bil·i·ty \di-ˌlek-tə-ˈbil-ət-ē\ *n* **1 :** DELECTABLENESS **2 :** something delectable — usu. used in pl.

de·lec·ta·ble \di-ˈlek-tə-bəl\ *adj* [ME, fr. MF, fr. L *delectabilis,* fr. *delectare* to delight] **1 :** highly pleasing **:** DELIGHTFUL **2 :** DELICIOUS — **de·lec·ta·ble·ness** *n* — **de·lec·ta·bly** \-blē\ *adv*

de·lec·ta·tion \ˌdē-ˌlek-ˈtā-shən\ *n* **1 :** DELIGHT **2 :** ENJOYMENT **syn** see PLEASURE

del·e·ga·ble \ˈdel-i-gə-bəl\ *adj* **:** capable of being delegated

del·e·ga·cy \-gə-sē\ *n* **1 a :** the act of delegating **b :** appointment as delegate **2 :** a body of delegates **:** BOARD

1**del·e·gate** \ˈdel-i-gət, -ˌgāt\ *n* [ME *delegat,* fr. ML *delegatus,* fr. L, pp. of *delegare* to delegate, fr. *de-* + *legare* to send — more at LEGATE] **:** a person acting for another: as **a :** a representative to a convention or conference **b :** a representative of a U.S. territory in the House of Representatives **c :** a member of the lower house of the legislature of Maryland, Virginia, or West Virginia

2**del·e·gate** \-ˌgāt\ *vt* **1 :** to entrust to another ⟨~ one's authority⟩ **2 :** to appoint as one's delegate

del·e·ga·tion \ˌdel-i-ˈgā-shən\ *n* **1 :** the act of empowering to act for another **2 :** one or more persons chosen to represent others

de·lete \di-ˈlēt\ *vt* [L *deletus,* pp. of *delēre* to wipe out, destroy, fr. *de-* + *-lēre* (akin to L *linere* to smear)] **:** to eliminate esp. by blotting out, cutting out, or erasing **syn** see ERASE

del·e·te·ri·ous \ˌdel-ə-ˈtir-ē-əs\ *adj* [Gk *dēlētērios,* fr. *dēleisthai* to hurt] **:** HURTFUL, NOXIOUS **syn** see PERNICIOUS — **del·e·te·ri·ous·ly** *adv* — **del·e·te·ri·ous·ness** *n*

de·le·tion \di-ˈlē-shən\ *n* [L *deletion-, deletio* destruction, fr. *deletus*] **1 :** an act of deleting **2 a :** something deleted **b :** DEFICIENCY 2b; *esp* **:** a large deficiency not including either end of a chromosome

delft \ˈdelft\ *or* **delft·ware** \ˈdelf-ˌtwa(ə)r, -ˌtwe(ə)r\ *n* [*Delft,* Netherlands] **1 :** a Dutch brown pottery covered with an opaque white glaze upon which the predominantly blue decoration is painted **2 :** glazed pottery esp. when blue and white

1**de·lib·er·ate** \di-ˈlib-(ə-)rət\ *adj* [L *deliberatus,* pp. of *deliberare* to weigh in mind, ponder, irreg. fr. *de-* + *libra* scale, pound] **1 :** characterized by or resulting from careful and thorough consideration **2 :** characterized by awareness of the consequences **:** WILLFUL **3 :** slow, unhurried, and steady **syn** see VOLUNTARY — **de·lib·er·ate·ly** *adv* — **de·lib·er·ate·ness** *n*

2**de·lib·er·ate** \-ˈlib-ə-ˌrāt\ *vt* **:** to think about deliberately ~ *vi* **:** to ponder issues and decisions carefully **syn** see THINK

de·lib·er·a·tion \di-ˌlib-ə-ˈrā-shən\ *n* **1 :** the act of deliberating **2 :** a discussion and consideration by a number of persons of the reasons for and against a measure **3 :** DELIBERATENESS — **de·lib·er·a·tive** \di-ˈlib-ə-ˌrāt-iv, -ˈlib-(ə-)rət-\ *adj* — **de·lib·er·a·tive·ly** *adv* — **de·lib·er·a·tive·ness** *n*

del·i·ca·cy \ˈdel-i-kə-sē\ *n* **1** *obs* **a :** LUXURIOUSNESS **b :** INDULGENCE **2 :** something pleasing to eat that is considered rare or luxurious **3 a :** FINENESS, DAINTINESS **b :** FRAILTY **4 :** nicety or subtle expressiveness of touch **5 a :** precise and refined perception and discrimination **b :** extreme sensitivity **:** PRECISION **6 a :** nice sensibility in feeling or conduct **b :** SQUEAMISHNESS **7 :** the quality or state of requiring delicate treatment

1**del·i·cate** \-kət\ *adj* [ME *delicat,* fr. L *delicatus* delicate, addicted to pleasure; akin to L *delicere* to allure] **1 :** pleasing to the senses: **a :** generally pleasant **b :** pleasing to the sense of taste or smell esp. in a mild or subtle way **c :** marked by daintiness or charm of color, lines, or proportions **2 :** marked by keen sensitivity or fine discrimination: as **a :** FASTIDIOUS **b :** SQUEAMISH **c :** SCRUPULOUS **3 a :** marked by minute precision **b :** exhibiting extreme sensitivity **4 :** precariously balanced **5 a :** marked by meticulous technique or operation or by execution with adroit finesse **b :** marked by fineness of structure, workmanship, or texture **c** (1) **:** easily torn or hurt (2) **:** WEAK, SICKLY **d :** marked by fine subtlety ⟨~ irony⟩ **e :** marked by tact; *also* **:** requiring tact **syn** see CHOICE — **del·i·cate·ly** *adv* — **del·i·cate·ness** *n*

2**delicate** *n* **1** *obs* **:** DELIGHT, LUXURY **2** *archaic* **:** a table delicacy

del·i·ca·tes·sen \ˌdel-i-kə-ˈtes-ᵊn\ *n pl* [obs. G, (now *delikatessen*), pl. of *delicatesse* delicacy, fr. F *délicatesse,* prob. fr. OIt *delicatezza,* fr. *delicato* delicate, fr. L *delicatus*] **1 :** ready-to-eat food products (as cooked meats and prepared salads) **2** *sing, pl* **delicatessens** [*delicatessen (store)*] **:** a store where delicatessen are sold

de·li·cious \di-ˈlish-əs\ *adj* [ME, fr. OF, fr. LL *deliciosus,* fr. L *deliciae* delight, fr. *delicere* to allure] **1 :** affording great pleasure **:** DELIGHTFUL **2 :** appealing to one of the bodily senses esp. of taste or smell — **de·li·cious·ly** *adv* — **de·li·cious·ness** *n*

de·lict \di-ˈlikt\ *n* [L *delictum* fault, fr. neut. of *delictus,* pp. of *delinquere*] **:** an offense against the law

1**de·light** \di-ˈlīt\ *n* **1 :** a high degree of gratification **:** JOY; *also* **:** extreme satisfaction **2 :** something that gives great pleasure **3** *archaic* **:** the power of affording pleasurable emotion **syn** see PLEASURE

2**delight** *vb* [ME *deliten,* fr. OF *delitier,* fr. L *delectare,* fr. *delectus,* pp. of *delicere* to allure, fr. *de-* + *lacere* to allure; akin to OE *lǣl* switch] *vi* **1 :** to take great pleasure **2 :** to give keen enjoyment ~ *vt* **:** to give joy or satisfaction to — **de·light·er** *n*

delighted *adj* **1** *obs* **:** DELIGHTFUL **2 :** highly pleased — **de·light·ed·ly** *adv* — **de·light·ed·ness** *n*

de·light·ful \di-ˈlīt-fəl\ *adj* **:** highly pleasing — **de·light·ful·ly** *adv* — **de·light·ful·ness** *n*

de·light·some \-ˈlīt-səm\ *adj* **:** very pleasing **:** DELIGHTFUL — **de·light·some·ly** *adv*

De·li·lah \di-ˈlī-lə\ *n* [Heb *Dĕlīlāh*] **:** the mistress and betrayer of Samson

de·lim·it \di-ˈlim-ət\ *vt* [F *délimiter,* fr. L *delimitare,* fr. *de-* + *limitare* to limit, fr. *limit-, limes* boundary, limit — more at LIMB] **1 :** to fix the limits of ⟨~ a frontier⟩ **2 :** BOUND, DEFINE

de·lim·i·tate \di-ˈlim-ə-ˌtāt\ *vt* **:** DELIMIT — **de·lim·i·ta·tion** \-ˌlim-ə-ˈtā-shən\ *n* — **de·lim·i·ta·tive** \-ˈlim-ə-ˌtāt-iv\ *adj*

de·lin·eate \di-ˈlin-ē-ˌāt\ *vt* [L *delineatus,* pp. of *delineare,* fr. *de-* + *linea* line] **1 a :** to indicate by lines drawn in the form or figure of **:** PORTRAY **b :** to represent accurately **2 :** to describe in usu. sharp or vivid detail — **de·lin·ea·tor** \-ˈlin-ē-ˌāt-ər\ *n*

de·lin·ea·tion \-ˌlin-ē-ˈā-shən\ *n* **1 :** the act of representing, portraying, or describing graphically or verbally **2 :** something made by delineating — **de·lin·ea·tive** \-ˈlin-ē-ˌāt-iv\ *adj*

de·lin·quen·cy \di-ˈliŋ-kwən-sē, -ˈlin-\ *n* **1 :** the quality or state of being delinquent **2 :** a psychological tendency to commit offenses against the law **3 :** a debt on which payment is in arrears

1**de·lin·quent** \-kwənt\ *n* **:** a delinquent person

2**delinquent** *adj* [L *delinquent-, delinquens,* prp. of *delinquere* to fail, offend, fr. *de-* + *linquere* to leave — more at LOAN] **1 :** offending by neglect or violation of duty or of law **2 :** being in arrears in payment — **de·lin·quent·ly** *adv*

del·i·quesce \ˌdel-i-ˈkwes\ *vi* [L *deliquescere,* fr. *de-* + *liquescere,* incho. of *liquēre* to be fluid — more at LIQUID] **1 :** to melt away: **a :** to dissolve gradually and become liquid by attracting and absorbing moisture from the air **b :** to become soft or liquid with age — used of plant structures (as mushrooms) **2 :** to divide repeatedly ending in fine divisions — used esp. of the veins of a leaf — **del·i·ques·cence** \-ˈkwes-ᵊn(t)s\ *n* — **del·i·ques·cent** \-ᵊnt\ *adj*

de·lir·i·ous \di-ˈlir-ē-əs\ *adj* **1 :** of, relating to, or characteristic of delirium **2 :** affected with or marked by delirium — **de·lir·i·ous·ly** *adv* — **de·lir·i·ous·ness** *n*

de·lir·i·um \-ˈlir-ē-əm\ *n* [L, fr. *delirare* to be crazy, fr. *de-* + *lira* furrow] **1 :** a mental disturbance characterized by confusion, disordered speech, and hallucinations **2 :** frenzied excitement

delirium tre·mens \-ˈtrē-mənz\ *n* [NL, lit., trembling delirium] **:** a violent delirium with tremors that is induced by excessive and prolonged use of alcoholic liquors

de·liv·er \di-ˈliv-ər\ *vt* **de·liv·er·ing** \-ˈliv-(ə-)riŋ\ [ME *deliveren,* fr. OF *delivrer,* fr. LL *deliberare,* fr. L *de-* + *liberare* to liberate] **1 :** to set free **2 :** to hand over **:** CONVEY **3 :** to assist in giving birth; *also* **:** to aid in the birth of **4 :** UTTER, RELATE **5 :** to send to an intended destination **6 :** to bring (as votes) to the support of a candidate or cause **syn** see RESCUE — **de·liv·er·able** \-ˈliv-(ə-)rə-bəl\ *adj* — **de·liv·er·er** \-ˈliv-ər-ər\ *n*

de·liv·er·ance \di-ˈliv-(ə-)rən(t)s\ *n* **1 :** the act of delivering or state of being delivered: as **a :** LIBERATION, RESCUE **b** *archaic* **:** UTTERANCE **2 :** something delivered or communicated; *esp* **:** an opinion or decision expressed publicly (as the verdict of a jury)

de·liv·ery \di-ˈliv-(ə-)rē\ *n* **1 :** a delivering from restraint **2 a :** the act of handing over **b :** the physical and legal transfer of a shipment from consignor to consignee **c :** the act of putting into the legal possession of another **d :** something delivered at one time or in one unit **3 :** the act of giving birth **4 :** a delivering esp. of a speech; *also* **:** manner or style of uttering in speech or song **5 :** the act or manner of sending forth or throwing

dell \ˈdel\ *n* [ME *delle;* akin to MHG *telle* ravine, OE *dæl* valley] **:** a secluded hollow or small valley usu. covered with trees or turf

de·louse \(ˈ)dē-ˈlau̇s, -ˈlau̇z\ *vt* **:** to remove lice from

Del·phi·an \ˈdel-fē-ən\ *or* **Del·phic** \-fik\ *adj* **1 :** of or relating to ancient Delphi or its oracle **2 :** AMBIGUOUS, OBSCURE

del·phin·i·um \del-ˈfin-ē-əm\ *n* [NL, genus name, fr. Gk *delphinion* larkspur, dim. of *delphin-, delphis* dolphin] **:** any of a large genus (*Delphinium*) of the crowfoot family of chiefly perennial erect branching herbs that have palmately divided leaves and irregular flowers in showy spikes and include several that are poisonous

Del·phi·nus \del-ˈfī-nəs\ *n* [L (gen. *Delphini*), lit., dolphin — more at DOLPHIN] **:** a northern constellation nearly west of Pegasus

1**del·ta** \ˈdel-tə\ *n* [ME *deltha,* fr. Gk *delta,* of Sem origin; akin to Heb *dāleth* daleth] **1 :** the fourth letter of the Greek alphabet — symbol Δ or δ **2 :** something shaped like a capital Δ; *esp* **:** the alluvial deposit at the mouth of a river **3 :** an increment of a variable — symbol Δ — **del·ta·ic** \del-ˈtā-ik\ *adj*

2**delta** *or* **δ-** *adj* **:** fourth in position in the structure of an organic molecule from a particular group or atom

Delta — a communications code word for the letter *d*
delta ray *n* : an electron ejected by an ionizing particle in its passage through matter
1**del·toid** \'del-ˌtȯid\ *or* **del·toi·de·us** \del-'tȯid-ē-əs\ *n, pl* **del·toids** *or* **del·toi·dei** \-'tȯi-dē-ˌī\ [*deltoid* fr. NL *deltoides*, fr. Gk *deltoeidēs* shaped like a delta, fr. *delta; deltoideus*, NL, alter. of *deltoides*] : a large triangular muscle that covers the shoulder joint and serves to raise the arm laterally
2**deltoid** *adj* : shaped like a capital delta : TRIANGULAR ⟨a ~ leaf⟩
de·lude \di-'lüd\ *vt* [ME *deluden*, fr. L *deludere*, fr. *de-* + *ludere* to play] **1** : to mislead the mind or judgment of : impose on : DECEIVE, TRICK **2** *obs* **a** : FRUSTRATE, DISAPPOINT **b** : EVADE, ELUDE **syn** see DECEIVE — **de·lud·er** *n* — **de·lud·ing·ly** \-iŋ-lē\ *adv*
1**del·uge** \'del-(ˌ)yüj\ *n* [ME, fr. MF, fr. L *diluvium*, fr. *diluere* to wash away, fr. *dis-* + *lavere* to wash] **1 a** : an overflowing of the land by water **b** : a drenching rain **2** : an irresistible rush
2**del·uge** *vt* **1** : to overflow with water : INUNDATE **2** : SWAMP
de·lu·sion \di-'lü-zhən\ *n* [ME, fr. L *delusion-, delusio*, fr. *delusus* pp. of *deludere*] **1 a** : the act of deluding : the state of being deluded **b** : an abnormal mental state characterized by occurrence of delusions **2 a** : something that is falsely or delusively believed or propagated **b** : a false belief regarding the self or persons or objects outside the self that persists despite the facts and is common in some psychotic states — **de·lu·sion·al** \-'lüzh-nəl, -'lü-zhən-ᵊl\ *adj*

syn DELUSION, ILLUSION, HALLUCINATION, MIRAGE mean something accepted as true or real that is actually false or unreal. DELUSION implies self-deception concerning facts or situations and usu. a disordered state of mind; ILLUSION implies an ascription of truth or reality to something that seems to normal perception to be true or real but in fact is not; HALLUCINATION implies an image that has no physical basis but is the result of disordered nerves or mental derangement; MIRAGE, literally an optical illusion presented to normal vision, suggests by extension a goal that is unattainable because it exists only in dreams or hopes

de·lu·sive \-'lü-siv, -'lü-ziv\ *adj* **1** : apt to delude **2** : constituting a delusion — **de·lu·sive·ly** *adv* — **de·lu·sive·ness** *n*
de·lu·so·ry \-sə-rē, -zə-rē\ *adj* : DECEPTIVE, DELUSIVE
de·luxe \di-'lu̇ks, -'ləks, -'lüks\ *adj* [F *de luxe*, lit., of luxury] : notably luxurious or elegant ⟨a ~ edition⟩
1**delve** \'delv\ *vb* [ME *delven*, fr. OE *delfan*; akin to OHG *telban* to dig] *vt, archaic* : EXCAVATE ~ *vi* **1** : to dig or labor with a spade **2** : to seek laboriously for information — **delv·er** *n*
2**delve** *n, archaic* : CAVE, HOLLOW
de·mag·ne·tize \(ˈ)dē-'mag-nə-ˌtīz\ *vt* : to deprive of magnetic properties — **de·mag·ne·tiz·er** *n*
dem·a·gog·ic \ˌdem-ə-'gäj-ik, -'gäg-\ *adj* : of, relating to, or characteristic of a demagogue — **dem·a·gog·i·cal** \-i-kəl\ *adj* — **dem·a·gog·i·cal·ly** \-i-k(ə-)lē\ *adv*
dem·a·gog·ism \'dem-ə-ˌgäg-ˌiz-əm\ *n* : the practices or principles of a demagogue
dem·a·gogue *or* **dem·a·gog** \'dem-ə-ˌgäg\ *n* [Gk *dēmagōgos*, fr. *dēmos* people (akin to Gk *daiesthai* to divide) + *agōgos* leading, fr. *agein* to lead] **1** : a leader championing the cause of the common people in ancient times **2** : a leader who makes use of popular prejudices and false claims and promises to gain power — **dem·a·gogu·ery** \-ˌgäg-(ə-)rē\ *n* — **dem·a·gogy** \-ˌgäj-ē, -ˌgäg-ē\ *n*
1**de·mand** \di-'mand\ *n* **1 a** : an act of demanding or asking esp. with authority **b** : something claimed as due **2** *archaic* : QUESTION **3 a** : an expressed desire for ownership or use **b** : willingness and ability to purchase a commodity or service **c** : the quantity of a commodity or service wanted at a specified price and time **4 a** : a seeking or state of being sought after **b** : urgent need **5** : the requirement of work or of the expenditure of a resource — **on demand** : upon presentation and request for payment
2**demand** *vb* [ME *demaunden*, fr. MF *demander*, fr. ML *demandare*, fr. L *de-* + *mandare* to enjoin] *vi* : to make a demand : ASK ~ *vt* **1** : to ask for peremptorily or urgently **2 a** : to ask for legally as a rightful owner **b** : to claim as due, just, or fit **c** : to ask for authoritatively **3 a** : to ask authoritatively or earnestly to be informed of **b** : to require to come : SUMMON **4** : to call for as useful or necessary — **de·mand·able** \-'man-də-bəl\ *adj* — **de·mand·er** *n*

syn CLAIM, REQUIRE, EXACT: DEMAND implies peremptoriness and insistence and often the right to make requests that are to be regarded as commands; CLAIM implies a demand for the delivery or concession of something due as one's own or one's right; REQUIRE suggests the imperativeness that arises from inner necessity, compulsion of law or regulation, or the exigencies of the situation; EXACT implies not only demanding but getting what one demands

de·mand·ant \di-'man-dənt\ *n* **1** : the plaintiff in a real action **2** : one who makes a demand or claim
demand deposit *n* : a bank deposit that can be withdrawn without notice
demanding *adj* : EXACTING — **de·mand·ing·ly** \-'man-diŋ-lē\ *adv*
demand loan *n* : CALL LOAN
demand note *n* : a note payable on demand
de·man·toid \di-'man-ˌtȯid\ *n* [G, fr. obs. G *demant* diamond, fr. MHG *diemant*, fr. OF *diamant*] : a green andradite used as a gem
de·mar·cate \di-'mär-ˌkāt, 'dē-ˌmär-\ *vt* [back-formation fr. *demarcation*, fr. Sp *demarcación* & Pg *demarcação*, fr. *demarcar* to delimit, fr. *de-* + *marcar* to mark, fr. It *marcare*, of Gmc origin] **1** : to mark the limits of **2** : to set apart : SEPARATE — **de·mar·ca·tion** *also* **de·mar·ka·tion** \ˌdē-ˌmär-'kā-shən\ *n*
de·marche \dā-'märsh\ *n* [F *démarche*, lit., gait, fr. MF, fr. *demarcher* to march, fr. OF *demarchier*, fr. *de-* + *marchier* to march] **1 a** : a course of action : MANEUVER **b** : a diplomatic move or maneuver **2 a** : a diplomatic representation **b** : a representation of views to a public official
de·mark \di-'märk\ *vt* : DEMARCATE
deme \'dēm\ *n* [Gk *dēmos*, lit., people] **1** : a unit of local government in ancient Attica **2** : a local population of closely related organisms — usu. used in combination ⟨*gamodeme*⟩
1**de·mean** \di-'mēn\ *vt* [ME *demenen*, fr. OF *demener* to conduct, fr. *de-* + *mener* to drive, fr. L *minare*, fr. *minari* to threaten — more at MOUNT] : to conduct or behave (oneself) usu. in a proper manner
2**demean** *n, archaic* : DEMEANOR
3**demean** *vt* [*de-* + *mean*] : DEGRADE, DEBASE **syn** see ABASE
de·mea·nor \di-'mē-nər\ *n* : outward behavior **syn** see BEARING
de·ment·ed \di-'ment-əd\ *adj* : MAD, INSANE — **de·ment·ed·ly** *adv* — **de·ment·ed·ness** *n*
de·men·tia \di-'men-chə\ *n* [L, fr. *dement-, demens* mad, fr. *de-* + *ment-, mens* mind] **1** : a condition of deteriorated mentality **2** : MADNESS, INSANITY **syn** see INSANITY — **de·men·tial** \-chəl\ *adj*
dementia prae·cox \-'prē-ˌkäks\ *n* [NL, lit., premature dementia] : SCHIZOPHRENIA
de·mer·it \(ˈ)dē-'mer-ət\ *n* [ME, fr. MF *demerite*, fr. *de-* + *merite* merit] **1** *obs* : OFFENSE **2 a** : a quality that deserves blame : FAULT **b** : lack of merit **3** : a mark usu. entailing a loss of privilege given to an offender
de·mesne \di-'mān, -'mēn\ *n* [ME, alter. of *demeyne*, fr. OF *demaine* — more at DOMAIN] **1** : legal possession of land as one's own **2** : manorial land actually possessed by the lord and not held by tenants **3 a** : the land attached to a mansion **b** : landed property : ESTATE **c** : REGION, TERRITORY **4** : REALM, DOMAIN
De·me·ter \di-'mēt-ər\ *n* [L, fr. Gk *Dēmētēr*] : the goddess of agriculture in Greek mythology
demi- *prefix* [ME, fr. *demi*, fr. MF, fr. L *dimidius*, prob. back-formation fr. *dimidiare* to halve] **1** : half ⟨*demi*bastion⟩ **2** : one that partly belongs to (a specified type or class) ⟨*demi*god⟩
demi·god \'dem-ē-ˌgäd\ *n* **1** : a mythological being with more power than a mortal but less than a god **2** : a person so outstanding that he seems to approach the divine
demi·john \'dem-ē-ˌjän\ *n* [by folk etymology fr. F *dame-jeanne*, lit., Lady Jane] : a narrow-necked bottle of glass or stoneware enclosed in wickerwork and holding from one to 10 gallons
de·mil·i·ta·ri·za·tion \(ˌ)dē-ˌmil-ə-tə-rə-'zā-shən\ *n* : the act, process, or result of demilitarizing
de·mil·i·ta·rize \(ˈ)dē-'mil-ə-tə-ˌrīz\ *vt* : to do away with the military organization and potential of
demi·mon·daine \ˌdem-ē-ˌmän-'dān\ *n* [F *demi-mondaine*, fr. fem. of *demi-mondain*, fr. *demi-monde*] : a woman of the demimonde
demi·monde \'dem-ē-ˌmänd\ *n* [F *demi-monde*, fr. *demi-* + *monde* world, fr. L *mundus* — more at MUNDANE] **1 a** : a class of women on the fringes of respectable society supported by wealthy lovers **b** : PROSTITUTES **2** : DEMIMONDAINE **3** : a group marked by doubtful propriety or lack of success
demi·rep \'dem-ē-ˌrep\ *n* [*demi-* + *rep* (reprobate)] : DEMIMONDAINE
1**de·mise** \di-'mīz\ *vt* **1** : to convey (as an estate) by will or lease **2** *obs* : CONVEY, GIVE **3** : to transmit by succession or inheritance
2**demise** *n* [MF, fem. of *demis*, pp. of *demettre* to dismiss, fr. L *demittere* to send down, fr. *de-* + *mittere* to send — more at SMITE] **1** : the conveyance of an estate **2** : transfer of the sovereignty to a successor **3 a** : DEATH **b** : a cessation of existence or activity
demi·semi·qua·ver \ˌdem-ē-'sem-ē-ˌkwā-vər\ *n* : THIRTY-SECOND NOTE
de·mis·sion \di-'mish-ən\ *n* [MF, fr. L *demission-, demissio* lowering, fr. *demissus*, pp. of *demittere*] : RESIGNATION, ABDICATION
de·mit \di-'mit\ *vb* **de·mit·ted; de·mit·ting** [MF *demettre*] *vt* **1** *archaic* : DISMISS **2** : RESIGN ~ *vi* : to withdraw from office or membership
demi·tasse \'dem-ē-ˌtas, -ˌtäs\ *n* [F *demi-tasse*, fr. *demi-* + *tasse* cup] : a small cup of black coffee; *also* : the cup used to serve it
demi·urge \'dem-ē-ˌərj\ *n* [LL *demiurgus*, fr. Gk *dēmiourgos*, lit., one who works for the people, fr. *dēmios* of the people (fr. *dēmos* people) + *-ourgos* worker (fr. *ergon* work) — more at DEMAGOGUE, WORK] **1** *cap* **a** : a Platonic subordinate deity who fashions the sensible world in the light of eternal ideas **b** : a Gnostic subordinate deity who is the creator of the material world **2** : something that is an autonomous creative force or decisive power — **demi·urge·ous** \ˌdem-ē-'ər-jəs\ *adj* — **demi·ur·gic** \-jik\ *or* **demi·ur·gi·cal** \-ji-kəl\ *adj* — **demi·ur·gi·cal·ly** \-ji-k(ə-)lē\ *adv*
1**de·mob** \(ˈ)dē-'mäb\ *vt, chiefly Brit* : DEMOBILIZE
2**demob** *n, chiefly Brit* : DEMOBILIZATION
de·mo·bi·li·za·tion \di-ˌmō-bə-lə-'zā-shən\ *n* : the act or process of demobilizing
de·mo·bi·lize \di-'mō-bə-ˌlīz\ *vt* **1** : DISBAND **2** : to discharge from military service
de·moc·ra·cy \di-'mäk-rə-sē\ *n* [MF *democratie*, fr. LL *democratia*, fr. Gk *dēmokratia*, fr. *dēmos* + *-kratia* -cracy] **1 a** : government by the people; *esp* : rule of the majority **b** : a government in which the supreme power is vested in the people and exercised by them directly or indirectly through a system of representation usu. involving periodically held free elections **2** : a political unit that has a democratic government **3** *cap* : the principles and policies of the Democratic party in the U.S. **4** : the common people esp. when constituting the source of political authority **5** : the absence of hereditary or arbitrary class distinctions or privileges
dem·o·crat \'dem-ə-ˌkrat\ *n* **1 a** : an adherent of democracy **b** : one who practices social equality **2** *cap* : a member of the Democratic party of the U.S.
dem·o·crat·ic \ˌdem-ə-'krat-ik\ *adj* **1** : of, relating to, or favoring democracy **2** *often cap* : of or relating to one of the two major political parties in the U.S. evolving in the early 19th century from the anti-Federalists and the Democratic-Republican party and associated in modern times with policies of broad social reform and internationalism **3** : of, relating to, or appealing to the broad masses of the people ⟨~ art⟩ **4** : favoring social equality : not snobbish — **dem·o·crat·i·cal·ly** \-i-k(ə-)lē\ *adv*
Democratic–Republican *adj* : of or relating to a major American political party of the early 19th century favoring a strict interpretation of the constitution to restrict the powers of the federal government and emphasizing states' rights
de·moc·ra·ti·za·tion \di-ˌmäk-rət-ə-'zā-shən\ *n* : the act or process of making or becoming democratic
de·moc·ra·tize \di-'mäk-rə-ˌtīz\ *vt* : to make democratic
dé·mo·dé \ˌdā-ˌmō-'dā\ *adj* [F, fr. *dé-* de- + *mode*] : no longer fashionable : OUT-OF-DATE
de·mod·ed \(ˈ)dē-'mōd-əd\ *adj* : DEMODÉ
de·mod·u·late \(ˈ)dē-'mäj-ə-ˌlāt\ *vt* : to extract the intelligence from (a modulated radio signal)
de·mod·u·la·tion \(ˌ)dē-ˌmäj-ə-'lā-shən\ *n* : extraction of the transmitted sound or visual images from a modulated radio signal

De·mo·gor·gon \'dē-mə-,gȯr-gən\ *n* [LL] **:** a mysterious, terrible, and evil divinity who in ancient mythology commanded the spirits of the netherworld

de·mog·ra·pher \di-'mäg-rə-fər\ *n* **:** a specialist in demography

de·mo·graph·ic \,dē-mə-'graf-ik, ,dem-ə-\ *adj* **:** of or relating to demography — **de·mo·graph·i·cal·ly** \-i-k(ə-)lē\ *adv*

de·mog·ra·phy \di-'mäg-rə-fē\ *n* [F *démographie*, fr. Gk *dēmos* people + F *-graphie* -graphy] **:** the statistical study of human populations esp. with reference to size and density, distribution, and vital statistics

dem·oi·selle \,dem-(w)ə-'zel\ *n* [F, fr. OF *dameisele*] **1 :** a young lady **2 :** a small Old World crane (*Anthropoides virgo*) with long secondaries and breast feathers **3 :** DAMSELFLY

de·mol·ish \di-'mäl-ish\ *vt* [MF *demoliss-*, stem of *demolir*, fr. L *demoliri*, fr. *de-* + *moliri* to construct, fr. *moles* mass] **1 a :** to tear down **:** RAZE **b :** to break to pieces **:** SMASH **2 a :** to do away with **:** DESTROY **b :** to put into a very weak position — **de·mol·ish·er** *n* — **de·mol·ish·ment** \-ish-mənt\ *n*

de·mo·li·tion \,dem-ə-'lish-ən, ,dē-mə-\ *n* **1 :** the act of demolishing; *specif* **:** destruction in war by means of explosives **2** *pl* **:** explosives for destruction in war — **de·mo·li·tion·ist** \-'lish-(ə-)nəst\ *n*

de·mon *or* **dae·mon** \'dē-mən\ *n, often attrib* [ME *demon*, fr. LL & L; LL *daemon* evil spirit, fr. L, divinity, spirit, fr. Gk *daimōn*] **1** *usu daemon* **:** an attendant power or spirit **:** GENIUS **2 a :** an evil spirit **b :** an evil or undesirable emotion, trait, or state **3** *usu daemon* **:** a supernatural being of Greek mythology intermediate between gods and men **4 :** one that has unusual drive or effectiveness — **de·mo·ni·an** \di-'mō-nē-ən\ *adj* — **de·mon·ic** \-'män-ik\ *also* **de·mon·i·cal** \-'män-i-kəl\ *adj* — **de·mon·i·cal·ly** \-i-k(ə-)lē\ *adv* — **de·mon·iza·tion** \,dē-mə-nə-'zā-shən\ *n* — **de·mon·ize** \'dē-mə-,nīz\ *vt*

de·mon·e·ti·za·tion \(,)dē-,män-ət-ə-'zā-shən, -,mən-\ *n* **:** the action of demonetizing

de·mon·e·tize \(')dē-'män-ə-,tīz, -'mən-\ *vt* [F *démonétiser*, fr. *dé-* de- + L *moneta* coin] **1 :** to stop using (a metal) as a monetary standard **2 :** to deprive of value for official payment

1**de·mo·ni·ac** \di-'mō-nē-,ak\ *also* **de·mo·ni·a·cal** \,dē-mə-'nī-ə-kəl\ *adj* [ME *demoniak*, fr. LL *daemoniacus*, fr. Gk *daimoniakos*, fr. *daimon-*, *daimōn*] **1 :** possessed by a demon **2 :** of, relating to, or suggestive of a demon — **de·mo·ni·a·cal·ly** \-'nī-ə-k(ə-)lē\ *adv*

2**demoniac** *n* **:** one regarded as possessed by a demon

de·mon·ol·o·gy \,dē-mə-'näl-ə-jē\ *n* **1 :** the study of demons **2 :** belief in demons **3 :** a catalog of enemies

de·mon·stra·bil·i·ty \di-,män(t)-strə-'bil-ət-ē, ,dem-ən-strə-\ *n* **:** the quality of being demonstrable

de·mon·stra·ble \di-'män(t)-strə-bəl, 'dem-ən-strə-\ *adj* **1 :** capable of being demonstrated **2 :** APPARENT, EVIDENT — **de·mon·stra·ble·ness** *n* — **de·mon·stra·bly** \-blē\ *adv*

dem·on·strate \'dem-ən-,strāt\ *vb* [L *demonstratus*, pp. of *demonstrare*, fr. *de-* + *monstrare* to show] *vt* **1 :** to show clearly **2 a :** to prove or make clear by reasoning or evidence **b :** to illustrate and explain esp. with many examples **3 :** to show or prove to a customer ~ *vi* **:** to make a demonstration **syn** see SHOW

dem·on·stra·tion \,dem-ən-'strā-shən\ *n* **1 :** an outward expression or display **2 :** an act, process, or means of demonstrating to the intelligence: as **a** (1) **:** conclusive evidence **:** PROOF (2) **:** a proof in which the conclusion is the immediate sequence of reasoning from premises **b :** a showing to a prospective buyer of the merits of a product **3 :** a show of armed force **4 :** a public display of group feelings toward a person or cause — **dem·on·stra·tion·al** \-shnəl, -shən-ᵊl\ *adj* — **dem·on·stra·tion·ist** \-sh(ə-)nəst\ *n*

1**de·mon·stra·tive** \di-'män(t)-strət-iv\ *adj* **1 a :** demonstrating as real or true **b :** characterized or established by demonstration **2 :** pointing out the one referred to and distinguishing it from others of the same class ⟨~ pronouns⟩ **3 :** marked by display of feeling — **de·mon·stra·tive·ly** *adv* — **de·mon·stra·tive·ness** *n*

2**demonstrative** *n* **:** a demonstrative word or morpheme

dem·on·stra·tor \'dem-ən-,strāt-ər\ *n* **1 :** one that demonstrates **2 :** a manufactured product used for demonstrations to customers

de·mor·al·iza·tion \di-,mȯr-ə-lə-'zā-shən, ,dē-, -,mär-\ *n* **1 :** the act or process of demoralizing **2 :** a demoralized state

de·mor·al·ize \di-'mȯr-ə-,līz, 'dē-, -'mär-\ *vt* **1 :** to corrupt the morals of **2 a :** to weaken the morale of **b :** to destroy the normal functioning of **c :** to throw into disorder — **de·mor·al·iz·er** *n*

de·mos \'dē-,mäs\ *n* [Gk *dēmos* — more at DEMAGOGUE] **1 :** the common people of an ancient Greek state **2 :** POPULACE

de·mote \di-'mōt, 'dē-\ *vt* [*de-* + *-mote* (as in *promote*)] **:** to reduce to a lower grade or rank — **de·mo·tion** \-'mō-shən\ *n*

de·mot·ic \di-'mät-ik\ *adj* [Gk *dēmotikos*, fr. *dēmotēs* commoner fr. *dēmos*] **1 :** POPULAR 1 **2 :** of, relating to, or written in a simplified form of the ancient Egyptian hieratic writing **3 :** of or relating to the form of Modern Greek that is based on colloquial use

de·mount \(')dē-'mau̇nt\ *vt* **1 :** to remove from a mounted position **2 :** DISASSEMBLE — **de·mount·able** \-ə-bəl\ *adj*

1**de·mul·cent** \di-'məl-sənt\ *adj* [L *demulcent-*, *demulcens*, prp. of *demulcēre* to soothe, fr. *de-* + *mulcēre* to soothe] **:** SOOTHING

2**demulcent** *n* **:** a usu. mucilaginous or oily substance (as tragacanth) capable of soothing or protecting an abraded mucous membrane

1**de·mur** \di-'mər\ *vi* **de·murred; de·mur·ring** [ME *demeoren* to linger, fr. OF *demorer*, fr. L *demorari*, fr. *de-* + *morari* to linger, fr. *mora* delay — more at MEMORY] **1 :** to interpose a demurrer **2 :** to take exception **:** OBJECT **3** *archaic* **:** DELAY, HESITATE

2**demur** *n* **1 :** HESITATION **2 :** OBJECTION, PROTEST **syn** see QUALM

de·mure \di-'myu̇(ə)r\ *adj* [ME] **1 :** SOBER, MODEST **2 :** affectedly modest, reserved, or serious — **de·mure·ly** *adv* — **de·mure·ness** *n*

de·mur·rage \di-'mər-ij, -'mə-rij\ *n* **1 :** the detention of a ship by the freighter beyond the time allowed for loading, unloading, or sailing **2 :** a charge for detaining a ship, freight car, or truck

de·mur·ral \di-'mər-əl, -'mə-rəl\ *n* **:** an act or instance of demurring

1**de·mur·rer** \di-'mər-ər, -'mə-rər\ *n* [MF *demorer*, v.] **1 :** a pleading by a party to a legal action that assumes the truth of the matter alleged by the opposite party and sets up that it is insufficient in law to sustain his claim or that there is some other defect on the face of the pleadings constituting a legal reason why the opposing party should not be allowed to proceed further **2 :** OBJECTION

2**de·mur·rer** \-'mər-ər\ *n* [1*demur*] **:** one that demurs

de·my \di-'mī\ *n* [ME *demi* half — more at DEMI-] **:** a size of paper typically 16 × 21 inches

de·my·e·lin·ate \(')dē-'mī-ə-lə-,nāt\ *vt* **:** to remove or destroy the myelin of — **de·my·e·lin·ation** \(,)dē-,mī-ə-lə-'nā-shən\ *n*

de·my·thol·o·gize \,dē-mə-'thäl-ə-,jīz\ *vt* **:** to divest of mythological forms in order to uncover the meaning underlying them

1**den** \'den\ *n* [ME, fr. OE *denn*; akin to OE *denu* valley, OHG *tenni* threshing floor, Gk *thenar* palm of the hand] **1 :** the lair of a wild usu. predatory animal **2 a** (1) **:** a hollow or cavern used esp. as a hideout (2) **:** a center of secret activity **b :** a small usu. squalid dwelling **3 :** a comfortable usu. secluded room

2**den** *vb* **denned; den·ning** *vi* **:** to live in or retire to a den ~ *vt* **:** to drive into a den

de·nar·i·us \di-'nar-ē-əs, -'ner-\ *n, pl* **de·nar·ii** \-ē-,ī, -ē-,ē\ [ME, fr. L — more at DENIER] **1 :** a small silver coin of ancient Rome **2 :** a gold coin of the Roman Empire equivalent to 25 denarii

de·na·tion·al·iza·tion \(,)dē-,nash-nə-lə-'zā-shən, -,nash-ən-ᵊl-ə-'zā-\ *n* **1 :** the act of denationalizing **2 :** the state of being denationalized

de·na·tion·al·ize \(')dē-'nash-nə-,līz, -'nash-ən-ᵊl-,īz\ *vt* **1 :** to divest of national character or rights **2 :** to remove from ownership or control by the national government

de·nat·u·ral·iza·tion \(,)dē-,nach-(ə-)rə-lə-'zā-shən\ *n* **1 :** the act of denaturalizing **2 :** the state of being denaturalized

de·nat·u·ral·ize \(')dē-'nach-(ə-)rə-,līz\ *vt* **1 :** to make unnatural **2 :** to deprive of the rights and duties of a citizen

de·na·tur·ant \(')dē-'nāch-(ə-)rənt\ *n* **:** a denaturing agent

de·na·tur·ation \(,)dē-,nā-chə-'rā-shən\ *n* **:** the process of denaturing

de·na·ture \(')dē-'nā-chər\ *vt* **de·na·tur·ing** \-'nāch-(ə-)riŋ\ **:** to deprive of natural qualities: as **a :** to make (alcohol) unfit for drinking without impairing usefulness for other purposes **b :** to modify (as a native protein) esp. by heat, acid, alkali, or ultraviolet radiation so that all of the original properties are removed or diminished **c :** to add nonfissionable material to (fissionable material) so as to make unsuitable for use in an atomic bomb

dendr- *or* **dendro-** *comb form* [Gk, fr. *dendron*; akin to Gk *drys* tree — more at TREE] **:** tree ⟨*dendro*philous⟩ **:** resembling a tree ⟨*dendr*ite⟩

den·dri·form \'den-drə-,fȯrm\ *adj* **:** resembling a tree in structure

den·drite \'den-,drīt\ *n* **1 :** a branching figure resembling a tree produced on or in a mineral by a foreign mineral; *also* **:** the mineral so marked **2 :** a crystallized arborescent form **3 :** any of the usu. branching protoplasmic processes that conduct impulses toward the body of a nerve cell — **den·drit·ic** \den-'drit-ik\ *also* **den·drit·i·cal** \-i-kəl\ *adj* — **den·drit·i·cal·ly** \-i-k(ə-)lē\ *adv*

den·dro·chron·o·log·i·cal \'den-(,)drō-,krän-ᵊl-'äj-i-kəl\ *adj* **:** of or relating to dendrochronology — **den·dro·chron·o·log·i·cal·ly** \-k(ə-)lē\ *adv*

den·dro·chro·nol·o·gy \,den-(,)drō-krə-'näl-ə-jē\ *n* **:** the science of dating events and variations in environment in former periods by comparative study of growth rings in trees and aged wood

den·droid \'den-,drȯid\ *adj* [Gk *dendroeidēs*, fr. *dendron*] **:** resembling a tree in form **:** ARBORESCENT

den·dro·log·ic \,den-drə-'läj-ik\ *adj* **:** relating to dendrology — **den·dro·log·i·cal** \-i-kəl\ *adj*

den·drol·o·gist \den-'dräl-ə-jəst\ *n* **:** a specialist in dendrology

den·drol·o·gy \-jē\ *n* **:** the study of trees

dene \'dēn\ *n* [ME, fr. OE *denu*] *Brit* **:** VALLEY

Dé·né \dā-'nā\ *n, pl* **Déné** *or* **Dénés** [F, fr. Déné] **1 a :** an Athapaskan people of the interior of Alaska and northwestern Canada **b :** a member of this people **2 :** the language of the Déné people

Den·eb \'den-,eb, -əb\ *n* [Ar *dhanab al-dajāj*, lit., the tail of the hen] **:** a star of the first magnitude in Cygnus

den·e·ga·tion \,den-i-'gā-shən\ *n* [ME *denegacioun*, fr. MF or L; MF *denegation*, fr. L *denegation-*, *denegatio*, fr. *denegatus*, pp. of *denegare* to deny — more at DENY] **:** DENIAL

den·gue \'deŋ-gē; 'deŋ-,gā, 'den-\ *n* [Sp] **:** an acute infectious disease characterized by headache, severe joint pain, and a rash

de·ni·able \di-'nī-ə-bəl\ *adj* **:** capable of being denied

de·ni·al \di-'nī(-ə)l\ *n* **1 :** refusal to satisfy a request or desire **2 a** (1) **:** refusal to admit the truth or reality (2) **:** assertion that something alleged is false **b :** DISAVOWAL **3 :** the opposing by the defendant of an allegation of the opposite party in a law suit **4 :** restriction on one's own activity or desires

de·nic·o·tin·ize \(')dē-'nik-ə-,tē-,nīz\ *vt* **:** to remove part of the nicotine from (tobacco)

1**de·ni·er** \di-'nī(-ə)r\ *n* **:** one that denies

2**de·nier** *n* [ME *denere*, fr. MF *denier*, fr. L *denarius*, coin worth ten asses, fr. *denarius* containing ten, fr. *deni* ten each, fr. *decem* ten] **1** \də-'ni(ə)r, dən-'yā\ **:** a small orig. silver coin of France and western Europe from the 8th to the 19th century **2** \'den-yər\ **:** a unit of fineness for silk, rayon, or nylon yarn equal to the fineness of a yarn weighing one gram for each 9000 meters

den·i·grate \'den-i-,grāt\ *vt* [L *denigratus*, pp. of *denigrare*, fr. *de-* + *nigrare* to blacken, fr. *nigr-*, *niger* black] **:** to cast aspersions on **:** DEFAME — **den·i·gra·tion** \,den-i-'grā-shən\ *n* — **den·i·gra·tor** \'den-i-,grāt-ər\ *n* — **den·i·gra·to·ry** \-grə-,tōr-ē, -,tȯr-\ *adj*

den·im \'den-əm\ *n* [F (*serge*) *de Nîmes* serge of Nîmes, France] **1 a :** a firm durable twilled usu. cotton fabric woven with colored warp and white filling threads **b :** a similar fabric woven in colored stripes **2** *pl* **:** overalls or trousers usu. of blue denim

de·ni·tri·fi·ca·tion \(,)dē-,nī-trə-fə-'kā-shən\ *n* **:** an act or process of denitrifying; *specif* **:** reduction of nitrates or nitrites commonly by bacteria and usu. resulting in the escape of nitrogen into the air

de·ni·tri·fy \(')dē-'nī-trə-,fī\ *vt* **1 :** to remove nitrogen or its compound from **2 :** to convert (a nitrate or a nitrite) into a compound of a lower state of oxidation

den·i·zen \'den-ə-zən\ *n* [ME *denysen*, fr. MF *denzein*, fr. OF, inner, fr. *denz* within, fr. LL *deintus*, fr. L *de-* + *intus* within — more at ENT-] **1 :** INHABITANT **2 :** one admitted to residence in a foreign country; *esp* **:** an alien admitted to rights of citizenship **3 a :** a naturalized plant or animal **b :** one that frequents a place

de·nom·i·nate \di-'näm-ə-,nāt\ *vt* [L *denominatus*, pp. of *denominare*, fr. *de-* + *nominare* to name — more at NOMINATE] **:** to give a name to **:** DESIGNATE

de·nom·i·nate number \di-,näm-ə-nət-\ *n* [L *denominatus*] **:** a number (as 7 in *7 feet*) that specifies a quantity in terms of a unit of measurement

de·nom·i·na·tion \di-,näm-ə-'nā-shən\ *n* **1 :** an act of denominat-

ing **2 :** NAME, DESIGNATION; *esp* **:** a general name for a category **3 :** a religious organization uniting in a single legal and administrative body a number of local congregations **4 :** a value or size of a series of values or sizes (as of money) — **de·nom·i·na·tion·al** \-shnəl, -shən-ᵊl\ *adj* — **de·nom·i·na·tion·al·ly** \-ē\ *adv*

de·nom·i·na·tion·al·ism \-shnəl-ˌiz-əm, -shən-ᵊl-\ *n* **1 :** devotion to denominational principles or interests **2 :** narrow emphasizing of denominational differences **:** SECTARIANISM

de·nom·i·na·tive \di-ˈnäm-(ə-)nət-iv\ *adj* [L *de* from + *nominnomen* name] **:** derived from a noun or adjective — **denominative** *n*

de·nom·i·na·tor \di-ˈnäm-ə-ˌnāt-ər\ *n* **1 :** the part of a fraction that is below the line signifying division and that in fractions with 1 as the numerator indicates into how many parts the unit is divided **:** DIVISOR **2 a :** a common trait **b :** the average level **:** STANDARD

de·no·ta·tion \ˌdē-nō-ˈtā-shən\ *n* **1 :** an act or process of denoting **2 a :** MEANING; *esp* **:** a direct specific meaning as distinct from connotations **b :** the things to which a name applies **3 :** a denoting term **:** NAME **4 :** SIGN, INDICATION ⟨visible ~*s* of divine wrath⟩

de·no·ta·tive \ˈdē-nō-ˌtāt-iv, di-ˈnōt-ət-iv\ *adj* **1 :** denoting or tending to denote **2 :** relating to denotation

de·note \di-ˈnōt\ *vt* [MF *denoter*, fr. L *denotare*, fr. *de-* + *notare* to note] **1 :** to serve as an indication of **2 :** to serve as an arbitrary mark for **3 :** to make known **:** ANNOUNCE **4 a :** to serve as linguistic expression of the notion of **:** MEAN **b :** to serve as a linguistic indication of **:** NAME — compare CONNOTE — **de·note·ment** \-ˈnōt-mənt\ *n* — **de·no·tive** \-ˈnōt-iv\ *adj*

syn DENOTE, CONNOTE: to DENOTE is to name or indicate a known object or concept or a definable class of objects or concepts; to CONNOTE is to imply the attributes or ideas suggested by or associated with a term ⟨"home" *denotes* the place where one lives but *connotes* safety, comfort, privacy, intimacy⟩ **syn** see in addition MEAN

de·noue·ment \ˌdā-nü-ˈmäⁿ, dā-ˈnü-ˌmäⁿ\ *n* [F *dénouement*, lit., untying, fr. MF *desnouement*, fr. *desnouer* to untie, fr. OF *desnoer*, fr. *des-* de- + *noer* to tie, fr. L *nodare*, fr. *nodus* knot] **1 :** the final outcome or unraveling of the main dramatic complication in a literary work **2 :** the outcome of a complex sequence of events

de·nounce \di-ˈnau̇n(t)s\ *vt* [ME *denouncen*, fr. OF *denoncier* to proclaim, fr. L *denuntiare*, fr. *de-* + *nuntiare* to report — more at ANNOUNCE] **1 :** to pronounce blameworthy or evil **2** *archaic* **a :** PROCLAIM **b :** to announce threateningly **3 :** to inform against **:** ACCUSE **4** *obs* **:** PORTEND **5 :** to announce formally the termination of (as a treaty) **syn** see CRITICIZE — **de·nounce·ment** \-ˈnau̇n(t)-smənt\ *n* — **de·nounc·er** *n*

de no·vo \di-ˈnō-(ˌ)vō, dā-\ *adv* [L] **:** ANEW, AGAIN

dense \ˈden(t)s\ *adj* [L *densus;* akin to Gk *dasys* thick with hair or leaves] **1 :** marked by compactness or crowding together of parts **2 a :** DULL, STUPID **b :** EXTREME ⟨~ ignorance⟩ **3 :** having between any two elements at least one element **4 :** having high or relatively high opacity **syn** see CLOSE, STUPID — **dense·ly** *adv* — **dense·ness** \ˈden(t)-snəs\ *n*

den·si·fy \ˈden(t)-sə-ˌfī\ *vt* **:** to make denser; *specif* **:** to increase the density of (wood) by pressure usu. with impregnation of a resin

den·sim·e·ter \den-ˈsim-ət-ər\ *n* [L *densus* + ISV *-meter*] **:** an instrument for determining density or specific gravity — **den·si·met·ric** \ˌden(t)-sə-ˈme-trik\ *adj*

den·si·tom·e·ter \ˌden(t)-sə-ˈtäm-ət-ər\ *n* **:** DENSIMETER — **den·si·to·met·ric** \ˌden(t)-sət-ə-ˈme-trik\ *adj* — **den·si·tom·e·try** \ˌden(t)-sə-ˈtäm-ə-trē\ *n*

den·si·ty \ˈden(t)-sət-ē\ *n* **1 :** the quality or state of being dense **2 :** the quantity per unit volume, unit area, or unit length: as **a :** the mass of a substance per unit volume **b :** the average number of individuals or units per space unit **3 :** STUPIDITY **4 a :** the degree of opacity of a translucent medium **b :** the common logarithm of the opacity

¹dent \ˈdent\ *n* [ME, blow, alter. of *dint*] **1 :** a depression or hollow made by a blow or by pressure **2 a :** an impression or effect made usu. against resistance **b :** initial progress — **dent** *vb*

²dent *n* [F, lit., tooth, fr. L *dent-*, *dens*] **:** TOOTH 3a

dent- *or* **denti-** *or* **dento-** *comb form* [ME *denti-*, fr. L, fr. *dent-*, *dens* tooth — more at TOOTH] **1 :** tooth **:** teeth ⟨*dent*algia⟩ ⟨*denti*form⟩ **2 :** dental and ⟨*dento*surgical⟩

¹den·tal \ˈdent-ᵊl\ *adj* [L *dentalis*, fr. *dent-*, *dens*] **1 :** of or relating to the teeth or dentistry **2 :** articulated with the tip or blade of the tongue against or near the upper front teeth — **den·tal·ly** \-ē\ *adv*

²dental *n* **:** a dental consonant

dental floss *n* **:** a flat waxed thread used to clean between the teeth

dental hygienist *n* **:** one who assists a dentist esp. in cleaning teeth

den·ta·li·um \den-ˈtā-lē-əm\ *n, pl* **den·ta·lia** \-lē-ə\ [NL, genus name, fr. L *dentalis*] **:** any of a genus (*Dentalium*) of widely distributed tooth shells; *broadly* **:** TOOTH SHELL

dental technician *n* **:** a technician who makes dental appliances

den·tate \ˈden-ˌtāt\ *or* **den·tat·ed** \-ˌtāt-əd\ *adj* [L *dentatus*, fr. *dent-*, *dens*] **:** having teeth or pointed conical projections ⟨multi*dentate*⟩ — **den·tate·ly** *adv* — **den·ta·tion** \den-ˈtā-shən\ *n*

dent corn *n* **:** an Indian corn having kernels that contain both hard and soft starch and become indented at maturity

den·ti·cle \ˈdent-i-kəl\ *n* [ME, fr. L *denticulus*, dim. of *dent-*, *dens*] **:** a small tooth or other conical pointed projection

den·tic·u·late \den-ˈtik-yə-lət\ *or* **den·tic·u·lat·ed** \-ˌlāt-əd\ *adj* **1 a :** covered with small pointed projections ⟨a ~ shell⟩; *esp* **:** SERRATE **b :** finely dentate **2 :** cut into dentils — **den·tic·u·late·ly** *adv* — **den·tic·u·la·tion** \(ˌ)den-ˌtik-yə-ˈlā-shən\ *n*

den·ti·form \ˈdent-ə-ˌfȯrm\ *adj* **1 :** shaped like a tooth **2 :** divided into dentate processes

den·ti·frice \ˈdent-ə-frəs\ *n* [MF, fr. L *dentifricium*, fr. *denti-* + *fricare* to rub] **:** a powder, paste, or liquid for cleaning the teeth

den·tig·er·ous \den-ˈtij-ə-rəs\ *adj* **:** bearing dentate structures

den·til \ˈdent-ᵊl\ *n* [obs. F *dentille*, fr. MF, dim. of *dent*] **:** one of a series of small projecting rectangular blocks esp. under a cornice

den·tin \ˈdent-ᵊn\ *or* **den·tine** \ˈden-ˌtēn, den-ˈtēn\ *n* **:** a calcareous material like bone but harder and denser that composes the principal mass of a tooth — **den·tin·al** \den-ˈtēn-ᵊl, ˈdent-ᵊn-əl\ *adj*

den·tist \ˈdent-əst\ *n* [F *dentiste*, fr. *dent*] **:** one who treats the teeth and associated tissues and makes and inserts false teeth

den·tist·ry \ˈdent-ə-strē\ *n* **:** the art or profession of a dentist

den·ti·tion \den-ˈtish-ən\ *n* [L *dentition-*, *dentitio*, fr. *dentitus*, pp. of *dentire* to cut teeth, fr. *dent-*, *dens*] **1 :** the development and cutting of teeth **2 :** the number, kind, and arrangement of teeth **3 :** the character of the teeth as determined by their form and arrangement

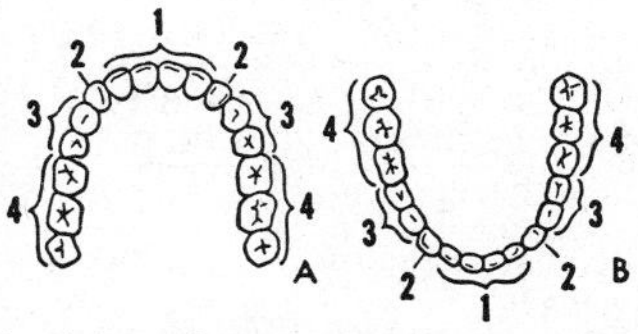

dentition of adult human: upper, *A;* lower, *B; 1* incisors, *2* canines, *3* bicuspids, *4* molars

den·tu·lous \ˈden-chə-ləs\ *adj* [back-formation fr. *edentulous*] **:** having teeth

den·ture \ˈden-chər\ *n* [F, fr. MF, fr. *dent*] **1 :** a set of teeth **2 :** an artificial replacement for one or more teeth; *esp* **:** a set of false teeth

de·nu·da·tion \ˌdē-(ˌ)n(y)ü-ˈdā-shən, ˌden-yü-\ *n* **:** an act or process of denuding — **de·nu·da·tion·al** \-shnəl, -shən-ᵊl\ *adj*

de·nude \di-ˈn(y)üd\ *vt* [L *denudare*, fr. *de-* + *nudus* bare] **1 a :** to strip of all covering **b :** to lay bare by erosion **c :** to strip (land) of forests **2 :** to divest of an important part — **de·nud·er** *n*

de·nu·mer·a·ble \di-ˈn(y)üm-(ə-)rə-bəl\ *adj* **:** capable of being put into one-to-one correspondence with the positive integers

de·nun·ci·a·tion \di-ˌnən(t)-sē-ˈā-shən\ *n* **:** an act of denouncing — **de·nun·ci·a·tive** \di-ˈnən(t)-sē-ˌāt-iv\ *adj*

de·nun·ci·a·to·ry \di-ˈnən(t)-sē-ə-ˌtōr-ē, -ˌtȯr-\ *adj* **:** marked by or given to denunciation

de·ny \di-ˈnī\ *vt* [ME *denyen*, fr. OF *denier*, fr. L *denegare*, fr. *de-* + *negare* to deny] **1 :** to declare untrue **2 :** to disclaim connection with or responsibility for **:** DISAVOW **3 a :** to give a negative answer to **b :** to refuse to grant **c :** to restrain (oneself) from gratification of desires **4** *archaic* **:** DECLINE **5 :** to refuse to accept the existence, truth, or validity of — **de·ny·ing·ly** \-iŋ-lē\ *adv*

syn GAINSAY, CONTRADICT, NEGATIVE, IMPUGN, CONTRAVENE: DENY implies a refusal to accept a statement as true or valid; GAINSAY implies opposition by disputing the truth of something said; CONTRADICT implies an open or flat denial and suggests that the contrary is true; NEGATIVE implies as little as possible beyond a mere refusal to assent or approve; IMPUGN stresses an attack upon the truth of a statement or upon the integrity of the person making it; CONTRAVENE stresses a conflict or logical incompatibility between something said or prescribed and a present act or state of affairs

de·o·dar \ˈdē-ə-ˌdär\ *or* **de·o·da·ra** \ˌdē-ə-ˈdär-ə\ *n* [Hindi *deodār*, fr. Skt *devadāru*, lit., timber of the gods, fr. *deva* god + *dāru* wood] **:** an East Indian cedar (*Cedrus deodara*)

de·odor·ant \dē-ˈōd-ə-rənt\ *n* **:** a preparation that destroys or masks unpleasant odors — **deodorant** *adj*

de·odor·ize \-ˈōd-ə-ˌrīz\ *vt* **:** to eliminate or prevent the offensive odor of — **de·odor·iz·er** *n*

de·on·tol·o·gy \ˌdē-ˌän-ˈtäl-ə-jē\ *n* [Gk *deont-*, *deon* that which is obligatory, fr. neut. of prp. of *dein* to lack, be needful — more at DEUTER-] **:** the theory or study of moral obligation

Deo vo·len·te \ˌdā-(ˌ)ō-və-ˈlent-ē, ˌdē-\ [L] **:** God being willing

de·ox·i·dize \(ˈ)dē-ˈäk-sə-ˌdīz\ *vt* **:** to remove oxygen from — **de·ox·i·diz·er** *n*

deoxy- *or* **desoxy-** *comb form* [ISV] **:** containing less oxygen in the molecule than the compound to which it is closely related ⟨*deoxy*ribonucleic acid⟩

de·oxy·cor·ti·cos·ter·one \dē-ˌäk-sē-ˌkȯrt-i-ˈkäs-tə-ˌrōn, -i-kō-ˈsti(ə)r-ˌōn\ *n* [ISV] **:** a steroid hormone $C_{21}H_{30}O_3$ of the adrenal cortex

de·ox·y·ge·nate \(ˈ)dē-ˈäk-si-jə-ˌnāt, ˌdē-ˌäk-ˈsij-ə-\ *vt* **:** to remove oxygen from — **de·ox·y·ge·na·tion** \(ˌ)dē-ˌäk-si-jə-ˈnā-shən, ˌdē-ˌäk-ˌsij-ə-\ *n*

de·ox·y·ge·nat·ed *adj* **:** having the hemoglobin in the reduced state

de·ox·y·ri·bo·nu·cle·ic acid \dē-ˌäk-sē-ˈrī-bō-n(y)u̇-ˌklē-ik-, -ˌklā-\ *n* [*deoxy-* + *ribonucleic acid* (a nucleic acid yielding ribose)] **:** any of various nucleic acids found esp. in cell nuclei and as a major constituent of chromatin

de·part \di-ˈpärt\ *vb* [ME *departen* to divide, go away, fr. OF *departir*, fr. *de-* + *partir* to divide, fr. L *partire*, fr. *part-*, *pars* part] *vi* **1 a :** to go away **:** LEAVE **b :** DIE **2 :** to turn aside **:** DEVIATE ~ *vt* **:** to go away from **:** LEAVE **syn** see GO, SWERVE

de·part·ed *adj* **1 :** BYGONE **2 :** no longer living **syn** see DEAD

de·part·ment \di-ˈpärt-mənt\ *n* [F *département*, fr. MF, fr. *departir*] **1 :** a distinct sphere **:** PROVINCE **2 :** a functional or territorial division: as **a :** a major administrative division of a government **b :** a major territorial administrative subdivision **c :** a division of a college or school giving instruction in a particular subject **d :** a major division of a business **e :** a section of a department store **f :** a territorial subdivision made for the administration and training of military units — **de·part·men·tal** \di-ˌpärt-ˈment-ᵊl, ˌdē-\ *adj* — **de·part·men·tal·ly** \-ᵊl-ē\ *adv*

de·part·men·tal·ize \-ᵊl-ˌīz\ *vt* **:** to divide into departments

department store *n* **:** a store keeping a wide variety of goods arranged in several departments

de·par·ture \di-ˈpär-chər\ *n* **1 a** (1) **:** the act of going away (2) *archaic* **:** DEATH **b :** a ship's position in latitude and longitude at the beginning of a voyage as a point from which to begin dead reckoning **c :** a setting out (as on a new course) **2 :** the distance due east or west made by a ship in its course **3 :** DIVERGENCE

de·pau·per·ate \di-ˈpȯ-pə-rət\ *adj* [ME *depauperat*, fr. ML *depauperatus*, pp. of *depauperare* to impoverish, fr. L *de-* + *pauperare* to impoverish, fr. *pauper* poor] **:** falling short of natural development or size — **de·pau·per·a·tion** \di-ˌpȯ-pə-ˈrā-shən\ *n*

de·pend \di-ˈpend\ *vi* [ME *dependen*, fr. MF *dependre*, modif. of L *dependēre*, fr. *de-* + *pendēre* to hang] **1 a :** to be contingent **b :** to exist by virtue of a necessary relation **2 :** to be pending or undecided **3 a :** to place reliance or trust **b :** to be dependent esp. for financial support **4 :** to hang down **syn** see RELY

de·pend·abil·i·ty \di-ˌpen-də-ˈbil-ət-ē\ *n* **:** the quality or state of being dependable

de·pend·able \di-ˈpen-də-bəl\ *adj* **:** capable of being depended on **:** RELIABLE — **de·pend·able·ness** *n* — **de·pend·ably** \-blē\ *adv*

de·pen·dence *also* **de·pen·dance** \di-ˈpen-dən(t)s\ *n* **1 :** the quality or state of being dependent; *esp* **:** the quality or state of being influenced by or subject to another **2 :** RELIANCE, TRUST **3 :** something on which one relies

de·pen·den·cy \-dən-sē\ *n* **1 :** DEPENDENCE 1 **2 :** something that is dependent on something else; *specif* **:** a territorial unit under the jurisdiction of a nation but not formally annexed by it

[1]**de·pen·dent** \di-'pen-dənt\ *adj* [ME *dependant*, fr. MF, prp. of *dependre*] **1 :** hanging down **2 a :** determined or conditioned by another **b :** relying on another for support **c :** subject to another's jurisdiction **d :** SUBORDINATE 3a — **de·pen·dent·ly** *adv*

[2]**dependent** *also* **de·pen·dant** *n* **1** *archaic* **:** DEPENDENCY **2 :** one that is dependent; *esp* **:** a person who relies on another for support

de·perm \(')dē-'pərm\ *vt* [*de-* + *perm*anent magnetism] **:** to reduce the magnetism of (a ship's steel hull) as a precaution against magnetically operated mines

de·per·son·al·iza·tion \(,)dē-,pər-snə-lə-'zā-shən, -,pərs-ᵊn-ə-lə-\ *n* **1 a :** an act or process of depersonalizing **b :** the quality or state of being depersonalized **2 :** loss of the sense of personal identity

de·per·son·al·ize \(')dē-'pər-snə-,līz, -'pərs-ᵊn-ə-\ *vt* **1 :** to deprive of personality **2 :** to make impersonal

de·pict \di-'pikt\ *vt* [L *depictus*, pp. of *depingere*, fr. *de-* + *pingere* to paint] **1 :** to represent by a picture **2 :** to portray in words — **de·pic·tion** \-'pik-shən\ *n* — **de·pic·tor** \-'pik-tər\ *n*

de·pic·ture \-'pik-chər\ *vt* [alter. of *picture*] **1 :** DEPICT **2 :** IMAGINE

de·pig·men·ta·tion \(,)dē-,pig-mən-'tā-shən, -,men-\ *n* **:** loss of normal pigmentation

dep·i·late \'dep-ə-,lāt\ *vt* [L *depilatus*, pp. of *depilare*, fr. *de-* + *pilus* hair — more at PILE] **:** to remove hair from — **dep·i·la·tion** \,dep-ə-'lā-shən\ *n*

de·pil·a·to·ry \di-'pil-ə-,tōr-ē, -,tȯr-\ *n* **:** an agent for removing hair, wool, or bristles — **depilatory** *adj*

de·plane \(')dē-'plān\ *vi* **:** to get off an airplane

de·plet·able \di-'plēt-ə-bəl\ *adj* **:** capable of being depleted

de·plete \di-'plēt\ *vt* [L *depletus*, pp. of *deplēre*, fr. *de-* + *plēre* to fill] **1 :** to empty of a principal substance **2 :** to lessen markedly in quantity, content, power, or value — **de·ple·tive** \-'plēt-iv\ *adj*

syn DEPLETE, DRAIN, EXHAUST, IMPOVERISH, BANKRUPT mean to deprive of something essential to existence or potency. DEPLETE implies a reduction in number or quantity so as to endanger the ability to function; DRAIN implies a gradual withdrawal and ultimate deprivation of what is necessary to a thing's existence; EXHAUST stresses a complete but not necessarily final emptying rather than implying, as DEPLETE does, a disastrous loss; IMPOVERISH suggests a deprivation of something essential to vigorous well-being; BANKRUPT suggests impoverishment to the point of imminent collapse

de·ple·tion \di-'plē-shən\ *n* **1 :** an act or process of depleting **2 :** the state of being depleted

de·plor·able \di-'plōr-ə-bəl, -'plȯr-\ *adj* **1 :** LAMENTABLE **2 :** BAD, WRETCHED — **de·plor·able·ness** *n* — **de·plor·ably** \-blē\ *adv*

de·plore \di-'plō(ə)r, -'plȯ(ə)r\ *vt* [MF or L; MF *deplorer*, fr. L *deplorare*, fr. *de-* + *plorare* to wail] **1 a :** to feel or express grief for **b :** to regret strongly **2 :** to consider unfortunate or deserving of deprecation — **de·plor·er** *n* — **de·plor·ing·ly** \-iŋ-lē\ *adv*

syn DEPLORE, LAMENT, BEWAIL, BEMOAN mean to express sorrow or keen regret for or over something but they are not now used seriously to describe personal distress or actual weeping. DEPLORE implies regret for the loss or impairment of something of value and often connotes a moral judgment; LAMENT implies mourning for something past and gone; BEWAIL and BEMOAN imply sorrow, disappointment, or protest finding outlet in words or cries, BEWAIL commonly suggesting loudness, and BEMOAN lugubriousness, in uttering complaints or expressing regret

de·ploy \di-'plȯi\ *vb* [F *déployer*, fr. L *displicare* to scatter — more at DISPLAY] *vt* **1 a :** to extend (a military unit) esp. in width **b :** to place in battle formation or appropriate positions **2 :** to spread out or arrange esp. strategically ~ *vi* **:** to move in deployment

de·ploy·ment \-'plȯi-mənt\ *n* **:** an act of deploying

de·plume \(')dē-'plüm\ *vt* [ME *deplumen*, fr. MF *deplumer*, fr. ML *deplumare*, fr. L *de-* + *pluma* feather] **1 :** to pluck off the feathers of **2 :** to strip of possessions, honors, or attributes

de·po·lar·iza·tion \(,)dē-,pō-lə-rə-'zā-shən\ *n* **1 :** the process of depolarizing **2 :** the state of being depolarized

de·po·lar·ize \(')dē-'pō-lə-,rīz\ *vt* **1 :** to cause to become partially or wholly unpolarized **2 :** to prevent or remove polarization of **3 :** DEMAGNETIZE — **de·po·lar·iz·er** *n*

de·pone \di-'pōn\ *vb* [ML *deponere*, fr. L, to put down, fr. *de-* + *ponere* to put — more at POSITION] **:** TESTIFY

[1]**de·po·nent** \di-'pō-nənt\ *adj* [LL *deponent-*, *deponens*, fr. L, prp. of *deponere*] **:** occurring with passive or middle voice forms but with active voice meaning ⟨the ~ verbs in Latin and Greek⟩

[2]**deponent** *n* **1 :** a deponent verb **2 :** one who gives evidence

de·pop·u·late \(')dē-'päp-yə-,lāt\ *vt* [L *depopulatus*, pp. of *depopulari*, fr. *de-* + *populari* to ravage] **1** *obs* **:** RAVAGE **2 :** to remove the inhabitants of — **de·pop·u·la·tion** \(,)dē-,päp-yə-'lā-shən\ *n* — **de·pop·u·la·tor** \(')dē-'päp-yə-,lāt-ər\ *n*

de·port \di-'pō(ə)rt, -'pȯ(ə)rt\ *vt* [MF *deporter*, fr. L *deportare* to carry away, fr. *de-* + *portare* to carry — more at FARE] **1 :** CONDUCT, BEHAVE **2** [L *deportare*] **a :** to carry away **b :** to send out of the country by legal deportation **syn** see BANISH, BEHAVE

de·port·able \di-'pōrt-ə-bəl, -'pȯrt-\ *adj* **1 :** subject to deportation **2 :** punishable by deportation ⟨~ offenses⟩

de·por·ta·tion \,dē-,pōr-'tā-shən, -,pȯr-, -pər-\ *n* **1 :** an act or instance of deporting **2 :** the removal from a country of an alien whose presence is unlawful or prejudicial

de·por·tee \,dē-,pōr-'tē, -,pȯr-\ *n* **:** one who has been deported or is under sentence of deportation

de·port·ment \di-'pōrt-mənt, -'pȯrt-\ *n* **:** BEHAVIOR, CONDUCT **syn** see BEARING

de·pos·al \di-'pō-zəl\ *n* **:** an act of deposing from office

de·pose \di-'pōz\ *vb* [ME *deposen*, fr. OF *deposer*, fr. LL *deponere* (perf. indic. *deposui*), fr. L, to put down] *vt* **1 :** to remove from a throne or other high position **2 :** to put down **:** DEPOSIT **3** [ME *deposen*, fr. ML *deponere*, fr. LL] **:** to testify to under oath or by affidavit ~ *vi* **:** to bear witness

[1]**de·pos·it** \di-'päz-ət\ *vb* **de·pos·it·ed** \-'päz-ət-əd, -'päz-təd\ **de·pos·it·ing** \-'päz-ət-iŋ, -'päz-tiŋ\ [L *depositus*, pp. of *deponere*] *vt* **1 :** to place esp. for safekeeping or as a pledge; *specif* **:** to put in a bank **2 a :** to lay down **:** PLACE **b :** to let fall (as sediment) ~ *vi* **:** to become deposited **:** SETTLE — **de·pos·i·tor** \-'päz-ət-ər, -'päz-tər\ *n*

[2]**deposit** *n* **1 :** the state of being deposited **2 :** something placed for safekeeping: as **a :** money deposited in a bank **b :** money given as a pledge **3 :** a place of deposit **:** DEPOSITORY **4 :** an act of depositing **5 a :** something laid down; *esp* **:** matter deposited by a natural process **b :** a natural accumulation

de·pos·i·tary \di-'päz-ə-,ter-ē\ *n* **1 :** a person to whom something is entrusted **2 :** DEPOSITORY 2

de·po·si·tion \,dep-ə-'zish-ən, ,dē-pə-\ *n* **1 :** an act of removing from a position of authority **2 a :** a testifying esp. before a court **b :** DECLARATION; *specif* **:** testimony taken down in writing under oath **3 :** an act or process of depositing **4 :** something deposited **:** DEPOSIT — **de·po·si·tion·al** \-'zish-nəl, -ən-ᵊl\ *adj*

de·pos·i·to·ry \di-'päz-ə-,tōr-ē, -,tȯr-\ *n* **1 :** DEPOSITARY 1 **2 :** a place where something is deposited esp. for safekeeping

de·pot *oftenest in senses 1 & 2* 'dep-(,)ō, *oftenest in sense 3* 'dē-(,)pō\ *n* [F *dépôt*, fr. ML *depositum*, fr. L, neut. of *depositus*] **1 a :** a place for the storage of military supplies **b :** a place for the reception and forwarding of military replacements **2 :** a place of deposit for goods **:** STOREHOUSE **3 :** a building for railroad, bus, or airplane passengers or freight **:** STATION

de·pra·va·tion \,dep-rə-'vā-shən, ,dē-,prā-\ *n* **1 :** an act or process of depraving **2 :** the state of being depraved

de·prave \di-'prāv\ *vt* [ME *depraven*, fr. MF *depraver*, fr. L *depravare* to pervert, fr. *de-* + *pravus* crooked, bad] **1** *archaic* **:** to speak ill of **:** MALIGN **2 :** to make bad **:** CORRUPT **syn** see DEBASE — **de·prave·ment** \-mənt\ *n* — **de·prav·er** *n*

de·praved \di-'prāvd\ *adj* **:** marked by corruption or evil; *esp* **:** PERVERTED — **de·praved·ly** \-'prā-vəd-lē, -'prāv-dlē\ *adv* — **de·praved·ness** \-'prā-vəd-nəs, -'prāv(d)-nəs\ *n*

de·prav·i·ty \di-'prav-ət-ē\ *n* **1 :** the quality or state of being depraved **2 :** a corrupt act or practice

dep·re·cate \'dep-ri-,kāt\ *vt* [L *deprecatus*, pp. of *deprecari* to avert by prayer, fr. *de-* + *precari* to pray] **1 :** to express disapproval of **2 :** DEPRECIATE **syn** see DISAPPROVE — **dep·re·cat·ing·ly** \-iŋ-lē\ *adv* — **dep·re·ca·tion** \,dep-ri-'kā-shən\ *n*

dep·re·ca·to·ry \'dep-ri-kə-,tōr-ē, -,tȯr-\ *adj* **1 :** serving to deprecate **2 :** expressing deprecation **:** APOLOGETIC

de·pre·cia·ble \di-'prē-sh(ē-)ə-bəl\ *adj* **:** capable of depreciation

de·pre·ci·ate \di-'prē-shē-,āt\ *vb* [LL *depretiatus*, pp. of *depretiare*, fr. L *de-* + *pretium* price — more at PRICE] *vt* **1 :** to lower the price or estimated value of **2 :** to represent as of little value **:** DISPARAGE ~ *vi* **:** to fall in value **syn** see DECRY — **de·pre·ci·at·ing·ly** \-iŋ-lē\ *adv* — **de·pre·ci·a·tor** \-,āt-ər\ *n*

de·pre·ci·a·tion \di-,prē-shē-'ā-shən\ *n* **1 :** an act or process of depreciating **2 :** the state of being depreciated

de·pre·ci·a·tive \di-'prē-shē-,āt-iv, -sh(ē-)ət-\ *adj* **:** DEPRECIATORY

de·pre·cia·to·ry \di-'prē-sh(ē-)ə-,tōr-ē, -,tȯr-\ *adj* **:** tending to depreciate

dep·re·date \'dep-rə-,dāt\ *vb* [LL *depraedatus*, pp. of *depraedari*, fr. L *de-* + *praedari* to plunder — more at PREY] **:** PLUNDER, RAVAGE — **dep·re·da·tion** \,dep-rə-'dā-shən\ *n* — **de·pre·da·tor** \'dep-rə-,dāt-ər, di-'pred-ət-\ *n* — **de·pre·da·to·ry** \di-'pred-ə-,tōr-ē, 'dep-ri-də-, -,tȯr-\ *adj*

de·press \di-'pres\ *vt* [ME *depressen*, fr. MF *depresser*, fr. L *depressus*, pp. of *deprimere* to press down, fr. *de-* + *premere* to press] **1** *obs* **:** REPRESS, SUBJUGATE **2 a :** to press down **b :** to cause to sink to a lower position **3 :** to lessen the activity or strength of **4 :** SADDEN, DISCOURAGE **5 :** to lessen in market value — **de·press·ible** \-ə-bəl\ *adj* — **de·press·ing·ly** \-iŋ-lē\ *adv*

syn DEPRESS, OPPRESS mean to press or weigh down heavily. DEPRESS implies a failure to withstand or bear up under a weight and stresses the resulting state of lowered activity or of dullness or dejection ⟨*depressed* by failure⟩ OPPRESS emphasizes the weight that is pressing down and that may or may not be successfully borne or withstood ⟨*oppressed* by sorrow⟩

de·pres·sant \di-'pres-ᵊnt\ *n* **:** one that depresses; *specif* **:** an agent that reduces bodily functional activity — **depressant** *adj*

de·pressed *adj* **1 :** low in spirits **:** SAD **2 a :** vertically flattened ⟨a ~ cactus⟩ **b :** having the central portion lower than the margin **c :** lying flat or prostrate **d :** dorsoventrally flattened **3 :** suffering from economic depression; *specif* **:** UNDERPRIVILEGED

de·pres·sion \di-'presh-ən\ *n* **1 a :** the angular distance of a celestial object below the horizon **b :** the angular distance of an object beneath the horizontal plane **2 :** an act of depressing or a state of being depressed: as **a :** a pressing down **:** LOWERING **b** (1) **:** a state of feeling sad **:** DEJECTION (2) **:** a psychoneurotic or psychotic disorder marked by sadness, inactivity, and self-depreciation **c** (1) **:** a reduction in activity, amount, quality, or force (2) **:** a lowering of vitality or functional activity **3 :** a depressed place or part **:** HOLLOW **4 :** LOW 1b **5 :** a period of low general economic activity marked esp. by unemployment **syn** see SADNESS

de·pres·sive \di-'pres-iv\ *adj* **1 :** tending to depress **2 :** of or relating to psychological depression — **de·pres·sive·ly** *adv*

de·pres·sor \-'pres-ər\ *n* [LL, fr. L *depressus*] **:** one that depresses: as **a :** a muscle that draws down a part **b :** a device for pressing a part down or aside **c :** a nerve or nerve fiber that decreases the activity or the tone of the organ or part it innervates

de·pri·va·tion \,dep-rə-'vā-shən, ,dē-,prī-\ *n* **1 :** an act or instance of depriving **:** LOSS **2 :** the state of being deprived **:** PRIVATION; *specif* **:** removal from an office, dignity, or benefice

de·prive \di-'prīv\ *vt* [ME *depriven*, fr. ML *deprivare*, fr. L *de-* + *privare* to deprive] **1** *obs* **:** REMOVE **2 :** to take something away from **3 :** to remove from office **4 :** to withhold something from

depth \'depth\ *n, pl* **depths** \'dep(t)s, 'depths\ [ME, prob. fr. *dep* deep] **1 a** (1) **:** a deep place in a body of water (2) **:** a part that is far from the outside or surface ⟨the ~*s* of the woods⟩ (3) **:** ABYSS **b** (1) **:** a remote region (as of thought) (2) **:** the middle of a time (as winter) (3) **:** an extreme state (as of misery) (4) **:** the worst part **2 a :** the perpendicular measurement downward from a surface **b :** the direct linear measurement from the point of viewing usu. from front to back **3 :** the quality of being deep **4 :** the degree of departure from colorlessness of a bulky color or from white of a surface color — **depth·less** \'depth-ləs\ *adj*

depth charge *n* **:** an explosive projectile for use underwater esp. against submarines — called also *depth bomb*

depth perception *n* **:** the ability to judge the distance of objects and the spatial relationship of objects at different distances

depth psychology *n* **:** PSYCHOANALYSIS

dep·u·ta·tion \,dep-yə-'tā-shən\ *n* **1 :** the act of appointing a deputy **2 :** a group of people appointed to represent others

de·pute \di-'pyüt\ *vt* [ME *deputen* to appoint, fr. MF *deputer*, fr.

LL *deputare* to assign, fr. L, to consider (as), fr. *de-* + *putare* to consider — more at PAVE] **:** DELEGATE

dep·u·tize \ˈdep-yə-ˌtīz\ *vt* **:** to appoint as deputy ~ *vi* **:** to act as deputy

dep·u·ty \ˈdep-yət-ē\ *n often attrib* [ME, fr. MF *deputé*, pp. of *deputer*] **1 a :** a person appointed as a substitute with power to act **b :** a second-in-command or assistant who usu. takes charge when his superior is absent **2 :** a member of the lower house of some legislative assemblies

de·rac·i·nate \di-ˈras-ᵊn-ˌāt\ *vt* [F *déraciner*, fr. MF *desraciner*, fr. *des-* de- + *racine* root, fr. LL *radicina*, fr. L *radic-*, *radix* — more at ROOT] **:** UPROOT — **de·rac·i·na·tion** \-ˌras-ᵊn-ˈā-shən\ *n*

de·rail \di-ˈrā(ə)l\ *vb* [F *dérailler*, fr. *dé-* de- + *rail*, fr. E] *vt* **1 :** to cause to run off the rails **2 :** to throw off course ~ *vi* **:** to leave the rails — **de·rail·ment** \-mənt\ *n*

de·range \di-ˈrānj\ *vt* [F *déranger*, fr. OF *desrengier*, fr. *de-* + *reng* place] **1 :** DISARRANGE **2 :** to disturb the operation or functions of **3 :** to make insane — **de·range·ment** \-mənt\ *n*

der·by \ˈdər-bē, *esp Brit* ˈdär-\ *n* [Edward Stanley †1834, 12th earl of *Derby*] **1** *cap* **a :** a race for three-year-old horses instituted in 1780 and run annually at Epsom Downs, England **b :** any of several horse races held annually and usu. restricted to three-year-olds **2 :** a race or contest open to all comers **3 :** a man's stiff felt hat with dome-shaped crown and narrow brim

1**der·e·lict** \ˈder-ə-ˌlikt\ *adj* [L *derelictus*, pp. of *derelinquere* to abandon, fr. *de-* + *relinquere* to leave — more at RELINQUISH] **1 :** abandoned esp. by the owner or occupant **:** RUN-DOWN **2 :** lacking a sense of duty **:** NEGLIGENT

2**derelict** *n* **1 a :** something voluntarily abandoned; *specif* **:** a ship abandoned on the high seas **b :** a tract of land left dry by receding water **2 :** a person no longer able to support himself **:** BUM

der·e·lic·tion \ˌder-ə-ˈlik-shən\ *n* **1 a :** an intentional abandonment **b :** the state of being abandoned **2 :** a recession of water leaving permanently dry land **3 a :** intentional or conscious neglect **:** DELINQUENCY **b :** FAULT, SHORTCOMING

de·ride \di-ˈrīd\ *vt* [L *deridēre*, fr. *de-* + *ridēre* to laugh] **1 :** to laugh at contemptuously **2 :** to subject to ridicule **syn** see RIDICULE — **de·rid·er** *n* — **de·rid·ing·ly** \-iŋ-lē\ *adv*

de ri·gueur \də-(ˌ)rē-ˈgər\ *adj* [F] **:** prescribed or required by fashion, etiquette, or custom **:** PROPER

de·ri·sion \di-ˈrizh-ən\ *n* [ME, fr. MF, fr. LL *derision-*, *derisio*, fr. L *derisus*, pp. of *deridēre*] **1 a :** an act of deriding **b :** a state of being derided **2 :** an object of ridicule or scorn

de·ri·sive \di-ˈrī-siv\ *adj* **:** expressing or causing derision — **de·ri·sive·ly** *adv* — **de·ri·sive·ness** *n*

de·ri·so·ry \di-ˈrī-sə-rē, -ˈrī-zə-\ *adj* **1 :** expressing derision **:** DERISIVE **2 :** worthy of derision **:** RIDICULOUS

de·riv·able \di-ˈrī-və-bəl\ *adj* **:** capable of being derived

der·i·vate \ˈder-ə-ˌvāt\ *n* **:** DERIVATIVE

der·i·va·tion \ˌder-ə-ˈvā-shən\ *n* **1 a** (1) **:** the formation of a word from an earlier word or base (as by the addition of an affix) (2) **:** an act of ascertaining or stating the derivation of a word (3) **:** ETYMOLOGY 1 **b :** the relation of a word to its base **2 a :** SOURCE, ORIGIN **b :** ORIGINATION, DESCENT **3 :** something derived **:** DERIVATIVE **4 :** an act or process of deriving **5 :** a sequence of statements showing that a result is a necessary consequence of previously accepted statements — **der·i·va·tion·al** \-shnəl, -shən-ᵊl\ *adj*

1**de·riv·a·tive** \di-ˈriv-ət-iv\ *adj* **1 :** formed by derivation **2 :** made up of or marked by derived elements — **de·riv·a·tive·ly** *adv*

2**derivative** *n* **1 :** a word formed by derivation **2 :** something derived **3 :** the limit of the ratio of the change in a function to the corresponding change in its independent variable as the latter change approaches zero **4 a :** a chemical substance so related structurally to another substance as to be theoretically derivable from it **b :** a substance that can be made from another substance in one or more steps

de·rive \di-ˈrīv\ *vb* [ME *deriven*, fr. MF *deriver*, fr. L *derivare*, fr. *de-* + *rivus* stream] *vt* **1 a :** to take or receive esp. from a specified source **b :** to obtain from a specified source; *specif* **:** to obtain (as a chemical substance) actually or theoretically from a parent substance **2 :** INFER, DEDUCE **3** *archaic* **:** BRING **4 :** to trace the derivation of ~ *vi* **:** ORIGINATE, STEM **syn** see SPRING — **de·riv·er** *n*

derm \ˈdərm\ *n* [NL *derma* & *dermis*] **1 :** DERMIS **2 :** SKIN 2a **3 :** CUTICLE 1a

derm- *or* **derma-** *or* **dermo-** *comb form* [NL, fr. Gk *derm-*, *dermo-*, fr. *derma*, fr. *derein* to skin] **:** skin ⟨*derm*al⟩ ⟨*dermo*tropic⟩

-derm \ˌdərm\ *n comb form* [prob. fr. F *-derme*, fr. Gk *derma*] **:** skin **:** covering ⟨ecto*derm*⟩

der·ma \ˈdər-mə\ *n* [NL, fr. Gk] **:** DERMIS

-der·ma \ˈdər-mə\ *n comb form, pl* **-der·mas** *or* **-der·ma·ta** \-mət-ə\ [NL, fr. Gk *dermat-*, *derma* skin] **:** skin or skin ailment of a (specified) type ⟨sclero*derma*⟩

der·mal \ˈdər-məl\ *adj* **1 :** of or relating to skin and esp. to the dermis **:** CUTANEOUS **2 :** EPIDERMAL

der·map·ter·an \(ˌ)dər-ˈmap-tə-rən\ *n* [NL *Dermaptera*, order name, fr. *derm-* + Gk *pteron* wing] **:** any of an order (Dermaptera) of insects consisting of the earwigs and usu. a few related forms — **dermapteran** *adj* — **der·map·ter·ous** \-rəs\ *adj*

dermat- *or* **dermato-** *comb form* [Gk, fr. *dermat-*, *derma*] **:** skin ⟨*dermat*itis⟩ ⟨*dermato*logy⟩

der·ma·ti·tis \ˌdər-mə-ˈtīt-əs\ *n* **:** inflammation of the skin

der·mat·o·gen \(ˌ)dər-ˈmat-ə-jən\ *n* [ISV] **:** the outer primary meristem of a plant or plant part

der·ma·toid \ˈdər-mə-ˌtȯid\ *adj* **:** resembling skin

der·ma·to·log·ic \(ˌ)dər-ˌmat-ᵊl-ˈäj-ik, ˌdər-mət-\ *or* **der·ma·to·log·i·cal** \-ˈäj-i-kəl\ *adj* **:** of or relating to dermatology

der·ma·tol·o·gist \ˌdər-mə-ˈtäl-ə-jəst\ *n* **:** a specialist in dermatology

der·ma·tol·o·gy \-jē\ *n* **:** a branch of science dealing with the skin, its structure, functions, and diseases

der·ma·tome \ˈdər-mə-ˌtōm\ *n* [ISV *dermat-*] **:** the lateral wall of a somite from which the dermis is produced — **der·ma·tom·ic** \ˌdər-mə-ˈtäm-ik, -ˈtō-mik\ *adj*

der·mato·phyte \(ˌ)dər-ˈmat-ə-ˌfīt\ *n* [ISV] **:** a fungus parasitic on the skin or skin derivatives (as hair or nails) — **der·mato·phyt·ic** \(ˌ)dər-ˌmat-ə-ˈfit-ik\ *adj*

der·ma·to·sis \ˌdər-mə-ˈtō-səs\ *n, pl* **der·ma·to·ses** \-ˈtō-ˌsēz\ **:** a disease of the skin

-der·ma·tous \ˈdər-mət-əs\ *adj comb form* [Gk *dermat-*, *derma* skin] **:** having a (specified) type of skin ⟨sclero*dermatous*⟩

der·mis \ˈdər-məs\ *n* [NL, fr. LL *-dermis*] **:** the sensitive vascular inner mesodermic layer of the skin — called also *corium*, *cutis*

-der·mis \ˈdər-məs\ *n comb form* [LL, fr. Gk, fr. *derma*] **:** layer of skin or tissue ⟨endo*dermis*⟩

der·moid \ˈdər-ˌmȯid\ *also* **der·moi·dal** \(ˌ)dər-ˈmȯid-ᵊl\ *adj* **1 :** made up of cutaneous elements and esp. ectodermal derivatives ⟨a ~ tumor⟩ **2 :** resembling skin

der·mop·ter·an \(ˌ)dər-ˈmäp-tə-rən\ *n* [NL *Dermoptera*, order of mammals, fr. *derm-* + Gk *pteron*] **:** FLYING LEMUR — **dermopteran** *adj* — **der·mop·ter·ous** \-rəs\ *adj*

der·mo·trop·ic \ˌdər-mə-ˈträp-ik\ *adj* **:** attracted to, localizing in, or entering by way of the skin ⟨~ viruses⟩

der·nier cri \ˌdern-ˌyā-ˈkrē\ *n* [F, lit., last cry] **:** the newest fashion

der·o·gate \ˈder-ə-ˌgāt\ *vb* [LL *derogatus*, pp. of *derogare*, fr. L, to annul (a law), detract, fr. *de-* + *rogare* to ask, propose (a law) — more at RIGHT] *vt* **:** to cause to seem inferior **:** DISPARAGE ~ *vi* **1 :** to take away a part so as to impair **:** DETRACT **2 :** to act beneath one's position or character — **der·o·ga·tion** \ˌder-ə-ˈgā-shən\ *n* — **de·ro·ga·tive** \di-ˈräg-ət-iv, ˈder-ə-ˌgāt-\ *adj*

de·rog·a·to·ri·ly \di-ˌräg-ə-ˈtōr-ə-lē, -ˈtȯr-\ *adv* **:** in a derogatory manner

de·rog·a·to·ry \di-ˈräg-ə-ˌtōr-ē, -ˌtȯr-ē\ *adj* **1 :** DETRACTING, DEGRADING **2 :** expressive of a low opinion **:** DISPARAGING

der·rick \ˈder-ik\ *n* [obs. *derrick* hangman, gallows, fr. *Derick*, name of 17th cent. E hangman] **1 :** a hoisting apparatus employing a tackle rigged at the end of a beam **2 :** a framework or tower over a deep drill hole (as of an oil well) for supporting boring tackle or for hoisting and lowering

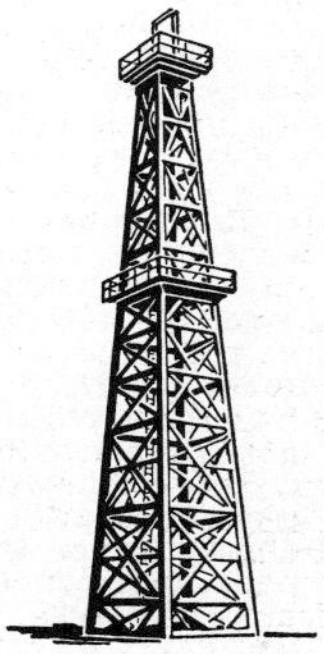
derrick of oil well

der·ri·ere *or* **der·ri·ère** \ˌder-ē-ˈe(ə)r\ *n* [F *derrière*, fr. *derrière*, adj., hinder, fr. OF *deriere* adv., behind, fr. L *de retro*, fr. *de* from + *retro* back — more at DE-, RETRO-] **:** BUTTOCKS

der·ring–do \ˌder-iŋ-ˈdü\ *n* [ME *dorring don* daring to do, fr. *dorring* (gerund of *dorren* to dare) + *don* to do] **:** daring action **:** DARING

der·rin·ger \ˈder-ən-jər\ *n* [Henry *Deringer*, 19th cent. Am inventor] **:** a short-barreled pocket pistol

der·ris \ˈder-əs\ *n* [NL, genus name, fr. Gk, skin, fr. *derein* to skin — more at TEAR] **1 :** any of a large genus (*Derris*) of leguminous tropical Old World shrubs and woody vines including sources of native fish and arrow poisons and commercial sources of rotenone **2 :** a preparation of derris roots and stems used as an insecticide

der·vish \ˈdər-vish\ *n* [Turk *derviş*, lit., beggar, fr. Per *darvēsh*] **:** a member of a Muslim religious order noted for devotional exercises (as bodily movements leading to a trance)

de·salt \(ˈ)dē-ˈsȯlt\ *vt* **:** to remove salt from — **de·salt·er** *n*

1**des·cant** \ˈdes-ˌkant\ *n* [ME *dyscant*, fr. ONF & ML; ONF *descant*, fr. ML *discantus*, fr. L *dis-* + *cantus* song — more at CHANT] **1 a :** a melody or counterpoint sung above the plainsong of the tenor **b :** the art of composing or improvising contrapuntal part music; *also* **:** the music so composed or improvised **c :** the upper voice (as soprano, treble) in part music **d :** a superimposed counterpoint to a hymn tune or other simple melody sung typically by some or all of the sopranos **2 :** a song or strain of melody **3 a :** a musical prelude in which a theme is varied **b :** discourse or comment on a theme felt to resemble variations on a musical air

2**des·cant** \ˈdes-ˌkant, des-ˈ\ *vi* **1 a :** to sing or play a descant **b :** SING, WARBLE **2 :** to talk or write at considerable length **:** DILATE

de·scend \di-ˈsend\ *vb* [ME *descenden*, fr. OF *descendre*, fr. L *descendere*, fr. *de-* + *scandere* to climb — more at SCAN] *vi* **1 :** to pass from a higher place or level to a lower one ⟨~*ed* from the platform⟩ **2 :** to pass in discussion from what is logically prior or more comprehensive **3 a :** to come down from a stock or source **:** DERIVE ⟨~*ed* from an ancient family⟩ **b :** to pass by inheritance ⟨an heirloom that has ~*ed* in the family⟩ **c :** to pass by transmission ⟨songs ~*ed* from early ballads⟩ **4 :** to incline, lead, or extend downward ⟨the road ~*s* to the river⟩ **5 :** to swoop or pounce down or make a sudden attack ⟨the plague ~*ed* upon them⟩ **6 :** to proceed in a sequence or gradation from higher to lower or from more remote to nearer or more recent **7 a :** to sink in status or dignity **:** STOOP **b :** to worsen and sink in condition or estimation ~ *vt* **1 :** to pass, move, or climb down or down along **2 :** to extend down along — **de·scend·ible** \-ˈsen-də-bəl\ *adj*

1**de·scen·dant** *or* **de·scen·dent** \di-ˈsen-dənt\ *adj* [MF & L; MF *descendant*, fr. L *descendent-*, *descendens*, prp. of *descendere*] **1 :** DESCENDING **2 :** proceeding from an ancestor or source

2**descendant** *or* **descendent** *n* [F & L; F *descendant*, fr. LL *descendent-*, *descendens*, fr. L, prp. of *descendere*] **1 :** one descended from another or from a common stock **2 :** one deriving directly from a precursor or prototype

de·scend·er \di-ˈsen-dər, ˈdē-ˌ\ *n* **:** the part of a lowercase letter that descends below x height; *also* **:** a letter that has such a part

de·scen·sion \di-ˈsen-chən\ *n, archaic* **:** DESCENT 1

de·scent \di-ˈsent\ *n* [ME, fr. MF *descente*, fr. *descendre*] **1 :** the act or process of descending from a higher to a lower level or state **2 :** a downward step (as in station or value) **:** DECLINE **3 a :** derivation from an ancestor **:** BIRTH, LINEAGE **b :** transmission or devolution of an estate by inheritance usu. in the descending line **c :** the fact or process of originating from an ancestral stock **d :** the shaping or development in nature and character by transmission from a source **:** DERIVATION **4 a :** an inclination downward **:** SLOPE **b :** a descending way (as a downgrade or stairway) **c** *obs* **:** the lowest part **5 a :** a sudden disconcerting appearance **b :** a hostile raid or predatory assault **6 :** a step downward in a scale of gradation; *specif* **:** one generation in an ancestral line or genealogical scale

de·scrib·able \di-'skrī-bə-bəl\ *adj* **:** capable of being described

de·scribe \di-'skrīb\ *vt* [L *describere*, fr. *de-* + *scribere* to write — more at SCRIBE] **1 :** to represent or give an account of in words **2 :** to represent by a figure, model, or picture **:** DELINEATE **3 :** to trace or traverse the outline of ⟨~ a circle⟩ **4** *obs* **:** DISTRIBUTE **5** *archaic* **:** OBSERVE, PERCEIVE — **de·scrib·er** *n*

de·scrip·tion \di-'skrip-shən\ *n* [ME *descripcioun*, fr. MF & L; MF *description*, fr. L *description-*, *descriptio*, fr. *descriptus*, pp. of *describere*] **1 a :** an act of describing; *specif* **:** discourse intended to give a mental image of something experienced (as a scene, person, or sensation) **b :** a descriptive statement or account **2 :** kind or character esp. as determined by salient features **syn** see TYPE

de·scrip·tive \-'skrip-tiv\ *adj* **1 :** serving to describe ⟨a ~ account⟩ **2 :** referring to, constituting, or grounded in matters of observation or experience **3 a** *of a modifying word* **:** expressing the quality, kind, or condition of what is denoted by the modified term ⟨*hot* in "hot water" is a ~ adjective⟩ **b :** NONRESTRICTIVE **4 :** of, relating to, or dealing with the structure of a language at a particular time usu. with exclusion of historical and comparative data ⟨~ linguistics⟩ — **de·scrip·tive·ly** *adv* — **de·scrip·tive·ness** *n*

descriptive geometry *n* **:** geometry treated in terms of projections; *specif* **:** the theory of projecting an exactly defined body so as to deduce projective and metrical properties from its projections

de·scrip·tor \di-'skrip-tər\ *n* **:** a key word or phrase used in data processing to identify an item (as a subject or a document)

1**de·scry** \di-'skrī\ *vt* **de·scried; de·scry·ing** [ME *descrien*, fr. OF *descrier* to proclaim, decry] **1 a :** to catch sight of **b :** to find out **:** DISCOVER **2** *obs* **:** to make known **:** REVEAL

2**descry** *n, obs* **:** discovery or view from afar

Des·de·mo·na \,dez-də-'mō-nə\ *n* **:** the wife of Othello in Shakespeare's *Othello*

des·e·crate \'des-i-,krāt\ *vt* [*de-* + *-secrate* (as in *consecrate*)] **1 :** to violate the sanctity of **:** PROFANE **2 :** to treat irreverently or contemptuously — **des·e·crat·er** *or* **des·e·cra·tor** \-,krāt-ər\ *n*

des·e·cra·tion \,des-i-'krā-shən\ *n* **:** an act or instance of desecrating **:** the state of being desecrated **syn** see PROFANATION

de·seg·re·gate \(')dē-'seg-ri-,gāt\ *vt* **:** to eliminate segregation in; *specif* **:** to free of any law, provision, or practice requiring isolation of the members of a particular race in separate units ⟨~ the armed services⟩ ~ *vi* **:** to bring about desegregation — **de·seg·re·ga·tion** \(,)dē-,seg-ri-'gā-shən\ *n*

de·sen·si·ti·za·tion \(,)dē-,sen(t)-sət-ə-'zā-shən, -,sen(t)-stə-'zā-\ *n* **:** the process of desensitizing

de·sen·si·tize \(')dē-'sen(t)-sə-,tīz\ *vt* **1 :** to make (a sensitized or hypersensitive individual) insensitive or nonreactive to a sensitizing agent **2 :** to make (a photographic material) less sensitive or completely insensitive to radiation **3 :** to make emotionally insensitive or callous — **de·sen·si·tiz·er** *n*

1**des·ert** \'dez-ərt\ *n* [ME, fr. OF, fr. LL *desertum*, fr. L, neut. of *desertus*, pp. of *deserere* to desert, fr. *de-* + *serere* to join together — more at SERIES] **1** *archaic* **:** a wild uninhabited and uncultivated tract **2 :** an arid barren tract incapable of supporting any considerable population without an artificial water supply **3 :** a desolating or forbidding prospect — **de·ser·tic** \di-'zərt-ik\ *adj*

2**des·ert** \'dez-ərt\ *adj* **1** *archaic* **:** FORSAKEN **2 :** desolate and sparsely occupied or unoccupied **3 :** of or relating to a desert

3**de·sert** \di-'zərt\ *n* [ME *deserte*, fr. OF, fr. fem. of *desert*, pp. of *deservir* to deserve] **1 :** the quality or fact of being deserving of reward or punishment **2 :** deserved reward or punishment **3 :** EXCELLENCE, WORTH

4**de·sert** \di-'zərt\ *vb* [F *déserter*, fr. LL *desertare*, fr. L *desertus*] *vt* **1 :** to withdraw from **:** LEAVE **2 a :** to leave in the lurch **:** ABANDON **b :** to abandon (military service) without leave **3 :** to fail (one) in time of need ~ *vi* **:** to quit one's post, allegiance, or service without leave; *specif* **:** to absent oneself without leave from a military post, station, or duty with intent to remain away permanently **syn** see ABANDON — **deserter** *n*

de·ser·tion \di-'zər-shən\ *n* **1 :** an act of deserting; *esp* **:** the abandonment without consent or legal justification of a person, post, or relationship and the duties and obligations connected therewith **2 :** a state of being deserted or forsaken **:** DESOLATION

desert soil *n* **:** a soil that develops under sparse shrub vegetation in warm to cool arid climates with a light-colored surface soil usu. underlain by calcareous material and a hardpan layer

de·serve \di-'zərv\ *vb* [ME *deserven*, fr. OF *deservir*, fr. L *deservire* to serve zealously, fr. *de-* + *servire* to serve] *vt* **:** to be worthy of (as good or evil) **:** MERIT ⟨~*s* another chance⟩ ~ *vi* **:** to be worthy, fit, or suitable for some reward or requital — **de·serv·er** *n*

de·served \-'zərvd\ *adj* **:** such as one deserves ⟨a ~ reputation⟩ — **de·served·ly** \-'zər-vəd-lē, -'zərv-dlē\ *adv* — **de·serv·edness** \-'zər-vəd-nəs, -'zərv(d)-nəs\ *n*

1**de·serv·ing** *n* **:** DESERT, MERIT

2**deserving** *adj* **:** MERITORIOUS, WORTHY; *specif* **:** meriting financial aid

de·sex \(')dē-'seks\ *vt* **:** DESEXUALIZE 1

de·sex·u·al·iza·tion \(,)dē-,seksh-(ə-)wə-lə-'zā-shən, -,sek-shə-lə-\ *n* **:** the act or an instance of desexualizing

de·sex·u·al·ize \(')dē-'seksh-(ə-)wə-,līz, -'sek-shə-,līz\ *vt* **1 :** to deprive of sexual characters or power **2 :** to divest of sexual quality

des·ha·bille \,des-ə-'bē(ə)l, -'bil, -'bē\ *var of* DISHABILLE

des·ic·cant \'des-i-kənt\ *n* **:** a drying agent

des·ic·cate \-,kāt\ *vb* [L *desiccatus*, pp. of *desiccare* to dry up, fr. *de-* + *siccare* to dry, fr. *siccus* dry — more at SACK] *vt* **1 :** to dry up or cause to dry up **2 :** to preserve (a food) by drying **:** DEHYDRATE **3 :** to drain of emotional or intellectual vitality ~ *vi* **:** to become dried up — **des·ic·ca·tion** \,des-i-'kā-shən\ *n* — **de·sic·ca·tive** \'des-i-,kāt-iv, di-'sik-ət-\ *adj* — **des·ic·ca·tor** \'des-i-,kāt-ər\ *n*

de·sid·er·ate \di-'sid-ə-,rāt, -'zid-\ *vt* [L *desideratus*, pp. of *desiderare* to desire] **:** to entertain or express a longing for or a wish to have or attain — **de·sid·er·a·tion** \-,sid-ə-'rā-shən, -,zid-\ *n* — **de·sid·er·a·tive** \-'sid-ə-,rāt-iv, -'sid-(ə-)rət-, -'zid-\ *adj*

de·sid·er·a·tum \-,sid-ə-'rät-əm, -,zid-, -'rāt-\ *n, pl* **de·sid·er·a·ta** \-ə\ [L, neut. of *desideratus*] **:** something desired as essential

1**de·sign** \di-'zīn\ *vb* [MF *designer*, fr. L *designare*, fr. *de-* + *signare* to mark, mark out — more at SIGN] *vt* **1 a :** to conceive and plan out in the mind **b :** DEVOTE, CONSIGN **c :** to have as a purpose **:** INTEND **d :** to devise for a specific function or end **2** *archaic* **:** to indicate with a distinctive mark, sign, or name **3 a :** to make a drawing, pattern, or sketch of **b :** to draw the plans for **c :** to create, fashion, execute, or construct according to plan **:** DEVISE, CONTRIVE ~ *vi* **1 :** to conceive or execute a plan **2 :** to draw, lay out, or prepare a design — **de·sign·er** *n*

2**design** *n* **1 :** a mental project or scheme in which means to an end are laid down **2 a :** a particular purpose held in view by an individual or group **b :** deliberate purposive planning **3 a :** a deliberate undercover project or scheme **:** PLOT **b** *pl* **:** aggressive or evil intent — used with *on* or *against* **4 :** a preliminary sketch or outline showing the main features of something to be executed **:** DELINEATION **5 :** an underlying scheme that governs functioning, developing, or unfolding **:** PATTERN, MOTIF **6 :** the arrangement of elements that make up a work of art, a machine, or other man-made object **7 :** a decorative pattern **syn** see INTENTION, PLAN

1**des·ig·nate** \'dez-ig-,nāt, -nət\ *adj* [L *designatus*, pp. of *designare*] **:** chosen for an office but not yet installed ⟨ambassador ~⟩

2**des·ig·nate** \-,nāt\ *vt* **1 a :** to point out the location of **b :** to make known directly **c :** to distinguish as to class **d :** SPECIFY, STIPULATE **2 :** to call by a distinctive title, term, or expression **3 :** to indicate and set apart for a specific purpose, office, or duty **4 :** DENOTE — **des·ig·na·tive** \-,nāt-iv\ *adj* — **des·ig·na·tor** \-,nāt-ər\ *n* — **des·ig·na·to·ry** \-nə-,tōr-ē, -,tȯr-\ *adj*

des·ig·na·tion \,dez-ig-'nā-shən\ *n* **1 :** the act of indicating or identifying **2 :** a distinguishing name, sign, or title **3 :** appointment to or selection for an office, post, or service **4 :** the relation between a sign and the thing signified

des·ig·nee \,dez-ig-'nē\ *n* **:** one who is designated

designing *adj* **1 :** practicing forethought **2 :** CRAFTY, SCHEMING

de·sign·ment \-'zīn-mənt\ *n, obs* **:** PLAN, PURPOSE

de·sir·abil·i·ty \di-,zī-rə-'bil-ət-ē\ *n* **1 :** the quality, fact, or degree of being desirable **2** *pl* **:** a desirable condition

1**de·sir·able** \di-'zī-rə-bəl\ *adj* **1 :** having pleasing qualities or properties **:** ATTRACTIVE ⟨a ~ woman⟩ **2 :** worth seeking or doing as advantageous, beneficial, or wise **:** ADVISABLE ⟨~ legislation⟩ — **de·sir·able·ness** *n* — **de·sir·ably** \-blē\ *adv*

2**desirable** *n* **:** one that is desirable

1**de·sire** \di-'zī(ə)r\ *vb* [ME *desiren*, fr. OF *desirer*, fr. L *desiderare*, fr. *de-* + *sider-*, *sidus* star] *vt* **1 :** to long or hope for **2 a :** to express a wish for **:** REQUEST **b :** to express a wish to **:** ASK **3** *obs* **:** INVITE **4** *archaic* **:** to feel the loss of ~ *vi* **:** to have or feel desire

syn WISH, WANT, CRAVE, COVET: DESIRE, WISH, and WANT are often interchangeable though DESIRE or WISH is often chosen as giving more dignity or a more respectful tone to a request. In more general use DESIRE emphasizes strength of feeling and often implies strong intention; WISH is less strong and often connotes a vague or passing longing for the unattainable; WANT implies a felt need or lack; CRAVE suggests strongly the force of physical appetite or emotional need; COVET implies a strong eager desire often inordinate and envious and often for what belongs to another

2**desire** *n* **1 :** conscious impulse toward an object or experience that promises enjoyment or satisfaction in its attainment **2 a :** LONGING, CRAVING **b :** sexual attraction or appetite **3 :** a usu. formal request or petition for some action **4 :** something desired

de·sir·ous \di-'zī(ə)r-əs\ *adj* **:** impelled or governed by desire **:** SOLICITOUS — **de·sir·ous·ly** *adv* — **de·sir·ous·ness** *n*

de·sist \di-'zist, -'sist\ *vi* [MF *desister*, fr. L *desistere*, fr. *de-* + *sistere* to stand, stop; akin to L *stare* to stand] **:** to cease to proceed or act **syn** see STOP — **de·sis·tance** \-'zis-tən(t)s, -'sis-\ *n*

desk \'desk\ *n* [ME *deske*, fr. ML *desca*, modif. of OIt *desco* table, fr. L *discus* dish, disc — more at DISH] **1 a :** a table, frame, or case with a sloping or horizontal surface esp. for writing and reading and often with drawers, compartments, and pigeonholes **b :** a reading table or lectern to support the book from which the liturgical service is read **c :** a counter, stand, or booth at which a person performs his duties **d :** a music stand **2 :** a division of an organization specializing in a particular phase of activity

desk·man \'desk-,man, -mən\ *n* **:** one that works at a desk; *specif* **:** a newspaperman who processes news and prepares copy

desm- *or* **desmo-** *comb form* [NL, fr. Gk, fr. *desmos*, fr. *dein* to bind — more at DIADEM] **:** bond **:** ligament ⟨*desmocyte*⟩

des·man \'dez-mən\ *n, pl* **desmans** [short for Sw *desmansråtta*, fr. *desman* musk + *råtta* rat] **:** an aquatic insectivorous mammal (*Desmana moschata*) of Russia that resembles a mole

des·mid \'dez-məd\ *n* [deriv. of Gk *desmos*] **:** any of numerous unicellular or colonial green algae (order Zygnematales)

1**des·o·late** \'des-ə-lət, 'dez-\ *adj* [ME *desolat*, fr. L *desolatus*, pp. of *desolare* to abandon, fr. *de-* + *solus* alone — more at SOLE] **1 :** devoid of inhabitants and visitors **:** DESERTED **2 :** FORSAKEN, LONELY **3 a :** showing the effects of abandonment and neglect **:** DILAPIDATED **b :** BARREN, LIFELESS **c :** CHEERLESS, GLOOMY **syn** see ALONE — **des·o·late·ly** *adv* — **des·o·late·ness** *n*

2**des·o·late** \-,lāt\ *vt* **:** to make desolate: **a :** to deprive of inhabitants **b :** to lay waste **c :** FORSAKE **d :** to make wretched — **des·o·lat·er** *or* **des·o·la·tor** \-,lāt-ər\ *n* — **des·o·lat·ing·ly** \-,lāt-iŋ-lē\ *adv*

des·o·la·tion \,des-ə-'lā-shən, ,dez-\ *n* **1 :** the action of desolating **2 :** the condition of being desolated **:** DEVASTATION, RUIN **3 :** barren wasteland **4 a :** GRIEF, SADNESS **b :** LONELINESS

desoxy- — see DEOXY-

des·oxy·cor·ti·co·ste·rone \de-,zäk-sē-,kȯrt-i-'käs-tə-,rōn, de-,säk-sē-, -i-kō-'sti(ə)r-,ōn\ *n* **:** DEOXYCORTICOSTERONE

des·oxy·ri·bo·nu·cle·ic acid \-'rī-bō-n(y)ü-,klē-ik-, -,klā-\ *n* **:** DEOXYRIBONUCLEIC ACID

1**de·spair** \di-'spa(ə)r, -'spe(ə)r\ *vb* [ME *despeiren*, fr. MF *desperer*, fr. L *desperare*, fr. *de-* + *sperare* to hope] *vi* **:** to lose all hope or confidence ~ *vt, obs* **:** to lose hope for

2**despair** *n* **:** utter loss of hope or a cause of such loss

de·spair·ing *adj* **:** given to, arising from, or marked by despair **syn** see DESPONDENT — **de·spair·ing·ly** \-iŋ-lē\ *adv*

des·patch \dis-'pach\ *var of* DISPATCH

des·per·a·do \,des-pə-'räd-(,)ō, -'rād-\ *n, pl* **des·per·a·does** *or* **des·per·a·dos** [prob. alter. of obs. *desperate* desperado, fr. *desperate*, adj.] **:** a bold or violent criminal; *esp* **:** a bandit of the western frontier

des·per·ate \'des-p(ə-)rət, -pərt\ *adj* [L *desperatus*, pp. of *desperare*] **1 :** having lost hope **2 a :** moved by or proceeding from despair **b :** suffering extreme need or anxiety ⟨~ for money⟩ ⟨~ for something to do⟩ **3 :** causing despair ⟨a ~ situation⟩ **4 :** of extreme intensity **:** OVERPOWERING **5 :** SHOCKING, OUTRAGEOUS **syn** see DESPONDENT — **des·per·ate·ly** *adv* — **des·per·ate·ness** *n*

des·per·a·tion \,des-pə-'rā-shən\ *n* **1 :** a loss of hope and surrender to despair **2 :** a state of hopelessness leading to rashness

de·spi·ca·ble \di-'spik-ə-bəl, 'des-(,)pik-\ *adj* [LL *despicabilis*, fr. L

despicari to despise] : deserving to be despised **syn** see CONTEMPTIBLE — **de·spi·ca·ble·ness** *n* — **de·spi·ca·bly** \-blē\ *adv*

de·spir·i·tu·al·ize \(')dē-'spir-ich-(ə-)wə-,līz, -ich-ə-,līz\ *vt* : to deprive of spiritual character or influence

de·spise \di-'spīz\ *vt* [ME *despisen*, fr. OF *despis-*, stem of *despire*, fr. L *despicere*, fr. *de-* + *specere* to look — more at SPY] **1** : to look down on with contempt or aversion ⟨*despised* the weak⟩ **2** : to regard as negligible, worthless, or distasteful — **de·spise·ment** \-'spīz-mənt\ *n* — **de·spis·er** \-'spī-zər\ *n*

syn CONTEMN, SCORN, DISDAIN, SCOUT: DESPISE may imply any emotional attitude ranging from indifferent disdain to loathing; CONTEMN implies a harsher but more intellectual or impersonal judgment; SCORN may suggest either lively and indignant or profound and passionate contempt; DISDAIN implies an arrogant or supercilious aversion to what is regarded as unworthy; SCOUT implies a derisive refusal to accept something as having any validity, efficacy, or credibility

[1]**de·spite** \di-'spīt\ *n* [ME, fr. OF *despit*, fr. L *despectus*, fr. *despectus*, pp. of *despicere*] **1** : the feeling or attitude of despising : CONTEMPT **2** : MALICE, SPITE **3 a** : an act showing contempt or defiance **b** : HARM, INJURY — **in despite of** : in spite of

[2]**despite** *vt, obs* : to vex or injure spitefully

[3]**despite** *prep* : in spite of : NOTWITHSTANDING ⟨ran ~ his injury⟩

de·spite·ful \di-'spīt-fəl\ *adj* : expressing malice or hate — **de·spite·ful·ly** \-fə-lē\ *adv* — **de·spite·ful·ness** *n*

de·spit·eous \dis-'pit-ē-əs\ *adj, archaic* : feeling or showing despite : MALICIOUS — **de·spit·eous·ly** *adv, archaic*

de·spoil \di-'spȯi(ə)l\ *vt* [ME *despoylen*, fr. OF *despoillier*, fr. L *despoliare*, fr. *de-* + *spoliare* to strip, rob — more at SPOIL] : to strip of belongings, possessions, or value : PILLAGE **syn** see RAVAGE — **de·spoil·er** *n* — **de·spoil·ment** \-'spȯi(ə)l-mənt\ *n*

de·spo·li·a·tion \di-,spō-lē-'ā-shən\ *n* [LL *despoliation-, despoliatio*, fr. *despoliatus*, pp. of *despoliare*] : the act of plundering : the condition of being despoiled : SPOLIATION

[1]**de·spond** \di-'spänd\ *vi* [L *despondēre*, fr. *de-* + *spondēre* to promise solemnly] : to become discouraged or disheartened

[2]**despond** *n* : DESPONDENCY

de·spon·dence \di-'spän-dən(t)s\ *n* : DESPONDENCY

de·spon·den·cy \-dən-sē\ *n* : the state of being despondent : DEJECTION, HOPELESSNESS

de·spon·dent \-dənt\ *adj* [L *despondent-, despondens*, prp. of *despondēre*] : feeling extreme discouragement, dejection, or depression ⟨~ about his health⟩ — **de·spon·dent·ly** *adv*

syn DESPONDENT, DESPAIRING, DESPERATE, HOPELESS mean having lost all or nearly all hope. DESPONDENT implies a deep dejection arising from a conviction of the uselessness of further effort; DESPAIRING suggests the slipping away of all hope and often an accompanying despondency; DESPERATE implies despair that prompts reckless action or convulsive struggle in the face of defeat or frustration; HOPELESS suggests despair and the cessation of effort or resistance and often implies acceptance or resignation

des·pot \'des-pət, -,pät\ *n* [MF *despote*, fr. Gk *despotēs;* akin to Skt *dampati* lord of the house; both fr. a prehistoric IE compound whose constituents are akin to L *domus* house and to L *potis* able — more at TIMBER, POTENT] **1 a** : a Byzantine emperor or prince **b** : a bishop or patriarch of the Eastern Orthodox Church **c** : an Italian hereditary prince or military leader during the Renaissance **2 a** : a ruler with absolute power and authority : AUTOCRAT **b** : a person exercising power abusively, oppressively, or tyrannously

des·pot·ic \des-'pät-ik, dis-\ *adj* : of, relating to, or having the character of a despot — **des·pot·i·cal·ly** \-i-k(ə-)lē\ *adv*

des·po·tism \'des-pə-,tiz-əm\ *n* **1 a** : rule by a despot **b** : despotic exercise of power **2 a** : a system of government in which the ruler has unlimited power : ABSOLUTISM **b** : a despotic state

des·qua·mate \'des-kwə-,māt\ *vi* [L *desquamatus*, pp. of *desquamare*, fr. *de-* + *squama* scale — more at SQUALOR] : to peel off in scales — **des·qua·ma·tion** \,des-kwə-'mā-shən\ *n*

des·sert \di-'zərt\ *n, often attrib* [MF, fr. *desservir* to clear the table, fr. *des-* de- + *servir* to serve, fr. L *servire*] **1** : a course of fruit, pastry, pudding, ice cream, or cheese served at the close of a meal **2** *Brit* : a fresh fruit served after a sweet course

des·sert·spoon \-,spün\ *n* : a spoon intermediate in size between a teaspoon and a tablespoon used in eating dessert

dessert wine *n* : a usu. sweet wine containing over 14 percent alcohol by volume and often served with dessert or between meals

de·sta·bi·lize \(')dē-'stā-bə-,līz\ *vt* : to make unstable

de·stain \(')dē-'stān\ *vt* : to selectively remove stain from (a specimen for microscopic study)

de·ster·i·lize \(')dē-'ster-ə-,līz\ *vt* : to release (gold) from an insulated condition in the treasury to useful service

de Stijl \də-'stī(ə)l, -'stā(ə)l\ *n* [D *De Stijl*, lit., the style, magazine published by members of the school] : an influential school of art founded in Holland in 1917 typically using rectangular forms and the primary colors plus black and white and asymmetric balance

des·ti·na·tion \,des-tə-'nā-shən\ *n* **1** : an act of appointing, setting aside for a purpose, or predetermining **2** : purpose for which something is destined **3** : a place which is set for the end of a journey or to which something is sent

des·tine \'des-tən\ *vt* [ME *destinen*, fr. OF *destiner*, fr. L *destinare*, fr. *de-* + *-stinare* (akin to L *stare* to stand) — more at STAND] **1** : to decree beforehand : PREDETERMINE **2 a** : to designate, assign, or dedicate in advance **b** : to direct, devise, or set apart for a specific purpose

des·ti·ny \'des-tə-nē\ *n, pl* **des·ti·nies** [ME *destinee*, fr. MF, fr. fem. of *destiné*, pp. of *destiner*] **1** : something to which a person or thing is destined : FORTUNE **2** : a predetermined course of events often held to be a resistless power or agency **syn** see FATE

des·ti·tute \'des-tə-,t(y)üt\ *adj* [ME, fr. L *destitutus*, pp. of *destituere* to abandon, deprive, fr. *de-* + *statuere* to set up] **1** : lacking something needed or desirable **2** : lacking possessions and resources; *esp* : suffering extreme want — **des·ti·tute·ness** *n*

des·ti·tu·tion \,des-tə-'t(y)ü-shən\ *n* : the state of being destitute; *esp* : extreme poverty **syn** see POVERTY

des·trier \'des-trē-ər, də-'stri(ə)r\ *n* [ME, fr. OF, fr. *destre* right hand, fr. L *dextra*, fr. fem. of *dexter*] *archaic* : WAR-HORSE

de·stroy \di-'strȯi\ *vb* [ME *destroyen*, fr. OF *destruire*, fr. (assumed) VL *destrugere*, alter. of L *destruere*, fr. *de-* + *struere* to build — more at STRUCTURE] *vt* **1** : to ruin the structure, organic existence, or condition of : DEMOLISH **2 a** : to put out of existence : KILL **b** : NEUTRALIZE **c** : to subject to a crushing defeat : ANNIHILATE ~ *vi* : to cause destruction

de·stroy·er \-'strȯi(-ə)r\ *n* **1** : a destroying agent or agency **2** : a small fast warship armed with usu. 5-inch guns, depth charges, torpedoes, mines, and sometimes guided missiles

destroyer escort *n* : a warship like a destroyer but smaller

destroying angel *n* : a variably colored poisonous mushroom (*Amanita phalloides*) sometimes mistaken for the common edible agarics; *also* : a related poisonous mushroom (*A. verna*)

de·struct \di-'strəkt\ *n* [short for *destruction*] : the deliberate destruction of a rocket after launching esp. during a test

de·struc·ti·bil·i·ty \di-,strək-tə-'bil-ət-ē\ *n* : the quality of being destructible

de·struc·ti·ble \di-'strək-tə-bəl\ *adj* : capable of being destroyed

de·struc·tion \di-'strək-shən\ *n* [ME *destruccioun*, fr. MF *destruction*, fr. L *destruction-, destructio*, fr. *destructus*, pp. of *destruere*] **1** : the action or process of destroying something **2** : the state or fact of being destroyed : RUIN **3** : a destroying agency

de·struc·tion·ist \-sh(ə-)nəst\ *n* : one who delights in or advocates destruction

de·struc·tive \di-'strək-tiv\ *adj* **1** : causing destruction : RUINOUS ⟨~ storm⟩ **2** : designed or tending to destroy ⟨~ criticism⟩ — **de·struc·tive·ly** *adv* — **de·struc·tive·ness** *n*

destructive distillation *n* : decomposition of a substance (as wood, coal, or a hydrocarbon oil) by heat in a closed container and collection of the volatile products produced

de·struc·tiv·i·ty \-,strək-'tiv-ət-ē ,dē-\ *n* : capacity for destruction

de·struc·tor \di-'strək-tər\ *n* **1** : a furnace for burning refuse : INCINERATOR **2** : a device for destroying a missile in flight

de·sue·tude \'des-wi-,t(y)üd, di-'sü-ə-,t(y)üd\ *n* [F or L; F *désuétude*, fr. L *desuetudo*, fr. *desuetus*, pp. of *desuescere* to become unaccustomed, fr. *de-* + *suescere* to become accustomed; akin to L *sui* of oneself] : discontinuance from use or exercise : DISUSE

de·sul·fur·ize \(')dē-'səl-f(y)ə-,rīz\ *vt* : to remove sulfur or sulfur compounds from — **de·sul·fur·iz·er** *n*

des·ul·to·ri·ly \,des-əl-'tōr-ə-lē, -'tȯr-\ *adv* : in a desultory manner

des·ul·to·ri·ness \'des-əl-,tōr-ē-nəs, -,tȯr-\ *n* : AIMLESSNESS

des·ul·to·ry \'des-əl-,tōr-ē, -,tȯr-\ *adj* [L *desultorius*, fr. *desultus*, pp. of *desilire* to leap down, fr. *de-* + *salire* to leap — more at SALLY] **1** : marked by lack of definite plan, regularity, or purpose **2** : not connected with the main subject **syn** see RANDOM

de·tach \di-'tach\ *vt* [F *détacher*, fr. OF *destachier*, fr. *des-* de- + *-tachier* (as in *atachier* to attach)] **1** : to separate esp. from a larger mass and usu. without violence or damage **2** : DISENGAGE, WITHDRAW — **de·tach·abil·i·ty** \di-,tach-ə-'bil-ət-ē\ *n* — **de·tach·able** \di-'tach-ə-bəl\ *adj* — **de·tach·ably** \-blē\ *adv*

de·tached \di-'tacht\ *adj* **1** : standing by itself : SEPARATE, UNCONNECTED; *specif* : not sharing any wall with another building ⟨~ house⟩ **2** : ALOOF, UNCONCERNED ⟨a ~ view of the affair⟩ **syn** see INDIFFERENT — **de·tached·ly** \-'tach-əd-lē, -'tach-tlē\ *adv* — **de·tached·ness** \-'tach-əd-nəs, -'tach(t)-nəs\ *n*

detached service *n* : military service away from one's assigned organization

de·tach·ment \di-'tach-mənt\ *n* **1** : the action or process of detaching : SEPARATION **2 a** : the dispatch of a body of troops or part of a fleet from the main body for a special mission or service **b** : the portion so dispatched **c** : a permanently organized separate unit usu. smaller than a platoon and different in composition from normal units **3 a** : indifference to worldly concerns : ALOOFNESS, UNWORLDLINESS **b** : freedom from bias or prejudice

[1]**de·tail** \di-'tā(ə)l, 'dē-,tāl\ *n* [F *détail*, fr. OF *detail* slice, piece fr. *detaillier* to cut in pieces, fr. *de-* + *taillier* to cut — more at TAILOR] **1** : extended treatment of or attention to particular items **2** : a part of a whole: as **a** : a small and subordinate part : PARTICULAR, CIRCUMSTANCE **b** : a portion considered independently of the parts considered together **c** : a minor part (as the cornice, caps of the buttresses, capitals of a building) **3 a** : selection for a particular task (as in military service) of a person or a body of persons **b** : the person or body selected or the task to be performed **4** : the small elements of a photographic image corresponding to those of the subject **syn** see ITEM

[2]**detail** *vt* **1** : to report minutely and distinctly **2** : ENUMERATE, SPECIFY **3** : to assign to a particular task **4** : to furnish with the smaller elements of design and finish ⟨beautifully ~*ed* hats⟩ ~ *vi* : to make detail drawings — **de·tail·er** *n*

de·tailed \di-'tā(ə)ld, 'dē-,tāld\ *adj* : marked by abundant detail or by thoroughness in treating small items or parts ⟨the ~ study of history⟩ **syn** see CIRCUMSTANTIAL — **de·tailed·ly** \di-'tāl(-ə)d-lē, 'dē-,\ *adv* — **de·tailed·ness** \di-'tā-ləd-nəs, -'tāl(d)-, 'dē-,\ *n*

detail man *n* : a representative of a drug manufacturer who introduces new drugs to professional dispensers

de·tain \di-'tān\ *vt* [ME *deteynen*, fr. MF *detenir*, fr. L *detinēre*, fr. *de-* + *tenēre* to hold] **1** : to hold or keep in or as if in custody **2** *obs* : to keep back (as something due) : WITHHOLD **3** : to restrain esp. from proceeding : STOP **syn** see DELAY, KEEP — **de·tain·ee** \di-,tā-'nē, ,dē-\ *n* — **de·tain·ment** \-'tān-mənt\ *n*

de·tain·er \di-'tā-nər\ *n* [AF *detener*, fr. *detener* to detain, fr. L *detinēre*] **1** : the act of keeping something in one's possession; *specif* : the withholding from the rightful owner of something which has lawfully come into the possession of the holder **2** : detention in custody **3** : a writ authorizing the keeper of a prison to continue to keep a person in custody

de·tect \di-'tekt\ *vt* [ME *detecten*, fr. L *detectus*, pp. of *detegere* to uncover, detect, fr. *de-* + *tegere* to cover — more at THATCH] **1** : to discover the true esp. hidden or disguised character of **2** : to discover or determine the existence, presence, or fact of **3 a** : RECTIFY 4 **b** : DEMODULATE — **de·tect·able** \-'tek-tə-bəl\ *adj*

de·tect·a·phone \-'tek-tə-,fōn\ *n* : a telephonic apparatus with an attached microphone transmitter used esp. for listening secretly

de·tec·tion \di-'tek-shən\ *n* **1** : the act of detecting or the state or fact of being detected : DISCOVERY **2** : DEMODULATION

[1]**de·tec·tive** \di-'tek-tiv\ *adj* : fitted for, employed for, or concerned with detection ⟨~ ability⟩ ⟨~ fiction⟩

[2]**detective** *n* : one employed or engaged in detecting lawbreakers or getting information that is not readily or publicly accessible

de·tec·tor \di-ˈtek-tər\ *n* : one that detects: as **a** : an indicator showing the depth of the water in a boiler **b** : a device for detecting the presence of electric waves or of radioactivity **c** : a rectifier of high-frequency current used esp. for extracting the intelligence from a radio signal

de·tent \ˈdē-ˌtent, di-ˈtent\ *n* [F *détente*, fr. MF *destente*, fr. *destendre* to slacken, fr. OF, fr. *des-* de- + *tendre* to stretch, fr. L *tendere* — more at THIN] : a mechanism that locks or unlocks a movement (as of a clock)

dé·tente \dā-ˈtänt, -ˈtäⁿt\ *n* [F] : a relaxation of strained relations or tensions (as between nations)

de·ten·tion \di-ˈten-chən\ *n* [MF or LL; MF, fr. LL *detention-*, *detentio*, fr. L *detentus*, pp. of *detinēre* to detain] **1** : the act or fact of detaining: **a** : a holding in custody **b** : a holding back **2** : the state of being detained; *esp* : a period of temporary custody prior to disposition by a court

de·ter \di-ˈtər\ *vt* **de·terred; de·ter·ring** [L *deterrēre*, fr. *de-* + *terrēre* to frighten] **1** : to turn aside, discourage, or prevent from acting (as by fear) **2** : INHIBIT — **de·ter·ment** \-ˈtər-mənt\ *n*

de·terge \di-ˈtərj\ *vt* [F or L; F *déterger*, fr. L *detergēre*, fr. *de-* + *tergēre* to wipe — more at TERSE] : to wash off : CLEANSE

de·ter·gen·cy \di-ˈtər-jən-sē\ *n* : cleansing quality or power

[1]**de·ter·gent** \-jənt\ *adj* : CLEANSING

[2]**detergent** *n* : a cleansing agent: as **a** : SOAP **b** : any of numerous synthetic water-soluble or liquid organic preparations that are chemically different from soaps but resemble them in the ability to emulsify oils and hold dirt in suspension **c** : an oil-soluble substance that holds insoluble foreign matter in suspension and is used in lubricating oils and dry-cleaning solvents

de·te·ri·o·rate \di-ˈtir-ē-ə-ˌrāt\ *vb* [LL *deterioratus*, pp. of *deteriorare*, fr. L *deterior* worse, fr. *de-* + *-ter* (suffix as in L *uter* which of two) + *-ior*] *vt* : to make inferior in quality or value : IMPAIR ~ *vi* **1** : to grow worse **2** : DEGENERATE

de·te·ri·o·ra·tion \di-ˌtir-ē-ə-ˈrā-shən\ *n* : the action or process of deteriorating : the state of having deteriorated

syn DETERIORATION, DEGENERATION, DECADENCE, DECLINE mean the falling from a higher to a lower level in quality, character, or vitality. DETERIORATION implies impairment of vigor, resilience, or usefulness; DEGENERATION stresses physical, intellectual, or esp. moral retrogression; DECADENCE presupposes a reaching and passing the peak of development and implies a turn downward with a consequent loss in vitality or energy; DECLINE differs from DECADENCE in suggesting a more markedly downward direction and greater momentum, more obvious evidence of deterioration, and less likelihood of a return to earlier vigor or state of excellence

de·te·ri·o·ra·tive \di-ˈtir-ē-ə-ˌrāt-iv\ *adj* : tending to deteriorate

de·ter·min·able \-ˈtərm-(ə-)nə-bəl\ *adj* **1** : capable of being determined, definitely ascertained, or decided upon : JUDICABLE **2** : liable to be terminated : TERMINABLE — **de·ter·min·able·ness** *n* — **de·ter·min·ably** \-blē\ *adv*

de·ter·mi·na·cy \-nə-sē\ *n* **1** : the quality or state of being determinate **2 a** : the state of being definitely and unequivocally characterized : EXACTNESS **b** : the state of being determined

de·ter·mi·nant \-ˈtərm-(ə-)nənt\ *n* **1** : something that determines or conditions : FACTOR **2** : a square array of numbers bordered on either side by a straight line with a value that is the algebraic sum of all the products that can be formed by taking as factors one element in succession from each row and column and giving to each product a positive or negative sign depending upon whether the number of permutations necessary to place the indices representing each factor's position in its row or column in the order of the natural numbers is odd or even **3** : GENE; *broadly* : a comparable subordinate agent (as a plasmagene) **syn** see CAUSE

de·ter·mi·nate \di-ˈtər-mə-nət\ *adj* [ME, fr. L *determinatus*, pp. of *determinare*] **1** : having defined limits : ESTABLISHED **2** : definitely settled : ARBITRARY **3** : conclusively determined : DEFINITIVE **4** : CYMOSE **5** *of an egg* : undergoing determinate cleavage — **de·ter·mi·nate·ly** *adv* — **de·ter·mi·nate·ness** *n*

determinate cleavage *n* : cleavage of an egg in which each division irreversibly separates portions of the zygote with specific potencies for further development

determinate growth *n* : growth (as in a cymose inflorescence) in which the axis does not continue to elongate indefinitely

de·ter·mi·na·tion \di-ˌtər-mə-ˈnā-shən\ *n* **1 a** : a judicial decision settling and ending a controversy **b** : the resolving of a question by argument or reasoning **2** *archaic* : TERMINATION **3 a** : the act of deciding definitely and firmly; *also* : the result of such an act of decision **b** : the power or habit of deciding definitely and firmly **4** : a fixing of the position, magnitude, or character of something: as **a** : the act, process, or result of an accurate measurement **b** : an identification of the taxonomic position of a plant or animal **5 a** : the definition of a concept by its essential constituents **b** : the addition of a differentia to a concept to limit its denotation **6** : direction or tendency to a certain end

[1]**de·ter·mi·na·tive** \-ˈtərm-ə-ˌnāt-iv, -(ə-)nət-\ *adj* : having power or tendency to determine : LIMITING, SHAPING **syn** see CONCLUSIVE — **de·ter·mi·na·tive·ly** *adv* — **de·ter·mi·na·tive·ness** *n*

[2]**determinative** *n* : one that serves to determine

de·ter·mi·na·tor \di-ˈtər-mə-ˌnāt-ər\ *n* : DETERMINER

de·ter·mine \di-ˈtər-mən\ *vb* **de·ter·min·ing** \-ˈtərm-(ə-)niŋ\ [ME *determinen*, fr. MF *determiner*, fr. L *determinare*, fr. *de-* + *terminare* to limit, fr. *terminus* boundary, limit] *vt* **1 a** : to fix conclusively or authoritatively **b** : to decide by judicial sentence **c** : to settle or decide by choice of alternatives or possibilities **d** : RESOLVE **2 a** : to fix the form or character of beforehand : ORDAIN ⟨two points ~ a straight line⟩ **b** : to bring about as a result : REGULATE ⟨demand ~*s* the price⟩ **3 a** : to fix the boundaries of **b** : to limit in extent or scope **c** : to put or set an end to : TERMINATE ⟨~ an estate⟩ **4 a** : to obtain definite and firsthand knowledge of ⟨~ a position at sea⟩ **b** : to discover the taxonomic position or the generic and specific names of ~ *vi* **1** : to come to a decision **2** : to come to an end or become void **syn** see DECIDE, DISCOVER

de·ter·mined \-ˈtər-mənd\ *adj* **1** : DECIDED, RESOLVED **2** : FIRM, RESOLUTE — **de·ter·mined·ly** \-mən-dlē, -mə-nəd-lē\ *adv* — **de·ter·mined·ness** \-mən(d)-nəs\ *n*

de·ter·min·er \-ˈtərm-(ə-)nər\ *n* : one that determines: as **a** : GENE, DETERMINANT **b** : a word (as *his* in "his new car") belonging to a group of limiting noun modifiers characterized by occurrence before descriptive adjectives modifying the same noun

de·ter·min·ism \-ə-ˌniz-əm\ *n* **1 a** : a doctrine that acts of the will, occurrences in nature, or social or psychological phenomena are determined by antecedent causes **b** : a belief in predestination **2** : the quality or state of being determined — **de·ter·min·ist** \-(ə-)nəst\ *n or adj* — **de·ter·min·is·tic** \di-ˌtər-mə-ˈnis-tik\ *adj* — **de·ter·min·is·ti·cal·ly** \-ˈnis-ti-k(ə-)lē\ *adv*

de·ter·rence \di-ˈtər-ən(t)s, -ˈter-, -ˈtə-rən(t)s\ *n* : the act or process of deterring

de·ter·rent \-ənt, -rənt\ *adj* [L *deterrent-*, *deterrens*, prp. of *deterrēre* to deter] **1** : serving to deter **2** : relating to deterrence — **deterrent** *n* — **de·ter·rent·ly** *adv*

de·ter·sive \di-ˈtər-siv, -ziv\ *adj* [MF *detersif*, fr. L *detersus*, pp. of *detergēre* to deterge] : CLEANSING, DETERGENT — **de·ter·sive** *n*

de·test \di-ˈtest\ *vt* [ME *detesten*, fr. L *detestari*, lit., to curse while calling a deity to witness, fr. *de-* + *testari* to call to witness — more at TESTAMENT] **1** : to dislike intensely : LOATHE, ABHOR **2** *obs* : CURSE, DENOUNCE **syn** see HATE — **de·test·er** \-ˈtes-tər\ *n*

de·test·able \di-ˈtes-tə-bəl\ *adj* : arousing or meriting intense dislike : ABOMINABLE ⟨~ vices⟩ **syn** see HATEFUL — **de·test·able·ness** *n* — **de·test·ably** \-blē\ *adv*

de·tes·ta·tion \ˌdē-ˌtes-ˈtā-shən\ *n* **1** : extreme hatred or dislike : ABHORRENCE, LOATHING **2** : an object of hatred or contempt

de·throne \di-ˈthrōn\ *vt* : to remove from a throne : DEPOSE — **de·throne·ment** \-mənt\ *n* — **de·thron·er** *n*

det·i·nue \ˈdet-ᵊn-ˌ(y)ü\ *n* [ME *detenewe*, fr. MF *detenue* detention, fr. fem. of *detenu*, pp. of *detenir* to detain] **1** : detention of something due; *esp* : the unlawful detention of a personal chattel from another **2** : a common-law action for the recovery of a personal chattel wrongfully detained or of its value

det·o·na·ble \ˈdet-ᵊn-ə-bəl, -ə-nə-\ *adj* : capable of being detonated

det·o·nat·able \ˈdet-ᵊn-ˌāt-ə-bəl, -ə-ˌnāt-\ *adj* : DETONABLE

det·o·nate \ˈdet-ᵊn-ˌāt, ˈdet-ə-ˌnāt\ *vb* [L *detonatus*, pp. of *detonare* to thunder down, fr. *de-* + *tonare* to thunder — more at THUNDER] *vi* : to explode with sudden violence ~ *vt* : to cause to detonate — **det·o·na·tion** \ˌdet-ᵊn-ˈā-shən, -ə-ˈnā-\ *n*

det·o·na·tor \ˈdet-ᵊn-ˌāt-ər, -ə-ˌnāt-\ *n* : a device or small quantity of explosive used for detonating a high explosive

[1]**de·tour** \ˈdē-ˌtu̇(ə)r, di-ˈtu̇(ə)r\ *n* [F *détour*, fr. OF *destor*, fr. *destorner* to divert, fr. *des-* de- + *torner* to turn — more at TURN] : a deviation from a direct course or the usual procedure; *specif* : a roundabout way temporarily replacing part of a route

[2]**detour** *vi* : to proceed by a detour ⟨~ around a pit⟩ ~ *vt* **1** : to send by a circuitous route **2** : to avoid by going around : BYPASS

de·tox·i·cate \(ˈ)dē-ˈtäk-sə-ˌkāt\ *vt* [*de-* + L *toxicum* poison] : DETOXIFY — **de·tox·i·ca·tion** \(ˌ)dē-ˌtäk-sə-ˈkā-shən\ *n*

de·tox·i·fi·ca·tion \(ˌ)dē-ˌtäk-sə-fə-ˈkā-shən\ *n* : the act of detoxifying : the state of being detoxified

de·tox·i·fy \(ˈ)dē-ˈtäk-sə-ˌfī\ *vt* : to remove the poison or effect of poison from

de·tract \di-ˈtrakt\ *vb* [ME *detracten*, fr. L *detractus*, pp. of *detrahere* to withdraw, disparage, fr. *de-* + *trahere* to draw] *vt* **1** *archaic* : to speak ill of **2** *archaic* : to take away **3** : DIVERT ⟨~ attention⟩ ~ *vi* : to take away something — **de·trac·tor** \-ˈtrak-tər\ *n*

de·trac·tion \di-ˈtrak-shən\ *n* **1** : a lessening of reputation or esteem esp. by envious, malicious, or petty criticism : BELITTLING, DISPARAGEMENT **2** : a taking away : SUBTRACTION — **de·trac·tive** \-ˈtrak-tiv\ *adj* — **de·trac·tive·ly** *adv*

de·train \(ˈ)dē-ˈtrān\ *vi* : to get off a railroad train ~ *vt* : to remove from a railroad train — **de·train·ment** \-mənt\ *n*

de·trib·al·iza·tion \(ˌ)dē-ˌtrī-bə-lə-ˈzā-shən\ *n* : the breaking down of a tribal organization esp. through culture contact

de·trib·al·ize \(ˈ)dē-ˈtrī-bə-ˌlīz\ *vt* : to estrange from a tribe

det·ri·ment \ˈde-trə-mənt\ *n* [ME, fr. MF or L; MF, fr. L *detrimentum*, fr. *deterere* to wear away, impair, fr. *de-* + *terere* to rub — more at THROW] : injury or damage or its cause : HURT

[1]**det·ri·men·tal** \ˌde-trə-ˈment-ᵊl\ *adj* : causing detriment : HARMFUL, DAMAGING **syn** see PERNICIOUS — **det·ri·men·tal·ly** *adv*

[2]**detrimental** *n* : an undesirable or harmful person or thing

de·tri·tal \di-ˈtrīt-ᵊl\ *adj* : of, relating to, or resulting from detritus

de·tri·tion \di-ˈtrish-ən\ *n* : a wearing off or away

de·tri·tus \di-ˈtrīt-əs\ *n*, *pl* **de·tri·tus** \-ˈtrīt-əs, -ˈtrī-ˌtüs\ [F *détritus*, fr. L *detritus*, pp. of *deterere*] **1** : loose material that results directly from rock disintegration esp. when composed of rock fragments **2** : a product of disintegration or wearing away

de trop \də-ˈtrō\ *adj* [F] : too much or too many : SUPERFLUOUS

de·trude \di-ˈtrüd\ *vt* [L *detrudere*, fr. *de-* + *trudere* to push] : to force down, out, or away — **de·tru·sion** \-ˈtrü-zhən\ *n*

Deu·ca·lion \d(y)ü-ˈkāl-yən\ *n* [L, fr. Gk *Deukaliōn*] : a son of Prometheus, survivor with his wife Pyrrha of a great flood sent by Zeus, and founder of the renewed human race

[1]**deuce** \ˈd(y)üs\ *n* [MF *deus* two, fr. L *duos*, acc. masc. of *duo* two — more at TWO] **1 a** (1) : the face of a die that bears two spots (2) : a playing card bearing an index number two **b** : a cast of dice yielding a point of two **2** : a tie in tennis with each side having a score of 40 **3** [obs. E *deuce* bad luck] **a** : DEVIL, DICKENS — used chiefly as a mild oath **b** : something notable of its kind

[2]**deuce** *vt* : to bring the score of (a tennis game or set) to deuce

deuc·ed \ˈd(y)ü-səd\ *adj* : DARNED, CONFOUNDED ⟨in a ~ fix⟩ — **deuced** *or* **deucedly** *adv*

deuces wild *n* : a card game (as poker) in which each deuce may represent any card designated by its holder

de·us ex ma·chi·na \ˌdā-ə-ˌsek-ˈsmak-ə-nə, ˌdē-\ *n* [NL, a god from a machine, trans. of Gk *theos ek mēchanēs*] : a person or thing that appears or is introduced suddenly and unexpectedly and provides a contrived solution to an apparently insoluble difficulty

deut- *or* **deuto-** *comb form* [ISV, fr. *deuter-*] : second : secondary ⟨*deuto*nymph⟩

[1]**deuter-** *or* **deutero-** *comb form* [alter. of ME *deutro-*, modif. of LL *deutero-*, fr. Gk *deuter-*, *deutero-*, fr. *deuteros*; prob. akin to L *dudum* formerly] : second : secondary ⟨*deutero*genesis⟩

[2]**deuter-** *or* **deutero-** *comb form* [ISV] : deuterium ⟨*deuter*ated⟩

deu·ter·ag·o·nist \ˌd(y)üt-ə-ˈrag-ə-nəst\ *n* [Gk *deuteragōnistēs*, fr. *deuter-* + *agōnistēs* combatant, actor — more at PROTAGONIST] **1** : the actor taking the part of second importance in a classical Greek drama **2** : a person who serves as a foil to another

deu·ter·an·ope \ˈd(y)üt-ə-rə-ˌnōp\ *n* : an individual affected with deuteranopia

deu·ter·an·opia \ˌd(y)üt-ə-rə-ˈnō-pē-ə\ *n* [NL, fr. [1]*deuter-* + [2]*a-* + *-opia*] : color blindness marked by confusion of purplish red and green

deu·te·ri·um \d(y)ü-ˈtir-ē-əm\ *n* [NL, fr. Gk *deuteros* second] **:** the hydrogen isotope that is of twice the mass of ordinary hydrogen and that occurs in water — called also *heavy hydrogen*

deuterium oxide *n* **:** heavy water D_2O composed only of deuterium and oxygen

deu·tero·ca·non·i·cal \ˌd(y)üt-ə-rō-kə-ˈnän-i-kəl\ *adj* [NL *deuterocanonicus*, fr. ¹*deuter-* + LL *canonicus* canonical] **:** of, relating to, or constituting the part of the Roman Catholic canon of scripture that contains writings whose authenticity has been questioned

deu·ter·og·a·my \ˌd(y)üt-ə-ˈräg-ə-mē\ *n* [LGk *deuterogamia*, fr. Gk *deuter-* + *-gamia* -gamy] **:** DIGAMY

deu·tero·gen·e·sis \ˌd(y)üt-ə-rō-ˈjen-ə-səs\ *n* **:** the appearance of a new adaptive character late in life

deu·ter·on \ˈd(y)üt-ə-ˌrän\ *n* [*deuterium*] **:** the nucleus of the deuterium atom that consists of one proton and one neutron — called also *deu·ton* \ˈd(y)ü-ˌtän\

Deu·ter·o·nom·ic \ˌd(y)üt-ə-rə-ˈnäm-ik\ *adj* [*Deuteronomy*, fifth book of the Old Testament, fr. ME *Deutronomie*, fr. LL *Deuteronomium*, fr. Gk *Deuteronomion*, fr. *deuter-* + *nomos* law — more at NIMBLE] **:** of or relating to the biblical book of Deuteronomy or marked by its prophetic and hortatory emphasis

Deu·ter·on·o·mist \ˌd(y)üt-ə-ˈrän-ə-məst\ *n* **:** one of the writers or editors of a Deuteronomic third strand often distinguished in the earlier books of the Old Testament — **Deu·ter·on·o·mis·tic** \-ˌrän-ə-ˈmis-tik\ *adj*

deu·to·plasm \ˈd(y)üt-ə-ˌplaz-əm\ *n* [ISV] **:** the nutritive inclusions of protoplasm; *esp* **:** the yolk reserves of an egg — **deu·to·plas·mic** \ˌd(y)üt-ə-ˈplaz-mik\ *adj*

deut·sche mark \ˌdȯi-chə-ˈmärk\ *n* [G] — see MONEY table

deut·zia \ˈd(y)üt-sē-ə\ *n* [NL, fr. Jean *Deutz* †1784? D patron of botanical research] **:** any of a genus (*Deutzia*) of the saxifrage family of ornamental shrubs with white or pink flowers

de·val·u·ate \(ˈ)dē-ˈval-yə-ˌwāt\ *vb* **:** DEVALUE

de·val·u·a·tion \(ˌ)dē-ˌval-yə-ˈwā-shən\ *n* **1 :** an official reduction in the exchange value of a currency by a lowering of its gold equivalency **2 :** a lessening esp. of status or stature **:** DECLINE

de·val·ue \(ˈ)dē-ˈval-(ˌ)yü, -yə-w\ *vt* **1 :** to institute the devaluation of (money) **2 :** to cause or be responsible for a devaluation of (as a person or a literary work) **∼** *vi* **:** to institute devaluation

De·va·na·ga·ri \ˌdā-və-ˈnäg-ə-rē\ *n* [Skt *devanāgarī*, fr. *deva* divine + *nāgarī* script of the city; akin to L *divus* divine — more at DEITY] **:** an alphabet usu. employed for Sanskrit and also used as a literary hand for various modern languages of India

dev·as·tate \ˈdev-ə-ˌstāt\ *vt* [L *devastatus*, pp. of *devastare*, fr. *de-* + *vastare* to lay waste — more at WASTE] **1 :** to lay waste **2 :** OVERPOWER, OVERWHELM **syn** see RAVAGE — **dev·as·tat·ing·ly** \-ˌstāt-iŋ-lē\ *adv* — **dev·as·ta·tor** \-ˌstāt-ər\ *n*

dev·as·ta·tion \ˌdev-ə-ˈstā-shən\ *n* **:** the action of devastating **:** the state of being devastated **:** DESOLATION

dev·as·ta·tive \ˈdev-ə-ˌstāt-iv\ *adj* **:** tending to cause devastation

de·vel·op \di-ˈvel-əp\ *vb* [F *développer*, fr. OF *desvoloper*, fr. *des-* de- + *voloper* to wrap] *vt* **1 a :** to set forth or make clear by degrees or in detail **:** EXPOUND **b :** to make visible or manifest **c :** to treat with an agent to cause the appearance of color **d :** to subject (exposed photograph material) to a usu. chemical treatment to produce a visible image; *also* **:** to make visible by such a method **e :** to elaborate by the unfolding of a musical idea and by the working out of rhythmic and harmonic changes in the theme **2 :** to evolve the possibilities of **3 a** (1) **:** to make active (2) **:** to promote the growth of ⟨∼*ed* his muscles⟩ **b :** to make available or usable ⟨∼ its resources⟩ **c :** to move (a chess piece) from the original position to one providing more opportunity for effective use **4 a :** to cause to unfold gradually ⟨∼*ed* his argument⟩ **b :** to expand by a process of growth **c :** to cause to grow and differentiate along lines natural to its kind ⟨rain and sun ∼ the grain⟩ **5 :** to acquire gradually ⟨∼ a taste for olives⟩ **6 :** to superimpose (a three-dimensional surface) on a plane without stretching **∼** *vi* **1 a :** to go through a process of natural growth, differentiation, or evolution by successive changes ⟨a blossom ∼*s* from a bud⟩ **b :** to acquire secondary sex characters **c :** EVOLVE, DIFFERENTIATE; *broadly* **:** GROW **2 a :** to become gradually manifest **b :** to become apparent **3 :** to develop one's pieces in chess — **de·vel·op·able** \-ˈvel-ə-pə-bəl\ *adj*

de·vel·op·er \-ə-pər\ *n* **:** one that develops; *specif* **:** a chemical used to develop exposed photographic materials

de·vel·op·ment \di-ˈvel-əp-mənt\ *n* **1 :** the act, process, or result of developing **2 :** the state of being developed — **de·vel·op·men·tal** \-ˌvel-əp-ˈment-ᵊl\ *adj* — **de·vel·op·men·tal·ly** \-ᵊl-ē\ *adv*

de·verb·a·tive \-bət-iv\ *adj* **1 :** derived from a verb ⟨the ∼ noun *developer* is derived from *develop*⟩ **2 :** used in derivation from a verb ⟨the ∼ suffix *-er* in *developer*⟩ — **deverbative** *n*

de·vest \di-ˈvest\ *vt* [MF *desvestir*, fr. ML *disvestire*, fr. L *dis-* + *vestire* to clothe — more at VEST] **:** DIVEST

de·vi·ance \ˈdē-vē-ən(t)s\ *or* **de·vi·an·cy** \-ən-sē\ *n* **:** deviant quality, state, or behavior

de·vi·ant \-ənt\ *adj* **1 :** deviating esp. from some accepted norm **2 :** characterized by deviation — **deviant** *n*

¹de·vi·ate \ˈdē-vē-ˌāt\ *vb* [LL *deviatus*, pp. of *deviare*, fr. L *de-* + *via* way — more at VIA] *vi* **1 :** to turn aside esp. from an established way **2 :** to stray esp. from a standard, principle, or topic **∼** *vt* **:** to cause to turn out of a previous course **syn** see SWERVE — **de·vi·a·tor** \-ˌāt-ər\ *n*

²de·vi·ate \-vē-ət, -vē-ˌāt\ *adj* **:** characterized by or given to significant departure from the behavioral norms of a particular society

³de·vi·ate \-vē-ət, -vē-ˌāt\ *n* **:** one that deviates from a norm; *esp* **:** a person who differs markedly from his group norm

de·vi·a·tion \ˌdē-vē-ˈā-shən\ *n* **:** an act or instance of deviating: as **a :** deflection of the needle of a compass caused by local magnetic influences (as in a ship) **b :** the difference between a value in a frequency distribution and a fixed number **c :** evolutionary differentiation involving interpolation of new stages in the ancestral pattern of morphogenesis **d :** departure from an established ideology or party line **e :** noticeable or marked departure from accepted norms of behavior — **de·vi·a·tion·ism** \-shə-ˌniz-əm\ *n* — **de·vi·a·tion·ist** \-sh(ə-)nəst\ *n*

de·vice \di-ˈvīs\ *n* [ME *devis*, *devise*, fr. OF, division, intention, fr. *deviser* to divide, regulate, tell — more at DEVISE] **1 :** something devised or contrived: as **a :** a scheme to deceive **:** STRATAGEM **b :** something fanciful, elaborate, or intricate in design **c :** something in a literary work designed to achieve a particular artistic effect **d** *archaic* **:** MASQUE, SPECTACLE **e :** a piece of equipment or a mechanism designed to serve a special purpose or perform a special function **2 :** DESIRE, WILL ⟨left to his own ∼*s*⟩ **3 :** an emblematic design used esp. as a heraldic bearing **4** *archaic* **:** DEVISING

¹dev·il \ˈdev-əl\ *n* [ME *devel*, fr. OE *dēofol*, fr. LL *diabolus*, fr. Gk *diabolos*, lit., slanderer, fr. *diaballein* to throw across, slander, fr. *dia-* + *ballein* to throw; akin to OHG *quellan* to well, gush] **1** *often cap* **:** the personal supreme spirit of evil often represented in Jewish and Christian belief as the tempter of mankind, the leader of all apostate angels, and ruler of hell — often used with *the* as a mild imprecation or expression of surprise, vexation, or emphasis **2 :** DEMON **3 a :** an extremely and malignantly wicked person **:** FIEND **b** *archaic* **:** a great evil **4 :** a person of notable energy, recklessness, and dashing spirit **5 a :** a person in a pitiable position or condition — usu. used with *poor* **b :** PRINTER'S DEVIL **6 :** something very provoking, difficult, or trying **7 :** any of various machines or devices **8** *Christian Science* **:** the opposite of Truth **:** a belief in sin, sickness, and death **:** EVIL, ERROR

²devil *vb* **dev·iled** *or* **dev·illed**; **dev·il·ing** *or* **dev·il·ling** \ˈdev-(ə-)liŋ\ *vt* **1 :** TEASE, ANNOY **2 :** to chop (food) fine and highly season ⟨∼*ed* eggs⟩ **3 :** to tear to pieces in a devil ⟨∼ rags⟩ **∼** *vi* **:** to serve or function as a devil

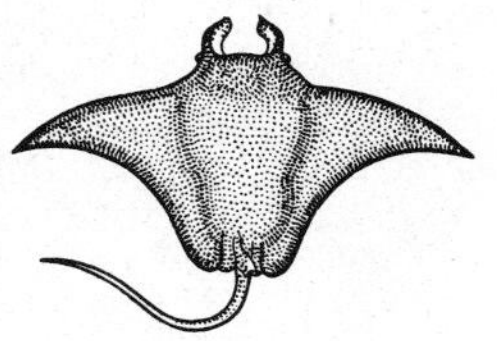
devilfish

dev·il·fish \ˈdev-əl-ˌfish\ *n* **1 :** any of several extremely large rays (genera *Manta* and *Mobula*) widely distributed in warm seas **2 :** OCTOPUS; *broadly* **:** any large cephalopod

dev·il·ish \ˈdev-(ə-)lish\ *adj* **1 :** of, relating to, or characteristic of the devil ⟨∼ tricks⟩ **2 :** EXTREME, EXCESSIVE ⟨in a ∼ hurry⟩ — **devilish** *adv* — **dev·il·ish·ly** *adv* — **dev·il·ish·ness** *n*

dev·il·kin \ˈdev-əl-kən\ *n* **:** a little devil **:** IMP

dev·il–may–care \ˌdev-əl-(ˌ)mā-ˈke(ə)r, -ˈka(ə)r\ *adj* **1 :** careless of authority **:** RECKLESS **2 :** RAKISH, INFORMAL

dev·il·ment \ˈdev-əl-mənt, -ˌment\ *n* **1 :** devilish conduct **2 :** reckless mischief

dev·il·ry \ˈdev-əl-rē\ *or* **dev·il·try** \-əl-trē\ *n*, *pl* **dev·il·ries** *or* **dev·il·tries** **1 a :** action performed with the help of the devil **:** WITCHCRAFT **b :** gross or malignant cruelty **:** WICKEDNESS **c :** reckless unrestrained conduct **:** MISCHIEF **2 :** an act of devilry

devil's advocate *n* [trans. of NL *advocatus diaboli*] **1 :** a Roman Catholic official whose duty is to point out defects in the evidence on which a demand for beatification or canonization rests **2 :** a person who champions the worse cause for the sake of argument

devil's darning needle *n* **1 :** DRAGONFLY **2 :** DAMSELFLY

dev·il's food cake \ˈdev-əlz-ˌfüd-ˌkāk\ *n* **:** a rich chocolate cake

devil's paintbrush *n* **:** any of various hawkweeds that are naturalized weeds in the eastern U.S.

dev·il·wood \ˈdev-əl-ˌwu̇d\ *n* **:** a small tree (*Osmanthus americanus*) of the southern U.S. that is related to the olive

de·vi·ous \ˈdē-vē-əs\ *adj* [L *devius*, fr. *de* from + *via* way — more at DE-, VIA] **1 :** located off the highroad **:** REMOTE **2 a :** deviating from a straight line **:** ROUNDABOUT **b :** moving without a fixed course **:** ERRANT ⟨∼ breezes⟩ **3 a :** deviating from a right, accepted, or common course **:** ERRING **b :** not straightforward **c :** TRICKY **syn** see CROOKED — **de·vi·ous·ly** *adv* — **de·vi·ous·ness** *n*

de·vis·able \di-ˈvī-zə-bəl\ *adj* **:** capable of being devised

de·vis·al \-zəl\ *n* **:** the act of devising

¹de·vise \di-ˈvīz\ *vt* [ME *devisen*, fr. OF *deviser* to divide, regulate, tell, modif. of (assumed) VL *divisare*, fr. L *divisus*, pp. of *dividere* to divide] **1 a :** to form in the mind by new combinations or applications of ideas or principles **:** INVENT **b** *archaic* **:** SUPPOSE **c :** to plan to obtain or bring about **:** PLOT **2 :** to give (real estate) by will — compare BEQUEATH — **de·vis·er** *n*

²devise *n* **1 :** the act of giving or disposing of real property by will **2 :** a will or clause of a will disposing of real property **3 :** property given by will

de·vi·see \ˌdev-ə-ˈzē, di-ˌvī-ˈzē\ *n* **:** one to whom a devise of property is made

de·vi·sor \ˌdev-ə-ˈzȯ(ə)r; di-ˈvī-zər, -ˌvī-ˈzȯ(ə)r\ *n* **:** one who devises property in a will

de·vi·tal·ize \(ˈ)dē-ˈvīt-ᵊl-ˌīz\ *vt* **:** to deprive of life or vitality

de·vit·ri·fy \(ˈ)dē-ˈvi-trə-ˌfī\ *vt* [F *dévitrifier*, fr. *dé-* de- + *vitrifier* to vitrify] **:** to deprive of glassy luster and transparency; *esp* **:** to change (as a glass) from a vitreous to a crystalline condition

de·vo·cal·ize \(ˈ)dē-ˈvō-kə-ˌlīz\ *vt* **:** DEVOICE

de·voice \(ˈ)dē-ˈvȯis\ *vt* **:** to pronounce without vibration of the vocal cords (a sound sometimes voiced)

de·void \di-ˈvȯid\ *adj* [ME, prob. short for *devoided*, pp. of *devoiden* to vacate, fr. MF *desvuidier* to empty, fr. OF, fr. *des-* dis- + *vuidier* to empty — more at VOID] **:** not having or using **:** DESTITUTE

de·voir \dəv-ˈwär, ˈdev-ˌwär\ *n* [ME, alter. of *dever*, fr. OF *deveir*, fr. *devoir*, *deveir* to owe, be obliged, fr. L *debēre* — more at DEBT] **1 :** DUTY, RESPONSIBILITY **2 :** a formal act of civility or respect

de·vo·lu·tion \ˌdev-ə-ˈlü-shən *also* ˌdē-və-\ *n* [ML *devolution-*, *devolutio*, fr. L *devolutus*, pp. of *devolvere*] **1 :** transference from one individual to another: as **a :** a passing or devolving (as of rights) upon a successor **b :** delegation or conferral to a subordinate **c :** the surrender of powers to local authorities by a central government **2 :** retrograde evolution **:** DEGENERATION — **de·vo·lu·tion·ary** \-shə-ˌner-ē\ *adj* — **de·vo·lu·tion·ist** \-sh(ə-)nəst\ *n*

de·volve \di-ˈvälv, -ˈvȯlv\ *vb* [ME *devolven*, fr. L *devolvere*, fr. *de-* + *volvere* to roll — more at VOLUBLE] *vt* **1** *archaic* **:** to cause to roll onward or downward **2 :** to transfer from one person to another **:** hand down **∼** *vi* **1 :** to pass by transmission or succession **2 :** to flow or roll onward or downward

dev·on \ˈdev-ən\ *n*, *often cap* [*Devon*, England] **:** any of a breed of vigorous red dual-purpose cattle of English origin

De·vo·ni·an \di-ˈvō-nē-ən\ *adj* [*Devon*, England] **1 :** of or relating to Devonshire, England **2 :** of, relating to, or being the period of the Paleozoic era between the Silurian and the Mississippian or the corresponding system of rocks — **Devonian** *n*

de·vote \di-ˈvōt\ *vt* [L *devotus*, pp. of *devovēre*, fr. *de-* + *vovēre* to vow] **1 :** to dedicate by a solemn act **2 a :** to give up

wholly or purposefully **b :** to center the attention or activities of (oneself) — **de·vote·ment** \di-'vōt-mənt\ *n*

syn DEVOTE, DEDICATE, CONSECRATE, HALLOW mean to set apart for a particular use or end. DEVOTE applies chiefly to personal activity and suggests motives as impelling as a vow; DEDICATE implies solemn and exclusive devotion to a sacred or serious use; CONSECRATE even more strongly than DEDICATE implies investing with a solemn and sacred character; HALLOW may be equivalent to CONSECRATE or it may imply intrinsic rather than conferred holiness

de·vot·ed *adj* **1 :** ARDENT, DEVOUT **2 :** AFFECTIONATE — **de·vot·ed·ly** *adv* — **de·vot·ed·ness** *n*

dev·o·tee \,dev-ə-'tē, -'tā\ *n* **1 :** a person preoccupied with religious duties and ceremonies **2 :** an ardent follower, supporter, or enthusiast

de·vo·tion \di-'vō-shən\ *n* **1 a :** religious fervor **:** PIETY **b :** an act of prayer or supplication — usu. used in pl. **c :** a religious exercise or practice other than the regular corporate worship of a congregation; *specif* **:** one directed in Roman Catholic piety to a particular object of faith **2 a :** the act of devoting or quality of being devoted **b :** ardent love or affection **syn** see FIDELITY

[1]**de·vo·tion·al** \-shnəl, -shən-ᵊl\ *adj* **:** of, relating to, or characterized by devotion — **de·vo·tion·al·ly** \-ē\ *adv*

[2]**devotional** *n* **:** a short worship service

de·vour \di-'vaů(ə)r\ *vt* [ME *devouren,* fr. MF *devourer,* fr. L *devorare,* fr. *de-* + *vorare* to devour — more at VORACIOUS] **1 :** to eat up greedily or ravenously **2 a :** to seize upon and destroy **b :** to use up wastefully ⟨~*ed* his wife's fortune⟩ **3 :** to prey upon **4 :** to take in eagerly by the senses or mind — **de·vour·er** *n*

de·vout \di-'vaůt\ *adj* [ME *devot,* fr. OF, fr. LL *devotus,* fr. L, pp. of *devovēre*] **1 :** devoted to religion or to religious duties or exercises **2 :** expressing devotion or piety **3 :** warmly devoted **:** SINCERE — **de·vout·ly** *adv* — **de·vout·ness** *n*

syn PIOUS, RELIGIOUS, PIETISTIC, SANCTIMONIOUS: DEVOUT stresses a mental attitude that leads to frequent and sincere though not always outwardly evident prayer and worship; PIOUS applies to the faithful performance of religious duties and maintenance of outwardly religious attitudes, frequently with a connotation of hypocrisy; RELIGIOUS may imply devoutness and piety but it emphasizes faith in a deity and adherence to a way of life in keeping with that faith; PIETISTIC implies an insistence on the emotional as opposed to the intellectual aspects of religion; SANCTIMONIOUS implies pretentions to holiness or smug appearance of piety

dew \'d(y)ü\ *n* [ME, fr. OE *dēaw;* akin to OHG *tou* dew, Gk *thein* to run] **1 :** moisture condensed upon the surfaces of cool bodies esp. at night **2 :** something resembling dew in purity, freshness, or power to refresh **3 :** moisture esp. when appearing in minute droplets: as **a :** TEARS **b :** SWEAT **c :** droplets of water produced by a plant in transpiration — **dew** *vt*

de·wan \di-'wän\ *n* [Hindi *dīwān,* fr. Per, account book] **:** an Indian official; *esp* **:** the prime minister of an Indian state

Dew·ar flask \,d(y)ü-ər-\ *n* [Sir James *Dewar* †1923 Sc chemist & physicist] **:** a glass or metal container with an evacuated space between the walls and often silvered on the inside to prevent heat transfer used esp. for storing liquefied gases

dew·ber·ry \'d(y)ü-,ber-ē\ *n* **1 :** any of several sweet edible berries related to and resembling blackberries **2 :** a trailing or decumbent bramble (genus *Rubus*) that bears dewberries

dew·claw \'d(y)ü-,klȯ\ *n* **:** a vestigial digit not reaching to the ground on the foot of a mammal or a claw or hoof terminating such a digit — **dew·clawed** \-,klȯd\ *adj*

dew·drop \'d(y)ü-,dräp\ *n* **:** a drop of dew

Dew·ey decimal classification \,d(y)ü-ē-\ *n* [Melvil *Dewey* †1931 Am librarian] **:** a system of classifying books and other publications whereby main classes are designated by a three-digit number and subdivisions are shown by numbers after a decimal point

dew·fall \'d(y)ü-,fȯl\ *n* **:** formation of dew; *also* **:** the time when dew begins to deposit

dew·i·ly \'d(y)ü-ə-lē\ *adv* **:** in a dewy manner

dew·i·ness \'d(y)ü-ē-nəs\ *n* **:** a dewy state

dew·lap \'d(y)ü-,lap\ *n* **:** a hanging fold of skin under the neck esp. of a bovine animal — **dew·lapped** \-,lapt\ *adj*

dew point *n* **:** the temperature at which a vapor begins to condense

dew worm *n* **:** an earthworm suitable for use as bait

dewy \'d(y)ü-ē\ *adj* **:** moist with, affected by, or suggestive of dew

dewy–eyed \,d(y)ü-ē-'īd\ *adj* **:** exhibiting childlike innocence and trust

dex·io·trop·ic \,dek-sē-ə-'träp-ik\ *or* **dex·i·ot·ro·pous** \-sē-'ä-trə-pəs\ *adj* [Gk *dexios* situated on the right + E *-tropic* or *-tropous*] **:** turning to the right **:** DEXTRAL

dex·ter \'dek-stər\ *adj* [L; akin to Gk *dexios* situated on the right, L *decēre* to be fitting] **1 :** relating to or situated on the right **2 :** being or relating to the side of a heraldic shield or escutcheon at the right of the person wearing it **3 :** appearing or facing toward the right and considered of good omen — **dexter** *adv*

dex·ter·i·ty \dek-'ster-ət-ē\ *n* [MF or L; MF *dexterité,* fr. L *dexteritat-, dexteritas,* fr. *dexter*] **1 :** readiness and grace in physical activity; *esp* **:** skill and ease in using the hands **2 :** mental skill or quickness **:** ADROITNESS **3 :** RIGHT-HANDEDNESS

dex·ter·ous *or* **dex·trous** \'dek-st(ə-)rəs\ *adj* [L *dextr-, dexter* dextral, skillful] **1 :** skillful and competent with the hands **2 :** mentally adroit and skillful **:** EXPERT **3 :** done with dexterity **:** ARTFUL — **dex·ter·ous·ly** *adv* — **dex·ter·ous·ness** *n*

syn DEXTEROUS, ADROIT, DEFT mean ready and skilled in physical movement. DEXTEROUS implies expertness with consequent facility and quickness in manipulation; ADROIT implies dexterity but may also stress resourcefulness or artfulness or inventiveness; DEFT emphasizes lightness, neatness, and sureness of touch or handling

dextr- *or* **dextro-** *comb form* [LL, fr. L *dextr-, dexter*] **1 :** right **:** on or toward the right ⟨*dextro*rotatory⟩ **2** *usu* *dextro-* **:** dextrorotatory ⟨*dextro*-tartaric acid⟩

dex·tral \'dek-strəl\ *adj* **:** of or relating to the right **:** inclined to the right: as **a :** RIGHT-HANDED **b** *of a flatfish* **:** having the right side uppermost **c** *of a gastropod shell* **:** having the whorls turning from the left toward the right as viewed with the apex toward the observer or having the aperture open toward the observer to the right of the axis when held with the spire uppermost — **dex·tral·i·ty** \dek-'stral-ət-ē\ *n* — **dex·tral·ly** \'dek-strə-lē\ *adv*

dex·tran \'dek-,stran, -strən\ *n* **:** any of numerous complex carbohydrates $(C_6H_{10}O_5)_n$ that yield only glucose on hydrolysis: as **a :** any such compound of high molecular weight obtained by fermentation of sugar **b :** any such compound of reduced molecular weight obtained by acid hydrolysis of native dextran and used as a plasma substitute

dex·trin \'dek-strən\ *also* **dex·trine** \-,strēn, -strən\ *n* [F *dextrine,* fr. *dextr-*] **:** any of various soluble gummy polysaccharides obtained from starch by the action of heat, acids, or enzymes and used as adhesives, as sizes for paper and textiles, and in syrups and beer

dex·tro \'dek-(,)strō\ *adj* [*dextr-*] **:** DEXTROROTATORY

dex·tro–glu·cose \,dek-strə-'glü-,kōs, -,kōz\ *n* **:** DEXTROSE

dex·tro·gy·rate \,dek-strə-'jī(ə)r-,āt, -ət\ *or* **dex·tro·gyre** \'dek-strə-,jī(ə)r\ *adj* [*dextrogyre* ISV *dextr-* + L *gyrus* gyre] **:** DEXTROROTATORY

dex·tro·ro·ta·tion \,dek-strə-rō-'tā-shən\ *n* **:** right-handed or clockwise rotation — used of the plane of polarization of light

dex·tro·ro·ta·to·ry \-'rōt-ə-,tōr-ē, -,tȯr-\ *also* **dex·tro·ro·ta·ry** \-'rōt-ə-rē\ *adj* **:** turning clockwise or toward the right; *esp* **:** rotating the plane of polarization of light toward the right ⟨~ crystals⟩

dex·trorse \'dek-,strȯ(ə)rs\ *adj* [NL *dextrorsus,* fr. L, toward the right, fr. *dextr-* + *versus,* pp. of *vertere* to turn] **1** *of a plant or its parts* **:** twining spirally upward around an axis from left to right — compare SINISTRORSE **2 :** DEXTRAL c — **dex·trorse·ly** *adv*

dex·trose \'dek-,strōs, -,strōz\ *n* **:** dextrorotatory glucose

dey \'dā\ *n* [F, fr. Turk *dayı,* lit., maternal uncle] **:** a ruling official of the Ottoman empire in northern Africa

dhar·ma \'dər-mə\ *n* [Skt, fr. *dhārayati* he holds; akin to L *firmus* firm] **1** *Hinduism* **:** custom or law regarded as duty **2** *Hinduism & Buddhism* **a :** the basic principles of cosmic or individual existence **:** NATURE **b :** conformity to one's duty and nature

dhole \'dōl\ *n* [perh. fr. Kanarese *tōḷa* wolf] **:** a fierce wild dog (*Cuon dukhunensis*) of India that hunts in packs

dho·ti \'dōt-ē\ *or* **dhoo·tie** \'düt-ē\ *n* [Hindi *dhotī*] **1 :** a loincloth worn by Hindu men **2 :** a fabric used for dhotis

dhow \'daů\ *n* [Ar *dāwa*] **:** an Arab lateen-rigged boat usu. having a long overhang forward, a high poop, and an open waist

Dhu'l–Hij·ja \,dü(-ə)l-'hij-(,)ä\ *n* [Ar *Dhū-l-ḥijjah,* lit., the one of the pilgrimage] **:** the 12th month of the Muhammadan year

Dhu'l–Qa'·dah \-'käd-(,)ä\ *n* [Ar *Dhū-l-qa'dah,* lit., the one of the sitting] **:** the 11th month of the Muhammadan year

di- *comb form* [ME, fr. MF, fr. L, fr. Gk; akin to OE *twi-*] **1 :** twice **:** twofold **:** double ⟨*di*chromatic⟩ **2 :** containing two atoms, radicals, or groups ⟨*di*chloride⟩

dia- *also* **di-** *prefix* [ME, fr. OF, fr. L, fr. Gk, through, apart, fr. *dia;* akin to L *dis-*] **:** through ⟨*dia*positive⟩ **:** across ⟨*di*actinic⟩

di·a·base \'dī-ə-,bās\ *n* [F, fr. Gk *diabasis* act of crossing over, fr. *diabainein* to cross over, fr. *dia-* + *bainein* to go — more at COME] **1** *archaic* **:** DIORITE **2** *chiefly Brit* **:** an altered basalt **3 :** a fine-grained rock of the composition of gabbro but with an ophitic texture — **di·a·ba·sic** \,dī-ə-'bā-sik\ *adj*

di·a·be·tes \,dī-ə-'bēt-ēz, -'bēt-əs\ *n* [L, fr. Gk *diabētēs,* fr. *diabainein*] **:** any of various abnormal conditions characterized by the secretion and excretion of excessive amounts of urine

diabetes in·sip·i·dus \-in-'sip-əd-əs\ *n* [NL, lit., insipid diabetes] **:** a disorder of the pituitary gland characterized by intense thirst and the excretion of large amounts of urine

diabetes mel·li·tus \-'mel-ət-əs\ *n* [NL, lit., honey-sweet diabetes] **:** a familial constitutional disorder of carbohydrate metabolism characterized by inadequate secretion or utilization of insulin, polyuria and excessive amounts of sugar in the blood and urine, and by thirst, hunger, and loss of weight

di·a·bet·ic \,dī-ə-'bet-ik\ *adj* **:** of or relating to diabetes or diabetics — **diabetic** *n*

di·a·ble·rie \dē-'äb-lə-(,)rē, -'ab-\ *n* [F, fr. OF, fr. *diable* devil, fr. LL *diabolus* — more at DEVIL] **1 a :** black magic **:** SORCERY **b :** a representation of black magic or of dealings with the devil **2 :** demon lore **3 a :** mischievous conduct or manner **b :** WICKEDNESS

diabol- *or* **diabolo-** *comb form* [ME *deabol-,* fr. MF *diabol-,* fr. LL, fr. Gk, fr. *diabolos* — more at DEVIL] **:** devil ⟨*diabol*ism⟩

di·a·bol·ic \,dī-ə-'bäl-ik\ *adj* [ME *deabolik,* fr. MF *diabolique,* fr. LL *diabolicus,* fr. *diabolus*] **:** of, relating to, or characteristic of the devil **:** FIENDISH — **di·a·bol·i·cal** \-'bäl-i-kəl\ *adj* — **di·a·bol·i·cal·ly** \-i-k(ə-)lē\ *adv* — **di·a·bol·i·cal·ness** \-i-kəl-nəs\ *n*

di·ab·o·lism \dī-'ab-ə-,liz-əm\ *n* **1 a :** dealings with or possession by the devil **b :** evil character or conduct **2 :** belief in or worship of devils — **di·ab·o·list** \-ləst\ *n*

di·ab·o·lize \-,līz\ *vt* **:** to represent as or make diabolical

dia·chron·ic \,dī-ə-'krän-ik\ *adj* **:** of, relating to, or dealing with phenomena esp. of language as they occur or change over a period of time — **dia·chron·i·cal·ly** \-'krän-i-k(ə-)lē\ *adv*

di·ach·ro·ny \dī-'ak-rə-nē\ *n* [ISV *dia-* + *-chrony* (as in *synchrony*)] **1 :** diachronic analysis **2 :** change extending through time

[1]**di·ac·id** \(')dī-'as-əd\ *or* **di·acid·ic** \,dī-ə-'sid-ik\ *adj* **1 :** able to react with two molecules of a monobasic acid or one of a dibasic acid to form a salt or ester — used esp. of bases **2 :** containing two hydrogen atoms replaceable by basic atoms or radicals

[2]**diacid** *n* [ISV] **:** an acid with two acid hydrogen atoms

di·ac·o·nal \dī-'ak-ən-ᵊl, dē-\ *adj* [LL *diaconalis,* fr. *diaconus* deacon — more at DEACON] **:** of or relating to a deacon

di·ac·o·nate \-'ak-ə-nət, dē-\ *n* **1 :** the office or period of office of a deacon **2 :** an official body of deacons

[1]**di·a·crit·ic** \,dī-ə-'krit-ik\ *or* **di·a·crit·i·cal** \-'krit-i-kəl\ *adj* [Gk *diakritikos* separative, fr. *diakrinein* to distinguish, fr. *dia-* + *krinein* to separate] **1 :** serving as a diacritic **2** *usu* *diacritical* **a :** serving to distinguish **:** DISTINCTIVE **b :** capable of distinguishing

[2]**diacritic** *n* **:** a modifying mark near or through an orthographic or phonetic character or combination of characters indicating a phonetic or semantic value different from that given the unmarked or otherwise marked character or group of characters

di·ac·tin·ic \,dī-,ak-'tin-ik\ *adj* [*dia-* + Gk *aktin-, aktis* ray — more at ACTIN-] **:** capable of transmitting actinic rays — **di·ac·ti·nism** \dī-'ak-tə-,niz-əm\ *n*

di·adel·phous \,dī-ə-'del-fəs\ *adj* [*di-* + *-adelphous*] **:** united by the filaments into two fascicles — used of stamens

di·a·dem \'dī-ə-,dem, -dəm\ *n* [ME *diademe,* fr. OF, fr. L *diadema,* fr. Gk *diadēma,* fr. *diadein* to bind around, fr. *dia-* + *dein* to bind] **1 :** CROWN; *specif* **:** a headband worn as a badge of royalty **2 :** regal power or dignity

di·ad·ro·mous \dī-'ad-rə-məs\ *adj, of a fish* **:** migratory between salt and fresh waters

di·aer·e·sis \dī-'er-ə-səs\ *n, pl* **di·aer·e·ses** \-'er-ə-,sēz\ [LL *diaeresis,* fr. Gk *diairesis,* fr. *diairein* to divide, fr. *dia-* + *hairein* to

take] **1 :** the division of one syllable into two esp. by separating the vowel elements of a diphthong or by resolving a *w* or *y* sound into a vowel **2 :** a mark ·· placed over a vowel to indicate that the vowel is pronounced in a separate syllable (as in *naïve, Brontë*) **3 :** the break in a verse caused by the coincidence of the end of a foot with the end of a word — **di·ae·ret·ic** \ˌdī-ə-ˈret-ik\ *adj*

di·ag·eo·tro·pism \ˌdī-ə-jē-ˈä-trə-ˌpiz-əm\ *or* **di·ag·eo·tro·py** \-pē\ *n* **:** the tendency of growing organs (as branches or roots) to extend the axis at right angles to the line of gravity

di·ag·nose \ˈdī-ig-ˌnōs, -ˌnōz\ *vb* [back-formation fr. *diagnosis*] *vt* **:** to make a diagnosis of ~ *vi* **:** to make a diagnosis

di·ag·no·sis \ˌdī-ig-ˈnō-səs\ *n, pl* **di·ag·no·ses** \-ˈnō-ˌsēz\ [NL, fr. Gk *diagnōsis*, fr. *diagignōskein* to distinguish, fr. *dia-* + *gignōskein* to know — more at KNOW] **1 :** the art or act of identifying a disease from its signs and symptoms **2 :** a concise technical description of a taxon **3 a :** investigation or analysis of the cause or nature of a condition, situation, or problem **b :** a statement or conclusion concerning the nature or cause of some phenomenon

1**di·ag·nos·tic** \-ˈnäs-tik\ *adj* **:** of or relating to diagnosis — **di·ag·nos·ti·cal·ly** \-ti-k(ə-)lē\ *adv*

2**diagnostic** *n* **1 :** the art or practice of diagnosis — often used in pl. **2 :** a distinguishing mark — **di·ag·nos·ti·cian** \-ˌnäs-ˈtish-ən\ *n*

1**di·ag·o·nal** \dī-ˈag-ən-ᵊl\ *adj* [L *diagonalis*, fr. Gk *diagōnios* from angle to angle, fr. *dia-* + *gōnia* angle; akin to Gk *gony* knee] **1 a :** joining two nonadjacent vertices of a rectilinear or polyhedral figure **b :** passing through two nonadjacent edges of a polyhedron **2 a :** obliquely from the vertical **b :** having diagonal markings or parts — **di·ag·o·nal·ly** \-ˈag-ən-ᵊl-ē, -ˈag-nə-lē\ *adv*

2**diagonal** *n* **1 :** a diagonal straight line or plane **2 a** (1) **:** a diagonal direction (2) **:** a diagonal row, arrangement, or pattern **b :** a twilled fabric esp. of wool **c :** something placed diagonally **3 :** a mark / used typically to denote "or" (as in *and/or*), "and or" (as in *straggler/deserter*), or "per" (as in *feet/second*) — called also *solidus, virgule*

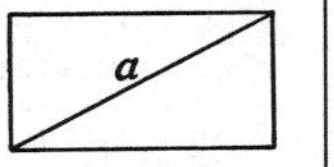

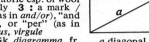

a diagonal

1**di·a·gram** \ˈdī-ə-ˌgram\ *n* [Gk *diagramma*, fr. *diagraphein* to mark out by lines, fr. *dia-* + *graphein* to write — more at CARVE] **1 :** a line drawing made for mathematical or scientific purposes **2 :** a graphic design that explains rather than represents — **di·a·gram·mat·ic** \ˌdī-ə-grə-ˈmat-ik\ *also* **di·a·gram·mat·i·cal** \-ˈmat-i-kəl\ *adj* — **di·a·gram·mat·i·cal·ly** \-i-k(ə-)lē\ *adv*

2**diagram** *vt* **di·a·gramed** \-ˌgramd\ *or* **di·a·grammed; di·a·gram·ing** \-ˌgram-iŋ\ *or* **di·a·gram·ming :** to represent by or put into the form of a diagram

dia·ki·ne·sis \ˌdī-ə-kə-ˈnē-səs, -(ˌ)kī-\ *n, pl* **dia·ki·ne·ses** \-ˈnē-ˌsēz\ [NL, fr. *dia-* + Gk *kinēsis* motion, fr. *kinein* to move; akin to L *ciēre* to move] **:** the final stage of the meiotic prophase marked by contraction of the bivalents — **dia·ki·net·ic** \-ˈnet-ik\ *adj*

1**di·al** \ˈdī(-ə)l\ *n* [ME, fr. L *dies* day] **1 :** the face of a sundial **2** *obs* **:** any of various timepieces **3 :** the graduated face of a timepiece **4 a :** a face upon which some measurement or other number is registered usu. by means of graduations and a pointer **b :** a disk that may be turned to make electrical connections or to regulate the operation of a machine and that usu. has marks around its border to serve as a guide for the operation

2**dial** *vb* **di·aled** *or* **di·alled; di·al·ing** *or* **di·al·ling** *vt* **1 :** to measure with a dial **2 a :** to manipulate a telephone dial so as to call **b :** to manipulate a dial so as to operate, regulate, or select ~ *vi* **1 :** to manipulate a dial **2 :** to make a call on a dial telephone

di·a·lect \ˈdī-ə-ˌlekt\ *n, often attrib* [MF *dialecte*, fr. L *dialectus*, fr. Gk *dialektos* conversation, dialect, fr. *dialegesthai* to converse] **1 a :** a regional variety of language distinguished by features of vocabulary, grammar, and pronunciation from other regional varieties and constituting together with them a single language ⟨the Doric ~ of ancient Greek⟩ **b :** one of two or more cognate languages ⟨French and Italian are Romance ~*s*⟩ **c :** a regional variety of a language usu. transmitted orally and differing distinctively from the standard language ⟨the Lancashire ~ of English⟩ **d :** a variety of a language used by the members of an occupational group ⟨the ~ of the atomic physicist⟩ **e :** the customary language of a social class ⟨peasant ~⟩ **2 :** manner or means of expressing oneself **:** PHRASEOLOGY — **di·a·lec·tal** \ˌdī-ə-ˈlek-tᵊl\ *adj* — **di·a·lec·tal·ly** \-tᵊl-ē\ *adv*

syn DIALECT, VERNACULAR, LINGO, JARGON, CANT, ARGOT, SLANG mean a form of language that is not recognized as standard. DIALECT applies commonly to a form of language persisting regionally or among the uneducated; VERNACULAR applies to the everyday speech of the people in contrast to that of learned men; LINGO is a mildly contemptuous term for any language not readily understood; JARGON applies to a technical or esoteric language used by a profession, trade, or cult; it may also be a stronger designation than LINGO for language or usage that sounds outlandish; CANT is applied derogatorily to language that is both peculiar to a group or class and intrinsically lacking in clarity or precision of expression ⟨journalistic *cant*⟩; ARGOT is applied to a peculiar language of a clique or other closely knit group ⟨thieves' *argot*⟩; SLANG designates a class of mostly recently coined and frequently short-lived terms or usages informally preferred to standard language as being forceful, novel, or voguish

dialect atlas *n* **:** LINGUISTIC ATLAS

dialect geography *n* **:** LINGUISTIC GEOGRAPHY

di·a·lec·tic \ˌdī-ə-ˈlek-tik\ *n* [ME *dialetik*, fr. MF *dialetique*, fr. L *dialectica*, fr. Gk *dialektikē*, fr. fem. of *dialektikos* of conversation, fr. *dialektos*] **1 :** discussion and reasoning by dialogue as a method of intellectual investigation **2 a :** the Hegelian process of change in which an entity passes over into and is preserved and fulfilled by its opposite; *also* **:** the critical investigation of this process **b** (1) *usu pl but sing or pl in constr* **:** development through the stages of thesis, antithesis, and synthesis in accordance with the laws of dialectical materialism (2) **:** the investigation of this process; *also* **:** the theoretical application of this process esp. in the social sciences **3** *usu pl but sing or pl in constr* **a :** any systematic reasoning, exposition, or argument esp. in literature that juxtaposes opposed or contradictory ideas and usu. seeks to resolve their conflict **b :** play of ideas **4 :** the dialectical tension or opposition between two interacting forces or elements

di·a·lec·ti·cal \ˌdī-ə-ˈlek-ti-kəl\ *also* **di·a·lec·tic** \-tik\ *adj* **1 a :** of, relating to, or in accordance with dialectic ⟨~ method⟩ **b :** practicing, devoted to, or employing dialectic ⟨a ~ philosopher⟩ **2 :** DIALECTAL — **di·a·lec·ti·cal·ly** \-ti-k(ə-)lē\ *adv*

dialectical materialism *n* **:** the Marxian theory that maintains the material basis of a reality constantly changing in a dialectical process and the priority of matter over mind

di·a·lec·ti·cian \ˌdī-ə-ˌlek-ˈtish-ən\ *n* **1 :** one who is skilled in or practices dialectic **2 :** a student of dialects

di·a·lec·to·log·i·cal \ˌdī-ə-ˌlek-tə-ˈläj-i-kəl\ *adj* **:** of or relating to dialectology — **di·a·lec·to·log·i·cal·ly** \-k(ə-)lē\ *adv*

di·a·lec·tol·o·gist \-ˈtäl-ə-jəst\ *n* **:** a specialist in dialectology

di·a·lec·tol·o·gy \-jē\ *n* [ISV] **1 :** the systematic study of dialect **2 :** the body of data available for study of a dialect

di·a·log·ic \ˌdī-ə-ˈläj-ik\ *adj* **:** of, relating to, or characterized by dialogue ⟨~ writing⟩ — **di·a·log·i·cal** \-ˈläj-i-kəl\ *adj* — **di·a·log·i·cal·ly** \-i-k(ə-)lē\ *adv*

di·a·lo·gist \dī-ˈal-ə-jəst; ˈdī-ə-ˌlȯg-əst, -ˌläg-\ *n* **1 :** one who participates in a dialogue **2 :** a writer of dialogues — **di·a·lo·gis·tic** \ˌdī-ə-lō-ˈjis-tik; -ˌlȯ-ˈgis-, -ˌlä-ˈgis-\ *adj*

1**di·a·logue** *or* **di·a·log** \ˈdī-ə-ˌlȯg, -ˌläg\ *n* [ME, fr. OF, fr. L *dialogus*, fr. Gk *dialogos*, fr. *dialegesthai* to converse, fr. *dia-* + *legein* to speak] **1 :** a written composition in which two or more characters are represented as conversing **2 a :** a conversation between two or more persons **b :** an exchange of ideas and opinions **3 :** the conversational element of literary or dramatic composition **4 :** a musical arrangement suggestive of a conversation

2**dialogue** *vi* **:** to take part in a dialogue ~ *vt* **:** to express in dialogue

di·al·y·sis \dī-ˈal-ə-səs\ *n, pl* **di·al·y·ses** \-ə-ˌsēz\ [NL, fr. Gk, separation, fr. *dialyein* to dissolve, fr. *dia-* + *lyein* to loosen] **:** the separation of substances in solution by means of their unequal diffusion through semipermeable membranes; *esp* **:** such a separation of colloids from soluble substances — **di·a·lyt·ic** \ˌdī-ə-ˈlit-ik\ *adj*

di·a·lyze \ˈdī-ə-ˌlīz\ *vt* **:** to subject to dialysis ~ *vi* **:** to undergo dialysis — **di·a·lyz·er** \-ˌlī-zər\ *n*

dia·mag·net \ˈdī-ə-ˌmag-nət\ *or* **dia·mag·net·ic** \ˌdī-ə-ˌmag-ˈnet-ik\ *n* [*diamagnet* back-formation fr. *diamagnetic*, adj.] **:** a diamagnetic substance

dia·mag·net·ic *adj* **:** having a magnetic permeability less than that of a vacuum — **dia·mag·ne·tism** \-ˈmag-nə-ˌtiz-əm\ *n*

di·am·e·ter \dī-ˈam-ət-ər\ *n* [ME *diametre*, fr. MF, fr. L *diametros*, fr. Gk, fr. *dia-* + *metron* measure] **1 :** a chord passing through the center of a figure or body **2 :** the length of a straight line through the center of an object — **di·am·e·tral** \-ˈam-ə-trəl\ *adj*

di·a·met·ric \ˌdī-ə-ˈme-trik\ *adj* **1 :** DIAMETRAL **2 :** completely opposed or opposite ⟨in ~ contradiction to his claims⟩ — **di·a·met·ri·cal** \-tri-kəl\ *adj* — **di·a·met·ri·cal·ly** \-tri-k(ə-)lē\ *adv*

di·amine \ˈdī-ə-ˌmēn, dī-ˈam-ən\ *n* [ISV] **:** a compound containing two amino groups

1**di·a·mond** \ˈdī-(ə-)mənd\ *n, often attrib* [ME *diamaunde*, fr. MF *diamant*, fr. LL *diamant-, diamas*, alter. of L *adamant-, adamas*, hardest metal, diamond, fr. Gk] **1 a :** native crystalline carbon that is usu. nearly colorless, that when transparent and free from flaws is highly valued as a precious stone, and that is used industrially as an abrasive powder and in rock drills because it is the hardest substance known; *also* **:** a piece of this substance **b :** crystallized carbon produced artificially **2 :** something that resembles a diamond **3 :** a square or rhombus-shaped configuration usu. having a distinctive orientation **4 a :** a red lozenge impressed on a playing card; *also* **:** a card marked with such lozenges **b** *pl but sing or pl in constr* **:** the suit comprising cards so marked **5 a :** INFIELD **b :** the entire playing field in baseball or softball

2**diamond** *vt* **:** to adorn with or as if with diamonds

1**di·a·mond·back** \ˈdī-(ə-)mən(d)-ˌbak\ *also* **di·a·mond–backed** \ˌdī-(ə-)mən(d)-ˈbakt\ *adj* **:** having marks like diamonds or lozenges on the back

2**diamondback** *n* **:** a large and deadly rattlesnake (*Crotalus adamanteus*) of the southern U.S.

diamondback terrapin *n* **:** any of several terrapins (genus *Malaclemys*) formerly widely distributed in salt marshes along the Atlantic and Gulf coasts but now much restricted

di·a·mond·if·er·ous \ˌdī-(ə-)mən-ˈdif-(ə-)rəs\ *adj* **:** yielding diamonds ⟨~ earth⟩

Di·ana \dī-ˈan-ə\ *n* [L] **:** the goddess of the moon, wild animals, and hunting in Roman mythology

di·an·drous \(ˈ)dī-ˈan-drəs\ *adj* **:** having two stamens

di·an·thus \dī-ˈan(t)-thəs\ *n* [NL, genus name, fr. Gk *dios* heavenly + *anthos* flower — more at DEITY, ANTHOLOGY] **:** any of a large Old World genus (*Dianthus*) of the pink family including the pinks and carnations

di·a·pa·son \ˌdī-ə-ˈpāz-ᵊn, -ˈpās-\ *n* [ME, fr. L, fr. Gk (*hē*) *dia pasōn* (*chordōn symphōnia*) the concord through all the notes, fr. *dia* through + *pasōn*, gen. fem. pl. of *pas* all] **1 a** (1) **:** a burst of harmonious sound (2) **:** any full deep outburst of sound **b :** one of two principal flue stops in the organ extending through the complete scale of the instrument **c** (1) **:** the entire compass of musical tones (2) **:** RANGE, SCOPE **2 a :** TUNING FORK **b :** a standard of pitch

dia·pause \ˈdī-ə-ˌpȯz\ *n* [Gk *diapausis* pause, fr. *diapauein* to pause, fr. *dia-* + *pauein* to stop — more at PAUSE] **:** a period of spontaneous dormancy between periods of activity (as in an insect)

di·a·pe·de·sis \ˌdī-ə-pə-ˈdē-səs\ *n, pl* **di·a·pe·de·ses** \-ˈdē-ˌsēz\ [NL, fr. Gk *diapēdēsis* act of oozing through, fr. *diapēdan* to ooze through, fr. *dia-* + *pēdan* to leap] **:** the passage of blood cells through capillary walls into the tissues — **di·a·pe·det·ic** \-ˈdet-ik\ *adj*

1**di·a·per** \ˈdī-(ə-)pər\ *n* [ME *diapre*, fr. MF, fr. ML *diasprum*] **1 :** a fabric with a distinctive pattern: **a :** a rich silk fabric **b :** a soft usu. white linen or cotton fabric used for tablecloths or towels **2 :** a basic garment for infants consisting of a folded cloth or other absorbent material drawn up between the legs and fastened about the waist **3 :** an allover pattern consisting of one or more small repeated units of design (as geometric figures) connecting with one another or growing out of one another with continuously flowing or straight lines

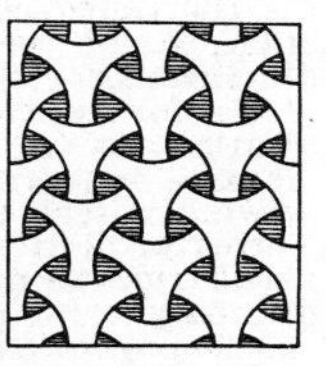

diaper 3

²diaper *vt* **di·a·per·ing** \-p(ə-)riŋ\ **1 :** to ornament with diaper designs **2 :** to put on or change the diaper of (an infant)
di·a·pha·ne·i·ty \(,)dī-,af-ə-'nē-ət-ē, ,dī-ə-fə-\ *n* **:** the quality or state of being diaphanous
di·aph·a·nous \dī-'af-ə-nəs\ *adj* [ML *diaphanus,* fr. Gk *diaphanēs,* fr. *diaphainein* to show through, fr. *dia-* + *phainein* to show] **1 :** characterized by such fineness of texture as to permit seeing through **2 :** characterized by extreme delicacy of form **:** ETHEREAL ⟨~ landscapes⟩ — **di·aph·a·nous·ly** *adv* — **di·aph·a·nous·ness** *n*
dia·phone \'dī-ə-,fōn\ *n* **:** a fog signal similar to a siren but producing a blast of two tones
di·a·pho·re·sis \,dī-ə-fə-'rē-səs\ *n, pl* **di·a·pho·re·ses** \-'rē-,sēz\ [LL, fr. Gk *diaphorēsis,* fr. *diaphorein* to dissipate by perspiration, fr. *dia-* + *pherein* to carry — more at BEAR] **:** PERSPIRATION; *esp* **:** profuse perspiration artificially induced
di·a·pho·ret·ic \-'ret-ik\ *adj* **:** having the power to increase perspiration — **diaphoretic** *n*
di·a·phragm \'dī-ə-,fram\ *n* [ME *diafragma,* fr. LL *diaphragma,* fr. Gk, fr. *diaphrassein* to barricade, fr. *dia-* + *phrassein* to enclose] **1 :** a body partition of muscle and connective tissue; *specif* **:** the partition separating the chest and abdominal cavities in mammals **2 :** a dividing membrane or thin partition esp. in a tube **3 a :** a more or less rigid partition in the body or shell of an invertebrate **b :** a transverse septum in a plant stem **4 :** a device that limits the aperture of a lens or optical system **5 :** a thin flexible disk that vibrates (as in a microphone) — **di·a·phrag·mat·ic** \,dī-ə-,frag-'mat-ik\ *adj* — **di·a·phrag·mat·i·cal·ly** \-'mat-i-k(ə-)lē\ *adv*
di·a·phy·se·al \(,)dī-,af-ə-'sē-əl, -'zē-; ,dī-ə-'fiz-ē-\ *or* **di·a·phys·i·al** \,dī-ə-'fiz-ē-əl\ *adj* **:** of, relating to, or involving a diaphysis
di·aph·y·sis \dī-'af-ə-səs\ *n, pl* **di·aph·y·ses** \-'af-ə-,sēz\ [NL, fr. Gk, spinous process of the tibia, fr. *diaphyesthai* to grow between, fr. *dia-* + *phyein* to bring forth] **:** the shaft of a long bone
di·apoph·y·sis \,dī-ə-'päf-ə-səs\ *n, pl* **di·apoph·y·ses** \-'päf-ə-,sēz\ [NL] **:** a transverse process of a vertebra that is an outgrowth of the neural arch on the dorsal side; *esp* **:** one of the dorsal pair of such processes when two or more pairs are present
dia·pos·i·tive \,dī-ə-'päz-ət-iv, -'päz-tiv\ *n* **:** a transparent photographic positive (as a lantern slide)
di·ap·sid \dī-'ap-səd\ *adj* [deriv. of Gk *di-* + *hapsid-, hapsis* arch — more at APSIS] **:** of, relating to, or including reptiles (as the crocodiles) with two pairs of temporal openings in the skull
di·ar·chy *var of* DYARCHY
di·a·rist \'dī-ə-rəst\ *n* **:** one who keeps a diary
di·ar·rhea *or* **di·ar·rhoea** \,dī-ə-'rē-ə\ *n* [ME *diaria,* fr. LL *diarrhoea,* fr. Gk *diarrhoia,* fr. *diarrhein* to flow through, fr. *dia-* + *rhein* to flow — more at STREAM] **:** an abnormal frequency of intestinal discharge — **di·ar·rhe·al** \-'rē-əl\ *or* **di·ar·rhe·ic** \-'rē-ik\ *also* **di·ar·rhet·ic** \-'ret-ik\ *adj*
di·ar·thro·sis \,dī-,är-'thrō-səs\ *n, pl* **di·ar·thro·ses** \-'thrō-,sēz\ [NL, fr. Gk *diarthrōsis,* fr. *diarthroun* to joint, fr. *dia-* + *arthroun* to fasten by a joint, fr. *arthron* joint] **1 :** articulation that permits free movement **2 :** a freely movable joint
di·a·ry \'dī-(ə-)rē\ *n* [L *diarium,* fr. *dies* day — more at DEITY] **1 :** a record of events, transactions, or observations kept daily or at frequent intervals **:** JOURNAL; *esp* **:** a daily record of personal activities, reflections, or feelings **2 :** a book intended or used for a diary
di·as·po·ra \dī-'as-p(ə-)rə\ *n* [Gk, dispersion, fr. *diaspeirein* to scatter, fr. *dia-* + *speirein* to sow] **1** *cap* **a :** the settling of scattered colonies of Jews outside Palestine after the Babylonian exile **b :** the area outside Palestine settled by Jews **c :** the Jews living outside Palestine or modern Israel **2 :** a dispersion abroad
di·a·spore \'dī-ə-,spō(ə)r, ,spȯ(ə)r\ *n* [F, fr. Gk *diaspora*] **:** a mineral consisting of aluminum hydrogen oxide $HAlO_2$
di·a·stase \'dī-ə-,stās, -,stāz\ *n* [F, fr. Gk *diastasis* separation, fr. *diistanai* to separate, fr. *dia-* + *histanai* to cause to stand] **1 :** AMYLASE; *esp* **:** a mixture of amylases from malt **2 :** ENZYME
di·as·ta·sis \dī-'as-tə-səs\ *n, pl* **di·as·ta·ses** \-'as-tə-,sēz\ [NL, fr. Gk, interval] **:** the rest phase of cardiac diastole occurring between filling of the ventricle and the start of auricular contraction
di·a·stat·ic \,dī-ə-'stat-ik\ *adj* **:** relating to or having the properties of diastase; *esp* **:** converting starch into sugar
di·a·ste·ma \,dī-ə-'stē-mə\ *n, pl* **di·a·ste·ma·ta** \-mət-ə\ [NL, fr. LL, interval, fr. Gk *diastēma,* fr. *diistanai*] **:** a space between teeth in a jaw — **di·a·ste·mat·ic** \-sti-'mat-ik\ *adj*
di·as·ter \'dī-,as-tər\ *n* [ISV] **:** a stage in mitosis in which the split and separated chromosomes group themselves near the poles of the spindle — **di·as·tral** \dī-'as-trəl\ *adj*
di·as·to·le \dī-'as-tə-(,)lē\ *n* [Gk *diastolē* dilatation, fr. *diastellein* to expand, fr. *dia-* + *stellein* to send] **:** a rhythmically recurrent expansion; *esp* **:** the dilatation of the cavities of the heart during which they fill with blood — **di·a·stol·ic** \,dī-ə-'stäl-ik\ *adj*
di·a·stroph·ic \,dī-ə-'sträf-ik\ *adj* **:** of, relating to, or caused by diastrophism
di·as·tro·phism \dī-'as-trə-,fiz-əm\ *n* [Gk *diastrophē* twisting, fr. *diastrephein* to distort, fr. *dia-* + *strephein* to twist] **:** the process of deformation that produces in the earth's crust its continents and ocean basins, plateaus and mountains, folds of strata, and faults
di·a·tes·sa·ron \,dī-ə-'tes-ə-rən\ *n* [ME, fr. L, fr. Gk (*hē*) *dia tessarōn* (*chordōn symphōnia*) the concord through four notes, fr. *dia* through + *tessarōn,* gen. of *tessares* four] **:** a harmony of the four Gospels edited and arranged into a single connected narrative
dia·ther·ma·nous \,dī-ə-'thər-mə-nəs\ *adj* **:** DIATHERMIC 1
dia·ther·mic \,dī-ə-'thər-mik\ *adj* **1 :** transmitting infrared radiation **2 :** of or relating to diathermy ⟨~ treatment⟩
dia·ther·my \'dī-ə-,thər-mē\ *n* [ISV] **:** the generation of heat in tissue for medical or surgical purposes by electric currents
di·ath·e·sis \dī-'ath-ə-səs\ *n, pl* **di·ath·e·ses** \-'ath-ə-,sēz\ [NL, fr. Gk, lit., arrangement, fr. *diatithenai* to arrange, fr. *dia-* + *tithenai* to set] **1 :** a constitutional predisposition toward an abnormality or disease **2 :** a disposition toward or aptitude for a particular mental development — **di·a·thet·ic** \,dī-ə-'thet-ik\ *adj*
di·a·tom \'dī-ə-,täm\ *n* [deriv. of Gk *diatomos* cut in half, fr. *diatemnein* to cut through, fr. *dia-* + *temnein* to cut] **:** any of a class (Bacillariophyceae) of minute planktonic unicellular or colonial algae with silicified skeletons that form diatomite
di·a·to·ma·ceous \,dī-ət-ə-'mā-shəs, (,)dī-,at-\ *adj* **:** consisting of or abounding in diatoms or their siliceous remains ⟨~ silica⟩
diatomaceous earth *n* **:** DIATOMITE
di·atom·ic \,dī-ə-'täm-ik\ *adj* [ISV] **1 :** consisting of two atoms **:** having two atoms in the molecule **2 :** having two replaceable atoms or radicals
di·at·o·mite \dī-'at-ə-,mīt\ *n* **:** a light friable siliceous material derived chiefly from diatom remains and used esp. as a filter
dia·ton·ic \,dī-ə-'tän-ik\ *adj* [LL *diatonicus,* fr. Gk *diatonikos,* fr. *diatonos* stretching, fr. *diateinein* to stretch out, fr. *dia-* + *teinein* to stretch — more at THIN] **:** relating to a standard major or minor scale of eight tones to the octave without chromatic deviation — **dia·ton·i·cal·ly** \-'tän-i-k(ə-)lē\ *adv*
di·a·tribe \'dī-ə-,trīb\ *n* [L *diatriba,* fr. Gk *diatribē* pastime, discourse, fr. *diatribein* to spend (time), wear away, fr. *dia-* + *tribein* to rub] **1** *archaic* **:** a prolonged discourse **2 :** a bitter and abusive speech or writing **3 :** ironical or satirical criticism
di·a·trop·ic \,dī-ə-'träp-ik\ *adj* **:** characterized by diatropism
di·at·ro·pism \dī-'a-trə-,piz-əm\ *n* [ISV] **:** the tropistic tendency of plant organs to place themselves transversely to the line of action of a stimulus
di·a·zine \'dī-ə-,zēn, dī-'az-ᵊn\ *n* [ISV *di-* + *az-* + *-ine*] **:** any of three parent compounds $C_4H_4N_2$ containing a ring composed of four carbon atoms and two nitrogen atoms
di·azo \dī-'az-(,)ō\ *adj* [ISV *diaz-, diazo-,* fr. *di-* + *az-*] **1 :** relating to or containing the group N_2 composed of two nitrogen atoms united to a single carbon atom of an organic radical **2 :** relating to or containing diazonium — often used in combination
diazo dye *n* **:** a developed dye
di·a·zo·ni·um \,dī-ə-'zō-nē-əm\ *n* [ISV] **:** the univalent cation $-N_2^+$ composed of two nitrogen atoms united to carbon in one organic radical
dib \'dib\ *vi* **dibbed; dib·bing** [perh. fr. obs. *dib* (to dab)] **:** to fish by letting the bait bob and dip lightly
di·ba·sic \(')dī-'bā-sik\ *adj* **1 :** having two hydrogen atoms replaceable by basic atoms or radicals — used of acids **2 :** containing two atoms of a univalent metal or their equivalent **3 :** having two basic hydroxyl groups — used of bases and basic salts — **di·ba·sic·i·ty** \,dī-(,)bā-'sis-ət-ē\ *n*
dib·ber \'dib-ər\ *n* **:** DIBBLE
¹**dib·ble** \'dib-əl\ *n* [ME *debylle*] **:** a small hand implement used to make holes in the ground for plants, seeds, or bulbs
²**dibble** *vt* **dib·bling** \'dib-(ə-)liŋ\ **1 :** to plant with a dibble **2 :** to make holes in (soil) with or as if with a dibble
³**dibble** *vi* [freq. of *dib*] **:** DIB
di·bran·chi·ate \dī-'braŋ-kē-ət\ *adj* [deriv. of Gk *di-* + *branchia*] **:** of or relating to a group (Dibranchia) of cephalopod mollusks including the squids and octopuses and having 2 gills, 2 auricles, 2 nephridia, an apparatus for emitting an inky fluid, and either 8 or 10 cephalic arms bearing suckers or hooks
dibs \'dibz\ *n pl* [short for *dibstones* (jacks), fr. obs. *dib* (to dab)] **1** *slang* **:** money esp. in small amounts **2** *slang* **:** CLAIM, RIGHTS
di·car·box·yl·ic \,dī-,kär-,bäk-'sil-ik\ *adj* **:** containing two carboxyl groups in the molecule
di·cast \'dī-,kast\ *n* [Gk *dikastēs,* fr. *dikazein* to judge, fr. *dikē* judgment — more at DICTION] **:** an ancient Athenian performing the functions of both judge and juryman at a trial
¹**dice** \'dīs\ *n, pl* **dice** [ME *dyce,* fr. *dees, dyce,* pl. of *dee* die] **1 :** a small cube marked distinctively on each face with one to six spots and used usu. in pairs in various games and in gambling by being shaken and thrown to come to rest at random on a flat surface **2 :** a gambling game played with dice — **no dice :** nothing doing **:** no use
²**dice** *vb* [ME *dycen,* fr. *dyce*] *vt* **1 a :** to cut into small cubes **b :** to ornament with square markings ⟨*diced* leather⟩ **2 a :** to bring by playing dice ⟨~ himself into debt⟩ **b :** to lose by dicing ~ *vi* **:** to play games with dice — **dic·er** *n*
di·cen·tra \dī-'sen-trə\ *n* [NL *Dicentra,* genus name, fr. *di-* + Gk *kentron* sharp point] **:** any of a genus (*Dicentra*) of the fumitory family of herbs with dissected leaves and irregular flowers
dich- *or* **dicho-** *comb form* [LL, fr. Gk, fr. *dicha;* akin to Gk *di-*] **:** in two **:** apart ⟨*dicho*gamous⟩
di·cha·sial \dī-'kā-zh(ē-)əl, -zē-əl\ *adj* **:** of, relating to, or constituting a dichasium
di·cha·si·um \-z(h)ē-əm\ *n, pl* **di·cha·sia** \-z(h)ē-ə\ [NL, fr. Gk *dichasis* halving, fr. *dichazein* to halve, fr. *dicha*] **:** a cymose inflorescence that produces two main axes
di·chla·myd·eous \,dī-klə-'mid-ē-əs\ *adj* [*di-* + Gk *chlamyd-, chlamys* mantle] **:** having both calyx and corolla
di·chlo·ride \(')dī-'klō(ə)r-,īd, -'klȯ(ə)r-\ *n* **:** a binary compound containing two atoms of chlorine combined with an element or radical
di·chog·a·mous \dī-'käg-ə-məs\ *or* **di·cho·gam·ic** \,dī-kə-'gam-ik\ *adj, of a hermaphroditic organism* **:** characterized by production at different times of male and female reproductive elements that ensures cross-fertilization — **di·chog·a·my** \dī-'käg-ə-mē\ *n*
di·chot·o·mist \dī-'kät-ə-məst\ *n* [Gk *dichotomia*] **:** one that dichotomizes
di·chot·o·mi·za·tion \(,)dī-,kät-ə-mə-'zā-shən\ *n* **:** an act of dichotomizing **:** the condition of being dichotomized
di·chot·o·mize \dī-'kät-ə-,mīz\ *vb* [LL *dichotomos*] *vt* **:** to divide into two parts, classes, or groups ~ *vi* **:** to exhibit dichotomy
di·chot·o·mous \-məs\ *adj* [LL *dichotomos,* fr. Gk, fr. *dich-* + *temnein* to cut] **1 :** dividing into two parts **2 :** relating to, involving, or proceeding from dichotomy — **di·chot·o·mous·ly** *adv*
di·chot·o·my \dī-'kät-ə-mē\ *n* [Gk *dichotomia,* fr. *dichotomos*] **1 :** a division or the process of dividing into two esp. mutually exclusive or contradictory groups **2 :** the phase of the moon or an inferior planet in which just half its disk appears illuminated **3 a :** FORKING; *esp* **:** repeated bifurcation **b :** a system of branching in which the main axis forks repeatedly into two branches **c :** branching of an ancestral line into two equal diverging branches
di·chro·ic \dī-'krō-ik\ *adj* [Gk *dichroos* two-colored, fr. *di-* + *chrōs* color] **1 :** having the property of dichroism **2 :** DICHROMATIC
di·chro·ism \'dī-krə-,wiz-əm\ *n* **1 :** the property according to which the colors are unlike when a crystal is viewed in the direction of two different axes **2 a :** the property of a solid of differing in color with the thickness of the transmitting layer or of a liquid with the degree of concentration of the solution **b :** the property of a surface of reflecting light of one color and transmitting light of other colors **3 :** DICHROMATISM
di·chro·mat \'dī-krō-,mat, (')dī-'krō-\ *n* [back-formation fr. *dichromatic*] **:** one affected with dichromatism

di·chro·mate \(')dī-'krō-,māt\ *n* [ISV] **:** a salt of dichromic acid — called also *bichromate*

di·chro·mat·ic \,dī-krō-'mat-ik\ *adj* [*di-* + *chromatic*] **1 :** having or exhibiting two colors **2 :** having two color varieties or color phases independently of age or sex ⟨a ~ bird⟩ **3 :** of, relating to, or exhibiting dichromatism

di·chro·ma·tism \dī-'krō-mə-,tiz-əm\ *n* **1 :** the state or condition of being dichromatic **2 :** partial color blindness in which only two colors are perceptible

di·chro·mic acid \,dī-,krō-mik-\ *n* **:** an acid $H_2Cr_2O_7$ known only in solution and esp. in the form of its salts

di·chro·scope \'dī-krə-,skōp\ *n* **:** an instrument for examining crystals for dichroism

dick \'dik\ *n* [*Dick*, nickname for *Richard*] **1** *chiefly Brit* **:** FELLOW, CHAP **2** [by shortening & alter.] **:** DETECTIVE

dick·cis·sel \dik-'sis-əl\ *n* [imit.] **:** a common migratory black-throated finch (*Spiza americana*) of the central U. S.

dick·ens \'dik-ənz\ *n* [euphemism] **:** DEVIL, DEUCE

Dick·en·si·an \dik-'en-zē-ən\ *adj* **:** of, relating to, or characteristic of Dickens or his writings

¹dick·er \'dik-ər\ *n* [ME *dyker;* akin to MHG *techer;* both fr. a prehistoric WGmc word borrowed fr. L *decuria* quantity of ten, fr. *decem* ten] **:** the number or quantity of 10 esp. of hides or skins

²dicker *vi* **dick·er·ing** \'dik-(ə-)riŋ\ [origin unknown] **:** BARGAIN — **dicker** *n*

dick·ey *or* **dicky** \'dik-ē\ *n* [*Dicky*, nickname for *Richard*] **1 :** any of various articles of clothing: as **a :** a man's separate or detachable shirtfront **b :** a small fabric insert worn to fill in the neckline **2 :** a small bird **3** *chiefly Brit* **a :** the driver's seat in a carriage **b :** a seat at the back of a carriage or automobile.

Dick test \'dik-\ *n* [George F. *Dick* †1967 and Gladys H. *Dick* †1963 Am physicians] **:** a test to determine susceptibility or immunity to scarlet fever by an injection of scarlet fever toxin

di·cli·nous \(')dī-'klī-nəs\ *adj* **:** having the stamens and pistils in separate flowers — **di·cli·ny** \'dī-,klī-nē\ *n*

di·cot \'dī-,kät\ *also* **di·cot·yl** \-,kät-ᵊl\ *n* **:** DICOTYLEDON

di·cot·y·le·don \,dī-,kät-ᵊl-'ēd-ᵊn\ *n* [deriv. of NL *di-* + *cotyledon*] **:** a plant with two seed leaves **:** a member of the one (Dicotyledones) of the two subclasses of angiospermous plants that comprises those with two cotyledons — **di·cot·y·le·don·ous** \-ᵊn-əs\ *adj*

di·cou·ma·rin \dī-'k(y)ü-mə-rən\ *n* [fr. *di-* + *coumarin*] **:** a crystalline compound $C_{19}H_{12}O_6$ obtained from spoiled sweet clover hay and used as an anticoagulant

di·crot·ic \dī-'krät-ik\ *adj* [Gk *dikrotos* having a double beat] **:** being or relating to the second expansion of the artery that occurs during the diastole of the heart — **di·cro·tism** \'dī-krə-,tiz-əm\ *n*

Dic·ta·phone \'dik-tə-,fōn\ *trademark* — used for a dictating machine

¹dic·tate \'dik-,tāt, dik-'tāt\ *vb* [L *dictatus*, pp. of *dictare* to assert, dictate, fr. *dictus*, pp. of *dicere* to say] *vi* **1 :** to give dictation **2 :** to speak or act domineeringly **:** PRESCRIBE ~ *vt* **1 :** to speak or read for a person to transcribe or for a machine to record **2 a :** to issue as an order **b :** to command or impose authoritatively

²dic·tate \'dik-,tāt\ *n* **1 a :** an authoritative rule, prescription, or injunction **b :** a ruling principle **2 :** a command by one in authority

dictating machine *n* **:** a machine used esp. for the recording of dictated matter

dic·ta·tion \dik-'tā-shən\ *n* **1 a :** PRESCRIPTION **b :** arbitrary command **2 a :** the act or manner of uttering words to be written by another **b** (1) **:** the performing of music to be reproduced by a student (2) **:** music so reproduced

dic·ta·tor \'dik-,tāt-ər, dik-'tāt-\ *n* [L, fr. *dictatus*] **1 a :** a person granted absolute emergency power; *esp* **:** one appointed by the senate of ancient Rome **b :** one enjoying complete autocratic control; *esp* **:** a supreme sometimes autocratic arbiter **c :** one ruling absolutely and often brutally and oppressively **2 :** one that dictates — **dic·ta·tress** \'dik-,tā-trəs, dik-'tā-\ *n*

dic·ta·to·ri·al \,dik-tə-'tōr-ē-əl, -'tȯr-\ *adj* **1 a :** of, relating to, or befitting a dictator ⟨~ power⟩ **b :** ruled by a dictator **2 :** DESPOTIC — **dic·ta·to·ri·al·ly** \-ē-ə-lē\ *adv* — **dic·ta·to·ri·al·ness** *n*

syn DICTATORIAL, MAGISTERIAL, DOGMATIC, DOCTRINAIRE, ORACULAR mean imposing one's will or opinions on others. DICTATORIAL stresses autocratic, high-handed methods and a domineering manner; MAGISTERIAL stresses assumption or use of prerogatives appropriate to a magistrate or schoolmaster in forcing acceptance of one's opinions; DOGMATIC implies the attitude of one who lays down principles as true and beyond dispute; DOCTRINAIRE implies a disposition to follow abstract theories in framing laws or policies affecting people; ORACULAR implies the manner of one who delivers opinions in cryptic phrases or with pompous dogmatism

dic·ta·tor·ship \dik-'tāt-ər-,ship\ *n* **1 :** the office of dictator **2 :** autocratic rule, control, or leadership **3 a :** a form of government in which absolute power is concentrated in a dictator or a small clique **b :** a government or other organization in which absolute power is so concentrated **c :** an area with such a government

dictatorship of the proletariat : the assumption of political power by the proletariat held in Marxism to be an essential part of the transition from capitalism to communism

dic·tion \'dik-shən\ *n* [L *diction-*, *dictio* speaking, style, fr. *dictus*, pp. of *dicere* to say; akin to OE *tēon* to accuse, L *dicare* to proclaim, dedicate, Gk *deiknynai* to show, *dikē* judgement, right] **1** *obs* **:** verbal description **2 :** choice of words esp. with regard to correctness, clearness, or effectiveness **3 a :** vocal expression **:** ENUNCIATION **b :** pronunciation and enunciation of words in singing

dic·tio·nary \'dik-shə-,ner-ē\ *n* [ML *dictionarium*, fr. LL *diction-*, *dictio* word, fr. L, speaking] **1 :** a reference book containing words usu. alphabetically arranged along with information about their forms, pronunciations, functions, etymologies, meanings, and syntactical and idiomatic uses **2 :** a reference book listing alphabetically terms or names important to a particular subject or activity along with discussion of their meanings and applications **3 :** a general comprehensive list, collection, or repository of information alphabetically arranged

Dic·to·graph \'dik-tə-,graf\ *trademark* — used for a telephonic device for picking up sounds in one room and transmitting them to another or recording them

dic·tum \'dik-təm\ *n, pl* **dic·ta** \-tə\ *also* **dic·tums** [L, fr. neut. of *dictus*] **1 a :** an authoritative pronouncement **b :** a formal statement of a principle, proposition, or opinion **2 :** a judicial opinion on a point other than the precise issue involved in determining a case

dicty- *or* **dictyo-** *comb form* [NL, fr. Gk *dikty-*, *diktyo-*, fr. *diktyon*, fr. *dikein* to throw] **:** net ⟨*dictyostele*⟩

di·cy·clic \(')dī-'sī-klik, -'sik-lik\ *adj* **1 :** BICYCLIC 2 **2 :** having two maxima of population each year — **di·cy·cly** \'dī-,sī-klē\ *n*

did *past of* DO

di·dac·tic \dī-'dak-tik\ *adj* [Gk *didaktikos*, fr. *didaskein* to teach] **1 a :** fitted or intended to teach **b :** intended to convey instruction and information as well as pleasure and entertainment **2 :** making moral observations — **di·dac·ti·cal** \-ti-kəl\ *adj* — **di·dac·ti·cal·ly** \-ti-k(ə-)lē\ *adv* — **di·dac·ti·cism** \-tə-,siz-əm\ *n*

di·dac·tics \-tiks\ *n pl but sing or pl in constr* **:** systematic instruction **:** PEDAGOGY, TEACHINGS

di·dap·per \'dī-,dap-ər\ *n* [ME *dydoppar*] **:** a dabchick or other small grebe

did·dle \'did-ᵊl\ *vb* **did·dling** \'did-liŋ, -ᵊl-iŋ\ [origin unknown] *vi* **1** *chiefly Scot* **:** JIGGLE **2 :** DAWDLE, FOOL ~ *vt* **1** *chiefly dial* **:** to move with short rapid motions **2 :** to waste (as time) in trifling **3 :** HOAX, SWINDLE — **did·dler** \'did-lər, -ᵊl-ər\ *n*

di·del·phic \dī-'del-fik\ *adj* [*di-* + Gk *delphys*] **1 a :** having or relating to a double uterus **b :** having the female genital tract doubled — used esp. of some worms **2** [NL *Didelphia*] **:** MARSUPIAL

didn't \'did-ᵊnt\ **:** did not

di·do \'dīd-(,)ō\ *n, pl* **didoes** *or* **didos** [origin unknown] **1 :** a foolish or mischievous act **2 :** something frivolous or showy

Di·do \'dīd-(,)ō\ *n* [L, fr. Gk *Deidō*] **:** a queen of Carthage who according to the *Aeneid* entertains Aeneas, falls in love with him, and on his departure stabs herself

didst \(')didst, (')ditst\ *archaic past 2d sing of* DO

di·dym·i·um \dī-'dim-ē-əm\ *n* [NL, fr. Gk *didymos*] **:** a mixture of rare-earth elements chiefly neodymium and praseodymium

did·y·mous \'did-ə-məs\ *adj* [Gk *didymos* double, twin (adj. & n.), testicle, fr. *dyo* two — more at TWO] **:** growing in pairs **:** TWIN

di·dyn·a·mous \dī-'din-ə-məs\ *adj* [deriv. of Gk *di-* + *dynamis* power — more at DYNAMIC] **:** having four stamens disposed in pairs of unequal length — **di·dyn·a·my** \-mē\ *n*

¹die \'dī\ *vi* **died; dy·ing** \'dī-iŋ\ [ME *dien*, fr. or akin to ON *deyja* to die; akin to OHG *touwen* to die, OIr *duine* human being] **1 :** to pass from physical life **:** EXPIRE ⟨*dying* of old age⟩ **2 a :** to pass out of existence **:** CEASE **b :** to disappear or subside gradually ⟨the wind *died* down⟩ **3 a :** to suffer or face the pains of death **b :** to come to or as if to the point of death **:** SINK **c :** LANGUISH ⟨*dying* from fatigue⟩ **d :** to long keenly or desperately ⟨*dying* to go⟩ **4 :** to cease to be subject ⟨let them ~ to sin⟩ **5 a :** to pass into an inferior state or situation **b :** STOP ⟨the motor *died*⟩

²die \'dī\ *n, pl* **dice** \'dīs\ *or* **dies** \'dīz\ [ME *dee*, fr. MF *dé*] **1** *pl dice* **:** DICE 1 **2** *pl dice* **:** a small cubical piece — usu. used in pl. **3** *pl usu dice* **:** something determined by or as if by a cast of dice **:** CHANCE **4** *pl dies* **:** DADO 1a **5** *pl dies* **:** any of various tools or devices for imparting a desired shape, form, or finish to a material or for impressing an object or material: as **a** (1) **:** the larger of a pair of cutting or shaping tools that when moved toward each other produce a certain desired form in or impress a desired device on an object by pressure or by a blow (2) **:** a device composed of a pair of such tools **b :** a hollow internally threaded screw-cutting tool used for forming screw threads **c :** a cutter to cut out blanks **d :** a mold into which some form of metal is forced **e :** a perforated block through which metal or plastic is drawn or extruded

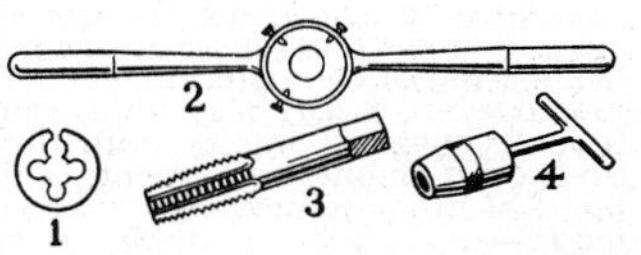

die 5b: four pieces of a tap-and-die set: *1* adjustable round split die, *2* diestock, *3* tap, *4* tap wrench

³die *vt* **died; die·ing :** to cut or shape with a die

die·back \'dī-,bak\ *n* **:** a condition in woody plants in which peripheral parts are killed esp. by parasites

di·ecious *var of* DIOECIOUS

die down *vi* **:** to undergo death of the aboveground portions

die·hard \'dī-,härd\ *n* **:** one who resists against hopeless odds; *esp* **:** an irreconcilable opponent

die–hard \'dī-,härd\ *adj* **1 :** offering extreme resistance to change **2 :** completely and determinedly fixed — **die–hard·ism** \-,iz-əm\ *n*

diel·drin \'dē(ə)l-drən\ *n* [*Diels-Alder* reaction, after Otto *Diels* †1954 & Kurt *Alder* †1958 G chemists] **:** a white crystalline insecticide $C_{12}H_8Cl_6O$

di·elec·tric \,dī-ə-'lek-trik\ *n* [*dia-* + *electric*] **:** a nonconductor of direct electric current — **dielectric** *adj*

dielectric heating *n* **:** the rapid and uniform heating throughout a nonconducting material by means of a high-frequency electromagnetic field

di·en·ce·phal·ic \(,)dī-,en(t)-sə-'fal-ik\ *adj* **:** of, relating to, or involving the diencephalon

di·en·ceph·a·lon \,dī-,en-'sef-ə-,län, -lən\ *n* [NL, fr. *dia-* + *encephalon*] **:** the posterior subdivision of the forebrain

di·er·e·sis *var of* DIAERESIS

die·sel \'dē-zəl, -səl\ *n, often attrib, sometimes cap* [Rudolph *Diesel* †1913 G inventor] **:** a vehicle driven by a diesel engine

diesel engine *n* **:** an internal-combustion engine in which air is compressed to a temperature sufficiently high to ignite fuel injected into the cylinder where the combustion actuates a piston

die·sel·ize \'dē-zə-,līz, 'dē-sə-\ *vt* **:** to equip with a diesel engine or with electric locomotives having electric generators powered by diesel engines

die·sink·er \'dī-,siŋ-kər\ *n* **:** one that makes cutting and shaping dies — **die·sink·ing** *n*

Di·es Irae \,dē-,ā-'sē-,rā\ *n* [ML, day of wrath; fr. the first words of the hymn] **:** a medieval Latin hymn on the Day of Judgment sung in requiem masses

di·esis \'dī-ə-səs\ *n, pl* **di·eses** \'dī-ə-ˌsēz\ [L, quarter tone, fr. Gk, fr. *diienai* to send through, fr. *dia-* + *hienai* to send — more at JET] **:** DOUBLE DAGGER

die·stock \'dī-ˌstäk\ *n* **:** a stock to hold dies used for cutting threads

di·es·trous \dī-'es-trəs\ *or* **di·es·tru·al** \-trə-wəl\ *adj* [NL *diestrus* period of sexual quiescence, fr. *dia-* + *estrus*] **:** of, relating to, or having a period of sexual quiescence that intervenes between two periods of estrus — **di·es·trus** \-trəs\ *n*

1di·et \'dī-ət\ *n* [ME *diete*, fr. OF, fr. L *diaeta* prescribed diet, fr. Gk, lit., manner of living, fr. *dia-* + *-aita* (akin to Gk *aisa* share)] **1 a :** food and drink regularly provided or consumed **b :** habitual course of feeding **c :** a prescribed course or allowance of food **2 :** something provided esp. habitually (as for use or enjoyment)

2diet *vt* **1 :** to cause to take food **:** FEED **2 :** to cause to eat and drink sparingly or according to prescribed rules **~** *vi* **:** to eat sparingly or according to prescribed rules — **di·et·er** *n*

3diet *n* [ML *dieta*, day's journey, assembly, fr. L *dies* day — more at DEITY] **1 :** a formal deliberative assembly of princes or estates **2 :** any of various national or provincial legislatures

1di·etary \'dī-ə-ˌter-ē\ *n* **:** a quantity of food provided or eaten by an individual, group, or population

2dietary *adj* **:** of or relating to a diet or to the rules of diet

dietary law *n* **:** one of the laws observed by Orthodox Jews that permit or prohibit certain foods and combinations of foods

di·etet·ic \ˌdī-ə-'tet-ik\ *adj* **1 :** of or relating to diet **2 :** adapted for use in special diets — **di·etet·i·cal·ly** \-i-k(ə-)lē\ *adv*

di·etet·ics \-'tet-iks\ *n pl but sing or pl in constr* **:** the science or art of applying the principles of nutrition to feeding

di·eth·yl·stil·bes·trol \ˌdī-ˌeth-əl-ˌstil-'bes-ˌtrȯl, -ˌtrōl\ *n* [ISV] **:** a colorless crystalline synthetic compound $C_{18}H_{20}O_2$ used as a potent estrogen — called also *stilbestrol*

di·eti·tian *or* **di·eti·cian** \ˌdī-ə-'tish-ən\ *n* [*dietitian* irreg. fr. *1diet*] **:** a person qualified in or practicing dietetics

dif·fer \'dif-ər\ *vi* **dif·fer·ing** \'dif-(ə-)riŋ\ [ME *differen*, fr. MF or L; MF *differer* to postpone, be different, fr. L *differre*, fr. *dis-* + *ferre* to carry] **1 a :** to be unlike or distinct in nature, form, or characteristics **b :** to change from time to time or from one instance to another **:** VARY **2 :** to be of unlike or opposite opinion **:** DISAGREE **3** *archaic* **:** DISPUTE

1dif·fer·ence \'dif-ərn(t)s, 'dif-(ə-)rən(t)s\ *n* **1 a :** the quality or state of being different **b :** an instance of differing in nature, form, or quality **c** *archaic* **:** a characteristic that distinguishes one from another or from the average **d :** the element or factor that separates or distinguishes contrasting situations **2 :** distinction or discrimination in preference **3 a :** disagreement in opinion **:** DISSENSION **b :** an instance or cause of disagreement **4 :** the degree or amount by which things differ in quantity or measure **5 :** a significant change in or effect on a situation

2difference *vt* **:** to make different

dif·fer·ent \'dif-ərnt, 'dif-(ə-)rənt\ *adj* [MF, fr. L *different-*, *differens*, prp. of *differre*] **1 :** partly or totally unlike in nature, form, or quality **:** DISSIMILAR ⟨could hardly be more ~⟩ **2 :** not the same: as **a :** DISTINCT ⟨~ age groups⟩ **b :** VARIOUS ⟨~ members of the class⟩ **c :** ANOTHER ⟨tried a ~ book⟩ **3 :** UNUSUAL, SPECIAL

syn DIFFERENT, DIVERSE, DIVERGENT, DISPARATE, VARIOUS mean unlike in kind or character. DIFFERENT may imply little more than separateness but it may also imply contrast or contrariness ⟨*different* foods⟩ DIVERSE implies both distinctness and marked contrast; DIVERGENT implies movement away from each other and unlikelihood of ultimate meeting or reconciliation; DISPARATE emphasizes incongruity or incompatibility; VARIOUS stresses the number of sorts or kinds ⟨*various* methods have been tried⟩

dif·fer·en·tia \ˌdif-ə-'ren-ch(ē-)ə\ *n, pl* **dif·fer·en·ti·ae** \-chē-ˌē, -chē-ˌī\ [L, difference, fr. *different-*, *differens*] **1 :** the property or mark distinguishing a species from other species of the same genus **2 :** the element, feature, or factor that distinguishes one entity, state, or class from another

dif·fer·en·tia·bil·i·ty \ˌdif-ə-ˌren-ch(ē-)ə-'bil-ət-ē\ *n* **:** the property or quality of being differentiable

dif·fer·en·tia·ble \-'ren-ch(ē-)ə-bəl\ *adj* **:** capable of being differentiated

1dif·fer·en·tial \ˌdif-ə-'ren-chəl\ *adj* **1 a :** of, relating to, or constituting a difference **:** DISTINGUISHING **b :** making a distinction between individuals or classes **c :** based upon or resulting from a differential **d :** functioning or proceeding differently or at a different rate **2 :** relating to or involving a differential or differentiation **3 a :** relating to quantitative differences **b :** producing effects by reason of such differences — **dif·fer·en·tial·ly** \-'rench-(ə-)lē\ *adv*

2differential *n* **1 a :** the product of the derivative of a function of one variable by the increment of the independent variable **b :** the sum of the products of each partial derivative of a function of several variables by the arbitrary increments of the corresponding variables **2 a :** the difference between transportation rates over different routes allowed to carriers to equalize traffic distribution **b :** an amount added to or deducted from a transportation rate **3 :** a difference in wage rates reflecting differences in working conditions, worker status, or job standards **4 :** the amount or degree by which comparable individuals or classes differ

differential calculus *n* **:** a branch of mathematics dealing chiefly with the rate of change of functions with respect to their variables

differential equation *n* **:** an equation containing differentials or derivatives of functions

differential gear *n* **:** an arrangement of gears forming an epicyclic train for connecting two shafts or axles in the same line, dividing the driving force equally between them, and permitting one shaft to revolve faster than the other — called also *differential gearing*

dif·fer·en·ti·ate \ˌdif-ə-'ren-chē-ˌāt\ *vt* **1 :** to obtain the mathematical derivative of **2 :** to mark or show a difference in **3 :** to develop differential characteristics in **4 :** to cause differentiation of in the course of development **5 :** to express the specific difference of **:** DISCRIMINATE **~** *vi* **1 :** to recognize a difference **2 :** to become distinct or different in character **3 :** to undergo differentiation

dif·fer·en·ti·a·tion \-ˌren-chē-'ā-shən\ *n* **1 :** the act or process of differentiating **2 :** development from the one to the many, the simple to the complex, or the homogeneous to the heterogeneous **3 a :** modification of body parts for performance of particular functions **b :** the sum of the processes whereby apparently indifferent cells, tissues, and structures attain their adult form and function

dif·fer·ent·ly \'dif-ərnt-lē, 'dif-(ə-)rənt-\ *adv* **1 :** in a different manner **2 :** OTHERWISE

dif·fi·cile *adj* [MF, fr. L *difficilis*, fr. *dis-* + *facilis* easy — more at FACILE] **1** \də-'fis-əl\ *obs* **:** DIFFICULT **2** \ˌdē-fi-'sē(ə)l\ **:** STUBBORN

dif·fi·cult \'dif-i-(ˌ)kəlt\ *adj* [back-formation fr. *difficulty*] **1 :** hard to do, make, or carry out **:** ARDUOUS ⟨a ~ climb⟩ **2 a :** hard to deal with, manage, or overcome ⟨a ~ child⟩ **b :** hard to understand **:** PUZZLING ⟨~ reading⟩ **syn** see HARD — **dif·fi·cult·ly** *adv*

dif·fi·cul·ty \-ˌkəl-tē, -kəl-\ *n* [ME *difficulte*, fr. L *difficultas*, irreg. fr. *difficilis*] **1 :** the quality or state of being difficult **2 :** something difficult **:** IMPEDIMENT **3 :** OBJECTION **4 :** embarrassment of affairs

syn HARDSHIP, RIGOR, VICISSITUDE: DIFFICULTY applies to any condition or task almost beyond one's ability to deal with and requiring skill, perseverance, and patience to surmount or solve; HARDSHIP stresses suffering, toil, or privation without necessarily implying any effort to overcome or patience in enduring; RIGOR suggests a hardship necessarily imposed upon one (as by an austere religion, a trying climate, an exacting undertaking, an oppressive government); VICISSITUDE applies to a difficulty or hardship incident to life or a career or course of action and usu. beyond one's control

dif·fi·dence \'dif-ə-dən(t)s, -ˌden(t)s\ *n* **:** the quality or state of being diffident

dif·fi·dent \-dənt, -ˌdent\ *adj* [L *diffident-*, *diffidens*, prp. of *diffidere* to distrust, fr. *dis-* + *fidere* to trust — more at BIDE] **1** *archaic* **:** DISTRUSTFUL **2 :** lacking confidence **:** TIMID **3 :** RESERVED, UNASSERTIVE **syn** see SHY — **dif·fi·dent·ly** *adv*

dif·fract \dif-'rakt\ *vt* [back-formation fr. *diffraction*] **:** to cause to undergo diffraction

dif·frac·tion \-'rak-shən\ *n* [NL *diffraction-*, *diffractio*, fr. L *diffractus*, pp. of *diffringere* to break apart, fr. *dis-* + *frangere* to break — more at BREAK] **:** a modification which light undergoes in passing by the edges of opaque bodies or through narrow slits or in being reflected from ruled surfaces and in which the rays appear to be deflected and produce fringes of parallel light and dark or colored bands; *also* **:** a similar modification of other waves

diffraction grating *n* **:** GRATING 3

1dif·fuse \dif-'yüs\ *adj* [L *diffusus*, pp. of *diffundere* to spread out, fr. *dis-* + *fundere* to pour] **1 a :** poured or spread out **b :** not concentrated or restrained **2 :** VERBOSE, PROLIX **3 a :** spreading widely or loosely **b :** SCATTERED **4 :** moving in many directions **syn** see WORDY — **dif·fuse·ly** *adv* — **dif·fuse·ness** *n*

2dif·fuse \dif-'yüz\ *vb* [MF or L; MF *diffuser*, fr. L *diffusus*, pp.] *vt* **1 a :** to pour out and permit or cause to spread freely **b :** EXTEND, SCATTER **c :** to spread thinly or wastefully **2 :** to subject to diffusion **3 :** to break up and distribute (incident light) by reflection **~** *vi* **1 :** to spread out or become transmitted esp. by contact **2 :** to undergo diffusion

dif·fus·er *also* **dif·fu·sor** \-'yü-zər\ *n* **:** one that diffuses; *specif* **:** a device for reducing the velocity and increasing the static pressure of a fluid passing through a system

dif·fus·ible \dif-'yü-zə-bəl\ *adj* **:** capable of diffusing or of being diffused

dif·fu·sion \dif-'yü-zhən\ *n* **1 :** the action of diffusing or state of being diffused **2 :** DIFFUSENESS, PROLIXITY **3 a :** the process whereby particles of liquids, gases, or solids intermingle as the result of their spontaneous movement and in dissolved substances move from a region of higher to one of lower concentration **b** (1) **:** reflection of light by a rough reflecting surface (2) **:** transmission of light through a translucent material **4 :** the softening of sharp outlines in a photographic image — **dif·fu·sion·al** *adj* \-'yüzh-nəl, -ən-ᵊl\

dif·fu·sive \dif-'yü-siv, -ziv\ *adj* **:** tending to diffuse **:** characterized by diffusion — **dif·fu·sive·ly** *adv* — **dif·fu·sive·ness** *n*

1dig \'dig\ *vb* **dug** \'dəg\ **dig·ging** [ME *diggen*] *vi* **1 :** to turn up, loosen, or remove earth **:** DELVE **2 :** to work hard or laboriously **3 :** to advance by or as if by removing or pushing aside material **~** *vt* **1 a :** to break up (earth) with an implement **b :** to turn over **:** PIERCE **2 :** to bring to the surface by digging **:** UNEARTH **3 :** to hollow out or form by removing earth **:** EXCAVATE **4 :** to drive down so as to penetrate **:** THRUST **5 :** POKE, PROD **6** *slang* **a :** to pay attention to **b :** UNDERSTAND, APPRECIATE

2dig *n* **1 a :** THRUST, POKE **b :** a cutting remark **2** *pl, Brit* **:** DIGGINGS 3 **3 :** an archaeological excavation site; *also* **:** the excavation itself

di·ga·met·ic \ˌdī-gə-'met-ik\ *adj* **:** forming two kinds of germ cells; *esp* **:** heterozygous for sex

dig·a·my \'dig-ə-mē\ *n* [LL *digamia*, fr. LGk, fr. Gk *digamos* married to two people, fr. *di-* + *-gamos* -gamous] **:** a second marriage after the termination of the first

di·gas·tric \dī-'gas-trik\ *adj* [NL *digastricus*, fr. *di-* + *gastricus* gastric] **:** of, relating to, or being a muscle with two bellies separated by a median tendon

di·gen·e·sis \dī-'jen-ə-səs\ *n* [NL] **:** successive reproduction by sexual and asexual methods

di·ge·net·ic \ˌdī-jə-'net-ik\ *adj* **1 :** of or relating to digenesis **2 :** of or relating to a subclass (Digenea) of trematode worms in which sexual reproduction as an internal parasite of a vertebrate alternates with asexual reproduction in a mollusk

1di·gest \'dī-ˌjest\ *n* [ME *Digest* compilation of Roman laws ordered by Justinian, fr. LL *Digesta*, pl., fr. L, collection of writings arranged under headings, fr. neut. pl. of *digestus*, pp. of *digerere* to arrange, distribute, digest, fr. *dis-* + *gerere* to carry] **1 :** a summation or condensation of a body of information: as **a :** a systematic compilation of legal rules, statutes, or decisions **b :** a literary abridgment **2 :** a product of digestion **syn** see COMPENDIUM

2di·gest \dī-'jest, də-\ *vb* [ME *digesten*, fr. L *digestus*] *vt* **1 :** to distribute or arrange systematically **:** CLASSIFY **2 :** to think over and arrange systematically in the mind **:** COMPREHEND **3 :** to convert (food) into absorbable form **4 :** to appropriate or assimilate mentally **5 :** to bear patiently **:** BROOK **6 a :** to soften or decompose by heat and moisture or chemicals **b :** to extract soluble ingredients from by warming with a liquid **7 :** to compress into a short summary **~** *vi* **1 :** to digest food **2 :** to become digested

di·gest·er \-tər\ *n* **1 :** one that digests or makes a digest **2 :** a vessel for digesting esp. plant or animal materials

di·gest·ibil·i·ty \-ˌjes-tə-'bil-ət-ē\ *n* **1 :** the fitness of a foodstuff for digestion **2 :** the percentage of a foodstuff taken into the digestive tract that is absorbed into the body

di·gest·ible \-'jes-tə-bəl\ *adj* **:** capable of being digested

di·ges·tion \dī-'jes(h)-chən, də-\ *n* **:** the action, process, or power

of digesting: as **a :** the process of making food absorbable by dissolving it and breaking it down into simpler chemical compounds that occurs in the living body chiefly through the action of enzymes secreted into the alimentary canal **b :** the process in sewage treatment by which organic matter in sludge is decomposed by anaerobic bacteria with the release of a burnable mixture of gases

1**di·ges·tive** \-'jes-tiv\ *n* **:** something that aids digestion

2**digestive** *adj* **1 :** relating to digestion **2 :** having the power to cause or promote digestion ⟨~ ferments⟩ — **di·ges·tive·ly** *adv* — **di·ges·tive·ness** *n*

digestive gland *n* **:** a gland secreting digestive enzymes

dig·ger \'dig-ər\ *n* **1 a :** one that digs **b :** a tool or machine for digging **2** *cap* **:** a No. American Indian who digs roots for food

digger wasp *n* **:** a burrowing wasp; *esp* **:** a usu. solitary wasp (superfamily Sphecoidea) that digs nest burrows in the soil and provisions them with insects or spiders paralyzed by stinging

dig·gings *n pl* **1 :** material dug out **2 :** a place of excavating esp. for ore, metals, or precious stones **3 :** PREMISES, QUARTERS

dight \'dīt\ *vt* **dight·ed** *or* **dight; dight·ing** [ME *dighten*, fr. OE *dihtan* to arrange, compose, fr. a prehistoric WGmc word borrowed fr. L *dictare* to dictate, compose] *archaic* **:** DRESS, ADORN

dig in *vi* **1 :** to dig defensive trenches **2 :** to hold stubbornly to a position **3 a :** to go resolutely to work **b :** to begin eating

dig·it \'dij-ət\ *n* [ME, fr. L *digitus* finger, toe] **1 a :** any of the arabic numerals 1 to 9 and usu. the symbol 0 **b :** one of the elements that combine to form numbers in a system other than the decimal system **2 :** a unit of length based on the breadth of a finger and equal in English measure to ¾ inch **3 :** FINGER, TOE

1**dig·i·tal** \'dij-ət-ᵊl\ *adj* **1 :** of or relating to the fingers or toes **:** DIGITATE **2 :** done with a finger **3 :** of or relating to calculation by numerical methods or by discrete units — **dig·i·tal·ly** \-ᵊl-ē\ *adv*

2**digital** *n* **:** a key (as of an organ) to be played by the finger

digital computer *n* **:** a computer that operates with numbers expressed directly as digits in a decimal, binary, or other system — compare ANALOG COMPUTER

dig·i·tal·in \ˌdij-ə-'tal-ən\ *n* [NL *Digitalis*] **1 :** a white crystalline steroid glycoside $C_{36}H_{56}O_{14}$ obtained from seeds of the common foxglove **2 :** a mixture of the glycosides of digitalis leaves or seeds

dig·i·tal·is \-'tal-əs\ *n* [NL, genus name, fr. L, of a finger, fr. *digitus*; fr. its finger-shaped corolla] **1 :** FOXGLOVE **2 :** the dried leaf of the common foxglove containing important glycosides and serving as a powerful cardiac stimulant and a diuretic

dig·i·tal·i·za·tion \-ˌtal-ə-'zā-shən\ *n* **:** the administration of digitalis until the desired physiologic adjustment is attained

dig·i·ta·lize \'dij-ət-ᵊl-ˌīz, ˌdij-ə-'tal-\ *vt* [*digitalis*] **:** to subject to digitalization

dig·i·tate \'dij-ə-ˌtāt\ *adj* **1 :** having digits **2 :** resembling a finger; *specif* **:** having divisions arranged like fingers of a hand ⟨~ leaf⟩ — **dig·i·tate·ly** *adv* — **dig·i·ta·tion** \ˌdij-ə-'tā-shən\ *n*

digiti- *comb form* [F, fr. L *digitus*] **:** digit **:** finger ⟨*digiti*form⟩

dig·i·ti·grade \'dij-ət-ə-ˌgrād\ *adj* [F, fr. *digiti-* + *-grade*] **:** walking on the digits with the posterior of the foot more or less raised

digi·tox·in \ˌdij-ə-'täk-sən\ *n* [ISV, blend of NL *Digitalis* and ISV *toxin*] **:** a poisonous glycoside $C_{41}H_{64}O_{13}$ occurring as the most active principle of digitalis; *also* **:** a mixture of digitalis glycosides consisting chiefly of digitoxin

dig·ni·fied \'dig-nə-ˌfīd\ *adj* **:** showing or expressing dignity

dig·ni·fy \'dig-nə-ˌfī\ *vt* [MF *dignifier*, fr. LL *dignificare*, fr. L *dignus* worthy] **1 :** to give distinction to **:** ENNOBLE **2 :** to confer dignity upon by changing name, appearance, or character

dig·ni·tary \'dig-nə-ˌter-ē\ *n* **:** one who possesses exalted rank or holds a position of dignity or honor — **dignitary** *adj*

dig·ni·ty \'dig-nət-ē\ *n* [ME *dignete*, fr. OF *digneté*, fr. L *dignitat-*, *dignitas*, fr. *dignus*] **1 :** the quality or state of being worthy, honored, or esteemed **2 a :** high rank, office, or position **b :** a legal title of nobility or honor **3** *archaic* **:** DIGNITARY **4 :** formal reserve of manner or language **syn** see DECORUM

di·graph \'dī-ˌgraf\ *n* **1 :** a group of two successive letters whose phonetic value is a single sound (as *ea* in *bread*) or whose value is not the sum of a value borne by each in other occurrences (as *ch* in *chin*) **2 :** a group of two successive letters — **di·graph·ic** \dī-'graf-ik\ *adj* — **di·graph·i·cal·ly** \-'graf-i-k(ə-)lē\ *adv*

di·gress \dī-'gres, də-\ *vi* [L *digressus*, pp. of *digredi*, fr. *dis-* + *gradi* to step] **:** to turn aside esp. from the main subject of attention or course of argument in writing or speaking **syn** see SWERVE

di·gres·sion \-'gresh-ən\ *n* **1** *archaic* **:** a going aside **2 :** the act or an instance of digressing in a discourse or other usu. organized literary work — **di·gres·sion·al** \-'gresh-nəl, -ən-ᵊl\ *adj*

di·gres·sive \-'gres-iv\ *adj* **:** characterized by digressions ⟨a ~ book⟩ — **di·gres·sive·ly** *adv* — **di·gres·sive·ness** *n*

1**di·he·dral** \dī-'hē-drəl\ *adj* **1 :** having or formed by two plane faces ⟨~ angle⟩ **2 a** *of an airplane* **:** having wings that make with one another a dihedral angle esp. when the angle between the upper sides is less than 180° **b** *of airplane wing pairs* **:** inclined at a dihedral angle to each other

2**dihedral** *n* **1 :** a figure formed by two intersecting planes **2 :** the angle between an aircraft supporting surface and a horizontal transverse line; *esp* **:** the angle between (1) an upwardly inclined wing or (2) a downwardly inclined wing and such a line

di·hy·brid \(ˈ)dī-'hī-brəd\ *adj* [ISV] **:** of, relating to, or being an individual or strain that is heterozygous for two genetic factors

di·hy·dro·chlo·ride \ˌdī-ˌhī-drə-'klō(ə)r-ˌīd, -'klȯ(ə)r-\ *n* **:** a chemical compound with two molecules of hydrochloric acid

di·kast *var of* DICAST

dik–dik \'dik-ˌdik\ *n* [native name in East Africa] **:** any of several small East African antelopes (genera *Madoqua, Rhynchotragus*)

1**dike** \'dīk\ *n* [ME, fr. OE *dīc* ditch, dike; akin to MHG *tīch* pond, dike, L *figere* to fasten, pierce] **1 :** an artificial watercourse **:** DITCH **2 a** *dial Brit* **:** a wall or fence of turf or stone **b :** a bank usu. of earth constructed to control or confine water **:** LEVEE **c :** a barrier preventing passage esp. of something undesirable **3 a :** a raised causeway **b :** a tabular body of igneous rock that has been injected while molten into a fissure

2**dike** *vt* **:** to surround or protect with a dike; *also* **:** to drain by a dike — **dik·er** *n*

dik·tat \dik-'tät\ *n* [G, lit., something dictated, fr. NL *dictatum*, fr. L, neut. of *dictatus*, pp. of *dictare* to dictate] **:** a harsh settlement unilaterally imposed (as on a defeated nation)

di·lap·i·date \də-'lap-ə-ˌdāt\ *vb* [L *dilapidatus*, pp. of *dilapidare* to squander, destroy, fr. *dis-* + *lapidare* to throw stones, fr. *lapid-*, *lapis* stone — more at LAPIDARY] *vt* **1 :** to bring into a condition of decay or partial ruin by neglect or misuse **2** *archaic* **:** SQUANDER ~ *vi* **:** to become dilapidated — **di·lap·i·da·tion** \-ˌlap-ə-'dā-shən\ *n* — **di·lap·i·da·tor** \-'lap-ə-ˌdāt-ər\ *n*

di·lap·i·dat·ed *adj* **:** fallen into partial ruin or decay

di·lat·abil·i·ty \dī-ˌlāt-ə-'bil-ət-ē, dil-ˌāt-\ *n* **:** the property of being dilatable

di·lat·able \dī-'lāt-ə-bəl, dil-'āt-\ *adj* **:** capable of being dilated

di·la·tan·cy \dī-'lāt-ᵊn-sē, dil-'āt-\ *n* **:** the property of being dilatant

di·la·tant \-ᵊnt\ *adj* **:** increasing in viscosity and setting to a solid as a result of deformation by expansion, pressure, or agitation

di·la·ta·tion \ˌdil-ə-'tā-shən, ˌdī-lə-\ *n* **1 :** amplification in writing or speech **2 a :** the condition of being stretched beyond normal dimensions esp. as a result of overwork or disease ⟨~ of the heart⟩ or of abnormal relaxation ⟨~ of the stomach⟩ **b :** DILATION 2 **3 :** the action of expanding **:** the state of being expanded **4 :** a dilated part or formation — **di·la·ta·tion·al** \-shnəl, -shən-ᵊl\ *adj*

di·late \dī-'lāt, 'dī-ˌlāt, dil-'āt\ *vb* [ME *dilaten*, fr. MF *dilater*, fr. L *dilatare*, lit., to spread wide, fr. *dis-* + *latus* wide — more at LATITUDE] *vt* **1** *archaic* **:** to describe or set forth at length or in detail **2 :** to enlarge or expand in bulk or extent **:** DISTEND ~ *vi* **1 :** to comment at length **:** DISCOURSE **2 :** to become wide **:** SWELL **syn** see EXPAND — **di·la·tor** \-ər\ *n*

di·lat·ed *adj* **1 :** expanded laterally **2** *of an insect part* **:** having a broad expanded border **3 :** expanded normally or abnormally in all dimensions — **di·lat·ed·ly** *adv* — **di·lat·ed·ness** *n*

di·la·tion \dī-'lā-shən, dil-'ā-\ *n* **1 :** the act of dilating **:** the state of being dilated **:** EXPANSION, DILATATION **2 :** the action of stretching or enlarging an organ or part of the body

di·la·tive \-'lāt-iv\ *adj* **:** causing dilation **:** tending to dilate

di·la·tom·e·ter \ˌdil-ə-'täm-ət-ər, ˌdī-lə-\ *n* [ISV] **:** an instrument for measuring thermal expansion — **di·la·to·met·ric** \-tə-'me-trik\ *adj* — **di·la·tom·e·try** \-'täm-ə-trē\ *n*

dil·a·to·ri·ly \ˌdil-ə-'tōr-ə-lē, -'tȯr-\ *adv* **:** in a dilatory manner

dil·a·to·ri·ness \'dil-ə-ˌtōr-ē-nəs, -ˌtȯr-\ *n* **:** the quality or state of being dilatory

dil·a·to·ry \'dil-ə-ˌtōr-ē, -ˌtȯr-\ *adj* [LL *dilatorius*, fr. L *dilatus* (pp. of *differre* to postpone, differ), fr. *dis-* + *latus*, pp. of *ferre* to carry — more at DIFFER, TOLERATE] **1 :** tending or intended to cause delay ⟨~ tactics⟩ **2 :** characterized by procrastination **:** TARDY

di·lem·ma \də-'lem-ə\ *n* [LL, fr. LGk *dilēmmat-*, *dilēmma*, prob. back-formation fr. Gk *dilēmmatos* involving two assumptions, fr. *di-* + *lēmmat-*, *lēmma* assumption] **1 :** an argument presenting two or more alternatives equally conclusive against an opponent **2 a :** a choice or a situation involving choice between equally unsatisfactory alternatives **b :** a problem seemingly incapable of a satisfactory solution **syn** see PREDICAMENT — **dil·em·mat·ic** \ˌdil-ə-'mat-ik\ *adj*

dil·et·tante \ˌdil-ə-'tänt(-ē), -'tant(-ē)\ *n, pl* **dil·et·tantes** *or* **dil·et·tan·ti** \-'tänt-ē, -'tant-ē\ [It, fr. prp. of *dilettare* to delight, fr. L *dilectare*] **1 :** an admirer or lover of the arts **2 :** a person who cultivates an art or branch of knowledge as a pastime esp. sporadically or superficially **syn** see AMATEUR — **dilettante** *adj*

dil·et·tant·ish \-'tänt-ish, -'tant-\ *adj* **:** of, relating to, or characteristic of a dilettante

dil·et·tan·tism \-'tän-ˌtiz-əm, -'tan-\ *n* **:** dilettantish quality or procedure — **dil·et·tan·tist** \-'tänt-əst, -'tant-\ *adj*

1**dil·i·gence** \'dil-ə-jən(t)s\ *n* **1 a :** persevering application **:** ASSIDUITY **b** *obs* **:** SPEED, HASTE **2 :** the attention and care legally expected or required of a person

2**dil·i·gence** \'dil-ə-ˌzhäⁿs, 'dil-ə-jən(t)s\ *n* [F, lit., haste, fr. MF, persevering application, fr. L *diligentia*, fr. *diligent-*, *diligens*] **:** STAGECOACH

dil·i·gent \'dil-ə-jənt\ *adj* [ME, fr. MF, fr. L *diligent-*, *diligens*, fr. prp. of *diligere* to esteem, love, fr. *di-* + *legere* to select — more at LEGEND] **:** characterized by steady, earnest, and energetic application and effort **:** PAINSTAKING **syn** see BUSY — **dil·i·gent·ly** *adv*

dill \'dil\ *n* [ME *dile*, fr. OE; akin to OHG *tilli* dill] **1 :** any of several plants of the carrot family; *esp* **:** a European herb (*Anethum graveolens*) with aromatic foliage and seeds both of which are used in flavoring pickles and other foods **2 :** a dill pickle

dil·ly \'dil-ē\ *n, pl* **dillies** [obs. slang *dilly*, adj. (delightful), irreg. fr. E *delightful*] *slang* **:** one that is remarkable or outstanding

dil·ly bag \'dil-ē-\ *n* [Australian *dhilla* hair] **:** an Australian mesh bag of native fibers used for carrying various articles

dil·ly·dal·ly \'dil-ē-ˌdal-ē\ *vi* [redupl. of *dally*] **:** to waste time by loitering or delay **:** DAWDLE

1**dil·u·ent** \'dil-yə-wənt\ *n* [L *diluent-*, *diluens*, prp. of *diluere*] **:** a diluting agent

2**diluent** *adj* [L *diluent-*, *diluens*] **:** making thinner or less concentrated by admixture **:** DILUTING

1**di·lute** \dī-'lüt, də-\ *vt* [L *dilutus*, pp. of *diluere* to wash away, dilute, partly fr. *di-* + *lavere* to wash, partly fr. *di-* + *luere* to release, atone for] **1 :** to make thinner or more liquid by admixture **2 :** to diminish the strength, flavor, or brilliance of by admixture **3 :** ATTENUATE — **di·lut·er** *or* **di·lu·tor** \-'lüt-ər\ *n*

2**dilute** *adj* **:** DILUTED, WEAK — **di·lute·ness** *n*

di·lu·tion \dī-'lü-shən, də-\ *n* **1 :** the action of diluting **:** the state of being diluted **2 :** something (as a solution) that is diluted

di·lu·vi·al \də-'lü-vē-əl, dī-\ *or* **di·lu·vi·an** \-vē-ən\ *adj* [LL *diluvialis*, fr. L *diluvium* deluge] **:** of, relating to, or effected by a flood

1**dim** \'dim\ *adj* **dim·mer; dim·mest** [ME, fr. OE; akin to OHG *timber* dark, Skt *dhamati* he blows] **1 a :** emitting a limited or insufficient amount of light **b :** DULL, LUSTERLESS **c :** lacking pronounced, clear-cut, or vigorous quality or character **2 a :** seen indistinctly or without clear outlines or details **b :** perceived by the senses or mind indistinctly or weakly **c :** having little prospect of favorable result or outcome ⟨a ~ future⟩ **d :** characterized by an unfavorable, skeptical, or pessimistic attitude — usu. used in the phrase *take a dim view of* **3 :** not perceiving clearly and distinctly **syn** see DARK — **dim·ly** *adv* — **dim·ness** *n*

2**dim** *vb* **dimmed; dim·ming** *vt* **1 :** to make dim or lusterless

2 : to reduce the light from (headlights) by switching to the low beam ~ *vi* **:** to become dim

3**dim** *n* **1** *archaic* **:** DIMNESS, DUSK **2 a :** a small light on an automobile for use in parking **b :** LOW BEAM

dime \'dīm\ *n* [ME, tenth part, tithe, fr. MF, fr. L *decima*, fr. fem. of *decimus* tenth, fr. *decem* ten — more at TEN] **1 a :** a coin of the U.S. worth 1/10 dollar **b :** a petty sum of money **2 :** a Canadian ten-cent piece

di·men·hy·dri·nate \,dī-,men-'hī-drə-,nāt\ *n* [*di-* + *m*ethyl + amin*e* + *hydr-* + amin*e* + *-ate*] **:** a crystalline compound $C_{24}H_{28}ClN_5O_3$ used in the prevention or treatment of motion sickness

dime novel *n* **:** an inexpensive melodramatic novel

1**di·men·sion** \də-'men-chən, dī-\ *n* [ME, fr. MF, fr. L *dimension-, dimensio*, fr. *dimensus*, pp. of *dimetiri* to measure out, fr. *dis-* + *metiri* to measure — more at MEASURE] **1 a** (1) **:** extension in one direction; *specif* **:** one of three or four coordinates determining a position in space or space and time (2) **:** an element represented in an equation by a symbol that functions analogously to symbols representing the three spatial dimensions and regarded as a constituent of a geometric space **b :** magnitude of extension in one direction or in all directions **c :** the range over which or the degree to which something extends **:** SCOPE **2** *obs* **:** bodily form or proportions **3 :** wood or stone cut to pieces of specified size — **di·men·sion·al** \-'mench-nəl, -'men-chən-ᵊl\ *adj* — **di·men·sion·al·i·ty** \-,men-chə-'nal-ət-ē\ *n* — **di·men·sion·al·ly** *adv*

2**dimension** *vt* **di·men·sion·ing** \-'mench-(ə-)niŋ\ **1 :** to form to the required dimensions **2 :** to indicate the dimensions on

di·mer·ic \dī-'mer-ik\ *adj* [NL *dimerus*] **1 :** consisting of two parts ⟨a ~ chromosome⟩ **2 :** involving or mediated by two factors

dim·er·ism \'dim-ə-,riz-əm\ *n* [ISV] **:** the quality or state of being dimerous

dim·er·ous \'dim-ə-rəs\ *adj* [NL *dimerus*, fr. L *di-* + NL *-merus* -merous] **:** consisting of two parts: as **a** *of an insect* **:** having the tarsi two-jointed **b** *of a flower* **:** having two members in each whorl

dim·e·ter \'dim-ət-ər\ *n* [LL, fr. Gk *dimetros*, adj., being a dimeter, fr. *di-* + *metron* measure — more at MEASURE] **:** a verse consisting of two accentual feet or of two dipodies

di·min·ish \də-'min-ish\ *vb* [ME *deminishen*, alter. of *diminuen*, fr. MF *diminuer*, fr. LL *diminuere*, alter. of L *deminuere*, fr. *de-* + *minuere* to lessen] *vt* **1 :** to make less or cause to appear less **2 :** to lessen the authority, dignity, or reputation of **:** BELITTLE **3 :** to cause to taper ~ *vi* **1 :** DWINDLE **2 :** TAPER **syn** see DECREASE — **di·min·ish·able** \-ə-bəl\ *adj* — **di·min·ish·ment** \-mənt\ *n*

di·min·ished *adj, of a musical interval* **:** made one half step less than perfect or minor ⟨a ~ fifth⟩

diminishing returns *n pl* **:** a rate of yield that beyond a certain point fails to increase in proportion to additional investments

di·min·u·en·do \də-,min-(y)ə-'wen-(,)dō\ *adj* (*or adv*) [It, lit. *diminishing*, fr. LL *diminuendum*, gerund of *diminuere*] **:** DECRESCENDO — **diminuendo** *n, pl* **diminuendos** *or* **diminuendoes**

dim·i·nu·tion \,dim-ə-'n(y)ü-shən\ *n* [ME *diminucioun*, fr. MF *diminution*, fr. ML *diminution-, diminutio*, alter. of L *deminution-, deminutio*, fr. *deminutus*, pp. of *deminuere*] **:** the act, process, or an instance of diminishing **:** DECREASE

1**di·min·u·tive** \də-'min-yət-iv\ *n* [ME *diminutif*, fr. ML *diminutivum*, alter. of LL *deminutivum*, fr. neut. of *deminutivus*] **1 :** a diminutive word, affix, or name **2 :** a diminutive individual

2**diminutive** *adj* **1 :** indicating small size and sometimes the state or quality of being familiarly known, lovable, pitiable, or contemptible — used of affixes (as *-ette*, *-kin*, *-ling*) and of words formed with them (as *kitchenette*, *ladykin*, *witling*); compare AUGMENTATIVE **2 :** extremely small **:** TINY **syn** see SMALL — **di·min·u·tive·ly** *adv* — **di·min·u·tive·ness** *n*

dim·i·ty \'dim-ət-ē\ *n, pl* **dimities** [alter. of ME *demyt*, prob. fr. MGk *dimitos* of double thread, fr. Gk *di-* + *mitos* warp thread] **:** a sheer usu. corded cotton fabric of plain weave in checks or stripes

dim·mer \'dim-ər\ *n* **1 :** a device for causing an electric light to burn less brightly **2** *pl* **a :** small lights on an automobile for use in parking **b :** headlights on low beam

di·mor·phic \dī-'mȯr-fik\ *adj* **1 a :** DIMORPHOUS 1 **b :** occurring in two distinct forms ⟨~ leaves of emergent plants⟩ ⟨a sexually ~ butterfly⟩ **2 :** combining qualities of two kinds of individuals in one

di·mor·phism \-,fiz-əm\ *n* [ISV] **:** the condition or property of being dimorphic or dimorphous: as **a :** difference between two individuals that might be expected to be similar or identical **b :** crystallization of a chemical compound in two different forms

di·mor·pho·the·ca \(,)dī-,mȯr-fə-'thē-kə\ *n* [NL *Dimorphotheca*, genus name, fr. Gk *dimorphos* + NL *theca*] **:** any of a genus (*Dimorphotheca*) of southern African composite herbs or subshrubs with showy terminal solitary flower heads and conspicuously toothed leaves

di·mor·phous \dī-'mȯr-fəs\ *adj* [Gk *dimorphos* having two forms, fr. *di-* + *-morphos* -morphous] **1 :** crystallizing in two different forms **2 :** DIMORPHIC 1b

dim·out \'dim-,au̇t\ *n* **:** a restriction limiting the use or showing of lights at night esp. during the threat of an air raid; *also* **:** a condition of partial darkness produced by such restriction

1**dim·ple** \'dim-pəl\ *n* [ME *dympull*; akin to OHG *tumphilo* whirlpool, OE *dyppan* to dip — more at DIP] **1 :** a slight natural indentation in the surface of some part of the human body **2 :** a depression or indentation on any surface — **dim·ply** \-p(ə-)lē\ *adj*

2**dimple** *vb* **dim·pling** \-p(ə-)liŋ\ *vt* **:** to mark with dimples ~ *vi* **:** to exhibit or form dimples

dim·wit \'dim-,wit\ *n* **:** a stupid or mentally slow person

dim–wit·ted \-'wit-əd\ *adj* **:** not mentally bright **:** STUPID — **dim–wit·ted·ly** *adv* — **dim–wit·ted·ness** *n*

1**din** \'din\ *n* [ME, fr. OE *dyne*; akin to ON *dynr* din, Skt *dhvanati* it roars] **:** a loud noise; *esp* **:** a welter of discordant sounds

2**din** *vb* **dinned**; **din·ning** *vt* **1 :** to assail or deafen with loud noise **2 :** to impress by insistent repetition ~ *vi* **:** to make a loud noise

di·nar \di-'när, 'dē-,när\ *n* [Ar *dīnār*, fr. Gk *dēnarion* denarius, fr. L *denarius*] **1 :** a gold coin first struck in the late 7th century A.D. that became the basic monetary unit in Muslim territories **2 —** see MONEY table

1**dine** \'dīn\ *vb* [ME *dinen*, fr. OF *diner*, fr. (assumed) VL *disjejunare* to break one's fast, fr. L *dis-* + LL *jejunare* to fast, fr. L *jejunus* fasting] *vi* **:** to take dinner ~ *vt* **:** to give a dinner to **:** FEED

2**dine** *n, Scot* **:** DINNER

din·er \'dī-nər\ *n* **1 :** one that dines **2 a :** DINING CAR **b :** a restaurant built in the shape of a railroad dining car

di·nette \dī-'net\ *n* **:** a small space usu. off a kitchen or pantry used for informal dining; *also* **:** furniture for such a space

ding *vb* [prob. imit.] *vt* **:** to talk or impress with tiresome repetition ~ *vi* **:** to make a ringing sound **:** CLANG

1**ding·dong** \'diŋ-,dȯŋ, -,däŋ\ *n* [imit.] **:** the ringing sound produced by repeated strokes on a bell or some other metallic object

2**dingdong** *vi* **1 :** to make a dingdong sound **2 :** to repeat a sound or action tediously or insistently

3**dingdong** *adj* **1 :** of, relating to, or resembling the ringing sound made by a bell **2 :** marked by a rapid exchange or alternation

din·ghy \'diŋ-(k)ē\ *n* [Bengali *ḍiṅgi* & Hindi *ḍiṅgī*] **1 :** an East Indian rowboat or sailboat **2 :** a ship's small boat **3 :** a rowboat used as a tender **4 :** a rubber life raft

din·gi·ly \'din-jə-lē\ *adv* **:** in a dingy manner

din·gi·ness \-jē-nəs\ *n* **:** the condition of being dingy

din·gle \'diŋ-gəl\ *n* [ME, abyss] **:** a small wooded valley

din·gle·ber·ry \'diŋ-gəl-,ber-ē\ *n* [origin unknown] **:** a shrub (*Vaccinium erythrocarpus*) of the southeastern U.S.; *also* **:** its globose dark red edible berry

din·go \'diŋ-(,)gō\ *n, pl* **dingoes** [native name in Australia] **:** a reddish brown wild dog (*Canis dingo*) of Australia

din·gus \'diŋ-(g)əs\ *n* [D or G; D *dinges*, prob. fr. G *dings*, fr. gen. of *ding* thing, fr. OHG — more at THING] **:** something (as a gadget) whose common name is unknown or forgotten

din·gy \'din-jē\ *adj* **din·gi·er**; **din·gi·est** [origin unknown] **1 :** DIRTY, DISCOLORED **2 :** SHABBY, SQUALID

dining car *n* **:** a railroad car in which meals are served

di·ni·tro·ben·zene \(,)dī-,nī-trō-'ben-,zēn, -,ben-'zēn\ *n* [ISV] **:** any of three isomeric toxic compounds $C_6H_4(NO_2)_2$ formed by nitration of benzene or nitrobenzene; *esp* **:** the yellow meta-isomer used chiefly as a dye intermediate

din·key *or* **din·ky** \'diŋ-kē\ *n* [prob. fr. *dinky*] **:** a small locomotive used esp. for hauling freight, logging, and shunting

din·ky \'diŋ-kē\ *adj* [Sc *dink* neat] **:** SMALL, INSIGNIFICANT

din·ner \'din-ər\ *n* [ME *diner*, fr. OF, fr. *diner* to dine] **1 a :** the principal meal of the day **b :** a formal feast or banquet **2 :** TABLE D'HÔTE 2

dinner jacket *n* **:** TUXEDO

di·no·flag·el·late \,dī-nō-'flaj-ə-lət, -,lāt; -flə-'jel-ət\ *n* [deriv. o Gk *dinos* rotation, eddy + NL *flagellum*] **:** any of an order (Dinoflagellata) of chiefly marine planktonic usu. solitary plantlike flagellates that include luminescent forms, forms important in marine food chains, and forms causing red tide

di·no·saur \'dī-nə-,sȯ(ə)r\ *n* [deriv. of Gk *deinos* terrible + *sauros* lizard — more at DIRE, SAURIAN] **1 :** any of a group (Dinosauria) of extinct chiefly terrestrial carnivorous or herbivorous reptiles **2 :** any of various large extinct reptiles — **di·no·sau·ri·an** \,dī-nə-'sȯr-ē-ən\ *adj or n* — **di·no·sau·ric** \-'sȯr-ik\ *adj*

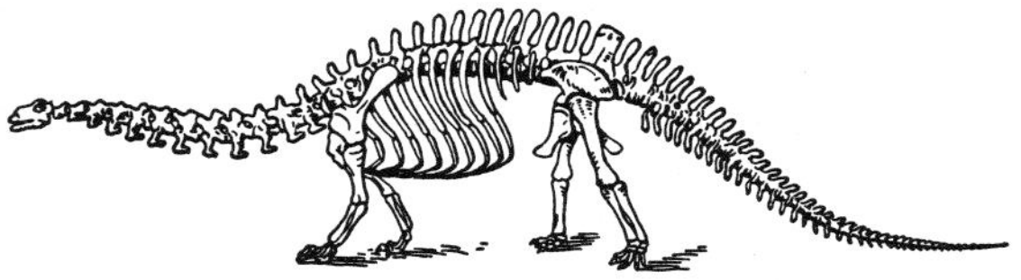

dinosaur skeleton restored

di·no·there \'dī-nə-,thi(ə)r\ *n* [NL *Deinotherium*, genus name, fr. Gk *deinos* + NL *-therium*] **:** any of a genus (*Deinotherium*) of extinct proboscidean mammals with a pair of downward-directed tusks

1**dint** \'dint\ *n* [ME, fr. OE *dynt*] **1** *archaic* **:** BLOW, STROKE **2 :** FORCE, POWER — used chiefly in the phrase *by dint of* **3 :** DENT

2**dint** *vt* **1 :** to make a dint in **2 :** to impress or drive in with force

1**di·oc·e·san** \dī-'äs-ə-sən\ *adj* **:** of or relating to a diocese

2**diocesan** *n* **:** a bishop having jurisdiction over a diocese

di·o·cese \'dī-ə-səs, -,sēz, -,sēs\ *n, pl* **di·o·ces·es** \-sə-səz, -,sē-zəz, -,sē-səz, -ə-,sēz\ [ME *diocise*, fr. MF, fr. LL *diocesis*, alter. of *dioecesis*, fr. L, administrative division, fr. Gk *dioikēsis* administration, administrative division, fr. *dioikein* to keep house, govern, fr. *dia-* + *oikein* to dwell, manage, fr. *oikos* house — more at VICINITY] **:** the territorial jurisdiction of a bishop

di·ode \'dī-,ōd\ *n* [ISV] **1 :** a two-electrode electron tube having a cathode and an anode **2 :** a rectifier consisting of a semiconducting crystal with two terminals and analogous to an electron tube diode

di·oe·cious \(')dī-'ē-shəs\ *adj* [deriv. of Gk *di-* + *oikos* house] **1 :** having male reproductive organs in one individual and female in another **2 :** having staminate and pistillate flowers borne on different individuals — **di·oe·cious·ly** *adv* — **di·oe·cism** \-'ē-,siz-əm\ *n*

di·oi·cous \-'ȯi-kəs\ *adj* [NL *dioicus*, fr. *di-* + Gk *oikos*] **:** having archegonia and antheridia on separate plants

Di·o·me·des \,dī-ə-'mēd-ēz\ *n* [L, fr. Gk *Diomēdēs*] **:** a Greek warrior in the Trojan War

Di·o·ny·sia \,dī-ə-'nizh-ē-ə, -'nis(h)-\ *n pl* [L, fr. Gk, fr. neut. pl. of *dionysios* of Dionysus fr. *Dionysos*] **:** any of the ancient Greek festivals in honor of Dionysus; *esp* **:** an autumn festival held in Attica from which the Greek drama is held to have developed

Di·o·nys·i·ac \-'nis-ē-,ak\ *adj* [L *dionysiacus*, fr. Gk *dionysiakos*, fr. *Dionysos*] **:** DIONYSIAN 2

Di·o·ny·sian *adj* **1** \,dī-ə-'nis(h)-ē-ən, -'nish-ən, -'nī-sē-ən\ **:** of or relating to Dionysius **2** \-'nizh-ən, -'nish-ən, -'nī-sē-ən\ **a :** devoted to the worship of Dionysus **b :** of a sensuous, frenzied, or orgiastic character

Di·o·ny·sus \,dī-ə-'nī-səs\ *n* [L, fr. Gk *Dionysos*] **:** the god of wine in Greek mythology

di·op·side \dī-'äp-,sīd\ *n* [F, fr. *di-* + Gk *opsis* appearance] **:** a green to white pyroxene containing little or no aluminum

di·op·ter *also* **di·op·tre** \dī-'äp-tər\ *n* [*diopter* (an optical instrument), fr. MF *dioptre*, fr. L *dioptra*, fr. Gk, fr. *dia-* + *opsesthai* to be going to see] **:** a unit of measurement of the refractive power of lenses equal to the reciprocal of the focal length in meters

di·op·tom·e·ter \(,)dī-,äp-'täm-ət-ər\ *n* **:** an instrument used in measuring the accommodation and refraction of the eye — **di·op·tom·e·try** \-'täm-ə-trē\ *n*

di·op·tric \dī-'äp-trik\ *adj* [Gk *dioptrikos* of a diopter (instru-

ment), fr. *dioptra*] **1 :** that effects or serves in refraction of a beam of light **:** REFRACTIVE; *specif* **:** that assists vision by refracting and focalizing light **2 :** produced by means of refraction

di·o·ra·ma \ˌdī-ə-ˈram-ə, -ˈräm-\ *n* [F, fr. *dia-* + *-orama* (as in *panorama*, fr. E)] **1 :** a scenic representation in which a partly translucent painting is seen from a distance through an opening **2 a :** a scenic representation in which sculptured figures and lifelike details are displayed usu. in miniature so as to blend indistinguishably with a realistic painted background **b :** a life-size exhibit of a wildlife specimen or scene with realistic natural surroundings and a painted background — **di·o·ram·ic** \-ˈram-ik\ *adj*

di·o·rite \ˈdī-ə-ˌrīt\ *n* [F, irreg. fr. Gk *diorizein* to distinguish, fr. *dia-* + *horizein* to define — more at HORIZON] **:** a granular crystalline igneous rock commonly of acid plagioclase and hornblende, pyroxene, or biotite — **di·o·rit·ic** \ˌdī-ə-ˈrit-ik\ *adj*

Di·os·cu·ri \dī-ˈäs-kyə-ˌrī, ˌdī-ə-ˈskyu̇(ə)r-ˌī\ *n pl* [Gk *Dioskouroi*, lit., sons of Zeus, fr. *Dios* (gen. of *Zeus;* akin to L *divus* divine) + *kouroi*, pl. of *koros, kouros* boy, son] **:** the twins Castor and Pollux reunited after Castor's death by Zeus's decree that they live in the upper and lower worlds on alternate days

di·ox·ide \(ˈ)dī-ˈäk-ˌsīd\ *n* [ISV] **:** an oxide containing two atoms of oxygen in the molecule ⟨carbon ~⟩

¹dip \ˈdip\ *vb* **dipped; dip·ping** [ME *dippen*, fr. OE *dyppan;* akin to OHG *tupfen* to wash, Lith *dubus* deep] *vt* **1 a :** to plunge or immerse momentarily or partially under the surface (as of a liquid) so as to moisten, cool, or coat **b :** to thrust in a way to suggest immersion **c :** to immerse (as a hog) in an antiseptic or parasiticidal solution **2 :** to lift a portion of by reaching below the surface with something shaped to hold liquid **:** LADLE **3 a** *archaic* **:** INVOLVE **b :** MORTGAGE **4 :** to lower and then raise again ⟨~ a flag in salute⟩ ~ *vi* **1 a :** to plunge into a liquid and quickly emerge **b :** to immerse something into a processing liquid or finishing material **2 a :** to drop down or out of sight esp. suddenly **b** *of a plane* **:** to drop suddenly before climbing **c :** to decline or decrease moderately and usu. temporarily ⟨prices *dipped*⟩ **3 :** to reach down inside or below a surface esp. to withdraw a part of the contents **4 :** to delve casually or tentatively into something; *specif* **:** to read superficially **5 :** to incline downward from the plane of the horizon

²dip *n* **1 :** an act of dipping: as **a :** a brief plunge into the water for sport or exercise **b :** an exercise on the parallel bars in which the performer rests on his hands, lets his arms bend until his chin is level with the bars, and then raises himself by straightening his arms **2 :** inclination downward: **a :** PITCH **b :** a sharp downward course **:** DROP **c :** the angle that a stratum or similar geological feature makes with a horizontal plane **3 :** the angle formed with the horizon by a magnetic needle free to rotate in the vertical plane **4 :** HOLLOW, DEPRESSION **5 :** something obtained by or used in dipping **6 :** a liquid preparation into which something may be dipped **7** *slang* **:** PICKPOCKET

di·phase \ˈdī-ˌfāz\ *or* **di·pha·sic** \(ˈ)dī-ˈfā-zik\ *adj* **:** having two phases

di·phe·nyl \(ˈ)dī-ˈfen-ᵊl, -ˈfēn-\ *n* **:** BIPHENYL

di·phe·nyl·amine \(ˌ)dī-ˌfen-ᵊl-ə-ˈmēn, -ˌfēn-, -ᵊl-ˈam-ən\ *n* [ISV] **:** a crystalline pleasant-smelling compound $(C_6H_5)_2NH$ used chiefly in the manufacture of dyes and in stabilizing explosives

di·phos·gene \(ˈ)dī-ˈfäz-ˌjēn\ *n* [ISV] **:** a liquid compound $ClCOOCCl_3$ used in World War I as a poison gas

diph·the·ria \dif-ˈthir-ē-ə, dip-\ *n* [NL, fr. F *diphthérie*, fr. Gk *diphthera* leather; fr. the toughness of the false membrane] **:** an acute febrile contagious disease marked by the formation of a false membrane esp. in the throat and caused by a bacterium which produces a toxin causing inflammation of the heart and nervous system — **diph·the·ri·al** \-ē-əl\ *or* **diph·the·ri·an** \-ē-ən\ *adj* — **diph·the·rit·ic** \ˌdif-thə-ˈrit-ik, ˌdip-\ *adj*

diph·thong \ˈdif-ˌthȯŋ, ˈdip-\ *n* [ME *diptonge*, fr. MF *diptongue*, fr. LL *dipthongus*, fr. Gk *diphthongos*, fr. *di-* + *phthongos* voice, sound] **1 :** a gliding monosyllabic speech item that starts at or near the articulatory position for one vowel and moves to or toward the position for another (as the vowel combination that forms the last part of *toy*) **2 :** DIGRAPH **3 :** a form of the ligature æ or œ — **diph·thon·gal** \dif-ˈthȯŋ-(g)əl, dip-\ *adj*

diph·thong·iza·tion \(ˌ)dif-ˌthȯŋ-ə-ˈzā-shən, (ˌ)dip-\ *n* **:** the act of diphthongizing **:** the state of being diphthongized

diph·thong·ize \ˈdif-ˌthȯŋ-ˌīz, ˈdip-\ *vi, of a simple vowel* **:** to change into a diphthong ~ *vt* **:** to pronounce as a diphthong

diphy- *or* **diphyo-** *comb form* [NL, fr. Gk *diphy-*, fr. *diphyēs*, fr. *di-* + *phyein* to bring forth] **:** double **:** bipartite ⟨*diphy*odont⟩

diphy·cer·cal \ˌdif-i-ˈsər-kəl\ *adj* **1** *of a tail fin* **:** having the upper and lower portions alike or nearly so and the vertebral column extending to the tip **2 :** having a diphycercal tail fin —**diphy·cer·cy** \ˈdif-i-ˌsər-sē, -ˌsər-kē\ *n*

di·phy·let·ic \ˌdī-(ˌ)fī-ˈlet-ik\ *adj* **:** derived from two lines of descent ⟨~ dinosaurs⟩

di·phyl·lous \(ˈ)dī-ˈfil-əs\ *adj* [NL *diphyllus*, fr. *di-* + *-phyllus* -phyllous] **:** having two leaves

di·phy·odont \(ˈ)dī-ˈfī-ə-ˌdänt\ *adj* [ISV] **:** marked by the development of deciduous and permanent sets of teeth successively

dipl- *or* **diplo-** *comb form* [Gk, fr. *diploos* — more at DOUBLE] **1 :** double **:** twofold ⟨*diplo*pia⟩ **2 :** diploid ⟨*diplo*phase⟩

di·ple·gia \dī-ˈplē-j(ē-)ə\ *n* [NL] **:** paralysis of corresponding parts on both sides of the body

di·plex \ˈdī-ˌpleks\ *adj* [alter. of *duplex*] **:** relating to or being simultaneous transmission or reception of two radio signals

dip·lo·ba·cil·lus \ˌdip-lō-bə-ˈsil-əs\ *n* [NL] **:** any of various small aerobic gram-negative bacilli parasitic on mucous membranes

dip·lo·blas·tic \ˌdip-lō-ˈblas-tik\ *adj* **:** having two germ layers — used of an embryo or lower invertebrate that lacks a true mesoderm

dip·lo·coc·cal \-ˈkäk-əl\ *or* **dip·lo·coc·cic** \-ˈkäk-(s)ik\ *adj* **:** of, relating to, or caused by diplococci

dip·lo·coc·cus \-ˈkäk-əs\ *n* [NL, genus name] **:** any of a genus (*Diplococcus*) of gram-positive encapsulated bacteria that occur usu. in pairs, are parasitic, and include serious pathogens

di·plod·o·cus \də-ˈpläd-ə-kəs, dī-\ *n* [NL, genus name, fr. *dipl-* + Gk *dokos* beam, fr. *dekesthai, dechesthai* to receive; akin to L *decēre* to be fitting — more at DECENT] **:** any of a genus (*Diplodocus*) of very large herbivorous dinosaurs from Colorado and Wyoming

dip·loe \ˈdip-lə-ˌwē\ *n* [NL, fr. Gk *diploē*, fr. *diploos* double] **:** cancellous bony tissue between the external and internal layers of the skull — **di·plo·ic** \də-ˈplō-ik, dī-\ *adj*

¹dip·loid \ˈdip-ˌlȯid\ *adj* **:** double or twofold in appearance or arrangement; *esp* **:** having the basic chromosome number doubled — **dip·loi·dy** \-ˌlȯid-ē\ *n*

²diploid *n* **1 :** a diploid cell **2 :** an individual or generation characterized by the diploid chromosome number

di·plo·ma \də-ˈplō-mə\ *n, pl* **diplomas** [L, passport, diploma, fr. Gk *diplōma* folded paper, passport, fr. *diploun* to double, fr. *diploos*] **1** *or pl* **di·plo·ma·ta** \-mət-ə\ **:** an official or state document **:** CHARTER **2 :** a writing usu. under seal conferring some honor or privilege **3 :** a document bearing record of graduation from or of a degree conferred by an educational institution

di·plo·ma·cy \də-ˈplō-mə-sē\ *n* **1 :** the art and practice of conducting negotiations between nations **2 :** skill in handling affairs without arousing hostility **:** TACT

dip·lo·mat \ˈdip-lə-ˌmat\ *n* [F *diplomate*, back-formation fr. *diplomatique*] **:** one employed or skilled in diplomacy

dip·lo·mat·ic \ˌdip-lə-ˈmat-ik\ *adj* [in sense 1, fr. NL *diplomaticus*, fr. L *diplomat-, diploma;* in other senses, fr. F *diplomatique* connected with documents regulating international relations, fr. NL *diplomaticus*] **1 a :** PALEOGRAPHIC **b :** exactly reproducing the original ⟨a ~ edition⟩ **2 a :** concerned with or skilled in international relations **b :** of or relating to those conducting international relations ⟨~ immunity⟩ **3 :** employing tact and conciliation **syn** see SUAVE — **dip·lo·mat·i·cal·ly** \-i-k(ə-)lē\ *adv*

di·plo·ma·tist \də-ˈplō-mət-əst\ *n* **:** DIPLOMAT

dip·lont \ˈdip-ˌlänt\ *n* [ISV] **:** an organism with somatic cells having the diploid chromosome number — compare HAPLONT — **dip·lon·tic** \dip-ˈlänt-ik\ *adj*

dip·lo·phase \ˈdip-lō-ˌfāz\ *n* **:** a diploid phase in a life cycle

dip·lo·pia \dip-ˈlō-pē-ə\ *n* [NL] **:** double vision of an object owing to unequal action of the eye muscles — **dip·lo·pic** \-ˈlō-pik, -ˈläp-ik\ *adj*

dip·lo·pod \ˈdip-lə-ˌpäd\ *n* [deriv. of Gk *dipl-* + *pod-, pous* foot — more at FOOT] **:** MILLIPEDE — **dip·lop·o·dous** \dip-ˈläp-əd-əs\ *adj*

dip·lo·sis \dip-ˈlō-səs\ *n* [NL, fr. Gk *diplōsis* action of doubling, fr. *diploun*] **:** restoration of the somatic chromosome number by fusion of two gametes in fertilization

dip·no·an \ˈdip-nə-wən\ *adj* [deriv. of Gk *dipnoos*, fr. *di-* + *pnoē* breath, fr. *pnein* to breathe] **:** of or relating to a group (Dipnoi) of fishes with pulmonary circulation, gills, and lungs — **dipnoan** *n*

dip·o·dy \ˈdip-əd-ē\ *n* [LL *dipodia*, fr. Gk, fr. *dipod-, dipous* having two feet, fr. *di-* + *pod-, pous*] **:** a prosodic unit or measure of two feet

di·po·lar \ˈdī-ˌpō-lər\ *adj* **:** of, relating to, or having a dipole

di·pole \ˈdī-ˌpōl\ *n* [ISV] **1 a :** a pair of equal and opposite electric charges or magnetic poles of opposite sign separated by a small distance **b :** a body or system (as a molecule) having such charges **2 :** a radio antenna consisting of two horizontal rods in line with each other with their ends slightly separated

dip·per \ˈdip-ər\ *n* [ME *dippere*, a diving bird, fr. *dippen* to dip] **1 :** one that dips: as **a :** a worker who dips articles **b :** something (as a long-handled cup) used for dipping **2** *cap* **a :** the seven principal stars in the constellation of Ursa Major arranged in a form resembling a dipper — called also *Big Dipper* **b :** the seven principal stars in Ursa Minor similarly arranged with the North Star forming the outer end of the handle — called also *Little Dipper* **3 :** any of several birds (as a bufflehead) skilled in diving

di·pro·pel·lant \ˌdī-prə-ˈpel-ənt\ *n* **:** BIPROPELLANT

dip·so·ma·nia \ˌdip-sə-ˈmā-nē-ə, -nyə\ *n* [NL, fr. Gk *dipsa* + LL *mania*] **:** an uncontrollable craving for alcoholic liquors — **dip·so·ma·ni·ac** \-nē-ˌak\ *n* — **dip·so·ma·ni·a·cal** \ˌdip-sō-mə-ˈnī-ə-kəl\ *adj*

dip·stick \ˈdip-ˌstik\ *n* **:** a graduated rod for indicating depth

dip·ter·an \ˈdip-tə-rən\ *adj* [deriv. of Gk *dipteros*] **:** of, relating to, or being a two-winged fly — **dipteran** *n*

dip·ter·on \ˈdip-tə-ˌrän\ *n, pl* **dip·tera** \-rə\ [Gk, neut. of *dipteros*] **:** TWO-WINGED FLY

dip·ter·ous \-rəs\ *adj* [NL *dipterus*, fr. Gk *dipteros*, fr. *di-* + *pteron* wing — more at FEATHER] **1 :** having two wings or winglike appendages **2 :** of or relating to the two-winged flies

dip·tych \ˈdip-(ˌ)tik\ *n* [LL *diptycha*, pl., fr. Gk, fr. neut. pl. of *diptychos* folded in two, fr. *di-* + *ptychē* fold] **1 :** a 2-leaved hinged tablet folding together to protect writing on its waxed surfaces **2 :** a picture or series of pictures (as an altarpiece) painted on two hinged tablets **3 :** a work made up of two matching parts

dir·dum \ˈdi(ə)rd-əm, ˈdərd-\ *n* [ME (northern dial.) *durdan*, fr. ScGael, grumbling, hum, dim. of *durd* hum] *Scot* **:** BLAME

dire \ˈdī(ə)r\ *adj* [L *dirus;* akin to Gk *deinos* terrible, Skt *dveṣti* he hates] **1 a :** exciting horror ⟨~ suffering⟩ **b :** DISMAL **2 :** warning of disaster ⟨a ~ forecast⟩ **3 a :** desperately urgent ⟨~ need⟩ **b :** EXTREME ⟨~ poverty⟩ — **dire·ly** *adv* — **dire·ness** *n*

¹di·rect \də-ˈrekt, dī-\ *vb* [ME *directen*, fr. L *directus*, pp. of *dirigere* to set straight, direct] *vt* **1 a** *obs* **:** to write to a person **b :** to mark with the name and address of the intended recipient **c :** to impart orally **d :** to adapt in expression so as to have particular applicability **2 :** to cause to turn, move, or point undeviatingly or to follow a straight course **3 :** to point, extend, or project in a specified line or course **4 :** to show or point out the way for **5 a :** to regulate the activities or course of **b :** to carry out the organizing, energizing, and supervising of **c :** to dominate and determine the course of **d :** to train and lead performances of **6 :** to request or enjoin with authority ~ *vi* **1 :** to point out, prescribe, or determine a course or procedure **2 :** to act as director **syn** see COMMAND, CONDUCT

²direct *adj* [ME, fr. L *directus*, fr. pp. of *dirigere*] **1 :** proceeding from one point to another in time or space without deviation or interruption **:** STRAIGHT **2 a :** stemming immediately from a source ⟨~ result⟩ **b :** being or passing in a straight line of descent from parent to offspring **:** LINEAL ⟨~ ancestor⟩ **c :** having no compromising or impairing element ⟨~ insult⟩ **3 :** characterized by close logical, causal, or consequential relationship ⟨~ evidence⟩ **4 :** NATURAL, STRAIGHTFORWARD ⟨~ manner⟩ **5 a :** marked by absence of an intervening agency, instrumentality, or influence **b :** effected by the action of the people or the electorate and not by representatives **c :** consisting of or reproducing the exact words of a speaker **6 :** capable of dyeing without the aid of a mordant **:** SUBSTANTIVE **7** *of a celestial body* **:** moving in the general planetary

direction from west to east — **direct** *adv* — **di·rect·ness** \-'rek(t)-nəs\ *n*

syn DIRECT, IMMEDIATE mean uninterrupted. DIRECT suggests unbroken connection or a straight bearing of one upon or toward another ⟨*direct* sunlight⟩ IMMEDIATE suggests the absence of any intervening object, medium, or influence ⟨*immediate* successor⟩

direct action *n* **:** action that seeks to achieve an end directly and by the most immediately effective means (as boycott or strike)

direct current *n* **:** an electric current flowing in one direction only and substantially constant in value

di·rect·ed *adj* **:** having a positive or negative sense ⟨~ line segment⟩

di·rec·tion \də-'rek-shən, dī-\ *n* **1 a :** guidance or supervision of action or conduct **b :** the art and technique of directing an orchestra or theatrical production **c :** a word, phrase, or sign indicating the appropriate tempo, mood, or intensity of a passage or movement in music **2** *archaic* **:** SUPERSCRIPTION **3 a :** something imposed as authoritative instruction or bidding **:** ORDER **b :** an explicit instruction **4 :** the line or course on which something is moving or is aimed to move or along which something is pointing or facing **5 a :** a channel or direct course of thought or action **b :** TENDENCY, TREND **c :** guiding or governing purpose **6** *archaic* **:** DIRECTORATE 1

di·rec·tion·al \-shnəl, -shən-ᵊl\ *adj* **1 :** relating to or indicating direction in space: **a :** suitable for detecting the direction from which radio signals come or for sending out radio signals in one direction only **b :** operating most effectively in a particular direction **2 :** relating to direction or guidance esp. of thought or effort

direction finder *n* **:** a radio receiving device for determining the direction of incoming radio waves typically consisting of a coil antenna rotating freely on a vertical axis

direction indicator *n* **:** a compass that assists an airplane pilot in flying a predetermined course by direct reading and comparison of two indicators one of which is set for the desired heading while the other shows the actual heading so that when the two indicators point alike the airplane is flying the desired course

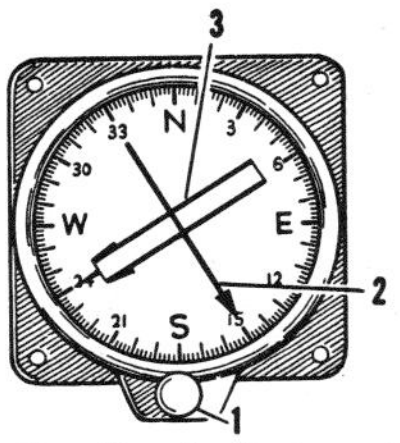

direction indicator: *1* index setting knob, *2* pointer, *3* index

1**di·rec·tive** \də-'rek-tiv, dī-\ *adj* **1 :** serving or qualified to guide or govern **2 :** serving to point direction; *specif* **:** DIRECTIONAL 1b

2**directive** *n* **:** something that serves to direct, guide, and usu. impel toward an action, attainment, or goal; *specif* **:** an authoritative instrument issued by a high-level official body or competent official

di·rec·tiv·i·ty \də-,rek-'tiv-ət-ē, (,)dī-\ *n* **:** the property of being directional

direct lighting *n* **:** lighting in which the greater part of the light goes directly from the source to the area lit

1**di·rect·ly** \də-'rek-(t)lē, dī-, *in sense 2* də-'rek-lē *or* 'drek-lē\ *adv* **1 :** in a direct manner **2 :** without delay **:** IMMEDIATELY

2**di·rect·ly** \də-'rek-(t)lē, dī-; 'drek-lē\ *conj, chiefly Brit* **:** immediately after **:** as soon as

direct object *n* **:** a grammatical object representing the primary goal or the result of the action of its verb ⟨*me* in "he hit me" and *house* in "we built a house" are *direct objects*⟩

di·rec·tor \də-'rek-tər, dī-\ *n* **:** one that directs: as **a :** the head of an organized group or administrative unit (as a bureau or school) **b :** one of a group of persons entrusted with the overall direction of a corporate enterprise **c :** one that supervises the production of a show (as for stage or screen) with responsibility for action, lighting, music, and rehearsals **d :** CONDUCTOR c

di·rec·tor·ate \də-'rek-t(ə-)rət, dī-\ *n* **1 :** the office of director **2 :** a board of directors (as of a corporation)

di·rec·to·ri·al \də-,rek-'tōr-ē-əl, (,)dī-, -'tȯr-\ *adj* **1 :** serving to direct **2 :** of or relating to a director or to theatrical direction **3 :** of, relating to, or administered by a directory

1**di·rec·to·ry** \də-'rek-t(ə-)rē, dī-\ *adj* **:** serving to direct; *specif* **:** providing advisory but not compulsory guidance

2**directory** *n* [ML *directorium*, fr. neut. of LL *directorius* directorial, fr. L *directus*, pp.] **1 a :** a book or collection of directions, rules, or ordinances **b :** an alphabetical or classified list containing names and addresses **2 :** a body of directors

direct primary *n* **:** a primary at which direct nominations of candidates for office are made

di·rec·tress \də-'rek-trəs, dī-\ *n* **:** a female director

di·rec·trix \-triks\ *n* [ML, fem. of LL *director*, fr. L *directus*, pp.] **1** *archaic* **:** DIRECTRESS **2 a :** a fixed line by relation to which a conic section is described **b :** a line or curve with which a generatrix of a surface remains in contact

direct tax *n* **:** a tax exacted directly from the person on whom the ultimate burden of the tax is expected to fall

dire·ful \'dī(ə)r-fəl\ *adj* **:** producing dire effects: **a :** DREADFUL **b :** WOEFUL **c :** OMINOUS — **dire·ful·ly** \-fə-lē\ *adv*

dirge \'dərj\ *n* [ME *dirige*, the Office of the Dead, fr. the first word of a LL antiphon, fr. L, imper. of *dirigere*] **1 :** a song or hymn of grief or lamentation; *esp* **:** one intended to accompany funeral or memorial rites **2 :** any slow, solemn, and mournful piece of music

dir·ham \də-'ram\ *n* [Ar, fr. L *drachma* drachma] — see MONEY table

1**di·ri·gi·ble** \'dir-ə-jə-bəl, də-'rij-ə-\ *adj* [L *dirigere*] **:** STEERABLE

2**dirigible** *n* [*dirigible* (*balloon*)] **:** AIRSHIP

dirk \'dərk\ *n* [Sc *durk*] **:** a long straight-bladed dagger — **dirk** *vt*

dirl \'dir(ə)l, 'dərl\ *vi* [prob. alter. of *thirl*] *Scot* **:** TREMBLE, QUIVER

dirndl \'dərn-dᵊl\ *n* [short for G *dirndlkleid*, fr. G dial. *dirndl* girl + G *kleid* dress] **1 :** a dress style with tight bodice, short sleeves, low neck, and gathered skirt **2 :** a full skirt with a tight waistband

dirt \'dərt\ *n, often attrib* [ME *drit*, fr. ON; akin to OE *drītan* to defecate, L *foria* diarrhea] **1 a :** EXCREMENT **b :** a filthy or soiling substance (as mud, dust, or grime) **c** *archaic* **:** something worthless **2 a :** loose or packed soil or sand **:** EARTH **b** (1) **:** alluvial earth in placer mining (2) **:** slate and waste in coal mines **3 a :** an abject or filthy state **:** SQUALOR **b :** CORRUPTION, CHICANERY **c :** licentiousness of language or theme **d :** scandalous or malicious gossip

dirt·i·ly \'dərt-ᵊl-ē\ *adv* **:** in a dirty manner

dirt·i·ness \'dərt-ē-nəs\ *n* **:** the quality or state of being dirty

1**dirty** \'dərt-ē\ *adj* **1 a :** not clean or pure ⟨~ linen⟩ **b :** likely to befoul or defile with dirt ⟨~ job⟩ **c :** tedious, disagreeable, and unrecognized or thankless ⟨assistants did the ~ work⟩ **d :** contaminated with infecting organisms ⟨~ wounds⟩ **2 a :** BASE, SORDID ⟨war is a ~ business⟩ **b :** UNSPORTSMANLIKE **c :** highly regrettable **:** GRIEVOUS ⟨~ shame⟩ **3 :** INDECENT, SMUTTY **4 :** FOGGY, STORMY **5 a** *of color* **:** not clear and bright **:** DULLISH **b :** characterized by a husky, rasping, or raw tonal quality **6 :** conveying ill-natured resentment **7 :** having considerable fallout

syn DIRTY, FILTHY, FOUL, NASTY, SQUALID mean conspicuously unclean or impure. DIRTY emphasizes the fact of the presence of dirt rather than an emotional reaction; FILTHY adds the suggestion of offensiveness and usu. of dirt that disfigures or clutters up; FOUL implies extreme offensiveness and an accumulation of what is rotten or stinking; NASTY applies to what is actually foul or is repugnant to one accustomed to or expecting cleanliness, freshness, or sweetness; SQUALID implies extreme dirtiness and extreme slovenliness or neglect. All these terms apply to obscenity or to morally reprehensible acts; the first four often to rainy or foggy weather

2**dirty** *vt* **1 :** to make dirty **2 a :** to stain with dishonor **b :** to debase by distorting the real nature of ~ *vi* **:** to become soiled

dis- *prefix* [ME *dis-*, *des-*, fr. OF & L; OF *des-*, *dis-*, fr. L *dis-*, lit., apart; akin to OE *te-* apart, L *duo* two — more at TWO] **1 a :** do the opposite of ⟨*dis*establish⟩ **b :** deprive of (a specified quality, rank, or object) ⟨*dis*able⟩ ⟨*dis*prince⟩ ⟨*dis*frock⟩ **c :** exclude or expel from ⟨*dis*bar⟩ **2 :** opposite or absence of ⟨*dis*union⟩ ⟨*dis*affection⟩ **3 :** not ⟨*dis*agreeable⟩ **4 :** completely ⟨*dis*annul⟩ **5** [by folk etymology] **:** DYS- ⟨*dis*function⟩

Dis \'dis\ *n* [L] **:** the god of the underworld in Roman mythology

dis·abil·i·ty \,dis-ə-'bil-ət-ē\ *n* **1 a :** the condition of being disabled **b :** inability to pursue an occupation because of physical or mental impairment **2 a :** lack of legal qualification to do something **b :** a nonlegal disqualification, restriction, or disadvantage

dis·able \dis-'ā-bəl, diz-\ *vt* **dis·abling** \-b(ə-)liŋ\ **1 :** to deprive of legal right, qualification, or capacity **2 :** to make incapable or ineffective; *esp* **:** to deprive of physical, moral, or intellectual strength **syn** see WEAKEN — **dis·able·ment** \-bəl-mənt\ *n*

dis·abuse \,dis-ə-'byüz\ *vt* [F *désabuser*, fr. *dés-* dis- + *abuser* to abuse] **:** to free from error or fallacy

di·sac·cha·ride \(')dī-'sak-ə-,rīd\ *n* **:** any of a class of sugars (as sucrose) that yield on hydrolysis two monosaccharide molecules

1**dis·ac·cord** \,dis-ə-'kȯ(ə)rd\ *vi* [ME *disacorden*, fr. MF *desacorder*, fr. *desacort* disagreement, fr. *des-* dis- + *acort* accord] **:** DISAGREE

2**disaccord** *n* **:** lack of harmony **:** DISAGREEMENT

dis·ac·cus·tom \,dis-ə-'kəs-təm\ *vt* [MF *desaccoustumer*, fr. OF *desacostumer*, fr. *des-* + *acostumer* to accustom] **:** to make no longer accustomed

1**dis·ad·van·tage** \,dis-əd-'vant-ij\ *n* [ME *disavauntage*, fr. MF *desavantage*, fr. OF, fr. *des-* + *avantage* advantage] **1 :** loss or damage esp. to reputation, credit, or finances **:** DETRIMENT **2 a :** an unfavorable, inferior, or prejudicial condition **b :** HANDICAP

2**disadvantage** *vt* **:** to place at a disadvantage **:** HARM

dis·ad·van·ta·geous \(,)dis-,ad-,van-'tā-jəs, -vən-; ,dis-əd-,van-\ *adj* **1 :** constituting a disadvantage **2 :** DISPARAGING — **dis·ad·van·ta·geous·ly** *adv* — **dis·ad·van·ta·geous·ness** *n*

dis·af·fect \,dis-ə-'fekt\ *vt* **:** to alienate the affection or loyalty of **syn** see ESTRANGE — **dis·af·fec·tion** \,dis-ə-'fek-shən\ *n*

dis·af·fil·i·ate \,dis-ə-'fil-ē-,āt\ *vt* **:** DISASSOCIATE ~ *vi* **:** to terminate an affiliation — **dis·af·fil·i·a·tion** \-,fil-ē-'ā-shən\ *n*

dis·af·firm \,dis-ə-'fərm\ *vt* **1 :** CONTRADICT **2 :** to refuse to confirm **:** ANNUL, REPUDIATE — **dis·af·fir·mance** \-'fər-mən(t)s\ *n* — **dis·af·fir·ma·tion** \(,)dis-,af-ər-'mā-shən\ *n*

dis·agree \,dis-ə-'grē\ *vi* [ME *disagreen*, fr. MF *desagreer*, fr. *des-* + *agreer* to agree] **1 :** to fail to agree ⟨the two accounts ~⟩ **2 :** to differ in opinion **3 :** to be unsuitable ⟨fried foods ~ with me⟩

dis·agree·able \-'grē-ə-bəl\ *adj* **1** *obs* **:** DISAGREEING **2 :** causing discomfort **:** UNPLEASANT, OFFENSIVE **3 :** marked by ill temper **:** PEEVISH — **dis·agree·able·ness** *n* — **dis·agree·ably** \-blē\ *adv*

dis·agree·ment \,dis-ə-'grē-mənt\ *n* **1 :** the act of disagreeing **2 a :** the state of being at variance **:** DISPARITY **b :** QUARREL

dis·al·low \,dis-ə-'laù\ *vt* **1 :** to deny the force, truth, or validity of **2 :** to refuse to allow **:** REJECT, VETO — **dis·al·low·ance** \-ən(t)s\ *n*

dis·an·nul \,dis-ə-'nəl\ *vt* **:** ANNUL

dis·ap·pear \,dis-ə-'pi(ə)r\ *vi* **1 :** to pass from view suddenly or gradually **2 :** to cease to be — **dis·ap·pear·ance** \-'pir-ən(t)s\ *n*

dis·ap·point \,dis-ə-'pȯint\ *vt* [MF *desapointier*, fr. *des-* dis- + *apointier* to arrange] **:** to fail to come up to the expectation or hope of **:** FRUSTRATE

dis·ap·point·ed *adj* **1 :** BALKED, THWARTED **2** *obs* **:** UNEQUIPPED

dis·ap·point·ment \,dis-ə-'pȯint-mənt\ *n* **1 :** the act or an instance of disappointing **:** the state or emotion of being disappointed **2 :** one that disappoints

dis·ap·pro·ba·tion \(,)dis-,ap-rə-'bā-shən\ *n* **:** the act or state of disapproving **:** the state of being disapproved **:** CONDEMNATION

dis·ap·prov·al \,dis-ə-'prü-vəl\ *n* **:** DISAPPROBATION, CENSURE

dis·ap·prove \-'prüv\ *vt* **1 :** to pass unfavorable judgment upon **:** CONDEMN **2 :** to refuse approval to **:** REJECT ~ *vi* **:** to feel or express disapproval — **dis·ap·prov·ing·ly** \-'prü-viŋ-lē\ *adv*

syn DISAPPROVE and DEPRECATE mean to feel or express an objection. DISAPPROVE implies dislike or distaste but not necessarily condemnation; DEPRECATE strongly implies regret and some degree of condemnation and often carries a suggestion of belittling

dis·arm \(')dis-'ärm, (')diz-\ *vb* [ME *desarmen*, fr. MF *desarmer*, fr. OF, fr. *des-* + *armer* to arm] *vt* **1 a :** to divest of arms **b :** to deprive of a means of attack or defense **c :** to make harmless **2 a :** to deprive of means, reason, or disposition to be hostile **b :** to win over ~ *vi* **1 :** to lay aside arms **2 :** to give up or reduce a military establishment — **dis·ar·ma·ment** \-'är-mə-mənt\ *n*

dis·arm·ing *adj* **:** allaying criticism or hostility **:** INGRATIATING

dis·ar·range \,dis-ə-'rānj\ *vt* **:** to disturb the arrangement or order of — **dis·ar·range·ment** \-mənt\ *n*

1**dis·ar·ray** \,dis-ə-'rā\ *n* **1 :** a lack of order or sequence **:** CONFUSION, DISORDER **2 :** disorderly dress **:** DISHABILLE

2**disarray** *vt* [ME *disarayen*, fr. MF *desarroyer*, fr. OF *desareer*, fr. *des-* + *areer* to array] **1 :** to throw into disorder **2 :** UNDRESS

dis·ar·tic·u·late \,dis-(,)är-'tik-yə-,lāt\ *vi* **:** to become disjointed ~ *vt* **:** DISJOINT — **dis·ar·tic·u·la·tion** \-,tik-yə-'lā-shən\ *n*

dis·as·sem·ble \,dis-ə-'sem-bəl\ *vt* **:** to take apart ⟨~ a watch⟩ — **dis·as·sem·bly** \-blē\ *n*

dis·as·so·ci·ate \-'sō-s(h)ē-,āt\ *vt* **:** to detach from association **:** DISSOCIATE — **dis·as·so·ci·a·tion** \-,sō-sē-'ā-shən, -shē-\ *n*

di·sas·ter \diz-'as-tər *or* dis-\ *n* [MF & OIt; MF *desastre*, fr. OIt

disastro, fr. *dis-* (fr. L) + *astro* star, fr. L *astrum*] **1** *obs* **:** an unfavorable aspect of a planet or star **2 :** a sudden or great misfortune
syn CALAMITY, CATASTROPHE, CATACLYSM: DISASTER implies an unforeseen mischance bringing with it destruction of life or property or utter defeat; CALAMITY implies a grievous misfortune causing usu. widespread distress and misery; CATASTROPHE implies generally a disastrous conclusion to a series of events; CATACLYSM connotes overwhelming or shattering natural or social forces
di·sas·trous \diz-ˈas-trəs *also* dis-\ *adj* **:** attended by or producing suffering or disaster **:** CALAMITOUS — **di·sas·trous·ly** *adv*
dis·avow \ˌdis-ə-ˈvau̇\ *vt* [ME *desavowen*, fr. MF *desavouer*, fr. OF, fr. *des-* dis- + *avouer* to avow] **:** to refuse to acknowledge **:** deny responsibility for **:** REPUDIATE — **dis·avow·al** \-ˈvau̇(-ə)l\ *n*
dis·band \dis-ˈband\ *vb* [MF *desbander*, fr. *des-* + *bande* band] *vt* **:** to break up the organization of **:** DISSOLVE ~ *vi* **:** to break up as an organization **:** DISPERSE — **dis·band·ment** \-ˈban(d)-mənt\ *n*
disbar *vt* **:** to expel from the bar or the legal profession **:** deprive of legal status and privileges — **dis·bar·ment** \-mənt\ *n*
dis·be·lief \ˌdis-bi-ˈlēf\ *n* **:** the act of disbelieving **:** mental rejection of a statement as untrue **syn** see UNBELIEF
dis·be·lieve \-ˈlēv\ *vt* **:** to hold not to be true or real ~ *vi* **:** to withhold or reject belief — **dis·be·liev·er** *n*
dis·branch \(ˈ)dis-ˈbranch\ *vt* [MF *desbrancher*, fr. *des-* + *branche* branch] **:** to tear off (as a branch)
dis·bud \(ˈ)dis-ˈbəd\ *vt* **1 :** to thin out flower buds to improve the quality of bloom of **2 :** to dehorn (cattle) by destroying the undeveloped horn bud
dis·bur·den \(ˈ)dis-ˈbərd-ᵊn\ *vt* **1 a :** to rid of a burden ⟨~ a pack animal⟩ **b :** UNBURDEN ⟨~ your conscience⟩ **2 :** UNLOAD ~ *vi* **:** DISCHARGE ⟨vessels ~*ing*⟩ — **dis·bur·den·ment** \-mənt\ *n*
dis·burse \dis-ˈbərs\ *vt* [MF *desbourser*, fr. OF *desborser*, fr. *des-* + *borser* to get money, fr. *borse* purse, fr. ML *bursa* — more at PURSE] **1 a :** to pay out **:** expend esp. from a fund **b :** DEFRAY **2 :** DISTRIBUTE ⟨~ property by will⟩ — **dis·burs·er** *n*
dis·burse·ment \-ˈbər-smənt\ *n* **:** the act of disbursing; *also* **:** funds paid out
disc *var of* DISK
disc- *or* **disci-** *or* **disco-** *comb form* [L, fr. Gk *disk-*, *disko-*, fr. *diskos*] **1 :** disk ⟨*disci*gerous⟩ **2 :** phonograph record ⟨*disco*phile⟩
dis·calced \(ˈ)dis-ˈkalst\ *adj* [part trans. of L *discalceatus*, fr. *dis-* + *calceatus*, pp. of *calceare* to put on shoes, fr. *calceus* shoe, fr. *calc-*, *calx* heel — more at CALK] **:** UNSHOD, BAREFOOTED ⟨~ friars⟩
dis·cant \ˈdis-ˌkant\ *var of* DESCANT
¹dis·card \dis-ˈkärd, ˈdis-ˌkärd\ *vt* **1 a :** to let go (a playing card) from one's hand **b :** to play (a card) from a suit other than trump but different from the one led **2 :** to get rid of as useless or unpleasant ~ *vi* **:** to discard a playing card
syn CAST, SHED, SLOUGH, SCRAP, JUNK: DISCARD implies the letting go or throwing away of something that has become presently useless or superfluous though often not intrinsically valueless; CAST, esp. when used with *off*, *away*, and *out*, implies a forceful rejection or repudiation; SHED and SLOUGH imply a throwing off of something both useless and encumbering and often suggest a consequent renewal of vitality or luster; SCRAP and JUNK imply throwing away or breaking up as worthless in existent form
²dis·card \ˈdis-ˌkärd\ *n* **1 a :** the act of discarding in a card game **b :** a card discarded **2 :** a person or thing cast off or rejected
dis·cern \dis-ˈərn, diz-\ *vb* [ME *discernen*, fr. MF *discerner*, fr. L *discernere* to separate, distinguish between, fr. *dis-* apart + *cernere* to sift] *vt* **1 a :** to detect with the eyes **b :** to detect with other senses than vision **2 :** to come to know or recognize mentally **3 :** to recognize or identify as separate and distinct **:** DISCRIMINATE ~ *vi* **:** to see or understand the difference — **dis·cern·er** *n* — **dis·cern·ible** \-ˈər-nə-bəl\ *adj* — **dis·cern·ibly** \-blē\ *adv*
dis·cern·ing *adj* **:** revealing insight and understanding **:** DISCRIMINATING ⟨a ~ critic⟩ — **dis·cern·ing·ly** \-ˈər-niŋ-lē\ *adv*
dis·cern·ment \dis-ˈərn-mənt, diz-\ *n* **1 :** an act of discerning **2 :** skill in discerning or discriminating **:** keenness of insight
syn DISCERNMENT, DISCRIMINATION, PERCEPTION, PENETRATION, INSIGHT, ACUMEN mean a power to see what is not evident to the average mind. DISCERNMENT stresses accuracy esp. in reading character or motives; DISCRIMINATION stresses the power to distinguish and select what is true or appropriate or genuinely excellent; PERCEPTION implies quick and often sympathetic discernment, as of shades of feeling; PENETRATION implies a searching mind that goes beyond what is obvious or superficial; INSIGHT suggests depth of discernment; ACUMEN implies characteristic penetration combined with keen practical judgment
¹dis·charge \dis(h)-ˈchärj, ˈdis(h)-ˌ\ *vb* [ME *dischargen*, fr. MF *descharger*, fr. LL *discarricare*, fr. L *dis-* + LL *carricare* to load] *vt* **1 :** to relieve of a charge, load, or burden: **a :** UNLOAD **b :** to release from an obligation **2 a :** to let go **:** clear out **b :** SHOOT ⟨~ an arrow⟩ **c :** to release from confinement, custody, or care ⟨~ a prisoner⟩ **d :** to give outlet or vent to **:** EMIT **3 a** (1) **:** to dismiss from employment (2) **:** to release from service or duty ⟨~ a soldier⟩ **b :** to get rid of (as a debt) by paying **:** FULFILL **c :** to set aside **:** ANNUL **d :** to order (a legislative committee) to end consideration of a bill in order to bring it before the house for action **4 a :** to receive and distribute (as the weight of a wall above an opening) **b :** to relieve from the weight of a wall **5 :** to bleach out or remove (color or dye) in dyeing and printing textiles **6 :** to cancel the record of the loan of (a library book) upon return ~ *vi* **1 :** to throw off or deliver a load, charge, or burden **2 a :** to go off **:** FIRE **b :** RUN ⟨some dyes ~⟩ **c :** to emit or give vent to fluid or other contents **syn** see FREE, PERFORM — **dis·charge·able** \-ə-bəl\ *adj* — **dis·charg·ee** \(ˌ)dis(h)-ˌchär-ˈjē\ *n* — **dis·charg·er** \dis(h)-ˈchär-jər, ˈdis(h)-ˌ\ *n*
²dis·charge \ˈdis(h)-ˌchärj, dis(h)-ˈ\ *n* **1 a :** the act of relieving of something that oppresses **:** RELEASE **b :** something that discharges or releases; *esp* **:** a certification of release or payment **2 :** the state or fact of being discharged or relieved **3 :** the act of discharging or unloading **4 :** legal release from confinement **5 :** a firing off **6 a :** a flowing or issuing out; *also* **:** a rate of flow **b :** something that is emitted **7 :** the act of removing an obligation or liability **8 a :** release or dismissal esp. from an office or employment **b :** complete separation from military service **9 :** the equalization of a difference of electric potential between two points
discharge lamp *n* **:** an electric lamp in which discharge of electricity between electrodes causes luminosity of the enclosed vapor or gas
dis·ci·flo·ral \ˌdis-(k)i-ˈflōr-əl, -ˈflȯr-\ *adj* **:** having flowers with the receptacle enlarged into a conspicuous disc
dis·ci·form \ˈdis-(k)ə-ˌfȯrm\ *adj* **:** round or oval in shape
dis·ci·ple \dis-ˈī-pəl\ *n* [ME, fr. OE *discipul* & OF *desciple*, fr. LL and L; LL *discipulus* follower of Jesus Christ in his lifetime, fr. L, pupil] **1 :** one who accepts and assists in spreading the doctrines of another: as **a :** APOSTLE 1 **b :** a convinced adherent of a school or individual **2** *cap* **:** a member of the Disciples of Christ founded in the U.S. in 1809 that holds the Bible alone to be the rule of faith and practice, baptizes by immersion, and has a congregational polity **syn** see FOLLOWER, SCHOLAR — **dis·ci·ple·ship** \-ˌship\ *n*
dis·ci·plin·able \ˌdis-ə-ˈplin-ə-bəl; ˈdis-ə-plən-, -(ˌ)plin-\ *adj* **1 :** TEACHABLE, DOCILE **2 :** DISCIPLINARY
dis·ci·plin·al \ˈdis-ə-plən-ᵊl, -(ˌ)plin-\ *adj* **:** of or relating to discipline
dis·ci·pli·nar·i·an \ˌdis-ə-plə-ˈner-ē-ən\ *n* **:** one who disciplines or enforces order — **disciplinarian** *adj*
dis·ci·plin·ary \ˈdis-ə-plə-ˌner-ē\ *adj* **1 a :** of or relating to discipline **b :** designed to correct or punish breaches of discipline ⟨took ~ action⟩ **2 :** of or relating to a particular field of study
¹dis·ci·pline \ˈdis-ə-plən, -(ˌ)plin\ *n* [ME, fr. MF & L; MF, fr. L *disciplina* teaching, learning, fr. *discipulus* pupil] **1** *obs* **:** INSTRUCTION **2 :** a subject that is taught **:** a field of study **3 :** training that corrects, molds, or perfects the mental faculties or moral character **4 :** PUNISHMENT **5 a :** control gained by enforcing obedience or order **b :** orderly or prescribed conduct or pattern of behavior **c :** SELF-CONTROL **6 :** a rule or system of rules governing conduct
²discipline *vt* **1 :** to punish or penalize for the sake of discipline **2 :** to train or develop by instruction and exercise esp. in self-control **3 a :** to bring (a group) under control ⟨~ troops⟩ **b :** to impose order upon **syn** see PUNISH, TEACH — **dis·ci·plin·er** *n*
disc jockey *n* **:** a person who conducts and announces a radio or television program of musical recordings often with interspersed comments not relating to music
dis·claim \dis-ˈklām\ *vb* [AF *disclaimer*, fr. *dis-* + *claimer* to claim, fr. OF *clamer*] *vi* **1 :** to make a disclaimer **2 a** *obs* **:** to disavow all part or share **b :** to utter denial ~ *vt* **1 :** to renounce a legal claim to **2 :** DENY, DISAVOW
dis·claim·er \-ˈklā-mər\ *n* [AF, fr. *disclaimer*, v.] **1 a :** a denial or disavowal of legal claim **:** relinquishment of or formal refusal to accept an interest or estate **b :** a writing that embodies a legal disclaimer **2 a :** DISAVOWAL, DENIAL **b :** REPUDIATION
dis·cla·ma·tion \ˌdis-klə-ˈmā-shən\ *n* **:** DISAVOWAL, RENUNCIATION
disc·like *var of* DISKLIKE
dis·cli·max \(ˈ)dis-ˈklī-ˌmaks\ *n* **:** a relatively stable ecological community often including kinds of organisms foreign to the region and displacing the climax because of disturbance esp. by man
¹dis·close \dis-ˈklōz\ *vt* [ME *disclosen*, fr. MF *desclos-*, stem of *desclore* to disclose, fr. ML *disclaudere* to open, fr. L *dis-* + *claudere* to close] **1** *obs* **:** to open up **2 a :** to expose to view **b** *archaic* **:** HATCH **c :** DIVULGE **syn** see REVEAL — **dis·clos·er** *n*
²disclose *n, obs* **:** DISCLOSURE
dis·clo·sure \dis-ˈklō-zhər\ *n* **1 :** the act or an instance of disclosing **:** EXPOSURE **2 :** something that is disclosed **:** REVELATION
disco- — see DISC-
dis·cog·ra·pher \dis-ˈkäg-rə-fər\ *n* **:** one that compiles discographies
dis·cog·ra·phy \-fē\ *n* [F *discographie*, fr. *disc-* + *-graphie* -graphy] **:** a descriptive compilation of phonograph records by groups
dis·coid \ˈdis-ˌkȯid\ *adj* [LL *discoides* quoit-shaped, fr. Gk *diskoeidēs*, fr. *diskos* disk] **1 :** resembling a disk or discus **:** being flat and circular **2 :** relating to or having a disk: as **a** *of a composite floret* **:** situated in the floral disk **b** *of a composite flower head* **:** having only tubular florets
dis·coi·dal \dis-ˈkȯid-ᵊl\ *adj* **:** of, resembling, or producing a disk: as **a** *of a gastropod shell* **:** having the whorls form a flat coil **b :** having the villi restricted to one or more disklike areas
dis·col·or \(ˈ)dis-ˈkəl-ər\ *vb* [ME *discolouren*, fr. MF *descolourer*, fr. LL *discolorari*, fr. L *discolor* of another color, fr. *dis-* + *color*] *vt* **:** to alter or change the hue or color of ~ *vi* **:** to change color **:** STAIN, FADE
dis·col·or·ation \(ˌ)dis-ˌkəl-ə-ˈrā-shən\ *n* **1 :** the act of discoloring **:** the state of being discolored **2 :** STAIN
dis·com·bob·u·late \ˌdis-kəm-ˈbäb-(y)ə-ˌlāt\ *vt* [prob. alter. of *discompose*] **:** UPSET, CONFUSE
¹dis·com·fit \dis-ˈkəm(p)-fət, *esp South* ˌdis-kəm-ˈfit\ *vt* [ME *discomfiten*, fr. OF *desconfit*, pp. of *desconfire*, fr. *des-* + *confire* to prepare — more at COMFIT] **1 a** *archaic* **:** to defeat in battle **b :** OVERCOME, THWART **2 :** DISCONCERT **syn** see EMBARRASS
²discomfit *n, archaic* **:** DISCOMFITURE
dis·com·fi·ture \dis-ˈkəm(p)-fə-ˌchu̇(ə)r, -chər, -ˌt(y)u̇(ə)r\ *n* **:** the act of discomfiting **:** the state of being discomfited
¹dis·com·fort \dis-ˈkəm(p)-fərt\ *vt* [ME *discomforten*, fr. MF *desconforter*, fr. OF, fr. *des-* + *conforter* to comfort] **1** *archaic* **:** DISMAY **2 :** to make uncomfortable or uneasy — **dis·com·fort·able** \dis-ˈkəm(p)(f)-tə-bəl, -ˈkəm(p)-fərt-ə-\ *adj, archaic*
²discomfort *n* **1** *archaic* **:** DISTRESS, GRIEF **2 :** UNEASINESS
dis·com·mend \ˌdis-kə-ˈmend\ *vt* **1 :** DISAPPROVE, DISPRAISE **2 :** to cause to be viewed unfavorably — **dis·com·mend·able** \-ˈmen-də-bəl\ *adj* — **dis·com·men·da·tion** \(ˌ)dis-ˌkäm-ən-ˈdā-shən, -ˌkäm-ˌen-\ *n, archaic*
dis·com·mode \ˌdis-kə-ˈmōd\ *vt* [MF *discommoder*, fr. *dis-* + *commode* convenient] **:** to cause inconvenience to
dis·com·mod·i·ty \-ˈmäd-ət-ē\ *n, archaic* **:** INCONVENIENCE
dis·com·pose \ˌdis-kəm-ˈpōz\ *vt* **1 :** to destroy the composure of **2 :** to disturb the order of — **dis·com·po·sure** \-ˈpō-zhər\ *n*
syn DISCOMPOSE, DISQUIET, DISTURB, PERTURB, AGITATE, UPSET, FLUSTER mean to destroy capacity for collected thought or decisive action. DISCOMPOSE implies some degree of loss of self-control or self-confidence esp. through emotional stress; DISQUIET suggests loss of sense of security or peace of mind; DISTURB implies interference with one's mental processes caused by worry, perplexity, or interruption; PERTURB implies deep disturbance and unsettlement of mind and emotions; AGITATE suggests obvious external signs of nervous or emotional excitement; UPSET implies the disturbance of normal or habitual functioning by disappointment, distress, or

grief; FLUSTER suggests bewildered agitation caused by unexpected or sudden demands or commands

dis·con·cert \ˌdis-kən-ˈsərt\ *vt* [obs. F *disconcerter*, alter. of MF *desconcerter*, fr. *des-* + *concerter* to concert] **1 :** to throw into confusion **2 :** to disturb the composure of **syn** see EMBARRASS — **dis·con·cert·ing** *adj* — **dis·con·cert·ing·ly** \-iŋ-lē\ *adv*

dis·con·for·mi·ty \ˌdis-kən-ˈfȯr-mət-ē\ *n* **1** *archaic* **:** NONCONFORMITY **2 :** a break in a sequence of sedimentary rocks all of which have approximately the same dip

dis·con·nect \ˌdis-kə-ˈnekt\ *vt* **:** to sever the connection of or between — **dis·con·nec·tion** \-ˈnek-shən\ *n*

dis·con·nect·ed *adj* **:** not connected **:** INCOHERENT — **dis·con·nect·ed·ly** *adv* — **dis·con·nect·ed·ness** *n*

dis·con·so·late \dis-ˈkän(t)-s(ə-)lət\ *adj* [ME, fr. ML *disconsolatus*, fr. L *dis-* + *consolatus*, pp. of *consolari* to console] **1 :** lacking consolation **:** hopelessly sad **2 :** causing dejection **:** CHEERLESS — **dis·con·so·late·ly** *adv* — **dis·con·so·late·ness** *n* — **dis·con·so·la·tion** \(ˌ)dis-ˌkän(t)-sə-ˈlā-shən\ *n*

1dis·con·tent \ˌdis-kən-ˈtent\ *adj* **:** DISCONTENTED

2discontent *n* **:** one who is discontented **:** MALCONTENT

3discontent *vt* **:** to make discontented — **dis·con·tent·ment** \-mənt\ *n*

4discontent *n* **:** lack of contentment: **a :** a sense of grievance **:** DISSATISFACTION **b :** restless yearning

dis·con·tent·ed *adj* **:** DISSATISFIED, UNSATISFIED, MALCONTENT — **dis·con·tent·ed·ly** *adv* — **dis·con·tent·ed·ness** *n*

dis·con·tin·u·ance \ˌdis-kən-ˈtin-yə-wən(t)s\ *n* **1 :** the act or an instance of discontinuing **2 :** the interruption or termination of a legal action by failure to continue or by the plaintiff's entry of a discontinuing order

dis·con·tin·ue \ˌdis-kən-ˈtin-(ˌ)yü, -yə(-w)\ *vb* [ME *discontinuen*, fr. MF *discontinuer*, fr. ML *discontinuare*, fr. L *dis-* + *continuare* to continue] *vt* **1 :** to break the continuity of **:** cease to operate, use, or take **2 :** to abandon or terminate by a legal discontinuance ~ *vi* **:** END; *specif* **:** to cease publication **syn** see STOP

dis·con·ti·nu·ity \(ˌ)dis-ˌkänt-ᵊn-ˈ(y)ü-ət-ē\ *n* **1 :** lack of continuity or cohesion **2 :** GAP 5 **3 :** a value of an argument at which a function is not continuous

dis·con·tin·u·ous \ˌdis-kən-ˈtin-yə-wəs\ *adj* **1 a :** not continuous **:** DISCRETE **b :** lacking sequence or coherence **2 :** having one or more discontinuities ⟨~ variable⟩ — **dis·con·tin·u·ous·ly** *adv*

dis·co·phile \ˈdis-kə-ˌfīl\ *n* **:** one who is devoted to the study and collecting of phonograph records

1dis·cord \ˈdis-ˌkȯ(ə)rd\ *n* **:** lack of agreement or harmony: **a :** DISUNITY, DISSENSION **b :** CONFLICT **c :** OPPOSITION, CONTRAST **d** (1) **:** a combination of musical sounds which strike the ear harshly (2) **:** DISSONANCE **e :** any harsh or unpleasant sound

syn STRIFE, CONFLICT, CONTENTION, DISSENSION, VARIANCE: DISCORD implies an intrinsic or essential lack of harmony producing quarreling, factiousness, or antagonism; STRIFE emphasizes a struggle for superiority rather than the incongruity or incompatibility of the persons or things involved; CONFLICT usu. stresses the action of forces in opposition but in static applications implies an irreconcilability as of duties or desires; CONTENTION applies to strife or competition that shows itself in quarreling, disputing, or controversy; DISSENSION implies strife or discord and stresses a division into factions; VARIANCE implies a clash between persons or things owing to a difference in nature, opinion, or interest

2dis·cord \ˈdis-ˌkȯ(ə)rd, dis-ˈkȯ(ə)rd\ *vi* [ME *discorden*, fr. OF *discorder*, fr. L *discordare*, fr. *discord-*, *discors* discordant, fr. *dis-* + *cord-*, *cor* heart — more at HEART] **:** DISAGREE, CLASH

dis·cor·dance \dis-ˈkȯrd-ᵊn(t)s\ *also* **dis·cor·dan·cy** \-ᵊn-sē\ *n* **1 :** the state or an instance of being discordant **2 :** DISSONANCE

dis·cor·dant \-ᵊnt\ *adj* **1 a :** being at variance **:** DISAGREEING **b :** QUARRELSOME **2 :** relating to a discord — **dis·cor·dant·ly** *adv*

dis·co·theque \ˌdis-kə-ˈtek\ *n* [F *discothèque*, fr. *disque* disk, record + *-o-* + *-thèque* (as in *bibliothèque* library)] **:** a usu. small intimate nightclub for dancing esp. to recorded music

1dis·count \ˈdis-ˌkau̇nt\ *n* **1 :** a reduction made from the gross amount or value of something: as **a** (1) **:** a reduction made from a regular or list price (2) **:** a proportionate deduction from a debt account usu. made for cash or prompt payment **b :** a deduction made for interest in advancing money upon or purchasing a bill or note not due **:** payment in advance **2 :** the act of discounting **3 :** a deduction taken or allowance made

2dis·count \ˈdis-ˌkau̇nt, dis-ˈkau̇nt\ *vb* [modif. of F *décompter*, fr. OF *desconter*, fr. ML *discomputare*, fr. L *dis-* + *computare* to count] *vt* **1 a :** to make a deduction from usu. for cash or prompt payment **b :** to sell or offer for sale at a discount **2 :** to lend money on after deducting the discount **3 a :** to leave out of account **:** DISREGARD **b :** to underestimate the importance of **:** MINIMIZE **c** (1) **:** to make allowance for bias or exaggeration in (2) **:** to view with doubt **:** DISBELIEVE **d :** to take into account (as a future event) in present calculations ~ *vi* **:** to give or make discounts

1dis·coun·te·nance \dis-ˈkau̇nt-ᵊn-ən(t)s, -ˈkau̇n-tə-nən(t)s, -ˈkau̇nt-nən(t)s\ *vt* **1 :** DISCONCERT **2 :** to look with disfavor on

2discountenance *n* **:** DISFAVOR, DISAPPROVAL

discount rate *n* **1 :** the interest on an annual basis deducted in advance on a bank or other loan **2 :** the charge levied by a central bank for advances and rediscounts

dis·cour·age \dis-ˈkər-ij, -ˈkə-rij\ *vt* [MF *descorager*, fr. OF *descoragier*, fr. *des-* dis- + *corage* courage] **1 :** to deprive of courage or confidence **:** DISHEARTEN **2 a :** to hinder by disfavoring **:** DETER **b :** to attempt to dissuade — **dis·cour·ag·er** *n*

dis·cour·age·ment \-mənt\ *n* **1 :** an act of discouraging **:** the state of being discouraged **2 :** something that discourages

dis·cour·ag·ing *adj* **:** DISHEARTENING, DEPRESSING, HINDERING — **dis·cour·ag·ing·ly** \-iŋ-lē\ *adv*

1dis·course \ˈdis-ˌkō(ə)rs, -ˌkȯ(ə)rs, dis-ˈ\ *n* [ME *discours*, fr. ML & LL *discursus;* ML, argument, fr. LL, conversation, fr. L, act of running about, fr. *discursus*, pp. of *discurrere* to run about, fr. *dis-* + *currere* to run] **1** *archaic* **:** the capacity of orderly thought or procedure **:** RATIONALITY **2 :** verbal interchange of ideas; *often* **:** CONVERSATION **3 :** formal and orderly and usu. extended expression of thought on a subject **4** *obs* **:** social familiarity

2dis·course \dis-ˈkō(ə)rs, -ˈkȯ(ə)rs, ˈdis-ˌ\ *vi* **1 :** to express oneself in esp. oral discourse **2 :** TALK, CONVERSE ~ *vt*, *archaic* **:** to give forth **:** UTTER — **dis·cours·er** *n*

dis·cour·te·ous \(ˈ)dis-ˈkərt-ē-əs\ *adj* **:** lacking courtesy **:** UNCIVIL, RUDE — **dis·cour·te·ous·ly** *adv* — **dis·cour·te·ous·ness** *n*

dis·cour·te·sy \-ˈkərt-ə-sē\ *n* **:** RUDENESS; *also* **:** a rude act

dis·cov·er \dis-ˈkəv-ər\ *vb* **dis·cov·er·ing** \-ˈkəv-(ə-)riŋ\ [ME *discoveren*, fr. OF *descovrir*, fr. LL *discooperire*, fr. L *dis-* + *cooperire* to cover — more at COVER] *vt* **1 a** to make known or visible **b** *archaic* **:** DISPLAY **2 :** to obtain sight or knowledge of for the first time **:** FIND ~ *vi* **:** to make a discovery — **dis·cov·er·able** \-(ə-)rə-bəl\ *adj* — **dis·cov·er·er** \-ər-ər\ *n*

syn ASCERTAIN, DETERMINE, UNEARTH, LEARN: DISCOVER presupposes exploration, investigation, or chance encounter and always implies the previous existence of what becomes known; ASCERTAIN implies effort to find the facts or the truth proceeding from awareness of ignorance or uncertainty; DETERMINE emphasizes the intent to establish the facts definitely or precisely; UNEARTH implies bringing to light something forgotten or hidden; LEARN may imply acquiring knowledge with little effort or conscious intention (as by simply being told); it may imply study and practice, but usu. does not stress active search **syn** see in addition INVENT, REVEAL

dis·cov·ery \dis-ˈkəv-(ə-)rē\ *n* **1 a :** the act or process of discovering **b** (1) *archaic* **:** DISCLOSURE (2) *obs* **:** DISPLAY **c** *obs* **:** EXPLORATION **2 :** something discovered

1dis·cred·it \(ˈ)dis-ˈkred-ət\ *vt* **1 :** to refuse to accept as true or accurate **:** DISBELIEVE **2 :** to cause disbelief in the accuracy or authority of **3 :** to deprive of good repute **:** DISGRACE

2discredit *n* **1 :** loss of credit or reputation **2 :** lack or loss of belief or confidence

dis·cred·it·able \-ə-bəl\ *adj* **:** injurious to reputation — **dis·cred·it·ably** \-blē\ *adv*

dis·creet \dis-ˈkrēt\ *adj* [ME, fr. MF *discret*, fr. ML *discretus*, fr. L, pp. of *discernere* to separate, distinguish between] **1 :** having or showing discernment or good judgment in conduct and esp. in speech **:** PRUDENT; *esp* **:** capable of preserving prudent silence **2 :** UNOBTRUSIVE, MODEST — **dis·creet·ly** *adv* — **dis·creet·ness** *n*

dis·crep·an·cy \dis-ˈkrep-ən-sē\ *n* **1 :** the quality or state of being discrepant **:** DIFFERENCE **2 :** an instance of being discrepant

dis·crep·ant \-ənt\ *adj* [L *discrepant-*, *discrepans*, prp. of *discrepare* to sound discordantly, fr. *dis-* + *crepare* to rattle, creak] **:** being at variance **:** DISAGREEING — **dis·crep·ant·ly** *adv*

dis·crete \dis-ˈkrēt, ˈdis-ˌ\ *adj* [ME, fr. L *discretus*] **1 :** constituting a separate entity **:** individually distinct **2 :** consisting of distinct or unconnected elements **:** NONCONTINUOUS **syn** see DISTINCT — **dis·crete·ly** *adv* — **dis·crete·ness** *n*

dis·cre·tion \dis-ˈkresh-ən\ *n* **1 :** the quality of being discreet **:** CIRCUMSPECTION; *esp* **:** cautious reserve in speech **2 :** ability to make responsible decisions **3 a :** individual choice or judgment **b :** power of free decision or latitude of choice within certain legal bounds — **dis·cre·tion·ary** \-ˈkresh-ə-ˌner-ē\ *adj*

dis·crim·i·na·ble \-ˈkrim-(ə-)nə-bəl\ *adj* **:** capable of being discriminated — **dis·crim·i·na·bly** \-blē\ *adv*

dis·crim·i·nant \-ˈkrim-(ə-)nənt\ *n* **:** a mathematical expression providing a criterion for the behavior of another more complicated expression, relation, or set of relations

dis·crim·i·nate \dis-ˈkrim-ə-ˌnāt\ *vb* [L *discriminatus*, pp. of *discriminare*, fr. *discrimin-*, *discrimen* distinction, fr. *discernere* to distinguish between] *vt* **1 a :** to mark or perceive the distinguishing or peculiar features of **b :** DISTINGUISH, DIFFERENTIATE **2 :** to distinguish by discerning or exposing differences; *esp* **:** to distinguish (one like object) from another ~ *vi* **1 a :** to make a distinction **b :** to use good judgment **2 :** to make a difference in treatment or favor on a basis other than individual merit

dis·crim·i·nat·ing *adj* **1 :** making a distinction **:** DISTINGUISHING **2 :** marked by discrimination: **a :** DISCERNING, JUDICIOUS **b :** DISCRIMINATORY — **dis·crim·i·nat·ing·ly** \-iŋ-lē\ *adv*

dis·crim·i·na·tion \dis-ˌkrim-ə-ˈnā-shən\ *n* **1 :** the act of discriminating **:** DIFFERENTIATION **2 :** the quality or power of finely distinguishing **3 :** the act, practice, or an instance of discriminating categorically rather than individually **syn** see DISCERNMENT — **dis·crim·i·na·tion·al** \-shnəl, -shən-ᵊl\ *adj*

dis·crim·i·na·tive \dis-ˈkrim-ə-ˌnāt-iv, -ˈkrim-(ə-)nət-\ *adj* **1 :** making distinctions **2 :** DISCRIMINATORY — **dis·crim·i·na·tive·ly** *adv*

dis·crim·i·na·tor \-ˈkrim-ə-ˌnāt-ər\ *n* **:** one that discriminates; *specif* **:** a circuit that can be adjusted to accept or reject signals of different characteristics (as amplitude or frequency)

dis·crim·i·na·to·ry \dis-ˈkrim-(ə-)nə-ˌtōr-ē, -ˌtȯr-\ *adj* **1 :** applying or favoring discrimination in treatment **2 :** DISCRIMINATIVE 1

dis·cur·sive \dis-ˈkər-siv\ *adj* [ML *discursivus*, fr. L *discursus*, pp. of *discurrere* to run about — more at DISCOURSE] **1 :** passing from one topic to another **:** DIGRESSIVE **2 :** marked by analytical reasoning — **dis·cur·sive·ly** *adv* — **dis·cur·sive·ness** *n*

dis·cus \ˈdis-kəs\ *n*, *pl* **dis·cus·es** [L — more at DISH] **1 a :** a disk (as of wood or rubber) thicker in the center than at the perimeter that is hurled for distance **b :** a field event in which a discus of about 4½ pounds is hurled **2 :** DISK 2, 3

dis·cuss \dis-ˈkəs\ *vt* [ME *discussen*, fr. L *discussus*, pp. of *discutere*, fr. *dis-* apart + *quatere* to shake] **1** *obs* **:** DISPEL **2 a :** to investigate by reasoning or argument **b :** to present in detail **c :** to talk about **3** *obs* **:** DECLARE **4 :** to consume with zest — **dis·cuss·able** *or* **dis·cuss·ible** \-ə-bəl\ *adj* — **dis·cuss·er** *n*

syn DISCUSS, ARGUE, DEBATE, DISPUTE mean to discourse about in order to reach conclusions or to convince. DISCUSS implies a sifting of possibilities esp. by presenting considerations pro and con; ARGUE implies the offering of reasons or evidence in support of convictions already held; DEBATE suggests formal or public argument between opposing parties; it may also apply to deliberation with oneself; DISPUTE implies contentious or heated argument

dis·cus·sant \dis-ˈkəs-ᵊnt\ *n* **:** one who takes part in a formal discussion or symposium

dis·cus·sion \dis-ˈkəsh-ən\ *n* **1 :** consideration of a question in open usu. informal debate **2 :** a formal treatment of a topic

1dis·dain \dis-ˈdān\ *n* [ME *desdeyne*, fr. OF *desdeign*, fr. *desdeignier*] **:** a feeling of contempt and aversion **:** SCORN

2disdain *vt* [ME *desdeynen*, fr. MF *desdeignier*, fr. (assumed) VL *disdignare*, fr. L *dis-* + *dignare* to deign — more at DEIGN] **1 :** to look with scorn on **2 :** to refuse or refrain from because of disdain **3 :** to treat disdainfully **syn** see DESPISE

dis·dain·ful \dis-ˈdān-fəl\ *adj* **:** full of or expressing disdain **syn** see PROUD — **dis·dain·ful·ly** \-fə-lē\ *adv* — **dis·dain·ful·ness** *n*

dis·ease \diz-ˈēz\ *n* [ME *disese*, fr. MF *desaise*, fr. *des-* dis- + *aise* ease] **1** *obs* **:** TROUBLE **2 a :** an impairment of the normal state of the living animal or plant body that affects the performance

of the vital functions : SICKNESS **b** : a particular instance or kind of such impairment : MALADY — **dis·eased** \-'ēzd\ *adj*
dis·econ·o·my \,dis-i-'kän-ə-mē\ *n* **1** : a lack of economy : an increase in costs **2** : a factor responsible for an increase in cost
dis·em·bark \,dis-əm-'bärk\ *vb* [MF *desembarquer,* fr. *des-* + *embarquer* to embark] *vt* : to put ashore from a ship ~ *vi* : to go ashore out of a ship; *also* : to get out of a vehicle — **dis·em·bar·ka·tion** \(,)dis-,em-,bär-'kā-shən, -bər-\ *n*
dis·em·bar·rass \,dis-əm-'bar-əs\ *vt* : to free from something troublesome or superfluous **syn** see EXTRICATE
dis·em·body \,dis-əm-'bäd-ē\ *vt* : to divest of the body, corporeal existence, or reality
dis·em·bogue \,dis-əm-'bōg\ *vb* [modif. of Sp *desembocar,* fr. *des-* dis- (fr. L *dis-*) + *embocar* to put into the mouth, fr. *en* in (fr. L *in*) + *boca* mouth, fr. L *bucca* — more at POCK] *vi* : to flow or come forth as if from a channel ~ *vt* : to pour out : EMPTY
dis·em·bow·el \,dis-əm-'baù(-ə)l\ *vt* **1** : to take out the bowels of : EVISCERATE **2** : to remove the substance of — **dis·em·bow·el·ment** \-mənt\ *n*
dis·en·chant \,dis-ᵊn-'chant\ *vt* [MF *desenchanter,* fr. *des-* + *enchanter* to enchant] : to free from enchantment : DISILLUSION — **dis·en·chant·er** *n* — **dis·en·chant·ing** *adj* — **dis·en·chant·ing·ly** \-iŋ-lē\ *adv* — **dis·en·chant·ment** \-mənt\ *n*
dis·en·cum·ber \,dis-ᵊn-'kəm-bər\ *vt* [MF *desencombrer,* fr. *des-* + *encombrer* to encumber] : to free from encumbrance : DISBURDEN **syn** see EXTRICATE
dis·en·dow \,dis-ᵊn-'daù\ *vt* : to strip of endowment — **dis·en·dow·er** \-'daù(-ə)r\ *n* — **dis·en·dow·ment** \-'daù-mənt\ *n*
dis·en·fran·chise \,dis-ᵊn-'fran-,chīz\ *vt* : DISFRANCHISE — **dis·en·fran·chise·ment** \-,chīz-mənt, -chəz-\ *n*
dis·en·gage \,dis-ᵊn-'gāj\ *vb* [F *désengager,* fr. MF, fr. *des-* + *engager* to engage] *vt* : to release from something that engages ~ *vi* : to release or detach oneself — **dis·en·gage·ment** \-mənt\ *n*
dis·en·tail \,dis-ᵊn-'tā(ə)l\ *vt* : to free from entail
dis·en·tan·gle \,dis-ᵊn-'taŋ-gəl\ *vt* : to free from entanglement : UNRAVEL ~ *vi* : to become disentangled **syn** see EXTRICATE — **dis·en·tan·gle·ment** \-mənt\ *n*
dis·en·thrall \,dis-ᵊn-'thròl\ *vt* : to free from bondage : LIBERATE
dis·equil·i·brate \,dis-i-'kwil-ə-,brāt\ *vt* : to put out of balance — **dis·equil·i·bra·tion** \-,kwil-ə-'brā-shən\ *n*
dis·equi·lib·ri·um \(,)dis-,ē-kwə-'lib-rē-əm, -,ek-wə-\ *n* : loss or lack of equilibrium; *esp* : a condition of economic imbalance
dis·es·tab·lish \,dis-ə-'stab-lish\ *vt* : to end the establishment of; *esp* : to deprive of the status and privileges of an established church — **dis·es·tab·lish·ment** \-mənt\ *n*
1**dis·es·teem** \,dis-ə-'stēm\ *vt* : to regard with disfavor
2**disesteem** *n* : DISFAVOR, DISREPUTE
di·seuse \dē-'zə(r)z, -'züz\ *n, pl* **di·seuses** \-'zə(r)z(-əz), -'züz(-əz)\ [F, fem. of *diseur,* fr. OF, fr. *dire* to say, fr. L *dicere*] : a skilled and usu. professional woman reciter
1**dis·fa·vor** \(')dis-'fā-vər\ *n* [prob. fr. MF *desfaveur,* fr. *des-* dis- + *faveur* favor, fr. OF *favor*] **1** : DISAPPROVAL, DISLIKE **2** : the state or fact of being deprived of favor **3** : DISADVANTAGE
2**disfavor** *vt* : to withhold or withdraw favor from
dis·fea·ture \(')dis-'fē-chər\ *vt* : to mar the features of **syn** see DEFACE — **dis·fea·ture·ment** \-mənt\ *n*
dis·fig·ure \dis-'fig-yər, *esp Brit* -'fig-ər\ *vt* [ME *disfiguren,* fr. MF *desfigurer,* fr. *des-* + *figure*] **1** : to spoil the appearance of **2** *obs* : DISGUISE **syn** see DEFACE — **dis·fig·ure·ment** \-mənt\ *n*
dis·fran·chise \(')dis-'fran-,chīz\ *vt* : to deprive of a franchise, of a legal right, or of some privilege or immunity; *esp* : to deprive of the right to vote — **dis·fran·chise·ment** \-,chīz-mənt, -chəz-\ *n*
dis·frock \(')dis-'fräk\ *vt* : UNFROCK
dis·fur·nish \(')dis-'fər-nish\ *vt* [MF *desfourniss-,* stem of *desfournir,* fr. *des-* + *fournir* to furnish — more at FURNISH] : to make destitute of possessions : DIVEST — **dis·fur·nish·ment** \-mənt\ *n*
dis·gorge \(')dis-'gò(ə)rj\ *vb* [MF *desgorger,* fr. *des-* + *gorge*] *vt* **1 a** : to discharge by the throat and mouth : VOMIT **b** : to discharge violently, confusedly, or as a result of force **2** : to discharge the contents of (as the stomach) ~ *vi* : to discharge contents
1**dis·grace** \dis-'grās\ *vt* **1** : to bring reproach or shame to **2** : to put to shame or out of favor — **dis·grac·er** *n*
2**disgrace** *n* [MF, fr. OIt *disgrazia,* fr. *dis-* (fr. L) + *grazia* grace, fr. L *gratia* — more at GRACE] **1 a** : loss of grace, favor, or honor **b** : the condition of one fallen from grace or honor **2** : something causing a fall from grace or bringing dishonor
syn DISHONOR, DISREPUTE, SHAME, INFAMY, IGNOMINY, OPPROBRIUM: DISGRACE implies a loss of favor or esteem once enjoyed or a severe humiliation not necessarily deserved; DISHONOR often equals DISGRACE but may imply loss of self-esteem; DISREPUTE stresses loss of one's good name or the attachment of a bad name or reputation; SHAME stresses a painful or humiliating disgrace often suffered because of another's act or behavior and often implies feelings of guilt and remorse; INFAMY stresses notoriety and well-deserved extreme contempt; IGNOMINY applies chiefly to the humiliation of defeat or insult usu. without implication of moral blame; OPPROBRIUM adds to DISGRACE the implication of severe reproach or condemnation
dis·grace·ful \dis-'grās-fəl\ *adj* : bringing or involving shame or disgrace — **dis·grace·ful·ly** \-fə-lē\ *adv* — **dis·grace·ful·ness** *n*
dis·grun·tle \dis-'grənt-ᵊl\ *vt* **dis·grun·tling** \-'grənt-liŋ, -ᵊl-iŋ\ [*dis-* + *gruntle* (to grumble), fr. ME *gruntlen,* freq. of *grunten* to grunt] : to put in bad humor — **dis·grun·tle·ment** \-ᵊl-mənt\ *n*
1**dis·guise** \dis-'gīz\ *vt* [ME *disgisen,* fr. MF *desguiser,* fr. OF, fr. *des-* + *guise*] **1 a** : to change the customary dress or appearance of **b** : to furnish with a false appearance or an assumed identity **2** *obs* : DISFIGURE **3** : to obscure the existence or true state or character of : CONCEAL — **dis·guis·ed·ly** \-'gīz(-ə)d-lē\ *adv* — **dis·guise·ment** \-'gīz-mənt\ *n* — **dis·guis·er** *n*
syn CLOAK, MASK, DISSEMBLE: DISGUISE typically implies a deceptive change of dress and physical appearance but may extend to a change in manner of speech or behavior that serves to conceal a motive or attitude; CLOAK suggests a means of hiding a movement or intention completely; MASK suggests the prevention of recognition of a thing's true character, nature, or presence usu. by some obvious means and does not always imply pretense or deception; DISSEMBLE stresses pretense for the purpose of misleading as well as hiding esp. with regard to feelings or opinions
2**disguise** *n* **1** : apparel assumed to conceal one's identity or counterfeit another's **2 a** : an outward form misrepresenting the true nature or identity of a person or thing **b** : PRETENSE **3** : the act of disguising
1**dis·gust** \dis-'gəst\ *n* : marked aversion excited by exposure to something highly distasteful or loathsome : REPUGNANCE
2**disgust** *vb* [MF *desgouster,* fr. *des-* dis- + *goust* taste, fr. L *gustus;* akin to L *gustare* to taste — more at CHOOSE] *vt* **1** : to provoke to loathing, repugnance, or aversion : be offensive to **2** : to cause (one) to lose an interest or intention through exciting distaste ~ *vi* : to cause disgust — **dis·gust·ed** *adj* — **dis·gust·ed·ly** *adv*
dis·gust·ful \-'gəst-fəl\ *adj* **1** : provoking disgust **2** : resulting from or accompanied by disgust — **dis·gust·ful·ly** \-fə-lē\ *adv*
dis·gust·ing *adj* : REVOLTING — **dis·gust·ing·ly** \-'gəs-tiŋ-lē\ *adv*
1**dish** \'dish\ *n* [ME, fr. OE *disc* plate; akin to OHG *tisc* plate, table; both fr. a prehistoric WGmc word borrowed fr. L *discus* quoit, disk, dish, fr. Gk *diskos,* fr. *dikein* to throw] **1** : a more or less concave vessel from which food is served **2 a** (1) : the food served in a dish ⟨a ~ of strawberries⟩ (2) : food prepared in a particular way **b** : something resembling a dish of food **3** : amount held by a dish : **4 a** : any of various shallow concave vessels; *broadly* : something that in shallow concavity resembles a dish **b** : the state of being concave or the degree of concavity
2**dish** *vt* **1** : to put into a dish **2** : to make concave like a dish
dis·ha·bille \,dis-ə-'bē(ə)l, -'bil, -'bē\ *n* [F *déshabillé,* fr. pp. of *déshabiller* to undress, fr. *dés-* dis- + *habiller* to dress — more at HABILIMENT] **1 a** *archaic* : NEGLIGEE **b** : the state of being dressed in a loose or careless style **2** : UNTIDINESS, DISORDER
dis·har·mon·ic \,dis-(,)här-'män-ik\ *or* **dis·har·mo·ni·ous** \-'mō-nē-əs\ *adj* **1** : lacking or defective in harmony **2 a** : having a combination of bodily characters that results in an unusual form or appearance **b** : ALLOMETRIC
dis·har·mo·nize \(')dis-'här-mə-,nīz\ *vt* : to make disharmonic
dis·har·mo·ny \-nē\ *n* : lack of harmony : DISCORD
dish·cloth \'dish-,klòth\ *n* : a cloth for washing dishes
dishcloth gourd *n* : the fruit of any of several gourds (genus *Luffa*) having a fibrous interior that is dried and used like a sponge
dish·clout \'dish-,klaùt\ *n, Brit* : DISHCLOTH
dis·heart·en \(')dis-'härt-ᵊn\ *vt* : to deprive of courage and hope — **dis·heart·en·ing** \-'härt-niŋ, -ᵊn-iŋ\ *adj* — **dis·heart·en·ing·ly** \-lē\ *adv* — **dis·heart·en·ment** \-'härt-ᵊn-mənt\ *n*
dished \'disht\ *adj* **1** : CONCAVE **2** *of a pair of vehicle wheels* : nearer together at the bottom than at the top
di·shev·el \dish-'ev-əl\ *vt* **di·shev·eled** *or* **di·shev·elled; di·shev·el·ing** *or* **di·shev·el·ling** \-'ev-(ə-)liŋ\ [back-formation fr. *disheveled*] : to let hang or fall loosely
di·shev·eled *or* **di·shev·elled** *adj* [ME *discheveled,* part trans. of MF *deschevelé,* fr. pp. of *descheveler* to disarrange the hair, fr. *des-* + *chevel* hair, fr. L *capillus*] : marked by loose disorder or disarray
dis·hon·est \(')dis-'än-əst\ *adj* [ME, fr. MF *deshoneste,* fr. *des-* + *honeste* honest] **1** *obs* : SHAMEFUL, UNCHASTE **2** : characterized by lack of truth, honesty, or trustworthiness — **dis·hon·est·ly** *adv*
syn DISHONEST, DECEITFUL, MENDACIOUS, LYING, UNTRUTHFUL mean unworthy of trust or belief. DISHONEST implies a willful perversion of truth in order to deceive, cheat, or defraud; DECEITFUL usu. implies an intent to mislead and commonly suggests a false appearance or double-dealing in behavior; MENDACIOUS is less forthright than LYING and may suggest bland or even harmlessly mischievous deceit; LYING implies a specific act or instance rather than a habit or tendency of telling untruths; UNTRUTHFUL is a less brutal term than LYING and in application to accounts or description may lack any suggestion of fraudulent motive
dis·hon·es·ty \-ə-stē\ *n* **1** : lack of honesty or integrity : disposition to defraud or deceive **2** : a dishonest act : FRAUD
1**dis·hon·or** \(')dis-'än-ər\ *n* [ME *dishonour,* fr. OF *deshonor,* fr. *des-* + *honor*] **1** : lack or loss of honor or reputation **2** : the state of one who has lost honor or prestige : SHAME **3 a** : a dishonorable thing or action **b** : a cause of disgrace **4** : the nonpayment or nonacceptance of commercial paper by the party on whom it is drawn **syn** see DISGRACE — **dis·hon·or·er** \-'än-ər-ər\ *n*
2**dishonor** *vt* **1 a** : to deprive of honor **b** : to bring shame on **2** : to refuse to accept or pay (as a draft, bill, check, or note)
dis·hon·or·able \(')dis-'än-(ə-)rə-bəl, -'än-ər-bəl\ *adj* **1** : lacking honor : SHAMEFUL ⟨~ conduct⟩ **2** *obs* : not honored — **dis·hon·or·able·ness** *n* — **dis·hon·or·ably** \-blē\ *adv*
dish out *vt* **1** : to serve (food) from a dish **2** : to give usu. freely
dish·rag \'dish-,rag\ *n* : DISHCLOTH
dish towel *n* : a cloth for drying dishes
dish·wash·er \-,wòsh-ər, -,wäsh-ər\ *n* **1** : a worker employed to wash dishes **2** : a machine for washing dishes
dish·wa·ter \-,wòt-ər, -,wät-\ *n* : water in which dishes have been or are to be washed
1**dis·il·lu·sion** \,dis-ə-'lü-zhən\ *n* : DISENCHANTMENT
2**disillusion** *vt* **dis·il·lu·sion·ing** \-'lüzh-(ə-)niŋ\ : to free from or deprive of illusion — **dis·il·lu·sion·ment** \-'lü-zhən-mənt\ *n*
dis·in·cen·tive \,dis-ᵊn-'sent-iv\ *n* : DETERRENT
dis·in·cli·na·tion \(,)dis-,in-klə-'nā-shən, -,iŋ-\ *n* : a state of unwillingness : slight aversion : DISTASTE
dis·in·cline \,dis-ᵊn-'klīn\ *vt* : to make unwilling
dis·in·clined *adj* : unwilling because of mild dislike or disapproval
syn DISINCLINED, HESITANT, RELUCTANT, LOATH, AVERSE mean lacking the will or the desire to do something indicated; DISINCLINED implies lack of taste for or inclination toward and often active disapproval of the thing suggested; HESITANT implies a holding back through fear, uncertainty, or disinclination; RELUCTANT implies a holding back through unwillingness; LOATH implies hesitancy because not in accord with one's opinions, predilections, or liking; AVERSE implies a holding back from or avoiding because of distaste or repugnance
dis·in·fect \,dis-ᵊn-'fekt\ *vt* [MF *desinfecter,* fr. *des-* + *infecter* to infect] : to free from infection esp. by destroying harmful microorganisms; *broadly* : CLEANSE — **dis·in·fec·tion** \-'fek-shən\ *n*
dis·in·fec·tant \-'fek-tənt\ *n* : an agent that frees from infection; *esp* : a chemical that destroys vegetative forms of harmful microorganisms but not ordinarily bacterial spores
dis·in·fest \,dis-ᵊn-'fest\ *vt* : to rid of insects, rodents, or other small animals — **dis·in·fes·ta·tion** \(,)dis-,in-,fes-'tā-shən\ *n*

ə abut; ᵊ kitten; ər further; a back; ā bake; ä cot, cart; aù out; ch chin; e less; ē easy; g gift; i trip; ī life
j joke; ŋ sing; ō flow; ò flaw; òi coin; th thin; th this; ü loot; ù foot; y yet; yü few; yù furious; zh vision

dis·in·fes·tant \ˌdis-ᵊn-ˈfes-tənt\ *n* **:** a disinfesting agent

dis·in·fla·tion \ˌdis-ᵊn-ˈflā-shən\ *n* **:** a reversal of inflationary pressures — **dis·in·fla·tion·ary** \-shə-ˌner-ē\ *adj*

dis·in·gen·u·ous \ˌdis-ᵊn-ˈjen-yə-wəs\ *adj* **:** lacking in candor; *also* **:** giving a false appearance of simple frankness **:** CALCULATING — **dis·in·gen·u·ous·ly** *adv* — **dis·in·gen·u·ous·ness** *n*

dis·in·her·it \ˌdis-ᵊn-ˈher-ət\ *vt* **1 a :** to deprive of the right to inherit **b :** to prevent deliberately (as by making a will) from inheriting **2 :** to deprive of natural or human rights or of special privileges previously held — **dis·in·her·i·tance** \-ˈher-ət-ən(t)s\ *n*

dis·in·te·grate \(ˈ)dis-ˈint-ə-ˌgrāt\ *vt* **1 :** to break or decompose into constituent elements, parts, or small particles **2 :** to destroy the unity or integrity of ~ *vi* **1 :** to break or separate into constituent elements or parts **2 :** to lose unity or integrity by or as if by breaking into parts **3 :** to undergo a change in composition ⟨an atomic nucleus that ~s because of radioactivity⟩ — **dis·in·te·gra·tion** \(ˌ)dis-ˌint-ə-ˈgrā-shən\ *n* — **dis·in·te·gra·tive** \(ˈ)dis-ˈint-ə-ˌgrāt-iv\ *adj* — **dis·in·te·gra·tor** \-ˌgrāt-ər\ *n*

dis·in·ter \ˌdis-ᵊn-ˈtər\ *vt* **1 :** to take out of the grave or tomb **2 :** to bring to light **:** UNEARTH — **dis·in·ter·ment** \-mənt\ *n*

1**dis·in·ter·est** \(ˈ)dis-ˈin-trəst; -ˈint-ə-rəst, -ə-ˌrest, -ərst; -ˈin-ˌtrest\ *vt* **:** to divest of interest

2**disinterest** *n* **1 :** DISADVANTAGE **2 :** lack of self-interest **:** DISINTERESTEDNESS **3 :** lack of interest **:** APATHY

dis·in·ter·est·ed *adj* **1 :** UNINTERESTED **2 :** free from selfish motive or interest **:** UNBIASED ⟨a ~ decision⟩ **syn** see INDIFFERENT — **dis·in·ter·est·ed·ly** *adv* — **dis·in·ter·est·ed·ness** *n*

dis·in·vest·ment \ˌdis-ᵊn-ˈves(t)-mənt\ *n* **:** consumption of capital

dis·join \(ˈ)dis-ˈjȯin\ *vb* [MF *desjoindre*, fr. L *disjungere*, fr. *dis-* + *jungere* to join] *vt* **:** to end the joining of ~ *vi* **:** to become detached

1**dis·joint** \-ˈjȯint\ *adj* [ME *disjoynt*, fr. MF *desjoint*, pp. of *desjoindre*] *obs* **:** out of joint **:** DISJOINTED

2**disjoint** *vt* **1 :** to separate the parts of **2 :** to take apart at the joints ~ *vi* **:** to part at the joints

dis·joint·ed *adj* **1 :** separated at or as if at the joint **2 :** DISCONNECTED, DISORDERED ⟨a ~ society⟩; *esp* **:** INCOHERENT ⟨~ conversation⟩ — **dis·joint·ed·ly** *adv* — **dis·joint·ed·ness** *n*

1**dis·junct** \dis-ˈjəŋ(k)t\ *adj* [L *disjunctus*, pp. of *disjungere* to disjoin] **:** marked by separation of or from usu. contiguous parts or individuals: as **a :** DISCONTINUOUS **b :** relating to melodic progression by intervals larger than a major second **c** *of an insect* **:** having head, thorax, and abdomen separated by deep constrictions

2**dis·junct** \ˈdis-ˌjəŋ(k)t\ *n* **:** any of the alternatives comprising a logical disjunction

dis·junc·tion \dis-ˈjəŋ(k)-shən\ *n* **1 :** DISUNION, SEPARATION **2 a :** a complex logical proposition that asserts one or more of its terms **b :** a proposition that asserts one and only one of its terms

1**dis·junc·tive** \-ˈjəŋ(k)-tiv\ *n* **:** a disjunctive conjunction

2**disjunctive** *adj* **1 :** tending to disjoin **2 a :** expressing an alternative or opposition between the meanings of the words connected ⟨the ~ conjunction *or*⟩ **b :** expressed by mutually exclusive alternatives joined by *or* ⟨~ pleading⟩ **3** *of a pronoun form* **:** stressed and not attached to the verb as an enclitic or proclitic — **dis·junc·tive·ly** *adv*

1**disk** *or* **disc** \ˈdisk\ *n, often attrib* [L *discus* — more at DISH] **1** *archaic* **:** DISCUS 1 **2 a :** the central part of the flower head of a typical composite made up of closely packed tubular flowers **b** *usu disc* **:** an enlargement of the torus surrounding, beneath, or above the pistil of a flower **3 :** any of various rounded and flattened animal anatomical structures **4 a :** a thin circular object **b** *usu disc* **:** a phonograph record **5** *usu disc* **:** one of the concave circular steel tools with sharpened edge making up the working part of a disc harrow or plow; *also* **:** an implement employing such tools

2**disk** *or* **disc** *vt* **1 :** to cultivate with a disc harrow or similar implement **2** *usu disc* **:** to record on a phonograph disc

disk flower *n* **:** one of the tubular flowers in the disk of a composite plant — called also *disk floret*

disk·like *or* **disc·like** \ˈdis-ˌklīk\ *adj* **:** circular and nearly flat

disk wheel *n* **:** a wheel presenting a solid surface from hub to rim

dis·lik·able *or* **dis·like·able** \(ˈ)dis-ˈlī-kə-bəl\ *adj* **:** UNLIKABLE

1**dis·like** \(ˈ)dis-ˈlīk\ *vt* **1** *archaic* **:** DISPLEASE **2 :** to regard with dislike **:** DISAPPROVE **3** *obs* **:** to show aversion to — **dis·lik·er** *n*

2**dislike** *n* **1 :** a feeling of distaste or disapproval **2** *obs* **:** DISCORD

dis·limn \(ˈ)dis-ˈlim\ *vb* **:** DIM

dis·lo·cate \ˈdis-lō-ˌkāt, (ˈ)dis-ˈlō-\ *vt* [ML *dislocatus*, pp. of *dislocare*, fr. L *dis-* + *locare* to locate] **1 :** to put out of place; *specif* **:** to displace (a bone) from normal connections with another bone **2 :** DISRUPT

dis·lo·ca·tion \ˌdis-(ˌ)lō-ˈkā-shən, -lə-\ *n* **:** the act of dislocating **:** the state of being dislocated: as **a :** displacement of one or more bones at a joint **b :** disruption of an established order

dis·lodge \(ˈ)dis-ˈläj\ *vb* [ME *disloggen*, fr. MF *desloger*, fr. *des-* + *loger* to lodge, fr. *loge* lodge] *vt* **1 :** to force out of a resting place **2 :** to drive from a position of hiding, defense, or advantage ~ *vi* **:** to leave a lodging place

dis·loy·al \(ˈ)dis-ˈlȯi(-ə)l\ *adj* [MF *desloial*, fr. OF, fr. *des-* + *loial* loyal] **:** lacking in loyalty **syn** see FAITHLESS — **dis·loy·al·ly** \-ˈlȯi-ə-lē\ *adv*

dis·loy·al·ty \-ˈlȯi(-ə)l-tē\ *n* **:** lack of loyalty

dis·mal \ˈdiz-məl\ *adj* [ME, fr. *dismal*, n., days marked as unlucky in medieval calendars, fr. AF, fr. ML *dies mali*, lit., evil days] **1** *obs* **:** DISASTROUS, DREADFUL **2 :** showing or causing gloom or depression **3 :** lacking interest or merit — **dis·mal·ly** \-mə-lē\ *adv*

dis·man·tle \(ˈ)dis-ˈmant-ᵊl\ *vt* **dis·man·tling** \-ˈmant-liŋ, -ᵊl-iŋ\ [MF *desmanteler*, fr. *des-* + *mantel* mantle] **1 :** to strip of dress or covering **:** DIVEST **2 :** to strip of furniture and equipment **3 :** to take to pieces — **dis·man·tle·ment** \-ˈmant-ᵊl-mənt\ *n*

dis·mast \(ˈ)dis-ˈmast\ *vt* **:** to remove or break off the mast of

1**dis·may** \dis-ˈmā, diz-\ *vt* [ME *dismayen*, fr. (assumed) OF *desmaiier*, fr. OF *des-* + *-maiier* (as in *esmaiier* to dismay), fr. (assumed) VL *-magare*, of Gmc origin] **:** to take away the courage or resolution of with alarm — **dis·may·ing·ly** \-iŋ-lē\ *adv*

syn APPALL, HORRIFY, DAUNT: DISMAY implies loss of power to carry on because of sudden fear or anxiety or great perplexity; APPALL implies an overwhelming or paralyzing dread or terror or sense of helplessness before something monstrous or shocking; HORRIFY may imply a shuddering revulsion from the ghastly or gruesome or hideous but it is often merely equal to *shock;* DAUNT suggests a cowing, subduing, disheartening, or frightening in a venture requiring courage

2**dismay** *n* **1 :** sudden loss of courage or resolution from alarm or fear **2 a :** sudden disappointment **b :** PERTURBATION

dis·mem·ber \(ˈ)dis-ˈmem-bər\ *vt* **dis·mem·ber·ing** \-b(ə-)riŋ\ [ME *dismembren*, fr. OF *desmembrer*, fr. *des-* + *membre* member] **1 :** to cut off or disjoin the limbs, members, or parts of **2 :** to break up or tear into pieces — **dis·mem·ber·ment** \-bər-mənt\ *n*

dis·miss \dis-ˈmis\ *vt* [modif. of L *dimissus*, pp. of *dimittere*, fr. *dis-* apart + *mittere* to send — more at DIS-, SMITE] **1 :** to permit or cause to leave **2 :** to send or remove from office, service, or employment **:** DISCHARGE **3 a :** to bar from attention or serious consideration **b :** to put out of judicial consideration **syn** see EJECT

dis·miss·al \-ˈmis-əl\ *n* **:** the act of dismissing **:** the fact or state of being dismissed

dis·mis·sion \-ˈmish-ən\ *n* **:** DISMISSAL

1**dis·mount** \(ˈ)dis-ˈmau̇nt\ *vb* [prob. modif. of MF *desmonter*, fr. *des-* + *monter* to mount] *vi* **1** *obs* **:** DESCEND **2 :** to alight from or as if from a horse ~ *vt* **1 :** to throw down or remove from a mount or an elevated position; *esp* **:** UNHORSE **2 :** DISASSEMBLE

2**dismount** *n* **:** the act of dismounting

dis·obe·di·ence \ˌdis-ə-ˈbēd-ē-ən(t)s\ *n* **:** refusal or neglect to obey

dis·obe·di·ent \-ənt\ *adj* [ME, fr. MF *desobedient*, fr. *des-* + *obedient*] **:** refusing or neglecting to obey — **dis·obe·di·ent·ly** *adv*

dis·obey \ˌdis-ə-ˈbā\ *vb* [ME *disobeyen*, fr. MF *desobeir*, fr. *des-* + *obeir* to obey] *vt* **:** to fail to obey ~ *vi* **:** to be disobedient

dis·oblige \ˌdis-ə-ˈblīj\ *vt* [F *désobliger*, fr. MF, fr. *des-* + *obliger* to oblige] **1 :** to go counter to the wishes of **2 :** to put out

di·so·mic \(ˈ)dī-ˈsō-mik\ *adj* [*di-* + *-somic*] **:** having one or more chromosomes duplicated but not an entire genome duplicated

1**dis·or·der** \(ˈ)dis-ˈȯrd-ər\ *vt* **1 :** to disturb the order of **2 :** to disturb the regular or normal functions of

2**disorder** *n* **1 a :** lack of order **b :** a disturbing, neglecting, or breaking away from a due order **2 :** breach of the peace or public order **3 :** an abnormal physical or mental condition **:** AILMENT

dis·or·dered *adj* **1** *obs* **:** morally reprehensible **:** UNRULY **2 a :** marked by disorder **b :** not functioning in a normal orderly healthy way — **dis·or·dered·ly** *adv* — **dis·or·dered·ness** *n*

dis·or·der·li·ness \(ˈ)dis-ˈȯrd-ər-lē-nəs\ *n* **:** the quality or state of being disorderly

dis·or·der·ly \-lē\ *adj* **1 a :** UNRULY, TURBULENT **b** (1) **:** constituting a public nuisance by being offensive to public order or decency (2) **:** guilty of disorderly conduct **2 :** marked by disorder

disorderly conduct *n* **:** a petty offense chiefly against public order and decency that falls short of an indictable misdemeanor

dis·or·ga·ni·za·tion \(ˌ)dis-ˌȯrg-(ə-)nə-ˈzā-shən\ *n* **:** the act of disorganizing **:** the state of being disorganized

dis·or·ga·nize \(ˈ)dis-ˈȯr-gə-ˌnīz\ *vt* [F *désorganiser*, fr. *dés-* dis- + *organiser* to organize] **:** to destroy the organic structure or regular or systematic arrangement of **:** CONFUSE

dis·ori·ent \(ˈ)dis-ˈōr-ē-ˌent, -ˈȯr-\ *vt* [F *désorienter*, fr. *dés-* dis- + *orienter* to orient, fr. MF, fr. *orient*, n.] **1 a :** to cause to lose bearings **:** displace from normal position or relationship **b :** to cause to lose the sense of time, place, or identity **2 :** CONFUSE

dis·ori·en·tate \-ē-ən-ˌtāt, -ē-ˌen-\ *vt* **:** DISORIENT — **dis·ori·en·ta·tion** \(ˌ)dis-ˌōr-ē-ən-ˈtā-shən, -ˌȯr-, -ē-en-\ *n*

dis·own \(ˈ)dis-ˈōn\ *vt* **1 :** to refuse to acknowledge as one's own **2 a :** DISCLAIM **b :** to deny the validity or authority of — **dis·own·ment** \-mənt\ *n*

dis·par·age \dis-ˈpar-ij\ *vt* [ME *disparagen* to degrade by marriage below one's class, disparage, fr. MF *desparagier* to marry below one's class, fr. OF, fr. *des-* dis- + *parage* extraction, lineage, fr. *per* peer] **1 :** to lower in rank or reputation **:** DEGRADE **2** *obs* **:** DISCOURAGE **3 :** to speak slightingly of **:** DEPRECIATE **syn** see DECRY — **dis·par·ag·ing** *adj* — **dis·par·ag·ing·ly** \-iŋ-lē\ *adv*

dis·par·age·ment \-ij-mənt\ *n* **1 :** a lowering of esteem or standing **2 :** the act of disparaging

dis·pa·rate \dis-ˈpar-ət, ˈdis-p(ə-)rət\ *adj* [L *disparatus*, pp. of *disparare* to separate, fr. *dis-* + *parare* to prepare — more at PARE] **:** distinct in quality or character **:** DISSIMILAR **syn** see DIFFERENT — **dis·pa·rate·ly** *adv* — **dis·pa·rate·ness** *n*

dis·par·i·ty \dis-ˈpar-ət-ē\ *n* [MF *desparité*, fr. LL *disparitat-*, *disparitas*, fr. L *dis-* + LL *paritat-*, *paritas* parity] **:** the state of being disparate **:** DIFFERENCE

dis·part \(ˈ)dis-ˈpärt\ *vb* [It & L; It *dispartire*, fr. L, fr. *dis-* + *partire* to divide — more at PART] *archaic* **:** SEPARATE, DIVIDE

dis·pas·sion·ate \(ˈ)dis-ˈpash-(ə-)nət\ *adj* **:** not influenced by strong feeling **:** CALM **syn** see FAIR — **dis·pas·sion·ate·ly** *adv*

1**dis·patch** \dis-ˈpach\ *vb* [Sp *despachar* or It *dispacciare*, fr. Prov *despachar* to get rid of, fr. MF *despeechier* to set free, fr. OF, fr. *des-* + *-peechier*] *vt* **1 :** to send off or away with promptness or speed esp. on official business **2 a :** to put to death **b** *obs* **:** DEPRIVE **3 :** to dispose of (as a task) rapidly or efficiently ~ *vi, archaic* **:** to make haste **:** HURRY **syn** see KILL — **dis·patch·er** *n*

2**dispatch** *n* **1 :** the act of dispatching: as **a** *obs* **:** DISMISSAL **b :** the act of putting to death **c** (1) **:** prompt settlement (as of an item of business) (2) **:** quick riddance **d :** a sending off **:** SHIPMENT **2 a :** a message sent with speed; *esp* **:** an important official message sent by a diplomatic, military, or naval officer **b :** a news item sent in by a correspondent to a newspaper **3 :** promptness and efficiency in performance or transmission **syn** see HASTE

dis·pel \dis-ˈpel\ *vt* **dis·pelled; dis·pel·ling** [L *dispellere*, fr. *dis-* + *pellere* to drive, beat — more at FELT] **:** to drive away by scattering **:** DISSIPATE **syn** see SCATTER

dis·pens·abil·i·ty \(ˌ)dis-ˌpen(t)-sə-ˈbil-ət-ē\ *n* **:** the quality or state of being dispensable

dis·pens·able \dis-ˈpen(t)-sə-bəl\ *adj* **:** capable of being dispensed with **:** UNESSENTIAL

dis·pen·sa·ry \dis-ˈpen(t)s-(ə-)rē\ *n* **:** a place where medical or dental aid is dispensed

dis·pen·sa·tion \ˌdis-pən-ˈsā-shən, -ˌpen-\ *n* **1 a :** a general state or ordering of things; *specif* **:** a system of revealed commands and promises regulating human affairs **b :** a particular arrangement or provision esp. of providence or nature **2 a :** an exemption from a law or from an impediment, vow, or oath **b :** a formal authorization **3 a :** the act of dispensing **b :** something dispensed or distributed — **dis·pen·sa·tion·al** \-shnəl, -shən-ᵊl\ *adj*

dis·pen·sa·to·ry \dis-ˈpen(t)-sə-ˌtōr-ē, -ˌtȯr-\ *n* **1 :** a medicinal formulary **2** *archaic* **:** DISPENSARY

dis·pense \dis-ˈpen(t)s\ *vb* [ME *dispensen*, fr. ML & L; ML *dispensare* to grant dispensation, fr. L, to distribute, fr. *dispensus*, pp. of *dispendere* to weigh out, fr. *dis-* + *pendere* to weigh] *vt* **1 a :** to deal

out in portions **b :** ADMINISTER ⟨~ justice⟩ **2 :** to give dispensation to **:** EXEMPT **3 :** to prepare and distribute (medicines) **~** *vi, archaic* **:** to grant dispensation **syn** see DISTRIBUTE — **dispense with 1 :** to suspend the operation of **2 :** to do without

dis·pens·er \-ˈpen(t)-sər\ *n* **:** one that dispenses: as **a :** a container that extrudes, sprays, or feeds out in convenient units **b :** a usu. mechanical device for vending merchandise

dis·peo·ple \(ˈ)dis-ˈpē-pəl\ *vt* **:** DEPOPULATE

dis·pers·al \dis-ˈpər-səl\ *n* **:** the act or result of dispersing

dis·perse \dis-ˈpərs\ *vb* [ME *dysparsen*, fr. MF *disperser*, fr. L *dispersus*, pp. of *dispergere* to scatter, fr. *dis-* + *spargere* to scatter] *vt* **1 a :** to cause to break up and go in different ways **b :** to cause to become spread widely **c :** DISPEL **2 :** to spread or distribute from a fixed or constant source: as **a :** DISSEMINATE **b :** to subject (as light) to dispersion **c :** to distribute more or less evenly throughout a medium **~** *vi* **1 :** to break up and move or scatter in different directions **2 :** DISSIPATE, VANISH **syn** see SCATTER — **dis·pers·er** \-ˈpər-sər\ *n* — **dis·pers·ible** \-sə-bəl\ *adj*

disperse system *n* **:** a two-phase system consisting of a dispersion medium and a dispersed phase

dis·per·sion \dis-ˈpər-zhən, -shən\ *n* **1** *cap* **:** DIASPORA 1a **2 :** the act or process of dispersing **:** the state of being dispersed **3 :** the scattering of the values of a frequency distribution from an average **4 :** the separation of light into colors by refraction or diffraction with formation of a spectrum; *also* **:** the separation of nonhomogeneous radiation into components in accordance with some characteristic (as energy) **5 a :** a dispersed substance **b :** a system consisting of a dispersed substance and the medium in which it is dispersed

dis·per·sive \-ˈpər-siv, -ziv\ *adj* **:** of or relating to dispersion **:** tending to disperse — **dis·per·sive·ly** *adv* — **dis·per·sive·ness** *n*

dis·per·soid \-ˈpər-ˌsȯid\ *n* **1 :** DISPERSE SYSTEM **2 :** finely divided particles, droplets, or bubbles of one substance dispersed in another

dispir·it \(ˈ)dis-ˈpir-ət\ *vt* [*dis-* + *spirit*] **:** to deprive of cheerful or sanguine spirits — **dispir·it·ed** *adj* — **dispir·it·ed·ly** *adv* — **dispir·it·ed·ness** *n*

dis·pit·eous \dis-ˈpit-ē-əs\ *adj* [alter. of *despiteous*] *archaic* **:** CRUEL

dis·place \(ˈ)dis-ˈplās\ *vt* [prob. fr. MF *desplacer*, fr. *des-* dis- + *place*] **1 a :** to remove from the usual or proper place; *specif* **:** to expel or force to flee from home or homeland **b :** to remove from an office **c** *obs* **:** BANISH **2 :** to take the place of **:** SUPPLANT **syn** see REPLACE — **dis·place·able** \-ˈplā-sə-bəl\ *adj*

displaced person *n* **:** a person expelled or impelled to flee from his country of nationality or habitual residence

dis·place·ment \dis-ˈplā-smənt\ *n* **1 :** the act or process of displacing **:** the state of being displaced **2 a :** the volume or weight of a fluid displaced by a floating body of equal weight **b :** the difference between the initial position of a body and any later position **c :** the volume displaced by a piston in a single stroke

dis·plant \dis-ˈplant\ *vt* [MF *desplanter*, fr. *des-* + *planter* to plant, fr. LL *plantare*] *obs* **:** DISPLACE, SUPPLANT

1**dis·play** \dis-ˈplā\ *vb* [ME *displayen*, fr. AF *despleier*, fr. L *displicare* to scatter, fr. *dis-* + *plicare* to fold] *vt* **1 :** to spread or stretch out **2 a :** to spread before the view **b :** to set in display **3** *obs* **:** DESCRY **~** *vi, obs* **:** to show off **syn** see SHOW

2**display** *n, often attrib* **1 a :** a displaying of something; *specif* **:** a device that gives information in visual form in communications **b :** ostentatious show **c :** type composition designed to catch the eye; *also* **:** printed matter so composed **d :** an eye-catching arrangement by which something is exhibited **2 :** a pattern of behavior exhibited esp. by male birds in the breeding season

dis·please \(ˈ)dis-ˈplēz\ *vb* [ME *displesen*, fr. MF *desplaisir*, fr. (assumed) VL *displacēre*, fr. L *dis-* + *placēre* to please] *vt* **1 :** to incur the disapproval of esp. as accompanied by annoyance or dislike **2 :** to be offensive to **~** *vi* **:** to give displeasure

dis·plea·sure \(ˈ)dis-ˈplezh-ər, -ˈplā-zhər\ *n* **1 :** the feeling of one that is displeased **:** DISFAVOR **2 a :** DISCOMFORT **b :** UNHAPPINESS

dis·plode \dis-ˈplōd\ *vb* [L *displodere*, fr. *dis-* + *plaudere* to clap, applaud] *archaic* **:** EXPLODE — **dis·plo·sion** \-ˈplō-zhən\ *n*

1**disport** \dis-ˈpō(ə)rt, -ˈpȯ(ə)rt\ *n, archaic* **:** SPORT, PASTIME

2**disport** *vb* [ME *disporten*, fr. MF *desporter*, fr. *des-* + *porter* to carry] *vt* **1 :** DIVERT, AMUSE **2 :** DISPLAY **~** *vi* **:** FROLIC

dis·pos·abil·i·ty \(ˌ)dis-ˌpō-zə-ˈbil-ət-ē\ *n* **:** the quality or state of being disposable

dis·pos·able \dis-ˈpō-zə-bəl\ *adj* **1 :** subject to or available for disposal ⟨~ income⟩ **2 :** easily disposed of ⟨~ towels⟩

dis·pos·al \dis-ˈpō-zəl\ *n* **1 :** the act or process of disposing: as **a :** orderly placement or distribution **b :** REGULATION, ADMINISTRATION **c :** BESTOWAL **d :** a discarding or throwing away **:** DESTRUCTION **2 :** the power or authority to dispose of

1**dis·pose** \dis-ˈpōz\ *vb* [ME *disposen*, fr. MF *disposer*, fr. L *disponere* to arrange (perf. indic. *disposui*), fr. *dis-* + *ponere* to put] *vt* **1 a :** to give a tendency to **:** INCLINE **b :** PREPARE **2 a :** to put in place **:** ARRANGE **b** *obs* **:** REGULATE **c** *archaic* **:** BESTOW **~** *vi* **1 :** to settle a matter finally **2** *obs* **:** to come to terms **syn** see INCLINE — **dis·pos·er** *n* — **dispose of 1 :** to place, distribute, or arrange esp. in an orderly way **2 a :** to transfer to the control of another **b** (1) **:** to get rid of (2) **:** to deal with conclusively

2**dispose** *n* **1** *obs* **:** DISPOSAL **2** *obs* **a :** DISPOSITION **b :** DEMEANOR

dis·po·si·tion \ˌdis-pə-ˈzish-ən\ *n* [ME, fr. MF, fr. L *disposition-*, *dispositio*, fr. *dispositus*, pp. of *disponere*] **1 :** the act or the power of disposing or the state of being disposed: as **a :** ADMINISTRATION, CONTROL **b** (1) **:** a giving over to the care or possession of another (2) **:** the power of so placing or ridding oneself of (3) **:** the transfer of property from one to another **c :** an ordering or arranging in an orderly way **2 a :** prevailing tendency, mood, or inclination **b :** temperamental makeup **c :** the tendency of something to act in a certain manner under given circumstances

syn DISPOSITION, TEMPERAMENT, TEMPER, CHARACTER, PERSONALITY mean the dominant quality or qualities distinguishing a person or group. DISPOSITION implies customary moods and attitude toward the life around one; TEMPERAMENT implies a pattern of innate characteristics associated with one's specific physical and nervous organization; TEMPER implies the qualities acquired through experience that determine how a person or a group meets difficulties or handles situations; CHARACTER applies to the aggregate of moral qualities by which a person is judged apart from his intelligence, competence, or special talents; PERSONALITY applies to an aggregate of qualities that distinguish one as a person

dis·pos·sess \ˌdis-pə-ˈzes, -ˈses\ *vt* [MF *despossesser*, fr. *des-* dis- + *possesser* to possess] **:** to put out of possession or occupancy — **dis·pos·ses·sor** \-ər\ *n*

dis·pos·ses·sion \-ˈzesh-ən, -ˈsesh-\ *n* **:** the act of dispossessing or the state of being dispossessed; *specif* **:** legal ouster

dis·po·sure \dis-ˈpō-zhər\ *n, archaic* **:** DISPOSAL, DISPOSITION

1**dis·praise** \(ˈ)dis-ˈprāz\ *vt* [ME *dispraisen*, fr. OF *despreisier*, fr. *des-* dis- + *preisier* to praise] **:** to comment on with disapproval or censure — **dis·prais·er** *n* — **dis·prais·ing·ly** \-ˈprā-ziŋ-lē\ *adv*

2**dispraise** *n* **:** the act of dispraising **:** DISPARAGEMENT

dispread \dis-ˈpred\ *vb* **:** to spread abroad or out **:** EXPAND

dis·prize \(ˈ)dis-ˈprīz\ *vt* [MF *despriser*, fr. OF *despreisier* to dispraise] *obs* **:** UNDERVALUE, SCORN

dis·proof \(ˈ)dis-ˈprüf\ *n* **1 :** the action of disproving **2 :** evidence that disproves

1**dis·pro·por·tion** \ˌdis-prə-ˈpōr-shən, -ˈpȯr-\ *n* **:** lack of proportion, symmetry, or proper relation **:** DISPARITY; *also* **:** an instance of such disparity — **dis·pro·por·tion·al** \-shnəl, -shən-ᵊl\ *adj*

2**disproportion** *vt* **:** to make out of proportion **:** MISMATCH

dis·pro·por·tion·ate \-sh(ə-)nət\ *adj* **:** being out of proportion **:** UNSYMMETRICAL — **dis·pro·por·tion·ate·ly** *adv*

dis·prov·able \(ˈ)dis-ˈprü-və-bəl\ *adj* **:** capable of being disproved

dis·prove \(ˈ)dis-ˈprüv\ *vt* [ME *disproven*, fr. MF *desprover*, fr. *des-* + *prover* to prove] **:** to prove to be false **:** REFUTE

syn REFUTE, CONFUTE, REBUT, CONTROVERT: DISPROVE implies the demonstration by any method of the falseness or invalidness of a claim or argument; REFUTE stresses a logical method of disproving; CONFUTE implies reducing an opponent to silence by an overwhelming argument; REBUT suggests formality in the act of answering an argument and does not necessarily imply success in disproving; CONTROVERT stresses the act of opposing with denial or an answering argument and, like REBUT, the attempt to refute an opposing argument without implying success in disproving

dis·put·abil·i·ty \(ˌ)dis-ˌpyüt-ə-ˈbil-ət-ē, ˌdis-pyət-\ *n* **:** the quality or state of being disputable

dis·put·able \dis-ˈpyüt-ə-bəl, ˈdis-pyət-\ *adj* **:** DEBATABLE

dis·pu·tant \dis-ˈpyüt-ᵊnt, ˈdis-pyət-ənt\ *n* **:** DISPUTER

dis·pu·ta·tion \ˌdis-pyə-ˈtā-shən, -(ˌ)pyü-ˈtā-\ *n* **1 :** the act of disputing **:** DEBATE **2 :** an academic exercise in oral defense of a thesis by formal logic

dis·pu·ta·tious \-shəs\ *adj* **1 :** inclined to dispute **2 :** CONTROVERSIAL — **dis·pu·ta·tious·ly** *adv* — **dis·pu·ta·tious·ness** *n*

1**dis·pute** \dis-ˈpyüt\ *vb* [ME *disputen*, fr. OF *desputer*, fr. L *disputare* to discuss, fr. *dis-* + *putare* to think] *vi* **1 :** to engage in argument **:** DEBATE **2 :** WRANGLE **~** *vt* **1 a :** to make the subject of disputation **b :** to call into question **2 a :** to struggle against **b :** to struggle over **:** CONTEST **syn** see DISCUSS — **dis·put·er** *n*

2**dis·pute** \dis-ˈpyüt, ˈdis-ˌpyüt\ *n* **1 a :** verbal controversy **:** DEBATE **b :** QUARREL **2** *obs* **:** physical combat

dis·qual·i·fi·ca·tion \(ˌ)dis-ˌkwäl-ə-fə-ˈkā-shən\ *n* **1 :** the act of disqualifying **:** the state of being disqualified ⟨~ from office⟩ **2 :** something that disqualifies or incapacitates

dis·qual·i·fy \(ˈ)dis-ˈkwäl-ə-ˌfī\ *vt* **1 :** to deprive of the required qualities, properties, or conditions **:** make unfit **2 :** to deprive of a power, right, or privilege; *specif* **:** to make ineligible **3 :** to debar from further competition for violation of the rules

dis·quan·ti·ty \(ˈ)dis-ˈkwän(t)-ət-ē\ *vt, obs* **:** DIMINISH, LESSEN

1**dis·qui·et** \(ˈ)dis-ˈkwī-ət\ *vt* **:** to take away the peace or tranquillity of **:** DISTURB, ALARM **syn** see DISCOMPOSE — **dis·qui·et·ing** *adj* — **dis·qui·et·ing·ly** \-iŋ-lē\ *adv*

2**disquiet** *n* **:** the lack of peace or tranquillity **:** ANXIETY

3**disquiet** *adj, archaic* **:** DISQUIETED, UNEASY — **dis·qui·et·ly** *adv*

dis·qui·etude \(ˈ)dis-ˈkwī-ə-ˌt(y)üd\ *n* **:** AGITATION, ANXIETY

dis·qui·si·tion \ˌdis-kwə-ˈzish-ən\ *n* [L *disquisition-*, *disquisitio*, fr. *disquisitus*, pp. of *disquirere* to inquire diligently, fr. *dis-* + *quaerere* to seek — more at QUEST] **:** a formal inquiry into or discussion of a subject **:** DISCOURSE

dis·rate \(ˈ)dis-ˈrāt\ *vt* **:** to reduce in rank **:** DEMOTE

1**dis·re·gard** \ˌdis-ri-ˈgärd\ *vt* **:** to pay no attention to **:** treat as unworthy of regard or notice **syn** see NEGLECT

2**disregard** *n* **:** the act of disregarding **:** the state of being disregarded **:** NEGLECT — **dis·re·gard·ful** \-fəl\ *adj*

dis·re·la·tion \ˌdis-ri-ˈlā-shən\ *n* **:** lack of a fitting or proportionate connection or relationship

1**dis·rel·ish** \(ˈ)dis-ˈrel-ish\ *vt* **:** to find unpalatable or distasteful

2**disrelish** *n* **:** lack of relish **:** DISTASTE, DISLIKE

dis·re·mem·ber \ˌdis-ri-ˈmem-bər\ *vt* **:** FORGET

dis·re·pair \ˌdis-ri-ˈpa(ə)r, -ˈpe(ə)r\ *n* **:** the state of being in need of repair

dis·rep·u·ta·bil·i·ty \(ˌ)dis-ˌrep-yət-ə-ˈbil-ət-ē\ *n* **:** the quality or state of being disreputable

dis·rep·u·ta·ble \(ˈ)dis-ˈrep-yət-ə-bəl\ *adj* **:** not reputable or decent — **dis·rep·u·ta·ble·ness** *n* — **dis·rep·u·ta·bly** \-blē\ *adv*

dis·re·pute \ˌdis-ri-ˈpyüt\ *n* **:** loss or lack of reputation **:** low esteem **:** DISCREDIT **syn** see DISGRACE

1**dis·re·spect** \ˌdis-ri-ˈspekt\ *vt* **:** to have disrespect for

2**disrespect** *n* **:** lack of respect or reverence **:** DISCOURTESY

dis·re·spect·able \ˌdis-ri-ˈspek-tə-bəl\ *adj* **:** not respectable

dis·re·spect·ful \ˌdis-ri-ˈspek(t)-fəl\ *adj* **:** lacking proper respect — **dis·re·spect·ful·ly** \-fə-lē\ *adv* — **dis·re·spect·ful·ness** *n*

dis·robe \(ˈ)dis-ˈrōb\ *vb* [MF *desrober*, fr. *des-* dis- + *robe* garment — more at ROBE] *vt* **:** UNDRESS **~** *vi* **:** to undress oneself

dis·rupt \dis-ˈrəpt\ *vt* [L *disruptus*, pp. of *disrumpere*, fr. *dis-* + *rumpere* to break — more at RUPTURE] **1 a :** to break apart **:** RUPTURE **b :** to throw into disorder **2 :** to cause to break down — **dis·rupt·er** *n* — **dis·rup·tion** \-ˈrəp-shən\ *n*

dis·rup·tive \dis-ˈrəp-tiv\ *adj* **:** causing or tending to cause disruption — **dis·rup·tive·ly** *adv* — **dis·rup·tive·ness** *n*

dis·sat·is·fac·tion \(ˌ)dis-ˌ(s)at-əs-ˈfak-shən\ *n* **:** the quality or state of being dissatisfied **:** DISCONTENT

dis·sat·is·fac·to·ry \-ˈfak-t(ə-)rē\ *adj* **:** causing dissatisfaction

dis·sat·is·fy \(ˈ)dis-ˈ(s)at-əs-ˌfī\ *vt* **:** to fail to satisfy **:** DISPLEASE

dis·save \(ˈ)dis-ˈ(s)āv\ *vi* **:** to use savings for current expenses

dis·seat \(ˈ)dis-ˈ(s)ēt\ *vt, archaic* **:** UNSEAT

dis·sect \dis-'ekt; dī-'sekt, 'dī-,\ *vb* [L *dissectus*, pp. of *dissecare* to cut apart, fr. *dis-* + *secare* to cut — more at SAW] *vt* **1** : to separate into pieces : expose the several parts (as of an animal) for scientific examination **2** : to analyze and interpret minutely ~ *vi* : to make a dissection **syn** see ANALYZE — **dis·sec·tor** \-ər\ *n*

dis·sect·ed *adj* : cut deeply into fine lobes ⟨a ~ leaf⟩

dis·sec·tion \dis-'ek-shən; dī-'sek-, 'dī-,\ *n* **1** : the act or process of dissecting : the state of being dissected **2** : an anatomical specimen prepared by dissecting

dis·seise *or* **dis·seize** \(')dis-'(s)ēz\ *vt* [ME *disseisen*, fr. ML *disseisiare* & AF *disseisir*, fr. OF *dessaisir*, fr. *des-* + *saisir* to put in possession of — more at SEIZE] : to deprive esp. wrongfully of seisin : DISPOSSESS — **dis·sei·sin** *or* **dis·sei·zin** \-'(s)ēz-ᵊn\ *n*

dis·sem·ble \dis-'em-bəl\ *vb* **dis·sem·bling** \-b(ə-)liŋ\ [alter. of obs. *dissimule*, fr. ME *dissimulen*, fr. MF *dissimuler*, fr. L *dissimulare* — more at DISSIMULATE] *vt* **1** : to hide under a false appearance **2** : to put on the appearance of : SIMULATE ~ *vi* : to put on a false appearance : conceal facts, intentions, or feelings under some pretense **syn** see DISGUISE — **dis·sem·bler** \-b(ə-)lər\ *n*

dis·sem·i·nate \dis-'em-ə-,nāt\ *vb* [L *disseminatus*, pp. of *disseminare*, fr. *dis-* + *seminare* to sow, fr. *semin-*, *semen* seed] *vt* **1** : to spread abroad as though sowing seed ⟨~ ideas⟩ **2** : to disperse throughout ~ *vi* : to spread widely — **dis·sem·i·na·tion** \-,em-ə-'nā-shən\ *n* — **dis·sem·i·na·tor** \-'em-ə-,nāt-ər\ *n*

dis·sem·i·nule \dis-'em-ə-,nyü(ə)l\ *n* : a part or organ (as a seed or spore) of a plant that ensures propagation

dis·sen·sion \dis-'en-chən\ *n* [ME, fr. MF, fr. L *dissension-*, *dissensio*, fr. *dissensus*, pp. of *dissentire*] : disagreement in opinion; *esp* : partisan and contentious quarreling **syn** see DISCORD

1**dis·sent** \dis-'ent\ *vi* [ME *dissenten*, fr. L *dissentire*, fr. *dis-* + *sentire* to feel] **1** : to withhold assent **2** : to differ in opinion

2**dissent** *n* : difference of opinion: as **a** : religious nonconformity **b** : a justice's nonconcurrence with a decision of the majority

dis·sent·er \dis-'ent-ər\ *n* **1** : one that dissents **2** *cap* : an English Nonconformist

dis·sen·tient \dis-'en-ch(ē-)ənt\ *adj* [L *dissentient-*, *dissentiens*, prp. of *dissentire*] : expressing dissent — **dissentient** *n*

Dis·sent·ing *adj* : NONCONFORMIST

dis·sep·i·ment \dis-'ep-ə-mənt\ *n* [L *dissaepimentum* partition, fr. *dissaepire* to divide, fr. *dis-* + *saepire* to fence in — more at SEPTUM] : a dividing tissue : SEPTUM; *esp* : a partition between cells of a compound plant ovary

dis·sert \dis-'ərt\ *vi* [L *dissertus*, pp. of *disserere*, fr. *dis-* + *serere* to join, arrange — more at SERIES] : DISCOURSE

dis·ser·tate \'dis-ər-,tāt\ *vi* [L *dissertatus*, pp. of *dissertare*, fr. *dissertus*] : DISSERT — **dis·ser·ta·tor** \-,tāt-ər\ *n*

dis·ser·ta·tion \,dis-ər-'tā-shən\ *n* : an extended usu. written treatment of a subject; *specif* : one submitted for a doctorate

dis·serve \(')dis-'(s)ərv\ *vt* : to serve badly or falsely : HARM

dis·ser·vice \(')dis-'(s)ər-vəs\ *n* : ill service : INJURY

dis·sev·er \dis-'ev-ər\ *vb* [ME *disseveren*, fr. OF *dessevrer*, fr. LL *disseparare*, fr. L *dis-* + *separare* to separate] *vt* : SEVER, SEPARATE ~ *vi* : to come apart : DISUNITE — **dis·sev·er·ance** \-'ev-(ə-)rən(t)s\ *n* — **dis·sev·er·ment** \-'ev-ər-mənt\ *n*

dis·si·dence \'dis-əd-ən(t)s\ *n* : DISSENT, DISAGREEMENT

dis·si·dent \-ənt\ *adj* [L *dissident-*, *dissidens*, prp. of *dissidēre* to sit apart, disagree, fr. *dis-* + *sedēre* to sit — more at SIT] : differing with an opinion or a group : DISAFFECTED — **dissident** *n*

dis·sim·i·lar \(')dis-'(s)im-(ə-)lər\ *adj* : UNLIKE — **dis·sim·i·lar·i·ty** \(,)dis-,(s)im-ə-'lar-ət-ē\ *n* — **dis·sim·i·lar·ly** *adv*

dis·sim·i·late \(')dis-'im-ə-,lāt\ *vb* [*dis-* + *-similate* (as in *assimilate*)] *vt* : to make dissimilar ~ *vi* : to become dissimilar — **dis·sim·i·la·tive** \-,lāt-iv\ *adj* — **dis·sim·i·la·to·ry** \(')dis-'im-(ə-)lə-,tōr-ē, -,tȯr-\ *adj*

dis·sim·i·la·tion \(,)dis-,im-ə-'lā-shən\ *n* : the act of making or the process of becoming dissimilar: as **a** : CATABOLISM **b** : the development of dissimilarity between two identical or closely related sounds in a word

dis·si·mil·i·tude \,dis-(s)ə-'mil-ə-,t(y)üd\ *n* [L *dissimilitudo*, fr. *dissimilis* unlike, fr. *dis-* + *similis* like] : lack of resemblance

dis·sim·u·late \(')dis-'im-yə-,lāt\ *vb* [L *dissimulatus*, pp. of *dissimulare*, fr. *dis-* + *simulare* to simulate] *vt* : to hide under a false appearance : DISSEMBLE ~ *vi* : to engage in dissembling — **dis·sim·u·la·tion** \(,)dis-,im-yə-'lā-shən\ *n* — **dis·sim·u·la·tor** \(')dis-'im-yə-,lāt-ər\ *n*

dis·si·pate \'dis-ə-,pāt\ *vb* [L *dissipatus*, pp. of *dissipare*, fr. *dis-* + *supare* to throw; akin to ON *svāf* spear, Skt *svapu* broom] *vt* **1 a** : to break up and drive off (as a crowd) **b** : to cause to spread out or spread thin to the point of vanishing : DISSOLVE **2 a** : to expend aimlessly or foolishly **b** : SQUANDER ~ *vi* **1** : to separate into parts and scatter or vanish **2** : to be extravagant or dissolute in the pursuit of pleasure; *esp* : to drink to excess **syn** see SCATTER — **dis·si·pat·er** *n* — **dis·si·pa·tive** \-,pāt-iv\ *adj*

dis·si·pat·ed *adj* : given to or marked by dissipation : DISSOLUTE — **dis·si·pat·ed·ly** *adv* — **dis·si·pat·ed·ness** *n*

dis·si·pa·tion \,dis-ə-'pā-shən\ *n* **1** : the act of dissipating : the state of being dissipated: **a** : DISPERSION, DIFFUSION **b** *archaic* : DISINTEGRATION **c** : wasteful expenditure **d** : intemperate living; *esp* : excessive drinking **2** : idle diversion : AMUSEMENT

dis·so·cia·bil·i·ty \(,)dis-,ō-sh(ē-)ə-'bil-ət-ē, -sē-ə-\ *n* : the quality of being dissociable

dis·so·cia·ble \(')dis-'ō-sh(ē-)ə-bəl, -sē-ə-\ *adj* : SEPARABLE

dis·so·cial \(')dis-'(s)ō-shəl\ *adj* : SELFISH

dis·so·ciant \dis-'ō-s(h)ē-ənt, -'ō-shənt\ *adj* : producing or resulting from dissociation; *specif* : MUTANT

dis·so·ci·ate \(')dis-'ō-s(h)ē-,āt\ *vb* [L *dissociatus*, pp. of *dissociare*, fr. *dis-* + *sociare* to join, fr. *socius* companion — more at SOCIAL] *vt* **1** : to separate from association or union with another : DISCONNECT **2** : DISUNITE; *specif* : to subject to chemical dissociation ~ *vi* **1** : to undergo dissociation **2** : to mutate esp. reversibly

dis·so·ci·a·tion \(,)dis-,ō-sē-'ā-shən, -shē-\ *n* **1** : the act or process of dissociating : the state of being dissociated: as **a** : the process by which a chemical combination breaks up into simpler constituents — used esp. of the action of heat or other forms of energy on gases and of solvents on dissolved substances **b** : the separation of an idea or activity from the main stream of consciousness or of behavior esp. as a mechanism of ego defense **2** : the property inherent in some biological stocks of differentiating into two or more distinct and relatively permanent strains; *also* : such a strain — **dis·so·cia·tive** \(')dis-'ō-s(h)ē-,āt-iv, -shət-iv\ *adj*

dis·sol·u·bil·i·ty \dis-,äl-yə-'bil-ət-ē\ *n* : the quality or state of being dissoluble

dis·sol·u·ble \dis-'äl-yə-bəl\ *adj* [L *dissolubilis*, fr. *dissolvere* to dissolve] : capable of being dissolved or disintegrated

dis·so·lute \'dis-ə-,lüt, -lət\ *adj* [L *dissolutus*, fr. pp. of *dissolvere* to loosen, dissolve] : lacking restraint; *esp* : loose in morals or conduct — **dis·so·lute·ly** *adv* — **dis·so·lute·ness** *n*

dis·so·lu·tion \,dis-ə-'lü-shən\ *n* **1** : the act or process of dissolving: as **a** : separation into component parts **b** : DECAY; *esp* : DEATH **c** : termination or destruction by breaking down, disrupting, or dispersing **d** : LIQUEFACTION **2** *obs* : DISSOLUTENESS

dis·solv·able \diz-'äl-və-bəl, -'ȯl-\ *adj* : capable of being dissolved

1**dis·solve** \diz-'älv, -'ȯlv\ *vb* [ME *dissolven*, fr. L *dissolvere*, fr. *dis-* + *solvere* to loosen — more at SOLVE] *vt* **1 a** : to cause to disperse or disappear : DESTROY **b** : to separate into component parts : DISINTEGRATE **c** : to bring to an end : TERMINATE ⟨~ parliament⟩ **2 a** : to cause to pass into solution ⟨~ sugar in water⟩ **b** : MELT, LIQUEFY **c** : to cause to be emotionally moved **d** : to fade out (a motion-picture shot) in a dissolve **3** *archaic* : DETACH, LOOSEN **4** : to clear up ⟨~ the mystery⟩ ~ *vi* **1 a** : to become dissipated or decomposed **b** : to break up : DISPERSE **c** : to fade away **2 a** : to become fluid : MELT **b** : to pass into solution **c** : to be overcome emotionally **d** : to resolve itself as if by dissolution **syn** see ADJOURN — **dis·solv·er** *n*

2**dissolve** *n* : a gradual superimposing of one motion-picture or television shot upon another on a screen

dis·sol·vent \diz-'äl-vənt, -'ȯl-\ *adj* : SOLVENT 2 — **dissolvent** *n*

dis·so·nance \'dis-ə-nən(t)s\ *n* **1** : a mingling of discordant sounds; *specif* : a clashing musical interval **2** : lack of agreement : DISCORD **3** : an unresolved musical note or chord; *specif* : an interval not included in a major or minor triad or its inversions

dis·so·nant \-nənt\ *adj* [MF or L; MF, fr. L *dissonant-*, *dissonans*, prp. of *dissonare* to be discordant, fr. *dis-* + *sonare* to sound — more at SOUND] **1** : marked by dissonance : DISCORDANT **2** : INCONGRUOUS **3** : harmonically unresolved — **dis·so·nant·ly** *adv*

dis·spir·it \(')dis-'(s)pir-ət\ *var of* DISPIRIT

dis·spread \dis-'pred\ *var of* DISPREAD

dis·suade \dis-'wād\ *vt* [MF or L; MF *dissuader*, fr. L *dissuadēre*, fr. *dis-* + *suadēre* to urge — more at SUASION] **1 a** *archaic* : to advise against (an action) **b** : to advise (a person) against something **2** : to turn from something by persuasion — **dis·suad·er** *n*

dis·sua·sion \dis-'wā-zhən\ *n* [MF or L; MF, fr. L *dissuasion-*, *dissuasio*, fr. *dissuasus*, pp. of *dissuadēre*] : the act of dissuading

dis·sua·sive \dis-'wā-siv, -ziv\ *adj* : tending to dissuade — **dis·sua·sive·ly** *adv* — **dis·sua·sive·ness** *n*

dis·syl·lab·ic \,dis-ə-'lab-ik, ,dī-sə-\, **dis·syl·la·ble** \'dis-,il-ə-bəl, (')dis-'(s)il-; 'dī-,sil-, (')dī-'sil-\ *var of* DISYLLABIC, DISYLLABLE

dis·sym·met·ric \,dis-(s)ə-'me-trik\ *adj* : characterized by dissymmetry

dis·sym·me·try \(')dis-'(s)im-ə-trē\ *n* : the absence of or the lack of symmetry; *specif* : ENANTIOMORPHISM

1**dis·taff** \'dis-,taf\ *n*, *pl* **distaffs** \-,tafs, -,tavz\ [ME *distaf*, fr. OE *distæf*, fr. *dis-* (akin to MLG *dise* bunch of flax) + *stæf* staff] **1 a** : a staff for holding the flax, tow, or wool in spinning **b** : woman's work or domain **2** : the female branch or side of a family

2**distaff** *adj* : FEMALE

dis·tain \dis-'tān\ *vt* [ME *disteynen*, fr. MF *desteindre* to take away the color of, fr. OF, fr. *des-* dis- + *teindre* to dye, fr. L *tingere* to wet, dye — more at TINGE] **1** *archaic* : STAIN **2** *archaic* : DISHONOR

dis·tal \'dist-ᵊl\ *adj* [*distant* + *-al*] : far from the point of attachment or origin — compare PROXIMAL — **dis·tal·ly** \-ᵊl-ē\ *adv*

1**dis·tance** \'dis-tən(t)s\ *n* **1** *obs* : DISCORD **2 a** : separation in time **b** : the degree or amount of separation between two points, lines, surfaces, or objects measured along the shortest path joining them **c** : an extent of area or an advance along a route measured linearly **d** : an extent of advance away or along from a point considered primary or original **e** : EXPANSE **f** *in racing* (1) : COURSE, ROUTE (2) : an extent of the track marked by a post or flag which a horse in a heat race must reach by the time the winner crosses the finish line to be qualified for later heats **3** : the quality or state of being distant: as **a** : spatial remoteness **b** : COLDNESS, RESERVE **c** : DIFFERENCE, DISPARITY **4** : a distant point or region

2**distance** *vt* **1** : to place or keep at a distance **2** : to leave far behind : OUTSTRIP **3** : to declare disqualified in racing because of losing a heat by a distance

dis·tant \'dis-tənt\ *adj* [ME, fr. MF, fr. L *distant-*, *distans*, prp. of *distare* to stand apart, be distant, fr. *dis-* + *stare* to stand] **1 a** : separated in space : AWAY **b** : situated at a great distance : FAR-OFF **c** : separated by a great distance from each other : far apart **2** : separated in a relationship other than spatial ⟨a ~ relative⟩ **3** : different in kind **4** : reserved or aloof in personal relationship : COLD ⟨~ politeness⟩ **5 a** : coming from or going to a distance ⟨~ voyages⟩ **b** : concerned with or directed toward things at a distance ⟨~ thoughts⟩ — **dis·tant·ly** *adv* — **dis·tant·ness** *n*

syn DISTANT, FAR, FARAWAY, FAR-OFF, REMOTE, REMOVED mean not close in space, time, or relationship. DISTANT stresses separation and implies an obvious interval whether long or short; FAR more often suggests an interval in space and implies a relatively long distance away; FARAWAY and FAR-OFF mean extremely far and are usu. preferred to FAR for indicating distance in time; REMOTE suggests a far removal from one's point of view, time, or location and connotes a consequent lessening of importance; REMOVED carries an even stronger implication of separateness and therefore suggests a contrast not only in time and space but often in character or quality

1**dis·taste** \(')dis-'tāst\ *vt* **1** *archaic* : to feel aversion to **2** *archaic* : OFFEND, DISPLEASE ~ *vi*, *obs* : to taste offensive

2**distaste** *n* **1 a** : dislike of food or drink **b** : DISINCLINATION, AVERSION **2** *obs* : ANNOYANCE, DISCOMFORT

dis·taste·ful \-'tāst-fəl\ *adj* **1 a** : unpleasant to the taste : LOATHSOME **b** : OFFENSIVE, DISAGREEABLE **2** : showing distaste or aversion **syn** see REPUGNANT — **dis·taste·ful·ly** \-fə-lē\ *adv* — **dis·taste·ful·ness** *n*

1**dis·tem·per** \dis-'tem-pər\ *vt* [ME *distempren*, fr. LL *distemperare* to temper badly, fr. L *dis-* + *temperare* to temper] **1** : to throw out of order **2** *archaic* : UNSETTLE, DERANGE

2**distemper** *n* **1** : bad humor or temper **2** : a disordered or abnormal bodily state usu. of a lower animal: as **a** : a highly contagious virus disease esp. of dogs marked by fever and by respiratory and sometimes nervous symptoms **b** : STRANGLES **c** : PANLEU-

COPENIA **d :** a severe frequently fatal infectious nasopharyngeal inflammation of rabbits **3 :** political or social disorder — **dis·tem·per·ate** \dis-'tem-p(ə-)rət\ *adj*

³distemper *vt* [ME *distemperen,* fr. MF *destemprer,* fr. L *dis-* + *temperare*] **1** *obs* **:** to dilute with or soak, steep, or dissolve in a liquid **2 a :** to mix (ingredients) to produce distemper **b :** to paint in or with distemper

⁴distemper *n* **1 :** a process of painting in which the pigments are mixed with an emulsion of egg yolk, with size, or with white of egg, or with size only as a vehicle and which is usu. used for scene painting or mural decoration **2 a :** the paint or the prepared ground used in the distemper process **b :** a painting done in distemper **3 :** any of a number of paints using water as a vehicle

dis·tem·per·a·ture \dis-'tem-pə(r)-,chu̇(ə)r, -p(ə-)rə-, -chər, -,t(y)u̇(ə)r\ *n* **:** a disordered condition **:** mental or bodily derangement

dis·tem·per·oid \dis-'tem-pə-,ròid\ *adj* **:** resembling distemper; *specif* **:** of, relating to, or being an attenuated canine distemper virus used to develop immunity to natural distemper infection

dis·tend \dis-'tend\ *vb* [ME *distenden,* fr. L *distendere,* fr. *dis-* + *tendere* to stretch] *vt* **1** *archaic* **:** EXTEND **2 :** to enlarge from internal pressure **:** SWELL ~ *vi* **:** to become expanded **syn** see EXPAND

dis·ten·si·ble \dis-'ten(t)-sə-bəl\ *adj* [LL *distensus,* pp. of L *distendere*] **:** capable of being distended

dis·ten·sion *or* **dis·ten·tion** \dis-'ten-chən\ *n* [L *distention-, distentio,* fr. *distentus,* pp. of *distendere*] **:** the act of distending or the state of being distended esp. unduly or abnormally

dis·tent \dis-'tent\ *adj, obs* **:** spread out **:** DISTENDED

dis·tich \'dis-(,)tik\ *n* [L *distichon,* fr. Gk, fr. neut. of *distichos* having two rows, fr. *di-* + *stichos* row, verse; akin to Gk *steichein* to go — more at STAIR] **:** a strophic unit of two lines

dis·ti·chous \'dis-ti-kəs\ *adj* [LL *distichus,* fr. Gk *distichos*] **1 :** disposed in two vertical rows ⟨~ leaves⟩ **2 :** divided into two segments ⟨~ antennae⟩ — **dis·ti·chous·ly** *adv*

dis·till *also* **dis·til** \dis-'til\ *vb* **dis·tilled; dis·till·ing; dis·tills** *also* **dis·tils** [ME *distillen,* fr. MF *distiller,* fr. LL *distillare,* alter. of L *destillare,* fr. *de-* + *stillare* to drip, fr. *stilla* drop; akin to OE *stān* stone — more at STONE] *vt* **1 :** to let fall, exude, or precipitate in drops or in a wet mist **2 a :** to subject to or transform by distillation **b :** to obtain by or as if by distillation **c :** to extract the essence of **:** CONCENTRATE ~ *vi* **1 a :** to fall or materialize in drops or in a fine moisture **:** DROP **b :** to appear slowly or in small quantities at a time **2 a :** to undergo distillation **b :** to condense or drop from a still after distillation

dis·til·late \'dis-tə-,lāt, dis-'til-ət\ *n* **1 :** a liquid product condensed from vapor during distillation **2 :** something resembling a distillate

dis·til·la·tion \,dis-tə-'lā-shən\ *n* **1 :** a process that consists of driving gas or vapor from liquids or solids by heating and condensing to liquid products and that is used esp. for purification, fractionation, or the formation of new substances **2 :** DISTILLATE

dis·till·er \dis-'til-ər\ *n* **:** one that distills esp. alcoholic liquors

dis·till·ery \dis-'til-(ə-)rē\ *n* **:** the works where distilling is done

dis·til·ment \dis-'til-mənt\ *n, archaic* **:** DISTILLATE

dis·tinct \dis-'tiŋ(k)t\ *adj* [ME, fr. MF, fr. L *distinctus,* fr. pp. of *distinguere*] **1 :** distinguished from others **2 a :** capable of being easily perceived **:** CLEAR **b :** well defined **3** *archaic* **:** notably decorated **4 a :** NOTABLE **b :** DECIDED — **dis·tinct·ly** \-'tiŋ(k)-tlē, -'tiŋ-klē\ *adv* — **dis·tinct·ness** \-'tiŋt-nəs, -'tiŋk-nəs\ *n*

syn DISTINCT, SEPARATE, SEVERAL, DISCRETE all refer to two or more things either not the same or not blended or united. DISTINCT indicates that something is distinguished by the mind or eye as being apart from or different from others; SEPARATE often stresses lack of connection or a difference in identity between two things; SEVERAL indicates distinctness, difference, or separation from similar items: it implies that a group is to be considered one member at a time; DISCRETE strongly emphasizes individuality and lack of physical connection despite apparent similarity or seeming continuity **syn** see in addition EVIDENT

dis·tinc·tion \dis-'tiŋ(k)-shən\ *n* **1 a** *archaic* **:** DIVISION **b :** CLASS **2 a :** the act of distinguishing a difference **:** DISCRIMINATION, DIFFERENTIATION **b :** the object or result of distinguishing **:** CONTRAST **3 :** a distinguishing mark **4 :** the quality or state of being distinguishable **5 a :** the quality or state of being distinguished **b :** special honor or recognition **c :** WORTHINESS

dis·tinc·tive \dis-'tiŋ(k)-tiv\ *adj* **1 a :** serving to distinguish **b :** having or giving style or distinction **2 :** capable of differentiating meaning in otherwise identical utterance **syn** see CHARACTERISTIC — **dis·tinc·tive·ly** *adv* — **dis·tinc·tive·ness** *n*

dis·tin·gué \,dēs-,taŋ-'gā, ,dis-; di-'staŋ-(,)gā\ *adj* [F, fr. pp. of *distinguer*] **:** distinguished esp. in manner or bearing

dis·tin·guish \dis-'tiŋ-gwish\ *vb* [MF *distinguer,* fr. L *distinguere,* lit., to separate by pricking, fr. *dis-* + *-stinguere* (akin to L *instigare* to urge on) — more at STICK] *vt* **1 :** to perceive as being separate or different **2 a :** to mark as separate or different **b :** to separate into kinds, classes, or categories **c :** to set above or apart from others **d :** CHARACTERIZE **3 a :** DISCERN **b :** to single out ~ *vi* **:** to perceive a difference — **dis·tin·guish·able** \-ə-bəl\ *adj* — **dis·tin·guish·ably** \-blē\ *adv*

dis·tin·guished *adj* **1 :** marked by eminence, distinction, or excellence **2 :** befitting an eminent person **syn** see FAMOUS

Distinguished Conduct Medal *n* **:** a British military decoration awarded for distinguished conduct in the field

Distinguished Flying Cross *n* **1 :** a U.S. military decoration awarded for heroism or extraordinary achievement while participating in an aerial flight **2 :** a British military decoration awarded for acts of gallantry when flying in operations against an enemy

Distinguished Service Cross *n* **1 :** a U.S. Army decoration awarded for extraordinary heroism during operations against an armed enemy **2 :** a British military decoration awarded for distinguished service against the enemy

Distinguished Service Medal *n* **1 :** a U.S. military decoration awarded for exceptionally meritorious service to the government in a wartime duty of great responsibility **2 :** a British military decoration awarded for distinguished conduct in war

Distinguished Service Order *n* **:** a British military decoration awarded for especial services in action

di·stome \'dī-,stōm\ *n* [deriv. of Gk *di-* + *stomat-, stoma* mouth] **:** any of various trematode worms with both oral and ventral suckers

dis·tort \dis-'tȯ(ə)rt\ *vt* [L *distortus,* pp. of *distorquēre,* fr. *dis-* + *torquēre* to twist] **1 :** to twist out of the true meaning or proportion **2 :** to twist out of a natural, normal, or original shape or condition **3 :** PERVERT **syn** see DEFORM — **dis·tort·er** *n*

dis·tor·tion \dis-'tȯr-shən\ *n* **1 :** the act of distorting **2 :** the quality or state of being distorted or a product of distortion: as **a :** a lack of proportionality in an image resulting from defects in the optical system **b :** falsified reproduction caused by change in wave form of a signal — **dis·tor·tion·al** \-shnəl, -shən-ᵊl\ *adj*

¹dis·tract \dis-'trakt, 'dis-,\ *adj, archaic* **:** INSANE, MAD

²dis·tract \dis-'trakt\ *vt* [ME *distracten,* fr. L *distractus,* pp. of *distrahere,* lit., to draw apart, fr. *dis-* + *trahere* to draw — more at DRAW] **1 a :** to turn aside **:** DIVERT **b :** to draw (as the attention) to a different object or in divergent directions at once **2 :** to stir up or confuse with conflicting emotions or motives **:** HARASS — **dis·tract·ing·ly** \-'trak-tiŋ-lē\ *adv* **syn** see PUZZLE

dis·trac·tion \dis-'trak-shən\ *n* **1 :** the act of distracting or the state of being distracted; *esp* **:** mental confusion **2 :** something that distracts; *esp* **:** AMUSEMENT — **dis·trac·tive** \-'trak-tiv\ *adj*

dis·train \dis-'trān\ *vb* [ME *distreynen,* fr. OF *destreindre,* fr. ML *distringere,* fr. L, to draw apart, detain, fr. *dis-* + *stringere* to bind tight — more at STRAIN] *vt* **1 :** to levy a distress upon **2 :** to seize by distress ~ *vi* **:** to levy a distress — **dis·train·able** \-'trā-nə-bəl\ *adj* — **dis·train·er** *or* **dis·trai·nor** \-'trā-nər\ *n*

dis·traint \-'trānt\ *n* [*distrain* + *-t* (as in *constraint*)] **:** the act or proceeding of distraining

dis·trait \di-'strā\ *adj* [F, fr. L *distractus*] **:** ABSENTMINDED; *esp* **:** inattentive or distracted because of anxiety or apprehension

dis·traught \dis-'trȯt\ *adj* [ME, fr. L *distractus*] **1 :** agitated with doubt or mental conflict **2 :** CRAZED — **dis·traught·ly** *adv*

¹dis·tress \dis-'tres\ *n* [ME *destresse,* fr. OF, fr. (assumed) VL *districtia,* fr. L *districtus,* pp. of *distringere*] **1 a :** seizure and detention of the goods of another as pledge or to obtain satisfaction of a claim by the sale of the goods seized; *broadly;* an act of distraining **b :** the thing distrained **2** *obs* **:** CONSTRAINT **3 a :** anguish of body or mind **:** TROUBLE **b :** a painful situation **:** MISFORTUNE **4 :** a state of danger or desperate need

syn DISTRESS, SUFFERING, MISERY, AGONY mean the state of being in great trouble. DISTRESS implies an external and usu. temporary cause of great physical or mental strain and stress; SUFFERING implies conscious endurance of pain or distress and often a stoical acceptance of it; MISERY stresses the unhappiness attending esp. sickness, poverty, or loss, and often connotes sordidness, abjectness, or dull passivity; AGONY suggests pain too intense to be borne

²distress *vt* **1 :** to subject to great strain or difficulties **2 :** to cause to worry or be troubled **:** UPSET **3** *archaic* **:** to force or overcome by inflicting pain — **dis·tress·ing·ly** \-iŋ-lē\ *adv*

³distress *adj* **1 :** offered for sale at a sacrifice ⟨~ merchandise⟩ **2 :** involving distress goods ⟨a ~ sale⟩

dis·tress·ful \dis-'tres-fəl\ *adj* **:** causing distress **:** full of distress — **dis·tress·ful·ly** \-fə-lē\ *adv* — **dis·tress·ful·ness** *n*

dis·trib·u·tary \dis-'trib-yə-,ter-ē\ *n* **:** a river branch flowing away from the main stream

dis·trib·ute \dis-'trib-yət\ *vt* [ME *distributen,* fr. L *distributus,* pp. of *distribuere,* fr. *dis-* + *tribuere* to allot — more at TRIBUTE] **1 :** to divide among several or many **:** APPORTION **2 a :** to spread out so as to cover something **:** SCATTER **b :** DELIVER ⟨~ magazines to subscribers⟩ **c :** to use (a term) so as to convey information about every member of the class named ⟨the proposition "all men are mortal" ~*s* "man" but not "mortal"⟩ **3 a :** to divide or separate esp. into kinds **b :** to return the units of (as typeset matter) to the proper storage places — **dis·trib·u·tee** \dis-,trib-yə-'tē\ *n*

syn DISPENSE, DIVIDE, DEAL, DOLE: DISTRIBUTE may apply to any manner of separating into parts and spreading out, equally or systematically or merely at random; DISPENSE suggests the giving of a carefully weighed or measured portion to each of a group; DIVIDE stresses the initial separation of a whole into parts before giving out or delivering; DEAL implies the delivery piece by piece in turn to members of a group; DOLE implies a dispensing of alms to the needy but may apply to any cautious dispensing or periodic giving

dis·tri·bu·tion \,dis-trə-'byü-shən\ *n* **1 a :** the act or process of distributing **b :** the apportionment by a court of the personal property of an intestate **2 a :** the position, arrangement, or frequency of occurrence (as of the members of a group) over an area or throughout a space or unit of time **b :** the natural geographic range of an organism **3 a :** something distributed **b :** FREQUENCY DISTRIBUTION **4 a :** a device by which something is distributed **b :** the pattern of branching and termination of a ramifying structure (as a nerve) **5 :** the marketing or merchandising of commodities — **dis·tri·bu·tion·al** \-shnəl, -shən-ᵊl\ *adj*

dis·trib·u·tive \dis-'trib-yət-iv\ *adj* **1 :** of or relating to distribution: as **a :** dealing a proper share to each of a group **b :** diffusing more or less evenly **2** *of a word* **:** referring singly and without exception to the members of a group ⟨*each, either,* and *none* are ~⟩ **3 :** producing the same element when operating on a whole as when operating on each part and collecting the results ⟨multiplication is ~ relative to addition⟩ — **dis·trib·u·tive·ly** *adv* — **dis·trib·u·tive·ness** *n*

dis·trib·u·tor \dis-'trib-yət-ər\ *n* **1 :** one that distributes **2 :** one that markets a commodity; *esp* **:** WHOLESALER **3 :** an apparatus for directing the secondary current from the induction coil to the various spark plugs of an engine in their proper firing order

¹dis·trict \'dis-(,)trikt\ *n, often attrib* [F, fr. ML *districtus* jurisdiction, district, fr. *districtus,* pp. of *distringere* to distrain] **1 :** a territorial division marked off or defined (as for electoral purposes) **2 :** an area, region, or section with a distinguishing character

²district *vt* **:** to divide or organize into districts

district attorney *n* **:** the prosecuting officer of a judicial district

district superintendent *n* **:** a church official supervising a district

¹dis·trust \(')dis-'trəst\ *vt* **:** to have no confidence in **:** SUSPECT

²distrust *n* **:** the lack or absence of trust **:** SUSPICION, WARINESS

dis·trust·ful \-'trəst-fəl\ *adj* **:** having or showing distrust — **dis·trust·ful·ly** \-fə-lē\ *adv* — **dis·trust·ful·ness** *n*

dis·turb \dis-'tərb\ *vb* [ME *disturben, destourben,* fr. OF & L; OF *destourber,* fr. L *disturbare,* fr. *dis-* + *turbare* to throw into disorder

— more at TURBID] *vt* **1 a :** to interfere with **:** INTERRUPT **b :** to alter the position or arrangement of **c :** to break up or damage (as by shaking or jarring) **2 a :** to destroy the tranquillity or composure of **b :** to throw into disorder **c :** ALARM **d :** to put to inconvenience ~ *vi* **:** to cause disturbance **syn** see DISCOMPOSE — **dis·turb·er** *n*

dis·tur·bance \dis-'tər-bən(t)s\ *n* **1 :** the act of disturbing **:** the state of being disturbed **2 :** a local variation from the average or normal wind conditions

dis·turbed *adj* **:** showing symptoms of emotional illness

di·sul·fide \(')dī-'səl-,fīd\ *n* **:** a compound containing two atoms of sulfur combined with an element or radical

dis·union \dish-'ü-nyən, (')dis(h)-'yü-\ *n* **1 :** the termination or destruction of union **:** SEPARATION **2 :** DISUNITY

dis·union·ist \-nyə-nəst\ *n* **:** one who favors disunion; *specif* **:** an American secessionist

dis·unite \,dish-ü-'nīt, ,dis(h)-yü-\ *vt* **:** DIVIDE, SEPARATE

dis·uni·ty \dish-'ü-nət-ē, (')dis(h)-'yü-\ *n* **:** lack of unity; *esp* **:** DISSENSION

1**dis·use** \dish-'üz, (')dis(h)-'yüz\ *vt* **:** to discontinue the use or practice of

2**dis·use** \-'üs, -'yüs\ *n* **:** cessation of use or practice

dis·util·i·ty \,dish-ü-'til-ət-ē, ,dis(h)-yü-\ *n* **:** ability to cause fatigue, inconvenience, discomfort, or pain ⟨~ of labor⟩

1**dis·val·ue** \(')dis-'val-(,)yü, -yə-w\ *vt* **1** *archaic* **:** UNDERVALUE, DEPRECIATE **2 :** to consider of little value **:** DISESTEEM

2**disvalue** *n* **1 :** DISESTEEM, DISREGARD **2 :** a negative value

di·syl·lab·ic \,dī-sə-'lab-ik, ,dis-ə-\ *adj* **:** having two syllables

di·syl·la·ble \'dī-,sil-ə-bəl, (')dī-'sil-; 'dis-,il-, (')dis-'(s)il-\ *n* [part trans. of MF *dissilabe*, fr. L *disyllabus* having two syllables, fr. Gk *disyllabos*, fr. *di-* + *syllabē* syllable] **:** a linguistic form consisting of two syllables

dit \'dit\ *n* [imit.] **:** a dot in radio or telegraphic code

1**ditch** \'dich\ *n* [ME *dich*, fr. OE *dīc* dike, ditch] **:** a long narrow excavation dug in the earth for defense, drainage, or irrigation

2**ditch** *vt* **1 a :** to enclose with a ditch **b :** to dig a ditch in **2 :** to cause (a train) to derail **:** drive (a car) into a ditch **3 :** to get rid of **:** DISCARD **4 :** to make a forced landing of (an airplane) on water

ditch reed *n* **:** a tall No. American reed (*Phragmites communis*) with broad flat leaves — called also *giant reed*

dite \'dīt\ *n* [alter. of *doit*] *dial* **:** MITE, BIT

1**dith·er** \'di*th*-ər\ *vi* **dith·er·ing** \'di*th*-(ə-)riŋ\ [ME *didderen*] **1 :** SHIVER, TREMBLE **2 :** to act nervously or indecisively **:** VACILLATE

2**dither** *n* **:** a highly nervous, excited, or agitated state **:** EXCITEMENT, CONFUSION — **dith·ery** \'di*th*-ə-rē\ *adj*

dith·y·ramb \'dith-i-,ram(b)\ *n*, *pl* **dithyrambs** \-,ramz\ [Gk *dithyrambos*] **1 :** a usu. irregular short poem or chant in a wild, inspired strain **2 :** a statement or writing in an exalted or enthusiastic vein — **dith·y·ram·bic** \,dith-i-'ram-bik\ *adj*

dit·ta·ny \'dit-ən-ē\ *n* [ME *ditoyne*, fr. MF *ditayne*, fr. L *dictamnum*, fr. Gk *diktamnon*] **:** an herb (*Origanum dictamnus*) native to Crete with pink flowers

1**dit·to** \'dit-(,)ō\ *n*, *pl* **dittos** [It dial., pp. of It *dire* to say, fr. L *dicere* — more at DICTION] **1 :** a thing mentioned previously or above — used to avoid repeating a word; often symbolized by inverted commas or apostrophes **2 :** a ditto mark

2**ditto** *vt* **:** to repeat the action or statement of

3**ditto** *adv* **:** as before or aforesaid **:** in the same manner

dit·ty \'dit-ē\ *n* [ME *ditee*, fr. OF *ditié* poem, fr. pp. of *ditier* to compose, fr. L *dictare* to dictate, compose] **:** a song or short poem intended to be sung; *esp* **:** one that is simple and unaffected

dit·ty bag \'dit-ē-\ *n* **:** a small bag used esp. by sailors to hold small articles of gear (as thread, needles, tape)

ditty box *n* **:** a box used for the same purpose as a ditty bag

di·ure·sis \,dī-yù-'rē-səs\ *n*, *pl* **di·ure·ses** \-'rē-,sēz\ [NL] **:** an increased excretion of urine

di·uret·ic \,dī-yù-'ret-ik\ *adj* [ME, fr. MF or LL; MF *diuretique*, fr. LL *diureticus*, fr. Gk *diourētikos*, fr. *diourein* to urinate, fr. *dia-* + *ourein* to urinate — more at URINE] **:** tending to increase the flow of urine — **diuretic** *n* — **di·uret·i·cal·ly** \-i-k(ə-)lē\ *adv*

1**di·ur·nal** \dī-'ərn-əl\ *adj* [ME, fr. L *diurnalis* — more at JOURNAL] **1 a :** recurring every day ⟨~ task⟩ **b :** having a daily cycle ⟨~ rotation of the heavens⟩ **2 a :** of, relating to, or occurring in the daytime ⟨the city's ~ noises⟩ **b :** opening during the day and closing at night **syn** see DAILY — **di·ur·nal·ly** \-əl-ē\ *adv*

2**diurnal** *n* **1** *archaic* **:** DAYBOOK, DIARY **2** *archaic* **:** JOURNAL

di·va \'dē-və\ *n*, *pl* **di·vas** *or* **di·ve** \-(,)vā\ [It, lit., goddess, fr. L, fem. of *divus* divine, god — more at DEITY] **:** PRIMA DONNA 1

di·va·gate \'dī-və-,gāt, 'div-ə-\ *vi* [LL *divagatus*, pp. of *divagari*, fr. L *dis-* + *vagari* to wander — more at VAGARY] **1 :** to wander about **2 :** DIVERGE — **di·va·ga·tion** \,dī-və-'gā-shən, ,div-ə-\ *n*

di·va·lent \(')dī-'vā-lənt\ *adj* **:** BIVALENT

di·van \'dī-,van, *esp in senses other than 3 also* di-'van, di-'vän, dī-'van\ *n* [Turk, fr. Per *dīwān* account book] **1 a :** the privy council of the Ottoman Empire **b :** COUNCIL **2 a :** a council chamber **b :** a smoking room **3 :** a large couch or sofa usu. without back or arms often designed for use as a bed **4 :** a collection of poems in Persian or Arabic usu. by one author

di·var·i·cate \dī-'var-ə-,kāt, də-'var-\ *vi* [L *divaricatus*, pp. of *divaricare*, fr. *dis-* + *varicare* to straddle — more at PREVARICATE] **:** to spread apart **:** branch off **:** DIVERGE

di·var·i·ca·tion \(,)dī-,var-ə-'kā-shən, də-,var-\ *n* **1 :** the action, process, or fact of divaricating **2 :** a divergence of opinion

1**dive** \'dīv\ *vb* **dived** \'dīvd\ *or* **dove** \'dōv\ **dived; div·ing** \'dī-viŋ\ [ME *diven, duven*, fr. OE *dȳfan* to dip & *dūfan* to dive; akin to OE *dyppan* to dip — more at DIP] *vi* **1 a :** to plunge into water headfirst; *specif* **:** to execute a dive **b :** SUBMERGE **2 a :** to descend or fall precipitously **b :** to plunge one's hand into something **c** *of an airplane* **:** to descend in a dive **3 a :** to plunge into some matter or activity **b :** DART, LUNGE ⟨*dived* for his legs⟩ ~ *vt* **1 :** to thrust into something **2 :** to cause to descend

2**dive** *n* **1 :** the act or an instance of diving: as **a** (1) **:** a plunge into water executed in a prescribed manner (2) **:** a submerging of a submarine (3) **:** a steep descent of an airplane at greater than the maximum horizontal speed **b :** a sharp decline **2 :** a disreputable bar **3** *slang* **:** a faked knockout

dive–bomb \'dīv-,bäm\ *vt* **:** to bomb by making a steep dive toward the target before releasing the bomb — **dive–bomb·er** *n*

div·er \'dī-vər\ *n* **1 :** one that dives **2 a :** a person who stays under water for long periods by having air supplied from the surface or by carrying a supply of compressed air **b :** any of various diving birds; *esp* **:** LOON

di·verge \də-'vərj, dī-\ *vb* [ML *divergere*, fr. L *dis-* + *vergere* to incline — more at WRENCH] *vi* **1 a :** to move or extend in different directions from a common point **:** draw apart **b :** to become or be different in character or form **:** differ in opinion **2 :** to turn aside from a path or course **:** DEVIATE ~ *vt* **:** DEFLECT **syn** see SWERVE

di·ver·gence \-'vər-jən(t)s\ *n* **1 a :** a drawing apart (as of lines extending from a common center) **b :** DIFFERENCE, DISAGREEMENT **c :** the acquisition of dissimilar characters by related organisms in unlike environments **2 :** a deviation from a course or standard

di·ver·gent \-jənt\ *adj* [L *divergent-, divergens*, prp. of *divergere*] **1 a :** diverging from each other **b :** differing from each other or from a standard **:** DEVIANT **2 :** of or relating to an infinite sequence that does not have a limit or to an infinite series the sum of whose initial terms does not have a limit **3 :** causing divergence of rays ⟨a ~ lens⟩ **syn** see DIFFERENT — **di·ver·gent·ly** *adv*

di·vers \'dī-vərz\ *adj* [ME *divers, diverse*] **:** VARIOUS

di·verse \dī-'vərs, də-, 'dī-,\ *adj* [ME *divers, diverse*, fr. OF & L; OF *divers*, fr. L *diversus*, fr. pp. of *divertere*] **1 :** differing from one another **:** UNLIKE **2 :** having various forms or qualities **syn** see DIFFERENT — **di·verse·ly** *adv* — **di·verse·ness** *n*

di·ver·si·fi·ca·tion \də-,vər-sə-fə-'kā-shən, (,)dī-\ *n* **:** the act or process of diversifying **:** the state of being diversified

di·ver·si·fy \də-'vər-sə-,fī, dī-\ *vt* **1 :** to make diverse **:** VARIEGATE ⟨~ a course of study⟩ **2 :** to distribute among different kinds of securities **3 :** to increase the variety of the products of ~ *vi* **1 :** to produce variety **2 :** to engage in varied operations

di·ver·sion \-'vər-zhən, -shən\ *n* **1 :** the act or an instance of diverting from a course, activity, or use **:** DEVIATION **2 :** something that diverts or amuses **:** PASTIME **3 :** an attack or feint that draws the attention and force of an enemy from the point of the principal operation — **di·ver·sion·ary** \-zhə-,ner-ē, -shə-\ *adj*

di·ver·sion·ist \-zhə-nəst, -shə-\ *n* **1 :** one characterized by political deviation **2 :** one engaged in diversionary activities

di·ver·si·ty \də-'vər-sət-ē, dī-\ *n* **1 :** the condition of being different or having differences **2 :** an instance or a point of difference

di·vert \də-'vərt, dī-\ *vb* [ME *diverten*, fr. MF & L; MF *divertir*, fr. L *divertere* to turn in opposite directions, fr. *dis-* + *vertere* to turn — more at WORTH] *vi* **:** to turn aside **:** DEVIATE ~ *vt* **1 a :** to turn from one course or use to another **:** DEFLECT **b :** DISTRACT **2 :** to give pleasure to **syn** see AMUSE

di·ver·tic·u·li·tis \,dī-vər-,tik-yə-'līt-əs\ *n* **:** inflammation of a diverticulum

di·ver·tic·u·lo·sis \-'lō-səs\ *n* **:** an intestinal disorder characterized by the presence of many diverticula

di·ver·tic·u·lum \,dī-vər-'tik-yə-ləm\ *n*, *pl* **di·ver·tic·u·la** \-lə\ [NL, fr. L, bypath, prob. alter. of *deverticulum*, fr. *devertere* to turn aside, fr. *de-* + *vertere*] **1 :** a pocket or closed branch opening off a main passage **2 :** an abnormal pouch or sac opening from a hollow organ (as the intestine or bladder)

di·ver·ti·men·to \di-,vərt-ə-'ment-(,)ō, -,vert-\ *n*, *pl* **di·ver·ti·men·ti** \-'ment-(,)ē\ *or* **divertimentos** [It, lit., diversion, fr. *divertire* to divert, amuse, fr. F *divertir*] **1 :** an instrumental chamber work in several movements **2 :** DIVERTISSEMENT 1

di·ver·tisse·ment \di-'vərt-əs-mənt, -əz-mənt, *F* dē-ver-tēs-mä^{n}\ *n*, *pl* **divertissements** \-mən(t)s, -mä^{n}(z)\ [F, lit., diversion, fr. *divertiss-* (stem of *divertir*)] **1 :** a ballet suite used as an interlude **2 :** DIVERTIMENTO 1 **3 :** DIVERSION, ENTERTAINMENT

Di·ves \'dī-,vēz\ *n* [ME, fr. L, rich, rich man] **1 :** the rich man in the parable recorded in Lk 16:19–31 **2 :** a rich man

di·vest \dī-'vest, də-\ *vt* [alter. of *devest*] **1 a :** to undress or strip esp. of clothing, ornament, or equipment **b :** to deprive or dispossess esp. of property, authority, or title **c :** RID, FREE **2 :** to take away from a person

1**di·vide** \də-'vīd\ *vb* [ME *dividen*, fr. L *dividere*, fr. *dis-* + *-videre* to separate — more at WIDOW] *vt* **1 a :** to separate into two or more parts, areas, or groups **b :** to separate into classes, categories, or divisions **c :** CLEAVE, PART **2 a :** to separate into portions and give out in shares **:** DISTRIBUTE **b :** to possess, enjoy, or make use of in common **c :** APPORTION **3 a :** to cause to be separate, distinct, or apart from one another **b :** to separate into opposing sides or parties **c :** to cause (a parliamentary body) to vote by division **4 a :** to mark divisions on **:** GRADUATE ⟨~ a sextant⟩ **b** (1) **:** to subject to mathematical division (2) **:** to locate one or more points on (a line or its extension) ~ *vi* **1 :** to perform mathematical division **2 a** (1) **:** to become separated into parts (2) **:** to branch out **b :** to become separated or disunited esp. in opinion or interest **c :** to vote by division **syn** see DISTRIBUTE, SEPARATE

2**divide** *n* **1 :** an act of dividing **2 a :** a dividing ridge between drainage areas **:** WATERSHED **b :** a point or line of division

di·vid·ed *adj* **1 a :** separated into parts or pieces **b** *of a leaf* **:** cut into distinct parts by incisions extending to the base or to the midrib **c** *of a road* **:** having the opposing streams of traffic separated **2 a :** disagreeing with each other **:** DISUNITED **b :** directed or moved toward conflicting interests, states, or objects

div·i·dend \'div-ə-,dend, -əd-ənd\ *n* [ME *divident*, fr. L *dividendus*, gerundive of *dividere*] **1 :** an individual share of something distributed: as **a :** a share of profits distributed to stockholders **b :** a share of surplus allocated to a policyholder in a participating insurance policy **c :** a proportional payment to a creditor of a bankrupt estate **2 :** BONUS **3 a :** a number to be divided **b :** a sum or fund to be divided and distributed

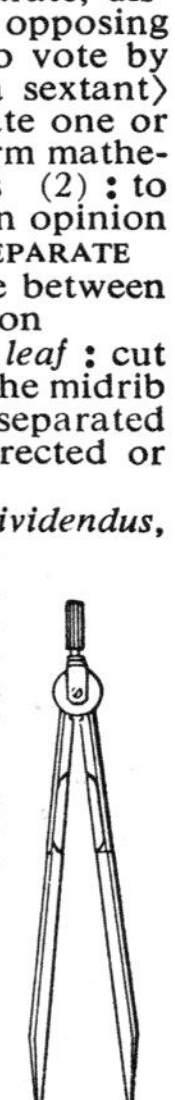
dividers

di·vid·er \də-'vīd-ər\ *n* **1 :** one that divides **2** *pl* **:** an instrument for measuring or marking (as in dividing lines and transferring dimensions) **3 :** something serving as a partition between separate spaces within a larger area

di·vi–di·vi \,dē-vē-'dē-vē\ *n* [Sp *dividivi* of Cariban origin; akin to Cumanagoto *diwidiwi* divi-divi] **:** a small leguminous tree (*Caesalpinia coriaria*) of tropical America with twisted astringent pods that yield a large proportion of tannin

div·i·na·tion \,div-ə-'nā-shən\ *n* [ME *divinacioun*, fr. L *divination-, divinatio*, fr. *divinatus*, pp. of *divinare*] **1 :** the art or practice that seeks to foresee or foretell future events or discover hidden knowledge usu. by means of augury or by the aid of supernatural powers **2 :** unusual insight or intuitive perception — **di·vi·na·to·ry** \də-'vin-ə-,tōr-ē, də-'vī-nə-, 'div-ə-nə-, -,tòr-\ *adj*

1di·vine \də-'vīn\ *adj* [ME *divin*, fr. MF, fr. L *divinus*, fr. *divus* god — more at DEITY] **1 a :** of, relating to, or proceeding directly from deity ⟨the ~ right of kings⟩ **b :** being deity **c :** directed to deity **2 a :** supremely good **:** SUPERB **b :** GODLIKE, HEAVENLY — **di·vine·ly** *adv*

2divine *n* [ME, fr. ML *divinus*, fr. L, soothsayer, fr. *divinus*, adj.] **1 :** CLERGYMAN **2 :** THEOLOGIAN

3divine *vb* [ME *divinen*, fr. MF & L; MF *diviner*, fr. L *divinare*, fr. *divinus*, n.] *vt* **:** to discover intuitively **:** INFER ~ *vi* **1 :** to practice divination **:** PROPHESY **2 :** to perceive intuitively **:** CONJECTURE **syn** see FORESEE — **di·vin·er** *n*

Divine Liturgy *n* **:** the Eastern Orthodox eucharistic rite

Divine Office *n* **:** the office of the breviary for the canonical hours that clerics in major orders and many religious say daily

diving bell *n* **:** a diving apparatus consisting of a container open only at the bottom and supplied with compressed air by a hose

diving duck *n* **:** any of various ducks that frequent deep waters and obtain their food by diving

divining rod *n* **:** a forked rod believed to divine the presence of water or minerals by dipping downward when held over a vein

di·vin·i·ty \də-'vin-ət-ē\ *n* **1 :** the quality or state of being divine **2 a** *often cap* **:** 2GOD **b** (1) **:** GOD (2) **:** GODDESS **c :** DEMIGOD **3 :** THEOLOGY

di·vis·i·bil·i·ty \də-,viz-ə-'bil-ət-ē\ *n* **:** the state of being divisible

di·vis·i·ble \də-'viz-ə-bəl\ *adj* **:** capable of being divided

di·vi·sion \də-'vizh-ən\ *n* [ME, fr. MF, fr. L *division-*, *divisio*, fr. *divisus*, pp. of *dividere* to divide] **1 a :** the act or process of dividing **:** the state of being divided **b :** the act, process, or an instance of distributing among a number **:** DISTRIBUTION **c** *obs* **:** a method of arranging or disposing **2 :** one of the parts, sections, or groupings into which a whole is divided **3 a :** the elementary organic unit of combined arms that is tactically and administratively a self-contained unit capable of independent action **b :** a military unit made up normally of five battle groups **c** (1) **:** the basic unit of men for administration aboard ship and ashore (2) **:** a tactical subdivision of a squadron of ships **4 a :** a portion of a territorial unit marked off for administrative, judicial, or other purposes **b :** an administrative or operating unit of a governmental, business, or educational organization **5 :** a group of organisms forming part of a larger group; *specif* **:** a primary category of the plant kingdom **6 :** a competitive class or category **7 a :** something that divides, separates, or marks off **b :** the act, process, or an instance of separating or keeping apart **:** SEPARATION **8 :** the condition or an instance of being divided in opinion or interest **:** DISAGREEMENT **9 :** the physical separation into different lobbies of the members of a parliamentary body voting for and against a question **10 :** the operation of finding how many times one number or quantity is contained in another **11 :** plant propagation by dividing parts and planting segments capable of producing roots and shoots **syn** see PART — **di·vi·sion·al** \-'vizh-nəl, -ən-ᵊl\ *adj*

di·vi·sion·ism \-'vizh-ə-,niz-əm\ *n, often cap* **:** the neo-impressionist theory or practice of juxtaposing on the canvas small strokes of pure colors to be mixed by the eye of the observer — **di·vi·sion·ist** \-'vizh-(ə-)nəst\ *n or adj*

di·vi·sive \də-'vī-siv; -'viz-iv, -'vis-\ *adj* **:** creating disunity or dissension — **di·vi·sive·ly** *adv* — **di·vi·sive·ness** *n*

di·vi·sor \də-'vī-zər\ *n* **:** the number by which a dividend is divided

1di·vorce \də-'vō(ə)rs, -'vȯ(ə)rs\ *n* [ME *divorse*, fr. MF, fr. L *divortium*, fr. *divertere*, *divortere* to divert, to leave one's husband] **1 :** a legal dissolution of a marriage **2 :** SEPARATION, SEVERANCE

2divorce *vt* **1 a :** to get rid of (one's spouse) by divorce **b :** to dissolve the marriage contract between **2 :** SEPARATE, DISUNITE **syn** see SEPARATE

di·vor·cée \də-,vōr-'sā, -,vȯr-, -'sē; -'vōr-,sā, -'vȯr-, -,sē\ *n* [F, fr. fem. of *divorcé*, pp. of *divorcer* to divorce, fr. MF *divorse*] **:** a divorced woman

di·vorce·ment \də-'vōr-smənt, -'vȯr-\ *n* **:** DIVORCE 2

div·ot \'div-ət\ *n* [origin unknown] **1** *Scot* **:** a square of turf or sod **2 :** a piece of turf dug from a golf fairway in making a stroke

di·vulge \də-'vəlj, dī-\ *vt* [ME *divulgen*, fr. L *divulgare*, fr. *dis-* + *vulgare* to make known] **1** *archaic* **:** to make public **:** PROCLAIM **2 :** to make known (as a secret) **syn** see REVEAL — **di·vul·gence** \-'vəl-jən(t)s\ *n*

di·vul·sion \dī-'vəl-shən\ *n* [L *divulsion-*, *divulsio*, fr. *divulsus*, pp. of *divellere* to tear apart, fr. *dis-* + *vellere* to pluck — more at VULNERABLE] **:** a tearing apart

Dix·ie \'dik-sē\ *n* [name for the Southern states in the song *Dixie* (1859) by Daniel D. Emmett] **:** the Southern states of the U. S.

Dix·ie·crat \-,krat\ *n* **:** a dissident southern Democrat; *specif* **:** a supporter of a 1948 presidential ticket opposing the civil rights stand of the Democrats — **Dix·ie·crat·ic** \,dik-sē-'krat-ik\ *adj*

di·zen \'dīz-ᵊn, 'diz-ᵊn\ *vt* [earlier *disen* to dress a distaff with flax, fr. MD] *archaic* **:** BEDIZEN

di·zy·got·ic \,dī-(,)zī-'gät-ik\ *adj, of twins* **:** FRATERNAL

diz·zi·ly \'diz-ə-lē\ *adv* **:** in a dizzy manner

diz·zi·ness \'diz-ē-nəs\ *n* **:** the condition of being dizzy **:** VERTIGO

1diz·zy \'diz-ē\ *adj* [ME *disy*, fr. OE *dysig* stupid; akin to OHG *tusig* stupid, L *furere* to rage — more at DUST] **1 :** FOOLISH, SILLY **2 a :** having a whirling sensation in the head with a tendency to fall **b :** mentally confused **3 a :** causing giddiness or mental confusion **b :** caused by or marked by giddiness **c :** extremely rapid

2dizzy *vt* **1 :** to make dizzy or giddy **2 :** BEWILDER

djin *or* **djinn** \'jin\ *or* **djin·ni** *var of* JINN

D layer *n* **:** a layer that may exist within the D region of the ionosphere; *also* **:** D REGION

1do \(')dü, də(-w)\ *vb* **did** \(')did, dəd\ **done** \'dən\ **do·ing** \'dü-iŋ\ **does** \(')dəz\ [ME *don*, fr. OE *dōn*; akin to OHG *tuon* to do, L *-dere* to put, *facere* to make, do, Gk *tithenai* to place, set] *vt* **1 :** to bring to pass **:** carry out **2 :** PUT — used chiefly in *do to death* **3 a :** PERFORM, EXECUTE ⟨~ some work⟩ **b :** COMMIT ⟨crimes *done* deliberately⟩ **4 a :** to bring about **:** EFFECT ⟨sleep will ~ you good⟩ **b :** RENDER, PAY ⟨~ honor to his memory⟩ **5 :** to bring to an end **:** FINISH — used in the past participle **6 :** to put forth **:** EXERT ⟨*did* his best to win the race⟩ **7 :** to bring into existence **:** PRODUCE ⟨~ a biography on the general⟩ **8 :** to play the part of **9 :** to treat unfairly; *esp* **:** CHEAT ⟨*did* him out of his inheritance⟩ **10 a :** to deal with or put in order by cleaning, arranging, or preparing for use ⟨~ the dinner dishes⟩ **b :** DECORATE **11 a :** to work at esp. as a vocation ⟨what to ~ after college⟩ **b :** to prepare or work out esp. by studying ⟨~*ing* his homework⟩ **12 a :** to pass over (as distance) **:** TRAVERSE **b :** to travel at a speed of ⟨~*ing* 80 on the turnpike⟩ **13 :** TOUR ⟨~*ing* 12 countries in 12 days⟩ **14 :** to serve out (as a term) in prison **15 :** to serve the needs of **:** SUIT ⟨worms will ~ us for bait⟩ **16** — used as a substitute verb to avoid repetition ⟨if you must make such a racket, ~ it somewhere else⟩ ~ *vi* **1 :** ACT, BEHAVE ⟨~ as I say⟩ **2 a :** to get along **:** FARE ⟨~ well in school⟩ **b :** to carry on **:** MANAGE ⟨we can ~ without your help⟩ **c :** to make good use ⟨~ with a cup of coffee⟩ **3 :** to take place **:** HAPPEN ⟨what's ~*ing* across the street⟩ **4 :** to come to or make an end **:** FINISH — used in the past participle **5 :** to be active or busy ⟨up and ~*ing* before dawn⟩ **6 :** to answer the purpose **:** SERVE ⟨half of that will ~⟩ **7 :** to be fitting **:** conform to custom or propriety ⟨won't ~ to be late⟩ **8** — used as a substitute verb to avoid repetition ⟨did you clean the stove? I *did*⟩ **9** — used in the imperative after an imperative to add emphasis ⟨be quiet, ~⟩ ~ *verbal auxiliary* **1** — used with the infinitive without *to* in legal and parliamentary language ⟨~ hereby bequeath⟩ and in poetry ⟨give what she *did* crave —Shak.⟩ **2** — used with the infinitive without *to* for emphasis ⟨I ~ say⟩ and esp. to form an imperative ⟨~ be careful⟩; regularly so used in negative sentences ⟨*don't* be silly⟩ — **do away** *archaic* **:** to put an end to — **do away with 1 :** to put an end to **:** ABOLISH **2 :** to put to death **:** KILL — **do by :** to deal with **:** TREAT — **do for :** to bring about the death or ruin of — **to do :** necessary to be done

2do \'dü\ *n, pl* **dos** *or* **do's** \'düz\ **1** *chiefly dial* **:** FUSS, ADO **2** *archaic* **:** DEED, DUTY **3** *chiefly Brit* **a :** a festive get-together **b :** BATTLE **4 :** a command or entreaty to do something **5** *Brit* **:** CHEAT, SWINDLE

3do \'dō\ *n* [It] **:** the first tone of the diatonic scale in solmization

do·able \'dü-ə-bəl\ *adj* **:** capable of being done **:** PRACTICABLE

dob·bin \'däb-ən\ *n* [*Dobbin*, nickname for *Robert*] **1 :** a farm horse **2 :** a quiet plodding horse

Do·bell's solution \'dō-,belz-\ *n* [Horace B. *Dobell* †1917 E physician] **:** an aqueous solution of sodium borate, sodium bicarbonate, glycerin, and phenol used as a nose or throat spray

Do·ber·man pin·scher \,dō-bər-mən-'pin-chər\ *n* [G *Dobermann-pinscher*, fr. Ludwig *Dobermann*, 19th cent. G dog breeder + G *pinscher*, a breed of hunting dog] **:** a short-haired medium-sized working dog of a breed of German origin

dob·son \'däb-sən\ *n* [prob. fr. the name *Dobson*] **:** HELLGRAMMITE

dob·son·fly \-,flī\ *n* **:** a winged insect (family Corydalidae) with very long slender mandibles in the male and a large carnivorous aquatic larva — compare HELLGRAMMITE

do·cent \'dōs-ᵊnt, dō(t)-'sent\ *n* [obs. G (now *dozent*), fr. L *docent-*, *docens*, prp. of *docēre*] **:** TEACHER, LECTURER

do·ce·tic \dō-'sēt-ik, -'set-\ *adj* [Gk *Dokētai* Docetists, fr. *dokein* to seem] **:** of or relating to Docetism or the Docetists

Do·ce·tism \dō-'sēt-,iz-əm, 'dō-sə-,tiz-\ *n* **:** a belief opposed as heresy in early Christianity that Christ only seemed to have a human body and to suffer and die on the cross — **Do·ce·tist** \-'sēt-əst, -sə-təst\ *n*

doch-an-dor·rach *or* **doch-an-dor·ris** \,däk-ən-'dō-rəs\ *n* [ScGael & IrGael *deoch an doruis*, lit., drink of the door] *Scot & Irish* **:** a parting drink **:** STIRRUP CUP

doc·ile \'däs-əl\ *adj* [L *docilis*, fr. *docēre* to teach; akin to L *decēre* to be fitting — more at DECENT] **1 :** easily taught **:** TEACHABLE **2 :** easily led or managed **:** TRACTABLE **syn** see OBEDIENT — **doc·ile·ly** \'däs-ə(l)-lē\ *adv* — **do·cil·i·ty** \dä-'sil-ət-ē, dō-\ *n*

1dock \'däk\ *n* [ME, fr. OE *docce*; akin to MD *docke* dock, ScGael *dogha* burdock] **1 :** any of a genus (*Rumex*) of the buckwheat family of coarse weedy plants that have long taproots and are used as potherbs and in folk medicine **2 :** any of various weedy plants

2dock *n* [ME *dok*, fr. OE *-docca* (as in *fingirdocca* finger muscle); akin to OHG *tocka* doll, ON *dokka* bundle] **1 :** the solid part of an animal's tail as distinguished from the hair **2 :** the cropped tail of an animal after clipping the hair or cropping the end

3dock *vt* **1 :** to cut off the end of a body part of, *specif* **:** to remove part of the tail of **2 a :** to take away a part of **:** REDUCE **b :** to subject (as wages) to a deduction **3 :** to deprive of a benefit ordinarily due esp. as a penalty for a fault ⟨~*ed* for tardiness⟩

4dock *n* [prob. fr. MD *docke* dock, ditch, fr. L *duction-*, *ductio* act of leading — more at DOUCHE] **1 :** a usu. artificial basin or enclosure for the reception of ships that is equipped with means for controlling the water height **2 :** the waterway extending between two piers for the reception of ships **3 :** a wharf or platform for the loading or unloading of materials **4 :** scaffolding for the inspection and repair of aircraft; *broadly* **:** HANGAR

5dock *vt* **:** to haul or guide into a dock ~ *vi* **:** to come into dock

6dock *n* [Flem *docke* cage] **:** the place in a criminal court where a prisoner stands or sits during trial

dock·age \'däk-ij\ *n* **1 :** a charge for the use of a dock **2 :** docking facilities **3 :** the docking of ships

1dock·er \'däk-ər\ *n* **:** one that docks (as the tails of animals)

2docker *n* **:** one connected with docks; *specif* **:** a dock laborer

1dock·et \'däk-ət\ *n* [ME *doggette*] **1 :** a brief written summary of a document **:** ABSTRACT **2 a** (1) **:** a formal abridged record of the proceedings in a legal action (2) **:** a register of such records **b** (1) **:** a list of legal causes to be tried (2) **:** a calendar of business matters to be acted on **:** AGENDA **3 :** an identifying statement about a document placed on its outer surface or cover

2docket *vt* **1 :** to inscribe (as a document) with an identifying statement **2 :** to make a brief abstract of (as a legal matter) and inscribe it in a list **3 :** to place on the docket for legal action

dock·hand \'däk-,hand\ *n* **:** LONGSHOREMAN

dock·yard \'däk-,yärd\ *n* **1 :** a storage place for naval stores or timber for shipbuilding with facilities for building or repairing ships **2** *Brit* **:** NAVY YARD

1doc·tor \'däk-tər\ *n* [ME *doctour* teacher, doctor, fr. MF & ML; MF, fr. ML *doctor*, fr. L, teacher, fr. *doctus*, pp. of *docēre*] **1 a :** an eminent theologian declared a sound expounder of doctrine by the Roman Catholic Church — called also *doctor of the church* **b :** a learned or authoritative teacher **c :** a person who has earned one of the highest academic degrees (as a PhD) conferred by a university **d :** a person awarded an honorary doctorate (as an LLD or LittD) by a college or university **2 a :** one skilled or specializ-

ing in healing arts; *esp* **:** a physician, surgeon, dentist, or veterinarian licensed to practice his profession **b :** MEDICINE MAN **3 :** material added to produce a desired effect **4 :** a usu. makeshift and emergency mechanical contrivance or attachment for remedying a difficulty **5 :** any of several brightly colored artificial flies — **doc·tor·al** \-t(ə-)rəl\ *adj* — **doc·tor·ship** \-tər-,ship\ *n*

2**doctor** *vb* **doc·tor·ing** \-t(ə-)riŋ\ *vt* **1 a :** to give medical treatment to **b :** to restore to good condition **:** REPAIR **2 a :** to adapt or modify for a desired end **b :** to alter deceptively ~ *vi* **1 :** to practice medicine **2** *dial* **:** to take medicine

doc·tor·ate \'däk-t(ə-)rət\ *n* **:** the degree, title, or rank of a doctor

1**doc·tri·naire** \,däk-trə-'na(ə)r, -'ne(ə)r\ *n* [F, fr. *doctrine*] **:** one who attempts to put into effect an abstract doctrine or theory with little or no regard for practical difficulties

2**doctrinaire** *adj* **:** relating to or characteristic of a doctrinaire **:** DOGMATIC **syn** see DICTATORIAL — **doc·tri·nair·ism** \-,iz-əm\ *n*

doc·tri·nal \'däk-trən-ᵊl, däk-'trīn-\ *adj* **:** of, relating to, or preoccupied with doctrine — **doc·tri·nal·ly** \-ᵊl-ē\ *adv*

doc·trine \'däk-trən\ *n* [ME, fr. MF & L; MF, fr. L *doctrina*, fr. *doctor*] **1** *archaic* **:** TEACHING, INSTRUCTION **2 a :** something that is taught **b :** a principle or position or the body of principles in a branch of knowledge or system of belief **:** DOGMA **c :** a principle of law established through past decisions **d :** a statement of fundamental government policy esp. in international relations

syn DOCTRINE, DOGMA, TENET mean a principle accepted as authoritative. DOCTRINE implies a principle accepted by a body of believers or adherents to a philosophy or school; DOGMA implies a doctrine that is laid down as true and beyond dispute; TENET stresses acceptance and belief rather than teaching and applies to a principle held or adhered to

doctrine of descent : a theory in biology: all animals and plants are direct descendants of previous animals or plants

1**doc·u·ment** \'däk-yə-mənt\ *n* [ME, fr. MF, fr. LL & L; LL *documentum* official paper, fr. L, lesson, proof, fr. *docēre* to teach — more at DOCILE] **1 a** *archaic* **:** PROOF, EVIDENCE **b :** an original or official paper relied upon as the basis, proof, or support of something **2 a :** a writing conveying information **b :** a material substance having on it a representation of the thoughts of men by means of some conventional mark or symbol **c :** DOCUMENTARY — **doc·u·men·tal** \,däk-yə-'ment-ᵊl\ *adj*

2**doc·u·ment** \'däk-yə-,ment\ *vt* **1 :** to furnish documentary evidence of **2 :** to furnish with documents **3 :** to provide with factual or substantial support for statements made or a hypothesis proposed; *esp* **:** to equip with exact references to authoritative supporting information — **doc·u·ment·able** \-ə-bəl, ,däk-yə-'\ *adj*

doc·u·men·tar·i·an \,däk-yə-mən-'ter-ē-ən, -,men-\ *n* **:** one who employs or advocates documentary presentation (as in photographic art or fiction)

doc·u·men·tar·i·ly \-'ter-ə-lē\ *adv* **:** in a documentary manner

1**doc·u·men·ta·ry** \,däk-yə-'ment-ə-rē, -'men-trē\ *adj* **1 :** contained or certified in writing **2 :** of, relating to, or employing documentation in literature or art; *broadly* **:** FACTUAL, OBJECTIVE

2**documentary** *n* **:** a documentary presentation (as a film or novel)

doc·u·men·ta·tion \,däk-yə-mən-'tā-shən, -,men-\ *n* **1 :** the act or an instance of furnishing or authenticating with documents **2 a :** the provision of documents in substantiation; *also* **:** documentary evidence **b** (1) **:** the use of historical documents (2) **:** conformity to historical or objective facts (3) **:** the provision of footnotes, appendices, or addenda referring to or containing documentary evidence **3 :** the assembling, coding, and disseminating of recorded knowledge treated as an integral procedure

1**dod·der** \'däd-ər\ *n* [ME *doder;* akin to OE *dydring* yolk, Norw *dudra* to tremble, L *fumus* smoke — more at FUME] **:** any of a genus (*Cuscuta*) of dicotyledonous leafless elongated wiry herbs that are deficient in chlorophyll and parasitic on other plants

2**dodder** *vi* **dod·der·ing** \'däd-(ə-)riŋ\ [ME *dadiren*] **1 :** to tremble or shake from weakness or age **2 :** to progress feebly

dod·dered \'däd-ərd\ *adj* [prob. alter. of *dodded*, fr. pp. of E dial. *dod* to lop, fr. ME *dodden*] **1 :** deprived of branches through age or decay ⟨a ~ oak⟩ **2 :** ENFEEBLED, INFIRM

dod·der·ing \'däd-(ə-)riŋ\ *adj* **:** FOOLISH, SENILE ⟨a ~ old man⟩

dod·dery \-(ə-)rē\ *adj* **:** DODDERED, DODDERING

dodeca- *or* **dodec-** *comb form* [L, fr. Gk *dōdeka-*, *dōdek-*, fr. *dōdeka*, *dyōdeka*, fr. *dyō*, *dyo* two + *deka* ten] **:** twelve ⟨*dodeca*phonic⟩

do·deca·gon \dō-'dek-ə-,gän\ *n* [Gk *dōdekagōnon*, fr. *dōdeka-* + *-gōnon* -gon] **:** a polygon of 12 angles and 12 sides

do·deca·he·dron \(,)dō-,dek-ə-'hē-drən\ *n, pl* **dodecahedrons** *or* **do·deca·he·dra** \-drə\ [Gk *dōdekaedron*, fr. *dōdeka-* + *-edron* -hedron] **:** a solid having 12 plane faces

do·deca·phon·ic \(,)dō-,dek-ə-'fän-ik\ *adj* [*dodeca-* + *phon-* + *-ic*] **1 :** composed through the mechanical application of a particular numerical arrangement of the notes of the chromatic scale **2 :** of or relating to the composition of dodecaphonic music — **do·deca·pho·nism** \dō-'dek-ə-,fō-,niz-əm, ,dō-di-'kaf-ə-,niz-\ *n* — **do·deca·pho·nist** \-nəst\ *n* — **do·deca·pho·ny** \-nē\ *n*

1**dodge** \'däj\ *vb* [origin unknown] *vi* **1 :** to evade a duty or issue esp. by trickery or deceit **2 a :** to move to and fro or from place to place usu. in an irregular course **b :** to make a sudden movement in a new direction (as to evade a blow) ~ *vt* **1 :** to evade (as a duty) usu. indirectly and by trickery **2 a :** to evade by a sudden or repeated shift of position **b :** to avoid an encounter with

2**dodge** *n* **1 :** an act of evading by sudden bodily movement **2 a :** an artful device to evade, deceive, or trick **b :** EXPEDIENT, SCHEME

dodg·er \'däj-ər\ *n* **1 :** one that dodges; *esp* **:** one who uses tricky devices **2 :** a small handbill **3 :** a cake made of cornmeal

dodg·ery \'däj-(ə-)rē\ *n* **:** EVASION, TRICKERY

dodgy \'däj-ē\ *adj* **:** EVASIVE, TRICKY

do·do \'dōd-(,)ō\ *n, pl* **dodoes** *or* **dodos** [Pg *doudo*, fr. *doudo* silly, stupid] **1 a :** a heavy flightless extinct bird (*Raphus cucullatus*, syn. *Didus ineptus*) related to the pigeons but larger than a turkey formerly present on the island of Mauritius **b :** a similar and apparently closely related extinct bird of the neighboring island of Réunion **2 :** one hopelessly behind the times

doe \'dō\ *n, pl* **does** *or* **doe** [ME *do*, fr. OE *dā;* akin to G dial. *tē* doe] **:** the adult female fallow deer; *broadly* **:** the female esp. when adult of any of various mammals of which the male is called buck

do·er \'dü-ər\ *n* **:** one that does ⟨a thinker or a ~⟩

doe·skin \'dō-,skin\ *n* **1 :** the skin of does or leather made of it; *also* **:** soft leather from sheep or lambskins **2 :** a compact coating and sportswear fabric napped and felted for a smooth surface

doesn't \'dəz-ᵊnt\ **:** does not

do·est \'dü-əst\ *archaic pres 2d sing of* DO

do·eth \'dü-əth\ *archaic pres 3d sing of* DO

doff \'däf, 'dȯf\ *vt* [ME *doffen*, fr. *don* to do + *of* off] **1 :** to take off (one's clothes); *esp* **:** to take off or lift up (the hat) **2 :** to rid oneself of

1**dog** \'dȯg\ *n, often attrib* [ME, fr. OE *docga*] **1 a :** a highly variable carnivorous domesticated mammal (*Canis familiaris*) prob. descended from the common wolf; *broadly* **:** any animal of the dog family (Canidae) to which this mammal belongs **b :** a male dog **2 a :** a worthless fellow **b :** CHAP, FELLOW ⟨a gay ~⟩ **3 a :** any of various usu. simple mechanical devices for holding, gripping, or fastening consisting of a spike, rod, or bar **b :** ANDIRON **4 a :** SUN DOG **b :** WATER DOG 4 **c :** FOGBOW **5 :** affected stylishness or dignity **6** *cap* **:** either of the constellations Canis Major or Canis Minor **7** *pl, slang* **:** FEET **8** *slang* **:** something inferior of its kind **9** *pl* **:** RUIN ⟨go to the ~*s*⟩ **10** *cap* **:** any of various American Indian peoples — **dog·like** \'dȯ-,glīk\ *adj*

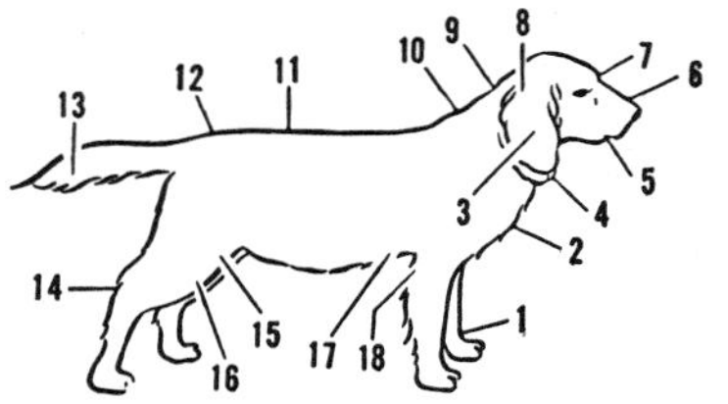

dog: *1* pastern, *2* chest, *3* leather, *4* dewlap, *5* flews, *6* muzzle, *7* stop, *8* occiput *9* crest, *10* withers, *11* loin, *12* rump, *13* feather, *14* hock, *15* stifle, *16* knee, *17* brisket, *18* elbow

2**dog** *vt* **dogged; dog·ging 1 a :** to hunt or track like a hound **b :** to worry as if by dogs **:** HOUND **2 :** to fasten with a dog

3**dog** *adv* **:** EXTREMELY, UTTERLY ⟨*dog*-tired⟩

Dog \'dȯg\ — a communications code word for the letter *d*

dog·bane \'dȯg-,bān\ *n* **:** any of a genus (*Apocynum* of the family Apocynaceae, the dogbane family) comprising chiefly tropical and often poisonous plants with milky juice and usu. showy flowers

dog·ber·ry \-,ber-ē\ *n* **1 :** any of various small fruits (as the chokeberry) usu. considered inferior or unfit for human consumption; *esp* **:** the fruit of the red dogwood **2 :** a plant bearing dogberries

dog·cart \'dȯg-,kärt\ *n* **1 :** a cart drawn by a dog **2 :** a light usu. one-horse carriage commonly two-wheeled with two transverse seats set back to back

dog·catch·er \-,kach-ər, -,kech-\ *n* **:** a community official assigned to catch and get rid of stray dogs

dog collar *n* **1 :** a collar for a dog **2** *slang* **:** CLERICAL COLLAR **3 :** a wide flexible snug-fitting necklace

dog days *n pl* [fr. their being reckoned from the heliacal rising of the Dog Star (Sirius)] **1 :** the period between early July and early September when the hot sultry weather of summer usu. occurs in the northern hemisphere **2 :** a period of stagnation or inactivity

doge \'dōj\ *n* [It dial., fr. L *duc-*, *dux* leader — more at DUKE] **:** the chief magistrate in the republics of Venice and Genoa

dog–ear \'dȯ-,gi(ə)r\ *n* **:** the corner of a leaf esp. of a book turned down like the ear of a fox terrier — **dog–ear** *vt*

dog–eared \'dȯ-,gi(ə)rd\ *adj* **1 :** having dog-ears ⟨a ~ book⟩ **2 :** SHABBY, WORN

dog–eat–dog \,dȯ-,gēt-'dȯg\ *adj* **:** marked by ruthless self-interest ⟨~ competition⟩

dog·face \'dȯg-,fās\ *n, slang* **:** SOLDIER; *esp* **:** INFANTRYMAN

dog family *n* **:** a natural family (Canidae of the order Carnivora) comprising the dogs, wolves, foxes, and related animals

dog fennel *n* **1 :** a strong-scented European chamomile (*Anthemis cotula*) naturalized along roadsides in the U.S. **2 :** an annual composite weed (*Eupatorium capillifolium*) with dissected leaves and a lax inflorescence

dog·fight \'dȯg-,fīt\ *n* **1 :** a fight between or as if between dogs; *broadly* **:** a fiercely disputed contest **2 :** a fight between two or more fighter planes usu. at close quarters — **dogfight** *vi*

dog·fish \'dȯg-,fish\ *n* **:** any of various small sharks (as of the families Squalidae, Carcharhinidae, and Scyliorhinidae) that often appear in schools near shore, are destructive to fish, and have livers valued for oil and flesh often made into fertilizer

dog·ged \'dȯ-gəd\ *adj* **:** stubbornly determined **:** TENACIOUS **syn** see OBSTINATE — **dog·ged·ly** *adv* — **dog·ged·ness** *n*

1**dog·ger·el** \'dȯg(-ə-)rəl, 'däg-(ə-)\ *adj* [ME *dogerel*] **:** loosely styled and irregular in measure esp. for burlesque or comic effect

2**doggerel** *n* **:** doggerel verse

dog·gery \'dȯ-gə-rē\ *n* **1 :** doglike behavior **2 a :** DOGS **b :** RABBLE, MOB **3** *slang* **:** a cheap saloon **:** DIVE

dog·gish \'dȯ-gish\ *adj* **1 :** resembling a dog esp. in bad qualities **:** CURRISH **2 :** stylish in a showy way — **dog·gish·ly** *adv* — **dog·gish·ness** *n*

dog·go \'dȯ-(,)gō\ *adv* [prob. fr. 1*dog*] *slang* **:** in hiding — used chiefly in the phrase *to lie doggo*

1**dog·gone** \'däg-,gän, 'dȯg-,gȯn\ *vb* [euphemism for *God damn*] **:** DAMN

2**doggone** *or* **dog·goned** \-,gänd, -,gȯnd\ *adj* (*or adv*) **:** DAMNED

3**doggone** *n* **:** DAMN

1**dog·gy** \'dȯ-gē\ *adj* **1 :** resembling a dog **2 :** STYLISH, SHOWY

2**dog·gy** *or* **dog·gie** \'dȯ-gē\ *n* **:** a small dog

dog·house \'dȯg-,haủs\ *n* **:** a shelter for a dog — **in the doghouse :** in a state of disfavor

do·gie \'dō-gē\ *n* [origin unknown] *chiefly West* **:** a motherless calf in a range herd

dog in the manger [fr. the fable of the dog who prevented an ox from eating hay which he did not want himself] **:** a person who selfishly withholds from others something useless to himself

1**dog·leg** \'dȯ-,gleg, -,glāg\ *n* **:** something having an abrupt angle

2**dogleg** *also* **dog·legged** \-'gleg(-ə)d, -'glāg(-ə)d\ *adj* **:** crooked or bent like a dog's hind leg

dog·ma \'dȯg-mə, 'däg-\ *n, pl* **dogmas** *also* **dog·ma·ta** \-mət-ə\ [L *dogmat-*, *dogma*, fr. Gk, fr. *dokein* to seem] **1 a :** something held as an established opinion; *esp* **:** a definite authoritative tenet **b :** a code of such tenets ⟨pedagogical ~⟩ **c :** a point of view or tenet put forth as authoritative without adequate grounds **2 :** a doctrine or body of doctrines concerning faith or morals formally stated and authoritatively proclaimed by a church **syn** see DOCTRINE

dog·mat·ic \dȯg-'mat-ik, däg-\ *adj* **1 :** characterized by or given to the use of dogmatism ⟨a ~ critic⟩ **2 :** of or relating to dogma **syn** see DICTATORIAL — **dog·mat·i·cal** \-i-kəl\ *adj* — **dog·mat·i·cal·ly** \-i-k(ə-)lē\ *adv* — **dog·mat·i·cal·ness** \-i-kəl-nəs\ *n*

dog·mat·ics \-'mat-iks\ *n pl but sing or pl in constr* **:** a branch of theology that seeks to interpret the dogmas of a religious faith

dogmatic theology *n* **:** DOGMATICS

dog·ma·tism \'dȯg-mə-,tiz-əm, 'däg-\ *n* **1 :** positiveness in assertion of opinion esp. when unwarranted or arrogant **2 :** a viewpoint or system of ideas based on insufficiently examined premises

dog·ma·tist \-mət-əst\ *n* **:** one who dogmatizes

dog·ma·ti·za·tion \,dȯg-mət-ə-'zā-shən, ,däg-\ *n* **:** an act or instance of dogmatizing

dog·ma·tize \'dȯg-mə-,tīz, 'däg-\ *vb* [F *dogmatiser*, fr. LL *dogmatizare*, fr. Gk *dogmatizein*, fr. *dogmat-, dogma*] *vi* **:** to speak or write dogmatically ~ *vt* **:** to state as a dogma or dogmatically — **dog·ma·tiz·er** *n*

do–good \'dü-,gu̇d\ *adj* **:** designed sometimes impracticably and too zealously toward bettering the conditions under which others live — **do–good·ing** \-iŋ\ *n* — **do–good·ism** \-,iz-əm\ *n*

do–good·er \-ər\ *n* **:** an earnest usu. impractical-minded humanitarian bent on promoting welfare work or reform

dog paddle *n* **:** an elementary form of swimming in which the arms paddle in the water and the legs maintain a kicking motion — **dog–pad·dle** \'dȯg-,pad-ᵊl\ *vi*

Dog Star *n* **1 :** SIRIUS **2 :** PROCYON

dog tag *n* **1 :** a metal disk or plate on a dog collar bearing a license registration number **2 :** a military identification tag

dog·tooth \'dȯg-,tüth\ *n* **1 :** CANINE 1, EYETOOTH **2 :** an architectural ornament common in early English Gothic consisting usu. of four leaves radiating from a raised point at the center

dogtooth violet *n* **:** any of a genus (*Erythronium*) of small spring-flowering bulbous herbs of the lily family

1dog·trot \'dȯg-,trät\ *n* **1 :** a quick easy gait suggesting that of a dog **2** *South & Midland* **:** a roofed passage similar to a breezeway; *esp* **:** one connecting two parts of a cabin

2dogtrot *vi* **:** to move or progress at a dogtrot

dog·watch \'dȯ-,gwäch\ *n* **1 :** either of two watches of two hours on shipboard that extend from 4 to 6 and from 6 to 8 p.m. **2 :** any of various night shifts; *esp* **:** the last shift

dog·wood \'dȯ-,gwu̇d\ *n* **:** any of a genus (*Cornus*) of trees and shrubs (family Cornaceae, the dogwood family) with heads of small flowers and often showy involucres

doi·ly \'dȯi-lē\ *n* [*Doily* or *Doyley fl* 1712 London draper] **1 :** a small napkin **2 :** a small often decorative mat

do in *vt* **1 a :** to bring about the defeat or destruction of **:** RUIN **b :** to bring about the death of **:** KILL **c :** to wear out **2 :** CHEAT

do·ing \'dü-iŋ\ *n* **1 :** the act of performing or executing **:** ACTION **2** *pl* **a :** things that are done or that occur **b** *dial* **:** social activities

doit \'dȯit\ *n* [D *duit;* akin to ON *thveiti* small coin, *thveita* to hew] **1 :** an old Dutch coin equal to about ½ farthing **2 :** TRIFLE

do–it–yourself \,dü-ə-chər-'self\ *adj* **:** of, relating to, or designed for use in construction, repair, or artistic work done by an amateur or hobbyist ⟨~ tools⟩ ⟨~ car model kit⟩

dol·ce \'dōl-(,)chā\ *adj* (*or adv*) [It, lit., sweet, fr. L *dulcis* — more at DULCET] **:** SOFT, SMOOTH — used as a direction in music — **dol·ce·men·te** \,dōl-chā-'ment-ē, -'men-(,)tā\ *adv*

dol·ce far nien·te \'dōl-chē-,fär-nē-'ent-ē\ *n* [It, lit., sweet doing nothing] **:** delightful relaxation in carefree idleness

dol·drums \'dōl-drəmz, 'däl-, 'dȯl-\ *n pl* [prob. akin to OE *dol* foolish] **1 :** a spell of listlessness or despondency **2 :** a part of the ocean near the equator abounding in calms, squalls, and light shifting winds **3 :** a state of inactivity, stagnation, or slump

1dole \'dōl\ *n* [ME, fr. OE *dāl* portion] **1** *archaic* **:** one's allotted share, portion, or destiny **2 a** (1) **:** a giving or distribution of food, money, or clothing to the needy (2) **:** a grant of government funds to the unemployed **b :** something distributed at intervals to the needy **c :** something portioned out and distributed

2dole *vt* **1 :** to give or distribute as a charity **2 :** to give or deliver in small portions **:** PARCEL — used with *out* **syn** see DISTRIBUTE

3dole *n* [ME *dol*, fr. OF, fr. LL *dolus*, alter. of L *dolor*] *archaic* **:** GRIEF, SORROW

dole·ful \'dōl-fəl\ *adj* **1 :** causing grief or affliction **2 :** full of grief **:** DISCONSOLATE **3 :** expressing grief **:** SAD — **dole·ful·ly** \-fə-lē\ *adv* — **dole·ful·ness** *n*

dol·er·ite \'däl-ə-,rīt\ *n* [F *dolérite*, fr. Gk *doleros* deceitful, fr. *dolos* deceit; fr. its being easily mistaken for diorite — more at TALE] **1 :** any of various coarse basalts **2** *Brit* **:** DIABASE 3 **3 :** any of various dark igneous rocks whose constituents are not determinable megascopically — **dol·er·it·ic** \,däl-ə-'rit-ik\ *adj*

dole·some \'dōl-səm\ *adj* **:** DOLEFUL

dolich- *or* **dolicho-** *comb form* [Gk, fr. *dolichos*] **:** long

dol·i·cho·ce·phal·ic \,däl-i-kō-sə-'fal-ik\ *adj* [NL *dolichocephalus* dolichocephalic individual, fr. *dolich-* + *-cephalus* (fr. Gk *kephalē* head) — more at CEPHALIC] **:** having a relatively long head with a cephalic index of less than 75 — **dol·i·cho·ceph·a·lism** \-'sef-ə-,liz-əm\ *n* — **dol·i·cho·ceph·a·ly** \-'sef-ə-lē\ *n*

dol·i·cho·cra·ni·al \-'krā-nē-əl\ *also* **dol·i·cho·cra·nic** \-nik\ *adj* [ISV] **:** having a relatively long head with a cranial index of less than 75 — **dol·i·cho·cra·ny** \'däl-i-kō-,krā-nē\ *n*

doll \'däl, 'dȯl\ *n, often attrib* [prob. fr. *Doll*, nickname for *Dorothy*] **1 :** a small-scale figure of a human being used esp. as a child's plaything **2 a :** a pretty but empty-headed young woman **b** *slang* **:** WOMAN **c** *slang* **:** DARLING, SWEETHEART — **doll·ish** \-ish\ *adj* — **doll·ish·ly** *adv* — **doll·ish·ness** *n*

dol·lar \'däl-ər\ *n, often attrib* [D or LG *daler*, fr. G *taler*, short for *joachimstaler*, fr. Sankt *Joachimsthal*, Bohemia, where talers were first made] **1 :** TALER **2 :** any of numerous coins patterned after the taler (as a Spanish piece of eight) **3 a :** any of various basic monetary units (as in the U.S. and Canada) — see MONEY table **b :** a coin, note, or token representing one dollar

dollar diplomacy *n* **1 :** diplomacy based on economic factors **2 :** diplomacy held to be designed primarily to further private financial and commercial interests

dollar mark *n* **:** a mark $ or $ placed before a number to indicate that it stands for dollars — called also *dollar sign*

dol·lop \'däl-əp\ *n* [origin unknown] **:** LUMP, BLOB

doll up *vt* **:** to dress or adorn formally or elegantly

1dol·ly \'däl-ē, 'dȯ-lē\ *n* **1 :** DOLL **2 a :** a wooden-pronged instrument for beating and stirring clothes in the process of washing them in a tub **b :** a device turning on a vertical axis by a handle or winch for stirring ore to be washed **3 :** a heavy bar with a cupped head for holding against the head of a rivet while the other end is being headed **4 :** a compact narrow-gauge railroad locomotive for moving construction trains and for switching **5 a :** a platform on a roller or on wheels or casters for transporting heavy objects **b :** a wheeled platform for a television or motion-picture camera

2dolly *vt* **1 :** to treat with a dolly **2 :** to move or convey on a dolly ~ *vi* **:** to move a motion-picture or television dolly about while shooting a scene

dol·man \'dōl-mən, 'dȯl-, 'däl-\ *n, pl* **dolmans** [F *doliman*, fr. Turk *dolama*, a Turkish robe] **:** a woman's coat made with dolman sleeves

dolman sleeve *n* **:** a sleeve very wide at the armhole and tight at the wrist often cut in one piece with the bodice

dol·men \'dōl-mən, 'dȯl-, 'däl-\ *n* [F, fr. Bret *tolmen*, fr. *tol* table + *men* stone] **:** a prehistoric monument consisting of two or more upright stones supporting a horizontal stone slab found esp. in Britain and France and thought to be a tomb

do·lo·mite \'dō-lə-,mīt, 'däl-ə-\ *n* [F, fr. Déodat de *Dolomieu* †1801 F geologist] **1 :** a mineral $CaMg(CO_3)_2$ consisting of a calcium magnesium carbonate found in crystals and in extensive beds as a compact limestone **2 :** a limestone or marble rich in magnesium carbonate — **do·lo·mit·ic** \,dō-lə-'mit-ik, ,däl-ə-\ *adj*

do·lor *or chiefly Brit* **do·lour** \'dō-lər, 'däl-ər\ *n* [ME *dolour*, fr. MF, fr. L *dolor* pain, grief, fr. *dolēre* to feel pain, grieve — more at CONDOLE] **:** mental suffering or anguish **:** SORROW

do·lor·ous \'dō-lə-rəs, 'däl-ə-\ *adj* **:** causing, marked by, or expressive of misery or grief — **do·lor·ous·ly** *adv* — **do·lor·ous·ness** *n*

dol·phin \'däl-fən, 'dȯl-\ *n* [ME, fr. MF *dophin, daufin*, fr. OF *dalfin*, fr. OProv, fr. ML *dalfinus*, alter. of L *delphinus*, fr. Gk *delphin-, delphis;* akin to Gk *delphys* womb, Skt *garbha*] **1 a :** any of various small toothed whales (family Delphinidae) with the snout more or less elongated into a beak and the neck vertebrae partially fused **b :** PORPOISE 1 **2 :** either of two active pelagic percoid food fishes (genus *Coryphaena*) of tropical and temperate seas **3** *cap* **:** DELPHINUS **4 :** a spar or buoy for mooring boats

dolphin striker *n* **:** a vertical spar under the end of the bowsprit of a sailboat to extend and support the martingale

dolt \'dōlt\ *n* [prob. akin to OE *dol* foolish] **:** a stupid fellow — **dolt·ish** \'dōl-tish\ *adj* — **dolt·ish·ly** *adv* — **dolt·ish·ness** *n*

Dom [L *dominus* master] **1** \(,)däm\ — used as a title for some monks and canons regular **2** \(,)dōⁿ\ — used as a title prefixed to the Christian name of a Portuguese or Brazilian man of rank

-dom \dəm\ *n suffix* [ME, fr. OE *-dōm;* akin to OHG *-tuom* -dom, OE *dōm* judgment] **1 a :** dignity **:** office ⟨duke*dom*⟩ **b :** realm **:** jurisdiction ⟨king*dom*⟩ **c :** geographical area ⟨Anglo-Saxon*dom*⟩ **2 :** state or fact of being ⟨free*dom*⟩ **3 :** those having a (specified) office, occupation, interest, or character ⟨official*dom*⟩

do·main \dō-'mān, də-\ *n* [MF *domaine, demaine*, fr. L *dominium*, fr. *dominus*] **1 a :** complete and absolute ownership of land — compare EMINENT DOMAIN **b :** land so owned **2 :** a territory over which dominion is exercised **3 :** a sphere of influence or activity **4 :** the set of elements to which a mathematical or logical variable is limited; *specif* **:** the set on which a function is defined

1dome \'dōm\ *n* [F, It, & L; F *dôme* dome, cathedral, fr. It *duomo* cathedral, fr. ML *domus* church, fr. L, house — more at TIMBER] **1** *archaic* **:** a stately building **:** MANSION **2 :** a large hemispherical roof or ceiling **3 :** a natural formation or other structure that resembles the dome or cupola of a building **4 a :** a form of crystal composed of planes parallel to a lateral axis which meet above in a horizontal edge like a roof **b :** a form of crystal composed of only two faces intersecting along and astride of a symmetry plane

2dome *vt* **1 :** to cover with or as if with a dome **2 :** to form into a dome ~ *vi* **:** to swell upward or outward like a dome

Domes·day Book \'dümz-,dā-, 'dōmz-\ *n* [ME, fr. *domesday* doomsday] **:** a record of a survey of English lands made by order of William the Conqueror about 1086

1do·mes·tic \də-'mes-tik\ *adj* [MF *domestique*, fr. L *domesticus*, fr. *domus*] **1 :** of or relating to the household or the family **2 :** relating and limited to one's own country or the country under consideration **3 :** INDIGENOUS **4 a :** living near or about the habitations of man **b :** DOMESTICATED, TAME **5 :** devoted to home duties and pleasures — **do·mes·ti·cal·ly** \-ti-k(ə-)lē\ *adv*

2domestic *n* **1 :** a household servant **2 :** an article of domestic manufacture — usu. used in pl.

domestic animal *n* **:** any of various animals (as the horse, sheep) domesticated by man so as to live and breed in a tame condition

do·mes·ti·cate \də-'mes-ti-,kāt\ *vt* **1 :** to bring into domestic use **:** ADOPT **2 :** to fit for domestic life **3 :** to adapt to life in intimate association with and to the advantage of man **4 :** to bring to the level of ordinary people — **do·mes·ti·ca·tion** \-,mes-ti-'kā-shən\ *n*

domestic fowl *n* **1 :** POULTRY **2 :** a bird of one of the breeds developed from the jungle fowl (*Gallus gallus*) esp. for meat or egg production **:** CHICKEN

do·mes·tic·i·ty \,dō-,mes-'tis-ət-ē, də-, ,dä-\ *n* **1 :** the quality or state of being domestic or domesticated **2 :** domestic activities or life **3** *pl* **:** domestic affairs

domestic prelate *n* **:** a priest having permanent honorary membership in the papal household and ranking above a papal chamberlain

domestic science *n* **:** instruction and training in domestic management and the household arts (as cooking and sewing)

dom·i·cal \'dō-mi-kəl, 'däm-i-\ *adj* **:** relating to, shaped like, or having a dome

1do·mi·cile \'däm-ə-,sīl, 'dō-mə-; 'däm-ə-səl\ *or* **dom·i·cil** \'däm-ə-səl\ *n* [MF, fr. L *domicilium*, fr. *domus*] **1 :** the place of residence of an individual or a family **:** ABODE **2 a :** the place with which a person has a settled connection for determination of his civil status or other legal purposes because it is actually or legally his permanent and principal home **b :** RESIDENCE 2a(1) **c :** RESIDENCE 2b — **do·mi·cil·i·ary** \,däm-ə-'sil-ē-,er-ē, ,dō-mə-\ *adj*

2domicile *vt* **:** to establish in or provide with a domicile

do·mi·cil·i·ate \,däm-ə-'sil-ē-,āt, ,dō-mə-\ *vb* [L *domicilium*] *vt* **:** DOMICILE ~ *vi* **:** RESIDE — **do·mi·cil·i·a·tion** \-,sil-ē-'ā-shən\ *n*

dom·i·nance \'däm-(ə-)nən(t)s\ *n* **:** the fact or state of being dominant **:** AUTHORITY

ə abut; ᵊ kitten; ər further; a back; ā bake; ä cot, cart; au̇ out; ch chin; e less; ē easy; g gift; i trip; ī life
j joke; ŋ sing; ō flow; ȯ flaw; ȯi coin; th thin; t͟h this; ü loot; u̇ foot; y yet; yü few; yu̇ furious; zh vision

1dom·i·nant \'nənt\ *adj* [MF or L; MF, fr. L *dominant-, dominans,* prp. of *dominari*] **1 :** commanding, controlling, or prevailing over all others **2 :** overlooking and commanding from a superior elevation **3 :** of, relating to, or exerting ecological dominance **4** *of paired bodily structures* **:** being the more effective or predominant one in action ⟨~ eye⟩ **5** *of an allele* **:** predominating over a contrasting allele in its manifestation — **dom·i·nant·ly** *adv*

syn DOMINANT, PREDOMINANT, PARAMOUNT, PREPONDERANT, SOVEREIGN mean superior to all others in power, influence, or importance. DOMINANT applies to something that is uppermost because ruling or controlling ⟨a *dominant* social class⟩; PREDOMINANT applies to something that exerts, often temporarily, the most marked influence ⟨a *predominant* emotion⟩; PARAMOUNT implies supremacy in importance, rank, or jurisdiction; PREPONDERANT applies to an element or factor that outweighs all others in influence or effect ⟨*preponderant* evidence in his favor⟩; SOVEREIGN indicates quality or rank to which everything else is clearly subordinate or inferior

2dominant *n* **1 a :** a dominant genetic character or factor **b :** any of one or more kinds of organism (as a species) in an ecological association that exerts a controlling influence on the environment and thereby largely determines what other kinds of organisms share in the association **2 :** the fifth note of the diatonic scale

dom·i·nate \'däm-ə-,nāt\ *vb* [L *dominatus,* pp. of *dominari,* fr. *dominus* master] *vt* **1 :** RULE **2 :** to exert the supreme determining or guiding influence on **3 :** to overlook from a superior elevation or command because of superior height **4 :** to have a commanding or preeminent place or position in ⟨name brands ~ the market⟩ ~ *vi* **1 :** to have or exert mastery, control, or preeminence **2 :** to occupy a more elevated or superior position — **dom·i·na·tive** \-,nāt-iv\ *adj* — **dom·i·na·tor** \-,nāt-ər\ *n*

dom·i·na·tion \,däm-ə-'nā-shən\ *n* **1 :** supremacy or preeminence over another **2 :** exercise of mastery or preponderant influence

dom·i·neer \,däm-ə-'ni(ə)r\ *vb* [D *domineren,* fr. F *dominer,* fr. L *dominari*] *vi* **:** to exercise arbitrary or overbearing rule ~ *vt* **:** to tyrannize over

dom·i·neer·ing *adj* **:** inclined to domineer **syn** see MASTERFUL — **dom·i·neer·ing·ly** \-iŋ-lē\ *adv* — **dom·i·neer·ing·ness** *n*

do·min·i·cal \də-'min-i-kəl\ *adj* [LL *dominicalis,* fr. *dominicus (dies)* the Lord's day, fr. L *dominicus* of a lord, fr. *dominus* lord, master] **1 :** of or relating to Jesus Christ as Lord **2 :** of or relating to the Lord's day

dominical letter *n* **:** the letter designating Sundays in a given year (as for finding the date of Easter) when the first seven letters of the alphabet are applied consecutively to the days of the year beginning with *A* on Jan. 1 and skipping the intercalary day in leap year

Do·min·i·can \də-'min-i-kən\ *n* [St. *Dominic* †1221 Sp priest] **:** a member of a Roman Catholic mendicant order founded in 1215 under a modified rule of St. Augustine and noted esp. for preaching — **Dominican** *adj*

dom·i·nick \'dam-ə-(,)nik, -,nek\ *or* **dom·i·nick·er** \-,nek-ər, -,nik-\ *n, often cap* **:** DOMINIQUE

do·mi·nie *1 oftenest* 'däm-ə-nē, *2 oftenest* 'dō-mə-\ *n* [L *domine,* voc. of *dominus*] **1** *chiefly Scot* **:** PEDAGOGUE **2 :** CLERGYMAN

do·min·ion \də-'min-yən\ *n* [ME *dominioun,* fr. MF *dominion,* modif. of L *dominium,* fr. *dominus*] **1 :** supreme authority **:** SOVEREIGNTY **2 :** DOMAIN **3 :** an angel of the fourth highest rank **4** *often cap* **:** a self-governing nation of the British Commonwealth other than the United Kingdom that acknowledges the British monarch as chief of state **5 :** absolute ownership **syn** see POWER

Dominion Day *n* **:** July 1 observed in Canada as a legal holiday in commemoration of the proclamation of dominion status in 1867

dom·i·nique \'däm-ə-(,)nik, -,nek\ *n* [*Dominique* (Dominica), one of the Windward islands, West Indies] **1** *cap* **:** an American breed of domestic fowls with rose combs, yellow legs, and barred plumage **2 :** a bird of the Dominique breed; *broadly* **:** a barred fowl

dom·i·no \'däm-ə-,nō\ *n, pl* **dominoes** *or* **dominos** [F, prob. fr. L (in the ritual formula *benedicamus Domino* let us bless the Lord)] **1 :** a long loose hooded cloak usu. worn with a half mask as a masquerade costume **2 :** a half mask worn with a masquerade costume **3 :** a person wearing a domino **4** [F, fr. It] **a :** a flat rectangular block (as of wood or plastic) the face of which is divided into two equal parts that are blank or bear from one to usu. six dots arranged as on dice faces **b** *pl but usu sing in constr* **:** any of several games played with a set of usu. 28 dominoes

1don \'dän\ *n* [Sp, fr. L *dominus* master — more at DAME] **1 :** a Spanish nobleman or gentleman — used as a title prefixed to the Christian name **2 a** *archaic* **:** a person of consequence **:** GRANDEE **b :** a head, tutor, or fellow in a college of Oxford or Cambridge

2don \'dän\ *vt* **donned; don·ning** [*do* + *on*] **1 :** to put on (an article of wear) **2 :** to envelop oneself in **:** ASSUME

1do·ña \,dō-nyə\ *n* [Sp, fr. L *domina* lady] **:** a Spanish woman of rank — used as a title prefixed to the Christian name

2do·na \,dō-nə\ *n* [Pg, fr. L *domina*] **:** a Portuguese or Brazilian woman of rank — used as a title prefixed to the Christian name

Do·nar \'dō-,när\ *n* [OHG] **:** the Germanic god of thunder

do·nate \'dō-,nāt, dō-'nāt\ *vb* [back-formation fr. *donation*] *vt* **:** to make a gift of **:** CONTRIBUTE ~ *vi* **:** to make a donation **syn** see GIVE

do·na·tion \dō-'nā-shən\ *n* [ME *donatyowne,* fr. L *donation-, donatio,* fr. *donatus,* pp. of *donare* to present, fr. *donum* gift; akin to L *dare* to give] **1 :** the action of making a gift esp. to a charity or public institution **2 :** a free contribution **:** GIFT

Do·na·tism \'dän-ə-,tiz-əm, 'dō-nə-\ *n* [*Donatus,* 4th cent. bishop of Carthage] **:** the doctrines of a Christian sect arising in No. Africa in 311 and holding that sanctity is essential for the administration of sacraments and church membership — **Do·na·tist** \-təst\ *n*

1do·na·tive \'dō-nət-iv, 'dän-ət-\ *n* **:** a special gift or donation

2do·na·tive *same or* 'dō-,nāt-, dō-'nāt-\ *adj* [L *donativus,* fr. *donatus*] **:** characterized by, capable of, or subject to donation ⟨a ~ trust⟩

do·na·tor \'dō-,nāt-ər, dō-'nāt-\ *n* **:** DONOR

1done \'dən\ *past part of* DO

2done *adj* **1 :** conformable to social convention **2 :** arrived at or brought to an end **3 :** physically exhausted **:** SPENT **4 :** gone by **:** OVER **5 :** doomed to failure, defeat, or death **6 :** cooked sufficiently

do·nee \dō-'nē\ *n* [*donor*] **:** a recipient of a gift

don·jon \'dän-jən, 'dən-\ *n* [ME — more at DUNGEON] **:** a massive chief tower in ancient castles

Don Juan \(')dän-'(h)wän, dän-'jü-ən\ *n* [Sp] **1 :** a profligate nobleman of Spanish legend **2 :** LIBERTINE, RAKE

don·key \'däŋ-kē, 'dəŋ-, 'dȯŋ-\ *n* [perh. fr. *1dun* + *-key* (as in *monkey*)] **1 :** the domestic ass **2 :** a stupid or obstinate person

donkey engine *n* **1 :** a small usu. portable auxiliary engine **2 :** a small locomotive used in switching

don·key·work \-,wərk\ *n* **:** plodding and routine work **:** DRUDGERY

don·na \,dän-ə, ,dȯn-\ *n, pl* **don·ne** \-(,)ā\ [It, fr. L *domina*] **:** an Italian woman esp. of rank — used as a title prefixed to the Christian name

don·née \dȯ-'nā, (,)də-\ *n, pl* **données** \-'nā(z)\ [F, fr. fem. of *donné,* pp. of *donner* to give, fr. L *donare* to donate] **:** the set of assumptions upon which a work of fiction or drama proceeds

don·nish \'dän-ish\ *adj* **:** relating to or characteristic of a university don **:** PEDANTIC — **don·nish·ly** *adv* — **don·nish·ness** *n*

don·ny·brook \'dän-ē-,bru̇k\ *n, often cap* [*Donnybrook* Fair, annual Irish event known for its brawls] **:** an uproarious brawl

do·nor \'dō-nər, -,nȯ(ə)r\ *n* [MF *doneur,* fr. L *donator,* fr. *donatus*] **1 :** one that gives, donates, or presents **2 :** one used as a source of biological material — **do·nor·ship** \-,ship\ *n*

1do-noth·ing \'dü-,nəth-iŋ\ *n* **:** a shiftless or habitually lazy person

2do-nothing *adj* **:** marked by inactivity; *specif* **:** marked by lack of initiative, disinclination to disturb the status quo, or failure to make positive progress — **do-noth·ing·ism** \-iŋ-,iz-əm\ *n*

Don Qui·xote \,dän-kē-'(h)ōt-ē, dän-'kwik-sət\ *n* [Sp] **:** the idealistic and impractical hero of Cervantes' *Don Quixote*

don·sie *or* **don·sy** \'dän(t)-sē\ *adj* [perh. fr. ScGael *donas* evil, harm] **1** *dial Brit* **:** UNLUCKY **2** *Scot* **a :** QUICK-TEMPERED **b :** SAUCY

1don't \(')dōnt\ **1 :** do not **2 :** does not — often used by cultivated speakers though the construction is sometimes objected to

2don't \'dōnt\ *n* **:** a command or entreaty not to do something

doo·dad \'dü-,dad\ *n* [origin unknown] **:** a small article whose common name is unknown or forgotten **:** GADGET

1doo·dle \'düd-ᵊl\ *vb* **doo·dling** \'düd-liŋ, -ᵊl-iŋ\ [perh. fr. *doodle* (to ridicule)] *vi* **1 :** to make a doodle **2 :** DAWDLE, TRIFLE ~ *vt* **:** to produce by doodling — **doo·dler** \'düd-lər, -ᵊl-ər\ *n*

2doodle *n* **:** an aimless scribble, design, or sketch

doo·dle·bug \'düd-ᵊl-,bəg\ *n* [prob. fr. *doodle* (fool) + *bug*] **1 :** the larva of an ant lion; *broadly* **:** any of several other insects **2 :** a device for finding underground minerals

doo·hick·ey \'dü-,hik-ē\ *n* [prob. fr. *doodad* + *hickey*] **:** DOODAD

1doom \'düm\ *n* [ME, fr. OE *dōm;* akin to OHG *tuom* condition, state, OE *dōn* to do] **1 :** a law or ordinance esp. in Anglo-Saxon England **2 a :** JUDGMENT, DECISION; *esp* **:** a judicial condemnation or sentence **b** (1) **:** JUDGMENT 3a (2) **:** JUDGMENT DAY 1 **3 a :** DESTINY; *esp* **:** unhappy destiny **b :** DEATH, RUIN **syn** see FATE

2doom *vt* **1 :** to give judgment against **:** CONDEMN **2 a :** to fix the fate of **:** DESTINE **b :** to make certain the failure or destruction of

dooms·day \'dümz-,dā\ *n* **:** JUDGMENT DAY

door \'dō(ə)r, 'dȯ(ə)r\ *n* [ME *dure, dor,* fr. OE *duru* door & *dor* gate; akin to OHG *turi* door, L *fores*] **1 :** a usu. swinging or sliding barrier by which an entry is closed and opened; *also* **:** a similar part of a piece of furniture **2 :** DOORWAY **3 :** a means of access

door·jamb \-,jam\ *n* **:** an upright piece forming the side of a door opening

door·keep·er \-,kē-pər\ *n* **:** one that tends a door

door·knob \-,näb\ *n* **:** a knob that releases a door latch

door·man \-,man, -mən\ *n* **:** DOORKEEPER

door·mat \-,mat\ *n* **1 :** a mat placed before or inside a door for wiping dirt from the shoes **2 :** a constant and unprotesting sufferer

door·nail \-,nāl, -'nā(ə)l\ *n* **:** a large-headed nail

door·plate \-,plāt\ *n* **:** a nameplate on a door

door·post \-,pōst\ *n* **:** DOORJAMB

door·sill \-,sil\ *n* **:** SILL b

door·step \-,step\ *n* **:** a step before an outer door

door·way \-,wā\ *n* **1 :** the opening that a door closes **2 :** a means of gaining access

door·yard \-,yärd\ *n* **:** a yard outside the door of a house

1dope \'dōp\ *n* [D *doop* sauce, fr. *dopen* to dip; akin to OE *dyppan* to dip — more at DIP] **1 a :** a thick liquid or pasty preparation **b :** a preparation for giving a desired quality to a substance or surface; *specif* **:** an antiknock added to gasoline **2 :** absorbent or adsorbent material used in various manufacturing processes (as the making of dynamite) **3 a** (1) **:** a narcotic preparation; *specif* **:** OPIUM (2) **:** a preparation given to a racehorse to stimulate it temporarily (3) *chiefly South* **:** a cola drink **b** (1) **:** a narcotic addict (2) **:** a stupid person **4 :** information esp. from a reliable source

2dope *vt* **1 :** to treat or affect with dope; *specif* **:** to give a narcotic to **2 :** to find a solution for ~ *vi* **:** to take dope — **dop·er** *n*

dope·ster \'dōp-stər\ *n* **:** a forecaster of the outcome of uncertain public events

dop·ey \'dō-pē\ *adj* **dop·i·er; dop·i·est 1 a :** dulled by alcohol or a narcotic **b :** SLUGGISH, STUPEFIED **2 :** DULL, STUPID — **dop·i·ness** *n*

dop·pel·gäng·er *or* **dop·pel·gang·er** \,däp-əl-'gaŋ-ər\ *n* [G *doppelgänger,* fr. *doppel-* double + *-gänger* goer] **:** a ghostly counterpart of a living person

Dopp·ler effect \'däp-lər-\ *n* [Christian J. *Doppler* †1853 Austrian physicist] **:** a change in the frequency with which waves (as of sound or light) from a given source reach an observer when the source and the observer are in rapid motion with respect to each other by which the frequency increases or decreases according to the speed at which the distance is decreasing or increasing

dor·bee·tle \'dȯr-,bēt-ᵊl\ *n* [*dor* (buzzing insect)] **:** any of various beetles that fly with a buzzing sound; *specif* **:** a common European dung beetle (*Geotrupes stercorarius*)

Dor·cas \'dȯr-kəs\ *n* [Gk *Dorkas*] **:** a Christian woman of New Testament times who made clothing for the poor

dor·hawk \'dȯ(ə)r-,hȯk\ *n* [*dor* (buzzing insect); fr. its diet] **:** the common European nightjar (*Caprimulgus europaeus*)

Do·ri·an \'dōr-ē-ən, 'dȯr-\ *n* [L *dorius* of Doris, fr. Gk *dōrios,* fr. *Dōris,* region of ancient Greece] **:** one of an ancient Hellenic race that completed the overthrow of Mycenaean civilization and settled esp. in the Peloponnesus and Crete — **Dorian** *adj*

1Dor·ic \'dȯr-ik, 'där-\ *adj* **1 :** of, relating to, or constituting Doric **2 :** of, relating to, or characteristic of the Dorians **3 :** belonging to the oldest and simplest Greek architectural order

2Doric *n* **:** a dialect of ancient Greek spoken esp. in the Peloponnesus, Crete, Sicily, and southern Italy

dorm \'dȯ(ə)rm\ *n* : DORMITORY

dor·man·cy \'dȯr-mən-sē\ *n* : the quality or state of being dormant

dor·mant \'dȯr-mənt\ *adj* [ME, fixed, stationary, fr. MF, fr. prp. of *dormir* to sleep, fr. L *dormire;* akin to Skt *drāti* he sleeps] **1 :** represented on a coat of arms in a lying position with the head on the forepaws **2 :** marked by a suspension of activity: as **a :** temporarily devoid of external activity ⟨a ~ volcano⟩ **b :** temporarily in abeyance yet capable of being activated or resumed ⟨a ~ judgment⟩ **3 a :** SLEEPING, DROWSING **b :** having the faculties suspended **:** SLUGGISH **c :** having biological activity suspended: as (1) **:** being in a state of suspended animation (2) **:** not actively growing and typically protected **4 :** associated with, carried out, or applied during dormancy ⟨~ grafting⟩ **syn** see LATENT

dor·mer \'dȯr-mər\ *n* [MF *dormeor* dormitory, fr. L *dormitorium*] **:** a window vertical in a roof; *also* **:** the roofed structure containing such a window

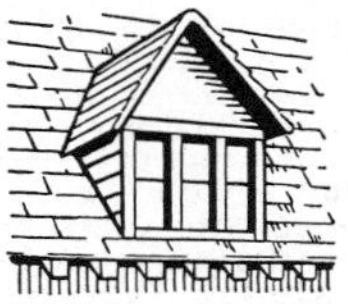
dormer

dor·mie *or* **dor·my** \'dȯr-mē\ *adj* [origin unknown] **:** being up as many holes in golf as remain to be played

dor·mi·to·ry \'dȯr-mə-,tōr-ē, -,tȯr-\ *n* [L *dormitorium,* fr. *dormitus,* pp. of *dormire*] **1 :** a room for sleeping; *esp* **:** a large room containing a number of beds **2 :** a residence hall providing sleeping rooms

dor·mouse \'dȯ(ə)r-,mau̇s\ *n, pl* **dor·mice** \-,mīs\ [ME *dormowse,* perh. fr. MF *dormir* + ME *mous* mouse] **:** any of numerous small Old World rodents (family Gliridae) that resemble small squirrels

dor·nick \'dȯr-nik, 'dä(r)n-ik\ *n* [prob. fr. IrGael *dornōg*] **:** a small stone or chunk of rock

do·ron·i·cum \də-'rän-i-kəm\ *n* [NL, genus name, fr. Ar *darūnaj,* a plant of this genus] **:** any of a genus (*Doronicum*) of Eurasian perennial composite herbs including several cultivated for their showy yellow flower heads

dorp \'dȯ(ə)rp\ *n* [D, fr. MD; akin to OHG *dorf*] **:** VILLAGE

dor·per \'dȯr-pər, 'dȯ(ə)r-,pər\ *n* [*Dor*set Horn + Blackhead *Per*sian (a breed of sheep)] **:** any of a breed of mutton-type sheep with white body and black face developed in southern Africa

dors- *or* **dorsi-** *or* **dorso-** *comb form* [LL *dors-,* fr. L *dorsum*] **1 :** back ⟨*dors*ad⟩ **2 :** dorsal and ⟨*dorso*lateral⟩

dor·sad \'dȯ(ə)r-,sad\ *adv* **:** toward the back **:** DORSALLY

[1]**dor·sal** \'dȯr-səl\ *adj* [LL *dorsalis,* fr. L *dorsum* back] **1 :** relating to or situated near or on the back esp. of an animal or of one of its parts **2 :** ABAXIAL — **dor·sal·ly** \-sə-lē\ *adv*

[2]**dorsal** *n* **:** a dorsally located part; *esp* **:** a thoracic vertebra

dorsal lip *n* **:** the margin of the fold of blastula wall that delineates the dorsal limit of the blastopore, constitutes the primary organizer, and forms the point of origin of chordamesoderm

dorsal root *n* **:** the one of the two roots of a spinal nerve that passes dorsally to the spinal cord and consists of sensory fibers

dor·set horn \'dȯr-sət-\ *n, often cap D&H* [*Dorset,* England] **:** any of an English breed of sheep that have very large horns

dor·si·ven·tral \,dȯr-si-'ven-trəl\ *adj* **1 :** having distinct dorsal and ventral surfaces **2 :** DORSOVENTRAL 1 — **dor·si·ven·tral·i·ty** \-,ven-'tral-ət-ē\ *n* — **dor·si·ven·tral·ly** \-'ven-trə-lē\ *adv*

dor·so·lat·er·al \,dȯr-(,)sō-'lat-ə-rəl, -'la-trəl\ *adj* **:** of, relating to, or involving both the back and sides

dor·so·ven·tral \,dȯr-(,)sō-'ven-trəl\ *adj* [ISV] **1 :** extending from the dorsal toward the ventral side **2 :** DORSIVENTRAL 1 — **dor·so·ven·tral·ly** \-trə-lē\ *adv*

dor·sum \'dȯr-səm\ *n, pl* **dor·sa** \-sə\ [L] **1 :** BACK; *esp* **:** the entire dorsal surface of an animal **2 :** the upper surface of an appendage or part

do·ry \'dōr-ē, 'dȯr-\ *n* [Miskito *dóri* dugout] **:** a flat-bottomed boat with high flaring sides, sharp bow, and deep V-shaped transom

dos·age \'dō-sij\ *n* **1 a :** the amount of a therapeutic dose **b** (1) **:** the giving of such a dose (2) **:** regulation or determination of doses **2 a :** the addition of an ingredient or the application of an agent in a measured dose **b :** the presence and relative representation or strength of a factor or agent **3 :** a dealing out

[1]**dose** \'dōs\ *n* [F, fr. LL *dosis,* fr. Gk, lit., act of giving, fr. *didonai* to give — more at DATE] **1 a :** the measured quantity of a therapeutic agent to be taken at one time **b :** the quantity of radiation administered or absorbed **2 :** a portion of a substance added during a process **3 :** a portion of an experience to which one is exposed

[2]**dose** *vt* **1 :** to give a dose to; *esp* **:** to give medicine to **2 :** to divide (as a medicine) into doses **3 :** to treat with an application or agent

do–si–do \,dō-(,)sē-'dō\ *n* [F *dos-à-dos* back to back] **:** a square-dance figure in which the dancers passing by right shoulder circle each other back to back

do·sim·e·ter \dō-'sim-ət-ər\ *n* [LL *dosis* + ISV *-meter*] **:** an instrument for measuring doses of X rays or of radioactivity — **do·si·met·ric** \,dō-sə-'me-trik\ *adj* — **do·sim·e·try** \dō-'sim-ə-trē\ *n*

[1]**doss** \'däs\ *vi* [origin unknown] *chiefly Brit* **:** to sleep or bed down in any convenient place

[2]**doss** *n, chiefly Brit* **:** a crude or makeshift bed

dos·sal \'däs-əl\ *or* **dor·sal** \'dȯr-səl\ *or* **dos·sel** \'däs-əl\ *n* [ML *dossale, dorsale,* fr. neut. of LL *dorsalis* dorsal] **:** an ornamental cloth for the back of a throne or chair

dos·sier \'dȯs-,yā, 'däs-ē-,ā\ *n* [F, bundle of documents labeled on the back, dossier, fr. *dos* back, fr. L *dorsum*] **:** a bundle of papers containing a detailed report or detailed information

dost \(')dəst\ *archaic pres 2d sing of* DO

[1]**dot** \'dät\ *n* [(assumed) ME, fr. OE *dott* head of a boil; akin to OHG *tutta* nipple] **1 :** a small spot **:** SPECK **2 a :** a small point made with a pointed instrument **b** (1) **:** a point after a note or rest in music indicating augmentation of the time value by one half (2) **:** a point over or under a note indicating that it is to be played staccato **3 :** a precise point in time or space **4 :** a short click or buzz forming a letter or part of a letter (as in the Morse code)

[2]**dot** *vb* **dot·ted; dot·ting** *vt* **1 :** to mark with a dot **2 :** to scatter or distribute like dots **3 :** to cover with dots ~ *vi* **:** to make a dot — **dot·ter** *n*

[3]**dot** *n* [F, fr. L *dot-, dos* dowry] **:** DOWRY 2a — **do·tal** \'dōt-ᵊl\ *adj*

dot·age \'dōt-ij\ *n* **:** a state of feeblemindedness esp. in old age

dot·ard \'dōt-ərd\ *n* **:** a person in his dotage

dote \'dōt\ *vi* [ME *doten;* akin to MLG *dotten* to be foolish] **1 :** to be feebleminded esp. from old age **2 :** to show excessive or foolish affection or fondness — **dot·er** *n* — **dot·ing·ly** \-iŋ-lē\ *adv*

doth \(')dəth\ *archaic pres 3d sing of* DO

dot·ted swiss \,dät-əd-'swis\ *n* **:** a light muslin ornamented with evenly spaced raised dots

dot·ter·el \'dät-ə-rəl, 'dä-trəl\ *n* [ME *dotrelle,* irreg. fr. *doten*] **:** a Eurasian plover (*Charadrius morinellus*) formerly common in England; *also* **:** any of various congeners chiefly of eastern Asia, Australia, and So. America

dot·tle \'dät-ᵊl\ *n* [ME *dottel* plug, fr. (assumed) ME *dot*] **:** unburnt and partially burnt tobacco caked in the bowl of a pipe

[1]**dot·ty** \'dät-ē\ *adj* **:** composed of or marked by dots

[2]**dotty** *adj* [alter. of Sc *dottle* fool, fr. ME *dotel,* fr. *doten*] **1 :** unsteady in gait **2 :** mentally unbalanced **:** CRAZY **3 :** ABSURD

Dou·ay Version \dü-'ā-\ *n* [*Douay,* France] **:** an English translation of the Vulgate used by Roman Catholics

[1]**dou·ble** \'dəb-əl\ *adj* [ME, fr. OF, fr. L *duplus,* fr. *duo* two + *-plus* multiplied by; akin to Gk di*ploos* double, OE *fealdan* to fold] **1 :** having a twofold relation or character **:** DUAL **2 :** consisting of two usu. combined members or parts **3 :** being twice as great or as many **4 :** marked by duplicity **:** DECEITFUL **5 :** folded in two **6 :** having more than the normal number of floral leaves often at the expense of the sporophylls — **dou·ble·ness** *n*

[2]**double** *n* **1 :** something twice the usual size, strength, speed, quantity, or value: as **a :** a double amount **b :** a two-base hit in baseball **2 :** COUNTERPART, DUPLICATE: as **a :** WRAITH **b** (1) **:** UNDERSTUDY (2) **:** one who resembles an actor and takes his place in scenes calling for special skills **3 a :** a sharp turn (as in running) **:** REVERSAL **b :** an evasive shift **4 :** something consisting of two paired members: as **a :** FOLD **b :** a combined bet placed on two different contests **c :** two consecutive strikes in bowling **5** *pl* **:** a game between two pairs of players **6 :** an act of doubling in a card game

[3]**double** *adv* **1 :** to twice the extent or amount **2 :** two together

[4]**double** *vb* **dou·bling** \'dəb-(ə-)liŋ\ *vt* **1 :** to make twice as great or as many: as **a :** to increase by adding an equal amount **b :** to amount to twice the number of **c :** to make a call in bridge that increases the value of odd tricks or undertricks at (an opponent's bid) **d** (1) **:** to advance (a base runner in baseball) by a two-base hit (2) **:** to put out (a base runner) in completing a double play **2 a :** to make of two thicknesses **:** FOLD **b :** CLENCH **c :** to cause to stoop **3 a :** to avoid by doubling **:** ELUDE **b :** to sail around (as a cape) by reversing direction **4 a :** to replace in a dramatic role **b :** to play (dramatic roles) by doubling ~ *vi* **1 a :** to become twice as much or as many **b :** to double a bid (as in bridge) **c :** to make a two-base hit in baseball **2 a :** to turn sharply and suddenly; *esp* **:** to turn back on one's course **b :** to follow a circuitous course **3 :** to become bent or folded usu. in the middle **4 a :** to serve an additional purpose or perform an additional duty **b :** to play a dramatic role as a double — **dou·bler** \'dəb-(ə-)lər\ *n*

double bar *n* **:** two adjacent vertical lines or a heavy single line separating principal sections of a musical composition

double bass *n* **:** the largest instrument of the viol family

double bassoon *n* **:** CONTRABASSOON

double boiler *n* **:** a cooking utensil consisting of two saucepans fitting into each other so that the contents of the upper can be cooked by boiling water in the lower

dou·ble–breast·ed \,dəb-əl-'bres-təd\ *adj* **1 :** having one half of the front lapped over the other and usu. a double row of buttons and a single row of buttonholes **2 :** having a double-breasted coat

double counterpoint *n* **:** two-part counterpoint so constructed that either part may be above or below the other

double cross *n* **1 a :** an act of winning or trying to win a fight or match after agreeing to lose it **b :** an act of betraying or cheating an associate **2 :** a cross between first-generation hybrids of four separate inbred lines (as in the production of hybrid seed corn)

dou·ble–cross \,dəb-əl-'krȯs\ *vt* **:** to deceive by double-dealing **:** BETRAY — **dou·ble–cross·er** *n*

double dagger *n* **:** the character ‡ used commonly as the third in the series of reference marks — called also *diesis*

dou·ble–deal·er \,dəb-əl-'dē-lər\ *n* **:** one who practices double-dealing

[1]**dou·ble–deal·ing** \-liŋ\ *n* **:** action contradictory to a professed attitude **:** DUPLICITY **syn** see DECEPTION

[2]**double–dealing** *adj* **:** given to or marked by duplicity

dou·ble–deck \'dəb-əl-,dek\ *or* **dou·ble–decked** \,dəb-əl-'dekt\ *adj* **:** having two stories, decks, or levels

dou·ble–deck·er \,dəb-əl-'dek-ər\ *n* **:** a double-deck structure

dou·ble–dome \'dəb-əl-,dōm\ *n* **:** EGGHEAD

dou·ble en·ten·dre \,düb-(ə-),läⁿ-'täⁿdrᵊ, ,dəb-\ *n, pl* **double entendres** *same*\ [obs. F, lit., double meaning] **1 :** ambiguity of meaning arising from language that lends itself to more than one interpretation **2 :** a word or expression capable of two interpretations one of which often has a risqué connotation

double entry *n* **:** a method of bookkeeping that recognizes both the receiving and the giving sides of a business transaction by debiting the amount of the transaction to one account and crediting it to another account so that the total debits equal the total credits

dou·ble–faced \,dəb-əl-'fāst\ *adj* **1 :** having two faces or sides designed for use **2 a :** AMBIGUOUS **b :** HYPOCRITICAL

dou·ble·head·er \,dəb-əl-'hed-ər\ *n* **1 :** a train pulled by two locomotives **2 :** two games played consecutively on the same day by the same teams or by different pairs of teams

double hyphen *n* **:** a punctuation mark ⸗ used in place of a hyphen at the end of a line to indicate that the word so divided is normally hyphenated

dou·ble–joint·ed \,dəb-əl-'jȯint-əd\ *adj* **:** having a joint that permits exceptional degree of freedom of motion of the parts joined

double negative *n* **1 :** a now substandard syntactic construction containing two negatives and having a negative meaning **2 :** a reiterated denial that equals an affirmative

dou·ble–park \,dəb-əl-'pärk\ *vb* **:** to park beside a row of automobiles already parked parallel to the curb

double play *n* **:** a play in baseball by which two players are put out

dou·ble–quick \'dəb-əl-,kwik\ *n* **:** DOUBLE TIME — **double–quick** *vi*

double reed *n* : two cane reeds bound and vibrating against each other and used as the mouthpiece of instruments of the oboe family
double refraction *n* : BIREFRINGENCE
double rhyme *n* : end rhyme involving two syllables
double salt *n* **1** : a salt (as an alum) yielding on hydrolysis two different cations or anions **2** : a salt regarded as a molecular combination of two distinct salts
dou·ble–space \ˌdəb-əl-ˈspās\ *vt* : to type (copy) leaving alternate lines blank ~ *vi* : to type on every second line
double standard *n* **1** : BIMETALLISM **2** : a set of principles that applies differently and usu. more rigorously to one group of people or circumstances than to another
double star *n* **1** : BINARY STAR **2** : two stars in very nearly the same line of sight but seen as physically separate by means of a telescope
dou·blet \ˈdəb-lət\ *n* [ME, fr. MF, fr. *double*] **1** : a man's close-fitting jacket worn in Europe esp. during the Renaissance **2 a** (1) : something consisting of two identical or similar parts (2) : a set of two identical or similar things; *specif* : two thrown dice with the same number of spots on the upper face **b** : one of a pair; *specif* : one of two or more words (as *guard* and *ward*) in the same language derived by different routes of transmission from the same source
dou·ble take \ˈdəb-əl-ˌtāk\ *n* : a delayed reaction to a surprising or significant situation
dou·ble–talk \ˈdəb-əl-ˌtȯk\ *n* **1** : language that appears to be earnest and meaningful but in fact is a mixture of sense and nonsense **2** : inflated, involved, and often deliberately ambiguous language
Double Ten *n* [trans. of Chin (Pek) *shuang[1] shih[2]*; fr. its being the tenth day of the tenth month] : October 10 observed by Nationalist China in commemoration of the revolution of 1911
dou·ble·think \ˈdəb-əl-ˌthiŋk\ *n* : the believing in two contradictory ideas simultaneously
double time *n* **1** : a marching cadence of 180 36-inch steps per minute **2** : payment of a worker at twice his regular wage rate
dou·ble–time \ˈdəb-əl-ˌtīm\ *vi* : to move at double time
dou·ble–tongue \ˌdəb-əl-ˈtəŋ\ *vi* : to cause the tongue to alternate rapidly between the positions for *t* and *k* so as to produce a fast succession of detached notes on a wind instrument
dou·ble·tree \ˈdəb-əl-(ˌ)trē\ *n* : an equalizing bar for use with a two-horse team
double twill *n* : a twill weave with intersecting diagonal lines going in opposite directions
dou·ble–u *as at* w\ *n* : the letter *w*
double up *vi* : to share accommodations designed for one
dou·bloon \ˌdə-ˈblün\ *n* [Sp *doblón*, aug. of *dobla*, an old Spanish coin, fr. L *dupla*, fem. of *duplus* double — more at DOUBLE] : an old gold coin of Spain and Spanish America worth 16 pieces of eight
dou·bly \ˈdəb-(ə-)lē\ *adv* **1** : to twice the degree **2** : in a two-fold manner
1**doubt** \ˈdau̇t\ *vb* [ME *douten*, fr. OF *douter* to doubt, fr. L *dubitare;* akin to L *dubius* dubious — more at DUBIOUS] *vt* **1** *archaic* : FEAR **2** : to be uncertain about **3 a** : to lack confidence in : DISTRUST **b** : to consider unlikely ~ *vi* : to be uncertain — **doubt·able** \ˈdau̇t-ə-bəl\ *adj* — **doubt·er** *n* — **doubt·ing·ly** \-iŋ-lē\ *adv*
2**doubt** *n* **1 a** : uncertainty of belief or opinion **b** : a deliberate suspension of judgment **2** : the condition of being objectively uncertain **3 a** : a lack of confidence : DISTRUST **b** : an inclination not to believe or accept **syn** see UNCERTAINTY
doubt·ful \ˈdau̇t-fəl\ *adj* **1** : marked by uncertainty or lack of clarity **2 a** : lacking a definite opinion, conviction, or determination **b** (1) : uncertain in outcome : UNDECIDED (2) : not predictable **3** : marked by qualities that raise doubts about worth, honesty, or validity — **doubt·ful·ly** \-fə-lē\ *adv* — **doubt·ful·ness** *n*
syn DUBIOUS, PROBLEMATIC, QUESTIONABLE: DOUBTFUL and DUBIOUS indicate uncertainty in reference to persons or unpredictability in reference to events and situations. DOUBTFUL implies simply a lack of certainty or conviction; DUBIOUS stresses the unlikelihood of an ultimately favorable outcome or judgment; PROBLEMATIC describes a situation having an entirely unpredictable outcome; DOUBTFUL, applied as an estimation or judgment, may question worth, honesty, or validity so strongly as to imply their absence or insufficiency; DUBIOUS stresses usu. well-grounded suspicion or mistrust; QUESTIONABLE may mean simply open to question but often connotes falsity unsoundness, or immorality that is strongly suspected but may be asserted only in guarded statements or hints
doubting Thom·as \-ˈtäm-əs\ *n* [*Thomas*, apostle of Jesus who doubted Jesus' resurrection until he had proof of it (Jn 20:24–29)] : a habitually doubtful person
1**doubt·less** \ˈdau̇t-ləs\ *adv* **1** : without doubt **2** : PROBABLY
2**doubtless** *adj* : free from doubt : CERTAIN — **doubt·less·ly** *adv* — **doubt·less·ness** *n*
douce \ˈdüs\ *adj* [ME, sweet, pleasant, fr. MF, fr. fem. of *douz*, fr. L *dulcis*] *chiefly Scot* : SOBER, SEDATE — **douce·ly** *adv, chiefly Scot*
dou·ceur \dü-ˈsər\ *n* [F, pleasantness, fr. LL *dulcor* sweetness, fr. L *dulcis* sweet] **1** *archaic* : AMIABILITY **2** : a conciliatory gift
douche \ˈdüsh\ *n* [F, fr. It *doccia*, fr. *docciare* to douche, fr. *doccia* water pipe, prob. back-formation fr. *doccione* conduit, fr. L *duction-*, *ductio* action of leading, fr. *ductus*, pp. of *ducere* to lead — more at TOW] **1 a** : a jet or current esp. of water directed against a part or into a cavity of the body **b** : an act of cleansing with a douche **2** : a device for giving douches — **douche** *vb*
dough \ˈdō\ *n* [ME *dogh*, fr. OE *dāg*] **1** : a mixture of flour and other ingredients stiff enough to knead or roll **2** : something resembling dough esp. in consistency **3** : MONEY **4** : DOUGHBOY
dough·boy \-ˌbȯi\ *n* : INFANTRYMAN
dough·face \-ˌfās\ *n* **1** : a northern congressman not opposed to slavery in the South **2** : a northerner sympathetic to the South before or during the Civil War — **dough–faced** \-ˈfāst\ *adj*
dough·foot \-ˌfu̇t\ *n, pl* **doughfeet** *or* **doughfoots** : INFANTRYMAN
dough·nut \-(ˌ)nət\ *n* : a small usu. ring-shaped cake fried in fat
dough·ti·ly \ˈdau̇t-ᵊl-ē\ *adv* : in a doughty manner
dough·ti·ness \ˈdau̇t-ē-nəs\ *n* : the quality or state of being doughty
dough·ty \ˈdau̇t-ē\ *adj* [ME, fr. OE *dohtig*] : ABLE, VALIANT
doughy \ˈdō-ē\ *adj* : resembling dough : PASTY
Doug·las fir \ˌdəg-ləs-\ *n* [David *Douglas* †1834 Sc botanist] : a tall evergreen timber tree (*Pseudotsuga taxifolia*) of the western U.S. having thick bark, pitchy wood, and pendulous cones — called also *Douglas spruce*
Dou·kho·bor \ˈdü-kə-ˌbȯ(ə)r\ *n* [Russ *dukhoborets*, fr. *dukh* spirit + *borets* wrestler] : a member of a Christian sect of 18th century Russian origin emphasizing the duty of obeying the inner light and rejecting church or civil authority
do up *vt* **1 a** : to make ready for use **b** : to put in order **2 a** : to wrap up **b** : to put up : CAN **3** : CLOTHE **4** : to wear out
dour \ˈdau̇(ə)r, ˈdu̇(ə)r\ *adj* [ME, fr. L *durus* hard — more at DURING] **1** : STERN, HARSH **2** : OBSTINATE, UNYIELDING **3** : GLOOMY, SULLEN — **dour·ly** *adv* — **dour·ness** *n*
1**douse** \ˈdüs, ˈdau̇s\ *n* [origin unknown] *Brit* : BLOW, STROKE
2**douse** \ˈdau̇s\ *vt* **1 a** : to take in ⟨~ a sail⟩ **b** : SLACKEN **2** : DOFF
3**douse** \ˈdau̇s, ˈdau̇z\ *vb* [prob. fr. obs. E *douse* (to smite), fr. 1*douse*] *vt* **1** : to plunge into water **2 a** : to throw a liquid on : DRENCH **b** : SLOSH **3** : EXTINGUISH ~ *vi* : to fall or become plunged into water — **dous·er** *n*
4**douse** \ˈdau̇s, ˈdau̇z\ *n* : DOWNPOUR, DRENCHING
1**dove** \ˈdəv\ *n* [ME, fr. (assumed) OE *dūfe;* akin to OHG *tūba* dove, and prob. to OE *dēaf* deaf] **1** : any of numerous pigeons; *esp* : a small wild pigeon **2** : a pure and gentle woman or child **3** : an individual who takes a conciliatory attitude (as in a dispute) and advocates negotiations and compromise — **dov·ish** \ˈdəv-ish\ *adj*
2**dove** \ˈdōv\ *past of* DIVE
dove·cote \ˈdəv-ˌkōt, -ˌkät\ *or* **dove·cot** \-ˌkät\ *n* : a small compartmented raised house or box for domestic pigeons
dove·kie \ˈdəv-kē\ *n* [dim. of *dove*] : a small short-billed auk (*Plautus alle*) breeding on arctic coasts and ranging south in winter
Do·ver's powder \ˈdō-vərz-\ *n* [Thomas *Dover* †1742 E physician] : a powder of ipecac and opium compounded in the U.S. with lactose and in England with potassium sulfate and used as an anodyne and diaphoretic
1**dove·tail** \ˈdəv-ˌtāl\ *n* : something resembling a dove's tail; *esp* : a flaring tenon and a mortise into which it fits tightly making an interlocking joint between two pieces
2**dovetail** *vt* **1 a** : to join by means of dovetails **b** : to cut to a dovetail **2 a** : to fit skillfully to form a whole **b** : to fit together with ~ *vi* : to fit together into a whole

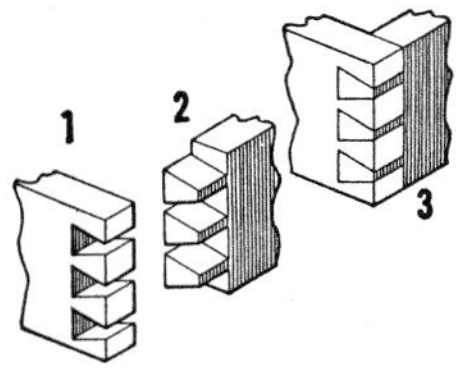

dovetail: *1* mortises, *2* tenons, *3* joint

dow \ˈdau̇\ *vi* **dought** \ˈdau̇t\ *or* **dowed** \ˈdau̇d\ **dow·ing** [ME *dow*, *deih* have worth, am able, fr. OE *dēah*, *dēag;* akin to OHG *toug* is worthy, is useful] *chiefly Scot* : to be able or capable
dow·a·ger \ˈdau̇-i-jər\ *n, often attrib* [MF *douagiere*, fr. *douage* dower, fr. *douer* to endow, fr. L *dotare*, fr. *dot-*, *dos* gift, dower] **1** : a widow holding property or a title received from her deceased husband **2** : an elderly woman of imposing appearance
dowd·i·ly \ˈdau̇d-ᵊl-ē\ *adv* : in a dowdy manner
dowd·i·ness \ˈdau̇d-ē-nəs\ *n* : the quality or state of being dowdy
1**dowdy** \ˈdau̇d-ē\ *n* [dim. of *dowd* (dowdy), fr. ME *doude*] **1** : a dowdy woman **2** : PANDOWDY
2**dowdy** *adj* **1** : lacking neatness and charm : SHABBY **2 a** : lacking smartness or taste **b** : OLD-FASHIONED — **dowdy·ish** \-ish\ *adj*
dow·el \ˈdau̇(-ə)l\ *n* [ME *dowle;* akin to OHG *tubili* plug, LGk *typhos* wedge] **1** : a pin fitting into a hole in an abutting piece to prevent motion or slipping; *also* : a round rod or stick used esp. for cutting up into dowels **2** : a piece of wood driven into a wall so that other pieces can be nailed to it — **dowel** *vt*
1**dow·er** \ˈdau̇(-ə)r\ *n* [ME *dowere*, fr. MF *douaire*, modif. of ML *dotarium*] **1** : the part of or interest in the real estate of a deceased husband given by law to his widow during her life **2** : DOWRY
2**dower** *vt* : to supply with a dower or dowry : ENDOW
dow·itch·er \ˈdau̇-i-chər\ *n, pl* **dowitchers** *also* **dowitcher** [of Iroquoian origin; akin to Mohawk *tawis* dowitcher] : a long-billed snipe (*Limnodromus griseus*) intermediate in characters between the typical snipes (genus *Capella*) and the sandpipers
1**down** \ˈdau̇n\ *n* [ME *doun* hill, fr. OE *dūn;* akin to ON *dūnn* down of feathers] **1** *archaic* **a** : HILL **b** : DUNE **2** : an undulating usu. treeless upland with sparse soil — usu. used in pl. **3** *often cap* : a sheep of any breed originating in the downs of southern England
2**down** *adv* [ME *doun*, fr. OE *dūne*, short for *adūne*, *of dūne*, fr. *a-* (fr. *of*), *of* off, from + *dūne*, dat. of *dūn* hill] **1 a** (1) : toward or in a lower physical position (2) : to a lying or sitting position (3) : toward or to the ground, floor, or bottom **b** : on the spot : in cash ⟨paid $10 ~⟩ **c** : on paper ⟨put ~ what he says⟩ **d** : so as to overtake or find the source of ⟨tracked the rumor ~⟩ **e** : FULLY, COMPLETELY **2** : in a direction that is the opposite of up: as **a** : toward or in the south **b** : toward or in the center of a city **c** : away from a city or other center of activity **3** : to or toward a lower position in a series **4** : to or in a lower or worse condition or status **5** : from a past time **6** : to or in a state of less activity or prominence **7** : from a thinner to a thicker consistency
3**down** *adj* **1 a** (1) : occupying a low position; *specif* : lying on the ground ⟨~ timber⟩ (2) : directed or going downward **b** : lower in price **c** : not being in play in football because of wholly stopped progress or because the officials stop the play ⟨a ~ ball⟩ **d** : trailing an opponent (as in points scored) **2 a** : being in a state of reduced or low activity **b** (1) : DEPRESSED, DEJECTED (2) : SICK ⟨~ with flu⟩ (3) : having a low opinion or dislike ⟨~ on him⟩ **3** : FINISHED, DONE ⟨eight ~ and two to go⟩ **4** : being the part paid at the time of purchase or delivery ⟨a ~ payment⟩
4**down** *prep* : down along, through, toward, in, into, or on
5**down** *n* **1** : DESCENT, DEPRESSION **2 a** : an instance of putting down **b** (1) : the termination of an attempt to advance a football on the referee's signal (2) : a complete play to advance the ball or its duration (3) : one of a series of four attempts to advance a football 10 yards **3** : DISLIKE, GRUDGE
6**down** *vt* : to cause to go or come down ~ *vi* : to go down
7**down** *n* [ME *doun*, fr. ON *dūnn*] **1** : a covering of soft fluffy feathers **2** : something soft and fluffy like down
1**down·beat** \ˈdau̇n-ˌbēt\ *n* **1** : the downward stroke of a conductor indicating the principally accented note of a measure of music; *also* : any first beat **2** : a decline in activity or prosperity
2**downbeat** *adj* : PESSIMISTIC, GLOOMY
down–bow \ˈdau̇n-ˌbō\ *n* : a stroke in playing a bowed instrument from the heel toward the point of the bow
down·cast \ˈdau̇n-ˌkast\ *adj* : cast down; *esp* : DEJECTED
down·fall \ˈdau̇n-ˌfȯl\ *n* **1 a** : a sudden fall (as from high rank)

b : a fall (as of snow) esp. when sudden or heavy **2** : something that causes a downfall — **down·fall·en** \-ˌfȯ-lən\ *adj*
down·grade \ˈdau̇n-ˌgrād\ *n* **1** : a downward grade (as of a road) **2** : a descent toward an inferior state — **downgrade** *vt*
down·haul \ˈdau̇n-ˌhȯl\ *n* : a rope or line for hauling down or holding down a sail or spar
down·heart·ed \ˈdau̇n-ˈhärt-əd\ *adj* : DEJECTED — **down·heart·ed·ly** *adv* — **down·heart·ed·ness** *n*
¹down·hill \ˈdau̇n-ˌhil\ *n* **1** : a descending gradient **2** : a skiing race down a trail
²down·hill \-ˈhil\ *adv* **1** : toward the bottom of a hill **2** : toward a lower or inferior state or level
³down·hill \-ˌhil\ *adj* **1** : sloping downhill **2** : of or relating to skiing downhill
down·pour \-ˌpō(ə)r, -ˌpȯ(ə)r\ *n* : a pouring or streaming downward; *esp* : a heavy rain
down·range \-ˈrānj\ *adv* (*or adj*) : away from a launching site and along the course of the test range ⟨a missile landing 5000 miles ~⟩
¹down·right \-ˌrīt\ *adv* **1** *archaic* : straight down **2** : THOROUGHLY ⟨~ mean⟩ **3** : in plain terms
²downright *adj* **1** *archaic* : directed vertically downward **2** : ABSOLUTE, THOROUGH ⟨a ~ lie⟩ **3** : PLAIN, BLUNT ⟨a ~ man⟩ — **down·right·ly** *adv* — **down·right·ness** *n*
down·stage \ˈdau̇n-ˈstāj\ *adv* (*or adj*) : toward or at the front of a theatrical stage — **down·stage** \-ˌstāj\ *n*
¹down·stairs \ˈdau̇n-ˈsta(ə)rz, -ˈste(ə)rz\ *adv* : down the stairs : on or to a lower floor
²downstairs \-ˌsta(ə)rz, -ˌste(ə)rz\ *adj* : situated on the main, lower, or ground floor of a building
³downstairs \ˈdau̇n-ˈ, ˈdau̇n-ˌ\ *n pl but sing or pl in constr* : the lower floor of a building
down·stream \ˈdau̇n-ˈstrēm\ *adv* (*or adj*) : in the direction of flow of a stream
down·stroke \-ˌstrōk\ *n* : a stroke made in a downward direction
down·swing \-ˌswiŋ\ *n* **1** : a swing downward **2** : a downward trend esp. in business activity
down·time \ˈdau̇n-ˌtīm\ *n* : time during which a machine, department, or factory is inactive during normal operating hours
down–to–earth \ˌdau̇n-tə-ˈ(w)ərth\ *adj* : PRACTICAL, REALISTIC
¹down·town \ˈdau̇n-ˈtau̇n\ *adv* : to, toward, or in the lower part or business center of a town or city
²down·town \-ˌtau̇n\ *adj* **1** : situated downtown **2** : of or relating to the business center of a town or city
³down·town \-ˌtau̇n\ *n* : an urban business center
down·trend \ˈdau̇n-ˌtrend\ *n* : DOWNTURN
down·trod·den \ˈdau̇n-ˈträd-ᵊn\ *adj* : ABUSED, OPPRESSED
down·turn \-ˌtərn\ *n* **1** : a turning downward **2** : a downward economic movement; *specif* : a decline in business activity
¹down·ward \ˈdau̇n-wərd\ *also* **down·wards** \-wərdz\ *adv* **1 a** : from a higher place to a lower **b** : toward a direction that is the opposite of up **2** : from a higher to a lower condition **3 a** : from an earlier time **b** : from an ancestor or predecessor
²downward *adj* **1** : moving or extending downward **2** : descending from a head, origin, or source — **down·ward·ly** *adv* — **down·ward·ness** *n*
down·wind \ˈdau̇n-ˈwind\ *adv* (*or adj*) : in the direction that the wind is blowing : LEEWARD
downy \ˈdau̇-nē\ *adj* **1** : resembling a bird's down **2** : covered with down **3 a** : made of down **b** : SOFT, SOOTHING
downy mildew *n* **1** : any of various parasitic lower fungi (family Peronosporaceae) that produces whitish masses of sporangiophores or conidiophores on the undersurface of the leaves of the host **2** : a plant disease caused by a downy mildew
dow·ry \ˈdau̇(ə)r-ē\ *n* [ME *dowarie*, fr. AF, irreg. fr. ML *dotarium*, fr. L *dot-*, *dos* gift, marriage portion; akin to L *dare* to give] **1** *archaic* : DOWER 1 **2 a** : the money, goods, or estate that a woman brings to her husband in marriage **b** : a sum of money required of postulants by cloistered nuns **3** : a gift of money or property by a man to or for his bride **4** : a natural gift
dow·sa·bel \ˈdau̇-sə-ˈbel, -zə-\ *n* [*Dowsabel*, fem. name] *obs* : SWEETHEART
¹dowse *var of* DOUSE
²dowse \ˈdau̇z\ *vb* [origin unknown] *vi* : to use a divining rod ~ *vt* : to find by dowsing — **dows·er** *n*
dox·ol·o·gy \däk-ˈsäl-ə-jē\ *n* [ML *doxologia*, fr. LGk, fr. Gk *doxa* opinion, glory (fr. *dokein* to seem, seem good) + *-logia* -logy — more at DECENT] : an expression of praise to God
doxy \ˈdäk-sē\ *n* [perh. modif. of obs. D *docke* doll, fr. MD] **1** : a woman of loose morals : PROSTITUTE **2** : MISTRESS 5a
doy·en \dȯi-ˈ(y)en, ˈdȯi-(y)ən, dwä-ˈyaⁿ\ *n* [F, fr. LL *decanus* dean] **1** : the senior man of a body or group **2 a** : the oldest one of a category **b** : the highest-ranking one of its kind
doy·enne \dȯi-ˈ(y)en, dwä-ˈyen\ *n* [F, fem. of *doyen*] : the senior woman of a group
doyley *or* **doyly** *var of* DOILY
¹doze \ˈdōz\ *vb* [prob. of Scand origin] *vt* : to pass drowsily ~ *vi* **1 a** : to sleep lightly **b** : to fall asleep unintentionally or effortlessly **2** : to be in a dull or stupefied condition — **doze** *n*
²doze *vt* [prob. back-formation fr. *dozer* (bulldozer)] : BULLDOZE 2
doz·en \ˈdəz-ᵊn\ *n, pl* **dozens** *or* **dozen** *often attrib* [ME *dozeine*, fr. OF *dozaine*, fr. *doze* twelve, fr. L *duodecim*, fr. *duo* two + *decem* ten — more at TWO, TEN] : a group of 12 — **doz·enth** \-ᵊn(t)th\ *adj*
¹doz·er \ˈdō-zər\ *n* : one that dozes
²dozer *n* : BULLDOZER 2
DP \(ˈ)dē-ˈpē\ *n, pl* **DP's** *or* **DPs** : DISPLACED PERSON
¹drab \ˈdrab\ *n* [perh. of Celt origin] **1** : SLATTERN **2** : HARLOT
²drab *vi* **drabbed**; **drab·bing** : to associate with prostitutes
³drab *n* [MF *drap* cloth, fr. LL *drappus*] **1** : any of various cloths of a dull brown or gray color; *esp* : a thick woolen coating or a heavy cotton **2 a** : a light olive brown **b** : a dull, lifeless, or faded appearance or quality
⁴drab *adj* **drab·ber**; **drab·best** **1 a** : of the dull brown color of drab **b** : of the color drab **2** : characterized by dullness and monotony : CHEERLESS — **drab·ly** *adv* — **drab·ness** *n*
drab·bet \ˈdrab-ət\ *n, dial Eng* : a coarse unbleached linen fabric
drab·ble \ˈdrab-əl\ *vb* **drab·bling** \-(ə-)liŋ\ [ME *drabelen*] *vt* : DRAGGLE ~ *vi* : to become wet and muddy
dra·cae·na \drə-ˈsē-nə\ *n* [NL, fr. LL, she-serpent, fr. Gk *drakaina*, fem. of *drakōn* serpent] : any of two genera (*Dracaena* and *Cordyline*) of Old World tropical shrubs or trees of the lily family with naked branches ending in tufts of sword-shaped leaves
drachm \ˈdram\ *n* [alter. of ME *dragme* — more at DRAM] **1** : DRACHMA **2** : DRAM
drach·ma \ˈdrak-mə\ *n, pl* **drach·mas** *or* **drach·mae** \-(ˌ)mē, -ˌmī\ *or* **drach·mai** \-ˌmī\ [L, fr. Gk *drachmē* — more at DRAM] **1 a** : any of various ancient Greek units of weight **b** : any of various modern units of weight; *esp* : DRAM 1 **2 a** : an ancient Greek silver coin equivalent to 6 obols **b** — see MONEY table
Dra·co \ˈdrā-(ˌ)kō\ *n* [L (gen. *Draconis*), lit., dragon — more at DRAGON] : a northern circumpolar constellation within which is the north pole of the ecliptic
dra·co·ni·an \drā-ˈkō-nē-ən, drə-\ *adj, often cap* [L *Dracon-*, *Draco fl*621 B.C. Athenian lawgiver, fr. Gk *Drakōn*] **1** : of, relating to, or characteristic of Draco or the severe code of laws held to have been framed by him **2** : extremely harsh or cruel : RIGOROUS
¹dra·con·ic \drə-ˈkän-ik\ *adj* [L *dracon-*, *draco*] : of, relating to, or resembling a dragon
²dra·con·ic \drā-ˈkän-ik, drə-\ *adj* : DRACONIAN
¹draft *or chiefly Brit* **draught** \ˈdraft, ˈdråft\ *n* [ME *draght*; akin to OE *dragan* to draw — more at DRAW] **1** : the act of drawing a net; *also* : the quantity of fish taken at one drawing **2 a** : the act of moving loads by drawing or pulling : PULL **b** : a team of animals together with what they draw **3 a** : the force required to pull an implement **b** : load or load-pulling capacity **4 a** : the act or an instance of drinking or inhaling; *also* : the portion drunk or inhaled in one such act **b** : a portion poured out or mixed for drinking : DOSE **5 a** : DELINEATION, REPRESENTATION; *specif* : a construction plan **b** : SCHEME, DESIGN **c** : a preliminary sketch, outline, or version **6** : the act, result, or plan of drawing out or stretching **7 a** : the act of drawing (as from a cask) **b** : a portion of liquid so drawn **8** : an allowance granted a buyer for loss in weight **9** : the depth of water a ship draws esp. when loaded **10 a** : the detaching or selecting of an individual from a group esp. for compulsory military service **b** : a group of individuals so selected **11 a** : an order for the payment of money drawn by one person or bank on another **b** : the act or an instance of drawing from or making demands upon something : DEMAND **12 a** : a current of air in a closed-in space **b** : a device for regulating the flow of air (as in a fireplace) **13** : ANGLE, TAPER; *specif* : the taper given to a pattern or die so that the work can be easily withdrawn **14** : a narrow border along the edge of a stone or across its face serving as a stonecutter's guide **15** : a system whereby exclusive rights to selected new players are apportioned among professional teams — **on draft** : ready to be drawn from a receptacle ⟨beer *on draft*⟩
²draft *or chiefly Brit* **draught** *adj* **1** : used for drawing loads ⟨~ animals⟩ **2** : constituting a preliminary or tentative version, sketch, or outline ⟨a ~ treaty⟩ **3** : being on draft; *also* : DRAWN
³draft *vt* **1** : to detach or select for some purpose usu. on a compulsory basis; *specif* : to conscript for military service **2 a** : to draw the preliminary sketch, version, or plan of **b** : COMPOSE, PREPARE **3** *or chiefly Brit* **draught** : to draw up, off, or away — **draft·ee** \draf-ˈtē, dråf-\ *n* — **draft·er** \ˈdraf-tər, ˈdråf-\ *n*
draft horse *n* : a horse adapted for drawing heavy loads
draft·i·ly \ˈdraf-tə-lē, ˈdråf-\ *adv* : in a drafty manner
draft·i·ness \-tē-nəs\ *n* : the condition of being drafty
drafts·man \ˈdraf(t)-smən, ˈdråf(t)-\ *n* **1** : one who draws legal documents or other writings **2** : one who draws plans and sketches **3** : an artist who excels in drawing — **drafts·man·ship** \-ˌship\ *n*
drafty \ˈdraf-tē, ˈdråf-\ *adj* : relating to or exposed to a draft
¹drag \ˈdrag\ *n* **1** : something that is dragged, pulled, or drawn along or over a surface: as **a** : HARROW **b** : a sledge for conveying heavy bodies **c** : CONVEYANCE **2** : something used to drag with; *esp* : a device for dragging under water or along the bottom to detect or obtain objects **3 a** : something (as a sea anchor) that retards motion **b** (1) : the retarding force acting on a body (as an airplane) moving through a fluid (as air) parallel and opposite to the direction of motion (2) : friction between engine parts **c** : something that hinders or obstructs progress **4 a** : an object drawn over the ground to leave a scented trail **b** : a clog fastened to a trap to prevent the escape of a trapped animal **5 a** : the act or an instance of dragging or drawing: as (1) : a drawing along or over a surface with effort or pressure (2) : motion effected with slowness or difficulty; *also* : the condition of having or seeming to have such motion (3) : a draw on a pipe, cigarette, or cigar : PUFF; *also* : a draft of liquid **b** : a movement, inclination, or retardation caused by or as if by dragging **c** *slang* : influence securing special favor or partiality **6** : something characterized by slow retarded motion **7** *slang* : STREET, ROAD **8** *slang* : a girl that one is escorting **9** *slang* : a speed contest between automobiles
²drag *vb* **dragged**; **drag·ging** [ME *draggen*, fr. ON *draga* or OE *dragan*] *vt* **1 a** (1) : to draw slowly or heavily : HAUL (2) : to cause to move with painful slowness or difficulty **b** : to force into or out of some situation, condition, or course of action **c** (1) : to pass (time) in lingering pain, tedium, or unhappiness (2) : PROTRACT ⟨~ a story out⟩ **2 a** : to explore with a drag **b** : to catch with a dragnet or trawl **3** : to hit (a bunt) esp. by pulling the bat back at the moment of impact ~ *vi* **1** : to hang or lag behind **2** : to fish or search with a drag **3** : to trail along on the ground **4** : to move on or proceed laboriously or tediously ⟨the book ~*s*⟩ **5** : DRAW ⟨~ on a cigarette⟩ **syn** see PULL — **drag·ging·ly** \-iŋ-lē\ *adv*
dra·gée \dra-ˈzhā, -ˈjē\ *n* [F, fr. MF *dragie* — more at DREDGE] **1 a** : a sugar-coated nut **b** : a silver-covered candy for decorating cakes **2** : a sugar-coated medicated confection
drag·ger \ˈdrag-ər\ *n* : one that drags; *specif* : a fishing boat operating a trawl or dragnet
drag·gle \ˈdrag-əl\ *vb* **drag·gling** \-(ə-)liŋ\ [freq. of *drag*] *vt* : to make wet and dirty by dragging ~ *vi* **1** : to become wet or dirty by being dragged or trailed **2** : STRAGGLE
drag·gle–tail \ˈdrag-əl-ˌtāl\ *n* : SLATTERN
drag·gy \ˈdrag-ē\ *adj* : SLUGGISH, DULL
drag·line \ˈdrag-ˌlīn\ *n* **1** : a line used in or for dragging **2** : an excavating machine

ə abut; ᵊ kitten; ər further; a back; ā bake; ä cot, cart; au̇ out; ch chin; e less; ē easy; g gift; i trip; ī life
j joke; ŋ sing; ō flow; ȯ flaw; ȯi coin; th thin; t͟h this; ü loot; u̇ foot; y yet; yü few; yu̇ furious; zh vision

drag link *n* **:** a rod connecting the steering-gear lever to the steering knuckle in an automotive vehicle

drag·man \'drag-mən\ *n* **:** a man who drags something

drag·net \'drag-,net\ *n* **1 a :** a net drawn along the bottom of a body of water **:** TRAWL **b :** a net used on the ground (as to capture small game) **2 :** a network of measures for apprehension

drag·o·man \'drag-ə-mən\ *n, pl* **drag·o·mans** *or* **drag·o·men** [ME *drogman*, fr. MF, fr. OIt *dragomanno*, fr. MGk *dragomanos*, fr. Ar *tarjumān*, fr. Aram *tūrgĕmānā*] **:** an interpreter chiefly of Arabic, Turkish, or Persian employed esp. in the Near East

drag·on \'drag-ən\ *n* [ME, fr. OF, fr. L *dracon-*, *draco* serpent, dragon, fr. Gk *drakōn* serpent; akin to OE *torht* bright, Gk *derkesthai* to see, look at] **1** *archaic* **:** a huge serpent **2 :** a fabulous animal usu. represented as a monstrous winged and scaly serpent or saurian with a crested head and enormous claws **3 :** a violent, combative, or very strict person **4 a :** a short musket formerly carried hooked to a soldier's belt; *also* **:** a soldier carrying such a musket **b :** an artillery tractor **5 :** any of numerous small brilliantly colored arboreal lizards (genus *Draco*) of the East Indies and southern Asia having the hind ribs on each side prolonged and covered with a web of skin **6** *cap* **:** DRACO

drag·on·et \,drag-ə-'net, 'drag-ə-nət\ *n* **1 :** a little dragon **2 :** any of various small often brightly colored scaleless marine fishes constituting a family (Callionymidae) and including a well-known European fish (*Callionymus lyra*) sometimes used as food

drag·on·fly \'drag-ən-,flī\ *n* **:** any of an order (Odonata) of large harmless insects that have long net-veined wings and feed esp. on flies, gnats, and mosquitoes

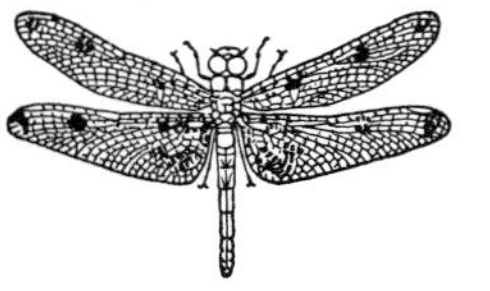

dragonfly

drag·on·head \-,hed\ *or* **drag·on's–head** \-ənz-\ *n* **:** any of several mints (genus *Dracocephalum*); *esp* **:** a No. American plant (*D. parviflorum*)

drag·on·ish \'drag-ə-nish\ *adj* **:** resembling a dragon

dragon lizard *n* **:** an Indonesian monitor lizard (*Varanus komodoensis*) that is the largest of all known lizards and reaches 11 feet in length

dragon's blood *n* **:** any of several resinous mostly dark-red plant products; *specif* **:** a resin from the fruit of a palm (genus *Daemonorops*) used for coloring varnish and in photoengraving

¹dra·goon \drə-'gün, dra-\ *n* [F *dragon* dragon, dragoon, fr. MF] **:** a member of a European military unit formerly composed of heavily armed mounted troops

²dragoon *vt* **1 :** to reduce to subjection or persecute by harsh use of troops **2 :** to force or attempt to force into submission by violent measures **:** HARASS

drag·rope \'drag-,rōp\ *n* **:** a rope that drags or is used for dragging

¹drain \'drān\ *vb* [ME *draynen*, fr. OE *drēahnian*] *vt* **1** *obs* **:** FILTER **2 a :** to draw off (liquid) gradually or completely **b :** to cause the gradual disappearance of **c :** to exhaust physically or emotionally **3 a :** to make gradually dry **b :** to carry away the surface water of **c :** EMPTY, EXHAUST **~** *vi* **1 a :** to flow off gradually **b :** to disappear gradually **:** DWINDLE **2 :** to become emptied or freed of liquid by its flowing or dropping **3 :** to discharge surface or surplus water **syn** see DEPLETE — **drain·er** *n*

²drain *n* **1 :** a means by which liquid or other matter is drained **2 a :** the act of draining **b :** a gradual outflow or withdrawal **:** DEPLETION **3 :** something that causes depletion **:** BURDEN

drain·age \'drā-nij\ *n* **1 :** the act, process, or mode of draining; *also* **:** something drained off **2 :** a device for draining **:** DRAIN; *also* **:** a system of drains **3 :** an area or district drained

drain·pipe \'drān-,pīp\ *n* **:** a pipe for drainage

¹drake \'drāk\ *n* [ME, dragon, fr. OE *draca*] **1 :** a small piece of artillery of the 17th and 18th centuries **2 :** MAYFLY

²drake *n* [ME] **:** the male of a wild or domestic duck

dram \'dram\ *n* [ME *dragme*, fr. MF & LL; MF, dram, drachma, fr. LL *dragma*, fr. L *drachma*, fr. Gk *drachmē*, lit., handful, fr. *drassesthai* to grasp] **1 a** — see MEASURE table **b :** FLUIDRAM **2 a :** a small portion of something to drink **b :** a small amount

dra·ma \'dräm-ə, 'dram-\ *n* [LL *dramat-*, *drama*, fr. Gk, deed, drama, fr. *dran* to do, act; prob. akin to Lith *daryti* to do] **1 :** a composition in verse or prose intended to portray life or character or to tell a story through action and dialogue and designed for theatrical performance **:** PLAY **2 :** dramatic art, literature, or affairs **3 a :** a state, situation, or series of events involving interesting or intense conflict of forces **b :** dramatic state, effect, or quality

Dram·a·mine \'dram-ə-,mēn\ *trademark* — used for dimenhydrinate

dra·mat·ic \drə-'mat-ik\ *adj* **1 :** of or relating to the drama **2 a :** suitable to or characteristic of the drama **:** VIVID **b :** striking in appearance or effect — **dra·mat·i·cal·ly** \-i-k(ə-)lē\ *adv*

syn THEATRICAL, DRAMATURGIC, MELODRAMATIC, HISTRIONIC: DRAMATIC applies to speech or action having the power of deeply stirring the imagination or the emotions; THEATRICAL suggests a blatant appeal to the emotions esp. by marked artificiality of voice, gesture, or action; DRAMATURGIC stresses the technical fitness for effective stage performance; MELODRAMATIC suggests an exaggerated emotionalism or an inappropriate theatricalism; HISTRIONIC suggests speech or behavior appropriate to the stage but not to real life

dramatic monologue *n* **:** a literary work in which a character reveals himself in a monologue usu. addressed to a second person

dra·mat·ics \drə-'mat-iks\ *n pl but sing or pl in constr* **1 a :** theatricals esp. as an extracurricular activity in school or college **b :** theatrical technique **2 :** dramatic behavior or expression

dra·ma·tis per·so·nae \,dram-ət-ə-spər-'sō-(,)nē, ,dräm-, -,nī\ *n pl* [NL] **:** the characters or actors in a drama

dra·ma·tist \'dram-ət-əst, 'dräm-\ *n* **:** PLAYWRIGHT

dra·ma·ti·za·tion \,dram-ət-ə-'zā-shən, ,dräm-\ *n* **:** the act, process, or product of dramatizing

dra·ma·tize \'dram-ə-,tīz, 'dräm-\ *vt* **1 :** to adapt for theatrical presentation **2 :** to present or represent in a dramatic manner **~** *vi* **1 :** to be suitable for dramatization **2 :** to dramatize oneself

dra·ma·tur·gic \,dram-ə-'tər-jik, ,dräm-\ *adj* **:** of or relating to dramaturgy ⟨~ theory⟩ **syn** see DRAMATIC — **dra·ma·tur·gi·cal** \-ji-kəl\ *adj* — **dra·ma·tur·gi·cal·ly** \-ji-k(ə-)lē\ *adv*

dra·ma·tur·gy \'dram-ə-,tər-jē, 'dräm-\ *n* [G *dramaturgie*, fr. Gk *dramatourgia* dramatic composition, fr. *dramatourgos* dramatist, fr. *dramat-*, *drama* + *-ourgos* worker, fr. *ergon* work] **:** the art or technique of dramatic composition and theatrical representation

dram·mock \'dram-ək\ *n* [ScGael *dramag* foul mixture] *chiefly Scot* **:** raw oatmeal mixed with cold water

dram·shop \'dram-,shäp\ *n, archaic* **:** BARROOM

drank *past of* DRINK

¹drape \'drāp\ *vb* [ME *drapen* to weave, fr. MF *draper*, fr. *drap* cloth — more at DRAB] *vt* **1 :** to cover or adorn with or as if with folds of cloth **2 :** to cause to hang or stretch out loosely or carelessly **3 :** to arrange in flowing lines or folds ⟨a cleverly *draped* suit⟩ **~** *vi* **:** to become arranged in folds

²drape *n* **1 a :** a drapery esp. for a window **:** CURTAIN **b :** a sterile covering used in an operating room — usu. used in pl. **2 :** arrangement in or of folds **3 :** the cut or hang of clothing

drap·er \'drā-pər\ *n* **1** *Brit* **:** a dealer in cloth and sometimes also in clothing and dry goods **2 :** one that drapes

drap·ery \'drā-p(ə-)rē\ *n* **1** *Brit* **:** DRY GOODS **2** *Brit* **:** the occupation of a draper **3 a :** a decorative piece of material usu. hung in loose folds and arranged in a graceful design **b :** hangings of heavy fabric for use as a curtain **c :** loose coverings for furniture **4 :** the draping or arranging of materials

dras·tic \'dras-tik\ *adj* [Gk *drastikos*, fr. *dran* to do] **1 :** acting rapidly or violently **2 :** SEVERE — **dras·ti·cal·ly** \-ti-k(ə-)lē\ *adv*

draught *chiefly Brit var of* DRAFT

draughts \'draf(t)s, 'dräf(t)s\ *n pl but sing or pl in constr* [ME *draghtes*, fr. pl. of *draght* draft, move in chess] *Brit* **:** CHECKERS

Dra·vid·i·an \drə-'vid-ē-ən\ *n* [Skt *Drāviḍa*] **1 :** an individual of an ancient Australoid race of southern India **2 :** any or all of the Dravidian languages — **Dravidian** *adj*

Dravidian languages *n pl* **:** a language family in India, Ceylon, and West Pakistan with no established relationship to any other

¹draw \'drȯ\ *vb* **drew** \'drü\ **drawn** \'drȯn\ **draw·ing** [ME *drawen*, *dragen*, fr. OE *dragan*; akin to ON *draga* to draw, drag and perh. to L *trahere* to pull, draw] *vt* **1 :** to cause to move continuously toward or after a force applied in advance **:** HAUL, DRAG **2 :** to cause to go in a certain direction (as by leading) ⟨*drew* him aside⟩ **3 a :** ATTRACT, ENTICE ⟨honey ~*s* flies⟩ **b :** PROVOKE, ROUSE ⟨*drew* enemy fire⟩ **4 :** INHALE **5 a :** to bring or pull out ⟨~ a sword⟩ **b :** to force out from cover or possession ⟨~ trumps⟩ **c :** to extract the essence from ⟨~ tea⟩ **d :** EVISCERATE **6 :** to require (a specified depth) to float in **7 a :** ACCUMULATE, GAIN ⟨~*ing* interest⟩ **b :** to take (money) from a place of deposit **c :** WITHDRAW **d :** to receive regularly from a source ⟨~ a salary⟩ **8 a :** to take (cards) from a stack or the dealer **b :** to receive or take at random ⟨*drew* a winning number⟩ **9 :** to bend (a bow) by pulling back the string **10 :** to cause to shrink or pucker **11 :** to strike (a ball) so as to impart a backward spin **12 :** to leave (a contest) undecided **:** TIE **13 a :** to produce a likeness of by making lines on a surface **:** DELINEATE **b :** to write out in due form ⟨~ a will⟩ **c :** to design or describe in detail **:** FORMULATE ⟨~ comparisons⟩ **14 :** DEDUCE ⟨~ a conclusion⟩ **15 :** to spread or elongate (metal) by hammering or by pulling through dies **~** *vi* **1 :** to move or go steadily or gradually ⟨night ~*s* near⟩ **2 :** to exert an attractive force **3 a :** to pull back a bowstring **b :** to bring out a weapon ⟨*drew*, aimed, and fired⟩ **4 a :** to produce or allow a draft ⟨chimney ~*s* well⟩ **b :** to swell out in a wind ⟨all sails ~*ing*⟩ **5 a :** to wrinkle or pucker up **:** SHRINK **b :** to change shape by pulling or stretching **6 a :** to cause blood or pus to localize at one point **b :** STEEP **7 :** to create a likeness or a picture in outlines **:** SKETCH **8 :** to come out even in a contest **9 a :** to make a written demand for payment of money or deposit **b :** to obtain supplies **syn** see PULL

²draw *n* **1 :** the act, process, or result of drawing **2 :** something that is drawn: as **a :** a card drawn to replace a discard in poker **b :** a lot or chance drawn at random **c :** the movable part of a drawbridge **3 :** a contest left undecided or deadlocked **:** TIE **4 :** something that draws attention or patronage **5 a :** the distance from the string to the back of a drawn bow **b :** the force required to draw a bow fully **6 :** a gully shallower than a ravine **7 :** the deal in draw poker to improve the players' hands after discarding

draw away *vi* **:** to move ahead (as of an opponent in a race)

draw·back \'drȯ-,bak\ *n* **1 :** a refund of duties esp. on an imported product subsequently exported or used to produce a product for export **2 :** an objectionable feature **:** HINDRANCE

draw·bar \'drȯ-,bär\ *n* **1 :** a railroad coupler **2 :** a beam across the rear of a tractor to which implements are hitched

draw·bore \-,bō(ə)r, -,bȯ(ə)r\ *n* **:** a bore for a mortise pin placed so as to draw the tenon and thus make the joint tighter

draw·bridge \-,brij\ *n* **:** a bridge made to be raised up, let down, or drawn aside so as to permit or hinder passage

draw·ee \drȯ-'ē\ *n* **:** the person on whom an order or bill of exchange is drawn

draw·er \'drȯ(-ə)r\ *n* **1 :** one that draws: as **a :** a person who draws liquor **b :** DRAFTSMAN **c :** one who draws a bill of exchange or order for payment or makes a promissory note **2 :** a sliding box or receptacle opened by pulling out and closed by pushing in **3** *pl* **:** an undergarment for the lower body

draw·ing \'drȯ(-)iŋ\ *n* **1 :** an act or instance of drawing; *specif* **:** an occasion when something is decided by drawing lots **2 :** the act, art, or technique of representing an object or outlining a figure, plan, or sketch by means of lines **3 :** something drawn or subject to drawing: as **a :** an amount drawn from a fund **b :** a representation formed by drawing **:** SKETCH

drawing card *n* **:** something that attracts attention or patronage

drawing room *n* [short for *withdrawing room*] **1 a :** a formal reception room **b :** a private room on a railroad passenger car with three berths and an enclosed toilet **2 :** a formal reception

draw·knife \'drȯ-,nīf\ *n* **:** a woodworker's tool having a blade with a handle at each end used to shave off surfaces — called also *drawshave*

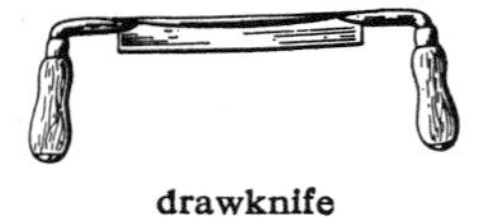

drawknife

¹drawl \'drȯl\ *vb* [prob. freq. of *draw*] *vi* **:** to speak slowly with vowels greatly prolonged **~** *vt* **:** to utter in a slow lengthened tone — **drawl·er** *n* — **drawl·ing·ly** \'drȯ-liŋ-lē\ *adv*

²drawl *n* **:** a drawling manner of speaking

drawn butter *n* **:** melted butter often with seasoning

drawn·work \'drȯn-,wərk\ *n* **:** decoration on cloth made by drawing out threads according to a pattern

draw off *vt* **:** REMOVE, WITHDRAW **~** *vi* **:** to move apart

draw on *vi* **:** APPROACH **~** *vt* **:** to bring on **:** CAUSE

draw out *vt* **1 :** REMOVE, EXTRACT **2 :** to cause to speak out freely
draw·plate \ˈdrȯ-ˌplāt\ *n* **:** a die with holes through which wires are drawn
draw poker *n* **:** poker in which each player is dealt five cards face down and after betting may discard cards and get replacements
draw·string \ˈdrȯ-ˌstriŋ\ *n* **:** a string, cord, or tape inserted into hems or casings or laced through eyelets for use in closing a bag or controlling fullness in garments or curtains
draw·tube \-ˌt(y)üb\ *n* **:** a telescoping tube (as for the eyepiece of a microscope)
draw up *vt* **1 :** to arrange (as a body of troops) in order **2 :** to draft in due form **3 :** to straighten (oneself) to an erect posture **4 :** to bring to a halt **～** *vi* **:** STOP
dray \ˈdrā\ *n* [ME *draye*, a wheelless vehicle, fr. OE *dræge* dragnet; akin to OE *dragan* to pull] **:** a vehicle used to haul goods; *specif* **:** a strong low cart or wagon without sides — **dray** *vb*
dray·age \ˈdrā-ij\ *n* **:** the work or cost of draying
dray·man \ˈdrā-mən\ *n* **:** one whose work is draying
1**dread** \ˈdred\ *vb* [ME *dreden*, fr. OE *drǣdan*] *vt* **1 a :** to fear greatly **b** *archaic* **:** REVERENCE **2 :** to feel extreme reluctance to meet or face **～** *vi* **:** to be apprehensive or fearful
2**dread** *n* **1 a :** great fear esp. in the face of impending evil **b** *archaic* **:** AWE **2 :** one causing fear or awe **syn** see FEAR
3**dread** *adj* **1 :** causing great fear or anxiety **2 :** inspiring awe
1**dread·ful** \ˈdred-fəl\ *adj* **1 a :** inspiring dread **:** FRIGHTENING **b :** inspiring awe or reverence **2 :** extremely distasteful, unpleasant, or shocking **3 :** EXTREME ⟨～ disorder⟩ **syn** see FEARFUL — **dread·ful·ly** \-f(ə-)lē\ *adv* — **dread·ful·ness** \-fəl-nəs\ *n*
2**dreadful** *n* **:** a cheap and sensational story or periodical
dread·nought \ˈdred-ˌnȯt, -ˌnät\ *n* **1 :** a warm garment of thick cloth; *also* **:** the cloth **2** [*Dreadnought*, Brit. battleship] **:** a battleship whose main armament consists entirely of big guns all of the same caliber
1**dream** \ˈdrēm\ *n* [ME *dreem*, fr. OE *drēam* noise, joy] **1 :** a series of thoughts, images, or emotions occurring during sleep **2 a :** a visionary creation of the imagination **:** DAYDREAM **b :** a state of mind marked by abstraction or release from reality **:** REVERIE **c :** an object seen in a dreamlike state **:** VISION **3 :** something notable for its beauty, excellence, or enjoyable quality **4 :** a goal or purpose ardently desired **:** IDEAL — **dream·ful** \-fəl\ *adj* — **dream·ful·ly** \-fə-lē\ *adv* — **dream·ful·ness** *n*
2**dream** \ˈdrēm\ *vb* **dreamed** \ˈdrem(p)t, ˈdrēmd\ *or* **dreamt** \ˈdrem(p)t\ **dream·ing** \ˈdrē-miŋ\ *vi* **1 :** to have a dream **2 :** to indulge in daydreams or fantasies **3 :** to conceive as possible, fitting, or proper — used with *of* **4 :** to appear tranquil or dreamy **～** *vt* **1 :** to have a dream of **2 :** to consider as a possibility **:** IMAGINE **3 :** to pass (time) in reverie or inaction
dream·er \ˈdrē-mər\ *n* **1 :** one who dreams **2 a :** one who lives in a world of fancy and imagination **b :** one who has ideas or conceives projects regarded as impractical **:** VISIONARY
dream·i·ly \ˈdrē-mə-lē\ *adv* **:** in a dreamy manner **:** VAGUELY
dream·i·ness \-mē-nəs\ *n* **:** the quality or state of being dreamy
dream·land \ˈdrēm-ˌland\ *n* **:** an unreal delightful country existing only in imagination or in dreams **:** NEVER-NEVER LAND
dream·less \-ləs\ *adj* **:** having no dreams ⟨a ～ sleep⟩ — **dream·less·ly** *adv* — **dream·less·ness** *n*
dream·like \-ˌlīk\ *adj* **:** resembling a dream **:** UNREAL
dream up *vt* **:** DEVISE, CONCOCT
dream·world \ˈdrēm-ˌwərld\ *n* **:** DREAMLAND; *also* **:** a world of illusion or fantasy
dreamy \ˈdrē-mē\ *adj* **1 a :** full of dreams **b :** VAGUE **2 :** given to dreaming or fantasy **3 a :** having the quality or characteristics of a dream **b :** quiet and soothing **c :** DELIGHTFUL, PLEASING
drear \ˈdri(ə)r\ *adj* **:** DREARY
drea·ri·ly \ˈdrir-ə-lē\ *adv* **:** in a dreary manner
drea·ri·ness \ˈdrir-ē-nəs\ *n* **:** the quality or state of being dreary
drea·ry \ˈdri(ə)r-ē\ *adj* [ME *drery*, fr. OE *drēorig* sad, bloody, fr. *drēor* gore; akin to OHG *trūrēn* to be sad] **1 :** DOLEFUL, SAD **2 :** causing feelings of cheerlessness **:** GLOOMY
1**dredge** \ˈdrej\ *n* [prob. fr. Sc *dreg-* (in *dregbot* dredge boat)] **1 :** an apparatus usu. in the form of an oblong iron frame with an attached bag net used esp. for gathering fish and shellfish **2 :** a machine for removing earth usu. by buckets on an endless chain or a suction tube **3 :** a barge used in dredging
2**dredge** *vt* **:** to dig, gather, or pull out with or as if with a dredge — often used with *up* **～** *vi* **:** to search with or as if with a dredge — **dredg·er** *n*
3**dredge** *vt* [obs. *dredge*, n., sweetmeat, fr. ME *drage*, *drege*, fr. MF *dragie*, modif. of L *tragemata* sweetmeats, fr. Gk *tragēmata*, pl. of *tragēma* sweetmeat, fr. *trōgein* to gnaw — more at TERSE] **:** to coat (food) by sprinkling (as with flour) — **dredg·er** *n*
dree \ˈdrē\ *vt* **dreed; dree·ing** [ME *dreen*, fr. OE *drēogan* — more at DRUDGE] *chiefly Scot* **:** ENDURE, SUFFER
dreg \ˈdreg\ *n* [ME, fr. ON *dregg;* akin to L *fraces* dregs of oil, Gk *thrassein* to trouble] **1 :** sediment contained in a liquid or precipitated from it **:** LEES — usu. used in pl. **2 :** the most undesirable part— usu. used in pl. **3 :** the last remaining part **:** VESTIGE
D region *n* **:** the lowest part of the ionosphere occurring between 25 and 40 miles above the surface of the earth
1**drench** \ˈdrench\ *n* **1 a :** DRINK, DRAFT **b :** a poisonous or medicinal drink; *specif* **:** a large dose of medicine mixed with liquid and put down the throat of an animal **2 a :** something that drenches **b :** a quantity sufficient to drench or saturate
2**drench** *vt* [ME *drenchen*, fr. OE *drencan;* akin to OE *drincan* to drink] **1 a** *archaic* **:** to force to drink **b :** to administer a drench to (an animal) **2 :** to steep or saturate by immersion in liquid **3 :** to soak or cover thoroughly with liquid that falls or is precipitated **4 :** to fill completely as if by soaking or precipitation **:** SATURATE **syn** see SOAK— **drench·er** *n*
1**dress** \ˈdres\ *vb* [ME *dressen*, fr. MF *dresser*, fr. (assumed) VL *directiare*, fr. L *directus* direct, pp. of *dirigere* to direct, fr. *dis-* + *regere* to lead straight — more at RIGHT] *vt* **1 a :** to make or set straight **b :** to arrange (as troops) in a straight line and at proper intervals **2** *archaic* **:** to dress down **3 a :** to put clothes on **b :** to provide with clothing **4 :** to add decorative details or accessories to **:** EMBELLISH **5 :** to put in order for use or service **6 a :** to apply dressings or medicaments to **b (1) :** to arrange (the hair) by combing, brushing, or curling **(2) :** to groom and curry (an animal) **c (1) :** to kill and prepare for market **(2) :** CULTIVATE, TEND; *esp* **:** to apply manure or fertilizer to **～** *vi* **1 a :** to put on clothing **b :** to put on or wear formal, elaborate, or fancy clothes **2** *of a food animal* **:** to weigh after being dressed **3 :** to align oneself with the next soldier in a line to make the line straight — **dress ship 1 :** to ornament a ship while in port by hoisting national ensigns at the mastheads and running a line of signal flags and pennants from bow to stern **2 :** to ornament a ship by hoisting national ensigns at the mastheads and the ship's largest ensign at the flagstaff
2**dress** *n* **1 :** APPAREL, CLOTHING **2 :** an outer garment for a woman or child **:** FROCK **3 :** covering, adornment, or appearance appropriate or peculiar to a particular time **4 :** a particular form of presentation **:** GUISE
3**dress** *adj* **1 :** relating to or used for a dress **2 :** suitable for a formal occasion **3 :** requiring or permitting formal dress ⟨a ～ affair⟩
dres·sage \drə-ˈsäzh, dre-\ *n* **:** the execution by a horse of complex maneuvers in response to barely perceptible movements of a rider's hands, legs, and weight
dress circle *n* **:** the first or lowest curved tier of seats in a theater
dress down *vt* **:** to reprove severely — **dressing down** *n*
1**dress·er** \ˈdres-ər\ *n* **1** *obs* **:** a table or sideboard for preparing and serving food **2 :** a cupboard to hold dishes and cooking utensils **3 :** a chest of drawers or bureau with a mirror
2**dresser** *n* **:** one that dresses
dress·i·ness \ˈdres-ē-nəs\ *n* **:** the quality or state of being dressy
dress·ing *n* **1 a :** the act or process of one who dresses **b :** an instance of such act or process **2 a :** a sauce for adding to a dish **b :** a seasoned mixture usu. used as a stuffing (as for poultry) **3 a :** material applied to cover a lesion **b :** fertilizing material
dressing gown *n* **:** a robe worn esp. while dressing or resting
dressing room *n* **:** a room used chiefly for dressing; *esp* **:** a room in a theater for changing costumes and makeup
dressing station *n* **:** a station for giving first aid to the wounded
dressing table *n* **:** a low table often fitted with drawers and a mirror in front of which one sits while dressing
1**dress·mak·er** \ˈdres-ˌmā-kər\ *n* **:** one that does dressmaking
2**dressmaker** *adj, of women's clothes* **:** having softness, rounded lines, and intricate detailing ⟨a ～ suit⟩
dress·mak·ing \-kiŋ\ *n* **:** the process or occupation of making dresses
dress parade *n* **:** a formal ceremonial parade in dress uniform
dress rehearsal *n* **:** a full rehearsal of a play in costume and with stage properties shortly before the first performance
dress shirt *n* **:** a man's white shirt esp. for wear with evening dress
dress suit *n* **:** a suit worn for full dress
dress uniform *n* **:** a uniform for formal wear
dressy \ˈdres-ē\ *adj* **1 :** showy in dress **2 :** STYLISH, SMART
drew *past of* DRAW
drib \ˈdrib\ *n* [prob. back-formation fr. *dribble* & *driblet*] **:** a small amount **:** FRAGMENT — usu. used in pl.
1**drib·ble** \ˈdrib-əl\ *vb* **drib·bling** \-(ə-)liŋ\ [freq. of *drib* (to dribble)] *vi* **1 :** to fall or flow in drops or in a thin intermittent stream **:** TRICKLE **2 :** to let saliva trickle from a corner of the mouth **:** DROOL **3 :** to come or issue little by little **4 a :** to dribble a ball or puck **b :** to proceed by dribbling **～** *vt* **1 :** to let or cause to fall in drops little by little **2 a :** to issue sporadically and in small bits **b :** FRITTER **3 :** to propel by successive slight taps or bounces with hand, foot, or stick — **drib·bler** \-(ə-)lər\ *n*
2**dribble** *n* **1 a :** a small trickling stream or flow **b :** a drizzling shower **2 :** a tiny or insignificant bit or quantity **3 :** an act or instance of dribbling a ball or puck
drib·let \ˈdrib-lət\ *n* **1 :** a trifling sum or part **2 :** a falling drop
dried–fruit beetle *n* **:** a small broad brown beetle (*Carpophilus hemipterus*) that is a cosmopolitan pest on stored products
dried–up \ˈdrī-ˈdəp\ *adj* **:** WIZENED
1**drier** *comparative of* DRY
2**dri·er** *also* **dry·er** \ˈdrī(-ə)r\ *n* **1 :** something that extracts or absorbs moisture **2 :** a substance that accelerates drying (as of oils, paints, and printing inks) **3** *usu* **dryer :** a device for drying
driest *superlative of* DRY
1**drift** \ˈdrift\ *n* [ME; akin to OE *drīfan* to drive — more at DRIVE] **1 a :** the act of driving something along **b :** the flow or the velocity of the current of a river or ocean stream **2 :** something driven, propelled, or urged along or drawn together in a clump by or as if by a natural agency: as **a :** wind-driven snow, rain, cloud, dust, or smoke usu. at or near the ground surface **b (1) :** a mass of matter (as sand) deposited together by or as if by wind or water **(2) :** a helter-skelter accumulation **c :** DROVE, FLOCK **d :** something (as driftwood) washed ashore **e :** rock debris deposited by natural agents; *specif* **:** a deposit of clay, sand, gravel, and boulders transported by a glacier or by running water from a glacier **3 a :** a general underlying design or tendency **b :** the meaning, import, or purport of what is spoken or written **4 :** something driven down upon or forced into a body: as **a :** a tool for ramming down or driving something **b :** a pin for stretching and aligning rivet holes **5 :** the motion or action of drifting spatially usu. under external influence: as **a :** a ship's deviation from its course caused by currents **b :** one of the slower movements of oceanic circulation **c :** the lateral motion of an airplane due to air currents **d :** an easy moderate more or less steady flow or sweep along a spatial course **e :** a gradual shift in attitude, opinion, or position **f :** an aimless course; *esp* **:** a foregoing of any attempt at direction or control **g :** a deviation from a true reproduction, representation, or reading **6 a :** a nearly horizontal mine passageway driven on or parallel to the course of a vein or rock stratum **b :** a small crosscut in a mine connecting two larger tunnels **7 a :** an assumed trend toward a general change in the structure of a language over a period of time **b :** change in genotypes of small populations due to random loss or multiplication of gene groups **c :** a gradual change in the zero reading of an instrument or in any quantitive characteristic that is supposed to remain constant **syn** see TENDENCY
2**drift** *vi* **1 a :** to become driven or carried along by a current of water, wind, or air **b :** to move or float smoothly and effortlessly

2 a : to move along the line of least resistance b : to travel about in a random way esp. in search of work c : to become carried along subject to no guidance or control 3 a : to accumulate in a mass or become piled up in heaps by wind or water b : to become covered with a drift 4 a : to vary or deviate from a set adjustment b : to vary sluggishly ~ *vt* 1 a : to cause to be driven in a current b *West* : to drive (livestock) slowly esp. to allow grazing 2 a : to cause to drift b : to cover with drifts — **drift·er** *n* — **drift·ing·ly** \'drif-tiŋ-lē\ *adv*

drift·age \'drif-tij\ *n* 1 : a drifting of some object esp. through action of wind or water 2 : deviation from a set course due to drifting 3 : something that drifts

drift·weed \'drif-,twēd\ *n* : a seaweed (as of the genus *Laminaria*) that tends to break free and drift ashore

drift·wood \'drif-,twu̇d\ *n* 1 : wood drifted or floated by water 2 : something that drifts aimlessly : FLOTSAM 2, WRECKAGE 3

drifty \'drif-tē\ *adj* : full of drifts or tending to form drifts

1**drill** \'dril\ *vb* [D *drillen;* akin to OHG *drāen* to turn] *vt* 1 : to pierce or bore with or as if with a drill 2 a : to instruct thoroughly b : to impart or communicate by repetition c : to train or exercise in military evolutions and the use of weapons ~ *vi* 1 : to make a hole with a drill 2 : to engage in an exercise 3 : to act like or have the effect of a drill **syn** see PRACTICE — **drill·er** *n*

2**drill** *n* 1 : an instrument with an edged or pointed end for making holes in hard substances by revolving or by a succession of blows; *also* : such an instrument with the machine for operating it 2 : the act or exercise of training soldiers in military skill and discipline 3 a : a physical or mental exercise aimed at perfecting facility and skill esp. by regular practice b : a formal exercise by a team of marchers c *chiefly Brit* : the approved or correct procedure for accomplishing something efficiently 4 : a marine snail (*Urosalpinx cinerea*) destructive to oysters by boring through their shells and feeding on the soft parts; *broadly* : any of several mollusks related to the drill 5 : a drilling sound

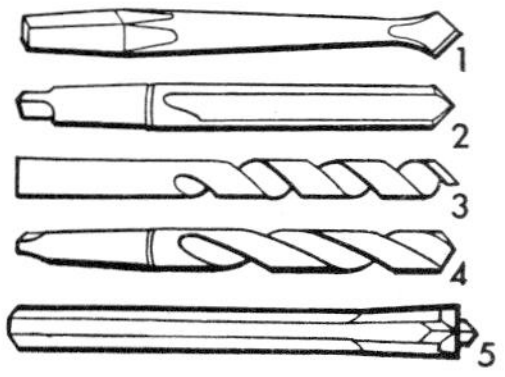

drills 1: *1* flat, *2* straight-flute, *3* single-twist, *4* two-groove, *5* star

3**drill** *n* [prob. native name in West Africa] : a West African baboon (*Mandrillus leucophaeus*) closely related to the typical mandrills

4**drill** *n* [perh. fr. *drill* (rill)] 1 a : a shallow furrow or trench into which seed is sown b : a row of seed sown in such a furrow 2 : a planting implement that makes holes or furrows, drops in the seed and sometimes fertilizer, and covers them with earth

5**drill** *vt* 1 : to sow (seeds) by dropping along a shallow furrow 2 a : to sow with seed or set with seedlings inserted in drills b : to distribute seed or fertilizer in by means of a drill

6**drill** *n* [short for *drilling*] : a durable cotton fabric in twill weave

dril·ling \'dril-iŋ\ *n* [modif. of G *drillich,* fr. MHG *drilich* fabric woven with a threefold thread, fr. OHG *drilīh* made up of three threads, fr. L *trilic-, trilix,* fr. *tri-* + *licium* thread] : 6DRILL

drill·mas·ter \'dril-,mas-tər\ *n* 1 : an instructor in military drill 2 : an instructor or director who maintains severe discipline

drill press *n* : an upright drilling machine in which the drill is pressed to the work by a hand lever or by power

drily *var of* DRYLY

1**drink** \'driŋk\ *vb* **drank** \'draŋk\ **drunk** \'drəŋk\ *or* **drank; drink·ing** [ME *drinken,* fr. OE *drincan;* akin to OHG *trinkan* to drink] *vt* 1 a : SWALLOW, IMBIBE b : to take in or suck up : ABSORB c : to take in or receive in a way suggestive of a liquid being swallowed 2 : to give or join in (a toast) 3 a : to spend in or on consumption of alcoholic beverages b : to bring to a specified state by taking drink ~ *vi* 1 a : to take liquid into the mouth for swallowing b : to receive into one's consciousness 2 : to partake of alcoholic beverages 3 : to make or join in a toast

2**drink** *n* 1 a : liquid suitable for swallowing b : alcoholic liquor 2 : a draft or portion of liquid 3 : excessive consumption of alcoholic beverages 4 : a sizable body of water — used with *the*

1**drink·able** \'driŋ-kə-bəl\ *adj* : suitable or safe for drinking

2**drinkable** *n* : a liquid suitable for drinking : BEVERAGE

drink·er \'driŋ-kər\ *n* 1 a : one that drinks b : one that drinks alcoholic beverages esp. to excess 2 : a device that provides water for domestic animals or poultry

1**drip** \'drip\ *vb* **dripped** *or* **dript; drip·ping** [ME *drippen,* fr. OE *dryppan;* akin to OE *dropa* drop] *vt* : to let fall in drops ~ *vi* 1 a : to let fall drops of moisture or liquid b : to overflow with or as if with moisture 2 : to fall in or as if in drops — **drip·per** *n*

2**drip** *n* 1 a : a falling in drops b : liquid that falls, overflows, or is extruded in drops 2 : the sound made by or as if by falling drops 3 : a part of a cornice or other member that projects to throw off rainwater; *also* : an overlapping metal strip serving the same purpose 4 : a device for the administration of a fluid at a slow rate esp. into a vein; *also* : a material so administered 5 *slang* : sloppy sentiment 6 *slang* : someone looked on as tiresomely dull

drip–dry \'drip-'drī\ *vi* : to dry with few or no wrinkles when hung dripping wet — **drip–dry** \-,drī\ *adj*

drip pan *n* : a pan for catching drippings — called also *dripping pan*

1**drip·ping** \'drip-iŋ\ *n* : fat and juices drawn from meat during cooking — often used in pl.

2**dripping** *adv* : EXTREMELY ⟨~ wet⟩

drip·py \'drip-ē\ *adj* 1 : RAINY, DRIZZLY 2 : MAWKISH

drip·stone \'drip-,stōn\ *n* 1 : a stone drip (as along an eaves) 2 : calcium carbonate in the form of stalactites or stalagmites

1**drive** \'drīv\ *vb* **drove** \'drōv\ **driv·en** \'driv-ən\ **driv·ing** \'drī-viŋ\ [ME *driven,* fr. OE *drīfan;* akin to OHG *trīban* to drive] *vt* 1 a : to impart a forward motion to by physical force b : to repulse, remove, or cause to go by force, authority, or influence ⟨~ the enemy back⟩ c : to set or keep in motion or operation 2 a : to direct the motions and course of (a draft animal) b : to operate the mechanism and controls and direct the course of (as a vehicle) c : to convey in a vehicle d : to float (logs) down a stream 3 : to carry on or through energetically ⟨*driving* a roaring trade⟩ 4 a : to exert inescapable or coercive pressure on : FORCE b : to compel to undergo or suffer a change of state c : to urge relentlessly to continuous exertion d : to press or force into an activity, course, or direction e : to project, inject, or impress incisively 5 a : to cause to move in a desired direction b : to search (a district) for game 6 : to force (a passage) by pressing or digging 7 a : to propel (an object of play) swiftly b : to hit (a golf ball) from the tee esp. with a driver c : to cause (a run or runner) to be scored in baseball — usu. used with *in* ~ *vi* 1 a : to dash, plunge, or surge ahead rapidly or violently b : to rush along with force against an obstruction 2 : to strive determinedly on a course or toward an objective 3 a : to operate and steer a vehicle b : to have oneself carried in a vehicle 4 : to drive an object of play **syn** see MOVE, RIDE

2**drive** *n* 1 : an act of driving: a : a trip in a carriage or automobile b : a collection and driving together of animals; *also* : the animals gathered c : a driving of cattle or sheep overland d : a hunt or shoot in which the game is driven within the hunter's range e : the guiding of logs downstream to a mill; *also* : the floating logs amassed in a drive f (1) : the act or an instance of driving an object of play (2) : the flight of a ball 2 a : a private road : DRIVEWAY 2 b : a public road for driving (as in a park) 3 : an offensive, aggressive, or expansionist move; *esp* : a strong military attack against enemy-held terrain 4 : the state of being hurried and under pressure 5 : a strong systematic group effort : CAMPAIGN 6 a : an urgent, basic, or instinctual need b : an impelling culturally acquired concern, interest, or longing c : dynamic quality 7 a : the means for giving motion to a machine or machine part b : the means by which the propulsive power of an automobile is applied to the road c : the means by which the propulsion of an automotive vehicle is controlled and directed — **drive** *adj*

drive–in \'drī-,vin\ *n* : a place of business so laid out that patrons can be accommodated while remaining in their automobiles

1**driv·el** \'driv-əl\ *vb* **driv·eled** *or* **driv·elled; driv·el·ing** *or* **driv·el·ling** \-(ə-)liŋ\ [ME *drivelen,* fr. OE *dreflian;* akin to ON *draf* malt dregs, OE *deorc* dark] *vi* 1 : to let saliva dribble from the mouth : SLAVER 2 : to talk stupidly and carelessly ~ *vt* 1 : to utter in an infantile or imbecilic way 2 : to waste or fritter in a childish fashion — **driv·el·er** *or* **driv·el·ler** \-(ə-)lər\ *n*

2**drivel** *n* 1 *archaic* : saliva trickling from the mouth 2 : NONSENSE

driv·er \'drī-vər\ *n* : one that drives: as a : COACHMAN b : the operator of a motor vehicle c : an implement (as a hammer) for driving d : a mechanical piece for imparting motion to another piece e : a golf club with a wooden head and nearly straight face used in driving — called also *number one wood*

driver ant *n* : ARMY ANT; *specif* : any of various African and Asian ants (*Dorylus* or related genera) that move in vast armies

driver's seat *n* : the position of top authority or dominance

drive shaft *n* : a shaft that transmits mechanical power

drive·way \'drīv-,wā\ *n* 1 : a road or way along which animals are driven 2 : a private road giving access from a public way to a building on abutting grounds

1**driv·ing** *adj* 1 a : communicating force ⟨a ~ wheel⟩ b : exercising pressure : DYNAMIC 2 a : having great force ⟨a ~ storm⟩ b : acting with vigor — **driv·ing·ly** \'drī-viŋ-lē\ *adv*

2**driving** *n* : management of a vehicle on the road

1**driz·zle** \'driz-əl\ *vb* **driz·zling** \-(ə-)liŋ\ [perh. alter. of ME *drysnen* to fall, fr. OE *-drysnian* to disappear; akin to Goth *driusan* to fall] *vi* : to rain in very small drops or lightly : SPRINKLE ~ *vt* 1 : to shed or let fall in minute drops or particles 2 : to make wet with minute drops — **driz·zling·ly** \-(ə-)liŋ-lē\ *adv*

2**drizzle** *n* : a fine misty rain — **driz·zly** \'driz-(ə-)lē\ *adj*

drogue \'drōg\ *n* [prob. alter. of 1*drag*] 1 : SEA ANCHOR 2 : a cylindrical or funnel-shaped device towed as a target by an airplane or a small parachute for stabilizing or decelerating something (as an astronaut's capsule) 3 : a funnel-shaped device at the end of a hose of a tanker airplane in flight used in refueling to receive the probe of another airplane

droit \'drȯit, drə-'wä\ *n* [MF, fr. ML *directum,* fr. LL, neut. of *directus* just, fr. L, direct] : a legal right ⟨~s of admiralty⟩

1**droll** \'drōl\ *adj* [F *drôle,* fr. *drôle* scamp, fr. MF *drolle,* fr. MD, imp] : having a humorous, whimsical, or odd quality **syn** see LAUGHABLE — **droll·ness** \'drōl-nəs\ *n* — **drol·ly** \'drō(l)-lē\ *adv*

2**droll** *n* : one that amuses or diverts : WAG, JESTER

3**droll** *vi, archaic* : to make fun : JEST, SPORT

droll·ery \'drōl-(ə-)rē\ *n* 1 : something that is droll: as a : a comic picture or drawing b : a usu. brief comic show or entertainment c : an amusing story or manner : JEST 2 : the act or an instance of jesting or burlesquing 3 : whimsical humor

-drome \,drōm\ *n comb form* [*hippodrome*] 1 : racecourse ⟨motor*drome*⟩ 2 : large specially prepared place ⟨aero*drome*⟩

drom·e·dary \'dräm-ə-,der-ē *also* 'drəm-\ *n, pl* **drom·e·dar·ies** [ME *dromedarie,* fr. MF *dromedaire,* fr. LL *dromedarius,* fr. L *dromad-, dromas,* fr. Gk, running; akin to Gk *dramein* to run, *dromos* racecourse, OE *treppan* to tread] 1 : a camel of unusual speed bred and trained esp. for riding 2 : the one-humped camel (*Camelus dromedarius*) of western Asia and northern Africa

drom·ond \'dräm-ənd\ *n* [ME, fr. MF *dromont,* fr. LL *dromon-, dromo* light ship, fr. Gk *dromōn,* fr. *dramein* to run] : a large medieval fast-sailing galley or cutter

-d·ro·mous \d-rə-məs\ *adj comb form* [NL *-dromus,* fr. Gk *-dromos* (akin to Gk *dramein*)] : running ⟨cata*dromous*⟩

1**drone** \'drōn\ *n* [ME, fr. OE *drān;* akin to OHG *treno* drone] 1 : the male of a bee (as the honeybee) that has no sting and gathers no honey 2 : one that lives on the labors of others : PARASITE 3 : a pilotless airplane or ship controlled by radio signals

2**drone** *vi* 1 a : to make a sustained deep murmuring, humming, or buzzing sound b : to talk in a persistently dull or monotonous tone 2 : to pass, proceed, or act in a dull, drowsy, or indifferent manner ~ *vt* 1 : to utter or pronounce with a drone 2 : to pass or spend dully — **dron·er** *n* — **dron·ing·ly** \'drō-niŋ-lē\ *adv*

3**drone** *n* 1 a : BAGPIPE b : one of the usu. three pipes on a bagpipe that sound fixed continuous tones 2 : a deep sustained or monotonous sound : HUM 3 : an unvarying sustained bass note

1**drool** \'drül\ *vb* [perh. alter. of *drivel*] *vi* 1 a : to water at the mouth b : DRIVEL 1 2 : to make an effusive show of pleasure 3 : to talk nonsense ~ *vt* : to express sentimentally or effusively

2**drool** *n* : DRIVEL

droop \'drüp\ *vb* [ME *drupen,* fr. ON *drūpa;* akin to OE *dropa* drop — more at DROP] *vi* 1 : to hang or incline downward 2 : to sink gradually 3 : to become depressed or weakened : LANGUISH ~ *vt* : to let droop — **droop** *n* — **droop·ing·ly** \'drü-piŋ-lē\ *adv*

droopy \'drü-pē\ *adj* 1 : drooping or tending to droop 2 : GLOOMY

1**drop** \'dräp\ *n* [ME, fr. OE *dropa;* akin to Goth *driusan* to fall — more at DREARY] 1 a (1) : the quantity of fluid that falls in one

spherical mass (2) *pl* **:** a dose of medicine measured by drops; *specif* **:** a solution for dilating the pupil of the eye **b :** a small quantity of drink **c :** the smallest practical unit of liquid measure **2 :** something that resembles a liquid drop: as **a :** a pendent ornament attached to a piece of jewelry; *also* **:** an earring with such a pendant **b :** a small globular candy **3** [2*drop*] **a :** the act or an instance of dropping **:** FALL **b :** a decline in quantity or quality **c :** a descent by parachute; *also* **:** the men or equipment dropped by parachute **4 a :** the distance from a higher to a lower level or through which something drops **b :** a fall of electric potential **5 :** a slot into which something is to be dropped **6** [2*drop*] **:** something that drops, hangs, or falls: as **a :** a movable plate that covers the keyhole of a lock **b :** an unframed piece of cloth scenery in a theater; *also* **:** DROP CURTAIN **c :** a hinged platform on a gallows **d :** a fallen fruit **7 :** the advantage of having an opponent covered with a firearm — usu. used in the phrase *get the drop on*

2drop *vb* **dropped; drop·ping** *vi* **1 :** to fall in drops **2 a** (1) **:** to fall unexpectedly or suddenly (2) **:** to descend from one line or level to another **b :** to fall in a state of collapse or death **c** *of a card* **:** to become played by reason of the obligation to follow suit **3 :** to move with a favoring wind or current — usu. used with *down* **4 :** to enter as if without conscious effort of will into some state, condition, or activity ⟨*dropped* into sleep⟩ **5 a :** to cease to be of concern **:** LAPSE ⟨let the matter ~⟩ **b :** to become less ⟨production *dropped*⟩ — often used with *off* **c :** to withdraw from participation or membership **:** QUIT — usu. used with *out* ~ *vt* **1 :** to let fall or cause to fall **2 a :** to lower or cause to descend from one level to another **b :** to lower (wheels) in preparation for landing an airplane **c :** to cause to lessen or decrease **:** REDUCE ⟨*dropped* his speed⟩ **3 :** to set down from a ship or vehicle **:** UNLOAD; *also* **:** AIR-DROP **4 :** to cause (the voice) to be less loud **5 a :** to bring down with a shot or a blow **b :** to cause (a high card) to fall **c :** to toss or roll (a ball) into a hole or basket **6 a :** to give up (as an idea) **b :** to leave incomplete ⟨~ a sentence in the middle⟩ **c :** to break off an association or connection with **:** DISMISS ⟨~ a failing student⟩ **7 a :** to leave (a letter) unsounded ⟨~ the *r* in *farm*⟩ **b :** to leave out in writing **8 a :** to utter or mention in a casual way ⟨~ a suggestion⟩ **b :** to send by mail **9** *of an animal* **:** to give birth to **10 :** LOSE ⟨*dropped* 3 games⟩ — **drop back :** to move toward the rear of an advancing line or column — **drop behind :** to fail to keep abreast — **drop by :** to pay a brief casual visit — **drop in :** to pay an unexpected visit

drop curtain *n* **:** a stage curtain lowered instead of drawn

drop–forge \'dräp-'fō(ə)rj, -'fȯ(ə)rj\ *vt* **:** to forge between dies by a drop hammer or punch press — **drop forger** *n*

drop forging *n* **:** a forging made by the force of a dropped weight

drop hammer *n* **:** a power hammer raised and then released to drop on metal resting on an anvil or die

drop·head \'dräp-,hed\ *n* **:** a device for a desk or table that enables an attached typewriter or sewing machine to be swung or dropped down to leave a flat table top

drop·kick \-'kik\ *n* **:** a kick made by dropping a football to the ground and kicking it at the moment it starts to rebound

drop–kick \-'kik\ *vi* **:** to make a dropkick ~ *vt* **:** to score (a goal) with a dropkick — **drop·kick·er** *n*

drop leaf *n* **:** a hinged leaf on a table that can be folded down

drop·let \'dräp-lət\ *n* **:** a tiny drop

droplet infection *n* **:** infection transmitted by airborne droplets of sputum containing infectious organisms

drop letter *n* **:** a letter to be delivered from the office where posted

drop·light \'dräp-,līt\ *n* **:** an electric light suspended by a cord

drop off *vi* **1 :** to fall asleep **2 :** DIE

drop–off \'dräp-,ȯf\ *n* **:** a very steep or perpendicular descent

drop·out \-,au̇t\ *n* **:** one who drops out (as of a high school)

drop·page \'dräp-ij\ *n* **:** the part of a fruit crop that falls from the tree before it is ready for picking

dropped egg *n* **:** a poached egg

drop·per \'dräp-ər\ *n* **1 :** one that drops **2 a :** a short glass tube fitted with a rubber bulb and used to measure liquids by drops **b :** a glass tube of small diameter for ejecting liquid in drops

drop·ping *n* **1 :** something dropped **2** *pl* **:** animal dung

drop press *n* **1 :** PUNCH PRESS **2 :** DROP HAMMER

drop shot *n* **1 :** a tennis shot that drops quickly after crossing the net **2 :** shot made by dropping molten shot metal from a height

drop·si·cal \'dräp-si-kəl\ *adj* **1 :** relating to or affected with dropsy **2 :** PUFFY, SWOLLEN, TURGID — **drop·si·cal·ly** \-k(ə-)lē\ *adv* — **drop·si·cal·ness** \-kəl-nəs\ *n*

drop·sonde \'dräp-,sänd\ *n* [*drop* + radio*sonde*] **:** a radiosonde dropped by parachute from a high-flying airplane

drop·sy \'dräp-sē\ *n* [ME *dropesie*, short for *ydropesie*, fr. OF, fr. L *hydropisis*, modif. of Gk *hydrōps*, fr. *hydōr* water] **:** EDEMA

dros·era \'dräs-ə-rə\ *n* [NL, genus name, fr. Gk, fem. of *droseros* dewy, fr. *drosos* dew] **:** any of a genus (*Drosera*) of low perennial or biennial insectivorous plants of the sundew family

drosh·ky \'dräsh-kē\ *n* [Russ *drozhki*, fr. *droga* pole of a wagon] **:** any of various 2- or 4-wheeled carriages used esp. in Russia

dro·soph·i·la \drō-'säf-ə-lə\ *n* [NL, genus name, fr. Gk *drosos* + NL *-phila*, fem. of *-philus* -phil] **:** any of a genus (*Drosophila*) of small two-winged flies used in the study of basic mechanisms of inheritance

dross \'dräs, 'drȯs\ *n* [ME *dros*, fr. OE *drōs* dregs] **1 :** the scum that forms on the surface of molten metal **2 :** waste or foreign matter **:** IMPURITY — **drossy** \-ē\ *adj*

drought *or* **drouth** \'drau̇th, 'drau̇t\ *n* [ME, fr. OE *drūgath*, fr. *drūgian* to dry up] **1 :** a prolonged period of dryness **2 :** a prolonged or chronic shortage — **droughty** \-ē\ *adj*

1drove \'drōv\ *n* [ME, fr. OE *drāf*, fr. *drīfan* to drive — more at DRIVE] **1 :** a group of animals driven or moving in a body **2 a :** a crowd of people moving or acting together **b :** a large group of like things **3 a :** a chisel used to form a grooved or roughly shaped surface on stone **b :** the grooved surface so formed

2drove *past of* DRIVE

drov·er \'drō-vər\ *n* **:** one that drives cattle or sheep

drown \'drau̇n\ *or substand* **drownd** \'drau̇nd\ *vb* **drowned** \'drau̇nd\ *or substand* **drownd·ed** \'drau̇n-dəd\ **drown·ing** \'drau̇-niŋ\ *or substand* **drownd·ing** \'drau̇n-diŋ\ [ME *drounen*] *vi* **:** to become drowned ~ *vt* **1 a :** to suffocate by submersion esp. in water **b :** to cover with water **:** INUNDATE **2 :** OVERCOME, OVERPOWER

1drowse \'drau̇z\ *vb* [prob. akin to Goth *driusan* to fall] *vi* **1 :** to fall into a light slumber **2 :** to be inactive ~ *vt* **1 :** to make drowsy or inactive **2 :** to pass (time) drowsily or in drowsing

2drowse *n* **:** the act or an instance of drowsing **:** DOZE

drows·i·ly \'drau̇-zə-lē\ *adv* **:** in a drowsy manner

drows·i·ness \-zē-nəs\ *n* **:** the quality or state of being drowsy

drowsy \'drau̇-zē\ *adj* **1 a :** ready to fall asleep **b :** tending to induce drowsiness **c :** INDOLENT, LETHARGIC **2 :** giving the appearance of inactivity

drub \'drəb\ *vb* **drubbed; drub·bing** [perh. fr. Ar *ḍaraba*] *vt* **1 :** to beat severely **:** BELABOR **2 :** to defeat decisively ~ *vi* **:** DRUM, STAMP — **drub·ber** *n*

1drudge \'drəj\ *vb* [ME *druggen;* prob. akin to OE *drēogan* to work, endure, L *firmus* firm] *vi* **:** to do hard, menial, or monotonous work ~ *vt* **:** to force to drudge — **drudg·er** *n*

2drudge *n* **1 :** one who is obliged to do menial work **2 :** one whose work is routine and boring **:** HACK

drudg·ery \'drəj-(ə-)rē\ *n* **:** tiresome or menial work **syn** see WORK

1drug \'drəg\ *n* [ME *drogge*] **1 a** *obs* **:** a substance used in dyeing or chemical operations **b :** a substance used as a medicine or in making medicines **2 :** something little sought after ⟨a ~ on the market⟩ **3 :** a narcotic substance or preparation

2drug *vb* **drugged; drug·ging** *vt* **1 :** to affect with a drug; *esp* **:** to stupefy by a narcotic drug **2 :** to administer a drug to **3 :** to lull or stupefy as if with a drug ~ *vi* **:** to take drugs for narcotic effect

drug·get \'drəg-ət\ *n* [MF *droguet*, dim. of *drogue* trash, drug] **1 :** a wool or partly wool fabric formerly used for clothing **2 :** a coarse durable cloth used chiefly as a floor covering **3 :** a rug having a cotton warp and a wool filling

drug·gist \'drəg-əst\ *n* **1 :** one who sells drugs and medicines **2 :** PHARMACIST **3 :** one who owns or manages a drugstore

drug·store \'drəg-,stō(ə)r, -,stȯ(ə)r\ *n* **:** a retail shop where medicines and miscellaneous articles are sold **:** PHARMACY

dru·id \'drü-əd\ *n, often cap* [L *druides, druidae*, pl., fr. Gaulish *druides;* akin to OE *trēow* tree] **:** one of an ancient Celtic priesthood appearing in Irish and Welsh sagas and Christian legends as magicians and wizards — **dru·id·ess** \-əs\ *n, often cap* — **dru·id·ic** \drü-'id-ik\ *or* **dru·id·i·cal** \-i-kəl\ *adj, often cap*

dru·id·ism \'drü-ə-,diz-əm\ *n, often cap* **:** the system of religion, philosophy, and instruction of the druids

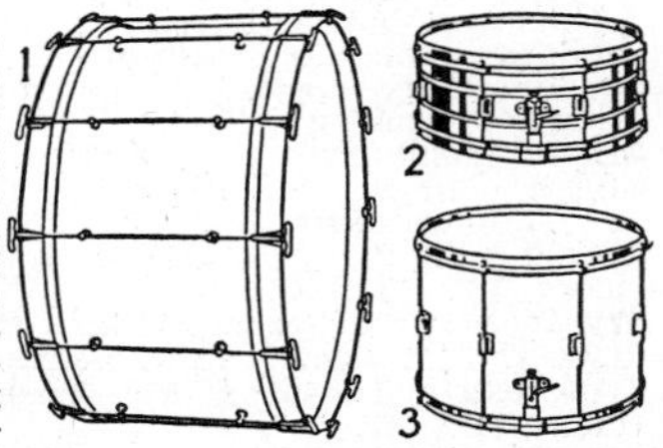

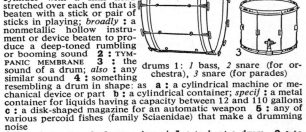

drums 1: *1* bass, *2* snare (for orchestra), *3* snare (for parades)

1drum \'drəm\ *n, often attrib* [prob. fr. D *trom;* akin to MHG *trumme* drum] **1 :** a musical percussion instrument usu. consisting of a hollow cylinder with a skin head stretched over each end that is beaten with a stick or pair of sticks in playing; *broadly* **:** a nonmetallic hollow instrument or device beaten to produce a deep-toned rumbling or booming sound **2 :** TYMPANIC MEMBRANE **3 :** the sound of a drum; *also* **:** any similar sound **4 :** something resembling a drum in shape: as **a :** a cylindrical machine or mechanical device or part **b :** a cylindrical container; *specif* **:** a metal container for liquids having a capacity between 12 and 110 gallons **c :** a disk-shaped magazine for an automatic weapon **5 :** any of various percoid fishes (family Sciaenidae) that make a drumming noise

2drum *vb* **drummed; drum·ming** *vi* **1 :** to beat a drum **2 :** to make a succession of strokes or vibrations that produce sounds like drumbeats **3 :** to sound rhythmically **4 :** to stir up interest **:** SOLICIT ~ *vt* **1 :** to summon or enlist by or as if by beating a drum **2 :** to dismiss ignominiously **:** EXPEL — usu. used with *out* **3 :** to drive or force by steady effort or reiteration **4 a :** to strike or tap repeatedly **b :** to produce (rhythmic sounds) by such action

3drum *n* [ScGael *druim* back, ridge, fr. OIr *druimm*] **1** *chiefly Scot* **:** a long narrow hill or ridge **2 :** DRUMLIN

drum·beat \'drəm-,bēt\ *n* **:** a stroke on a drum or its sound

drum·beat·er \-,bēt-ər\ *n* **:** a vociferous supporter of a cause — **drum·beat·ing** \-iŋ\ *n*

drum·fire \'drəm-,fī(ə)r\ *n* **1 :** artillery firing so continuous as to sound like a drum **2 :** something suggestive of drumfire **:** BARRAGE

drum·head \-,hed\ *n* **1 :** the skin stretched over each end of a drum **2 :** the top of a capstan that is pierced with sockets

drumhead court–martial *n* [fr. the use of a drumhead as a table] **:** a summary court-martial to try offenses on the battlefield

drum·lin \'drəm-lən\ *n* [IrGael *druim* back, ridge (fr. OIr *druimm*) + E *-lin* (alter. of *-ling*)] **:** an elongate or oval hill of glacial drift

drum major *n* **:** the marching leader of a band or drum corps

drum ma·jor·ette \,drəm-,mā-jə-'ret\ *n* **:** a female drum major

drum·mer \'drəm-ər\ *n* **1 :** one that plays a drum **2 :** TRAVELING SALESMAN

drum·stick \'drəm-,stik\ *n* **1 :** a stick for beating a drum **2 :** the segment of a fowl's leg between the thigh and tarsus

1drunk \'drəŋk\ *adj* [ME *drunke*, alter. of *drunken*] **1 :** having the faculties impaired by alcohol **2 :** dominated by some feeling as if by alcohol **3 :** of, relating to, or caused by intoxication

syn DRUNK, DRUNKEN, INTOXICATED, INEBRIATED, TIPSY, TIGHT mean considerably affected by alcohol. DRUNK is the simple, inclusive term, used predicatively and implying neither censure nor apology; DRUNKEN, used attributively, is also a plain term but may suggest habitual excessive drinking; INTOXICATED and INEBRIATED both offer a way of avoiding the blunt effect of DRUNK, INTOXICATED being often applied to one who is slightly drunk, INEBRIATED suggesting the hilarious or noisy phases of insobriety; TIPSY and TIGHT are likely to apply to one infrequently or unexpectedly affected and stress the comic rather than offensive aspects of drunkenness

2drunk *n* **1 :** a period of excessive drinking **2 :** DRUNKARD

drunk·ard \'drəŋ-kərd\ *n* **:** one who is habitually drunk

drunk·en \'drəŋ-kən\ *adj* [ME, fr. OE *druncen*, fr. pp. of *drincan*

drincan to drink] **1 :** DRUNK 1 **2** *obs* **:** DRENCHED **3 a :** given to habitual excessive use of alcohol **b :** of, relating to, or attended by drunkenness **c :** resulting from or as if from intoxication **4 :** unsteady or lurching as if from intoxication **syn** see DRUNK — **drunk·en·ly** *adv* — **drunk·en·ness** \-kən-nəs\ *n*

drunk·o·me·ter \ˌdrəŋ-ˈkäm-ət-ər, ˈdrəŋ-kə-ˌmēt-\ *n* **:** a device for measuring blood alcohol content by chemical analysis of the breath

dru·pa·ceous \drü-ˈpā-shəs\ *adj* **1 :** of or relating to a drupe **2 :** bearing drupes

drupe \ˈdrüp\ *n* [NL *drupa*, fr. L, overripe olive, fr. Gk *dryppa* olive] **:** a one-seeded indehiscent fruit having a hard bony endocarp, a fleshy mesocarp, and a thin epicarp that is flexible (as in the cherry) or dry and almost leathery (as in the almond)

drupe·let \ˈdrü-plət\ *n* **:** a small drupe; *specif* **:** one of the individual parts of an aggregate fruit (as the raspberry)

Druze *or* **Druse** \ˈdrüz\ *n* [Ar *Durūz*, pl., fr. Muḥammed ibn-Ismʿaīlal- *Darazīy* †1019 Muslim religious leader] **:** a member of a nominally Muslim sect of the mountains of Lebanon and Syria

[1]**dry** \ˈdrī\ *adj* **dri·er** \ˈdrī(-ə)r\ **dri·est** \ˈdrī-əst\ [ME, fr. OE *drȳge;* akin to OHG *truckan* dry, and perh. to ON *draugr* dry wood] **1 :** free from water or liquid **2 :** characterized by loss or lack of water: as **a :** lacking precipitation and humidity **b :** lacking freshness **:** STALE **c :** ANHYDROUS **3 a :** not being in or under water ⟨~ land⟩ **b :** using no liquid ⟨~ masonry⟩ **c :** served without butter **d :** DEHYDRATED **e** *of natural gas* **:** containing no recoverable gasoline or other liquid hydrocarbon **f :** functioning without lubrication ⟨~ clutch⟩ **4 a :** THIRSTY **b :** marked by the absence of alcoholic beverages **c :** no longer liquid or sticky ⟨the ink is ~⟩ **5 a :** depleted of liquid contents **:** EMPTY ⟨~ well⟩ **b :** devoid of running water **6 :** not giving milk **7 a :** not shedding tears **b :** marked by the absence or scantiness of secretions, effusions, or other forms of moisture ⟨~ cough⟩ **8 :** practiced without some essential ⟨~ firing⟩ **9 a :** solid as opposed to liquid ⟨~ groceries⟩ **b :** SLACK 6 **10 :** not manifesting or communicating warmth, enthusiasm, or tender feeling **:** SEVERE ⟨~ style of painting⟩ **11 a :** not yielding what is expected or desired **:** BARREN **b :** RESERVED, ALOOF **12 :** marked by a matter-of-fact, ironic, or terse manner of expression ⟨~ humor⟩ **13 :** having no personal bias or emotional concern ⟨~ light of reason⟩ **14 :** UNINTERESTING, WEARISOME ⟨~ passages of description⟩ **15 a :** not sweet **:** SEC **b :** lacking smooth sound qualities **16 :** relating to the prohibition of the manufacture or distribution of alcoholic beverages
syn DRY, ARID mean lacking moisture. DRY may suggest absence of moisture in any degree and applies equally to a normal or an abnormal condition; ARID always implies abnormality or at least undesirability, suggesting such an extreme of dryness that fertility is entirely lacking

[2]**dry** *vb* **dried; dry·ing** *vt* **:** to make dry **~** *vi* **:** to become dry

[3]**dry** *n, pl* **drys 1 :** DRYNESS **2 :** something dry; *esp* **:** a dry place **3 :** PROHIBITIONIST

dry·ad \ˈdrī-əd, -ˌad\ *n* [L *dryad-*, *dryas*, fr. Gk, fr. *drys* tree — more at TREE] **:** WOOD NYMPH 1

dry·as·dust \ˈdrī-əz-ˌdəst\ *adj* **:** BORING, PROSAIC — **dryasdust** *n*

dry cell *n* **:** a voltaic cell whose contents are not spillable

dry–clean \ˈdrī-ˌklēn\ *vt* **:** to subject to dry cleaning — **dry clean·er** \-ˌklē-nər\ *n*

dry clean·ing \-ˌklē-niŋ\ *n* **:** the cleansing of fabrics with substantially nonaqueous organic solvents (as petroleum naphtha)

dry dock \ˈdrī-ˌdäk\ *n* **:** a dock that can be kept dry for use during the construction or repairing of ships

dry–dock \-ˌdäk\ *vt* **:** to place in a dry dock

dry·er *var of* DRIER

dry farm \ˈdrī-ˈfärm\ *n* **:** a nonirrigated farm on dry land operated on the basis of moisture-conserving tillage and drought-resistant crops — **dry–farm** \-ˈfärm\ *vt* — **dry farm·er** \-ˈfär-mər\ *n* — **dry farm·ing** \-ˈfär-miŋ\ *n*

dry fly *n* **:** an artificial angling fly designed to float upon the surface of the water

dry gangrene *n* **:** gangrene that develops in the presence of arterial obstruction, is sharply localized, and is characterized by dryness of the dead tissue which is sharply demarcated from adjacent tissue by a line of inflammation

dry goods \ˈdrī-ˌgu̇dz\ *n pl* **:** textiles, ready-to-wear clothing, and notions as distinguished from other goods

Dry Ice *trademark* — used for solidified carbon dioxide usu. in the form of blocks that at −78.5° C changes directly to a gas and that is used chiefly as a refrigerant

drying oil *n* **:** an oil that changes readily to a hard tough elastic substance when exposed in a thin film to air

dry kiln *n* **:** a heated chamber for drying and seasoning cut lumber

dry·lot \ˈdrī-ˈlät\ *n* **:** an enclosure of limited size usu. bare of vegetation and used for fattening livestock

dry·ly \ˈdrī-lē\ *adv* **:** in a dry manner

dry measure *n* **:** a series of units of capacity for dry commodities — see MEASURE table, METRIC SYSTEM table

dry·ness \ˈdrī-nəs\ *n* **:** the quality or state of being dry

dry nurse *n* **:** a nurse who cares for but does not suckle an infant

dry–nurse \ˈdrī-ˈnərs\ *vt* **:** to act as dry nurse to

dryo·pith·e·cine \ˌdrī-ō-ˈpith-ə-ˌsīn\ *n* [deriv. of Gk *drys* tree + *pithēkos* ape] **:** any of a subfamily (Dryopithecinae) of Miocene and Pliocene Old World anthropoid apes sometimes regarded as ancestors of both man and modern anthropoids — **dryopithecine** *adj*

dry pleurisy *n* **:** pleurisy in which the exudation is mainly fibrinous

dry·point \ˈdrī-ˌpȯint\ *n* **:** an engraving made with a needle or other pointed instrument instead of a burin directly into the metal plate without the use of acid as in etching

dry rot \ˈdrī-ˈrät\ *n* **1 a :** a decay of seasoned timber caused by fungi that consume the cellulose of wood leaving a soft skeleton which is readily reduced to powder **b :** a fungous rot of plant tissue in which the affected areas are dry and often firmer than normal or more or less mummified **2 :** a fungus causing dry rot **3 :** decay from within caused esp. by resistance to new forces

dry–rot \-ˈrät\ *vt* **:** to affect with dry rot **~** *vi* **:** to become affected with dry rot

dry run *n* **1 :** a practice firing without ammunition **2 :** TRIAL

dry·salt·er \-ˌsȯl-tər\ *n, Brit* **:** a dealer in crude dry chemicals and dyes — **dry·salt·ery** \-tə-rē\ *n, Brit*

dry–shod \ˈdrī-ˈshäd\ *adj* **:** having dry shoes or feet

dry socket *n* **:** a tooth socket in which after extraction a blood clot fails to form or disintegrates without organizing

dry wash *n* **:** laundry washed and dried but not ironed

d.t.'s \(ˈ)dē-ˈtēz\ *n pl, often cap D&T* **:** DELIRIUM TREMENS

du·ad \ˈd(y)ü-ˌad\ *n* [irreg. fr. Gk *dyad-*, *dyas* two] **:** PAIR

[1]**du·al** \ˈd(y)ü-əl\ *adj* [L *dualis*, fr. *duo* two — more at TWO] **1** *of grammatical number* **:** denoting reference to two **2 a :** consisting of two parts or elements or having two like parts **:** DOUBLE **b :** having a double character or nature — **du·al·i·ty** \d(y)ü-ˈal-ət-ē\ *n* — **du·al·ly** \ˈd(y)ü-ə(l)-lē\ *adv*

[2]**dual** *n* **:** the dual number of a language or a form in it

du·al·ism \ˈd(y)ü-ə-ˌliz-əm\ *n* **1 :** a theory that considers reality to consist of two irreducible elements or modes **2 :** the quality or state of being dual **3 a :** a doctrine that the universe is under the dominion of two opposing principles one of which is good and the other evil **b :** a view of man as constituted of two irreducible elements — **du·al·ist** \-ləst\ *n* — **du·al·is·tic** \ˌd(y)ü-ə-ˈlis-tik\ *adj* — **du·al·is·ti·cal·ly** \-ti-k(ə-)lē\ *adv*

du·al·ize \ˈd(y)ü-ə-ˌlīz\ *vt* **:** to make dual

du·al–pur·pose \ˌd(y)ü-əl-ˈpər-pəs\ *adj* **1 :** intended for or serving two purposes **2 :** bred for two purposes

[1]**dub** \ˈdəb\ *vb* **dubbed; dub·bing** [ME *dubben*, fr. OE *dubbian;* akin to ON *dubba* to dub, OHG *tubili* plug] *vt* **1 a :** to confer knighthood upon **b :** to dignify or give new character to **c :** NICKNAME **2 :** to trim or remove the comb and wattles of **3 a :** to hit poorly in golf **b :** to execute poorly **~** *vi* **:** THRUST, POKE

[2]**dub** *n* **:** a clumsy unskillful person **:** DUFFER

[3]**dub** *n* [ME (Sc dial.) *dubbe*] *chiefly Scot* **:** POOL, PUDDLE

[4]**dub** *vt* **dubbed; dub·bing** [by shortening & alter. fr. *double*] **1 :** to provide with a new sound track **2 :** to add (sound effects) to a film or to a radio or television production **3 :** to transpose (sound already recorded) to a new record

dub·ber \ˈdəb-ər\ *n* **:** one that dubs

dub·bin \ˈdəb-ən\ *also* **dub·bing** \-ən, -iŋ\ *n* [*dubbing*, gerund of *dub* (to dress leather)] **:** a dressing of oil and tallow for leather

du·bi·ety \d(y)ü-ˈbī-ət-ē\ *n* [LL *dubietas*, fr. L *dubius*] **1 :** DUBIOUSNESS, UNCERTAINTY **2 :** a matter of doubt **syn** see UNCERTAINTY

du·bi·os·i·ty \ˌd(y)ü-bē-ˈäs-ət-ē\ *n* **:** DOUBT **syn** see UNCERTAINTY

du·bi·ous \ˈd(y)ü-bē-əs\ *adj* [L *dubius*, fr. *dubare* to vacillate; akin to L *duo* two — more at TWO] **1 :** occasioning doubt **:** EQUIVOCAL **2 :** unsettled in opinion **3 :** of doubtful promise or uncertain outcome **4 :** questionable as to value, quality, or origin **syn** see DOUBTFUL — **du·bi·ous·ly** *adv* — **du·bi·ous·ness** *n*

du·bi·ta·ble \ˈd(y)ü-bət-ə-bəl\ *adj* [L *dubitabilis*, fr. *dubitare* to doubt — more at DOUBT] **:** open to doubt or question

du·bi·ta·tion \ˌd(y)ü-bə-ˈtā-shən\ *n, archaic* **:** DOUBT

du·cal \ˈd(y)ü-kəl\ *adj* [MF, fr. LL *ducalis* of a leader, fr. L *duc-*, *dux* leader — more at DUKE] **:** of or relating to a duke or dukedom — **du·cal·ly** \-kə-lē\ *adv*

duc·at \ˈdək-ət\ *n* [ME, fr. MF, fr. OIt *ducato* coin with the doge's portrait on it, fr. *duca* doge, fr. LGk *douk-*, *doux* leader, fr. L *duc-*, *dux*] **:** a gold coin of various European countries

du·ce \ˈdü-(ˌ)chā\ *n* [It (*Il*) *Duce*, lit., the leader, title of Benito Mussolini, fr. L *duc-*, *dux*] **:** LEADER 2c(5)

duch·ess \ˈdəch-əs\ *n* [ME *duchesse*, fr. MF, fr. *duc* duke] **:** the wife of a duke or a woman holding a ducal title in her own right

duchy \ˈdəch-ē\ *n* [ME *duche*, fr. MF *duché*, fr. *duc*] **:** the territory of a duke or duchess **:** DUKEDOM

[1]**duck** \ˈdək\ *n, pl* **ducks** *often attrib* [ME *doke*, fr. OE *dūce*] **1** *or pl* **duck a :** any of various swimming birds (family Anatidae, the duck family) in which the neck and legs are short, the body more or less depressed, the bill often broad and flat, and the sexes almost always different from each other in plumage **b :** the flesh of any of these birds used as food **2 :** a female duck **3** *chiefly Brit* **:** DARLING **4** *slang* **:** PERSON, CREATURE

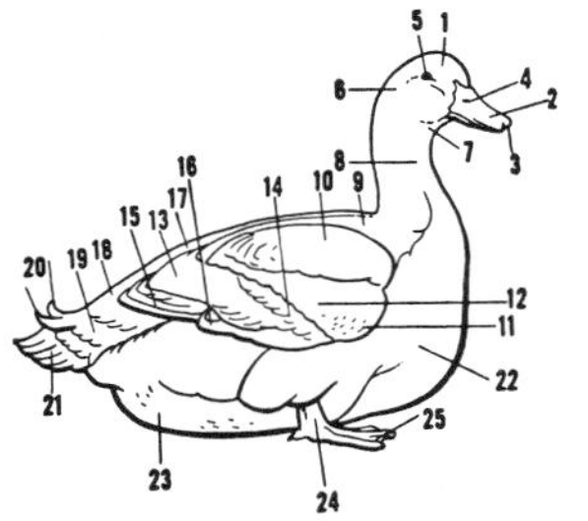

diagram of male duck: *1* head, *2* bill, *3* beam, *4* nostril, *5* eye, *6* ear, *7* throat, *8* neck, *9* cape, *10* shoulder, *11* wing front, *12* wing bow, *13* secondaries, *14* coverts, *15* primaries, *16* flight coverts, *17* saddle, *18* rump, *19* tail coverts, *20* drake feathers, *21* tail, *22* breast, *23* fluff, *24* shank, *25* web

[2]**duck** *vb* [ME *douken;* akin to OHG *tūhhan* to dive, OE *dūce* duck] *vt* **1 :** to thrust under water **2 :** to lower (as the head) quickly **:** BOW **3 :** AVOID, EVADE ⟨~ the issue⟩ **~** *vi* **1 a :** to plunge under the surface of water **b :** to descend suddenly **:** DIP **2 a :** to lower the head or body suddenly **b :** BOW, BOB **3 a :** to move quickly **:** DODGE **b :** to evade a duty, question, or responsibility — **duck·er** *n*

[3]**duck** *n* **:** an instance of ducking

[4]**duck** *n* [D *doek* cloth; akin to OHG *tuoh* cloth, and perh. to Skt *dhvaja* flag] **1 :** a durable closely woven usu. cotton fabric **2** *pl* **:** light clothes made of duck

[5]**duck** *n* [*DUKW*, its code designation] **:** an amphibious truck

duck·bill \ˈdək-ˌbil\ *n* **1 :** PLATYPUS **2 :** a paddlefish (*Polyodon spathula*)

duck·board \ˈdək-ˌbō(ə)rd, -ˌbȯ(ə)rd\ *n* **:** a boardwalk or slatted flooring laid on a wet, muddy, or cold surface — usu. used in pl.

duck call *n* **:** a device for imitating the calls of ducks

duckfooted *adv* **:** with feet pointed outward **:** FLAT-FOOTED

ducking stool *n* **:** a seat attached to a plank and formerly used to plunge culprits tied to it into water

duck·ling \ˈdək-liŋ\ *n* **:** a young duck

duck·pin \-ˌpin\ *n* **1 :** a small bowling pin shorter than a tenpin but proportionately wider at mid-diameter **2** *pl but sing in constr* **:** a bowling game using duckpins

ducks and drakes *or* **duck and drake** *n* **:** the pastime of skimming flat stones or shells along the surface of calm water — **play ducks and drakes with** *or* **make ducks and drakes of :** SQUANDER

duck sickness *n* **:** a highly destructive botulism affecting esp. wild ducks in the western U.S.

duck soup *n* **:** something easy to do

duck·weed \ˈdək-ˌwēd\ *n* **:** a small floating aquatic monocoty-

ledonous plant (family Lemnaceae, the duckweed family)

ducky \'dək-ē\ *adj* **1 :** SATISFACTORY, FINE **2 :** DARLING, CUTE

1**duct** \'dəkt\ *n* [NL *ductus*, fr. ML, aqueduct, fr. L, act of leading fr. *ductus*, pp. of *ducere* to lead — more at TOW] **1 :** a bodily tube or vessel esp. when carrying the secretion of a gland **2 a :** a pipe, tube, or channel that conveys a substance **b :** a pipe or tubular runway for carrying an electric power line, telephone cables, or other conductors **3 a :** a continuous tube formed in plant tissue by a row of elongated cells that have lost their intervening end walls **b :** an elongated cavity formed by disintegration or separation of cells — **duct·less** \'dək-tləs\ *adj*

2**duct** *vt* **:** to convey (as a gas) through a duct

duc·tile \'dək-tᵊl\ *adj* [MF & L; MF, fr. L *ductilis*, fr. *ductus*, pp.] **1 :** capable of being fashioned into a new form **2 a :** capable of being drawn out or hammered thin ⟨~ metal⟩ **b :** capable of being molded **3 :** easily led or influenced **syn** see PLASTIC — **duc·til·i·ty** \,dək-'til-ət-ē\ *n*

duct·ing \'dək-tiŋ\ *n* **:** a system of ducts; *also* **:** the material composing a duct

ductless gland *n* **:** an endocrine gland

duct·ule \'dək-(,)t(y)ü(ə)l\ *n* **:** a small duct

1**dud** \'dəd\ *n* [ME *dudde*] **1** *pl* **a :** CLOTHES **b :** personal belongings **2 :** FAILURE **3 :** a missile that fails to explode

2**dud** *adj* **:** of little or no worth **:** VALUELESS ⟨~ checks⟩

dud·die *or* **dud·dy** \'dəd-ē\ *adj, Scot* **:** RAGGED, TATTERED

dude \'d(y)üd\ *n* [origin unknown] **1 :** a man extremely fastidious in dress and manner **:** DANDY **2 :** a city man; *esp* **:** an easterner in the West — **dud·ish** \'d(y)üd-ish\ *adj* — **dud·ish·ly** *adv*

du·deen \dü-'dēn, -'th̲ēn\ *n* [IrGael *dūidīn*, dim. of *dūd* pipe] **:** a short tobacco pipe made of clay

dude ranch *n* **:** a vacation resort offering horseback riding and other activities typical of western ranches

1**dud·geon** \'dəj-ən\ *n* [ME *dogeon*, fr. AF *digeon*] **1** *obs* **:** a wood used esp. for dagger hilts **2 a** *archaic* **:** a dagger with a handle of dudgeon **b** *obs* **:** a haft made of dudgeon

2**dudgeon** *n* [origin unknown] **:** ILL HUMOR, RESENTMENT **syn** see OFFENSE

1**due** \'d(y)ü\ *adj* [ME, fr. MF *deu*, pp. of *devoir* to owe, fr. L *debēre* — more at DEBT] **1 :** owed or owing as a debt **2 a :** owed or owing as a natural or moral right **b :** according to accepted notions or procedures **:** APPROPRIATE **3 a :** satisfying or capable of satisfying a need, obligation, or duty **:** ADEQUATE **b :** REGULAR, LAWFUL ⟨~ proof of loss⟩ **4 :** ATTRIBUTABLE, ASCRIBABLE — used with *to* **5 :** having reached the date at which payment is required **:** PAYABLE **6 :** required or expected in the prescribed, normal, or logical course of events **:** SCHEDULED — **due·ness** *n*

2**due** *n* **:** something due or owed: **a :** something that rightfully belongs to one **b :** a payment or obligation required by law or custom **:** DEBT **c** *pl* **:** FEES, CHARGES

3**due** *adv* **1** *obs* **:** DULY **2 :** DIRECTLY, EXACTLY ⟨~ north⟩

1**du·el** \'d(y)ü-əl\ *n* [ML *duellum*, fr. OL, war] **1 :** a combat between two persons; *specif* **:** a formal combat with weapons fought between two persons in the presence of witnesses **2 :** a conflict between antagonistic persons, ideas, or forces

2**duel** *vb* **du·eled** *or* **du·elled; du·el·ing** *or* **du·el·ling :** to fight in a duel — **du·el·er** *or* **du·el·ler** *n* — **du·el·ist** *or* **du·el·list** \'d(y)ü-ə-ləst\ *n*

du·el·lo \d(y)ü-'el-(,)ō\ *n* [It, fr. ML *duellum*] **1 :** the rules or practice of dueling **2 :** DUEL

du·en·na \d(y)ü-'en-ə\ *n* [Sp *dueña*, fr. L *domina* mistress] **1 :** an elderly woman serving as governess and companion to the younger ladies in a Spanish or a Portuguese family **2 :** CHAPERON

due process of law : a course of legal proceedings carried out regularly and in accordance with established rules and principles

du·et \d(y)ü-'et\ *n* [It *duetto*, dim. of *duo*] **:** a composition for two performers — **duet** *vi* **du·et·ted; du·et·ting**

due to \'d(y)üt-ə(-w)\ *prep* **:** because of

duff \'dəf\ *n* [E dial., alter. of *dough*] **1 :** a steamed pudding usu. containing raisins and currants **2 :** the partly decayed organic matter on the forest floor **3 :** fine coal **:** SLACK

duf·fel *or* **duf·fle** \'dəf-əl\ *n* [D *duffel*, fr. *Duffel*, Belgium] **1 :** a coarse heavy woolen material with a thick nap **2 :** transportable personal belongings, equipment, and supplies

duffel bag *n* **:** a large cylindrical fabric bag for personal belongings

duf·fer \'dəf-ər\ *n* [origin unknown] **1** *slang* **a :** a peddler esp. of cheap flashy articles **b :** something worthless **2 :** an incompetent, ineffectual, or clumsy person

1**dug** *past of* DIG

2**dug** \'dəg\ *n* [perh. of Scand origin; akin to OSw *dæggia* to suckle; akin to OE *delu* nipple] **:** UDDER, BREAST; *also* **:** TEAT, NIPPLE

du·gong \'dü-,gäŋ, -,gȯŋ\ *n* [NL, genus name, fr. Malay & Tag *duyong* sea cow] **:** any of a monotypic genus (*Dugong*) of aquatic herbivorous mammals that with the manatees constitute an order (Sirenia) and have a bilobate tail and upper incisors altered into tusks in the male — called also *sea cow*

dug·out \'dəg-,au̇t\ *n* **1 :** a boat made by hollowing out a large log **2 :** a shelter dug in a hillside or dug in the ground and roofed with sod; *specif* **:** one in the side of a trench for quarters, storage, or protection **3 :** a low shelter facing a baseball diamond and containing the players' bench

dui·ker \'dī-kər\ *n* [Afrik, lit., diver, fr. *duik* to dive, fr. MD *dūken*; akin to OHG *tūhhan* to dive — more at DUCK] **:** any of several small African antelopes (*Cephalophus* or related genera)

duke \'d(y)ük\ *n* [ME, fr. OF *duc*, fr. L *duc-, dux*, fr. *ducere* to lead — more at TOW] **1 :** a sovereign ruler of a continental European duchy **2 :** a nobleman of the highest hereditary rank; *esp* **:** a member of the highest grade of the British peerage **3** *slang* **:** FIST, HAND — usu. used in pl. **4 :** any of several prob. hybrid cultivated cherries between sweet cherries and sour cherries in character — **duke·dom** \-dəm\ *n*

Du·kho·bor *var of* DOUKHOBOR

1**dul·cet** \'dəl-sət\ *adj* [ME *doucet*, fr. MF, fr. *douz* sweet, fr. L *dulcis*] **1** *archaic* **:** sweet to the taste **2 a :** sweet to the ear **:** MELODIOUS **b :** AGREEABLE, SOOTHING — **dul·cet·ly** *adv*

2**dulcet** *n* **:** a pipe-organ stop like the dulciana but an octave higher

dul·ci·ana \,dəl-sē-'an-ə\ *n* [NL, fr. ML, bassoon, fr. L *dulcis*] **:** a labial pipe-organ stop with a tone of soft sweet string quality

dul·ci·fy \'dəl-sə-,fī\ *vt* [LL *dulcificare*, fr. L *dulcis*] **1 :** to make sweet **2 :** to make agreeable **:** MOLLIFY

dul·ci·mer \'dəl-sə-mər\ *n* [ME *dowcemere*, fr. MF *doulcemer*, fr. OIt *dolcimelo*] **:** a wire-stringed instrument of trapezoidal shape played with light hammers held in the hands

dul·ci·nea \,dəl-sə-'nē-ə, -'sin-ē-ə\ *n* [Sp, fr. *Dulcinea* del Toboso, beloved of Don Quixote] **:** SWEETHEART

dull \'dəl\ *adj* [ME *dul*; akin to OE *dol* foolish and prob. to L *fumus* smoke — more at FUME] **1 :** mentally slow **:** STUPID **2 a :** slow in perception or sensibility **:** INSENSIBLE **b :** lacking zest or vivacity **:** LISTLESS **3 a :** slow in action **:** SLUGGISH **b :** marked by little business activity ⟨~ season⟩ **4 :** lacking sharpness of edge or point **5 :** lacking brilliance or luster **6 a :** not clear **:** INDISTINCT **b :** not resonant or ringing **7** *of a color* **:** low in saturation and low in lightness **8 :** CLOUDY, OVERCAST **9 :** TEDIOUS, UNINTERESTING — **dull** *vb* — **dull·ness** *or* **dul·ness** \'dəl-nəs\ *n* — **dul·ly** \'dəl-(l)ē\ *adv*

syn BLUNT, OBTUSE: DULL applies physically to an edge or point that has lost its original sharpness through use; figuratively it suggests loss of original or usual quickness, zest, or pungency; BLUNT applies to an edge or end not designed to be sharp or keen; it suggests innate or inherent lack of sharpness or quickness of feeling or perception; OBTUSE applies to the shape of something whose point is broader than a right angle; it suggests that which is inordinately blunt or insensitive in perception or imagination ⟨*obtuse* audience⟩ **syn** see in addition STUPID

dull·ard \'dəl-ərd\ *n* **:** a stupid person

dull·ish \'dəl-ish\ *adj* **:** somewhat dull

dulse \'dəls\ *n* [ScGael & IrGael *duileasg*; akin to W *delysg* dulse] **:** any of several coarse red seaweeds (esp. *Rhodymenia palmata*) found esp. in northern latitudes and used as a food condiment

du·ly \'d(y)ü-lē\ *adv* **:** in a due manner, time, or degree

du·ma \'dü-mə, -(,)mä\ *n* [Russ, of Gmc origin; akin to OE *dōm* judgment — more at DOOM] **:** a representative council in Russia; *specif* **:** the principal legislative assembly in czarist Russia

1**dumb** \'dəm\ *adj* [ME, fr. OE; akin to OHG *tumb* mute, OE *dēaf* deaf — more at DEAF] **1 :** destitute of the power of speech **2 :** naturally incapable of speech ⟨~ animals⟩ **3 :** not expressed in uttered words ⟨~ grief⟩ **4 a :** not willing to speak **b :** not having the usual accompaniment of speech or sound **5 :** lacking some usual attribute or accompaniment; *esp* **:** having no means of self-propulsion ⟨~ barge⟩ **6 :** STUPID, FOOLISH **syn** see STUPID — **dumb·ly** \'dəm-lē\ *adv* — **dumb·ness** *n*

2**dumb** *vt* **:** to make silent **:** DEADEN

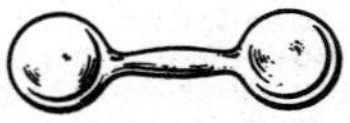

dumbbell

dumb·bell \'dəm-,bel\ *n* **1 :** a weight that consists of two identical spheres connected by a short bar serving as a handle and that is used usu. in pairs for calisthenic exercise **2 :** one that is dull and stupid **:** DUMMY

dumb·found *or* **dum·found** \,dəm-'fau̇nd\ *vt* [*dumb* + *-found* (as in *confound*)] **:** to strike dumb with astonishment **syn** see PUZZLE

dumb·found·er *or* **dum·found·er** \-'fau̇n-dər\ *vt* **:** DUMBFOUND

dumb show *n* **1 :** a part of a play presented in pantomime **2 :** signs and gestures without words **:** PANTOMIME

dumb·struck \'dəm-,strək\ *adj* **:** made silent by astonishment

dumb·wait·er \'dəm-'wāt-ər\ *n* **1 :** a portable serving table or stand **2 :** a small elevator used for conveying food and dishes or small goods from one story of a building to another

dum·dum \'dəm-,dəm\ *n* [*Dum-Dum*, India] **:** a soft-nosed bullet that expands upon hitting an object

1**dum·my** \'dəm-ē\ *n* **1 a :** one who is incapable of speaking **b :** one who is habitually silent **c :** one who is stupid **2 a :** the exposed hand in bridge played by the declarer in addition to his own hand **b :** a bridge player whose hand is a dummy **3 :** an imitation, copy, or likeness of something used as a substitute **4 :** one seeming to act for himself but in reality acting for or at the direction of another **5 :** something usu. mechanically operated that serves to replace or aid a human being's work **6 :** a pattern arrangement of matter to be reproduced esp. by printing

2**dummy** *adj* **1 a :** having the appearance of being real but lacking capacity to function **:** ARTIFICIAL **b :** existing in name only **:** FICTITIOUS **2 :** apparently acting for oneself while really acting for or at the direction of another ⟨a ~ director⟩

1**dump** \'dəmp\ *n* [prob. fr. D *domp* haze, fr. MD *damp*] **:** a dull gloomy state of mind **:** DESPONDENCY ⟨in the ~*s*⟩

2**dump** *vb* [perh. fr. D *dompen* to immerse, topple; akin to OE *dyppan* to dip — more at DIP] *vt* **1 a :** to let fall in a heap or mass **b :** to get rid of unceremoniously or irresponsibly **2** *slang* **:** to knock down **:** BEAT **3 :** to sell in quantity at a very low price; *specif* **:** to sell abroad at less than the market price at home ~ *vi* **1 :** to fall abruptly **:** PLUNGE **2 :** to dump refuse — **dump·er** *n*

3**dump** *n, often attrib* **1 a :** an accumulation of refuse or other discarded materials **b :** a place where such materials are dumped **2 a :** a quantity of reserve materials accumulated at one place **b :** a place where such materials are stored; *esp* **:** a place for the temporary storage of military supplies in the field **3 :** a disorderly, slovenly, or dilapidated place

dump·i·ly \'dəm-pə-lē\ *adv* **:** in a dumpy manner

dump·i·ness \-pē-nəs\ *n* **:** the quality or state of being dumpy

dump·ish \-pish\ *adj* **:** SAD, MELANCHOLY — **dump·ish·ly** *adv* — **dump·ish·ness** *n*

dump·ling \-pliŋ\ *n* [perh. alter. of *lump*] **1 a :** a small mass of leavened dough cooked by boiling or steaming **b :** a dessert made by wrapping fruit in biscuit dough and baking **2 :** something shapeless like a dumpling; *specif* **:** a short fat person or animal

dump truck *n* **:** a truck for transporting and dumping loose materials

dumpy *adj* [E dial. *dump* (lump)] **:** short and thick in build **:** SQUAT

dumpy level *n* **:** a surveyor's level with a short usu. invertible telescope rigidly fixed and rotating only in a horizontal plane

1**dun** \'dən\ *adj* [ME, fr. OE *dunn* — more at DUSK] **1 a :** having a dun color **b** *of a horse* **:** exhibiting reduced hair pigmentation **2 :** marked by dullness and drabness — **dun·ness** \'dən-nəs\ *n*

2**dun** *n* **1 :** a dun horse **2 :** a variable color averaging a nearly neutral slightly brownish dark gray **3 a :** a subadult mayfly; *also* **:** an artificial fly tied to imitate such an insect **b :** CADDIS FLY

3**dun** *vt* **dunned; dun·ning** [origin unknown] **1 :** to make persistent demands upon for payment **2 :** to plague or pester constantly

4dun *n* **1 :** one who duns **2 :** an urgent request; *esp* **:** a demand for payment

Dun·can Phyfe \ˌdəŋ-kən-ˈfīf\ *adj* [*Duncan Phyfe* †1854 Sc-Am cabinetmaker] **:** of, relating to, or constituting furniture designed and built by or in the style of Duncan Phyfe

dunce \ˈdən(t)s\ *n* [John *Duns* Scotus †*ab*1308 Sc scholastic theologian, whose once accepted writings were ridiculed in the 16th cent.] **:** a dull-witted and stupid person

dun·der·head \ˈdən-dər-ˌhed\ *n* [perh. fr. D *donder* thunder + E *head;* akin to OHG *thonar* thunder — more at THUNDER] **:** DUNCE, BLOCKHEAD — **dun·der·head·ed** \ˌdən-dər-ˈhed-əd\ *adj*

dun·drea·ries \ˌdən-ˈdri(ə)r-ēz\ *n pl, often cap* [Lord *Dundreary,* character in the play *Our American Cousin* (1858), by Tom Taylor] **:** long flowing side-whiskers

dune \ˈd(y)ün\ *n* [F, fr. OF, fr. MD; akin to OE *dūn* down — more at DOWN] **:** a hill or ridge of sand piled up by the wind

dung \ˈdəŋ\ *n* [ME, fr. OE; akin to ON *dyngja* manure pile, Lith *dengti* to cover] **1 :** the excrement of an animal **:** MANURE **2 :** something vile or loathsome — **dung** *vt* — **dungy** \ˈdəŋ-ē\ *adj*

dun·ga·ree \ˌdəŋ-gə-ˈrē\ *n* [Hindi *dūgrī*] **1 :** a heavy coarse durable cotton twill woven from colored yarns; *specif* **:** blue denim **2** *pl* **:** heavy cotton work clothes made usu. of blue dungaree

dung beetle *n* **:** a beetle (as a dorbeetle or tumblebug) that rolls balls of dung in which to lay eggs and on which the larvae feed

dun·geon \ˈdən-jən\ *n* [ME *donjon,* fr. MF, fr. (assumed) ML *dominion-, dominio,* fr. L *dominus* lord — more at DAME] **1 :** DONJON **2 :** a close dark prison or vault commonly underground

dung·hill \ˈdəŋ-ˌhil\ *n* **1 :** a heap of dung **2 :** a vile or degraded situation, condition, or thing

dunk \ˈdəŋk\ *vb* [PaG *dunke,* fr. MHG *dunken,* fr. OHG *dunkōn*] *vt* **1 :** to dip into liquid while eating **2 :** to dip or submerge temporarily in liquid ~ *vi* **:** to submerge oneself in water

Dun·ker \ˈdəŋ-kər\ *or* **Dun·kard** \-kərd\ *n* [PaG *Dunker,* fr. *dunke*] **:** a member of the Church of the Brethren or any of several other orig. German Baptist denominations practicing trine immersion, love feasts, simplicity of life, and avoidance of oaths

dun·lin \ˈdən-lən\ *n, pl* **dunlins** *or* **dunlin** [¹*dun* + *-lin* (alter. of *-ling*)] **:** a small widely distributed sandpiper (*Erolia alpina*) largely cinnamon to rusty brown above and white below

dun·nage \ˈdən-ij\ *n* [origin unknown] **1 :** loose materials used around a cargo to prevent damage; *also* **:** padding in a shipping container to protect contents against breakage **2 :** BAGGAGE

duo \ˈd(y)ü-(ˌ)ō\ *n* [It, fr. L, two] **1 :** DUET; *specif* **:** a composition for two performers at two pianos **2 :** PAIR

duo- *comb form* [L *duo*] **:** two

duo·de·cil·lion \ˌd(y)ü-(ˌ)ō-di-ˈsil-yən\ *n, often attrib* [L *duodec*im twelve + E *-illion* (as in *million*)] — see NUMBER table

duo·dec·i·mal \ˌd(y)ü-ə-ˈdes-ə-məl\ *adj* [L *duodecim* — more at DOZEN] **:** of, relating to, or proceeding by twelve or the scale of twelves — **duodecimal** *n*

duo·dec·i·mo \-ə-ˌmō\ *n* [L, abl. of *duodecimus* twelfth, fr. *duodecim*] **:** TWELVEMO

duoden- *or* **duodeno-** *comb form* [NL, fr. ML *duodenum*] **:** duodenum ⟨*duoden*itis⟩ ⟨*duodeno*gram⟩

du·o·de·nal \ˌd(y)ü-ə-ˈdēn-ᵊl, d(y)ü-ˈäd-ᵊn-əl\ *adj* **:** of or relating to the duodenum

du·o·de·num \ˌd(y)ü-ə-ˈdē-nəm, d(y)ü-ˈäd-ᵊn-əm\ *n, pl* **du·o·de·na** \-ˈdē-nə, -ᵊn-ə\ *or* **duodenums** [ME, fr. ML, fr. L *duodeni* twelve each, fr. *duodecim* twelve; fr. its length, about 12 fingers' breadth] **:** the first part of the small intestine extending from the pylorus to the jejunum

duo·logue \ˈd(y)ü-ə-ˌlȯg, -ˌläg\ *n* **:** a dialogue between two persons

du·op·o·ly \d(y)ü-ˈäp-ə-lē\ *n* [*duo-* + *-poly* (as in *monopoly*)] **:** an oligopoly limited to two sellers

du·op·so·ny \-ˈäp-sə-nē\ *n* [*duo-* + *-opsony* (as in *oligopsony*)] **:** an oligopsony limited to two buyers

dup \ˈdəp\ *vt* [contr. of *do up*] *archaic* **:** OPEN

1dupe \ˈd(y)üp\ *n* [F, fr. MF *duppe,* prob. alter. of *huppe* hoopoe] **:** one who is easily deceived or cheated **:** FOOL

2dupe *vt* **:** to make a dupe of **:** DECEIVE — **dup·er** *n*

syn DUPE, GULL, TRICK, HOAX mean to deceive by underhanded means. DUPE suggests unwariness in the person deluded; GULL stresses credulousness or readiness to be imposed on (as through greed) on the part of the victim; TRICK implies an intent to delude by means of a ruse or fraud but does not always imply a vicious intent; HOAX often applies to a tricking merely for fun or with the aim of demonstrating the extent of human gullibility; HOAX often implies, also, an elaborate or painstaking imposture

3dupe *n or vb* **:** DUPLICATE

dup·ery \ˈd(y)ü-p(ə-)rē\ *n* **:** the act or practice of duping **:** the condition of being duped

du·ple \ˈd(y)ü-pəl\ *adj* [L *duplus* double] **1 :** having two units or members **2 a :** marked by two beats per measure ⟨~ meter⟩ **b** *of rhythm* **:** consisting of a meter based on disyllabic feet

1du·plex \ˈd(y)ü-ˌpleks\ *adj* [L, fr. *duo* two + *-plex* -fold — more at TWO, SIMPLE] **1 :** DOUBLE, TWOFOLD; *specif* **:** having two parts that operate at the same time or in the same way ⟨a ~ lathe⟩ **2 :** allowing telecommunication in opposite directions simultaneously

2duplex *n* **:** something duplex; *esp* **:** a two-family house

duplex apartment *n* **:** an apartment having rooms on two floors

1du·pli·cate \ˈd(y)ü-pli-kət\ *adj* [ME, fr. L *duplicatus,* pp. of *duplicare* to double, fr. *duplic-, duplex*] **1 a :** consisting of or existing in two corresponding or identical parts or examples **b :** being the same as another **2 :** of or relating to a card game in which players play identical hands in order to compare scores

2duplicate *n* **1 :** either of two things that exactly resemble or correspond to each other; *specif* **:** a legal instrument essentially identical with another and having equal validity as an original **2 :** COPY, COUNTERPART **syn** see REPRODUCTION

3du·pli·cate \ˈd(y)ü-pli-ˌkāt\ *vt* **1 :** to make double or twofold **2 :** to make a duplicate of

du·pli·ca·tion \ˌd(y)ü-pli-ˈkā-shən\ *n* **1 a :** an act or process of duplicating **b :** the quality or state of being duplicated **2 :** DUPLICATE, COUNTERPART — **du·pli·ca·tive** \ˈd(y)ü-pli-ˌkāt-iv\ *adj*

du·pli·ca·tor \ˈd(y)ü-pli-ˌkāt-ər\ *n* **:** one that duplicates; *specif* **:** a machine for making copies of typed, drawn, or printed matter

du·plic·i·ty \d(y)ù-ˈplis-ət-ē\ *n* **1 :** doubleness of thought, speech, or action; *esp* **:** deception by pretending to feel and act one way while acting another **2 :** the quality or state of being double or twofold **3 :** the technically incorrect use of two or more distinct items (as claims, charges, or defenses) in a single legal action

du·ra·bil·i·ty \ˌd(y)ùr-ə-ˈbil-ət-ē\ *n* **:** the quality or state of being durable

du·ra·ble \ˈd(y)ùr-ə-bəl\ *adj* [ME, fr. MF, fr. L *durabilis,* fr. *durare* to last] **:** able to endure **syn** see LASTING — **du·ra·ble·ness** *n* — **du·ra·bly** \-blē\ *adv*

durable goods *n pl* **:** goods of relatively long usefulness

Du·ral·u·min \d(y)ù-ˈral-yə-mən, ˌd(y)ùr-ə-ˈlü-mən\ *trademark* — used for an alloy of aluminum, copper, manganese, and magnesium comparable in strength and hardness to soft steel

du·ra ma·ter \ˈd(y)ùr-ə-ˌmāt-ər, -ˌmät-\ *n* [ME, fr. ML, lit., hard mother] **:** the tough fibrous membrane that envelops the brain and spinal cord external to the arachnoid and pia mater

du·ra·men \d(y)ù-ˈrā-mən\ *n* [NL, fr. L, hardness, fr. *durare* to harden] **:** HEARTWOOD

du·rance \ˈd(y)ùr-ən(t)s\ *n* [MF, fr. *durer*] **:** IMPRISONMENT

du·ra·tion \d(y)ù-ˈrā-shən\ *n* **1 :** continuance in time **2 :** the time during which something exists or lasts

dur·bar \ˈdər-ˌbär\ *n* [Hindi *darbār,* fr. Per, fr. *dar* door + *bār* admission, audience] **1 :** court held by a native Indian prince **2 :** a formal reception marked by pledges of fealty given to a native Indian or African prince by his subjects or to the British monarch by native princes

du·ress \d(y)ù-ˈres\ *n* [ME *duresse,* fr. MF *duresce* hardness, severity, fr. L *duritia,* fr. *durus*] **1 :** forcible restraint or restriction **2 :** compulsion by threat; *specif* **:** unlawful constraint

Dur·ham \ˈdər-əm, ˈdə-rəm, ˈdùr-əm\ *n* [*Durham* co., England] **:** SHORTHORN

du·ri·an \ˈdùr-ē-ən, -ē-ˌän\ *n* [Malay] **1 :** a large oval tasty but foul-smelling fruit with a prickly rind **2 :** an East Indian tree (*Durio zibethinus*) of the silk-cotton family that bears durians

dur·ing \ˌd(y)ùr-iŋ\ *prep* [ME, fr. prp. of *duren* to last, fr. OF *durer,* fr. L *durare* to harden, endure, fr. *durus* hard; perh. akin to Skt *dāru* wood — more at TREE] **1 :** throughout the duration of ⟨swims every day ~ the summer⟩ **2 :** at a point in the course of **:** IN ⟨takes his vacation ~ July⟩

dur·mast \ˈdər-ˌmast\ *n* [perh. alter. of *dun mast,* fr. ¹*dun* + *mast*] **:** a European oak (*Quercus sessiliflora* or *Q. petraea*) valued esp. for its dark heavy tough elastic wood

durn \ˈdərn\ **durned** \ˈdərn(d)\ *var of* DARN, DARNED

du·ro \ˈdù(ə)r-(ˌ)ō\ *n* [Sp, short for *peso duro* hard peso] **:** a Spanish or Spanish American peso or silver dollar

du·roc \ˈd(y)ù(ə)r-ˌäk\ *n* [*Duroc,* 19th cent. Am stallion] *often cap* **:** any of a breed of large vigorous red American hogs

du·rom·e·ter \d(y)ù-ˈräm-ət-ər\ *n* **:** an instrument for measuring hardness

dur·ra \ˈdùr-ə\ *n* [Ar *dhurah*] **:** any of several grain sorghums widely grown in warm dry regions

du·rum wheat \ˌd(y)ùr-əm-, ˌdər-əm-, ˌdə-rəm-\ *n* [NL *durum,* fr. L, neut. of *durus* hard] **:** a wheat (*Triticum durum*) that yields a glutenous flour used esp. in macaroni and spaghetti

1dusk \ˈdəsk\ *adj* [ME *dosk,* alter. of OE *dox;* akin to L *fuscus* dark brown, OE *dunn* dun, *dūst* dust] **:** DUSKY

2dusk *vi* **:** to become dark ~ *vt* **:** to make dark or gloomy

3dusk *n* **1 :** the darker part of twilight esp. at night **2 :** GLOOM

dusk·i·ly \ˈdəs-kə-lē\ *adv* **:** in a dusky manner

dusk·i·ness \-kē-nəs\ *n* **:** the quality or state of being dusky

dusky \ˈdəs-kē\ *adj* **1 :** somewhat dark in color; *specif* **:** having dark skin **2 :** marked by slight or deficient light **:** SHADOWY

syn DUSKY, SWARTHY, TAWNY mean dark and dull. DUSKY implies a nearly complete absence of both light and color; SWARTHY and TAWNY apply to darkness of color only, SWARTHY to a shade verging on or suggesting blackness, TAWNY to a tan or yellowish brown color **syn** see in addition DARK

1dust \ˈdəst\ *n* [ME, fr. OE *dūst;* akin to L *furere* to rage, Gk *thyein*] **1 :** fine dry pulverized particles of earth or other matter **2 :** the particles into which something disintegrates **3 a :** something worthless **b :** a state of humiliation **4 a :** the earth esp. as a place of burial **b :** the surface of the ground **5 a :** a cloud of dust **b :** CONFUSION, DISTURBANCE **6** *archaic* **:** a single particle (as of earth) **7** *Brit* **:** sweepings or other refuse ready for collection — **dust·less** \-ləs\ *adj* — **dust·like** \-ˌlīk\ *adj*

2dust *vt* **1** *archaic* **:** to make dusty **2 a :** to make free of dust **b :** to prepare to use again **3 a :** to sprinkle with fine particles **b :** to sprinkle in the form of dust ~ *vi* **1** *of a bird* **:** to work dust into the feathers **2 :** to remove dust **3 :** to give off dust

dust·bin \ˈdəs(t)-ˌbin\ *n, Brit* **:** a trash or garbage can

dust bowl *n* **:** a region that suffers from prolonged droughts and dust storms — **dust bowl·er** \-ˌbō-lər\ *n*

dust devil *n* **:** a small whirlwind containing sand or dust

dust·er \ˈdəs-tər\ *n* **1 :** one that removes dust **2 a :** a lightweight overgarment to protect clothing from dust **b :** a dress-length housecoat **3 :** one that scatters fine particles; *specif* **:** a device for applying insecticidal or fungicidal dusts to crops

dust·i·ly \ˈdəs-tə-lē\ *adv* **:** in a dusty manner

dust·i·ness \-tē-nəs\ *n* **:** the quality or state of being dusty

dust jacket *n* **:** a paper cover for a book

dust·man \ˈdəs(t)-mən\ *n, Brit* **:** a trash or garbage collector

dust·pan \ˈdəs(t)-ˌpan\ *n* **:** a shovel-shaped pan for sweepings

dust storm *n* **1 :** a dust-laden whirlwind that moves across an arid region and is usu. associated with hot dry air and attended by high electrical tension **2 :** strong winds bearing clouds of dust

dust·up \ˈdəs-ˌtəp\ *n* **:** QUARREL, ROW

dusty \ˈdəs-tē\ *adj* **1 :** filled, covered, or abounding with dust **2 :** consisting of dust **:** POWDERY **3 :** resembling dust

dusty miller *n* **:** any of several plants (as a mullein pink) having ashy-gray or white tomentose leaves

dutch \ˈdəch\ *adv, often cap* **:** with each person paying his own way

1Dutch \ˈdəch\ *adj* [ME *Duch,* fr. MD *duutsch;* akin to OHG *diutisc* German, Goth *thiudisko* gentile, *thiuda* people, Oscan *touto* city] **1 a** *archaic* **:** of or relating to the Germanic peoples of Germany, Austria, Switzerland, and the Low Countries **b :** of or relating to the Netherlands or its inhabitants **c** *slang* **:** GERMAN **2 a** *archaic* **:** of, relating to, or in any of the Germanic languages of Germany, Austria, Switzerland, and the Low Countries **b :** of, relating to, or in the Dutch of the Netherlands **3 :** of or relating to the Pennsylvania Dutch or their language — **Dutch·ly** *adv*

2Dutch *n* **1 a** *archaic* (1) **:** any of the Germanic languages of Germany, Austria, Switzerland, and the Low Countries (2) **:** GERMAN 2

b : the Germanic language of the Netherlands **2 Dutch** *pl* **a** *archaic* **:** the Germanic peoples of Germany, Austria, Switzerland, and the Low Countries **b** *archaic* **:** GERMANS 1a, 1b **c :** the people of the Netherlands **3 :** PENNSYLVANIA DUTCH **4** *slang* **:** DANDER ⟨his *Dutch* is up⟩ **5 :** DISFAVOR, TROUBLE ⟨in *Dutch* with his boss⟩

Dutch cheese *n* **:** COTTAGE CHEESE

Dutch clover *n* **:** WHITE DUTCH CLOVER

Dutch courage *n* **:** courage due to intoxicants

Dutch door *n* **:** a door divided horizontally so that the lower or upper part can be shut separately

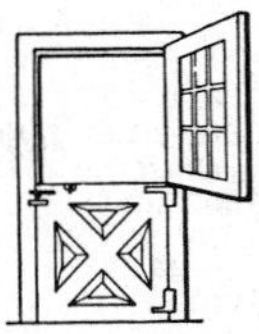

Dutch door

Dutch elm disease *n* **:** a disease of elms caused by a fungus (*Ceratostomella ulmi*) and characterized by yellowing of the foliage, defoliation, and death

Dutch hoe *n* **:** SCUFFLE HOE

dutch·man \'dəch-mən\ *n* **1** *cap* **a** *archaic* **:** a member of any of the Germanic peoples of Germany, Austria, Switzerland, and the Low Countries **b :** a native or inhabitant of the Netherlands **c :** a person of Dutch descent **d** *slang* **:** GERMAN 1a, 1b **2 :** a device for hiding or counteracting structural defects

Dutch·man's–breech·es \,dəch-mənz-'brich-əz\ *n pl but sing or pl in constr* **:** a delicate spring-flowering herb (*Dicentra cucullaria*) of the fumitory family occurring in the eastern U.S. and having finely divided leaves and cream-white double-spurred flowers

Dutch oven *n* **1 :** a metal shield for roasting before an open fire **2 :** a brick oven in which cooking is done by the preheated walls **3 a :** a cast-iron kettle with a tight cover that is used for baking in an open fire **b :** a heavy pot with a tight-fitting domed cover

Dutch treat *n* **:** a treat for which each person pays his own way

Dutch uncle *n* **:** one who admonishes sternly and bluntly

du·te·ous \'d(y)üt-ē-əs\ *adj* [irreg. fr. *duty*] **:** DUTIFUL, OBEDIENT

du·ti·able \'d(y)üt-ē-ə-bəl\ *adj* **:** subject to a duty ⟨~ imports⟩

du·ti·ful \'d(y)üt-i-fəl\ *adj* **1 :** filled with or motivated by a sense of duty ⟨a ~ son⟩ **2 :** proceeding from or expressive of a sense of duty ⟨~ affection⟩ — **du·ti·ful·ly** \-fə-lē\ *adv* — **du·ti·ful·ness** *n*

du·ty \'d(y)üt-ē\ *n* [ME *duete*, fr. AF *dueté*, fr. OF *deu* due] **1 :** conduct due to parents and superiors **:** RESPECT **2 a :** the action required by one's position or occupation **b :** assigned service or business; *specif* **:** active military service **3 a :** a moral or legal obligation **b :** the force of moral obligation **4 :** TAX; *esp* **:** a tax on imports **5 a** (1) **:** the work done by a machine under given conditions (2) **:** a measure of efficiency expressed in terms of the amount of work done in relation to the energy consumed **b** (1) **:** the service required (as of an electrical machine) under specified conditions of load and rest (2) **:** USE, SERVICE **6 :** the quantity of irrigation water required to fill the needs of the area of a particular crop **syn** see FUNCTION, OBLIGATION, TASK

du·um·vir \d(y)ü-'əm-vər\ *n* [L, fr. *duum* (gen. of *duo* two) + *vir* man] **1 :** one of two Roman officers or magistrates constituting a board or court **2 :** one of two men jointly holding power

du·um·vi·rate \-və-rət\ *n* **1 :** two people associated in high office **2 :** government or control by two people

duve·tyn \'d(y)ü-və-,tēn, 'dəv-,tēn\ *n* [F *duvetine*, fr. *duvet* down, fr. MF, alter. of (assumed) MF *dumet*, dim. of OF *dun*, *dum* down, fr. ON *dūnn* — more at DOWN] **:** a smooth lustrous velvety fabric

1dwarf \'dwȯ(ə)rf\ *n, pl* **dwarfs** \'dwȯ(ə)rfs\ *or* **dwarves** \'dwȯ(ə)rvz\ *often attrib* [ME *dwerg*, *dwerf*, fr. OE *dweorg*, *dweorh*; akin to OHG *twerg* dwarf] **1 :** a person much below the usual in stature **2 :** an animal or plant much below normal size **3 :** a small legendary manlike being usu. misshapen and ugly and skilled as an artificer **4 :** a star (as the sun) of ordinary or low luminosity and relatively small mass and size — **dwarf·ish** \'dwȯr-fish\ *adj* — **dwarf·ness** *n*

2dwarf *vt* **1 :** to make into a dwarf **2 :** to stunt the development of **3 :** to cause to appear smaller **~** *vi* **:** to become smaller

dwell \'dwel\ *vi* **dwelt** \'dwelt\ *or* **dwelled** \'dweld, 'dwelt\ **dwell·ing** [ME *dwellen*, fr. OE *dwellan* to go astray, hinder; akin to OHG *twellen* to tarry] **1 :** to remain for a time **2 a :** to live as a resident **:** RESIDE **b :** EXIST, LIE **3 a :** to keep the attention directed **:** LINGER **b :** to expatiate insistently — **dwell·er** *n*

dwell·ing *n* **:** a building or other shelter in which people live **:** HOUSE

dwin·dle \'dwin-dᵊl\ *vb* **dwin·dling** \-(d)liŋ, -dᵊl-iŋ\ [prob. freq. of *dwine* (to waste away)] *vi* **:** to become steadily less **:** SHRINK **~** *vt* **:** to make steadily less **syn** see DECREASE

DX \(')dē-'eks\ *n* **:** DISTANCE — used of long-distance radio transmission

dy- *or* **dyo-** *comb form* [LL, fr. Gk, fr. *dyo*] **:** two ⟨*dy*archy⟩

dy·ad \'dī-,ad, -əd\ *n* [LL *dyad-*, *dyas*, fr. Gk, fr. *dyo*] **1 :** PAIR **2 :** a meiotic chromosome after separation of the two homologous members of a tetrad — **dy·ad·ic** \dī-'ad-ik\ *adj*

Dy·ak *var of* DAYAK

dy·ar·chy \'dī-,är-kē\ *n* **:** a government with two sets of authorities

dyb·buk \'dib-ək\ *n* [LHeb *dibbūq*] **:** a wandering soul believed in Jewish folklore to enter and possess a person

1dye \'dī\ *n* [ME *dehe*, fr. OE *dēah*, *dēag*; akin to L *fumus* smoke] **1 :** color from dyeing **2 :** a soluble or insoluble coloring matter

2dye *vb* **dyed**; **dye·ing** *vt* **1 :** to impart a new and often permanent color to esp. by impregnating with a dye **2 :** to impart (a color) by dyeing **~** *vi* **:** to take up or impart color in dyeing — **dy·er** \'dī(-ə)r\ *n*

dyed–in–the–wool \,dīd-ᵊn-thə-'wu̇l\ *adj* **:** UNCOMPROMISING

dy·er's–broom \,dī(-ə)rz-'brüm, -'bru̇m\ *n* **:** WOODWAXEN

dy·er's–weed \'dī(-ə)rz-,wēd\ *n* **:** any of several dye-yielding plants

dye·stuff \'dī-,stəf\ *n* **:** DYE 2

dye·weed \'dī-,wēd\ *n* **1 :** WOODWAXEN **2 :** a small American weedy composite herb (*Eclipta alba*) with yellowish white flowers

dye·wood \-,wu̇d\ *n* **:** a wood (as logwood or fustic) from which coloring matter is extracted for dyeing

dying *pres part of* DIE

dyke *var of* DIKE

dynam- *or* **dynamo-** *comb form* [prob. fr. F, fr. Gk, fr. *dynamis*] **:** power ⟨*dynamo*graph⟩

1dy·nam·ic \dī-'nam-ik\ *adj* [F *dynamique*, fr. Gk *dynamikos* powerful, fr. *dynamis* power, fr. *dynasthai* to be able] **1 a :** of or relating to physical force or energy **b :** of or relating to dynamics **:** ACTIVE **2 a :** marked by continuous usu. productive activity or change **b :** marked by energy **:** FORCEFUL — **dy·nam·i·cal** \-i-kəl\ *adj* — **dy·nam·i·cal·ly** \-i-k(ə-)lē\ *adv*

2dynamic *n* **1 a :** DYNAMICS 2 **b :** a dynamic force **2 :** DYNAMICS 3

dy·nam·ics \dī-'nam-iks\ *n pl but sing or pl in constr* **1 :** a branch of mechanics that deals with forces and their relation primarily to the motion but sometimes also to the equilibrium of bodies of matter **2 :** the driving physical, moral, or intellectual forces of any area or the laws relating to them **3 :** the pattern of change or growth of an object or phenomenon **4 :** variation and contrast in force or intensity (as in music)

dy·na·mism \'dī-nə-,miz-əm\ *n* **1 a :** a theory that explains the universe in terms of forces and their interplay **b :** DYNAMICS 3 **2 :** a dynamic or expansionist quality — **dy·na·mist** \-məst\ *n* — **dy·na·mis·tic** \,dī-nə-'mis-tik\ *adj*

1dy·na·mite \'dī-nə-,mīt\ *n* **1 :** a blasting explosive that is made of nitroglycerin absorbed in a porous material and that sometimes contains ammonium nitrate or cellulose nitrate; *also* **:** a blasting explosive that contains no nitroglycerin **2 :** one that has explosive force — **dy·na·mit·ic** \,dī-nə-'mit-ik\ *adj*

2dynamite *vt* **1 :** to blow up with dynamite **2 :** to cause the complete failure or destruction of — **dy·na·mit·er** *n*

dy·na·mo \'dī-nə-,mō\ *n* [short for *dynamoelectric machine*] **1 :** GENERATOR 3 **2 :** a forceful energetic individual

dy·na·mo·elec·tric \,dī-nə-mō-ə-'lek-trik\ *adj* [ISV] **:** relating to the conversion by induction of mechanical energy into electrical energy or vice versa

dy·na·mom·e·ter \,dī-nə-'mäm-ət-ər\ *n* [F *dynamomètre*, fr. *dynam-* + *-mètre* -meter] **1 :** an instrument for measuring mechanical force **2 :** an apparatus for measuring mechanical power (as of an engine) — **dy·na·mo·met·ric** \,dī-nə-mō-'me-trik\ *adj* — **dy·na·mom·e·try** \,dī-nə-'mäm-ə-trē\ *n*

dy·na·mo·tor \'dī-nə-,mōt-ər\ *n* [*dynamo* + *motor*] **:** a motor generator combining the electric motor and generator

dy·nast \'dī-,nast, -nəst\ *n* [L *dynastes*, fr. Gk *dynastēs*, fr. *dynasthai* to be able, have power] **:** RULER

dy·nas·tic \dī-'nas-tik\ *adj* **:** of or relating to a dynasty — **dy·nas·ti·cal·ly** \-ti-k(ə-)lē\ *adv*

dy·nas·ty \'dī-nə-stē, -,nas-tē, *esp Brit* 'din-ə-stē\ *n* **1 :** a succession of rulers of the same line of descent **2 :** a powerful group or family that maintains its position for a considerable time

dy·na·tron \'dī-nə-,trän\ *n* [Gk *dynamis* power] **:** a vacuum tube in which the secondary emission of electrons from the plate results in a decrease in the plate current as the plate voltage increases

dyne \'dīn\ *n* [F, fr. Gk *dynamis*] **:** the unit of force in the cgs system equal to the force that would give a free mass of one gram an acceleration of one centimeter per second per second

dy·node \'dī-,nōd\ *n* [Gk *dynamis*] **:** an electrode in an electron tube that functions to produce secondary emission of electrons

dys- *prefix* [ME *dis-* bad, difficult, fr. MF & L; MF *dis-*, fr. L *dys-*, fr. Gk; akin to OE *tō-*, *te-* apart, Skt *dus-* bad, difficult] **1 :** abnormal ⟨*dys*hidrosis⟩ **2 :** difficult ⟨*dys*phagia⟩ — compare EU- **3 :** impaired ⟨*dys*function⟩ **4 :** bad ⟨*dys*logistic⟩ — compare EU-

dys·cra·sia \dis-'krā-zh(ē-)ə\ *n* [NL, fr. ML, bad mixture of humors, fr. Gk *dyskrasia*, fr. *dys-* + *krasis* mixture — more at CRASIS] **:** an abnormal condition of the body

dys·en·ter·ic \,dis-ᵊn-'ter-ik\ *adj* **:** of or relating to dysentery

dys·en·tery \'dis-ᵊn-,ter-ē\ *n* [ME *dissenterie*, fr. L *dysenteria*, fr. Gk, fr. *dys-* + *enteron* intestine — more at INTER-] **1 :** a disease characterized by severe diarrhea with passage of mucus and blood and usu. caused by infection **2 :** DIARRHEA

dys·func·tion \(')dis-'fəŋ(k)-shən\ *n* **:** impaired or abnormal functioning — **dys·func·tion·al** \-shnəl, -shən-ᵊl\ *adj*

dys·gen·ic \(')dis-'jen-ik\ *adj* **1 :** detrimental to the hereditary qualities of a stock **2 :** biologically defective or deficient

dys·gen·ics \-iks\ *n pl but sing in constr* **:** the study of racial degeneration

dys·lex·ia \dis-'lek-sē-ə\ *n* [NL, fr. *dys-* + Gk *lexis* word, speech] **:** a disturbance of the ability to read

dys·lo·gis·tic \,dis-lə-'jis-tik\ *adj* [*dys-* + *-logistic* (as in *eulogistic*)] **:** UNCOMPLIMENTARY — **dys·lo·gis·ti·cal·ly** \-ti-k(ə-)lē\ *adv*

dys·men·or·rhea \(,)dis-,men-ə-'rē-ə\ *n* [NL] **:** painful menstruation — **dys·men·or·rhe·al** \-'rē-əl\ *or* **dys·men·or·rhe·ic** \-'rē-ik\ *adj*

dys·pep·sia \dis-'pep-shə, -sē-ə\ *n* [L, fr. Gk, fr. *dys-* + *pepsis* digestion, fr. *peptein*, *pessein* to cook, digest] **:** INDIGESTION

1dys·pep·tic \-'pep-tik\ *adj* **1 :** relating to or having dyspepsia **2 :** GLOOMY, CROSS — **dys·pep·ti·cal·ly** \-ti-k(ə-)lē\ *adv*

2dyspeptic *n* **:** a person having dyspepsia

dys·pha·gia \dis-'fā-j(ē-)ə\ *n* [NL] **:** difficulty in swallowing — **dys·phag·ic** \-'faj-ik\ *adj*

dys·pha·sia \dis-'fā-zh(ē-)ə\ *n* [NL] **:** loss of or deficiency in the power to use or understand language caused by injury to or disease of the brain — **dys·pha·sic** \-'fā-zik\ *n or adj*

dys·pho·nia \dis-'fō-nē-ə\ *n* [NL] **:** defective use of the voice — **dys·phon·ic** \-'fän-ik\ *adj*

dys·pho·ria \dis-'fōr-ē-ə, -'fȯr-\ *n* [NL, fr. Gk, fr. *dysphoros* hard to bear, fr. *dys-* + *pherein* to bear — more at BEAR] **:** a state of feeling unwell or unhappy — **dys·phor·ic** \-'fȯr-ik, -'fär-\ *adj*

dys·pla·sia \dis-'plā-zh(ē-)ə\ *n* [NL] **:** abnormal growth or development (as of organs or cells); *broadly* **:** abnormal anatomic structure due to such growth — **dys·plas·tic** \-'plas-tik\ *adj*

dys·pnea \'dis(p)-nē-ə, dis(p)-'nē-ə\ *n* [L *dyspnoea*, fr. Gk *dyspnoia*, fr. *dyspnoos* short of breath, fr. *dys-* + *pnein*, to breathe] **:** difficult or labored respiration — **dys·pne·ic** \dis(p)-'nē-ik\ *adj*

dys·pro·si·um \dis-'prō-zē-əm, -zh(ē-)əm\ *n* [NL, fr. Gk *dysprositos* hard to get at, fr. *dys-* + *prositos* approachable, fr. *prosienai* to approach, fr. *pros-* + *ienai* to go] **:** an element of the rare-earth group that forms highly magnetic compounds — see ELEMENT table

dys·tro·phic \dis-'träf-ik, -'trō-fik\ *adj* **1 :** relating to or caused by faulty nutrition **2** *of a lake* **:** brownish with much dissolved humic matter, a small bottom fauna, and a high oxygen consumption

dys·tro·phy \'dis-trə-fē\ *n* [NL *dystrophia*, fr. *dys-* + *-trophia* -trophy] **:** imperfect nutrition; *specif* **:** any of several neuromuscular disorders — compare MUSCULAR DYSTROPHY

dys·uria \dish-'(y)u̇r-ē-ə, dis-'yu̇r-\ *n* [NL, fr. Gk *dysouria*, fr. *dys-* + *-ouria* -uria] **:** difficult or painful discharge of urine

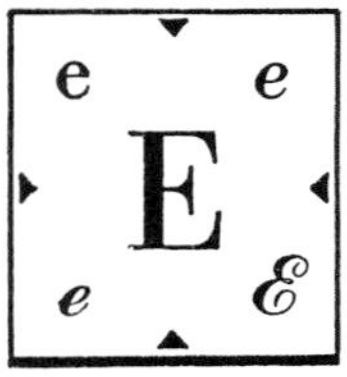

e \'ē\ *n, often cap, often attrib* **1 a :** the fifth letter of the English alphabet **b :** a graphic representation of this letter **c :** a speech counterpart of orthographic *e* **2 :** the tone E **3 :** a graphic device for reproducing the letter *e* **4 :** one designated *e* esp. as the fifth in order or class; *specif* **:** the base of the system of natural logarithms having the approximate numerical value 2.71828 **5 a :** a grade rating a student's work as poor and usu. constituting a conditional pass **b :** one graded or rated with an E **6 :** something shaped like the letter E

e- *prefix* [ME, fr. OF & L; OF, out, forth, away, fr. L, fr. *ex-*] **1 a :** not ⟨*e*carinate⟩ **b :** missing **:** absent ⟨*e*dental⟩ **2 :** out **:** on the outside ⟨*e*scribe⟩ **3 :** thoroughly ⟨*e*vaporize⟩ **4 :** forth ⟨*e*radiate⟩ **5 :** away ⟨*e*luvium⟩

1**each** \'ēch\ *adj* [ME *ech*, fr. OE *ǣlc;* akin to OHG *iogilīh* each; both fr. a prehistoric WGmc compound whose first and second constituents respectively are represented by OE *ā* always and by OE *gelīc* alike] **:** being one of two or more distinct individuals having a similar relation and often constituting an aggregate

2**each** *pron* **1 :** each one **2 :** all considered one by one

3**each** *adv* **:** to or for each **:** APIECE

each other *pron* **:** each of two or more in reciprocal action or relation ⟨looked at *each other* in surprise⟩

ea·ger \'ē-gər\ *adj* [ME *egre*, fr. OF *aigre*, fr. L *acer*] **1 a** *archaic* **:** KEEN, SHARP **b** *obs* **:** SOUR **2 :** marked by keen, enthusiastic, or impatient desire or interest — **ea·ger·ly** *adv* — **ea·ger·ness** *n*

syn AVID, KEEN, ANXIOUS, ATHIRST: EAGER implies ardor and enthusiasm and sometimes impatience at delay or restraint; AVID adds to EAGER the implication of insatiability or greed; KEEN suggests intensity of interest and quick responsiveness in action; ANXIOUS emphasizes fear of frustration or failure or disappointment; ATHIRST stresses yearning but not, as AVID does, insatiability nor does it connote, as EAGER and KEEN do, readiness for action

eager beaver *n* **:** one who is unduly zealous in performing his assigned duties and in volunteering for more

ea·gle \'ē-gəl\ *n* [ME *egle*, fr. OF *aigle*, fr. L *aquila*] **1 :** any of various large diurnal birds of prey of the accipiter family noted for their strength, size, graceful figure, keenness of vision, and powers of flight **2 :** any of various esp. emblematic or symbolic figures or representations of an eagle: as **a :** the standard of the ancient Romans **b :** the seal or standard of a nation (as the U.S.) having an eagle as emblem **c :** one of a pair of silver insignia of rank worn by a military colonel or a naval captain **3 :** a ten-dollar gold coin of the U.S. bearing an eagle on the reverse **4 :** a golf score of two strokes less than par on a hole — compare BIRDIE

ea·glet \'ē-glət\ *n* **:** a young eagle

ea·gre \'ē-gər\ *n* [origin unknown] **:** a tidal bore

eal·dor·man \'al-dər-mən\ *n* [OE — more at ALDERMAN] **:** the chief officer in a shire or other district in Anglo-Saxon England

-ean — see -AN

1**ear** \'i(ə)r\ *n* [ME *ere*, fr. OE *ēare;* akin to OHG *ōra* ear, L *auris*, Gk *ous*] **1 a :** the characteristic vertebrate organ of hearing and equilibrium consisting in the typical mammal of a sound-collecting outer ear separated by a membranous drum from a sound-transmitting middle ear that in turn is separated from a sensory inner ear by membranous fenestrae **b :** any of various organs capable of detecting vibratory motion **2 :** the external ear of man and most mammals **3 a :** the sense or act of hearing **b :** acuity of hearing **c :** sensitivity to musical tone and pitch **4 :** something resembling in shape or position a mammalian ear: as **a :** a projecting part (as a lug or handle) **b :** either of a pair of tufts of lengthened feathers on the head of some birds **5 a :** sympathetic attention **b :** AWARENESS, NOTICE

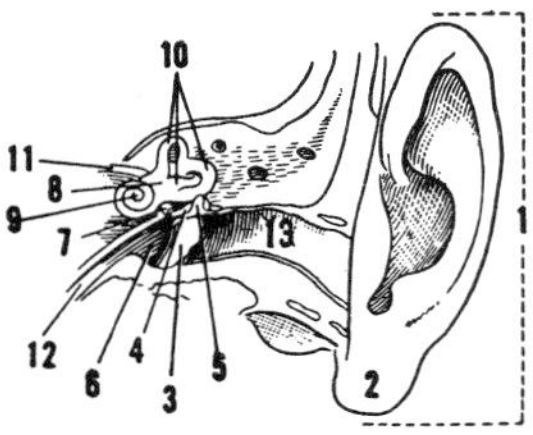

ear: *1* pinna, *2* lobe, *3* tympanic membrane, *4* incus, *5* malleus, *6* tympanum, *7* stapes, *8* vestibule, *9* cochlea, *10* semicircular canals, *11* auditory nerve, *12* eustachian tube, *13* auditory meatus

2**ear** *n* [ME *er*, fr. OE *ēar;* akin to OHG *ahir* ear, OE *ecg* edge — more at EDGE] **:** the fruiting spike of a cereal (as Indian corn) including both the seeds and protective structures — **ear** *vi*

ear·ache \'i(ə)r-,āk\ *n* **:** an ache or pain in the ear

ear·drop \'i(ə)r-,dräp\ *n* **:** EARRING; *esp* **:** one with a pendant

ear·drum \-,drəm\ *n* **:** TYMPANIC MEMBRANE

eared \'i(ə)rd\ *adj* **1 :** having ears **2 :** having external ears

eared seal *n* **:** any of various seals constituting the eared-seal family (Otariidae), including the sea lions and fur seals, and having independent mobile hind limbs and small well-developed external ears

ear·ful \'i(ə)r-,fu̇l\ *n* **:** an outpouring of news or gossip

ear·ing \'i(ə)r-iŋ\ *n* [perh. fr. 1*ear*] **:** a line used to fasten a corner of a sail to the yard or gaff or to haul a reef cringle to the yard

earl \'ər(-ə)l\ *n* [ME *erl*, fr. OE *eorl* warrior, nobleman; akin to ON *jarl* warrior, nobleman] **:** a member of the third grade of the British peerage ranking below a marquess and above a viscount

ear·less seal \,i(ə)r-ləs-\ *n* **:** any of various seals constituting the earless-seal family (Phocidae), including the hair seals, and having the hind limbs reduced to swimming flippers and no external ears

ear·li·ness \'ər-lē-nəs\ *n* **:** the quality or state of being early

earl marshal *n* **:** a great officer of state in England serving chiefly as a royal attendant on great ceremonial occasions, as marshal of state processions, and as head of the College of Arms

ear·lobe \'i(ə)r-,lōb\ *n* **:** the pendent part of the ear of man or some fowls

1**ear·ly** \'ər-lē\ *adv* [ME *erly*, fr. OE *ǣrlīce*, fr. *ǣr* early, soon — more at ERE] **1 :** near the beginning of a period of time or of a process or series **2 a :** before the usual time **b** *archaic* **:** SOON **c :** sooner than related forms

2**early** *adj* **1 a :** of, relating to, or occurring near the beginning of a period of time or of a development or series **b** (1) **:** distant in past time (2) **:** PRIMITIVE **2 a :** occurring before the usual time **b :** occurring in the near future **c :** maturing or producing sooner than related forms

1**ear·mark** \'i(ə)r-,märk\ *n* **1 :** a mark of identification on the ear of an animal **2 :** a distinguishing or identifying mark

2**earmark** *vt* **1 :** to mark with or as if with an earmark **2 :** to designate for a specific owner, use, or destination

ear·muff \-,məf\ *n* **:** one of a pair of ear coverings connected by a flexible band and worn as protection against cold

1**earn** \'ərn\ *vt* [ME *ernen*, fr. OE *earnian*] **1 :** to receive as return for work done or services rendered **2 :** to come to be duly worthy of or entitled or suited to **syn** see GET — **earn·er** *n*

2**earn** *vb* [prob. alter. of *yearn*] *obs* **:** YEARN, GRIEVE

1**ear·nest** \'ər-nəst\ *n* [ME *ernest*, fr. OE *eornost;* akin to OHG *ernust* earnest] **:** a serious and intent mental state ⟨in ~⟩

2**earnest** *adj* **1 :** characterized by or proceeding from an intense and serious state of mind **2 :** GRAVE, IMPORTANT **syn** see SERIOUS — **ear·nest·ly** *adv* — **ear·nest·ness** \-nəst-nəs, -nə-snəs\ *n*

3**earnest** *n* [ME *ernes*, *ernest*, fr. OF *erres*, pl. of *erre* earnest, fr. L *arra*, short for *arrabo*, fr. Gk *arrhabōn*, fr. Heb *'ērābhōn*] **1 :** something of value given by a buyer to a seller to bind a bargain **2 :** a token of what is to come **:** PLEDGE

earn·ings \'ər-niŋz\ *n pl* **1 :** something earned **2 :** the balance of revenue after deduction of related costs and expenses

ear·phone \'i(ə)r-,fōn\ *n* **:** a device that converts electrical energy into sound waves and is worn over or inserted into the ear

ear·ring \'i(ə)r-(,)iŋ, -,riŋ\ *n* **:** an ornament for the earlobe

ear shell *n* **:** ABALONE

ear·shot \'i(ə)r-,shät\ *n* **:** the range within which the unaided voice may be heard

ear·split·ting \-,split-iŋ\ *adj* **:** distressingly loud or shrill

1**earth** \'ərth\ *n* [ME *erthe*, fr. OE *eorthe;* akin to OHG *erda* earth, Gk *eraze* to the ground] **1 :** the fragmental material composing part of the surface of the globe; *esp* **:** cultivable soil **2 :** the sphere of mortal life as distinguished from spheres of spirit life — compare HEAVEN, HELL **3 a :** areas of land as distinguished from sea and air **b :** the solid footing formed of soil **:** GROUND **4** *often cap* **:** the planet upon which we live, third in order of distance from the sun — see PLANET table **5 a :** the people of the planet Earth **b :** the mortal body of man **c :** the pursuits and interests and pleasures of earthly life as distinguished from spiritual concerns **6 :** the lair of a burrowing animal **7 :** a difficultly reducible metallic oxide (as alumina) formerly classed as an element

syn EARTH, WORLD, UNIVERSE mean the entire area in which man thinks of himself as living. EARTH is the usual designation of the material global body, the planet of the sun, but it often means the immediate scene of present existence in contrast to the unastronomical regions heaven and hell; WORLD is often used as equal to EARTH, but may apply to the whole space present to experience including the earth and all visible celestial bodies; UNIVERSE denotes the entire system of created things and physical phenomena regarded as a unit in its arrangement and operation

— **on earth :** among many possibilities — used as an intensive

2**earth** *vt* **1 :** to drive to hiding in the earth **2 :** to draw soil about (plants) ~ *vi, of a hunted animal* **:** to hide in the ground

earth·born \-,bȯ(ə)rn\ *adj* **1 :** born on this earth **:** MORTAL **2 :** arising from the earth or from earthly life ⟨~ cares⟩

earth·bound \-,bau̇nd\ *adj* **1 a :** fast in or to the soil ⟨~ roots⟩ **b :** restricted to land or to the surface of the earth **2 a :** bound by earthly interests **b :** UNIMAGINATIVE, PEDESTRIAN

earth·en \'ər-thən, -*th*ən\ *adj* **1 :** made of earth **2 :** EARTHLY

earth·en·ware \-,wa(ə)r, -,we(ə)r\ *n* **:** ware made of slightly porous opaque clay fired at low heat

earth·i·ness \'ər-thē-nəs, -*th*ē-\ *n* **:** the quality or state of being earthy

earth·li·ness \'ərth-lē-nəs\ *n* **:** the quality or state of being earthly

earth·ling \-liŋ\ *n* **1 :** an inhabitant of the earth **2 :** WORLDLING

earth·ly \'ərth-lē\ *adj* **1 a :** characteristic of or belonging to this earth **b :** relating to man's actual life on this earth **2 :** POSSIBLE

syn TERRESTRIAL, MUNDANE, WORLDLY: EARTHLY is used chiefly in opposition to *heavenly* ⟨*earthly* love⟩ TERRESTRIAL in opposition to *celestial*, or in distinction to *marine*, *aerial*, or *arboreal;* MUNDANE and WORLDLY both imply a relation to the immediate concerns and activities of men, MUNDANE used in opposition esp. to *eternal* ⟨*mundane* discussion of finances⟩ WORLDLY in opposition to *spiritual* ⟨*worldly* satisfactions⟩

earth·quake \-,kwāk\ *n* **:** a shaking or trembling of the earth that is volcanic or tectonic in origin

earth science *n* **:** any of the sciences that deal with the earth or with one or more of its parts

earth·shak·ing \-,shā-kiŋ\ *adj* **:** of fundamental importance

earth·shine \-,shīn\ *n* **:** sunlight reflected by the earth that illuminates the dark part of the moon — called also *earthlight*

earth·star \-,stär\ *n* **:** a globose fungus (genus *Geastrum*) with a double wall whose outer layer splits into the shape of a star

earth·ward \'ərth-wərd\ *or* **earth·wards** \-wərdz\ *adv* **:** toward the earth

earth·work \-,wərk\ *n* **1 :** an embankment or other construction made of earth; *esp* **:** one used as a field fortification **2 :** the operations connected with excavations and embankments of earth

earth·worm \-,wərm\ *n* **:** a terrestrial annelid worm (class Oligochaeta); *esp* **:** any of numerous widely distributed hermaphroditic worms that constitute a family (Lumbricidae) and that move through the soil by means of setae

earthy \'ər-thē, -*th*ē\ *adj* **1 :** consisting of or resembling earth ⟨an ~ flavor⟩ **2** *archaic* **:** EARTHLY, WORLDLY **3 a :** DOWN-TO-EARTH, PRACTICAL **b :** UNREFINED, GROSS ⟨~ humor⟩

ear·wax \'i(ə)r-,waks\ *n* **:** CERUMEN

1**ear·wig** \-,wig\ *n* [ME *erwigge*, fr. OE *ēarwicga*, fr. *ēare* ear + *wicga* insect — more at VETCH] **:** any of numerous insects (order Dermaptera) having slender many-jointed antennae and a pair of large forceps at the end of the body

2**earwig** *vt* **ear·wigged; ear·wig·ging :** to annoy or attempt to influence by private talk

ear·worm \'i(ə)r-,wərm\ *n* **:** a larval insect (as the corn earworm) that feeds in the developing maize ear

1**ease** \'ēz\ *n* [ME *ese*, fr. OF *aise* convenience, comfort, fr. L *adjacent-*, *adjacens* neighborhood, fr. neut. of prp. of *adjacēre* to lie near] **1 :** the state of being comfortable: as **a :** freedom from pain or discomfort **b :** freedom from care **c :** freedom from labor or difficulty **d :** freedom from embarrassment or constraint **:** NATURALNESS **2 :** relief from discomfort or obligation **3 :** FACILITY,

EFFORTLESSNESS — **at ease** **1** *of a man in military ranks* **:** standing silently with the right foot in place **2** *of a man marching* **:** silent but relaxed from attention and free to break step

2ease *vt* **1 :** to free from something that pains, disquiets, or burdens **2 :** to make less painful **:** ALLEVIATE ⟨~ his suffering⟩ **3 a :** to lessen the pressure or tension of esp. by slackening, lifting, or shifting **b :** to moderate or reduce esp. in amount or intensity **4 :** to make less difficult ⟨~ credit⟩ **5 a :** to put the helm of (a ship) alee **b :** to let (a helm or rudder) come back a little after having been put hard over ~ *vi* **1 :** to give freedom or relief **2 :** to move or pass with freedom **3 :** MODERATE, SLACKEN

ease·ful \'ēz-fəl\ *adj* **:** RESTFUL — **ease·ful·ly** \-fə-lē\ *adv*

ea·sel \'ē-zəl\ *n* [D *ezel* ass; akin to OE *esol* ass; both fr. a prehistoric EGmc-WGmc word borrowed fr. L *asinus* ass] **:** a frame for supporting something (as an artist's canvas)

ease·ment \'ēz-mənt\ *n* **1 :** an act or means of easing or relieving **2 :** a nonprofitable interest in land owned by another that entitles its holder to a specific limited use or enjoyment

eas·i·ly \'ēz-(ə-)lē\ *adv* **1 :** in an easy manner **2 :** by far

eas·i·ness \'ē-zē-nəs\ *n* **:** the quality or state of being easy

1east \'ēst\ *adv* [ME *est*, fr. OE *ēast;* akin to OHG *ōstar* to the east, L *aurora* dawn, Gk *ēōs, heōs*] **:** to, toward, or in the east

2east *adj* **1 :** situated toward or at the east **2 :** coming from the east

3east *n* **1 a :** the general direction of sunrise **:** the direction toward the right of one facing north **b :** the place on the horizon where the sun rises when it is near one of the equinoxes **c :** the cardinal point directly opposite to west **2** *cap* **:** regions lying to the east of a specified or implied point of orientation **3 :** the altar end of a church

east·bound \'ēs(t)-,baund\ *adj* **:** traveling or headed east

east by north : a compass point that is one point north of due east **:** N78°45′E

east by south : a compass point that is one point south of due east **:** S78°45′E

Eas·ter \'ē-stər\ *n* [ME *estre*, fr. OE *ēastre;* akin to OHG *ōstarun* (pl.) Easter; both fr. the prehistoric WGmc name of a pagan spring festival akin to OE *ēast* east] **:** a feast observed on the first Sunday after the full moon on or next after the vernal equinox in commemoration of Christ's resurrection

EASTER DATES

YEAR	ASH WEDNESDAY	EASTER	YEAR	ASH WEDNESDAY	EASTER
1962	Mar 7	Apr 22	1972	Feb 16	Apr 2
1963	Feb 27	Apr 14	1973	Mar 7	Apr 22
1964	Feb 12	Mar 29	1974	Feb 27	Apr 14
1965	Mar 3	Apr 18	1975	Feb 12	Mar 30
1966	Feb 23	Apr 10	1976	Mar 3	Apr 18
1967	Feb 8	Mar 26	1977	Feb 23	Apr 10
1968	Feb 28	Apr 14	1978	Feb 8	Mar 26
1969	Feb 19	Apr 6	1979	Feb 28	Apr 15
1970	Feb 11	Mar 29	1980	Feb 20	Apr 6
1971	Feb 24	Apr 11	1981	Mar 4	Apr 19

Easter egg *n* **:** an egg used to celebrate Easter: as **a :** an egg dyed in bright colors **b :** a symbolic representation of an egg

Easter lily *n* **:** any of several white cultivated lilies that bloom in early spring

east·er·ly \'ē-stər-lē\ *adv* (*or adj*) [obs. *easter* (eastern)] **1 :** from the east **2 :** toward the east

Easter Monday *n* **:** the Monday after Easter observed as a legal holiday in parts of the British Commonwealth

east·ern \'ē-stərn\ *adj* [ME *estern*, fr. OE *ēasterne;* akin to OHG *ōstrōni* eastern, OE *ēast* east] **1** *often cap* **:** of, relating to, or characteristic of a region usu. designated East **2** *cap* **a :** of, relating to, or being the Christian churches originating in the church of the Eastern Roman Empire **b :** Eastern Orthodox **3 a :** lying toward the east **b :** coming from the east — **east·ern·most** \-,mōst\ *adj*

East·ern·er \'ē-stə(r)-nər\ *n* **:** a native or inhabitant of the East; *esp* **:** a native or resident of the eastern part of the U.S.

eastern hemisphere *n* **:** the half of the earth to the east of the Atlantic ocean including Europe, Asia, and Africa

Eastern Orthodox *adj* **:** of or consisting of the Eastern churches that form a loose federation according primacy of honor to the patriarch of Constantinople and adhering to the decisions of the first seven ecumenical councils and to the Byzantine rite

eastern time *n, often cap E* **:** the time of the 5th time zone west of Greenwich that includes the eastern U.S.

Eas·ter·tide \'ē-stər-,tīd\ *n* **:** the period from Easter to Ascension Day, to Whitsunday, or to Trinity Sunday

east·ing \'ē-stiŋ\ *n* **1 :** difference in longitude to the east from the last preceding point of reckoning **2 :** easterly progress

east–northeast *n* — see COMPASS CARD

east–southeast *n* — see COMPASS CARD

1east·ward \'ēs-twərd\ *adv* (or *adj*) **:** toward the east

2eastward *n* **:** eastward direction or part ⟨sail to the ~⟩

east·wards \'ēs-twərdz\ *adv* **:** EASTWARD

1easy \'ē-zē\ *adj* [ME *esy*, fr. OF *aaisié*, pp. of *aaisier* to ease, fr. *a-* ad- (fr. L *ad-*) + *aise* ease] **1 :** causing or involving little difficulty or discomfort ⟨~ problem⟩ **2 a :** not severe **:** LENIENT **b :** not steep or abrupt ⟨~ slope⟩ **c :** not difficult to endure or undergo ⟨~ penalty⟩ **d :** readily prevailed on ⟨~ prey⟩ **e** (1) **:** plentiful in supply at low or declining interest rates ⟨~ money⟩ (2) **:** less in demand and usu. lower in price ⟨bonds were *easier*⟩ **f :** read and understood without difficulty ⟨~ language⟩ **3 a :** marked by peace and comfort ⟨~ life⟩ **b :** not hurried or strenuous ⟨~ pace⟩ **4 a :** free from pain, annoyance, or anxiety **b :** marked by social ease ⟨~ manners⟩ **c :** showing a disinclination to energetic individual action or resolute independent thought ⟨~ disposition⟩ **5 a :** giving ease, comfort, or relaxation ⟨~ furniture⟩ **b :** PLEASING, PLEASANT ⟨~ circumstances⟩ **c :** fitting comfortably ⟨an ~ shoe⟩ **d :** marked by ready facility ⟨~ flowing style⟩ **e :** felt or attained to readily, naturally, and spontaneously ⟨~ emotions⟩

syn EASY, FACILE, SIMPLE, LIGHT, EFFORTLESS, SMOOTH mean not demanding effort or involving difficulty. EASY is applicable either to persons or things imposing tasks or to activity required by such tasks; FACILE often adds to EASY the connotation of undue haste or shallowness; SIMPLE stresses ease in understanding or dealing with because lacking in intricacy; LIGHT stresses freedom from what is burdensome, and often suggests quickness of movement; EFFORTLESS stresses the appearance of ease and usu. implies the prior attainment of artistry or expertness; SMOOTH stresses the absence or removal of all difficulties or hardships or obstacles **syn** see in addition COMFORTABLE

2easy *adv* **1 :** EASILY **2 :** SLOWLY, CAUTIOUSLY

easy·go·ing \,ē-zē-'gō-iŋ\ *adj* **1 :** taking life easily: as **a :** PLACID **b :** indolent and careless **c :** morally lax **2 :** UNHURRIED, COMFORTABLE — **easy·go·ing·ness** *n*

eat \'ēt\ *vb* **ate** \'āt, *chiefly Brit or substand* 'et\ **eat·en** \'ēt-ᵊn\ **eat·ing** \'ēt-iŋ\ [ME *eten*, fr. OE *etan;* akin to OHG *ezzan* to eat, L *edere*, Gk *edmenai*] *vt* **1 :** to take in through the mouth as food **:** ingest, chew, and swallow in turn **2 :** to destroy, use up, or waste by or as if by eating **:** DEVOUR **3 :** to consume gradually **:** CORRODE ~ *vi* **1 :** to take food or a meal **2 :** to affect something by gradual destruction or consumption — used with *into* — **eat·er** *n* — **eat crow :** to accept what one has fought against — **eat humble pie :** to apologize or retract under pressure — **eat one's words :** to retract what one has said

1eat·able \'ēt-ə-bəl\ *adj* **:** fit to be eaten

2eatable *n* **1 :** something to eat **2** *pl* **:** FOOD

eath \'ēth\ *adv* (*or adj*) [ME *ethe*, fr. OE *ēathe;* akin to OHG *ōdi* easy and perh. to L *avēre* to long for — more at AVID] *Scot* **:** EASY

eat·ing \'ēt-iŋ\ *adj* **1 :** used for eating **2 :** fit to be eaten raw

eau de co·logne \,ōd-ə-kə-'lōn\ *n, pl* **eaux de cologne** \,ō(z)d-ə-\ [F, lit., Cologne water, fr. *Cologne*, Germany] **:** COLOGNE

eau–de–vie \,ōd-ə-'vē\ *n, pl* **eaux–de–vie** \,ō(z)d-ə-\ [F, lit., water of life, trans. of ML *aqua vitae*] **:** BRANDY

eaves \'ēvz\ *n pl but sing or pl in constr* [ME *eves* (sing.), fr. OE *efes;* akin to OHG *obasa* portico, OE *ūp* up — more at UP] **:** the lower border of a roof that overhangs the wall

eaves·drop \'ēvz-,dräp\ *vi* [prob. back-formation fr. *eavesdropper*, lit., one standing under the drip from the eaves] **:** to listen secretly to what is said in private — **eaves·drop·per** *n*

1ebb \'eb\ *n* [ME *ebbe*, fr. OE *ebba;* akin to MD *ebbe* ebb, OE *of* from — more at OF] **1 :** the reflux of the tide toward the sea **2 :** a point or condition of decline

2ebb *vi* **1 :** to recede from the flood **2 :** to fall from a higher to a lower level or from a better to a worse state **syn** see ABATE

eb·bet \'eb-ət\ *n* [ME *evete*, fr. OE *efete*] **:** a common green newt (*Triturus viridescens*) of the eastern U.S.

ebb tide *n* **1 :** the tide while ebbing or at ebb **2 :** a period or state of decline

eb·on \'eb-ən\ *adj* **:** EBONY

eb·o·nite \'eb-ə-,nīt\ *n* **:** hard rubber esp. when black or unfilled

eb·o·nize \-,nīz\ *vt* **:** to stain black in imitation of ebony

1eb·o·ny \'eb-ə-nē\ *n* [prob. fr. LL *hebeninus* of ebony, fr. Gk *ebeninos*, fr. *ebenos* ebony, fr. Egypt *hbnj*] **1 :** a hard heavy wood yielded by various Old World tropical dicotyledonous trees (genus *Diospyros*) of the ebony family (Ebonaceae) **2 a :** a tree yielding ebony **b :** any of several trees yielding wood resembling ebony

2ebony *adj* **1 :** made of or resembling ebony **2 :** BLACK, DARK

ebul·lience \i-'bùl-yən(t)s, -'bəl-\ *n* **:** the quality of lively or enthusiastic expression of thoughts or feelings **:** EXUBERANCE

ebul·lient \-yənt\ *adj* [L *ebullient-, ebulliens*, prp. of *ebullire* to bubble out, fr. *e-* + *bullire* to bubble, boil — more at BOIL] **1 :** BOILING, AGITATED **2 :** characterized by ebullience — **ebul·lient·ly** *adv*

eb·ul·li·tion \,eb-ə-'lish-ən\ *n* **1 :** the act, process, or state of boiling or bubbling up **2 :** a sudden violent outburst or display

eb·ur·nat·ed \'eb-ər-,nāt-əd\ *adj* [L *eburnus* of ivory, fr. *ebur* ivory] **:** hard and dense like ivory — **eb·ur·na·tion** \,eb-ər-'nā-shən\ *n*

ec- *or* **eco-** *comb form* [LL *oeco-* household, fr. Gk *oik-, oiko-*, fr. *oikos* house] **:** habitat or environment ⟨*ecospecies*⟩

ecar·i·nate \(')ē-'kar-ə-,nāt, -nət\ *adj* **:** lacking a keel ⟨an ~ flower⟩

1ec·cen·tric \ik-'sen-trik, ek-\ *adj* [ML *eccentricus*, fr. Gk *ekkentros*, fr. *ex* out of + *kentron* center] **1 :** not having the same center ⟨~ spheres⟩ **2 :** deviating from some established pattern or from conventional or accepted usage or conduct **3 a :** deviating from a circular path **b :** located elsewhere than at the geometrical center **syn** see STRANGE — **ec·cen·tri·cal·ly** \-tri-k(ə-)lē\ *adv*

2eccentric *n* **1 :** a mechanical device consisting of a disk through which a shaft is keyed eccentrically and a circular strap which works freely round the rim of the disk for communicating its motion to one end of a rod whose other end is constrained to move in a straight line so as to produce reciprocating motion **2 :** an eccentric person

ec·cen·tric·i·ty \,ek-,sen-'tris-ət-ē\ *n* **1 a :** the quality or state of being eccentric **b :** deviation from an established pattern, rule, or norm; *esp* **:** odd or whimsical behavior **2 :** the ratio of the distances from any point of a conic section to a focus and the corresponding directrix

syn ECCENTRICITY, IDIOSYNCRASY mean a strange trait, trick, or habit. ECCENTRICITY stresses divergence from the usual or customary and suggests at least mild mental aberration; IDIOSYNCRASY stresses the following of one's particular bent or temperament and connotes strong individuality and independence of action

ec·chy·mo·sis \,ek-i-'mō-səs\ *n* [NL, fr. Gk *ekchymōsis*] **:** the escape of blood into the tissues from ruptured blood vessels — **ec·chy·mot·ic** \-'mät-ik\ *adj*

ecclesi- *or* **ecclesio-** *comb form* [ME *ecclesi-*, fr. LL *ecclesia*, fr. Gk *ekklēsia* assembly of citizens, church, fr. *ekkalein* to call forth, summon, fr. *ex* + *kalein* to call] **:** church ⟨*ecclesiography*⟩

ec·cle·si·as·tic \ik-,lē-zē-'as-tik, e-,klē-\ *n* **:** CLERGYMAN

ec·cle·si·as·ti·cal \-'as-ti-kəl\ *or* **ec·cle·si·as·tic** \-tik\ *adj* [*ecclesiastical* fr. ME, fr. LL *ecclesiasticus; ecclesiastic* fr. MF *ecclesiastique*, fr. LL *ecclesiasticus*, fr. LGk *ekklēsiastikos*, fr. Gk, of an assembly of citizens, fr. *ekklēsiastēs* member of an assembly, fr. *ekklēsia*] **1 :** of or relating to a church esp. as a formal and established institution ⟨~ law⟩ **2 :** suitable for use in a church ⟨~ vestments⟩ — **ec·cle·si·as·ti·cal·ly** \-ti-k(ə-)lē\ *adv*

ec·cle·si·as·ti·cism \-'as-tə-,siz-əm\ *n* **:** excessive attachment to ecclesiastical forms and practices

ec·cle·si·ol·o·gy \-zē-'äl-ə-jē\ *n* **1 :** the study of church architecture and adornment **2 :** theological doctrine relating to the church

ec·crine \'ek-rən, -,rīn, -,rēn\ *adj* [ISV *ec-* (fr. Gk *ex* out) + Gk *krinein* to separate] **:** producing a fluid secretion without removing

cytoplasm from the secreting cells **:** produced by an eccrine gland

ec·cri·nol·o·gy \,ek-rə-'näl-ə-jē\ *n* [F *eccrinologie*] **:** a branch of physiology that deals with secretion and secretory organs

ec·dys·i·ast \ek-'diz-ē-,ast, -ē-əst\ *n* **:** STRIPTEASER

ec·dy·sis \'ek-də-səs\ *n, pl* **ec·dy·ses** \-də-,sēz\ [NL, fr. Gk *ekdysis* act of getting out] **:** the act of molting or shedding an outer cuticular layer (as in insects and crustaceans)

ece·sis \i-'sē-səs, -'kē-\ *n* [NL, fr. Gk *oikēsis* inhabitation] **:** the establishment of a plant or animal in a new habitat

¹**ech·e·lon** \'esh-ə-,län\ *n* [F *échelon*, lit., rung of a ladder] **1 a** (1) **:** an arrangement of a body of troops with its units each somewhat to the left or right of the one in the rear like a series of steps (2) **:** a formation of units or individuals resembling such an echelon (3) **:** a flight formation in which each airplane flies at a certain elevation above or below and at a certain distance behind and to the right or left of the airplane ahead **b :** any of several military units in echelon formation **2 a :** one of a series of levels or grades in an organization or field of activity **b :** a group of individuals having a particular responsibility or occupying a particular level or grade

echelon 1a(3): 1, 2, line of bearing

²**echelon** *vb* **:** to form in echelon

ech·e·ve·ria \,ech-ə-və-'rē-ə\ *n* [NL, genus name, fr. *Echeveria*, 19th cent. Mex botanical illustrator] **:** any of a large genus (*Echeveria*) of tropical American succulent plants of the orpine family having axillary clusters of flowers with erect petals that spread only at the tips

echid·na \i-'kid-nə\ *n* [NL, fr. L, viper, fr. Gk] **:** an oviparous burrowing nocturnal mammal (*Tachyglossus aculeatus*) of Australia, Tasmania, and New Guinea that is somewhat larger than a hedgehog and has a spiny back, a long tapering snout, a toothless mouth with a long extensile tongue, and long heavy claws

echin- *or* **echino-** *comb form* [L, fr. Gk, fr. *echinos* sea urchin] **1 :** prickle ⟨*Echino*dermata⟩ **2 :** sea urchin ⟨*echin*ite⟩

echi·nate \i-'kī-nət, 'ek-ə-,nāt, -,nāt\ *adj* **:** SPINY

echi·nite \'ek-ə-,nīt, i-'kī-,nīt\ *n* **:** a fossil sea urchin

echi·no·coc·cus \i-,kī-nə-'käk-əs, ,ek-ə-nō-\ *n* [NL, genus name] **:** any of a genus (*Echinococcus*) of tapeworms that alternate a minute adult living as a commensal in the intestine of carnivores with a hydatid invading tissues esp. of the liver of cattle, sheep, swine, and man and acting as a dangerous pathogen

echi·no·derm \i-'kī-nə-,dərm, 'ek-ə-nō-\ *n* [NL *Echinodermata*, phylum name, fr. *echin-* + *-dermata* (fr. Gk *derma* skin)] **:** any of a phylum (Echinodermata) of radially symmetrical coelomate marine animals consisting of the starfishes, sea urchins, and related forms — **echi·no·der·ma·tous** \i-,kī-nə-'dər-mət-əs, ,ek-ə-nō-\ *adj*

echi·noid \i-'kī-,nȯid, 'ek-ə-,nȯid\ *n* **:** SEA URCHIN

echi·nu·late \i-'kin-yə-lət, -'kīn-, -,lāt\ *adj* **:** set with small spines or prickles — **echi·nu·la·tion** \i-,kin-yə-'lā-shən, i-,kīn-\ *n*

echi·nus \i-'kī-nəs\ *n, pl* **echi·ni** \-,nī\ [ME, fr. L, fr. Gk *echinos* hedgehog, sea urchin, architectural echinus] **1 :** SEA URCHIN **2 a :** the rounded molding forming the bell of the capital in the Greek Doric order **b :** a similar member in other orders

¹**echo** \'ek-(,)ō\ *n, pl* **ech·oes** [ME *ecco*, fr. MF & L; MF *echo*, fr. L, fr. Gk *ēchō*; akin to L *vagire* to wail, Gk *ēchē* sound] **1 a :** the repetition of a sound caused by reflection of sound waves **b :** the sound due to such reflection **2 a :** a repetition or imitation of another **:** REFLECTION **b :** REPERCUSSION, RESULT **c :** TRACE **d :** RESPONSE **3 :** one who closely imitates or repeats another's words, ideas, or acts **4 :** a soft repetition of a musical phrase **5 a :** the repetition of a received radio signal due esp. to reflection of part of the wave from an ionized layer of the atmosphere **b** (1) **:** the reflection of transmitted radar signals by an object (2) **:** the visual indication of this reflection on a radarscope

²**echo** *vb* **echo·ing** \'ek-(,)ō-iŋ, 'ek-ə-wiŋ\ *vi* **1 :** to resound with echoes **2 :** to produce an echo ~ *vt* **1 :** REPEAT, IMITATE **2 :** to send back or repeat (a sound) by the reflection of sound waves

Echo — a communications code word for the letter *e*

echo·ic \i-'kō-ik, e-\ *adj* **1 :** of or relating to an echo **2 :** formed in imitation of some natural sound **:** ONOMATOPOEIC

echo·la·lia \,ek-ō-'lā-lē-ə\ *n* [NL] **:** the often pathological repetition of what is said by other people as if echoing them

echo·lo·ca·tion \,ek-ō-lō-'kā-shən\ *n* **:** a process for locating distant or invisible objects by means of sound waves reflected back to the emitter by the objects

echo sounder *n* **:** SONIC DEPTH FINDER

éclair \ā-'kla(ə)r, -'kle(ə)r, 'ā-,kla(ə)r, -,kle(ə)r\ *n* [F, lit., lightning] **:** an oblong cream puff with whipped cream or custard filling

éclair·cisse·ment \ā-kler-sē-smäⁿ\ *n, pl* **éclaircissements** \-smäⁿ(z)\ [F] **:** CLARIFICATION, ENLIGHTENMENT

eclamp·sia \e-'klam(p)-sē-ə\ *n* [NL, fr. Gk *eklampsis* sudden flashing, fr. *eklampein* to shine forth, fr. *ex* out + *lampein* to shine] **:** a convulsive state; *esp* **:** an attack of convulsions during pregnancy or parturition — **eclamp·tic** \-'klam(p)-tik\ *adj*

éclat \ā-'klä\ *n* [F, splinter, burst, *éclat*] **1 :** dazzling effect **:** BRILLIANCE **2 a :** ostentatious display **:** PUBLICITY **b** *archaic* **:** NOTORIETY **3 a :** brilliant or conspicuous success **b :** ACCLAIM, APPLAUSE

¹**eclec·tic** \e-'klek-tik, i-\ *adj* [Gk *eklektikos*, fr. *eklegein* to select, fr. *ex* + *legein* to gather] **1 :** selecting what appears to be best in various doctrines, methods, or styles **2 :** composed of elements drawn from various sources — **eclec·ti·cal·ly** \-ti-k(ə-)lē\ *adv*

²**eclectic** *n* **:** one who uses an eclectic method or approach

eclec·ti·cism \-'klek-tə-,siz-əm\ *n* **:** the theory or practice of an eclectic method

¹**eclipse** \i-'klips\ *n* [ME, fr. OF, fr. L *eclipsis*, fr. Gk *ekleipsis*, fr. *ekleipein* to omit,

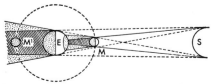

eclipse: sun, *S;* earth, *E;* moon in solar eclipse, *M;* moon in lunar eclipse, *M*¹

fail, suffer eclipse, fr. *ex* + *leipein* to leave — more at LOAN] **1 a :** the total or partial obscuration of one celestial body by another **b :** the passing into the shadow of a celestial body — compare OCCULTATION, TRANSIT **2 :** a falling into obscurity, decline, or disgrace

²**eclipse** *vt* **:** to cause an eclipse of: as **a :** OBSCURE, DARKEN **b :** to reduce in importance or repute **:** DISGRACE **c :** SURPASS

¹**eclip·tic** \i-'klip-tik\ *n* [ME *ecliptik*, fr. LL *ecliptica linea*, lit., line of eclipses] **1 :** the great circle of the celestial sphere that is the apparent path of the sun among the stars or of the earth as seen from the sun **:** the plane of the earth's orbit extended to meet the celestial sphere **2 :** a great circle drawn on a terrestrial globe making an angle of about 23° 27' with the equator and used for illustrating and solving astronomical problems

²**ecliptic** *adj* **:** of or relating to the ecliptic or an eclipse

ec·logue \'ek-,lȯg, -,läg\ *n* [ME *eclog*, fr. L *Eclogae*, title of Vergil's pastorals, fr. L, lit., selections, pl. of *ecloga*, fr. Gk *eklogē*, fr. *eklegein* to select] **:** a poem in which shepherds are introduced conversing **:** BUCOLIC, IDYLL

eclo·sion \i-'klō-zhən\ *n* [F *éclosion*] *of an insect* **:** the act of emerging from the pupal case or hatching from the egg

eco- — see EC-

eco·log·i·cal \,ek-ə-'läj-i-kəl, ,ē-kə-\ *adj* **:** of or relating to ecology — **eco·log·i·cal·ly** \-k(ə-)lē\ *adv*

ecol·o·gist \i-'käl-ə-jəst\ *n* **:** a specialist in ecology

ecol·o·gy \-jē\ *n* [G *ökologie*, fr. *ök- ec-* + *-logie* -logy] **1 :** a branch of science concerned with the interrelationship of organisms and their environments **2 :** the totality or pattern of relations between organisms and their environment

econo·met·rics \i-,kän-ə-'me-triks\ *n pl but sing in constr* [blend of *economics* and *metric*] **:** the application of statistical methods to the study of economic data and problems

eco·nom·ic \,ek-ə-'näm-ik, ,ē-kə-\ *adj* **1** *archaic* **:** of or relating to a household or its management **2** *archaic* **:** ECONOMICAL 2 **3 a :** of or relating to economics **b :** of, relating to, or based on the production, distribution, and consumption of goods and services **c :** of or relating to an economy **4 :** having practical or industrial significance or uses **:** affecting material resources **5 :** PROFITABLE

eco·nom·i·cal \-'näm-i-kəl\ *adj* **1** *archaic* **:** ECONOMIC **2 :** given to thrift **:** FRUGAL **3 :** operating with little waste or at a saving **syn** see SPARING — **eco·nom·i·cal·ly** \-i-k(ə-)lē\ *adv*

economic rent *n* **:** the return for the use of a factor in excess of the minimum required to bring forth its service

eco·nom·ics \,ek-ə-'näm-iks, ,ē-kə-\ *n pl but sing or pl in constr, often attrib* **1 :** a social science concerned chiefly with description and analysis of the production, distribution, and consumption of goods and services **2 :** economic aspect or significance

econ·o·mist \i-'kän-ə-məst\ *n* **1** *archaic* **:** one who practices economy **2 :** a specialist in economics

econ·o·mize \-,mīz\ *vi* **:** to practice economy **:** be frugal ~ *vt* **:** to use more economically **:** SAVE — **econ·o·miz·er** *n*

econ·o·my \i-'kän-ə-mē\ *n, pl* **economies** [MF *yconomie*, fr. ML *oeconomia*, fr. Gk *oikonomia*, fr. *oikonomos* household manager, fr. *oikos* house + *nemein* to manage — more at VICINITY, NIMBLE] **1** *archaic* **:** the management of household or private affairs and esp. expenses **2 a :** thrifty use of material resources **:** frugality in expenditures; *also* **:** an instance or a means of economizing **b :** the efficient and sparing use of the means available for the end proposed **3 :** the system of arrangement or mode of operation or functioning of something **:** ORGANIZATION **4 :** the structure of economic life in a country, area, or period; *specif* **:** an economic system

eco·spe·cies \'ek-ō-,spē-(,)shēz, 'ē-kō-, -(,)sēz\ *n* **:** a subdivision of a cenospecies capable of free gene interchange between its members without impairment of fertility but less capable of fertile crosses with members of other subdivisions and typically more or less equivalent to the taxonomic species — **eco·spe·cif·ic** \,ek-ō-spi-'sif-ik, ,ē-kō-\ *adj*

eco·sys·tem \'ek-ō-,sis-təm, 'ē-kō-\ *n* **:** a complex of ecological community and environment forming a functioning whole in nature

eco·tone \-,tōn\ *n* [*ec-* + Gk *tonos* tension — more at TONE] **:** a transition area between two adjacent ecological communities usu. exhibiting competition between organisms common to both

eco·type \-,tīp\ *n* **:** a subdivision of an ecospecies that comprises individuals intertfertile with each other and with members of other ecotypes of the same ecospecies but surviving as a distinct group through environmental selection and isolation and that is comparable with a taxonomic subspecies — **eco·typ·ic** \,ek-ō-'tip-ik, ,ē-kō-\ *adj* — **eco·typ·i·cal·ly** \-'tip-i-k(ə-)lē\ *adv*

ecru \'ek-(,)rü, 'ā-(,)krü\ *n* [F *écru* unbleached, fr. OF *escru*, fr. *es-* completely (fr. L *ex-*) + *cru* raw, fr. L *crudus*] **:** BEIGE 2

ec·sta·sy \'ek-stə-sē\ *n* [ME *extasie*, fr. MF, fr. LL *ecstasis*, fr. Gk *ekstasis*, fr. *existanai* to derange, fr. *ex* out + *histanai* to cause to stand] **1 a :** a state of being beyond reason and self-control **b** *archaic* **:** SWOON **2 :** a state of overwhelming emotion; *esp* **:** rapturous delight **3 :** TRANCE; *esp* **:** a mystic or prophetic trance **syn** ECSTASY, RAPTURE, TRANSPORT mean intense exaltation of mind and feelings. ECSTASY and RAPTURE both suggest a state of trance or near immobility produced by an overmastering emotion; ECSTASY may apply to any strong emotion (as joy, fear, rage, adoration); RAPTURE usu. implies intense bliss or beatitude. TRANSPORT applies to any powerful emotion that lifts one out of oneself and usu. provokes vehement expression or frenzied action

ec·stat·ic \ek-'stat-ik, ik-'stat-\ *adj* [ML *ecstaticus*, fr. Gk *ekstatikos*, fr. *existanai*] **:** of, relating to, or marked by ecstasy — **ec·stat·i·cal·ly** \-'stat-i-k(ə-)lē\ *adv*

ect- *or* **ecto-** *comb form* [NL, fr. Gk *ektos*, fr. *ektos* out — more at EX-] **:** outside **:** external ⟨*ectomere*⟩ — compare END-, EXO-

ec·to·blast \'ek-tə-,blast\ *n* [ISV] **:** EPIBLAST — **ec·to·blas·tic** \,ek-tə-'blas-tik\ *adj*

ec·to·chon·dral \,ek-tə-'kän-drəl\ *adj* **:** occurring on the surface of cartilage

ec·to·com·men·sal \,ek-(,)tō-kə-'men(t)-səl\ *n* **:** an organism that lives as a commensal on the body surface of another

ec·to·derm \'ek-tə-,dərm\ *n* [ISV *ect-* + Gk *derma* skin — more at DERM-] **1 :** the outer cellular membrane of a diploblastic animal **2 a :** the outermost of the three primary germ layers of an embryo **b :** a tissue (as neural tissue) derived from this germ layer — **ec·to·der·mal** \,ek-tə-'dər-məl\ *or* **ec·to·der·mic** \-mik\ *adj*

ec·to·gen·ic \-'jen-ik\ *adj* **:** ECTOGENOUS

ec·tog·e·nous \ek-'täj-ə-nəs\ *adj* **:** capable of development apart from the host — used chiefly of pathogenic bacteria

ec·to·mere \'ek-tə-,mi(ə)r\ *n* **:** a blastomere destined to form ectoderm — **ec·to·mer·ic** \,ek-tə-'mer-ik, -'mi(ə)r-\ *adj*
ec·to·morph \'ek-tə-,mȯrf\ *n* [*ecto*derm + *-morph*] **:** an ectomorphic individual
ec·to·mor·phic \,ek-tə-'mȯr-fik\ *adj* **:** characterized by predominance of the structures (as nerves) developed from the ectodermal layer of the embryo **:** of a light type of body build — **ec·to·mor·phi·cal·ly** \-fi-k(ə-)lē\ *adv* — **ec·to·mor·phy** \'ek-tə-,mȯr-fē\ *n*
-ec·to·my \'ek-tə-mē\ *n comb form* [NL *-ectomia*, fr. Gk *ektemnein* to cut out, fr. *ex* out + *temnein* to cut — more at TOME] **:** surgical removal ⟨gastr*ectomy*⟩
ec·to·par·a·site \,ek-(,)tō-'par-ə-,sīt\ *n* [ISV] **:** a parasite that lives on the exterior of its host — **ec·to·par·a·sit·ic** \-,par-ə-'sit-ik\ *adj*
ec·to·plasm \'ek-tə-,plaz-əm\ *n* **1 :** the outer relatively rigid granule-free layer of the cytoplasm usu. held to be a reversible gel **2 :** a substance held to produce spirit materialization and telekinesis — **ec·to·plas·mic** \,ek-tə-'plaz-mik\ *adj*
ec·to·therm \'ek-tə-,thərm\ *n* **:** a cold-blooded animal **:** POIKILOTHERM — **ec·to·ther·mic** \,ek-tə-'thər-mik\ *adj*
ec·u·men·i·cal \,ek-yə-'men-i-kəl\ *adj* [LL *oecumenicus*, fr. LGk *oikoumenikos*, fr. Gk *oikoumenē* the inhabited world, fr. fem. of *oikoumenos*, pres. pass. part. of *oikein* to inhabit, fr. *oikos* house] **1 :** worldwide or general in extent, influence, or application **2 a :** of, relating to, or representing the whole of a body of churches **b :** promoting or tending toward worldwide Christian unity or cooperation — **ec·u·me·nic·i·ty** \,ek-yə-mə-'nis-ət-ē\ *n* — **ecu·me·nism** \'ek-yə-mə-,niz-əm, e-'kyü-mə-\ *n*
ecumenical patriarch *n* **:** the patriarch of Constantinople as the dignitary given first honor in the Eastern Orthodox Church
ec·ze·ma \ig-'zē-mə, 'ek-sə-mə, 'eg-zə-\ *n* [NL, fr. Gk *ekzema*, fr. *ekzein* to erupt, fr. *ex* out + *zein* to boil — more at EX-, YEAST] **:** an inflammatory condition of the skin characterized by redness, itching, and oozing vesicular lesions which become scaly, crusted, or hardened — **ec·zem·a·tous** \ig-'zem-ət-əs, eg-, -'zē-mət-\ *adj*
1-ed \d *after a vowel or* b, g, j, l, m, n, ŋ, r, t͟h, v, z, zh; əd, id *after* d, t; t *after other sounds; exceptions are pronounced at their subentries or entries*\ *vb suffix or adj suffix* [ME, fr. OE *-ed, -od, -ad;* akin to OHG *-t*, pp. ending, L *-tus*, Gk *-tos*, suffix forming verbals] **1** — used to form the past participle of regular weak verbs ⟨end*ed*⟩ ⟨fad*ed*⟩ ⟨tri*ed*⟩ ⟨patt*ed*⟩ **2** — used to form adjectives of identical meaning from Latin-derived adjectives ending in *-ate* ⟨crenulat*ed*⟩ **3 a :** having **:** characterized by ⟨cultur*ed*⟩ ⟨two-legg*ed*⟩ **b :** having the characteristics of ⟨bigot*ed*⟩
2-ed *vb suffix* [ME *-ede, -de*, fr. OE *-de, -ede, -ode, -ade;* akin to OHG *-ta*, past ending (1st sing.) and prob. to OHG *-t*, pp. ending] — used to form the past tense of regular weak verbs ⟨judg*ed*⟩ ⟨deni*ed*⟩ ⟨dropp*ed*⟩
eda·cious \i-'dā-shəs\ *adj* [L *edac-, edax*, fr. *edere* to eat] **1 :** of or relating to eating **2 :** VORACIOUS — **edac·i·ty** \i-'das-ət-ē\ *n*
Edam \'ēd-əm, 'ē-,dam\ *n* [*Edam*, Netherlands] **:** a Dutch pressed cheese of yellow color and mild flavor made in balls
edaph·ic \i-'daf-ik\ *adj* [Gk *edaphos* bottom, ground] **1 :** of or relating to the soil **2 a :** resulting from or influenced by the soil rather than the climate **b :** AUTOCHTHONOUS — **edaph·i·cal·ly** \-'daf-i-k(ə-)lē\ *adv*
Ed·dic \'ed-ik\ *adj* [ON *Edda*] **:** of, relating to, or resembling the Old Norse *Edda* which is a 13th century collection of mythological, heroic, and aphoristic poems in alliterative verse
ed·dy \'ed-ē\ *n* [ME (Sc dial.) *ydy*, prob. fr. ON *itha;* akin to OHG *ith-* again, L *et* and] **1 a :** a current of water or air running contrary to the main current; *esp* **:** a small whirlpool **b :** a substance moving similarly **2 :** a contrary or circular current — **eddy** *vb*
edel·weiss \'ād-ᵊl-,wīs, -,vīs\ *n* [G, fr. *edel* noble + *weiss* white] **:** a small perennial composite herb (*Leontopodium alpinum*) having a dense woolly white pubescence and growing high in the Alps
ede·ma \i-'dē-mə\ *n* [NL, fr. Gk *oidēma* swelling, fr. *oidein* to swell; akin to OE *ātor* pus] **1 :** an abnormal accumulation of serous fluid in connective tissue or in a serous cavity **2 a :** watery swelling of plant organs or parts **b :** any of various plant diseases characterized by such swellings — **ede·ma·tous** \-'dem-ət-əs, -'dēm-\ *adj*
Eden \'ēd-ᵊn\ *n* [LL, fr. Heb *'Ēdhen*] **1 :** the garden where Adam and Eve are held to have first lived **2 :** PARADISE 2 — **Eden·ic** \i-'den-ik\ *adj*
1eden·tate \(')ē-'den-,tāt\ *adj* [L *edentatus*, pp. of *edentare* to make toothless, fr. *e-* + *dent-, dens* tooth — more at TOOTH] **1 :** lacking teeth **2 :** being an edentate
2edentate *n* **:** any of an order (Edentata) of mammals having few or no teeth and including the sloths, armadillos, and New World anteaters and formerly also the pangolins and the aardvark
eden·tu·lous \(')ē-'den-chə-ləs\ *adj* [L *edentulus*, fr. *e-* + *dent-, dens*] **:** TOOTHLESS
1edge \'ej\ *n* [ME *egge*, fr. OE *ecg;* akin to L *acer* sharp, Gk *akmē* point] **1 a :** the cutting side of a blade **b :** the sharpness of a blade **c :** penetrating power **:** KEENNESS **2 a :** the line where an object or area begins or ends; *also* **:** the narrow adjacent part **:** BORDER **b :** a point near the beginning or the end **c :** a favorable margin **:** ADVANTAGE **syn** see BORDER — **edged** \'ejd\ *adj* — **on edge :** ANXIOUS, NERVOUS
2edge *vt* **1 :** to give an edge to **2 :** to move or force gradually **3 :** to incline (a ski) sideways so that one edge cuts into the snow ~ *vi* **:** to advance by short moves — **edg·er** \'ej-ər\ *n*
edge tool *n* **:** a tool with a sharp cutting edge
edge·ways \'ej-,wāz\ *or* **edge·wise** \-,wīz\ *adv* **:** SIDEWAYS
edg·i·ly \'ej-ə-lē\ *adv* **:** in an edgy manner
edg·i·ness \'ej-ē-nəs\ *n* **:** the quality or state of being edgy
edg·ing *n* **:** something that forms an edge or border
edgy \'ej-ē\ *adj* **1 :** having an edge **:** SHARP **2 :** being on edge
edh \'et͟h\ *n* [Icel *eth*] **:** a letter ð used in Old English and in Icelandic to represent an interdental fricative and in some phonetic alphabets to represent the voiced interdental fricative (as in *then*)
ed·i·ble \'ed-ə-bəl\ *adj* [LL *edibilis*, fr. L *edere* to eat — more at EAT] **:** fit to be eaten **:** EATABLE — **edible** *n* — **ed·i·ble·ness** *n*
edict \'ē-,dikt\ *n* [L *edictum*, fr. neut. of *edictus*, pp. of *edicere* to decree, fr. *e-* + *dicere* to say — more at DICTION] **:** an official public proclamation having the force of law — **edic·tal** \i-'dik-tᵊl\ *adj*
ed·i·fi·ca·tion \,ed-ə-fə-'kā-shən\ *n* **:** an act or process of edifying — **edi·fi·ca·to·ry** \i-'dif-ə-kə-,tōr-ē, 'ed-ə-fə-kə-, -,tȯr-\ *adj*
ed·i·fice \'ed-ə-fəs\ *n* [ME, fr. MF, fr. L *aedificium*, fr. *aedificare*] **1 :** BUILDING; *esp* **:** a large building **2 :** a large abstract structure
ed·i·fy \'ed-ə-,fī\ *vt* [ME *edifien*, fr. MF *edifier*, fr. LL & L; LL *aedificare* to instruct or improve spiritually, fr. L, to erect a house, fr. *aedes* temple, house; akin to OE *ād* funeral pyre, L *aestas* summer] **1** *archaic* **a :** BUILD **b :** ESTABLISH **2 :** to instruct and improve esp. in moral and religious knowledge **:** ENLIGHTEN
ed·it \'ed-ət\ *vt* **1 a :** to prepare an edition of ⟨~*ed* Poe's works⟩ **b :** to assemble (as a moving picture) by cutting and rearranging **2 :** to direct the publication of **3 :** DELETE — usu. used with *out*
edi·tion \i-'dish-ən\ *n* [MF, fr. L *edition-, editio* publication, edition, fr. *editus*, pp. of *edere* to bring forth, publish, fr. *e-* + *-dere* to put or *-dere* (fr. *dare* to give) — more at DO, DATE] **1 a :** the form in which a text (as a printed book) is published **b (1) :** the whole number of copies published at one time **(2) :** one of the several issues of a newspaper for a single day **2 :** COPY, VERSION
ed·i·tor \'ed-ət-ər\ *n* **1 :** one that edits esp. as an occupation **2 :** a person who writes editorials — **ed·i·tor·ship** \-,ship\ *n*
1ed·i·to·ri·al \,ed-ə-'tōr-ē-əl, -'tȯr-\ *adj* **1 :** of or relating to an editor ⟨an ~ office⟩ **2 :** being or resembling an editorial ⟨an ~ statement⟩ — **ed·i·to·ri·al·ly** \-ē-ə-lē\ *adv*
2editorial *n* **:** a newspaper or magazine article that gives the opinions of its editors or publishers
ed·i·to·ri·al·ist \-ē-ə-ləst\ *n* **:** a writer of editorials
ed·i·to·ri·al·iza·tion \-,tōr-ē-ə-lə-'zā-shən, -,tȯr-\ *n* **:** the action of editorializing
ed·i·to·ri·al·ize \,ed-ə-'tōr-ē-ə-,līz, -'tȯr-\ *vi* **1 :** to express an opinion in the form of an editorial **2 :** to introduce opinion into the reporting of facts — **ed·i·to·ri·al·iz·er** *n*
Edom·ite \'ēd-ə-,mīt\ *n* [*Edom* (Esau), ancestor of the Edomites] **:** a member of a Semitic people living south of the Dead sea in biblical times
ed·u·ca·ble \'ej-ə-kə-bəl\ *also* **ed·u·cat·able** \-,kāt-ə-bəl\ *adj* **:** capable of being educated
ed·u·cate \'ej-ə-,kāt\ *vt* [ME *educaten* to rear, fr. L *educatus*, pp. of *educare* to rear, educate] **1 :** to provide schooling for **2 a :** to develop mentally and morally esp. by instruction **b :** TRAIN, INSTRUCT **syn** see TEACH — **ed·u·ca·tor** \-,kāt-ər\ *n*
ed·u·cat·ed *adj* **1 :** having an education; *esp* **:** having an education beyond the average **2 :** giving evidence of education
ed·u·ca·tion \,ej-ə-'kā-shən\ *n* **1 a :** the action or process of educating or of being educated; *also* **:** a stage of such a process **b :** the knowledge and development resulting from an educational process ⟨a man of little ~⟩ **2 :** the field of study that deals mainly with methods of teaching and learning in schools — **ed·u·ca·tion·al** \-shnəl, -shən-ᵊl\ *adj* — **ed·u·ca·tion·al·ly** \-ē\ *adv*
ed·u·ca·tion·ist \-sh(ə-)nəst\ *also* **ed·u·ca·tion·al·ist** \-shnə-ləst, -shən-ᵊl-əst\ *n* **1** *chiefly Brit* **:** a professional educator **2 :** an educational theorist
ed·u·ca·tive \'ej-ə-,kāt-iv\ *adj* **1 :** tending to educate **:** INSTRUCTIVE **2 :** of or relating to education
educe \i-'d(y)üs\ *vt* [L *educere* to draw out, fr. *e-* + *ducere* to lead] **1 :** to bring out (as something latent) **2 :** DEDUCE — **educ·ible** \-'d(y)ü-sə-bəl\ *adj* — **educ·tion** \i-'dək-shən\ *n*
syn EDUCE, EVOKE, ELICIT, EXTRACT, EXTORT mean to draw out something hidden, latent, or reserved. EDUCE implies the bringing out of something potential or latent; EVOKE implies a strong stimulus that arouses an emotion or an interest or recalls an image or memory; ELICIT usu. implies some effort or skill in drawing forth a response, but is often equal to EVOKE; EXTRACT implies the use of force or pressure in obtaining answers or information; EXTORT suggests a wringing or wresting from one strongly resisting
educ·tor \i-'dək-tər\ *n* [LL, one that leads out, fr. L *eductus*, pp. of *educere*] **:** one that educes; *specif* **:** EJECTOR 2
Ed·war·di·an \e-'dwärd-ē-ən, -'dwȯrd-\ *adj* **:** of, relating to, or characteristic of Edward VII of England or his age — **Edwardian** *n*
1-ee \'ē, ,ē, ē\ *n suffix* [ME *-e*, fr. MF *-é*, fr. *-é*, pp. ending, fr. L *-atus*] **1 :** recipient or beneficiary of (a specified action) ⟨appoint*ee*⟩ ⟨grant*ee*⟩ **2 :** person furnished with (a specified thing) ⟨patent*ee*⟩ **3 :** person that performs (a specified action) ⟨escap*ee*⟩
2-ee *n suffix* [prob. alter. of *-y*] **1 :** one associated with ⟨barg*ee*⟩ **2 :** a particular esp. small kind of ⟨boot*ee*⟩ **3 :** one resembling or suggestive of ⟨goat*ee*⟩
eel \'ē(ə)l\ *n* [ME *ele*, fr. OE *ǣl;* akin to OHG *āl* eel] **1 a :** any of numerous voracious elongate snakelike teleost fishes (order Apodes) that have a smooth slimy skin, lack pelvic fins, and have the median fins confluent around the tail **b :** any of numerous other elongate fishes (as of the order Symbranchii) **2 :** any of various nematodes — **eel·like** \'ē(ə)l-,līk\ *adj* — **eely** \'ē-lē\ *adj*
eel·grass \'ē(ə)l-,gras\ *n* **1 :** a submerged marine plant (*Zostera marina*) with very long narrow leaves abundant along the No. Atlantic coast and with related forms constituting a monocotyledonous family (Zosteraceae, the eelgrass family) **2 :** TAPE GRASS
eel·pout \-,paůt\ *n* **1 :** any of various marine fishes resembling blennies (family Zoarcidae) **2 :** BURBOT
eel·worm \-,wərm\ *n* **:** a nematode worm; *esp* **:** any of various small free-living or plant-parasitic roundworms
1-een \'ēn\ *n suffix* [prob. fr. *ratteen*] **:** inferior fabric resembling (a specified fabric) **:** imitation ⟨velvet*een*⟩
2-een *n suffix* [IrGael *-in*] *chiefly Irish* **:** small one **:** dear one **:** petty or contemptible one — in diminutive nouns ⟨buck*een*⟩
e'en \(')ēn\ *adv* **:** EVEN
-eer \'i(ə)r\ *n suffix* [MF *-ier*, fr. L *-arius* — more at -ARY] **1 :** one that is concerned with professionally, conducts, or produces ⟨auction*eer*⟩ ⟨pamphlet*eer*⟩ — often in words with derogatory meaning ⟨profit*eer*⟩ **2 :** contemptible one ⟨patriot*eer*⟩
e'er \(')e(ə)r, (')a(ə)r\ *adv* **:** EVER
ee·rie *also* **ee·ry** \'i(ə)r-ē\ *adj* [ME *eri*, fr. OE *earg* cowardly, wretched] **1** *chiefly Scot* **:** FRIGHTENED **2 a :** frightening because of strangeness or gloominess **b :** STRANGE, MYSTERIOUS **syn** see WEIRD — **ee·ri·ly** \'ir-ə-lē\ *adv* — **ee·ri·ness** \'ir-ē-nəs\ *n*
ef \'ef\ *n* **:** the letter *f*
ef·face \i-'fās, e-\ *vt* [MF *effacer*, fr. *ex-* + *face*] **1 :** to wipe out **:** OBLITERATE **2 :** to make indistinct by rubbing out **syn** see ERASE — **ef·face·able** \-'fā-sə-bəl\ *adj* — **ef·face·ment** \-'fā-smənt\ *n* — **ef·fac·er** *n*

1ef·fect \i-'fekt\ n [ME, fr. MF & L; MF, fr. L *effectus*, fr. *effectus*, pp. of *efficere* to bring about, fr. *ex-* + *facere* to make, do] **1 :** something produced by an agent or cause **:** RESULT **2 a :** PURPORT, INTENT **b :** basic meaning **:** ESSENCE **3 :** an outward sign **:** APPEARANCE **4 :** ACCOMPLISHMENT, FULFILLMENT **5 :** REALITY, FACT **6 :** power to bring about a result **:** INFLUENCE **7** *pl* **:** movable property **:** GOODS **8 a :** a distinctive impression **b :** the creation of a desired impression **9 :** the quality or state of being operative **:** OPERATION

syn EFFECT, CONSEQUENCE, RESULT, EVENT, ISSUE, OUTCOME mean a condition or occurrence traceable to a cause. EFFECT may be chosen to designate only those factors in a complex situation that may be definitely attributed to a known and immediate cause; CONSEQUENCE implies a looser or remoter connection with a cause and usu. implies that the cause is no longer operating; RESULT applies often to the last in a series of effects; an EVENT is a result that cannot be foreseen or is at least partly determined by conditions beyond human control; an ISSUE is often a result that provides an ending or solving of a difficulty; an OUTCOME is the final result of complex or conflicting causes or forces

2**effect** *vt* **1 :** to bring about **:** ACCOMPLISH **2 :** PRODUCE, MAKE **syn** see PERFORM — **ef·fect·er** *n*

1**ef·fec·tive** \i-'fek-tiv\ *adj* **1 a :** producing a decided, decisive, or desired effect **b :** IMPRESSIVE, STRIKING **2 :** ready for service or action **3 :** ACTUAL **4 :** being in effect **:** OPERATIVE — **ef·fec·tive·ly** *adv* — **ef·fec·tive·ness** *n*

syn EFFECTUAL, EFFICIENT, EFFICACIOUS: EFFECTIVE emphasizes the actual production of an effect when in use or in force; EFFECTUAL suggests the decisive accomplishment of a result or fulfillment of an intention; EFFICIENT suggests having given proof of power to produce results, esp. the achievement of maximum result with minimum effort; EFFICACIOUS implies possession of a special quality or virtue giving effective power

2**effective** *n* **:** one that is effective; *esp* **:** a soldier equipped for duty

ef·fec·tor \i-'fek-tər, -,tȯ(ə)r\ *n* **:** a bodily organ that becomes active in response to stimulation

ef·fec·tu·al \i-'fek-chə(-wə)l, -'feksh-wəl\ *adj* **:** producing or able to produce a desired effect **:** ADEQUATE **syn** see EFFECTIVE — **ef·fec·tu·al·i·ty** \i-,fek-chə-'wal-ət-ē\ *n* — **ef·fec·tu·al·ness** \-'fek-chə(-wə)l-nəs, -'feksh-wəl-\ *n*

ef·fec·tu·al·ly \i-'fek-chə-(wə-)lē, -'feksh-wə-\ *adv* **1 :** in an effectual manner **2 :** with great effect **:** COMPLETELY

ef·fec·tu·ate \i-'fek-chə-,wāt\ *vt* **:** EFFECT 1 — **ef·fec·tu·a·tion** \i-,fek-chə-'wā-shən\ *n*

ef·fem·i·na·cy \ə-'fem-ə-nə-sē\ *n* **:** the quality of being effeminate

ef·fem·i·nate \-nət\ *adj* [ME, fr. L *effeminatus*, fr. pp. of *effeminare* to make effeminate, fr. *ex-* + *femina* woman — more at FEMININE] **1 :** having unsuitable feminine qualities **:** UNMANLY **2 :** marked by weakness and love of ease ⟨an ~ civilization⟩ **syn** see FEMININE — **ef·fem·i·nate·ly** *adv* — **ef·fem·i·nate·ness** *n*

ef·fen·di \e-'fen-dē, ə-\ *n* [Turk *efendi* master, fr. NGk *aphentēs*, alter. of Gk *authentēs* — more at AUTHENTIC] **:** a man of property, authority, or education in an eastern Mediterranean country

ef·fer·ent \'ef-ə-rənt, -,er-ənt\ *adj* [F *efférent*, fr. L *efferent-*, *efferens*, prp. of *efferre* to carry outward, fr. *ex-* + *ferre* to carry] **:** conducting outward from a part or organ; *specif* **:** conveying nervous impulses to an effector — **ef·fer·ent** *n* — **ef·fer·ent·ly** *adv*

ef·fer·vesce \,ef-ər-'ves\ *vi* [L *effervescere*, fr. *ex-* + *fervescere* to begin to boil, fr. *fervēre* to boil — more at BURN] **1 :** to bubble, hiss, and foam as gas escapes **2 :** to show liveliness or exhilaration — **ef·fer·ves·cence** \-'ves-ᵊn(t)s\ *n* — **ef·fer·ves·cent** \-ᵊnt\ *adj* — **ef·fer·ves·cent·ly** *adv*

ef·fete \e-'fēt, i-\ *adj* [L *effetus*, fr. *ex-* + *fetus* fruitful] **1 :** no longer fertile **2 a :** worn out with age **:** EXHAUSTED **b :** marked by weakness or decadence — **ef·fete·ly** *adv* — **ef·fete·ness** *n*

ef·fi·ca·cious \,ef-ə-'kā-shəs\ *adj* [L *efficac-*, *efficax*, fr. *efficere*] **:** having the power to produce a desired effect **syn** see EFFECTIVE — **ef·fi·ca·cious·ly** *adv* — **ef·fi·ca·cious·ness** *n*

ef·fi·cac·i·ty \,ef-ə-'kas-ət-ē\ *n* **:** EFFECTIVENESS

ef·fi·ca·cy \'ef-i-kə-sē\ *n* **:** EFFECTIVENESS

ef·fi·cien·cy \i-'fish-ən-sē\ *n* **1 :** the quality or degree of being efficient **2 a :** efficient operation **b** (1) **:** effective operation as measured by a comparison of production with cost (as in energy, time, and money) (2) **:** the ratio of the useful energy delivered by a dynamic system to the energy supplied to it

efficiency engineer *n* **:** one who analyzes methods, procedures, and jobs in order to secure maximum efficiency

ef·fi·cient \i-'fish-ənt\ *adj* [ME, fr. MF or L; MF, fr. L *efficient-*, *efficiens*, fr. pp. of *efficere* to bring about] **1 :** immediately effecting **2 :** productive of desired effects; *esp* **:** productive without waste **syn** see EFFECTIVE — **ef·fi·cient·ly** *adv*

ef·fi·gy \'ef-ə-jē\ *n* [ME *effigie*, fr. L *effigies*, fr. *effingere* to form, fr. *ex-* + *fingere* to shape] **:** an image or representation esp. of a person; *specif* **:** a crude figure representing a hated person

ef·flo·resce \,ef-lə-'res\ *vi* [L *efflorescere*, fr. *ex-* + *florescere* to begin to blossom] **1 :** to burst forth **:** BLOOM **2 a :** to change to a powder from loss of water of crystallization **b :** to form or become covered with a powdery crust

ef·flo·res·cence \-'res-ᵊn(t)s\ *n* **1 :** the period or state of flowering **2 a :** the action or process of developing **b :** an instance of development **c :** fullness of manifestation **:** CULMINATION **3 :** the process or product of efflorescing chemically **4 :** a redness of the skin **:** ERUPTION — **ef·flo·res·cent** \-ᵊnt\ *adj*

ef·flu·ence \'ef-,lü-ən(t)s, -lə-wən(t)s\ *n* [L *effluere* to flow out, fr. *ex-* + *fluere* to flow] **1 :** something that flows out **2 :** an action or process of flowing out — **ef·flu·ent** \-ənt, -wənt\ *adj or n*

ef·flu·vi·um \e-'flü-vē-əm\ *n, pl* **ef·flu·via** \-vē-ə\ *often sing in constr or* **ef·flu·vi·ums** [L *effluvium* act of flowing out, fr. *effluere*] **:** an invisible emanation; *esp* **:** an offensive exhalation or smell

ef·flux \'ef-,ləks\ *n* [L *effluxus*, pp. of *effluere*] **1 :** EFFLUENCE **2 :** a passing away **:** EXPIRATION

ef·flux·ion \e-'flək-shən\ *n* **:** EFFLUX

ef·fort \'ef-ərt, -,ȯ(ə)rt\ *n* [MF, fr. OF *esfort*, fr. *esforcier* to force, fr. *ex-* + *forcier* to force] **1 :** conscious exertion of power **2 :** a serious attempt **:** TRY **3 :** something produced by exertion or trying **4 :** effective force as distinguished from the possible resistance called into action by such a force

syn EFFORT, EXERTION, PAINS, TROUBLE mean the active use of energy in producing a result. EFFORT often suggests a single action or attempt and implies the calling up or directing of energy by the conscious will; EXERTION may describe the bringing into effect of any power of mind or body or it may suggest laborious and exhausting effort; PAINS implies toilsome or solicitous effort; TROUBLE implies effort that inconveniences or slows down

ef·fort·less \'ef-ərt-ləs\ *adj* **:** showing or requiring little or no effort **syn** see EASY — **ef·fort·less·ly** *adv* — **ef·fort·less·ness** *n*

ef·fron·tery \i-'frənt-ə-rē, e-\ *n* [F *effronterie*, deriv. of LL *effront-*, *effrons* shameless, fr. L *ex-* + *front-*, frons forehead — more at BRINK] **:** shameless boldness **:** INSOLENCE **syn** see TEMERITY

ef·ful·gence \i-'fu̇l-jən(t)s, e-, -'fəl-\ *n* [LL *effulgentia*, fr. L *effulgent-*, *effulgens*, prp. of *effulgēre* to shine forth, fr. *ex-* + *fulgēre* to shine] **:** radiant splendor **:** BRILLIANCE — **ef·ful·gent** \-jənt\ *adj*

1**ef·fuse** \i-'fyüz, e-\ *vb* [L *effusus*, pp. of *effundere*, fr. *ex-* + *fundere* to pour — more at FOUND] *vt* **1 :** to pour out (a liquid) **2 :** to give off **:** RADIATE ~ *vi* **:** to flow out **:** EMANATE

2**ef·fuse** \-'fyüs\ *adj* **1 :** poured out freely **:** OVERFLOWING **2 :** DIFFUSE; *specif* **:** spread out flat without definite form ⟨~ lichens⟩ **3 :** having the lips separated by a gap — used of a bivalve shell

ef·fu·sion \i-'fyü-zhən, e-\ *n* **1 :** an act of effusing **2 :** unrestrained expression **3 a :** the escape of a fluid from its vessels by rupture or exudation **b :** the fluid that escapes

ef·fu·sive \i-'fyü-siv, e-, -ziv\ *adj* **1** *archaic* **:** pouring freely **2 :** excessively demonstrative **:** GUSHING **3 :** characterized or formed by a nonexplosive outpouring of lava — **ef·fu·sive·ly** *adv* — **ef·fu·sive·ness** *n*

eft \'eft\ *n* [ME *evete*, *ewte*, fr. OE *efete*] **:** NEWT

eft·soons \eft-'sünz\ *adv* [ME *eftsones*, fr. *eft* after (fr. OE) + *sone* soon + *s*, adv. suffix; akin to OE *æfter* after] *archaic* **:** soon after

egad \i-'gad\ *interj* [prob. euphemism for *oh God*] — used as a mild oath

egal \'ē-gəl\ *adj* [ME, fr. MF, fr. L *aequalis*] *obs* **:** EQUAL

egal·i·tar·i·an \i-,gal-ə-'ter-ē-ən\ *adj* [F *égalitaire*, fr. *égalité* equality, fr. L *aequalitat-*, *aequalitas*, fr. *aequalis*] **:** asserting, promoting, or marked by egalitarianism — **egalitarian** *n*

egal·i·tar·i·an·ism \-ē-ə-,niz-əm\ *n* **1 :** a belief in human equality esp. with respect to social, political, and economic rights and privileges **2 :** a social philosophy advocating the removal of inequalities among men

Ege·ria \i-'jir-ē-ə\ *n* [L] **1 :** a nymph who advised the legendary Roman king Numa Pompilius **2 :** a woman adviser or companion

egest \i-'jest\ *vt* [L *egestus*, pp. of *egerere* to carry outside, discharge, fr. *e-* + *gerere* to carry — more at CAST] **:** EXCRETE — **eges·tion** \-'jes(h)-chən\ *n* — **eges·tive** \-'jes-tiv\ *adj*

eges·ta \i-'jes-tə\ *n pl* [NL, fr. L, neut. pl. of *egestus*] **:** something egested

1**egg** \'eg, 'āg\ *vt* [ME *eggen*, fr. ON *eggja*; akin to OE *ecg* edge — more at EDGE] **:** to incite to action

2**egg** *n, often attrib* [ME *egge*, fr. ON *egg*; akin to OE *ǣg* egg, L *ovum*, Gk *ōion*] **1 a :** the hard-shelled reproductive body produced by a bird and esp. by domestic poultry **b :** an animal reproductive body consisting of an ovum together with its nutritive and protective envelopes and being capable of developing into a new individual capable of independent existence **c :** OVUM **2 :** something resembling an egg **3** *slang* **:** FELLOW, GUY

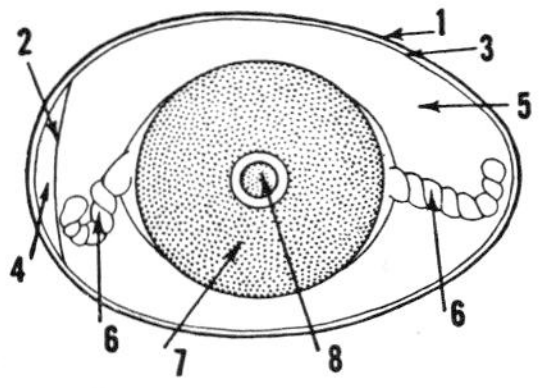

egg of a hen: *1* shell, *2* inner shell membrane, and *3* outer shell membrane enclosing air space *4*, *5* albumen or white, *6* chalazas, *7* yolk, *8* blastodisc

3**egg** *vt* **1 :** to cover with egg **2 :** to pelt with eggs

egg and dart *n* **:** a carved ornamental design in relief consisting of an egg-shaped figure alternating with a figure somewhat like an elongated javelin or arrowhead

egg·head \'eg-,hed, 'āg-\ *n* **:** INTELLECTUAL, HIGHBROW

egg·nog \-,näg\ *n* **:** a drink consisting of eggs beaten up with sugar, milk or cream, and often alcoholic liquor

egg·plant \-,plant\ *n* **1 a :** a widely cultivated perennial herb (*Solanum melongena*) yielding edible fruit **b :** the usu. smooth ovoid fruit of the eggplant **2 :** a dark grayish or blackish purple

1**egg·shell** \'eg-,shel, 'āg-\ *n* **1 :** the hard exterior covering of an egg **2 :** the color of a bird's egg and esp. of a hen's egg

2**eggshell** *adj* **1 :** thin and fragile **2 :** slightly glossy

egis \'ē-jəs\ *var of* AEGIS

eg·lan·tine \'eg-lən-,tīn, -,tēn\ *n* [ME *eglentyn*, fr. MF *aiglent*, fr. (assumed) VL *aculentum*, fr. L *acus* needle] **:** SWEETBRIER

ego \'ē-(,)gō *also* 'eg-(,)ō\ *n* [NL, fr. L, I — more at I] **1 :** the self esp. as contrasted with another self or the world **2 a :** EGOTISM **b :** SELF-ESTEEM **3 :** the conscious part of the personality that is derived from the id through contacts with reality and that mediates the demands of the id, superego, and external reality

ego·cen·tric \,ē-gō-'sen-trik *also* ,eg-ō-\ *adj* **1 :** concerned with the individual rather than society **2 :** taking the ego as the starting point in philosophy **3 a :** limited in outlook or concern to one's own activities or needs **b :** SELFISH — **egocentric** *n* — **ego·cen·tric·i·ty** \-,sen-'tris-ət-ē\ *n* — **ego·cen·trism** \-'sen-,triz-əm\ *n*

ego ideal *n* **:** the positive standards, ideals, and ambitions assimilated from the superego

ego·ism \'ē-gə-,wiz-əm *also* 'eg-ə-\ *n* **1 :** a doctrine that all the elements of knowledge are in the ego and its relations **2 a :** an ethical doctrine that individual self-interest is the actual motive of all conscious action **b :** an ethical doctrine that individual self-interest is the valid end of all action **3 :** EGOTISM

ego·ist \-wəst\ *n* **1 :** a believer in egoism **2 :** an egocentric or egotistic person — **ego·is·tic** \,ē-gə-'wis-tik *also* ,eg-ə-\ *also* **ego·is·ti·cal** \-ti-kəl\ *adj* — **ego·is·ti·cal·ly** \-ti-k(ə-)lē\ *adv*

ego·tism \'ē-gə-,tiz-əm *also* 'eg-ə-\ *n* [L *ego* + E *-tism* (as in *idiotism*)] **1 a :** excessive use of the first person singular personal pronoun **b :** the practice of talking about oneself too much **2 :** an exaggerated sense of self-importance

ego·tist \-təst\ *n* **:** one characterized by egotism — **ego·tis·tic** \,ē-gə-'tis-tik *also* ,eg-ə-\ *or* **ego·tis·ti·cal** \-'tis-ti-kəl\ *adj* — **ego·tis·ti·cal·ly** \-'tis-ti-k(ə-)lē\ *adv*

egre·gious \i-'grē-jəs\ *adj* [L *egregius*, fr. *e-* + *greg-*, *grex* herd — more at GREGARIOUS] **1** *archaic* **:** DISTINGUISHED **2 :** conspicuously bad **:** FLAGRANT — **egre·gious·ly** *adv* — **egre·gious·ness** *n*

1**egress** \'ē-,gres\ *n* [L *egressus*, fr. *egressus*, pp. of *egredi* to go out,

fr. *e-* + *gradi* to go] **1 :** the act or right of going or coming out; *specif* **:** the emergence of a celestial object from eclipse, occultation, or transit **2 :** a place or means of going out **:** EXIT

²**egress** \ē-'gres\ *vi* **:** to go out **:** ISSUE

egres·sion \ē-'gresh-ən\ *n* **:** EGRESS, EMERGENCE

egret \'ē-grət, i-'gret, 'eg-rət, 'ē-,gret\ *n* [ME, fr. MF *aigrette*, fr. OProv *aigreta*, of Gmc origin; akin to OHG *heigaro* heron] **:** any of various herons that bear long plumes during the breeding season

¹**Egyp·tian** \i-'jip-shən\ *adj* **:** of, relating to, or characteristic of Egypt or the Egyptians

²**Egyptian** *n* **1 :** a native or inhabitant of Egypt **2 :** the Afro-Asiatic language of the ancient Egyptians from earliest times to about the 3d century A.D.

Egyptian cotton *n* **:** a fine long-staple often somewhat brownish cotton grown chiefly in Egypt

Egypto- *comb form* [prob. fr. F *Égypto-*, fr. Gk *Aigypto-*, fr. *Aigyptos*] **:** Egypt ⟨*Egyptology*⟩

Egyp·tol·o·gist \,ē-(,)jip-'täl-ə-jəst\ *n* **:** a specialist in Egyptology

Egyp·tol·o·gy \-jē\ *n* **:** the study of Egyptian antiquities

eh \'ā, 'e, 'a(i), *also with* h *preceding and/or with nasalization*\ *interj* [ME *ey*] — used to ask for confirmation or to express inquiry

ei·der \'īd-ər\ *n* [D, G, or Sw, fr. Icel *æthur*, fr. ON *æthr*] **1 :** any of several large northern sea ducks (*Somateria* or related genera) having fine soft down that is used by the female for lining the nest **2 :** EIDERDOWN 1

ei·der·down \-,daůn\ *n* [prob. fr. G *eiderdaune*, fr. Icel *æthardūnn*, fr. *æthur* + *dūnn* down] **1 :** the down of the eider **2 :** a comforter filled with eiderdown

ei·det·ic \ī-'det-ik\ *adj* [Gk *eidētikos* of a form, fr. *eidos* form] **:** of or relating to voluntarily producible visual images having almost photographic accuracy — **ei·det·i·cal·ly** \-i-k(ə-)lē\ *adv*

ei·do·lon \ī-'dō-lən\ *n, pl* **eidolons** \-lənz\ *or* **ei·do·la** \-lə\ [Gk *eidōlon*] **1 :** an unsubstantial image **:** PHANTOM **2 :** IDEAL

eight \'āt\ *n* [ME *eighte*, fr. *eighte*, adj., fr. OE *eahta*; akin to OHG *ahto* eight, L *octo*, Gk *oktō*] **1** — see NUMBER table **2 :** the eighth in a set or series ⟨wears an ∼⟩ **3 :** FIGURE EIGHT **4 :** something having eight units or members: as **a :** an eight-oared racing boat or crew **b :** an eight-cylinder engine or automobile — **eight** *adj or pron*

eight ball *n* **:** a black pool ball numbered 8 — **behind the eight ball :** in a highly disadvantageous position or baffling situation

eigh·teen \(')ā(t)-'tēn\ *n* [ME *eightetene*, adj., fr. OE *eahtatīene*; akin to OE *tīen* ten] — see NUMBER table — **eighteen** *adj or pron* — **eigh·teenth** \-'tēn(t)th\ *adj* — **eighteenth** *n, pl* **eighteenths** \-'tēn(t)s, -'tēn(t)ths\

eigh·teen·mo \ā(t)-'tēn-(,)mō\ *n* **:** the size of a piece of paper cut 18 from a sheet; *also* **:** a book, a page, or paper of this size

eighth \'ātth\ *n, pl* **eighths** \'āts, 'ātths\ — see NUMBER table — **eighth** *adj or adv*

eighth note *n* **:** a musical note with the time value of one eighth of a whole note

eight·i·eth \'āt-ē-əth\ *n* — see NUMBER table — **eightieth** *adj*

eighty \'āt-ē\ *n* [ME *eighty*, adj, fr. OE *eahtatig*, short for *hundeahtatig*, fr. *hundeahtatig*, n., group of eighty, fr. *hund* hundred + *eahta* eight + *-tig* group of ten; akin to OE *tīen* ten] **1** — see NUMBER table **2** *pl* **:** the numbers 80 to 89 inclusive; *specif* **:** the years 80 to 89 in a lifetime or century — **eighty** *adj or pron*

-ein *or* **-eine** *n suffix* [ISV, alter. of *-in*, *-ine*] **:** compound distinguished from a compound with a name ending in *-in* or *-ine* — usu. *-eine* in names of bases and *-ein* in names of other compounds ⟨phthal*ein*⟩

Ein·stein·ian \īn-'stī-nē-ən\ *adj* **:** of or relating to Albert Einstein or his theories

ein·stei·ni·um \-nē-əm\ *n* [NL, fr. Albert *Einstein* †1955 Am physicist & mathematician] **:** a radioactive element produced artificially — see ELEMENT table

ei·stedd·fod \ī-'steth-,vȯd\ *n* [W, lit., session, fr. *eistedd* to sit + *bod* being] **:** a Welsh competitive festival of the arts esp. in singing — **ei·stedd·fod·ic** \,ī-,steth-'vȯd-ik\ *adj*

¹**ei·ther** \'ē-thər *also* 'ī-\ *adj* [ME, fr. OE *ǣghwæther* both, each, fr. *ā* always + *ge-*, collective prefix + *hwæther* which of two, whether] **1 :** the one and the other of two **:** EACH ⟨flowers blooming on ∼ side of the walk⟩ **2 :** the one or the other of two ⟨take ∼ road⟩

²**either** *pron* **:** the one or the other

³**either** *conj* — used as a function word before two or more coordinate words, phrases, or clauses joined usu. by *or* to indicate that what immediately follows is the first of two or more alternatives

⁴**either** *adv* **1 :** LIKEWISE, MOREOVER — used for emphasis after a negative ⟨not wise or handsome ∼⟩ **2 :** for that matter — used for emphasis after an alternative following a question or conditional clause esp. where negation is implied ⟨who answers for the Irish parliament? or army ∼? —Robert Browning⟩

¹**ejac·u·late** \i-'jak-yə-,lāt\ *vb* [L *ejaculatus*, pp. of *ejaculari* to throw out, fr. *e-* + *jaculari* to throw, fr. *jaculum* dart, fr. *jacere* to throw] *vt* **1 :** to eject from a living body; *specif* **:** to eject (semen) in orgasm **2 :** to utter suddenly and vehemently ∼ *vi* **:** to eject a fluid

²**ejac·u·late** \-lət\ *n* **:** the semen released by one ejaculation

ejac·u·la·tion \i-,jak-yə-'lā-shən\ *n* **1 :** an act of ejaculating; *specif* **:** a sudden discharging of a fluid from a duct **2 :** something ejaculated; *esp* **:** a short sudden emotional utterance

ejac·u·la·to·ry \i-'jak-yə-lə-,tōr-ē, -,tȯr-\ *adj* **1 :** casting or throwing out; *specif* **:** associated with or concerned in physiological ejaculation ⟨∼ vessels⟩ **2 :** marked by or given to vocal ejaculation

eject \i-'jekt\ *vt* [ME *ejecten*, fr. L *ejectus*, pp. of *eicere*, fr. *e-* + *jacere*] **1 a :** to drive out esp. by physical force **b :** to evict from property **2 :** to throw out or off from within — **eject·able** \-'jek-tə-bəl\ *adj* — **ejec·tion** \-'jek-shən\ *n* — **ejec·tive** \-'jek-tiv\ *adj*

syn EJECT, EXPEL, OUST, EVICT, DISMISS mean to drive or force out. EJECT carries an esp. strong implication of throwing or thrusting out from within as a physical action; EXPEL implies usu. a voluntary compulsion to get rid of; OUST implies removal or dispossession by power of the law or by compulsion of necessity; EVICT chiefly applies to turning out of house and home; DISMISS implies a getting rid of something unpleasant or troublesome simply by refusing to consider it further

ejec·ta \i-'jek-tə\ *n pl but sing or pl in constr* [NL, fr. L, neut. pl. of *ejectus*] **:** material thrown out (as from a volcano)

ejection seat *n* **:** an emergency escape seat for propelling an occupant out and away from an airplane by means of an explosive charge

eject·ment \i-'jek(t)-mənt\ *n* **1 :** DISPOSSESSION **2 :** an action for the recovery of possession of real property and damages and costs

ejec·tor \i-'jek-tər\ *n* **1 :** one that ejects **2 :** a jet pump for withdrawing a gas, fluid, or powdery substance from a space

¹**eke** \'ēk\ *adv* [ME, fr. OE *ēac*; akin to OHG *ouh* also, L *aut* or, Gk *au* again] *archaic* **:** ALSO

²**eke** *vt* [ME *eken*, fr. OE *īecan*, *ēcan*; akin to OHG *ouhhōn* to add, L *augēre* to increase, Gk *auxein*] *archaic* **:** INCREASE, LENGTHEN

eke out *vt* **1 a :** to supplement so as to make up for the deficiencies of **b :** to make (a supply) last by economy **2 :** to make (as a living) by laborious or precarious means

¹**el** \'el\ *n* **:** the letter *l*

²**el** *n, often cap, often attrib* **:** ELEVATED RAILROAD

¹**elab·o·rate** \i-'lab-(ə-)rət\ *adj* [L *elaboratus*, fr. pp. of *elaborare* to work out, acquire by labor, fr. *e-* + *laborare* to work] **1 :** planned or carried out with great care **:** DETAILED ⟨∼ calculations⟩ **2 :** marked by complexity, fullness of detail, or ornateness **3 :** PAINSTAKING — **elab·o·rate·ly** *adv* — **elab·o·rate·ness** *n*

²**elab·o·rate** \i-'lab-ə-,rāt\ *vt* **1 :** to produce by labor **2 :** to build up (complex organic compounds) from simple ingredients **3 :** to work out in detail **:** DEVELOP ∼ *vi* **1 :** to become elaborate **2 :** to give details — **elab·o·ra·tion** \-,lab-ə-'rā-shən\ *n* — **elab·o·ra·tive** \-'lab-ə-,rāt-iv\ *adj*

Elaine \i-'lān\ *n* **:** any of several women in Arthurian legend; *esp* **:** one who dies for unrequited love of Lancelot

Elam·ite \'ē-lə-,mīt\ *n* **:** a language of unknown affinities used in Elam approximately from the 25th to the 4th centuries B.C.

élan \ā-'län\ *n* [F, fr. MF *eslan* rush, fr. *(s')eslancer* to rush, fr. *ex-* + *lancer* to hurl — more at LANCE] **:** ARDOR, DASH

eland \'ē-lənd, -,land\ *n* [Afrik, elk, fr. D, fr. obs. G *elend*, fr. Lith *elnis*] **:** either of two large African antelopes (genus *Taurotragus*) bovine in form with short spirally twisted horns in both sexes

élan vi·tal \,ā-,län-vē-'täl\ *n* [F] **:** the vital force or impulse of life; *specif* **:** a creative principle held by Bergson to be immanent in all organisms and responsible for evolution

el·a·pid \'el-ə-pəd\ *n* [NL *Elap-*, *Elaps*, genus of snakes, fr. MGk, a fish, alter. of Gk *elops*] **:** any of a family (Elapidae) of venomous snakes with grooved fangs

¹**elapse** \i-'laps\ *vi* [L *elapsus*, pp. of *elabi*, fr. *e-* + *labi* to slip — more at SLEEP] **:** to slip or glide away **:** PASS

²**elapse** *n, of time* **:** PASSAGE, EXPIRATION

elas·mo·branch \i-'laz-mə-,braŋk\ *adj* [deriv. of Gk *elasmos* metal plate (fr. *elaunein*) + L *branchia* gill] **:** of or relating to a class (Chondrichthyes) of fishes having lamellate gills and comprising the sharks, rays, chimaeras, and various extinct related fishes — **elasmobranch** *n*

¹**elas·tic** \i-'las-tik\ *adj* [NL *elasticus*, fr. LGk *elastos* ductile, beaten, fr. Gk *elaunein* to drive, beat out; akin to OIr *luid* he went] **1 a** *of a solid* **:** capable of recovering size and shape after deformation **b** *of a gas* **:** capable of indefinite expansion **2 :** capable of recovering quickly esp. from depression or disappointment **3 :** capable of being easily stretched or expanded and resuming former shape **:** FLEXIBLE **4 a :** capable of ready change or easy expansion or contraction **b :** receptive to new ideas **:** ADAPTABLE — **elas·ti·cal·ly** \-ti-k(ə-)lē\ *adv*

syn RESILIENT, SPRINGY, FLEXIBLE, SUPPLE: ELASTIC implies the property of resisting deformation by stretching; RESILIENT implies the ability to recover shape quickly when the deforming force or pressure is removed; SPRINGY stresses both the ease with which something yields to pressure and the quickness of its return to original shape; FLEXIBLE applies to something which may or may not be resilient or elastic but which can be bent or folded without breaking; SUPPLE applies to something that can be readily bent, twisted, or folded without any sign of injury

²**elastic** *n* **1 a :** an elastic fabric usu. made of yarns containing rubber **b :** something made from such fabric **2 a :** easily stretched rubber usu. prepared in cords, strings, or bands **b :** a rubber band

elas·tic·i·ty \i-,las-'tis-ət-ē, ,ē-,las-, -'tis-tē\ *n* **:** the quality or state of being elastic: as **a :** the capability of a strained body to recover its size and shape after deformation **:** SPRINGINESS **b :** RESILIENCE **c :** ADAPTABILITY

elas·ti·cized \i-'las-tə-,sīzd\ *adj* **:** made with elastic thread or inserts

elas·tin \-tən\ *n* [ISV, fr. NL *elasticus*] **:** a protein similar to collagen that is the chief constituent of elastic fibers

elas·to·mer \-tə-mər\ *n* [*elastic* + *-o-* + *-mer*] **:** any of various elastic substances resembling rubber ⟨polyvinyl ∼*s*⟩ — **elas·to·mer·ic** \i-,las-tə-'mer-ik\ *adj*

¹**elate** \i-'lāt\ *adj* **:** lifted up esp. in spirits **:** ELATED

²**elate** *vt* [L *elatus* (pp. of *efferre* to carry out, elevate), fr. *e-* + *latus*, pp. of *ferre* to carry — more at TOLERATE, BEAR] **:** to fill with joy or pride — **elat·ed·ly** \-'lāt-əd-lē\ *adv* — **elat·ed·ness** *n*

el·a·ter \'el-ət-ər\ *n* [NL, genus of beetles, fr. Gk *elatēr* driver, fr. *elaunein*] **1 :** CLICK BEETLE **2 :** a filamentous plant structure functioning in the distribution of a product (as spores)

elat·er·ite \i-'lat-ə-,rīt\ *n* [G *elaterit*, fr. Gk *elatēr*] **:** a dark brown elastic mineral resin occurring in soft flexible masses

ela·tion \i-'lā-shən\ *n* **1 :** the quality or state of being elated **2 :** pathological euphoria

E layer *n* **:** a layer of the ionosphere occurring at about 60 miles above the earth's surface and capable of reflecting radio waves

¹**el·bow** \'el-(,)bō\ *n* [ME *elbowe*, fr. OE *elboga*; akin to OHG *elinbogo* elbow; both fr. a prehistoric NGmc-WGmc compound whose constituents are akin to OE *eln* ell & OE *boga* bow — more at ELL, BOW] **1 a :** the joint of the arm **b :** a corresponding joint in the anterior limb of a lower vertebrate **2 :** something resembling an elbow; *specif* **:** an angular pipe fitting

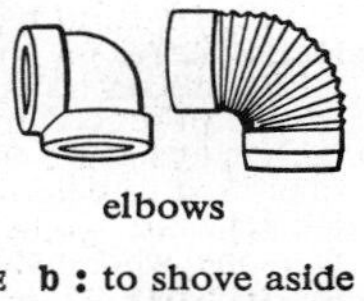

elbows

²**elbow** *vt* **1 a :** to push with the elbow **:** JOSTLE **b :** to shove aside

by pushing with the elbow **2 a :** to force (as one's way) by pushing with the elbow **b :** to force (as one's way) rudely ~ *vi* **1 :** to advance by pushing with the elbow **2 :** to make an angle **:** TURN
elbow grease *n* **:** energy vigorously exerted esp. in physical labor
el·bow·room \\-ˌrüm, -ˌru̇m\\ *n* **1 a :** room for moving the elbows freely **b :** adequate space for work or operation **2 :** free scope
eld \\ˈeld\\ *n* [ME, fr. OE *ieldo;* akin to OE *eald* old — more at OLD] **1** *archaic* **:** old age **2** *archaic* **:** old times **:** ANTIQUITY
[1]**el·der** \\ˈel-dər\\ *n* [ME *eldre,* fr. OE *ellærn;* prob. akin to OE *alor* alder — more at ALDER] **:** any of a genus (*Sambucus*) of shrubs or trees of the honeysuckle family bearing flat clusters of small white or pink flowers and black or red drupes resembling berries
[2]**elder** *adj* [ME, fr. OE *ieldra,* compar. of *eald* old] **1 :** of earlier birth or greater age **2 :** of or relating to earlier times **:** FORMER **3** *obs* **:** of or relating to a more advanced time of life **4 :** prior or superior in rank, office, or validity — **el·der·ship** \\-ˌship\\ *n*
[3]**elder** *n* **1 :** one living in an earlier period **2 a :** one who is older **:** SENIOR **b** *archaic* **:** an aged person **3 :** one having authority by virtue of age and experience **4 :** any of various church officers as **a :** PRESBYTER 1 **b :** a permanent officer elected by a Presbyterian congregation and ordained to serve on the session and assist the pastor at communion **c :** MINISTER 2a, 2b **d :** a Mormon ordained to the Melchizedek priesthood — **el·der·ship** \\-ˌship\\ *n*
el·der·ber·ry \\ˈel-də(r)-ˌber-ē\\ *n* **1 :** the edible berrylike drupe of an elder **2 :** [1]ELDER
el·der·li·ness \\ˈel-dər-lē-nəs\\ *n* **:** the quality or state of being elderly
el·der·ly \\ˈel-dər-lē\\ *adj* **1 :** rather old; *specif* **:** past middle age **2 :** of, relating to, or characteristic of later life
elder statesman *n* **:** an eminent senior member of a group or organization; *esp* **:** a retired statesman who unofficially advises current leaders
el·dest \\ˈel-dəst\\ *adj* **:** OLDEST
eldest hand *n* **:** the card player who first receives cards in the deal
El Do·ra·do \\ˌel-də-ˈräd-(ˌ)ō, -ˈrād-\\ *n* [Sp, lit., the gilded one] **1 :** a city or country of fabulous riches held by 16th-century explorers to exist in So. America **2 :** a place of fabulous wealth, abundance, or opportunity
el·dritch \\ˈel-drich\\ *adj* [perh. fr. (assumed) ME *elfriche* fairyland, fr. ME *elf* + *riche* kingdom, fr. OE *rīce*] **:** WEIRD, EERIE
El·e·at·ic \\ˌel-ē-ˈat-ik\\ *adj* [L *Eleaticus,* fr. Gk *Eleatikos,* fr. *Elea* (Velia), ancient town in So. Italy] **:** of or relating to a school of Greek philosophers founded by Parmenides, developed by Zeno, and marked by belief in the unity of being and the unreality of motion or change — **Eleatic** *n* — **El·e·at·i·cism** \\-ˈat-ə-ˌsiz-əm\\ *n*
ele·cam·pane \\ˌel-i-ˌkam-ˈpān\\ *n* [ME *elena campana,* fr. ML *enula campana,* lit., field elecampane, fr. *inula, enula* elecampane + *campana* of the field] **:** a large coarse European composite herb (*Inula helenium*) with yellow ray flowers naturalized in the U.S.
[1]**elect** \\i-ˈlekt\\ *adj* [ME, fr. L *electus* choice, fr. pp. of *eligere* to select, fr. *e-* + *legere* to choose] **1 :** carefully selected **:** CHOSEN **2 :** chosen for eternal life through divine mercy **3 :** chosen for office or position but not yet installed ⟨president-*elect*⟩
[2]**elect** *n, pl* **elect :** an elect person
[3]**elect** *vt* **1 :** to select usu. by vote for an office, position, or membership **2 :** CHOOSE, SELECT ~ *vi* **:** to make a selection **:** CHOOSE
elec·tion \\i-ˈlek-shən\\ *n* **1 a :** an act or process of electing **b :** the fact of being elected **2 :** predestination to eternal life **3 :** the right, power, or privilege of making a choice **syn** see CHOICE
elec·tion·eer \\i-ˌlek-shə-ˈni(ə)r\\ *vi* [*election* + *-eer* (as in *auctioneer,* v.)] **:** to take an active part in an election; *specif* **:** to work for the election of a candidate or party — **elec·tion·eer·er** \\-ˈnir-ər\\ *n*
[1]**elec·tive** \\i-ˈlek-tiv\\ *adj* **1 a :** chosen or filled by popular election **b :** of or relating to election **c :** based on the right or principle of election **2 :** permitting a choice **:** OPTIONAL **3 a :** tending to operate on one substance rather than another **b :** favorably inclined **:** SYMPATHETIC — **elec·tive·ly** *adv* — **elec·tive·ness** *n*
[2]**elec·tive** *n* **:** an elective course or subject
elec·tor \\i-ˈlek-tər, -ˌtȯ(ə)r\\ *n* **1 :** one qualified to vote in an election **2 :** one entitled to participate in an election: as **a :** one of the German princes entitled to take part in choosing the Holy Roman Emperor **b :** a member of the electoral college in the U.S.
elec·tor·al \\i-ˈlek-t(ə-)rəl\\ *adj* **1 :** of or relating to an elector ⟨the ~ vote⟩ **2 :** of or relating to election ⟨an ~ system⟩
electoral college *n* **:** a body of electors; *esp* **:** one that elects the president and vice-president of the U.S.
elec·tor·ate \\i-ˈlek-t(ə-)rət\\ *n* **1 :** the territory, jurisdiction, or dignity of a German elector **2 :** a body of people entitled to vote
electr- *or* **electro-** *comb form* [NL *electricus*] **1 a :** electricity ⟨*electro*meter⟩ **b :** electric ⟨*electr*ode⟩ **:** electric and ⟨*electro*chemical⟩ **:** electrically ⟨*electro*positive⟩ **2 :** electrolytic ⟨*electro*analysis⟩ **3 :** electron ⟨*electro*valence⟩
Elec·tra \\i-ˈlek-trə\\ *n* [L, fr. Gk *Ēlektra*] **:** a sister of Orestes who urges her brother to avenge their father's murder
Electra complex *n* **:** the female counterpart of the Oedipus complex
elec·tress \\i-ˈlek-trəs\\ *n* **:** the wife or widow of a German elector
[1]**elec·tric** \\i-ˈlek-trik\\ *adj* [NL *electricus* produced from amber by friction, electric, fr. ML, of amber, fr. L *electrum* amber, electrum, fr. Gk *ēlektron;* akin to Gk *ēlektōr* beaming sun, Skt *ulkā* meteor] **1 :** of, relating to, or operated by electricity **2 :** ELECTRIFYING, THRILLING ⟨an ~ performance⟩ — **elec·tri·cal** \\-tri-kəl\\ *adj* — **elec·tri·cal·ly** \\-k(ə-)lē\\ *adv* — **elec·tri·cal·ness** \\-kəl-nəs\\ *n*
[2]**electric** *n* **1** *archaic* **:** a nonconductor of electricity used to excite or accumulate electricity **2 :** something operated by electricity
electrical transcription *n* **1 :** a phonograph record esp. designed for use in radiobroadcasting **2 :** a radio program broadcast from an electrical transcription
electric chair *n* **1 :** a chair used in legal electrocution **2 :** the penalty of death by electrocution
electric eel *n* **:** a large eel-shaped fish (*Electrophorus electricus*) of the Orinoco and Amazon basins said to disable large animals by shocks produced by its electric organs
electric eye *n* **1 :** PHOTOELECTRIC CELL **2 :** a miniature cathode-ray tube used to determine a condition (as of radio tuning)
elec·tri·cian \\i-ˌlek-ˈtrish-ən\\ *n* **1 :** a specialist in electricity **2 :** one who installs, operates, or repairs electrical equipment
elec·tric·i·ty \\i-ˌlek-ˈtris-ət-ē, -ˈtris-tē\\ *n* **1 a :** a fundamental entity of nature consisting of negative and positive kinds composed respectively of electrons and protons or possibly of electrons and positrons, observable in the attractions and repulsions of bodies electrified by friction and in natural phenomena (as lightning or the aurora borealis), and usu. utilized in the form of electric currents **b :** electric current **2 :** a science that deals with the phenomena and laws of electricity **3 :** keen contagious excitement
electric ray *n* **:** any of various rounded rays of warm seas with a short tail and a pair of electric organs
elec·tri·fi·ca·tion \\i-ˌlek-trə-fə-ˈkā-shən\\ *n* **1 :** an act or process of electrifying **2 :** the state of being electrified
elec·tri·fy \\i-ˈlek-trə-ˌfī\\ *vt* **1 a :** to charge with electricity **b** (1) **:** to equip for use of electric power (2) **:** to supply with electric power **2 :** to excite intensely or suddenly as if by an electric shock
elec·tro·anal·y·sis \\i-ˌlek-(ˌ)trō-ə-ˈnal-ə-səs\\ *n* **:** chemical analysis by electrolytic methods — **elec·tro·an·a·lyt·ic** \\-ˌan-ᵊl-ˈit-ik\\ *or* **elec·tro·an·a·lyt·i·cal** \\-ˈit-i-kəl\\ *adj*
elec·tro·car·dio·gram \\-ˈkärd-ē-ə-ˌgram\\ *n* **:** the tracing made by an electrocardiograph
elec·tro·car·dio·graph \\-ˌgraf\\ *n* **:** an instrument for recording the changes of electrical potential occurring during the heartbeat used esp. in diagnosing abnormalities of heart action — **elec·tro·car·dio·graph·ic** \\-ˌkärd-ē-ə-ˈgraf-ik\\ *adj* — **elec·tro·car·dio·graph·i·cal·ly** \\-i-k(ə-)lē\\ *adv* — **elec·tro·car·di·og·ra·phy** \\-ē-ˈäg-rə-fē\\ *n*
elec·tro·chem·i·cal \\-ˈkem-i-kəl\\ *adj* **:** of or relating to electrochemistry — **elec·tro·chem·i·cal·ly** \\-i-k(ə-)lē\\ *adv*
elec·tro·chem·is·try \\-ˈkem-ə-strē\\ *n* **:** a science that deals with the relation of electricity to chemical changes and with the interconversion of chemical and electrical energy
elec·tro·cute \\i-ˈlek-trə-ˌkyüt\\ *vt* [*electr-* + *-cute* (as in *execute*)] **1 :** to execute (a criminal) by electricity **2 :** to kill by electric shock — **elec·tro·cu·tion** \\i-ˌlek-trə-ˈkyü-shən\\ *n*
elec·trode \\i-ˈlek-ˌtrōd\\ *n* **:** a conductor used to establish electrical contact with a nonmetallic part of a circuit
[1]**elec·tro·de·pos·it** \\i-ˌlek-trō-di-ˈpäz-ət\\ *n* **:** a deposit formed on or at an electrode by electrolysis
[2]**electrodeposit** *vt* **:** to deposit (as a metal or rubber) by electrolysis — **elec·tro·de·po·si·tion** \\-ˌdep-ə-ˈzish-ən, -ˌdē-pə-\\ *n*
elec·tro·dy·nam·ic \\-(ˌ)dī-ˈnam-ik\\ *adj* [F *électrodynamique*] **:** of or relating to electrodynamics
elec·tro·dy·nam·ics \\-iks\\ *n pl but sing or pl in constr* **:** a branch of physics that deals with the effects arising from the interactions of electric currents with magnets, with other currents, or with themselves
elec·tro·dy·na·mom·e·ter \\-ˌdī-nə-ˈmäm-ət-ər\\ *n* [ISV] **:** an instrument that measures current by indicating the strength of the forces between a current flowing in fixed coils and one flowing in movable coils
elec·tro·en·ceph·a·lo·gram \\-en-ˈsef-ə-lō-ˌgram\\ *n* [ISV] **:** the tracing of brain waves made by an electroencephalograph
elec·tro·en·ceph·a·lo·graph \\-ˌgraf\\ *n* [ISV] **:** an apparatus for detecting and recording brain waves — **elec·tro·en·ceph·a·lo·graph·ic** \\-(ˌ)en-ˌsef-ə-lō-ˈgraf-ik\\ *adj* — **elec·tro·en·ceph·a·log·ra·phy** \\-ˌsef-ə-ˈläg-rə-fē\\ *n*
elec·tro·form \\i-ˈlek-trə-ˌfȯrm\\ *vt* **:** to form (shaped articles) by electrodeposition on a mold
elec·tro·graph \\-ˌgraf\\ *n* **1 :** an apparatus for the electrical transmission of pictures **2 :** a device used for the etching or transfer of pictures or designs by electrolytic means — **elec·tro·graph·ic** \\i-ˌlek-trə-ˈgraf-ik\\ *adj* — **elec·trog·ra·phy** \\-ˈträg-rə-fē\\ *n*
elec·tro·jet \\i-ˈlek-trə-ˌjet\\ *n* **:** an overhead concentration of electric current found in the regions of strong auroral displays and along the magnetic equator
elec·tro·ki·net·ic \\i-ˌlek-trō-kə-ˈnet-ik, -(ˌ)kī-\\ *adj* **:** of or relating to the motion of particles or liquids that results from or produces a difference of electric potential
elec·tro·ki·net·ics \\-ˈnet-iks\\ *n pl but sing in constr* **:** a branch of physics that deals with the motion of electricity or with the motion of electrified particles in electric and magnetic fields
elec·trol·y·sis \\i-ˌlek-ˈträl-ə-səs\\ *n* **1 a :** the producing of chemical changes by passage of an electric current through an electrolyte **b :** subjection to this action **2 :** the destruction of hair roots with an electric current
elec·tro·lyte \\i-ˈlek-trə-ˌlīt\\ *n* **1 :** a nonmetallic electric conductor in which current is carried by the movement of ions **2 :** a substance that when dissolved in a suitable solvent or when fused becomes an ionic conductor
elec·tro·lyt·ic \\i-ˌlek-trə-ˈlit-ik\\ *adj* **:** of or relating to electrolysis or an electrolyte; *also* **:** involving or produced by electrolysis — **elec·tro·lyt·i·cal·ly** \\-i-k(ə-)lē\\ *adv*
elec·tro·lyze \\i-ˈlek-trə-ˌlīz\\ *vt* **:** to subject to electrolysis
elec·tro·mag·net \\i-ˌlek-trō-ˈmag-nət\\ *n* **:** a core of magnetic material surrounded by a coil of wire through which an electric current is passed to magnetize the core

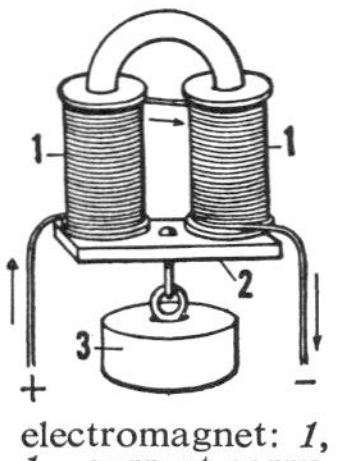

electromagnet: *1, 1,* current-carrying coils, *2* armature, *3* load

elec·tro·mag·net·ic \\-ˌmag-ˈnet-ik\\ *adj* **:** of, relating to, or produced by electromagnetism — **elec·tro·mag·net·i·cal·ly** \\-i-k(ə-)lē\\ *adv*
electromagnetic spectrum *n* **:** the entire range of wavelengths or frequencies of electromagnetic radiation extending from gamma rays to the longest radio waves and including visible light
electromagnetic wave *n* **:** one of the waves propagated by simultaneous periodic variations of electric and magnetic field intensity
elec·tro·mag·ne·tism \\-ˈmag-nə-ˌtiz-əm\\ *n* **1 :** magnetism developed by a current of electricity **2 :** a branch of physical science that deals with the physical relations between electricity and magnetism
elec·tro·met·al·lur·gy \\-ˈmet-ᵊl-ˌər-jē\\ *n* **:** a branch of metallurgy that deals with the application of electric current either for electrolytic deposition or as a source of heat
elec·trom·e·ter \\i-ˌlek-ˈträm-ət-ər\\ *n* **:** any of various instruments for detecting or measuring electric-potential differences or ionizing radiations by means of the forces of attraction or repulsion between charged bodies
elec·tro·mo·tive \\i-ˌlek-trə-ˈmōt-iv\\ *adj* **:** of, relating to, or tending to produce an electric current
electromotive force *n* **:** something that moves or tends to move

electricity **:** the amount of energy derived from an electrical source per unit quantity of electricity passing through the source

elec·tron \i-'lek-,trän\ *n* [*electr-* + *-on*] **:** an elementary particle consisting of a charge of negative electricity equal to about 1.602 $\times 10^{-19}$ coulomb and having a mass when at rest of about 9.107 $\times 10^{-28}$ gram or 1/1837 that of a proton

elec·tro·neg·a·tive \i-,lek-trō-'neg-ət-iv\ *adj* **1 :** charged with negative electricity **2 :** capable of acting as the negative electrode of a voltaic cell — **elec·tro·neg·a·tiv·i·ty** \-,neg-ə-'tiv-ət-ē\ *n*

electron gun *n* **:** the electron-emitting cathode and its surrounding assembly in a cathode-ray tube for directing, controlling, and focusing the stream of electrons to a spot of desired size

elec·tron·ic \i-,lek-'trän-ik\ *adj* **1 :** of or relating to electrons **2 :** of, relating to, or utilizing devices constructed or working by the methods or principles of electronics — **elec·tron·i·cal·ly** \-'trän-i-k(ə-)lē\ *adv*

elec·tron·ics \-'trän-iks\ *n pl but sing in constr* **:** a branch of physics that deals with the emission, behavior, and effects of electrons (as in electron tubes and transistors) and with electronic devices

electron lens *n* **:** a device for converging or diverging a beam of electrons by means of either an electric or a magnetic field

electron microscope *n* **:** an electron-optical instrument in which a beam of electrons focused by means of an electron lens is used to produce an enlarged image of a minute object on a fluorescent screen or photographic plate — **electron microscopy** *n*

electron multiplier *n* **:** a device that amplifies a corpuscular or photon emission by means of the emission of secondary electrons

elec·tron·o·graph·ic \i-,lek-,trän-ə-'graf-ik\ *adj* **:** done by or designed for electronography ⟨an ~ press⟩ ⟨~ printing⟩

elec·tro·nog·ra·phy \-trə-'näg-rə-fē\ *n* **:** a printing process in which the ink is transferred by electrostatic action across a gap between printing plate and impression cylinder

electron optics *n pl but sing or pl in constr* **:** a branch of electronics that deals with those properties of beams of electrons that are analogous to the properties of rays of light

electron tube *n* **:** an electronic device in which conduction by electrons takes place through a vacuum or a gaseous medium within a sealed glass or metal container and which has various common uses based on the controlled flow of electrons

electron volt *n* **:** a unit of energy equal to the energy gained by an electron in passing from a point of low potential to a point one volt higher in potential **:** 1.60 $\times 10^{-12}$ erg

elec·tro·pho·re·sis \i-,lek-trə-fə-'rē-səs\ *n* [NL] **:** the movement of suspended particles through a fluid under the action of an electromotive force applied to electrodes in contact with the suspension — **elec·tro·pho·ret·ic** \-'ret-ik\ *adj*

elec·troph·o·rus \i-,lek-'träf-ə-rəs\ *n, pl* **elec·troph·o·ri** \-,rī, -,rē\ [NL, fr. *electr-* + *-phorus* -phore (fr. Gk *-phoros*)] **:** an instrument for the production of electric charges by induction consisting of a disk that is negatively electrified by friction and a metal plate that becomes charged by induction when placed upon the disk

elec·tro·plate \i-'lek-trə-,plāt\ *vt* **1 :** to plate with an adherent continuous coating by electrodeposition **2 :** ELECTROTYPE

elec·tro·pos·i·tive \i-,lek-trō-'päz-ət-iv, -'päz-tiv\ *adj* **1 a :** charged with positive electricity **b :** capable of acting as the positive electrode of a voltaic cell **2 :** having a tendency to release electrons

elec·tro·scope \i-'lek-trə-,skōp\ *n* [prob. fr. F *électroscope*] **:** any of various instruments for detecting the presence of an electric charge on a body, for determining whether the charge is positive or negative, or for indicating and measuring intensity of radiation

elec·tro·shock therapy \-,shäk-\ *n* **:** the treatment of mental disorder by the induction of coma through use of an electric current

elec·tro·stat·ic \i-,lek-trə-'stat-ik\ *adj* [ISV] **:** of or relating to static electricity or electrostatics — **elec·tro·stat·i·cal·ly** \-i-k(ə-)lē\ *adv*

electrostatic generator *n* **:** an apparatus for the production of electrical discharges at high voltage commonly consisting of an insulated hollow conducting sphere that accumulates in its interior the charge continuously conveyed from a source of direct current by an endless belt of flexible nonconducting material

elec·tro·stat·ics \i-,lek-trə-'stat-iks\ *n pl but sing in constr* **:** physics that deals with phenomena due to attractions or repulsions of electric charges but not dependent upon their motion

electrostatic unit *n* **:** any of a system of electrical units based primarily upon forces of interaction between electric charges

elec·tro·sur·gery \i-,lek-trō-'sərj-(ə-)rē\ *n* **:** surgery by means of diathermy — **elec·tro·sur·gi·cal** \-'sər-ji-kəl\ *adj*

elec·tro·ther·a·py \-'ther-ə-pē\ *n* **:** treatment of disease by means of diathermy or electrically generated heat

elec·tro·ther·mal \-'thər-məl\ *or* **elec·tro·ther·mic** \-mik\ *adj* **:** relating to or combining electricity and heat; *specif* **:** relating to the generation of heat by electricity

elec·tro·ton·ic \i-,lek-trə-'tän-ik\ *adj* **:** relating to electrotonus

elec·trot·o·nus \i-,lek-'trät-ᵊn-əs\ *n* [NL] **:** altered sensitivity of a nerve when a constant current of electricity passes through

[1]**elec·tro·type** \i-'lek-trə-,tīp\ *n* **1 :** a duplicate printing surface made by pressure molding in a plastic material the surface to be reproduced and electrodepositing on it a thin shell that is then backed up with lead **2 :** a print made from an electrotype

[2]**electrotype** *vt* **:** to make an electrotype from (a printing surface) ~ *vi* **:** to be reproducible by electrotyping — **elec·tro·typ·er** *n*

elec·tro·va·lence \i-,lek-trō-'vā-lən(t)s\ *or* **elec·tro·va·len·cy** \-lən-sē\ *n* **:** valence characterized by the transfer of electrons from one atom to another with the formation of ions; *also* **:** the number of charges acquired by an atom by the loss or gain of electrons — **elec·tro·va·lent** \-lənt\ *adj*

elec·trum \i-'lek-trəm\ *n* [ME, fr. L — more at ELECTRIC] **:** a natural pale yellow alloy of gold and silver

elec·tu·ary \i-'lek-chə-,wer-ē\ *n* [ME *electuarie*, fr. L *electuarium*, prob. fr. Gk *ekleikton*, fr. *ekleichein* to lick up, fr. *ex-* + *leichein* to lick — more at LICK] **:** CONFECTION 2b

el·ee·mos·y·nary \,el-i-'mäs-ᵊn-,er-ē\ *adj* [ML *eleemosynarius*, fr. LL *eleemosyna* alms] **:** of, relating to, or supported by charity

el·e·gance \'el-i-gən(t)s\ *n* **1 a :** refined gracefulness **b :** tasteful richness of design or ornamentation **2 :** something that is elegant

el·e·gan·cy \-gən-sē\ *n* **:** ELEGANCE

el·e·gant \'el-i-gənt\ *adj* [MF or L; MF, fr. L *elegant-, elegans*; akin to L *eligere* to select — more at ELECT] **1 :** marked by elegance **2 :** EXCELLENT, SPLENDID **syn** see CHOICE — **el·e·gant·ly** *adv*

ele·gi·ac \,el-ə-'jī-ək, -'jī-,ak; i-'lē-jē-,ak\ *also* **el·e·gi·a·cal** \,el-ə-'jī-ə-kəl\ *adj* [LL *elegiacus*, fr. Gk *elegeiakos*, fr. *elegeion*] **1 a :** of, relating to, or consisting of two dactylic hexameter lines the second of which lacks the arses in the third and sixth feet **b** (1) **:** written in or consisting of elegiac couplets (2) **:** noted for having written poetry in such couplets **c :** of or relating to the period in Greece about the seventh century B.C. when poetry written in such couplets flourished **2 :** of, relating to, or comprising elegy or an elegy; *esp* **:** expressing sorrow often for something now past — **elegiac** *n*

elegiac stanza *n* **:** a quatrain in iambic pentameter with a rhyme scheme of *abab*

ele·git \i-'lē-jət\ *n* [L, he has chosen, fr. *eligere*] **:** a judicial writ of execution by which a defendant's goods and if necessary his lands are delivered for debt to the plaintiff until the debt is paid

el·e·gize \'el-ə-,jīz\ *vi* **:** to lament or celebrate in an elegy ~ *vt* **:** to write an elegy on

el·e·gy \'el-ə-jē\ *n, pl* **elegies** [L *elegia* poem in elegiac couplets, fr. Gk *elegeia, elegeion*, fr. *elegos* song of mourning] **1 a :** a song or poem expressing sorrow or lamentation esp. for one who is dead **b :** something resembling such a song or poem **2 :** a poem in elegiac couplets **3 a :** a pensive or reflective poem usu. nostalgic or melancholy **b :** a short pensive musical composition

el·e·ment \'el-ə-mənt\ *n* [ME, fr. OF & L; OF, fr. L *elementum*] **1 a :** one of the four substances air, water, fire, and earth formerly believed to compose the physical universe **b** *pl* **:** weather conditions caused by activities of the elements; *esp* **:** violent or severe weather **c :** the state or sphere natural or suited to a person or thing **2 :** a constituent part: as **a** *pl* **:** the simplest principles of a subject of study **:** RUDIMENTS **b** (1) **:** a part of a geometric magnitude (2) **:** a generator of a geometric figure (3) **:** a basic member of a mathematical class or set **c** (1) **:** one of the necessary data or values on which calculations or conclusions are based (2) **:** one of the factors determining the outcome of a process **d :** any of more than 100 fundamental substances that consist of atoms of only one kind and that singly or in combination constitute all matter **e :** a distinct part of a composite device **f :** a subdivision of a military unit **g :** MEMBER 4d **3** *pl* **:** the bread and wine used in the Eucharist

syn COMPONENT, CONSTITUENT, INGREDIENT, FACTOR: ELEMENT applies to anything that is a part of a compound or complex whole and often connotes irreducible simplicity; COMPONENT and CONSTITUENT may designate any of the substances (whether elements or compounds) or the qualities that enter into the makeup of a complex product; COMPONENT stresses its separate entity or distinguishable character; CONSTITUENT stresses its essential and formative character; INGREDIENT applies to any of the substances which when combined form a particular mixture (as a medicine, an alloy); FACTOR applies to any constituent or element whose presence helps actively to perform a certain kind of work or produce a definite result

CHEMICAL ELEMENTS
with international atomic weights

ELEMENT & SYMBOL	ATOMIC NUMBER	ATOMIC WEIGHT (O=16)	(C=12)
actinium (Ac)	89		
aluminum (Al)	13	26.98	26.9815
americium (Am)	95		
antimony (Sb)	51	121.76	121.75
argon (Ar)	18	39.944	39.948
arsenic (As)	33	74.91	74.9216
astatine (At)	85		
barium (Ba)	56	137.36	137.34
berkelium (Bk)	97		
beryllium (Be)	4	9.013	9.0122
bismuth (Bi)	83	209.00	208.980
boron (B)	5	10.82	10.811
bromine (Br)	35	79.916	79.909
cadmium (Cd)	48	112.41	112.40
calcium (Ca)	20	40.08	40.08
californium (Cf)	98		
carbon (C)	6	12.011	12.01115
cerium (Ce)	58	140.13	140.12
cesium (Cs)	55	132.91	132.905
chlorine (Cl)	17	35.457	35.453
chromium (Cr)	24	52.01	51.996
cobalt (Co)	27	58.94	58.9332
columbium (Cb)	(see niobium)		
copper (Cu)	29	63.54	63.54
curium (Cm)	96		
dysprosium (Dy)	66	162.51	162.50
einsteinium (Es)	99		
erbium (Er)	68	167.27	167.26
europium (Eu)	63	152.0	151.96
fermium (Fm)	100		
fluorine (F)	9	19.00	18.9984
francium (Fr)	87		
gadolinium (Gd)	64	157.26	157.25
gallium (Ga)	31	69.72	69.72
germanium (Ge)	32	72.60	72.59
gold (Au)	79	197.0	196.967
hafnium (Hf)	72	178.50	178.49
helium (He)	2	4.003	4.0026
holmium (Ho)	67	164.94	164.930
hydrogen (H)	1	1.008	1.00797
indium (In)	49	114.82	114.82
iodine (I)	53	126.91	126.9044
iridium (Ir)	77	192.2	192.2
iron (Fe)	26	55.85	55.847
krypton (Kr)	36	83.80	83.80
lanthanum (La)	57	138.92	138.91
lawrencium (Lr)	103		
lead (Pb)	82	207.21	207.19
lithium (Li)	3	6.940	6.939
lutetium (Lu)	71	174.99	174.97
magnesium (Mg)	12	24.32	24.312

ELEMENT & SYMBOL	ATOMIC NUMBER	ATOMIC WEIGHT (O=16)	(C=12)
manganese (Mn)	25	54.94	54.9380
mendelevium (Md)	101		
mercury (Hg)	80	200.61	200.59
molybdenum (Mo)	42	95.95	95.94
neodymium (Nd)	60	144.27	144.24
neon (Ne)	10	20.183	20.183
neptunium (Np)	93		
nickel (Ni)	28	58.71	58.71
niobium (Nb)	41	92.91	92.906
nitrogen (N)	7	14.008	14.0067
nobelium (No)	102		
osmium (Os)	76	190.2	190.2
oxygen (O)	8	16.000	15.9994
palladium (Pd)	46	106.4	106.4
phosphorus (P)	15	30.975	30.9738
platinum (Pt)	78	195.09	195.09
plutonium (Pu)	94		
polonium (Po)	84		
potassium (K)	19	39.100	39.102
praseodymium (Pr)	59	140.92	140.907
promethium (Pm)	61		
protactinium (Pa)	91		
radium (Ra)	88		
radon (Rn)	86		
rhenium (Re)	75	186.22	186.2
rhodium (Rh)	45	102.91	102.905
rubidium (Rb)	37	85.48	85.47
ruthenium (Ru)	44	101.1	101.07
samarium (Sm)	62	150.35	150.35
scandium (Sc)	21	44.96	44.956
selenium (Se)	34	78.96	78.96
silicon (Si)	14	28.09	28.086
silver (Ag)	47	107.880	107.870
sodium (Na)	11	22.991	22.9898
strontium (Sr)	38	87.63	87.62
sulfur (S)	16	32.066	32.064
tantalum (Ta)	73	180.95	180.948
technetium (Tc)	43		
tellurium (Te)	52	127.61	127.60
terbium (Tb)	65	158.93	158.924
thallium (Tl)	81	204.39	204.37
thorium (Th)	90	232.05	232.038
thulium (Tm)	69	168.94	168.934
tin (Sn)	50	118.70	118.69
titanium (Ti)	22	47.90	47.90
tungsten (W)	74	183.86	183.85
uranium (U)	92	238.07	238.03
vanadium (V)	23	50.95	50.942
wolfram (W)	(see tungsten)		
xenon (Xe)	54	131.30	131.30
ytterbium (Yb)	70	173.04	173.04
yttrium (Y)	39	88.92	88.905
zinc (Zn)	30	65.38	65.37
zirconium (Zr)	40	91.22	91.22

el•e•men•tal \\,el-ə-'ment-ᵊl\\ *adj* **1 a :** of, relating to, or being an element; *specif* **:** existing as an uncombined chemical element **b :** of, relating to, or being the ultimate constituent **c :** ELEMENTARY **d :** INTEGRAL, ESSENTIAL **2 :** of, relating to, or resembling a great force of nature — **elemental** *n* — **el•e•men•tal•ly** \\-ᵊl-ē\\ *adv*

ele•men•tar•i•ly \\,el-ə-(,)men-'ter-ə-lē, -mən-\\ *adv* **:** in an elementary manner

el•e•men•ta•ri•ness \\-'ment-ə-rē-nəs, -'men-trē-\\ *n* **:** the quality or state of being elementary

el•e•men•ta•ry \\,el-ə-'ment-ə-rē, -'men-trē\\ *adj* **1 a :** of or relating to the simplest principles of a subject **b :** of, relating to, or teaching the basic subjects of education ⟨~ school⟩ **2 :** ELEMENTAL 1a, 1b **3 :** ELEMENTAL 2

elementary particle *n* **:** any of the ultimate constituents of matter considered as extremely small charged or uncharged bodies

el•e•mi \\'el-ə-mē\\ *n* [NL *elimi*] **:** any of various fragrant oleoresins obtained from tropical trees (family Burseraceae) and used chiefly in varnishes, lacquers, and printing inks

elen•chus \\i-'leŋ-kəs\\ *n, pl* **elen•chi** \\-,kī, -,kē\\ [L, fr. Gk *elenchos*] **:** REFUTATION; *esp* **:** one in syllogistic form

el•e•phant \\'el-ə-fənt\\ *n* [ME, fr. OF & L; OF *olifant*, fr. L *elephantus*, fr. Gk *elephant-, elephas*] **:** any of various thickset mostly very large nearly hairless four-footed mammals constituting with related extinct forms the elephant family (Elephantidae) and having the snout prolonged into a muscular trunk and two incisors in the upper jaw developed esp. in the male into long tusks which furnish ivory; *broadly* **:** a related animal or fossil

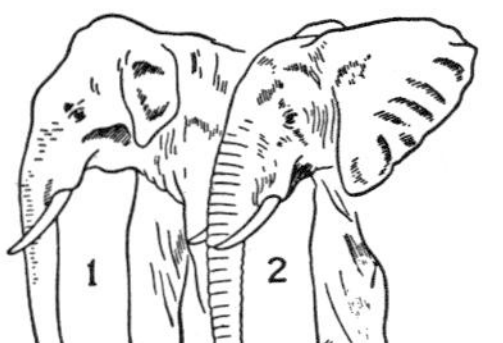

elephants: *1* Indian, *2* African

el•e•phan•ti•a•sis \\,el-ə-fən-'tī-ə-səs, -,fan-\\ *n, pl* **el•e•phan•ti•a•ses** \\-'tī-ə-,sēz\\ [NL, fr. L, a kind of leprosy, fr. Gk, fr. *elephant-, elephas*] **:** enlargement and thickening of tissues; *specif* **:** the enormous enlargement of a limb or the scrotum caused by obstruction of lymphatics by filarial worms

el•e•phan•tine \\,el-ə-'fan-,tēn, -,tīn; 'el-ə-fən-, -,fan-\\ *adj* **1 a :** having enormous size or strength **:** MASSIVE **b :** CLUMSY, PONDEROUS **2 :** of or relating to an elephant

El•eu•sin•i•an mysteries \\,el-yu̇-,sin-ē-ən-\\ *n pl* **:** religious mysteries celebrated at ancient Eleusis in worship of Demeter and Persephone

¹el•e•vate \\'el-ə-,vāt, -vət\\ *adj, archaic* **:** ELEVATED

²el•e•vate \\-,vāt\\ *vt* [ME *elevaten*, fr. L *elevatus*, pp. of *elevare*, fr. *e-* + *levare* to raise] **1 :** to lift up **:** RAISE **2 :** to raise in rank or status **:** EXALT **3 :** to improve morally, intellectually, or culturally **4 :** to raise the spirits of **:** ELATE **syn** see LIFT

el•e•vat•ed *adj* **1 :** raised esp. above the ground or other surface ⟨~ highway⟩ **2 a :** morally or intellectually on a high plane ⟨~ mind⟩ **b :** FORMAL, DIGNIFIED ⟨~ diction⟩ **3 :** EXHILARATED

elevated railroad *n* **:** an urban or interurban railroad operating chiefly on an elevated structure — called also *elevated railway*

el•e•va•tion \\,el-ə-'vā-shən\\ *n* **1 :** the height to which something is elevated: as **a :** the angular distance of a celestial object above the horizon **b :** the degree to which a gun is aimed above the horizon **c :** the height above the level of the sea **:** ALTITUDE **2 :** an act or instance of elevating **3 :** something that is elevated: as **a :** an elevated place or station **b :** a swelling esp. on the skin **4 :** the quality or state of being elevated **5 :** a geometrical projection on a vertical plane **syn** see HEIGHT

el•e•va•tor \\'el-ə-,vāt-ər\\ *n* **1 :** one that raises or lifts something up: as **a :** an endless belt or chain conveyor with cleats, scoops, or buckets for raising material **b :** a cage or platform and its hoisting machinery for conveying something to different levels **c :** a building for elevating, storing, discharging, and sometimes processing grain **2 :** a movable auxiliary airfoil usu. attached to the tail plane of an airplane for producing motion up or down

elev•en \\i-'lev-ən\\ *n* [ME *enleven*, fr. *enleven*, adj., fr. OE *endleofan*; akin to OHG *einlif* eleven; both fr. a prehistoric Gmc compound whose first element is akin to OE *ān* one, and whose second element is prob. akin to OE *lēon* to lend] **1** — see NUMBER table **2 :** the eleventh in a set or series **3 :** something having 11 units or members; *esp* **:** a football team — **eleven** *adj or pron*

elev•enth \\-ən(t)th\\ *n, pl* **elevenths** \\-ən(t)s, -ən(t)ths\\ — see NUMBER table — **eleventh** *adj or adv*

el•e•von \\'el-ə-,vän\\ *n* [*elevator* + *aileron*] **:** an airplane control surface that combines the functions of elevator and aileron

elf \\'elf\\ *n, pl* **elves** \\'elvz\\ [ME, fr. OE *ælf*; akin to ON *alfr* elf] **1 :** a small often mischievous fairy **2 a :** a small creature **:** DWARF; *esp* **:** a mischievous child **b :** a mischievous or malicious person — **elf•ish** \\'el-fish\\ *adj* — **elf•ish•ly** *adv*

elf•in \\'el-fən\\ *adj* [irreg. fr. *elf*] **1 :** of, relating to, or produced by an elf **2 :** resembling an elf; *esp* **:** having a strange charm

elf•lock \\'el-,fläk\\ *n* **:** hair matted as if by elves — usu. used in pl.

Eli \\'ē-,lī\\ *n* [Heb *'Ēlī*] **:** a judge and priest of ancient Israel

elic•it \\i-'lis-ət\\ *vt* [L *elicitus*, pp. of *elicere*, fr. *e-* + *lacere* to allure] **1 a :** to draw forth or bring out **b :** to derive by reason or argument **2 :** to call forth **:** EVOKE **syn** see EDUCE — **elic•i•ta•tion** \\i-,lis-ə-'tā-shən, ,ē-\\ *n* — **elic•i•tor** \\i-'lis-ət-ər\\ *n*

elide \\i-'līd\\ *vt* [L *elidere* to strike out, fr. *e-* + *laedere* to injure by striking] **1 a :** to suppress or alter by elision **b :** to strike out **2 a :** to leave out of consideration **b :** CURTAIL, ABRIDGE

el•i•gi•bil•i•ty \\,el-i-jə-'bil-ət-ē\\ *n* **:** the quality or state of being eligible ⟨~ of a candidate for office⟩

el•i•gi•ble \\'el-i-jə-bəl\\ *adj* [ME, fr. MF & LL; MF, fr. LL *eligibilis*, fr. L *eligere* to choose — more at ELECT] **1 a :** qualified to be chosen **b :** ENTITLED **2 :** worthy of being chosen **:** DESIRABLE — **eligible** *n* — **el•i•gi•bly** \\-blē\\ *adv*

Eli•jah \\i-'lī-jə\\ *n* [Heb *Ēlīyāh*] **:** a Hebrew prophet of the 9th century B.C.

elim•i•nate \\i-'lim-ə-,nāt\\ *vt* [L *eliminatus*, pp. of *eliminare*, fr. *e-* + *limin-, limen* threshold] **1 a :** to get rid of **:** EXPEL **b :** to set aside as unimportant **:** IGNORE **2 :** to expel from the living body **3 :** to cause to disappear by combining two or more equations **syn** see EXCLUDE — **elim•i•na•tion** \\i-,lim-ə-'nā-shən\\ *n* — **elim•i•na•tive** \\i-'lim-ə-,nāt-iv\\ *adj* — **elim•i•na•tor** \\-,nāt-ər\\ *n*

Eli•sha \\i-'lī-shə\\ *n* [Heb *Ělīshā'*] **:** a Hebrew prophet and disciple and successor of Elijah

eli•sion \\i-'lizh-ən\\ *n* [LL *elision-, elisio*, fr. L *elisus*, pp. of *elidere*] **1 :** the use of a speech form that lacks a final or initial sound that a variant speech form has (as the use of *'s* instead of *is* in English *there's*); *specif* **:** the omission of an unstressed vowel or syllable in a verse to achieve a uniform metrical pattern **2 :** the act or an instance of dropping out or omitting something **:** CUT

elite \\ā-'lēt, i-\\ *n* [F *élite*, fr. OF *eslite*, fr. fem. of *eslit*, pp. of *eslire* to choose, fr. L *eligere*] **1 a :** the choice part; *esp* **:** a socially superior group **b :** a powerful minority group **2 :** a typewriter type providing 12 characters to the linear inch and 6 lines to the vertical inch — **elite** *adj*

elit•ism \\-'lēt-,iz-əm\\ *n* **1 a :** leadership or rule by an elite **b :** belief in or advocacy of such elitism **2 :** consciousness of being or belonging to an elite — **elit•ist** \\-'lēt-əst\\ *n or adj*

elix•ir \\i-'lik-sər\\ *n* [ME, fr. ML, fr. Ar *al-iksīr* the elixir, fr. *al* the + *iksīr* elixir, prob. fr. Gk *xērion* desiccative powder, fr. *xēros* dry] **1 a :** a substance held capable of changing metals into gold **b** (1) **:** a substance held capable of prolonging life indefinitely (2) **:** CURE-ALL (3) **:** a sweetened liquid usu. containing alcohol that is used as a vehicle for medicinal agents **2 :** the essential principle

Eliz•a•be•than \\i-,liz-ə-'bē-thən\\ *adj* **:** of, relating to, or characteristic of Elizabeth I of England or her age — **Elizabethan** *n*

elk \\'elk\\ *n, pl* **elks** [ME, prob. fr. OE *eolh*; akin to OHG *elaho* elk, Gk *elaphos* deer] **1** *pl usu* **elk a :** the largest existing deer (*Alces alces*) of Europe and Asia resembling but not so large as the moose of No. America **b :** WAPITI **c :** any of various large Asiatic deer **2 :** soft tanned leather

elk•hound \\'elk-,hau̇nd, 'el-,kau̇nd\\ *n* **:** NORWEGIAN ELKHOUND

¹ell \\'el\\ *n* [ME *eln*, fr. OE] **1 :** a former English unit of length chiefly for cloth equal to 45 inches **2 :** any of various units of length similar in use to the English ell

²ell *n* [alter. of ¹*el*] **:** an extension at right angles to a building

el•lipse \\i-'lips, e-\\ *n* [Gk *elleipsis*] **1 a :** OVAL **b :** a closed plane curve generated by a point moving in such a way that the sums of its distances from two fixed points is a constant **:** a plane section of a right circular cone that is a closed curve **2 :** ELLIPSIS

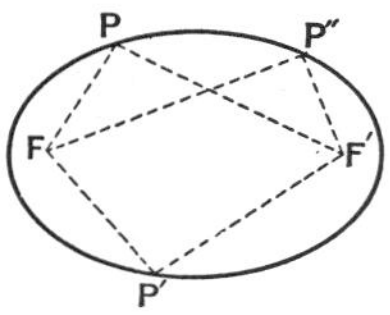

ellipse: *F, F′*, foci; *P, P′, P″*, any point on the curve; $FP+PF' = FP''+P''F' = FP'+P'F'$

el•lip•sis \\i-'lip-səs, e-\\ *n, pl* **el•lip•ses** \\-'lip-,sēz\\ [L, fr. Gk *elleipsis* ellipsis, ellipse, fr. *elleipein* to leave out, fall short, fr. *en* in + *leipein* to leave — more at IN, LOAN] **1 a :** the omission of one or more words that can be obviously understood and supplied to make a construction seem more complete (as in "the man he sees" for "the man that he sees") **b :** a leap or sudden passage without logical connectives from one topic to another **2 :** marks or a mark (as . . . or *** or —) showing omission esp. of letters or words

el·lip·soid \i-ˈlip-ˌsȯid, e-\ *n* **:** a surface all plane sections of which are ellipses or circles — **ellipsoid** *or* **el·lip·soi·dal** \i-ˌlip-ˈsȯid-ᵊl, (ˌ)e-\ *adj*

el·lip·tic \i-ˈlip-tik, e-\ *adj* [Gk *elleiptikos* defective, marked by ellipsis, fr. *elleipein*] **1 a :** of, relating to, or shaped like an ellipse **b :** of, relating to, or being a space in which no line parallel to a given line passes through a point not on the line **2 a :** of, relating to, or marked by ellipsis or an ellipsis **b** (1) **:** of, relating to, or marked by extreme economy of speech or writing (2) **:** of or relating to studied obscurity of literary style — **el·lip·ti·cal** \-ti-kəl\ *adj* — **el·lip·ti·cal·ly** \-ti-k(ə-)lē\ *adv*

el·lip·tic·i·ty \i-ˌlip-ˈtis-ət-ē, (ˌ)e-\ *n* **:** deviation of an ellipse or a spheroid from the form of a circle or a sphere

elm \ˈelm\ *n* [ME, fr. OE; akin to OHG *elme* elm, L *ulmus*] **1 :** any of a genus (*Ulmus* of the family Ulmaceae, the elm family) comprising large graceful trees with alternate stipulate leaves and small apetalous flowers **2 :** the wood of an elm

elm blight *n* **:** DUTCH ELM DISEASE

el·o·cu·tion \ˌel-ə-ˈkyü-shən\ *n* [ME *elocucioun*, fr. L *elocution-*, *elocutio*, fr. *elocutus*, pp. of *eloqui*] **1 :** the art of effective public speaking **2 :** a style of speaking esp. in public — **el·o·cu·tion·ary** \-shə-ˌner-ē\ *adj* — **el·o·cu·tion·ist** \-sh(ə-)nəst\ *n*

elo·dea \i-ˈlōd-ē-ə\ *n* [NL, genus name, fr. Gk *helōdēs* marshy, fr. *helos* marsh; akin to Skt *saras* pond] **:** any of a small American genus (*Elodea*) of submerged aquatic monocotyledonous herbs

eloign \i-ˈlȯin\ *vt* [ME *eloynen*, fr. MF *esloigner*, fr. OF, fr. *es-* ex (fr. L *ex-*) + *loing* (adv.) far, fr. L *longe*, fr. *longus* long] **:** to remove to a distant or unknown place ⟨~ goods liable to distress⟩

1**elon·gate** \i-ˈlȯŋ-ˌgāt\ *vb* [LL *elongatus*, pp. of *elongare*, fr. L *e-* + *longus* long] *vt* **:** to extend the length of ~ *vi* **:** to grow in length **syn** see EXTEND — **elon·ga·tion** \i-ˌlȯŋ-ˈgā-shən, ˌē-\ *n*

2**elongate** *adj* **1 :** stretched out **:** LENGTHENED **2 :** long in proportion to width **:** SLENDER

elon·gat·ed *adj* **:** ELONGATE

elope \i-ˈlōp\ *vi* [AF *aloper*] **1 a :** to run away from one's husband with a lover **b :** to run away secretly with the intention of getting married usu. without parental consent **2 :** to slip away **:** ESCAPE — **elope·ment** \-ˈlōp-mənt\ *n* — **elop·er** *n*

el·o·quence \ˈel-ə-kwən(t)s\ *n* **:** discourse marked by force and persuasiveness; *also* **:** the art or power of using such discourse

el·o·quent \-kwənt\ *adj* [ME, fr. MF, fr. L *eloquent-*, *eloquens*, fr. prp. of *eloqui* to speak out, fr. *e-* + *loqui* to speak] **1 :** marked by forceful and fluent expression **2 :** vividly or movingly expressive or revealing — **el·o·quent·ly** *adv*

1**else** \ˈels\ *adv* [ME *elles*, fr. OE; akin to L *alius* other, *alter* other of two] **1 a :** in a different manner or place or at a different time **b :** in an additional manner or place or at an additional time **2 :** if the facts are or were different **:** if not **:** OTHERWISE

2**else** *adj* **:** OTHER: **a :** being different in identity ⟨somebody ~⟩ **b :** being in addition ⟨what ~⟩

else·where \-ˌ(h)we(ə)r, -ˌ(h)wa(ə)r\ *adv* **:** in or to another place

elu·ci·date \i-ˈlü-sə-ˌdāt\ *vb* [LL *elucidatus*, pp. of *elucidare*, fr. L *e-* + *lucidus* lucid] *vt* **:** to make lucid esp. by explanation ~ *vi* **:** to give a clarifying explanation **syn** see EXPLAIN — **elu·ci·da·tion** \i-ˌlü-sə-ˈdā-shən\ *n* — **elu·ci·da·tive** \i-ˈlü-sə-ˌdāt-iv\ *adj* — **elu·ci·da·tor** \-ˌdāt-ər\ *n*

elude \i-ˈlüd\ *vt* [L *eludere*, fr. *e-* + *ludere* to play] **1 :** to avoid adroitly **:** EVADE **2 :** to escape the notice of **syn** see ESCAPE

El·ul \ˈel-əl\ *n* [Heb *Ělūl*] **:** the 12th month of the civil year or the 6th month of the ecclesiastical year in the Jewish calendar

elu·sion \i-ˈlü-zhən\ *n* [ML *elusion-*, *elusio*, fr. LL, deception, fr. L *elusus*, pp. of *eludere*] **:** an act of eluding: as **a :** an adroit escape **b :** an evasion esp. of a problem or an order

elu·sive \i-ˈlü-siv, -ˈlü-ziv\ *adj* **:** tending to elude **:** EVASIVE — **elu·sive·ly** *adv* — **elu·sive·ness** *n*

elute \i-ˈlüt\ *vt* [L *elutus*, pp. of *eluere* to wash out, fr. *e-* + *lavere* to wash] **:** EXTRACT; *specif* **:** to remove (adsorbed material) from an adsorbent by means of a solvent — **elu·tion** \-ˈlü-shən\ *n*

elu·tri·ate \i-ˈlü-trē-ˌāt\ *vt* [L *elutriatus*, pp. of *elutriare*, irreg. fr. *elutus*] **:** to purify, separate, or remove by washing — **elu·tri·a·tor** \-ˌāt-ər\ *n*

elu·vi·al \ē-ˈlü-vē-əl\ *adj* **1 :** of, relating to, or composed of eluvium **2 :** of or relating to eluviation or to eluviated materials or areas

elu·vi·ate \-vē-ˌāt\ *vi* **:** to undergo eluviation

elu·vi·a·tion \(ˌ)ē-ˌlü-vē-ˈā-shən\ *n* **:** the transportation of dissolved or suspended material within the soil by the movement of water when rainfall exceeds evaporation

elu·vi·um \ē-ˈlü-vē-əm\ *n* [NL, fr. L *eluere* to wash out] **1 :** rock debris produced by the weathering and disintegration of rock in situ **2 :** fine soil or sand deposited by wind

el·ver \ˈel-vər\ *n* [alter. of *eelfare* (migration of eels)] **:** a young eel

elves *pl of* ELF

el·vish \ˈel-vish\ *adj* **1 :** of or relating to elves **2 :** MISCHIEVOUS

ely·sian \i-ˈlizh-ən\ *adj, often cap* **1 :** of or relating to Elysium **2 :** BLISSFUL, DELIGHTFUL

Ely·si·um \i-ˈliz(h)-ē-əm\ *n* [L, fr. Gk *Ēlysion*] **1 :** the abode of the good after death in classical mythology **2 :** PARADISE 2

elytr- *or* **elytri-** *or* **elytro-** *comb form* [NL *elytron*] **:** elytron ⟨*elytr*oid⟩ ⟨*elytri*ferous⟩

el·y·tron \ˈel-ə-ˌträn\ *also* **el·y·trum** \-trəm\ *n, pl* **el·y·tra** \-trə\ [NL, fr. Gk *elytron* sheath, wing cover, fr. *eilyein* to roll, wrap] **:** one of the anterior wings in beetles and some other insects that serve to protect the posterior pair of functional wings

em \ˈem\ *n* **1 :** the letter *m* **2 :** the set dimension of an em quad used as a unit of measure **3 :** PICA

em- — see EN-

ema·ci·ate \i-ˈmā-shē-ˌāt\ *vb* [L *emaciatus*, pp. of *emaciare*, fr. *e-* + *macies* leanness, fr. *macer* lean] *vt* **1 :** to cause to lose flesh so as to become very thin **2 :** to make feeble ~ *vi* **:** to waste away physically — **ema·ci·a·tion** \i-ˌmā-s(h)ē-ˈā-shən\ *n*

em·a·nate \ˈem-ə-ˌnāt\ *vb* [L *emanatus*, pp. of *emanare*, fr. *e-* + *manare* to flow] *vi* **:** to come out from a source ~ *vt* **:** to give out **:** EMIT **syn** see SPRING

em·a·na·tion \ˌem-ə-ˈnā-shən\ *n* **1 a :** the action of emanating **b :** the origination of the world by a series of hierarchically descending radiations from the godhead through intermediate stages to matter **2 a :** something that emanates or is produced by emanation **:** EFFLUENCE **b :** a heavy gaseous element produced by radioactive disintegration ⟨radium ~⟩ — **em·a·na·tion·al** \-shnəl, -shən-ᵊl\ *adj* — **em·a·na·tive** \ˈem-ə-ˌnāt-iv\ *adj*

eman·ci·pate \i-ˈman(t)-sə-ˌpāt\ *vt* [L *emancipatus*, pp. of *emancipare*, fr. *e-* + *mancipare* to transfer ownership of, fr. *mancip-*, *manceps* purchaser, fr. *manus* hand + *capere* to take] **1 :** to release from paternal care and responsibility and make sui juris **2 :** to free from restraint, control, or the power of another; *esp* **:** to free from bondage **syn** see FREE — **eman·ci·pa·tor** \-ˌpāt-ər\ *n*

eman·ci·pa·tion \i-ˌman(t)-sə-ˈpā-shən\ *n* **:** the act or process of emancipating — **eman·ci·pa·tion·ist** \-sh(ə-)nəst\ *n*

emar·gin·ate \(ˈ)ē-ˈmär-jə-nət, -ˌnāt\ *or* **emar·gin·at·ed** \-ˌnāt-əd\ *adj* [L *emarginatus*, pp. of *emarginare* to deprive of a margin, fr. *e-* + *margin-*, *margo* margin] **:** having the margin notched

emas·cu·late \i-ˈmas-kyə-ˌlāt\ *vt* [L *emasculatus*, pp. of *emasculare*, fr. *e-* + *masculus* male] **1 :** to deprive of virile or procreative power **:** CASTRATE **2 :** to deprive of masculine vigor or spirit **:** WEAKEN **syn** see UNNERVE — **emas·cu·late** \-lət\ *adj* — **emas·cu·la·tion** \i-ˌmas-kyə-ˈlā-shən\ *n* — **emas·cu·la·tor** \i-ˈmas-kyə-ˌlāt-ər\ *n*

em·balm \im-ˈbäm, -ˈbälm\ *vt* [ME *embaumen*, fr. MF *embaumer*, fr. OF *embasmer*, fr. *en-* + *basme* balm— more at BALM] **1 :** to treat (a dead body) so as to protect from decay **2 :** to fill with sweet odors **:** PERFUME **3 :** to protect from decay or oblivion **:** PRESERVE — **em·balm·er** *n* — **em·balm·ment** \-ˈbä(l)m-mənt\ *n*

em·bank \im-ˈbaŋk\ *vt* **:** to enclose or confine by an embankment

em·bank·ment \-mənt\ *n* **1 :** the action of embanking **2 :** a raised structure to hold back water or to carry a roadway

em·bar·go \im-ˈbär-(ˌ)gō\ *n, pl* **embargoes** [Sp., fr. *embargar* to bar, fr. (assumed) VL *imbarricare*, fr. L *in-* + (assumed) VL *barra* bar] **1 :** an order of a government prohibiting the departure of commercial ships from its ports **2 :** a legal prohibition upon commerce **3 :** STOPPAGE, IMPEDIMENT; *esp* **:** PROHIBITION **4 :** a common carrier or public regulatory agency order prohibiting or restricting freight transportation — **embargo** *vt*

em·bark \im-ˈbärk\ *vb* [MF *embarquer*, fr. OProv *embarcar*, fr. *em-* (fr. L *im-*) + *barca* bark] *vt* **1 :** to cause to go on board a boat or airplane **2 :** to engage, enlist, or invest in an enterprise ~ *vi* **1 :** to go on board a boat or airplane for transportation **2 :** to make a start **:** COMMENCE — **em·bar·ka·tion** \ˌem-ˌbär-ˈkā-shən, -bər-\ *n* — **em·bark·ment** \-mənt\ *n*

em·bar·rass \im-ˈbar-əs\ *vt* [F *embarrasser*, fr. Sp *embarazar*, fr. Pg *embaraçar*] **1 a :** to hamper the movement of **b :** HINDER, IMPEDE **2 a :** to place in doubt, perplexity, or difficulties **b :** to involve in financial difficulties **c :** to cause to experience a state of self-conscious distress **3 :** to make intricate **:** COMPLICATE

syn DISCOMFIT, ABASH, DISCONCERT, RATTLE: EMBARRASS implies some influence that impedes thought, speech, or action and may be used of persons or of the things they plan or desire to do; DISCOMFIT implies a hampering or frustrating accompanied by confusion; ABASH presupposes some initial self-confidence that receives a sudden check by something that produces shyness, shame, or a conviction of inferiority; DISCONCERT implies an upsetting of equanimity or assurance producing uncertainty or hesitancy; RATTLE implies an agitation that impairs thought and judgment

em·bar·rass·ing·ly \-ə-siŋ-lē\ *adv* **:** to an embarrassing degree

em·bar·rass·ment \im-ˈbar-ə-smənt\ *n* **1 :** the state of being embarrassed: as **a :** confusion or discomposure of mind **b :** difficulty arising from the want of money to pay debts **c :** difficulty in functioning as a result of disease **2 a :** something that embarrasses **:** IMPEDIMENT **b :** an excessive quantity from which to select — used esp. in the phrase *embarrassment of riches*

em·bas·sa·dor \im-\ *var of* AMBASSADOR

em·bas·sage \ˈem-bə-sij\ *n* **1 :** the message or commission entrusted to an ambassador **2** *archaic* **:** EMBASSY

em·bas·sy \ˈem-bə-sē\ *n, often attrib* [MF *ambassee*, of Gmc origin; akin to OHG *ambaht* service] **1 a :** the function or position of an ambassador **b :** a mission abroad undertaken officially esp. by an ambassador **2 :** EMBASSAGE 1 **3 :** a body of diplomatic representatives; *specif* **:** one headed by an ambassador **4 :** the official residence and offices of an ambassador

1**em·bat·tle** \im-ˈbat-ᵊl\ *vt* **em·bat·tling** \-ˈbat-liŋ, -ᵊl-iŋ\ [ME *embatailen*, fr. MF *embatailler*, fr. *en-* + *batailler* to battle] **1 :** to arrange in order of battle **:** prepare for battle **2 :** FORTIFY

2**embattle** *vt* [ME *embatailen*, fr. *en-* + *batailen* to fortify with battlements — more at BATTLE] **:** to furnish with battlements

em·bat·tle·ment \-ˈbat-ᵊl-mənt\ *n* **:** BATTLEMENT

em·bay \im-ˈbā\ *vt* **:** to shut in or shelter esp. in a bay

em·bay·ment \-mənt\ *n* **1 :** formation of a bay **2 :** a bay or a conformation resembling a bay

Emb·den \ˈem-dən\ *n* [*Emden*, Germany] **:** a breed of large white domestic geese with an orange bill and deep orange shanks and toes

em·bed \im-ˈbed\ *vt* **1 a :** to enclose closely in a matrix **b :** to make something an integral part of **c :** to prepare (a microscopy specimen) for sectioning by infiltrating with and enclosing in a supporting substance **2 :** to surround closely ~ *vi* **:** to become embedded — **em·bed·ment** \-mənt\ *n*

em·bel·lish \im-ˈbel-ish\ *vt* [ME *embelisshen*, fr. MF *embeliss-*, stem of *embelir*, fr. *en-* + *bel* beautiful — more at BEAUTY] **1 :** to make beautiful with ornamentation **:** DECORATE **2 :** to heighten the attractiveness of by adding ornamental details **syn** see ADORN

em·bel·lish·ment \-mənt\ *n* **1 :** the act or process of embellishing **2 :** something serving to embellish **3 :** ORNAMENT 5

em·ber \ˈem-bər\ *n* [ME *eymere*, fr. ON *eimyrja*; akin to OE *æmerge* ashes] **1 :** a glowing fragment (as of coal) from a fire; *esp* **:** one smoldering in ashes **2** *pl* **:** the smoldering remains of a fire

ember day \ˈem-bər-\ *n* [ME, fr. OE *ymbrendæg*, fr. *ymbrene* circuit, anniversary + *dæg* day] **:** a Wednesday, Friday, or Saturday following the first Sunday in Lent, Whitsunday, September 14, or December 13 and set apart for fasting and prayer

em·bez·zle \im-ˈbez-əl\ *vt* **em·bez·zling** \-ˈbez-(ə-)liŋ\ [ME *embesilen*, fr. AF *embeseiller*, fr. MF *en-* + *besillier* to destroy] **:** to appropriate (as property entrusted to one's care) fraudulently to one's own use — **em·bez·zle·ment** \-ˈbez-əl-mənt\ *n* — **em·bez·zler** \-ˈbez-(ə-)lər\ *n*

em·bit·ter \im-ˈbit-ər\ *vt* **1 :** to make bitter **2 :** to excite bitter feelings in — **em·bit·ter·ment** \-mənt\ *n*

[1]**em·blaze** \im-ˈblāz\ *vt* [*en-* + *blaze* (to blazon)] **1** *archaic* **:** EMBLAZON 1 **2 :** to adorn sumptuously

[2]**emblaze** *vt* **1 :** to illuminate esp. by a blaze **2 :** to set ablaze

em·bla·zon \im-ˈblāz-ᵊn\ *vt* **em·bla·zon·ing** \-ˈblāz-niŋ, -ᵊn-iŋ\ **1 :** to inscribe or adorn with heraldic bearings or devices **2 a :** to deck in bright colors **b :** CELEBRATE, EXTOL — **em·bla·zon·er** \-ˈblāz-nər, -ᵊn-ər\ — **em·bla·zon·ment** \-ˈblāz-ᵊn-mənt\ *n* — **em·bla·zon·ry** \-ᵊn-rē\ *n*

[1]**em·blem** \ˈem-bləm\ *n* [ME, fr. L *emblema* inlaid work, fr. Gk *emblēmat-*, *emblēma*, fr. *emballein* to insert, fr. *en-* + *ballein* to throw — more at DEVIL] **1 :** a picture with a motto or set of verses intended as a moral lesson **2 :** an object or the figure of an object symbolizing and suggesting another object or an idea **3 a :** a symbolic object used as a heraldic device **b :** a device, symbol, or figure adopted and used as an identifying mark

[2]**emblem** *vt* **:** to represent by an emblem

em·blem·at·ic \ˌem-blə-ˈmat-ik\ *also* **em·blem·at·i·cal** \-i-kəl\ *adj* **:** of, relating to, or constituting an emblem **:** SYMBOLIC

em·blem·a·tize \em-ˈblem-ə-ˌtīz\ *or* **em·blem·ize** \ˈem-blə-ˌmīz\ *vt* **:** to represent by or as if by an emblem **:** SYMBOLIZE

em·ble·ments \ˈem-blə-mən(t)s\ *n pl* [ME *emblayment*, fr. MF *emblaement*, fr. *emblaer* to sow with grain, fr. *en-* + *blee* grain] **:** crops from annual cultivation legally belonging to the tenant

em·bod·i·er \im-ˈbäd-ē-ər\ *n* **:** one that embodies

em·bod·i·ment \im-ˈbäd-i-mənt\ *n* **1 :** the act of embodying or state of being embodied **2 :** a thing that embodies something

em·body \im-ˈbäd-ē\ *vt* **1 :** to give a body to (a spirit) **:** INCARNATE **2 a :** to deprive of spirituality **b :** to make concrete and perceptible **3 :** to cause to become a body or part of a body **:** INCORPORATE **4 :** to represent in human or animal form **:** PERSONIFY

embol- *or* **emboli-** *or* **embolo-** *comb form* [NL, fr. *embolus*] **:** embolus ⟨*embol*ectomy⟩

em·bold·en \im-ˈbōl-dən\ *vt* **:** to impart boldness or courage to

em·bo·lec·to·my \ˌem-bə-ˈlek-tə-mē\ *n* **:** surgical removal of an embolus

em·bol·ic \em-ˈbäl-ik\ *adj* **:** of or relating to an embolus or embolism

em·bo·lism \ˈem-bə-ˌliz-əm\ *n* [ME *embolisme*, fr. ML *embolismus*, fr. Gk *embol-* (fr. *emballein* to insert, intercalate)] **1 :** INTERCALATION **2 a :** the sudden obstruction of a blood vessel by an embolus **b :** EMBOLUS — **em·bo·lis·mic** \ˌem-bə-ˈliz-mik\ *adj*

em·bo·lus \ˈem-bə-ləs\ *n, pl* **em·bo·li** \-ˌlī, -ˌlē\ [NL, fr. Gk *embolos* wedge-shaped object, stopper, fr. *emballein*] **:** an abnormal particle (as an air bubble) circulating in the blood

em·bo·ly \ˈem-bə-lē\ *n* [Gk *embolē* insertion, fr. *emballein*] **:** gastrula formation by simple invagination of the blastula wall

em·bon·point \äⁿ-bōⁿ-pwaⁿ\ *n* [F, fr. MF, fr. *en bon point* in good condition] **:** plumpness of person **:** STOUTNESS

em·bo·som \im-ˈbu̇z-əm, -ˈbüz-\ *vt* **1** *archaic* **:** to take into or place in the bosom **2 :** CHERISH, SHELTER

[1]**em·boss** \im-ˈbäs, -ˈbȯs\ *vt* [ME *embosen* to become exhausted fr. being hunted] *obs* **:** to drive (as a hunted animal) to bay

[2]**emboss** *vt* [ME *embosen*, fr. MF *embocer*, fr. *en-* + *boce* boss] **1 :** to raise the surface of into bosses; *esp* **:** to ornament with raised work **2 :** to raise in relief from a surface **3 :** ADORN, EMBELLISH — **em·boss·er** *n* — **em·boss·ment** \-mənt\ *n*

em·bou·chure \ˌäm-bü-ˈshu̇(ə)r\ *n* [F, fr. (*s'*)*emboucher* to flow into, fr. *en-* + *bouche* mouth — more at DEBOUCH] **1 :** the position and use of the lips in producing a musical tone on a wind instrument **2 :** the mouthpiece of a musical instrument

em·bowed \im-ˈbōd\ *adj* **:** bent like a bow: as **a :** ARCHED, VAULTED **b :** curved outward to form a projecting recess

em·bow·el \im-ˈbau̇(-ə)l\ *vt* **1 :** DISEMBOWEL **2** *obs* **:** ENCLOSE

em·bow·er \im-ˈbau̇(-ə)r\ *vt* **:** to shelter or enclose in a bower

[1]**em·brace** \im-ˈbrās\ *vb* [ME *embracen*, fr. MF *embracer*, fr. OF *embracier*, fr. *en-* + *brace* two arms] *vt* **1 a :** to clasp in the arms **:** HUG **b :** CHERISH, LOVE **2 :** ENCIRCLE, ENCLOSE **3 a :** to take up esp. readily or gladly **b :** to avail oneself of **:** WELCOME **4 a :** to take in **:** INCLUDE **b :** to be equal or equivalent to ⟨his assets *embraced* ten dollars⟩ ~ *vi* **:** to participate in an embrace **syn** see ADOPT, INCLUDE — **em·brace·able** \-ˈbrā-sə-bəl\ *adj* — **em·brace·ment** \-ˈbrā-smənt\ *n* — **em·brac·er** *n*

[2]**embrace** *n* **1 :** a close encircling with the arms and pressure to the bosom **2 :** ENCIRCLEMENT, GRIP **3 :** ACCEPTANCE

em·bra·ceor \im-ˈbrā-sər\ *n* [AF, fr. MF *embraseor* instigator, fr. *embraser* to set on fire, fr. *en-* + *brase, brese* live coals] **:** one guilty of embracery

em·brac·ery \im-ˈbrās-(ə-)rē\ *n* [ME, fr. AF *embraceor*] **:** an attempt to influence a jury corruptly

em·branch·ment \im-ˈbranch-mənt\ *n* [F *embranchement*, fr. (*s'*)*embrancher* to branch out, fr. *en-* + *branche* branch] **1 :** a branching off or out (as of a valley) **2 :** BRANCH

em·bran·gle \im-ˈbraŋ-gəl\ *vt* [*en-* + *brangle* (squabble)] **:** CONFUSE, ENTANGLE — **em·bran·gle·ment** \-mənt\ *n*

em·bra·sure \im-ˈbrā-zhər\ *n* [F, fr. obs. *embraser* to widen an opening] **1 :** a recess of a door or window **2 :** an opening with sides flaring outward in a wall or parapet of a fortification usu. for allowing the firing of cannon

em·brit·tle \im-ˈbrit-ᵊl\ *vt* **:** to make brittle ~ *vi* **:** to become brittle — **em·brit·tle·ment** \-mənt\ *n*

em·bro·cate \ˈem-brə-ˌkāt\ *vt* [LL *embrocatus*, pp. of *embrocare*, fr. Gk *embrochē* lotion, fr. *embrechein* to embrocate, fr. *en-* + *brechein* to wet] **:** to moisten and rub (a part of the body) with a lotion

em·bro·ca·tion \ˌem-brə-ˈkā-shən\ *n* **:** LINIMENT

embroglio *var of* IMBROGLIO

em·broi·der \im-ˈbrȯid-ər\ *vb* **em·broi·der·ing** \-(ə-)riŋ\ [ME *embroderen*, fr. MF *embroder*, fr. *en-* + *broder* to embroider, of Gmc origin; akin to OE *brord* point, *byrst* bristle] *vt* **1 a :** to ornament with needlework **b :** to form with needlework **2 :** to elaborate on **:** EXAGGERATE ~ *vi* **1 :** to make embroidery **2 :** to provide embellishments **:** ELABORATE — **em·broi·der·er** \-ˈbrȯid-ər-ər\ *n*

em·broi·dery \im-ˈbrȯid-(ə-)rē\ *n, often attrib* **1 a :** the art or process of forming decorative designs with hand or machine needlework **b :** such a design or decoration **c :** an object decorated with embroidery **2 :** elaboration by use of decorative often fictitious detail **3 :** something pleasing or desirable but unimportant

em·broil \im-ˈbrȯi(ə)l\ *vt* [F *embrouiller*, fr. MF, fr. *en-* + *brouiller* to broil] **1 :** to throw into disorder or confusion **2 :** to involve in conflict or difficulties — **em·broil·ment** \-mənt\ *n*

em·brown \im-ˈbrau̇n\ *vt* **1 :** DARKEN **2 :** to cause to turn brown

embrue *var of* IMBRUE

embry- *or* **embryo-** *comb form* [LL, fr. Gk, fr. *embryon*] **:** embryo ⟨*embryo*geny⟩

em·bryo \ˈem-brē-ˌō\ *n, often attrib* [ML *embryon-*, *embryo*, fr. Gk *embryon*, fr. *en-* + *bryein* to swell; akin to Gk *bryon* moss] **1 a** *archaic* **:** a vertebrate at any stage of development prior to birth or hatching **b :** an animal in the early stages of growth and differentiation that are characterized by cleavage, the laying down of fundamental tissues, and the formation of primitive organs and organ systems; *esp* **:** the developing human individual from the time of implantation to the end of the eighth week after conception **2 :** the young sporophyte of a seed plant usu. comprising a rudimentary plant with plumule, radicle, and cotyledons **3 a :** something as yet undeveloped **b :** a beginning or undeveloped state of something — used esp. in the phrase *in embryo*

em·bryo·gen·ic \ˌem-brē-ō-ˈjen-ik\ *or* **em·bryo·ge·net·ic** \ˌem-brē-(ˌ)ō-jə-ˈnet-ik\ *adj* **:** of, relating to, or involved in embryogeny

em·bry·og·e·ny \ˌem-brē-ˈäj-ə-nē\ *or* **em·bryo·gen·e·sis** \ˌem-brē-ō-ˈjen-ə-səs\ *n* **:** the formation and development of the embryo

em·bry·o·log·ic \ˌem-brē-ə-ˈläj-ik\ *adj* **:** of or relating to embryology — **em·bry·o·log·i·cal** \-i-kəl\ *adj* — **em·bry·o·log·i·cal·ly** \-i-k(ə-)lē\ *adv*

em·bry·ol·o·gist \ˌem-brē-ˈäl-ə-jəst\ *n* **:** a specialist in embryology

em·bry·ol·o·gy \-jē\ *n* [F *embryologie*] **1 :** a branch of biology that relates to embryogeny **2 :** the features and phenomena exhibited in the formation and development of an embryo

embryon- *or* **embryoni-** *comb form* [ML *embryon-*, *embryo*] **:** embryo ⟨*embryon*ic⟩

em·bry·o·nal \ˈem-brē-ən-ᵊl\ *adj* **:** EMBRYONIC 1 — **em·bry·o·nal·ly** \-ᵊl-ē\ *adv*

em·bry·o·nat·ed \ˈem-brē-ə-ˌnāt-əd\ *adj* **:** having an embryo

em·bry·on·ic \ˌem-brē-ˈän-ik\ *adj* **1 :** of or relating to an embryo **2 :** INCIPIENT, RUDIMENTARY — **em·bry·on·i·cal·ly** \-i-k(ə-)lē\ *adv*

embryonic disk *n* **1 a :** BLASTODISC **b :** BLASTODERM **2 :** the part of the inner cell mass of a blastocyst from which the embryo of a placental mammal develops — called also *embryonic shield*

embryonic layer *n* **:** GERM LAYER

embryonic membrane *n* **:** a structure (as the amnion) that derives from the fertilized ovum but does not form a part of the embryo

em·bryo·phyte \ˈem-brē-ə-ˌfīt\ *n, in some classifications* **:** a plant (as a fern) producing an embryo and developing vascular tissues

embryo sac *n* **:** the female gametophyte of a seed plant consisting of a thin-walled sac within the nucellus that contains the egg nucleus and others which give rise to endosperm on fertilization

em·bry·ot·ic \ˌem-brē-ˈät-ik\ *adj* [*embryo* + *-tic* (as in *patriotic*)] **:** EMBRYONIC 2

[1]**em·cee** \ˈem-ˈsē\ *n* [*M.C.*] **:** MASTER OF CEREMONIES

[2]**emcee** *vb* **em·ceed; em·cee·ing** *vt* **:** to act as master of ceremonies of ~ *vi* **:** to act as master of ceremonies

Em·den *var of* EMBDEN

-eme \ˌēm\ *n suffix* [F *-ème* (fr. *phonème* speech sound, phoneme)] **:** significantly distinctive unit of language structure ⟨taxeme⟩

emend \ē-ˈmend\ *vt* [ME *emenden*, fr. L *emendare* — more at AMEND] **1** *archaic* **:** to free from defects **2 :** to correct usu. by textual alterations **syn** see CORRECT — **emend·able** \-ˈmen-də-bəl\ *adj*

emen·date \ˈē-ˌmen-ˌdāt, ˈem-ən-\ *vt* **:** EMEND 2 — **emen·da·tor** \-ˌdāt-ər\ *n* — **emen·da·to·ry** \ē-ˈmen-də-ˌtōr-ē, -ˌtȯr-\ *adj*

emen·da·tion \(ˌ)ē-ˌmen-ˈdā-shən, ˌem-ən-\ *n* **1 :** the act of emending **2 :** an alteration designed to correct or improve

[1]**em·er·ald** \ˈem-(ə-)rəld\ *n* [ME *emerallde*, fr. MF *esmeralde*, fr. (assumed) VL *smaralda*, fr. L *smaragdus*, fr. Gk *smaragdos*] **1 :** a rich green variety of beryl prized as a gemstone **2 :** any of various green gemstones (as synthetic corundum or demantoid)

[2]**emerald** *adj* **:** brightly or richly green

emerald green *n* **1 :** a clear bright green resembling that of the emerald **2 :** any of various strong greens

emerge \i-ˈmərj\ *vi* [L *emergere*, fr. *e-* + *mergere* to plunge] **1 :** to rise from or as if from an enveloping fluid **:** come out into view **2 :** to become manifest **3 :** to rise from an obscure or inferior condition **4 :** to come into being through evolution

emer·gence \i-ˈmər-jən(t)s\ *n* **1 :** the act or an instance of emerging **2 :** any of various superficial outgrowths of plant tissue usu. formed from both epidermis and immediately underlying tissues

emer·gen·cy \i-ˈmər-jən-sē\ *n* **1 :** an unforeseen combination of circumstances or the resulting state that calls for immediate action **2 :** a pressing need **:** EXIGENCY **syn** see JUNCTURE

[1]**emer·gent** \i-ˈmər-jənt\ *adj* [ME, fr. L *emergent-*, *emergens*, prp. of *emergere*] **1 :** rising out of or as if out of a fluid **2 a :** arising unexpectedly **b :** calling for prompt action **:** URGENT **3 :** arising as a natural or logical consequence

[2]**emergent** *n* **1 :** something emergent **2 :** a plant rooted in shallow water and having most of the vegetative growth above water

emergent evolution *n* **:** evolution characterized by the appearance at different levels of wholly new and unpredictable characters or qualities through a rearrangement of preexistent entities

emer·i·tus \i-ˈmer-ət-əs\ *adj* [L, pp. of *emereri* to serve out one's term, fr. *e-* + *mereri*, *merēre* to earn, deserve, serve] **1 :** holding after retirement an honorary title corresponding to that held last during active service **2 :** retired from an office or position — **emeritus** *n, pl* **emer·i·ti** \-ˈmer-ə-ˌtī, -ˌtē\

emersed \(ˈ)ē-ˈmərst\ *adj* **:** standing out of or rising above a surface (as of a fluid)

emer·sion \(ˈ)ē-ˈmər-zhən, -shən\ *n* [L *emersus*, pp. of *emergere*] **:** an act of emerging **:** EMERGENCE

em·ery \ˈem-(ə-)rē\ *n, often attrib* [ME, fr. MF *emeri*, fr. OIt *smiriglio*, fr. ML *smiriglum*, fr. Gk *smyrid-*, *smyris*] **:** a dark granular corundum used for grinding and polishing; *also* **:** a hard abrasive powder

emet·ic \i-ˈmet-ik\ *n* [L *emetica*, fr. Gk *emetikē*, fr. fem. of *emetikos* causing vomiting, fr. *emein* to vomit] **:** an agent that induces vomiting — **emetic** *adj* — **emet·i·cal·ly** \-i-k(ə-)lē\ *adv*

em·e·tine \'em-ə-ˌtēn\ *n* **:** an amorphous alkaloid $C_{29}H_{40}N_2O_4$ extracted from ipecac root and used as an emetic and expectorant

émeute \ā-mœ̄t\ *n, pl* **émeutes** *same*\ [F] **:** UPRISING

-emia *or* **-ae·mia** \'ē-mē-ə\ *also* **-he·mia** *or* **-hae·mia** \'hē-\ *n comb form* [NL *-emia, -aemia,* fr. Gk *-aimia,* fr. *haima* blood — more at HEM-] **1 :** condition of having (such) blood ⟨leuk*emia*⟩ **2 :** condition of having (a specified thing) in the blood ⟨ur*emia*⟩

¹em·i·grant \'em-i-grənt\ *n* **1 :** one who emigrates **2 :** a migrant plant or animal

syn EMIGRANT, IMMIGRANT mean one who leaves his country to settle in another. Both terms refer to the same person, EMIGRANT as leaving his country, IMMIGRANT as entering and settling in another country

²emigrant *adj* **:** departing from a country to settle elsewhere

em·i·grate \'em-ə-ˌgrāt\ *vi* [L *emigratus,* pp. of *emigrare,* fr. *e-* + *migrare* to migrate] **:** to leave a place of abode or a country for life or residence elsewhere — **em·i·gra·tion** \ˌem-ə-'grā-shən\ *n*

émi·gré *or* **emi·gré** \ˌem-ə-'grā, ˌā-mə-\ *n* [F *émigré,* fr. pp. of *émigrer* to emigrate, fr. L *emigrare*] **:** EMIGRANT; *esp* **:** a person forced to emigrate by political or other circumstances

em·i·nence \'em-ə-nən(t)s\ *n* **1 :** a condition or station of prominence or superiority by reason of rank or office or of personal attainments — used as a title for a cardinal **2 :** something eminent, prominent, or lofty: as **a :** a person of high rank or attainments **b :** a natural elevation

em·i·nen·cy \'em-ə-nən-sē\ *n* **:** EMINENCE

em·i·nent \'em-ə-nənt\ *adj* [ME, fr. MF or L; MF, fr. L *eminent-, eminens,* prp. of *eminēre* to stand out, fr. *e-* + *-minēre* (akin to L *mont-, mons* mountain)] **1 :** standing out so as to be readily perceived or noted **:** CONSPICUOUS **2 a :** PROJECTING **b :** LOFTY, TOWERING **3 :** exhibiting eminence esp. in standing above others in some quality or position **:** PROMINENT **syn** see FAMOUS — **em·i·nent·ly** *adv*

eminent domain *n* **:** a right of a government to take private property for public use by virtue of the superior dominion of the sovereign power over all lands within its jurisdiction

emir \i-'mi(ə)r, ā-\ *n* [Ar *amīr* commander] **:** a native ruler in parts of Asia and Africa — **emir·ate** \-'mi(ə)r-ət, -ˌāt\ *n*

em·is·sary \'em-ə-ˌser-ē\ *n* [L *emissarius,* fr. *emissus,* pp. of *emittere*] **1 :** one sent upon a mission as the agent of another **2 :** a spy or other secret agent

emis·sion \ē-'mish-ən\ *n* **1 a :** an act or instance of emitting **:** EMANATION **b** *archaic* **:** PUBLICATION **c :** a putting into circulation **d :** a flow of electrons from a surface **2 a :** something sent forth by emitting **b :** EFFLUVIUM — **emis·sive** \-'mis-iv\ *adj*

emis·siv·i·ty \ˌem-ə-'siv-ət-ē, ˌē-ˌmi-\ *n* **:** the relative power of a surface to emit heat by radiation

emit \ē-'mit\ *vt* **emit·ted; emit·ting** [L *emittere* to send out, fr. *e-* + *mittere* to send — more at SMITE] **1 a :** to throw or give off or out (as light) **b :** to send out **:** EJECT **2 a :** to issue with authority; *esp* **:** to put (as money) into circulation **b** *obs* **:** PUBLISH **3 a :** to give utterance to **:** EXPRESS **b :** to give voice to — **emit·ter** *n*

em·men·a·gogue \ə-'men-ə-ˌgäg, e-\ *n* [Gk *emmēna* menses (fr. neut. pl. of *emmēnos* monthly, fr. *en-* + *mēn* month) + E *-agogue* — more at MOON] **:** an agent that promotes the menstrual discharge

em·mer \'em-ər\ *n* [G, fr. OHG *amari*] **:** a hard red wheat (*Triticum dicoccum*) having spikelets with two kernels that remain in the glumes after threshing; *broadly* **:** a tetraploid wheat

em·met \'em-ət\ *n* [ME *emete*] *chiefly dial* **:** ANT

¹emol·lient \i-'mäl-yənt, -ē-ənt\ *adj* [L *emollient-, emolliens,* prp. of *emollire* to soften, fr. *e-* + *mollis* soft] **1 :** making soft or supple; *also* **:** soothing esp. to the skin or mucous membrane **2 :** MOLLIFYING

²emollient *n* **:** something that softens or soothes

emol·u·ment \i-'mäl-yə-mənt\ *n* [ME, fr. L *emolumentum,* lit., miller's fee, fr. *emolere* to grind up, fr. *e-* + *molere* to grind — more at MEAL] **1 :** the profit arising from office or employment usu. in the form of compensation or perquisites **2** *archaic* **:** ADVANTAGE **syn** see WAGE

emote \i-'mōt\ *vi* [back-formation fr. *emotion*] **:** to give expression to emotion esp. in or as if in a play or movie

emo·tion \i-'mō-shən\ *n* [MF, fr. *emouvoir* to stir up, fr. L *exmovēre* to move away, disturb, fr. *ex-* + *movēre* to move] **1 a** *obs* **:** DISTURBANCE **b :** EXCITEMENT **2 a :** the affective aspect of consciousness **:** FEELING **b :** a state of feeling **c :** a psychic and physical reaction subjectively experienced as strong feeling and physiologically involving changes that prepare the body for immediate vigorous action **syn** see FEELING

emo·tion·al \-shnəl, -shən-ᵊl\ *adj* **1 :** of or relating to emotion **2 :** dominated by or prone to emotion **3 :** appealing to or arousing emotion **4 :** markedly aroused or agitated in feeling or sensibilities — **emo·tion·al·ly** \-ē\ *adv*

emo·tion·al·ism \-shnə-ˌliz-əm, -shən-ᵊl-ˌiz-\ *n* **1 :** undue indulgence in or display of emotion **2 :** a tendency to regard things emotionally

emo·tion·al·ist \-shnə-ləst, -shən-ᵊl-əst\ *n* **1 :** one who tends to rely on emotion as opposed to reason; *esp* **:** one who bases a theory or policy on an emotional conviction **2 :** one given to emotionalism — **emo·tion·al·is·tic** \i-ˌmō-shnə-'lis-tik, -shən-ᵊl-'is-\ *adj*

emo·tion·al·i·ty \i-ˌmō-shə-'nal-ət-ē\ *n* **:** the quality or state of being emotional

emo·tion·al·ize \i-'mō-shnə-ˌlīz, -shən-ᵊl-ˌīz\ *vt* **:** to give an emotional quality to

emo·tion·less \i-'mō-shən-ləs\ *adj* **:** showing or expressing no emotion — **emo·tion·less·ness** *n*

emo·tive \i-'mōt-iv\ *adj* **1 :** of or relating to the emotions **2 :** appealing to or expressing emotion — **emo·tive·ly** *adv* — **emo·tiv·i·ty** \i-ˌmō-'tiv-ət-ē, ˌē-ˌmō-\ *n*

empanel *var of* IMPANEL

em·pa·thet·ic \ˌem-pə-'thet-ik\ *adj* **:** EMPATHIC

em·path·ic \em-'path-ik, im-\ *adj* **:** involving, characterized by, or based on empathy

em·pa·thy \'em-pə-thē\ *n* **1 :** the imaginative projection of a subjective state into an object so that the object appears to be infused with it **2 :** the capacity for participating in another's feelings or ideas

em·pen·nage \ˌäm-pə-'näzh, ˌem-\ *n* [F, feathers of an arrow, empennage] **:** the tail assembly of an airplane

em·per·or \'em-pər-ər, -prər\ *n* [ME, fr. OF *empereor,* fr. L *imperator,* lit., commander, fr. *imperatus,* pp. of *imperare* to command, fr. *in-* + *parare* to prepare, order — more at PARE] **:** the sovereign or supreme monarch of an empire

emperor butterfly *n* **:** any of several large richly colored butterflies (family Nymphalidae)

em·pery \'em-p(ə-)rē\ *n* [ME *emperie,* fr. OF, fr. *emperer* to command, fr. L *imperare*] **:** wide dominion **:** EMPIRE

em·pha·sis \'em(p)-fə-səs\ *n, pl* **em·pha·ses** \-fə-ˌsēz\ [L, fr. Gk, exposition, emphasis, fr. *emphainein* to indicate, fr. *en-* + *phainein* to show] **1 a :** a forcefulness of expression that gives special impressiveness or importance **b :** a particular prominence given in reading or speaking to one or more words or syllables **2 :** special consideration of or stress or insistence upon something

em·pha·size \'em(p)-fə-ˌsīz\ *vt* **:** to give emphasis to or place emphasis upon **:** STRESS

em·phat·ic \im-'fat-ik, em-\ *adj* [Gk *emphatikos,* fr. *emphainein*] **1 :** uttered with or marked by emphasis **2 :** tending to express oneself in forceful speech or to take decisive action **3 :** attracting special attention **4 :** constituting or belonging to a set of tense forms in English that consist of the auxiliary *do* followed by an infinitive without *to* and are used to facilitate rhetorical inversion, to take the place of a simple verb form normally in negative or interrogative sentences, or to emphasize — **em·phat·i·cal·ly** \-i-k(ə-)lē\ *adv*

em·phy·se·ma \ˌem(p)-fə-'sē-mə, -'zē-\ *n* [NL, fr. Gk *emphysēma* bodily inflation] **:** a condition characterized by air-filled expansions of body tissues; *specif* **:** a condition of the lung marked by distension and frequently by impairment of heart action — **em·phy·se·ma·tous** \-'sem-ət-əs, -'zem-, -'sēm-, -'zēm-\ *adj*

em·pire \'em-ˌpī(ə)r\ *n* [ME, fr. OF *empire, empirie,* fr. L *imperium* absolute authority, empire, fr. *imperare* to command] **1 a** (1) **:** a major political unit having a territory of great extent or a number of territories or peoples under a single sovereign authority; *esp* **:** one having an emperor as chief of state (2) **:** the territory of such a political unit **b :** something held to resemble a political empire; *esp* **:** an extensive territory or enterprise under single domination or control **2 :** imperial sovereignty, rule, or dominion

Em·pire \'äm-ˌpi(ə)r, 'em-ˌpī(ə)r\ *adj* [F, fr. (*le premier*) *Empire* the first Empire of France] **:** of, relating to, or characteristic of a style (as of clothing) popular in early 19th-century France

Em·pire Day \'em-ˌpī(ə)r-\ *n* **:** COMMONWEALTH DAY — used before the official adoption of *Commonwealth Day* in 1958

em·pir·ic \im-'pir-ik, em-\ *n* [L *empiricus,* fr. Gk *empeirikos* doctor relying on experience alone, fr. *empeiria* experience, fr. *en-* + *peiran* to attempt — more at FEAR] **1** *archaic* **:** CHARLATAN **2 :** one who relies upon practical experience

em·pir·i·cal \-i-kəl\ *or* **em·pir·ic** \-ik\ *adj* **1 :** relying on experience or observation alone often without due regard for system and theory **2 :** originating in or based on observation or experience **3 :** capable of being verified or disproved by observation or experiment ⟨~ laws⟩ — **em·pir·i·cal·ly** \-i-k(ə-)lē\ *adv*

empirical formula *n* **:** a chemical formula showing the simplest ratio of elements in a compound rather than the total number of atoms in the molecule

em·pir·i·cism \-'pir-ə-ˌsiz-əm\ *n* **1 a :** a former school of medical practice founded on experience without the aid of science or theory **b :** QUACKERY, CHARLATANRY **2 a :** the practice of relying upon observation and experiment esp. in the natural sciences **b :** a tenet arrived at empirically **3 a :** a theory that all knowledge originates in experience **b :** LOGICAL POSITIVISM — **em·pir·i·cist** \-səst\ *n*

em·place \im-'plās\ *vt* [back-formation fr. *emplacement*] **:** to put into position

em·place·ment \-'plā-smənt\ *n* [F, fr. MF *emplacer* to emplace, fr. *en-* + *place*] **1 :** the situation or location of something **2 :** a prepared position for weapons or military equipment **3 :** a putting into position **:** PLACEMENT

em·plane \im-'plān\ *var of* ENPLANE

¹em·ploy \im-'plȯi\ *vt* [ME *emploien,* fr. MF *emploier,* fr. L *implicare* to enfold, involve, implicate, fr. *in-* + *plicare* to fold — more at PLY] **1 a :** to make use of **b :** to occupy (as time) advantageously **c** (1) **:** to use or engage the services of (2) **:** to provide with a job that pays wages or a salary **2 :** to devote to or direct toward a particular activity or person

syn EMPLOY, HIRE mean to engage for work. EMPLOY stresses the use of a person's services; HIRE stresses the act of engaging a person's services for pay **syn** see in addition USE

²employ *n* **1** *archaic* **a :** USE **b :** OCCUPATION **2 :** the state of being employed esp. for wages or a salary

em·ploy·abil·i·ty \im-ˌplȯi-ə-'bil-ət-ē\ *n* **:** the quality or state of being employable

em·ploy·able \im-'plȯi-ə-bəl\ *adj* **:** capable of being employed

em·ploy·ee *or* **em·ploye** \im-ˌplȯ(i)-'ē, (ˌ)em-; im-'plȯ(i)-ˌē, em-\ *n* **:** one employed by another usu. for wages or salary and in a position below the executive level

em·ploy·er \im-'plȯi(-ə)r, -'plȯ-yər\ *n* **:** one that employs

em·ploy·ment \im-'plȯi-mənt\ *n* **1 :** USE, PURPOSE **2 a :** activity in which one engages or is employed **b :** an instance of such activity **3 :** the act of employing **:** the state of being employed **syn** see WORK

em·poi·son \im-'pȯiz-ᵊn\ *vt* [ME *empoysonen,* fr. MF *empoisoner,* fr. *en-* + *poison*] **1** *archaic* **:** POISON **2 :** EMBITTER — **em·poi·son·ment** \-mənt\ *n*

em·po·ri·um \im-'pōr-ē-əm, em-, -'pȯr-\ *n, pl* **emporiums** *also* **em·po·ria** \-ē-ə\ [L, fr. Gk *emporion,* fr. *emporos* traveler, trader, fr. *en* in + *poros* passage, journey] **1 a :** a place of trade; *esp* **:** a commercial center **b :** a usu. sizable place of business that serves customers **2 :** a store carrying a diversity of merchandise

em·pow·er \im-'paů(-ə)r\ *vt* **:** to give official authority or legal power to **syn** see ENABLE — **em·pow·er·ment** \-mənt\ *n*

em·press \'em-prəs\ *n* [ME *emperesse,* fr. OF, fem. of *empereor* emperor] **1 :** the wife or widow of an emperor **2 :** a woman who holds an imperial title in her own right

em·presse·ment \äⁿ-pres-mäⁿ\ *n* [F, fr. (*s'*)*empresser* to hurry, fr. *en-* + *presser* to press] **:** demonstrative warmth or cordiality

em·prise \em-'prīz\ *n* [ME, fr. MF, fr. OF, fr. *emprendre* to undertake, fr. (assumed) VL *imprehendere,* fr. L *in-* + *prehendere* to seize

1 : UNDERTAKING, ENTERPRISE; *esp* : an adventurous, daring, or chivalric enterprise **2** : ADVENTUROUSNESS, BOLDNESS

emp·ti·ly \'em(p)-tə-lē\ *adv* : in an empty manner

emp·ti·ness \-tē-nəs\ *n* : the quality or state of being empty

1**emp·ty** \'em(p)-tē\ *adj* [ME, fr. OE *ǣmettig* unoccupied, fr. *ǣmetta* leisure, fr. *ǣ-* without + *-metta* (fr. *mōtan* to have to)] **1 a** : containing nothing **b** : UNOCCUPIED **c** : UNINHABITED **d** : UNFREQUENTED **e** : not pregnant ⟨~ heifer⟩ **f** : NULL 4 **2 a** : lacking reality, substance, or value : HOLLOW ⟨an ~ pleasure⟩ **b** : destitute of effect or force **c** : devoid of sense : FOOLISH **3** : HUNGRY **4 a** : IDLE ⟨~ hours⟩ **b** : having no purpose or result : USELESS **5** : marked by the absence of human life, activity, or comfort

syn VACANT, BLANK, VOID, VACUOUS: EMPTY implies a complete lack or absence of usual content; VACANT implies absence of any occupant or tenant or inmate; BLANK stresses the lack of any significant, intelligible, or relieving features on a surface, esp. freedom from writing or marking; VOID implies the absence of anything whatever, utter emptiness; VACUOUS suggests the emptiness of a vacuum and esp. the lack of intelligence or significance **syn** see in addition VAIN

2**empty** *vt* **1 a** : to make empty : remove the contents of **b** : DEPRIVE, DIVEST **c** : to discharge (itself) of contents **2** : to remove from what holds or encloses **3** : to transfer by emptying ~ *vi* **1** : to become empty **2** : to discharge its contents

3**empty** *n* : something that is empty: as **a** : an empty container **b** : an unoccupied vehicle

emp·ty–hand·ed \,em(p)-tē-'han-dəd\ *adj* **1** : having or bringing nothing **2** : having acquired or gained nothing

emp·ty–head·ed \-'hed-əd\ *adj* : SCATTERBRAINED

em·pur·ple \im-'pər-pəl\ *vb* **em·pur·pling** \-'pər-p(ə-)liŋ\ *vt* : to tinge or color purple ~ *vi* : to become purple

em·py·ema \,em-,pī-'ē-mə, -pē-\ *n* [LL, fr. Gk *empyēma*] : the presence of pus in a bodily cavity — **em·py·emic** \-'ē-mik, -'em-ik\ *adj*

em·py·re·al \,em-,pī-'rē-əl, -pə-; em-'pir-ē-əl, -'pī-rē-\ *adj* [LL *empyrius, empyreus*, fr. LGk *empyrios*, fr. Gk *en* in + *pyr* fire] **1** : of or relating to the empyrean : CELESTIAL **2** : SUBLIME

1**em·py·re·an** \-ən\ *adj* : EMPYREAL

2**empyrean** *n* **1 a** : the highest heaven or heavenly sphere in ancient and medieval cosmology usu. consisting of fire or light **b** : the true and ultimate heavenly paradise **2** : FIRMAMENT, HEAVENS

emu \'ē-(,)myü\ *n* [modif. of Pg *ema* rhea] **1** : an Australian bird (*Dromiceius novae-hollandiae*) that is the largest existing bird next to the ostrich **2** : any of various tall flightless birds (as the rhea)

1**em·u·late** \'em-yə-,lāt\ *vt* [L *aemulatus*, pp. of *aemulari*, fr. *aemulus* rivaling] **1 a** : to strive to equal or excel **b** : IMITATE **2** : to equal or approach equality with — **em·u·la·tor** \-,lāt-ər\ *n*

2**em·u·late** \-lət\ *adj*, *obs* : EMULOUS

em·u·la·tion \,em-yə-'lā-shən\ *n* **1** : ambition or endeavor to equal or excel; *also* : IMITATION **2** *obs* : ambitious or envious rivalry — **em·u·la·tive** \'em-yə-,lāt-iv\ *adj* — **em·u·la·tive·ly** *adv*

em·u·lous \'em-yə-ləs\ *adj* **1 a** : ambitious or eager to emulate **b** : inspired by or deriving from a desire to emulate **2** *obs* : JEALOUS — **em·u·lous·ly** *adv* — **em·u·lous·ness** *n*

emul·si·fi·able \i-'məl-sə-,fī-ə-bəl\ *or* **emul·si·ble** \i-'məl-sə-bəl\ *adj* : capable of being emulsified ⟨~ oils⟩

emul·si·fi·ca·tion \i-,məl-sə-fə-'kā-shən\ *n* : the process of emulsifying

emul·si·fi·er \i-'məl-sə-,fī(-ə)r\ *n* : one that emulsifies; *esp* : a surface-active agent (as a soap) promoting the formation and stabilization of an emulsion

emul·si·fy \-,fī\ *vt* : to convert (as an oil) into an emulsion

emul·sion \i-'məl-shən\ *n* [NL *emulsion-, emulsio*, fr. L *emulsus*, pp. of *emulgēre* to milk out, fr. *e-* + *mulgēre* to milk; akin to OE *melcan* to milk, Gk *amelgein*] **1 a** : a system (as fat in milk) consisting of a liquid dispersed with or without an emulsifier in an immiscible liquid usu. in droplets of larger than colloidal size **b** : the state of such a system **2** : SUSPENSION 2b(3); *esp* : a suspension of a sensitive silver salt or salts in a viscous medium (as a gelatin solution) forming a coating on photographic plates, film, or paper — **emul·sive** \-'məl-siv\ *adj*

emul·soid \i-'məl-,sȯid\ *n* **1** : a colloidal system consisting of a liquid dispersed in a liquid **2** : a lyophilic sol (as a gelatin solution) — **emul·soi·dal** \-,məl-'sȯid-ᵊl\ *adj*

emunc·to·ry \i-'məŋ(k)-t(ə-)rē\ *n* [NL *emunctorium*, fr. L *emunctus*, pp. of *emungere* to clean the nose, fr. *e-* + *-mungere* (akin to *mucus*)] *archaic* : an organ that carries off body wastes

en \'en\ *n* **1** : the letter *n* **2** : the set dimension of an en quad

1**en-** *also* **em-** \e *also occurs in these prefixes although only* i *may be shown as in "engage"*\ *prefix* [ME, fr. OF, fr. L *in-, im-*, fr. *in*] **1** : put into or on to ⟨*en*cradle⟩ ⟨*en*throne⟩ : cover with ⟨*en*verdure⟩ : go into or on to ⟨*em*bus⟩ — in verbs formed from nouns **2** : cause to be ⟨*en*slave⟩ — in verbs formed from adjectives or nouns **3** : provide with ⟨*em*power⟩ — in verbs formed from nouns **4** : so as to cover ⟨*en*wrap⟩ : thoroughly ⟨*en*tangle⟩ — in verbs formed from verbs; in all senses usu. *em-* before *b, m,* or *p*

2**en-** *also* **em-** *prefix* [ME, fr. L, fr. Gk, fr. *en* in — more at IN] : in : within ⟨*en*zootic⟩ — usu. *em-* before *b, m,* or *p* ⟨*em*pathy⟩

1**-en** \ən, ᵊn\ *also* **-n** \n\ *adj suffix* [ME, fr. OE; akin to OHG *-īn* made of, L *-īnus* of or belonging to, Gk *-inos* made of, of or belonging to] : made of : consisting of ⟨earth*en*⟩ ⟨wool*en*⟩ ⟨silver*n*⟩

2**-en** *vb suffix* [ME *-nen*, fr. OE *-nian*; akin to OHG *-inōn* -en] **1 a** : cause to be ⟨sharp*en*⟩ **b** : cause to have ⟨length*en*⟩ **2 a** : come to be ⟨steep*en*⟩ **b** : come to have ⟨length*en*⟩

en·able \in-'ā-bəl\ *vt* **en·abling** \-b(ə-)liŋ\ **1 a** : to make able ⟨~ a person to earn a living⟩ **b** : to make possible, practical, or easy **2** : to give legal power, capacity, or sanction to

syn ENABLE, EMPOWER mean to make one able to do something. ENABLE implies provision of the means or opportunity for doing; EMPOWER implies the granting of power or delegation of authority to do

en·act \in-'akt\ *vt* **1** : to establish by legal and authoritative act; *specif* : to make (as a bill) into law **2** : to act out : REPRESENT — **en·ac·tor** \-'ak-tər\ *n*

en·act·ment \-'ak(t)-mənt\ *n* **1** : the act of enacting : the state of being enacted **2** : LAW, STATUTE

1**enam·el** \in-'am-əl\ *vt* **enam·eled** *or* **enam·elled**; **enam·el·ing** *or* **enam·el·ling** \-'am-(ə-)liŋ\ [ME *enamelen*, fr. MF *enamailler*, fr. *en-* + *esmail* enamel, of Gmc origin; akin to OHG *smelzan* to melt — more at SMELT] **1** : to cover or inlay with enamel **2** : to beautify with a colorful surface **3** : to form a glossy surface on

2**enamel** *n* **1** : a usu. opaque vitreous composition applied by fusion to the surface of metal, glass, or pottery **2** : a surface, exterior, or outer covering that resembles enamel **3** : a usu. glossy paint that flows out to a smooth hard coat when applied **4** : a calcareous substance that forms a thin layer capping the teeth

enam·el·ware \-,wa(ə)r, -,we(ə)r\ *n* : ware coated with enamel

en·am·or *or chiefly Brit* **en·am·our** \in-'am-ər\ *vt* **en·am·or·ing** \-(ə-)riŋ\ [ME *enamouren*, fr. OF *enamourer*, fr. *en-* + *amour* love — more at AMOUR] : to inflame with love

en·an·tio·morph \in-'ant-ē-ə-,mȯrf\ *n* [Gk *enantios* opposite (fr. *enanti* facing, fr. *en* in + *anti* against) + ISV *-morph*] : either of a pair of chemical compounds or crystals whose molecular structures have a mirror-image relationship to each other — **en·an·tio·mor·phic** \in-,ant-ē-ə-'mȯr-fik\ *adj* — **en·an·tio·mor·phism** \-,fiz-əm\ *n* — **en·an·tio·mor·phous** \-'mȯr-fəs\ *adj*

en·ar·thro·sis \,en-(,)är-'thrō-səs\ *n* [NL, fr. Gk *enarthrōsis*] : a ball-and-socket joint (as the hip joint)

en bloc \ä^n-'bläk\ *adv (or adj)* [F] : as a whole : in a mass

en·cae·nia \en-'sē-nyə\ *n pl but sing or pl in constr, often cap* [NL, fr. L, dedication festival, fr. Gk *enkainia*, fr. *en* in + *kainos* new] : an annual university ceremony (as at Oxford) of commemoration with recital of poems and essays and conferring of degrees

en·cage \in-'kāj\ *vt* : CAGE 1

en·camp \in-'kamp\ *vt* : to form into or place in a camp ~ *vi* : to form or occupy a camp

en·camp·ment \-mənt\ *n* **1 a** : the act of encamping **b** : the state of being encamped **2** : CAMP

en·cap·su·late \in-'kap-sə-,lāt\ *vt* : to encase in a capsule ~ *vi* : to become encapsulated — **en·cap·su·la·tion** \in-,kap-sə-'lā-shən\ *n*

en·cap·su·lat·ed *adj* : surrounded by a gelatinous or membranous envelope

en·case \in-'kās\ *vt* : to enclose in or as if in a case

en·case·ment \in-'kā-smənt\ *n* **1** : the act or process of encasing : the state of being encased **2** : the supposed enclosure in a living germ of the germs of all future generations that might develop from it

1**en·caus·tic** \in-'kȯ-stik\ *adj* [L *encausticus*, fr. Gk *enkaustikos*, fr. *enkaiein* to burn in, fr. *en-* + *kaiein* to burn] : of or relating to encaustic — **en·caus·ti·cal·ly** \-sti-k(ə-)lē\ *adv*

2**encaustic** *n* **1** : a paint mixed with melted beeswax and after application fixed by heat **2** : the method involving the use of encaustic

-ence \ən(t)s, ᵊn(t)s\ *n suffix* [ME, fr. OF, fr. L *-entia*, fr. *-ent-, -ens*, prp. ending + *-ia* -y] **1** : action or process ⟨emerg*ence*⟩ : instance of an action or process ⟨refer*ence*⟩ **2** : quality or state ⟨despond*ence*⟩

1**en·ceinte** \ä^n-'sant, än-\ *adj* [MF, fr. (assumed) VL *incienta*, alter. of L *incient-, inciens* being with young, fr. *in* + *-cient-, -ciens* (akin to Gk *kyein* to be pregnant)] : being with child : PREGNANT

2**enceinte** *n* [F, fr. OF, enclosing wall, fr. *enceindre* to surround, fr. L *incingere*, fr. *in-* + *cingere* to gird] : a line of fortification enclosing a castle or town; *also* : the area or town so enclosed

encephal- *or* **encephalo-** *comb form* [F *encéphal-*, fr. Gk *enkephal-*, fr. *enkephalos*] : brain ⟨*encephal*itis⟩ ⟨*encephalo*cele⟩

en·ce·phal·ic \,en(t)-sə-'fal-ik\ *adj* : of or relating to the brain; *also* : lying within the cranial cavity

en·ceph·a·lit·ic \(,)en-,sef-ə-'lit-ik\ *adj* : relating to, affected with, or characteristic of encephalitis

en·ceph·a·li·tis \-'līt-əs\ *n* : inflammation of the brain

en·ceph·a·lo·gram \en-'sef-ə-lō-,gram\ *n* [ISV] : an X-ray picture of the brain made by encephalography

en·ceph·a·lo·graph \-,graf\ *n* **1** : ENCEPHALOGRAM **2** : ELECTROENCEPHALOGRAPH

en·ceph·a·log·ra·phy \(,)en-,sef-ə-'läg-rə-fē\ *n* [ISV] : roentgenography of the brain after the cerebrospinal fluid has been replaced

en·ceph·a·lo·my·eli·tis \en-,sef-ə-lō-,mī-ə-'līt-əs\ *n* [NL] : concurrent inflammation of the brain and spinal cord; *specif* : any of several virus diseases of horses

en·ceph·a·lon \en-'sef-ə-,län, -lən\ *n, pl* **en·ceph·a·la** \-lə\ [NL, fr. Gk *enkephalos*, fr. *en* in + *kephalē* head] : the vertebrate brain

en·chain \in-'chān\ *vt* [ME *encheynen*, fr. MF *enchainer*, fr. OF, fr. *en-* + *chaeine* chain] **1** : to bind with or as if with chains **2** : to attract and hold (as the attention) — **en·chain·ment** \-mənt\ *n*

en·chant \in-'chant\ *vt* [ME *enchanten*, fr. MF *enchanter*, fr. L *incantare*, fr. *in-* + *cantare* to sing] **1** : to influence by charms and incantation : BEWITCH **2** : THRILL, ENRAPTURE **syn** see ATTRACT

en·chant·er \in-'chant-ər\ *n* : one that enchants; *esp* : SORCERER

en·chant·ing *adj* : CHARMING — **en·chant·ing·ly** \-iŋ-lē\ *adv*

en·chant·ment \in-'chant-mənt\ *n* **1 a** : the act or action of enchanting **b** : the quality or state of being enchanted **2** : something that enchants

en·chant·ress \in-'chan-trəs\ *n* **1** : a woman who practices magic : SORCERESS **2** : a fascinating woman

en·chase \in-'chās\ *vt* [ME *enchasen* to emboss, fr. MF *enchasser* to enshrine, set, fr. *en-* + *chasse* reliquary, fr. L *capsa* case] **1** : SET ⟨~ a gem⟩ **2** : ORNAMENT: as **a** : to cut or carve in relief **b** : INLAY

en·chi·la·da \,en-chə-'läd-ə\ *n* [AmerSp] : a tortilla rolled with meat filling and served with tomato sauce seasoned with chili

en·chi·rid·i·on \,en-(,)kī-'rid-ē-ən\ *n* [LL, fr. Gk *encheiridion*, fr. *en* in + *cheir* hand — more at IN, CHIR-] : HANDBOOK, MANUAL

-en·chy·ma \'eŋ-kə-mə, 'en-\ *n comb form, pl* **-en·chym·a·ta** \ən-'kim-ət-ə, -ᵊn-\ *or* **-enchymas** [NL, fr. *parenchyma*] : cellular tissue ⟨coll*enchyma*⟩

en·ci·pher \in-'sī-fər, en-\ *vt* : to convert (a message) into cipher

en·cir·cle \in-'sər-kəl\ *vt* **1** : to form a circle about : SURROUND **2** : to make a circuit about — **en·cir·cle·ment** \-mənt\ *n*

en·clasp \in-'klasp\ *vt* : to seize and hold : EMBRACE

en·clave \'en-,klāv, 'än-\ *n* [F, fr. MF, fr. *enclaver* to enclose, fr. (assumed) VL *inclavare* to lock up, fr. L *in-* + *clavis* key — more at CLAVICLE] **1** : a territorial or culturally distinct unit enclosed within foreign territory **2** : a small often relict community of one kind of plant in an opening of a larger plant community

en·clit·ic \en-'klit-ik\ *adj* [LL *encliticus*, fr. Gk *enklitikos*, fr. *enklinesthai* to lean on, fr. *en-* + *klinein* to lean — more at LEAN] *of a word or particle* : being without independent accent and treated in pronunciation as forming a part of the preceding word (as English *thee* in *prithee* and *not* in *cannot*) — **enclitic** *n*

en·close \in-'klōz\ *vt* [ME *enclosen*, prob. fr. *enclos* enclosed, fr. MF, pp. of *enclore* to enclose, fr. (assumed) VL *inclaudere*, alter. of

L *includere* — more at INCLUDE] **1 a :** to close in **:** SURROUND; *specif* **:** to fence off (common land) for individual use **b :** to hold in **:** CONFINE **2 :** to place in a parcel or envelope

en·clo·sure \in-ˈklō-zhər\ *n* **1 :** the act or action of enclosing **2 :** the quality or state of being enclosed **3 :** something that encloses **4 :** something enclosed

en·code \in-ˈkōd\ *vt* **:** to transfer from one system of communication into another; *esp* **:** to convert (a message) into code

en·co·mi·ast \en-ˈkō-mē-ˌast, -mē-əst\ *n* [Gk *enkōmiastēs*, fr. *enkōmiazein* to praise, fr. *enkōmion*] **:** one that praises **:** EULOGIST — **en·co·mi·as·tic** \(ˌ)en-ˌkō-mē-ˈas-tik\ *adj*

en·co·mi·um \en-ˈkō-mē-əm\ *n, pl* **encomiums** *or* **en·co·mia** \-mē-ə\ [L, fr. Gk *enkōmion*, fr. *en* in + *kōmos* revel, celebration — more at IN, COMEDY] **:** high or glowing praise

syn ENCOMIUM, EULOGY, PANEGYRIC, TRIBUTE, CITATION mean a formal expression of praise. ENCOMIUM implies enthusiasm and warmth in praising a person or a thing; EULOGY applies to a prepared speech or writing extolling the virtues and services of a person; PANEGYRIC suggests an elaborate often poetic compliment; TRIBUTE implies deeply felt praise conveyed either through words or through a significant act; CITATION applies to the formal praise accompanying the mention of a person in a military dispatch or in awarding an honorary degree

en·com·pass \in-ˈkəm-pəs, -ˈkäm-\ *vt* **1 a :** to form a circle about **:** ENCLOSE **b** *obs* **:** to go around **2 a :** ENVELOP **b :** INCLUDE **3 :** to bring about **:** ACCOMPLISH — **en·com·pass·ment** \-pə-smənt\ *n*

¹en·core \ˈän-ˌkō(ə)r, -ˌkȯ(ə)r\ *n* [F, still, again] **:** a demand for repetition or reappearance made by an audience; *also* **:** a further performance in response to such a demand

²encore *vt* **:** to request an encore of or by

¹en·coun·ter \in-ˈkau̇nt-ər\ *vt* **en·coun·ter·ing** \-ˈkau̇nt-ə-riŋ, -ˈkau̇n-triŋ\ [ME *encountren*, fr. OF *encontrer*, fr. ML *incontrare*, fr. LL *incontra* toward, fr. L *in-* + *contra* against] **1 a :** to meet as an adversary or enemy **b :** to engage in conflict with **2 :** to come upon face to face **:** MEET **3 :** to come upon unexpectedly

²encounter *n* **1 a :** a meeting between hostile factions or persons **b :** a sudden often violent clash **:** COMBAT **2 a :** a chance meeting **b :** a direct often momentary meeting

syn ENCOUNTER, SKIRMISH, BRUSH mean a minor battle. An ENCOUNTER may be unexpected and sometimes violent but not of long duration; a SKIRMISH is a slight and often preliminary encounter between light detachments; a BRUSH is a short but brisk skirmish

en·cour·age \in-ˈkər-ij, -ˈkə-rij\ *vt* [ME *encoragen*, fr. MF *encoragier*, fr. OF, fr. *en-* + *corage* courage] **1 :** to inspire with courage, spirit, or hope **:** HEARTEN **2 :** to spur on **:** STIMULATE **3 :** to give help or patronage to **:** FOSTER

en·cour·age·ment \-mənt\ *n* **1 :** the act of encouraging **:** the state of being encouraged **2 :** something that encourages

en·cour·ag·ing *adj* **:** giving hope or promise **:** FAVORING — **en·cour·ag·ing·ly** \-iŋ-lē\ *adv*

en·crim·son \in-ˈkrim-zən\ *vt* **:** to make or dye crimson

en·cri·nite \ˈeŋ-krə-ˌnīt, ˈen-\ *n* [NL *encrinites*] **:** CRINOID; *esp* **:** a fossil crinoid — **en·cri·nit·ic** \ˌeŋ-krə-ˈnit-ik, ˌen-\ *adj*

en·croach \in-ˈkrōch\ *vi* [ME *encrochen* to get, seize, fr. MF *encrochier*, fr. OF, fr. *en-* + *croc*, *croche* hook — more at CROCHET] **1 :** to enter by gradual steps or by stealth into the possessions or rights of another **2 :** to advance beyond desirable or normal limits **syn** see TRESPASS — **en·croach·ment** \mənt\ *n*

en·crust \in-ˈkrəst\ *vb* [prob. fr. L *incrustare*, fr. *in-* + *crusta* crust] *vt* **:** to cover, line, or overlay with a crust **∼** *vi* **:** to form a crust

en·crus·ta·tion \(ˌ)in-ˌkrəs-ˈtā-shən, ˌen-\ *var of* INCRUSTATION

en·cum·ber \in-ˈkəm-bər\ *vt* **en·cum·ber·ing** \-b(ə-)riŋ\ [ME *encombren*, fr. MF *encombrer*, fr. OF, fr. *en-* + (assumed) OF *combre* abatis] **1 :** to weigh down **:** BURDEN, OVERBURDEN **2 :** to impede or hamper the function or activity of **:** HINDER **3 :** to burden with debts, mortgages, or other legal claims ⟨∼ an estate⟩

en·cum·brance \in-ˈkəm-brən(t)s\ *n* **1 :** something that encumbers **:** IMPEDIMENT **2 :** a claim or lien upon an estate

en·cum·branc·er \-brən-sər\ *n* **:** one that holds an encumbrance

-en·cy \ən-sē, ᵊn-\ *n suffix* [ME *-encie*, fr. L *-entia* — more at -ENCE] **:** quality or state ⟨despond*ency*⟩

¹en·cyc·li·cal \in-ˈsik-li-kəl, en-\ *adj* [LL *encyclicus*, fr. Gk *enkyklios* circular, general, fr. *en* in + *kyklos* circle — more at IN, WHEEL] **:** addressed to all the individuals of a group **:** GENERAL

²encyclical *n* **:** an encyclical letter; *specif* **:** a papal letter to the bishops of the church as a whole or in one country

encyclopaedia, encyclopaedic *var of* ENCYCLOPEDIA, ENCYCLOPEDIC

en·cy·clo·pe·dia \in-ˌsī-klə-ˈpēd-ē-ə\ *n* [ML *encyclopaedia* course of general education, fr. Gk *enkyklios paideia* general education] **:** a work that contains information on all branches of knowledge or treats comprehensively a particular branch of knowledge usu. in articles arranged alphabetically by subject

en·cy·clo·pe·dic \-ˈpēd-ik\ *adj* **:** of, relating to, or suggestive of an encyclopedia or its methods of treating or covering a subject **:** COMPREHENSIVE — **en·cy·clo·pe·di·cal·ly** \-i-k(ə-)lē\ *adv*

en·cy·clo·pe·dism \-ˈpē-ˌdiz-əm\ *n* **:** encyclopedic knowledge

en·cy·clo·pe·dist \-ˈpēd-əst\ *n* **1 :** one who compiles or writes for an encyclopedia **2** *often cap* **:** one of the writers of a French encyclopedia (1751-80) who were identified with the Enlightenment and advocated deism and scientific rationalism

en·cyst \in-ˈsist, en-\ *vt* **:** to enclose in a cyst **∼** *vi* **:** to form or become enclosed in a cyst — **en·cyst·ment** \-ˈsis(t)-mənt\ *n*

en·cys·ta·tion \ˌen-ˌsis-ˈtā-shən\ *n* **:** ENCYSTMENT

¹end \ˈend\ *n* [ME *ende*, fr. OE; akin to OHG *enti* end, L *ante* before, Gk *anti* against] **1 a :** the part of an area that lies at the boundary **b** (1) **:** a point that marks the extent of something (2) **:** the point where something ceases to exist ⟨world without ∼⟩ **c :** the extreme or last part lengthwise **:** TIP **d :** the terminal unit of something spatial that is marked off by units **e :** a player stationed at the extremity of a line (as in football) **2 a :** cessation of a course of action, pursuit, or activity **b :** DEATH, DESTRUCTION **c** (1) **:** the ultimate state (2) **:** RESULT, ISSUE **d :** the complex of events, parts, or sections that forms an extremity, termination, or finish **3 :** something incomplete, fragmentary, or undersize **:** REMNANT **4 a :** the goal toward which an agent acts or should act **b :** the object by virtue of or for the sake of which an event takes place **5 a :** a share in an undertaking **b :** a particular phase of an undertaking or organization — **end·ed** \ˈen-dəd\ *adj*

syn END, TERMINATION, ENDING, TERMINUS mean the point or line beyond which something does not or cannot go. END is the inclusive term, implying the final limit in time or space, in extent of influence, or range of possibility; TERMINATION and ENDING apply to the end of something having predetermined limits or being complete or finished; ENDING often includes the portion leading to the actual final point; TERMINUS applies commonly to the point to which one moves or progresses **syn** see in addition INTENTION

²end *vt* **1 a :** to bring to an end **b :** DESTROY **2 :** to make up the end of **∼** *vi* **1 :** to come to an end **2 :** DIE **syn** see CLOSE

³end *vt* [prob. alter. of E dial. *in* (to harvest)] *dial Eng* **:** to put (grain or hay) into a barn or stack

end- *or* **endo-** *comb form* [F, fr. Gk, fr. *endon* within, fr. *en* in + *-don* (akin to L *domus* house) — more at IN, TIMBER] **1 :** within **:** inside ⟨*endo*skeleton⟩ — compare EXO- **2 :** taking in ⟨*endo*thermal⟩

en·dam·age \in-ˈdam-ij\ *vt* **:** to cause loss or damage to

end·amoe·ba \ˌen-də-ˈmē-bə\ *n* [NL, genus name] **:** any of a genus (*Endamoeba*) comprising amoebas parasitic in the intestines of insects and in some classifications various parasites of vertebrates including the amoeba (*E. histolytica*) that causes amebic dysentery in man — **end·amoe·bic** \-bik\ *adj*

en·dan·ger \in-ˈdān-jər\ *vt* **en·dan·ger·ing** \-ˈdānj-(ə-)riŋ\ **:** to bring into danger or peril — **en·dan·ger·ment** \-ˈdān-jər-mənt\ *n*

en·darch \ˈen-ˌdärk\ *adj* **:** formed or taking place from the center outward ⟨∼ xylem⟩ — **en·dar·chy** \-ˌdär-kē\ *n*

end·brain \ˈen(d)-ˌbrān\ *n* **:** the anterior subdivision of the forebrain

end bulb *n* **:** one of the bulbous bodies in which some of the sensory nerve fibers end in parts of the skin and mucous membranes

en·dear \in-ˈdi(ə)r\ *vt* **1** *obs* **:** to make higher in cost, value, or estimation **2 :** to make dear, beloved, or esteemed

en·dear·ment \in-ˈdi(ə)r-mənt\ *n* **1 :** the act or process of endearing **2 :** something that endears or manifests affection **:** CARESS

¹en·deav·or \in-ˈdev-ər\ *vb* **en·deav·or·ing** \-(ə-)riŋ\ [ME *endeveren* to exert oneself, fr. *en-* + *dever* duty — more at DEVOIR] *vt* **1** *archaic* **:** to strive to achieve or reach **2 :** TRY 5 **∼** *vi* **:** to work with set purpose **syn** see ATTEMPT

²endeavor *n* **:** a serious determined effort

¹en·dem·ic \en-ˈdem-ik\ *adj* [F *endémique*, fr. *endémie* endemic disease, fr. Gk *endēmia* action of dwelling, fr. *endēmos* endemic, fr. *en* in + *dēmos* people, populace] **1 :** belonging or native to a particular people or country **2 :** restricted to or native to a particular area or region **3 :** peculiar to a locality or region ⟨∼ diseases⟩ **syn** see NATIVE — **en·dem·i·cal·ly** \-i-k(ə-)lē\ *adv* — **en·de·mic·i·ty** \ˌen-ˌde-ˈmis-ət-ē, -də-\ *n* — **en·dem·ism** \en-ˈdem-ˌiz-əm\ *n*

²endemic *n* **:** NATIVE 2b

en·der·mic \en-ˈdər-mik\ *adj* **:** acting through the skin or by direct application to the skin — **en·der·mi·cal·ly** \-mi-k(ə-)lē\ *adv*

end·ing \ˈen-diŋ\ *n* **:** a thing that constitutes an end; *esp* **:** one or more letters or syllables added to a word base esp. in inflection **syn** see END

endite *archaic var of* INDITE

en·dive \ˈen-ˌdīv\ *n* [ME, fr. MF, fr. LL *endivia*, fr. LGk *entubion*, fr. L *intubus*] **1 :** an annual or biennial composite herb (*Cichorium endivia*) widely cultivated as a salad plant — called also *escarole* **2 :** the developing crown of chicory when blanched for use as salad

end·less \ˈen-(d)ləs\ *adj* **1 :** having no end **2 :** extremely numerous **3 :** united at the ends ⟨an ∼ chain⟩ — **end·less·ly** *adv* — **end·less·ness** *n*

end·long \ˈen-ˌdlȯŋ\ *adv* [ME *endelong*, alter. of *andlong*, fr. OE *andlang* along, fr. *andlang*, prep.] *archaic* **:** LENGTHWISE

end man *n* **:** a man at each end of the line of performers in a minstrel show who engages in comic repartee with the interlocutor

end·most \ˈen(d)-ˌmōst\ *adj* **:** situated at the very end **:** FARTHEST

en·do·bi·ot·ic \ˌen-dō-(ˌ)bī-ˈät-ik, -bē-\ *adj* [ISV] **:** dwelling within the tissues of a host

en·do·blast \ˈen-də-ˌblast\ *n* [ISV] **:** HYPOBLAST — **en·do·blas·tic** \ˌen-də-ˈblas-tik\ *adj*

en·do·car·di·al \ˌen-dō-ˈkärd-ē-əl\ *adj* **:** situated within the heart **:** of or relating to the endocardium

en·do·car·di·tis \ˌen-dō-(ˌ)kär-ˈdīt-əs\ *n* **:** inflammation of the lining of the heart and its valves

en·do·car·di·um \ˌen-dō-ˈkärd-ē-əm\ *n* [NL, fr. *end-* + Gk *kardia* heart] **:** a thin serous membrane lining the cavities of the heart

en·do·carp \ˈen-də-ˌkärp\ *n* [F *endocarpe*] **:** the inner layer of the pericarp of a fruit when it consists of two or more layers of different texture or consistency — **en·do·car·pal** \ˌen-də-ˈkär-pəl\ *or* **en·do·car·pic** \-pik\ *adj*

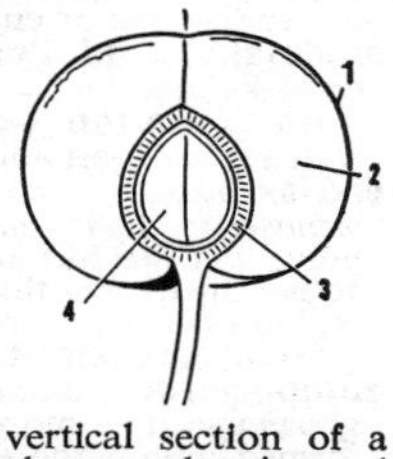

vertical section of a cherry, showing: *1* epicarp, *2* mesocarp, *3* endocarp, *4* seed; *1, 2,* and *3* together form the pericarp

en·do·cra·ni·um \ˌen-dō-ˈkrā-nē-əm\ *n, pl* **en·do·cra·nia** \-nē-ə\ [NL] **1 :** the processes of the inner surface of the cranium of an insect **2 :** the inner surface of the cranium

¹en·do·crine \ˈen-də-krən, -ˌkrīn, -ˌkrēn\ *adj* [ISV *end-* + Gk *krinein* to separate] **1 a :** secreting internally; *specif* **:** producing secretions that are distributed in the body by way of the bloodstream ⟨∼ glands⟩ **b :** of, relating to, or resembling that of an endocrine gland **2 :** HORMONAL

²endocrine *n* **1 :** HORMONE **2 :** an endocrine gland

en·do·cri·no·log·ic \ˌen-də-ˌkrin-ᵊl-ˈäj-ik, -ˌkrīn-, -ˌkrēn-\ *adj* **:** involving or relating to the endocrine glands or secretions or to endocrinology

en·do·cri·nol·o·gy \ˌen-də-kri-ˈnäl-ə-jē, -(ˌ)krī-\ *n* [ISV] **:** a branch of knowledge dealing with the endocrine glands

en·do·derm \ˈen-də-ˌdərm\ *n* [F *endoderme*, fr. *end-* + Gk *derma* skin] **:** the innermost of the germ layers of an embryo that is the source of the epithelium of the digestive tract and its derivatives **:** HYPOBLAST; *also* **:** a tissue that is derived from this germ layer — **en·do·der·mal** \ˌen-də-ˈdər-məl\ *or* **en·do·der·mic** \-mik\ *adj*

en·do·der·mis \ˌen-də-ˈdər-məs\ *n* [NL] **:** the innermost tissue of the cortex in many roots and stems

end·odon·tia \ˌen-də-'dän-ch(ē-)ə\ *n* [NL, fr. *end-* + *-odontia*] : a branch of dentistry concerned with diseases of the pulp — **end·odon·tic** \-'dänt-ik\ *adj* — **end·odon·tist** \-'dänt-əst\ *n*

end·odon·tics \-'dänt-iks\ *n pl but sing in constr* : ENDODONTIA

en·do·en·zyme \ˌen-(ˌ)dō-'en-ˌzīm\ *n* [ISV] : an intracellular enzyme

en·do·eryth·ro·cyt·ic \ˌen-(ˌ)dō-i-ˌrith-rə-'sit-ik\ *adj* : occurring within red blood cells — used chiefly of stages of malaria parasites

en·dog·a·mous \en-'däg-ə-məs\ *adj* : of, relating to, or characterized by endogamy

en·dog·a·my \-mē\ *n* 1 : marriage within a specific group as required by custom or law 2 : sexual reproduction between near relatives; *esp* : pollination of a flower by pollen from another flower of the same plant — compare AUTOGAMY

en·do·gen \'en-də-jən\ *n* [F *endogène*, fr. *end-* + *-gène* -gen] : a plant that develops by endogenous growth

en·dog·e·nous \en-'däj-ə-nəs\ *adj* 1 a : growing from or on the inside : developing within the cell wall b : originating within the body 2 : constituting or relating to metabolism of the nitrogenous constituents of cells and tissues — **en·dog·e·nous·ly** *adv*

en·dog·e·ny \-nē\ *n* : growth from within or from a deep layer

en·do·lymph \'en-də-ˌlim(p)f\ *n* [ISV] : the watery fluid in the membranous labyrinth of the ear

en·do·mic·tic \ˌen-də-'mik-tik\ *adj* : of or relating to endomixis

en·do·mix·is \-'mik-səs\ *n* [NL, fr. *end-* + Gk *mixis* act of mixing, fr. *mignynai* to mix — more at MIX] : a periodic nuclear reorganization in ciliated protozoans

en·do·morph \'en-də-ˌmȯrf\ *n* [ISV] 1 : a crystal of one species enclosed in one of another 2 [*endoderm* + *-morph*] : an endomorphic individual

en·do·mor·phic \ˌen-də-'mȯr-fik\ *adj* 1 a : of or relating to an endomorph b : of, relating to, or produced by endomorphism 2 [*endoderm* + *-morphic*] : characterized by predominance of the structures (as the internal organs) developed from the endodermal layer of the embryo — **en·do·mor·phy** \'en-də-ˌmȯr-fē\ *n*

en·do·mor·phism \ˌen-də-'mȯr-ˌfiz-əm\ *n* : a change produced in an intrusive rock by reaction with the wall rock

en·do·par·a·site \ˌen-(ˌ)dō-'par-ə-ˌsīt\ *n* [ISV] : a parasite that lives in the internal organs or tissues of its host

en·doph·a·gous \en-'däf-ə-gəs\ *adj* : feeding from within; *esp* : consuming vegetation or plant debris by burrowing in and disintegrating plant structures

en·do·phyte \'en-də-ˌfīt\ *n* [ISV] : a plant living within another plant — **en·do·phyt·ic** \ˌen-də-'fit-ik\ *adj*

en·do·plasm \'en-də-ˌplaz-əm\ *n* [ISV] : the inner relatively fluid part of the cytoplasm — **en·do·plas·mic** \ˌen-də-'plaz-mik\ *adj*

en·dop·o·dite \en-'däp-ə-ˌdīt\ *n* [ISV] : the mesial or internal branch of a typical limb of a crustacean — **en·dop·o·dit·ic** \ˌ(ˌ)en-ˌdäp-ə-'dit-ik\ *adj*

en·do·poly·ploid \ˌen-(ˌ)dō-'päl-i-ˌplȯid\ *adj* : of or relating to a polyploid state in which the chromosomes have divided repeatedly without mitosis or subsequent cell division — **en·do·poly·ploi·dy** \-ˌplȯid-ē\ *n*

end organ *n* : a structure forming the peripheral terminus of a path of nerve conduction and consisting of an effector or a receptor with its associated nerve terminations

en·dorse \in-'dȯr(ə)rs\ *vt* [alter. of obs. *endoss*, fr. ME *endosen*, fr. MF *endosser*, fr. OF, to put on the back, fr. *en-* + *dos* back, fr. L *dorsum*] 1 a : to write on the back of; *esp* : to sign one's name as payee on the back of (a check) to obtain the cash or credit represented on the face b : to inscribe (one's signature) on a check, bill, or note c : to inscribe (as an official document) with a title or memorandum d : to make over to another (the value represented in a check, bill, or note) by inscribing one's name on the document e : to acknowledge receipt of (a sum specified) by one's signature on a document 2 : to express definite approval of syn see APPROVE — **en·dors·ee** \in-ˌdȯr-'sē, ˌen-\ *n* — **en·dors·er** \in-'dȯr-sər\ *n*

en·dorse·ment \in-'dȯr-smənt\ *n* 1 : the act or process of endorsing 2 a : something that is written in the process of endorsing b : a provision added to an insurance contract altering its scope or application 3 : SANCTION, APPROVAL

en·do·scle·rite \ˌen-(ˌ)dō-'skli(ə)r-ˌīt\ *n* : a sclerite that is part of the internal skeleton of an insect or other arthropod

en·do·scope \'en-də-ˌskōp\ *n* [ISV] : an instrument for visualizing the interior of a hollow organ (as the rectum or urethra) — **en·dos·co·py** \en-'däs-kə-pē\ *n*

en·do·scop·ic \ˌen-də-'skäp-ik\ *adj* : of, relating to, or by means of the endoscope or endoscopy

en·do·skel·e·tal \ˌen-(ˌ)dō-'skel-ət-ᵊl\ *adj* : of or relating to an endoskeleton

en·do·skel·e·ton \-ət-ᵊn\ *n* : an internal skeleton or supporting framework in an animal

end·os·mo·sis \ˌen-ˌdäs-'mō-səs, -ˌdäz-\ *n* [alter. of obs. *endosmose*, fr. F, fr. *end-* + Gk *ōsmos* act of pushing, fr. *ōthein* to push; akin to Skt *vadhati* he strikes] : passage (as of a surface-active substance) through a membrane from a region of lower to a region of higher concentration — **end·os·mot·ic** \-'mät-ik\ *adj* — **end·os·mot·i·cal·ly** \-i-k(ə-)lē\ *adv*

en·do·sperm \'en-də-ˌspərm\ *n* [F *endosperme*, fr. *end-* + Gk *sperma* seed — more at SPERM] : a nutritive tissue in seed plants formed within the embryo sac — **en·do·sper·mic** \ˌen-də-'spər-mik\ *adj* — **en·do·sper·mous** \-məs\ *adj*

en·do·spore \'en-də-ˌspō(ə)r, -ˌspȯ(ə)r\ *n* [ISV] : an asexual spore developed within the cell esp. in bacteria — **en·do·spor·ic** \ˌen-də-'spōr-ik, -'spȯr-\ *adj* — **en·dos·po·rous** \-əs; ˌen-'däs-pə-rəs\ *adj*

end·os·te·al \en-'däs-tē-əl\ *adj* 1 : of or relating to the endosteum 2 : located within bone or cartilage — **end·os·te·al·ly** \-ə-lē\ *adv*

en·do·ster·nite \ˌen-dō-'stər-ˌnīt\ *n* [ISV] : a segment of the endoskeleton of an arthropod

end·os·te·um \en-'däs-tē-əm\ *n, pl* **end·os·tea** \-tē-ə\ [NL, fr. *end-* + Gk *osteon* bone — more at OSSEOUS] : the layer of vascular connective tissue lining the medullary cavities of bone

end·os·tra·cum \en-'däs-tri-kəm\ *n, pl* **end·os·tra·ca** \-kə\ [NL, fr. *end-* + Gk *ostrakon* shell] : the inner layer of a shell (as of a crustacean)

en·do·the·ci·um \ˌen-dō-'thē-s(h)ē-əm\ *n, pl* **en·do·the·cia** \-s(h)ē-ə\ [NL] : the inner lining of a mature anther

endotheli- *or* **endothelio-** *comb form* [ISV, fr. NL *endothelium*] : endothelium ⟨*endothelioma*⟩

en·do·the·li·al \ˌen-də-'thē-lē-əl\ *adj* : of, relating to, or produced from endothelium

en·do·the·li·um \-lē-əm\ *n, pl* **en·do·the·lia** \-lē-ə\ [NL, fr. *end-* + *epithelium*] 1 : an epithelium of mesoblastic origin composed of a single layer of thin flattened cells that lines internal body cavities 2 : the inner layer of the seed coat of some plants — **en·do·the·loid** \-'thē-ˌlȯid\ *adj*

en·do·therm \'en-də-ˌthərm\ *n* : a warm-blooded animal

en·do·ther·mic \ˌen-də-'thər-mik\ *or* **en·do·ther·mal** \-məl\ *adj* [ISV] : characterized by or formed with absorption of heat

en·do·tox·in \ˌen-dō-'täk-sən\ *n* [ISV] : a toxin of internal origin; *specif* : a poisonous substance present in bacteria (as of typhoid fever) but separable from the cell body only on its disintegration

en·do·tra·che·al \ˌen-(ˌ)dō-'trā-kē-əl\ *adj* 1 : placed within the trachea ⟨an ~ tube⟩ 2 : applied or effected through the trachea

en·dow \in-'daù\ *vt* [ME *endowen*, fr. AF *endouer*, fr. MF *en-* + *douer* to endow, fr. L *dotare*, fr. *dot-, dos* gift, dowry] 1 : to furnish with a dower 2 : to furnish with an income 3 a : to provide or equip gratuitously : ENRICH b : CREDIT 5a, INVEST 5

en·dow·ment \-mənt\ *n* 1 : the act or process of endowing 2 : something that is endowed; *specif* : the portion of an institution's income derived from donations 3 : natural capacity, power, or ability

en·do·zo·ic \ˌen-də-'zō-ik\ *adj* [ISV] : living within or involving passage through an animal ⟨~ distribution of weeds⟩

end·pa·per \'en(d)-ˌpā-pər\ *n* : a once-folded sheet of paper having one leaf pasted flat against the inside of the front or back cover of a book and the other pasted at the base to the first or last page

end plate *n* : a flat plate or structure at the end of something; *specif* : a complex terminal arborization of a motor nerve fiber

end run *n* 1 : a football play in which the ball carrier attempts to run wide around his own end 2 : an evasive trick

end–stopped \'en(d)-ˌstäpt\ *adj, of a verse* : marked by a logical or rhetorical pause at the end — compare RUN-ON

end table *n* : a small table used beside a larger piece of furniture

en·due \in-'d'(y)ü\ *vt* [ME *enduen*, fr. MF *enduire* to bring in, introduce, fr. L *inducere* — more at INDUCE] 1 a : PROVIDE, ENDOW b : IMBUE, TRANSFUSE 2 [ME *induen*, fr. L *induere*, fr. *ind-* in (fr. OL *indu, endo*) + *-uere* to put on] : to put on : DON

en·dur·able \in-'d(y)ùr-ə-bəl\ *adj* : capable of being endured — **en·dur·ably** \-blē\ *adv*

en·dur·ance \in-'d(y)ùr-ən(t)s\ *n* 1 : PERMANENCE, DURATION 2 : the ability to withstand hardship, adversity, or stress 3 : SUFFERING, TRIAL

en·dure \in-'d(y)ù(ə)r\ *vb* [ME *enduren*, fr. MF *endurer*, fr. (assumed) VL *indurare*, fr. L, to harden, fr. *in-* + *durare* to harden, endure — more at DURING] *vi* 1 : to continue in the same state : LAST 2 : to remain firm under suffering or misfortune without yielding ~ *vt* 1 : to undergo (as a hardship) esp. without giving in : SUFFER 2 : TOLERATE, PERMIT syn see BEAR, CONTINUE

en·dur·ing *adj* : LASTING, DURABLE — **en·dur·ing·ly** \-iŋ-lē\ *adv* — **en·dur·ing·ness** *n*

end·ways \'en-ˌdwāz\ *or* **end·wise** \-ˌdwīz\ *adv (or adj)* 1 : with the end forward 2 : LENGTHWISE 3 : at or on the end

En·dym·i·on \en-'dim-ē-ən\ *n* [L, fr. Gk *Endymiōn*] : a beautiful youth loved by Selene

-ene \ˌēn\ *n suffix* [ISV, fr. Gk *-ēnē*, fem. of *-ēnos*, adj. suffix] : unsaturated carbon compound ⟨*benzene*⟩; *esp* : carbon compound with one double bond ⟨*ethylene*⟩

en·e·ma \'en-ə-mə\ *n* [LL, fr. Gk, fr. *enienai* to inject, fr. *en-* + *hienai* to send] 1 : the injection of liquid into the intestine by way of the anus 2 : material for injection as an enema

en·e·my \'en-ə-mē\ *n, often attrib* [ME *enemi*, fr. OF, fr. L *inimicus*, fr. *in-* ¹*in-* + *amicus* friend] 1 : one that seeks the injury, overthrow, or failure of an opponent 2 : something harmful or deadly 3 a : a military adversary b : a hostile unit or force syn ENEMY, FOE mean one who shows hostility or ill will. ENEMY stresses antagonism showing itself in hatred or destructive attitude or action; FOE stresses active fighting or struggle but is used only figuratively of an enemy in war

en·er·get·ic \ˌen-ər-'jet-ik\ *adj* [Gk *energetikos*, fr. *energein* to be active, fr. *energos*] 1 : marked by energy : STRENUOUS 2 : operating with vigor or effect 3 : of or relating to energy ⟨~ equation⟩ syn see VIGOROUS — **en·er·get·i·cal·ly** \-i-k(ə-)lē\ *adv*

en·er·get·ics \-iks\ *n pl but sing in constr* : a branch of mechanics that deals primarily with energy and its transformations

en·er·gid \'en-ər-jəd, -ˌjid\ *n* [ISV, fr. Gk *energos*] : a nucleus and the body of cytoplasm with which it interacts

en·er·gize \'en-ər-ˌjīz\ *vi* : to put forth energy : ACT ~ *vt* 1 : to impart energy to 2 : to make energetic or vigorous 3 : to apply voltage to — **en·er·giz·er** *n*

en·er·gy \'en-ər-jē\ *n* [LL *energia*, fr. Gk *energeia* activity, fr. *energos* active, fr. *en* in + *ergon* work] 1 : vitality of expression 2 : the capacity of acting 3 : power forcefully exerted 4 : the capacity for doing work syn see POWER

energy level *n* : one of the stable states of constant energy that may be assumed by a physical system — called also *energy state*

¹en·er·vate \i-'nər-vət\ *adj* : ENERVATED

²en·er·vate \'en-ər-ˌvāt\ *vt* [L *enervatus*, pp. of *enervare*, fr. *e-* + *nervus* sinew] 1 : to lessen the vitality or strength of 2 : to reduce the mental or moral vigor of syn see UNNERVE — **en·er·va·tion** \ˌen-ər-'vā-shən\ *n*

en·fant ter·ri·ble \äⁿ-fäⁿ-te-'rēblᵊ\ *n* [F] : one whose inopportune remarks or unconventional actions cause embarrassment

en·fee·ble \in-'fē-bəl\ *vt* **en·fee·bling** \-b(ə-)liŋ\ [ME *enfeblen*, fr. MF *enfeblir*, fr. OF, fr. *en-* + *feble* feeble] : to make feeble syn see WEAKEN — **en·fee·ble·ment** \-bəl-mənt\ *n*

en·feoff \in-'fef, -'fēf\ *vt* [ME *enfeoffen*, fr. AF *enfeoffer*, fr. OF *en-* + *fief*] : to invest with a fief, fee, or other possession — **en·feoff·ment** \-mənt\ *n*

en·fet·ter \in-'fet-ər\ *vt* : to bind in fetters : ENCHAIN

¹en·fi·lade \'en-fə-ˌlād, -ˌläd\ *n* [F, fr. *enfiler* to thread, enfilade, fr. OF, to thread, fr. *en-* + *fil* thread] : a condition permitting the delivery of gunfire in a lengthwise direction at an objective

²enfilade *vt* : to rake or be in a position to rake with gunfire in a lengthwise direction

enflame *var of* INFLAME

en·fleu·rage \ˌäⁿ-ˌflər-'äzh\ *n* [F] : a process of extracting per-

fumes by exposing absorbents to the exhalations of flowers

en·fold \in-ˈfōld\ *vt* **1 a :** to cover with folds : ENVELOP **b :** CONTAIN **2 :** to clasp within the arms : EMBRACE

en·force \in-ˈfō(ə)rs, -ˈfȯ(ə)rs\ *vt* [ME *enforcen*, fr. MF *enforcier*, fr. OF, fr. *en-* + *force*] **1 :** to give force to : STRENGTHEN **2 :** to urge with energy **3 :** CONSTRAIN, COMPEL **4** *obs* **:** to effect or gain by force **5 :** to execute vigorously ⟨~ laws⟩ — **en·force·abil·i·ty** \-ˌfōr-sə-ˈbil-ət-ē, -ˌfȯr-\ *n* — **en·force·able** \-ˈfōr-sə-bəl, -ˈfȯr-\ *adj* — **en·force·ment** \-ˈfōr-smənt, -ˈfȯr-\ *n* — **en·forc·er** *n*

syn ENFORCE, IMPLEMENT mean to put into effect. ENFORCE refers chiefly to laws and statutes and implies the exercise of executive or police power; IMPLEMENT suggests the performance of acts necessary to bring into effect some agreed-on plan, measure, or policy

en·fran·chise \in-ˈfran-ˌchīz\ *vt* [ME *enfranchisen*, fr. MF *enfranchiss-*, stem of *enfranchir*, fr. OF, fr. *en-* + *franc* free — more at FRANK] **1 :** to set free (as from slavery) **2 :** to endow with a franchise: **a :** to admit to the privileges of a citizen; *specif* **:** admit to the right of suffrage **b :** to admit (a municipality) to political privileges or rights — **en·fran·chise·ment** \-ˌchīz-mənt, -chəz-\ *n*

en·gage \in-ˈgāj\ *vb* [ME *engagen*, fr. MF *engagier*, fr. OF, *en-* + *gage*] *vt* **1 :** to offer (as one's word) as security for a debt or cause **2 a** *obs* **:** INVOLVE, ENTANGLE **b :** to attract and hold by influence or power **c :** to interlock with : MESH; *also* **:** to cause to mesh **3 :** to bind (as oneself) to do something; *esp* **:** to bind by a pledge to marry **4 a :** to provide occupation for **b :** to arrange to obtain the use or services of : HIRE **5 a :** ENGROSS, OCCUPY **b :** to induce to participate **6 a :** to enter into contest with **b :** to bring together or interlock (weapons) ~ *vi* **1 a :** to pledge oneself : PROMISE **b :** GUARANTEE **2 a :** to begin and carry on an enterprise **b :** PARTICIPATE **3 :** to enter into conflict **4 :** to be or become in gear

en·gaged \in-ˈgājd\ *adj* **1 :** OCCUPIED, EMPLOYED **2 :** PLEDGED, BETROTHED **3 :** greatly interested : COMMITTED **4 :** partly embedded in a wall ⟨an ~ column⟩ **5 :** being in gear : MESHED

en·gage·ment \in-ˈgāj-mənt\ *n* **1 a :** the act of engaging or state of being engaged **b :** BETROTHAL **2 :** something that engages **3 a :** a promise to be present at a specified time and place **b :** employment esp. for a stated time **4 :** the state of being in gear **5 :** a hostile encounter between military forces **syn** see BATTLE

en·gag·ing *adj* **:** tending to draw favorable attention : ATTRACTIVE — **en·gag·ing·ly** \-ˈgā-jiŋ-lē\ *adv*

en·gar·land \in-ˈgär-lənd\ *vt* **:** to adorn with or as if with a garland

en·gen·der \in-ˈjen-dər\ *vb* **en·gen·der·ing** \-d(ə-)riŋ\ [ME *engendren*, fr. MF *engendrer*, fr. L *ingenerare*, fr. *in-* + *generare* to generate] *vt* **1 :** BEGET, PROCREATE **2 :** to cause to exist or to develop ⟨angry words ~ strife⟩ ~ *vi* **:** to assume form : ORIGINATE

¹en·gine \ˈen-jən\ *n* [ME *engin*, fr. OF, fr. L *ingenium* natural disposition, talent, fr. *in-* + *gignere* to beget] **1** *obs* **a :** INGENUITY **b :** evil contrivance : WILE **2** *archaic* **:** something used to effect a purpose : AGENT **3 a :** a mechanical tool: as (1) **:** an instrument or machine of war (2) *obs* **:** a torture implement **b :** MACHINERY **c :** any of various mechanical appliances — compare FIRE ENGINE **4 :** a machine for converting any of various forms of energy into mechanical force and motion **5 :** a railroad locomotive

²engine *vt* **:** to equip with an engine

¹en·gi·neer \ˌen-jə-ˈni(ə)r\ *n* **1 :** a member of a military group devoted to engineering work **2** *obs* **:** PLOTTER **3 a :** a designer or builder of engines **b :** a person who is trained in or follows as a profession a branch of engineering **c :** a person who carries through an enterprise by skillful or artful contrivance **4 :** a person who runs or supervises an engine or an apparatus

²engineer *vt* **1 :** to lay out, construct, or manage as an engineer **2 a :** CONTRIVE **b :** to guide the course of **syn** see GUIDE

en·gi·neer·ing *n, often attrib* **1 :** the art of managing engines **2 :** a science by which the properties of matter and the sources of energy in nature are made useful to man

en·gine·ry \ˈen-jən-rē\ *n* **1 :** instruments of war **2 :** machines and tools : MACHINERY

en·gird \in-ˈgərd\ *vt* **:** GIRD, ENCOMPASS

en·gir·dle \in-ˈgərd-ᵊl\ *vt* **:** GIRDLE

en·gla·cial \en-ˈglā-shəl\ *adj* **:** embedded in a glacier

¹En·glish \ˈiŋ-glish *also* ˈiŋ-lish\ *adj* [ME, fr. OE *englisc*, fr. *Engle* (pl.) Angles] **:** of, relating to, or characteristic of England, the English people, or the English language

²English *n* **1 a :** the language of the people of England and the U.S. and many areas now or formerly under British control **b :** a particular variety of English distinguished by peculiarities (as of pronunciation) **c :** English language, literature, or composition when a subject of study **2** *pl in constr* **:** the people of England **3 a :** an English translation **b :** idiomatic or intelligible English **4 :** spin around the vertical axis given to a ball by striking it to right or left of center (as in pool) or by the manner of releasing it (as in bowling)

³English *vt* **1 :** to translate into English **2 :** ANGLICIZE

English breakfast tea *n* **:** CONGOU; *broadly* **:** any similar black tea

English foxhound *n* **:** any of a breed of foxhounds developed in England and characterized by a large heavily boned form, rather short ears, and lightly fringed tail

English horn *n* **:** a double-reed woodwind instrument similar to the oboe but a fifth lower in pitch

En·glish·man \ˈiŋ-glish-mən *also* ˈiŋ-lish-\ *n* **:** a native or inhabitant of England

English muffin *n* **:** bread dough rolled and cut into rounds and baked on a griddle

English rabbit *n* **:** any of a breed of white domestic rabbits having distinctive dark markings

English setter *n* **:** any of a breed of bird dogs characterized by a moderately long flat silky coat of white or white with color and by feathering on the tail and legs

English shepherd *n* **:** any of a breed of vigorous medium-sized working dogs with a long and glossy black coat with usu. tan to brown markings developed in England for herding sheep and cattle

English sonnet *n* **:** a sonnet consisting of three quatrains and a couplet with a rhyme scheme of *abab, cdcd, efef, gg*

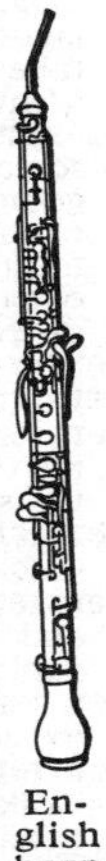

English horn

English springer *n* **:** any of a breed of springer spaniels held to have originated in Spain and characterized by deep-bodied muscular build and a moderately long straight or slightly wavy silky coat of usu. black and white hair

English toy spaniel *n* **:** any of a breed of small blocky spaniels with well-rounded upper skull projecting forward toward the short turned-up nose

English walnut *n* **:** a Eurasian walnut (*Juglans regia*) valued for its large edible nut and its hard richly figured wood; *also* **:** its fruit

En·glish·wom·an \ˈiŋ-glish-ˌwu̇m-ən *also* ˈiŋ-lish-\ *n* **:** a woman of English birth, nationality, or origin

en·glut \in-ˈglət\ *vt* [MF *engloutir*, fr. LL *inglutire*, fr. L *in-* + *glutire* to swallow — more at GLUTTON] **:** to gulp down : SWALLOW

en·gorge \in-ˈgȯ(ə)rj\ *vb* [MF *engorgier*, fr. OF, to devour, fr. *en-* + *gorge* throat] *vt* **:** GORGE, GLUT ~ *vi* **:** to suck blood to the limit of body capacity — **en·gorge·ment** \-mənt\ *n*

en·graft \in-ˈgraft\ *vt* **1 :** GRAFT 1, 2 **2 a :** ATTACH : IMPLANT **b :** INVIGORATE

en·grailed \in-ˈgrā(ə)ld\ *adj* [ME *engreled*, fr. MF *engreslé*, fr. *en-* + *gresle* slender, fr. L *gracilis*] **1 :** indented with small concave curves **2 :** made of or bordered by a circle of raised dots

engrain *vt* **:** INGRAIN

en·gram *also* **en·gramme** \ˈen-ˌgram\ *n* [ISV] **:** a memory trace; *specif* **:** a protoplasmic change in neural tissue hypothesized to account for persistence of memory — **en·gram·mic** \en-ˈgram-ik\ *adj*

en·grave \in-ˈgrāv\ *vt* [MF *engraver*, fr. *en-* + *graver* to grave, of Gmc origin; akin to OE *grafan* to grave] **1 a :** to form by incision (as upon wood or metal) **b :** to impress as if with a graver **2 a :** to cut figures, letters, or devices upon for printing; *also* **:** to print from an engraved plate **b :** PHOTOENGRAVE — **en·grav·er** *n*

en·grav·ing *n* **1 :** the act or process of one that engraves **2 :** something that is engraved: as **a :** an engraved printing surface **b :** engraved work **3 :** an impression from an engraved printing surface

en·gross \in-ˈgrōs\ *vt* [ME *engrossen*, fr. AF *engrosser*, prob. fr. ML *ingrossare*, fr. L *in* + ML *grossa* large handwriting, fr. L, fem. of *grossus* thick] **1 a :** to copy or write in a large hand **b :** to prepare the usu. final handwritten or printed text of (an official document) **2** [ME *engrossen*, fr. MF *en gros* in large quantities] **a :** to purchase large quantities of (as for speculation) **b** *obs* **:** AMASS **c :** to take the whole of : MONOPOLIZE — **en·gross·er** *n*

en·grossed \-ˈgrōst\ *adj* **:** completely occupied or absorbed ⟨a scholar ~ in research⟩

en·gross·ing *adj* **:** taking up the attention completely : ABSORBING

en·gross·ment \in-ˈgrō-smənt\ *n* **1 :** the act of engrossing **2 :** the state of being absorbed or occupied : PREOCCUPATION

en·gulf \in-ˈgəlf\ *vt* **1 :** to flow over and enclose : OVERWHELM **2 :** to take in (food) by or as if by flowing over and enclosing — **en·gulf·ment** \-mənt\ *n*

en·hance \in-ˈhan(t)s\ *vt* [ME *enhauncen*, fr. AF *enhauncer*, alter. of OF *enhaucier*, fr. (assumed) VL *inaltiare*, fr. L *in* + *altus* high — more at OLD] **1** *obs* **:** RAISE **2 :** to make greater (as in value, desirability, or attractiveness) : HEIGHTEN ⟨a hillside location *enhanced* by a broad vista⟩ **syn** see INTENSIFY — **en·hance·ment** \-ˈhan(t)-smənt\ *n*

en·har·mon·ic \ˌen-(ˌ)här-ˈmän-ik\ *adj* [F *enharmonique*, fr. MF, of a scale employing quarter tones, fr. Gk *enarmonios*, fr. *en* in + *harmonia* harmony, scale] **1 :** relating to a written change of notes that sound the same on all instruments using the tempered scale ⟨the ~ change from A flat to G sharp⟩ **2 :** relating to the difference in pitch that results from exact tuning of a diatonic scale and its transposition into another key — **en·har·mon·i·cal·ly** \-i-k(ə-)lē\ *adv*

enig·ma \i-ˈnig-mə\ *n* [L *aenigma*, fr. Gk *ainigmat-, ainigma*, fr. *ainissesthai* to speak in riddles, fr. *ainos* fable] **1 :** an obscure speech or writing **2 :** something hard to understand or explain **3 :** an inscrutable or mysterious person **syn** see MYSTERY

enig·mat·ic \ˌen-(ˌ)ig-ˈmat-ik, ˌē-(ˌ)nig-\ *adj* **:** relating to or resembling an enigma : PUZZLING **syn** see OBSCURE — **enig·mat·i·cal** \-i-kəl\ *adj* — **enig·mat·i·cal·ly** \-i-k(ə-)lē\ *adv*

en·isle \in-ˈī(ə)l\ *vt* **1 :** ISOLATE **2 :** to make an island of

en·jamb·ment *or* **en·jambe·ment** \in-ˈjam-mənt, äⁿ-zhäⁿb-mäⁿ\ *n* [F *enjambement*, fr. MF, encroachment, fr. *enjamber* to straddle, encroach on, fr. *en-* + *jambe* leg — more at JAMB] **:** the running over of a sentence from one verse or couplet into another so that closely related words fall in different lines — compare RUN-ON

en·join \in-ˈjȯin\ *vt* [ME *enjoinen*, fr. OF *enjoindre*, fr. L *injungere*, fr. *in-* + *jungere* to join — more at YOKE] **1 :** to direct or impose by authoritative order **2 :** FORBID, PROHIBIT **syn** see COMMAND

en·joy \in-ˈjȯi\ *vt* [MF *enjoir*, fr. OF, fr. *en-* + *joir* to enjoy, fr. L *gaudēre* to rejoice — more at JOY] **1 :** to take pleasure or satisfaction in **2 :** to have for one's use, benefit, or lot — **en·joy·able** \-ˈjȯi-ə-bəl\ *adj* — **en·joy·able·ness** *n* — **en·joy·ably** \-blē\ *adv*

en·joy·ment \in-ˈjȯi-mənt\ *n* **1 :** the action or state of enjoying **2 :** something that is enjoyed **syn** see PLEASURE

en·kin·dle \in-ˈkin-dᵊl\ *vb* **:** KINDLE

en·lace \in-ˈlās\ *vt* [ME *enlacen*, fr. MF *enlacier*, fr. OF, fr. *en-* + *lacier* to lace] **1 :** ENCIRCLE, ENFOLD **2 :** ENTWINE, INTERLACE

en·large \in-ˈlärj\ *vb* [ME *enlargen*, fr. MF *enlargier*, fr. OF, fr. *en-* + *large*] *vt* **1 :** to make larger : EXTEND **2 :** to give greater scope to : EXPAND **3 :** to set free ~ *vi* **1 :** to grow larger **2 :** to speak or write at length : ELABORATE **syn** see INCREASE — **en·large·able** \-ˈlär-jə-bəl\ *adj* — **en·larg·er** *n*

en·large·ment \in-ˈlärj-mənt\ *n* **1 :** an act or instance of enlarging or the state of being enlarged **2 :** a photographic print that is larger than the negative and is made by projecting through a lens an image of the negative upon a photographic printing surface

en·light·en \in-ˈlīt-ᵊn\ *vt* **en·light·en·ing** \-ˈlīt-niŋ, -ᵊn-iŋ\ **1** *archaic* **:** ILLUMINATE **2 a :** to furnish knowledge to : INSTRUCT **b :** to give spiritual insight to

en·light·en·ment \in-ˈlīt-ᵊn-mənt\ *n* **1 :** the act or means of enlightening : the state of being enlightened **2** *cap* **:** a philosophic movement of the 18th century marked by questioning of traditional doctrines and values, a tendency toward individualism, and an emphasis on the idea of universal human progress, the empirical method in science, and the free use of reason — used with *the*

en·list \in-ˈlist\ *vt* **1 :** to engage (a person) for duty in the armed forces **2 :** to secure the support and aid of ~ *vi* **1 :** to enroll oneself in the armed forces **2 :** to participate heartily (as in a cause, drive, crusade) — **en·list·ment** \-ˈlis(t)-mənt\ *n*

en·list·ed \-'lis-təd\ *adj* **:** of, relating to, or constituting the part of a military or naval force below commissioned or warrant officers

en·liv·en \in-'lī-vən\ *vt* **:** to give life, action, or spirit to **:** ANIMATE **syn** see QUICKEN

en masse \än-'mas, ä^n-\ *adv* [F] **:** in a body **:** as a whole

en·mesh \in-'mesh\ *vt* **:** to catch or entangle in or as if in meshes

en·mi·ty \'en-mət-ē\ *n* [ME *enmite*, fr. MF *enemité*, fr. OF *enemisté*, irreg. fr. *enemi* enemy] **:** HATRED; *esp* **:** mutual hatred

syn HOSTILITY, ANTIPATHY, ANTAGONISM, ANIMOSITY, RANCOR, ANIMUS: ENMITY suggests positive hatred which may be open or concealed; HOSTILITY suggests an enmity showing itself in attacks or aggression; ANTIPATHY and ANTAGONISM imply a natural or logical basis for one's hatred or dislike, ANTIPATHY suggesting repugnance, a desire to avoid or reject, and ANTAGONISM suggesting a clash of temperaments leading readily to hostility; ANIMOSITY and RANCOR suggest intense ill will and vindictiveness that threaten to kindle hostility; RANCOR is esp. applied to bitter brooding over a wrong; ANIMUS adds to animosity the implication of strong prejudice

en·ne·ad \'en-ē-,ad\ *n* [Gk *ennead-, enneas*, fr. *ennea* nine — more at NINE] **:** a group of nine

en·no·ble \in-'ō-bəl\ *vt* **en·no·bling** \-b(ə-)liŋ\ [ME *ennobelen*, fr. MF *ennoblir*, fr. OF, fr. *en-* + *noble*] **1 :** to make noble **:** ELEVATE **2 :** to raise to the rank of nobility — **en·no·ble·ment** \-bəl-mənt\ *n* — **en·no·bler** \-b(ə-)lər\ *n*

en·nui \'än-'wē\ *n* [F, fr. OF *enui* annoyance, fr. *enuier* to annoy] **:** a feeling of weariness and dissatisfaction

Enoch \'ē-nək, -nik\ *n* [Gk *Enōch*, fr. Heb *Ḥănōkh*] **1 :** an Old Testament patriarch and father of Methuselah **2 :** a son of Cain

enol \'ē-,nȯl, -,nōl\ *n* [ISV *ene-* (fr. *-ene*) + *-ol*] **:** an organic compound containing a hydroxyl group adjacent to a double bond and usu. characterized by the grouping >C:C(OH)– — **eno·lic** \ē-'nō-lik, -'näl-ik\ *adj*

enol·o·gy \ē-'näl-ə-jē\ *n* [Gk *oinos* wine + E *-logy* — more at WINE] **:** a science that deals with wine and wine making

enor·mi·ty \i-'nȯr-mət-ē\ *n* **1 :** the quality or state of being immoderate, monstrous, or outrageous; *esp* **:** great wickedness **2 :** a grave offense **3 :** HUGENESS, IMMENSITY

enor·mous \i-'nȯr-məs\ *adj* [L *enormis*, fr. *e, ex* out of + *norma* rule] **1** *archaic* **a :** ABNORMAL, INORDINATE **b :** exceedingly wicked **:** SHOCKING **2 :** marked by extraordinarily great size, number, or degree — **enor·mous·ly** *adv* — **enor·mous·ness** *n*

syn ENORMOUS, IMMENSE, HUGE, VAST, GIGANTIC, COLOSSAL, MAMMOTH mean exceedingly large or big. ENORMOUS suggests an exceeding of all ordinary bounds in size or amount or degree; IMMENSE implies an exceeding of usual standards or measurements without suggesting, as ENORMOUS often does, abnormality or monstrousness; HUGE commonly suggests an immensity of bulk or amount; VAST usu. suggests immensity of extent; GIGANTIC stresses the contrast with the size of others of the same kind; COLOSSAL applies esp. to a human creation of stupendous or incredible dimensions; MAMMOTH suggests both hugeness and ponderousness of bulk

1enough \i-'nəf; *after* t, d, s, z *often* ᵊn-'əf\ *adj* [ME *ynough*, fr. OE *genōg*; akin to OHG *ginuog* enough; both fr. a prehistoric Gmc compound whose first constituent is represented by OE *ge-* (perfective prefix) and whose second constituent is akin to L *nancisci* to get, Gk *enenkein* to carry] **:** occurring in such quantity, quality, or scope as to fully satisfy demands or needs **syn** see SUFFICIENT

2enough *adv* **1 :** in or to a degree or quantity that satisfies **:** SUFFICIENTLY **2 :** FULLY, QUITE **3 :** in a tolerable degree

3enough *n* **:** a quantity that is enough **:** SUFFICIENCY

enounce \ē-'nau̇n(t)s\ *vt* [F *énoncer*, fr. L *enuntiare* to report] **1 :** to set forth or state (as a proposition) **2 :** ENUNCIATE 2

enow \i-'nau̇\ *adv (or adj)* [ME *inow*, fr. OE *genōg*] *archaic* **:** ENOUGH

en pas·sant \ä^n-pä-sä^n\ *adv* [F] **:** in passing — used in chess of the capture of a pawn as it makes a first move of two squares by an enemy pawn in a position to threaten the first of these squares

en·phy·tot·ic \,en-(,)fī-'tät-ik\ *adj, of a plant disease* **:** occurring regularly in a district but only in moderate severity — **enphytotic** *n*

en·plane \in-'plān\ *vi* **:** to board an airplane

en prise \ä^n-prēz\ *adj* [F] *of a chess piece* **:** exposed to capture

en·quire \in-'kwī(ə)r\ **en·qui·ry** \'in-,kwī(ə)r-ē, in-'; 'in-kwə-rē, 'iŋ-\ *var of* INQUIRE, INQUIRY

en·rage \in-'rāj\ *vt* [MF *enrager* to become mad, fr. OF *enragier*, fr. *en-* + *rage*] **:** to fill with rage **:** ANGER

en·rapt \in-'rapt\ *adj* **:** RAPT, ENRAPTURED

en·rap·ture \in-'rap-chər\ *vt* **en·rap·tur·ing** \-'rap-chə-riŋ, -'rap-shriŋ\ **:** to fill with delight

en·reg·is·ter \in-'rej-ə-stər\ *vt* [MF *enregistrer*, fr. OF, fr. *en-* + *registre* register] **:** to put on record

en·rich \in-'rich\ *vt* [ME *enrichen*, fr. MF *enrichir*, fr. OF, fr. *en-* + *riche* rich] **1 :** to make rich or richer **2 :** ADORN, ORNAMENT **3 a :** to make richer in some quality **b :** to make (soil) more fertile **c :** to improve (a food) in nutritive value by adding vitamins and minerals in processing — **en·rich·er** *n* — **en·rich·ment** \-mənt\ *n*

en·robe \in-'rōb\ *vt* **:** to invest or adorn with or as if with a robe

en·roll *or* **en·rol** \in-'rōl\ *vb* **en·rolled; en·roll·ing** [ME *enrollen*, fr. MF *enroller*, fr. *en-* + *rolle* roll, register] *vt* **1 :** to insert, register, or enter in a list, catalog, or roll **2 :** to prepare in written or printed form a final perfect copy of (a bill passed by a legislature) **3 :** to roll or wrap up **~** *vi* **:** to enroll oneself or cause oneself to be enrolled — **en·roll·ment** *or* **en·rol·ment** \-mənt\ *n*

en·root \in-'rüt, -'ru̇t\ *vt* **:** to fix by or as if by roots **:** ESTABLISH

en route \än-'rüt, en-, in-, ä^n-\ *adv* [F] **:** on or along the way

en·sam·ple \in-'sam-pəl\ *n* [ME, fr. MF *ensample*, *example*] **:** EXAMPLE, INSTANCE

en·san·guine \in-'saŋ-gwən\ *vt* **1 :** BLOODY **2 :** CRIMSON

en·sate \'en-,sāt\ *adj* [L *ensis*] **:** ENSIFORM

en·sconce \in-'skän(t)s\ *vt* **1 :** SHELTER, CONCEAL **2 :** to settle comfortably or snugly

enscroll *var of* INSCROLL

en·sem·ble \än-'säm-bəl, ä^n-\ *n, often attrib* [F, fr. *ensemble* together, fr. L *insimul* at the same time, fr. *in-* + *simul* at the same time — more at SAME] **:** a group constituting an organic whole or producing together a single effect: as **a :** SET **b :** concerted music of two or more parts **c :** a complete costume of harmonizing or complementary pieces **d :** a group of supporting players, singers, or dancers; *esp* **:** CORPS DE BALLET

en·sheathe \in-'shēth\ *vt* **:** to cover with or as if with a sheath

en·shrine \in-'shrīn, *esp South* -'srīn\ *vt* **1 :** to enclose in or as if in a shrine **2 :** to preserve or cherish as sacred

en·shroud \in-'shrau̇d, *esp South* -'srau̇d\ *vt* **:** to cover or enclose with or as if with a shroud

en·si·form \'en(t)-sə-,fȯrm\ *adj* [F *ensiforme*, fr. L *ensis* sword + F *-forme* -form; akin to Skt *asi* sword] **:** having sharp edges and tapering to a slender point

en·sign \'en(t)-sən, *in senses other than 3b also* 'en-,sīn\ *n* [ME *ensigne*, fr. MF *enseigne*, fr. L *insignia* insignia, flags] **1 :** a flag flown as the symbol of nationality **2 a :** a badge of office, rank, or power **b :** EMBLEM, SIGN **3 a** *archaic* **:** STANDARD-BEARER **b :** the most junior naval commissioned officer ranking just below a lieutenant junior grade and above a chief warrant officer

en·si·lage \'en(t)-s(ə-)lij\ *n* **1 :** the process of preserving fodder by ensiling **2 :** SILAGE

en·sile \en-'sī(ə)l\ *vt* [F *ensiler*, fr. *en-* + *silo*, fr. Sp] **:** to prepare and store (fodder) for silage in a tight silo or pit

en·sky \in-'skī\ *vt* **:** to lift to or as if to the skies or heaven **:** EXALT

en·slave \in-'slāv\ *vt* **:** to reduce to or as if to slavery **:** SUBJUGATE — **en·slave·ment** \-mənt\ *n* — **en·slav·er** *n*

en·snare \in-'sna(ə)r, -'sne(ə)r\ *vt* **:** SNARE, ENTRAP **syn** see CATCH

en·snarl \in-'snär(ə)l\ *vt* **:** to involve in a snarl

en·soul \in-'sōl\ *vt* **:** to endow or imbue with a soul

en·sphere \in-'sfi(ə)r\ *vt* **:** to enclose in or as if in a sphere

en·sue \in-'sü\ *vi* [ME *ensuen*, fr. MF *ensuivre*, fr. OF, fr. *en-* + *suivre* to follow] **:** to take place afterward or as a result **syn** see FOLLOW

en suite \ä^n-'swēt\ *adv (or adj)* [F] **:** in a succession, series, or set

en·sure \in-'shu̇(ə)r\ *vt* [ME *ensuren*, fr. AF *enseurer*, prob. alter. of OF *aseürer*] **:** to make sure, certain, or safe **:** GUARANTEE

syn ENSURE, INSURE, ASSURE, SECURE mean to make an outcome sure. ENSURE implies a making certain and inevitable; INSURE stresses the taking of necessary measures beforehand to make a result certain or provide for any probable contingency; ASSURE implies a making sure in mind by removing all doubt and suspense; SECURE implies action taken to guard against attack or loss

en·swathe \in-'swäth, -'swȯth, -'swāth\ *vt* **:** SWATHE, ENWRAP

ent- *or* **ento-** *comb form* [NL, fr. Gk *entos* within; akin to L *intus* within, Gk *en* in — more at IN] **:** inner **:** within ⟨*ento*blast⟩

en·tab·la·ture \in-'tab-lə-,chu̇(ə)r, -chər, -,t(y)u̇(ə)r\ *n* [obs. F, modif. of It *intavolatura*, fr. *intavolare* to put on a board or table, fr. *in-* (fr. L) + *tavola* board, table, fr. L *tabula* — more at TABLE] **:** the upper section of a wall or story that usu. is supported on columns or pilasters and that in classical orders consists of architrave, frieze, and cornice; *also* **:** a similar part (as an elevated support for a machine part)

en·ta·ble·ment \in-'tā-bəl-mənt, ä^n-tȧ-blə-mä^n\ *n* [F, fr. OF, fr. *en-* + *table*] **:** a platform supporting a statue and above the dado

1en·tail \in-'tā(ə)l\ *vt* **1 :** to restrict (property) by limiting the inheritance to the owner's lineal descendants or to a particular class thereof **2 :** to attach as if by entail **3 :** to impose, involve, or imply as a necessary accompaniment or result — **en·tail·er** \-'tā-lər\ *n* — **en·tail·ment** \-'tā(ə)l-mənt\ *n*

2entail *n* **1 a :** an entailing esp. of lands **b :** an entailed estate **c :** the rule fixing the descent **2 :** something transmitted as if by entail

en·tan·gle \in-'taŋ-gəl\ *vt* **1 :** to make tangled, complicated, or confused **2 :** to involve in a tangle — **en·tan·gler** \-g(ə-)lər\ *n*

en·tan·gle·ment \in-'taŋ-gəl-mənt\ *n* **1 a :** the action of entangling **:** the state of being entangled **b :** something that entangles, confuses, or ensnares **2 :** the condition of being deeply involved

en·tel·e·chy \en-'tel-ə-kē\ *n* [LL *entelechia*, fr. Gk *entelecheia*] **1 :** the realization of form-giving cause as contrasted with potential existence **2 :** an immanent agency held by some vitalists to regulate or direct the vital processes of an organism

en·tente \än-'tänt\ *n* [F, fr. OF, intent, understanding — more at INTENT] **1 :** an international understanding providing for a common course of action **2 :** a coalition of parties to an entente

en·ter \'ent-ər\ *vb* **en·ter·ing** \'ent-ə-riŋ, 'en-triŋ\ [ME *entren*, fr. OF *entrer*, fr. L *intrare*, fr. *intra* within; akin to L *inter* between] *vi* **1 :** to go or come in **2 :** to come into a group **:** JOIN **3 a :** to make a beginning ⟨*~ed* into business⟩ **b :** to begin to consider a subject **4 :** to go upon land for the purpose of taking possession **5 :** to play a part **:** be a factor ⟨~ into a conversation⟩ **~** *vt* **1 :** to come or go into ⟨~ a room⟩ **2 :** INSCRIBE, REGISTER **3 :** to cause to be received or admitted ⟨~ a boy at a school⟩ **4 :** to put in **:** INSERT **5 a :** to make a beginning in **:** take up **b :** to pass within the limits of (a particular period of time) **6 :** to become a member of or an active participant in **7 :** to make report of (a ship or her cargo) to customs authorities **8 :** to place in proper form before a law court or upon record ⟨~ a writ⟩ **9 :** to go into or upon and take actual possession of **10 :** to put on record — **en·ter·able** \'ent-ə-rə-bəl, 'en-trə-\ *adj*

syn ENTER, PENETRATE, PIERCE, PROBE mean to make way into something. ENTER is the most general of these and may imply either going in or forcing a way in; PENETRATE carries a strong implication of an impelling force or compelling power that effects entrance; PIERCE adds to PENETRATE a clear implication or suggestion of an entering point or wedge; PROBE implies penetration for investigating or exploring something hidden from sight or knowledge

enter- *or* **entero-** *comb form* [Gk, fr. *enteron*] **:** intestine ⟨*enter*itis⟩

en·ter·al \'ent-ə-rəl\ *adj* **:** ENTERIC — **en·ter·al·ly** \-rə-lē\ *adv*

en·ter·ic \en-'ter-ik\ *adj* **1 :** of or relating to the enteron **2 :** of, relating to, or being a medicinal preparation treated to pass through the stomach unaltered and disintegrate in the intestines

en·ter·it·i·dis \,ent-ə-'rit-əd-əs\ *n* [NL (*Salmonella*) *enteritidis*, species of bacteria] **:** enteritis esp. in young animals

en·ter·i·tis \,ent-ə-'rīt-əs\ *n* **1 :** inflammation of the intestines and esp. of the human ileum **2 :** a disease of domestic animals (as panleucopenia of cats) marked by enteritis and diarrhea

en·tero·coc·cal \,ent-ə-rō-'käk-əl\ *adj* **:** of, relating to, or caused by enterococci

en·tero·coc·cus \-'käk-əs\ *n, pl* **en·tero·coc·ci** \-'käk-,(s)ī, -'käk-(,)(s)ē\ [NL, genus name] **:** STREPTOCOCCUS; *esp* **:** a streptococcus (as *Streptococcus faecalis*) normally present in the intestine

en·tero·coele *or* **en·tero·coel** \'ent-ə-rō-,sēl\ *n* **:** a coelom originating by outgrowth from the archenteron — **en·tero·coe·lic** \,ent-ə-rō-'sē-lik\ *adj* — **en·tero·coe·lous** \-ləs\ *adj*

en·tero·co·li·tis \,ent-ə-(,)rō-kə-'līt-əs\ *n* [NL] **:** enteritis affecting both the small and large intestine

en·tero·gas·trone \,ent-ə-rō-'gas-,trōn\ *n* [*enter-* + *gastr-* +

hormone] : a hormone of the upper intestinal mucosa with an inhibitory action on gastric motility and secretion

en·tero·hep·a·ti·tis \,ent-ə-(,)rō-,hep-ə-'tīt-əs\ *n* [NL] : BLACKHEAD 3

en·tero·ki·nase \,ent-ə-rō-'kīn-,ās, -'kin-, -,āz\ *n* [ISV] : an enzyme esp. of the upper intestinal mucosa that activates trypsinogen by converting it to trypsin

en·ter·on \'ent-ə-,rän, -rən\ *n* [NL, fr. Gk, intestine — more at INTER-] : the alimentary canal or system — used esp. of the embryo

en·ter·os·to·my \,ent-ə-'räs-tə-mē\ *n* [ISV] : a surgical formation of an opening into the intestine through the abdominal wall

en·ter·prise \'ent-ə(r)-,prīz\ *n* [ME *enterprise*, fr. MF *entreprise*, fr. *entreprendre* to undertake, fr. *entre-* inter- + *prendre* to take] **1** : a project or undertaking that is difficult, complicated, or risky **2 a** : a business organization **b** : a systematic purposeful activity **3** : readiness to engage in daring action : INITIATIVE

en·ter·pris·er \-,prī-zər\ *n* : one who undertakes an enterprise; *specif* : ENTREPRENEUR

en·ter·pris·ing \-,prī-ziŋ\ *adj* : marked by an independent energetic spirit and by readiness to undertake or experiment

en·ter·tain \,ent-ər-'tān\ *vb* [ME *entertinen*, fr. MF *entretenir*, fr. *entre-* inter- + *tenir* to hold] *vt* **1 a** *archaic* : MAINTAIN **b** *obs* : RECEIVE **2** : to show hospitality to **3 a** : to consider with favor **b** : CONSIDER **4** : to provide entertainment for ~ *vi* : to provide entertainment esp. for guests **syn** see AMUSE — **en·ter·tain·er** *n*

en·ter·tain·ment \,ent-ər-'tān-mənt\ *n* **1** : the act of entertaining **2 a** *archaic* : MAINTENANCE, PROVISION **b** *obs* : EMPLOYMENT **3** : something diverting or engaging; *esp* : a public performance

en·thal·py \'en-,thal-pē, en-'thal-\ *n* [*en-* + Gk *thalpein* to heat] : the sum of the internal energy of a body and the product of its volume multiplied by the pressure

en·thrall *or* **en·thral** \in-'thrȯl\ *vt* **en·thralled**; **en·thrall·ing** **1** : to hold in or reduce to slavery **2** : to hold spellbound : CHARM — **en·thrall·ment** *or* **en·thral·ment** \-mənt\ *n*

en·throne \in-'thrōn\ *vt* **1** : to seat ceremonially on a throne **2** : to place on high : EXALT — **en·throne·ment** \-mənt\ *n*

en·thuse \in-'th(y)üz\ *vb* [back-formation fr. *enthusiasm*] *vt* : to make enthusiastic ~ *vi* : to show enthusiasm

en·thu·si·asm \in-'th(y)ü-zē-,az-əm\ *n* [Gk *enthousiasmos*, fr. *enthousiazein* to be inspired, fr. *entheos* inspired, fr. *en-* + *theos* god] **1 a** : belief in special revelations of the Holy Spirit **b** : religious fanaticism **2 a** : strong excitement of feeling : FERVOR **b** : something inspiring zeal or fervor **syn** see PASSION

en·thu·si·ast \-,ast, -əst\ *n* : a person filled with enthusiasm

en·thu·si·as·tic \in-,th(y)ü-zē-'as-tik\ *adj* : filled with or marked by enthusiasm — **en·thu·si·as·ti·cal·ly** \-ti-k(ə-)lē\ *adv*

en·thy·meme \'en(t)-thi-,mēm\ *n* [L *enthymema*, fr. Gk *enthymēma*, fr. *enthymeisthai* to keep in mind, fr. *en-* + *thymos* mind, soul] : a syllogism in which one of the premises is implicit

en·tice \in-'tīs\ *vt* [ME *enticen*, fr. OF *enticier*, fr. (assumed) VL *intitiare*, fr. L *in-* + *titio* firebrand] : to draw on by arousing hope or desire : TEMPT **syn** see LURE — **en·tice·ment** \-'tī-smənt\ *n*

[1]**en·tire** \in-'tī(ə)r, 'en-,\ *adj* [ME, fr. MF *entir*, fr. L *integer*, lit., untouched, fr. *in-* + *tangere* to touch — more at TANGENT] **1** : having no element or part left out **2** : complete in degree : TOTAL **3 a** : consisting of one piece : HOMOGENOUS **b** : INTACT **4** : not castrated **5** : having the margin continuous **syn** see PERFECT, WHOLE — **entire** *adv* — **en·tire·ly** *adv* — **en·tire·ness** *n*

[2]**entire** *n* **1** *archaic* : the whole : ENTIRETY **2** : STALLION

en·tire·ty \in-'tī-rət-ē, -'tī(ə)rt-ē\ *n* **1** : the state of being entire or complete **2** : SUM TOTAL, WHOLE

en·ti·tle \in-'tīt-ᵊl\ *vt* **en·ti·tling** \-'tīt-liŋ, -ᵊl-iŋ\ [ME *entitlen*, fr. MF *entituler*, fr. LL *intitulare*, fr. L *in-* + *titulus* title] **1** : to give a title to : DESIGNATE **2 a** : to give a legal right to **b** : to qualify for something — **en·ti·tle·ment** \-'tīt-ᵊl-mənt\ *n*

en·ti·ty \'en(t)-ət-ē\ *n* [ML *entitas*, fr. L *ent-*, *ens* existing thing, fr. coined prp. of *esse* to be] **1 a** : BEING, EXISTENCE; *esp* : independent, separate, or self-contained existence **b** : the existence of a thing as contrasted with its attributes **2** : something that has separate and distinct existence and objective or conceptual reality

ento- — see ENT-

en·to·blast \'ent-ə-,blast\ *n* **1** : HYPOBLAST **2** : a blastomere producing endoderm — **en·to·blas·tic** \,ent-ə-'blas-tik\ *adj*

en·to·derm \'ent-ə-,dərm\ *n* : ENDODERM — **en·to·der·mal** \,ent-ə-'dər-məl\ *or* **en·to·der·mic** \-mik\ *adj*

en·toil \in-'tȯi(ə)l\ *vt* : ENTRAP, ENMESH

entom- *or* **entomo-** *comb form* [F, fr. Gk *entomon*] : insect ⟨*entomophagous*⟩

en·tomb \in-'tüm\ *vt* [ME *entoumben*, fr. MF *entomber*, fr. *en-* + *tombe* tomb] **1** : to deposit in a tomb : BURY **2** : to serve as a tomb for — **en·tomb·ment** \-'tüm-mənt\ *n*

en·to·mo·log·i·cal \,ent-ə-mə-'läj-i-kəl\ *adj* : of or relating to entomology — **en·to·mo·log·i·cal·ly** \-i-k(ə-)lē\ *adv*

en·to·mol·o·gist \,ent-ə-'mäl-ə-jəst\ *n* : a specialist in entomology

en·to·mol·o·gy \-jē\ *n* [F *entomologie*, fr. Gk *entomon* insect (fr. neut. of *entomos* cut up, fr. *en-* + *temnein* to cut) + F *-logie* -logy — more at TOME] : a branch of zoology that deals with insects

en·to·moph·a·gous \,ent-ə-'mäf-ə-gəs\ *adj* : feeding on insects

en·to·moph·i·lous \,ent-ə-'mäf-ə-ləs\ *adj* : normally pollinated by insects — **en·to·moph·i·ly** \-lē\ *n*

en·to·mos·tra·can \,ent-ə-'mäs-tri-kən\ *n* [deriv. of *entom-* + Gk *ostrakon* shell — more at OYSTER] : any of numerous simple typically small crustaceans (as branchiopods, ostracods, copepods, and barnacles) sometimes placed in a subclass (Entomostraca) — **entomostracan** *or* **en·to·mos·tra·cous** \-kəs\ *adj*

en·to·proct \'ent-ə-,präkt\ *n* [deriv. of *ent-* + Gk *prōktos* anus] : any of a phylum (Entoprocta) of animals lacking a true coelom and having the anus adjacent to the mouth — **entoproct** *or* **en·to·proc·tous** \,ent-ə-'präk-təs\ *adj*

en·tou·rage \,änt-ə-'räzh, ,än-(,)tü-\ *n* [F, fr. MF, fr. *entourer* to surround, fr. *entour* around, fr. *en* in (fr. L *in*) + *tour* circuit] **1** : one's attendants or associates **2** : SURROUNDINGS

en·to·zoa \,ent-ə-'zō-ə\ *n pl* [NL] : internal animal parasites; *esp* : the intestinal worms — **en·to·zo·an** \-'zō-ən\ *adj or n*

en·to·zo·ic \-'zō-ik\ *or* **en·to·zo·al** \-'zō-əl\ *adj* : living within an animal

en·tr'acte \'än-,trakt, 'äⁿ-, än-', äⁿ-'\ *n* [F, fr. *entre-* inter- + *acte* act] **1** : the interval between two acts of a play **2** : a dance, piece of music, or interlude performed between two acts of a play

en·trails \'en-trəlz, -,trālz\ *n pl* [ME *entrailles*, fr. MF, fr. ML *intralia*, alter. of L *interanea*, pl. of *interaneum* intestine, fr. neut. of *interaneus* interior] : GUTS, VISCERA; *broadly* : internal parts

[1]**en·train** \in-'trān\ *vt* [MF *entrainer*, fr. *en-* + *trainer* to draw, drag — more at TRAIN] **1** : to draw along with or after oneself **2** : to carry along or over esp. mechanically (as fine drops of liquid during distillation) **3** : to incorporate (air bubbles) into concrete — **en·train·er** *n* — **en·train·ment** \-'trān-mənt\ *n*

[2]**entrain** *vt* : to put aboard a train ~ *vi* : to go aboard a train

[1]**en·trance** \'en-trən(t)s\ *n* **1** : the act of entering **2** : the means or place of entry **3** : power or permission to enter : ADMISSION **4** : the point at which a voice or instrument part begins in ensemble music **5** : the first appearance of an actor in a scene

[2]**en·trance** \in-'tran(t)s\ *vt* **1** : to put into a trance **2** : to carry away with delight, wonder, or rapture — **en·trance·ment** \-'tran(t)-smənt\ *n* — **en·tranc·ing·ly** \-siŋ-lē\ *adv*

en·trant \'en-trənt\ *n* : one that enters esp. in a contest

en·trap \in-'trap\ *vt* [MF *entraper*, fr. *en-* + *trape* trap] **1** : to catch in or as if in a trap **2** : to lure into a compromising statement or act **syn** see CATCH — **en·trap·ment** \-mənt\ *n*

en·treat \in-'trēt\ *vb* [ME *entreten*, fr. MF *entraitier*, fr. *en-* + *traitier* to treat — more at TREAT] *vt* **1** *archaic* : to deal with : TREAT **2** : to ask earnestly or urgently ~ *vi* **1** *obs* : NEGOTIATE **b** : INTERCEDE **2** : PLEAD **syn** see BEG — **en·treat·ing·ly** \-iŋ-lē\ *adv* — **en·treat·ment** \-mənt\ *n*

en·treaty \in-'trēt-ē\ *n* : the act of entreating : PLEA

en·tre·chat \,än-trə-'shä\ *n* [F] : a leap in which a ballet dancer repeatedly crosses the legs and sometimes beats them together

en·trée *or* **en·tree** \'än-(,)trā\ *n* [F *entrée*, fr. OF] **1 a** : the act or manner of entering : ENTRANCE **b** : freedom of entry or access **2 a** : a dish served between the main courses or in England before the roast **b** : the principal dish of the meal in the U.S.

en·tre·mets *as sing* ,än-trə-'mā, *as pl* -'mā(z)\ *n pl but sing or pl in constr* [F, fr. OF *entremes*, fr. L *intermissus*, pp. of *intermittere* to intermit] : dishes served in addition to the main course of a meal

en·trench \in-'trench\ *vt* **1 a** : to place within or surround with a trench esp. for defense **b** : to place (oneself) in a strong defensive position **c** : to establish solidly : CONFIRM **2** : to cut into : FURROW; *specif* : to erode downward so as to form a trench ~ *vi* **1** : to dig or occupy a trench for defensive purposes **2** : ENCROACH — used with *on* or *upon* **syn** see TRESPASS — **en·trench·ment** \-mənt\ *n*

en·tre·pôt \,än-trə-'pō\ *n* [F] : a center of trade and transshipment

en·tre·pre·neur \,än-trə-p(r)ə-'nər, -'n(y)u̇(ə)r\ *n* [F, fr. OF, fr. *entreprendre* to undertake] : one who organizes, manages, and assumes the risks of a business or enterprise — **en·tre·pre·neur·ship** \-'nər-,ship, -'n(y)u̇(ə)r-\ *n*

en·tre·sol \'ent-ər-,säl, 'en-trə-, 'än-trə-, -,sȯl\ *n* [F] : MEZZANINE

en·tro·py \'en-trə-pē\ *n* [ISV] **1 a** : a measure of the unavailable energy in a closed thermodynamic system so related to the state of the system that a change in the measure varies with change in the ratio of the increment of heat taken in to the absolute temperature at which it is absorbed **b** : a measure of the disorder of a closed thermodynamic system in terms of a constant multiple of the natural logarithm of the probability of the occurrence of a particular molecular arrangement of the system that by suitable choice of a constant reduces to the measure of unavailable energy **2** : a measure of the amount of information in a message that is based on the logarithm of the number of possible equivalent messages **3** : the degradation of the matter and energy in the universe to an ultimate state of inert uniformity

en·trust \in-'trəst\ *vt* **1** : to confer a trust upon; *esp* : to deliver something in trust to **2** : to commit to another with confidence **syn** see COMMIT — **en·trust·ment** \-'trəs(t)-mənt\ *n*

en·try \'en-trē\ *n, pl* **entries** [ME *entre*, fr. OF *entree*, fr. fem. of *entré*, pp. of *entrer* to enter] **1** : the act of entering : ENTRANCE **2** : ADMISSION, ENTRÉE **3** : the place of entrance: as **a** : VESTIBULE, PASSAGE **b** : DOOR, GATE **4 a** : the act of making or entering a record **b** : something entered: as (1) : HEADWORD (2) : a headword with its definition or identification (3) : VOCABULARY ENTRY **5** : a person, thing, or group entered in a contest

en·twine \in-'twīn\ *vb* : to twine together or around

en·twist \in-'twist\ *vt* : ENTWINE

enu·cle·ate \(')ē-'n(y)ü-klē-,āt\ *vt* [L *enucleatus*, pp. of *enucleare*, lit., to remove the kernel from, fr. *e-* + *nucleus* kernel] **1** *archaic* : EXPLAIN **2** : to deprive of a nucleus **3** : to remove without cutting into — **enu·cle·ation** \(,)ē-,n(y)ü-klē-'ā-shən\ *n*

enu·mer·a·ble \i-'n(y)üm-(ə-)rə-bəl\ *adj* : DENUMERABLE

enu·mer·ate \i-'n(y)ü-mə-,rāt\ *vt* [L *enumeratus*, pp. of *enumerare*, fr. *e-* + *numerare* to count, fr. *numerus* number — more at NIMBLE] **1** : to ascertain the number of : COUNT **2** : to specify one after another : LIST — **enu·mer·a·tion** \-,n(y)ü-mə-'rā-shən\ *n* — **enu·mer·a·tive** \-'n(y)ü-mə-,rāt-iv, -'n(y)üm-(ə-)rət-\ *adj* — **enu·mer·a·tor** \-'n(y)ü-mə-,rāt-ər\ *n*

enun·cia·ble \ē-'nən(t)-sē-ə-bəl, -'nən-ch(ē-)ə-bəl\ *adj* : capable of being enunciated

enun·ci·ate \ē-'nən(t)-sē-,āt\ *vb* [L *enuntiatus*, pp. of *enuntiare* to report, declare, fr. *e-* + *nuntiare* to report — more at ANNOUNCE] *vt* **1 a** : to make a definite or systematic statement of **b** : ANNOUNCE, PROCLAIM **2** : ARTICULATE, PRONOUNCE ~ *vi* : to utter articulate sounds — **enun·ci·a·tion** \-,nən(t)-sē-'ā-shən\ *n* — **enun·ci·a·tor** \-'nən(t)-sē-,āt-ər\ *n*

en·ure *var of* INURE

en·ure·sis \,en-yü-'rē-səs\ *n* [NL, fr. Gk *enourein* to urinate in, wet the bed, fr. *en-* + *ourein* to urinate] : an involuntary discharge of urine : incontinence of urine — **en·uret·ic** \-'ret-ik\ *adj or n*

en·vel·op \in-'vel-əp\ *vt* [ME *envolupen*, fr. MF *envoluper*, *enveloper*, fr. OF *envoloper*, fr. *en-* + *voloper* to wrap] **1** : to enclose or enfold completely with or as if with a covering **2** : to mount an attack on (an enemy's flank) — **en·vel·op·ment** \-mənt\ *n*

en·ve·lope \'en-və-,lōp, 'än-\ *n* **1** : something that envelops : WRAPPER **2** : a flat usu. paper container (as for a letter) **3 a** : the outer covering of an aerostat **b** : the bag containing the gas in a balloon or airship **4** : a natural enclosing covering (as a membrane) **5 a** : a curve tangent to each of a family of curves **b** : a surface tangent to each of a family of surfaces

en·ven·om \in-ˈven-əm\ *vt* [ME *envenimen*, fr. OF *envenimer*, fr. *en-* + *venim* venom] **1 :** to make poisonous **2 :** EMBITTER

en·vi·able \ˈen-vē-ə-bəl\ *adj* **:** highly desirable — **en·vi·able·ness** *n* — **en·vi·ably** \-blē\ *adv*

en·vi·er \ˈen-vē-ər\ *n* **:** one that envies

en·vi·ous \ˈen-vē-əs\ *adj* **1 :** feeling or showing envy **2** *archaic* **a :** EMULOUS **b :** ENVIABLE — **en·vi·ous·ly** *adv* — **en·vi·ous·ness** *n*
syn JEALOUS: ENVIOUS suggests a grudging of another's possessions and accomplishments and a spiteful or malicious coveting of them; JEALOUS implies a grudging of something regarded as properly belonging to or peculiarly befitting to oneself; it may also indicate without derogation a vigilant guarding or maintaining

en·vi·ron \in-ˈvī-rən, -ˈvī(-ə)rn\ *vt* [ME *envirounen*, fr. MF *environner*, fr. *environ* around, fr. *en* in (fr. L *in*) + *viron* circle, fr. *virer* to turn, fr. (assumed) VL *virare*] **:** ENCIRCLE, SURROUND

en·vi·ron·ment \in-ˈvī-rən-mənt, -ˈvī(-ə)rn-\ *n* **1 :** something that environs **:** SURROUNDINGS **2 a :** the complex of climatic, edaphic, and biotic factors that act upon an organism or an ecological community and ultimately determine its form and survival **b :** the aggregate of social and cultural conditions that influence the life of an individual or community — **en·vi·ron·men·tal** \in-ˌvī-rən-ˈment-ᵊl, -ˌvī(-ə)rn-\ *adj* — **en·vi·ron·men·tal·ly** \-ᵊl-ē\ *adv*

en·vi·rons \in-ˈvī-rənz, -ˈvī(-ə)rnz, ˈen-və-rənz\ *n pl* **1 :** the districts around a city **2 a :** SURROUNDINGS **b :** VICINITY

en·vis·age \in-ˈviz-ij\ *vt* [F *envisager*, fr. *en-* + *visage*] **:** to have a mental picture of esp. in advance of realization **syn** see THINK

en·vi·sion \in-ˈvizh-ən\ *vt* **:** to picture to oneself **syn** see THINK

en·voi *or* **en·voy** \ˈen-ˌvȯi, ˈän-\ *n* [F *envoi*, lit., message, fr. OF *envei*, fr. *envoier* to send on one's way, fr. (assumed) VL *inviare*, fr. L *in-* + *via* way] **:** the usu. explanatory or commendatory concluding remarks to a poem, essay, or book; *specif* **:** a short fixed final stanza of a ballade serving as a summary or dedication

en·voy \ˈen-ˌvȯi, ˈän-\ *n* [F *envoyé*, fr. pp. of *envoyer* to send, fr. OF *envoier*] **1 a :** a minister plenipotentiary accredited to a foreign government who ranks between an ambassador and a minister resident — called also *envoy extraordinary* **b :** any person deputed to represent one government in its intercourse with another **2 :** MESSENGER, REPRESENTATIVE

1**en·vy** \ˈen-vē\ *n* [ME *envie*, fr. OF, fr. L *invidia*, fr. *invidus* envious, fr. *invidēre* to look askance at, envy, fr. *in-* + *vidēre* to see] **1** *obs* **:** MALICE **2 :** painful or resentful awareness of an advantage enjoyed by another joined with a desire to possess the same advantage **3 :** an object of envious notice or feeling

2**envy** *vt* **1 :** to feel envy toward or on account of **2** *obs* **:** BEGRUDGE ~ *vi, obs* **:** to feel or show envy — **en·vy·ing·ly** \-iŋ-lē\ *adv*

en·wheel \in-ˈhwē(ə)l, -ˈwē(ə)l\ *vt, obs* **:** ENCIRCLE

en·wind \in-ˈwīnd\ *vt* **:** to wind in or about **:** ENFOLD

en·womb \in-ˈwüm\ *vt* **:** to shut up in or as if in a womb

en·wrap \in-ˈrap\ *vt* **1 :** ENFOLD **2 a :** ENVELOP **b :** ENGROSS

en·wreathe \in-ˈrēth\ *vt* **:** WREATHE, ENVELOP

en·zo·ot·ic \ˌen-zə-ˈwät-ik\ *adj* [*en-* + *zo-*] *of animal diseases* **:** peculiar to or constantly present in a locality — **enzootic** *n*

en·zy·got·ic \ˌen-(ˌ)zī-ˈgät-ik\ *adj* [*en-* + *zyg-*] *of twins* **:** IDENTICAL

en·zy·mat·ic \ˌen-zə-ˈmat-ik, -(ˌ)zī-\ *also* **en·zy·mic** \en-ˈzī-mik, -ˈzim-ik\ *adj* **:** of, relating to, or produced by an enzyme — **en·zy·mat·i·cal·ly** *also* **en·zy·mi·cal·ly** \-(ə-)lē\ *adv*

en·zyme \ˈen-ˌzīm\ *n* [G *enzym*, fr. MGk *enzymos* leavened, fr. Gk *en-* + *zymē* leaven] **:** any of numerous complex proteinaceous substances that are produced by living cells and bring about or accelerate reactions at body temperatures without themselves undergoing marked destruction in the process

en·zy·mol·o·gist \ˌen-zə-ˈmäl-ə-jəst, -(ˌ)zī-\ *n* **:** a specialist in enzymology

en·zy·mol·o·gy \-jē\ *n* [ISV] **:** a branch of science that deals with enzymes, their nature, activity, and significance

eo- *comb form* [Gk *ēō-* dawn, fr. *ēōs*] **:** earliest **:** oldest ⟨*eo*lithic⟩

Eo·cene \ˈē-ə-ˌsēn\ *adj* **:** of, relating to, or being an epoch of the Tertiary between the Paleocene and the Oligocene or the corresponding system of rocks — **Eocene** *n*

eo·hip·pus \ˌē-ō-ˈhip-əs\ *n* [NL, genus name, fr. *eo-* + Gk *hippos* horse] **:** any of a genus (*Eohippus*) of small primitive 4-toed horses from the Lower Eocene of the western U.S.

eo·lian \ē-ˈō-lē-ən, -ˈōl-yən\ *adj* [L *Aeolus*, god of the winds] **:** borne, deposited, produced, or eroded by the wind

eo·lith \ˈē-ə-ˌlith\ *n* **:** a very crudely chipped flint

Eo·lith·ic \ˌē-ə-ˈlith-ik\ *adj* **:** of or relating to the early period of the Stone Age marked by the use of eoliths

eon \ˈē-ən, ˈē-ˌän\ *var of* AEON

Eos \ˈē-ˌäs\ *n* [Gk *Ēōs*] **:** the goddess of dawn in Greek mythology

eo·sin \ˈē-ə-sən\ *or* **eo·sine** \-sən, -ˌsēn\ *n* [ISV, fr. Gk *ēōs* dawn] **1 :** a red fluorescent dye $C_{20}H_8Br_4O_5$ obtained by the action of bromine on fluorescein and used esp. in cosmetics and as a toner; *also* **:** its red to brown sodium or potassium salt used esp. in pink or red organic pigments **2 :** any of several dyes related to eosin

eo·sin·o·phil \ˌē-ə-ˈsin-ə-ˌfil\ *or* **eo·sin·o·phile** \-ˌfīl\ *n* **:** a leukocyte or other granulocyte with cytoplasmic inclusions readily stained by eosin — **eo·sin·o·phil·ic** \-ˌsin-ə-ˈfil-ik\ *adj*

eosinophile *or* **eosinophil** *adj* **:** staining readily with eosin ⟨~ cells⟩

-eous *adj suffix* [L *-eus*; akin to Gk *-eos* composed of, Skt *-aya*] **:** like **:** resembling ⟨dichlamyd*eous*⟩

Eo·zo·ic \ˌē-ə-ˈzō-ik\ *adj or n* **1 :** PRECAMBRIAN **2 :** PROTEROZOIC

epact \ˈē-ˌpakt, ˈep-ˌakt\ *n* [MF *epacte*, fr. LL *epacta*, fr. Gk *epaktē*, fr. *epagein* to bring in, intercalate, fr. *epi-* + *agein* to drive] **:** a period added to harmonize the lunar with the solar calendar

ep·ar·chy \ˈep-ˌär-kē\ *n* [Gk *eparchia* province, fr. *eparchos* prefect, fr. *epi-* + *archos* ruler] **:** a diocese in an Eastern church

ep·au·let *also* **ep·au·lette** \ˌep-ə-ˈlet; ˈep-ə-ˌlet, -lət\ *n* [F *épaulette*, dim. of *épaule* shoulder, fr. LL *spatula* shoulder blade, spoon, dim. of L *spatha* spoon, sword] **:** something that ornaments or protects the shoulder; *specif* **:** an ornamental fringed shoulder pad

épée \ˈep-ˌā, ā-ˈpā\ *n* [F, fr. L *spatha*] **1 :** a fencing or dueling sword having a bowl-shaped guard and a rigid blade with no cutting edge that tapers to a sharp point blunted for fencing **2 :** the art or practice of fencing with the épée

épée·ist \-əst\ *n* **:** one that uses an épée

epei·ro·gen·ic \i-ˌpī-rə-ˈjen-ik\ *adj* **:** of or relating to epeirogeny

ep·ei·rog·e·ny \ˌep-ˌī-ˈräj-ə-nē\ *n* [Gk *ēpeiros* mainland, continent + E *-geny*] **:** the deformation of the earth's crust by which the broader features of relief are produced

ep·en·ceph·a·lon \ˌep-ˌen-ˈsef-ə-ˌlän, -lən\ *n* [NL] **1 :** METENCEPHALON **2 :** RHOMBENCEPHALON

epen·the·sis \i-ˈpen(t)-thə-səs, e-\ *n, pl* **epen·the·ses** \-thə-ˌsēz\ [LL, fr. Gk, fr. *epentithenai* to insert a letter, fr. *epi-* + *entithenai* to put in, fr. *en-* + *tithenai* to put] **:** the insertion or development of a sound or letter in the body of a word (as \ə\ in \ˈath-ə-ˌlēt\ *athlete*) — **ep·en·thet·ic** \ˌep-ən-ˈthet-ik\ *adj*

epergne \i-ˈpərn, ā-\ *n* [prob. fr. F *épargne* saving] **:** a composite centerpiece of silver or glass used esp. on a dinner table

ep·ex·e·ge·sis \ˌep-ˌek-sə-ˈjē-səs\ *n* [Gk *epexēgēsis*, fr. *epi-* + *exēgēsis*] **:** additional explanation or explanatory matter — **ep·ex·e·get·i·cal** \-ˈjet-i-kəl\ *or* **ep·ex·e·get·ic** \-ˈjet-ik\ *adj*

ephah \ˈē-fə, ˈef-ə\ *n* [Heb *ēphāh*, fr. Egypt *ʼpt*] **:** an ancient Hebrew unit of dry measure equal to 1⁄10 homer or a little over a bushel

ephebe \ˈef-ˌēb, i-ˈfēb\ *n* [L *ephebus*] **:** a young man; *esp* **:** EPHEBUS

ephe·bus \i-ˈfē-bəs, e-\ *n, pl* **ephe·bi** \-ˌbī\ [L, fr. Gk *ephēbos*, fr. *epi-* + *hēbē* youth, puberty] **:** a youth of ancient Greece; *esp* **:** an Athenian 18 or 19 years old in training for full citizenship

ephe·drine \i-ˈfed-rən, ˈef-ə-ˌdrēn\ *n* [NL *Ephedra*, genus of shrubs, fr. L, horsetail plant, fr. Gk, fr. *ephedros* sitting upon, fr. *epi-* + *hedra* seat — more at SIT] **:** a crystalline alkaloid $C_{10}H_{15}NO$ extracted from Chinese plants (genus *Ephedra* of the family Gnetaceae) or synthesized and used as a salt in relieving hay fever, asthma, and nasal congestion

ephem·era \i-ˈfem-(ə-)rə\ *n, pl* **ephem·er·as** *or* **ephem·er·ae** \-ə-ˌrē, -ˌrī\ [NL, genus of mayflies, fr. Gk *ephēmeron*] **1 :** MAYFLY, EPHEMERID **2 :** an ephemeral thing

1**ephem·er·al** \i-ˈfem-(ə-)rəl\ *adj* [Gk *ephēmeros* lasting a day, daily, fr. *epi-* + *hēmera* day] **1 :** lasting one day only **2 :** lasting a very short time **syn** see TRANSIENT — **ephem·er·al·ly** \-ē\ *adv*

2**ephemeral** *n* **:** something ephemeral; *specif* **:** a plant that grows, flowers, and dies in a few days

ephem·er·al·i·ty \i-ˌfem-ə-ˈral-ət-ē\ *n* **1 :** the quality or state of being ephemeral **2** *pl* **:** ephemeral things

ephem·er·id \i-ˈfem-ə-rəd\ *n* [deriv. of Gk *ephēmeron*] **:** MAYFLY — **ephemerid** *adj*

ephem·er·is \-ə-rəs\ *n, pl* **eph·e·mer·i·des** \ˌef-ə-ˈmer-ə-ˌdēz\ [L, diary, ephemeris, fr. Gk *ephēmeris*, fr. *ephēmeros*] **1 :** any tabular statement of the assigned places of a celestial body for regular intervals **2 :** EPHEMERAL

ephem·er·on \i-ˈfem-ə-ˌrän\ *n, pl* **ephem·era** \-ˈfem-(ə-)rə\ *also* **ephem·er·ons** \-ˈfem-ə-ˌränz\ [NL, fr. Gk *ephēmeron* mayfly, fr. neut. of *ephēmeros*] **1 :** EPHEMERID **2 :** EPHEMERAL

ephem·er·ous \i-ˈfem-(ə-)rəs\ *adj* **:** EPHEMERAL

eph·od \ˈef-ˌäd\ *n* [Heb *ēphōdh*] **1 :** a linen apron worn in ancient Hebrew rites; *esp* **:** a vestment for the high priest **2 :** an ancient Hebrew instrument of priestly divination

eph·or \ˈef-ər, -ˌȯ(ə)r\ *n* [L *ephorus*, fr. Gk *ephoros*, fr. *ephoran* to oversee, fr. *epi-* + *horan* to see] **:** one of five ancient Spartan magistrates having power over the king — **eph·or·ate** \ˈef-ə-ˌrāt\ *n*

Ephra·im \ˈē-frē-əm\ *n* [Heb *Ephrayim*] **:** a son of Joseph and ancestor of one of the tribes of Israel — **Ephra·im·ite** \-ə-ˌmīt\ *n or adj*

epi- *or* **ep-** *prefix* [ME, fr. MF & L; MF, fr. L, fr. Gk, fr. *epi* on, at, besides, after; akin to OE *eofot* crime] **1 :** upon ⟨*epi*phyte⟩ **:** besides ⟨*epi*phenomenon⟩ **:** near to ⟨*ep*encephalon⟩ **:** over ⟨*epi*center⟩ **:** outer ⟨*epi*blast⟩ **:** anterior ⟨*epi*sternum⟩ **:** after ⟨*epi*genesis⟩ **2 :** chemical entity related to (such) another ⟨*epi*cholesterol⟩

epi·blast \ˈep-ə-ˌblast\ *n* **:** the outer layer of the blastoderm **:** ECTODERM — **epi·blas·tic** \ˌep-ə-ˈblas-tik\ *adj*

ep·i·bol·ic \ˌep-ə-ˈbäl-ik\ *adj* **:** of, relating to, or produced by epiboly ⟨~ invagination⟩ ⟨~ growth⟩

epib·o·ly \i-ˈpib-ə-lē\ *n* [Gk *epibolē* addition, fr. *epiballein* to throw on, fr. *epi-* + *ballein* to throw — more at DEVIL] **:** the growing of one part about another; *esp* **:** such growth of the dorsal lip area during gastrulation

1**ep·ic** \ˈep-ik\ *adj* [L *epicus*, fr. Gk *epikos*, fr. *epos* word, speech, poem — more at VOICE] **1 :** of, relating to, or having the characteristics of an epic **2 a :** unusually long esp. in size or scope **b :** HEROIC — **ep·i·cal** \-i-kəl\ *adj* — **ep·i·cal·ly** \-i-k(ə-)lē\ *adv*

2**epic** *n* **1 :** a long narrative poem in elevated style recounting the deeds of a legendary or historical hero **2 :** a work of art that resembles or suggests an epic **3 :** a series of events or body of legend or tradition felt to form the proper subject of an epic

epi·ca·lyx \ˌep-ə-ˈkā-liks, -ˈkal-iks\ *n* **:** an involucre resembling the calyx but consisting of a whorl of bracts below the calyx or resulting from the union of the sepal appendages

epi·car·di·al \ˌep-ə-ˈkärd-ē-əl\ *adj* **:** of or relating to the epicardium

epi·car·di·um \-ē-əm\ *n* [NL, fr. *epi-* + Gk *kardia* heart] **:** the visceral part of the pericardium that closely invests the heart

epi·carp \ˈep-ə-ˌkärp\ *n* [F *épicarpe*, fr. *épi-* epi- + *-carpe* -carp] **:** the outermost layer of the pericarp of a fruit

ep·i·cene \ˈep-ə-ˌsēn\ *adj* [ME, fr. L *epicoenus*, fr. Gk *epikoinos*, fr. *epi-* + *koinos* common] **1** *of a noun* **:** having but one form to indicate either sex **2 a :** having characteristics typical of the other sex **:** INTERSEXUAL **b :** EFFEMINATE **3 :** lacking characteristics of either sex — **epicene** *n* — **ep·i·cen·ism** \-ˌsē-ˌniz-əm\ *n*

epi·cen·ter \ˈep-ə-ˌsent-ər\ *n* [NL *epicentrum*, fr. *epi-* + L *centrum* center] **1 :** the part of the earth's surface directly above the focus of an earthquake **2 :** CENTER 2

epi·cot·yl \ˈep-ə-ˌkät-ᵊl\ *n* [*epi-* + *cotyl*edon] **:** the portion of the axis of a plant embryo or seedling above the cotyledonary node

epi·cot·y·le·don·ary \ˌep-ə-ˌkät-ᵊl-ˈēd-ᵊn-ˌer-ē\ *adj* **:** situated above the cotyledons; *also* **:** of or relating to the epicotyl

epi·cra·ni·al \ˌep-ə-ˈkrā-nē-əl\ *adj* **:** situated on the cranium

epi·crit·ic \ˌep-ə-ˈkrit-ik\ *adj* [Gk *epikritikos* determinative, fr. *epikrinein* to decide, fr. *epi-* + *krinein* to judge — more at CERTAIN] **:** of, relating to, or being cutaneous sensory reception marked by accurate discrimination between small degrees of sensation

ep·i·cure \ˈep-i-ˌkyu̇(ə)r\ *n* [*Epicurus* †270 B.C. Gk philosopher] **1** *archaic* **:** one devoted to sensual pleasure **:** SYBARITE **2 :** one with sensitive and discriminating tastes in food or wine
syn EPICURE, GOURMET, GOURMAND, GLUTTON, BON VIVANT mean one who takes pleasure in eating and drinking. EPICURE implies fastidiousness and voluptuousness of taste; GOURMET implies being a connoisseur in food and drink and the discriminating enjoyment of them; GOURMAND suggests a hearty interest in good food; GLUTTON stresses greediness and insatiability of appetite; BON VIVANT stresses the enjoyment of fine food and drink in company

ep·i·cu·re·an \ˌep-i-kyu̇-ˈrē-ən, -ˈkyu̇r-ē-\ *adj* **1** *cap* **:** of or relating to Epicurus or Epicureanism **2 :** of, relating to, or suited to an epicure **syn** see SENSUOUS

Epicurean *n* **1 :** a follower of Epicurus **2** *often not cap* **:** EPICURE 2

ep·i·cu·re·an·ism \-ə-ˌniz-əm\ *n* **1** *cap* **a :** the philosophy of Epicurus who subscribed to a hedonistic ethics that considered an imperturbable emotional calm the highest good, held intellectual pleasures superior to others, and advocated the renunciation of momentary in favor of more permanent pleasures **b :** a mode of life in consonance with Epicureanism **2 :** EPICURISM

ep·i·cur·ism \ˈep-i-ˌkyu̇(ə)r-ˌiz-əm\ *n* **:** the practices or tastes of an epicure or an epicurean

epi·cy·cle \ˈep-ə-ˌsī-kəl\ *n* [ME *epicicle*, fr. LL *epicyclus*, fr. Gk *epikyklos*, fr. *epi-* + *kyklos* circle — more at WHEEL] **1** *in Ptolemaic astron* **:** a circle in which a planet moves and which has a center that is itself carried around at the same time on the circumference of a larger circle **2 :** a process going on within a larger one — **epi·cy·clic** \ˌep-ə-ˈsī-klik, -ˈsik-lik\ *adj*

epicyclic train *n* **:** a train designed to have one or more parts travel around the circumference of another fixed or revolving part

epi·cy·cloid \ˌep-ə-ˈsī-ˌklȯid\ *n* **:** a curve traced by a point on a circle that rolls on the outside of a fixed circle

[1]**ep·i·dem·ic** \ˌep-ə-ˈdem-ik\ *adj* [F *épidémique*, fr. MF, fr. *epidemie*, n., epidemic, fr. LL *epidemia*, fr. Gk *epidēmia* visit, epidemic, fr. *epidēmos* visiting, epidemic, fr. *epi-* + *dēmos* people] **1 a :** affecting many persons at once **b :** EPIPHYTOTIC **c :** EPIZOOTIC **2 :** excessively prevalent — **ep·i·dem·i·cal** \-i-kəl\ *adj* — **ep·i·dem·i·cal·ly** \-i-k(ə-)lē\ *adv* — **ep·i·de·mic·i·ty** \-ˌdem-ˈis-ət-ē\ *n*

[2]**epidemic** *n* **1 :** an outbreak of epidemic disease **2 :** an outbreak or product of sudden rapid spread, growth, or development; *specif* **:** a natural population suddenly and greatly enlarged

ep·i·de·mi·o·log·ic \ˌep-ə-ˌdē-mē-ə-ˈläj-ik, -ˌdem-ē-\ *adj* **:** of, relating to, or involving epidemiology — **ep·i·de·mi·o·log·i·cal** \-i-kəl\ *adj* — **ep·i·de·mi·o·log·i·cal·ly** \-i-k(ə-)lē\ *adv*

ep·i·de·mi·ol·o·gist \-ˈäl-ə-jəst\ *n* **:** a specialist in epidemiology

ep·i·de·mi·ol·o·gy \-jē\ *n* [LL *epidemia* + ISV *-logy*] **1 :** a science that deals with the incidence, distribution, and control of disease in a population **2 :** the sum of the factors controlling the presence or absence of a disease or pathogen

epi·den·drum \ˌep-ə-ˈden-drəm\ *or* **epi·den·dron** \-drən\ *n* [NL, genus name, fr. Gk *epi-* + *dendron* tree] **:** any of a large genus (*Epidendrum*) of chiefly epiphytic and tropical American orchids

epiderm- *or* **epidermo-** *comb form* [*epidermis*] **:** epidermis ⟨*epidermal*⟩

epi·der·mal \ˌep-ə-ˈdər-məl\ *also* **epi·der·mic** \-mik\ *adj* **:** of, relating to, or arising from the epidermis

epi·der·mis \-məs\ *n* [LL, fr. Gk, fr. *epi-* + *derma* skin] **1 a :** the outer epithelial layer of the external integument of the animal body that is derived from the embryonic epiblast; *specif* **:** the outer nonsensitive and nonvascular layer of the skin of a vertebrate that overlies the corium **b :** any of various animal integuments **2 :** a thin surface layer of primary tissue in higher plants

epi·der·moid \-ˌmȯid\ *also* **epi·der·moi·dal** \-ˌdər-ˈmȯid-ᵊl\ *adj* **:** resembling epidermis or epidermal cells **:** made up of elements like those of epidermis ⟨~ neoplasms⟩

epi·dia·scope \ˌep-ə-ˈdī-ə-ˌskōp\ *n* [ISV] **1 :** a projector for images of opaque objects or for images on transparencies **2 :** EPISCOPE

epi·did·y·mal \ˌep-ə-ˈdid-ə-məl\ *adj* **:** of or relating to the epididymis

epi·did·y·mis \-məs\ *n, pl* **epi·did·y·mi·des** \-mə-ˌdēz\ [NL, fr. Gk, fr. *epi-* + *didymos* testicle] **:** an elongated mass at the back of the testis composed of convoluted efferent tubes

ep·i·dote \ˈep-ə-ˌdōt\ *n* [F *épidote*, fr. Gk *epididonai* to give in addition, fr. *epi-* + *didonai* to give — more at DATE] **:** a yellowish green mineral $Ca_2(Al,Fe)_3Si_3O_{12}OH$ consisting of a silicate of calcium, aluminum, and iron

epi·gas·tric \ˌep-ə-ˈgas-trik\ *adj* **1 :** lying upon or over the stomach **2 :** of or relating to the anterior walls of the abdomen

epi·gas·tri·um \-trē-əm\ *n, pl* **epi·gas·tria** \-trē-ə\ [NL, fr. Gk *epigastrion*, fr. *epi-* + *gastr-*, *gastēr* stomach — more at GASTRIC] **:** the epigastric region

epi·ge·al \ˌep-ə-ˈjē-əl\ *or* **epi·ge·ous** \-ˈjē-əs\ *adj* [Gk *epigaios* upon the earth, fr. *epi-* + *gē* earth] **1 a** (1) **:** growing above the surface of the ground (2) *of a cotyledon* **:** forced above ground by elongation of the hypocotyl **b :** marked by the production of epigeal cotyledons **2 :** living near or on the surface of the ground

ep·i·gene \ˈep-ə-ˌjēn\ *adj* [*epi-* + *-gene* (as in *hypogene*)] **:** formed, originating, or taking place on or not far below the earth's surface

epi·gen·e·sis \ˌep-ə-ˈjen-ə-səs\ *n* [NL] **1 :** development involving gradual diversification and differentiation of an initially undifferentiated entity (as a spore) **2 :** change in the mineral character of a rock owing to outside influences

epi·ge·net·ic \-jə-ˈnet-ik\ *adj* **1 :** of, relating to, or produced by epigenesis **2** *or* **epi·gen·ic** \-ˈjen-ik\ *of deposit or structure* **:** formed after the laying down of the enclosing rock

epig·e·nous \i-ˈpij-ə-nəs, e-\ *adj* [ISV] **:** growing upon the surface of a leaf or other plant organ

epi·glot·tal \ˌep-ə-ˈglät-ᵊl\ *also* **epi·glot·tic** \-ˈglät-ik\ *adj* **:** of, relating to, or produced with the aid of the epiglottis

epi·glot·tis \-ˈglät-əs\ *n* [NL, fr. Gk *epiglōttis*, fr. *epi-* + *glōttis* glottis] **:** a thin plate of yellow elastic cartilage behind the tongue and in front of the glottis that covers the glottis during swallowing

ep·i·gone \ˈep-ə-ˌgōn\ *n* [G *epigone*, fr. Gk *epigonos* successor, fr. *epigignesthai* to be born after, fr. *epi-* + *gignesthai* to be born] **:** an imitative follower; *esp* **:** an inferior imitator of a creative thinker or artist — **ep·i·gon·ic** \ˌep-ə-ˈgän-ik\ *or* **epig·o·nous** \i-ˈpig-ə-nəs, e-\ *adj* — **epig·o·nism** \-ˈpig-ə-ˌniz-əm\ *n*

ep·i·gram \ˈep-ə-ˌgram\ *n* [ME *epigrame*, fr. L *epigrammat-*, *epigramma*, fr. Gk, fr. *epigraphein* to write on, inscribe, fr. *epi-* + *graphein* to write — more at CARVE] **1 :** a short poem dealing concisely, pointedly, and often satirically with a single thought or event and often ending with an ingenious turn of thought **2 :** a terse, sage, or witty often paradoxical saying **3 :** epigrammatic expression — **ep·i·gram·mat·ic** \ˌep-i-grə-ˈmat-ik\ *also* **ep·i·gram·mat·i·cal** \-ˈmat-i-kəl\ *adj* — **ep·i·gram·mat·i·cal·ly** \-i-k(ə-)lē\ *adv* — **ep·i·gram·ma·tism** \ˌep-ə-ˈgram-ə-ˌtiz-əm\ *n* — **ep·i·gram·ma·tist** \-ˈgram-ət-əst\ *n*

ep·i·gram·ma·tize \ˌep-ə-ˈgram-ə-ˌtīz\ *vt* **1 :** to express epigrammatically **2 :** to make an epigram about ~ *vi* **:** to make an epigram — **ep·i·gram·ma·tiz·er** *n*

ep·i·graph \ˈep-ə-ˌgraf\ *n* [Gk *epigraphē*, fr. *epigraphein*] **1 :** an engraved inscription **2 :** a quotation set at the beginning of a literary work or a division of it to suggest its theme

epig·ra·pher \i-ˈpig-rə-fər, e-\ *n* **:** EPIGRAPHIST

ep·i·graph·ic \ˌep-ə-ˈgraf-ik\ *adj* **:** of or relating to epigraphs or epigraphy — **ep·i·graph·i·cal** \-i-kəl\ *adj* — **ep·i·graph·i·cal·ly** \-i-k(ə-)lē\ *adv*

epig·ra·phist \i-ˈpig-rə-fəst, e-\ *n* **:** a specialist in epigraphy

epig·ra·phy \-fē\ *n* **1 :** EPIGRAPHS, INSCRIPTIONS **2 :** the study of inscriptions; *esp* **:** the deciphering of ancient inscriptions

epig·y·nous \i-ˈpij-ə-nəs, e-\ *adj* **1** *of a floral organ* **:** adnate to the surface of the ovary and appearing to grow from the top of it **2 :** having epigynous floral organs — **epig·y·ny** \-nē\ *n*

ep·i·lep·sy \ˈep-ə-ˌlep-sē\ *n* [MF *epilepsie*, fr. LL *epilepsia*, fr. Gk *epilēpsia*, fr. *epilambanein* to seize, fr. *epi-* + *lambanein* to take, seize] **:** any of various disorders marked by disturbed electrical rhythms of the central nervous system and typically manifested by convulsive attacks usu. with clouding of consciousness

epilept- *or* **epilepti-** *or* **epilepto-** *comb form* [Gk *epilēpt-*, fr. *epilēptos* seized by epilepsy, fr. *epilambanein*] **:** epilepsy ⟨*epileptoid*⟩

ep·i·lep·tic \ˌep-ə-ˈlep-tik\ *adj* **:** relating to, affected with, or having the characteristics of epilepsy — **epileptic** *n* — **ep·i·lep·ti·cal·ly** \-ti-k(ə-)lē\ *adv*

ep·i·lep·ti·form \ˌep-ə-ˈlep-tə-ˌfȯrm\ *adj* **:** resembling that of epilepsy ⟨an ~ convulsion⟩

ep·i·lep·toid \-ˌtȯid\ *adj* **1 :** EPILEPTIFORM **2 :** exhibiting symptoms resembling those of epilepsy

ep·i·logue \ˈep-ə-ˌlȯg, -ˌläg\ *n* [ME *epiloge*, fr. MF *epilogue*, fr. L *epilogus*, fr. Gk *epilogos*, fr. *epilegein* to say in addition, fr. *epi-* + *legein* to say] **1 :** a concluding section that rounds out the design of a literary work **2 a :** a speech often in verse addressed to the audience by an actor at the end of a play **b :** the actor speaking such an epilogue

ep·i·mere \ˈep-ə-ˌmi(ə)r\ *n* [ISV] **:** the dorsal part of a mesodermal segment of a chordate embryo

epi·mor·pho·sis \ˌep-ə-ˈmȯr-fə-səs\ *n* [NL, fr. *epi-* + Gk *morphōsis* formation, fr. *morphoun* to form, fr. *morphē* form — more at FORM] **:** regeneration of a part or organism involving extensive cell proliferation followed by differentiation

epi·my·si·um \ˌep-ə-ˈmiz(h)-ē-əm\ *n* [NL, fr. *epi-* + Gk *mys* mouse, muscle] **:** the external connective-tissue sheath of a muscle

epi·neph·rine *also* **epi·neph·rin** \ˌep-ə-ˈnef-ˌrēn, -rən\ *n* [ISV *epi-* + Gk *nephros* kidney] **:** a colorless crystalline feebly basic sympathomimetic adrenal hormone $C_9H_{13}NO_3$ used medicinally esp. as a heart stimulant, a vasoconstrictor, and a muscle relaxant

epi·neu·ri·um \ˌep-ə-ˈn(y)u̇r-ē-əm\ *n* [NL] **:** the external connective-tissue sheath of a nerve trunk

epiph·a·ny \i-ˈpif-ə-nē\ *n* [ME *epiphanie*, fr. MF, fr. LL *epiphania*, fr. LGk, pl., prob. alter. of Gk *epiphaneia* appearance, manifestation, fr. *epiphainein* to manifest, fr. *epi-* + *phainein* to show — more at FANCY] **1** *cap* **:** a feast on January 6 in commemoration of the coming of the Magi as the first manifestation of Christ to the Gentiles or in the Eastern Church the baptism of Christ **2 :** an appearance or manifestation esp. of a divine being

epi·phe·nom·e·nal \ˌep-ə-fi-ˈnäm-ən-ᵊl\ *adj* **:** of or relating to an epiphenomenon **:** DERIVATIVE — **epi·phe·nom·e·nal·ly** \-ᵊl-ē\ *adv*

epi·phe·nom·e·nal·ism \-ᵊl-ˌiz-əm\ *n* **:** a doctrine that mental processes are epiphenomena of brain processes

epi·phe·nom·e·non \-ˈnäm-ə-ˌnän, -nən\ *n* **:** a secondary phenomenon accompanying another and caused by it

ep·i·phragm \ˈep-ə-ˌfram\ *n* [Gk *epiphragma* covering] **:** a closing membrane or septum (as of a snail shell or a moss capsule)

epi·phy·se·al \i-ˌpif-ə-ˈsē-əl, -ˈzē-; ˌep-ə-ˈfiz-ē-\ *also* **ep·i·phys·i·al** \ˌep-ə-ˈfiz-ē-əl\ *adj* **:** of or relating to an epiphysis

epiph·y·sis \i-ˈpif-ə-səs\ *n, pl* **epiph·y·ses** \-ə-ˌsēz\ [NL, fr. Gk, growth, fr. *epiphyesthai* to grow on, fr. *epi-* + *phyesthai* to grow, pass. of *phyein* to bring forth] **1 :** a part or process of a bone that ossifies separately and later becomes ankylosed to the main part of the bone; *esp* **:** an end of a long bone **2 :** PINEAL BODY

epi·phyte \ˈep-ə-ˌfīt\ *n* **:** a plant that derives its moisture and nutrients from the air and rain and grows usu. on another plant

epi·phyt·ic \ˌep-ə-ˈfit-ik\ *adj* **1 :** of, relating to, or being an epiphyte **2 :** living on the surface of plants — **epi·phyt·i·cal·ly** \-ˈfit-i-k(ə-)lē\ *adv*

ep·i·phy·tol·o·gy \ˌep-ə-ˌfī-ˈtäl-ə-jē\ *n* **1 :** a science that deals with character, ecology, and causes of outbreak of plant diseases **2 :** the sum of the factors controlling the occurrence of a disease or pathogen of plants

ep·i·phy·tot·ic \-ˈtät-ik\ *adj* [*epi-* + Gk *phyton* plant] **:** of, relating to, or being a plant disease that tends to recur sporadically and to affect large numbers of susceptible plants — **epiphytotic** *n*

epi·ro·gen·ic, ep·i·rog·e·ny *var of* EPEIROGENIC, EPEIROGENY

epi·scia \i-ˈpish-(ē-)ə\ *n* [NL, genus name, fr. Gk *episkios* shaded, fr. *epi-* + *skia* shadow] **:** any of a genus (*Episcia*) of tropical American herbs with hairy foliage related to the African violet

epis·co·pa·cy \i-ˈpis-kə-pə-sē\ *n* **1 :** government of the church by bishops or by a hierarchy **2 :** EPISCOPATE

epis·co·pal \i-ˈpis-kə-pəl\ *adj* [ME, fr. LL *episcopalis*, fr. *episcopus* bishop — more at BISHOP] **1 :** of or relating to a bishop **2 :** of, having, or constituting government by bishops **3** *cap* **:** of or relating to the Protestant Episcopal Church representing the Anglican communion in the U.S. — **epis·co·pal·ly** \-p(ə-)lē\ *adv*

Epis·co·pa·lian \i-ˌpis-kə-ˈpāl-yən\ *n* **1 :** an adherent of the episcopal form of church government **2 :** a member of an episcopal church (as the Protestant Episcopal Church) — **Episcopalian** *adj* — **Epis·co·pa·lian·ism** \-yə-ˌniz-əm\ *n*

epis·co·pate \i-ˈpis-kə-pət, -ˌpāt\ *n* **1 :** the rank, office, or term of bishop **2 :** DIOCESE **3 :** the body of bishops (as in a country)

epi·scope \ˈep-ə-ˌskōp\ *n* [ISV] **:** a projector for images of opaque objects (as photographs)

ep·i·sode \ˈep-ə-ˌsōd\ *n* [Gk *epeisodion*, fr. neut. of *epeisodios* coming in besides, fr. *epi-* + *eisodios* coming in, fr. *eis* into (akin to Gk *en* in) + *hodos* road, journey — more at IN, CEDE] **1 :** a usu.

brief unit of action in a dramatic or literary work: as **a :** the part of an ancient Greek tragedy between two choric songs **b :** a developed situation that is integral to but separable from a continuous narrative : INCIDENT **c :** one of a series of loosely connected stories or scenes **d :** the part of a serial presented at one performance **2 :** an event that is distinctive and separate although part of a larger series **3 :** a digressive subdivision in a musical composition **syn** see OCCURRENCE — **ep·i·sod·ic** \ˌep-ə-ˈsäd-ik\ *also* **ep·i·sod·i·cal** \-i-kəl\ *adj* — **ep·i·sod·i·cal·ly** \-i-k(ə-)lē\ *adv*

epis·ta·sis \i-ˈpis-tə-səs\ *or* **epis·ta·sy** \-sē\ *n* [NL *epistasis*, fr. Gk, act of stopping, fr. *ephistanai* to stop, fr. *epi-* + *histanai* to cause to stand — more at STAND] **:** suppression of the effect of a gene by a nonallelic gene — **ep·i·stat·ic** \ˌep-ə-ˈstat-ik\ *adj*

ep·i·stax·is \ˌep-ə-ˈstak-səs\ *n* [NL, fr. Gk, fr. *epistazein* to drip on, to bleed at the nose again, fr. *epi-* + *stazein* to drip — more at STAGNATE] **:** NOSEBLEED

ep·i·ste·mic \ˌep-ə-ˈstē-mik\ *adj* **:** of or relating to knowledge or knowing **:** COGNITIVE — **ep·i·ste·mi·cal·ly** \-mi-k(ə-)lē\ *adv*

epis·te·mo·log·i·cal \i-ˌpis-tə-mə-ˈläj-i-kəl\ *adj* **:** of or relating to epistemology — **epis·te·mo·log·i·cal·ly** \-k(ə-)lē\ *adv*

epis·te·mol·o·gy \-ˈmäl-ə-jē\ *n* [Gk *epistēmē* knowledge, fr. *epistanai* to understand, know, fr. *epi-* + *histanai*] **:** the study or a theory of the nature and grounds of knowledge esp. with reference to its limits and validity

epi·ster·num \ˌep-ə-ˈstər-nəm\ *n* [NL] **1 :** an anterior element of or associated with the sternum **2 :** a lateral division or piece of a somite of an arthropod **3 :** MANUBRIUM

epis·tle \i-ˈpis-əl\ *n* [ME, letter, Epistle, fr. OF, fr. L *epistula*, *epistola* letter, fr. Gk *epistolē* message, letter, fr. *epistellein* to send to, fr. *epi-* + *stellein* to send] **1** *cap* **a :** one of the letters of the New Testament **b :** a liturgical lection usu. from one of the New Testament Epistles **2 a :** LETTER; *esp* **:** a formal or elegant letter **b :** a composition in the form of a letter — **epis·tler** \-ˈpis-(ə-)lər\ *n*

epis·to·lary \i-ˈpis-tə-ˌler-ē\ *adj* **1 :** of, relating to, or suitable to a letter **2 :** contained in or carried on by letters **3 :** written in the form of a series of letters ⟨~ novel⟩

epis·to·ler \i-ˈpis-tə-lər\ *n* **:** the reader of the liturgical Epistle esp. in Anglican churches

epi·style \ˈep-ə-ˌstīl\ *n* [L *epistylium*, fr. Gk *epistylion*, fr. *epi-* + Gk *stylos* pillar — more at STEER] **:** ARCHITRAVE 1

ep·i·taph \ˈep-ə-ˌtaf\ *n* [ME *epitaphe*, fr. MF, fr. ML *epitaphium*, fr. L, funeral oration, fr. Gk *epitaphion*, fr. *epi-* + *taphos* tomb, funeral] **1 :** an inscription on or at a tomb or a grave in memory of the one buried there **2 :** a brief statement commemorating or epitomizing a deceased person or something past — **ep·i·taph·ial** \ˌep-ə-ˈtaf-ē-əl\ *or* **ep·i·taph·ic** \-ˈtaf-ik\ *adj*

epit·a·sis \i-ˈpit-ə-səs\ *n* [Gk, increased intensity, fr. *epiteinein* to stretch tighter, fr. *epi-* + *teinein* to stretch — more at THIN] **:** the development of a play leading to the catastrophe

ep·i·tha·la·mi·um \ˌep-ə-thə-ˈlā-mē-əm\ *or* **ep·i·tha·la·mi·on** \-mē-ən\ *n, pl* **epithalamiums** *or* **ep·i·tha·la·mia** \-mē-ə\ [L & Gk; L *epithalamium*, fr. Gk *epithalamion*, fr. *epi-* + *thalamos* room, bridal chamber] **:** a song or poem in honor of a bride and bridegroom

epitheli- *or* **epithelio-** *comb form* [NL *epithelium*] **:** epithelium

ep·i·the·li·al \ˌep-ə-ˈthē-lē-əl\ *adj* **:** of or relating to epithelium

ep·i·the·li·oid \-lē-ˌȯid\ *adj* **:** resembling epithelium ⟨~ cells⟩

ep·i·the·li·o·ma \-ˌthē-lē-ˈō-mə\ *n* **:** a benign or malignant tumor derived from epithelial tissue — **ep·i·the·li·o·ma·tous** \-ˈäm-ət-əs, -ˈō-mət-\ *adj*

ep·i·the·li·um \ˌep-ə-ˈthē-lē-əm\ *n* [NL, fr. *epi-* + Gk *thēlē* nipple — more at FEMININE] **1 :** a membranous cellular tissue that covers a free surface or lines a tube or cavity of an animal body and serves esp. to enclose and protect the other parts of the body, to produce secretions and excretions, and to function in assimilation **2 :** a usu. thin layer of parenchyma that lines a cavity or tube of a plant

ep·i·the·lize \ˌep-ə-ˈthē-ˌlīz\ *also* **ep·i·the·li·al·ize** \-lē-ə-ˌlīz\ *vt* **:** to cover with or convert to epithelium ⟨*epithelized* lesions⟩

ep·i·thet \ˈep-ə-ˌthet *also* -thət\ *n* [L *epitheton*, fr. Gk, fr. neut. of *epithetos* added, fr. *epitithenai* to put on, add, fr. *epi-* + *tithenai* to put] **1 a :** a characterizing word or phrase accompanying or occurring in place of the name of a person or thing **b :** a disparaging or abusive word or phrase **c :** the part of a taxonomic name identifying a subordinate unit within a genus **2** *obs* **:** TERM — **ep·i·thet·ic** \ˌep-ə-ˈthet-ik\ *or* **ep·i·thet·i·cal** \-i-kəl\ *adj*

epit·o·me \i-ˈpit-ə-mē\ *n* [L, fr. Gk *epitomē*, fr. *epitemnein* to cut short, fr. *epi-* + *temnein* to cut — more at TOME] **1 a :** a summary of a written work **b :** a brief presentation or statement of something **2 :** a typical representation or ideal expression **:** EMBODIMENT **3 :** brief or miniature form **syn** see ABRIDGMENT

epit·o·mize \-ˌmīz\ *vt* **1 :** to make or give an epitome of **2 :** to serve as the typical representation or ideal expression of

epi·zo·ic \ˌep-ə-ˈzō-ik\ *adj* **:** dwelling upon the body of an animal ⟨an ~ plant⟩ — **epi·zo·ism** \-ˌiz-əm\ *n* — **epi·zo·ite** \-ˌīt\ *n*

[1]**epi·zo·ot·ic** \ˌep-ə-zə-ˈwät-ik\ *adj* **:** of, relating to, or being a disease that affects many animals of one kind at the same time — **epi·zo·ot·i·cal·ly** \-i-k(ə-)lē\ *adv*

[2]**epizootic** *n* **:** an epizootic disease

epi·zo·ot·i·ol·o·gy \ˌep-ə-zə-ˌwät-ē-ˈäl-ə-jē\ *or* **epi·zo·otol·o·gy** \-ˌzō-ə-ˈtäl-ə-jē\ *or* **epi·zo·ol·o·gy** \-zə-ˈwäl-ə-jē\ *n* **1 :** a science that deals with the character, ecology, and causes of outbreaks of animal diseases **2 :** the sum of the factors controlling the occurrence of a disease or pathogen of animals

e plu·ri·bus unum \ˌē-ˌplu̇r-ə-bəs-ˈyü-nəm; ˌā-ˌplu̇r-, -bə-ˈsü-\ [L, one out of many] **:** one composed of many — used on the seal of the U.S. and on several U.S. coins

ep·och \ˈep-ək, ˈep-ˌäk *also* ˈē-ˌpäk\ *n* [ML *epocha*, fr. Gk *epochē* cessation, fixed point, fr. *epechein* to pause, hold back, fr. *epi-* + *echein* to hold — more at SCHEME] **1 :** an instant of time or a date selected as a point of reference in astronomy **2 a :** an event or a time marked by an event that begins a new period or development **b :** a memorable event or date **c :** TIME 8a **3 a :** an extended period of time usu. characterized by a distinctive development or by a memorable series of events **b :** a division of geologic time less than a period and greater than an age **syn** see PERIOD — **ep·och·al** \ˈep-ə-kəl, ˈep-ˌäk-əl\ *adj* — **ep·och·al·ly** \-ə-lē\ *adv*

ep·ode \ˈep-ˌōd\ *n* [L *epodos*, fr. Gk *epōidos*, fr. *epōidos* sung or said after, fr. *epi-* + *aidein* to sing] **1 :** a lyric poem in which a long verse is followed by a shorter one **2 :** the third part of triadically constructed Greek odes following the strophe and the antistrophe

ep·o·nym \ˈep-ə-ˌnim\ *n* [Gk *epōnymos*, fr. *epōnymos* eponymous, fr. *epi-* + *onyma* name — more at NAME] **1 :** the person for whom something is named or supposedly named **2 :** one whose name is so prominently connected with something as to be a figurative designation for it — **ep·o·nym·ic** \ˌep-ə-ˈnim-ik\ *adj* — **epon·y·mous** \i-ˈpän-ə-məs, e-\ *adj*

epon·y·my \i-ˈpän-ə-mē, e-\ *n* **:** the explanation of a proper name by supposing a fictitious eponym

ep·o·pee \ˈep-ə-ˌpē\ *n* [F *épopée*, fr. Gk *epopoiia*, fr. *epos* + *poiein* to make — more at POET] **:** EPIC; *esp* **:** an epic poem

ep·os \ˈep-ˌäs\ *n* [Gk, word, epic poem] **1 :** a number of poems that treat an epic theme but are not formally united **2 :** EPIC

ep·ox·ide \(ˈ)ep-ˈäk-ˌsīd\ *n* **:** an epoxy compound

ep·ox·i·dize \-sə-ˌdīz\ *vt* **:** to convert into an epoxide

ep·oxy \-sē\ *adj* **:** containing oxygen attached to two different atoms already united in some other way; *specif* **:** containing a 3-membered ring consisting of one oxygen and two carbon atoms — **epoxy** *n*

epoxy resin *n* **:** a flexible usu. thermosetting resin made by polymerization of an epoxide and used chiefly in coatings and adhesives

ep·si·lon \ˈep-sə-ˌlän, -lən\ *n* [Gk *e psilon*, lit., simple e] **1 :** the 5th letter of the Greek alphabet — symbol Ε or ϵ **2 :** a usu. small positive number

Ep·som salt \ˌep-səm-\ *n* [*Epsom*, England] **:** a bitter colorless or white crystalline salt $MgSO_4.7H_2O$ that is a hydrated magnesium sulfate with cathartic properties — usu. used in pl.

equa·bil·i·ty \ˌek-wə-ˈbil-ət-ē, ˌē-kwə-\ *n* **:** the quality or condition of being equable

equa·ble \ˈek-wə-bəl, ˈē-kwə-\ *adj* [L *aequabilis*, fr. *aequare* to make level or equal, fr. *aequus*] **1 :** marked by lack of variation or change **:** UNIFORM **2 :** marked by lack of noticeable, unpleasant, or extreme variation or inequality **syn** see STEADY — **equa·ble·ness** *n* — **equa·bly** \-blē\ *adv*

[1]**equal** \ˈē-kwəl\ *adj* [ME, fr. L *aequalis*, fr. *aequus* level, equal] **1 a** (1) **:** of the same measure, quantity, amount, or number as another **:** LIKE (2) **:** identical in mathematical value or logical denotation **:** EQUIVALENT **b :** like in quality, nature, or status **c :** UNIFORM **2 :** regarding or affecting all objects in the same way **:** IMPARTIAL **3 :** free from extremes: as **a :** tranquil of mind or mood **b :** not showing variation in appearance, structure, or proportion **4 a :** capable of meeting the requirements of a situation or a task **b :** SUITABLE **syn** see SAME

[2]**equal** *n* **1 :** one that is equal **2 :** an equal quantity

[3]**equal** *vt* **equaled** *or* **equalled; equal·ing** *or* **equal·ling** **1** *archaic* **:** EQUALIZE **2 :** to be equal to; *specif* **:** to be identical in value to **3 :** to make or produce something equal to **:** MATCH

equal–area *adj, of a map projection* **:** maintaining constant ratio of size between quadrilaterals formed by the meridians and parallels and the quadrilaterals of the globe thereby preserving true areal extent of forms represented

equal·i·tar·i·an \i-ˌkwäl-ə-ˈter-ē-ən\ *adj or n* **:** EGALITARIAN — **equal·i·tar·i·an·ism** \-ē-ə-ˌniz-əm\ *n*

equal·i·ty \i-ˈkwäl-ət-ē\ *n* **1 :** the quality or state of being equal **2 :** EQUATION 2a

equal·iza·tion \ˌē-kwə-lə-ˈzā-shən\ *n* **:** the act of equalizing **:** the state of being equalized

equal·ize \ˈē-kwə-ˌlīz\ *vt* **1 :** to make equal **2 a :** to compensate for **b :** to make uniform; *specif* **:** to distribute evenly or uniformly **c :** to adjust or correct the frequency characteristics of

equal·iz·er \-ˌlī-zər\ *n* **:** one that equalizes esp. by equal distribution (as of force)

equal·ly \ˈē-kwə-lē\ *adv* **1 :** in an equal manner **:** EVENLY **2 :** to an equal degree **:** ALIKE

equa·nim·i·ty \ˌē-kwə-ˈnim-ət-ē, ˌek-wə-\ *n* [L *aequanimitas*, fr. *aequo animo* with even mind] **1 :** evenness of mind esp. under stress **:** COMPOSURE **2 :** right disposition **:** BALANCE

syn COMPOSURE, SANGFROID, PHLEGM: EQUANIMITY suggests a habit of mind that is only rarely disturbed under great strain; COMPOSURE implies the controlling of emotional or mental agitation by an effort of will or as a matter of habit; SANGFROID implies great coolness and steadiness under strain; PHLEGM implies insensitiveness and suggests apathy rather than self-control

equate \i-ˈkwāt\ *vb* [ME *equaten*, fr. L *aequatus*, pp. of *aequare*] *vt* **1 a :** to make equal **:** EQUALIZE **b :** to make such an allowance or correction in as will reduce to a common standard or obtain a correct result **2 :** to treat, represent, or regard as equal, equivalent, or comparable ~ *vi* **:** to correspond as equal

equa·tion \i-ˈkwā-zhən, -shən\ *n* **1 a :** the act or process of equating **b** (1) **:** an element affecting a process **:** FACTOR (2) **:** a complex of variable factors **c :** a state of being equated; *specif* **:** a state of association or identification of two or more things **2 a :** a usu. formal statement of the equality or equivalence of mathematical or logical expressions **b :** an expression representing a chemical reaction quantitatively by means of chemical symbols placed on the left for reacting substances and on the right for products of the sign → or = or of the sign ⇆ or ⇄ if the reaction is reversible

equa·tion·al \i-ˈkwāzh-nəl, -ˈkwāsh-, -ən-ᵊl\ *adj* **1 :** of, using, or involving equation or equations **2 :** having a subject and predicate not linked by a verb — **equa·tion·al·ly** *adv*

equa·tor \i-ˈkwāt-ər, ˈē-ˌkwāt-\ *n* [ME, fr. ML *aequator*, lit., equalizer, fr. L *aequatus*; fr. its containing the equinoxes] **1 :** the great circle of the celestial sphere whose plane is perpendicular to the axis of the earth **2 :** a great circle of the earth that is everywhere equally distant from the two poles and divides the earth's surface into the northern and southern hemispheres **3 :** a circle or circular band dividing the surface of a body into two usu. equal and symmetrical parts **4 :** GREAT CIRCLE

[1]**equa·to·ri·al** \ˌē-kwə-ˈtōr-ē-əl, ˌek-wə-, -ˈtȯr-\ *adj* **1 a :** of, located at, or relating to the equator or an equator **b :** of, originating in, or suggesting the region around the geographic equator **2 :** being or having a support that includes two axles at right angles to each other with one parallel to the earth's axis of rotation

[2]**equatorial** *n* **:** an equatorial telescope

equer·ry \ˈek-wə-rē, i-ˈkwer-ē\ *n* [obs. *escuirie*, *equerry* stable, fr. MF *escuirie* office of a squire, stable, fr. *escuier* squire] **1 :** an officer of princes or nobles charged with the care of their horses **2 :** one of the officers of the British royal household in personal attendance on the sovereign or another member of the royal family

[1]**eques·tri·an** \i-ˈkwes-trē-ən\ *adj* [L *equestr-*, *equester* of a horseman, fr. *eques* horseman, fr. *equus* horse — more at EQUINE]

1 a : of, relating to, or featuring horseback riding b *archaic* : riding on horseback : MOUNTED c : representing a person on horseback ⟨an ~ statue⟩ 2 : of, relating to, or composed of knights
2**equestrian** *n* : one who rides on horseback
eques·tri·enne \i-ˌkwes-trē-ˈen\ *n* [2equestrian + -enne (as in *tragedienne*)] : a female equestrian
equi- *comb form* [ME, fr. MF, fr. L *aequi-*, fr. *aequus* equal] : equal ⟨*equi*poise⟩ : equally ⟨*equi*probable⟩
equi·an·gu·lar \ˌē-kwi-ˈaŋ-gyə-lər\ *adj* : having all or corresponding angles equal
equi·ca·lor·ic \ˌē-kwə-kə-ˈlȯr-ik, -ˈlär-\ *adj* : capable of yielding equal amounts of energy in the body ⟨~ diets⟩
equi·dis·tance \ˌē-kwə-ˈdis-tən(t)s\ *n* : equal distance
equi·dis·tant \-tənt\ *adj* [MF or LL; MF, fr. LL *aequidistant-*, *aequidistans*, fr. L *aequi-* + *distant-*, *distans*, prp. of *distare* to stand apart] 1 : equally distant 2 : representing map distances true to scale in all directions — **equi·dis·tant·ly** *adv*
equi·lat·er·al \ˌē-kwə-ˈlat-ə-rəl, -ˈla-trəl\ *adj* [LL *aequilateralis*, fr. L *aequi-* + *later-*, *latus* side — more at LATERAL] 1 a : having all sides equal ⟨~ triangle⟩ b : having all the faces equal ⟨~ polyhedron⟩ 2 : bilaterally symmetrical
equil·i·brant \i-ˈkwil-ə-brənt\ *n* : a counterbalancing force or system of forces
equil·i·brate \-ˌbrāt\ *vt* : to bring into or keep in equilibrium : BALANCE ~ *vi* : to bring about, come to, or be in equilibrium — **equil·i·bra·tion** \i-ˌkwil-ə-ˈbrā-shən\ *n* — **equil·i·bra·tor** \i-ˈkwil-ə-ˌbrāt-ər\ *n* — **equil·i·bra·to·ry** \-brə-ˌtōr-ē, -ˌtȯr-\ *adj*
equi·li·brist \ˌē-kwə-ˈlib-rəst, ˌek-wə-; i-ˈkwil-ə-brəst\ *n* : one who balances himself in unnatural positions and hazardous movements — **equil·i·bris·tic** \i-ˌkwil-ə-ˈbris-tik\ *adj*
equi·lib·ri·um \ˌē-kwə-ˈlib-rē-əm, ˌek-wə-\ *n, pl* **equilibriums** *or* **equi·lib·ria** \-rē-ə\ [L *aequilibrium*, fr. *aequilibris* in equilibrium, fr. *aequi-* + *libra* weight, balance] 1 : a static or dynamic state of balance between opposing forces or actions 2 : a state of adjustment between opposing or divergent influences or elements 3 : the normal oriented state of the animal body in respect to its environment
equi·mo·lal \ˌē-kwə-ˈmō-ləl\ *adj* 1 : having equal molal concentration 2 : EQUIMOLAR 1
equi·mo·lar \-lər\ *adj* 1 : of or relating to an equal number of moles ⟨an ~ mixture⟩ 2 : having equal molar concentration
equine \ˈē-ˌkwīn, ˈek-ˌwīn\ *adj* [L *equinus*, fr. *equus* horse; akin to OE *eoh* horse, Gk *hippos*] : of, relating to, or resembling a horse or the horse family — **equine** *n* — **equine·ly** *adv*
1**equi·noc·tial** \ˌē-kwə-ˈnäk-shəl, ˌek-wə-\ *adj* 1 : relating to an equinox or to a state or the time of equal day and night 2 : relating to the regions or climate of the equinoctial line or equator 3 : relating to the time when the sun passes an equinoctial point
2**equinoctial** *n* 1 : EQUATOR 1 2 : an equinoctial storm
equinoctial circle *n* : EQUATOR 1 — called also *equinoctial line*
equi·nox \ˈē-kwə-ˌnäks, ˈek-wə-\ *n* [ME, fr. MF or ML; MF *equinoxe*, fr. ML *equinoxium*, alter. of L *aequinoctium*, fr. *aequi-* equi- + *noct-*, *nox* night — more at NIGHT] 1 : either of the two times each year when the sun crosses the equator and day and night are everywhere of equal length, being about March 21 and September 23 2 : either of the two points on the celestial sphere where the celestial equator intersects the ecliptic
equip \i-ˈkwip\ *vt* **equipped**; **equip·ping** [MF *equiper*, of Gmc origin; akin to OE *scip* ship] 1 : to furnish for service or action : PREPARE 2 : DRESS, ARRAY — **syn** see FURNISH
eq·ui·page \ˈek-wə-pij\ *n* 1 a : material or articles used in equipment : OUTFIT b *archaic* (1) : a set of small articles (as for table service) (2) : ETUI c : TRAPPINGS 2 *archaic* : RETINUE 3 a : a horse-drawn carriage with its servants b : such a carriage alone
equip·ment \i-ˈkwip-mənt\ *n* 1 a : the equipping of a person or thing b : the state of being equipped 2 a : the set of articles or physical resources serving to equip a person or thing: as (1) : the implements used in an operation or activity : APPARATUS (2) : all the fixed assets other than land and buildings of a business enterprise (3) : the rolling stock of a railway b : a piece of such equipment 3 : mental or emotional traits or resources : ENDOWMENT
1**equi·poise** \ˈek-wə-ˌpȯiz, ˈē-kwə-\ *n* 1 : a state of equilibrium 2 : COUNTERBALANCE
2**equipoise** *vt* 1 : to serve as an equipoise to 2 : to put or hold in equipoise
equi·pol·lence \ˌē-kwə-ˈpäl-ən(t)s\ *also* **equi·pol·len·cy** \-ən-sē\ *n* : the quality of being equipollent
equi·pol·lent \-ənt\ *adj* [ME, fr. MF, fr. L *aequipollent-*, *aequipollens*, fr. *aequi-* equi- + *pollent-*, *pollens*, prp. of *pollēre* to be able] 1 : equal in force, power, or validity 2 : the same in effect or signification — **equipollent** *n* — **equi·pol·lent·ly** *adv*
equi·pon·der·ant \ˌē-kwə-ˈpän-də-rənt\ *adj* : evenly balanced
equi·pon·der·ate \-ˌrāt\ *vb* [ML *aequiponderatus*, pp. of *equiponderare*, fr. L *aequi-* + *ponderare* to weigh, ponder] *vi* : to be equal in weight or force ~ *vt* : to equal or make equal in weight
equi·po·tent \ˌē-kwə-ˈpōt-ᵊnt\ *adj* : having equal effects or capacities ⟨~ genes⟩
equi·po·ten·tial \-pə-ˈten-chəl\ *adj* : having the same electrical potential ⟨~ points⟩ : of uniform potential throughout
eq·ui·se·tum \ˌek-wə-ˈsēt-əm\ *n, pl* **equisetums** *or* **eq·ui·se·ta** \-ˈsēt-ə\ [NL, genus name, fr. L *equisaetum* horsetail (plant), fr. *equus* horse + *saeta* bristle] : any of a genus (*Equisetum*) of lower tracheophytes comprising perennial plants that spread by creeping rhizomes, are homosporous and asexual, and have leaves reduced to nodal sheaths on the hollow jointed grooved shoots
eq·ui·ta·ble \ˈek-wət-ə-bəl\ *adj* 1 : having or exhibiting equity : JUST 2 : existing or valid in equity as distinguished from law **syn** see FAIR — **eq·ui·ta·ble·ness** *n* — **eq·ui·ta·bly** \-blē\ *adv*
eq·ui·tant \ˈek-wət-ənt\ *adj* [L *equitant-*, *equitans*, prp. of *equitare* to ride on horseback, fr. *equit-*, *eques* horseman] *of leaves* : overlapping each other transversely at the base (as in an iris)
eq·ui·ta·tion \ˌek-wə-ˈtā-shən\ *n* : the act or art of riding on horseback
eq·ui·ty \ˈek-wət-ē\ *n* [ME *equite*, fr. MF *equité*, fr. L *aequitat-*, *aequitas*, fr. *aequus* equal, fair] 1 a : justice according to natural law or right; *specif* : IMPARTIALITY b : something that is equitable 2 a : a system of law originating in the English chancery and comprising a settled and formal body of legal and procedural rules and doctrines that supplement, aid, or override common and statute law and are designed to protect rights and enforce duties fixed by substantive law b : trial or remedial justice under or by the rules and doctrines of equity c : a body of legal doctrines and rules developed to enlarge, supplement, or override a narrow rigid system of law 3 a : a right, claim, or interest existing or valid in equity b : the money value of a property or of an interest in a property in excess of claims or liens against it c : a risk interest or ownership right in property
equity capital *n* : VENTURE CAPITAL
equiv·a·lence \i-ˈkwiv(-ə)-lən(t)s\ *also* **equiv·a·len·cy** \-lən-sē\ *n* 1 a : the state or property of being equivalent b (1) : the relation holding between two statements if they are either both true or both false (2) : the relation holding between two statements if to affirm one and to deny the other would result in a contradiction 2 : a presentation of terms as equivalent 3 : equality in metrical value of a regular foot and one in which there are substitutions
equiv·a·lent \-lənt\ *adj* [ME, fr. MF or LL; MF, fr. LL *aequivalent-*, *aequivalens*, prp. of *aequivalēre* to have equal power, fr. L *aequi-* + *valēre* to be strong] 1 : equal in force, amount, or value; *also* : equal in area or volume but not admitting of superposition ⟨a square ~ to a triangle⟩ 2 : like in signification or import 3 : corresponding or virtually identical esp. in effect or function 4 *obs* : equal in might or authority 5 : having the same chemical combining capacity **syn** see SAME — **equivalent** *n* — **equiv·a·lent·ly** *adv*
equiv·o·cal \i-ˈkwiv-ə-kəl\ *adj* [LL *aequivocus*, fr. *aequi-* equi- + *voc-*, *vox* voice] 1 a : having two or more significations : AMBIGUOUS b : uncertain as an indication or sign 2 a : of uncertain nature or classification b : of uncertain disposition toward a person or thing : UNDECIDED c : of doubtful advantage, genuineness, or moral rectitude ⟨~ behavior⟩ **syn** see OBSCURE — **equiv·o·cal·i·ty** \i-ˌkwiv-ə-ˈkal-ət-ē\ *n* — **equiv·o·cal·ly** \i-ˈkwiv-ə-k(ə-)lē\ *adv* — **equiv·o·cal·ness** \-kəl-nəs\ *n*
equiv·o·cate \i-ˈkwiv-ə-ˌkāt\ *vi* 1 : to use equivocal language esp. with intent to deceive PREVARICATE 2 : to avoid committing oneself in what one says **syn** see LIE — **equiv·o·ca·tion** \i-ˌkwiv-ə-ˈkā-shən\ *n* — **equiv·o·ca·tor** \i-ˈkwiv-ə-ˌkāt-ər\ *n*
equi·voque *or* **equi·voke** \ˈek-wə-ˌvōk, ˈē-kwə-\ *n* [F *équivoque*, fr. *équivoque* equivocal, fr. LL *aequivocus*] 1 : an equivocal word or phrase; *specif* : PUN 2 a : double meaning b : WORDPLAY
1**-er** \ər; *after some vowels, often* r; *after* ŋ, *usu* gər\ *adj suffix or adv suffix* [ME *-er*, *-ere*, *-re*, fr. OE *-ra* (in adjectives), *-or* (in adverbs); akin to OHG *-iro*, adj. compar. suffix, L *-ior*, Gk *-iōn*] — used to form the comparative degree of adjectives and adverbs of one syllable ⟨hott*er*⟩ ⟨dri*er*⟩ and of some adjectives and adverbs of two syllables ⟨complet*er*⟩ and sometimes of longer ones
2**-er** \ər; *after some vowels, often* r\ *also* **-ier** \ē-ər, yər\ *or* **-yer** \yər\ *n suffix* [ME *-er*, *-ere*, *-ier*, *-iere*; partly fr. OE *-ere* (akin to OHG *-āri*; both fr. a prehistoric Gmc suffix borrowed fr. L *-arius*); partly fr. OF *-ier*, *-iere*, fr. L *-arius*, *-aria*, *-arium* -ary; partly fr. MF *-ere*, fr. L *-ator* -or — more at -ARY, -OR] 1 a : person occupationally connected with ⟨hatt*er*⟩ ⟨furr*ier*⟩ ⟨law*yer*⟩ b : person or thing belonging to or associated with ⟨head*er*⟩ ⟨old-tim*er*⟩ c : native of : resident of ⟨cottag*er*⟩ ⟨New York*er*⟩ d : one that has ⟨three-deck*er*⟩ e : one that produces or yields ⟨pork*er*⟩ 2 a : one that does or performs (a specified action) ⟨report*er*⟩ — sometimes added to both elements of a compound ⟨build*er*-upp*er*⟩ b : one that is a suitable object of (a specified action) ⟨broil*er*⟩ 3 : one that is ⟨foreign*er*⟩ — *-yer* in a few words after *w*, *-ier* in a few words after other letters, otherwise *-er*
era \ˈi(ə)r-ə, ˈer-ə, ˈē-rə\ *n* [LL *aera*, fr. L, counters, pl. of *aer-*, *aes* copper, money — more at ORE] 1 : a system of chronological notation computed from a given date as basis 2 a : a fixed point in time from which a series of years is reckoned b : a memorable or important date or event; *esp* : one that begins a new period in the history of a person or thing 3 a : a period set off or typified by some prominent figure or characteristic feature b : a stage in the development of a person or thing; *specif* : one of the five major divisions of geologic time ⟨Paleozoic ~⟩ **syn** see PERIOD
era·di·ate \(ˈ)ē-ˈrād-ē-ˌāt\ *vt* : RADIATE 1 — **era·di·a·tion** \(ˌ)ē-ˌrād-ē-ˈā-shən\ *n*
erad·i·ca·ble \i-ˈrad-i-kə-bəl\ *adj* : capable of being eradicated
erad·i·cate \i-ˈrad-ə-ˌkāt\ *vt* [L *eradicatus*, pp. of *eradicare*, fr. *e-* + *radic-*, *radix* root] 1 : to pull up by the roots 2 : ERASE, ELIMINATE **syn** see EXTERMINATE — **erad·i·ca·tion** \-ˌrad-ə-ˈkā-shən\ *n* — **erad·i·ca·tive** \-ˈrad-ə-ˌkāt-iv\ *adj* — **erad·i·ca·tor** \-ˌkāt-ər\ *n*
eras·abil·i·ty \i-ˌrā-sə-ˈbil-ət-ē\ *n* : the property or degree of being erasable
eras·able \i-ˈrā-sə-bəl\ *adj* : capable of being erased
erase \i-ˈrās\ *vb* [L *erasus*, pp. of *eradere*, fr. *e-* + *radere* to scratch, scrape — more at RAT] *vt* 1 a : to rub or scrape out (as written, painted, or engraved letters) b : to remove (recorded matter) from a magnetic tape or wire 2 : to remove from existence or memory as if by erasing ~ *vi* : to yield to being erased

syn EXPUNGE, CANCEL, EFFACE, OBLITERATE, BLOT (*out*), DELETE: ERASE implies the act of rubbing or wiping out (letters or impressions) often in preparation for correction or new matter; EXPUNGE stresses a removal or destruction that leaves no trace; CANCEL implies an action (as marking, revoking, or neutralizing) that makes a thing no longer effective or usable; EFFACE implies the removal of an impression by damage to or wearing off of the surface; OBLITERATE and BLOT (*out*) both imply a covering up or smearing over that removes all traces of a thing's existence; DELETE implies a deliberate exclusion, or a marking to direct exclusion, of written matter

eras·er \i-ˈrā-sər\ *n* : one that erases; *specif* : a sharp instrument or a piece of rubber or cloth used to erase marks (as of ink or chalk)
Eras·tian \i-ˈras-tē-ən, -ˈras-chən\ *adj* [Thomas *Erastus* †1583 German-Swiss physician and Zwinglian theologian] : of, characterized by, or advocating the doctrine of state supremacy in ecclesiastical affairs — **Erastian** *n* — **Eras·tian·ism** \-ˌiz-əm\ *n*
era·sure \i-ˈrā-shər *also* -zhər\ *n* : an act or instance of erasing
Er·a·to \ˈer-ə-ˌtō\ *n* [Gk *Eratō*] : the Greek Muse of lyric and love poetry
er·bi·um \ˈər-bē-əm\ *n* [NL, fr. *Ytterby*, Sweden] : a trivalent metallic element of the rare-earth group that occurs with yttrium — see ELEMENT table

1ere \(,)e(ə)r, (,)a(ə)r\ *prep* [ME *er*, fr. OE *ǣr*, fr. *ǣr*, adv., early, soon; akin to OHG *ēr* earlier, Gk *ēri* early] **:** 2BEFORE 2
2ere *conj* **:** 3BEFORE ⟨go back ~ it is too late⟩
Er·e·bus \'er-ə-bəs\ *n* [L, fr. Gk *Erebos*] **:** a dark place through which according to Greek mythology souls pass on their way to Hades
1erect \i-'rekt\ *adj* [ME, fr. L *erectus*, pp. of *erigere* to erect, fr. *e-* + *regere* to lead straight, guide — more at RIGHT] **1 a :** vertical in position; *specif* **:** not spreading or decumbent **b :** standing up or out from the body **c :** characterized by firm or rigid straightness in bodily posture ⟨~ bearing⟩ **2** *archaic* **:** directed upward **3** *obs* **:** ALERT, WATCHFUL — **erect·ly** \-'rek-(t)lē\ *adv* — **erect·ness** \-'rek(t)-nəs\ *n*
2erect *vt* **1 a** (1) **:** to put up by the fitting together of materials or parts **:** BUILD (2) **:** to fix in an upright position (3) **:** to cause to stand up or out **b** *archaic* **:** to direct upward **c :** to change (an image) from an inverted to a normal position **2 :** to elevate in status **3 :** to set up **:** ESTABLISH **4** *obs* **:** ENCOURAGE, EMBOLDEN **5 :** to construct (as a perpendicular) upon a given base
erec·tile \i-'rek-tᵊl, -,tīl\ *adj* **:** capable of being raised to an erect position; *esp* **:** CAVERNOUS 3 — **erec·til·i·ty** \i-,rek-'til-ət-ē\ *n*
erec·tion \i-'rek-shən\ *n* **1 :** the act or process of erecting **:** CONSTRUCTION **2 a :** the state marked by firm turgid form and erect position of a previously flaccid bodily part containing cavernous tissue when that tissue becomes dilated with blood **b :** an occurrence of such a state in the penis or clitoris **3 :** something erected
erec·tor \i-'rek-tər\ *n* **:** one that erects; *specif* **:** a muscle that raises or keeps a part erect
E region *n* **:** the part of the ionosphere occurring between 40 and 90 miles above the surface of the earth and containing the daytime E layer and the sporadic E layer
ere·long \e(ə)r-'lȯŋ, a(ə)r-\ *adv* **:** before long **:** SOON
er·e·mite \'er-ə-,mīt\ *n* [ME] **:** HERMIT; *esp* **:** a religious recluse — **er·e·mit·ic** \,er-ə-'mit-ik\ *or* **er·e·mit·i·cal** \-i-kəl\ *adj* — **er·e·mit·ism** \'er-ə-,mīt-,iz-əm\ *n*
er·em·urus \,er-ə-'myu̇r-əs\ *n, pl* **er·em·uri** \-'myu̇(ə)r-,ī\ [NL, genus name, fr. Gk *erēmos* solitary + *oura* tail — more at RETINA, SQUIRREL] **:** FOXTAIL LILY
ere·now \e(ə)r-'nau̇, a(ə)r-\ *adv* **:** HERETOFORE
erep·sin \i-'rep-sən\ *n* [ISV *er-* (prob. fr. L *eripere* to sweep away, fr. *e-* + *rapere* to sweep) + *pepsin* — more at RAPID] **:** a proteolytic fraction obtained esp. from the intestinal juice and known to be a mixture of peptidases
er·e·thism \'er-ə-,thiz-əm\ *n* [F *éréthisme*, fr. Gk *erethismos* irritation, fr. *erethizein* to irritate; akin to Gk *ornynai* to rouse — more at RISE] **:** abnormal irritability or responsiveness to stimulation — **er·e·this·mic** \,er-ə-'thiz-mik\ *adj*
ere·while \er-'(h)wī(ə)l, ar-\ *also* **ere·whiles** \-'(h)wī(ə)lz\ *adv, archaic* **:** HERETOFORE
erg \'ərg\ *n* [Gk *ergon* work — more at WORK] **:** a cgs unit of work equal to the work done by a force of one dyne acting through a distance of one centimeter
erg- *or* **ergo-** *comb form* [Gk, fr. *ergon*] **:** work ⟨*ergo*phobia⟩
er·go \'e(ə)r-(,)gō, 'ər-\ *adv* [L, fr. (assumed) OL *e rogo* from the direction (of)] **:** THEREFORE, HENCE
ergo- *comb form* [F, fr. *ergot*] **:** ergot ⟨*ergo*sterol⟩
er·go·graph \'ər-gə-,graf\ *n* [ISV] **:** an apparatus for measuring the work capacity of a muscle
er·gom·e·ter \,ər-'gäm-ət-ər\ *n* **:** an apparatus for measuring the work performed by a group of muscles
er·go·no·vine \,ər-gə-'nō-,vēn\ *n* [*ergo-* + L *nov*us new — more at NEW] **:** an alkaloid $C_{19}H_{23}N_3O_2$ from ergot with similar pharmacological action but reduced toxicity
er·gos·ter·ol \,ər-'gäs-tə-,rȯl, -,rōl\ *n* [ISV] **:** a crystalline steroid alcohol $C_{28}H_{43}OH$ that occurs esp. in yeast, molds, and ergot and is converted by ultraviolet irradiation ultimately into vitamin D_2
er·got \'ər-gət, -,gät\ *n* [F, lit., cock's spur] **1 a :** the black or dark purple sclerotium of fungi of the genus *Claviceps* that occurs as a club-shaped body replacing the seed of a grass (as rye) **b :** a fungus of the genus *Claviceps* **2 :** a disease of rye and other cereals caused by fungi of the genus *Claviceps* and characterized by the presence of ergots in the seed heads **3 a :** the dried sclerotia of an ergot fungus grown on rye and containing several alkaloids (as ergonovine, ergotamine) **b :** any of such alkaloids used medicinally for their contractile effect on smooth muscle (as of peripheral arterioles) — **er·got·ic** \,ər-'gät-ik\ *adj*
er·got·a·mine \,ər-'gät-ə-,mēn\ *n* [ISV] **:** an alkaloid $C_{33}H_{35}N_5O_5$ from ergot that has the pharmacological action of ergot and is used esp. in treating migraine
er·got·ism \'ər-gət-,iz-əm\ *n* **:** a toxic condition produced by eating grain, grain products (as rye bread), or grasses infected with ergot fungus or by chronic excessive use of the drug ergot
er·got·ized \-,īzd\ *adj* **:** containing ergot ⟨~ grain⟩
er·i·ca \'er-i-kə\ *n* [NL, genus name, fr. L *erice* heather, fr. Gk *ereikē*] **:** any of a large genus of the heath family of low much-branched evergreen shrubs — **er·i·ca·ceous** \,er-ə-'kā-shəs\ *adj*
er·i·coid \'er-ə-,kȯid\ *adj* **:** resembling heath
Erie \'i(ə)r-ē\ *n* **1 :** a member of an Iroquoian people of the Lake Erie region **2 :** the language of the Erie people
Er·in \'er-ən\ *n* [OIr *Ērinn*, dat. of *Ēriu* Ireland] **:** Ireland
Eri·nys \i-'rin-əs, -'rī-nəs\ *n, pl* **Eriny·es** \-'rin-ē-,ēz\ [Gk] **:** one of the Furies in Greek mythology
Eris \'ir-əs, 'er-\ *n* [Gk] **:** the Greek goddess of discord
eris·tic \i-'ris-tik, e-\ *adj* [Gk *eristikos* fond of wrangling, fr. *erizein* to wrangle, fr. *eris* strife] **:** characterized by disputatious often subtle and specious reasoning — **eristic** *n* — **eris·ti·cal** \-ti-kəl\ *adj*
Er·len·mey·er flask \,ər-lən-,mī(-ə)r-, ,er-lən-\ *n* [Emil *Erlenmeyer* †1909 G chemist] **:** a flat-bottomed conical laboratory flask
er·mine \'ər-mən\ *n, pl* **ermines** [ME, fr. OF, of Gmc origin] **1** *or pl* **ermine a :** any of several weasels that assume white winter pelage usu. with more or less black on the tail; *esp* **:** a large European weasel (*Mustela erminea*) **b :** the white fur of the ermine in winter pelage **2 :** a rank or office whose ceremonial or official robe is ornamented with ermine
er·mined \-mənd\ *adj* **:** clothed or adorned with ermine
erne *or* **ern** \'ərn, 'e(ə)rn\ *n* [ME, fr. OE *earn*; akin to OHG *arn* eagle, Gk *ornis* bird] **:** EAGLE; *esp* **:** a white-tailed sea eagle (*Haliaeetus albicilla*)
erode \i-'rōd\ *vb* [L *erodere* to eat away, fr. *e-* + *rodere* to gnaw — more at RAT] *vt* **1 :** to diminish or destroy by degrees: **a :** to eat into or away by slow destruction of substance **:** CORRODE **b :** to wear away by the action of water, wind, or glacial ice **c :** to cause to deteriorate or disappear as if by eating or wearing away **2 :** to produce or form by eroding ~ *vi* **:** to undergo erosion
erod·ible \i-'rōd-ə-bəl\ *adj* **:** capable of or subject to being eroded
erog·e·nous \i-'räj-ə-nəs\ *also* **er·o·gen·ic** \,er-ə-'jen-ik\ *adj* [Gk *erōs* + E *-genous*, *-genic*] **1 :** sexually sensitive **2 :** sexually stimulating
Eros \'e(ə)r-,äs, 'i(ə)r-\ *n* [Gk *Erōs*, fr. *erōs* love; akin to Gk *erasthai* to love, desire] **1 :** the god of love in Greek mythology **2 :** the aggregate of pleasure-directed life instincts whose energy is derived from libido **3** *often not cap* **:** love directed toward self-realization
erose \i-'rōs\ *adj* [L *erosus*, pp. of *erodere*] **:** IRREGULAR, UNEVEN; *specif* **:** having the margin irregularly notched as if gnawed ⟨an ~ leaf⟩ — **erose·ly** *adv*
ero·si·ble \i-'rō-zə-bəl, -'rō-sə-\ *adj* **:** ERODIBLE
ero·sion \i-'rō-zhən\ *n* **1 :** the process of eroding **:** the state of being eroded **2 :** an instance or product of the process of eroding — **ero·sion·al** \-'rōzh-nəl, -'rō-zhən-ᵊl\ *adj*
ero·sive \i-'rō-siv, -ziv\ *adj* **:** tending to erode — **ero·sive·ness** *or* **ero·siv·i·ty** \i-,rō-'siv-ət-ē\ *n*
erot·ic \i-'rät-ik\ *adj* [Gk *erōtikos*, fr. *erōt-*, *erōs*] **1 :** of, devoted to, or tending to arouse sexual love or desire **2 :** strongly affected by sexual desire — **erotic** *n* — **erot·i·cal** \-i-kəl\ *adj* — **erot·i·cal·ly** \-i-k(ə-)lē\ *adv*
erot·i·ca \i-'rät-i-kə\ *n pl* [NL, fr. Gk *erōtika*, neut. pl. of *erōtikos*] **:** literary or artistic items having an erotic theme or quality
erot·i·cism \i-'rät-ə-,siz-əm\ *also* **er·o·tism** \'er-ə-,tiz-əm\ *n* **1 :** erotic theme or quality **2 :** a state of sexual arousal **3 a :** sexual impulse or desire **b :** abnormally insistent sexual passion
ero·to·gen·ic \i-,rōt-ə-'jen-ik\ *adj* **:** EROGENOUS
err \'e(ə)r, 'ər\ *vi* [ME *erren*, fr. OF *errer*, fr. L *errare*; akin to OE *ierre* wandering, angry, ON *rās* race] **1** *archaic* **:** STRAY **2 a :** to make a mistake **b :** to violate an accepted standard of conduct
er·ran·cy \'er-ən-sē\ *n* **:** the state or an instance of erring
er·rand \'er-ənd\ *n* [ME *erend* message, business, fr. OE *ǣrend*; akin to OHG *ārunti* message] **1** *archaic* **a :** an oral message entrusted to a person **b :** EMBASSY, MISSION **2 a :** a short trip taken to attend to some business esp. for another **b :** the object or purpose of such a trip
er·rant \'er-ənt\ *adj* [ME *erraunt*, fr. MF *errant*, prp. of *errer* to err & *errer* to travel, fr. ML *iterare*, fr. L *iter* road, journey] **1 :** traveling or given to traveling ⟨an ~ knight⟩ **2 a :** straying outside the proper path or bounds ⟨an ~ calf⟩ **b :** moving about aimlessly or irregularly ⟨an ~ breeze⟩ **c :** deviating from what is true or correct ⟨an ~ child⟩ **3** *obs* **:** ARRANT — **er·rant·ly** *adv*
er·rant·ry \'er-ən-trē\ *n* **:** the quality, condition, or fact of wandering; *esp* **:** a roving in search of knightly adventure
er·ra·ta \e-'rät-ə, -'rāt-, -'rat-\ *n* [fr. pl. of *erratum*] **:** a list of corrigenda or a page bearing such a list
er·rat·ic \ir-'at-ik\ *adj* [ME, fr. MF or L; MF *erratique*, fr. L *erraticus*, fr. *erratus*, pp. of *errare*] **1 a :** having no fixed course **:** WANDERING ⟨an ~ comet⟩ **b** *archaic* **:** NOMADIC **2 :** transported from an original resting place esp. by a glacier ⟨~ boulder⟩ **3 a :** characterized by lack of consistency, regularity, or uniformity **b :** deviating from what is ordinary or standard **:** ECCENTRIC **syn** see STRANGE — **erratic** *n* — **er·rat·i·cal** \-i-kəl\ *adj* — **er·rat·i·cal·ly** \-i-k(ə-)lē\ *adv* — **er·rat·i·cism** \-'at-ə-,siz-əm\ *n*
er·ra·tum \e-'rät-əm, -'rāt-, -rat-\ *n, pl* **er·ra·ta** \-ə\ [L, fr. neut. of *erratus*] **:** CORRIGENDUM
er·ro·ne·ous \ir-'ō-nē-əs, e-'rō-\ *adj* [ME, fr. L *erroneus*, fr. *erron-*, *erro* wanderer, fr. *errare*] **1** *archaic* **:** WANDERING **2 :** containing or characterized by error **:** MISTAKEN — **er·ro·ne·ous·ly** *adv* — **er·ro·ne·ous·ness** *n*
er·ror \'er-ər\ *n* [ME *errour*, fr. OF, fr. L *error*, fr. *errare*] **1 a :** an act or condition of often ignorant or imprudent deviation from a code of behavior **b :** an act involving an unintentional deviation from truth or accuracy **c** (1) **:** an act that through ignorance, deficiency, or accident departs from or fails to achieve what should be done (2) **:** a defensive misplay other than a wild pitch or passed ball made by a baseball player when normal play would have resulted in an out or prevented an advance by a base runner **d :** a mistake in the proceedings of a court of record in matters of law or of fact **2 a :** the quality or state of erring **b** *Christian Science* **:** illusion about the nature of reality that is the cause of human suffering **:** the contradiction of truth **c :** an instance of false belief **3 :** something produced by mistake **4 a :** the difference between an observed or calculated value and a true value; *specif* **:** variation in measurements, calculations, or observations of a quantity due to mistakes or to uncontrollable factors **b :** the amount of deviation from a standard or specification — **er·ror·less** \'er-ər-ləs\ *adj*
syn ERROR, MISTAKE, BLUNDER, SLIP, LAPSE mean a departure from what is true, right, or proper. ERROR may imply carelessness or wilfulness in failing to follow a true course or a model, but it may suggest an inaccuracy where accuracy is impossible; MISTAKE implies misconception or inadvertence and is seldom a harsh term; BLUNDER commonly implies stupidity or ignorance and usu. culpability; SLIP carries a strong implication of inadvertence or accident producing trivial mistakes; LAPSE implies forgetfulness, weakness, or inattention
er·satz \'e(ə)r-,zäts, er-'\ *adj* [G *ersatz-*, fr. *ersatz*, n., substitute] **:** SUBSTITUTE, SYNTHETIC ⟨~ flour⟩ — **ersatz** *n*
Erse \'ərs\ *n* [ME (Sc) *Erisch*, adj., Irish, alter. of *Irish*] **1 :** SCOTTISH GAELIC **2 :** IRISH GAELIC — **Erse** *adj*
erst \'ərst\ *adv* [ME *erest* earliest, formerly, fr. OE *ǣrest*, superl. of *ǣr* early — more at ERE] *archaic* **:** FORMERLY
1erst·while \'ərst-,(h)wīl\ *adv* **:** in the past **:** FORMERLY
2erstwhile *adj* **:** FORMER, PREVIOUS
eruct \i-'rəkt\ *vb* [L *eructare*, fr. *e-* + *ructare* to belch, fr. *-ructus*, pp. of *-rugere* to belch; akin to L *rugire* to roar] **:** BELCH — **eruc·tate** \i-'rək-,tāt\ *vb* — **eruc·ta·tion** \i-,rək-'tā-shən, ,ē-,rək-\ *n*
er·u·dite \'er-(y)ə-,dīt\ *adj* [ME *erudit*, fr. L *eruditus*, fr. pp. of *erudire* to instruct, fr. *e-* + *rudis* rude, ignorant] **:** possessing or displaying erudition **:** LEARNED — **er·u·dite·ly** *adv*
er·u·di·tion \,er-(y)ə-'dish-ən\ *n* **:** extensive knowledge acquired chiefly from books **:** LEARNING
erum·pent \i-'rəm-pənt\ *adj* [L *erumpent-*, *erumpens*, prp. of *erumpere*] **:** bursting forth ⟨~ fungi⟩
erupt \i-'rəpt\ *vb* [L *eruptus*, pp. of *erumpere* to burst forth, fr. *e-* +

rumpere to break] *vi* **1 a :** to force out or release suddenly and often violently something pent up **b :** to burst from limits or restraint **c :** to become active or violent **:** EXPLODE **2 :** to break out (as with a skin eruption) ~ *vt* **:** to force out or release usu. suddenly and violently — **erupt·ible** \-ˈrəp-tə-bəl\ *adj*

erup·tion \i-ˈrəp-shən\ *n* **1 a :** an act, process, or instance of erupting **b :** the breaking out of a rash on the skin or mucous membrane **2 a :** a product of erupting **b :** an erupted rash or one of its lesions — **erup·tive** \-ˈrəp-tiv\ *adj*

-ery \(ə-)rē\ *n suffix* [ME *-erie*, fr. OF, fr. *-ier* -er + *-ie* -y] **1 :** qualities collectively **:** character **:** -NESS ⟨snobb*ery*⟩ **2 :** art **:** practice ⟨cook*ery*⟩ **3 :** place of doing, keeping, producing, or selling (the thing specified) ⟨fish*ery*⟩ ⟨bak*ery*⟩ **4 :** collection **:** aggregate ⟨fin*ery*⟩ **5 :** state or condition ⟨slav*ery*⟩

eryn·go \i-ˈriŋ-(ˌ)gō\ *n* [modif. of L *eryngion* sea holly, fr. Gk *ēryngion*] *obs* **:** candied sea-holly root made to be used as an aphrodisiac

er·y·sip·e·las \ˌer-ə-ˈsip-(ə-)ləs, ˌir-\ *n* [ME *erisipila*, fr. L *erysipelas*, fr. Gk, fr. *erysi-* (akin to Gk *erythros* red) + *-pelas* (akin to L *pellis* skin)] **:** an acute febrile disease associated with intense edematous local inflammation of the skin and subcutaneous tissues caused by a hemolytic streptococcus

er·y·the·ma \ˌer-ə-ˈthē-mə\ *n* [NL, fr. Gk *erythēma*, fr. *erythainein* to redden, fr. *erythros*] **:** abnormal redness of the skin due to capillary congestion (as in inflammation) — **er·y·the·ma·tous** \ˌer-ə-ˈthem-ət-əs, -ˈthē-mət-\ *adj*

erythr- *or* **erythro-** *comb form* [Gk, fr. *erythros*] **1 :** red ⟨*erythro*cyte⟩ **2 :** erythrocyte ⟨*erythr*oid⟩

er·y·thrism \ˈer-ə-ˌthriz-əm\ *n* **:** a condition marked by exceptional prevalence of red pigmentation (as in skin or hair) — **er·y·thris·mal** \ˌer-ə-ˈthriz-məl\ *adj* — **er·y·thris·tic** \-ˈthris-tik\ *adj*

er·y·thrite \ˈer-ə-ˌthrīt\ *n* **:** a mineral $Co_3(AsO_4)_2.8H_2O$ consisting of a hydrous cobalt arsenate occurring esp. in monoclinic crystals

eryth·ro·blast \i-ˈrith-rə-ˌblast\ *n* [ISV] **:** a polychromatic nucleated cell occurring in red marrow as the first specifically identifiable stage in red blood-cell formation; *broadly* **:** a cell ancestral to red blood cells — **eryth·ro·blas·tic** \-ˌrith-rə-ˈblas-tik\ *adj*

eryth·ro·cyte \i-ˈrith-rə-ˌsīt\ *n* [ISV] **:** RED BLOOD CELL — **eryth·ro·cyt·ic** \-ˌrith-rə-ˈsit-ik\ *adj*

eryth·ro·cyt·om·e·ter \i-ˌrith-rə-ˌsīt-ˈäm-ət-ər\ *n* **:** HEMACYTOMETER

er·y·throid \ˈer-ə-ˌthrȯid\ *adj* **:** relating to erythrocytes or their precursors

eryth·ro·my·cin \i-ˌrith-rə-ˈmīs-ᵊn\ *n* **:** an antibiotic produced by an actinomycete (*Streptomyces erythreus*) active against amebiasis

er·y·thron \ˈer-ə-ˌthrän\ *n* [NL, fr. Gk, neut. of *erythros*] **:** the red blood cells and their precursors in the bone marrow

eryth·ro·poi·e·sis \i-ˌrith-rə-ˌpȯi-ˈē-səs\ *n* [NL, fr. *erythr-* + Gk *poiēsis* creation] **:** the production of red blood cells (as from the bone marrow) — **eryth·ro·poi·et·ic** \-ˌpȯi-ˈet-ik\ *adj*

eryth·ro·sin *also* **eryth·ro·sine** \i-ˈrith-rə-sən, -ˌsēn\ *n* [ISV *erythr-* + *eosin*] **:** any of several dyes made by iodination of fluorescein that yield reddish shades

1**-es** \əz, iz *after* s, z, sh, ch; z *after* v *or a vowel*\ *n pl suffix* [ME *-es*, *-s* — more at 1-s] **1** — used to form the plural of most nouns that end in *s* ⟨glass*es*⟩, *z* ⟨fuzz*es*⟩, *sh* ⟨bush*es*⟩, *ch* ⟨peach*es*⟩, or a final *y* that changes to *i* ⟨lad*ies*⟩ and of some nouns ending in *f* that changes to *v* ⟨loav*es*⟩; compare 1-s 1 **2 :** 1-s 2

2**-es** *vb suffix* [ME — more at 2-s] — used to form the third person singular present of most verbs that end in *s* ⟨bless*es*⟩, *z* ⟨fizz*es*⟩, *sh* ⟨hush*es*⟩, *ch* ⟨catch*es*⟩, or a final *y* that changes to *i* ⟨def*ies*⟩

Esau \ˈē-(ˌ)sȯ\ *n* [L, fr. Gk *Ēsau*, fr. Heb *ʽĒsāw*] **:** the elder son of Isaac and Rebekah and brother of Jacob

es·ca·drille \ˈes-kə-ˌdril, -ˌdrē\ *n* [F, flotilla, escadrille, fr. Sp *escuadrilla*, dim. of *escuadra* squadron, squad — more at SQUAD] **:** a unit of a European air command containing usu. six airplanes

es·ca·lade \ˈes-kə-ˌlād, -ˌläd\ *n* [F, fr. It *scalata*, fr. *scalare* to scale, fr. *scala* ladder, fr. LL] **:** an act of scaling esp. the walls of a fortification — **escalade** *vt* — **es·ca·lad·er** *n*

es·ca·late \ˈes-kə-ˌlāt\ *vb* [back-formation fr. *escalator*] *vi* **:** to increase in extent, volume, or scope ~ *vt* **:** EXPAND 1 — **es·ca·la·tion** \ˌes-kə-ˈlā-shən\ *n*

1**es·ca·la·tor** \ˈes-kə-ˌlāt-ər\ *n* [fr. *Escalator*, a trademark] **1 :** a power-driven set of stairs arranged like an endless belt that ascend or descend continuously **2 :** an escalator clause or provision

2**escalator** *adj* **:** providing for a periodic proportional upward or downward adjustment (as of prices or wages) ⟨an ~ clause⟩

es·cal·lop \is-ˈkäl-əp, -ˈkal-\ *var of* SCALLOP

es·cap·able \is-ˈkā-pə-bəl\ *adj* **:** capable of being escaped

es·ca·pade \ˈes-kə-ˌpād\ *n* [MF, fr. OIt *scappata*, fr. *scappare* to escape, fr. (assumed) VL *excappare*] **:** a usu. adventurous action that runs counter to approved or ordinary conduct

1**es·cape** \is-ˈkāp\ *vb* [ME *escapen*, fr. ONF *escaper*, fr. (assumed) VL *excappare*, fr. L *ex-* + LL *cappa* head covering, cloak] *vi* **1 a :** to get away (as by flight) **b :** to issue from confinement ⟨gas is *escaping*⟩ **c** *of a plant* **:** to run wild from cultivation **2 :** to avoid a threatening evil ~ *vt* **1 :** to get out of the way of **:** AVOID **2 :** to fail to be noticed or recallable by ⟨his name ~*s* me⟩ **3 a :** to issue from **b :** to be uttered involuntarily by — **es·cap·er** *n*

syn AVOID, EVADE, ELUDE, SHUN, ESCHEW: ESCAPE stresses the fact of getting away or being passed by not necessarily through effort or by conscious intent; AVOID stresses forethought and caution in keeping clear of danger or difficulty; EVADE implies adroitness, ingenuity, or lack of scruple in escaping or avoiding; ELUDE implies a slippery or baffling quality in the person or thing that escapes; SHUN often implies an avoiding as a matter of habitual practice or policy and may imply repugnance or abhorrence; ESCHEW implies an avoiding or abstaining from as unwise or distasteful

2**escape** *n* **1 :** an act or instance of escaping: as **a :** flight from confinement **b :** evasion of something undesirable **c :** leakage or outflow esp. of a fluid **d :** distraction or relief from routine or reality **2 :** a means of escape **3 :** a cultivated plant run wild

3**escape** *adj* **:** providing a means of escape ⟨an ~ clause⟩

es·cap·ee \(ˌ)es-ˌkā-ˈpē, is- *also* ˌes-kə-ˈpē\ *n* **:** one that has escaped; *esp* **:** an escaped prisoner

escape mechanism *n* **:** a mode of behavior or thinking adopted to evade unpleasant facts or responsibilities

es·cape·ment \is-ˈkāp-mənt\ *n* **1 a :** a device in a timepiece which controls the motion of the train of wheelwork and through which the energy of the power source is delivered to the pendulum or balance by means of impulses that permit a tooth to escape from a pallet at regular intervals **b :** a ratchet device (as the spacing mechanism of a typewriter) that permits motion in one direction only in equal steps **2 a :** the act of escaping **b :** a way of escape **:** VENT

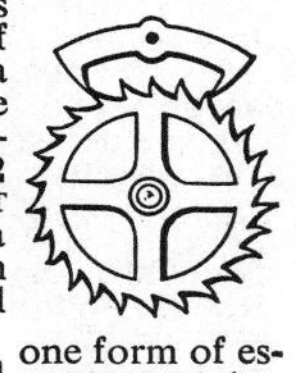

one form of escapement 1a

escape velocity *n* **:** the minimum velocity that a moving body (as a rocket) must have to escape from the gravitational field of the earth or of a celestial body and move outward into space

es·cap·ism \is-ˈkā-ˌpiz-əm\ *n* **:** habitual diversion of the mind to purely imaginative activity or entertainment to escape from reality or routine — **es·cap·ist** \-pəst\ *adj or n*

es·ca·role \ˈes-kə-ˌrōl\ *n* [F, fr. LL *escariola*, fr. L *escarius* of food, fr. *esca* food, fr. *edere* to eat — more at EAT] **:** ENDIVE 1

es·carp \is-ˈkärp\ *n or vt* [F *escarpe*, n., fr. It *scarpa*] **:** SCARP

es·carp·ment \-mənt\ *n* **1 :** a steep slope in front of a fortification **2 a :** a long cliff **b :** a steep slope separating two comparatively level or more gently sloping surfaces

-es·cence \ˈes-ᵊn(t)s\ *n suffix* [MF, fr. L *-escentia*, fr. *-escent-*, *-escens* + *-ia* -y] **:** process of becoming ⟨hyal*escence*⟩

-es·cent \ˈes-ᵊnt\ *adj suffix* [MF, fr. L *-escent-*, *-escens*, prp. suffix of incho. verbs in *-escere*] **1 :** beginning **:** beginning to be **:** slightly ⟨alkal*escent*⟩ **2 :** reflecting or emitting light (in a specified way) ⟨fluor*escent*⟩

1**es·char** \ˈes-ˌkär, -kər\ *n* [ME *escare* — more at SCAR] **:** a scab formed esp. after a burn

2**eschar** *var of* ESKER

es·cha·rot·ic \ˌes-kə-ˈrät-ik\ *adj* [F or LL; F *escharotique*, fr. LL *escharoticus*, fr. Gk *escharōtikos*, fr. *escharoun* to form an eschar, fr. *eschara* eschar] **:** producing an eschar — **escharotic** *n*

es·cha·to·log·i·cal \ˌes-ˌkat-ᵊl-ˈäj-i-kəl, ˌes-kət-\ *adj* **:** of or relating to the end of the world or the events associated with it in religious expectation — **es·cha·to·log·i·cal·ly** \-i-k(ə-)lē\ *adv*

es·cha·tol·o·gy \ˌes-kə-ˈtäl-ə-jē\ *n* [Gk *eschatos* last, farthest] **:** belief about or in the end of the world or the last things (as the second coming of Christ, resurrection, Judgment, the new age)

1**es·cheat** \is(h)-ˈchēt\ *n* [ME *eschete*, fr. OF, reversion of property, fr. *escheoir* to fall, devolve, fr. (assumed) VL *excadēre*, fr. L *ex-* + (assumed) VL *cadēre* to fall, fr. L *cadere* — more at CHANCE] **1 :** escheated property **2 a :** the reversion of lands in English feudal law to the lord of the fee upon the failure of heirs capable of inheriting under the original grant **b :** the reversion of property to the crown in England or to the state in the U.S. by failure of persons legally entitled to hold the property

2**escheat** *vt* **:** to cause to revert by escheat ~ *vi* **:** to revert by escheat — **es·cheat·able** \-ˈchēt-ə-bəl\ *adj*

es·chew \is(h)-ˈchü\ *vt* [ME *eschewen*, fr. MF *eschiuver*, of Gmc origin] **:** SHUN, AVOID **syn** see ESCAPE — **es·chew·al** \-əl\ *n*

es·co·lar \ˌes-kə-ˈlär\ *n, pl* **escolar** *or* **escolars** [Sp, lit., scholar, fr. ML *scholaris*] **:** a large widely distributed rough-scaled fish (*Ruvettus pretiosus*) that resembles a mackerel

1**es·cort** \ˈes-ˌkȯ(ə)rt\ *n* [F *escorte*, fr. It *scorta*, fr. *scorgere* to guide, fr. (assumed) VL *excorrigere*, fr. L *ex-* + *corrigere* to make straight, correct — more at CORRECT] **1 a** (1) **:** a person or group of persons accompanying another to give protection or show courtesy (2) **:** the man who goes on a date with a woman **b :** a protective screen of warships or fighter planes or a single ship or plane used to fend off enemy attack from one or more vulnerable craft **2 :** accompaniment by a person or an armed protector (as a ship)

2**es·cort** \is-ˈkȯ(ə)rt, es-, ˈes-ˌ\ *vt* **:** to accompany as an escort **syn** see ACCOMPANY

es·cot \is-ˈkät\ *vt* [MF *escoter*, fr. *escot* contribution, of Gmc origin; akin to ON *skot* contribution] *obs* **:** SUPPORT, MAINTAIN

es·cri·toire \ˈes-krə-ˌtwär\ *n* [obs. F, writing desk, scriptorium, fr. ML *scriptorium*] **:** a writing table or desk; *specif* **:** SECRETARY 5b

1**es·crow** \ˈes-ˌkrō, es-ˈ\ *n* [MF *escroue* scroll] **1 :** a deed, a bond, money, or a piece of property delivered to a third person to be delivered by him to the grantee only upon the fulfillment of a condition **2 :** a fund or deposit designed to serve as an escrow

2**es·crow** \es-ˈkrō, ˈes-ˌ\ *vt* **:** to place in escrow

es·cu·do \is-ˈküd-(ˌ)ō\ *n* [Sp & Pg, lit., shield] **1 :** any of various former gold or silver coins of Hispanic countries **2** — see MONEY table

es·cu·lent \ˈes-kyə-lənt\ *adj* [L *esculentus*, fr. *esca* food, fr. *edere* to eat — more at EAT] **:** EDIBLE — **esculent** *n*

es·cutch·eon \is-ˈkəch-ən\ *n* [ME *escochon*, fr. MF *escuchon*, fr. (assumed) VL *scution-*, *scutio*, fr. L *scutum* shield — more at ESQUIRE] **1 :** a defined area on which armorial bearings are displayed usu. consisting of a shield **:** COAT OF ARMS **2 :** a protective or ornamental shield (as around a keyhole) **3 :** the part of a ship's stern on which the name is displayed

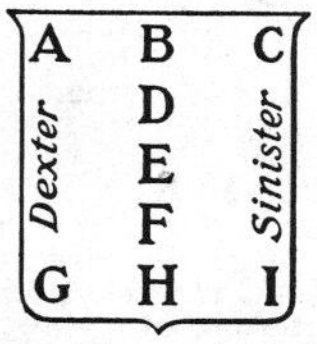

escutcheon 1a: *A* dexter chief point; *B* middle chief point; *C* sinister chief point; *D* honor point; *E* fess point; *F* nombril; *G* dexter base point; *H* middle base point; *I* sinister base point

1**-ese** \ˈēz, ˈēs\ *adj suffix* [Pg *-ês* & It *-ese*, fr. L *-ensis*] **:** of, relating to, or originating in (a certain place or country) ⟨Japan*ese*⟩

2**-ese** *n suffix, pl* **-ese 1 :** native or resident of (a specified place or country) ⟨Chin*ese*⟩ **2 a :** language of (a particular place, country, or nationality) ⟨Siam*ese*⟩ **b :** speech, literary style, or diction peculiar to (a specified place, person, or group) — usu. in words applied in depreciation ⟨journal*ese*⟩

es·er·ine \ˈes-ə-ˌrēn\ *n* [F *ésérine*] **:** PHYSOSTIGMINE

es·ker \ˈes-kər\ *n* [IrGael *eiscir* ridge] **:** a long narrow ridge or mound of sand, gravel, and boulders deposited by a stream flowing on, within, or beneath a stagnant glacier

Es·ki·mo \ˈes-kə-ˌmō\ *n* [Dan, of Algonquian origin; akin to Cree

askimowew he eats it raw] **1** *pl* **Eskimo** *or* **Eskimos a :** a group of peoples of northern Canada, Greenland, Alaska, and eastern Siberia **b :** a member of such people **2 :** the language of the Eskimo people — **Es·ki·mo·an** \,es-kə-'mō-ən\ *adj*

Eskimo dog *n* **1 :** a broad-chested powerful dog of a breed native to Greenland and Labrador characterized by a heavy double coat **2 :** a sled dog of American origin

eso·pha·geal \i-,säf-ə-'jē-əl *also* ,ē-sə-'faj-(ē-)əl\ *adj* **:** of or relating to the esophagus

esoph·a·gus \i-'säf-ə-gəs\ *n, pl* **esoph·a·gi** \-,gī, -,jī, -,gē\ [ME *ysophagus*, fr. Gk *oisophagos*, fr. *oisein* to be going to carry + *phagein* to eat — more at BAKSHEESH] **:** a muscular tube that leads from the pharynx to the stomach, passes down the neck between the trachea and the spinal column, and in man is about nine inches long

es·o·ter·ic \,es-ə-'ter-ik\ *adj* [LL *esotericus*, fr. Gk *esōterikos*, fr. *esōterō*, compar. of *eisō*, *esō* within, fr. *eis* into, fr. *en* in — more at IN] **1 a :** designed for or understood by the specially initiated alone **b :** of or relating to knowledge that is restricted to a small group **2 a :** limited to a small circle ⟨~ pursuits⟩ **b :** PRIVATE, CONFIDENTIAL ⟨an ~ purpose⟩ — **es·o·ter·i·cal·ly** \-i-k(ə-)lē\ *adv*

es·o·ter·i·ca \-i-kə\ *n pl* [NL, fr. Gk *esōterika*, neut. pl. of *esōterikos*] **:** esoteric items

es·pa·drille \'es-pə-,dril\ *n* [F] **:** a flat sandal usu. having a fabric upper and a flexible sole

1es·pal·ier \is-'pal-yər, -,yā\ *n* [F, deriv. of It *spalla* shoulder, fr. LL *spatula* shoulder blade] **1 :** a plant (as a fruit tree) trained to grow flat against a support (as a wall or trellis) **2 :** a railing or trellis on which fruit trees or shrubs are trained to grow flat

2espalier *vt* **1 :** to train as an espalier **2 :** to furnish with an espalier

es·par·to \is-'pärt-(,)ō\ *n* [Sp, fr. L *spartum*, fr. Gk *sparton*] **:** either of two Spanish and Algerian grasses (*Stipa tenacissima* and *Lygeum spartum*) used esp. to make cordage, shoes, and paper

es·pe·cial \is-'pesh-əl\ *adj* [ME, fr. MF] **:** SPECIAL, PARTICULAR **syn** see SPECIAL — **es·pe·cial·ly** \-'pesh-(ə-)lē\ *adv*

es·per·ance \'es-p(ə-)rən(t)s, ,es-pə-'rän(t)-sə\ *n* [ME *esperaunce*, fr. MF *esperance*] *obs* **:** HOPE, EXPECTATION

Es·pe·ran·to \,es-pə-'rant-(,)ō, -'ränt-\ *n* [Dr. *Esperanto*, pseudonym of L.L. Zamenhof †1917 Pol oculist, its inventor] **:** an artificial international language based as far as possible on words common to the chief European languages

es·pi·al \is-'pī(-ə)l\ *n* **1 :** OBSERVATION **2 :** NOTICE, DISCOVERY

es·piè·gle \es-pyeglᵊ\ *adj* [F] **:** ROGUISH, FROLICSOME

es·pi·o·nage \'es-pē-ə-,näzh, -nij, -,näj; e-'spē-ə-nij\ *n* [F *espionnage*, fr. MF, fr. *espionner* to spy, fr. *espion* spy, fr. OIt *spione*, fr. *spia*, of Gmc origin; akin to OHG *spehōn* to spy — more at SPY] **:** the practice of spying or the use of spies esp. to obtain information about the plans and activities of a foreign government

es·pla·nade \'es-plə-,näd, -,nād\ *n* [F, fr. It *spianata*, fr. *spianare* to level, fr. L *explanare*] **:** a level open stretch of paved or grassy ground; *esp* **:** one designed for walking or driving along a shore

es·pous·al \is-'paù-zəl, -səl\ *n* **1 a :** BETROTHAL **b :** WEDDING **c :** MARRIAGE **2 :** a taking up of a cause or belief as a supporter

es·pouse \is-'paùz, -'paùs\ *vt* [ME *espousen*, fr. MF *espouser*, fr. LL *sponsare* to betroth, fr. L *sponsus*, pp. of *spondēre* to promise, betroth — more at SPOUSE] **1 :** MARRY **2 :** to take up the cause of **:** SUPPORT **syn** see ADOPT — **es·pous·er** *n*

espres·so \e-'spres-(,)ō\ *n* [It (*caffè*) *espresso*, lit., pressed out coffee] **:** coffee brewed by forcing steam through finely ground darkly roasted coffee beans

es·prit \is-'prē\ *n* [F, fr. L *spiritus* spirit] **:** vivacious cleverness or wit

es·prit de corps \is-,prēd-ə-'kō(ə)r, -'kò(ə)r\ *n* [F] **:** the common spirit existing in the members of a group and inspiring enthusiasm, devotion, and strong regard for the honor of the group

es·py \is-'pī\ *vt* [ME *espien*, fr. OF *espier*] **:** to catch sight of

-esque \'esk\ *adj suffix* [F, fr. It *-esco*, of Gmc origin; akin to OHG *-isc* -ish] **:** in the manner or style of **:** like ⟨statuesque⟩

Es·qui·mau \'es-kə-,mō\ *n, pl* **Esquimau** *or* **Es·qui·maux** \-,mō(z)\ [F, of Algonquian origin] **:** ESKIMO

es·quire \'es-,kwī(ə)r, is-'\ *n* [ME, fr. MF *esquier* squire, fr. LL *scutarius*, fr. L *scutum* shield; akin to OHG *sceida* sheath] **1 :** a member of the English gentry ranking below a knight **2 :** a candidate for knighthood serving as shield bearer and attendant to a knight **3** — used as a title of courtesy usu. placed in its abbreviated form after the surname **4** *archaic* **:** a landed proprietor

ess \'es\ *n* **:** the letter *s*

-ess \əs, is, *also* ,es\ *n suffix* [ME *-esse*, fr. OF, fr. LL *-issa*, fr. Gk] **:** female ⟨giantess⟩

1es·say \e-'sā, 'es-,ā\ *vt* **1 a :** to put to a test **b :** 2ASSAY 2a **2 :** to make an effort to perform **syn** see ATTEMPT — **es·say·er** *n*

2es·say *in sense 2* 'es-,ā, *in other senses also* e-'sā\ *n* [MF *essai*, fr. LL *exagium* act of weighing, fr. *ex-* + *agere* to drive — more at AGENT] **1 a :** EFFORT, ATTEMPT; *esp* **:** an initial tentative effort **b :** the result or product of an attempt **2 a :** an analytic or interpretative literary composition usu. dealing with its subject from a limited or personal point of view **b :** something resembling such a composition **3 :** TRIAL, TEST **4 :** a proof of an unaccepted design for a stamp or piece of paper money

es·say·ist \'es-,ā-əst\ *n* **:** a writer of essays

es·sence \'es-ᵊn(t)s\ *n* [ME, fr. MF & L; MF, fr. L *essentia*, fr. *esse* to be — more at IS] **1 a :** the permanent as contrasted with the accidental element of being **b :** the individual, real, or ultimate nature of a thing esp. as opposed to its existence **c :** the property necessary to the nature of a thing **d :** the most significant property of a thing **2 :** something that exists **:** ENTITY **3 a** (1) **:** a volatile substance or constituent (as of perfume) (2) **:** a constituent or derivative (as an extract or essential oil) possessing the special qualities (as of a plant or drug) in concentrated form; *also* **:** a preparation (as an alcoholic solution) of such an essence or a synthetic substitute **b :** ODOR, PERFUME **c :** something that resembles an extract in possessing a quality in concentrated form

Es·sene \is-'ēn, 'es-,ēn\ *n* [Gk *Essēnos*] **:** a member of a monastic brotherhood of Jews in Palestine from the 2d century B.C. to the 2d century A.D. — **Es·se·ni·an** \is-'ē-nē-ən\ *or* **Es·se·nic** \-'en-ik, -'ē-nik\ *adj*

1es·sen·tial \i-'sen-chəl\ *adj* **1 :** of, relating to, or constituting essence **:** INHERENT **2 :** of the utmost importance **:** BASIC, INDISPENSABLE, NECESSARY ⟨~ foods⟩ ⟨an ~ requirement for admission to college⟩ **3 :** containing or constituting a volatile essence that imparts the characteristic odor of a plant ⟨~ oil⟩ **4 :** IDIOPATHIC — **es·sen·ti·al·i·ty** \i-,sen-chē-'al-ət-ē\ *n* — **es·sen·tial·ly** \i-'sench-(ə-)lē\ *adv* — **es·sen·tial·ness** \i-'sen-chəl-nəs\ *n*

syn ESSENTIAL, FUNDAMENTAL, VITAL, CARDINAL mean so important as to be indispensable. ESSENTIAL implies belonging to the very nature of a thing and therefore incapable of removal without destroying the thing itself or its character; FUNDAMENTAL applies to something that is a foundation without which an entire system or complex whole would collapse; VITAL suggests something that is as necessary to a thing's continued existence or operation as air, food, and water are to living things; CARDINAL suggests something on which an outcome turns or depends

2essential *n* **1 :** something basic ⟨~s of astronomy⟩ **2 :** something necessary, indispensable, or unavoidable

essential amino acid *n* **:** an amino acid (as lysine) that is required for normal health and growth, is either not manufactured in the body or manufactured in insufficient quantities, and is usually supplied by dietary protein

es·sen·tial·ism \i-'sen-chə-,liz-əm\ *n* **1 :** a theory that ideas and skills basic to our culture should be taught to all alike by time-tested methods **2 a :** REALISM **b :** a theory that gives priority to essence over existence — **es·sen·tial·ist** \-ləst\ *adj or n*

es·soin \is-'òin\ *n* [ME *essoine*, fr. MF, fr. ML *essonium*, fr. L *ex-* + LL *sonium* care, worry] **1 :** an excuse for not appearing in an English law court at the appointed time **2** *obs* **:** EXCUSE, DELAY

es·so·nite \'es-ᵊn-,īt\ *n* [F, fr. Gk *hēsson* inferior; fr. its being less hard than true hyacinth] **:** a yellow to brown garnet

1-est \əst, ist\ *adj suffix or adv suffix* [ME, fr. OE *-st*, *-est*, *-ost*; akin to OHG *-isto* (adj. superl. suffix), Gk *-istos*] — used to form the superlative degree of adjectives and adverbs of one syllable ⟨fattest⟩ ⟨latest⟩, of some adjectives and adverbs of two syllables ⟨luckiest⟩ ⟨oftenest⟩, and less often of longer ones ⟨beggarliest⟩

2-est \əst, ist\ *or* **-st** \st\ *suffix* [ME, fr. OE *-est*, *-ast*, *-st*; akin to OHG *-ist*, *-ōst*, *-ēst*, 2d sing. ending] — used to form the archaic 2d person singular of English verbs (with *thou*) ⟨gettest⟩ ⟨didst⟩

es·tab·lish \is-'tab-lish\ *vb* [ME *establissen*, fr. MF *establiss-*, stem of *establir*, fr. L *stabilire*, fr. *stabilis* stable] *vt* **1 :** to make firm or stable **2 :** to institute (as a law) permanently by enactment or agreement **3** *obs* **:** SETTLE 7 **4 a :** to bring into existence **:** FOUND ⟨~ed a republic⟩ **b :** to bring about **:** EFFECT **5 a :** to set on a firm basis ⟨~ his son in business⟩ **b :** to put into a favorable position **c :** to gain full recognition or acceptance of **6 :** to make (a church) a national institution **7 :** to put beyond doubt **:** PROVE ~ *vi, of a plant* **:** to become naturalized — **es·tab·lish·er** *n*

established church *n* **:** a church recognized by law as the official church of a nation and supported by civil authority

es·tab·lish·ment \is-'tab-lish-mənt\ *n* **1 :** something established: as **a :** a settled arrangement; *esp* **:** a code of laws **b :** ESTABLISHED CHURCH **c :** a permanent civil or military organization **d :** a place of business or residence with its furnishings and staff **e :** a public or private institution **f :** an established order of society; *also* **:** the social, economic, and political leaders of such an order **2 a :** an act of establishing **b :** the state of being established

es·ta·mi·net \e-stà-mē-nā\ *n, pl* **estaminets** \-nā(z)\ [F] **:** a small café

es·tate \is-'tāt\ *n* [ME *estat*, fr. MF — more at STATE] **1 :** STATE, CONDITION **2 :** social standing or rank esp. of a high order **3 :** a social or political class; *specif* **:** one of the great classes (as the nobility, the clergy, and the commons) formerly vested with distinct political powers **4 a :** the degree, quality, nature, and extent of one's interest in land or other property **b** (1) **:** POSSESSIONS, PROPERTY; *specif* **:** a person's property in land and tenements (2) **:** the assets and liabilities left by a person at death **c :** a landed property usu. with a large house on it — **estate** *vt, archaic*

1es·teem \is-'tēm\ *n* **1** *archaic* **:** WORTH, VALUE **2** *archaic* **:** OPINION, JUDGMENT **3 :** high regard

2esteem *vt* [ME *estemen* to estimate, fr. MF *estimer*, fr. L *aestimare*] **1** *archaic* **:** APPRAISE **2 a :** REGARD, CONSIDER ⟨~ it a privilege⟩ **b :** THINK, BELIEVE **3 :** to set a high value on **syn** see REGARD

es·ter \'es-tər\ *n* [G, fr. *essigäther* ethyl acetate, fr. *essig* vinegar + *äther* ether] **:** an often fragrant compound formed by the reaction between an acid and an alcohol or phenol with elimination of water

es·ter·ase \'es-tə-,rās, -,rāz\ *n* **:** an enzyme that accelerates the hydrolysis or synthesis of esters

es·ter·i·fy \e-'ster-ə-,fī\ *vt* **:** to convert into an ester

Es·ther \'es-tər\ *n* [L, fr. Heb *Estēr*] **:** the Jewish heroine of the Old Testament book of Esther

es·the·sia \es-'thē-zh(ē-)ə\ *n* [NL, back-formation fr. *anesthesia*] **:** capacity for sensation and feeling **:** SENSIBILITY

esthesio- *or* **aesthesio-** *comb form* [Gk *aisthēsis*] **:** sensation ⟨*esthesio*logy⟩

es·the·si·om·e·ter \es-,thē-zē-'äm-ət-ər, -,thē-sē-\ *n* **:** an instrument for measuring sensory discrimination; *esp* **:** one for determining the distance by which two points pressed against the skin must be separated in order that they may be felt as separate

es·the·sis \es-'thē-səs\ *n* [NL, fr. Gk *aisthēsis*, fr. *aisthanesthai* to perceive] **:** SENSATION; *esp* **:** rudimentary sensation

esthete, esthetic *var of* AESTHETE, AESTHETIC

es·ti·ma·ble \'es-tə-mə-bəl\ *adj* **1** *archaic* **:** VALUABLE **2 :** worthy of esteem — **es·ti·ma·ble·ness** *n*

1es·ti·mate \'es-tə-,māt\ *vt* [L *aestimatus*, pp. of *aestimare* to value, estimate] **1** *archaic* **a :** ESTEEM **b :** APPRAISE **2 a :** to judge tentatively or approximately the value, worth, or significance of **b :** to determine roughly the size, extent, or nature of **c :** to produce a statement of the approximate cost of **3 :** JUDGE, CONCLUDE — **es·ti·ma·tive** \-,māt-iv\ *adj* — **es·ti·ma·tor** \-,māt-ər\ *n*

syn APPRAISE, EVALUATE, VALUE, RATE, ASSESS: ESTIMATE implies a judgment, considered or casual, that precedes or takes the place of actual measuring or counting or testing out; APPRAISE commonly implies the fixing by an expert of the monetary worth of a thing, but it may be used of any critical judgment; EVALUATE suggests an attempt to determine either the relative or intrinsic worth of something in terms other than monetary; VALUE equals APPRAISE but without implying expertness of judgment; RATE adds to ESTIMATE the implication of fixing a scale of values; ASSESS implies a critical appraisal for the purpose of understanding or interpreting, or as a guide in taking action **syn** see in addition CALCULATE

2es·ti·mate \'es-tə-mət\ *n* **1 :** the act of appraising or valuing **:** CALCULATION **2 :** an opinion or judgment of the nature, character, or quality of a thing **3 a :** a rough or approximate calculation **b :** a numerical value obtained from a statistical sample and assigned to a population parameter **4 :** a statement of the cost of a job

es·ti·ma·tion \,es-tə-'mā-shən\ *n* **1 :** JUDGMENT, OPINION **2 a :** the act of estimating **b :** ESTIMATE **3 :** ESTEEM, HONOR

estival, estivate *var of* AESTIVAL, AESTIVATE

Es·to·nian \e-'stō-nē-ən, -nyən\ *n* **1 :** a member of a Finno-Ugric-speaking people of Estonia **2 :** the Finno-Ugric language of the Estonian people — **Estonian** *adj*

es·top \e-'stäp\ *vt* [ME *estoppen*, fr. MF *estouper*] **1** *archaic* **:** to stop up **2 :** STOP, BAR; *specif* **:** to impede by estoppel

es·top·pel \e-'stäp-əl\ *n* [prob. fr. MF *estoupail* bung, fr. *estouper*] **:** a bar to alleging or denying a fact because of one's own previous actions or words to the contrary

es·tra·di·ol \,es-trə-'dī-,ȯl, -,ōl\ *n* [ISV *estra-* (fr. *estrin*) + *di-* + *-ol*] **:** an estrogenic hormone that is a phenolic steroid alcohol $C_{18}H_{24}O_2$ usu. made synthetically and is used esp. in treating menopausal symptoms

es·trange \is-'trānj\ *vt* [MF *estranger*, fr. ML *extraneare*, fr. L *extraneus* strange] **1 :** to remove from customary environment or associations **2 :** to arouse enmity or indifference in where there had formerly been love, affection, or friendliness **:** ALIENATE — **es·trange·ment** \-'trānj-mənt\ *n* — **es·trang·er** *n*

syn ALIENATE, DISAFFECT, WEAN: ESTRANGE implies the development of indifference or hostility with consequent separation or divorcement; ALIENATE may or may not suggest separation but always implies loss of affection or interest and often a diversion of that affection or interest to another; DISAFFECT refers esp. to those from whom loyalty is expected and stresses the effects (as rebellion or discontent) of alienation without actual separation; WEAN implies separation from something having a strong hold on one

1**es·tray** \is-'trā\ *vi* [MF *estraier*] *archaic* **:** STRAY

2**estray** *n* **:** STRAY 1

es·trin \'es-trən\ *n* [NL *estrus*] **:** an estrogenic hormone; *esp* **:** ESTRONE

es·tri·ol \'es-,trī-,ȯl, e-'strī-, -,ōl\ *n* [*estrin* + *tri-* + *-ol*] **:** a crystalline estrogenic hormone that is a glycol $C_{18}H_{24}O_3$ usu. obtained from the urine of pregnant women

es·tro·gen \'es-trə-jən\ *n* [NL *estrus* + ISV *-o-* + *-gen*] **:** a substance (as a sex hormone) tending to promote estrus and stimulate the development of secondary sex characteristics in the female

es·tro·gen·ic \,es-trə-'jen-ik\ *adj* **1 :** promoting estrus **2 :** of, relating to, or caused by an estrogen — **es·tro·gen·i·cal·ly** \-'jen-i-k(ə-)lē\ *adv*

es·trone \'es-,trōn\ *n* [ISV, fr. *estrin*] **:** an estrogenic hormone that is a ketone $C_{18}H_{22}O_2$, is usu. obtained from the urine of pregnant females, and is used similarly to estradiol

es·trous \'es-trəs\ *adj* **1 :** of, relating to, or characteristic of estrus **2 :** being in heat

estrous cycle *n* **:** the correlated phenomena of the endocrine and generative systems of a female mammal from the beginning of one period of estrus to the beginning of the next

es·trus \'es-trəs\ *or* **es·trum** \-trəm\ *n* [NL, fr. L *oestrus* gadfly, frenzy, fr. Gk *oistros* — more at IRE] **1 a :** a regularly recurrent state of sexual excitability during which the female of most mammals will accept the male and is capable of conceiving **:** HEAT **b :** a single occurrence of this state **2 :** ESTROUS CYCLE

es·tu·a·rine \'es(h)-chə-wə-,rīn\ *adj* **:** of, relating to, or formed in an estuary ⟨~ currents⟩

es·tu·ary \'es(h)-chə-,wer-ē\ *n, often attrib* [L *aestuarium*, fr. *aestus* boiling, tide; akin to L *aestas* summer — more at AESTIVAL] **:** a water passage where the tide meets a river current; *esp* **:** an arm of the sea at the lower end of a river

esu·ri·ence \i-'su̇r-ē-ən(t)s\ *or* **esu·ri·en·cy** \-ən-sē\ *n* **:** the quality or state of being esurient

esu·ri·ent \-ənt\ *adj* [L *esurient-, esuriens*, prp. of *esurire* to be hungry] **:** HUNGRY, GREEDY — **esu·ri·ent·ly** *adv*

-et \'et, ,et, ət, it\ *n suffix* [ME, fr. OF *-et*, masc., & *-ete*, fem., fr. LL *-itus* & *-ita*] **1 :** small one ⟨baron*et*⟩ ⟨cellar*et*⟩ **2 :** group ⟨oct*et*⟩

eta \'āt-ə, 'ēt-ə\ *n* [LL, fr. Gk *ēta*, of Sem origin; akin to Heb *ḥēth* heth] **:** the 7th letter of the Greek alphabet — symbol Η or η

éta·gère *or* **eta·gere** \,ā-,tä-'zhe(ə)r\ *n* [F *étagère*] **:** an elaborate whatnot often with a large mirror at the back and sometimes with an enclosed cabinet as a base

eta·mine \'āt-ə-,mēn\ *n* [F *étamine*] **:** a light cotton or worsted fabric with an open mesh

etat·ism \ā-'tät-,iz-əm\ *n* [F *étatisme*, fr. *état* state, fr. OF *estat*] **:** STATE SOCIALISM — **etat·ist** \-'tät-əst\ *adj*

et cet·era \et-'set-ə-rə, -'se-trə\ [L] **:** and others esp. of the same kind **:** and so forth

et·cet·era *n* **1 :** a number of unspecified additional persons or things **2** *pl* **:** additional items **:** ODDS AND ENDS

1**etch** \'ech\ *vb* [D *etsen*, fr. G *ätzen*, lit., to feed, fr. OHG *azzen*] *vt* **1 :** to produce esp. on metal or glass by the corrosive action of an acid; *also* **:** to subject to such etching **2 :** to delineate or impress clearly ~ *vi* **:** to practice etching — **etch·er** *n*

2**etch** *n* **:** a chemical agent used in etching

etch·ing *n* **1 a :** the act or process of etching **b :** the art of producing pictures or designs by printing from an etched metal plate **2 a :** an etched design **b :** an impression from an etched plate

Ete·o·cles \i-'tē-ə-,klēz\ *n* [L, fr. Gk *Eteoklēs*] **:** a son of Oedipus and intended victim of the expedition of the Seven against Thebes

1**eter·nal** \i-'tərn-ᵊl\ *adj* [ME, fr. MF, fr. LL *aeternalis*, fr. L *aeternus* eternal; akin to L *aevum* age] **1 a :** having infinite duration **:** EVERLASTING **b :** of or relating to eternity **c :** characterized by abiding fellowship with God **2 a :** continued without intermission **:** PERPETUAL **b :** seemingly endless **3** *archaic* **:** INFERNAL **4 :** TIMELESS — **eter·nal·ly** \-ᵊl-ē\ *adv* — **eter·nal·ness** *n*

2**eternal** *n* **1** *cap* **:** 2GOD — used with *the* **2 :** something eternal

eterne \i-'tərn\ *adj* [ME, MF, fr. L *aeternus*] *archaic* **:** ETERNAL

eter·ni·ty \i-'tər-nət-ē\ *n* [ME *eternite*, fr. MF *eternité*, fr. L *aeternitat-, aeternitas*, fr. *aeternus*] **1 :** the quality or state of being eternal **2 :** infinite time **3** *pl* **:** AGES **4 :** the state after death **:** IMMORTALITY **5 :** a seemingly endless or immeasurable time

eter·nize \i-'tər-,nīz\ *vt* **1 a :** to make eternal **b :** to prolong indefinitely **2 :** IMMORTALIZE

ete·sian \i-'tē-zhən\ *adj, often cap* [L *etesius*, fr. Gk *etēsios*, fr. *etos* year — more at WETHER] **:** recurring annually — used of summer winds that blow over the Mediterranean — **etesian** *n, often cap*

eth \'et͟h\ *var of* EDH

eth- *or* **etho-** *comb form* [ISV] **:** ethyl ⟨*eth*aldehyde⟩ ⟨*etho*chloride⟩

1**-eth** \əth, ith\ *or* **-th** \th\ *vb suffix* [ME, fr. OE *-eth, -ath, -th;* akin to OHG *-it, -ōt, -ēt*, 3d sing. ending, L *-t, -it*] — used to form the archaic third person singular present of verbs ⟨go*eth*⟩ ⟨do*th*⟩

2**-eth** — see -TH

eth·ane \'eth-,ān\ *n* [ISV, fr. *ethyl*] **:** a colorless odorless gaseous hydrocarbon CH_3CH_3 found in natural gas and used esp. as a fuel

eth·a·nol \'eth-ə-,nȯl, -,nōl\ *n* **:** ALCOHOL 1

eth·ene \'eth-,ēn\ *n* **:** ETHYLENE

ether \'ē-thər\ *n* [ME, fr. L *aether*, fr. Gk *aithēr*, fr. *aithein* to ignite, blaze] **1 a :** the rarefied element formerly believed to fill the upper regions of space **b :** the upper regions of space **:** HEAVENS **2 a :** a medium that in the undulatory theory of light permeates all space and transmits transverse waves **b :** the medium that transmits radio waves **3 a :** a light volatile flammable liquid $(C_2H_5)_2O$ obtained by the distillation of alcohol with sulfuric acid and used chiefly as a solvent and anesthetic **b :** any of various organic compounds characterized by an oxygen atom attached to two carbon atoms

ethe·re·al \i-'thir-ē-əl\ *adj* **1 a :** of or relating to the upper regions **b :** CELESTIAL, HEAVENLY **2 a :** IMMATERIAL, IMPALPABLE **b :** marked by unusual delicacy and refinement **3 :** relating to, containing, or resembling a chemical ether — **ethe·re·al·i·ty** \i-,thir-ē-'al-ət-ē\ *n* — **ethe·re·al·ly** \i-'thir-ē-ə-lē\ *adv* — **ethe·re·al·ness** *n*

ethe·re·al·ize \i-'thir-ē-ə-,līz\ *vt* **:** to make ethereal

ether extract *n* **:** the part of a complex organic material that is soluble in ether and consists chiefly of fats and fatty acids

ethe·ric \i-'ther-ik, -'thir-\ *adj* **:** ETHEREAL

ether·iza·tion \,ē-th(ə-)rə-'zā-shən\ *n* **:** the administration of ether

ether·ize \'ē-thə-,rīz\ *vt* **1 :** to treat or anesthetize with ether **2 :** to make numb as if by anesthetizing — **ether·iz·er** *n*

eth·ic \'eth-ik\ *n* [ME *ethik*, fr. MF *ethique*, fr. L *ethice*, fr. Gk *ēthikē*, fr. *ēthikos*] **1** *pl but sing or pl in constr* **:** the discipline dealing with what is good and bad and with moral duty and obligation **2 a :** a set of moral principles or values **b :** a theory or system of moral values **c** *pl but sing or pl in constr* **:** the principles of conduct governing an individual or a group

1**eth·i·cal** \'eth-i-kəl\ *or* **eth·ic** \-ik\ *adj* [ME *etik*, fr. L *ethicus*, fr. Gk *ēthikos*, fr. *ēthos* character] **1 :** of or relating to ethics **2 :** conforming to accepted esp. professional standards of conduct **3** *of a drug* **:** restricted to sale only on a doctor's prescription **syn** see MORAL — **eth·i·cal·i·ty** \,eth-i-'kal-ət-ē\ *n* — **eth·i·cal·ly** \'eth-i-k(ə-)lē\ *adv* — **eth·i·cal·ness** \-kəl-nəs\ *n*

2**ethical** *n* **:** an ethical drug

Ethi·op \'ē-thē-,äp\ *or* **Ethi·ope** \-,ōp\ *n* [ME *Ethiope*, fr. L *Aethiops*, fr. Gk *Aithiops*] *archaic* **:** ETHIOPIAN

Ethi·o·pi·an \,ē-thē-'ō-pē-ən\ *n* **1 :** a member of any of the mythical or actual peoples usu. described by the ancient Greeks as dark-skinned and living far to the south **2 :** NEGRO **3 :** a native or inhabitant of Ethiopia — **Ethiopian** *adj*

1**Ethi·o·pic** \-'äp-ik, -'ō-pik\ *adj* **1 :** ETHIOPIAN **2 a :** of, relating to, or constituting the language Ethiopic **b :** of, relating to, or constituting a group of related Semitic languages spoken in Ethiopia

2**Ethiopic** *n* **1 :** a Semitic language formerly spoken in Ethiopia and still used as the liturgical language of the Christian church in Ethiopia **2 :** the Ethiopic group of Semitic languages

eth·moid \'eth-,mȯid\ *or* **eth·moi·dal** \eth-'mȯid-ᵊl\ *adj* [F *ethmoïde*, fr. Gk *ethmoeidēs*, lit., like a strainer, fr. *ēthmos* strainer] **:** of, relating to, adjoining, or being one or more bones of the walls and septum of the nasal cavity — **ethmoid** *n*

eth·nic \'eth-nik\ *adj* [ME, fr. LL *ethnicus*, fr. Gk *ethnikos* national, gentile, fr. *ethnos* nation, people] **1 :** neither Christian nor Jewish **:** HEATHEN **2 :** of or relating to races or large groups of people classed according to common traits and customs

eth·ni·cal \-ni-kəl\ *adj* **1 :** ETHNIC **2 :** ETHNOLOGIC — **eth·ni·cal·ly** \-ni-k(ə-)lē\ *adv*

ethno- *comb form* [F, fr. Gk *ethno-, ethn-*, fr. *ethnos*] **:** race **:** people **:** cultural group ⟨*ethno*biology⟩

eth·no·cen·tric \,eth-nō-'sen-trik\ *adj* **1 :** having race as a central interest **2 :** regarding one's own group as superior — **eth·no·cen·tri·cal·ly** \-tri-k(ə-)lē\ *adv* — **eth·no·cen·trism** \-,triz-əm\ *n*

eth·nog·ra·pher \eth-'näg-rə-fər\ *n* **:** a specialist in ethnography

eth·no·graph·ic \,eth-nə-'graf-ik\ *adj* **:** of or relating to ethnography — **eth·no·graph·i·cal** \-i-kəl\ *adj* — **eth·no·graph·i·cal·ly** \-i-k(ə-)lē\ *adv*

eth·nog·ra·phy \eth-'näg-rə-fē\ *n* [F *ethnographie*, fr. *ethno-* + *-graphie* -graphy] **:** ETHNOLOGY; *specif* **:** descriptive anthropology

eth·no·log·ic \,eth-nə-'läj-ik\ *adj* **:** of or relating to ethnology — **eth·no·log·i·cal** \-i-kəl\ *adj* — **eth·no·log·i·cal·ly** \-k(ə-)lē\ *adv*

eth·nol·o·gist \eth-'näl-ə-jəst\ *n* **:** a specialist in ethnology

eth·nol·o·gy \-jē\ *n* **1 :** a science that deals with the division of mankind into races and their origin, distribution, relations, and characteristics **2 :** anthropology dealing chiefly with the comparative and analytical study of cultures **:** cultural anthropology

ethol·o·gy \ē-'thäl-ə-jē\ *n* **1 :** a branch of knowledge dealing with human ethos and with its formation and evolution **2 a :** the scientific and objective study of animal behavior, sometimes as contrasted with comparative psychology **b :** ECOLOGY, BIONOMICS

ethos \'ē-,thäs\ *n* [NL, fr. Gk *ēthos* custom, character] **:** distinguishing character, tone, or guiding beliefs

ethyl \'eth-əl\ *n* [ISV *eth*er + *-yl*] **:** a univalent hydrocarbon radical C_2H_5 or CH_3CH_2 — **ethyl·ic** \e-'thil-ik\ *adj*

ethyl acetate *n* **:** a colorless fragrant volatile flammable liquid ester $CH_3COOC_2H_5$ of ethyl alcohol and acetic acid

ethyl alcohol *n* **:** ALCOHOL 1

eth·yl·ate \'eth-ə-,lāt\ *vt* **:** to introduce the ethyl group into (a compound) — **eth·yl·ation** \,eth-ə-'lā-shən\ *n*

ethyl cellulose *n* **:** any of various thermoplastic substances made by ethylating alkali cellulose and used esp. in plastics and lacquers

ethyl chloride *n* **:** a colorless pungent flammable gaseous or volatile liquid compound C_2H_5Cl used esp. as a local surface anesthetic

eth·yl·ene \'eth-ə-,lēn\ *n* **1 :** a colorless flammable gaseous unsaturated hydrocarbon $CH_2{=}CH_2$ found in coal gas or obtained by pyrolysis of petroleum hydrocarbons **2 :** a bivalent hydrocarbon radical $-CH_2CH_2-$ derived from ethane

ethylene glycol *n* **:** a thick liquid alcohol $HOCH_2CH_2OH$

ethyl ether *n* **:** ETHER 3a

-et·ic \'et-ik\ *adj suffix* [L & Gk; L *-eticus*, fr. Gk *-etikos, -ētikos*,

fr. *-etos, -ētos,* ending of certain verbals] **:** -IC ⟨limn*etic*⟩ — often in adjectives corresponding to nouns ending in *-esis* ⟨gen*etic*⟩

eti·o·late \'ēt-ē-ə-,lāt\ *vt* [F *étioler*] **1 :** to bleach and alter the natural development of (a green plant) by excluding sunlight **2 a :** to make pale and sickly **b :** to take away the natural vigor of — **eti·o·la·tion** \,ēt-ē-ə-'lā-shən\ *n*

eti·o·log·ic \,ēt-ē-ə-'läj-ik\ *adj* **1 :** assigning or seeking to assign a cause **2 :** of or relating to etiology — **eti·o·log·i·cal** \-i-kəl\ *adj* — **eti·o·log·i·cal·ly** \-i-k(ə-)lē\ *adv*

eti·ol·o·gy \,ēt-ē-'äl-ə-jē\ *n* [ML *aetiologia* statement of causes, fr. Gk *aitiologia,* fr. *aitia* cause; akin to L *aemulus* rivaling] **1 :** CAUSE, ORIGIN; *specif* **:** all of the causes of a disease or abnormal condition **2 :** a branch of knowledge dealing with causes

et·i·quette \'et-i-kət, -,ket\ *n* [F *étiquette,* lit., ticket — more at TICKET] **:** the forms required by good breeding or prescribed by authority to be observed in social or official life **syn** see DECORUM

Eton collar \,ēt-ᵊn-\ *n* [*Eton* College, English public school] **:** a large stiff turnover collar

Eton jacket *n* **:** a short black jacket with long sleeves, wide lapels, and an open front

Etru·ri·an \i-'trůr-ē-ən\ *n* [*Etruria*] **:** ETRUSCAN — **Etrurian** *adj*

¹**Etrus·can** \i-'trəs-kən\ *adj* [L *etruscus;* akin to L *Etruria,* ancient country in central Italy] **:** of, relating to, or characteristic of Etruria, the Etruscans, or the Etruscan language

²**Etruscan** *n* **1 :** a native or inhabitant of ancient Etruria **2 :** the language of the Etruscans which is of unknown affiliation

-ette \'et, ,et, ət, it\ *n suffix* [ME, fr. MF, fem. dim. suffix, fr. OF *-ete* — more at -ET] **1 :** little one ⟨kitchen*ette*⟩ **2 :** group ⟨oct*ette*⟩ **3 :** female ⟨farmer*ette*⟩ **4 :** imitation ⟨beaver*ette*⟩

étude \'ā-,t(y)üd\ *n* [F, lit., study, fr. MF *estude, estudie*] **1 :** a piece of music for the practice of a point of technique **2 :** a composition built on a technical motive but played for its artistic value

etui \ā-'twē, 'ā-,twē\ *n* [F *étui*] **:** a small ornamental case

et·y·mo·log·i·cal \,et-ə-mə-'läj-i-kəl\ *adj* **:** of, relating to, or being in accord with etymology — **et·y·mo·log·i·cal·ly** \-k(ə-)lē\ *adv*

et·y·mol·o·gist \-'mäl-ə-jəst\ *n* **:** a specialist in etymology

et·y·mol·o·gize \-,jīz\ *vt* **:** to discover, formulate, or state an etymology for ~ *vi* **:** to study or formulate etymologies

et·y·mol·o·gy \-jē\ *n* [ME *ethimologie,* fr. L *etymologia,* fr. Gk, fr. *etymon* + *-logia* -logy] **1 :** the history of a linguistic form (as a word) shown by tracing its development since its earliest recorded occurrence in the language where it is found, by tracing its transmission from one language to another, by analyzing it into its component parts, by identifying its cognates in other languages, or by tracing it and its cognates to a common ancestral form in an ancestral language **2 :** a branch of linguistics concerned with etymologies

et·y·mon \'et-ə-,män\ *n, pl* **et·y·ma** \-mə\ *also* **etymons** [L, fr. Gk, literal meaning of a word according to its origin, fr. *etymos* true; akin to Gk *eteos* true] **1 a :** an earlier form of a word in the same language or an ancestral language **b :** a word in a foreign language that is the source of a particular loanword **2 :** a word or morpheme from which words are formed by composition or derivation

eu- *comb form* [ME, fr. L, fr. Gk, fr. *ey, eu,* fr. neut. of *eys* good; akin to Hitt *asus* good and perh. to L *esse* to be] **1 a :** well **:** easily ⟨*eu*plastic⟩ — compare DYS- **b :** good ⟨*eu*daemon⟩ — compare DYS- **2 a :** true ⟨*eu*chromosome⟩ ⟨*eu*globulin⟩ **b :** truly ⟨*eu*coelomate⟩

eu·caine \'yü-,kān\ *n* [ISV] **:** a local anesthetic $C_{15}N_{21}NO_2$ derived from piperidine

eu·ca·lypt \'yü-kə-,lipt\ *n* **:** EUCALYPTUS

eu·ca·lyp·tole *or* **eu·ca·lyp·tol** \,yü-kə-'lip-,tōl, -,tōl\ *n* **:** CINEOLE

eu·ca·lyp·tus \-kə-'lip-təs\ *n, pl* **eu·ca·lyp·ti** \-,tī, -,tē\ *or* **eu·ca·lyp·tus·es** [NL, genus name, fr. *eu-* + Gk *kalyptos* covered, fr. *kalyptein* to conceal; fr. the conical covering of the buds] **:** any of a genus (*Eucalyptus*) of mostly Australian evergreen trees or rarely shrubs of the myrtle family having rigid entire leaves and umbellate flowers and yielding gums, resins, oils, and useful woods

Eu·cha·rist \'yü-k(ə-)rəst\ *n* [ME *eukarist,* fr. MF *eucharistie,* fr. LL *eucharistia,* fr. Gk, Eucharist, gratitude, fr. *eucharistos* grateful, fr. *eu-* + *charizesthai* to show favor, fr. *charis* favor, grace, gratitude; akin to Gk *chairein* to rejoice] **1 :** COMMUNION 2a; *specif* **:** a Roman Catholic sacrament renewing Christ's propitiatory sacrifice of his body and blood **2** *Christian Science* **:** spiritual communion with God — **eu·cha·ris·tic** \,yü-kə-'ris-tik\ *adj, often cap*

¹**eu·chre** \'yü-kər\ *n* [origin unknown] **1 :** a card game in which each player is dealt five cards and the player making trump must take three tricks to win a hand **2 :** the action of euchring an opponent

²**euchre** *vt* **eu·chring** \-k(ə-)riŋ\ **1 :** to prevent from winning three tricks in euchre **2 :** CHEAT, TRICK

eu·chro·mat·ic \,yü-krō-'mat-ik\ *adj* **:** of or relating to euchromatin

eu·chro·ma·tin \(')yü-'krō-mət-ən\ *n* [G, fr. *eu-* + *chromatin*] **:** the genetically active portion of chromatin held to be largely made up of genes

eu·chro·mo·some \(')yü-'krō-mə-,sōm\ *n* **:** AUTOSOME

eu·cil·i·ate \yü-'sil-ē-ət\ *n* [deriv. of NL *eu-* + *cilium*] **:** any of a subclass (Euciliata) of ciliated protozoans with a trophic macronucleus and a reproductive micronucleus — **euciliate** *adj*

eu·clase \'yü-,klās, -,klāz\ *n* [F, fr. *eu-* (fr. L) + Gk *klasis* breaking, fr. *klan* to break — more at HALT] **:** a mineral $BeAlSiO_4(OH)$ consisting of a brittle silicate of beryllium and aluminum in pale-yellow, green, or blue prismatic crystals

eu·clid·e·an *also* **eu·clid·i·an** \yü-'klid-ē-ən\ *adj, often cap* **:** of or relating to the geometry of Euclid or a geometry based on similar axioms

eu·dae·mo·nism \yü-'dē-mə-,niz-əm\ *or* **eu·dai·mo·nism** \-'dī-\ *n* [Gk *eudaimonia* happiness, fr. *eudaimōn* having a good attendant spirit, happy, fr. *eu-* + *daimōn* spirit] **:** a theory that defines moral obligation by reference to personal well-being through a life governed by reason — **eu·dae·mo·nist** \-nəst\ *n* — **eu·dae·mo·nis·tic** \yü-,dē-mə-'nis-tik, ,yü-\ *adj*

eu·di·om·e·ter \,yüd-ē-'äm-ət-ər\ *n* [It *eudiometro,* fr. Gk *eudia* fair weather (fr. *eu-* + *-dia* weather — akin to L *dies* day) + It *-metro* -meter, fr. Gk *metron* measure] **:** an instrument for the volumetric measurement and analysis of gases — **eu·dio·met·ric** \,yüd-ē-ə-'me-trik\ *adj* — **eu·dio·met·ri·cal·ly** \-tri-k(ə-)lē\ *adv*

eu·gen·ic \yü-'jen-ik\ *adj* [Gk *eugenēs* wellborn, fr. *eu-* + *-genēs*] **1 :** relating to or fitted for the production of good offspring **2 :** of or relating to eugenics — **eu·gen·i·cal·ly** \-i-k(ə-)lē\ *adv*

eu·gen·i·cist \-'jen-ə-səst\ *n* **:** a student or advocate of eugenics

eu·gen·ics \yü-'jen-iks\ *n pl but sing or pl in constr* **:** a science that deals with the improvement (as by control of human mating) of hereditary qualities of a race or breed

eu·ge·nol \'yü-jə-,nȯl, -,nōl\ *n* [F *eugénol,* fr. NL *Eugenia,* genus of tropical trees] **:** a colorless aromatic liquid phenol $C_{10}H_{12}O_2$ found esp. in clove oil and used chiefly in flavors and perfumes

eu·gle·na \yü-'glē-nə\ *n* [NL, genus name, fr. *eu-* + Gk *glēnē* eyeball, socket of a joint; prob. akin to Gk *glainoi* ornaments — more at CLEAN] **:** any of a genus (*Euglena*) of green freshwater flagellates often classed as algae

eu·gle·noid \-,nȯid\ *adj* **:** of, related to, or like euglenas

euglenoid movement *n* **:** writhing usu. nonprogressive protoplasmic movement of plastic-bodied euglenoid flagellates

eu·he·mer·ism \yü-'hē-mə-,riz-əm, -'hem-ə-\ *n* [*Euhemerus,* 4th cent. B.C. Gk mythographer] **:** interpretation of myths as traditional accounts of historical persons and events — **eu·he·mer·ist** \-rəst\ *n* — **eu·he·mer·is·tic** \-,hē-mə-'ris-tik, -,hem-ə-\ *adj* — **eu·he·mer·is·ti·cal·ly** \-ti-k(ə-)lē\ *adv* — **eu·he·mer·ize** \-'hē-mə-,rīz, -'hem-ə-\ *vt*

eu·la·chon \'yü-lə-,kän\ *n, pl* **eulachon** *or* **eulachons** [Chinook Jargon *ulâkân*] **:** CANDLEFISH 1

eu·la·mel·li·branch \,yü-lə-'mel-ə-,braŋk\ *n* [NL *Eulamellibranchia,* order name, fr. *eu-* + *Lamellibranchia,* class of mollusks — more at LAMELLIBRANCH] **:** any of an order (Eulamellibranchia) of lamellibranchiate bivalve mollusks with filamentous gills forming two continuous flattened layers on each side of the body — **eu·la·mel·li·bran·chi·ate** \-,mel-ə-'braŋ-kē-ət\ *adj or n*

eu·lo·gist \'yü-lə-jəst\ *n* **:** one that eulogizes

eu·lo·gis·tic \,yü-lə-'jis-tik\ *adj* **:** of, relating to, or characterized by eulogy **:** LAUDATORY — **eu·lo·gis·ti·cal·ly** \-ti-k(ə-)lē\ *adv*

eu·lo·gi·um \yü-'lō-jē-əm\ *n, pl* **eu·lo·gia** \-jē-ə\ *or* **eu·lo·gi·ums** [ML] **:** EULOGY

eu·lo·gize \'yü-lə-,jīz\ *vt* **:** to speak or write in high praise of **:** EXTOL — **eu·lo·giz·er** *n*

eu·lo·gy \'yü-lə-jē\ *n* [ME *euloge,* fr. ML *eulogium,* fr. Gk *eulogia* praise, fr. *eu-* + *-logia* -logy] **1 :** a commendatory formal statement or set oration **2 :** high praise **syn** see ENCOMIUM

Eu·men·i·des \yü-'men-ə-,dēz\ *n pl* [L, fr. Gk] **:** ERINYES

eu·mor·phic \(')yü-'mȯr-fik\ *adj* **:** MESOMORPHIC, ATHLETIC 3

eu·nuch \'yü-nək\ *n* [ME *eunuk,* fr. L *eunuchus,* fr. Gk *eunouchos,* fr. *eunē* bed + *echein* to have, have charge of — more at SCHEME] **1 :** a castrated man placed in charge of a harem or employed as a chamberlain in a palace **2 :** a man or boy deprived of the testes or external genitals — **eu·nuch·ism** \-nə-,kiz-əm\ *n*

eu·on·y·mus \yü-'än-ə-məs\ *n* [NL, genus name, fr. L *euonymos* spindle tree, fr. Gk *euōnymos,* fr. *euōnymos* having an auspicious name, fr. *eu-* + *onyma* name] **:** any of a genus (*Euonymus*) of evergreen shrubs, small trees, or vines of the staff tree family

eu·pa·trid \yü-'pa-trəd, 'yü-pə-\ *n, pl* **eu·pat·ri·dae** \yü-'pa-trə-,dē\ *often cap* [Gk *eupatridēs,* fr. *eu-* + *patr-, patēr* father — more at FATHER] **:** one of the hereditary aristocrats of ancient Athens

eu·pep·sia \yü-'pep-shə, -sē-ə\ *n* [NL, fr. *eu-* + *-pepsia* (as in *dyspepsia*)] **:** good digestion

eu·pep·tic \-'pep-tik\ *adj* **1 :** of, relating to, or having good digestion **2 :** CHEERFUL, OPTIMISTIC

eu·phe·mism \'yü-fə-,miz-əm\ *n* [Gk *euphēmismos,* fr. *euphēmos* auspicious, sounding good, fr. *eu-* + *phēmē* speech, fr. *phanai* to speak — more at BAN] **:** the substitution of an agreeable or inoffensive expression for one that may offend or suggest something unpleasant; *also* **:** the expression so substituted (as *pass away* for *die*) — **eu·phe·mis·tic** \,yü-fə-'mis-tik\ *adj* — **eu·phe·mis·ti·cal·ly** \-ti-k(ə-)lē\ *adv* — **eu·phe·mize** \'yü-fə-,mīz\ *vb*

eu·phon·ic \yü-'fän-ik\ *adj* **:** of, relating to, or according with the principles of euphony — **eu·phon·i·cal·ly** \-i-k(ə-)lē\ *adv*

eu·pho·ni·ous \yü-'fō-nē-əs\ *adj* **:** pleasing in sound — **eu·pho·ni·ous·ly** *adv* — **eu·pho·ni·ous·ness** *n*

eu·pho·ni·um \-nē-əm\ *n* [Gk *euphōnos* + E *-ium* (as in *harmonium*)] **:** a tenor tuba like a baritone but mellower in tone

eu·pho·nize \'yü-fə-,nīz\ *vt* **:** to make euphonious

eu·pho·ny \'yü-fə-nē\ *n* [F *euphonie,* fr. LL *euphonia,* fr. Gk *euphōnia,* fr. *euphōnos* sweet-voiced, musical, fr. *eu-* + *phōnē* voice — more at BAN] **1 :** pleasing or sweet sound; *esp* **:** the acoustic effect produced by words so formed or combined as to please the ear **2 :** a harmonious succession of words having a pleasing sound

eu·phor·bia \yü-'fȯr-bē-ə\ *n* [NL, genus name, alter. of L *euphorbea* euphorbia, fr. *Euphorbus,* 1st cent. A.D. physician] **:** a typical milky-juiced spurge (genus *Euphorbia*)

eu·pho·ria \yü-'fȯr-ē-ə, -'fȯr-\ *n* [NL, fr. Gk, fr. *euphoros* healthy, fr. *eu-* + *pherein* to bear — more at BEAR] **:** an often unaccountable feeling of well-being or elation — **eu·phor·ic** \-'fȯr-ik, -'fär-\ *adj*

eu·pho·tic \yü-'fōt-ik\ *adj* [ISV] **:** of, relating to, or constituting the upper layers of a body of water into which sufficient light penetrates to permit growth of green plants

Eu·phros·y·ne \yü-'fräs-ᵊn-(,)ē\ *n* [L, fr. Gk *Euphrosynē*] **:** one of the three Graces

eu·phu·ism \'yü-fyə-,wiz-əm\ *n* [*Euphues,* character in prose romances by John Lyly] **1 :** an elegant Elizabethan literary style marked by excessive use of balance, antithesis, and alliteration and of similes drawn from mythology and nature **2 :** artificial elegance of language — **eu·phu·ist** \-wəst\ *n* — **eu·phu·is·tic** \,yü-fyə-'wis-tik\ *adj* — **eu·phu·is·ti·cal·ly** \-ti-k(ə-)lē\ *adv*

eu·plas·tic \yü-'plas-tik\ *adj* **:** adapted to the formation of tissue **:** BLASTEMATIC

eu·ploid \'yü-,plȯid\ *adj* [ISV] **:** having a chromosome number that is an exact multiple of the monoploid number — **euploid** *n* — **eu·ploi·dy** \-,plȯid-ē\ *n*

eup·nea *also* **eup·noea** \'yüp-nē-ə, yüp-'nē-ə\ *n* [NL, fr. Gk *eupnoia,* fr. *eupnous* breathing freely, fr. *eu-* + *pnein* to breathe — more at SNEEZE] **:** normal respiration — **eup·ne·ic** \yüp-'nē-ik\ *adj*

Eur- *or* **Euro-** *comb form* [*Europe*] **:** European and ⟨*Eur*american⟩

Eur·asian \yü-'rā-zhən, -shən\ *adj* **1 :** of or relating to Europe and Asia **2 :** of a mixed European and Asiatic origin — **Eurasian** *n*

eu·re·ka \yü-'rē-kə\ *interj* [Gk *heurēka* I have found, fr. *heuriskein* to find; fr. the exclamation attributed to Archimedes on discovering a method for determining the purity of gold — more at HEURISTIC] — used to express triumph on a discovery

Eu·rip·i·de·an \yü-,rip-ə-'dē-ən\ *adj* **:** of, relating to, or characteristic of Euripides or his tragedies

eu·ro \'yu̇(ə)r-(,)ō\ *n* [native name in Australia] **:** a large reddish gray kangaroo (*Macrobus robustus*)

Eu·ro·dol·lar \'yu̇(ə)r-(,)ō-,däl-ər\ *n* [*Europe* + *dollar*] **:** a U.S. dollar held (as by a bank) outside the U. S. and esp. in Europe

Eu·ro·pa \yu̇-'rō-pə\ *n* [L, fr. Gk *Eurōpē*] **:** a Phoenician princess carried off by Zeus in the form of a white bull and by him mother of Minos, Rhadamanthus, and Sarpedon

Eu·ro·pe·an \,yu̇r-ə-'pē-ən\ *adj* **1 :** of or relating to Europe or its inhabitants **2 :** native to Europe — **European** *n*

European plan *n* **:** a hotel rate whereby guests are charged a fixed sum for lodging and service

European red mite *n* **:** a small bright or brownish red oval mite (*Panonychus ulmi*) that is a destructive orchard pest

eu·ro·pi·um \yu̇-'rō-pē-əm\ *n* [NL, fr. *Europe*] **:** a bivalent and trivalent metallic element of the rare-earth group found in monazite sand — see ELEMENT table

eury- *comb form* [NL, fr. Gk, fr. *eurys*; akin to Skt *uru* broad, wide] **:** broad **:** wide ⟨*eury*bathic⟩

eu·ry·bath·ic \,yu̇r-i-'bath-ik\ *adj* [*eury-* + Gk *bathos* depth] **:** living on the bottom of a body of water at varying depths

Eu·ryd·i·ce \yu̇-'rid-ə-(,)sē\ *n* [L, fr. Gk *Eurydikē*] **:** the wife of Orpheus

eu·ry·ha·line \,yu̇r-i-'hā-,līn, -'hal-,īn\ *adj* [ISV *eury-* + Gk *halinos* of salt, fr. *hals* salt] **:** able to live in waters of a wide range of salinity

eu·ryp·ter·id \yu̇-'rip-tə-rəd\ *n* [deriv. of Gk *eury-* + *pteron* wing] **:** any of an order (Eurypterida) of usu. large aquatic Paleozoic arthropods related to the king crabs — **eurypterid** *adj*

eu·ry·therm \'yu̇r-i-,thərm\ *n* [prob. fr. G *eurytherm* eurythermal, fr. *eury-* + Gk *thermē* heat] **:** an organism that tolerates a wide range of temperature — **eu·ry·ther·mal** \,yu̇r-i-'thər-məl\ *or* **eu·ry·ther·mic** \-mik\ *or* **eu·ry·ther·mous** \-məs\ *adj*

eu·ryth·mic *or* **eu·rhyth·mic** \yu̇-'rith-mik\ *adj* **1 :** HARMONIOUS **2 :** of or relating to eurythmy or eurythmics

eu·ryth·mics *or* **eu·rhyth·mics** \-miks\ *n pl but sing or pl in constr* **:** the art of harmonious bodily movement esp. through expressive timed movements in response to improvised music

eu·ryth·my *or* **eu·rhyth·my** \-mē\ *n* [G *eurhythmie*, fr. L *eurythmia* rhythmical movement, fr. Gk, fr. *eurythmos* rhythmical, fr. *eu-* + *rhythmos* rhythm] **:** a system of harmonious body movement to the rhythm of spoken words

eu·ry·top·ic \,yu̇r-i-'täp-ik\ *adj* [prob. fr. G *eurytop*, fr. *eury-* + Gk *topos* place] **:** having a wide range of tolerance to variation of environmental factors — **eu·ry·to·pic·i·ty** \-tō-'pis-ət-ē, -tä-\ *n*

eu·sta·chian tube \yu̇-,stā-shən-, -,stā-kē-ən-\ *n, often cap E* [Bartolommeo *Eustachio* †1574 It anatomist] **:** a bony and cartilaginous tube connecting the middle ear with the nasopharynx and equalizing air pressure on both sides of the tympanic membrane

eu·stat·ic \yu̇-'stat-ik\ *adj* [ISV] **:** relating to or characterized by worldwide change of sea level

eu·stele \'yü-,stēl, yu̇-'stē-lē\ *n* **:** a stele in which the vascular cylinder is broken at leaf emergences and by interfascicular areas

eu·tec·tic \yu̇-'tek-tik\ *adj* [Gk *eutēktos* easily melted, fr. *eu-* + *tēktos* melted, fr. *tēkein* to melt] **1** *of an alloy or solution* **:** having the lowest melting point possible **2 :** of or relating to a eutectic alloy or solution or its melting or freezing point — **eutectic** *n* — **eu·tec·toid** \-,tȯid\ *adj or n*

Eu·ter·pe \yu̇-'tər-pē\ *n* [L, fr. Gk *Euterpē*] **:** the Greek Muse of music

eu·tha·na·sia \,yü-thə-'nā-zh(ē-)ə\ *n* [Gk, easy death, fr. *eu-* + *thanatos* death] **:** the act or practice of killing individuals (as persons or domestic animals) that are hopelessly sick or injured for reasons of mercy — **eu·tha·na·sic** \-zik, -sik\ *adj*

eu·then·ics \yu̇-'then-iks\ *n pl but sing or pl in constr* [Gk *euthenein* to thrive, fr. *eu-* + *-thenein* (akin to Skt *āhanas* swelling)] **:** a science that deals with development of human well-being by improvement of living conditions — **eu·the·nist** \yu̇-'then-əst, 'yü-thə-nəst\ *n*

eu·the·ri·an \yu̇-'thir-ē-ən\ *adj* [deriv. of NL *eu-* + Gk *thērion* beast] **:** of or relating to a major division (Eutheria) of mammals comprising the placental mammals — **eutherian** *n*

eu·tro·phic \yu̇-'träf-ik, -'trō-fik\ *adj* [prob. fr. G *eutroph* eutrophic, fr. Gk *eutrophos* well nourished, nourishing, fr. *eu-* + *trephein* to nourish] *of a lake* **:** rich in dissolved nutrients but often shallow and with seasonal oxygen deficiency — **eu·tro·phy** \'yü-trə-fē\ *n*

eux·e·nite \'yük-sə-,nīt\ *n* [G *euxenit*, fr. Gk *euxenos* hospitable, fr. *eu-* + *xenos* guest, stranger; fr. its rare elements] **:** a brownish black mineral (Y,Ca,Ce,U,Th) (Cb,Ta,Ti)$_2$O$_6$ consisting of oxide of calcium, cerium, columbium, tantalum, titanium, and uranium

evac·u·ate \i-'vak-yə-,wāt\ *vb* [L *evacuatus*, pp. of *evacuare*, fr. *e-* + *vacuus* empty — more at VACUUM] *vt* **1 :** to make empty **2 :** to discharge through the excretory passages **:** VOID **3 :** to remove something from esp. by pumping **4 a :** to remove esp. from a military zone or dangerous area **b :** to withdraw from military occupation of **c :** VACATE ~ *vi* **1 :** to withdraw from a place in an organized way esp. for protection **2 :** to pass urine or feces from the body — **evac·u·a·tive** \-,wāt-iv\ *adj*

evac·u·a·tion \i-,vak-yə-'wā-shən\ *n* **1 :** the act or process of evacuating **2 :** something evacuated or discharged

evac·u·ee \i-,vak-yə-'wē\ *n* **:** an evacuated person

evad·able \i-'vād-ə-bəl\ *adj* **:** capable of being evaded

evade \i-'vād\ *vb* [MF & L; MF *evader*, fr. L *evadere*, fr. *e-* + *vadere* to go, walk — more at WADE] *vi* **1 :** to slip away **2 :** to take refuge in evasion ~ *vt* **1 :** to elude by dexterity or stratagem **:** ESCAPE **2 a :** to avoid facing up to **b :** to avoid the performance of **:** CIRCUMVENT; *specif* **:** to fail to pay (taxes) **c :** to avoid answering directly **:** turn aside **syn** see ESCAPE — **evad·er** *n*

evag·i·nate \i-'vaj-ə-,nāt\ *vt* [L *evaginatus*, pp. of *evaginare* to unsheathe, fr. *e-* + *vagina* sheath, vagina] **:** to turn inside out — **evag·i·na·tion** \i-,vaj-ə-'nā-shən\ *n*

eval·u·ate \i-'val-yə-,wāt\ *vt* [back-formation fr. *evaluation*] **1 :** to determine or fix the value of **2 :** to examine and judge **syn** see ESTIMATE — **eval·u·a·tion** \-,val-yə-'wā-shən\ *n* — **eval·u·a·tive** \-'val-yə-,wāt-iv\ *adj*

ev·a·nesce \,ev-ə-'nes\ *vi* [L *evanescere*] **:** to dissipate like vapor

ev·a·nes·cence \,ev-ə-'nes-ᵊn(t)s\ *n* **1 :** the process or fact of evanescing **2 :** evanescent quality

ev·a·nes·cent \-ᵊnt\ *adj* [L *evanescent-*, *evanescens*, prp. of *evanescere*] **:** tending to vanish like vapor **syn** see TRANSIENT

1evan·gel \i-'van-jəl\ *n* [ME *evangile*, fr. MF, fr. LL *evangelium*, fr. Gk *euangelion* good news, gospel, fr. *euangelos* bringing good news, fr. *eu-* + *angelos* messenger] **:** GOSPEL

2evangel *n* **:** EVANGELIST

evan·gel·i·cal \,ē-,van-'jel-i-kəl, ,ev-ən-\ *also* **evan·gel·ic** \-ik\ *adj* **1 :** of, relating to, or in agreement with the Christian gospel esp. as it is presented in the four Gospels **2 :** PROTESTANT **3 :** emphasizing salvation by faith in the atoning death of Jesus Christ through personal conversion, the authority of Scripture, and the importance of preaching as contrasted with ritual **4 a** *cap* **:** of or relating to the Evangelical Church in Germany **b** *often cap* **:** FUNDAMENTALIST **c** *often cap* **:** Low Church **5 :** EVANGELISTIC, ZEALOUS — **Evan·gel·i·cal·ism** \-i-kə-,liz-əm\ *n* — **evan·gel·i·cal·ly** \-i-k(ə-)lē\ *adv*

Evangelical *n* **:** one holding evangelical principles or belonging to an evangelical party or church

evan·ge·lism \i-'van-jə-,liz-əm\ *n* **1 :** the winning or revival of personal commitments to Christ **2 :** militant or crusading zeal — **evan·ge·lis·tic** \i-,van-jə-'lis-tik\ *adj* — **evan·ge·lis·ti·cal·ly** \-ti-k(ə-)lē\ *adv*

evan·ge·list \-ləst\ *n* **1** *often cap* **:** a writer of any of the four Gospels **2 :** one who evangelizes; *specif* **:** a Protestant minister or layman who preaches at special services

evan·ge·lize \i-'van-jə-,līz\ *vt* **1 :** to preach the gospel to **2 :** to convert to Christianity ~ *vi* **:** to preach the gospel

evan·ish \i-'van-ish\ *vi* [ME *evanisshen*, fr. MF *evaniss-*, stem of *evanir*] **:** VANISH — **evan·ish·ment** \-mənt\ *n*

evap·o·rate \i-'vap-ə-,rāt\ *vb* [ME *evaporaten*, fr. L *evaporatus*, pp. of *evaporare*, fr. *e-* + *vapor* steam, vapor] *vi* **1 a :** to pass off in vapor or in invisible minute particles **b** (1) **:** to pass off or away **:** DISAPPEAR (2) **:** to diminish quickly **2 :** to give forth vapor ~ *vt* **1 a :** to convert into vapor; *also* **:** to dissipate or draw off in vapor or fumes **b :** to deposit (as a metal) in the form of a film by sublimation **2 a :** to expel moisture from **b :** EXPEL ⟨~ electrons⟩ — **evap·o·ra·tion** \i-,vap-ə-'rā-shən\ *n* — **evap·o·ra·tive** \i-'vap-ə-,rāt-iv\ *adj* — **evap·o·ra·tive·ly** *adv* — **evap·o·ra·tiv·i·ty** \i-,vap-ə-rə-'tiv-ət-ē\ *n* — **evap·o·ra·tor** \i-'vap-ə-,rāt-ər\ *n*

evaporated milk *n* **:** milk concentrated by evaporation without the addition of sugar to one half or less of its bulk and usu. to a specified amount of milk fat and milk solids

evapo·trans·pi·ra·tion \i-'vap-(,)ō-,tran(t)-spə-'rā-shən\ *n* [*evaporation* + *transpiration*] **:** loss of water from the soil both by evaporation and by transpiration from the plants growing thereon

eva·sion \i-'vā-zhən\ *n* [ME, fr. MF or LL; MF, fr. LL *evasion-*, *evasio*, fr. L *evasus*, pp. of *evadere* to evade] **1 :** the act or an instance of evading **:** ESCAPE **2 :** a means of evading

eva·sive \i-'vā-siv, -ziv\ *adj* **:** marked by a tendency or purpose to evade **:** EQUIVOCAL — **eva·sive·ly** *adv* — **eva·sive·ness** *n*

eve \'ēv\ *n* [ME *eve*, *even*] **1 :** EVENING **2 :** the evening or the day before a special day **3 :** the period immediately preceding

Eve \'ēv\ *n* [OE *Ēfe*, fr. LL *Eva*, fr. Heb *Ḥawwāh*] **:** Adam's wife

evec·tion \i-'vek-shən\ *n* [L *evection-*, *evectio* rising, fr. *evectus*, pp. of *evehere* to carry out, raise up, fr. *e-* + *vehere* to carry] **:** perturbation of the moon's orbital motion due to the attraction of the sun

1even \'ē-vən\ *n* [ME *even*, *eve*, fr. OE *ǣfen*] *archaic* **:** EVENING

2even *adj* [ME, fr. OE *efen*; akin to OHG *eban* even] **1 a :** having a horizontal surface **:** FLAT ⟨~ ground⟩ **b :** being without break, indentation, roughness, or other irregularity **:** SMOOTH **c :** being in the same plane or line **2 a :** being without variation **:** UNIFORM **b :** LEVEL 4 **3 a** *obs* **:** CANDID **b :** EQUAL, FAIR **c** (1) **:** SQUARE, QUITS (2) **:** fully revenged **d :** BALANCED; *specif* **:** showing neither profit nor loss **4 a :** being one of the sequence of natural numbers beginning with two and counting by twos that are exactly divisible by two **b :** marked by an even number **5 :** EXACT, PRECISE **syn** see LEVEL, STEADY — **even·ly** *adv* — **even·ness** \-vən-nəs\ *n*

3even *adv* [ME, fr. OE *efne*, fr. *efen*, adj.] **1 a :** EXACTLY, PRECISELY **b :** FULLY, QUITE **c :** at the very time **2 a :** TRULY, INDEED **b** — used as an intensive to indicate something unexpected **c** — used as an intensive to stress the comparative degree

4even *vb* **even·ing** \'ēv-(ə-)niŋ\ *vt* **:** to make even ~ *vi* **:** to become even — **even·er** \'ēv-(ə-)nər\ *n*

even·fall \'ē-vən-,fȯl\ *n* **:** the beginning of evening **:** DUSK

even·hand·ed \,ē-vən-'han-dəd\ *adj* **:** FAIR, IMPARTIAL

eve·ning \'ēv-niŋ\ *n, often attrib* [ME, fr. OE *ǣfnung*, fr. *ǣfnian* to grow toward evening, fr. *ǣfen* evening; akin to OHG *āband* evening and perh. to Gk *epi* on] **1 a :** the latter part and close of the day and early part of the night **b** *chiefly South & Midland* **:** AFTERNOON **c :** the period from sunset or the evening meal to bedtime **2 :** the latter portion **3 :** the period of an evening's entertainment

evening dress *n* **:** dress for evening social occasions

evening prayer *n, often cap E&P* **:** EVENSONG 2

evening primrose *n* **:** any of several dicotyledonous plants of a family (Onagraceae, the evening-primrose family) and esp. of the type genus (*Oenothera*); *esp* **:** a coarse biennial herb (*O. biennis*) with yellow flowers that open in the evening

eve·nings \'ēv-niŋz\ *adv* **:** in the evening repeatedly **:** on any evening ⟨goes bowling ~⟩

evening star *n* **1 :** a bright planet (as Venus) seen in the western sky at or after sunset **2 :** any planet that rises before midnight

even·song \'ē-vən-,sȯŋ\ *n, often cap* [ME, fr. OE *ǣfensang*, fr. *ǣfen* even + *sang* song] **1 :** VESPERS 1 **2 :** an evening worship service in the Anglican communion

event \i-'vent\ *n* [MF or L; MF, fr. L *eventus*, fr. *eventus*, pp. of *evenire* to happen, fr. *e-* + *venire* to come] **1 a :** something that happens **b :** a noteworthy happening **c :** a social occasion or activity **2 a** *archaic* **:** OUTCOME **b :** the issue of a legal action as finally determined **c :** CONTINGENCY, EVENTUALITY **3 :** any of the contests in a program of sports **4 :** the fundamental entity of observed physical reality represented by a point designated by three coordinates of place and one of time in the space-time continuum postulated by the theory of relativity **syn** see EFFECT, OCCURRENCE — **at all events :** in any case — **in any event :** in any case — **in the event :** as it turns out

event·ful \-fəl\ *adj* **1 :** full of or rich in events **2 :** MOMENTOUS — **event·ful·ly** \-fə-lē\ *adv* — **event·ful·ness** *n*

even·tide \'ē-vən-,tīd\ *n* **:** the time of evening **:** EVENING

even·tu·al \i-'vench-(ə-)wəl, -'ven-chəl\ *adj* **1** *archaic* **:** CONTIN-

GENT, CONDITIONAL **2 :** taking place at an unspecified later time **:** ULTIMATE ⟨~ success⟩ **syn** see LAST — **even·tu·al·ly** \-ē\ *adv*
even·tu·al·i·ty \i-ˌven-chə-ˈwal-ət-ē\ *n* **:** POSSIBILITY
even·tu·ate \i-ˈven-chə-ˌwāt\ *vi* **:** to come out finally
ev·er \ˈev-ər\ *adv* [ME, fr. OE *ǣfre*] **1 :** ALWAYS **2 a :** at any time **b :** in any way **3** — used as an intensive esp. with *so*
ev·er·bloom·ing \ˌev-ər-ˈblü-miŋ\ *adj* **:** blooming more or less continuously throughout the growing season
[1]**ev·er·green** \ˈev-ər-ˌgrēn\ *adj* **1 :** remaining verdant — compare DECIDUOUS **2 :** ever retaining its freshness **:** PERENNIAL
[2]**evergreen** *n* **1 :** an evergreen plant; *also* **:** CONIFER **2** *pl* **:** twigs and branches of evergreen plants used for decoration
[1]**ev·er·last·ing** \ˌev-ər-ˈlas-tiŋ\ *adj* **1 :** lasting or enduring through all time **:** ETERNAL **2 a** (1) **:** continuing long or indefinitely **:** PERPETUAL (2) *of a plant* **:** retaining its form or color for a long time when dried **b :** TEDIOUS **3 :** wearing indefinitely **:** DURABLE — **ev·er·last·ing·ly** \-tiŋ-lē\ *adv* — **ev·er·last·ing·ness** *n*
[2]**everlasting** *n* **1** *cap* **:** [2]GOD **2 :** ETERNITY ⟨from ~⟩ **3 a :** any of several chiefly composite plants with flowers that can be dried without loss of form or color **b :** the flower of an everlasting
ev·er·more \ˌev-ər-ˈmō(ə)r, -ˈmȯ(ə)r\ *adv* **1 :** ALWAYS, FOREVER **2 :** in the future
ever·si·ble \i-ˈvər-sə-bəl\ *adj* **:** capable of being everted
ever·sion \i-ˈvər-zhən, -shən\ *n* [ME, fr. MF, fr. L *eversion-, eversio,* fr. *eversus,* pp. of *evertere*] **:** the act of everting **:** the state of being everted
evert \i-ˈvərt\ *vt* [L *evertere,* fr. *e-* + *vertere* to turn — more at WORTH] **1 :** OVERTHROW, UPSET **2 :** to turn outward or inside out
ever·tor \i-ˈvərt-ər\ *n* **:** a muscle that rotates a part outward
ev·ery \ˈev-rē\ *adj* [ME *everich, every,* fr. OE *ǣfre ǣlc,* fr. *ǣfre* ever + *ǣlc* each] **1 :** being each individual or part of a group without exception **2** *obs* **:** being all taken severally **3 :** being each within a range of possibilities **4 :** COMPLETE, ENTIRE
ev·ery·body \ˈev-ri-ˌbäd-ē\ *pron* **:** every person **:** EVERYONE
ev·ery·day \ˈev-rē-ˌdā\ *adj* **:** encountered or used routinely or typically **:** ORDINARY
ev·ery·one \-(ˌ)wən\ *pron* **:** EVERYBODY
ev·ery·thing \ˈev-rē-ˌthiŋ\ *pron* **1 a :** all that exists **b :** all that relates to the subject **2 :** a most important or excellent thing
ev·ery·where \-ˌ(h)we(ə)r, -ˌ(h)wa(ə)r\ *adv* **:** in every place or part
evict \i-ˈvikt\ *vt* [ME *evicten,* fr. LL *evictus,* pp. of *evincere,* fr. L, to vanquish, win a point — more at EVINCE] **1 a :** to recover (property) from a person by legal process **b :** to put out (a person) from property by legal process **2 :** to force out **:** EXPEL **syn** see EJECT — **evic·tion** \i-ˈvik-shən\ *n* — **evic·tor** \i-ˈvik-tər\ *n*
[1]**ev·i·dence** \ˈev-əd-ən(t)s, -ə-ˌden(t)s\ *n* **1 a :** an outward sign **:** INDICATION **b :** something that furnishes proof **:** TESTIMONY; *specif* **:** something legally submitted to a tribunal to ascertain the truth of a matter **2 :** one who bears witness; *esp* **:** one who voluntarily confesses a crime and testifies for the prosecution against his accomplices — **in evidence :** to be seen **:** CONSPICUOUS
[2]**evidence** *vt* **:** to offer evidence of **:** PROVE, EVINCE **syn** see SHOW
ev·i·dent \ˈev-əd-ənt, -ə-ˌdent\ *adj* [ME, fr. MF, fr. L *evident-, evidens,* fr. *e-* + *vident-, videns,* prp. of *vidēre* to see — more at WIT] **:** clear to the vision and understanding — **ev·i·dent·ly** *adv*
syn EVIDENT, MANIFEST, PATENT, DISTINCT, OBVIOUS, APPARENT, PLAIN, CLEAR mean readily perceived or apprehended. EVIDENT implies presence of visible signs which serve as indications of a person's intention or state of mind or of the probable nature of a past or coming event or action; MANIFEST implies an external display so evident that little or no inference is required; PATENT applies to a cause, effect, or significant feature that is clear and unmistakable once attention has been directed to it; DISTINCT implies such sharpness of outline or definition that no unusual effort to see or hear or comprehend is required; OBVIOUS implies such ease in discovering or accounting for that it often suggests conspicuousness or little need for perspicacity in the observer; APPARENT is very close to EVIDENT except that it may imply more conscious exercise of inference; PLAIN and CLEAR imply the quality of being unmistakable, PLAIN because of lack of intricacy, complexity, or elaboration, CLEAR because of an absence of anything that confuses the mind or obscures the pattern
ev·i·den·tial \ˌev-ə-ˈden-chəl\ *adj* **:** being, relating to, or affording evidence — **ev·i·den·tial·ly** \-ˈdench-(ə-)lē\ *adv*
[1]**evil** \ˈē-vəl\ *adj* **evil·er** *or* **evil·ler; evil·est** *or* **evil·lest** [ME, fr. OE *yfel;* akin to OHG *ubil* evil] **1 a :** not good morally **:** WICKED **b :** arising from actual or imputed bad character or conduct **2 a** *archaic* **:** INFERIOR **b :** causing discomfort or repulsion **:** OFFENSIVE **c :** DISAGREEABLE **3 a :** causing harm **:** PERNICIOUS **b :** marked by misfortune **:** UNLUCKY **syn** see BAD — **evil** *adv, archaic* — **evil·ly** \-və(l)-lē\ *adv*
[2]**evil** *n* **1 :** something that brings sorrow, distress, or calamity **2 a :** the fact of suffering and misfortune **b :** a cosmic evil force — **evil·do·er** \ˌē-vəl-ˈdü-ər\ *n* — **evil·do·ing** \-ˈdü-iŋ\ *n*
evil eye *n* **:** an eye or glance held capable of inflicting harm
evil–mind·ed \ˌē-vəl-ˈmīn-dəd\ *adj* **:** having an evil disposition or evil thoughts — **evil–mind·ed·ly** *adv* — **evil–mind·ed·ness** *n*
evince \i-ˈvin(t)s\ *vt* [L *evincere* to vanquish, win a point, fr. *e-* + *vincere* to conquer — more at VICTOR] **1 :** to constitute evidence of **:** SHOW **2 :** to display clearly **:** REVEAL **syn** see SHOW — **evinc·ible** \i-ˈvin(t)-sə-bəl\ *adj*
evis·cer·ate \i-ˈvis-ə-ˌrāt\ *vb* [L *evisceratus,* pp. of *eviscerare,* fr. *e-* + *viscera*] *vt* **1 a :** to take out the entrails of **:** DISEMBOWEL **b :** to deprive of vital content or force **2 :** to remove an organ from (a patient) or the contents of (an organ) **~** *vi* **:** to protrude through a surgical incision or suffer protrusion of a part through an incision — **evis·cer·a·tion** \i-ˌvis-ə-ˈrā-shən\ *n*
ev·i·ta·ble \ˈev-ət-ə-bəl\ *adj* **:** AVOIDABLE
evo·ca·ble \ˈev-ə-kə-bəl, i-ˈvō-kə-\ *adj* **:** capable of being evoked
evo·ca·tion \ˌē-vō-ˈkā-shən, ˌev-ə-\ *n* [L *evocation-, evocatio,* fr. *evocatus,* pp. of *evocare*] **1 :** the act or fact of evoking **:** SUMMONING: as **a :** the summoning of a spirit **b :** imaginative re-creation **2 :** INDUCTION 4e; *specif* **:** initiation of development of a primary embryonic axis — **evo·ca·tor** \ˈē-vō-ˌkāt-ər, ˈev-ə-\ *n*
evoc·a·tive \i-ˈväk-ət-iv\ *adj* **:** tending or serving to evoke ⟨an ~ description⟩ — **evoc·a·tive·ly** *adv* — **evoc·a·tive·ness** *n*
evoke \i-ˈvōk\ *vt* [F *évoquer,* fr. L *evocare,* fr. *e-* + *vocare* to call — more at VOCATION] **1 a :** to call forth or up **:** SUMMON **b :** INVOKE **2 :** ELICIT **3 :** to re-create imaginatively **syn** see EDUCE
evo·lute \ˈev-ə-ˌlüt *also* ˈē-və-\ *n* **:** the locus of the center of curvature or the envelope of the normals of a curve
evo·lu·tion \ˌev-ə-ˈlü-shən *also* ˌē-və-\ *n* [L *evolution-, evolutio* unrolling, fr. *evolutus,* pp. of *evolvere*] **1 a :** a process of change in a certain direction **:** UNFOLDING **b** (1) **:** a process of continuous change from a lower, simpler, or worse to a higher, more complex, or better state **:** GROWTH (2) **:** a process of gradual and relatively peaceful social, political, and economic advance **c :** something evolved **2 :** one of a set of prescribed movements **3 :** the process of working out or developing **4 :** the extraction of a mathematical root **5 a :** PHYLOGENY **b :** the process by which through a series of changes or steps a living organism has acquired its distinguishing morphological and physiological characters **c :** a theory that the various types of animals and plants have their origin in other preexisting types and that the distinguishable differences are due to modifications in successive generations **6 :** a process in which the whole universe is a progression of interrelated phenomena — **evo·lu·tion·ary** \-shə-ˌner-ē\ *adj* — **evo·lu·tion·ism** \-shə-ˌniz-əm\ *n* — **evo·lu·tion·ist** \-sh(ə-)nəst\ *n or adj*
evolve \i-ˈvälv, -ˈvȯlv\ *vb* [L *evolvere* to unroll, fr. *e-* + *volvere* to roll] *vt* **1 :** to give off **:** EMIT **2 a :** DERIVE, EDUCE **b :** to work out **:** DEVELOP **c :** to produce by natural evolutionary processes **~** *vi* **:** to undergo evolutionary change — **evolvement** \-mənt\ *n*
evon·y·mus \i-ˈvän-ə-məs\ *n* **:** EUONYMUS
evul·sion \i-ˈvəl-shən\ *n* [L *evulsion-, evulsio,* fr. *evulsus,* pp. of *evellere* to pluck out, fr. *e-* + *vellere* to pluck] **:** EXTRACTION
ev·zone \ˈev-ˌzōn\ *n* [NGk *euzōnos,* fr. Gk, active, lit., well girt, fr. *eu-* + *zōnē* girdle] **:** a member of a select Greek infantry unit
ewe \ˈyü\ *n* [ME, fr. OE *ēowu*] **:** the female of the sheep esp. when mature; *also* **:** the female of various related animals
ewe–neck \-ˈnek\ *n* **:** a thin neck having an insufficient, faulty, or concave arch and occurring as a defect in dogs and horses — **ewe–necked** \-ˈnekt\ *adj*
ew·er \ˈyü-ər, ˈyu̇(-ə)r\ *n* [ME, fr. AF, fr. OF *evier,* fr. (assumed) VL *aquarium,* fr. L, neut. of *aquarius* of water, fr. *aqua* water — more at ISLAND] **:** a vase-shaped pitcher or jug

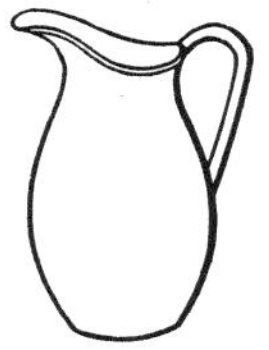

ewer

[1]**ex** \ˈeks\ *n* **:** the letter *x*
[2]**ex** \(ˌ)eks\ *prep* [L] **1 :** out of **:** FROM: as **a :** from a specified place or source **b :** from a specified dam **2 :** free from **:** WITHOUT: as **a :** without an indicated value or right — used esp. of securities **b :** free of charges precedent to removal from the specified place with purchaser to provide means of subsequent transportation ⟨~ dock⟩
[1]**ex-** \e *also occurs in this prefix where only* i *is shown below (as in "express") and* ks *sometimes occurs where only* gz *is shown (as in "exact")*\ *prefix* [ME, fr. OF & L; OF, fr. L (also, intensive prefix), fr. *ex* out of, from; akin to Gk *ex, ex-* out of, from, OSlav *iz*] **1 :** out of **:** outside ⟨*ex*clave⟩ **2 :** not ⟨*ex*stipulate⟩ **3** \(ˌ)eks, ˈeks\ [ME, fr. LL, fr. L] **:** former ⟨*ex*-president⟩ ⟨*ex*-child actor⟩
[2]**ex-** — see EXO-
ex·ac·er·bate \ig-ˈzas-ər-ˌbāt, ek-ˈsas-\ *vt* [L *exacerbatus,* pp. of *exacerbare,* fr. *ex-* + *acerbus* harsh, bitter, fr. *acer* sharp — more at EDGE] **:** to make more violent, bitter, or severe — **ex·ac·er·ba·tion** \ig-ˌzas-ər-ˈbā-shən, (ˌ)ek-ˌsas-\ *n*
[1]**ex·act** \ig-ˈzakt\ *vt* [ME *exacten,* fr. L *exactus,* pp. of *exigere* to drive out, demand, measure, fr. *ex-* + *agere* to drive — more at AGENT] **1 :** to demand and compel **:** EXTORT **2 :** to call for as necessary, appropriate, or desirable **syn** see DEMAND — **ex·act·able** \-ˈzak-tə-bəl\ *adj* — **ex·ac·tor** *also* **ex·act·er** \-tər\ *n*
[2]**exact** *adj* [L *exactus,* fr. pp. of *exigere*] **1 :** exhibiting or marked by strict, particular, and complete accordance with fact **2 :** marked by thorough consideration or minute measurement of small factual details — **exact·ness** \-ˈzak(t)-nəs\ *n* **syn** see CORRECT
ex·act·ing *adj* **1 :** tryingly or unremittingly severe in making demands **2 :** requiring careful attention and precise accuracy **syn** see ONEROUS — **ex·act·ing·ly** \-tiŋ-lē\ *adv* — **ex·act·ing·ness** *n*
ex·ac·tion \ig-ˈzak-shən\ *n* **1 a :** the act or process of exacting **b :** EXTORTION **2 :** something exacted; *esp* **:** a fee, reward, or contribution demanded or levied with severity or injustice
ex·ac·ti·tude \ig-ˈzak-tə-ˌt(y)üd\ *n* **:** the quality or an instance of being exact
ex·act·ly \ig-ˈzak-(t)lē\ *adv* **1 a :** in an exact manner **:** PRECISELY **b :** ENTIRELY, ALTOGETHER **2 :** quite so
ex·a·cum \ˈek-sə-kəm\ *n* [NL, genus name, fr. L, a kind of centaury, fr. Gaulish] **:** any of a genus (*Exacum*) of tropical Asiatic and African plants of the gentian family
ex·ag·ger·ate \ig-ˈzaj-ə-ˌrāt\ *vb* [L *exaggeratus,* pp. of *exaggerare,* lit., to heap up fr. *ex-* + *agger* heap, fr. *aggerere* to carry toward, fr. *ad-* + *gerere* to carry] *vt* **1 :** to enlarge beyond bounds or the truth **:** OVERSTATE **2 :** to enlarge or increase esp. beyond the normal **~** *vi* **:** to misrepresent by overstating — **ex·ag·ger·a·tion** \ig-ˌzaj-ə-ˈrā-shən\ *n* — **ex·ag·ger·a·tive** \-ˈzaj-ə-ˌrāt-iv, -ˈzaj-(ə-)rət-\ *adj* — **ex·ag·ger·a·tor** \-ˌrāt-ər\ *n* — **ex·ag·ger·a·to·ry** \-ˈzaj-(ə-)rə-ˌtōr-ē, -ˌtȯr-\ *adj*
ex·alt \ig-ˈzȯlt\ *vb* [ME *exalten,* fr. MF & L; MF *exalter,* fr. L *exaltare,* fr. *ex-* + *altus* high — more at OLD] *vt* **1 :** to raise high **:** ELEVATE **2 :** to raise in rank, power, or character **3 :** to elevate by praise or in estimation **:** GLORIFY **4** *obs* **:** ELATE **5 :** to enhance the activity of **:** INTENSIFY **~** *vi* **:** to induce exaltation — **ex·alt·er** *n*
ex·al·ta·tion \ˌeg-ˌzȯl-ˈtā-shən, ˌek-ˌsȯl-\ *n* **1 :** an act of exalting **:** the state of being exalted **2 a :** marked or excessive intensification of a mental state or of the activity of a bodily part or function **b :** an abnormal sense of well-being, power, or importance
ex·am \ig-ˈzam\ *n* **:** EXAMINATION
ex·a·men \ig-ˈzā-mən\ *n* [L, tongue of a balance, examination, fr. *exigere*] **1 :** EXAMINATION **2 :** a critical study
ex·am·in·able \ig-ˈzam-(ə-)nə-bəl\ *adj* **:** suitable for examination
ex·am·i·nant \-ˈzam-ə-nənt\ *n* **:** one who examines
ex·am·i·na·tion \ig-ˌzam-ə-ˈnā-shən\ *n* **1 :** the act or process of examining **:** state of being examined **2 :** an exercise designed to examine progress or test qualification or knowledge **3 :** a formal interrogation — **ex·am·i·na·tion·al** \-shnəl, -shən-ᵊl\ *adj*
ex·am·i·na·to·ri·al \-nə-ˈtōr-ē-əl, -ˈtȯr-\ *adj* **:** of or relating to an examiner or examination
ex·am·ine \ig-ˈzam-ən\ *vt* **ex·am·in·ing** \-(ə-)niŋ\ [ME *examinen,* fr. MF *examiner,* fr. L *examinare,* fr. *examen*] **1 a :** to inspect

closely **b :** to test the condition of **c :** to inquire into carefully **:** INVESTIGATE **2 a :** to interrogate closely **b :** to try or test by question in order to determine progress, fitness, or knowledge **syn** see SCRUTINIZE — **ex·am·in·ee** \-ˌzam-ə-ˈnē\ *n* — **ex·am·in·er** \-ˈzam-(ə-)nər\ *n*

1ex·am·ple \ig-ˈzam-pəl\ *n* [ME, fr. MF, fr. L *exemplum*, fr. *eximere* to take out, fr. *ex-* + *emere* to take — more at REDEEM] **1 :** a particular single item, fact, incident, or aspect that is representative of all of a group or type **2 :** someone or something that serves as a pattern to be imitated or not to be imitated ⟨a good ~⟩ ⟨a bad ~⟩ **3 :** a parallel or closely similar case esp. when serving as a precedent or model **4 a :** a punishment inflicted on someone as a warning to others **b :** an individual so punished **5 :** an instance (as a problem to be solved) serving to illustrate a rule or precept or to act as an exercise in the application of a rule **syn** see INSTANCE, MODEL

2example *vt* **ex·am·pling** \-p(ə-)liŋ\ **1 :** to serve or use as an example of **2** *archaic* **:** to be or set an example to

ex·an·i·mate \eg-ˈzan-ə-mət\ *adj* [L *exanimatus*, pp. of *exanimare* to deprive of life or spirit, fr. *ex-* + *anima* breath, soul — more at ANIMATE] **1 :** lacking animation **:** SPIRITLESS **2 :** lifeless or appearing lifeless

ex·an·them \ig-ˈzan(t)-thəm\ *also* **ex·an·the·ma** \ˌeg-ˌzan-ˈthē-mə\ *n, pl* **exanthems** *also* **ex·an·the·ma·ta** \ˌeg-ˌzan-ˈthem-ət-ə, -ˈthē-mət-\ *or* **exanthemas** [LL *exanthema*, fr. Gk *exanthēma*, fr. *exanthein* to bloom, break out, fr. *ex-* + *anthos* flower — more at ANTHOLOGY] **:** an eruptive disease (as measles) or its symptomatic eruption — **ex·an·them·a·tous** \ˌeg-ˌzan-ˈthem-ət-əs\ *adj*

1ex·arch \ˈek-ˌsärk\ *n* [LL *exarchus*, fr. LGk *exarchos*, fr. Gk, leader, fr. *exarchein* to begin, take the lead, fr. *ex-* + *archein* to rule, begin] **1 :** a Byzantine viceroy **2 :** an Eastern bishop ranking below a patriarch and above a metropolitan; *specif* **:** the head of an independent church — **ex·ar·chal** \ek-ˈsär-kəl\ *adj* — **ex·arch·ate** \ˈek-ˌsär-kət\ *n* — **ex·ar·chy** \ˈek-ˌsär-kē\ *n*

2exarch *adj* [*exo-* + *-arch*] **:** formed or taking place from the periphery toward the center ⟨~ xylem⟩

1ex·as·per·ate \ig-ˈzas-pə-ˌrāt\ *vt* [L *exasperatus*, pp. of *exasperare*, fr. *ex-* + *asper* rough] **1 a :** to excite or inflame the anger of **:** ENRAGE **b :** to cause irritation or annoyance to **2** *obs* **:** to make grievous or more grievous or malignant **syn** see IRRITATE

2ex·as·per·ate \-rət\ *adj* **1 :** EXASPERATED **2 :** roughened with irregular prickles or elevations ⟨~ seed coats⟩

ex·as·per·a·tion \ig-ˌzas-pə-ˈrā-shən\ *n* **1 :** the state of being exasperated **2 :** the act or an instance of exasperating

Ex·cal·i·bur \ek-ˈskal-ə-bər\ *n* [OF *Escalibor*, fr. ML *Caliburnus*] **:** the sword of King Arthur

ex ca·the·dra \ˌek-skə-ˈthē-drə\ *adv* (*or adj*) [NL, lit., from the chair] **:** by virtue of or in the exercise of one's office

ex·ca·vate \ˈek-skə-ˌvāt\ *vb* [L *excavatus*, pp. of *excavare*, fr. *ex-* + *cavare* to make hollow] *vt* **1 :** to form a cavity or hole in **2 :** to form by hollowing **3 :** to dig out and remove **4 :** to expose to view by digging away a covering ~ *vi* **:** to make excavations

ex·ca·va·tion \ˌek-skə-ˈvā-shən\ *n* **1 :** the act or process of excavating **2 :** a cavity formed by cutting, digging, or scooping

ex·ca·va·tor \ˈek-skə-ˌvāt-ər\ *n* **:** one that excavates; *esp* **:** a power-operated shovel

ex·ceed \ik-ˈsēd\ *vb* [ME *exceden*, fr. MF *exceder*, fr. L *excedere*, fr. *ex-* + *cedere* to go] *vt* **1 :** to extend outside of ⟨river will ~ its banks⟩ **2 :** to be greater than or superior to **:** SURPASS **3 :** to go beyond a limit set by ⟨~*ed* his authority⟩ ~ *vi* **1** *obs* **:** OVERDO **2 :** PREDOMINATE

syn SURPASS, TRANSCEND, EXCEL, OUTDO, OUTSTRIP: EXCEED implies going beyond a limit set by authority or established by custom or by prior achievement; SURPASS suggests superiority in quality, merit, or skill; TRANSCEND implies a rising or extending notably above or beyond ordinary limits; EXCEL implies preeminence in achievement or quality and may suggest superiority to all others; OUTDO applies to a bettering or exceeding what has been done before; OUTSTRIP suggests surpassing in a race or competition

ex·ceed·ing *adj* **:** exceptional in amount, quality, or degree

ex·ceed·ing·ly \ik-ˈsēd-iŋ-lē\ *or* **ex·ceed·ing** *adv* **:** EXTREMELY

ex·cel \ik-ˈsel\ *vb* **ex·celled; ex·cel·ling** [ME *excellen*, fr. L *excellere*, fr. *ex-* + *-cellere* to rise, project; akin to L *collis* hill — more at HILL] *vt* **:** SURPASS, OUTDO ~ *vi* **:** to be distinguishable by superiority **:** surpass others ⟨~*s* in mathematics⟩ **syn** see EXCEED

ex·cel·lence \ˈek-s(ə-)lən(t)s\ *n* **1 :** the quality of being excellent **2 :** an excellent or valuable quality **:** VIRTUE **3 :** EXCELLENCY 2

ex·cel·len·cy \-s(ə-)lən-sē\ *n* **1 :** EXCELLENCE; *esp* **:** outstanding or valuable quality — usu. used in pl. **2** — used as a title for certain high dignitaries of state (as a governor or an ambassador) and church (as a Roman Catholic archbishop or bishop)

ex·cel·lent \ˈek-s(ə-)lənt\ *adj* [ME, fr. MF, fr. L *excellent-, excellens*, fr. prp. of *excellere*] **1** *archaic* **:** SUPERIOR **2 :** very good of its kind **:** eminently good **:** FIRST-CLASS — **ex·cel·lent·ly** *adv*

ex·cel·si·or \ik-ˈsel-sē-ər\ *n* [trade name, fr. L, higher, compar. of *excelsus* high, fr. pp. of *excellere*] **:** fine curled wood shavings used esp. for packing fragile items

1ex·cept \ik-ˈsept\ *vb* [ME *excepten*, fr. MF *excepter*, fr. L *exceptare*, fr. *exceptus*, pp. of *excipere* to take out, except, fr. *ex-* + *capere* to take — more at HEAVE] *vt* **:** to take or leave out from a number or a whole **:** EXCLUDE ~ *vi* **:** to take exception **:** OBJECT

2except *also* **ex·cept·ing** *prep* **1 :** with the exclusion or exception of ⟨daily ~ Sundays⟩ **2 :** otherwise than or other than ⟨take no orders ~ from me⟩

3except *also* **excepting** *conj* **1 :** on any other condition than that **:** UNLESS ⟨~ you repent⟩ **2 :** ONLY ⟨I would go ~ it's too far⟩

except for *prep* **:** but for ⟨*except for* you I would be dead⟩

ex·cep·tion \ik-ˈsep-shən\ *n* **1 :** the act of excepting **:** EXCLUSION **2 :** one that is excepted **3 :** something offered as objection or taken as objectionable **4 :** an oral or written legal objection

ex·cep·tion·able \ik-ˈsep-sh(ə-)nə-bəl\ *adj* **:** likely to cause objection **:** OBJECTIONABLE **syn** see EXCEPTIONAL — **ex·cep·tion·ably** \-blē\ *adv*

ex·cep·tion·al \ik-ˈsep-shnəl, -shən-ᵊl\ *adj* **1 :** forming an exception **:** RARE **2 :** better than average **:** SUPERIOR — **ex·cep·tion·al·i·ty** \-ˌsep-shə-ˈnal-ət-ē\ *n* — **ex·cep·tion·al·ly** \-ˈsep-shnə-lē, -shən-ᵊl-ē\ *adv* — **ex·cep·tion·al·ness** *n*

syn EXCEPTIONAL and EXCEPTIONABLE are frequently confused. Something is EXCEPTIONAL that is itself an exception and is therefore out of the ordinary; something is EXCEPTIONABLE to which exception may be taken and is therefore objectionable or offensive

ex·cep·tive \ik-ˈsep-tiv\ *adj* **1 :** relating to, containing, or constituting exception **2** *archaic* **:** CAPTIOUS

1ex·cerpt \ek-ˈsərpt, eg-ˈzərpt, ˈek-ˌ, ˈeg-ˌ\ *vt* [L *excerptus*, pp. of *excerpere*, fr. *ex-* + *carpere* to gather, pluck] **:** to select for quoting **:** EXTRACT — **ex·cerp·tion** \ek-ˈsərp-shən, eg-ˈzərp-\ *n*

2ex·cerpt \ˈek-ˌsərpt, ˈeg-ˌzərpt\ *n* **:** a passage selected or copied **:** EXTRACT

1ex·cess \ik-ˈses, ˈek-ˌ\ *n* [ME, fr. MF or LL; MF *exces*, fr. LL *excessus*, fr. L, departure, projection, fr. *excessus*, pp. of *excedere* to exceed] **1 a :** a state of surpassing limits **:** SUPERFLUITY **b :** something that exceeds what is usual, proper, or specified **c :** the amount or degree by which one thing or quantity exceeds another **2 :** undue or immoderate indulgence **:** INTEMPERANCE

2excess *adj* **:** more than the usual, proper, or specified amount

ex·ces·sive \ik-ˈses-iv\ *adj* **:** exceeding the usual, proper, or normal — **ex·ces·sive·ly** *adv* — **ex·ces·sive·ness** *n*

syn EXCESSIVE, IMMODERATE, INORDINATE, EXTRAVAGANT, EXORBITANT, EXTREME mean going beyond a normal limit. EXCESSIVE implies an amount or degree too great to be reasonable or acceptable; IMMODERATE implies lack of desirable or necessary restraint; INORDINATE implies an exceeding of the limits dictated by reason or good judgment; EXTRAVAGANT implies an indifference to restraints imposed by truth, prudence, or good taste; EXORBITANT implies a departure from accepted standards regarding amount or degree; EXTREME may imply an approach to the farthest limit possible or conceivable but commonly means only to a notably high degree

1ex·change \iks-ˈchānj, ˈeks-ˌ\ *n* [ME *exchaunge*, fr. MF *eschange*, fr. *eschangier* to exchange, fr. (assumed) VL *excambiare*, fr. L *ex-* + *cambiare* to exchange — more at CHANGE] **1 :** the act of giving or taking one thing in return for another **:** TRADE **2 a :** the act of substituting one thing for another **b :** reciprocal giving and receiving **3 :** something offered, given, or received in an exchange; *also* **:** an item or article reprinted from a newspaper **4 a :** funds payable currently at a distant point either in a foreign currency or in domestic currency **b** (1) **:** interchange or conversion of the money of two countries or of current and uncurrent money with allowance for difference in value (2) **:** the amount of one currency that will buy a given amount of another (3) **:** the amount of the difference in value between two currencies or between values at two places **5 :** a place where things or services are exchanged: as **a :** an organized market or center for trading in securities or commodities **b :** a store or shop specializing in merchandise usu. of a particular type **c :** a cooperative store or society **d :** a central office in which telephone lines are connected to permit communication

2exchange *vt* **1 a :** to part with, give, or transfer in consideration of something received as an equivalent **b :** to have replaced by other merchandise **2 :** to part with for a substitute **3 :** BARTER, SWAP ~ *vi* **1 :** to pass or become received in exchange **2 :** to engage in an exchange — **ex·change·able** \-ə-bəl\ *adj* — **ex·chang·er** *n*

ex·chang·ee \ˌeks-ˌchān-ˈjē, iks-\ *n* **:** a participant in an exchange program

exchange professor *n* **:** a professor teaching at an institution other than his own sometimes in exchange with that institution

exchange rate *n* **:** the ratio at which the principal unit of two currencies may be traded

exchange student *n* **:** a student from a usu. foreign country received into an institution in exchange for one sent to that country

ex·che·quer \ˈeks-ˌchek-ər, iks-ˈ\ *n* [ME *escheker*, fr. AF, fr. OF *eschequier* chessboard, counting table] **1** *cap* **:** a department or office of state in medieval England charged with the collection and management of the royal revenue and judicial determination of all revenue causes **2** *cap* **:** a former superior court having jurisdiction in England and Wales primarily over revenue matters and now forming a division of the Court of King's Bench **3** *often cap* **a :** the department or office of state in Great Britain and Northern Ireland charged with the receipt and care of the national revenue **b :** the national banking account of this realm **4 :** TREASURY; *esp* **:** a national or royal treasury **5 :** pecuniary resources **:** FUNDS

ex·cide \ek-ˈsīd\ *vt* [L *excidere*] **:** to cut out **:** EXCISE

ex·cip·i·ent \ik-ˈsip-ē-ənt\ *n* [L *excipient-, excipiens*, prp. of *excipere* to take out, take up — more at EXCEPT] **:** an inert substance that forms a vehicle (as for a drug)

ex·cis·able \ˈek-ˌsī-zə-bəl, -ˌsī-sə-, ek-ˈ\ *adj* **:** subject to excise

1ex·cise \ˈek-ˌsīz, -ˌsīs\ *n* [obs. D *excijs* (now *accijus*), fr. MD, prob. modif. of OF *assise* session, assessment — more at ASSIZE] **1 :** an internal tax levied on the manufacture, sale, or consumption of a commodity within a country **2 :** any of various taxes on privileges often assessed in the form of a license or other fee

2excise *vt* **:** to impose an excise upon

3ex·cise \ek-ˈsīz\ *vt* [L *excisus*, pp. of *excidere*, fr. *ex-* + *caedere* to cut] **:** to remove by cutting out — **ex·ci·sion** \-ˈsizh-ən\ *n*

ex·cise·man \ˈek-ˌsīz-mən, -ˌsī-smən\ *n* **:** an officer who inspects and rates articles liable to excise under British law

ex·cit·abil·i·ty \ik-ˌsīt-ə-ˈbil-ət-ē\ *n* **:** the quality or state of being excitable

ex·cit·able \ik-ˈsīt-ə-bəl\ *adj* **:** capable of being readily roused into action or a state of excitement or irritability; *specif* **:** capable of being activated by and reacting to stimuli — **ex·cit·able·ness** *n*

ex·ci·tant \ik-ˈsīt-ᵊnt, ˈek-sət-ənt\ *adj* **:** tending to excite or augment — **excitant** *n*

ex·ci·ta·tion \ˌek-ˌsī-ˈtā-shən, ˌek-sə-\ *n* **:** EXCITEMENT; *esp* **:** the irritability induced in protoplasm by a stimulus

ex·cit·ative \ik-ˈsīt-ət-iv\ *adj* **:** tending or able to excite

ex·cit·ato·ry \-ə-ˌtōr-ē, -ˌtȯr-\ *adj* **1 :** EXCITATIVE **2 :** exhibiting or marked by excitement or excitation

ex·cite \ik-ˈsīt\ *vt* [ME *exciten*, fr. MF *exciter*, fr. L *excitare*, fr. *ex-* + *citare* to rouse — more at CITE] **1 a :** to call to activity **b :** to rouse to feeling **2 a :** ENERGIZE **b :** to produce a magnetic field in **3 :** to increase the activity of (as a living organism) **:** STIMULATE **4 :** to raise (as an atom) to a higher energy level **syn** see PROVOKE

ex·cit·ed *adj* **:** having or showing strong feeling — **ex·cit·ed·ly** *adv*

ex·cite·ment \ik-ˈsīt-mənt\ *n* **1 :** the act of exciting **:** the state of being excited **2 :** something that excites or rouses

ex·cit·er \-ˈsīt-ər\ *n* **1 :** one that excites **2 a :** a dynamo or

ə abut; ᵊ kitten; ər further; a back; ā bake; ä cot, cart; aů out; ch chin; e less; ē easy; g gift; i trip; ī life
j joke; ŋ sing; ō flow; ȯ flaw; ȯi coin; th thin; th this; ü loot; ů foot; y yet; yü few; yů furious; zh vision

battery that supplies the electric current used to produce the magnetic field in another dynamo or motor **b :** an electrical oscillator that generates the carrier frequency
ex·cit·ing *adj* **:** producing excitement — **ex·cit·ing·ly** \-iŋ-lē\ *adv*
ex·ci·tor \ik-ˈsīt-ər\ *n* **1** *archaic* **:** EXCITER **2 :** an afferent nerve arousing increased action of the part it supplies
ex·claim \iks-ˈklām\ *vb* [MF *exclamer*, fr. L *exclamare*, fr. *ex-* + *clamare* to cry out] *vi* **1 :** to cry out or speak in strong or sudden emotion **2 :** to speak loudly or vehemently ~ *vt* **:** to utter sharply, passionately, or vehemently **:** PROCLAIM — **ex·claim·er** *n*
ex·cla·ma·tion \ˌeks-klə-ˈmā-shən\ *n* **1 :** a sharp or sudden utterance **:** OUTCRY **2 :** vehement expression of protest or complaint
exclamation point *n* **:** a mark ! used esp. after an interjection or exclamation to indicate forceful utterance or strong feeling
ex·clam·a·to·ry \iks-ˈklam-ə-ˌtōr-ē, -ˌtȯr-\ *adj* **:** containing, expressing, using, or relating to exclamation ⟨an ~ phrase⟩
ex·clave \ˈeks-ˌklāv\ *n* [*ex-* + *-clave* (as in *enclave*)] **:** a portion of a country separated from the main part and constituting an enclave in respect to the surrounding territory
ex·clo·sure \eks-ˈklō-zhər\ *n* [*ex-* + *-closure* (as in *enclosure*)] **:** an area from which intruders are excluded esp. by fencing
ex·clud·abil·i·ty \iks-ˌklüd-ə-ˈbil-ət-ē\ *n* **:** the condition of being excludable
ex·clud·able *or* **ex·clud·ible** \iks-ˈklüd-ə-bəl\ *adj* **:** subject to exclusion ⟨~ income⟩
ex·clude \iks-ˈklüd\ *vt* [ME *excluden*, fr. L *excludere*, fr. *ex-* + *claudere* to close] **1 a :** to shut out **b :** to bar from participation, consideration, or inclusion **2 :** to put out — **ex·clud·er** *n*
syn DEBAR, ELIMINATE, SUSPEND: EXCLUDE implies keeping out what is already outside; DEBAR implies setting up a barrier that is effectual in excluding a person or class from what is open or accessible to others; ELIMINATE implies the getting rid of what is already within esp. as a constituent part or element; SUSPEND implies temporary and commonly disciplinary removal from membership in a school or organization
ex·clu·sion \iks-ˈklü-zhən\ *n* [L *exclusion-*, *exclusio*, fr. *exclusus*, pp. of *excludere*] **1 :** the act or an instance of excluding **2 :** the state of being excluded — **ex·clu·sion·ary** \-zhə-ˌner-ē\ *adj*
ex·clu·sion·ist \iks-ˈklüzh-(ə-)nəst\ *n* **:** one who would exclude another from some right or privilege — **exclusionist** *adj*
exclusion principle *n* **:** a principle in physics: no two electrons in an atom or molecule will be exactly equivalent
ex·clu·sive \iks-ˈklü-siv, -ziv\ *adj* **1 a :** excluding or having power to exclude **b :** limiting or limited to possession, control, or use by a single individual or group **2 a :** excluding others from participation **b :** snobbishly aloof **3 a :** accepting or soliciting only a socially restricted patronage **b :** STYLISH, FASHIONABLE **4 a :** SINGLE, SOLE ⟨~ jurisdiction⟩ **b :** UNDIVIDED, WHOLE ⟨his ~ attention⟩ — **exclusive** *n* — **ex·clu·sive·ly** *adv* — **ex·clu·sive·ness** *n*
exclusive of *prep* **:** not taking into account ⟨*exclusive of* artillery⟩
ex·clu·siv·i·ty \ˌeks-ˌklü-ˈsiv-ət-ē, -ˈziv-\ *n* **1 :** EXCLUSIVENESS **2 :** exclusive rights or services
ex·cog·i·tate \ek-ˈskäj-ə-ˌtāt\ *vt* [L *excogitatus*, pp. of *excogitare*, fr. *ex-* + *cogitare* to cogitate] **:** to think out **:** DEVISE — **ex·cog·i·ta·tion** \(ˌ)ek-ˌskäj-ə-ˈtā-shən\ *n* — **ex·cog·i·ta·tive** \ek-ˈskäj-ə-ˌtāt-iv\ *adj*
1**ex·com·mu·ni·cate** \ˌek-skə-ˈmyü-nə-ˌkāt\ *vt* [ME *excommunicaten*, fr. LL *excommunicatus*, pp. of *excommunicare*, fr. L *ex-* + LL *communicare* to communicate] **:** to subject to excommunication — **ex·com·mu·ni·ca·tor** \-ˌkāt-ər\ *n*
2**ex·com·mu·ni·cate** \-ni-kət\ *adj* **:** EXCOMMUNICATED — **excommunicate** *n*
ex·com·mu·ni·ca·tion \-ˌmyü-nə-ˈkā-shən\ *n* **1 :** an ecclesiastical censure depriving a person of the rights of church membership **2 :** exclusion from fellowship in a group or community — **ex·com·mu·ni·ca·tive** \-ˈmyü-nə-ˌkāt-iv, -ni-kət-\ *adj*
ex·co·ri·ate \ek-ˈskōr-ē-ˌāt, -ˈskȯr-\ *vt* [ME *excoriaten*, fr. LL *excoriatus*, pp. of *excoriare*, fr. L *ex-* + *corium* skin, hide — more at CUIRASS] **1 :** to wear off the skin of **:** ABRADE **2 :** to censure scathingly — **ex·co·ri·a·tion** \(ˌ)ek-ˌskōr-ē-ˈā-shən, -ˌskȯr-\ *n*
ex·cre·ment \ˈek-skrə-mənt\ *n* [L *excrementum*, fr. *excernere*] **:** waste matter discharged from the body; *esp* **:** waste discharged from the alimentary canal — **ex·cre·men·tal** \ˌek-skrə-ˈment-ᵊl\ *or* **ex·cre·men·ti·tious** \-ˌmen-ˈtish-əs\ *adj*
ex·cres·cence \ek-ˈskres-ᵊn(t)s\ *n* **:** an often immoderate or abnormal outgrowth or enlargement
ex·cres·cen·cy \-ᵊn-sē\ *n* **:** EXCRESCENCE
ex·cres·cent \-ᵊnt\ *adj* [L *excrescent-*, *excrescens*, prp. of *excrescere* to grow out, fr. *ex-* + *crescere* to grow] **1 :** growing out or forming an outgrowth; *esp* **:** forming an abnormal, excessive, or useless outgrowth **2 :** EPENTHETIC — **ex·cres·cent·ly** *adv*
ex·cre·ta \ek-ˈskrēt-ə\ *n pl* [NL, fr. L, neut. pl. of *excretus*] **:** waste matter eliminated or separated from an organism; *esp* **:** EXCRETIONS — **ex·cre·tal** \-ˈskrēt-ᵊl\ *adj*
ex·crete \ek-ˈskrēt\ *vt* [L *excretus*, pp. of *excernere* to sift out, discharge, fr. *ex-* + *cernere* to sift — more at CERTAIN] **:** to separate and eliminate or discharge from the blood or tissues or from the active protoplasm — **ex·cret·er** *n*
ex·cre·tion \ek-ˈskrē-shən\ *n* **1 :** the act or process of excreting **2 :** something excreted; *esp* **:** useless, superfluous, or harmful material (as urea) eliminated from the body that differs from a secretion in not being produced to perform a useful function
ex·cre·to·ry \ˈek-skrə-ˌtōr-ē, -ˌtȯr-\ *adj* **:** of, relating to, or serving for excretion
ex·cru·ci·ate \ik-ˈskrü-shē-ˌāt\ *vt* [L *excruciatus*, pp. of *excruciare*, fr. *ex-* + *cruciare* to crucify, fr. *cruc-*, *crux* cross] **1 :** to inflict intense pain on **:** TORTURE **2 :** to subject to intense mental distress
ex·cru·ci·at·ing *adj* **1 :** causing great pain or anguish **:** AGONIZING **2 :** very intense **:** EXTREME — **ex·cru·ci·at·ing·ly** \-iŋ-lē\ *adv*
ex·cru·ci·a·tion \ik-ˌskrü-s(h)ē-ˈā-shən, (ˌ)ek-\ *n* **:** the act of excruciating **:** the state or an instance of being excruciated
ex·cul·pate \ˈek-(ˌ)skəl-ˌpāt, ek-ˈskəl-\ *vt* [(assumed) ML *exculpatus*, pp. of *exculpare*, fr. L *ex* + *culpa* blame] **:** to clear from alleged fault or guilt — **ex·cul·pa·tion** \ˌek-(ˌ)skəl-ˈpā-shən\ *n*
syn ABSOLVE, EXONERATE, ACQUIT, VINDICATE: EXCULPATE implies a clearing from blame or fault often in a matter of small importance; ABSOLVE implies a release either from an obligation that binds the conscience or from the consequences of disobeying the law or committing a sin; EXONERATE implies a complete clearance from an accusation or charge and from any attendant suspicion of blame or guilt; ACQUIT implies a formal decision in one's favor with respect to a definite charge; VINDICATE may refer to things as well as persons that have been subjected to critical attack or imputation of guilt, weakness, or folly, and implies a clearing effected by proving the unfairness of such criticism or blame
ex·cul·pa·to·ry \ek-ˈskəl-pə-ˌtōr-ē, -ˌtȯr-\ *adj* **:** tending or serving to exculpate
ex·cur·rent \ek-ˈskər-ənt, -ˈskə-rənt\ *adj* [L *excurrent-*, *excurrens*, prp. of *excurrere* to run out, extend, fr. *ex-* + *currere* to run] **:** running or flowing out: as **a** (1) **:** having the axis prolonged to form an undivided main stem or trunk (2) **:** projecting beyond the apex **b :** characterized by a current that flows outward
ex·cur·sion \ik-ˈskər-zhən\ *n*, *often attrib* [L *excursion-*, *excursio*, fr. *excursus*, pp. of *excurrere*] **1 a :** a going out or forth **:** EXPEDITION **b** (1) **:** a usu. brief pleasure trip (2) **:** a trip at special reduced rates **2 :** deviation from a direct or proper course; *esp* **:** DIGRESSION **3 a :** a movement outward or from a mean position or axis; *also* **:** the distance traversed **:** AMPLITUDE **b :** one complete movement of expansion and contraction of the lungs and their membranes
ex·cur·sion·ist \-ˈkərzh-(ə-)nəst\ *n* **:** a person who goes on an excursion
ex·cur·sive \ik-ˈskər-siv\ *adj* **:** constituting a digression **:** characterized by digression — **ex·cur·sive·ly** *adv* — **ex·cur·sive·ness** *n*
ex·cur·sus \ik-ˈskər-səs\ *n*, *pl* **ex·cur·sus·es** *also* **ex·cur·sus** \-səs, -ˌsüs\ [L, digression, fr. *excursus*, pp.] **:** an appendix or digression that contains an exposition of some point or topic
ex·cus·able \ik-ˈskyü-zə-bəl\ *adj* **:** capable of being excused **:** PARDONABLE — **ex·cus·able·ness** *n* — **ex·cus·ably** \-blē\ *adv*
ex·cu·sa·to·ry \-zə-ˌtōr-ē, -ˌtȯr-\ *adj* **:** making or containing excuse
1**ex·cuse** \ik-ˈskyüz\ *vt* [ME *excusen*, fr. OF *excuser*, fr. L *excusare*, fr. *ex-* + *causa* cause, explanation] **1 a :** to make apology for **b :** to try to remove blame from **2 :** to accept an excuse for **:** PARDON **3 :** to grant exemption or release to ⟨the class was *excused*⟩ **4 :** to serve as excuse for **:** JUSTIFY — **ex·cus·er** *n*
syn CONDONE, PARDON, FORGIVE: EXCUSE implies a passing over of a fault, omission, or failure without censure or due punishment in view of extenuating circumstances; CONDONE suggests an accepting without protest or censure some reprehensible act or condition; PARDON implies the freeing from the penalty due for admitted or proved offense; FORGIVE implies the giving up not only of any claim to requital or retribution but also of any resentment or desire for revenge
2**ex·cuse** \ik-ˈskyüs\ *n* **1 :** the act of excusing **2 a :** something offered as grounds for being excused **b** *pl* **:** an expression of regret for failure to do something **c :** a note of explanation of an absence **3 :** JUSTIFICATION, REASON **syn** see APOLOGY
ex·e·at \ˈek-sē-ˌat\ *n* [L, let him go out, fr. *exire* to go out, fr. *ex-* + *ire* to go] *Brit* **:** a permit for temporary absence from a college
ex·ec \ig-ˈzek\ *n* **:** EXECUTIVE OFFICER
ex·e·cra·ble \ˈek-si-krə-bəl\ *adj* **1 :** deserving to be execrated **:** DETESTABLE **2 :** very bad **:** WRETCHED — **ex·e·cra·ble·ness** *n* — **ex·e·cra·bly** \-blē\ *adv*
ex·e·crate \ˈek-sə-ˌkrāt\ *vt* [L *exsecratus*, pp. of *exsecrari*, fr. *ex* + *sacr-*, *sacer* sacred] **1** *archaic* **:** to put under a curse **2 :** to declare to be evil or detestable **:** DENOUNCE **3 :** to detest utterly — **ex·e·cra·tive** \-ˌkrāt-iv\ *adj* — **ex·e·cra·tor** \-ˌkrāt-ər\ *n*
syn EXECRATE, CURSE, DAMN, ANATHEMATIZE mean to denounce violently. EXECRATE implies intense loathing and usu. passionate fury; CURSE and DAMN imply angry denunciation by blasphemous oaths or profane imprecations; ANATHEMATIZE implies solemn denunciation of an evil or an injustice
ex·e·cra·tion \ˌek-sə-ˈkrā-shən\ *n* **1 :** the act of cursing or denouncing; *also* **:** the curse so uttered **2 :** an object of curses
ex·e·cut·able \ˈek-sə-ˌkyüt-ə-bəl\ *adj* **:** capable of execution
ex·ec·u·tant \ig-ˈzek-yət-ənt\ *n* **:** one who executes or performs; *esp* **:** one skilled in the technique of an art **:** PERFORMER
ex·e·cute \ˈek-sə-ˌkyüt\ *vt* [ME *executen*, fr. MF *executer*, back-formation fr. *execution*] **1 :** to put into effect **:** carry out **:** PERFORM **2 :** to do what is provided or required by ⟨~ a decree⟩ **3 :** to put to death in compliance with a legal sentence **4 :** to make or produce esp. by carrying out a design **5 :** to perform what is required to give validity to ⟨~ a deed⟩ — **ex·e·cut·er** *n*
syn EXECUTE, ADMINISTER mean to carry out the declared intent of another (as a people, a legislature). EXECUTE stresses the enforcing of the specific provisions of a law, a will, a commission or command; ADMINISTER implies the continuing exercise of deputed authority in pursuance of only generally indicated goals rather than specifically prescribed means of attaining them **syn** see in addition KILL, PERFORM
ex·e·cu·tion \ˌek-sə-ˈkyü-shən\ *n* [ME, fr. MF, fr. L *exsecution-*, *executio*, fr. *exsecutus*, pp. of *exsequi* to execute, fr. *ex-* + *sequi* to follow — more at SUE] **1 :** the act or process of executing **:** PERFORMANCE **2 :** a putting to death as a legal penalty **3 :** a judicial writ empowering an officer to carry out a judgment **4 :** the act or mode or result of performance **5 :** effective or destructive action
ex·e·cu·tion·er \-sh(ə-)nər\ *n* **:** one who executes; *esp* **:** one who puts to death
1**ex·ec·u·tive** \ig-ˈzek-(y)ət-iv\ *adj* **1 :** designed for or relating to execution **2 :** of or relating to the execution of the laws and the conduct of public affairs **3 :** of or relating to an executive
2**executive** *n* **1 :** the executive branch of a government; *also* **:** the persons who constitute the executive magistracy of a state **2 :** an individual or group constituting the agency that controls or directs an organization **3 :** one who holds a position of administrative or managerial responsibility
executive agreement *n* **:** an agreement between the U.S. and a foreign government made by the executive
executive council *n* **1 :** a council constituted to advise or share in the functions of a political executive **2 :** a council that exercises supreme executive power
executive officer *n* **:** the officer second in command of a military or naval organization
executive order *n* **:** REGULATION 2b
executive session *n* **:** a usu. closed session esp. of a legislative body
ex·ec·u·tor \ig-ˈzek-(y)ət-ər, *in sense 1a also* ˈek-sə-ˌkyüt-\ *n* [ME, fr. OF, fr. L *executor*, fr. *exsecutus*] **1 a :** one who executes something **b** *obs* **:** EXECUTIONER **2 :** the person appointed by a testator to execute his will — **ex·ec·u·to·ri·al** \ig-ˌzek-(y)ə-ˈtōr-ē-əl, -ˈtȯr-\ *adj* — **ex·ec·u·trix** \ig-ˈzek-(y)ə-triks\ *n*

ex·ec·u·to·ry \ig-ˈzek-(y)ə-ˌtōr-ē, -ˌtȯr-\ *adj* **1 :** relating to administration **2 :** designed or of such a nature as to be executed in time to come or to take effect on a future contingency

ex·e·ge·sis \ˌek-sə-ˈjē-səs\ *n, pl* **ex·e·ge·ses** \-ˈjē-ˌsēz\ [NL, fr. Gk *exēgēsis*, fr. *exēgeisthai* to explain, interpret, fr. *ex-* + *hēgeisthai* to lead] **:** explanation or critical interpretation of a text

ex·e·gete \ˈek-sə-ˌjēt\ *n* [Gk *exēgētēs*, fr. *exēgeisthai*] **:** one who practices exegesis

ex·e·get·ic \ˌek-sə-ˈjet-ik\ *adj* [Gk *exēgētikos*, fr. *exēgeisthai*] **:** of or relating to exegesis — **ex·e·get·i·cal** \-i-kəl\ *adj* — **ex·e·get·i·cal·ly** \-i-k(ə-)lē\ *adv*

ex·e·get·ist \-ˈjet-əst\ *n* **:** EXEGETE

ex·em·plar \ig-ˈzem-ˌplär, -plər\ *n* [ME, fr. L, fr. *exemplum* example] **:** something that serves as a model or example: as **a :** an ideal model **b :** a typical or standard specimen **c :** a copy of a book or writing **d :** IDEA 1a **syn** see MODEL

ex·em·plar·i·ly \ˌeg-zəm-ˈpler-ə-lē\ *adv* **:** in an exemplary manner

ex·em·pla·ri·ness \ig-ˈzem-plə-rē-nəs\ *n* **:** the quality or state of being exemplary

ex·em·pla·ry \ig-ˈzem-plə-rē\ *adj* **1 a :** serving as a pattern **b :** deserving imitation **:** COMMENDABLE **2 :** serving as a warning **:** MONITORY **3 :** serving as an example, instance, or illustration

ex·em·pli·fi·ca·tion \ig-ˌzem-plə-fə-ˈkā-shən\ *n* **1 :** an exemplified copy of a document **2 a :** the act or process of exemplifying **b :** a case in point **:** EXAMPLE

ex·em·pli·fy \ig-ˈzem-plə-ˌfī\ *vt* [ME *exemplifien*, fr. MF *exemplifier*, fr. ML *exemplificare*, fr. L *exemplum*] **1 a :** to show or illustrate by example **b :** to serve as an example of **2 :** to make an attested copy or transcript of (a document) under seal

ex·em·pli gra·tia \ig-ˌzem-plē-ˈgrät-ē-ˌä\ *adv* [L] **:** for example

ex·em·plum \ig-ˈzem-pləm\ *n, pl* **ex·em·pla** \-plə\ [L] **1 :** EXAMPLE, MODEL **2 :** an anecdote or short narrative used to point a moral or sustain an argument

¹**ex·empt** \ig-ˈzem(p)t\ *adj* [ME, fr. L *exemptus*, pp. of *eximere* to take out — more at EXAMPLE] **1** *obs* **:** set apart **2 :** free or released from some liability to which others are subject

²**exempt** *n* **:** one exempted or freed from duty

³**exempt** *vt* **1** *obs* **:** to set apart **2 :** to release or deliver from some liability or requirement to which others are subject **:** EXCUSE

ex·emp·tion \ig-ˈzem(p)-shən\ *n* **1 :** the act of exempting or state of being exempt **:** IMMUNITY **2 :** a cause for exempting

ex·en·ter·ate \ek-ˈsent-ə-ˌrāt\ *vt* [L *exenteratus*, pp. of *exenterare* to disembowel, modif. of Gk *exenterizein*, fr. *ex-* + *enteron* intestine — more at INTER-] **:** to remove the contents of (as the orbit, pelvis) — **ex·en·ter·a·tion** \(ˌ)ek-ˌsent-ə-ˈrā-shən\ *n*

ex·e·quy \ˈek-sə-kwē\ *n* [ME *exequies*, sing. & pl., fr. MF & L; MF, pl., fr. L *exsequiae*, fr. *exsequi* to follow out, execute — more at EXECUTION] **:** a funeral rite — usu. used in pl.

ex·er·cis·able \ˈek-sər-ˌsī-zə-bəl\ *adj* **:** capable of being exercised

¹**ex·er·cise** \ˈek-sər-ˌsīz\ *n* [ME, fr. MF *exercice*, fr. L *exercitium*, fr. *exercitus*, pp. of *exercēre* to drive on, keep busy, fr. *ex-* + *arcēre* to enclose, hold off — more at ARK] **1 a :** the act of bringing into play or realizing in action **:** USE **b :** the discharge of an official function or professional occupation **2 a :** regular or repeated appropriate use of a faculty, power, or bodily organ **b :** bodily exertion for the sake of developing and maintaining physical fitness **3 :** something performed or practiced in order to develop, improve, or display a specific power or skill **4 a :** a maneuver, operation, or drill carried out for training and discipline **b** *pl* **:** a program including speeches, announcements of awards and honors, and various traditional practices of secular or religious character

²**exercise** *vt* **1 :** to bring to bear **:** EXERT ⟨~ influence⟩ **2 a :** to use repeatedly in order to strengthen or develop **b :** to train (as troops) by drills and maneuvers **c :** to put through exercises **3 a :** to engage the attention and effort of **b :** to cause anxiety, alarm, or indignation in ~ *vi* **:** to take exercise **syn** see PRACTICE — **ex·er·cis·er** *n*

ex·er·ci·ta·tion \ig-ˌzər-sə-ˈtā-shən\ *n* [ME *exercitacioun*, fr. L *exercitation-*, *exercitatio*, fr. *exercitatus*, pp. of *exercitare* to exercise diligently, fr. *exercitus*, pp. of *exercēre*] *archaic* **:** EXERCISE

ex·ergue \ˈek-ˌsərg, ˈeg-ˌzərg\ *n* [F, fr. NL *exergum*, fr. Gk *ex* out of + *ergon* work] **:** a space on a coin, token, or medal usu. on the reverse below the central part of the design

ex·ert \ig-ˈzərt\ *vt* [L *exsertus*, pp. of *exserere* to thrust out, fr. *ex-* + *serere* to join] **1 a :** to put forth (as strength) **b :** to put (oneself) into action or to tiring effort **2 :** to bring to bear esp. with sustained effort or lasting effect **3 :** EMPLOY, WIELD

ex·er·tion \ig-ˈzər-shən\ *n* **:** the act or an instance of exerting; *esp* **:** a laborious or perceptible effort **syn** see EFFORT

ex·e·unt \ˈek-sē-(ˌ)ənt, -ˌu̇nt\ [L, they go out, fr. *exire* to go out — more at EXEAT] — used as a stage direction to specify that all or certain named characters leave the stage

ex·fo·li·ate \(ˈ)eks-ˈfō-lē-ˌāt\ *vb* [LL *exfoliatus*, pp. of *exfoliare* to strip of leaves, fr. L *ex-* + *folium* leaf — more at BLADE] *vt* **1 :** to cast off in scales, laminae, or splinters **2 :** to remove the surface of in scales or laminae **3 :** to spread or extend by or as if by opening out leaves ~ *vi* **1 :** to split into or give off scales, laminae, or body cells **2 :** to come off in a thin piece **3 :** to grow by or as if by producing or unfolding leaves — **ex·fo·li·a·tion** \(ˌ)eks-ˌfō-lē-ˈā-shən\ *n* — **ex·fo·li·a·tive** \eks-ˈfō-lē-ˌāt-iv\ *adj*

ex·hal·ant *or* **ex·hal·ent** \eks-ˈhā-lənt, ek-ˈsā-\ *adj* **:** bearing out or outward **:** EMISSIVE

ex·ha·la·tion \ˌeks-(h)ə-ˈlā-shən, ˌek-sə-\ *n* **1 :** an act of exhaling **2 :** something exhaled

ex·hale \eks-ˈhā(ə)l, ek-ˈsā(ə)l\ *vb* [ME *exalen*, fr. L *exhalare*, fr. *ex-* + *halare* to breathe; akin to L *anima* breath — more at ANIMATE] *vt* **1 a :** to breathe out **b :** to give forth (gaseous matter) **:** EMIT **2** *archaic* **:** to cause to be emitted in vapor ~ *vi* **1 :** to rise or be given off as vapor **2 :** to emit breath or vapor

¹**ex·haust** \ig-ˈzȯst\ *vb* [L *exhaustus*, pp. of *exhaurire*, fr. *ex-* + *haurire* to draw; akin to MHG *œsen* to empty, Gk *auein* to take] *vt* **1 a :** to draw off or let out completely **b :** to empty by drawing off the contents; *specif* **:** to create a vacuum in **2 a :** to use up **:** wholly expend ⟨~*ed* his patience⟩ ⟨carelessly ~*ing* the timber⟩ ⟨~*ed* our funds in a week⟩ **b :** to tire extremely or completely ⟨~*ed* by overwork⟩ **c :** to deprive of a valuable quality or constituent ⟨~ a photographic developer⟩ ⟨~ a soil of fertility⟩ **3 a :** to develop (a subject) completely **b :** to try out the whole number of ~ *vi* **:** DISCHARGE, EMPTY **syn** see DEPLETE, TIRE — **ex·haust·er** *n* — **ex·haust·ibil·i·ty** \-ˌzȯ-stə-ˈbil-ət-ē\ *n* — **ex·haust·ible** \-ˈzȯ-stə-bəl\ *adj*

²**exhaust** *n* **1 a :** the escape of used steam or gas from an engine **b :** the gas thus escaping **2 a :** the conduit through which used gases escape **b :** an arrangement for withdrawing fumes, dusts, or odors from an enclosure

ex·haus·tion \ig-ˈzȯs-chən\ *n* **:** the act or process of exhausting **:** the state of being exhausted

ex·haus·tive \ig-ˈzȯ-stiv\ *adj* **1 :** serving or tending to exhaust **2 :** testing all possibilities or considering all elements — **ex·haus·tive·ly** *adv* — **ex·haus·tive·ness** *n*

ex·haust·less \ig-ˈzȯst-ləs\ *adj* **:** not to be exhausted **:** INEXHAUSTIBLE — **ex·haust·less·ly** *adv* — **ex·haust·less·ness** *n*

¹**ex·hib·it** \ig-ˈzib-ət\ *vb* [ME *exhibiten*, fr. L *exhibitus*, pp. of *exhibēre*, fr. *ex-* + *habēre* to have, hold — more at GIVE] *vt* **1 :** to present to view: as **a :** to show or display outwardly esp. by visible signs or actions ⟨~*ed* no fear⟩ **b :** to show publicly esp. for purposes of competition or demonstration **2 :** to submit (as a document) to a court or officer in course of proceedings; *also* **:** to present or offer officially or in legal form **3 :** to administer as a remedy ~ *vi* **:** to display something for public inspection **syn** see SHOW — **ex·hib·i·tor** *also* **ex·hib·it·er** \-ˈzib-ət-ər\ *n*

²**exhibit** *n* **1 :** an act or instance of exhibiting **2 :** something exhibited **3 :** a document or material object produced and identified in court or before an examiner for use as evidence

ex·hi·bi·tion \ˌek-sə-ˈbish-ən\ *n* **1 :** an act or instance of exhibiting **2** *Brit* **:** a grant drawn from the funds of a school or university to help maintain a student **3 :** a public showing (as of works of art, objects of manufacture, or athletic skill)

ex·hi·bi·tion·er \-ˈbish-(ə-)nər\ *n, Brit* **:** one who holds an exhibition (sense 2)

ex·hi·bi·tion·ism \-ˈbish-ə-ˌniz-əm\ *n* **1 a :** a perversion marked by a tendency to indecent exposure **b :** an act of such exposure **2 :** the act or practice of behaving so as to attract attention to oneself — **ex·hi·bi·tion·ist** \-ˈbish-(ə-)nəst\ *n* — **exhibitionist** *or* **ex·hi·bi·tion·is·tic** \-ˌbish-ə-ˈnis-tik\ *adj*

ex·hib·i·tive \ig-ˈzib-ət-iv\ *adj* **:** having the function of exhibiting

ex·hib·i·to·ry \-ˈzib-ə-ˌtōr-ē, -ˌtȯr-\ *adj* **:** relating to or intended for exhibition

ex·hil·a·rant \ig-ˈzil-ə-rənt\ *adj* **:** EXHILARATING

ex·hil·a·rate \ig-ˈzil-ə-ˌrāt\ *vt* [L *exhilaratus*, pp. of *exhilarare*, fr. *ex-* + *hilarare* to gladden, fr. *hilarus* cheerful] **1 :** to make cheerful **:** ENLIVEN **2 :** REFRESH, STIMULATE — **ex·hil·a·rat·ing** *adj*

ex·hil·a·ra·tion \ig-ˌzil-ə-ˈrā-shən\ *n* **1 :** the action of exhilarating **2 :** the feeling or the state of being exhilarated

ex·hil·a·ra·tive \ig-ˈzil-ə-ˌrāt-iv\ *adj* **:** tending to exhilarate

ex·hort \ig-ˈzȯ(ə)rt\ *vb* [ME *exhorten*, fr. MF *exhorter*, fr. L *exhortari*, fr. *ex-* + *hortari* to incite] *vt* **:** to incite by argument or advice ~ *vi* **:** to give warnings or advice — **ex·hort·er** *n*

ex·hor·ta·tion \ˌeks-ˌȯr-ˈtā-shən, ˌegz-, -ər-\ *n* **1 :** an act or instance of exhorting **2 :** language intended to incite and encourage

ex·hort·ative \ig-ˈzȯrt-ət-iv\ *adj* **:** serving to exhort **:** HORTATIVE

ex·hort·ato·ry \-ə-ˌtōr-ē, -ˌtȯr-\ *adj* **:** HORTATORY

ex·hu·ma·tion \ˌeks-(ˌ)(h)yü-ˈmā-shən, ˌegz-(ˌ)(y)ü-\ *n* **:** the act or process of exhuming

ex·hume \igz-ˈ(y)üm, iks-ˈ(h)yüm\ *vt* [F or ML; F *exhumer*, fr. ML *exhumare*, fr. L *ex-* out of + *humus* earth] **1 :** DISINTER **2 :** to bring back from neglect or obscurity — **ex·hum·er** *n*

ex·i·gen·cy \ˈek-sə-jən-sē, ig-ˈzij-ən-\ *also* **ex·i·gence** \ˈek-sə-jən(t)s\ *n* **1 :** the quality or state of being exigent **2 :** such need or necessity as belongs to the occasion — usu. used in pl. **syn** see JUNCTURE, NEED

ex·i·gent \ˈek-sə-jənt\ *adj* [L *exigent-*, *exigens*, prp. of *exigere* to demand] **1 :** requiring immediate aid or action **2 :** requiring or calling for much **:** DEMANDING — **ex·i·gent·ly** *adv*

ex·i·gi·ble \ˈek-sə-jə-bəl\ *adj* **:** liable to be exacted

ex·i·gu·ity \ˌek-sə-ˈgyü-ət-ē, ˌeg-zə-\ *n* **:** SCANTINESS, SMALLNESS

ex·ig·u·ous \eg-ˈzig-yə-wəs\ *adj* [L *exiguus*, fr. *exigere*] **:** scanty in amount **syn** see MEAGER — **ex·ig·u·ous·ly** *adv* — **ex·ig·u·ous·ness** *n*

¹**ex·ile** \ˈeg-ˌzīl, ˈek-ˌsīl\ *n* [ME *exil*, fr. MF, fr. L *exilium*] **1 a :** forced removal from one's native country **b :** voluntary absence from one's country **2 a :** a person expelled from his country by authority **b :** one who separates himself from his home

²**exile** *vt* **:** to banish or expel from one's own country or home **syn** see BANISH

ex·il·ic \eg-ˈzil-ik\ *adj* **:** of or relating to exile

ex·im·i·ous \eg-ˈzim-ē-əs\ *adj* [L *eximius*, fr. *eximere* to take out — more at EXAMPLE] *archaic* **:** CHOICE, EXCELLENT

ex·ist \ig-ˈzist\ *vi* [L *exsistere* to come into being, exist, fr. *ex-* + *sistere* to stand; akin to L *stare* to stand — more at STAND] **1 a :** to have real being whether material or spiritual **b :** to have being in space and time **c :** to have being in a specified place or with respect to understood limitations or conditions **d :** to have contingent but free and responsible being **2 :** to continue to be **:** LIVE

ex·is·tence \ig-ˈzis-tən(t)s\ *n* **1 a :** reality as opposed to appearance **b :** reality as presented in experience **c** (1) **:** the totality of existent things (2) **:** a particular being **d :** sentient or living being **:** LIFE **2 a :** the state or fact of having being esp. independently of consciousness or knowledge **b :** being with respect to a limiting condition or under a particular aspect **c :** the condition of a person aware of his radically contingent yet free and responsible nature **3 :** continued or repeated manifestation

ex·is·tent \-tənt\ *adj* [L *exsistent-*, *exsistens*, prp. of *exsistere*] **1 :** having being **:** EXISTING **2 :** existing now **:** EXTANT — **existent** *n*

ex·is·ten·tial \ˌeg-(ˌ)zis-ˈten-chəl, ˌek-(ˌ)sis-\ *adj* **1 :** of, relating to, or affirming existence ⟨~ propositions⟩ **2 a :** grounded in existence or the experience of existence **:** EMPIRICAL **b :** having being in time and space **3** [trans. of Dan *eksistentiel* & G *existential*] **a :** concerned with or involving an individual as radically free and responsible **b :** EXISTENTIALIST — **ex·is·ten·tial·ly** \-ˈtench-(ə-)lē\ *adv*

ex·is·ten·tial·ism \-ˈten-chə-ˌliz-əm\ *n* **:** a chiefly 20th century philosophy that is centered upon the analysis of existence specif.

of individual human beings, that regards human existence as not exhaustively describable or understandable in idealistic or scientific terms, and that stresses the freedom and responsibility of the individual, the irreducible uniqueness of an ethical or religious situation, and usu. the isolation and subjective experiences (as of anxiety, guilt, dread, anguish) of an individual therein

¹**ex·is·ten·tial·ist** \-ləst\ *n* **:** an adherent of existentialism

²**existentialist** *adj* **1 :** of or relating to existentialism or existentialists **2 :** EXISTENTIAL 3a — **ex·is·ten·tial·is·tic** \-,ten-chə-'lis-tik\ *adj* — **ex·is·ten·tial·is·ti·cal·ly** \-ti-k(ə-)lē\ *adv*

existential operator *n* **:** a quantifier that asserts at least one value of a variable — called also *existential quantifier*

¹**ex·it** \'eg-zət, 'ek-sət\ [L, he goes out, fr. *exire* to go out — more at EXEAT] — used as a stage direction to specify who goes off stage

²**exit** *n* [L *exitus*, fr. *exitus*, pp. of *exire*] **1** [¹*exit*] **:** a departure from a stage **2 a :** the act of going out or going away **b :** DEATH **3 :** a way out of an enclosed place or space — **exit** *vi*

ex li·bris \ek-'slē-brəs, -,brēs\ *n, pl* **ex libris** [NL, from the books; used before the owner's name on bookplates] **:** BOOKPLATE

Ex·moor \'ek-,smu̇(ə)r, -,smō(ə)r, -,smȯ(ə)r\ *n* [*Exmoor*, England] **1 :** any of a breed of horned sheep of Devonshire in England valued esp. for mutton **2 :** any of a breed of hardy heavy-maned ponies native to the Exmoor district

exo- *or* **ex-** *comb form* [Gk *exō* out, outside, fr. *ex* out of — more at EX-] **1 :** outside ⟨*exo*gamy⟩ **:** outer ⟨*exo*skeleton⟩ — compare ECT-, END- **2 :** turning out ⟨*exo*ergic⟩

exo·bi·ol·o·gist \'ek-(,)sō-bī-'äl-ə-jəst\ *n* **:** a specialist in extraterrestrial biology — **exo·bi·ol·o·gy** \-jē\ *n*

exo·carp \'ek-sō-,kärp\ *n* [ISV] **:** EPICARP

exo·crine \'ek-sə-krən, -,krīn, -,krēn\ *adj* [ISV *exo-* + Gk *krinein* to separate] **:** secreting externally ⟨~ glands⟩

exo·der·mis \,ek-sō-'dər-məs\ *n* [NL] **:** a layer of the outer living cortical cells that take over the functions of the epidermis in roots lacking secondary thickening

ex·odon·tia \,ek-sə-'dän-ch(ē-)ə\ *n* [NL, fr. *ex-* + *-odontia*] **:** a branch of dentistry that deals with the extraction of teeth — **ex·odon·tist** \-'dänt-əst\ *n*

ex·o·dus \'ek-səd-əs, 'eg-zəd-\ *n* [*Exodus*, Old Testament book that tells of the departure of the Israelites fr. Egypt] **:** a mass departure **:** EMIGRATION

exo·en·zyme \,ek-(,)sō-'en-,zīm\ *n* [ISV] **:** an extracellular enzyme

exo·er·gic \,ek-sə-'wər-jik\ *adj* **:** releasing energy ⟨~ reaction⟩

exo·eryth·ro·cyt·ic \,ek-(,)sō-i-,rith-rə-'sit-ik\ *adj* **:** occurring outside the red blood cells — used of stages of malaria parasites

ex of·fi·cio \,ek-sə-'fish-ē-,ō\ *adv (or adj)* [LL] **:** by virtue or because of an office ⟨*ex officio* chairman⟩

ex·og·a·mous \ek-'säg-ə-məs\ *or* **exo·gam·ic** \,ek-sə-'gam-ik\ *adj* **:** of, relating to, or characterized by exogamy

ex·og·a·my \ek-'säg-ə-mē\ *n* **1 :** marriage outside of a specific group esp. as required by custom or law **2 :** sexual reproduction between organisms not closely related

ex·og·e·nous \ek-'säj-ə-nəs\ *adj* [F *exogène* exogenous, fr. *exo-* + *-gène* (fr. Gk *-genēs* born) — more at -GEN] **:** originating from or due to external causes: as **a :** growing from or on the outside ⟨~ spores⟩ **b** *of disease* **:** having a cause external to the body **c :** of, relating to, or produced by the metabolism of nitrogenous substances obtained from food — **ex·og·e·nous·ly** *adv*

ex·on·er·ate \ig-'zän-ə-,rāt\ *vt* [ME *exoneraten*, fr. L *exoneratus*, pp. of *exonerare* to unburden, fr. *ex-* + *oner-*, *onus* load] **1 :** to relieve of a responsibility, obligation, or hardship **2 :** to clear from accusation or blame **syn** see EXCULPATE — **ex·on·er·a·tion** \-,zän-ə-'rā-shən\ *n* — **ex·on·er·a·tive** \-'zän-ə-,rāt-iv\ *adj*

ex·oph·thal·mic \,ek-,säf-'thal-mik, -,säp-'thal-\ *adj* **:** relating to or characterized by exophthalmos

ex·oph·thal·mos \-məs, -,mäs\ *also* **ex·oph·thal·mus** \-məs\ *n* [NL, fr. Gk *exophthalmos* having prominent eyes, fr. *ex* out + *ophthalmos* eye] **:** abnormal protrusion of the eyeball

ex·o·ra·ble \'eks-(ə-)rə-bəl, 'egz-ə-rə-\ *adj* [L *exorabilis* — more at INEXORABLE] **:** capable of being moved by entreaty

ex·or·bi·tance \ig-'zȯr-bət-ən(t)s\ *n* **1 :** an exorbitant action or procedure; *esp* **:** excessive or gross deviation from rule, right, or propriety **2 :** tendency or disposition to be exorbitant

ex·or·bi·tant \-ənt\ *adj* [ME, fr. MF, fr. LL *exorbitant-*, *exorbitans*, prp. of *exorbitare* to deviate, fr. L *ex-* + *orbita* track, rut — more at ORB] **1 :** not coming within the orbit or scope of the law **2 :** exceeding in intensity, quality, or size the customary or appropriate limits **syn** see EXCESSIVE — **ex·or·bi·tant·ly** *adv*

ex·or·cise \'ek-,sȯr-,sīz, -sər-\ *vt* [ME *exorcisen*, fr. MF *exorciser*, fr. LL *exorcizare*, fr. Gk *exorkizein*, fr. *ex-* + *horkizein* to bind by oath, adjure, fr. *horkos* oath; akin to Gk *herkos* fence, L *sarcire* to mend] **1 a :** to expel by adjuration **b :** to get rid of as if by adjuration **2 :** to free of an evil spirit — **ex·or·cis·er** *n*

ex·or·cism \-,siz-əm\ *n* **1 :** the act or practice of exorcising **2 :** a spell or formula used in exorcising — **ex·or·cist** \-,sist, -səst\ *n*

ex·or·di·al \eg-'zȯrd-ē-əl\ *adj* **:** INTRODUCTORY

ex·or·di·um \-ē-əm\ *n, pl* **exordiums** *or* **ex·or·dia** \-ē-ə\ [L, fr. *exordiri* to begin, fr. *ex-* + *ordiri* to begin — more at ORDER] **:** a beginning or introduction esp. to a discourse or composition

exo·skel·e·tal \,ek-(,)sō-'skel-ət-ᵊl\ *adj* **:** of or relating to an exoskeleton

exo·skel·e·ton \-ət-ᵊn\ *n* **1 :** an external supportive covering of an animal **2 :** bony or horny parts of a vertebrate produced from epidermal tissues

ex·os·mo·sis \,ek-,säs-'mō-səs, ,ek-,säz-\ *n* [alter. of obs. *exosmose*, fr. F, fr. *ex-* + Gk *ōsmos* act of pushing — more at ENDOSMOSIS] **:** passage of material through a membrane from a region of higher to a region of lower concentration — **ex·os·mot·ic** \-'mät-ik\ *adj*

exo·sphere \'ek-sō-,sfi(ə)r\ *n* [ISV] **:** the outer fringe region of the atmosphere

exo·spore \'ek-sə-,spō(ə)r, -,spȯ(ə)r\ *n* [ISV] **:** an asexual spore formed by abstriction from a parent cell

ex·os·to·sis \,ek-,säs-'tō-səs\ *n* [NL, fr. Gk *exostōsis*, fr. *ex* out of + *osteon* bone — more at EX-, OSSEOUS] **:** a spur or bony outgrowth from a bone or the root of a tooth

ex·o·ter·ic \,ek-sə-'ter-ik\ *adj* [L & Gk; L *exotericus*, fr. Gk *exōterikos*, lit., external, fr. *exōterō* more outside, compar. of *exō* outside — more at EXO-] **1 a :** suitable to be imparted to the public ⟨the ~ doctrine⟩ **b :** belonging to the outer or less initiate circle **2 :** relating to the outside — **ex·o·ter·i·cal·ly** \-i-k(ə-)lē\ *adv*

exo·ther·mic \,ek-sō-'thər-mik\ *or* **exo·ther·mal** \-məl\ *adj* [ISV] **:** characterized by or formed with evolution of heat

ex·ot·ic \ig-'zät-ik\ *adj* [L *exoticus*, fr. Gk *exōtikos*, fr. *exō*] **1 :** introduced from another country **2** *archaic* **:** OUTLANDISH, ALIEN **3 :** strikingly or excitingly different or unusual — **exotic** *n* — **ex·ot·i·cal·ly** \-i-k(ə-)lē\ *adv* — **ex·ot·ic·ness** \-ik-nəs\ *n*

ex·ot·i·cism \ig-'zät-ə-,siz-əm\ *also* **ex·o·tism** \'ek-sə-,tiz-əm, 'eg-zə-\ *n* **1 :** the quality or state of being exotic **2 :** EXOTIC

exo·tox·in \,ek-sō-'täk-sən\ *n* [ISV] **:** a soluble poisonous substance passing into the medium during growth of a microorganism

ex·pand \ik-'spand\ *vb* [ME *expaunden*, fr. L *expandere*, fr. *ex-* + *pandere* to spread — more at FATHOM] *vt* **1 :** to increase the extent, number, or scope of **:** ENLARGE **2 a :** to express fully or in detail **b :** to write out in full ~ *vi* **1 :** to open out **2 :** to increase in extent, number, or scope **3 :** to speak or write fully or in detail **4 :** to feel generous or optimistic — **ex·pand·able** \-ə-bəl\ *adj*

syn EXPAND, AMPLIFY, SWELL, DISTEND, INFLATE, DILATE mean to increase in size or volume. EXPAND may apply whether the increase comes from within or without, or in any manner such as growth, unfolding, addition of parts; AMPLIFY implies the extension or enlargement of something inadequate; SWELL implies gradual expansion beyond a thing's original or normal limits; DISTEND implies expansion caused by pressure from within forcing extension outward; INFLATE implies expanding by introduction of air or something insubstantial and suggests a resulting vulnerability and liability to sudden collapse; DILATE applies esp. to expansion of circumference

ex·pand·er \ik-'span-dər\ *n* **:** one that expands; *specif* **:** any of several colloidal substances of high molecular weight used as a blood or plasma substitute for increasing the blood volume

ex·panse \ik-'span(t)s\ *n* [NL *expansum*, fr. L, neut. of *expansus*, pp. of *expandere*] **:** something spread out typically over a wide area: as **a :** FIRMAMENT **b :** an extensive stretch of land or sea

ex·pan·si·ble \ik-'span(t)-sə-bəl\ *adj* **:** capable of being expanded

ex·pan·sile \ik-'span(t)-səl, -'span-,sīl\ *adj* **:** of, relating to, or capable of expansion

ex·pan·sion \ik-'span-chən\ *n* **1 :** the act or process of expanding **2 :** the quality or state of being expanded **3 :** EXPANSE **4 :** the increase in volume of working fluid (as steam) in an engine cylinder after cutoff or in an internal-combustion engine after explosion **5 a :** an expanded part **b :** something that results from an act of expanding **6 :** the result of carrying out an indicated operation **:** the expression of a function in the form of a series

ex·pan·sion·ary \-chə-,ner-ē\ *adj* **:** tending toward expansion

ex·pan·sion·ism \-,niz-əm\ *n* **:** a policy or practice of usu. territorial expansion by a nation — **ex·pan·sion·ist** \'spanch-(ə-)nəst\ *n* — **expansionist** *or* **ex·pan·sion·is·tic** \-,span-chə-'nis-tik\ *adj*

ex·pan·sive \ik-'span(t)-siv\ *adj* **1 :** having a capacity or a tendency to expand **2 :** causing or tending to cause expansion **3 a :** characterized by high spirits or benevolent inclinations **b :** marked by or indicative of exaggerated euphoria and delusions of self-importance **4 :** having considerable extent **5 :** characterized by largeness or magnificence of scale ⟨~ living⟩ — **ex·pan·sive·ly** *adv* — **ex·pan·sive·ness** *n*

ex·pan·siv·i·ty \,ek-,span-'siv-ət-ē, ik-\ *n* **:** EXPANSIVENESS; *esp* **:** the capacity to expand

ex par·te \(')ek-'spärt-ē\ *adj (or adv)* [ML] **1 :** on or from one side only — used of legal proceedings **2 :** from a one-sided or partisan point of view

ex·pa·ti·ate \ek-'spā-shē-,āt\ *vi* [L *exspatiatus*, pp. of *exspatiari* to wander, digress, fr. *ex* + *spatium* space, course — more at SPEED] **1 :** to move about freely or at will **:** WANDER **2 :** to speak or write at length or in detail — **ex·pa·ti·a·tion** \(,)ek-,spā-shē-'ā-shən\ *n*

¹**ex·pa·tri·ate** \ek-'spā-trē-,āt\ *vb* [ML *expatriatus*, pp. of *expatriare* to leave one's own country, fr. L *ex* + *patria* native country, fr. fem. of *patrius* of a father, fr. *patr-*, *pater* father — more at FATHER] *vt* **1 :** to drive into exile **:** BANISH **2 :** to withdraw (oneself) from residence in or allegiance to one's native country ~ *vi* **:** to leave one's native country; *specif* **:** to renounce allegiance to one's native country — **ex·pa·tri·a·tion** \(,)ek-,spā-trē-'ā-shən\ *n*

²**ex·pa·tri·ate** \ek-'spā-trē-,āt, -trē-ət\ *adj* **:** living in a foreign country **:** EXPATRIATED — **ex·pa·tri·ate** \-,āt, -ət\ *n*

ex·pect \ik-'spekt\ *vb* [L *exspectare* to look forward to, fr. *ex-* + *spectare* to look at, fr. *spectus*, pp. of *specere* to look — more at SPY] *vi* **1** *archaic* **:** WAIT, STAY **2 :** to look forward **3 :** to be pregnant ~ *vt* **1** *archaic* **:** AWAIT **2 :** SUPPOSE, THINK **3 :** to anticipate or look forward to the coming or occurrence of **4 a :** to consider probable or certain ⟨~ to be forgiven⟩ **b :** to consider reasonable, due, or necessary **c :** to consider obligated or in duty bound — **ex·pect·able** \-'spek-tə-bəl\ *adj* — **ex·pect·ably** \-blē\ *adv*

syn EXPECT, HOPE, LOOK mean to await some occurrence or outcome. EXPECT implies a high degree of certainty and usu. involves the idea of preparing or envisioning; HOPE implies little certainty but suggests confidence or assurance in the possibility that what one desires or longs for will happen; LOOK suggests a degree of expectancy and watchfulness rather than confidence or certainty

ex·pec·tan·cy \ik-'spek-tən-sē\ *or* **ex·pec·tance** \-tən(t)s\ *n* **1 :** the act, action, or state of expecting **2 :** the state of being expected **3 a :** something expected **b :** the expected amount (as of the number of years of life) based on statistical probability

ex·pec·tant \-tənt\ *adj* **1 :** characterized by expectation **2 :** expecting the birth of a child — **expectant** *n* — **ex·pec·tant·ly** *adv*

ex·pec·ta·tion \,ek-,spek-'tā-shən, ik-\ *n* **1 :** the act or state of expecting **2 :** prospect of the future **:** ANTICIPATION **3 a :** something expected **b :** prospects of inheritance — usu. used in pl. **4 :** the state of being expected **5 a :** EXPECTANCY 3b **b :** the product of the probability that an event will occur and the amount to be received if it does occur — called also *mathematical expectation*

ex·pec·ta·tive \ik-'spek-tət-iv\ *adj* **:** relating to or constituting an object of expectation

expected value *n* **:** the mean value of a random variable

ex·pec·to·rant \ik-'spek-tə-rənt\ *adj* **:** tending to promote discharge of mucus from the respiratory tract — **expectorant** *n*

ex·pec·to·rate \-tə-,rāt\ *vb* [prob. fr. (assumed) NL *expectoratus*, pp. of *expectorare*, fr. L, to cast out of the mind, fr. *ex-* + *pector-*, *pectus* breast, soul] *vt* **1 :** to eject from the throat or lungs by coughing or hawking and spitting **2 :** SPIT ~ *vi* **1 :** to discharge matter from the throat or lungs by coughing or hawking and spitting **2 :** SPIT — **ex·pec·to·ra·tion** \-,spek-tə-'rā-shən\ *n*

ex·pe·di·en·cy \ik-'spēd-ē-ən-sē\ *or* **ex·pe·di·ence** \-ən(t)s\ *n* **1** *obs* **:** HASTE, DISPATCH **2 :** the quality or state of being suited to the end in view **3 :** cultivation of or adherence to expedient

means and methods **4 :** a means of achieving a particular end **:** EXPEDIENT — **ex·pe·di·en·tial** \ik-,spēd-ē-'en-chəl\ *adj*

1ex·pe·di·ent \ik-'spēd-ē-ənt\ *adj* [ME, fr. MF or L; MF, fr. L *expedient-, expediens* prp. of *expedire* to extricate, arrange, be advantageous, fr. *ex-* + *ped-, pes* foot] **1 :** suitable for achieving a particular end **2 :** characterized by concern with what is opportune; *specif* **:** governed by self-interest — **ex·pe·di·ent·ly** *adv*

syn POLITIC, ADVISABLE: EXPEDIENT usu. implies what is immediately advantageous without regard for ethics or concern with consistent principles; POLITIC stresses judiciousness and tactical value but usu. implies a lack of candor or sincerity in some degree; ADVISABLE applies to what is practical, prudent, or advantageous but lacks the derogatory implication of EXPEDIENT and POLITIC

2expedient *n* **1 :** something expedient **2 :** a means devised or used in an exigency **:** MAKESHIFT **syn** see RESOURCE

ex·pe·dite \'ek-spə-,dīt\ *vt* [L *expeditus*, pp. of *expedire*] **1 :** to execute promptly **2 :** to accelerate the process or progress of **:** FACILITATE **3 :** to send out **:** DISPATCH

ex·pe·dit·er *also* **ex·pe·di·tor** \-,dīt-ər\ *n* **:** one that expedites; *specif* **:** one employed to ensure adequate supplies of raw materials and equipment or to coordinate the flow of materials, tools, parts, and processed goods within a plant

ex·pe·di·tion \,ek-spə-'dish-ən\ *n* **1 a :** a journey or excursion undertaken for a specific purpose **b :** the group of persons making such a journey **2 :** efficient promptness **:** SPEED **3 :** a sending or setting forth **syn** see HASTE

ex·pe·di·tion·ary \-'dish-ə-,ner-ē\ *adj* **:** of, relating to, or constituting an expedition; *specif* **:** sent on military service abroad

ex·pe·di·tious \,ek-spə-'dish-əs\ *adj* **:** characterized by or acting with promptness and efficiency **:** SPEEDY **syn** see FAST — **ex·pe·di·tious·ly** *adv* — **ex·pe·di·tious·ness** *n*

ex·pel \ik-'spel\ *vt* **ex·pelled; ex·pel·ling** [ME *expellen*, fr. L *expellere*, fr. *ex-* + *pellere* to drive — more at FELT] **1 :** to force out ⟨~ air from the lungs⟩ **:** EJECT **2 :** to drive away; *specif* **:** DEPORT **3 :** to cut off from membership ⟨*expelled* from college⟩ **syn** see EJECT — **ex·pel·la·ble** \-'spel-ə-bəl\ *adj* — **ex·pel·lee** \,ek-,spel-'ē\ *n* — **ex·pel·ler** \ik-'spel-ər\ *n*

ex·pel·lant *or* **ex·pel·lent** \ik-'spel-ənt\ *adj* [L *expellent-, expellens*, prp. of *expellere*] **:** tending or serving to expel ⟨an ~ medicine⟩ **:** EXPULSIVE — **expellant** *n*

ex·pend \ik-'spend\ *vt* [ME *expenden*, fr. L *expendere* to weigh out, expend, fr. *ex-* + *pendere* to weigh — more at SPAN] **1 :** to pay out **:** SPEND **2 :** to consume by use **:** use up — **ex·pend·er** *n*

ex·pend·abil·i·ty \ik-,spen-də-'bil-ət-ē\ *n* **:** the quality or state of being expendable

1ex·pend·able \ik-'spen-də-bəl\ *adj* **:** that may be expended: as **a :** normally used up or consumed in service **b :** more economically replaced than rescued, salvaged, or protected; *specif* **:** deliberately sacrificed to accomplish a military mission

2expendable *n* **:** one that is expendable — usu. used in pl.

ex·pen·di·ture \ik-'spen-di-chər, -də-,chů(ə)r, -də-,t(y)ů(ə)r\ *n* [irreg. fr. *expend*] **1 :** the act or process of expending **2 :** something expended **:** DISBURSEMENT, EXPENSE

ex·pense \ik-'spen(t)s\ *n* [ME, fr. AF or LL; AF, fr. LL *expensa*, fr. L, fem. of *expensus*, pp. of *expendere*] **1 a** *archaic* **:** the act or practice of expending money **:** SPENDING **b (1)** *archaic* **:** the act or process of using up **:** CONSUMPTION **(2)** *obs* **:** LOSS **2 a :** something expended to secure a benefit or bring about a result **b :** financial burden or outlay **:** COST **c :** the charges incurred by an employee in connection with the performance of his duties — usu. used in pl. **d :** an item of business outlay chargeable against revenue for a specific period **3 :** a cause or occasion of expenditure **4 :** SACRIFICE — usu. used in the phrase *at the expense of*

expense account *n* **:** an account of expenses reimbursable to an employee

ex·pen·sive \ik-'spen(t)-siv\ *adj* **1 :** occasioning expense **2 :** high-priced **:** DEAR **syn** see COSTLY — **ex·pen·sive·ly** *adv* — **ex·pen·sive·ness** *n*

1ex·pe·ri·ence \ik-'spir-ē-ən(t)s\ *n* [ME, fr. MF, fr. L *experientia* act of trying, fr. *experient-, experiens*, prp. of *experiri* to try, fr. *ex-* + *-periri* (akin to *periculum* attempt)] **1 a :** the usu. conscious perception or apprehension of reality or of an external, bodily, or psychic event **b :** facts or events or the totality of facts or events observed **2 a :** direct participation in events **b :** the state or result of being engaged in an activity or in affairs ⟨business ~⟩ **c :** knowledge, skill, or practice derived from direct observation of or participation in events **3 a :** the conscious events that make up an individual life **b :** the events that make up the conscious past of a community or nation or mankind generally **4 :** something personally encountered, undergone, or lived through

2experience *vt* **1 :** to have experience of **:** UNDERGO **2 :** to learn by experience — **experience religion :** to undergo religious conversion

ex·pe·ri·enced \-ən(t)st\ *adj* **:** made skillful or wise through observation of or participation in a particular activity or in affairs generally **:** PRACTICED ⟨an ~ driver⟩

ex·pe·ri·en·tial \ik-,spir-ē-'en-chəl\ *adj* **:** derived from, based on, or relating to experience **:** EMPIRICAL — **ex·pe·ri·en·tial·ly** \-chə-lē\ *adv*

1ex·per·i·ment \ik-'sper-ə-mənt *also* -'spir-\ *n* [ME, fr. MF, fr. L *experimentum*, fr. *experiri*] **1 a :** TEST, TRIAL **b :** a tentative procedure or policy **c :** an operation carried out under controlled conditions in order to discover an unknown effect or law, to test or establish a hypothesis, or to illustrate a known law **2** *obs* **:** EXPERIENCE **3 :** the process of testing **:** EXPERIMENTATION

2ex·per·i·ment \-,ment\ *vi* **:** to make experiments — **ex·per·i·men·ta·tion** \ik-,sper-ə-mən-'tā-shən, -,men- *also* -,spir-\ *n* — **ex·per·i·ment·er** \-'sper-ə-,ment-ər *also* -'spir-\ *n*

ex·per·i·men·tal \ik-,sper-ə-'ment-ᵊl *also* -,spir-\ *adj* **1 :** of, relating to, or based on experience **:** EMPIRICAL **2 :** founded on or derived from experiment **3 :** serving the ends of or used as a means of experimentation **4 :** relating to or having the characteristics of experiment **:** TENTATIVE — **ex·per·i·men·tal·ly** \-ᵊl-ē\ *adv*

ex·per·i·men·tal·ism \-ᵊl-,iz-əm\ *n* **:** reliance on or advocacy of experimental or empirical principles and procedures; *specif* **:** INSTRUMENTALISM

ex·per·i·men·tal·ist \-ᵊl-əst\ *n* **:** one who experiments; *specif* **:** a person conducting scientific experiments

experiment station *n* **:** an establishment for scientific research (as in agriculture) where experiments are carried out, studies of practical application are made, and information is disseminated

1ex·pert \'ek-,spərt, ik-'\ *adj* [ME, fr. MF & L; MF, fr. L *expertus*, fr. pp. of *experiri*] **1** *obs* **:** EXPERIENCED **2 :** having, involving, or displaying special skill or knowledge derived from training or experience **syn** see PROFICIENT — **ex·pert·ly** *adv* — **ex·pert·ness** *n*

2ex·pert \'ek-,spərt\ *n* [F, fr. *expert*, adj] **:** one who has acquired special skill in or knowledge of a particular subject **:** AUTHORITY

3ex·pert \'ek-,spərt\ *vt* **:** to serve as an expert for **~** *vi* **:** to serve as an expert

ex·per·tise \,ek-,spər-'tēz, -,sper-\ *n* [F, fr. MF, expertness, fr. *expert*] **1 :** expert opinion or commentary **2 :** expertness in a particular field **:** KNOW-HOW

ex·pert·ism \'ek-,spərt-,iz-əm\ *n* **:** EXPERTISE 2

ex·pert·ize \-,īz\ *vi* **:** to give a professional opinion usu. after careful study **~** *vt* **:** to examine and give expert judgment on

ex·pi·a·ble \'ek-spē-ə-bəl\ *adj* **:** capable of being expiated

ex·pi·ate \'ek-spē-,āt\ *vb* [L *expiatus*, pp. of *expiare* to atone for, fr. *ex-* + *piare* to atone for, appease] *vt* **1** *obs* **:** to put an end to **2 a :** to atone for **b :** to pay the penalty for **c :** to make amends for **~** *vi* **:** to make expiation — **ex·pi·a·tor** \-,āt-ər\ *n*

ex·pi·a·tion \,ek-spē-'ā-shən\ *n* **1 :** the act of making atonement **2 :** the means by which atonement is made

ex·pi·a·to·ry \'ek-spē-ə-,tōr-ē, -,tòr-\ *adj* **:** serving to expiate

ex·pi·ra·tion \,ek-spə-'rā-shən\ *n* **1 a :** the act or process of releasing air from the lungs through the nose or mouth **b** *archaic* **:** the last emission of breath **:** DEATH **2 :** the fact of coming to an end **:** TERMINATION **3 :** something produced by breathing out

ex·pir·ato·ry \ek-'spī-rə-,tōr-ē, -,tòr-\ *adj* **:** of, relating to, or employed in the expiration of air from the lungs

ex·pire \ik-'spī(ə)r, *oftenest for vi3 and vt2* ek-\ *vb* [ME *expiren*, fr. MF or L; MF *expirer*, fr. L *exspirare*, fr. *ex-* + *spirare* to breathe] *vi* **1 :** to breathe one's last breath **:** DIE **2 :** to come to an end **3 :** to emit the breath **~** *vt* **1** *obs* **:** CONCLUDE **2 :** to breathe out from or as if from the lungs **3** *archaic* **:** to give off

ex·pi·ry \ik-'spī(ə)-rē, 'ek-spə-rē\ *n* **1 a :** exhalation of breath **b :** DEATH **2 :** TERMINATION; *esp* **:** the termination of a time or period fixed by law, contract, or agreement

ex·plain \ik-'splān\ *vb* [ME *explanen*, fr. L *explanare*, lit., to make level, fr. *ex-* + *planus* level, flat] *vt* **1 :** to make plain or understandable **2 :** to give the reason for or cause of **3 :** to show the logical development or relationships of **~** *vi* **:** to give an explanation — **ex·plain·able** \-'splā-nə-bəl\ *adj* — **ex·plain·er** *n*

syn EXPLAIN, EXPOUND, EXPLICATE, ELUCIDATE, INTERPRET mean to make something clear or understandable. EXPLAIN implies a making plain or intelligible what is not immediately obvious or entirely known; EXPOUND implies a careful often elaborate explanation; EXPLICATE adds the idea of a developed or detailed analysis; ELUCIDATE stresses the throwing of light upon as by offering details or motives previously obscure or only implicit; INTERPRET adds to EXPLAIN the use of imagination or sympathy or special knowledge in dealing with something that presents more than logical difficulty

ex·pla·na·tion \,ek-splə-'nā-shən\ *n* **1 :** the act or process of explaining **2 :** something that explains **3 :** a mutual discussion designed to correct a misunderstanding or reconcile differences

ex·plan·a·tive \ik-'splan-ət-iv\ *adj* **:** EXPLANATORY — **ex·plan·a·tive·ly** *adv*

ex·plan·a·to·ri·ly \ik-,splan-ə-'tōr-ə-lē, -'tòr-\ *adv* **:** in an explanatory manner

ex·plan·a·to·ry \ik-'splan-ə-,tōr-ē, -,tòr-\ *adj* **:** serving or disposed to explain ⟨~ notes⟩

ex·plant \(')ek-'splant\ *vt* **:** to remove (living tissue) to a place or medium outside the natural habitat esp. in tissue culture — **ex·plan·ta·tion** \,ek-,splan-'tā-shən\ *n*

1ex·ple·tive \'ek-splət-iv, *esp Brit* ik-'splē-tiv\ *adj* [LL *expletivus*, fr. L *expletus*, pp. of *explēre* to fill out, fr. *ex-* + *plēre* to fill] **1 :** serving to fill up ⟨~ phrases⟩ **2 :** marked by the use of expletives

2expletive *n* **1 a :** a syllable, word, or phrase inserted to fill a vacancy (as in a sentence or a metrical line) without adding to the sense; *esp* **:** a word (as *it* in "it is easy to say so" or "make it clear which you prefer") that occupies the position of the subject or object of a verb in normal English word order and anticipates a subsequent word or phrase that supplies the needed meaningful content **b :** an exclamatory word or phrase; *esp* **:** one that is obscene or profane **2 :** one that serves as a filler

ex·ple·to·ry \'ek-splə-,tōr-ē, -,tòr-\ *adj* **:** EXPLETIVE

ex·pli·ca·ble \ek-'splik-ə-bəl, 'ek-(,)splik-\ *adj* **:** capable of being explained

ex·pli·cate \'ek-splə-,kāt\ *vt* [L *explicatus*, pp. of *explicare*, lit., to unfold, fr. *ex-* + *plicare* to fold] **1 :** to give a detailed explanation of **2 :** to develop the implications of **syn** see EXPLAIN — **ex·pli·ca·tion** \,ek-splə-'kā-shən\ *n* — **ex·pli·ca·tive** \ek-'splik-ət-iv, 'ek-splə-,kāt-\ *adj* — **ex·pli·ca·tor** \'ek-splə-,kāt-ər\ *n*

ex·pli·ca·tion de texte \ek-splē-kä-syōⁿ-də-tekst, -syōⁿd-tekst\ *n, pl* **explications de texte** *same*\ [F, lit., explanation of the text] **:** a method of literary criticism involving a detailed analysis of each part of a work

ex·pli·ca·to·ry \ek-'splik-ə-,tōr-ē, 'ek-(,)splik-, -,tòr-\ *adj* **:** EXPLICATIVE

ex·plic·it \ik-'splis-ət\ *adj* [F or ML; F *explicite*, fr. ML *explicitus*, fr. L, pp. of *explicare*] **1 :** characterized by full clear expression **2 :** fully developed or formulated **3 :** unreserved and unambiguous in expression **4 :** externally visible **5 :** involving direct payment ⟨~ costs⟩ — **ex·plic·it·ly** *adv* — **ex·plic·it·ness** *n*

syn EXPRESS, SPECIFIC, DEFINITE: EXPLICIT implies such plainness and distinctness that there is no room for ambiguity or reason for difficulty in interpretation; EXPRESS implies explicitness and utterance with directness or force; SPECIFIC implies precision in reference or particularization in statement of the details covered or included; DEFINITE stresses precise and determinate limitations and the absence of uncertainty, indecision, or ambiguity

explicit function *n* **:** a mathematical function defined by an expression containing only independent variables

ex·plode \ik-ˈsplōd\ *vb* [L *explodere* to drive off the stage by clapping, fr. *ex-* + *plaudere* to clap] *vt* **1** *archaic* **:** to drive from the stage by noisy disapproval **2 :** to bring into disrepute or discredit **3 :** to cause to explode or burst noisily ~ *vi* **1 :** to burst forth with sudden violence or noise ⟨~ with wrath⟩ **2 a :** to burn suddenly so that there is violent expansion of hot gases with great disruptive force and a loud noise; *also* **:** to undergo a rapid atomic nuclear reaction with similar but more violent results **b :** to burst violently as a result of pressure from within — **ex·plod·er** *n*

ex·plod·ed *adj* **:** showing the parts separated but in correct relationship to each other ⟨an ~ view of a carburetor⟩

ex·plod·ent \ik-ˈsplōd-ᵊnt\ *n* [L *explodent-, explodens,* prp. of *explodere*] **:** EXPLOSIVE

1ex·ploit \ˈek-ˌsplȯit, ik-ˈ\ *n* [ME, outcome, success, fr. OF, fr. L *explicitum,* neut. of *explicitus,* pp.] **:** DEED, ACT; *esp* **:** a notable or heroic act **syn** see FEAT

2ex·ploit \ik-ˈsplȯit, ˈek-ˌ\ *vt* **1 a :** to turn to economic account ⟨~ a mine⟩ **b :** to take advantage of **:** UTILIZE ⟨~*ing* the qualities of the material⟩ **2 :** to make use of meanly or unjustly for one's own advantage — **ex·ploit·able** \-ə-bəl\ *adj* — **ex·ploit·er** *n*

ex·ploi·ta·tion \ˌek-ˌsplȯi-ˈtā-shən\ *n* **1 :** an act of exploiting: as **a :** utilization or working of a natural resource **b :** an unjust or improper use of another person for one's own profit or advantage **c :** coaction between organisms in which one is benefited at the expense of the other **2 :** PUBLICITY, ADVERTISING — **ex·ploit·ative** \ik-ˈsplȯit-ət-iv\ *adj* — **ex·ploit·ative·ly** *adv*

ex·plo·ra·tion \ˌek-splə-ˈrā-shən, -ˌsplōr-ˈā-, -ˌsplȯ-ˈrā-\ *n* **:** the act or an instance of exploring

ex·plor·ative \ik-ˈsplōr-ət-iv, -ˈsplȯr-\ *adj* **:** EXPLORATORY

ex·plor·ato·ry \-ə-ˌtōr-ē, -ˌtȯr-\ *adj* **:** of or relating to exploration

ex·plore \ik-ˈsplō(ə)r, -ˈsplȯ(ə)r\ *vb* [L *explorare,* fr. *ex-* + *plorare* to cry out] *vt* **1** *obs* **:** to seek for or after **2 a :** to search through or into **b :** to examine minutely esp. for diagnostic purposes **c :** to penetrate into or range over for purposes of geographical discovery ~ *vi* **:** to make or conduct a systematic search

ex·plor·er \ik-ˈsplōr-ər, -ˈsplȯr-\ *n* **:** one that explores; *esp* **:** a person who travels in search of geographical or scientific information

ex·plo·sion \ik-ˈsplō-zhən\ *n* [L *explosion-, explosio* act of driving off by clapping, fr. *explosus,* pp. of *explodere*] **1 :** the act or an instance of exploding: as **a :** a large-scale, rapid, and spectacular expansion, outbreak, or other upheaval **b :** a violent outburst of feeling **2 :** the release of stoppage-impounded breath that occurs in one kind of articulation of stop consonants

1ex·plo·sive \ik-ˈsplō-siv, -ziv\ *adj* **1 :** relating to, characterized by, or operated by explosion ⟨an ~ engine⟩ **2 :** tending to explode ⟨~ person⟩ — **ex·plo·sive·ly** *adv* — **ex·plo·sive·ness** *n*

2explosive *n* **1 :** an explosive substance **2 :** a consonant characterized by explosion in its articulation when it occurs in certain environments **:** STOP

ex·po·nent \ik-ˈspō-nənt, ˈek-ˌspō-\ *n* [L *exponent-, exponens,* prp. of *exponere*] **1 :** a symbol written above and to the right of a mathematical expression to indicate the operation of raising to a power ⟨in the expression a^3, the ~ *3* indicates that *a* is to be multiplied by itself twice⟩ **2 a :** one that expounds or interprets **b :** one that champions, advocates, or exemplifies

ex·po·nen·tial \ˌek-spə-ˈnen-chəl\ *adj* **1 :** of or relating to an exponent **2 :** involving a variable exponent ⟨10^x is an ~ function⟩ **3 :** expressible or approximately expressible by an exponential equation ⟨~ curve⟩ — **ex·po·nen·tial·ly** \-chə-lē\ *adv*

1ex·port \ek-ˈspō(ə)rt, -ˈspȯ(ə)rt, ˈek-ˌ\ *vb* [L *exportare,* fr. *ex-* + *portare* to carry] *vt* **1 :** to carry away **:** REMOVE **2 :** to carry or send (as a commodity) to some other country or place ~ *vi* **:** to export something abroad — **ex·port·able** \-ə-bəl\ *adj*

2ex·port \ˈek-ˌspō(ə)rt, -ˌspȯ(ə)rt\ *n* **1 :** something exported; *specif* **:** a commodity conveyed from one country or region to another for purposes of trade **2 :** an act of exporting **:** EXPORTATION

3export \ˈek-ˌ\ *adj* **:** of or relating to exportation or exports

ex·por·ta·tion \ˌek-ˌspōr-ˈtā-shən, -ˌspȯr-, -spər-\ *n* **:** an act of exporting; *also* **:** a commodity exported

ex·port·er \ek-ˈspōrt-ər, -ˈspȯrt-, ˈek-ˌ\ *n* **:** one that exports; *specif* **:** a wholesaler who sells to merchants or industrial consumers in foreign countries

1ex·pose \ik-ˈspōz\ *vt* [ME *exposen,* fr. MF *exposer,* fr. L *exponere* to set forth, explain (perf. indic. *exposui*), fr. *ex-* + *ponere* to put, place — more at POSITION] **1 a :** to deprive of shelter, protection, or care ⟨~ troops needlessly⟩ **b :** to submit or subject to an action or influence; *specif* **:** to subject (a sensitive photographic film, plate, or paper) to the action of radiant energy **c :** to abandon (an infant) esp. by leaving in the open **:** DESERT **2 :** to lay open to view: as **a :** to offer publicly for sale **b :** to exhibit for public veneration **c :** to reveal the face of (a playing card) **3 a :** to bring to light (as something shameful) **:** UNMASK **b :** to disclose the faults or crimes of ⟨~ a murderer⟩ **syn** see SHOW — **ex·pos·er** *n*

2ex·po·sé *or* **ex·po·se** \ˌek-(ˌ)spō-ˈzā, -spə-\ *n* [F *exposé,* fr. pp. of *exposer*] **1 :** a formal recital or exposition of facts **:** STATEMENT **2 :** an exposure of something discreditable

ex·posed \ik-ˈspōzd\ *adj* **1 :** open to view ⟨an ~ card⟩ **2 :** not shielded or protected ⟨an ~ electric wire⟩ **syn** see LIABLE

ex·pos·it \ik-ˈspäz-ət\ *vt* [L *expositus,* pp. of *exponere*] **:** EXPOUND

ex·po·si·tion \ˌek-spə-ˈzish-ən\ *n* **1 :** a setting forth of the meaning or purpose (as of a writing) **2 a :** discourse or an example of it designed to convey information or explain what is difficult to understand **b** (1) **:** the first part of a musical composition in sonata form (2) **:** the opening section of a fugue **3 :** an act or an instance of exposing: as **a :** abandonment of an infant **b :** a public exhibition or show — **ex·po·si·tion·al** \-ˈzish-nəl, -ən-ᵊl\ *adj*

ex·pos·i·tive \ik-ˈspäz-ət-iv\ *adj* **:** DESCRIPTIVE, EXPOSITORY

ex·pos·i·tor \-ət-ər\ *n* [ME *expositour,* fr. MF *expositeur,* fr. LL *expositor,* fr. L *expositus*] **:** one who expounds or explains

ex·pos·i·to·ry \ik-ˈspäz-ə-ˌtōr-ē, -ˌtȯr-\ *adj* **:** of, relating to, or containing exposition ⟨~ writing⟩

1ex post fac·to \ˌek-ˌspōst-ˈfak-(ˌ)tō\ *adj* [LL, from a thing done afterward] **1 :** done, made, or formulated after the fact ⟨*ex post facto* approval⟩ **2 :** disregarding or altering the previous status or setting of the event or thing concerning which a conclusion is reached or at which action is directed ⟨*ex post facto* laws⟩

2ex post facto *adv* **:** after the fact **:** RETROACTIVELY

ex·pos·tu·late \ik-ˈspäs-chə-ˌlāt\ *vb* [L *expostulatus,* pp. of *expostulare* to demand, dispute, fr. *ex-* + *postulare* to ask for] *vt, obs* **:** DISCUSS, EXAMINE ~ *vi* **:** to reason earnestly with a person for purposes of dissuasion or remonstrance **syn** see OBJECT

ex·pos·tu·la·tion \ik-ˌspäs-chə-ˈlā-shən\ *n* **:** an act or an instance of expostulating **:** REMONSTRANCE — **ex·pos·tu·la·to·ry** \-ˈspäs-chə-lə-ˌtōr-ē, -ˌtȯr-\ *adj*

ex·po·sure \ik-ˈspō-zhər\ *n* **1 :** the act or an instance of exposing: as **a :** disclosure to view **b** (1) **:** UNMASKING (2) **:** PRESENTATION, EXPOSITION **c :** an act of abandoning esp. in the open **d** (1) **:** the act of exposing a sensitized photographic material (2) **:** a section of a film for an individual picture (3) **:** the total amount of light or other radiant energy received per unit area on the sensitized material usu. expressed for cameras in terms of the time and the lens *f*-number **2 a :** a condition or an instance of being exposed; *specif* **:** the condition of being exposed to the elements **b :** a position with respect to the points of the compass or to climatic or weather influences ⟨a western ~⟩

exposure meter *n* **:** a device for indicating correct photographic exposure under varying conditions of illumination

ex·pound \ik-ˈspau̇nd\ *vb* [ME *expounden,* fr. MF *expondre,* fr. L *exponere* to explain] *vt* **1 a :** to set forth **:** STATE **b :** to defend with argument **2 :** to make clear the meaning of **:** INTERPRET ~ *vi* **:** to make a statement **syn** see EXPLAIN — **ex·pound·er** *n*

1ex·press \ik-ˈspres\ *adj* [ME, fr. MF *expres,* fr. L *expressus,* pp. of *exprimere* to press out, express, fr. *ex-* + *premere* to press — more at PRESS] **1 a :** directly and distinctly stated **:** EXPLICIT **b :** EXACT, PRECISE **2 a :** designed for or adapted to its purpose **b :** of a particular sort **:** SPECIFIC **3 a :** traveling at high speed; *specif* **:** traveling with few or no stops ⟨~ train⟩ **b :** adapted or suitable for travel at high speed **c** *Brit* **:** designated to be delivered without delay by special messenger **syn** see EXPLICIT

2express *adv* **1** *obs* **:** EXPRESSLY **2 :** by express ⟨send a package ~⟩

3express *n* **1 a** *Brit* **:** a messenger sent on a special errand **b** *Brit* **:** a dispatch conveyed by a special messenger **c** (1) **:** a system for the prompt and safe transportation of parcels, money, or goods at rates higher than standard freight charges (2) **:** a company operating such a merchandise freight service (3) **:** the goods or shipments so transported **d** *Brit* **:** SPECIAL DELIVERY **2 :** an express vehicle

4express *vt* [ME *expressen,* fr. MF & L; MF *expresser,* fr. OF, fr. *expres,* adj., fr. L *expressus,* pp.] **1 a :** DELINEATE, DEPICT **b :** to represent in words **:** STATE **c :** to make known **:** SHOW **d :** to make known the opinions or feeling of (oneself) **e :** to give expression to the artistic or creative impulses or abilities of (oneself) **f :** to represent by a sign or symbol **:** SYMBOLIZE **2 a :** to press or squeeze out **b :** to subject to pressure so as to extract something **3 :** to send by express — **ex·press·er** *n* — **ex·press·ible** \-ə-bəl\ *adj*

syn EXPRESS, VENT, UTTER, VOICE, BROACH, AIR mean to let out what one thinks or feels. EXPRESS suggests an impulse to reveal in any manner, as in words, gestures, actions, or in what one makes or produces; VENT stresses a strong inner compulsion to express esp. in words; UTTER implies the use of the voice not necessarily in articulate speech; VOICE does not necessarily imply vocal utterance but does imply expression or formulation in words; BROACH adds the implication of disclosing for the first time something long thought over or reserved for a suitable occasion; AIR implies an exposing or parading of one's views often in order to gain relief or sympathy or attention

ex·press·age \ik-ˈspres-ij\ *n* **:** a carrying of parcels by express; *also* **:** a charge for such carrying

ex·pres·sion \ik-ˈspresh-ən\ *n* **1 a :** an act, process, or instance of representing in words or some other medium **:** UTTERANCE **b** (1) **:** something that manifests, embodies, or symbolizes something else (2) **:** a significant word or phrase (3) **:** a mathematical or logical symbol or a meaningful combination of symbols (4) **:** the detectable effect of a gene; *also* **:** EXPRESSIVITY **2 a :** a mode, means, or use of significant representation or symbolism; *esp* **:** felicitous or vivid indication or depiction of mood or sentiment **b** (1) **:** the quality or fact of being expressive (2) **:** facial aspect or vocal intonation as indicative of feeling **3 :** an act or product of pressing out — **ex·pres·sion·al** \-ˈspresh-nəl, -ən-ᵊl\ *adj*

ex·pres·sion·ism \ik-ˈspresh-ə-ˌniz-əm\ *n* **:** a theory or practice in art of seeking to depict not objective reality but the subjective emotions and responses that objects and events arouse in the artist — **ex·pres·sion·ist** \-ˈspresh-(ə-)nəst\ *n or adj* — **ex·pres·sion·is·tic** \-ˌspresh-ə-ˈnis-tik\ *adj* — **ex·pres·sion·is·ti·cal·ly** \-ˈnis-ti-k(ə-)lē\ *adv*

ex·pres·sion·less \ik-ˈspresh-ən-ləs\ *adj* **:** lacking expression ⟨an ~ face⟩ — **ex·pres·sion·less·ly** *adv* — **ex·pres·sion·less·ness** *n*

ex·pres·sive \ik-ˈspres-iv\ *adj* **1 :** of or relating to expression **2 :** serving to express, utter, or represent **3 :** full of expression **:** SIGNIFICANT — **ex·pres·sive·ly** *adv* — **ex·pres·sive·ness** *n*

ex·pres·siv·i·ty \ˌek-ˌspres-ˈiv-ət-ē\ *n* **1 :** the relative capacity of a gene to modify the organism of which it is a part **2 :** the quality of being expressive

ex·press·ly \ik-ˈspres-lē\ *adv* **1 :** in an express manner **:** EXPLICITLY **2 :** for the express purpose **:** PARTICULARLY

ex·press·man \ik-ˈspres-ˌman, -mən\ *n* **:** a person employed in the express business

ex·press·way \ik-ˈspres-ˌwā\ *n* **:** a high-speed divided highway for through traffic with access partially or fully controlled and grade separations at important intersections with other roads

ex·pro·pri·ate \ek-ˈsprō-prē-ˌāt\ *vt* [ML *expropriatus,* pp. of *expropriare,* fr. L *ex-* + *proprius* own] **1 :** to deprive of possession or proprietary rights **2 :** to transfer (the property of another) to one's own possession — **ex·pro·pri·a·tor** \-ˌāt-ər\ *n*

ex·pro·pri·a·tion \(ˌ)ek-ˌsprō-prē-ˈā-shən\ *n* **:** the act of expropriating or the state of being expropriated; *specif* **:** the action of the state in taking or modifying the property rights of an individual in the exercise of its sovereignty

ex·pulse \ik-ˈspəls\ *vt* **:** EXPEL

ex·pul·sion \ik-ˈspəl-shən\ *n* [ME, fr. L *expulsion-, expulsio,* fr. *expulsus,* pp. of *expellere* to expel] **:** the act of expelling or the state of being expelled — **ex·pul·sive** \-ˈspəl-siv\ *adj*

ex·punc·tion \ik-ˈspəŋ(k)-shən\ *n* [L *expunctus,* pp. of *expungere*] **:** the act of expunging or the state of being expunged **:** ERASURE

ex·punge \ik-ˈspənj\ *vt* [L *expungere* to mark for deletion by dots, fr. *ex-* + *pungere* to prick] **1 :** to strike out, obliterate, or mark for deletion **2 :** ANNIHILATE **syn** see ERASE — **ex·pung·er** *n*

ex·pur·gate \'ek-spər-ˌgāt\ *vt* [L *expurgatus*, pp. of *expurgare*, fr. *ex-* + *purgare* to purge] **:** to cleanse of something morally harmful, offensive, or erroneous; *esp* **:** to expunge objectionable parts from before publication or presentation — **ex·pur·ga·tion** \ˌek-spər-'gā-shən\ *n* — **ex·pur·ga·tor** \'ek-spər-ˌgāt-ər\ *n*

ex·pur·ga·to·ri·al \ik-ˌspər-gə-'tōr-ē-əl, ˌek-, -'tȯr-\ *adj* **:** relating to expurgation or an expurgator **:** EXPURGATORY

ex·pur·ga·to·ry \ik-'spər-gə-ˌtōr-ē, -ˌtȯr-\ *adj* **:** serving to purify from something morally harmful, offensive, or erroneous

[1]**ex·qui·site** \ek-'skwiz-ət, 'ek-(ˌ)skwiz-\ *adj* [ME *exquisit*, fr. L *exquisitus*, fr. pp. of *exquirere* to search out, fr. *ex-* + *quaerere* to seek] **1 :** carefully selected **:** CHOICE **2** *archaic* **:** ACCURATE **3 a :** marked by flawless craftsmanship or by beautiful, ingenious, delicate, or elaborate execution **b :** keenly appreciative **:** DISCRIMINATING **c :** ACCOMPLISHED, PERFECTED **4 a :** pleasing through beauty, fitness, or perfection **b :** ACUTE, INTENSE **syn** see CHOICE — **ex·qui·site·ly** *adv* — **ex·qui·site·ness** *n*

[2]**exquisite** *n* **:** one who is too fastidious in dress or ornament

ex·san·gui·nate \ek(s)-'saŋ-gwə-ˌnāt\ *vt* [L *exsanguinatus* bloodless, fr. *ex-* + *sanguin-*, *sanguis* blood] **:** to drain of blood — **ex·san·gui·na·tion** \(ˌ)ek(s)-ˌsaŋ-gwə-'nā-shən\ *n*

ex·scind \ek-'sind\ *vt* [L *exscindere*, fr. *ex-* + *scindere* to cut, tear — more at SHED] **:** to cut off or out **:** EXCISE

ex·sect \(')ek(s)-'sekt\ *vt* [L *exsectus*, pp. of *exsecare*, fr. *ex-* + *secare* to cut] **:** to cut out — **ex·sec·tion** \ek-'sek-shən\ *n*

ex·sert \ek-'sərt\ *vt* [L *exsertus*, pp. of *exserere*] **:** to thrust out — **ex·ser·tile** \-'sərt-ᵊl, -'sər-ˌtīl\ *adj* — **ex·ser·tion** \-'sər-shən\ *n*

ex·sert·ed *adj* **:** projecting beyond an enclosing organ or part

ex·sic·cate \'ek-si-ˌkāt\ *vt* [L *exsiccatus*, pp. of *exsiccare*, fr. *ex-* + *siccare* to dry, fr. *siccus* dry — more at SACK] **:** to remove moisture from **:** DRY — **ex·sic·ca·tion** \ˌek-si-'kā-shən\ *n*

ex·stip·u·late \(')ek(s)-'stip-yə-lət\ *adj* **:** having no stipules

ex·tant \'ek-stənt, -ˌstant, ek-'stant\ *adj* [L *exstant-*, *exstans*, prp. of *exstare* to stand out, be in existence, fr. *ex-* + *stare* to stand — more at STAND] **1** *archaic* **:** standing out or above **2 a :** currently or actually existing **b :** not destroyed or lost

ex·tem·po·ral \ek-'stem-p(ə-)rəl\ *adj* [L *extemporalis*, fr. *ex tempore*] *archaic* **:** EXTEMPORANEOUS — **ex·tem·po·ral·ly** \-ē\ *adv*

ex·tem·po·ra·ne·ous \(ˌ)ek-ˌstem-pə-'rā-nē-əs\ *adj* [LL *extemporaneus*] **1 a** (1) **:** composed, performed, or uttered on the spur of the moment **:** IMPROMPTU (2) **:** carefully prepared but delivered without notes or text **b :** skilled at or given to extemporaneous utterance **2 :** provided, made, or put to use as an expedient — **ex·tem·po·ra·ne·ous·ly** *adv* — **ex·tem·po·ra·ne·ous·ness** *n*

ex·tem·po·rar·i·ly \ik-ˌstem-pə-'rer-ə-lē, (ˌ)ek-\ *adv* **:** EXTEMPORANEOUSLY

ex·tem·po·rary \ik-'stem-pə-ˌrer-ē\ *adj* **:** EXTEMPORANEOUS

ex·tem·po·re \ik-'stem-pə-(ˌ)rē\ *adv* [L *ex tempore*, fr. *ex* + *tempore*, abl. of *tempus* time] **:** EXTEMPORANEOUSLY — **extempore** *adj*

ex·tem·po·ri·za·tion \ik-ˌstem-pə-rə-'zā-shən\ *n* **1 :** the act of extemporizing **:** IMPROVISATION **2 :** something extemporized

ex·tem·po·rize \ik-'stem-pə-ˌrīz\ *vi* **1 :** to do something extemporaneously **:** IMPROVISE; *esp* **:** to speak extemporaneously **2 :** to get along in a makeshift manner ~ *vt* **:** to compose, perform, or utter extemporaneously **:** IMPROVISE — **ex·tem·po·riz·er** *n*

ex·tend \ik-'stend\ *vb* [ME *extenden*, fr. MF or L; MF *estendre*, fr. L *extendere*, fr. *ex-* + *tendere* to stretch — more at THIN] *vt* **1** [ME *extenden*, fr. ML *extendere* (fr. L) or AF *estendre*, fr. OF] **a** *Brit* **:** to assess the value of (as lands) **b** *Brit* **:** to take possession of by a writ of extent **c** *obs* **:** to take by force **2 :** to spread or stretch forth **:** UNBEND **3 a :** to stretch out to fullest length **b :** to cause (as a horse) to move at full stride **c :** to exert (oneself) to full capacity **d** (1) **:** to increase the bulk of (a product) by the addition of a cheaper substance (2) **:** ADULTERATE **4 a :** to make the offer of **:** PROFFER **b :** to make available **5 a :** to cause to reach **b :** to cause to be longer; *specif* **:** to prolong the time of payment of **c :** ADVANCE, FURTHER **6 a :** to cause to be of greater area or volume **:** ENLARGE **b :** to increase the scope, meaning, or application of **:** BROADEN **c** *archaic* **:** EXAGGERATE ~ *vi* **1 :** to stretch out in distance, space, or time **:** REACH **2 :** to span an interval of distance, space, or time — **ex·tend·ible** \-'sten-də-bəl\ *adj*

syn LENGTHEN, ELONGATE, PROLONG, PROTRACT: EXTEND and LENGTHEN both imply a drawing out in space or time, but LENGTHEN can apply to one direction or dimension only whereas EXTEND may imply increase in width or compass or area or range as well as length; ELONGATE suggests a stretching out resulting in a long narrow shape or in unusual length; PROLONG suggests chiefly increase in duration esp. beyond usual limits; PROTRACT adds to PROLONG the implications of needlessness, boredom, vexation, indefiniteness

ex·tend·ed *adj* **1 :** PROLONGED **2 a :** fully stretched out **b :** INTENSIVE **3 :** EXTENSIVE — **ex·tend·ed·ly** *adv* — **ex·tend·ed·ness** *n*

extended play *n* **:** a 45-rpm phonograph record with a playing time of about 6 to 8 minutes

ex·tend·er \ik-'sten-dər\ *n* **:** a substance added to a product esp. in the capacity of a diluent, adulterant, or modifier

ex·ten·si·bil·i·ty \ik-ˌsten(t)-sə-'bil-ət-ē\ *n* **:** capability of being extended

ex·ten·si·ble \ik-'sten(t)-sə-bəl\ *adj* **:** capable of being extended

ex·ten·sile \ik-'sten(t)-səl, -'sten-ˌsīl\ *adj* **:** EXTENSIBLE

ex·ten·sion \ik-'sten-chən\ *n* [ME, fr. MF or LL; MF, fr. LL *extension-*, *extensio*, fr. L *extensus*, pp. of *extendere*] **1 a :** the action of extending **:** state of being extended **b :** something extended **2 a :** the total range over which something extends **:** COMPASS **b :** DENOTATION 2 **3 a :** the stretching of a fractured or luxated limb so as to restore it to its natural position **b :** the straightening out of a flexed limb **4 :** a property whereby something occupies space **5 :** an increase in length of time; *specif* **:** an agreement on or concession of additional time **6 :** the making available of the educational resources of an institution by special programs (as correspondence courses) to persons otherwise unable to take advantage of such resources **7 a :** a part constituting an addition **b :** a section forming an additional length **c :** an extra telephone connected to the principal line

ex·ten·sion·al \ik-'stench-nəl, -'sten-chən-ᵊl\ *adj* **1 :** of, relating to, or marked by extension; *specif* **:** DENOTATIVE **2 :** concerned with objective reality — **ex·ten·sion·al·i·ty** \-ˌsten-chə-'nal-ət-ē\ *n* — **ex·ten·sion·al·ly** \-'stench-nə-lē, -'sten-chən-ᵊl-ē\ *adv*

ex·ten·si·ty \ik-'sten(t)-sət-ē\ *n* **1 a :** the quality of having extension **b :** degree of extension **:** RANGE **2 :** an attribute of sensation whereby space or size is perceived

ex·ten·sive \ik-'sten(t)-siv\ *adj* **1 :** EXTENSIONAL **2 :** having wide or considerable extent **3 :** of, relating to, or constituting farming in which large areas of land are utilized with minimum outlay and labor — **ex·ten·sive·ly** *adv* — **ex·ten·sive·ness** *n*

ex·ten·som·e·ter \ˌek-ˌsten-'säm-ət-ər\ *n* [*extension* + *-o-* + *-meter*] **:** an instrument for measuring minute deformations of test specimens caused by tension, compression, bending, or twisting

ex·ten·sor \ik-'sten(t)-sər\ *n* **:** a muscle serving to extend a limb or other bodily part

ex·tent \ik-'stent\ *n* [ME, fr. AF & MF; AF *extente* land valuation, fr. MF, area, surveying of land, fr. *extendre* to extend] **1** *archaic* **:** valuation (as of land) in Great Britain esp. for taxation **2 a :** seizure in execution of a writ of extent in Great Britain or the condition of being so seized **b :** a writ giving to a creditor temporary possession of his debtor's property **3 a** (1) **:** the range or distance over which something extends (2) **:** the point, degree, or limit to which something extends **b :** the amount of space which something occupies **c :** an extended tract or region

ex·ten·u·ate \ik-'sten-yə-ˌwāt\ *vt* [L *extenuatus*, pp. of *extenuare*, fr. *ex-* + *tenuis* thin — more at THIN] **1 a** *archaic* **:** to make light of **b :** to lessen or to try to lessen the seriousness or extent of by making partial excuses **:** MITIGATE **c** *obs* **:** DISPARAGE **2** *archaic* **a :** to make thin or emaciated **b :** to lessen the strength or effect of — **ex·ten·u·a·tor** \-ˌwāt-ər\ *n* — **ex·ten·u·a·to·ry** \-wə-ˌtōr-ē, -ˌtȯr-\ *adj*

ex·ten·u·at·ing *adj* **:** that extenuates ⟨an ~ circumstance⟩

ex·ten·u·a·tion \ik-ˌsten-yə-'wā-shən\ *n* **1 :** the act of extenuating or state of being extenuated; *esp* **:** partial justification **2 :** something extenuating; *esp* **:** a partial excuse

[1]**ex·te·ri·or** \ek-'stir-ē-ər\ *adj* [L, compar. of *exter*, *exterus* being on the outside, foreign, fr. *ex*] **1 :** EXTERNAL, OUTER **2 a :** happening or coming from outside **b :** suitable for use on outside surfaces — **ex·te·ri·or·ly** *adv*

[2]**exterior** *n* **1 a :** an exterior part or surface **:** OUTSIDE **b :** outward manner or appearance **2 :** a representation of an outdoor scene

exterior angle *n* **1 :** the angle between a side of a polygon and an adjacent side prolonged **2 :** an angle between a line crossing two parallel lines and either of the latter on the outside

ex·te·ri·or·i·ty \(ˌ)ek-ˌstir-ē-'ȯr-ət-ē, -'är-\ *n* **:** the quality or state of being exterior or exteriorized **:** EXTERNALITY

ex·te·ri·or·iza·tion \ek-ˌstir-ē-ə-rə-'zā-shən\ *n* **:** the act of exteriorizing or the state of being exteriorized

ex·te·ri·or·ize \ek-'stir-ē-ə-ˌrīz\ *vt* **1 :** EXTERNALIZE **2 :** to bring out of the abdomen (as for surgery)

ex·ter·mi·nate \ik-'stər-mə-ˌnāt\ *vt* [L *exterminatus*, pp. of *exterminare*, fr. *ex-* + *terminus* boundary — more at TERM] **:** to get rid of completely **:** ANNIHILATE — **ex·ter·mi·na·tion** \-ˌstər-mə-'nā-shən\ *n* — **ex·ter·mi·na·tor** \-'stər-mə-ˌnāt-ər\ *n*

syn EXTERMINATE, EXTIRPATE, ERADICATE, UPROOT mean to effect the destruction or abolition of something. EXTERMINATE implies complete and immediate extinction by killing off all individuals; EXTIRPATE implies extinction of a race, family, species, or sometimes of an idea or doctrine by destruction or removal of its means of propagation; ERADICATE implies the driving out or elimination of something that has established itself; UPROOT implies a forcible or violent removal and stresses displacement or dislodgment rather than immediate destruction

ex·ter·mi·na·to·ry \ik-'stər-mə-nə-ˌtōr-ē, -ˌtȯr-\ *adj* **:** of, relating to, or marked by extermination

ex·ter·mine \ik-'stər-mən\ *vt*, *obs* **:** EXTERMINATE

[1]**ex·tern** \ek-'stərn\ *adj* [MF or L; MF *externe*, fr. L *externus*] *archaic* **:** EXTERNAL, OUTER

[2]**ex·tern** *also* **ex·terne** \'ek-ˌstərn\ *n* **:** a person connected with an institution but not living or boarding in it; *specif* **:** a nonresident doctor or medical student at a hospital

[1]**ex·ter·nal** \ek-'stərn-ᵊl\ *adj* [ME, fr. L *externus* external, fr. *exter*] **1 a :** capable of being perceived outwardly ⟨~ signs of a disease⟩ **b** (1) **:** having merely the outward appearance of something **:** SUPERFICIAL (2) **:** not intrinsic or essential ⟨~ circumstances⟩ **2 a :** of, relating to, or connected with the outside or an outer part **b :** applied or applicable to the outside **3 a** (1) **:** situated outside, apart, or beyond; *specif* **:** situated away from the mesial plane (2) **:** arising or acting from outside ⟨~ force⟩ **b :** of or relating to dealings or relationships with foreign countries **c :** having existence independent of the mind ⟨~ reality⟩ — **ex·ter·nal·ly** \-ᵊl-ē\ *adv*

[2]**external** *n* **:** something that is external: as **a** *archaic* **:** an outer part **b :** an external feature or aspect — usu. used in pl.

external–combustion engine *n* **:** a heat engine (as a steam engine) that derives its heat from fuel consumed outside the engine cylinder

ex·ter·nal·ism \ek-'stərn-ᵊl-ˌiz-əm\ *n* **1 :** EXTERNALITY 1 **2 :** attention to externals; *esp* **:** excessive preoccupation with externals

ex·ter·nal·i·ty \ˌek-ˌstər-'nal-ət-ē\ *n* **1 :** the quality or state of being external or externalized **2 :** something that is external

ex·ter·nal·iza·tion \ek-ˌstərn-ᵊl-ə-'zā-shən\ *n* **1 a :** the action or process of externalizing **b :** the quality or state of being externalized **2 :** something externalized **:** EMBODIMENT

ex·ter·nal·ize \ek-'stərn-ᵊl-ˌīz\ *vt* **1 :** to make external or externally manifest **:** EMBODY **2 :** to attribute to causes outside the self **:** RATIONALIZE ⟨~ his failure⟩

external respiration *n* **:** exchange of gases between the external environment and a distributing system of the animal body or between the alveoli of the lungs and the blood

ex·tero·cep·tive \ˌek-stə-rō-'sep-tiv\ *adj* [L *exter* + E *-o-* + *-ceptive* (as in *receptive*)] **:** activated by, relating to, or being stimuli impinging on the organism from outside

ex·tero·cep·tor \-tər\ *n* [NL, fr. L *exter* + NL *-o-* + *-ceptor* (as in *receptor*)] **:** a sense organ excited by exteroceptive stimuli

ex·ter·ri·to·ri·al \ˌek-ˌster-ə-'tōr-ē-əl, -'tȯr-\ *adj* **:** EXTRATERRITORIAL — **ex·ter·ri·to·ri·al·i·ty** \-ˌtōr-ē-'al-ət-ē, -ˌtȯr-\ *n*

[1]**ex·tinct** \ik-'stiŋ(k)t, 'ek-ˌ\ *adj* [ME, fr. L *exstinctus*, pp. of *exstinguere*] **1 a :** no longer burning **b :** no longer active ⟨an ~

volcano⟩ **2 :** no longer existing ⟨an ~ animal⟩ **3 a :** gone out of use **:** SUPERSEDED **b :** having no qualified claimant ⟨an ~ title⟩
2**extinct** *vt, archaic* **:** EXTINGUISH
ex·tinc·tion \ik-ˈstiŋ(k)-shən\ *n* **1 :** the act of making extinct or causing to be extinguished **2 :** the condition or fact of being extinct or extinguished
ex·tinc·tive \ik-ˈstiŋ(k)-tiv\ *adj* **:** tending or serving to extinguish or make extinct
ex·tin·guish \ik-ˈstiŋ-gwish\ *vt* [L *exstinguere* (fr. *ex-* + *stinguere* to extinguish) + E *-ish* (as in *abolish*); akin to L in*stigare* to incite — more at STICK] **1 a :** to cause to cease burning **:** QUENCH **b** (1) **:** to cause to die out **:** DESTROY (2) **:** to reduce to silence or ineffectiveness **c :** to dim the brightness of **:** ECLIPSE **2 a :** to cause to be void **:** NULLIFY ⟨~ a claim⟩ **b :** to get rid of usu. by payment ⟨~ a debt⟩ **syn** see ABOLISH — **ex·tin·guish·able** \-ə-bəl\ *adj* — **ex·tin·guish·er** \-ər\ *n* — **ex·tin·guish·ment** \-mənt\ *n*
ex·tir·pate \ˈek-stər-ˌpāt, ek-ˈstər-\ *vt* [L *exstirpatus*, pp. *exstirpare*, fr. *ex-* + *stirp-*, *stirps* trunk, root — more at TORPID] **1 a :** to pull up by the root **b :** to wipe out **2 :** to cut out by surgery **syn** see EXTERMINATE — **ex·tir·pa·tion** \ˌek-(ˌ)stər-ˈpā-shən\ *n* — **ex·tir·pa·tive** \ˈek-stər-ˌpāt-iv, ek-ˈstər-pət-\ *adj* — **ex·tir·pa·tor** \-ˌpāt-ər\ *n*
ex·tol *also* **ex·toll** \ik-ˈstōl\ *vt* **ex·tolled; ex·tol·ling** [ME *extollen*, fr. L *extollere*, fr. *ex-* + *tollere* to lift up] **:** to praise highly **:** GLORIFY — **ex·tol·ler** *n* — **ex·tol·ment** \-ˈstōl-mənt\ *n*
ex·tor·sion \ek-ˈstȯr-shən, ˈek-ˌ\ *n* **:** outward rotation (as of a body part) about an axis or fixed point
ex·tort \ik-ˈstȯ(ə)rt\ *vt* [L *extortus*, pp. of *extorquēre* to wrench out, extort, fr. *ex-* + *torquēre* to twist] **:** to obtain from a person by force or undue or illegal power or ingenuity **:** WRING **syn** see EDUCE — **ex·tort·er** *n* — **ex·tor·tive** \-ˈstȯrt-iv\ *adj*
ex·tor·tion \ik-ˈstȯr-shən\ *n* **1 :** the act or practice of extorting esp. money or other property; *specif* **:** the offense committed by an official engaging in such practice **2 :** something extorted; *esp* **:** a gross overcharge
ex·tor·tion·ary \-shə-ˌner-ē\ *adj, archaic* **:** EXTORTIONATE
ex·tor·tion·ate \ik-ˈstȯr-sh(ə-)nət\ *adj* **1 :** characterized by extortion **2 :** EXCESSIVE, EXORBITANT — **ex·tor·tion·ate·ly** *adv*
ex·tor·tion·er \-sh(ə-)nər\ *n* **:** one that practices extortion
ex·tor·tion·ist \-sh(ə-)nəst\ *n* **:** EXTORTIONER
1**ex·tra** \ˈek-strə\ *adj* [prob. short for *extraordinary*] **1 a :** more than is due, usual, or necessary **:** ADDITIONAL ⟨~ work⟩ **b :** subject to an additional charge **2 :** SUPERIOR ⟨~ quality⟩
2**extra** *n* **1 :** something extra or additional: as **a :** an added charge **b :** a special edition of a newspaper **c :** an additional worker; *specif* **:** one hired to act in a group scene in a motion picture or stage production **2 :** something of superior quality or grade
3**extra** *adv* **:** beyond the usual size, extent, or degree ⟨~ long⟩
extra- *prefix* [ME, fr. L, fr. *extra*, adv. & prep., outside, except, beyond, fr. *exter* being on the outside — more at EXTERIOR] **:** outside **:** beyond ⟨*extra*judicial⟩
extra–base hit *n* **:** a hit in baseball good for more than one base
ex·tra·cel·lu·lar \ˌek-strə-ˈsel-yə-lər\ *adj* **:** situated or occurring outside a cell or the cells of the body — **ex·tra·cel·lu·lar·ly** *adv*
1**ex·tract** \ik-ˈstrakt, *oftenest in sense 5* ˈek-ˌ\ *vt* [ME *extracten*, fr. L *extractus*, pp. of *extrahere*, fr. *ex-* + *trahere* to draw] **1 a :** to draw forth; *esp* **:** to pull out forcibly **b :** to obtain by much effort from someone unwilling **2 :** to withdraw (as a juice or fraction) by physical or chemical process; *also* **:** to treat with a solvent so as to remove a soluble substance **3 :** to separate (a metal) from an ore **4 :** to determine (a mathematical root) by calculation **5 :** to select (excerpts) and copy out or cite **syn** see EDUCE — **ex·tract·able** *or* **ex·tract·ible** \-ə-bəl\ *adj* — **ex·trac·tor** \-ər\ *n*
2**ex·tract** \ˈek-ˌstrakt\ *n* **1 :** a selection from a writing or discourse **:** EXCERPT **2 :** a product (as an essence or concentrate) prepared by extracting; *esp* **:** a solution (as in alcohol) of essential constituents of a complex material (as meat or an aromatic plant)
ex·trac·tion \ik-ˈstrak-shən\ *n* **1 :** the act or process of extracting **2 :** ORIGIN, LINEAGE **3 :** something extracted
1**ex·trac·tive** \ik-ˈstrak-tiv\ *adj* **1 a :** of, relating to, or involving extraction ⟨~ processes⟩ **b :** tending toward or resulting in withdrawal of natural resources by extraction with no provision for replenishment ⟨~ agriculture⟩ **2 :** capable of being extracted
2**extractive** *n* **:** something extracted or extractable **:** EXTRACT
ex·tra·cur·ric·u·lar \ˌek-strə-kə-ˈrik-yə-lər\ *adj* **1 :** not falling within the scope of a regular curriculum; *specif* **:** of or relating to officially or semiofficially approved and usu. organized student activities (as athletics) connected with school and usu. carrying no academic credit **2 :** lying outside one's regular duties or routine
ex·tra·dit·able \ˈek-strə-ˌdīt-ə-bəl\ *adj* **1 :** subject or liable to extradition **2 :** making liable to extradition ⟨an ~ offense⟩
ex·tra·dite \ˈek-strə-ˌdīt\ *vt* [back-formation fr. *extradition*] **1 :** to deliver up to extradition **2 :** to obtain the extradition of
ex·tra·di·tion \ˌek-strə-ˈdish-ən\ *n* [F, fr. *ex-* + L *tradition-*, *traditio* act of handing over] **:** the surrender of an alleged criminal usu. under the provisions of a treaty or statute by one state or other authority to another having jurisdiction to try the charge
ex·tra·dos \ˈek-strə-ˌdäs, -ˌdō; ek-ˈstrā-ˌdäs\ *n, pl* **ex·tra·dos** \-ˌdōz, -ˌdäs\ *or* **ex·tra·dos·es** \-ˌdäs-əz\ [F, fr. L *extra* + F *dos* back — more at DOSSIER] **:** the exterior curve of an arch
ex·tra·ga·lac·tic \ˌek-strə-gə-ˈlak-tik\ *adj* [ISV] **:** lying or coming from outside the Milky Way
ex·tra·ju·di·cial \-jü-ˈdish-əl\ *adj* **:** out of or beyond the proper authority of a court or judge — **ex·tra·ju·di·cial·ly** \-(ə-)lē\ *adv*
ex·tra·le·gal \-ˈlē-gəl\ *adj* **:** not regulated or sanctioned by law — **ex·tra·le·gal·ly** \-gə-lē\ *adv*
ex·tra·lim·it·al \-ˈlim-ət-ᵊl\ *adj* **:** not present in a given area — used of kinds of organisms (as species)
ex·tral·i·ty \ek-ˈstral-ət-ē\ *n* [by contr.] **:** EXTRATERRITORIALITY
ex·tra·mar·i·tal \ˌek-strə-ˈmar-ət-ᵊl\ *adj* **:** ADULTEROUS
ex·tra·mun·dane \ˌek-strə-ˌmən-ˈdān, -ˈmən-ˌ\ *adj* [LL *extramundanus*, fr. L *extra* + *mundus* the world] **:** situated in or relating to a region beyond the material world
ex·tra·mu·ral \-ˈmyu̇r-əl\ *adj* **1 :** existing or functioning outside or beyond the walls, boundaries, or precincts of an organized unit **2 :** relating to or taking part in informal interscholastic contests arranged for competition between special groups or classes rather than varsities — **ex·tra·mu·ral·ly** \-ə-lē\ *adv*
ex·tra·ne·ous \ek-ˈstrā-nē-əs\ *adj* [L *extraneus*] **1 :** existing or coming from the outside **2 a :** not forming an essential or vital part **:** ACCIDENTAL **b :** having no relevance **syn** see EXTRINSIC — **ex·tra·ne·ous·ly** *adv* — **ex·tra·ne·ous·ness** *n*
ex·tra·nu·cle·ar \ˌek-strə-ˈn(y)ü-klē-ər\ *adj* **:** situated in or affecting the parts of a cell external to the nucleus **:** CYTOPLASMIC
ex·traor·di·nar·i·ly \ik-ˌstrȯrd-ᵊn-ˈer-ə-lē, ˌek-strə-ˌȯrd-\ *adv* **:** in an extraordinary manner or degree
ex·traor·di·nar·i·ness \ik-ˈstrȯrd-ᵊn-ˌer-ē-nəs, ˌek-strə-ˈȯrd-\ *n* **:** the quality, state, or fact of being extraordinary
ex·traor·di·nary \ik-ˈstrȯrd-ᵊn-ˌer-ē, ˌek-strə-ˈȯrd-\ *adj* [ME *extraordinarie*, fr. L *extraordinarius*, fr. *extra ordinem* out of course, fr. *extra* + *ordinem*, acc. of *ordin-*, *ordo* order] **1 a :** going beyond what is usual, regular, or customary ⟨~ powers⟩ **b :** exceptional to a very marked extent **:** REMARKABLE ⟨~ beauty⟩ **2 :** employed for or sent on a special function or service ⟨an ambassador ~⟩
extra point *n* **1 :** a point scored in football after a touchdown by drop-kicking or place-kicking **2** *pl* **:** a score of two points scored after a touchdown by advancing the ball across the goal line in one play
ex·trap·o·late \ik-ˈstrap-ə-ˌlāt\ *vb* [L *extra* outside + E *-polate* (as in *interpolate*) — more at EXTRA-] *vt* **1 :** to infer (values of a variable in an unobserved interval) from values within an already observed interval **2 a :** to project, extend, or expand (known data or experience) into an area not known or experienced so as to arrive at a usu. conjectural knowledge of the unknown area by inferences based on an assumed continuity, correspondence, or other parallelism between it and what is known **b :** to gain knowledge of (an area not known or experienced) by extrapolating ~ *vi* **:** to perform the act or process of extrapolating — **ex·trap·o·la·tion** \ik-ˌstrap-ə-ˈlā-shən\ *n* — **ex·trap·o·la·tive** \-ˈstrap-ə-ˌlāt-iv\ *adj* — **ex·trap·o·la·tor** \-ˌlāt-ər\ *n*
ex·tra·sen·so·ry \ˌek-strə-ˈsen(t)s-(ə-)rē\ *adj* **:** residing beyond or outside the ordinary senses ⟨instances of ~ perception⟩
ex·tra·sys·to·le \-ˈsis-tə-(ˌ)lē\ *n* [NL] **:** a premature beat of one of the chambers of the heart that leads to momentary arrhythmia — **ex·tra·sys·tol·ic** \-(ˌ)sis-ˈtäl-ik\ *adj*
ex·tra·ter·res·tri·al \-tə-ˈres-t(r)ē-əl, -res(h)-chəl\ *adj* **:** originating or existing outside the earth or its atmosphere
ex·tra·ter·ri·to·ri·al \-ˌter-ə-ˈtōr-ē-əl, -ˈtȯr-\ *adj* **:** located outside the territorial limits of a jurisdiction
ex·tra·ter·ri·to·ri·al·i·ty \-ˌtōr-ē-ˈal-ət-ē, -ˌtȯr-\ *n* **:** exemption from the application or jurisdiction of local law or tribunals
ex·tra·uter·ine \ˌek-strə-ˈyüt-ə-rən, -ˌrīn\ *adj* [ISV] **:** situated or occurring outside the uterus
ex·trav·a·gance \ik-ˈstrav-i-gən(t)s\ *n* **1 a :** an instance of excess or prodigality; *esp* **:** an excessive outlay of money **b :** something extravagant **2 :** the quality or fact of being extravagant
ex·trav·a·gan·cy \-gən-sē\ *n* **:** EXTRAVAGANCE
ex·trav·a·gant \ik-ˈstrav-i-gənt\ *adj* [ME, fr. MF, fr. ML *extravagant-*, *extravagans*, fr. L *extra-* + *vagant-*, *vagans*, prp. of *vagari* to wander about] **1 a** *archaic* **:** WANDERING **b** *obs* **:** STRANGE, CURIOUS **2 a :** exceeding the limits of reason or necessity ⟨~ claims⟩ **b :** lacking in moderation balance, and restraint ⟨~ praise⟩ **c :** extremely or excessively elaborate **3 a :** spending much more than necessary **b :** PROFUSE **4 :** unreasonably high in price **syn** see EXCESSIVE — **ex·trav·a·gant·ly** *adv*
ex·trav·a·gan·za \ik-ˌstrav-ə-ˈgan-zə\ *n* [It *estravaganza*, lit., extravagance, fr. *estravagante* extravagant, fr. ML *extravagant-*, *extravagans*] **1 :** a literary or musical work marked by extreme freedom of style and structure and usu. by elements of burlesque or parody **2 :** a lavish or spectacular show or event
ex·trav·a·gate \ik-ˈstrav-ə-ˌgāt\ *vi* **1** *archaic* **:** WANDER **2** *archaic* **:** to go beyond proper limits
1**ex·trav·a·sate** \ik-ˈstrav-ə-ˌsāt\ *vb* [L *extra* + *vas* vessel] *vt* **:** to force out or cause to escape from a proper vessel or channel ~ *vi* **1 :** to pass by infiltration or effusion from a proper vessel or channel (as a blood vessel) into surrounding tissue **2 :** to erupt in liquid form from a vent — **ex·trav·a·sa·tion** \-ˌstrav-ə-ˈsā-shən\ *n*
2**extravasate** *n* **:** an extravasated fluid (as blood)
ex·tra·vas·cu·lar \ˌek-strə-ˈvas-kyə-lər\ *adj* **:** destitute of or not contained in body vessels
ex·tra·ve·hic·u·lar \-vē-ˈhik-yə-lər\ *adj* **:** taking place outside a vehicle (as a spacecraft) ⟨~ activity⟩
1**ex·treme** \ik-ˈstrēm\ *adj* [ME, fr. MF, fr. L *extremus*, superl. of *exter*, *exterus* being on the outside] **1 a :** existing in the highest or the greatest possible degree ⟨~ poverty⟩ **b :** going to great or exaggerated lengths **c :** exceeding the ordinary, usual, or expected **2** *archaic* **:** LAST **3 :** situated at the farthest possible point from a center **4 a :** most advanced **:** UTMOST **b :** MAXIMUM **syn** see EXCESSIVE — **ex·treme·ly** *adv* — **ex·treme·ness** *n*
2**extreme** *n* **1 :** an extreme state or condition **2 a :** something situated at or marking one end or the other of a range **b :** the first term or the last term of a mathematical proportion **c :** the major term or minor term of a syllogism **3 a :** a very pronounced or excessive degree **b :** MAXIMUM **4 :** an extreme measure or expedient
extremely high frequency *n* **:** a radio frequency in the highest range of the radio spectrum — see RADIO FREQUENCY table
extreme unction \ik-ˌstrē-ˈməŋ(k)-shən, ˌek-(ˌ)strē-\ *n* **:** a Roman Catholic sacrament in which a priest anoints a critically ill or injured person and prays for his recovery and salvation
ex·trem·ism \ik-ˈstrē-ˌmiz-əm\ *n* **:** the quality or state of being extreme; *specif* **:** RADICALISM — **ex·trem·ist** \-məst\ *n or adj*
ex·trem·i·ty \ik-ˈstrem-ət-ē\ *n* **1 a :** the farthest or most remote part, section, or point **b :** a limb of the body; *esp* **:** a human hand or foot **2 a :** extreme danger or critical need **b :** a moment marked by imminent destruction or death **3 :** the utmost degree (as of emotion or pain) **4 :** a drastic or desperate act or measure
ex·tre·mum \ik-ˈstrē-məm\ *n, pl* **ex·tre·ma** \-mə\ [NL, fr. L, neut. of *extremus*] **:** a maximum or a minimum of a mathematical function
ex·tri·ca·ble \ek-ˈstrik-ə-bəl, ˈek-(ˌ)strik-\ *adj* **:** capable of being extricated
ex·tri·cate \ˈek-strə-ˌkāt\ *vt* [L *extricatus*, pp. of *extricare*, fr. *ex-* + *tricae* trifles, perplexities] **1 a** *archaic* **:** UNRAVEL **b :** to distinguish from a related thing **2 :** to free or remove from an entanglement or difficulty — **ex·tri·ca·tion** \ˌek-strə-ˈkā-shən\ *n*
syn EXTRICATE, DISENTANGLE, UNTANGLE, DISENCUMBER, DISEMBARRASS mean to free from what binds or holds back. EXTRICATE implies the use of force or ingenuity in freeing from a difficult position or situation; DISENTANGLE and UNTANGLE suggest painstaking separation of a thing from other things; DISENCUMBER implies a

release from something that clogs or weighs down; DISEMBARRASS suggests a release from something that impedes or hinders

ex·trin·sic \ek-'strin-zik, -'strin(t)-sik\ *adj* [F & LL; F *extrinsèque* fr. LL *extrinsecus*, fr. L, adv., from without; akin to L *exter* outward and to L *sequi* to follow] **1 a :** not forming part of or belonging to a thing **b :** originating from or on the outside; *specif* **:** originating outside a part and acting upon the part as a whole **2 :** EXTERNAL — **ex·trin·si·cal·ly** \-zi-k(ə-)lē, -si-\ *adv* **syn** EXTRINSIC, EXTRANEOUS, FOREIGN, ALIEN mean external to a thing, its essential nature, or its original character. EXTRINSIC applies to what is distinctly outside the thing in question or is not contained in or derived from its essential nature; EXTRANEOUS applies to what is on or comes from the outside and may or may not be capable of becoming an essential part; FOREIGN applies to what is so different as to be rejected or repelled or, if admitted, to be incapable of becoming identified or assimilated by the thing in question; ALIEN is stronger than FOREIGN in suggesting opposition, repugnance, or irreconcilability

extrinsic factor *n* **:** a dietary substance held to interact with the intrinsic factor of the gastric secretion to prevent pernicious anemia

extro- *prefix* [alter. of L *extra-*] **:** outward ⟨*extrovert*⟩ — compare INTRO-

ex·trorse \'ek-,strȯ(ə)rs\ *adj* [prob. fr. (assumed) NL *extrorsus*, fr. LL, adv., outward, fr. L *extra-* + *-orsus* (as in *introrsus*)] **:** turned away from the axis of growth ⟨an ~ anther⟩ — **ex·trorse·ly** *adv*

ex·tro·ver·sion *also* **ex·tra·ver·sion** \,ek-strə-'vər-zhən, -shən\ *n* [G, fr. *extro-* or *extra-* + L *versus*, pp. of *vertere* to turn] **:** the act, state, or habit of directing attention toward and obtaining gratification from what is outside the self — **ex·tro·ver·sive** \-siv, -ziv\ *adj* — **ex·tro·ver·sive·ly** *adv*

1ex·tro·vert *also* **ex·tra·vert** \'ek-strə-,vərt\ *adj* [modif. of G *extrovertiert*, *extravertiert*, fr. *extro-* or *extra-* + L *vertere*] **:** EXTROVERTED

2extrovert *also* **extravert** *n* **:** one whose attention and interests are directed wholly or predominantly toward what is outside the self

ex·tro·vert·ed *also* **ex·tra·vert·ed** \-,vərt-əd\ *adj* **:** marked by extroversion

ex·trude \ik-'strüd\ *vb* [L *extrudere*, fr. *ex-* + *trudere* to thrust] *vt* **1 :** to force, press, or push out **2 :** to shape (as metal) by forcing through a die ~ *vi* **:** to become extruded — **ex·trud·er** *n*

ex·tru·sion \ik-'strü-zhən\ *n* [ML *extrusion-, extrusio*, fr. L *extrusus*, pp. of *extrudere*] **:** the act or process of extruding; *also* **:** a form produced by this process

ex·tru·sive \ik-'strü-siv, -ziv\ *adj* **:** formed by crystallization of lava poured out at the earth's surface ⟨~ rock⟩

ex·tu·bate \ek-'st(y)ü-,bāt, 'ek-,\ *vt* **:** to take a tube out of (as the larynx)

ex·u·ber·ance \ig-'zü-b(ə-)rən(t)s\ *n* **1 :** the quality or state of being exuberant **2 :** an exuberant act or expression

ex·u·ber·ant \ig-'zü-b(ə-)rənt\ *adj* [ME, fr. MF, fr. L *exuberant-, exuberans*, prp. of *exuberare* to be abundant, fr. *ex-* + *uber* fruitful, fr. *uber* udder — more at UDDER] **1 a** (1) **:** joyously unrestrained and enthusiastic (2) **:** extremely inflated **:** PROFUSE **b :** extreme or excessive in degree, size, or extent **2 :** produced in extreme abundance **:** PLENTIFUL **syn** see PROFUSE — **ex·u·ber·ant·ly** *adv*

ex·u·ber·ate \ig-'zü-bə-,rāt\ *vi* **1** *archaic* **:** OVERFLOW **2 :** to be exuberant or show exuberance

ex·u·date \'eks-ə-,dāt, 'egz-; ig-'züd-ət, -,āt\ *n* **:** exuded matter

ex·u·da·tion \,eks-ə-'dā-shən, ,egz-\ *n* **1 :** the process of exuding **2 :** EXUDATE — **ex·u·da·tive** \ig-'züd-ət-iv\ *adj*

ex·ude \ig-'züd\ *vb* [L *exsudare*, fr. *ex-* + *sudare* to sweat] *vi* **1 :** to ooze out **2 :** to undergo diffusion ~ *vt* **1 :** to cause to ooze out **2 :** to cause to spread out in all directions ⟨*exuding* charm⟩

ex·ult \ig-'zəlt\ *vi* [MF *exulter*, fr. L *exsultare*, lit., to leap up, fr. *ex-* + *saltare* to leap] **1** *obs* **:** to leap for joy **2 :** to be extremely joyful **:** REJOICE — **ex·ult·ing·ly** \-'zəl-tiŋ-lē\ *adv*

ex·ul·tance \ig-'zəlt-°n(t)s\ *or* **ex·ul·tan·cy** \-°n-sē\ *n* **:** EXULTATION

ex·ul·tant \ig-'zəlt-°nt\ *adj* **:** filled with or expressing extreme joy **:** JUBILANT — **ex·ul·tant·ly** *adv*

ex·ul·ta·tion \,ek-(,)səl-'tā-shən, ,eg-(,)zəl-\ *n* **:** the act of exulting **:** the state of being exultant

ex·urb \'ek-,sərb, 'eg-,zərb\ *n* [*ex-* + *-urb* (as in *suburb*)] **:** a region or district outside a city and usu. beyond its suburbs inhabited chiefly by well-to-do families

ex·ur·ban·ite \ek-'sər-bə-,nīt, eg-'zər-\ *n* **:** one who lives in an exurb

ex·ur·bia \-bē-ə\ *n* **:** the generalized region of exurbs

ex·u·vi·ae \ig-'zü-vē-,ē, -,ī\ *n pl* [L, fr. *exuere* to take off, fr. *ex-* + *-uere* to put on; akin to ORuss *izuti* to take off footwear] **:** the natural coverings of animals (as the skins of snakes) after they have been sloughed off — **ex·u·vi·al** \-vē-əl\ *adj*

ex·u·vi·ate \-,āt\ *vb* **:** MOLT — **ex·u·vi·a·tion** \-,zü-vē-'ā-shən\ *n*

1ex·vo·to \(')eks-'vōt-(,)ō\ *n* [L *ex voto* according to a vow] **:** a votive offering

2ex-voto *adj* **:** VOTIVE

-ey — see -Y

ey·as \'ī-əs\ *n* [ME, alter. (by incorrect division of *a neias*) of *neias*, fr. MF *niais* fresh from the nest, fr. (assumed) VL *nidax* nestling, fr. L *nidus* nest — more at NEST] **:** an unfledged bird; *specif* **:** a nestling hawk

1eye \'ī\ *n* [ME, fr. OE *ēage*; akin to OHG *ouga* eye, L *oculus*, Gk *ōps* eye, face] **1 a :** an organ of sight; *esp* **:** a nearly spherical

hollow organ lined with a sensitive retina and lodged in a bony orbit in the skull that is the vertebrate organ of sight and is normally paired **b :** all the visible structures within and surrounding the orbit and including eyelids, eyelashes, and eyebrows **c** (1) **:** the faculty of seeing with eyes (2) **:** the faculty of intellectual perception or appreciation **d :** LOOK, GLANCE **e :** an attentive look **f :** POINT OF VIEW, JUDGMENT **2 :** something having an appearance suggestive of an eye: as **a :** the hole through the head of a needle **b :** a usu. circular marking (as on a peacock's tail) **c :** LOOP; *esp* **:** a loop or other catch to receive a hook **d :** an undeveloped bud (as on a potato) **e :** an area like a hole in the center of a tropical cyclone marked by only light winds or complete calm with no precipitation **f :** the center of a flower esp. when differently colored or marked; *specif* **:** the disk of a composite **3 :** something central **:** CENTER **4 :** the direction *from* which the wind is blowing **5** *slang* **:** DETECTIVE ⟨a private ~⟩ — **eyed** \'īd\ *adj* — **eye·less** \'ī-ləs\ *adj* — **eye·like** \'ī-,līk\ *adj* — **all eyes :** marked by rapt attention — **with an eye to :** with a view to

2eye *vb* **eyed; eye·ing** *or* **ey·ing** *vt* **1 a :** to fix the eyes on **b :** to watch sharply **2 :** to furnish with an eye ~ *vi*, *obs* **:** SEEM, LOOK

eye·ball \'ī-,bȯl\ *n* **1 :** the more or less globular capsule of the vertebrate eye formed by the sclera and cornea together with their contained structures **2 :** the eye proper

eye bank *n* **:** a storage place for human corneas from the newly dead for transplanting to the eyes of those blind through corneal defects

eye·bolt \'ī-,bōlt\ *n* **:** a bolt with a looped head

eye·bright \'ī-,brīt\ *n* **1 :** any of several herbs (genus *Euphrasia*) of the figwort family **2 :** the scarlet pimpernel

eye·brow \'ī-,braú\ *n* **:** the ridge over the eye or hair growing on it

eye-catch·er \'ī-,kach-ər, -,kech-\ *n* **:** something strongly attracting the eye — **eye-catch·ing** \-iŋ\ *adj*

eye·cup \'ī-,kəp\ *n* **:** a small oval cup with a rim curved to fit the orbit of the eye used for applying liquid remedies to the eyes

eye dialect *n* **:** the use of spellings in the representation of speech that are based on pronunciation

eye·drop·per \'ī-,dräp-ər\ *n* **:** DROPPER 2a

eye·ful \'ī-,fúl\ *n* **1 :** a full or completely satisfying view **2 :** one that is visually attractive; *esp* **:** a strikingly beautiful woman

eye·glass \'ī-,glas\ *n* **1 a :** EYEPIECE **b :** a lens worn to aid vision; *specif* **:** MONOCLE **c** *pl* **:** GLASSES, SPECTACLES **2 :** EYECUP

eye·hole \'ī-,hōl\ *n* **1 :** ORBIT 1 **2 :** PEEPHOLE

eye·lash \'ī-,lash\ *n* **:** the fringe of hair edging the eyelid; *esp* **:** a single hair of this fringe

eye·let \'ī-lət\ *n* [ME *oilet*, fr. MF *oillet*, dim. of *oil* eye, fr. L *oculus*] **1 a :** a small hole designed to receive a cord or used for decoration (as in embroidery) **b :** a small typically metal ring to reinforce an eyelet **:** GROMMET **2 :** PEEPHOLE, LOOPHOLE

eye·lid \'ī-,lid\ *n* **:** one of the movable lids of skin and muscle that can be closed over the eyeball

ey·en \'ī-ən\ *archaic pl of* EYE

eye-open·er \'ī-,ōp-(ə-)nər\ *n* **1 :** a drink intended to wake one up **2 :** something startling or surprising — **eye-open·ing** \-niŋ\ *adj*

eye·piece \'ī-,pēs\ *n* **:** the lens or combination of lenses at the eye end of an optical instrument

eye rhyme *n* **:** an imperfect rhyme that appears to have identical vowel sounds from similarity of spelling (as *move* and *love*)

eye·shot \'ī-,shät\ *n* **:** the range of the eye **:** VIEW

eye·sight \'ī-,sīt\ *n* **1 :** SIGHT **2** *archaic* **:** OBSERVATION

eye·sore \'ī-,sō(ə)r, -,sȯ(ə)r\ *n* **:** something offensive to the sight

eye·spot \'ī-,spät\ *n* **1 :** a simple visual organ of pigment or pigmented cells covering a sensory termination **2 :** a spot of color

eye·stalk \'ī-,stȯk\ *n* **:** one of the movable peduncles bearing an eye at the tip in a decapod crustacean

eye·strain \'ī-,strān\ *n* **:** weariness or a strained state of the eye

eye·strings \'ī-,striŋz\ *n pl, obs* **:** organic eye attachments formerly believed to break at death or blindness

eye·tooth \'ī-'tüth\ *n* **:** a canine tooth of the upper jaw

eye·wash \'ī-,wȯsh, -,wäsh\ *n* **1 :** an eye lotion **2 :** misleading or deceptive statements, actions, or procedures

eye·wink \'ī-,wiŋk\ *n* **1 :** a wink of the eye **2** *obs* **:** LOOK, GLANCE

eye·wit·ness \'ī-'wit-nəs\ *n* **:** one who sees an occurrence or an object; *esp* **:** one who gives a report on what he has seen

eyre \'a(ə)r, 'e(ə)r\ *n* [ME *eire*, fr. AF, fr. OF *erre* trip, fr. *errer* to travel] **1 :** periodic circuit ⟨medieval English justices in ~⟩ **2 :** a medieval English court held by itinerant royal justices

ey·rie \'ī(ə)r-ē, *or like* AERIE\ *var of* AERIE

ey·rir \'ā-,ri(ə)r\ *n, pl* **au·rar** \'aú-,rär\ [Icel, fr. ON, money (in pl.)] — see *krona* at MONEY table

Eze·kiel \i-'zēk-yəl\ *n* [LL *Ezechiel*, fr. Heb *Yĕḥezqēl*] **:** a major Hebrew prophet of the 6th century B.C.

Ez·ra \'ez-rə\ *n* [LL, fr. Heb *'Ezrā*] **:** a Hebrew priest of the 5th century B.C.

eye 1a: *1* optic nerve, *2* blind spot, *3* sclera, *4* anterior chamber, *5* cornea, *6* lens, *7* pupil, *8* iris, *9* posterior chamber, *10* suspensory ligament, *11* conjunctiva, *12* choroid coat, *13* macula and fovea, *14* ciliary muscle

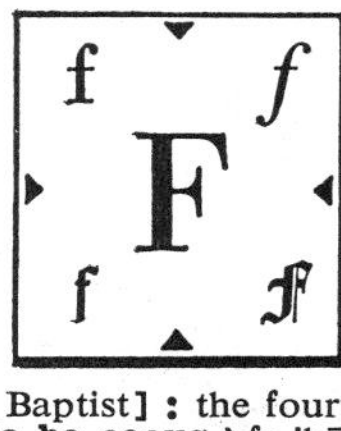

f \'ef\ *n, often cap, often attrib* **1 a :** the sixth letter of the English alphabet **b :** a graphic representation of this letter **c :** a speech counterpart of orthographic *f* **2 :** the tone F **3 :** a graphic device for reproducing the letter *f* **4 :** one designated *f* esp. as the sixth in order or class **5 a :** a grade rating a student's work as failing **b :** one graded or rated with an F **6 :** something shaped like the letter F
fa \'fä\ *n* [ME, fr. ML, fr. the syllable sung to this note in a medieval hymn to St. John the Baptist] **:** the fourth tone of the diatonic scale in solmization
fa·ba·ceous \fə-'bā-shəs\ *adj* [NL *Fabaceae*, family of legumes, fr. *Faba*, type genus, fr. L, bean] **1 :** of or relating to the legume family **:** LEGUMINOUS **2 :** relating to, like, or being a bean
Fa·bi·an \'fā-bē-ən\ *adj* **1 a :** of, relating to, or in the manner of the Roman general Quintus Fabius Maximus known for his defeat of Hannibal in the Second Punic War by the avoidance of decisive contests **b :** CAUTIOUS, DILATORY **2** [the *Fabian* Society; fr. the members' belief in slow rather than revolutionary change in government] **:** of, relating to, or being a society of socialists organized in England in 1884 to spread socialist principles gradually — **Fabian** *n* — **Fa·bi·an·ism** \-ə-,niz-əm\ *n*
¹fa·ble \'fā-bəl\ *n* [ME, fr. MF, fr. L *fabula* conversation, story, play, fr. *fari* to speak — more at BAN] **:** a fictitious narrative or statement: as **a :** a legendary story of supernatural happenings **b :** a narration intended to enforce a useful truth; *esp* **:** one in which animals speak and act like human beings **c :** FALSEHOOD, LIE
²fable *vb* **fa·bling** \-b(ə-)liŋ\ *vi, archaic* **:** to tell fables ~ *vt* **:** to talk or write about as if true — **fa·bler** \-b(ə-)lər\ *n*
fa·bled \'fā-bəld\ *adj* **1 :** FICTITIOUS **2 :** told or celebrated in fable
fab·li·au \'fab-lē-,ō\ *n, pl* **fab·li·aux** \-,ō(z)\ [F, fr. OF, dim. of *fable*] **:** a short usu. comic, frankly coarse, and often cynical tale in verse popular in the 12th and 13th centuries
fab·ric \'fab-rik\ *n* [MF *fabrique*, fr. L *fabrica* workshop, structure — more at FORGE] **1 a :** STRUCTURE, BUILDING **b :** underlying structure **:** FRAMEWORK **2 :** an act of constructing **:** ERECTION; *specif* **:** the construction and maintenance of a church building **3 a :** structural plan or style of construction **b :** TEXTURE, QUALITY — used chiefly of textiles **4 a :** CLOTH 1a **b :** a material that resembles cloth **5 :** the appearance or pattern produced by the shapes and arrangement of the crystal grains in a rock
fab·ri·cant \'fab-ri-kənt\ *n* **:** MANUFACTURER
fab·ri·cate \'fab-ri-,kāt\ *vt* [ME *fabricaten*, fr. L *fabricatus*, pp. of *fabricari*, fr. *fabrica*] **1 :** CONSTRUCT, MANUFACTURE; *specif* **:** to construct from standardized parts **2 :** INVENT, CREATE **3 :** to make up for the purpose of deception **syn** see MAKE — **fab·ri·ca·tion** \,fab-ri-'kā-shən\ *n* — **fab·ri·ca·tor** \'fab-ri-,kāt-ər\ *n*
Fab·ri·koid \'fab-ri-,kȯid\ *trademark* — used for imitation leather made from pyroxylin-treated cloth and used for bookbinding, luggage, and upholstery
fab·u·list \'fab-yə-ləst\ *n* **1 :** a creator or writer of fables **2 :** LIAR
fab·u·lous \-ləs\ *adj* [L *fabulosus*, fr. *fabula*] **1 :** resembling a fable **2 :** told in or based on fable **3 :** INCREDIBLE, MARVELOUS **syn** see FICTITIOUS — **fab·u·lous·ly** *adv* — **fab·u·lous·ness** *n*
fa·cade *also* **fa·çade** \fə-'säd\ *n* [F *façade*, fr. It *facciata*, fr. *faccia* face, fr. (assumed) VL *facia*] **1 :** the front of a building usu. given special architectural treatment **2 :** a false, superficial, or artificial appearance or effect
¹face \'fās\ *n, often attrib* [ME, fr. OF, fr. (assumed) VL *facia*, fr. L *facies* make, form, face, fr. *facere* to make, do — more at DO] **1 :** the front part of the human head including the chin, mouth, nose, cheeks, eyes, and usu. the forehead **2** *archaic* **:** PRESENCE, SIGHT **3 a :** facial expression **b :** GRIMACE **4 a :** outward appearance **b :** DISGUISE, PRETENSE **c** (1) **:** ASSURANCE, CONFIDENCE (2) **:** EFFRONTERY **d :** DIGNITY, PRESTIGE **5 :** SURFACE: **a** (1) **:** a front, upper, or outer surface (2) **:** the front of something having two or four sides (3) **:** FACADE (4) **:** an exposed surface of rock (5) **:** any of the plane surfaces that bound a geometric solid **b :** a surface specially prepared: as (1) **:** the principal dressed surface (as of a disk) (2) **:** the right side (as of cloth or leather) (3) **:** an inscribed, printed, or marked side **c** (1) **:** the surface (as of type) that receives the ink and transfers it to the paper (2) **:** any style of type **6 :** the end or wall of a mine tunnel, drift, or excavation at which work is progressing
syn FACE, COUNTENANCE, VISAGE, PHYSIOGNOMY denote the front part of the head from forehead to chin. FACE is the simple, direct, but also the inclusive term; COUNTENANCE applies to a face as seen and as revealing a mood or attitude; VISAGE suggests attention to shape and proportions and sometimes expression; PHYSIOGNOMY suggests attention to the contours and characteristic expression as indicative of race, temperament, or qualities of mind or character
²face *vt* **1 :** to confront impudently **2 a :** to line near the edge esp. with a different material **b :** to cover the front or surface of ⟨*faced* the building with marble⟩ **3 :** to bring face to face **4 a :** to stand or sit with the face toward **b :** to front on **5 a :** to oppose firmly **b :** to master by confronting with determination **6 :** to turn face upward **7 :** to make the surface of (as a stone) flat or smooth **8 :** to cause (troops) to face in a particular direction on command ~ *vi* **1 :** to have the face or front turned in a specified direction **2 :** to turn the face in a specified direction
face card *n* **:** a king, queen, or jack in a deck of cards
face·down \'fās-'daun\ *adv* **:** with the face downward
face–hard·en \'fās-,härd-ᵊn\ *vt* **:** to harden the surface of (as steel)
face–lift·ing \'fā-,slif-tiŋ\ *n* **1 :** a plastic operation for removal of facial defects (as wrinkles) typical of aging **2 :** an alteration or restyling intended to modernize
face·plate \'fā-,splāt\ *n* **:** a disk fixed with its face at right angles to the live spindle of a lathe for the attachment of the work
fac·er \'fā-sər\ *n* **1 :** a stunning check or defeat **2 :** one that faces; *specif* **:** a cutter for facing a surface
fac·et \'fas-ət\ *n* [F *facette*, dim. of *face*] **1 :** a small plane surface (as on a cut gem) **2 :** ASPECT, PHASE **3 :** the external corneal surface of an ommatidium **4 :** a smooth flat circumscribed anatomical surface **5 :** a fillet between the flutes of a column **syn** see PHASE — **fac·et·ed** *or* **fac·et·ted** \'fas-ət-əd\ *adj*
fa·cete \fə-'sēt\ *adj* [L *facetus*] *archaic* **:** FACETIOUS, WITTY
fa·ce·ti·ae \fə-'sē-shē-,ē\ *n pl* [L, fr. pl. of *facetia* jest, fr. *facetus*] **:** witty or humorous writings or sayings
fa·ce·tious \fə-'sē-shəs\ *adj* [MF *facetieux*, fr. *facetie* jest, fr. L *facetia*] **:** HUMOROUS, JOCULAR **syn** see WITTY — **fa·ce·tious·ly** *adv* — **fa·ce·tious·ness** *n*
face up *vi* **:** to meet without shrinking
face·up \'fā-'səp\ *adv* **:** with the face upward
face value *n* **1 :** the value indicated on the face **2 :** the apparent value or significance
fa·cia \'fā-sh(ē-)ə\ *var of* FASCIA
¹fa·cial \'fā-shəl\ *adj* **1 :** of or relating to the face **2 :** concerned with or used in improving the appearance of the face — **fa·cial·ly** \-shə-lē\ *adv*
²facial *n* **:** a facial treatment
facial index *n* **:** the ratio of the breadth of the face to its length multiplied by 100
-fa·cient \'fā-shənt\ *adj comb form* [L *-facient-*, *-faciens* (as in *calefacient-*, *calefaciens* making warm, prp. of *calefacere* to warm) — more at CHAFE] **:** making **:** causing ⟨somni*facient*⟩
fa·cies \'fā-sh(ē-,)ēz\ *n, pl* **facies** [NL, fr. L, face] **1 :** an appearance and expression of the face characteristic of a particular condition **2 a :** general appearance **b :** a particular local aspect or modification of an ecological community **3 :** a rock or group of rocks that differs from comparable rocks (as in composition)
fac·ile \'fas-əl\ *adj* [MF, fr. L *facilis*, fr. *facere* to do — more at DO] **1 a** (1) **:** easily accomplished or attained (2) **:** SPECIOUS, SUPERFICIAL **b :** used or comprehended with ease **c :** readily manifested and often lacking sincerity or depth **2 :** mild or pleasing in manner or disposition **3 a :** READY, FLUENT **b :** ASSURED, POISED **syn** see EASY — **fac·ile·ly** \-ə(l)-lē\ *adv* — **fac·ile·ness** \-əl-nəs\ *n*
fa·cil·i·tate \fə-'sil-ə-,tāt\ *vt* **:** to make easier — **fa·cil·i·ta·tion** \-,sil-ə-'tā-shən\ *n*
fa·cil·i·ty \fə-'sil-ət-ē\ *n* **1 :** the quality of being easily performed **2 :** ease in performance **:** APTITUDE **3 :** readiness of compliance **4 a :** something that facilitates an action, operation, or course of conduct — usu. used in pl. **b :** something (as a hospital) that is built, installed, or established to serve a particular purpose
fac·ing \'fā-siŋ\ *n* **1 a :** a lining at the edge esp. of a garment **b** *pl* **:** the collar, cuffs, and trimmings of a uniform coat **2 :** an ornamental or protective layer **3 :** material for facing
fac·sim·i·le \fak-'sim-ə-lē\ *n, often attrib* [L *fac simile* make similar] **1 :** an exact copy **2 :** the process of transmitting (as printed matter or still pictures) by wire or radio for reproduction **syn** see REPRODUCTION
fact \'fakt\ *n* [L *factum*, fr. neut. of *factus*, pp. of *facere*] **1 :** a thing done: as **a :** CRIME ⟨accessory after the ~⟩ **b** *obs* **:** FEAT **c** *archaic* **:** ACTION **2** *archaic* **:** PERFORMANCE, DOING **3 :** the quality of being actual **:** ACTUALITY **4 a :** something that has actual existence **b :** an actual occurrence **:** EVENT **5 :** a piece of information presented as having objective reality
fac·tion \'fak-shən\ *n* [MF & L; MF, fr. L *faction-*, *factio* act of making, faction] **1 :** a usu. selfish or contentious group **:** CLIQUE **2 :** party spirit esp. when marked by dissension — **fac·tion·al** \-shnəl, -shən-ᵊl\ *adj* — **fac·tion·al·ly** \-ē\ *adv*
-fac·tion \'fak-shən\ *n comb form* [ME *-faccioun*, fr. MF & L; MF *-faction*, fr. L *-faction-*, *-factio* (as in *satisfaction-*, *satisfactio* satisfaction)] **:** making **:** -FICATION ⟨petri*faction*⟩
fac·tion·al·ism \'fak-shnə-,liz-əm, -shən-ᵊl-,iz-\ *n* **1 :** adherence to a faction **2 :** a condition marked by factional differences
fac·tious \'fak-shəs\ *adj* [MF or L; MF *factieux*, fr. L *factiosus*, fr. *factio*] **:** of or relating to faction: as **a :** caused by faction ⟨~ disputes⟩ **b :** inclined to faction or the formation of factions; *specif* **:** SEDITIOUS — **fac·tious·ly** *adv* — **fac·tious·ness** *n*
fac·ti·tious \fak-'tish-əs\ *adj* [L *facticius*, fr. *factus*, pp. of *facere* to make, do — more at DO] **1 :** produced artificially **2 a :** formed by or adapted to an artificial or conventional standard **b :** produced by special effort **:** SHAM **syn** see ARTIFICIAL — **fac·ti·tious·ly** *adv* — **fac·ti·tious·ness** *n*
fac·ti·tive \'fak-tət-iv\ *adj* [NL *factitivus*, irreg. fr. L *factus*] **:** of or relating to a transitive verb that in some constructions requires besides its object an objective complement — **fac·ti·tive·ly** *adv*
-fac·tive \'fak-tiv\ *adj comb form* [MF *-factif*, fr. *-faction*] **:** making **:** causing ⟨petri*factive*⟩
¹fac·tor \'fak-tər\ *n* [ME, fr. MF *facteur*, fr. L *factor* doer, fr. *factus*] **1 :** one who acts or transacts business for another: as **a :** COMMISSION MERCHANT **b :** an agent in charge of a trading post **c :** one that lends money to producers and dealers (as on the security of accounts receivable) **2 a :** something that actively contributes to the production of a result **:** INGREDIENT **b :** a good or service used in the process of production **3 a :** GENE **b :** a presumed equivalent of a gene **4 a :** any of the numbers or symbols in mathematics that when multiplied together form a product **b :** a quantity by which a given quantity is multiplied or divided in order to indicate a difference in measurement **c :** the number by which a given time is multiplied in photography to give the complete time for exposure or development **d :** a number that converts by multiplication the weight of one substance into the chemically equivalent weight of another substance **syn** see ELEMENT — **fac·tor·ship** \-,ship\ *n*
²factor *vb* **fac·tor·ing** \-t(ə-)riŋ\ *vt* **:** to resolve into factors ~ *vi* **:** to work as a factor — **fac·tor·able** \-t(ə-)rə-bəl\ *adj*
fac·tor·age \-t(ə-)rij\ *n* **1 :** the charges made by a factor for his services **2 :** the business of a factor
¹fac·to·ri·al \fak-'tōr-ē-əl, -'tȯr-\ *n* **:** the product of all the positive integers from one to a given number
²factorial *adj* **:** of or relating to a factor or a factorial
fac·tor·iza·tion \,fak-t(ə-)rə-'zā-shən\ *n* **:** an act or process of factoring
fac·tor·ize \'fak-tə-,rīz\ *vt* **:** FACTOR
fac·to·ry \'fak-t(ə-)rē\ *n* **1 :** a station where resident factors trade **2 :** a building or set of buildings with facilities for manufacturing
fac·to·tum \fak-'tōt-əm\ *n* [NL, lit., do everything, fr. L *fac* do + *totum* everything] **:** an employee with various duties
fac·tu·al \'fak-chə(-wə)l, 'faksh-wəl\ *adj* **1 :** of or relating to facts **2 :** restricted to or based on fact — **fac·tu·al·i·ty** \,fak-chə-'wal-ət-ē\ *n* — **fac·tu·al·ly** \'fak-chə(-wə)-lē, 'faksh-wə-\ *adv* — **fac·tu·al·ness** *n*
fac·tu·al·ism \'fak-chə-(wə-),liz-əm, 'faksh-wə-,\ *n* **1 :** adherence or dedication to facts **2 :** a theory emphasizing the importance of facts — **fac·tu·al·ist** \-ləst\ *n*
fac·ture \'fak-chər\ *n* [ME, fr. MF, fr. L *factura* action of making, fr. *factus*] **:** the action or manner of making

fac·u·la \'fak-yə-lə\ *n, pl* **fac·u·lae** \-,lē, -,lī\ [NL, fr. L, dim. of *fac-, fax* torch] **:** any of the bright regions of the sun's photosphere seen most easily near the sun's edge

fac·ul·ta·tive \'fak-əl-,tāt-iv\ *adj* **1 a :** of or relating to the grant of permission, authority, or privilege **b :** OPTIONAL **2 :** of or relating to a mental faculty **3 a :** having opposite reactions under different conditions **b :** able to live or thrive under more than one set of conditions — **fac·ul·ta·tive·ly** *adv*

fac·ul·ty \'fak-əl-tē\ *n* [ME *faculte*, fr. MF *faculté*, fr. ML & L; ML *facultat-, facultas* branch of learning or teaching, fr. L, ability, abundance, fr. *facilis* facile] **1 :** ABILITY, POWER: as **a** (1) **:** personal capacity (2) **:** a natural aptitude **b :** a physical power or function **c :** one of the powers of the mind formerly held by psychologists to form a basis for the explanation of all mental phenomena **2 a :** a branch of teaching or learning in an educational institution **b** *archaic* **:** something in which one is trained or qualified **3 a :** the members of a profession **b :** the teaching and administrative staff and those members of the administration having academic rank in an educational institution **4 :** power, authority, or prerogative given or conferred **syn** see GIFT

fad \'fad\ *n* [origin unknown] **:** a practice or interest followed for a time with exaggerated zeal **:** CRAZE **syn** see FASHION — **fad·dish** \'fad-ish\ *adj* — **fad·dism** \'fad-,iz-əm\ *n* — **fad·dist** \'fad-əst\ *n*

1**fade** \'fād\ *vb* [ME *faden*, fr. MF *fader*, fr. *fade* feeble, insipid, fr. (assumed) VL *fatidus*, alter. of L *fatuus* fatuous, insipid] *vi* **1 :** to lose freshness or vitality **:** WITHER **2 :** to lose freshness or brilliance of color **3 :** to sink away **:** VANISH **4 :** to change gradually in loudness or visibility — used of a motion-picture image or of an electronics signal and usu. with *in* or *out* **~** *vt* **:** to cause to fade

2**fade** *n* **:** a gradual changing of one picture to another in a motion-picture or television sequence

3**fade** \'fäd\ *adj* [F, fr. MF] **:** INSIPID, COMMONPLACE

fade·away \'fād-ə-,wā\ *n* **1 :** an act or instance of fading away **2 a :** SCREWBALL 1 **b :** a slide in which a base runner throws his body sideways to avoid the tag

fade·less \'fād-ləs\ *adj* **:** not susceptible to fading — **fade·less·ly** *adv*

fa·do \'fäth-(,)ü\ *n* [Pg, lit., fate, fr. L *fatum*] **:** a plaintive Portuguese folk song

fae·cal, fae·ces *var of* FECAL, FECES

fa·er·ie *also* **fa·ery** \'fā-(ə-)rē, 'fa(ə)r-ē, 'fe(ə)r-ē\ *n* [MF *faerie*] **1 :** the realm of fairies **2 :** FAIRY — **faery** *adj*

Faero·ese \,far-ə-'wēz, ,fer-, -'wēs\ *n, pl* **Faeroese 1 a :** the Germanic people inhabiting the Faeroes **b :** a member of this people **2 :** the Germanic language of the Faeroese people — **Faeroese** *adj*

Faf·nir \'fäv-,ni(ə)r, 'fäf-, -nər\ *n* [ON *Fāfnir*] **:** a dragon in Norse mythology slain by Sigurd

1**fag** \'fag\ *vb* **fagged; fag·ging** [obs. *fag* to droop, perh. fr. *fag* (fag end)] *vi* **1 :** to work hard **:** DRUDGE **2 :** to act as a fag **~** *vt* **:** to tire by strenuous activity **:** EXHAUST **syn** see TIRE

2**fag** *n* **1** *chiefly Brit* **:** TOIL, DRUDGERY **2 a :** an English public-school boy who acts as servant to another **b :** MENIAL, DRUDGE

3**fag** *n* [*fag end*] **:** CIGARETTE

fag end *n* [earlier *fag*, fr. ME *fagge* flap] **1 a :** the last part or coarser end of a web of cloth **b :** the untwisted end of a rope **2 a :** a poor or worn-out end **:** REMNANT **b :** the extreme end

1**fag·ot** *or* **fag·got** \'fag-ət\ *n* [ME *fagot*, fr. MF] **:** BUNDLE: as **a :** a bundle of sticks **b :** a bundle of pieces of wrought iron to be shaped by rolling or hammering at high temperature

2**fagot** *or* **faggot** *vt* **1 :** to make a fagot of **2 :** to bind in a fagot

fag·ot·ing *or* **fag·got·ing** *n* **1 :** an embroidery produced by pulling out horizontal threads from a fabric and tying the remaining cross threads into groups of an hourglass shape **2 :** an openwork stitch joining hemmed edges

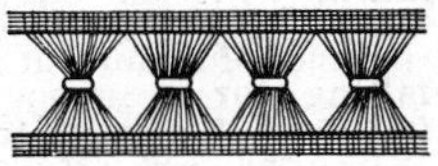

fagoting 1

Fahr·en·heit \'far-ən-,hīt\ *adj* [Gabriel D. *Fahrenheit* †1736 G physicist] **:** relating or conforming to a thermometric scale on which under standard atmospheric pressure the boiling point of water is at 212 degrees above the zero of the scale, the freezing point is at 32 degrees above zero, and the zero point approximates the temperature produced by mixing equal quantities by weight of snow and common salt

fa·ience *or* **fa·ïence** \fā-'än(t)s, fī-, -'äⁿs\ *n* [F, fr. *Faenza*, Italy] **:** earthenware decorated with opaque colored glazes

1**fail** \'fā(ə)l\ *vb* [ME *failen*, fr. OF *faillir*, fr. (assumed) VL *fallire*, alter. of L *fallere* to deceive, disappoint; prob. akin to Gk *phēlos* deceitful] *vi* **1 a :** to lose strength **:** WEAKEN **b :** to fade or die away **c :** to stop functioning **2 a :** to fall short ⟨*~ed* in his duty⟩ **b :** to be or become absent or inadequate ⟨the water supply *~ed*⟩ **c :** to be unsuccessful (as in passing an examination) **d :** to become bankrupt or insolvent **~** *vt* **1 :** DISAPPOINT, DESERT **2 :** to be deficient in **3 :** to leave undone **:** NEGLECT **4 a :** to be unsuccessful in passing **b :** to grade (as a student) as not passing — **fail·ing·ly** \'fā-liŋ-lē\ *adv*

2**fail** *n* **:** FAILURE — usu. used in the phrase *without fail*

1**fail·ing** \'fā-liŋ\ *n* **:** WEAKNESS, SHORTCOMING **syn** see FAULT

2**failing** *prep* **:** in absence or default of

faille \'fī(ə)l\ *n* [F] **:** a somewhat shiny closely woven silk, rayon, or cotton fabric characterized by slight ribs in the weft

fail–safe \'fā(ə)l-,sāf\ *adj* **1 :** incorporating some feature for automatically counteracting the effect of an anticipated possible source of failure **2 :** being or relating to a safeguard that prevents continuing on a bombing mission according to a preconceived plan

fail·ure \'fā(ə)l-yər\ *n* [alter. of earlier *failer*, fr. AF, fr. OF *faillir* to fail] **1 a :** omission of occurrence or performance; *specif* **:** a failing to perform a duty or expected action **b :** a state of inability to perform a normal function ⟨heart **~**⟩ **2 a :** lack of success **b :** a failing in business **:** BANKRUPTCY **3 a :** a falling short **:** DEFICIENCY **b :** DETERIORATION, DECAY **4 :** one that has failed

1**fain** \'fān\ *adj* [ME *fagen, fayn*, fr. OE *fægen;* akin to ON *fegiun* happy, OE *fæger* fair] **1** *archaic* **:** PLEASED, HAPPY **2** *archaic* **:** INCLINED **3** *archaic* **a :** WILLING **b :** OBLIGED, COMPELLED

2**fain** *adv* **1** *archaic* **:** WILLINGLY **2** *archaic* **:** RATHER

1**fai·né·ant** \'fā-nē-ənt, fā-nā-'äⁿ\ *n, pl* **fainéants** \-ən(t)s, -'äⁿ(z)\ [F, fr. MF *fait-nient*, lit., does nothing, by folk etymology fr. *faignant*, fr. prp. of *faindre, feindre*] **:** an irresponsible idler

2**fainéant** *or* **fai·ne·ant** *adj* **:** having the character of a fainéant

1**faint** \'fānt\ *adj* [ME *faint, feint*, fr. OF, fr. pp. of *faindre, feindre* to feign, shirk — more at FEIGN] **1 :** lacking courage and spirit **:** COWARDLY **2 :** weak, dizzy, and likely to faint **3 a :** lacking strength **b :** performed weakly or languidly **4 :** producing a sensation of faintness **5 :** lacking distinctness **:** DIM — **faint·ish** \'fānt-ish\ *adj* — **faint·ish·ness** *n* — **faint·ly** *adv* — **faint·ness** *n*

2**faint** *vi* **1** *archaic* **:** to lose courage or spirit **2** *archaic* **:** to become weak **3 :** to lose consciousness because of a temporary decrease in the blood supply to the brain **4 :** to lose brightness

3**faint** *n* **:** an act or condition of fainting **:** SYNCOPE

faint·heart·ed \'fānt-'härt-əd\ *adj* **:** lacking courage or resolution **:** TIMID — **faint·heart·ed·ly** *adv* — **faint·heart·ed·ness** *n*

1**fair** \'fa(ə)r, 'fe(ə)r\ *adj* [ME *fager, fair* fr. OE *fæger;* akin to OHG *fagar* beautiful and perh. to Lith *puošti* to decorate] **1 :** attractive in appearance **:** BEAUTIFUL **2 :** superficially pleasing **:** SPECIOUS **3 a :** CLEAN, PURE **b :** CLEAR, LEGIBLE **4 a :** not stormy or foul **:** CLOUDLESS **b :** free or nearly free from precipitation **5 :** AMPLE ⟨a **~** estate⟩ **6 a :** marked by impartiality and honesty **:** JUST **b :** conforming with the established rules **:** ALLOWED **c :** open to legitimate pursuit or attack ⟨**~** game⟩ **7 a :** PROMISING, LIKELY **b :** favorable to a ship's course ⟨a **~** wind⟩ **8** *archaic* **:** free of obstacles **9 :** not dark **:** BLOND **10 :** ADEQUATE — **fair·ness** *n*

syn FAIR, JUST, EQUITABLE, IMPARTIAL, UNBIASED, DISPASSIONATE, OBJECTIVE mean free from favor toward either or any side. FAIR implies an elimination of one's own feelings, prejudices, and desires so as to achieve a proper balance of conflicting interests; JUST implies an exact following of a standard of what is right and proper; EQUITABLE, less rigid than JUST, implies equal treatment of all concerned; IMPARTIAL stresses an absence of favor or prejudice in making a judgment; UNBIASED implies even more strongly an absence of all prejudice or prepossession; DISPASSIONATE suggests freedom from the influence of strong feeling and often implies coolness or even coldness in judgment; OBJECTIVE stresses a tendency to view events or persons as apart from oneself and one's own interest, opinion, likes, or dislikes **syn** see in addition BEAUTIFUL

2**fair** *n* **1** *obs* **:** FAIRNESS, BEAUTY **2 :** something that is fair or fortunate **3** *archaic* **:** WOMAN; *esp* **:** SWEETHEART

3**fair** *adv* **:** FAIRLY

4**fair** *vi, of the weather* **:** CLEAR **~** *vt* **:** to join so that the external surfaces blend smoothly

5**fair** *n* [ME *feire*, fr. OF, fr. ML *feria* weekday, fair, fr. LL, festal day, fr. L *feriae* (pl.) holidays — more at FEAST] **1 :** a gathering of buyers and sellers at a particular place and time for trade **2 :** a competitive exhibition (as of farm products) **3 :** a sale of a collection of articles usu. for a charitable purpose

fair ball *n* **:** a batted baseball that settles within the foul lines in the infield, that first touches the ground within the foul lines in the outfield, or that is within the foul lines when bounding to the outfield past first or third base or when going beyond the outfield for a home run

fair catch *n* **:** a catch of a kicked football by a player who gives a prescribed signal, may not advance the ball, and may not be tackled

fair copy *n* **:** a neat and exact copy esp. of a corrected draft

fair·ground \'fa(ə)r-,graùnd, 'fe(ə)r-\ *n* **:** an area where outdoor fairs, circuses, or exhibitions are held

1**fair·ing** \'fa(ə)r-iŋ, 'fe(ə)r-\ *n* **1** *Brit* **a :** a present bought or given at a fair **b :** GIFT **2** *Brit* **:** DESERTS

2**fairing** *n* **:** a member or structure whose primary function is to produce a smooth outline and reduce drag

fair·ish \'fa(ə)r-ish, 'fe(ə)r-\ *adj* **:** fairly good — **fair·ish·ly** *adv*

fair·lead \'fa(ə)r-,lēd, 'fe(ə)r-\ *n* **1** *also* **fair·lead·er :** a block, ring, or strip of plank with holes that serves as a guide for the running rigging or any ship's rope and keeps it from chafing **2 :** a course of running ship's rope that avoids all chafing

fair·ly \'fa(ə)r-lē, 'fe(ə)r-\ *adv* **1 a :** HANDSOMELY **b :** BECOMINGLY, SUITABLY **2** *obs* **a :** GENTLY, QUIETLY **b :** COURTEOUSLY **3 :** QUITE, COMPLETELY **4 a :** in a proper or legal manner **b :** IMPARTIALLY **5 :** PLAINLY, DISTINCTLY **6 :** MODERATELY, TOLERABLY

fair–mind·ed \'fa(ə)r-'mīn-dəd, 'fe(ə)r-\ *adj* **:** UNPREJUDICED, JUST — **fair–mind·ed·ness** *n*

fair–spok·en \-'spō-kən\ *adj* **1 :** using fair speech **2 :** COURTEOUS

fair trade *n* **:** trade in conformity with a fair-trade agreement

fair–trade \'fa(ə)r-'trād, 'fe(ə)r-\ *vt* **:** to market (a commodity) in compliance with the provisions of a fair-trade agreement — **fair trader** *n*

fair–trade agreement *n* **:** an agreement between a producer and a seller that commodities bearing a trademark, label, or brand name belonging to the producer be sold at or above a specified price

fair·way \'fa(ə)r-,wā, 'fe(ə)r-\ *n* **1 a :** a navigable part of a river, bay, or harbor **b :** an open path or space **2 :** the mowed part of a golf course between a tee and a green

fair–weath·er \-'weth-ər\ *adj* **1 :** suitable for, done during, or made in fair weather **2 :** loyal only during a time of success

fairy \'fa(ə)r-ē, 'fe(ə)r-\ *n* [ME *fairie* fairyland, fairy people, fr. OF *faerie*, fr. *feie, fee* fairy, fr. L *Fata*, goddess of fate, fr. *fatum* fate] **:** a mythical being of folklore and romance usu. having diminutive human form and magic powers — **fairy** *adj* — **fairy·like** \-,līk\ *adj*

fairy·ism \-,iz-əm\ *n, archaic* **:** power to enchant

fairy·land \-,land\ *n* **1 :** the land of fairies **2 :** a place of delicate beauty or magical charm

fairy ring *n* **1 :** a ring of mushrooms produced at the periphery of mycelium which has grown centrifugally from an initial growth point; *also* **:** a ring of luxuriant vegetation associated with these mushrooms **2 :** a mushroom (esp. *Marasmius oreades*) that commonly grows in fairy rings

fairy tale *n* **1 :** a simple narrative that deals with supernatural beings and is told for the amusement of children — called also *fairy story* **2 :** a made-up story usu. designed to mislead

fairy–tale *adj* **:** characteristic of or suitable to a fairy tale; *esp* **:** marked by unusual grace or beauty

fait ac·com·pli \fā-tà-kōⁿ-plē\ *n, pl* **faits accomplis** \fā-tà-kōⁿ-plē(z)\ [F, accomplished fact] **:** a thing accomplished and presumably irreversible

1**faith** \'fāth\ *n, pl* **faiths** \'fāths, 'fāthz\ [ME *feith*, fr. OF *feid, foi*, fr. L *fides;* akin to L *fidere* to trust — more at BIDE] **1 a :** allegiance

to duty or a person : LOYALTY **b** : fidelity to one's promises **2 a** (1) : belief and trust in and loyalty to God (2) : belief in the traditional doctrines of a religion **b** (1) : firm belief in something for which there is no proof (2) : complete confidence **3** : something that is believed esp. with strong conviction; *esp* : a system of religious beliefs **syn** see BELIEF — **in faith** : by my faith

²faith *vt, archaic* : BELIEVE, TRUST

¹faith·ful \'fāth-fəl\ *adj* **1** *obs* : full of faith **2** : steadfast in affection or allegiance **3** : firm in adherence to promises or in observance of duty : CONSCIENTIOUS **4** : given with strong assurance : BINDING ⟨~ promise⟩ **5** : true to the facts or to an original — **faith·ful·ly** \-fə-lē\ *adv* — **faith·ful·ness** *n*

syn LOYAL, CONSTANT, STAUNCH, STEADFAST, RESOLUTE: FAITHFUL implies unswerving adherence to a person or thing or to the oath or pledge or promise by which a tie was contracted; LOYAL implies a firm resistance to any temptation to desert or betray; CONSTANT stresses continuing firmness of emotional attachment without necessarily implying strict obedience to promises or vows; STAUNCH suggests fortitude and resolution in adherence and imperviousness to influences that would weaken it; STEADFAST implies a steady and unwavering course in love, allegiance, or conviction; RESOLUTE implies firm determination to adhere to a cause or purpose

²faithful *n, pl* **faithful** *or* **faithfuls** : one that is faithful: as **a** : church members in full communion and good standing — used with *the* **b** : the body of adherents of the Muslim religion — used with *the* **c** : a loyal follower or member ⟨party ~s⟩

faith·less \'fāth-ləs\ *adj* **1** : marked by absence of faith **2** : not worthy of trust or reliance : DISLOYAL — **faith·less·ly** *adv* — **faith·less·ness** *n*

syn FALSE, DISLOYAL, TRAITOROUS, TREACHEROUS, PERFIDIOUS: FAITHLESS applies to any failure to keep a promise or pledge or any breach of allegiance or loyalty; FALSE stresses the fact of failing to be true in any manner ranging from fickleness to cold treachery; DISLOYAL implies a lack of complete faithfulness in thought or words or actions to a friend, cause, leader, or country; TRAITOROUS implies either actual treason or a serious betrayal of trust; TREACHEROUS implies readiness to betray trust or confidence more commonly through lack of scruple than through weakness; PERFIDIOUS adds to FAITHLESS the implication of an incapacity for fidelity or reliability

fai·tour \'fāt-ər\ *n* [ME, fr. AF, fr. OF *faitor* perpetrator, fr. L *factor* doer — more at FACTOR] *archaic* : CHEAT, IMPOSTOR

¹fake \'fāk\ *vt* [ME *faken*] : to coil in fakes

²fake *n* : one loop of a coil (as of ship's rope) coiled free for running

³fake *vb* [origin unknown] *vt* **1** : to alter, manipulate, or treat so as to impart a false character or appearance to **2** : COUNTERFEIT, SIMULATE ~ *vi* : to engage in faking something : PRETEND — **fak·er** *n* — **fak·ery** \'fā-k(ə-)rē\ *n*

⁴fake *n* **1** : COUNTERFEIT, IMITATION: as **a** : a worthless imitation passed off as genuine **b** : IMPOSTOR, CHARLATAN **2** : a device or apparatus used by a magician to achieve the illusion of magic in a trick **syn** see IMPOSTURE

⁵fake *adj* : COUNTERFEIT, SHAM

fa·kir *n* [Ar *faqīr*, lit., poor man] **1** \fə-'ki(ə)r\ **a** : a Muslim mendicant : DERVISH **b** : an itinerant Hindu ascetic or wonder-worker **2** \'fā-kər\ : FAKER; *esp* : SWINDLER

fa la \fä-'lä\ *n* [*fa-la*, meaningless syllables often occurring in its refrain] : a 16th and 17th century part-song

Fa·lan·gist \fə-'lan-jəst, 'fā-,\ *n* [Sp *Falangista*, fr. *Falange española* Spanish Phalanx, a fascist organization] : a member of the fascist political party governing Spain after the civil war of 1936–39

fal·cate \'fal-,kāt, 'fȯl-\ *also* **fal·cat·ed** \-,kāt-əd\ *adj* [L *falcatus*, fr. *falc-, falx* sickle, scythe] : hooked or curved like a sickle

fal·chion \'fȯl-chən\ *n* [ME *fauchoun*, fr. OF *fauchon*, fr. *fauchier* to mow, fr. (assumed) VL *falcare*, fr. L *falc-, falx*] **1** : a broad-bladed slightly curved sword of medieval times **2** *archaic* : SWORD

fal·ci·form \'fal-sə-,fȯrm, 'fȯl-\ *adj* [L *falc-, falx* + E *-iform*] : having the shape of a scythe or sickle

fal·con \'fal-kən, 'fȯl- *also* 'fȯ-kən\ *n* [ME, fr. OF, fr. LL *falcon-, falco*, prob. of Gmc origin; akin to OHG *falcho* falcon] **1 a** : any of various hawks trained for use in falconry; *esp* : PEREGRINE — used technically only of a female; compare TIERCEL **b** : any of various hawks (family Falconidae) distinguished by long wings and a notch and tooth on the edge of the upper mandible **c** : HAWK 1 **2** : a light cannon used from the 15th to the 17th centuries

fal·con·er \-kə-nər\ *n* **1** : one who hunts with hawks **2** : a breeder or trainer of hawks for hunting

fal·con·et \,fal-kə-'net, ,fȯl- *also* ,fȯ-kə-\ *n* **1** : a very small cannon used in the 16th and 17th centuries **2** : any of several very small Asiatic falcons constituting a genus (*Microhierax*)

fal·con-gen·tle \,fal-kən-'jent-ᵊl, ,fȯ(l)-\ *n* [ME *faucon gentil* peregrine falcon, fr. MF, lit., noble falcon] : the female peregrine falcon

fal·con·ry \'fal-kən-rē, 'fȯl- *also* 'fȯ-kən-\ *n* **1** : the art of training falcons to pursue game **2** : the sport of hunting with falcons

fal·de·ral \'fäl-də-,räl\ *var of* FOLDEROL

fald·stool \'fȯl(d)-,stül\ *n* [ML *faldistolium*, of Gmc origin; akin to OHG *faltistuol* folding chair, fr. a prehistoric WGmc compound whose first constituent is akin to OHG *faldan* to fold and whose second constituent is represented by OHG *stuol* chair — more at FOLD, STOOL] **1** : a folding stool or chair; *specif* : one used by a bishop **2** : a folding stool or small desk at which one kneels during devotions; *esp* : one used by the sovereign of England at his coronation **3** : the desk from which the litany is read in Anglican churches

¹fall \'fȯl\ *vb* **fell** \'fel\ **fall·en** \'fȯ-lən *or esp in poetry* 'fȯln\ **fall·ing** [ME *fallen*, fr. OE *feallan*; akin to OHG *fallan* to fall and perh. to Lith *pulti*] *vi* **1 a** : to descend freely by the force of gravity **b** : to hang freely **c** : to drop oneself to a lower position **d** : to come as if by descending **2** : to become born — usu. used of lambs **3 a** : to become of lower degree or level **b** : to drop in pitch or volume **c** : to become uttered **d** : to become lowered ⟨her eyes *fell*⟩ **4 a** : to leave an erect position suddenly and involuntarily **b** : STUMBLE, STRAY **c** : to drop down wounded or dead; *esp* : to die in battle **d** : to suffer military capture **e** : to lose office ⟨the party *fell* from power⟩ **f** : to suffer ruin, defeat, or failure **5** : to commit an immoral act; *esp* : to lose one's chastity **6 a** : to move or extend in a downward direction **b** : SUBSIDE, ABATE **c** : to decline in quality, activity, or quantity **d** : to lose weight — used with *off* or *away* **e** : to assume a look of shame, disappointment, or dejection **7** : to decline in financial value or price **8 a** : to occur at a certain time **b** : to come by chance **c** : to come or pass by lot, assignment, or inheritance : DEVOLVE **d** : to have its place or station ⟨the accent ~s on the second syllable⟩ **9** : to come within the limits, scope, or jurisdiction of something **10** : to pass suddenly and passively into a state of body or mind **11** : to set about heartily or actively ⟨*fell* to work⟩ **12** : STRIKE, IMPINGE ~ *vt* : FELL 1 — **fall behind 1** : to lag behind **2** : to be in arrears — **fall flat** : to produce no response or result — **fall for 1** : to fall in love with **2** : to become a victim of — **fall foul 1** : to have a collision — used chiefly of ships **2** : to have a quarrel : CLASH — often used with *of* — **fall from grace 1** : to lapse morally : SIN **2** : BACKSLIDE — **fall home** : to curve inward — used of the timbers or upper parts of a ship's side — **fall into line** : to comply with a certain course of action — **fall over oneself** : to display excessive eagerness — **fall short 1** : to be deficient **2** : to fail to attain

²fall *n* **1** : the act of falling by the force of gravity **2 a** : a falling out, off, or away : DROPPING **b** : the season when leaves fall from trees : AUTUMN **c** : a thing or quantity that falls **d** (1) : BIRTH (2) : the quantity born — usu. used of lambs **3 a** : a costume decoration of lace or thin fabric arranged to hang loosely and gracefully **b** : a very wide turned-down collar worn in the 17th century **c** : the part of a turned-over collar from the crease to the outer edge **d** : a wide front flap on trousers (as those worn by sailors) **e** : the freely hanging lower edge of the skirt of a coat **f** : one of the three outer and often drooping segments of the flower of an iris **4** : a hoisting-tackle rope or chain; *esp* : the part of it to which the power is applied **5 a** : loss of greatness : COLLAPSE **b** : the surrender or capture of a besieged place **c** : lapse or departure from innocence or goodness **d** : loss of a woman's chastity **6 a** : the descent of land or a hill : SLOPE **b** : precipitous descent of water : WATERFALL — usu. used in pl. but sing. or pl. in constr. **c** : a musical cadence **d** : a falling-pitch intonation in speech **7** : a decrease in size, quantity, or degree; *specif* : a decrease in price or value **8 a** : the distance which something falls **b** : INCLINATION, PITCH **9 a** : the act of felling **b** : the quantity of trees cut down **c** (1) : an act of forcing a wrestler's shoulders to the mat (2) : a bout of wrestling **10** *Scot* : FORTUNE, LOT

³fall *adj* : of or relating to fall ⟨~ coat⟩

fal·la·cious \fə-'lā-shəs\ *adj* **1** : embodying a fallacy **2 a** : DECEPTIVE, MISLEADING **b** : DELUSIVE, DISAPPOINTING — **fal·la·cious·ly** *adv* — **fal·la·cious·ness** *n*

fal·la·cy \'fal-ə-sē\ *n* [L *fallacia*, fr. *fallac-, fallax* deceitful, fr. *fallere* to deceive — more at FAIL] **1 a** *obs* : GUILE, TRICKERY **b** : deceptive appearance : DECEPTION **2 a** : a false idea **b** : erroneous or fallacious character : ERRONEOUSNESS **3** : an argument failing to satisfy the conditions of valid or correct inference

fal-lal \fa-'lal, 'fal-'lal\ *n* [perh. alter. of *falbala* (furbelow)] : a fancy ornament esp. in dress — **fal·lal·ery** \fa-'lal-ə-rē\ *n*

fall away *vi* **1 a** : to withdraw friendship or support **b** : to renounce one's faith **2 a** : to diminish in size **b** : to drift off a course

fall back *vi* : RETREAT, RECEDE — **fall back on** *or* **fall back upon** : to have recourse to

fall·back \'fȯl-,bak\ *n* **1** : something on which one can fall back : RESERVE **2** : a falling back : RETREAT

fall·er \'fȯ-lər\ *n* **1** : a logger who fells trees **2** : a machine part that acts by falling

fall·fish \'fȯl-,fish\ *n* : any of several common No. American cyprinoid fishes; *esp* : a fish (*Semotilus corporalis*) of the streams of northeastern No. America — compare CHUB

fall guy *n* **1** : one that is easily duped **2** : SCAPEGOAT

fal·li·bil·i·ty \,fal-ə-'bil-ət-ē\ *n* : liability to err

fal·li·ble \'fal-ə-bəl\ *adj* [ME, fr. ML *fallibilis*, fr. L *fallere*] **1** : liable to be erroneous **2** : capable of making a mistake — **fal·li·bly** \-blē\ *adv*

fall in *vi* : to take one's proper place in a military formation

fall·ing-out \,fȯ-liŋ-'au̇t\ *n, pl* **fallings-out** *or* **falling-outs** : an instance of falling out : QUARREL

falling star *n* : METEOR 2a

fall off *vi* **1** : TREND 1b **2** : to deviate to leeward of the point to which the head was directed

fall·off \'fȯ-,lȯf\ *n* : DECLINE

fal·lo·pi·an tube \fə-,lō-pē-ən-\ *n, often cap F* [Gabriel *Fallopius* †1562 It anatomist] : either of the pair of tubes conducting the egg from the ovary to the uterus

fall out *vi* **1** : HAPPEN **2** : QUARREL **3 a** : to leave one's place in the ranks **b** : to leave a building to meet a military formation

fall·out \'fȯ-,lau̇t\ *n* : the often radioactive particles stirred up by or resulting from a nuclear explosion and descending through the atmosphere

¹fal·low \'fal-(,)ō, -ə(-w)\ *adj* [ME *falow*, fr. OE *fealu*; akin to OHG *falo* pale, fallow, L *pallēre* to be pale, Gk *polios* gray] : of a light yellowish brown

²fallow *n* [ME *falwe, falow*, fr. OE *fealg* — more at FELLY] **1** *obs* : plowed land **2** : usu. cultivated land allowed to lie idle during the growing season **3** : the state or period of being fallow **4** : the tilling of land without sowing it for a season

³fallow *vt* : to plow, harrow, and break up (land) without seeding to destroy weeds and conserve soil moisture

⁴fallow *adj* **1** : left untilled or unsown after plowing **2** : DORMANT, INACTIVE — **fal·low·ness** *n*

fallow deer *n* : a small European deer (*Dama dama*) with broad antlers and a pale yellow coat spotted white in the summer

fall to *vi* : to set about doing something esp. actively

¹false \'fȯls\ *adj* [ME *fals*, fr. OE & L; OF, fr. L *falsus*, fr. pp. of *fallere*] **1** : not genuine ⟨~ documents⟩ ⟨~ teeth⟩ **2 a** : intentionally untrue ⟨~ testimony⟩ **b** : adjusted or made so as to deceive ⟨~ scales⟩ **c** : tending to mislead ⟨~ promise⟩ **3** : not true ⟨~ concepts⟩ **4 a** : not faithful or loyal : TREACHEROUS **b** *obs* : not solid **5 a** : not essential or permanent **b** : fitting over a main part to strengthen it, to protect it, or to disguise its appearance **6** : of a kind related to or resembling another kind that is usu. designated by the unqualified vernacular ⟨~ oats⟩ **7** : inaccurate in pitch ⟨a ~ note⟩ **8 a** : based on mistaken ideas ⟨~ pride⟩ **b** : inconsistent with the true facts ⟨a ~ position⟩ — **false·ly** *adv* — **false·ness** *n*

syn FALSE, WRONG mean neither true nor right. FALSE in nearly all its senses carries an implication of deceiving or of being deceived; WRONG implies usu. no more than a simple negation of or deviation from rightness or correctness **syn** see in addition FAITHLESS

²false *adv* : FAITHLESSLY, TREACHEROUSLY ⟨his wife played him ~⟩

false·hood \'fȯls-,hu̇d\ *n* **1 a** : an untrue statement : LIE **b** : something contrary to truth **2** : absence of truth or accuracy : FALSITY **3** : the practice of lying : MENDACITY

false horizon *n* **:** HORIZON 1c
false imprisonment *n* **:** imprisonment of a person contrary to law
false rib *n* **:** a rib whose cartilages unite indirectly or not at all with the sternum
[1]**fal·set·to** \fȯl-'set-(,)ō\ *n, often attrib* [It, fr. dim. of *falso* false, fr. L *falsus*] **1 :** an artificially high voice; *specif* **:** an artificially produced singing voice that overlaps and extends above the range of the full voice esp. of a tenor **2 :** a singer who uses falsetto
[2]**falsetto** *adv* **:** in falsetto
fals·ie \'fȯl-sē\ *n* **:** a breast-shaped usu. fabric or rubber cup used to pad a brassiere — usu. used in pl.
fal·si·fi·ca·tion \,fȯls-(ə-)fə-'kā-shən\ *n* **:** an act or instance of falsifying
fal·si·fi·er \'fȯl-sə-,fī(-ə)r\ *n* **:** one that falsifies
fal·si·fy \'fȯl-sə-,fī\ *vb* [ME *falsifien*, fr. MF *falsifier*, fr. ML *falsificare*, fr. L *falsus*] *vt* **1 :** to prove or declare false **2 :** to make false: as **a :** to make false by mutilation or addition ⟨~ a will⟩ **b :** to represent falsely **:** MISREPRESENT **3 :** to prevent the fulfillment of ~ *vi* **:** to tell lies **:** LIE
fal·si·ty \'fȯl-sət-ē, -stē\ *n* **1 :** something false **:** LIE **2 :** the quality or state of being false
Fal·staff·ian \fȯl-'staf-ē-ən\ *adj* [Sir John *Falstaff*, character in Shakespeare's *Merry Wives of Windsor* and *Henry IV*] **:** of, relating to, or characteristic of Falstaff
falt·boat \'fält-,bōt, 'fȯlt-\ *n* [part trans. of G *faltboot* folding boat, fr. *falten* to fold (fr. OHG *faldan*) + *boot* boat] **:** a small collapsible canoe made of rubberized sailcloth stretched over a framework
[1]**fal·ter** \'fȯl-tər\ *vb* **fal·ter·ing** \-t(ə-)riŋ\ [ME *falteren*] *vi* **1 a :** to walk unsteadily **:** STUMBLE **b :** to give way **:** TOTTER **c :** to move waveringly or hesitatingly **2 :** to speak brokenly or weakly **:** STAMMER **3 :** to hesitate in purpose or action **:** WAVER ~ *vt* **:** to utter hesitatingly or brokenly **syn** see HESITATE — **fal·ter·er** \-tər-ər\ *n* — **fal·ter·ing·ly** \-t(ə-)riŋ-lē\ *adv*
[2]**falter** *n* **:** an act or instance of faltering
[1]**fame** \'fām\ *n* [ME, fr. OF, fr. L *fama* report, fame; akin to L *fari* to speak — more at BAN] **1 a :** public estimation **:** REPUTATION **b :** popular acclaim **:** RENOWN **2** *archaic* **:** RUMOR
[2]**fame** *vt* **1 :** REPORT, REPUTE **2 :** to make famous
famed \'fāmd\ *adj* **:** FAMOUS
fa·mil·ial \fə-'mil-yəl\ *adj* [F, fr. L *familia*] **:** of, relating to, or characteristic of a family
[1]**fa·mil·iar** \fə-'mil-yər\ *n* **1 :** an intimate associate **:** COMPANION **2 :** a member of the household of a high official **3 :** a spirit often embodied in an animal and held to attend and serve or guard a person **4 :** one who frequents a place
[2]**familiar** *adj* [ME *familier*, fr. OF, fr. L *familiaris*, fr. *familia*] **1 :** closely acquainted **:** INTIMATE **2** *obs* **:** AFFABLE, SOCIABLE **3 a :** of or relating to a family **b :** frequented by families **4 a :** being free and easy **b :** marked by informality ⟨~ essay⟩ **c :** overly free and unrestrained **:** PRESUMPTUOUS **d :** moderately tame **5 a :** frequently seen or experienced **b :** of everyday occurrence
syn INTIMATE: FAMILIAR suggests the ease, informality, absence of reserve or constraint natural among members of a family or acquaintances of long standing; INTIMATE stresses the closeness and intensity rather than the mere frequency of personal association and suggests either deep mutual understanding or the sharing of deeply personal thoughts and feeling **syn** see in addition COMMON
fa·mil·iar·i·ty \fə-,mil-'yar-ət-ē, -,mil-ē-'(y)ar-\ *n* **1 :** a state of being familiar **:** INTIMACY **2 a :** absence of ceremony **:** INFORMALITY **b :** an unduly informal act or expression **:** IMPROPRIETY **c :** a sexual liberty **3 :** close acquaintance with something
fa·mil·iar·iza·tion \fə-,mil-yə-rə-'zā-shən\ *n* **:** the act or process of familiarizing
fa·mil·iar·ize \fə-'mil-yə-,rīz\ *vt* **1 :** to make known or familiar **2 :** to make well acquainted
fa·mil·iar·ly *adv* **:** in a familiar manner
familiar spirit *n* **1 :** a spirit or demon that serves or prompts an individual **2 :** the spirit of a dead person invoked by a medium to advise or prophesy
[1]**fam·i·ly** \'fam-(ə-)lē\ *n* [ME *familie*, fr. L *familia* household (including servants as well as kin of the householder), fr. *famulus* servant; perh. akin to Skt *dhāman* dwelling place] **1 :** FELLOWSHIP **2 a :** a group of persons of common ancestry **:** CLAN **b :** a people or group of peoples regarded as deriving from a common stock **:** RACE **3 :** a group of individuals living under one roof and usu. under one head **:** HOUSEHOLD **4 a :** a group of things related by common characteristics or properties **b :** a group of soils that have similar profiles and include one or more series **5 :** the basic unit in society having as its nucleus two or more adults living together and cooperating in the care and rearing of their own or adopted children **6 a :** a group of related plants or animals forming a category ranking above a genus and below an order and usu. comprising several to many genera **b** *in livestock breeding* (1) **:** the descendants or line of a particular individual esp. of some outstanding female (2) **:** an identifiable strain within a breed **c :** an ecological community consisting of a single kind of organism and usu. being of limited extent and representing an early stage of a succession **7 :** a set of curves or surfaces whose equations differ only in parameters
[2]**family** *adj* **:** of or relating to a family
family Bible *n* **:** a large Bible usu. having special pages for recording births, marriages, and deaths
family circle *n* **:** a gallery in a theater or opera house usu. located above or behind a gallery containing more expensive seats
family man *n* **1 :** a man with a wife and children dependent upon him **2 :** a responsible man of domestic habits
family name *n* **1 :** SURNAME 2 **2 :** the name of an individual that identifies him with his family
family tree *n* **1 :** GENEALOGY **2 :** a genealogical diagram
fam·ine \'fam-ən\ *n* [ME, fr. MF, fr. (assumed) VL *famina*, fr. L *fames* hunger] **1 :** an extreme scarcity of food **2** *archaic* **:** STARVATION **3** *archaic* **:** a ravenous appetite **4 :** a great shortage
fam·ish \'fam-ish\ *vb* [ME *famishen*, prob. alter. of *famen*, fr. MF *afamer*, fr. (assumed) VL *affamare*, fr. L *ad-* + *fames*] *vt* **1 :** to cause to suffer severely from hunger **2** *archaic* **:** to cause to starve to death ~ *vi* **1** *archaic* **:** STARVE **2** *archaic* **:** to suffer for lack of something necessary — **fam·ish·ment** \-mənt\ *n*
fa·mous \'fā-məs\ *adj* [ME, fr. MF *fameux*, fr. L *famosus*, fr. *fama* fame] **1 a :** widely known **b :** honored for achievement **2 :** EXCELLENT, FIRST-RATE — **fa·mous·ly** *adv* — **fa·mous·ness** *n*
syn RENOWNED, CELEBRATED, NOTED, NOTORIOUS, DISTINGUISHED, EMINENT, ILLUSTRIOUS: FAMOUS implies little more than the fact of being, sometimes briefly, widely and popularly known; RENOWNED implies more glory and acclamation, CELEBRATED more notice and attention esp. in print; NOTED suggests well-deserved public attention; NOTORIOUS frequently adds to FAMOUS an implication of questionableness or evil; DISTINGUISHED implies acknowledged excellence or superiority; EMINENT implies even greater conspicuousness for outstanding quality or character; ILLUSTRIOUS stresses enduring honor and glory attached to a deed or person
fam·u·lus \'fam-yə-ləs\ *n, pl* **fam·u·li** \-,lī, -,lē\ [G, assistant to a professor, fr. L, servant] **:** a private secretary or attendant
[1]**fan** \'fan\ *n* [ME, fr. OE *fann*, fr. L *vannus* — more at WINNOW] **1 :** any of various devices for winnowing grain **2 :** an instrument for producing a current of air: as **a :** a device for cooling the person usu. shaped like a segment of a circle and composed of material (as feathers, paper) mounted on thin rods or slats moving about a pivot so that the device may be closed compactly when not in use **b :** a device for producing a current of air that consists of a series of vanes radiating from a hub rotated on its axle by a motor **3 :** something resembling an open fan — **fan·like** \-,līk\ *adj*
[2]**fan** *vb* **fanned; fan·ning** *vt* **1 a :** to drive away the chaff of by means of a current of air **b :** to eliminate by winnowing **2 :** to move or impel (air) with a fan **3 :** to blow or breathe upon **4 a :** to direct a current of air upon with a fan **b :** to stir up to activity as if by fanning **:** STIMULATE **5** *archaic* **:** WAVE **6** *slang* **:** SPANK **7 :** to spread like a fan **8 :** to strike (a batter) out in baseball **9 :** to fire by squeezing the trigger and striking the hammer to the rear with the free hand ~ *vi* **1 :** to move like a fan **2 :** to spread like a fan **3** *of a baseball batter* **:** to strike out
[3]**fan** *n* [prob. short for *fanatic*] **1 :** an enthusiastic devotee (as of a sport) usu. as a spectator **2 :** an ardent admirer (as of a celebrity)
fa·nat·ic \fə-'nat-ik\ *adj* [L *fanaticus* inspired by a deity, frenzied, fr. *fanum* temple] **:** marked by excessive enthusiasm and intense uncritical devotion — **fanatic** *n* — **fa·nat·i·cal** \-i-kəl\ *adj* — **fa·nat·i·cal·ly** \-i-k(ə-)lē\ *adv* — **fa·nat·i·cal·ness** \-kəl-nəs\ *n*
fa·nat·i·cism \fə-'nat-ə-,siz-əm\ *n* **:** fanatic outlook or behavior
fa·nat·i·cize \-,sīz\ *vt* **:** to cause to become fanatic
fan·ci·er \'fan(t)-sē-ər\ *n* **:** one that has a special liking or interest; *esp* **:** a person who breeds or grows a particular animal or plant for points of excellence
fan·ci·ful \'fan(t)-si-fəl\ *adj* **1 :** marked by fancy or unrestrained imagination rather than by reason and experience **2 :** existing in fancy only **3 :** marked by or as if by fancy or whim **syn** see IMAGINARY — **fan·ci·ful·ly** \-f(ə-)lē\ *adv* — **fan·ci·ful·ness** \-fəl-nəs\ *n*
fan·ci·ly \'fan(t)-sə-lē\ *adv* **1 :** with fancy or imagination esp. when studied or affected **2 :** ELABORATELY, ORNATELY
fan·ci·ness \-sē-nəs\ *n* **:** fancy quality or form
[1]**fan·cy** \'fan(t)-sē\ *n* [ME *fantasie*, *fantsy* fantasy, fancy, fr. MF *fantasie*, fr. L *phantasia*, fr. Gk, appearance, imagination, fr. *phantazein* to present to the mind (middle voice, to imagine), fr. *phainein* to show; akin to OE *gebōned* polished, Gk *phōs* light] **1 a :** a liking formed by caprice rather than reason **:** INCLINATION **b :** amorous fondness **:** LOVE **2 a :** NOTION, WHIM **b :** a mental image or representation **3** *archaic* **:** fantastic quality or state **4 a :** imagination esp. of a capricious or delusive sort **b :** the power of conception and representation used in artistic expression (as by a poet) **5 :** TASTE, JUDGMENT **6 a :** devotees of some particular art, practice, or amusement **b :** the object of interest of such a fancy; *esp* **:** PUGILISM **syn** see IMAGINATION
[2]**fancy** *vt* **1 :** to have a fancy for **:** LIKE **2 :** to form a conception of **:** IMAGINE **3 :** to believe without any evidence **syn** see THINK
[3]**fancy** *adj* **1 :** dependent or based on fancy **:** WHIMSICAL **2 a :** not plain **:** ORNAMENTAL **b :** of particular excellence or highest grade **c** *of an animal or plant* **:** bred for special qualities esp. such as lack practical utility **3 :** based on conceptions of the fancy ⟨~ sketches⟩ **4 a :** dealing in fancy goods **b :** above real value or the usual market price; *esp* **:** EXTRAVAGANT **5 :** executed with technical skill and superior grace **6 :** PARTI-COLORED
fancy dress *n* **:** a costume chosen to suit the wearer's fancy
fan·cy–free \'fan(t)-sē-,frē\ *adj* **1 :** free to imagine or fancy **2 :** free from amorous attachment or engagement
fancy man *n* **:** a woman's paramour; *also* **:** PIMP
fancy woman *n* **:** a woman of dubious morals; *specif* **:** PROSTITUTE
fan·cy·work \'fan(t)-sē-,wərk\ *n* **:** decorative needlework
fan·dan·go \fan-'daŋ-(,)gō\ *n* [Sp] **1 :** a lively Spanish or Spanish-American dance; *also* **:** music for this dance **2 :** TOMFOOLERY
fane \'fān\ *n* [ME, fr. L *fanum* — more at FEAST] **:** TEMPLE
fan·fare \'fan-,fa(ə)r, -,fe(ə)r\ *n* [F] **1 :** a flourish of trumpets **2 :** a showy outward display
fan·far·o·nade \,fan-,far-ə-'nād, -'näd\ *n* [F *fanfaronnade*, fr. Sp *fanfarronada*, fr. *fanfarrón* braggart] **:** empty boasting **:** BLUSTER
fang \'faŋ\ *n* [ME, fr. OE; akin to OHG *fang* seizure, OE *fōn* to seize — more at PACT] **1 a :** a long sharp tooth: as (1) **:** one by which an animal's prey is seized and held or torn (2) **:** one of the long hollow or grooved and often erectile teeth of a venomous snake **b :** one of the chelicerae of a spider at the tip of which a poison gland opens **2 :** the root of a tooth or one of the processes or prongs into which a root divides **3 :** a projecting tooth or prong — **fanged** \'faŋd\ *adj*

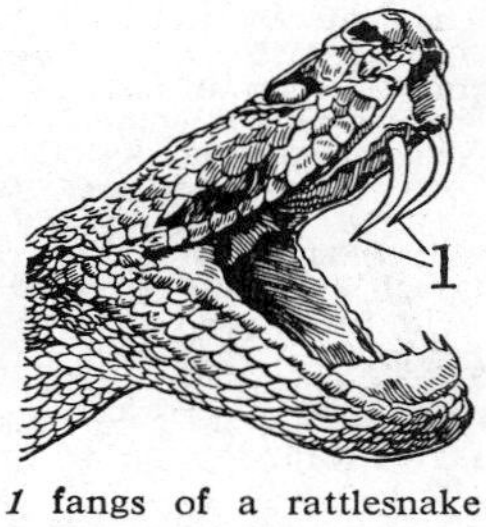

1 fangs of a rattlesnake

fan·ion \'fan-yən\ *n* [F, fr. *fanon* maniple, pennon, of Gmc origin; akin to OHG *fano* cloth — more at VANE] **:** a small flag used by soldiers and surveyors to mark positions
fan–jet \'fan-,jet\ *n* **1 :** a jet engine having a ducted fan that draws in extra air to provide extra thrust **2 :** an airplane powered by a fan-jet engine
fan·light \'fan-,līt\ *n* **:** a semicircular window with radiating sash bars like the ribs of a fan placed over a door or window
fan·ner \'fan-ər\ *n* **:** one that fans
fan·tail \'fan-,tāl\ *n, often attrib* **1 :** a fan-shaped tail or end

2 : a domestic pigeon having a broad rounded tail often with 30 or 40 feathers 3 : an architectural part resembling a fan; *specif* : a centering (as of an arch) of radiating struts 4 : a counter or after overhang of a ship shaped like a duck's bill
fan–tan \'fan-,tan\ *n* [Chin *fan¹-t'an¹*] 1 : a Chinese gambling game 2 : a card game
fan·ta·sia \fan-'tā-zhə, -z(h)ē-ə; ,fant-ə-'zē-ə\ *also* **fan·ta·sie** \,fant-ə-'zē, ,fänt-\ *n* [It *fantasia*, lit., fancy, fr. L *phantasia* — more at FANCY] 1 a : a free instrumental composition not in strict form (as the development section of sonata form) b : a potpourri of operatic arias or familiar airs 2 : a work (as a poem or play) in which the author's fancy roves unrestricted
fan·ta·sied \'fant-ə-sēd, -zēd\ *adj* 1 : existing only in the imagination : FANCIED 2 *obs* : full of fancies or strange whims
fantasm *var of* PHANTASM
fan·tast \'fan-,tast\ *n* [G, fr. ML *fantasta*, prob. back-formation fr. LL *phantasticus*] 1 : VISIONARY 2 : a fantastic person
¹**fan·tas·tic** \fan-'tas-tik, fən-\ *adj* [ME *fantastic, fantastical*, fr. MF & LL; MF *fantastique*, fr. LL *phantasticus*, fr. Gk *phantastikos* producing mental images, fr. *phantazein* to present to the mind] 1 a : based on fantasy : IMAGINARY b : conceived or seemingly conceived by unrestrained fancy c : exceedingly or unbelievably great 2 : marked by extravagant fantasy or extreme individuality : ECCENTRIC — **fan·tas·ti·cal** \-ti-kəl\ *adj* — **fan·tas·ti·cal·i·ty** \(,)fan-,tas-ti-'kal-ət-ē, fən-\ *n* — **fan·tas·ti·cal·ly** \fan-'tas-ti-k(ə-)lē, fən-\ *adv* — **fan·tas·ti·cal·ness** \-kəl-nəs\ *n*
syn BIZARRE, GROTESQUE: FANTASTIC may connote unrestrained extravagance in conception or merely ingenuity of decorative invention; BIZARRE applies to the sensationally queer or strange and implies violence of contrast or incongruity of combination; GROTESQUE may apply to what is conventionally ugly but artistically effective or it may connote ludicrous awkwardness or incongruity often with sinister or tragic overtones **syn** see in addition IMAGINARY
²**fantastic** *n, archaic* : ECCENTRIC 2
fan·tas·ti·co \fan-'tas-ti-,kō, fən-\ *n* [It, fantastic (adj.), fr. LL *phantasticus*] : a ridiculously fantastic individual
¹**fan·ta·sy** \'fant-ə-sē, -ə-zē\ *n* [ME *fantasie* — more at FANCY] 1 *obs* : HALLUCINATION 2 : FANCY; *esp* : the free play of creative imagination 3 a : a creation of the imaginative faculty; *broadly* : a fanciful design or invention b : a chimerical or fantastic notion c : FANTASIA 1 4 : CAPRICE 5 *usu* **phan·ta·sy** : the power, process, or result of creating mental images modified by need, wish, or desire ⟨the ~ of daydreams⟩ **syn** see IMAGINATION
²**fantasy** *vt* : to portray in the mind : FANCY ~ *vi* : to indulge in reverie : DAYDREAM
fan·toc·ci·ni \,fänt-ə-'chē-nē, ,fant-\ *n pl* [It, pl. of *fantoccino*, dim. of *fantoccio* doll, aug. of *fante* child, fr. L *infant-, infans* infant] 1 : puppets moved by strings or mechanical devices 2 : puppet shows using fantoccini
fan·tod \'fan-,täd\ *n* [perh. alter. of E dial. *fantique, fanteeg*] 1 a : a state of irritability and tension b *pl* : FIDGETS 2 : FIT
fantom *var of* PHANTOM
fan tracery *n* : decorative tracery on vaulting in which the ribs diverge like the rays of a fan
¹**far** \'fär\ *adv* **far·ther** \-thər\ *or* **fur·ther** \'fər-\ **far·thest** *or* **fur·thest** \-thəst\ [ME *fer*, fr. OE *feorr*; akin to OHG *ferro* far, OE *faran* to go — more at FARE] 1 : at or to a considerable distance in space 2 : by a broad interval : WIDELY 3 : to or at a definite distance, point, or degree ⟨as ~ as I know⟩ 4 a : to an advanced point or extent : a long way b : to a great extent : MUCH ⟨~ better methods⟩ 5 : at a considerable distance in time — **by far** : GREATLY — **far and away** : DECIDEDLY
²**far** *adj* **farther** *or* **further**; **farthest** *or* **furthest** 1 a : remote in space : DISTANT b : distinctly different in quality or relationship c : remote in time 2 a : LONG ⟨a ~ journey⟩ b : of notable extent : COMPREHENSIVE 3 : the more distant of two **syn** see DISTANT
far·ad \'far-,ad, -əd\ *n* [Michael *Faraday* †1867 E physicist] : the unit of capacitance equal to the capacitance of a capacitor between whose plates there appears a potential of one volt when it is charged by one coulomb of electricity
far·a·day \'far-ə-,dā, -əd-ē\ *n* [Michael *Faraday*] : the quantity of electricity transferred in electrolysis per equivalent weight of an element or ion equal to about 96,500 coulombs
fa·rad·ic \fə-'rad-ik\ *adj* : of or relating to an asymmetric alternating current of electricity produced by an induction coil
far·a·dism \'far-ə-,diz-əm\ *also* **far·a·di·za·tion** \,far-əd-ə-'zā-shən\ *n* : the application of a faradic current of electricity (as for therapeutic purposes)
far·a·dize \'far-ə-,dīz\ *vt* : to treat by faradism — **far·a·diz·er** *n*
far·an·dole \'far-ən-,dōl\ *n* [F *farandole*, fr. Prov *farandoulo*] : a lively Provençal chain dance in sextuple measure
far·away \,fär-ə-,wā\ *adj* 1 : lying at a great distance : REMOTE 2 : DREAMY, ABSTRACTED **syn** see DISTANT
¹**farce** \'färs\ *vt* [ME *farsen*, fr. MF *farcir*, fr. L *farcire*; akin to Gk *phrassein* to enclose] 1 : STUFF 2 : to make more acceptable (as a literary work) by padding or spicing
²**farce** *n* [ME *farse*, fr. MF *farce*, fr. (assumed) VL *farsa*, fr. L, fem of *farsus*, pp. of *farcire*] 1 : a savory stuffing : FORCEMEAT 2 : a light dramatic composition marked by broadly satirical comedy and improbable plot 3 : the broad humor characteristic of farce or pretense : MOCKERY 4 : ridiculous or empty show
far·ceur \fär-'sər\ *n* [F, fr. MF, fr. *farcer* to joke, fr. OF, fr. *farce*] 1 : JOKER, WAG 2 : a writer or actor of farce
far·ci *or* **far·cie** \fär-'sē\ *adj* [F, fr. pp. of *farcir*] : stuffed esp. with forcemeat ⟨oysters ~⟩
far·ci·cal \'fär-si-kəl\ *adj* 1 : of, relating to, or resembling farce : LUDICROUS 2 : laughably inept : ABSURD — **far·ci·cal·i·ty** \,fär-si-'kal-ət-ē\ *n* — **far·ci·cal·ly** \'fär-si-k(ə-)lē\ *adv*
far·cy \'fär-sē\ *n* [ME *farsin, farsi*, fr. MF *farcin*, fr. LL *farcimen*, fr. L, sausage, fr. *farcire*] 1 : GLANDERS; *esp* : cutaneous glanders 2 : a chronic ultimately fatal actinomycosis of cattle
¹**fard** \'färd\ *vt* [ME *farden*, fr. MF *farder*; akin to OHG *faro* colored] 1 : to paint (the face) with cosmetics 2 *archaic* : to gloss over
²**fard** *n, archaic* : paint used on the face
far·del \'färd-ᵊl\ *n* [ME, fr. MF, prob. fr. Ar *fardah*] 1 : BUNDLE 2 *archaic* : BURDEN
¹**fare** \'fa(ə)r, 'fe(ə)r\ *vi* [ME *faren*, fr. OE *faran*; akin to OHG *faran* to go, L *portare* to carry, Gk *poros* passage, journey] 1 : GO, TRAVEL 2 : to get along : SUCCEED 3 : EAT, DINE
²**fare** *n* [ME, journey, passage, supply of food, fr. OE *faru, fær*; akin to OE *faran* to go] 1 a : the price charged to transport a person b : a paying passenger on a public conveyance 2 a : range of food : DIET b : material provided for consumption or enjoyment
far·er \'far-ər, 'fer-\ *n* : TRAVELER — used esp. in combination ⟨way*farer*⟩
fare–thee–well \,far-(,)thē-'wel, ,fer-\ *or* **fare–you–well** \-yə-, -yü-, -yē-\ *n* 1 : a state of perfection 2 : the utmost degree
¹**fare·well** \fa(ə)r-'wel, fe(ə)r-\ *v imper* : get along well — used interjectionally to or by one departing
²**farewell** *n* 1 : a wish of welfare at parting : GOOD-BYE 2 a : an act of departure : LEAVE-TAKING b : a formal occasion honoring a person about to leave or retire
³**fare·well** \,fa(ə)r-,wel, ,fe(ə)r-\ *adj* : PARTING, FINAL ⟨a ~ concert⟩
far·fetched \'fär-'fecht\ *adj* 1 : brought from a remote time or place 2 : not easily or naturally deduced or introduced : IMPROBABLE — **far·fetched·ness** \-'fech(t)-nəs, -'fech-əd-nəs\ *n*
far–flung \-'fləŋ\ *adj* : widely spread or distributed
fa·ri·na \fə-'rē-nə\ *n* [L, meal, flour, fr. *far* spelt] 1 : a fine meal of vegetable matter used chiefly for puddings or as a breakfast cereal 2 : any of various powdery or mealy substances
far·i·na·ceous \,far-ə-'nā-shəs\ *adj* 1 : containing or rich in starch 2 : having a mealy texture or surface — **far·i·na·ceous·ly** *adv*
fa·ri·nha \fə-'rēn-yə\ *n* [Pg, flour, cassava meal, fr. L *farina*] : cassava meal
far·i·nose \'far-ə-,nōs\ *adj* 1 : yielding or resembling farina 2 : covered with a whitish mealy powder — **far·i·nose·ly** *adv*
far·kle·ber·ry \'fär-kəl-,ber-ē\ *n* [prob. alter. of *whortleberry*] : a shrub or small tree (*Vaccinium arboreum*) of the heath family of the southeastern U.S. having a black berry with stony seeds
farl *or* **farle** \'fär(ə)l\ *n* [contr. of Sc *fardel*, lit., fourth part, fr. ME (Sc), fr. *ferde del*; fr. *ferde* fourth + *del* part] *Scot* : a small scone
¹**farm** \'färm\ *n, often attrib* [ME *ferme* rent, lease, fr. OF, lease, fr. *fermer* to fix, make a contract, fr. L *firmare* to make firm, fr. *firmus* firm] 1 *obs* : a sum or due fixed in amount and payable at fixed intervals 2 : a letting out of revenues or taxes for a fixed sum to one authorized to collect and retain them 3 : a district or division of a country leased out for the collection of government revenues 4 : a tract of land devoted to agricultural purposes 5 a : a plot of land devoted to the raising of domestic or other animals b : a tract of water reserved for the artificial cultivation of some aquatic life form 6 : a minor-league baseball club associated with a major-league club as a subsidiary to which recruits are assigned until needed or for further training
²**farm** *vt* 1 *obs* : RENT 2 : to collect and take the fees or profits of on payment of a fixed sum 3 : to give up to another on condition of receiving in return a fixed sum 4 a : to devote to agriculture b : to manage and cultivate as a farm ~ *vi* : to engage in raising crops or livestock
farm·er \'fär-mər\ *n* 1 : a person who pays a fixed sum for some privilege or source of income 2 : a person who cultivates land or crops or raises livestock
farm·er·ette \,fär-mə-'ret\ *n* : a female farmer or farmhand
farm·hand \'färm-,hand\ *n* : a farm laborer; *esp* : a hired laborer on a farm
farm·house \-,haủs\ *n* : the dwelling on a farm
farm·ing *n* : the practice of agriculture
farm·land \'färm-,land\ *n* : land used or suitable for farming
farm out *vt* 1 : to turn over for performance or use usu. on contract 2 a : to put into the hands of a private individual for care in return for a fee b : to send to a farm team 3 : to exhaust (land) by farming esp. under a monoculture system
farm·stead \'färm-,sted\ *also* **farm·stead·ing** \-iŋ\ *n* : the buildings and adjacent service areas of a farm
farm·yard \-,yärd\ *n* : space around or enclosed by farm buildings; *esp* : BARNYARD
faro \'fa(ə)r-(,)ō, 'fe(ə)r-\ *n* [prob. alter. of earlier *pharaoh*, trans. of F *pharaon*] : a banking game in which players bet on cards drawn from a dealing box
Faro·ese *var of* FAEROESE
far–off \'fär-'óf\ *adj* : remote in time or space **syn** see DISTANT
fa·rouche \fə-'rüsh\ *adj* [F, wild, shy, fr. LL *forasticus* belonging outside, fr. L *foras* outdoors; akin to L *fores* door — more at DOOR] : marked by shyness and lack of polish; *also* : WILD
far–out \'fär-'aủt\ *adj* : marked by a considerable departure from the conventional or traditional : EXTREME
far point *n* : the point farthest from the eye at which an object is accurately focused on the retina at full accommodation
far·rag·i·nous \fə-'raj-ə-nəs\ *adj* : formed of various materials
far·ra·go \fə-'räg-(,)ō, -'rā-(,)gō\ *n, pl* **farragoes** [L *farragin-, farrago* mixed fodder, mixture, fr. *far* spelt — more at BARLEY] : a confused collection : MIXTURE
far–reach·ing \'fär-'rē-chiŋ\ *adj* : having a wide range or effect
far·ri·er \'far-ē-ər\ *n* [alter. of ME *ferrour*, fr. MF *ferrour* blacksmith, fr. OF *ferreor*, fr. *ferrer* to fit with iron, fr. (assumed) VL *ferrare*, fr. L *ferrum* iron] : one that attends to or shoes horses
¹**far·row** \'far-(,)ō, -ə(-w)\ *vb* [ME *farwen*, fr. (assumed) OE *feargian*, fr. OE *fearh* young pig; akin to OHG *farah* young pig, L *porcus* pig] *vt* : to give birth to (a farrow) ~ *vi, of swine* : to bring forth young — often used with *down*
²**farrow** *n* 1 : a litter of pigs 2 : an act of farrowing
³**farrow** *adj* [ME (Sc) *ferow*; prob. akin to OE *fearr* bull, ox — more at PARE] *of a cow* : not in calf : not settled
far·see·ing \'fär-'sē-iŋ\ *adj* : FARSIGHTED 1
far·sight·ed \-'sīt-əd\ *adj* 1 a : seeing or able to see to a great distance b : having foresight or good judgment : SAGACIOUS 2 : HYPEROPIC — **far·sight·ed·ly** *adv* — **far·sight·ed·ness** *n*
¹**far·ther** \'fär-thər\ *adv* [ME *ferther*, alter. of *further*] 1 : at or to a greater distance or more advanced point 2 : more completely
²**farther** *adj* 1 : more distant : REMOTER 2 : ²FURTHER 2
syn FARTHER, FURTHER are often used interchangeably, but FARTHER implies greater distance from a point in space or less often in time, and FURTHER applies to advance not only in space or time but also in degree or in quantity ⟨move out *farther* from the city; no *further* discussion is needed⟩
far·ther·most \-,mōst\ *adj* : most distant : FARTHEST
¹**far·thest** \'fär-thəst\ *adj* : most distant in space or time

[2]**farthest** *adv* **1 :** to or at the greatest distance in space or time **:** REMOTEST **2 :** to the most advanced point **3 :** by the greatest degree or extent **:** MOST

far·thing \'fär-thiŋ\ *n* [ME *ferthing,* fr. OE *fēorthung;* akin to MHG *vierdunc* fourth part, OE *fēortha* fourth] **1 a :** a British monetary unit equal to ¼ of a penny **b :** a coin representing this unit **2 :** something of small value **:** MITE

far·thin·gale \'fär-thən-,gāl, -thiŋ-\ *n* [modif. of MF *verdugale,* fr. OSp *verdugado,* fr. *verdugo* young shoot of a tree, fr. *verde* green, fr. L *viridis* — more at VERDANT] **:** a support (as of hoops) worn esp. in the 16th century beneath a skirt to swell it out at the hip line

fas·ces \'fas-,ēz\ *n pl but sing or pl in constr* [L, fr. pl. of *fascis* bundle; akin to L *fascia*] **:** a bundle of rods and among them an ax with projecting blade borne before ancient Roman magistrates as a badge of authority

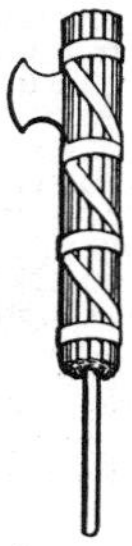

fasces

fas·cia \'fash-(ē-)ə, 'fāsh-\ *n, pl* **fas·ci·ae** \-ē-,ē\ *or* **fascias** [It, fr. L, band, bandage; akin to MIr *basc* necklace] **1 :** a flat horizontal member of an order or building having the form of a flat band or broad fillet; *esp* **:** one of the three bands making up the architrave in the Ionic order **2 :** a broad and well-defined band of color **3 :** a sheet of connective tissue covering or binding together body structures; *also* **:** tissue of this character — **fas·cial** \'fash-(ē-)əl, 'fāsh-\ *adj*

fas·ci·ate \'fash-ē-,āt\ *or* **fas·ci·at·ed** \-,āt-əd\ *adj* **1 :** banded or striped; *esp* **:** broadly banded with color **2 a :** FASCICLED **b :** exhibiting fasciation

fas·ci·a·tion \,fas(h)-ē-'ā-shən\ *n* **:** a malformation of plant stems commonly manifested as enlargement and flattening as if several were fused

fas·ci·cle \'fas-i-kəl\ *n* [L *fasciculus,* dim. of *fascis*] **1 :** a small bundle: as **a :** an inflorescence consisting of a compacted cyme less capitate than a glomerule **b :** FASCICULUS 1 **2 :** one of the divisions of a book published in parts — **fas·ci·cled** \-kəld\ *adj*

fas·cic·u·lar \fə-'sik-yə-lər, fa-\ *adj* **:** of, relating to, or consisting of fascicles — **fas·cic·u·lar·ly** *adv*

fas·cic·u·late \-lət\ *or* **fas·cic·u·lat·ed** \-,lāt-əd\ *adj* **:** FASCICULAR — **fas·cic·u·late·ly** *adv* — **fas·cic·u·la·tion** \fə-,sik-yə-'lā-shən, (,)fa-\ *n*

fas·ci·cule \'fas-i-,kyü(ə)l\ *n* [F, fr. L *fasciculus*] **1 :** FASCICLE 2 **2 :** FASCICULUS 1

fas·cic·u·lus \fə-'sik-yə-ləs, fa-\ *n, pl* **fas·cic·u·li** \-,lī\ [NL, fr. L] **1 :** a slender bundle of anatomical fibers **2 :** FASCICLE 2

fas·ci·nate \'fas-ᵊn-,āt\ *vb* [L *fascinatus,* pp. of *fascinare,* fr. *fascinum* witchcraft] *vt* **1** *obs* **:** BEWITCH **2 a :** to transfix and hold spellbound by an irresistible power **b :** to command the interest of **:** ALLURE ~ *vi* **:** to be irresistibly attractive **syn** see ATTRACT

fas·ci·nat·ing *adj* **:** extremely interesting or charming **:** CAPTIVATING — **fas·ci·nat·ing·ly** \-iŋ-lē\ *adv*

fas·ci·na·tion \,fas-ᵊn-'ā-shən\ *n* **1 :** the quality or power of fascinating **2 :** the state of being fascinated

fas·ci·na·tor \'fas-ᵊn-,āt-ər\ *n* **1 :** one that fascinates **2 :** a woman's light head scarf usu. of crochet or lace

fas·cine \fa-'sēn, fə-\ *n* [F, fr. L *fascina,* fr. *fascis*] **:** a long bundle of sticks of wood bound together and used for such purposes as filling ditches and making parapets

fas·cism \'fash-,iz-əm, 'fas-,iz-\ *n* [It *fascismo,* fr. *fascio* bundle, fasces, group, fr. L *fascis* bundle & *fasces* fasces] **1** *often cap* **:** the body of principles held by Fascisti **2 :** a political philosophy, movement, or regime that exalts nation and race and stands for a centralized autocratic government headed by a dictatorial leader, severe economic and social regimentation, and forcible suppression of opposition — **fas·cist** \-əst\ *n or adj, often cap* — **fas·cis·tic** \fa-'shis-tik *also* -'sis-\ *adj, often cap* — **fas·cis·ti·cal·ly** \-ti-k(ə-)lē\ *adv, often cap*

Fa·sci·sta \fä-'shē-(,)stä\ *n, pl* **Fa·sci·sti** \-(,)stē\ [It, fr. *fascio*] **:** a member of an Italian political organization under Mussolini governing Italy 1922-1943 according to the principles of fascism

fash \'fash\ *vb* [MF *fascher,* fr. (assumed) VL *fastidiare* to disgust, fr. L *fastidium* disgust] *chiefly Scot* **:** VEX — **fash** *n, chiefly Scot*

[1]**fash·ion** \'fash-ən\ *n* [ME *facioun, fasoun* shape, manner, fr. OF *façon,* fr. L *faction-, factio* act of making, faction, fr. *factus,* pp. of *facere* to make] **1 a :** the make or form of something **b** *archaic* **:** KIND, SORT **2 :** MANNER, WAY **3 a :** a prevailing custom, usage, or style **b** (1) **:** the prevailing style (as in dress) during a particular time (2) **:** a garment in such a style **c :** social standing or prominence esp. as signalized by dress or conduct

syn FASHION, STYLE, MODE, VOGUE, FAD, RAGE, CRAZE mean the accepted usage by those wishing to be regarded as up-to-date. FASHION is the most general term and applies to any way of dressing, behaving, writing, performing that is favored at any one time or place; STYLE often implies a distinctive fashion adopted by people of wealth or taste; MODE suggests the fashion of the moment among those anxious to appear elegant and sophisticated; VOGUE stresses the prevalence or wide acceptance of a fashion; FAD suggests caprice in taking up or in dropping a fashion; RAGE and CRAZE stress intense or senseless enthusiasm in adopting or pursuing a fad **syn** see in addition METHOD

[2]**fashion** *vt* **fash·ion·ing** \'fash-(ə-)niŋ\ **1 a :** to give shape or form to **:** MOLD **b :** ALTER, TRANSFORM **c :** to mold into a particular character by influencing or training **2 :** FIT, ADAPT **3** *obs* **:** CONTRIVE **syn** see MAKE — **fash·ion·er** \-(ə-)nər\ *n*

[1]**fash·ion·able** \'fash-(ə-)nə-bəl\ *adj* **1 :** conforming to the custom, fashion, or established mode **2 :** of or relating to the world of fashion — **fash·ion·able·ness** *n* — **fash·ion·ably** \-blē\ *adv*

[2]**fashionable** *n* **:** a fashionable person

fash·ion·mon·ger \'fash-ən-,məŋ-gər, -,mäŋ-\ *n* **:** one that studies, imitates, or sets the fashion

fashion plate *n* **1 :** an illustration of a clothing style **2 :** a person who dresses in the newest fashion

[1]**fast** \'fast\ *adj* [ME, fr. OE *fæst;* akin to OHG *festi* firm, ON *fastr,* Arm *hast*] **1 a :** firmly fixed **b :** tightly shut **c :** adhering firmly **d :** not easily freed **e :** closely bound to something **f :** STABLE **2 :** firmly loyal **3** *obs* **:** COMPACT, DENSE **4 a :** characterized by quick motion, operation, or effect: (1) **:** moving or able to move rapidly **:** SWIFT (2) **:** taking a comparatively short time (3) **:** imparting quickness of motion ⟨a ~ bowler⟩ (4) **:** accomplished quickly (5) **:** agile of mind **b :** conducive to rapidity of play or action ⟨a ~ track⟩ **c** (1) *of a timepiece or weighing device* **:** indicating in advance of what is correct (2) **:** according to daylight saving time **d :** contributing to a shortening of exposure time ⟨~ lens⟩ **5 a :** securely attached **b :** TENACIOUS **6 a** *archaic* **:** sound asleep **b** *of sleep* **:** not easily disturbed **7 a :** permanently dyed **b :** proof against fading by a particular agency ⟨sun*fast*⟩ **8 a :** DISSIPATED **b :** daringly unconventional esp. in sexual matters **9 :** resistant to change and esp. to destructive action ⟨acid-*fast* bacteria⟩

syn RAPID, SWIFT, FLEET, QUICK, SPEEDY, HASTY, EXPEDITIOUS: FAST and RAPID are very close in meaning, but FAST applies particularly to the thing that moves ⟨*fast* horse⟩ RAPID to the movement itself ⟨*rapid* current⟩ SWIFT suggests great rapidity coupled with ease of movement; FLEET adds the implication of lightness and nimbleness; QUICK suggests promptness and the taking of little time; SPEEDY implies quickness of successful accomplishment; it may also suggest unusual velocity; HASTY suggests hurry and precipitousness and often connotes carelessness; EXPEDITIOUS suggests efficiency together with rapidity of accomplishment

[2]**fast** *adv* **1 :** in a firm or fixed manner **2 :** QUICKLY, RAPIDLY **3 :** RECKLESSLY, DISSIPATEDLY **4 :** ahead of a correct time or posted schedule **5** *archaic* **:** CLOSE, NEAR

[3]**fast** *vi* [ME *fasten,* fr. OE *fæstan*] **1 :** to abstain from food **2 :** to eat sparingly or abstain from some foods

[4]**fast** *n* **1 :** the practice of fasting **2 :** a time of fasting

[5]**fast** *n* [alter. of ME *fest,* fr. ON *festr* rope, mooring cable, fr. *fastr* firm] **:** something that fastens or holds a fastening

fast·back \'fas(t)-,bak\ *n* **:** an automobile roof with a long curving downward slope to the rear; *also* **:** an automobile with such a roof

fas·ten \'fas-ᵊn\ *vb* **fas·ten·ing** \'fas-niŋ, -ᵊn-iŋ\ [ME *fastnen,* fr. OE *fæstnian* to make fast; akin to OHG *festinōn* to make fast, OE *fæst* fast] *vt* **1 a :** to attach esp. by pinning, tying, or nailing **b :** to make fast and secure **c :** to fix firmly or securely **d :** to secure against opening **2 :** to fix or set steadily **3 :** to take a firm grip with **4 a :** to attach (oneself) persistently and usu. objectionably **b :** IMPOSE ~ *vi* **1 :** to become fast or fixed **2 a :** take a firm grip or hold **b :** to focus attention — **fas·ten·er** \-nər, -ᵊn-ər\ *n*

syn FASTEN, FIX, ATTACH, AFFIX mean to make something stay firmly in place. FASTEN implies an action such as tying, buttoning, nailing, locking, or otherwise securing; FIX usu. implies a driving in, implanting, or embedding; ATTACH suggests a connecting or uniting by a bond, link, or tie in order to keep things together; AFFIX implies an imposing of one thing on another by gluing, impressing, or nailing

fas·ten·ing *n* **:** something that fastens **:** FASTENER

fas·tid·i·ous \fa-'stid-ē-əs\ *adj* [ME, fr. L *fastidiosus,* fr. *fastidium* disgust, prob. fr. *fastus* arrogance + *taedium* irksomeness; akin to L *fastigium* top] **1** *archaic* **:** SCORNFUL **2 a :** overly difficult to please **b :** showing or demanding excessive delicacy or care **3 :** having complex nutritional requirements ⟨~ microorganisms⟩ **syn** see NICE — **fas·tid·i·ous·ly** *adv* — **fas·tid·i·ous·ness** *n*

fas·tig·i·ate \fa-'stij-ē-ət\ *or* **fas·tig·i·at·ed** \-ē-,āt-əd\ *adj* [prob. fr. (assumed) NL *fastigiatus,* fr. L *fastigium*] **:** narrowing toward the top: **a :** having upright usu. clustered branches **b :** united into a conical bundle — **fas·tig·i·ate·ly** *adv*

fas·tig·i·um \-ē-əm\ *n* [NL, fr. L, top, gable end] **:** the period of greatest intensity (as of a disease)

fast·ness \'fas(t)-nəs\ *n* **1 :** the quality or state of being fast: as **a :** FIXEDNESS **b :** SWIFTNESS **c :** colorfast quality **d :** resistance (as of an organism) to the action of a usu. toxic substance **2 a :** a fortified or secure place **b :** a remote and secluded place

[1]**fat** \'fat\ *adj* **fat·ter; fat·test** [ME, fr. OE *fǣtt,* pp. of *fǣtan* to cram; akin to OHG *feizit* fat, L *opimus* fat, copious] **1 :** notable for having an unusual amount of fat: **a :** PLUMP **b :** OBESE **c** *of a meat animal* **:** fattened for market **d** *of food* **:** OILY, GREASY **2 a :** well filled out **:** BIG **b :** well stocked **:** ABUNDANT **3 a :** richly rewarding or profitable **b** *slang* **:** practically nonexistent ⟨a ~ chance⟩ **c :** SLOTHFUL **4 :** PRODUCTIVE, FERTILE ⟨a ~ year for crops⟩ **5 a** *of soil* **:** containing minerals that cause a greasy feel **b** *of wood* **:** having a high resin content **6 :** STUPID, FOOLISH — **fat·ness** *n*

[2]**fat** *n* **1 :** animal tissue consisting chiefly of cells distended with greasy or oily matter **2 a :** oily or greasy matter making up the bulk of adipose tissue and often abundant in seeds **b :** any of numerous compounds of carbon, hydrogen, and oxygen that are glycerides of fatty acids, the chief constituents of plant and animal fat, and a major class of energy-rich food, that are soluble in organic solvents (as ether) but not in water, and that are widely used industrially **c :** a solid or semisolid fat as distinguished from an oil **3 :** the best or richest part **4 :** the condition of fatness **:** OBESITY **5 :** something in excess **:** SUPERFLUITY

[3]**fat** *var of* PHAT

[4]**fat** *vt* **fat·ted; fat·ting :** to make fat **:** FATTEN

fa·tal \'fāt-ᵊl\ *adj* [ME, fr. MF & L; MF, fr. L *fatalis,* fr. *fatum*] **1** *obs* **:** FATED **2 :** FATEFUL ⟨a ~ hour⟩ **3 a :** of or relating to fate **b :** resembling fate in foretelling destiny **:** PROPHETIC **c :** resembling fate in proceeding according to a fixed sequence **d :** determining one's fate **4 a :** causing death **b :** bringing ruin **syn** see DEADLY

fa·tal·ism \-,iz-əm\ *n* **:** a doctrine that events are fixed in advance for all time in such a manner that human beings are powerless to change them; *also* **:** a belief in or attitude determined by this doctrine — **fa·tal·ist** \-əst\ *n* — **fa·tal·is·tic** \,fāt-ᵊl-'is-tik\ *adj* — **fa·tal·is·ti·cal·ly** \-ti-k(ə-)lē\ *adv*

fa·tal·i·ty \fā-'tal-ət-ē, fə-\ *n* **1 :** something established by fate **2 a :** the quality or state of causing death or destruction **:** DEADLINESS **b :** the quality or condition of being destined for disaster **3 a :** FATE 1 **b :** FATALISM **4 :** the agent or agency of fate **5 :** death resulting from a disaster

fa·tal·ly \'fāt-ᵊl-ē\ *adv* **1 :** in a way determined by fate **2 :** in a manner resulting in death or disaster **:** MORTALLY, DISASTROUSLY

fa·ta mor·ga·na \,fät-ə-,mȯr-'gän-ə\ *n* [It, lit., Morgan the fay, sorceress of Arthurian legend] **:** MIRAGE

fat·back \'fat-,bak\ *n* **:** the strip of fat from the back of a hog carcass usu. cured by drying and salting

[1]**fate** \'fāt\ *n* [ME, fr. MF or L; MF, fr. L *fatum,* lit., what has been spoken, fr. neut. of *fatus,* pp. of *fari* to speak] **1 :** the principle or determining cause or will by which things in general are supposed to come to be as they are or events to happen as they do **:** DESTINY **2 a :** whatever is destined or decreed **b :** DISASTER; *esp* **:** DEATH **3 :** final outcome **4** *cap, pl* **:** the three goddesses of classical my-

thology who determine the course of human life
syn FATE, DESTINY, LOT, PORTION, DOOM mean a predetermined state or end. FATE implies an inevitable and usu. an adverse outcome, condition, or end; DESTINY implies something foreordained and inescapable but rarely suggests of itself something to be feared; it more often suggests a great or noble course or end; LOT and PORTION imply a distribution by fate or destiny, LOT suggesting blind chance, PORTION implying the apportioning of good and evil; DOOM distinctly implies a grim or calamitous fate

[2]fate *vt* **:** DESTINE; *also* **:** DOOM

fat·ed *adj* **:** decreed, controlled, or marked by fate

fate·ful \'fāt-fəl\ *adj* **1** *of an utterance* **:** OMINOUS, PROPHETIC **2 a :** involving momentous consequences **:** DECISIVE **b :** DEADLY, CATASTROPHIC **3 :** controlled by fate **:** FOREORDAINED **syn** see OMINOUS — **fate·ful·ly** \-fə-lē\ *adv* — **fate·ful·ness** *n*

[1]fa·ther \'fä*th*-ər\ *n* [ME *fader*, fr. OE *fæder*; akin to OHG *fater* father, L *pater*, Gk *patēr*] **1 a :** a man who has begotten a child **:** SIRE **b** *cap* (1) **:** [2]GOD (2) **:** the first person of the Trinity **2 :** FOREFATHER **3 a :** one related to another in a way suggesting that of father to child **b :** an old man — used as a respectful form of address **4** *often cap* **:** a pre-Scholastic Christian writer accepted by the church as an authoritative witness to its teaching and practice — called also *church father* **5 a :** ORIGINATOR **b :** SOURCE **c :** PROTOTYPE **6 :** a priest of the regular clergy; *broadly* **:** PRIEST — used esp. as a title **7 :** one of the leading men (as of a city) — usu. used in pl.

[2]father *vt* **fa·ther·ing** \'fä*th*-(ə-)riŋ\ **1 a :** BEGET **b :** to make oneself the founder, producer, or author of **c :** to accept responsibility for **2 :** to fix the paternity or origin of **3 :** FOIST

Father Christmas *n, chiefly Brit* **:** SANTA CLAUS

fa·ther·hood \'fä*th*-ər-,hu̇d\ *n* **:** the state of being a father

father image *n* **:** an idealization of one's father often projected onto someone to whom one then looks for guidance and protection

fa·ther-in-law \'fä*th*-ə-rən-,lȯ, -ərn-,lȯ\ *n, pl* **fa·thers-in-law** \-ər-zən-\ **1 :** the father of one's spouse **2 :** STEPFATHER

fa·ther·land \'fä*th*-ər-,land\ *n* **1 :** one's native land or country **2 :** the native land or country of one's father or ancestors

fa·ther·less \-ləs\ *adj* **:** having no father **:** ORPHANED

fa·ther·like \-,līk\ *adj (or adv)* **:** FATHERLY

fa·ther·li·ness \-lē-nəs\ *n* **:** paternal quality

fa·ther·ly \'fä*th*-ər-lē\ *adj* **1 :** of, relating to, or befitting a father **2 :** resembling a father (as in affection or care) — **fatherly** *adv*

Father's Day *n* **:** the third Sunday in June appointed for the honoring of fathers

[1]fath·om \'fa*th*-əm\ *n* [ME *fadme*, fr. OE *fæthm* outstretched arms, length of the outstretched arms; akin to ON *fathmr* fathom, L *patēre* to be open, *pandere* to spread out, Gk *petannynai*] **1 :** a unit of length equal to 6 feet used esp. for measuring the depth of water **2 :** COMPREHENSION

[2]fathom *vt* **1 :** to measure by a sounding line **2 :** to penetrate and come to understand **~** *vi* **:** to take soundings; *also* **:** PROBE — **fath·om·able** \'fa*th*-ə-mə-bəl\ *adj*

Fa·thom·e·ter \fa-'*th*äm-ət-ər, 'fa*th*-ə(m)-,mēt-\ *trademark* — used for a sonic depth finder

fath·om·less \'fa*th*-əm-ləs\ *adj* **:** incapable of being fathomed — **fath·om·less·ly** *adv* — **fath·om·less·ness** *n*

fa·tid·ic \fā-'tid-ik, fə-\ *adj* [L *fatidicus*, fr. *fatum* fate + *dicere* to say] **:** of or relating to prophecy — **fa·tid·i·cal** \-i-kəl\ *adj*

fat·i·ga·bil·i·ty \,fat-i-gə-'bil-ət-ē\ *n* **:** susceptibility to fatigue

fat·i·ga·ble \'fat-i-gə-bəl\ *adj* **:** susceptible to fatigue

[1]fa·tigue \fə-'tēg\ *n* [F, fr. MF, fr. *fatiguer* to fatigue, fr. L *fatigare*; akin to L *affatim* sufficiently and prob. to L *fames* hunger] **1 a** (1) **:** weariness from labor or exertion (2) **:** nervous exhaustion **b :** the temporary loss of power to respond induced in a sensory receptor or motor end organ by continued stimulation **2 a :** LABOR **b :** manual or menial work performed by military personnel **c** *pl* **:** the uniform or work clothing worn on fatigue and in the field **3 :** the tendency of a material to break under repeated stress

[2]fatigue *vt* **1 :** to weary with labor or exertion **2 :** to induce a condition of fatigue in **~** *vi* **:** to suffer fatigue **syn** see TIRE

fat·ling \'fat-liŋ\ *n* **:** a young animal fattened for slaughter

fat·ly *adv* **1 :** RICHLY **2 :** in the manner of one that is fat

fats·hed·era \fat-'sed-ə-rə, fats-'hed-\ *n* [NL *Fatsia*, genus of shrubs + *Hedera*, genus of vines, fr. L, ivy] **:** a vigorous upright hybrid ornament foliage plant (*Hedera helix* × *Aralia elata*) with glossy deeply lobed palmate leaves

fat-sol·u·ble \'fat-,säl-yə-bəl\ *adj* **:** soluble in fats or fat solvents

fat·ten \'fat-ᵊn\ *vb* **fat·ten·ing** \'fat-niŋ, -ᵊn-iŋ\ *vt* **1 a :** to make fat, fleshy, or plump **b :** to make more substantial **2 :** to make fertile **~** *vi* **:** to grow fat — **fat·ten·er** \'fat-nər, -ᵊn-ər\ *n*

fat·ti·ness \'fat-ē-nəs\ *n* **:** the quality or state of being fatty

fat·tish \'fat-ish\ *adj* **:** somewhat fat

fat·ty \'fat-ē\ *adj* **1 :** containing fat esp. in unusual amounts; *also* **:** unduly stout **:** CORPULENT **2 :** GREASY

fatty acid *n* **1 :** any of numerous saturated aliphatic monocarboxylic acids $C_nH_{2n+1}COOH$ including many that occur naturally usu. in the form of esters in fats, waxes, and essential oils **2 :** any of the saturated or unsaturated monocarboxylic acids usu. with an even number of carbon atoms that occur naturally in the form of glycerides in fats and fatty oils

fa·tu·ity \fə-'t(y)ü-ət-ē, fa-\ *n* [MF *fatuité* foolishness, fr. L *fatuitat-, fatuitas*, fr. *fatuus*] **1 a :** something foolish or stupid **b :** FOOLISHNESS, STUPIDITY **2** *archaic* **:** IMBECILITY, DEMENTIA

fat·u·ous \'fach-(ə-)wəs\ *adj* [L *fatuus* foolish — more at BATTLE] **:** complacently or inanely foolish **:** SILLY **syn** see SIMPLE — **fat·u·ous·ly** *adv* — **fat·u·ous·ness** *n*

fat-wit·ted \'fat-'wit-əd\ *adj* **:** STUPID, IDIOTIC

fau·bourg \fō-'bu̇(ə)r\ *n* [ME *fabour*, fr. MF *fauxbourg*, alter. of *forsbourg*, fr. OF *forsborc*, fr. *fors* outside + *borc* town] **1 :** SUBURB; *esp* **:** a suburb of a French city **2 :** a city quarter

fau·ces \'fȯ-,sēz\ *n pl but sing or pl in constr* [L, pl., throat, fauces] **:** the narrow passage from the mouth to the pharynx situated between the soft palate and the base of the tongue — **fau·cial** \'fȯ-shəl\ *adj*

fau·cet \'fȯ-sət, 'fäs-ət\ *n* [ME, bung, faucet, fr. MF *fausset* bung, fr. *fausser* to damage, fr. LL *falsare* to falsify, fr. L *falsus* false] **:** a fixture for drawing a liquid from a pipe, cask, or other vessel

faugh *a strong p-sound or lip trill; often read as* 'fȯ\ *interj* — used to express contempt, disgust, or abhorrence

[1]fault \'fȯlt\ *n* [ME *faute*, fr. OF, fr. (assumed) VL *fallita*, fr. fem. of *fallitus*, pp. of L *fallere* to deceive, disappoint — more at FAIL] **1** *obs* **:** LACK **2 a :** WEAKNESS, FAILING; *esp* **:** a moral weakness less serious than a vice **b :** a physical or intellectual imperfection or impairment **c :** an error in a racket game **3 a :** MISDEMEANOR **b :** MISTAKE **4 :** responsibility for wrongdoing or failure **5 :** a fracture in the earth's crust accompanied by a displacement of one side of the fracture with respect to the other and in a direction parallel to the fracture

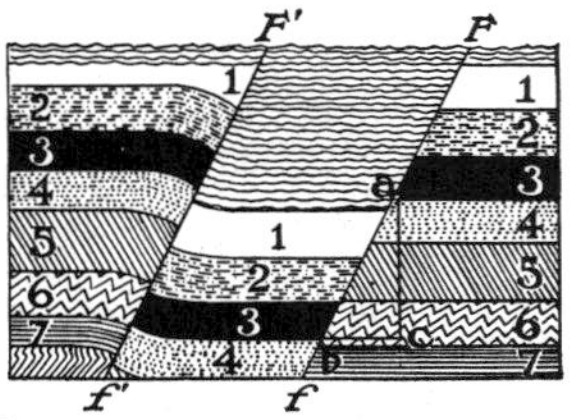

faults 5: *F* normal; *F'* reverse; *Ff, F'f'* fault planes; inclination in the direction *af* measured by the angle *fac* is the hade; *ac* throw; *bc* heave; *ab* displacement; parts having the same number are of the same stratum

syn FAULT, FAILING, FRAILTY, FOIBLE, VICE mean an imperfection or weakness of character. FAULT implies a failure, not necessarily culpable, to reach some standard of perfection in disposition, action, or habit; FAILING suggests a shortcoming in character, usu. minor in degree, of which one may be unaware; FRAILTY implies a general or chronic proneness to yield to temptation; FOIBLE applies to a harmless weakness or idiosyncrasy more likely to be endearing than disfiguring; VICE is a general term for any imperfection or weakness; it often implies a normal quality or appetite carried to excess
— **at fault 1 :** unable to find the scent and continue chase **:** PUZZLED **2 :** open to blame **:** RESPONSIBLE — **to a fault :** EXCESSIVELY

[2]fault *vi* **1 :** to commit a fault **:** ERR **2 :** to fracture so as to produce a geologic fault **~** *vt* **1 :** to find a fault in **2 :** to produce a geologic fault in

fault·find·er \-,fīn-dər\ *n* **:** one given to faultfinding

[1]fault·find·ing \-diŋ\ *n* **:** CRITICISM; *esp* **:** petty, nagging, or unreasonable censure

[2]faultfinding *adj* **:** disposed to find fault **:** CAPTIOUS **syn** see CRITICAL

fault·i·ly \'fȯl-tə-lē\ *adv* **:** in a faulty or blamable manner

fault·i·ness \-tē-nəs\ *n* **:** the quality or state of being faulty

fault·less \'fȯlt-ləs\ *adj* **:** having no fault **:** IRREPROACHABLE — **fault·less·ly** *adv* — **fault·less·ness** *n*

faulty \'fȯl-tē\ *adj* **:** marked by fault, blemish, or defect **:** IMPERFECT

faun \'fȯn, 'fän\ *n* [ME, fr. L *faunus*, fr. *Faunus*] **:** an ancient Italian deity of fields and herds having human shape, with pointed ears, small horns, and sometimes a goat's tail

fau·na \'fȯn-ə, 'fän-\ *n, pl* **faunas** *also* **fau·nae** \-,ē, -,ī\ [NL, fr. LL *Fauna*, sister of Faunus] **1 :** animals or animal life; *esp* **:** the animals or animal life of a region, period, or geological stratum **2 :** the animals or animal life developed or adapted for living in a specified environment — **fau·nal** \-ᵊl\ *adj* — **fau·nal·ly** \-ᵊl-ē\ *adv*

fau·nis·tic \fȯ-'nis-tik, fä-\ *adj* **:** of or relating to zoogeography **:** FAUNAL — **fau·nis·ti·cal** \-ti-kəl\ *adj* — **fau·nis·ti·cal·ly** \-ti-k(ə-)lē\ *adv*

Fau·nus \'fȯn-əs, 'fän-\ *n* [L] **:** the god of animals in Roman mythology

Faust \'fau̇st\ *n* [G] **:** a German magician and astrologer held to have sold his soul to the devil in exchange for worldly experience and power — **Faust·ian** \'fau̇-stē-ən\ *adj*

fau·vism \'fō-,viz-əm\ *n, often cap* [F *fauvisme*, fr. *fauve* wild animal, fr. *fauve* tawny, wild, of Gmc origin; akin to OHG *falo* fallow] **:** a movement in painting typified by the work of Matisse and characterized by vivid colors, free treatment of form, and a resulting vibrant and decorative effect — **fau·vist** \-vəst\ *n*

faux pas \(')fō-'pä\ *n, pl* **faux pas** \-'pä(z)\ [F, lit., false step] **:** BLUNDER; *esp* **:** a social blunder

fa·va bean \,fäv-ə-\ *n* [It *fava*, fr. L *faba* bean] **:** BROAD BEAN

fa·vo·ni·an \fə-'vō-nē-ən\ *adj* [L *favonianus*, fr. *Favonius*, the west wind] **:** of or relating to the west wind **:** MILD

[1]fa·vor *or chiefly Brit* **fa·vour** \'fā-vər\ *n* [ME, friendly regard, attractiveness, fr. OF *favor* friendly regard, fr. L, fr. *favēre* to be favorable; akin to OHG *gouma* attention, OSlav *gověti* to revere] **1** *archaic* **a :** APPEARANCE **b** (1) **:** COUNTENANCE (2) **:** a facial feature **2 a** (1) **:** friendly regard shown toward another esp. by a superior (2) **:** APPROVAL, APPROBATION **b :** PARTIALITY **c** *archaic* **:** LENIENCY **d** *archaic* **:** PERMISSION **e :** POPULARITY **3 a :** gracious kindness; *also* **:** an act of such kindness **b** *archaic* **:** HELP, ASSISTANCE **c** *pl* **:** effort in one's behalf or interest **:** ATTENTION **4 a :** a token of love (as a ribbon) usu. worn conspicuously **b :** a small gift or decorative item given out at a party **c :** BADGE **5 a :** a special privilege or right granted or conceded **b :** sexual privileges — usu. used in pl. **6** *archaic* **:** LETTER **7 :** BEHALF, INTEREST
syn GOODWILL, COUNTENANCE: FAVOR suggests an active interest and usu. implies partiality or preference; GOODWILL implies positive friendliness and a willingness to contribute to the success or welfare of a person, group, or cause; COUNTENANCE stresses approval or sanction but does not necessarily imply helpfulness or friendliness
— **in favor of 1 a :** in accord or sympathy with **b :** for the acquittal of **c :** in support of **2 :** to the order of

[2]favor *or chiefly Brit* **favour** *vt* **fa·vor·ing** \'fāv-(ə-)riŋ\ **1 a :** to regard or treat with favor **b** (1) **:** to do a kindness for **:** OBLIGE (2) **:** ENDOW **c :** to treat gently or carefully **:** SPARE **2 :** to show partiality toward **:** PREFER **3 a :** to give support or confirmation to **:** SUSTAIN **b :** to afford advantages for success to **:** FACILITATE **4 :** to bear a resemblance to — **fa·vor·er** \'fā-vər-ər\ *n*

fa·vor·able \'fāv-(ə-)rə-bəl, 'fā-vər-bəl\ *adj* **1 a :** disposed to favor **:** PARTIAL **b :** expressing approval **:** COMMENDATORY **c :** giving a result that is in one's favor ⟨~ comparison⟩ **d :** AFFIRMATIVE **2 :** winning approval **:** PLEASING **3 a :** tending to promote or facilitate **:** ADVANTAGEOUS ⟨~ wind⟩ **b :** marked by success — **fa·vor·able·ness** *n* — **fa·vor·ably** \-blē\ *adv*
syn FAVORABLE, AUSPICIOUS, PROPITIOUS mean pointing toward a happy outcome. FAVORABLE implies definitely that the persons involved are approving or helpful or that the circumstances are advantageous; AUSPICIOUS applies rather to something taken as a sign or omen promising success before or at the beginning of an event; PROPITIOUS may also apply to beginnings but often implies a continuing favorable condition

fa·vored \'fā-vərd\ *adj* **1 :** endowed with special advantages or

gifts **2 :** having an appearance or features of a particular kind ⟨hard-*favored*⟩ **3 :** providing preferential treatment

¹fa·vor·ite \'fāv-(ə-)rət\ *n* [It *favorito*, pp. of *favorire* to favor, fr. *favore* favor, fr. L *favor*] **1 :** something treated or regarded with special favor or liking; *specif* **:** one unusually loved, trusted, or provided with favors by a person of high rank or authority **2 :** a competitor (as a horse in a race) judged most likely to win

²favorite *adj* **:** constituting a favorite; *specif* **:** markedly popular

favorite son *n* **:** a man favored by the delegates of his state as presidential candidate at a national political convention

fa·vor·it·ism \'fāv-(ə-)rət-,iz-əm\ *n* **1 :** the showing of special favor **:** PARTIALITY **2 :** the state or fact of being a favorite

fa·vus \'fā-vəs\ *n* [NL, fr. L, honeycomb] **:** a contagious skin disease caused by a fungus (as *Achorion schoenleinii*) occurring in man and many domestic animals and fowls

¹fawn \'fȯn, 'fän\ *vi* [ME *faunen*, fr. OE *fagnian* to rejoice, fr. *fægen, fagan* glad — more at FAIN] **1 :** to show affection — used esp. of a dog **2 :** to court favor by a cringing or flattering manner **:** GROVEL — **fawn·er** *n* — **fawn·ing·ly** \-iŋ-lē\ *adv*

syn TOADY, TRUCKLE, CRINGE, COWER: FAWN implies seeking favor by servile flattery or exaggerated attention; TOADY suggests the attempt to ingratiate oneself by an abjectly menial or subservient attitude; TRUCKLE implies the subordination of oneself and one's desires or judgment to those of a superior; CRINGE suggests a bowing or shrinking in fear or servility; COWER suggests a display of abject fear in the face of threatening or domineering

²fawn *n* [ME *foun*, fr. MF *feon, faon* young of an animal, fr. (assumed) VL *feton-, feto*, fr. L *fetus* offspring] **1 :** a young deer; *esp* **:** one still unweaned or retaining a distinctive baby coat **2 :** KID 1 **3 :** a variable color averaging a light grayish brown

fawn lily *n* **:** DOGTOOTH VIOLET

¹fay \'fā\ *vb* [ME *feien*, fr. OE *fēgan;* akin to OHG *fuogen* to fit, L *pangere* to fasten] **:** to fit or join closely or tightly

²fay *n* [ME *fai, fei*, fr. OF *feid, fei* — more at FAITH] *obs* **:** FAITH

³fay *n* [ME *faie*, fr. MF *feie, fee*] **:** FAIRY, ELF — **fay** *adj*

faze \'fāz\ *vt* [alter. of *feeze* (to drive away, frighten), fr. ME *fesen*, fr. OE *fēsian* to drive away] **:** to disturb the composure of

F clef *n* **:** BASS CLEF

fe·al \'fē(-ə)l\ *adj* [MF, fr. OF, alter. of *feeil*, fr. L *fidelis*, fr. *fides* faith — more at FAITH] *archaic* **:** FAITHFUL, LOYAL

fe·al·ty \'fē(-ə)l-tē\ *n* [alter. of ME *feute*, fr. OF *feelté, fealté*, fr. L *fidelitat-, fidelitas* — more at FIDELITY] **1 a :** the fidelity of a vassal or feudal tenant to his lord **b :** the obligation of such fidelity **2 :** FAITHFULNESS, ALLEGIANCE **syn** see FIDELITY

¹fear \'fi(ə)r\ *n* [ME *fer*, fr. OE *fǣr* sudden danger; akin to L *periculum* attempt, peril, Gk *peiran* to attempt, OE *faran* to go — more at FARE] **1 a :** an unpleasant often strong emotion caused by anticipation or awareness of danger **b :** an instance of this emotion; *specif* **:** a state marked by this emotion **2 :** anxious concern **:** SOLICITUDE **3 :** profound reverence and awe esp. toward God **4 :** reason for alarm **:** DANGER

syn FEAR, DREAD, FRIGHT, ALARM, PANIC, TERROR, TREPIDATION mean painful agitation in the presence or anticipation of danger. FEAR is the most general term and implies anxiety and usu. loss of courage; DREAD usu. adds the idea of intense reluctance to face or meet a person or situation and suggests aversion as well as anxiety; FRIGHT implies the shock of sudden, startling fear; ALARM suggests sudden and intense apprehension; PANIC implies unreasoning and overmastering fear causing hysterical activity; TERROR implies the most extreme degree of fear; TREPIDATION adds to DREAD the implications of timidity, trembling, and hesitation

²fear *vt* **1** *archaic* **:** FRIGHTEN **2** *archaic* **:** to feel fear in (oneself) **3 :** to have a reverential awe of ⟨~ God⟩ **4 :** to be afraid of ~ *vi* **:** to be afraid or apprehensive — **fear·er** *n*

fear·ful \'fi(ə)r-fəl\ *adj* **1 :** causing fear **2 a :** full of fear **b :** indicating or arising from fear ⟨a ~ glance⟩ **3 :** extremely bad, intense, or large — **fear·ful·ly** \-fə-lē\ *adv* — **fear·ful·ness** *n*

syn AWFUL, DREADFUL, FRIGHTFUL, TERRIBLE, TERRIFIC, APPALLING: in conversational use these words are all nearly interchangeable as mere intensives. Used seriously, FEARFUL applies to what produces fear, agitation, or loss of courage; AWFUL implies striking with an overpowering awareness of transcendent force, might, or significance; DREADFUL suggests a power to make one shudder with mingled fear and aversion; FRIGHTFUL implies a startling or outrageous quality; TERRIBLE suggests painfulness too great to be endured; TERRIFIC implies the power to stun or strike terror with the release or display of great or explosive force; APPALLING describes what terrifies and also dismays or dumbfounds

syn FEARFUL, APPREHENSIVE, AFRAID mean disturbed by fear. FEARFUL implies a timorous, worrying, or imaginative temperament more often than a real cause for fear; APPREHENSIVE implies an immediate state of mind produced by having good grounds for fear; AFRAID may or may not imply good grounds but usu. suggests weakness or cowardice

fear·less \'fi(ə)r-ləs\ *adj* **:** free from fear **:** BRAVE — **fear·less·ly** *adv* — **fear·less·ness** *n*

fear·some \'fi(ə)r-səm\ *adj* **1 :** causing fear **2 :** TIMID, TIMOROUS — **fear·some·ly** *adv* — **fear·some·ness** *n*

fea·si·bil·i·ty \,fē-zə-'bil-ət-ē\ *n* **:** the quality of being feasible

fea·si·ble \'fē-zə-bəl\ *adj* [ME *faisible*, fr. MF, fr. *fais-*, stem of *faire* to make, do, fr. L *facere*] **1 :** capable of being done or carried out ⟨a ~ plan⟩ **2 :** capable of being used or dealt with successfully **:** SUITABLE **3 :** REASONABLE, LIKELY **syn** see POSSIBLE — **fea·si·ble·ness** *n* — **fea·si·bly** \-blē\ *adv*

¹feast \'fēst\ *n* [ME *feste* festival, feast, fr. OF, festival, fr. L *festa*, pl. of *festum* festival, fr. neut. of *festus* solemn, festal; akin to L *feriae* holidays, *fanum* temple, Arm *dikʻ* gods] **1 a :** an elaborate meal often accompanied by a ceremony or entertainment **:** BANQUET **b :** something that gives unusual or abundant pleasure **2 :** a periodic religious observance commemorating an event or honoring a deity, person, or thing

²feast *vi* **1 :** to take part in a feast **2 :** to enjoy an unusual pleasure ~ *vt* **1 :** to present with a feast **2 :** DELIGHT, GRATIFY — **feast·er** *n*

feast·ful \'fēst-fəl\ *adj, archaic* **:** FESTIVE, FESTAL

¹feat \'fēt\ *adj* [ME *fete, fayt*, fr. MF *fait*, pp. of *faire*] **1** *archaic* **:** BECOMING, NEAT **2** *archaic* **:** SMART, DEXTEROUS

²feat *n* [ME *fait*, fr. MF, fr. L *factum*, fr. neut. of *factus*, pp. of *facere* to make, do] **1 :** ACT, DEED **2 a :** a deed notable esp. for courage **b :** an act or product of skill, endurance, or ingenuity

syn FEAT, EXPLOIT, ACHIEVEMENT mean a remarkable deed. FEAT implies strength or dexterity or daring; EXPLOIT suggests an adventurous or heroic act; ACHIEVEMENT implies hard-won success in the face of difficulty or opposition

¹feath·er \'feth-ər\ *n* [ME *fether*, fr. OE, akin to OHG *fedara* wing, L *petere* to go to, seek, Gk *petesthai* to fly, *piptein* to fall, *pteron* wing] **1 a :** one of the light horny epidermal outgrowths that form the external covering of the body of birds and that consist of a shaft bearing on each side a series of barbs which bear barbules which in turn bear barbicels commonly ending in hooked hamuli and interlocking with the barbules of an adjacent barb to link the barbs into a continuous vane **b :** PLUME **c :** the vane of an arrow **2 a :** PLUMAGE **b :** KIND, NATURE **c :** ATTIRE, DRESS **d :** CONDITION, MOOD **3 :** a feathery tuft or fringe of hair (as on the leg of a dog) **4 :** a projecting strip, rib, fin, or flange **5 :** a feathery flaw in the eye or in a precious stone **6 :** the act of feathering an oar — **feath·ered** \-ərd\ *adj* — **a feather in one's cap :** a mark of distinction **:** HONOR

²feather *vb* **feath·er·ing** \-(ə-)riŋ\ *vt* **1 a :** to furnish (as an arrow) with a feather **b :** to cover, clothe, or adorn with feathers **2 a :** to turn (an oar blade) almost horizontal when lifting from the water at the end of a stroke to reduce air resistance **b (1) :** to change the angle of (airplane propeller blades) so that the chords become approximately parallel to the line of flight; *also* **:** to change the angle of airplane propeller blades of (an engine) in such a manner **(2) :** to change the angle of (a rotor blade of a rotary-wing aircraft) periodically in forward flight **3 :** to reduce the edge of to a featheredge **4 :** to cut (as air) with or as if with a wing **5 :** to join by a tongue and groove ~ *vi* **1 :** to grow or form feathers **2 :** to move, spread, or grow like feathers **3 :** to feather an oar or an airplane propeller blade — **feather one's nest :** to provide for oneself esp. reprehensibly while in a position of trust

¹feath·er·bed \'feth-ər-,bed\ *adj* **:** calling for, sanctioning, or resulting from featherbedding

²featherbed *vi* **1 a :** to require more workmen than are needed **b :** to limit production under a featherbed rule **2 :** to do featherbed work or put in time under a featherbed rule ~ *vt* **1 :** to bring under a featherbed rule **2 :** to assist (as an industry) by government aid

feath·er·bed·ding *n* **:** the requiring of an employer usu. under a union rule or safety statute to pay more employees than are needed or to limit production

feath·er·brain \-,brān\ *n* **:** a foolish scatterbrained person

feath·er·brained \-,brānd\ *adj* **:** FOOLISH, FRIVOLOUS

feath·er·edge \'feth-ə-,rej\ *n* **:** a very thin sharp edge; *esp* **:** one that is easily broken or bent over — **featheredge** *vt*

feath·er·head \'feth-ər-,hed\ *n* **:** a foolish or scatterbrained person — **feath·er·head·ed** \,feth-ər-'hed-əd\ *adj*

feath·er·less \'feth-ər-ləs\ *adj* **:** having no feathers

feather star *n* **:** COMATULID

feath·er·stitch \'feth-ər-,stich\ *n* **:** an embroidery stitch consisting of a line of diagonal blanket stitches worked alternately to the left and right — **featherstitch** *vb*

feath·er·weight \-,wāt\ *n* **1 :** a very light weight; *specif* **:** the lightest weight a racehorse may carry in a handicap **2 :** one that is very light in weight: as **a :** a boxer weighing more than 118 but not over 126 pounds **b :** a wrestler weighing more than 123 but not over 134 pounds

feath·ery \'feth-(ə-)rē\ *adj* **:** resembling, suggesting, or covered with feathers

¹feat·ly \'fēt-lē\ *adv* [ME *fetly*, fr. *fete* feat (adj.)] **1 :** SUITABLY, PROPERLY **2 :** GRACEFULLY, NIMBLY **3 :** CLEVERLY, SKILLFULLY

²featly *adj* **:** GRACEFUL, NEAT

¹fea·ture \'fē-chər\ *n* [ME *feture*, fr. MF, fr. L *factura* act of making, fr. *factus*, pp. of *facere* to make — more at DO] **1 a :** the structure, form, or appearance esp. of a person **b** *obs* **:** physical beauty **2 a :** the makeup or appearance of the face or its parts **b :** a part of the face **:** LINEAMENT **3 :** a prominent part or characteristic **4 :** a special attraction: as **a :** the principal motion picture shown on a program with other pictures **b :** a distinctive article, story, or special department in a newspaper or magazine **c :** something offered to the public or advertised as particularly attractive

²feature *vb* **fea·tur·ing** \'fēch-(ə-)riŋ\ *vt* **1** *chiefly dial* **:** to resemble in features **2 :** to outline the features of **3 :** to mark as a feature **4 :** to make a feature of ~ *vi* **:** to play an important part

fea·tured \'fē-chərd\ *adj* **1 a :** formed into or expressed by features **b :** having facial features of a particular kind ⟨a heavy-*featured* man⟩ **2 :** displayed, advertised, or presented as a special attraction

fea·ture·less \'fē-chər-ləs\ *adj* **:** having no distinctive features

feaze \'fēz, 'fāz\ *var of* FAZE

febri- *comb form* [LL, fr. L *febris*] **:** fever ⟨*febri*fic⟩

fe·brif·ic \fi-'brif-ik\ *adj, archaic* **:** FEVERISH

fe·brif·u·gal \fi-'brif-(y)i-gəl\ *adj* **:** mitigating or removing fever

feb·ri·fuge \'feb-rə-,fyüj\ *n* [F *fébrifuge*, prob. fr. (assumed) NL *febrifuga*, fr. LL *febrifuga, febrifugia* centaury, fr. *febri-* + *-fuga* -fuge] **:** ANTIPYRETIC — **febrifuge** *adj*

fe·brile \'feb-rəl, 'fēb-, -,rīl\ *adj* [ML *febrilis*, fr. L *febris* fever — more at FEVER] **:** of or relating to fever **:** FEVERISH

Feb·ru·ary \'feb-(y)ə-,wer-ē, 'feb-rə-\ *n* [ME *Februarie*, fr. L *Februarius*, fr. *Februa*, pl., feast of purification; perh. akin to L *fumus* smoke] **:** the 2d month of the Gregorian calendar

fe·cal \'fē-kəl\ *adj* **:** of, relating to, or constituting feces

fe·ces \'fē-(,)sēz\ *n pl* [ME, fr. L *faec-, faex* (sing.) dregs] **:** bodily waste discharged through the anus **:** EXCREMENT

feck \'fek\ *n* [ME (Sc) *fek*, alter. of ME *effect*] **1** *chiefly Scot* **a :** MAJORITY **b :** PART **c :** QUANTITY **2** *chiefly Scot* **:** VALUE

feck·et \'fek-ət\ *n* [origin unknown] *Scot* **:** a garment with sleeves used as an undershirt or a jacket

feck·less \'fek-ləs\ *adj* **1 :** INEFFECTUAL, WEAK **2 :** WORTHLESS, IRRESPONSIBLE — **feck·less·ly** *adv* — **feck·less·ness** *n*

feck·ly \'fek-lē\ *adv, chiefly Scot* **:** ALMOST, NEARLY

fec·u·lence \'fek-yə-lən(t)s\ *n* **1 :** something that is feculent **2 :** the quality or state of being feculent

fec·u·lent \-lənt\ *adj* [ME, fr. L *faeculentus*, fr. *faec-, faex*] **:** foul with impurities **:** FECAL

fe·cund \'fē-kənd, 'fek-ənd\ *adj* [ME, fr. MF *fecond*, fr. L *fecundus*

— more at FEMININE] **1 :** fruitful in offspring or vegetation **:** PROLIFIC **2 :** intellectually productive or inventive to a marked degree **syn** see FERTILE — **fe·cun·di·ty** \fi-ˈkən-dət-ē\ *n*

fe·cun·date \ˈfek-ən-ˌdāt, ˈfē-kən-\ *vt* [L *fecundatus*, pp. of *fecundare*, fr. *fecundus*] **1 :** to make fruitful or prolific **2 :** to make fertile — **fe·cun·da·tion** \ˌfek-ən-ˈdā-shən, ˌfē-kən-\ *n*

fed·er·al \ˈfed-(ə-)rəl\ *adj* [L *foeder-*, *foedus* compact, league; akin to L *fidere* to trust — more at BIDE] **1** *archaic* **:** of or relating to a compact or treaty **2 a :** formed by a compact between political units that surrender their individual sovereignty to a central authority but retain limited residuary powers of government **b :** of or constituting a form of government in which power is distributed between a central authority and a number of constituent territorial units **c :** of or relating to the central government of a federation as distinguished from the governments of the constituent units **3** *cap* **:** advocating or friendly to the principle of a federal government with strong centralized powers; *esp* **:** of or relating to the American Federalists **4** *often cap* **:** of, relating to, or loyal to the federal government or the Union armies of the U.S. in the American Civil War — **fed·er·al·ly** \-(ə-)rə-lē\ *adv*

Federal *n* **1 :** a supporter of the government of the U.S. in the Civil War; *specif* **:** a soldier in the federal armies **2 :** a federal agent or officer

federal district *n* **:** a district set apart as the seat of the central government of a federation

fed·er·al·ism \ˈfed-(ə-)rə-ˌliz-əm\ *n* **1 a** *often cap* **:** the federal principle of organization **b :** support or advocacy of this principle **2** *cap* **:** the principles of the Federalists

fed·er·al·ist \-ləst\ *n* **1 :** an advocate of federalism: as **a** *often cap* **:** an advocate of a federal union between the American colonies after the Revolution and of the adoption of the U.S. Constitution **b** *often cap* **:** WORLD FEDERALIST **2** *cap* **:** a member of a major political party in the early years of the U.S. favoring a strong centralized national government — **federalist** *adj, often cap*

fed·er·al·iza·tion \ˌfed-(ə-)rə-lə-ˈzā-shən\ *n* **1 :** the act of federalizing **2 :** the state of being federalized

fed·er·al·ize \ˈfed-(ə-)rə-ˌlīz\ *vt* **1 :** to unite in or under a federal system **2 :** to bring under the jurisdiction of a federal government

Federal Reserve bank *n* **:** one of 12 banks set up under the Federal Reserve system to serve as a bank of reserve and discount for affiliated banks in its district

¹**fed·er·ate** \ˈfed-(ə-)rət\ *adj* [L *foederatus*, fr. *foeder-*, *foedus*] **:** united in an alliance or federation

²**fed·er·ate** \ˈfed-ə-ˌrāt\ *vb* **:** to join in a federation

federated church *n* **:** a local church uniting two or more congregations that maintain denominational ties

fed·er·a·tion \ˌfed-ə-ˈrā-shən\ *n* **1 :** the act of federating; *esp* **:** the formation of a federal union **2 :** something formed by federation: as **a :** a federal government **b :** a union of organizations

fed·er·a·tive \ˈfed-ə-ˌrāt-iv, ˈfed-(ə-)rət-\ *adj* **1 :** concerned with foreign affairs and national security **2 :** FEDERAL — **fed·er·a·tive·ly** *adv*

fe·do·ra \fi-ˈdōr-ə, -ˈdȯr-\ *n* [*Fédora*, drama by V. Sardou] **:** a low soft felt hat with the crown creased lengthwise

fed up *adj* **1 :** SATIATED, SURFEITED **2 :** BORED, TIRED

¹**fee** \ˈfē\ *n* [ME, fr. OF *fé*, *fief*, of Gmc origin; akin to OE *feoh* cattle, property, OHG *fihu* cattle; akin to L *pecus* cattle, *pecunia* money, *pectere* to comb] **1 a (1) :** an estate in land held in feudal law from a lord on condition of homage and service **(2) :** a piece of land so held **b :** an inherited or heritable estate in land **2 a (1) :** a fixed charge **(2) :** a charge for a professional service **b :** TIP **syn** see WAGE — **in fee :** in absolute and legal possession

²**fee** *vt* **feed; fee·ing 1** *chiefly Scot* **:** HIRE **2 :** TIP

fee·ble \ˈfē-bəl\ *adj* **fee·bler** \-b(ə-)lər\ **fee·blest** \-b(ə-)ləst\ [ME *feble*, fr. OF, fr. L *flebilis* lamentable, wretched, fr. *flēre* to weep] **1 a :** markedly lacking in strength **b :** indicating weakness **2 a :** deficient in qualities or resources that indicate vigor, authority, force, or efficiency **b :** INADEQUATE, INFERIOR **syn** see WEAK — **fee·ble·ness** \-bəl-nəs\ *n* — **fee·bly** \-blē\ *adv*

fee·ble·mind·ed \ˌfē-bəl-ˈmīn-dəd\ *adj* **1** *obs* **:** IRRESOLUTE, VACILLATING **2 :** mentally deficient **3 :** FOOLISH, STUPID — **fee·ble·mind·ed·ly** *adv* — **fee·ble·mind·ed·ness** *n*

fee·blish \ˈfē-b(ə-)lish\ *adj* **:** somewhat feeble

¹**feed** \ˈfēd\ *vb* **fed** \ˈfed\ **feed·ing** [ME *feden*, fr. OE *fēdan*; akin to OE *fōda* food — more at FOOD] *vt* **1 a :** to give food to **b :** to give as food **2 :** to furnish esp. with something essential to the growth, sustenance, maintenance, or operation of **3 :** to produce or serve as food for **4 a :** to give satisfaction to **:** GRATIFY **b :** SUPPORT, ENCOURAGE **5 a :** to supply for use or consumption **b (1) :** to supply (a signal) to an electronic circuit **(2) :** to send by wire to a transmitting station for broadcast **6 :** to supply with cues and situations that make a role more effective ~ *vi* **1 a :** to consume food **:** EAT **b :** PREY — used with *on*, *upon*, or *off* **2 :** to become nourished or satisfied as if by food **3 :** to move into a machine or opening in order to be used or processed

²**feed** *n* **1 a :** an act of eating **b :** MEAL; *esp* **:** a large meal **2 a :** food for livestock; *specif* **:** a mixture or preparation for feeding livestock **b :** the amount given at each feeding **3 a :** material supplied (as to a furnace) **b :** a mechanism by which the action of feeding is effected **c :** the motion or process of carrying forward the material to be operated upon (as in a machine)

feed·back \ˈfēd-ˌbak\ *n* **1 :** the return to the input of a part of the output of a machine, system, or process **2 :** the partial reversion of the effects of a process to its source or to a preceding stage

feed·er \ˈfēd-ər\ *n, often attrib* **:** one that feeds: as **a :** a device or apparatus for supplying food **b (1) :** TRIBUTARY **(2) :** a source of supply **(3) :** a heavy wire conductor supplying electricity to an electric distribution system **(4) :** a branch transportation line **c :** an animal being fattened or suitable for fattening **d :** an actor or role that serves as a foil for another

feed·stuff \-ˌstəf\ *n* **:** FEED 2a; *also* **:** any of the constituent nutrients of an animal ration

¹**feel** \ˈfē(ə)l\ *vb* **felt** \ˈfelt\ **feel·ing** [ME *felen*, fr. OE *fēlan*, akin to OHG *fuolen* to feel, L *palpare* to caress, and perh. to Gk *pallein* to brandish — more at POLEMIC] *vt* **1 a (1) :** to touch in order to have a tactile sensation **(2) :** to examine or test by touching **b :** to perceive by a physical sensation coming from discrete end organs (as of the skin or muscles) **2 a :** to undergo passive experience of **b :** to suffer from **3 :** to ascertain by cautious trial — often used with *out* **4 a :** to have an awareness of **b :** BELIEVE, THINK ~ *vi* **1 a :** to receive or be able to receive a tactile sensation **b :** to search for something with the fingers **2 :** to be conscious of an inward impression, state of mind, or physical condition **3 :** to seem esp. to the sense of touch **4 :** to have sympathy or pity

²**feel** *n* **1 :** the sense of touch **2 :** SENSATION, FEELING **3 a :** the quality of a thing as imparted through touch **b :** typical or peculiar quality or atmosphere **4 :** intuitive knowledge or ability

feel·er \ˈfē-lər\ *n* **:** one that feels: as **a :** a tactile process (as a tentacle) of an animal **b :** something (as a proposal) ventured to ascertain the views of others

¹**feel·ing** *n* **1 a :** the one of the five senses of which the skin contains the chief end organs and of which the sensations of touch and temperature are characteristic **:** TOUCH **b :** a sensation experienced through this sense **2 a :** EMOTION **b** *pl* **:** susceptibility to impression **:** SENSIBILITIES **3 a :** the undifferentiated background of one's awareness considered apart from any identifiable sensation, perception, or thought **b :** the overall quality of one's awareness **c :** conscious recognition **:** SENSE **4 a :** OPINION, BELIEF **b :** unreasoned opinion **:** SENTIMENT **c :** PRESENTIMENT **5 :** capacity to respond emotionally esp. with the higher emotions **6 :** the character ascribed to something as a result of one's impression or emotional state **:** ATMOSPHERE **7 a :** the quality of a work of art that embodies and conveys the emotion of the artist **b :** sympathetic aesthetic response **8 :** FEEL 4

syn AFFECTION, EMOTION, SENTIMENT, PASSION: FEELING denotes any partly mental, partly physical response marked by pleasure, pain, attraction, repulsion; it may suggest the mere existence of a response without implying anything concerning the nature or intensity of it; AFFECTION applies to such feelings as are also inclinations or likings; EMOTION carries a stronger implication of excitement or agitation; SENTIMENT often implies an emotion inspired by an idea; it may often suggest emotion that is out of proportion to the cause and so considered to be artificial or insincere; PASSION suggests a very powerful or controlling emotion

²**feeling** *adj* **1 a :** SENTIENT, SENSITIVE **b :** easily moved emotionally **2** *obs* **:** deeply felt **3 :** expressing emotion or sensitivity — **feel·ing·ly** \ˈfē-liŋ-lē\ *adv* — **feel·ing·ness** *n*

fee simple *n, pl* **fees simple :** a fee without limitation to any class of heirs or restrictions on transfer of ownership

fee splitting *n* **:** payment by a specialist of a part of his fee to the referring physician

feet *pl of* FOOT

fee tail *n, pl* **fees tail :** a fee limited to a particular class of heirs

feeze \ˈfēz, ˈfāz\ *n* [ME *veze*, fr. *fesen*, *vesen* to drive away — more at FAZE] **1** *chiefly dial* **:** RUSH **2** *dial* **:** a state of alarm or excitement

feign \ˈfān\ *vb* [ME *feignen*, fr. OF *feign-*, stem of *feindre*, fr. L *fingere* to shape, feign — more at DOUGH] *vt* **1 a :** to represent by a false appearance of **:** SHAM **b :** to assert as if true **:** PRETEND **2** *archaic* **a :** INVENT, IMAGINE **b :** to give fictional representation to **3** *obs* **:** DISGUISE, CONCEAL ~ *vi* **:** PRETEND, DISSEMBLE **syn** see ASSUME — **feign·er** *n*

feigned *adj* **1 :** FICTITIOUS **2 :** not genuine or real

¹**feint** \ˈfānt\ *n* [F *feinte*, fr. OF, fr. *feint*, pp. of *feindre*] **:** something feigned; *specif* **:** a mock blow or attack on or toward one part in order to distract attention from the point one really intends to attack **syn** see TRICK

²**feint** *vi* **:** to make a feint ~ *vt* **1 :** to lure or deceive with a feint **2 :** to make a pretense of

fei·rie \ˈfē-rē\ *adj* [ME (Sc) *fery*, fr. ME *fere* strong — more at FERE] *Scot* **:** NIMBLE, STRONG

feist \ˈfīst\ *n* [obs. *fisting hound*, fr. obs. *fist* (to break wind)] *chiefly dial* **:** a small dog

feisty \ˈfī-stē\ *adj, chiefly South & Midland* **:** being in a state of excitement or agitation: as **a :** full of nervous energy **:** FIDGETY **b :** touchy and quarrelsome **c :** frisky and exuberant

feld·spar \ˈfel(d)-ˌspär\ *n* [modif. of obs. G *feldspath* (now *feldspat*), fr. G *feld* field + obs. G *spath* (now *spat*) spar] **:** any of a group of crystalline minerals that consist of aluminum silicates with either potassium, sodium, calcium, or barium and that are an essential constituent of nearly all crystalline rocks (hardness 6–6.5, sp. gr. 2.5–2.9) — **feld·spath·ic** \fel(d)-ˈspath-ik\ *also* **feld·spath·ose** \ˈfel(d)-ˌspath-ˌōs\ *adj*

fe·li·cif·ic \ˌfē-lə-ˈsif-ik\ *adj* [L *felic-*, *felix*] **:** causing or intended to cause happiness

¹**fe·lic·i·tate** \fi-ˈlis-ə-ˌtāt\ *adj* [LL *felicitatus*, pp. of *felicitare* to make happy, fr. L *felicitas*] *obs* **:** made happy

²**felicitate** *vt* **1** *archaic* **:** to make happy **2 a :** to consider happy or fortunate **b :** to offer congratulations to — **fe·lic·i·ta·tion** \fi-ˌlis-ə-ˈtā-shən\ *n* — **fe·lic·i·ta·tor** \-ˈlis-ə-ˌtāt-ər\ *n*

syn CONGRATULATE: FELICITATE is the more formal term, denoting the simple offering of good wishes and hopes for happiness; CONGRATULATE is intimate, familiar, or informal, and more often implies acknowledgment of achievement or good fortune

fe·lic·i·tous \fi-ˈlis-ət-əs\ *adj* **1 :** very well suited or expressed **:** APT ⟨a ~ remark⟩ **2 :** having a talent for apt expression ⟨a ~ speaker⟩ **syn** see FIT — **fe·lic·i·tous·ly** *adv* — **fe·lic·i·tous·ness** *n*

fe·lic·i·ty \fi-ˈlis-ət-ē\ *n* [ME *felicite*, fr. MF *felicité*, fr. L *felicitat-*, *felicitas*, fr. *felic-*, *felix* fruitful, happy] **1 a :** the quality or state of being happy; *esp* **:** great happiness **b :** an instance of happiness **2 :** something that causes happiness **3 :** a pleasing faculty esp. in art or language **:** APTNESS **4 :** an apt expression

fe·lid \ˈfē-ləd\ *n* [NL *Felidae*, family name, fr. *Felis*, genus of cats, fr. L, cat] **:** CAT 1b — **felid** *adj*

fe·line \ˈfē-ˌlīn\ *adj* [L *felinus*, fr. *felis*] **1 :** of or relating to cats or the cat family **2 :** resembling a cat: as **a :** SLY, TREACHEROUS **b :** STEALTHY — **feline** *n* — **fe·line·ly** *adv* — **fe·lin·i·ty** \fē-ˈlin-ət-ē\ *n*

feline distemper *n* **1 :** PANLEUCOPENIA **2 :** a gastrointestinal disease of cats closely related to panleucopenia

¹**fell** \ˈfel\ *n* [ME, fr. OE; akin to OHG *fel* skin, L *pellis*] **:** SKIN, HIDE, PELT

²**fell** *vt* [ME *fellen*, fr. OE *fellan*; akin to OE *feallan* to fall — more at FALL] **1 a :** to cut, beat, or knock down **b :** KILL **2 :** to sew (a seam) by folding one raw edge under the other and sewing flat on the wrong side — **fell·able** \ˈfel-ə-bəl\ *adj* — **fell·er** *n*

³**fell** *past of* FALL

⁴**fell** *adj* [ME *fel*, fr. OF — more at FELON] **1 a :** FIERCE, CRUEL **b :** very destructive or painful **:** DEADLY **c :** TERRIBLE, AWFUL **2** *Scot* **:** SHARP, PUNGENT — **fell·ness** *n* — **fel·ly** \ˈfel-lē\ *adv*

fel·lah \'fel-ə, fə-'lä\ *n, pl* **fel·la·hin** *or* **fel·la·heen** \ˌfel-ə-'hēn, fə-ˌlä-'hēn\ [Ar *fallāḥ*] : a peasant or agricultural laborer in Egypt, Syria, and other Arab countries

fel·la·tio \fə-'lā-shē-ˌō, fe-, -'lät-ē-\ *also* **fel·la·tion** \-'lā-shən\ *n* [NL *fellation-, fellatio*, fr. L *fellatus*, pp. of *felare, fellare*, lit., to suck — more at FEMININE] : oral stimulation of the penis

fell·mon·ger \'fel-ˌməŋ-gər, -ˌmäŋ-\ *n, Brit* : one who removes hair or wool from hides in preparation for leather making — **fell·mon·gered** \-gərd\ *adj, Brit* — **fell·mon·ger·ing** \-g(ə-)riŋ\ *or* **fell·mon·gery** \-g(ə-)rē\ *n, Brit*

1**fel·low** \'fel-(ˌ)ō, -ə(-w)\ *n* [ME *felawe*, fr. OE *fēolaga*, fr. ON *fēlagi*, fr. *fēlag* partnership, fr. *fē* cattle, money + *lag* act of laying] **1** : COMRADE, ASSOCIATE **2 a** : an equal in rank, power, or character : PEER **b** : one of a pair : MATE **3** : a member of a group having common characteristics; *specif* : a member of an incorporated literary or scientific society **4 a** *obs* : a person of one of the lower social classes **b** : a worthless or low man or boy **c** : MAN, BOY **d** : BOYFRIEND, BEAU **5** : an incorporated member of a college or collegiate foundation esp. in a British university **6** : a person appointed to a position granting a stipend and allowing for advanced study

2**fellow** *adj* : being a companion, mate, or associate

fel·low·ly \-ō-lē, -ə-lē\ *adj* : SOCIABLE — **fellowly** *adv*

fel·low·man \ˌfel-ō-'man, -ə-\ *n* : a kindred human being

fellow servant *n* : an employee working with another employee under such circumstances that each one if negligent may expose the other to harm which the employer cannot reasonably be expected to guard against or be held legally liable for

1**fel·low·ship** \'fel-ō-ˌship, -ə-\ *n* **1** : COMPANIONSHIP, COMPANY **2 a** : community of interest, activity, feeling, or experience **b** : the state of being a fellow or associate **3** : a company of equals or friends : ASSOCIATION **4** : intimate personal intercourse **5** : FRIENDLINESS, COMRADESHIP **6** *obs* : MEMBERSHIP, PARTNERSHIP **7 a** : the position of a fellow (as of a university) **b** : the stipend of a fellow **c** : a foundation for the providing of such a stipend

2**fellowship** *vi* : to join in fellowship esp. with a church member ~ *vt* : to admit to fellowship (as in a church)

fellow traveler *n* [trans. of Russ *poputchik*] : one that sympathizes with and often furthers the ideals and program of an organized group (as the Communist party) without membership in the group or regular participation in its activities — **fel·low–trav·el·ing** \ˌfel-ō-'trav-(ə-)liŋ, ˌfel-ə-\ *adj*

fel·ly \'fel-ē\ *or* **fel·loe** \-(ˌ)ō\ *n* [ME *fely, felive*, fr. OE *felg*; akin to OHG *felga* felly, OE *fealg* piece of plowed land] : the exterior rim or a segment of the rim of a wheel supported by the spokes

felo–de–se \ˌfel-(ˌ)ōd-ə-'sā, -'sē\ *n, pl* **fe·lo·nes–de–se** \fə-ˌlō-(ˌ)nēz-də-\ *or* **felos–de–se** \ˌfel-(ˌ)ōz-də-\ [ML *felo de se, fello de se*, lit., evildoer upon himself] **1** : one who deliberately kills himself or dies from the effects of his commission of an unlawful malicious act **2** : an act of deliberate self-destruction : SUICIDE

1**fel·on** \'fel-ən\ *adj* [ME, fr. OF *felon, fel*, fr. ML *fellon-, fello* evildoer, villain] **1** *archaic* **a** : CRUEL **b** : EVIL **2** *archaic* : WILD

2**felon** *n* **1** : one who has committed a felony **2** *archaic* : VILLAIN

3**felon** *n* : a deep usu. suppurative inflammation of the finger or toe esp. near the end or around the nail

fe·lo·ni·ous \fə-'lō-nē-əs\ *adj* **1** *archaic* : very evil : VILLAINOUS **2** : of, relating to, or having the quality of a felony — **fe·lo·ni·ous·ly** *adv* — **fe·lo·ni·ous·ness** *n*

fel·on·ry \'fel-ən-rē\ *n* : FELONS; *specif* : the convict population of a penal colony

fel·o·ny \'fel-ə-nē\ *n* **1** : an act on the part of a feudal vassal involving the forfeiture of his fee **2 a** : a grave crime formerly differing from a misdemeanor under English common law by involving forfeiture in addition to any other punishment **b** : a grave crime expressly declared to be a felony by the common law or by statute **c** : a crime declared a felony by statute because of the punishment imposed

fel·site \'fel-ˌsīt\ *n* [*felspar*] : a dense igneous rock that consists almost entirely of feldspar and quartz — **fel·sit·ic** \fel-'sit-ik\ *adj*

fel·spar *var of* FELDSPAR

1**felt** \'felt\ *n* [ME, fr. OE; akin to OHG *filz* felt, L *pellere* to drive, beat, Gk *pelas* near] **1 a** : a cloth made of wool and fur often mixed with natural or synthetic fibers through the action of heat, moisture, chemicals, and pressure **b** : a firm woven cloth of wool or cotton heavily napped and shrunk **2** : an article made of felt **3** : a material resembling felt: as **a** : a heavy paper of organic or asbestos fibers impregnated with asphalt and used in building construction **b** : semirigid pressed fiber insulation used in building

2**felt** *vt* **1** : to make into felt or a similar substance **2** : to cause to adhere and mat together **3** : to cover with felt

3**felt** *past of* FEEL

felt·ing *n* **1** : the process by which felt is made **2** : FELT

fe·luc·ca \fə-'lü-kə, -'lək-ə\ *n* [It *feluca*] : a narrow fast lateen-rigged sailing ship chiefly of the Mediterranean area

1**fe·male** \'fē-ˌmāl\ *n* [ME, alter. of *femel, femelle*, fr. MF & ML; MF *femelle*, fr. ML *femella*, fr. L, girl, dim. of *femina*] **1** : an individual that bears young or produces eggs as distinguished from one that begets young; *esp* : a woman or girl as distinguished from a man or boy **2** : a pistillate plant

syn WOMAN, LADY: FEMALE is the regular term where mere classification of persons, animals, or plants is intended, but is used of persons only in contempt or derision; WOMAN is the generally accepted term applying to all adult female persons regardless of rank or character; LADY specifically designates a woman of rank and connotes the qualities of dress, manner, and social behavior commonly associated with women of the privileged classes

2**female** *adj* **1 a** : of, relating to, or being the sex that bears young or produces eggs **b** : PISTILLATE **2** : designed with a hollow into which a corresponding male part fits (~ coupling of a hose) **syn** see FEMININE — **fe·male·ness** *n*

1**fem·i·nine** \'fem-ə-nən\ *adj* [ME, fr. MF *feminin*, fr. L *femininus*, fr. *femina* woman; akin to OE *delu* nipple, L *filius* son, *felix, fetus*, & *fecundus* fruitful, *felare* to suck, Gk *thēlē* nipple] **1** : FEMALE 1a **2** : characteristic of or appropriate or peculiar to women **3** : of, relating to, or constituting the gender that ordinarily includes most words or grammatical forms referring to females **4 a** : having an unstressed and usu. hypermetric final syllable (~ ending) **b** *of rhyme* : occurring in the last metrically stressed syllable and a final light syllable (as in *motion, ocean*) **c** : having the final chord occurring on a weak beat (music in ~ cadences) — **fem·i·nine·ly** *adv* — **fem·i·nine·ness** \-nə(n)-nəs\ *n*

syn FEMALE, WOMANLY, WOMANLIKE, WOMANISH, EFFEMINATE, LADYLIKE: FEMININE applies to qualities or attitudes characteristic of women and not shared by men; FEMALE stresses the fact of sex; used otherwise than scientifically or statistically it has a contemptuous or patronizing suggestion; WOMANLY suggests qualities esp. associated with the ideal wife or mother; WOMANLIKE suggests faults and foibles thought typical of women; WOMANISH implies weakness and emotionalism and is used chiefly in reference to a man; EFFEMINATE emphasizes the softer or more delicate aspects of a woman's attitudes and behavior and applies chiefly to men, implying a lack of virility or masculinity; LADYLIKE suggests decorous propriety or, in reference to boys and men, may impute primness, daintiness, or lack of expected masculine force and strength

2**feminine** *n* **1** : the female principle (eternal ~) **2 a** : a noun, pronoun, adjective, or inflectional form or class of the feminine gender **b** : the feminine gender

fem·i·nin·i·ty \ˌfem-ə-'nin-ət-ē\ *n* **1** : the quality or nature of the female sex **2** : EFFEMINACY **3** : WOMEN, WOMANKIND

fem·i·nism \'fem-ə-ˌniz-əm\ *n* **1** : the theory of the political, economic, and social equality of the sexes **2** : organized activity on behalf of women's rights and interests — **fem·i·nist** \-nəst\ *n or adj* — **fem·i·nis·tic** \ˌfem-ə-'nis-tik\ *adj*

fe·min·i·ty \fe-'min-ət-ē\ *n* : FEMININITY

fem·i·ni·za·tion \ˌfem-ə-nə-'zā-shən\ *n* : the process or condition of being feminized

fem·i·nize \'fem-ə-ˌnīz\ *vt* : to give a feminine quality to

femme fa·tale \ˌfem-fə-'tal, -'täl\ *n, pl* **femmes fa·tales** \ˌfem-fə-'tal(z), -'täl(z)\ [F, lit., disastrous woman] **1** : a seductive woman who lures men into dangerous or compromising situations : SIREN **2** : a woman who attracts men by an aura of charm and mystery

fem·o·ral \'fem-(ə-)rəl\ *adj* : of or relating to the femur or thigh

fe·mur \'fē-mər\ *n, pl* **fe·murs** *or* **fem·o·ra** \'fem-(ə-)rə\ [NL *femor-, femur*, fr. L, thigh] **1** : the proximal bone of the hind or lower limb — called also *thigh·bone* \'thī-'bōn, -ˌbōn\ **2** : the segment of an insect's leg that is third from the body

1**fen** \'fen\ *n* [ME, fr. OE *fenn*; akin to OHG *fenna* fen, Skt *paṅka* mud] : low land covered wholly or partly with water unless artificially drained

2**fen** \'fən\ *n, pl* **fen** [Chin (Pek) *fên*1] — see *yuan* at MONEY table

1**fence** \'fen(t)s\ *n, often attrib* [ME *fens*, short for *defens* defense] **1** *archaic* : a means of protection : DEFENSE **2** : a barrier intended to prevent escape or intrusion or to mark a boundary; *esp* : such a barrier made of posts and wire or boards **3** : FENCING 1 **4 a** : a receiver of stolen goods **b** : a place where stolen goods are bought — **fence·less** \'fen(t)-sləs\ *adj* — **fence·less·ness** *n* — **on the fence** : in a position of neutrality or indecision

2**fence** *vt* **1 a** : to enclose with a fence **b** (1) : to keep in or out with a fence (2) : to ward off **2** : to provide a defense for ~ *vi* **1 a** : to practice fencing **b** (1) : to use tactics of attack and defense resembling those of fencing (2) : to parry arguments by shifting ground **2** *archaic* : to provide protection — **fenc·er** *n*

fenc·ing *n* **1** : the art or practice of attack and defense with the sword or foil **2 a** (1) : FENCE 2 (2) : the fences of a property or region **b** : material used for building fences

1**fend** \'fend\ *vb* [ME *fenden*, short for *defenden*] *vt* **1** : DEFEND **2** : to keep or ward off : REPEL **3** *dial Brit* : to provide for : SUPPORT ~ *vi* **1** *dial Brit* : to make an effort : STRUGGLE **2 a** : to try to get along without help : SHIFT **b** : to provide a livelihood

2**fend** *n, chiefly Scot* : an effort or attempt esp. for oneself

fend·er \'fen-dər\ *n* : a device that protects: as **a** : a cushion to lessen shock **b** : RAILING **c** : a device in front of locomotives and streetcars to lessen injury to animals or pedestrians in case of collision **d** : a guard over the wheel of a motor vehicle **e** : a low metal frame or a screen before an open fireplace

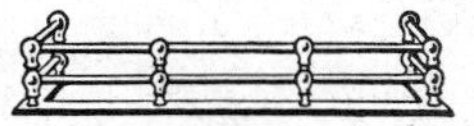

fender e

fe·nes·tra \fi-'nes-trə\ *n, pl* **fe·nes·trae** \-ˌtrē, -ˌtrī\ [NL, fr. L, window] **1** : a small opening; *esp* : either of two apertures in the bone between the middle and inner ear **2** : an opening cut in bone **3** : a transparent spot — **fe·nes·tral** \-trəl\ *adj*

fe·nes·trate \fi-'nes-ˌtrāt, 'fen-ə-ˌstrāt\ *adj* [L *fenestratus*, fr. *fenestra*] : FENESTRATED 2

fe·nes·trat·ed \-ˌtrāt-əd, -ˌstrāt-əd\ *adj* **1** : provided with or characterized by windows **2 a** : having one or more openings or transparent spots **b** : RETICULATE (~ leaves)

fen·es·tra·tion \ˌfen-ə-'strā-shən\ *n* **1** : the arrangement, proportioning, and design of windows and doors in a building **2** : an opening in a surface **3** : the operation of cutting an opening in the bony labyrinth between the inner ear and tympanum to replace natural fenestrae that are not functional

Fe·ni·an \'fē-nē-ən\ *n* [IrGael *Fēinne*, pl. of *Fiann*, legendary band of Irish warriors] **1** : one of a legendary band of warriors defending Ireland in the 2d and 3d centuries A.D. **2** : a member of a secret 19th century Irish and Irish-American organization dedicated to the overthrow of British rule in Ireland — **Fenian** *adj* — **Fe·ni·an·ism** \-nē-ə-ˌniz-əm\ *n*

fen·nec \'fen-ik\ *n* [Ar *fanak*] : a small pale-fawn African fox (*Fennecus zerda*) with large ears

fen·nel \'fen-ᵊl\ *n* [ME *fenel*, fr. OE *finugl*, fr. (assumed) VL *fenuculum*, fr. L *feniculum* fennel, dim. of *fenum* hay; perh. akin to L *fetus* fruitful — more at FEMININE] : a perennial European herb (*Foeniculum vulgare*) of the carrot family adventive in No. America and cultivated for its aromatic seeds

fen·ny \'fen-ē\ *adj* [ME, fr. OE *fennig*, fr. *fenn* fen] **1** : having the characteristics of a fen : BOGGY **2** : peculiar to or found in a fen

fenu·greek \'fen-yə-ˌgrēk\ *n* [ME *fenugrek*, fr. MF *fenugrec*, fr. L *fenum Graecum*, lit., Greek hay] : a leguminous annual Asiatic herb (*Trigonella foenumgraecum*) with aromatic seeds

feoff·ee \fe-'fē, fē-'fē\ *n* : the person to whom a feoffment is made

feoff·ment \'fef-mənt, 'fēf-\ *n* [ME *feoffement*, fr. AF, fr. *feoffer* to invest with a fee, fr. OF *fief* fee] : the granting of a fee

feof·for \'fef-ər, 'fēf-, -ˌȯ(ə)r; fe-'fȯ(ə)r, fē-\ *or* **feoff·er** \'fef-ər, 'fēf-\ *n* : one who makes a feoffment

-fer \fər\ *n comb form* [F & L; F *-fère,* fr. L *-fer* bearing, one that bears, fr. *ferre* to carry — more at BEAR] **:** one that bears ⟨aqui*fer*⟩

fe·rae na·tu·rae \'fer-,ī-nə-'tu̇(ə)r-,ī\ *adj* [L, of a wild nature] **:** wild by nature and not usu. tamed

fe·ral \'fir-əl, 'fer-\ *adj* [ML *feralis,* fr. L *fera* wild animal, fr. fem. of *ferus* wild — more at FIERCE] **1 :** of, relating to, or suggestive of a wild beast **:** SAVAGE **2 :** not domesticated or cultivated **:** WILD

fer·bam \'fər-,bam\ *n* [*fer*ric dimethyl-dithiocar*bam*ate] **:** an agricultural fungicide $FeC_9H_{18}N_3S_6$ used esp. on fruit trees

fer-de-lance \,ferd-ᵊl-'an(t)s, -'än(t)s\ *n, pl* **fer-de-lance** [F, lit., lance iron, spearhead] **:** a large extremely venomous pit viper (*Bothrops atrox*) of Central and So. America

fere \'fi(ə)r\ *n* [ME, fr. OE *gefēra;* akin to OE *faran* to go, travel] **1** *archaic* **:** COMPANION, COMRADE **2** *archaic* **:** SPOUSE

fe·ria \'fir-ē-ə, 'fer-\ *n* [ML — more at FAIR] **:** a weekday of the Roman Catholic or Anglican church calendar on which no feast is celebrated — **fe·ri·al** \-ē-əl\ *adj*

fe·rine \'fi(ə)r-,īn\ *adj* [L *ferinus,* fr. *fera*] **:** FERAL

fer·i·ty \'fer-ət-ē\ *n* [L *feritas,* fr. *ferus*] **:** the quality or state of being feral

fer·lie *also* **fer·ly** \'fer-lē\ *n* [ME, fr. *ferly* strange, fr. OE *fǣrlīc* unexpected, fr. *fǣr* sudden danger] *Scot* **:** WONDER

fer·ma·ta \fer-'mät-ə\ *n* [It, lit., stop, fr. *fermare* to stop, fr. L *firmare* to make firm] **:** a prolongation at the discretion of the performer of a musical note, chord, or rest beyond its given time value; *also* **:** the sign ⌢ or ⌣ denoting such a prolongation

¹fer·ment \(,)fər-'ment\ *vi* **1 :** to undergo fermentation **2 :** to be in a state of agitation or intense activity ~ *vt* **1 :** to cause to undergo fermentation **2 :** to work up (as into a state of agitation) **:** FOMENT — **fer·ment·able** \-'ment-ə-bəl\ *adj* — **fer·ment·er** *n*

²fer·ment \'fər-,ment *also* (,)fər-'ment\ *n* [ME, fr. L *fermentum* yeast] **1 :** an agent capable of bringing about fermentation **2 a :** FERMENTATION 1 **b :** a state of unrest **:** AGITATION

fer·men·ta·tion \,fər-mən-'tā-shən, -,men-\ *n* **1 :** a chemical change with effervescence; *esp* **:** a transformation of an organic substance by the action of ferments **2 :** FERMENT 2b

fer·men·tative \(,)fər-'ment-ət-iv\ *adj* **1 :** causing fermentation **2 :** of, relating to, or produced by fermentation **3 :** capable of undergoing fermentation

fer·mi·um \'fer-mē-əm, 'fər-\ *n* [Enrico *Fermi*] **:** a radioactive metallic element artificially produced (as by bombardment of plutonium with neutrons) — see ELEMENT table

fern \'fərn\ *n* [ME, fr. OE *fearn;* akin to OHG *farn* fern, Skt *parṇa* wing, leaf] **:** any of numerous flowerless seedless plants constituting a class (Filicineae) of lower vascular plants; *esp* **:** any of an order (Filicales) resembling seed plants in being differentiated into root, stem, and leaflike fronds and in having vascular tissue but differing in reproducing by spores — **fern·like** \'fərn-,līk\ *adj* — **ferny** \'fər-nē\ *adj*

fern·ery \'fərn-(ə-)rē\ *n* **1 :** a place or stand where ferns grow **2 :** a collection of growing ferns

fern seed *n* **:** the dustlike asexual spores of ferns formerly taken for seeds and thought to make the possessor invisible

fe·ro·cious \fə-'rō-shəs\ *adj* [L *feroc-, ferox,* lit., fierce looking, fr. *ferus* + *-oc-, -ox* (akin to Gk *ōps* eye) — more at EYE] **1 :** FIERCE, SAVAGE **2 :** unbearably intense **:** EXTREME ⟨~ heat⟩ **syn** see FIERCE — **fe·ro·cious·ly** *adv* — **fe·ro·cious·ness** *n*

fe·roc·i·ty \fə-'räs-ət-ē\ *n* **:** the quality or state of being ferocious

-f·er·ous \f-(ə-)rəs\ *adj comb form* [ME, fr. L *-fer* & MF *-fere* (fr. L *-fer*)] **:** bearing **:** producing ⟨carboni*ferous*⟩

fer·rate \'fe(ə)r-,āt\ *n* [ISV, fr. L *ferrum* iron] **:** a compound containing iron and oxygen in the anion; *esp* **:** a red salt analogous to the chromates and sulfates

¹fer·ret \'fer-ət\ *n* [ME *furet, ferret,* fr. MF *furet,* fr. (assumed) VL *furittus,* lit., little thief, dim. of L *fur* thief] **1 :** a partially domesticated usu. albino European polecat sometimes treated as a separate species (*Mustela furo*) used esp. for hunting rodents **2 :** an active and persistent searcher — **fer·rety** \-ət-ē\ *adj*

²ferret *vi* **1 :** to hunt with ferrets **2 :** to search about ~ *vt* **1 a** (1) **:** to hunt (as game) with ferrets (2) **:** DRIVE, EXPEL **b :** to find and bring to light by searching — usu. used with *out* **2 :** HARRY, WORRY — **fer·ret·er** *n*

³ferret *n* [prob. modif. of It *fioretti* floss silk, fr. pl. of *fioretto,* dim. of *fiore* flower, fr. L *flor-, flos* — more at BLOW] **:** a narrow cotton, silk, or wool tape — called also *ferreting*

ferri- *comb form* [L, fr. *ferrum*] **1 :** iron ⟨*ferri*ferous⟩ **2 :** ferric iron ⟨*ferri*cyanic⟩

fer·ri·age \'fer-ē-ij\ *n* **1 :** the fare paid for a ferry passage **2 :** the act or business of transporting by ferry

fer·ric \'fer-ik\ *adj* **1 :** of, relating to, or containing iron **2 :** being or containing iron with a higher valence esp. three than in ferrous compounds

ferric oxide *n* **:** the red or black oxide of iron Fe_2O_3 found in nature as hematite and as rust and also obtained synthetically and used as a pigment and for polishing

fer·ri·cy·an·ic acid \,fer-,ī-,sī-,an-ik-, ,fer-i-\ *n* **:** a brown crystalline unstable acid $H_3Fe(CN)_6$

fer·ri·cy·a·nide \-'sī-ə-,nīd\ *n* [ISV] **:** a salt of ferricyanic acid

fer·rif·er·ous \fə-'rif-(ə-)rəs, fe-\ *adj* **:** containing or yielding iron

Fer·ris wheel \'fer-əs-\ *n* [G. W. G. *Ferris* †1896 Am engineer] **:** an amusement device consisting of a large upright power-driven wheel carrying seats that remain horizontal around its rim

fer·rite \'fe(ə)r-,īt\ *n* **1 :** an iron compound that is a salt of a ferric hydroxide acting in its capacity of an acid **2 :** a solid solution in which alpha iron is the solvent — **fer·rit·ic** \fə-'rit-ik, fe-\ *adj*

ferro- *comb form* [ML, fr. L *ferrum*] **1 :** iron ⟨*ferro*concrete⟩ **2 :** iron and ⟨*ferro*nickel⟩ — chiefly in names of alloys **3 :** ferrous iron ⟨*ferro*cyanic⟩

fer·ro·al·loy \,fer-ō-'al-,ȯi, -ə-'lȯi\ *n* **:** a crude alloy of iron with one or more other elements (as metals)

fer·ro·con·crete \-'kän-,krēt, -,kän-'\ *n* **:** REINFORCED CONCRETE

fer·ro·cy·an·ic acid \,fer-ō-,sī-,an-ik-\ *n* [ISV] **:** a white crystalline acid $H_4Fe(CN)_6$

fer·ro·cy·a·nide \-'sī-ə-,nīd\ *n* **:** a salt of ferrocyanic acid

fer·ro·elec·tric \,fer-ō-i-'lek-trik\ *n* **:** a crystalline substance that exhibits spontaneous electric polarization, electric hysteresis, and piezoelectricity

fer·ro·mag·ne·sian \-,mag-'nē-shən, -zhən\ *adj* **:** containing iron and magnesium

fer·ro·mag·net·ic \-'net-ik\ *adj* **:** of or relating to substances with an abnormally high magnetic permeability, a definite saturation point, and appreciable residual magnetism and hysteresis — **ferromagnetic** *n* — **fer·ro·mag·ne·tism** \-'mag-nə-,tiz-əm\ *n*

¹fer·ro·type \'fer-ə-,tīp\ *n* **1 :** a positive photograph made by a collodion process on a thin iron plate having a darkened surface **2 :** the process by which a ferrotype is made

²ferrotype *vt* **:** to give a gloss to (a photographic print) by squeegeeing facedown while wet on a ferrotype plate and allowing to dry

fer·rous \'fer-əs\ *adj* [NL *ferrosus,* fr. L *ferrum*] **1 :** of, relating to, or containing iron **2 :** being or containing bivalent iron

ferrous oxide *n* **:** the monoxide of iron FeO

ferrous sulfate *n* **:** an astringent salt $FeSO_4$ used in making pigments and ink, in treating industrial wastes, and in medicine

fer·ru·gi·nous \fə-'rü-jə-nəs, fe-\ *or* **fer·ru·gin·e·ous** \,fer-(y)u̇-'jin-ē-əs\ *adj* [L *ferrugineus, ferruginus,* fr. *ferrugin-, ferrugo* iron rust, fr. *ferrum*] **1 :** of, relating to, or containing iron **2 :** resembling iron rust in color

¹fer·rule \'fer-əl\ *n* [alter. of ME *virole,* fr. MF, fr. L *viriola,* dim. of *viria* bracelet, of Celtic origin; akin to OIr *fiar* oblique — more at VEER] **1 :** a ring or cap usu. of metal put around a slender shaft (as a cane or a tool handle) to strengthen it or prevent splitting **2 :** a short tube or bushing for making a tight joint (as between pipes)

²ferrule *vt* **:** to supply with a ferrule

¹fer·ry \'fer-ē\ *vb* [ME *ferien,* fr. OE *ferian* to carry, convey; akin to OE *faran* to go] *vt* **1 a :** to carry by boat over a body of water **b :** to cross by a ferry **2 a :** to convey from one place to another **b :** to fly (an airplane) from the factory or other shipping point to a designated delivery point or from one base to another **c :** to transport in an airplane ~ *vi* **:** to cross water in a boat

²ferry *n* **1 :** a place where persons or things are carried across a river or other body of water in a boat **2 :** FERRYBOAT **3 :** a franchise or right to operate a ferry service across a body of water **4 :** an organized service and route for flying airplanes esp. across a sea or continent for delivery to the user — **fer·ry·man** \-mən\ *n*

fer·ry·boat \-,bōt\ *n* **:** a boat used to ferry passengers, vehicles, or goods

fer·tile \'fərt-ᵊl\ *adj* [ME, fr. MF & L; MF, fr. L *fertilis,* fr. *ferre* to carry, bear — more at BEAR] **1 a :** producing or bearing fruit in great quantities **:** PRODUCTIVE, INVENTIVE **b** *obs* **:** PLENTIFUL **2 a** (1) **:** capable of sustaining abundant plant growth ⟨~ soil⟩ (2) **:** affording abundant possibilities for development **b :** capable of growing or developing ⟨~ egg⟩ **c** (1) **:** capable of producing fruit (2) *of an anther* **:** containing pollen (3) **:** developing spores or spore-bearing organs **d :** capable of breeding or reproducing **3 :** capable of being converted into fissionable material ⟨~ uranium 238⟩ — **fer·tile·ly** \-ᵊl-(l)ē\ *adv* — **fer·tile·ness** \-ᵊl-nəs\ *n*

syn FECUND, FRUITFUL, PROLIFIC: FERTILE implies the power to reproduce in kind or to assist in reproduction and growth; applied to a brain, or to an idea, it suggests readiness of invention and development; FECUND emphasizes abundance or rapidity in bearing fruit or offspring; FRUITFUL adds to FERTILE and FECUND the implication of desirable or useful results; PROLIFIC stresses rapidity of spreading or multiplying by or as if by natural reproduction

fer·til·i·ty \(,)fər-'til-ət-ē\ *n* **1 :** the quality or state of being fertile **2 :** the birthrate of a population

fer·til·iz·able \'fərt-ᵊl-,ī-zə-bəl\ *adj* **:** capable of being fertilized

fer·til·iza·tion \,fərt-ᵊl-ə-'zā-shən\ *n* **:** an act or process of making fertile: as **a :** the application of fertilizer **b** (1) **:** an act or process of fecundation, insemination, impregnation, or pollination (2) **:** the process of union of two germ cells whereby the somatic chromosome number is restored and the development of a new individual is initiated — **fer·til·iza·tion·al** \-shnəl, -shən-ᵊl\ *adj*

fer·til·ize \'fərt-ᵊl-,īz\ *vt* **:** to make fertile: as **a :** to cause the fertilization of **b :** to apply a fertilizer to ⟨~ land⟩

fer·til·iz·er \-,ī-zər\ *n* **:** one that fertilizes; *specif* **:** a substance (as manure or a chemical mixture) used to make soil more fertile

fer·u·la \'fer-(y)ə-lə\ *n* [NL, genus name, fr. L, giant fennel] **:** any of a genus (*Ferula*) of Old World plants of the carrot family yielding various gum resins (as galbanum and asafetida)

fer·ule \'fer-əl\ *also* **fer·u·la** \'fer-(y)ə-lə\ *n* [L *ferula* giant fennel, ferule] **1 :** an instrument (as a rod) used to punish children; *specif* **:** a flat piece of wood **2 :** school discipline

fer·ven·cy \'fər-vən-sē\ *n* **:** FERVOR

fer·vent \'fər-vənt\ *adj* [ME, fr. MF & L; MF, fr. L *fervent-, fervens,* prp. of *fervēre* to boil, glow — more at BURN] **1 :** very hot **:** GLOWING **2 :** marked by great warmth of feeling **:** ARDENT **syn** see IMPASSIONED — **fer·vent·ly** *adv*

fer·vid \'fər-vəd\ *adj* [L *fervidus,* fr. *fervēre*] **1 :** very hot **:** BURNING **2 :** ARDENT, ZEALOUS **syn** see IMPASSIONED — **fer·vid·ly** *adv* — **fer·vid·ness** *n*

fer·vor *also chiefly Brit* **fer·vour** \'fər-vər\ *n* [ME *fervour,* fr. MF & L; MF *ferveur,* fr. L *fervor,* fr. *fervēre*] **1 :** intense heat **2 :** intensity of feeling or expression **:** PASSION **syn** see PASSION

fes·cen·nine \'fes-ᵊn-,īn, -,ēn\ *adj* [L *fescennini* (*versus*), ribald songs sung at rustic weddings, prob. fr. *fescenninus* of Fescennium, fr. *Fescennium* town in Etruria] **:** SCURRILOUS, OBSCENE

fes·cue \'fes-(,)kyü\ *n* [ME *festu* stalk, straw, fr. MF, fr. LL *festucum,* fr. L *festuca*] **1 :** a small pointer (as a stick) used to point out letters to children learning to read **2 :** a tufted perennial grass (genus *Festuca*) with panicled spikelets

fess *also* **fesse** \'fes\ *n* [ME *fesse,* fr. MF *faisse,* fr. L *fascia* band] **:** a broad horizontal bar across the middle of a heraldic field

-fest \,fest\ *n comb form* [G, fr. *fest* celebration, fr. L *festum*] **:** meeting or occasion marked by (such) activity ⟨talk*fest*⟩

fes·tal \'fest-ᵊl\ *adj* [L *festum* festival — more at FEAST] **:** of or relating to a feast or festival **:** FESTIVE — **fes·tal·ly** \-ᵊl-ē\ *adv*

¹fes·ter \'fes-tər\ *n* [ME, fr. MF *festre,* fr. L *fistula* pipe, fistulous ulcer] **:** a suppurating sore **:** PUSTULE

²fester *vb* **fes·ter·ing** \-t(ə-)riŋ\ *vi* **1 :** to generate pus **2 :** PUTREFY, ROT **3 :** to cause increasing poisoning or irritation **:** RANKLE ~ *vt* **:** to make inflamed or corrupt

¹fes·ti·nate \'fes-tə-,nāt, -nət\ *adj* [L *festinatus,* pp. of *festinare* to hasten — more at BORZOI] **:** HASTY — **fes·ti·nate·ly** *adv*

²fes·ti·nate \-,nāt\ *vb* **:** HASTEN

¹fes·ti·val \'fes-tə-vəl\ *adj* [ME, fr. MF, fr. L *festivus* festive] **:** of, relating to, appropriate to, or set apart as a festival

²festival *n* **1 a :** a time of celebration marked by special observances **b :** FEAST 2 **2 :** a periodic season or program of cultural events or entertainment **3 :** CONVIVIALITY, GAIETY

Festival of Lights : HANUKKAH
fes·tive \'fes-tiv\ *adj* [L *festivus*, fr. *festum*] **1** : of, relating to, or suitable for a feast or festival **2** : JOYOUS, GAY — **fes·tive·ly** *adv* — **fes·tive·ness** *n*
fes·tiv·i·ty \fes-'tiv-ət-ē, fəs-\ *n* **1** : FESTIVAL 1 **2** : the quality or state of being festive : GAIETY **3** : festive activity
¹fes·toon \fes-'tün\ *n* [F *feston*, fr. It *festone*, fr. *festa* festival, fr. L] **1** : a decorative chain or strip hanging between two points **2** : a carved, molded, or painted ornament representing a decorative chain **3** : one of the somewhat quadrangular segments bordering the body of some ticks

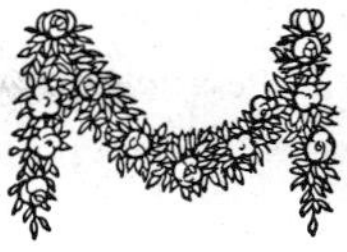
festoon 1

²festoon *vt* **1** : to hang or form festoons on **2** : to shape into festoons
fes·toon·ery \fes-'tü-nə-rē\ *n* : an arrangement of festoons
fest·schrift \'fest-,shrift\ *n, pl* **fest·schrif·ten** \-,shrif-tən\ *or* **fest·schrifts** \-,shrif(t)s\ *often cap* [G, fr. *fest* festival, celebration + *schrift* writing] : a volume of writings by different authors presented as a tribute or memorial esp. to a scholar
fe·tal \'fēt-ᵊl\ *adj* : of, relating to, or being a fetus
fe·ta·tion \fē-'tā-shən\ *n* : the formation of a fetus : PREGNANCY
¹fetch \'fech\ *vb* [ME *fecchen*, fr. OE *fetian*, *feccan*; akin to OE *fōt* foot — more at FOOT] *vt* **1 a** : to go or come after and bring or take back **b** : DERIVE, DEDUCE **2 a** : to cause to come **b** : to bring in (as a price) : REALIZE **c** : INTEREST, ATTRACT **3 a** : to give (a blow) by striking : DEAL **b** *chiefly dial* : to bring about : ACCOMPLISH **c** (1) : to take in (as a breath) : DRAW (2) : to bring forth (as a sound) : HEAVE ⟨~ a sigh⟩ **4 a** : to reach by sailing esp. against the wind or tide **b** : to arrive at : REACH ~ *vi* **1** : to get and bring something; *specif* : to retrieve killed game **2** : to take a roundabout way : CIRCLE **3 a** : to hold a course on a body of water **b** : VEER — **fetch·er** *n*
²fetch *n* **1** : an act or instance of fetching **2** : TRICK, STRATAGEM
³fetch *n* [origin unknown] **1** : DOPPELGÄNGER **2** : GHOST
fetch·ing *adj* : ATTRACTIVE, PLEASING — **fetch·ing·ly** \-iŋ-lē\ *adv*
fetch up *vt* **1** : to bring up or out : PRODUCE **2** : to make up (as leeway) **3** : to bring to a stop ~ *vi* : to come to a standstill, stopping place, or result : ARRIVE
¹fete *or* **fête** \'fāt\ *n* [F *fête* fr. OF *feste*] **1** : FESTIVAL **2 a** : a lavish often outdoor entertainment **b** : an elaborate usu. large party
²fete *or* **fête** *vt* **1** : to honor or commemorate with a fete **2** : to pay high honor to
fête cham·pê·tre \,fāt-,shäm-'petrᵊ, -,shä^{n}-\ *n, pl* **fêtes champê·tres** *same*\ [F, lit., rural festival] : an outdoor entertainment
fet·er·i·ta \,fet-ə-'rēt-ə\ *n* [Sudanese Ar] : any of various grain sorghums with compact oval heads of large soft white seeds
feti- *or* **feto-** *also* **foeti-** *or* **foeto-** *comb form* [NL *fetus*] : fetus ⟨*feti*cide⟩
fe·ti·cide \'fēt-ə-,sīd\ *n* : the act of killing a fetus
fet·id \'fet-əd, *esp Brit* 'fē-tid\ *adj* [ME, fr. L *foetidus*, fr. *foetēre* to stink; akin to L *fumus* smoke] : having an offensive smell : STINKING **syn** see MALODOROUS — **fet·id·ly** *adv* — **fet·id·ness** *n*
fe·tish *or* **fe·tich** \'fet-ish, 'fēt-\ *n* [F & Pg; F *fétiche*, fr. Pg *feitiço*, fr. *feitiço* artificial, false, fr. L *facticius* factitious] **1 a** : an object believed among a primitive people to have magical power to protect or aid its owner; *broadly* : any material object regarded with superstitious or extravagant trust or reverence **b** : an object of irrational reverence or obsessive devotion : PREPOSSESSION **c** : an object or a body part that arouses libido often to the exclusion of genital impulses **2** : a rite or cult of fetish worshipers
syn FETISH, TALISMAN, CHARM, AMULET mean an object believed useful in averting evil or bringing good. FETISH is literally applied to such an object regarded as sacred or magical among a primitive people; it applies by extension to something often intangible that is cherished unreasonably or obsessively; TALISMAN applies to something having extraordinary and seemingly magical powers; CHARM applies to an object or form of words believed effective in repelling evil spirits or in attracting their opposite; it may often imply something markedly efficacious in any manner; AMULET applies esp. to an inscribed ornament worn on the person
fe·tish·ism \-ish-,iz-əm\ *n* **1** : belief in magical fetishes **2** : extravagant irrational devotion **3** : the pathological displacement of erotic interest and satisfaction to a fetish — **fe·tish·ist** \-əst\ *n* — **fe·tish·is·tic** \,fet-ish-'is-tik, ,fēt-\ *adj*
fet·lock \'fet-,läk\ *n* [ME *fitlok*, *fetlak*; akin to OE *fōt* foot] **1 a** : a projection bearing a tuft of hair on the back of the leg above the hoof of a horse or similar animal **b** : the tuft of hair itself **2** : the joint of the limb at the fetlock
fe·tor \'fēt-ər, 'fē-,tȯ(ə)r\ *n* [ME *fetoure*, fr. L *foetor*, fr. *foetēre*] : STENCH
¹fet·ter \'fet-ər\ *n* [ME *feter*, fr. OE; akin to OE *fōt* foot] **1** : a chain or shackle for the feet **2** : something that confines : RESTRAINT
²fetter *vt* **1** : to put fetters on : SHACKLE **2** : to restrain from motion or action : CONFINE **syn** see HAMPER
¹fet·tle \'fet-ᵊl\ *vt* **fet·tling** \'fet-liŋ, -ᵊl-iŋ\ [ME *fetlen* to shape, prepare; prob. akin to OE *fæt* vessel — more at VAT] : to cover or line the hearth of (as a reverberatory furnace) with fettling
²fettle *n* **1** : a state of fitness or order : CONDITION **2** : FETTLING
fet·tling \'fet-liŋ, -ᵊl-iŋ\ *n* : loose material (as ore or sand) thrown on the hearth of a furnace to protect it
fe·tus \'fēt-əs\ *n* [NL, fr. L, act of bearing young, offspring; akin to L *fetus* newly delivered, fruitful — more at FEMININE] : an unborn or unhatched vertebrate esp. after attaining the basic structural plan of its kind; *specif* : a developing human from usu. three months after conception to birth
¹feud \'fyüd\ *n* [alter. of ME *feide*, fr. MF, of Gmc origin; akin to OHG *fēhida* hostility, feud, OE *fāh* hostile — more at FOE] : a prolonged quarrel; *esp* : a lasting state of hostilities between families or clans marked by violent attacks for revenge — **feud** *vi*
²feud *n* [ML *feodum*, *feudum*, of Gmc origin] : FEE 1a
¹feu·dal \'fyüd-ᵊl\ *adj* **1** : of, relating to, or having the characteristics of a medieval fee **2** : of, relating to, or suggestive of feudalism ⟨~ law⟩ — **feu·dal·ly** \-ᵊl-ē\ *adv*
²feud·al \'fyüd-ᵊl\ *adj* : of or relating to a prolonged quarrel
feu·dal·ism \'fyüd-ᵊl-,iz-əm\ *n* **1** : the system of political organization prevailing in Europe from the 9th to about the 15th centuries having as its basis the relation of lord to vassal with all land held in fee and as chief characteristics homage, the service of tenants under arms and in court, wardship, and forfeiture **2** : any of various political or social systems similar to medieval feudalism — **feu·dal·ist** \-ᵊl-əst\ *n* — **feu·dal·is·tic** \,fyüd-ᵊl-'is-tik\ *adj*
feu·dal·i·ty \fyü-'dal-ət-ē\ *n* **1** : the quality or state of being feudal **2** : a feudal holding, domain, or concentration of power
feu·dal·iza·tion \,fyüd-ᵊl-ə-'zā-shən\ *n* : an act or process of feudalizing
feu·dal·ize \'fyüd-ᵊl-,īz\ *vt* : to make feudal
¹feu·da·to·ry \'fyüd-ə-,tōr-ē, -,tȯr-\ *adj* [ML *feudatorius*, fr. *feudatus*, pp. of *feudare* to enfeoff, fr. *feudum*] **1** : owing feudal allegiance **2** : being under the overlordship of a foreign state
²feudatory *n* **1** : one holding lands by feudal tenure **2** : a dependent lordship : FEE
¹feud·ist \'fyüd-əst\ *n* : a specialist in feudal law
²feudist *n* : one who feuds
feuil·le·ton \,fə(r)-ē-'tō^{n}\ *n* [F, fr. *feuillet* sheet of paper, fr. OF *foillet*, dim. of *foille* leaf — more at FOIL] **1** : a part of a European newspaper or magazine devoted to material designed to entertain the general reader **2** : something (as an installment of a novel) printed in a feuilleton **3 a** : a novel printed in installments **b** : a work of fiction catering to popular taste **4** : a short literary composition often having a familiar tone and reminiscent content — **feuil·le·ton·ism** \,fə(r)-ē-'to^{n}-,niz-əm\ *n* — **feuil·le·ton·ist** \-'to^{n}-nəst\ *n*
fe·ver \'fē-vər\ *n* [ME, fr. OE *fēfer*, fr. L *febris*; akin to L *fovēre* to warm] **1 a** : a rise of body temperature above the normal **b** : any of various diseases of which fever is a prominent symptom **2 a** : a state of heightened or intense emotion or activity **b** : a contagious usu. transient enthusiasm — **fever** *vb* **fe·ver·ing** \'fēv-(ə-)riŋ\
fever blister *n* : COLD SORE
fe·ver·few \'fē-vər-,fyü\ *n* [ME, fr. (assumed) AF *fevrefue*, fr. LL *febrifugia* centaury — more at FEBRIFUGE] : a perennial European composite herb (*Chrysanthemum parthenium*)
fe·ver·ish \'fēv-(ə-)rish\ *adj* **1 a** : having the symptoms of a fever **b** : indicating or relating to fever **c** : tending to cause fever **2** : marked by intense emotion, activity, or instability — **fe·ver·ish·ly** *adv* — **fe·ver·ish·ness** *n*
fe·ver·ous \'fēv-(ə-)rəs\ *adj* : FEVERISH — **fe·ver·ous·ly** *adv*
fever tree *n* : any of several shrubs or trees that are thought to indicate regions free from fever or that yield remedies for fever: as **a** : a blue gum (*Eucalyptus globulus*) **b** : an ornamental tree (*Pinckneya pubens*) of the southeastern U.S.
fe·ver·weed \'fē-vər-,wēd\ *n* : any of several plants (genus *Eryngium*) of coarse bristly herbs of the carrot family
fe·ver·wort \-,wərt, -,wȯ(ə)rt\ *n* : BONESET
¹few \'fyü\ *pron, pl in constr* [ME *fewe*, pron. & adj., fr. OE *fēawa*; akin to OHG *fō* little, L *paucus* little, *pauper* poor, Gk *paid-*, *pais* child, Skt *putra* son] : not many persons or things ⟨~ were present⟩ ⟨~ of his stories are true⟩
²few *adj* **1** : consisting of or amounting to a small number ⟨one of his ~ pleasures⟩ **2** : not many but some ⟨caught a ~ fish⟩ — **few·ness** *n*
³few *n, pl in constr* **1** : a small number of units or individuals ⟨a ~ of them⟩ **2** : a special limited number ⟨the discriminating ~⟩
few·er *pron, pl in constr* : a smaller number of persons or things
few·trils \'fyü-trəlz\ *n pl* [origin unknown] *dial Eng* : TRIFLES
fey \'fā\ *adj* [ME *feye*, fr. OE *fǣge*; akin to OHG *feigi* fey and perh. to OE *fāh* hostile, outlawed — more at FOE] **1 a** *chiefly Scot* : fated to die : DOOMED **b** : marked by a foreboding of death or calamity **2 a** : able to see into the future : VISIONARY **b** : marked by an otherworldly air or attitude : ELFIN **c** : CRAZY, TOUCHED
fez \'fez\ *n, pl* **fez·zes** *also* **fez·es** [F, fr. *Fez*, Morocco] : a brimless cone-shaped flat-crowned hat that usu. has a tassel, is usu. made of red felt, and is worn esp. by men in eastern Mediterranean countries
fia·cre \fē-'äkrᵊ\ *n, pl* **fiacres** *same*\ [F, fr. the Hotel St. *Fiacre*, Paris] : a small hackney coach
fi·an·cé \,fē-,än-'sā, fē-'än-,sā\ *n* [F, fr. MF, fr. pp. of *fiancer* to promise, betroth, fr. OF *fiancier*, fr. *fiance* promise, trust, fr. *fier* to trust, fr. (assumed) VL *fidare*, alter. of L *fidere* — more at BIDE] : a man engaged to be married
fi·an·cée \,fē-,än-'sā, fē-'än-,sā\ *n* [F, fem. of *fiancé*] : a woman engaged to be married
fi·as·co \fē-'as-(,)kō\ *n, pl* **fiascoes** [F, fr. It, lit., bottle, of Gmc origin; akin to OHG *flaska* bottle] : a complete failure
fi·at \'fī-,at, 'fē-,ät\ *n* [L, let it be done, 3d sing. pres. subj. of *fieri* to become, be done — more at BE] **1** : a command that creates **2** : AUTHORIZATION, SANCTION **3** : an authoritative order or decree
fiat money *n* : money (as paper currency) not convertible into coin or specie of equivalent value
¹fib \'fib\ *n* [perh. by shortening & alter. fr. *fable*] : a trivial lie
²fib *vi* **fibbed**; **fib·bing** : to tell a fib **syn** see LIE — **fib·ber** *n*
³fib *vb* **fibbed**; **fib·bing** [origin unknown] *Brit* : BEAT, PUMMEL
fi·ber *or* **fi·bre** \'fī-bər\ *n* [F *fibre*, fr. L *fibra*] **1** : a thread or a structure or object resembling a thread: as **a** (1) : a slender root (as of a grass) (2) : an elongated tapering thick-walled plant cell void at maturity that imparts elasticity, flexibility, and tensile strength **b** (1) : the axis cylinder of a nerve cell with its sheath (2) : one of the filaments composing most of the intercellular matrix of connective tissue (3) : one of the elongated contractile cells of muscle tissue **c** : a slender and greatly elongated natural or synthetic filament (as of wool, cotton, asbestos, gold, glass, or rayon) typically capable of being spun into yarn **2** : material made of fibers; *specif* : VULCANIZED FIBER **3 a** : an element that gives texture or substance **b** : basic toughness : STRENGTH **c** : essential structure — **fi·bered** \-bərd\ *adj*
fi·ber·board \'fī-bər-,bō(ə)rd, -,bȯ(ə)rd\ *n* : a material made by compressing fibers (as of wood) into stiff sheets
fiber glass *n* : glass in fibrous form used in making various products
fi·ber·ize \'fī-bə-,rīz\ *vb* : to break into fibers
fibr- *or* **fibro-** *comb form* [L *fibra*] : fiber : fibrous tissue ⟨*fibr*oid⟩ : fibrous and ⟨*fibro*vascular⟩
fi·bril \'fīb-rəl, 'fib-\ *n* [L *fibrilla*, dim. of *fibra*] : a small filament or fiber; *specif* : ROOT HAIR — **fi·bril·lar** \-rə-lər\ *adj* — **fi·bril-**

li·form \fī-ˈbril-ə-ˌfȯrm, fə-\ *adj* — **fi·bril·lose** \ˈfīb-rə-ˌlōs, ˈfib-\ *adj*

fi·bril·la·tion \ˌfib-rə-ˈlā-shən, ˌfīb-\ *n* **1 :** an act or process of forming fibrils **2 a :** muscular twitching involving individual muscle fibers acting without coordination **b :** very rapid irregular contractions of the muscle fibers of the heart resulting in a lack of synchronism between heartbeat and pulse beat

fi·brin \ˈfī-brən\ *n* **:** a white insoluble fibrous protein formed from fibrinogen by the action of thrombin esp. in the clotting of blood

fi·brin·o·gen \fī-ˈbrin-ə-jən\ *n* [ISV] **:** a globulin that is produced in the liver, that is present esp. in blood plasma, and that is converted into fibrin during clotting of blood

fi·bri·nol·y·sin \ˌfī-brə-ˈnäl-ə-sən\ *n* [ISV] **1 :** PLASMIN **2 :** STREPTOKINASE

fi·bri·nol·y·sis \-səs\ *n* [NL] **:** the usu. enzymatic breakdown of fibrin — **fi·bri·no·lyt·ic** \ˌfī-brə-nō-ˈlit-ik\ *adj*

fi·brin·ous \ˈfī-brə-nəs\ *adj* **:** marked by the presence of fibrin

fi·bro·blast \ˈfī-brə-ˌblast\ *n* [ISV] **:** a mesenchyme cell giving rise to connective tissue — **fi·bro·blas·tic** \ˌfī-brə-ˈblas-tik\ *adj*

fi·bro·cyte \ˈfī-brə-ˌsīt\ *n* [ISV] **:** a spindle-shaped cell of fibrous tissue — **fi·bro·cyt·ic** \ˌfī-brə-ˈsit-ik\ *adj*

[1]**fi·broid** \ˈfī-ˌbrȯid\ *adj* **:** resembling, forming, or consisting of fibrous tissue

[2]**fibroid** *n* **:** a benign tumor esp. of the uterine wall

fi·bro·in \ˈfī-brə-wən\ *n* [F *fibroïne*, fr. *fibr-* + *-ine* -in] **:** an insoluble protein comprising the filaments of the raw silk fiber

fi·bro·ma \fī-ˈbrō-mə\ *n, pl* **fibromas** *also* **fi·bro·ma·ta** \-mət-ə\ **:** a benign tumor consisting mainly of fibrous tissue — **fi·bro·ma·tous** \-ˈbräm-ət-əs, -ˈbrō-mət-\ *adj*

fi·bro·sis \fī-ˈbrō-səs\ *n* **:** a condition marked by increase of interstitial fibrous tissue — **fi·brot·ic** \-ˈbrät-ik\ *adj*

fi·bro·si·tis \ˌfī-brə-ˈsīt-əs\ *n* [NL, fr. *fibrosus* fibrous, fr. ISV *fibrous*] **:** a rheumatic disorder of fibrous tissue

fi·brous \ˈfī-brəs\ *adj* [F *fibreux*, fr. *fibre* fiber, fr. L *fibra*] **1 a :** containing, consisting of, or resembling fibers **b :** characterized by fibrosis **c :** capable of being separated into fibers ⟨a ~ mineral⟩ **2 :** TOUGH, SINEWY — **fi·brous·ly** *adv* — **fi·brous·ness** *n*

fi·bro·vas·cu·lar \ˌfī-brō-ˈvas-kyə-lər\ *adj* **:** having or consisting of fibers and conducting cells (as vessels)

fib·u·la \ˈfib-yə-lə\ *n, pl* **fib·u·lae** \-ˌlē, -ˌlī\ *or* **fibulas** [L] **1 :** a clasp resembling a safety pin used by the ancient Greeks and Romans **2 :** the outer and usu. the smaller of the two bones of the hind limb below the knee — **fib·u·lar** \-lər\ *adj*

-fic \fik\ *adj suffix* [MF & L; MF *-fique*, fr. L *-ficus*, fr. *facere* to make — more at DO] **:** making **:** causing ⟨felici*fic*⟩

-fi·ca·tion \fə-ˈkā-shən\ *n comb form* [ME *-ficacioun*, fr. MF & L; MF *-fication*, fr. L *-fication-*, *-ficatio*, fr. *-ficatus*, pp. ending of verbs ending in *-ficare* to make, fr. *-ficus*] **:** making **:** production ⟨rei*fication*⟩

fice \ˈfīs\ *var of* FEIST

fiche \ˈfēsh\ *n* [short for *microfiche*] **:** a flat piece of microfilm that contains several rows of images (as of printed matter) **:** MICROFICHE

fichu \ˈfish-(ˌ)ü\ *n* [F, fr. pp. of *ficher* to stick in, throw on, fr. (assumed) VL *figicare*, fr. L *figere* to fasten, pierce — more at DIKE] **:** a woman's light triangular scarf that is draped over the shoulders and fastened in front or worn to fill in a low neckline

fick·le \ˈfik-əl\ *adj* [ME *fikel* deceitful, inconstant, fr. OE *ficol* deceitful; akin to OE be*fician* to deceive, L *pigēre* to irk and prob. to OE *fāh* hostile — more at FOE] **:** marked by erratic changeableness esp. in affections **syn** see INCONSTANT — **fick·le·ness** *n*

fi·co \ˈfē-(ˌ)kō\ *n, pl* **ficoes** [obs. *fico*, obscene gesture of contempt, modif. of It *fica* fig, vulva, gesture of contempt, fr. (assumed) VL *fica* fig — more at FIG] **:** FIG 2

fic·tile \ˈfik-tᵊl\ *adj* [L *fictilis* molded of clay, fr. *fictus*] **1 :** molded or moldable of earth, clay, or other soft material **2 :** of or relating to pottery or earthenware

fic·tion \ˈfik-shən\ *n* [ME *ficcioun*, fr. MF *fiction*, fr. L *fiction-*, *fictio* act of fashioning, fiction, fr. *fictus*, pp. of *fingere* to shape, fashion, feign — more at DOUGH] **1 a :** something invented by the imagination or feigned; *specif* **:** an invented story **b :** fictitious literature (as novels or short stories) **2 :** an assumption of a possibility as a fact irrespective of the question of its truth **3 :** the action of feigning or of creating with the imagination — **fic·tion·al** \-shnəl, -shən-ᵊl\ *adj* — **fic·tion·al·ly** \-ē\ *adv*

fic·tion·al·iza·tion \ˌfik-shnə-lə-ˈzā-shən, -shən-ᵊl-ə-ˈzā-\ *or* **fic·tion·iza·tion** \-shə-nə-ˈzā-\ *n* **:** an act, process, or product of fictionalizing

fic·tion·al·ize \ˈfik-shnə-ˌlīz, -shən-ᵊl-ˌīz\ *or* **fic·tion·ize** \-shə-ˌnīz\ *vt* **:** to make into fiction

fic·tion·eer \ˌfik-shə-ˈni(ə)r\ *n* **:** one who writes fiction esp. in quantity and without high standards — **fic·tion·eer·ing** *n*

fic·tion·ist \ˈfik-sh(ə-)nəst\ *n* **:** a writer of fiction; *esp* **:** NOVELIST

fic·ti·tious \fik-ˈtish-əs\ *adj* [L *ficticius* artificial, feigned, fr. *fictus*] **1 :** of, relating to, or characteristic of fiction **:** IMAGINARY **2 :** conventionally or hypothetically assumed **3 :** FEIGNED, SIMULATED — **fic·ti·tious·ly** *adv* — **fic·ti·tious·ness** *n*

syn FABULOUS, LEGENDARY, MYTHICAL, APOCRYPHAL: FICTITIOUS implies fabrication and suggests artificiality or contrivance more than deliberate falsification or deception; FABULOUS stresses the marvelous or incredible character of something without distinctly implying impossibility or actual nonexistence; LEGENDARY suggests the elaboration of invented details and distortion of historical facts produced by popular tradition; MYTHICAL implies a purely fanciful explanation of facts or the creation of beings and events out of the imagination; APOCRYPHAL implies an unknown or dubious source or origin for an account circulated as true or genuine

fic·tive \ˈfik-tiv\ *adj* **1 :** IMAGINARY, FEIGNED **2 :** of, relating to, or capable of imaginative creation — **fic·tive·ly** *adv*

fid \ˈfid\ *n* [origin unknown] **1 :** a square bar of wood or iron used to support a topmast **2 :** a pin usu. of hard wood that tapers to a point and is used in opening the strands of a rope

-fid \fəd, ˌfid\ *adj comb form* [L *-fidus*, fr. *findere* to split] **:** divided into (so many) parts ⟨sexi*fid*⟩ or (such) parts ⟨pinnati*fid*⟩

[1]**fid·dle** \ˈfid-ᵊl\ *n* [ME *fidel*, fr. OE *fithele*, prob. fr. ML *vitula*] **1 :** VIOLIN **2 :** a device to keep dishes from sliding off a table aboard ship

[2]**fiddle** *vb* **fid·dling** \ˈfid-liŋ, -ᵊl-iŋ\ *vi* **1 :** to play on a fiddle **2 a :** to move the hands or fingers restlessly **b :** to spend time in aimless activity **:** PUTTER **c :** MEDDLE, TAMPER ~ *vt* **:** to play (as a tune) on a fiddle — **fid·dler** \ˈfid-lər, -ᵊl-ər\ *n*

fiddle away *vt* **:** to fritter away

fid·dle·back \ˈfid-ᵊl-ˌbak\ *n, often attrib* **:** something resembling a fiddle

fid·dle–fad·dle \ˈfid-ᵊl-ˌfad-ᵊl\ *n* [redupl. of *fiddle* (fiddlesticks)] **:** NONSENSE — **fid·dle–fad·dler** \-lər, -ᵊl-ər\ *n*

fid·dle·head \ˈfid-ᵊl-ˌhed\ *n* **:** an ornament on a ship's bow curved like the scroll at the head of a violin

fiddler crab *n* **:** a burrowing crab (genus *Uca*) that has one claw much enlarged in the male

fid·dle·stick \ˈfid-ᵊl-ˌstik\ *n* **1 :** a violin bow **2 a :** something of little value **b** *pl* **:** NONSENSE — used as an interjection

fid·dling *adj* **:** TRIFLING, PETTY

fi·de·ism \ˈfēd-(ˌ)ā-ˌiz-əm\ *n* [prob. fr. F *fidéisme*, fr. L *fides* faith] **:** reliance on faith rather than reason esp. in metaphysics — **fi·de·ist** \-ə-əst\ *n* — **fi·de·is·tic** \ˌfēd-(ˌ)ā-ˈis-tik\ *adj*

fi·del·i·ty \fə-ˈdel-ət-ē, fī-\ *n* [ME *fidelite*, fr. MF *fidelité*, fr. L *fidelitat-*, *fidelitas*, fr. *fidelis* faithful, fr. *fides* faith — more at BIDE] **1 a :** the quality or state of being faithful **b :** accuracy in details **:** EXACTNESS **2 :** the degree to which an electronic device (as a radio or phonograph) accurately reproduces its effect (as sound)

syn ALLEGIANCE, FEALTY, LOYALTY, DEVOTION, PIETY: FIDELITY implies strict and continuing faithfulness to an obligation, trust, or duty; ALLEGIANCE suggests an adherence like that of a medieval vassal to his lord or of a citizen to his country; FEALTY implies a fidelity acknowledged by the individual and as compelling as a sworn vow; LOYALTY implies a faithfulness that is steadfast in the face of any temptation to renounce, desert, or betray; DEVOTION stresses zeal and service amounting to self-dedication; PIETY stresses fidelity to obligations regarded as natural and fundamental and the observance of duties required by such fidelity

fidge \ˈfij\ *vi* [prob. alter. of E dial. *fitch*, fr. ME *fichen*] *chiefly Scot* **:** FIDGET — **fidge** *n, dial chiefly Brit*

[1]**fid·get** \ˈfij-ət\ *n* [irreg. fr. *fidge*] **1 :** uneasiness or restlessness as shown by nervous movements — usu. used in pl. **2** [[2]*fidget*] **:** one that fidgets

[2]**fidget** *vi* **:** to move or act restlessly or nervously ~ *vt* **:** to cause to move or act nervously

fid·get·i·ness \ˈfij-ət-ē-nəs\ *n* **:** the quality or state of being fidgety

fid·gety \ˈfij-ət-ē\ *adj* **1 :** inclined to fidget **2 :** making unnecessary fuss **:** FUSSY

fi·du·cial \fə-ˈd(y)ü-shəl, fī-\ *adj* **1 :** taken as standard of reference ⟨a ~ mark⟩ **2 :** founded on faith or trust **3 :** having the nature of a trust **:** FIDUCIARY — **fi·du·cial·ly** \-shə-lē\ *adv*

[1]**fi·du·ciary** \fə-ˈd(y)ü-shē-ˌer-ē, fī-, -shə-rē\ *n* **:** one that holds a fiduciary relation or acts in a fiduciary capacity

[2]**fiduciary** *adj* [L *fiduciarius*, fr. *fiducia* confidence, trust, fr. *fidere*] **:** of, relating to, or involving a confidence or trust: as **a :** held or founded in trust or confidence **b :** holding in trust **c :** depending on public confidence for value or currency ⟨~ fiat money⟩

fie \ˈfī\ *interj* [ME *fi*, fr. OF] — used to express disgust or shock

fief \ˈfēf\ *n* [F — more at FEE] **1 :** a feudal estate **:** FEE **2 :** something over which one has rights or exercises control

[1]**field** \ˈfē(ə)ld\ *n* [ME, fr. OE *feld;* akin to OHG *feld* field, OE *flōr* floor] **1 a :** an open land area free of woods and buildings **b** (1) **:** an area of cleared enclosed land used for cultivation or pasture (2) **:** land containing a natural resource ⟨coal ~⟩ **c :** the place where a battle is fought; *also* **:** BATTLE **d :** a large unbroken expanse (as of ice) **2 a :** an area or division of an activity **b :** the sphere of practical operation outside a laboratory, office, or factory **c :** an area for military exercises or maneuvers **d** (1) **:** an area for sports (2) **:** the part of a sports area enclosed by a racing track **3 :** a space on which something is drawn or projected: as **a :** the space on the surface of a coin, medal, or seal that does not contain the design **b :** the ground of each division in a flag **c :** the whole surface of an escutcheon **4 :** the individuals that make up all or part of a sports activity **5 :** a complex of forces that serve as causative agents in human behavior **6 a :** a set of mathematical elements that is subject to two binary operations the second of which is distributive relative to the first and both of which yield an element and that constitutes a commutative group under the first operation and also under the second if the zero or unit element under the first is omitted **b :** a region or space in which a given effect (as magnetism) exists **7 :** the area visible through the lens of an optical instrument **8 :** a series of drain tiles and an absorption area

[2]**field** *vt* **1 a :** to handle (as a batted ball) while playing in the field **b :** to answer satisfactorily ⟨~ a tough question⟩ **2 :** to put into the field ~ *vi* **:** to play as a fielder

[3]**field** *adj* **:** of or relating to a field: as **a :** growing in or inhabiting the fields or open country **b :** made, conducted, or used in the field ⟨~ operations⟩ **c :** operating or active in the field

field artillery *n* **:** artillery other than antiaircraft artillery used with armies in the field

field corn *n* **:** an Indian corn (as dent corn or flint corn) with starchy kernels grown for feeding stock or for market grain

field day *n* **1 a :** a day for military exercises or maneuvers **b :** an outdoor meeting or social gathering **c :** a day of sports and athletic competition **2 :** a time of unusual pleasure or unexpected success

field·er \ˈfēl-dər\ *n* **:** one that fields; *esp* **:** a player stationed in the field (as in baseball)

fielder's choice *n* **:** an attempt by a fielder when handling a batted ball to retire a base runner other than the batter when a play to first base would retire the batter

field event *n* **:** an event in a track meet other than a race

field·fare \ˈfē(ə)ld-ˌfa(ə)r, -ˌfe(ə)r\ *n* [ME *feldefare*, fr. OE *feldeware*, fr. *feld* + *-ware* dweller] **:** a medium-sized Eurasian thrush (*Turdus pilaris*) with ash-colored head and chestnut wings

field glass *n* **:** a hand-held optical instrument for use outdoors usu. consisting of two telescopes on a single frame with a focusing device — usu. used in pl.

field goal *n* **1 :** a score in football made by drop-kicking or place-kicking the ball over the crossbar from ordinary play **2 :** a basket in basketball made while the ball is in play

field grade *n* **:** the military rank of major, lieutenant colonel, or colonel

field house *n* **1 :** a building at an athletic field for housing equipment or providing dressing facilities **2 :** a building enclosing a large area suitable for various forms of athletics

field magnet *n* **:** a magnet for producing and maintaining a magnetic field esp. in a generator or electric motor

field marshal *n* **:** an officer (as in the British army) of the highest rank
field officer *n* **:** a field-grade officer
field of force : FIELD 6b
field of honor 1 : a place where a duel is fought **2 :** BATTLEFIELD
field pea *n* **:** a small-seeded pea (*Pisum sativum* var. *arvense*) widely grown for forage and food
field·piece \'fē(ə)ld-,pēs\ *n* **:** a gun or howitzer for use in the field
field theory *n* **:** a detailed mathematical description of the assumed physical properties of a region under some influence (as gravitation)
field trial *n* **:** a trial of sporting dogs in actual performance
field winding *n* **:** the winding of the field magnet of a dynamo or motor
fiend \'fēnd\ *n* [ME, fr. OE *fīend;* akin to OHG *fīant* enemy] **1 a :** DEVIL **b :** DEMON **c :** a person of great wickedness or maliciousness **2 :** a person excessively devoted to a pursuit or study **:** FANATIC **3 :** a person who uses immoderate quantities of something **:** ADDICT **4 :** a person remarkably clever at something
fiend·ish \'fēn-dish\ *adj* **1 :** perversely diabolical **2 :** extremely cruel or wicked **3 :** excessively bad, unpleasant, or difficult — **fiend·ish·ly** *adv* — **fiend·ish·ness** *n*
fierce \'fi(ə)rs\ *adj* [ME *fiers,* fr. OF, fr. L *ferus* wild, savage; akin to *thēr* wild animal] **1 a :** violently hostile or aggressive in temperament **b :** given to fighting or killing **:** PUGNACIOUS **2 a :** marked by unrestrained zeal or vehemence **b :** extremely vexatious, disappointing, or intense **3 :** furiously active or determined **4 :** wild or menacing in aspect — **fierce·ly** *adv* — **fierceness** *n*
syn FIERCE, FEROCIOUS, BARBAROUS, SAVAGE, CRUEL mean showing fury or malignity in looks or actions. FIERCE applies to men and animals that inspire terror because of their wild and menacing aspect or fury in attack; FEROCIOUS implies extreme fierceness and unrestrained violence and brutality; BARBAROUS implies a ferocity or mercilessness regarded as unworthy of civilized men; SAVAGE implies the absence of inhibitions restraining civilized men filled with rage, lust, or other violent passion; CRUEL implies indifference to suffering and even positive pleasure in inflicting it
fi·eri fa·ci·as \,fē-ə-rē-'fāk-ē-,äs\ *n* [L, cause (it) to be done] **:** a writ authorizing the sheriff to obtain satisfaction of a judgment in debt or damages from the goods and chattels of the defendant
fi·eri·ness \'fī(-ə)-rē-nəs\ *n* **:** the quality or state of being fiery
fi·ery \'fī-(ə-)rē\ *adj* [ME, fr. *fire, fier* fire] **1 a :** consisting of fire **b :** BURNING, BLAZING **c :** using or carried out with fire **d :** liable to catch fire or explode **:** FLAMMABLE **2 a :** hot like a fire **b** (1) **:** INFLAMED (2) **:** feverish and flushed **3 a :** of the color of fire **:** RED **b :** intensely or unnaturally red **4 a :** full of or exuding emotion or spirit **b :** easily provoked **:** IRRITABLE — **fiery** *adv*
fi·es·ta \fē-'es-tə\ *n* [Sp, fr. L *festa* — more at FEAST] **:** FESTIVAL; *specif* **:** a saint's day celebrated in Spain and Latin America with processions and dances
fife \'fīf\ *n* [G *pfeife* pipe, fife, fr. OHG *pfīfa* — more at PIPE] **:** a small transverse flute with shrill tone used chiefly to accompany the drum

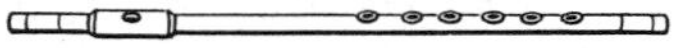
fife

fife rail *n* **:** a rail about the mast near the deck to which running rigging is belayed
fif·teen \fif-'tēn\ *n* [ME *fiftene,* adj., fr. OE *fīftēne;* akin to OE *tīen* ten] **1** — see NUMBER table **2 :** the first point scored by a side in a game of tennis — called also *five* — **fifteen** *adj or pron* — **fif·teenth** \-'tēn(t)th\ *adj* — **fifteenth** *n, pl* **fif·teenths** \-'tēn(t)s, -'tēn(t)ths\
fifth \'fif(t)th, 'fift\ *n, pl* **fifths** \'fifths, 'fif(t)s\ **1** — see NUMBER table **2 a :** the musical interval embracing five diatonic degrees **b :** DOMINANT 2 **c :** the harmonic combination of two tones at this interval **3 :** a unit of measure for liquor equal to one fifth of a U.S. gallon **4** *cap* **:** the Fifth Amendment of the U.S. Constitution — **fifth** *adj or adv* — **fifth·ly** *adv*
fifth column *n* [name applied to rebel sympathizers in Madrid in 1936 when four rebel columns were advancing on the city] **:** a group of secret sympathizers or supporters of an enemy that engage in espionage or sabotage within defense lines or national borders — **fifth columnism** *n* — **fifth columnist** *n*
fifth wheel *n* **1 a :** a horizontal wheel or segment of a wheel that consists of two parts rotating on each other above the fore axle of a carriage and that forms support to prevent tipping **b :** a similar coupling between tractor and trailer of a semitrailer **2 :** a spare wheel **3 :** one that is superfluous, unnecessary, or burdensome
fif·ti·eth \'fif-tē-əth\ *n* — see NUMBER table — **fiftieth** *adj*
fif·ty \'fif-tē\ *n* [ME, fr. *fifty,* adj., fr. OE *fīftig,* fr. *fīftig,* n., group of 50, fr. *fīf* five + *-tig* group of ten — more at EIGHTY] **1** — see NUMBER table **2** *pl* **:** the numbers 50 to 59; *specif* **:** the years 50 to 59 in a lifetime or history — **fifty** *adj or pron*
fif·ty-fif·ty \,fif-tē-'fif-tē\ *adj* **1 :** shared, assumed, or borne equally **2 :** half favorable and half unfavorable — **fifty-fifty** *adv*
¹fig \'fig\ *n* [ME *fige,* fr. OF, fr. OProv *figa,* fr. (assumed) VL *fica,* fr. L *ficus* fig tree, fig] **1 a :** an oblong or pear-shaped fruit that is a syconium **b :** any of a genus (*Ficus*) of trees of the mulberry family bearing fruits that are syconia; *esp* **:** a widely cultivated tree (*F. carica*) that produces edible figs **2 :** a contemptibly worthless trifle ⟨not worth a ~⟩

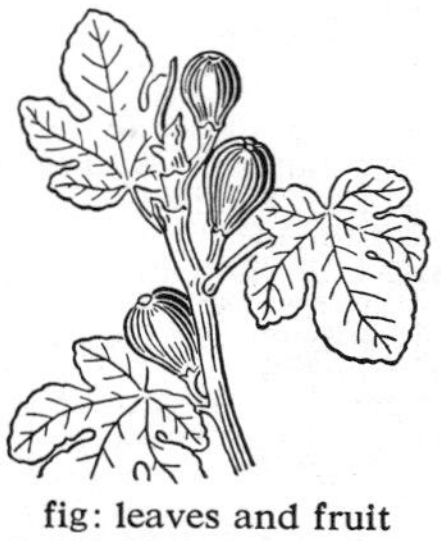
fig: leaves and fruit

²fig *n* [*fig* (to adorn)] **:** DRESS, ARRAY
¹fight \'fīt\ *vb* **fought** \'fȯt\ **fight·ing** [ME *fighten,* fr. OE *feohtan;* akin to OHG *fehtan* to fight, L *pectere* to comb — more at FEE] *vi* **1 a :** to contend in battle or physical combat; *esp* **:** to strive to overcome a person by blows **b :** to engage in prizefighting **:** BOX **2 :** to put forth a determined effort ~ *vt* **1 a** (1) **:** to contend against in battle or physical combat (2) **:** to box against in the ring **b** (1) **:** to attempt to prevent the success or effectiveness of (2) **:** to oppose the passage or development **2 a :** to carry on **:** WAGE **b :** to take part in (as a boxing match) **3 :** to struggle to endure or survive **4 a :** to gain by struggle ⟨~*s* his way through⟩ **b :** to resolve by struggle **5 a** (1) **:** to manage (a ship) in a battle or storm (2) **:** to cause to contend **b :** to manage in an unnecessarily rough or awkward manner — **fight shy of :** to avoid facing or meeting
²fight *n* **1 a :** a combat or hostile encounter **:** BATTLE **b :** a boxing match **c :** a verbal disagreement **2 :** a struggle for a goal or an objective **3 :** strength or disposition for fighting **:** PUGNACITY
fight·er \'fīt-ər\ *n* **:** one that fights: as **a** (1) **:** WARRIOR, SOLDIER (2) **:** a pugnacious or game individual (3) **:** PRIZEFIGHTER, BOXER **b :** an airplane of high speed and maneuverability with armament designed to destroy enemy aircraft
fig leaf *n* **1 :** the leaf of a fig tree **2 :** something that conceals or camouflages usu. inadequately or dishonestly
fig marigold *n* **:** any of several carpetweeds (genus *Mesembryanthemum*) with showy white or pink flowers
fig·ment \'fig-mənt\ *n* [ME, fr. L *figmentum,* fr. *fingere* to shape — more at DOUGH] **:** something made up, fabricated, or contrived
fig·ur·al \'fig-(y)ə-rəl\ *adj* **:** of, relating to, or consisting of human or animal figures
fig·u·ra·tion \,fig-(y)ə-'rā-shən\ *n* **1 :** the act or process of creating or providing a figure **2 :** FORM, OUTLINE **3 :** an act or instance of representation in figures and shapes **4 :** ornamentation of a musical passage by using decorative and usu. repetitive figures
fig·u·ra·tive \'fig-(y)ə-rət-iv, 'fig-(y)ərt-iv\ *adj* **1 a :** representing by a figure or resemblance **:** EMBLEMATIC **b :** of or relating to graphic representation **2 :** expressing one thing in terms normally denoting another with which it may be regarded as analogous **:** METAPHORICAL **3 :** characterized by figures of speech — **fig·u·ra·tive·ly** *adv* — **fig·u·ra·tive·ness** *n*
¹fig·ure \'fig-yər, *esp Brit* 'fig-ər\ *n* [ME, fr. OF, fr. L *figura,* fr. *fingere*] **1 a :** a number symbol **:** NUMERAL **b** *pl* **:** arithmetical calculations **c :** a written or printed character **d :** value esp. as expressed in numbers **:** PRICE **2 a :** the external shape or outline of something **b :** bodily shape or form esp. of a person **c :** an object noticeable only as a shape or form **3 a :** the graphic representation of a form esp. of a person **b :** a diagram or pictorial illustration of textual matter **c :** a geometric diagram **4 :** a person, thing, or action representative of another **5 :** an intentional deviation from the ordinary form or syntactical relation of words **6 :** the form of a syllogism with respect to the relative position of the middle term **7 :** PATTERN, DESIGN **8 :** appearance made or impression produced ⟨the couple cut quite a ~⟩ **9 a :** a series of movements in a dance **b :** an outline representation of a form traced by a series of evolutions **10 :** a prominent personality **:** PERSONAGE **11 :** a short coherent group of tones or chords that may grow into a phrase, theme, or composition **syn** see FORM
²figure *vt* **1 :** to represent by or as if by a figure or outline **:** PORTRAY **2 :** to decorate with a pattern; *specif* **:** to write figures over or under (the bass) in order to indicate the accompanying chords **3 :** to indicate or represent by numerals **4 a :** CALCULATE **b :** CONCLUDE, DECIDE **c :** REGARD, CONSIDER ~ *vi* **1 :** to be or appear important or conspicuous **2 :** to perform a figure in dancing **3 :** COMPUTE, CALCULATE — **fig·ur·er** \-(y)ər-ər\ *n* — **figure on 1 :** to take into consideration **2 :** to rely on **3 :** PLAN
fig·ured *adj* **1 :** REPRESENTED, PORTRAYED **2 :** decorated with or formed into a figure **3 :** indicated by figures esp. in music
figure eight *n* **:** something resembling the arabic numeral eight in form or shape: as **a :** a small knot **b :** an embroidery stitch **c :** a dance pattern **d :** a skater's figure
fig·ure·head \'fig-yər-,hed, *esp Brit* 'fig-ər-\ *n* **1 :** the figure on a ship's bow **2 :** a head or chief in name only
figure of speech : a form of expression (as a simile or metaphor) used to convey meaning or heighten effect often by comparing or identifying one thing with another that has a meaning or connotation familiar to the reader or listener
figure out *vt* **1 :** DISCOVER, DETERMINE **2 :** SOLVE, FATHOM
figure skating *n* **:** skating in which the skater executes figures
fig·u·rine \,fig-(y)ə-'rēn\ *n* **:** a small carved or molded figure
fig·wort \'fig-,wərt, -,wȯ(ə)rt\ *n* **:** any of a genus (*Scrophularia* of the family Scrophulariaceae, the figwort family) of chiefly herbaceous plants with leaves having no stipules, an irregular bilabiate corolla, and a 2-celled ovary
Fi·ji·an \'fē-(,)jē-ən\ *n* **1 :** a member of a Melanesian people of the Fiji islands **2 :** the Austronesian language of the Fijians — **Fijian** *adj*
fila *pl of* FILUM
fil·a·ment \'fil-ə-mənt\ *n* [MF, fr. ML *filamentum,* fr. LL *filare*] **:** a single thread or a thin flexible threadlike object, process, or appendage: as **a :** a tenuous conductor (as of carbon or metal) made incandescent by the passage of an electric current; *specif* **:** a cathode in the form of a metal wire in an electron tube **b :** the anther-bearing stalk of a stamen — **fil·a·men·ta·ry** \,fil-ə-'ment-ə-rē, -'men-trē\ *adj* — **fil·a·men·tous** \-'ment-əs\ *adj*
fi·lar \'fī-lər\ *adj* [L *filum* thread] **:** of or relating to a thread or line; *esp* **:** having threads across the field of view
fi·lar·ia \fə-'lar-ē-ə, -'ler-\ *n, pl* **fi·lar·i·ae** \-ē-,ē\ [NL, fr. L *filum*] **:** any of numerous slender filamentous nematodes (of *Filaria* and related genera) that as adults are parasites in the blood or tissues of mammals and as larvae usu. develop in biting insects — **fi·lar·i·al** \-ē-əl\ *adj* — **fi·lar·i·id** \-ē-əd\ *adj or n*
fil·a·ri·a·sis \,fil-ə-'rī-ə-səs\ *n* **:** infestation with or disease caused by filariae
fil·a·ture \'fil-ə-,chu̇(ə)r, -chər\ *n* [F, fr. LL *filatus,* pp. of *filare*] **1 :** the reeling of silk from cocoons **2 :** a reel for drawing off silk from cocoons **3 :** a factory where silk is reeled
fil·bert \'fil-bərt\ *n* [ME, fr. AF *philber,* fr. St. *Philibert* †684 Frankish abbot whose feast day falls in the nutting season] **1 :** either of two European hazels (*Corylus avellana pontica* and *C. maxima*); *also* **:** the sweet thick-shelled nut of the filbert **2 :** HAZELNUT
filch \'filch\ *vt* [ME *filchen*] **:** to steal furtively **:** PILFER **syn** see STEAL
¹file \'fī(ə)l\ *n* [ME, fr. OE *fēol;* akin to OHG *fīla* file] **1 :** a tool usu. of hardened steel with cutting ridges for forming or smoothing surfaces esp. of metal **2 :** a shrewd or crafty person

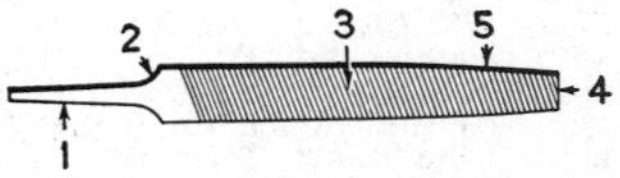

file 1: *1* tang, *2* heel, *3* face, *4* tip, *5* edge

2file *vt* **1 :** to rub, smooth, or cut away with a file **2 :** to refine or smooth esp. by careful revision
3file *vt* [ME *filen*, fr. OE *fȳlan*, fr. *fūl* foul] *chiefly dial* **:** DEFILE, CORRUPT
4file *vb* [ME *filen*, fr. MF *filer* to string documents on a string or wire, fr. *fil* thread, fr. L *filum*; akin to Arm *jil* sinew] *vt* **1 :** to arrange in order for preservation or reference **2 a :** to place among official records as prescribed by law **b :** to send (copy) to a newspaper **c :** to return to the office of the clerk of a court without action on the merits **3 :** to perform the first act of (as a lawsuit) ~ *vi* **:** to register as a candidate esp. in a primary election
5file *n* **1 :** a container or other device by which papers are kept usu. in order **2 a** *archaic* **:** ROLL, LIST **b :** a collection of papers or publications usu. arranged or classified
6file *n* [MF, fr. *filer* to spin, fr. LL *filare*, fr. L *filum*] **1 :** a row of persons, animals, or things arranged one behind the other **2 :** a row of squares extending vertically across a chessboard
7file *vi* **:** to march or proceed in file
file·fish \ˈfī(ə)l-ˌfish\ *n* **:** any of various fishes (as a triggerfish) with rough granular leathery skins
fi·let \fi-ˈlā\ *n* [F, lit., net] **:** a lace with a square mesh and geometric designs
fi·let mi·gnon \ˌfil-(ˌ)ā-mēn-ˈyō^n, fi-ˌlā-\ *n, pl* **filets mignons** *same or* -ˈyō^{n}z\ [F, lit., dainty fillet] **:** a fillet of beef cut from the thick end of a beef tenderloin
fili- *or* **filo-** *comb form* [L *filum*] **:** thread ⟨*fili*form⟩
fil·ial \ˈfil-ē-əl, ˈfil-yəl\ *adj* [ME, fr. LL *filialis*, fr. L *filius* son] **1 :** of, relating to, or befitting a son or daughter **2 :** having or assuming the relation of a child or offspring — **fil·ial·ly** \-ē\ *adv*
filial generation *n* **:** a generation in a cross successive to a parental generation
fil·i·a·tion \ˌfil-ē-ˈā-shən\ *n* **1 a :** filial relationship esp. of a son to his father **b :** the adjudication of paternity **:** AFFILIATION **2 :** an offshoot or branch of a culture or language **3 a :** descent or derivation esp. from a culture or language **b :** the act or process of determining such relationship
1fil·i·bus·ter \ˈfil-ə-ˌbəs-tər\ *n* [Sp *filibustero*, lit., freebooter] **1 :** an irregular military adventurer; *specif* **:** an American engaged in fomenting insurrections in Latin America in the mid-19th century **2** [*2filibuster*] **a :** the use of extreme dilatory tactics in an attempt to delay or prevent action esp. in a legislative assembly **b :** an instance of this practice — **fil·i·bus·ter·er** \-tər-ər\ *n*
2filibuster *vb* **fil·i·bus·ter·ing** \-t(ə-)riŋ\ *vi* **1 :** to carry out insurrectionist or revolutionary activities in a foreign country **2 :** to engage in a filibuster ~ *vt* **:** to subject to a filibuster
fi·li·form \ˈfil-ə-ˌfȯrm, ˈfī-lə-\ *adj* **:** shaped like a filament
1fil·i·gree \ˈfil-ə-ˌgrē\ *n, often attrib* [F *filigrane*, fr. It *filigrana*, fr. L *filum* + *granum* grain] **1 :** ornamental work esp. of fine wire of gold, silver, or copper applied chiefly to gold and silver surfaces **2 a :** ornamental openwork of delicate or intricate design **b :** a pattern or design resembling such openwork
2filigree *vt* **fil·i·greed; fil·i·gree·ing :** to adorn with or as if with filigree
fil·ing *n* **1 :** an act or instance of using a file **2 :** a fragment rubbed off in filing ⟨iron ~*s*⟩
Fil·i·pi·no \ˌfil-ə-ˈpē-(ˌ)nō\ *n* [Sp] **1 :** a native of the Philippine islands; *specif* **:** a member of a Christianized Philippine people **2 :** a citizen of the Republic of the Philippines — **Filipino** *adj*
1fill \ˈfil\ *vb* [ME *fillen*, fr. OE *fyllan*; akin to OE *full*] *vt* **1 a :** to put into as much as can be held or conveniently contained **b :** to supply with a full complement **c** (1) **:** to cause to swell or billow (2) **:** to trim (a sail) to catch the wind **d :** to raise the level of with fill **e :** to repair the cavities of (teeth) **f :** to stop up **:** OBSTRUCT **2 a :** FEED, SATIATE **b :** SATISFY, FULFILL ⟨~*s* all requirements⟩ **3 a :** to occupy the whole of **b :** to spread through **4 a :** OCCUPY, HOLD **b :** to place a person in **5 :** to supply as directed **6 :** to cover the surface of with a layer of precious metal ~ *vi* **:** to become full — **fill one's shoes :** to take one's place or position — **fill the bill :** to serve the purpose satisfactorily
2fill *n* **1 :** a full supply; *esp* **:** a quantity that satisfies or satiates **2 :** material used to fill a receptacle, cavity, or passage
fill away *vi* **1 :** to trim a sail to catch the wind **2 :** to proceed on the course esp. after being brought up in the wind
1fill·er \ˈfil-ər\ *n* **:** one that fills: as **a :** a substance added to augment another **b :** a composition used to fill the pores and grain of a wood or other surface before painting or varnishing **c :** a plate or other piece used to cover or fill in a space between two parts of a structure **d :** tobacco used to form the core of a cigar
2fil·ler \ˈfil-ˌe(ə)r\ *n, pl* **fillers** *or* **filler** [Hung *fillér*] — see *forint* at MONEY table
1fil·let \ˈfil-ət, *in sense 2b also* fi-ˈlā, ˈfil-(ˌ)ā\ *also* **fi·let** \fi-ˈlā, ˈfil-(ˌ)ā\ *n* [ME *filet*, fr. MF, dim. of *fil* thread — more at FILE] **1 :** a ribbon or narrow strip of material used esp. as a headband **2 :** a thin narrow strip of any material: as **a :** a band of anatomical fibers; *specif* **:** LEMNISCUS **b :** a piece or slice of boneless meat or fish; *specif* **:** the tenderloin of beef **3 a :** a concave junction formed where two surfaces meet **b :** a curved strip fitted into the angle of such a junction **4 :** a narrow flat architectural member: **a :** a flat molding separating others **b :** the space between two flutings in a shaft **5 :** an ornament impressed on a book cover
2fil·let \ˈfil-ət, *in sense 2 also* fi-ˈlā, ˈfil-(ˌ)ā\ *vt* **1:** to bind or adorn with or as if with a fillet **2 :** to cut into fillets
fill in *vt* **1 :** to furnish with specified information **2 :** to enrich with detail ~ *vi* **:** to fill a vacancy usu. temporarily **:** SUBSTITUTE
fill–in \ˈfil-ˌin\ *n* **:** someone or something that fills in
fill·ing *n* **1 :** an act or instance of filling **2 :** something used to fill a cavity, container, or depression **3 :** something that completes: as **a :** the yarn interlacing the warp in a fabric; *also* **:** yarn for the shuttle **b :** a food mixture used to fill pastry or sandwiches
filling station *n* **:** a retail station for servicing motor vehicles esp. with gasoline and oil
1fil·lip \ˈfil-əp\ *n* [prob. of imit. origin] **1 a :** a blow or gesture made by the sudden forcible straightening of a finger curled up against the thumb **b :** BUFFET **2 :** something tending to arouse or excite
2fillip *vt* **1 a :** to strike or tap with a fillip **b :** to make a fillip with **2 :** to project quickly by or as if by a fillip **3 :** to urge on
fil·lis·ter \ˈfil-ə-stər\ *n* [origin unknown] **:** an adjustable rabbet plane
fill out *vi* **:** to put on flesh
fil·ly \ˈfil-ē\ *n* [ME *fyly*, fr. ON *fylja*; akin to OE *fola* foal] **1 :** a young female horse usu. of less than four years **2 :** GIRL
1film \ˈfilm\ *n, often attrib* [ME *filme*, fr. OE *filmen*; akin to Gk *pelma* sole of the foot, OE *fell* skin — more at FELL] **1 a :** a thin skin or membranous covering **:** PELLICLE **b :** an abnormal growth on or in the eye **2 a :** HAZE, MIST **b :** a thin covering or coating **3 a :** an exceedingly thin layer **:** LAMINA **b** (1) **:** a thin flexible transparent sheet used as a wrapping (2) **:** such a sheet of cellulose acetate or cellulose nitrate coated with a light-sensitive emulsion for taking photographs **4 :** MOTION PICTURE
2film *vt* **1 :** to cover with or as if with a film **2 :** to make a motion picture of or from ⟨~ a scene⟩ ⟨~ a novel⟩ ~ *vi* **1 :** to become covered or obscured with a film **2 a :** to be suitable for photographing **b :** to make a motion picture
film·dom \ˈfilm-dəm\ *n* **1 :** the motion-picture industry **2 :** the personnel of the motion-picture industry
film·ic \ˈfil-mik\ *adj* **:** of, relating to, or resembling motion pictures — **film·i·cal·ly** \-mi-k(ə-)lē\ *adv*
film·i·ness \ˈfil-mē-nəs\ *n* **:** the quality or state of being filmy
film·strip \ˈfilm-ˌstrip\ *n* **:** a strip of usu. 35 mm. film bearing photographs, diagrams, or graphic matter for still projection
filmy \ˈfil-mē\ *adj* **1 :** of, resembling, or composed of film **2 :** covered with a haze or film
filo- — see FILI-
fi·lo·po·di·um \ˌfil-ə-ˈpōd-ē-əm, ˌfī-lə-\ *n* [NL] **:** a filamentous chiefly ectoplasmic pseudopodium
fi·lose \ˈfī-ˌlōs\ *adj* [NL *filum*] **1 :** FILAMENTOUS **2 :** terminating in a threadlike process
fils \ˈfils\ *n, pl* **fils** [Ar] — see *dinar* at MONEY table
1fil·ter \ˈfil-tər\ *n, often attrib* [ME *filtre*, fr. ML *filtrum*, piece of felt used as a filter, of Gmc origin; akin to OHG *filz* felt — more at FELT] **1 :** a porous article or mass through which a gas or liquid is passed to separate out matter in suspension **2 :** an apparatus containing a filter medium **3 :** a device or material for suppressing or minimizing waves or oscillations of certain frequencies (as of electricity, light, or sound)
2filter *vb* **fil·ter·ing** \-t(ə-)riŋ\ *vt* **1 :** to subject to the action of a filter **2 :** to remove by means of a filter ~ *vi* **:** to pass or move through a filter
fil·ter·able *also* **fil·tra·ble** \ˈfil-t(ə-)rə-bəl\ *adj* **:** capable of being filtered or of passing through a filter
filterable virus *n* **:** a virus so small that a fluid containing it remains virulent after passing through a filter
filter bed *n* **:** a bed of sand or gravel for filtering water or sewage
filter paper *n* **:** porous unsized paper used esp. for filtering
filter tip *n* **:** a cigar or cigarette tip designed to filter the smoke before it enters the smoker's mouth; *also* **:** a cigar or cigarette provided with such a tip — **fil·ter–tipped** \ˌfil-tər-ˈtipt\ *adj*
filth \ˈfilth\ *n* [ME, fr. OE *fȳlth*, fr. *fūl* foul] **1 :** foul or putrid matter; *esp* **:** loathsome dirt or refuse **2 a :** moral corruption or defilement **b :** something that tends to corrupt or defile **:** OBSCENITY
filth·i·ly \ˈfil-thə-lē\ *adv* **:** in a filthy manner
filth·i·ness \-thē-nəs\ *n* **:** the quality or state of being filthy
filthy \ˈfil-thē\ *adj* **1 :** covered with or containing filth **2 a :** UNDERHANDED, VILE **b :** OBSCENE **syn** see DIRTY
1fil·trate \ˈfil-ˌtrāt\ *vb* [ML *filtratus*, pp. of *filtrare*, fr. *filtrum*] **:** FILTER — **fil·tra·tion** \fil-ˈtrā-shən\ *n*
2filtrate *n* **:** something passed through a filter
fi·lum \ˈfī-ləm\ *n, pl* **fi·la** \-lə\ [NL, fr. L — more at FILE] **:** a filamentous structure **:** FILAMENT
fim·bria \ˈfim-brē-ə\ *n, pl* **fim·bri·ae** \-brē-ˌē, -ˌī\ [NL, fr. L, fringe] **:** a bordering fringe esp. at the entrance of the fallopian tubes — **fim·bri·al** \-brē-əl\ *adj*
fim·bri·ate \-brē-ˌāt\ *or* **fim·bri·at·ed** \-ˌāt-əd\ *adj* **:** having the edge or extremity bordered by slender processes **:** FRINGED — **fim·bri·a·tion** \ˌfim-brē-ˈā-shən\ *n*
1fin \ˈfin\ *n* [ME *finn*, fr. OE; akin to L *spina* thorn, spine] **1 :** an external membranous process of an aquatic animal (as a fish) used in propelling or guiding the body **2 :** something resembling a fin esp. in appearance or function: **a :** HAND, ARM **b** (1) **:** an appendage of a boat (2) **:** an airfoil attached to an airplane for directional stability (3) **:** one of a pair of usu. ornamental projections at the rear of an automobile **c :** FLIPPER 1b **d :** any of the projecting ribs on a radiator or an engine cylinder — **fin·like** \ˈfin-ˌlīk\ *adj* — **finned** \ˈfind\ *adj*
2fin *vb* **finned; fin·ning** *vi* **:** to show the fins above the water ~ *vt* **:** to equip with fins
3fin *n* [Yiddish *finf* five, fr. OHG] *slang* **:** a five-dollar bill
fi·na·gle \fə-ˈnā-gəl\ *vb* **fi·na·gling** \-g(ə-)liŋ\ [perh. alter. of *fainaigue* (to renege)] *vt* **1 :** to arrange for **:** WANGLE **2 :** to obtain by trickery **:** SWINDLE ~ *vi* **:** to use devious dishonest methods to achieve one's ends — **fi·na·gler** \-g(ə-)lər\ *n*
1fi·nal \ˈfīn-ᵊl\ *adj* [ME, fr. MF, fr. L *finalis*, fr. *finis* boundary, end] **1 a :** not to be altered or undone **:** CONCLUSIVE **b :** of or relating to a concluding court action or proceeding ⟨~ decree⟩ **2 :** constituting the ultimate in degree or development ⟨the ~ climax⟩ **3 :** of or relating to the ultimate purpose or result of a process ⟨the ~ goal of life⟩ **4 :** relating to or occurring at the end or conclusion **syn** see LAST — **fi·nal·ly** \ˈfīn-ᵊl-ē, ˈfīn-lē\ *adv*
2final *n* **:** something final: as **a :** a deciding match, game, or trial **b :** the last examination in a course
fi·na·le \fə-ˈnal-ē, fi-ˈnäl-\ *n* [It, fr. *finale*, adj., final, fr. L *finalis*] **:** the close or termination of something: as **a :** the last section of an instrumental musical composition **b :** the closing part or number in any public performance **c :** the close of a series or action
fi·nal·ist \ˈfīn-ᵊl-əst\ *n* **:** a contestant in the finals of a competition
fi·nal·i·ty \fī-ˈnal-ət-ē, fə-\ *n* **1 a :** the character or condition of being final, settled, or complete **b :** the condition of being at an ultimate point esp. of development or authority **2 :** something final; *esp* **:** an ultimate fact, action, or belief
fi·nal·iza·tion \ˌfīn-ᵊl-ə-ˈzā-shən\ *n* **:** an act or instance of finalizing
fi·nal·ize \ˈfīn-ᵊl-ˌīz\ *vt* **:** to put in final or finished form
1fi·nance \fə-ˈnan(t)s, ˈfī-ˌ, fī-ˈ\ *n* [ME, payment, ransom, fr. MF, fr. *finer* to end, pay, fr. *fin* end — more at FINE] **1** *pl* **:** money or other liquid resources esp. of a government or business **2 :** the system that includes the circulation of money, the granting of credit, the making of investments, and the provision of banking facilities **3 :** the obtaining of funds or capital **:** FINANCING

2finance *vt* **1 a :** to raise or provide funds or capital for **b :** to furnish with necessary funds **2 :** to sell or supply on credit

fi·nan·cial \fə-'nan-chəl, fī-\ *adj* **:** relating to finance or financiers — **fi·nan·cial·ly** \-'nanch-(ə-)lē\ *adv*

syn FINANCIAL, MONETARY, PECUNIARY, FISCAL mean of or relating to money. FINANCIAL implies money matters conducted on a large scale or involving some degree of complexity; MONETARY refers to money as coined, distributed, or circulating; PECUNIARY implies reference to money matters affecting the individual; FISCAL refers to money as providing revenue for the state or to the financial affairs of an institution or corporation

1fi·nan·cier \,fin-ən-'si(ə)r, fə-,nan-, ,fī-,nan-\ *n* **1 :** one who specializes in raising and expending public moneys **2 :** one who deals with finance and investment on a large scale

2financier *vi* **:** to conduct financial operations often by sharp or reprehensible practices

fi·nanc·ing *n* **:** the act or process or an instance of raising or providing funds; *also* **:** the funds thus raised or provided

fin·back \'fin-,bak\ *n* **:** a whalebone whale (genus *Balaenoptera*) **:** RORQUAL; *esp* **:** a common whale (*B. physalus*) of the Atlantic coast of the U.S. that attains a length of over 60 feet

finch \'finch\ *n* [ME, fr. OE *finc;* akin to OHG *fincho* finch, Gk *spiza* chaffinch] **:** any of numerous songbirds (family Fringillidae) including the sparrows, grosbeaks, crossbills, goldfinches, linnets, buntings, and related birds having a short stout conical bill adapted for crushing seeds

1find \'fīnd\ *vb* **found** \'faund\ **find·ing** [ME *finden,* fr. OE *findan;* akin to OHG *findan* to find, L *pont-, pons* bridge, Gk *pontos* sea, Skt *patha* way, course] *vt* **1 a :** to come upon often accidentally **:** ENCOUNTER **b :** to meet with (a particular reception) ⟨hoped to ~ favor⟩ **2 a :** to come upon by searching or effort **b :** to discover by study or experiment **c :** to obtain by effort or management ⟨~ the time to study⟩ **d :** to arrive at **:** REACH ⟨the bullet *found* its mark⟩ **e :** to discover by sounding **3 a :** EXPERIENCE, DETECT ⟨~ much pleasure in his company⟩ **b :** to perceive (oneself) to be in a certain place or condition ⟨*found* himself in a dilemma⟩ **c :** to gain or regain the use or power of ⟨trying to ~ his tongue⟩ **d :** to bring (oneself) to a realization of one's powers or sphere of activity **4 a :** PROVIDE, SUPPLY **b :** to furnish (room and board) esp. as a condition of employment **5 :** to settle upon and make a statement about (as a conclusion) ⟨~ a verdict⟩ **~** *vi* **:** to determine a case judicially by a verdict ⟨~ for the defendant⟩ — **find fault :** to criticize unfavorably

2find *n* **1 :** an act or instance of finding **2 :** something found; *esp* **:** a valuable item of discovery

find·er \'fīn-dər\ *n* **1 :** one that finds **2 :** a small astronomical telescope of low power and wide field attached to a larger telescope for finding an object **3 :** a device on a camera for showing the area of the subject to be included in the picture

fin de siè·cle \,faⁿ-də-sē-'yekl°\ *adj* [F, end of the century] **:** of, relating to, or resembling the close of the 19th century and esp. its literary and artistic climate of sophistication, world-weariness, and fashionable despair

find·ing *n* **1 a :** the act of one that finds **b :** FIND 2 **2** *pl* **:** small tools or trimmings used by artisans in various trades **3 a :** the result of a judicial examination or inquiry **b :** the results of an investigation

find out *vt* **1 a :** to learn by study or observation **b :** DETECT, DISCOVER **2 a :** to catch in a theft or offense **b :** to ascertain the true character of

1fine \'fīn\ *n* [ME, fr. OF *fin,* fr. L *finis* boundary, end] **1** *obs* **:** END, CONCLUSION **2 :** a compromise of a fictitious suit used as a form of conveyance of lands **3 a :** a sum imposed as punishment for an offense **b :** a forfeiture or penalty paid to an injured party in a civil action — **in fine :** in short

2fine *vt* **:** to set a fine on by judgment of a court

3fine *adj* [ME *fin,* fr. OF, fr. L *finis,* n., end, limit] **1 a :** free from impurity **b** *of a metal* **:** having a stated proportion of pure metal in the composition **2 a** (1) **:** very thin in gauge or texture (2) **:** not coarse ⟨~ sand⟩ **b :** physically trained or hardened close to the limit of efficiency **3 :** subtle or sensitive in perception or discrimination ⟨a ~ instrument⟩ ⟨a ~ distinction⟩ **4 :** superior in quality, conception, or appearance **5 :** marked by or affecting elegance or refinement **6 :** very well **:** EXCELLENT — **fine·ness** \'fīn-nəs\ *n*

4fine *adv* **:** FINELY

5fine *vt* **1 :** PURIFY, CLARIFY ⟨~ and filter wine⟩ **2 :** to make finer in quality or size **~** *vi* **1 :** to become pure or clear ⟨the ale will ~⟩ **2 :** to become smaller in lines or proportions **:** DIMINISH

6fi·ne \'fē-(,)nā\ *n* [It, fr. L *finis* end] **:** END — used as a direction in music to mark the closing point after a repeat

fine art *n* **1 a :** art (as painting, sculpture, music) concerned primarily with the creation of beautiful objects — usu. used in pl. **b :** the objects themselves **2 :** an activity requiring a fine skill

fine·ly \'fīn-lē\ *adv* **:** in a fine manner

fin·ery \'fīn-(ə-)rē\ *n* **:** ORNAMENT, DECORATION; *esp* **:** showy clothing and jewels

fines \'fīnz\ *n pl* [3*fine*] **:** finely crushed or powdered material (as ore or coal); *also* **:** very small particles in a mixture of various sizes

fine·spun \'fīn-'spən\ *adj* **1 :** developed with extreme care or delicacy **2 :** developed in excessively fine or subtle detail

1fi·nesse \fə-'nes\ *n* [ME, fr. MF, fr. *fin*] **1 :** fineness or subtlety esp. of skill or discrimination **2 a :** adroit maneuvering **b :** TRICK, STRATAGEM **3 :** the withholding of one's highest card or trump on the assumption that a lower card will take the trick because the taking card is in the hand of an opponent who has already played

2finesse *vi* **:** to make a finesse in playing cards **~** *vt* **1 :** to play (a card) as a finesse **2 a :** to bring about by adroit maneuvering **b :** EVADE, TRICK

1fin·ger \'fiŋ-gər\ *n* [ME, fr. OE; akin to OHG *fingar* finger] **1 :** one of the five terminating members of the hand; *esp* **:** one other than the thumb **2 a :** something that resembles or does the work of a finger **b :** a part of a glove into which a finger is inserted **c :** a projecting piece (as a pawl for a ratchet) brought into contact with an object to affect its motion **3 :** the breadth of a finger

2finger *vb* **fin·ger·ing** \-g(ə-)riŋ\ *vt* **1 a :** to play (a musical instrument) with the fingers **b :** to play with a specific fingering **c :** to mark the notes of (a music score) as a guide in playing **2 :** to touch or feel with the fingers **:** HANDLE **3 :** to point out **:** IDENTIFY **4 :** to extend into or penetrate in the shape of a finger **~** *vi* **1 :** to touch or handle something ⟨~*s* through the cards⟩ **2 a :** to use the fingers in playing a musical instrument **b :** to have a certain fingering **3 :** to extend in the shape or manner of a finger

fin·ger·board \'fiŋ-gər-,bō(ə)rd, -,bȯ(ə)rd\ *n* **1 :** the part of a stringed instrument against which the fingers press the strings to vary the pitch **2 :** the keyboard of a piano or organ **:** MANUAL

finger bowl *n* **:** a basin to hold water for rinsing the fingers at table

fin·gered \'fiŋ-gərd\ *adj* **1 :** having fingers **2 :** DIGITATE 2

fin·ger·ing *n* **1 :** the act or process of handling or touching with the fingers **2 a :** the act or method of using the fingers in playing an instrument **b :** the marking of the method of fingering

fin·ger·ling \'fiŋ-gər-liŋ\ *n* **:** a small fish esp. up to one year of age

fin·ger·nail \'fiŋ-gər-,nāl, ,fiŋ-gər-'nā(ə)l\ *n* **:** the nail of a finger

finger painting *n* **1 :** a technique of spreading pigment on wet paper chiefly with the fingers **2 :** a picture produced by finger painting

fin·ger·post \'fiŋ-gər-,pōst\ *n* **1 :** a post bearing one or more signs often terminating in a pointing finger **2 :** something serving as a guide to understanding or knowledge

fin·ger·print \-,print\ *n* **:** the impression of a fingertip on any surface; *esp* **:** an ink impression of the lines upon the fingertip taken for purpose of identification — **fingerprint** *vb*

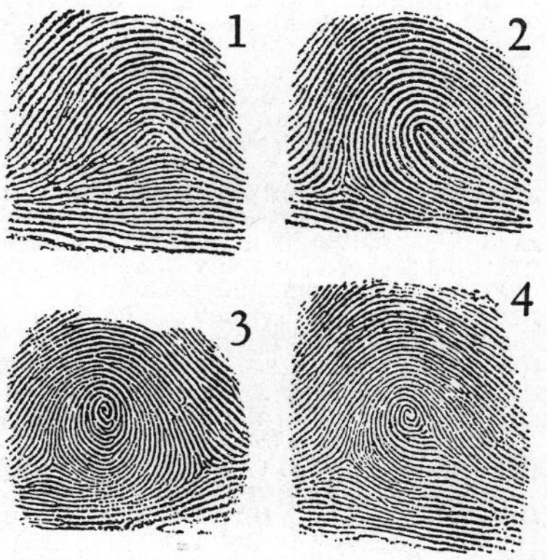

fingerprints: *1* arch, *2* loop, *3* whorl, *4* composite

fin·ger·tip \-,tip\ *n* **1 :** the tip of a finger **2 :** a protective covering for the end of a finger — **at one's fingertips :** instantly or readily available

finger wave *n* **:** a method of setting hair by dampening with water or wave solution and forming waves or curls with the fingers and a comb

fin·i·al \'fin-ē-əl\ *n* [ME, fr. *final, finial* final] **1 :** a usu. foliated ornament forming an upper extremity esp. in Gothic architecture **2 :** a crowning ornament or detail

fin·i·cal \'fin-i-kəl\ *adj* [prob. fr. 3*fine*] **:** FINICKY **syn** see NICE — **fin·i·cal·ly** \-k(ə-)lē\ *adv* — **fin·i·cal·ness** \-kəl-nəs\ *n*

fin·ick·i·ness \'fin-i-kē-nəs\ *n* **:** the quality or state of being finicky

fin·ick·ing \-kiŋ, -kən\ *adj* [alter. of *finical*] **:** FINICKY

fin·icky \'fin-i-kē\ *adj* [alter. of *finicking*] **:** excessively nice, exacting, or meticulous in taste or standards

fi·nis \'fin-əs, 'fī-nəs\ *n* [ME, fr. L] **:** END, CONCLUSION

1fin·ish \'fin-ish\ *vb* [ME *finisshen,* fr. MF *finiss-,* stem of *finir,* fr. L *finire,* fr. *finis*] *vt* **1 a :** to bring to an end **:** TERMINATE **b :** to use or dispose of entirely **2 a :** to bring to completion or issue **:** PERFECT **b :** to put a final coat or surface on **3 a :** to bring to an end the significance or effectiveness of **b :** to bring about the death of **~** *vi* **1 :** to come to an end **:** TERMINATE **2 :** to come to the end of a course, task, or undertaking **syn** see CLOSE — **fin·ish·er** *n*

2finish *n* **1 a :** the final stage **:** END **b :** the cause of one's ruin **2 :** something that completes or perfects: as **a :** the fine or decorative work required for a building **b :** a finishing material used in painting **c :** the final treatment or coating of a surface **3 :** the result or product of a finishing process **4 :** the quality or state of being perfected

fin·ished *adj* **1 :** brought to conclusion **2 :** of the highest quality **3 :** brought to an ineffective or defeated condition

finishing school *n* **:** a private school for girls that emphasizes cultural studies and prepares students esp. for social activities

fi·nite \'fī-,nīt\ *adj* [ME *finit,* fr. L *finitus,* pp. of *finire*] **1 a :** having definite or definable limits **b :** having a limited nature or existence **2 a :** having a character completely determinable in theory or in fact by enumeration, measurement, or conceptualization **b :** neither infinite nor infinitesimal **3 :** less than an arbitrary positive integer and greater than the negative of that integer **4** *of a verb or verb form* **:** showing distinction of grammatical person and number — **finite** *n* — **fi·nite·ly** *adv* — **fi·nite·ness** *n*

fi·ni·tude \'fin-ə-,t(y)üd, 'fī-nə-\ *n* **:** finite quality or state

fink \'fiŋk\ *n* [origin unknown] **1** *slang* **:** INFORMER 2 **2** *slang* **:** STRIKEBREAKER **3** *slang* **:** an objectionable person — used as a generalized term of abuse

Finn \'fin\ *n* [Sw *Finne*] **1 :** a member of a people speaking Finnish or a Finnic language **2 a :** a native or inhabitant of Finland **b :** one that is of Finnish descent

fin·nan had·die \,fin-ən-'had-ē\ *or* **finnan haddock** *n* [*finnan* alter. of *findon,* fr. *Findon,* Scotland] **:** smoked haddock

Fin·nic \'fin-ik\ *adj* **1 :** of or relating to the Finns **2 :** of, relating to, or constituting the branch of the Finno-Ugric subfamily of the Uralic family of languages that includes Finnish, Estonian, Lapp, and various other languages

1Finn·ish \'fin-ish\ *adj* **:** of, relating to, or characteristic of Finland, the Finns, or Finnish

2Finnish *n* **:** a Finno-Ugric language spoken in Finland, Karelia, and small areas of Sweden and Norway

Fin·no-Ugric \,fin-,ō-'(y)ü-grik\ *adj* **1 :** of or relating to any of various peoples including the Finnish, Hungarian, and Bulgarian peoples and the Lapps and Estonians **2 :** of, relating to, or constituting a subfamily of the Uralic family of languages comprising various languages spoken in Hungary, Lapland, Finland, Estonia, and northwestern U.S.S.R. — **Finno-Ugric** *n*

fin·ny \'fin-ē\ *adj* **1 :** provided with or characterized by fins **2 :** relating to or being fish

fiord *var of* FJORD

fip·ple flute \,fip-əl-\ *n* [origin unknown] **:** a wind instrument (as

the recorder) in which air is blown through a flue in the mouthpiece
fir \'fər\ *n, often attrib* [ME, fr. OE *fyrh;* akin to OHG *forha* fir, L *quercus* oak] **1 a :** any of a genus (*Abies*) of typically large symmetrical trees of the pine family including some that yield useful lumber or resins **b :** any of various other evergreen coniferous trees (as a Douglas fir) **2 :** the wood of a fir
[1]**fire** \'fī(-ə)r\ *n, often attrib* [ME, fr. OE *fȳr;* akin to OHG *fiur* fire, Gk *pyr*] **1 a** (1) **:** the phenomenon of combustion manifested in light, flame, and heat (2) **:** one of the four elements of the alchemists **b** (1) **:** burning passion **:** ARDOR (2) **:** liveliness of imagination **:** INSPIRATION **2 :** fuel in combustion **3 a :** a destructive burning **b** (1) **:** death or torture by fire (2) **:** severe trial or ordeal **4 :** BRILLIANCY, LUMINOSITY **5 a :** the discharge of firearms **b :** intense verbal attack **c :** a rapidly delivered series (as of remarks) — **fire·less** \-ləs\ *adj* — **on fire :** BURNING, EAGER
[2]**fire** *vt* **1 a :** to set on fire **:** KINDLE **b** (1) **:** to give life or spirit to **:** INSPIRE (2) **:** to fill with passion **:** INFLAME **c :** to light up as if by fire **2 a :** to drive out or away by or as if by fire **b :** to discharge from a position **3 a** (1) **:** to cause to explode **:** DETONATE (2) **:** to propel from a gun **:** DISCHARGE, LAUNCH (3) **:** to score (a number) in a game or contest **b :** to throw with speed **:** HURL **c :** to utter with force and rapidity **4 :** to apply fire or fuel to: as **a :** to process by applying heat **b :** to feed or serve the fire of ~ *vi* **1 a :** to take fire **:** KINDLE **b** *of an internal-combustion engine* **:** to have the explosive charge ignite at the proper time **2 :** to become irritated or angry **3 a :** to discharge a firearm **b :** to emit or let fly an object **4 :** to tend a fire — **fir·er** \'fīr-ər\ *n*
fire·arm \'fī(ə)r-,ärm\ *n* **:** a weapon from which a shot is discharged by gunpowder — usu. used only of small arms
fire·ball \'fī(ə)r-,bȯl\ *n* **1 :** a ball of fire **2 :** a brilliant meteor that may trail bright sparks **3 :** the highly luminous cloud of vapor and dust created by a nuclear explosion
fire·bird \-,bərd\ *n* **:** any of several small birds (as the Baltimore oriole or the scarlet tanager) having brilliant orange or red plumage
fire blight *n* **:** a destructive highly infectious bacterial disease of apples, pears, and related fruits
fire·boat \-,bōt\ *n* **:** a ship equipped with fire-fighting apparatus
fire·box \-,bäks\ *n* **1 :** a chamber (as of a furnace or steam boiler) that contains a fire **2 :** a box containing an apparatus for transmitting an alarm to a fire station
fire·brand \-,brand\ *n* **1 :** a piece of burning wood **2 :** a person who creates unrest or strife **:** AGITATOR
fire·break \-,brāk\ *n* **:** a barrier of cleared or plowed land intended to check a forest or grass fire
fire·brick \-,brik\ *n* **:** a refractory brick capable of sustaining high temperature that is used esp. for lining furnaces or fireplaces
fire·bug \-,bəg\ *n* **:** INCENDIARY, PYROMANIAC
fire·clay \-,klā\ *n* **:** clay capable of withstanding high temperatures that is used esp. for firebrick and crucibles
fire control *n* **1 :** the planning, preparation, and delivery of gunfire on targets **2 :** the control or extinction of fires
fire·crack·er \-,krak-ər\ *n* **:** a usu. paper cylinder containing an explosive and a fuse and usu. discharged to make a noise
fire–cured \-'kyů(ə)rd\ *adj* **:** cured over open fires in direct contact with the smoke ⟨~ tobacco⟩
fire·damp \'fī(ə)r-,damp\ *n* **:** a combustible mine gas that consists chiefly of methane; *also* **:** the explosive mixture of this gas with air
fire·drake \-,drāk\ *n* [ME *firdrake*, fr. OE *fȳrdraca*, fr. *fȳr* + *draca* dragon — more at DRAKE] **:** a fire-breathing dragon
fire drill *n* **:** a practice drill in extinguishing fires or in the conduct and manner of exit in case of fire
fire–eat·er \'fī(ə)r-,ēt-ər\ *n* **1 :** a performer who pretends to eat fire **2 :** a violent or pugnacious person
fire engine *n* **:** a usu. mobile apparatus for directing an extinguishing agent upon fires
fire escape *n* **:** a device for escape from a burning building; *esp* **:** a metal stairway attached to the outside of a building
fire extinguisher *n* **:** a portable or wheeled apparatus for putting out small fires by ejecting fire-extinguishing chemicals
fire·fly \'fī(ə)r-,flī\ *n* **:** a winged nocturnal insect usu. producing a bright soft intermittent light by oxidation of luciferin; *esp* **:** the male of various elongated flattened beetles (family Lampyridae)
fire·guard \-,gärd\ *n* **1 :** FIRE SCREEN **2 :** FIREBREAK **3 :** one who watches for the outbreak of fire; *also* **:** one whose duty is to extinguish fires
fire·house \-,hau̇s\ *n* **:** FIRE STATION
fire irons *n pl* **:** implements for tending a fire esp. in a fireplace
fire·light \'fī(ə)r-,līt\ *n* **:** the light of a fire esp. in a fireplace
fire·lock \-,läk\ *n* **1 :** a gunlock employing a slow match to ignite the powder charge; *also* **:** a gun having such a lock **2 a :** FLINTLOCK **b :** WHEEL LOCK
fire·man \-mən\ *n* **1 :** a member of a company organized to fight fires **2 :** one who tends or feeds fires **:** STOKER **3 :** an enlisted man in the navy who works with engineering machinery **4 :** a relief pitcher in baseball
fire opal *n* **:** GIRASOL 2
fire·place \'fī(ə)r-,plās\ *n* **1 :** a framed rectangular opening made in a chimney to hold an open fire **:** HEARTH **2 :** an outdoor structure of brick or stone made for an open fire
fire·plug \-,pləg\ *n* **:** HYDRANT
fire·pow·er \-,pau̇(-ə)r\ *n* **1 :** the relative capacity for delivering fire on a target **2 :** the aggregate of effective missiles that can be placed upon a target
[1]**fire·proof** \-'prüf\ *adj* **:** proof against or resistant to fire
[2]**fireproof** *vt* **:** to make fireproof
fire sale *n* **:** a sale of merchandise damaged by fire
fire screen *n* **:** an often ornamental screen before a fireplace
fire ship *n* **:** a ship carrying combustibles or explosives sent among the enemy's ships or works to set them on fire
fire·side \'fī(ə)r-,sīd\ *n* **1 :** a place near the fire or hearth **2 :** HOME
fire station *n* **:** a building housing fire apparatus and usu. firemen
fire·stone \-,stōn\ *n* **1 :** pyrite formerly used for striking fire; *also* **:** FLINT **2 :** a stone that will endure high heat
fire tower *n* **:** a tower from which a watch for fires is maintained
fire·trap \-,trap\ *n* **:** a building or place apt to catch on fire or difficult to escape from in case of fire
fire wall *n* **:** a wall constructed to prevent the spread of fire
fire·wa·ter \'fī(ə)r-,wȯt-ər, -,wät-\ *n* **:** strong alcoholic beverage
fire·weed \-,wēd\ *n* **:** any of several weeds (as the jimsonweed or orange hawkweed) troublesome in clearings or burned districts
fire·wood \-,wu̇d\ *n* **:** wood cut for fuel
fire·work \-,wərk\ *n* **1 :** a device for producing a striking display (as of light, noise, or smoke) by the combustion of explosive or flammable compositions **2** *pl* **:** a display of fireworks **3** *pl* **:** a display of temper or intense conflict
fir·ing *n* **1 :** the act or process of one that fires **2 :** the process of maturing ceramic products by the application of heat **3 :** FIREWOOD, FUEL **4 :** the scorching of plants esp. by unfavorable soil conditions
firing line *n* **1 :** a line from which fire is delivered against a target **2 :** the forefront of an activity
firing pin *n* **:** the pin that strikes the cartridge primer in the breech mechanism of a firearm
firing squad *n* **1 :** a detachment detailed to fire volleys over the grave of one buried with military honors **2 :** a detachment detailed to carry out a sentence of death by shooting
fir·kin \'fər-kən\ *n* [ME, deriv. of MD *veerdel* fourth] **1 :** a small wooden vessel or cask **2 :** any of various British units of capacity usu. equal to ¼ barrel
[1]**firm** \'fərm\ *adj* [ME *ferm*, fr. MF, fr. L *firmus;* akin to Gk *thronos* chair, throne] **1 a :** securely or solidly fixed in place **b :** SOLID, VIGOROUS **c :** having a solid or compact texture **2 a** (1) **:** not subject to change or revision (2) **:** not subject to price weakness **3 :** STEADY **b :** not easily moved or disturbed **:** STEADFAST **c :** WELL-FOUNDED **3 :** indicating firmness or resolution ⟨~ mouth⟩ — **firm·ly** *adv* — **firm·ness** *n*
syn HARD, SOLID: FIRM implies such compactness and coherence and often elasticity of substance as to resist pulling, distorting, pressing; it connotes stability and resoluteness; HARD implies impenetrability and nearly complete but inelastic resistance to pressure or tension; it may connote stubbornness or lack of feeling; SOLID implies a texture of uniform density so as to be not only firm but heavy; figuratively it implies substantiality, reliability, soundness, or sobriety
[2]**firm** *vt* **1 :** to make secure or fast **:** FIX **2 :** to make solid or compact **3 :** SETTLE, CONFIRM ⟨~ a contract⟩ ~ *vi* **:** to become firm
[3]**firm** *n* [G *firma*, fr. It, signature, deriv. of L *firmare* to make firm, confirm, fr. *firmus*] **1 :** the name, title, or style under which a company transacts business **2 :** a partnership of two or more persons not recognized as a legal person distinct from the members composing it **3 :** a business unit or enterprise
fir·ma·ment \'fər-mə-mənt\ *n* [ME, fr. LL & L; LL *firmamentum*, fr. L, support, fr. *firmare*] **1 :** the vault or arch of the sky **:** HEAVENS **2** *obs* **:** BASIS — **fir·ma·men·tal** \,fər-mə-'ment-ᵊl\ *adj*
fir·mer chisel \'fər-mər-,\ *n* [F *fermoir* chisel, alter. of MF *formoir*, fr. *former* to form] **:** a woodworking chisel with a thin flat blade
firn \'fi(ə)rn\ *n* [G] **:** NÉVÉ
fir·ry \'fər-ē\ *adj* **:** made of or abounding in firs
[1]**first** \'fərst\ *adj* [ME, fr. OE *fyrst;* akin to OHG *furist* first, OE *faran* to go] **1** — see NUMBER table **2 :** preceding all others in time, order, or importance: as **a :** EARLIEST **b :** being a type of grammatical declension or conjugation conventionally placed first **c :** being the lowest forward gear or speed in an automotive vehicle **d :** highest or most prominent in carrying the melody ⟨~ violin⟩
[2]**first** *adv* **1 a :** before another in time, space, or importance **b :** for the first time **2 :** in preference to something else **:** SOONER
[3]**first** *n* **1** — see NUMBER table **2 :** something that is first: as **a :** the first occurrence or item of a kind **b :** the first gear or speed in an automotive vehicle **c :** the highest or chief voice or instrument of a group **d :** an article of commerce of the finest grade **e :** the winning place in a competition or contest
first aid *n* **:** emergency care or treatment given to an ill or injured person before regular medical aid can be obtained
first base *n* **1 :** the base that must be touched first by a base runner in baseball **2 :** the player position for defending the area around first base
first·born \'fərs(t)-'bȯ(ə)rn\ *adj* **:** first brought forth **:** ELDEST — **firstborn** *n*
first cause *n* **:** the self-created source of all causality
first class *n* **:** the first or highest group in a classification: as **a :** the highest of usu. three classes of accommodations in a passenger ship **b :** a class of mail that comprises letters, postcards, or matter sealed against inspection — **first–class** *adj or adv*
first floor *n* **1 :** GROUND FLOOR **2** *Brit* **:** the floor next above the ground floor
first·fruits \'fərs(t)-'früts\ *n pl* **1 :** the earliest gathered fruits offered to the Deity in acknowledgment of the gift of fruitfulness **2 :** the earliest products or results of an endeavor
first·hand \'fərst-'hand\ *adj* **:** coming directly from the original source — **firsthand** *adv*
first lady *n, often cap F&L* **1 :** the wife or hostess of the chief executive of a country or jurisdiction **2 :** the leading woman of an art or profession
first lieutenant *n* **1 :** a commissioned officer in the army, air force, or marine corps ranking above a second lieutenant and below a captain **2 :** a naval officer responsible for a ship's upkeep
first·ling \'fərst-liŋ\ *n* **1 :** the first of a class or kind **2 :** the first produce or result of something
first·ly \-lē\ *adv* **:** in the first place **:** FIRST
first mortgage *n* **:** a mortgage that has priority as a lien over all mortgages and liens except those imposed by law
first offender *n* **:** one legally convicted for the first time
first papers *n pl* **:** papers declaring intention filed by an applicant for citizenship as the first step in the naturalization process
first person *n* **1 a :** a set of linguistic forms (as verb forms, pronouns, and inflectional affixes) referring to the speaker or writer of the utterance in which they occur **b :** a linguistic form belonging to such a set **c :** reference of a linguistic form to the speaker or writer of the utterance in which it occurs **2 :** a style of discourse marked by general use of verbs and pronouns of the first person
[1]**first–rate** \'fər-'strāt\ *adj* **:** of the first order of size, importance, or quality — **first–rat·er** \-'strāt-ər\ *n*
[2]**first–rate** *adv* **:** very well
First Reader *n* **:** a Christian Scientist chosen to conduct meetings for a specified time and specif. to read aloud from the writings of Mary Baker Eddy
first reading *n* **:** the formal reading of a legislative bill upon introduction usu. by title only

first sergeant *n* **1 :** a noncommissioned officer serving as chief enlisted assistant to the commander of a company or equivalent military unit **2 :** a master sergeant in the army or marine corps
first–string \ˈfərs(t)-ˈstriŋ\ *adj* **1 :** being a regular as distinguished from a substitute **2 :** FIRST-RATE
first water *n* **1 :** the purest luster **2 :** the highest grade, degree, or quality
firth \ˈfərth\ *n* [ME, fr. ON *fjörthr* — more at FORD] **:** ESTUARY
fisc \ˈfisk\ *n* **:** a state or royal treasury
¹fis·cal \ˈfis-kəl\ *adj* [L *fiscalis*, fr. *fiscus* basket, treasury; akin to Gk *pithos* wine jar] **1 :** of or relating to taxation, public revenues, or public debt ⟨~ policy⟩ **2 :** of or relating to financial matters ⟨~ agent⟩ **syn** see FINANCIAL — **fis·cal·ly** \-kə-lē\ *adv*
²fiscal *n* **:** REVENUE STAMP
fiscal year *n* **:** an accounting period of 12 months
¹fish \ˈfish\ *n, pl* **fish** *or* **fish·es** [ME, fr. OE *fisc;* akin to OHG *fisc* fish, L *piscis*] **1 a :** an aquatic animal — usu. used in combina-

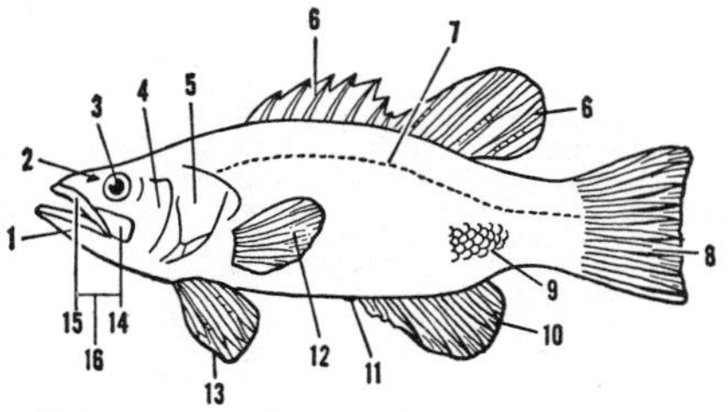

fish: *1* mandible, *2* external naris, *3* eye, *4* cheek, *5* operculum, *6,6*, dorsal fins, *7* lateral line, *8* caudal fin, *9* scales, *10* anal fin, *11* anus, *12* pectoral fin, *13* pelvic fin, *14* maxilla, *15* premaxilla, *16* upper jaw

tion ⟨star*fish*⟩ ⟨cuttle*fish*⟩ **b :** any of numerous cold-blooded strictly aquatic craniate vertebrates that have typically an elongated somewhat spindle-shaped body terminating in a broad caudal fin, limbs in the form of fins when present at all, and a 2-chambered heart by which blood is sent through thoracic gills to be oxygenated **2 :** the flesh of fish used as food **3 :** PERSON ⟨a queer ~⟩ **4 :** something that resembles a fish: as **a :** a purchase used to fish the anchor **b :** a piece of wood or iron fastened alongside another member to strengthen it — **fish·like** \ˈfish-ˌlīk\ *adj*
²fish *vi* **1 :** to attempt to catch fish **2 :** to seek something by roundabout means ⟨~*ing* for praise⟩ **3 a :** to search for something underwater (as with a hook) **b :** to engage in a search by groping or feeling ~ *vt* **1 :** to try to catch fish in ⟨~ the stream⟩ **2 a :** to catch or try to catch **b :** to draw forth as if fishing
fish·able \ˈfish-ə-bəl\ *adj* **:** suitable, promising, or legally open for fishing
fish–and–chips \ˌfish-ən-ˈchips\ *n pl* **:** fried fish and french fried potatoes
fish cake *n* **:** a round fried cake made of shredded fish and mashed potato — called also *fish ball*
fish·er \ˈfish-ər\ *n* **1 :** one that fishes **2 a :** a large dark brown No. American arboreal carnivorous mammal (*Martes pennanti*) related to the weasels **b :** the fur or pelt of this animal
fish·er·man \-mən\ *n* **1 :** one who engages in fishing as an occupation or for pleasure **2 :** a ship used in commercial fishing
fisherman's bend *n* **:** a knot made by passing the end twice round a spar or through a ring and then back under both turns
fish·ery \ˈfish-(ə-)rē\ *n* **1 :** the act, process, occupation, or season of taking fish or other sea products **:** FISHING **2 :** a place for catching fish or taking other sea products **3 :** a fishing establishment; *also* **:** its fishermen **4 :** the legal right to take fish at a particular place or in particular waters **5 :** the technology of fishery
fish·hook \ˈfish-ˌhu̇k\ *n* **:** a usu. barbed hook for catching fish
fish·ing *n* **1 :** the act of one that fishes **2 :** a place for catching fish
fishing expedition *n* **1 :** a legal interrogation or examination to discover information for a later proceeding **2 :** an investigation that does not stick to a stated objective and that uses questionable methods to uncover incriminating evidence
fish joint *n* **:** a butt joint of timbers or rails in which the two abutting members are held in alignment by one or more fishplates
fish meal *n* **:** ground dried fish and fish waste used as fertilizer and animal food
fish·mon·ger \ˈfish-ˌməŋ-gər, -ˌmäŋ-\ *n, chiefly Brit* **:** a fish dealer
fish·plate \-ˌplāt\ *n* **:** a steel plate used to lap a butt joint
fish stick *n* **:** a small elongated fillet of fish breaded and fried
fish story *n* **:** an extravagant or incredible story
fish·tail \ˈfish-ˌtāl\ *vi* **:** to swing the tail of an airplane from side to side to reduce speed esp. when landing
fish·wife \-ˌwīf\ *n* **1 :** a woman who sells fish **2 :** a scurrilously abusive woman
fishy \ˈfish-ē\ *adj* **1 :** of or resembling fish esp. in taste or odor **2 :** inspiring doubt or suspicion **:** QUESTIONABLE
fis·sile \ˈfis-əl, ˈfis-ˌīl\ *adj* **1 :** capable of being split or divided **2 :** FISSIONABLE — **fis·sil·i·ty** \fis-ˈil-ət-ē\ *n*
¹fis·sion \ˈfish-ən, ˈfizh-\ *n* [L *fission-, fissio*, fr. *fissus*, pp. of *findere* to split — more at BITE] **1 :** a splitting or breaking up into parts **2 :** reproduction by spontaneous division of the body into two or more parts each of which grows into a complete organism **3 a :** the splitting of a molecule into simpler molecules **b :** the splitting of an atomic nucleus resulting in the release of large amounts of energy — **fis·sion·al** \-ᵊl\ *adj*
²fission *vb* **fis·sion·ing** \ˈfish-(ə-)niŋ, ˈfizh-\ *vt* **:** to cause to undergo fission ~ *vi* **:** to undergo fission
fis·sion·able \ˈfish-(ə-)nə-bəl, ˈfizh-\ *adj* **:** capable of undergoing fission — **fissionable** *n*
fission bomb *n* **:** ATOM BOMB 1
fis·sip·a·rous \fis-ˈip-ə-rəs\ *adj* [L *fissus* + E *-parous*] **1 :** producing new biological units or individuals by fission **2 :** tending to break up into parts **:** DIVISIVE — **fis·sip·a·rous·ly** *adv* — **fis·sip·a·rous·ness** *n*
fis·si·ped \ˈfis-ə-ˌped\ *adj* [LL *fissiped-, fissipes*, fr. L *fissus* + *ped-, pes* foot] **:** having the toes separated to the base — **fissiped** *n*
¹fis·sure \ˈfish-ər\ *n* **1 :** a narrow opening or crack of some length and depth usu. occurring from some breaking or parting **2 :** a separation or disagreement in thought or viewpoint **:** SCHISM **3 a :** a natural cleft between body parts or in the substance of an organ **b :** a break or lesion in tissue usu. at the junction of skin and mucous membrane
²fissure *vt* **:** to break into fissures **:** CLEAVE ~ *vi* **:** CRACK, DIVIDE
¹fist \ˈfist\ *n* [ME, fr. OE *fȳst;* akin to OHG *fūst* fist, OSlav *pęstĭ*] **1 :** the hand clenched with fingers doubled into the palm **2 :** CLUTCH, GRASP **3 :** INDEX 6
²fist *vt* **1 :** to clench into a fist **2 :** to grip with the fist **:** HANDLE
fist·ic \ˈfis-tik\ *adj* **:** of or relating to boxing or to fist fighting
fist·i·cuffs \ˈfis-ti-ˌkəfs\ *n pl* [alter. of *fisty cuff*, fr. *fisty* (fistic) + *cuff*] **:** a fight with usu. bare fists
fis·tu·la \ˈfis(h)-chə-lə\ *n, pl* **fistulas** *or* **fis·tu·lae** \-ˌlē, -ˌlī\ [ME, fr. L, pipe, fistula] **:** an abnormal passage leading from an abscess or hollow organ to the body surface or from one hollow organ to another
fis·tu·lous \-ləs\ *adj* **1 :** of, relating to, or having the form or nature of a fistula **2 :** hollow like a pipe or reed
fistulous withers *n pl but sing or pl in constr* **:** a deep-seated chronic inflammation of the withers of the horse in which bloody fluid is discharged
¹fit \ˈfit\ *n* [ME, fr. OE *fitt;* akin to OS *fittea* division of a poem, OHG *fizza* skein] *archaic* **:** a division of a poem or song
²fit *n* [ME, fr. OE *fitt* strife] **1 a :** a stroke of a disease producing convulsions or unconsciousness **:** PAROXYSM **b :** a sudden but transient attack of a physical disturbance **2 :** a sudden burst or flurry (as of activity) **3 :** an emotional outburst — **by fits** *or* **by fits and starts :** in an impulsive and irregular manner
³fit *adj* **fit·ter; fit·test** [ME; akin to ME *fitten*] **1 :** adapted to an end or design **:** APPROPRIATE ⟨water ~ for drinking⟩ **2 :** BECOMING, PROPER **3 a :** READY, PREPARED **b :** APT, DISPOSED ⟨~ to jump overboard⟩ **4 :** QUALIFIED, COMPETENT **5 :** sound physically and mentally **:** HEALTHY — **fit·ly** *adv* — **fit·ness** *n*
syn SUITABLE, MEET, PROPER, APPROPRIATE, FITTING, APT, HAPPY, FELICITOUS: FIT stresses adaptability and sometimes special readiness for use or action; SUITABLE implies an answering to requirements or demands; MEET suggests a just proportioning; PROPER suggests a suitability through essential nature or accordance with custom; APPROPRIATE implies eminent or distinctive fitness; FITTING implies harmony of mood or tone; APT connotes a fitness marked by nicety and discrimination; HAPPY suggests what is effectively or successfully appropriate; FELICITOUS suggests an aptness that is opportune, telling, or graceful
— **fit to be tied :** angry or irritated
⁴fit *vb* **fit·ted** *also* **fit; fit·ting** [ME *fitten*, fr. or akin to MD *vitten* to be suitable; akin to OHG *fizza* skein] *vt* **1 :** to be suitable for or to **:** BEFIT **2 a :** to be correctly adjusted to or shaped for **b :** to insert or adjust until correctly in place **c :** to make a place or room for **3 :** to be in agreement or accord with ⟨the theory ~*s* all the facts⟩ **4 a :** to put into a condition of readiness **:** PREPARE **b :** to bring to a required form and size **:** ADJUST **c :** to cause to conform to or suit something else **5 :** SUPPLY, EQUIP ~ *vi* **1** *archaic* **:** to be seemly, proper, or suitable **2 :** to conform to a particular shape or size **3 :** to be in harmony or accord **:** BELONG — **fit·ter** *n*
⁵fit *n* **1 a :** the quality, state, or manner of being fitted or adapted **b :** the degree of closeness with which surfaces are brought together in an assembly of parts **2 :** a piece of clothing that fits
⁶fit *dial past of* FIGHT
fitch \ˈfich\ *or* **fitch·ew** \ˈfich-(ˌ)ü\ *n* [ME *fiche, ficheux*, fr. MF or MD; MF *fichau*, fr. MD *vitsau*] **1 :** POLECAT 1 **2 :** the fur or pelt of the polecat
fitch·et \ˈfich-ət\ *n* **:** POLECAT 1
fit·ful \ˈfit-fəl\ *adj* **1** *obs* **:** characterized by fits or paroxysms ⟨life's ~ fever —Shak.⟩ **2 :** having a spasmodic or intermittent character **:** RESTLESS — **fit·ful·ly** \-fə-lē\ *adv* — **fit·ful·ness** *n*
syn FITFUL, SPASMODIC, CONVULSIVE mean lacking steadiness or regularity in movement. FITFUL implies intermittence, a succession of starts and stops or risings and fallings; SPASMODIC adds to FITFUL the implication of violent activity alternating with inactivity; CONVULSIVE suggests the breaking of regularity or quiet by uncontrolled movement
fit·ment \ˈfit-mənt\ *n* [*⁴fit*] **1 :** EQUIPMENT **2** *pl* **:** FITTINGS
¹fit·ting *adj* **:** APPROPRIATE, SUITABLE **syn** see FIT — **fit·ting·ly** \-iŋ-lē\ *adv* — **fit·ting·ness** *n*
²fitting *n* **1 :** an act or process of one that fits; *specif* **:** a trying on of clothes in the process of being made or altered **2 :** a small often standardized accessory part ⟨a plumbing ~⟩ ⟨an electrical ~⟩
five \ˈfīv\ *n* [ME, fr. *five*, adj., fr. OE *fīf;* akin to OHG *finf* five, L *quinque*, Gk *pente*] **1 —** see NUMBER table **2 :** the fifth in a set or series ⟨the ~ of hearts⟩ **3 :** something having five units or members; *esp* **:** a male basketball team **4 :** a five-dollar bill **5 :** FIFTEEN 2 — **five** *adj or pron*
five–and–ten \ˌfī-vən-ˈten\ *also* **five–and–dime** \-ˈdīm\ *n* **1 :** a store selling articles priced at 5 or 10 cents **2 :** a variety store selling chiefly inexpensive articles of merchandise
five–fin·ger \ˈfīv-ˌfiŋ-gər\ *n* **1 :** CINQUEFOIL 1 **2 :** BIRD'S-FOOT TREFOIL **3 :** VIRGINIA CREEPER
fiv·er \ˈfī-vər\ *n* **1** *slang* **:** a five-dollar bill **2** *slang* **:** a five-pound note
five–star \ˈfīv-ˈstär\ *adj* **:** being of top military rank usu. denoted by five stars
¹fix \ˈfiks\ *vb* [ME *fixen*, fr. L *fixus*, pp. of *figere* to fasten — more at DIKE] *vt* **1 a :** to make firm, stable, or fast **b :** to give a permanent or final form to: as (1) **:** to change into a stable compound or available form ⟨bacteria that ~ nitrogen⟩ (2) **:** to kill, harden, and preserve for microscopic study (3) **:** to make the image of (a photographic film) permanent by removing unused salts **c :** AFFIX, ATTACH **2 :** to hold or direct steadily ⟨~*es* his eyes on the horizon⟩ **3 a :** to set or place definitely **:** ESTABLISH **b :** ASSIGN ⟨~ blame⟩ **4 :** to set in order **:** ADJUST **5 :** to get ready **:** PREPARE **6 a :** REPAIR, MEND **b :** RESTORE, CURE **c :** SPAY, CASTRATE **7 a :** to get even with **b :** to influence the actions, outcome, or effect of by improper or illegal methods ~ *vi* **:** to become firm, stable, or fixed
syn see FASTEN — **fix·able** \ˈfik-sə-bəl\ *adj*

2**fix** *n* **1 :** a position of difficulty or embarrassment **:** PREDICAMENT **2 a :** the position (as of a ship) determined by bearings, observations, or radio **b :** a determination of one's position **3 a :** an act of obtaining special privilege or immunity from the law by bribery or collusion **b :** BRIBE **4** *slang* **:** a shot of a narcotic **syn** see PREDICAMENT

fix·ate \ˈfik-ˌsāt\ *vt* **1 :** FIX **2 :** to focus one's gaze on **3 :** to direct (the libido) toward an infantile form of gratification ~ *vi* **1 :** to focus or concentrate one's gaze or attention **2 :** to undergo arrestment at a stage of development

fix·a·tion \fik-ˈsā-shən\ *n* **:** the act, process, or result of fixing or fixating: as **a :** a habit formation **b :** an obsessive or unhealthy preoccupation or attachment **c :** a persistent concentration of libidinal energies upon pregenital objects

fix·a·tive \ˈfik-sət-iv\ *n* **:** something that fixes or sets: as **a :** a substance added to a perfume esp. to prevent too rapid evaporation **b :** a varnish used esp. for the protection of crayon drawings **c :** a substance used to fix living tissue — **fixative** *adj*

fixed \ˈfikst\ *adj* **1 a :** securely placed or fastened **:** STATIONARY **b** (1) **:** NONVOLATILE; *specif* **:** constituting an oil obtained from a plant or a marine animal (2) **:** COMBINED **c** (1) **:** not subject to change or fluctuation **:** SETTLED (2) **:** firmly set in the mind (3) **:** having a final or crystallized form or character (4) **:** recurring on the same date from year to year **d :** CONCENTRATED, IMMOBILE ⟨a ~ stare⟩ **2 :** supplied with a definite amount of something needed or desirable; *esp* **:** supplied with money — **fixed·ly** \ˈfik-səd-lē, ˈfiks-tlē\ *adv* — **fixed·ness** \ˈfik-səd-nəs, ˈfiks(t)-nəs\ *n*

fixed charge *n* **:** a regularly recurring expense that is constant and does not fluctuate with business volume

fixed star *n* **:** a star so distant that its motion can be measured only by very precise observations over long periods

fix·er \ˈfik-sər\ *n* **:** one that fixes: as **a :** one that intervenes to enable a person to circumvent the law or obtain a political favor **b :** one that adjusts matters or disputes by negotiation

fix·ing \-siŋ, *2 is often* -sən\ *n* **1 :** the act or process of one that fixes **2** *pl* **:** TRIMMINGS

fix·i·ty \ˈfik-sət-ē\ *n* **1 :** the quality or state of being fixed or stable **2 :** something that is fixed **:** FIXTURE

fix·ture \ˈfiks-chər\ *n* [modif. of LL *fixura*, fr. L *fixus*] **1 a :** the act or process of fixing **b :** the state of being fixed **2 :** something that is fixed in place: as **a :** a chattel so annexed to realty that it may be regarded as legally a part of it **b :** a permanent appendage or structural part **3 :** an element or feature usu. present in some particular setting; *esp* **:** a person long associated with a place or activity **4 :** a settled date or time esp. for a sporting or festive event; *also* **:** such an event esp. as a regularly scheduled affair

1**fizz** \ˈfiz\ *vi* [prob. of imit. origin] **1 :** to make a hissing or sputtering sound **:** EFFERVESCE **2 :** to exhibit excitement or exhilaration

2**fizz** *n* **1 a :** a hissing sound **b :** LIVELINESS, SPIRIT **2 :** an effervescent beverage — **fizzy** \-ē\ *adj*

1**fiz·zle** \ˈfiz-əl\ *vi* **fiz·zling** \-(ə-)liŋ\ [prob. alter. of *fist* (to break wind)] **1 :** FIZZ **2 :** to fail or end feebly esp. after a promising start

2**fizzle** *n* **:** an abortive effort **:** FAILURE

fjeld \fē-ˈel, ˈfyel\ *n* [Dan] **:** a barren plateau of the Scandinavian upland

fjord \fē-ˈȯ(ə)rd, ˈfyȯ(ə)rd\ *n* [Norw *fjord*, fr. ON *fjörthr* — more at FORD] **:** a narrow inlet of the sea between cliffs or steep slopes

flab·ber·gast \ˈflab-ər-ˌgast\ *vt* [origin unknown] **:** to overwhelm with shock, surprise or wonder **:** ASTOUND **syn** see SURPRISE

flab·bi·ly \ˈflab-ə-lē\ *adv* **:** in a flabby manner

flab·bi·ness \ˈflab-ē-nəs\ *n* **:** the quality or state of being flabby

flab·by \ˈflab-ē\ *adj* [alter. of *flappy*] **1 :** lacking resilience or firmness **:** FLACCID **2 :** weak and ineffective **:** FEEBLE **syn** see LIMP

fla·bel·late \flə-ˈbel-ət, ˈflab-ə-ˌlāt\ *or* **fla·bel·li·form** \flə-ˈbel-ə-ˌfȯrm\ *adj* **:** shaped like a fan

flabelli- *comb form* [L, fr. *flabellum*] **:** fan ⟨*flabelli*form⟩

fla·bel·lum \flə-ˈbel-əm\ *n, pl* **fla·bel·la** \-ə\ [NL, fr. L, fan] **:** a body organ or part resembling a fan

flac·cid \ˈflak-səd, ˈflas-əd\ *adj* [L *flaccidus*, fr. *flaccus* flabby] **1 :** LIMP, FLABBY **2** *of a plant part* **:** deficient in turgor **syn** see LIMP — **flac·cid·i·ty** \fla(k)-ˈsid-ət-ē\ *n* — **flac·cid·ly** *adv*

fla·con \ˈflak-ən, -ˌän; fla-kōⁿ\ *n* [F, fr. MF, bottle — more at FLAGON] **:** a small usu. ornamental bottle with a tight cap

1**flag** \ˈflag\ *n* [ME *flagge* reed, rush] **:** any of various monocotyledonous plants with long ensiform leaves: as **a :** IRIS; *esp* **:** a wild iris **b :** SWEET FLAG **c :** CATTAIL

2**flag** *n* [ME *flagge*, fr. ON *flaga* slab; akin to OE *flēan* to flay — more at FLAY] **:** a hard evenly stratified stone that splits into flat pieces suitable for paving; *also* **:** a piece of such stone

3**flag** *vt* **flagged; flag·ging :** to lay (as a pavement) with flags

4**flag** *n* [perh. fr. 1*flag*] **1 :** a usu. rectangular piece of fabric of distinctive design that is used as a symbol or as a signaling device **2 a :** something used like a flag to signal or attract attention **b :** one of the cross strokes of a musical note less than a quarter note in value **3 a :** FLAGSHIP **b :** an admiral functioning in his office of command **c :** NATIONALITY

5**flag** *vt* **flagged; flag·ging 1 :** to put a flag on **2 :** to signal with or as if with a flag; *esp* **:** to signal to stop ⟨~ me a taxi⟩

6**flag** *vi* **flagged; flag·ging** [origin unknown] **1 a :** to hang loose without stiffness **b** *of a plant* **:** to droop esp. from lack of water **2 a :** to become unsteady, feeble, or spiritless **:** DROOP ⟨his interest *flagged*⟩ **b :** to decline in interest or attraction ⟨the topic *flagged*⟩

flag day *n* **1** *cap F&D* **:** June 14 observed in various states in commemoration of the adoption in 1777 of the official U.S. flag **2** *Brit* **:** a day on which charitable contributions are solicited in exchange for small flags

fla·gel·lant \ˈflaj-ə-lənt, flə-ˈjel-ənt\ *n* **:** one that whips; *specif* **:** a person who scourges himself as a public penance — **flagellant** *adj* — **fla·gel·lant·ism** \-lən-ˌtiz-əm, -ən-ˌtiz\ *n*

fla·gel·lar \flə-ˈjel-ər\ *adj* **:** of or relating to a flagellum

1**flag·el·late** \ˈflaj-ə-ˌlāt\ *vt* [L *flagellatus*, pp. of *flagellare*, fr. *flagellum*, dim. of *flagrum* whip; akin to ON *blaka* to wave] **1 :** WHIP **2 :** to drive or punish as if by whipping

2**fla·gel·late** \ˈflaj-ə-lət, -ˌlāt; flə-ˈjel-ət\ *adj* [NL *flagellatus*, fr. *flagellum*] **1 a** *or* **flag·el·lat·ed** \ˈflaj-ə-ˌlāt-əd\ **:** having flagella **b :** shaped like a flagellum **2** [3*flagellate*] **:** of, relating to, or caused by flagellates

3**flagellate** *like* 2\ *n* [NL *Flagellata*, class of unicellular organisms, fr. neut. pl. of *flagellatus*] **:** a flagellate protozoan or alga

1**flag·el·la·tion** \ˌflaj-ə-ˈlā-shən\ *n* **:** the act or practice of flagellating

2**flagellation** *n* **:** the formation or arrangement of flagella

fla·gel·lum \flə-ˈjel-əm\ *n, pl* **fla·gel·la** \-ə\ *also* **flagellums** [NL, fr. L, whip, shoot of a plant] **:** any of various elongated filiform appendages: as **a :** the slender distal part of an antenna **b :** a long tapering process that projects singly or in groups from a cell and is the primary organ of motion of many microorganisms **c :** a long slender shoot

fla·geo·let \ˌflaj-ə-ˈlet, -ˈlā\ *n* [F, fr. OF *flajolet*, fr. *flajol* flute, fr. (assumed) VL *flabeolum*, fr. L *flare* to blow — more at BLOW] **:** a small fipple flute resembling the treble recorder

1**flag·ging** \ˈflag-iŋ\ *adj* **1 :** LANGUID, WEAK **2 :** DWINDLING, WEAKENING — **flag·ging·ly** \-iŋ-lē\ *adv*

2**flagging** *n* **:** a pavement or walk of flagstones

flag·gy \ˈflag-ē\ *adj* **:** abounding with flags or other reedy plants

fla·gi·tious \flə-ˈjish-əs\ *adj* [ME *flagicious*, fr. L *flagitiosus*, fr. *flagitium* shameful thing; akin to L *flagrum* whip] **:** marked by outrageous or scandalous crime or vice **:** VILLAINOUS **syn** see VICIOUS — **fla·gi·tious·ly** *adv* — **fla·gi·tious·ness** *n*

flag·man \ˈflag-mən\ *n* **:** one who signals with or as if with a flag

flag officer *n* **:** a naval officer of flag rank

flag of truce : a white flag carried or displayed to an enemy as an invitation to conference or parley

flag·on \ˈflag-ən\ *n* [ME, fr. MF *flascon*, *flacon* bottle, fr. LL *flascon-*, *flasco* — more at FLASK] **1 a :** a large usu. metal or pottery vessel with handle and spout and often a lid **b :** a large bulging short-necked bottle **2 :** the contents of a flagon

flag·pole \ˈflag-ˌpōl\ *n* **:** a pole to raise a flag on

fla·gran·cy \ˈflā-grən-sē\ *also* **fla·grance** \-grən(t)s\ *n* **:** the quality or state of being flagrant

flag rank *n* **:** any of the ranks in the navy above a captain

fla·grant \ˈflā-grənt\ *adj* [L *flagrant-*, *flagrans*, prp. of *flagrare* to burn — more at BLACK] **1** *archaic* **:** FLAMING, GLOWING **2 :** extremely or purposefully conspicuous — **fla·grant·ly** *adv*

syn FLAGRANT, GLARING, GROSS, RANK mean conspicuously bad or objectionable. FLAGRANT applies to offenses or errors so bad that they cannot escape notice or be condoned ⟨*flagrant* disobedience⟩ GLARING implies painful or damaging obtrusiveness ⟨a *glaring* fault⟩ GROSS implies the exceeding of reasonable or excusable limits ⟨*gross* carelessness⟩ RANK applies to what is openly and extremely objectionable and utterly condemned ⟨*rank* dishonesty⟩

fla·gran·te de·lic·to *or* **in flagrante delicto** \(ˌin-)flə-ˌgrant-ē-di-ˈlik-(ˌ)tō\ *adv* [ML, lit., while the crime is blazing] **:** in the very act of committing a misdeed

flag·ship \ˈflag-ˌship\ *n* **:** the ship that carries the commander of a fleet or subdivision thereof and flies his flag

flag·staff \-ˌstaf\ *n* **:** a staff on which a flag is hoisted

flag·stone \-ˌstōn\ *n* **:** 2FLAG

flag stop *n* **:** a point at which a vehicle in public transportation stops only on prearrangement or signal

flag-wav·ing \-ˌwā-viŋ\ *n* **:** passionate appeal to patriotic or partisan sentiment **:** CHAUVINISM

1**flail** \ˈflā(ə)l\ *n* [ME *fleil*, *flail*, partly fr. (assumed) OE *flegel* (akin to OHG *flegil* flail; both fr. a prehistoric WGmc word borrowed fr. LL *flagellum* flail, fr. L, whip) & partly fr. MF *flaiel*, fr. LL *flagellum* — more at FLAGELLATE] **:** a hand threshing implement consisting of a wooden handle at the end of which a stouter and shorter stick is so hung as to swing freely

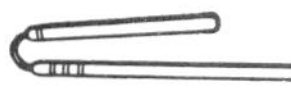
flail

2**flail** *vt* **1 :** to strike with or as if with a flail **2 :** to thresh with a flail ~ *vi* **:** to engage in flailing **:** THRASH ⟨~*ed* away at each other⟩

flair \ˈfla(ə)r, ˈfle(ə)r\ *n* [F, lit., sense of smell, fr. OF, odor, fr. *flairier* to give off an odor, fr. LL *flagrare*, fr. L *fragrare*] **1 :** discriminating sense **2 :** natural aptitude **:** BENT **syn** see LEANING

flak \ˈflak\ *n, pl* **flak** [G, fr. *flieger*abwehr*k*anonen, fr. *flieger* flyer + *abwehr* defense + *kanonen* cannons] **1 :** antiaircraft guns **2 :** the bursting shells fired from flak

1**flake** \ˈflāk\ *n* [ME, hurdle, fr. ON *flaki*; akin to OHG *flah* smooth, Gk *pelagos* sea, L *placēre* to please — more at PLEASE] **:** a stage, platform, or tray for drying fish or produce

2**flake** *n* [ME, of Scand origin; akin to Norw *flak* disk] **1 :** a small loose mass or bit **2 :** a thin flattened piece or layer **:** CHIP

3**flake** *vi* **:** to separate into flakes ~ *vt* **1 :** to form into flakes **:** CHIP **2 :** to cover with or as if with flakes — **flak·er** *n*

flak·i·ness \ˈflā-kē-nəs\ *n* **:** the quality or state of being flaky

flaky \ˈflā-kē\ *adj* **1 :** consisting of flakes **2 :** tending to flake

1**flam** \ˈflam\ *n* [prob. short for *flimflam*] **1 :** FALSEHOOD, TRICK **2 :** HUMBUG, NONSENSE — **flam** *vb* **flammed; flam·ming**

2**flam** *n* [prob. imit.] **:** a drumbeat of two strokes of which the first is a very quick grace note

flam·beau \ˈflam-ˌbō\ *n, pl* **flam·beaux** \-ˌbōz\ *or* **flambeaus** [F, fr. MF, fr. *flambe* flame] **:** a flaming torch; *broadly* **:** TORCH

flam·boy·ance \flam-ˈbȯi-ən(t)s\ *also* **flam·boy·an·cy** \-ən-sē\ *n* **:** the quality or state of being flamboyant

1**flam·boy·ant** \-ənt\ *adj* [F, fr. prp. of *flamboyer* to flame, fr. OF, fr. *flambe*] **1** *often cap* **:** characterized by waving curves suggesting flames ⟨~ window tracery⟩ **2 :** FLORID, ORNATE; *also* **:** RESPLENDENT **3 :** given to dashing display **:** SHOWY — **flam·boy·ant·ly** *adv*

2**flamboyant** *n* **:** ROYAL POINCIANA

1**flame** \ˈflām\ *n* [ME *flaume*, *flaumbe*, fr. MF *flamme* (fr. L *flamma*) & *flambe*, fr. OF, fr. *flamble*, fr. L *flammula*, dim. of *flamma* flame; akin to L *flagrare* to burn] **1 :** the glowing gaseous part of a fire **2 a :** a state of blazing combustion **b :** a condition or appearance suggesting a flame **c :** BRILLIANCE, LUMINESCENCE **3 :** burning zeal or passion **4 :** SWEETHEART **syn** see BLAZE

2**flame** *vi* **1 :** to burn with a flame **:** BLAZE **2 :** to burst or break out violently or passionately **3 :** to shine brightly **:** GLOW ~ *vt* **1 :** to send or convey by means of flame **2 :** to treat or affect with flame; *esp* **:** to cleanse, sterilize, or destroy by fire — **flam·er** *n*

flame cell *n* **:** a hollow cell with a tuft of vibratile cilia of the excretory system of various lower invertebrates

flame cultivator *n* **:** a flamethrower to destroy small weeds

fla·men \ˈflā-mən\ *n, pl* **flamens** *or* **flam·i·nes** \ˈflam-ə-ˌnēz\ [ME *flamin*, fr. L *flamin-*, *flamen*] **:** PRIEST; *esp* **:** a priest of a Roman god

fla·men·co \flə-'meŋ-(,)kō\ *n* [Sp, Flemish, like a gypsy, fr. MD *Vlaminc* Fleming] **:** a vigorous rhythmic dance style of the Andalusian gypsies

flame·out \'flā-,maůt\ *n* **:** the cessation of operation of a jet airplane engine

flame·proof \'flām-'prüf\ *adj* **1 :** resistant to the action of flame **2 :** not burning on contact with flame

flame·throw·er \-,thrō(-ə)r\ *n* **:** a device that expels from a nozzle a burning stream of liquid or semiliquid fuel under pressure

flame tree *n* **:** any of several trees or shrubs with showy scarlet or yellow flowers

flam·ing \'flā-miŋ\ *adj* **1 :** BLAZING **2 :** suggesting a flame in brilliance or wavy outline **3 :** ARDENT, PASSIONATE — **flam·ing·ly** \-miŋ-lē\ *adv*

fla·min·go \flə-'miŋ-(,)gō\ *n, pl* **flamingos** *also* **flamingoes** [obs. Sp *flamengo* (now *flamenco*), fr. MD *Vlaminc* Fleming] **:** any of several aquatic birds (family Phoenicopteridae) with long legs and neck, webbed feet, a broad lamellated bill resembling that of a duck but abruptly bent downward, and usu. rosy-white plumage with scarlet wing coverts and black wing quills

flam·ma·bil·i·ty \,flam-ə-'bil-ət-ē\ *n* **:** ability to support combustion; *esp* **:** a high capacity for combustion

flam·ma·ble \'flam-ə-bəl\ *adj* [L *flammare* to flame, set on fire, fr. *flamma*] **:** capable of being easily ignited and of burning with extreme rapidity — **flammable** *n*

flâ·ne·rie \,flän-(ə-)'rē\ *n* [F] **:** AIMLESSNESS, IDLENESS

fla·neur \flä-'nər\ *n* [F *flâneur* idler] **:** an aimless person: as **a :** MAN-ABOUT-TOWN **b :** TRIFLER

[1]**flange** \'flanj\ *n* [perh. alter. of *flanch* (a curving charge on a heraldic shield)] **:** a rib or rim for strength, for guiding, or for attachment to another object

[2]**flange** *vt* **:** to furnish with a flange — **flang·er** \'flan-jər\ *n*

[1]**flank** \'flaŋk\ *n* [ME, fr. OF *flanc*, of Gmc origin; akin to OHG *hlanca* loin, flank — more at LANK] **1 a :** the fleshy part of the side between the ribs and the hip; *broadly* **:** the side of a quadruped **b :** a cut of meat from this part of an animal **2 a :** SIDE **b :** the right or left of a formation

[2]**flank** *vt* **1 :** to protect a flank of **2 a :** to attack or threaten the flank of **b :** to turn the flank of **3 a :** to be situated at the side of **:** BORDER **b :** to place something on each side of — **flank·er** *n*

flan·nel \'flan-ᵊl\ *n, often attrib* [ME *flaunneol* woolen cloth or garment] **1 a :** a soft twilled wool or worsted fabric with a loose texture and a slightly napped surface **b :** a stout cotton fabric usu. napped on one side **2** *pl* **a :** flannel underwear **b :** outer garments of flannel; *esp* **:** men's trousers — **flan·nel·ly** \-ᵊl-ē\ *adj*

flan·nel·ette \,flan-ᵊl-'et\ *n* **:** a napped cotton flannel

[1]**flap** \'flap\ *n* [ME *flappe*] **1 :** a stroke with something broad **:** SLAP **2** *obs* **:** something broad and flat used for striking **3 :** something that is broad, limber, or flat and usu. thin and that hangs loose or projects freely: as **a :** a piece on a garment that hangs free **b :** a piece of tissue partly severed from its place of origin for use in surgical grafting **c :** an extended part forming the closure (as of an envelope) **d :** a movable auxiliary airfoil usu. attached to an airplane wing's trailing edge **4 :** the motion of something broad and limber **5 :** a state of excitement or panicky confusion

[2]**flap** *vb* **flapped; flap·ping** *vt* **1 :** to beat with or as if with a flap **2 :** to toss sharply **:** FLING **3 :** to move or cause to move in flaps ~ *vi* **1 :** to sway loosely usu. with a noise of striking and esp. when moved by wind **2 a :** to beat or pulsate wings or something suggesting wings **b :** to progress by flapping **3 :** to flutter ineffectively

flap·doo·dle \'flap-,düd-ᵊl\ *n* [origin unknown] **:** NONSENSE

flap·jack \-,jak\ *n* **:** GRIDDLE CAKE

flap·per \'flap-ər\ *n* **1 a :** one that flaps **b :** something used in flapping or striking **c :** FLIPPER 1 **2 :** a young woman; *esp* **:** one who shows bold freedom from conventions in conduct and dress

flap·py \'flap-ē\ *adj* **1 :** SLACK, FLABBY **2 :** FLAPPING

[1]**flare** \'fla(ə)r, 'fle(ə)r\ *vb* [origin unknown] *vi* **1 a :** to stream in the wind **b :** to burn with an unsteady flame **2 a :** to shine with a sudden light **b :** to become suddenly excited or angry ⟨~ up⟩ **3 :** to open or spread outward ~ *vt* **1 :** to display flaringly **2 :** to cause to flare **3 :** to signal with a flare or by flaring

[2]**flare** *n* **1 :** an unsteady glaring light **2 a :** a fire or blaze of light used to signal, illuminate, or attract attention; *also* **:** a device or composition used to produce such a flare **b :** a temporary outburst of energy from a small area of the sun's surface **3 :** a sudden outburst (as of sound, excitement, or anger) **4 :** a spreading outward; *also* **:** a place or part that spreads **5 :** light resulting from reflection (as between lens surfaces) or an effect of this light (as a fogged or dense area in a photographic negative) **syn** see BLAZE

flare·back \-,bak\ *n* **:** a burst of flame back or out (as from a furnace) in a direction opposite to that of normal operation

flare–up \-,əp\ *n* **1 :** a sudden bursting into flame or light **2 :** a sudden outburst or intensification

flar·ing *adj* **1 a :** flaming brightly or unsteadily **b :** GAUDY **2 :** opening or spreading outward — **flar·ing·ly** \-iŋ-lē\ *adv*

[1]**flash** \'flash\ *vb* [ME *flaschen*, of imit. origin] *vi* **1 :** RUSH, DASH — used of flowing water **2 :** to break forth in or like a sudden flame or flare **3 a :** to appear suddenly **b :** to move with great speed **4 a :** to break forth or out so as to make a sudden display **b :** to act or speak vehemently and suddenly esp. in anger **5 :** to gleam or glow intermittently ~ *vt* **1 a** *archaic* **:** SPLASH **b :** to fill by a sudden inflow of water **2 a :** to cause the sudden appearance of (light) **b :** to cause to burst violently into flame; *also* **:** to burn for determining character of residue **c** (1) **:** to cause (light) to reflect (2) **:** to cause (as a mirror) to reflect light **d :** to convey by means of flashes of light **3 a :** to make known or cause to appear with great speed **b :** to show off **c :** to expose to view suddenly and briefly **4 :** to cover with or form into a thin layer: as **a :** to protect against rain by covering with sheet metal or a substitute **b :** to coat with a thin layer **5 :** to subject to exposure to light before development in order to modify detail or tone — **flash·er** *n*

syn FLASH, GLEAM, GLANCE, GLINT, SPARKLE, GLITTER, GLISTEN, GLIMMER, SHIMMER mean to send forth light. FLASH implies a sudden and transient outburst of bright light; GLEAM suggests a steady light seen through an obscuring medium or against a dark background; GLANCE suggests a bright darting light reflected from a quickly moving surface; GLINT implies a cold-glancing light; SPARKLE suggests innumerable moving points of bright light; GLITTER connotes a brilliant sparkling or gleaming, but often connotes a cold or menacing quality; GLISTEN applies to the soft sparkle from a wet or oily surface; GLIMMER suggests a faint, or wavering gleam; SHIMMER implies a soft tremulous gleaming or a blurred reflection

[2]**flash** *n* **1 a :** a sudden burst of light **b :** a movement of a flag in signaling **2 :** a sudden and brilliant burst (as of wit) **3 :** a brief time **4 a :** SHOW, DISPLAY; *esp* **:** a vulgar ostentatious display **b** *archaic* **:** a showy ostentatious person **c :** one that attracts notice; *esp* **:** an outstanding athlete **5** *obs* **:** thieves' slang **6 :** a rush of water released to permit passage of a boat **7 :** something flashed: as **a :** GLIMPSE, LOOK **b :** SMILE **c :** a first brief news report **d :** FLASHLIGHT 2,3 **e :** a quick-spreading flame or momentary intense outburst of radiant heat

[3]**flash** *adj* **1 a :** FLASHY, SHOWY **b :** SPORTY, FAST **c :** of, relating to, or characteristic of persons considered social outcasts ⟨~ language⟩ **2 :** of sudden origin and short duration

flash·back \'flash-,bak\ *n* **1 :** interruption of chronological sequence in a literary or theatrical work by interjection of events of earlier occurrence **2 :** a recession of flame to an unwanted position (as into a blowpipe)

flash·board \-,bō(ə)rd, -,bȯ(ə)rd\ *n* **:** one or more boards projecting above the top of a dam to increase the depth of the water

flash·bulb \-,bəlb\ *n* **:** an electric flash lamp in which metal foil or wire is burned

flash card *n* **:** a card bearing words, numbers, or pictures briefly displayed (as by a teacher to a class during reading drills)

flash·cube \'flash-,kyüb\ *n* **:** a cubical device that incorporates four flashbulbs and is attached to a camera

flash flood *n* **:** a local flood of great volume and short duration generally resulting from heavy rainfall in the immediate vicinity — **flash·flood** \'flash-'fləd\ *vt*

flash·gun \-,gən\ *n* **1 :** a device for holding and igniting flashlight powder **2 :** a device for holding and operating a flashbulb

flash·i·ly \'flash-ə-lē\ *adv* **:** in a flashy manner or style

flash·i·ness \'flash-ē-nəs\ *n* **:** the quality or state of being flashy

flash·ing *n* **:** sheet metal used in waterproofing roof valleys or hips or the angle between a chimney and a roof

flash lamp *n* **:** a usu. electric lamp for producing a brief but intense flash of light for taking photographs

flash·light \'flash-,līt\ *n* **1 :** a flash of light or a light that flashes; *esp* **:** a scintillating light or a light of regularly varying brightness in a lighthouse **2 a :** a sudden bright artificial light used in taking photographic pictures **b :** a photograph taken by such a light **3 :** a small battery-operated portable electric light

flash·over \'flash-,ō-vər\ *n* **:** an abnormal electrical discharge (as through the air to the ground from a high potential source)

flash point \-,pȯint\ *n* **:** the lowest temperature at which vapors above a volatile combustible substance ignite in air when exposed to flame

flash·tube \'flash-,t(y)üb\ *n* **:** STROBOTRON

flashy \'flash-ē\ *adj* **1 :** INSIPID **2 :** momentarily dazzling **3 a :** superficially attractive **:** BRIGHT **b :** SHOWY **syn** see GAUDY

flask \'flask\ *n, often attrib* [MF *flasque* powder flask, deriv. of LL *flascon-, flasco* bottle, prob. of Gmc origin; akin to OHG *flaska* bottle] **1 :** a container often somewhat narrowed toward the outlet and often fitted with a closure; *esp* **:** a broad flattened necked vessel used esp. to carry alcoholic beverages on the person **2 :** a frame that holds molding sand used in a foundry

[1]**flat** \'flat\ *adj* **flat·ter; flat·test** [ME, fr. ON *flatr;* akin to OHG *flaz* flat, Gk *platys* — more at PLACE] **1 :** having a continuous horizontal surface **2 a :** lying at full length or spread out upon the ground **:** PROSTRATE **b :** resting with a surface against something **3 :** having a relatively smooth or even surface **4 :** arranged or laid out so as to be level or even **5 :** having the major surfaces essentially parallel and distinctly greater than the minor surfaces ⟨a ~ piece of wood⟩ **6 a :** clearly unmistakable **:** DOWNRIGHT **b :** ABSOLUTE, FIXED; *also* **:** EXACT, PRECISE **7 a :** lacking in animation, zest, or vigor **:** DULL **b :** lacking savor **:** INSIPID **c :** DEFLATED — used of tires **8 a :** lower than the proper pitch **b** (1) **:** lower by a half step ⟨tone of A ~⟩ (2) **:** having a flat in the signature ⟨the key of B ~⟩ **c** *of the vowel a* **:** pronounced as in *bad* or *bat* **9 :** having a low trajectory **10 :** not having an inflectional ending or sign — used esp. of an infinitive without the sign *to* or of an adverb with no adverbial ending **11** *of a sail* **:** TAUT **12 a :** uniform in hue or shade **b** *of a painting* **:** having little or no illusion of depth **c** *of a photograph or negative* **:** lacking contrast **d** *of a photographic lighting arrangement* **:** not emphasizing shadows or contours **e :** free from gloss **syn** see INSIPID, LEVEL — **flat·ly** *adv* — **flat·ness** *n*

[2]**flat** *n* **1 :** a level surface of land with little or no relief **:** PLAIN **2 :** a flat part or surface **3 a :** a musical note or tone one half step lower than a specified note or tone **b :** a character ♭ on a line or space of the musical staff indicating a half step drop in pitch **4 :** something flat: as **a :** a shallow box in which seedlings are started **b :** a flat-bottomed boat **c :** a flat piece of theatrical scenery **d :** a shoe or slipper having a flat heel or no heel **5 :** a deflated tire

[3]**flat** *adv* **1 :** in a flat manner **:** FLATLY: as **a :** on or against a flat surface **b :** at full length **c :** DIRECTLY **d :** COMPLETELY **e :** below the proper musical pitch **2 :** without interest charge

[4]**flat** *vb* **flat·ted; flat·ting** *vt* **1 :** FLATTEN **2 :** to lower in pitch esp. by a half step ~ *vi* **:** to sing or play below the true pitch

[5]**flat** *n* **1 :** a floor or story in a building **2 :** an apartment on one floor

[1]**flat·bed** \,flat-,bed\ *adj* **:** having a horizontal bed on which a horizontal printing surface rests

[2]**flat·bed** \'flat-,\ *n* **:** a motortruck or trailer with a body in the form of a platform or shallow box

flat·boat \'flat-,bōt\ *n* **:** a boat with a flat bottom and square ends used for transportation of bulky freight esp. in shallow waters

flat·cap \-,kap\ *n* **1 :** a round low-crowned cap worn in 16th and 17th century London **2 :** a wearer of a flatcap; *esp* **:** a Londoner

flat·car \-,kär\ *n* **:** a railroad freight car without permanent raised sides, ends, or covering

flat·fish \-,fish\ *n* **:** any of an order (Heterosomata) of marine teleost fishes (as the halibuts, flounders, turbots, and soles) that as adults swim on one side of the laterally compressed body and have both eyes on the upper side

flat·foot \-,fu̇t (*always so in sense 3*), -'fu̇t\ *n, pl* **flat·feet** **1 :** a condition in which the arch of the instep is flattened so that the entire

sole rests upon the ground **2 :** a foot affected with flatfoot **3 :** a person having or held likely to have flatfeet: as **a** *or pl* **flatfoots** *slang* **:** POLICEMAN; *esp* **:** a patrolman walking a regular beat **b** *slang* **:** SAILOR

¹**flat–foot·ed** \ˈflat-ˈfu̇t-əd\ *adj* **1 :** affected with flatfoot; *broadly* **:** walking with a dragging or shambling gait **2 a :** firm and well balanced on the feet **b :** DETERMINED, FORTHRIGHT **3 :** UNREADY — **flat–foot·ed·ly** *adv* — **flat–foot·ed·ness** *n*

²**flat–footed** *adv* **:** in an open and determined manner **:** FLATLY

flat–hat \ˈflat-ˌhat\ *vi* [fr. an alleged incident in which a pedestrian's hat was crushed by a low-flying plane] **:** to fly low in an airplane in a reckless manner **:** HEDGEHOP — **flat–hat·ter** *n*

Flat·head \ˈflat-ˌhed\ *n, pl* **Flatheads** *or* **Flathead 1 :** a member of any of several Indian peoples of No. America that formerly practiced head-flattening **2 :** a member of a Salishan people of western Montana **3** *not cap* **:** any of various fishes with more or less flat heads

flat·iron \ˈflat-ˌī(-ə)rn\ *n* **:** an iron for ironing clothes

flat knot *n* **:** REEF KNOT

flat·ling \ˈflat-liŋ\ *or* **flat·lings** \-liŋz\ *adv, dial Brit* **:** with a flat side or edge

flat silver *n* **:** eating or serving utensils made of or plated with silver

flat·ten \ˈflat-ᵊn\ *vb* **flat·ten·ing** \ˈflat-niŋ, -ᵊn-iŋ\ *vt* **1 :** to make flat: as **a :** LEVEL, SMOOTH **b :** to lay low **:** RUIN **2 :** to make (as paint) lusterless ~ *vi* **1 :** to become flat or flatter **2 a :** to manipulate an airplane so as to bring its longitudinal axis parallel with the ground — used with *out* **b** *of an airplane* **:** to assume such a position — **flat·ten·er** \ˈflat-nər, -ᵊn-ər\ *n*

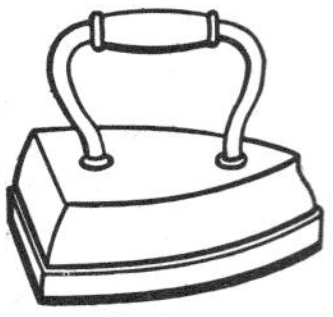

flatiron

¹**flat·ter** \ˈflat-ər\ *vb* [ME *flateren,* fr. OF *flater* to lick, flatter, of Gmc origin; akin to OHG *flaz* flat] *vt* **1 :** to praise excessively esp. from motives of self-interest **2 a** *archaic* **:** to make more pleasant **:** BEGUILE **b :** to raise the hope of or gratify esp. by false or specious representations **3 a :** to portray too favorably **b :** to display to advantage ~ *vi* **:** to use flattery — **flat·ter·er** \-ər-ər\ *n* — **flat·ter·ing·ly** \-ə-riŋ-lē\ *adv*

²**flatter** *n* **:** one that flattens: as **a :** a drawplate with a narrow rectangular orifice for drawing flat strips **b :** a flat-faced swage used in smithing

flat·tery \ˈflat-ə-rē\ *n* **1 a :** the act or practice of flattering **b** (1) **:** something that flatters (2) **:** insincere or excessive praise **2** *obs* **:** a pleasing self-deception

flat·top \ˈflat-ˌtäp\ *n* **:** something with a flat or flattened upper surface; *esp* **:** AIRCRAFT CARRIER

flat·u·lence \ˈflach-ə-lən(t)s\ *also* **flat·u·len·cy** \-lən-sē\ *n* **:** the quality or state of being flatulent

flat·u·lent \-lənt\ *adj* [MF, fr. L *flatus* act of blowing, wind, fr. *flatus,* pp. of *flare* to blow — more at BLOW] **1 a :** marked by or affected with gases generated in the intestine or stomach **b :** likely to cause digestive flatulence **2 :** pretentious without real worth or substance **:** TURGID **syn** see INFLATED — **flat·u·lent·ly** *adv*

fla·tus \ˈflāt-əs\ *n* [L] **:** gas generated in the stomach or bowels

flat·ware \ˈflat-ˌwa(ə)r, -ˌwe(ə)r\ *n* **:** tableware more or less flat and usu. formed or cast in a single piece; *esp* **:** FLAT SILVER

flat·wise \-ˌwīz\ *or* **flat·ways** \-ˌwāz\ *adv* **:** with the flat side downward or next to another object

flat·work \-ˌwərk\ *n* **:** articles that in laundering can be finished mechanically as distinguished from those requiring hand ironing

flat·worm \-ˌwərm\ *n* **:** PLATYHELMINTH; *esp* **:** TURBELLARIAN

flaunt \ˈflȯnt, ˈflänt\ *vb* [prob. of Scand origin; akin to ON *flana* to rush around — more at PLANET] *vi* **1 :** to wave or flutter showily **2 :** to display or obtrude oneself to public notice ~ *vt* **:** to display ostentatiously or impudently **:** PARADE **syn** see SHOW — **flaunt** *n* — **flaunt·ing·ly** \-iŋ-lē\ *adv* — **flaunty** \ˈflȯnt-ē, ˈflänt-\ *adj*

flau·tist \ˈflȯt-əst, ˈflau̇t-\ *n* [It *flautista,* fr. *flauto* flute, fr. OProv *flaut*] **:** FLUTIST

fla·va·none \ˈflāv-ə-ˌnōn\ *n* [L *flavus* + ISV *-ane* + *-one*] **:** a colorless crystalline ketone $C_{15}H_{12}O_2$; *also* **:** any of the derivatives of this ketone many of which occur in plants often in the form of glycosides

fla·vin \ˈflā-vən\ *n* [ISV, fr. L *flavus* yellow — more at BLUE] **:** a yellow water-soluble nitrogenous pigment derived from isoalloxazine and occurring in the form of nucleotides as coenzymes of flavoproteins; *esp* **:** RIBOFLAVIN

fla·vine \ˈflā-ˌvēn\ *n* [ISV, fr. L *flavus*] **:** a yellow acridine dye (as acriflavine) often used medicinally for its antiseptic properties

fla·vone \ˈflā-ˌvōn\ *n* [ISV, fr. L *flavus*] **:** a colorless crystalline ketone $C_{15}H_{10}O_2$ found on the leaves, stems, and seed capsules of many primroses; *also* **:** any of the derivatives of this ketone many of which occur as yellow plant pigments in the form of glycosides — **fla·vo·noid** \ˈflā-və-ˌnȯid\ *adj or n*

fla·vo·nol \ˈflā-və-ˌnȯl, -ˌnōl\ *n* **:** any of various hydroxy derivatives of flavone

fla·vo·pro·tein \ˌflā-ˌvō-ˈprō-ˌtēn, -ˈprōt-ē-ən\ *n* [ISV *flav*in + *-o-* + *protein*] **:** a dehydrogenase that contains a flavin and often a metal and plays a major role in biological oxidations

¹**fla·vor** *or chiefly Brit* **fla·vour** \ˈflā-vər\ *n* [ME, fr. MF *flaor, flavor,* fr. (assumed) VL *flator,* fr. L *flare* to blow] **1 a** *archaic* **:** ODOR, FRAGRANCE **b :** the quality of something that affects the sense of taste **:** SAVOR **c :** the blend of taste and smell sensations evoked by a substance in the mouth **2 :** a substance that flavors **3 :** characteristic or predominant quality **syn** see TASTE — **fla·vored** \-vərd\ *adj*

²**flavor** *or chiefly Brit* **flavour** *vt* **fla·vor·ing** \ˈflāv-(ə-)riŋ\ **:** to give or add flavor to

fla·vor·ful \ˈflā-vər-fəl\ *adj* **:** full of flavor **:** SAVORY — **fla·vor·ful·ly** \-fə-lē\ *adv*

fla·vor·ing *n* **:** FLAVOR 2

fla·vor·less \ˈflā-vər-ləs\ *adj* **:** lacking in flavor **:** FLAT ⟨~ platitudes⟩

fla·vor·some \-səm\ *adj* **:** FLAVORFUL

¹**flaw** \ˈflȯ\ *n* [ME, prob. of Scand origin; akin to Sw *flaga* flake, flaw; akin to OE *flēan* to flay] **1** *obs* **:** FRAGMENT **2 :** a faulty part **:** CRACK **3 :** FAULT, DEFECT; *esp* **:** a fault in a legal paper that may nullify it **syn** see BLEMISH — **flaw·less** \-ləs\ *adj* — **flaw·less·ly** *adv* — **flaw·less·ness** *n*

²**flaw** *vt* **:** to make flaws in **:** CRACK ~ *vi* **:** to become defective

³**flaw** *n* [of Scand origin; akin to Norw *flaga* gust; akin to L *plangere* to beat — more at PLAINT] **1 :** a sudden brief burst of wind; *also* **:** a spell of stormy weather **2** *obs* **:** an outburst esp. of passion

flax \ˈflaks\ *n, often attrib* [ME, fr. OE *fleax;* akin to OHG *flahs* flax, L *plectere* to braid] **1 :** any of a genus (*Linum* of the family Linaceae, the flax family) of herbs; *esp* **:** a slender erect annual (*L. usitatissimum*) with blue flowers commonly cultivated for its bast fiber and seed **2 :** the fiber of the flax plant esp. when prepared for spinning **3 :** any of several plants resembling flax

flax·en \ˈflak-sən\ *adj* **1 :** made of flax **2 :** resembling flax esp. in pale soft strawy color

flax·seed \ˈflak-ˌsēd\ *n* **:** the seed of flax used as a source of oil and medicinally as a demulcent and emollient

flaxy \ˈflak-sē\ *adj* **:** resembling flax esp. in texture **:** FLAXEN

flay \ˈflā\ *vt* [ME *flen,* fr. OE *flēan;* akin to ON *flā* to flay, Lith *plėšti* to tear] **1 :** to strip off the skin or surface of **:** SKIN **2 a :** to strip of possessions **:** FLEECE **b :** to criticize harshly **:** EXCORIATE

F layer *n* **1 :** the highest and most densely ionized regular layer of the ionosphere occurring at night within the F region **2 :** the forest soil zone marked by abundant plant remains undergoing decay

flea \ˈflē\ *n* [ME *fle,* fr. OE *flēa;* akin to OHG *flōh* flea] **1 :** any of an order (Siphonaptera) of wingless bloodsucking insects that have a hard laterally compressed body and legs adapted to leaping and feed on warm-blooded animals **2 :** FLEA BEETLE — **flea in one's ear :** an irritating hint or warning **:** REBUKE

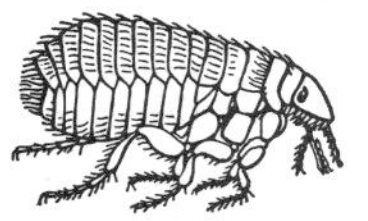

dog flea

flea·bane \-ˌbān\ *n* **:** any of various composite plants (as of the genera *Erigeron* and *Artemisia*) supposed to drive away fleas

flea beetle *n* **:** any of various small beetles (as of the genera *Altica* and *Epitrix*) with legs adapted for leaping that feed on foliage and sometimes serve as vectors of virus diseases of plants

flea·bite \ˈflē-ˌbīt\ *n* **1 :** the bite of a flea; *also* **:** the red spot caused by such a bite **2 :** a trifling pain or annoyance

flea–bit·ten \-ˌbit-ᵊn\ *adj* **1 :** bitten by or infested with fleas **2** *of a horse* **:** having a white or gray coat flecked with bay or sorrel

flea·hop·per \-ˌhäp-ər\ *n* **:** any of various small jumping bugs that feed on cultivated plants

flea market *n* **:** a street market for cheap or secondhand articles

flea weevil *n* **:** any of various small broad weevils with legs adapted for leaping and with larvae that are leaf miners

flea·wort \ˈflē-ˌwərt, -ˌwȯ(ə)rt\ *n* **:** an Old World plantain (*Plantago psyllium*) whose seeds swell and become gelatinous when moist

flèche \ˈflāsh, ˈflesh\ *n* [F, lit., arrow] **:** SPIRE; *esp* **:** a slender spire above the intersection of the nave and transepts of a church

¹**fleck** \ˈflek\ *vt* [back-formation fr. *flecked* spotted, fr. ME, prob. fr. ON *flekkōttr,* fr. *flekkr* spot] **:** STREAK, SPOT

²**fleck** *n* **1 :** SPOT, MARK **2 :** FLAKE, PARTICLE

flec·tion \ˈflek-shən\ *n* [alter. of *flexion,* fr. L *flexion-, flexio,* fr. *flexus,* pp. of *flectere* to bend] **1 :** the act of flexing or bending **2 :** a part bent **:** BEND **3 :** INFLECTION 3 **4** *usu* **flex·ion a :** a bending of a joint between the bones of a limb by which the angle between the bones is diminished **b :** a forward raising of the arm or leg by a movement at the shoulder or hip joint — **flec·tion·al** \-shnəl, -shən-ᵊl\ *adj*

fledge \ˈflej\ *vb* [*fledge* (capable of flying), fr. ME *flegge,* fr. OE *-flycge;* akin to OHG *flucki* capable of flying, OE *flēogan* to fly] *vi* **1** *of a bird* **:** to acquire the feathers necessary for flight **2** *of an insect* **:** to attain the winged adult stage ~ *vt* **1 :** to rear until ready for flight or independent activity **2 :** to cover with or as if with feathers or down **3 :** to furnish with feathers

fledg·ling \ˈflej-liŋ\ *n* **1 :** a young bird just fledged **2 :** an immature or inexperienced person

flee \ˈflē\ *vb* **fled** \ˈfled\ **flee·ing** [ME *flen,* fr. OE *flēon;* akin to OHG *fliohan* to flee] *vi* **1 :** to run away from danger or evil **:** FLY **2 :** to pass away swiftly **:** VANISH ~ *vt* **:** to run away from **:** SHUN

¹**fleece** \ˈflēs\ *n* [ME *flees,* fr. OE *flēos;* akin to MHG *vlius* fleece, L *pluma* feather, down] **1 a :** the coat of wool covering a sheep or similar animal **b :** the quantity of wool shorn at one time **2 a :** any of various soft or woolly coverings **b :** a soft bulky deep-piled knitted or woven fabric used chiefly for clothing

²**fleece** *vt* **1 :** to remove the fleece from **:** SHEAR **2 :** to strip of money or property by fraud or extortion **3 :** to dot or cover with fleecy masses

fleeced \ˈflēst\ *adj* **1 :** covered with or as if with a fleece **2** *of a textile* **:** having a soft nap

fleech \ˈflēch\ *vb* [ME (Sc) *flechen*] *dial* **:** COAX, WHEEDLE

fleecy \ˈflē-sē\ *adj* **:** covered with, made of, or resembling fleece

¹**fleer** \ˈfli(ə)r\ *vi* [ME *fleryen,* of Scand origin; akin to Norw *flire* to giggle — more at FLIMFLAM] **:** to laugh or grimace in a coarse manner **:** SNEER **syn** see SCOFF — **fleer·ing·ly** \-iŋ-lē\ *adv*

²**fleer** *n* **:** a word or look of derision or mockery

¹**fleet** \ˈflēt\ *vb* [ME *fleten,* fr. OE *flēotan;* akin to OHG *fliozzan* to float, OE *flōwan* to flow] *vi* **1** *dial Brit* **:** FLOAT **2** *obs* **:** DRIFT **3 a** *archaic* **:** FLOW **b :** to fade away **:** VANISH **4 :** to fly swiftly **:** FLIT ~ *vt* **1 :** to cause (time) to pass **2** [alter. of *flit*] **:** to move or change in position ⟨~ a hawser⟩ **syn** see WHILE

²**fleet** *n* [ME *flete,* fr. OE *flēot* estuary, river; akin to MHG *vliez* river, OE *flēotan* to float] *dial Eng* **:** a shallow inlet **:** CREEK

³**fleet** *n* [ME *flete,* fr. OE *flēot* ship, fr. *flēotan*] **1 :** a number of warships under a single command **2 :** a group (as of ships, planes, or trucks) operated under unified control

⁴**fleet** *adj* [prob. fr. ¹*fleet*] **1 :** swift in motion **:** NIMBLE **2 :** EVANESCENT, FLEETING **syn** see FAST — **fleet·ly** *adv* — **fleet·ness** *n*

fleet admiral *n* **:** an admiral of the highest rank whose insignia is five stars

fleet·ing *adj* **:** passing swiftly **:** TRANSITORY **syn** see TRANSIENT — **fleet·ing·ly** \-iŋ-lē\ *adv* — **fleet·ing·ness** *n*

Fleet Street \ˈflēt-\ *n* [*Fleet Street,* London, England, center of the London newspaper district] **:** the London press

Flem·ing \ˈflem-iŋ\ *n* [ME, fr. MD *Vlaminc,* fr. *Vlam-* (as in *Vlamland* Flanders)] **:** a member of the Germanic people inhabiting northern Belgium and the Nord department of France

¹**Flem·ish** \ˈflem-ish\ *adj* **:** of, relating to, or characteristic of Flanders or the Flemings or their language

²**Flemish** *n* **1 :** the Germanic language of the Flemings **2** *pl* **:** FLEMINGS **3 :** a rabbit of a breed prob. of Belgian origin that is characterized by large size, vigor, and solid coat color in black, white, or gray — called also *Flemish giant*

flense \ˈflen(t)s\ *vt* [D *flensen* or Dan & Norw *flense*] **:** to strip (as a whale) of blubber or skin

[1]**flesh** \'flesh\ *n, often attrib* [ME, fr. OE *flǣsc;* akin to OHG *fleisk* flesh] **1 a :** the soft parts of the body of an animal and esp. of a vertebrate; *esp* **:** the parts composed chiefly of skeletal muscle as distinguished from visceral structures, bone, and integuments **b :** sleek well-fatted condition of body **c :** SKIN **2 a :** edible parts of an animal **b :** flesh of a mammal or bird that is an article of diet **3 a :** the physical being of man **b :** human nature **4 a :** human beings **b :** living beings **c :** STOCK, KINDRED **5 :** a fleshy plant part used as food; *also* **:** the fleshy part of a fruit **6** *Christian Science* **:** an illusion that matter has sensation — **fleshed** \'flesht\ *adj*

[2]**flesh** *vt* **1 a :** to feed (as a hawk) with flesh from the kill to encourage interest in the chase **b :** to initiate or habituate esp. by giving a foretaste **2** *archaic* **:** GRATIFY **3 :** to clothe or cover with or as if with flesh; *broadly* **:** to give substance to **4 :** to free from flesh ∼ *vi* **:** to become fleshy — often used with *up* or *out*

flesh fly *n* **:** a two-winged fly whose maggots feed on flesh

flesh·i·ness \'flesh-ē-nəs\ *n* **:** the state of being fleshy **:** CORPULENCE

flesh·ing \'flesh-iŋ\ *n* **1** *pl* **:** close-fitting usu. flesh-colored tights **2** *pl* **:** material removed in fleshing a hide or skin **3 a :** the distribution of the lean and fat on an animal **b :** the capacity of an animal to put on fat

flesh·ly \'flesh-lē\ *adj* **1 a :** CORPOREAL, BODILY **b :** CARNAL, SENSUAL; *esp* **:** LASCIVIOUS **c :** not spiritual **:** WORLDLY **2 :** FLESHY, PLUMP **3 :** SENSUOUS **syn** see CARNAL

flesh·ment \'flesh-mənt\ *n* [[2]*flesh*] *obs* **:** excitement attending a successful beginning

flesh·pots \'flesh-,päts\ *n pl* **1 :** bodily comfort **2 :** a place of luxurious entertainment

fleshy \'flesh-ē\ *adj* **1 a :** marked by, consisting of, or resembling flesh **b :** marked by abundant flesh; *esp* **:** CORPULENT **2 a :** SUCCULENT, PULPY **b :** not thin, dry, or membranaceous

fletch \'flech\ *vt* [back-formation fr. *fletcher*] **:** FEATHER

fletch·er \'flech-ər\ *n* [ME *flecchere*, fr. OF *flechier*, fr. *fleche* arrow] **:** a maker of arrows

Fletch·er·ism \'flech-ə-,riz-əm\ *n* [Horace *Fletcher* †1919 Am nutritionist] **:** the practice of eating in small amounts and only when hungry and of chewing one's food thoroughly

fleur–de–lis *or* **fleur–de–lys** \,flərd-ᵊl-'ē, ,flu̇rd-\ *n, pl* **fleurs–de–lis** *or* **fleur–de–lis** *or* **fleurs–de–lys** *or* **fleur–de–lys** \,flərd-ᵊl-'ē(z), ,flu̇rd-\ [ME *flourdelis*, fr. MF *flor de lis*, lit., lily flower] **1 :** IRIS 3 **2 :** a conventionalized iris in art and heraldry

fleur-de-lis 2

fleu·ry \'flu̇(ə)r-ē\ *adj* [alter. of ME *flory*, fr. OF *floré*, fr. *flor* flower — more at FLOWER] *of a heraldic cross* **:** having the ends of the arms broadening out into the heads of fleurs-de-lis — see CROSS illustration

flew *past of* FLY

flews \'flüz\ *n pl* [origin unknown] **:** the pendulous lateral parts of a dog's upper lip

[1]**flex** \'fleks\ *vb* [L *flexus*, pp. of *flectere*] *vt* **1 :** to bend esp. repeatedly **2 :** to cause flexion of ∼ *vi* **:** BEND

[2]**flex** *n* **1 :** an act or instance of flexing **2** [short for *flexible cord*] *chiefly Brit* **:** electric cord

flex·i·bil·i·ty \,flek-sə-'bil-ət-ē\ *n* **:** flexible quality or state

flex·i·ble \'flek-sə-bəl\ *adj* **1 :** capable of being flexed **:** PLIANT **2 :** yielding to influence **:** TRACTABLE **3 :** capable of responding or conforming to changing or new situations **syn** see ELASTIC — **flex·i·bly** \-blē\ *adv*

flex·ile \'flek-səl, -,sīl\ *adj* **:** FLEXIBLE

flexion *var of* FLECTION

flex·or \'flek-sər\ *n* **:** a muscle that produces flexion

flex·u·os·i·ty \,flek-shə-'wäs-ət-ē\ *n* **1 :** the quality or state of being flexuous **2 :** a winding part

flex·u·ous \'fleksh-(ə-)wəs\ *adj* [L *flexuosus*, fr. *flexus* bend, fr. *flexus*, pp.] **:** having turns or windings — **flex·u·ous·ly** *adv*

flex·ur·al \'flek-sh(ə-)rəl\ *adj* **1 :** of, relating to, or resulting from flexure **2 :** characterized by flexure

flex·ure \'flek-shər\ *n* **1 :** the quality or state of being flexed **:** FLECTION **2 :** TURN, FOLD

fley \'flā\ *vt* [ME *flayen*, fr. OE *āflēgan*, fr. *ā-*, perfective prefix + *-flēgan* to put to flight] *Scot* **:** FRIGHTEN

flib·ber·ti·gib·bet \,flib-ərt-ē-'jib-ət\ *n* [ME *flepergebet*] **:** a silly restless person — **flib·ber·ti·gib·bety** \-ət-ē\ *adj*

flic \'flēk\ *n* [F] **:** a Parisian policeman

[1]**flick** \'flik\ *n* [imit.] **1 :** a light sharp jerky stroke or movement **2 :** a sound produced by a flick **3 :** DAUB, SPLOTCH

[2]**flick** *vt* **1 a :** to strike lightly with a quick sharp motion **b :** to remove with light blows **2 :** to cause to move with a flick ∼ *vi* **1 :** FLUTTER **2 :** to direct flicks at something

[3]**flick** *n* [short for [2]*flicker*] **:** MOVIE — usu. used in pl.

[1]**flick·er** \'flik-ər\ *vb* **flick·er·ing** \-(ə-)riŋ\ [ME *flikeren*, fr. OE *flicorian*] *vi* **1 a :** to waver unsteadily **:** FLUTTER **b :** to move in a quick glancing manner **2 :** to burn fitfully or with a fluctuating light **3 :** to appear in a tremulous incomplete form ∼ *vt* **1 :** to cause to flicker **2 :** to produce by flickering

[2]**flicker** *n* **1 a :** an act of flickering **b :** a sudden brief movement **c :** a momentary quickening **2 :** a wavering light **3 :** MOVIE — often used in pl. — **flick·ery** \'flik-(ə-)rē\ *adj*

[3]**flicker** *n* [prob. fr. [2]*flick*] **:** a common large brightly marked woodpecker (*Colaptes auratus*) of eastern No. America; *also* **:** any of several related birds of the southern and western U.S.

flick·er·tail \'flik-ər-,tāl\ *n* **:** a ground squirrel (*Citellus richardsoni*) chiefly of the north-central U.S. and adjacent Canada

fli·er *or* **fly·er** \'flī(-ə)r\ *n* **1 :** one that flies; *specif* **:** AIRMAN **2 :** a reckless or speculative venture **3 :** an advertising circular for mass distribution **4 :** a step in a straight flight of steps

[1]**flight** \'flīt\ *n* [ME, fr. OE *flyht;* akin to MD *vlucht* flight, OE *flēogan* to fly] **1 a :** an act or instance of passing through the air by the use of wings **b :** the ability to fly **2 a :** a passing through the air or through space outside the earth's atmosphere **b :** the distance covered in such a flight **c :** swift movement **3 a :** a trip made by or in an airplane **b :** an airplane making a scheduled flight **4 :** a group of similar beings or objects flying through the air together **5 :** a brilliant, imaginative, or unrestrained exercise or display **6 :** a continuous series of stairs from one landing or floor to another **7 :** a unit of the U. S. Air Force below a squadron — **flight·less** \-ləs\ *adj*

[2]**flight** *vi* **:** to rise, settle, or fly in a flock ∼ *vt* **:** [1]FLUSH

[3]**flight** *n* [ME *fluht, fliht;* akin to OHG *fluht* flight, OE *flēon* to flee] **1 :** an act or instance of running away **2 :** withdrawal or transfer of capital to avoid loss

flight control *n* **1 :** the control from a ground station of an airplane esp. by radio **2 :** system of control devices of an airplane

flight deck *n* **1 :** the uppermost complete deck of an aircraft carrier **2 :** the forward compartment in some airplanes

flight engineer *n* **:** a flight crewman responsible for mechanical operation

flight feather *n* **:** one of the quills of a bird's wing or tail that support it in flight — compare CONTOUR FEATHER

flight·i·ness \'flīt-ē-nəs\ *n* **:** the quality or state of being flighty **syn** see LIGHTNESS

flight line *n* **:** a parking and servicing area for airplanes

flight path *n* **:** the path of the center of gravity of an airplane in flight

flight pay *n* **:** an additional allowance paid to military personnel on flight status

flight status *n* **:** the status of a person in the military participating in regular authorized aircraft flights

flight strip *n* **:** an emergency landing field beside a highway

flight surgeon *n* **:** an air force medical officer trained in aeromedicine

flight–test \'flīt-,test\ *vt* **:** to test (an airplane) in flight

flighty \'flīt-ē\ *adj* **1 :** SWIFT **2** *archaic* **:** WHIMSICAL **3 a :** easily excited **:** SKITTISH **b :** lacking stability **:** IRRESPONSIBLE **c :** SILLY

[1]**flim·flam** \'flim-,flam\ *n* [prob. of Scand origin; akin to ON *flim* mockery] **1 :** DECEPTION, FRAUD **2 :** HANKY-PANKY

[2]**flimflam** *vt* **:** to subject to a flimflam — **flim·flam·mer** *n*

flim·si·ly \'flim-zə-lē\ *adv* **:** in a flimsy manner

flim·si·ness \-zē-nəs\ *n* **:** the quality or state of being flimsy

[1]**flim·sy** \'flim-zē\ *adj* [perh. alter. of [1]*film* + *-sy* (as in *tricksy*)] **1 a :** lacking strength or substance **b :** of inferior materials and workmanship **2 :** having little worth or plausibility **syn** see LIMP

[2]**flimsy** *n* **1 :** a lightweight paper used esp. for multiple copies **2 :** a document printed on flimsy

flinch \'flinch\ *vi* [MF *flenchir* to bend] **:** to shrink from or as if from physical pain **:** WINCE; *specif* **:** to tense the muscles involuntarily in fear **syn** see RECOIL — **flinch** *n* — **flinch·er** *n*

flin·ders \'flin-dərz\ *n pl* [ME *flendris*] **:** SPLINTERS, FRAGMENTS

[1]**fling** \'fliŋ\ *vb* **flung** \'fləŋ\ **fling·ing** [ME *flingen*, of Scand origin; akin to ON *flengja* to whip, *flā* to flay — more at FLAY] *vi* **1 :** to move in a brusque or headlong manner **2 :** to kick or plunge vigorously **3** *Scot* **:** CAPER ∼ *vt* **1 a :** to throw with force or recklessness **b :** to cast aside **:** DISCARD **2 :** to place or send suddenly and unceremoniously **3 :** SPREAD, DIFFUSE **4 :** to give unrestrainedly **syn** see THROW — **fling·er** *n*

[2]**fling** *n* **1 :** an act or instance of flinging **2 :** a casual try **:** ATTEMPT **3 :** a period devoted to self-indulgence; *esp* **:** AFFAIR 3a

flint \'flint\ *n, often attrib* [ME, fr. OE; akin to OHG *flins* pebble, hard stone] **1 :** a massive hard quartz that strikes fire with steel **2 :** something used for striking fires; *specif* **:** an iron and cerium alloy used in cigarette lighters **3 :** something resembling flint in hardness — **flint** *vt* — **flint·like** \-,līk\ *adj*

flint corn *n* **:** an Indian corn (*Zea mays indurata*) having hard horny usu. rounded kernels with the soft endosperm enclosed by a hard outer layer

flint glass *n* **:** heavy brilliant glass that contains lead oxide, has a relatively high index of refraction, and is used for optical structures

flint·i·ly \'flint-ᵊl-ē\ *adv* **:** in a flinty manner

flint·i·ness \'flint-ē-nəs\ *n* **:** the quality or state of being flinty

flint·lock \'flint-,läk\ *n* **1 :** a lock for a gun or pistol of the 17th and 18th centuries having a flint in the hammer for striking a spark to ignite the charge **2 :** a firearm fitted with a flintlock

flinty \'flint-ē\ *adj* **1 :** composed of or covered with flint **2 :** UNYIELDING, STERN

[1]**flip** \'flip\ *vb* **flipped; flip·ping** [prob. imit.] *vt* **1 a :** to toss with a sharp movement so as to cause to turn over in the air **b :** THROW **2 :** FLICK 1 **3 :** to turn over ∼ *vi* **1 a :** to make a twitching or flicking movement **b :** to strike at something with such a movement **2 :** to move jerkily **3 :** LEAF 2 **4** *slang* **:** to react violently

[2]**flip** *n* **1 :** an act or instance of flipping **2 :** the motion used in flipping **3 :** a somersault esp. when performed in the air **4 :** a short quick football pass **5 :** any of several mixed drinks

[3]**flip** *adj* **:** FLIPPANT, IMPERTINENT

flip–flop \'flip-,fläp\ *n* **1 :** the sound or motion of something flapping loosely **2 a :** a backward handspring **b :** a sudden reversal of direction or point of view — **flip-flop** *vi*

flip·pan·cy \'flip-ən-sē\ *n* **:** the quality or state of being flippant **syn** see LIGHTNESS

flip·pant \'flip-ənt\ *adj* [prob. fr. [1]*flip*] **1** *archaic* **:** GLIB, TALKATIVE **2 :** lacking proper respect or seriousness — **flip·pant·ly** *adv*

flip·per \'flip-ər\ *n* **1 a :** a broad flat limb (as of a seal) adapted for swimming **b :** a flat rubber shoe with the front expanded into a paddle used in skin diving **2 :** one that flips

[1]**flirt** \'flərt\ *vb* [origin unknown] *vt* **1 :** FLICK **2 :** to move in a jerky manner ∼ *vi* **1 :** to move erratically **:** FLIT **2 a :** to behave amorously without serious intent **b :** TOY **syn** see TRIFLE — **flir·ta·tion** \,flər-'tā-shən\ *n* — **flirt·er** *n* — **flirty** \'flərt-ē\ *adj*

[2]**flirt** *n* **1 :** an act or instance of flirting **2 :** a person who flirts

flir·ta·tious \,flər-'tā-shəs\ *adj* **:** inclined to flirt **:** COQUETTISH — **flir·ta·tious·ness** *n*

flit \'flit\ *vi* **flit·ted; flit·ting** [ME *flitten*, of Scand origin; akin to ON *flytjask* to move, OE *flēotan* to float] **1 :** to pass quickly or abruptly from one place to another **2** *archaic* **:** ALTER, SHIFT **3 :** to move in an erratic fluttering manner — **flit** *n*

flitch \'flich\ *n* [ME *flicche*, fr. OE *flicce*] **1 :** a side of pork cured and smoked as bacon **2 a :** a longitudinal section of a log **b :** a bundle of sheets of veneer laid together in sequence **3 :** one of the parts secured together to make a girder or beam

[1]**flit·ter** \'flit-ər\ *vi* [freq. of *flit*] **:** FLUTTER, FLICKER

[2]**flitter** *n* **:** one that flits

fliv·ver \'fliv-ər\ *n* [origin unknown] **:** a small cheap usu. old automobile

[1]**float** \'flōt\ *n* [ME *flote* boat, float, fr. OE *flota* ship; akin to OHG *flōz* raft, stream, OE *flēotan* to float — more at FLEET] **1 :** an act or

instance of floating **2 :** something that floats in or on the surface of a fluid: as **a :** a cork or bob buoying up the baited end of a fishing line **b :** a floating platform anchored near a shoreline for use by swimmers or boats **c :** a hollow ball that floats at the end of a lever in a cistern, tank, or boiler and regulates the liquid level **d :** a sac containing air or gas and buoying up the body of a plant or animal **:** PNEUMATOPHORE **e :** a watertight structure giving an airplane buoyancy on water **3 :** a tool or apparatus for smoothing a surface **4 :** a government grant of a fixed amount of land not yet located by survey out of a larger specific tract **5 a :** a vehicle with a platform used to carry an exhibit in a parade **b :** the vehicle and exhibit together **6 :** an amount of money represented by checks outstanding and in process of collection **7 :** a drink consisting of ice cream floating in a beverage — **floaty** \'flōt-ē\ *adj*

2**float** *vi* **1 :** to rest on the surface of or be suspended in a fluid **2 a :** to drift on or through or as if on or through a liquid **b :** WANDER **3 :** to lack firmness of purpose **:** VACILLATE ~ *vt* **1 :** to cause to float in or on the surface of a liquid **2 :** to support (a structure) on a mat or raft foundation when the ground gives poor support **3 :** FLOOD **4 a :** to gain support for **b :** to place (securities) on the market **c :** to establish (an enterprise) by floating securities **d :** NEGOTIATE ⟨~ a loan⟩

float·age *var of* FLOTAGE

floa·ta·tion *var of* FLOTATION

float·er \'flōt-ər\ *n* **1 a :** one that floats **b :** a person who floats something **2 a :** a person who votes illegally in various polling places **b :** a person who represents an irregular constituency **3 a :** a person without a permanent residence or regular employment **:** VAGRANT **b :** an employee without a specific job **4 :** a slow baseball pitch with little or no spin

float·ing *adj* **1 :** buoyed on or in a fluid **2 a :** free from the usual attachment ⟨~ rib⟩ **b :** located out of the normal position ⟨~ kidney⟩ **3 a :** continually drifting or changing position ⟨~ population⟩ **b :** not presently committed or invested ⟨~ capital⟩ **c :** short-term and usu. not funded ⟨~ debt⟩ **4 :** connected or constructed so as to operate and adjust smoothly ⟨~ axle⟩

floating dock *n* **:** a dock that floats on the water and can be partly submerged to permit entry of a ship and raised to keep the ship high and dry

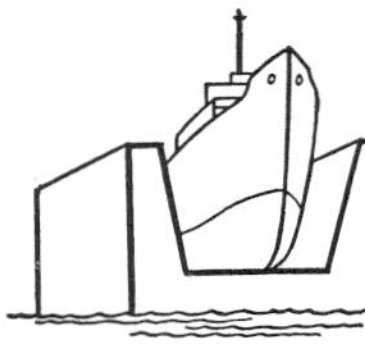
floating dock

floating island *n* **:** a dessert consisting of custard with floating masses of whipped white of egg

float·plane \'flōt-,plān\ *n* **:** a seaplane supported on the water by one or more floats

1**floc** \'fläk\ *n* [short for *floccule*] **1 :** a flocculent mass formed by the aggregation of a number of fine suspended particles **2 :** 3FLOCK 1,2,3

2**floc** *vb* **flocced** \'fläkt\ **floc·cing** \'fläk-iŋ\ *vi* **:** to aggregate into flocs ~ *vt* **:** to cause to floc

floc·cose \'fläk-,ōs\ *adj* [LL *floccosus*, fr. L *floccus*] **:** having tufts of soft woolly hairs ⟨~ plants⟩

1**floc·cu·late** \'fläk-yə-lət, -,lāt\ *adj* **:** bearing small tufts of hairs

2**floc·cu·late** \-,lāt\ *vt* **:** to cause to aggregate into a flocculent mass ⟨~ clay⟩ ~ *vi* **:** to become flocculated — **floc·cu·la·tion** \,fläk-yə-'lā-shən\ *n* — **floc·cu·la·tor** \'fläk-yə-,lāt-ər\ *n*

3**floc·cu·late** \-lət, -,lāt\ *n* **:** something that has flocculated

floc·cule \'fläk-(,)yü(ə)l\ *n* [LL *flocculus*] **:** a small loosely aggregated mass of material suspended in or precipitated from a liquid

floc·cu·lence \'fläk-yə-lən(t)s\ *n* **:** a flocculent quality or state

floc·cu·lent \-lənt\ *adj* [L *floccus* + E *-ulent*] **1 :** resembling wool esp. in loose fluffy organization **2 :** covered with woolly material **3 :** having a soft waxy covering

floc·cu·lus \-ləs\ *n, pl* **floc·cu·li** \-,lī, -,lē\ [LL, dim. of L *floccus* flock of wool; akin to OHG *blaha* coarse linen] **1 :** a small loosely aggregated mass **2 :** a bright or dark patch on the sun

1**flock** \'fläk\ *n* [ME, fr. OE *flocc* crowd, band; akin to ON *flokkr* crowd, band] **1 :** a group of birds or mammals assembled or herded together **2 :** a group under the guidance of a leader; *specif* **:** a church congregation in relation to the pastor **3 :** a large number

2**flock** *vi* **:** to gather or move in a crowd

3**flock** *n* [ME] **1 :** a tuft of wool or cotton fiber **2 :** woolen or cotton refuse used for stuffing furniture and mattresses **3 :** very short or pulverized fiber used to form a pattern on cloth or paper or a protective covering on metal **4 :** FLOC

4**flock** *vt* **1 :** to fill with flock **2 :** to decorate with flock

flock·ing \'fläk-iŋ\ *n* **:** a design in flock

floe \'flō\ *n* [prob. fr. Norw *flo* flat layer] **1 :** floating ice formed in a large sheet on the surface of a body of water **2 :** ICE FLOE

flog \'fläg\ *vt* **flogged; flog·ging** [perh. modif. of L *flagellare* to whip — more at FLAGELLATE] **1 :** to beat with a rod or whip **:** LASH **2 :** to criticize harshly **3 :** to force into action **:** DRIVE — **flog·ger** *n*

1**flood** \'fləd\ *n* [ME, fr. OE *flōd;* akin to OHG *fluot* flood, OE *flōwan* to flow] **1 :** a rising and overflowing of a body of water esp. onto normally dry land **2 :** the flowing in of the tide **3 :** an overwhelming quantity or volume **4 :** FLOODLIGHT

2**flood** *vt* **1 :** to cover with a flood **:** INUNDATE **2 :** to fill abundantly or excessively; *specif* **:** to supply with an excess of fuel ~ *vi* **1 :** to pour forth in a flood **2 :** to become filled with a flood — **flood·er** *n*

flood·gate \'fləd-,gāt\ *n* **1 :** a gate for shutting out, admitting, or releasing a body of water **:** SLUICE **2 :** something serving to restrain an outburst

1**flood·light** \-,līt\ *n* **1 a :** artificial illumination in a broad beam **b :** a source of such illumination **2 :** a lighting unit for projecting a beam of light

2**floodlight** *vt* **:** to illuminate by means of one or more floodlights

flood·plain \-,plān\ *n* **1 :** level land that may be submerged by floodwaters **2 :** a plain built up by stream deposition

flood tide *n* **1 :** a rising tide **2 a :** an overwhelming quantity **b :** a high point **:** PEAK

flood·wa·ter \'fləd-,wȯt-ər, -,wät-\ *n* **:** the water of a flood

flood·way \-,wā\ *n* **:** a channel for diverting floodwaters

floo·ey \'flü-ē\ *adv* (*or adj*) [origin unknown] **:** AWRY, ASKEW

1**floor** \'flō(ə)r, 'flȯ(ə)r\ *n, often attrib* [ME *flor*, fr. OE *flōr;* akin to OHG *fluor* meadow, L *planus* level, Gk *planasthai* to wander] **1 :** the part of a room on which one stands **2 a :** the lower inside surface of a hollow structure **b :** a ground surface **3 a :** a structure dividing a building into stories; *also* **:** STORY **b :** the occupants of such a floor **4 :** the surface of a structure on which one travels **5 a :** a main level space (as in a legislative chamber) distinguished from a platform or gallery **b :** the members of an assembly **c** (1) **:** the attention of an assembly (2) **:** the right to address an assembly **6 :** a lower limit **:** BASE

2**floor** *vt* **1 :** to cover with a floor or flooring **2 a :** to knock to the floor **b :** SHOCK, OVERWHELM **c :** DEFEAT **3 :** to press (the accelerator of a vehicle) to the floorboard — **floor·er** *n*

floor·age \'flōr-ij, 'flȯr-\ *n* **:** floor space

floor·board \'flō(ə)r-,bō(ə)rd, 'flȯ(ə)r-,bȯ(ə)rd\ *n* **1 :** a board in a floor **2 :** the floor of an automobile

floor furnace *n* **:** a small furnace located close below the floor

floor·ing \'flōr-iŋ, 'flȯr-\ *n* **1 :** FLOOR **2 :** material for floors

floor lamp *n* **:** a tall lamp that stands on the floor

floor leader *n* **:** a member of a legislative body chosen by his party to have charge of its organization and strategy on the floor

floor-length \'flō(ə)r-'leŋ(k)th, 'flȯ(ə)r-\ *adj* **:** reaching to the floor

floor show *n* **:** a series of acts presented in a nightclub

floor·walk·er \-,wȯ-kər\ *n* **:** a supervisor of a section in a retail store

floo·zy \'flü-zē\ *n* [origin unknown] **:** a tawdry or immoral woman; *specif* **:** PROSTITUTE

1**flop** \'fläp\ *vb* **flopped; flop·ping** [alter. of 2*flap*] *vi* **1 :** to swing or bounce loosely **2 :** to throw or move oneself in a heavy, clumsy, or relaxed manner **3 :** to change suddenly **4 :** to go to bed **5 :** to fail completely ~ *vt* **:** to move or drop heavily and noisily — **flop·per** *n*

2**flop** *n* **1 :** an act or sound of flopping **2 :** a complete failure **:** DUD

3**flop** *adv* **:** RIGHT, SQUARELY ⟨fell ~ on his face⟩

flop·house \'fläp-,hau̇s\ *n* **:** a cheap rooming house or hotel

flop·over \-,ō-vər\ *n* **:** a defect in television reception in which a succession of frames appears to traverse the screen vertically

flop·py \'fläp-ē\ *adj* **:** tending to flop; *esp* **:** soft and flexible

flo·ra \'flōr-ə, 'flȯr-\ *n, pl* **floras** *also* **flo·rae** \'flō(ə)r-,ē, 'flȯ(ə)r-, -,ī\ [NL, fr. *Flora*, Roman goddess of flowers] **1** *cap* **:** the goddess of flowers in Roman mythology **2 :** a treatise on or list of the plants of an area or period **3 :** plant life; *esp* **:** the plant life characteristic of a region, period, or special environment — compare FAUNA

flo·ral \'flōr-əl, 'flȯr-\ *adj* [L *flor-*, *flos* flower — more at BLOW] **:** of or relating to flowers or a flora — **flo·ral·ly** \-ə-lē\ *adv*

floral leaf *n* **1 :** a modified leaf (as a sepal or petal) of the perianth of a flower **2 :** BRACT

flo·res·cence \flō-'res-ən(t)s, flə-\ *n* [NL *florescentia*, fr. L *florescent-*, *florescens*, prp. of *florescere*, incho. of *florēre* to blossom, flourish — more at FLOURISH] **:** a state or period of flourishing — **flo·res·cent** \-ənt\ *adj*

flo·ret \'flōr-ət, 'flȯr-\ *n* [ME *flourette*, fr. MF *flouret*, dim. of *flour* flower] **:** a small flower; *esp* **:** one of the small flowers forming the head of a composite plant

flori- *comb form* [L, fr. *flor-*, *flos*] **:** flower or flowers ⟨*flori*culture⟩ **:** something resembling a flower or flowers ⟨*flori*ated⟩

flo·ri·at·ed \'flōr-ē-,āt-əd, 'flȯr-\ *adj* **:** having floral ornaments or a floral form — **flo·ri·a·tion** \,flōr-ē-'ā-shən, ,flȯr-\ *n*

flo·ri·bun·da \,flōr-ə-'bən-də, ,flȯr-\ *n* [NL, fem. of *floribundus* flowering freely] **:** any of various bush roses with large flowers in open clusters that derive from crosses of polyantha and tea roses

flo·ri·cul·tur·al \,flōr-ə-'kəlch-(ə-)rəl, ,flȯr-\ *adj* **:** of or relating to floriculture — **flo·ri·cul·tur·al·ly** \-ē\ *adv*

flo·ri·cul·ture \'flōr-ə-,kəl-chər, 'flȯr-\ *n* **:** the cultivation and management of ornamental and flowering plants — **flo·ri·cul·tur·ist** \,flōr-ə-'kəlch-(ə-)rəst, ,flȯr-\ *n*

flor·id \'flȯr-əd, 'flär-\ *adj* [L *floridus* blooming, flowery, fr. *florēre*] **1 a** *obs* **:** covered with flowers **b :** excessively flowery in style **:** ORNATE **2 :** tinged with red **:** RUDDY **3** *archaic* **:** HEALTHY — **flo·rid·i·ty** \flə-'rid-ət-ē, flȯ-\ *n* — **flor·id·ly** \'flȯr-əd-lē, 'flär-\ *adv* — **flor·id·ness** *n*

flo·rif·er·ous \flȯ-'rif-(ə-)rəs\ *adj* [L *florifer*, fr. *flori-*] **:** bearing flowers; *esp* **:** blooming freely — **flo·rif·er·ous·ly** *adv* — **flo·rif·er·ous·ness** *n*

flo·ri·gen \'flōr-ə-jən, 'flȯr-, 'flär-\ *n* [ISV] **:** a hormone or hormonal agent that promotes flowering — **flo·ri·gen·ic** \,flōr-ə-'jen-ik, ,flȯr-, ,flär-\ *adj*

flo·ri·le·gi·um \,flōr-ə-'lē-jē-əm, ,flȯr-, ,flär-\ *n, pl* **flo·ri·le·gia** \-jē-ə\ [NL, fr. L *florilegus* culling flowers, fr. *flori-* + *legere* to gather — more at LEGEND] **:** a volume of writings **:** ANTHOLOGY

flo·rin \'flȯr-ən, 'flär-, 'flōr-\ *n* [ME, fr. MF, fr. OIt *fiorino*, fr. *fiore* flower, fr. L *flor-*, *flos;* fr. the lily on the coins] **1 a :** an old gold coin first struck at Florence in 1252 **b :** any of various gold coins of European countries patterned after the Florentine florin **2 a :** a British silver coin worth two shillings **b :** any of several similar coins issued in British Commonwealth countries **3 :** GULDEN **4 :** FORINT

flo·rist \'flōr-əst, 'flȯr-, 'flär-\ *n* **:** one who sells flowers and ornamental plants — **flo·rist·ry** \-ə-strē\ *n*

flo·ris·tic \flȯ-'ris-tik\ *adj* **:** of or relating to flowers, a flora, or floristics — **flo·ris·ti·cal·ly** \-ti-k(ə-)lē\ *adv*

flo·ris·tics \-tiks\ *n pl but sing or pl in constr* **:** a branch of phytogeography that deals numerically with plants and plant groups

-flo·rous \'flōr-əs, 'flȯr-\ *adj comb form* [LL *-florus*, fr. L *flor-*, *flos*] **:** having or bearing (such or so many) flowers ⟨uni*florous*⟩

flo·ru·it \'flȯr-(y)ə-wət, 'flär-\ *n* [L, he flourished, fr. *florēre* to flourish] **:** a period of flourishing

floss \'fläs, 'flȯs\ *n* [fr. or akin to D *vlos;* akin to MHG *vlus*, *vlius* fleece — more at FLEECE] **1 :** waste or short silk fibers that cannot be reeled **2 a :** soft thread of silk or mercerized cotton for embroidery **b :** a lightweight wool knitting yarn **3 :** fluffy fibrous material; *esp* **:** SILK COTTON

floss·flow·er \-,flau̇(-ə)r\ *n* **:** AGERATUM

flossy \'fläs-ē, 'flȯs-\ *adj* **1 a :** of, relating to, or having the characteristics of floss **b :** DOWNY **2 :** STYLISH, GLAMOROUS

flo·ta \'flōt-ə\ *n* [Sp] **:** a fleet of Spanish ships

flo·tage \'flōt-ij\ *n* [2*float*] **1 :** FLOTATION 1 **2 :** material that floats

flo·ta·tion \flō-'tā-shən\ *n* [2*float*] **1 :** the act, process, or state of floating **2 :** an act or instance of financing (as an issue of stock) **3 :** the separation of the particles of a mass of pulverized ore according to their relative capacity for floating on a given liquid; *also* **:** any of various similar processes involving the relative capacity of materials for floating

flo·til·la \flō-'til-ə\ *n* [Sp, dim. of *flota* fleet, fr. OF *flote*, fr. ON *floti;* akin to OE *flota* ship, fleet] **1 :** a fleet of ships; *specif* **:** a navy organizational unit consisting of two or more squadrons of small warships **2 :** a group resembling a flotilla of ships

flot·sam \'flät-səm\ *n* [AF *floteson*, fr. OF *floter* to float, of Gmc origin; akin to OE *flotian* to float, *flota* ship] **1 :** floating wreckage of a ship or its cargo **2 a :** vagrant impoverished people **b :** unimportant miscellaneous material

1flounce \'flau̇n(t)s\ *vi* [perh. of Scand origin; akin to Norw *flunsa* to hurry] **1 a :** to move with exaggerated jerky motions **b :** to go with sudden determination **2 :** FLOUNDER, STRUGGLE — **flouncy** \'flau̇n(t)-sē\ *adj*

2flounce *n* **:** an act or instance of flouncing

3flounce *n* [alter. of earlier *frounce*, fr. ME *frouncen* to curl] **:** a strip of fabric attached by one edge — **flouncy** \'flau̇n(t)-sē\ *adj*

4flounce *vt* **:** to trim with flounces

flounc·ing \'flau̇n(t)-siŋ\ *n* **:** material used for flounces

1floun·der \'flau̇n-dər\ *n, pl* **flounder** *or* **flounders** [ME, of Scand origin; akin to ON *flythra* flounder, *flatr* flat] **:** FLATFISH; *esp* **:** one of either of two families (Pleuronectidae and Bothidae) that include important marine food fishes

2flounder *vi* **floun·der·ing** \-d(ə-)riŋ\ [prob. alter. of *founder*] **1 :** to struggle to move or obtain footing **2 :** to proceed clumsily

1flour \'flau̇(ə)r\ *n, often attrib* [ME — more at FLOWER] **1 a :** finely ground meal of wheat usu. largely freed from bran **b :** a similar meal of any cereal grain or edible seed or other product **2 :** a fine soft powder — **floury** \'flau̇(ə)r-ē\ *adj*

2flour *vt* **:** to coat with or as if with flour ~ *vi* **:** to break up into particles

1flour·ish \'flər-ish, 'flə-rish\ *vb* [ME *florisshen*, fr. MF *floriss-*, stem of *florir*, fr. (assumed) VL *florire*, alter. of L *florēre*, fr. *flor-*, *flos* flower] *vi* **1 :** to grow luxuriantly **:** THRIVE **2 a :** to achieve success **:** PROSPER **b :** to be in a state of activity or production ⟨~*ed* around 1850⟩ **c :** to reach a height of development or influence **3 :** to make bold and sweeping gestures ~ *vt* **:** to wield with dramatic gestures **:** BRANDISH **syn** see SWING — **flour·ish·er** *n*

2flourish *n* **1 :** a period of thriving **2 a :** an extraneous florid embellishment or passage **b :** an act or instance of brandishing **:** WAVE **c :** a dramatic action

1flout \'flau̇t\ *vb* [prob. fr. ME *flouten* to play the flute, fr. *floute* flute] *vt* **:** to treat with contemptuous disregard **:** SCORN ~ *vi* **:** to indulge in scornful behavior **syn** see SCOFF — **flout·er** *n*

2flout *n* **1 :** INSULT **2 :** MOCKERY

1flow \'flō\ *vb* [ME *flowen*, fr. OE *flōwan;* akin to OHG *flouwen* to rinse, wash, L *pluere* to rain, Gk *plein* to sail, float] *vi* **1 a** (1) **:** to issue or move in a stream (2) **:** CIRCULATE **b :** to move with a continual change of place among the constituent particles ⟨the molasses ~*ed* slowly⟩ **2 :** RISE ⟨the tide ebbs and ~*s*⟩ **3 :** ABOUND **4 a :** to proceed smoothly and readily **b :** to have a smooth uninterrupted continuity **5 :** to hang loose and billowing **6 :** COME, ARISE **7 :** to deform under stress without cracking or rupturing — used esp. of minerals and rocks **8 :** MENSTRUATE ~ *vt* **1 a :** to cause to flow **b :** to cover with water **:** FLOOD **2 :** to discharge in a flow **syn** see SPRING — **flow·ing·ly** \-iŋ-lē\ *adv*

2flow *n* **1 :** an act of flowing **2 :** FLOOD 1, 2 **3 a :** a smooth uninterrupted movement **b :** STREAM **4 :** the quantity that flows in a certain time **5 a :** MENSTRUATION **b :** YIELD, PRODUCTION **6 a :** the motion characteristic of fluids **b :** a continuous transfer of energy

flow·age \'flō-ij\ *n* **1 a :** an overflowing onto adjacent land **b :** a body of water formed by overflowing or damming **c :** floodwater esp. of a stream **2 :** gradual deformation of a body of plastic solid (as rock) by intermolecular shear

flow·chart \-,chärt\ *n* **:** a diagram or outline showing progress of material through a manufacturing process or the succession of operations in a complicated activity

1flow·er \'flau̇(-ə)r\ *n* [ME *flour* flower, best of anything, flour fr. OF *flor*, *flour*, fr. L *flor-*, *flos*] **1 a :** BLOSSOM, INFLORESCENCE **b :** a shoot of the sporophyte of a higher plant that is modified for reproduction and consists of a shortened axis bearing modified leaves **c :** a plant cultivated or esteemed for its blossoms **2 a :** the best part or example **b :** the finest most vigorous period **c :** a state of blooming or flourishing **3** *pl* **:** a finely divided powder produced esp. by condensation or sublimation ⟨~*s* of sulfur⟩ — **flow·ered** \'flau̇(-ə)rd\ *adj* — **flow·er·less** \'flau̇(-ə)r-ləs\ *adj* — **flow·er·like** \-,līk\ *adj*

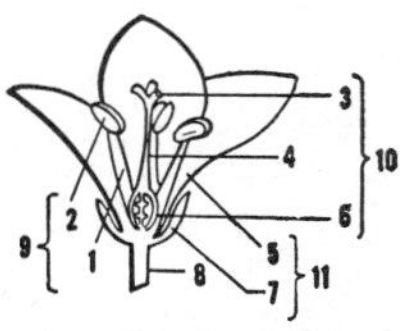

a flower in section: *1* filament, *2* anther, *3* stigma, *4* style, *5* petal, *6* ovary, *7* sepal, *8* pedicel, *9* stamen, *10* pistil, *11* perianth

2flower *vi* **1 :** to produce flowers **:** BLOSSOM **2 a :** DEVELOP ⟨~*ed* into young womanhood⟩ **b :** FLOURISH ~ *vt* **1 :** to cause to bear flowers **2 :** to decorate with floral designs — **flow·er·er** \'flau̇r-ər, 'flau̇-ər-ər\ *n*

flow·er·age \'flau̇-(ə-)rij\ *n* **:** a flowering state

flower bud *n* **:** a plant bud that produces only a flower

flow·er·et \'flau̇-(ə-)rət\ *n* **:** FLORET

flower girl *n* **:** a little girl who carries flowers at a wedding

flower head *n* **:** a capitulum having sessile flowers so arranged that the whole inflorescence looks like a single flower

flow·er·i·ness \'flau̇-(ə-)rē-nəs\ *n* **:** the quality or state of being flowery

flow·er·pot \'flau̇(-ə)r-,pät\ *n* **:** a pot in which to grow plants

flow·ery \'flau̇-(ə-)rē\ *adj* **1 :** of, relating to, or resembling flowers **2 :** marked by or given to rhetorical elegance

1flown *past part of* FLY

2flown \'flōn\ *adj* [archaic pp. of 1*flow*] **:** filled to excess

flow·stone \'flō-,stōn\ *n* **:** travertine found where water flowing in a very thin sheet over rocks has deposited mineral matter

flu \'flü\ *n* **1 :** INFLUENZA **2 :** any of several virus diseases marked esp. by respiratory symptoms

1flub \'fləb\ *vb* **flubbed; flub·bing** [origin unknown] *vt* **:** to make a mess of **:** BOTCH ~ *vi* **:** BLUNDER

2flub *n* **:** an act or instance of flubbing

flub·dub \'fləb-,dəb\ *n* [origin unknown] **:** CLAPTRAP, BUNKUM

fluc·tu·ant \'flək-chə-wənt\ *adj* **1 :** moving in waves **2 :** VARIABLE, UNSTABLE **3 :** being movable and compressible ⟨a ~ abscess⟩

fluc·tu·ate \'flək-chə-,wāt\ *vb* [L *fluctuatus*, pp. of *fluctuare*, fr. *fluctus* flow, wave, fr. *fluctus*, pp. of *fluere*] *vi* **1 :** to ebb and flow in waves **2 :** to shift back and forth uncertainly ~ *vt* **:** to cause to fluctuate **syn** see SWING — **fluc·tu·a·tion** \,flək-chə-'wā-shən\ *n*

flue \'flü\ *n* [origin unknown] **:** an enclosed passageway for directing a current: as **a :** a channel in a chimney for conveying flame and smoke to the outer air **b :** a pipe for conveying flame and hot gases around or through water in a steam boiler **c :** an air channel to the lip of a wind instrument

flu·en·cy \'flü-ən-sē\ *n* **:** the quality or state of being fluent

flu·ent \'flü-ənt\ *adj* [L *fluent-*, *fluens*, prp. of *fluere*] **1 :** capable of flowing **:** FLUID **2 a :** ready or facile in speech ⟨~ in Spanish⟩ **b :** effortlessly smooth and rapid **:** POLISHED — **flu·ent·ly** *adv*

flue pipe *n* **:** an organ pipe whose tone is produced by an air current striking the lip and causing the air within to vibrate

flue stop *n* **:** an organ stop made up of flue pipes

1fluff \'fləf\ *n* [prob. alter. of *flue* (fluff)] **1 :** NAP, DOWN **2 :** something fluffy **3 :** something inconsequential **4 :** BLUNDER; *esp* **:** an actor's lapse of memory

2fluff *vi* **1 :** to become fluffy **2 :** to make a mistake; *esp* **:** to forget or bungle one's lines in a play ~ *vt* **1 :** to make fluffy **2 a :** to spoil by a mistake **:** BOTCH **b :** to deliver badly or forget (one's lines) in a play

fluff·i·ness \'fləf-ē-nəs\ *n* **:** the quality or state of being fluffy

fluffy \'fləf-ē\ *adj* **1 a :** covered with or resembling fluff **b :** being light and soft or airy ⟨a ~ omelet⟩ **2 :** FATUOUS, SILLY

1flu·id \'flü-əd\ *adj* [F or L; F *fluide*, fr. L *fluidus*, fr. *fluere* to flow; akin to Gk *phlyzein* to boil over, L *flare* to blow — more at BLOW] **1 a :** having particles that easily move without a separation of the mass and easily yield to pressure **b :** likely or tending to change or move **2 :** characterized by or employing a smooth easy style **3 a :** available for a different use **b :** easily converted into cash **syn** see LIQUID — **flu·id·ly** *adv* — **flu·id·ness** *n*

2fluid *n* **:** a substance tending to flow or conform to the outline of its container — **flu·id·al** \'flü-əd-ᵊl\ *adj* — **flu·id·al·ly** \-ᵊl-ē\ *adv*

fluid drive *n* **:** an automotive power coupling that operates on a hydraulic turbine principle with the flywheel having a set of turbine blades connected directly to it and driving them in oil thereby turning another set of turbine blades attached to the transmission gears

flu·id·ex·tract \,flü-ə-'dek-,strakt\ *n* **:** an alcohol preparation of a vegetable drug containing the active constituents of one gram of the dry drug in each milliliter

flu·id·i·ty \flü-'id-ət-ē\ *n* **1 :** the quality or state of being fluid **2 :** the physical property of a substance that enables it to flow

flu·id·iza·tion \,flü-əd-ə-'zā-shən\ *n* **:** the process of fluidizing **:** the state of being fluidized

flu·id·ize \'flü-ə-,dīz\ *vt* **:** to suspend in a rapidly moving stream of gas for transportation ⟨~ flour⟩ — **flu·id·iz·er** *n*

fluid mechanics *n pl but sing or pl in constr* **:** a branch of mechanics dealing with the properties of liquids and gases

flu·id·ounce \,flü-ə-'dau̇n(t)s\ *n* **1 :** a U.S. unit of liquid capacity equal to 1⁄16 pint — see MEASURE table **2 :** a British unit of liquid capacity equal to 1⁄20 pint — see MEASURE table

flu·idram \,flü-ə(d)-'dram\ *n* [blend of 1*fluid* and *dram*] **:** a unit of liquid capacity equal to 1⁄8 fluidounce — see MEASURE table

1fluke \'flük\ *n* [ME, fr. OE *flōc;* akin to OHG *flah* smooth — more at FLAKE] **1 :** FLATFISH **2 :** a flattened digenetic trematode worm; *broadly* **:** TREMATODE

2fluke *n* [perh. fr. 1*fluke*] **1 :** the part of an anchor that fastens in the ground **2 :** a barbed head (as of a harpoon) **3 :** one of the lobes of a whale's tail

3fluke *n* [origin unknown] **1 :** an accidentally successful stroke at billiards or pool **2 :** a stroke of luck

fluky \'flü-kē\ *adj* **1 :** happening by or depending on chance **2 :** UNCERTAIN, CHANGEABLE ⟨~ wind⟩

flume \'flüm\ *n* [prob. fr. ME *flum* river, fr. OF, fr. L *flumen*, fr. *fluere*] **1 :** a ravine or gorge with a stream running through it **2 :** an inclined channel for conveying water (as for power)

flum·mery \'fləm-(ə-)rē\ *n* [W *llymru*] **1 a :** a soft jelly or porridge made with flour or meal **b :** any of several sweet desserts **2 :** MUMMERY, MUMBO JUMBO

flum·mox \'fləm-əks, -iks\ *vt* [origin unknown] **:** CONFUSE

flung *past of* FLING

1flunk \'fləŋk\ *vb* [perh. blend of *flinch* and *funk*] *vi* **:** to fail in an examination or course ~ *vt* **1 :** to give a failing grade to **2 :** to get a failing grade in — **flunk·er** *n*

2flunk *n* **:** an act or instance of flunking

flunk out *vi* **:** to be dismissed from a school or college for failure ~ *vt* **:** to dismiss from a school or college for failure

flun·ky *or* **flun·key** \'fləŋ-kē\ *n* [Sc, of unknown origin] **1 a :** a liveried servant **b :** one performing menial duties **2 :** YES-MAN

flu·or \'flü-,ȯ(ə)r, 'flü-ər, 'flu̇(-ə)r\ *n* [NL, mineral belonging to a group used as fluxes and including fluorite, fr. L, flow, fr. *fluere* — more at FLUID] **:** FLUORITE

fluor- *or* **fluoro-** *comb form* [F, fr. *fluorine*] **1 :** fluorine ⟨*fluor*ide⟩ **2** *also* **fluori- :** fluorescence ⟨*fluoro*scope⟩ ⟨*fluori*meter⟩

flu·o·resce \(,)flu̇(-ə)r-'es, flōr-, flȯr-\ *vi* [back-formation fr. *fluorescence*] **:** to produce, undergo, or exhibit fluorescence

flu·o·res·ce·in \-'es-ē-ən\ *n* **:** a yellow or red crystalline dye $C_{20}H_{12}O_5$ with a bright yellow-green fluorescence in alkaline solution

flu·o·res·cence \-'es-ᵊn(t)s\ *n* **:** emission of or the property of emitting electromagnetic radiation usu. as visible light resulting from and only during the absorption of radiation from some other source; *also* **:** the radiation emitted — **flu·o·res·cent** \-ᵊnt\ *adj*

fluorescent lamp *n* **:** a tubular electric lamp having a coating of fluorescent material on its inner surface and containing mercury vapor whose bombardment by electrons from the cathode provides ultraviolet light which causes the material to emit visible light

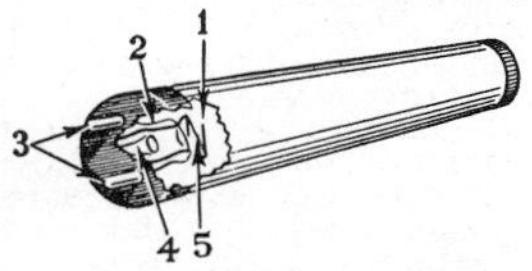

fluorescent lamp: *1* anode, *2* stem press, *3* base pins, *4* exhaust tubes, *5* cathode

flu·o·ri·date \'flu̇r-ə-,dāt, 'flōr-, 'flȯr-\ *vt* **:** to add a fluoride to — **flu·o·ri·da·tion** \,flu̇r-ə-'dā-shən, ,flōr-, ,flȯr-\ *n*

flu·o·ride \'flü(-ə)r-,īd\ *n* **:** a binary compound of fluorine usu. with another element or a radical
flu·o·rin·ate \'flür-ə-,nāt, 'flōr-, 'flòr-\ *vt* **:** to treat or cause to combine with fluorine or a compound of fluorine — **flu·o·rin·a·tion** \,flür-ə-'nā-shən, ,flōr-, ,flòr-\ *n*
flu·o·rine \'flü(-ə)r-,ēn, -ən\ *n* [F, fr. NL *fluor*] **:** a nonmetallic univalent halogen element that is normally a pale yellowish flammable irritating toxic gas — see ELEMENT table
flu·o·rite \'flü(-ə)r-,īt\ *n* [It] **:** a transparent or translucent mineral of different colors that consists of calcium fluoride and is used as a flux
flu·o·ro·car·bon \,flü(-ə)r-ō-'kär-bən\ *n* **:** any of various chemically inert compounds of carbon and fluorine used chiefly as lubricants and in making resins and plastics
flu·o·rog·ra·phy \(,)flü(-ə)r-'äg-rə-fē\ *n* **:** PHOTOFLUOROGRAPHY
flu·o·rom·e·ter \(,)flü(-ə)r-'äm-ət-ər\ *or* **flu·o·rim·e·ter** \-'im-\ *n* **:** an instrument for measuring fluorescence and related phenomena (as intensity of radiation) — **flu·o·ro·met·ric** \,flü(-ə)r-ə-'me-trik\ *adj* — **flu·o·rom·e·try** \(,)flü(-ə)r-'äm-ə-trē\ *n*
1flu·o·ro·scope \'flür-ə-,skōp\ *n* [ISV] **:** an instrument used for observing the internal structure of an opaque object (as the living body) by means of X rays — **flu·o·ro·scop·ic** \,flür-ə-'skäp-ik\ *adj* — **flu·o·ro·scop·i·cal·ly** \-i-k(ə-)lē\ *adv* — **flu·o·ros·co·pist** \(,)flü(-ə)r-'äs-kə-pəst\ *n* — **flu·o·ros·co·py** \-pē\ *n*
2fluoroscope *vt* **:** to examine by fluoroscopy
flu·o·ro·sis \(,)flü(-ə)r-'ō-səs\ *n* **:** an abnormal condition caused by fluorine or its compounds — **flu·o·rot·ic** \-'ät-ik\ *adj*
flu·or·spar \'flü(-ə)r-,spär\ *n* **:** FLUORITE
1flur·ry \'flər-ē, 'flə-rē\ *n* [prob. fr. *flurr* (to throw scatteringly)] **1 a :** a gust of wind **b :** a brief light snowfall **2 :** nervous commotion **:** BUSTLE **3 :** a brief advance or decline in prices **:** a short-lived outburst of trading activity **syn** see STIR
2flurry *vt* **:** to cause to become agitated and confused ~ *vi* **:** to become flurried
1flush \'fləsh\ *vb* [ME *flusshen*] *vi* **:** to take wing suddenly ~ *vt* **:** to cause (a bird) to flush
2flush *n* [perh. modif. of L *fluxus* — more at FLUX] **1 :** a sudden flow **2 :** a sudden increase or expansion; *esp* **:** a surge of emotion **3 a :** a tinge of red **:** BLUSH **b :** a fresh and vigorous state **4 :** a transitory sensation of extreme heat
3flush *vi* **1 :** to flow and spread suddenly and freely **2 a :** to glow brightly **b :** BLUSH ~ *vt* **1 a :** to cause to flow **b :** to pour liquid over or through; *esp* **:** to wash out with a rush of liquid **2 :** INFLAME, EXCITE **3 :** to cause to blush **4 :** to prepare (sheep) for breeding by special feeding
4flush *adj* **1 a :** filled to overflowing **b :** AFFLUENT **2 a :** full of life and vigor **:** LUSTY **b :** of a ruddy healthy color **3 :** readily available **:** ABUNDANT **4 a :** having or forming a continuous plane ⟨~ paneling⟩ **b :** directly abutting or immediately adjacent: as (1) **:** set even with an edge of a type page or column (2) **:** arranged edge to edge so as to fit snugly — **flush·ness** *n*
5flush *adv* **1 :** in a flush manner **2 :** SQUARELY
6flush *vt* **:** to make flush
7flush *n* [MF *flus, fluz*, fr. L *fluxus* flow] **1 :** a hand of playing cards all of the same suit; *specif* **:** a poker hand with all five cards of the same suit but not in sequence **2 :** a series of three or more slalom gates set vertically on a slope
1flus·ter \'fləs-tər\ *vb* **flus·ter·ing** \-t(ə-)riŋ\ [prob. of Scand origin; akin to Icel *flaustur* hurry] *vt* **1 :** to make tipsy **2 :** to put into a state of agitated confusion **:** UPSET ~ *vi* **:** to move or behave in an agitated or confused manner **syn** see DISCOMPOSE
2fluster *n* **:** a state of agitated confusion
1flute \'flüt\ *n* [ME *floute*, fr. MF *flahute*, fr. OProv *flaut*] **1 a :** RECORDER 3 **b :** a keyed woodwind instrument consisting of a hollow cylinder stopped at one end and with a side embouchure **c :** an organ flue pipe with a flutelike tone or a stop composed of such pipes **2 a :** a grooved pleat **b :** a rounded groove; *specif* **:** one of the vertical parallel grooves on a classical architectural column — **flute·like** \-,līk\ *adj* — **fluty** \'flüt-ē\ *adj*
2flute *vi* **1 :** to play a flute **2 :** to produce a flutelike sound ~ *vt* **1 :** to utter with a flutelike sound **2 :** to form flutes in — **flut·er** *n*
flut·ing \'flüt-iŋ\ *n* **:** fluted material or decoration
flut·ist \'flüt-əst\ *n* **:** a flute player
1flut·ter \'flət-ər\ *vb* [ME *floteren* to float, flutter, fr. OE *floterian*, freq. of *flotian* to float; akin to OE *flēotan* to float — more at FLEET] *vi* **1 :** to flap the wings rapidly **2 a :** to move with quick wavering or flapping motions **b :** to vibrate in irregular spasms **3 :** to move about or behave in an agitated aimless manner ~ *vt* **:** to cause to flutter — **flut·ter·er** \-ər-ər\ *n* — **flut·tery** \-ə-rē\ *adj*
2flutter *n* **1 :** an act of fluttering **2 a :** a state of nervous confusion or excitement **b :** FLURRY, COMMOTION **c :** abnormal spasmodic fluttering of a body part **3 a :** a distortion in reproduced sound similar to but of a higher pitch than wow **b :** fluctuation in the brightness of a television image **4 :** an unwanted oscillation set up by natural forces
flut·ter·board \'flət-ər-,bō(ə)rd, -,bò(ə)rd\ *n* **:** a rectangular board used by swimmers in practicing leg strokes
flutter kick *n* **:** an alternating whipping motion of the legs used in various swimming styles
flu·vi·al \'flü-vē-əl\ *adj* [L *fluvialis*, fr. *fluvius* river, fr. *fluere*] **1 :** of, relating to, or living in streams **2 :** produced by stream action
flu·vi·a·tile \'flü-vē-ə-,tīl\ *adj* [MF, fr. L *fluviatilis*, irreg. fr. *fluvius*] **:** FLUVIAL
1flux \'fləks\ *n* [ME, fr. MF & ML; MF, fr. ML *fluxus*, fr. L, flow, fr. *fluxus*, pp. of *fluere* to flow — more at FLUID] **1 :** a flowing of fluid from the body; *esp* **:** an excessive abnormal discharge from the bowels **2 :** a continuous moving on or passing by (as of a stream) **3 :** a continued flow **:** FLOOD **4 a :** INFLUX **b :** CHANGE, FLUCTUATION **5 a :** a substance used to promote fusion esp. of metals or minerals **b :** a substance (as rosin) applied to surfaces to be joined to clean and free them from oxide and promote their union **6 :** the rate of transfer of fluid, particles, or energy across a given surface
2flux *vt* **1 :** to cause to become fluid **2 :** to treat with a flux ~ *vi* **:** to become fluid **:** FUSE
flux gate *n* **:** a device used to indicate the direction of the terrestrial magnetic field
flux·ion \'flək-shən\ *n* **1 :** constant change **2** *pl, archaic* **:** INFINITESIMAL CALCULUS — **flux·ion·al** \-shnəl, -shən-ᵊl\ *adj*

1fly \'flī\ *vb* **flew** \'flü\ **flown** \'flōn\ **fly·ing** [ME *flien*, fr. OE *flēogan*; akin to OHG *fliogan* to fly, OE *flōwan* to flow] *vi* **1 a :** to move in or pass through the air with wings **b :** to move through the air or before the wind **c :** to float, wave, or soar in the air **2 a :** to take flight **:** FLEE **b :** to fade and disappear **:** VANISH **3 :** to move or pass swiftly **4 :** to become expended or dissipated rapidly **5 :** to pursue or attack in flight **6** *past or past part* **flied :** to hit a fly in baseball **7 :** to operate or travel in an airplane ~ *vt* **1 a :** to cause to fly or float in the air **b :** to operate (an airplane) in flight **c :** to journey over by flying **2 a :** to flee or escape from **b :** AVOID, SHUN **3 :** to transport by airplane — **fly at :** to assail suddenly and violently — **fly blind :** to fly an airplane solely by instruments — **fly contact :** to fly an airplane with the aid of visible landmarks or reference points — **fly high :** to be elated — **fly in the face of** *or* **fly in the teeth of :** to act forthrightly or brazenly in defiance or disobedience of
2fly *n, pl* **flies 1 :** the action or process of flying **:** FLIGHT **2 a :** a device consisting of two or more radial vanes capable of rotating on a spindle to act as a fan or to govern the speed of clockwork or very light machinery **b :** FLYWHEEL **3 a :** a horse-drawn public coach or delivery wagon **b** *chiefly Brit* **:** a light covered carriage or cab **4** *pl* **:** the space over a theater stage **5 :** something attached by one edge: as **a :** a garment closing concealed by a fold of cloth extending over the fastener **b :** the outer canvas of a tent with double top **c** (1) **:** the length of an extended flag from its staff or support (2) **:** the outer or loose end of a flag **6 :** a baseball hit high into the air **7 :** FLYLEAF — **on the fly :** in motion: as **a :** continuously active **:** very busy **b :** while still in the air
3fly *n, pl* **flies** [ME *flie*, fr. OE *flēoge*; akin to OHG *flioga* fly, OE *flēogan* to fly] **1 :** a winged insect **2 :** a winged or rarely wingless insect (order Diptera); *esp* **:** a large stout-bodied two-winged fly **3 :** a fishhook dressed to suggest an insect — **fly in the ointment :** a detracting factor or element
4fly *adj* [prob. fr. 1*fly*] *slang Brit* **:** KEEN, ARTFUL

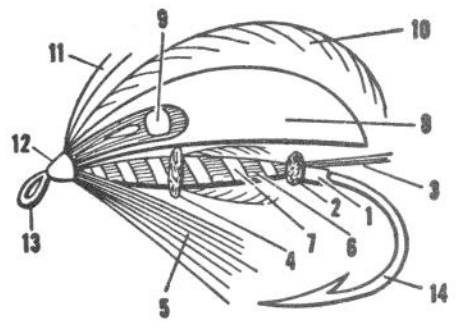

fly 3: *1* tag, *2* butt, *3* tail, *4* joint, *5* hackle, *6* body, *7* ribbing, *8* wing, *9* cheek, *10* topping, *11* horns, *12* head, *13* eye, *14* hook

fly·able \'flī-ə-bəl\ *adj* **:** suitable for flying or for being flown
fly agaric *n* **:** a poisonous mushroom (*Amanita muscaria*) with a usu. bright red cap
fly ash *n* **:** fine solid particles of noncombustible ash carried out of a bed of solid fuel by the draft
fly·away \'flī-ə-,wā\ *adj* **1 :** ready to fly ⟨~ aircraft⟩ **2 :** of or relating to an airplane that is ready to fly ⟨~ price⟩
fly·belt \'flī-,belt\ *n* **:** an area infested with tsetse fly
1fly·blow \-,blō\ *n* [3*fly* + *blow* (deposit of insect eggs)] **1 :** an egg or young larva deposited by a flesh fly or blowfly **2 :** FLYSTRIKE
2flyblow *vt* **1 :** to deposit flyblows in **2 :** TAINT, CONTAMINATE
fly·blown \-,blōn\ *adj* **:** SEEDY, MOTH-EATEN
fly·boat \-,bōt\ *n* [modif. of D *vlieboot*, fr. *Vlie*, channel between North sea & Zuider Zee + *boot* boat] **:** any of various fast boats
fly–boy \-,bòi\ *n, slang* **:** a member of the air force
fly·by \-,bī\ *n* **:** a usu. low-altitude flight past a predesignated place by one or more airplanes
fly–by–night \'flī-bə-,nīt\ *n* **1 :** one that operates only long enough to make a quick profit **2 :** one that has an ephemeral existence or attraction — **fly–by–night** *adj*
fly casting *n* **:** the casting of artificial flies in angling
fly·catch·er \'flī-,kach-ər, -,kech-\ *n* **:** a bird (order Passeriformes) that feeds on insects taken on the wing
fly dope *n* **1 :** a dressing that makes angling flies water-resistant so that they will float **2 :** an insect repellent
fly·er *var of* FLIER
fly gallery *n* **:** a narrow raised platform at the side of a theater stage from which flying scenery lines are operated
1fly·ing *adj* **1 a :** rapidly moving **b :** HASTY **2 :** intended for ready movement or action ⟨~ squad of police⟩ **3 :** having stylized wings
2flying *n* **1 :** travel by air **2 :** the operation of an aircraft
flying boat *n* **:** a seaplane with a hull adapted for floating
flying bridge *n* **:** the highest navigational bridge on a ship
flying buttress *n* **:** a masonry structure typically consisting of a straight inclined bar carried on an arch and a solid pier or buttress against which it abuts that receives the thrust of a roof or vault
flying colors *n pl* **:** complete success
Flying Dutchman *n* **1 :** a legendary Dutch mariner condemned to sail the seas until Judgment Day **2 :** a spectral ship held by sailors to haunt the seas near the Cape of Good Hope in stormy weather
flying field *n* **:** a field with a graded area for airplane landings and takeoffs
flying fish *n* **:** any of numerous fishes (family Exocoetidae) chiefly of tropical and warm seas that have long pectoral fins suggesting wings and are able to move some distance through the air
flying fox *n* **:** FRUIT BAT
flying gurnard *n* **:** any of several marine fishes (family Dactylopteridae) that resemble gurnards and have large pectoral fins allowing them to glide above the water for short distances
flying jib *n* **:** a sail outside the jib on an extension of the jibboom
flying lemur *n* **:** an East Indian or a Philippine arboreal nocturnal mammal (genus *Cynocephalus*) that is about the size of a cat with a broad fold of skin from the neck to the tail on each side that embraces the limbs and forms a parachute used in making long sailing leaps and that is usu. isolated in a distinct order (Dermoptera)
flying machine *n* **:** an apparatus for navigating the air
flying mare *n* **:** a wrestling maneuver in which the aggressor seizes his opponent's wrist, turns about, and jerks him over his back
flying saucer *n* **:** any of various unidentified moving objects repeatedly reported as seen in the air and usu. alleged to be saucer-shaped or disk-shaped — called also *flying disk*
flying squirrel *n* **:** a squirrel with folds of skin connecting the forelegs and hind legs enabling it to make long gliding leaps
fly·leaf \'flī-,lēf\ *n* **:** one of the free endpapers of a book
fly·over \-,ō-vər\ *n* **1 :** a low-altitude flight over a public gathering or place by one or more airplanes **2** *Brit* **:** OVERPASS

fly·pa·per \-ˌpā-pər\ *n* **:** paper poisoned or coated with a sticky substance for killing flies
fly·past \-ˌpast\ *n, Brit* **:** FLYBY
fly sheet *n* **:** a small loose advertising sheet **:** HANDBILL
fly·speck \-ˌspek\ *n* **1 :** a speck made by fly excrement **2 :** something small and insignificant — **flyspeck** *vt*
fly–strike \-ˌstrīk\ *n* **:** infestation with fly maggots
flyt·ing \ˈflīt-iŋ\ *n* [gerund of E dial. *flyte* to quarrel] **:** a dispute or exchange of personal abuse in verse form (as in an epic)
fly·way \ˈflī-ˌwā\ *n* **:** an established air route of migratory birds
fly·weight \-ˌwāt\ *n* **:** a boxer weighing 112 pounds or less
fly·wheel \-ˌhwēl, -ˌwēl\ *n* **:** a heavy wheel for opposing and moderating by its inertia any fluctuation of speed in the machinery with which it revolves
fly whisk *n* **:** a whisk for brushing away flies
f–num·ber \ˈef-ˌnəm-bər\ *n* [*f*ocal length] **:** a number following the symbol f/ that expresses the effectiveness of the aperture of a camera lens in relation to brightness of image so that the smaller the number the brighter the image and therefore the shorter the exposure required
foal \ˈfōl\ *n* [ME *fole,* fr. OE *fola;* akin to L *pullus* young of an animal, Gk *pais* child — more at FEW] **:** the young of an animal of the horse family; *esp* **:** one under one year — **foal** *vb*
[1]**foam** \ˈfōm\ *n* [ME *fome,* fr. OE *fām;* akin to OHG *feim* foam, L *spuma* foam, *pumex* pumice] **1 :** a light frothy mass of fine bubbles formed in or on the surface of a liquid: as **a :** such a mass formed in salivating or sweating **b :** a stabilized froth produced chemically or mechanically and used esp. in fighting oil fires **c :** a material in a lightweight cellular form resulting from introduction of gas bubbles during manufacture **2 :** SEA **3 :** something resembling foam
[2]**foam** *vi* **1 a :** to produce or form foam **b :** to froth at the mouth esp. in anger; *broadly* **:** to be angry **2 :** to gush out in foam **~** *vt* **1 :** to cause to foam; *specif* **:** to cause air bubbles to form in **2 :** to convert (as a plastic) into a foam
foam·i·ly \ˈfō-mə-lē\ *adv* **:** in a foamy manner
foam·i·ness \-mē-nəs\ *n* **:** the quality or state of being foamy
foam rubber *n* **:** spongy rubber of fine texture made from latex by foaming (as by whipping) before vulcanization
foamy \ˈfō-mē\ *adj* **1 :** covered with foam **:** FROTHY **2 :** full of, consisting of, or resembling foam
[1]**fob** \ˈfäb\ *vt* **fobbed; fob·bing** [ME *fobben*] *archaic* **:** DECEIVE, CHEAT
[2]**fob** *n* [perh. akin to G dial. *fuppe* pocket] **1 :** a small pocket just below the front waistband of men's trousers **2 :** a short chain or ribbon connecting a watch carried in a fob pocket and an ornament hanging outside **3 :** an ornament attached to a fob chain
[3]**fob** *vt* **fobbed; fob·bing :** to put into one's fob **:** POCKET
fob off *vt* **1 :** to put off with a trick or excuse **2 :** to pass or offer as genuine **3 :** to put aside
fo·cal \ˈfō-kəl\ *adj* **:** of, relating to, or having a focus — **fo·cal·ly** \-kə-lē\ *adv*
focal infection *n* **:** a persistent bacterial infection of some organ or region; *esp* **:** one causing symptoms elsewhere in the body
fo·cal·iza·tion \ˌfō-kə-lə-ˈzā-shən\ *n* **:** the act of focalizing **:** the state of being focalized
fo·cal·ize \ˈfō-kə-ˌlīz\ *vt* **1 :** to bring to a focus **2 :** to adjust the focus of **3 :** LOCALIZE **~** *vi* **:** to become focalized
focal length *n* **:** the distance of the focus from the surface of a lens or concave mirror
fo'·c'sle *var of* FORECASTLE
[1]**fo·cus** \ˈfō-kəs\ *n, pl* **fo·cus·es** *or* **fo·ci** \-ˌsī\ [NL, fr. L, hearth] **1 :** a point at which rays converge or from which they diverge or appear to diverge; *specif* **:** the point where the geometrical lines or their prolongations conforming to the rays diverging from or converging toward another point intersect and give rise to an image after reflection by a mirror or refraction by a lens or optical system **2 a :** FOCAL LENGTH **b :** adjustment for distinct vision; *also* **:** the area that may be seen distinctly or resolved into a clear image **3 :** one of the points that with the corresponding directrix defines a conic section **4 :** a localized area of disease or the chief site of a generalized disease or infection **5 :** a center of activity, attraction, or attention **6 :** the place of origin of an earthquake — **in focus :** having or giving the proper sharpness of outline due to good focusing — **out of focus :** not in focus

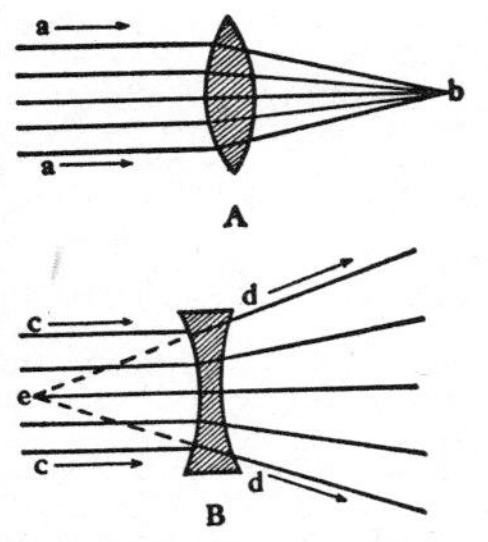

focus 1: fig. *A,* convex lens: light rays *a, a,* converge to form principal focus, *b;* fig. *B,* concave lens: light rays *c, c,* refracted as at *d, d,* and form virtual focus, *e*

[2]**focus** *vb* **fo·cused** *also* **fo·cussed; fo·cus·ing** *also* **fo·cus·sing** *vt* **1 :** to bring to a focus **:** CONCENTRATE **2 :** to cause to be concentrated **3 a :** to adjust the focus of **b :** to bring into focus **~** *vi* **1 :** to come to a focus **:** CONVERGE **2 :** to adjust one's eye or a camera to a particular range
fod·der \ˈfäd-ər\ *n* [ME, fr. OE *fōdor*] **1 :** something fed to domestic animals; *esp* **:** coarse food for cattle, horses, or sheep **2 :** something to be consumed — **fodder** *vt* **fod·der·ing** \-(ə-)riŋ\
fod·gel \ˈfäj-əl\ *adj* [origin unknown] *Scot* **:** BUXOM
foe \ˈfō\ *n* [ME *fo,* fr. OE *fāh,* fr. *fāh* hostile; akin to OHG *gifēh* hostile] **1 :** one who has personal enmity for another **:** ENEMY **2 :** an enemy in war **:** ADVERSARY **3 :** one who opposes on principle **4 :** something prejudicial or injurious **syn** see ENEMY
foehn *or* **föhn** \ˈfə(r)n, ˈfān\ *n* [G *föhn*] **:** a warm dry wind blowing down the side of a mountain
foe·man \ˈfō-mən\ *n* **:** an enemy in war **:** FOE
foe·tal, foe·tus *var of* FETAL, FETUS
foeti- *or* **foeto-** — see FETI-
foe·tid \ˈfēt-əd\ *var of* FETID
[1]**fog** \ˈfȯg, ˈfäg\ *n* [ME, rank grass] **1** *dial* **a :** dead or decaying grass in the winter **b :** a second growth of grass **2** *dial* **:** MOSS
[2]**fog** *n* [prob. of Scand origin; akin to Dan *fog* spray, shower; akin to L *pustula* blister, pimple, Gk *physan* to blow] **1 a :** vapor condensed to fine particles of water suspended in the lower atmosphere that differs from cloud only in being near the ground **b :** a fine spray or a foam for fire fighting **2 :** a murky condition of the atmosphere or a substance causing it **3 :** a state of mental confusion **4 :** a density in a developed photographic image caused by chemical action or stray radiation **syn** see HAZE
[3]**fog** *vb* **fogged; fog·ging** *vt* **1 :** to cover or envelop with or as if with fog **2 :** to make obscure or confusing **3 :** to make confused **4 :** to produce fog on (as a photographic film) during development **~** *vi* **1 :** to become covered or thick with fog **2 a :** to become blurred by a covering of fog or mist **b :** to become indistinct through exposure to light or radiation
fog·bound \-ˌbau̇nd\ *adj* **1 :** covered with or surrounded by fog ⟨~ coast⟩ **2 :** unable to move because of fog ⟨~ ship⟩
fog·bow \-ˌbō\ *n* **:** a nebulous arc or circle of white or yellowish light sometimes seen in fog — called also *fogdog*
fog·gage \ˈfȯg-ij, ˈfäg-\ *n, chiefly Scot* **:** FOG, MOSS
fog·gi·ly \-ə-lē\ *adv* **:** in a foggy manner
fog·gi·ness \-ē-nəs\ *n* **:** the quality or state of being foggy
fog·gy \ˈfȯg-ē, ˈfäg-\ *adj* **1 a :** filled or abounding with fog **b :** covered or made opaque by moisture or grime **2 :** MUDDLED
fog·horn \-ˌhȯ(ə)rn\ *n* **1 :** a horn sounded in a fog to give warning **2 :** a loud hoarse voice
fog·less \-ləs\ *adj* **:** marked by the absence of fog
fo·gy *also* **fo·gey** \ˈfō-gē\ *n* [origin unknown] **:** a person with old-fashioned ideas — usu. used with *old* — **fo·gy·ish** \-ish\ *adj* — **fo·gy·ism** \-ˌiz-əm\ *n*
foi·ble \ˈfȯi-bəl\ *n* [obs. F (now *faible*), fr. obs. *foible* weak, fr. OF *feble* feeble] **1 :** the part of a sword or foil blade between the middle and point **2 :** a minor flaw or shortcoming in personal character or behavior **:** WEAKNESS **syn** see FAULT
foie gras \fwä-ˈgrä\ *n* [F] **:** fat liver esp. of a goose usu. in the form of a pâté
[1]**foil** \ˈfȯi(ə)l\ *vt* [ME *foilen* to trample, full cloth, fr. MF *fouler* — more at FULL] **1** *obs* **:** TRAMPLE **2 a :** to prevent from attaining an end **:** DEFEAT **b :** to bring to naught **syn** see FRUSTRATE
[2]**foil** *n* **1** *archaic* **:** DEFEAT **2** *archaic* **:** the track or trail of an animal **3 a :** a fencing weapon with a flat guard and a light flexible blade tapering to a blunt point **b** *pl* **:** the art or practice of fencing with foils
[3]**foil** *n* [ME, fr. MF *foille* (fr. L *folia,* pl. of *folium*) & *foil,* fr. L *folium* — more at BLADE] **1 :** a plant leaf — used in compounds **2 a :** an indentation between cusps in Gothic tracery **b :** one of several arcs that enclose a complex figure **3 a :** very thin sheet metal **b :** a thin coat of tin or silver laid on the back of a mirror **4 :** a thin piece of metal or other material put under a paste or inferior stone to add color or brilliancy **5 :** one that serves as a contrast to another

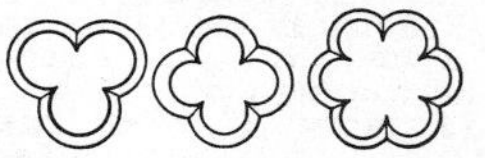
foils 2a

[4]**foil** *vt* **1 :** to back or cover with foil **2 :** to enhance by contrast
foiled \ˈfȯi(ə)ld\ *adj* **:** ornamented with foils ⟨a ~ arch⟩
foils·man \ˈfȯi(ə)lz-mən\ *n* **:** one who fences with a foil **:** FENCER
[1]**foin** \ˈfȯin\ *vi* [ME *foinen,* fr. *foin* fork for spearing fish, fr. MF *foisne*] *archaic* **:** to thrust with a sword or spear **:** LUNGE
[2]**foin** *n* **:** a pass in fencing **:** LUNGE
foi·son \ˈfȯiz-ᵊn\ *n* [ME *foisoun,* fr. MF *foison*] **1** *archaic* **:** rich harvest **2** *chiefly Scot* **:** physical energy or strength **3** *pl, obs* **:** RESOURCES
foist \ˈfȯist\ *vt* [prob. fr. obs. D *vuisten* to take into one's hand, fr. MD *vuysten,* fr. *vuyst* fist; akin to OE *fȳst* fist] **1 a :** to introduce or insert surreptitiously or without warrant **b :** to force another to accept esp. by stealth or deceit **2 :** to pass off as genuine or worthy
fo·la·cin \ˈfō-lə-sən\ *n* [*fol*ic *ac*id + *-in*] **:** FOLIC ACID
[1]**fold** \ˈfōld\ *n* [ME, fr. OE *falod;* akin to MLG *vālt* enclosure] **1 :** an enclosure for sheep **2 a :** a flock of sheep **b :** a group of people adhering to a common faith, belief, or enthusiasm
[2]**fold** *vt* **:** to pen up or confine (as sheep) in a fold
[3]**fold** *vb* [ME *folden,* fr. OE *fealdan;* akin to OHG *faldan* to fold, Gk di*plasios* twofold] *vt* **1 :** to lay one part over another part of ⟨~ a letter⟩ **2 :** to reduce the length or bulk of by doubling over ⟨~ his legs⟩ **3 :** to clasp together **:** ENTWINE ⟨~ his hands⟩ **4 :** to clasp or enwrap closely **:** EMBRACE **5 :** to incorporate (a food ingredient) into a mixture by repeated overturnings without stirring or beating **6 :** to bring to an end **~** *vi* **1 :** to become doubled or pleated **2 :** to fail completely **:** COLLAPSE
[4]**fold** *n* **1 :** a doubling or folding over **2 :** a part doubled or laid over another part **:** PLEAT **3 :** something that is folded together or that enfolds **4 a :** a bend or flexure produced in rock by forces operative after the depositing or consolidation of the rock **b** *chiefly Brit* **:** an undulation in the landscape **5 :** a margin apparently formed by the doubling upon itself of a membrane or other flat anatomical structure
-fold \ˌfōld, ˈfōld\ *suffix* [ME, fr. OE *-feald;* akin to OHG *-falt* -fold, OE *fealdan*] **1 :** multiplied by (a specified number) **:** times — in adjectives ⟨a twelve*fold* increase⟩ and adverbs ⟨repay you ten*fold*⟩ **2 :** having (so many) parts ⟨three*fold* aspect of the problem⟩
fold·away \ˈfōl-də-ˌwā\ *adj* **:** designed to fold out of the way or out of sight ⟨~ doors⟩ ⟨~ bed⟩
fold·boat \ˈfōl(d)-ˌbōt\ *n* **:** FALTBOAT — **fold·boat·er** \-ˌbōt-ər\ *n* — **fold·boat·ing** *n*
fold·er \ˈfōl-dər\ *n* **1 :** one that folds **2 :** a printed circular folded usu. so that the printed matter does not cross the fold **3 :** a folded cover or large envelope for holding or filing loose papers
fol·de·rol \ˈfäl-də-ˌräl\ *n* [*fol-de-rol,* a refrain in some old songs] **1 :** a useless ornament or accessory **:** TRIFLE **2 :** NONSENSE
folding door *n* **:** a door in sections that can be folded back
folding money *n* **:** PAPER MONEY
fo·li·a·ceous \ˌfō-lē-ˈā-shəs\ *adj* **1 :** of, relating to, or resembling a foliage leaf **2 :** consisting of thin laminae ⟨~ spar⟩
fo·liage \ˈfō-l(ē-)ij, -lyij\ *n* [MF *fuellage,* fr. *foille* leaf] **1 :** the mass of leaves of a plant **2 :** a representation of leaves, flowers, and branches for architectural ornamentation — **fo·liaged** *adj*
foliage leaf *n* **:** an ordinary green leaf as distinguished from a floral leaf, scale, or bract
foliage plant *n* **:** a plant grown primarily for its decorative foliage
fo·li·ar \ˈfō-lē-ər\ *adj* **:** of or relating or applied to leaves

1fo·li·ate \'fō-lē-ət\ *adj* [L *foliatus* leafy fr. *folium* leaf — more at BLADE] **1 :** shaped like a leaf **2 :** furnished with or composed of leaves **:** LEAFY ⟨3-*foliate*⟩ **3 :** FOLIOLATE

2fo·li·ate \-lē-,āt\ *vt* **1 :** to beat into a leaf or thin foil **2 :** to spread over with a thin coat of tin amalgam **3 :** to number the leaves of (as a manuscript) **4 a :** to form (as an arch) into foils **b :** to ornament (as a pedestal) with foliage ~ *vi* **:** to divide into laminae or leaves — **fo·li·at·ed** *adj*

fo·li·a·tion \,fō-lē-'ā-shən\ *n* **1 a :** the process of forming into a leaf **b :** the state of being in leaf **c :** VERNATION **2 :** the act of numbering the leaves of a book; *also* **:** the total count of leaves so numbered **3 a :** ornamentation with foliage **b :** a decoration resembling a leaf **4 :** the enrichment of an opening by foils **5 :** the act of beating a metal into a thin plate or foil **6 :** foliated texture

fo·lic acid \,fō-li-'kas-əd\ *n* [L *folium*] **:** a crystalline vitamin $C_{19}H_{19}N_7O_6$ of the B complex used in the treatment of nutritional anemias and sprue

fo·lie à deux \fò-lē-à-dœ\ *n* [F, lit., double madness] **:** the presence of the same or similar delusional ideas in two persons closely associated with one another

fo·li·ic·o·lous \,fō-lē-'ik-ə-ləs\ *adj* [L *folium* + ISV *-colous*] **:** growing or parasitic upon leaves

1fo·lio \'fō-lē-,ō\ *n* [ME, fr. L, abl. of *folium*] **1 a :** a leaf esp. of a manuscript or book **b :** a leaf number **c :** a page number **d :** an identifying reference in accounting used in posting **2 a :** a sheet of paper folded once **b :** a case or folder for loose papers **3 a :** the size of a piece of paper cut two from a sheet; *also* **:** paper or a page of this size **b :** a book printed on folio pages **c :** a book of the largest size **4 :** a certain number of words taken as a unit or division in a document for purposes of measurement or reference

2folio *vt* **:** to put a serial number on each leaf or page of

fo·li·o·late \'fō-lē-ə-,lāt\ *adj* [*foliole* (leaflet)] **:** relating to, having, or consisting of leaflets — usu. used in combination

fo·li·ose \'fō-lē-,ōs\ *or* **fo·li·ous** \-lē-əs\ *adj* **1 :** LEAFY **2 :** resembling a leaf

fo·li·um \'fō-lē-əm\ *n, pl* **fo·lia** \-lē-ə\ [NL, fr. L, leaf] **:** a thin layer occurring esp. in metamorphic rocks

1folk \'fōk\ *n, pl* **folk** *or* **folks** [ME, fr. OE *folc;* akin to OHG *folc* people] **1** *archaic* **:** a group of kindred tribes forming a nation **:** PEOPLE **2 :** the great proportion of the members of a people that determines the group character and that tends to preserve its characteristic form of civilization and its customs, arts and crafts, legends, traditions, and superstitions from generation to generation **3 :** a certain kind or class of people **4 :** people generally **5 :** the persons of one's own family **:** RELATIVES

2folk *adj* **1 :** originated or widely used among the common people ⟨~ music⟩ **2 :** of or relating to the common people

folk etymology *n* **:** the transformation of words so as to give them an apparent relationship to other better-known or better-understood words (as the change of *chaise longue* to *chaise lounge*)

folk·ish \'fō-kish\ *adj* **:** FOLKLIKE — **folk·ish·ness** *n*

folk·like \'fō-,klīk\ *adj* **:** having a folk character

folk·lore \'fō-,klō(ə)r, -,klò(ə)r\ *n* **1 :** traditional customs, tales, or sayings preserved orally among a people **2 :** a comparative science that investigates the life and spirit of a people as revealed in their folklore — **folk·lor·ic** \-,klōr-ik, -,klòr-\ *adj* — **folk·lor·ist** \-əst\ *n* — **folk·lor·is·tic** \,fō-,klōr-'is-tik, -,klòr-\ *adj*

folk·lor·ish \'fō-,klōr-ish, -,klòr-\ *adj* **:** FOLKISH

folk·moot \'fōk-,müt\ *or* **folk·mote** \-,mōt\ *n* **:** a general assembly of the people (as of a shire) in early England

folks·i·ly \'fōk-sə-lē\ *adv* **:** in a folksy manner

folks·i·ness \-sē-nəs\ *n* **:** the quality of being folksy

folksy \'fōk-sē\ *adj* **1 :** SOCIABLE, FRIENDLY **2 :** informal, casual, or familiar in manner or style

folk·tale \'fōk-,tāl\ *n* **:** a characteristically anonymous, timeless, and placeless tale circulated orally among a people

folk·way \'fō-,kwā\ *n* **:** a mode of thinking, feeling, or acting common to a people or to a social group

fol·li·cle \'fäl-i-kəl\ *n* [NL *folliculus*, fr. L, dim. of *follis* bag — more at FOOL] **1 a :** a small anatomical cavity or deep narrow-mouthed depression **b :** a small lymph node **2 :** a dry dehiscent one-celled, many-seeded, and monocarpellary fruit that opens along only one suture — **fol·lic·u·lar** \fə-'lik-yə-lər, fä-\ *adj* — **fol·lic·u·late** \-lət\ *also* **fol·lic·u·lat·ed** \-,lāt-əd\ *adj*

follicle mite *n* **:** any of several minute mites (genus *Demodex*) parasitic in hair follicles

follicle–stimulating hormone *n* **:** a hormone from the anterior lobe of the pituitary body that stimulates the growth of Graafian follicles and activates sperm-forming cells

fol·lic·u·lin \fə-'lik-yə-lən, fä-\ *n* **:** ESTROGEN; *esp* **:** ESTRONE

1fol·low \'fäl-(,)ō, -ə(-w)\ *vb* [ME *folwen*, fr. OE *folgian;* akin to OHG *folgēn* to follow] *vt* **1 :** to go, proceed, or come after ⟨~*ed* the guide⟩ **2 a :** to pursue in an effort to overtake **b :** to seek to attain ⟨~ knowledge⟩ **3 :** to accept as authority **:** OBEY **4 :** to copy after **:** IMITATE **5 a :** to walk or proceed along ⟨~ a path⟩ **b :** to engage in **:** PURSUE ⟨men who ~ the sea⟩ **6 a :** to come or take place after in time, sequence, or order **b :** to cause to be followed ⟨~*ed* dinner with a liqueur⟩ **7 :** to come into existence or take place as a result or consequence of ⟨disaster ~*ed* the blunder⟩ **8 a :** to watch steadily ⟨~*ed* the ball over the fence⟩ **b :** to keep the mind on ⟨~ a speech⟩ **c :** to attend closely to ~ *vi* **1 :** to go or come after a person or thing in place, time, or sequence **2 :** to result or occur as a consequence, effect, or inference

syn FOLLOW, SUCCEED, ENSUE, SUPERVENE mean to come after something or someone. FOLLOW may apply to a coming after in time, position, or logical sequence; SUCCEED implies a coming after immediately in a sequence determined by natural order, inheritance, election, or laws of rank; ENSUE commonly suggests a logical consequence or naturally expected development; SUPERVENE suggests the following or beginning of something unforeseen or unpredictable **syn** see in addition CHASE

— **follow suit 1 :** to play a card of the same suit as the card led **2 :** to follow an example set

2follow *n* **1 :** the act or process of following **2 a :** a shot in billiards made by striking the cue ball above its center **b :** the forward spin so imparted to the ball

fol·low·er \'fäl-ə-wər\ *n* **1 a :** one in the service of another **:** RETAINER **b :** one that follows the opinions or teachings of another **:** DISCIPLE **c :** one that imitates another **2** *archaic* **:** one that chases **3 :** a sheet added to the first sheet of an indenture or other deed **4 :** a machine part that receives motion from another part

syn ADHERENT, DISCIPLE, PARTISAN, SATELLITE: FOLLOWER applies to one who attaches himself to the person or to the opinions or teachings of another, and usu. implies nothing beyond this; ADHERENT suggests a close and persistent attachment; DISCIPLE implies a devoted allegiance to the teachings of one chosen as a master; PARTISAN suggests a zealous often prejudiced attachment; SATELLITE suggests either constant attendance and sycophancy or a marked subservience or subordination to one stronger or dominating

fol·low·er·ship \-,ship\ *n* **1 :** FOLLOWING **2 :** the capacity to follow a leader

1fol·low·ing *adj* **1 :** next after **:** SUCCEEDING ⟨the ~ day⟩ **2 :** that immediately follows ⟨trains will leave at the ~ times⟩

2following *n* **:** a group of followers, adherents, or partisans

3following *prep* **:** subsequent to ⟨~ the lecture tea was served⟩

follow out *vt* **1 :** to follow to the end or to a conclusion **2 :** to carry out **:** EXECUTE

follow through *vi* **1 :** to continue a stroke or motion to the end of its arc **2 :** to press on in an activity or process esp. to a conclusion

fol·low–through \'fäl-ō-,thrü, ,fäl-ō-', -ə-\ *n* **1 :** the act of following through **2 :** the part of the stroke following the striking of a ball **3 :** the act of carrying out to an end an activity planned or begun

follow up *vt* **1 :** to pursue closely and steadily **2 :** to strengthen the effect of by further action **:** EXPLOIT **3 :** to seek or give further details about (a news story) **4 :** to maintain contact with (a patient) after diagnosis or therapy

fol·low–up \'fäl-ə-,wəp\ *n* **1 :** a system of pursuing an initial effort by supplementary action **2 :** reexamination of or maintenance of contact with a patient at prescribed intervals following diagnosis or treatment **3 :** a news story presenting new information on a story published earlier — **follow–up** *adj*

fol·ly \'fäl-ē\ *n* [ME *folie*, fr. OF, fr. *fol* fool] **1 :** lack of good sense or normal prudence and foresight **2 :** a foolish act or idea **3 a** *obs* **:** EVIL, WICKEDNESS; *esp* **:** LEWDNESS **b :** criminally or tragically foolish actions or conduct **4 :** an excessively costly or unprofitable undertaking; *esp* **:** a ruinously costly often unfinished building

Fol·som \'fōl-səm\ *adj* [*Folsom*, N.M.] **:** of or relating to a prehistoric culture of No. America on the east side of the Rocky mountains characterized esp. by a leaf-shaped flint projectile point

fo·ment \fō-'ment\ *vt* [ME *fomenten*, fr. LL *fomentare*, fr. L *fomentum* fomentation, fr. *fovēre* to warm, fondle, foment] **1 :** to treat with moist heat (as for easing pain) **2 :** to nurse to life or activity **:** INSTIGATE ⟨~ riots⟩ **syn** see INCITE — **fo·ment·er** *n*

fo·men·ta·tion \,fō-mən-'tā-shən, -,men-\ *n* **1 a :** the application of hot moist substances to the body to ease pain **b :** the material so applied **2 :** the act of fomenting **:** INSTIGATION

1fond \'fänd\ *adj* [ME, fr. *fonne* fool] **1 :** FOOLISH, SILLY ⟨~ pride⟩ **2 a :** prizing highly **:** DESIROUS ⟨~ of praise⟩ **b :** strongly attracted or predisposed ⟨~ of music⟩ **3 a :** foolishly tender **:** INDULGENT ⟨a ~ mother⟩ **b :** LOVING, AFFECTIONATE ⟨a ~ wife⟩ **4 :** doted on **:** DEAR ⟨his ~*est* hopes⟩

2fond *vi, obs* **:** to be foolish **:** DOTE

3fond \'fōⁿ\ *n, pl* **fonds** \'fōⁿ(z)\ [F — more at FUND] **1 :** BACKGROUND, BASIS **2** *obs* **:** FUND

fon·dant \'fän-dənt\ *n* [F, fr. prp. of *fondre* to melt — more at FOUND] **1 :** a creamy preparation of sugar used as a basis for candies or icings **2 :** a candy consisting chiefly of fondant

fon·dle \'fän-dᵊl\ *vb* **fon·dling** \-(d)liŋ, -dᵊl-iŋ\ [freq. of obs. *fond*] *vt* **1** *obs* **:** PAMPER **2 :** to handle tenderly, lovingly, or lingeringly ~ *vi* **:** to show affection or desire by caressing **syn** see CARESS — **fon·dler** \-(d)lər, -dᵊl-ər\ *n*

fond·ling \'fän-(d)liŋ\ *n* [obs. *fond* (to fondle)] **:** a person or thing fondled or caressed **:** PET

fond·ly \'fän-(d)lē\ *adv* **1** *archaic* **:** FOOLISHLY **2 :** in a fond manner **:** AFFECTIONATELY **3 :** in a willingly credulous manner

fond·ness \'fän(d)-nəs\ *n* **1** *obs* **:** FOOLISHNESS, FOLLY **2 :** tender affection **3 :** APPETITE, RELISH

fon·due *also* **fon·du** \fän-'d(y)ü\ *n* [F *fondue*, fr. fem. of *fondu*, pp. of *fondre*] **1 :** a preparation of melted cheese usu. flavored with wine or brandy **2 :** a soufflé made with bread crumbs

F_1 layer \'ef-'wən-\ *n* **:** the lower of the two layers into which the F region of the ionosphere splits in the daytime occurring at varying heights from about 90 to 150 miles above the earth's surface

fons et ori·go \,fōn(t)-,set-ə-'rē-(,)gō\ *n* [LL] **:** source and origin

1font \'fänt\ *n* [ME, fr. OE, fr. LL *font-*, *fons*, fr. L, fountain] **1 a :** a receptacle for baptismal water **b :** a receptacle for holy water **2 :** FOUNTAIN, SOURCE — **font·al** \'fänt-ᵊl\ *adj*

2font *n* [MF *fonte* act of founding, fr. (assumed) VL *fundita*, fem. of *funditus*, pp. of L *fundere* to found, pour — more at FOUND] **:** an assortment of type all of one size and style

fon·ta·nel *also* **fon·ta·nelle** \,fänt-ᵊn-'el\ *n* [ME *fontinelle*, a bodily hollow or pit, fr. MF *fontenele*, dim. of *fontaine* fountain] **:** a membrane-covered opening in bone or between bones; *specif* **:** one of the intervals closed by membranous structures between the uncompleted angles of the parietal bones and the neighboring bones of a fetal or young skull

food \'füd\ *n, often attrib* [ME *fode*, fr. OE *fōda;* akin to OHG *fuotar* food, fodder, L *panis* bread, *pascere* to feed] **1 a :** material consisting essentially of protein, carbohydrate, and fat used in the body of an organism to sustain growth, repair, and vital processes and to furnish energy; *also* **:** such food together with supplementary substances (as minerals, vitamins, and condiments) **b :** inorganic substances absorbed by plants in gaseous form or in water solution **2 :** nutriment in solid form **3 :** something that nourishes, sustains, or supplies

food chain *n* **:** a sequence of organisms in which each uses the next usu. lower member of the sequence as a food source

food cycle *n* **:** a group of food chains constituting all or most of the food relations that enable an ecological community to survive

food·less \'füd-ləs\ *adj* **:** lacking food — **food·less·ness** *n*

food poisoning *n* **:** an acute gastrointestinal disorder caused by bacteria or their toxic products or by chemical residues in food

food·stuff \'füd-,stəf\ *n* **:** a substance with food value; *specif* **:** the raw material of food before or after processing

foo·fa·raw \'fü-fə-,rò\ *n* [origin unknown] **1 :** frills and flashy finery **2 :** a disturbance or to-do over a trifle **:** FUSS

1fool \'fül\ *n* [ME, fr. OF *fol*, fr. LL *follis*, fr. L, bellows, bag; akin to L *flare* to blow — more at BLOW] **1 :** a person lacking in judgment or prudence **2 a :** a retainer formerly kept in great house-

holds to provide casual entertainment and commonly dressed in motley with cap, bells, and bauble **b :** one who is victimized or made to appear foolish **:** DUPE **3 a :** a harmlessly deranged person or one lacking in common powers of understanding **:** IDIOT **b :** one with a marked propensity or talent for a certain activity ⟨a letter-writing ~⟩ **4 a :** mashed fruit and cream **b :** a dessert made of pulped fruit covered with a custard and cream

syn FOOL, IDIOT, IMBECILE, MORON, SIMPLETON, NATURAL mean one who is mentally defective. FOOL is the general term and may often suggest derangement rather than feebleness of mind, or merely some degree of lack of good sense or judgment; IDIOT, IMBECILE, and MORON designate technically three grades of mental insufficiency; an IDIOT is incapable of coherent speech and of avoiding ordinary hazards and so requires constant care; an IMBECILE is incapable of earning a living but can be educated to attend to his simpler wants and avoid ordinary dangers; a MORON can learn a simple trade but requires constant supervision in work and play; SIMPLETON is often a term of indulgent contempt and implies silliness or lack of sophistication or of normal shrewdness; NATURAL, now rare, applies to any congenitally feeble-minded person

2**fool** *vi* **1 a :** to spend time idly or aimlessly **b :** to meddle or tamper thoughtlessly or ignorantly ⟨don't ~ with that gun⟩ **2 a :** to play or improvise a comic role **b :** to speak in jest **:** JOKE ⟨I was only ~*ing*⟩ **3 :** to contend or fight without serious intent or with less than full strength **:** TOY **~** *vt* **1 :** to make a fool of **:** DECEIVE **2** *obs* **:** INFATUATE **3 :** to spend on trifles or without advantage **:** FRITTER — used with *away*

3**fool** *adj* **:** FOOLISH, SILLY ⟨barking his ~ head off⟩

fool·ery \ˈfül-(ə-)rē\ *n* **1 :** the habit or practice of folly or fooling **2 :** an act of folly or fooling

fool·har·di·ly \ˈfül-ˌhärd-ᵊl-ē\ *adv* **:** in a foolhardy manner

fool·har·di·ness \-ˌhärd-ē-nəs\ *n* **:** the quality or state of being foolhardy

fool·har·dy \-ē\ *adj* **:** foolishly adventurous and bold **:** RASH

fool·ish \ˈfü-lish\ *adj* **1 :** marked by or proceeding from folly **2 a :** ABSURD, RIDICULOUS **b :** NONPLUSSED, ABASHED **3 :** TRIFLING, HUMBLE **syn** see SIMPLE — **fool·ish·ly** *adv* — **fool·ish·ness** *n*

fool·proof \ˈfül-ˈprüf\ *adj* **:** so simple, plain, or reliable as to leave no opportunity for error, misuse, or failure

fools·cap *or* **fool's cap** \ˈfül-ˌskap\ *n* **1 :** a cap or hood usu. with bells worn by jesters **2 :** a conical cap for slow or lazy students **3** [fr. the watermark of a fool's cap formerly applied to such paper] *usu foolscap* **:** a size of paper typically 16x13 inches

fool's errand *n* **:** a needless or profitless errand

fool's gold *n* **1 :** PYRITE **2 :** CHALCOPYRITE

fool's paradise *n* **:** a state of delusory happiness

fool's parsley *n* **:** a poisonous European weed (*Aethusa cynapium*) of the carrot family resembling parsley

1**foot** \ˈfu̇t\ *n, pl* **feet** \ˈfēt\ *also* **foot** [ME *fot*, fr. OE *fōt*; akin to L *ped-*, *pes* foot, Gk *pod-*, *pous*] **1 :** the terminal part of the vertebrate leg upon which an individual stands **2 :** an invertebrate organ of locomotion or attachment; *esp* **:** a ventral muscular surface or process of a mollusk **3 :** any of various units of length based on the length of the human foot; *esp* **:** a unit equal to ⅓ yard and comprising 12 inches ⟨a 10-*foot* pole⟩ ⟨6 *feet* tall⟩ — see MEASURE table **4 :** the basic unit of verse meter consisting of any of various fixed combinations or groups of stressed and unstressed or long and short syllables **5 a :** motion or power of walking or running **:** STEP **b :** SWIFTNESS, SPEED **6 :** something resembling a foot in position or use: as **a :** the lower end of the leg of a chair or table **b :** one of the areas of the base of a piece of printing type **c :** a piece on a sewing machine that presses the cloth against the feed **7** *foot pl, chiefly Brit* **:** INFANTRY **8 :** the lower edge (as of a sail) **9 :** the lowest part **:** BOTTOM **10 :** the end that is lower or opposite the head **11 foots** *pl but sing or pl in constr* **:** material deposited esp. in aging or refining **:** DREGS — **foot·like** \-ˌlīk\ *adj*

2**foot** *vi* **1 :** DANCE **2 :** to go on foot **3 :** to make speed **:** MOVE **~** *vt* **1 a :** to perform the movements of (a dance) **b :** to walk, run, or dance on, over, or through **2** *archaic* **a :** KICK **b :** REJECT **3** *archaic* **:** ESTABLISH **4 a :** to add up **b :** to pay or stand credit for **5 :** to make or renew the foot of (as a stocking)

foot·age \ˈfu̇t-ij\ *n* **:** length or quantity expressed in feet: as **a :** BOARD FEET **b :** the total number of running feet of film used

foot-and-mouth disease *n* **:** an acute contagious febrile virus disease esp. of cloven-footed animals marked by ulcerating vesicles in the mouth, about the hoofs, and on the udder and teats

foot·ball \ˈfu̇t-ˌbȯl\ *n* **1 :** any of several games played with a football on a rectangular field having two goalposts at each end by two teams whose object is to get the ball over a goal line or between goalposts: as **a** *Brit* **:** SOCCER **b** *Brit* **:** RUGBY **c :** a game played between two teams of 11 players each in which the ball is in possession of one side at a time and is advanced by running or passing **2 a :** an inflated oval ball used in the game of football **b** *Brit* **:** a soccer ball **3 :** something tossed or kicked about **:** PLAYTHING

foot·board \ˈfu̇t-ˌbō(ə)rd, -ˌbȯ(ə)rd\ *n* **1 :** a narrow platform on which to stand or brace the feet **2 :** a board forming the foot of a bed

foot·boy \-ˌbȯi\ *n* **:** a serving boy **:** PAGE, ATTENDANT

foot brake *n* **:** a brake operated by foot pressure

foot·bridge \ˈfu̇t-ˌbrij\ *n* **:** a bridge for pedestrians

foot-can·dle \ˈfu̇t-ˈkan-dᵊl\ *n* **:** a unit of illuminance on a surface that is everywhere one foot from a uniform point source of light of one candle and equal to one lumen per square foot

foot·cloth \-ˌklȯth\ *n* **1 :** an ornamental cloth draped over the back of a horse to reach the ground on each side **2** *obs* **:** CARPET

foot·ed \ˈfu̇t-əd\ *adj* **1 :** having a foot ⟨~ creatures⟩ **2 :** having such or so many feet ⟨fleet-*footed*⟩ ⟨four-*footed*⟩

foot·er \ˈfu̇t-ər\ *n* **1 :** PEDESTRIAN **2 :** one that is a specified number of feet in height, length, or breadth ⟨a six-*footer*⟩

foot·fall \ˈfu̇t-ˌfȯl\ *n* **:** STEP

foot fault *n* **:** a fault called against a server in tennis by reason of his failure to keep both feet behind the base line

foot·gear \ˈfu̇t-ˌgi(ə)r\ *n* **:** covering for the feet (as shoes)

foot·hill \-ˌhil\ *n* **:** a hill at the foot of higher hills

foot·hold \-ˌhōld\ *n* **1 :** a hold for the feet **:** FOOTING **2 :** a position serving a military force as a base for further advance

foot·ing \ˈfu̇t-iŋ\ *n* **1 :** a stable position or placing of the feet **2 :** a surface or its condition with respect to one walking or running on it; *specif* **:** the condition of a racetrack **3 :** the act of moving on foot **:** STEP, TREAD **4 a :** a place or space for standing **:** FOOTHOLD **b :** established position **:** STATUS **5 :** BASIS **6 :** an enlargement at the lower end of a foundation wall, pier, or column to distribute the load **7 :** the sum of a column of figures

foo·tle \ˈfüt-ᵊl\ *vi* **foo·tling** \ˈfüt-liŋ, -ᵊl-iŋ\ [alter. of *footer* (to footle)] **1 :** to waste time **:** TRIFLE, FOOL **2 :** to talk or act foolishly — **footle** *n* — **foo·tler** \ˈfüt-lər, -ᵊl-ər\ *n*

foot·less \ˈfu̇t-ləs\ *adj* **1 a :** having no feet **b :** lacking foundation **:** UNSUBSTANTIAL **2 :** STUPID, INEPT ⟨a ~ and futile plan⟩ — **foot·less·ly** *adv* — **foot·less·ness** *n*

foot·lights \-ˌlīts\ *n pl* **1 :** a row of lights set across the front of a stage floor **2 :** the stage as a profession

foo·tling \ˈfüt-liŋ, -ᵊl-iŋ\ *adj* [*footle*] **1 :** lacking judgment or ability **:** INEPT **2 :** lacking use or value **:** TRIVIAL

foot·lock·er \ˈfu̇t-ˌläk-ər\ *n* **:** a small flat trunk designed to be placed at the foot of a bed (as in barracks)

foot·loose \-ˌlüs\ *adj* **:** having no ties **:** FREE, UNTRAMMELED

foot·man \ˈfu̇t-mən\ *n* **1 a** *archaic* **:** a traveler on foot **:** PEDESTRIAN **b :** INFANTRYMAN **2 a :** a servant in livery formerly attending a rider or required to run before his master's carriage **b :** a house servant that serves at table, tends the door, and runs errands

foot·mark \-ˌmärk\ *n* **:** FOOTPRINT

foot·note \-ˌnōt\ *n* **1 :** a note of reference, explanation, or comment placed below the text on a printed page **2 :** something subordinate or added to a larger statement or event — **footnote** *vt*

foot·pace \-ˌpās\ *n* **1 :** a walking pace **2 :** PLATFORM, DAIS

foot·pad \-ˌpad\ *n* [*foot* + *pad* (highwayman)] **:** one who robs a pedestrian

foot·path \-ˌpath, -ˌpȧth\ *n* **:** a narrow path for pedestrians

foot-pound \-ˈpau̇nd\ *n, pl* **foot-pounds :** a unit of work equal to the work done by a pound-force acting through a distance of one foot in the direction of the force

foot-pound·al \-ˈpau̇n-dᵊl\ *n* **:** the absolute unit of work equal to the work done by a force of one poundal acting through a distance of one foot in the direction of the force

foot-pound-second *adj* **:** being or relating to a system of units based upon the foot as the unit of length, the pound as the unit of weight or mass, and the second as the unit of time

foot·print \ˈfu̇t-ˌprint\ *n* **:** an impression of the foot

foot·race \-ˌrās\ *n* **:** a race run on foot

foot·rest \-ˌrest\ *n* **:** a support for the feet

foot·rope \-ˌrōp\ *n* **1 :** a rope rigged below a yard for men to stand on **2 :** the part of a boltrope sewed to the lower edge of a sail

foot rot *n* **1 :** a plant disease marked by rot of the stem near the ground **2 :** a progressive inflammation of the feet of sheep or cattle

foot·slog \ˈfu̇t-ˌsläg\ *vi* **:** to march or tramp through mud — **foot·slog·ger** *n*

foot soldier *n* **:** INFANTRYMAN

foot·sore \ˈfu̇t-ˌsō(ə)r, -ˌsȯ(ə)r\ *adj* **:** having sore or tender feet (as from much walking) — **foot·sore·ness** *n*

foot·stall \-ˌstȯl\ *n* **:** the plinth, base, or pedestal of a pillar

foot·step \-ˌstep\ *n* **1 a :** TREAD **b :** distance covered by a step **:** PACE **2 :** the mark of the foot **:** TRACK **3 :** a step on which to ascend or descend

foot·stock \-ˌstäk\ *n* **:** TAILSTOCK

foot·stone \-ˌstōn\ *n* **:** a stone placed at the foot of a grave

foot·stool \-ˌstül\ *n* **:** a low stool to support the feet

foot-ton \-ˈtən\ *n* **:** a unit of energy equal to the work done in raising one ton against the force of gravity through the height of one foot

foot·wall \-ˌwȯl\ *n* **1 :** the lower wall of a vein, ore deposit, or coal seam in a mine **2 :** the lower wall of an inclined fault

foot·way \-ˌwā\ *n* **:** a narrow way or path for pedestrians

foot·wear \-ˌwa(ə)r, -ˌwe(ə)r\ *n* **:** wearing apparel for the feet (as shoes or boots) usu. excluding hosiery

foot·work \-ˌwərk\ *n* **1 :** the management of the feet and work done with them (as in boxing) **2 :** the activity of moving from place to place

foo·ty \ˈfüt-ē\ *adj* [F *foutu*] **1** *chiefly dial* **:** INSIGNIFICANT, PALTRY ⟨a ~ little town⟩ **2** *chiefly dial* **:** poorly kept **:** SHABBY

1**foo·zle** \ˈfü-zəl\ *vt* **foo·zling** \ˈfüz-(ə-)liŋ\ [perh. fr. G dial. *fuseln* to work carelessly] **:** to manage or play awkwardly **:** BUNGLE

2**foozle** *n* **:** an act of foozling; *esp* **:** a bungling golf stroke

1**fop** \ˈfäp\ *n* [ME; akin to ME *fobben* to deceive, MHG *voppen*] **1** *obs* **:** a foolish or silly person **2 :** a man who is devoted to or vain of his appearance or dress **:** COXCOMB, DANDY

2**fop** *vt* **fopped; fop·ping** *obs* **:** FOOL, DUPE

fop·pery \ˈfäp-(ə-)rē\ *n* **1 :** foolish character or action **:** FOLLY **2 :** the behavior, dress, or other mark of a fop

fop·pish \ˈfäp-ish\ *adj* **1** *obs* **:** FOOLISH, SILLY **2 :** characteristic of a fop in dress or manners — **fop·pish·ly** *adv* — **fop·pish·ness** *n*

1**for** \fər, (ˈ)fȯ(ə)r\ *prep* [ME, fr. OE; akin to L *per* through, *prae* before, *pro* before, for, ahead, Gk *pro*, OE *faran* to go — more at FARE] **1 a** — used as a function word to indicate purpose ⟨money ~ studying⟩ **b** — used as a function word to indicate an intended destination ⟨left ~ home⟩ **c** — used as a function word to indicate the object toward which one's desire or activity is directed ⟨now ~ a good rest⟩ **2 a :** as being **:** AS ⟨take him ~ a fool⟩ **b** — used as a function word to indicate an actual or implied enumeration or selection ⟨~ one thing, the price is too high⟩ **3 :** because of ⟨cried ~ joy⟩ **4 a** — used as a function word to indicate a recipient (as of an action that fills a need) **b :** in support of ⟨fighting ~ their country⟩ **c** — used as a function word to indicate appropriateness or belonging ⟨medicine ~ a cold⟩ **d** — used as a function word with a following noun or pronoun to introduce an infinitive construction equivalent to such noun clauses as *that he should, that he might* ⟨shouted the news ~ all to hear⟩ **5 a :** in place of **b :** in exchange as the equivalent of ⟨paid $10 ~ a hat⟩ **c :** on behalf of **:** REPRESENTING **6 :** in spite of **7 :** CONCERNING ⟨a stickler ~ detail⟩ **8** — used as a function word to indicate equality or proportion ⟨point ~ point⟩ ⟨tall ~ his age⟩ **9** — used as a function word to indicate duration of time or extent of space **10 :** in honor of **:** AFTER

2**for** *conj* **:** for this reason or on this ground

for- *prefix* [ME, fr. OE; akin to OHG *fur-* for-, OE *for*] **1 :** so as to

involve prohibition, exclusion, omission, failure, neglect, or refusal ⟨*for*say⟩ **2 :** destructively or detrimentally ⟨*for*storm⟩ **3 :** completely **:** excessively **:** to exhaustion **:** to pieces ⟨*for*spent⟩

fora *pl of* FORUM

1for·age \'fȯr-ij, 'fär-\ *n* [ME, fr. MF, fr. OF, fr. *forre* fodder, of Gmc origin; akin to OHG *fuotar* food, fodder — more at FOOD] **1 :** food for animals esp. when taken by browsing or grazing **2** [*2forage*] **:** the act of foraging **:** search for provisions

2forage *vt* **1 a :** to strip of provisions **:** collect forage from **b** *archaic* **:** SPOIL, PLUNDER **2 :** to secure by foraging ⟨*foraged* a chicken for the feast⟩ ~ *vi* **1 :** to wander in search of forage or food **2 :** to secure forage (as for horses) by stripping the country **3 :** RAVAGE, RAID **4 :** to make a search **:** RUMMAGE — **for·ag·er** *n*

forage acre *n* **:** a unit of grazing value equivalent to one acre of land entirely covered with herbage that can be completely utilized by grazing animals

fo·ram \'fōr-əm, 'fȯr-\ *n* **:** FORAMINIFER

fo·ra·men \fə-'rā-mən\ *n, pl* **fo·ram·i·na** \-'ram-ə-nə\ *or* **fo·ra·mens** \-'rā-mənz\ [L *foramin-, foramen*, fr. *forare* to bore — more at BORE] **:** a small opening, perforation, or orifice **:** FENESTRA — **fo·ram·i·nal** \fə-'ram-ən-ᵊl\ *or* **fo·ram·i·nous** \-ə-nəs\ *adj*

fo·ra·men mag·num \fə-,rā-mən-'mag-nəm\ *n* [NL, lit., great opening] **:** the opening in the skull through which the spinal cord passes to become the medulla oblongata

for·a·min·i·fer \,fȯr-ə-'min-ə-fər, ,fär-\ *n* **:** any of an order (Foraminifera) of large chiefly marine rhizopods usu. having calcareous shells that often are perforated with minute holes for protrusion of slender pseudopodia and form the bulk of chalk and nummulitic limestone — **fo·ra·mi·nif·er·al** \fə-,ram-ə-'nif-(ə-)rəl; ,fȯr-ə-mə-'nif-, ,fär-\ *or* **fo·ra·mi·nif·er·ous** \-(ə-)rəs\ *adj*

for and *conj, obs* **:** and also

for·as·much as \'fȯr-əz-,məch-əz\ *conj* **:** in consideration that **:** seeing that **:** SINCE

1for·ay \'fȯr-,ā\ *vb* [ME *forrayen*, fr. MF *forrer*, fr. *forre*] *vt, archaic* **:** to ravage in search of spoils **:** PILLAGE ~ *vi* **:** to make a raid ⟨~*ed* briefly into enemy territory⟩ — **for·ay·er** *n*

2foray *n* **:** a sudden or irregular invasion or attack for war or spoils **:** RAID

forb \'fȯ(ə)rb\ *n* [Gk *phorbē* fodder, food, fr. *pherbein* to graze; akin to OE *beorgan* to taste] **:** an herb other than grass **:** WEED

1for·bear \fȯr-'ba(ə)r, fər-, -'be(ə)r\ *vb* **for·bore** \-'bō(ə)r, -'bȯ(ə)r\ **for·borne** \-'bō(ə)rn, -'bȯ(ə)rn\ **for·bear·ing** [ME *forberen*, fr. OE *forberan*, fr. *for-* + *beran* to bear] *vt* **1** *obs* **:** to bear with **:** ENDURE **2** *obs* **:** to leave alone **:** SHUN ⟨~ his presence —Shak.⟩ **3** *obs* **:** to do without **4 :** to refrain from **:** abstain or desist from ~ *vi* **1 :** to hold back **:** ABSTAIN **2 :** to control oneself when provoked **:** be patient **syn** see REFRAIN — **for·bear·er** *n*

2forbear *var of* FOREBEAR

for·bear·ance \fȯr-'bar-ən(t)s, fər-, -'ber-\ *n* **1 :** a refraining from the enforcement of something that is due **2 :** the act of forbearing **:** PATIENCE **3 :** the quality of being forbearing **:** LENIENCY

1for·bid \fər-'bid, fȯr-\ *vt* **for·bade** \-'bad, -'bād\ *or* **for·bad** \-'bad\ **for·bid·den** \-'bid-ᵊn\ **for·bid·ding** [ME *forbidden*, fr. OE *forbēodan*, fr. *for-* + *bēodan* to bid — more at BID] **1 :** to command against **:** PROHIBIT **2 a :** to exclude or warn off by express command **b :** to bar from use ⟨cameras are *forbidden*⟩ **3 :** to hinder or prevent as if by an effectual command — **for·bid·der** *n*

syn PROHIBIT, INTERDICT, INHIBIT: FORBID implies absolute proscription and expected obedience and suggests the restraint of a parent, physician, or teacher; PROHIBIT implies more generality and impersonality and suggests statutes or ordinances; INTERDICT implies prohibition by civil or ecclesiastical authority usu. for a given time or a declared purpose; INHIBIT implies the imposition of restraint or restriction by authority or by the exigencies of time or situation or the operation of often involuntary self-restraint

2forbid *adj, archaic* **:** ACCURSED ⟨he shall live a man ~ —Shak.⟩

for·bid·dance \fər-'bid-ᵊn(t)s, fȯr-\ *n* **:** the act of forbidding

for·bid·ding *adj* **1 :** such as to make approach or passage difficult or impossible **2 :** DISAGREEABLE, REPELLENT — **for·bid·ding·ly** \-iŋ-lē\ *adv* — **for·bid·ding·ness** *n*

forbode *var of* FOREBODE

1for·by *or* **for·bye** \fȯr-'bī\ *prep* [ME *forby*, prep. & adv., fr. *fore-* + *by*] **1** *archaic* **a :** PAST **b :** NEAR **2** *chiefly Scot* **:** BESIDES

2forby *or* **forbye** *adv, chiefly Scot* **:** in addition **:** BESIDES

1force \'fō(ə)rs, 'fȯ(ə)rs\ *n, often attrib* [ME, fr. MF, fr. (assumed) VL *fortia*, fr. L *fortis* strong] **1 a :** strength or energy exerted or brought to bear **:** cause of motion or change ⟨~*s* of nature⟩ **:** active power **b :** moral or mental strength **c** (1) **:** capacity to persuade or convince (2) **:** legal efficacy ⟨that law is still in ~⟩ **2 a :** military strength **b** (1) **:** a body (as of troops or ships) assigned to a military purpose (2) *pl* **:** the whole military strength (as of a nation) **c :** a body of persons available for a particular end ⟨labor ~⟩ **d :** an individual or group having the power of effective action **3 :** violence, compulsion, or constraint exerted upon or against a person or thing **4 :** an agency or influence that if applied to a free body results chiefly in an acceleration of the body and sometimes in elastic deformation and other effects **syn** see POWER — **force·less** \-ləs\ *adj*

2force *vt* **1 :** to do violence to; *esp* **:** RAPE **2 :** to compel by physical, moral, or intellectual means **:** COERCE **3 :** to make or cause through natural or logical necessity ⟨*forced* to admit he was right⟩ **4 a :** to attain to or effect against resistance or inertia ⟨~ your way through⟩ **b :** to impose or thrust urgently, importunately, or inexorably **5 :** to achieve or win by strength in struggle or violence: **a :** to win one's way into ⟨~ a castle⟩ ⟨*forced* the mountain passes⟩ **b :** to break open or through ⟨~ a lock⟩ **6 a :** to raise or accelerate to the utmost ⟨*forcing* the pace⟩ **b :** to produce only with unnatural or unwilling effort ⟨*forced* laughter⟩ **c :** to wrench, strain, or use (language) with marked unnaturalness and lack of ease **7 a :** to hasten the rate of progress or growth of ⟨a *forced* march⟩ **b :** to bring (as plants) to maturity out of the normal season ⟨*forcing* lilies for the Easter trade⟩ **8 :** to induce (as a particular bid or play by another player) in a card game by some conventional act, play, bid, or response **9 a :** to cause (a runner in baseball) to be put out through the necessity of leaving a base and attempting to advance to the next one **b :** to cause (a run) to be scored in baseball by giving a base on balls when the bases are full — **forc·er** *n*

syn COMPEL, COERCE, CONSTRAIN, OBLIGE: FORCE is the general term and implies the overcoming of resistance by the exertion of strength, power, weight, stress, or duress; COMPEL typically requires a personal object and suggests the working of an irresistible force; COERCE suggests overcoming resistance or unwillingness by actual or threatened violence or pressure; CONSTRAIN suggests the effect of a force or circumstance that limits freedom of action or choice; OBLIGE implies the constraint of necessity, law, or duty

— **force one's hand :** to cause one to act precipitously **:** force one to reveal his purpose or intention

forced \'fō(ə)rst, 'fȯ(ə)rst\ *adj* **1 :** compelled by force **:** INVOLUNTARY **2 :** done or produced with effort, exertion, or pressure — **forced·ly** \'fōr-səd-lē, 'fȯr-; 'fōrst-lē, 'fȯrst-\ *adv*

force feed *n* **:** a lubricating system (as in an internal-combustion engine) in which the lubricant is supplied under pressure

force–feed \'fōrs-'fēd, 'fȯrs-\ *vt* **:** to feed (as an animal) by forcible administration of food

force·ful \'fōrs-fəl, 'fȯrs-\ *adj* **:** possessing or filled with force **:** VIGOROUS — **force·ful·ly** \-fə-lē\ *adv* — **force·ful·ness** *n*

force ma·jeure \,fōr-smä-'zhər, ,fȯr-\ *n* [F] **:** superior or irresistible force

force·meat \'fōr-,smēt, 'fȯr-\ *n* [*force* (alter. of *farce*) + *meat*] **:** finely chopped and highly seasoned meat or fish that is either served alone or used as a stuffing — called also *farce*

for·ceps \'fȯr-səps\ *n, pl* **forceps** [L, fr. *formus* warm + *capere* to take — more at WARM, HEAVE] **:** an instrument for grasping, holding firmly, or exerting traction upon objects esp. for delicate operations (as by jewelers or surgeons) — **for·ceps·like** \-,līk\ *adj*

force pump *n* **:** a pump with a solid piston for drawing and forcing through valves a liquid (as water) to a considerable height above the pump or under a considerable pressure

forc·ible \'fōr-sə-bəl, 'fȯr-\ *adj* **1 :** effected by force used against opposition or resistance **2 :** characterized by force, efficiency, or energy **:** POWERFUL — **forc·i·ble·ness** *n* — **forc·i·bly** \-blē\ *adv*

1ford \'fō(ə)rd, 'fȯ(ə)rd\ *n* [ME, fr. OE; akin to ON *fjǫrthr* fiord, L *portus* port, OE *faran* to go — more at FARE] **:** a shallow part of a body of water that may be crossed by wading

2ford *vt* **:** to cross (a body of water) by wading — **ford·able** \'fōrd-ə-bəl, 'fȯrd-\ *adj*

for·do *or* **fore·do** \fȯr-'dü, fōr-\ *vt* [ME *fordon*, fr. OE *fordōn*, fr. *for-* + *dōn* to do] **1** *archaic* **:** to do away with **:** DESTROY **2 :** to overcome with fatigue **:** EXHAUST ⟨quite *fordone* with the heat⟩

1fore \'fō(ə)r, 'fȯ(ə)r\ *adv* [ME, fr. OE; akin to OE *for*] **1** *obs* **:** FORMERLY **2 :** in, toward, or adjacent to the front **:** FORWARD

2fore *also* **'fore** *prep* **1** *chiefly dial* **:** BEFORE **2 :** in the presence of

3fore *adj* [*fore-*] **1 :** prior in order of occurrence **:** FORMER **2 :** situated in front of something else **:** FORWARD

4fore *n* **1 :** FRONT **2 :** something that occupies a front position

5fore *interj* [prob. short for *before*] — used by a golfer to warn anyone within range of the probable line of flight of his ball

fore- *comb form* [ME *for-, fore-*, fr. OE *fore-*, fr. *fore*, adv.] **1 a :** earlier **:** beforehand ⟨*fore*see⟩ **b :** occurring earlier **:** occurring beforehand ⟨*fore*payment⟩ **2 a :** situated at the front **:** in front ⟨*fore*leg⟩ **b :** front part of (something specified) ⟨*fore*arm⟩

fore and aft *adv* **1 :** lengthwise of a ship **:** from stem to stern **2 :** in, at, or toward both the bow and stern

fore–and–aft \,fōr-ə-'naft, ,fȯr-\ *adj* **1 :** lying, running, or acting in the general line of the length of a ship or other construction **:** LONGITUDINAL **2 :** having no square sails

fore–and–aft·er \-'naf-tər\ *n* **:** a ship with a fore-and-aft rig; *esp* **:** SCHOONER

fore–and–aft rig *n* **:** a sailing-ship rig in which most or all of the sails are not attached to yards but are bent to gaffs or set on the masts or on stays amidships

1fore·arm \(')fōr-'ärm, (')fȯr-\ *vt* **:** to arm in advance **:** PREPARE

2fore·arm \'fōr-,ärm, 'fȯr-\ *n* **:** the part of the arm between the elbow and the wrist; *also* **:** the corresponding part in other vertebrates

fore·bear *or* **for·bear** \'fōr-,ba(ə)r, 'fȯr-, -,be(ə)r\ *n* [ME (Sc) *forebear*, fr. *fore-* + *-bear* (fr. *been* to be)] **:** ANCESTOR, FOREFATHER — usu. used in pl.

fore·bode *also* **for·bode** \fōr-'bōd, fȯr-\ *vt* **1 :** FORETELL, PORTEND ⟨such heavy air ~*s* storm⟩ **2 :** to have an inward conviction of (as coming ill or misfortune) ~ *vi* **:** AUGUR, PREDICT — **fore·bod·er** *n*

1fore·bod·ing *n* **:** an omen, prediction, or presentiment esp. of coming evil **:** PORTENT

2foreboding *adj* **:** indicative of or marked by foreboding — **fore·bod·ing·ly** \-iŋ-lē\ *adv* — **fore·bod·ing·ness** *n*

fore·brain \'fōr-,brān, 'fȯr-\ *n* **1 :** the anterior of the three primary divisions of the developing vertebrate brain **2 a :** the part of the brain of the adult that develops from the embryonic forebrain and includes the telencephalon and diencephalon **b :** TELENCEPHALON

1fore·cast \'fōr-,kast, 'fȯr-\ *vb* **forecast** *or* **fore·cast·ed; fore·cast·ing** *vt* **1** *archaic* **:** to plan ahead **:** SCHEME **2 a :** to calculate or predict (some future event or condition) usu. as a result of rational study and analysis of available pertinent data; *esp* **:** to predict (weather conditions) on the basis of correlated meteorological observations **b :** to indicate as likely to occur **3 :** to serve as a forecast of **:** PRESAGE ~ *vi* **:** to calculate the future **syn** see FORETELL — **fore·cast·er** *n*

2forecast *n* **1** *obs* **a :** previous determination **b :** PLAN, DESIGN **2** *archaic* **:** foresight of consequences and provision against them **:** FORETHOUGHT **3 :** a prophecy, estimate, or prediction of a future happening or condition

fore·cas·tle \'fōk-səl; 'fōr-,kas-əl, 'fȯr-\ *n* **1 :** the part of the upper deck of a ship forward of the foremast or of the fore channels **2 :** the forward part of a merchantman where the sailors live

fore·close \fōr-'klōz, fȯr-\ *vb* [ME *forclosen*, fr. OF *forclos*, pp. of *forclore*, fr. *fors* outside (fr. L *foris*) + *clore* to close — more at FORUM] *vt* **1 :** to shut out **:** DEBAR **2 :** to hold exclusively **3 :** to deal with or close in advance **4 :** to subject to foreclosure proceedings ~ *vi* **:** to foreclose a mortgage

fore·clo·sure \-'klō-zhər\ *n* **:** an act or instance of foreclosing; *specif* **:** a legal proceeding that bars or extinguishes a mortgagor's right of redeeming a mortgaged estate

fore·deck \'fōr-,dek, 'fȯr-\ *n* **:** the forepart of a ship's main deck

foredo *var of* FORDO

1fore·doom \'fōr-,düm, 'fȯr-\ *n, archaic* **:** consignment in advance to a particular fate **:** DESTINY

2fore·doom \fōr-'düm, fȯr-\ *vt* **:** to doom beforehand

fore·face \'fōr-,fās, 'fȯr-\ *n* **:** the part of the head of a quadruped that is in front of the eyes

fore·fa·ther \'fōr-,fät͟h-ər, 'fȯr-\ *n* **1 :** ANCESTOR 1a **2 :** a person

of an earlier period and common heritage
fore·feel \(')fōr-'fē(ə)l, (')fȯr-\ *vt* **:** to have a presentiment of
forefend *var of* FORFEND
fore·fin·ger \'fōr-,fiŋ-gər, 'fȯr-\ *n* **:** the finger next to the thumb — called also *index finger*
fore·foot \'fōr-,fu̇t, 'fȯr-\ *n* **1 :** one of the anterior feet of a quadruped or multiped **2 :** the forward part of a ship where the stem and keel meet
fore·front \-,frənt\ *n* **:** the foremost part or place **:** VANGUARD
foregather *var of* FORGATHER
1**fore·go** \fōr-'gō, fȯr-\ *vt* **:** to go before **:** PRECEDE — **fore·go·er** \-'gō(-ə)r\ *n*
2**forego** *var of* FORGO
fore·go·ing \-'gō-iŋ, -'gȯ(-)iŋ\ *adj* **:** going before **syn** see PRECEDING
fore·gone \'fōr-,gȯn, 'fȯr- *also* -,gän\ *adj* **:** PREVIOUS, PAST
foregone conclusion *n* **1 :** a conclusion that has preceded argument or examination **2 :** an inevitable result **:** CERTAINTY
fore·ground \'fōr-,grau̇nd, 'fȯr-\ *n* **1 :** the part of a scene or representation that is nearest to and in front of the spectator **2 :** a position of prominence **:** FOREFRONT
fore·gut \-,gət\ *n* **:** the anterior part of the alimentary canal of a vertebrate embryo that develops into the pharynx, esophagus, stomach, and extreme anterior part of the intestine
1**fore·hand** \'fōr-,hand, 'fȯr-\ *n* **1** *archaic* **:** superior position **:** ADVANTAGE **2 :** the part of a horse that is before the rider **3 :** a forehand stroke (as in tennis or racquets); *also* **:** the side on which such strokes are made

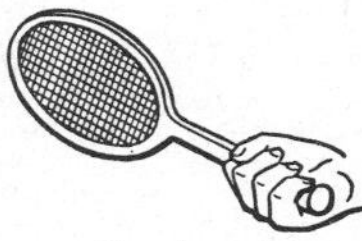
forehand 3

2**forehand** *adv* **:** with a forehand stroke
3**forehand** *adj* **1** *obs* **:** done or given in advance **:** PRIOR **2 :** made with the palm of the hand turned in the direction in which the hand is moving ⟨a ~ tennis stroke⟩
fore·hand·ed \'fōr-'han-dəd, 'fȯr-\ *adj* **1 a :** mindful of the future **:** THRIFTY, PRUDENT **b :** comfortably off **:** WELL-TO-DO **2 :** FOREHAND 2 — **fore·hand·ed·ly** *adv* — **fore·hand·ed·ness** *n*
fore·head \'fȯr-əd, 'fär-; 'fōr-,hed, 'fȯr-\ *n* **1 :** the part of the face above the eyes **2 :** the front or forepart of something
fore·hoof \'fōr-,hu̇f, 'fȯr-, -,hüf\ *n* **:** the hoof of a forefoot
for·eign \'fȯr-ən, 'fär-\ *adj* [ME *forein*, fr. OF, fr. LL *foranus* on the outside, fr. L *foris* outside — more at FORUM] **1 :** situated outside a place or country; *esp* **:** situated outside one's own country **2 :** born in, belonging to, or characteristic of some place or country other than the one under consideration **3 :** of, relating to, or proceeding from some other person or material thing than the one under consideration **4 :** alien in character **:** not connected or pertinent **5 :** related to or dealing with other nations **6 :** occurring in an abnormal situation in the living body and commonly introduced from without **7 :** not being within the jurisdiction of a political unit (as a state) **syn** see EXTRINSIC — **for·eign·ness** \-ən-nəs\ *n*
foreign bill *n* **:** a bill of exchange not both drawn and payable within a particular jurisdiction
for·eign·er \'fȯr-ə-nər, 'fär-\ *n* **1 :** a person belonging to or owing allegiance to a foreign country **:** ALIEN **2** *chiefly dial* **:** STRANGER
foreign exchange *n* **1 :** a process of settling accounts or debts between persons residing in different countries **2 :** foreign currency or current short-term credit instruments payable in such currency
for·eign·ism \'fȯr-ə-,niz-əm, 'fär-\ *n* **:** something peculiar to a foreign language or people; *specif* **:** a foreign idiom or custom
foreign minister *n* **:** a governmental minister for foreign affairs
1**fore·judge** *or* **for·judge** \fər-'jəj, fōr-, fȯr-\ *vt* [ME *forjuggen*, fr. MF *forjugier*, fr. *fors* outside (fr. L *foris*) + *jugier* to judge] **:** to expel, oust, or put out by judgment of a court
2**fore·judge** \(')fōr-'jəj, (')fȯr-\ *vt* **:** PREJUDGE
fore·know \(')fōr-'nō, (')fȯr-\ *vt* **:** to have previous knowledge of **:** know beforehand **syn** see FORESEE — **fore·knowl·edge** \-'näl-ij\ *n*
fore·la·dy \'fōr-,lād-ē, 'fȯr-\ *n* **:** a woman who acts as a foreman
fore·land \'fōr-lənd, 'fȯr-\ *n* **:** PROMONTORY, HEADLAND
fore·leg \'fōr-,leg, 'fȯr-, -,lāg\ *n* **:** a front leg
fore·limb \-,lim\ *n* **:** an arm, fin, wing, or leg that is or is homologous to a foreleg
fore·lock \-,läk\ *n* **:** a lock of hair growing from the front of the head
fore·man \'fōr-mən, 'fȯr-\ *n* **:** a first or chief man: as **a :** a member of a jury who acts as chairman and spokesman **b (1) :** a chief and often specially trained workman who works with and commonly leads a gang or crew **(2) :** a person in authority over a group of workers, a particular operation, or a section of a plant — **foreman·ship** \-,ship\ *n*
fore·mast \-,mast, -məst\ *n* **:** the mast nearest the bow of a ship
fore·milk \-,milk\ *n* **1 :** first-drawn milk **2 :** COLOSTRUM
1**fore·most** \'fōr-,mōst, 'fȯr-\ *adj* [ME *formest*, fr. OE, superl. of *forma* first; akin to OHG *fruma* advantage, OE *fore* fore] **1 :** first in a series or progression **2 :** of first rank or position **:** PREEMINENT
2**foremost** *adv* **:** in the first place
fore·moth·er \'fōr-,məth-ər, 'fȯr-\ *n* **:** a female ancestor
fore·name \-,nām\ *n* **:** a first name
fore·named \-,nāmd\ *adj* **:** previously named **:** AFORESAID
fore·noon \'fōr-,nün, 'fȯr-, , fōr-', fȯr-'\ *n* **:** the early part of the day ending with noon **:** MORNING
1**fo·ren·sic** \fə-'ren(t)-sik, -'ren-zik\ *adj* [L *forensis* public, forensic, fr. *forum*] **1 :** belonging to, used in, or suitable to courts of judicature or to public discussion and debate **2 :** ARGUMENTATIVE, RHETORICAL — **fo·ren·si·cal·ly** \-si-k(ə-)lē, -zi-\ *adv*
2**forensic** *n* **1 :** an argumentative exercise **2** *pl but sing or pl in constr* **:** the art or study of argumentative discourse
fore·or·dain \,fōr-ȯr-'dān, ,fȯr-\ *vt* **:** to dispose or appoint in advance **:** PREDESTINE — **fore·or·di·na·tion** \-,ȯrd-ᵊn-'ā-shən\ *n*
fore·part \'fōr-,pärt, 'fȯr-\ *n* **1 :** the anterior part of something **2 :** the earlier part of a period of time
fore·passed *or* **fore·past** \-,past\ *adj* **:** BYGONE
fore·paw \-,pȯ\ *n* **:** the paw of a foreleg
fore·peak \-,pēk\ *n* **:** the extreme forward lower compartment or tank used for trimming or storage in a ship
fore·quar·ter \-,kwȯ(r)t-ər\ *n* **:** the front half of a lateral half of the body or carcass of a quadruped ⟨a ~ of beef⟩
fore·reach \fōr-'rēch, fȯr-\ *vi, of a ship* **:** to gain ground in tacking ~ *vt* **:** to gain on or overhaul and go ahead of when close-hauled
fore·run \-'rən\ *vt* **1 :** to run before **2 :** to come before as a token of something to follow **3 :** FORESTALL, ANTICIPATE
fore·run·ner \'fōr-,rən-ər, 'fȯr-\ *n* **1 :** one going or sent before to give notice of the approach of others: as **a :** a premonitory sign or symptom **b :** a skier who runs the course before the start of a race **2 :** PREDECESSOR, FOREBEAR
syn FORERUNNER, PRECURSOR, HARBINGER, HERALD mean one who goes before or announces the coming of another. FORERUNNER is applicable to anything that serves as a sign or presage; PRECURSOR applies to a person or thing paving the way for the success or accomplishment of another; HARBINGER and HERALD both apply, chiefly figuratively, to one that proclaims or announces the coming or arrival of a notable event
fore·said \'fōr-,sed, 'fȯr-\ *adj, archaic* **:** AFORESAID
fore·sail \'fōr-,sāl, 'fȯr-, -səl\ *n* **1 :** a sail carried on the foreyard of a square-rigged ship that is the lowest sail on the foremast **2 :** the lower sail set abaft a schooner's foremast **3 :** FORESTAYSAIL
fore·see \fōr-'sē, fȯr-\ *vt* **:** to see (as a development) beforehand **:** FOREKNOW — **fore·see·able** \-'sē-ə-bəl, fər-\ *adj* — **fore·se·er** \fōr-'sē-ər, fȯr-, -'si(-ə)r\ *n*
syn FORESEE, FOREKNOW, DIVINE, APPREHEND, ANTICIPATE mean to know beforehand. FORESEE implies nothing about how the knowledge is derived and may apply to ordinary reasoning and experience; FOREKNOW usu. implies supernatural assistance, as through revelation; DIVINE adds to FORESEE the suggestion of exceptional wisdom or discernment; APPREHEND implies foresight mingled with uncertainty, anxiety, or dread; ANTICIPATE implies taking action about or responding emotionally to something before it happens
fore·shad·ow \fōr-'shad-(,)ō, fȯr-, -'shad-ə(-w)\ *vt* **:** to represent or typify beforehand **:** PREFIGURE — **fore·shad·ow·er** \-ə-wər\ *n*
fore·shank \'fōr-,shaŋk, 'fȯr-\ *n* **:** a beef shin
fore·sheet \-,shēt\ *n* **1 :** one of the sheets of a foresail **2** *pl* **:** the forward part of an open boat
fore·shore \-,shō(ə)r, -,shȯ(ə)r\ *n* **1 :** a strip of land margining a body of water **2 :** the part of a seashore between high-water and low-water marks
fore·short·en \fōr-'shȯrt-ᵊn, fȯr-\ *vt* **1 :** to shorten by proportionately contracting in the direction of depth so that an illusion of projection or extension in space is obtained **2 :** to make more compact
fore·show \fōr-'shō, fȯr-\ *vt* **1 :** FORETELL **2 :** to show beforehand
fore·side \'fōr-,sīd, 'fȯr-\ *n* **:** the front side or part **:** FRONT
fore·sight \'fōr-,sīt, 'fȯr-\ *n* **1 :** an act or the power of foreseeing **:** PRESCIENCE **2 :** an act of looking forward; *also* **:** a view forward **3 :** action in reference to the future **:** PRUDENCE — **fore·sight·ed** \-əd\ *adj* — **fore·sight·ed·ly** *adv* — **fore·sight·ed·ness** *n*
fore·skin \'fōr-,skin, 'fȯr-\ *n* **:** a fold of skin that covers the glans of the penis — called also *prepuce*
fore·speak \fōr-'spēk, fȯr-\ *vt* **1 :** FORETELL, PREDICT **2 :** to arrange for in advance
1**for·est** \'fȯr-əst, 'fär-\ *n, often attrib* [ME, fr. OF, fr. ML *forestis*, fr. L *foris* outside] **1 :** a tract of wooded land in England formerly owned by the sovereign and used for game **2 :** a dense growth of trees and underbrush covering a large tract **3 :** something resembling a forest esp. in profusion — **for·est·al** \-əst-ᵊl\ *or* **fo·res·ti·al** \fə-'res-tē-əl, fȯ-, -'res(h)-chəl\ *adj* — **for·es·ta·tion** \,fȯr-ə-'stā-shən, ,fär-\ *n*
2**forest** *vt* **:** to cover with trees or forest
fore·stage \'fōr-,stāj, 'fȯr-\ *n* **:** APRON 2g
fore·stall \fōr-'stȯl, fȯr-\ *vt* [ME *forstallen*, fr. *forstall* act of waylaying, fr. OE *foresteall*, fr. *fore-* + *steall* position, stall] **1** *archaic* **:** INTERCEPT **2 :** to exclude, hinder, or prevent by prior occupation or measures **3 :** to get ahead of **:** ANTICIPATE **4** *obs* **:** OBSTRUCT, BESET **5 :** to prevent the normal trading in by buying or diverting goods or by persuading persons to raise prices **syn** see PREVENT — **fore·stall·er** *n* — **fore·stall·ment** \-'stȯl-mənt\ *n*
fore·stay \'fōr-,stā, 'fȯr-\ *n* **:** a stay from the foremast head to the deck of a ship
fore·stay·sail \-,sāl, -səl\ *n* **:** the triangular aftermost headsail of a schooner, ketch, or yawl set on hanks on the forestay
for·est·er \'fȯr-ə-stər, 'fär-\ *n* **1 :** a person trained in forestry **2 :** an inhabitant of a forest **3 :** any of various woodland moths (family Agaristidae)
forest floor *n* **:** the richly organic layer of soil and debris characteristic of forested land
forest green *n* **:** a dark yellowish or moderate olive green
for·est·ry \'fȯr-ə-strē, 'fär-\ *n* **1 :** forest land **2 a :** the science of developing, caring for, or cultivating forests **b :** the management of growing timber
foreswear *var of* FORSWEAR
foresworn *var of* FORSWORN
1**fore·taste** \'fōr-,tāst, 'fȯr-\ *n* **:** an advance indication or warning **syn** see PROSPECT
2**fore·taste** \fōr-'tāst, fȯr-', 'fōr-, , 'fȯr-,\ *vt* **:** to taste beforehand **:** ANTICIPATE
fore·tell \fōr-'tel, fȯr-\ *vt* **:** to tell beforehand **:** PREDICT — **fore·tell·er** *n*
syn FORETELL, PREDICT, FORECAST, PROPHESY, PROGNOSTICATE mean to tell beforehand. FORETELL applies to the telling of the coming of a future event by any procedure or any source of information; PREDICT commonly implies inference from facts or accepted laws of nature; FORECAST adds the implication of anticipating eventualities and differs from PREDICT in being usually concerned with probabilities rather than certainties; PROPHESY connotes inspired or mystic knowledge of the future especially as the fulfilling of divine threats or promises; PROGNOSTICATE suggests the learned or skilled interpretation of signs or symptoms
1**fore·thought** \'fōr-,thȯt, 'fȯr-\ *n* **1 :** a thinking or planning out in advance **:** PREMEDITATION **2 :** consideration for the future
2**forethought** *adj* **:** thought of or planned beforehand **:** DELIBERATE
fore·thought·ful \-fəl\ *adj* **:** full of or having forethought — **fore·thought·ful·ly** \-fə-lē\ *adv* — **fore·thought·ful·ness** *n*

fore·time \'fōr-,tīm, 'fȯr-\ *n* **:** former or past time
1**fore·to·ken** \'fōr-,tō-kən, 'fȯr-\ *n* **:** a premonitory sign
2**fore·to·ken** \fōr-'tō-kən, fȯr-\ *vt* **fore·to·ken·ing** \-'tōk-(ə-)niŋ\ **:** to warn of in advance
fore·top \'fōr-,täp, 'fȯr-, *in sense 2 often* 'fōrt-əp *or* 'fȯrt-\ *n* **1 :** hair on the forepart of the head; *esp* **:** the forelock of a horse **2 :** the platform at the head of a ship's foremast
fore–top·gal·lant \'fōr-,täp-,gal-ənt, 'fōrt-ə-,gal-, 'fȯr(t)-\ *adj* **:** being the part next above the fore-topmast
fore·top·man \'fōr-,täp-mən, 'fōrt-əp-, 'fȯr(t)-\ *n* **:** a sailor on duty on the foremast and above
fore–top·mast \'fōr-,täp-məst, 'fōrt-əp-,mast, 'fȯr(t)-\ *n* **:** a mast next above the foremast
fore–top·sail \'fōr-,täp-səl, 'fōrt-əp-,sāl, 'fȯr(t)-\ *n* **:** the sail above the foresail
for·ev·er \fə-'rev-ər, fȯ-\ *adv* **1 :** for a limitless time **2 :** at all times
for·ev·er·more \-,rev-ə(r)-'mō(ə)r, -'mȯ(ə)r\ *adv* **:** FOREVER
for·ev·er·ness \-'rev-ər-nəs\ *n* **:** ETERNITY
fore·warn \fōr-'wȯ(ə)rn, fȯr-\ *vt* **:** to warn in advance **syn** see WARN
fore wing *n* **:** either of the anterior wings of a 4-winged insect
fore·wom·an \'fōr-,wu̇m-ən, 'fȯr-\ *n* **:** FORELADY
fore·word \'fōr-(,)wərd, 'fȯr-\ *n* **:** PREFACE
foreworn *var of* FORWORN
fore·yard \'fōr-,yärd, 'fȯr-\ *n* **:** the lowest yard on a foremast
1**for·feit** \'fȯr-fət\ *n* [ME *forfait*, fr. MF, fr. pp. of *forfaire* to commit a crime, forfeit, prob. fr. *fors* outside (fr. L *foris*) + *faire* to do, fr. L *facere*] **1 a :** something forfeited **b :** PENALTY **2 :** FORFEITURE **3 a :** something deposited and then redeemed on payment of a fine **b** *pl* **:** a game in which forfeits are exacted
2**forfeit** *vt* **1 :** to lose or lose the right to by some error, offense, or crime **2 :** to subject to confiscation as a forfeit — **for·feit·able** \-ə-bəl\ *adj* — **for·feit·er** *n*
3**forfeit** *adj* **:** forfeited or subject to forfeiture
for·fei·ture \'fȯr-fə-,chu̇(ə)r, -chər, -,t(y)u̇(ə)r\ *n* **1 :** the act of forfeiting **2 :** something that is forfeited **:** PENALTY
for·fend *also* **fore·fend** \fȯr-'fend, fōr-\ *vt* **1 a** *archaic* **:** FORBID **b :** to ward off **:** PREVENT **2 :** PROTECT, PRESERVE
for·gath·er *or* **fore·gath·er** \fȯr-'gath-ər, fōr-, -'geth-\ *vi* **1 :** to come together **:** ASSEMBLE **2 :** to meet someone usu. by chance
1**forge** \'fō(ə)rj, 'fȯ(ə)rj\ *n* [ME, fr. OF, fr. L *fabrica*, fr. *fabr-*, *faber* smith — more at DAFT] **1 :** a furnace or a shop with its furnace where metal is heated and wrought **:** SMITHY **2 :** a workshop where wrought iron is produced or where iron is made malleable
2**forge** *vt* **1 a :** to form (as metal) by heating and hammering **b :** to form (metal) by a mechanical or hydraulic press **2 :** to form or shape out in any way **:** FASHION **3 :** to make or imitate falsely esp. with intent to defraud **:** COUNTERFEIT ~ *vi* **1 :** to work at a forge **2 :** to commit forgery **syn** see MAKE
3**forge** *vi* [origin unknown] **1 :** to move forward slowly and steadily **2 :** to move with a sudden increase of speed and power
forg·er \'fōr-jər, 'fȯr-\ *n* **1 a :** FALSIFIER; *specif* **:** a creator of false tales **b :** a person guilty of forgery **2 :** one that forges
forg·ery \'fōrj-(ə-)rē, 'fȯrj-\ *n* **1** *archaic* **:** INVENTION **2 :** an act of forging; *esp* **:** the crime of falsely and fraudulently making or altering a writing or other instrument **3 :** something forged
for·get \fər-'get, fȯr-\ *vb* **for·got** \-'gät\ **for·got·ten** \-'gät-ᵊn\ *or* **forgot; for·get·ting** [ME *forgeten*, fr. OE *forgietan*, fr. *for-* + *-gietan* (akin to ON *geta* to get)] *vt* **1 a :** to lose the remembrance of **b** *obs* **:** to cease from doing **2 :** to treat with inattention or disregard **:** NEGLECT ⟨*forgot* his old friends⟩ **3 :** to put out of mind ⟨~ it⟩ ~ *vi* **1 :** to cease remembering or noticing **2 :** to fail to become mindful at the proper time ⟨~ about paying the bill⟩ **syn** see NEGLECT — **for·get·ter** *n* — **forget oneself :** to lose one's dignity, temper, or self-control
for·get·ful \-'get-fəl\ *adj* **1 :** likely to forget **2 :** CARELESS, NEGLECTFUL **3 :** inducing oblivion ⟨~ sleep⟩ — **for·get·ful·ly** \-fə-lē\ *adv* — **for·get·ful·ness** *n*
syn OBLIVIOUS, UNMINDFUL: FORGETFUL usually implies a heedless or negligent habit of failing to keep in mind; OBLIVIOUS suggests a failure to notice or remember due to external causes or conditions or to a determination to ignore; UNMINDFUL may suggest inattention and heedlessness or a deliberate ignoring
for·ge·tive \'fōr-jət-iv, 'fȯr-\ *adj* [prob. fr. 2*forge* + *-tive* (as in *inventive*)] **:** INVENTIVE, IMAGINATIVE
for·get–me–not \fər-'get-mē-,nät, fȯr-\ *n* **:** any of a genus (*Myosotis*) of small herbs of the borage family having bright-blue or white flowers usu. in a curving spike
for·get·ta·ble \fər-'get-ə-bəl, fȯr-\ *adj* **:** likely to be forgotten
forg·ing *n* **1 :** the act of a forger **2 :** a piece of forged work
for·giv·able \fər-'giv-ə-bəl, fȯr-\ *adj* **:** capable of being forgiven
for·give \fər-'giv, fȯr-\ *vb* **for·gave** \-'gāv\ **for·giv·en** \-'giv-ən\ **for·giv·ing** [ME *forgiven*, fr. OE *forgifan*, fr. *for-* + *gifan* to give] *vt* **1 :** to cease to feel resentment against (an offender) **:** PARDON ⟨~ one's enemies⟩ **2 a :** to give up resentment of or claim to requital for ⟨~ an insult⟩ **b :** to grant relief from payment of ~ *vi* **:** to grant forgiveness **syn** see EXCUSE — **for·giv·er** *n*
for·give·ness \-'giv-nəs\ *n* **:** the act of forgiving **:** PARDON
for·giv·ing *adj* **1 :** willing or able to forgive **2 :** characterized by forgiveness — **for·giv·ing·ly** \-iŋ-lē\ *adv* — **for·giv·ing·ness** *n*
for·go *or* **fore·go** \fȯr-'gō, fōr-\ *vt* [ME *forgon*, fr. OE *forgān* to pass by, forgo, fr. *for-* + *gān* to go] **1** *archaic* **:** FORSAKE **2 :** to abstain from **:** RENOUNCE — **for·go·er** \-'gō(-ə)r\ *n*
fo·rint \'fō-,rint\ *n* [Hung] — see MONEY table
forjudge *var of* FOREJUDGE
1**fork** \'fȯ(ə)rk\ *n* [ME *forke*, fr. OE & ONF; OE *forca* & ONF *forque*, fr. L *furca*] **1 :** an implement with two or more prongs used esp. for taking up (as in eating), pitching, or digging **2 :** a forked part, tool, or piece of equipment **3 a :** a division into branches or the place where something divides into branches **b :** CONFLUENCE **4 a :** a branch of a fork **b :** ALTERNATIVE, CHOICE
2**fork** *vi* **:** to divide into two or more branches ⟨the road ~*s*⟩ ~ *vt* **1 :** to give the form of a fork to ⟨~*ing* her fingers⟩ **2 :** to raise or pitch with a fork ⟨~ hay⟩ **3 :** to attack (two chessmen) simultaneously **4 :** PAY, CONTRIBUTE — **fork·er** *n*
forked \'fȯ(ə)rkt, 'fȯr-kəd\ *adj* **1 :** resembling a fork esp. in having one end divided into two or more branches or points ⟨~ lightning⟩ **2 :** shaped like a fork or having a forked part ⟨a ~ road⟩
fork·ful \'fȯrk-,fu̇l\ *n, pl* **forkfuls** \'fȯrk-,fu̇lz\ *or* **forks·ful** \'fȯrks-,fu̇l\ **:** as much as a fork will hold
fork·lift \'fȯrk-,klift\ *n* **:** a machine for hoisting heavy objects by means of steel fingers inserted under the load
forky \'fȯr-kē\ *adj* **:** FORKED ⟨a ~ beard⟩
for·lorn \fər-'lȯ(ə)rn\ *adj* [ME *forloren*, fr. OE, pp. of *forlēosan* to lose, fr. *for-* + *lēosan* to lose] **1 a :** FORSAKEN, BEREFT **b :** DESERTED **2 :** MISERABLE, WRETCHED **3 :** nearly hopeless **syn** see ALONE — **for·lorn·ly** *adv* — **for·lorn·ness** \-'lȯrn-nəs\ *n*
forlorn hope *n* [by folk etymology fr. D *verloren hoop*, lit., lost band] **1 :** a body of men selected to perform a perilous service **2 :** a desperate or extremely difficult enterprise
1**form** \'fȯ(ə)rm\ *n* [ME *forme*, fr. OF, fr. L *forma*] **1 a :** the shape and structure of something as distinguished from its material **b :** a body (as of a person) esp. in its external appearance or as distinguished from the face **c** *archaic* **:** BEAUTY **2 :** the essential nature of a thing as distinguished from its matter: as **a :** IDEA 1a **b :** the component of a thing that determines its kind **3 a :** established method of expression or proceeding **:** procedure according to rule or rote **b :** a prescribed and set order of words **:** FORMULA **4 :** a printed or typed document with blank spaces for insertion of required or requested information ⟨tax ~⟩ **5 a :** conduct regulated by extraneous controls (as of custom or etiquette) **:** CEREMONY, CONVENTIONALITY; *sometimes* **:** show without substance **b :** manner or style of performing or accomplishing according to recognized standards of technique **6 a :** the resting place of a hare **b :** a long seat **:** BENCH **7 a :** a supporting frame model of the human figure used for displaying clothes **b :** a mold in which concrete is placed to set **8 :** the printing type or other matter arranged and secured in a chase ready for printing **9 :** one of the different modes of existence, action, or manifestation of a particular thing or substance **:** KIND, SORT, VARIETY **10 a :** orderly method of arrangement (as in the presentation of ideas) **:** manner of coordinating elements (as of an artistic production or course of reasoning); *sometimes* **:** a particular kind or instance of such arrangement ⟨the sonnet is a poetical ~⟩ **b :** PATTERN, SCHEMA ⟨arguments of the same logical ~⟩ **c :** the structural element, plan, or design of a work of art — compare CONTENT **d :** a visible and measurable unit defined by a contour **:** a bounded surface or volume **11 :** a grade in a British secondary school or in some American private schools **12 a :** known ability to perform **b :** condition suitable for performing (as in athletic competition) **13 a :** LINGUISTIC FORM **b :** one of the different aspects a word may take as a result of inflection or change of spelling or pronunciation ⟨verbal ~*s*⟩
syn FIGURE, SHAPE, CONFORMATION, CONFIGURATION: FORM usu. suggests reference to both internal structure and external outline and often the principle that gives unity to the whole; FIGURE applies chiefly to the form as determined by bounding or enclosing lines; SHAPE like FIGURE suggests an outline but carries a stronger implication of the enclosed body or mass; CONFORMATION implies structure composed of related parts; CONFIGURATION refers to the disposition and arrangement of component parts
2**form** *vt* **1 :** to give form or shape to **:** FASHION **2 a :** to give a particular shape to **:** shape or mold into a certain state or after a particular model **:** ARRANGE **b :** to model by instruction and discipline ⟨a mind ~*ed* by classical education⟩ **3 :** DEVELOP, ACQUIRE ⟨~ a habit⟩ **4 :** to serve to make up or constitute **:** be a usu. essential or basic element of **5 a :** to assume an inflection so as to produce (as a tense) ⟨~*s* the past in *-ed*⟩ **b :** to combine to make (a compound word) **c :** to make up **:** CONSTITUTE ⟨~ a clause⟩ **6 :** to arrange in order **:** draw up ~ *vi* **1 :** to become formed or shaped **2 :** to take form **:** come into existence **:** ARISE **3 :** to take on a definite form, shape, or arrangement **syn** see MAKE — **form on :** to take up a formation next to
form- *or* **formo-** *comb form* [*formic*] **:** formic acid ⟨*form*ate⟩
-form \,fȯrm\ *adj comb form* [MF & L; MF *-forme*, fr. L *-formis*, fr. *forma*] **:** in the form or shape of **:** resembling ⟨ovi*form*⟩
1**for·mal** \'fȯr-məl\ *adj* **1 a :** belonging to or being the essential constitution or structure ⟨~ cause⟩ **b :** relating to, concerned with, or constituting the outward form of something as distinguished from its content **2 a :** following or according with established form, custom, or rule **:** CONVENTIONAL **b :** done in due form **:** CEREMONIAL **3 a :** based on conventional forms and rules **b :** characterized by punctilious respect for form **:** METHODICAL **c :** rigidly ceremonious **:** PRIM **4 :** having the appearance without the substance **syn** see CEREMONIAL — **for·mal·ly** \-mə-lē\ *adv*
2**formal** *n* **:** something formal in character
form·al·de·hyde \fȯr-'mal-də-,hīd, fər-\ *n* [ISV] **:** a colorless pungent irritating gas HCHO that is made by oxidation of methanol or of gaseous hydrocarbons and used chiefly as a disinfectant and preservative and in synthesizing other compounds and resins
For·ma·lin \'fȯr-mə-lən, -,lēn\ *trademark* — used for a clear aqueous solution of formaldehyde containing a small amount of methanol
for·mal·ism \'fȯr-mə-,liz-əm\ *n* **:** the practice or the doctrine of strict adherence to prescribed or external forms (as in religion or art); *also* **:** an instance of this — **for·mal·ist** \-ləst\ *n or adj* — **for·mal·is·tic** \,fȯr-mə-'lis-tik\ *adj* — **for·mal·is·ti·cal·ly** \-ti-k(ə-)lē\ *adv*
for·mal·i·ty \fȯr-'mal-ət-ē\ *n* **1 :** the quality or state of being formal **2 :** compliance with formal or conventional rules **:** CEREMONY **3 :** an established form that is required or conventional
for·mal·iza·tion \,fȯr-mə-lə-'zā-shən\ *n* **:** an act of formalizing **:** the state of being formalized
for·mal·ize \'fȯr-mə-,līz\ *vt* **1 :** to give a certain or definite form to **:** SHAPE **2 a :** to make formal **b :** to give formal status or approval to — **for·mal·iz·er** *n*
formal logic *n* **:** a system of logic (as Aristotelian logic or symbolic logic) that abstracts the forms of thought from its content to establish abstract criteria of consistency
for·mant \'fȯr-mənt, -,mant\ *n* **:** a characteristic component of the quality of a speech sound; *specif* **:** any of several resonance bands held to determine the phonetic quality of a vowel
1**for·mat** \'fȯr-,mat\ *n* [F or G; F, fr. G, fr. L *formatus*, pp. of *formare* to form, fr. *forma*] **1 :** the shape, size, and general makeup of a publication **2 :** general plan of organization or arrangement
2**format** *vt* **for·mat·ted; for·mat·ting :** to produce in a specified form or style ⟨*formatted* output of a computer⟩
for·mate \-,māt\ *n* **:** a salt or ester of formic acid
for·ma·tion \fȯr-'mā-shən\ *n* **1 :** an act of giving form or shape to something or of taking form **:** DEVELOPMENT **2 :** something that is

formed **3 :** the manner in which a thing is formed **:** STRUCTURE **4 :** the largest unit in an ecological community comprising two or more associations and their precursors **5 :** any sedimentary bed or consecutive series of beds sufficiently homogeneous or distinctive to be a unit **6 :** an arrangement of a body or group of persons in some prescribed manner or for a particular purpose — **for·ma·tion·al** \-shnəl, -shən-ᵊl\ *adj*

1for·ma·tive \'fȯr-mət-iv\ *adj* **1 a :** giving or capable of giving form **:** CONSTRUCTIVE ⟨a ~ influence⟩ **b** *of an affix or other word element* **:** used in word formation or inflection **2 :** capable of alteration by growth and development; *also* **:** producing new cells and tissues **3 :** of, relating to, or characterized by formative effects or formation ⟨~ years⟩ — **for·ma·tive·ly** *adv* — **for·ma·tive·ness** *n*

2formative *n* **:** the element in a word that serves to give the word appropriate form and is not part of the base

form class *n* **:** a class of linguistic forms that can be used in the same position in a construction and that have one or more morphological or syntactical features in common

for·mée \fȯr-'mā\ *adj* [ME *forme*, fr. MF *formé*] *of a heraldic cross* **:** having the arms narrow at the center and expanding toward the ends — see CROSS illustration

1for·mer \'fȯr-mər\ *adj* [ME, fr. *forme* first, fr. OE *forma* — more at FOREMOST] **1 :** coming before in time; *esp* **:** of, relating to, or occurring in the past ⟨~ correspondence⟩ **2 :** preceding in place or arrangement **:** FOREGOING ⟨~ part of the chapter⟩ **3 :** first mentioned or in order of two things mentioned or understood ⟨of these two evils the ~ is the lesser⟩ **syn** see PRECEDING

2form·er \'fȯr-mər\ *n* **:** one that forms

for·mer·ly \-mə(r)-lē\ *adv* **1** *obs* **:** just before **2 :** in time past

form·fit·ting \'fȯrm-,fit-iŋ\ *adj* **:** conforming to the outline of the body **:** CLOSE-FITTING ⟨a ~ sweater⟩

form genus *n* **:** an artificial taxonomic category established for organisms (as imperfect fungi) of obscure true relationships

for·mic \'fȯr-mik\ *adj* [L *formica* ant — more at PISMIRE] **:** derived from formic acid

For·mi·ca \fȯr-'mī-kə, fər-\ *trademark* — used for any of various laminated plastic products used esp. for surface finish

formic acid *n* **:** a colorless pungent fuming vesicatory liquid acid HCOOH found in ants and some other insects and in many plants or made by acidification of sodium formate and used chiefly in dyeing and finishing textiles

for·mi·cary \'fȯr-mə-,ker-ē\ *n* [ML *formicarium*, fr. L *formica*] **:** an ant nest

for·mi·da·bil·i·ty \,fȯr-məd-ə-'bil-ət-ē\ *n* **:** formidable quality

for·mi·da·ble \'fȯr-məd-ə-bəl *also* fȯr-'mid-\ *adj* [ME, fr. L *formidabilis*, fr. *formidare* to fear, fr. *formido* fear; akin to Gk *mormō* she-monster] **1 :** exciting fear ⟨a ~ prospect⟩ **2 :** having qualities that discourage approach or attack **3 :** tending to inspire awe or wonder — **for·mi·da·ble·ness** *n* — **for·mi·da·bly** \-blē\ *adv*

form·less \'fȯrm-ləs\ *adj* **:** having no regular form or shape — **form·less·ly** *adv* — **form·less·ness** *n*

for·mu·la \'fȯr-myə-lə\ *n, pl* **formulas** *also* **for·mu·lae** \-,lē, -,lī\ [L, dim. of *forma* form] **1 a :** a set form of words for use in a ceremony or ritual **b :** a conventionalized statement intended to express some fundamental truth or principle **2 a :** RECIPE, PRESCRIPTION **b :** a milk mixture or substitute for feeding an infant **3 a :** a general fact, rule, or principle expressed in symbols **b :** a symbolic expression of the composition or constitution of a substance **c :** a group of numerical symbols associated to express briefly a single concept **d :** a combination of signs in a logical calculus **4 :** a prescribed or set form or method — **for·mu·la·ic** \,fȯr-myə-'lā-ik\ *adj* — **for·mu·la·i·cal·ly** \-'lā-ə-k(ə-)lē\ *adv*

for·mu·la·ri·za·tion \,fȯr-myə-lə-rə-'zā-shən\ *n* **:** an act or product of formularizing

for·mu·la·rize \'fȯr-myə-lə-,rīz\ *vt* **:** to state in or reduce to a formula **:** FORMULATE — **for·mu·la·riz·er** *n*

for·mu·lary \'fȯr-myə-,ler-ē\ *n* **1 :** a book or other collection of stated and prescribed forms **2 :** a prescribed form or model **:** FORMULA **3 :** a book containing a list of medicinal substances and formulas — **formulary** *adj*

for·mu·late \'fȯr-myə-,lāt\ *vt* **1 a :** to reduce to or express in a formula **b :** to put into a systematized statement or expression **c :** DEVISE **2 a :** to develop a formula for the preparation of (as a soap or a plastic) **b :** to prepare according to a formula — **for·mu·la·tor** \-,lāt-ər\ *n*

for·mu·la·tion \,fȯr-myə-'lā-shən\ *n* **:** an act or the product of formulating

for·mu·lism \'fȯr-myə-,liz-əm\ *n* **:** attachment to or reliance on formulas — **for·mu·lis·tic** \,fȯr-myə-'lis-tik\ *adj*

for·mu·li·za·tion \,fȯr-myə-lə-'zā-shən\ *n* **:** FORMULATION

for·mu·lize \'fȯr-myə-,līz\ *vt* **:** FORMULATE 1

form word *n* **:** FUNCTION WORD

for·myl \'fȯr-,mil\ *n* [ISV] **:** the radical HCO— of formic acid that is also characteristic of aldehydes

1for·ni·cate \'fȯr-nə-,kāt\ *vi* [LL *fornicatus*, pp. of *fornicare*, fr. L *fornic-*, *fornix* arch, vault, brothel] **:** to commit fornication — **for·ni·ca·tor** \-,kāt-ər\ *n*

2for·ni·cate \'fȯr-ni-kət, -nə-,kāt\ *also* **for·ni·cat·ed** \-nə-,kāt-əd\ *adj* [L *fornicatus*, fr. *fornic-*, *fornix*] **:** having an arched or vaulted form ⟨broad ~ leaves⟩; *also* **:** having fornices

for·ni·ca·tion \,fȯr-nə-'kā-shən\ *n* **1 :** human sexual intercourse other than between a man and his wife **:** sexual intercourse between a spouse and an unmarried person **:** sexual intercourse between unmarried people — used in some translations (as AV, DV) of the Bible (as in Mt 5:32) for *unchastity* (as in RSV) or *immorality* (as in NCE) to cover all sexual intercourse except between husband and wife or concubine **2 :** sexual intercourse on the part of an unmarried person accomplished with consent and not deemed adultery

for·nix \'fȯr-niks\ *n, pl* **for·ni·ces** \-nə-,sēz\ [NL, fr. L] **:** an anatomical arch or fold

for·rad·er *also* **for·rard·er** \'fär-əd-ər\ *adv* [E dial., compar. of E *forward*] *chiefly Brit* **:** further ahead

for·sake \fər-'sāk, fȯr-\ *vt* **for·sook** \-'sùk\ **for·sak·en** \-'sā-kən\ **for·sak·ing** [ME *forsaken*, fr. OE *forsacan*, fr. *for-* + *sacan* to dispute, accuse — more at SAKE] **1 :** to give up **:** RENOUNCE **2 :** to quit or leave entirely **syn** see ABANDON

for·sooth \fər-'süth\ *adv* [ME *for soth*, fr. OE *forsōth*, fr. *for* + *sōth* sooth] **:** in truth **:** INDEED

for·spent \fər-'spent\ *adj, archaic* **:** worn out **:** EXHAUSTED

for·swear *or* **fore·swear** \fȯr-'swa(ə)r, fōr-, -'swe(ə)r\ *vt* **1 a :** to reject or renounce upon oath **b :** to renounce earnestly **2 :** to deny upon oath **3 :** PERJURE ⟨~ himself⟩ **~** *vi* **:** to swear falsely **syn** see ABJURE

for·sworn *or* **fore·sworn** \-'swō(ə)rn, -'swȯ(ə)rn\ *adj* **:** PERJURED

for·syth·ia \fər-'sith-ē-ə\ *n* [NL, genus name, fr. William *Forsyth* †1804 Brit botanist] **:** any of a genus (*Forsythia*) of ornamental shrubs of the olive family with opposite leaves and yellow bell-shaped flowers appearing before the leaves in early spring

1fort \'fō(ə)rt, 'fȯ(ə)rt\ *n* [ME *forte*, fr. MF *fort*, fr. *fort* strong, fr. L *fortis*] **:** a strong or fortified place; *esp* **:** a fortified place occupied only by troops and surrounded with such works as a ditch, rampart, and parapet **:** FORTIFICATION

2fort *vt* **:** FORTIFY **~** *vi* **:** to construct or assemble behind fortifications

for·ta·lice \'fȯrt-ᵊl-əs\ *n* [ME, fr. ML *fortalitia* — more at FORTRESS] **1** *archaic* **:** FORTRESS **2** *archaic* **:** a small fort

1forte \'fō(ə)rt, 'fȯ(ə)rt; 'fȯr-,tā\ *n* [MF *fort*, fr. *fort* strong] **1 :** one's strong point **2 :** the strong part of the blade of a sword from the middle to the hilt

2for·te \'fȯr-,tā, 'fȯrt-ē\ *adv* (*or adj*) [It, fr. *forte* strong, fr. L *fortis*] **:** LOUDLY, POWERFULLY — used as a direction in music

3for·te \'fȯr-,tā, 'fȯrt-ē\ *n* **:** a tone or passage played forte

1forth \'fō(ə)rth, 'fȯ(ə)rth\ *adv* [ME, fr. OE; akin to OE *for*] **1 :** onward in time, place, or order **:** FORWARD ⟨from that day ~⟩ **2 :** out into notice or view ⟨put ~ leaves⟩ **3** *obs* **:** AWAY, ABROAD

2forth *prep, archaic* **:** forth from **:** out of

1forth·com·ing \(')fōrth-'kəm-iŋ, (')fȯrth-\ *adj* [obs *forthcome* (to come forth)] **1 :** being about to appear **:** APPROACHING ⟨the ~ holidays⟩ **2 :** readily available or approachable

2forthcoming *n* **:** a coming forth **:** APPROACH

forth of *prep* **:** out of **:** out from

1forth·right \'fōr-,thrīt, 'fȯr-\ *adv* **1 a :** directly forth or ahead **b :** without hesitation **:** FRANKLY **2** *archaic* **:** at once

2forthright *adj* **:** proceeding straight on **:** STRAIGHTFORWARD — **forth·right·ly** *adv* — **forth·right·ness** *n*

3forthright *n* **:** a straight path

forth·with \(')fōrth-'with, (')fȯrth-, -'with\ *adv* **:** IMMEDIATELY

for·ti·eth \'fȯrt-ē-əth\ *n* — see NUMBER table — **fortieth** *adj*

for·ti·fi·ca·tion \,fȯrt-ə-fə-'kā-shən\ *n* **1 :** an act or process of fortifying **2 :** something that fortifies, defends, or strengthens; *esp* **:** works erected to defend a place or position

for·ti·fi·er \'fȯrt-ə-,fī(-ə)r\ *n* **:** one that fortifies

for·ti·fy \-,fī\ *vb* [ME *fortifien*, fr. MF *fortifier*, fr. LL *fortificare*, fr. L *fortis* strong] *vt* **:** to make strong: as **a :** to strengthen and secure (as a town) by forts or batteries **b :** to give physical strength, courage, or endurance to **:** INVIGORATE **c :** to add mental or moral strength to **:** ENCOURAGE **d :** to add material to for strengthening or enriching **~** *vi* **:** to erect fortifications

for·tis \'fȯrt-əs\ *adj* [NL, fr. L] **:** produced with relatively great articulatory tenseness and strong expiration ⟨\t\ in *toe* is ~, \d\ in *doe* is lenis⟩

1for·tis·si·mo \fȯr-'tis-ə-,mō\ *adv* (*or adj*) [It, superl. of *forte*] **:** very loud — used as a direction in music

2fortissimo *n, pl* **fortissimos** *or* **for·tis·si·mi** \-,mē\ **:** a very loud passage, sound, or tone

for·ti·tude \'fȯrt-ə-,t(y)üd\ *n* [ME, fr. L *fortitudin-*, *fortitudo*, fr. *fortis*] **1** *obs* **:** STRENGTH **2 :** strength of mind that enables a person to encounter danger or bear pain or adversity with courage

syn FORTITUDE, GRIT, BACKBONE, PLUCK, GUTS, SAND mean courage and staying power. FORTITUDE stresses firmness in enduring physical or mental hardships and suffering; GRIT stresses unyielding resolution and indomitableness in the face of hardship or danger; BACKBONE suggests the ability to withstand intimidation or domineering; PLUCK suggests courage and tenacity in fighting on esp. against odds; GUTS implies fortitude and stamina essential to facing and coping with what alarms or repels or discourages; SAND is close to GRIT but sometimes suggests also boldness or effrontery

for·ti·tu·di·nous \,fȯrt-ə-'t(y)üd-nəs, -ᵊn-əs\ *adj* **:** COURAGEOUS

fort·night \'fȯrt-,nīt, 'fȯrt-\ *n* [ME *fourtenight*, alter. of *fourtene night*, fr. OE *fēowertȳne niht* fourteen nights] **:** the space of 14 days **:** two weeks

1fort·night·ly \-lē\ *adj* **:** occurring or appearing once in a fortnight

2fortnightly *adv* **:** once in a fortnight

3fortnightly *n* **:** a publication issued fortnightly

1for·tress \'fȯr-trəs\ *n* [ME *forteresse*, fr. MF *forteresce*, fr. ML *fortalitia*, fr. L *fortis* strong] **:** a fortified place **:** STRONGHOLD; *esp* **:** a large and permanent fortification sometimes including a town

2fortress *vt* **:** FORTIFY

for·tu·itous \fȯr-'t(y)ü-ət-əs, fər-\ *adj* [L *fortuitus*; akin to L *fort-*, *fors*] **1 :** occurring by chance **2 :** FORTUNATE, LUCKY **syn** see ACCIDENTAL — **for·tu·itous·ly** *adv* — **for·tu·itous·ness** *n*

for·tu·ity \-ət-ē\ *n* [irreg. fr. *fortuitous*] **1 :** the quality or state of being fortuitous **2 :** a chance event or occurrence

for·tu·nate \'fȯrch-(ə-)nət\ *adj* **1 :** bringing some good thing not foreseen as certain **:** AUSPICIOUS **2 :** receiving some unexpected good **syn** see LUCKY — **for·tu·nate·ly** *adv* — **for·tu·nate·ness** *n*

1for·tune \'fȯr-chən\ *n* [ME, fr. MF, fr. L *fortuna*; akin to L *fort-*, *fors* chance, luck, *ferre* to carry — more at BEAR] **1** *often cap* **:** a hypothetical force or personified power that unpredictably determines events and issues favorably or unfavorably **2** *obs* **:** ACCIDENT, INCIDENT **3 a :** favorable issue **:** SUCCESS **b :** good or bad luck happening to a person **4 :** DESTINY, FATE **5 a :** possession of material goods **:** WEALTH **b :** a store of material possessions

2fortune *vt* **1** *obs* **:** to give good or bad fortune to **2** *archaic* **:** to provide with a fortune **~** *vi, archaic* **:** HAPPEN, CHANCE

fortune hunter *n* **:** a person that seeks wealth esp. by marriage

for·tune–tell·er \-,tel-ər\ *n* **:** one that professes to foretell future events — **for·tune–tell·ing** \-iŋ\ *n or adj*

for·ty \'fȯrt-ē\ *n* [ME *fourty*, adj., fr. OE *fēowertig*, fr. *fēowertig* group of 40, fr. *fēower* four + *-tig* group of 10 — more at EIGHTY] **1** — see NUMBER table **2 :** the third point scored by a side in a

game of tennis **3** *pl* **:** the numbers 40 to 49; *specif* **:** the years 40 to 49 in a lifetime or century — **forty** *adj or pron*
for·ty–eight·mo \ˌfȯrt-ē-ˈāt-(ˌ)mō\ *n* **:** the size of a piece of paper cut 48 from a sheet; *also* **:** a book, a page, or paper of this size
for·ty–five \ˌfȯrt-ē-ˈfīv\ *n* **1** — see NUMBER table **2 :** a 45 caliber pistol — usu. written .45 **3 :** a microgroove phonograph record designed to be played at 45 revolutions per minute — usu. written 45 — **forty–five** *adj or pron*
Forty Hours *n pl but sing or pl in constr* **:** a Roman Catholic devotion in which the churches of a diocese in two-day turns maintain continuous daytime prayer before the exposed Blessed Sacrament
for·ty–nin·er \ˌfȯrt-ē-ˈnī-nər\ *n* **:** one taking part in the rush to California for gold in 1849
forty winks *n pl but sing or pl in constr* **:** a short sleep **:** NAP
fo·rum \ˈfōr-əm, ˈfȯr-\ *n, pl* **forums** *also* **fo·ra** \-ə\ [L; akin to L *foris* outside, *fores* door — more at DOOR] **1 a :** the marketplace or public place of an ancient Roman city forming the center of judicial and public business **b :** a public meeting place for open discussion **c :** a medium of open discussion **2 :** a judicial body or assembly **:** COURT **3 a :** a public meeting or lecture involving audience discussion **b :** a program (as on radio or television) involving discussion of a problem usu. by several authorities
1**for·ward** \ˈfȯr-wərd, *South also* ˈfär-\ *adj* [ME, fr. OE *foreweard* fr. *fore-* + *-weard* -ward] **1 a :** near, being at, or belonging to the forepart **b :** situated in advance **2 a :** strongly inclined **:** READY **b :** tending to push oneself **:** BRASH ⟨a flashy ~ young woman⟩ **3 :** notably advanced or developed **:** PRECOCIOUS **4 :** moving, tending, or leading toward a position in front **5 :** EXTREME, RADICAL **6 :** of, relating to, or getting ready for the future ⟨~ buying of produce⟩ — **for·ward·ly** *adv* — **for·ward·ness** *n*
2**forward** *adv* **:** to or toward what is before or in front
3**forward** *n* **:** a mainly offensive player in any of several games (as basketball) stationed at or near the front of his side or team
4**forward** *vt* **1 :** to help onward **:** ADVANCE **2 a :** to send forward **:** TRANSMIT **b :** to send or ship onward from an intermediate post or station in transit **syn** see ADVANCE
for·ward·er \-wərd-ər\ *n* **:** one that forwards; *specif* **:** an agent who performs services (as receiving, transshipping, or delivering) designed to assure and facilitate the passage of goods of his principal
for·ward·ing \-iŋ\ *n* **:** the act of one that forwards; *esp* **:** the business of a forwarder of goods
forward pass *n* **:** a pass in football made in the direction of the opponents' goal
for·wards \-wərdz\ *adv* **:** FORWARD
1**for·why** \fər-ˈ(h)wī\ *adv, chiefly dial* **:** WHY, WHEREFORE
2**forwhy** *conj, archaic* **:** BECAUSE, SINCE
for·worn *also* **fore·worn** \fər-ˈwō(ə)rn, -ˈwȯ(ə)rn\ *adj, archaic* **:** worn out
for·zan·do \fȯrt-ˈsän-(ˌ)dō\ *adj (or adv)* [It] **:** SFORZANDO
fos·sa \ˈfäs-ə\ *n, pl* **fos·sae** \-ˌē, -ˌī\ [NL, fr. L] **:** an anatomical pit or depression — **fos·sate** \-ˌāt\ *adj*
fosse *or* **foss** \ˈfäs\ *n* [ME *fosse*, fr. OF, fr. L *fossa*, fr. fem. of *fossus*] **:** DITCH, MOAT
1**fos·sil** \ˈfäs-əl\ *n* [L *fossilis* dug up, fr. *fossus*, pp. of *fodere* to dig — more at BED] **1 :** any remains, impression, or trace of an animal or plant of past geological ages that has been preserved in the earth's crust **2 a :** a person whose views are outmoded **:** FOGY **b :** something that has become rigidly fixed **3 :** an old word or word element preserved only by idiom (as *fro* in *to and fro*)
2**fossil** *adj* **1 :** extracted from the earth ⟨~ fuels such as coal⟩ **2 :** being or resembling a fossil
fos·sil·if·er·ous \ˌfäs-ə-ˈlif-(ə-)rəs\ *adj* **:** containing fossils
fos·sil·iza·tion \ˌfäs-(ə-)lə-ˈzā-shən\ *n* **:** the process of fossilizing **:** the state of becoming fossilized
fos·sil·ize \ˈfäs-ə-ˌlīz\ *vt* **1 :** to convert into a fossil **2 :** to make outmoded, rigid, or fixed **~** *vi* **:** to become changed into a fossil
fos·so·ri·al \fä-ˈsōr-ē-əl, -ˈsȯr-\ *adj* [ML *fossorius*, fr. L *fossus*, pp.] **:** adapted to digging ⟨a ~ foot⟩
1**fos·ter** \ˈfȯs-tər, ˈfäs-\ *adj* [ME, fr. OE *fōstor-*, fr. *fōstor* food, feeding; akin to OE *fōda* food] **:** affording, receiving, or sharing nurture or parental care though not related by blood or legal ties
2**foster** *vt* **fos·ter·ing** \-t(ə-)riŋ\ **1 :** to give parental care to **:** NURTURE **2 :** to promote the growth or development of **:** ENCOURAGE — **fos·ter·er** \-tər-ər\ *n*
fos·ter·age \-tə-rij\ *n* **:** the act or custom of fostering
fos·ter·ling \-tər-liŋ\ *n* **:** a foster child
fou \ˈfü\ *adj* [ME (Sc) *fow* full, fr. ME *full*] *Scot* **:** DRUNK
fou·droy·ant \fü-ˈdrȯi-ənt, fü-drwä-yäⁿ\ *adj* [F] **:** THUNDERING, DAZZLING
fought *past of* FIGHT
1**foul** \ˈfau̇(ə)l\ *adj* [ME, fr. OE *fūl;* akin to OHG *fūl* rotten, L *pus* pus, *putēre* to stink, Gk *pyon* pus] **1 a :** offensive to the senses **:** LOATHSOME **b :** charged or covered with offensive matter **2 :** full of dirt **:** MUDDY **3 :** morally or spiritually odious **:** DETESTABLE **4 a :** OBSCENE, PROFANE **b :** ABUSIVE **5 a :** being wet and stormy **b :** obstructive to navigation **6** *dial Brit* **:** HOMELY, UGLY **7 a :** TREACHEROUS, DISHONORABLE ⟨fair means or ~⟩ **b :** constituting an infringement of rules in a game or sport **8 a :** marked up or defaced by changes ⟨~ manuscript⟩ **b** *of a proof* **:** pulled before the latest alterations in type **9 :** encrusted, clogged, or choked with a foreign substance **10 :** being odorous and impure **:** POLLUTED **11 :** ENTANGLED **12 :** being outside the foul lines in baseball ⟨~ grounder⟩ **syn** see DIRTY — **foul·ly** \ˈfau̇(l)-lē\ *adv*
2**foul** *n* **1** *archaic* **:** bad luck **2 :** an entanglement or collision esp. in angling or sailing **3 a :** an infringement of the rules in a game or sport **b :** FREE THROW **4 :** FOUL BALL
3**foul** *adv* **:** FOULLY
4**foul** *vi* **1 :** to become or be foul: as **a :** DECOMPOSE, ROT **b :** to become encrusted, clogged, or choked with a foreign substance **c :** to become entangled or come into collision **2 :** to commit a violation of the rules in a sport or game **3 :** to hit a foul ball **~** *vt* **1 :** to make foul: as **a :** to make dirty **:** POLLUTE **b :** to become entangled or come into collision with **c :** to encrust with a foreign substance **d :** OBSTRUCT, BLOCK **2 :** DISHONOR, DISCREDIT **3 :** to commit a foul against **4 :** to hit (a baseball) foul
fou·lard \fü-ˈlärd\ *n* [F] **1 a :** a lightweight plain-woven or twilled silk usu. decorated with a printed pattern **b :** an imitation of this fabric **2 :** an article of clothing (as a scarf) made of foulard
foul ball *n* **:** a baseball batted into foul territory
foul·brood \ˈfau̇l-ˌbrüd\ *n* **:** a destructive bacterial disease of the larvae of the honeybee
foul·ing *n* **:** DEPOSIT, INCRUSTATION
foul line *n* **1 :** either of two straight lines extending from the rear corner of home plate through the outer corners of first and third base respectively and prolonged to the boundary of a baseball field **2 :** a line across a bowling alley that a player must not step over when delivering the ball
foul·mouthed \ˈfau̇l-ˈmau̇t͟hd, -ˈmau̇tht\ *adj* **:** given to the use of obscene, profane, or abusive language
foul·ness \ˈfau̇l-nəs\ *n* **1 :** the quality or state of being foul **2 :** something that is foul
foul play *n* **:** morally objectionable conduct or dealing; *specif* **:** VIOLENCE
foul tip *n* [*foul* + *tip* (tap)] **:** a pitched ball in baseball that is slightly deflected by the bat; *specif* **:** a tipped pitch legally caught by the catcher and counting as a full strike with the ball remaining in play
1**found** *past of* FIND
2**found** \ˈfau̇nd\ *n* **:** free food and lodging in addition to wages
3**found** *vt* [ME *founden*, fr. OF *fonder*, fr. L *fundare*, fr. *fundus* bottom — more at BOTTOM] **1 :** to take the first steps in building **2 :** to set or ground on something solid **:** BASE **3 :** to establish (as an institution) often with provision for future maintenance
4**found** *vt* [MF *fondre* to pour, melt, fr. L *fundere;* akin to OE *gēotan* to pour, Gk *chein*] **:** to melt (metal) and pour into a mold
foun·da·tion \fau̇n-ˈdā-shən\ *n* **1 :** the act of founding **2 :** the basis upon which something stands or is supported **3 a :** funds given for the permanent support of an institution **:** ENDOWMENT **b :** an organization or institution established by endowment with provision for future maintenance **4 :** an underlying natural or prepared base or support; *esp* **:** the whole masonry substructure of a building **5 a :** a body or ground upon which something is built up or overlaid **b :** a woman's supporting undergarment **:** CORSET **syn** see BASE — **foun·da·tion·al** \-shnəl, -shən-ᵊl\ *adj*
1**found·er** \ˈfau̇n-dər\ *n* **:** one that founds or establishes
2**foun·der** \ˈfau̇n-dər\ *vb* **foun·der·ing** \-d(ə-)riŋ\ [ME *foundren* to send to the bottom, collapse, fr. MF *fondrer*, deriv. of L *fundus*] *vi* **1 :** to become disabled; *esp* **:** to go lame **2 :** to give way **:** COLLAPSE **3 :** to sink below the surface of the water **4 :** to come to grief **:** FAIL **~** *vt* **:** to disable esp. by excessive feeding
3**foun·der** *n* [2*founder*] **:** the condition of a foundered horse
4**found·er** *n* **:** one that founds metal; *specif* **:** TYPEFOUNDER
foun·der·ous *or* **foun·drous** \ˈfau̇n-d(ə-)rəs\ *adj* [2*founder*] **:** MIRY, SWAMPY
found·ling \ˈfau̇n-(d)liŋ\ *n* **:** an infant found after its unknown parents have deserted it
found·ry \ˈfau̇n-drē\ *n* **1 :** the act, process, or art of casting metals; *also* **:** CASTINGS **2 :** an establishment where founding is carried on
foundry proof *n* **:** a proof taken from a form that has been locked up and made ready for plating
1**fount** \ˈfau̇nt\ *n* [MF *font*, fr. L *font-*, *fons*] **:** FOUNTAIN
2**fount** \ˈfänt, ˈfau̇nt\ *n* [F *fonte*] *Brit* **:** a type font
foun·tain \ˈfau̇nt-ᵊn\ *n* [ME, fr. MF *fontaine*, fr. LL *fontana*, fr. L, fem. of *fontanus* of a spring, fr. *font-*, *fons*] **1 :** a spring of water issuing from the earth **2 :** SOURCE **3 :** an artificially produced jet of water; *also* **:** the structure from which it rises **4 :** a reservoir containing a liquid that can be drawn off as needed
foun·tain·head \-ˌhed\ *n* **1 :** a spring that is the source of a stream **2 :** principal source **:** ORIGIN
fountain pen *n* **:** a pen containing a reservoir that automatically feeds the writing point with ink
four \ˈfō(ə)r, ˈfȯ(ə)r\ *n* [ME, fr. *four* adj., fr. OE *fēower;* akin to OHG *fior* four, L *quattuor*, Gk *tessares, tettares*] **1** — see NUMBER table **2 :** the fourth in a set or series ⟨the ~ of hearts⟩ **3 :** something having four units or members ⟨rows on the school ~⟩ — **four** *adj or pron*
four·chée \fu̇(ə)r-ˈshā\ *adj* [F] *of a heraldic cross* **:** having the end of each arm forked — see CROSS illustration
four–cycle *adj* **:** having a four-stroke cycle ⟨a ~ engine⟩
four–dimensional *adj* **:** relating to or having four dimensions ⟨~ space-time continuum⟩; *esp* **:** consisting of or relating to elements requiring four coordinates to determine them
four·dri·nier \ˌfōr-drə-ˈni(ə)r, ˌfȯr-; fu̇r-ˈdrin-ē-ər, fōr-, fȯr-\ *n* [Henry *Fourdrinier* †1854 & Sealy *Fourdrinier* †1847 E papermakers] **:** a machine for making paper in an endless web
four flush *n* **:** four cards of the same suit in a five-card poker hand
four–flush \ˈfōr-ˌfləsh, ˈfȯr-\ *vi* **:** to bluff in poker holding a four flush; *broadly* **:** to make a false claim **:** BLUFF — **four–flush·er** *n*
four·fold \-ˌfōld, -ˈfōld\ *adj* **1 :** having four units or members **2 :** being four times as great or as many — **four·fold** \-ˈfōld\ *adv*
four–foot·ed \-ˈfu̇t-əd\ *adj* **:** QUADRUPED
four·gon \fu̇r-ˈgōⁿ\ *n, pl* **fourgons** \-ˈgōⁿ(z)\ [F] **:** a wagon for carrying baggage
four–hand \ˈfōr-ˌhand, ˈfȯr-\ *adj* **:** FOUR-HANDED
four–hand·ed \-ˈhan-dəd\ *adj* **1 a :** QUADRUMANOUS **b :** designed for four hands **2 :** engaged in by four persons
Four Horsemen *n pl* [fr. the apocalyptic vision in Rev 6:2–8] **:** war, famine, pestilence, and death personified as the four major plagues of mankind
Four Hundred *or* **400** *n* **:** the exclusive social set of a community — used with *the*
Fou·ri·er·ism \ˈfu̇r-ē-ə-ˌriz-əm, -ē-ˌā-ˌiz-\ *n* [F *fouriérisme*, fr. F.M.C. *Fourier* †1837 F social scientist] **:** a system for reorganizing society into cooperative communities of small groups living in common — **Fou·ri·er·ist** \-ē-ə-rəst, -ē-ˌā-əst\ *n*
Fou·ri·er series \ˌfu̇r-ē-ˌā-\ *n* [Baron J.B.J. *Fourier* †1830 F geometrician & physicist] **:** an infinite series in which the terms are constants multiplied by sine or cosine functions of integer multiples of the variable and which is used in the analysis of periodic functions
four–in–hand \ˈfōr-ən-ˌhand, ˈfȯr-\ *n* **1 a :** a team of four horses driven by one person **b :** a vehicle drawn by such a team **2 :** a necktie tied in a slipknot with long ends overlapping vertically in front
four–o'clock \-ə-ˌkläk\ *n* **:** any of a genus (*Mirabilis*) of chiefly American annual or perennial herbs (family Nyctaginaceae, the four-o'clock family) having apetalous flowers with a showy involucre simulating a calyx; *esp* **:** a garden plant (*M. jalapa*) with fra-

grant yellow, red, or white flowers opening late in the afternoon
four-post·er \-'pō-stər\ *n* **:** a bed with tall often carved corner posts orig. designed to support curtains or a canopy
four·ra·gère \ˌfu̇r-ə-'zhe(ə)r\ *n* [F] **:** a braided cord worn usu. around the left shoulder; *esp* **:** such a cord awarded to a military unit
four·score \'fōr-ˌskō(ə)r, 'fȯr-ˌskȯ(ə)r\ *adj* **:** being four times twenty **:** EIGHTY
four·some \'fōr-səm, 'fȯr-\ *n* **1 a :** a group of four persons or things **:** QUARTET **b :** two mixed couples **2 :** a golf match between two pairs of partners
four·square \-'skwa(ə)r, -'skwe(ə)r\ *adj* **1 :** SQUARE **2 :** marked by boldness and conviction **:** FORTHRIGHT — **foursquare** *adv*
four·teen \(')fōr(t)-'tēn, (')fȯr(t)-\ *n* [ME *fourtene*, fr. OE *fēowertīene*, fr. *fēowertīene*, adj.; akin to OE *tīen* ten] — see NUMBER table — **fourteen** *adj or pron* — **four·teenth** \-'tēn(t)th\ *adj* — **fourteenth** *n, pl* **fourteenths** \-'tēn(t)s, -'tēn(t)ths\
four·teen·er \-'tē-nər\ *n* **:** a verse consisting of 14 syllables or esp. of 7 iambic feet
fourth \'fō(ə)rth, 'fȯ(ə)rth\ *n* **1** — see NUMBER table **2 a :** the musical interval embracing four diatonic degrees **b :** SUBDOMINANT **a c :** the harmonic combination of two tones a fourth apart **3 :** the 4th forward gear or speed of a motor vehicle **4** *cap* **:** INDEPENDENCE DAY — **fourth** *adj or adv* — **fourth·ly** *adv*
fourth dimension *n* **:** a dimension in addition to length, breadth, and depth; *specif* **:** a coordinate in addition to three rectangular coordinates esp. when interpreted as the time coordinate in a space-time continuum — **fourth–dimensional** *adj*
fourth estate *n, often cap F&E* **:** the public press
Fourth of July : INDEPENDENCE DAY
four-way \'fōr-'wā, 'fȯr-\ *adj* **1 :** allowing passage in any of four directions **2 :** including four participants
four-wheel \'fōr-ˌhwēl, 'fȯr-, -ˌwēl\ *or* **four-wheeled** \-'hwē(ə)ld, -'wē(ə)ld\ *adj* **1 :** having four wheels **2 :** acting on or by means of four wheels of an automotive vehicle ⟨~ drive⟩
four-wheel·er \-'hwē-lər, -'wē-\ *n* **:** a four-wheel vehicle
fo·vea \'fō-vē-ə\ *n, pl* **fo·ve·ae** \-vē-ˌē, -vē-ˌī\ [NL, fr. L, pit] **:** a small fossa; *esp* **:** a rodless area of the retina affording acute vision — **fo·ve·al** \-vē-əl\ *adj* — **fo·ve·ate** \-vē-ˌāt\ *adj* — **fo·ve·iform** \-vē-ə-ˌfȯrm\ *adj*
¹**fowl** \'fau̇(ə)l\ *n, pl* **fowl** *or* **fowls** [ME *foul*, fr. OE *fugel;* akin to OHG *fogal* bird] **1 :** a bird of any kind **2 a :** a domestic cock or hen; *esp* **:** an adult hen **b :** any of several domesticated or wild gallinaceous birds **3 :** the meat of fowls used as food
²**fowl** *vi* **:** to seek, catch, or kill wildfowl — **fowl·er** *n*
fowling piece *n* **:** a light gun for shooting birds or small quadrupeds
¹**fox** \'fäks\ *n, pl* **fox·es** *or* **fox** *often attrib* [ME, fr. OE; akin to OHG *fuhs* fox, Skt *puccha* tail] **1 a :** any of various alert carnivorous mammals (esp. genus *Vulpes*) of the dog family related to but smaller than wolves with shorter legs, more pointed muzzle, large erect ears, and long bushy tail **b :** the fur of a fox **2 :** a clever crafty person **3** *archaic* **:** SWORD **4** *cap* **:** a member of an Indian people formerly living in Wisconsin **5 :** rope yarns twisted and tarred to make small cordage used for lashings or for weaving mats
²**fox** *vt* **1 a :** to trick by ingenuity or cunning **:** OUTWIT **b :** BAFFLE **2** *obs* **:** INTOXICATE **3 a :** to repair (a shoe) by renewing the upper **b :** to add a strip of something to **:** TRIM
foxed \'fäkst\ *adj* **:** discolored with yellowish brown stains
fox fire *n* **:** an eerie phosphorescent light (as of decaying wood); *also* **:** a luminous fungus (as *Armillaria mellea*) that causes decaying wood to glow
fox·glove \'fäks-ˌgləv\ *n* **:** any of a genus (*Digitalis*) of the figwort family of erect herbs; *esp* **:** a common European biennial or perennial (*D. purpurea*) cultivated for its showy racemes of dotted white or purple tubular flowers and as a source of digitalis

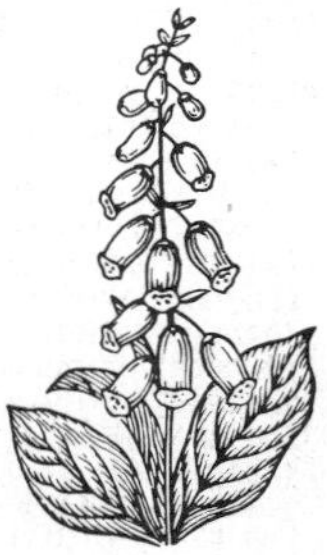
foxglove

fox grape *n* **:** any of several native grapes of eastern No. America with sour or musky fruit
fox·hole \'fäks-ˌhōl\ *n* **:** a pit dug hastily during combat for individual cover against enemy fire
fox·hound \-ˌhau̇nd\ *n* **:** any of various large swift powerful hounds of great endurance used in hunting foxes and developed to form several breeds and many distinctive strains
fox·i·ly \'fäk-sə-lē\ *adv* **:** in a foxy manner
fox·i·ness \-sē-nəs\ *n* **:** the quality or state of being foxy
fox·tail lily \ˌfäk-ˌstāl-\ *n* **:** any of a genus (*Eremurus*) of the lily family of perennial herbs with tall racemes of showy bloom
foxtail millet *n* **:** a coarse drought-resistant but frost-sensitive annual grass (*Setaria italica*) grown for grain, hay, and forage
fox terrier *n* **:** a small lively terrier formerly used to dig out foxes and known in smooth-haired and wirehaired varieties
¹**fox-trot** \'fäk-ˌsträt\ *n* **1 :** a short broken slow trotting gait in which the hind foot of the horse hits the ground a trifle before the diagonally opposite forefoot **2 :** a ballroom dance in duple time that includes slow walking steps, quick running steps, and two-steps
²**fox-trot** *vi* **:** to dance the fox-trot
Foxtrot — a communications code word for the letter *f*
foxy \'fäk-sē\ *adj* **1 a :** resembling a fox in appearance or disposition **:** WILY **b :** alert and knowing **:** CLEVER **2 :** having the color of a fox **3 :** FOXED **syn** see SLY
foy \'fȯi\ *n* [D dial. *fooi* feast at end of the harvest] *chiefly Scot* **:** a farewell feast or gift
foy·er \'fȯi(-ə)r, 'fȯi-ˌ(y)ā\ *n* [F, lit., fireplace, fr. ML *focarius*, fr. L *focus* hearth] **:** an anteroom or lobby esp. of a theater; *also* **:** entrance hallway **:** VESTIBULE
Fra \(ˌ)frä\ *n* [It, short for *frate*, fr. L *frater* — more at BROTHER] **:** BROTHER — used as a title preceding the name of an Italian monk or friar
fra·cas \'frāk-əs, 'frak, *Brit* 'frak-ˌä\ *n, pl* **fra·cas·es** \-ə-səz\ *or Brit* **frac·as** \-ˌäz\ [F, din, row, fr. It *fracasso*, fr. *fracassare* to shatter] **:** a noisy quarrel **:** BRAWL
fract·ed \'frak-təd\ *adj* [L *fractus*] *obs* **:** BROKEN
frac·tion \'frak-shən\ *n* [ME *fraccioun*, fr. LL *fraction-, fractio* act of breaking, fr. L *fractus*, pp. of *frangere* to break — more at BREAK] **1 a :** a numerical representation (as ¾, ⅝, 3.234) of two numbers whose quotient is to be determined **b** (1) **:** a piece broken off **:** FRAGMENT (2) **:** PORTION, SECTION **2** *archaic* **a :** RUPTURE, BREAK **b :** DISCORD **3 :** one of several portions (as of a distillate) separable by fractionation
frac·tion·al \-shnəl, -shən-ᵊl\ *adj* **1 :** of, relating to, or being a fraction **2 :** relatively small **:** INCONSIDERABLE **3 :** of, relating to, or involving a process for separating components of a mixture through differences in physical or chemical properties — **frac·tion·al·ly** \-ē\ *adv*
fractional currency *n* **1 :** paper money in denominations of less than one dollar issued by the U.S. 1863–76 **2 :** currency in denominations less than the basic monetary unit
frac·tion·al·ize \-shnə-ˌlīz, -shən-ᵊl-ˌīz\ *vt* **:** to break up into parts or sections
frac·tion·ate \'frak-shə-ˌnāt\ *vt* **1 :** to separate into different portions **2 :** to divide or break up — **frac·tion·ation** \ˌfrak-shə-'nā-shən\ *n* — **frac·tion·ator** \'frak-shə-ˌnāt-ər\ *n*
frac·tious \'frak-shəs\ *adj* **1 :** tending to be troublesome **:** REFRACTORY **2 :** QUARRELSOME, IRRITABLE — **frac·tious·ly** *adv* — **frac·tious·ness** *n*
¹**frac·ture** \'frak-chər\ *n* **1 a :** the act or process of breaking or the state of being broken; *specif* **:** the breaking of hard tissue (as bone) **b :** the rupture of soft tissue **2 :** the result of fracturing **:** BREAK **3 :** the texture of a freshly broken surface of a mineral
syn FRACTURE, RUPTURE mean a break in tissue. FRACTURE commonly applies to the cracking of hard substances (as bones), RUPTURE to the tearing or bursting of soft ones (as blood vessels)
²**fracture** *vb* **frac·tur·ing** \-chə-riŋ, -shriŋ\ *vt* **1 a :** to cause a fracture in **:** BREAK **b :** RUPTURE, TEAR **2 a :** to damage or destroy as if by rupturing **b :** to break up **:** FRACTIONATE ~ *vi* **:** to undergo fracture
frae \(')frā\ *prep* [ME (northern) *fra, frae*, fr. ON *frā;* akin to OE *from*] *Scot* **:** FROM
frag·ile \'fraj-əl, -ˌīl\ *adj* [MF, fr. L *fragilis*] **1 :** easily broken or destroyed **:** FRAIL **2 :** TENUOUS, SLIGHT — **fra·gil·i·ty** \frə-'jil-ət-ē\ *n*
syn FRAGILE, FRANGIBLE, BRITTLE, CRISP, FRIABLE mean breaking easily. FRAGILE implies extreme delicacy of material or construction and need for careful handling; FRANGIBLE implies susceptibility to being broken without implying weakness or delicacy; BRITTLE implies hardness together with lack of elasticity or flexibility or toughness; CRISP implies a firmness and brittleness desirable esp. in some foods; FRIABLE applies to substances that are easily crumbled or pulverized **syn** see in addition WEAK
¹**frag·ment** \'frag-mənt\ *n* [ME, fr. L *fragmentum*, fr. *frangere* to break — more at BREAK] **:** a part broken off, detached, or incomplete **syn** see PART
²**frag·ment** \-ˌment\ *vb* **:** to break into fragments **:** FRAGMENTIZE
frag·men·tal \frag-'ment-ᵊl\ *adj* **:** FRAGMENTARY — **frag·men·tal·ly** \-ᵊl-ē\ *adv*
frag·men·tar·i·ness \'frag-mən-ˌter-ē-nəs\ *n* **:** the quality or state of being fragmentary
frag·men·tary \'frag-mən-ˌter-ē\ *adj* **:** consisting of fragments
frag·men·tate \'frag-mən-ˌtāt\ *vb* **:** to break into pieces **:** FRAGMENTIZE — **frag·men·ta·tion** \ˌfrag-mən-'tā-shən, -ˌmen-\ *n*
frag·men·tize \'frag-mən-ˌtīz\ *vt* **:** to break up or apart into fragments ~ *vi* **:** to fall to pieces
fra·grance \'frā-grən(t)s\ *n* **1 :** the quality or state of having a sweet odor **2 a :** a sweet or delicate odor **b :** the odor of perfume, cologne, or toilet water
syn FRAGRANCE, PERFUME, SCENT, INCENSE, REDOLENCE, BOUQUET mean a sweet or pleasant odor. FRAGRANCE suggests the odors of flowers or other growing things; PERFUME may suggest a stronger or heavier odor and applies esp. to a prepared or synthetic liquid; SCENT is very close to PERFUME but of wider application because more neutral in connotation; INCENSE applies to the smoke from burning spices and gums and suggests an esp. pleasing odor; REDOLENCE implies a mixture of fragrant or pungent odors; BOUQUET implies the distinctive delicate odor of a good wine
fra·gran·cy \-grən-sē\ *n, archaic* **:** FRAGRANCE
fra·grant \'frā-grənt\ *adj* [ME, fr. L *fragrant-, fragrans*, fr. prp. of *fragrare* to be fragrant; akin to MHG *bræhen* to smell] **:** marked by fragrance — **fra·grant·ly** *adv*
¹**frail** \'frā(ə)l\ *n* [ME *frayel*, fr. MF *fraiel*] **:** a basket typically made of rushes and used for shipping (as of figs or raisins)
²**frail** *adj* [ME, fr. MF *fraile*, fr. L *fragilis* fragile, fr. *frangere*] **1 :** easily led into evil ⟨~ humanity⟩ **2 :** easily broken or destroyed **:** FRAGILE **3 a :** physically weak **b :** SLIGHT, UNSUBSTANTIAL **syn** see WEAK — **frail·ly** \'frā(ə)l-lē\ *adv* — **frail·ness** *n*
frail·ty \'frā(-ə)l-tē\ *n* **1 :** the quality or state of being frail **2 :** a fault due to weakness esp. of moral character **syn** see FAULT
fraise \'frāz\ *n* [F] **:** an obstacle of pointed stakes driven into the ramparts of a fortification in a horizontal or inclined position
¹**frame** \'frām\ *vb* [ME *framen* to benefit, construct, fr. OE *framian* to benefit, make progress; akin to ON *fram* forward, OE *from* from] *vi* **1** *archaic* **:** PROCEED, GO **2** *obs* **:** MANAGE ~ *vt* **1 a :** PLAN, CONTRIVE **b :** to give expression to **:** FORMULATE **c :** SHAPE, CONSTRUCT **d :** to draw up (as a document) **2 :** to fit or adjust for a purpose **:** ARRANGE **3** *obs* **:** PRODUCE **4 :** to construct by fitting and uniting the parts of the skeleton of (a structure) **5 :** to enclose in a frame **6 a :** to devise falsely (as a criminal charge) **b :** to contrive the evidence against (an innocent man) so that a verdict of guilty is assured **c :** to prearrange (as a contest) so that a particular outcome is assured — **fram·er** *n*
²**frame** *n* **1 :** something composed of parts fitted together and united; *esp* **:** the bodily structure **2 a :** the constructional system that gives shape or strength **b :** such a skeleton not filled in or covered **3 a :** an open case or structure made for admitting, enclosing, or supporting something ⟨a window ~⟩ **b :** a machine built upon or within a framework ⟨a spinning ~⟩ **c :** a structural unit in an automobile chassis supported on the axles and supporting the rest of the chassis and the body **4** *obs* **:** the act or manner of framing **5 :** a particular state or disposition (as of the mind) **:** MOOD **6 a :** an enclosing border **b :** the matter or area enclosed in such a border: as (1) **:** one of the squares in which scores for each round are recorded (as in bowling); *also* **:** a round in bowling (2) **:** boxed

matter in a newspaper; *esp* **:** a box of a comic strip (3) **:** one picture of the series on a length of motion-picture or other film (4) **:** a complete image being transmitted by television **c :** a limiting, typical, or esp. appropriate set of circumstances **d :** an event that forms the background for the action of a novel or play

3**frame** *adj* **:** having a wood frame ⟨~ houses⟩

frame of reference 1 : an arbitrary set of axes with reference to which the position or motion of something is described or physical laws are formulated **2 :** a set or system (as of facts or ideas) serving to orient or give particular meaning

frame–up \'frā-ˌməp\ *n* **1 :** an act or series of actions in which someone is framed **2 :** an action that is framed

1**frame·work** \'frām-ˌwərk\ *n* **1 a :** a skeletal, openwork, or structural frame **b :** a basic structure (as of ideas) **2 :** FRAME OF REFERENCE **3 :** the larger branches of a tree that determine its shape

2**framework** *vt* **:** to graft scions of another variety on the framework of (a tree)

fram·ing \'frā-miŋ\ *n* **:** FRAME, FRAMEWORK

franc \'fraŋk\ *n* [F] — see MONEY table

1**fran·chise** \'fran-ˌchīz\ *n* [ME, fr. OF, fr. *franchir* to free, fr. *franc* free] **1 :** freedom or immunity from some burden or restriction vested in a person or group **2 a :** a special privilege granted to an individual or group; *esp* **:** the right to be and exercise the powers of a corporation **b :** a constitutional or statutory right or privilege; *esp* **:** the right to vote

2**franchise** *vt* **:** ENFRANCHISE, FREE

1**Fran·cis·can** \fran-'sis-kən\ *adj* [ML *Franciscus* Francis] **:** of or relating to St. Francis of Assisi or the Franciscans

2**Franciscan** *n* **:** a member of the Order of Friars Minor observing the unmodified rule of the first order of St. Francis of Assisi and engaging in preaching and missionary, charitable, and other work

fran·ci·um \'fran(t)-sē-əm\ *n* [NL, fr. *France*] **:** a radioactive element of the alkali-metal group discovered as a disintegration product of actinium and obtained artificially by the bombardment of thorium with protons — see ELEMENT table

Franco- *comb form* [ML, fr. *Francus* Frenchman, fr. LL, Frank] **:** French and ⟨*Franco*-German⟩ **:** French ⟨*Franco*phile⟩

fran·co·lin \'fraŋ-k(ə-)lən\ *n* [F, fr. It *francolino*] **:** any of numerous partridges (*Francolinus* and related genera) of southern Asia and Africa

Fran·co·phile \'fraŋ-kə-ˌfīl\ *or* **Fran·co·phil** \-ˌfil\ *adj* **:** markedly friendly to France or French culture — **Francophile** *n*

franc–ti·reur \ˌfräⁿ-(ˌ)tē-'rər\ *n* [F, fr. *franc* free + *tireur* shooter] **:** a civilian fighter or sniper

fran·gi·bil·i·ty \ˌfran-jə-'bil-ət-ē\ *n* **:** the quality or state of being frangible

fran·gi·ble \'fran-jə-bəl\ *adj* [ME, fr. MF & ML; MF, fr. ML *frangibilis*, fr. L *frangere* to break] **:** BREAKABLE **syn** see FRAGILE

fran·gi·pane \'fran-jə-ˌpān\ *n* [F, fr. It, fr. Marquis Muzio *Frangipane*, 16th cent. It nobleman] **:** FRANGIPANI

fran·gi·pa·ni \ˌfran-jə-'pan-ē, -'pän-\ *n, pl* **frangipani** *or* **frangipanis** [modif. of It *frangipane*] **1 :** a perfume derived from or imitating the odor of the flower of the red jasmine **2 :** a tropical American shrub or small tree (genus *Plumeria*) of the dogbane family (as red jasmine)

1**frank** \'fraŋk\ *adj* [ME, fr. OF *franc*, fr. ML *francus*, fr. LL *Francus* Frank] **1** *obs* **:** FREE **2** *archaic* **:** LIBERAL, GENEROUS **3 :** marked by free, forthright, and sincere expression ⟨a ~ reply⟩ **4 :** clinically evident **:** UNMISTAKABLE ⟨~ pus⟩ — **frank·ness** *n*

syn FRANK, CANDID, OPEN, PLAIN mean showing willingness to tell what one feels or thinks. FRANK stresses lack of shyness or secretiveness or of evasiveness from considerations of tact or expedience; CANDID suggests expression marked by sincerity and honesty esp. in offering unwelcome criticism or opinion; OPEN implies frankness but suggests more indiscretion than FRANK and less earnestness than CANDID; PLAIN suggests outspokenness, downrightness, and freedom from affectation or subtlety in expression

2**frank** *vt* **1 a :** to mark (a piece of mail) with an official signature or sign indicating the right of the sender to free mailing **b :** to mail free **c :** to affix to (mail) a stamp or a marking indicating the payment of postage **2 :** to enable to pass or go freely or easily — **frank·er** *n*

3**frank** *n* **1 a :** the signature of the sender on a piece of franked mail serving in place of a postage stamp **b :** a mark or stamp on a piece of mail indicating postage paid **c :** a franked envelope **2 :** the privilege of sending mail free of charge

Frank \'fraŋk\ *n* [ME, partly fr. OE *Franca;* partly fr. OF *Franc*, fr. LL *Francus*, of Gmc origin; akin to OHG *Franko* Frank, OE *Franca*] **:** a member of a West Germanic people entering the Roman provinces in A.D. 253, occupying the Netherlands and most of Gaul, and establishing themselves along the Rhine

Fran·ken·stein \'fraŋ-kən-ˌstīn, -ˌstēn\ *n* **1 :** a student of physiology in Mary W. Shelley's novel *Frankenstein* whose life is ruined by a monster he creates **2 :** a work or agency that ruins its originator **3 :** a monster in the shape of a man

frank·furt·er *or* **frank·fort·er** \'fraŋk-fə(r)t-ər, -ˌfərt-\ *or* **frank·furt** *or* **frank·fort** \-fərt\ *n* [G *frankfurter* of Frankfurt, fr. *Frankfurt* am Main, Germany] **:** a sausage (as of beef or beef and pork) cured and cooked and stuffed in a casing or skinless

frank·in·cense \'fraŋ-kən-ˌsen(t)s\ *n* **:** a fragrant gum resin from chiefly East African or Arabian trees (genus *Boswellia* of the family Burseraceae) that is an important incense resin

1**Frank·ish** \'fraŋ-kish\ *adj* **:** of or relating to the Franks

2**Frankish** *n* **:** the Germanic language of the Franks

frank·lin \'fraŋ-klən\ *n* [ME *frankeleyn*, fr. AF *fraunclein*, fr. OF *franc*] **:** a free medieval English landowner not of noble birth

frank·lin·ite \-klə-ˌnīt\ *n* [*Franklin*, N.J.] **:** a black slightly magnetic mineral $ZnFe_2O_4$ consisting of an oxide of iron and zinc

Frank·lin stove \ˌfraŋ-klən-\ *n* [Benjamin *Franklin*, its inventor] **:** a metal heating stove resembling an open fireplace but designed to be set out in a room

frank·ly *adv* **1 :** in a frank manner **2 :** in truth **:** INDEED

frank·pledge \'fraŋk-ˌplej\ *n* **:** an Anglo-Saxon system under which each adult male member of a tithing was responsible for the good conduct of the others; *also* **:** the member himself or the tithing

fran·se·ria \fran-'sir-ē-ə\ *n* [NL, genus name, fr. Antonio *Franseri*, 18th cent. Sp botanist] **:** any of a genus (*Franseria*) of annual or perennial composite herbs or shrubs

fran·tic \'frant-ik\ *adj* [ME *frenetik, frantik* — more at FRENETIC] **1** *archaic* **:** mentally deranged **2 :** marked by uncontrollable emotion **:** FRENZIED — **fran·ti·cal·ly** \-i-k(ə-)lē\ *adv* — **fran·tic·ly** \-i-klē\ *adv* — **fran·tic·ness** \-ik-nəs\ *n*

frap \'frap\ *vt* **frapped; frap·ping** [ME *frapen* to strike, beat, fr. MF *fraper*] **:** to draw tight

1**frap·pé** *or* **frap·pe** \fra-'pā\ *adj* [F *frappé*, fr. pp. of *frapper* to strike, chill, fr. MF *fraper* to strike] **:** ICED, FROZEN

2**frap·pé** \fra-'pā\ *or* **frappe** \'frap, fra-'pā\ *n* **1 :** a frappé mixture or drink **2 :** a thick milk shake

fra·ter·nal \frə-'tərn-ᵊl\ *adj* [ME, fr. ML *fraternalis*, fr. L *fraternus* fr. *frater* brother] **1 a :** of, relating to, or involving brothers **b :** of, relating to, or being a fraternity or society **2 :** derived from two ova **:** DIZYGOTIC **3 :** FRIENDLY, BROTHERLY — **fra·ter·nal·ism** \-ᵊl-ˌiz-əm\ *n* — **fra·ter·nal·ly** \-ᵊl-ē\ *adv*

fra·ter·ni·ty \frə-'tər-nət-ē\ *n* **1 :** a group of people associated or formally organized for a common purpose, interest, or pleasure: as **a :** a fraternal order **b :** GUILD **c :** a student organization formed chiefly for social purposes having secret rites and a name consisting of Greek letters **2 :** the quality or state of being brothers **:** BROTHERLINESS **3 :** men of the same class, profession, character, or tastes **4 a :** the entire progeny of a single mating **b :** a group of siblings

frat·er·ni·za·tion \ˌfrat-ər-nə-'zā-shən\ *n* **:** the act of fraternizing

frat·er·nize \'frat-ər-ˌnīz\ *vi* **1 :** to associate or mingle as brothers or on fraternal terms **2 a :** to associate on intimate terms with members of a hostile group esp. when contrary to military orders **b :** to be friendly or amiable — **frat·er·niz·er** *n*

frat·ri·ci·dal \ˌfra-trə-'sīd-ᵊl\ *adj* **:** of, relating to, or resulting in fratricide

frat·ri·cide \'fra-trə-ˌsīd\ *n* [in sense 1, fr. ME, fr. MF or L; MF, fr. L *fratricida*, fr. *fratr-, frater* brother + *-cida* -cide; in sense 2, fr. MF or L; MF, fr. L *fratricidium*, fr. *fratr-, frater* + *-cidium* -cide] **1 :** one that murders or kills his own brother or sister **2 :** the act of a fratricide

Frau \'frau̇\ *n, pl* **Frau·en** \'frau̇(-ə)n\ [G, woman, wife, fr. OHG *frouwa* mistress, lady; akin to OE *frēa* lord] **:** a German married woman **:** WIFE — used as a title equivalent to *Mrs.*

fraud \'frȯd\ *n* [ME *fraude*, fr. MF, fr. L *fraud-, fraus;* akin to Skt *dhvarati* he bends, injures] **1 a :** DECEIT, TRICKERY; *specif* **:** intentional perversion of truth in order to induce another to part with something of value or to surrender a legal right **b :** an act of deceiving or misrepresenting **:** TRICK **2 a :** one who is not what he pretends to be **:** IMPOSTOR **b :** one who defrauds **:** CHEAT **syn** see DECEPTION, IMPOSTURE

fraud·u·lence \'frȯ-jə-lən(t)s\ *n* **:** the quality or state of being fraudulent

fraud·u·lent \-lənt\ *adj* **:** characterized by, based on, or done by fraud **:** DECEITFUL — **fraud·u·lent·ly** *adv* — **fraud·u·lent·ness** *n*

1**fraught** \'frȯkt\ *n* [ME, freight, load, fr. MD or MLG *vracht, vrecht*] *chiefly Scot* **:** LOAD, CARGO

2**fraught** *vt* **fraught·ed** *or* **fraught; fraught·ing** [ME *fraughten*, fr. 1*fraught*] *chiefly Scot* **:** LOAD, FREIGHT

3**fraught** \'frȯt\ *adj* [ME, fr. pp. of *fraughten*] **1** *archaic* **a :** FREIGHTED **b :** SUPPLIED **2 a :** ACCOMPANIED **b :** bearing promise or menace **:** PREGNANT ⟨words ~ with meaning⟩

fräu·lein \'frȯi-ˌlīn\ *n* [G] **1** *cap* **:** an unmarried German girl or woman — used as a title equivalent to *Miss* **2 :** a German governess

frax·i·nel·la \ˌfrak-sə-'nel-ə\ *n* [NL, dim. of L *fraxinus* ash tree] **:** a Eurasian perennial herb (*Dictamnus albus*) of the rue family with flowers that exhale a flammable vapor in hot weather

1**fray** \'frā\ *vt* [ME *fraien*, short for *affraien* to affray] *archaic* **:** SCARE; *also* **:** to frighten away

2**fray** *n* **:** BRAWL, FIGHT; *also* **:** DISPUTE, DEBATE

3**fray** *vb* [MF *froyer, frayer* to rub, fr. L *fricare*] *vt* **1 a :** to wear (as an edge of cloth) by rubbing **:** FRET **b :** to separate the threads at the edge of **2 :** STRAIN, IRRITATE ~ *vi* **:** to wear out or into shreds

4**fray** *n* **:** a raveled place or worn spot (as on fabric)

fray·ing *n* **:** something rubbed or worn off by fraying

1**fraz·zle** \'fraz-əl\ *vb* **fraz·zling** \'fraz-(ə-)liŋ\ [alter. of E dial. *fazle* (to tangle, fray)] *vt* **1 :** 3FRAY **2 a :** to put in a state of extreme physical or nervous fatigue **b :** UPSET ~ *vi* **:** to become frazzled

2**frazzle** *n* **:** the state of being frazzled

1**freak** \'frēk\ *n* [origin unknown] **1 a :** a sudden turn of the mind **:** WHIM **b :** a seemingly capricious action or event **2** *archaic* **:** WHIMSICALITY **3 :** something markedly unusual or abnormal; *esp* **:** one with a physical oddity who appears in a circus sideshow **syn** see CAPRICE

2**freak** *adj* **:** having the character of a freak ⟨a ~ accident⟩

3**freak** *vt* **:** to streak esp. with color

freak·ish \'frē-kish\ *adj* **1 :** WHIMSICAL, CAPRICIOUS **2 :** being or befitting a freak — **freak·ish·ly** *adv* — **freak·ish·ness** *n*

1**freck·le** \'frek-əl\ *n* [ME *freken, frekel*, of Scand origin; akin to ON *freknōttr* freckled; akin to OE *spearca* spark] **:** a small brownish spot in the skin usu. due to precipitation of pigment on exposure to sunlight — **freck·ly** \'frek-(ə-)lē\ *adv*

2**freckle** *vb* **freck·ling** \'frek-(ə-)liŋ\ *vt* **:** to sprinkle or mark with freckles or small spots ~ *vi* **:** to become marked with freckles

1**free** \'frē\ *adj* **fre·er; fre·est** [ME, fr. OE *frēo;* akin to OHG *frī* free, Gk *prays* gentle] **1 a :** having the legal and political rights of a citizen **b :** enjoying civil and political liberty ⟨~ citizens⟩ **c :** enjoying political independence or freedom from outside domination **d :** not dependent on others **:** SELF-RELIANT **2 a :** not determined by anything beyond its own nature or being ⟨a ~ agent⟩ **b :** determined by the choice of the actor or by his wishes ⟨~ actions⟩ **c :** made, done, or given voluntarily or spontaneously **:** SPONTANEOUS **3 a :** exempt, relieved, or released esp. from a burdensome, noxious, or deplorable condition or obligation ⟨~ from pain⟩ **b :** not bound, confined, or detained by force ⟨prisoner was now ~⟩ **4 a :** having no trade restrictions ⟨~ port⟩ **b :** not subject to government regulation **c** *of foreign exchange* **:** not subject to restriction or official control **5 :** having no obligations (as to work) or commitments (as to duty or custom) ⟨~ evening⟩ **6 :** having a scope not restricted by qualification ⟨~ variable⟩ **7 a** (1) **:** not obstructed or impeded **:** CLEAR ⟨~ and open highway⟩ (2) **:** not being used or occupied ⟨waved with his ~ hand⟩ **b :** not hampered or restricted in its normal operation **:** LOOSE **c :** allowed to be executed without interference from the opposing side ⟨~ kick⟩ **8 a :** not fastened ⟨~ end of the rope⟩ **b :** not confined to a particular position or place **c :** capable of moving or turning in any direction ⟨~ particle⟩ **d :** performed without apparatus ⟨~

tumbling⟩ 9 a : not parsimonious ⟨~ spending⟩ b : OUTSPOKEN c : availing oneself of something without stint d : FRANK, OPEN e : overly familiar or forward in action or attitude f : LICENTIOUS 10 : not costing or charging anything 11 a : not united or combined with something else : SEPARATED ⟨~ ore⟩ b : NATIVE 8b ⟨~ oxygen⟩ c : not permanently attached but able to move about d *of accent* : not occurring on the same syllable in all words e *of a linguistic form* : capable of being used alone with meaning ⟨the word *hats* is a ~ form⟩ 12 a : not literal or exact ⟨~ translation⟩ b : not restricted by or conforming to conventional forms ⟨~ skating⟩ 13 : FAVORABLE — used of a wind blowing from a direction more than six points from straight ahead 14 : not allowing slavery 15 : open to all comers — **free·ly** *adv*

syn FREE, INDEPENDENT, SOVEREIGN, AUTONOMOUS mean not subject to the rule or control of another. FREE stresses the complete absence of external rule and the full right to make all of one's own decisions; INDEPENDENT implies a standing alone; applied to a state it implies lack of connection with any other having power to interfere with its citizens, laws, or policies; SOVEREIGN stresses the absence of a superior power and implies supremacy within a thing's own domain or sphere; AUTONOMOUS stresses independence in matters pertaining to self-government, but usu. implies at the same time a recognition of sovereignty of a higher or central power in foreign relations and policy

2**free** *adv* 1 : FREELY 2 : without charge ⟨admitted ~⟩ 3 : with the wind more than six points from dead ahead ⟨sailing ~⟩

3**free** *vt* **freed; free·ing** 1 a : to cause to be free b : RELIEVE, RID c : DISENTANGLE, CLEAR 2 *obs* : BANISH

syn FREE, RELEASE, LIBERATE, EMANCIPATE, MANUMIT, DISCHARGE mean to set loose from restraint or constraint. FREE implies a usu. permanent removal from whatever binds, confines, entangles, or oppresses; RELEASE suggests a setting loose from confinement, restraint, or a state of pressure or tension, often without implication of permanent liberation; LIBERATE stresses particularly the resulting state of liberty; EMANCIPATE implies the liberation of a person from subjection or domination; MANUMIT implies emancipation from slavery; DISCHARGE may imply liberation or merely ejection or emission from confinement or a containing that is not necessarily restraint

free alongside ship *or* **free alongside vessel** *adv* (*or adj*) : with delivery at the side of the ship free of charges where the buyer's liability begins

free·board \'frē-,bō(ə)rd, -,bȯ(ə)rd\ *n* 1 : the distance between the waterline and the freeboard deck of a ship 2 : the space between the surface of the ground and the undercarriage of an automobile

freeboard deck *n* : the deck below which all bulkheads are made watertight

free·boot·er \-ər\ *n* [D *vrijbuiter*, fr. *vrijbuit* plunder, fr. *vrij* free + *buit* booty] : PLUNDERER, PIRATE

free·born \'frē-'bȯ(ə)rn\ *adj* 1 : not born in vassalage or slavery 2 : relating to or befitting one that is freeborn

free capital *n* 1 : capital that has numerous possible or actual uses as opposed to capital confined to a specialized use 2 : capital available for investment

freed·man \'frēd-mən\ *n* : a man freed from slavery

free·dom \'frēd-əm\ *n* 1 : the quality or state of being free: as a : the absence of necessity, coercion, or constraint in choice or action b : liberation from slavery or restraint or from the power of another : INDEPENDENCE c : EXEMPTION, RELEASE d : EASE, FACILITY e : FRANKNESS, OUTSPOKENNESS f : improper familiarity g : boldness of conception or execution h : unrestricted use 2 a : a political right b : FRANCHISE, PRIVILEGE

syn FREEDOM, LIBERTY, LICENSE mean the power or condition of acting without compulsion. FREEDOM has a broad range and may imply total absence of restraint even as imposed by necessity, or moderate absence of restraint, or merely an unawareness of being unduly hampered or frustrated; LIBERTY implies the power to choose what one does or says as distinguished from lack of inhibition in doing or saying; it may also imply more strongly than FREEDOM a release from restraint or compulsion; LICENSE implies liberty that consists in breaking laws or rules either as an abuse or as the exercise of special privilege

freedom of the seas : the right of a merchant ship to travel any waters except territorial waters either in peace or war

free enterprise *n* : freedom of private business to organize and operate for profit in a competitive system without interference by government beyond regulation necessary to protect public interest and keep the national economy in balance

free–for–all \'frē-fə-,rȯl\ *n* : a competition, dispute, or fight open to all comers and usu. with no rules : BRAWL — **free–for–all** *adj*

free gold *n* : gold or gold certificates held in excess of legal reserve requirements

free·hand \'frē-,hand\ *adj* : done without mechanical aids or devices : FREE ⟨~ drawing⟩ — **freehand** *adv*

free hand *n* : freedom of action or decision

free·hand·ed \'frē-'han-dəd\ *adj* : OPENHANDED, GENEROUS — **free·hand·ed·ly** *adv*

free·heart·ed \-'härt-əd\ *adj* 1 : FRANK, UNRESERVED 2 : GENEROUS — **free·heart·ed·ly** *adv*

free·hold \'frē-,hōld\ *n* 1 : a tenure of real property by which an estate of inheritance in fee simple or fee tail or for life is held : an estate held by such tenure — compare FEE 1 2 : a tenure of an office or dignity similar to a freehold — **free·hold·er** *n*

free lance *n* 1 a : a knight or roving soldier available for hire by a state or commander b : one who acts on his own responsibility without regard to authority 2 : one who pursues a profession under no long-term contractual commitments to any one employer

1**free–lance** \'frē-'lan(t)s\ *adj* : of, relating to, or befitting a free lance : INDEPENDENT

2**free–lance** *vi* : to act as a free lance ~ *vt* : to offer or contract for the purchase of in the manner of a free lance — **free–lanc·er** *n*

free–liv·ing \-'liv-iŋ\ *adj* 1 : marked by more than usual freedom in the gratification of appetites 2 : neither parasitic nor symbiotic

free love *n* : sexual intercourse or cohabitation without a legal wedding

free·man \'frē-mən\ *n* 1 : one enjoying civil or political liberty 2 : one having the full rights of a citizen

free·mar·tin \-,märt-ᵊn\ *n* [origin unknown] : a sexually imperfect usu. sterile female calf twinborn with a male

Free·ma·son \-'mās-ᵊn\ *n* : a member of a widespread secret fraternal society called Free and Accepted Masons

free·ma·son·ry \-rē\ *n* 1 *cap* : the principles, institutions, or practices of Freemasons — called also *Masonry* 2 : natural or instinctive fellowship or sympathy

free·ness *n* : FREEDOM

free on board *adv* (*or adj*) : without charge for delivery to and placing on board a carrier at a specified point

free port *n* : an enclosed port or section of a port where goods are received and shipped free of customs duty

fre·er \'frē-ər\ *n* : one that frees ⟨the ~ of the slaves⟩

free radical *n* : an atom or a group of atoms having at least one unpaired electron and participating in various reactions

free·sia \'frē-zh(ē-)ə\ *n* [NL, genus name, fr. F. H. T. *Freese* †1876 G physician] : any of a genus (*Freesia*) of the iris family of sweet-scented African herbs with red, white, or yellow flowers

free silver *n* : the free coinage of silver often at a fixed ratio with gold

free soil *n* : U.S. territory where prior to the Civil War slavery was prohibited

free–soil \'frē-,sȯil\ *adj* 1 : characterized by free soil ⟨~ states⟩ 2 *cap F&S* : opposing the extension of slavery into U.S. territories and the admission of slave states into the Union prior to the Civil War; *specif* : of, relating to, or constituting a minor U.S. political party having these aims — **Free–Soil·er** \-'sȯi-lər\ *n*

free–spo·ken \-'spō-kən\ *adj* : speaking freely : OUTSPOKEN

fre·est \'frē-əst\ *superlative of* FREE

freestanding *adj* : standing alone or on its own foundation free of architectural or supporting frame or attachment

free·stone \'frē-,stōn\ *n* 1 : a stone that may be cut freely without splitting 2 a : a fruit stone to which the flesh does not cling b : a fruit having such a stone

free–swim·ming \-'swim-iŋ\ *adj* : able to swim about because not attached

free·think·er \-'thiŋ-kər\ *n* : one that forms opinions on the basis of reason independently of authority; *esp* : one who doubts or denies religious dogma syn see ATHEIST — **free·think·ing** \-kiŋ\ *n or adj*

free thought *n* : free thinking or unorthodox thought; *specif* : 18th century deism

free throw *n* : an unhindered shot in basketball made from behind a set line and usu. awarded because of a foul by an opponent

free trade *n* : trade based upon the unrestricted international exchange of goods with tariffs used only as a source of revenue

free verse *n* : verse whose meter is irregular in some respect or whose rhythm is not metrical

free·way \'frē-,wā\ *n* 1 : an expressway with fully controlled access 2 : a toll-free highway

1**free·wheel** \-'(h)wē(ə)l\ *n* 1 : a power-transmission system in a motor vehicle with a device that permits the propeller shaft to run freely when its speed is greater than that of the engine shaft 2 : a clutch fitted in the rear hub of a bicycle that permits the rear wheel to run on free from the rear sprocket when the pedals are stopped

2**freewheel** *vi* : to move, live, or drift along freely or irresponsibly

free will *n* 1 : the power asserted of moral beings of choosing within limitations or with respect to some matters without restraint of physical or divine necessity or causal law 2 : the ability to choose between alternatives so that the choice and action are to an extent creatively determined by the conscious subject

free·will \,frē-,wil\ *adj* : VOLUNTARY, SPONTANEOUS

Freewill Baptist *n* : a member of a Baptist group holding Arminian doctrines and practicing open communion and anointing

free world *n* : the part of the world where democracy and capitalism or moderate socialism rather than totalitarian or Communist political and economic systems prevail

1**freeze** \'frēz\ *vb* **froze** \'frōz\ **fro·zen** \'frōz-ᵊn\ **freez·ing** [ME *fresen*, fr. OE *frēosan*; akin to OHG *friosan* to freeze, L *pruina* hoarfrost] *vi* 1 : to become congealed into ice by cold : SOLIDIFY 2 a : to become chilled with cold ⟨almost *froze* to death⟩ b : to become coldly formal in manner 3 : to adhere solidly by freezing 4 : to become clogged with ice ⟨the water pipes *froze*⟩ 5 : to become fixed or motionless; *esp* : to become incapable of acting or speaking ~ *vt* 1 : to harden into ice 2 a : to make extremely cold : CHILL b : to act toward in a stiff and formal way 3 a : to act on usu. destructively by frost b : to anesthetize by cold 4 : to cause to grip tightly or remain in immovable contact 5 a : to cause to become fixed, immovable, or unalterable b : to forbid further manufacture, use, or sale of (a raw material) c : to immobilize by governmental regulation the expenditure, withdrawal, or exchange of (foreign-owned bank balances)

2**freeze** *n* 1 : a state of weather marked by low temperature 2 a : an act or instance of freezing b : the state of being frozen

freeze–dry \'frēz-,drī\ *vt* : to dry in a frozen state under high vacuum esp. for preservation

freez·er \'frē-zər\ *n* : one that freezes or keeps cool; *esp* : an insulated compartment or room for keeping food at a subfreezing temperature or for freezing perishable food rapidly

freezing point *n* : the temperature at which a liquid solidifies ⟨the *freezing point* of water is 0° C or 32° F⟩

free zone *n* : an area within which goods may be received and stored without payment of duty

F region *n* : the highest region of the ionosphere occurring from 90 to more than 250 miles above the earth

1**freight** \'frāt\ *n*, *often attrib* [ME, fr. MD or MLG *vracht*, *vrecht*] 1 : the compensation paid for the transportation of goods 2 a : something that is loaded for transportation : CARGO b : LOAD, BURDEN 3 a : the ordinary transportation of goods afforded by a common carrier and distinguished from express b : a train designed or used for such transportation

2**freight** *vt* 1 a : to load with goods for transportation b : BURDEN, CHARGE 2 : to transport or ship by freight

freight·age \'frāt-ij\ *n* : FREIGHT

freight·er \-ər\ *n* 1 : one that loads or charters and loads a ship 2 : SHIPPER 3 : a ship or airplane used chiefly to carry freight

frem·i·tus \'frem-ət-əs\ *n* [NL, fr. L, murmur, fr. *fremitus*, pp.

of *fremere* to murmur; akin to OE *bremman* to roar] **:** a sensation felt by a hand placed on the chest vibrating during speech

french \'french\ *vt, often cap* **:** to cut (snap beans) in thin lengthwise strips before cooking

¹**French** \'french\ *adj* [ME, fr. OE *frencisc*, fr. *Franca* Frank] **:** of, relating to, or characteristic of France, its people, or their language — **French·man** \-mən\ *n* — **French·wom·an** \-ˌwu̇m-ən\ *n*

²**French** *n* **1 :** a Romance language that developed out of the Vulgar Latin of Transalpine Gaul and became the literary and official language of France **2** *pl in constr* **:** the French people

French bulldog *n* **:** any of a breed of small compact heavy-boned bat-eared dog developed in France supposedly from a crossing of small English bulldogs with native dogs

French Canadian *n* **:** one of the descendants of French settlers in lower Canada

French–Canadian *adj* **:** of, relating to, or characteristic of the French Canadians

French chalk *n* **:** a soft white granular variety of steatite used esp. for drawing lines on cloth and for removing grease in dry cleaning

French chop *n* **:** a rib chop with the meat trimmed from the end of the rib

French door *n* **:** a light door with glazed rectangular panels extending the full length; *also* **:** one of a pair of such doors in a single frame

French dressing *n* **:** a salad dressing of oil and vinegar or lemon juice seasoned with salt, pepper, mustard, or other condiments

French endive *n* **:** ENDIVE 2

¹**french fry** *vt, often cap 1st F* [back-formation fr. *French fried (potatoes)*] **:** to fry (as strips of potato) in deep fat until brown

²**french fry** *n, often cap 1st F* **:** a strip of potato fried in deep fat — usu. used in pl.

French heel *n* **:** a woman's shoe heel that is usu. high, pitched well forward, and markedly curved

French horn *n* **:** a brass wind instrument consisting of a long curved conical tube with a narrow funnel-shaped mouthpiece at one end and a flaring bell at the other

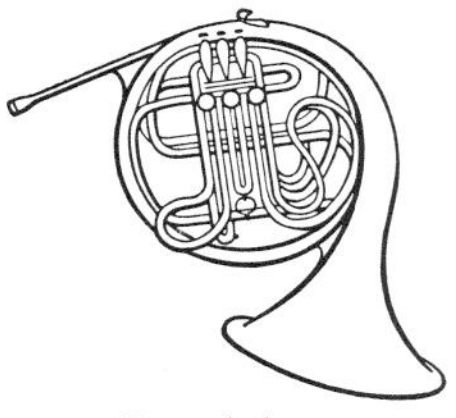

French horn

french·ifi·ca·tion \ˌfren-chə-fə-'kā-shən\ *n, often cap* **:** the act of frenchifying **:** the state of being frenchified

french·ify \'fren-chə-ˌfī\ *vt, often cap* **:** to make French

French leave *n* **:** an informal, hasty, or secret departure

French pastry *n* **:** fancy pastry baked in individual portions and filled

French telephone *n* **:** HANDSET

French toast *n* **:** bread dipped in egg and milk and sautéed

French window *n* **1 :** a French door placed in an exterior wall **2 :** a casement window

fre·net·ic \fri-'net-ik\ *adj* [ME *frenetik* insane, fr. MF *frenetique*, fr. L *phreneticus*, modif. of Gk *phrenitikos*, fr. *phrenitis* inflammation of the brain, fr. *phren-*, *phrēn* diaphragm, mind] **:** FRENZIED, FRANTIC — **fre·net·i·cal·ly** \-'net-i-k(ə-)lē\ *adv*

fre·num \'frē-nəm\ *n, pl* **frenums** *or* **fre·na** \-nə\ [L, lit., bridle; akin to L *firmus* firm] **:** a connecting fold of membrane serving to support or restrain

fren·zied \'fren-zēd\ *adj* **:** marked by frenzy— **fren·zied·ly** *adv*

¹**fren·zy** \'fren-zē\ *n* [ME *frenesie*, fr. MF, fr. ML *phrenesia*, alter. of L *phrenesis*, fr. *phreneticus*] **1 a :** a temporary madness **b :** a violent mental or emotional agitation **2 :** intense usu. wild and often disorderly compulsive or agitated activity

²**frenzy** *vt* **:** to affect with frenzy

Fre·on \'frē-ˌän\ *trademark* — used for any of various nonflammable gaseous and liquid fluorinated hydrocarbons used as refrigerants and as propellants for aerosols

fre·quence \'frē-kwən(t)s\ *n* **:** FREQUENCY

fre·quen·cy \-kwən-sē\ *n* **1 :** the fact or condition of occurring frequently **2 a :** the number of times that a periodic function repeats the same sequence of values during a unit variation of the independent variable **b :** the number of individuals in a single class when objects are classified according to variations in a set of one or more specified attributes **3 :** the number of repetitions of a periodic process in a unit of time: as **a :** the number of complete alternations per second of an alternating current **b :** the number of sound waves per second produced by a sounding body **c :** the number of complete oscillations per second of an electromagnetic wave

frequency distribution *n* **:** an arrangement of statistical data that exhibits the frequency of the occurrence of the values of a variable

frequency modulation *n* **:** modulation of the frequency of the carrier wave in accordance with speech or a signal; *specif* **:** the system of broadcasting using this method of modulation

¹**fre·quent** \'frē-kwənt\ *adj* [ME, fr. MF or L; MF, fr. L *frequent-*, *frequens*] **1** *obs* **:** THRONGED **2 a :** COMMON, USUAL **b :** happening at short intervals **3 :** HABITUAL, PERSISTENT **4** *archaic* **:** INTIMATE, FAMILIAR — **fre·quent·ness** *n*

²**fre·quent** \frē-'kwent, 'frē-kwənt\ *vt* **1 :** to associate with, be in, or resort to often or habitually **2** *archaic* **:** to read systematically or habitually — **fre·quent·er** *n*

fre·quen·ta·tion \ˌfrē-ˌkwen-'tā-shən, -kwən-\ *n* **:** the act or habit of frequenting

¹**fre·quen·ta·tive** \frē-'kwent-ət-iv\ *adj* **:** denoting repeated or recurrent action or state — used of a verb aspect, verb form, or meaning

²**frequentative** *n* **:** a frequentative verb or verb form

fre·quent·ly \'frē-kwənt-lē\ *adv* **:** at frequent or short intervals

¹**fres·co** \'fres-(ˌ)kō\ *n, pl* **frescoes** *or* **frescos** [It, fr. *fresco* fresh, of Gmc origin; akin to OHG *frisc*] **1 :** the art of painting on freshly spread moist lime plaster with pigments suspended in a water vehicle **2 :** a painting executed in fresco

²**fresco** *vt* **:** to paint in fresco

¹**fresh** \'fresh\ *adj* [ME, fr. OF *freis*, of Gmc origin; akin to OHG *frisc* fresh; akin to OE *fersc* fresh] **1 a :** not salt ⟨~ water⟩ **b** (1) **:** PURE, INVIGORATING ⟨~ air⟩ (2) *of wind* **:** STRONG **2 a :** not stored or preserved ⟨~ vegetables⟩ **b :** having its original qualities unimpaired: as (1) **:** full of or renewed in vigor or readiness for action **:** REFRESHED (2) **:** not stale, sour, or decayed ⟨~ bread⟩ (3) **:** not faded (4) **:** not worn or rumpled **:** SPRUCE **3 a** (1) **:** experienced, made, or received newly or anew (2) **:** ADDITIONAL, ANOTHER ⟨make a ~ start⟩ **b :** ORIGINAL, VIVID **c :** INEXPERIENCED, RAW **d :** newly or just come or arrived ⟨~ from school⟩ **e :** having the milk flow recently established ⟨a ~ cow⟩ **4** [prob. by folk etymology fr. G *frech*] **:** disposed to take liberties **:** IMPUDENT **syn** see NEW — **fresh·ly** *adv* — **fresh·ness** *n*

²**fresh** *adv* **:** just recently **:** FRESHLY ⟨a ~ laid egg⟩

³**fresh** *n* **1 :** an increased flow or rush (as of water) **:** FRESHET **2 :** a stream of fresh water running into salt water

fresh breeze *n* **:** wind having a speed of 19 to 24 miles per hour

fresh·en \'fresh-ən\ *vb* **fresh·en·ing** \'fresh-(ə-)niŋ\ *vi* **1 :** to grow or become fresh: as **a** *of wind* **:** to increase in strength **b :** to become fresh in appearance or vitality **c** *of water* **:** to lose saltiness **2** *of a milch animal* **:** to come into milk **~** *vt* **:** to make fresh; *also* **:** REFRESH, REVIVE

fresh·et \'fresh-ət\ *n* **1** *archaic* **:** STREAM 1 **2 :** a great rise or overflowing of a stream caused by heavy rains or melted snow

fresh gale *n* **:** wind having a speed of 39 to 46 miles per hour

fresh·man \'fresh-mən\ *n, often attrib* **1 :** NOVICE, NEWCOMER **2 :** a student in his first year or having chiefly first-year standing

fresh·wa·ter \ˌfresh-ˌwȯt-ər, -ˌwät-\ *adj* **1 :** of, relating to, or living in fresh water **2 :** accustomed to navigating only in fresh waters; *also* **:** UNSKILLED

¹**fret** \'fret\ *vb* **fret·ted; fret·ting** [ME *freten* to devour, fret, fr. OE *fretan* to devour; akin to OHG *frezzan* to devour, *ezzan* to eat] *vt* **1 :** to cause to suffer emotional strain **:** VEX **2 a :** to eat or gnaw into **:** CORRODE; *also* **:** FRAY **b :** RUB, CHAFE **c :** to make by wearing away a substance ⟨the stream *fretted* a channel⟩ **3 :** to pass (as time) in fretting **4 :** AGITATE, RIPPLE **~** *vi* **1 a :** to eat into something **b :** to affect something as if by gnawing or biting **:** GRATE **2 a :** WEAR, CORRODE **b :** CHAFE **c :** FRAY **3 a :** to become vexed or worried **b** *of running water* **:** to become agitated

²**fret** *n* **1 a :** the action of wearing away **:** EROSION **b :** a worn or eroded spot **2 :** an agitation of mind **:** IRRITATION

³**fret** *vt* **fret·ted; fret·ting** [ME *fretten*, fr. MF *freter* to bind with a ferrule, fret, fr. OF, fr. *frete* ferrule] **1 a :** to decorate with interlaced designs **b :** to form a pattern upon **2 :** to enrich with embossed or pierced carved patterns

⁴**fret** *n* **1 :** an ornamental network; *esp* **:** a woman's headdress **2 :** an ornament or ornamental work often in relief consisting of small straight bars intersecting one another in right or oblique angles

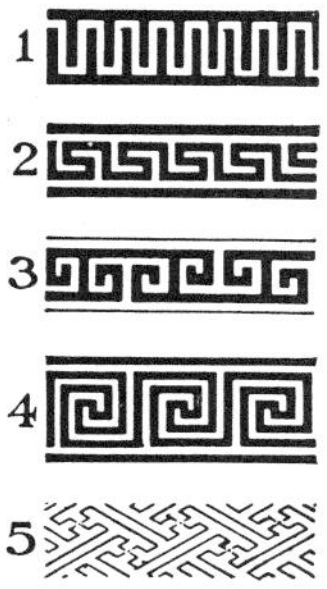

frets 2: *1, 2, 3, 4,* Greek *5* Japanese

⁵**fret** *n* [prob. fr. MF *frete* ferrule] **:** one of a series of ridges fixed across the fingerboard of a stringed musical instrument

⁶**fret** *vt* **fret·ted; fret·ting :** to furnish with frets

fret·ful \'fret-fəl\ *adj* **1 :** disposed to fret **:** IRRITABLE **2 a** *of water* **:** TROUBLED **b** *of wind* **:** GUSTY — **fret·ful·ly** \-fə-lē\ *adv* — **fret·ful·ness** *n*

fret·saw \'fret-ˌsȯ\ *n* **:** a narrow-bladed fine-toothed saw for cutting curved outlines

fret·work \-ˌwərk\ *n* **1 :** decoration consisting of work adorned with frets **2 :** ornamental openwork or work in relief

Freud·ian \'frȯid-ē-ən\ *adj* **:** of, relating to, or according with the psychoanalytic theories or practices of Freud — **Freudian** *n* — **Freud·ian·ism** \-ē-ə-ˌniz-əm\ *n*

Frey \'frā\ *n* [ON *Freyr*] **:** the god of fertility and crops and of peace and prosperity in Norse mythology

Freya \'frā-ə\ *n* [ON *Freyja*] **:** the goddess of love and beauty in Norse mythology

fri·a·bil·i·ty \ˌfrī-ə-'bil-ət-ē\ *n* **:** the condition of being friable

fri·a·ble \'frī-ə-bəl\ *adj* [MF or L; MF, fr. L *friabilis*, fr. *friare* to crumble] **:** easily crumbled or pulverized **syn** see FRAGILE — **fri·a·ble·ness** *n*

fri·ar \'frī(-ə)r\ *n* [ME *frere*, *fryer*, fr. OF *frere*, lit., brother, fr. L *fratr-*, *frater* — more at BROTHER] **:** a member of a mendicant order **syn** see RELIGIOUS

fri·ar·ly \-lē\ *adj* **:** resembling a friar **:** relating to friars

friar's lantern *n* **:** IGNIS FATUUS

fri·ary \'frī-(ə-)rē\ *n* **:** a monastery of friars

¹**frib·ble** \'frib-əl\ *vb* **frib·bling** \-(ə-)liŋ\ [origin unknown] *vi* **:** TRIFLE, DODDER **~** *vt* **:** to trifle or fool away

²**fribble** *n* **:** a frivolous person, thing, or idea **:** TRIFLER — **fribble** *adj*

fric·an·deau \'frik-ən-ˌdō\ *n* [F] **:** larded veal roasted and glazed in its own juices

¹**fric·as·see** \'frik-ə-ˌsē, ˌfrik-ə-'\ *n* [MF, fr. fem. of *fricassé*, pp. of *fricasser* to fricassee] **:** a dish made of chicken, veal, or other meat cut into pieces and stewed in a gravy

²**fricassee** *vt* **fric·as·seed; fric·as·see·ing :** to cook as a fricassee

¹**fric·a·tive** \'frik-ət-iv\ *adj* [L *fricatus*, pp. of *fricare*] **:** characterized by frictional passage of the expired voiced or voiceless breath against a narrowing at some point in the vocal tract ⟨\f v th t͟h s z sh zh h\ are ~⟩

²**fricative** *n* **:** a fricative consonant

fric·tion \'frik-shən\ *n* [MF or L; MF, fr. L *friction-*, *frictio*, fr. *frictus*, pp. of *fricare* to rub; akin to L *friare* to crumble, Skt *bhrīṇanti* they injure] **1 a :** the rubbing of one body against another **b :** resistance to relative motion between two bodies in contact **2 :** the clashing between two persons or parties of opposed views **:** DISAGREEMENT — **fric·tion·less** \-ləs\ *adj*

fric·tion·al \-shnəl, -shən-ᵊl\ *adj* **1 :** of or relating to friction **2 :** moved or produced by friction — **fric·tion·al·ly** \-ē\ *adv*

friction clutch *n* **:** a clutch in which connection is made through sliding friction

friction drive *n* **:** an automobile power-transmission system that transmits motion by surface friction instead of teeth and provides a full range of variation in desired speed ratios

friction match *n* **:** a match that is ignited by friction

friction tape *n* **:** a usu. cloth tape impregnated with water-resistant insulating material and an adhesive and used esp. to protect, insulate, and support electrical conductors

Fri·day \'frīd-ē\ *n* [ME, fr. OE *frīgedæg*; akin to OHG *frīatag*;

both fr. a prehistoric WGmc compound whose components are akin to OHG *Frīa*, goddess of love and to OE *dæg* day] **:** the sixth day of the week — **Fri·days** \-ēz\ *adv*
fridge *also* **frig** \ˈfrij\ *n* [by shortening & alter.] *chiefly Brit* **:** REFRIGERATOR
fried·cake \ˈfrīd-ˌkāk\ *n* **:** DOUGHNUT, CRULLER
1**friend** \ˈfrend\ *n* [ME *frend*, fr. OE *frēond*; akin to OHG *friunt* friend; both fr. the prp. of a prehistoric Gmc verb represented by OE *frēon* to love; akin to OE *frēo* free] **1 a :** one attached to another by affection or esteem **b :** ACQUAINTANCE **2 a :** one not hostile **b :** one that is of the same nation or group **3 :** one that favors something **4** *obs* **:** PARAMOUR **5** *cap* **:** a member of a group that stress Inner Light, reject ostentation, outward rites, and an ordained ministry, and oppose war — called also *Quaker*
2**friend** *vt* **:** to act as the friend of **:** BEFRIEND
friend·less \ˈfren-(d)ləs\ *adj* **:** having no friends — **friend·less·ness** *n*
friend·li·ly \-(d)lə-lē\ *adv* **:** in a friendly manner
friend·li·ness \-(d)lē-nəs\ *n* **:** the quality or state of being friendly
1**friend·ly** \ˈfren-(d)lē\ *adj* **:** of, relating to, or befitting a friend: as **a :** showing kindly interest and goodwill **b :** not hostile **c :** inclined to favor **d :** COMFORTING, CHEERFUL **syn** see AMICABLE
2**friendly** *adv* **:** in a friendly manner **:** AMICABLY
friend·ship \ˈfren(d)-ˌship\ *n* **1 :** the state of being friends **2 :** FRIENDLINESS **3** *obs* **:** AID
fri·er *var of* FRYER
Frie·sian \ˈfrē-zhən\ *n, chiefly Brit* **:** HOLSTEIN-FRIESIAN
1**frieze** \ˈfrēz *or* (*compare* FRISÉ) frē-ˈzā\ *n* [ME *frise*, fr. MF, fr. MD *vriese*] **1 :** a heavy durable coarse wool and shoddy fabric with a rough surface **2 :** a pile surface of uncut loops or of patterned cut and uncut loops
2**frieze** \ˈfrēz\ *n* [MF, perh. fr. ML *phrygium*, *frisium* embroidered cloth, fr. L *phrygium*, fr. neut. of *Phrygius* Phrygian, fr. *Phrygia*] **1 :** the part of an entablature between the architrave and the cornice **2 :** a sculptured or richly ornamented band (as on a building)
frig·ate \ˈfrig-ət\ *n* [MF, fr. OIt *fregata*] **1 :** a light boat propelled orig. by oars but later by sails **2 :** a square-rigged war vessel intermediate between a corvette and a ship of the line **3 :** a British or Canadian escort ship between a corvette and a destroyer in size **4 :** a U.S. warship of 5000 to 7000 tons that is smaller than a cruiser and larger than a destroyer
frigate bird *n* **:** any of several strong-winged seabirds (family Fregatidae) noted for their rapacious habits
Frig·ga \ˈfrig-ə\ *n* [ON *Frigg*] **:** the goddess of the sky in Norse mythology who shares dominion in heaven with her husband Odin
1**fright** \ˈfrīt\ *n* [ME, fr. OE *fyrhto*, *fryhto*; akin to OHG *forhta* fear] **1 :** fear excited by sudden danger **:** ALARM **2 :** something strange, ugly, or shocking ⟨his beard was a ~⟩ **syn** see FEAR
2**fright** *vt* **:** to alarm suddenly **:** FRIGHTEN
fright·en \ˈfrīt-ᵊn\ *vb* **fright·en·ing** \ˈfrīt-niŋ, -ᵊn-iŋ\ *vt* **1 :** to make afraid **:** TERRIFY **2 :** to drive away or out by frightening ~ *vi* **:** to become frightened — **fright·en·ing·ly** \-niŋ-lē, -ᵊn-iŋ-\ *adv*
fright·ful \ˈfrīt-fəl\ *adj* **1 :** causing fear or alarm **:** TERRIFYING **2 :** causing shock or horror **:** STARTLING **3 :** EXTREME ⟨~ thirst⟩ **syn** see FEARFUL — **fright·ful·ly** \-fə-lē\ *adv* — **fright·ful·ness** *n*
frig·id \ˈfrij-əd\ *adj* [L *frigidus*, fr. *frigēre* to be cold; akin to L *frigus* frost, cold, Gk *rhigos*] **1 a :** intensely cold **b :** lacking warmth or ardor **:** INDIFFERENT **2 :** INSIPID **3 :** abnormally averse to sexual intercourse — **frig·id·ly** *adv* — **frig·id·ness** *n*
Frig·i·daire \ˌfrij-ə-ˈda(ə)r, -ˈde(ə)r\ *trademark* — used for a mechanical refrigerator
fri·gid·i·ty \frij-ˈid-ət-ē\ *n* **:** the quality or state of being frigid; *specif* **:** marked or abnormal sexual indifference esp. in a woman
frigid zone *n* **:** the area or region between the arctic circle and the north pole or between the antarctic circle and the south pole
frig·o·rif·ic \ˌfrig-ə-ˈrif-ik\ *adj* [L *frigorificus*, fr. *frigor-*, *frigus* frost] **:** causing cold **:** CHILLING
fri·jol \frē-ˈhōl\ *also* **fri·jo·le** \-ˈhō-lē\ *n, pl* **fri·jo·les** \frē-ˈhō-lēz, ˈfrē-\ [Sp *frijol*] *chiefly Southwest* **:** BEAN 1b
1**frill** \ˈfril\ *vt* **:** to provide or decorate with a frill
2**frill** *n* [perh. fr. Flem *frul*] **1 a :** a gathered, pleated, or bias-cut fabric edging used on clothing **b :** a strip of paper curled at one end and rolled to be slipped over the bone end (as of a chop) in serving **2 a :** a ruff of hair or feathers about the neck of an animal **b :** AFFECTATION, AIR **c :** something decorative but not essential **:** EXTRAVAGANCE — **frilly** \ˈfril-ē\ *adj*
1**fringe** \ˈfrinj\ *n, often attrib* [ME *frenge*, fr. MF, fr. (assumed) VL *frimbia*, fr. L *fimbriae* (pl.)] **1 :** an ornamental border consisting of short straight or twisted threads or strips hanging from cut or raveled edges or from a separate band **2 a :** something resembling a fringe **:** BORDER **b :** one of various light or dark bands produced by the interference or diffraction of light **3 a :** something that is marginal, additional, or secondary to some activity, process, or subject matter **b :** a group with marginal or extremist views
2**fringe** *vt* **1 :** to furnish or adorn with a fringe **2 :** to serve as a fringe for
fringe area *n* **:** a region in which reception from a given broadcasting station is weak or subject to serious distortion
fringe benefit *n* **:** an employment benefit granted by an employer that involves a money cost without affecting basic wage rates
fringy \ˈfrin-jē\ *adj* **:** adorned with or resembling fringes
1**frip·pery** \ˈfrip-(ə-)rē\ *n* [MF *friperie*, deriv. of ML *faluppa* piece of straw] **1** *obs* **a :** cast-off clothes **b :** a place where old clothes are sold **2 a :** FINERY; *esp* **:** something showy, tawdry, or nonessential **b :** affected elegance **:** OSTENTATION
2**frippery** *adj* **:** TRIFLING, TAWDRY
fri·sé \frē-ˈzā\ *n* [F, fr. pp. of *friser* to curl] **:** FRIEZE
Frise aileron \ˈfrēz-\ *n* [Leslie George *Frise* b1897 E engineer] **:** an aileron having a nose portion projecting ahead of the hinge axis and a lower surface in line with the lower surface of the wing
fri·sette \frē-ˈzet\ *n* [F] *archaic* **:** a fringe of hair or curls worn on the forehead by women
fri·seur \frē-ˈzər\ *n* [F] **:** HAIRDRESSER
1**Fri·sian** \ˈfrizh-ən, ˈfrē-zhən\ *adj* [L *Frisii* Frisians] **:** of, relating to, or characteristic of Friesland, the Frisians, or Frisian
2**Frisian** *n* **1 :** a member of a people that inhabit principally the Netherlands province of Friesland and the Frisian islands in the North sea **2 :** the Germanic language of the Frisian people
1**frisk** \ˈfrisk\ *vb* [obs. *frisk* (lively)] *vi* **:** to leap, skip, or dance in a lively or playful way **:** GAMBOL ~ *vt* **:** to search esp. for concealed weapons by running the hand rapidly over the clothing and through the pockets — **frisk·er** *n*
2**frisk** *n* **1 a** *archaic* **:** CARACOLE, CAPER **b :** GAMBOL, ROMP **c :** a gay time **2 :** an act of frisking
frisk·i·ly \ˈfris-kə-lē\ *adv* **:** in a frisky manner
frisk·i·ness \-kē-nəs\ *n* **:** the quality or state of being frisky
frisky \ˈfris-kē\ *adj* **:** inclined to frisk **:** FROLICSOME
fris·son \frē-ˈsōⁿ\ *n, pl* **frissons** \-ˈsōⁿ(z)\ [F] **:** SHUDDER, THRILL
1**frit** \ˈfrit\ *n* [It *fritta*] **1 :** the calcined or partly fused materials of which glass is made **2 :** glass variously compounded that is quenched and ground as a basis for glazes or enamels
2**frit** *vt* **frit·ted**; **frit·ting :** to prepare (materials for glass) by heat
frith \ˈfrith\ *n* **:** FIRTH
frit·il·lar·ia \ˌfrit-ᵊl-ˈer-ē-ə, -ˈar-\ *n* [NL, fr. L *fritillus* dice cup; fr. the markings of the petals] **:** any of a genus (*Fritillaria*) of bulbous herbs of the lily family with mottled or checkered flowers
frit·il·lary \ˈfrit-ᵊl-ˌer-ē\ *n* [NL *fritillaria*] **1 :** FRITILLARIA **2 :** any of numerous spotted butterflies (*Argynnis* and related genera)
1**frit·ter** \ˈfrit-ər\ *n* [ME *fritour*, fr. MF *friture*, fr. (assumed) VL *frictura*, fr. *frictus*, pp. of *frigere* to fry — more at FRY] **:** a small quantity of fried or sautéed batter often containing fruit or meat
2**fritter** *vb* [*fritter*, n. (fragment, shred)] *vt* **1 :** to reduce or waste piecemeal ⟨~*ing* away his time on trifles⟩ **2 :** to break into small fragments ~ *vi* **:** DISSIPATE, DWINDLE — **frit·ter·er** \-ər-ər\ *n*
friv·ol \ˈfriv-əl\ *vi* **friv·oled** *or* **friv·olled**; **friv·ol·ing** *or* **friv·ol·ling** \-(ə-)liŋ\ [back-formation fr. *frivolous*] **:** to act frivolously **:** TRIFLE — **friv·ol·er** *or* **friv·ol·ler** \-(ə-)lər\ *n*
fri·vol·i·ty \friv-ˈäl-ət-ē\ *n* **1 :** the quality or state of being frivolous **2 :** a frivolous act or thing **syn** see LIGHTNESS
friv·o·lous \ˈfriv-(ə-)ləs\ *adj* [ME, fr. L *frivolus*] **1 :** of little weight or importance **2 a :** lacking in seriousness **:** PLAYFUL **b :** marked by unbecoming levity — **friv·o·lous·ly** *adv* — **friv·o·lous·ness** *n*
1**frizz** \ˈfriz\ *vb* [F *friser*] *vt* **:** to form into small tight curls ~ *vi* **:** to become frizzled
2**frizz** *n* **1 :** a tight curl **2 :** hair that is tightly curled
3**frizz** *vb* [alter. of 1FRY] **:** to fry or sear with a sizzling noise **:** SIZZLE
frizz·i·ly \ˈfriz-ə-lē\ *adv* **:** in a frizzy manner
frizz·i·ness \ˈfriz-ē-nəs\ *n* **:** the quality or state of being frizzy
1**friz·zle** \ˈfriz-əl\ *vb* **friz·zling** \-(ə-)liŋ\ [prob. akin to OE *frīs* curly, OFris *frīsle* curl] **:** FRIZZ, CURL
2**frizzle** *n* **:** a crisp curl
3**frizzle** *vb* [1*fry* + *sizzle*] *vt* **1 :** to fry until crisp and curled **2 :** BURN, SCORCH ~ *vi* **:** to cook with a sizzling noise
friz·zly \ˈfriz-(ə-)lē\ *or* **frizzy** \ˈfriz-ē\ *adj* **:** tightly curled
1**fro** \frə, (ˈ)frō\ *prep* [ME, fr. ON *frā*; akin to OE *from*] *dial Brit* **:** FROM
2**fro** \ˈfrō\ *adv* **:** BACK, AWAY — used in the phrase *to and fro*
1**frock** \ˈfräk\ *n* [ME *frok*, fr. MF *froc*, of Gmc origin; akin to OHG *hroch* mantle, coat] **1 :** an outer garment worn by monks and friars **:** HABIT **2 :** an outer garment worn chiefly by men: **a :** a long loose mantle **b :** a workman's outer shirt; *esp* **:** SMOCK FROCK **c :** a woolen jersey worn esp. by sailors **3 :** a woman's dress
2**frock** *vt* **1 :** to clothe in a frock **2 :** to make a cleric of
frock coat *n* **:** a man's usu. double-breasted coat having knee-length skirts front and back
froe \ˈfrō\ *n* [perh. alter. of obs. *froward* turned away, fr. ME; fr. the position of the handle] **:** a cleaving tool for splitting cask staves and shingles from the block
frog \ˈfrȯg, ˈfräg\ *n* [ME *frogge*, fr. OE *frogga*; akin to OHG *frosk* frog, Skt *pravate* he jumps up] **1 a :** any of various smooth-skinned web-footed largely aquatic tailless agile leaping amphibians (as of the suborder Diplasiocoela) — compare TOAD **b :** a condition in the throat that produces hoarseness ⟨had a ~ in his throat⟩ **2 :** the triangular elastic horny pad in the middle of the sole of the foot of a horse **3 a** (1) **:** a loop attached to a belt to hold a weapon or tool (2) **:** an ornamental braiding for fastening the front of a garment that consists of a button and a loop through which it passes **b :** a device permitting the wheels on one rail of a track to cross an intersecting rail **c :** the nut of a violin bow

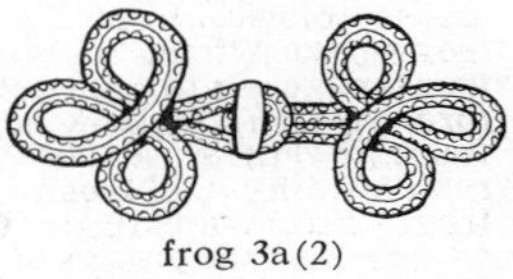

frog 3a(2)

frog·eye \-ˌī\ *n* **:** any of numerous leaf diseases characterized by concentric rings about the diseased spots
frog·hop·per \-ˌhäp-ər\ *n* **:** SPITTLEBUG
frog·man \-ˌman, -mən\ *n* **:** a person equipped for extended periods of underwater swimming usu. for reconnaissance and demolition
frog spit *n* **1 :** CUCKOO SPIT 1 — called also *frog spittle* **2 :** an alga that forms slimy masses on quiet water
1**frol·ic** \ˈfräl-ik\ *adj* [D *vroolijk*, fr. MD *vrolijc*, fr. *vro* happy; akin to OHG *frō* happy, OE *frogga* frog] **:** full of fun **:** MERRY
2**frolic** *vi* **frol·icked**; **frol·ick·ing 1 :** to make merry **2 :** to play about happily **:** ROMP
3**frolic** *n* **1 :** a playful mischievous action **2 a :** FUN, MERRIMENT **b :** PARTY
frol·ic·some \ˈfräl-ik-səm\ *adj* **:** full of gaiety **:** SPORTIVE
from \(ˈ)frəm, ˈfräm *also* fəm\ *prep* [ME, fr. OE; akin to OHG *fram*, adv., forth, away, OE *faran* to go — more at FARE] **1** — used as a function word to indicate a starting point: as (1) a place where a physical movement begins ⟨came here ~ the city⟩ (2) a starting point in a statement of limits ⟨cost ~ $5 to $10⟩ **2** — used as a function word to indicate separation: as (1) physical separation (2) an act or condition of removal, abstention, exclusion, release, or differentiation **3** — used as a function word to indicate the source, cause, agent, or basis
frond \ˈfränd\ *n* [L *frond-*, *frons* foliage] **1 :** LEAF; *esp* **:** the leaf of a palm **2 a :** a thallus or thalloid shoot resembling a leaf **b :** the leaf of a fern — **frond·ed** \ˈfrän-dəd\ *adj*
fron·dose \ˈfrän-ˌdōs\ *adj* **:** bearing or resembling fronds — **fron·dose·ly** *adv*
1**front** \ˈfrənt\ *n* [ME, fr. OF, fr. L *front-*, *frons* — more at BRINK]

1 a : FOREHEAD; *also* **:** the whole face **b** (1) **:** demeanor or bearing esp. in the face of danger or other trial (2) **:** external and often feigned appearance (3) **:** an artificial or self-important manner **2 a** (1) **:** VANGUARD (2) **:** a line of battle (3) *often cap* **:** a zone of conflict between armies (4) **:** lateral space occupied by a military unit **b** (1) **:** a stand in reference to some issue **:** POLICY — usu. used with *change* (2) **:** a sphere of activity (3) **:** a movement linking divergent elements to achieve certain common objectives; *esp* **:** a Communist dominated political coalition **3 :** a side of a building; *esp* **:** the side that contains the principal entrance **4 a :** the forward part or surface **b** (1) **:** FRONTAGE (2) **:** a beach promenade at a seaside resort **c :** DICKEY 1a **d :** the boundary between two dissimilar air masses **5** *archaic* **:** BEGINNING **6 a** (1) **:** a position ahead of a person or of the foremost part of a thing (2) — used as a call by a hotel desk clerk in summoning a bellboy **b :** a position of leadership or superiority **7 a :** a person, group, or thing used to mask the identity or true character or activity of the actual controlling agent **b :** a person who serves as the nominal head or spokesman of an enterprise or group to lend it prestige

2front *vi* **1 :** FACE **2 :** to serve as a front ⟨~*ing* for special interests⟩ ~ *vt* **1 a :** CONFRONT **b :** to appear before **2 :** to be in front of **3 :** to supply a front to **4 :** to face toward **5 :** to articulate (a sound) with the tongue farther forward

3front *adj* **1 :** of, relating to, or situated at the front **2 :** articulated at or toward the front of the oral passage ⟨~ vowels⟩ — **front** *adv*

front·age \ˈfrənt-ij\ *n* **1 a :** a piece of land that fronts **b :** the land between the front of a building and the street **2 :** the front side of a building **3 :** the act or fact of facing a given way

1fron·tal \ˈfrənt-ᵊl\ *n* **1** [ME *frontel*, fr. ML *frontellum*, dim. of L *front-, frons*] **:** a cloth hanging over the front of an altar **2 :** FACADE

2frontal *adj* [NL *frontalis*, fr. L *front-, frons*] **1 :** of, relating to, or adjacent to the forehead or the frontal bone **2 a :** of, relating to, or situated at the front **b :** directed against the front or at the main point or issue **:** DIRECT ⟨~ assault⟩ — **fron·tal·ly** \-ᵊl-ē\ *adv*

frontal bone *n* **:** either of a pair of membrane bones forming the forehead

frontal lobe *n* **:** the anterior division of each cerebral hemisphere

fron·tier \ˌfrən-ˈti(ə)r, ˈfrən-ˌ, frän-ˈ, ˈfrän-ˌ\ *n* [ME *fronter*, fr. MF *frontiere*, fr. *front*] **1 a :** a border between two countries **b** *obs* **:** a stronghold upon a frontier **2 a :** a region that forms the margin of settled or developed territory **b :** the farthermost limits of knowledge or achievement **c :** a new field that offers scope for activity — **frontier** *adj*

fron·tiers·man \-ˈti(ə)rz-mən\ *n* **:** a man living on the frontier

fron·tis·piece \ˈfrənt-ə-ˌspēs\ *n* [MF *frontispice*, fr. LL *frontispicium*, lit., view of the front, fr. L *front-, frons* + *-i-* + *specere* to look at — more at SPY] **1 a :** the principal front of a building **b :** a decorated pediment over a portico or window **2 :** an illustration preceding and usu. facing the title page of a book or magazine

front·less \ˈfrənt-ləs\ *adj, archaic* **:** SHAMELESS

front·let \-lət\ *n* **1** [ME *frontlette*, fr. MF *frontelet*, dim. of *frontel*, fr. L *frontale*, fr. *front-, frons*] **:** a band or phylactery worn on the forehead **2 :** FOREHEAD; *esp* **:** the forehead of a bird when distinctively marked

front man *n* **:** a person serving as a front or figurehead

front matter *n* **:** matter preceding the main text of a book

fronto- *comb form* [ISV, fr. L *front-, frons*] **1 :** frontal and ⟨*fronto*parietal⟩ **2** [ˈ*front*] **:** boundary of an air mass ⟨*fronto*genesis⟩

front office *n* **:** the policy-making officials of an organization

front·o·gen·e·sis \ˌfrənt-ō-ˈjen-ə-səs\ *n* [NL] **:** the coming together into a distinct front of two dissimilar air masses that commonly react upon each other to induce cloud and precipitation

front·ol·y·sis \ˌfrənt-ˈäl-ə-səs\ *n* [NL] **:** a process tending to destroy a meteorological front

1front-page \ˈfrənt-ˈpāj\ *adj* **:** very newsworthy

2front-page *vt* **:** to print or report on the front page of a newspaper

frore \ˈfrō(ə)r, ˈfrȯ(ə)r\ *adj* [ME *froren*, fr. OE, pp. of *frēosan* to freeze] **:** FROSTY, FROZEN

frosh \ˈfräsh\ *n, pl* **frosh** [by shortening & alter.] **:** FRESHMAN

1frost \ˈfrȯst\ *n* [ME, fr. OE; akin to OHG *frost*, OE *frēosan* to freeze] **1 a :** the process of freezing **b :** the temperature that causes freezing **c :** a covering of minute ice crystals on a cold surface **2 a :** coldness of deportment or temperament **b :** FAILURE

2frost *vt* **1 a :** to cover with or as if with frost; *esp* **:** to put icing on (cake) **b :** to produce a fine-grained slightly roughened surface on (as metal or glass) **2 :** to injure or kill (as plants) by frost ~ *vi* **:** to become frosted **:** FREEZE

1frost·bite \ˈfrȯs(t)-ˌbīt\ *vt* **:** to blight or nip with frost

2frostbite *n* **:** the freezing or the local effect of a partial freezing of some part of the body

frost·ed \ˈfrȯ-stəd\ *adj* **:** QUICK-FROZEN ⟨~ vegetables⟩

frost heave *n* **:** an upthrust of ground or pavement caused by freezing of moist soil

frost·i·ly \ˈfrȯ-stə-lē\ *adv* **:** in a frosty manner

frost·i·ness \-stē-nəs\ *n* **:** the quality or state of being frosty

frost·ing \ˈfrȯ-stiŋ\ *n* **1 a :** ICING **b :** a trimming on a garment **2 :** lusterless finish of metal or glass **:** MAT

frost·work \ˈfrȯs-ˌtwərk\ *n* **1 :** the figures that moisture sometimes forms in freezing (as on a windowpane) **2 :** ornamentation imitative of the figures of frostwork

frosty \ˈfrȯ-stē\ *adj* **1 :** attended with or producing frost **:** FREEZING **2 :** covered or appearing as if covered with frost **:** HOARY **3 :** marked by coolness or extreme reserve in manner

1froth \ˈfrȯth\ *n, pl* **froths** \ˈfrȯths, ˈfrȯt͟hz\ [ME, fr. ON *frotha*; akin to OE *āfrēothan* to froth] **1 a :** bubbles formed in or on a liquid **:** FOAM **b :** a foamy slaver sometimes accompanying disease or exhaustion **2 :** something unsubstantial or of little value

2froth \ˈfrȯth, ˈfrȯt͟h\ *vt* **1 :** to cause to foam **2 :** VENT, VOICE **3 :** to cover with froth ~ *vi* **:** to throw froth out or up **:** FOAM

froth·i·ly \ˈfrȯ-thə-lē, -t͟hə-\ *adv* **:** in a frothy manner

froth·i·ness \-thē-nəs, -t͟hē-\ *n* **:** the quality or state of being frothy

frothy \ˈfrȯ-thē, -t͟hē\ *adj* **1 :** full of or consisting of froth **2 a :** gaily frivolous or light in content or treatment **b :** made of light thin material

frou·frou \ˈfrü-(ˌ)frü\ *n* [F, of imit. origin] **1 :** a rustling esp. of a woman's skirts **2 :** frilly ornamentation esp. in women's clothing

frow \ˈfrō\ *var of* FROE

fro·ward \ˈfrō-(w)ərd\ *adj* [ME, turned away, froward, fr. *fro* + *-ward*] **1 :** habitually disposed to disobedience and opposition **2** *archaic* **:** ADVERSE **syn** see CONTRARY — **fro·ward·ly** *adv* — **fro·ward·ness** *n*

1frown \ˈfrau̇n\ *vb* [ME *frounen*, fr. MF *froigner* to snort, frown, of Celt origin; akin to W *ffroen* nostril] *vi* **1 :** to contract the brow in displeasure or concentration **2 :** to give evidence of displeasure or disapproval by or as if by facial expression ~ *vt* **:** to show displeasure with or disapproval of esp. by facial expression — **frown·er** *n* — **frown·ing·ly** \ˈfrau̇-niŋ-lē\ *adv*

syn SCOWL, GLOWER, LOWER: FROWN implies conveying disapproval or displeasure by contracting the brows; SCOWL suggests a similar facial expression but conveying rather a bad humor, sullenness, or resentful puzzlement; GLOWER implies a more direct staring or glaring than FROWN or SCOWL, as in expressing contempt or defiance; LOWER suggests a menacing blackness or gloomy anger

2frown *n* **1 :** a wrinkling of the brow in displeasure or concentration **2 :** an expression of displeasure

frows·ty \ˈfrau̇-stē\ *adj* [alter. of *frowzy*] *chiefly Brit* **:** MUSTY

frow·zy *or* **frow·sy** \ˈfrau̇-zē\ *adj* [origin unknown] **1 :** having a slovenly or uncared-for appearance **2 :** MUSTY, STALE

froze *past of* FREEZE

fro·zen \ˈfrōz-ᵊn\ *adj* **1 a :** affected or crusted over by freezing **b :** subject to long and severe cold ⟨~ north⟩ **c :** CHILLED, REFRIGERATED ⟨~ fish⟩ **2 a** (1) **:** drained or incapable of emotion (2) **:** expressing or characterized by cold unfriendliness **b :** incapable of being changed, moved, or undone; *specif* **:** debarred by official action from movement or from change in status ⟨wages were ~⟩ **c :** not available for present use ⟨~ capital⟩ — **fro·zen·ly** *adv* — **fro·zen·ness** \-ᵊn-(n)əs\ *n*

frozen food *n* **:** food that has been subjected to rapid freezing and is kept frozen until used

fruc·ti·fi·ca·tion \ˌfrək-tə-fə-ˈkā-shən, ˌfru̇k-\ *n* **1 :** the forming or producing of fruit **2 a :** FRUIT 1d **b :** SPOROPHORE

fruc·ti·fy \ˈfrək-tə-ˌfī, ˈfru̇k-\ *vi* **:** to bear fruit ~ *vt* **:** to make fruitful or productive

fruc·tose \ˈfrək-ˌtōs, ˈfrük-, ˈfru̇k-, -ˌtōz\ *n* **1 :** a sugar $C_6H_{12}O_6$ known in three forms that are optically different with respect to polarized light **2 :** the very sweet soluble levorotatory D-form of fructose that occurs esp. in fruit juices and honey

fruc·tu·ous \ˈfrək-chə-wəs, ˈfru̇k-\ *adj* **:** FRUITFUL

fru·gal \ˈfrü-gəl\ *adj* [MF or L; MF, fr. L *frugalis* virtuous, frugal, alter. of *frugi*, fr. dat. of *frug-, frux* fruit, value; akin to L *frui* to enjoy] **:** characterized by or reflecting economy in the expenditure of resources **syn** see SPARING — **fru·gal·i·ty** \frü-ˈgal-ət-ē\ *n* — **fru·gal·ly** \ˈfrü-gə-lē\ *adv*

fru·giv·o·rous \frü-ˈjiv-ə-rəs\ *adj* [L *frug-, frux* + E *-vorous*] **:** feeding on fruit

1fruit \ˈfrüt\ *n, often attrib* [ME, fr. OF, fr. L *fructus* fruit, use, fr. *fructus*, pp. of *frui* to enjoy, have the use of — more at BROOK] **1 a :** a product of plant growth — usu. used in pl. **b** (1) **:** the usu. edible reproductive body of a seed plant; *esp* **:** one having a sweet pulp associated with the seed (2) **:** a succulent plant part used chiefly in a dessert or sweet course **c :** a dish, quantity, or diet of fruits **d :** a product of fertilization in a plant with its modified envelopes or appendages; *specif* **:** the ripened ovary of a seed plant and its contents **2 :** OFFSPRING, PROGENY **3 :** CONSEQUENCE, RESULT

2fruit *vi* **:** to bear fruit ~ *vt* **:** to cause to bear fruit

fruit·age \ˈfrüt-ij\ *n* **1 a :** the condition or process of bearing fruit **b :** FRUIT **2 :** the product or result of an action

fruit bat *n* **:** any of a suborder (Megachiroptera) of large Old World fruit-eating bats of warm regions

fruit·cake \ˈfrüt-ˌkāk\ *n* **:** a rich cake containing nuts, dried or candied fruits, and spices

fruit·er·er \ˈfrüt-ər-ər\ *n* [ME, modif. of MF *fruitier*, fr. *fruit*] **:** one that deals in fruit

fruit fly *n* **:** any of various small two-winged flies whose larvae feed on fruit or decaying vegetable matter

fruit·ful \ˈfrüt-fəl\ *adj* **1 a :** yielding or producing fruit **b :** conducive to an abundant yield **2 :** abundantly productive **syn** see FERTILE — **fruit·ful·ly** \-fə-lē\ *adv* — **fruit·ful·ness** *n*

fruiting body *n* **:** a plant organ specialized for producing spores

fru·ition \frü-ˈish-ən\ *n* [ME *fruicioun*, fr. MF or LL; MF *fruition*, fr. LL *fruition-, fruitio*, fr. L *fruitus*, alter. of *fructus*, pp.] **1 :** pleasurable use or possession **:** ENJOYMENT **2 a :** the state of bearing fruit **b :** REALIZATION, ACCOMPLISHMENT **syn** see PLEASURE

fruit·less \ˈfrüt-ləs\ *adj* **1 :** lacking or not bearing fruit **2 :** productive of no good effect **:** UNSUCCESSFUL **syn** see FUTILE — **fruit·less·ly** *adv* — **fruit·less·ness** *n*

fruit sugar *n* **:** FRUCTOSE 2

fruity \ˈfrüt-ē\ *adj* **1 a :** relating to or resembling a fruit **b :** rich in flavor ⟨~ wine⟩ **2 a :** extremely effective, interesting, or enjoyable **b :** sweet or sentimental esp. to excess

fru·men·ta·ceous \ˌfrü-mən-ˈtā-shəs\ *adj* [LL *frumentaceus*, fr. L *frumentum* grain, fr. *frui*] **:** made of or resembling grain (as wheat)

fru·men·ty \ˈfrü-mən-tē\ *n* [ME, fr. MF *frumentee*, fr. *frument* grain, fr. L *frumentum*] **:** a dish of wheat boiled in milk and usu. flavored with sugar, spice, and raisins

frump \ˈfrəmp\ *n* [prob. fr. *frumple* (to wrinkle)] **1 :** a dowdy unattractive girl or woman **2 :** a staid, drab, old-fashioned person — **frump·ish** \ˈfrəm-pish\ *adj* — **frumpy** \-pē\ *adj*

1frus·trate \ˈfrəs-ˌtrāt\ *vt* [ME *frustraten*, fr. L *frustratus*, pp. of *frustrare* to deceive, frustrate, fr. *frustra* in error, in vain; akin to L *fraus* fraud — more at FRAUD] **1 a :** to balk or defeat in an endeavor **b :** to induce feelings of discouragement in **2 a :** to bring to nothing **b :** to make invalid or of no effect **:** NULLIFY

syn THWART, FOIL, BAFFLE, BALK, CIRCUMVENT, OUTWIT: FRUSTRATE implies making vain or ineffectual all efforts however vigorous or persistent; THWART suggests frustration by running counter to or crossing one making headway; FOIL implies checking or defeating so as to discourage further effort; BAFFLE implies frustration by confusing or puzzling; BALK suggests the interposing of obstacles or hindrances; CIRCUMVENT implies frustration by a particular stratagem, OUTWIT by craft and cunning

2frustrate *adj* **:** FRUSTRATED

frus·tra·tion \(ˌ)frəs-ˈtrā-shən\ *n* **1 :** the act of frustrating **2 a :** the state or an instance of being frustrated **:** DISAPPOINTMENT **b :** a deep chronic sense or state of insecurity and dissatisfaction arising from unresolved problems **3 :** something that frustrates

frus·tule \ˈfrəs-ˌchü(ə)l, -ˌt(y)ü(ə)l\ *n* [F, fr. L *frustulum*, dim. of *frustum*] **:** the 2-valved siliceous shell of a diatom

frus·tum \ˈfrəs-təm\ *n, pl* **frustums** *or* **frus·ta** \-tə\ [NL, fr. L, piece, bit — more at BRUISE] **:** the part of a cone-shaped solid next to the base and formed by cutting off the top by a plane parallel to the base; *also* **:** the part of a solid intersected between two usu. parallel planes

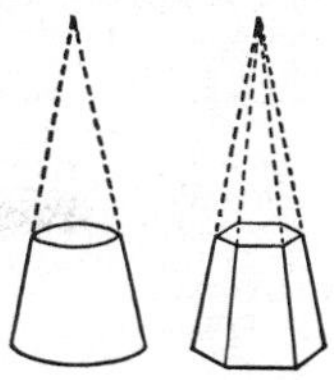

frustums

fru·tes·cence \frü-ˈtes-ᵊn(t)s\ *n* [L *frutex*] **:** shrubby habit of growth — **fru·tes·cent** \-ᵊnt\ *adj*

fru·ti·cose \ˈfrüt-i-ˌkōs\ *adj* [L *fruticosus*, fr. *frutic-*, *frutex* shrub; akin to OHG *broz* bud, OIr *broth* whisker] **:** occurring in the form of or resembling a shrub **:** SHRUBBY

1**fry** \ˈfrī\ *vb* **fried; fry·ing** [ME *frien*, fr. OF *frire*, fr. L *frigere;* akin to Gk *phrygein* to roast, fry, Skt *bhṛjjati* he roasts] *vt* **:** to cook in a pan or on a griddle over a fire esp. with the use of fat ~ *vi* **:** to undergo frying

2**fry** *n, pl* **fries** **1 :** a dish of something fried **2 :** a social gathering where food is fried and eaten

3**fry** *n, pl* **fry** [ME, prob. fr. ONF *fri*, fr. OF *frier*, *froyer* to rub, spawn] **1 a :** recently hatched fishes **b :** the young of other animals **2 :** very small adult fishes **3 :** members of a group or class ⟨small ~⟩

fry·er \ˈfrī(-ə)r\ *n* **:** something intended for or used in frying: as **a :** a young chicken **b :** a deep utensil for frying foods

f-stop \ˈef-ˌstäp\ *n* [*f*, symbol for *focal length*] **:** a camera lens aperture setting indicated by an f-number

F_2 layer \ˈef-ˈtü-\ *n* **:** the upper of the two layers into which the F region of the ionosphere splits in the daytime at varying heights from about 150 to 250 miles above the earth

fubsy \ˈfəb-zē\ *adj* [obs. E *fubs* (chubby person)] **:** being chubby and somewhat squat

fuch·sia \ˈfyü-shə\ *n* [NL, genus name, fr. Leonhard *Fuchs* †1566 G botanist] **1 :** any of a genus (*Fuchsia*) of decorative shrubs of the evening-primrose family having showy nodding flowers usu. in deep pinks, reds, and purples **2 :** a vivid reddish purple

fuch·sine *or* **fuch·sin** \ˈfyük-sən, -ˌsēn\ *n* [F *fuchsine*, prob. fr. NL *Fuchsia;* fr. its color] **:** a dye that is produced by oxidation of a mixture of aniline and toluidines and yields a brilliant bluish red

1**fu·coid** \ˈfyü-ˌkȯid\ *adj* **:** relating to or resembling the rockweeds

2**fucoid** *n* **:** a fucoid seaweed or fossil

fu·cus \ˈfyü-kəs\ *n* [L, archil, rouge, fr. Gk *phykos* seaweed, archil, rouge, of Sem origin; akin to Heb *pūkh* antimony used as a cosmetic] **1** *obs* **:** a face paint **2** [NL, genus name, fr. L] **:** any of a genus (*Fucus*) of cartilaginous brown algae used in the kelp industry; *broadly* **:** any of various brown algae

fud \ˈfəd\ *n* **:** FUDDY-DUDDY

fud·dle \ˈfəd-ᵊl\ *vb* **fud·dling** \ˈfəd-liŋ, -ᵊl-iŋ\ [origin unknown] *vi* **:** to take part in a drinking bout **:** TIPPLE ~ *vt* **1 :** to make drunk **2 :** to make confused **:** MUDDLE

fud·dy–dud·dy \ˈfəd-ē-ˌdəd-ē\ *n* [perh. redupl. of Sc *fuddy* short-tailed animal, tail, fr. *fud* tail] **:** one who is old-fashioned, pompous, unimaginative, or concerned about trifles — **fuddy–duddy** *adj*

1**fudge** \ˈfəj\ *vb* [origin unknown] *vi* **1 :** to act dishonestly **2 :** to fail to live up to something **3 :** to avoid commitment **:** HEDGE ~ *vt* **1 a :** to devise as a substitute or without adequate basis **:** FAKE **b :** FALSIFY **2 :** to fail to come to grips with

2**fudge** *n* **1 :** foolish nonsense **2 :** an item typeset and inserted directly on the printing press **3 :** a soft creamy candy made typically of sugar, milk, butter, and flavoring

Fue·gi·an \fü-ˈā-gē-ən\ *n* **:** an Indian of Tierra del Fuego

1**fu·el** \ˈfyü(-ə)l, ˈfyü(-ə)l\ *n, often attrib* [ME *fewel*, fr. OF *fouaille*, fr. *feu* fire, fr. LL *focus*, fr. L, hearth — more at FOCUS] **1 a :** a material used to produce heat or power by burning **b :** nutritive material **c :** a material from which atomic energy can be liberated esp. in a reactor **2 :** a source of sustenance or incentive

2**fuel** *vb* **fu·eled** *or* **fu·elled; fu·el·ing** *or* **fu·el·ling** *vt* **1 :** to provide with fuel **2 :** SUPPORT, STIMULATE ~ *vi* **:** to take in fuel

fuel cell *n* **:** a cell that continuously changes the chemical energy of a fuel and oxidant to electrical energy

fuel oil *n* **:** an oil that is used for fuel and usu. has a higher flash point than kerosine

1**fug** \ˈfəg\ *n* [prob. alter. of 2*fog*] **:** an odorous emanation; *esp* **:** the stuffy atmosphere of a poorly ventilated space — **fug·gy** \ˈfəg-ē\ *adj*

2**fug** *vb* **fugged; fug·ging** *vi* **:** to loll indoors in a stuffy atmosphere ~ *vt* **:** to make stuffy and odorous

fu·ga·cious \fyü-ˈgā-shəs\ *adj* [L *fugac-*, *fugax*, fr. *fugere*] **1 :** lasting a short time **:** EVANESCENT **2 :** disappearing before the usual time — used chiefly of plant parts (as stipules) other than floral organs — **fu·gac·i·ty** \-ˈgas-ət-ē\ *n*

fu·gal \ˈfyü-gəl\ *adj* **:** of, relating to, or in the style of a musical fugue — **fu·gal·ly** \-gə-lē\ *adv*

-fuge \ˌfyüj\ *n comb form* [F, fr. LL *-fuga*, fr. L *fugare* to put to flight, fr. *fuga*] **:** one that drives away ⟨insecti*fuge*⟩

1**fu·gi·tive** \ˈfyü-jət-iv\ *adj* [ME, fr. MF & L; MF *fugitif*, fr. L *fugitivus*, fr. *fugitus*, pp. of *fugere* to flee; akin to Gk *pheugein* to flee and prob. to OHG *biogan* to bend — more at BOW] **1 :** running away or intending flight ⟨~ slave⟩ ⟨~ debtor⟩ **2 :** moving from place to place **:** WANDERING **3 a :** being of short duration **b :** difficult to grasp or retain **:** ELUSIVE **c :** likely to evaporate, deteriorate, change, fade, or disappear **4 :** being of transient interest **syn** see TRANSIENT — **fu·gi·tive·ly** *adv* — **fu·gi·tive·ness** *n*

2**fugitive** *n* **1 :** one who flees or tries to escape; *specif* **:** REFUGEE **2 :** something elusive or hard to find

fu·gle \ˈfyü-gəl\ *vi* [back-formation fr. *fugleman*] *archaic* **:** to act as fugleman

fu·gle·man \ˈfyü-gəl-mən\ *n* [modif. of G *flügelmann*, fr. *flügel* wing + *mann* man] **1 :** a trained soldier formerly posted in front of a line of men at drill to serve as a model in their exercises **2 :** one who heads a group; *specif* **:** a political manager

fugue \ˈfyüg\ *n* [prob. fr. It *fuga* flight, fugue, fr. L, flight, fr. *fugere*] **:** a polyphonic musical composition in which one or two themes are imitated by successively entering voices and contrapuntally developed — **fugue** *vb* — **fugu·ist** \ˈfyü-gəst\ *n*

füh·rer *or* **fueh·rer** \ˈfyu̇r-ər, ˈfir-\ *n* [G *führer* leader, guide, fr. MHG *vüerer* bearer, fr. *vüeren* to lead, bear, fr. OHG *fuoren* to lead; akin to OE *faran* to go — more at FARE] **1 a :** LEADER 2c(5) — used chiefly of the leader of the German Nazis **b :** a lesser Nazi party official **2 :** a leader exercising tyrannical authority

fu·ji \ˈf(y)ü-(ˌ)jē\ *n* [*Fuji* mountain, Japan] **:** a spun silk clothing fabric in plain weave orig. made in Japan

1**-ful** \fəl\ *adj suffix, sometimes* **-ful·ler;** *sometimes* **-ful·lest** [ME, fr. OE, fr. *full*, adj] **1 :** full of ⟨event*ful*⟩ **2 :** characterized by ⟨peace*ful*⟩ **3 :** having the qualities of ⟨master*ful*⟩ **4 :** -ABLE ⟨mourn*ful*⟩

2**-ful** \ˌfu̇l\ *n suffix* **:** number or quantity that fills or would fill ⟨room*ful*⟩

Fu·la *or* **Fu·lah** \ˈfü-lə\ *n, pl* **Fula** *or* **Fulas** *or* **Fulah** *or* **Fulahs** **1 :** a Sudanese people of African Negroid stock and Mediterranean Caucasoid admixture **2 :** a member of the Fula people

Fu·la·ni \ˈfü-ˌlän-ē, fü-ˈ\ *n, pl* **Fulani** *or* **Fulanis** **1 a :** FULA 1; *esp* **:** the Fula of northern Nigeria and adjacent areas **b :** a member of the Fulani people **2 :** the language of the Fula people

ful·crum \ˈfu̇l-krəm, ˈfəl-\ *n, pl* **fulcrums** *or* **ful·cra** \-krə\ [LL, fr. L, bedpost, fr. *fulcire* to prop] **1 a :** PROP; *specif* **:** the support about which a lever turns **b :** one that supplies capability for action **2 :** a part of an animal that serves as a hinge or support

ful·fill *or* **ful·fil** \fu̇l-ˈfil\ *vt* **ful·filled; ful·fill·ing** [ME *fulfillen*, fr. OE *fullfyllan*, fr. *full* + *fyllan* to fill] **1 a :** to put into effect **b :** to bring to an end **c :** to measure up to **:** SATISFY **2 a :** to convert into reality **b :** to develop the full potentialities of **syn** see PERFORM — **ful·fill·er** *n* — **ful·fill·ment** \-mənt\ *n*

ful·gent \ˈfu̇l-jənt, ˈfəl-\ *adj* [ME, fr. L *fulgent-*, *fulgens*, prp. of *fulgēre* to shine; akin to L *flagrare* to burn — more at BLACK] **:** dazzlingly bright — **ful·gent·ly** *adv*

ful·gu·rant \ˈfu̇l-gyə-rənt, ˈfəl-\ *adj* **:** flashing like lightning

ful·gu·rate \-gyə-ˌrāt\ *vt* [L *fulguratus*, pp. of *fulgurare* to flash with lightning, fr. *fulgur* lightning, fr. *fulgēre*] **:** to emit flashes of

ful·gu·ra·tion \ˌfu̇l-gyə-ˈrā-shən, ˌfəl-\ *n* **:** the act or process of flashing as lightning

ful·gu·rite \ˈfu̇l-gyə-ˌrīt, ˈfəl-\ *n* [ISV, fr. L *fulgur*] **:** a vitrified crust produced by the fusion of sand or rock by lightning

ful·gu·rous \-rəs\ *adj* [L *fulgur*] **:** emitting flashes of or like lightning

ful·ham \ˈfu̇l-əm\ *n* [alter. of earlier *fullan*, perh. fr. *full* + *one*] **:** a loaded dice

fu·lig·i·nous \fyu̇-ˈlij-ə-nəs\ *adj* [LL *fuliginosus*, fr. L *fuligin-*, *fuligo* soot; akin to L *fumus* smoke] **1 a :** SOOTY **b :** OBSCURE, MURKY **2 :** having a dark or dusky color — **fu·lig·i·nous·ly** *adv*

1**full** \ˈfu̇l\ *adj* [ME, fr. OE; akin to OHG *fol* full, L *plenus* full, *plēre* to fill, Gk *plērēs* full, *plēthein* to be full] **1 :** containing as much or as many as is possible or normal ⟨a bin ~ of corn⟩ **2 a :** complete esp. in number, amount, or duration ⟨his ~ share⟩ **b :** having all the distinguishing characteristics ⟨a ~ member⟩ **c :** being at the highest degree **:** MAXIMUM ⟨~ strength⟩ **3 a :** convexly rounded in outline ⟨a ~ figure⟩ **b :** having an abundance of material esp. in the form of gathered, pleated, or flared parts ⟨a ~ skirt⟩ **4 a :** possessing or containing an abundance ⟨a ~ life⟩ **b :** rich in detail ⟨a ~ report⟩ **5 :** satisfied esp. with food or drink **6 :** completely weary ⟨~ of work and worry⟩ **7 :** having both parents in common ⟨~ sisters⟩ **8 :** having volume or depth of sound ⟨~ tones⟩ **9 :** completely occupied esp. with a thought or plan ⟨~ of his own concerns⟩ **10 :** possessing a rich or pronounced quality ⟨a food of ~ flavor⟩ — **full·ness** *also* **ful·ness** *n*

syn COMPLETE, PLENARY, REPLETE: FULL is usu. interchangeable with any of the other three; it may imply either the inclusion of all that is needed or the presence of all that can be held or contained; COMPLETE means full in the sense of having everything needed; PLENARY adds to COMPLETE the implication of fullness without qualification; REPLETE implies being filled to the brim or to satiety

2**full** *adv* **1 a :** VERY, EXTREMELY **b :** ENTIRELY **2 a :** EXACTLY **b :** STRAIGHT, SQUARELY ⟨hit him ~ in the face⟩

3**full** *n* **1 a :** the utmost extent ⟨enjoy to the ~⟩ **b :** the highest or fullest state or degree **2 :** the requisite or complete amount

4**full** *vi, of the moon* **:** to become full ~ *vt* **:** to make full in sewing

5**full** *vt* [ME *fullen*, fr. MF *fouler*, fr. (assumed) VL *fullare*, fr. L *fullo* fuller] **:** to shrink and thicken (woolen cloth) by moistening, heating, and pressing

full·back \ˈfu̇l-ˌbak\ *n* **:** a football back used primarily for line plunges and blocking on offense and as a linebacker on defense

full blood *n* **1** \-ˈbləd\ **:** descent from parents both of one pure breed **2** \-ˌbləd\ **:** an individual of full blood

full–blood·ed \ˈfu̇l-ˈbləd-əd\ *adj* **1 :** of unmixed ancestry **:** PUREBRED **2 :** FLORID, RUDDY **3 :** FORCEFUL ⟨~ prose style⟩ **4 a :** lacking no particulars **:** GENUINE **b :** containing fullness of substance **:** RICH — **full–blood·ed·ness** *n*

full–blown \-ˈblōn\ *adj* **1 a :** being at the height of bloom **b :** fully mature **2 :** possessing all the usual or necessary features

full–bod·ied \-ˈbäd-ēd\ *adj* **1 :** having a large body **2 :** marked by richness and fullness **3 :** having importance or meaningfulness

full dress *n* **:** the style of dress prescribed for ceremonial or formal social occasions

full–dress \ˈfu̇l-ˈdres\ *adj* **1 :** complete down to the last formal detail **2 :** carried out by all possible means

1**full·er** \ˈfu̇l-ər\ *n* **:** one that fulls cloth

2**ful·ler** \ˈfu̇l-ər\ *n* [*fuller* (to form a groove in)] **:** a blacksmithing hammer for grooving and spreading iron

fuller's earth *n* **:** a clayish earthy substance used in fulling cloth, as a filter medium, and as a catalyst

full–fash·ioned \ˈfu̇l-ˈfash-ənd\ *adj* **:** employing or produced by a knitting process for shaping to conform to body lines ⟨~ hosiery⟩

full–fledged \-ˈflejd\ *adj* **1 :** fully developed **:** MATURE **2 :** having full plumage **3 :** having attained complete status ⟨~ lawyer⟩

full house *n* **:** a poker hand containing three of a kind and a pair

full–length \ˈfu̇l-ˈleŋ(k)th\ *adj* **1 :** showing or adapted to the entire length esp. of the human figure **2 :** having a length as great as that which is normal or standard for an object of its kind

full moon *n* **:** the moon with its whole apparent disk illuminated

full·mouthed \ˈfu̇l-ˈmau̇thd, -ˈmau̇tht\ *adj* **1 :** having a full mouth; *esp* **:** having a full complement of teeth **2 :** uttered with full power or sound **:** LOUD

full–scale \-ˈskā(ə)l\ *adj* **1 :** identical to an original in proportion and size ⟨~ drawing⟩ **2 :** involving full use of available resources

full stop *n* : PERIOD 4a
full tilt *adv* [2tilt] : at high speed
full time *n* : the amount of time considered the normal or standard amount for working during a given period
full–time \ˌfu̇l-ˌtīm\ *adj* : employed for or involving full time
ful·ly \ˈfu̇l-(l)ē\ *adv* **1** : in a full manner or degree : COMPLETELY **2** : at least ⟨~ nine tenths of us⟩
ful·mar \ˈfu̇l-mər, -ˌmär\ *n* [of Scand origin; akin to ON *fūlmār* fulmar, fr. *fūll* foul + *mār* gull] : an Arctic seabird (*Fulmarus glacialis*) closely related to the petrels; *also* : any of several related birds of southern seas
ful·mi·nant \ˈfu̇l-mə-nənt, ˈfəl-\ *adj* : FULMINATING 3
1**ful·mi·nate** \-ˌnāt\ *vb* [ME *fulminaten*, fr. ML *fulminatus*, pp. of *fulminare*, fr. L, to flash with lightning, strike with lightning, fr. *fulmin-*, *fulmen* lightning; akin to L *flagrare* to burn — more at BLACK] *vt* **1** : to utter or send out with denunciation **2** : to cause to explode ~ *vi* **1** : to send forth censures or invectives **2** : to make a sudden loud noise : EXPLODE — **ful·mi·na·tion** \ˌfu̇l-mə-ˈnā-shən, ˌfəl-\ *n* — **ful·mi·na·tor** \ˈfu̇l-mə-ˌnāt-ər, ˈfəl-\ *n*
2**fulminate** *n* : an often explosive salt [as mercury fulminate $Hg(ONC)_2$] of fulminic acid
ful·mi·nat·ing *adj* **1** : exploding with a vivid flash **2** : hurling denunciations or menaces **3** : coming on suddenly with great severity
ful·mine \ˈfu̇l-mən, ˈfəl-\ *vb*, *archaic* : FULMINATE
ful·min·ic acid \(ˌ)fu̇l-ˌmin-ik-, ˌfəl-\ *n* [ISV, fr. L *fulmin-*, *fulmen* lightning] : an unstable acid CNOH isomeric with cyanic acid and known chiefly in the form of highly explosive salts
ful·some \ˈfu̇l-səm\ *adj* [ME *fulsom* copious, cloying, fr. *full* + *-som* -some] **1** : offensive to sense, appetite, or moral or aesthetic sensibility : DISGUSTING **2** : offensive from insincerity or baseness of motive — **ful·some·ly** *adv* — **ful·some·ness** *n*
ful·vous \ˈfu̇l-vəs, ˈfəl-\ *adj* [L *fulvus*; perh. akin to L *flavus* yellow — more at BLUE] : of a dull brownish yellow : TAWNY
fu·mar·ic acid \fyu̇-ˌmar-ik-, ˌfyü-\ *n* [ISV, fr. NL *Fumaria*, genus of herbs, fr. LL, fumitory, fr. L *fumus*] : a crystalline acid HOOCCH=CHCOOH found in various plants or made synthetically and used esp. in making resins
fu·ma·role \ˈfyü-mə-ˌrōl\ *n* [It *fumarola*, modif. of LL *fumariolum*, fr. L *fumarium* smoke chamber for aging wine, fr. *fumus*] : a hole in a volcanic region from which hot gases and vapors issue — **fu·ma·rol·ic** \ˌfyü-mə-ˈrō-lik, -ˈräl-ik\ *adj*
1**fum·ble** \ˈfəm-bəl\ *vb* **fum·bling** \-b(ə-)liŋ\ [prob. of Scand origin; akin to Sw *fumla* to fumble] *vi* **1 a** : to grope for or handle something clumsily **b** : to make awkward attempts to do or find something **c** : to search by trial and error **d** : BLUNDER **2** : to feel one's way or move awkwardly **3 a** : to drop or juggle or fail to play cleanly a grounder **b** : to lose hold of a football while handling or running with it ~ *vt* **1** : to bring about by clumsy manipulation **2 a** : to feel of or handle clumsily **b** : to deal with in a blundering way : BUNGLE **3** : to make (one's way) in a clumsy manner **4 a** : MISPLAY ⟨~ a grounder⟩ **b** : to lose hold of (a football) while handling or running — **fum·bler** \-b(ə-)lər\ *n*
2**fumble** *n* **1** : an act or instance of fumbling **2** : a fumbled ball
1**fume** \ˈfyüm\ *n* [ME, fr. MF *fum*, fr. L *fumus*; akin to OHG *toumen* to be fragrant, Gk *thymos* mind, spirit] **1** : a smoke, vapor, or gas esp. when irritating or offensive ⟨engine exhaust ~*s*⟩ **2** : something that impairs one's reasoning **3** : a state of excited irritation or anger — **fumy** \ˈfyü-mē\ *adj*
2**fume** *vt* **1** : to expose to or treat with fumes **2** : to give off in fumes ⟨*fuming* thick black smoke⟩ ~ *vi* **1 a** : to emit fumes **b** : to act as if generating fumes **2** : to rise in or as if in fumes
fu·mi·gant \ˈfyü-mi-gənt\ *n* : a substance used for fumigation
fu·mi·gate \ˈfyü-mə-ˌgāt\ *vt* [L *fumigatus*, pp. of *fumigare*, fr. *fumus* + *-igare* (akin to L *agere* to drive) — more at AGENT] : to apply smoke, vapor, or gas to esp. for the purpose of disinfecting or of destroying pests — **fu·mi·ga·tion** \ˌfyü-mə-ˈgā-shən\ *n* — **fu·mi·ga·tor** \ˈfyü-mə-ˌgāt-ər\ *n*
fu·mi·to·ry \ˈfyü-mə-ˌtōr-ē, -ˌtȯr-\ *n* [ME *fumeterre*, fr. MF, fr. ML *fumus terrae*, lit., smoke of the earth, fr. L *fumus* + *terrae*, gen. of *terra* earth — more at TERRACE] : any of a genus (*Fumaria* of the family Fumariaceae, the fumitory family) of erect or climbing herbs; *esp* : a common European herb (*F. officinalis*)
1**fun** \ˈfən\ *n* [E dial. *fun* to hoax, perh. alter. of ME *fonnen*, fr. *fonne* dupe] **1** : what provides amusement or enjoyment; *specif* : playful often boisterous action or speech **2** : AMUSEMENT, ENJOYMENT **3** : violent or excited activity or argument — **fun** *adj*
syn FUN, JEST, SPORT, GAME, PLAY mean action or speech that provides amusement or arouses laughter. FUN usu. implies laughter or gaiety but may imply merely a lack of serious or ulterior purpose; JEST implies lack of earnestness in what is said or done and may suggest hoaxing or teasing; SPORT applies esp. to the arousing of laughter against someone; GAME is close to SPORT, and often stresses mischievous or malicious fun; PLAY stresses the opposition to *earnest* without implying any element of malice or mischief
2**fun** *vi* **funned**; **fun·ning** : to indulge in banter or play : JOKE
fu·nam·bu·list \fyu̇-ˈnam-byə-ləst\ *n* [L *funambulus*, fr. *funis* rope + *ambulare* to walk — more at AMBLE] : ROPEWALKER, ROPEDANCER
1**func·tion** \ˈfəŋ(k)-shən\ *n* [L *function-*, *functio* performance, fr. *functus*, pp. of *fungi* to perform; prob. akin to Skt *bhuṅkte* he enjoys] **1** : professional or official position : OCCUPATION **2** : the action for which a person or thing is specially fitted or used or for which a thing exists **3** : an impressive, elaborate, or formal ceremony or social gathering **4** : one of a group of related actions contributing to a larger action; *esp* : the normal and specific contribution of a bodily part to the economy of a living organism **5 a** : a mathematical entity that assigns to each element of one set at least one element of the same or another set **b** : a quality, trait, or fact dependent on and varying with another **c** : SENTENTIAL FUNCTION — **func·tion·less** \-ləs\ *adj*
syn FUNCTION, OFFICE, DUTY, PROVINCE mean the acts or operations expected of a person or thing. FUNCTION is comprehensively applicable to the proper or characteristic action of a person, living thing, manufactured or created thing; OFFICE applies to the work or more often service expected from one in a particular relation to others or having a special fitness or training ⟨needs the *offices* of an editor⟩; DUTY applies to a task imposed by one's occupation, rank, status, or calling; PROVINCE applies to any duty or function that comes within one's jurisdiction, powers, or competence
2**function** *vi* **func·tion·ing** \-sh(ə-)niŋ\ **1** : to have a function : SERVE ⟨an attributive noun ~*s* as an adjective⟩ **2** : to be in action : OPERATE ⟨a government ~*s* through numerous divisions⟩
func·tion·al \ˈfəŋ(k)-shnəl, -shən-əl\ *adj* **1 a** : of, connected with, or being a function **b** : affecting functions but not structure **2** : used to contribute to the development or maintenance of a larger whole; *also* : designed or developed chiefly from the point of view of use **3** : performing or able to perform its regular function **4** : placing related functions (as in an industry) under the direction of a specialist — **func·tion·al·ly** \-ē\ *adv*
func·tion·al·ism \-shnə-ˌliz-əm, -shən-əl-ˌiz-\ *n* : a philosophy of design (as in architecture) holding that form should be adapted to use, material, and structure; *broadly* : a doctrine or practice that emphasizes practical utility or functional relations — **func·tion·al·ist** \-shnə-ləst, -shən-əl-əst\ *n* — **functionalist** *or* **func·tion·al·is·tic** \ˌfəŋ(k)-shnə-ˈlis-tik, -shən-əl-ˈis-\ *adj*
functional shift *n* : the process by which a word or form comes to be used in a second or third grammatical function
func·tion·ary \ˈfəŋ(k)-shə-ˌner-ē\ *n* : one who serves in a certain function; *esp* : OFFICIAL
function word *n* : a word expressing primarily grammatical relationship
func·tor \ˈfəŋ(k)-tər\ *n* : an expression (as ± or *not*) that has a purely syntactic function : OPERATOR
1**fund** \ˈfənd\ *n* [L *fundus* bottom, piece of landed property — more at BOTTOM] **1** : an available quantity of material or intangible resources : SUPPLY **2 a** : a sum of money or other resources the principal or interest of which is set apart for a specific objective **b** : money on deposit on which checks or drafts can be drawn — usu. used in pl. **c** : CAPITAL **d** *pl* : the stock of the British national debt — usu. used with *the* **3** *pl* : available pecuniary resources **4** : an organization administering a special fund
2**fund** *vt* **1** : to make provision of resources for discharging the interest or principal of **2** : to place in a fund : ACCUMULATE **3** : to convert into a debt that is payable either at a distant date or at no definite date and that bears a fixed interest ⟨~ a floating debt⟩
fun·da·ment \ˈfən-də-mənt\ *n* [ME, fr. OF *fondement*, fr. L *fundamentum*, fr. *fundare* to found, fr. *fundus*] **1 a** *obs* : the base on which a structure is erected **b** : an underlying ground, theory, or principle **2 a** : BUTTOCKS **b** : ANUS **3** : the part of a land surface that has not been altered by human activities
1**fun·da·men·tal** \ˌfən-də-ˈment-əl\ *adj* **1 a** : serving as an original or generating source : PRIMARY **b** : serving as a basis supporting existence or determining essential structure or function : BASIC **2 a** : of or relating to essential structure, function, or facts : RADICAL ⟨~ change⟩; *specif* : of or dealing with general principles rather than practical application ⟨~ science⟩ **b** : FUNDAMENTALIST **3 a** *of a musical chord or its position* : having the root in the bass **b** : of, relating to, or produced by the lowest component of a complex vibration **4** : of central importance : PRINCIPAL ⟨~ purpose⟩
syn see ESSENTIAL — **fun·da·men·tal·ly** \-əl-ē\ *adv*
2**fundamental** *n* **1** : something fundamental; *esp* : one of the minimum constituents without which a thing or a system would not be what it is **2 a** : the prime tone of a harmonic series **b** : the root of a chord **3** : the harmonic component of a wave that has the lowest frequency and commonly the greatest amplitude
fun·da·men·tal·ism \-əl-ˌiz-əm\ *n* **1 a** *often cap* : a movement in 20th century Protestantism emphasizing as fundamental the literal inerrancy of the Scriptures, the second coming of Jesus Christ, the virgin birth, physical resurrection, and substitutionary atonement **b** : the beliefs of this movement **c** : adherence to such beliefs **2** : a movement or attitude similar to Protestant fundamentalism — **fun·da·men·tal·ist** \-əl-əst\ *n* — **fundamentalist** *or* **fun·da·men·tal·is·tic** \-ˌment-əl-ˈis-tik\ *adj*
fundamental law *n* : the organic or basic law of a political unit as distinguished from legislative acts; *specif* : CONSTITUTION
fundamental particle *n* : ELEMENTARY PARTICLE
fun·dic \ˈfən-dik\ *adj* : of or relating to a fundus
fun·dus \ˈfən-dəs\ *n*, *pl* **fun·di** \-ˌdī, -ˌdē\ [NL, fr. L, bottom] : the bottom of or part opposite the aperture of the internal surface of a hollow organ: as **a** : the greater curvature of the stomach **b** : the lower back part of the bladder **c** : the large upper end of the uterus **d** : the part of the eye opposite the pupil
1**fu·ner·al** \ˈfyün-(ə-)rəl\ *adj* [ME, fr. LL *funeralis*, fr. L *funer-*, *funus* funeral (n.); perh. akin to ON *deyja* to die — more at DIE] **1** : of, relating to, or constituting a funeral **2** : FUNEREAL 2
2**funeral** *n* **1** : the observances held for a dead person usu. before burial or cremation **2** *chiefly dial* : a funeral sermon **3** : a funeral party in transit **4** : a matter of concern
funeral director *n* : one whose profession is the management of funerals and who is usu. an embalmer
funeral home *n* : an establishment with facilities for the preparation of the dead for burial or cremation, for the viewing of the body, and for funerals — called also *funeral parlor*
fu·ner·ary \ˈfyü-nə-ˌrer-ē\ *adj* : of, used for, or associated with burial ⟨a pharaoh's ~ chamber⟩
fu·ne·re·al \fyu̇-ˈnir-ē-əl\ *adj* [L *funereus*, fr. *funer-*, *funus*] **1** : of or relating to a funeral **2** : befitting or suggesting a funeral — **fu·ne·re·al·ly** \-ə-lē\ *adv*
fun·gal \ˈfəŋ-gəl\ *adj* : FUNGOUS
fungi- *comb form* [L *fungus*] : fungus ⟨*fungi*form⟩
fun·gi·bil·i·ty \ˌfən-jə-ˈbil-ət-ē\ *n* : the quality or state of being fungible
1**fun·gi·ble** \ˈfən-jə-bəl\ *n* : fungible goods — usu. used in pl.
2**fungible** *adj* [NL *fungibilis*, fr. L *fungi* to perform — more at FUNCTION] **1** : of such a kind or nature that one specimen or part may be used in place of another specimen or equal part in the satisfaction of an obligation **2** : INTERCHANGEABLE
fun·gi·ci·dal \ˌfən-jə-ˈsīd-əl, ˌfəŋ-gə-\ *adj* : destroying fungi; *broadly* : inhibiting the growth of fungi — **fun·gi·ci·dal·ly** \-əl-ē\ *adv*
fun·gi·cide \ˈfən-jə-ˌsīd, ˈfəŋ-gə-\ *n* [ISV] : an agent that destroys or is hostile to fungi
fun·gi·form \ˈfən-jə-ˌfȯrm, ˈfəŋ-gə-\ *adj* : shaped like a mushroom
fun·go \ˈfəŋ-(ˌ)gō\ *n*, *pl* **fungoes** [origin unknown] : a fly ball hit by a player who tosses a ball in the air and hits it as it comes down
fun·goid \ˈfəŋ-ˌgȯid\ *adj* : resembling, characteristic of, or being a fungus — **fungoid** *n*
fun·gous \ˈfəŋ-gəs\ *adj* **1** : of, relating to, or having the characteristics of fungi **2** : caused by a fungus
fun·gus \ˈfəŋ-gəs\ *n*, *pl* **fun·gi** \ˈfən-ˌjī, ˈfəŋ-ˌgī\ *also* **fun·gus·es** *often attrib* [L] **1** : any of a major group (Fungi) of saprophytic

and parasitic lower plants that lack chlorophyll and include molds, rusts, mildews, smuts, mushrooms, and usu. bacteria **2 :** infection with a fungus

fun house *n* **:** a building in an amusement park that contains various devices designed to startle or amuse

1fu·nic·u·lar \fyu̇-ˈnik-yə-lər, fə-\ *adj* [L *funiculus* small rope] **1 :** dependent on the tension of a cord or cable **2 :** having the form of or associated with a cord **3** [NL *funiculus*] **:** of, relating to, or being a funiculus

2funicular *n* **:** a cable railway ascending a mountain; *esp* **:** one in which an ascending car counterbalances a descending car

fu·nic·u·lus \-ləs\ *n, pl* **fu·nic·u·li** \-ˌlī, -ˌlē\ [NL, fr. L, dim. of *funis* rope] **1 :** a bodily structure suggesting a cord: as **a :** UMBILICAL CORD **b :** a bundle of nerve fibers **c :** SPERMATIC CORD **2 :** the stalk of a plant ovule

1funk \ˈfəŋk\ *n* [prob. fr. obs. Flem *fonck*] **1 :** a state of paralyzing fear or extreme depression **2** [2*funk*] **:** one that funks **:** COWARD

2funk *vi* **:** to become frightened and shrink back **~** *vt* **1 :** to be afraid of **:** DREAD **2 :** to shrink from undertaking or facing

funk hole *n* **1 :** DUGOUT 2 **2 :** a place of safe retreat

fun·kia \ˈfəŋ-kē-ə, ˈfu̇ŋ-\ *n* [NL, genus of herbs, irreg. fr. C. H. *Funck* †1839 G botanist] **:** PLANTAIN LILY

1funky \ˈfəŋ-kē\ *adj* **:** being in a state of funk **:** PANICKY

2funky *adj* [*funk* (offensive odor)] **1 :** having an offensive odor **:** FOUL **2 :** having the style and feeling of blues ⟨~ piano playing⟩

1fun·nel \ˈfən-ᵊl\ *n* [ME *fonel*, fr. OProv *fonilh*, fr. ML *fundibulum*, short for L *infundibulum*, fr. *infundere* to pour in, fr. *in-* + *fundere* to pour — more at FOUND] **1 a :** a utensil that is usu. a hollow cone with a tube extending from the point and is designed to catch and direct a downward flow **b :** something shaped like a funnel **2 :** a stack or flue for the escape of smoke or for ventilation

2funnel *vb* **fun·neled** *also* **fun·nelled; fun·nel·ing** *also* **fun·nel·ling** *vi* **1 :** to have or take the shape of a funnel **2 :** to pass through or as if through a funnel **~** *vt* **:** to cause to funnel; *esp* **:** to move to a focal point or into a central channel

fun·nel·form \ˈfən-ᵊl-ˌfȯrm\ *adj* **:** INFUNDIBULIFORM

fun·ni·ly \ˈfən-ᵊl-ē\ *adv* **:** in a funny manner **:** ODDLY

fun·ni·ness \ˈfən-ē-nəs\ *n* **:** the quality or state of being funny

1fun·ny \ˈfən-ē\ *adj* **1 a :** affording light mirth and laughter **:** AMUSING **b :** seeking or intended to amuse **:** FACETIOUS **2 :** differing from the ordinary in a suspicious way **:** QUEER **3 :** involving trickery or deception **syn** see LAUGHABLE

2funny *n* **:** a comic strip or a comic section of a periodical

funny bone *n* [fr. the tingling felt when it is struck] **1 :** the place at the back of the elbow where the ulnar nerve rests against a prominence of the humerus **2 :** a sense of humor

1fur \ˈfər\ *vb* **furred; fur·ring** [ME *furren*, fr. MF *fourrer*, fr. OF *forrer*, fr. *fuerre* sheath, of Gmc origin; akin to OHG *fuotar* sheath; akin to Gk *pōy* herd, Skt *pāti* he protects] *vt* **1 :** to cover, line, trim, or clothe with fur **2 :** to coat or clog as if with fur **3 :** to apply furring to **~** *vi* **:** to become coated or clogged as if with fur

2fur *n, often attrib* **1 :** a piece of the dressed pelt of an animal used to make, trim, or line wearing apparel **2 :** an article of clothing made of or with fur **3 :** the hairy coat of a mammal esp. when fine, soft, and thick; *also* **:** such a coat with the skin **4 :** a coating resembling fur: as **a :** a coat of epithelial debris on the tongue **b :** the thick pile of a fabric (as chenille) — **fur·less** \ˈfər-ləs\ *adj*

fu·ran \ˈfyu̇(ə)r-ˌan, fyu̇-ˈran\ *also* **fu·rane** \ˈfyu̇(ə)r-ˌān, fyu̇-ˈrān\ *n* [ISV, fr. *furfural*] **:** a flammable liquid C_4H_4O that is obtained from wood oils of pines or made synthetically and is used esp. in the manufacture of nylon

fur·be·low \ˈfər-bə-ˌlō\ *n* [by folk etymology fr. F dial. *farbella*] **1 :** a pleated or gathered piece of material **:** RUFFLE; *specif* **:** a flounce on women's clothing **2 :** something that suggests a furbelow esp. in being showy or superfluous — **furbelow** *vt*

fur·bish \ˈfər-bish\ *vt* [ME *furbisshen*, fr. MF *fourbiss-*, stem of *fourbir*, of Gmc origin; akin to OHG *furben* to polish] **1 :** to make lustrous **:** POLISH **2 :** RENOVATE, REVIVE — **fur·bish·er** *n, archaic*

1fur·cate \ˈfər-ˌkāt\ *adj* [LL *furcatus*, fr. L *furca* fork] **:** branching like a fork **:** FORKED — **fur·cate·ly** *adv*

2furcate *vi* **:** to branch like a fork — **fur·ca·tion** \ˌfər-ˈkā-shən\ *n*

fur·cu·la \ˈfər-kyə-lə\ *n, pl* **fur·cu·lae** \-ˌlē, -ˌlī\ [NL, fr. L, forked prop, dim. of *furca*] **:** a forked process or part; *esp* **:** WISHBONE — **fur·cu·lar** \-lər\ *adj*

fur·cu·lum \-ləm\ *n, pl* **fur·cu·la** \-lə\ [NL, fr. L *furca*] **:** FURCULA

fur·fu·ra·ceous \ˌfər-f(y)ə-ˈrā-shəs\ *adj* [LL *furfuraceus*, fr. L *furfur* bran] **:** consisting of or covered with flaky particles

fur·fu·ral \ˈfər-f(y)ə-ˌral\ *also* **fur·fur·al·de·hyde** \ˌfər-f(y)ə-ˈral-də-ˌhīd\ *n* [L *furfur* + ISV *aldehyde*] **:** a liquid aldehyde C_4H_3OCHO of penetrating odor that is usu. made from plant materials by digestion with acid and used esp. in making furan or phenolic resins and as a solvent

fur·fu·ran \ˈfər-f(y)ə-ˌran\ *n* **:** FURAN

fu·ri·ous \ˈfyu̇r-ē-əs\ *adj* **1 a :** exhibiting or goaded by anger **b :** appearing or moving as if angry **c :** full of noise, excitement, or activity **2 :** INTENSE — **fu·ri·ous·ly** *adv*

1furl \ˈfər(-ə)l\ *vb* [MF *ferler*, fr. ONF *ferlier* to tie tightly, fr. OF *fer, ferm* tight (fr. L *firmus* firm) + *lier* to tie, fr. L *ligare* — more at LIGATURE] *vt* **:** to wrap or roll (as a sail or a flag) close to or around something **~** *vi* **:** to curl or fold as in being furled

2furl *n* **1 :** the act of furling **2 :** a furled coil

fur·long \ˈfər-ˌlȯŋ\ *n* [ME, fr. OE *furlang*, fr. *furh* furrow + *lang* long] **:** a unit of distance equal to 220 yards

1fur·lough \ˈfər-(ˌ)lō\ *n* [D *verlof*, lit., permission, fr. MD, fr. *ver-* for- + *lof* permission; akin to OE *for-* and to MHG *loube* permission — more at FOR-, LEAVE] **:** a leave of absence from duty granted esp. to a soldier; *also* **:** a document authorizing such a leave of absence

2furlough *vt* **1 :** to grant a furlough to **2 :** to lay off from work

fur·mi·ty \ˈfər-mət-ē\ *var of* FRUMENTY

fur·nace \ˈfər-nəs\ *n* [ME *furnas*, fr. OF *fornaise*, fr. L *fornac-, fornax*; akin to L *formus* warm — more at WARM] **:** an enclosed structure in which heat is produced (as for heating a house)

fur·nish \ˈfər-nish\ *vt* [ME *furnisshen*, fr. MF *fourniss-*, stem of *fournir* to complete, equip, of Gmc origin; akin to OHG *frummen* to further] **1 :** to provide with what is needed; *esp* **:** to equip with furniture **2 :** SUPPLY, GIVE — **fur·nish·er** *n*

syn EQUIP, OUTFIT, APPOINT, ACCOUTER, ARM: FURNISH implies the provision of any or all essentials for performing a function; EQUIP suggests the provision of something making for efficiency in action or use; OUTFIT implies provision of a complete list or set of articles as for a journey, an expedition, a special occupation; APPOINT implies provision of complete and usu. elegant or elaborate equipment or furnishings; ACCOUTER suggests the supplying of personal dress or equipment for a special activity; ARM implies provision for effective action or operation esp. in war

fur·nish·ing *n* **1 :** an article or accessory of dress — usu. used in pl. **2 :** an object that tends to increase comfort or utility; *specif* **:** an article of furniture for the interior of a building — usu. used in pl.

fur·ni·ture \ˈfər-ni-chər\ *n* [MF *fourniture*, fr. *fournir*] **1 :** equipment that is necessary, useful, or desirable: as **a** *archaic* **:** the trappings of a horse **b :** movable articles used in readying a room for occupancy or use **2 :** pieces of wood or metal less than type high placed in printing forms to fill in blank spaces

fu·ror \ˈfyu̇(ə)r-ˌȯ(ə)r, -ˌō(ə)r\ *n* [MF & L; MF, fr. L, fr. *furere* to rage — more at DUST] **1 :** an angry or maniacal fit **:** RAGE **2 :** FURY 4 **3 :** a fashionable craze **:** VOGUE **4 a :** furious or hectic activity **b :** an outburst of public excitement or indignation **:** UPROAR

fu·rore \-ˌō(ə)r, -ˌȯ(ə)r\ *n* [It, fr. L *furor*] **1 :** FUROR 3 **2 :** FUROR 4b

furred \ˈfərd\ *adj* **1 :** lined, trimmed, or faced with fur **2 :** coated as if with fur; *specif* **:** having a coating consisting chiefly of mucus and dead epithelial cells ⟨a ~ tongue⟩ **3 :** bearing or wearing fur **4 :** provided with furring ⟨~ wall⟩

fur·ri·er \ˈfər-ē-ər, ˈfə-rē-\ *n* **1 :** a fur dealer **2 a :** one that dresses furs **b :** one that makes, repairs, alters, or cleans fur garments

fur·ri·ery \-ə-rē\ *n* **1 :** the fur business **2 :** fur craftsmanship

fur·ring \ˈfər-iŋ\ *n* **1 :** a fur trimming or lining **2 a :** the application of thin wood, brick, or metal to joists, studs, or walls to form a level surface or an air space **b :** the material used in this process

1fur·row \ˈfər-(ˌ)ō, -ə(-w); ˈfə-(ˌ)rō, -rə(-w)\ *n* [ME *furgh, forow*, fr. OE *furh*; akin to OHG *furuh* furrow, L *porca*] **1 a :** a trench in the earth made by a plow **b :** rural land **:** FIELD **2 :** something that resembles the track of a plow: as **a :** a natural depression **:** GROOVE **b :** a deep wrinkle

2furrow *vt* **:** to make furrows, grooves, or wrinkles in **~** *vi* **:** to make or form furrows, grooves, or wrinkles

fur·ry \ˈfər-ē\ *adj* **1 :** consisting of or resembling fur **2 :** covered with fur **3 :** clogged as if with fur

1fur·ther \ˈfər-t͟hər\ *adv* [ME, fr. OE *furthor*; akin to OHG *furthar* further; both compars. fr. the root of OE *forth*] **1 :** 1FARTHER 1 **2 :** in addition **:** MOREOVER **3 :** to a greater degree or extent

2further *adj* **1 :** 2FARTHER 1 **2 :** going or extending beyond **:** ADDITIONAL ⟨~ volumes⟩ ⟨~ education⟩ **syn** see FARTHER

3further *vt* **fur·ther·ing** \ˈfərt͟h-(ə-)riŋ\ **:** to help forward **:** PROMOTE **syn** see ADVANCE — **fur·ther·er** \ˈfər-t͟hər-ər\ *n*

fur·ther·ance \ˈfərt͟h-(ə-)rən(t)s\ *n* **:** the act of furthering **:** ADVANCEMENT

fur·ther·more \ˈfər-t͟hə(r)-ˌmō(ə)r, -ˌmȯ(ə)r\ *adv* **:** in addition to what precedes **:** BESIDES

fur·ther·most \-ˌmōst\ *adj* **:** most distant **:** FARTHEST

fur·thest \ˈfər-t͟həst\ *adv* (*or adj*) **:** FARTHEST

fur·tive \ˈfərt-iv\ *adj* [F or L; F *furtif*, fr. L *furtivus*, fr. *furtum* theft, fr. *fur* thief] **1 a :** done by stealth **:** SURREPTITIOUS **b :** expressive of stealth **:** SLY **2 :** STOLEN **syn** see SECRET — **fur·tive·ly** *adv* — **fur·tive·ness** *n*

fu·run·cle \ˈfyu̇(ə)r-ˌəŋ-kəl\ *n* [L *furunculus* petty thief, sucker, furuncle, dim. of *furon-*, *furo* ferret, thief, fr. *fur*] **:** a localized inflammatory swelling of the skin and underlying tissues that is caused by infection by a bacterium in a hair follicle or skin gland and that discharges pus and a central core of dead tissue **:** BOIL — **fu·run·cu·lar** \fyu̇-ˈrəŋ-kyə-lər\ *adj* — **fu·run·cu·lous** \-ləs\ *adj*

fu·run·cu·lo·sis \fyu̇-ˌrəŋ-kyə-ˈlō-səs\ *n* **:** the condition of having or tending to develop multiple furuncles

fu·ry \ˈfyu̇(ə)r-ē\ *n* [ME *furie*, fr. MF & L; MF, fr. L *furia*, fr. *furere* to rage — more at DUST] **1 :** violent anger **:** RAGE **2 a** *cap* **:** one of the avenging spirits in classical mythology **b :** an avenging spirit **c :** one who resembles an avenging spirit; *esp* **:** a spiteful woman **3 :** extreme fierceness or violence **4 :** a state of inspired exaltation **:** FRENZY **syn** see ANGER

furze \ˈfərz\ *n* [ME *firse*, fr. OE *fyrs*] **:** a spiny yellow-flowered evergreen leguminous European shrub (*Ulex europaeus*); *broadly* **:** any of several related plants (genera *Ulex* and *Genista*) — **furzy** \ˈfər-zē\ *adj*

fus·cous \ˈfəs-kəs\ *adj* [L *fuscus* — more at DUSK] **:** of any of several colors averaging a brownish gray

1fuse \ˈfyüz\ *n* [It *fuso* spindle, fr. L *fusus*, of unknown origin] **1 :** a continuous train of a combustible substance enclosed in a cord or cable for setting off an explosive charge by transmitting fire to it **2** *usu* **fuze :** a mechanical or electrical detonating device for setting off the bursting charge of a projectile, bomb, or torpedo

2fuse *or* **fuze** *vt* **:** to equip with a fuse

3fuse *vb* [L *fusus*, pp. of *fundere* to pour, melt — more at FOUND] *vt* **1 a :** to reduce to a liquid or plastic state by heat **b :** to blend by melting together **2 :** BLEND, INTEGRATE **~** *vi* **1 :** to become fluid with heat; *also* **:** to fail because of the blowing of a fuse **2 :** to become blended **syn** see MIX

4fuse *n* **:** an electrical safety device consisting of or including a wire or strip of fusible metal that melts and interrupts the circuit when the current becomes too strong

fused quartz *n* **:** QUARTZ GLASS

fu·see \fyü-ˈzē\ *n* [F *fusée*, lit., spindleful of yarn, fr. OF, fr. *fus* spindle, fr. L *fusus*] **1 :** a conical spirally grooved pulley in a timepiece from which a cord or chain unwinds onto a barrel containing the spring and which by its increasing diameter compensates for the lessening power of the spring **2 :** 1FUSE 1 **3 :** a friction match with a bulbous head not easily blown out **4 :** a red signal flare used esp. for protecting stalled trains and trucks

fu·se·lage \ˈfyü-sə-ˌläzh, -zə-\ *n* [F, fr. *fuselé* spindle-shaped, fr. MF, fr. *fusel*, dim. of *fus*] **:** the central body portion of an airplane designed to accommodate the crew and the passengers or cargo

fu·sel oil \ˈfyü-zəl-\ *n* [G *fusel* bad liquor] **:** an acrid oily liquid occurring in insufficiently distilled alcoholic liquors and consisting chiefly of amyl alcohol; *also* **:** commercial pentyl alcohol

fusi- *comb form* [L *fusus*] **:** spindle ⟨*fusi*form⟩

fus·ibil·i·ty \ˌfyü-zə-ˈbil-ət-ē\ *n* **:** the quality, state, or degree of being fusible
fus·ible \ˈfyü-zə-bəl\ *adj* **:** capable of being fused and esp. liquefied by heat
fusible metal *n* **:** an alloy having a melting point usu. below 300°F and used esp. for boiler safety plugs and automatic-sprinkler fuses
fu·si·form \ˈfyü-zə-ˌfȯrm\ *adj* **:** tapering toward each end
¹**fu·sil** \ˈfyü-zəl\ *or* **fu·sile** \ˈfyü-zəl, -ˌzīl\ *adj* [ME, fr. L *fusilis*, fr. *fusus*, pp.] **1** *archaic* **a :** made by melting and pouring into forms **:** CAST **b :** liquefied by heat **2** *archaic* **:** FUSIBLE
²**fusil** *n* [F, lit., steel for striking fire, fr. OF *foisil*, fr. (assumed) VL *focilis*, fr. LL *focus* fire — more at FUEL] **:** a light flintlock musket
fu·sil·ier *or* **fu·sil·eer** \ˌfyü-zə-ˈli(ə)r\ *n* [F *fusilier*, fr. *fusil*] **1 :** a soldier armed with a fusil **2 :** a member of a British regiment formerly armed with fusils
¹**fu·sil·lade** \ˈfyü-sə-ˌläd, -ˌläd, ˌfyü-sə-ˈ, -zə-\ *n* [F, fr. *fusiller* to shoot, fr. *fusil*] **1 :** a number of shots fired simultaneously or in rapid succession **2 :** a spirited outburst esp. of criticism
²**fusillade** *vt* **:** to attack or shoot down by a fusillade
fu·sion \ˈfyü-zhən\ *n, often attrib* [L *fusion-*, *fusio*, fr. *fusus*, pp.] **1 a :** the act or process of liquefying or rendering plastic by heat **b :** the liquid or plastic state induced by heat **2 :** a union by melting: as **a :** a merging of diverse elements into a unified whole **b :** a political partnership **:** COALITION **c :** the union of atomic nuclei to form heavier nuclei resulting in the release of enormous quantities of energy when certain light elements unite
fusion bomb *n* **:** a bomb in which nuclei of a light chemical element unite to form nuclei of heavier elements with a release of energy; *esp* **:** HYDROGEN BOMB
fu·sion·ist \ˈfyüzh-(ə-)nəst\ *n* **:** one who promotes or takes part in a coalition esp. of political parties
¹**fuss** \ˈfəs\ *n* [perh. of imit. origin] **1 a :** needless bustle or excitement **:** COMMOTION **b :** effusive praise **2 a :** a state of agitation esp. over a trivial matter **b :** OBJECTION, PROTEST **c :** an angry dispute **syn** see STIR
²**fuss** *vi* **1 a :** to create or be in a state of restless activity; *specif* **:** to shower flattering attentions **b :** to pay undue attention to small details **2 a :** to become upset **:** WORRY **b :** COMPLAIN, ARGUE ~ *vt* **:** AGITATE, UPSET — **fuss·er** *n*
fuss·bud·get \ˈfəs-ˌbəj-ət\ *n* **:** one who fusses about trifles
fuss·i·ly \ˈfəs-ə-lē\ *adv* **:** in a fussy manner
fuss·i·ness \ˈfəs-ē-nəs\ *n* **:** the quality or state of being fussy
fussy \ˈfəs-ē\ *adj* **1 :** easily upset **:** IRRITABLE **2 a :** requiring or giving close attention to details **b :** revealing a concern for niceties **:** FASTIDIOUS
fus·tian \ˈfəs-chən\ *n* [ME, fr. OF *fustaine*, fr. ML *fustaneum*, prob. fr. *fustis* tree trunk, fr. L, club] **1 a :** a strong cotton and linen fabric **b :** a class of cotton fabrics usu. having a pile face and twill weave **2 :** pretentious writing or speech **syn** see BOMBAST — **fustian** *adj*
fus·tic \ˈfəs-tik\ *n* [ME *fustik*, fr. MF *fustoc*, fr. Ar *fustuq*, fr. Gk *pistakē* pistachio tree — more at PISTACHIO] **1 :** the wood of a tropical American tree (*Chlorophora tinctoria*) of the mulberry family that yields a yellow dye; *also* **:** any of several similar dyewoods **2 :** a tree yielding fustic
fus·ti·gate \ˈfəs-tə-ˌgāt\ *vt* [LL *fustigatus*, pp. of *fustigare*, fr. L *fustis* + *-igare* (akin to *agere* to drive) — more at AGENT] **1 :** CUDGEL **2 :** to criticize severely — **fus·ti·ga·tion** \ˌfəs-tə-ˈgā-shən\ *n*
fus·ti·ly \ˈfəs-tə-lē\ *adv* **:** in a fusty manner
fus·ti·ness \-tē-nəs\ *n* **:** the quality or state of being fusty
fus·ty \ˈfəs-tē\ *adj* [ME, fr. *fust* wine cask, fr. MF, club, cask, fr. L *fustis*] **1** *Brit* **:** impaired by age or dampness **:** MOLDY **2 :** saturated with dust and stale odors **:** MUSTY **3 :** old-fashioned or rigidly conservative **syn** see MALODOROUS
fu·thark \ˈfü-ˌthärk\ *also* **fu·thorc** *or* **fu·thork** \-ˌthȯ(ə)rk\ *n* [fr. the first six letters, *f*, *u*, *þ* (*th*), *o* (or *a*), *r*, *c* (-k)] **:** the runic alphabet
fu·tile \ˈfyüt-ᵊl, ˈfyü-ˌtīl\ *adj* [MF or L; MF, fr. L *futilis* that pours out easily, useless, fr. *fut-* (akin to *fundere* to pour) — more at FOUND] **1 :** serving no useful purpose **2 :** occupied with trifles **:** FRIVOLOUS — **fu·tile·ly** \-ᵊl-(l)ē, -ˌtīl-lē\ *adv* — **fu·tile·ness** *n* — **fu·til·i·ty** \fyü-ˈtil-ət-ē\ *n*

syn VAIN, FRUITLESS: FUTILE may connote completeness of failure or unwisdom of undertaking; VAIN usu. implies simple failure to achieve a desired result; FRUITLESS comes close to VAIN but often suggests long and arduous effort or severe disappointment

fu·til·i·tar·i·an \fyü-ˌtil-ə-ˈter-ē-ən, ˌfyü-\ *n* [blend of *futile* and *utilitarian*] **:** one who believes that human striving is futile — **futilitarian** *adj* — **fu·til·i·tar·i·an·ism** \-ē-ə-ˌniz-əm\ *n*
fut·tock \ˈfət-ək\ *n* [prob. alter. of *foothook* (futtock)] **:** one of the curved timbers scarfed together to form the lower part of the compound rib of a ship
futtock shroud *n* **:** a short iron rod connecting the topmast rigging with the lower mast
¹**fu·ture** \ˈfyü-chər\ *adj* [ME, fr. OF & L; OF *futur*, fr. L *futurus* about to be — more at BE] **1 :** that is to be; *specif* **:** existing after death **2 :** of, relating to, or constituting a verb tense formed in English with *will* and *shall* and expressive of time yet to come
²**future** *n* **1 a :** time that is to come **b :** what is going to happen **2 :** an expectation of advancement or progressive development **3 :** a stock or commodity bought and sold for delivery at a future time — usu. used in pl. **4 a :** the future tense of a language **b :** a verb form in the future tense
fu·ture·less \-ləs\ *adj* **:** having no prospect of future success
future perfect *adj* **:** of, relating to, or constituting a verb tense that is traditionally formed in English with *will have* and *shall have* and that expresses completion of an action by a specified time that is yet to come — **future perfect** *n*
fu·tur·ism \ˈfyü-chə-ˌriz-əm\ *n* **:** a movement in art, music, and literature begun in Italy about 1910 and marked esp. by an effort to give formal expression to the dynamic energy and movement of mechanical processes — **fu·tur·ist** \ˈfyüch-(ə-)rəst\ *n*
fu·tur·is·tic \ˌfyü-chə-ˈris-tik\ *adj* **:** of or relating to the future or to futurism — **fu·tur·is·ti·cal·ly** \-ti-k(ə-)lē\ *adv*
fu·tu·ri·ty \fyü-ˈt(y)u̇r-ət-ē, -ˈchu̇r-\ *n* **1 :** FUTURE **2 :** the quality or state of being future **3** *pl* **:** future events or prospects
futurity race *n* **1 :** a horse race usu. for two-year-olds in which the competitors are nominated at birth or before **2 :** a race or competition for which entries are made well in advance of the event
fuze, fu·zee *var of* FUSE, FUSEE
¹**fuzz** \ˈfəz\ *n* [prob. back-formation fr. *fuzzy*] **:** fine light particles or fibers (as of down or fluff)
²**fuzz** *vi* **:** to fly off in or become covered with fluffy particles ~ *vt* **1 :** to make fuzzy **2 :** to envelop in a haze **:** BLUR
fuzz·i·ly \ˈfəz-ə-lē\ *adv* **:** in a fuzzy manner
fuzz·i·ness \ˈfəz-ē-nəs\ *n* **:** the quality or state of being fuzzy
fuzzy \ˈfəz-ē\ *adj* [perh. fr. LG *fussig* loose, spongy; akin to OHG *fūl* rotten — more at FOUL] **1 :** covered with or resembling fuzz **2 :** not clear **:** INDISTINCT
-fy \ˌfī\ *vb suffix* [ME *-fien*, fr. OF *-fier*, fr. L *-ficare*, fr. *-ficus* -fic] **1 :** make **:** form into ⟨dandi*fy*⟩ **2 :** invest with the attributes of **:** make similar to ⟨citi*fy*⟩
fyce \ˈfīs\ *var of* FEIST
fyke \ˈfīk\ *n* [D *fuik*] **:** a long bag net kept open by hoops
fyl·fot \ˈfil-ˌfät\ *n* [ME, device used to fill the lower part of a painted glass window, fr. *fillen* to fill + *fot* foot] **:** SWASTIKA

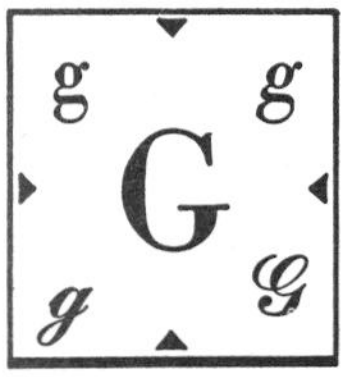
letter G

g \ˈjē\ *n, often cap, often attrib* **1 a :** the seventh letter of the English alphabet **b :** a graphic representation of this letter **c :** a speech counterpart of orthographic *g* **2 :** the tone G **3 :** a graphic device for reproducing the letter *g* **4 :** one designated *g* esp. as the seventh in order or class **5** [gravity] **:** a unit of force equal to the force exerted by gravity on a body at rest and used to indicate the force to which a body is subjected when accelerated **6** [grand] *slang* **:** a sum of $1000 **7 :** something shaped like the capital letter G
¹**gab** \ˈgab\ *vi* **gabbed; gab·bing** [prob. short for *gabble*] **:** to talk in a rapid or thoughtless manner **:** CHATTER
²**gab** *n* **:** TALK; *esp* **:** idle talk
gab·ar·dine \ˈgab-ər-ˌdēn\ *n* [MF *gaverdine*] **1 :** GABERDINE **2 a :** a firm hard-finish durable fabric twilled with diagonal ribs on the right side and made of various fibers **b :** a garment of gabardine
gab·ber \ˈgab-ər\ *n* **:** one that talks much, habitually, and usu. idly
gab·ble \ˈgab-əl\ *vb* **gab·bling** \-(ə-)liŋ\ [prob. of imit. origin] *vi* **1 :** to talk fast or foolishly **:** JABBER **2 :** to utter inarticulate or animal sounds ~ *vt* **:** to say with incoherent rapidity **:** BABBLE — **gabble** *n* — **gab·bler** \-(ə-)lər\ *n*
gab·bro \ˈgab-(ˌ)rō\ *n* [It] **:** a granular igneous rock composed essentially of calcic plagioclase, a ferromagnesian mineral, and accessory minerals — **gab·bro·ic** \ga-ˈbrō-ik\ *adj*
gab·broid \ˈgab-ˌrȯid\ *adj* **:** resembling gabbro
gab·by \ˈgab-ē\ *adj* **:** TALKATIVE, GARRULOUS
ga·belle \gə-ˈbel\ *n* [ME, fr. MF, fr. OIt *gabella* tax, fr. Ar *qabālah*] **:** a tax on salt levied in France prior to 1790
gab·er·dine \ˈgab-ər-ˌdēn\ *n* [MF *gaverdine*] **1 a :** a coarse long coat or smock worn chiefly by Jews in medieval times **b :** an English laborer's smock **c :** GARMENT **2 :** GABARDINE
gab·er·lun·zie \ˌgab-ər-ˈlən-zē\ *n* [origin unknown] **1** *Scot* **:** BEGGAR, MENDICANT **2** *Scot* **:** VAGRANT
gab·fest \ˈgab-ˌfest\ *n* **1 :** an informal gathering for general talk **2 :** an extended conversation
ga·bi·on \ˈgā-bē-ən\ *n* [MF, fr. OIt *gabbione*, lit., large cage, aug. of *gabbia* cage, fr. L *cavea* — more at CAGE] **:** a hollow wickerwork or iron cylinder filled with earth and used in building fieldworks or in mining
ga·ble \ˈgā-bəl\ *n* [ME, fr. MF, of Gmc origin; akin to ON *gafl* gable — more at CEPHALIC] **1 a :** the vertical triangular end of a building from cornice or eaves to ridge **b :** the similar end of a gambrel roof **c :** the end wall of a building **2 :** a triangular furniture or building part

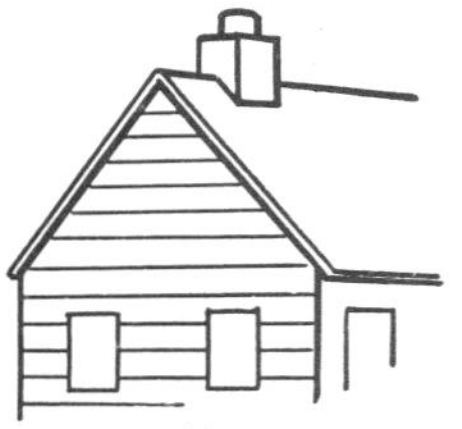
gable 1a

ga·bled \-bəld\ *adj* **:** built with a gable
gable roof *n* **:** a double-sloping roof that forms a gable at each end
gab·oon \gä-ˈbün\ *n* [alter. of ¹*gob* + *-oon* (as in *spittoon*)] *dial* **:** CUSPIDOR, SPITTOON
Ga·bri·el \ˈgā-brē-əl\ *n* [Heb *Gabhrī'ēl*] **:** one of the archangels
ga·by \ˈgā-bē\ *n* [perh. of Scand origin; akin to ON *gapa* to gape — more at GAPE] *dial chiefly Eng* **:** SIMPLETON
¹**gad** \ˈgad\ *n* [ME, spike, fr. ON *gaddr*; akin to OE *geard* rod — more at YARD] **1 :** a chisel or pointed iron or steel bar for loosening ore or rock **2** *dial* **:** ROD, STICK
²**gad** *vi* **gad·ded; gad·ding** [ME *gadden*] **:** to be on the go to little purpose — **gad·der** *n*
³**gad** *interj* [euphemism for *God*] — used as a mild oath
Gad \ˈgad\ *n* [Heb *Gādh*] **:** a son of Jacob and ancestor of one of the tribes of Israel — **Gad·ite** \-ˌīt\ *n*
gad·about \ˈgad-ə-ˌbau̇t\ *n* **:** a person who flits about in social activity — **gadabout** *adj*
gad·a·rene \ˈgad-ə-ˌrēn\ *adj, often cap* [fr. the demon-possessed *Gadarene* swine (Mt 8:28) that rushed into the sea] **:** HEADLONG, PRECIPITATE
gad·fly \ˈgad-ˌflī\ *n* **1 :** any of various flies (as a horsefly, botfly, or warble fly) that bite or annoy livestock **2 :** a person who annoys or stirs up from lethargy

gad·get \'gaj-ət\ *n* [origin unknown] **:** DEVICE, CONTRIVANCE — **gad·ge·teer** \ˌgaj-ə-'ti(ə)r\ *n* — **gad·get·ry** \'gaj-ə-trē\ *n* — **gad·gety** \-ət-ē\ *adj*

ga·doid \'gād-ˌȯid, 'gad-\ *adj* [NL *Gadus*, genus of fishes, fr. Gk *gados*, a fish] **:** resembling or related to the cods — **gadoid** *n*

gad·o·lin·ite \'gad-ᵊl-ə-ˌnīt\ *n* [G *gadolinit*, fr. Johann *Gadolin* †1852 Finn chemist] **:** a black or brown mineral $Be_2FeY_4Si_2O_{13}$ that is a source of rare earths and consists of silicate of iron, beryllium, yttrium, cerium, and erbium

gad·o·lin·i·um \ˌgad-ᵊl-'in-ē-əm\ *n* [NL, fr. J. *Gadolin*] **:** a trivalent magnetic metallic element of the rare-earth group occurring in combination in gadolinite and several other minerals — see ELEMENT table

ga·droon \gə-'drün\ *n* [F *godron* round plait, gadroon] **1 :** the ornamental notching or carving of a rounded molding **2 :** a short often oval fluting or reeding used in decoration — **ga·droon·ing** *n*

gad·wall \'gad-ˌwȯl\ *n, pl* **gadwalls** *or* **gadwall** [origin unknown] **:** a grayish brown dabbling duck (*Anas strepera*) about the size of the mallard

Gaea \'jē-ə\ *n* [Gk *Gaia*] **:** earth as a goddess and mother of the Titans in Greek mythology

-gaea *or* **-gea** \'jē-ə\ *n comb form* [NL, fr. Gk *gaia*, *gē* earth] **:** geographical area ⟨Neo*gaea*⟩

Gael \'gā(ə)l\ *n* [ScGael *Gàidheal* & IrGael *Gaedheal*] **1 :** a Scottish Highlander **2 :** a Celtic esp. Gaelic-speaking inhabitant of Ireland, Scotland, or the Isle of Man

Gael·ic \'gā-lik\ *adj* **1 :** of or relating to the Gaels and esp. the Celtic Highlanders of Scotland **2 :** of, relating to, or constituting the Goidelic speech of the Celts in Ireland, the Isle of Man, and the Scottish Highlands — **Gaelic** *n*

1**gaff** \'gaf\ *n* [F *gaffe*, fr. Prov *gaf*] **1 a :** a spear or spearhead for taking fish or turtles **b :** a handled hook for holding or lifting heavy fish **c :** a metal spur for a gamecock **d :** a butcher's hook **e :** a climbing iron or its steel point used by a telephone lineman **2 :** the spar upon which the head of a fore-and-aft sail is extended **3 a :** HOAX, FRAUD **b :** GIMMICK, TRICK **4 :** rough treatment **:** ABUSE **5 :** GAFFE

2**gaff** *vt* **1 a :** to strike or secure with a gaff **b :** to fit (a gamecock) with a gaff **2 :** DECEIVE, TRICK; *also* **:** FLEECE **3 :** to fix for the purpose of cheating **:** GIMMICK

3**gaff** *n* [origin unknown] *Brit* **:** a cheap theater or music hall

gaffe \'gaf\ *n* [F, gaff, gaffe] **:** a social blunder **:** FAUX PAS

gaf·fer \'gaf-ər\ *n* [prob. alter. of *godfather*] **1 :** an old man **2** *Brit* **a :** EMPLOYER **b :** FOREMAN, OVERSEER **3 :** a head glassblower **4 :** a lighting electrician on a motion-picture or television set

gaff–top·sail \'gaf-'täp-ˌsāl, -səl\ *n* **:** a usu. triangular topsail with its foot extended upon the gaff and its luff upon the topmast

1**gag** \'gag\ *vb* **gagged; gag·ging** [ME *gaggen* to strangle, of imit. origin] *vt* **1 a :** to stop the mouth of with something inserted **b :** to pry or hold open with a gag **c :** to prevent from free speech **2 :** to cause to retch **3 :** OBSTRUCT, CHOKE **4 :** to provide with quips or pranks ⟨~ a show⟩ **~** *vi* **1 :** HEAVE, RETCH **2 :** BALK, STOP **3 :** to make quips

2**gag** *n* **1 :** something thrust into the mouth to keep it open **2 a :** something thrust into the mouth to prevent speech or outcry **b :** CLOTURE **c :** a check to free speech **3 :** a laugh-provoking remark or act **4 :** HOAX, TRICK

ga·ga \'gä-ˌgä\ *adj* [F, fr. *gaga* fool, of imit. origin] **1 :** CRAZY, FOOLISH **2 :** INFATUATED

1**gage** \'gāj\ *n* [ME, fr. MF, of Gmc origin; akin to OHG *wetti* pledge — more at WED] **1 :** a token of defiance; *specif* **:** a glove or cap cast on the ground to be taken up by an opponent as a pledge of combat **2 :** something deposited as a pledge of performance

2**gage** *vt* **1** *archaic* **:** PLEDGE **2** *archaic* **:** STAKE, RISK

3**gage** *var of* GAUGE

4**gage** *n* **:** GREENGAGE

gag·ger \'gag-ər\ *n* **1 :** one that gags **2 :** JOKER, GAGMAN

gag·gle \'gag-əl\ *n* [ME *gagyll*, fr. *gagelen* to cackle] **1 :** FLOCK; *esp* **:** a flock of geese when not in flight **2 :** AGGREGATION, CLUSTER

gag·man \'gag-ˌman\ *n* **1 :** a gag writer **2 :** a comedian who uses gags

gag rule *n* **:** a rule restricting freedom of debate or expression esp. in a legislative body

gag·ster \'gag-stər\ *n* **:** GAGMAN; *also* **:** PRACTICAL JOKER

gahn·ite \'gän-ˌīt\ *n* [G *gahnit*, fr. J. G. *Gahn* †1818 Sw chemist] **:** a usu. dark green mineral $ZnAl_2O_4$ consisting of an oxide of zinc and aluminum

gai·ety \'gā-ət-ē\ *n* **1 :** MERRYMAKING **2 :** gay spirits or manner **3 :** FINERY

gail·lar·dia \gə-'lärd-(ē-)ə\ *n* [NL, genus name, fr. *Gaillard* de Marentonneau, 18th cent. F botanist] **:** any of a genus (*Gaillardia*) of chiefly western American composite herbs with showy flower heads

gai·ly \'gā-lē\ *adv* **:** in a gay manner

1**gain** \'gān\ *n* [ME *gayne*, fr. MF *gaigne*, *gain*, fr. OF *gaaigne*, *gaaing*, fr. *gaaignier* to till, earn, gain, of Gmc origin; akin to OHG *weidanōn* to hunt for food, L *vis* power — more at VIM] **1 :** INCREASE, PROFIT **2 :** the obtaining of profit or possessions **3 a :** an increase in amount, magnitude, or degree **b :** the ratio of increase of output over input in an amplifier

2**gain** *vt* **1 a :** to get possession of **:** EARN **b :** to win in competition or conflict **c :** to get by a natural development or process **:** ACHIEVE ⟨~ strength⟩ **d :** MAKE ⟨~ a friend⟩ **e** (1) **:** to arrive at ⟨~*ed* the river that night⟩ (2) **:** TRAVERSE, COVER ⟨~*ed* 10 yards on the play⟩ **2 :** to win to one's side **:** PERSUADE **3 :** ATTRACT ⟨~ attention⟩ **4 :** to increase in ⟨~ momentum⟩ **5** *of a timepiece* **:** to run fast by the amount of ⟨~*s* a minute a day⟩ **~** *vi* **1 :** to get advantage **:** PROFIT **2 a :** INCREASE **b :** to increase in weight **c :** to improve in health **3** *of a timepiece* **:** to run fast **syn** see GET, REACH — **gain ground :** to make progress

3**gain** *n* [origin unknown] **1 :** a beveled shoulder above a tenon **2 :** a notch or mortise for insertion of a girder or joist

gain·er \'gā-nər\ *n* **1 :** one that gains **2 :** a fancy dive in which the diver from a forward position rotates backward and enters the water feet first and facing away from the board

gain·ful \'gān-fəl\ *adj* **:** productive of gain **:** PROFITABLE — **gain·ful·ly** \-fə-lē\ *adv* — **gain·ful·ness** *n*

gain·giv·ing \'gān-ˌgiv-iŋ\ *n* [*gain-* (against) + *giving*] *archaic* **:** MISGIVING

gain·less \'gān-ləs\ *adj* **:** PROFITLESS — **gain·less·ness** *n*

gain·ly \'gān-lē\ *adj* [*gain* (handy)] **:** GRACEFUL, SHAPELY

gain·say \gān-'sā\ *vt* **gain·said** \-'sād, -'sed\ **gain·say·ing** [ME *gainsayen*, fr. *gain-* against (fr. OE *gēan-*) + *sayen* to say — more at AGAIN] **1 :** DENY, DISPUTE **2 :** to speak against **:** CONTRADICT **syn** see DENY — **gain·say·er** *n*

1**gait** \'gāt\ *n* [ME *gait*, *gate* gate, way] **1 :** a manner of walking or moving on foot **2 :** a sequence of foot movements (as a walk, trot, pace, or canter) by which a horse moves forward **3 :** a manner or rate of movement

2**gait** *vt* **1 :** to train (a horse) to use a particular gait or set of gaits **2 :** to lead (a show dog) before a judge to display carriage and movement

3**gait** *n* [prob. alter. of 1*gate*] **1 :** the distance between two adjoining carriages of a lace-making frame **2** *Brit* **:** a full repeat of a pattern in harness weaving of woolens

gait·ed \'gāt-əd\ *adj* **:** having a particular gait ⟨slow-*gaited*⟩

gai·ter \'gāt-ər\ *n* [F *guêtre*] **1 :** a cloth or leather leg covering reaching from the instep to ankle, mid-calf, or knee **2 a :** an ankle-high shoe with elastic gores in the sides **b :** an overshoe with fabric upper

1**gal** \'gal\ *n* [by alter.] **:** GIRL

2**gal** *n* [*Galileo* †1642 It astronomer] **:** a unit of acceleration equivalent to one centimeter per second per second — used esp. for values of gravity

ga·la \'gā-lə, 'gal-ə\ *n* [It, fr. MF *gale* festivity, pleasure — more at GALLANT] **1** *archaic* **:** festive dress or decoration **2 :** a gay celebration **:** FESTIVITY — **gala** *adj*

galact- *or* **galacto-** *comb form* [L *galact-*, fr. Gk *galakt-*, *galakto-*, fr. *galakt-*, *gala*] **:** milk ⟨*galacto*poiesis⟩

ga·lac·tic \gə-'lak-tik\ *adj* **:** of or relating to a galaxy

galactic noise *n* **:** radio-frequency radiation from the Milky Way

ga·lac·to·poi·e·sis \gə-ˌlak-tə-ˌpȯi-'ē-səs\ *n* [NL] **:** formation and secretion of milk — **ga·lac·to·poi·et·ic** \-'et-ik\ *adj or n*

ga·lac·tose \gə-'lak-ˌtōs, -ˌtōz\ *n* [F, fr. *galact-*] **:** a sugar $C_6H_{12}O_6$ less soluble and less sweet than glucose

ga·lac·to·side \gə-'lak-tə-ˌsīd\ *n* **:** a glycoside that yields galactose on hydrolysis

ga·lah \gə-'lä\ *n* [native name in Australia] **:** a showy Australian cockatoo (*Kakatoë roseicapilla*) that is a destructive pest in wheat-growing areas and is often kept as a cage bird

Gal·a·had \'gal-ə-ˌhad\ *n* **:** a knight of the Round Table who finds the Holy Grail

gal·an·tine \'gal-ən-ˌtēn\ *n* [F] **:** a dish of poultry, fish, game, or other meat, boned, stuffed, cooked, pressed, covered with aspic, and served cold

ga·lan·ty show \gə-'lant-ē-\ *n* [perh. fr. It *galante* gallant, fr. MF *galant*] **:** SHADOW PLAY

Gal·a·tea \ˌgal-ə-'tē-ə\ *n* [L, fr. Gk *Galateia*] **:** an ivory statue of a maiden carved by Pygmalion according to Greek legend and given life by Aphrodite in response to the sculptor's prayer

gal·a·vant *var of* GALLIVANT

ga·lax \'gā-ˌlaks\ *n* [NL, genus name] **:** any of a genus (*Galax*) of evergreen herbs related to the true heaths with leaves widely used for decorations

gal·axy \'gal-ək-sē\ *n* [ME *galaxie*, *galaxias*, fr. LL *galaxias*, fr. Gk, fr. *galakt-*, *gala* milk; akin to L *lac* milk] **1 a** *often cap* **:** MILKY WAY GALAXY **b :** one of billions of systems each including stars, nebulae, star clusters, globular clusters, and interstellar matter that make up the universe **2 :** an assemblage of brilliant or notable persons or things

gal·ba·num \'gal-bə-nəm\ *n* [ME, fr. L, fr. Gk *chalbanē*, fr. Heb *ḥelbĕnāh*] **:** a yellowish to green or brown aromatic bitter gum resin derived from several Asiatic plants and used for medicinal purposes and in incense

1**gale** \'gā(ə)l\ *n* [origin unknown] **1 a :** a strong current of air; *specif* **:** a wind of from 32 to 63 miles per hour **b** *archaic* **:** BREEZE **2 :** an emotional outburst **:** GUST

2**gale** *n* [prob. alter. of 1*gavel*] *Brit* **:** a periodical payment of rent

ga·lea \'gā-lē-ə\ *n* [NL, fr. L, helmet] **:** an anatomical part suggesting a helmet; *esp* **:** the upper lip of the corolla of a mint — **ga·le·ate** \'gā-lē-ˌāt\ *also* **ga·le·at·ed** \-ˌāt-əd\ *adj* — **ga·le·iform** \gə-'lē-ə-ˌfȯrm, 'gā-lē-\ *adj*

ga·le·na \gə-'lē-nə\ *n* [L, lead ore] **:** a bluish gray mineral PbS with metallic luster consisting of lead sulfide, showing highly perfect cubic cleavage, and constituting the principal ore of lead

Ga·len·ic \gā-'len-ik\ *adj* **:** of or relating to Galen or his medical principles or method — **Ga·len·i·cal** \-i-kəl\ *adj*

galenical *n* **:** a medicinal preparation usu. of vegetable origin made by extracting the desired principle without other constituents

Ga·len·ism \'gā-lə-ˌniz-əm\ *n* **:** the Galenic system of medical practice

Gal·i·le·an \ˌgal-ə-'lē-ən, -'lā-\ *adj* **:** of or relating to Galileo Galilei, founder of experimental physics and astronomy

gal·i·lee \'gal-ə-ˌlē, ˌgal-ə-'\ *n* [AF, fr. ML *galilaea*] **:** a chapel or porch at the entrance of an English church

gal·i·ma·ti·as \ˌgal-ə-'mā-shē-əs, -mə-'tyä\ *n* [F] **:** confused and meaningless talk **:** GIBBERISH

gal·in·gale \'gal-ən-ˌgāl, -iŋ-\ *n* [ME, a kind of ginger, fr. MF *galingal*, fr. Ar *khalanjān*] **:** an Old World sedge (*Cyperus longus*) with an aromatic root; *broadly* **:** any of various related plants

gal·i·ot *var of* GALLIOT

gal·i·pot \'gal-ə-ˌpät, -ˌpō\ *n* [F] **:** the crude turpentine oleoresin exuded from a southern European pine (*Pinus pinaster*)

1**gall** \'gȯl\ *n* [ME, fr. OE *gealla*; akin to Gk *cholē*, *cholos* gall, wrath, OE *geolu* yellow — more at YELLOW] **1 a :** BILE; *esp* **:** bile obtained from an animal and used in the arts or medicine **b :** something bitter to endure **c :** bitterness of spirit **:** RANCOR **2 :** EFFRONTERY, IMPUDENCE **syn** see TEMERITY

2**gall** *n* [ME *galle*, fr. OE *gealla*, fr. L *galla* gallnut] **1 a :** a skin sore caused by chronic irritation **b :** a cause or state of exasperation **2** *archaic* **:** FLAW

3**gall** *vt* **1 a :** to fret and wear away by friction **:** CHAFE **b :** IRRITATE, VEX **2 :** HARASS **~** *vi* **1 :** to become sore or worn by rubbing **2 :** SEIZE 2

G H

ə abut; ᵊ kitten; ər further; a back; ā bake; ä cot, cart; aů out; ch chin; e less; ē easy; g gift; i trip; ī life
j joke; ŋ sing; ō flow; ȯ flaw; ȯi coin; th thin; th this; ü loot; ů foot; y yet; yü few; yů furious; zh vision

4gall *n* [ME *galle*, fr. MF, fr. L *galla*] **1 :** a swelling of plant tissue usu. due to fungi or other parasites and sometimes forming an important source of tannin **2 :** a small generally flattened pellet of clay found in some sandstones and sandy shales

Gal·la \'gal-ə\ *n, pl* **Galla** *or* **Gallas** **1 a :** any of several groups of Cushitic-speaking peoples occupying British East Africa and southern Ethiopia **b :** a member of any of these groups **2 :** the Cushitic language of the Galla

1gal·lant \gə-'lant, gə-'länt, 'gal-ənt\ *n* **1 :** a young man of fashion **2 a :** LADIES' MAN **b :** SUITOR **c :** PARAMOUR

2gal·lant \'gal-ənt (*usu in sense 3b*); gə-'lant, gə-'länt (*usu in sense 4*)\ *adj* [ME *galaunt*, fr. MF *galant*, fr. prp. of *galer* to have a good time, fr. *gale* pleasure, of Gmc origin; akin to OE *wela* weal — more at WEAL] **1 :** showy in dress or bearing **:** SMART **2** *archaic* **:** GRAND **3 a :** SPLENDID, STATELY **b :** SPIRITED, BRAVE **c :** CHIVALROUS, NOBLE **4 a :** attentive to ladies **b :** given to amorous intrigue **syn** see CIVIL — **gal·lant·ly** *adv*

3gal·lant \gə-'lant, -'länt\ *vt* **1 :** to pay court to (a lady) **:** ATTEND **2** *obs* **:** to manipulate (a fan) in a modish manner **~** *vi* **:** to pay court to ladies

gal·lant·ry \'gal-ən-trē\ *n* **1** *archaic* **:** gallant appearance **2 a :** an act of marked courtesy **b :** courteous attention to a lady **c :** amorous attention or pursuit **3 :** conspicuous bravery **syn** see HEROISM

gall·blad·der \'gȯl-,blad-ər\ *n* **:** a membranous muscular sac in which bile from the liver is stored

gal·le·ass \'gal-ē-əs, -,as\ *n* [MF *galeasse*] **:** a large fast war galley of southern Europe in the 16th and 17th centuries

gal·lein \'gal-ē-ən, 'gal-,ēn\ *n* [*gall*ic acid + phthal*ein*] **:** a metallic-green crystalline phthalein dye $C_{20}H_{12}O_7$ used esp. in dyeing violet and as an indicator

gal·le·on \'gal-ē-ən\ *n* [OSp *galeón*, fr. MF *galion*, fr. OF *galie* galley] **:** a heavy square-rigged sailing ship of the 15th to early 18th centuries used for war or commerce esp. by the Spanish

gal·ler·ied \'gal-(ə-)rēd\ *adj* **:** having a gallery

gal·lery \'gal-(ə-)rē\ *n* [ME *galerie*, fr. ML *galeria*] **1 a :** a roofed promenade **:** COLONNADE **b :** CORRIDOR **2 a :** an outdoor balcony **b** *South & Midland* **:** PORCH, VERANDA **c** (1) **:** a platform at the quarters or stern of a ship (2) **:** a gun platform or emplacement on a ship **d :** a railed walk around the upper part of an engine to facilitate oiling or inspection **3 a :** a long and narrow passage, apartment, or corridor **b :** a subterranean passageway in a cave or military mining system; *also* **:** a working drift or level in mining **c :** an underground passage made by a mole or ant or a passage made in wood by an insect **4 a :** a room or building devoted to the exhibition of works of art **b :** an institution or business exhibiting or dealing in works of art **c :** a collection of specimens worth showing **5 a :** a structure projecting from one or more interior walls of an auditorium to accommodate additional people; *esp* **:** the highest balcony in a theater commonly having the cheapest seats **b :** the part of a theater audience seated in the top gallery **c :** the undiscriminating general public **d :** the spectators at a tennis or golf match **6 :** a photographer's studio

ga·lle·ta \gə-'yet-ə, gī-'et-ə\ *n* [Sp, hardtack] **:** either of two perennial forage grasses (*Hilaria rigida* and *H. jamesii*) used for hay in southwestern U.S. and Mexico

gal·ley \'gal-ē\ *n* [ME *galeie*, fr. OF *galie*, deriv. of MGk *galea*] **1 :** a large low medieval ship propelled by sails and oars and used in the Mediterranean for war and trading **2 :** a seagoing ship of classical antiquity propelled chiefly by oars **3 :** a large open rowing boat formerly used in England **4 :** the kitchen and cooking apparatus esp. of a ship or airplane **5 :** an oblong tray commonly of pressed steel with upright sides to hold set type

galley proof *n* **:** a proof from type on a galley before it is made up in pages; *also* **:** such proofs

galley slave *n* **1 :** a slave or criminal acting as a rower on a galley **2 :** DRUDGE 1

gal·ley-west \,gal-ē-'west\ *adv* [prob. alter. of E dial. *collywest* (badly askew)] **:** into destruction or confusion ⟨knocked ~⟩

gall·fly \'gȯl-,flī\ *n* **:** an insect that deposits its eggs in plants and causes galls in which the larvae feed

1gal·liard \'gal-yərd\ *n* [ME *gaillard*, fr. MF] **1** *archaic* **:** GAY, LIVELY **2** *archaic* **:** HARDY, VALIANT

2galliard *n* **:** a gay dance with five steps to a phrase popular in the 16th and 17th centuries

Gal·lic \'gal-ik\ *adj* [L *Gallicus*, fr. *Gallia* Gaul] **:** of or relating to Gaul or France

gal·lic acid \,gal-ik-, ,gȯ-lik-\ *n* [F *gallique*, fr. *galle* gall] **:** a white crystalline acid $C_7H_6O_5.H_2O$ found widely in plants or combined in tannins and used esp. in dyes and writing ink and as a photographic developer

Gal·li·can \'gal-i-kən\ *adj* **1 :** GALLIC **2** *often not cap* **:** of or relating to Gallicanism — **Gallican** *n*

Gal·li·can·ism \-kə-,niz-əm\ *n* **:** a movement originating in France and advocating administrative independence from papal control for the Roman Catholic Church in each nation

gal·li·cism \'gal-ə-,siz-əm\ *n, often cap* **1 :** a characteristic French idiom or expression appearing in another language **2 :** a French trait

gal·li·cize \-,sīz\ *vb* **:** to conform to a French mode or idiom

gall·ic·o·lous \gȯ-'lik-ə-ləs\ *adj* **:** producing and inhabiting galls

gal·li·gas·kins \,gal-i-'gas-kənz\ *n pl* [prob. modif. of MF *garguesques*, fr. OSp *greguescos*, fr. *griego* Greek, fr. L *Graecus*] **1 a :** loose wide hose or breeches worn in the 16th and 17th centuries **b :** very loose trousers **2** *chiefly dial* **:** LEGGINGS

gal·li·mau·fry \,gal-ə-'mȯ-frē\ *n* [MF *galimafree* hash] **:** MEDLEY, JUMBLE

gal·li·na·ceous \,gal-ə-'nā-shəs\ *adj* [L *gallinaceus* of domestic fowl, fr. *gallina* hen, fr. *gallus* cock] **:** of or relating to an order (Galliformes) of heavy-bodied largely terrestrial birds including the pheasants, turkeys, grouse, and the common domestic fowl

gall·ing \'gȯ-liŋ\ *adj* **:** CHAFING, VEXING

gal·li·nip·per \'gal-ə-,nip-ər\ *n* [origin unknown] **:** a very large American mosquito (*Psorophora ciliata*); *also* **:** CRANE FLY

gal·li·nule \'gal-ə-,n(y)ü(ə)l\ *n* [NL *Gallinula*, genus of birds, fr. L, pullet, dim. of *gallina*] **:** any of several aquatic birds of the rail family with unlobed feet and a frontal shield on the head

gal·li·ot \'gal-ē-ət\ *n* [ME *galiote*, fr. MF, fr. ML *galeota*, dim. of *galea* galley, fr. MGk] **1 :** a small swift galley formerly used in the Mediterranean **2** [D *galjoot*, fr. MF *galiote*] **:** a long narrow light-draft Dutch merchant sailing ship

gal·li·pot \'gal-i-,pät\ *n* [ME *galy pott*] **1 :** a small ceramic vessel used by apothecaries **2 :** DRUGGIST

gal·li·um \'gal-ē-əm\ *n* [NL, fr. L *gallus* (intended as trans. of Paul *Lecoq* de Boisbaudran †*ab*1912 F chemist)] **:** a rare bluish white usu. trivalent metallic element that is hard and brittle at low temperatures but melts just above room temperature and expands on freezing — see ELEMENT table

gal·li·vant \'gal-ə-,vant\ *vi* [perh. alter. of 3*gallant*] **1 :** to go about ostentatiously with the opposite sex **2 :** to travel or roam about for pleasure

gall·iv·o·rous \gȯ-'liv-ə-rəs\ *adj* **:** feeding on galls or gall tissue (as the larvae of gall insects)

gall mite *n* **:** any of various minute 4-legged mites (family Eriophyidae) that form galls on plants

gall·nut \'gȯl-,nət\ *n* [4*gall*] **:** a gall resembling a nut

gal·lon \'gal-ən\ *n* [ME *galon*, a liquid measure, fr. ONF, fr. ML *galeta* pail, a liquid measure] — see MEASURE table

gal·lon·age \'gal-ə-nij\ *n* **:** amount in gallons

gal·loon \gə-'lün\ *n* [F *galon*] **:** a narrow trimming esp. of lace or embroidery or metallic thread

1gal·lop \'gal-əp\ *n* [MF *galop*] **1 :** a springing gait of a quadruped; *specif* **:** a fast natural 3-beat gait of the horse — compare CANTER, RUN **2 :** a ride or run at a gallop

2gallop *vi* **1 :** to move or ride at a gallop **2 :** to run fast **~** *vt* **1 :** to cause to gallop **2 :** to transport at a gallop — **gal·lop·er** *n*

gal·lo·pade \,gal-ə-'pād, -'päd\ *n* **:** GALOP

Gal·lo·phile \'gal-ə-,fīl\ *n* [L *Gallus* Gaul + E *-phile*] **:** FRANCOPHILE — **Gallophile** *adj*

Gal·lo·way \'gal-ə-,wā\ *n* [*Galloway*, Scotland] **:** any of a breed of hardy medium-sized hornless chiefly black beef cattle native to southwestern Scotland

gal·low·glass \'gal-ō-,glas\ *n* [IrGael *gallōglach*, fr. *gall* foreigner + *ōglach* soldier] **1 :** a mercenary or retainer of an Irish chief **2 :** an armed Irish foot soldier

1gal·lows \'gal-(,)ōz, -əz, *in sense 3 also* -əs\ *n, pl* **gallows** *or* **gal·lows·es** [ME *galwes*, pl. of *galwe*, fr. OE *gealga*; akin to OHG *galgo* gallows, Arm *jatk* twig] **1 :** a frame usu. of two upright posts and a crossbeam from which criminals are hanged — called also *gallows tree* **2 :** a structure consisting of an upright frame with a crosspiece **3** *chiefly dial* **:** SUSPENDER 2a

2gallows *adj* **:** deserving the gallows

gallows bird *n* **:** a person who deserves hanging

gall·stone \'gȯl-,stōn\ *n* **:** a calculus formed in the gallbladder or biliary passages

gal·lus \'gal-əs\ *n* [alter. of 1*gallows*] *chiefly dial* **:** SUSPENDER 2a — usu. used in pl.

gal·lused \'gal-əst\ *adj, chiefly dial* **:** wearing galluses

gall wasp *n* **:** a hymenopterous gallfly (family Cynipidae)

gal·ly \'gal-ē\ *vt* [origin unknown] *chiefly dial* **:** FRIGHTEN, TERRIFY

Ga·lois theory \'gal-,wä-\ *n* [Évariste *Galois* †1832 F mathematician] **:** a part of the theory of groups concerned with the reduction of the solution of a given polynomial equation to that of an equation of the third or fourth degree

ga·loot \gə-'lüt\ *n* [origin unknown] *slang* **:** a disreputable-looking man **:** FELLOW

ga·lop \'gal-əp, ga-'lō\ *n* [F] **:** a lively dance in duple measure; *also* **:** its music

ga·lore \gə-'lō(ə)r, -'lȯ(ə)r\ *adj* [IrGael *go leor* enough] **:** ABUNDANT, PLENTIFUL — used postpositively

ga·losh \gə-'läsh\ *n* [ME *galoche*, fr. MF] **1** *obs* **:** a shoe with a heavy sole **2 :** a high overshoe worn esp. in snow and slush — **ga·loshed** \-'läsht\ *adj*

ga·lumph \gə-'ləm(p)f\ *vi* [prob. alter. of 1*gallop*] **:** to move with a clumsy bumping tread **:** BOUND

gal·van·ic \gal-'van-ik\ *adj* **1 :** of, relating to, or producing a direct current of electricity **2 a :** having an electric effect **:** STIMULATING **b :** JERKY, NERVOUS — **gal·van·i·cal·ly** \-i-k(ə-)lē\ *adv*

galvanic couple *n* **:** a pair of dissimilar substances (as metals) capable of acting together as an electric source when brought in contact with an electrolyte

gal·va·nism \'gal-və-,niz-əm\ *n* [F or It; F *galvanisme*, fr. It *galvanismo*, fr. Luigi *Galvani* †1798 It physician and physicist] **1 :** a direct current of electricity esp. when produced by chemical action **2 :** the therapeutic use of direct electric current **3 :** FORCEFULNESS

gal·va·ni·za·tion \,gal-və-nə-'zā-shən\ *n* **:** the act or process of galvanizing

gal·va·nize \'gal-və-,nīz\ *vt* **1 a :** to subject to the action of an electric current **b :** to stimulate or excite by an electric shock ⟨~ a muscle⟩ **2 :** to coat with zinc — **gal·va·niz·er** *n*

galvano- *comb form* [*galvanic*] **:** galvanic current ⟨*galvano*meter⟩

gal·va·nom·e·ter \,gal-və-'näm-ət-ər\ *n* **:** an instrument for detecting or measuring a small electric current by movements of a magnetic needle or of a coil in a magnetic field — **gal·va·no·met·ric** \,gal-və-nō-'me-trik\ *adj*

gal·vano·scope \gal-'van-ə-,skōp, 'gal-və-nō-\ *n* **:** an instrument for detecting the presence and direction of an electric current by the deflection of a magnetic needle

gal·yak \'gal-,yak\ *n* [native name in Uzbekistan, U.S.S.R.] **:** a short-haired flat or slightly moiré fur derived from the pelt of a stillborn lamb or kid

1gam \'gam\ *n* [prob. fr. F dial. *gambe*, fr. ONF, fr. LL *gamba*] *slang* **:** LEG

2gam *n* [perh. short for obs. *gammon* (talk)] **1 :** a visit or friendly conversation at sea or ashore esp. between whalers **2 :** a school of whales

3gam *vb* **gammed; gam·ming** *vi* **:** to engage in a gam **~** *vt* **1 :** to have a gam with **2 :** to spend talking

gam- *or* **gamo-** *comb form* [NL, fr. Gk, marriage, fr. *gamos* — more at BIGAMY] **1 :** united **:** joined ⟨*gamo*sepalous⟩ **2 :** sexual **:** sexuality ⟨*gam*ic⟩ ⟨*gamo*genesis⟩

gamba *n* **:** VIOLA DA GAMBA

1gam·ba·do \gam-'bād-(,)ō\ *n, pl* **gambadoes** *also* **gambados** [perh. modif. of It *gambale*, fr. *gamba*] **:** a horseman's legging

2gambado *n, pl* **gambadoes** *also* **gambados** [modif. of F *gambade*] **1 :** a spring of a horse **2 :** CAPER, GAMBOL

gam·bier *also* **gam·bir** \'gam-,bi(ə)r\ *n* [Malay *gambir*] **:** a yellowish catechu obtained from a Malayan woody vine, chewed with the

betel nut, and exported for tanning and dyeing
gam·bit \'gam-bət\ *n* [It *gambetto,* lit., act of tripping someone, fr. *gamba* leg, fr. LL *gamba, camba,* modif. of Gk *kampē* bend — more at CAMP] **1 :** a chess opening in which a player risks one or more minor pieces to gain an advantage in position **2 a :** a remark intended to start a conversation or score a point **b :** a calculated move **:** STRATAGEM
[1]**gam·ble** \'gam-bəl\ *vb* **gam·bling** \-b(ə-)liŋ\ [prob. back-formation fr. *gambler,* prob. alter. of obs. *gamner,* fr. obs. *gamen* (to play)] *vi* **1 a :** to play a game for money or other stakes **b :** to bet on an uncertain outcome **2 :** to stake something on a contingency **:** SPECULATE ~ *vt* **1 :** to risk by gambling **:** WAGER **2 :** VENTURE, HAZARD — **gam·bler** \-blər\ *n*
[2]**gamble** *n* **1 :** the playing of a game of chance for stakes **2 a :** an act having an element of risk **b :** something chancy
gam·boge \gam-'bōj, -'büzh\ *n* [NL *gambogium,* alter. of *cambugium,* irreg. fr. *Cambodia*] **1 :** an orange to brown gum resin from southeast Asian trees (genus *Garcinia,* family Guttiferae) that is used as a yellow pigment and cathartic **2 :** a strong yellow
[1]**gam·bol** \'gam-bəl\ *n* [modif. of MF *gambade* spring of a horse, gambol, prob. fr. OProv *camba* leg, fr. LL] **:** a skipping or leaping about in play **:** PRANK
[2]**gambol** *vi* **gam·boled** *or* **gam·bolled; gam·bol·ing** *or* **gam·bol·ling** \-b(ə-)liŋ\ **:** to skip about in play **:** FRISK — **gam·bol·ler** \-b(ə-)lər\ *n*
gam·brel \'gam-brəl\ *n* [ONF *gamberel,* fr. *gambe* leg, fr. LL *gamba*] **1 :** a stick or iron for suspending slaughtered animals **2 :** the hock of an animal
gambrel roof *n* **:** a curb roof of the same section in all parts with a lower steeper slope and an upper flatter one
gam·bu·sia \gam-'byü-zh(ē-)ə\ *n* [NL, genus name, modif. of AmerSp *gambusino* gambusia] **:** any of a genus (*Gambusia*) of topminnows introduced as valuable exterminators of mosquito larvae in warm fresh waters
[1]**game** \'gām\ *n* [ME, fr. OE *gamen;* akin to OHG *gaman* amusement] **1 a** (1) **:** AMUSEMENT, DIVERSION (2) **:** the equipment for a game **b :** FUN, SPORT **2 a :** a procedure for gaining an end **b** (1) **:** RACKET (2) **:** a field of gainful activity **:** LINE **3 a** (1) **:** a physical or mental competition conducted according to rules with the participants in direct opposition to each other (2) **:** a division of a larger contest (3) **:** the number of points necessary to win (4) **:** the manner of playing in a contest (5) **:** the set of rules governing a game **b :** a situation involving opposing interests given specific information and allowed a choice of moves with the object of maximizing their wins and minimizing their losses **4 a** (1) **:** animals under pursuit or taken in hunting; *esp* **:** wild animals hunted for sport or food (2) **:** the flesh of game animals **b** *archaic* **:** PLUCK **c :** an object of ridicule or attack — often used in the phrase *fair game* **syn** see FUN
[2]**game** *vi* **:** to play for a stake ~ *vt, archaic* **:** to lose or squander by gambling
[3]**game** *adj* **1 :** having a resolute unyielding spirit ⟨~ to the end⟩ **2 :** of or relating to game ⟨~ laws⟩
[4]**game** *adj* [perh. fr. [3]*game*] **:** LAME ⟨a ~ leg⟩
game·cock \'gām-,käk\ *n* **:** a male game fowl
game fish *n* **1 :** a fish of the family Salmonidae **2 :** SPORT FISH; *esp* **:** a fish made a legal catch by law
game fowl *n* **:** a domestic fowl of a strain developed for the production of fighting cocks
game·keep·er \-,kē-pər\ *n* **:** one that has charge of the breeding and protection of game animals or birds on a private preserve
gam·elan \'gam-ə-,lan\ *n* [Jav] **1 :** a Javanese instrument resembling the xylophone **2 :** a flute, string, and percussion orchestra of southeast Asia
game·ly \'gām-lē\ *adv* **:** in a plucky manner
game·ness \'gām-nəs\ *n* **:** ENDURANCE, PLUCK
games·man·ship \'gāmz-mən-,ship\ *n* **:** the art of winning games by doubtful expedients without actually violating the rules
game·some \'gām-səm\ *adj* **:** GAY, FROLICSOME — **game·some·ly** *adv* — **game·some·ness** *n*
game·ster \'gām-stər\ *n* **:** a person who plays games; *esp* **:** GAMBLER
gamet- *or* **gameto-** *comb form* [NL, fr. *gameta*] **:** gamete ⟨*gameto*phore⟩
gam·etan·gi·um \,gam-ə-'tan-jē-əm\ *n, pl* **gam·etan·gia** \-jē-ə\ [NL, fr. *gamet-* + Gk *angeion* vessel — more at ANGI-] **:** a cell or organ in which gametes are developed
ga·mete \gə-'mēt, 'gam-,ēt\ *n* [NL *gameta,* fr. Gk *gametēs* husband, fr. *gamein* to marry, fr. *gamos* marriage — more at BIGAMY] **:** a mature germ cell possessing a haploid chromosome set and capable of initiating formation of a new individual by fusion with another gamete — **ga·met·ic** \gə-'met-ik\ *adj* — **ga·met·i·cal·ly** \-i-k(ə-)lē\ *adv*
game theory *n* **:** THEORY OF GAMES
ga·meto·cyte \gə-'mēt-ə-,sīt\ *n* [ISV] **:** a cell that divides to produce gametes
ga·meto·gen·e·sis \gə-,mēt-ə-'jen-ə-səs\ *n* [NL] **:** the production of gametes — **ga·meto·gen·ic** \-'jen-ik\ *or* **gam·etog·e·nous** \,gam-ə-'täj-ə-nəs\ *adj* — **gam·etog·e·ny** \-nē\ *n*
ga·meto·phore \gə-'mēt-ə-,fō(ə)r, -,fȯ(ə)r\ *n* **:** a modified branch bearing gametangia — **ga·meto·phor·ic** \-,mēt-ə-'fȯr-ik, -'fär-\ *adj*
ga·meto·phyte \gə-'mēt-ə-,fīt\ *n* [ISV] **:** the individual or generation of a plant exhibiting alternation of generations that bears sex organs — **ga·meto·phyt·ic** \-,mēt-ə-'fit-ik\ *adj*
gam·ic \'gam-ik\ *adj* **:** requiring fertilization
-gam·ic \'gam-ik\ *adj comb form* [ISV, fr. Gk *-gamos* -gamous] **:** having (such) reproductive organs ⟨cleisto*gamic*⟩
gam·i·ly \'gā-mə-lē\ *adv* **:** in a gamy manner **:** PLUCKILY
gam·in \'gam-ən\ *n* [F] **1 :** a boy who runs the streets **:** URCHIN **2 :** GAMINE 2
ga·mine \ga-'mēn\ *n* [F, fem. of *gamin*] **1 :** a girl who runs the streets **:** TOMBOY **2 :** a girl of elfin appeal
gam·i·ness \'gā-mē-nəs\ *n* **:** the quality or state of being gamy
gam·ing \'gā-miŋ\ *n* **:** the practice of gambling
[1]**gam·ma** \'gam-ə\ *n* [ME, fr. LL, fr. Gk, of Sem origin; akin to Heb *gīmel* gimel] **1 :** the third letter of the Greek alphabet — symbol Γ or γ **2 :** the degree of contrast of a developed photographic image or of a television image **3 :** MICROGRAM
[2]**gamma** *or* γ- *adj* **:** third in position in the structure of an organic molecule from a particular group or atom
gamma globulin *n* **:** a fraction of blood plasma rich in antibodies
gamma nasal *n, in ancient and modern Greek* **:** gamma pronounced \ŋ\, before κ, χ, ξ, or another gamma
gamma ray *n* **1 :** a photon or radiation quantum emitted spontaneously by a radioactive substance **2 :** a continuous stream of gamma rays — called also *gamma radiation*
gam·mer \'gam-ər\ *n* [prob. alter. of *godmother*] **:** an old woman — compare GAFFER
Gam·mex·ane \ga-'mek-,sān\ *trademark* — used for lindane
[1]**gam·mon** \'gam-ən\ *n* [ONF *gambon* ham, aug. of *gambe* leg — more at GAM] **1 :** a ham or flitch of cured bacon **2 :** the lower end of a side of bacon
[2]**gammon** *vt* [*gammon,* n. (fastening of the bowsprit)] **:** to fasten (a bowsprit) to the stem of a ship with rope or iron
[3]**gammon** *n* [perh. alter. of ME *gamen* game] **1** *archaic* **:** BACKGAMMON **2 :** the winning of a backgammon game before the loser bears off any men
[4]**gammon** *vt* **:** to beat by scoring a gammon
[5]**gammon** *n* [obs. *gammon* (talk)] **:** talk intended to deceive **:** HUMBUG
[6]**gammon** *vi* **1 :** to talk gammon **2 :** PRETEND, FEIGN ~ *vt* **:** DECEIVE, FOOL
gamo- — see GAM-
gamo·deme \'gam-ə-,dēm\ *n* **:** a more or less isolated breeding community of organisms
gamo·gen·e·sis \,gam-ə-'jen-ə-səs\ *n* [NL] **:** sexual reproduction — **gamo·ge·net·ic** \-jə-'net-ik\ *adj* — **gamo·ge·net·i·cal·ly** \-i-k(ə-)lē\ *adv*
gamo·pet·al·ous \,gam-ə-'pet-ᵊl-əs\ *adj* **:** having the corolla composed of united petals
gamo·phyl·lous \-'fil-əs\ *adj* **:** having united leaves or leaflike parts
gamo·sep·al·ous \-'sep-ə-ləs\ *adj* **:** having the sepals united
-g·a·mous \g-ə-məs\ *adj comb form* [Gk *-gamos,* fr. *gamos* marriage — more at BIGAMY] **1 :** characterized by having or practicing (such) a marriage or (such or so many) marriages ⟨exo*gamous*⟩ **2 :** -GAMIC ⟨hetero*gamous*⟩
gamp \'gamp\ *n* [Sarah *Gamp,* nurse with a large umbrella in *Martin Chuzzlewit* by Charles Dickens] *Brit* **:** a large umbrella
gam·ut \'gam-ət\ *n* [ML *gamma,* lowest note of Guido's scale (fr. LL, third letter of the Greek alphabet) + *ut*] **1 :** the whole series of recognized musical notes **2 :** an entire range or series
gamy *or* **gam·ey** \'gā-mē\ *adj* **gam·i·er; gam·i·est** **1 :** BRAVE, PLUCKY — used esp. of animals **2 a :** having the flavor of game; *esp* **:** having the flavor of game near tainting **b :** SMELLY **3 a :** SCANDALOUS, SPICY **b :** CORRUPT, DISREPUTABLE
-g·a·my \g-ə-mē\ *n comb form* [ME *-gamie,* fr. LL *-gamia,* fr. Gk — more at BIGAMY] **1 :** marriage ⟨exo*gamy*⟩ **2 :** union for propagation or reproduction ⟨allo*gamy*⟩
gan *past of* GIN
Gan·da \'gan-də\ *n, pl* **Ganda** *or* **Gandas** **1 a :** a Bantu-speaking people of Uganda **b :** a member of this people **2 :** the Bantu language of the Ganda people used as the official language of Uganda
[1]**gan·der** \'gan-dər\ *n* [ME, fr. OE *gandra;* akin to OE *gōs* goose] **1 :** the adult male goose **2 :** SIMPLETON
[2]**gander** *vi, dial* **:** WANDER, RAMBLE
[3]**gander** *n, slang* **:** LOOK, GLANCE
Gan·dhi·an \'gän-dē-ən, 'gan-\ *adj* **:** of or relating to the Indian political and spiritual leader Mohandas K. Gandhi or his principle of nonviolence
gan·dy dancer \'gan-dē-\ *n* [perh. fr. the *Gandy* Manufacturing Company, Chicago, Illinois, toolmakers] **1 :** a laborer in a railroad section gang **2 :** an itinerant or seasonal laborer
ga·nef \'gän-əf\ *n* [Yiddish *ganef,* fr. Heb *gannābh* thief] *slang* **:** THIEF, RASCAL
[1]**gang** \'gaŋ\ *n* [ME, fr. OE; akin to OHG *gang* act of going, Skt *jaṅghā* shank] **1** *dial Brit* **:** JOURNEY, WAY **2 a** (1) **:** OUTFIT, SET (2) **:** a combination of similar implements or devices arranged for convenience to act together ⟨a ~ of saws⟩ **b :** GROUP: as (1) **:** a group of persons working together (2) **:** a group of persons working to unlawful or antisocial ends
[2]**gang** *vt* **1 :** to attack in a gang **2 a :** to assemble or operate simultaneously as a group **b :** to arrange in or produce as a gang (as type pages) ~ *vi* **:** to move or act as a gang
gang·er \'gaŋ-ər\ *n, Brit* **:** the foreman of a gang of workmen
gang hook *n* **:** two or three fishhooks with their shanks joined together
gang·land \'gaŋ-,land\ *n* **:** the world of organized crime
gangli- *or* **ganglio-** *comb form* [NL, fr. Gk *ganglion*] **:** ganglion ⟨*gangli*ectomy⟩ ⟨*ganglio*plexus⟩
gan·gling \'gaŋ-gliŋ, -glən\ *adj* [perh. irreg. fr. Sc *gangrel* vagrant, lanky person] **:** LANKY, SPINDLING
gan·gli·on \'gaŋ-glē-ən\ *n, pl* **gan·glia** \-glē-ə\ *also* **ganglions** [LL, fr. Gk] **1 a :** a small cystic tumor connected either with a joint membrane or tendon sheath **b :** a mass of nerve tissue containing nerve cells external to the brain or spinal cord; *also* **:** NUCLEUS 2b **2 :** a focus of strength or energy — **gan·gli·on·at·ed** \'gaŋ-glē-ə-,nāt-əd\ *adj* — **gan·gli·on·ic** \,gaŋ-glē-'än-ik\ *adj*
gan·gly \'gaŋ-glē\ *adj* **:** GANGLING, LANKY
gang·plank \'gaŋ-,plaŋk\ *n* **:** a movable bridge used in boarding or leaving a ship at a pier
gang·plow \-,plau̇\ *n* **:** a plow built to turn parallel furrows
gang·rel \'gaŋ-(ə-)rəl\ *n* [ME, irreg. fr. *gangen* to go, fr. OE *gangan;* akin to OE *gang*] *Scot* **:** VAGRANT
[1]**gan·grene** \'gaŋ-,grēn, gaŋ-', 'gan-,, gan-'\ *n* [L *gangraena,* fr. Gk *gangraina;* akin to Gk *gran* to gnaw] **1 :** local death of soft tissues due to loss of blood supply **2 :** a mortal evil — **gan·gre·nous** \'gaŋ-grə-nəs\ *adj*
[2]**gangrene** *vt* **:** to make gangrenous ~ *vi* **:** to become gangrenous
gang·ster \'gaŋ(k)-stər\ *n* **:** a member of a gang of criminals **:** RACKETEER — **gang·ster·ism** \-stə-,riz-əm\ *n*

gangue \ˈgaŋ\ *n* [F, fr. G *gang* vein of metal, fr. OHG, act of going] **:** the worthless rock or vein matter in which valuable metals or minerals occur

gang up *vi* **1 :** MEET, GATHER **2 :** to make a joint assault **3 :** to exert group pressure

gang·way \ˈgaŋ-ˌwā\ *n* **1 :** PASSAGEWAY; *esp* **:** a temporary way of planks **2 a :** either of the sides of the upper deck of a ship **b :** the opening by which a ship is boarded **c :** GANGPLANK **3** *Brit* **:** AISLE **4 :** a main level or haulageway in a mine **5 a :** a cross aisle dividing the front benches from the back benches in the British House of Commons **b :** an aisle in the British House of Commons that separates government and opposition benches **6 :** a clear passage through a crowd — often used as an interjection

gan·is·ter *or* **gan·nis·ter** \ˈgan-ə-stər\ *n* [origin unknown] **1 :** a fine-grained quartzite used in the manufacture of refractory brick **2 :** a mixture of ground quartz and fireclay used for lining metallurgical furnaces

gan·net \ˈgan-ət\ *n, pl* **gannets** *also* **gannet** [ME *ganet*, fr. OE *ganot;* akin to OE *gōs* goose] **:** any of several large fish-eating seabirds (family Sulidae) that remain at sea for long periods and breed in large colonies chiefly on offshore islands

gan·oid \ˈgan-ˌȯid\ *adj* [deriv. of Gk *ganos* brightness; akin to Gk *gēthein* to rejoice — more at JOY] **:** of or relating to a subclass (Ganoidei) of living and extinct teleost fishes (as the sturgeons) with usu. hard rhombic enameled scales — **ganoid** *n* — **ga·noi·de·an** \ga-ˈnȯid-ē-ən\ *adj or n*

gante·lope *or* **gant·lope** \ˈgant-ˌlōp, -ᵊl-ˌōp\ *n* [modif. of Sw *gatlopp*, fr. OSw *gatulop*, fr. *gata* road + *lop* course] *archaic* **:** GAUNTLET

1**gant·let** \ˈgȯnt-lət, ˈgänt-\ *var of* GAUNTLET

2**gant·let** \ˈgȯnt-lət, ˈgänt-\ *n* [2*gauntlet*] **:** a stretch of railroad track where two lines of track overlap so that one rail of each track is within the rails of the other in order to obviate switching

3**gantlet** *vt* **:** to run (railroad tracks) together so as to make a gantlet

gant·line \ˈgant-ˌlīn\ *n* [perh. alter. of *girtline* (gantline)] **:** a line rove through a block aloft on a ship and used for hoisting

gan·try \ˈgan-trē\ *n* [perh. modif. of ONF *gantier*, fr. L *cantherius* trellis] **1 :** a frame for supporting barrels **2 a :** a platform made to carry a traveling crane and supported by towers or side frames running on parallel tracks; *also* **:** a movable structure with platforms at different levels used for erecting and servicing rockets before launching **b :** a structure spanning several railroad tracks and displaying signals for each

Gan·y·mede \ˈgan-ə-ˌmēd\ *n* [L *Ganymedes*, fr. Gk *Ganymēdēs*] **1 :** a beautiful youth in classical mythology carried off to Olympus to be the cupbearer of the gods **2 :** a youth who serves liquors **:** CUPBEARER **3 :** the fourth satellite of Jupiter

gaol \ˈjā(ə)l\ *chiefly Brit var of* JAIL

1**gap** \ˈgap\ *n* [ME, fr. ON, chasm, hole; akin to ON *gapa*] **1 a :** a break in a wall, hedge, or line of military defense **b :** an assailable position **2 a :** a mountain pass **b :** RAVINE **3 :** SPARK GAP **4 :** a separation in space **5 :** a break in continuity **:** HIATUS **6 :** lack of balance **:** DISPARITY ⟨the ~ between imports and exports⟩ — **gap·py** \-ē\ *adj*

2**gap** *vb* **gapped; gap·ping** *vt* **:** to make an opening in ~ *vi* **:** to fall or stand open

1**gape** \ˈgāp *also* ˈgap\ *vi* [ME *gapen*, fr. ON *gapa;* akin to L *hiare* to gape, yawn — more at YAWN] **1 a :** to open the mouth wide **b :** to open or part widely **2 :** to stare openmouthed **3 :** YAWN **syn** see GAZE — **gap·er** *n* — **gap·ing·ly** \ˈgāp-iŋ-lē, ˈgap-\ *adv*

2**gape** *n* **1 :** an act of gaping: **a :** YAWN **b :** an openmouthed stare **2 :** an unfilled space or extent **3 a :** the median margin-to-margin length of the open mouth **b :** the line along which the mandibles of a bird close **c :** the width of an opening **4** *pl but sing in constr* **a :** a disease of young birds in which gapeworms invade and irritate the trachea **b :** a fit of yawning

gape·seed \-ˌsēd\ *n, dial Brit* **:** something that attracts stares

gape·worm \-ˌwərm\ *n* **:** a nematode worm (*Syngamus trachea*) that causes gapes of birds

gapped scale *n* **:** a musical scale omitting some notes

1**gar** \ˈgär\ *interj* [euphemism for *God*] — used as a mild oath

2**gar** *n* [short for *garfish*] **:** any of various fishes that have an elongate body resembling that of a pike and long and narrow jaws: as **a :** NEEDLEFISH **b :** any of several predaceous No. American freshwater ganoid fishes with rank tough flesh

1**ga·rage** \gə-ˈräzh, -ˈräj\ *n* [F, act of docking, garage, fr. *garer* to dock, of Gmc origin; akin to OHG *biwarōn* to protect — more at WARE] **:** a shelter or repair shop for automotive vehicles

2**garage** *vt* **:** to keep or put in a garage

ga·rage·man \-ˌman\ *n* **:** a garage worker

Ga·rand rifle \gə-ˌran-ˈdrī-fəl, ˌgar-ən-\ *n* [John C. *Garand* b1888 Am inventor] **:** a rapid-fire semiautomatic rifle

garb \ˈgärb\ *n* [MF or OIt; MF *garbe* graceful contour, grace, fr. OIt *garbo* grace] **1** *obs* **:** FASHION, MANNER **2 a :** style of apparel **b :** CLOTHING, DRESS — **garb** *vt*

gar·bage \ˈgär-bij\ *n* [ME, animal entrails] **1 :** food waste **:** REFUSE **2 :** trashy writing or speech

1**gar·ble** \ˈgär-bəl\ *vt* **gar·bling** \-b(ə-)liŋ\ [ME *garbelen*, fr. OIt *garbellare* to sift, fr. Ar *ghirbāl* sieve, fr. LL *cribellum;* akin to L *cernere* to sift — more at CERTAIN] **1** *archaic* **:** CULL **2 :** to sift impurities from **3 :** DISTORT, CONFUSE — **gar·bler** \-b(ə-)lər\ *n*

2**garble** *n* **1 :** the impurities removed from spices in sifting **2 :** DISTORTION, JUMBLE

gar·board \ˈgär-ˌbō(ə)rd, -ˌbȯ(ə)rd\ *n* [obs. D *gaarboord*] **:** the strake next to a ship's keel

gar·boil \-ˌbȯil\ *n* [MF *garbouil*] **:** CONFUSION, TURMOIL

gar·çon \gär-ˈsōⁿ\ *n, pl* **garçons** \-ˈsōⁿ(z)\ [F, boy, servant] **:** WAITER

garde–man·ger \ˌgärd-(ə-)ˌmäⁿ-ˈzhā\ *n, pl* **garde–mangers** \-ˈzhā(z)\ [F] **:** the cold meat department of a large kitchen; *also* **:** the chef in charge of it

1**gar·den** \ˈgärd-ᵊn\ *n* [ME *gardin*, fr. ONF, of Gmc origin; akin to OHG *gart* enclosure — more at YARD] **1 a :** a plot of ground where herbs, fruits, flowers, or vegetables are cultivated **b :** a rich well-cultivated region **2 a :** a public recreation area or park ⟨a botanical ~⟩ **b :** an open-air eating or drinking place

2**garden** *vb* **gar·den·ing** \ˈgärd-niŋ, -ᵊn-iŋ\ *vi* **:** to lay out or work in a garden ~ *vt* **1 :** to make into a garden **2 :** to ornament with gardens — **gar·den·er** \ˈgärd-nər, -ᵊn-ər\ *n*

3**garden** *adj* **1 :** of, relating to, or frequenting a garden **2 a :** of a kind grown in the open as distinguished from one more delicate ⟨~ plant⟩ **b :** ORDINARY, COMMONPLACE

garden apartment *n* **:** any of various multiple-unit dwellings having considerable lawn or garden space

garden city *n* **:** a planned residential community with park and planted areas

garden cress *n* **:** an Asiatic annual herb (*Lepidium sativum*) of the mustard family sometimes cultivated for its pungent basal leaves

garden heliotrope *n* **1 :** a tall rhizomatous Old World valerian (*Valeriana officinalis*) widely cultivated for its fragrant tiny flowers and roots which yield the drug valerian **2 :** a shrubby Peruvian heliotrope (*Heliotropium arborescens*) with fragrant usu. lilac or violet flowers

gar·de·nia \gär-ˈdē-nyə, -nē-ə\ *n* [NL, genus name, fr. Alexander *Garden* †1791 Sc naturalist] **:** any of a large genus (*Gardenia*) of Old World tropical trees and shrubs of the madder family with showy fragrant white or yellow flowers

garden–variety *adj* **:** GARDEN 2b

garde·robe \ˈgär-ˌdrōb\ *n* [ME, fr. MF; akin to ONF *warderobe* wardrobe] **1 :** a wardrobe or its contents **2 :** a private room **:** BEDROOM **3 :** PRIVY

gar·dy·loo \ˌgärd-ē-ˈlü\ *n* [perh. fr. F *garde à l'eau!* look out for the water!] **:** a warning cry formerly used on throwing slops into the streets from the windows in Edinburgh

Gar·eth \ˈgar-əth\ *n* **:** a knight of the Round Table and nephew of King Arthur

gar·fish \ˈgär-ˌfish\ *n* [ME *garfysshe*] **:** GAR

Gar·gan·tua \gär-ˈganch-(ə-)wə\ *n* [F] **:** a gigantic king in Rabelais' *Gargantua* having a great capacity for food and drink — **gar·gan·tu·an** \-wən\ *adj, often cap*

gar·get \ˈgär-gət\ *n* [prob. fr. ME, throat, fr. MF *gargate*; akin to MF *gargouiller*] **:** mastitis of domestic animals; *esp* **:** chronic bovine mastitis with gross changes in the form and texture of the udder — **gar·gety** \-gət-ē\ *adj*

1**gar·gle** \ˈgär-gəl\ *vb* **gar·gling** \-g(ə-)liŋ\ [MF *gargouiller* to gargle, of imit. origin] *vt* **1 a :** to hold (a liquid) in the mouth or throat and agitate with air from the lungs **b :** to cleanse or disinfect (the oral cavity) in this manner **2 :** to utter with a gargling sound ~ *vi* **1 :** to use a gargle **2 :** to speak or sing as if gargling

2**gargle** *n* **1 :** a liquid used in gargling **2 :** a gargling sound

gar·goyle \ˈgär-ˌgȯil\ *n* [ME *gargoyl*, fr. MF *gargouille;* akin to MF *gargouiller*] **1 a :** a spout in the form of a grotesque human or animal figure projecting from a roof gutter to throw rainwater clear of a building **b :** a grotesquely carved figure **2 :** a person with an ugly face — **gar·goyled** \-ˌgȯild\ *adj*

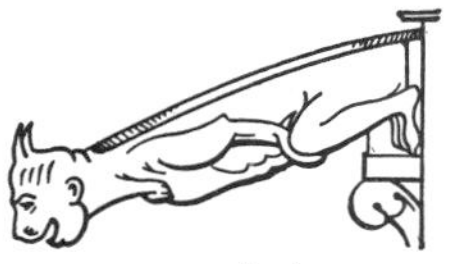

gargoyle 1a

gar·i·bal·di \ˌgar-ə-ˈbȯl-dē\ *n* [Giuseppe *Garibaldi* †1882 It patriot] **:** a woman's blouse copied from the red shirt worn by the Italian patriot Garibaldi

gar·ish \ˈga(ə)r-ish, ˈge(ə)r-\ *adj* [origin unknown] **1 :** clothed in vivid colors **2 a :** excessively vivid **:** FLASHY **b :** offensively bright **:** GLARING **3 :** tastelessly showy **syn** see GAUDY — **gar·ish·ly** *adv* — **gar·ish·ness** *n*

1**gar·land** \ˈgär-lənd\ *n* [ME, fr. MF *garlande*] **1 :** WREATH, CHAPLET **2 :** a grommet or ring of rope used aboard ship in hoisting or to prevent chafing **3 :** ANTHOLOGY, COLLECTION

2**garland** *vt* **:** to form into or deck with a garland

gar·lic \ˈgär-lik\ *n, often attrib* [ME *garlek*, fr. OE *gārlēac*, fr. *gār* spear + *lēac* leek — more at GORE] **:** a European bulbous herb (*Allium sativum*) of the lily family widely cultivated for its pungent compound bulbs much used in cookery; *also* **:** one of the bulbs — **gar·licky** \-li-kē\ *adj*

garlic salt *n* **:** a seasoning of ground dried garlic and salt

1**gar·ment** \ˈgär-mənt\ *n* [ME, fr. MF *garnement*, fr. OF, fr. *garnir* to equip] **:** an article of clothing

2**garment** *vt* **:** to clothe with or as if with a garment

1**gar·ner** \ˈgär-nər\ *n* [ME, fr. OF *grenier*, fr. L *granarium*, fr. *granum* grain] **1 :** GRANARY **2 :** a grain bin

2**garner** *vt* **gar·ner·ing** \ˈgärn-(ə-)riŋ\ **1 a :** to gather into storage **b :** to deposit as if in a granary **2 a :** to acquire by effort **:** EARN **b :** ACCUMULATE, COLLECT

1**gar·net** \ˈgär-nət\ *n* [ME *grenat*, fr. MF, fr. *grenat*, adj., red like a pomegranate, fr. (*pome*) *grenate* pomegranate] **1 :** a brittle and more or less transparent usu. red silicate mineral that has a vitreous luster, occurs mainly in crystals but also massive and in grains, is found commonly in gneiss and mica schist, and is used as a semiprecious stone and as an abrasive (hardness 6.5–7.5, sp. gr. 3.15–4.3) **2 :** a variable color averaging a dark red

2**garnet** *n* [ME *garnett*] **:** a tackle usu. rigged on the mainstay of a sailing ship for hoisting cargo

gar·net·if·er·ous \ˌgär-nət-ˈif-(ə-)rəs\ *adj* **:** containing garnets

garnet paper *n* **:** an abrasive paper with crushed garnet as the abrasive

gar·ni·er·ite \ˈgär-nē-ə-ˌrīt\ *n* [Jules *Garnier* †1904 F geologist] **:** a silicate mineral prob. $(Mg,Ni)_3Si_2O_5(OH)_4$ consisting of hydrous nickel magnesium and constituting an important ore of nickel

1**gar·nish** \ˈgär-nish\ *vt* [ME *garnishen*, fr. MF *garniss-*, stem of *garnir* to warn, equip, garnish, of Gmc origin; akin to OHG *warnōn* to take heed — more at WARN] **1 a :** DECORATE, EMBELLISH **b :** to add decorative or savory touches to (food) **2 :** to equip with accessories **:** FURNISH **3 :** GARNISHEE **syn** see ADORN

2**garnish** *n* **1 :** EMBELLISHMENT, ORNAMENT **2 :** a savory and usu. decorative condiment **3** *slang* **a :** an unauthorized fee formerly extorted from a new inmate by the keeper of an English jail **b :** a similar payment required of a new workman

1**gar·nish·ee** \ˌgär-nə-ˈshē\ *n* **:** one who is served with a garnishment

2**garnishee** *vt* **gar·nish·eed; gar·nish·ee·ing 1 :** to serve with a garnishment **2 :** to take (as a debtor's wages) by legal authority

gar·nish·ment \ˈgär-nish-mənt\ *n* **1 :** GARNISH **2 :** a legal summons or warning concerning the attachment of property to satisfy a debt **3 :** a stoppage of a specified sum from wages to satisfy a creditor

gar·ni·ture \ˈgär-ni-chər, -nə-ˌchü(ə)r\ *n* [MF, equipment, alter. of OF *garnesture*, fr. *garnir*] **:** EMBELLISHMENT, TRIMMING

gar·pike \ˈgär-ˌpīk\ *n* **:** GAR b

gar·ret \ˈgar-ət\ *n* [ME *garette* watchtower, fr. MF *garite*, perh.

fr. OProv *garida*, fr. *garir* to protect, of Gmc origin; akin to OHG *werien*] : a room or unfinished part of a house just under the roof

¹**gar·ri·son** \'gar-ə-sən\ *n* [ME *garisoun* protection, fr. OF *garison*, fr. *garir* to protect, of Gmc origin; akin to OHG *werien* to defend — more at WEIR] **1** : a military post; *esp* : a permanent military installation **2** : the troops stationed at a garrison

²**garrison** *vt* **gar·ri·son·ing** \'gar-ə-s(ə-)niŋ\ **1** : to station troops in **2 a** : to assign as a garrison **b** : to occupy with troops

Gar·ri·son finish \,gar-ə-sən-\ *n* [prob. fr. Snapper *Garrison* 19th cent. Am jockey] : a finish in which the winner comes from behind at the end

garrison house *n* **1** : a house fortified against Indian attack **2** : BLOCKHOUSE **3** : a house of colonial times having the second story overhanging the first in the front elevation

garrison state *n* : a state organized on a primarily military basis

gar·ron \'gar-ən\ *n* [IrGael *gearrān* & ScGael *gearran*, gelding] *Scot & Irish* : a small sturdy work horse

¹**gar·rote** *or* **ga·rotte** \gə-'rät, -'rōt\ *n* [Sp *garrote*] **1 a** : a method of execution by strangling with an iron collar **b** : the iron collar used **2 a** : strangulation esp. with robbery as the motive **b** : an implement for this purpose

²**garrote** *or* **garotte** *vt* **1** : to execute with or as if with a garrote **2** : to strangle and rob — **gar·rot·er** *n*

gar·ru·li·ty \gə-'rü-lət-ē\ *n* : LOQUACITY, TALKATIVENESS

gar·ru·lous \'gar-ə-ləs *also* -yə-\ *adj* [L *garrulus*, fr. *garrire* to chatter — more at CARE] : CHATTERING, TALKATIVE **syn** see TALKATIVE — **gar·ru·lous·ly** *adv* — **gar·ru·lous·ness** *n*

¹**gar·ter** \'gärt-ər\ *n* [ME, fr. ONF *gartier*, fr. *garet* bend of the knee, of Celt origin; akin to OIr *gairri* calves of the legs] **1 a** : a band worn to hold up a stocking or sock **b** : a strap hanging from a girdle or corset to support a stocking **c** : a band worn to hold up a shirt sleeve **2** *cap* **a** : the British Order of the Garter **b** : the blue velvet garter that is its badge **c** : membership in the order

²**garter** *vt* : to support with or as if with a garter

garter snake *n* : any of numerous harmless viviparous American snakes (genus *Thamnophis*) with longitudinal stripes on the back

garth \'gärth\ *n* [ME, fr. ON *garthr* yard; akin to OHG *gart* enclosure — more at YARD] *archaic* : a small yard or enclosure

gar·vey \'gär-vē\ *n* : a small scow of the New Jersey coast

¹**gas** \'gas\ *n, pl* **gas·es** *also* **gas·ses** [NL, alter. of *chaos* air, fr. L, chaos] **1** : a fluid (as air) that has neither independent shape nor volume but tends to expand indefinitely **2 a** : a gas or gaseous mixture with the exception of atmospheric air: as (1) : a gas or gaseous mixture used to produce anesthesia (2) : a combustible gaseous mixture (as for fuel) **b** : a substance that can be used to produce a poisonous, asphyxiating, or irritant atmosphere **3** *slang* : empty talk : BOMBAST **4** : GASOLINE

²**gas** *vb* **gassed; gas·sing** *vt* **1 a** : to treat chemically with gas **b** : to poison with gas **2** *slang* : to address with idle talk **3** : to supply with gas or esp. gasoline ⟨~ up the automobile⟩ ~ *vi* **1** : to give off gas **2** *slang* : to talk idly **3** : to fill the tank (as of an automobile) with gasoline — often used with *up*

gas·bag \'gas-,bag\ *n* **1** : a bag for holding gas **2** : an idle talker

gas·boat \'gas-,bōt\ *n* : a boat powered by a converted automobile engine

gas chamber *n* : a chamber in which prisoners are executed by poison gas

gas·con \'gas-kən\ *n* **1** *cap* : a native of Gascony **2** : a boastful swaggering person — **Gascon** *adj*

gas·con·ade \,gas-kə-'nād\ *n* [F *gasconnade*, fr. *gasconner* to boast, fr. *gascon* gascon, boaster] : BOASTING, BRAVADO — **gasconade** *vi* — **gas·con·ad·er** *n*

gas·eous \'gas-ē-əs, 'gash-əs\ *adj* **1 a** : having the form of or being gas; *also* : of or relating to gases **b** : SUPERHEATED **2** : lacking substance or solidity : TENUOUS — **gas·eous·ness** *n*

gas fitter *n* : a workman who installs or repairs gas pipes and appliances

¹**gash** \'gash\ *vb* [ME *garsen*, fr. ONF *garser*, fr. (assumed) VL *charissare*, fr. Gk *charassein* to scratch, engrave] *vt* : to make a long deep cut in ~ *vi* : to make a gash : CUT — **gash** *n*

²**gash** *adj* [origin unknown] **1** *chiefly Scot* : KNOWING, WITTY **2** *chiefly Scot* : well dressed : TRIM

gas·hold·er \'gas-,hōl-dər\ *n* : a container for gas; *esp* : a large cylindrical tank for storing fuel gas under pressure commonly having two parts one of which telescopes into the other

gas·house \-,haủs\ *n* : GASWORKS

gas·ifi·ca·tion \,gas-ə-fə-'kā-shən\ *n* : the act or process of gasifying

gas·ify \'gas-ə-,fī\ *vt* : to convert into gas ~ *vi* : to become gaseous

gas·ket \'gas-kət\ *n* [prob. alter. of F *garcette*] **1** : a line or band used to lash a furled sail **2 a** : plaited hemp or tallowed rope for packing pistons or making pipe or other joints fluid-tight **b** : packing for the same purpose made of other material (as rubber)

gas·kin \'gas-kən\ *n* [prob. short for *galligaskins*] **1** *obs* : HOSE, BREECHES **2** : a part of the hind leg of a quadruped between the stifle and the hock

gas·light \'gas-,līt\ *n* **1** : light made by burning illuminating gas **2** : a gas flame or gas lighting fixture

gas·lit \-,lit\ *adj* : illuminated by gaslight

gas log *n* : a hollow perforated imitation log used as a gas burner in a fireplace

gas mask *n* : a mask connected to a chemical air filter and used to protect the face and lungs against poison gases; *broadly* : RESPIRATOR 1

gas·ogene \'gas-ə-,jēn\ *n* [F *gazogène*, fr. *gaz* gas (fr. NL *gas*) + *-o-* + *-gène* -gen] **1** : an apparatus carried by a vehicle to produce gas for fuel by partial burning of charcoal or wood **2** : a portable apparatus for carbonating liquids

gas oil *n* : a hydrocarbon oil used as a fuel oil; *esp* : a petroleum distillate intermediate in boiling range and viscosity between kerosine and lubricating oil

gas·olier \,gas-ə-'li(ə)r\ *n* [alter. of *gaselier*, fr. *gas* + *-elier* (as in *chandelier*)] : a gaslight chandelier

gas·o·line *or* **gas·o·lene** \,gas-ə-'lēn, 'gas-ə-,lēn\ *n* [¹*gas* + *-ol* + *-ine* or *-ene*] : a volatile flammable liquid hydrocarbon mixture used as a fuel esp. for internal-combustion engines and blended from several products of natural gas and petroleum — **gas·o·lin·ic** \,gas-ə-'lē-nik, -'lin-ik\ *adj*

gas·om·e·ter \ga-'säm-ət-ər\ *n* [F *gazomètre*, fr. *gaz* + *-o-* + *-mètre* -meter] **1** : a laboratory apparatus for holding and measuring gases **2** : GASHOLDER

gasp \'gasp\ *vb* [ME *gaspen*; akin to ON *geispa* to yawn] *vi* **1** : to catch the breath with shock or other emotion **2** : to breathe laboriously : PANT ~ *vt* : to utter in a gasping manner — **gasp** *n*

gasp·er \'gas-pər\ *n, slang Brit* : CIGARETTE

gas plant *n* : FRAXINELLA

gas·ser \'gas-ər\ *n* **1** : an oil well that yields gas **2** *slang* : a talkative person **3** *slang* : something outstanding

gas·si·ness \'gas-ē-nəs\ *n* : the quality or state of being gassy

gas station *n* : FILLING STATION

gas·sy \'gas-ē\ *adj* **1** : full of or containing gas **2** : having the characteristics of gas **3** : WINDY, FLATULENT

gast \'gast\ *vt* [ME *gasten*, fr. *gast*, *gost* ghost] *obs* : SCARE

gaster- *or* **gastero-** *comb form* [NL, fr. Gk *gastero-* belly, fr. *gastr-*, *gaster-*, *gastēr*] : ventral area ⟨*Gastero*poda⟩

gas·tight \'gas-'tīt\ *adj* : impervious to gas — **gas·tight·ness** *n*

gast·ness \'gas(t)-nəs\ *n, obs* : FRIGHT, TERROR

gastr- *or* **gastro-** *also* **gastri-** *comb form* [Gk, fr. *gastr-*, *gastēr*] **1** : belly ⟨*Gastro*poda⟩ : stomach ⟨*gastr*itis⟩ **2** : gastric and ⟨*gastro*intestinal⟩

gas·traea *also* **gas·trea** \ga-'strē-ə\ *n* [NL, fr. Gk *gastr-*, *gastēr*] : a hypothetical metazoan ancestral form corresponding in organization to a simple invaginated gastrula — **gas·trae·al** \-əl\ *adj*

gas·tral \'gas-trəl\ *adj* : of or relating to the stomach or digestive tract

gas·trec·to·my \ga-'strek-tə-mē\ *n* [ISV] : surgical removal of all or part of the stomach

gas·tric \'gas-trik\ *adj* [Gk *gastr-*, *gastēr*, alter. of (assumed) Gk *grastēr*, fr. Gk *gran* to gnaw, eat] : of or relating to the stomach

gastric juice *n* : a thin watery acid digestive fluid secreted by glands in the mucous membrane of the stomach

gastric ulcer *n* : a peptic ulcer situated in the stomach

gas·trin \'gas-trən\ *n* : a hormone probably identical with histamine that induces secretion of gastric juice

gas·tri·tis \ga-'strīt-əs\ *n* : inflammation esp. of the mucous membrane of the stomach

gas·tro·coel *also* **gas·tro·coele** \'gas-trə-,sēl\ *n* [F *gastrocèle*, fr. *gastr-* + *-cèle* -coele] : ARCHENTERON

gas·tro·en·ter·ol·o·gist \,gas-(,)trō-,ent-ə-'räl-ə-jəst\ *n* : a specialist in gastroenterology

gas·tro·en·ter·ol·o·gy \-jē\ *n* [ISV] : the study of the diseases and pathology of the stomach and intestines

gas·tro·gen·ic \,gas-trə-'jen-ik\ *or* **gas·trog·e·nous** \ga-'sträj-ə-nəs\ *adj* : of gastric origin ⟨~ anemia⟩

gas·tro·in·tes·ti·nal \,gas-(,)trō-in-'tes-tən-ᵊl\ *adj* : of or relating to both stomach and intestine

gas·tro·nome \'gas-trə-,nōm\ *n* [F, back-formation fr. *gastronomie*] : EPICURE, GOURMET

gas·tro·nom·ic \,gas-trə-'näm-ik\ *adj* : of or relating to gastronomy — **gas·tro·nom·i·cal** \-i-kəl\ *adj* — **gas·tro·nom·i·cal·ly** \-i-k(ə-)lē\ *adv*

gas·tron·o·mist \ga-'strän-ə-məst\ *n* : GASTRONOME

gas·tron·o·my \-mē\ *n* [F *gastronomie*, fr. Gk *Gastronomia*, title of a 4th cent. B.C. poem, fr. *gastro-* belly + *-nomia* -nomy] **1** : good eating or its lore **2** : culinary customs or style

gas·tro·pod \'gas-trə-,päd\ *n* [NL *Gastropoda*, class name] : any of a large class (Gastropoda) of mollusks (as snails) often with a univalve shell and usu. a distinct head bearing sensory organs — **gastropod** *also* **gas·trop·o·dan** \ga-'sträp-əd-ən\ *or* **gas·trop·o·dous** \-əd-əs\ *adj*

gas·tro·scope \'gas-trə-,skōp\ *n* [ISV] : an instrument for viewing the interior of the stomach — **gas·tro·scop·ic** \,gas-trə-'skäp-ik\ *adj* — **gas·tros·co·pist** \ga-'sträs-kə-pəst\ *n* — **gas·tros·co·py** \-pē\ *n*

gas·tro·trich \'gas-trə-,trik\ *n* [deriv. of Gk *gastr-* + *trich-*, *thrix* hair — more at TRICH-] : any of a small group (Gastrotricha) of minute freshwater multicellular animals superficially resembling infusorians — **gas·trot·ri·chan** \ga-'strä-tri-kən\ *adj or n*

gas·tro·vas·cu·lar \,gas-(,)trō-'vas-kyə-lər\ *adj* [ISV] : functioning in both digestion and circulation

gas·tru·la \'gas-trə-lə\ *n, pl* **gastrulas** *or* **gas·tru·lae** \-,lē, -,lī\ [NL, fr. *gastr-*] : an early metazoan embryo consisting of a hollow 2-layered cellular cup made up of an outer epiblast and an inner hypoblast that meet along the marginal line of a blastopore and jointly enclose the archenteron — **gas·tru·lar** \-lər\ *adj*

gas·tru·late \-,lāt\ *vi* : to become or form a gastrula — **gas·tru·la·tion** \,gas-trə-'lā-shən\ *n*

gas turbine *n* : an engine in which turbine blades are driven by hot gases whose pressure and velocity are intensified by compressed air introduced into the combustion chamber

gas·works \'gas-,wərks\ *n pl but sing in constr* : a plant for manufacturing gas

¹**gat** \(')gat\ *archaic past of* GET

²**gat** \'gat\ *n* [prob. fr. D, lit., hole; akin to OE *geat*] : a natural or artificial channel or passage

³**gat** *n* [short for *Gatling gun*] *slang* : PISTOL

¹**gate** \'gāt\ *n, often attrib* [ME, fr. OE *geat*; akin to ON *gat* opening, Gk *chezein* to defecate] **1** : an opening in a wall or fence **2** : a city or castle entrance often with towers or other defensive structures **3** : the frame or door that closes a gate **4 a** : a means of entrance or exit **b** : a pass or defile in mountains **c** : an opening between two markers through which a skier must pass in a slalom race **5 a** : a door, valve, or other device for controlling the passage esp. of fluid **b** : a signal that makes an electronic circuit operative for a short period **6** : a channel in a foundry mold through which the molten metal flows into the cavity made by the pattern **7** : the total admission receipts or the number of spectators at a sports event **8** *slang* : DISMISSAL ⟨gave him the ~⟩ — **gate·keep·er** \-,kē-pər\ *n* — **gate·way** \'gāt-,wā\ *n*

²**gate** *vt* **1** : to supply with a gate **2** *Brit* : CAMPUS **3** : to control by means of a gate

ə abut; ᵊ kitten; ər further; a back; ā bake; ä cot, cart; aủ out; ch chin; e less; ē easy; g gift; i trip; ī life
j joke; ŋ sing; ō flow; ȯ flaw; ȯi coin; th thin; th this; ü loot; ủ foot; y yet; yü few; yủ furious; zh vision

[3]**gate** *n* [ME, fr. ON *gata* road; akin to OHG *gazza* road] **1** *archaic* **:** WAY, PATH **2** *dial* **:** METHOD, STYLE

gate–crash·er \'gāt-ˌkrash-ər\ *n* **:** one who enters, attends, or participates without ticket or invitation — **gate–crash·ing** \-iŋ\ *n*

gate·fold \-ˌfōld\ *n* **:** a folded insert (as a map) in a book or other publication larger in some dimension than the page

gate·leg table \ˌgāt-ˌleg-, -ˌlāg-\ *n* **:** a table with drop leaves supported by movable paired legs

gate·post \'gāt-ˌpōst\ *n* **:** the post to which a gate is hung or the one against which it closes

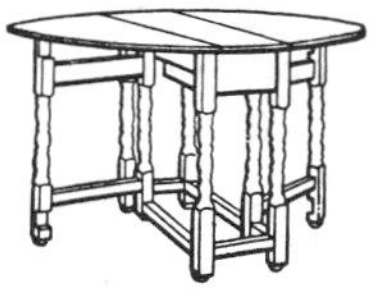
gateleg table

[1]**gath·er** \'gath-ər, 'geth-\ *vb* **gath·er·ing** \-(ə-)riŋ\ [ME *gaderen*, fr. OE *gaderian;* akin to Skt *gadh* to hold fast — more at GOOD] *vt* **1 :** to bring together **:** COLLECT **2 a :** PICK, HARVEST **b :** to pick up little by little **c :** to gain by gradual increase ⟨~ speed⟩ **d :** to accumulate and place in order or readiness ⟨~*ed* up his tools⟩ **e :** to assemble (volume signatures) in sequence for binding **3 :** to serve as a center of attraction for **4 :** to effect the collection of (as tax) **5 a :** to summon up **b :** to prepare (as oneself) by mustering strength **6 a :** to bring together the parts of **b :** to draw about or close to something ⟨~*ing* his cloak about him⟩ **c :** to pull (fabric) along a line of stitching so as to draw into puckers **d :** to haul in **7 :** GUESS, DEDUCE ~ *vi* **1 a :** to come together in a body **b :** to cluster around a focus of attraction **2 a :** to swell and fill with pus **b :** GROW, INCREASE — **gath·er·er** \-ər-ər\ *n*

syn COLLECT, ASSEMBLE, CONGREGATE: GATHER is the most general term for bringing or coming together and lacks definite connotation except when it suggests a picking or harvesting; COLLECT often implies careful selection or orderly arrangement; ASSEMBLE implies an ordered union or organization of persons or things and a definite purpose in their coming or being brought together; CONGREGATE implies a spontaneous flocking together into a crowd or huddle **syn** see in addition INFER

[2]**gather** *n* **1 :** something gathered; *esp* **:** a puckering in cloth made by gathering **2 :** an act or instance of gathering

gath·er·ing *n* **1 a :** ASSEMBLY, MEETING **b :** a suppurating swelling **:** ABSCESS **2 :** the collecting of food and raw materials from the wild **3 :** COLLECTION, COMPILATION **4 :** a gather in cloth

Gat·ling gun \ˌgat-liŋ-\ *n* [Richard J. *Gatling* †1903 Am inventor] **:** an early machine gun with a revolving cluster of barrels fired once each per revolution

gauche \'gōsh\ *adj* [F, lit., left] **:** lacking social experience or grace **:** CRUDE **syn** see AWKWARD — **gauche·ness** \'gōsh-nəs\ *n* — **gau·che·rie** \ˌgōsh-(ə-)'rē\ *n*

gau·cho \'gaů-(ˌ)chō\ *n* [AmerSp] **:** a cowboy of the So. American pampas

gaud \'gȯd, 'gäd\ *n* [ME *gaude*] **:** ORNAMENT, TRINKET

gaud·ery \-ə-rē\ *n* **:** showy ornament; *esp* **:** personal finery

gaud·i·ly \'gȯd-ᵊl-ē, 'gäd-\ *adv* **:** in a gaudy manner **:** SHOWILY

gaud·i·ness \'gȯd-ē-nəs, 'gäd-\ *n* **:** SHOWINESS

[1]**gaudy** \-ē\ *adj* **:** ostentatiously or tastelessly ornamented

syn TAWDRY, GARISH, FLASHY, MERETRICIOUS: GAUDY implies a tasteless use of overly bright colors or lavish ornamentation; TAWDRY implies both gaudiness and cheapness of quality; GARISH stresses an unpleasant brightness; FLASHY implies momentarily brilliant performance or display that is likely to prove shallow or vulgar; MERETRICIOUS applies to what is superficially attractive or plausible but lacking sincerity or sound basis

[2]**gau·dy** \'gȯd-ē, 'gäd-\ *n* [prob. fr. L *gaudium* joy — more at JOY] **:** a feast or entertainment esp. in the form of an annual college dinner in a British university

gauf·fer \'gäf-ər, 'gȯf-, 'gōf-\ *var of* GOFFER

[1]**gauge** \'gāj\ *n* [ME *gauge*, fr. ONF] **1 a :** measurement according to some standard or system **b :** DIMENSIONS, SIZE **2 a :** an instrument for measuring or testing **b :** an instrument for measuring a dimension or for testing mechanical accuracy **c :** an instrument with a graduated scale or dial for measuring or indicating quantity **3 :** relative position of a ship with reference to another ship and the wind **4 a :** the distance between the rails of a railroad **b :** the distance between a pair of wheels on an axle **5 :** the quantity of plaster of paris used with mortar to accelerate its setting **6 :** the size of a shotgun expressed as the number of lead balls each just fitting the interior diameter of the barrel required to make a pound ⟨a 12-*gauge* shotgun⟩ **7 a :** the thickness of sheet metal or the diameter of wire, a hypodermic needle, or a screw **b :** the fineness of a knitted fabric in loops per 1½ inch **syn** see STANDARD

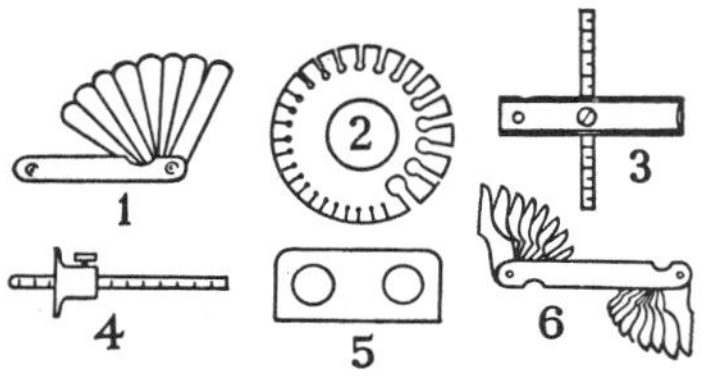

gauges 2b: *1* thickness, *2* wire or sheet metal, *3* depth, *4* marking, *5* go no-go, *6* thread

[2]**gauge** *vt* **1 a :** to measure the size, dimensions, or other measurable quantity of exactly **b :** to determine the capacity or contents of **c :** ESTIMATE, JUDGE **2 a :** to check for conformity to specifications or limits **b :** to measure off or set out **3 :** to mix (plaster) in definite proportions **4 :** to dress (as bricks) to size by rubbing or chipping — **gauge·able** \'gā-jə-bəl\ *adj* — **gauge·ably** \-blē\ *adv*

gaug·er \'gā-jər\ *n* **1 :** one that gauges **2** *chiefly Brit* **:** an exciseman who inspects dutiable bulk goods

Gaul \'gȯl\ *n* **1 :** a Celt of ancient Gaul **2 :** FRENCHMAN

[1]**Gaul·ish** \'gȯ-lish\ *adj* **:** of or relating to the Gauls or their language or land

[2]**Gaulish** *n* **:** the Celtic language of the ancient Gauls

Gaull·ism \'gō-ˌliz-əm\ *n* **1 :** a French political movement during World War II led by Charles de Gaulle in opposition to the Vichy regime **2 :** a postwar French political movement led by Charles de Gaulle — **Gaull·ist** \-ləst\ *n*

gault \'gȯlt\ *n* [prob. of Scand origin; akin to ON *gald* hard-packed snow] **:** a heavy thick clay soil

gaum \'gȯm, 'gäm\ *vt* [perh. alter. of [4]*gum*] *dial* **:** SMUDGE, SMEAR

gaunt \'gȯnt, 'gänt\ *adj* [ME] **1 :** being thin and angular **2 :** attenuated by suffering or weariness **3 :** BARREN, DESOLATE **syn** see LEAN — **gaunt·ly** *adv* — **gaunt·ness** *n*

[1]**gaunt·let** \'gȯnt-lət, 'gänt-\ *n* [ME, fr. MF *gantelet*, dim. of *gant* glove, of Gmc origin; akin to MD *want* mitten, ON *vöttr* gloves] **1 :** a glove to protect the hand worn with medieval armor **2 :** any of various protective gloves used esp. in industry **3 :** a challenge to combat with **4 :** a dress glove extending above the wrist — **gaunt·let·ed** \-lət-əd\ *adj*

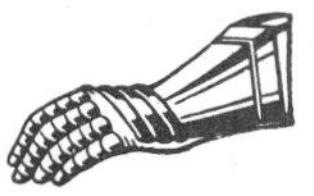
gauntlet 1

[2]**gaunt·let** \'gȯnt-lət, 'gänt-\ *n* [by folk etymology fr. *gantelope*] **1 :** a double file of men facing each other and armed with clubs or other weapons with which to strike at an individual who is made to run between them **2 :** a cross fire of any kind; *also* **:** ORDEAL

gaur \'gaů(ə)r\ *n* [Hindi, fr. Skt *gaura;* akin to Skt *go* bull, cow — more at COW] **:** a large East Indian wild ox (*Bibos gaurus*) with a broad forehead and short thick conical horns

gauss \'gaůs\ *n, pl* **gauss** *also* **gauss·es** [Karl F. *Gauss* †1855 G mathematician] **:** the cgs unit of magnetic induction equal to the magnetic flux density that will induce an electromotive force of one one-hundred millionth of a volt in each linear centimeter of a wire moving laterally with a speed of one centimeter per second at right angles to a magnetic flux

gauze \'gȯz\ *n* [MF *gaze*] **1 a :** a thin often transparent fabric used chiefly for clothing or draperies **b :** a loosely woven cotton surgical dressing **c :** a firm woven fabric of metal or plastic filaments **2 :** HAZE, MIST — **gauze·like** \-ˌlīk\ *adj* — **gauz·i·ly** \'gȯ-zə-lē\ *adv* — **gauz·i·ness** \-zē-nəs\ *n* — **gauzy** \-zē\ *adj*

ga·vage \gə-'väzh\ *n* [F] **:** introduction of material into the stomach by a tube

gave *past of* GIVE

[1]**gav·el** \'gav-əl\ *n* [ME, fr. OE *gafol;* akin to OE *giefan* to give] **:** rent or tribute in ancient and medieval England

[2]**gavel** *n* [origin unknown] **1 :** a mason's setting maul **2 :** the mallet of a presiding officer or auctioneer

[3]**gavel** *vt* **gav·eled** *or* **gav·elled; gav·el·ing** *or* **gav·el·ling** \-(ə-)liŋ\ **:** to bring or force by use of a gavel

gav·el·kind \'gav-əl-ˌkīnd\ *n* [ME *gavelkynde*, fr. [1]*gavel* + *kinde* kind] **:** a tenure of land existing chiefly in Kent from Anglo-Saxon times until 1925 and providing for division of an intestate's estate equally among the sons or other heirs

gave·lock \'gav-lək\ *n* [ME *gavelok*, fr. OE *gafeluc*, of Celt origin; akin to W *gaflach* javelin] *dial Brit* **:** an iron crowbar

ga·votte \gə-'vät\ *n* [F, fr. MF, fr. OProv *gavato*] **1 :** a dance of French peasant origin marked by the raising rather than sliding of the feet **2 :** a tune for the gavotte in moderately quick 4/4 time — **gavotte** *vi*

Ga·wain \gə-'wān, 'gä-ˌwān, 'gaů-ən\ *n* **:** a nephew of King Arthur and knight of the Round Table

[1]**gawk** \'gȯk\ *vi* [perh. alter. of obs. *gaw* (to stare)] **:** to gape or stare stupidly

[2]**gawk** *n* [prob. fr. E dial. *gawk* (left-handed)] **:** LOUT

gawk·ish \'gȯ-kish\ *adj* **:** AWKWARD, DULL — **gawk·ish·ly** *adv* — **gawk·ish·ness** *n*

gawky \'gȯ-kē\ *adj* **:** AWKWARD, CLUMSY — **gawky** *n*

gaw·sie *or* **gaw·sy** \'gȯ-sē\ *adj* [origin unknown] *chiefly Scot* **:** prosperous and jolly looking

[1]**gay** \'gā\ *adj* [ME, fr. MF *gai*] **1 :** happily excited **:** MERRY **2 a :** BRIGHT, LIVELY **b :** brilliant in color **3 :** given to social pleasures; *also* **:** LICENTIOUS **4 :** HOMOSEXUAL **syn** see LIVELY — **gay** *adv* — **gay·ness** *n*

[2]**gay** *n* **:** HOMOSEXUAL

gay·ety *var of* GAIETY

gayly *var of* GAILY

ga·za·bo \gə-'zā-(ˌ)bō\ *n* [origin unknown] *slang* **:** FELLOW, GUY

[1]**gaze** \'gāz\ *vi* [ME *gazen*] **:** to fix the eyes in a steady and intent look and often with eagerness or studious attention — **gaz·er** *n*

syn GAZE, GAPE, STARE, GLARE, PEER, GLOAT mean to look (at) long and attentively. GAZE implies fixed and prolonged attention (as in wonder, admiration, or abstractedness); GAPE suggests an openmouthed often stupid wonder; STARE implies a direct open-eyed gazing denoting curiosity, disbelief, insolence; GLARE is a fierce or angry staring; PEER suggests a looking narrowly and curiously as if through a small opening; GLOAT implies a prolonged gazing expressing undue or malignant satisfaction

[2]**gaze** *n* **:** a fixed intent look

ga·ze·bo \gə-'zā-(ˌ)bō, -'zē-\ *n* [perh. fr. [1]*gaze* + L *-ebo* (as in *videbo* I shall see)] **:** BELVEDERE

gaze·hound \'gāz-ˌhaůnd\ *n* **:** a dog that hunts by sight rather than by scent; *esp* **:** GREYHOUND

ga·zelle \gə-'zel\ *n, pl* **gazelles** *also* **gazelle** [F, fr. MF, fr. Ar *ghazāl*] **:** any of numerous small, graceful, and swift African and Asiatic antelopes (of *Gazella* and related genera) noted for their soft lustrous eyes

[1]**ga·zette** \gə-'zet\ *n* [F, fr. It *gazetta*] **1 :** NEWSPAPER **2 :** an official journal **3** *Brit* **:** an announcement in an official gazette

[2]**gazette** *vt* **1** *chiefly Brit* **:** to announce or publish in a gazette **2** *Brit* **:** to announce the appointment or status of in an official gazette

gaz·et·teer \ˌgaz-ə-'ti(ə)r\ *n* **1** *archaic* **:** JOURNALIST, PUBLICIST **2** [*The Gazetteer's: or, Newsman's Interpreter*, a geographical index edited by Laurence Echard] **:** a geographical dictionary

gaz·o·gene \'gaz-ə-ˌjēn\ *var of* GASOGENE

G clef *n* **:** TREBLE CLEF

ge- *or* **geo-** *comb form* [ME *geo-*, fr. MF & L; MF, fr. L, fr. Gk *gē-*, *geō-*, fr. *gē*] **1 :** earth **:** ground **:** soil ⟨*ge*anticline⟩ ⟨*geo*phyte⟩ **2 :** geographical **:** geography and ⟨*geo*politics⟩

-gea — see -GAEA

ge·an·ti·cline \jē-'ant-i-ˌklīn\ *also* **ge·an·ti·cli·nal** \(ˌ)jē-ˌant-i-'klīn-ᵊl\ *n* **:** a great upward flexure of the earth's crust — compare GEOSYNCLINE

[1]**gear** \'gi(ə)r\ *n* [ME *gere*, fr. OE *gearwe;* akin to OHG *garuwi* equipment, clothing, OE *gearu* ready — more at YARE] **1 a :** CLOTHING, GARMENTS **b :** movable property **:** GOODS **2 :** EQUIPMENT, PARAPHERNALIA **3 a :** the rigging of a ship or boat **b :** the harness esp. of horses **4** *dial chiefly Brit* **:** absurd talk **:** NONSENSE **5** *dial chiefly Brit* **:** DOINGS **6 a** (1) **:** a mechanism that performs a specific function in a complete machine ⟨steering ~⟩ (2) **:** a toothed wheel (3) **:** working relation or adjustment ⟨in ~⟩ **b :** one of two or more

adjustments of a motor-vehicle transmission that determine mechanical advantage, relative speed, and direction of travel — **gear·less** \-ləs\ *adj*

2gear *vt* **1 a :** to provide with gearing **b :** to connect by gearing **c :** to put into gear **2 a :** to make ready for effective operation **b :** to adjust so as to match or blend with something ~ *vi* **1** *of machinery* **:** to be in or come into gear **2 :** to become adjusted so as to match or blend

gear·box \'gi(ə)r-,bäks\ *n* **:** TRANSMISSION 3

gear·ing *n* **1 :** the act or process of providing or fitting with gears **2 :** the parts by which motion is transmitted from one portion of machinery to another

gear·shift \'gi(ə)r-,shift\ *n* **:** a mechanism by which the transmission gears in a power-transmission system are engaged and disengaged

gear wheel *n* **:** a toothed wheel that gears with another piece of a mechanism; *specif* **:** COGWHEEL

Geat \'gēt, 'yaət\ *n* [OE *Gēat*] **:** a member of a Scandinavian people of southern Sweden subjugated by the Swedes in the 6th century — **Geat·ish** \-ish\ *adj*

gecko \'gek-(,)ō\ *n, pl* **geck·os** *or* **geck·oes** [Malay *ge'kok*, of imit. origin] **:** any of numerous small harmless chiefly tropical and nocturnal insectivorous lizards (family Gekkonidae)

1gee \'jē\ *v imper* [origin unknown] — used as a direction to turn to the right or move ahead; compare 5HAW ~ *vi* **geed; gee·ing :** to turn to the right side

2gee *n* **1 :** the letter *g* **2** [guy] *slang* **:** MAN, GUY **3** [grand] *slang* **:** a thousand dollars

3gee *interj* [euphemism for *Jesus*] — used as an introductory expletive or to express surprise or enthusiasm

gee·gaw \'jē-(,)gȯ, 'gē-\ *var of* GEWGAW

geek \'gēk\ *n* [prob. fr. E dial. *geek*, *geck* fool, fr. LG *geck*, fr. MLG] **:** a carnival performer often billed as a wild man whose act usu. includes biting the head off a live chicken or snake

geese *pl of* GOOSE

geest \'gāst, 'gēst\ *n* [G] **1 :** alluvial matter not of recent origin on the surface of land **2 :** loose material (as earth or soil) formed by decay of rocks in a place

Ge·ez \gē-'ez\ *n* [Ethiopic *ge'ez*] **:** ETHIOPIC 1

gee·zer \'gē-zər\ *n* [prob. alter. of Sc *guiser* (one in disguise)] *slang* **:** a queer, odd, or eccentric man

ge·fil·te fish \gə-'fil-tə-,\ *n* [Yiddish, lit., filled fish] **:** a Jewish dish of stewed or baked fish stuffed with a mixture of the fish flesh, bread crumbs, eggs, and seasoning or prepared as balls or oval cakes boiled in a fish stock

ge·gen·schein \'gā-gən-,shīn\ *n, often cap* [G, fr. *gegen* against, counter- + *schein* shine] **:** a faint light about 20° across on the celestial sphere opposite the sun probably associated in origin with the zodiacal light

Ge·hen·na \gi-'hen-ə\ *n* [LL, fr. Gk *Geenna*, fr. Heb *Gê' Hinnōm*, lit., valley of Hinnom] **1 :** HELL 1a(2) **2 :** a place or state of misery

Gei·ger counter \,gī-gər-'\ *or* **Gei·ger–Mül·ler counter** \-'myül-ər-, , -'mil-, -'məl-\ *n* [Hans *Geiger* †1945 G physicist and W. *Müller*, 20th cent. G physicist] **1 :** GEIGER-MÜLLER TUBE **2 :** an instrument consisting of a Geiger-Müller tube and the electronic equipment used in conjunction with it to record the momentary current pulsations in the tube gas

Geiger–Müller tube *or* **Geiger tube** *n* [H. *Geiger* and W. *Müller*] **:** a gas-filled counting tube with a cylindrical cathode and axial wire electrode for detecting the presence of cosmic rays or radioactive substances by means of the ionizing particles that penetrate its envelope and set up momentary current pulsations in the gas

gei·sha \'gā-shə, 'gē-\ *n, pl* **geisha** *or* **geishas** [Jap, fr. *gei* art + *-sha* person] **:** a Japanese girl who is trained to provide entertaining and lighthearted company esp. for a man or a group of men

1gel \'jel\ *n* [*gelatin*] **:** a colloid in a more solid form than a sol

2gel *vi* **gelled; gel·ling :** to change into or take on the form of a gel — **gel·able** \'jel-ə-bəl\ *adj*

ge·län·de·sprung \gə-'len-də-,s(h)prüŋ\ *n* [G, fr. *gelände* open field + *sprung* jump] **:** a jump in skiing made from a low crouching position with the aid of both ski poles and usu. over an obstacle

gel·ate \'jel-,āt\ *vi* **:** GEL

gel·a·tin *also* **gel·a·tine** \'jel-ət-ᵊn\ *n* [F *gélatine* edible jelly, gelatin, fr. It *gelatina*, fr. *gelato*, pp. of *gelare* to freeze, fr. L — more at COLD] **1 :** glutinous material obtained from animal tissues by boiling; *esp* **:** a colloidal protein used as a food, in photography, and in medicine **2 a :** any of various substances resembling gelatin **b :** an edible jelly formed with gelatin **c :** a thin colored transparent sheet used to color a stage light

ge·la·ti·ni·za·tion \jə-,lat-ᵊn-ə-'zā-shən, ,jel-ə-tə-nə-\ *n* **:** the process of gelatinizing

ge·la·ti·nize \jə-'lat-ᵊn-,īz, 'jel-ə-tə-,nīz\ *vt* **1 :** to convert into a gelatinous form or into a jelly **2 :** to coat or treat with gelatin ~ *vi* **:** to become gelatinous or change into a jelly

ge·lat·i·nous \jə-'lat-nəs, -ᵊn-əs\ *adj* **1 :** resembling gelatin or jelly **:** VISCOUS ⟨a ~ precipitate⟩ **2 :** of, relating to, or containing gelatin — **ge·lat·i·nous·ly** *adv* — **ge·lat·i·nous·ness** *n*

1ge·la·tion \ji-'lā-shən\ *n* [L *gelation-, gelatio*, fr. *gelatus*, pp. of *gelare*] **:** the action or process of freezing

2ge·la·tion \je-'lā-shən\ *n* [1*gel* + *-ation*] **:** the formation of a gel from a sol

1geld \'geld\ *vt* [ME *gelden*, fr. ON *gelda;* akin to OE *gelte* young sow, Gk *gallos* eunuch, priest of Cybele] **1 :** CASTRATE; *also* **:** SPAY **2 a :** DEPRIVE **b :** to lessen the force of **c :** EXPURGATE

2geld *n* [OE *gield*, *geld* service, tribute; akin to OE *gieldan* to pay, yield] **:** the crown tax paid under Anglo-Saxon and Norman kings

geld·ing \'gel-diŋ\ *n* [ME, fr. ON *geldingr*, fr. *gelda*] **1 :** a castrated animal; *specif* **:** a castrated male horse **2 :** EUNUCH

gel·id \'jel-əd\ *adj* [L *gelidus*, fr. *gelu* frost, cold] **:** extremely cold **:** ICY — **ge·lid·i·ty** \jə-'lid-ət-ē, je-\ *n* — **gel·id·ly** *adv*

gel·ig·nite \'jel-ig-,nīt\ *n* [*gelatin* + L *ignis* fire + E *-ite* — more at IGNITE] **:** a dynamite in which the adsorbent base is largely potassium nitrate or a similar nitrate usu. with some wood pulp

gelt \'gelt\ *n* [D & G *geld* & Yiddish *gelt;* all akin to OE *geld* service, tribute] *slang* **:** MONEY

1gem \'jem\ *n* [ME *gemme*, fr. MF, fr. L *gemma* bud, gem] **1 a :** JEWEL **b :** a precious or sometimes semiprecious stone cut and polished for ornament **2 a :** something prized esp. for great beauty or perfection **b :** a highly prized or well-beloved person **3 :** MUFFIN

2gem *vt* **gemmed; gem·ming :** to adorn with or as if with gems

Ge·ma·ra \gə-'mär-ə, -'mȯr-\ *n* [Aram *gĕmārā* completion] **:** a commentary on the Mishnah forming the second part of the Talmud — **Ge·ma·ric** \-ik\ *adj* — **Ge·ma·rist** \-əst\ *n*

1gem·i·nate \'jem-ə-nət, -,nāt\ *adj* [L *geminatus*, pp. of *geminare* to double, fr. *geminus* twin] **:** arranged in pairs **:** DUPLICATE — **gem·i·nate·ly** *adv*

2gem·i·nate \-,nāt\ *vt* **:** DOUBLE ~ *vi* **:** to become double or paired — **gem·i·na·tion** \,jem-ə-'nā-shən\ *n*

Gem·i·ni \'jem-ə-(,)nē, -,nī; 'gem-ə-,nē\ *n pl but sing in constr* [L (gen. *Geminorum*), lit., the twins (Castor and Pollux)] **1 :** the 3d zodiacal constellation pictorially represented as the twins Castor and Pollux sitting together and located on the opposite side of the Milky Way from Taurus and Orion **2 :** the 3d sign of the zodiac

gem·ma \'jem-ə\ *n, pl* **gem·mae** \-,ē\ [L] **:** BUD; *broadly* **:** an asexual reproductive body that becomes detached from a parent plant — **gem·ma·ceous** \je-'mā-shəs\ *adj* — **gem·ma·tion** \-shən\ *n*

gem·mate \'jem-,āt\ *adj* **1 :** having gemmae **2 :** reproducing by a bud

gem·mip·a·rous \je-'mip-ə-rəs\ *adj* **:** producing or reproducing by buds — **gem·mip·a·rous·ly** *adv*

gem·mo·log·i·cal *or* **gem·olog·i·cal** \,jem-ə-'läj-i-kəl\ *adj* **:** of or relating to a gem or gemmology

gem·mol·o·gist *or* **gem·ol·o·gist** \je-'mäl-ə-jəst\ *n* **:** a specialist in gems

gem·mol·o·gy *or* **gem·ol·o·gy** \-jē\ *n* [L *gemma* gem] **:** the science of gems

gem·mu·la·tion \,jem-yə-'lā-shən\ *n* **:** formation of or reproduction by gemmules

gem·mule \'jem-(,)yü(ə)l\ *n* [F, fr. L *gemmula*, dim. of *gemma* bud] **:** a small bud: **a :** a minute particle held in the theory of pangenesis to mediate the production in a new individual of cells like that in which it originated **b :** an internal resistant reproductive bud (as of a sponge) — **gem·mu·lif·er·ous** \,jem-yü-'lif-(ə-)rəs\ *adj*

gem·my \'jem-ē\ *adj* **1 :** having the characteristics desired in a gemstone **2 :** GLITTERING, BRIGHT

ge·mot *or* **ge·mote** \gə-'mōt\ *n* [OE *gemōt*, fr. *ge-* (perfective prefix) + *mōt* assembly — more at CO-, MOOT] **:** a judicial or legislative assembly in England before the Norman conquest

gems·bok \'gemz-,bäk\ *n* [Afrik, lit., male chamois, fr. G *gemsbock*, fr. *gems* chamois + *bock* male goat] **:** a large and strikingly marked oryx (*Oryx gazella*) formerly abundant in southern Africa

gem·stone \'jem-,stōn\ *n* **:** a mineral or petrified material that can when cut and polished be used in jewelry

1gen- *or* **geno-** *comb form* [Gk *genos* birth, race, kind — more at KIN] **1 :** race ⟨*geno*cide⟩ **2 :** gene **:** kind ⟨*geno*type⟩

2gen- *or* **geno-** *comb form* **:** gene ⟨*geno*cline⟩

-gen \jən *also esp when two unstressed syllables precede* ,jen\ *also* **-gene** \,jēn\ *n comb form* [F *-gène*, fr. Gk *-genēs* born; akin to Gk *genos* birth] **1 :** producer ⟨andro*gen*⟩ **2 :** one that is (so) produced ⟨culti*gen*⟩ ⟨phos*gene*⟩

gen·darme \'zhän-,därm, 'jän-\ *n* [F, fr. MF, back-formation fr. *gensdarmes*, pl. of *gent d'armes*, lit., armed people] **1 :** one of a body of soldiers esp. in France serving as an armed police force for the maintenance of public order **2** *slang* **:** POLICEMAN

gen·dar·mer·ie *or* **gen·dar·mery** \jän-'där(r)m-ə-rē, zhän-\ *n* [MF *gendarmerie*, fr. *gendarme*] **:** a body of gendarmes

1gen·der \'jen-dər\ *n* [ME *gendre*, fr. MF *genre, gendre*, fr. L *gener-, genus* birth, race, kind, gender — more at KIN] **1 :** SEX **2 a :** any of two or more subclasses within a grammatical class of a language (as noun, pronoun, adjective, verb) that are partly arbitrary but also partly based on distinguishable characteristics such as shape, social rank, manner of existence, or sex and that determine agreement with and selection of other words or grammatical forms **b :** membership of a word or a grammatical form in such a subclass **c :** an inflectional form showing membership in such a subclass

2gender *vb* **gen·der·ing** \-d(ə-)riŋ\ [ME *gendren*, fr. MF *gendrer*, fr. L *generare* — more at GENERATE] **:** ENGENDER

gene \'jēn\ *n* [G *gen*, short for *pangen*, fr. *pan-* + *-gen*] **:** an element of the germ plasm that transmits a hereditary character and forms a specific part of a self-perpetuating deoxyribonucleic acid in the cell nucleus

ge·ne·a·log·i·cal \,jē-nē-ə-'läj-i-kəl, ,jen-ē-\ *adj* **:** of or relating to genealogy — **ge·ne·a·log·i·cal·ly** \-i-k(ə-)lē\ *adv*

ge·ne·al·o·gist \,jē-nē-'äl-ə-jəst, ,jen-ē-, -'al-\ *n* **:** a person who traces or studies the descent of persons or families

ge·ne·al·o·gy \-jē\ *n* [ME *genealogie*, fr. MF, fr. LL *genealogia*, fr. Gk, fr. *genea* race, family + *-logia* -logy; akin to Gk *genos* race] **1 :** an account of the descent of a person, family, or group from an ancestor or from older forms **2 :** regular descent of a person, family, or group of organisms from a progenitor or older form **:** PEDIGREE **3 :** the study of family pedigrees

gene mutation *n* **:** mutation due to fundamental intramolecular reorganization of a gene

genera *pl of* GENUS

gen·er·a·ble \'jen-(ə-)rə-bəl\ *adj* **:** capable of being generated

1gen·er·al \'jen-(ə-)rəl\ *adj* [ME, fr. MF, fr. L *generalis*, fr. *gener-, genus* kind, class — more at KIN] **1 :** involving or applicable to the whole **2 :** involving, relating to, or applicable to every member of a class, kind, or group **3 a :** applicable to or characteristic of the majority of individuals involved **:** PREVALENT **b :** concerned or dealing with universal rather than particular aspects **4 :** relating to, determined by, or concerned with main elements rather than limited details ⟨bearing a ~ resemblance to the original⟩ **5 :** not confined by specialization or careful limitation **6 :** belonging to the common nature of a group of like individuals **:** GENERIC **7 :** holding superior rank **syn** see UNIVERSAL

2general *n* **1 :** something that involves or is applicable to the whole **2** *archaic* **:** the general public **:** PEOPLE **3 :** SUPERIOR GENERAL **4 a :** GENERAL OFFICER **b (1) :** a commissioned officer in the army or air force ranking above a lieutenant general and below a general of the army or a general of the air force **(2) :** a commis-

sioned officer of the highest rank in the marine corps — **in general** : for the most part : GENERALLY

general assembly *n* **1 :** the highest governing body in a religious denomination (as the United Presbyterian Church) **2 :** a legislative assembly; *esp* **:** a U.S. state legislature **3** *cap G&A* **:** the supreme deliberative body of the United Nations

General Court *n* **:** a legislative assembly; *specif* **:** the state legislature in Massachusetts and New Hampshire

general delivery *n* **:** a department of a post office that handles the delivery of mail at a post office window to persons who call for it

general election *n* **:** an election usu. held at regular intervals in which candidates are chosen in all or most constituencies of a nation or state

gen•er•a•lis•si•mo \,jen-(ə-)rə-'lis-ə-,mō\ *n, pl* **generalissimos** [It, fr. *generale* general] **:** the chief commander of an army **:** COMMANDER IN CHIEF

gen•er•al•ist \'jen-(ə-)rə-ləst\ *n* **:** one who is conversant with several different fields or aptitudes

gen•er•al•i•ty \,jen-ə-'ral-ət-ē\ *n* **1 :** the quality or state of being general **2 a :** GENERALIZATION 2 **b :** a vague or inadequate statement **3 :** the greatest part **:** BULK

gen•er•al•iza•tion \,jen-(ə-)rə-lə-'zā-shən\ *n* **1 :** the act or process of generalizing **2 :** a general statement, law, principle, or proposition

gen•er•al•ize \'jen-(ə-)rə-,līz\ *vt* **1 :** to give a general form to **2 a :** to derive or induce (a general conception or principle) from particulars **b :** to draw a general conclusion from **3 :** to give general applicability to ⟨~ a law⟩; *also* **:** to make indefinite ~ *vi* **1 :** to form generalizations; *also* **:** to make vague or indefinite statements **2 :** to extend throughout the body — **gen•er•al•iz•er** *n*

gen•er•al•ized *adj* **:** made general; *esp* **:** not highly differentiated biologically nor strictly adapted to a particular environment

gen•er•al•ly \'jen-(ə-)rə-lē, 'jen-ər-lē\ *adv* **:** in a general manner: as **a :** in disregard of specific instances and with regard to an overall picture ⟨~ speaking⟩ **b :** as a rule **:** USUALLY

general officer *n* **:** any of the officers in the army, air force, or marine corps above colonel

general of the air force : a general of the highest rank in the air force whose insignia is five stars

general of the army : a general of the highest rank in the army whose insignia is five stars

general order *n* **1 :** any of the orders that include permanent directive matter issued by a military headquarters **2 :** any of the permanent military guard orders that govern the duties of a sentry

general paresis *n* **:** insanity caused by syphilitic alteration of the brain that leads to dementia and paralysis

general practitioner *n* **:** a physician or veterinarian who does not limit his practice to a specialty

general-purpose *adj* **:** suitable to be used for two or more basic purposes

general semantics *n pl but sing or pl in constr* **:** a doctrine and educational discipline intended to improve habits of response of human beings to their environment and one another esp. by training in the more critical use of words and other symbols

gen•er•al•ship \'jen-(ə-)rəl-,ship\ *n* **1 :** office or tenure of office of a general **2 :** military skill in a high commander **3 :** LEADERSHIP

general staff *n* **:** a group of officers in an army division or similar or larger unit who assist their commander in planning, coordinating, and supervising operations

general store *n* **:** a retail store that carries a wide variety of goods but is not divided into departments

general will *n* **:** the collective will of a community that is the embodiment or expression of its common interest

gen•er•ate \'jen-ə-,rāt\ *vt* [L *generatus*, pp. of *generare*, fr. *gener-*, *genus* birth — more at KIN] **:** to bring into existence: as **a :** PROCREATE, BEGET **b :** to originate by a vital or chemical process **:** PRODUCE **c :** to trace out mathematically by a moving point, line, or surface — **gen•er•a•tive** \-ə-,rāt-iv, -(ə-)rət-\ *adj*

gen•er•a•tion \,jen-ə-'rā-shən\ *n* **1 a :** a body of living beings constituting a single step in the line of descent from an ancestor **b :** a group of individuals born and living contemporaneously **c :** a group of individuals having contemporaneously a status (as that of students in a school) which each one holds only for a limited period **d :** a type or class of objects developed from an earlier type **2 :** the average span of time between the birth of parents and that of their offspring **3 a :** the act or process of producing offspring **:** PROCREATION **b :** origination by a mathematical, chemical, or other process **:** PRODUCTION; *specif* **:** formation of a geometrical figure by motion of another **c :** the process of coming into being

generative cell *n* **:** a sexual reproductive cell **:** GAMETE

gen•er•a•tor \'jen-ə-,rāt-ər\ *n* **1 :** one that generates **2 :** an apparatus in which vapor or gas is formed **3 :** a machine by which mechanical energy is changed into electrical energy **4 :** GENERATRIX

gen•er•a•trix \,jen-ə-'rā-triks\ *n, pl* **gen•er•a•tri•ces** \-trə-,sēz, -ə-rə-'trī-(,)sēz\ **:** a point, line, or surface whose motion generates a line, surface, or solid

ge•ner•ic \jə-'ner-ik\ *adj* [F *générique*, fr. L *gener-*, *genus* birth, kind, class] **1 a :** relating to or characteristic of a whole group or class **:** GENERAL **b :** not protected by trademark registration **2 :** relating to or having the rank of a biological genus **syn** see UNIVERSAL — **ge•ner•i•cal•ly** \-i-k(ə-)lē\ *adv*

gen•er•os•i•ty \,jen-ə-'räs-ət-ē, -'räs-tē\ *n* **1 a :** liberality in spirit or act; *esp* **:** liberality in giving **b :** a generous act **2 :** ABUNDANCE

gen•er•ous \'jen-(ə-)rəs\ *adj* [MF or L; MF *genereus*, fr. L *generosus*, fr. *gener-*, *genus* birth, family] **1** *archaic* **:** HIGHBORN **2 a :** characterized by a noble or forbearing spirit **:** MAGNANIMOUS, KINDLY **b :** liberal in giving **:** OPENHANDED **c :** marked by abundance or ample proportions **:** COPIOUS **d :** full flavored ⟨~ wine⟩ **syn** see LIBERAL — **gen•er•ous•ly** *adv* — **gen•er•ous•ness** *n*

gen•e•sis \'jen-ə-səs\ *n, pl* **gen•e•ses** \-ə-,sēz\ [L, fr. Gk, fr. *gignesthai* to be born — more at KIN] **:** the origin or coming into being of something

gen•et \'jen-ət\ *n* [ME *genete*, fr. MF, fr. Ar *jarnayt*] **:** any of several small Old World carnivorous mammals (genus *Genetta*) related to the civets but with scent glands less developed and claws fully retractile

ge•net•ic \jə-'net-ik\ *adj* [*genesis*] **1 :** relating to or determined by the origin, development, or causal antecedents of something **2 a :** of, relating to, or involving genetics **b :** GENIC — **ge•net•i•cal** \-i-kəl\ *adj* — **ge•net•i•cal•ly** \-i-k(ə-)lē\ *adv*

-ge•net•ic \jə-'net-ik\ *adj comb form* **:** -GENIC 1, 2 ⟨psycho*genetic*⟩ ⟨spermato*genetic*⟩

genetic code *n* **:** the self-reproducing record of the specific protein pattern of an organism which is apparently stored in the nuclear deoxyribonucleic acid

ge•net•i•cist \jə-'net-ə-səst\ *n* **:** a specialist in genetics

ge•net•ics \jə-'net-iks\ *n pl but sing in constr* **1 a :** a branch of biology that deals with the heredity and variation of organisms and with the mechanisms by which these are effected **b :** a treatise or textbook on this subject **2 :** the genetic makeup and phenomena of an organism, type, group, or condition **3 :** GENESIS

ge•ne•va \jə-'nē-və\ *n* [modif. of obs. D *genever* (now *jenever*), lit., juniper, deriv. of L *juniperus*] **:** a strongly alcoholic liquor flavored with juniper berries and made in the Netherlands

Ge•ne•va bands \jə-,nē-və-\ *n pl* [*Geneva*, Switzerland; fr. their use by the Calvinist clergy of Geneva] **:** two strips of white cloth suspended from the front of a clerical collar and sometimes used by Protestant clergymen

Geneva convention *n* **:** one of a series of agreements concerning the treatment of prisoners of war and of the sick, wounded, and dead in battle first made at Geneva, Switzerland, in 1864 and subsequently accepted in later revisions by the majority of nations

Geneva cross *n* [fr. its adoption by the Geneva convention] **:** RED CROSS

Geneva gown *n* [fr. its use by the Calvinist clergy of Geneva] **:** a loose large-sleeved black academic gown widely used as a vestment by Protestant clergymen

Ge•ne•van \jə-'nē-vən\ *adj* **1 :** of or relating to Geneva, Switzerland **2 :** CALVINISTIC — **Genevan** *n*

[1]**ge•nial** \'jē-nyəl, -nē-əl\ *adj* [L *genialis*, fr. *genius*] **1** *obs* **:** of or relating to marriage or generation **2 a :** favorable to growth or comfort **:** MILD ⟨~ sunshine⟩ **b :** marked by or diffusing sympathy or friendliness **:** KINDLY **3** *obs* **:** NATIVE, INBORN **4 :** displaying or marked by genius **syn** see GRACIOUS — **ge•nial•i•ty** \,jē-nē-'al-ət-ē, jēn-'yal-\ *n* — **ge•nial•ly** \'jē-nyə-lē, -nē-ə-lē\ *adv* — **ge•nial•ness** *n*

[2]**ge•ni•al** \ji-'nī(-ə)l\ *adj* [Gk *geneion* chin, fr. *genys* jaw — more at CHIN] **:** of or relating to the chin

gen•ic \'jē-nik\ *adj* **:** of, relating to, or being a gene — **gen•i•cal•ly** \-ni-k(ə-)lē\ *adv*

-gen•ic \'jen-ik\ *adj comb form* [ISV *-gen* & *-geny* + *-ic*] **1 :** producing **:** forming ⟨ero*genic*⟩ **2 :** produced by **:** formed from ⟨phyto*genic*⟩ **3** [*photogenic*] **:** suitable for production or reproduction by (such) a medium ⟨tele*genic*⟩

ge•nic•u•late \jə-'nik-yə-lət\ *or* **ge•nic•u•lat•ed** \-,lāt-əd\ *adj* [L *geniculatus*, fr. *geniculum*, dim. of *genu* knee — more at KNEE] **:** bent abruptly at an angle like a bent knee — **ge•nic•u•late•ly** *adv*

ge•nie \'jē-nē, 'jen-ē\ *n, pl* **ge•nies** *also* **ge•nii** \'jē-nē-,ī\ [F *génie*, fr. Ar *jinnīy*] **:** JINN

gen•i•tal \'jen-ə-t[ə]l\ *adj* [ME, fr. L *genitalis*, fr. *genitus*, pp. of *gignere* to beget — more at KIN] **1 :** GENERATIVE **2 :** of, relating to, or being a sexual organ

gen•i•ta•lia \,jen-ə-'tā-lē-ə, -'tāl-yə\ *n pl* [L, fr. neut. pl. of *genitalis*] **:** the organs of the reproductive system; *esp* **:** the external genital organs — **gen•i•tal•ic** \-'tal-ik\ *adj*

gen•i•tals \'jen-ə-t[ə]lz\ *n pl* **:** GENITALIA

gen•i•ti•val \,jen-ə-'tī-vəl\ *adj* **:** of, relating to, or formed with or from the genitive case — **gen•i•ti•val•ly** \-və-lē\ *adv*

gen•i•tive \'jen-ət-iv\ *adj* [ME, fr. L *genetivus*, *genitivus*, lit., of generation (erroneous translation of Gk *genikos* genitive), fr. *genitus*] **1 :** of, relating to, or constituting a grammatical case marking typically a relationship of possessor or source — compare POSSESSIVE **2 :** not characterized by case inflection but nevertheless expressing a relationship that in some inflected languages is often marked by a genitive case — used esp. of English prepositional phrases introduced by *of* — **genitive** *n*

genito- *comb form* [*genital*] **:** genital and ⟨*genito*urinary⟩

gen•i•to•uri•nary \,jen-ə-tō-'yür-ə-,ner-ē\ *adj* **:** of or relating to the genital and urinary organs or functions

gen•i•ture \'jen-ə-,chü(ə)r, -chər, -,t(y)ü(ə)r\ *n* **:** NATIVITY, BIRTH

ge•nius \'jē-nyəs, -nē-əs\ *n, pl* **ge•nius•es** *or* **ge•nii** \-nē-,ī\ [L, tutelary spirit, fondness for social enjoyment, fr. *gignere* to beget] **1** *pl* **genii :** an attendant spirit of a person or place **2 :** a strong leaning or inclination **:** PENCHANT **3 a :** a peculiar, distinctive, or identifying character or spirit **b :** the associations and traditions of a place **c :** a personification or embodiment esp. of a quality or condition **4** *pl usu* **genii a :** an elemental spirit **:** JINN **b :** a person who influences another for good or bad ⟨his evil ~⟩ **5** *pl usu* **geniuses a :** a single strongly marked capacity or aptitude **b :** extraordinary intellectual power esp. as manifested in creative activity **c :** a person endowed with transcendent mental superiority; *specif* **:** a person with a very high intelligence quotient **syn** see GIFT

ge•nius lo•ci \,jē-nyə-'slō-,sī, -nē-ə-, -'slō-,kē\ *n* [L] **1 :** a tutelary deity of a place **2 :** the pervading spirit of a place

geno- — see GEN-

geno•ci•dal \,jen-ə-'sīd-[ə]l\ *adj* **:** tending toward or producing genocide ⟨~ acts⟩

geno•cide \'jen-ə-,sīd\ *n* **:** the deliberate and systematic destruction of a racial, political, or cultural group

ge•nome \'jē-,nōm\ *or* **ge•nom** \-,näm\ *n* [G *genom*, fr. *gen-* [2]gen- + *chromosom* chromosome] **:** one haploid set of chromosomes with the genes they contain — **ge•no•mic** \ji-'nō-mik, -'näm-ik\ *adj*

ge•no•spe•cies \,jē-nō-'spē-(,)shēz, -(,)sēz\ *n* **:** the sum of the genotypes of a taxonomic species

ge•no•type \'jē-nə-,tīp, 'jen-ə-\ *n* **1** [[1]gen-] **:** TYPE SPECIES **2** [[2]gen-] **a :** the genetic constitution of an individual or group **b :** a class or group of individuals sharing a specified genetic makeup — **ge•no•typ•ic** \,jē-nə-'tip-ik, ,jen-ə-\ *also* **ge•no•typ•i•cal** \-i-kəl\ *adj* — **ge•no•typ•i•cal•ly** \-i-k(ə-)lē\ *adv* — **ge•no•ty•pic•i•ty** \-,tī-'pis-ət-ē\ *n*

-g•e•nous \j-ə-nəs\ *adj comb form* [-*gen* + -*ous*] **1 :** producing **:** yielding ⟨pyro*genous*⟩ **2 :** having (such) an origin ⟨hypo*genous*⟩

genre \'zhä(n)n-rə, 'zhän(-ə)r, 'zhä(n)ŋ-rə\ *n, often attrib* [F, fr. MF *genre* kind, gender — more at GENDER] **1 :** KIND, SORT **2 a :** paintings that depict scenes or events from everyday life usu.

realistically; *also* : the school or style of painting featured by the use of such subject matter **b** : a distinctive type or category of literary composition

gen·ro \'gen-'rō\ *n pl, often cap* [Jap *genrō*] : the elder statesmen of Japan

gens \'jenz, 'gen(t)s\ *n, pl* **gen·tes** \'jen-ˌtēz, 'gen-ˌtās\ [L *gent-, gens* — more at GENTLE] **1** : a Roman clan embracing the families of the same stock in the male line with the members having a common name and being united in worship of their common ancestor **2** : CLAN; *esp* : a patrilineal clan **3** : a distinguishable group of related organisms

¹gent \'jent\ *adj* [ME, noble, graceful, fr. OF, fr. L *genitus*, pp. of *gignere* to beget — more at KIN] *archaic* : GRACEFUL, PRETTY

²gent *n* [short for *gentleman*] : MAN, FELLOW

gen·teel \jen-'tē(ə)l\ *adj* [MF *gentil* gentle] **1 a** : having an aristocratic quality or flavor : STYLISH **b** : of or relating to the gentry or upper class **c** : elegant or graceful in manner, appearance, or shape **d** : free from vulgarity or rudeness : POLITE **2 a** : maintaining or striving to maintain the appearance of superior or middle-class social status or respectability **b** (1) : marked by false delicacy, prudery, or affectation (2) : conventionally or insipidly pretty ⟨timid and ~ artistic style⟩ — **gen·teel·ly** \-'tē(ə)l-lē\ *adv* — **gen·teel·ness** *n*

gen·tian \'jen-chən\ *n* [ME *gencian*, fr. MF *gentiane*, fr. L *gentiana*] **1** : any of two genera (*Gentiana* and *Dasystephana*) of herbs of a family (Gentianaceae, the gentian family) with opposite smooth leaves and showy usu. blue flowers **2** : the rhizome and roots of the yellow gentian (*Gentiana lutea*) used as a tonic and stomachic

gen·tia·nel·la \ˌjen-ch(ē-)ə-'nel-ə\ *n* [NL, dim. of L *gentiana*] : any of several gentians; *esp* : an often cultivated blue-flowered alpine gentian (*Gentiana acaulis*)

gentian violet *n, often cap G&V* : a dye consisting of one or more methyl derivatives of pararosaniline used as a biological stain, as a bactericide, fungicide, and anthelmintic, and in the treatment of burns

¹gen·tile \'jen-ˌtīl\ *n* [ME, fr. LL *gentilis*, fr. L *gent-, gens* nation] **1** *often cap* : a person of a non-Jewish nation or of non-Jewish faith; *esp* : a Christian as distinguished from a Jew **2** : HEATHEN, PAGAN **3** *often cap* : a non-Mormon

²gentile *adj* **1** *often cap* **a** : of or relating to the nations at large as distinguished from the Jews; *also* : of or relating to Christians as distinguished from the Jews **b** : of or relating to non-Mormons **2** : PAGAN, HEATHEN **3** [L *gentilis*] : relating to a tribe or clan **4** : denoting a people or country ⟨*Canadian* and *Irish* are ~ nouns⟩

gen·ti·lesse \ˌjent-ᵊl-'es\ *n* [ME, fr. MF, fr. *gentil*] *archaic* : decorum of conduct befitting a member of the gentry

gen·til·i·ty \jen-'til-ət-ē\ *n* **1 a** : the condition of belonging to the gentry **b** : the members of the upper class : GENTRY **2 a** (1) : decorum of conduct : COURTESY (2) : attitudes or activity marked by false delicacy, prudery, or affectation **b** (1) : superior social status or prestige evidenced by manners, possessions, or mode of life (2) : the maintenance of the appearance of superior or middle-class social status esp. in the face of decayed prosperity

gen·tis·ic acid \(ˌ)jen-ˌtis-ik-, -ˌtiz-\ *n* [ISV fr. *gentisin* (a pigment obtained from gentian root)] : a crystalline acid $C_7H_7O_4$ used medicinally as an analgesic and diaphoretic

¹gen·tle \'jent-ᵊl\ *adj* [ME *gentil*, fr. OF, fr. L *gentilis* of a clan, of the same clan, fr. *gent-, gens* clan, nation; akin to L *gignere* to beget — more at KIN] **1 a** : belonging to a family of high social station **b** *archaic* : CHIVALROUS **c** : HONORABLE, DISTINGUISHED; *specif* : of or relating to a gentleman **d** : KIND, AMIABLE ⟨~ reader⟩ **e** : suited to a person of high social station **2 a** : TRACTABLE, DOCILE **b** : not harsh, stern, or violent : MILD **3** : SOFT, DELICATE **4** : MODERATE **syn** see SOFT — **gent·ly** \'jent-lē\ *adv*

²gentle *n* : a person of gentle birth or status

³gentle *vt* **gen·tling** \'jent-liŋ, -ᵊl-iŋ\ **1** : to raise from the commonalty : ENNOBLE **2 a** : to make mild, docile, soft, or moderate **b** : MOLLIFY, PLACATE **c** : to stroke soothingly : PET

gentle breeze *n* : wind having a speed of 8 to 12 miles per hour

gen·tle·folk \'jent-ᵊl-ˌfōk\ *also* **gen·tle·folks** \-ˌfōks\ *n pl* : persons of gentle or good family and breeding

gen·tle·man \'jent-ᵊl-mən\ *n, often attrib* **1 a** : a man of noble or gentle birth **b** : a man belonging to the gentry (sense 2b) **c** (1) : a man who combines gentle birth or rank with chivalrous qualities (2) : a man whose conduct conforms to a high standard of propriety or correct behavior **d** (1) : a man of independent means who does not engage in any occupation or profession for gain (2) : a man who does not engage in any menial occupation or in manual labor for gain **2** : VALET — often used in the phrase *gentleman's gentleman* **3** : a man of any social class or condition

gen·tle·man–at–arms \-mə-nət-'ärmz\ *n, pl* **gentlemen–at–arms** : one of a military corps of 40 gentlemen who attend the British sovereign on state occasions

gen·tle·man–com·mon·er \-mən-'käm-ə-nər\ *n, pl* **gentlemen–commoners** : one of a privileged class of commoners formerly required to pay higher fees than ordinary commoners at the universities of Oxford and Cambridge

gen·tle·man·like \'jent-ᵊl-mən-ˌlīk\ *adj* : resembling or appropriate to a gentleman — **gen·tle·man·like·ness** *n*

gen·tle·man·li·ness \-mən-lē-nəs\ *n* : the quality or state of being gentlemanly

gen·tle·man·ly \-lē\ *adj* : characteristic of or having the character of a gentleman

gentleman of fortune : ADVENTURER

gentleman's agreement *or* **gentlemen's agreement** *n* : an agreement secured only by the honor of the participants

gen·tle·ness \'jent-ᵊl-nəs\ *n* : the quality or state of being gentle; *esp* : mildness of manners or disposition

gentle sex *n* : the female sex : women in general

gen·tle·wom·an \'jent-ᵊl-ˌwu̇m-ən\ *n* **1 a** : a woman of noble or gentle birth **b** : a woman attendant upon a lady of rank **2** : a woman of refined manners or good breeding : LADY

Gen·too \'jen-(ˌ)tü\ *n* [Pg *gentio*, lit., gentile, fr. LL *gentilis*] *archaic* : HINDU

gen·trice \'jen-trəs\ *n* [ME *gentrise*, fr. OF *genterise*, alter. of *gentelise*, fr. *gentil* gentle] *archaic* : gentility of birth : RANK

gen·try \'jen-trē\ *n* [ME *gentrie*, alter. of *gentrise*] **1 a** *obs* : the qualities appropriate to a person of gentle birth; *esp* : COURTESY **b** : the condition or rank of a gentleman **2 a** : upper or ruling class : ARISTOCRACY **b** : a class whose members are entitled to bear a coat of arms though not of noble rank; *esp* : the landed proprietors having such status **3** : people of a specified class or kind : FOLKS

gen·u·flect \'jen-yə-ˌflekt\ *vi* [LL *genuflectere*, fr. L *genu* knee + *flectere* to bend — more at KNEE] **1 a** : to bend the knee **b** : to touch the knee to the floor or ground esp. in worship **2** : to be servilely obedient or respectful : KOWTOW

gen·u·flec·tion *also* **gen·u·flex·ion** \ˌjen-yə-'flek-shən\ *n* : the act or an instance of genuflecting

gen·u·ine \'jen-yə-wən\ *adj* [L *genuinus* native, genuine; akin to L *gignere* to beget — more at KIN] **1 a** : actually having the reputed or apparent qualities or character : TRUE ⟨~ idealist⟩ **b** : actually produced by or proceeding from the alleged source or author **c** : sincerely and honestly felt or experienced **2** : of or relating to the original stock **3** : free from hypocrisy or pretense **syn** see AUTHENTIC — **gen·u·ine·ly** *adv* — **gen·u·ine·ness** \-wən-nəs\ *n*

ge·nus \'jē-nəs\ *n, pl* **gen·era** \'jen-ə-rə\ [L *gener-, genus* birth, race, kind — more at KIN] **1** : a class, kind, or group marked by common characteristics or by one common characteristic; *specif* : a category of biological classification ranking between the family and the species, comprising structurally or phylogenetically related species or an isolated species exhibiting unusual differentiation, and being designated by a Latin or latinized capitalized singular noun **2** : a class of objects divided into several subordinate species

-g·e·ny \j-ə-nē\ *n comb form* [Gk *-geneia* act of being born, fr. *-genēs* born — more at -GEN] : generation : production ⟨bio*geny*⟩

geo- — see GE-

geo·cen·tric \ˌjē-ō-'sen-trik\ *adj* **1 a** : relating to, measured from, or as if observed from the earth's center **b** : having or relating to the earth as center — compare HELIOCENTRIC **2** : taking or based on the earth as the center of perspective and valuation — **geo·cen·tri·cal·ly** \-tri-k(ə-)lē\ *adv*

geo·chem·i·cal \-'kem-i-kəl\ *adj* : of, relating to, or using the methods of geochemistry — **geo·chem·i·cal·ly** \-k(ə-)lē\ *adv*

geo·chem·is·try \-'kem-ə-strē\ *n* : a science that deals with the chemical composition of and chemical changes in the crust of the earth

geo·chro·no·log·i·cal \ˌjē-(ˌ)ō-ˌkrän-ᵊl-'äj-i-kəl, -ˌkrōn-\ *or* **geo·chro·no·log·ic** \-'äj-ik\ *adj* : of or relating to geochronology

geo·chro·nol·o·gy \-krə-'näl-ə-jē\ *n* : the chronology of the past as indicated by geologic data

geo·chro·no·met·ric \-ˌkrän-ə-'me-trik, -ˌkrō-nə-\ *adj* : of or relating to geochronometry

geo·chro·nom·e·try \-krə-'näm-ə-trē\ *n* : the measurement of past time by geochronological methods

ge·ode \'jē-ˌōd\ *n* [L *geodes*, a gem, fr. Gk *geōdēs* earthlike, fr. *gē* earth] **1** : a nodule of stone having a cavity lined with crystals or mineral matter **2** : the cavity in a geode

¹geo·de·sic \ˌjē-ə-'des-ik, -'dē-sik\ *adj* **1** : GEODETIC **2** : made of light straight structural elements largely in tension ⟨a ~ dome⟩

²geodesic *n* : the shortest line between two points on a mathematically derived surface

ge·od·e·sist \jē-'äd-ə-səst\ *n* : a specialist in geodesy

ge·od·e·sy \-sē\ *n* [Gk *geōdaisia*, fr. *geō-* ge- + *daiesthai* to divide — more at TIDE] : a branch of applied mathematics that determines the exact positions of points and the figures and areas of large portions of the earth's surface, the shape and size of the earth, and the variations of terrestrial gravity and magnetism

geo·det·ic \ˌjē-ə-'det-ik\ *adj* **1** : of, relating to, or determined by geodesy **2** : relating to the geometry of geodetic lines — **geo·det·i·cal** \-i-kəl\ *adj* — **geo·det·i·cal·ly** \-i-k(ə-)lē\ *adv*

geo·duck \'gü-ē-ˌdək\ *n* [Chinook Jargon *go-duck*] : an edible clam (*Panope generosa*) of the Pacific coast weighing over 5 pounds

ge·og·no·sy \jē-'äg-nə-sē\ *n* [ISV] : a branch of geology that deals with the materials of the earth and its general exterior and interior constitution

ge·og·ra·pher \jē-'äg-rə-fər\ *n* : a specialist in geography

geo·graph·ic \ˌjē-ə-'graf-ik\ *adj* **1** : of or relating to geography **2** : belonging to or characteristic of a particular region — **geo·graph·i·cal** \-i-kəl\ *adj* — **geo·graph·i·cal·ly** \-i-k(ə-)lē\ *adv*

geographical mile *n* : NAUTICAL MILE

ge·og·ra·phy \jē-'äg-rə-fē\ *n, often attrib* [L *geographia*, fr. Gk *geōgraphia*, fr. *geographein* to describe the earth's surface, fr. *geō-* + *graphein* to write — more at CARVE] **1** : a science that deals with the earth and its life; *esp* : the description of land, sea, air, and the distribution of plant and animal life including man and his industries **2** : the geographic features of an area **3** : a treatise on geography **4** : a delineation or systematic arrangement of constituent elements : CONFIGURATION

ge·oid \'jē-ˌȯid\ *n* [G, fr. Gk *geoeidēs* earthlike, fr. *gē*] : the surface within or around the earth that is everywhere normal to the direction of gravity and coincides with mean sea level in the oceans

geo·log·ic \ˌjē-ə-'läj-ik\ *adj* : of, relating to, or based on geology — **geo·log·i·cal** \-i-kəl\ *adj* — **geo·log·i·cal·ly** \-i-k(ə-)lē\ *adv*

ge·ol·o·gist \jē-'äl-ə-jəst\ *n* : a specialist in geology

ge·ol·o·gize \-ˌjīz\ *vi* : to study geology or make geologic investigations

ge·ol·o·gy \jē-'äl-ə-jē\ *n, often attrib* [NL *geologia*, fr. *ge-* + *-logia* -logy] **1 a** : a science that deals with the history of the earth and its life esp. as recorded in rocks **b** : a study of the solid matter of a celestial body (as the moon) **2** : geologic features **3** : a treatise on geology

geo·mag·net·ic \ˌjē-(ˌ)ō-(ˌ)mag-'net-ik\ *adj* : of or relating to terrestrial magnetism — **geo·mag·ne·tism** \-'mag-nə-ˌtiz-əm\ *n*

geo·man·cer \'jē-ə-ˌman(t)-sər\ *n* : one that practices geomancy

geo·man·cy \-sē\ *n* [ME *geomancie*, fr. MF, fr. ML *geomantia*, fr. LGk *geōmanteia*, fr. Gk *geō-* + *-manteia* -mancy] : divination by means of figures or lines — **geo·man·tic** \ˌjē-ə-'mant-ik\ *adj*

ge·om·e·ter \jē-'äm-ət-ər\ *n* : a specialist in geometry

geo·met·ric \ˌjē-ə-'me-trik\ *adj* **1** : of, relating to, or according to the methods or principles of geometry **2** *cap* : of or relating to a style of ancient Greek pottery characterized by geometric decorative motifs **3** : utilizing rectilinear or simple curvilinear motifs or outlines in design — **geo·met·ri·cal** \-tri-kəl\ *adj* — **geo·met·ri·cal·ly** \-tri-k(ə-)lē\ *adv*

geo·me·tri·cian \(,)jē-,äm-ə-'trish-ən, ,jē-ə-mə-\ *n* : GEOMETER
geometric mean *n* **1** : a term between the first and last terms of a geometric progression **2** : the *n*th root of the product of *n* numbers
geometric progression *n* : a progression (as 1, ½, ¼) in which the ratio of a term to its predecessor is always the same
geo·me·trid \jē-'äm-ə-trəd, ,jē-ə-'me-\ *n* [deriv. of Gk *geōmetrēs* geometer, fr. *geōmetrein*] : any of a family (Geometridae) of medium-sized moths with large wings and larvae that are loopers — **geometrid** *adj*
ge·om·e·trize \jē-'äm-ə-,trīz\ *vi* : to work by or as if by geometric methods or laws ~ *vt* **1** : to represent geometrically **2** : to make conform to geometric principles and laws
ge·om·e·try \jē-'äm-ə-trē\ *n, often attrib* [ME *geometrie*, fr. MF, fr. L *geometria*, fr. Gk *geōmetria*, fr. *geōmetrein* to measure the earth, fr. *geō-* ge- + *metron* measure — more at MEASURE] **1 a** : a branch of mathematics that deals with the measurement, properties, and relationships of points, lines, angles, surfaces, and solids **b** : a particular type or system of geometry **c** : a treatise on geometry **2 a** : CONFIGURATION **b** : surface shape **3** : an arrangement of objects or parts that suggests geometrical figures
geo·mor·phic \,jē-ə-'mȯr-fik\ *adj* : of or relating to the form of the earth or its surface features
geo·mor·pho·log·ic \-,mȯr-fə-'läj-ik\ *adj* : of or relating to geomorphology — **geo·mor·pho·log·i·cal** \-i-kəl\ *adj*
geo·mor·phol·o·gy \-(,)mȯr-'fäl-ə-jē\ *n* [ISV] **1** : a science that deals with the land and submarine relief features of the earth's surface and seeks a genetic interpretation of them **2 a** : the features dealt with in geomorphology **b** : a treatise on geomorphology
ge·oph·a·gy \jē-'äf-ə-jē\ *n* [ISV] : a practice of eating earthy substances (as clay) widespread among primitive or depressed peoples on a scanty or unbalanced diet
geo·phys·i·cal \,jē-ə-'fiz-i-kəl\ *adj* : of, relating to, or based on geophysics
geo·phys·i·cist \-'fiz-(ə-)səst\ *n* : a specialist in geophysics
geo·phys·ics \-'fiz-iks\ *n pl but sing or pl in constr* [ISV] : the physics of the earth including the fields of meteorology, hydrology, oceanography, seismology, volcanology, magnetism, radioactivity, and geodesy
geo·phyte \'jē-ə-,fīt\ *n* : a perennial plant that bears its overwintering buds below the surface of the soil
geo·po·lit·i·cal \,jē-ō-pə-'lit-i-kəl\ *adj* : of, relating to, or based on geopolitics — **geo·po·lit·i·cal·ly** \-k(ə-)lē\ *adv*
geo·pol·i·ti·cian \-,päl-ə-'tish-ən\ *n* : a specialist in geopolitics
geo·pol·i·tics \-'päl-ə-,tiks\ *n pl but sing in constr* **1** : a study of the influence of such physical factors as geography, economics, and demography on the politics and esp. the foreign policy of a state **2** : a Nazi expansionist doctrine emphasizing strategic frontiers, lebensraum, and racial, economic, and social pressures as factors demanding reallocation of the earth's surface and resources **3** : a governmental policy guided by geopolitics **4** : the combination of political and geographic factors characterizing a particular state or region
geo·pon·ic \,jē-ə-'pän-ik\ *adj* [Gk *geōponikos*, fr. *geōponein* to plow, fr. *geō-* + *ponein* to toil, fr. *ponos* labor] : AGRICULTURAL — **geo·pon·ics** \-iks\ *n pl but sing or pl in constr*
George \'jȯ(ə)rj\ *n* [St. *George* †*ab* A.D. 303, patron saint of England] **1** : either of two of the insignia of the British Order of the Garter **2** : a British coin bearing the image of St. George
geor·gette \jȯr-'jet\ *n* [fr. *Georgette*, a trademark] : a thin strong clothing crepe of fibers woven from hard twisted yarns to produce a dull pebbly surface
[1]**Geor·gian** \'jȯr-jən\ *n* **1** : a native or inhabitant of Georgia in the Caucasus **2** : the language of the Georgian people
[2]**Georgian** *adj* : of, relating to, or constituting Georgia in the Caucasus, the Georgians, or Georgian
[3]**Georgian** *n* : a native or resident of the state of Georgia
[4]**Georgian** *adj* : of, relating to, or characteristic of the state of Georgia or its people
[5]**Georgian** *adj* **1** : of, relating to, or characteristic of the reigns of the first four Georges of Great Britain **2** : of, relating to, or characteristic of the reign of George V of Great Britain
[6]**Georgian** *n* **1** : one belonging to either of the Georgian periods **2** : Georgian taste or style
Geor·gia pine \,jȯr-jə-\ *n* : LONGLEAF PINE
[1]**geor·gic** \'jȯr-jik\ *n* [the *Georgics*, poem by Vergil] : a poem dealing with agriculture
[2]**georgic** *adj* [L *georgicus*, fr. Gk *geōrgikos*, fr. *geōrgos* farmer, fr. *geō-* ge- + *ergon* work — more at WORK] : of or relating to agriculture
geo·sci·ence \,jē-ō-'sī-ən(t)s\ *n* **1** : the sciences (as geology, geophysics, and geochemistry) dealing with the earth **2** : any of the geosciences
geo·stra·te·gic \-strə-'tē-jik\ *adj* : of or relating to geostrategy
geo·strat·e·gist \-'strat-ə-jəst\ *n* : a specialist in geostrategy
geo·strat·e·gy \-jē\ *n* **1** : a branch of geopolitics that deals with strategy **2** : the combination of geopolitical and strategic factors characterizing a particular geographic region **3** : the use by a government of strategy based upon geopolitics
geo·stroph·ic \,jē-ō-'sträf-ik\ *adj* [*ge-* + Gk *strophikos* turned, fr. *strophē* turning — more at STROPHE] : of or relating to deflective force due to the rotation of the earth
geo·syn·cli·nal \-(,)sin-'klīn-ᵊl\ *adj* : of or relating to a geosyncline
geo·syn·cline \-'sin-,klīn\ *or* **geosynclinal** *n* : a great downward flexure of the earth's crust — compare GEANTICLINE
geo·tac·tic \,jē-ō-'tak-tik\ *adj* : of or relating to geotaxis — **geo·tac·ti·cal·ly** \-ti-k(ə-)lē\ *adv*
geo·tax·is \-'tak-səs\ *n* [NL] : a taxis in which the force of gravity is the directive factor
geo·tec·ton·ic \-,tek-'tän-ik\ *adj* : of or relating to the form, arrangement, and structure of rock masses of the earth's crust
geo·ther·mal \-'thər-məl\ *or* **geo·ther·mic** \-mik\ *adj* [ISV] : of or relating to the heat of the earth's interior
geo·trop·ic \,jē-ə-'träp-ik\ *adj* : of or relating to geotropism — **geo·trop·i·cal·ly** \-i-k(ə-)lē\ *adv*
ge·ot·ro·pism \jē-'ä-trə-,piz-əm\ *n* [ISV] **1** : tropism in which gravity is the orienting factor **2** : tropism in which turning or movement is toward rather than away from the earth
ge·rah \'gir-ə\ *n* [Heb *gērāh*, lit., grain] : an ancient Hebrew unit of weight equal to 1/20 shekel
ge·ra·ni·ol \jə-'rā-nē-,ȯl, -,ōl\ *n* [ISV, fr. NL *Geranium*] : a fragrant liquid unsaturated alcohol $C_{10}H_{17}OH$ used chiefly in perfumes and soap
ge·ra·ni·um \jə-'rā-nē-əm, -nyəm\ *n* [NL, genus name, fr. L, geranium, fr. Gk *geranion*, fr. dim. of *geranos* crane — more at CRANE] **1** : any of a widely distributed genus (*Geranium* of the family Geraniaceae, the geranium family) of plants having regular flowers without spurs and with glands that alternate with the petals **2** : PELARGONIUM **3** : a vivid or strong red
ge·rar·dia \jə-'rärd-ē-ə\ *n* [NL, genus name, fr. John *Gerard* †1612 E botanist] : any of a genus (*Gerardia*) of often root-parasitic herbs of the figwort family having showy pink, purple, or yellow flowers
ger·bera \'gər-bə-rə\ *n* [NL, genus name, fr. Traugott *Gerber* †1743 G naturalist] : any of a genus (*Gerbera*) of Old World composite herbs having basal tufted leaves and showy heads of yellow, pink, or orange flowers with prominent rays
ger·bil *or* **ger·bille** \'jər-bəl\ *n* [F *gerbille*, fr. NL *Gerbillus*, genus name, dim. of *jerboa*] : any of numerous Old World burrowing desert rodents (of *Gerbillus* and related genera) with long hind legs adapted for leaping
ge·rent \'jir-ənt\ *n* [L *gerent-, gerens*, prp. of *gerere* to bear — more at CAST] : one that rules or manages
gerfalcon *var of* GYRFALCON
ger·i·at·ric \,jer-ē-'a-trik\ *adj* [Gk *gēras* old age + E *-iatric*] : of or relating to geriatrics, the aged, or the process of aging
ger·i·a·tri·cian \,jer-ē-ə-'trish-ən\ *or* **ge·ri·a·trist** \,jer-ē-'a-trəst, jə-'rī-ə-\ *n* : a specialist in geriatrics
ger·i·at·rics \,jer-ē-'a-triks\ *n pl but sing in constr* : a branch of medicine that deals with the problems and diseases of old age and aging people — compare GERONTOLOGY
germ \'jərm\ *n, often attrib* [F *germe*, fr. L *germin-, germen*, fr. *gignere* to beget — more at KIN] **1** : a small mass of living substance capable of developing into an organism or one of its parts **2** : something that serves or may serve as an origin : RUDIMENT **3** : MICROORGANISM; *esp* : a microorganism causing disease
[1]**ger·man** \'jər-mən\ *adj* [ME *germain*, fr. MF, fr. L *germanus* having the same parents, irreg. fr. *germen*] : having the same parents or the same grandparents on either the maternal or paternal side — usu. used after the noun which it modifies and joined to it by a hyphen ⟨brother-*german*⟩ ⟨cousin-*german*⟩
[2]**german** *n, obs* : a near relative
[1]**Ger·man** \'jər-mən\ *n* [ML *Germanus*, fr. L, any member of the Germanic peoples] **1 a** : a native or inhabitant of Germany **b** : a person of German descent **c** : one who speaks German outside Germany (as a Swiss German) **2 a** : the Germanic language spoken mainly in Germany, Austria, and parts of Switzerland **b** : the literary and official language of Germany **3** *often not cap* **a** : a dance consisting of capriciously involved figures intermingled with waltzes **b** *chiefly Midland* : a dancing party; *specif* : one at which the german is danced
[2]**German** *adj* : of, relating to, or characteristic of Germany, the Germans, or German
German Baptist Brethren *n pl* : DUNKERS — not used officially since 1908
ger·man·der \(,)jər-'man-dər\ *n* [deriv. of Gk *chamaidrys*, fr. *chamai* on the ground + *drys* tree — more at HUMBLE, TREE] **1** : a plant of a genus (*Teucrium*) of the mint family **2** : any of several plants (genus *Veronica*) of the figwort family
ger·mane \(,)jər-'mān\ *adj* [ME *germain*, lit., having the same parents, fr. MF] **1** *obs* : closely akin **2** : having a significant connection : PERTINENT **syn** see RELEVANT — **ger·mane·ly** *adv*
[1]**Ger·man·ic** \(,)jər-'man-ik\ *adj* **1** : GERMAN **2** : of, relating to, or characteristic of the Germanic-speaking peoples **3** : of, relating to, or constituting Germanic
[2]**Germanic** *n* : a branch of the Indo-European language family containing English, German, Dutch, Afrikaans, Flemish, Frisian, the Scandinavian languages, and Gothic — see INDO-EUROPEAN LANGUAGES table
Ger·man·ism \'jər-mə-,niz-əm\ *n* **1** : a characteristic feature of German occurring in another language **2** : partiality for Germany or German customs **3** : the practices or objectives characteristic of the Germans
Ger·man·ist \'jər-mə-nəst\ *n* : a specialist in German or Germanic language, literature, or culture
ger·ma·ni·um \(,)jər-'mā-nē-əm\ *n* [NL, fr. ML *Germania* Germany] : a grayish white hard brittle metalloid element that resembles silicon and is used as a semiconductor — see ELEMENT table
ger·man·iza·tion \,jərm-(ə-)nə-'zā-shən\ *n, often cap* : the act or process of germanizing : the state of being germanized
ger·man·ize \'jər-mə-,nīz\ *vb, often cap, vt* **1** *archaic* : to translate into German **2** : to cause to acquire German characteristics ~ *vi* : to have or acquire German customs or predilections
German measles *n pl but sing or pl in constr* : an acute contagious virus disease milder than typical measles but damaging to the fetus when occurring early in pregnancy
Germano- *comb form* : German ⟨*Germano*phile⟩ : German and ⟨*Germano*-Russian⟩
German shepherd *n* : a shepherd dog of a breed originating in northern Europe that is intelligent and responsive and is often used in police work and as a guide dog for the blind
German silver *n* : NICKEL SILVER
germ cell *n* : an egg or sperm cell or one of their antecedent cells
ger·men \'jər-mən\ *n* [L] *archaic* : GERM 1, 2
ger·mi·ci·dal \,jər-mə-'sīd-ᵊl\ *adj* : of or relating to a germicide; *also* : destroying germs
ger·mi·cide \'jər-mə-,sīd\ *n* : an agent that destroys germs
ger·mi·nal \'jərm-nəl, -ən-ᵊl\ *adj* [F, fr. L *germin-, germen* — more at GERM] **1 a** : being in the earliest stage of development **b** : CREATIVE, PRODUCTIVE **2** : of, relating to, or having the characteristics of a germ cell or early embryo — **ger·mi·nal·ly** \-ē\ *adv*
germinal area *n* : the part of the blastoderm that forms the embryo proper of an amniote vertebrate
germinal disc *n* **1** : BLASTODISC **2** : GERMINAL AREA
germinal vesicle *n* : the enlarged nucleus of the egg before completion of the reduction divisions

ger·mi·nant \'jərm-(ə-)nənt\ *adj* **:** having the capacity to grow or develop

ger·mi·nate \'jər-mə-ˌnāt\ *vb* [L *germinatus,* pp. of *germinare* to sprout, fr. *germin-, germen* bud, germ] *vt* **:** to cause to sprout or develop ~ *vi* **1 :** to begin to grow **:** SPROUT **2 :** to come into being **:** EVOLVE — **ger·mi·na·tion** \ˌjər-mə-'nā-shən\ *n* — **ger·mi·na·tive** \'jər-mə-ˌnāt-iv\ *adj*

germ layer *n* **:** any of the three primary layers of cells differentiated in most embryos during and immediately following gastrulation

germ plasm *n* **1 :** germ cells and their precursors serving as the bearers of heredity and being fundamentally independent of other cells **2 :** the hereditary material of the germ cells **:** GENES

germ theory *n* **:** a theory in medicine: infections, contagious diseases, and various other conditions result from the action of microorganisms

germ warfare *n* **:** the use of harmful bacteria as weapons in war

geront- *or* **geronto-** *comb form* [F *géront-, géronto-,* fr. Gk *geront-, geronto-,* fr. *geront-, gerōn* old man; akin to Gk *gēras* old age — more at CORN] **:** old age ⟨*geronto*logy⟩

ger·on·toc·ra·cy \ˌjer-ən-'täk-rə-sē\ *n* [F *gérontocratie,* fr. *géront-* + *-cratie* -cracy] **:** rule by elders

ger·on·to·log·i·cal \ˌjer-ˌänt-ᵊl-'äj-i-kəl, jə-ˌränt-\ *adj* **:** of or relating to gerontology

ger·on·tol·o·gist \ˌjer-ən-'täl-ə-jəst\ *n* **:** a specialist in gerontology

ger·on·tol·o·gy \-ə-jē\ *n* [ISV] **:** a branch of knowledge dealing with aging and the problems of the aged — compare GERIATRICS

ge·ron·to·mor·pho·sis \jə-ˌränt-ə-'mȯr-fə-səs\ *n* [NL] **:** phylogenetic change involving specialization of the adult with decreased capacity for further change indicative of racial senescence

-ge·rous \j-(ə-)rəs\ *adj comb form* [L *-ger,* fr. *gerere* to bear — more at CAST] **:** bearing **:** producing ⟨denti*gerous*⟩

¹ger·ry·man·der \ˌjer-ē-'man-dər, 'jer-ē-, *also* ˌger-, 'ger-\ *n* [Elbridge *Gerry* †1814 Am statesman + sala*mander;* fr. the shape of an election district formed during Gerry's governorship] **1 :** the act or method of gerrymandering **2 :** a district or pattern of districts varying greatly in size or population as a result of gerrymandering

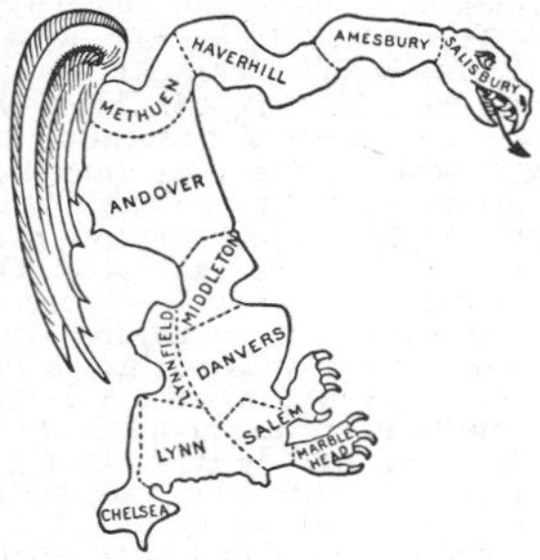

gerrymander 2

²gerrymander *vt* **ger·ry·man·der·ing** \-d(ə-)riŋ\ **1 :** to divide (a territorial unit) into election districts to give one political party an electoral majority in a large number of districts while concentrating the voting strength of the opposition in as few districts as possible **2 :** to divide (an area) into political units to give special advantages to one group ⟨~ a school district⟩

ger·und \'jer-ənd\ *n* [LL *gerundium,* fr. L *gerundus,* gerundive of *gerere* to bear — more at CAST] **1 :** a verbal noun in Latin that expresses the action of the verb as generalized or in continuance **2 :** any of several linguistic forms analogous to the Latin gerund in languages other than Latin; *esp* **:** the English verbal noun in *-ing* that has the function of a substantive and at the same time shows the verbal features of tense, voice, and capacity to take adverbial qualifiers and to govern objects

ge·run·dive \jə-'rən-div\ *n* **1 :** the Latin adjective that serves as the future passive participle, expresses necessity or fitness, and has the same suffix as the gerund **2 :** a verbal adjective in a language other than Latin analogous to the gerundive

Ger·y·on \'ger-ē-ən, 'jer-\ *n* [L, fr. Gk *Gēryōn*] **:** a three-bodied winged monster of Greek mythology slain by Hercules

ges·so \'jes-(ˌ)ō\ *n* [It, lit., gypsum, fr. L *gypsum*] **1 :** plaster of paris or gypsum prepared with glue for use in painting or making bas-reliefs **2 :** a paste prepared by mixing whiting with size or glue and spread upon a surface to fit it for painting or gilding

gest *or* **geste** \'jest\ *n* [ME *geste* — more at JEST] **1 :** ADVENTURE, EXPLOIT **2 :** a tale of adventures; *esp* **:** a romance in verse

ge·stalt \gə-'shtält\ *n, pl* **ge·stal·ten** \-ᵊn\ *or* **gestalts** [G, lit., shape, form] **:** a structure or configuration of physical, biological, or psychological phenomena so integrated as to constitute a functional unit with properties not derivable from its parts in summation

Gestalt psychology *n* **:** the study of perception and behavior from the standpoint of an organism's response to configurational wholes with stress on the identity of psychological and physiological events and rejection of atomistic or elemental analysis of stimulus, percept, and response

ge·sta·po \gə-'stäp-(ˌ)ō\ *n* [G, fr. *Ge*heime *Sta*ats *po*lizei, lit., secret state police] **:** a secret-police organization operating esp. against persons suspected of treason or sedition and employing methods held to be underhanded and terrorist

ges·tate \'jes-ˌtāt\ *vt* [back-formation fr. *gestation*] **1 :** to carry in the uterus during pregnancy **2 :** to conceive and gradually develop in the mind

ges·ta·tion \je-'stā-shən\ *n* [L *gestation-, gestatio,* fr. *gestatus,* pp. of *gestare* to bear, fr. *gestus,* pp. of *gerere* to bear — more at CAST] **1 :** the carrying of young in the uterus **:** PREGNANCY **2 :** conception and development esp. in the mind — **ges·ta·tion·al** \-shnəl, -shən-ᵊl\ *adj*

geste *also* **gest** \'jest\ *n* [MF *geste,* fr. L *gestus,* fr. *gestus,* pp. of *gerere*] **1** *archaic* **:** DEPORTMENT **2** *archaic* **:** GESTURE

ges·tic \'jes-tik\ *adj* **:** relating to or consisting of bodily movements or gestures

ges·tic·u·late \je-'stik-yə-ˌlāt\ *vi* [L *gesticulatus,* pp. of *gesticulari,* fr. (assumed) L *gesticulus,* dim. of L *gestus*] **:** to make gestures esp. when speaking — **ges·tic·u·la·tion** \(ˌ)jes-ˌtik-yə-'lā-shən\ *n* — **ges·tic·u·la·tive** \je-'stik-yə-ˌlāt-iv\ *adj* — **ges·tic·u·la·tor** \-ˌlāt-ər\ *n* — **ges·tic·u·la·to·ry** \-lə-ˌtōr-ē, -ˌtȯr-\ *adj*

¹ges·ture \'jes(h)-chər\ *n* [ML *gestura* mode of action, fr. L *gestus,* pp.] **1** *archaic* **:** CARRIAGE, BEARING **2 :** the use of motions of the limbs or body as a means of expression **3 :** a movement usu. of the body or limbs that expresses or emphasizes an idea, sentiment, or attitude **4 :** something said or done by way of formality or courtesy, as a symbol or token, or for its effect on the attitudes of others

²gesture *vi* **:** to make a gesture ~ *vt* **:** to express or direct by a gesture

ge·sund·heit \gə-'zu̇nt-ˌhīt\ *interj* [G, lit., health] — used to wish good health esp. to one who has just sneezed

¹get \(')get; *often* git, *without stress, when a heavily stressed syllable follows, as in "get up"*\ *vb* **got** \(')gät\ **got** *or* **got·ten** \'gät-ᵊn\ **get·ting** [ME *geten,* fr. ON *geta* to get, beget; akin to OE *bigietan* to beget, L pre*hendere* to seize, grasp, Gk *chandanein* to hold, contain] *vt* **1 a :** to gain possession of **b :** EARN **2 a :** to obtain or receive by way of benefit or profit **b :** to achieve as a result of military activity **3 :** to obtain by concession or entreaty **4 a :** to seek out and obtain ⟨hoped to ~ dinner at the inn⟩ **b :** FETCH **5 :** BEGET **6 a :** to succeed in bringing or conveying **b :** to cause to move ⟨~ him out of the house⟩ **c :** to cause to be in a certain position or condition ⟨*got* his feet wet⟩ **d :** to make ready **:** PREPARE **7 a :** SEIZE **b :** OVERCOME **c :** to have an emotional effect on **d :** PUZZLE **e :** IRRITATE **f :** to take vengeance on; *specif* **:** KILL **g :** HIT **8 a :** to be subjected to ⟨*got* a bad fall⟩ **b :** to receive by way of punishment **c :** to suffer a specified injury to **9 a :** MEMORIZE **b :** to find out by calculation **c :** HEAR **d :** UNDERSTAND **10 :** PERSUADE, INDUCE **11 a :** HAVE — used in the present perfect tense form with present meaning ⟨I've *got* no money⟩ **b :** to have as an obligation or necessity — used in the present perfect tense form with present meaning ⟨he has *got* to come⟩ **12 :** to establish communication with **13 :** to put out in baseball ~ *vi* **1 a :** to succeed in coming or going ⟨~ to the city⟩ **b :** to reach a certain condition ⟨*got* to sleep after midnight⟩ **2 :** to acquire wealth **3 :** to be able **:** CONTRIVE **4 :** BECOME ⟨*got* married last week⟩ **5 :** to leave immediately ⟨told them to ~⟩

syn GET, OBTAIN, PROCURE, SECURE, ACQUIRE, GAIN, WIN, EARN mean to come into possession of. GET is a very general term and may or may not imply effort or initiative; OBTAIN suggests the attainment of something sought for with some expenditure of time and effort; PROCURE implies effort in obtaining something for oneself or for another; SECURE implies difficulty in obtaining and keeping in possession or under one's control; ACQUIRE often suggests an addition to what is already possessed; GAIN adds to OBTAIN the implication of struggle and usu. of material value in the thing obtained; WIN adds to GAIN the suggestion of favoring qualities or circumstances playing a part in the gaining; EARN implies a correspondence between the effort and what one gets by effort — **get after :** to pursue with exhortation, reprimand, or attack — **get ahead :** to achieve success — **get around 1 :** to get the better of **:** CIRCUMVENT **2 :** EVADE — **get at 1 :** to reach effectively **2 :** to influence corruptly **:** BRIBE **3 :** to turn one's attention to **4 :** to try to prove or make clear ⟨what is he *getting at*⟩ — **get away with :** to perform without suffering unpleasant consequences — **get even :** to get revenge — **get even with :** to repay in kind — **get it :** to receive a scolding or punishment — **get on :** to produce an unfortunate effect on **:** UPSET — **get one's goat :** to make one angry or annoyed — **get over 1 a :** OVERCOME, SURMOUNT **b :** to recover from **2 :** to move or travel across — **get somewhere :** to be successful — **get there :** to be successful — **get through 1 :** to reach the end of **:** COMPLETE **2 :** to while away — **get to 1 :** BEGIN **2 :** to have an effect on **:** INFLUENCE — **get together 1 :** to bring together **:** ACCUMULATE **2 :** to come together **:** ASSEMBLE **3 :** to reach agreement — **get wind of :** to become aware of

²get \'get\ *n* **1 a :** something begotten: (1) **:** OFFSPRING (2) **:** the entire progeny of a male animal **b :** LINEAGE **2 :** a difficult return of a shot in a game

get along *vi* **1 a :** to proceed toward a destination **:** PROGRESS **b :** to approach an advanced stage; *esp* **:** to approach old age **2 :** to meet one's needs **:** MANAGE **3 :** to be or remain on congenial terms

get·at·able \get-'at-ə-bəl\ *adj* **:** ACCESSIBLE

get·away \'get-ə-ˌwā\ *n* **:** an act or instance of getting away: as **a :** START **b :** ESCAPE

get by *vi* **1 :** to avoid failure or catastrophe **2 :** to proceed without being discovered, criticized, or punished

Geth·sem·a·ne \geth-'sem-ə-nē\ *n* [Gk *Gethsēmanē*] **1 :** the garden outside Jerusalem mentioned in Mk 14 as the scene of the agony and arrest of Jesus **2 :** a place or occasion of great esp. mental or spiritual suffering

get on *vi* **1 :** to get along **2 :** to gain knowledge or understanding ⟨*got on* to the racket⟩

get round *vb* **:** to get around

get·ter \'get-ər\ *n* **:** one that gets; *esp* **:** a substance introduced into a vacuum tube or incandescent electric lamp to remove traces of gas

get–to·geth·er \'get-tə-ˌgeth-ər\ *n* **:** MEETING; *esp* **:** an informal social gathering

get·up \'get-ˌəp\ *n* **1 :** general composition or structure **2 :** OUTFIT, COSTUME

get up *vi* **1 a :** to arise from bed **b :** to rise to one's feet **c :** CLIMB, ASCEND **2 :** to go ahead or faster — used in the imperative as a command to horses ~ *vt* **1 :** to make preparations for **:** ORGANIZE **2 :** to arrange as to external appearance **:** DRESS **3 :** to acquire a knowledge of **4 :** to create in oneself

ge·um \'jē-əm\ *n* [L] **:** AVENS

gew·gaw \'g(y)ü-(ˌ)gȯ\ *n* [origin unknown] **:** a showy trifle **:** BAUBLE

gey \(')gā\ *adv* [alter. of *gay,* adv.] *chiefly Scot* **:** VERY, QUITE

gey·ser \'gī-zər, *Brit sometimes* 'gā- *or* 'gē- *in sense 1 & usu* 'gē- *in sense 2*\ *n* [Icel *geysir* gusher, fr. *geysa* to rush forth, fr. ON; akin to OE *gēotan* to pour — more at FOUND] **1 :** a spring that throws forth intermittent jets of heated water and steam **2** *Brit* **:** an apparatus for heating water rapidly esp. by injected steam

gey·ser·ite \-zə-ˌrīt\ *n* [F *geysérite,* fr. *geyser,* fr. Icel *geysir*] **:** a hydrous silica that constitutes one variety of opal and is deposited around some hot springs and geysers in white or grayish concretionary masses

ghar·ry \'gar-ē, 'gär-\ *n* [Hindi *gāṛī*] **:** a horse-drawn cab used esp. in India and Egypt

ghast \'gast\ *adj, archaic* **:** GHASTLY

ghast·ful \-fəl\ *adj, archaic* **:** FRIGHTFUL — **ghast·ful·ly** *adv, obs*

ghast·li·ness \'gast-lē-nəs\ *n* **:** the quality or state of being ghastly

ghast·ly \'gast-lē\ *adj* [ME *gastly*, fr. OE *gāstlīc* spiritual] **1 :** terrifyingly horrible to the senses **2 :** resembling a ghost **3** *obs* **:** TERRIFIED **4 :** TERRIBLE ⟨~ wreck⟩ **5 :** very great ⟨~ mistake⟩ — **ghastly** *adv*

syn GRISLY, GRUESOME, MACABRE, LURID: GHASTLY suggests the terrifying aspects of corpses and ghosts; GRISLY and GRUESOME suggest additionally the results of extreme violence or cruelty; MACABRE implies a morbid preoccupation with the physical aspects of death; LURID adds to GRUESOME the suggestion of shuddering fascination with violent death and esp. with murder

ghat \'gȯt, 'gät\ *n* [Hindi *ghāṭ*] **:** a landing place with stairs descending to a river in India

ghee *or* **ghi** \'gē\ *n* [Hindi *ghī*, fr. Skt *ghṛta;* akin toMIr *gert* milk] **:** a semifluid clarified butter made esp. in India

gher·kin \'gər-kən\ *n* [D *gurken*, pl. of *gurk* cucumber, deriv. of Pol *ogurek*, fr. MGk *agouros*] **1 :** a small prickly cucumber used for pickling; *also* **:** the slender annual vine (*Cucumis anguria*) that bears it **2 :** the immature fruit of the common cucumber

ghet·to \'get-(,)ō\ *n, pl* **ghettos** *or* **ghettoes** [It] **1 :** a quarter of a city in which Jews are required to live; *broadly* **:** a quarter of a city in which members of a minority group live because of social, legal, or economic pressure — **ghetto** *vt* — **ghet·to·iza·tion** \,get-(,)ō-ə-'zā-shən\ *n* — **ghet·to·ize** \'get-(,)ō-,īz\ *vt*

Ghib·el·line \'gib-ə-,lēn, -,līn, -lən\ *n* [It *Ghibellino*] **:** a member of an aristocratic political party in medieval Italy supporting the authority of the German emperors — compare GUELF

ghillie *var of* GILLIE

1ghost \'gōst\ *n, often attrib* [ME *gost, gast*, fr. OE *gāst;* akin to OHG *geist* spirit, Skt *heḍa* anger] **1 :** the seat of life or intelligence **:** SOUL ⟨give up the ~⟩ **2 :** a disembodied soul; *esp* **:** the soul of a dead person believed to be an inhabitant of the unseen world or to appear to the living in bodily likeness **3 :** SPIRIT, DEMON **4 a :** a faint shadowy trace **b :** the least bit **:** IOTA **5 :** a false image in a photographic negative or on a television screen caused esp. by reflection **6 :** one who ghostwrites — **ghost·like** \-,līk\ *adj* — **ghosty** \'gō-stē\ *adj*

2ghost *vt* **1 :** to haunt like a ghost **2 :** GHOSTWRITE ~ *vi* **1 :** to move silently like a ghost **2 :** GHOSTWRITE

ghost dance *n* **:** a group dance for communication with the spirits of the dead characteristic of an Amerindian messianic cult

ghost·li·ness \'gōst-lē-nəs\ *n* **:** the quality or state of being ghostly

ghost·ly \-lē\ *adj* **1 :** of or relating to the soul **:** SPIRITUAL **2 :** of, relating to, or having the characteristics of a ghost **:** SPECTRAL **3 :** of or relating to a ghost-writer — **ghostly** *adv*

ghost town *n* **:** a deserted but once-flourishing town

ghost word *n* **:** a word form never in established usage

ghost·write \'gō-,strīt\ *vb* [back-formation fr. *ghost-writer*] *vi* **:** to write for and in the name of another ~ *vt* **:** to write for another who is the presumed author — **ghost–writ·er** *n*

ghoul \'gül\ *n* [Ar *ghūl*] **1 :** a legendary evil being that robs graves and feeds on corpses **2 :** one suggestive of a ghoul — **ghoul·ish** \'gü-lish\ *adj* — **ghoul·ish·ly** *adv* — **ghoul·ish·ness** *n*

1GI \(')jē-'ī\ *adj* [galvanized *iron*; fr. abbr. used in listing such articles as garbage cans, but taken as abbr. for *government issue*] **1 :** provided by an official U.S. military supply department **2 :** of, relating to, or characteristic of U.S. military personnel **3 :** conforming to military regulations or customs

2GI *n* **:** a member or former member of the U.S. armed forces; *esp* **:** an enlisted man

3GI *vt* **GI'd** \-'īd\ **GI'ing** \-'ī-iŋ\ **:** to prepare for military inspection by cleaning

4GI *adv* **:** in strict conformity with military regulations or customs

1gi·ant \'jī-ənt\ *n* [ME *giaunt*, fr. MF *geant*, L *gigant-, gigas*, fr. Gk] **1 :** a legendary being of great stature and strength and of more than mortal but less than godlike power **2 a :** a living being of great size **b :** a person of extraordinary powers **3 :** something unusually large or powerful — **gi·ant·ess** \-əs\ *n* — **gi·ant·like** \-,līk\ *adj*

2giant *adj* **:** characterized by extremely large size, proportion, or power

gi·ant·ism \'jī-ənt-,iz-əm\ *n* **1 :** the quality or state of being a giant **2 :** GIGANTISM 2

giant star *n* **:** a star of great intrinsic luminosity and of large mass

giaour \'jaù(ə)r\ *n* [Turk *gâvur*] **:** one outside the Muslim faith **:** INFIDEL

1gib \'gib\ *n* [ME, fr. *Gib*, nickname for *Gilbert*] **:** a male cat; *specif* **:** a castrated male cat

2gib *n* [origin unknown] **:** a plate of metal or other material machined to hold other parts in place, to afford a bearing surface, or to provide means for taking up wear

3gib *vt* **gibbed; gib·bing :** to fasten with a gib

gib·ber \'jib-ər\ *vi* **gib·ber·ing** \-(ə-)riŋ\ [imit.] **:** to speak rapidly, inarticulately, and often foolishly **:** CHATTER — **gibber** *n*

gib·ber·el·lic acid \,jib-ə-,rel-ik-\ *n* **:** a crystalline acid $C_{18}H_{21}O_4COOH$ associated with and similar in effect to the gibberellins

gib·ber·el·lin \,jib-ə-'rel-ən\ *n* [NL *Gibberella*, genus name] **:** any of several plant-growth regulators produced by a fungus (*Gibberella fujikuroi*) that in low concentrations promote shoot growth

gib·ber·ish \'jib-(ə-)rish, 'gib-\ *n* [prob. fr. *gibber*] **:** unintelligible or meaningless language: **a :** a technical or esoteric language **b :** pretentious or needlessly obscure language

1gib·bet \'jib-ət\ *n* [ME *gibet*, fr. OF] **:** GALLOWS; *esp* **:** an upright post with a projecting arm for hanging the bodies of executed criminals as a warning

2gibbet *vt* **1 a :** to hang on a gibbet **b :** to expose to infamy or public scorn **2 :** to execute by hanging on a gibbet

gib·bon \'gib-ən\ *n* [F] **:** any of several tailless apes (genera *Hylobates* and *Symphalangus*) of southeastern Asia and the East Indies that are the smallest and most arboreal anthropoid apes

gib·bos·i·ty \jib-'äs-ət-ē, gib-\ *n* **:** PROTUBERANCE, SWELLING

gib·bous \'jib-əs, 'gib-\ *adj* [ME, fr. MF *gibbeux*, fr. LL *gibbosus* humpbacked, fr. L *gibbus* hump] **1 a :** marked by convexity **:** PROTUBERANT **b** *of the moon or a planet* **:** seen with more than half but not all of the apparent disk illuminated **c :** swollen on one side **2 :** having a hump **:** HUMPBACKED — **gib·bous·ly** *adv* — **gib·bous·ness** *n*

gibe \'jīb\ *vb* [perh. fr. MF *giber* to shake, handle roughly] *vi* **:** to utter taunting words ~ *vt* **:** to reproach with taunting words **syn** see SCOFF — **gibe** *n* — **gib·er** *n*

gib·let \'jib-lət\ *n* [ME *gibelet* entrails, garbage, fr. MF, stew of wildfowl] **:** the edible viscera of a fowl or other bird — usu. used in pl.

Gi·bral·tar \jə-'brȯl-tər\ *n* [*Gibraltar*, fortress in the Brit. colony of Gibraltar] **:** an impregnable stronghold

Gib·son \'gib-sən\ *n* [fr. the name *Gibson*] **:** a cocktail made of gin and dry vermouth and garnished with a small onion

gid \'gid\ *n* [back-formation fr. *giddy*] **:** a disease esp. of sheep caused by the larva of a tapeworm (*Multiceps multiceps*) in the brain

gid·dap \gid-'ap\ *v imper* [alter. of *get up*] — a command to a horse to go ahead or go faster

gid·di·ly \'gid-ᵊl-ē\ *adv* **:** in a giddy manner

gid·di·ness \'gid-ē-nəs\ *n* **:** the quality or state of being giddy

gid·dy \'gid-ē\ *adj* [ME *gidy* mad, foolish, fr. OE *gydig* possessed, mad; akin to OE *god*] **1 :** lightheartedly silly **:** FRIVOLOUS **2 a :** DIZZY **b :** causing dizziness **c :** whirling rapidly — **giddy** *vb* **gid·died; gid·dy·ing**

Gid·e·on \'gid-ē-ən\ *n* [Heb *Gidh'ōn*] **:** a biblical hero noted for his defeat of the Midianites and his 40-year rule over Israel

gie \'gē\ *chiefly Scot var of* GIVE

1gift \'gift\ *n, often attrib* [ME, fr. ON, something given, talent; akin to OE *giefan* to give] **1 :** a notable capacity or talent **2 :** something voluntarily transferred by one person to another without compensation **3 :** the act, right, or power of giving

syn FACULTY, APTITUDE, BENT, TALENT, GENIUS, KNACK: GIFT often implies special favor by God or nature; FACULTY applies to an innate or less often acquired ability for a particular accomplishment or function; APTITUDE implies a natural liking for some activity and the likelihood of success in it; BENT is nearly equal to APTITUDE but stresses inclination perhaps more than specific ability; TALENT suggests a marked special ability without implying a mind of extraordinary power; GENIUS suggests impressive inborn creative ability; KNACK implies a comparatively trivial but special ability making for ease and dexterity in performance

2gift *vt* **1 :** to endow with some power, quality, or attribute **2** *chiefly Brit* **:** PRESENT

gift·ed \'gif-təd\ *adj* **1 :** having great natural ability **:** TALENTED ⟨~ children⟩ **2 :** revealing a special gift ⟨~ voices⟩

gift wrap *vt* **:** to wrap (merchandise intended as a gift) in specially attractive or fancy wrapping usu. with ribbons

1gig \'gig\ *n* [ME *gigg* top, perh. of Scand origin; akin to ON *geiga* to turn aside; akin to OE *geonian* to yawn — more at YAWN] **1 :** something that whirls or is whirled: as **a** *obs* **:** TOP, WHIRLIGIG **b :** a 3-digit selection in a numbers game **2 :** one that is odd **3 a :** a long light ship's boat propelled by oars, sail, or motor **b :** a rowboat designed for speed rather than for work **4 :** a light two-wheeled one-horse carriage

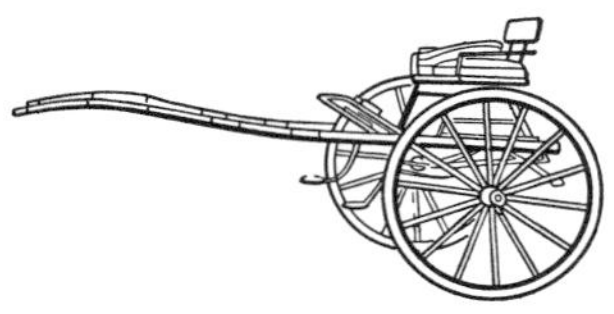

gig 4

2gig *vi* **gigged; gig·ging :** to travel in a gig

3gig *n* [short for earlier *fizgig, fishgig*, of unknown origin] **1 :** a pronged spear for catching fish **2 :** an arrangement of hooks to be drawn through a school of fish when they will not bite in order to hook them in the bodies

4gig *vb* **gigged; gig·ging** *vt* **1 :** to spear with a gig **2 a** *chiefly West* **:** SPUR, JAB **b :** GOAD, PROVOKE ~ *vi* **:** to fish with a gig

5gig *n* [origin unknown] **:** a military demerit

6gig *vt* **gigged; gig·ging :** to give a military gig to

giga- \'jig-ə\ *comb form* [ISV, fr. Gk *gigas* giant] **:** billion ⟨*giga*cycle⟩ ⟨*giga*volt⟩

gigant- *or* **giganto-** *comb form* [Gk, fr. *gigant-, gigas*] **:** giant ⟨*gigant*ism⟩

gi·gan·tesque \,jī-,gan-'tesk\ *adj* **:** of enormous proportions

gi·gan·tic \jī-'gant-ik\ *adj* **1 a :** resembling a giant ⟨~ stature⟩ **b :** greater in size than the usual or expected ⟨~ wave⟩ **2 :** extremely large or great ⟨~ industry⟩ **syn** see ENORMOUS — **gi·gan·ti·cal·ly** \-i-k(ə-)lē\ *adv*

gi·gan·tism \jī-'gan-,tiz-əm\ *n* **1 :** GIANTISM 1 **2 :** development to abnormally large size **3 :** excessive vegetative growth often accompanied by the inhibiting of reproduction

gi·gas \'jī-,gas\ *adj* [NL, fr. L, giant, fr. Gk] *of a polyploid plant* **:** having thicker stem, taller growth, darker thicker leaves, and larger flowers and seeds than a corresponding diploid

gig·gle \'gig-əl\ *vb* **gig·gling** \-(ə-)liŋ\ [imit.] *vi* **:** to laugh with repeated short catches of the breath **:** laugh in a silly manner ~ *vt* **:** to utter with a giggle — **giggle** *n* — **gig·gler** \-(ə-)lər\ *n* — **gig·gling·ly** \'gig-liŋ-lē\ *adv* — **gig·gly** \-(ə-)lē\ *adj*

gig·o·lo \'jig-ə-,lō\ *n, pl* **gigolos** [F] **1 :** a man living on the earnings of a woman **2 :** a professional dancing partner or male escort

gi·got \'jig-ət, zhē-'gō\ *n, pl* **gi·gots** \-əts, -'gō(z)\ [MF, dim. of *gigue* fiddle; fr. its shape — more at JIG] **1 :** a leg (as of lamb) esp. when cooked **2 :** a leg-of-mutton sleeve

Gi·la monster \,hē-lə-\ *n* [*Gila* river, Arizona] **:** a large orange and black venomous lizard (*Heloderma suspectum*) of the southwestern U.S.; *also* **:** a related lizard (*H. horridum*) of Mexico

gil·bert \'gil-bərt\ *n* [William *Gilbert* †1603 E physicist] **:** the cgs unit of magnetomotive force equivalent to $10 \div 4\pi$ ampere-turn

1gild \'gild\ *vt* **gild·ed** \'gil-dəd\ *or* **gilt** \'gilt\ **gild·ing** [ME *gilden*, fr. OE *gyldan;* akin to OE *gold*] **1 :** to overlay with or as if with a thin covering of gold **2 a :** to give money to **b :** to give an often deceptive attractive appearance to **c** *archaic* **:** to make bloody — **gild·er** *n* — **gild·ing** *n* — **gild the lily :** to add unnecessary ornamentation to something beautiful in its own right

2gild *var of* GUILD

1gill \'jil\ *n* [ME *gille*] — see MEASURE table

2gill \'gil\ *n* [ME *gile, gille*] **1 :** an organ (as of a fish) for obtaining oxygen from water **2 a :** WATTLE 2a **b :** the flesh under or about the chin or jaws — usu. used in pl. **c :** one of the radiating plates forming the undersurface of the cap of a mushroom fungus — **gilled** \'gild\ *adj*

3gill \'gil\ *vt* **:** to catch (fish) in a gill net ~ *vi, of fish* **:** to become entangled in a gill net — **gill·er** *n*

4gill \'gil\ *n* [ME *gille*, fr. ON *gil*] **1** *Brit* **:** RAVINE **2** *Brit* **:** a narrow stream or rivulet

5gill \'jil\ *n, often cap* [ME, fr. *Gill,* nickname for *Gillian*] : GIRL, SWEETHEART

gil·lie *or* **gil·ly** *or* **ghil·lie** \'gil-ē\ *n* [ScGael *gille* & IrGael *giolla* boy] **1** : a male attendant on a Scottish Highland chief **2** *Scot & Irish* : a fishing and hunting guide **3** *usu* **ghillie** : a low-cut shoe with decorative lacing — **gillie** *vi*

gill net *n* : a flat net suspended vertically in the water with meshes that allow the head of a fish to pass but entangle it as it seeks to withdraw — **gill–net** \'gil-,net\ *vt* — **gill–net·ter** \-,net-ər\ *n*

gill slit *n* : a branchial cleft

gil·ly·flow·er \'jil-ē-,flau̇(-ə)r\ *n* [by folk etymology fr. ME *gilofre* clove, fr. MF *girofle, gilofre,* fr. L *caryophyllum,* fr. Gk *karyophyllon,* fr. *karyon* nut + *phyllon* leaf — more at CAREEN, BLADE] **1 a** : an Old World pink (*Dianthus caryophyllus*) widely cultivated for its clove-scented flowers — called also *clove pink* **b** : any of several related plants (genus *Dianthus*) **2** : STOCK 7 **3** : WALLFLOWER 1a

Gil·son·ite \'gil-sə-,nīt\ *trademark* — used for uintaite

1gilt \'gilt\ *adj* [ME, fr. pp. of *gilden* to gild] : covered with gold or gilt : of the color of gold

2gilt *n* **1** : gold or something that resembles gold laid on a surface **2** *slang* : MONEY **3** : superficial brilliance

3gilt *n* [ME *gylte,* fr. ON *gyltr;* akin to OE *gelte* young sow — more at GELD] : a young female swine

gilt–edged \'gil-'tejd\ *or* **gilt–edge** \-'tej\ *adj* **1** : having a gilt edge **2** : of the best quality

gilt·head \'gilt-,hed\ *n* : any of several marine fishes: as **a** : a percoid food fish (*Sparus auratus*) of the Mediterranean **b** : a cunner (*Crenilabrus melops*) of the British coasts

gim·bal \'gim-bəl, 'jim-\ *or* **gimbal ring** *n* [alter. of obs. *gemel* (double ring)] : a device that permits a body to incline freely in any direction or suspends it so that it will remain level when its support is tipped — usu. used in pl.

gim·crack \'jim-,krak\ *n* [origin unknown] : a showy object of little use or value : GEWGAW — **gimcrack** *adj* — **gim·crack·ery** \-(ə-)rē\ *n*

gim·el \'gim-əl\ *n* [Heb *gīmel*] : the third letter of the Hebrew alphabet — symbol ג

1gim·let \'gim-lət\ *n* [ME, fr. MF *guimbelet*] : a small tool with a screw point, grooved shank, and cross handle for boring holes

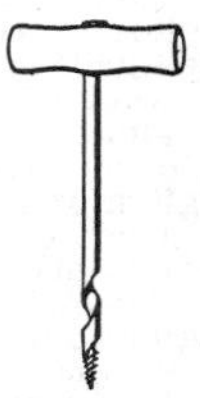

gimlet

2gimlet *adj* : having a piercing or penetrating quality

3gimlet *vt* : to pierce with a gimlet

gim·mal \'gim-əl, 'jim-\ *n* [alter. of obs. *gemel* (double ring)] **1** *pl* : joined work (as in a clock) whose parts move within each other **2** : a pair or series of interlocked rings

gim·mick \'gim-ik\ *n* [origin unknown] **1 a** : a mechanical device for secretly and dishonestly controlling gambling apparatus **b** : an ingenious or novel mechanical device : GADGET **2 a** : an important feature that is not immediately apparent : CATCH **b** : a new and ingenious scheme or angle — **gimmick** *vt* — **gim·mick·ry** \-i-krē\ *n* — **gim·micky** \-i-kē\ *adj*

1gimp \'gimp\ *n* [perh. fr. D] : an ornamental flat braid or round cord used as a trimming

2gimp *n* [origin unknown] : SPIRIT, VIM

3gimp *n* [origin unknown] : CRIPPLE; *also* : LIMP — **gimpy** \'gim-pē\ *adj*

4gimp *vi* : LIMP, HOBBLE

1gin \'gin\ *vb* **gan** \'gan\ **gin·ning** [ME *ginnen,* short for *beginnen*] *archaic* : BEGIN

2gin \'jin\ *n* [ME *gin,* modif. of OF *engin* — more at ENGINE] : any of various tools or mechanical devices: as **a** : a snare or trap for game **b** : a machine for raising or moving heavy weights **c** : a cotton gin

3gin \'jin\ *vt* **ginned; gin·ning** **1** : SNARE **2** : to separate (cotton fiber) from seeds and waste material — **gin·ner** *n* — **gin·ning** *n*

4gin \(,)gin\ *conj* [perh. alter. of Sc & E dial. *gif,* fr. ME *yif, if*] *dial* : IF

5gin \'jin\ *n* [by shortening & alter. fr. *geneva*] **1** : a strong alcoholic liquor made by distilling a mash of grain with juniper berries **2** : a liquor similar to gin made from plain spirit flavored with an aromatic — **gin·ny** \'jin-ē\ *adj*

1gin·ger \'jin-jər\ *n, often attrib* [ME, fr. OE *gingifer,* fr. ML *gingiber,* alter. of L *zingiber,* fr. Gk *zingiberi*] **1** : any of a genus (*Zingiber,* esp. *Z. officinale*) of tropical Asiatic and Polynesian herbs of a family (Zingiberaceae, the ginger family) with pungent aromatic rhizomes used as a condiment and as a stimulant and a carminative; *also* : the rhizome of this plant **2** : high spirit : PEP **3** : a strong brown — **gin·gery** \'jinj-(ə-)rē\ *adj*

2ginger *vt* **gin·ger·ing** \'jinj-(ə-)riŋ\ : to make lively : pep up

ginger ale *n* : a sweetened carbonated nonalcoholic beverage flavored mainly with ginger extract

ginger beer *n* : a sweetened carbonated nonalcoholic beverage heavily flavored with ginger or capsicum or both

gin·ger·bread \'jin-jər-,bred\ *n* **1** : a cake made with molasses and flavored with ginger **2** : tawdry, gaudy, or superfluous ornament — **gingerbread** *adj* — **gin·ger·bready** \-ē\ *adj*

gin·ger·li·ness \'jin-jər-lē-nəs\ *n* : the quality of being gingerly

gin·ger·ly \-lē\ *adj* [perh. fr. 1*ginger*] : very cautious or careful — **gingerly** *adv*

gin·ger·snap \-,snap\ *n* : a thin brittle cookie sweetened with molasses and flavored with ginger

ging·ham \'giŋ-əm\ *n* [modif. of Malay *genggang* checkered cloth] : a clothing fabric usu. of yarn-dyed cotton in plain weave

gingiv- *or* **gingivo-** *comb form* [L *gingiva*] : gum : gums ⟨*gingiv*itis⟩

gin·gi·va \jin-'jī-və\ *n, pl* **gin·gi·vae** \-,vē\ [L — more at CONGER EEL] : 1GUM — **gin·gi·val** \jin-'jī-vəl, 'jin-jə-\ *adj*

gin·gi·vi·tis \,jin-jə-'vīt-əs\ *n* : inflammation of the gums

gink \'giŋk\ *n* [origin unknown] *slang* : PERSON, GUY

gink·go *also* **ging·ko** \'giŋ-(,)kō *also* 'giŋk-(,)gō\ *n, pl* **ginkgoes** [NL *Ginkgo,* genus name, fr. Jap *ginkyo*] : a showy gymnospermous tree (*Ginkgo biloba*) of eastern China with fan-shaped leaves and yellow fruit

gin mill *n* : BAR, SALOON

gin rummy *n* [5*gin*] : a rummy game for two players in which each player is dealt 10 cards and in which a player may win a hand by matching all his cards or may end play when his unmatched cards count up to less than 10

gin·seng \'jin-,saŋ, -,seŋ\ *n* [Chin (Pek) *jen²-shen¹*] **1 a** : a Chinese perennial herb (*Panax schinseng*) of a widely distributed family (Araliaceae, the ginseng family) having 5-foliolate leaves, scarlet berries, and an aromatic root valued locally as a medicine **b** : any of several related plants; *esp* : a similar No. American herb (*P. quinquefolium*) **2** : the root of a ginseng

Gipsy *var of* GYPSY

gi·raffe \jə-'raf\ *n, pl* **giraffes** [It *giraffa,* fr. Ar *zirāfah*] **1** *or pl* **giraffe** : a large fleet African ruminant mammal (*Giraffa camelopardalis*) that is the tallest of living quadrupeds and has a very long neck and a black-blotched fawn or cream coat **2** *cap* : CAMELOPARD 2 — **gi·raff·ish** \-'raf-ish\ *adj*

gir·an·dole \'jir-ən-,dōl\ *n* [F & It; F, fr. It *girandola,* fr. *girare* to turn, fr. LL *gyrare,* fr. L *gyrus* gyre] **1** : a radiating and showy composition **2** : an ornamental branched candle holder

gir·a·sol *or* **gir·a·sole** \'jir-ə-,sȯl, -,sōl, -,säl\ *n* [It *girasole,* fr. *girare* + *sole* sun, fr. L *sol* — more at SOLAR] **1** : JERUSALEM ARTICHOKE **2** : an opal of varying color that gives out fiery reflections in bright light

1gird \'gərd\ *vb* **gird·ed** \'gərd-əd\ *or* **girt** \'gərt\ **gird·ing** [ME *girden,* fr. OE *gyrdan;* akin to OE *geard* yard] *vt* **1 a** : to encircle or bind with a flexible band **b** : to make fast **c** : SURROUND **2** : PROVIDE, EQUIP; *esp* : to invest with the sword of knighthood **3** : to prepare (oneself) for action ~ *vi* : to prepare for action

2gird \'gərd, 'gi(ə)rd\ *vb* [ME *girden* to strike, thrust] : GIBE

3gird \'gərd, 'gi(ə)rd\ *n* : a sarcastic remark

gird·er \'gərd-ər\ *n* [1*gird*] : a horizontal main structural member that supports vertical loads, that sometimes consists of several pieces, and that may be made of one or more materials

1gir·dle \'gərd-ᵊl\ *n* [ME *girdel,* fr. OE *gyrdel;* akin to OHG *gurtil* girdle, OE *gyrdan* to gird] **1** : something that encircles or confines: as **a** : an article of dress encircling the body usu. at the waist **b** : a woman's close-fitting undergarment often boned and usu. elasticized that extends from the waist to below the hips **c** : a bony arch for the support of a limb **d** : a ring made by the removal of the bark and cambium around a plant stem **2** : the edge of a brilliant that is grasped by the setting

2girdle *vt* **gir·dling** \'gərd-liŋ, -ᵊl-iŋ\ **1** : to encircle with a girdle **2** : to move around : CIRCLE **3** : to cut a girdle around (a plant) usu. to kill by interrupting the circulation of water and nutrients

gir·dler \'gərd-lər, -ᵊl-ər\ *n* **1** : a maker of girdles **2** : one that girdles; *esp* : an insect that feeds on bark and gnaws grooves about stems and twigs

girl \'gər(-ə)l\ *n, often attrib* [ME *gurle, girle* young person of either sex] **1 a** : a female child **b** : a young unmarried woman **c** : a single or married woman of any age **2 a** : a female servant or employee **b** : SWEETHEART **c** : DAUGHTER — **girl·hood** \-,hu̇d\ *n*

girl Friday *n* [*girl* + *Friday* as in *man Friday*] : a female assistant (as in an office) entrusted with a wide variety of tasks

girl friend *n* **1** : a female friend **2** : a frequent or regular female companion of a boy or man **3** : a female paramour

girl guide *n* : a member of the British Girl Guides

girl·ie *or* **girly** \'gər-lē\ *adj* : featuring scantily clothed girls ⟨~ magazines⟩ ⟨~ show⟩

girl·ish \'gər-lish\ *adj* : of, relating to, or having the characteristics of a girl or girlhood — **girl·ish·ly** *adv* — **girl·ish·ness** *n*

girl scout *n* : a member of the Girl Scouts of the United States of America

girn \'gi(ə)rn\ *vi* [ME *girnen,* alter. of *grinnen* to grin, snarl] *chiefly Scot* : SNARL — **girn** *n, chiefly Scot*

Gi·rond·ist \jə-'rän-dəst, zhi-\ *n* [F *girondiste,* fr. *Gironde,* a political party, fr. *Gironde,* department of France represented by its leaders] : a member of the moderate republican party in the French legislative assembly in 1791

girt \'gərt\ *vb* [ME *girten,* alter. of *girden*] *vt* **1** : GIRD **2** : to fasten by means of a girth ~ *vi* : to measure in girth

1girth \'gərth\ *n* [ME, fr. ON *gjörth;* akin to OE *gyrdan* to gird] **1** : a band or strap that encircles the body of an animal to fasten something (as a saddle) upon its back **2 a** : a measure round a body **b** : SIZE, DIMENSIONS

2girth *vt* **1** : ENCIRCLE **2** : to bind or fasten with a girth **3** : to measure the girth of

gi·sarme \giz-'ärm, jiz-\ *n* [ME, fr. OF] : a medieval weapon mounted on a long staff and carried by foot soldiers

gist \'jist\ *n* [AF, it lies, fr. MF, fr. *gesir* to lie, fr. L *jacēre*] **1** : the ground of a legal action **2** : the main point of a matter : ESSENCE

git·tern \'git-ərn\ *n* [ME *giterne,* fr. MF *guiterne,* modif. of OSp *guitarra* guitar] : a medieval stringed instrument of the guitar family

1give \'giv\ *vb* **gave** \'gāv\ **giv·en** \'giv-ən\ **giv·ing** [ME *given,* of Scand origin; akin to OSw *giva* to give; akin to OE *giefan, gifan* to give, L *habēre* to have, hold] *vt* **1** : to make a present of **2 a** : to grant or bestow by formal action **b** : to accord or yield to another ⟨*gave* him her confidence⟩ **3 a** : to put into the possession of another for his use : HAND **b** (1) : to administer as a sacrament (2) : to administer as a medicine **c** : to commit to the trust or keeping of another **d** : to transfer from one's authority or custody **e** : to execute and deliver ⟨all employees must ~ bond⟩ **f** : to offer for conveyance or transmittal ⟨~ my regards to your family⟩ **4 a** : to offer to the action of another : PROFFER ⟨*gave* his hand to the visitor⟩ **b** : to yield to a man in sexual intercourse **5 a** : to present in public performance ⟨~ a concert⟩ **b** : to present to view or observation ⟨*gave* the signal to start⟩ **6** : to provide by way of entertainment ⟨~ a party⟩ **7** : to propose as a toast **8 a** : to designate as a share or portion : ALLOT **b** : to make assignment of (a name) **c** : to set forth as an actual or hypothetical datum : ASSUME **d** : ATTRIBUTE, ASCRIBE ⟨*gave* all the glory to God⟩ **9 a** : to yield as a product, consequence, or effect : PRODUCE ⟨cows ~ milk⟩ ⟨84 divided by 12 ~*s* 7⟩ **b** : to bring forth : BEAR **10 a** : to yield possession of by way of exchange : PAY **b** : to dispose of for a price : SELL **11 a** : to deliver by some bodily action ⟨*gave* him a push⟩ **b** : EXECUTE **c** : to inflict as punishment **d** : to award by formal verdict ⟨judgment was *given* against the plaintiff⟩ **12** : to offer for consideration, acceptance, or use ⟨~*s* no reason for his absence⟩

13 a : SACRIFICE **b :** CONSIGN, COMMEND **c :** to apply freely or fully **:** DEVOTE **d :** to offer as a pledge ⟨I ~ you my word⟩ **14 a :** OCCASION ⟨mountains always *gave* him pleasure⟩ **b :** to cause a person to catch by contagion, infection, or exposure **15 :** PERMIT, CONCEDE **16 :** to care to the extent of ⟨didn't ~ a hang⟩ **~** *vi* **1 :** to make gifts or presents **:** CONTRIBUTE, DONATE **2 a :** to yield to physical force or strain **b :** to collapse from the application of force or pressure **3 a** *of weather* **:** to become mild **b** *of frozen ground* **:** THAW **4 :** to afford a view or passage **:** OPEN

syn PRESENT, DONATE, BESTOW, CONFER, AFFORD: GIVE is the general term applicable to passing over, delivering, transmitting in any manner; PRESENT suggests more ceremony and implies a degree of value or complexity in what is given; DONATE implies a publicized giving as to charity; BESTOW implies a settling of something on one as a gift and often suggests condescension in the giver; CONFER applies to the giving of an intangible thing of permanent value (as an honor, privilege, rank); AFFORD implies a giving or supplying that is a natural consequence of the character of the thing that gives — **give a good account of :** to acquit (oneself) well — **give ground :** to withdraw before superior force **:** RETREAT — **give the gun :** to open the throttle of **:** speed up — **give tongue** *of hounds* **:** to begin barking on the scent — **give way 1 a :** RETREAT **b :** to yield the right of way **2 :** to yield oneself without restraint or control **3 a :** COLLAPSE, FAIL **b :** CONCEDE **4 :** to yield place **5 :** to begin to row

[2]**give** *n* **1 :** capacity or tendency to yield to force or strain **2 :** the quality or state of being springy

give–and–take \ˌgiv-ən-ˈtāk\ *n* **1 :** the practice of making mutual concessions **:** COMPROMISE **2 :** good-natured exchange of ideas

give away *vt* **1 :** to make a present of **2 :** to deliver (a bride) to the bridegroom at a wedding **3 a :** BETRAY **b :** DISCLOSE, REVEAL **4 :** to give (as weight) by way of a handicap

give•away \ˈgiv-ə-ˌwā\ *n* **1 :** an unintentional revelation or betrayal **2 :** something given away free; *specif* **:** PREMIUM **3 :** a radio or television program on which prizes are given away

give back *vi* **:** RETIRE, RETREAT

give in *vt* **:** DELIVER, SUBMIT ⟨*gave in* his resignation⟩ **~** *vi* **:** to yield under insistence or entreaty **:** SURRENDER

giv•en \ˈgiv-ən\ *adj* **1 :** PRESENTED, BESTOWED **2 :** PRONE, DISPOSED ⟨~ to swearing⟩ **3** *of an official document* **:** EXECUTED, DATED **4 a :** FIXED, SPECIFIED **b :** ASSUMED, GRANTED **5 :** immediately present in experience — **given** *n*

given name *n* **:** CHRISTIAN NAME

give off *vt* **1 :** to send out as a branch **2 :** EMIT **~** *vi* **:** to branch off

give out *vt* **1 a :** DECLARE, PUBLISH **b :** to read aloud the words of for congregational singing **2 :** EMIT **3 :** ISSUE ⟨*gave out* new uniforms⟩ **~** *vi* **1 :** to become exhausted **:** COLLAPSE **2 :** to break down

give over *vt* **1 :** CEASE **2 a :** to yield without restraint or control **:** ABANDON **b :** to set apart for a particular purpose or use **:** DEVOTE **3** *archaic* **:** to pronounce incurable **4 :** ENTRUST **~** *vi* **:** to bring an activity to an end **:** STOP

giv•er \ˈgiv-ər\ *n* **:** one that gives **:** DONOR

give up *vt* **1 :** SURRENDER **2 :** to desist from **3 a :** to abandon (oneself) to a particular feeling, influence, or activity **b :** to devote to a particular purpose or use **4 :** to declare incurable or insoluble **5 :** to despair of seeing **~** *vi* **:** to withdraw from an activity or course of action

giz•mo *or* **gis•mo** \ˈgiz-(ˌ)mō\ *n* [origin unknown] **:** GADGET

giz•zard \ˈgiz-ərd\ *n* [alter. of ME *giser*, fr. ONF *guisier*, fr. L *gigeria* (pl.) giblets] **1 :** the muscular enlargement of the alimentary canal of birds that immediately follows the crop and has usu. thick muscular walls and a tough horny lining for grinding the food **2 :** INNARDS

gla•bel•la \glə-ˈbel-ə\ *n, pl* **gla•bel•lae** \-ˈbel-ˌē, -ˌī\ [NL, fr. L, fem. of *glabellus* hairless, dim. of *glaber*] **:** the smooth prominence between the eyebrows — **gla•bel•lar** \-ˈbel-ər\ *adj*

gla•bres•cent \glā-ˈbres-ᵊnt\ *adj* **:** somewhat glabrous

gla•brous \ˈglā-brəs\ *adj* [L *glabr-*, *glaber* smooth, bald — more at GLAD] **:** SMOOTH; *esp* **:** having a surface without hairs or projections — **gla•brous•ness** *n*

gla•cé \gla-ˈsā\ *adj* [F, fr. pp. of *glacer* to freeze, ice, glaze, fr. L *glaciare*, fr. *glacies*] **1 :** made or finished so as to have a smooth glossy surface **2 :** coated with a glaze **:** CANDIED

gla•cial \ˈglā-shəl\ *adj* [L *glacialis*, fr. *glacies*] **1 a :** extremely cold **:** FRIGID **b :** devoid of warmth and cordiality **c :** coldly imperturbable **2 a :** of, relating to, or produced by glaciers **b :** suggestive of the very slow movement of glaciers **c** (1) **:** of, relating to, or being any of those parts of geologic time from Precambrian onward when a much larger portion of the earth was covered by glaciers than at present (2) *cap* **:** PLEISTOCENE **3 :** resembling ice ⟨~ acetic acid⟩ — **gla•cial•ly** \-shə-lē\ *adv*

gla•cial•ist \-shə-ləst\ *n* **1 :** GLACIOLOGIST **2 :** one who supports the glacier theory

gla•ci•ate \ˈglā-shē-ˌāt\ *vt* **1 :** FREEZE **2 :** to subject to glacial action; *also* **:** to produce glacial effects in or on — **gla•ci•a•tion** \ˌglā-s(h)ē-ˈā-shən\ *n*

gla•cier \ˈglā-shər\ *n* [F dial., fr. MF dial., fr. MF *glace* ice, fr. L *glacies;* akin to L *gelu* frost — more at COLD] **:** a large body of ice moving slowly down a slope or valley or spreading outward on a land surface

glacier theory *n* **:** a theory in glaciology: drift was deposited through the agency of glaciers in the glacial epoch

gla•ci•ol•o•gist \ˌglā-s(h)ē-ˈäl-ə-jəst\ *n* **:** a specialist in glaciology

gla•ci•ol•o•gy \-jē\ *n* [ISV *glacier* + *-o-* + *-logy*] **1 :** any of the branches of science dealing with snow or ice accumulation, glaciation, or glacial epochs **2 :** the glacial features of a region

gla•cis \gla-ˈsē, ˈglas-əs\ *n, pl* **gla•cis** \gla-ˈsēz\ *also* **glac•is•es** \ˈglas-ə-səz\ [F, fr. *glacer* to freeze, slide] **1 a :** a gentle slope **:** INCLINE **b :** a slope that runs downward from a fortification **2 :** a buffer area

[1]**glad** \ˈglad\ *adj* **glad•der; glad•dest** [ME, shining, glad, fr. OE *glæd;* akin to OHG *glat* shining, smooth, L *glaber* smooth, bald] **1** *archaic* **:** having a cheerful or happy disposition by nature **2 a :** experiencing pleasure, joy, or delight **:** made happy **b :** GRATIFIED, PLEASED **c :** very willing **3 a :** marked by, expressive of, or caused by happiness and joy **b :** causing happiness and joy **:** PLEASANT **4 :** full of brightness and cheerfulness — **glad•ly** *adv* — **glad•ness** *n*

syn HAPPY, CHEERFUL, LIGHTHEARTED, JOYFUL, JOYOUS: GLAD and HAPPY may express gratification but GLAD usu. implies delight, HAPPY a sense of well-being and complete content; CHEERFUL suggests a strong and spontaneous flow of good spirits; LIGHTHEARTED implies freedom from care, worry, or discontent; JOYFUL and JOYOUS imply exultant rejoicing

[2]**glad** *vb* **glad•ded; glad•ding** *archaic* **:** GLADDEN

[3]**glad** *n* **:** GLADIOLUS 1

glad•den \ˈglad-ᵊn\ *vb* **glad•den•ing** \ˈglad-niŋ, -ᵊn-iŋ\ *vt* **:** to make glad **~** *vi, archaic* **:** to be glad

glade \ˈglād\ *n* [perh. fr. [1]*glad*] **:** an open space surrounded by woods — **glady** \ˈglād-ē\ *adj*

glad hand *n* **:** a warm welcome or greeting often prompted by ulterior reasons — **glad–hand** \ˈglad-ˈhand\ *vb* — **glad–hand•er** *n*

glad•i•a•tor \ˈglad-ē-ˌāt-ər\ *n* [L, fr. *gladius* sword, of Celt origin; akin to W *cleddyf* sword; akin to L *clades* destruction, Gk *klados* sprout, branch — more at HALT] **1 :** a person engaged in a fight to the death for public entertainment in ancient Rome **2 :** a person engaging in a public fight or controversy **3 :** a trained fighter; *specif* **:** PRIZEFIGHTER — **glad•i•a•to•ri•al** \ˌglad-ē-ə-ˈtōr-ē-əl, -ˈtȯr-\ *adj*

glad•i•o•la \ˌglad-ē-ˈō-lə\ *n* [back-formation fr. *gladiolus*, taken as a pl.] **:** GLADIOLUS 1

gla•di•o•lus \ˌglad-ē-ˈō-ləs *also* glə-ˈdī-ə-ləs\ *n, pl* **gla•di•o•li** \-ˈō-(ˌ)lē, -ˈō-ˌlī; -ə-ˌlī\ [NL, genus name, fr. L, small sword, dim. of *gladius*] **1** *or pl* **gladiolus** *or* **gla•di•o•lus•es :** any of a genus (*Gladiolus*) of chiefly African plants of the iris family with erect sword-shaped leaves and spikes of brilliantly colored irregular flowers arising from flattened corms **2 :** the large middle portion of the sternum

glad•some \ˈglad-səm\ *adj* **:** giving or showing joy **:** CHEERFUL — **glad•some•ly** *adv* — **glad•some•ness** *n*

glad•stone \ˈglad-ˌstōn, *chiefly Brit* -stən\ *n, often cap* [W. E. Gladstone †1898 Brit. statesman] **:** a traveling bag with flexible sides on a rigid frame that opens flat into two compartments

glai•kit *or* **glai•ket** \ˈglā-kət\ *adj* [ME (Sc) *glaikit*] *chiefly Scot* **:** FOOLISH, GIDDY

glair *or* **glaire** \ˈgla(ə)r, ˈgle(ə)r\ *n* [ME *gleyre* egg white, fr. MF *glaire*, modif. of (assumed) VL *claria*, fr. L *clarus* clear — more at CLEAR] **1 :** a sizing liquid made from egg white **2 :** a viscid substance suggestive of an egg white

glairy \-ē\ *adj* **:** having the characteristics of or overlaid with glair

glaive \ˈglāv\ *n* [ME, fr. MF, javelin, sword, modif. of L *gladius* sword] *archaic* **:** SWORD; *esp* **:** BROADSWORD

glam•or•iza•tion \ˌglam-(ə-)rə-ˈzā-shən\ *n* **:** the act of glamorizing or the process of being glamorized

glam•or•ize *also* **glam•our•ize** \ˈglam-ə-ˌrīz\ *vt* **1 :** to make glamorous **2 :** ROMANTICIZE, GLORIFY — **glam•or•iz•er** *n*

glam•or•ous *also* **glam•our•ous** \ˈglam-(ə-)rəs\ *adj* **:** full of glamour — **glam•or•ous•ly** *adv* — **glam•or•ous•ness** *n*

glam•our *or* **glam•or** \ˈglam-ər\ *n* [Sc *glamour*, alter. of E *grammar;* fr. the popular association of erudition with occult practices] **1 :** a magic spell **2 :** a romantic, exciting, and often illusory attractiveness; *esp* **:** alluring or fascinating personal attraction — **glamour** *vt* **glam•our•ing** \-(ə-)riŋ\

[1]**glance** \ˈglan(t)s\ *vb* [ME *glencen*, *glenchen*] *vi* **1 :** to strike a surface obliquely so as to go off at an angle ⟨bullet *glanced* off the wall⟩ **2 a :** to flash or gleam with quick intermittent rays of light ⟨brooks *glancing* in the sun⟩ **b :** to make sudden quick movements ⟨dragonflies *glancing* over the pond⟩ **3 a :** to touch briefly or indirectly on a subject ⟨~*s* at the customs of ancient cultures⟩ **b :** to refer briefly to something by way of censure or satire **4 a** *of the eyes* **:** to move swiftly from one thing to another **b :** to take a quick look at something **~** *vt* **1** *archaic* **a :** to take a quick look at **b :** to catch a glimpse of **2 :** to give an oblique path of direction to: **a :** to throw or shoot so that the object glances from a surface **b** *archaic* **:** to aim (as an innuendo) indirectly **:** INSINUATE **syn** see FLASH

[2]**glance** *n* **1 a :** a quick intermittent flash or gleam **b** *archaic* **:** a sudden quick movement **2 a** *archaic* **:** a rapid oblique movement **b :** a deflected impact or blow **3 a :** a swift movement of the eyes **b :** a quick or cursory look **4** *archaic* **a :** GIBE **b :** ALLUSION

[3]**glance** *n* [G *glanz* luster, glanz; akin to OHG *glanz* bright — more at GLINT] **:** any of several mineral sulfides usu. dark colored with a metallic luster

glanc•ing \ˈglan(t)-siŋ\ *adj* **1 :** INCIDENTAL, INDIRECT **2 :** CASUAL, OFFHAND — **glanc•ing•ly** \-siŋ-lē\ *adv*

[1]**gland** \ˈgland\ *n* [F *glande*, fr. OF, glandular swelling on the neck, gland, modif. of L *gland-*, *glans* acorn; akin to Gk *balanos* acorn] **1 a :** a cell or group of cells that selectively removes materials from the blood, concentrates or alters them, and secretes them for further use in the body or for elimination from the body **b :** any of various animal structures suggestive of glands though not secretory in function ⟨lymph ~⟩ **2 :** any of various secreting organs (as a nectary) of plants

[2]**gland** *n* [origin unknown] **1 :** a device for preventing leakage of fluid past a joint in machinery **2 :** the movable part of a stuffing box by which the packing is compressed

glan•dered \ˈglan-dərd\ *adj* **:** affected with glanders

glan•ders \-dərz\ *n pl but sing or pl in constr* [MF *glandre* glandular swelling on the neck, fr. L *glandulae*, fr. pl. of *glandula*, dim. of *gland-*, *glans*] **:** a contagious and destructive disease esp. of horses caused by a bacterium (*Actinobacillus mallei*) and characterized by caseating nodular lesions that tend to break down and form ulcers

glan•du•lar \ˈglan-jə-lər\ *adj* **1 a :** of, relating to, or involving glands, gland cells, or their products **b :** having the characteristics or function of a gland **2 a :** INNATE, INHERENT **b :** PHYSICAL, SEXUAL — **glan•du•lar•ly** *adv*

glans \ˈglanz\ *n, pl* **glan•des** \ˈglan-ˌdēz\ [L *gland-*, *glans*, lit., acorn] **1 a :** a conical vascular body forming the extremity of the penis **b :** a similar body of the clitoris **2 :** a nut enclosed by an involucre

[1]**glare** \ˈgla(ə)r, ˈgle(ə)r\ *vb* [ME *glaren;* akin to OE *glæs*] *vi* **1 a :** to shine with a harsh uncomfortably brilliant light **b :** to stand out offensively **:** OBTRUDE **2 :** to stare angrily or fiercely **~** *vt* **1 :** to express (as hostility) by staring angrily **2** *archaic* **:** to cause to be sharply reflected **syn** see GAZE

[2]**glare** *n* **1 a :** a harsh uncomfortably bright light; *specif* **:** painfully bright sunlight **b :** cheap showy brilliance **:** GARISHNESS **2 :** an angry or fierce stare **syn** see BLAZE

[3]**glare** *n* [prob. fr. [2]*glare*] **:** a surface or sheet of ice with a smooth slippery surface

glar·ing *adj* **1 :** having a fixed look of hostility, fierceness, or anger **2 a :** shining with or reflecting an uncomfortably bright light **b** (1) **:** GARISH (2) **:** vulgarly ostentatious **3 :** painfully obvious ⟨~ error⟩ **syn** see FLAGRANT — **glar·ing·ly** \-iŋ-lē\ *adv* — **glar·ing·ness** *n*

glary \'gla(ə)r-ē, 'gle(ə)r-\ *adj* **:** having a dazzling brightness **:** GLARING

1glass \'glas\ *n, often attrib* [ME *glas,* fr. OE *glæs;* akin to OE *geolu* yellow — more at YELLOW] **1 a :** an amorphous inorganic usu. transparent or translucent substance consisting of a mixture of silicates or sometimes borates or phosphates formed by fusion of silica or of oxides of boron or phosphorus with a flux and a stabilizer into a mass that cools to a rigid condition without crystallization **b :** a substance resembling glass **2 a :** something made of glass: as (1) **:** TUMBLER (2) **:** MIRROR (3) **:** BAROMETER **b** (1) **:** an optical instrument or device that has one or more lenses and is designed to aid in the viewing of objects not readily seen (2) *pl* **:** a device used to correct defects of vision or to protect the eyes that consists typically of a pair of glass lenses and the frame by which they are held in place — called also *eyeglasses, spectacles* **3 :** the quantity held by a glass container **4 :** GLASSWARE — **glass·mak·er** \-,mā-kər\ *n* — **glass·mak·ing** \-kiŋ\ *n*

2glass *vt* **1 a :** GLAZE 1 **b :** to put in a glass container **2 :** to make glassy **3 a :** REFLECT **b :** to see mirrored **4 :** to scan with an optical instrument esp. for game ~ *vi* **1 :** to become glassy **2 :** to look for game through an optical instrument

glass·blow·er \-,blō(-ə)r\ *n* **:** one skilled in glassblowing

glass·blow·ing \-,blō-iŋ\ *n* **:** the art of shaping a mass of glass that has been softened by heat by blowing air into it through a tube

glass eye *n* **1 :** an artificial eye made of glass **2 :** an eye having a pale, whitish, or colorless iris — **glass–eyed** \-'īd\ *adj*

glass·ful \'glas-,fu̇l\ *n* **:** the quantity held by a glass

glass·house \'glas-,hau̇s\ *n* **1 :** GLASSWORKS **2** *chiefly Brit* **:** GREENHOUSE

glass·i·ly \'glas-ə-lē\ *adv* **:** in a glassy manner

glass·ine \gla-'sēn\ *n* **:** a thin dense paper highly resistant to the passage of air and grease

glass·i·ness \'glas-ē-nəs\ *n* **:** the quality or state of being glassy

glass·man \'glas-,man, -mən\ *n* **:** a dealer in or maker of glass

glass snake *n* **:** a limbless lizard (*Ophisaurus ventralis*) of the southern U.S. resembling a snake and having a fragile tail that readily breaks into pieces; *also* **:** any of several similar Old World lizards

glass·ware \'glas-,wa(ə)r, -,we(ə)r\ *n* **:** articles made of glass

glass wool *n* **:** glass fibers in a mass resembling wool and being used esp. for thermal insulation and air filters

glass·work \'glas-,wərk\ *n* **1 a :** the manufacture of glass or glassware; *also* **:** GLAZIERY **b** *pl* **:** a place where glass is made **2 :** GLASSWARE — **glass·work·er** \-,wər-kər\ *n*

glass·wort \-,wərt, -,wȯ(ə)rt\ *n* [fr. its former use in the manufacture of glass] **1 :** any of a genus (*Salicornia*) of woody succulent-leaved herbs of the goosefoot family **2 :** a saltwort (*Salsola kali*)

glassy \'glas-ē\ *adj* **1 :** resembling glass **2 :** DULL, LIFELESS ⟨~ eyes⟩

Glau·ber's salt \,glau̇-bər(z)-'sȯlt\ *or* **Glauber salt** \-bər-\ *n* [Johann R. *Glauber* †1668 G chemist] **:** a colorless crystalline sodium salt $Na_2SO_4.10H_2O$ used esp. as a cathartic — sometimes used in pl.

glau·co·ma \glȯ-'kō-mə, glau̇-\ *n* [L, cataract, fr. Gk *glaukōma,* fr. *glaukos*] **:** a disease of the eye marked by increased pressure within the eyeball, damage to the optic disk, and gradual loss of vision

glau·co·nite \'glȯ-kə-,nīt\ *n* [G *glaukonit,* irreg. fr. Gk *glaukos*] **:** a mineral consisting of a dull green earthy iron potassium silicate occurring abundantly in greensand — **glau·co·nit·ic** \,glȯ-kə-'nit-ik\ *adj*

glau·cous \'glȯ-kəs\ *adj* [L *glaucus* gleaming, gray, fr. Gk *glaukos*] **1 a :** of a pale yellow green color **b :** of a light bluish gray or bluish white color **2 :** having a powdery or waxy coating that gives a frosted appearance and tends to rub off ⟨~ fruits⟩ — **glau·cous·ness** *n*

1glaze \'glāz\ *vb* [ME *glasen,* fr. *glas* glass] *vt* **1 :** to furnish or fit with glass **2 a :** to coat with or as if with glass **b :** to apply a glaze to **3 :** to give a smooth glossy surface to ~ *vi* **1 :** to become glazed **2 :** to form a glaze — **glaz·er** *n*

2glaze *n* **1 :** a smooth slippery coating of thin ice **2 a :** a transparent or translucent substance used as a coating to produce a glossy or lustrous appearance applied to food on which it hardens **b :** a transparent or translucent color applied to modify the effect of a painted surface **c :** a smooth glossy or lustrous surface or finish **3 :** a glassy film

3glaze *vi* [prob. blend of *glare* and *gaze*] *archaic* **:** STARE

gla·zier \'glā-zhər, -zē-ər\ *n* **:** one who sets glass — **gla·ziery** \'glāzh-(ə-)rē, 'glā-zē-ə-rē\ *n*

glaz·ing \'glā-ziŋ\ *n* **1 :** the act, process, or trade of using or applying glaze **2 a :** GLASSWORK **b :** GLAZE

1gleam \'glēm\ *n* [ME *gleem,* fr. OE *glǣm;* akin to OE *geolu* yellow — more at YELLOW] **1 a :** a transient appearance of subdued or partly obscured light **b :** a small bright light **:** GLINT **2 :** a brief or faint appearance or occurrence **:** TRACE ⟨~ of hope⟩ — **gleamy** \'glē-mē\ *adj*

2gleam *vi* **1 :** to shine with subdued light or moderate brightness **2 :** to appear briefly or faintly ~ *vt* **:** to cause to gleam **syn** see FLASH

glean \'glēn\ *vb* [ME *glenen,* fr. MF *glener,* fr. LL *glennare;* akin to MIr *digliunn* I glean, OHG *glanz* bright — more at GLINT] *vi* **1 :** to gather grain or other produce left by reapers **2 :** to gather information or other material bit by bit ~ *vt* **1 a :** to pick up after a reaper **b :** to strip (as a field) of the leavings of reapers **2 a :** to gather (as information) bit by bit **b :** to pick over **3 :** to find out **:** LEARN, ASCERTAIN — **glean·able** \'glē-nə-bəl\ *adj* — **glean·er** *n*

glean·ings \'glē-niŋz\ *n pl* **:** things acquired by gleaning

glebe \'glēb\ *n* [L *gleba* clod, land — more at CLIP] **1** *archaic* **:** LAND; *specif* **:** a plot of cultivated land **2 :** land belonging or yielding revenue to a parish church or ecclesiastical benefice

glede \'glēd\ *n* [ME, fr. OE *glida;* akin to OE *glīdan* to glide] **:** any of several birds of prey (as the European kite)

glee \'glē\ *n* [ME, fr. OE *glēo* entertainment, music; akin to ON *glȳ* joy, Gk *chleuē* joke] **1 :** exultant high-spirited joy **:** MERRIMENT **2 :** an unaccompanied song for three or more solo usu. male voices **syn** see MIRTH

glee club *n* **:** a chorus organized for singing usu. short choral pieces

gleed \'glēd\ *n* [ME, fr. OE *glēd;* akin to OE *glōwan* to glow] *dial Brit* **:** a glowing coal

glee·ful \'glē-fəl\ *adj* **:** full of glee **:** MERRY — **glee·ful·ly** \-fə-lē\ *adv* — **glee·ful·ness** *n*

gleek \'glēk\ *n* [origin unknown] *archaic* **:** GIBE, TRICK — **gleek** *vb, archaic*

glee·man \'glē-mən\ *n* **:** MINSTREL

glee·some \-səm\ *adj, archaic* **:** GLEEFUL

gleet \'glēt\ *n* [ME *glet* slimy or mucous matter, fr. MF *glete,* fr. L *glittus* viscous; akin to LL *glut-, glus* glue — more at CLAY] **:** a chronic inflammation of a bodily orifice usu. accompanied by an abnormal discharge; *also* **:** the discharge itself — **gleety** \-ē\ *adj*

gleg \'gleg\ *adj* [ME, fr. ON *glöggr* clear-sighted] *Scot* **:** QUICK, SHARP

glei·za·tion \glā-'zā-shən\ *n* **:** development of or conversion into gley

glen \'glen\ *n* [ME (Sc), valley, fr. (assumed) ScGael *glenn;* akin to MIr *glend* valley] **:** a secluded narrow valley

glen·gar·ry \glen-'gar-ē\ *n, often cap* [*Glengarry,* valley in Scotland] **:** a woolen cap of Scottish origin

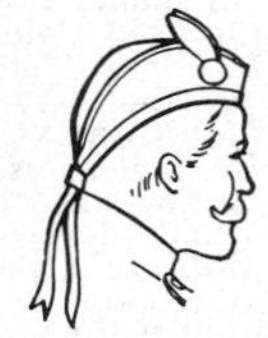

glengarry

gley \'glā\ *n* [Russ *gleĭ* clay; akin to OE *clǣg* clay — more at CLAY] **:** a sticky clay layer formed under the surface of some waterlogged soils

gli·a·din \'glī-əd-ən\ *n* [It *gliadina,* fr. MGk *glia* glue — more at CLAY] **:** PROLAMIN; *esp* **:** one obtained by alcoholic extraction of gluten from wheat and rye

glib \'glib\ *adj* **glib·ber; glib·best** [prob. modif. of LG *glibberig* slippery] **1** *archaic* **:** SMOOTH, SLIPPERY **2 a :** marked by ease and informality **b :** SUPERFICIAL, SLICK **3 :** marked by ease and fluency in speaking or writing — **glib·ly** *adv* — **glib·ness** *n*

1glide \'glīd\ *vb* [ME *gliden,* fr. OE *glīdan;* akin to OHG *glītan* to glide] *vi* **1 :** to move smoothly, continuously, and effortlessly **2 :** to pass gradually and imperceptibly **3** *of an airplane* **:** to descend at a normal angle without engine power sufficient for level flight **4** *of the tongue* **:** to change position in the articulation of a glide ~ *vt* **:** to cause to glide

2glide *n* **1 :** the act or action of gliding **2 :** a calm stretch of shallow water flowing smoothly **3 a :** PORTAMENTO **b :** a nonsignificant sound produced by the passing of the vocal organs to or from the articulatory position of a speech sound

glid·er \'glīd-ər\ *n* **1 :** one that glides: as **a :** an aircraft without an engine **b :** a porch seat suspended from an upright framework by short chains or straps **2 :** something that aids gliding

glim \'glim\ *n* [perh. short for 2*glimmer*] **1 :** GLIMMER **2** *slang* **:** a brief look **:** GLANCE **3 :** LIGHT

1glim·mer \'glim-ər\ *vi* **glim·mer·ing** \-(ə-)riŋ\ [ME *glimeren;* akin to OE *glǣm* gleam] **1 a :** to shine faintly or unsteadily **b :** to shimmer softly **2 :** to appear indistinctly with a faintly luminous quality **syn** see FLASH

2glimmer *n* **1 a :** a feeble or intermittent light **b :** a soft shimmer **2 a :** a dim perception or faint idea **:** INKLING **b :** a small amount **:** BIT

glim·mer·ing *n* **:** GLIMMER

1glimpse \'glim(p)s\ *vb* [ME *glimsen;* akin to MHG *glimsen* to glimmer, OE *glǣm* gleam] *vi* **1** *archaic* **:** GLIMMER **2 :** to take a brief look ~ *vt* **:** to get a brief look at — **glimps·er** *n*

2glimpse *n* **1 :** GLIMMER **2 :** a brief fleeting view or look

1glint \'glint\ *vb* [ME *glinten* to dart obliquely, glint, alter. of *glenten,* of Scand origin; akin to Sw dial. *glänta* to clear up; akin to OHG *glanz* bright, OE *geolu* yellow — more at YELLOW] *vi* **1 a** *archaic* **:** to glance off an object **b** *of rays of light* **:** to strike a reflecting surface obliquely and dart out at an angle **2 :** to shine by reflection: **a :** to shine with tiny bright flashes **:** SPARKLE **b :** GLITTER **c :** GLEAM **3 :** PEEP **4 :** to appear briefly or faintly ~ *vt* **:** to cause to glint **syn** see FLASH

2glint *n* **1 :** a tiny bright flash of light **:** SPARKLE **2** *archaic* **:** GLANCE **3 :** a brief or faint manifestation

1glis·sade \glis-'äd\ *vi* [F, n., slide, glissade, fr. *glisser* to slide, fr. OF *glicier,* alter. of *glier,* of Gmc origin; akin to OHG *glītan* to glide] **1 :** to slide without skis or other devices down a snow-covered slope **2 :** to perform a ballet glissade — **glis·sad·er** *n*

2glissade *n* **1 :** the action of glissading **2 :** a gliding step in ballet

glis·san·do \gli-'sän-(,)dō\ *n, pl* **glis·san·di** \-(,)dē\ *or* **glis·sandos** [prob. modif. of F *glissade*] **:** a rapid sliding up or down the musical scale

1glis·ten \'glis-ᵊn\ *vi* **glis·ten·ing** \'glis-niŋ, -ᵊn-iŋ\ [ME *glistnen,* fr. OE *glisnian;* akin to OE *glisian* to glitter, *geolu* yellow — more at YELLOW] **:** to shine by reflection with a sparkling radiance or with the mild luster of a wet or oiled surface **syn** see FLASH

2glisten *n* **:** GLITTER, SPARKLE

glis·ter \'glis-tər\ *vi* **glis·ter·ing** \-t(ə-)riŋ\ [ME *glistren;* akin to OE *glisian*] **:** GLISTEN — **glister** *n*

1glit·ter \'glit-ər\ *vi* [ME *gliteren,* fr. ON *glitra;* akin to OE *geolu* yellow] **1 a :** to shine by reflection with brilliant or metallic luster ⟨~*ing* sequins⟩ **b :** SPARKLE **c :** to shine with a hard cold glassy brilliance ⟨little eyes ~*ed* cruelly⟩ **2 :** to be brilliantly attractive in a superficial way **syn** see FLASH

2glitter *n* **1 :** sparkling brilliancy, showiness, or attractiveness **2 :** small glittering objects used for ornamentation — **glit·tery** \'glit-ə-rē\ *adj*

gloam \'glōm\ *n* [Sc *gloam* to become twilight, back-formation fr. *gloaming*] *archaic* **:** TWILIGHT

gloam·ing \'glō-miŋ\ *n* [ME (Sc) *gloming,* fr. OE *glōming,* fr. *glōm* twilight; akin to OE *glōwan* to glow] **:** TWILIGHT, DUSK

1gloat \'glōt\ *vi* [prob. of Scand origin; akin to ON *glotta* to grin scornfully; akin to OE *geolu* yellow] **1 :** to look or gaze at something admiringly or affectionately **2 :** to gaze at or think

about something with great self-satisfaction, gratification, or joy ⟨∼*ing* over his gold⟩ **3 :** to linger over or dwell upon something with malicious pleasure **syn** see GAZE — **gloat·er** *n*

2**gloat** *n* **1 :** the act of gloating **2 :** a feeling of triumphant or malicious satisfaction

glob \'gläb\ *n* [perh. blend of *globe* and *blob*] **1 :** a small drop **:** BLOB **2 :** a usu. large and rounded lump

glob·al \'glō-bəl\ *adj* **1 :** SPHERICAL **2 :** WORLDWIDE ⟨a system of ∼ communication⟩ **3 :** COMPREHENSIVE, UNIVERSAL — **glob·al·ly** \-bə-lē\ *adv*

glo·bate \'glō-ˌbāt\ *adj* **:** GLOBULAR 1a

1**globe** \'glōb\ *n* [MF, fr. L *globus* — more at CLIP] **:** something spherical or rounded: as **a :** a spherical representation of the earth or heavens **b :** EARTH **c :** ORB 5

2**globe** *vt, archaic* **:** to form into a globe

globe·fish \'glōb-ˌfish\ *n* **:** any of numerous chiefly tropical marine spiny-finned fishes of a family (Tetraodontidae) which can distend themselves to a globular form and most of which are highly poisonous

globe·flow·er \-ˌflau̇(-ə)r\ *n* **:** any of a genus (*Trollius*) of plants of the crowfoot family with globose yellow flowers

globe–trot·ter \-ˌträt-ər\ *n* **:** one that travels widely — **globe–trot·ting** \-iŋ\ *n or adj*

glo·bin \'glō-bən\ *n* [ISV, back-formation fr. *hemoglobin*] **:** a colorless protein obtained by removal of heme from a hemoglobin or similar conjugated protein

glo·boid \'glō-ˌbȯid\ *n or adj* **:** SPHEROID

glo·bose \'glō-ˌbōs\ *adj* **:** GLOBULAR 1a — **glo·bose·ly** *adv* — **glo·bos·i·ty** \glō-'bäs-ət-ē\ *n*

glob·u·lar \'gläb-yə-lər\ *adj* [partly fr. L *globus* + E *-ular;* partly fr. L *globulus* + E *-ar*] **1 a :** having the shape of a globe or globule **b :** WORLDWIDE **2 :** having or consisting of globules — **glob·u·lar·ly** *adv* — **glob·u·lar·ness** *n*

glob·ule \'gläb-(ˌ)yü(ə)l\ *n* [F, fr. L *globulus*, dim. of *globus*] **:** a tiny globe or ball

glob·u·lin \'gläb-yə-lən\ *n* **:** any of a class of simple proteins (as myosin) insoluble in pure water but soluble in dilute salt solutions that occur widely in plant and animal tissues

glo·chid·i·ate \glō-'kid-ē-ət\ *adj* **1** *or* **glo·chid·i·al** \-ē-əl\ **:** having glochidia **2 :** having barbed tips ⟨∼ leaves⟩

glo·chid·i·um \-ē-əm\ *n, pl* **glo·chid·ia** \-ē-ə\ [NL, fr. Gk *glōchis* projecting point + NL *-idium*] **1 :** a barbed hair or spine (as on a cactus) **2 :** a larval freshwater mussel (family Unionidae) that develops as an external parasite on fish

glock·en·spiel \'gläk-ən-ˌs(h)pēl\ *n* [G, fr. *glocke* bell + *spiel* play] **:** a percussion musical instrument consisting of a series of graduated metal bars tuned to the chromatic scale and played with two hammers

glom \'gläm\ *vt* **glommed; glom·ming** [prob. alter. of E dial. *glaum* to grab] **1** *slang* **:** TAKE, STEAL **2** *slang* **:** SEIZE, CATCH — **glom on to** *slang* **:** to take possession of

glom·er·ate \'gläm-ə-rət\ *adj* [L *glomeratus*, pp. of *glomerare* to wind into a ball, fr. *glomer-*, *glomus* ball — more at CLAM] **:** AGGLOMERATE, CONGLOMERATE — **glom·er·a·tion** \ˌgläm-ə-'rā-shən\ *n*

glo·mer·u·lar \glä-'mer-(y)ə-lər\ *adj* **:** of, relating to, or produced by a glomerulus ⟨∼ nephritis⟩

glo·mer·u·late \-lət\ *adj* **:** arranged in small compact clusters

glom·er·ule \'gläm-ə-ˌrül, -ər-ˌyü(ə)l\ *n* [NL *glomerulus*] **1 :** a compacted cyme like the flower head of a composite **2 :** GLOMERULUS

glo·mer·u·lo·ne·phri·tis \glä-ˌmer-(y)ə-lō-ni-'frīt-əs\ *n* **:** nephritis marked by inflammation of the capillaries of the renal glomeruli

glo·mer·u·lus \glä-'mer-(y)ə-ləs\ *n, pl* **glo·mer·u·li** \-ˌlī, -ˌlē\ [NL, glomerulus, glomerule, dim. of L *glomer-*, *glomus* ball] **:** a small convoluted or intertwined mass; *esp* **:** a tuft of capillaries at the point of origin of each vertebrate nephron

1**gloom** \'glüm\ *vb* [ME *gloumen;* akin to OE *geolu* yellow — more at YELLOW] *vi* **1 :** to look sullen or despondent **2 :** to be or become overcast **3 :** to loom up dimly or somberly ∼ *vt* **1 :** SADDEN **2 :** to make dark, murky, or somber

2**gloom** *n* **1 a :** partial or total darkness **b :** a dark place **2 a :** lowness of spirits **:** DEJECTION **b :** an atmosphere of despondency **syn** see SADNESS

gloom·i·ly \'glü-mə-lē\ *adv* **:** in a gloomy manner

gloom·i·ness \-mē-nəs\ *n* **:** the quality or state of being gloomy

gloomy \'glü-mē\ *adj* **1 a :** partially or totally dark; *esp* **:** dismally and depressingly dark ⟨∼ weather⟩ **b :** having a frowning or scowling appearance **:** FORBIDDING **c :** low in spirits **:** MELANCHOLY **2 a :** causing gloom **:** DEPRESSING ⟨a ∼ story⟩ **b :** marked by little or no hopefulness **:** PESSIMISTIC ⟨∼ prophecies⟩ **syn** see DARK, SULLEN

Glo·ria \'glōr-ē-ə, 'glȯr-\ *n* [L, glory] **:** one of several Christian doxologies beginning in the original Latin with *gloria*

glo·ri·fi·ca·tion \ˌglōr-ə-fə-'kā-shən, ˌglȯr-\ *n* **:** the act of glorifying or the state of being glorified

glo·ri·fi·er \'glōr-ə-ˌfī(-ə)r, 'glȯr-\ *n* **:** one that glorifies

glo·ri·fy \-ˌfī\ *vt* **1 :** to make glorious by bestowing glory upon; *esp* **:** to elevate to celestial glory **2 :** to shed radiance or splendor on **3 :** to make glorious by presentation in a favorable aspect **4 :** to give glory to (as in worship)

glo·ri·ous \'glōr-ē-əs, 'glȯr-\ *adj* **1 a :** possessing or deserving glory **:** ILLUSTRIOUS **b :** conferring glory ⟨∼ victory⟩ **2 :** RESPLENDENT, MAGNIFICENT **3 :** DELIGHTFUL, WONDERFUL **syn** see SPLENDID — **glo·ri·ous·ly** *adv* — **glo·ri·ous·ness** *n*

1**glo·ry** \'glōr-ē, 'glȯr-\ *n* [ME *glorie*, fr. MF & L; MF, fr. L *gloria*] **1 a :** praise, honor, or distinction extended by common consent **:** RENOWN **b :** worshipful praise, honor, and thanksgiving **2 a :** something that secures praise or renown **b :** a highly commendable asset **3 a** (1) **:** RESPLENDENCE, MAGNIFICENCE (2) **:** something marked by beauty or resplendence **b :** the splendor and beatific happiness of heaven **4 :** a height of prosperity or achievement **5 :** a ring or spot of light: as **a :** AUREOLE **b :** CORONA 2a, 2b

2**glory** *vi* **:** to rejoice proudly **:** EXULT

1**gloss** \'gläs, 'glȯs\ *n* [prob. of Scand origin; akin to Icel *glossa* to glow; akin to OE *geolu* yellow] **1 :** a superficial luster or brightness **:** POLISH **2 :** a deceptively attractive appearance **:** SEMBLANCE

2**gloss** *vt* **1 a :** to give a deceptive appearance to ⟨∼ the matter over⟩ **b :** to hide by a plausible pretext or quick superficial discussion ⟨∼ over inadequacies⟩ **2 :** to give gloss to

3**gloss** *n* [ME *glose*, fr. OF, fr. L *glossa* unusual word requiring explanation, fr. Gk *glōssa, glōtta* tongue, language, unusual word; akin to Gk *glōchis* projecting point] **1 a :** a brief explanation (as in the margin or between the lines of a text) of a difficult or obscure word or expression **b :** a false interpretation **2 a :** GLOSSARY **b :** an interlinear translation **c :** a continuous commentary accompanying a text

4**gloss** *vt* **1 :** to furnish glosses for **2 :** to make a false or perverse interpretation of **syn** see ANNOTATE

gloss- *or* **glosso-** *comb form* [L, fr. Gk *glōss-*, *glōsso-*, fr. *glōssa*] **1 :** tongue ⟨*gloss*algia⟩ **2 :** language ⟨*glosso*logy⟩

glos·sa \'gläs-ə, 'glȯs-\ *n, pl* **glos·sae** \-ˌē, -ˌī\ *also* **glossas** [NL, fr. Gk *glōssa*] **:** a tongue or lingual structure esp. in an insect; *esp* **:** the median distal lobe of the labium of an insect

glos·sal \-əl\ *adj* **:** of or relating to the tongue

glos·sar·i·al \glä-'sar-ē-əl, glȯ-, -'ser-\ *adj* **:** of, relating to, or having the characteristics of a glossary

glos·sa·rist \'gläs-ə-rəst, 'glȯs-\ *n* **1 :** one that makes textual glosses **2 :** a compiler of a glossary

glos·sa·ry \-(ə-)rē\ *n* **:** a collection of textual glosses or of terms limited to a special area of knowledge or usage

glos·sa·tor \'gläs-ˌāt-ər, 'glȯs-\ *n* **:** GLOSSARIST

gloss·i·ly \'gläs-ə-lē, 'glȯs-\ *adv* **:** in a glossy manner

glos·si·na \glä-'sī-nə, glȯ-, -'sē-\ *n* [NL, genus name, fr. Gk *glōssa* tongue; fr. its long proboscis] **:** TSETSE

gloss·i·ness \'gläs-ē-nəs, 'glȯs-\ *n* **:** the quality or state of being glossy

glos·sog·ra·pher \glä-'säg-rə-fər, glȯ-\ *n* [Gk *glōssographos*, fr. *glōssa* + *graphein* to write — more at CARVE] **:** GLOSSARIST

glos·so·pha·ryn·geal \ˌgläs-(ˌ)ō-fə-'rin-j(ē-)əl, ˌglȯs-, -ˌfar-ən-'jē-əl\ *adj* **:** of or relating to both tongue and pharynx

glossopharyngeal nerve *n* **:** a mixed nerve that is either of the 9th pair of cranial nerves and supplies chiefly the pharynx, posterior tongue, and parotid gland

glossy \'gläs-ē, 'glȯs-\ *adj* **1 :** having a superficial luster or brightness **2 :** SPECIOUS; *esp* **:** having a false air of sophistication

glott- *or* **glotto-** *comb form* [Gk *glōtt-*, *glōtto-* tongue, fr. *glōssa, glōtta*] **:** language ⟨*glotto*logy⟩

glot·tal \'glät-ᵊl\ *adj* **:** of, relating to, or produced in or by the glottis ⟨∼ constriction⟩

glottal stop *n* **:** a speech sound or phenomenon of speech produced by interruption of the breath stream by closure of the glottis

glot·tis \'glät-əs\ *n, pl* **glot·tis·es** *or* **glot·ti·des** \-ə-ˌdēz\ [Gk *glōttid-*, *glōttis*, fr. *glōtta* tongue — more at GLOSS] **:** the elongated space between the vocal folds; *also* **:** the structures that surround this space — compare EPIGLOTTIS

glot·to·chro·nol·o·gy \ˌglät-(ˌ)ō-krə-'näl-ə-jē\ *n* **:** the study of the time during which two or more languages have evolved separately from a common source

glout \'glüt, 'glau̇t\ *vi* [ME *glouten*, prob. of Scand origin; akin to ON *glotta* to grin scornfully — more at GLOAT] *archaic* **:** FROWN, SCOWL

glove \'gləv\ *n* [ME, fr. OE *glōf;* akin to ON *glōfi* glove] **1 a :** a covering for the hand having separate sections for each finger **b :** GAUNTLET **2 a :** a padded leather covering for the hand used in baseball — compare MITT **b :** BOXING GLOVE — **glove** *vt*

glove compartment *n* **:** a small storage cabinet in the dashboard of an automobile

glov·er \'gləv-ər\ *n* **:** one that makes or sells gloves

1**glow** \'glō\ *vi* [ME *glowen*, fr. OE *glōwan;* akin to OE *geolu* yellow — more at YELLOW] **1 a :** to shine with or as if with an intense heat **b** (1) **:** to have a rich warm typically ruddy color (2) **:** FLUSH, BLUSH **2 a :** to experience a sensation of or as if of heat **b :** to show exuberance or elation ⟨∼ with pride⟩ **syn** see BLAZE

2**glow** *n* **1 :** brightness or warmth of color; *esp* **:** REDNESS **2 a :** warmth of feeling or emotion **b :** a sensation of warmth **3 :** light such as is emitted by a solid body heated to luminosity **:** INCANDESCENCE

1**glow·er** \'glau̇(-ə)r\ *vi* [ME (Sc) *glowren;* perh. of Scand origin; akin to Norw dial. *glyra* to look askance; Icel *glossa* to glow — more at GLOW] **1** *dial Brit* **:** to stare in amazement **2 :** to look or stare with sullen annoyance or anger **syn** see FROWN

2**glower** *n* **1** *dial Brit* **:** an amazed stare **2 :** a sullen brooding look marked by annoyance or anger

glow lamp *n* **:** a gas-discharge electric lamp in which most of the light proceeds from the glow of the gas near the cathode

glow plug *n* **:** a small electric heating element placed inside a diesel-engine cylinder to preheat the air and facilitate starting

glow·worm \'glō-ˌwərm\ *n* **:** any of various luminous insects with wings rudimentary or lacking; *esp* **:** a wingless female or larva of a beetle (family Lampyridae) that emits light from the abdomen

glox·in·ia \gläk-'sin-ē-ə\ *n* [NL, genus name, fr. B. P. *Gloxin* 18th cent. G botanist] **:** any of a genus (*Sinningia*) of Brazilian tuberous herbs of a family (Gesneriaceae, the gloxinia family); *esp* **:** a plant (*S. speciosa*) widely cultivated for its showy bell-shaped flowers

1**gloze** \'glōz\ *vb* [ME *glosen* to gloss, flatter, fr. *glose* gloss] *vi, archaic* **:** to use flattery ∼ *vt, archaic* **:** 4GLOSS *vt* 1

2**gloze** *vt* **:** 2GLOSS 1 — often used with *over*

glu·co·nate \'glü-kə-ˌnāt\ *n* **:** a salt of gluconic acid

glu·con·ic acid \(ˌ)glü-ˌkän-ik-\ *n* [ISV, irreg. fr. *glucose* + *-ic*] **:** a crystalline acid $C_6H_{12}O_7$ obtained by oxidation of glucose and used chiefly in cleaning metals

glu·cose \'glü-ˌkōs, -ˌkōz\ *n* [F, modif. of Gk *gleukos* must, sweet wine; akin to Gk *glykys* sweet] **1 :** a sugar $C_6H_{12}O_6$ known in dextrorotatory, levorotatory, and racemic forms; *esp* **:** the sweet colorless soluble dextrorotatory form that occurs widely in nature and is the usual form in which carbohydrate is assimilated by animals **2 :** a starch syrup

glu·co·side \'glü-kə-ˌsīd\ *n* **:** GLYCOSIDE; *esp* **:** a glycoside that yields glucose on hydrolysis — **glu·co·sid·ic** \ˌglü-kə-'sid-ik\ *adj* — **glu·co·sid·i·cal·ly** \-i-k(ə-)lē\ *adv*

1**glue** \'glü\ *n* [ME *glu*, fr. MF, fr. LL *glut-*, *glus* — more at CLAY] **1 :** a hard protein substance largely gelatin that absorbs water to form a viscous solution with strong adhesive properties and is obtained by cooking down collagenous materials (as hides, bones); *also* **:** a solution of such glue used for sticking things together **2 :** any of various other strong adhesive substances or solutions

— **glu·ey** \-ē\ *adj* **glu·i·er**; **glu·i·est** — **glu·i·ly** \'glü-ə-lē\ *adv*

2**glue** *vt* **glued**; **glu·ing** *also* **glue·ing** : to make fast with or as if with glue

glum \'gləm\ *adj* **glum·mer**; **glum·mest** [prob. akin to ME *gloumen* to gloom] **1** : broodingly morose ⟨became ~ when they heard the news⟩ **2** : DREARY, GLOOMY ⟨a ~ countenance⟩ **syn** see SULLEN — **glum·ly** *adv* — **glum·ness** *n*

glu·ma·ceous \glü-'mā-shəs\ *adj* : consisting or having the character of glumes ⟨~ flowers⟩

glume \'glüm\ *n* [NL *gluma*, fr. L, hull, husk; akin to L *glubere* to peel — more at CLEAVE] : a chaffy bract; *specif* : either of two empty bracts at the base of the spikelet in grasses — **glu·mif·er·ous** \glü-'mif-(ə-)rəs\ *adj*

1**glut** \'glət\ *vb* **glut·ted**; **glut·ting** [ME *glouten*] *vt* **1** : to fill esp. with food to satiety : SATIATE **2** : to flood with goods so that supply exceeds demand ~ *vi* : to eat gluttonously **syn** see SATIATE

2**glut** *n* **1** *archaic* : the act or process of glutting **2** : an excessive quantity : OVERSUPPLY

3**glut** *vt* **glut·ted**; **glut·ting** [prob. fr. obs. *glut*, n. (swallow)] *archaic* : to swallow greedily

glu·ta·mate \'glüt-ə-,māt\ *n* : a salt or ester of glutamic acid

glu·tam·ic acid \(,)glü-,tam-ik-\ *n* [ISV *gluten* + *amino* + *-ic*] : a crystalline amino acid $C_5H_9NO_4$ widely distributed in plant and animal proteins and used in the form of a sodium salt as a seasoning

glu·ta·mine \'glüt-ə-,mēn\ *n* [ISV *gluten* + *amine*] : a crystalline amino acid $C_5H_{10}N_2O_3$ found both free and in proteins in plants and animals that yields glutamic acid and ammonia on hydrolysis

glu·te·al \'glüt-ē-əl, glü-'tē-\ *adj* : of or relating to the gluteus muscles

glu·ten \'glüt-ᵊn\ *n* [L *glutin-*, *gluten* glue; akin to LL *glut-*, *glus* glue] : a tenacious elastic protein substance esp. of wheat flour that gives cohesiveness to dough — **glu·ten·ous** \'glüt-nəs, -ᵊn-əs\ *adj*

glu·te·us \'glüt-ē-əs, glü-'tē-\ *n, pl* **glu·tei** \'glüt-ē-,ī, -ē-,ē; glü-'tē-,ī\ [NL *glutaeus*, *gluteus*, fr. Gk *gloutos* buttock — more at CLOUD] : any of the large muscles of the buttocks

glu·ti·nous \'glüt-nəs, -ᵊn-əs\ *adj* [MF or L; MF *glutineux*, fr. L *glutinosus*, fr. *glutin-*, *gluten*] : having the quality of glue : GUMMY — **glu·ti·nous·ly** *adv* — **glu·ti·nous·ness** *n*

glut·ton \'glət-ᵊn\ *n* [ME *glotoun*, fr. OF *gloton*, fr. L *glutton-*, *glutto*; akin to L *gluttire* to swallow, *gula* throat, OE *ceole*] **1 a** : one that eats too much **b** : one that has a great capacity for accepting or enduring something ⟨a ~ for work⟩ **2 a** : a shaggy thickset carnivorous mammal (*Gulo gulo*) of the family Mustelidae of northern Europe and Asia related to the marten and the sable **b** : WOLVERINE 1 **syn** see EPICURE

glut·ton·ous \'glət-nəs, -ᵊn-əs\ *adj* : marked by or given to gluttony — **glut·ton·ous·ly** *adv* — **glut·ton·ous·ness** *n*

glut·tony \'glət-nē, -ᵊn-ē\ *n* : excess in eating or drinking

glyc- *or* **glyco-** *comb form* [ISV, fr. Gk *glyk-* sweet, fr. *glykys*] : sugar ⟨*glyco*protein⟩

glycer- *or* **glycero-** *comb form* [ISV, fr. *glycerin*] **1** : glycerol ⟨*glycer*yl⟩ **2** : related to glycerol or glyceric acid ⟨*glycer*aldehyde⟩

glyc·er·al·de·hyde \,glis-ə-'ral-də-,hīd\ *n* : a sweet crystalline compound $C_3H_6O_3$ formed by the breakdown of sugars that yields glycerol on reduction

glyc·er·ate \'glis-ə-,rāt, -rət\ *n* : a salt or ester of glyceric acid

gly·cer·ic acid \glis-,er-ik-\ *n* [ISV, fr. *glycerine*] : a syrupy acid $C_3H_6O_4$ obtainable by oxidation of glycerol or glyceraldehyde

glyc·er·ide \'glis-ə-,rīd\ *n* : an ester of glycerol esp. with fatty acids — **glyc·er·id·ic** \,glis-ə-'rid-ik\ *adj*

glyc·er·in *or* **glyc·er·ine** \'glis-(ə-)rən\ *n* [F *glycérine*, fr. Gk *glykeros* sweet; akin to Gk *glykys*] : GLYCEROL

glyc·er·in·ate \'glis-(ə-)rə-,nāt\ *vt* : to treat with or preserve in glycerin — **glyc·er·in·ation** \,glis-(ə-)rə-'nā-shən\ *n*

glyc·er·ol \'glis-ə-,ról, -,rōl\ *n* [*glycer*ine + *-ol*] : a sweet syrupy hygroscopic trihydroxy alcohol $C_3H_8O_3$ usu. obtained by the saponification of fats and used esp. as a solvent and plasticizer

glyc·er·yl \'glis-(ə-)rəl\ *n* : a radical derived from glycerol by removal of hydroxide; *esp* : a trivalent radical CH_2CHCH_2

gly·cine \'glī-,sēn, 'glīs-ᵊn\ *n* : a sweet crystalline amino acid $C_2H_5NO_2$ formed esp. by hydrolysis of proteins

gly·co·gen \'glī-kə-jən\ *n* : a white amorphous tasteless polysaccharide $(C_6H_{10}O_5)x$ that is the chief storage carbohydrate of animals

gly·co·gen·e·sis \,glī-kə-'jen-ə-səs\ *n* [NL] **1** : formation of sugar from glycogen **2** : formation of glycogen — **gly·co·ge·net·ic** \-jə-'net-ik\ *adj*

gly·col \'glī-,kól, -,kōl\ *n* : ETHYLENE GLYCOL; *broadly* : any of numerous related alcohols

gly·col·ic acid \(,)glī-,käl-ik-\ *n* : a translucent crystalline compound $C_2H_4O_3$ found esp. in unripe grapes and sugar beets

gly·col·y·sis \glī-'käl-ə-səs\ *n* [NL] : the enzymatic breakdown of glucose, glycogen, or other carbohydrate by way of phosphate derivatives — **gly·co·lyt·ic** \,glī-kə-'lit-ik\ *adj* — **gly·co·lyt·i·cal·ly** \-i-k(ə-)lē\ *adv*

gly·co·pro·tein \,glī-(,)kō-'prō-,tēn, -'prōt-ē-ən\ *n* : a conjugated protein containing usu. small amounts of a substance other than nucleic acid with a carbohydrate group

gly·co·side \'glī-kə-,sīd\ *n* [ISV, fr. *glycose*, alter. of *glucose*] : any of numerous acetal derivatives of sugars that on hydrolysis yield a sugar (as glucose) — **gly·co·sid·ic** \,glī-kə-'sid-ik\ *adj* — **gly·co·sid·i·cal·ly** \-i-k(ə-)lē\ *adv*

gly·cos·uria \,glī-kō-'s(h)ùr-ē-ə, -'z(h)ùr-; -(,)kōs-'yùr-, -(,)kōz-\ *n* [NL] : the presence in the urine of abnormal amounts of sugar — **gly·cos·uric** \-ik\ *adj*

glyph \'glif\ *n* [Gk *glyphē* carved work, fr. *glyphein* to carve — more at CLEAVE] **1** : an ornamental vertical groove esp. in a Doric frieze **2** : a symbolic figure or a character usu. incised or carved in relief — **glyph·ic** \-ik\ *adj*

Glyp·tal \'glip-tᵊl\ *trademark* — used for an alkyd

glyp·tic \-tik\ *n, often attrib* [prob. fr. F *glyptique*, fr. Gk *glyptikē*, fr. *glyphein*] : the art or process of carving or engraving esp. on gems

G–man \'jē-,man\ *n* [prob. fr. *g*overnment *man*] : a special agent of the Federal Bureau of Investigation

gnar *or* **gnarr** \'när\ *vi* [imit.] : SNARL, GROWL

1**gnarl** \'när(ə)l\ *vi* [prob. freq. of *gnar*] : GROWL, SNARL

2**gnarl** *vt* [back-formation fr. *gnarled*] : to twist into a state of deformity **syn** see DEFORM

3**gnarl** *n* : a hard protuberance with twisted grain on a tree — **gnarly** \'när-lē\ *adj*

gnarled \'när(ə)ld\ *adj* [prob. alter. of *knurled*] **1** : full of knots or gnarls : KNOTTY **2** : crabbed in disposition

gnash \'nash\ *vt* [alter. of ME *gnasten*] : to strike or grind (the teeth) together — **gnash** *n*

gnat \'nat\ *n* [ME, fr. OE *gnæt*; akin to OE *gnagan* to gnaw] : any of various small usu. biting two-winged flies — **gnat·ty** \-ē\ *adj*

gnath- *or* **gnatho-** *comb form* [NL, fr. Gk *gnath-*, fr. *gnathos*; akin to Gk *genys* jaw — more at CHIN] : jaw ⟨*gnatho*plasty⟩

gnath·ic \'nath-ik\ *or* **gna·thal** \'nā-thəl, 'nath-əl\ *adj* : of or relating to the jaw

gna·thite \'nā-,thīt, 'na-\ *n* : a mouth appendage of an arthropod

-gna·thous *adj comb form* [NL *-gnathus*, fr. Gk *gnathos*] : having (such) a jaw ⟨opistho*gnathous*⟩

gnaw \'nó\ *vb* [ME *gnawen*, fr. OE *gnagan*; akin to OHG *gnagan* to gnaw] *vt* **1 a** : to bite or chew on with the teeth; *esp* : to wear away by persistent biting or nibbling ⟨dog ~*ing* a bone⟩ **b** : to make by gnawing ⟨rats ~*ed* a hole⟩ **2 a** : to be a source of vexation to : PLAGUE **b** : to affect like gnawing **3** : ERODE, CORRODE ~ *vi* **1** : to bite or nibble persistently **2** : to destroy or reduce as if by gnawing — **gnaw·er** \'nó(-ə)r\ *n*

gneiss \'nīs\ *n* [G *gneis*] : a laminated or foliated metamorphic rock corresponding in composition to granite or some other feldspathic plutonic rock — **gneiss·ic** \'nī-sik\ *adj* — **gneiss·oid** \-,sóid\ *adj* — **gneiss·ose** \-,sōs\ *adj*

1**gnome** \'nōm\ *n* [Gk *gnōmē*, fr. *gignōskein* to know — more at KNOW] : MAXIM, APHORISM

2**gnome** *n* [F, fr. NL *gnomus*] **1** : a subterranean often deformed dwarf of folklore who usu. guards precious ore or treasure **2** : an elemental being in the theory of Paracelsus inhabiting earth — **gnom·ish** \'nō-mish\ *adj*

gno·mic \'nō-mik\ *adj* **1** : APHORISTIC ⟨~ poetry⟩ **2** : given to the composition of gnomic poetry

gno·mon \'nō-,män, -mən\ *n* [L, fr. Gk *gnōmōn* interpreter, pointer on a sundial, fr. *gignōskein*] **1** : an object that by the position or length of its shadow serves as an indicator esp. of the hour of the day: as **a** : the style of an ordinary sundial **b** : a column or shaft erected perpendicular to the horizon **2** : the remainder of a parallelogram after the removal of a similar parallelogram containing one of its corners

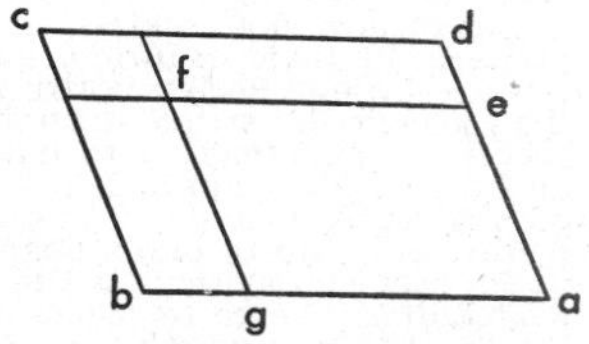

bcdefg gnomon 2

gno·mon·ic \nō-'män-ik\ *adj* : of or relating to the gnomon or its use in telling time

gno·sis \'nō-səs\ *n* [Gk *gnōsis*, lit., knowledge, fr. *gignōskein*] : immediate knowledge of spiritual truth held by the ancient Gnostics to be attainable through faith alone

-gno·sis \(g-)'nō-səs\ *n comb form, pl* **-gno·ses** \-,sēz\ [L, fr. Gk *gnōsis*] : knowledge : recognition ⟨psycho*gnosis*⟩

Gnos·tic \'näs-tik\ *n* [LL *gnosticus*, fr. Gk *gnōstikos* of knowledge, fr. *gignōskein*] : an adherent of Gnosticism — **Gnostic** *adj*

gnos·ti·cism \'näs-tə-,siz-əm\ *n, often cap* : the thought and practice of various cults of late pre-Christian and early Christian centuries distinguished by the conviction that matter is evil and that emancipation comes through gnosis

gnu \'n(y)ü\ *n, pl* **gnu** *or* **gnus** [modif. of Bushman *nqu*] : any of several large African antelopes (genera *Connochaetes* and *Gorgon*) with a head like that of an ox, short mane, long tail, and horns in both sexes that curve downward and outward

1**go** \'gō\ *vb* **went** \'went\ **gone** \'gòn *also* 'gän\ **go·ing** \'gō-iŋ, 'gò(-)iŋ; *"going to" indicating intent is often* 'gō-nə *or* 'gò-nə\ **goes** \'gōz\ [ME *gon*, fr. OE *gān*; akin to OHG *gān* to go, Gk *kichanein* to reach, attain] *vi* **1** : to move on a course : PROCEED — compare STOP ⟨~ slow⟩ ⟨*went* by train⟩ **2** : LEAVE, DEPART — compare COME **3 a** : to take a certain course or follow a certain procedure **b** : to pass by a process like journeying ⟨the message *went* by wire⟩ **c** : to proceed without delay — used esp. to intensify a complementary verb ⟨why did he have to ~ and spoil everything⟩ **d** (1) : to extend from point to point or in a certain direction : RUN ⟨his land ~*es* almost to the river⟩ (2) : to give access : LEAD ⟨that door ~*es* to the cellar⟩ **4** *obs* : WALK **5** : to be habitually in a certain state or condition ⟨~ bareheaded⟩ ⟨~ armed after dark⟩ **6 a** : to become lost, consumed, or spent **b** : DIE **c** : to slip away : ELAPSE ⟨the evening *went* pleasantly enough⟩ **d** : to come to be given up or discarded **e** : to pass by sale ⟨*went* for a good price⟩ **f** : to become impaired or weakened ⟨his hearing started to ~⟩ **g** : to give way esp. under great force or pressure : BREAK **7 a** : to take place : HAPPEN ⟨what's ~*ing* on⟩ **b** : to have course or issue : FARE ⟨see how life ~*es*⟩ **c** : to be in general or on an average ⟨cheap, as yachts ~⟩ **d** : to be or become esp. as the result of a contest ⟨decision *went* against him⟩ **e** : to turn out well : SUCCEED **8 a** : to apply oneself ⟨*went* to fighting among themselves⟩ **b** : to put or subject oneself ⟨*went* to unnecessary expense⟩ **c** *chiefly South & Midland* : INTEND ⟨I didn't ~ to do it⟩ **9** : to have recourse to another for corroboration, vindication, or decision : RESORT ⟨~ to court to recover damages⟩ **10 a** : to begin an action or motion ⟨here ~*es*⟩ **b** : to maintain or perform a certain action or motion ⟨drums had been ~*ing* strong⟩ **c** : to function in the proper or expected manner ⟨trying to get the motor to ~⟩ **11 a** : to have currency ⟨now ~*s* by another name⟩ **b** : to pass from person to person : CIRCULATE ⟨the report ~*es*⟩ **12 a** : to act in accordance or harmony ⟨a good rule to ~ by⟩ **b** : to come to be determined ⟨dreams ~ by contraries⟩ **c** : to come to be applied or appropriated ⟨part of the budget ~*es* for military purposes⟩ **d** : to pass by award, assignment, or lot ⟨the prize *went* to a sophomore⟩ **e** : to contribute to an end or result ⟨qualities that ~ to make a hero⟩ **13** : to be about, intending, or expecting something ⟨is ~*ing* to leave town⟩ **14 a** : EXTEND ⟨his knowledge fails to ~ very deep⟩ **b** : to come or arrive at a certain state or condition

⟨~ to sleep⟩ **c :** to come to be ⟨the tire *went* flat⟩ **15 a :** to be in phrasing or expression **:** READ ⟨as the phrase *~es*⟩ **b :** to be capable of being sung or played ⟨the tune *~es* like this⟩ **16 :** to be compatible, suitable, or becoming **:** HARMONIZE ⟨claret *~es* with beef⟩ **17 a :** to be capable of passing, extending, or being contained or inserted ⟨will these clothes ~ in your suitcase?⟩ **b :** to have a usual or proper place or position **:** BELONG ⟨these books ~ on the top shelf⟩ **c :** to be capable of being contained in another quantity ⟨5 *~es* into 60 12 times⟩ **18 :** to have a tendency **:** CONDUCE ⟨it *~es* to show he can be trusted⟩ **19 a** (1) **:** to carry authority ⟨what she said *went*⟩ (2) **:** to be acceptable, satisfactory, or adequate ⟨anything *~es* here⟩ **b :** to hold true **:** be valid **~** *vt* **1 :** to proceed along or according to **:** FOLLOW ⟨if I were *~ing* his way⟩ **2 :** TRAVERSE **3 a :** to make a wager of **:** BET ⟨~ a dollar on the outcome⟩ **b :** to make an offer of **:** BID ⟨willing to ~ $50 for the clock⟩ **4 a :** to assume the function or obligation of ⟨promised to ~ bail for his friend⟩ **b :** to participate to the extent of ⟨decided to ~ halves if either of them found the treasure⟩ **5 :** YIELD, WEIGH ⟨striped bass that would ~ a hundred pounds⟩ **6 a :** to put up with **b :** AFFORD ⟨can't ~ the price⟩ **c :** ENJOY ⟨I could ~ a soda⟩
syn LEAVE, DEPART, QUIT, WITHDRAW, RETIRE: GO is the general term for moving out of or away from and is the simple opposite of *come;* LEAVE stresses the fact of separation from someone or something; DEPART implies a setting forth from with some suggestion of formality; it is opposite to *arrive;* QUIT adds to LEAVE the suggestion of freeing, ridding, or disentangling; WITHDRAW suggests a deliberate removal for good reason; RETIRE may add to WITHDRAW an implication of relinquishment, retreat, or recession
— **go about :** to set about **:** UNDERTAKE — **go after :** SEEK, PURSUE — **go all the way :** to enter into complete agreement — **go at 1 a :** to make an attack on **b :** to make an approach to **2 :** UNDERTAKE — **go back on 1 :** ABANDON **2 :** BETRAY **3 :** FAIL — **go begging :** to be in little demand — **go by the board 1 :** to be carried over a ship's side **2 :** to be discarded — **go down the line :** to give wholehearted support — **go for 1 :** to pass for or serve as **2 :** to try to secure **3 a :** FAVOR, ACCEPT **b :** to have an interest in or liking for **4 :** ATTACK, ASSAIL — **go for broke :** to put forth all one's strength or resources — **go great guns :** to achieve great success — **go hang :** to cease to be of interest or concern — **go it 1 :** to behave in a reckless, excited, or improper manner **2 :** to proceed in a rapid or furious manner **3 :** to conduct one's affairs **:** ACT — **go one better :** OUTDO, SURPASS — **go over 1 :** EXAMINE **2 a :** REPEAT **b :** STUDY, REVIEW — **go places :** to be on the way to success — **go steady :** to date one person exclusively and frequently — **go through 1 :** to subject to thorough examination, consideration, or study **2 :** EXPERIENCE, UNDERGO **3 :** to carry out **:** PERFORM — **go to one's head 1 :** to cause one to become confused, excited, or dizzy **2 :** to cause one to become conceited or overconfident — **go to pieces :** to become shattered in nerves or health — **go to town 1 :** to work or act rapidly or efficiently **2 :** to be markedly successful — **go with :** DATE — **to go :** REMAINING, LEFT ⟨five minutes *to go* before the train leaves⟩

2**go** \'gō\ *n, pl* **goes 1 :** the act or manner of going **2 :** the height of fashion **3 :** a turn of affairs **:** OCCURRENCE **4 :** the quantity used or furnished at one time **5 :** ENERGY, VIGOR **6 :** ATTEMPT, TRY **7 :** a spell of activity — **no go :** to no avail **:** USELESS — **on the go :** constantly or restlessly active

3**go** *adj* **:** being in good and ready condition ⟨all systems ~⟩

4**go** *n* [Jap] **:** a Japanese game played with stones on a board checkered by 19 vertical lines and 19 horizontal lines to make 361 intersections

1**goad** \'gōd\ *n* [ME *gode,* fr. OE *gād* spear, goad; akin to Langobardic *gaida* spear, Skt *hinoti* he urges on] **1 :** a pointed rod used to urge on an animal **2 a :** something that pricks like a goad **:** THORN **b :** something that urges **:** SPUR **syn** see MOTIVE

2**goad** *vt* **:** to drive with a goad

1**go–ahead** \'gō-ə-,hed\ *adj* **1 :** ENTERPRISING, PROGRESSIVE **2 :** indicating that one may proceed ⟨~ signal⟩

2**go–ahead** *n* **:** GREEN LIGHT

1**goal** \'gōl, *chiefly in uncultivated or children's speech* 'gül\ *n* [ME *gol* boundary, limit] **1 :** the terminal point of a race **2 :** the end toward which effort is directed **:** AIM **3 a :** an area or object toward which players in various games attempt to advance a ball or puck to score points **b :** the score resulting from such an act **syn** see INTENTION

2**goal** *vi* **:** to seek or score a goal

goal·keep·er \-,kē-pər\ *n* **:** a player who defends the goal in various games — called also *goal·ie* \'gō-lē\, *goal·tend·er* \'gōl-,ten-dər\

go along *vi* **1 :** to move along **:** PROCEED **2 :** to go or travel as a companion **3 :** to act in cooperation

goal·post \'gōl-,pōst\ *n* **:** one of two vertical posts that with a crossbar constitute the goal in various games

Goa powder \'gō-ə-\ *n* [*Goa,* India] **:** a bitter powder found in the wood of a Brazilian leguminous tree (*Vataireopsis araroba*) and valued as the chief source of the drug chrysarobin

goat \'gōt\ *n, pl* **goats** [ME *gote,* fr. OE *gāt;* akin to OHG *geiz* goat, L *haedus* kid] **1** *or pl* **goat :** any of various hollow-horned ruminant mammals (esp. of the genus *Capra*) related to the sheep but of lighter build and with backwardly arching horns, a short tail, and usu. straight hair **2 :** a licentious man **:** LECHER **3 :** SCAPEGOAT — **goat·ish** \'gōt-ish\ *adj* — **goat·like** \-,līk\ *adj*

goat antelope *n* **:** any of several mammals related to the goats but in some respects resembling the antelopes

goa·tee \gō-'tē\ *n* **:** a small trim beard on a man's chin

goat·fish \'gōt-,fish\ *n* **:** MULLET 2

goat·skin \-,skin\ *n* **:** the skin of a goat

goat·suck·er \-,sək-ər\ *n* **:** any of various medium-sized long-winged crepuscular or nocturnal birds (as the whippoorwills and nighthawks) constituting a family (Caprimulgidae), having a short wide bill, short legs, and soft mottled plumage, and feeding on insects which they catch on the wing

1**gob** \'gäb\ *n* [ME *gobbe,* fr. MF *gobe* large piece of food, back-formation fr. *gobet*] **1 :** LUMP **2 :** a large amount — usu. used in pl.

2**gob** *n* [origin unknown] **:** SAILOR

gob·bet \'gäb-ət\ *n* [ME *gobet,* fr. MF, mouthful, piece] **1 :** a piece or portion usu. of meat **2 :** LUMP, MASS

1**gob·ble** \'gäb-əl\ *vt* **gob·bling** \-(ə-)liŋ\ [prob. irreg. fr. 1*gob*] **1 :** to swallow or eat greedily **2 :** to take eagerly **:** GRAB

2**gobble** *vi* [imit.] **:** to make the natural guttural noise of a male turkey — **gobble** *n*

gob·ble·dy·gook *or* **gob·ble·de·gook** \,gäb-əl-dē-'gu̇k, -'gük\ *n* [irreg. fr. *gobble,* n.] **:** wordy and generally unintelligible jargon

gob·bler \'gäb-lər\ *n* **:** a male turkey

Go·be·lin \'gō-bə-lən, 'gäb-ə-\ *adj* [*Gobelin* dyehouse and tapestry works, Paris, France] **:** relating to or characteristic of tapestry produced at the Gobelin works in Paris — **Gobelin** *n*

go–be·tween \'gō-bə-,twēn\ *n* **:** an intermediate agent **:** BROKER

1**gob·let** \'gäb-lət\ *n* [ME *gobelet,* fr. MF] **1** *archaic* **:** a bowl-shaped drinking vessel without handles **2 :** a drinking glass with a foot and stem — compare TUMBLER

2**goblet** *n, obs* **:** GOBBET

gob·lin \'gäb-lən\ *n* [ME *gobelin,* fr. MF, fr. ML *gobelinus,* deriv. of Gk *kobalos* rogue] **:** an ugly or grotesque sprite that is mischievous and sometimes evil and malicious

go·bo \'gō-(,)bō\ *n, pl* **gobos** *also* **goboes** [origin unknown] **1 :** a dark strip (as of wallboard) to shield a motion-picture or television camera from light **2 :** a device to shield a microphone from sound

go·by \'gō-bē\ *n, pl* **gobies** *also* **goby** [L *gobius* gudgeon, fr. Gk *kōbios*] **:** any of numerous spiny-finned fishes (family Gobiidae) with the pelvic fins thoracic and often united to form a sucking disk

go–cart \'gō-,kärt\ *n* **1 a :** WALKER **b :** STROLLER **2 :** HANDCART **3 :** a light open carriage

1**god** \'gäd *also* 'gȯd\ *n* [ME, fr. OE; akin to OHG *got* god] **1 :** a being or object believed to have more than natural attributes and powers and to require man's worship; *specif* **:** one controlling a particular aspect or part of reality **2 :** a person or thing of supreme value **3 :** a powerful ruler

2**God** *n* **:** the supreme or ultimate reality: as **a :** the Being perfect in power, wisdom, and goodness whom men worship as creator and ruler of the universe **b** *Christian Science* **:** the incorporeal divine Principle ruling over all as eternal Spirit **:** infinite Mind

3**god** *vt* **god·ded; god·ding :** IDOLIZE, DEIFY

god·child \-,chīld\ *n* **:** one for whom a person becomes sponsor at baptism

god·daugh·ter \'gäd-,dȯt-ər *also* 'gȯd-\ *n* **:** a female godchild

god·dess \'gäd-əs\ *n* **1 :** a female god **2 :** a woman whose great charm or beauty arouses adoration

go–dev·il \'gō-,dev-əl\ *n* **:** any of various devices: as **a :** a weight formerly dropped in a bored hole (as of an oil well) to explode a cartridge previously lowered **b :** a cleaning scraper rotated and propelled through a pipeline by the force of the flowing oil **c :** a handcar or small gasoline car used on a railroad for transporting laborers and supplies

1**god·fa·ther** \'gäd-,fäth-ər *also* 'gȯd-\ *n* **1 :** a man who sponsors a child at baptism **2 :** one having a relation to someone or something analogous to that of a male sponsor to his godchild

2**godfather** *vt* **:** to act as godfather to

god·head \-,hed\ *n* **1 :** divine nature or essence **:** DIVINITY **2** *cap* **a :** DEITY 1b **b :** the nature of God esp. as existing in three persons — used with *the*

god·hood \-,hu̇d\ *n* **:** DIVINITY

Go·di·va \gə-'dī-və\ *n* **:** a Saxon lady noted in legend for riding naked through the streets of Coventry to relieve the town of a burdensome tax levied by her husband

god·less \'gäd-ləs *also* 'gȯd-\ *adj* **:** not acknowledging a deity or divine law — **god·less·ness** *n*

god·like \-,līk\ *adj, sometimes cap* **:** resembling or having the qualities of God or a god **:** DIVINE — **god·like·ness** *n*

god·li·ness \-lē-nəs\ *n* **:** the quality or state of being godly

god·ling \-liŋ\ *n* **:** an inferior or local god

god·ly \-lē\ *adj* **1 :** DIVINE **2 :** devoutly conforming to the will of God — **godly** *adv*

god·moth·er \-,məth-ər\ *n* **:** a woman who sponsors a child at baptism

go·down \'gō-,dau̇n\ *n* [Malay *gudang*] **:** a warehouse in an oriental country

go down *vi* **1 :** to undergo defeat **2 :** to find acceptance ⟨will the plan *go down* with the farmers⟩ **3** *Brit* **:** to leave a university

god·par·ent \'gäd-,par-ənt, -,per- *also* 'gȯd-\ *n* **:** a sponsor at baptism

God's acre *n* **:** CHURCHYARD

god·send \'gäd-,send *also* 'gȯd-\ *n* [back-formation fr. *god-sent*] **:** a desirable or needed thing or event that comes unexpectedly

god·son \-,sən\ *n* **:** a male godchild

God·speed \-'spēd\ *n* [ME *god speid,* fr. the phrase *God spede you* God prosper you] **:** a prosperous journey **:** SUCCESS ⟨bade him ~⟩

god·wit \-,wit\ *n* [origin unknown] **:** any of a genus (*Limosa*) of long-billed wading birds related to the snipes but similar to curlews

go·er \'gō(-ə)r\ *n* **:** one that goes

goe·thite \'gə(r)t-,īt, 'gāt-\ *n* [G *göthit,* fr. J. W. von *Goethe* †1832 G poet] **:** a mineral $HFeO_2$ that consists of an iron hydrogen oxide and is the commonest constituent of many forms of natural rust

gof·fer \'gäf-ər, 'gȯf-\ *vt* [F *gaufrer*] **:** CRIMP, FLUTE — **goffer** *n*

go–get·ter \'gō-,get-ər\ *n* **:** an often aggressively enterprising person **:** HUSTLER — **go–get·ting** \-,get-iŋ\ *adj or n*

1**gog·gle** \'gäg-əl\ *vi* **gog·gling** \-(ə-)liŋ\ [ME *gogelen* to squint] **:** to stare with wide or protuberant eyes — **gog·gler** \-(ə-)lər\ *n*

2**goggle** *adj, of the eyes* **:** PROTUBERANT, STARING — **gog·gly** \'gäg-(ə-)lē\ *adj*

gog·gle–eye \'gäg-ə-,lī\ *n* **:** a fish with large prominent eyes

gog·gle–eyed \,gäg-ə-'līd\ *adj* **:** having bulging or rolling eyes

gog·gles \'gäg-əlz\ *n pl* **:** protective spectacles typically with shields at the side

go–go \'gō-,gō\ *adj* [*a-go-go*] **1 a :** of, relating to, or being a discotheque or the music or dances performed there **b :** employed to dance in a discotheque ⟨~ girls⟩ **2 a :** LIVELY, FREEWHEELING ⟨~ baseball⟩ **b :** very up-to-date **:** HIP

1**Goi·del·ic** \gȯi-'del-ik\ *adj* [MIr *Gōidel* Gael] **1 :** of, relating to, or characteristic of the Gaels **2 :** of, relating to, or constituting Goidelic

2**Goidelic** *n* **:** the branch of the Celtic languages that includes Irish Gaelic, Scottish Gaelic, and Manx

go in *vi* **1 a :** ENTER **b :** to approach in attacking **2 a :** to take part in a game or contest **b :** to call the opening bet in poker **:** STAY **3** *of a heavenly body* **:** to become obscured by a cloud **4 :** to form a union or alliance **:** JOIN — **go in for 1 :** to give support to **:** ADVOCATE **2 a :** to make one's particular interest or specialty **b :** to have or show an interest in or liking for **3 :** to engage in

¹go·ing *n* **1 a :** the act or action of going **b :** DEPARTURE **2** *pl* **:** BEHAVIOR, ACTIONS **3 :** the condition of the ground (as for walking) **4 :** advance toward an objective **:** PROGRESS

²going *adj* **1 a :** that goes **b :** MOVING, WORKING **2 :** EXISTING, LIVING **3 :** CURRENT, PREVAILING ⟨~ price⟩ **4 :** conducting business with the expectation of indefinite continuance ⟨~ concern⟩ — **going on :** drawing near to **:** APPROACHING

go·ings–on \ˌgō-iŋ-ˈzȯn, (ˌ)gȯ(-)iŋ-, -ˈzän\ *n pl* **:** ACTIONS, EVENTS

goi·ter *also* **goi·tre** \ˈgȯit-ər\ *n* [F *goitre,* fr. MF, back-formation fr. *goitron* throat, fr. (assumed) VL *guttrion-, guttrio,* fr. L *guttur* — more at COT] **:** an enlargement of the thyroid gland visible as a swelling of the front of the neck — compare HYPERTHYROIDISM, HYPOTHYROIDISM — **goi·trous** \ˈgȯi-trəs, ˈgȯit-ə-rəs\ *adj*

goi·tro·gen·ic \ˌgȯi-trə-ˈjen-ik\ *also* **goi·ter·o·gen·ic** \ˌgȯit-ə-rō-ˈjen-\ *adj* **:** producing or tending to produce goiter — **goi·tro·ge·nic·i·ty** \ˌgȯi-trə-jə-ˈnis-ət-ē\ *n*

Gol·con·da \gäl-ˈkän-də\ *n* [*Golconda,* India, famous for its diamonds] **:** a rich mine; *broadly* **:** a source of great wealth

gold \ˈgōld\ *n, often attrib* [ME, fr. OE; akin to OE *geolu* yellow — more at YELLOW] **1 :** a malleable ductile yellow trivalent and univalent metallic element that occurs chiefly free or in a few minerals and is used esp. in coins, jewelry, and dentures — see ELEMENT table **2 a** (1) **:** gold coins (2) **:** a gold piece **b :** MONEY **c :** GOLD STANDARD **3 :** a variable color averaging deep yellow

gold–and–sil·ver plant \ˌgōl-dən-ˈsil-vər-\ *n* **:** HONESTY

gold·beat·er \ˈgōl(d)-ˌbēt-ər\ *n* **:** one that beats gold into gold leaf

gold·beat·ing \-ˌbēt-iŋ\ *n* **:** the act, art, or process of hammering gold into thin leaves

gold·brick \ˈgōl(d)-ˌbrik\ *n* **1 :** a worthless brick that appears to be of gold **2 :** a soldier or other person who shirks assigned work — **goldbrick** *vi*

Gold Democrat *n* **:** a member of the Democratic party favoring the gold standard; *esp* **:** one supporting an independent ticket in the presidential election of 1896

gold digger *n* **1 :** one that digs gold **2 :** a woman who uses feminine charm to extract money or gifts from men

gold·en \ˈgōl-dən\ *adj* **1 :** consisting of, relating to, or containing gold **2 a :** having the color of gold **b :** BLOND 1a **3 :** SHINING, LUSTROUS **4 :** of a high degree of excellence **:** SUPERB **5 :** FLOURISHING, PROSPEROUS ⟨~ age⟩ **6 a :** radiantly youthful and vigorous **b :** possessing talents that promise worldly success ⟨~ boys of the airlines⟩ **7 :** FAVORABLE, ADVANTAGEOUS ⟨~ opportunity⟩ **8 :** MELLOW, RESONANT ⟨smooth ~ tenor⟩ — **gold·en·ly** *adv* — **gold·en·ness** \-dən-nəs\ *n*

gold·en·eye \ˈgōl-də-ˌnī\ *n* **1 a :** a large-headed swift-flying holarctic diving duck (*Bucephala clangula*) having the male strikingly marked in black and white **b :** a closely related duck **2 :** a lacewing (family Chrysopidae) with yellow eyes

Golden Fleece *n* **:** a fleece of gold placed by the king of Colchis in a dragon-guarded grove and recovered by the Argonauts

golden glow *n* **:** a tall branching composite herb (*Rudbeckia laciniata hortensia*) with showy yellow much-doubled flower heads

Golden Horde *n* [fr. the golden tent of the Mongol ruler] **:** a body of Mongol Tatars overrunning eastern Europe in the 13th century and dominating Russia until 1486

golden mean *n* **:** the medium between extremes **:** MODERATION

golden nematode *n* **:** a small yellowish Old World nematode worm (*Heterodera rostochiensis*) established locally as a pest of potatoes in eastern No. America

gold·en·rain tree \ˌgōl-dən-ˈrān-\ *n* **:** a round-headed leguminous tree (*Koelreuteria paniculata*) having very long showy clusters of yellow flowers

golden retriever *n* **:** a medium-sized golden-coated retriever developed by interbreeding Russian shepherd dogs with bloodhounds

gold·en·rod \ˈgōl-dən-ˌräd\ *n* **:** any of numerous chiefly No. American composite biennial or perennial plants (esp. of the genus *Solidago*) with stems resembling wands and heads of small yellow or sometimes white flowers often clustered in panicles — compare RAYLESS GOLDENROD

golden rule *n* **1 :** a rule stating that one should do to others as he would have others do to him **2 :** a guiding principle

gold·en·seal \ˈgōl-dən-ˌsēl\ *n* **:** a perennial American herb (*Hydrastis canadensis*) of the crowfoot family with a thick knotted yellow rootstock that yields hydrastine and large rounded leaves

golden yellow *n* **1 :** a vivid or light yellow **2 :** a moderate to strong orange yellow

gold·field \ˈgōl(d)-ˌfēld\ *n* **:** a gold-mining district

gold–filled \-ˈfild\ *adj* **:** covered with a layer of gold so as to constitute filled gold ⟨~ bracelet⟩

gold·finch \-ˌfinch\ *n* **1 :** a small largely red, black, and yellow European finch (*Carduelis carduelis*) often kept as a cage bird **2 :** any of several small American finches (genus *Spinus*) typically having the male in summer plumage variably yellow with black wings, tail, and crown

gold·fish \-ˌfish\ *n* **1 :** a small usu. golden yellow or orange cyprinid fish (*Carassius auratus*) much used as an aquarium and pond fish **2** *slang* **:** canned salmon

gold foil *n* **:** gold beaten or rolled out very thin; *specif* **:** gold in sheets thicker than gold leaf

gold leaf *n* **:** a sheet of gold ordinarily varying from four to five millionths of an inch in thickness that is used esp. for gilding

gold of pleasure : an annual herb (*Camelina sativa*) of the mustard family formerly grown for its oil-rich seeds

gold·smith \ˈgōl(d)-ˌsmith\ *n* **:** one who makes or deals in articles of gold

gold standard *n* **:** a monetary standard under which the basic unit of currency is defined by a stated quantity of gold and that is usu. characterized by the coinage and circulation of gold, unrestricted convertibility of other money into gold, and the free export and import of gold for the settlement of international obligations

gold·stone \ˈgōl(d)-ˌstōn\ *n* **:** aventurine spangled close and fine with particles of gold-colored material

go·lem \ˈgō-ləm\ *n* [Yiddish *goylem*] **:** an artificial human being of Hebrew folklore endowed with life

golf \ˈgälf, ˈgȯlf, ˈgäf, ˈgȯf\ *n, often attrib* [ME (Sc)] **:** a game whose

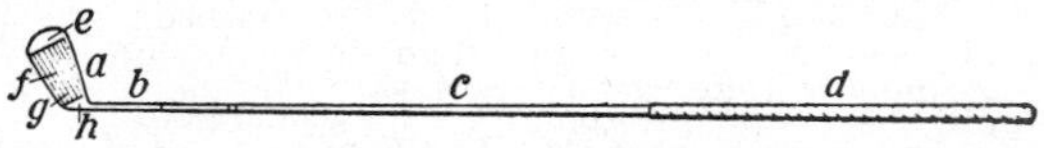

golf club (iron): *a* head, *b* hosel, *c* shaft, *d* grip, *e* toe, *f* face, *g* heel, *h* neck

object is to sink a ball into each of the 9 or 18 successive holes on a course by using as few strokes as possible and avoiding various obstacles — **golf** *vi* — **golf·er** *n*

Golf — a communications code word for the letter *g*

Gol·gi apparatus \ˈgȯl-(ˌ)jē-\ *n* [Camillo *Golgi* †1926 It physician] **:** a cytoplasmic component that prob. plays a part in elaboration and secretion of cell products and appears either as a net or as discrete particles

Golgi body *n* **:** a discrete particle of the Golgi apparatus as observed in a stained preparation

go·liard \ˈgōl-yərd, -ˌyärd\ *n* [F] **:** a wandering student of the 12th or 13th century given to the writing of satiric Latin verse and to convivial living and minstrelsy — **go·liar·dic** \gōl-ˈyärd-ik\ *adj*

Go·li·ath \gə-ˈlī-əth\ *n* [LL, fr. Heb *Golyath*] **:** a Philistine giant held in the Bible to have been killed by David with a sling

gol·li·wog *or* **gol·li·wogg** \ˈgäl-ē-ˌwäg\ *n* [*Golliwogg,* an animated doll in children's fiction by Bertha Upton] **1 :** a grotesque black doll **2 :** a grotesque person

gom·er·al *or* **gom·er·il** \ˈgäm-(ə-)rəl\ *n* [origin unknown] *Scot* **:** SIMPLETON, FOOL

gom·pho·sis \gäm-ˈfō-səs\ *n* [NL, fr. Gk *gomphōsis,* lit., a bolting together] **:** an immovable articulation in which a hard part is received into a bone cavity (as the teeth into the jaws)

gon- *or* **gono-** *comb form* [Gk, fr. *gonos* procreation, seed, fr. *gignesthai* to be born — more at KIN] **:** sexual **:** generative **:** semen **:** seed ⟨*gono*duct⟩

-gon \ˌgän *also* -gən\ *n comb form* [NL *-gonum,* fr. Gk *-gōnon,* fr. *gōnia* angle; akin to Gk *gony* knee — more at KNEE] **:** figure having (so many) angles ⟨deca*gon*⟩

go·nad \ˈgō-ˌnad\ *n* [NL *gonad-, gonas,* fr. Gk *gonos*] **:** a primary sex gland **:** OVARY, TESTIS — **go·nad·al** \gō-ˈnad-ᵊl\ *adj*

go·na·do·tro·phic \(ˌ)gō-ˌnad-ə-ˈträf-ik, ˌgän-əd-ō-, -ˈtrō-fik\ *or* **go·na·do·trop·ic** \-ˈträp-ik\ *adj* [ISV] **:** acting on or stimulating the gonads — **go·na·do·tro·phin** \-ˈtrō-fən\ *n*

Gond \ˈgänd\ *n* **:** a member of a Dravidian or pre-Dravidian people of central India

Gondi \ˈgän-dē\ *n* **:** the Dravidian language of the Gonds

gon·do·la \ˈgän-də-lə (*usual for sense 1*), gän-ˈdō-\ *n* [It, fr. ML *gondula,* dim. of (assumed) VL *condua*] **1 :** a long narrow flat-bottomed boat with a high prow and stern used on the canals of Venice **2 :** a heavy flat-bottomed boat used on New England rivers and on the Ohio and Mississippi rivers **3 :** a railroad car with no top, flat bottom, and fixed sides used chiefly for hauling heavy bulk commodities **4 a :** an elongated car attached to the underside of an airship **b :** an often spherical airtight enclosure suspended from a balloon for carrying passengers or instruments **5 :** an upholstered chair whose back curves forward at both sides to form the arms **6 :** a fixture approachable from all sides used in self-service retail stores to display merchandise **7 :** a motortruck or trailer having a large hopper-shaped container for transporting mixed concrete

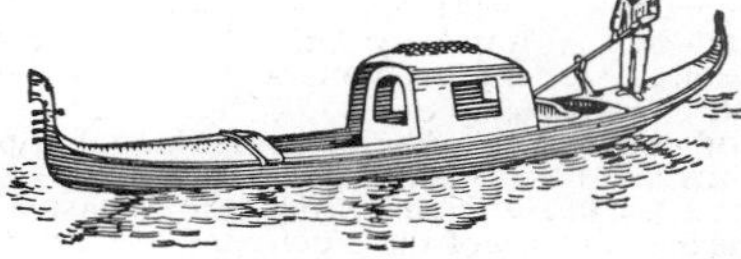

gondola 1

gon·do·lier \ˌgän-də-ˈli(ə)r\ *n* **:** one who propels a gondola

gone \ˈgȯn *also* ˈgän\ *adj* [fr. pp. of *go*] **1 :** PAST **2 a :** INVOLVED, ABSORBED ⟨far ~ in hysteria⟩ **b :** INFATUATED **c :** PREGNANT **3 a :** DEAD **b :** LOST, RUINED **c :** SINKING **4** *slang* **:** GREAT ⟨real ~ guy⟩

gon·er \ˈgȯ-nər *also* ˈgän-ər\ *n* **:** one whose case is hopeless

gon·fa·lon \ˈgän-fə-ˌlän, -lən\ *n* [It *gonfalone*] **1 :** the ensign of certain princes or states (as the medieval republics of Italy) **2 :** a flag that hangs from a crosspiece or frame

gon·fa·lon·ier \ˌgän-fə-ˌlä-ˈni(ə)r, -lə-\ *n* **:** one who bears a gonfalon

gong \ˈgäŋ, ˈgȯŋ\ *n* [Malay & Jav, of imit. origin] **1 :** a disk-shaped percussion instrument that produces a resounding tone **2 a :** a flat saucer-shaped bell **b :** a wire rod wound in a flat spiral used to sound the time or chime or alarm (as in a clock)

Gon·go·rism \ˈgäŋ-gə-ˌriz-əm\ *n* [Sp *gongorismo,* fr. Luis de *Góngora* y Argote †1627 Sp poet] **:** a literary style characterized by studied obscurity and by use of various ornate devices — **gon·go·ris·tic** \ˌgäŋ-gə-ˈris-tik\ *adj*

goni- *or* **gonio-** *comb form* [Gk *gōnia*] **:** corner **:** angle ⟨*gonio*meter⟩

go·nid·i·al \gō-ˈnid-ē-əl\ *adj* **:** of or relating to a gonidium

go·nid·i·um \-ē-əm\ *n, pl* **go·nid·ia** \-ē-ə\ **1 :** an asexual reproductive cell or group of cells in or on a gametophyte **2 :** a green chlorophyll-bearing cell within the thallus of a lichen

go·ni·om·e·ter \ˌgō-nē-ˈäm-ət-ər\ *n* **1 :** an instrument for measuring angles **2 :** DIRECTION FINDER — **go·nio·met·ric** \ˌgō-nē-ə-ˈme-trik\ *adj* — **go·ni·om·e·try** \ˌgō-nē-ˈäm-ə-trē\ *n*

go·ni·um \ˈgō-nē-əm\ *n, pl* **go·nia** \-nē-ə\ *also* **go·ni·ums** [NL, fr. Gk *gonos* procreation — more at GON-] **:** an undifferentiated primitive germ cell

gono·coc·cal \ˌgän-ə-ˈkäk-əl\ *or* **gono·coc·cic** \-ˈkäk-(s)ik\ *adj* **:** or, relating to, or caused by gonococci

gono·coc·cus \-ˈkäk-əs\ *n, pl* **gono·coc·ci** \-ˈkäk-ˌ(s)ī, -ˈkäk-(ˌ)(s)ē\ [NL] **:** a pus-producing bacterium (*Neisseria gonorrhoeae*) that causes gonorrhea

gono·cyte \ˈgän-ə-ˌsīt\ *n* [ISV] **:** a cell that produces gametes; *esp* **:** GAMETOCYTE

gono·gen·e·sis \ˌgän-ō-ˈjen-ə-səs\ *n* [NL] **:** the maturation of germ cells **:** OOGENESIS, SPERMATOGENESIS

gon·oph \'gän-əf\ *var of* GANEF
gono·phore \'gän-ə-,fō(ə)r, -,fȯ(ə)r\ *n* [ISV] **1 :** a sporophyll-bearing prolongation of a plant axis **2 :** an attached reproductive zooid of a hydroid colony — **gono·phor·ic** \,gän-ə-'fōr-ik, -'fȯr-\ *adj* — **go·noph·o·rous** \gə-'näf-ə-rəs, gä-\ *adj*
gono·pore \'gän-ə-,pō(ə)r, -,pȯ(ə)r\ *n* **:** a genital pore
gon·or·rhea \,gän-ə-'rē-ə\ *n* [NL, fr. LL, morbid loss of semen, fr. Gk *gonorrhoia,* fr. *gon-* + *-rrhoia* -rrhea] **:** a contagious inflammation of the genital mucous membrane caused by the gonococcus — **gon·or·rhe·al** \-'rē-əl\ *adj*
-g·o·ny \g-ə-nē\ *n comb form* [L *-gonia,* fr. Gk, fr. *gonos*] **:** generation **:** reproduction **:** manner of coming into being ⟨sporo*gony*⟩
goo \'gü\ *n* [perh. alter. of *glue*] **1 :** a viscid or sticky substance **2 :** cloying sentimentality — **goo·ey** \'gü-ē\ *adj* **goo·i·er; goo·i·est**
goo·ber \'gü-bər, 'gu̇b-ər\ *n* [of African origin; akin to Kongo *nguba* peanut] *dial* **:** PEANUT
[1]**good** \'gu̇d\ *adj* **bet·ter** \'bet-ər\ **best** \'best\ [ME, fr. OE *gōd;* akin to OHG *guot* good, Skt *gadh* to hold fast] **1 a** (1) **:** of a favorable character or tendency ⟨~ news⟩ (2) **:** BOUNTIFUL, FERTILE ⟨~ land⟩ (3) **:** COMELY, ATTRACTIVE ⟨~ looks⟩ **b** (1) **:** SUITABLE, FIT ⟨~ to eat⟩ (2) **:** SOUND, WHOLE ⟨one ~ arm⟩ (3) **:** not depreciated ⟨bad money drives out ~⟩ (4) **:** commercially reliable ⟨~ risk⟩ (5) **:** certain to last or live ⟨~ for another year⟩ (6) **:** certain to pay or contribute ⟨~ for a hundred dollars⟩ (7) **:** certain to elicit a specified result ⟨always ~ for a laugh⟩ **c** (1) **:** AGREEABLE, PLEASANT (2) **:** SALUTARY, WHOLESOME ⟨~ for a cold⟩ **d** (1) **:** CONSIDERABLE, AMPLE ⟨~ margin⟩ (2) **:** FULL ⟨~ measure⟩ **e** (1) **:** WELL-FOUNDED, COGENT ⟨~ reasons⟩ (2) **:** TRUE ⟨holds ~ for society at large⟩ (3) **:** ACTUALIZED, REAL ⟨made ~ his promises⟩ (4) **:** RECOGNIZED, HONORED ⟨in ~ standing⟩ (5) **:** legally valid or effectual ⟨~ title⟩ **f** (1) **:** ADEQUATE, SATISFACTORY ⟨~ care⟩ (2) **:** conforming to a standard ⟨~ English⟩ (3) **:** DISCRIMINATING, CHOICE ⟨~ taste⟩ (4) **:** containing less fat and being less tender than higher grades — used of meat and esp. of beef **2 a** (1) **:** COMMENDABLE, VIRTUOUS, JUST ⟨~ man⟩ (2) **:** RIGHT ⟨~ conduct⟩ (3) **:** KIND, BENEVOLENT ⟨~ intentions⟩ **b :** UPPER-CLASS ⟨~ family⟩ **c :** COMPETENT, SKILLFUL ⟨~ doctor⟩ **d :** LOYAL ⟨~ party man⟩ ⟨~ Catholic⟩ — **good·ish** \'gu̇d-ish\ *adj* — **as good as :** in effect **:** VIRTUALLY ⟨*as good as* dead⟩ — **good and :** VERY, ENTIRELY ⟨was *good and* mad⟩
[2]**good** *n* **1 a :** something that is good **b** (1) **:** something conforming to the moral order of the universe (2) **:** praiseworthy character **:** GOODNESS **c :** a good element or portion **2 :** PROSPERITY, BENEFIT ⟨~ of the community⟩ **3 a :** something that has economic utility or satisfies an economic want **b** *pl* **:** personal property having intrinsic value usu. excluding money, securities, and negotiable instruments **c** *pl* **:** CLOTH **d** *pl* **:** WARES, COMMODITIES **4 :** good persons — used with *the* **5** *pl* **:** proof of wrongdoing
[3]**good** *adv* **:** WELL
good book *n, often cap G&B* **:** BIBLE
good-bye *or* **good-by** \gu̇d-'bī, gə(d)-\ *n* [alter. of *God be with you*] **:** a concluding remark at parting — often used interjectionally
good fellow *n* **:** a hearty companionable person — **good-fel·low·ship** \gu̇d-'fel-ō-,ship, -'fel-ə-\ *n*
Good Friday *n* **:** the Friday before Easter observed in churches as the anniversary of the crucifixion of Christ and in some states of the U.S. as a legal holiday
good-heart·ed \'gu̇d-'härt-əd\ *adj* **:** having a kindly generous disposition — **good-heart·ed·ly** *adv* — **good-heart·ed·ness** *n*
good-hu·mored \-'hyü-mərd, -'yü-\ *adj* **:** GOOD-NATURED, CHEERFUL — **good-hu·mored·ly** *adv* — **good-hu·mored·ness** *n*
good·ly \'gu̇d-lē\ *adj* **1 :** COMELY, HANDSOME **2 :** CONSIDERABLE
good·man \'gu̇d-mən\ *n* **1** *archaic* **:** the head of a household **:** HUSBAND **2** *archaic* **:** MISTER
good-na·tured \'gu̇d-'nā-chərd\ *adj* **:** of a pleasant cheerful disposition — **good-na·tured·ly** *adv* — **good-na·tured·ness** *n*
good-neighbor *adj* **:** marked by principles of friendship, cooperation, and noninterference in the internal affairs of another country ⟨~ policy⟩
good·ness \'gu̇d-nəs\ *n* **:** EXCELLENCE, VIRTUE
good-tem·pered \'gu̇d-'tem-pərd\ *adj* **:** having an even temper — **good-tem·pered·ly** *adv* — **good-tem·pered·ness** *n*
good·wife \'gu̇d-,wīf\ *n* **1** *archaic* **:** the mistress of a household **2** *archaic* — used as a title equivalent to *Mrs.*
good·will \'gu̇d-'wil\ *n* **1 a :** kindly feeling **:** BENEVOLENCE **b :** the favor or advantage in the way of custom that a business has acquired beyond the mere value of what it sells **2 a :** cheerful consent **b :** willing effort **syn** see FAVOR
[1]**goody** \'gu̇d-ē\ *n* [alter. of *goodwife*] *archaic* **:** a usu. married woman of lowly station — used as a title preceding a surname
[2]**goody** *n* **:** something that is particularly good to eat or otherwise attractive
goody-goody \,gu̇d-ē-'gu̇d-ē\ *adj* **:** affectedly good — **goody-goody** *n*
[1]**goof** \'güf\ *n* [prob. alter. of E dial. *goff* (simpleton)] **1 :** a ridiculous stupid person **2 :** BLUNDER
[2]**goof** *vi* **1 :** BLUNDER **2** *slang* **:** IDLE, LOAF — often used with *off* ~ *vt* **:** to make a mess of **:** BUNGLE
go off *vi* **1 :** EXPLODE **2 :** to burst forth in a sudden or noisy manner **3 :** to undergo decline or deterioration **4 :** to follow the expected or desired course **:** PROCEED **5 :** to make a characteristic noise **:** SOUND
goof·i·ness \'gü-fē-nəs\ *n* **:** the quality or state of being goofy
goofy \'gü-fē\ *adj* **:** CRAZY, SILLY
goo·gol \'gü-,gȯl\ *n* [coined by a child] **:** the figure 1 followed by 100 zeroes equal to 10^{100}
goo·gol·plex \-,pleks\ *n* [*googol* + *-plex* (as in *duplex*)] **:** the figure 1 followed by a googol of zeroes equal to 10$^{10^{100}}$
goo-goo \'gü-(,)gü\ *n* [fr. *good government*] **:** a member or advocate of a political reform movement
gook \'gu̇k, 'gük\ *n* [perh. alter. of *goo*] **:** GOO
goon \'gün\ *n* [partly short for E dial. *gooney* (simpleton), partly fr. Alice the *Goon,* subhuman comic-strip creature by E.C. Segar] **1 :** a man hired to terrorize or eliminate opponents **2** *slang* **:** DOPE, SAP
goo·san·der \gü-'san-dər\ *n* [origin unknown] **:** the common merganser (*Mergus merganser*) of the northern hemisphere

[1]**goose** \'güs\ *n, pl* **geese** \'gēs\ [ME *gos,* fr. OE *gōs;* akin to OHG *gans* goose, L *anser*] **1 a :** any of numerous birds (family Anatidae) intermediate between the swans and ducks with long necks, feathered lores, and reticulate tarsi **b :** a female goose as distinguished from a gander **2 :** SIMPLETON, DOLT **3** *pl* **goos·es :** a tailor's smoothing iron with a gooseneck handle **4** *pl* **goos·es :** a poke between the buttocks
[2]**goose** *vt* **:** to poke between the buttocks
goose·ber·ry \'güs-,ber-ē, 'güz-, -b(ə-)rē, *chiefly Brit* 'gu̇z-\ *n* **1 a :** the acid usu. prickly fruit of any of several shrubs (genus *Ribes*) of the rose family **b :** a shrub bearing gooseberries **2 :** CURRANT 2
goose egg *n* **:** ZERO, NOTHING
goose·flesh \'güs-,flesh\ *n* **:** a roughness of the skin produced by erection of its papillae usu. from cold or fear
goose·foot \-,fu̇t\ *n, pl* **goose·foots :** any of a genus (*Chenopodium*) or family (Chenopodiaceae, the goosefoot family) of glabrous herbs with utricular fruit
goose·neck \'gü-,snek\ *n, often attrib* **:** something (as a flexible jointed metal pipe) curved like the neck of a goose or U-shaped — **goose·necked** \-,snekt\ *adj*

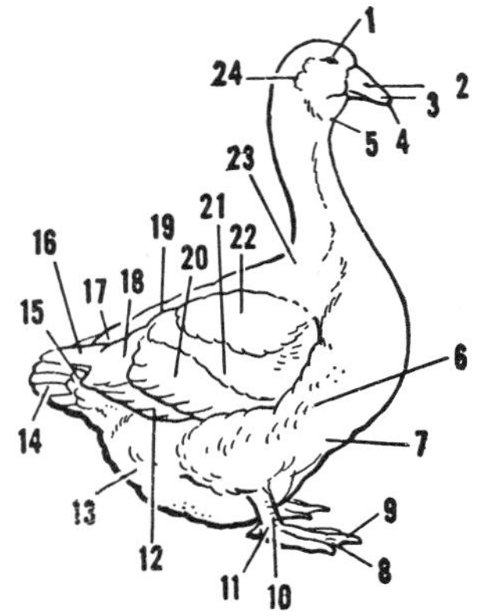

goose: *1* eye, *2* nostril, *3* bill, *4* bean, *5* dewlap, *6* breast, *7* keel, *8* web, *9* toes, *10* shank, *11* foot, *12* pinion coverts, *13* fluff, *14* tail feathers, *15* tail coverts, *16* wing flight feathers, *17* rump, *18* wing secondaries, *19* saddle, *20* wing coverts, *21* wing bow, *22* shoulder, *23* cape, *24* ear

goose step *n* **:** a straight-legged stiff-kneed step used by troops of some armies when passing in review — **goose-step·per** \'güs-,step-ər\ *n*
goos·ey \'gü-sē\ *adj* **goos·i·er; goos·i·est 1 :** belonging to or resembling a goose **2 :** FOOLISH, STUPID
go out *vi* **1 a :** to go forth, abroad, or outdoors; *specif* **:** to leave one's house **b** (1) **:** to take the field as a soldier (2) **:** to participate as a principal in a duel **c :** to travel as or as if a colonist or immigrant **d :** to work away from home **e :** to play the first nine holes of an 18-hole golf match **2 a :** to come to an end **b :** to become extinguished ⟨the hall light *went out*⟩ **c :** to give up office **:** RESIGN **d :** to become obsolete **3 :** to go on strike **4 :** BREAK, COLLAPSE **5 :** to become a candidate ⟨*went out* for the football team⟩
go over *vi* **1 :** to go on a journey **2 :** to become converted **3 :** to receive approval **:** SUCCEED
go·pher \'gō-fər\ *n* [origin unknown] **1 :** a burrowing edible land tortoise (*Gopherus polyphemus*) of the southern U.S.; *broadly* **:** any of several related land tortoises **2 a :** any of several burrowing rodents (family Geomyidae) of western No. America, Central America, and the southern U.S. the size of a large rat with large cheek pouches opening beside the mouth **b :** any of numerous small ground squirrels (genus *Citellus*) of the prairie region of No. America closely related to the chipmunks
gopher snake *n* **1 :** INDIGO SNAKE **2 :** BULL SNAKE
Gor·di·an knot \,gȯrd-ē-ən-\ *n* **1 :** a knot tied by Gordius, king of Phrygia, held to be capable of being untied only by the future ruler of Asia, and cut by Alexander the Great with his sword **2 :** an intricate problem; *esp* **:** a problem insoluble in its own terms
Gor·don setter \,gȯrd-ᵊn-\ *n* [Alexander, 4th Duke of *Gordon* †1827 Sc sportsman] **:** any of a breed of large long-haired bird dogs deep black with tan, chestnut, or mahogany markings
[1]**gore** \'gō(ə)r, 'gȯ(ə)r\ *n* [ME, filth, fr. OE *gor;* akin to OE *wearm* warm] **:** BLOOD; *esp* **:** clotted blood
[2]**gore** *n* [ME, fr. OE *gāra;* akin to OE *gār* spear, Gk *chaios* shepherd's staff] **1 :** a small usu. triangular piece of land **2 :** a tapering or triangular piece (as of cloth in a skirt)
[3]**gore** *vt* **1 :** to cut into a tapering triangular form **2 :** to provide with a gore
[4]**gore** *vt* **:** to pierce or wound with a horn or tusk
[1]**gorge** \'gȯ(ə)rj\ *n* [ME, fr. MF, fr. LL *gurga,* alter. of L *gurges* throat, whirlpool — more at VORACIOUS] **1 :** THROAT **2 a :** a hawk's crop **b :** STOMACH, BELLY **3 :** the entrance into a bastion or other outwork of a fort **4 :** a narrow passage **5 :** a mass of matter that chokes up a passage
[2]**gorge** *vi* **:** to eat greedily or to repletion ~ *vt* **1 :** to stuff to capacity **:** GLUT **2 :** to swallow greedily **syn** see SATIATE — **gorg·er** *n*
gor·geous \'gȯr-jəs\ *adj* [ME *gorgayse,* fr. MF *gorgias* elegant, fr. *gorgias* neckerchief, fr. *gorge*] **:** resplendently beautiful — **syn** see SPLENDID — **gor·geous·ly** *adv* — **gor·geous·ness** *n*
gor·get \'gȯr-jət\ *n* **1 :** a piece of armor defending the throat **2 a :** an ornamental collar **b :** a part of a wimple covering the throat and shoulders **3 :** a specially colored patch on the throat
gor·gon \'gȯr-gən\ *n* [L *Gorgon-, Gorgo,* fr. Gk *Gorgōn*] **1** *cap* **:** any of three snaky-haired sisters in Greek mythology whose glance turns the beholder to stone **2 :** an ugly or repulsive woman — **Gor·go·nian** \gȯr-'gō-nē-ən, -nyən\ *adj*
gor·go·nian \gȯr-'gō-nē-ən, -nyən\ *n* [deriv. of L *gorgonia* coral, fr. *Gorgon-, Gorgo*] **:** any of an order (Gorgonacea) of colonial anthozoans with a usu. horny and branching axial skeleton — **gorgonian** *adj*
gor·gon·ize \'gȯr-gə-,nīz\ *vt* **:** STUPEFY, PETRIFY
Gor·gon·zo·la \,gȯr-gən-'zō-lə\ *n* [It, fr. *Gorgonzola,* Italy] **:** a blue cheese of Italian origin usu. made of cow's milk
go·ril·la \gə-'ril-ə\ *n* [deriv. of Gk *Gorillai,* an African tribe of hairy women] **1 :** an anthropoid ape (*Gorilla gorilla*) of west equatorial Africa related to the chimpanzee but less erect and much larger **2 a :** an ugly or brutal man **b :** THUG, GOON
gor·man·dize \'gȯr-mən-,dīz\ *vi* [*gormand,* alter. of *gourmand*] **:** to eat gluttonously or ravenously ~ *vt* **:** to eat greedily **:** DEVOUR — **gor·man·diz·er** *n*

gorse \'gȯ(ə)rs\ *n* [ME *gorst,* fr. OE — more at HORROR] **1 :** FURZE **2 :** JUNIPER — **gorsy** \'gȯr-sē\ *adj*

gory \'gō(ə)r-ē, 'gȯ(ə)r-\ *adj* **1 :** covered with gore **:** BLOODSTAINED **2 :** BLOODCURDLING, SENSATIONAL

gos·hawk \'gäs-,hȯk\ *n* [ME *goshawke,* fr. OE *gōshafoc,* fr. *gōs* goose + *hafoc* hawk] **:** any of several long-tailed short-winged accipitrine hawks noted for their powerful flight, activity, and vigor

gos·ling \'gäz-liŋ, 'gȯz-, -lən\ *n* [ME, fr. *gos* goose] **1 :** a young goose **2 :** a foolish or callow person

1gos·pel \'gäs-pəl\ *n* [ME, fr. OE *gōdspel,* fr. *gōd* good + *spell* tale — more at SPELL] **1 a** *often cap* **:** the good news concerning Christ, the kingdom of God, and salvation **b** *cap* **:** one of the first four New Testament books telling of the life, death, and resurrection of Jesus Christ; *also* **:** a similar apocryphal book **c :** an interpretation of the Christian message **2** *cap* **:** a lection from one of the New Testament Gospels **3 :** the message or teachings of a religious teacher **4 :** something accepted as infallible truth

2gospel *adj* **1 :** relating to or in accordance with the gospel **:** EVANGELICAL **2 :** EVANGELISTIC ⟨a ~ team⟩ **3 :** of or relating to religious songs associated with evangelism and popular devotion ⟨a ~ singer⟩

gos·pel·er *or* **gos·pel·ler** \'gäs-pə-lər\ *n* **1 :** one who preaches or propounds a gospel **2 :** one who reads or sings the liturgical Gospel

gos·port \'gäs-,pō(ə)rt, -,pȯ(ə)rt\ *n* [*Gosport,* England] **:** a flexible one-way speaking tube for communication between separate cockpits of an airplane

gos·sa·mer \'gäs-ə-mər, 'gäz-(ə-)mər\ *n* [ME *gossomer,* fr. *gos* goose + *somer* summer] **1 :** a film of cobwebs floating in air in calm clear weather **2 :** something light, delicate, or tenuous — **gossamer** *adj* — **gos·sa·mery** \-mə-rē\ *adj*

gos·san \'gäs-ᵊn\ *n* [Corn *gossen*] **:** decomposed rock or vein material of reddish or rusty color resulting from oxidized pyrites

1gos·sip \'gäs-əp\ *n* [ME *gossib,* fr. OE *godsibb,* fr. *god* + *sibb* kinsman, fr. *sibb* related] **1 a** *dial Brit* **:** GODPARENT **b :** COMPANION, CRONY **c :** a person who habitually reveals personal or sensational facts **2 a :** rumor or report of an intimate nature **b :** a chatty talk — **gos·sip·ry** \-ə-prē\ *n* — **gos·sipy** \-ə-pē\ *adj*

2gossip *vi* **:** to relate gossip — **gos·sip·er** *n*

gos·sy·pol \'gäs-ə-,pȯl, -,pōl\ *n* [ISV, deriv. of L *gossypion* cotton] **:** a toxic phenolic pigment $C_{30}H_{30}O$ in cottonseed

got *past of* GET

Goth \'gäth\ *n* [LL *Gothi,* pl.] **1 :** a member of a Germanic people that in the early centuries of the Christian era overran the Roman Empire **2 :** a person lacking culture or refinement **:** BARBARIAN

1Goth·ic \'gäth-ik\ *adj* **1 a :** of, relating to, or resembling the Goths, their civilization, or their language **b :** TEUTONIC, GERMANIC **c** (1) **:** MEDIEVAL (2) **:** UNCOUTH, BARBAROUS **2 a :** of, relating to, or having the characteristics of a style of architecture developed in northern France and spreading through western Europe from the middle of the 12th century to the early 16th century that is characterized by the converging of weights and strains at isolated points upon slender vertical piers and counterbalancing buttresses and by pointed arches and vaulting **b :** of or relating to an architectural style reflecting the influence of the medieval Gothic **3** *not cap* **:** of or relating to a literary style characterized by violence, desolation, and decay — **goth·ic·al·ly** \-i-k(ə-)lē\ *adv* — **Goth·ic·ness** *n*

2Gothic *n* **1 :** the East Germanic language of the Goths **2 :** Gothic art style or decoration; *specif* **:** the Gothic architectural style **3 a :** BLACK LETTER **b :** SANS SERIF

Gothic arch *n* **:** a pointed arch; *esp* **:** one with a joint instead of a keystone at its apex

Goth·i·cism \'gäth-ə-,siz-əm\ *n* **1 :** barbarous lack of taste or elegance **2 :** conformity to or practice of Gothic style — **Goth·i·cist** \-səst\ *n*

goth·i·cize \-,sīz\ *vt, often cap* **:** to make Gothic

gö·thite *var of* GOETHITE

gotten *past part of* GET

gouache \'gwäsh, gü-'äsh\ *n* [F, deriv. of L *aquatio* act of fetching water, fr. *aquatus,* pp. of *aquari* to fetch water, fr. *aqua* water — more at ISLAND] **1 :** a method of painting with opaque colors that have been ground in water and mingled with a preparation of gum **2 a :** a picture painted by gouache **b :** the pigment used in gouache

Gou·da \'gaủd-ə, 'güd-, 'haủd-\ *n* [*Gouda,* Netherlands] **:** a usu. mild cheese of Dutch origin shaped in flattened balls and often covered with a red protective coating

1gouge \'gaủj\ *n* [ME *gowge,* fr. MF *gouge,* fr. LL *gulbia,* of Celt origin; akin to OIr *gulban* sting] **1 :** a chisel with a concavo-convex cross section **2 a :** the act of gouging **b :** a groove or cavity scooped out **3 :** an excessive or improper exaction **:** EXTORTION

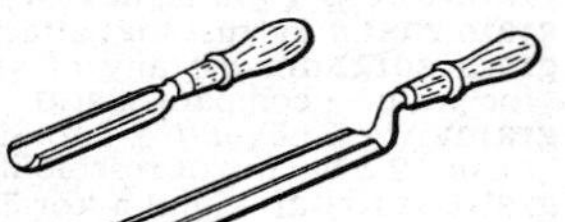

gouges 1

2gouge *vt* **1 :** to scoop out with a gouge **2 a :** to force out (an eye) with the thumb **b :** to thrust the thumb into the eye of **3 :** to subject to extortion — **goug·er** *n*

gou·lash \'gü-,läsh, -,lash\ *n* [Hung *gulyás* herdsman's stew] **:** a beef stew with onion, paprika, and caraway

gourd \'gō(ə)rd, 'gȯ(ə)rd, 'gủ(ə)rd\ *n* [ME *gourde,* fr. MF, fr. L *cucurbita*] **1 :** any of a family (Cucurbitaceae, the gourd family) of chiefly herbaceous tendril-bearing vines including the cucumber, melon, squash, and pumpkin **2 :** the fruit of a gourd **:** PEPO; *esp* **:** any of various hard-rinded inedible fruits of plants of two genera (*Lagenaria* and *Cucurbita*) often used for ornament or for vessels and utensils

gourde \'gủ(ə)rd\ *n* [AmerF] — see MONEY table

gour·mand \'gủ(ə)r-,mänd, gủr-'; 'gủ(ə)r-mənd\ *n* [MF *gourmant*] **1 :** one who is excessively fond of eating and drinking **2 :** a luxurious eater **:** GOURMET **syn** see EPICURE — **gour·mand·ism** \'gủ(ə)r-,män-,diz-əm, -mən-\ *n*

gour·met \'gủ(ə)r-,mā, gủr-'\ *n* [F, fr. MF, alter. of OF *gromet* boy servant] **:** a connoisseur in eating and drinking **syn** see EPICURE

gout \'gaủt\ *n* [ME *goute,* fr. OF, gout, drop, fr. L *gutta* drop] **1 :** a metabolic disease marked by a painful inflammation of the joints, deposits of urates in and around the joints, and usu. an excessive amount of uric acid in the blood **2 :** CLOT, BLOB — **gouty** \-ē\ *adj*

gov·ern \'gəv-ərn\ *vb* [ME *governen,* fr. OF *governer,* fr. L *gubernare* to steer, govern, fr. Gk *kybernan*] *vt* **1 a :** to exercise continuous sovereign authority over; *esp* **:** to control and direct the making and administration of policy in **b :** to rule without sovereign power usu. without having the authority to determine basic policy **2 a** *archaic* **:** MANIPULATE **b :** to control the speed of by automatic means **3 a :** to control, direct, or strongly influence the actions and conduct of **b :** DETERMINE, REGULATE **c :** to hold in check **:** RESTRAIN **4 :** to require (a word) to be in a certain case or mood ⟨in English a transitive verb ~*s* a noun in the common case⟩ **5 :** to constitute a rule or law for ~ *vi* **1 :** to prevail or have decisive influence **:** CONTROL **2 :** to exercise authority — **gov·ern·able** \-ər-nə-bəl\ *adj*

syn GOVERN, RULE mean to exercise power or authority in controlling others. GOVERN implies the aim of keeping in a straight course or smooth operation for the good of the individual and the whole; RULE more often suggests the exercise of despotic or arbitrary power

gov·er·nance \'gəv-ər-nən(t)s\ *n* **:** GOVERNMENT

gov·ern·ess \'gəv-ər-nəs\ *n* **1 :** a woman who governs **2 :** a woman entrusted with the care and supervision of a child esp. in a private household **3 :** the wife of a governor

gov·ern·ment \'gəv-ər(n)-mənt, 'gəv-ᵊm-ənt\ *n, often attrib* **1** *obs* **:** DISCRETION **2 :** the act or process of governing; *specif* **:** authoritative direction or control **3 a :** the office, authority, or function of governing **b** *obs* **:** the term during which a governing official holds office **4 a :** the continuous exercise of authority over and the performance of functions for a political unit **:** RULE **b :** the political function of policy making as distinguished from the administration of policy decisions **5 a :** the organization, machinery, or agency through which a political unit exercises authority and performs functions and which is usu. classified according to the distribution of power within it **b :** the complex of political institutions, laws, and customs through which the function of governing is carried out in a specific political unit **6 :** the body of persons that constitutes the governing authority of a political unit or organization: as **a :** the officials comprising the governing body of a political unit and constituting the organization as an active agency **b** *cap* **:** the executive branch of the U.S. federal government including the political officials and usu. the permanent civil service employees **c** *cap* **:** a small group of persons holding simultaneously the principal political executive offices of a nation or other political unit and responsible for the direction and supervision of public affairs: (1) **:** such a group in a parliamentary system constituted by the cabinet or by the ministry (2) **:** ADMINISTRATION 4b **7 :** POLITICAL SCIENCE — **gov·ern·men·tal** \,gəv-ər(n)-'ment-ᵊl\ *adj* — **gov·ern·men·tal·ly** \-ᵊl-ē\ *adv*

gov·ern·men·tal·ism \,gəv-ər(n)-'ment-ᵊl-,iz-əm\ *n* **1 :** a theory advocating extension of the sphere and degree of government activity **2 :** the tendency toward extension of the role of government — **gov·ern·men·tal·ist** \-ᵊl-əst\ *n*

gov·ern·men·tal·ize \-ᵊl-,īz\ *vt* **:** to subject to the regulation or control of a government

gov·er·nor \'gəv-(ə-)nər *also* 'gəv-ər-nər\ *n* **1 :** one that governs: as **a :** one that exercises authority esp. over an area or group **b :** an official elected or appointed to act as ruler, chief executive, or nominal head of a political unit **c :** COMMANDANT **d :** the managing director and usu. the principal officer of an institution or organization **e :** a member of a group that directs or controls an institution or society **2 :** TUTOR **3 a** *slang* **:** one looked upon as governing **b :** MISTER **4 a :** an automatic attachment to a machine for automatic control or limitation of speed **b :** a device giving automatic control (as of pressure or temperature)

gov·er·nor-gen·er·al \-'jen-(ə-)rəl\ *n, pl* **governors-general** *or* **governor-generals :** a governor of high rank; *esp* **:** one who governs a large territory or has deputy governors under him — **gov·er·nor-gen·er·al·ship** \-(ə-)rəl-,ship\ *n*

governor's council *n* **:** an executive or legislative council chosen to advise or assist a governor

gov·er·nor·ship \'gəv-(ə-)nər-,ship, 'gəv-ər-nər-\ *n* **1 :** the office of governor **2 :** the period of incumbency of a governor

gow·an \'gaủ-ən\ *n* [prob. alter. of ME *gollan*] *chiefly Scot* **:** DAISY 1a; *broadly* **:** a white or yellow field flower — **gow·any** \-ə-nē\ *adj*

gown \'gaủn\ *n* [ME, fr. MF *goune,* fr. LL *gunna,* a fur or leather garment] **1 a :** a loose flowing outer garment formerly worn by men **b :** a distinctive robe worn by a professional or academic person **c :** a woman's dress **d :** a loose garment for lounging or resting **e :** a coverall worn in an operating room **2 a :** an office or profession symbolized by a distinctive robe **b :** a body of college students and faculty — **gown** *vt*

gowns·man \'gaủnz-mən\ *n* **:** a professional or academic person

goy \'gȯi\ *n, pl* **goy·im** \'gȯi-əm\ *or* **goys** [Yiddish, fr. Heb *gōy* people, nation] **:** GENTILE 1 — **goy·ish** \'gȯi-ish\ *adj*

Graaf·ian follicle \,gräf-ē-ən-, ,graf-\ *n* [Regnier de *Graaf* †1673 D anatomist] **:** a vesicle in a mammal ovary enclosing a developing egg

1grab \'grab\ *vb* **grabbed; grab·bing** [obs. D or LG *grabben;* akin to ME *graspen* to grasp, Skt *gṛbhṇāti* he seizes] *vt* **1 :** CLUTCH, SNATCH **2 :** to get unscrupulously **3 :** to take hastily ~ *vi* **1 :** to make a grab **:** SNATCH **2** *of a horse* **:** OVERREACH **syn** see TAKE — **grab·ber** *n*

2grab *n* **1 a :** a sudden snatch **b :** a lawless seizure **c :** something grabbed **2 a :** a device for clutching an object **b :** CLAMSHELL — **up for grabs** *slang* **:** available to a winner or taker

3grab *adj* **1 :** intended to be grabbed ⟨a ~ rail⟩ **2 :** taken at random

4grab *n* [Ar *ghurāb,* lit., raven] **:** an oriental coasting ship of light draft and broad beam having lateen sails and usu. two masts

grab·ble \'grab-əl\ *vi* **grab·bling** \-(ə-)liŋ\ [D *grabbelen,* fr. MD, freq. of *grabben*] **1 :** to search with the hand **:** GROPE **2 :** to lie or fall prone **:** SPRAWL — **grab·bler** \-(ə-)lər\ *n*

grab·by \'grab-ē\ *adj* **:** GRASPING, GREEDY

gra·ben \'gräb-ən\ *n* [G, ditch] **:** a depressed segment of the earth's crust bounded on at least two sides by faults

grab off *vt* **:** to take forcibly or hastily

¹grace \'grās\ *n* [ME, fr. OF, fr. L *gratia* favor, charm, thanks, fr. *gratus* pleasing, grateful; akin to OHG *queran* to sigh, Skt *grṇāti* he praises] **1 a :** unmerited divine assistance given man for his regeneration or sanctification **b :** a state of sanctification enjoyed through divine grace **c :** a virtue coming from God **2 :** a short prayer at a meal asking a blessing or giving thanks **3 a :** KINDNESS, FAVOR **b** *archaic* **:** MERCY, PARDON **c :** a special favor **:** PRIVILEGE **d :** REPRIEVE, MARGIN **e :** APPROVAL, ACCEPTANCE ⟨stayed in his good ~*s*⟩ **4 a :** a charming trait or accomplishment **b** (1) **:** ATTRACTIVENESS, BEAUTY (2) **:** fitness or proportion of line or expression (3) **:** ease of movement or charm of bearing **5 :** a musical trill, turn, or appoggiatura **6 —** used as a title for a duke, a duchess, or an archbishop **7 :** sense of propriety or right; *also* **:** CONSIDERATENESS, THOUGHTFULNESS **8** *pl, cap* **:** three sister goddesses in Greek mythology who are the givers of charm and beauty **syn** see MERCY — **grace·ful** \'grās-fəl\ *adj* — **grace·ful·ly** \-fə-lē\ *adv* — **grace·ful·ness** *n*

²grace *vt* **1 :** HONOR **2 :** ADORN, EMBELLISH **3 :** to add grace notes or other musical ornamentation to

grace cup *n* **:** a cup used in drinking a final health after the grace at the end of a meal or a health drunk from it

grace·less \'grā-sləs\ *adj* **1 :** UNREGENERATE **2 a :** lacking a sense of propriety **b :** devoid of attractive qualities **3 :** artistically inept or unbeautiful — **grace·less·ly** *adv* — **grace·less·ness** *n*

grace note *n* **:** a musical note added as an ornament; *esp* **:** APPOGGIATURA

grac·ile \'gras-əl, -,īl\ *adj* [L *gracilis*] **1 :** SLENDER, SLIGHT **2 :** GRACEFUL — **grac·ile·ness** *n* — **gra·cil·i·ty** \grə-'sil-ət-ē\ *n*

gra·ci·o·so \,gräs-ē-'ō-(,)sō, -(,)zō\ *n* [Sp] **:** a buffoon in Spanish comedy

gra·cious \'grā-shəs\ *adj* [ME, fr. MF *gracieus*, fr. L *gratiosus* enjoying favor, agreeable, fr. *gratia*] **1 a** *obs* **:** GODLY **b :** *archaic* **:** PLEASING, ACCEPTABLE **2 a :** marked by kindness and courtesy **b :** GRACEFUL **c :** marked by tact and delicacy **:** URBANE **d :** characterized by charm, good taste, and generosity of spirit **3 :** MERCIFUL, COMPASSIONATE — used conventionally of royalty and high nobility — **gra·cious·ly** *adv* — **gra·cious·ness** *n*

syn CORDIAL, AFFABLE, GENIAL, SOCIABLE: GRACIOUS implies courtesy and kindliness and often a degree of condescension toward strangers and social inferiors; CORDIAL suggests warmth and heartiness; AFFABLE implies easy approachability and readiness to respond pleasantly to conversation or requests or proposals; GENIAL implies qualities such as warm sympathy or a sense of humor that makes for good cheer ⟨a *genial* host⟩; SOCIABLE suggests a genuine liking for or even a need for frequent companionship

grack·le \'grak-əl\ *n* [deriv. of L *graculus* jackdaw] **1 :** any of various Old World starlings (as the hill mynas) **2 :** any of several rather large American blackbirds (family Icteridae) having glossy iridescent black plumage

gra·date \'grā-,dāt\ *vb* [back-formation fr. *gradation*] *vi* **:** to shade into the next color, note, or stage ~ *vt* **:** to arrange in a progression, scale, or series

gra·da·tion \grā-'dā-shən, grə-\ *n* **1 a :** a series forming successive stages **b :** a step or place in an ordered scale **2 :** an advance by regular degrees **3 :** a color scale — **gra·da·tion·al** \-shnəl, -shən-ᵊl\ *adj* — **gra·da·tion·al·ly** \-ē\ *adv*

¹grade \'grād\ *n* [F, fr. L *gradus* step, degree; akin to L *gradi* to step, go, Lith *gridyti* to go, wander] **1 a** (1) **:** a stage in a process (2) **:** a position in a scale of ranks or qualities **b :** a class organized for the work of a particular year of a school course **c :** a military or naval rank **d :** a degree of intensity in illness ⟨~ III carcinoma⟩ **2 a :** a class of things of the same stage or degree **b :** a mark indicating a degree of accomplishment in school **c :** a standard of food quality ⟨prime-*grade* beef⟩ **3 a :** the degree of inclination of a road or slope; *also* **:** a sloping road **b :** a datum or reference level; *esp* **:** ground level **c :** ELEVATION 1c **4 :** a domestic animal with one parent purebred and the other of inferior breeding

²grade *vt* **1 a :** to arrange in grades **:** SORT **b :** to arrange in a scale or series **2 :** to level off to a smooth horizontal or sloping surface **3 :** to improve by breeding females to purebred males ~ *vi* **1 a :** to form a series **b :** BLEND **2 :** to be of a particular grade

-grade \,grād\ *adj comb form* [F, fr. L *-gradus*, fr. *gradi*] **:** walking ⟨planti*grade*⟩

grade crossing *n* **:** a crossing of highways, railroad tracks, or pedestrian walks or combinations of these on the same level

grad·er \'grād-ər\ *n* **1 :** one that grades **2 :** a machine for leveling earth **3 :** a pupil in an elementary or secondary school grade ⟨a 5th ~⟩

grade school *n* **:** a public school including the first six or the first eight grades

grade separation *n* **:** a highway or railroad crossing using an underpass or overpass

gra·di·ent \'grād-ē-ənt\ *n* [L *gradient-*, *gradiens*, prp. of *gradi*] **1 a :** the rate of regular or graded ascent or descent **:** INCLINATION **b :** a part sloping upward or downward **2 :** change in the value of a quantity per unit distance in a specified direction ⟨vertical temperature ~⟩ **3 :** a graded difference in physiological activity along an axis (as of the body or an embryonic field)

gra·din \'grād-ᵊn\ *or* **gra·dine** \'grā-,dēn, grə-'\ *n* [F *gradin*] **:** one of a series of tiered steps or seats

¹grad·u·al \'graj-(ə-)wəl, 'graj-əl\ *n* [fr. its being sung on the steps of the altar] **1 :** the response and versicle following the Epistle of the Mass **2 :** a book containing the choral parts of the Mass

²gradual *adj* **1 :** proceeding by steps or degrees **2 :** moving, changing, or developing by fine, slight, or often imperceptible degrees — **grad·u·al·ly** *adv* — **grad·u·al·ness** *n*

grad·u·al·ism \-,iz-əm\ *n* **:** the policy of approaching a desired end by gradual stages — **grad·u·al·ist** \-əst\ *n or adj*

¹grad·u·ate \'graj-(ə-)wət, -ə-,wāt\ *n* **1 :** a holder of an academic degree or diploma **2 :** a graduated cup, cylinder, or flask for measuring

²graduate *adj* **1 a :** holding an academic degree or diploma **b :** of or relating to studies beyond the first or bachelor's degree **2 :** arranged by degrees **:** GRADUATED

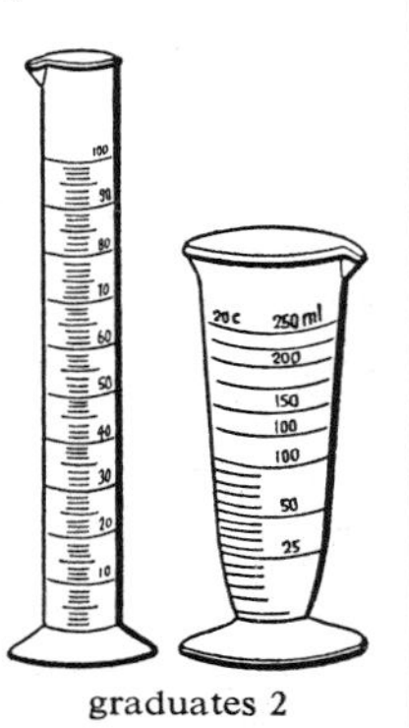

graduates 2

³grad·u·ate \'graj-ə-,wāt\ *vt* **1 :** to grant an academic degree or diploma to **2 :** to admit to a particular standing or grade **3 a :** to mark with degrees of measurement **b :** to divide into grades or intervals ~ *vi* **1 :** to receive an academic degree or diploma **2 :** to change gradually — **grad·u·a·tor** \-,wāt-ər\ *n*

grad·u·a·tion \,graj-ə-'wā-shən\ *n* **1 :** a mark on an instrument or vessel indicating degrees or quantity; *also* **:** these marks **2 a :** the award or acceptance of an academic degree or diploma **b :** COMMENCEMENT **3 :** arrangement in degrees or ranks

gra·dus \'grād-əs\ *n* [*Gradus ad Parnassum* (L, lit., a step to Parnassus)] **:** a dictionary used as an aid in the writing of Greek or Latin poetry

Grae·ae \'grē-,ē, 'grī-,ī\ *n pl* [L, fr. Gk *Graiai*] **:** three daughters of a sea deity in Greek mythology who are guardians of their sisters the Gorgons and have but one eye and one tooth among them

Graeco- — see GRECO-

graf·fi·to \grə-'fēt-(,)ō\ *n, pl* **graf·fi·ti** \-(,)ē\ [It] **:** a rude inscription or drawing found on rocks or walls

¹graft \'graft\ *vb* [ME *graften*, alter. of *graffen*, fr. *graffe* graft, fr. MF *grafe*, fr. ML *graphium*, fr. L, stylus, fr. Gk *grapheion*, fr. *graphein* to write — more at CARVE] *vt* **1 a :** to cause (a scion) to unite with a stock; *also* **:** to unite by joining scion and stock **b :** to propagate (a plant) by grafting **2 :** to unite closely **3 :** to implant (living tissue) surgically **4 :** to get (illicit gain) by graft ~ *vi* **1 :** to become grafted **2 :** to perform grafting **3 :** to practice graft — **graft·er** *n*

²graft *n* **1 a :** a grafted plant **b :** SCION 1 **c :** the point of insertion

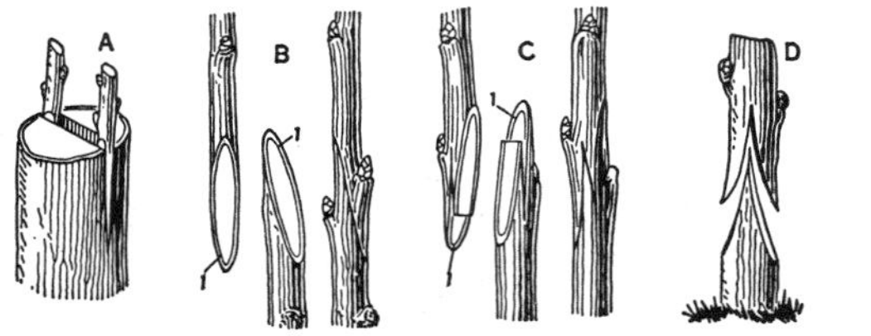

graft 1c: *A* cleft, *B* splice, *C* whip, *D* saddle, *1* cambium

of a scion upon a stock **2 a :** the act of grafting **b :** something grafted; *specif* **:** living tissue used in grafting **3 :** the taking of money or other gain in dishonest or questionable ways; *also* **:** illegal or unfair gain

graft·age \'graf-tij\ *n* **:** the principles and practice of grafting

gra·ham flour \,grā-əm-, (,)gra(-ə)m-\ *n* [Sylvester *Graham* †1851 Am dietary reformer] **:** WHOLE WHEAT FLOUR

grail \'grā(ə)l\ *n* [ME *graal*, fr. MF, bowl, grail, fr. ML *gradalis*] **1** *cap* **:** the cup or platter used according to medieval legend by Christ at the Last Supper and thereafter the object of knightly quests — called also *Holy Grail* **2 :** the object of an extended or difficult quest

¹grain \'grān\ *n* [ME, partly fr. MF *grain* cereal grain, fr. L *granum*; partly fr. MF *graine* seed, kermes, fr. L *grana*, pl. of *granum* — more at CORN] **1 a** (1) *obs* **:** a single small hard seed (2) **:** a seed or fruit of a cereal grass **b :** the seeds or fruits of various food plants including the cereal grasses and in commercial and statutory usage other plants **c :** plants producing grain **2 a :** a small hard particle or crystal **b :** a minute portion or particle **c :** fine crystallization **3 a :** kermes or a scarlet dye made from it **b :** cochineal or a brilliant scarlet dye made from it **c :** a fast dye **d** *archaic* **:** COLOR, TINT **4 a :** a granulated surface or appearance **b :** the outer or hair side of a skin or hide **5 :** a unit of weight based on the weight of a grain of wheat taken as an average of the weight of grains from the middle of the ear — see MEASURE table **6 a :** the stratification of the wood fibers in a piece of wood **b :** a texture due to constituent particles or fibers **7 :** tactile quality **8 a :** natural disposition **:** TEMPER **b :** basic quality or kind — **grained** \'grānd\ *adj* — **with a grain of salt :** SKEPTICALLY ⟨take his predictions *with a grain of salt*⟩

²grain *vt* **1 :** INGRAIN **2 :** to form into grains **:** GRANULATE **3 :** to paint in imitation of the grain of wood or stone ~ *vi* **:** to become granular **:** GRANULATE — **grain·er** *n*

grain alcohol *n* **:** ALCOHOL 1

grain·field \'grān-,fēld\ *n* **:** a field where grain is grown

grain·i·ness \'grā-nē-nəs\ *n* **:** the quality or state of being grainy

grain rust *n* **:** a rust that attacks a cereal grass

grain sorghum *n* **:** any of several sorghums cultivated primarily for grain — compare SORGO

grainy \'grā-nē\ *adj* **1 :** consisting of or resembling grains **:** GRANULAR **2 :** having or resembling the grain of wood

gral·la·to·ri·al \,gral-ə-'tōr-ē-əl, -'tȯr-\ *adj* [deriv. of L *grallae* stilts; akin to L *gradus* step — more at GRADE] **:** of or relating to the wading birds

¹gram \'gram\ *n* [obs. Pg (now *grão*), grain, fr. L *granum*] **:** any of several leguminous plants (as a chick-pea) grown esp. for their seed

²gram *or* **gramme** \'gram\ *n* [F *gramme*, fr. LL *gramma*, a small weight, fr. Gk *grammat-*, *gramma* letter, writing, a small weight, fr. *graphein* to write — more at CARVE] **:** a metric unit of mass and weight equal to 1/1000 kilogram and nearly equal to one cubic centimeter of water at its maximum density — see METRIC SYSTEM table

-gram \,gram\ *n comb form* [L *-gramma*, fr. Gk, fr. *gramma*] **:** drawing **:** writing **:** record ⟨chrono*gram*⟩ ⟨tele*gram*⟩

grama \'gram-ə\ *n* [Sp] **:** a pasture grass (genus *Bouteloua*) of the western U.S.

gram·a·rye \'gram-ə-rē\ *n* [ME, fr. MF *gramaire* grammar, grammar book, book of sorcery] **:** MAGIC

gram atom *n* **:** the weight in grams of a chemical element that is equal numerically to its atomic weight ⟨a *gram atom* of oxygen is 16 grams⟩ — called also *gram-atomic weight*

gra·mer·cy \grə-'mər-sē\ *interj* [ME *grand mercy*, fr. MF *grand merci* great thanks] *archaic* — used to express gratitude or astonishment

gram·i·ci·din \,gram-ə-'sīd-ᵊn\ *n* [*gram*-positive + *-i-* + *-cide* +

-in] : a toxic crystalline polypeptide antibiotic produced by a soil bacterium (*Bacillus brevis*) and used against gram-positive bacteria in local infections

gra·min·e·ous \grə-ˈmin-ē-əs\ *adj* [L *gramineus*, fr. *gramin-*, *gramen* grass] : of or relating to a grass — **gra·min·e·ous·ness** *n*

gram·mar \ˈgram-ər\ *n* [ME *gramere*, fr. MF *gramaire*, modif. of L *grammatica*, fr. Gk *grammatikē*, fr. fem. of *grammatikos* of letters, fr. *grammat-*, *gramma*] **1 a :** the study of the classes of words, their inflections, and their functions and relations in the sentence **b :** a study of what is to be preferred and what avoided in inflection and syntax **2 :** the phenomena of language with which grammar deals **3 a :** a grammar textbook **b :** speech or writing evaluated according to its conformity to grammatical rules **4 :** the principles or rules of an art, science, or technique — **gram·mar·i·an** \grə-ˈmer-ē-ən, -ˈmar-\ *n*

grammar school *n* **1 a :** a secondary school emphasizing Latin and Greek in preparation for college **b :** a British college preparatory school **2 :** a school intermediate between the primary grades and high school **3 :** ELEMENTARY SCHOOL

gram·mat·i·cal \grə-ˈmat-i-kəl\ *adj* **1 :** of or relating to grammar **2 :** conforming to the rules of grammar — **gram·mat·i·cal·ly** \-k(ə-)lē\ *adv* — **gram·mat·i·cal·ness** \-kəl-nəs\ *n*

grammatical meaning *n* **:** the part of meaning that varies from one inflectional form to another (as from *plays* to *played* to *playing*) — compare LEXICAL MEANING

gram–mo·lec·u·lar \ˌgram-mə-ˈlek-yə-lər\ *or* **gram–mo·lar** \ˈgram-ˈmō-lər\ *adj* **:** of, relating to, or containing a gram molecule

gram molecule *n* **:** the quantity of a chemical compound or element that has a weight in grams numerically equal to the molecular weight — called also *gram-molecular weight*

gram–neg·a·tive \ˈgram-ˈneg-ət-iv\ *adj* **:** not holding the purple dye when stained by gram's method — used chiefly of bacteria

Gram·o·phone \ˈgram-ə-ˌfōn\ *trademark* — used for a phonograph

gram–pos·i·tive \-ˈpäz-ət-iv, -ˈpäz-tiv\ *adj* **:** holding the purple dye when stained by gram's method — used chiefly of bacteria

gram·pus \ˈgram-pəs\ *n* [alter. of ME *graspey*, *grapay*, fr. MF *graspeis*, fr. *gras* fat (fr. L *crassus*) + *peis* fish, fr. L *piscis* — more at FISH] **1 :** a cetacean (*Grampus griseus*) related to the blackfish; *broadly* **:** any of various small cetaceans (as the blackfish or killer whale) **2 :** the giant whip scorpion (*Mastigoproctus giganteus*) of the southern U.S.

gram's method \ˈgramz-\ *n* [Hans C. J. *Gram* †1938 Dan physician] **:** a method for the differential staining of bacteria

gram–vari·able \ˈgram-ˈver-ē-ə-bəl, -ˈvar-\ *adj* **:** staining irregularly or inconsistently by gram's method

gran·a·dil·la \ˌgran-ə-ˈdil-ə, -ˈdē-(y)ə\ *n* [Sp] **:** the oblong fruit of various passionflowers (esp. *Passiflora quadrangularis* of tropical America) widely used as a dessert

gra·na·ry \ˈgrān-(ə-)rē, ˈgran-\ *n* [L *granarium*, fr. *granum* grain] **1 a :** a storehouse for threshed grain **b :** a region producing grain in abundance **2 :** a chief source or storehouse

1**grand** \ˈgrand\ *adj* [MF, large, great, grand, fr. L *grandis*] **1 a :** having more importance than others **:** FOREMOST **b :** having higher rank than others bearing the same general designation ⟨a ~ duke⟩ **2 a :** INCLUSIVE, COMPREHENSIVE **b :** DEFINITIVE, INCONTROVERTIBLE ⟨~ example⟩ **3 :** MAIN, PRINCIPAL **4 :** of large size, extent, or scope **5 a :** MAGNIFICENT, SUMPTUOUS **b :** marked by a regal form and dignity **c :** fine or imposing in appearance or impression **:** STATELY **d :** LOFTY, SUBLIME ⟨the ~ style⟩ **6 a :** pretending to social superiority **:** SUPERCILIOUS **b :** intended to impress ⟨a man of ~ gestures and pretentious statements⟩ **7 :** very good **:** WONDERFUL ⟨a ~ time⟩ ⟨~ old man⟩ — **grand·ly** \ˈgran-(d)lē\ *adv* — **grand·ness** \ˈgran(d)-nəs\ *n*

syn GRAND, MAGNIFICENT, IMPOSING, STATELY, MAJESTIC, GRANDIOSE mean large and impressive. GRAND adds to greatness of size the implications of handsomeness and dignity; MAGNIFICENT implies an impressive largeness proportionate to scale without sacrifice of dignity or good taste; IMPOSING implies impressive size and dignity; STATELY may suggest poised dignity, erectness of bearing, handsomeness of proportions, ceremonious deliberation of movement; MAJESTIC combines the implications of IMPOSING and STATELY and usu. adds a suggestion of solemn grandeur; GRANDIOSE implies a size or scope exceeding ordinary experience but is most commonly applied derogatorily to inflated pretension or absurd exaggeration

2**grand** *n, slang* **:** a thousand dollars

gran·dam \ˈgran-ˌdam, -dəm\ *or* **gran·dame** \-ˌdām, -dəm\ *n* [ME *graundam*, fr. AF *graund dame*, lit., great lady] **1 :** GRANDMOTHER **2 :** an old woman

grand·aunt \ˈgran-ˈdant, -ˈdȧnt\ *n* **:** the aunt of one's father or mother

grand·ba·by \ˈgran(d)-ˌbā-bē\ *n* **:** an infant grandchild

grand·child \-ˌchīld\ *n* **:** a son's or daughter's child

grand·daugh·ter \ˈgran-ˌdȯt-ər\ *n* **:** the daughter of one's son or daughter

grand duchess *n* **1 :** the wife or widow of a grand duke **2 :** a woman who rules a grand duchy in her own right

grand duchy *n* **:** the territory or dominion of a grand duke or grand duchess

grand duke *n* **1 :** the sovereign duke of any of various European states **2 :** a son or male descendant of a Russian czar in the male line

grande dame \grän(d)-dȧm\ *n* [F] **:** a usu. elderly woman of great prestige or ability

gran·dee \gran-ˈdē\ *n* [Sp *grande*, fr. *grande*, adj., large, great, fr. L *grandis*] **:** a man of elevated rank or station; *esp* **:** a Spanish or Portuguese nobleman of the first rank

gran·deur \ˈgran-jər, -ˌdyu̇(ə)r, -ˌju̇(ə)r\ *n* [ME, fr. MF, fr. *grand*] **1 :** the quality or state of being grand ⟨the glory that was Greece and the ~ that was Rome —E.A.Poe⟩ **2 :** an instance or example of grandeur

grand·fa·ther \ˈgran(d)-ˌfäth-ər\ *n* **:** a father's or mother's father; *also* **:** ANCESTOR 1a

grandfather clause *n* **:** a clause creating an exemption based on circumstances previously existing; *esp* **:** a provision in several southern state constitutions designed to enfranchise poor whites and disfranchise Negroes by waiving high voting requirements for descendants of men voting before 1867

grandfather clock *n* [fr. the song *My Grandfather's Clock* (1878) by Henry C. Work] **:** a tall pendulum clock standing directly on the floor — called also *grandfather's clock*

gran·dil·o·quence \gran-ˈdil-ə-kwən(t)s\ *n* [prob. fr. MF, fr. L *grandiloquus* using lofty language, fr. *grandis* + *loqui* to speak] **:** lofty or pompous eloquence **:** BOMBAST — **gran·dil·o·quent** \-kwənt\ *adj* — **gran·dil·o·quent·ly** *adv*

gran·di·ose \ˈgran-dē-ˌōs, ˌgran-dē-ˈ\ *adj* [F, fr. It *grandioso*, fr. *grande* great, fr. L *grandis*] **1 :** impressive because of uncommon largeness, scope, effect, or grandeur **2 :** characterized by affectation of grandeur or splendor or by absurd exaggeration **syn** see GRAND — **gran·di·ose·ly** *adv* — **gran·di·ose·ness** *n* — **gran·di·os·i·ty** \ˌgran-dē-ˈäs-ət-ē\ *n*

gran·di·o·so \ˌgrän-dē-ˈō-(ˌ)sō, ˌgran-, -(ˌ)zō\ *adv (or adj)* [It] **:** in a broad and noble style — used as a direction in music

grand jury *n* **:** a jury usu. of 12 to 23 persons specially or periodically impaneled chiefly to examine in private sessions accusations against persons charged with crime and on just cause to find bills of indictment

Grand Lama *n* **:** DALAI LAMA

grand larceny *n* **:** larceny of property of a value greater than that fixed as constituting petit larceny

grand mal \ˈgran(d)-ˈmäl, ˈgrän-, -ˈmal\ *n* [F, lit., great illness] **:** severe epilepsy

grand·moth·er \ˈgran(d)-ˌməth-ər\ *n* **:** the mother of one's father or mother; *also* **:** a female ancestor

grand·neph·ew \-ˈnef-(ˌ)yü, *chiefly Brit* -ˈnev-\ *n* **:** a grandson of one's brother or sister

grand·niece \-ˈnēs\ *n* **:** a granddaughter of one's brother or sister

grand opera *n* **:** opera in which the plot is elaborated as in serious drama and the entire text set to music

grand·par·ent \ˈgran(d)-ˌpar-ənt, -ˌper-\ *n* **:** a parent's parent

grand piano *n* **:** a piano with horizontal frame and strings

grand·sire \ˈgran(d)-ˌsī(ə)r\ *or* **grand·sir** \ˈgran(t)-sər\ *n* **1** *dial* **:** GRANDFATHER **2** *archaic* **:** FOREFATHER **3** *archaic* **:** an aged man

grand slam *n* **1 :** the winning of all the tricks of one hand in a card game (as bridge) **2 :** a clean sweep or total success

grand·son \ˈgran(d)-ˌsən\ *n* **:** the son of one's son or daughter

1**grand·stand** \ˈgran(d)-ˌstand\ *n* **1 :** a usu. roofed stand for spectators at a racecourse or stadium **2 :** AUDIENCE

2**grandstand** *vi* **:** to play or act so as to impress onlookers — **grand·stand·er** *n*

grand tour *n* **:** an extended European tour formerly a usual part of the education of youth of the British aristocracy

grand·un·cle \ˈgran-ˈdəŋ-kəl\ *n* **:** a father's or mother's uncle

grange \ˈgrānj\ *n* [ME, fr. MF, fr. ML *granica*, fr. L *granum* grain] **1** *archaic* **:** GRANARY, BARN **2 :** FARM; *esp* **:** a farmhouse with outbuildings **3** *cap* **:** one of the lodges of a national fraternal association of farmers; *also* **:** the association itself

grang·er \ˈgrān-jər\ *n* **:** a member of a Grange

1**gran·ger·ism** \ˈgrān-jə-ˌriz-əm\ *n* **:** the practice of grangerizing

2**grang·er·ism** \ˈgrān-jə-ˌriz-əm\ *n* **:** the policy or methods of the grangers

gran·ger·ize \ˈgrān-jə-ˌrīz\ *vt* [James *Granger* †1776 E biographer; fr. his method of illustrating his *Biographical History of England* (1769)] **:** to illustrate by inserting engravings or photographs collected from other books; *also* **:** to mutilate (books) to obtain material for such illustration — **gran·ger·iz·er** *n*

grani- *comb form* [L, fr. *granum*] **:** grain **:** seeds ⟨*granivorous*⟩

gran·ite \ˈgran-ət\ *n* [It *granito*, fr. pp. of *granire* to granulate, fr. *grano* grain, fr. L *granum*] **1 :** a very hard natural igneous rock formation of visibly crystalline texture formed essentially of quartz and orthoclase or microcline and used for building and for monuments **2 :** unyielding firmness or endurance — **gra·nit·ic** \gra-ˈnit-ik\ *adj* — **gran·it·oid** \ˈgran-ət-ˌȯid\ *adj*

granite paper *n* **:** a paper containing a small proportion of deeply colored mottling fibers

gran·ite·ware \ˈgran-ət-ˌwa(ə)r, -ˌwe(ə)r\ *n* **:** enameled iron kitchenware

gra·niv·o·rous \grə-ˈniv-ə-rəs, grā-\ *adj* **:** feeding on seeds or grain

gran·ny *or* **gran·nie** \ˈgran-ē\ *n* [by shortening & alter.] **1 a :** GRANDMOTHER **b :** a fussy person **2** *South & Midland* **:** MIDWIFE

granny knot *n* **:** an easily jammed and insecure knot often made by the inexperienced instead of a square knot

grano- *comb form* [G, fr. *granit*, fr. It *granito*] **:** granite **:** granitic ⟨*granogabbro*⟩

grano·di·o·rite \ˌgran-ō-ˈdī-ə-ˌrīt\ *n* **:** a granular intrusive quartzose igneous rock intermediate between granite and quartz diorite with plagioclase predominant over orthoclase

grano·lith \ˈgran-ə-ˌlith\ *n* **:** an artificial stone of crushed granite and cement — **grano·lith·ic** \ˌgran-ə-ˈlith-ik\ *adj*

grano·phyre \ˈgran-ə-ˌfī(ə)r\ *n* [ISV] **:** a porphyritic igneous rock chiefly of feldspar and quartz with granular groundmass — **grano·phyr·ic** \ˌgran-ə-ˈfir-ik\ *adj*

1**grant** \ˈgrant\ *vt* [ME *granten*, fr. OF *creanter*, *graanter*, fr. (assumed) VL *credentare*, fr. L *credent-*, *credens*, prp. of *credere* to believe — more at CREED] **1 a :** to consent to carry out or allow fulfillment of **b :** to permit as a right, privilege, or favor **2 :** BESTOW, CONFER; *specif* **:** give the possession or title of by a deed **3 a :** to be willing to concede **b :** to assume to be true — **grant·able** \-ə-bəl\ *adj* — **grant·er** \-ər\ *n* — **grant·or** \ˈgrant-ər, -ˌȯ(ə)r; grant-ˈȯ(ə)r\ *n*

syn GRANT, CONCEDE, VOUCHSAFE, ACCORD, AWARD mean to give as a favor or a right. GRANT may apply to giving to a petitioner, often a subordinate or inferior, something sought that could be withheld; CONCEDE implies a yielding with reluctance to a rightful or compelling claim; VOUCHSAFE implies a granting as a courtesy or as an act of gracious condescension; ACCORD implies the sometimes reluctant granting of what is due to someone because of his station or character; AWARD applies to the granting of something merited or earned

2**grant** *n* **1 :** the act of granting **2 :** something granted; *esp* **:** a gift for a particular purpose **3 a :** a transfer of property by deed or writing **b :** the instrument by which such a transfer is made; *also* **:** the property so transferred **4 :** a minor territorial division of Maine, New Hampshire, or Vermont orig. granted by the state to an individual or institution

grant·ee \grant-'ē\ *n* **:** one to whom a grant is made

grant–in–aid \,grant-ᵊn-'ād\ *n, pl* **grants–in–aid** \,gran(t)-sə-'nād\ **1 :** a grant or subsidy from public funds paid by a central to a local government in aid of a public undertaking **2 :** a grant or subsidy to a school or individual for an educational or artistic project

granul- *or* **granuli-** *or* **granulo-** *comb form* [LL *granulum*] **:** granule ⟨*granul*ose⟩

gran·u·lar \'gran-yə-lər\ *adj* **:** consisting of or appearing to consist of granules **:** having a grainy texture — **gran·u·lar·i·ty** \,gran-yə-'lar-ət-ē\ *n* — **gran·u·lar·ly** *adv*

gran·u·late \'gran-yə-,lāt\ *vt* **:** to form or crystallize into grains or granules ~ *vi* **:** to collect into grains or granules — **gran·u·la·tive** \-,lāt-iv\ *adj* — **gran·u·la·tor** \-,lāt-ər\ *n*

gran·u·la·tion \,gran-yə-'lā-shən\ *n* **1 :** the act or process of granulating **:** the condition of being granulated **2 :** one of the minute red granules of new capillaries formed on the surface of a wound in healing **3 :** GRANULE 2

granulation tissue *n* **:** tissue made up of granulations that temporarily replaces lost tissue in a wound

gran·ule \'gran-(,)yü(ə)l\ *n* [LL *granulum*, dim. of L *granum* grain] **1 :** a small particle; *esp* **:** one of numerous particles forming a larger unit **2 :** one of the small short-lived brilliant spots on the sun's seething photosphere

gran·u·lite \'gran-yə-,līt\ *n* **:** a banded or laminated whitish granular rock consisting of feldspar, quartz, and small red garnets and occurring with crystalline schists — **gran·u·lit·ic** \,gran-yə-'lit-ik\ *adj*

gran·u·lo·cyte \'gran-yə-lō-,sīt\ *n* [ISV] **:** a cell with granule-containing cytoplasm — **gran·u·lo·cyt·ic** \,gran-yə-lō-'sit-ik\ *adj*

gran·u·lo·cy·to·poi·e·sis \,gran-yə-lō-,sīt-ə-(,)pȯi-'ē-səs\ *n* [NL] **:** the formation of blood granulocytes typically in the bone marrow

gran·u·lo·ma \,gran-yə-'lō-mə\ *n* **:** a mass or nodule of chronically inflamed tissue with granulations that is usu. associated with an infective process — **gran·u·lo·ma·tous** \-'läm-ət-əs, -'lōm-\ *adj*

gran·u·lose \'gran-yə-,lōs\ *adj* **:** GRANULAR; *esp* **:** having the surface roughened with granules

grape \'grāp\ *n* [ME, fr. OF *crape*, *grape* hook, grape stalk, bunch of grapes, grape, of Gmc origin; akin to OHG *krāpfo* hook — more at CRAVE] **1 :** a smooth-skinned juicy berry eaten dried or fresh as a fruit or fermented to produce wine **2 :** any of numerous woody plants (genus *Vitis*) of a family (Vitaceae, the grape family) that usu. climb by tendrils, produce clustered fruits that are grapes, and are nearly cosmopolitan in cultivation **3 :** GRAPESHOT

grape·fruit \'grāp-,früt\ *n* **1 :** a large citrus fruit with a bitter yellow rind and inner skin and a highly flavored somewhat acid juicy pulp **2 :** a small roundheaded tree (*Citrus paradisi*) that produces grapefruit and is prob. derived from the shaddock

grape hyacinth *n* **:** any of several small bulbous spring-flowering herbs (genus *Muscari*) of the lily family with racemes of usu. blue flowers

grape·shot \'grāp-,shät\ *n* **:** a cluster of small iron balls used as a cannon charge

grape sugar *n* **:** dextrorotatory glucose

grape·vine \'grāp-,vīn\ *n* **1 :** GRAPE 2 **2 a :** RUMOR, REPORT; *esp* **:** a baseless rumor **b** (1) **:** an informal means of circulating information or gossip (2) **:** a secret source of information

1graph \'graf\ *n* [short for *graphic formula*] **1 :** a diagram that represents the variation of a variable in comparison with that of one or more other variables **2 :** the collection of all points whose coordinates satisfy a given functional relation

2graph *vt* **1 :** to represent by a graph **2 :** to plot upon a graph

3graph *n* [prob. fr. *-graph*] **1 :** a spelling of a word **2 :** a single occurrence of a letter of an alphabet in any of its various shapes (as D, d) **3 :** a letter or combination of letters taken as a minimum unit in determining the phonemes of a language from written records

-graph \,graf\ *n comb form* [MF *-graphe*, fr. L *-graphum*, fr. Gk *-graphon*, fr. neut. of *-graphos* written, fr. *graphein* to write] **1 :** something written ⟨mono*graph*⟩ **2** [F *-graphe*, fr. LL *-graphus*] **:** instrument for making or transmitting records ⟨chrono*graph*⟩

graph·eme \'graf-,ēm\ *n* **1 :** a letter of an alphabet **2 :** the sum of all written letters and letter combinations that represent one phoneme ⟨the *p* of *pin*, the *pp* of *hopping*, and the *gh* of *hiccough* are members of one ~⟩ — **gra·phe·mic** \gra-'fē-mik\ *adj* — **gra·phe·mi·cal·ly** \-mi-k(ə-)lē\ *adv* — **gra·phe·mics** \-miks\ *n pl but sing or pl in constr*

-g·ra·pher \g-rə-fər\ *n comb form* [LL *-graphus*, fr. Gk *-graphos*, fr. *graphein*] **:** one that writes about (specified) material or in a (specified) way ⟨cranio*grapher*⟩

1graph·ic \'graf-ik\ *adj* [L *graphicus*, fr. Gk *graphikos*, fr. *graphein*] **1 :** written, drawn, or engraved **2 a :** marked by or capable of clear and lively description or striking imaginative power **b :** sharply outlined or delineated **3 a :** of or relating to the pictorial arts **b :** of, relating to, or involving such reproductive methods as those of engraving, etching, lithography, photography, serigraphy, and woodcut **c :** of or relating to the art of printing **d :** relating or according to graphics **4 :** having mineral crystals resembling written or printed characters **5 :** of, relating to, or represented by a graph **6 :** of or relating to the written or printed word or the symbols or devices used in writing or printing to represent sound or convey meaning — **graph·i·cal** \-i-kəl\ *adj* — **graph·i·cal·ly** \-i-k(ə-)lē\ *adv* — **graph·ic·ness** *n*

syn GRAPHIC, VIVID, PICTURESQUE, PICTORIAL mean giving a clear visual impression in words. GRAPHIC stresses the evoking of a clear lifelike picture; VIVID suggests an impressing on the mind the vigorous aliveness of something; PICTURESQUE suggests the presentation of a striking or effective picture often without regard to reality; PICTORIAL implies representation in the manner of painting with emphasis upon colors, shapes, and spatial relations

2graphic *n* **1 a :** a product of graphic art **b** *pl* **:** the graphic media **2 :** a picture, map, or graph used for illustration or demonstration

-graph·ic \'graf-ik\ *or* **-graph·i·cal** \-i-kəl\ *adj comb form* [LL *-graphicus*, fr. Gk *-graphikos*, fr. *graphikos*] **1 :** written or transmitted in a (specified) way ⟨stylo*graphic*⟩ **2 :** of or relating to writing in a (specified) field or on a (specified) subject ⟨oro*graphic*⟩

graphic arts *n pl* **:** the fine and applied arts of representation, decoration, and writing or printing on flat surfaces together with the techniques and crafts associated with each

graph·ics \'graf-iks\ *n pl but sing or pl in constr* **:** the art or science of drawing a representation of an object upon a two-dimensional surface according to mathematical rules of projection

graph·ite \'graf-,īt\ *n* [G *graphit*, fr. Gk *graphein* to write] **:** a soft black lustrous carbon that conducts electricity and is used in lead pencils, crucibles, electrolytic anodes, as a lubricant, and as a moderator in atomic-energy plants (hardness 1–2, sp. gr. 2.09–2.23) — **gra·phit·ic** \gra-'fit-ik\ *adj*

graph·it·iza·tion \,graf-,īt-ə-'zā-shən\ *n* **:** the process of graphitizing

graph·i·tize \'graf-ə-,tīz, -,īt-,īz\ *vt* **1 :** to convert into graphite **2 :** to impregnate or coat with graphite

grapho- *comb form* [F, fr. MF, fr. Gk, fr. *graphē*, fr. *graphein* to write] **:** writing ⟨*grapho*motor⟩

gra·phol·o·gist \gra-'fäl-ə-jəst\ *n* **:** a specialist in graphology

gra·phol·o·gy \-jē\ *n* [F *graphologie*, fr. *grapho-* + *-logie* -logy] **:** the study of handwriting esp. for the purpose of character analysis

Graph·o·phone \'graf-ə-,fōn\ *trademark* — used for a phonograph using wax records

graph paper *n* **:** paper ruled for drawing graphs

-g·ra·phy \g-rə-fē\ *n comb form* [L *-graphia*, fr. Gk, fr. *graphein*] **1 :** writing or representation in a (specified) manner or by a (specified) means or of a (specified) object ⟨phono*graphy*⟩ ⟨photo*graphy*⟩ ⟨steno*graphy*⟩ **2 :** writing on a (specified) subject or in a (specified) field ⟨organo*graphy*⟩

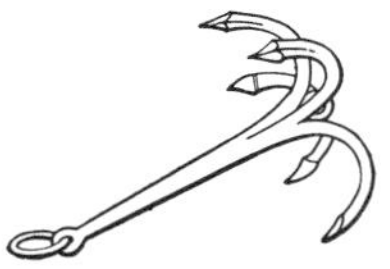
grapnel

grap·nel \'grap-nᵊl\ *n* [ME *grapenel*, fr. (assumed) MF *grapinel*, dim. of *grapin*, dim. of *grape* hook — more at GRAPE] **:** a small anchor with four or five flukes or claws used in dragging or grappling operations and for anchoring a dory or skiff

grap·pa \'gräp-ə\ *n* [It] **:** a dry colorless Italian brandy made from the distilled residue of a wine press

1grap·ple \'grap-əl\ *n* [MF *grappelle*, dim. of *grape* hook — more at GRAPE] **1 a :** an instrument with iron claws used to fasten an enemy ship alongside before boarding **b :** GRAPNEL **2 :** a hand-to-hand struggle **3 :** a bucket similar to a clamshell

2grapple *vb* **grap·pling** \'grap-(ə-)liŋ\ *vt* **1 :** to seize with or as if with a grapple **2 :** to come to grips with **:** WRESTLE **3 :** to bind closely ~ *vi* **1 :** to make a ship fast with a grapple **2 :** to come to grips **:** WRESTLE **3 :** to use a grapple — **grap·pler** \-(ə-)lər\ *n*

grap·pling *n* **1 :** GRAPPLE 1a **2 :** GRAPNEL

grappling iron *n* **:** a hooked iron for anchoring a boat, grappling ships to each other, or recovering sunken objects — called also *grappling hook*

grapy \'grā-pē\ *adj* **1 :** of or relating to grapes or the vine **2 :** having a grape taste as well as a wine taste — used of wines

1grasp \'grasp\ *vb* [ME *graspen* — more at GRAB] *vi* **:** to make the motion of seizing **:** CLUTCH ~ *vt* **1 :** to take or seize eagerly **2 :** to clasp or embrace with or as if with the fingers or arms **3 :** to lay hold of with the mind **:** COMPREHEND **syn** see TAKE — **grasp·able** \'gras-pə-bəl\ *adj* — **grasp·er** *n*

2grasp *n* **1 a :** HANDLE **b :** the fluke of an anchor **c :** EMBRACE **2 :** HOLD, CONTROL **3 a :** the reach of the arms **b :** the power of seizing and holding **4 :** COMPREHENSION ⟨showed remarkable ~⟩

grasp·ing *adj* **:** AVARICIOUS **syn** see COVETOUS — **grasp·ing·ly** \'gras-piŋ-lē\ *adv* — **grasp·ing·ness** *n*

1grass \'gras\ *n, often attrib* [ME *gras*, fr. OE *græs*; akin to OHG *gras* grass, OE *grōwan* to grow] **1 :** herbage suitable or used for grazing animals **2 :** any of a large family (Gramineae) of monocotyledonous mostly herbaceous plants with jointed stems, slender sheathing leaves, and flowers borne in spikelets of bracts **3 :** land on which grass is grown ⟨keep off the ~⟩ **4 :** a leaf or plant of grass — used only in pl. **5 :** a state or place of retirement **6 :** electronic noise on a radarscope that takes the form of vertical lines resembling lawn grass **7 :** MARIJUANA — **grass·land** \-,land\ *n* — **grass·like** \-,līk\ *adj* — **grass·plot** \-,plät\ *n*

2grass *vt* **1 :** to feed (livestock) on grass sometimes without grain or other concentrates **2 :** to cover with grass; *esp* **:** to seed to grass ~ *vi* **:** to produce grass

grass green *n* **1 :** a moderate to strong yellowish green **2 :** a moderate yellow green

grass·hop·per \'gras-,häp-ər\ *n* **1 :** any of numerous plant-eating orthopterous insects (suborder Saltatoria) having the hind legs adapted for leaping and sometimes engaging in migratory flights in which whole regions may be stripped of vegetation **2 :** a light unarmed scouting and liaison airplane

grass roots *n pl but sing or pl in constr* **1 :** soil at or near the surface **2 :** society at the local level esp. in rural areas as distinguished from the centers of political leadership **3 :** the very foundation or source

grass tree *n* **1 :** any of a genus (*Xanthorrhoea*) of Australian plants of the lily family with a thick woody trunk bearing a cluster of stiff linear leaves and a terminal spike of small flowers **2 :** any of several Australasian trees of grasslike foliage (as a ti)

grass widow *n* **1** *chiefly dial* **a :** a discarded mistress **b :** a woman who has had an illegitimate child **2 a :** a woman divorced or separated from her husband **b :** a woman whose husband is temporarily away from her

grass widower *n* **1 :** a man divorced or separated from his wife **2 :** a man whose wife is temporarily away from him

grassy \'gras-ē\ *adj* **1 a :** covered or abounding with grass **b :** consisting of or having a flavor or odor of grass **2 :** resembling grass esp. in color

grat *past of* GREET

1grate \'grāt\ *n* [ME, fr. ML *crata*, *grata* hurdle, modif. of L *cratis* — more at HURDLE] **1** *obs* **:** CAGE, PRISON **2 :** a frame of parallel bars or a lattice of crossed ones blocking a passage **3 a :** a frame or basket of iron bars to hold a stove or furnace fire **b :** FIREPLACE **4 :** a screen or sieve for grading ore

2grate *vt* **:** to furnish with a grate

3grate *vb* [ME *graten*, fr. MF *grater* to scratch, of Gmc origin; akin to OHG *krazzōn* to scratch] *vt* **1** *archaic* **:** ABRADE **2 :** to pulverize by rubbing with something rough **3 :** FRET, IRRITATE **4 a :** to gnash or grind noisily **b :** to cause to make a rasping sound **c :** to utter in a harsh voice ~ *vi* **1 :** to rub or rasp noisily **2 :** to cause irritation **:** JAR — **grat·er** *n*

grate·ful \'grāt-fəl\ *adj* [obs. *grate* pleasing, thankful, fr. L *gratus* — more at GRACE] **1 a :** appreciative of benefits received **b :** expressing gratitude **2 a :** affording pleasure or contentment

: PLEASING **b** : pleasing by reason of comfort supplied or discomfort alleviated — **grate·ful·ly** \-fə-lē\ *adv* — **grate·ful·ness** *n*
syn GRATEFUL, THANKFUL mean feeling or expressing gratitude. GRATEFUL commonly applies to a proper sense of favors received from one's fellowmen; THANKFUL may apply to a more generalized acknowledgment of what is vaguely felt to be providential **syn** see in addition PLEASANT

grat·i·cule \'grat-i-,kyü(ə)l\ *n* [F, fr. L *craticula* fine latticework, dim. of *cratis*] **1** : a scale on transparent material in the focal plane of an optical instrument for the location and measurement of objects **2** : the network of lines of latitude and longitude upon which a map is drawn

grat·i·fi·ca·tion \,grat-ə-fə-'kā-shən\ *n* **1** : the act of gratifying : the state of being gratified **2** *archaic* : REWARD, RECOMPENSE; *esp* : GRATUITY **3** : a source of satisfaction or pleasure

grat·i·fy \'grat-ə-,fī\ *vt* [MF *gratifier*, fr. L *gratificari*, lit., to make oneself pleasing, fr. *gratus* + *-ificari*, pass. of *-ificare* -ify] **1** *archaic* : REMUNERATE **2** : to give or be a source of pleasure or satisfaction to **3** : to confer a favor on : INDULGE

grat·i·fy·ing *adj* : PLEASING, SATISFYING **syn** see PLEASANT

gra·tin \'grat-ᵊn, 'grät-\ *n* [F, fr. MF, fr. *grater* to scratch] : a brown crust formed upon food cooked with a covering of buttered crumbs or grated cheese

grat·ing \'grāt-iŋ\ *n* **1** : a partition, covering, or frame of parallel bars or crossbars : GRATE **2** : a wooden or metal lattice used to close or floor any of various openings **3** : a system of close equidistant and parallel lines or bars ruled on a polished surface to produce spectra by diffraction

gra·tis \'grat-əs, 'grāt-\ *adv (or adj)* [ME, fr. L *gratiis*, *gratis*, fr. abl. pl. of *gratia* favor — more at GRACE] : without charge or recompense : FREE

grat·i·tude \'grat-ə-,t(y)üd\ *n* [ME, fr. MF or ML; MF, fr. ML *gratitudo*, fr. L *gratus* grateful] : the state of being grateful : THANKFULNESS

gra·tu·itous \grə-'t(y)ü-ət-əs\ *adj* [L *gratuitus*, fr. *gratus*] **1 a** : given unearned or without recompense **b** : costing nothing : FREE **c** : not involving a return benefit, compensation, or consideration **2** : UNCALLED-FOR, UNWARRANTED **syn** see SUPEREROGATORY — **gra·tu·itous·ly** *adv* — **gra·tu·itous·ness** *n*

gratuitous contract *n* : a contract for the benefit of only one of the parties

gra·tu·ity \grə-'t(y)ü-ət-ē\ *n* : something given voluntarily or beyond obligation; *esp* : TIP

grat·u·lant \'grach-ə-lənt\ *adj* : showing gratification : CONGRATULATORY

grat·u·late \'grach-ə-,lāt\ *vt* [L *gratulatus*, pp. of *gratulari* — more at CONGRATULATE] *archaic* : CONGRATULATE — **grat·u·la·tion** \,grach-ə-'lā-shən\ *n* — **grat·u·la·to·ry** \'grach-ə-lə-,tōr-ē, -,tȯr-\ *adj*

grau·pel \'grau̇-pəl\ *n* [G] : granular snow pellets — called also *soft hail*

Grau·stark \'grau̇-,stärk, 'grȯ-\ *n* [*Graustark*, imaginary country in the novel *Graustark* (1901) by George B. McCutcheon] : an imaginary land of high romance; *also* : a highly romantic piece of writing — **Grau·stark·ian** \grau̇-'stär-kē-ən, grȯ-\ *adj*

gra·va·men \grə-'vām-ən, -'väm-\ *n, pl* **gravamens** *or* **gra·va·mi·na** \-'vam-ə-nə, -'vām-, -'väm-\ [LL, burden, fr. L *gravare* to burden, fr. *gravis*] : the material or significant part of a grievance or complaint

1**grave** \'grāv\ *vt* **graved**; **grav·en** \'grā-vən\ *or* **graved**; **grav·ing** [ME *graven*, fr. OE *grafan*; akin to OHG *graban* to dig, OSlav *pogreti* to bury] **1** *archaic* : DIG, EXCAVATE **2 a** : to carve or shape with a chisel : SCULPTURE **b** : to carve or cut (as letters or figures) into a hard surface **3** : to impress or fix (as a thought) deeply

2**grave** *n* [ME, fr. OE *græf*; akin to OHG *grab* grave, OE *grafan* to dig] : an excavation for burial of a body; *broadly* : TOMB

3**grave** *vt* [ME *graven*] : to clean and pay with pitch (as a ship's bottom)

4**grave** \'grāv, *in sense 5 also* 'gräv\ *adj* [MF, fr. L *gravis* heavy, grave — more at GRIEVE] **1 a** *obs* : AUTHORITATIVE, WEIGHTY **b** : meriting serious consideration : IMPORTANT **c** : threatening great harm or danger : MORTAL **2** : dignified in bearing or demeanor **3** : drab in color : SOMBER **4** : low-pitched in sound **5 a** *of an accent mark* : having the form ` **b** : marked with a grave accent **c** : of the variety indicated by a grave accent **syn** see SERIOUS — **grave·ly** *adv* — **grave·ness** *n*

5**grave** \'grāv, 'gräv\ *n* : a grave accent ` used to show that a vowel is pronounced with a fall of pitch (as in ancient Greek), that a vowel has a certain quality (as over *e* in French), that a final *e* is stressed and close and that a final *o* is stressed and open (as in Italian), that a syllable has a degree of stress between maximum and minimum (as in phonetic transcription), or that the *e* of the English ending *-ed* in a line of poetry is to be pronounced \ə\, \i\, or \e\ for the sake of the meter (as in "this cursèd day")

6**gra·ve** \'gräv-(,)ā\ *adv (or adj)* [It, lit., grave, fr. L *gravis*] : slowly and solemnly — used as a direction in music

grave·clothes \'grāv-,klō(th)z\ *n pl* : the clothes in which a dead person is buried

1**grav·el** \'grav-əl\ *n* [ME, fr. MF *gravele*, fr. OF, dim. of *grave*, *greve* pebbly ground, beach] **1** *obs* : SAND **2** : loose rounded fragments of rock **3** : a deposit of small calculous concretions in the kidneys and urinary bladder

2**gravel** *adj* : GRAVELLY 2 — used of the human voice

3**gravel** *vt* **grav·eled** *or* **grav·elled**; **grav·el·ing** *or* **grav·el·ling** \'grav-(ə-)liŋ\ **1** : to cover or spread with gravel **2 a** : PERPLEX, CONFOUND **b** : IRRITATE, NETTLE

grav·el–blind \'grav-əl-,blīnd\ *adj* [suggested by *sand-blind*] : having very weak vision

grave·less \'grāv-ləs\ *adj* **1** : UNBURIED ⟨these ~ bones⟩ **2** : not requiring graves : DEATHLESS ⟨the ~ home of the blessed⟩

grav·el·ly \'grav-(ə-)lē\ *adj* **1** : of, containing, or covered with gravel **2** : having a harsh grating sound ⟨a ~ voice⟩

grav·er \'grā-vər\ *n* **1** : ENGRAVER, SCULPTOR **2** : any of various cutting or shaving tools

Graves' disease \'grāvz(-əz)-\ *n* [Robert J. *Graves* †1853 Ir physician] : HYPERTHYROIDISM; *specif* : exophthalmic goiter

grave·stone \'grāv-,stōn\ *n* : a burial monument

grave·yard \-,yärd\ *n* : CEMETERY

gravi- *comb form* [MF, fr. L, fr. *gravis*] : heavy

grav·id \'grav-əd\ *adj* [L *gravidus*, fr. *gravis* heavy] : PREGNANT — **gra·vid·i·ty** \gra-'vid-ət-ē\ *n* — **grav·id·ly** \'grav-əd-lē\ *adv* — **grav·id·ness** *n*

grav·i·da \'grav-əd-ə\ *n* [L, fr. fem. of *gravidus*] : a pregnant woman

gra·vim·e·ter \gra-'vim-ət-ər, 'grav-ə-,mēt-\ *n* [F *gravimètre*, fr. *gravi-* + *-mètre* -meter] : a device similar to a hydrometer for determining specific gravity

gravi·met·ric \,grav-ə-'me-trik\ *adj* **1** : of or relating to measurement by weight **2** : of or relating to variations in the gravitational field determined by means of a gravimeter — **gravi·met·ri·cal·ly** \-tri-k(ə-)lē\ *adv*

gra·vim·e·try \gra-'vim-ə-trē\ *n* : the measurement of weight or density

graving dock *n* : DRY DOCK

grav·i·tate \'grav-ə-,tāt\ *vi* **1** : to move under the influence of gravitation **2 a** : to move toward something **b** : to become attracted ~ *vt* : to move by gravitation

grav·i·ta·tion \,grav-ə-'tā-shən\ *n* **1 a** : a force manifested by acceleration toward each other of two free material particles or bodies or of radiant-energy quanta **b** : the action or process of gravitating **2** : an attraction to something — **grav·i·ta·tion·al** \-shnəl, -shən-ᵊl\ *adj* — **grav·i·ta·tion·al·ly** \-ē\ *adv* — **grav·i·ta·tive** \'grav-ə-,tāt-iv\ *adj*

grav·i·ty \'grav-ət-ē\ *n* [MF or L; MF *gravité*, fr. L *gravitat-*, *gravitas*, fr. *gravis*] **1 a** : dignity or sobriety of bearing **b** : IMPORTANCE, SIGNIFICANCE; *esp* : SERIOUSNESS **2** : PONDERABILITY **3** : WEIGHT — used chiefly in the phrase *center of gravity* **4 a** : the gravitational attraction of the earth's mass for bodies at or near its surface; *broadly* : GRAVITATION **b** : ACCELERATION OF GRAVITY **c** : SPECIFIC GRAVITY — **gravity** *adj*

gra·vure \grə-'vyu̇(ə)r, grā-\ *n* [F, fr. *graver* to grave, of Gmc origin; akin to OHG *graban* to dig, engrave — more at GRAVE] **1 a** : a process for producing an intaglio printing plate on wood or copper **b** : a gravure plate or print **2** : PHOTOGRAVURE

gra·vy \'grā-vē\ *n* [ME *gravey*, fr. MF *gravé*] **1** : a sauce made from the thickened and seasoned juices of cooked meat **2 a** : a soft snap **b** : unearned or illicit gain : GRAFT

gravy train *n, slang* : a much exploited source of easy money; *also* : a soft snap

1**gray** \'grā\ *adj* [ME, fr. OE *grǣg*; akin to OHG *grāo* gray, OSlav *zĭrěti* to see] **1** : of the color gray; *also* : dull in color **2** : having the hair gray : HOARY **3** : clothed in gray **4** : dull in mood or outlook **5** : bordering on black-market practices — **gray·ly** *adv* — **gray·ness** *n*

2**gray** *n* **1** : something (as a horse, garment, cloth, spot) of a gray color **2** : a neutral or achromatic color ranging between black and white

3**gray** *vt* : to make gray ~ *vi* : to become gray

gray·beard \'grā-,bi(ə)rd\ *n* : an old man

gray·fish \-,fish\ *n* **1** : a young pollack **2** : DOGFISH

gray hen *n* : a female black grouse

gray·ish \'grā-ish\ *adj* **1** : somewhat gray **2** *of a color* : low in saturation

gray·ling \'grā-liŋ\ *n, pl* **grayling** *also* **graylings** : any of several freshwater salmonoid fishes (genus *Thymallus*) valued as food and sport fishes

gray matter *n* **1** : neural tissue esp. of the brain and spinal cord that contains nerve-cell bodies as well as nerve fibers and has a brownish gray color **2** : BRAINS, INTELLECT

gray trout *n* : a common weakfish (*Cynoscion regalis*) of the Atlantic coast of the U.S.

gray·wacke \'grā-,wak(-ə)\ *n* [1*gray* + *wacke* (graywacke), fr. G] : a coarse usu. dark gray sandstone or fine-grained conglomerate composed of firmly cemented rounded fragments (as of quartz and feldspars)

1**graze** \'grāz\ *vb* [ME *grasen*, fr. OE *grasian*, fr. *græs* grass] *vi* : to feed on growing herbage ~ *vt* **1 a** : to crop and eat in the field **b** : to feed on the herbage of **2 a** : to put to graze ⟨*grazed* his cows on the meadow⟩ **b** : to put cattle to graze on **3** : to supply herbage for the grazing of

2**graze** *n* **1** : an act of grazing **2** : herbage for grazing

3**graze** *vb* [perh. fr. 1*graze*] *vt* **1** : to touch lightly in passing **2** : ABRADE, SCRATCH ~ *vi* : to touch or rub against something in passing

4**graze** *n* : a scraping along a surface or an abrasion made by it; *esp* : a superficial abrasion of the skin

gra·zier \'grā-zhər\ *n* : a person who grazes cattle; *broadly* : RANCHER

1**grease** \'grēs\ *n* [ME *grese*, fr. OF *craisse*, *graisse*, fr. (assumed) VL *crassia*, fr. L *crassus* fat] **1 a** : rendered animal fat **b** : oily matter **c** : a thick lubricant **2** : wool as shorn and before cleansing — **in the grease** *of wool or fur* : in the natural uncleaned condition

2**grease** \'grēs, 'grēz\ *vt* **1** : to smear or daub with grease **2** : to lubricate with grease **3** : to soil with grease — **greas·er** *n* — **grease the hand** *or* **grease the palm** : BRIBE

grease·paint \'grē-,spānt\ *n* : theater makeup

grease·wood \'grē-,swu̇d\ *n* : a low stiff shrub (*Sarcobatus vermiculatus*) of the goosefoot family common in alkaline soils in the western U.S.; *also* : any of various related or similar shrubs

greas·i·ly \'grē-sə-lē, -zə-\ *adv* : in a greasy manner

greas·i·ness \-sē-nəs, -zē-\ *n* : the quality or state of being greasy

greasy \'grē-sē, -zē\ *adj* **1 a** : smeared or soiled with grease **b** : oily in appearance, texture, or manner **c** : SLIPPERY **2** : containing an unusual amount of grease

1**great** \'grāt, *South also* 'gre(ə)t\ *adj* [ME *grete*, fr. OE *grēat*; akin to OHG *grōz* large] **1 a** : large in size : BIG **b** : of a kind characterized by relative largeness — used in plant and animal names **c** : ELABORATE, AMPLE ⟨~ detail⟩ **2 a** : large in number : NUMEROUS ⟨~ multitudes⟩ **b** : PREDOMINANT ⟨the ~ majority⟩ **3** : remarkable in magnitude, degree, or effectiveness ⟨~ bloodshed⟩ **4** : full of emotion ⟨~ with anger⟩ **5 a** : EMINENT, DISTINGUISHED **b** : ARISTOCRATIC, GRAND ⟨~ ladies⟩ **6** : long continued ⟨~ while⟩ **7** : MAIN, PRINCIPAL **8** : more remote in a family relationship by a single generation than a specified relative ⟨*great*-grandfather⟩

ə abut; ᵊ kitten; ər further; a back; ā bake; ä cot, cart; au̇ out; ch chin; e less; ē easy; g gift; i trip; ī life
j joke; ŋ sing; ō flow; ȯ flaw; ȯi coin; th thin; th this; ü loot; u̇ foot; y yet; yü few; yu̇ furious; zh vision

9 **:** markedly superior in character or quality; *esp* **:** NOBLE ⟨∼ of soul⟩ **10 a :** remarkably skilled ⟨∼ at tennis⟩ **b :** enthusiastic about ⟨∼ on science fiction⟩ **11** — used as a generalized term of approval ⟨had a ∼ time⟩ ⟨it was just ∼⟩ **syn** see LARGE — **great** *adv* — **great·ly** *adv* — **great·ness** *n*

2**great** *n* **:** one that is great

great ape *n* **:** any of the recent anthropoid apes

great–aunt *n* **:** GRANDAUNT

Great Bear *n* **:** the constellation Ursa Major

great circle *n* **:** a circle formed on the surface of a sphere by the intersection of a plane that passes through the center of the sphere; *specif* **:** such a circle on the surface of the earth an arc of which constitutes the shortest distance between any two terrestrial points

great·coat \ˈgrāt-ˌkōt\ *n* **:** a heavy overcoat

Great Dane *n* **:** any of a breed of tall massive powerful smooth-coated dogs

great divide *n* [the *Great Divide*, No. American watershed] **1 :** a watershed between major drainage systems **2 :** a significant point of division; *esp* **:** DEATH ⟨he crossed the *great divide* bravely⟩

great·en \ˈgrāt-ᵊn\ *vb* **great·en·ing** \ˈgrāt-niŋ, -ᵊn-iŋ\ *vt* **:** to make greater ∼ *vi* **:** to become greater

great·heart·ed \ˈgrāt-ˈhärt-əd\ *adj* **1 :** COURAGEOUS **2 :** MAGNANIMOUS — **great·heart·ed·ly** *adv* — **great·heart·ed·ness** *n*

great–nephew *n* **:** GRANDNEPHEW

great–niece *n* **:** GRANDNIECE

great power *n* **:** one of the nations that figure most decisively in international affairs

Great Pyr·e·nees \-ˈpir-ə-ˌnēz\ *n* **:** any of a breed of large heavy-coated white dogs that resemble the Newfoundland

Great Russian *n* **:** a member of the Russian-speaking people of the central and northeastern U.S.S.R.

great seal *n* **:** a large seal that constitutes an emblem of sovereignty and is used esp. for the authentication of important documents

great soil group *n* **:** a group of soils that is characterized by common characteristics usu. developed under the influence of environmental factors (as vegetation and climate) active over a considerable geographic range and that comprises one or more families of soil

great–uncle *n* **:** GRANDUNCLE

great year *n* **:** the period of about 25,800 years of one complete cycle of precession of the equinoxes

greave \ˈgrēv\ *n* [ME *greve*, fr. MF] **:** armor for the leg below the knee — usu. used in pl.

grebe \ˈgrēb\ *n* [F *grèbe*] **:** any of a family (Colymbidae) of swimming and diving birds closely related to the loons but having lobate toes — compare DABCHICK

Gre·cian \ˈgrē-shən\ *adj* [L *Graecia* Greece] **:** GREEK — **Grecian** *n* — **gre·cian·ize** \-shə-ˌnīz\ *vt, often cap*

Gre·cism \ˈgrē-ˌsiz-əm\ *n* **1 :** a Greek idiom **2 :** a quality or style imitative of Greek art or culture

gre·cize \-ˌsīz\ *vt, often cap* **:** to make Greek or Hellenistic in character

Greco- *or* **Graeco-** *comb form* [L *Graeco-*, fr. *Graecus*] **1 :** Greece **:** Greeks ⟨*Grecophile*⟩ ⟨*Grecomania*⟩ **2 :** Greek and ⟨*Graeco-Roman*⟩

1**gree** \ˈgrē\ *n* [ME, fr. MF *gré* step, degree, fr. L *gradus* — more at GRADE] *Scot* **:** MASTERY, SUPERIORITY

2**gree** *vb* [ME *greem*, short for *agreen*] *dial* **:** AGREE

greed \ˈgrēd\ *n* [back-formation fr. *greedy*] **:** inordinate or reprehensible acquisitiveness **:** AVARICE

greed·i·ly \ˈgrēd-ᵊl-ē\ *adv* **:** in a greedy manner

greed·i·ness \ˈgrēd-ē-nəs\ *n* **:** the quality or state of being greedy

greedy \ˈgrēd-ē\ *adj* [ME *gredy*, fr. OE *grǣdig*; akin to OHG *grātag* greedy] **1 :** having a strong desire for food or drink **2 :** marked by greed **3 :** EAGER, KEEN **syn** see COVETOUS

1**Greek** \ˈgrēk\ *n* [ME *Greke*, fr. OE *Grēca*, fr. L *Graecus*, fr. Gk *Graikos*] **1 a :** a native or inhabitant of ancient or modern Greece **b :** a person of Greek descent **2 a :** the language used by the Greeks from prehistoric times to the present constituting a branch of Indo-European **b :** ancient Greek as used from the time of the earliest records to the end of the 2d century A.D. **c** *not cap* [trans. of L *Graecum* (in the medieval phrase *Graecum est; non potest legi* It is Greek; it cannot be read)] **:** something unintelligible

2**Greek** *adj* **1 :** of, relating to, or characteristic of Greece, the Greeks, or Greek ⟨∼ architecture⟩ **2 a :** Eastern Orthodox **b :** of or relating to an Eastern church using the Byzantine rite in Greek **c :** of or relating to the established Orthodox church of Greece

Greek Catholic *n* **1 :** a member of an Eastern church **2 :** a member of an Eastern rite of the Roman Catholic Church

Greek cross *n* — see CROSS illustration

Greek fire *n* **:** an incendiary composition used in warfare by the Byzantine Greeks and said to have burst into flame on wetting

Greek Orthodox *adj* **:** Eastern Orthodox; *specif* **:** GREEK 2c

1**green** \ˈgrēn\ *adj* [ME *grene*, fr. OE *grēne*; akin to OE *grōwan* to grow] **1 :** of the color green **2 a :** covered by green growth or foliage **b :** pleasantly alluring **c** *of a season* **:** TEMPERATE **d :** consisting of green plants or green vegetables **3 :** YOUTHFUL, VIGOROUS **4 :** not ripened or matured **:** IMMATURE ⟨∼ apples⟩ ⟨tender ∼ grasses⟩ **5 :** FRESH, NEW **6 :** marked by a sickly appearance ⟨∼ with envy⟩ **7 a :** not fully processed or treated: as (1) **:** not aged ⟨∼ liquor⟩ (2) **:** not dressed or tanned ⟨∼ hides⟩ (3) **:** freshly sawed **:** UNSEASONED **b :** not in condition for a particular use **c** (1) *of a female fish* **:** not ready to spawn (2) **:** not quite ready to shed ⟨∼ crab⟩ **8 a :** lacking training, knowledge, or experience **b :** GULLIBLE, NAIVE **c :** not fully qualified for or experienced in a particular function ⟨∼ horse⟩ **syn** see RUDE — **green·ly** *adv*

2**green** *vi* **:** to become green

3**green** *n* **1 :** a color whose hue is somewhat less yellow than that of growing fresh grass or of the emerald or is that of the part of the spectrum lying between blue and yellow **2 :** something of a green color **3 :** green vegetation: as **a** *pl* **:** leafy parts of plants for use as decoration **b** *pl* (1) **:** leafy herbs (as spinach, dandelions, Swiss chard) that are boiled or steamed as a vegetable **:** POTHERB (2) **:** GREEN VEGETABLE **4 :** a grassy plain or plot; *specif* **:** PUTTING GREEN — **greeny** \ˈgrē-nē\ *adj*

green alga *n* **:** an alga in which the chlorophyll is not masked by other pigments; *specif* **:** such an alga of a division (Chlorophyta)

green·back \ˈgrēn-ˌbak\ *n* **:** a legal-tender note issued by the U.S. government

green·back·er \-ər\ *n* **1** *cap* **:** a member of a post-Civil War American political party opposing reduction in the amount of paper money in circulation **2 :** one who advocates a paper currency backed only by the U.S. government — **green·back·ism** \-ˌiz-əm\ *n*

green bean *n* **:** a kidney bean with the pods green when suitably matured for use as snap beans

green·belt \ˈgrēn-ˌbelt\ *n* **:** a belt of parkways or farmlands that encircles a community and is designed to prevent undesirable encroachments

green·bri·er \-ˌbrī(-ə)r\ *n* **:** any of a genus (*Smilax*) of plants of the lily family; *esp* **:** a prickly vine (*S. rotundifolia*) of the eastern U.S. with umbels of small greenish flowers

green·bug \-ˌbəg\ *n* **:** a green aphid (*Toxoptera graminum*) very destructive to small grains

green corn *n* **:** the young tender ears of Indian corn suitable for cooking

green dragon *n* **1 :** a European arum (*Dracunculus vulgaris*) resembling the cuckoopint **2 :** an American arum (*Arisaema dracontium*) with digitate leaves, slender greenish yellow spathe, and elongated spadix

green·ery \ˈgrēn-(ə-)rē\ *n* **1 :** green foliage or plants **2 :** GREEN 3a

green–eyed \ˈgrē-ˈnīd\ *adj* **:** JEALOUS

green·finch \ˈgrēn-ˌfinch\ *n* **:** a very common European finch (*Chloris chloris*) having olive-green and yellow plumage

green·fly \-ˌflī\ *n, Brit* **:** APHID

green·gage \-ˌgāj\ *n* [*green* + Sir William *Gage* †1820 E botanist] **:** any of several rather small rounded greenish or greenish yellow cultivated plums

green·gro·cer \ˈgrēn-ˌgrō-sər\ *n, chiefly Brit* **:** a retailer of fresh vegetables and fruit — **green·gro·cery** \-ˌgrōs-(ə-)rē\ *n*

green·heart \-ˌhärt\ *n* **:** any of several tropical American trees furnishing somewhat greenish usu. hard wood; *also* **:** the wood of a greenheart

green·horn \-ˌhȯ(ə)rn\ *n* [obs. *greenhorn* (animal with young horns)] **:** an inexperienced or unsophisticated person

green·house \-ˌhau̇s\ *n* **1 :** a glassed enclosure used for the cultivation or protection of tender plants **2 :** a clear plastic shell covering a section of an airplane

green·ing \ˈgrē-niŋ\ *n* **:** any of several green-skinned apples

green·ish \ˈgrē-nish\ *adj* **:** somewhat green — **green·ish·ness** *n*

green·let \ˈgrēn-lət\ *n* **:** VIREO

green light *n* [fr. the green traffic light which signals permission to proceed] **:** authority or permission to undertake a project

green·ling \ˈgrēn-liŋ\ *n* **1 a :** any of several food fishes (family Hexagrammidae) of the rocky coasts of the northern Pacific; *esp* **:** a common food and sport fish (*Hexagrammos decagrammus*) **b :** LINGCOD **2 :** POLLACK

green manure *n* **:** an herbaceous crop (as clover) plowed under while green to enrich the soil

green mold *n* **:** a green or green-spored mold (as of the genera *Penicillium* or *Aspergillus*)

Green Mountain boy *n* [*Green Mountain Boys*, Vermont militia during the American Revolution, fr. the *Green Mountains*, Vt.] **:** a male native or resident of Vermont — used as a nickname

green·ness \ˈgrēn-nəs\ *n* **:** the quality or state of being green

gree·nock·ite \ˈgrē-nə-ˌkīt\ *n* [Charles M. Cathcart, Lord *Greenock* †1859 E soldier] **:** a mineral CdS consisting of native cadmium sulfide occurring in yellow translucent hexagonal crystals or as an earthy incrustation

green onion *n* **:** a young onion pulled before the bulb has enlarged and used esp. in salads

green·room \ˈgrēn-ˌrüm, -ˌru̇m\ *n* **:** a room in a theater or concert hall where actors or musicians relax before, between, or after appearances

green·sand \ˈgrēn-ˌsand\ *n* **:** a sedimentary deposit that consists largely of dark greenish grains of glauconite often mingled with clay or sand

green·shank \-ˌshaŋk\ *n* **:** an Old World sandpiper (*Tringa nebularia*) related to the yellowlegs of America

green·sick \-ˌsik\ *adj* [back-formation fr. *greensickness* (chlorosis)] **:** affected with chlorosis — **green·sick·ness** *n*

green snake *n* **:** either of two bright green harmless largely insectivorous No. American colubrid snakes (*Liopeltis vernalis* and *Ophiodrys aestivus*)

green soap *n* **:** a soft soap made from vegetable oils and used esp. in skin diseases

green·stone \ˈgrēn-ˌstōn\ *n* **1 :** any of numerous usu. altered dark green compact rocks (as diorite) **2 :** NEPHRITE

green·sward \-ˌswȯ(ə)rd\ *n* **:** turf green with growing grass

green thumb *n* **:** an unusual ability to make plants grow — **green–thumbed** \ˈgrēn-ˈthəmd\ *adj*

green turtle *n* **:** a large sea turtle (*Chelonia mydas*) with a smooth greenish or olive-colored shell, highly nutritious eggs, and flesh used for food

green vegetable *n* **:** a vegetable whose foliage or foliage-bearing stalks are the chief edible part

Green·wich time \ˈgrin-ij-, ˈgren-, -ich-\ *n* [*Greenwich*, England] **:** the mean solar time of the meridian of Greenwich used as the prime basis of standard time throughout the world

green·wood \ˈgrēn-ˌwu̇d\ *n* **:** a forest green with foliage

1**greet** \ˈgrēt\ *vt* [ME *greten*, fr. OE *grētan*; akin to OE *grǣtan*] **1 :** to address with expressions of kind wishes **:** HAIL **2 :** to meet or react to in a specified manner ⟨the candidate was ∼*ed* with catcalls⟩ **3 :** to be perceived by ⟨a sight ∼*ed* her eyes⟩ — **greet·er** *n*

2**greet** *vi* **grat** \ˈgrat\ **grut·ten** \ˈgrət-ᵊn\ [ME *greten*, fr. OE *grǣtan*; akin to ON *grāta* to weep] *Scot* **:** WEEP, LAMENT

greet·ing *n* **1 :** a salutation at meeting **2 :** a compliment from one absent

greg·a·rine \ˈgreg-ə-ˌrīn\ *n* [deriv. of L *gregarius*] **:** any of a large order (Gregarinida) of parasitic vermiform sporozoan protozoans that usu. occur in insects and other invertebrates — **gregarine** *or* **greg·a·rin·i·an** \ˌgreg-ə-ˈrin-ē-ən\ *adj*

gre·gar·i·ous \gri-ˈgar-ē-əs, -ˈger-\ *adj* [L *gregarius* of a flock or herd, fr. *greg-*, *grex* flock, herd; akin to Gk *ageirein* to collect, *agora* assembly] **1 :** tending to associate with others of one's kind **:** SOCIAL **2 a** *of a plant* **:** growing in a cluster or a colony **b :** living in contiguous nests but not forming a true colony — used esp. of wasps and bees — **gre·gar·i·ous·ly** *adv* — **gre·gar·i·ous·ness** *n*

[1]**Gre·go·ri·an** \gri-'gōr-ē-ən, -'gȯr-\ *adj* **:** of or relating to Pope Gregory XIII or the Gregorian calendar
[2]**Gregorian** *adj* **1 :** of or relating to Pope Gregory I **2 :** of, relating to, or having the characteristics of Gregorian chant
[3]**Gregorian** *adj* [St. *Gregory* the Illuminator †332] **:** of or relating to the Armenian national church
Gregorian calendar *n* **:** a calendar in general use introduced by Pope Gregory XIII in 1582 to correct an error in the Julian calendar with the date Oct. 5 called Oct. 15, adopted in Great Britain and the American colonies in 1752, and marked by the restriction of centesimal years as leap years to those divisible by 400 — see CALENDAR table
Gregorian chant *n* **:** a monodic and rhythmically free liturgical chant of the Roman Catholic Church
grei·sen \'grīz-ᵊn\ *n* [G] **:** a crystalline rock consisting of quartz and mica that is common in Cornwall and Saxony
grem·lin \'grem-lən\ *n* [perh. modif. of IrGael *gruaimīn* ill-humored little fellow] **:** a small gnome held to be responsible for malfunction of equipment esp. in an airplane
gre·nade \grə-'nād\ *n* [MF, pomegranate, fr. LL *granata*, fr. L, fem. of *granatus* seedy, fr. *granum* grain — more at CORN] **1 :** a missile consisting of a container fitted with priming and bursting charges and filled with a destructive agent **2 :** a glass bottle or globe that contains volatile chemicals and can be burst by throwing (as for extinguishing a fire)
gren·a·dier \,gren-ə-'di(ə)r\ *n* **1 :** a member of a European regiment formerly armed with grenades **2 :** any of various deep-sea fishes (family Macruridae) that are related to the cods and have an elongate tapering body and compressed pointed tail
gren·a·dine \,gren-ə-'dēn, 'gren-ə-,\ *n* [F, fr. *grenade*] **1 :** a plain or figured open-weave fabric of various fibers **2 :** a syrup flavored with pomegranates and used in mixed drinks
Gresh·am's law \,gresh-əmz-\ *n* [Sir Thomas *Gresham* †1579 E financier] **:** an observation in economics: when two coins are equal in debt-paying value but unequal in intrinsic value, the one having the lesser intrinsic value tends to remain in circulation and the other to be hoarded or exported as bullion
gres·so·ri·al \gre-'sōr-ē-əl, -'sȯr-\ *adj* [L *gressus*, pp. of *gradi* to step] **:** adapted for walking ⟨~ feet of some birds⟩
Gret·na Green \,gret-nə-'grēn\ *n* [*Gretna Green*, Scotland] **:** a place where many eloping couples are married
grew *past of* GROW
grew·some *var of* GRUESOME
grey *var of* GRAY
grey friar *n, often cap G&F* **:** a Franciscan friar
grey·hound \'grā-,haund\ *n* [ME *grehound*, fr. OE *grīghund*, fr. *grīg-* (akin to ON *grey* bitch) + *hund* hound] **:** a tall slender graceful smooth-coated dog of a breed characterized by swiftness and keen sight and used for coursing game and racing; *also* **:** any of several related dogs
grey·lag \-,lag\ *n* **:** the common gray wild goose (*Anser anser* syn. *A. cinereus*) of Europe
grib·ble \'grib-əl\ *n* [prob. dim. of [2]*grub*] **:** a small marine isopod crustacean (*Limnoria lignorum* or *L. terebrans*) that destroys submerged timber
grid \'grid\ *n* [back-formation fr. *gridiron*] **1 :** GRATING **2 a** (1) **:** a perforated or ridged metal plate used as a conductor in a storage battery (2) **:** an electrode consisting of a mesh or a spiral of fine wire in an electron tube **b :** a network of uniformly spaced horizontal and perpendicular lines for locating points by means of coordinates **c :** GRIDIRON 2
grid·dle \'grid-ᵊl\ *n* [ME *gredil* gridiron, fr. ONF, fr. L *craticulum*, dim. of *cratis* wickerwork — more at HURDLE] **:** a flat surface or pan on which food is cooked by dry heat
griddle cake *n* **:** a flat cake made of thin batter and cooked on both sides on a griddle
grid·iron \'grid-,ī(-ə)rn\ *n* [ME *gredire*] **1 :** a grated metal frame for broiling food **2 :** something consisting of or covered with a network; *esp* **:** a football field
grief \'grēf\ *n* [ME *gref*, fr. OF, heavy, grave, fr. (assumed) VL *grevis*, alter. of L *gravis*] **1** *obs* **:** GRIEVANCE 3 **2 a :** emotional suffering caused by or as if by bereavement **b :** a cause of such suffering **3 a :** MISHAP, MISADVENTURE **b :** an unfortunate outcome **:** DISASTER **syn** see SORROW
griev·ance \'grē-vən(t)s\ *n* **1** *obs* **:** SUFFERING, DISTRESS **2 :** a cause of distress felt to afford reason for complaint or resistance (as an unsatisfactory working condition) **3 :** the formal expression of a grievance **:** COMPLAINT **syn** see INJUSTICE
griev·ant \-vənt\ *n* **:** one who submits a grievance for arbitration
grieve \'grēv\ *vb* [ME *greven*, fr. OF *grever*, fr. L *gravare* to burden, fr. *gravis* heavy, grave; akin to Goth *kaurjos*, pl., heavy, Gk *barys*, Skt *guru*] *vt* **:** to cause to suffer **:** DISTRESS **~** *vi* **:** to feel grief **:** SORROW — **griev·er** *n*
griev·ous \'grē-vəs\ *adj* **1 :** OPPRESSIVE, ONEROUS **2 :** causing or characterized by esp. severe pain, suffering, or sorrow **3 :** SERIOUS, GRAVE ⟨~ fault⟩ — **griev·ous·ly** *adv* — **griev·ous·ness** *n*
grif·fin *or* **grif·fon** \'grif-ən\ *n* [ME *griffon*, fr. MF *grifon*, fr. *grif*, fr. L *gryphus*, fr. Gk *gryp-*, *gryps*, fr. *grypos* curved; akin to OE *cradol* cradle] **:** a fabulous animal typically half eagle and half lion
grif·fon \'grif-ən\ *n* [F, lit., griffin] **1 :** any of a breed of small short-faced compact dogs of Belgian origin **2 :** any of a breed of medium-sized long-headed sporting dogs with downy undercoat and harsh wiry outer coat
grift \'grift\ *vt* [*grift*, n., perh. alter. of *graft*] *slang* **:** to obtain (money) by swindling or cheating — **grift** *n* — **grift·er** *n*
grig \'grig\ *n* [ME *grege*] **:** a gay lively person
gri·gri *var of* GRIS-GRIS
[1]**grill** \'gril\ *vt* **1 :** to broil on a grill **2 a :** to torment as if by broiling **b :** to question intensely **syn** see AFFLICT — **grill·er** *n*
[2]**grill** *n* [F *gril*, fr. L *craticulum* — more at GRIDDLE] **1 :** a cooking utensil of parallel bars on which food is exposed to heat **2 :** food that is broiled usu. on a grill **3 :** a restaurant featuring broiled foods
gril·lage \'gril-ij, gril-'äzh\ *n* **:** a framework of timbers for support in marshy or treacherous soil
grille *or* **grill** \'gril\ *n* [F *grille*, alter. of OF *greille*, fr. L *craticula*, dim. of *cratis* wickerwork — more at HURDLE] **1 :** a grating forming a barrier or screen **2 :** an opening covered with a grille **3 :** a square opening in the corner at the farther end of a court-tennis court on the hazard side
grill·work \'gril-,wərk\ *n* **:** work constituting or resembling a grille
grilse \'grils\ *n, pl* **grilse** [ME *grills*] **:** a young mature Atlantic salmon returning from the sea to spawn for the first time; *broadly* **:** any of various salmon at such a stage of development
grim \'grim\ *adj* **grim·mer; grim·mest** [ME, fr. OE *grimm*; akin to OHG *grimm* fierce, Gk *chromados* action of gnashing] **1 :** SAVAGE, FIERCE **2 a :** of harsh and forbidding aspect **b :** ghastly, repellent, or sinister in character — **grim·ly** *adv* — **grim·ness** *n*
gri·mace \'grim-əs, grim-'ās\ *n* [F, fr. MF, alter. of *grimache*, of Gmc origin; akin to OE *grīma*] **:** a facial expression usu. of disgust or disapproval — **grimace** *vi* — **gri·mac·er** *n*
gri·mal·kin \grim-'al-kən, -'ȯ(l)-\ *n* [*gray* + *malkin*] **:** CAT 1a; *esp* **:** an old female cat
grime \'grīm\ *n* [Flem *grijm*, fr. MD *grime* soot, mask; akin to OE *grīma* mask, Gk *chriein* to anoint — more at CHRISM] **:** soot, smut, or dirt adhering to or embedded in a surface; *broadly* **:** accumulated dirtiness and disorder — **grime** *vt*
grim·i·ness \'grī-mē-nəs\ *n* **:** the quality or state of being grimy
Grimm's law \'grimz-\ *n* [Jacob *Grimm* †1863 G philologist] **:** a statement in historical linguistics: Proto-Indo-European voiceless stops became Proto-Germanic voiceless fricatives (as in Greek *pyr*, *treis*, *kardia* compared with English *fire*, *three*, *heart*), Proto-Indo-European voiced stops became Proto-Germanic voiceless stops (as in Old Slavic *jablŭko*, Greek *dyo*, *genos* compared with English *apple*, *two*, *kin*), and Proto-Indo-European voiced aspirated stops became Proto-Germanic voiced fricatives (as in Sanskrit *nābhi*, *madhya* "mid", Latin *helvus* compared with English *navel*, Old Norse *mithr* "mid", English *yellow*)
grimy \'grī-mē\ *adj* **:** full of or covered with grime **:** DIRTY
grin \'grin\ *vi* **grinned; grin·ning** [ME *grennen*, fr. OE *grennian;* akin to OHG *grennen* to snarl] **:** to draw back the lips so as to show the teeth esp. in amusement or laughter — **grin** *n* — **grin·ner** *n*
[1]**grind** \'grīnd\ *vb* **ground** \'graund\ **grind·ing** [ME *grinden*, fr. OE *grindan;* akin to L *frendere* to crush, grind, Gk *chondros* grain, OE *grēot* grit] *vt* **1 :** to reduce to powder by friction (as in a mill or with the teeth) **2 :** to wear down, polish, or sharpen by friction **:** WHET **3 :** to press with a grating noise **:** GRIT ⟨~ the teeth⟩ **4 :** OPPRESS, HARASS **5 :** to operate or produce by turning a crank **~** *vi* **1 :** to perform the operation of grinding **2 :** to become pulverized, polished, or sharpened by friction **3 :** to move with difficulty or friction **4 :** DRUDGE; *esp* **:** to study hard **5 :** to rotate the hips suggestively — **grind·ing·ly** \'grīn-diŋ-lē\ *adv*
[2]**grind** *n* **1 :** an act of grinding **2 a :** monotonous labor or routine; *esp* **:** intensive study **b :** a student who studies excessively **3 :** the result of grinding; *esp* **:** the size of particle obtained by grinding **syn** see WORK
grind·er \'grīn-dər\ *n* **1 a :** MOLAR **b** *pl* **:** TEETH **2 :** one that grinds **3 :** a machine or device for grinding **4** *chiefly NewEng* **:** two slabs of bread cut lengthwise and filled usu. with meat, cheese, tomato, and lettuce
grind·stone \'grīn-,stōn\ *n* **1 :** MILLSTONE 1 **2 :** a flat circular stone of natural sandstone that revolves on an axle and is used for grinding, shaping, or smoothing

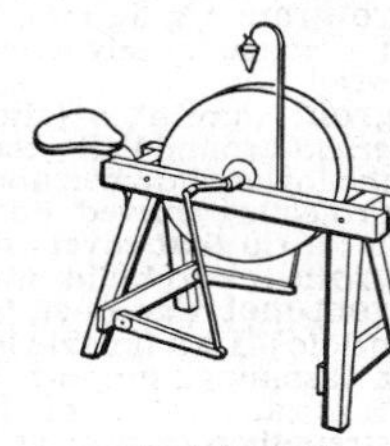
grindstone 2

grin·go \'griŋ-(,)gō\ *n* [Sp, alter. of *griego* Greek, stranger, fr. L *Graecus* Greek] **:** a foreigner in Spain or Latin America esp. when of English or American origin — often used disparagingly
[1]**grip** \'grip\ *vt* **gripped; grip·ping** [ME *grippen*, fr. OE *grippan;* akin to OE *grīpan*] **:** to seize firmly — **grip·per** *n*
[2]**grip** *n* **1 a :** a strong or tenacious grasp **b :** strength in gripping **c** (1) **:** a mode of clasping the hand by which members of a secret order recognize or greet one another (2) **:** arrangement of the hands in grasping **2 a :** CONTROL, MASTERY, UNDERSTANDING **b :** APPREHENSION **3 :** a part or device for gripping **4 :** a part by which something is grasped; *esp* **:** HANDLE **5 :** SUITCASE
[1]**gripe** \'grīp\ *vb* [ME *gripen*, fr. OE *grīpan;* akin to OHG *grīfan* to grasp, Lith *griebti*] *vt* **1 :** SEIZE, GRIP **2 a :** AFFLICT, DISTRESS **b :** IRRITATE, VEX **3 :** to cause pinching and spasmodic pain in the bowels of **~** *vi* **1 :** to experience griping pains **2 :** to complain with sustained grumbling — **grip·er** *n*
[2]**gripe** *n* **1 :** CLUTCH, GRASP; *broadly* **:** CONTROL, MASTERY **2 :** GRIEVANCE, COMPLAINT **3 :** a pinching spasmodic intestinal pain — usu. used in pl. **4 :** HANDLE, GRIP **5 :** a device (as a brake) for grasping or holding
grippe \'grip\ *n* [F, lit., seizure] **:** an acute febrile contagious virus disease identical with or resembling influenza — **grippy** \'grip-ē\ *adj*
grip·sack \'grip-,sak\ *n* **:** TRAVELING BAG
gri·saille \gri-'zī\ *n* [F] **:** decorative painting in gray monochrome esp. on glass
Gri·sel·da \griz-'el-də\ *n* [It] **:** a woman noted in medieval literature for her meekness and patience
gris·eous \'griz-ē-əs\ *adj* [ML *griseus*, of Gmc origin; akin to OHG *grīs* gray] **:** of a light color or white mottled with black or brown **:** GRIZZLED
gri·sette \gri-'zet\ *n* [F] **:** a young French working-class woman
gris-gris \'grē-(,)grē\ *n, pl* **gris-gris** \-(,)grēz\ [of African origin; akin to Bulanda *grigri* amulet] **:** an amulet or incantation used chiefly by people of African Negro ancestry
gris·li·ness \'griz-lē-nəs\ *n* **:** the quality or state of being grisly
gris·ly \'griz-lē\ *adj* [ME, fr. OE *grislic*, fr. *gris-* (akin to OE *āgrīsan* to fear); akin to OHG *grīsenlīh* terrible] **:** HORRIBLE, GRUESOME **syn** see GHASTLY
grist \'grist\ *n* [ME, fr. OE *grīst;* akin to OE *grindan* to grind] **1 a :** grain or a batch of grain for grinding **b :** the product obtained from a grist of grain including the flour or meal and the grain offals **2 :** something turned to advantage
gris·tle \'gris-əl\ *n* [ME *gristil*, fr. OE *gristle;* akin to MLG *gristel* gristle] **:** CARTILAGE — **gris·tly** \'gris-(ə-)lē\ *adj*

gris·tli·ness \-(ə)-lē-nəs\ *n* **:** the quality or state of being gristly
grist·mill \'grist-,mil\ *n* **:** a mill for grinding grain
¹**grit** \'grit\ *n* [ME *gryt*, fr. OE *grytt;* akin to OE *grēot*] **1** *obs* **:** CHAFF **2** *pl but sing or pl in constr* **:** coarsely ground hulled grain — compare HOMINY
²**grit** *n* [ME *grete*, fr. OE *grēot;* akin to OHG *grioz* sand, L *furfur* bran, Gk *chrōs* skin] **1 a** *obs* **:** SAND, GRAVEL **b :** a hard sharp granule (as of sand); *also* **:** material (as many abrasives) composed of such granules **2 :** any of several sandstones **3 :** the structure of a stone that adapts it to grinding **4 :** firmness of mind or spirit **:** unyielding courage **syn** see FORTITUDE
³**grit** *vb* **grit·ted; grit·ting** *vi* **:** to give forth a grating sound ~ *vt* **1 :** to cover or spread with grit; *esp* **:** to smooth (as marble) by means of a coarse abrasive **2 :** to cause (as one's teeth) to grind or grate
grith \'grith\ *n* [ME, fr. OE, fr. ON, security] **:** peace, security, or sanctuary imposed or guaranteed in early England under various special conditions
grit·ti·ness \'grit-ē-nəs\ *n* **:** the quality or state of being gritty
grit·ty \'grit-ē\ *adj* **1 :** containing or resembling grit **2 :** courageously persistent **:** PLUCKY
gri·vet \'griv-ət, gri-'vā\ *n* [F] **:** a white and olive green monkey (*Cercopithecus aethiops*) of the upper Nile and Abyssinia
¹**griz·zle** \'griz-əl\ *n* [ME *grisel*, adj., gray, fr. MF, fr. *gris*, of Gmc origin; akin to OHG *grīs* gray] **1** *archaic* **:** gray hair **2 a :** a roan coat pattern or color **b :** a gray or roan animal
²**grizzle** *vb* **griz·zling** \-(ə-)liŋ\ *vt* **:** to make grayish ~ *vi* **:** to become grayish
griz·zled \'griz-əld\ *adj* **:** sprinkled, streaked, or mixed with gray
griz·zly \'griz-lē\ *adj* **:** GRIZZLED
grizzly bear *n* **:** a very large powerful typically brownish yellow bear (*Ursus horribilis*) of the uplands of western No. America
groan \'grōn\ *vb* [ME *gronen*, fr. OE *grānian;* akin to OHG *grīnan* to growl] *vi* **1 :** to utter a deep moan indicative of pain, grief, or annoyance **2 :** to make a harsh sound under sudden or prolonged strain ~ *vt* **:** to utter or express with groaning — **groan** *n* — **groan·er** *n*
¹**groat** \'grōt\ *n* [ME *grotes*, pl., fr. OE *grotan;* akin to OE *grēot*] **1** *usu pl but sing or pl in constr* **:** hulled grain broken into fragments larger than grits **2 :** a grain (as of oats) exclusive of the hull
²**groat** *n* [ME *groot*, fr. MD] **:** a former British coin worth fourpence
gro·cer \'grō-sər\ *n* [ME, fr. MF *grossier* wholesaler, fr. *gros* coarse, wholesale — more at GROSS] **:** a dealer in staple foodstuffs and other commodities
gro·cery \'grōs-(ə-)rē\ *n* **1** *pl* **:** commodities sold by a grocer — usu. sing. in Brit. usage **2 :** a grocer's store
grog \'gräg\ *n* [Old *Grog*, nickname of Edward Vernon †1757 E admiral responsible for diluting the sailors' rum] **:** spirituous liquor; *specif* **:** liquor (as rum) cut with water — **grog·gery** \-(ə-)rē\ *n* — **grog·shop** \'gräg-,shäp\ *n*
grog·gi·ly \'gräg-ə-lē\ *adv* **:** in a groggy manner
grog·gi·ness \-ē-nəs\ *n* **:** the quality or state of being groggy
grog·gy \'gräg-ē\ *adj* [*grog*] **:** weak and unsteady in action
gro·gram \'gräg-rəm, 'grō-grəm\ *n* [MF *gros grain* coarse texture] **:** a coarse loosely woven fabric of silk, silk and mohair, or silk and wool
¹**groin** \'grȯin\ *n* [alter. of ME *grynde*, fr. OE, abyss; akin to OE *grund* ground] **1 :** the fold or depression marking the juncture of the lower abdomen and thigh; *also* **:** the region of this line **2 a :** the projecting curved line along which two intersecting vaults meet **b :** a rib that covers this edge
²**groin** *vt* **:** to build or equip with groins
grom·met \'gräm-ət, 'grəm-\ *n* [perh. fr. obs. F *gormette* curb of a bridle] **1 :** a flexible loop that serves as a fastening, support, or reinforcement **2 :** an eyelet of firm material to strengthen or protect an opening or to insulate or protect something passed through it

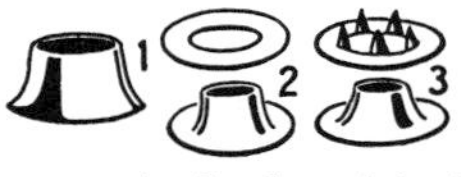
grommets 2: *1* eyelet, *2* with washer, *3* with teeth

grom·well \'gräm-,wel, -wəl\ *n* [ME *gromil*, fr. MF] **:** any of a genus (*Lithospermum*) of plants of the borage family having polished white stony nutlets
¹**groom** \'grüm, 'grům\ *n* [ME *grom*] **1** *archaic* **:** MAN, FELLOW **2 a** (1) *archaic* **:** MANSERVANT (2) **:** one of several officers of the English royal household **b :** a man or boy in charge of horses **3 :** BRIDEGROOM
²**groom** *vt* **1 :** to clean and care for (an animal) **2 :** to make neat or attractive **:** POLISH ~ *vi* **:** to groom oneself
grooms·man \'grümz-mən, 'grůmz-\ *n* **:** a male friend who attends a bridegroom at his wedding
groove \'grüv\ *n* [ME *groof;* akin to OE *grafan* to dig — more at GRAVE] **1 :** a long narrow channel or depression **2 a :** a fixed routine **:** RUT **b :** a situation suited to one's abilities or interests **:** NICHE **3 :** top form ⟨a great talker when he is in the ~⟩ — **groove** *vt* — **groov·er** *n*
grope \'grōp\ *vb* [ME *gropen*, fr. OE *grāpian;* akin to OE *grīpan* to seize] *vi* **:** to feel about blindly or uncertainly in search ~ *vt* **:** to find (as one's way) by groping — **grope** *n* — **groper** *n*
gros·beak \'grōs-,bēk\ *n* [part trans. of F *grosbec*, fr. *gros* thick + *bec* beak] **:** any of several finches of Europe or America having large stout conical bills
gro·schen \'grō-shən, 'grȯ-\ *n, pl* **groschen** [G] — see *schilling* at MONEY table
gros·grain \'grō-,grān\ *n* [F *gros grain*] **:** a silk or rayon fabric with crosswise cotton ribs
¹**gross** \'grōs\ *adj* [ME, fr. MF *gros* thick, coarse, fr. L *grossus*] **1 a** *archaic* **:** immediately obvious **b** (1) **:** glaringly noticeable ⟨~ error⟩ (2) **:** OUT-AND-OUT, UTTER ⟨~ fool⟩ **c :** visible without the aid of a microscope **2 a :** BIG, BULKY; *esp* **:** excessively fat **b :** growing or spreading with excessive luxuriance **3 a :** of, relating to, or dealing with general aspects or broad distinctions **b :** consisting of an overall total exclusive of deductions ⟨~ earnings⟩ **4 :** EARTHY, CARNAL ⟨~*er* part of human nature⟩ **5 :** not fastidious in taste **:** UNDISCRIMINATING **6 :** lacking knowledge or culture **:** UNREFINED **7 :** OBSCENE ⟨a ~ expletive⟩ **syn** see COARSE, FLAGRANT, WHOLE — **gross·ly** *adv* — **grossness** *n*
²**gross** *n* **1 a** *obs* **:** AMOUNT **b :** an overall total exclusive of deductions **2** *archaic* **:** main body **:** MASS
³**gross** *vt* **:** to earn (an overall total) exclusive of deductions — **gross·er** *n*
⁴**gross** *n, pl* **gross** [ME *groce*, fr. MF *grosse*, fr. fem. of *gros*] **:** an aggregate of 12 dozen things ⟨~ of pencils⟩
gros·su·la·rite \'gräs(h)-ə-lə-,rīt\ *n* [G *grossularit*, fr. NL *Grossularia*, genus of shrubs] **:** a colorless or green, yellow, brown, or red garnet $Ca_3Al_2(SiO_4)_3$
grosz \'grȯsh\ *n, pl* **gro·szy** \'grȯ-shē\ [Pol] — see *zloty* at MONEY table
grot \'grät\ *n* [MF *grotte*, fr. It *grotta*] **:** GROTTO
¹**gro·tesque** \grō-'tesk\ *n* [MF & OIt; MF, fr. OIt (*pittura*) *grottesca*, lit., cave painting, fem. of *grottesco* of a cave, fr. *grotta*] **1 :** a piece of decorative art characterized by fanciful or fantastic human and animal forms often interwoven with foliage or similar figures that may distort the natural into absurdity, ugliness, or caricature **2 :** something that is grotesque
²**grotesque** *adj* **:** of, relating to, or having the characteristics of grotesque: as **a :** FANCIFUL, BIZARRE **b :** absurdly incongruous **c :** departing markedly from the natural, the expected, or the typical **syn** see FANTASTIC — **gro·tesque·ly** *adv* — **gro·tesque·ness** *n*
gro·tes·que·rie \-'tes-kə-rē\ *n* [*grotesque* + *-erie* -ery] **1 :** something that is grotesque **2 :** GROTESQUENESS
grot·to \'grät-(,)ō\ *n, pl* **grottoes** *also* **grottos** [It *grotta*, *grotto*, fr. L *crypta* cavern, crypt] **1 :** CAVE **2 :** an artificial recess or structure made to resemble a natural cave
grouch \'grau̇ch\ *n* [prob. alter. of *grutch* (grudge)] **1 a :** a fit of bad temper **b :** GRUDGE **2 :** an habitually irritable or complaining person — **grouch** *vi* — **grouch·i·ly** \'grau̇-chə-lē\ *adv* — **grouch·i·ness** \-chē-nəs\ *n* — **grouchy** \-chē\ *adj*
¹**ground** \'grau̇nd\ *n* [ME, fr. OE *grund;* akin to OHG *grunt* ground, Gk *chrainein* to touch slightly] **1 a :** the bottom of a body of water **b** *pl* (1) **:** SEDIMENT 1 (2) **:** ground coffee beans after brewing **2 a :** a basis for belief, action, or argument **b** (1) **:** a fundamental logical condition (2) **:** a basic metaphysical cause **3 a :** a surrounding area **:** BACKGROUND **b :** material that serves as a substratum **4 a :** the surface of the earth **b :** an area used for a particular purpose ⟨parade ~⟩ **c** *pl* **:** the area around and belonging to a house or other building **d :** an area to be won or defended in or as if in battle **e :** a subject of study or discourse **5 a :** SOIL, EARTH **b :** a special soil **c :** rock or formation through which mine workings are driven **6 a :** an object that makes an electrical connection with the earth **b :** a large conducting body (as the earth) used as a common return for an electric circuit and as an arbitrary zero of potential **c :** electric connection with a ground **syn** see BASE
²**ground** *vt* **1 :** to bring to or place on the ground **2 a :** to provide a reason or justification for **b :** to instruct in fundamentals **3 :** to connect electrically with a ground **4 :** to restrict to the ground ⟨~ a pilot⟩ ~ *vi* **1 :** to have a ground or basis **:** RELY **2 :** to run aground **3 :** to hit a grounder
³**ground** *past of* GRIND
ground bass *n* **:** a short bass passage continually repeated below constantly changing melody and harmony
ground–cher·ry \'grau̇n(d)-'cher-ē\ *n* **:** a plant (genus *Physalis*) of the nightshade family with pulpy fruits in papery husks; *also* **:** the fruit of such a plant
ground cover *n* **1 :** the small plants in a forest except young trees **2 a :** a planting of low plants (as ivy) that covers the ground in place of turf **b :** a plant adapted for such use
ground crew *n* **:** the mechanics and technicians who maintain and service an airplane
ground·er \'grau̇n-dər\ *n* **:** a batted ball in baseball that strikes the ground almost immediately
ground fir *n* **:** a club moss (as *Lycopodium selago* or *L. obscurum*) having a stiff erect habit
ground floor *n* **:** the floor of a house most nearly on a level with the ground — compare FIRST FLOOR
ground glass *n* **:** glass with a light-diffusing surface produced by etching or abrading
ground·hog \'grau̇nd-,hȯg, -,häg\ *n* **:** WOODCHUCK
Groundhog Day *n* [fr. the legend that the groundhog comes out and is frightened back into hibernation if he sees his shadow] **:** February 2 that traditionally indicates six more weeks of winter if sunny or an early spring if cloudy
ground itch *n* **:** an itching inflammation of the skin marking the point of entrance into the body of larval hookworms
ground ivy *n* **:** a trailing mint (*Nepeta hederacea*) with rounded leaves and blue-purple flowers
ground·less \'grau̇n-(d)ləs\ *adj* **:** having no foundation — **ground·less·ly** *adv* — **ground·less·ness** *n*
ground·ling \'grau̇n-(d)liŋ\ *n* **1 a :** a spectator in the cheaper part of a theater **b :** a person of inferior taste **2 :** one that lives or works on or near the ground
ground loop *n* **:** a sharp uncontrollable turn made by an airplane in landing, taking off, or taxiing
ground·mass \'grau̇n(d)-,mas\ *n* **:** the fine-grained base of a porphyry in which the larger distinct crystals are embedded
ground meristem *n* **:** the part of a primary apical meristem remaining after differentiation of dermatogen and procambium
ground·nut \'grau̇n(d)-,nət\ *n* **1 a :** any of several plants having edible tuberous roots; *esp* **:** a No. American leguminous vine (*Apios tuberosa*) with pinnate leaves and clusters of brownish purple fragrant flowers **b :** the root of a groundnut **2** *chiefly Brit* **:** PEANUT
ground pine *n* **1 :** a European bugle (*Ajuga chamaepitys*) with a resinous odor **2 :** any of several club mosses (esp. *Lycopodium clavatum* and *L. complanatum*) with long creeping stems and erect branches **:** GROUND FIR
ground plan *n* **1 :** a plan of a floor of a building as distinguished from an elevation **2 :** a first or basic plan
ground rent *n* **:** the rent paid by a lessee for the use of land esp. for building
ground rule *n* **:** a rule of procedure
¹**ground·sel** \'grau̇n(d)-səl\ *n* [ME *groundeswele*, fr. OE *grundeswelge*, fr. *grund* ground + *swelgan* to swallow — more at SWALLOW] **:** any of a large genus (*Senecio*) of composite plants with mostly yellow flower heads
²**groundsel** *n* [ME *ground sille*, fr. *ground* + *sille* sill] **:** a foundation timber
ground·sheet \'grau̇n(d)-,shēt\ *n* **:** a waterproof sheet placed on the ground for protection from moisture — called also *ground cloth*

ground state *n* **:** the energy level of a system of interacting elementary particles having the least energy of all its possible states — called also *ground level*
ground swell *n* **1 :** a broad deep undulation of the ocean caused by an often distant gale or seismic disturbance **2 :** a rapid spontaneous growth (as of political opinion)
ground·wa·ter \'graůn-,dwȯt-ər, -,dwät-\ *n* **:** water within the earth that supplies wells and springs
ground wave *n* **:** a radio wave that is propagated along the surface of the earth
ground·work \'graůn-,dwərk\ *n* **:** FOUNDATION, BASIS **syn** see BASE
1**group** \'grüp\ *n* [F *groupe*, fr. It *gruppo*, of Gmc origin; akin to OHG *kropf* craw — more at CROP] **1 :** two or more figures forming a complete unit in a composition **2 a :** a number of individuals assembled together or having common interests **b :** an assemblage of objects regarded as a unit **c** (1) **:** a military unit consisting of a headquarters and attached battalions (2) **:** a unit of the U.S. Air Force higher than a squadron and lower than a wing **3 a :** an assemblage of related organisms — often used to avoid taxonomic connotations when the kind or degree of relationship is not clearly defined **b** (1) **:** an assemblage of atoms forming part of a molecule ⟨a methyl ~ (CH_3)⟩ (2) **:** an assemblage of elements forming one of the vertical columns of the periodic table **c :** a stratigraphic division comprising rocks deposited during an era **4 :** a set of elements and an associative operation on pairs of elements yielding elements of the set of such nature that for any two elements there exists a third element of a kind that operation on the first and third yields the second
2**group** *vt* **1 :** to combine in a group **2 :** to assign to a group **:** CLASSIFY ~ *vi* **1 :** to form a group **2 :** to belong to a group
group dynamics *n pl but sing or pl in constr* **:** the interacting forces within a small human group; *also* **:** the sociological study of these forces
grou·per \'grü-pər\ *n, pl* **groupers** *also* **grouper** [Pg *garoupa*] **1 :** any of numerous fishes (family Serranidae and esp. genera *Epinephelus* and *Mycteroperea*) that are typically large solitary bottom fishes of warm seas **2 :** any of several rockfishes (family Scorpaenidae)
group·ing \'grü-piŋ\ *n* **1 :** the act or process of combining in groups **2 :** a set of objects combined in a group ⟨furniture ~⟩
1**grouse** \'graůs\ *n, pl* **grouse** [origin unknown] **:** any of numerous birds (family Tetraonidae) that have a plump body, strong feathered legs, and plumage less brilliant than that of pheasants usu. with reddish brown or other protective color and include many important game birds
2**grouse** *vi* [origin unknown] **:** COMPLAIN, GRUMBLE — **grous·er** *n*
grout \'graůt\ *n* [OE *grūt* coarse meal; akin to OE *grytt* grit] **1 :** LEES **2 a :** thin mortar **b :** PLASTER — **grout** *vt* — **grout·er** *n*
grove \'grōv\ *n* [ME, fr. OE *grāf*] **1 :** a small wood without underwood ⟨a picnic ~⟩ **2 :** a planting of fruit or nut trees
grov·el \'gräv-əl, 'grəv-\ *vi* **grov·eled** *or* **grov·elled; grov·el·ing** *or* **grov·el·ling** \-(ə-)liŋ\ [back-formation fr. *groveling* prone, fr. *groveling*, adv., fr. ME, fr. *gruf*, adv., on the face (fr. ON *ā grūfu*) + *-ling;* akin to OE *crēopan* to creep] **1 :** to creep with the face to the ground **:** CRAWL **2 a :** to lie or creep with the body prostrate in token of subservience or abasement **b :** to abase oneself — **grov·el·er** *or* **grov·el·ler** \-(ə-)lər\ *n*
grow \'grō\ *vb* **grew** \'grü\ **grown** \'grōn\ **grow·ing** [ME *growen*, fr. OE *grōwan;* akin to OHG *gruowan* to grow] *vi* **1 a :** to spring up and develop to maturity **b :** to be able to grow in some place or situation ⟨trees that ~ only in the tropics⟩ **c :** to assume some relation through or as if through a process of natural growth ⟨a tree with limbs *grown* together⟩ ⟨ferns *~ing* from the rocks⟩ **2 a :** to increase in size by addition of material either by assimilation into the living organism or by accretion in a natural inorganic process (as crystallization) **b :** INCREASE, EXPAND ⟨*~s* in wisdom⟩ **3 a :** RESULT, ORIGINATE **b :** to come into existence **:** ARISE **4 a :** to pass into a condition **:** BECOME ⟨*grew* pale⟩ **b :** to obtain influence ⟨habit *~s* on a man⟩ ~ *vt* **1 :** to cause to grow **:** PRODUCE ⟨~ wheat⟩ **2 :** DEVELOP 5 — **grow·er** \'grō(-ə)r\ *n*
growing pains *n pl* **1 :** pains in the legs of growing children having no demonstrable relation to growth **2 :** the stresses and strains attending a new project
growing point *n* **:** the undifferentiated end of a plant shoot from which additional shoot tissues differentiate
growl \'graů(ə)l\ *vb* [prob. imit.] *vi* **1 a :** RUMBLE **b :** to utter a deep guttural threatening sound ⟨the dog *~ed* at the stranger⟩ **2 :** to complain angrily ~ *vt* **:** to utter with a growl — **growl** *n*
growl·er *n* **1 :** one that growls **2 :** a small iceberg **3 :** an electromagnetic device with two adjustable pole pieces used for finding short-circuited coils and for magnetizing and demagnetizing
growl·ing *adj* **:** marked by a growl ⟨a low ~ voice⟩ ⟨listened to the ~ thunder⟩ — **growl·ing·ly** \'graů-liŋ-lē\ *adv*
grown \'grōn\ *adj* **1 :** fully grown **:** MATURE ⟨~ man⟩ **2 :** covered or surrounded with vegetation ⟨land well ~ with trees⟩ **3 a :** cultivated or produced in a specified way or locality — used in combination ⟨shade-*grown* tobacco⟩ **b :** overgrown with — used in combination ⟨a weed-*grown* patio⟩
1**grown-up** \'grō-,nəp\ *adj* **:** ADULT ⟨~ books⟩
2**grown-up** *n* **:** ADULT
growth \'grōth\ *n* **1 a** (1) **:** a stage in the process of growing **:** SIZE (2) **:** full growth **b :** the process of growing **c :** progressive development **:** EVOLUTION **d :** EMERGENCE **e :** INCREASE, EXPANSION **2 a :** something that grows or has grown **b :** an abnormal proliferation of tissue (as a tumor) **c :** OUTGROWTH **d :** the result of growth **:** PRODUCT **3 :** PRODUCTION, ORIGIN
growth factor *n* **:** a substance (as a vitamin) that promotes the growth of an organism
growth ring *n* **:** a layer of wood (as an annual ring) produced during a single period of growth
GR-S \,jē-,är-'es\ *n* [government *r*ubber + *s*tyrene] **:** a synthetic rubber made by copolymerizing emulsions of butadiene and styrene and used esp. in tires
1**grub** \'grəb\ *vb* **grubbed; grub·bing** [ME *grubben;* akin to OE *grafan* to dig — more at GRAVE] *vt* **1 :** to clear by digging up roots and stumps **2 :** to dig up by or as if by the roots ~ *vi* **1 a :** to dig in the ground usu. for a hidden object **b :** to search about **:** RUMMAGE **2 :** TOIL, DRUDGE — **grub·ber** *n*
2**grub** *n* [ME *grubbe*, fr. *grubben*] **1 :** a soft thick wormlike larva of an insect **2 a :** DRUDGE **b :** a slovenly person **3 :** FOOD
grub·bi·ly \'grəb-ə-lē\ *adv* **:** in a grubby manner
grub·bi·ness \'grəb-ē-nəs\ *n* **:** the quality or state of being grubby
grub·by \'grəb-ē\ *adj* **1 :** infested with fly maggots **2 :** DIRTY, SLOVENLY **3 :** BASE, CONTEMPTIBLE
grub·stake \'grəb-,stāk\ *n* **:** supplies or funds furnished a mining prospector on promise of a share in his discoveries — **grubstake** *vt* — **grub·stak·er** *n*
Grub Street \'grəb-\ *n* [*Grub Street*, London, formerly inhabited by literary hacks] **:** mediocre and disdained writers **:** literary hacks
1**grudge** \'grəj\ *vt* [ME *grucchen, grudgen* to grumble, complain, fr. OF *groucier*, of Gmc origin; akin to MHG *grogezen* to howl] **:** to be unwilling to give or admit **:** BEGRUDGE — **grudg·er** *n* — **grudg·ing·ly** \-iŋ-lē\ *adv*
2**grudge** *n* **:** a feeling of deep-seated resentment or ill will **syn** see MALICE
gru·el \'grü(-ə)l\ *n* [ME *grewel*, fr. MF *gruel*, of Gmc origin; akin to OE *grūt* grout] **1 :** a thin porridge **2** *chiefly Brit* **:** PUNISHMENT
gru·el·ing *or* **gru·el·ling** \'grü-(ə-)liŋ\ *adj* [fr. prp. of obs. *gruel* (to exhaust)] **:** trying to the point of exhaustion **:** PUNISHING
grue·some \'grü-səm\ *adj* [alter. of earlier *growsome*, fr. E dial. *grow, grue* to shiver, fr. ME *gruen*, prob. fr. MD *grūwen;* akin to OHG *ingrūēn* to shiver] **:** inspiring horror or repulsion **:** GRISLY **syn** see GHASTLY — **grue·some·ly** *adv* — **grue·some·ness** *n*
gruff \'grəf\ *adj* [D *grof;* akin to OHG *grob* coarse, *hruf* scurf — more at DANDRUFF] **1 :** rough or stern in manner, speech, or aspect **2 :** being deep and harsh **:** HOARSE **syn** see BLUFF — **gruff·ly** *adv* — **gruff·ness** *n*
grum \'grəm\ *adj* **grum·mer; grum·mest** [prob. blend of *grim* and *glum*] **:** MOROSE, GLUM
grum·ble \'grəm-bəl\ *vb* **grum·bling** \-b(ə-)liŋ\ [prob. fr. MF *grommeler* deriv. of MD *grommen;* akin to OHG *grimm* grim] *vi* **1 :** to mutter in discontent **2 a :** GROWL **b :** RUMBLE ~ *vt* **:** to express with grumbling — **grumble** *n* — **grum·bler** \-b(ə-)lər\ *n* — **grum·bly** \-b(ə-)lē\ *adj*
grum·met \'grəm-ət\ *var of* GROMMET
grump \'grəmp\ *n* [obs. E *grumps* (snubs, slights)] **1** *pl* **:** a fit of ill humor **2 :** a person given to complaining — **grump** *vi* — **grump·i·ly** \'grəm-pə-lē\ *adv* — **grump·i·ness** \-pē-nəs\ *n* — **grumpy** \-pē\ *adj*
grun·ion \'grən-yən\ *n* [prob. fr. Sp *gruñón* grunter] **:** a silversides (*Leuresthes tenuis*) of the California coast notable for the regularity with which it comes inshore to spawn at nearly full moon
1**grunt** \'grənt\ *vb* [ME *grunten*, fr. OE *grunnettan*, freq. of *grunian*, of imit. origin] *vi* **:** to make the characteristic throat sound of a hog or a similar sound ~ *vt* **:** to utter with a grunt — **grunt·er** *n*
2**grunt** *n* **1 a :** the deep short sound characteristic of a hog **b :** a similar sound **2** [fr. the noise it makes when taken from the water] **:** any of numerous chiefly tropical marine percoid fishes (family Pomadasidae) related to the snappers
grutch \'grəch\ *vt* [ME *grucchen*] *obs* **:** BEGRUDGE
grutten *past part of* GREET
Gru·yère \grü-'ye(ə)r, grē-'(y)e(ə)r\ *n* [*Gruyère*, district in Switzerland] **:** a pale yellow pressed whole-milk cheese of nutty flavor and usu. with small holes
gryph·on *var of* GRIFFIN
G-string \'jē-,striŋ\ *n* [origin unknown] **:** a strip of cloth passed between the legs and supported by a waist cord; *esp* **:** one worn as part of a burlesque costume
G suit *n* [gravity *suit*] **:** an aviator's suit designed to counteract the physiological effects of acceleration
guai·ac \'g(w)ī-,ak\ *n* [NL *Guaiacum*] **:** GUAIACUM 2
guai·a·cum \'g(w)ī-ə-kəm\ *n* [NL, genus name, fr. Sp *guayaco*, fr. Taino *guayacan*] **1 :** any of a genus (*Guaiacum*) of tropical American trees and shrubs of the bean-caper family having pinnate leaves, mostly blue flowers, and capsular fruit **2 a :** the hard greenish brown wood of a guaiacum (esp. *Guaiacum officinale*) **b :** a resin with a faint balsamic odor obtained from the trunk of two guaiacums (*G. officinale* and *G. sanctum*)
guan \'gwän\ *n* [AmerSp] **:** any of various large tropical American lowland-forest birds (family Cracidae) that somewhat resemble turkeys
gua·na·co \gwə-'näk-(,)ō\ *n, pl* **guanacos** *also* **guanaco** [Sp, fr. Quechua *huanacu*] **:** a So. American mammal (*Lama guanicoe*) with a soft thick fawn-colored coat that is related to the camel but lacks a dorsal hump
gua·ni·dine \'gwän-ə-,dēn\ *n* [ISV, fr. *guanine*] **:** a strong deliquescent crystalline base $NH{:}C(NH_2)_2$ found esp. in young tissues and used in organic synthesis and medicine
gua·nine \'gwän-,ēn\ *n* **:** a purine base $C_5H_5N_5O$ found esp. in animal excrements and leguminous plants
gua·no \'gwän-(,)ō\ *n* [Sp, fr. Quechua *huanu* dung] **1 :** a substance composed chiefly of the excrement of seafowl and used as a fertilizer **2 :** a similar product (as of cannery waste)
gua·ra·ni \,gwär-ə-'nē\ *n* [Sp *guaraní*] **1 a** *pl* **guarani** *or* **guaranis** *cap* (1) **:** a Tupi-Guaranian people of Bolivia, Paraguay, and southern Brazil (2) **:** a member of this people **b** *cap* **:** the language of this people **2** *pl* **guaranis** *or* **guaranies** — see MONEY table
1**guar·an·tee** \,gar-ən-'tē, ,gär-\ *n* [prob. alter. of 1*guaranty*] **1 :** GUARANTOR **2 :** GUARANTY 1 **3 a :** an agreement by which one person undertakes to secure another in the possession or enjoyment of something **b :** an assurance of the quality of or of the length of use to be expected from a product offered for sale often with a promise of reimbursement **4 :** GUARANTY 3
2**guarantee** *vt* **1 :** to undertake to answer for the debt, default, or miscarriage of **2 :** to engage for the existence, permanence, or nature of ⟨~ the winning of three tricks⟩ **3 :** to give security to
guar·an·tor \,gar-ən-'tȯ(ə)r, 'gar-ən-tər, ,gär-, 'gär-\ *n* **1 :** one that guarantees **2 :** one that makes or gives a guaranty
1**guar·an·ty** \'gar-ən-tē, 'gär-\ *n* [MF *garantie*, fr. OF, fr. *garantir* to guarantee, fr. *garant* warrant, of Gmc origin; akin to OHG *werēnto* guarantor — more at WARRANT] **1 :** an undertaking to answer for the payment of a debt or the performance of a duty of another in case of the other's default or miscarriage **2 :** GUARANTEE 3a **3 :** something given as security **:** PLEDGE **4 :** GUARANTOR **5 :** the protection of a right afforded by legal provision (as in a constitution)

2**guaranty** *vt* : GUARANTEE

1**guard** \'gärd\ *n* [ME *garde*, fr. MF, fr. OF, fr. *garder* to guard, defend, of Gmc origin; akin to OHG *wartēn* to watch, take care — more at WARD] **1** *obs* : GUARDIANSHIP **2** : a posture of defense **3 a** : the act or duty of protecting or defending **b** : the state of being protected : PROTECTION **4** *archaic* : PRECAUTION **5 a** : a person or a body of men on sentinel duty **b** *pl* : troops attached to the person of the sovereign **c** (1) : BRAKEMAN (2) *Brit* : CONDUCTOR **6 a** : a position or player next to the center in a football line **b** : either of two primarily defensive players stationed to the rear of the court in basketball **7** : a protective or safety device; *specif* : a device for protecting a machine part or the operator of a machine

2**guard** *vt* **1** : to protect an edge of with an ornamental border **2 a** : to protect from danger : DEFEND **b** : to stand at the entrance of as if on guard or as a barrier **3** *archaic* : ESCORT **4 a** : to watch over so as to prevent escape, disclosure, or indiscretion **b** : to attempt to prevent (an opponent) from scoring ~ *vi* : to be on guard **syn** see DEFEND — **guard·er** *n* — **guard·house** \'gärd-,haùs\ *n* — **guard·room** \'gär-,drüm, -,drùm\ *n*

guard·ant \'gärd-ᵊnt\ *n*, *obs* : GUARDIAN

guard cell *n* : one of the two crescent-shaped epidermal cells that border and open and close a plant stoma

guard hair *n* : one of the long coarse hairs forming a protective coating over the underfur of a mammal

guard·ian \'gärd-ē-ən\ *n* **1** : one that guards : CUSTODIAN **2** : a superior of a Franciscan monastery **3** : one who has the care of the person or property of another — **guard·ian·ship** \-,ship\ *n*

guards·man \'gärdz-mən\ *n* : a member of the guards

Guar·ne·ri·us \gwär-'nir-ē-əs, -'ner-\ *n* [NL, fr. It *Guarneri*] : a violin made by one of the Italian Guarneri family in the 17th and 18th centuries

gua·va \'gwäv-ə\ *n* [modif. of Sp *guayaba*, of Arawakan origin; akin to Tupi *guayava* guava] **1** : any of several tropical American shrubs or small trees (genus *Psidium*) of the myrtle family; *esp* : a shrubby tree (*P. guajava*) widely cultivated for its sweet acid yellow fruit **2** : the fruit of a guava

gua·yu·le \(g)wī-'ü-lē\ *n* [AmerSp, fr. Nahuatl *cuauhuli*] : a much-branched composite subshrub (*Parthenium argentatum*) of Mexico and the southwestern U. S. that has been cultivated as a source of rubber

gu·ber·na·to·ri·al \,gü-bə(r)-nə-'tōr-ē-əl, ,gyü-, ,gùb-ə(r)-, -'tòr-\ *adj* [L *gubernator* governor, fr. *gubernatus*, pp. of *gubernare* to govern — more at GOVERN] : of or relating to a governor

guck \'gək\ *n* [perh. fr. *goo* + *muck*] *slang* : oozy sloppy dirt or debris

1**gud·geon** \'gəj-ən\ *n* [ME *gudyon*, fr. MF *goujon*] **1** : PIVOT, JOURNAL **2** : a socket for a rudder pintle

2**gudgeon** *n* [ME *gojune*, fr. MF *gouvion*, *gougon*, fr. L *gobion-*, *gobio*, alter. of *gobius* — more at GOBY] **1** : a small European freshwater fish (*Gobio gobio*) related to the carps and often used for food or bait **2 a** : any of various gobies **b** : any of several Australian fishes (family Eleotridae) **3** : any of various killifishes **4** : BURBOT

gudgeon pin *n* : WRIST PIN

Gud·run \'gùd-,rün\ *n* [ON *Guthrūn*] : the wife of Sigurd and later of Atli in Norse mythology

guel·der rose \,gel-də(r)-\ *n* [*Guelderland*, *Gelderland*, Netherlands] : a cultivated cranberry bush with large globose heads of sterile flowers

Guelf *or* **Guelph** \'gwelf\ *n* [It *Guelfo*] : a member of a papal and popular political party in medieval Italy opposing the authority of the German emperors — compare GHIBELLINE

gue·non \gə-'nōⁿ\ *n* [F] : any of various long-tailed chiefly arboreal African monkeys (*Cercopithecus* and related genera)

guer·don \'gərd-ᵊn\ *n* [ME, fr. MF, modif. of OHG *widarlōn*, fr. *widar* back + *lōn* reward — more at WITH, LUCRE] : REWARD, RECOMPENSE — **guerdon** *vt* **guer·don·ing** \'gərd-niŋ, -ᵊn-iŋ\

guern·sey \'gərn-zē\ *n* [*Guernsey*, Channel islands] : any of a breed of fawn and white dairy cattle that are larger than the jersey and produce rich yellowish milk

guer·ril·la *or* **gue·ril·la** \gə-'ril-ə\ *n* [Sp *guerrilla*, fr. dim. of *guerra* war, of Gmc origin; akin to OHG *werra* strife — more at WAR] **1** *archaic* : irregular warfare by independent bands **2** : one who engages in irregular warfare esp. as a member of an independent unit carrying out harassment and sabotage

guess \'ges\ *vb* [ME *gessen*, prob. of Scand origin; akin to ON *geta* to get, guess — more at GET] *vt* **1** : to form an opinion of from little or no evidence **2** : to conjecture correctly about **3** : BELIEVE, SUPPOSE ⟨I ~ you're right⟩ ~ *vi* : to make a guess **syn** see CONJECTURE — **guess** *n* — **guess·er** *n*

guess·ti·mate \'ges-tə-,māt\ *vt* [blend of *guess* and *estimate*] : to estimate without adequate information — **guess·ti·mate** \-mət\ *n*

guess·work \'ges-,wərk\ *n* : CONJECTURE

1**guest** \'gest\ *n* [ME *gest*, fr. ON *gestr*; akin to OE *gæst* guest, stranger, L *hostis* stranger, enemy] **1 a** : a person entertained in one's house **b** : a person to whom hospitality is extended **c** : a patron of a hotel, restaurant, or other establishment **2** : an organism (as an insect) sharing the dwelling of another; *esp* : INQUILINE **3** : a person not a regular member of a cast who appears on a program

2**guest** *vt* : to receive as a guest ~ *vi* : to appear as a guest

guff \'gəf\ *n* [prob. imit.] : HUMBUG; *broadly* : GOSSIP

guf·faw \(,)gə-'fò, 'gəf-,ò\ *n* [imit.] : a loud burst of laughter — **guf·faw** \(,)gə-'fò\ *vi*

gug·gle \'gəg-əl\ *vi* **gug·gling** \-(ə-)liŋ\ [imit.] : GURGLE — **guggle** *n*

guid·able \'gīd-ə-bəl\ *adj* : capable of being guided

guid·ance \'gīd-ᵊn(t)s\ *n* **1** : the act or process of guiding **2** : advice on vocational or educational problems given to students **3** : the process of controlling the course of a projectile by a built-in mechanism

1**guide** \'gīd\ *n* [ME, fr. MF, fr. OProv *guida*, of Gmc origin; akin to OE *wītan* to look after, *witan* to know — more at WIT] **1 a** : one who leads or directs another in his way **b** : one who exhibits and explains points of interest **c** : something that provides a person with guiding information **d** : SIGNPOST **e** : one who directs a person in his conduct or course of life **2 a** : a contrivance for steadying or directing the motion of something **b** : a ring or loop for holding the line of a fishing rod in position **c** : a sheet or a card with projecting tab for labeling inserted in a card index to facilitate reference **3** : a member of a unit upon whom the movements or alignments of a military command are regulated — used esp. in commands ⟨~ right⟩

2**guide** *vt* **1** : to act as a guide to : CONDUCT **2 a** : to regulate and manage : DIRECT **b** : to superintend the training or instruction of ~ *vi* : to act or work as a guide — **guid·er** *n*

syn LEAD, STEER, PILOT, ENGINEER: GUIDE implies intimate knowledge of the way and of all its difficulties and dangers; LEAD implies a going ahead to show the way and often to keep those that follow under control and in order; STEER implies an ability to keep to a chosen course and stresses the capacity of maneuvering correctly; PILOT suggests guidance over a dangerous, intricate, or complicated course; ENGINEER implies guidance by one who finds ways to avoid or overcome difficulties in achieving an end or carrying out a plan

guide·book \'gīd-,bùk\ *n* : a book of information for travelers

guided missile *n* : a missile whose course may be altered during flight (as by a target-seeking radar device)

guide·line \'gīd-,līn\ *n* : a line by which one is guided; *esp* : an outline (as by a government) of policy or conduct

guide word *n* : CATCHWORD 1b

gui·don \'gīd-,än, -ᵊn\ *n* [MF] **1** : a small flag; *esp* : one borne by a military unit as a unit marker **2** : one who carries a guidon

guid·will·ie \gœ̄-'dwil-ē\ *adj* [Sc *guidwill* goodwill] *Scot* : CORDIAL, CHEERING

guild \'gild\ *n* [ME *gilde*, fr. ON *gildi* payment, guild; akin to OE *gield* tribute, guild — more at GELD] **1** : an association of men with similar interests or pursuits; *esp* : a medieval association of merchants or craftsmen **2** : an ecological group of plants distinguished from ordinary herbs, shrubs, and trees by a special mode of life usu. involving some degree of dependence on other plants — **guild·ship** \'gil(d)-,ship\ *n* — **guilds·man** \'gil(d)z-mən\ *n*

guil·der \'gil-dər\ *n* [modif. of D *gulden*] : GULDEN

guild·hall \'gild-,hòl, -'hòl\ *n* : a hall where a guild or corporation usu. assembles : TOWN HALL

guild socialism *n* : an early 20th century English socialistic theory advocating state ownership of industry with control and management by guilds of workers

guile \'gī(ə)l\ *n* [ME, fr. OF] **1** : deceitful cunning : DUPLICITY **2** *obs* : STRATAGEM, TRICK — **guile·ful** \-fəl\ *adj* — **guile·ful·ly** \-fə-lē\ *adv* — **guile·ful·ness** *n*

guile·less \'gī(ə)l-ləs\ *adj* : INNOCENT, NAÏVE — **guile·less·ly** *adv* — **guile·less·ness** *n*

guil·le·mot \'gil-ə-,mät\ *n* [F, fr. MF, dim. of *Guillaume* William] : any of several narrow-billed auks of northern seas constituting two genera (*Uria* and *Cepphus*)

guil·loche \gil-'ōsh, gē-'(y)ōsh\ *n* [F *guillochis*] : an architectural ornament formed of interlaced bands with openings containing round devices

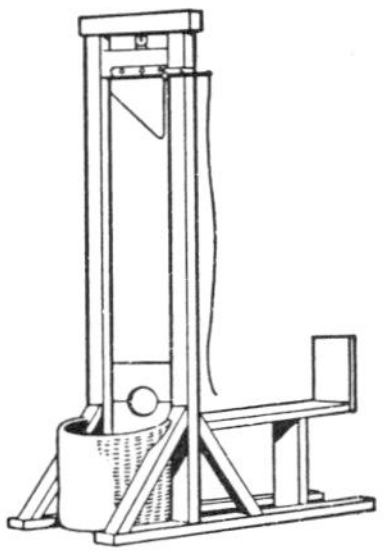

guillotine 1

guil·lo·tine \'gil-ə-,tēn, ,gil-ə-', ,gē-(y)ə-', 'gē-(y)ə-,\ *n* [F, fr. Joseph *Guillotin* †1814 F physician] **1** : a machine for beheading by means of a heavy blade that slides down in vertical guides **2** : an instrument that resembles a guillotine **3** : closure by the imposition of a predetermined time limit on the consideration of specific sections of a bill or portions of other legislative business — **guillotine** *vb*

guilt \'gilt\ *n* [ME, delinquency, guilt, fr. OE *gylt* delinquency] **1** : the fact of having committed a breach of conduct esp. violating law and involving a penalty; *broadly* : guilty conduct **2** : CULPABILITY **3** : a feeling of culpability for offenses

guilt·i·ly \'gil-tə-lē\ *adv* : in a guilty manner

guilt·i·ness \-tē-nəs\ *n* : the quality or state of being guilty

guilt·less \'gilt-ləs\ *adj* **1** : INNOCENT **2** : lacking experience or familiarity — **guilt·less·ly** *adv* — **guilt·less·ness** *n*

guilty \'gil-tē\ *adj* **1** : having committed a breach of conduct **2** *obs* : justly liable to or deserving of a penalty **3 a** : suggesting or involving guilt **b** : aware of or suffering from guilt **syn** see BLAMEWORTHY

guimpe \'gamp, 'gimp\ *n* [F, fr. OF *guimple*, of Gmc origin; akin to OE *wimpel* wimple] **1** : a blouse worn under a jumper or pinafore **2** : a wide cloth used to cover the neck and shoulders by some nuns **3** [by alter.] : 1GIMP

guin·ea \'gin-ē\ *n* [*Guinea*, region in West Africa, supposed source of the gold from which it was made] **1** : an English gold coin issued from 1663 to 1813 and fixed in 1717 at 21 shillings **2** : a unit of value equal to 21 shillings

guinea fowl *n* : a West African bird (*Numida meleagris*) related to the pheasants, raised for food in most parts of the world, and marked by a bare neck and head and slaty plumage speckled with white; *broadly* : any of several related birds of continental Africa and Madagascar

guinea hen *n* : a female guinea fowl; *broadly* : GUINEA FOWL

guinea pepper *n* **1 a** : the pungent aromatic fruit of a tropical African tree (*Xylopia aethiopica*) of the custard-apple family used as a condiment and in folk medicine **b** : any of several moderately hot peppers grown in Africa **2** : a plant bearing Guinea peppers

guinea pig *n* **1** : a small stout-bodied short-eared nearly tailless domesticated rodent (*Cavia cobaya*) often kept as a pet and widely used in biological research — called also *cavy* **2** : a subject of scientific research, experimentation, or testing

guinea worm *n* : a slender nematode worm (*Dracunculus medinensis*) attaining a length of several feet and occurring as an adult in the subcutaneous tissues of man and various mammals in warm countries

Guin·e·vere \'gwin-ə-,vi(ə)r\ *n* : the wife of King Arthur and mistress of Lancelot in Arthurian legend

gui·pure \gē-'p(y)ù(ə)r\ *n* [F] : a heavy large-patterned decorative lace

guise \'gīz\ *n* [ME, fr. OF, of Gmc origin; akin to OHG *wīsa* manner — more at WISE] **1** : a form or style of dress : COSTUME **2 a** *obs* : MANNER, FASHION **b** *archaic* : a customary way of speaking or behaving **3** : external appearance : SEMBLANCE

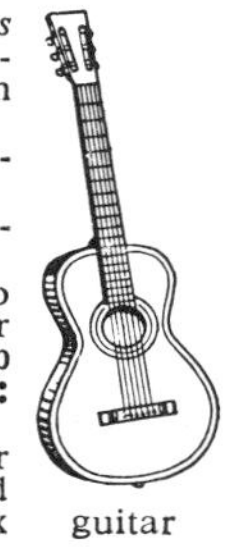

guitar

gui·tar \gə-'tär, gi-\ *n* [F *guitare*, fr. Sp *guitarra*, fr. Ar *qītār*, fr. Gk *kithara* cithara] : a flat-bodied stringed instrument with a long fretted neck and usu. six strings plucked with a plectrum or with the fingers

gui·tar·fish \-,fish\ *n* **:** any of several viviparous rays (family Rhinobatidae) somewhat resembling a guitar in outline when viewed from above

Gu·ja·ra·ti \,gü-jə-'rät-ē, ,gu̇j-ə-\ *n, pl* **Gujarati** [Hindi *gujarātī*, fr. *Gujarāt* Gujarat] **1 :** the language of Gujarat, Baroda, and neighboring regions in northwestern India **2** *or* **Guj·ra·ti** \gu̇j-'rät-, gu̇j-'rät-\ **:** a member of a people chiefly of Gujarat speaking the Gujarati language

gul \'gül\ *n* [Per] **:** ROSE

gu·lar \'g(y)ü-lər\ *adj* [L *gula* throat] **:** of, relating to, or situated on the throat

gulch \'gəlch\ *n* [perh. fr. E dial. *gulch* to gulp, fr. ME *gulchen*] **:** a deep or precipitous cleft **:** RAVINE; *esp* **:** one occupied by a torrent

gul·den \'gül-dən, 'gu̇l-\ *n, pl* **guldens** *or* **gulden** [ME (Sc), fr. MD *gulden florijn* golden florin] — see MONEY table

gules \'gyü(ə)lz\ *n, pl* **gules** [ME *goules*, fr. MF] **:** the heraldic color red

1**gulf** \'gəlf\ *n* [ME *goulf*, fr. MF *golfe*, fr. It *golfo*, fr. LL *colpus*, fr. Gk *kolpos* bosom, gulf; akin to OE *hwealf* vault, OHG *walbo*] **1 :** a part of an ocean or sea extending into the land **2 :** a deep chasm **:** ABYSS **3 :** WHIRLPOOL **4 :** an unbridgeable gap — **gulfy** \'gəl-fē\ *adj*

2**gulf** *vt* **:** ENGULF

gulf·weed \'gəlf-,wēd\ *n* [*Gulf* of Mexico] **:** any of several marine brown algae (genus *Sargassum*); *esp* **:** a branching olive-brown seaweed (*S. bacciferum*) of tropical American seas with numerous berrylike air vesicles

1**gull** \'gəl\ *n* [ME, of Celt origin; akin to W *gwylan* gull] **:** any of numerous long-winged web-footed aquatic birds (family Laridae); *esp* **:** a largely white bird (as of the genus *Larus*) that differs from a tern in usu. larger size, stouter build, thicker bill somewhat hooked at the tip, less pointed wings, and short unforked tail

2**gull** *vt* [obs. *gull* gullet, fr. ME *golle*, fr. MF *goule*] **:** to make a dupe of **:** DECEIVE **syn** see DUPE

3**gull** *n* **:** a person who is easily deceived or cheated **:** DUPE

gull·able \'gəl-ə-bəl\ *adj* **:** GULLIBLE

Gul·lah \'gəl-ə\ *n* **1 :** one of a group of Negroes inhabiting the sea islands and coastal districts of So. Carolina, Georgia, and northeastern Florida **2 :** the language of the Gullahs

gul·let \'gəl-ət\ *n* [ME *golet*, fr. MF *goulet*, dim. of *goule* throat, fr. L *gula* — more at GLUTTON] **1 :** ESOPHAGUS; *broadly* **:** THROAT **2 :** the space between adjacent saw teeth

gull·ibil·i·ty \,gəl-ə-'bil-ət-ē\ *n* **:** the quality or state of being gullible

gull·ible \'gəl-ə-bəl\ *adj* **:** easily deceived, cheated, or duped — **gull·ibly** \-blē\ *adv*

Gul·li·ver \'gəl-ə-vər\ *n* **:** an Englishman in Jonathan Swift's satire *Gulliver's Travels* who makes voyages to the imaginary lands of the Lilliputians, Brobdingnagians, Laputans, and Houyhnhnms

1**gul·ly** \'gu̇l-ē, 'gəl-\ *n* [short for E dial. *gully knife*] *dial Brit* **:** a large knife

2**gul·ly** \'gəl-ē\ *n* [obs. E *gully* (gullet)] **:** a trench worn in the earth by running water after rains — **gully** *vb*

gully erosion *n* **:** soil erosion produced by running water

gu·los·i·ty \g(y)ü-'läs-ət-ē\ *n* [ME *gulosite*, fr. LL *gulositas*, fr. L *gulosus* gluttonous, fr. *gula* gullet] **:** GREEDINESS

gulp \'gəlp\ *vb* [ME *gulpen*, fr. a MD or MLG word akin to D & Fris *gulpen* to bubble forth, drink deep; akin to OE *gielpan* to boast — more at YELP] *vt* **1 :** to swallow hurriedly or greedily or in one swallow **2 :** SUPPRESS ~ *vi* **:** to catch the breath as if in taking a long drink — **gulp** *n* — **gulp·er** *n*

1**gum** \'gəm\ *n* [ME *gome*, fr. OE *gōma* palate; akin to OHG *guomo* palate, Gk *chaos* abyss] **:** the tissue that surrounds the necks of teeth and covers the alveolar parts of the jaws; *broadly* **:** the alveolar portion of a jaw with its enveloping soft tissues

2**gum** *vt* **gummed; gum·ming 1 :** to enlarge gullets of (a saw) **2 :** to chew with the gums

3**gum** *n* [ME *gomme*, fr. OF, fr. L *cummi*, *gummi*, fr. Gk *kommi*, fr. Egypt *qmy.t*] **1 a :** any of numerous colloidal polysaccharide substances of plant origin that are gelatinous when moist but harden on drying and are salts of complex organic acids — compare MUCILAGE 1 **b :** any of various plant exudates (as a mucilage, oleoresin, or gum resin) **2 :** a substance or deposit resembling a plant gum (as in sticky or adhesive quality) **3 a :** a tree (as a sour gum or sapodilla) that yields gum **b** *Austral* **:** EUCALYPT **4** *also* **gum·wood** \-,wu̇d\ **:** the wood or lumber of a gum; *esp* **:** that of the sweet gum **5 :** CHEWING GUM — **gum·mif·er·ous** \,gə-'mif-(ə-)rəs\ *adj*

4**gum** *vb* **gummed; gum·ming** *vt* **:** to smear, seal, or clog with or as if with gum ⟨~ up the works⟩ ~ *vi* **1 :** to exude or form gum **2 :** to become gummy — **gum·mer** *n*

gum ammoniac *n* **:** AMMONIAC

gum arabic *n* **:** a water-soluble gum obtained from several acacias (esp. *Acacia senegal* and *A. arabica*) and used esp. in the manufacture of adhesives, in confectionery, and in pharmacy

gum·bo \'gəm-(,)bō\ *n* [AmerF *gombo*, of Bantu origin; akin to Umbundu *ochinggômbo* okra] **1 :** OKRA 1 **2 :** a soup thickened with okra pods and usu. containing vegetables with meat or seafoods **3 a :** any of various fine-grained silty soils esp. of the central U. S. that when wet become impervious and soapy or waxy and very sticky **b :** a heavy sticky mud **4** *often cap* [AmerF *gombo*, perh. fr. Kongo *nkômbô* runaway slave] **:** a patois used by Negroes and Creoles esp. in Louisiana — **gumbo** *adj*

gum·boil \'gəm-,bȯil\ *n* **:** an abscess in the gum

gum·drop \-,dräp\ *n* **:** a candy made usu. from corn syrup with gelatin or gum arabic and coated with sugar crystals

gum elemi *n* **:** ELEMI

gum·ma \'gəm-ə\ *n, pl* **gummas** *also* **gum·ma·ta** \'gəm-ət-ə\ [NL *gummat-*, *gumma*, fr. LL, gum, alter. of L *gummi*] **:** a tumor of gummy or rubbery consistency that is characteristic of the tertiary stage of syphilis — **gum·ma·tous** \-ət-əs\ *adj*

gum·mi·ness \'gəm-ē-nəs\ *n* **:** the quality or state of being gummy

gum·mite \'gəm-,īt\ *n* **:** a yellow to reddish brown mixture of hydrous oxides of uranium, thorium, and lead consisting perhaps largely of curite

gum·mo·sis \,gə-'mō-səs\ *n* **:** a pathological production of gummy exudate in a plant; *also* **:** a plant disease marked by gummosis

gum·mous \'gəm-əs\ *adj* **:** resembling or composed of gum **:** GUMMY

gum·my \'gəm-ē\ *adj* **1 a :** consisting of or containing gum **b :** covered with gum **2 :** VISCOUS, STICKY

gump·tion \'gəm(p)-shən\ *n* [origin unknown] **1 :** COMMON SENSE **2 :** ENTERPRISE, INITIATIVE **syn** see SENSE

gum resin *n* **:** a product consisting essentially of a mixture of gum and resin usu. obtained by making an incision in a plant and allowing the juice which exudes to solidify

gum·shoe \'gəm-,shü\ *n* **:** DETECTIVE — **gumshoe** *vi*

1**gun** \'gən\ *n* [ME *gonne*, *gunne*] **1 a :** a piece of ordnance usu. with high muzzle velocity and comparatively flat trajectory **b :** a portable firearm (as a rifle, pistol) **c :** a device that throws a projectile **2 a :** a discharge of a gun **b :** a signal marking a beginning or ending **3 :** one who is skilled with a gun **4 :** something suggesting a gun in shape or function **5 :** THROTTLE — **gunned** \'gənd\ *adj*

2**gun** *vb* **gunned; gun·ning** *vi* **:** to hunt with a gun ~ *vt* **1 a :** to fire on **b :** SHOOT **2 :** to open up the throttle of so as to increase speed ⟨~ the engine⟩

gun·boat \'gən-,bōt\ *n* **:** an armed ship of shallow draft

gun·cot·ton \-,kät-ᵊn\ *n* **:** CELLULOSE NITRATE; *esp* **:** an explosive higher-nitrated product used chiefly in smokeless powder

gun·dog \-,dȯg\ *n* **:** a dog trained to accompany sportsmen when they hunt with guns

gun·fight \-,fīt\ *n* **:** a duel with guns — **gun·fight·er** \-ər\ *n*

gun·fire \-,fī(ə)r\ *n* **:** the firing of guns

gun·flint \-,flint\ *n* **:** a small sharp flint to ignite the priming in a flintlock

gunk \'gəŋk\ *n* [prob. imit.] **:** filthy, sticky, or greasy matter

gun·lock \'gən-,läk\ *n* **:** a mechanism attached to or integral with a firearm by which the charge is ignited

gun·man \-mən\ *n* **1 :** a man armed with a gun; *esp* **:** a professional killer **2 :** a man noted for speed or skill in handling a gun

gun·met·al \'gən-,met-ᵊl\ *n* **1 :** a metal used for guns; *specif* **:** a bronze formerly much used as a material for cannon **2 :** an alloy or metal treated to imitate nearly black tarnished copper-alloy gunmetal

gun moll \-,mäl\ *n, slang* **:** the girl friend of a gangster

gun·nel \'gən-ᵊl\ *n* [origin unknown] **:** a small slimy elongate north Atlantic blenny (*Pholis gunnellus*)

gun·ner \'gən-ər\ *n* **1 :** a soldier or airman who operates or aims a gun **2 :** one that hunts with a gun **3 :** a warrant officer who supervises ordnance and ordnance stores

gun·nery \'gən-(ə-)rē\ *n* **:** the use of guns; *specif* **:** the science of the flight of projectiles and of the effective use of guns

gunnery sergeant *n* **:** a noncommissioned officer in the marine corps ranking above a staff sergeant and below a first sergeant

gun·ny \'gən-ē\ *n* [Hindi *ganī*] **1 :** coarse jute sacking **2 :** BURLAP

gun·ny·sack \-,sak\ *n* **:** a sack made of gunny or burlap

gun·pow·der \'gən-,pau̇d-ər\ *n* **:** an explosive mixture of potassium nitrate, charcoal, and sulfur used in gunnery and blasting; *broadly* **:** any of various powders used in guns as propelling charges

gun room *n* **:** quarters on a British warship orig. used by the gunner and his mates but now by midshipmen and junior officers

gun·run·ner \'gən-,rən-ər\ *n* **:** one that traffics in contraband arms and ammunition — **gun·run·ning** \-,rən-iŋ\ *n*

gun·sel \'gən(t)-səl\ *n* [slang *gunsel* (stupid person, traitor)] *slang* **:** GUNMAN

gun·shot \'gən-,shät\ *n* **1 :** shot or a projectile fired from a gun **2 :** the range of a gun **3 :** the firing of a gun

gun–shy \-,shī\ *adj* **1 :** afraid of the sound of a gun or of other loud noises **2 :** markedly distrustful

gun·sling·er \-,sliŋ-ər\ *n* **:** GUNMAN — **gun·sling·ing** \-,sliŋ-iŋ\ *n*

Gun·ter's chain \,gənt-ərz-\ *n* [Edmund *Gunter* †1626 E mathematician] **:** a chain 66 feet long that is the unit of length for surveys of U.S. public lands

Gun·ther \'gu̇nt-ər\ *n* [G] **:** a Burgundian king and husband of Brunhild in Germanic legend

gun·wale *or* **gun·nel** \'gən-ᵊl\ *n* [ME *gonnewale*, fr. *gonne* gun + *wale*; fr. its former use as a support for guns] **:** the part of a ship where topsides and deck meet

gup·py \'gəp-ē\ *n* [R.J.L. *Guppy* of Trinidad, donor of specimens to the British Museum] **:** a small topminnow (*Lebistes reticulatus*) of the Barbados, Trinidad, and Venezuela frequently kept as an aquarium fish

gurge \'gərj\ *n* [L *gurges* whirlpool — more at GORGE] *archaic* **:** SURGE, EDDY

gur·gle \'gər-gəl\ *vi* **gur·gling** \-g(ə-)liŋ\ [prob. imit.] **1 :** to flow in a broken irregular current **2 :** to make a sound like that of a gurgling liquid — **gurgle** *n*

Gur·kha \'gu̇(ə)r-kə, 'gər-\ *n* [*Ghurka*, member of race dominant in Nepal] **:** a soldier from Nepal in the British or Indian army

gur·nard \'gər-nərd\ *n, pl* **gurnard** *or* **gurnards** [ME, fr. MF *gornart*, irreg. fr. *grognier* to grunt, fr. L *grunnire*, of imit. origin] **:** any of various marine spiny-finned fishes (family Triglidae) with a spiny armored head and three pairs of modified fin rays used as feelers and in crawling

gur·ry \'gər-ē, 'gə-rē\ *n* [origin unknown] **:** fishing offal

gu·ru \gə-'rü\ *n* [Hindi *gurū*, fr. Skt *guru*, fr. *guru*, adj., heavy, venerable — more at GRIEVE] **:** a personal religious teacher and spiritual guide in Hinduism

gush \'gəsh\ *vb* [ME *guschen*] *vi* **1 :** to issue copiously or violently **2 :** to emit a sudden copious flow **3 :** to make an effusive display of affection or enthusiasm ~ *vt* **:** to emit in a copious free flow — **gush** *n*

gush·er \'gəsh-ər\ *n* **:** one that gushes; *specif* **:** an oil well with a copious natural flow

gushy \'gəsh-ē\ *adj* **:** marked by effusive sentimentality

gus·set \'gəs-ət\ *n* [ME, piece of armor covering the joints in a suit of armor, fr. MF *gouchet*] **:** a triangular insert (as in a seam of a sleeve) to give width or strength

1**gust** \'gəst\ *n* [ME *guste*, fr. L *gustus*; akin to L *gustare* to taste — more at CHOOSE] **1** *obs* **a :** the sensation of taste **b :** INCLINATION, LIKING **2** *obs* **:** an esp. pleasing flavor **3 :** ENJOYMENT, APPRECIATION — **gust** *vt* — **gust·able** \'gəs-tə-bəl\ *adj or n*

2gust *n* [prob. fr. ON *gustr;* akin to OHG *gussa* flood, OE *gēotan* to pour — more at FOUND] **1 :** a sudden brief rush of wind **2 :** a sudden outburst **:** SURGE — **gust·i·ly** \'gəs-tə-lē\ *adv* — **gust·i·ness** \-tē-nəs\ *n* — **gusty** \-tē\ *adj*

gus·ta·tion \ˌgəs-'tā-shən\ *n* [L *gustation-, gustatio,* fr. *gustatus,* pp. of *gustare*] **:** the act or sensation of tasting

gus·ta·tive \'gəs-tət-iv\ *adj* **:** GUSTATORY — **gus·ta·tive·ness** *n*

gus·ta·to·ri·al \ˌgəs-tə-'tōr-ē-əl, -'tȯr-\ *adj* **:** GUSTATORY

gus·ta·to·ry \'gəs-tə-ˌtōr-ē, -ˌtȯr-\ *adj* **:** relating to, associated with, or being the sense of taste

gus·to \'gəs-(ˌ)tō\ *n* [Sp, fr. L *gustus*] **1 a :** TASTE, LIKING **b :** enthusiastic and vigorous enjoyment or appreciation **c :** overabundant vitality **2** *archaic* **:** artistic style **syn** see TASTE

1gut \'gət\ *n* [ME, fr. OE *guttas,* pl.; akin to OE *gēotan* to pour] **1 a :** BOWELS, ENTRAILS — usu. used in pl. **b :** the alimentary canal or part of it (as the intestine or stomach) **c :** BELLY, ABDOMEN **2** *pl* **:** the inner essential parts **3 :** a narrow passage (as a strait) **4 :** the sac of silk taken from a silkworm ready to spin its cocoon and drawn out into a thread for use as a snell **5** *pl* **:** COURAGE **syn** see FORTITUDE

2gut *vt* **gut·ted; gut·ting 1 :** EVISCERATE **2 :** to destroy the inside of ⟨fire *gutted* the building⟩

gut·less \'gət-ləs\ *adj* **1 :** lacking courage **:** COWARDLY **2 :** lacking vitality — **gut·less·ness** *n*

gut·ta \'gət-ə, 'gu̇t-ə\ *n, pl* **gut·tae** \'gə-ˌtē, 'gu̇-, -ˌtī\ [L, lit., drop — more at GOUT] **:** one of a series of ornaments in the Doric entablature that is usu. in the form of a frustum of a cone

gut·ta–per·cha \ˌgət-ə-'pər-chə\ *n* [Malay *gĕtah-pĕrcha,* fr. *gĕtah* sap, latex + *pĕrcha,* tree producing gutta-percha] **:** a tough plastic substance from the latex of several Malaysian trees (genera *Payena* and *Palaquium*) of the sapodilla family resembling rubber but containing more resin and used esp. as insulation and in dentistry

gut·tate \'gə-ˌtāt\ *adj* [L *guttatus,* fr. *gutta*] **:** having small usu. colored spots or drops

1gut·ter \'gət-ər\ *n* [ME *goter,* fr. OF *goutiere,* fr. *goute* drop, fr. L *gutta*] **1 a :** a trough under an eaves to carry off water **b :** a low area (as at a roadside) to carry off surface water **c :** a similar narrow channel or groove **2 :** a white space along inside margins of facing pages **3 :** the lowest level of urban civilization

2gutter *vt* **:** to form gutters in ~ *vi* **1 a :** to flow in small streams **b** *of a candle* **:** to melt away through a channel out of the side of the cup hollowed out by the burning wick **2 :** to flicker in a draft

gut·ter·snipe \-ˌsnīp\ *n* **:** a person of the lowest moral or economic station; *esp* **:** URCHIN — **gut·ter·snip·ish** \-ˌsnī-pish\ *adj*

gut·tle \'gət-ᵊl\ *vb* **gut·tling** \'gət-liŋ, -ᵊl-iŋ\ [alter. of *guzzle*] **:** to eat greedily — **gut·tler** \-lər, -ᵊl-ər\ *n*

gut·tur·al \'gət-ə-rəl, 'gə-trəl\ *adj* [MF, prob. fr. ML *gutturalis,* fr. L *guttur* throat — more at COT] **1 :** of or relating to the throat **2 a :** articulated in the throat ⟨~ sounds⟩ **b :** being or marked by utterance that is strange, unpleasant, or disagreeable **c :** VELAR, PALATAL — **guttural** *n* — **gut·tur·al·ism** \'gət-ə-rə-ˌliz-əm, 'gə-trə-\ *n* — **gut·tur·al·i·ty** \ˌgət-ə-'ral-ət-ē\ *n* — **gut·tur·al·ly** \'gət-ə-rə-lē, 'gə-trə-lē\ *adv* — **gut·tur·al·ness** *n*

gut·tur·al·iza·tion \ˌgət-ə-rə-lə-'zā-shən, ˌgə-trə-lə-\ *n* **:** the act or process of gutturalizing **:** the state of being gutturalized

gut·tur·al·ize \'gət-ə-rə-ˌlīz, 'gə-trə-\ *vt* **1 :** to pronounce in a guttural manner **2 :** VELARIZE

gut·ty \'gət-ē\ *adj* **:** being vital, bold, and challenging ⟨~ realism⟩

1guy \'gī\ *n* [prob. fr. D *gei* brail] **:** a rope, chain, or rod attached to something as a brace or guide

2guy *vt* **:** to steady or reinforce with a guy

3guy *n* [*Guy* Fawkes] **1** *often cap* **:** a grotesque effigy of Guy Fawkes paraded and burned in England on Guy Fawkes Day **2** *chiefly Brit* **:** a person of grotesque appearance **3 :** MAN, FELLOW

4guy *vt* **:** to make fun of **:** RIDICULE

Guy Fawkes Day \'gī-'fȯks-\ *n* **:** November 5 observed in England in commemoration of the seizure of Guy Fawkes in 1605 for an attempt to blow up the houses of parliament

guz·zle \'gəz-əl\ *vb* **guz·zling** \-(ə-)liŋ\ [origin unknown] **:** to drink greedily — **guz·zler** \-(ə-)lər\ *n*

gwe·duc \'gü-ē-ˌdək\ *var of* GEODUCK

gybe \'jīb\ *var of* JIBE

gym \'jim\ *n* **:** GYMNASIUM

gym·kha·na \jim-'kän-ə, -'kan-\ *n* [prob. modif. of Hindi *gendkhāna* racket court] **:** a meet featuring sports contests (as racing)

gymn- *or* **gymno-** *comb form* [NL, fr. Gk, fr. *gymnos* — more at NAKED] **:** naked **:** bare ⟨*gymno*gynous⟩

gym·na·si·um *in sense 1* jim-'nā-zē-əm, *in sense 2* gim-'nä-zē-əm\ *n, pl* **gym·na·si·ums** *or* **gym·na·sia** \-zē-ə\ [L, exercise ground, school, fr. Gk *gymnasion,* fr. *gymnazein* to exercise naked, fr. *gymnos*] **1 :** a room or building for sports activities **2 :** a German secondary school designed to prepare students for the university

gym·nast \'jim-ˌnast, -nəst\ *n* [MF *gymnaste,* fr. Gk *gymnastēs* trainer, fr. *gymnazein*] **:** an expert in gymnastics

gym·nas·tic \jim-'nas-tik\ *adj* **:** of or relating to gymnastics **:** ATHLETIC — **gym·nas·ti·cal·ly** \-ti-k(ə-)lē\ *adv*

gym·nas·tics \-tiks\ *n pl but sing in constr* **:** physical exercises performed in or adapted to performance in a gymnasium

gym·nos·o·phist \jim-'näs-ə-fəst\ *n* [L *gymnosophista,* fr. Gk *gymnosophistēs,* fr. *gymn-* + *sophistēs* wise man, sophist] **:** one of a sect of naked ascetics of ancient India

gym·no·sperm \'jim-nə-ˌspərm\ *n* [deriv. of NL *gymn-* + Gk *sperma* seed — more at SPERM] **:** any of a class or subdivision (Gymnospermae) of vascular seed plants (as conifers) that produce naked seeds not enclosed in an ovary and in some instances have motile spermatozoids — **gym·no·sper·mous** \ˌjim-nə-'spər-məs\ *adj* — **gym·no·sper·my** \'jim-nə-ˌspər-mē\ *n*

gym·no·spore \'jim-nə-ˌspō(ə)r, -ˌspȯ(ə)r\ *n* **:** a spore not developing in a sporangium; *also* **:** a naked spore — **gym·no·spo·rous** \ˌjim-nə-'spōr-əs, -'spȯr-; jim-'näs-pə-rəs\ *adj*

gyn- *or* **gyno-** *comb form* [Gk *gyn-,* fr. *gynē*] **1 :** woman ⟨*gyn*iatrics⟩ ⟨*gyno*cracy⟩ **2 :** female reproductive organ **:** ovary ⟨*gyno*phore⟩ **:** pistil ⟨*gyno*dioecious⟩

gyn·an·dro·morph \jin-'an-drə-ˌmȯrf, gīn-\ *n* [ISV] **:** an abnormal individual exhibiting characters of both sexes in various parts of the body — **gyn·an·dro·mor·phic** \-ˌan-drə-'mȯr-fik\ *adj* — **gyn·an·dro·mor·phism** \-ˌfiz-əm\ *n* — **gyn·an·dro·mor·phous** \-fəs\ *adj* — **gyn·an·dro·mor·phy** \-'an-drə-ˌmȯr-fē\ *n*

gyn·an·drous \jin-'an-drəs, gīn-\ *adj* [Gk *gynandros* of doubtful sex, fr. *gynē* woman + *andr-, anēr* man — more at ANDR-] **1 :** having the androecium and gynoecium united in a column **2 :** characterized by gynandry

gyn·an·dry \-'an-drē\ *n* **:** HERMAPHRODITISM, INTERSEXUALITY; *specif* **:** the condition of a female in which the external genitalia simulate those of the male

-gyne \ˌjīn, -ˌgīn\ *n comb form* [Gk *gynē*] **1 :** woman **:** female ⟨pseudo*gyne*⟩ **2 :** female reproductive organ ⟨tricho*gyne*⟩

gynec- *or* **gyneco-** *also* **gynaec-** *or* **gynaeco-** *comb form* [Gk *gynaik-, gynaiko-,* fr. *gynaik-, gynē* woman] **:** woman ⟨*gynec*oid⟩

gy·ne·coc·ra·cy \ˌjin-i-'käk-rə-sē, ˌgīn-\ *n* [Gk *gynaikokratia,* fr. *gynaik-* + *-kratia* -cracy] **:** political supremacy of women — **gy·ne·co·crat** \jin-'ē-kə-ˌkrat, gīn-; 'jin-i-kō-ˌkrat, 'gīn-\ *n* — **gy·ne·co·crat·ic** \jin-ˌē-kə-'krat-ik, gīn-; ˌjin-i-kō-'krat-ik, ˌgīn-\ *adj*

gy·ne·coid \'jin-i-ˌkȯid, 'gīn-\ *adj* **:** having female characteristics; *also* **:** typical of a woman

gy·ne·co·log·ic \ˌjin-i-kə-'läj-ik, ˌgīn-\ *adj* **:** of, relating to, or falling in the province of gynecology — **gy·ne·co·log·i·cal** \-'läj-i-kəl\ *adj*

gy·ne·col·o·gist \-'käl-ə-jəst\ *n* **:** a specialist in gynecology

gy·ne·col·o·gy \-jē\ *n* [ISV] **:** a branch of medicine that deals with women, their diseases, and their hygiene

gy·noe·ci·um \jin-'ē-s(h)ē-əm, gīn-\ *n, pl* **gy·noe·cia** \-s(h)ē-ə\ [NL, alter. of L *gynaeceum* women's apartments, fr. Gk *gynaikeion,* fr. *gynaik-, gynē*] **1 :** the aggregate of carpels in a flower **:** PISTILS **2 :** the female inflorescence of a liverwort

gy·no·phore \'jin-ə-ˌfō(ə)r, 'gīn-, -ˌfȯ(ə)r\ *n* **:** a prolongation of the receptacle that bears the gynoecium at its apex (as in caper flowers) — **gy·no·phor·ic** \ˌjin-ə-'fȯr-ik, ˌgīn-, -'fär-\ *adj*

-g·y·nous \j-ə-nəs\ *adj comb form* [NL *-gynus,* fr. Gk *-gynos,* fr. *gynē* woman — more at QUEEN] **1 :** of, relating to, or having (such or so many) females ⟨hetero*gynous*⟩ **2 :** having (such or so many) styles or pistils ⟨tetra*gynous*⟩

-g·y·ny \j-ə-nē\ *n comb form* **1 :** existence of or condition of having (such or so many) females ⟨poly*gyny*⟩ **2 :** existence of or condition of having (such or so many) female organs and esp. pistils ⟨epi*gyny*⟩

1gyp \'jip\ *n* [prob. short for *gypsy*] **1** *Brit* **:** a college servant **2 a :** CHEAT, SWINDLER **b :** FRAUD, SWINDLE

2gyp *vb* **gypped; gyp·ping :** CHEAT

gyp·se·ous \'jip-sē-əs\ *adj* **:** resembling, containing, or consisting of gypsum

gyp·sif·er·ous \jip-'sif-(ə-)rəs\ *adj* **:** bearing gypsum

gyp·soph·i·la \jip-'säf-ə-lə\ *n* [NL, genus name, fr. L *gypsum* + *-phila* -phil] **:** any of a large genus (*Gypsophila*) of Old World herbs of the pink family having small delicate paniculate flowers

gyp·sum \'jip-səm\ *n* [L, fr. Gk *gypsos,* of Sem origin; akin to Ar *jibs* plaster] **1 :** a widely distributed mineral $CaSO_4.2H_2O$ consisting of hydrous calcium sulfate that is used esp. as a soil amendment and in making plaster of paris **2 :** PLASTERBOARD

Gyp·sy \'jip-sē\ *n* [by shortening & alter. fr. *Egyptian*] **1 :** one of a dark Caucasoid people coming orig. from India to Europe in the 14th or 15th century and living and maintaining a migratory way of life chiefly in Europe and the U.S. **2 :** ROMANY 2

gypsy *vi* **:** to live or roam like a gypsy

gypsy moth *n* **:** an Old World tussock moth (*Porthetria dispar*) introduced about 1869 into the U.S. that has a grayish brown mottled hairy caterpillar which is a destructive defoliator of many trees

gyr- *or* **gyro-** *comb form* [prob. fr. MF, fr. L, fr. Gk, fr. *gyros*] **1 :** ring **:** circle **:** spiral ⟨*gyro*magnetic⟩ **2 :** gyroscope ⟨*gyro*compass⟩

1gy·rate \'jī(ə)r-ˌāt\ *adj* **:** winding or coiled round **:** CONVOLUTED

2gyrate *vi* **1 :** to revolve around a point or axis **2 :** to oscillate with or as if with a circular or spiral motion — **gy·ra·tor** \-ˌāt-ər\ *n* — **gy·ra·to·ry** \'jī-rə-ˌtōr-ē, -ˌtȯr-\ *adj*

gy·ra·tion \jī-'rā-shən\ *n* **1 :** an act or instance of gyrating **2 :** something (as a coil of a shell) that is gyrate — **gy·ra·tion·al** \-shnəl, -shən-ᵊl\ *adj*

gyre \'jī(ə)r\ *n* [L *gyrus,* fr. Gk *gyros* — more at COWER] **:** a circular or spiral motion or form — **gyre** *vi*

gy·rene \'jī(ə)r-ˌēn\ *n* [prob. by alter.] *slang* **:** MARINE

gyr·fal·con \'jər-ˌfal-kən, -ˌfȯl- *also* -ˌfȯ-kən\ *n* [ME *gerfaucun,* fr. MF *girfaucon*] **:** any of various large arctic falcons that commonly constitute a subgenus (*Hierofalco*) and are more powerful though less active than the peregrine falcon

gy·ro \'jī(ə)r-(ˌ)ō\ *n* **1 :** GYROSCOPE **2 :** GYROCOMPASS

gy·ro·com·pass \'jī-rō-ˌkəm-pəs, -ˌkäm-\ *n* **:** a compass consisting of a continuously driven gyroscope whose spinning axis is confined to a horizontal plane so that the earth's rotation causes it to assume a position parallel to the earth's axis and thus point to the true north

gyro horizon *n* **:** ARTIFICIAL HORIZON 2

gy·ro·mag·net·ic \ˌjī-rō-(ˌ)mag-'net-ik\ *adj* **:** of or relating to the magnetic properties of a rotating electrical particle

gy·ro·plane \-ˌplān\ *n* [ISV] **:** an airplane balanced and supported by the aerodynamic forces acting on rapidly rotating horizontal or slightly inclined planes

gy·ro·scope \'jī-rə-ˌskōp\ *n* [F, fr. *gyr-* + *-scope;* fr. its original use to illustrate the rotation of the earth] **:** a wheel or disk mounted to spin rapidly about an axis and also free to rotate about one or both of two axes perpendicular to each other and to the axis of spin so that a rotation of one of the two mutually perpendicular axes results from application of torque to the other when the wheel is spinning and so that the entire apparatus offers considerable opposition depending on the angular momentum to any torque that would change the direction of the axis of spin — **gy·ro·scop·ic** \ˌjī-rə-'skäp-ik\ *adj* — **gy·ro·scop·i·cal·ly** \-i-k(ə-)lē\ *adv*

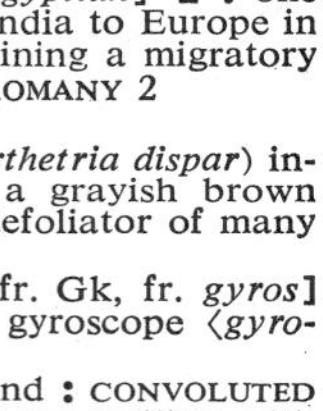

gyroscope

gy·ro·sta·bi·liz·er \ˌjī-rō-'stā-bə-ˌlī-zər\ *n* **:** a stabilizing device (as for a ship or airplane) consisting of a continuously driven gyro spinning about a vertical axis and pivoted so that its axis of spin may be tipped fore-and-aft in the vertical plane

gy·ro·stat \'jī-rə-ˌstat\ *n* **:** GYROSTABILIZER — **gy·ro·stat·ic** \ˌjī-rə-'stat-ik\ *adj* — **gy·ro·stat·i·cal·ly** \-'stat-i-k(ə-)lē\ *adv*

gy·rus \'jī-rəs\ *n, pl* **gy·ri** \'jī(ə)r-ˌī\ [NL, fr. L, circle — more at GYRE] **:** a convoluted ridge between anatomical grooves

gyve \'jīv\ *n* [ME] **:** FETTER — usu. used in pl. — **gyve** *vt*

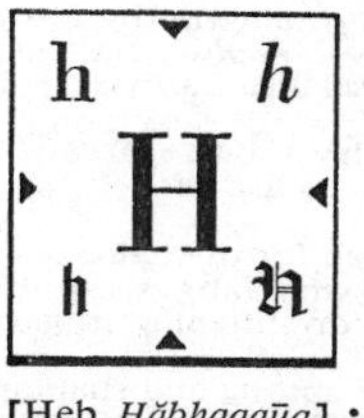

h \'āch\ *n, often cap, often attrib* **1 a :** the eighth letter of the English alphabet **b :** a graphic representation of this letter **c :** a speech counterpart of orthographic *h* **2 :** a graphic device for reproducing the letter *h* **3 :** one designated *h* esp. as the eighth in order or class **4 :** something shaped like the letter H

ha \'hä\ *interj* [ME] — used to express surprise, joy, or grief or sometimes doubt or hesitation

Ha·bak·kuk \'hab-ə-,kək, hə-'bak-ək\ *n* [Heb *Hăbhaqqūq*] **:** a Hebrew prophet of Old Testament times

ha·ba·ne·ra \,(h)äb-ə-'ner-ə\ *n* [Sp (*danza*) *habanera*, lit., Havanan dance] **1 :** a Cuban dance in slow duple time **2 :** the music for the habanera

hab·da·lah \,häv-də-'lä, häv-'dō-lə\ *n, often cap* [Heb *habhdālāh* separation] **:** a Jewish ceremony marking the close of a Sabbath or holy day

ha·be·as cor·pus \,hā-bē-ə-'skȯr-pəs\ *n* [ME, fr. ML, lit., you should have the body (the opening words of the writ)] **1 :** any of several common-law writs issued to bring a party before a court or judge; *esp* **:** HABEAS CORPUS AD SUBJICIENDUM **2 :** the right of a citizen to obtain a writ of habeas corpus as a protection against illegal imprisonment

habeas corpus ad sub·ji·ci·en·dum \-pə-,sad-səb-,yik-ē-'en-dəm\ *n* [NL, lit., you should have the body for submitting] **:** a writ for inquiring into the lawfulness of the restraint of a person who is imprisoned or detained in another's custody

hab·er·dash·er \'hab-ə(r)-,dash-ər\ *n* [ME *haberdassher*, fr. modif. of AF *hapertas* petty merchandise] **1** *Brit* **:** a dealer in small wares or notions **2 :** a dealer in men's furnishings

hab·er·dash·ery \-,dash-(ə-)rē\ *n* **1 :** goods sold by a haberdasher **2 :** a haberdasher's shop

ha·ber·geon \'hab-ər-jən, hə-'bər-j(ē-)ən\ *n* [ME *haubergeoun*, fr. MF *haubergeon*, dim. of *hauberc* hauberk] **1 :** a medieval jacket of mail shorter than a hauberk **2 :** HAUBERK

hab·ile \'hab-əl\ *adj* [F, fr. L *habilis* — more at ABLE] **:** ABLE, SKILLFUL

ha·bil·i·ment \hə-'bil-ə-mənt\ *n* [MF *habillement*, fr. *habiller* to dress a log, dress, fr. *bille* log — more at BILLET] **1** *pl* **:** TRAPPINGS, EQUIPMENT **2 a :** the dress characteristic of an occupation or occasion — usu. used in pl. **b :** CLOTHES — usu. used in pl.

ha·bil·i·tate \hə-'bil-ə-,tāt\ *vb* [LL *habilitatus*, pp. of *habilitare*, fr. L *habilitas* ability — more at ABILITY] *vt* **1** *archaic* **:** CAPACITATE **2 :** CLOTHE, DRESS ~ *vi* **:** to qualify oneself — **ha·bil·i·ta·tion** \hə-,bil-ə-'tā-shən\ *n*

[1]**hab·it** \'hab-ət\ *n* [ME, fr. OF, fr. L *habitus* condition, character, fr. *habitus*, pp. of *habēre* to have, hold — more at GIVE] **1** *archaic* **:** CLOTHING **2 a :** a costume characteristic of a calling, rank, or function **b :** RIDING HABIT **3 :** BEARING, CONDUCT **4 :** bodily appearance or makeup **:** PHYSIQUE **5 :** the prevailing disposition or character of a person's thoughts and feelings **:** mental makeup **6 :** a usual manner of behavior **:** CUSTOM **7 a :** a behavior pattern acquired by frequent repetition or physiologic exposure that shows itself in regularity or increased facility of performance **b :** an acquired mode of behavior that has become nearly or completely involuntary **8 :** characteristic mode of growth or occurrence **9** *of a crystal* **:** characteristic assemblage of forms at crystallization leading to a usual appearance **10 :** ADDICTION

syn HABIT, HABITUDE, PRACTICE, USAGE, CUSTOM, USE, WONT mean a way of acting that has become fixed through repetition. HABIT implies a doing unconsciously or without premeditation, often compulsively; HABITUDE implies a fixed attitude or usual state of mind; PRACTICE suggests an act or method followed with regularity and usu. through choice; USAGE suggests a customary action so generally followed that it has become a social norm; CUSTOM applies to a practice or usage so steadily associated with an individual or group as to have the force of unwritten law; USE and WONT are rare in speech, and differ in that USE stresses the fact of repeated action, WONT the manner of it

[2]**habit** *vt* **:** CLOTHE, DRESS

hab·it·abil·i·ty \,hab-ət-ə-'bil-ət-ē\ *n* **:** the state of being habitable

hab·it·able \'hab-ət-ə-bəl\ *adj* **:** capable of being inhabited — **hab·it·able·ness** *n* — **hab·it·ably** \-blē\ *adv*

ha·bi·tant *n* **1** \'hab-ət-ənt\ **:** INHABITANT, RESIDENT **2** \,(h)ab-i-'täⁿ, -'tänt, -'tant\ *or* **ha·bi·tan** \-'täⁿ\ **:** a settler or descendant of a settler of French origin belonging to the farming class in Canada

hab·i·tat \'hab-ə-,tat\ *n* [L, it inhabits, fr. *habitare*] **1 :** the place or type of site where a plant or animal naturally or normally lives and grows **2 :** the place where something is commonly found

hab·i·ta·tion \,hab-ə-'tā-shən\ *n* [ME *habitacioun*, fr. MF *habitation*, fr. L *habitation-*, *habitatio*, fr. *habitatus*, pp. of *habitare* to inhabit, fr. *habitus*, pp.] **1 :** the act of inhabiting **:** OCCUPANCY **2 :** a dwelling place **:** RESIDENCE **3 :** SETTLEMENT, COLONY

hab·it–form·ing \'hab-ət-,fȯr-miŋ\ *adj* **:** inducing the formation of an addiction

ha·bit·u·al \hə-'bich-(ə-)wəl, ha-, -'bich-əl\ *adj* **1 :** of the nature of a habit **:** according to habit **:** CUSTOMARY ⟨~ smoking⟩ **2 :** doing, practicing, or acting in some manner by force of habit ⟨~ drunkard⟩ **3 :** REGULAR ⟨~ topic⟩ **4 :** inherent in an individual ⟨~ grace⟩ **syn** see USUAL — **ha·bit·u·al·ly** \-ē\ *adv* — **ha·bit·u·al·ness** *n*

ha·bit·u·ate \hə-'bich-ə-,wāt, ha-\ *vt* **1 :** to make used to **:** ACCUSTOM **2** *archaic* **:** FREQUENT

ha·bit·u·a·tion \-,bich-ə-'wā-shən\ *n* **1 :** the act or process of making habitual or accustomed **2 a :** tolerance to the effects of a drug acquired through continued use **b :** psychologic dependence upon a drug after a period of use — compare ADDICTION

hab·i·tude \'hab-ə-,t(y)üd\ *n* **1** *archaic* **:** native or essential character **2** *obs* **:** habitual association **3 a :** habitual disposition or mode of behavior or procedure **b :** CUSTOM **syn** see HABIT

ha·bi·tué \hə-'bich-ə-,wā, ha-, -,bich-ə-'\ *n* [F, fr. pp. of *habituer* to frequent, fr. LL *habituare* to habituate, fr. L *habitus*] **:** one who frequents a place or class of places

hab·i·tus \'hab-ət-əs\ *n, pl* **hab·i·tus** \-ət-əs, -ə-,tüs\ [NL, fr. L] **:** HABIT; *specif* **:** body build and constitution esp. as related to predisposition to disease

Habs·burg \'haps-, 'häps-\ *var of* HAPSBURG

[1]**ha·chure** \ha-'shů(ə)r\ *n* [F] **:** a short line used for shading and denoting surfaces in relief (as in map drawing) and drawn in the direction of slope

[2]**hachure** *vt* **:** to shade with or show by hachures

ha·ci·en·da \,(h)äs-ē-'en-də, ,(h)as-\ *n* [Sp] **1 a :** a large estate in present or formerly Spanish-speaking countries **:** PLANTATION **b :** the main building of a farm or ranch **2** *chiefly Southwest* **:** a ranch dwelling typically with low rambling lines and wide porches

[1]**hack** \'hak\ *vb* [ME *hakken*, fr. OE *-haccian;* akin to OHG *hacchōn* to hack, OE *hōc* hook] *vt* **1 a :** to cut with repeated irregular or unskillful blows **b :** to sever with repeated blows **2 :** to clear by cutting away vegetation **3 :** to kick the shins of (an opposing player) in rugby ~ *vi* **1 :** to make cutting blows or rough cuts **:** CHOP **2 :** to cough in a short dry manner **3 a :** to kick at a rugby opponent's shins deliberately **b :** to strike or hold the arm of a basketball opponent with the hand — **hack·er** *n*

[2]**hack** *n* **1 :** an implement for hacking **2 :** NICK, NOTCH; *esp* **:** a blaze cut in a tree **3 :** a short dry cough **4 :** a hacking blow **5 :** a kick on the shins in rugby **6 :** restriction to quarters as punishment for naval officers

[3]**hack** *n* [short for *hackney*] **1 a** (1) **:** a horse let out for common hire (2) **:** a horse used in all kinds of work **b :** a horse worn out in service **:** JADE **c :** a light easy saddle horse; *esp* **:** a three-gaited saddle horse **2 a :** HACKNEY **b** (1) **:** TAXICAB (2) **:** CABDRIVER **3 :** one who forfeits individual freedom of action or professional integrity in exchange for wages or other assured reward; *esp* **:** a writer who works mainly for hire

[4]**hack** *adj* **1 :** working for hire **2 :** performed by, suited to, or characteristic of a hack **3 :** HACKNEYED, TRITE

[5]**hack** *vt* **1 :** to make trite and commonplace by frequent and indiscriminate use **2 :** to use as a hack ~ *vi* **1 :** to ride or drive at an ordinary pace or over the roads as distinguished from racing or riding across country **2 :** to operate a taxicab

hack·a·more \'hak-ə-,mō(ə)r, -,mȯ(ə)r\ *n* [by folk etymology fr. Sp *jaquima*] **:** a bridle with a loop capable of being tightened about the nose in place of a bit or with a slip noose passed over the lower jaw

hack·ber·ry \'hak-,ber-ē\ *n* [alter. of *hagberry* (European bird cherry)] **:** any of a genus (*Celtis*) of trees and shrubs of the elm family with small often edible berries; *also* **:** its wood

hack·but \'hak-(,)bət\ *or* **hag·but** \'hag-\ *n* [MF *haguebute*] **:** HARQUEBUS — **hack·bu·teer** \,hak-bə-'ti(ə)r\ *or* **hack·but·ter** \'hak-(,)bət-ər\ *n*

hack·ie \'hak-ē\ *n* **:** CABDRIVER

[1]**hack·le** \'hak-əl\ *n* [ME *hakell;* akin to OHG *hāko* hook — more at HOOK] **1 :** a comb or board with long metal teeth for dressing flax, hemp, or jute **2 a :** one of the long narrow feathers on the neck or saddle of a bird **b :** the neck plumage of the male domestic fowl **3** *pl* **a :** erectile hairs along the neck and back esp. of a dog **b :** TEMPER, DANDER **4 a :** an artificial fishing fly made chiefly of the filaments of a cock's neck feathers **b :** filaments of cock feather projecting downward from the head of an artificial fly

[2]**hackle** *vt* **hack·ling** \'hak-(ə-)liŋ\ **1 :** to comb out with a hackle **2 :** to furnish with a hackle — **hack·ler** \'hak-(ə-)lər\ *n*

[3]**hackle** *vt* [freq. of [1]*hack*] **:** to chop up or chop off roughly **:** HACK

[4]**hackle** *n* **:** fracture resulting in hackly edges

hack·ly \'hak-(ə-)lē\ *adj* **:** looking as if hacked **:** JAGGED

hack·man \'hak-mən\ *n* **:** CABDRIVER

hack·ma·tack \'hak-mə-,tak\ *n* [of Algonquian origin; akin to Abnaki *akemantak* snowshoe wood] **:** TAMARACK; *also* **:** any of several other trees (as a common juniper or poplar)

[1]**hack·ney** \'hak-nē\ *n* [ME *hakeney*] **1 a :** a horse suitable for ordinary riding or driving **b :** a trotting horse used chiefly for driving **c :** any of a breed of rather compact usu. chestnut, bay, or brown English horses with a conspicuously high knee and hock flexion in stepping **2** *obs* **:** one that works for hire **:** DRUDGE **3 :** a carriage or automobile kept for hire

[2]**hackney** *adj* **1 :** kept for public hire **2 :** HACKNEYED **3** *archaic* **:** done or suitable for doing by a drudge

[3]**hackney** *vt* **1 a :** to make common or frequent use of **b :** to make trite, vulgar, or commonplace **2** *archaic* **:** to make sophisticated or jaded

hackney coach *n* **:** a coach kept for hire; *esp* **:** a four-wheeled carriage drawn by two horses and having seats for six persons

hack·neyed \'hak-nēd\ *adj* **:** COMMONPLACE **syn** see TRITE

hack·saw \'hak-,sȯ\ *n* **:** a fine-tooth saw with blade under tension in a bow-shaped frame for cutting metal or other hard materials

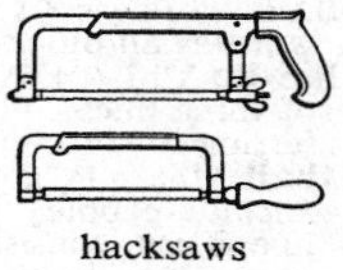

hacksaws

hack·work \-,wərk\ *n* **:** literary, artistic, or professional work done on order usu. according to formula and in conformity with commercial standards

had *past of* HAVE

had·dock \'had-ək\ *n, pl* **haddock** *also* **haddocks** [ME *haddok*] **:** an important food fish (*Melanogrammus aeglefinus*) that is usu. smaller than the related common cod and occurs on both sides of the Atlantic

[1]**hade** \'hād\ *vi* [origin unknown] **:** to deviate from the vertical (as of a vein, fault, or lode)

[2]**hade** *n* **:** the angle made by a rock fault plane or a vein with the vertical

Ha·des \'hād-(,)ēz\ *n* [Gk *Haidēs*] **1 :** the abode of the dead in Greek mythology **2 :** SHEOL **3** *often not cap* **:** HELL

hadj, hadji *var of* HAJJ, HAJJI

hadn't \'had-ᵊnt\ **:** had not

hadst \(')hadst, hədst, *or* t *for* d\ *archaic past 2d sing of* HAVE

hae \(')hā\ *chiefly Scot var of* HAVE

haem- *or* **haemo-** — see HEM-

haema- — see HEMA-

haemat- *or* **haemato-** — see HEMAT-

hae·ma·tox·y·lon \,hē-mə-'täk-sə-,län, ,hem-ə-\ *n* [NL, fr. *hemat-* + Gk *xylon* wood] **:** the wood or dye of logwood

-haemia — see -EMIA

haemoglobin *var of* HEMOGLOBIN

haet \'hāt\ *n* [contr. of Sc *hae it* (as in *Deil hae it!* Devil take it!)]

chiefly Scot : a small quantity : WHIT, BIT

haf·fet *or* **haf·fit** \'haf-ət\ *n* [ME (Sc) *halfheid*, fr. ME *half* + *hed* head] *Scot* : CHEEK, TEMPLE

haf·ni·um \'haf-nē-əm\ *n* [NL, fr. *Hafnia* (Copenhagen), Denmark] : a tetravalent metallic element resembling zirconium chemically, occurring in zirconium minerals, and useful because of its ready emission of electrons — see ELEMENT table

1haft \'haft\ *n* [ME, fr. OE *hæft*; akin to OE *hebban* to lift — more at HEAVE] : the handle of a weapon or tool

2haft *vt* : to set in or furnish with a haft

haf·ta·rah \,häf-tə-'rä, häf-'tō-rə\ *n*, *pl* **haf·ta·rot** \,häf-tə-'rōt\ *or* **haftarahs** [Heb *haphṭārāh* conclusion] : one of the biblical selections from the Books of the Prophets read after the parashah at the conclusion of the Jewish synagogue service

1hag \'hag\ *n* [ME *hagge*] **1** *archaic* **a** : a female demon **b** : an evil or frightening spirit : HOBGOBLIN **2** : WITCH **3** : an ugly, slatternly, or evil-looking old woman

2hag *n* [E dial., felled timber, of Scand origin; akin to ON *högg* stroke, blow; akin to OE *hēawan* to hew] **1** *dial Brit* : QUAGMIRE, BOG **2** *dial Brit* : a firm spot in a bog

Ha·gar \'hā-,gär, -gər\ *n* [Heb *Hāghār*] : a concubine of Abraham driven into the desert with her son Ishmael because of Sarah's jealousy

hag·born \'hag-,bō(ə)rn\ *adj* : born of a witch

hag·fish \-,fish\ *n* : any of several marine cyclostomes (order Hyperotreta) that are related to the lampreys and in general resemble eels but have a round mouth surrounded by eight tentacles and that feed upon fishes by boring into their bodies

Hag·ga·dah \hə-'gäd-ə, -'gōd-\ *n*, *pl* **Hag·ga·doth** \-'gäd-,ōt(h), -'gōd-\ [Heb *haggādhāh*] **1** : ancient Jewish lore forming esp. the nonlegal part of the Talmud **2** : the Jewish ritual for the Seder — **hag·ga·dic** \-'gad-ik, -'gäd-, -'gōd-\ *adj*, *often cap*

hag·ga·dist \hə-'gäd-əst, -'gōd-\ *n*, *often cap* **1** : a haggadic writer **2** : a student of the Haggadah — **hag·ga·dis·tic** \,hag-ə-'dis-tik\ *adj*, *often cap*

Hag·gai \'hag-ē-,ī, 'hag-,ī\ *n* [Heb *Haggai*] : a Hebrew prophet of the 6th century B.C.

1hag·gard \'hag-ərd\ *adj* [MF *hagard*] **1 a** *of a hawk* : not tamed **b** *obs* : WANTON, UNCHASTE **2 a** : wild in appearance **b** : having a worn or emaciated appearance : GAUNT — **hag·gard·ly** *adv* — **hag·gard·ness** *n*

2haggard *n* **1** : an adult hawk caught wild **2** *obs* : an intractable person; *esp* : a coy woman

hag·gis \'hag-əs\ *n* [ME *hagese*] : a pudding esp. popular in Scotland made of the heart, liver, and lungs of a sheep or a calf minced with suet, onions, oatmeal, and seasonings and boiled in the stomach of the animal

hag·gish \'hag-ish\ *adj* : resembling or characteristic of a hag

1hag·gle \'hag-əl\ *vb* **hag·gling** \-(ə-)liŋ\ [freq. of *hag* (to hew)] *vt* **1** : to cut roughly or clumsily : HACK **2** *archaic* : to annoy or exhaust with wrangling ~ *vi* : BARGAIN, WRANGLE — **hag·gler** \-(ə-)lər\ *n*

2haggle *n* : an act or instance of haggling

hagi- *or* **hagio-** *comb form* [LL, fr. Gk, fr. *hagios*] **1** : holy ⟨*hagio*scope⟩ **2** : saints ⟨*hagio*graphy⟩

Ha·gi·og·ra·pha \,hag-ē-'äg-rə-fə, ,hā-jē-\ *n pl but sing or pl in constr* [LL, fr. LGk, fr. *hagio-* + *graphein* to write — more at CARVE] : the third part of the Jewish scriptures — compare LAW, PROPHETS

ha·gi·og·ra·pher \-fər\ *n* : a writer of hagiography

ha·gio·graph·ic \,hag-ē-ə-'graf-ik, ,hā-jē-\ *adj* **1** : of or relating to Hagiographa **2** : of or relating to hagiography

ha·gi·og·ra·phy \,hag-ē-'äg-rə-fē, ,hā-jē-\ *n* **1** : biography of saints or venerated persons **2** : idealizing or idolizing biography

ha·gi·ol·a·try \-'äl-ə-trē\ *n* : the invocation or worship of saints

ha·gi·ol·o·gy \-'äl-ə-jē\ *n* **1** : literature dealing with venerated persons or writings **2** : a canon of saints

ha·gio·scope \'hag-ē-ə-,skōp, 'hā-jē-\ *n* : an opening in the interior walls of a cruciform church so placed as to afford a view of the altar to those in the transept — **ha·gio·scop·ic** \,hag-ē-ə-'skäp-ik, ,hā-jē-\ *adj*

hag·ride \'hag-,rīd\ *vt* : HARASS, TORMENT

hag·seed \-,sēd\ *n* : the offspring of a witch

hah *var of* HA

1ha-ha \(')hä-'hä\ *interj* [ME, fr. OE *ha ha*] — used to express amusement or derision

2ha-ha \'hä-,hä\ *n* [F *haha*] : SUNK FENCE

haik \'hīk\ *n* [Ar *ḥā'ik*] : a voluminous piece of usu. white cloth worn as an outer garment in northern Africa

hai·ku \'hī-(,)kü\ *n*, *pl* **haiku** [Jap] : an unrhymed Japanese poem of three lines containing 5, 7, and 5 syllables respectively and referring in some way to one of the seasons of the year

1hail \'hā(ə)l\ *n* [ME, fr. OE *hægl*; akin to OHG *hagal* hail, Gk *kachlēx* pebble] **1 a** : precipitation in the form of small balls or lumps usu. consisting of concentric layers of clear ice and compact snow **b** *archaic* : HAILSTORM **2** : something that gives the effect of falling hail

2hail *vi* **1** : to precipitate hail **2** : to pour down like hail ~ *vt* : to hurl or shower down forcibly ⟨~*ed* curses on him⟩

3hail *interj* [ME, fr. ON *heill*, fr. *heill* healthy — more at WHOLE] **1** — used to express acclamation **2** *archaic* — used as a salutation

4hail *vt* **1 a** : SALUTE, GREET **b** : to greet with enthusiastic approval : ACCLAIM **2** : to greet or summon by calling ~ *vi* : to call out; *esp* : to call a greeting to a passing ship — **hail·er** *n* — **hail from** : to come from

5hail *n* **1** : an exclamation of greeting or acclamation **2** : a calling to attract attention **3** : hailing distance

hail-fel·low \'hā(ə)l-,fel-(,)ō, -ə(-w)\ *or* **hail-fellow-well-met** \-,fel-ə-,wel-'met, -,fel-ō-\ *adj* [fr. the archaic salutations *hail, fellow!* & *hail, fellow! well met!*] : heartily informal : COMRADELY — **hail-fellow** *or* **hail-fellow-well-met** *n*

Hail Mary *n* : AVE MARIA

hail·stone \'hā(ə)l-,stōn\ *n* : a pellet of hail

hail·storm \-,stō(ə)rm\ *n* : a storm accompanied by hail

hair \'ha(ə)r, 'he(ə)r\ *n* [ME, fr. OE *hǣr*; akin to OHG *hār* hair] **1** : a slender threadlike outgrowth of the epidermis of an animal; *esp* : one of the usu. pigmented filaments that form the characteristic coat of a mammal **2 a** : the hairy covering of an animal or a body part; *esp* : the coating of hairs on a human head **b** : HAIRCLOTH **3 a** : a minute distance or amount : TRIFLE ⟨won by a ~⟩ **b** : a precise degree : NICETY ⟨aligned to a ~⟩ **4** *obs* : NATURE, CHARACTER **5** : a filamentous structure that resembles hair ⟨leaf ~⟩ — **haired** \'ha(ə)rd, 'he(ə)rd\ *adj*

1hair·breadth \'ha(ə)r-,bredth, 'he(ə)r-, -,bretth\ *or* **hairs·breadth** \'ha(ə)rz-, 'he(ə)rz-\ *n* : a very small distance or margin

2hairbreadth *adj* : very narrow : CLOSE

hair·brush \'ha(ə)r-,brəsh, 'he(ə)r-\ *n* : a brush for the hair

hair·cloth \-,klōth\ *n* : any of various stiff wiry fabrics esp. of horsehair or camel's hair used for upholstery or stiffening in garments

hair·cut \-,kət\ *n* : the act, process, or style of cutting and shaping the hair — **hair·cut·ter** \-,kət-ər\ *n* — **hair·cut·ting** \-,kət-iŋ\ *n*

hair·do \-(,)dü\ *n*, *pl* **hairdos** : a way of dressing a woman's hair

hair·dress·er \-,dres-ər\ *n* **1** : one who dresses or cuts women's hair **2** *Brit* : BARBER — **hair·dress·ing** \-,dres-iŋ\ *n*

hair·i·ness \'har-ē-nəs, 'her-\ *n* : the quality or state of being hairy

hair·less \'ha(ə)r-ləs, 'he(ə)r-\ *adj* : lacking hair — **hair·less·ness** *n*

hair·like \-,līk\ *adj* : resembling hair

hair·line \-,līn\ *n* **1** : a very slender line: as **a** : a tiny line or crack on a surface **b** : a fine line connecting thicker strokes in a printed letter **2 a** : a textile design consisting of lengthwise or crosswise lines usu. one thread wide **b** : a fabric with such a design **3** : the outline of the scalp or of the hair on the head — **hairline** *adj*

1hair·pin \-,pin\ *n* **1** : a pin to hold the hair in place; *specif* : a two-pronged U-shaped pin **2** : something shaped like a hairpin; *specif* : a sharp turn in a road

2hairpin *adj* : having the shape of a hairpin

hair-rais·er \'ha(ə)r-,rā-zər, 'he(ə)r-\ *n* : THRILLER

hair-rais·ing \-,rā-ziŋ\ *adj* : causing terror, excitement, or astonishment — **hair-rais·ing·ly** \-ziŋ-lē\ *adv*

hair seal *n* : an earless seal with a coarse hairy coat

hair shirt *n* : a shirt made of rough animal hair worn next to the skin as a penance

hair space *n* : a very thin space used in printing

hair·split·ter \'ha(ə)r-,split-ər, 'he(ə)r-\ *n* : one that makes excessively fine distinctions in reasoning : QUIBBLER — **hair·split·ting** *adj or n*

hair·spring \-,spriŋ\ *n* : a slender spiraled recoil spring that regulates the motion of the balance wheel of a timepiece

hair·streak \-,strēk\ *n* : any of various small butterflies (*Strymon* or a related genus) usu. having striped markings under the wings and thin filamentous projections from the hind wings

hair stroke *n* : a delicate stroke in writing or printing

hair trigger *n* : a gun trigger so adjusted as to permit the firearm to be fired by a very slight pressure

hair-trigger *adj* **1** : immediately responsive to the slightest stimulus **2** : delicately adjusted or easily disrupted

hair·worm \'ha(ə)r-,wərm, 'he(ə)r-\ *n* : any of various very slender elongated worms (as of the nematode genus *Capillaria*)

hairy \'ha(ə)r-ē, 'he(ə)r-\ *adj* **1 a** : covered with or as if with hair **b** : having a downy fuzz on the stems and leaves **2** : made of or resembling hair **3** *slang* : RUGGED, TRYING

hairy vetch *n* : a European vetch (*Vicia villosa*) extensively cultivated as a cover and early forage crop

Hai·tian \'hā-shən, 'hāt-ē-ən\ *n* : the French spoken by the great majority of the inhabitants of Haiti — called also *Haitian Creole*

hajj \'haj\ *n* [Ar *ḥajj*] : the pilgrimage to Mecca prescribed as a religious duty for Muslims

hajji \'haj-ē\ *n* [Ar *ḥajjī*, fr. *ḥajj*] : one who has made a pilgrimage to Mecca — often used as a title

hake \'hāk\ *n* [ME] : any of several marine food fishes (as of the genera *Merluccius* and *Urophycis*) that are related to the common Atlantic cod

ha·ken·kreuz \'häk-ən-,krȯits\ *n*, *often cap* [G, fr. *haken* hook + *kreuz* cross] : the swastika used as a symbol of German anti-Semitism or of Nazi Germany

1ha·kim \hə-'kēm\ *n* [Ar *ḥakīm*, lit., wise one] : a Muslim physician

2ha·kim \'häk-əm\ *n*, *pl* **hakim** *or* **hakims** [Ar *ḥākim*] : a Muslim ruler, governor, or judge

hal- *or* **halo-** *comb form* [F, fr. Gk, fr. *hals* — more at SALT] **1** : salt ⟨*halo*phyte⟩ **2** [ISV, fr. *halogen*] : halogen ⟨*hal*ide⟩

ha·la·kah \hä-'läk-ə, ,hä-lə-'kä\ *n*, *pl* **ha·la·koth** \hə-'läk-,ōt(h), ,hä-lə-'kōt(h)\ *or* **halakahs** *often cap* [Heb *hălākhāh*, lit., way] : the body of Jewish law supplementing the scriptural law and forming esp. the legal part of the Talmud — **ha·lak·ic** \hə-'lak-ik, -'läk-\ *adj*, *often cap*

ha·la·tion \hā-'lā-shən\ *n* [*halo* + *-ation*] **1** : the spreading of light beyond its proper boundaries in a developed photographic image **2** : a bright ring that sometimes surrounds a bright object on a television screen

hal·berd \'hal-bərd, 'hȯl-\ *or* **hal·bert** \-bərt\ *n* [ME *halberd*, fr. MF *hallebarde*] : a weapon esp. of the 15th and 16th centuries consisting typically of a battle-ax and pike mounted on a handle about six feet long — **hal·berd·ier** \,hal-bər-'di(ə)r, ,hȯl-\ *n*

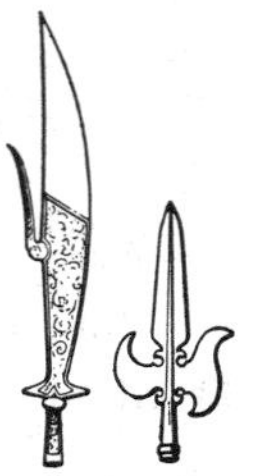
halberd heads

1hal·cy·on \'hal-sē-ən\ *n* [ME *alceon*, fr. L *halcyon*, fr. Gk *halkyōn*] **1** : a bird identified with the kingfisher and held in ancient legend to nest at sea about the time of the winter solstice and to calm the waves during incubation **2** : KINGFISHER

2halcyon *adj* **1** : of or relating to the halcyon or its nesting period **2 a** : CALM, PEACEFUL **b** : HAPPY, GOLDEN **c** : PROSPEROUS, AFFLUENT

1hale \'hā(ə)l\ *adj* [partly fr. ME (northern) *hale*, fr. OE *hāl*; partly fr. ME *hail*, fr. ON *heill* — more at WHOLE] : free from defect, disease, or infirmity : SOUND **syn** see HEALTHY

2hale *vt* [ME *halen*, fr. MF *haler* — more at HAUL] **1** : HAUL, PULL **2** : to compel to go

ha·ler \'häl-ər, -,e(ə)r\ *n*, *pl* **halers** *or* **ha·le·ru** \'häl-ə-,rü\ [Czech] — see *koruna* at MONEY table

1half \'haf, 'häf\ *n*, *pl* **halves** \'havz, 'hävz\ [ME, fr. OE *healf*; akin to L *scalpere* to cut, OE *sciell* shell] **1 a** : one of two equal parts into which a thing is divisible; *also* : a part of a thing approximately equal to the remainder **b** : half an hour — used in designation of time **2** : one of a pair: as **a** : PARTNER **b** : SEMESTER, TERM

c (1) : one of the two playing periods usu. separated by an interval that together make up the playing time of various games (2) : the turn of one team to bat in baseball 3 : HALF-DOLLAR 4 : HALFBACK — **by half** : by a great deal — **by halves** : in part : HALF-HEARTEDLY — **in half** : into two equal or nearly equal parts

²**half** *adj* **1 a** : being one of two equal parts ⟨a ~ share⟩ **b** (1) : amounting to nearly half (2) : PARTIAL, IMPERFECT ⟨~ measures⟩ **2** : extending or covering only half ⟨a ~ window⟩ — **half·ness** *n*

³**half** *adv* **1 a** : in an equal part or degree **b** : not completely : IMPERFECTLY ⟨~ persuaded⟩ **2** — used with a negative to imply the opposite of what is expressed ⟨her singing isn't ~ bad⟩

half–and–half \ˌhaf-ən-ˈhaf, ˌhȧf-ən-ˈhȧf\ *n* : something that is half one thing and half another; *specif* : a mixture of two malt beverages — **half–and–half** *adj* — **half–and–half** *adv*

half·back \ˈhaf-ˌbak, ˈhȧf-\ *n* **1** : one of the backs stationed near either flank in football **2** : a player stationed immediately behind the forward line (as in field hockey or soccer or rugby)

half–baked \-ˈbākt\ *adj* **1** : imperfectly baked : UNDERDONE **2 a** : not well planned **b** : lacking judgment, intelligence, or common sense

half binding *n* : a book binding in which one kind of material (as leather) covers the backbone, one quarter of the boards away from the backbone, and sometimes the corners while another kind of material covers the rest

half blood *n* **1 a** : the relation between persons having one parent but not both in common **b** : a person so related to another **2** : HALF-BREED **3** : GRADE 4

half–blood·ed \ˈhaf-ˈbləd-əd, ˈhȧf-\ *adj* : having half blood or being a half blood

half boot *n* : a boot with a top reaching above the ankle

half–bound \ˈhaf-ˈbau̇nd, ˈhȧf-\ *adj* : having a half binding

half–bred \-ˌbred\ *adj* : having one purebred parent — **half–bred** *n*

half–breed \-ˌbrēd\ *n* : the offspring of parents of different races; *esp* : the offspring of an American Indian and a white person — **half–breed** *adj*

half brother *n* : a brother by one parent only

half–caste \ˈhaf-ˌkast, ˈhȧf-\ *n* : one of mixed racial descent : HALF-BREED — **half–caste** *adj*

half–cell \-ˌsel\ *n* : a device consisting of a single electrode immersed in an electrolytic solution and thus developing a definite potential difference

half cock *n* **1** : the position of the hammer of a firearm when about half retracted and held by the sear so that it cannot be operated by a pull on the trigger **2** : a state of inadequate preparation or mental confusion

half–cocked \ˈhaf-ˈkäkt, ˈhȧf-\ *adj* **1** : being at half cock **2** : lacking adequate preparation or forethought

half crown *n* : a British coin worth 2*s* 6*d*

half dime *n* : a silver five-cent coin struck by the U.S. mint in 1792 and from 1794 to 1873

half–dol·lar \ˈhaf-ˈdäl-ər, ˈhȧf-\ *n* **1** : a coin representing one half of a dollar **2** : the sum of fifty cents

half eagle *n* : a five-dollar gold piece issued by the U.S. 1795–1916 and in 1929

half–ev·er·green \ˈhaf-ˈev-ər-ˌgrēn, ˈhȧf-\ *adj* **1** : having functional and persistent foliage during part of the winter or dry season **2** : tending to be evergreen in a mild climate but deciduous in a rigorous climate

half gainer *n* : a gainer in which the diver executes a half-backward somersault and enters the water headfirst and facing the board

half·heart·ed \ˈhaf-ˈhärt-əd, ˈhȧf-\ *adj* : lacking spirit or interest — **half·heart·ed·ly** *adv* — **half·heart·ed·ness** *n*

half hitch *n* : a simple knot so made as to be easily unfastened

half hour *n* **1** : thirty minutes **2** : the middle point of an hour — **half–hour·ly** \ˈhaf-ˈau̇(ə)r-lē, ˈhȧf-\ *adv* (*or adj*)

half–knot \ˈhaf-ˌnät, ˈhȧf-\ *n* : a knot joining the ends of two cords and used in tying other knots

half–length \ˈhaf-ˈleŋ(k)th, ˈhȧf-\ *n* : something (as a portrait) that is or represents only half the complete length

half–life \ˈhaf-ˌlīf, ˈhȧf-\ *n* : the time required for half of the atoms of a radioactive substance present to become disintegrated

half–light \-ˌlīt\ *n* : grayish light (as of dim interiors or evening)

half line *n* : a straight line extending from a point in one direction only

half–long \-ˈlȯŋ\ *adj, of a speech sound* : intermediate in duration between long and short

¹**half–mast** \-ˈmast\ *n* : a point some distance but not necessarily halfway down below the top of a mast or staff or the peak of a gaff

²**half–mast** *vt* : to cause to hang at half-mast

half–moon \-ˌmün\ *n* **1** : the moon when half its disk appears illuminated **2** : something shaped like a crescent **3** : LUNULE

half nelson *n* : a wrestling hold in which one arm is thrust under the corresponding arm of the opponent generally from behind and the hand placed upon the back of his neck

half note *n* : a musical note of half the value of a whole note

half·pen·ny \ˈhāp-(ə-)nē, *US also* ˈhaf-ˌpen-ē, ˈhȧf-\ *n, pl* **half·pence** \ˈhā-pən(t)s, ˈhāp-ᵊm(p)s, *US also* ˈhaf-ˌpen(t)s, ˈhȧf-\ *or* **halfpennies** **1** : a British coin representing one half of a penny **2** : the sum of half a penny **3** : a small amount — **halfpenny** *adj*

half–pint \ˈhaf-ˌpīnt, ˈhȧf-\ *adj, slang* : of less than average size : DIMINUTIVE — **half–pint** *n, slang*

half sister *n* : a sister by one parent only

half–slip \ˈhaf-ˌslip, ˈhȧf-\ *n* : PETTICOAT 1c

half sole *n* : a shoe sole extending from the shank forward

half–sole \ˈhaf-ˈsōl, ˈhȧf-\ *vt* : to put half soles on

half sovereign *n* : a British gold coin worth ten shillings

half–staff \ˈhaf-ˈstaf, ˈhȧf-\ *n* : HALF-MAST

half step *n* **1** : a walking step of 15 inches or in double time of 18 inches **2** : the pitch interval between any two adjacent keys on a keyboard instrument — called also *semitone*

half tide *n* : the time or state halfway between flood and ebb

half tim·ber \ˈhaf-ˈtim-bər, ˈhȧf-\ *or* **half–tim·bered** \-bərd\ *adj, of a building* : constructed of wood framing with spaces filled with masonry — **half–tim·ber·ing** \-b(ə-)riŋ\ *n*

half time *n* : an intermission marking the completion of half of a game or contest (as in football or basketball)

half title *n* : the title of a book standing alone on a usu. right-hand page immediately preceding the first page of text or at the head of the first page of text

half·tone \ˈhaf-ˌtōn, ˈhȧf-\ *n* **1** : HALF STEP 2 **2 a** : any of the shades of gray between the darkest and the lightest parts of a photographic image **b** : a photoengraving made from an image photographed through a screen having a lattice of horizontal and vertical lines and then etched so that the details of the image are reproduced in dots — **halftone** *adj*

half–track \-ˌtrak\ *n* **1** : an endless chain-track drive system that propels a vehicle supported in front by a pair of wheels **2** : a motor vehicle propelled by half-tracks; *specif* : one lightly armored for military use — **half–track** *or* **half–tracked** \-ˌtrakt\ *adj*

half–truth \-ˌtrüth\ *n* **1** : a statement that is only partially true **2** : a statement that mingles truth and falsehood with deliberate intent to deceive

half volley *n* : a stroke of a ball at the instant it rebounds from the ground

half–vol·ley \-ˈväl-ē\ *vb* : to hit with a half volley

half·way \ˈhaf-ˈwā, ˈhȧf-\ *adj* **1** : midway between two points **2** : PARTIAL — **halfway** *adv*

half–wit \-ˌwit\ *n* : a foolish or imbecilic person — **half–wit·ted** \-ˈwit-əd\ *adj*

half–world \-ˌwərld\ *n* : DEMIMONDE

hal·i·but \ˈhal-ə-bət, ˈhäl-\ *n, pl* **halibut** *also* **halibuts** [ME *halybutte*, fr. *haly, holy* holy + *butte* flatfish, fr. MD or MLG *but*; fr. its being eaten on holy days] : a marine food fish that is the largest flatfish and one of the largest teleost fishes, attains a weight of several hundred pounds in the female, and is now usu. held to form an Atlantic species (*Hippoglossus hippoglossus*) and a Pacific (*H. stenolepis*)

ha·lide \ˈhal-ˌīd, ˈhā-ˌlīd\ *n* : a binary compound of a halogen with a more electropositive element or radical

hal·i·dom \ˈhal-əd-əm\ *or* **hal·i·dome** \-ə-ˌdōm\ *n* [ME, fr. OE *hāligdōm*, fr. *hālig*] *archaic* : something held sacred

ha·lite \ˈhal-ˌīt, ˈhā-ˌlīt\ *n* : native salt

hal·i·to·sis \ˌhal-ə-ˈtō-səs\ *n* [NL, fr. L *halitus* breath, fr. *halare* to breathe — more at EXHALE] : a condition of having fetid breath

hall \ˈhȯl\ *n* [ME *halle*, fr. OE *heall*; akin to L *cella* small room, *celare* to conceal — more at HELL] **1 a** : the castle or house of a medieval king or noble **b** : the chief living room in such a structure **2** : the manor house of a landed proprietor **3** : a large usu. imposing building used for public or semipublic purposes **4 a** : a building used by a college or university for some special purpose **b** : a college or a division of a college at some universities **c** (1) : the common dining room of an English college (2) : a meal served there **5 a** : the entrance room of a building : LOBBY **b** : a corridor or passage in a building **6** : a large room for assembly : AUDITORIUM **7** : a place used for public entertainment

Hal·lel \hä-ˈlā(ə)l\ *n* [Heb *hallēl* praise] : a selection comprising Psalms 113–118 chanted during the Passover and other Jewish feasts

¹**hal·le·lu·jah** \ˌhal-ə-ˈlü-yə\ *interj* [Heb *halălūyāh* praise (ye) the Lord] — used to express praise, joy, or thanks

²**hallelujah** *n* : a shout or song of praise or thanksgiving

¹**hall·mark** \ˈhȯl-ˌmärk\ *n* [Goldsmiths' *Hall*, London, England, where gold and silver articles were assayed and stamped] **1 a** : an official mark stamped on gold and silver articles in England to attest their purity **b** : a mark or device placed or stamped upon an article of trade to indicate origin, purity, or genuineness **2** : a distinguishing characteristic, trait, or feature

²**hallmark** *vt* : to stamp with a hallmark

hal·lo \hə-ˈlō, ha-\ *or* **hal·loo** \-ˈlü\ *var of* HOLLO

hal·low \ˈhal-(ˌ)ō, -ə(-w)\ *vt* [ME *halowen*, fr. OE *hālgian*, fr. *hālig* holy — more at HOLY] **1** : to make holy or set apart for holy use **2** : to respect greatly : VENERATE **syn** see DEVOTE

hal·lowed \ˈhal-(ˌ)ōd, ˈhal-əd, *in the Lord's Prayer also* ˈhal-ə-wəd\ *adj* : CONSECRATED, SACRED

Hal·low·een \ˌhal-ə-ˈwēn, ˌhäl-\ *n* [short for *All Hallow Even*] : October 31 observed with merrymaking and the playing of pranks by children during the evening

Hal·low·mas \ˈhal-ō-ˌmas, ˈhal-ə-, -məs\ *n* [short for ME *Alholowmesse*, fr. OE *ealra halgena mæsse*, lit., all saints' mass] : ALL SAINTS' DAY

Hall·statt *or* **Hall·stadt** \ˈhȯl-ˌstat, ˈhäl-ˌs(h)tät\ *adj* [*Hallstatt*, Austria] : of or relating to the earlier period of the Iron Age in Europe

hal·lu·ci·nate \hə-ˈlüs-ᵊn-ˌāt\ *vb* [L *hallucinatus*, pp. of *hallucinari* to prate, dream] *vt* : to affect with visions or imaginary perceptions ~ *vi* : to have hallucinations

hal·lu·ci·na·tion \hə-ˌlüs-ᵊn-ˈā-shən\ *n* **1** : perception of objects with no reality usu. arising from disorder of the nervous system **2** : the object of a hallucinatory perception **syn** see DELUSION — **hal·lu·ci·na·tion·al** \-shnəl, -shən-ᵊl\ *adj* — **hal·lu·ci·na·tive** \-ˈlüs-ᵊn-ˌāt-iv\ *adj*

hal·lu·ci·na·to·ry \hə-ˈlüs-ᵊn-ə-ˌtōr-ē, -ˈlüs-nə-, -ˌtȯr-\ *adj* : partaking of or tending to produce hallucination ⟨~ dreams⟩

hal·lu·ci·no·gen \hə-ˈlüs-ᵊn-ə-jən\ *n* [*hallucination* + *-o-* + *-gen*] : a substance that induces hallucinations — **hal·lu·ci·no·gen·ic** \-ˌlüs-ᵊn-ə-ˈjen-ik\ *adj*

hal·lu·ci·no·sis \hə-ˌlüs-ᵊn-ˈō-səs\ *n* : a pathological mental state characterized by hallucinations

hal·lux \ˈhal-əks\ *n, pl* **hal·lu·ces** \ˈhal-(y)ə-ˌsēz\ [NL, fr. L *hallus, hallux*] : the first or preaxial digit of the hind limb

hall·way \ˈhȯl-ˌwā\ *n* **1** : an entrance hall **2** : CORRIDOR

¹**ha·lo** \ˈhā-(ˌ)lō\ *n, pl* **halos** *or* **haloes** [L *halos*, fr. Gk *halōs* threshing floor, disk, halo] **1** : a circle of light appearing to surround the sun or moon and resulting from refraction or reflection of light by ice particles in the atmosphere **2** : something resembling a halo: as **a** : NIMBUS **b** : a differentiated zone surrounding a central object **3** : the aura of glory, veneration, or sentiment surrounding an idealized person or thing

²**halo** *vt* : to form into or surround with a halo

halo- — see HAL-

halo·bi·ont \ˌhal-ō-ˈbī-ˌänt\ *n* [*hal-* + Gk *biount-, biōn*, prp. of *bioun* to live, fr. *bios* life — more at QUICK] : an organism that flourishes in a saline habitat

halo·gen \'hal-ə-jən\ *n* [Sw] **:** any of the five elements fluorine, chlorine, bromine, iodine, and astatine forming part of group VII A of the periodic table and existing in the free state normally as diatomic molecules — **ha·log·e·nous** \ha-'läj-ə-nəs\ *adj*

ha·lo·ge·nate \'hal-ə-jə-,nāt, ha-'läj-ə-\ *vt* **:** to treat or cause to combine with a halogen — **ha·lo·ge·na·tion** \,hal-ə-jə-'nā-shən, ha-,läj-ə-\ *n*

hal·o·ge·ton \,hal-ō-'jē-,tän\ *n* [NL, genus name, fr. *hal-* + Gk *geitōn* neighbor] **:** a coarse annual herb (*Halogeton glomeratus*) of the goosefoot family that is a noxious weed in western American ranges

halo·mor·phic \,hal-ə-'mȯr-fik\ *adj, of a soil* **:** developed in the presence of neutral or alkali salts or both — **halo·mor·phism** \-,fiz-əm\ *n*

halo·phile \'hal-ə-,fīl\ *n* [ISV] **:** an organism that flourishes in a salty environment — **halo·phil·ic** \,hal-ə-'fil-ik\ *or* **ha·loph·i·lous** \ha-'läf-ə-ləs\ *adj*

halo·phyte \'hal-ə-,fīt\ *n* [ISV] **:** a plant that grows in salty soil and usu. resembles a true xerophyte — **halo·phyt·ic** \,hal-ə-'fit-ik\ *adj*

[1]**halt** \'hȯlt\ *adj* [ME, fr. OE *healt;* akin to OHG *halz* lame, L *clades* destruction, Gk *klan* to break] **:** LAME

[2]**halt** *vi* **1 :** to walk or proceed lamely **:** LIMP **2 :** to stand in perplexity or doubt between alternate courses **:** WAVER **3 :** to display weakness or imperfection **:** FALTER

[3]**halt** *n* [G, fr. MHG, fr. *halt,* imper. of *halten* to hold, fr. OHG *haltan* — more at HOLD] **:** STOP

[4]**halt** *vi* **1 :** to cease marching or journeying **2 :** DISCONTINUE, TERMINATE ~ *vt* **1 :** to bring to a stop **2 :** to cause the discontinuance of **:** END

[1]**hal·ter** \'hȯl-tər\ *n* [ME, fr. OE *hælftre;* akin to OHG *halftra* halter, OE *hielfe* helve] **1 a :** a rope or strap for leading or tying an animal **b :** a headstall usu. with noseband and throatlatch to which a lead may be attached **2 :** a rope for hanging criminals **:** NOOSE; *also* **:** death by hanging **3 :** a woman's blouse typically held in place by straps around the neck and across the back and leaving the back, arms, and midriff bare

[2]**halter** *vt* **hal·ter·ing** \-t(ə-)riŋ\ **1 a :** to catch with or as if with a halter; *also* **:** to put a halter on **b :** HANG **2 :** to put restraint upon **:** HAMPER

[3]**hal·ter** \'hȯl-tər, 'hal-\ *or* **hal·tere** \-,ti(ə)r\ *n, pl* **hal·teres** \hȯl-'ti(ə)r-(,)ēz, hal-; 'hȯl-,ti(ə)rz, 'hal-\ [NL, fr. L, jumping weight, fr. Gk *haltēr,* fr. *hallesthai* to leap — more at SALLY] **:** one of a pair of club-shaped organs in a dipterous insect that are the modified second pair of wings and function as sensory flight instruments

hal·ter·break \'hȯl-tər-,brāk\ *vt* **:** to break (as a colt) to halter

halt·ing *adj* **:** LAME, LIMPING — **halt·ing·ly** \'hȯl-tiŋ-lē\ *adv*

halve \'hav, 'hȧv\ *vt* [ME *halven,* fr. *half*] **1 a :** to divide into two equal parts **b :** to reduce to one half ⟨*halving* the cost⟩ **c :** to share equally **2 :** to play (as a hole) in the same number of strokes as one's opponent at golf

halv·ers \'hav-ərz, 'hȧv-\ *n pl* **:** half shares **:** HALVES

halves *pl of* HALF

hal·yard *or* **hal·liard** \'hal-yərd\ *n* [ME *halier,* fr. *halen* to pull — more at HALE] **:** a rope or tackle for hoisting and lowering

[1]**ham** \'ham\ *n* [ME *hamme,* fr. OE *hamm;* akin to OHG *hamma* ham, Gk *knēmē* shinbone] **1 a :** the hollow of the knee **b :** a buttock with its associated thigh — usu. used in pl. **2 :** a cut of meat consisting of a thigh; *esp* **:** one from a hog **3** [short for *hamfatter,* fr. "The *Ham-fat* Man," Negro minstrel song] **a :** an unskillful but showy performer; *esp* **:** an inept actor esp. in a highly theatrical style **b :** an operator of an amateur radio station — **ham** *adj*

[2]**ham** *vb* **hammed; ham·ming** *vt* **:** to execute with exaggerated speech or gestures **:** OVERACT ~ *vi* **:** to overplay a part

Ham \'ham\ *n* **:** the youngest son of Noah

hama·dry·ad \,ham-ə-'drī-əd, -,ad\ *n* [L *hamadryad-, hamadryas,* fr. Gk, fr. *hama* together with + *dryad-, dryas* dryad] **1 :** WOOD NYMPH 1 **2 a :** a large venomous elapid snake (*Naja hannah*) of southeastern Asia and the Philippines — called also *king cobra* **b :** a baboon (*Papio hamadryas*) venerated by the ancient Egyptians — called also *sacred baboon*

ha·mal *also* **ham·mal** \hə-'mäl\ *n* [Ar *ḥammāl* porter] **:** a porter in Turkey and other eastern countries

Ha·man \'hā-mən\ *n* [Heb *Hāmān*] **:** an enemy of the Jews hanged according to the book of Esther for plotting their destruction

ha·mate \'hā-,māt\ *also* **ha·mat·ed** \-,māt-əd\ *adj* [L *hamatus,* fr. *hamus* hook] **:** shaped like a hook

ha·ma·tum \hə-'māt-əm, -'mät-\ *n, pl* **ha·ma·ta** \-ə\ [NL, fr. L, neut. of *hamatus*] **:** a bone on the inner side of the second row of the carpus in mammals

Ham·burg \'ham-,bərg\ *n* [*Hamburg,* Germany] **:** any of a European breed of rather small domestic fowls with rose combs and lead-blue legs

ham·burg·er \'ham-,bər-gər\ *or* **ham·burg** \-,bərg\ *n* **1 a :** ground beef **b :** a cooked patty of ground beef **2 :** a sandwich consisting of a patty of hamburger in a split round bun

[1]**hame** \'hām\ *n* [ME] **:** one of two curved projections which are attached to the collar of a draft horse and to which the traces are fastened

[2]**hame** *Scot var of* HOME

ham–fist·ed \'ham-'fis-təd\ *adj, chiefly Brit* **:** HAM-HANDED

ham–hand·ed \-'han-dəd\ *adj* **:** CLUMSY, HEAVY-HANDED

Ham·il·to·nian \,ham-əl-'tō-nē-ən, -nyən\ *adj* **:** of or relating to Alexander Hamilton or to Hamiltonianism — **Hamiltonian** *n*

Ham·il·to·nian·ism \-,iz-əm\ *n* **:** the political principles and ideas held by or associated with Alexander Hamilton and centering around a belief in a strong unitary central government, broad interpretation of the federal constitution, encouragement of an industrial and commercial economy, and a general distrust of the political capacity or wisdom of the common man

Ham·ite \'ham-,īt\ *n* [*Ham*] **:** a member of a group of chiefly northern African peoples that are mostly Muslims and are highly variable in appearance but mainly Caucasoid

[1]**Ham·it·ic** \ha-'mit-ik, hə-\ *adj* **:** of, relating to, or characteristic of the Hamites or one of the Hamitic languages

[2]**Hamitic** *n* **:** HAMITIC LANGUAGES

Hamitic languages *n pl* **:** the Berber, Cushitic, and sometimes Egyptian branches of the Afro-Asiatic languages

Ham·i·to–Se·mit·ic \,ham-ə-(,)tō-sə-'mit-ik\ *adj* **:** of, relating to, or constituting the Afro-Asiatic languages — **Hamito–Semitic** *n*

Hamito–Semitic languages *n pl* **:** AFRO-ASIATIC LANGUAGES

ham·let \'ham-lət\ *n* [ME, fr. MF *hamelet,* dim. of *ham,* of Gmc origin; akin to OE *hām* village, home] **:** a small village

Ham·let \'ham-lət\ *n* **:** a legendary prince of Denmark and hero of Shakespeare's tragedy *Hamlet*

[1]**ham·mer** \'ham-ər\ *n* [ME *hamer,* fr. OE *hamor;* akin to OHG *hamar* hammer, Gk *akmē* point, edge — more at EDGE] **1 a :** a hand tool consisting of a solid head set crosswise on a handle and used for pounding **b :** a power tool that often substitutes a metal block or a drill for the hammerhead **2 :** something that resembles a hammer in form or action: as **a :** a lever with a striking head for ringing a bell or striking a gong **b** (1) **:** an arm that strikes the cap in a percussion lock to ignite the propelling charge (2) **:** a part of the action of a modern gun that strikes the primer of the cartridge in firing or that strikes the firing pin to ignite the cartridge **c :** MALLEUS **d :** GAVEL **e** (1) **:** a padded mallet in a piano action for striking a string (2) **:** a hand mallet for playing on various percussion instruments (as a xylophone) **3 :** a metal sphere hurled in the hammer throw that usu. weighs 16 pounds — **under the hammer :** for sale at auction

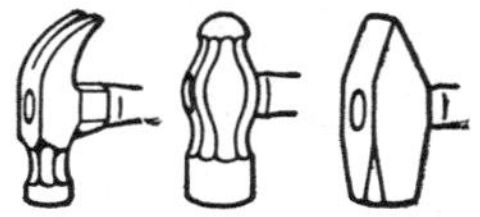
hammers

[2]**hammer** *vb* **ham·mer·ing** \'ham-(ə-)riŋ\ *vi* **1 :** to strike blows esp. repeatedly with or as if with a hammer **:** POUND **2 a :** to make repeated efforts **b :** to reiterate an opinion or attitude ~ *vt* **1 a :** to beat, drive, or shape with repeated blows of a hammer **b :** to fasten or build with a hammer **2 :** to strike or drive as if with a hammer **3 :** to produce or bring about as if by repeated blows ⟨~ out a policy⟩ — **ham·mer·er** \'ham-ər-ər\ *n*

hammer and sickle *n* **:** an emblem consisting of a crossed hammer and sickle used chiefly as a symbol of Russian Communism

hammer and tongs *adv* **:** with great force and violence

ham·mered *adj* **:** having surface indentations produced or appearing to have been produced by hammering ⟨~ copper⟩

ham·mer·head \'ham-ər-,hed\ *n* **1 :** the striking part of a hammer **2 :** BLOCKHEAD **3 :** something that resembles the striking part of a hammer; *specif* **:** any of various active voracious medium-sized sharks that have the eyes at the ends of lateral extensions of the flattened head and that with the shovelheads constitute a family (Sphyrnidae)

ham·mer·less \-ləs\ *adj* **:** having the hammer concealed ⟨~ gun⟩

ham·mer·lock \-,läk\ *n* **:** a wrestling hold in which an opponent's arm is held bent behind his back

ham·mer·toe \,ham-ər-'tō\ *n* **:** a toe (as the second) deformed by permanent angular flexion

[1]**ham·mock** \'ham-ək\ *n* [Sp *hamaca,* fr. Taino] **:** a swinging couch or bed usu. made of netting or canvas and slung by cords from supports at each end

[2]**hammock** *n* [origin unknown] **1 :** HUMMOCK **2 :** a fertile area in the southern U.S. and esp. Florida usu. higher than its surroundings and characterized by hardwood vegetation and deep humus-rich soil

ham·my \'ham-ē\ *adj* **:** characteristic of a ham actor

[1]**ham·per** \'ham-pər\ *vt* **ham·per·ing** \-p(ə-)riŋ\ [ME *hamperen*] **1 a :** to restrict the movement of by bonds or obstacles **:** IMPEDE **b :** to interfere with the operation of **:** DISRUPT **2 a :** CURB, RESTRAIN **b :** to interfere with **:** ENCUMBER

syn TRAMMEL, CLOG, FETTER, SHACKLE, MANACLE: HAMPER may imply the effect of any impeding or restraining influence; TRAMMEL suggests entangling by or confining within a net; CLOG usu. implies the slowing by something extraneous that clings, weighs down, obstructs, or gums up; FETTER suggest a restraining so severe that freedom to move or progress is almost lost; SHACKLE and MANACLE are similar to but stronger than FETTER and suggest total loss of freedom

[2]**hamper** *n* **1 :** something that impedes**:** OBSTRUCTION **2 :** TOP-HAMPER

[3]**hamper** *n* [ME *hampere,* alter. of *hanaper,* lit., case to hold goblets, fr. MF *hanapier,* fr. *hanap* goblet, of Gmc origin; akin to OE *hnæpp* bowl] **:** a large basket usu. with a cover for packing, storing, or transporting food and other articles

[1]**Hamp·shire** \'ham(p)-,shi(ə)r, -shər\ *n* [*Hampshire,* England] **:** any of an American breed of black white-belted swine with white forelegs, rather long head, and straight face

[2]**Hampshire** *n* **:** any of a British breed of medium-wooled mutton-type sheep that are large, thick-fleshed, and hornless — called also *Hampshire Down*

ham·ster \'ham(p)-stər\ *n* [G, fr. OHG *hamustro,* of Slavic origin; akin to OSlav *chomĕstorŭ* hamster] **:** any of numerous Old World rodents (*Cricetus* or a related genus) having very large cheek pouches

[1]**ham·string** \'ham-,striŋ\ *n* **1 :** either of two groups of tendons at the back of the human knee **2 :** a large tendon above and behind the hock of a quadruped

[2]**hamstring** *vt* **1 :** to cripple by cutting the leg tendons **2 :** to make ineffective or powerless **:** CRIPPLE

ham·u·lus \'ham-yə-ləs\ *n, pl* **ham·u·li** \-,lī, -,lē\ [NL, fr. L, dim. of *hamus* hook] **:** a hook or hooked process

ham·za *or* **ham·zah** \'ham-zə\ *n* [Ar *hamzah,* lit., compression] **:** the sign for a glottal stop in Arabic orthography usu. represented in English by an apostrophe

Han \'hän\ *n* **1 :** a Chinese dynasty dated 207B.C.–A.D.220 and marked by centralized control through an appointive bureaucracy, a revival of learning, and the penetration of Buddhism **2 :** the orthodox Chinese peoples esp. as distinguished from Mongol, Manchu, or other non-Chinese elements in the population **:** the Chinese race

hance \'han(t)s\ *n* [obs. E *hance* (lintel)] **1 :** a curved contour on a ship **2 a :** the arc of minimum radius at the springing of an elliptical or similar arch **b :** the haunch of an arch

[1]**hand** \'hand\ *n, often attrib* [ME, fr. OE; akin to OHG *hant* hand] **1 a** (1) **:** the terminal part of the vertebrate forelimb when modified (as in man) as a grasping organ (2) **:** the segment of the forelimb of a vertebrate above the fishes that corresponds to the hand (as the pinion of a bird) irrespective of its form or functional specialization **b :** a part serving the function of or resembling a hand: as (1) **:** the hind foot of an ape (2) **:** the chela of a crustacean **c :** something resembling a hand: as (1) **:** an indicator or pointer on a dial (2)

: a stylized figure of a hand with forefinger extended to point a direction or call attention to something; *specif* : INDEX 6 (3) : a cluster of bananas developed from a single flower group (4) : a bunch of large leaves tied together usu. with another leaf **2 a** : personal possession — usu. used in pl. **b** : CONTROL, DIRECTION **3 a** : SIDE, DIRECTION **b** : a side or aspect of an issue or argument **4** : a pledge esp. of betrothal or bestowal in marriage **5 a** : style of penmanship : HANDWRITING **b** : SIGNATURE **6 a** : SKILL, ABILITY **b** : an instrumental part ⟨had a ~ in the crime⟩ **7** : SOURCE ⟨at first ~⟩ **8** : a unit of measure equal to 4 inches used esp. for the height of horses **9 a** : assistance or aid esp. involving physical effort ⟨lend a ~⟩ **b** : PARTICIPATION, INTEREST **c** : a round of applause **10 a** (1) : a player in a card game or board game (2) : the cards or pieces held by a player **b** : a single round in a game **11 a** : one who performs or executes a particular work ⟨two portraits by the same ~⟩ **b** (1) : one employed at manual labor or general tasks ⟨a ranch ~⟩ (2) : WORKER, EMPLOYEE **c** : a member of a ship's crew ⟨all ~*s* on deck⟩ **d** : one skilled in a particular activity or field **12 a** : HANDIWORK **b** : style of execution : WORKMANSHIP ⟨the ~ of a master⟩ **c** : TOUCH, FEEL — **at hand** : near in time or place — **at the hands of** *or* **at the hand of** : by the act or instrumentality of — **by hand** : with the hands — **in hand 1 a** : in one's possession or control **b** : at one's disposal **2** : in preparation — **off one's hands** : out of one's care or charge — **on all hands** *or* **on every hand** : EVERYWHERE — **on hand 1** : in present possession **2** : about to appear : PENDING **3** : in attendance : PRESENT — **on one's hands** : in one's possession, care, or management — **out of hand 1** : without delay : FORTHWITH **2** : done with **3** : out of control — **to hand 1** : into possession **2** : within reach **3** : into control or subjection

2hand *vt* **1 a** *obs* : to manage with the hands : MANIPULATE; *also* : to lay hands on **b** : FURL **2** : to lead, guide, or assist with the hand ⟨~ a lady into a bus⟩ **3 a** : to give, pass, or transmit with the hand ⟨~ a letter to her⟩ **b** : PRESENT, PROVIDE ⟨~*ed* him a surprise⟩

hand and foot *adv* : TOTALLY, COMPLETELY

hand·bag \ˈhan(d)-ˌbag\ *n* **1** : TRAVELING BAG **2** : a woman's bag held in the hand or looped over the shoulder and used for carrying small personal articles and money

hand·ball \-ˌbȯl\ *n* **1** : a small rubber ball used in the game of handball **2** : a game played in a walled court or against a single wall or board by two or four players who use their hands to strike the ball

hand·bar·row \-ˌbar-(ˌ)ō, -ə(-w)\ *n* : a flat rectangular frame with handles at both ends that is carried by two persons

hand·bill \-ˌbil\ *n* : a small printed sheet to be distributed by hand

hand·book \-ˌbu̇k\ *n* **1 a** : a book capable of being conveniently carried as a ready reference : MANUAL **b** : a concise reference book covering a particular subject **2 a** : a bookmaker's book of bets **b** : a place where bookmaking is carried on

hand·breadth \-ˌbredth, -ˌbretth\ *n* : any of various units of length varying from about 2½ to 4 inches based on the breadth of a hand

hand·car \ˈhan(d)-ˌkär\ *n* : a small four-wheeled railroad car propelled by a hand-operated mechanism or by a small motor

hand·cart \-ˌkärt\ *n* : a cart drawn or pushed by hand

hand·clasp \-ˌklasp\ *n* : HANDSHAKE

1hand·craft \-ˌkraft\ *n* : HANDICRAFT

2handcraft *vt* : to fashion by handicraft

1hand·cuff \-ˌkəf\ *vt* : to apply handcuffs to : MANACLE

2handcuff *n* : a metal fastening that can be locked around a wrist and is usu. connected by a chain or bar with another such fastening — usu. used in pl.

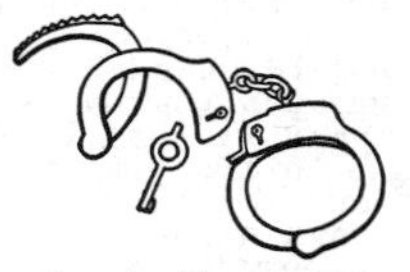

handcuffs, open and closed

hand down *vt* **1** : to transmit in succession **2** : to make official formulation of and express (the opinion of a court)

hand·ed \ˈhan-dəd\ *adj* **1** : having hands **2** : having or using such or so many hands ⟨a right-*handed* person⟩

hand·ed·ness \-nəs\ *n* : a tendency to use one hand rather than the other

hand·fast \ˈhan(d)-ˌfast\ *n, archaic* : a contract or covenant esp. of betrothal or marriage

hand·ful \ˈhan(d)-ˌfu̇l\ *n, pl* **handfuls** \-ˌfu̇lz\ *or* **hands·ful** \ˈhan(d)z-ˌfu̇l\ **1** : as much or as many as the hand will grasp **2** : a small quantity or number **3** : as much as one can manage

hand glass *n* : a small mirror with a handle

hand·grip \ˈhan(d)-ˌgrip\ *n* **1** : a grasping with the hand **2** : HANDLE **3** *pl* : hand-to-hand combat

hand·gun \-ˌgən\ *n* : a firearm held and fired with one hand

hand·hold \ˈhand-ˌhōld\ *n* **1** : HOLD, GRIP **2** : something to hold on to

1hand·i·cap \ˈhan-di-ˌkap\ *n* [obs. E *handicap* (a game in which forfeits were held in a cap), fr. *hand in cap*] **1** : a race or contest in which an artificial advantage is given or disadvantage imposed on a contestant to equalize chances of winning; *also* : the advantage given or disadvantage imposed **2** : a disadvantage that makes achievement unusually difficult

2handicap *vt* **hand·i·capped; hand·i·cap·ping 1 a** : to give a handicap to **b** : to assign handicaps to **2** : to put at a disadvantage

hand·i·cap·per \-ˌkap-ər\ *n* : one who predicts the winners in a horse race usu. for publication

hand·i·craft \ˈhan-di-ˌkraft\ *n* [ME *handi-crafte*, alter. of *handcraft*] **1 a** : manual skill **b** : an occupation requiring skill with the hands **2** : the articles fashioned by those engaged in handicraft **3** *archaic* : HANDICRAFTSMAN — **hand·i·craft·er** \-ˌkraf-tər\ *n* — **hand·i·crafts·man** \-ˌkraf(t)-smən\ *n*

Hand·ie–Talk·ie \ˌhan-dē-ˈtȯ-kē\ *trademark* — used for a small portable radio transmitter-receiver

hand·i·ly \ˈhan-də-lē\ *adv* : in a handy manner

hand·i·ness \-dē-nəs\ *n* : the quality or state of being handy

hand in glove *or* **hand and glove** *adv* : in extremely close relationship or agreement

hand in hand *adv* : in union : CONJOINTLY

hand·i·work \ˈhan-di-ˌwərk\ *n* [ME *handiwerk*, fr. OE *handgeweorc*, fr. *hand* + *geweorc*, fr. *ge-* (collective prefix) + *weorc* work] **1** : work done by the hands **2** : work done personally

hand·ker·chief \ˈhaŋ-kər-chəf, -(ˌ)chif, -ˌchēf\ *n, pl* **handkerchiefs** *also* **hand·ker·chieves** \-chəfs, -(ˌ)chifs, -ˌchēvz (*used by many who have sing.* -chəf *or* -(ˌ)chif), -ˌchēfs, -chəvz, -(ˌ)chivz\ **1** : a small usu. square piece of cloth used for various usu. personal purposes or as a costume accessory **2** : KERCHIEF 1

hand language *n* : communication by means of a manual alphabet

1han·dle \ˈhan-dᵊl\ *n* [ME *handel*, fr. OE *handle*; akin to OE *hand*] **1** : a part that is designed esp. to be grasped by the hand **2** : something that resembles a handle **3** *slang* : NAME **4** : the feel of a textile **5** : the total amount of money bet on a race, game, or event — **han·dled** \-dᵊld\ *adj* — **off the handle** : into a state of sudden and violent anger

2handle *vb* **han·dling** \ˈhan-(d)liŋ, -dᵊl-iŋ\ *vt* **1 a** : to touch, hold, or otherwise affect with the hand **b** : to manage with the hands ⟨~ a horse⟩ **2 a** : to deal with in writing or speaking or in the plastic arts **b** : CONTROL, DIRECT **c** : to train and act as second for (a prizefighter) **3** : to deal with, act on, or dispose of ⟨~ the day's mail⟩ **4** : to trade in ~ *vi* : to act, behave, or feel in a certain way when handled or directed ⟨car that ~*s* well⟩

syn HANDLE, MANIPULATE, WIELD mean to manage dexterously or effectively. HANDLE implies directing an acquired skill to the accomplishment of immediate ends; MANIPULATE implies adroit handling and often suggests the use of craft or of fraud; WIELD implies mastery and vigor in handling a tool or a weapon, or in exerting influence, authority, or power

han·dle·able \ˈhan-dᵊl-ə-bəl, -(d)lə-\ *adj* : capable of being handled

han·dle·bar \ˈhan-dᵊl-ˌbär\ *n* : a straight or bent bar with a handle at each end; *specif* : one used to steer a bicycle

han·dler \ˈhan-(d)lər, -dᵊl-ər\ *n* **1** : one that handles **2 a** : one in immediate physical charge of an animal; *esp* : one that holds and incites a dog, gamecock, or other animal in a match or hunt **b** : one that helps to train a prizefighter or acts as his second during a match

hand·less \ˈhan-(d)ləs\ *adj* **1** : having no hands **2** : inefficient in manual tasks : CLUMSY

han·dling *n* **1 a** : the action of one that handles something **b** : a process by which something is handled esp. in a commercial transaction **2** : the mode of treatment in a musical, literary, or art work

hand·list \ˈhan-ˌ(d)list\ *n* : a handy orig. fairly brief list (as of books) for purposes of reference or check

hand·made \ˈhan(d)-ˈmād\ *adj* : made by hand or a hand process

hand·maid \-ˌmād\ *or* **hand·maid·en** \-ᵊn\ *n* **1** : a female attendant **2** : SERVANT

hand–me–down \ˈhan(d)-mē-ˌdau̇n\ *adj* **1** : ready-made and usu. cheap and shoddy **2** : worn or put in use by one person or group after being discarded by another — **hand–me–down** *n*

hand·off \ˈhan-ˌdȯf\ *n* : a football play in which the ball is handed by one player to another nearby

hand on *vt* : to hand down (sense 1)

hand organ *n* : a barrel organ operated by a hand crank

hand·out \ˈhan-ˌdau̇t\ *n* **1** : a portion of food, clothing, or money given to or as if to a beggar **2** : a folder or circular of information for free distribution **3 a** : a release by a news service **b** : a prepared statement released to the press

hand over *vt* : to yield control of

hand over fist *adv* : quickly and in large amounts

hand·pick \ˈhan(d)-ˈpik\ *vt* : to select personally or for personal ends

hand·rail \ˈhan-ˌdrāl\ *n* : a narrow rail for grasping with the hand as a support

hand running *adv* : in unbroken succession : CONSECUTIVELY

hand·saw \ˈhan(d)-ˌsȯ\ *n* : a saw used with one hand

hands·breadth \ˈhan(d)z-ˌbredth, -ˌbretth\ *var of* HANDBREADTH

hands down *adv* : without question : EASILY

hands–down \ˈhan(d)z-ˈdau̇n\ *adj* : UNQUESTIONABLE

1hand·sel \ˈhan(t)-səl\ *n* [ME *hansell*] **1** : a gift made as a token of good wishes or luck esp. at the beginning of a new year **2** : something received first (as in a day of trading) and taken to be a token of good luck **3 a** : a first installment : earnest money **b** : EARNEST, FORETASTE

2handsel *vt* **hand·seled** *or* **hand·selled; hand·sel·ing** *or* **hand·sel·ling** \-s(ə-)liŋ\ **1** *chiefly Brit* : to give a handsel to **2** *chiefly Brit* : to inaugurate with a token or gesture of luck or pleasure **3** *chiefly Brit* : to use or do for the first time

hand·set \ˈhan(d)-ˌset\ *n* : a combined telephone transmitter and receiver mounted on a handle

hand·shake \-ˌshāk\ *n* : a clasping of right hands by two people (as in greeting or farewell)

hand·some \ˈhan(t)-səm\ *adj* [ME *handsom* easy to manipulate] **1** *chiefly dial* : APPROPRIATE, SUITABLE **2** : moderately large : SIZABLE **3** : marked by skill or cleverness : ADROIT **4** : marked by graciousness or generosity : LIBERAL **5** : having a pleasing and usu. impressive or dignified appearance **syn** see BEAUTIFUL — **hand·some·ly** *adv* — **hand·some·ness** *n*

hand·spike \ˈhan(d)-ˌspīk\ *n* [by folk etymology fr. D *handspaak*, fr. *hand* + *spaak* pole] : a bar used as a lever

hand·spring \-ˌspriŋ\ *n* : a feat of tumbling in which the body turns forward or backward in a full circle from a standing position and lands first on the hands and then on the feet

hand·stand \-ˌstand\ *n* : an act of supporting the body on the hands with the trunk and legs balanced in air

hand to hand \ˌhan-tə-ˈhand, -də-\ *adv* : at very close quarters

hand–to–hand *adj* : being at very close quarters

hand–to–mouth \-ˈmau̇th\ *adj* : having or providing nothing to spare : PRECARIOUS ⟨a ~ existence⟩

hand·wheel \ˈhan(d)-ˌhwēl, ˈhan-ˌdwēl\ *n* : a wheel worked by hand

hand·work \ˈhan-ˌdwərk\ *n* : work done with the hands

hand·wo·ven \-ˈdwō-vən\ *adj* : produced on a hand-operated loom

hand·write \-ˌdrīt\ *vt* [back-formation fr. *handwriting*] : to write by hand

hand·writ·ing \ˈhan-ˌdrīt-iŋ\ *n* **1** : writing done by hand; *esp* : the cast or form of writing peculiar to a particular person **2** : something written by hand : MANUSCRIPT

handy \ˈhan-dē\ *adj* **1 a** : conveniently near **b** : convenient for use **c** *of a ship* : easily handled **2** : clever in using the hands : DEXTEROUS

handy·man \-ˌman\ *n* : a man who does odd jobs

[1]hang \'haŋ\ *vb* **hung** \'həŋ\ *also* **hanged** \'haŋd\ **hang·ing** \'haŋ-iŋ\ [partly fr. ME *hon*, fr. OE *hōn*, v.t.; partly fr. ME *hangen*, fr. OE *hangian*, v.i. & v.t.; both akin to OHG *hāhan*, v.t., to hang, *hangēn*, v.i.] *vt* **1 a :** to fasten to some elevated point without support from below **:** SUSPEND **b :** to put to death by suspending from a cross, gibbet, or gallows ⟨~*ed* by the neck until dead⟩ — used as a mild oath **c :** to fasten so as to allow free motion within given limits upon a point of suspension ⟨~ a door⟩ **d :** to fit or fix in position or at a proper angle ⟨~ an ax to its helve⟩ **e :** to adjust the hem of (a skirt) so as to hang evenly and at a proper height **2 :** to cover, decorate, or furnish by hanging pictures, trophies, or drapery **3 :** to hold or bear in a suspended or inclined manner ⟨~ his head in shame⟩ **4 :** to fasten to a wall ⟨~ wallpaper⟩ **5 :** to deadlock (a jury) by refusing to join in a unanimous vote **6 :** to display (pictures) in a gallery **~** *vi* **1 a :** to remain suspended or fastened to some point above without support from below **:** DANGLE **b :** to die by hanging ⟨he ~*ed* for his crimes⟩ **2 :** to remain poised or stationary in the air ⟨clouds ~*ing* low overhead⟩ **3 :** to stay with persistence **4 :** to be imminent **:** IMPEND ⟨evils ~ over the nation⟩ **5 :** to fall or droop from a usu. tense or taut position **6 :** DEPEND ⟨election ~*s* on one vote⟩ **7 a** (1) **:** to take hold for support **:** CLING ⟨she *hung* on his arm⟩ (2) **:** to keep persistent contact ⟨dogs *hung* to the trail⟩ **b :** to be burdensome or oppressive ⟨time ~*s* on his hands⟩ **c :** LEAN **8 a :** to be in suspense **:** suffer delay ⟨the decision is still ~*ing*⟩ **b :** to occupy an uncertain mid-position **9 :** to lean, incline, or jut over or downward **10 :** to be in a state of rapt attention ⟨*hung* on his every word⟩ **11 :** LINGER, LOITER **12 :** to fit or fall from the figure in easy lines ⟨the coat ~*s* loosely⟩ — **hang·able** \'haŋ-ə-bəl\ *adj* — **hang fire 1 :** to be slow in the explosion of a charge after its primer has been discharged **2 :** DELAY, HESITATE — **hang one on 1** *slang* **:** to inflict a blow upon **2** *slang* **:** to get very drunk

[2]hang *n* **1 a :** the manner in which a thing hangs **b :** a position in gymnastics in which the center of gravity is below the point of support **2 :** DECLIVITY, SLOPE; *also* **:** DROOP **3 a :** peculiar and significant meaning **b :** the special method of doing, using, or dealing with something **:** KNACK **4 :** a hesitation or slackening in motion or in a course — **give a hang** *or* **care a hang :** to be concerned or worried

[1]han·gar \'haŋ-ər, 'haŋ-gər\ *n* [F] **:** SHELTER, SHED; *esp* **:** a covered and usu. enclosed area for housing and repairing aircraft

[2]hangar *vt* **:** to place or store in a hangar

hang around *vi* **1 :** to pass time or stay aimlessly **:** loiter idly **2 :** to spend one's time in company

hang back *vi* **1 :** to drag behind others **2 :** to be reluctant **:** HESITATE, FALTER

[1]hang·dog \'haŋ-ˌdȯg\ *adj* **1 :** ASHAMED, GUILTY **2 :** ABJECT, COWED

[2]hangdog *n* **:** a despicable or miserable person

hang·er \'haŋ-ər\ *n* **1 :** one that hangs or causes to be hung or hanged **2 :** something that hangs, overhangs, or is suspended: as **a :** a decorative strip of cloth **b :** a small sword formerly used by seamen **c** *chiefly Brit* **:** a small wood on steeply sloping land **3 :** a device by which or to which something is hung or hangs: as **a :** a strap on a sword belt by which a sword or dagger can be suspended **b :** a loop by which a garment is hung up **c :** a device that fits inside or around a garment for hanging from a hook or rod

hang·er–on \ˌhaŋ-ə-'rȯn, -'rän\ *n, pl* **hangers–on** [*hang on* + *-er*] **:** one that hangs around a person, place, or institution esp. for personal gain

[1]hang·ing *n* **1 :** an execution by strangling or breaking the neck by a suspended noose **2 :** something hung: as **a :** CURTAIN **b :** a covering (as a tapestry) for a wall **3 :** a downward slope **:** DECLIVITY

[2]hanging *adj* **1 :** situated or lying on steeply sloping ground **2 a :** OVERHANGING **b :** supported only by the wall on one side **3** *archaic* **:** downcast in appearance **4 :** adapted for sustaining a hanging object **5 :** deserving, likely to cause, or prone to inflict death by hanging

hanging indention *n* **:** indention of all the lines of a paragraph except the first

hang·man \'haŋ-mən\ *n* **:** one who hangs another; *esp* **:** a public executioner

hang·nail \-ˌnāl\ *n* [by folk etymology fr. *agnail*] **:** a bit of skin hanging loose at the side or root of a fingernail

hang off *vi* **:** to hang back

hang on *vi* **1 :** to keep hold **:** hold onto something **2 :** to persist tenaciously ⟨a cold that *hung on* all spring⟩ — **hang on to :** to hold, grip, or keep tenaciously ⟨learned to *hang on to* his money⟩

hang out *vi* **1 :** to protrude in a downward direction **2 a** *slang* **:** LIVE, RESIDE **b :** to spend one's time idly or in loitering around **~** *vt* **:** to display outside as an announcement to the public

hang·out \'haŋ-ˌau̇t\ *n* **:** a favorite or usual place of resort

hang·over \'haŋ-ˌō-vər\ *n* **1 :** something (as a surviving custom) that remains from what is past **2 a :** disagreeable physical effects following heavy consumption of alcohol **b :** disagreeable aftereffects from the use of drugs **c :** a letdown following great excitement or excess

hang together *vi* **1 :** to remain united **:** stand by one another **2 :** to form a consistent or coherent whole

hang up *vt* **1 a :** to place on a hook or hanger designed for the purpose ⟨told the child to *hang up* his coat⟩ **b :** to replace (a telephone receiver) on the cradle so that the connection is broken **2 :** to keep delayed, suspended, or held up ⟨the negotiations were *hung up* for a week⟩ **3 :** to cause to stick or snag immovably ⟨the ship was *hung up* on a sandbar⟩ **~** *vi* **1 :** to terminate a telephone conversation **2 :** to become stuck or snagged so as to be immovable

hank \'haŋk\ *n* [ME, of Scand origin; akin to ON *hönk* hank; akin to OE *hangian* to hang] **1 :** COIL, LOOP; *specif* **:** a coiled or looped bundle **2 :** a ring attached to the edge of a jib or staysail and running on a stay

han·ker \'haŋ-kər\ *vi* **han·ker·ing** \-k(ə-)riŋ\ [prob. fr. Flem *hankeren*, freq. of *hangen* to hang; akin to OE *hangian*] **:** to desire strongly or persistently **syn** see LONG — **han·ker·er** \-kər-ər\ *n*

han·ker·ing *n* **:** a strong or persistent desire

han·ky–pan·ky \ˌhaŋ-kē-'paŋ-kē\ *n* [alter. of *hocus-pocus*] **:** questionable or underhand activity **:** TRICKERY

[1]Han·o·ve·ri·an \ˌhan-ə-'vir-ē-ən, -'ver-\ *adj* [*Hanover*, Germany] **1 :** of, relating to, or supporting the German ducal house of Hanover **2 :** of, relating to, or supporting a British royal house furnishing sovereigns from 1714 to 1901

[2]Hanoverian *n* **1 :** a member or supporter of the ducal or of the British royal Hanoverian house **2 :** any of a breed of horses developed by crossing heavy cold-blooded German horses with Thoroughbreds

Han·sa \'han(t)-sə\ *or* **Hanse** \'han(t)s\ *n* [*Hansa* fr. ML, fr. MLG *hanse*; *Hanse* fr. ME, fr. MF, fr. MLG] **1 :** a medieval merchant guild or trading association **2 :** a league orig. constituted of merchants of various free German cities dealing abroad in the medieval period and later of the cities themselves and organized to secure greater safety and privileges in trading — **Han·se·at·ic** \ˌhan(t)-sē-'at-ik\ *n or adj*

Han·sard \'han(t)-sərd, 'han-ˌsärd\ *n* [Luke *Hansard* †1828 E printer] **:** the official published verbatim report of proceedings in the British parliament

han·sel *var of* HANDSEL

Han·sen's disease \'han(t)-sənz-\ *n* [Armauer *Hansen* †1912 Norw physician] **:** LEPROSY

han·som \'han(t)-səm\ *n* [Joseph A. *Hansom* †1882 E architect] **:** a light 2-wheeled covered carriage with the driver's seat elevated behind

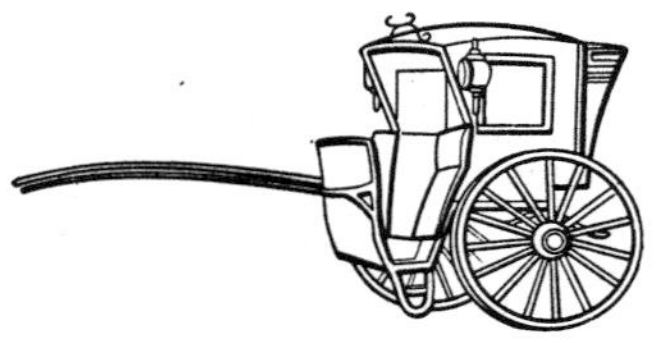

hansom

hant \'hant\ *dial var of* HAUNT

Ha·nuk·kah \'ḵän-ə-kə, 'hän-\ *n* [Heb *ḥănukkāh* dedication] **:** an 8-day Jewish holiday beginning on the 25th of Kislev and commemorating the rededication of the Temple of Jerusalem after its defilement by Antiochus of Syria

hao·le \'hau̇-lē, -(ˌ)lā\ *n* [Hawaiian] **:** one who is not a member of the native race of Hawaii; *esp* **:** WHITE

[1]hap \'hap\ *n* [ME, fr. ON *happ* good luck; akin to OE *gehæp* suitable, OSlav *kobĭ* augury] **1 :** HAPPENING **2 :** CHANCE, FORTUNE

[2]hap *vi* **happed; hap·ping :** HAPPEN

[3]hap *vt* **happed; hap·ping** [ME *happen*] *dial* **:** CLOTHE, COVER — **hap** *n*

ha·pax le·go·me·non \ˌhap-ˌak-sli-'gäm-ə-ˌnän, -nən\ *n, pl* **hapax le·go·me·na** \-nə\ [Gk, something said only once] **:** a word or form evidenced by a single occurrence

[1]hap·haz·ard \hap-'haz-ərd\ *n* [[1]*hap* + *hazard*] **:** CHANCE

[2]haphazard *adj* **:** marked by lack of plan, order, or direction **:** AIMLESS **syn** see RANDOM — **haphazard** *adv* — **hap·haz·ard·ly** *adv* — **hap·haz·ard·ness** *n*

hapl- *or* **haplo-** *comb form* [NL, fr. Gk, fr. *haploos*, fr. *ha-* one + *-ploos* multiplied by; akin to Gk *homos* same — more at SAME, DOUBLE] **1 :** single **:** simple **2** [*haploid*] **:** of or relating to the haploid generation or condition ⟨*haplosis*⟩

hap·less \'hap-ləs\ *adj* **:** having no luck **:** UNFORTUNATE — **hap·less·ly** *adv* — **hap·less·ness** *n*

hap·loid \'hap-ˌlȯid\ *adj* [ISV, fr. Gk *haploeidēs* single, fr. *haploos*] **1 :** having the gametic number of chromosomes or half the number characteristic of somatic cells **2 :** MONOPLOID — **haploid** *n* — **hap·loi·dy** \-ˌlȯid-ē\ *n*

hap·lont \'hap-ˌlänt\ *n* [ISV] **:** an organism with somatic cells having the haploid chromosome number and only the zygote diploid — **hap·lon·tic** \ha-'plänt-ik\ *adj*

hap·lo·sis \ha-'plō-səs\ *n* **:** the halving of the somatic chromosome number by meiosis

hap·ly \'hap-lē\ *adv* **:** by chance, luck, or accident

hap·pen \'hap-ən, -ᵊm\ *vi* **hap·pen·ing** \'hap-(ə-)niŋ\ [ME *happenen*, fr. *hap*] **1 :** to occur by chance **2 a :** to come into being **b :** to take place **:** OCCUR **3 :** CHANCE 1c ⟨~*ed* to hear⟩ **4 a :** to meet something by chance **b :** to appear by chance

syn HAPPEN, CHANCE, OCCUR, TRANSPIRE mean to come about. HAPPEN is the general term applying to whatever comes about with or without causation or intention; CHANCE implies happening without plan or apparent causation; OCCUR differs from HAPPEN in stressing presentation to sight or attention; TRANSPIRE specifically implies a coming out or becoming known ⟨what *happened* that day only *transpired* much later⟩ but is often nearly equal to OCCUR; it may suggest an event of some importance

hap·pen·chance \'hap-ən-ˌchan(t)s, 'hap-ᵊm-\ *n* **:** HAPPENSTANCE

hap·pen·ing *n* **1 :** OCCURRENCE **2 :** an apparently aimless and pointless staged performance intended to create startling chance effects

hap·pen·stance \'hap-ən-ˌstan(t)s, 'hap-ᵊm-\ *n* [*happen* + *circumstance*] **:** a circumstance regarded as due to chance

hap·pi·ly \'hap-ə-lē\ *adv* **1 :** FORTUNATELY, LUCKILY **2** *archaic* **:** by chance **3 :** in a happy manner or state **4 :** SUCCESSFULLY

hap·pi·ness \'hap-i-nəs\ *n* **1** *obs* **:** good fortune **:** PROSPERITY **2 a :** a state of well-being and contentment **:** JOY **b :** a pleasurable satisfaction **3 :** APTNESS, FELICITY

hap·py \'hap-ē\ *adj* [ME, fr. *hap*] **1 :** favored by luck or fortune **:** FORTUNATE **2 :** notably well adapted or fitting **:** FELICITOUS **3 a :** enjoying well-being and contentment **:** JOYOUS **b :** expressing or suggestive of happiness **:** PLEASANT **c :** PLEASED, GRATIFIED **4 a :** characterized by a dazed irresponsible state ⟨punch-*happy*⟩ **b :** impulsively or obsessively quick to use something ⟨trigger-*happy*⟩ **syn** see FIT, GLAD, LUCKY

hap·py–go–lucky \ˌhap-ē-(ˌ)gō-'lək-ē\ *adj* **:** blithely unconcerned **:** CAREFREE

[1]Haps·burg \'haps-ˌbərg, 'häps-ˌbu̇(ə)rg\ *adj* [*Hapsburg*, Aargau, Switzerland] **:** of or relating to a princely German family furnishing the rulers of Austria from 1278 to 1918 and of Spain from 1516 to 1700 and many of the Holy Roman emperors

[2]Hapsburg *n* **:** a member of the Hapsburg family; *esp* **:** a Hapsburg monarch

hap·ten \'hap-ˌten\ *also* **hap·tene** \-ˌtēn\ *n* [G *hapten*] **:** a substance other than an antigen that reacts in vitro with an antibody; *also* **:** one that in combination with a carrier antigen confers specificity or antigenicity or both — **hap·ten·ic** \hap-'ten-ik\ *adj*

hap·tic \'hap-tik\ *adj* [ISV, fr. Gk *haptein* to fasten] **:** relating to or based on the sense of touch — **hap·ti·cal** \-ti-kəl\ *adj*

hara–kiri \ˌhar-i-'ki(ə)r-ē, -'kar-ē\ *n* [Jap *harakiri*] **:** suicide by disembowelment formerly practiced by the Japanese samurai or decreed by a court in lieu of the death penalty

ha·rangue \hə-'raŋ\ *n* [ME *arang*, fr. MF *arenge*, fr. OIt *aringa*]

1 : a speech addressed to a public assembly **2** : a bombastic ranting speech or writing **3** : a didactic or hortatory talk or discussion : see LECTURE — **harangue** vb — **ha·rangu·er** \-'raŋ-ər\ n

ha·rass \hə-'ras, 'har-əs\ vt [F harasser, fr. MF, fr. harer to set a dog on, fr. OF hare, interj. used to incite dogs, of Gmc origin; akin to OHG hier here — more at HERE] **1** : to worry and impede by repeated raids **2 a** : EXHAUST, FATIGUE **b** : to annoy continually syn see WORRY — **ha·rass·er** n — **ha·rass·ment** \-mənt\ n

¹**har·bin·ger** \'här-bən-jər\ n [ME herbergere, fr. OF, host, fr. herberge hostelry, of Gmc origin; akin to OHG heriberga] **1** archaic : a person sent before to provide lodgings **2 a** : one who pioneers in or initiates a major change : PRECURSOR **b** : something that presages or foreshadows what is to come syn see FORERUNNER

²**harbinger** vt : to be a harbinger of : PRESAGE

¹**har·bor** or chiefly Brit **har·bour** \'här-bər\ n [ME herberge; akin to OHG heriberga army encampment, hostelry; both fr. a prehistoric WGmc-NGmc compound whose components are akin respectively to OHG heri army and to OHG bergan to shelter — more at HARRY, BURY] **1** : a place of security and comfort : REFUGE **2 a** : a part of a body of water protected and deep enough to furnish anchorage; esp : one with port facilities — **har·bor·less** \-ləs\ adj

²**harbor** or chiefly Brit **harbour** vb **har·bor·ing** \-b(ə-)riŋ\ vt **1 a** (1) : to give shelter or refuge to (2) : to keep possession of (an animal) **b** : to be the home or habitat of : CONTAIN **2** : to hold a thought or feeling of ~ vi **1** : to take shelter in or as if in a harbor **2** of an animal : to rest or hide away esp. habitually **b** : LIVE — **har·bor·er** \-bər-ər\ n

har·bor·age \-bə-rij\ n : SHELTER, HARBOR

harbor master n : an officer who executes the regulations respecting the use of a harbor

¹**hard** \'härd\ adj [ME, fr. OE heard; akin to OHG hart hard, Gk kratos strength] **1** : not easily penetrated : not easily yielding to pressure **2 a** of liquor (1) : having a harsh or acid taste (2) : STRONG; specif : having an alcoholic content of more than 22.5 percent **b** : characterized by the presence of salts that prevent lathering with soap ⟨~ water⟩ **3 a** : of or relating to radiation of relatively high penetrating power ⟨~ X rays⟩ **b** : having or producing relatively great photographic contrast ⟨a ~ negative⟩ **4 a** : metallic as distinct from paper ⟨~ money⟩ **b** of currency : convertible into gold : stable in value ⟨~ being high and firm ⟨~ prices⟩ **5 a** : TIGHT ⟨~ yarns⟩ **b** : NAPLESS ⟨~ woolens⟩ **6 a** : physically fit ⟨in good ~ condition⟩ **b** : HARDY : free of weakness or other flaw **7 a** (1) : FIRM, DEFINITE ⟨~ agreement⟩ (2) : FACTUAL, ACTUAL ⟨~ evidence⟩ **b** : CLOSE, SEARCHING ⟨~ look⟩ **c** : free from sentimentality or illusion : REALISTIC ⟨good ~ sense⟩ **8 a** (1) : difficult to bear or endure ⟨~ luck⟩ ⟨~ times⟩ (2) : OPPRESSIVE, UNJUST ⟨~ greedy landlord⟩ **b** : INCORRIGIBLE, TOUGH ⟨~ gang⟩ **c** (1) : harsh, severe, or offensive in tendency or effect ⟨said some ~ things⟩ (2) : RESENTFUL ⟨~ feelings⟩ (3) : STRICT, UNRELENTING ⟨drives a ~ bargain⟩ **d** : INCLEMENT ⟨~ winter⟩ **e** (1) : intense in force, manner, or degree ⟨~ blow⟩ (2) : ARDUOUS, STRENUOUS ⟨~ work⟩ (3) : performing or carrying on with great energy, intensity, or persistence ⟨~ worker⟩ **9 a** : characterized by sharp or harsh outline, rigid execution, and stiff drawing **b** : sharply defined : STARK ⟨~ shadows⟩ **c** : lacking in shading delicacy, or resonance ⟨~ singing tone⟩ **d** : sounding as in arcing and geese respectively — used of c and g **10 a** (1) : difficult to accomplish or resolve : TROUBLESOME ⟨~ problem⟩ (2) : difficult to comprehend or explain ⟨~ words⟩ **b** : having difficulty in doing something ⟨~ of hearing⟩

syn HARD, DIFFICULT, ARDUOUS mean demanding great exertion or effort. HARD implies the opposite of all that is easy; DIFFICULT implies the presence of obstacles to be surmounted or puzzles to be resolved and suggests the need of skill, patience, or courage; ARDUOUS stresses the need of laborious and persevering exertion syn see in addition FIRM

— **hard up 1** : short of money **2** : poorly provided

²**hard** adv **1 a** : with great or utmost effort or energy : STRENUOUSLY **b** : VIOLENTLY, FIERCELY **c** : to the full extent — used in nautical directions **d** : INTENTLY **2 a** : HARSHLY, SEVERELY **b** : with rancor, bitterness, or grief ⟨took his defeat ~⟩ **3** : TIGHTLY, FIRMLY **4** : to the point of hardness **5** : close in time or space

hard–and–fast \,härd-ᵊn-'fast\ adj : STRICT

hard·back \'härd-,bak\ n : a book bound in hard covers

hard·ball \-,bȯl\ n : BASEBALL

hard·bill \-,bil\ n : any of numerous birds with a hard strong bill adapted to cracking seeds and nuts — compare SOFT-BILL

hard–bit·ten \-'bit-ᵊn\ adj **1** : inclined to bite hard **2** : TOUGH

hard·board \-,bō(ə)rd, -,bȯ(ə)rd\ n : composition board made by compressing shredded wood chips often with a binder at high temperatures

hard–boiled \-'bȯi(ə)ld\ adj **1** of an egg : boiled until both white and yolk have solidified **2** : heavily starched **3 a** : lacking sentiment : CALLOUS **b** : HARDHEADED

hard cider n : fermented apple juice containing usu. less than 10 percent alcohol

hard clam n : a clam with a thick hard shell; specif : QUAHOG

hard coal n : ANTHRACITE

hard·en \'härd-ᵊn\ vb **hard·en·ing** \'härd-niŋ, -ᵊn-iŋ\ vt **1** : to make hard or harder : INDURATE **2** : to confirm in disposition, feelings, or action; esp : to make callous ⟨~ed his heart⟩ **3** : INURE, TOUGHEN ⟨~ troops⟩ ~ vi **1** : to become hard or harder **2 a** : to become confirmed or strengthened **b** : to assume an appearance of harshness or severity **3** : to become higher or less subject to fluctuations downward

hard·en·er \'härd-nər, -ᵊn-ər\ n : one that hardens; esp : a substance added (as to a paint or varnish) to harden the film

hard·en·ing n : something that hardens

hard goods n pl : DURABLE GOODS

hard·hack \'härd-,hak\ n : an American shrub (Spiraea tomentosa) with rusty hairy leaves and dense terminal panicles of pink or occas. white flowers

hard–hand·ed \-'han-dəd\ adj **1** : having hands made hard by labor **2** : STRICT, OPPRESSIVE — **hard–hand·ed·ness** n

hard·head \'härd-,hed\ n **1 a** : a hardheaded person **b** : BLOCKHEAD **2 a** : any of several fishes (as a sculpin) esp. with a spiny or bony head **b** : any of several ducks **3** : any of several weedy plants (as knapweed) with firm inflorescences

hard·head·ed \-'hed-əd\ adj **1** : STUBBORN, WILLFUL **2** : SOBER, REALISTIC — **hard·head·ed·ly** adv — **hard·head·ed·ness** n

hardhead sponge n : any of several commercial sponges of the West Indies and Central America with a harsh but elastic fiber

hard–heart·ed \'härd-'härt-əd\ adj : UNFEELING, PITILESS — **hard·heart·ed·ly** adv — **hard·heart·ed·ness** n

har·di·hood \'härd-ē-,hùd\ n **1 a** : resolute courage and fortitude **b** : disdainful insolence **2** : VIGOR, ROBUSTNESS syn see TEMERITY

har·di·ment \-mənt\ n [ME, fr. MF, fr. OF, fr. hardi bold, hardy] **1** archaic : HARDIHOOD **2** obs : a bold deed

har·di·ness \'härd-ē-nəs\ n : the quality or state of being hardy

hard labor n : compulsory labor of imprisoned criminals as a part of the prison discipline

hard·ly \'härd-lē\ adv **1** : with force : VIGOROUSLY **2** : SEVERELY, HARSHLY **3** : with difficulty : PAINFULLY **4** : not quite : BARELY

hard maple n : SUGAR MAPLE

hard–mouthed \'härd-'maùthd, -'maùtht\ adj, of an animal : not responding satisfactorily to pressure (as of a bit) on the mouth

hard·ness n **1** : the quality or state of being hard **2** : the cohesion of the particles on the surface of a mineral as determined by its capacity to scratch another or be itself scratched — compare MOHS' SCALE

hard–of–hear·ing \,härd-ə(v)-'hi(ə)r-iŋ\ adj : of or relating to a defective but functional sense of hearing

hard palate n : the bony anterior part of the palate forming the roof of the mouth

hard·pan \'härd-,pan\ n **1** : a cemented or compacted and often clayey layer in soil that is impenetrable by roots **2** : a fundamental part : BEDROCK

hard put adj : barely able

hard rubber n : a firm relatively inextensible rubber or rubber product; esp : a normally black horny substance made by vulcanizing natural rubber with high percentages of sulfur

hard sauce n : a creamed mixture of butter and powdered sugar often with added cream and flavoring

hard·scrab·ble \'härd-,skrab-əl\ adj : yielding or gaining a meager living by great labor

hard sell n : aggressive high-pressure salesmanship

hard–set \'härd-'set\ adj : TIGHT, FIXED

hard–shell \-,shel\ adj : CONFIRMED, UNCOMPROMISING

hard–shell clam also **hard–shelled clam** \,härd-,shel(d)-\ n : QUAHOG

hard–shell crab or **hard–shelled crab** n : a crab that has not recently shed its shell

hard·ship \'härd-,ship\ n **1** : SUFFERING, PRIVATION **2** : something that causes or entails suffering or privation syn see DIFFICULTY

hard·stand \-,stand\ n : a hard-surfaced area for parking an airplane

hard–sur·face \-'sər-fəs\ vt : to provide with a paved surface

hard·tack \'härd-,tak\ n **1** : a hard biscuit or bread made of flour and water without salt **2** : any of several mountain mahoganies

hard·top \-,täp\ n : an automobile styled to resemble a convertible but having a rigid top of metal or plastic

hard·ware \'här-,dwa(ə)r, -,dwe(ə)r\ n **1** : ware (as fittings, cutlery, tools, utensils, parts of machines) made of metal **2** : major items of military equipment or their components **3** : the physical components (as electronic and electrical devices) of a vehicle (as a spacecraft) or an apparatus (as a computer)

hard wheat n : a wheat with hard flinty kernels high in gluten that yield a strong flour esp. suitable for bread and macaroni

¹**hard·wood** \'här-,dwùd\ n **1** : the wood of an angiospermous tree as distinguished from that of a coniferous tree **2** : a tree that yields hardwood

²**hardwood** adj **1** : having or made of hardwood **2** : consisting of mature woody tissue

hard–wood·ed \'här-'dwùd-əd\ adj **1** : having hard wood that is difficult to work or finish **2** : HARDWOOD 1

har·dy \'härd-ē\ adj [ME hardi, fr. OF, fr. (assumed) OF hardir to make hard, of Gmc origin; akin to OE heard hard] **1** : BOLD, BRAVE **2** : AUDACIOUS, BRAZEN **3 a** : inured to fatigue or hardships : ROBUST **b** : capable of living outdoors over winter without artificial protection or of withstanding other adverse conditions

¹**hare** \'ha(ə)r, 'he(ə)r\ n, pl hare or hares [ME, fr. OE hara; akin to OHG haso hare, L canis hoary, gray] : any of various swift timid long-eared mammals (order Lagomorpha and esp. genus Lepus) having a divided upper lip, long hind legs, a short cocked tail, and the young open-eyed and furred at birth

²**hare** vi : RUN

hare and hounds n : a game in which some of the players scatter bits of paper for a trail and others try to find and catch them

hare·bell \'ha(ə)r-,bel, 'he(ə)r-\ n **1** : a slender blue-flowered herb (Campanula rotundifolia) **2** : WOOD HYACINTH

hare·brained \-'brānd\ adj : FLIGHTY

hare family n : the natural family (Leporidae of the order Lagomorpha) comprising the rabbits and the typical hares

hare·lip \-'lip\ n : a congenitally divided lip suggesting that of a hare; also : the deformity exhibited — **hare·lipped** \-'lipt\ adj

har·em \'har-əm, 'her-\ n [Ar ḥarīm, lit., something forbidden & ḥaram, lit., sanctuary] **1 a** : a usu. secluded house or part of a house allotted to women in a Muslim household **b** : the wives, concubines, female relatives, and servants occupying a harem **2** : a group of women associated with one man **3** : a group of females associated with one male — used of polygamous animals

har·i·cot \'(h)ar-i-,kō\ n [F] : the ripe seed or the unripe pod of any of several beans (genus Phaseolus and esp. P. vulgaris)

hark \'härk\ vi [ME herken; akin to OHG hōrechen to listen] : to pay close attention : LISTEN

hark back vi : to go back to something earlier

harken var of HEARKEN

har·le·quin \'här-li-k(w)ən\ n [It arlecchino, fr. MF Helquin, a demon] **1** cap : a character in comedy and pantomime with a shaved head, masked face, variegated tights, and wooden sword **2** : a variegated pattern

har·le·quin·ade \,här-li-k(w)ə-'nād\ n : a play or pantomime in which Harlequin has a leading role

har·lot \'här-lət\ n [ME, fr. OF herlot rogue] : PROSTITUTE

ə abut; ᵊ kitten; ər further; a back; ā bake; ä cot, cart; aù out; ch chin; e less; ē easy; g gift; i trip; ī life
j joke; ŋ sing; ō flow; ȯ flaw; ȯi coin; th thin; t̲h̲ this; ü loot; ù foot; y yet; yü few; yù furious; zh vision

har·lot·ry \-lə-trē\ *n* **1 :** PROSTITUTION **2 :** PROSTITUTE

1**harm** \'härm\ *n* [ME, fr. OE *hearm;* akin to OHG *harm* injury, OSlav *sramŭ* shame] **1 :** physical or mental damage **:** INJURY **2 :** MISCHIEF, HURT

2**harm** *vt* **:** to cause harm to **syn** see INJURE — **harm·er** *n*

har·mat·tan \ˌhär-mə-'tan, här-'mat-ᵊn\ *n* [Twi *haramata*] **:** a dust-laden wind on the Atlantic coast of Africa in some seasons

harm·ful \'härm-fəl\ *adj* **:** DAMAGING, INJURIOUS — **harm·ful·ly** \-fə-lē\ *adv* — **harm·ful·ness** *n*

harm·less \'härm-ləs\ *adj* **1 :** free from harm, liability, or loss **2 :** lacking capacity or intent to injure **:** INNOCUOUS — **harm·less·ly** *adv* — **harm·less·ness** *n*

1**har·mon·ic** \här-'män-ik\ *adj* **1 :** MUSICAL **2 :** of or relating to musical harmony or harmonics **3 :** pleasing to the ear **:** HARMONIOUS **4 :** expressible in terms of sine or cosine functions ⟨~ function⟩ **5 :** of an integrated nature **:** CONGRUOUS — **har·mon·i·cal** \-i-kəl\ *adj* — **har·mon·i·cal·ly** \-i-k(ə-)lē\ *adv* — **har·mon·i·cal·ness** \-i-kəl-nəs\ *n*

2**harmonic** *n* **1 a :** OVERTONE; *esp* **:** one whose vibration frequency is an integral multiple of that of the fundamental **b :** a flutelike tone produced on a stringed instrument by touching a vibrating string at a nodal point **2 :** a component frequency of a harmonic motion (as of an electromagnetic wave) that is an integral multiple of the fundamental frequency

har·mon·i·ca \här-'män-i-kə\ *n* [It *armonica*, fem. of *armonico* harmonious] **1 :** a musical instrument consisting of a series of hemispherical glasses played by touching the edges with a dampened finger **2 :** a small rectangular wind instrument with free metallic reeds recessed in air slots from which tones are sounded by exhaling and inhaling

harmonic analysis *n* **:** the expression of a periodic function as a sum of sines and cosines and specif. by means of a Fourier series

harmonic mean *n* **:** the reciprocal of the arithmetic mean of the reciprocals of a finite set of numbers

harmonic motion *n* **:** a periodic motion that has a single frequency or amplitude (as of a sounding violin string or swinging pendulum) or a vibratory motion that is composed of two or more such simple periodic motions

harmonic progression *n* **:** a progression the reciprocals of whose terms form an arithmetic progression

har·mon·ics \här-'män-iks\ *n pl but sing or pl in constr* **:** the study of the physical characteristics of musical sounds

har·mo·ni·ous \här-'mō-nē-əs\ *adj* **1 :** musically concordant **2 :** having the parts agreeably related **:** CONGRUOUS **3 :** marked by accord in sentiment or action — **har·mo·ni·ous·ly** *adv* — **har·mo·ni·ous·ness** *n*

har·mo·nist \'här-mə-nəst\ *n* **:** HARMONIZER — **har·mo·nis·tic** \ˌhär-mə-'nis-tik\ *adj* — **har·mo·nis·ti·cal·ly** \-ti-k(ə-)lē\ *adv*

har·mo·ni·um \här-'mō-nē-əm\ *n* [F, fr. MF *harmonie, armonie*] **:** REED ORGAN

har·mo·ni·za·tion \ˌhär-mə-nə-'zā-shən\ *n* **1 :** the quality or state of being in harmony **2 :** an act or instance of producing harmony

har·mo·nize \'här-mə-ˌnīz\ *vi* **1 :** to play or sing in harmony **2 :** to be in harmony ~ *vt* **1 :** to bring into consonance or accord **2 :** to provide or accompany with harmony **syn** see AGREE — **har·mo·niz·er** *n*

har·mo·ny \'här-mə-nē\ *n* [ME *armony*, fr. MF *armonie*, fr. L *harmonia*, fr. Gk, joint, harmony, fr. *harmos* joint — more at ARM] **1** *archaic* **:** tuneful sound **:** MELODY **2 a :** the combination of simultaneous musical notes in a chord **b :** the structure of music with respect to the composition and progression of chords **c :** the science of the structure, relation, and progression of chords **3 a :** pleasing or congruent arrangement of parts **b :** CORRESPONDENCE, ACCORD **c :** internal calm **:** TRANQUILLITY **4 a :** an interweaving of different accounts into a single narrative **b :** an arrangement of different accounts in parallel columns with corresponding passages side by side

har·mo·tome \'här-mə-ˌtōm\ *n* [F, fr. Gk *harmos* + *tomē* section, fr. *temnein* to cut — more at TOME] **:** a mineral $(Ba,K)(Al,Si)_2Si_6O_{16}.6H_2O$ consisting of a hydrous silicate of aluminum, barium, and potassium

1**har·ness** \'här-nəs\ *n* [ME *herneis* baggage, gear, fr. OF] **1 a** (1) **:** the gear other than a yoke of a draft animal (2) **:** GEAR, EQUIPMENT **b** (1) **:** occupational surroundings or routine (2) **:** close association **2 :** military equipment for horse or man **3 :** a part of a loom which holds and controls the heddles

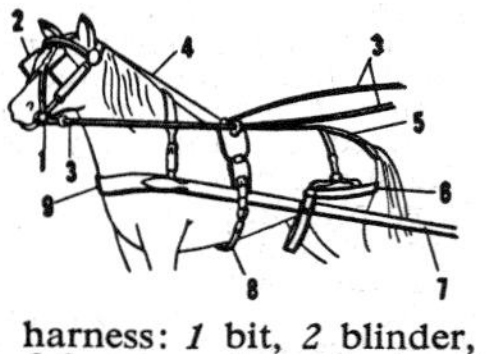

harness: *1* bit, *2* blinder, *3,3*, reins, *4* checkrein, *5* crupper, *6* breeching, *7* trace, *8* girth, *9* breast collar

2**harness** *vt* **1 :** to put a harness on **2 :** to tie together **:** YOKE **3 :** UTILIZE

harness horse *n* **:** a horse for racing or working in harness

1**harp** \'härp\ *n* [ME, fr. OE *hearpe;* akin to OHG *harpha* harp, Gk *karphos* dry stalk] **1 :** an instrument having many strings of graded length stretched across an open triangular frame with a curving top and played by plucking with the fingers **2 :** something that resembles a harp — **harp·ist** \'här-pəst\ *n*

2**harp** *vi* **1 :** to play on a harp **2 :** to dwell on or recur to a subject tiresomely or monotonously

harp·er \'här-pər\ *n* **1 :** HARPIST **2 :** one that harps

har·poon \här-'pün\ *n* [prob. fr. D *harpoen*, fr. OF *harpon* brooch, fr. *harper* to grapple] **:** a barbed spear or javelin used esp. in hunting large fish or whales — **harpoon** *vt* — **har·poon·er** *n*

harp·si·chord \'härp-si-ˌkȯ(ə)rd\ *n* [modif. of It *arpicordo*, fr. *arpa* harp + *corda* string] **:** a keyboard instrument resembling the grand piano and producing tones by the plucking of wire strings with quills or leather points

har·py \'här-pē\ *n* [L *Harpyia*, fr. Gk] **1** *cap* **:** a foul malign creature of classical mythology that is part woman and part bird **2 a :** a predatory person **:** LEECH **b :** a shrewish woman

har·que·bus \'här-kwi-(ˌ)bəs, -kə-bəs\ *n* [MF *harquebuse, arquebuse*] **:** an obsolete portable firearm — **har·que·bus·ier** \ˌhär-kwi-(ˌ)bə-'si(ə)r, -kə-bə-\ *n*

har·ri·dan \'har-əd-ᵊn\ *n* [perh. modif. of F *haridelle* old horse, gaunt woman] **:** a scolding old woman

1**har·ri·er** \'har-ē-ər\ *n* [irreg. fr. 1*hare*] **1 :** a hunting dog that resembles a small foxhound and is used esp. for hunting rabbits **2 :** a runner on a cross-country team

2**harrier** *n* **1 :** one that harries **2** [alter. of *harrower*, fr. 1*harrow*] **:** any of various slender hawks (genus *Circus*) with long angled wings and long legs that feed chiefly on small mammals, reptiles, and insects

1**har·row** \'har-(ˌ)ō, -ə(-w)\ *vt* [ME *harwen*, fr. OE *hergian*] *archaic* **:** PILLAGE, PLUNDER

2**harrow** *n* [ME *harwe*] **:** a cultivating implement set with spikes, spring teeth, or disks and used primarily for pulverizing and smoothing the soil

3**harrow** *vt* **1 :** to cultivate with a harrow **2 :** TORMENT, VEX — **har·row·er** \'har-ə-wər\ *n*

har·ry \'har-ē\ *vt* [ME *harien*, fr. OE *hergian;* akin to OHG *heriōn* to lay waste, *heri* army, Gk *koiranos* commander] **1 :** to make a pillaging or destructive raid on **2 :** to force to move along **3 :** to torment by or as if by constant attack **syn** see WORRY

harsh \'härsh\ *adj* [ME *harsk*, of Scand origin; akin to Norw *harsk* harsh] **1 :** disagreeable to the touch or other sense **2 :** causing discomfort or pain **3 :** unduly exacting **:** SEVERE **4 :** aesthetically jarring **syn** see ROUGH — **harsh·en** \'här-shən\ *vb* **harsh·en·ing** \-sh(ə-)niŋ\ — **harsh·ly** *adv* — **harsh·ness** *n*

hart \'härt\ *n* [ME *hert*, fr. OE *heort;* akin to L *cervus* hart, Gk *keras* horn — more at HORN] *chiefly Brit* **:** the male of the red deer esp. over five years old **:** STAG — compare HIND

harte·beest \'härt-(ə-)ˌbēst\ *n* [obs. Afrik (now *hartbees*), fr. D, fr. *hart* deer + *beest* beast] **:** a large nearly exterminated African antelope (*Alcelaphus caama*) with ringed divergent horns

harts·horn \'härts-ˌhȯ(ə)rn\ *n* [fr. the earlier use of hart's horns as the chief source of ammonia] **1** *chiefly dial* **:** AMMONIA WATER **2 :** a mixture of ammonium bicarbonate and carbamate

har·um–scar·um \ˌhar-əm-'skar-əm, ˌher-əm-'sker-\ *adj* [perh. alter. of *helter-skelter*] **:** RECKLESS, IRRESPONSIBLE — **harum–scarum** *adv*

ha·rus·pex \hə-'rəs-ˌpeks, 'har-əs-\ *n, pl* **ha·rus·pi·ces** \hə-'rəs-pə-ˌsēz\ [L] **:** a diviner in ancient Rome basing his predictions on inspection of the entrails of sacrificial animals

1**har·vest** \'här-vəst\ *n, often attrib* [ME *hervest*, fr. OE *hærfest;* akin to L *carpere* to pluck, gather, Gk *karpos* fruit, *keirein* to cut — more at SHEAR] **1 :** the season for gathering in agricultural crops **2 :** the act or process of gathering in a crop **3 a :** a mature crop of grain or fruit **:** YIELD **b :** the quantity of a natural product gathered in a single season **4 :** the product or reward of exertion

2**harvest** *vt* **1 a :** to gather in (a crop) **:** REAP **b :** to gather as if by harvesting **2 :** to win by achievement ~ *vi* **:** to gather in a food crop — **har·vest·able** \-və-stə-bəl\ *adj* — **har·vest·er** *n*

harvest bug *n* **:** CHIGGER 2

harvest fly *n* **:** CICADA

harvest home *n* **1 :** the gathering or the time of harvest **2 :** a feast at the close of harvest **3 :** a song sung by the reapers at the close of the harvest

har·vest·man \'här-vəs(t)-mən\ *n* **:** an arachnid (order Phalangida) that superficially resembles a true spider but has a small rounded body and very long slender legs — called also *daddy longlegs*

harvest moon *n* **:** the full moon nearest the time of the September equinox

has *pres 3d sing of* HAVE

has–been \'haz-ˌbin, *chiefly Brit* -ˌbēn\ *n* **:** one that has passed the peak of effectiveness or popularity

ha·sen·pfef·fer \'häz-ᵊn-ˌ(p)fef-ər\ *n* [G, fr. *hase* hare + *pfeffer* pepper] **:** a stew made of marinated rabbit meat

1**hash** \'hash\ *vt* [F *hacher*, fr. OF *hachier*, fr. *hache* battle-ax, of Gmc origin; akin to OHG *hāppa* sickle; akin to Gk *koptein* to cut — more at CAPON] **1 a :** to chop into small pieces **b :** CONFUSE, MUDDLE **2 :** to talk about **:** REVIEW

2**hash** *n* **1 :** chopped food; *specif* **:** chopped meat mixed with potatoes and browned **2 :** a restatement of something that is already known **3 :** HODGEPODGE, JUMBLE

Hash·im·ite *or* **Hash·em·ite** \'hash-ə-ˌmīt\ *n* [*Hashim*, great-grandfather of Muhammad] **:** a member of an Arabic family having common ancestry with Muhammad and founding dynasties in countries of the eastern Mediterranean

hash·ish \'hash-ˌēsh, -(ˌ)ish\ *n* [Ar *hashīsh*] **:** a narcotic drug derived from the hemp (*Cannabis sativa*) that is smoked, chewed, or drunk for its intoxicating effect

hash mark *n* **:** SERVICE STRIPE

Ha·sid *or* **Has·sid** \'has-əd, 'k̲äs-\ *n, pl* **Ha·si·dim** *or* **Has·si·dim** \'has-əd-əm, k̲ə-'sēd-\ [Heb *ḥāsīdh* pious] **1 :** a member of a Jewish sect of the second century B.C. opposed to Hellenism and devoted to the strict observance of the ritual law **2 :** a member of a Jewish mystical sect founded in Poland about 1750 in opposition to rationalism and ritual laxity — **Ha·sid·ic** \hə-'sid-ik, ha-\ *adj*

Has·i·dism \'has-ə-ˌdiz-əm\ *n* **1 :** the practices and beliefs of the Hasidim **2 :** the Hasidic movement

Has·mo·nae·ans *or* **Has·mo·ne·ans** \ˌhaz-mə-'nē-ənz\ *n pl* [LL *Asmonaeus* Hasmon, ancestor of the Maccabees, fr. Gk *Asamōnaios*] **:** MACCABEES

hasn't \'haz-ᵊnt\ **:** has not

hasp \'hasp\ *n* [ME, fr. OE *hæsp;* akin to MHG *haspe* hasp] **:** any of several devices for fastening; *esp* **:** a fastener esp. for a door or lid consisting of a hinged metal strap that fits over a staple and is secured by a pin or padlock — **hasp** *vt*

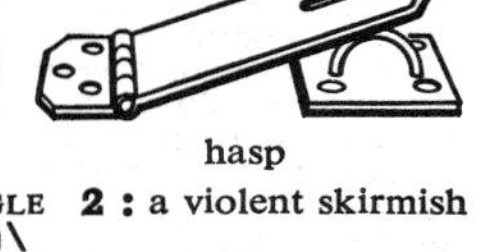
hasp

has·sle \'has-əl\ *n* [perh. fr. 2*haggle* + 2*tussle*] **1 :** a heated argument **:** WRANGLE **2 :** a violent skirmish **:** FIGHT — **hassle** *vi* **has·sling** \-(ə-)liŋ\

has·sock \'has-ək\ *n* [ME, sedge, fr. OE *hassuc*] **1 :** TUSSOCK **2 a :** a cushion to kneel upon in prayer **b :** a cushion that serves as a seat or leg rest

hast \(')hast, (h)əst\ *archaic pres 2d sing of* HAVE

has·tate \'has-ˌtāt\ *adj* [NL *hastatus*, fr. L *hasta* spear — more at YARD] **:** shaped like an arrow with flaring barbs ⟨~ leaf⟩ — **has·tate·ly** *adv*

1**haste** \'hāst\ *n* [ME, fr. OF, of Gmc origin; akin to OE *hǣst* violence] **1 :** rapidity of motion **:** SWIFTNESS **2 :** rash or headlong action **:** PRECIPITATENESS **3 :** undue eagerness to act **:** URGENCY
syn HURRY, SPEED, EXPEDITION, DISPATCH: HASTE implies urgency or precipitancy in persons; HURRY carries a stronger implication of

agitation, bustle, or confusion; SPEED suggests swiftness of movement of things or persons, or of performance, without bustle or confusion and usu. with success; EXPEDITION and DISPATCH both imply speed and efficiency, EXPEDITION suggesting ease and DISPATCH promptness

²**haste** *vt, archaic* **:** to urge on **:** HASTEN ~ *vi* **:** to move or act swiftly

has·ten \'hās-ᵊn\ *vb* **has·ten·ing** \'hās-niŋ, -ᵊn-iŋ\ *vt* **1 :** to urge on **2 :** ACCELERATE ~ *vi* **:** to move or act quickly **:** HURRY — **has·ten·er** \'hās-nər, -ᵊn-ər\ *n*

hast·i·ly \'hā-stə-lē\ *adv* **:** in haste **:** HURRIEDLY

hast·i·ness \-stē-nəs\ *n* **:** the quality or state of being hasty

hasty \'hā-stē\ *adj* **1 a** *archaic* **:** rapid in action or movement **:** SPEEDY **b :** done or made in a hurry **c :** fast and often superficial **2 :** EAGER, IMPATIENT **3 :** PRECIPITATE, RASH **4 :** prone to anger **:** IRRITABLE **syn** see FAST

hasty pudding *n* **1** *Brit* **:** a porridge of oatmeal or flour boiled in water **2** *NewEng* **:** cornmeal mush

hat \'hat\ *n* [ME, fr. OE *hæt;* akin to OHG *huot* head covering — more at HOOD] **1 :** a covering for the head usu. having a shaped crown and brim **2 a :** a distinctive head covering worn as a symbol of office **b :** OFFICE, POSITION — **hat in the ring :** an entry into or readiness to enter a contest

hat·box \-ˌbäks\ *n* **:** a round piece of luggage esp. for carrying hats

¹**hatch** \'hach\ *n* [ME *hache,* fr. OE *hæc;* akin to MD *hecke* trapdoor] **1 :** a small door or opening (as in an airplane) ⟨an escape ~⟩ **2 a :** an opening in the deck of a ship or in the floor or roof of a building **b :** the covering for such an opening **c :** HATCHWAY **d :** COMPARTMENT **3 :** FLOODGATE

²**hatch** *vb* [ME *hacchen;* akin to MHG *hecken* to mate] *vi* **1 :** to produce young by incubation **2 :** to emerge from an egg or chrysalis **3 :** to incubate eggs **:** BROOD ~ *vt* **1 :** to produce (young) from an egg by applying natural or artificial heat **:** INCUBATE **2 :** to bring into being **:** ORIGINATE; *esp* **:** to concoct in secret — **hatch·abil·i·ty** \ˌhach-ə-'bil-ət-ē\ *n* — **hatch·able** \'hach-ə-bəl\ *adj* — **hatch·er** *n*

³**hatch** *n* **1 :** an act or instance of hatching **2 :** a brood of hatched young

⁴**hatch** *vt* [ME *hachen,* fr. MF *hacher* to inlay, chop up] **1 :** to inlay in fine lines **2 :** to mark with fine closely spaced lines

⁵**hatch** *n* **:** STROKE, LINE; *esp* **:** one used to give the effect of shading

hatch·ery \'hach-(ə-)rē\ *n* **1 :** a place for hatching eggs **2 :** a place for the large-scale production of weanling feeder pigs

hatch·et \'hach-ət\ *n* [ME *hachet,* fr. MF *hachette,* dim. of *hache* battle-ax — more at HASH] **1 :** a short-handled ax with a hammerhead to be used with one hand **2 :** TOMAHAWK

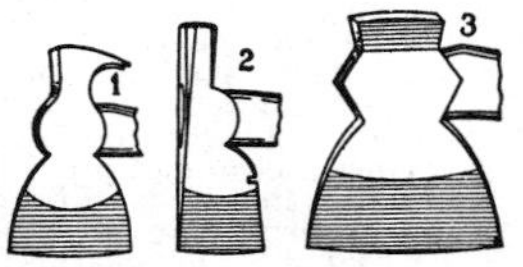

hatchets 1: *1* claw, *2* lathing *3* broad

hatchet face *n* **:** a thin sharp face — **hatch·et–faced** \ˌhach-ət-'fāst\ *adj*

hatchet man *n* **:** one hired for murder, coercion, or unscrupulous attack

hatch·ing *n* **:** the engraving or drawing of fine lines in close proximity chiefly to give an effect of shading; *also* **:** the pattern so created

hatch·ling \'hach-liŋ\ *n* **:** a recently hatched animal

hatch·ment \'hach-mənt\ *n* [perh. alter. of *achievement*] **:** a panel on which a coat of arms of a deceased person is temporarily displayed

hatch·way \'hach-ˌwā\ *n* **:** a passage giving access usu. by a ladder or stairs to an enclosed space (as a cellar); *also* **:** HATCH 2a

¹**hate** \'hāt\ *n* [ME, fr. OE *hete;* akin to OHG *haz* hate, Gk *kēdos* grief] **1 a :** intense hostility and aversion usu. deriving from fear, anger, or sense of injury **b :** an habitual emotional attitude of distaste coupled with sustained ill will **c :** a very strong dislike or antipathy **2 :** an object of hatred

²**hate** *vt* **1 :** to feel extreme enmity toward ⟨~*s* his country' enemies⟩ **2 a :** to have a strong aversion to **:** DETEST ⟨~ hypocrisy⟩ **b :** to find distasteful **:** DISLIKE ⟨~*s* cold weather⟩ ~ *vi* **:** to express or feel extreme enmity or active hostility — **hat·er** *n*

syn DETEST, ABHOR, ABOMINATE, LOATHE: HATE implies an emotional aversion often coupled with enmity or malice; DETEST suggests violent antipathy; ABHOR implies a deep often shuddering repugnance; ABOMINATE suggests strong detestation and often moral condemnation; LOATHE implies utter disgust and intolerance

hate·ful \'hāt-fəl\ *adj* **1 :** full of hate **:** MALICIOUS **2 :** exciting deserving hate — **hate·ful·ly** \-fə-lē\ *adv* — **hate·ful·ness** *n*

syn ODIOUS, ABHORRENT, DETESTABLE, ABOMINABLE: HATEFUL applies to something or someone that arouses active hatred and hostility; ODIOUS applies to that which arouses offense or repugnance; ABHORRENT characterizes that which outrages a sense of what is right, decent, just, or honorable; DETESTABLE suggests something deserving extreme contempt; ABOMINABLE suggests something fiercely condemned as vile or unnatural

hath \(')hath, (h)əth\ *archaic pres 3d sing of* HAVE

ha·tred \'hā-trəd\ *n* [ME, fr. *hate* + OE *rǣden* condition — more at KINDRED] **1 :** HATE **2 :** prejudiced hostility or animosity

hat·ter \'hat-ər\ *n* **:** one that makes, sells, or cleans and repairs hats

hau·berk \'hȯ-(ˌ)bərk\ *n* [ME, fr. OF *hauberc,* of Gmc origin; akin to OE *healsbeorg* neck armor] **:** a tunic of chain mail worn as defensive armor from the 12th to the 14th century

haugh \'hȯ(k̲)\ *n* [ME (Sc) *holch,* fr. OE *heolh* corner of land; akin to OE *holh* hole] *Scot* **:** a low-lying meadow by the side of a river

haugh·ti·ly \'hȯt-ᵊl-ē, 'hät-\ *adv* **:** in a haughty manner

haugh·ti·ness \'hȯt-ē-nəs, 'hät-\ *n* **:** the quality or state of being haughty

haugh·ty \'hȯt-ē, 'hät-\ *adj* [obs. *haught,* fr. ME *haute,* fr. MF *haut,* lit., high, fr. L *altus* — more at OLD] **:** disdainfully proud **:** ARROGANT **syn** see PROUD

¹**haul** \'hȯl\ *vb* [ME *halen* to pull, fr. OF *haler,* of Gmc origin; akin to MD *halen* to pull; akin to OE *geholian* to obtain] *vt* **1 :** to change the course of (a ship) esp. so as to sail closer to the wind **2 a :** to exert traction on **:** DRAW **b :** to obtain or move by hauling **c :** to transport in a vehicle **:** CART **3 :** HALE ~ *vi* **1 :** to exert traction **:** PULL **2 :** to furnish transportation **3** *of the wind* **:** SHIFT **syn** see PULL — **haul·er** *n*

²**haul** *n* **1 a :** the act or process of hauling **:** PULL **b :** a device for hauling **2 a :** the result of an effort to collect **:** TAKE **b :** the fish taken in a single draft of a net **3 a :** transportation by hauling **b :** the distance or route over which a load is transported **c :** a quantity transported **:** LOAD

haul·age \'hȯ-lij\ *n* **1 :** the act or process of hauling **2 :** a charge made for hauling — **haul·age·way** \-ˌwā\ *n*

haulm \'hȯm\ *n* [ME *halm,* fr. OE *healm;* akin to OHG *halm* stem, L *culmus* stalk, Gk *kalamos* reed] **1 :** the stems or tops of cultivated plants (as peas, beans, or potatoes) esp. after the crop has been gathered **2 :** a plant stem (as the culm of a grass)

haunch \'hȯnch, 'hänch\ *n* [ME *haunche,* fr. OF *hanche,* of Gmc origin; akin to MD *hanke* haunch] **1 a :** HIP 1a **b :** HINDQUARTER 2 — usu. used in pl. **2 :** HINDQUARTER 1 **3 :** either side of an arch between the springing and the crown

¹**haunt** \'hȯnt, 'hänt\ *vb* [ME *haunten,* fr. OF *hanter*] *vt* **1 a :** to visit often **:** FREQUENT **b :** to continually seek the company of **2 a :** to recur constantly and spontaneously to **b :** to reappear continually in **3 :** to visit or inhabit as a ghost ~ *vi* **1 :** to stay around or persist **:** LINGER **2 :** to appear habitually as a ghost — **haunt·er** *n* — **haunt·ing·ly** \-iŋ-lē\ *adv*

²**haunt** \'hȯnt, 'hänt, *2 is usu* 'hant\ *n* **1 :** a place habitually frequented **:** HOME **2** *chiefly dial* **:** GHOST

Hau·sa \'haů-sə, -zə\ *n, pl* **Hausa** *or* **Hausas 1 a :** a negroid people of the Sudan between Lake Chad and the Niger **b :** a member of this people **2 :** the language of the Hausa people widely used in west Africa as a trade language

haus·tel·late \hȯ-'stel-ət, 'hȯ-stə-ˌlāt\ *adj* **:** having a haustellum

haus·tel·lum \hȯ-'stel-əm\ *n, pl* **haus·tel·la** \-ə\ [NL, fr. L *haustus,* pp. of *haurire* to drink, draw — more at EXHAUST] **:** a proboscis (as of an insect) adapted to suck blood or juices of plants

haus·to·ri·al \hȯ-'stōr-ē-əl, -'stȯr-\ *adj* **:** having a haustorium **:** HAUSTELLATE

haus·to·ri·um \-ē-əm\ *n, pl* **haus·to·ria** \-ē-ə\ [NL, fr. L *haustus*] **:** a food-absorbing outgrowth of a hypha, stem, or other plant organ

haut·bois *or* **haut·boy** \'(h)ō-ˌbȯi\ *n, pl* **hautbois** \-ˌbȯiz\ *or* **hautboys** [MF *hautbois,* fr. *haut* high + *bois* wood] **:** OBOE

haute cou·ture \ˌōt-kü-'tů(ə)r\ *n* [F, lit., high sewing] **:** the establishments or designers that create fashions for women; *also* **:** the fashions created

haute école \ˌōt-ā-'kȯl, -'kəl\ *n* [F, lit., high school] **:** a highly stylized form of classical riding **:** advanced dressage

hau·teur \hȯ-'tər, (h)ō-\ *n* [F, fr. *haut* high — more at HAUGHTY] **:** HAUGHTINESS, ARROGANCE

Ha·vana \hə-'van-ə\ *n* [prob. fr. Sp *habano,* fr. *habano* of Havana, fr. La *Habana* (Havana), Cuba] **1 :** a cigar made from Cuban tobacco **2 :** tobacco raised in Cuba

¹**have** \(')hav, (h)əv, v; *before* "*to*" *usu* 'haf\ *vb* **had** \(')had, (h)əd, d\ **hav·ing** \'hav-iŋ\ **has** \(')haz, (h)əz, z, s; *before* "*to*" *usu* 'has\ [ME *haven,* fr. OE *habban;* akin to OHG *habēn* to have, *hevan* to lift — more at HEAVE] *vt* **1 a :** to hold in possession as property **b :** to hold in one's use, service, or affection or at one's disposal ⟨~ your cake and eat it too⟩ **c :** to consist of **:** CONTAIN **2 :** to feel obligation or necessity in regard to ⟨~ to go⟩ ⟨~ a letter to write⟩ **3 :** to stand in relationship to ⟨~ enemies⟩ **4 a :** to acquire or get possession of **:** OBTAIN ⟨best to be *had*⟩ **b :** RECEIVE ⟨*had* news⟩ **c :** ACCEPT; *specif* **:** to accept in marriage **5 a :** to be marked or characterized by ⟨~ red hair⟩ **b :** SHOW ⟨*had* the gall to refuse⟩ **c :** USE, EXERCISE ⟨~ mercy on us⟩ **6 a :** to experience esp. by submitting to, undergoing, or suffering ⟨~ a cold⟩ **b :** to carry on **:** PERFORM, TAKE ⟨~ a look at that cut⟩ ⟨~ a fight⟩ **c :** to entertain in the mind **:** CHERISH ⟨~ an opinion⟩ **7 a :** to cause to by persuasive or forceful means — used with the infinitive without *to* ⟨~ the children stay⟩ **b :** to cause to be **8 :** ALLOW ⟨we'll ~ no more of that⟩ **9 :** to be competent in ⟨*has* only a little French⟩ **10 a :** to hold in a position of disadvantage or certain defeat ⟨we ~ him now⟩ **b :** TRICK, FOOL ⟨been *had* by a partner⟩ **11 :** to be able to exercise ⟨I ~ my rights⟩ **12 :** BEGET, BEAR ⟨~ a baby⟩ **13 :** to partake of ⟨~ dinner⟩ **14 :** BRIBE, SUBORN ⟨can be *had* for a price⟩ ~ *verbal auxiliary* — used with the past participle to form the present perfect, past perfect, or future perfect ⟨*has* gone home⟩ ⟨*had* already eaten⟩ ⟨will ~ finished dinner by then⟩

syn HOLD, OWN, POSSESS: HAVE is the general term for any relation of belonging or of being controlled, kept, regarded, or experienced as one's own; HOLD suggests stronger control, grasp, or retention; it may imply occupancy as well as ownership; OWN implies a natural or legal right to regard as under one's full control; POSSESS is widely interchangeable with HAVE; it is similar to OWN but is applied more readily to intangibles such as power, knowledge, a quality — **have at** \ha-'vat\ **:** to go at or deal with **:** ATTACK — **have done :** FINISH, STOP — **have had it 1** *slang* **:** to have had or have done all one is going to be allowed to **2** *slang* **:** to have experienced, endured, or suffered all one can — **have it in for** \ˌhav-ət-'in-fər, -ˌfȯ(ə)r\ **:** to intend to do harm to — **have it out :** to settle a matter of contention by discussion or a fight — **have to do with 1 :** to deal with **2 :** to have in the way of connection or relation with or effect on

²**have** \'hav\ *n* **:** one that has material wealth as distinguished from one that is poor

have·lock \'hav-ˌläk, -lək\ *n* [Sir Henry *Havelock* †1857 E general] **:** a covering on a cap to protect the neck from the sun or bad weather

ha·ven \'hā-vən\ *n* [ME, fr. OE *hæfen;* akin to MHG *habene* harbor, OE *hebban* to lift — more at HEAVE] **1 :** HARBOR, PORT **2 :** a place of safety **:** ASYLUM — **haven** *vt*

have–not \'hav-ˌnät, -'nät\ *n* **:** one that is poor in material wealth as distinguished from one that is rich

haven't \'hav-ənt\ **:** have not

ha·vers \'hā-vərz\ *n pl* [*haver* (to hem and haw)] *chiefly Scot* **:** NONSENSE, POPPYCOCK

hav·er·sack \'hav-ər-ˌsak\ *n* [F *havresac,* fr. G *habersack* bag for oats, fr. *haber* oats + *sack* bag] **:** a bag similar to a knapsack but worn over one shoulder

hav·oc \'hav-ək, -ik\ *n* [ME *havok,* fr. AF, modif. of OF *havot* plunder] **1 :** wide and general destruction **:** DEVASTATION **2 :** great

confusion and disorder — **havoc** *vb* **hav·ocked; hav·ock·ing**

1haw \'hȯ\ *n* [ME *hawe,* fr. OE *haga* — more at HEDGE] **1 :** a hawthorn berry **2 :** HAWTHORN

2haw *n* [origin unknown] **:** NICTITATING MEMBRANE; *esp* **:** an inflamed nictitating membrane of a domesticated mammal

3haw *vi* [imit.] **1 :** to utter the sound represented by *haw* — usu. used with *hem* **2 :** EQUIVOCATE

4haw *n* **:** a vocalized pause in speaking

5haw *v imper* [origin unknown] — used as a direction to turn to the left; compare GEE **~** *vi* **:** to turn to the near or left side

Ha·wai·ian \hə-'wä-yən, -'wī-(y)ən, -'wȯ-yən\ *n* **1 :** a native or resident of Hawaii; *esp* **:** one of Polynesian ancestry **2 :** the Polynesian language of the Hawaiians — **Hawaiian** *adj*

Hawaiian guitar *n* **:** a flat-bodied stringed musical instrument with a long fretted neck and usu. 6 to 8 strings that are plucked

Hawaii time *n* **:** the time of the 10th time zone west of Greenwich that includes the Hawaiian islands

haw·finch \'hȯ-,finch\ *n* [1*haw*] **:** a Eurasian finch (*Coccothraustes coccothraustes*) with a large heavy bill and short thick neck and the male marked with black, white, and brown

1hawk \'hȯk\ *n* [ME *hauk,* fr. OE *hafoc;* akin to OHG *habuh* hawk, Russ *kobets,* a falcon] **1 :** any of numerous diurnal birds of prey belonging to a suborder (Falcones of the order Falconiformes) and including all the smaller members of this group; *esp* **:** ACCIPITER — compare OWL **2 :** a small board or metal sheet with a handle on the underside used to hold mortar **3 :** an individual who takes a militant attitude (as in a dispute) and advocates immediate vigorous action — **hawk·ish** *adj*

2hawk *vi* **1 :** to hunt birds by means of a trained hawk **2 :** to soar and strike like a hawk **~** *vt* **:** to hunt on the wing like a hawk

3hawk *vt* [back-formation fr. 2*hawker*] **:** to offer for sale by calling out in the street

4hawk *vb* [imit.] *vi* **:** to utter a harsh guttural sound in or as if in trying to clear the throat **~** *vt* **:** to raise by hawking ⟨~ up phlegm⟩

5hawk *n* **:** an audible effort to force up phlegm from the throat

1hawk·er \'hȯ-kər\ *n* **:** FALCONER

2hawk·er *n* [by folk etymology fr. LG *höker,* fr. MLG *hōker,* fr. *hōken* to peddle, squat; akin to OE *hēah* high] **:** one that hawks wares

Hawk·eye \'hȯ-,kī\ *n* **:** a native or resident of Iowa — used as a nickname

hawk·moth \'hȯk-,mȯth\ *n* **:** any of numerous rather large stout-bodied moths (family Sphingidae) with a long proboscis which at rest is kept coiled, long strong narrow fore wings more or less pointed at the ends, and small hind wings

hawks·bill \'hȯks-,bil\ *n* **:** a carnivorous sea turtle (*Eretmochelys imbricata*) having a shell that yields a valuable tortoiseshell

hawk·weed \'hȯ-,kwēd\ *n* **:** any of several composite plants (as of the genera *Hieracium, Picris,* and *Erechtites*) usu. having flower heads with red or orange rays

hawse \'hȯz\ *n* [ME *halse,* fr. ON *hals* neck, hawse — more at COLLAR] **1 a :** HAWSEHOLE **b :** the part of a ship's bow that contains the hawseholes **2 :** the arrangement of the anchor cables of a ship when both a port and starboard anchor are used **3 :** the distance between a ship's bow and her anchor

hawse·hole \-,hōl\ *n* **:** a hole in the bow of a ship through which a cable passes

haw·ser \'hȯ-zər\ *n* [ME, fr. AF *hauceour,* fr. MF *haucier* to hoist, fr. (assumed) VL *altiare,* fr. L *altus* high — more at OLD] **:** a large rope for towing, mooring, or securing a ship

hawser bend *n* **:** a method of joining the ends of two heavy ropes by means of seizings

haw·ser–laid \,hȯ-zər-'lād\ *adj* **:** CABLE-LAID

haw·thorn \'hȯ-,thȯ(ə)rn\ *n* [ME *hawethorn,* fr. OE *hagathorn,* fr. *haga* hawthorn + *thorn* — more at HEDGE] **:** any of a genus (*Crataegus*) of spring-flowering spiny shrubs (as the European *C. oxyacantha* and the American *C. coccinea*) of the rose family with glossy and often lobed leaves, white or pink fragrant flowers, and small red fruits

1hay \'hā\ *n* [ME *hey,* fr. OE *hīeg;* akin to OHG *hewi* hay, OE *hēawan* to hew] **1 :** grass mowed and cured for fodder **2 :** REWARD **3** *slang* **:** BED **4 :** a small sum of money

2hay *vi* **:** to cut, cure, and store for hay **~** *vt* **:** to feed with hay — **hay·er** *n*

hay·cock \'hā-,käk\ *n* **:** a conical pile of hay

hay fever *n* **:** an acute allergic nasal catarrh and conjunctivitis

hay·fork \'hā-,fȯ(ə)rk\ *n* **:** a hand or mechanically operated fork for loading or unloading hay

hay·loft \-,lȯft\ *n* **:** a loft for hay

hay·mak·er \'hā-,mā-kər\ *n* **1 :** HAYER **2 :** a powerful blow

hay·mow \-,maů\ *n* **:** a mow of or for hay

hay·rack \-,rak\ *n* **1 :** a frame mounted on the running gear of a wagon and used esp. in hauling hay or straw **2 :** a feeding rack that holds hay for livestock

hay·seed \-,sēd\ *n* **1 a :** seed shattered from hay **b :** clinging bits of straw or chaff from hay **2 :** BUMPKIN, YOKEL

hay·stack \-,stak\ *n* **:** a stack of hay

hay·wire \-,wī(ə)r\ *adj* [fr. the use of baling wire for makeshift repairs] **1 :** hastily or shoddily made **2 :** being out of order **3 :** emotionally or mentally upset **:** CRAZY

ha·zan \kə-'zän, 'käz-ᵊn\ *n, pl* **ha·za·nim** \kə-'zän-əm\ [LHeb *ḥazzān*] **1 :** a synagogue official of the talmudic period **2 :** CANTOR 2

1haz·ard \'haz-ərd\ *n* [ME, fr. MF *hasard,* fr. Ar *az-zahr* the die] **1 :** a game of chance like craps played with two dice **2 :** a source of danger **3 a :** CHANCE **b :** a chance event **:** ACCIDENT **4** *obs* **:** STAKE 3a **5 :** one of the winning openings in a court-tennis court **6 :** a golf-course obstacle — **at hazard :** at stake

2hazard *vt* **:** VENTURE, RISK

haz·ard·ous \'haz-ərd-əs\ *adj* **1 :** depending on hazard or chance **2 :** involving risk **syn** see DANGEROUS — **haz·ard·ous·ly** *adv* — **haz·ard·ous·ness** *n*

1haze \'hāz\ *vb* [prob. back-formation fr. *hazy*] *vi* **:** to become hazy or cloudy **~** *vt* **:** to make hazy, dull, or cloudy

2haze *n* [prob. back-formation fr. *hazy*] **1 :** fine dust, smoke, or light vapor causing lack of transparency **2 :** vagueness of mind or mental perception

syn MIST, FOG: HAZE suggests a diffusion of smoke or dust just sufficient to blur the vision but not obstruct it; MIST implies a fine suspension of water droplets reducing but not cutting off vision; FOG implies a denser condition than MIST with power to cut off vision entirely. Figuratively HAZE suggests vagueness, MIST dimness or uncertainty, FOG a blinding of mental or spiritual vision

3haze *vt* [origin unknown] **1 :** to harass by exacting unnecessary or disagreeable work **2 a :** to harass by banter, ridicule, or criticism **b :** to play abusive and humiliating tricks on by way of initiation **3** *West* **:** to drive (as cattle or horses) from horseback—**haz·er** *n*

1ha·zel \'hā-zəl\ *n* [ME *hasel,* fr. OE *hæsel;* akin to OHG *hasal* hazel, L *corulus*] **1 :** any of a genus (*Corylus*) of shrubs or small trees of the birch family (esp. the American *C. americana* and the European *C. cornuta*) bearing nuts enclosed in a leafy involucre **2 :** a light brown to strong yellowish brown

2hazel *adj* **1 :** consisting of hazels or of the wood of the hazel **2 :** of the color hazel

hazel hen *n* **:** a European woodland grouse (*Tetrastes bonasia*) related to the American ruffed grouse

ha·zel·nut \'hā-zəl-,nət\ *n* **:** the nut of a hazel

haz·i·ly \'hā-zə-lē\ *adv* **:** in a hazy manner

haz·i·ness \-zē-nəs\ *n* **:** the quality or state of being hazy

hazy \'hā-zē\ *adj* [origin unknown] **1 :** obscured or darkened by or as if by haze **2 :** VAGUE, INDEFINITE **3 :** CLOUDED

H–bomb \'āch-,bäm\ *n* **:** HYDROGEN BOMB

1he \(')hē, ē\ *pron* [ME, fr. OE *hē;* akin to OE *hēo* she, *hit* it, OHG *hē* he, L *cis, citra* on this side, Gk *ekeinos* that person] **1 :** that male one ⟨~ is my father⟩ — compare HIM, HIS, IT, SHE, THEY **2 :** that one whose sex is unknown or immaterial ⟨~ that runs may read⟩

2he \'hē\ *n, often attrib* **1 :** a male person or animal **2 :** one that is strongly masculine or virile ⟨a real *he*-man⟩

3he \'hā\ *n* [Heb *hē'*] **:** the 5th letter of the Hebrew alphabet — symbol ה

1head \'hed\ *n* [ME *hed,* fr. OE *hēafod;* akin to OHG *houbit* head, L *caput*] **1 :** the upper or anterior division of the body (as of a man or an insect) that contains the brain, the chief sense organs, and the mouth **2 a :** the seat of the intellect **:** MIND **b :** natural aptitude or talent **c :** mental or emotional control **:** POISE **d :** HEADACHE **3 :** the obverse of a coin **4 a :** each one among a number **:** INDIVIDUAL **b** *pl* **head :** a unit of number (as of domestic animals) **5 a :** the end that is upper or higher or opposite the foot **b :** the source of a stream **c :** either end of something (as a drum) whose two ends need not be distinguished **d :** a horizontal passage in a coal mine **6 :** DIRECTOR, LEADER: as **a :** HEADMASTER **b :** one in charge of a division or department in an office or institution **7 a :** CAPITULUM 2 **b :** the foliaged part of a plant esp. when consisting of a compact mass of leaves or close fructification **8 a :** the leading element of a military column or a procession **b :** HEADWAY **9 a :** the uppermost extremity or projecting part of an object **:** TOP **b :** the striking part of a weapon **c :** the oval part of a printed musical note **10 a :** a body of water kept in reserve at a height; *also* **:** the containing bank, dam, or wall **b :** a mass of water in motion **11 a :** the difference in elevation between two points in a body of fluid **b :** the resulting pressure of the fluid at the lower point expressible as this height; *broadly* **:** pressure of a fluid **12 a :** the bow and adjacent parts of a ship **b :** a ship's toilet **13 :** the place of leadership or of honor or of command **14 a** (1) **:** a word often in larger letters placed above a passage in order to introduce or categorize (2) **:** a separate part or topic **b :** a portion of a page or sheet that is above the first line of printing **15 a :** the topmost edge of a book **b :** the upper edge of a sail **16 :** the foam or scum that rises on a fermenting or effervescing liquid (as beer) **17 a :** the part of a boil, pimple, or abscess at which it is likely to break **b :** culminating point of action **:** CRISIS **18 :** a part or attachment of a machine or machine tool containing a device (as a cutter, drill); *also* **:** the part of an apparatus that performs the chief function or a particular function **19 :** an immediate constituent of an endocentric compound or construction having the same grammatical function as the whole (as the terms *polite old man, old man,* and *man* in "a polite old man") — **by the head :** drawing the greater depth of water forward — **off one's head :** CRAZY, DISTRACTED — **out of one's head :** DELIRIOUS — **over one's head 1 :** beyond one's comprehension **2 :** so as to pass over one's superior standing or authority

2head *adj* **1 :** of, relating to, or for the head **2 :** PRINCIPAL, CHIEF ⟨~ cook⟩ **3 :** situated at the head **4 :** coming from in front ⟨~ sea⟩

3head *vt* **1 :** BEHEAD **2 a :** to cut back the upper or terminal growth of (a plant or plant part) — often used with *back* **b :** to harvest (a cereal grass) by cutting off the heads **3 a :** to put a head on **:** fit a head to ⟨~ an arrow⟩ **b :** to form the head or top of ⟨tower ~*ed* by a spire⟩ **4 :** to put oneself at the head of **:** act as leader to ⟨~ a revolt⟩ **5 a :** to face or oppose head on ⟨~ the waves⟩ **b :** to get in front of so as to hinder, stop, or turn back **c :** to take a lead over (as in a race) **:** SURPASS **d :** to pass (a stream) by going round above the source **6 a :** to put something at the head of (as a list) **b :** to stand as the first or leading member of ⟨~*s* the list of heroes⟩ **7 :** to set the course of ⟨~ a ship northward⟩ **8 :** to drive (as a soccer ball) with the head **~** *vi* **1 :** to form a head ⟨this cabbage ~*s* early⟩ **2 :** to point or proceed in a certain direction ⟨the fleet was ~*ing* out⟩ **3 :** to have a source **:** ORIGINATE

head·ache \'hed-,āk\ *n* **1 :** pain in the head **2 :** a vexatious or baffling situation or problem — **head·achy** \-,ā-kē\ *adj*

head·band \'hed-,band\ *n* **1 :** a band worn on or around the head **2 :** a plain or decorative band printed or engraved at the head of a page or a chapter **3 :** a narrow strip of cloth sewn or glued by hand to a book at the extreme ends of the backbone

head·board \-,bō(ə)rd, -,bȯ(ə)rd\ *n* **:** a board forming the head (as of a bed)

head·cheese \-,chēz\ *n* **:** a product made from edible parts of the head, feet, and sometimes the tongue and heart esp. of a pig cut up fine, boiled, and pressed

head cold *n* **:** a common cold centered in the nasal passages and adjacent mucous tissues

head·dress \'he(d)-,dres\ *n* **:** an often elaborate covering for the head

head·ed \'hed-əd\ *adj* **1 :** having a head or a heading **2 :** having such a head or so many heads — often used in compounds

head·er \'hed-ər\ *n* **1 :** one that removes heads; *esp* **:** a grain-harvesting machine that cuts off the grain heads and elevates them to a wagon **2 a :** a brick

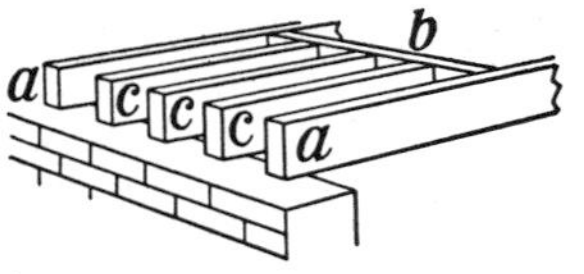

timbers, with header: *a,a* trimmers; *b* header; *c,c,c* tail beams

or stone laid in a wall with its end toward the face of the wall **b :** a beam fitted between trimmers and across the ends of tailpieces in a building frame **3 :** a fall or dive head foremost

head·first \'hed-'fərst\ *also* **head·fore·most** \-'fōr-,mōst, -'fȯr-\ *adv* **:** with the head foremost **:** HEADLONG — **headfirst** *adj*

head gate *n* **1 :** a gate at the upper end of a canal lock **2 :** a gate for controlling the water flowing into a race, sluice, or irrigation ditch

head·gear \'hed-,gi(ə)r\ *n* **:** a covering or protective device for the head

head·hunt \-,hənt\ *vi* **:** to decapitate enemies and preserve their heads as trophies — **headhunt** *n* — **head·hunt·er** *n* — **head·hunt·ing** *n*

head·i·ly \'hed-ᵊl-ē\ *adv* **:** in a heady manner

head·i·ness \'hed-ē-nəs\ *n* **:** the quality or state of being heady

head·ing \'hed-iŋ\ *n* **1 :** the compass direction in which the longitudinal axis of a ship or aircraft points **2 :** something that forms or serves as a head; *esp* **:** an inscription, headline, or title standing at the top or beginning (as of a letter or chapter) **3 :** DRIFT 6

head·land \'hed-lənd, -,land\ *n* **1 :** unplowed land at the ends of furrows or near a fence **2 :** a point of usu. high land jutting out into the sea **:** PROMONTORY

head·less \-ləs\ *adj* **1 a :** having no head **b :** BEHEADED **2 :** having no chief **3 :** lacking good sense or prudence **:** FOOLISH — **head·less·ness** *n*

head·light \-,līt\ *n* **:** a light with a reflector and special lens mounted on the front of an automotive vehicle

¹head·line \-,līn\ *n* **1 :** a head of a newspaper story or article usu. printed in large type and devised to summarize the story or article that follows **2 :** words set at the head of a passage or page to introduce or categorize

²headline *vt* **1 :** to provide with a headline **2 :** to publicize highly

head·lin·er \-,lī-nər\ *n* **:** a performer whose name is given prominent billing **:** STAR

head·lock \-,läk\ *n* **:** a wrestling hold in which one encircles his opponent's head with one arm

¹head·long \-'lȯŋ\ *adv* [ME *hedlong,* alter. of *hedling,* fr. *hed* head] **1 :** HEADFIRST **2 :** without deliberation **:** RECKLESSLY **3 :** without pause or delay

²head·long \-,lȯŋ\ *adj* **1 :** PRECIPITATE, RASH **2 :** plunging headforemost **3** *archaic* **:** STEEP, PRECIPITOUS **syn** see PRECIPITATE

head louse *n* **:** one of a variety (*Pediculus humanus capitis*) of the common louse that lives on the scalp of man

head·man *n* **1 a** \'hed-'man\ **:** OVERSEER, FOREMAN **b** \-'man, -,man\ **:** a lesser chief of a primitive community **2** \-mən\ **:** HEADSMAN

head·mas·ter \'hed-,mas-tər, -'mas-\ *n* **:** a man heading the staff of a private school **:** PRINCIPAL — **head·mas·ter·ship** \-,ship\ *n*

head·mis·tress \-,mis-trəs, -'mis-\ *n* **:** a woman heading the staff of a private school

head·most \'hed-,mōst\ *adj* **:** most advanced **:** LEADING

head·note \-,nōt\ *n* **:** a prefixed note of comment or explanation; *esp* **:** one prefixed to the report of a decided legal case

head–on \-'ȯn, -'än\ *adj* **1 :** having the front facing in the direction of motion or line of sight **2 :** FRONTAL

head over heels *adv* **1 a :** in or as if in a somersault **:** HELTER-SKELTER **b :** upside down **2 :** HOPELESSLY, DEEPLY

head·phone \'hed-,fōn\ *n* **:** an earphone held over the ear by a band worn on the head

head·piece \-,pēs\ *n* **1 :** a protective or defensive covering for the head **2 :** BRAINS, INTELLIGENCE **3 :** an ornament esp. at the beginning of a chapter

head·pin \-,pin\ *n* **:** a bowling pin that stands foremost in the arrangement of pins

head·quar·ters \'hed-,kwȯ(r)t-ərz, (')hed-'\ *n pl but sing or pl in constr* **1 :** a place from which a commander performs the functions of command **2 :** the administrative center of an enterprise

head·race \'hed-,rās\ *n* **:** a race for conveying water to a point of industrial application

head·rest \-,rest\ *n* **:** a support for the head

head·sail \'hed-,sāl, -səl\ *n* **:** a sail set forward of the foremast

head·set \-,set\ *n* **:** a pair of headphones

head·ship \-,ship\ *n* **:** the position, office, or dignity of a head

heads·man \'hedz-mən\ *n* **:** one that beheads **:** EXECUTIONER

head·spring \'hed-,spriŋ\ *n* **:** FOUNTAINHEAD, SOURCE

head·stall \'hed-,stȯl\ *n* **:** a part of a bridle or halter that encircles the head

head·stock \-,stäk\ *n* **:** a bearing or pedestal for a revolving or moving part; *specif* **:** a part of a lathe that holds the revolving spindle and its attachments

head·stone \-,stōn\ *n* **:** the stone at the head of a grave

head·stream \-,strēm\ *n* **:** a stream that is the source of a river

head·strong \-,strȯŋ\ *adj* **1 :** not easily restrained **:** WILLFUL **2 :** directed by ungovernable will **syn** see UNRULY

head·wait·er \'hed-'wāt-ər\ *n* **:** the head of the dining-room staff of a restaurant or hotel

head·wa·ter \-,wȯt-ər, -,wät-\ *n* **:** the source of a stream

head·way \-,wā\ *n* **1 a :** motion or rate of motion in a forward direction **b :** ADVANCE, PROGRESS **2 :** clear space (as under an arch) **3 :** the time interval between two vehicles traveling in the same direction on the same route

head wind *n* **:** a wind blowing in a direction opposite to a course esp. of a ship or aircraft

head·word \'hed-,wərd\ *n* **1 :** a word or term placed at the beginning (as of a chapter or entry) **2 :** a word qualified by a modifier

head·work \-,wərk\ *n* **:** mental labor; *esp* **:** clever thinking

heady \'hed-ē\ *adj* **1 a :** WILLFUL, RASH **b :** VIOLENT, IMPETUOUS **2 :** tending to make giddy **:** INTOXICATING **3 :** SHREWD

heal \'hē(ə)l\ *vb* [ME *helen,* fr. OE *hǣlan;* akin to OHG *heilen* to heal, OE *hāl* whole — more at WHOLE] *vt* **1 a :** to make sound or whole ⟨~ a wound⟩ **b :** to restore to health **2 a :** CURE, REMEDY **b :** to patch up (a breach or division) **3 :** to restore to original purity or integrity **~** *vi* **:** to return to a sound state **syn** see CURE

heal·er \'hē-lər\ *n* **1 :** one that heals **2 :** a Christian Science practitioner

health \'helth\ *n, often attrib* [ME *helthe,* fr. OE *hǣlth,* fr. *hāl*] **1 a :** the condition of being sound in body, mind, or soul; *esp* **:** freedom from physical disease or pain **b :** the general condition of the body ⟨in poor ~⟩ ⟨enjoys good ~⟩ **2 :** flourishing condition **:** WELL-BEING **3 :** a toast to someone's health or prosperity

health·ful \-fəl\ *adj* **1 :** beneficial to health of body or mind **2 :** HEALTHY — **health·ful·ly** \-fə-lē\ *adv* — **health·ful·ness** *n*

health·i·ly \'hel-thə-lē\ *adv* **:** in a healthy manner

health·i·ness \-thē-nəs\ *n* **:** the quality or state of being healthy

healthy \'hel-thē\ *adj* **1 :** enjoying good health **:** WELL **2 :** evincing health ⟨a ~ complexion⟩ **3 :** conducive to health **4 a :** PROSPEROUS, FLOURISHING **b :** not small or feeble **:** CONSIDERABLE

syn SOUND, WHOLESOME, ROBUST, HALE, WELL: HEALTHY implies full strength and vigor as well as freedom from signs of disease; SOUND emphasizes the absence of disease, weakness, or malfunction; WHOLESOME implies appearance and behavior indicating soundness and balance; ROBUST implies the opposite of all that is delicate or sickly; HALE applies particularly to robustness in old age; WELL implies merely freedom from disease or illness

¹heap \'hēp\ *n* [ME *heep,* fr. OE *hēap;* akin to OE *hēah* high] **1 :** a collection of things thrown one on another **:** PILE **2 :** a great number or large quantity **:** LOT

²heap *vt* **1 :** to throw or lay in a heap **2 :** to cast or bestow in large quantities **3 :** to fill (as a container) more than even full

hear \'hi(ə)r\ *vb* **heard** \'hərd\ **hear·ing** \'hi(ə)r-iŋ\ [ME *heren,* fr. OE *hīeran;* akin to OHG *hōren* to hear, L *cavēre* to be on guard, Gk *akouein* to hear] *vt* **1 :** to perceive or apprehend by the ear **2 :** to gain knowledge of by hearing **3 a :** to listen to with attention **:** HEED **b :** ATTEND **4 a :** to give a legal hearing to **b :** to take testimony from ⟨~ witnesses⟩ **~** *vi* **1 :** to have the capacity of apprehending sound **2 :** to gain information **:** LEARN **3 :** to entertain the idea ⟨wouldn't ~ of it⟩ — **hear·er** \'hir-ər\ *n*

hear·ing *n* **1 a :** the process, function, or power of perceiving sound; *specif* **:** the special sense by which noises and tones are received as stimuli **b :** EARSHOT **2 a :** opportunity to be heard, to present one's side of a case, or to be generally known or appreciated **b** (1) **:** a listening to arguments (2) **:** a preliminary examination in criminal procedure **c :** a session (as of a legislative committee) in which witnesses are heard and testimony is taken **3** *chiefly dial* **:** a piece of news **:** RUMOR

hearing aid *n* **:** an electronic device usu. worn by a person for amplifying sound before it reaches the receptor organs

hear·ken \'här-kən\ *vb* **hear·ken·ing** \'härk-(ə-)niŋ\ [ME *herknen,* fr. OE *heorcnian;* akin to OHG *hōrechen* to listen — more at HARK] *vi* **1 :** to give ear **:** LISTEN **2 :** to give respectful attention **~** *vt, archaic* **:** to give heed to **:** HEAR

hear·say \'hi(ə)r-,sā\ *n* **:** something heard from another **:** RUMOR

hearsay evidence *n* **:** evidence based not on a witness's personal knowledge but on matters told him by another

¹hearse \'hərs\ *n* [ME *herse,* fr. MF *herce* harrow, frame for holding candles, fr. L *hirpic-, hirpex* harrow] **1 a :** a triangular candelabrum for 15 candles used esp. at Tenebrae **b :** an elaborate framework erected over a coffin or tomb to which memorial verses or epitaphs are attached **2 a** *archaic* **:** COFFIN **b** *obs* **:** BIER 2 **3 :** a vehicle for conveying the dead to the grave

²hearse *vt* **1 a** *archaic* **:** to place on or in a hearse **b :** to convey in a hearse **2 :** BURY

¹heart \'härt\ *n* [ME *hert,* fr. OE *heorte;* akin to OHG *herza* heart, L *cord-, cor,* Gk *kardia*] **1 a :** a hollow muscular organ of vertebrate animals that by its rhythmic contraction acts as a force pump maintaining the circulation of the blood **b :** a structure in an invertebrate animal functionally analogous to the vertebrate heart **c :** BREAST, BOSOM **d :** something resembling a heart in shape; *specif* **:** a conventionalized representation of a heart **2 a :** a playing card marked with a conventionalized figure of a heart **b** *pl* **:** the suit comprising cards so marked **c** *pl but sing in constr* **:** a game in which the object is to avoid taking tricks containing hearts **3 a** (1) **:** the whole personality including intellectual as well as emotional functions or traits (2) *obs* **:** INTELLECT (3) **:** MEMORY, ROTE (4) **:** OPINION, ATTITUDE **b** (1) **:** the emotional or moral as distinguished from the intellectual nature (2) **:** generous disposition **:** COMPASSION (3) **:** TEMPERAMENT, MOOD (4) **:** GOODWILL **c :** LOVE, AFFECTIONS **d :** COURAGE, ARDOR **e** (1) **:** TASTE, LIKING (2) **:** fixed purpose or desire (3) **:** intense concern, solicitude, or preoccupation **f :** one's innermost being **4 :** PERSON **5 a :** the central or innermost part **:** CENTER **b :** the essential or most vital part of something — **to heart :** with deep concern

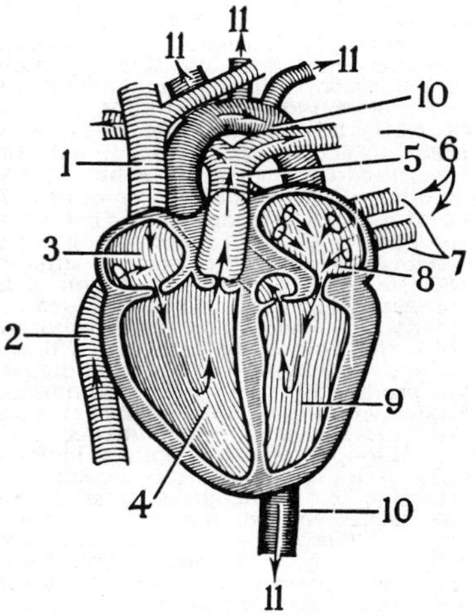

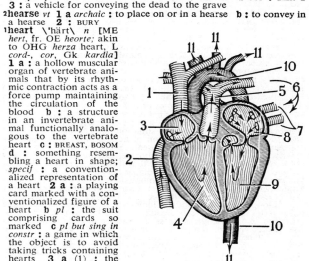

heart 1a: showing course of the blood coming from the extremities and entering from *1* superior vena cava, and from *2* inferior vena cava; to *3* right auricle; to *4* right ventricle; to *5* pulmonary artery; to *6* lungs (not shown); to *7* pulmonary veins; to *8* left auricle; to *9* left ventricle, to *10* aorta; leaving by *11* to the extremities (not shown)

²heart *vt* **1** *archaic* **:** HEARTEN **2 :** to fix or seat in the heart

heart·ache \'härt-,āk\ *n* **:** anguish of mind **:** SORROW

heart·beat \-,bēt\ *n* **1 :** one complete pulsation of the heart **2 :** the vital center or driving impulse

heart block *n* **:** incoordination of the heartbeat in which the auricles and ventricles beat independently

heart·break \'härt-,brāk\ *n* **:** crushing grief

heart·break·ing \-ˌbrā-kiŋ\ *adj* **:** causing intense sorrow or distress
heart·bro·ken \-ˌbrō-kən\ *adj* **:** overcome by sorrow **:** BROKEN-HEARTED
heart·burn \-ˌbərn\ *n* **:** a burning discomfort behind the lower part of the sternum usu. related to spasm of the lower end of the esophagus or of the upper part of the stomach
heart·burn·ing \-ˌbər-niŋ\ *n* **:** intense or rancorous jealousy or resentment
heart disease *n* **:** an abnormal organic condition of the heart or of the heart and circulation
heart·ed \ˈhärt-əd\ *adj* **1 :** having a specified kind of heart ⟨a faint-*hearted* leader⟩ **2 :** seated in the heart
heart·en \ˈhärt-ᵊn\ *vt* **heart·en·ing** \ˈhärt-niŋ, -ᵊn-iŋ\ **:** to give heart to **:** ENCOURAGE
heart·felt \-ˌfelt\ *adj* **:** deeply felt **:** EARNEST **syn** see SINCERE
heart-free \-ˌfrē\ *adj* **:** not in love
hearth \ˈhärth\ *n* [ME *herth*, fr. OE *heorth;* akin to OHG *herd* hearth, Skt *kūḍayāti* he singes] **1 a :** a brick, stone, or cement area in front of a fireplace **b :** the floor of a fireplace **c** (1) **:** the lowest section of a blast furnace (2) **:** the bottom of a refinery, reverberatory, or open-hearth furnace on which the ore or metal is exposed to the flame (3) **:** the inside bottom of a cupola **2 :** HOME, FIRESIDE
hearth·stone \-ˌstōn\ *n* **1 a :** stone forming a hearth **b :** FIRESIDE, HOME **2 :** a soft stone or composition of powdered stone and pipe clay used to whiten or scour hearths and doorsteps
heart·i·ly \ˈhärt-ᵊl-ē\ *adv* **1 :** in a hearty manner **2 a :** with all sincerity **:** WHOLEHEARTEDLY **b :** with zest or gusto **3 :** THOROUGHLY
heart·i·ness \ˈhärt-ē-nəs\ *n* **:** the quality or state of being hearty
heart·land \-ˌland\ *n* **:** a central and vital area; *esp* **:** the central land area of northern Eurasia held by geopoliticians to have strategic advantages for mastery of the world
heart·less \-ləs\ *adj* **1** *archaic* **:** SPIRITLESS **2 :** lacking feeling **:** CRUEL — **heart·less·ly** *adv* — **heart·less·ness** *n*
heart·rend·ing \ˈhärt-ˌren-diŋ\ *adj* **:** causing intense grief, anguish, or distress
hearts·ease \ˈhärt-ˌsēz\ *n* **1 :** peace of mind **:** TRANQUILLITY **2 :** any of various violas; *esp* **:** WILD PANSY
heart·sick \ˈhärt-ˌsik\ *adj* **:** very despondent **:** DEPRESSED — **heart·sick·ness** *n*
heart·some \ˈhert-səm\ *adj, chiefly Scot* **:** animating and enlivening — **heart·some·ly** *adv, chiefly Scot*
heart·sore \ˈhärt-ˌsō(ə)r, -ˌsȯ(ə)r\ *adj* **:** HEARTSICK
heart-strick·en \-ˌstrik-ən\ *or* **heart-struck** \-ˌstrək\ *adj* **:** stricken to the heart (as with grief or dismay)
heart·string \-ˌstriŋ\ *n* **1** *obs* **:** a nerve once believed to sustain the heart **2 :** the deepest emotions or affections ⟨pulled at his ~*s*⟩
heart·throb \-ˌthräb\ *n* **1 :** the throb of a heart **2 :** sentimental emotion **:** PASSION
heart-to-heart \ˌhärt-tə-ˌhärt\ *adj* **:** SINCERE, FRANK ⟨a ~ talk⟩
heart-whole \ˈhärt-ˌhōl\ *adj* **1 :** HEART-FREE **2 :** SINCERE, GENUINE
heart·wood \-ˌwu̇d\ *n* **:** the older harder nonliving central portion of wood that is usu. darker, denser, less permeable, and more durable than the surrounding sapwood — called also *duramen*
[1]**hearty** \ˈhärt-ē\ *adj* **1 a :** giving unqualified support **:** THOROUGHGOING **b :** enthusiastically or exuberantly cordial **:** JOVIAL **c :** expressed unrestrainedly **2 a :** exhibiting vigorous good health **b** (1) **:** consuming abundantly or with gusto (2) **:** ABUNDANT **c :** NOURISHING **3 :** VIGOROUS, VEHEMENT **syn** see SINCERE
[2]**hearty** *n* **:** a bold brave fellow **:** COMRADE; *also* **:** SAILOR
[1]**heat** \ˈhēt\ *vb* [ME *heten*, fr. OE *hǣtan;* akin to OE *hāt* hot] *vi* **1 :** to become warm or hot **2 :** to become hot and start to spoil ~ *vt* **1 :** to make warm or hot **2 :** EXCITE — **heat·ed·ly** *adv*
[2]**heat** *n* **1 a** (1) **:** a condition of being hot **:** WARMTH (2) **:** a marked or notable degree of hotness **b :** pathological excessive bodily temperature **c :** a hot place or situation **d** (1) **:** a period of heat (2) **:** a single complete operation of heating; *also* **:** the quantity of material so heated **e** (1) **:** added energy that causes substances to rise in temperature, fuse, evaporate, expand, or undergo any of various other related changes, that flows to a body by contact with or radiation from bodies at higher temperatures, and that can be produced in a body (as by compression) (2) **:** the energy associated with the random motions of the molecules, atoms, or smaller structural units of which matter is composed **f :** appearance, condition, or color of a body as indicating its temperature **g :** one of a series of intensities of heating **2 a :** intensity of feeling or reaction **b :** the height or stress of an action or condition **c :** sexual excitement esp. in a female mammal; *specif* **:** ESTRUS **3 :** pungency of flavor **4 :** a single continuous effort: as **a :** a single course in a race **b :** one of several preliminary races held to eliminate less competent contenders **c** (1) *slang* **:** the intensification of law-enforcement activity or investigation (2) **:** PRESSURE, COERCION — **heat·less** \ˈhēt-ləs\ *adj*
heat engine *n* **:** a mechanism for converting heat energy into mechanical energy
heat·er \ˈhēt-ər\ *n* **1 :** a contrivance that imparts heat or holds something to be heated **2 :** one whose work is to heat something
heat exhaustion *n* **:** a condition marked by weakness, nausea, dizziness, and profuse sweating that results from physical exertion in a hot environment — called also *heat prostration;* compare HEATSTROKE
heath \ˈhēth\ *n* [ME *heth*, fr. OE *hǣth;* akin to OHG *heida* heather, OW *coit* forest] **1 a :** any of a family (Ericaceae, the heath family) of shrubby dicotyledonous and often evergreen plants that thrive on open barren usu. acid and ill-drained soil; *esp* **:** an evergreen subshrub of either of two genera (*Erica* and *Calluna*) with whorls of needlelike leaves and clusters of small flowers **b :** any of various plants that resemble true heaths **2 a :** a tract of wasteland **b :** an extensive area of rather level open uncultivated land usu. with poor coarse soil, inferior drainage, and a surface rich in peat or peaty humus — **heath·less** \-ləs\ *adj* — **heath·like** \-ˌlīk\ *adj* — **heathy** \ˈhē-thē\ *adj*
heath·bird \ˈhēth-ˌbərd\ *n* **:** BLACK GROUSE
heath cock *n* **:** BLACKCOCK
[1]**hea·then** \ˈhē-t͟hən\ *adj* [ME *hethen*, fr. OE *hǣthen;* akin to OHG *heidan* heathen] **1 :** of or relating to the heathen, their religions, or their customs **:** PAGAN **2 :** STRANGE, UNCIVILIZED
[2]**heathen** *n, pl* **heathens** *or* **heathen 1 :** an unconverted member of a people or nation that does not acknowledge the God of the Bible **:** PAGAN **2 :** an uncivilized or irreligious person — **hea·then·dom** \-dəm\ *n* — **hea·then·ism** \-t͟hə-ˌniz-əm\ *n*
hea·then·ish \ˈhē-t͟hə-nish\ *adj* **:** resembling or characteristic of heathens **:** BARBAROUS — **hea·then·ish·ly** *adv*
hea·then·ize \-ˌnīz\ *vt* **:** to make heathen
[1]**heath·er** \ˈhet͟h-ər\ *n* [ME (northern) *hather*] **:** HEATH 1a; *esp* **:** a common heath (*Calluna vulgaris*) of northern and alpine regions that has small crowded sessile leaves and racemes of tiny usu. purplish pink flowers — **heath·ery** \ˈhet͟h-(ə-)rē\ *adj*
[2]**heather** *adj* **1 :** of, relating to, or resembling heather **2 :** having flecks of various colors ⟨a soft ~ tweed⟩
heath hen *n* **1 :** GRAY HEN **2 :** a now extinct grouse (*Tympanuchus cupido cupido*) of the northeastern U.S. — compare PRAIRIE CHICKEN
heat lightning *n* **:** vivid and extensive flashes of electric light without thunder seen near the horizon esp. at the close of a hot day and ascribed to far-off lightning reflected by high clouds
heat rash *n* **:** PRICKLY HEAT
heat·stroke \ˈhēt-ˌstrōk\ *n* **:** a condition marked esp. by cessation of sweating, extremely high body temperature, and collapse that results from prolonged exposure to high temperature — compare HEAT EXHAUSTION
heat unit *n* **1 :** BRITISH THERMAL UNIT **2 :** CALORIE
[1]**heave** \ˈhēv\ *vb* **heaved** *or* **hove** \ˈhōv\ **heav·ing** [ME *heven*, fr. OE *hebban;* akin to OHG *hevan* to lift, L *capere* to take] *vt* **1** *obs* **:** ELEVATE **2 :** to cause to be lifted upward or onward **3 :** THROW, CAST **4 :** to utter with obvious effort **5 a :** to cause to swell or rise **b :** to displace (as a rock stratum) esp. by a fault **6 :** HAUL, DRAW ~ *vi* **1 :** to rise or become thrown or raised up **2 :** to strain to do something **3 a :** to rise and fall rhythmically **b :** PANT **4 :** RETCH **5 a :** PULL, PUSH **b :** to move a ship in a specified direction or manner **c** *of a ship* **:** to move in an indicated way **syn** see LIFT — **heav·er** *n*
[2]**heave** *n* **1 a :** an effort to heave or raise **b :** HURL, CAST **2 :** an upward motion **:** RISING; *esp* **:** a rhythmical rising **3 :** the horizontal displacement by the faulting of a rock **4** *pl but sing or pl in constr* **:** chronic pulmonary emphysema of the horse resulting in difficult expiration, heaving of the flanks, and a persistent cough
heav·en \ˈhev-ən\ *n* [ME *heven*, fr. OE *heofon;* akin to OHG *himil* heaven] **1 :** the expanse of space that seems to be over the earth like a dome **:** FIRMAMENT — usu. used in pl. **2 a** *often cap* **:** the dwelling place of the Deity and the joyful abode of the blessed dead **b :** a spiritual state of everlasting communion with God **3** *cap* **:** [2]GOD **4 :** a place or condition of utmost happiness **5** *Christian Science* **:** a state of immortality in which sin is absent and all manifestations of Mind are harmoniously ordered under the divine Principle
heav·en·li·ness \-lē-nəs\ *n* **:** the quality or state of being heavenly
heav·en·ly \-lē\ *adj* **1 :** of or relating to heaven or the heavens **:** CELESTIAL **2 a :** SACRED, DIVINE **b :** DELIGHTFUL — **heavenly** *adv*
heav·en·ward \ˈhev-ən-wərd\ *adv* (*or adj*) **:** toward heaven
heav·en·wards \-wərdz\ *adv* **:** HEAVENWARD
heav·i·ly \ˈhev-ə-lē\ *adv* **1 :** in a heavy manner **2 :** slowly and laboriously **:** DULLY **3** *archaic* **:** SORROWFULLY, GRIEVOUSLY **4 :** to a great degree **:** SEVERELY
heav·i·ness \ˈhev-ē-nəs\ *n* **:** the quality or state of being heavy
Heav·i·side layer \ˌhev-ē-ˌsīd-\ *n* [Oliver *Heaviside* †1925 E physicist] **:** IONOSPHERE
[1]**heavy** \ˈhev-ē\ *adj* [ME *hevy*, fr. OE *hefig;* akin to OHG *hebīc* heavy, OE *hebban* to lift — more at HEAVE] **1 a :** having great weight **b :** having a high specific gravity **c** (1) *of an isotope* **:** having or being atoms of greater than normal mass (2) *of a compound* **:** containing heavy isotopes **2 :** hard to bear; *specif* **:** GRIEVOUS, AFFLICTIVE ⟨a ~ sorrow⟩ **3 :** of weighty import **:** SERIOUS **4 :** DEEP, PROFOUND **5 a :** borne down by something oppressive **:** BURDENED **b :** PREGNANT; *esp* **:** approaching parturition **6 a :** slow or dull from loss of vitality or resiliency **:** SLUGGISH **b :** lacking sparkle or vivacity **:** DRAB **c :** lacking mirth or gaiety **:** DOLEFUL **d :** characterized by declining prices **7 :** dulled with weariness **:** DROWSY **8 :** greater in quantity or quality than the average of its kind or class: as **a :** unusually large ⟨~ traffic⟩ **b :** of great force ⟨~ seas⟩ **c :** OVERCAST **d** (1) **:** impeding motion (2) **:** full of clay and inclined to hold water **e :** coming as if from a depth **:** LOUD **f :** THICK, COARSE **g :** OPPRESSIVE ⟨~ odor⟩ **h :** STEEP, ACUTE **i :** LABORIOUS, DIFFICULT **j :** of large capacity or output **9 a :** digested with difficulty because of excessive richness or seasoning ⟨~ fruitcake⟩ **b :** not properly raised or leavened ⟨~ bread⟩ **10 :** producing goods (as coal or steel) used in the production of other goods ⟨~ industry⟩ **11 a :** armed with guns of large caliber **b :** heavily armored **12 a :** having stress ⟨~ rhythm⟩ — used esp. of syllables in accentual verse **b :** being the strongest of three degrees of stress in speech **13 :** relating to theatrical parts of a grave or somber nature
syn WEIGHTY, PONDEROUS, CUMBROUS, CUMBERSOME: HEAVY implies having greater density or thickness, or sometimes power, than the average of its kind; WEIGHTY suggests having weight as a positive attribute; PONDEROUS implies having great weight because of size and massiveness with resulting great inertia; CUMBROUS and CUMBERSOME imply heaviness and bulkiness that make for difficulty in grasping, moving, carrying, or manipulating
[2]**heavy** *adv* **:** in a heavy manner **:** HEAVILY
[3]**heavy** *n* **1** *pl* **:** heavy cavalry **2 :** HEAVYWEIGHT 2 **3 a :** a theatrical role or an actor representing a dignified or imposing person **b :** VILLAIN 4
heavy-du·ty \ˌhev-ē-ˈd(y)üt-ē\ *adj* **:** able or designed to withstand unusual strain
heavy-foot·ed \-ˈfu̇t-əd\ *adj* **:** heavy and slow in movement **:** DULL ⟨~ literary style⟩
heavy-hand·ed \-ˈhan-dəd\ *adj* **1 :** CLUMSY, UNGRACEFUL **2 :** OPPRESSIVE, HARSH — **heavy-hand·ed·ly** *adv* — **heavy-hand·ed·ness** *n*
heavy·heart·ed \-ˈhärt-əd\ *adj* **:** SADDENED, DESPONDENT — **heavy·heart·ed·ly** *adv* — **heavy·heart·ed·ness** *n*
heavy hydrogen *n* **:** an isotope of hydrogen having a mass number greater than 1; *esp* **:** DEUTERIUM
heavy·set \ˌhev-ē-ˈset\ *adj* **:** stocky and compact and sometimes tending to stoutness in build
heavy spar *n* **:** BARITE
heavy water *n* **:** water containing more than the usual proportion

of heavy isotopes; *esp* : water enriched in deuterium

heavy·weight \'hev-ē-ˌwāt\ *n* **1** : one above average in weight **2** : one in the heaviest class of contestants: as **a** : a boxer weighing over 175 pounds **b** : a wrestler weighing over 175 pounds

heb·do·mad \'heb-də-ˌmad\ *n* [L *hebdomad-, hebdomas*, fr. Gk, fr. *hebdomos* seventh, fr. *hepta* seven] : a group of seven

heb·dom·a·dal \heb-'däm-əd-ᵊl\ *adj* : WEEKLY

heb·dom·a·dal·ly \-ᵊl-ē\ *adv* : every week

hebe- *comb form* [Gk *hēbē* youth — more at EPHEBUS] : puberty

He·be \'hē-bē\ *n* [L, fr. Gk *Hēbē*] : the Greek goddess of youth

he·be·phre·nia \ˌhē-bə-'fre-nē-ə, -'fren-ē-\ *n* [NL] : a schizophrenic reaction characterized by silliness, delusions, hallucinations, and regression — **he·be·phre·nic** \-'fren-ik, -'frē-nik\ *adj*

heb·e·tate \'heb-ə-ˌtāt\ *vt* [L *hebetatus*, pp. of *hebetare*, fr. *hebet-, hebes* dull] : to make dull or obtuse — **heb·e·ta·tion** \ˌheb-ə-'tā-shən\ *n*

heb·e·tude \'heb-ə-ˌt(y)üd\ *n* : DULLNESS, LETHARGY — **heb·e·tu·di·nous** \ˌheb-ə-'t(y)üd-nəs, -ᵊn-əs\ *adj*

He·bra·ic \hi-'brā-ik\ *adj* [ME *Ebrayke*, fr. LL *Hebraicus*, fr. Gk *Hebraikos*, fr. *Hebraios*] : of, relating to, or characteristic of the Hebrews or their language or culture — **He·bra·i·cal·ly** \-'brā-ə-k(ə-)lē\ *adv*

He·bra·ism \'hē-(ˌ)brā-ˌiz-əm\ *n* **1** : a Hebrew idiom occurring in another language **2** : the thought, spirit, or practice characteristic of the Hebrews **3** : the moral theory of life held to be characteristic of the Hebrews

He·bra·ist \-ˌbrā-əst\ *n* : a specialist in Hebrew and Hebraic studies

He·bra·is·tic \ˌhē-brā-'is-tik\ *adj* **1** : HEBRAIC **2** : marked by Hebraisms

he·bra·ize \'hē-brā-ˌīz\ *vb, often cap, vi* : to use Hebraisms ~ *vt* : to make Hebraic

He·brew \'hē-(ˌ)brü\ *n* [ME *Ebreu*, fr. OF, fr. LL *Hebraeus*, fr. L, adj., fr. Gk *Hebraios*, fr. Aram *'Ebrai*] **1** : a member of or descendant from one of a group of northern Semitic peoples including the Israelites; *esp* : ISRAELITE **2 a** : the Semitic language of the ancient Hebrews **b** : any of various later forms of this language — **Hebrew** *adj*

Hec·ate \'hek-ət-ē, *archaic* -ət\ *n* [L, fr. Gk *Hekatē*] : the goddess of the underworld in Greek mythology

hec·a·tomb \'hek-ə-ˌtōm\ *n* [L *hecatombe*, fr. Gk *hekatombē*, fr. *hekaton* hundred + *bous* cow — more at HUNDRED, COW] **1** : an ancient Greek and Roman sacrifice of 100 oxen or cattle **2** : the sacrifice or slaughter of many victims

heck·le \'hek-əl\ *vt* **heck·ling** \-(ə-)liŋ\ [ME *hekelen*, fr. *heckele* hackle; akin to OHG *hāko* hook — more at HOOK] : to harass and try to disconcert with questions, challenges, or gibes : BADGER **syn** see BAIT — **heck·ler** \-(ə-)lər\ *n*

hect- *or* **hecto-** *comb form* [F, irreg. fr. Gk *hekaton*] : hundred ⟨*hecto*graph⟩

hect·are \'hek-ˌta(ə)r, -ˌte(ə)r, -ˌtär\ *n* [F, fr. *hect-* + *are*] — see METRIC SYSTEM table

hec·tic \'hek-tik\ *adj* [ME *etyk*, fr. MF *etique*, fr. LL *hecticus*, fr. Gk *hektikos* habitual, consumptive, fr. *hekt-* (akin to *echein* to have) — more at SCHEME] **1** : of, relating to, or being a fluctuating but persistent fever (as in tuberculosis) **2** : having a hectic fever **3** : FLUSHED, RED **4** : marked by feverish activity : RESTLESS — **hec·ti·cal·ly** \-ti-k(ə-)lē\ *adv*

hec·to·gram \'hek-tə-ˌgram\ *n* [F *hectogramme*, fr. *hect-* + *gramme* gram] — see METRIC SYSTEM table

hec·to·graph \'hek-tə-ˌgraf\ *n* [G *hektograph*, fr. *hekto-* hect- + *-graph*] : a machine for making copies of a writing or drawing — **hectograph** *vt* — **hec·to·graph·ic** \ˌhek-tə-'graf-ik\ *adj*

hec·to·li·ter \'hek-tə-ˌlēt-ər\ *n* [F *hectolitre*, fr. *hect-* + *litre* liter] — see METRIC SYSTEM table

hec·to·me·ter \'hek-tə-ˌmēt-ər, hek-'täm-ət-ər\ *n* [F *hectomètre*, fr. *hect-* + *mètre* meter] — see METRIC SYSTEM table

1**hec·tor** \'hek-tər\ *n* [L, fr. Gk *Hektōr*] **1** *cap* : a son of Priam, husband of Andromache, and bravest of the Trojans in Homer's *Iliad* **2** : BULLY, BRAGGART

2**hector** *vb* **hec·tor·ing** \-t(ə-)riŋ\ *vi* : to play the bully : SWAGGER ~ *vt* : to intimidate by bluster or personal pressure **syn** see BAIT

Hec·u·ba \'hek-yə-bə\ *n* [L, fr. Gk *Hekabē*] : the wife of Priam and mother of Hector in Homer's *Iliad*

he'd \(ˌ)hēd, ēd\ : he had : he would

hed·dle \'hed-ᵊl\ *n* [prob. alter. of ME *helde*, fr. OE *hefeld*; akin to ON *hafald* heddle, OE *hebban* to lift — more at HEAVE] : one of the sets of parallel cords or wires that with their mounting compose the harness used to guide warp threads in a loom

he·der \'ḵād-ər, 'ḵed-\ *n* [Yiddish *kheyder*, fr. Heb *ḥedher* room] : an elementary Jewish school in which children are taught to read the Pentateuch, the Prayer Book, and other books in Hebrew

1**hedge** \'hej\ *n* [ME *hegge*, fr. OE *hecg*; akin to OE *haga* hedge, hawthorn, L *colum* sieve] **1 a** : a fence or boundary formed by a dense row of shrubs or low trees **b** : BARRIER, LIMIT **2 a** : a means of protection or defense (as against financial loss) **3** : a calculatedly noncommittal statement

2**hedge** *vt* **1** : to enclose or protect with or as if with a hedge : ENCIRCLE **2** : to hem in or obstruct with or as if with a barrier : HINDER **3** : to protect oneself from losing by a counterbalancing transaction ⟨~ a bet⟩ ~ *vi* **1** : to plant, form, or trim a hedge **2** : to evade the risk of commitment esp. by leaving open a way of retreat : TRIM **3 a** : to protect oneself financially; *specif* : to buy or sell commodity futures as a protection against loss due to price fluctuation **b** : to minimize the risk of a bet — **hedg·er** *n*

3**hedge** *adj* **1** : of, relating to, or designed for a hedge **2** : born, living, or made near or as if near hedges : ROADSIDE **3** : INFERIOR

hedge·hog \'hej-ˌhȯg, -ˌhäg\ *n* **1 a** : any of a genus (*Erinaceus*) of Old World nocturnal insectivorous mammals having both hair and spines that they present outwardly by rolling themselves up **b** : any of several spiny mammals (as a porcupine) **2** : a military defensive obstacle or stronghold

hedge·hop \-ˌhäp\ *vi* [back-formation fr. *hedgehopper*] : to fly an airplane close to the ground and rise over obstacles as they appear — **hedge·hop·per** *n*

hedge·pig \-ˌpig\ *n* : HEDGEHOG

hedge·row \-ˌrō\ *n* : a row of shrubs or trees enclosing or separating fields

he·don·ic \hi-'dän-ik\ *adj* **1** : of, relating to, or characterized by pleasure **2** : HEDONISTIC

he·do·nism \'hēd-ᵊn-ˌiz-əm\ *n* [Gk *hēdonē* pleasure; akin to Gk *hēdys* sweet — more at SWEET] **1** : the doctrine that pleasure or happiness is the sole or chief good in life — compare PSYCHOLOGICAL HEDONISM **2** : a way of life based on or suggesting the principles of hedonism — **he·do·nist** \-ᵊn-əst\ *n* — **he·do·nis·tic** \ˌhēd-ᵊn-'is-tik\ *adj*

hedonistic calculus *n* : a method of determining the rightness of an action by balancing the pleasures and pains that it would produce

-he·dral \'hē-drəl\ *adj comb form* [NL *-hedron*] : having (such) a surface or (such or so many) surfaces ⟨di*hedral*⟩

-he·dron \'hē-drən\ *n comb form, pl* **-hedrons** *or* **-he·dra** \-drə\ [NL, fr. Gk *-edron*, fr. *hedra* seat — more at SIT] : crystal or geometrical figure having a (specified) form or number of surfaces ⟨penta*hedron*⟩ ⟨trapezo*hedron*⟩

hee·bie–jee·bies \ˌhē-bē-'jē-bēz\ *n pl* [coined by Billy DeBeck] : JITTERS

1**heed** \'hēd\ *vb* [ME *heeden*, fr. OE *hēdan*; akin to OHG *huota* guard] *vi* : to pay attention ~ *vt* : to concern oneself with

2**heed** *n* : ATTENTION, NOTICE

heed·ful \'hēd-fəl\ *adj* : taking heed : CAREFUL — **heed·ful·ly** \-fə-lē\ *adv* — **heed·ful·ness** *n*

heed·less \-ləs\ *adj* : not taking heed : CARELESS — **heed·less·ly** *adv* — **heed·less·ness** *n*

hee–haw \'hē-ˌhȯ\ *n* [imit.] **1** : the bray of a donkey **2** : a loud rude laugh : GUFFAW — **hee–haw** *vi*

1**heel** \'hē(ə)l\ *n* [ME, fr. OE *hēla*; akin to ON *hæll* heel, OE *hōh* — more at HOCK] **1 a** : the back of the human foot below the ankle and behind the arch **b** : the back of the hind limb of other vertebrates homologous with the human heel **2** : an anatomical structure suggestive of the human heel **3 a** : one of the crusty ends of a loaf of bread **b** : one of the rind ends of a cheese **4 a** : the part (as of a shoe) that covers the human heel **b** : a solid attachment of a shoe or boot forming the back of the sole under the heel of the foot **5** : a rear, low, or bottom part: as **a** : the after end of a ship's keel or the lower end of a mast **b** : the base of a tuber or cutting of a plant used for propagation **c** : the base of a ladder **6** : a contemptible person — **heel·less** \'hē(ə)l-ləs\ *adj* — **by the heels** : in a tight grip — **down at heel** *or* **down at the heel** : in or into a rundown or shabby condition — **to heel 1** : close behind **2** : into agreement or line — **under heel** : under control or subjection

2**heel** *vt* **1 a** : to furnish with a heel **b** : to supply esp. with money **2** : to exert pressure on, propel, or strike with the heel ~ *vi* : to move along at the heels of someone

3**heel** *vb* [alter. of ME *heelden*, fr. OE *hieldan*; akin to OHG *hald* inclined, Lith *šalis* side, region] *vi* : to tilt to one side : TIP, LIST ~ *vt* : to cause to list

4**heel** *n* : LIST; *also* : the extent of a list

heel–and–toe \ˌhē-lən-'tō\ *adj* : marked by a stride in which the heel of one foot touches the ground before the toe of the other foot leaves it

heel·er \'hē-lər\ *n* **1** : one that heels **2 a** : a henchman of a local political boss **b** : a worker for a local party organization; *esp* : WARD HEELER

heel·piece \'hē(ə)l-ˌpēs\ *n* : a piece designed for or forming the heel

heel·post \-ˌpōst\ *n* : a post to which a gate or door is hinged

heel·tap \'hē(ə)l-ˌtap\ *n* : a small quantity of liquor remaining (as in a glass after drinking)

1**heft** \'heft\ *n* [irreg. fr. *heave*] **1** : WEIGHT, HEAVINESS **2** *archaic* : BULK

2**heft** *vt* **1** : to heave up : HOIST **2** : to test the weight of by lifting

hefty \'hef-tē\ *adj* **1** : quite heavy **2 a** : marked by bigness, bulk, and usu. strength **b** : POWERFUL, MIGHTY **c** : impressively large

he·gari \hi-'gar-ē, -'ger-\ *n* [Ar (Sudan) *hegiri*] : any of several Sudanese grain sorghums having chalky white seeds including one grown in the southwestern U.S.

He·ge·li·an \hā-'gā-lē-ən\ *adj* : of, relating to, or characteristic of Hegel, his philosophy, or his dialectic method — **Hegelian** *n*

He·ge·li·an·ism \-lē-ə-ˌniz-əm\ *n* : the philosophy of Hegel that equates the rational and the real and that uses dialectic to comprehend an absolute idea of which phenomena are partial representations

he·ge·mo·ny \hi-'jem-ə-nē, 'hej-ə-ˌmō-nē\ *n* [Gk *hēgemonia*, fr. *hēgemōn* leader, fr. *hēgeisthai* to lead — more at SEEK] : preponderant influence or authority esp. of one nation over others

he·gi·ra *also* **he·ji·ra** \hi-'jī-rə, 'hej-(ə-)rə\ *n* [the *Hegira*, flight of Muhammad from Mecca in A.D. 622, fr. ML, fr. Ar *hijrah*, lit., flight] : a journey esp. when undertaken to seek refuge away from a dangerous or undesirable environment : EXODUS

Hei·del·berg man \ˌhīd-ᵊl-ˌbərg-, -ˌbe(ə)rg-\ *n* [*Heidelberg*, Germany] : an early Pleistocene man known from a massive fossilized jaw with distinctly human dentition

heif·er \'hef-ər\ *n* [ME *hayfare*, fr. OE *hēahfore*] : a young cow; *esp* : one that has not had a calf

heigh \'hī, 'hā\ *interj* [origin unknown] : HEY

heigh–ho \-'hō\ *interj* — used typically to express boredom, weariness, or sadness or sometimes as a cry of encouragement

height \'hīt, 'hītth\ *n* [ME *heighthe*, fr. OE *hīehthu*; akin to OHG *hōhida* height, OE *hēah* high] **1 a** : the highest part : SUMMIT **b** : the highest or most advanced point : ZENITH **2 a** : the distance from the bottom to the top of something standing upright **b** : the extent of elevation above a level : ALTITUDE **3** : the condition of being tall or high **4 a** : an extent of land rising to a considerable degree above the surrounding country **b** : a high point or position **5** *obs* : an advanced social rank **6** : degree of geographical latitude **syn** STATURE, ELEVATION, ALTITUDE: HEIGHT may be used of any vertical distance great or small; STATURE applies only to animal bodies, esp. to the mature human body; ELEVATION and ALTITUDE imply height practicably determined only by angular measurement or atmospheric pressure

height·en \'hīt-ᵊn\ *vb* **height·en·ing** \'hīt-niŋ, -ᵊn-iŋ\ *vt* **1 a** : to increase the amount or degree of : AUGMENT **b** : to make brighter or more intense : DEEPEN **c** : to bring out more strongly : point up **d** : to make more acute : SHARPEN **2 a** : to raise high or higher : ELEVATE **b** : to raise above the ordinary or trite **3** *obs* : ELATE ~ *vi* **1** *archaic* : GROW, RISE **2 a** : to become great or greater in

ə abut; ᵊ kitten; ər further; a back; ā bake; ä cot, cart; aů out; ch chin; e less; ē easy; g gift; i trip; ī life; j joke; ŋ sing; ō flow; ȯ flaw; ȯi coin; th thin; t͟h this; ü loot; ů foot; y yet; yü few; yů furious; zh vision

amount, degree, or extent **b :** to become brighter or more intense **syn** see INTENSIFY

height to paper : the standard 0.9186 inch height of printing type in English-speaking countries

Heim·dal \'hām-,däl\ *n* [ON *Heimdallr*] **:** the guardian of Asgard in Norse mythology

hei·nous \'hā-nəs\ *adj* [ME, fr. MF *haineus*, fr. *haine* hate, fr. *hair* to hate, of Gmc origin; akin to OHG *haz* hate — more at HATE] **:** hatefully or shockingly evil **:** ABOMINABLE **syn** see OUTRAGEOUS — **hei·nous·ly** *adv* — **hei·nous·ness** *n*

[1]**heir** \'a(ə)r, 'e(ə)r\ *n* [ME, fr. OF, fr. L *hered-*, *heres;* akin to Gk *chēros* bereaved, OE *gān* to go] **1 :** one who inherits or is entitled to inherit property: as **a :** HEIR AT LAW **b :** one who receives the property of a deceased person esp. by operation of law or by virtue of a will **2 :** one who inherits or is entitled to succeed to a hereditary rank, title, or office **3 :** one who receives or is entitled to receive some endowment or quality from a parent or predecessor — **heir·ship** \-,ship\ *n*

[2]**heir** *vt, chiefly dial* **:** INHERIT

heir apparent *n, pl* **heirs apparent 1 :** an heir whose right to an inheritance is indefeasible in law if he survives the legal ancestor **2 :** HEIR PRESUMPTIVE **3 :** one whose succession esp. to a position or role appears certain under existing circumstances

heir at law : an heir in whom an intestate's real property is vested by operation of law

heir·ess \'ar-əs, 'er-\ *n* **:** a female heir; *esp* **:** a female heir to great wealth

heir·loom \'a(ə)r-,lüm, 'e(ə)r-\ *n* [ME *heirlome*, fr. *heir* + *lome* implement — more at LOOM] **1 :** a piece of property that descends to the heir as an inseparable part of an inheritance **2 :** something of special value handed on from one generation to another

heir presumptive *n, pl* **heirs presumptive :** an heir whose legal right to an inheritance may be defeated (as by the birth of a nearer relative)

[1]**heist** \'hīst\ *vt* [alter. of [1]*hoist*] **1** *chiefly dial* **:** HOIST **2** *slang* **a :** to commit armed robbery on **b :** STEAL

[2]**heist** *n, slang* **:** armed robbery **:** HOLDUP; *also* **:** THEFT

Hel \'hel\ *n* [ON] **:** the goddess of the dead and queen of the underworld in Norse mythology

held *past of* HOLD

Hel·en of Troy \,hel-ə-nəv-'tròi\ **:** the beautiful wife of Menelaus whose abduction by Paris brings about the Trojan War

heli- *or* **helio-** *comb form* [L, fr. Gk *hēli-*, *hēlio-*, fr. *hēlios* — more at SOLAR] **:** sun ⟨*helio*centric⟩

he·li·a·cal \hi-'lī-ə-kəl\ *adj* [LL *heliacus*, fr. Gk *hēliakos*, fr. *hēlios*] **:** relating to or near the sun — used esp. of the last setting of a star before and its first rising after invisibility due to conjunction with the sun — **he·li·a·cal·ly** \-ə-k(ə-)lē\ *adv*

helic- *or* **helico-** *comb form* [Gk *helik-*, *heliko-*, fr. *helik-*, *helix* spiral — more at HELIX] **:** helix **:** spiral ⟨*helical*⟩

he·li·cal \'hel-i-kəl, 'hē-li-\ *adj* **:** of, relating to, or having the form of a helix; *broadly* **:** SPIRAL 1a — **he·li·cal·ly** \-k(ə-)lē\ *adv*

[1]**he·li·coid** \'hel-ə-,kòid, 'hē-lə-\ *or* **he·li·coi·dal** \,hel-ə-'kòid-ᵊl, ,hē-lə-\ *adj* **1 :** forming or arranged in a spiral **2 :** having the form of a flat coil or flattened spiral ⟨~ snail shell⟩

[2]**helicoid** *n* **:** a surface resembling that of a screw thread

hel·i·con \'hel-ə-,kän, -i-kən\ *n* [prob. fr. Gk *helik-*, *helix* + E *-on* (as in *bombardon*)] **:** a large circular bass tuba used in military bands that is carried over the shoulder and around the body

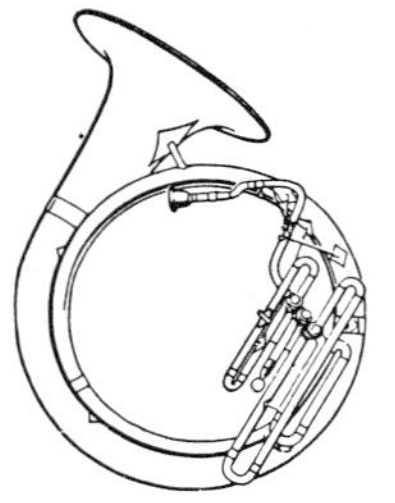
helicon

he·li·cop·ter \'hel-ə-,käp-tər, 'hē-lə-\ *n* [F *hélicoptère*, fr. Gk *heliko-* + *pteron* wing — more at FEATHER] **:** an aircraft whose support in the air is derived chiefly from the aerodynamic forces acting on one or more rotors turning about substantially vertical axes — **helicopter** *or* **he·li·copt** \-,käpt\ *vb*

he·lio·cen·tric \,hē-lē-ō-'sen-trik\ *adj* **:** referred to or measured from the sun's center or appearing as if seen from it **:** having or relating to the sun as a center — compare GEOCENTRIC

he·lio·chrome \'hē-lē-ə-,krōm\ *n* **:** a photograph in natural colors

he·lio·gram \-,gram\ *n* **:** a message transmitted by a heliograph

[1]**he·lio·graph** \-,graf\ *n* [ISV] **1 a :** PHOTOENGRAVING 2b **b :** PHOTOHELIOGRAPH **2 :** an apparatus for telegraphing by means of the sun's rays thrown from a mirror — **he·lio·graph·ic** \,hē-lē-ə-'graf-ik\ *adj* — **he·li·og·ra·phy** \,hē-lē-'äg-rə-fē\ *n*

[2]**heliograph** *vb* **:** to signal by means of a heliograph — **he·li·og·ra·pher** \,hē-lē-'äg-rə-fər\ *n*

he·lio·gra·vure \,hē-lē-ō-grə-'vyù(ə)r\ *n* [F *héliogravure*, fr. *hélio-* heli- + *gravure*] **:** PHOTOGRAVURE

he·li·ol·a·try \,hē-lē-'äl-ə-trē\ *n* **:** sun worship

he·li·om·e·ter \,hē-lē-'äm-ət-ər\ *n* [F *héliomètre*, fr. *hélio-* heli- + *-mètre* -meter] **:** a visual telescope that has a divided objective with two movable parts which give a double image and that was orig. designed for measuring the apparent diameter of the sun — **he·lio·met·ric** \,hē-lē-ō-'me-trik\ *adj* — **he·lio·met·ri·cal·ly** \-tri-k(ə-)lē\ *adv*

He·li·os \'hē-lē-,äs\ *n* [Gk *Hēlios*] **:** the sun-god in Greek mythology represented as driving a four-horse chariot through the heavens

he·lio·stat \'hē-lē-ə-,stat\ *n* [NL *heliostata*, fr. *heli-* + Gk *-statēs* -stat] **:** an instrument consisting of a mirror mounted on an axis moved by clockwork by which a sunbeam is steadily reflected in one direction

he·lio·tax·is \,hē-lē-ō-'tak-səs\ *n* [NL] **:** phototaxis in which sunlight is the stimulus

he·lio·trope \'hēl-yə-,trōp, -ē-ə-, *Brit usu* 'hel-\ *n* [L *heliotropium*, fr. Gk *hēliotropion*, fr. *hēlio-* heli- + *tropos* turn — more at TROPE] **1 a** *obs* **:** a plant that turns toward the sun **b :** any of a genus (*Heliotropium*) of herbs or shrubs of the borage family — compare GARDEN HELIOTROPE **2 :** BLOODSTONE **3 a :** a variable color averaging a moderate purple **b :** a moderate reddish purple

he·lio·tro·pic \,hē-lē-ə-'trōp-ik, -'träp-\ *adj* **:** characterized by heliotropism — **he·lio·tro·pi·cal·ly** \-i-k(ə-)lē\ *adv*

he·li·ot·ro·pism \,hē-lē-'ä-trə-,piz-əm\ *n* **:** phototropism in which sunlight is the orienting stimulus

he·lio·zo·an \,hē-lē-ə-'zō-ən\ *n* [NL *Heliozoa*, order name, fr. *heli-* + *-zoa*] **:** any of an order (Heliozoa) of free-living holozoic usu. freshwater rhizopod protozoans that reproduce by binary fission or budding — **heliozoan** *adj* — **he·lio·zo·ic** \-'zō-ik\ *adj*

he·li·port \'hel-ə-,pō(ə)rt, 'hē-lə-, -,pó(ə)rt\ *n* [*heli*copter + *port*] **:** a landing and takeoff place for a helicopter

he·li·um \'hē-lē-əm\ *n, often attrib* [NL, fr. Gk *hēlios*] **:** a light colorless inert gaseous element present in economically extractable amounts in various natural gases — see ELEMENT table

he·lix \'hē-liks\ *n, pl* **he·li·ces** \'hel-ə-,sēz, 'hē-lə-\ *also* **he·lix·es** \'hē-lik-səz\ [L, fr. Gk; akin to Gk *eilyein* to roll, wrap — more at VOLUBLE] **1 :** something spiral in form: as **a :** an ornamental volute **b :** a coil formed by winding wire around a uniform tube **2 :** the incurved rim of the external ear **3 :** a curve traced on a cylinder by the rotation of a point crossing its right sections at a constant oblique angle; *broadly* **:** SPIRAL 1b

hell \'hel\ *n, often attrib* [ME, fr. OE; akin to OHG *helan* to conceal, L *celare*, Gk *kalyptein*] **1 a** (1) **:** a nether world in which the dead continue to exist **:** HADES (2) **:** the nether realm of the devil and the demons in which the damned suffer everlasting punishment **b** *Christian Science* **:** ERROR 2b, SIN **2 a :** a place or state of torment or wickedness — often used as an interjection, an intensive, or a generalized term of abuse **b :** a place or state of turmoil or destruction **c :** severe scolding **d :** unrestrained fun or sportiveness **3 a** *archaic* **:** a tailor's receptacle **b :** HELLBOX

he'll \(,)hē(ə)l, hil, ēl, il\ **:** he will **:** he shall

hell·ben·der \'hel-,ben-dər\ *n* **:** a large voracious aquatic salamander (*Cryptobranchus alleganiensis*) of the Ohio valley

hell–bent \-,bent\ *adj* **1 :** stubbornly often recklessly determined **2 :** going full tilt

hell·box \-,bäks\ *n* **:** a receptacle into which a printer throws damaged or discarded type material

hell·broth \-,bròth\ *n* **:** a brew for working black magic

hell·cat \-,kat\ *n* **1 :** WITCH 1b(2) **2 :** TORMENTOR; *esp* **:** SHREW

hel·le·bore \'hel-ə-,bō(ə)r, -,bó(ə)r\ *n* [L *helleborus*, fr. Gk *helleboros*] **1 a :** any of a genus (*Helleborus*) of herbs of the crowfoot family **b :** a poisonous herb (genus *Veratrum*) of the lily family **2 a :** the dried rhizome and root of a hellebore (genus *Helleborus*) or a powder or extract of this formerly used in medicine **b :** the dried rhizome and root of a hellebore (*Veratrum album* or *V. viride*) or a powder or extract of this containing alkaloids used as a cardiac and respiratory depressant and as an insecticide

Hel·lene \'hel-,ēn\ *n* [Gk *Hellēn*] **:** GREEK — **Hel·len·ic** \he-'len-ik, hə-\ *adj*

Hel·le·nism \'hel-ə-,niz-əm\ *n* **1 :** GRECISM 1 **2 :** devotion to or imitation of esp. ancient Greek thought, customs, or styles **3 :** Greek civilization **4 :** a body of humanistic and classical ideals associated with ancient Greece

Hel·le·nist \-nəst\ *n* **1 :** a person living in Hellenistic times not Greek in ancestry but Greek in language, outlook, and way of life; *esp* **:** a hellenized Jew **2 :** a specialist in the language or culture of ancient Greece

Hel·le·nis·tic \,hel-ə-'nis-tik\ *adj* **1 :** of or relating to Greek history, culture, or art after Alexander the Great **2 :** of or relating to the Hellenists — **Hel·le·nis·ti·cal·ly** \-ti-k(ə-)lē\ *adv*

hel·le·ni·za·tion \,hel-ə-nə-'zā-shən\ *n, often cap* **1 :** the act or process of hellenizing **2 :** the quality or state of being hellenized

hel·le·nize \'hel-ə-,nīz\ *vb, often cap, vi* **:** to become Greek or Hellenistic ~ *vt* **:** to make Greek or Hellenistic in form or culture

hell·er \'hel-ər\ *n, chiefly dial* **:** HELLION

hel·leri \'hel-ə-,rī, -,rē\ *n* [NL, fr. C. *Heller*, 20th cent. tropical fish collector] **1 :** SWORDTAIL **2 :** any of various brightly colored topminnows developed in the aquarium by hybridization of swordtails and platys

hell·gram·mite \'hel-grə-,mīt\ *n* [origin unknown] **:** a long-lived carnivorous aquatic larva of a large No. American insect (*Corydalus cornutus*) or of a related insect much used as a fish bait

hell·hound \-,haùnd\ *n* **1 :** a dog represented in mythology as a guardian of the underworld **2 :** a fiendishly evil person

hel·lion \'hel-yən\ *n* [prob. alter. of *hallion* (scamp)] **:** a troublesome or mischievous person

hell·ish \'hel-ish\ *adj* **:** of, resembling, or befitting hell **:** DEVILISH — **hell·ish·ly** *adv* — **hell·ish·ness** *n*

hel·lo \hə-'lō, he-\ *n, pl* **hellos** [alter. of *hollo*] **:** an expression or gesture of greeting — used interjectionally in greeting, in answering the telephone, or to express surprise

[1]**helm** \'helm\ *n* [ME, fr. OE] **:** HELMET 1

[2]**helm** *vt* **:** to cover or furnish with a helmet

[3]**helm** *n* [ME *helme*, fr. OE *helma;* akin to OHG *helmo* tiller] **1 a :** a lever or wheel controlling the rudder of a ship for steering; *broadly* **:** the entire apparatus for steering a ship **b :** deviation of the position of the helm from the amidships position **2 :** a position of control **:** HEAD

[4]**helm** *vt* **:** to direct with or as if with a helm **:** STEER

hel·met \'hel-mət\ *n* [MF, dim. of *helme* helmet, of Gmc origin; akin to OE *helm* helmet, OHG *helan* to conceal — more at HELL] **1 :** a covering or enclosing headpiece of ancient or medieval armor **2 :** any of various protective head coverings usu. made of a hard material to resist impact **3 :** something resembling a helmet; *specif* **:** a hood-shaped upper sepal or petal of some flowers — **hel·met·like** \-,līk\ *adj*

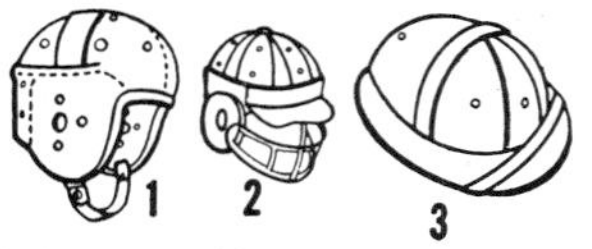
helmets 2: *1* football, *2* lacrosse, *3* polo

hel·minth \'hel-,min(t)th\ *n* [Gk *helminth-*, *helmis;* akin to Gk *eilyein* to roll — more at VOLUBLE] **:** WORM; *esp* **:** an intestinal worm — **hel·min·thic** \hel-'min(t)-thik\ *adj*

helminth- *or* **helmintho-** *comb form* [NL, fr. Gk *helminth-*, *helmis*] **:** helminth ⟨*helminth*iasis⟩ ⟨*helmintho*logy⟩

hel·min·thi·a·sis \,hel-,min-'thī-ə-səs\ *n* [NL] **:** infestation with or disease caused by parasitic worms

hel·min·thol·o·gy \,hel-,min-'thäl-ə-jē\ *n* **:** a branch of zoology concerned with helminths; *esp* **:** the study of parasitic worms

helms·man \'helmz-mən\ *n* **:** the man at the helm **:** STEERSMAN

hel·ot \'hel-ət\ *n* [L *Helotes*, pl., fr. Gk *Heilōtes*] **1** *cap* **:** a member of the lowest social class of ancient Sparta constituting a body of serfs **2 :** SERF, SLAVE — **hel·ot·ry** \'hel-ə-trē\ *n*

hel·ot·ism \'hel-ət-ˌiz-əm\ *n* **1 :** SERFDOM **2 :** a symbiotic relation in which one member functions as the slave of the other

1help \'help, *South also* 'hep\ *vb* [ME *helpen*, fr. OE *helpan;* akin to OHG *helfan* to help, Lith *šelpti*] *vt* **1 :** to give assistance to **:** AID **2 a :** REMEDY, RELIEVE **b** *archaic* **:** RESCUE, SAVE **c :** to get (oneself) out of a difficulty **3 a :** to be of use to **:** BENEFIT **b :** to further the advancement of **:** PROMOTE **4 a :** to change for the better **:** MEND **b :** to refrain from ⟨couldn't ~ laughing⟩ **c :** to keep from occurring **:** PREVENT **5 :** to serve with food or drink esp. at a meal **6 :** to appropriate for the use of (oneself) ~ *vi* **:** to be of use or benefit ⟨every little bit ~*s*⟩

syn HELP, AID, ASSIST mean to supply what is needed to accomplish an end. HELP carries a strong implication of advance toward an objective; AID suggests the evident need of help or relief and so imputes weakness to the one aided and strength to the one aiding; ASSIST suggests a secondary role in the assistant or a subordinate character in the assistance **syn** see in addition IMPROVE

— **cannot help but :** cannot but — **so help me :** I swear it

2help *n* **1 :** AID, ASSISTANCE **2 :** a source of aid **3 :** REMEDY, RELIEF **4 a :** one who is in the service of or who assists another **:** HELPER **b :** the services of a paid worker **5 :** HELPING

help·er *n* **:** one that helps; *specif* **:** a relatively unskilled worker who assists another esp. by manual labor

help·ful \-fəl\ *adj* **:** of service or assistance **:** USEFUL — **help·ful·ly** \-fə-lē\ *adv* — **help·ful·ness** *n*

help·ing *n* **:** a portion of food **:** SERVING

help·less \'hel-pləs\ *adj* **1 :** lacking protection or support **:** DEFENSELESS **2 :** lacking strength or effectiveness **:** POWERLESS — **help·less·ly** *adv* — **help·less·ness** *n*

help·mate \'help-ˌmāt\ *n* [by folk etymology fr. *helpmeet*] **:** one who is a companion and helper; *specif* **:** WIFE

help·meet \-ˌmēt\ *n* [2*help* + *meet*, adj.] **:** HELPMATE

1hel·ter–skel·ter \ˌhel-tər-'skel-tər\ *adv* [imit.] **1 :** in headlong disorder **:** PELL-MELL **2 :** in random order **:** HAPHAZARDLY

2helter–skelter *n* **:** a disorderly confusion **:** TURMOIL

3helter–skelter *adj* **1 :** confusedly hurried **:** PRECIPITATE **2 :** HIT-OR-MISS, HAPHAZARD

helve \'helv\ *n* [ME, fr. OE *hielfe;* akin to OE *healf* half] **:** a handle of a tool or weapon **:** HAFT

Hel·ve·tian \hel-'vē-shən\ *adj* **:** of or relating to the Helvetii or Helvetia **:** SWISS — **Helvetian** *n*

Hel·ve·tii \-shē-ˌī\ *n pl* [L] **:** an early Celtic people of western Switzerland in the time of Julius Caesar

1hem \'hem\ *n* [ME, fr. OE; akin to MHG *hemmen* to hem in, Arm *kamel* to press] **1 a :** a border of a cloth article doubled back and stitched down **b :** a similar border on an article of sheet metal, plastic, rubber, or leather **2 :** RIM, MARGIN

2hem *vt* **hemmed; hem·ming 1 a :** to finish with a hem **b :** BORDER, EDGE **2 :** to surround in a restrictive manner **:** CONFINE — usu. used with *in* ~ *vi* **:** to make a hem in sewing — **hem·mer** *n*

3hem \'hem; *as an interjection a throat-clearing sound*\ *n* [imit.] **:** a vocalized pause in speaking — often used interjectionally to call attention or to express hesitation or doubt

4hem \'hem\ *vi* **hemmed; hem·ming 1 :** to utter the sound represented by *hem* **2 :** EQUIVOCATE

hem- *or* **hemo-** *or* **haem-** *or* **haemo-** *comb form* [MF *hemo-*, fr. L *haem-*, *haemo-*, fr. Gk *haim-*, *haimo-*, fr. *haima*] **:** blood ⟨*hem*al⟩ ⟨*hemo*flagellate⟩

hema- *or* **haema-** *comb form* [NL, fr. Gk *haima*] **:** HEM- ⟨*hema*cytometer⟩

he·ma·cy·tom·e·ter \ˌhē-mə-(ˌ)sī-'täm-ət-ər, ˌhem-ə-\ *n* **:** an instrument for counting blood cells

hem·ag·glu·ti·nate \ˌhē-mə-'glüt-ᵊn-ˌāt, ˌhem-ə-\ *vt* **:** to cause hemagglutination of

hem·ag·glu·ti·na·tion \-ˌglüt-ᵊn-'ā-shən\ *n* [ISV] **:** agglutination of red blood cells

hem·ag·glu·ti·nin \-'glüt-ᵊn-ən\ *n* [ISV] **:** an agglutinin that causes hemagglutination

he·mal \'hē-məl\ *adj* **1 :** of or relating to the blood or blood vessels **2 :** relating to or situated on the side of the spinal cord where the heart and chief blood vessels are placed

he–man \'hē-'man\ *n* **:** an obviously strong virile man

hemat- *or* **hemato-** *or* **haemat-** *or* **haemato-** *comb form* [L *haemat-*, *haemato-*, fr. Gk *haimat-*, *haimato-*, fr. *haimat-*, *haima*] **:** HEM- ⟨*hemat*oid⟩ ⟨*hemato*genous⟩

he·ma·tal \'hem-ət-ᵊl, 'hē-mət-\ *adj* **:** HEMAL 1

he·ma·tein \ˌhē-mə-'tē-ən, ˌhem-ə-; 'hem-ə-ˌtēn\ *n* **:** a reddish brown crystalline compound $C_{16}H_{12}O_6$ constituting the essential dye in logwood extracts

he·mat·ic \hi-'mat-ik\ *adj* **1 :** of, relating to, or containing blood **2 :** affecting the blood

he·ma·tin \'hem-ət-ən, 'hē-mət-\ *n* **1 :** HEMATEIN **2 a :** a brownish black or bluish black derivative $C_{34}H_{32}N_4O_4FeOH$ of oxidized heme; *also* **:** any of several similar compounds **b :** HEME

he·ma·tin·ic \ˌhem-ə-'tin-ik, ˌhē-mə-\ *n* **:** an agent that tends to stimulate blood cell formation or to increase the hemoglobin in the blood — **hematinic** *adj*

he·ma·tite \'hem-ə-ˌtīt, 'hē-mə-\ *n* **:** a mineral Fe_2O_3 constituting an important iron ore and occurring in crystals or in a red earthy form

he·ma·to·blast \'hem-ət-ō-ˌblast, 'hē-mət-ō-, hi-'mat-ə-\ *n* [ISV] **1 :** BLOOD PLATELET **2 :** an immature blood cell — **he·ma·to·blas·tic** \ˌhem-ət-ō-'blas-tik, ˌhē-mət-ō-, hi-ˌmat-ə-\ *adj*

he·ma·to·crit \'hem-ət-ō-ˌkrit, 'hē-mət-ō-, hi-'mat-ə-\ *n* [ISV *hemat-* + Gk *kritēs* judge, fr. *krinein* to judge — more at CERTAIN] **1 :** an instrument for determining usu. by centrifugation the relative amounts of plasma and corpuscles in blood **2 :** a ratio of volume of packed red blood cells to volume of whole blood determined by a hematocrit

he·ma·tog·e·nous \ˌhem-ə-'täj-ə-nəs, ˌhē-mə-\ *adj* **1 :** producing blood **2 :** spread by or arising in the blood

he·ma·to·log·ic \ˌhem-ət-ə-'läj-ik, ˌhē-mət-\ *adj* **:** of or relating to blood or to hematology — **he·ma·to·log·i·cal** \-i-kəl\ *adj*

he·ma·tol·o·gist \ˌhem-ə-'täl-ə-jəst, ˌhē-mə-\ *n* **:** a specialist in hematology

he·ma·tol·o·gy \-jē\ *n* **:** a branch of biology that deals with the blood and blood-forming organs

he·ma·to·ma \ˌhē-mə-'tō-mə, ˌhem-ə-\ *n* **:** a tumor or swelling containing blood

he·ma·toph·a·gous \-'täf-ə-gəs\ *adj* [ISV] **:** feeding on blood

he·ma·to·poi·e·sis \ˌhem-ət-ō-(ˌ)pói-'ē-səs, ˌhē-mət-ō-, hi-ˌmat-ə-\ *n* [NL] **:** the formation of blood or of blood cells in the living body — **he·ma·to·poi·et·ic** \-'et-ik\ *adj*

he·ma·tox·y·lin \ˌhē-mə-'täk-sə-lən, ˌhem-ə-\ *n* [ISV, fr. NL *Haematoxylon*, genus of plants] **:** a crystalline phenolic compound $C_{16}H_{14}O_6$ found in logwood and used chiefly as a biological stain

he·ma·to·zo·on \ˌhem-ət-ə-'zō-ˌän, ˌhē-mət-\ *n, pl* **he·ma·to·zoa** \-'zō-ə\ [NL] **:** a blood-dwelling animal parasite

he·ma·tu·ria \ˌhē-mə-'t(y)u̇r-ē-ə, ˌhem-ə-\ *n* [NL] **:** the presence of blood or blood cells in the urine

heme \'hēm\ *n* [ISV, fr. *hematin*] **:** a deep red iron-containing pigment $C_{34}H_{32}N_4O_4Fe$ obtained from hemoglobin

hem·el·y·tron \he-'mel-ə-ˌträn\ *n* [NL, fr. *hemi-* + *elytron*] **:** one of the basally thickened anterior wings of various insects (as true bugs)

hem·er·a·lo·pia \ˌhem-ə-rə-'lō-pē-ə\ *n* [NL, fr. Gk *hēmeralōps*, fr. *hēmera* day + *alaos* blind + *ōps* eye — more at EPHEMERAL, EYE] **1 :** a defect of vision characterized by reduced visual capacity in bright lights **2 :** NIGHT BLINDNESS — **hem·er·a·lo·pic** \-'lō-pik, -'läp-ik\ *adj*

hem·ero·cal·lis \ˌhem-ə-rō-'kal-əs\ *n* [NL, fr. Gk *hēmerokalles*, fr. *hēmera* + *kallos* beauty — more at CALLIGRAPHY] **:** DAY LILY 1

hemi- *prefix* [ME, fr. L, fr. Gk *hēmi-*] **:** half ⟨*hemi*hedral⟩

-hemia — see -EMIA

he·mic \'hē-mik, 'hem-ik\ *adj* **:** of or relating to blood

hemi·cel·lu·lose \ˌhem-i-'sel-yə-ˌlōs, -ˌlōz\ *n* [ISV] **:** any of various plant polysaccharides less complex than cellulose and easily hydrolyzable to simple sugars and other products

hemi·cy·cle \'hem-i-ˌsī-kəl\ *n* [F *hémicycle*, fr. L *hemicyclium*, fr. Gk *hēmikyklion*, fr. *hēmi-* + *kyklos* circle — more at CYCLE] **:** a curved or semicircular structure or arrangement

hemi·cy·clic \ˌhem-i-'sī-klik, -'sik-lik\ *adj* **:** having floral leaves partly in whorls and partly in spirals

hemi·demi·semi·qua·ver \ˌhem-i-ˌdem-i-'sem-i-ˌkwā-vər\ *n* **:** SIXTY-FOURTH NOTE

hemi·he·dral \ˌhem-i-'hē-drəl\ *adj* [*hemi-* + *-hedron*] *of a crystal* **:** having half the faces required by complete symmetry — **hemi·he·dral·ly** \-drə-lē\ *adv*

hemi·hy·drate \-'hī-ˌdrāt\ *n* **:** a hydrate containing half a molecule of water to one of the compound forming the hydrate — **hemi·hy·drat·ed** \-ˌdrāt-əd\ *adj*

hemi·me·tab·o·lism \-mə-'tab-ə-ˌliz-əm\ *n* **:** incomplete metamorphosis esp. in various insects with aquatic larvae in which the young does not resemble the adult — **hemi·me·tab·o·lous** \-mə-'tab-ə-ləs\ *also* **hemi·met·a·bol·ic** \-ˌmet-ə-'bäl-ik\ *adj*

hemi·mor·phic \ˌhem-i-'mȯr-fik\ *adj* [ISV] **:** unsymmetrical in form as regards the two ends of an axis — **hemi·mor·phism** \-ˌfiz-əm\ *n*

hemi·mor·phite \-ˌfīt\ *n* **:** a mineral $Zn_4Si_2O_7OH.H_2O$ that is a basic zinc silicate in usu. colorless transparent orthorhombic crystals

he·min \'hē-mən\ *n* [ISV] **:** a red-brown to blue-black crystalline salt $C_{34}H_{32}N_4O_4FeCl$ derived from oxidized heme but usu. obtained in a characteristic crystalline form from hemoglobin

hemi·o·la \ˌhem-ē-'ō-lə\ *n* [LL *hemiolia*, fr. Gk *hēmiolia* ratio of one and a half to one, fr. *hēmi-* + *holos* whole — more at SAFE] **:** a musical rhythmic alteration consisting of three beats in place of two or two beats in place of three

hemi·par·a·site \ˌhem-i-'par-ə-ˌsīt\ *n* [ISV] **1 :** a facultative parasite **2 :** a parasitic plant (as the mistletoe) that contains some chlorophyll and is capable of photosynthesis — **hemi·par·a·sit·ic** \ˌpar-ə-'sit-ik\ *adj*

hemi·ple·gia \ˌhem-i-'plē-j(ē-)ə\ *n* [NL, fr. MGk *hēmiplēgia* paralysis, fr. Gk *hēmi-* + *-plēgia* -plegia] **:** paralysis of one lateral half of the body or part of it resulting from injury to the motor centers of the brain — **hemi·ple·gic** \-jik\ *adj or n*

he·mip·ter·an \hi-'mip-tə-rən\ *n* [deriv. of Gk *hēmi-* + *pteron* wing — more at FEATHER] **:** any of a large order (Hemiptera) of insects that comprise the true bugs and related insects, have mouthparts adapted to piercing and sucking and usu. two pairs of wings, undergo an incomplete metamorphosis, and include many important pests — **he·mip·ter·oid** \-ˌrȯid\ *adj* — **he·mip·ter·on** \-ˌrän\ *n* — **he·mip·ter·ous** \-rəs\ *adj*

hemi·sphere \'hem-ə-ˌsfi(ə)r\ *n* [ME *hemispere*, fr. L *hemisphaerium*, fr. Gk *hēmisphairion*, fr. *hēmi-* + *sphairion*, dim. of *sphaira* sphere] **1 a :** a half of the celestial sphere divided into two halves by the horizon, the celestial equator, or the ecliptic **b :** the northern or southern half of the earth divided by the equator or the eastern or western half divided by a meridian **c :** the inhabitants of a terrestrial hemisphere **2 :** REALM, PROVINCE **3 :** one of two half spheres formed by a plane through the sphere's center **4 :** a map or projection of a celestial or terrestrial hemisphere **5 :** CEREBRAL HEMISPHERE — **hemi·spher·ic** \ˌhem-ə-'sfi(ə)r-ik, -'sfer-\ *or* **hemi·spher·i·cal** \-i-kəl\ *adj*

hemi·stich \'hem-i-ˌstik\ *n* [L *hemistichium*, fr. Gk *hēmistichion*, fr. *hēmi-* + *stichos* line, verse; akin to Gk *steichein* to go — more at STAIR] **:** half a poetic verse usu. divided by a caesura

hemi·ter·pene \ˌhem-i-'tər-ˌpēn\ *n* [ISV] **:** a compound C_5H_8 whose formula represents half that of a terpene; *esp* **:** ISOPRENE

hem·line \'hem-ˌlīn\ *n* **:** the line formed by the lower edge of a dress, skirt, or coat

hem·lock \'hem-ˌläk\ *n* [ME *hemlok*, fr. OE *hemlic*] **1 a :** any of several poisonous herbs of the carrot family having finely cut leaves and small white flowers **b :** a poisonous drink made from the fruit of the hemlock — compare CONIINE **2 :** any of a genus (*Tsuga*) of evergreen coniferous trees of the pine family; *also* **:** the soft light splintery wood of a hemlock

hemo- — see HEM-

he·mo·blast \'hē-mə-ˌblast, 'hem-ə-\ *n* [ISV] **:** HEMATOBLAST

he·mo·cy·a·nin \ˌhē-mō-'sī-ə-nən, ˌhem-ō-\ *n* [ISV] **:** a colorless copper-containing respiratory pigment in solution in the blood plasma of various arthropods and mollusks

he·mo·cyte \'hē-mə-ˌsīt, 'hem-ə-\ *n* [ISV] **:** a blood cell esp. of an invertebrate animal

ə abut; ᵊ kitten; ər further; a back; ā bake; ä cot, cart; au̇ out; ch chin; e less; ē easy; g gift; i trip; ī life
j joke; ŋ sing; ō flow; ȯ flaw; ȯi coin; th thin; t͟h this; ü loot; u̇ foot; y yet; yü few; yu̇ furious; zh vision

he·mo·cy·tom·e·ter \ˌhē-mə-(ˌ)sī-ˈtäm-ət-ər, ˌhem-ə-\ *n* [ISV] : HEMACYTOMETER

he·mo·fla·gel·late \ˌhē-mō-ˈflaj-ə-lət, ˌhem-ō-, -ˌlāt; -flə-ˈjel-ət\ *n* : a flagellate (as a trypanosome) that is a blood parasite

he·mo·glo·bin \ˈhē-mə-ˌglō-bən, ˈhem-ə-, ˌhē-mə-ˈ, ˌhem-ə-ˈ\ *n* [ISV, short for earlier *hematoglobulin*] **1 a :** an iron-containing protein respiratory pigment occurring in the red blood cells of vertebrates **b :** a dark purplish crystallizable form of this pigment found chiefly in the venous blood of vertebrates that is a conjugated protein composed of heme and globin **2 :** any of numerous iron-containing respiratory pigments of invertebrates and some plants (as yeasts) — **he·mo·glo·bin·ic** \ˌhē-mə-glō-ˈbin-ik, ˌhem-ə-\ *adj* — **he·mo·glo·bin·ous** \-ˈglō-bə-nəs\ *adj*

he·mo·glo·bin·uria \-ˌglō-bə-ˈn(y)ür-ē-ə\ *n* [NL] : the presence of free hemoglobin in the urine — **he·mo·glo·bin·uric** \-ˈn(y)ü(ə)r-ik\ *adj*

he·mo·ly·sin \hi-ˈmäl-ə-sən; ˌhē-mə-ˈlīs-ᵊn, ˌhem-ə-\ *n* [ISV] : a substance that causes the dissolution of red blood cells

he·mol·y·sis \hi-ˈmäl-ə-səs\ *n* [NL] : liberation of hemoglobin from red blood cells — **he·mo·lyt·ic** \ˌhē-mə-ˈlit-ik, ˌhem-ə-\ *adj*

he·mo·lyze \ˈhē-mə-ˌlīz, ˈhem-ə-\ *vb* [irreg. fr. *hemolysis*] *vt* : to cause hemolysis of ~ *vi* : to undergo hemolysis

¹**he·mo·phile** \ˈhē-mə-ˌfīl, ˈhem-ə-\ *adj* : HEMOPHILIC

²**hemophile** *n* [ISV] **1 :** HEMOPHILIAC **2 :** a hemophilic organism

he·mo·phil·ia \ˌhē-mə-ˈfil-ē-ə, ˌhem-ə-\ *n* [NL] : a usu. hereditary tendency to uncontrollable bleeding — **he·mo·phil·i·ac** \-ē-ˌak\ *adj or n*

he·mo·phil·ic \-ˈfil-ik\ *adj* : blood-loving ⟨~ bacteria⟩

he·mop·ty·sis \hi-ˈmäp-tə-səs\ *n* [NL, fr. *hem-* + Gk *ptysis* act of spitting, fr. *ptyein* to spit — more at SPEW] : expectoration of blood from some part of the respiratory tract

¹**hem·or·rhage** \ˈhem-(ə-)rij\ *n* [F & L; F *hémorrhagie*, fr. L *haemorrhagia*, fr. Gk *haimorrhagia*, fr. *haimo-* hem- + *-rrhagia*] : a copious discharge of blood from the blood vessels — **hem·or·rhag·ic** \ˌhem-ə-ˈraj-ik\ *adj*

²**hemorrhage** *vi* : BLEED

hem·or·rhoid \ˈhem-(ə-)ˌrȯid\ *n* [MF *hemorrhoides*, pl., fr. L *haemorrhoidae*, fr. Gk *haimorrhoides*, fr. *haimorrhoos* flowing with blood, fr. *haimo-* hem- + *rhein* to flow — more at STREAM] : a mass of dilated tortuous veins in swollen tissue situated at or within the anal margin — usu. used in pl.; called also *piles* — **hem·or·rhoid·ec·to·my** \ˌhem-(ə-)ˌrȯi-ˈdek-tə-mē\ *n*

hem·or·rhoid·al \ˌhem-ə-ˈrȯid-ᵊl\ *adj* **1 :** of, relating to, or involving hemorrhoids **2 :** RECTAL — **hemorrhoidal** *n*

he·mo·sid·er·in \ˌhē-mō-ˈsid-ə-rən, ˌhem-ō-\ *n* [ISV] : a yellowish brown granular pigment formed by breakdown of hemoglobin and composed essentially of colloidal ferric oxide

he·mos·ta·sis \hi-ˈmäs-tə-səs\ *n* [NL, fr. Gk *haimostasis* styptic, fr. *haimo-* hem- + *-stasis*] : arrest of bleeding

he·mo·stat \ˈhē-mə-ˌstat, ˈhem-ə-\ *n* **1 :** HEMOSTATIC **2 :** an instrument for compressing a bleeding vessel

he·mo·stat·ic \ˌhē-mə-ˈstat-ik, ˌhem-ə-\ *n* : an agent that checks bleeding — **hemostatic** *adj*

hemp \ˈhemp\ *n* [ME, fr. OE *hænep*; akin to OHG *hanaf* hemp; both prob. fr. the source of Gk *kannabis* hemp] **1 a :** a tall widely cultivated Asiatic herb (*Cannabis sativa*) of the mulberry family with tough bast fiber used esp. for cordage **b :** the fiber of hemp **c :** a narcotic drug (as marijuana) from hemp **2 :** a fiber (as jute) from various plants; *also* **:** a plant yielding such fiber — **hemp·en** \ˈhem-pən\ *adj*

hemp nettle *n* : any of a genus (*Galeopsis*) of coarse Old World herbs of the mint family; *esp* **:** a bristly Eurasian herb (*G. tetrahit*) common in the U.S. as a weed

¹**hem·stitch** \ˈhem-ˌstich\ *vt* : to embroider (fabric) by drawing out parallel threads and stitching the exposed threads in groups to form various designs

²**hemstitch** *n* **1 :** decorative needlework similar to drawnwork **2 :** a stitch used in hemstitching

hemstitch

hen \ˈhen\ *n* [ME, fr. OE *henn*; akin to OE *hana* rooster — more at CHANT] **1 a :** a female domestic fowl esp. over a year old; *broadly* **:** a female bird **b :** the female of various mostly aquatic animals (as lobsters or fish) **2 :** WOMAN; *specif* **:** a fussy middle-aged woman

hen and chickens *n* : any of several plants having offsets, runners, or proliferous flowers: as **a :** HOUSELEEK **b :** GROUND IVY

hen·bane \ˈhen-ˌbān\ *n* : a poisonous fetid Old World herb (*Hyoscyamus niger*) of the nightshade family having sticky hairy dentate leaves and yellowish brown flowers and yielding a medicinal extract resembling belladonna

hence \ˈhen(t)s\ *adv* [ME *hennes*, *henne*, fr. OE *heonan*; akin to OHG *hinnan* away, OE *hēr* here] **1 :** from this place **:** AWAY; *specif* **:** from this world or life **2 a** *archaic* **:** HENCEFORTH **b :** from this time **3 :** THEREFORE **4 :** from this source or origin

hence·forth \ˈhen(t)s-ˌfō(ə)rth, -ˌfȯ(ə)rth, hen(t)s-ˈ\ *adv* : from this point on

hence·for·ward \hen(t)s-ˈfȯr-wərd\ *adv* : HENCEFORTH

hench·man \ˈhench-mən\ *n* [ME *hengestman* groom, fr. *hengest* stallion (fr. OE) + *man*; akin to OHG *hengist* gelding] **1** *obs* **:** a squire or page to a person of high rank **2 a :** a trusted follower **:** a right-hand man **b :** a political follower whose support is chiefly for personal advantage

hen·deca·syl·lab·ic \(ˌ)hen-ˌdek-ə-sə-ˈlab-ik\ *adj* [L *hendecasyllabus*, fr. Gk *hendeka* eleven (fr. *hen-*, *heis* one + *deka* ten) + *syllabē* syllable — more at SAME, TEN] : consisting of 11 syllables or composed of verses of 11 syllables — **hendecasyllabic** *n* — **hen·deca·syl·la·ble** \hen-ˈdek-ə-ˌsil-ə-bəl, (ˌ)hen-ˌdek-ə-ˈ\ *n*

hen·di·a·dys \hen-ˈdī-əd-əs\ *n* [LL, modif. of Gk *hen dia dyoin* one through two] : the expression of an idea by two nouns connected by *and* (as *cups and gold*) instead of by a noun and an adjective (as *golden cups*)

hen·e·quen *also* **hen·i·quen** \ˈhen-i-kən, ˌhen-i-ˈken\ *n* [Sp *henequén*] : a strong yellowish or reddish hard fiber obtained from the leaves of a tropical American agave chiefly in Yucatan and used esp. for binder twine; *also* **:** a plant (*Agave fourcroydes*) that yields henequen

¹**hen·na** \ˈhen-ə\ *n* [Ar *ḥinnā'*] **1 :** an Old World tropical shrub or small tree (*Lawsonia inermis*) of the loosestrife family with small opposite leaves and axillary panicles of fragrant white flowers **2 :** a reddish brown dye obtained from leaves of the henna plant and used esp. on hair

²**henna** *vt* : to dye (hair) with henna

hen·nery \ˈhen-ə-rē\ *n* : a poultry farm; *also* **:** an enclosure for poultry

heno·the·ism \ˈhen-ə-thē-ˌiz-əm\ *n* [G *henotheismus*, fr. Gk *hen-*, *heis* + *theos* god] : the worship of one god without denying the existence of other gods — **heno·the·ist** \-ˌthē-əst\ *n* — **heno·the·is·tic** \ˌhen-ə-thē-ˈis-tik\ *adj*

hen party *n* : a party for women only

hen·peck \ˈhen-ˌpek\ *vt* : to subject (one's husband) to persistent nagging and domination

hen·ry \ˈhen-rē\ *n, pl* **henrys** *or* **henries** [Joseph *Henry* †1878 Am physicist] : the practical mks unit of inductance equal to the self-inductance of a circuit or the mutual inductance of two circuits in which the variation of one ampere per second results in an induced electromotive force of one volt

hent \ˈhent\ *vt* [ME *henten*, fr. OE *hentan* — more at HUNT] *obs* : SEIZE

hen track *n* : an illegible or scarcely legible mark intended as handwriting — called also *hen scratch*

¹**hep** \ˈhep, ˈhəp, ˈhət\ *interj* [origin unknown] — used to mark a marching cadence

²**hep** \ˈhep\ *var of* HIP

hep·a·rin \ˈhep-ə-rən\ *n* [ISV, fr. Gk *hēpar* liver] : a polysaccharide sulfuric acid ester found esp. in liver that prolongs the clotting time of blood and is used medically

hep·a·rin·ize \-rə-ˌnīz\ *vt* : to treat with heparin

hepat- *or* **hepato-** *comb form* [L, fr. Gk *hēpat-*, *hēpato-*, fr. *hēpat-*, *hēpar*] : liver ⟨*hepat*ectomy⟩ ⟨*hepato*toxic⟩

¹**he·pat·ic** \hi-ˈpat-ik\ *adj* [L *hepaticus*, fr. Gk *hēpatikos*, fr. *hēpat-*, *hēpar*; akin to L *jecur* liver] : of, relating to, or resembling the liver

²**hepatic** *n* : LIVERWORT

he·pat·i·ca \hi-ˈpat-i-kə\ *n* [NL, genus name, fr. ML, liverwort, fr. L, fem. of *hepaticus*] : a plant or flower of a genus (*Hepatica*) of herbs of the crowfoot family with lobed leaves and delicate flowers

hep·a·ti·tis \ˌhep-ə-ˈtīt-əs\ *n* : inflammation of the liver

hep·a·to·tox·ic·i·ty \ˌhep-ət-ō-täk-ˈsis-ət-ē\ *n* **1 :** a state of toxic damage to the liver **2 :** a tendency or capacity to cause hepatotoxicity

hep·cat \ˈhep-ˌkat\ *n* : HIPSTER

He·phaes·tus \hi-ˈfes-təs\ *n* [Gk *Hēphaistos*] : the god of fire and of metalworking in Greek mythology

hepped up \ˈhep-ˈtəp\ *adj* : ENTHUSIASTIC

Hep·ple·white \ˈhep-əl-ˌhwīt, -ˌwīt\ *adj* [George *Hepplewhite* †1786 E cabinetmaker] : of, relating to, or imitating a style of furniture originating in late 18th century England

hepta- *or* **hept-** *comb form* [Gk, fr. *hepta* — more at SEVEN] **1 :** seven ⟨*hepta*meter⟩ **2 :** containing seven atoms, groups, or equivalents ⟨*hept*ane⟩

hep·tad \ˈhep-ˌtad\ *n* [Gk *heptad-*, *heptas*, fr. *hepta*] : a group of seven

hep·ta·gon \ˈhep-tə-ˌgän\ *n* [Gk *heptagōnos* heptagonal, fr. *hepta* + *gōnia* angle — more at -GON] : a polygon of seven angles and seven sides — **hep·tag·o·nal** \hep-ˈtag-ən-ᵊl\ *adj*

hep·tam·e·ter \hep-ˈtam-ət-ər\ *n* : a verse consisting of seven feet

hep·tane \ˈhep-ˌtān\ *n* : any of nine isomeric hydrocarbons C_7H_{16} of the methane series

Hep·tar·chy \ˈhep-ˌtär-kē\ *n* : a hypothetical confederacy of seven Anglo-Saxon kingdoms of the 7th and 8th centuries

Hep·ta·teuch \ˈhep-tə-ˌt(y)ük\ *n* [LL *heptateuchos*, fr. Gk, fr *hepta* + *teuchos* book — more at PENTATEUCH] : the first seven books of the Old Testament

hep·tose \ˈhep-ˌtōs, -ˌtōz\ *n* : any of the monosaccharides $C_7H_{14}O_7$ containing seven carbon atoms in the molecule

¹**her** \(h)ər, ˌhər\ *adj* [ME *hire*, fr. OE *hiere*, gen. of *hēo* she — more at HE] : of or relating to her or herself esp. as possessor, agent, or object of an action ⟨~ house⟩ ⟨~ research⟩ ⟨~ rescue⟩ — compare ¹SHE

²**her** \ər, (ˈ)hər\ *pron, objective case of* SHE

He·ra \ˈhir-ə, ˈhē-rə\ *n* [L, fr. Gk *Hēra*] : the queen of heaven in Greek mythology, sister and wife of Zeus, and goddess of women and marriage

Her·a·kles *or* **Her·a·cles** \ˈher-ə-ˌklēz\ *n* [Gk *Hēraklēs*] : HERCULES

¹**her·ald** \ˈher-əld\ *n* [ME, fr. MF *hiraut*, fr. an (assumed) Gmc compound whose 1st component is akin to OHG *heri* army, and whose 2d is akin to OHG *waltan* to rule — more at HARRY, WIELD] **1 a :** an official at a tournament of arms with duties including the making of announcements and the marshaling of combatants **b :** an officer with the status of ambassador acting as official messenger between leaders esp. in war **c :** an officer of a monarch or government responsible for devising and granting armorial bearings **2 :** an official crier or messenger **3 a :** HARBINGER **b :** ANNOUNCER, SPOKESMAN **syn** see FORERUNNER

²**herald** *vt* **1 :** to give notice of **:** ANNOUNCE **2 a :** PUBLICIZE **b :** HAIL, GREET

he·ral·dic \he-ˈral-dik, hə-\ *adj* : of or relating to heralds or heraldry — **he·ral·di·cal·ly** \-di-k(ə-)lē\ *adv*

her·ald·ry \ˈher-əl-drē\ *n* **1 :** the practice of devising, blazoning, and granting armorial insignia and of tracing and recording genealogies **2 a :** an armorial ensign **b :** INSIGNIA **3 :** PAGEANTRY

herb \ˈ(h)ərb\ *n, often attrib* [ME *herbe*, fr. OF, fr. L *herba*] **1 :** a seed-producing annual, biennial, or perennial that does not develop persistent woody tissue but dies down at the end of a growing season **2 :** a plant or plant part valued for its medicinal, savory, or aromatic qualities — **her·ba·ceous** \ˌ(h)ər-ˈbā-shəs\ *adj* — **herb·like** \ˈ(h)ər-ˌblīk\ *adj* — **herby** \ˈ(h)ər-bē\ *adj*

herb·age \ˈ(h)ər-bij\ *n* **1 :** grass and other herbaceous vegetation esp. when used for grazing **2 :** the succulent parts of herbaceous plants

¹**herb·al** \ˈ(h)ər-bəl\ *n* **1 :** a book about plants esp. with reference to their medicinal properties **2** *archaic* **:** HERBARIUM 1

²**herbal** *adj* : of, relating to, or made of herbs

herb·al·ist \-bə-ləst\ *n* **1 :** one that collects or grows herbs **2 :** HERB DOCTOR

her·bar·i·um \ˌ(h)ər-ˈbar-ē-əm, -ˈber-\ *n, pl* **her·bar·ia** \-ē-ə\ **1 :** a collection of dried plant specimens usu. mounted and systematically arranged for reference **2 :** a place that houses an herbarium
herb doctor *n* **:** one who practices healing by the use of herbs
her·bi·ci·dal \ˌ(h)ər-bə-ˈsīd-ᵊl\ *adj* **:** of, relating to, or being an herbicide
her·bi·cide \ˈ(h)ər-bə-ˌsīd\ *n* [L *herba* + ISV *-cide*] **:** an agent used to destroy or inhibit plant growth
her·bi·vore \ˈ(h)ər-bə-ˌvō(ə)r, -ˌvo̊(ə)r\ *n* [NL *Herbivora*, group of mammals, fr. neut. pl. of *herbivorus*] **:** a plant-eating animal; *esp* **:** UNGULATE
her·biv·o·rous \ˌ(h)ər-ˈbiv-ə-rəs\ *adj* [NL *herbivorus*, fr. L *herba* grass + *-vorus* -vorous] **1 :** feeding on plants **2 :** having a stout body and a long small intestine — **her·biv·o·rous·ly** *adv*
herb Rob·ert \ˌ(h)ərb-ˈräb-ərt\ *n* [prob. fr. *Robertus* (St. Robert †1067 F ecclesiastic)] **:** a sticky low geranium (*Geranium robertianum*) with small reddish purple flowers
Her·cu·le·an \ˌhər-kyə-ˈlē-ən, ˌhər-ˈkyü-lē-\ *adj* **1 :** of, relating to, or characteristic of Hercules **2** *often not cap* **:** of extraordinary power, size, or difficulty
Her·cu·les \ˈhər-kyə-ˌlēz\ *n* [L, fr. Gk *Hēraklēs*] **1 :** a hero of classical mythology noted for great strength and esp. for achieving twelve labors imposed on him by Hera **2** [L (gen. *Herculis*)] **:** a northern constellation between Corona Borealis and Lyra
Her·cu·les'–club \ˌhər-kyə-ˌlēz-ˈkləb\ *n* **1 :** a small prickly eastern U.S. tree (*Aralia spinosa*) of the ginseng family — called also *angelica tree* **2 :** a prickly shrub or tree (genus *Zanthoxylum*, esp. *Z. clava-herculis*) of the rue family
1**herd** \ˈhərd\ *n* [ME, fr. OE *heord;* akin to OHG *herta* herd, Gk *korthys* heap] **1 a :** a number of animals of one kind kept together under human control **b :** a congregation of gregarious wild animals **2 a :** a group of people usu. having a common bond **b :** the undistinguished unthinking masses of mankind **:** MOB
2**herd** *vi* **1 :** to assemble or move in a herd **2 :** to place oneself in a group **:** ASSOCIATE ~ *vt* **1 a :** to keep or move (animals) together **b :** to gather, lead, or drive as if in a herd **2 :** to place in a group
herd·er \ˈhərd-ər\ *n* **:** one that herds; *specif* **:** HERDSMAN
her·dic \ˈhərd-ik\ *n* [Peter *Herdic* †1888 Am inventor] **:** a small 19th century American horse-drawn cab having side seats and an entrance at the back
herds·man \ˈhərdz-mən\ *n* **1 :** a manager, breeder, or tender of livestock **2** *cap* **:** BOÖTES
1**here** \ˈhi(ə)r\ *adv* [ME, fr. OE *hēr;* akin to OHG *hier* here, OE *hē* he] **1 a :** in or at this place ⟨turn ~⟩ — often used interjectionally esp. in answering a roll call **b :** NOW ⟨~ it's morning already⟩ **2 :** at or in this point or particular ⟨~ we agree⟩ **3 :** in the present life or state **4 :** HITHER ⟨come ~⟩ **5** — used interjectionally in rebuke or encouragement
2**here** *adj* **1** — used for emphasis esp. after a demonstrative pronoun or after a noun modified by a demonstrative adjective ⟨this book ~⟩ **2** *substand* — used for emphasis after a demonstrative adjective but before the noun modified ⟨this ~ book⟩
3**here** *n* **:** this place ⟨let's get out of ~⟩
here·abouts \ˈhir-ə-ˌbau̇ts\ *or* **here·about** \-ˌbau̇t\ *adv* **:** in this vicinity
1**here·af·ter** \hir-ˈaf-tər\ *adv* **1 :** after this in sequence or in time **2 :** in some future time or state
2**hereafter** *n, often cap* **1 :** FUTURE **2 :** an existence beyond earthly life
3**hereafter** *adj, archaic* **:** FUTURE
here·away \ˈhi(ə)r-ə-ˌwā\ *or* **here·aways** \-ˌwāz\ *adv, dial* **:** HEREABOUT
here·by \hi(ə)r-ˈbī, ˈhi(ə)r-ˌ\ *adv* **:** by this means; *esp* **:** by means of this act or document
her·e·dit·a·ment \ˌher-ə-ˈdit-ə-mənt\ *n* [ML *hereditamentum*, fr. LL *hereditare*, fr. L *hered-*, *heres*] **:** heritable property
he·red·i·tary \hə-ˈred-ə-ˌter-ē\ *adj* **1 a :** genetically transmitted or transmittable from parent to offspring **b :** characteristic of or fostered by one's predecessors **2 a :** received or passing by inheritance or required to pass by inheritance **b :** having title or possession through inheritance **3 :** of a kind established by tradition **4 :** of or relating to inheritance or heredity **syn** see INNATE
he·red·i·ty \hə-ˈred-ət-ē\ *n* [MF *heredité*, fr. L *hereditat-*, *hereditas*, fr. *hered-*, *heres* heir — more at HEIR] **1 a :** INHERITANCE **b :** TRADITION **2 a :** the sum of the qualities and potentialities genetically derived from one's ancestors **b :** the transmission of qualities from ancestor to descendant through a mechanism lying primarily in the chromosomes of the germ cells
Her·e·ford \ˈhər-fərd *also* ˈher-ə-\ *n* [*Hereford* co., England] **:** any of an English breed of hardy red beef cattle with white faces and markings now extensively raised in the western U.S.
here·in \hir-ˈin\ *adv* **:** in this
here·in·above \(ˌ)hir-ˌin-ə-ˈbəv\ *adv* **:** above this
here·in·af·ter \ˌhir-ə-ˈnaf-tər\ *adv* **:** after this
here·in·be·fore \(ˌ)hir-ˌin-bi-ˈfō(ə)r, -ˈfo̊(ə)r\ *adv* **:** in the preceding part of this writing or document
here·in·be·low \-bi-ˈlō\ *adv* **:** below this
here·of \hir-ˈəv, -ˈäv\ *adv* **:** of this
here·on \-ˈo̊n, -ˈän\ *adv* **:** on this writing or document
He·re·ro \hə-ˈre(ə)r-(ˌ)ō, ˈher-ə-ˌrō\ *n, pl* **Herero** *or* **Hereros** **1 :** a Bantu people of the central part of southwest Africa **2 :** a member of the Herero people
he·re·si·arch \hə-ˈrē-zē-ˌärk, ˈher-ə-sē-\ *n* [LL *haeresiarcha*, fr. LGk *hairesiarchēs*, fr. *hairesis* + Gk *-archēs* -arch] **:** an originator or chief advocate of a heresy
her·e·sy \ˈher-ə-sē\ *n* [ME *heresie*, fr. OF, fr. LL *haeresis*, fr. LGk *hairesis*, fr. Gk, action of taking, choice, sect, fr. *hairein* to take] **1 a :** adherence to a religious opinion contrary to church dogma **b :** denial of a revealed truth by a baptized member of the Roman Catholic Church **c :** an opinion or doctrine contrary to church dogma **2 a :** dissent from a dominant theory or opinion in any field **b :** an opinion or doctrine contrary to the truth or to generally accepted beliefs
her·e·tic \ˈher-ə-ˌtik\ *n* **1 :** a dissenter from established church dogma; *esp* **:** a baptized member of the Roman Catholic Church who disavows a revealed truth **2 :** one that dissents from an accepted belief or doctrine of any kind
he·ret·i·cal \hə-ˈret-i-kəl\ *also* **he·re·tic** \ˈher-ə-ˌtik, hə-ˈret-ik\ *adj* **1 :** of, relating to, or characterized by heresy **2 :** of, relating to, or characterized by departure from accepted beliefs or standards **:** UNORTHODOX **syn** see HETERODOX — **he·ret·i·cal·ly** \hə-ˈret-i-k(ə-)lē\ *adv* — **he·ret·i·cal·ness** \-kəl-nəs\ *n*
here·to \hi(ə)r-ˈtü\ *adv* **:** to this writing or document
here·to·fore \ˈhirt-ə-ˌfō(ə)r, -ˌfo̊(ə)r, ˌhirt-ə-ˈ\ *adv* **:** up to this time **:** HITHERTO
here·un·der \hir-ˈən-dər\ *adv* **:** under or in accordance with this
here·un·to \hir-ˈən-(ˌ)tü, ˌhir-(ˌ)ən-ˈtü\ *adv* **:** to this; *esp* **:** to this writing or document
here·upon \ˈhir-ə-ˌpo̊n, -ˌpän, ˌhir-ə-ˈ\ *adv* **:** on this **:** immediately after this
here·with \hi(ə)r-ˈwith, -ˈwith\ *adv* **1 :** with this **:** enclosed in this **2 :** HEREBY
her·i·ot \ˈher-ē-ət\ *n* [ME, fr. OE *heregeatwe*, pl., military equipment, fr. *here* army + *geatwe* equipment; akin to OHG *heri* army — more at HARRY] **:** a feudal duty or tribute due under English law to a lord upon the death of a tenant
her·i·ta·bil·i·ty \ˌher-ət-ə-ˈbil-ət-ē\ *n* **:** the quality or state of being heritable
her·i·ta·ble \ˈher-ət-ə-bəl\ *adj* **1 :** capable of being inherited or of passing by inheritance **2 :** HEREDITARY
her·i·tage \ˈher-ət-ij\ *n* [ME, fr. MF, fr. *heriter* to inherit, fr. LL *hereditare*, fr. L *hered-*, *heres* heir — more at HEIR] **1 :** property that descends to an heir **2 a :** something transmitted by or acquired from a predecessor **:** LEGACY **b :** TRADITION **3 :** BIRTHRIGHT

syn HERITAGE, INHERITANCE, PATRIMONY, BIRTHRIGHT mean something received from a parent or predecessor. HERITAGE may imply anything passed on to heirs or succeeding generations but applies usu. to things other than actual property or money ⟨*heritage* of freedom⟩ INHERITANCE applies to that which passes from parent to child (as money, property, traits of character or feature); PATRIMONY applies esp. to property passed down in a direct line of descent; BIRTHRIGHT applies to property, rank, or privilege coming by right of birth and esp. by primogeniture

her·i·tor \ˈher-ət-ər\ *n* **:** INHERITOR
herm \ˈhərm\ *n* [L *hermes*, fr. Gk *hermēs* statue of Hermes, herm, fr. *Hermēs*] **:** a statue in the form of a square stone pillar surmounted by a bust or head esp. of Hermes — called also *herma*
her·maph·ro·dite \(ˌ)hər-ˈmaf-rə-ˌdīt\ *n* [ME *hermofrodite*, fr. L *hermaphroditus*, fr. Gk *hermaphroditos*, fr. *Hermaphroditos*] **1 a :** an animal or plant having both male and female reproductive organs **b :** HOMOSEXUAL **2 :** a combination of diverse elements; *specif* **:** HERMAPHRODITE BRIG — **hermaphrodite** *adj* — **her·maph·ro·dit·ic** \(ˌ)hər-ˌmaf-rə-ˈdit-ik\ *adj* — **her·maph·ro·dit·i·cal·ly** \-i-k(ə-)lē\ *adv* — **her·maph·ro·dit·ism** \(ˌ)hər-ˈmaf-rə-ˌdīt-ˌiz-əm\ *n*
hermaphrodite brig *n* **:** a 2-masted vessel square-rigged forward and schooner-rigged aft
Her·maph·ro·di·tus \(ˌ)hər-ˌmaf-rə-ˈdīt-əs\ *n* [Gk *Hermaphroditos*] **:** a son of Hermes and Aphrodite who according to Greek mythology becomes joined in one body with a nymph while bathing

hermaphrodite brig

her·me·neu·tic \ˌhər-mə-ˈn(y)üt-ik\ *adj* [Gk *hermēneutikos*, fr. *hermēneuein* to interpret, fr. *hermēneus* interpreter] **:** of or relating to hermeneutics **:** INTERPRETATIVE — **her·me·neu·ti·cal** \-i-kəl\ *adj*
her·me·neu·tics \-iks\ *n pl but sing or pl in constr* **:** the study of the methodological principles of interpretation (as of the Bible)
Her·mes \ˈhər-(ˌ)mēz\ *n* [L, fr. Gk *Hermēs*] **:** a Greek god who serves as herald and messenger of the other gods, presides over roads, commerce, invention, eloquence, cunning, and theft, and conducts the dead to Hades
Hermes Tris·me·gis·tus \-ˌtris-mə-ˈjis-təs\ *n* [Gk *Hermēs trismegistos*, lit., Hermes thrice greatest] **:** a legendary author of works embodying magical, astrological, and alchemical doctrines
her·met·ic \(ˌ)hər-ˈmet-ik\ *adj* [NL *hermeticus*, fr. *Hermet-*, *Hermes Trismegistus*] **1** *often cap* **a :** of or relating to the writings or teachings attributed to Hermes Trismegistus **b :** relating to or characterized by occultism or abstruseness **:** RECONDITE **2** [fr. the belief that Hermes Trismegistus invented a magic seal to keep vessels airtight] **a :** AIRTIGHT **b :** impervious to external influence — **her·met·i·cal** \-i-kəl\ *adj* — **her·met·i·cal·ly** \-i-k(ə-)lē\ *adv*
Her·me·tism \ˈhər-mə-ˌtiz-əm\ *n* **1 :** a system of ideas based on hermetic teachings **2** *often not cap* **:** adherence to hermetic doctrine — **Her·me·tist** \-məst-əst\ *n*
her·mit \ˈhər-mət\ *n* [ME *eremite*, fr. OF, fr. LL *eremita*, fr. LGk *erēmitēs*, fr. Gk, adj., living in the desert, fr. *erēmia* desert, fr. *erēmos* lonely — more at RETINA] **1 a :** one that retires from society and lives in solitude esp. for religious reasons **:** RECLUSE **b** *obs* **:** BEADSMAN **2 :** a spiced molasses cookie
her·mit·age \ˈhər-mət-ij\ *n* **1 a :** the habitation of a hermit **b :** HIDEAWAY **c :** MONASTERY **2 :** the life or condition of a hermit
Her·mi·tage \ˌ(h)er-mi-ˈtäzh\ *n* [Tain-l'*Ermitage*, commune in France] **1 :** a chiefly red Rhone valley wine **2 :** a wine similar to Hermitage
hermit crab *n* **:** any of numerous chiefly marine decapod crustaceans (families Paguridae and Parapaguridae) having soft asymmetrical abdomens and occupying the empty shells of gastropods
hern \ˈhe(ə)rn, ˈhərn\ *dial var of* HERON
her·nia \ˈhər-nē-ə\ *n, pl* **her·ni·as** *or* **her·ni·ae** \-nē-ˌē, -nē-ˌī\ [L — more at YARN] **:** a protrusion of an organ or part through connective tissue or through a wall of the cavity in which it is normally enclosed — called also *rupture* — **her·ni·al** \-nē-əl\ *adj*
her·ni·ate \ˈhər-nē-ˌāt\ *vi* **:** to protrude through an abnormal body opening — **her·ni·a·tion** \ˌhər-nē-ˈā-shən\ *n*
he·ro \ˈhē-(ˌ)rō, ˈhi(ə)r-(ˌ)ō\ *n, pl* **heroes** [L *heros*, fr. Gk *hērōs*] **1 a :** a mythological or legendary figure often of divine descent endowed with great strength or ability **b :** an illustrious warrior

c : a man admired for his achievements and qualities d : one that shows great courage 2 a : the principal male character in a literary or dramatic work b : the central figure in an event or period
Hero *n* [L, fr. Gk *Hērō*] : a priestess of Aphrodite loved by Leander
[1]**he·ro·ic** \hi-'rō-ik\ *adj* **1** : of, relating to, or resembling heroes esp. of antiquity **2 a** : exhibiting or marked by courage and daring **b** : GRAND, NOBLE **3 a** : of impressive size or power **b** : POTENT **4** : of, relating to, or constituting drama written during the Restoration in heroic couplets and concerned with a conflict between love and honor — **he·ro·ical** \-i-kəl\ *adj* — **he·ro·ical·ly** \-i-k(ə-)lē\ *adv*
[2]**heroic** *n* **1** : a heroic verse or poem **2** *pl* **a** : heroic behavior **b** : ostentatious hammy conduct or expression
heroic couplet *n* : a rhyming couplet in iambic pentameter
he·roi·com·ic \hi-,rō-i-'käm-ik\ *adj* [F *héroïcomique*, fr. *héroïque* heroic + *comique* comic] : comic by being ludicrously noble, bold, or elevated — **he·roi·com·i·cal** \-i-kəl\ *adj*
heroic stanza *n* : a rhymed quatrain in heroic verse with a rhyme scheme of *abab* — called also *heroic quatrain*
heroic verse *n* **1** : dactylic hexameter esp. of epic verse of classical times — called also *heroic meter* **2** : the iambic pentameter used in epic and other serious English poetry during the 17th and 18th centuries — called also *heroic line, heroic meter*
her·o·in \'her-ə-wən\ *n* [fr. *Heroin*, a trademark] : a strongly addictive narcotic $C_{21}H_{23}NO_5$ made from but more potent than morphine — **her·o·in·ism** \-wə-,niz-əm\ *n*
her·o·ine \'her-ə-wən\ *n* [L *heroina*, fr. Gk *hērōinē*, fem. of *hērōs*] **1 a** : a mythological or legendary woman having the qualities of a hero **b** : a woman admired and emulated for her achievements and qualities **2 a** : the principal female character in a literary or dramatic work **b** : the central female figure in an event or period
her·o·ism \'her-ə-,wiz-əm\ *n* **1** : heroic conduct **2** : the qualities of a hero
syn VALOR, PROWESS, GALLANTRY: HEROISM implies superlative courage esp. in fulfilling a high purpose against odds; VALOR implies illustrious bravery and audacity in fighting; PROWESS stresses skill as well as bravery; GALLANTRY implies dash and spirit as well as courage and gay indifference to danger or hardship
he·ro·ize \'hē-(,)rō-,īz, 'hir-(,)ō-; 'her-ə-,wīz\ *vt* : to make heroic
her·on \'her-ən\ *n, pl* **herons** *also* **heron** [ME *heiroun*, fr. MF *hairon*, of Gmc origin; akin to OHG *heigaro* heron, Gk *krizein* to creak, OHG *scrīan* to scream] : any of various long-necked wading birds (family Ardeidae) with a long tapering bill, large wings, and soft plumage

great blue heron

her·on·ry \-ən-rē\ *n* : a heron rookery
hero worship *n* **1** : veneration of a hero **2** : foolish or excessive adulation for an individual
hero-worship *vt* : to feel or express hero worship for — **hero-worshiper** *n*
her·pes \'hər-(,)pēz\ *n* [L, fr. Gk *herpēs*, fr. *herpein* to creep — more at SERPENT] : any of several virus diseases characterized by the formation of blisters on the skin or mucous membranes — **her·pet·ic** \(,)hər-'pet-ik\ *adj*
herpes sim·plex \-'sim-,pleks\ *n* [NL, lit., simple herpes] : a virus disease marked by groups of blisters on the skin or mucous membranes
herpes zos·ter \,hər-(,)pē(z)-'zōs-tər, -'zäs-\ *n* [NL, lit., girdle herpes] : an acute viral inflammation of the sensory ganglia of spinal and cranial nerves associated with a vesicular eruption and neuralgic pains — called also *shingles*
herpet- *or* **herpeto-** *comb form* [Gk *herpeton*, fr. neut. of *herpetos* creeping, fr. *herpein*] **1** : reptile or reptiles ⟨*herpeto*fauna⟩ ⟨*herpeto*logy⟩ **2** [L *herpet-, herpes*] : herpes ⟨*herpeti*form⟩
her·pe·to·log·ic \,hər-pət-ə-'läj-ik\ *adj* : of or relating to herpetology — **her·pe·to·log·i·cal** \-i-kəl\ *adj* — **her·pe·to·log·i·cal·ly** \-i-k(ə-)lē\ *adv*
her·pe·tol·o·gist \,hər-pə-'täl-ə-jəst\ *n* : a specialist in herpetology
her·pe·tol·o·gy \-jē\ *n* : a branch of zoology dealing with reptiles and amphibians
Herr \(,)he(ə)r\ *n, pl* **Her·ren** \,her-ən, (,)he(ə)rn\ [G] — used among German-speaking people as a title equivalent to *mister*
her·ren·volk \'her-ən-,fōk, -,fōlk\ *n, often cap* [G] : MASTER RACE
her·ring \'her-iŋ\ *n, pl* **herring** *or* **herrings** [ME *hering*, fr. OE *hǣring*; akin to OHG *hārinc* herring] : a valuable soft-rayed food fish (*Clupea harengus*) that is abundant in the temperate and colder parts of the north Atlantic and is preserved in the adult state by smoking or salting and in the young state is extensively canned and sold as sardines; *broadly* : a fish of the herring family (Clupeidae)
[1]**her·ring·bone** \'her-iŋ-,bōn\ *n, often attrib* **1** : a pattern made up of rows of parallel lines with adjacent rows slanting in reverse directions **2** : a twilled fabric with a herringbone pattern; *also* : a suit made of such a fabric **3** : a method in skiing of ascending a slope by herringboning
[2]**herringbone** *vt* **1** : to produce a herringbone pattern on **2** : to arrange in a herringbone pattern ~ *vi* **1** : to produce a herringbone pattern **2** : to ascend a slope by toeing out on skis and placing the weight on the inner edge
hers \'hərz\ *pron, sing or pl in constr* : her one : her ones — used without a following noun as a pronoun equivalent in meaning to the adjective *her*
her·self \(h)ər-'self\ *pron* **1** : that identical female one — compare [1]SHE; used reflexively, for emphasis, or in absolute constructions ⟨she considers ~ lucky⟩ ⟨she ~ did it⟩ ⟨~ an orphan, she understood the situation⟩ **2** : her normal, healthy, or sane condition or self **3** *Irish & Scot* : a woman of consequence; *esp* : the mistress of the house
hertz \'hərts, 'he(ə)rts\ *n* [Heinrich R. *Hertz* †1894 G physicist] : a unit of frequency equal to one cycle per second — abbr. *Hz*
hertz·ian wave \,hərt-sē-ən-, ,hert-\ *n* [Heinrich R. *Hertz* †1894 G physicist] : an electromagnetic wave produced by the oscillation of electricity in a conductor (as a radio antenna) and of a length ranging from a few millimeters to many kilometers
he's \(,)hēz, ēz\ : he is : he has
Hesh·van \'kesh-vən\ *n* [Heb *Ḥeshwān*] : the 2d month of the civil year or the 8th month of the ecclesiastical year in the Jewish calendar
hes·i·tance \'hez-ə-tən(t)s\ *n* : HESITANCY
hes·i·tan·cy \-tən-sē\ *n* **1** : the quality or state of being hesitant : INDECISION, RELUCTANCE **2** : an act or instance of hesitating
hes·i·tant \'hez-ə-tənt\ *adj* : tending to hesitate **syn** see DISINCLINED — **hes·i·tant·ly** *adv*
hes·i·tate \'hez-ə-,tāt\ *vi* [L *haesitatus*, pp. of *haesitare* to stick fast, hesitate, fr. *haesus*, pp. of *haerēre* to stick; akin to Lith *gaišti* to loiter] **1** : to hold back in doubt or indecision **2** : to delay momentarily **3** : STAMMER — **hes·i·tat·er** *n* — **hes·i·tat·ing·ly** \-,tāt-iŋ-lē\ *adv*
syn HESITATE, WAVER, VACILLATE, FALTER mean to show irresolution or uncertainty. HESITATE implies a pause before deciding or acting or choosing; WAVER implies hesitation after seeming to decide and so connotes weakness or a retreat; VACILLATE implies prolonged hesitation from inability to reach a firm decision; FALTER implies a wavering or stumbling and often connotes nervousness, lack of courage, or outright fear
hes·i·ta·tion \,hez-ə-'tā-shən\ *n* **1** : an act or instance of hesitating **2** : STAMMERING
Hes·pe·ri·an \he-'spir-ē-ən\ *adj* [L *Hesperia*, the west, fr. Gk, fr. fem. of *hesperios* of the evening, western, fr. *hesperos* evening — more at WEST] : WESTERN, OCCIDENTAL
Hes·per·i·des \he-'sper-ə-,dēz\ *n pl* [L, fr. Gk] **1** : the nymphs in classical mythology who guard with the aid of a dragon a garden in which golden apples grow **2** : a legendary garden at the western extremity of the world producing golden apples
hes·per·i·din \he-'sper-əd-ᵊn\ *n* [NL *hesperidium* orange, fr. L *Hesperides*] : a crystalline glycoside $C_{28}H_{34}O_{15}$ found in most citrus fruits and esp. in orange peel
Hes·per·us \'hes-p(ə-)rəs\ *n* [L, fr. Gk *Hesperos*] : EVENING STAR
hes·sian \'hesh-ən\ *n* **1** *cap* **a** : a native of Hesse **b** : a German mercenary serving in the British forces during the American Revolution; *broadly* : a mercenary soldier **2** : BURLAP
Hessian boot *n* : a high boot introduced into England by the Hessians early in the 19th century
Hessian fly *n* : a small two-winged fly (*Mayetiola destructor*) that is destructive to wheat in America
hess·ite \'hes-,īt\ *n* [G *hessit*, fr. Henry *Hess* †1850 Swiss chemist] : a mineral Ag_2Te consisting of a lead-gray sectile silver telluride
hes·so·nite \'hes-\ *var of* ESSONITE
hest \'hest\ *n* [ME *hest, hes*, fr. OE *hǣs*; akin to OE *hātan* to command — more at HIGHT] *archaic* : COMMAND, PRECEPT
Hes·tia \'hes-tē-ə, 'hes(h)-chə\ *n* [Gk] : the goddess of the hearth in Greek mythology
he·tae·ra \hi-'tir-ə\ *or* **he·tai·ra** \-'tī-rə\ *n, pl* **he·tae·rae** \-'ti(ə)r-(,)ē\ *or* **hetaeras** *or* **hetairas** *or* **he·tai·rai** \-'tī(ə)r-,ī\ [Gk *hetaira*, lit., companion, fem. of *hetairos*] **1** : one of a class of highly cultivated courtesans in ancient Greece **2** : DEMIMONDAINE
heter- *or* **hetero-** *comb form* [MF or LL; MF, fr. LL, fr. Gk, fr. *heteros*; akin to Gk *heis* one — more at SAME] **1** : other than usual : other : different ⟨*hetero*phyllous⟩ **2** : containing atoms of different kinds ⟨*hetero*cyclic⟩
het·ero·au·to·tro·phic \'het-ə-(,)rō-,ȯt-ə-'träf-ik, -'trō-fik\ *adj* : requiring a simple organic source of carbon but utilizing inorganic nitrogen for metabolism
het·ero·cer·cal \,het-ə-rō-'sər-kəl\ *adj* **1** : having the upper lobe larger than the lower with the end of the vertebral column prolonged and somewhat upturned in the upper lobe **2** : having or relating to a heterocercal tail fin
het·ero·chro·mat·ic \,het-ə-(,)rō-krə-'mat-ik\ *adj* **1** : of, relating to, or having different colors : having a more or less complex pattern of colors **2** : made up of various wavelengths or frequencies **3** [*heterochromatin*] : of or relating to heterochromatin — **het·ero·chro·ma·tism** \-ə-rō-'krō-mə-,tiz-əm\ *n*
het·ero·chro·ma·tin \-ə-rō-'krō-mət-ən\ *n* [G] : densely staining chromatin appearing as nodules in or along chromosomes
het·ero·chro·mo·some \,het-ə-(,)rō-'krō-mə-,sōm\ *n* [ISV] : SEX CHROMOSOME
het·er·och·tho·nous \,het-ə-'räk-thə-nəs\ *adj* [*heter-* + *-chthonous* (as in *autochthonous*)] : not indigenous : FOREIGN
[1]**het·ero·clite** \'het-ə-rə-,klīt\ *n* **1** : a word irregular in inflection; *esp* : a noun irregular in declension **2** : one that deviates from common rules or forms
[2]**heteroclite** *adj* [MF or LL; MF, fr. LL *heteroclitus*, fr. Gk *heteroklitos*, fr. *heter-* + *klinein* to lean, inflect — more at LEAN] : deviating from ordinary forms or rules
het·ero·crine \'het-ə-rə-,krin, -,krīn, -,krēn\ *adj* [*heter-* + *-crine* (as in *endocrine*)] : having both an endocrine and an exocrine secretion
het·ero·cy·clic \,het-ə-rō-'sī-klik, -'sik-lik\ *adj* [ISV] : relating to, characterized by, or being a ring composed of atoms of different elements — **heterocyclic** *n*
het·ero·dox \'het-ə-rə-,däks, 'he-trə-\ *adj* [LL *heterodoxus*, fr. Gk *heterodoxos*, fr. *heter-* + *doxa* opinion — more at DOXOLOGY] **1** : contrary to or different from some acknowledged standard **2** : holding unorthodox opinions or doctrines
syn HERETICAL: HETERODOX implies merely not being in conformity with orthodox teachings; HERETICAL has an additional implication of regarding such divergence as destructive of truth
het·ero·doxy \-,däk-sē\ *n* **1** : the quality or state of being heterodox **2** : a heterodox opinion or doctrine
[1]**het·ero·dyne** \'het-ə-rə-,dīn, 'he-trə-\ *adj* : of or relating to the production of an electrical beat between two radio frequencies of which one usu. is that of a received signal-carrying current and the other that of an uninterrupted current introduced into the apparatus
[2]**heterodyne** *vt* : to combine (a radio frequency) with a different frequency so that a beat is produced
het·er·oe·cious \,het-ə-'rē-shəs\ *adj* [*heter-* + Gk *oikia* house — more at VICINITY] : passing through the different stages in the life cycle on alternate and often unrelated hosts ⟨~ insects⟩ — **het·er·oe·cism** \-'rē-,siz-əm\ *n*
het·ero·ga·mete \,het-ə-rō-gə-'mēt, -'gam-,ēt\ *n* [ISV] : either of a pair of gametes that differ in form, size, or behavior and occur typically as large nonmotile oogametes and small motile sperms — **het·ero·ga·met·ic** \-gə-'met-ik\ *adj*
het·er·og·a·mous \,het-ə-'räg-ə-məs\ *adj* : exhibiting or characterized by diversity in the reproductive elements or processes: as

a : characterized by fusion of unlike gametes; *esp* **:** OOGAMOUS 1 **b :** exhibiting alternation of generations in which two kinds of sexual generation alternate **c :** bearing flowers of two kinds — **het·er·og·a·my** \-mē\ *n*

het·er·o·ge·ne·ity \ˌhet-ə-rō-jə-ˈnē-ət-ē, ˌhe-trō-\ *n* **:** the quality or state of being heterogeneous

het·er·o·ge·neous \ˌhet-ə-rə-ˈjē-nē-əs, ˌhe-trə-, -nyəs\ *adj* [ML *heterogeneus, heterogenus,* fr. Gk *heterogenēs,* fr. *heter-* + *genos* kind — more at KIN] **:** consisting of dissimilar ingredients or constituents **:** MIXED — **het·er·o·ge·neous·ly** *adv* — **het·er·o·ge·neous·ness** *n*

het·ero·gen·e·sis \ˌhet-ə-rō-ˈjen-ə-səs\ *n* [NL] **1 :** ABIOGENESIS **2 :** ALTERNATION OF GENERATIONS — **het·ero·ge·net·ic** \-jə-ˈnet-ik\ *adj*

het·er·og·e·nous \ˌhet-ə-ˈräj-ə-nəs\ *adj* **1 :** of other origin **:** not originating within the body **2 :** HETEROGENEOUS

het·er·og·e·ny \-nē\ *n* **:** a heterogenous collection or group

het·er·og·o·nous \-ˈräg-ə-nəs\ *or* **het·ero·gon·ic** \ˌhet-ə-rə-ˈgän-ik\ *adj* [*heter-* + Gk *-gonia* -gony] **1 :** having two or more kinds of perfect flowers **2 :** characterized by alternation of generations **3 :** ALLOMETRIC — **het·er·og·o·ny** \-ˈräg-ə-nē\ *n*

het·er·og·y·nous \ˌhet-ə-ˈräj-ə-nəs\ *adj* **:** having females of more than one kind

het·ero·lec·i·thal \ˌhet-ə-rō-ˈles-ə-thəl\ *adj* [*heter-* + Gk *lekithos* egg yolk] **:** having the yolk unequally distributed

het·er·ol·o·gous \ˌhet-ə-ˈräl-ə-gəs\ *adj* **1 :** characterized by heterology **2 :** derived from a different species — **het·er·ol·o·gous·ly** *adv*

het·er·ol·o·gy \-ˈräl-ə-jē\ *n* [ISV] **:** a lack of correspondence of apparently similar bodily parts due to differences in fundamental makeup or origin

het·er·ol·y·sis \ˌhet-ə-ˈräl-ə-səs\ *n* [NL] **1 :** destruction by an outside agent; *specif* **:** solution (as of a cell) by lysins or enzymes from another source **2 :** decomposition of a compound into two oppositely charged particles or ions — **het·er·o·lyt·ic** \ˌhet-ə-rə-ˈlit-ik\ *adj*

het·er·om·er·ous \ˌhet-ə-ˈräm-ə-rəs\ *adj* [*heter-* + Gk *meros* part — more at MERIT] **:** having one or more floral whorls the number of whose members differs from that of the remaining whorls

het·ero·meso·tro·phic \ˌhet-ə-rō-ˌmez-ə-ˈträf-ik, -ˌmes-, -ˈtrō-fik\ *adj* **:** requiring a single organic source of nitrogen and carbon for metabolism

het·ero·met·a·bol·ic \-ˌmet-ə-ˈbäl-ik\ *or* **het·ero·me·tab·o·lous** \-mə-ˈtab-ə-ləs\ *adj* **:** of, relating to, or exhibiting heterometabolism

het·ero·me·tab·o·lism \-mə-ˈtab-ə-ˌliz-əm\ *also* **het·ero·me·tab·o·ly** \-lē\ *n* **:** insect development with incomplete metamorphosis in which the nymph is basically like the adult and no pupa occurs

het·ero·meta·tro·phic \ˌhet-ə-rō-ˌmet-ə-ˈträf-ik, -ˈtrō-fik\ *adj* **:** requiring complex organic sources of carbon and nitrogen for metabolism — compare HOLOZOIC

het·ero·mor·phic \-ˈmȯr-fik\ *or* **het·ero·mor·phous** \-fəs\ *adj* [ISV] **:** deviating from the usual form **:** exhibiting diversity of form (as in different stages of a life cycle) — **het·ero·mor·phism** \-ˌfiz-əm\ *n*

het·er·on·o·mous \ˌhet-ə-ˈrän-ə-məs\ *adj* [*heter-* + *-nomous* (as in *autonomous*)] **1 :** specialized along different lines of growth or under different controlling forces **2 :** subject to external controls and impositions — **het·er·on·o·mous·ly** *adv*

het·er·on·o·my \-mē\ *n* [*heter-* + *-nomy* (as in *autonomy*)] **:** a subjection to something else; *esp* **:** a condition of lacking moral freedom or self-determination

het·ero·pet·al·ous \ˌhet-ə-rō-ˈpet-ᵊl-əs\ *adj* **:** having dissimilar petals

het·ero·phile \ˈhet-ə-rə-ˌfīl\ *adj* **:** reacting serologically with an antigen of another species

het·er·oph·o·ny \ˌhet-ə-ˈräf-ə-nē\ *n* [Gk *heterophōnia* diversity of note, fr. *heter-* + *-phōnia* -phony] **:** the performance of a melody by two or more individuals who add their own rhythmic or melodic modifications

het·ero·phyl·lous \ˌhet-ə-rō-ˈfil-əs\ *adj* **:** having the foliage leaves of more than one form on the same plant or stem — **het·ero·phyl·ly** \ˈhet-ə-rō-ˌfil-ē\ *n*

het·ero·phyte \ˈhet-ə-rə-ˌfīt\ *n* **:** a plant (as a parasite or saprophyte) that is dependent for food materials upon other organisms or their products — **het·ero·phyt·ic** \ˌhet-ə-rə-ˈfit-ik\ *adj*

het·ero·ploid \ˈhet-ə-rə-ˌplȯid\ *adj* [ISV] **:** having a chromosome number that is not a simple multiple of the haploid chromosome number — **heteroploid** *n* — **het·ero·ploi·dy** \-ˌplȯid-ē\ *n*

het·ero·po·lar \ˌhet-ə-rə-ˈpō-lər\ *adj* [ISV] **:** POLAR 5, IONIC — **het·ero·po·lar·i·ty** \-(ˌ)rō-pə-ˈlar-ət-ē\ *n*

het·er·op·ter·ous \ˌhet-ə-ˈräp-tə-rəs\ *adj* [deriv. of Gk *heter-* + *pteron* wing — more at FEATHER] **:** of or relating to an order or suborder (Heteroptera) comprising the true bugs

het·ero·sex·u·al \ˌhet-ə-rō-ˈseksh-(ə-)wəl, -ˈsek-shəl\ *adj* [ISV] **1 :** of or relating to or marked by sexual orientation toward members of the opposite sex **2 :** of or relating to different sexes — **heterosexual** *n* — **het·ero·sex·u·al·i·ty** \-ˌsek-shə-ˈwal-ət-ē\ *n*

het·er·o·sis \ˌhet-ə-ˈrō-səs\ *n* [NL] **:** a marked vigor or capacity for growth often shown by crossbred animals or plants — **het·er·ot·ic** \-ˈrät-ik\ *adj*

het·ero·spo·rous \ˌhet-ə-rə-ˈspōr-əs, -ˈspȯr-; -ˈräs-pə-rəs\ *adj* **1 :** producing asexual spores of more than one kind **2 :** producing microspores and megaspores — **het·ero·spo·ry** \ˈhet-ə-rə-ˌspōr-ē, -ˌspȯr-; ˌhet-ə-ˈräs-pə-rē\ *n*

het·ero·tro·phic \ˌhet-ə-rə-ˈträf-ik, -ˈtrō-fik\ *adj* **:** requiring complex organic compounds of nitrogen and carbon for metabolic synthesis — **het·ero·tro·phi·cal·ly** \-i-k(ə-)lē, -fi-\ *adv*

het·ero·typ·ic \ˌhet-ə-rō-ˈtip-ik\ *adj* **1 :** of or being the reduction division of meiosis as contrasted with typical mitotic division **2 :** of or being a genus containing groups of species showing various degrees of relationship — **het·ero·typ·i·cal** \-i-kəl\ *adj*

het·ero·zy·go·sis \ˌhet-ə-rō-ˌzī-ˈgō-səs\ *n* [NL] **1 :** a union of genetically dissimilar gametes forming a heterozygote **2 :** the state of being a heterozygote

het·ero·zy·gote \-ˈzī-ˌgōt\ *n* **:** an animal or plant containing genes for both members of at least one pair of allelomorphic characters — **het·ero·zy·gous** \-ˈzī-gəs\ *adj*

heth \ˈk̟āt(h), ˈk̟et(h)\ *n* [Heb *ḥēth*] **:** the 8th letter of the Hebrew alphabet — symbol ח

het·man \ˈhet-mən\ *n* [Pol] **:** a cossack leader

het up \ˈhet-ˈəp\ *adj* [*het,* dial. past of *heat*] *chiefly dial* **:** highly excited **:** UPSET

heu·land·ite \ˈhyü-lən-ˌdīt\ *n* [Henry *Heuland,* 19th cent. E mineral collector] **:** a zeolite $(Na,Ca)_{4-6}Al_6(Al,Si)_4Si_{26}O_{72}.24H_2O$ consisting of a hydrous aluminosilicate of sodium and calcium

[1]**heu·ris·tic** \hyü-ˈris-tik\ *adj* [G *heuristisch,* fr. NL *heuristicus,* fr. Gk *heuriskein* to discover; akin to OIr *fúar* I have found] **:** serving to guide, discover, or reveal; *specif* **:** valuable for empirical research but unproved or incapable of proof

[2]**heuristic** *n* **1 :** the study or practice of heuristic procedure **2 :** heuristic argument

hew \ˈhyü\ *vb* **hewed**; **hewed** *or* **hewn** \ˈhyün\ **hew·ing** [ME *hewen,* fr. OE *hēawan;* akin to OHG *houwan* to hew, L *cudere* to beat] *vt* **1 :** to cut with blows of a heavy cutting instrument **2 :** to fell by blows of an ax **3 :** to give form or shape to with or as if with heavy cutting blows ~ *vi* **1 :** to make cutting blows **2 :** to conform strictly **:** ADHERE — **hew·er** *n*

[1]**hex** \ˈheks\ *vb* [PaG *hexe,* fr. G *hexen,* fr. *hexe* witch] *vi* **:** to practice witchcraft ~ *vt* **1 :** to put a hex on **2 :** to affect as if by an evil spell **:** JINX — **hex·er** *n*

[2]**hex** *n* **1 :** SPELL, JINX **2 :** a person who practices witchcraft **:** WITCH

[3]**hex** *adj* **:** HEXAGONAL

hexa- *or* **hex-** *comb form* [Gk, fr. *hex* six — more at SIX] **1 :** six ⟨*hexa*merous⟩ **2 :** containing six atoms, groups, or equivalents ⟨*hex*ane⟩

hexa·bi·ose *or* **hexo·bi·ose** \ˌhek-sə-ˈbī-ˌōs, -ˌōz\ *n* **:** a disaccharide yielding two hexose molecules on hydrolysis

hexa·chlo·ro·eth·ane \ˌhek-sə-ˌklōr-ə-ˈweth-ˌān, -ˌklȯr-\ *or* **hexa·chlor·eth·ane** \-ˌklōr-ˈeth-, -ˌklȯr-\ *n* [ISV] **:** a toxic crystalline compound C_2Cl_6 used esp. in smoke bombs and in the control of liver flukes in ruminants

hexa·chlo·ro·phene \-ˈklōr-ə-ˌfēn, -ˈklȯr-\ *n* [*hexa-* + *chlor-* + *phenol*] **:** a crystalline phenolic bacteria-inhibiting agent $C_{13}Cl_6H_6O_2$ used esp. in soap

hexa·chord \ˈhek-sə-ˌkȯ(ə)rd\ *n* [*hexa-* + Gk *chordē* string — more at YARN] **:** a diatonic series of six tones having a semitone between the third and fourth

hex·ad \ˈhek-ˌsad\ *or* **hex·ade** \-ˌsād\ *n* [LL *hexad-, hexas,* fr. Gk, fr. *hex*] **:** a group or series of six — **hex·ad·ic** \hek-ˈsad-ik\ *adj*

hexa·gon \ˈhek-sə-ˌgän\ *n* [Gk *hexagōnon,* neut. of *hexagōnos* hexagonal, fr. *hexa-* + *gōnia* angle — more at -GON] **:** a polygon of six angles and six sides

hex·ag·o·nal \hek-ˈsag-ən-ᵊl\ *adj* **1 :** having six angles and six sides **2 :** having a hexagon as section or base **3 :** relating to or being a crystal system characterized by three equal lateral axes intersecting at angles of 60 degrees and a vertical axis of variable length at right angles — **hex·ag·o·nal·ly** \-ᵊl-ē\ *adv*

hexa·gram \ˈhek-sə-ˌgram\ *n* [ISV] **:** a figure formed by completing externally an equilateral triangle on each side of a regular hexagon

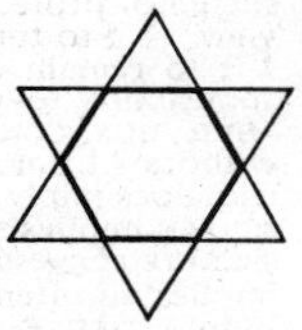

hexagram

hexa·he·dron \ˌhek-sə-ˈhē-drən\ *n, pl* **hexahe·drons** *also* **hexa·he·dra** \-drə\ [LL, fr. Gk *hexaedron,* fr. neut. of *hexaedros* of six surfaces, fr. *hexa-* + *hedra* seat — more at SIT] **:** a polyhedron of six faces

hexa·hy·drate \-ˈhī-ˌdrāt\ *n* **:** a chemical compound with six molecules of water — **hexa·hy·drat·ed** \-ˌdrāt-əd\ *adj*

hex·am·er·ous \hek-ˈsam-ə-rəs\ *adj* **:** having six parts or parts in multiples of six; *specif* **:** having floral whorls composed of six members

hex·am·e·ter \hek-ˈsam-ət-ər\ *n* [L, fr. Gk *hexametron,* fr. neut. of *hexametros* having six measures, fr. *hexa-* + *metron* measure — more at MEASURE] **:** a verse consisting of six feet

hexa·meth·y·lene·tet·ra·mine \ˌhek-sə-ˈmeth-ə-ˌlēn-ˈte-trə-ˌmēn\ *n* [ISV] **:** a crystalline compound $C_6H_{12}N_4$ used esp. as an accelerator in vulcanizing rubber, as an absorbent for phosgene, and as a diuretic

hex·ane \ˈhek-ˌsān\ *n* [ISV] **:** any of five isomeric volatile liquid paraffin hydrocarbons C_6H_{14} found in petroleum

hexa·ni·trate \ˌhek-sə-ˈnī-ˌtrāt, -trət\ *n* **:** a compound containing six nitrate groups in the molecule

hexa·ploid \ˈhek-sə-ˌplȯid\ *adj* [ISV] **:** arranged or appearing in sixes; *specif* **:** having or being six times the monoploid chromosome number — **hexaploid** *n* — **hexa·ploi·dy** \-ˌplȯid-ē\ *n*

[1]**hexa·pod** \ˈhek-sə-ˌpäd\ *n* [Gk *hexapod-, hexapous* having six feet, fr. *hexa-* + *pod-, pous* foot — more at FOOT] **:** INSECT 1b

[2]**hexapod** *adj* **1 :** six-footed **2 :** of or relating to insects

hex·ap·o·dous \hek-ˈsap-əd-əs\ *adj* **:** HEXAPOD

Hexa·teuch \ˈhek-sə-ˌt(y)ük\ *n* [*hexa-* + Gk *teuchos* book — more at PENTATEUCH] **:** the first six books of the Old Testament

hex·e·rei \ˌhek-sə-ˈrī\ *n* [PaG, fr. G] **:** WITCHCRAFT

hex·o·san \ˈhek-sə-ˌsan\ *n* **:** a polysaccharide yielding only hexoses on hydrolysis

hex·ose \ˈhek-ˌsōs, -ˌsōz\ *n* [ISV] **:** a monosaccharide $C_6H_{12}O_6$ containing six carbon atoms in the molecule

hex·yl \ˈhek-səl\ *n* [ISV] **:** an alkyl radical C_6H_{13} derived from a hexane

hex·yl·res·or·cin·ol \ˌhek-səl-rə-ˈzȯrs-ᵊn-ˌȯl, -ˌōl\ *n* **:** a crystalline phenol $C_{12}H_{18}O_2$ used as an antiseptic and anthelmintic

hey \ˈhā\ *interj* [ME] — used esp. to call attention or to express interrogation, surprise, or exultation

[1]**hey·day** \ˈhā-ˌdā\ *interj* [irreg. fr. *hey*] *archaic* — used to express exultation or wonder

[2]**heyday** *also* **hey·dey** *n* **1** *archaic* **:** high spirits **2 :** a period of greatest strength, vigor, or prosperity

Hez·e·ki·ah \ˌhez-ə-ˈkī-ə\ *n* [Heb *Ḥizqīyāh*] **:** a king of Judah of the 8th–7th centuries B.C.

hi \ˈhī(-ē)\ *interj* [ME *hy*] — used esp. as a greeting

hi·a·tus \hī-ˈāt-əs\ *n* [L, fr. *hiatus,* pp. of *hiare* to yawn — more at YAWN] **1 :** a break in an object **:** GAP **2 a :** a lapse in continuity **b :** the occurrence of two vowel sounds without pause or intervening consonantal sound

Hi·a·wa·tha \ˌhī-ə-ˈwȯ-thə, ˌhē-ə-, -ˈwäth-ə\ *n* **:** the Indian hero of Longfellow's poem *The Song of Hiawatha*
hi·ba·chi \hē-ˈbäch-ē\ *n* [Jap] **:** a charcoal brazier
hi·ber·nac·u·lum \ˌhī-bər-ˈnak-yə-ləm\ *n, pl* **hi·ber·nac·u·la** \-lə\ [NL, fr. L, winter residence, fr. *hibernare*] **1 :** the winter resting part of a plant **2 a :** a shelter occupied during the winter by a dormant animal (as an insect) **b :** an encysted bud in a freshwater bryozoan that survives the winter
hi·ber·nal \hī-ˈbərn-ᵊl\ *adj* **:** of or relating to winter **:** WINTRY
hi·ber·nate \ˈhī-bər-ˌnāt\ *vi* [L *hibernatus*, pp. of *hibernare* to pass the winter, fr. *hibernus* of winter; akin to L *hiems* winter, Gk *cheimōn*] **:** to pass the winter in a torpid or resting state — **hi·ber·na·tion** \ˌhī-bər-ˈnā-shən\ *n* — **hi·ber·na·tor** \ˈhī-bər-ˌnāt-ər\ *n*
Hi·ber·ni·an \hī-ˈbər-nē-ən\ *adj* [L *Hibernia* Ireland] **:** of, relating to, or characteristic of Ireland or the Irish — **Hibernian** *n* — **Hi·ber·ni·an·ism** \-nē-ə-ˌniz-əm\ *n*
Hi·ber·ni·cism \-nə-ˌsiz-əm\ *n* **:** something characteristically Irish
hi·bis·cus \hī-ˈbis-kəs, hə-\ *n* [NL, genus name, fr. L, marshmallow] **:** any of a large genus (*Hibiscus*) of herbs, shrubs, or small trees of the mallow family with dentate leaves and large showy flowers
¹**hic·cup** *also* **hic·cough** \ˈhik-(ˌ)əp\ *n* [imit.] **1 :** a spasmodic inbreathing with closure of the glottis accompanied by a peculiar sound **2 :** an attack of hiccuping — usu. used in pl. but sing. or pl. in constr.
²**hiccup** *also* **hiccough** *vi* **hic·cuped** *also* **hic·cupped; hic·cup·ing** *also* **hic·cup·ping :** to make a hiccup; *also* **:** to be affected with hiccups
hic ja·cet \(ˈ)hik-ˈjā-sət, (ˈ)hēk-ˈyäk-ət\ *n* [L, here lies] **:** EPITAPH
¹**hick** \ˈhik\ *n* [*Hick*, nickname for *Richard*] **:** an awkward provincial person
²**hick** *vi* **:** HICCUP
hick·ey \ˈhik-ē\ *n* [origin unknown] **1 a :** a threaded coupling between an electrical fixture and an outlet box **b :** a device for bending pipe and conduit **2 :** DEVICE, GADGET
hick·o·ry \ˈhik-(ə-)rē\ *n, often attrib* [short for obs. *pokahickory*, fr. *pawcohiccora* food prepared from pounded nuts (in some Algonquian language of Virginia)] **1 a :** any of a genus (*Carya*) of No. American hardwood trees of the walnut family often with sweet edible nuts **b :** the usu. tough pale wood of a hickory **2 :** a switch or cane (as of hickory wood) used esp. for punishing a child
hid \ˈhid\ *adj* **:** HIDDEN
hi·dal·go \hid-ˈal-(ˌ)gō, ē-ˈt͟häl-\ *n, often cap* [Sp] **:** a member of the lower nobility of Spain
hid·den·ite \ˈhid-ᵊn-ˌīt\ *n* [William E. *Hidden* †1918 Am mineralogist] **:** a transparent yellow to green spodumene valued as a gem
¹**hide** \ˈhīd\ *n* [ME, fr. OE *hīgid*] **:** any of various old English units of land area; *esp* **:** a unit of 120 acres
²**hide** *vb* **hid** \ˈhid\ **hid·den** \ˈhid-ᵊn\ *or* **hid; hid·ing** \ˈhīd-iŋ\ [ME *hiden*, fr. OE *hȳdan;* akin to Gk *keuthein* to conceal, OE *hȳd* hide, skin] *vt* **1 a :** to put out of sight **:** SECRETE **b :** to conceal for shelter or protection **:** SHIELD **2 :** to keep secret **3 :** to screen from view **4 :** to turn (the eyes or face) away in shame or anger ~ *vi* **1 :** to remain out of sight **2 :** to seek protection or evade responsibility ⟨~*s* behind dark glasses⟩ — **hid·er** \ˈhīd-ər\ *n*
syn HIDE, CONCEAL, SCREEN, SECRETE, BURY mean to withhold or withdraw from sight. HIDE may or may not suggest intent; CONCEAL usu. does imply intent and often specif. implies a refusal to divulge; SCREEN implies an interposing of something that prevents discovery; SECRETE suggests a depositing in a place unknown to others; BURY implies an often accidental covering up so as to hide completely
³**hide** *n* [ME, fr. OE *hȳd;* akin to OHG *hūt* hide, L *cutis* skin, Gk *kytos* hollow vessel] **:** the skin of an animal whether raw or dressed — used esp. of large heavy skins
⁴**hide** *vt* **hid·ed; hid·ing :** to give a beating to **:** FLOG
hide·away \ˈhīd-ə-ˌwā\ *n* **:** RETREAT, HIDEOUT
hide·bound \-ˌbau̇nd\ *adj* **1 a** *of a domestic animal* **:** having a dry skin lacking in pliancy and adhering closely to the underlying flesh **b** *of a tree* **:** having the bark so close and constricting that it impedes growth **2 :** obstinately conservative **:** NARROW
hid·eous \ˈhid-ē-əs\ *adj* [alter. of ME *hidous*, fr. OF, fr. *hisde*, *hide* terror] **1 :** offensive to the sense **:** UGLY **2 :** morally offensive **:** SHOCKING — **hid·eous·ly** *adv* — **hid·eous·ness** *n*
hide·out \ˈhī-ˌdau̇t\ *n* **:** a place of refuge or concealment

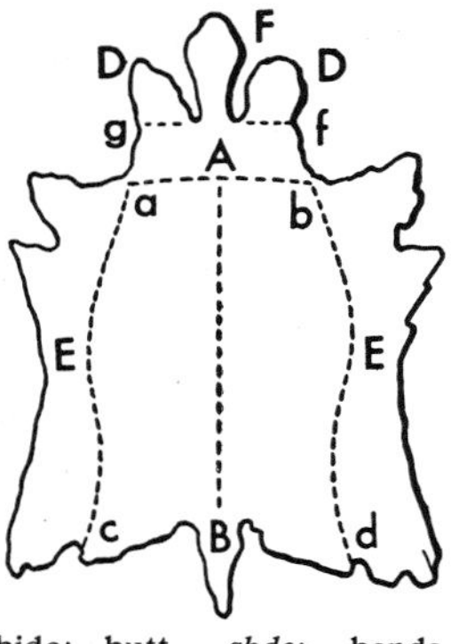

hide: butt, *abdc;* bends, *ABdb* and *ABca;* shoulder, *abfg;* belly, *E,E;* cheeks, *D,D;* head, F

hi·dro·sis \hid-ˈrō-səs, hī-ˈdrō-\ *n* [NL, fr. Gk *hidrōsis*, fr. *hidroun* to sweat, fr. *hidrōs* sweat — more at SWEAT] **:** excretion of sweat **:** PERSPIRATION — **hi·drot·ic** \-ˈrät-ik, -ˈdrät-\ *adj*
hie \ˈhī\ *vb* **hied; hy·ing** *or* **hie·ing** [ME *hien*, fr. OE *hīgian* to strive, hasten; akin to OSw *hikka* to pant, Skt *śīghra* quick] **:** HASTEN
hi·emal \ˈhī-ə-məl\ *adj* [L *hiemalis*, fr. *hiems* winter — more at HIBERNATE] **:** of or relating to winter **:** WINTRY
hier- *or* **hiero-** *comb form* [LL, fr. Gk, fr. *hieros* — more at IRE] **:** sacred **:** holy ⟨*hiero*logy⟩
hi·er·arch \ˈhī-(ə-)ˌrärk\ *n* [MF or ML; MF *hierarche*, fr. ML *hierarcha*, fr. Gk *hierarchēs*, fr. *hier-* + *-archēs* -arch] **1 :** a religious leader in a position of authority **2 :** a person high in a hierarchy — **hi·er·ar·chal** \ˌhī-(ə-)ˈrär-kəl\ *adj*
hi·er·ar·chi·cal \ˌhī-(ə-)ˈrär-ki-kəl\ *or* **hi·er·ar·chic** \-kik\ *adj* **:** of or relating to a hierarchy — **hi·er·ar·chi·cal·ly** \-ki-k(ə-)lē\ *adv*
hi·er·ar·chy \ˈhī-(ə-)ˌrär-kē\ *n* **1 :** a division of angels **2 a :** a ruling body of clergy organized into orders or ranks each subordinate to the one above it; *specif* **:** the bishops of a province or nation **b :** church government by a hierarchy **3 :** a body of persons in authority **4 a :** arrangement into a graded series **b :** persons or other entities arranged in a series

hi·er·at·ic \ˌhī-(ə-)ˈrat-ik\ *adj* [L *hieraticus* sacerdotal, fr. Gk *hieratikos*, deriv. of *hieros*] **1 :** constituting or belonging to a cursive form of ancient Egyptian writing simpler than the hieroglyphic **2 :** SACERDOTAL — **hi·er·at·i·cal·ly** \-i-k(ə-)lē\ *adv*
hi·ero·dule \ˈhī-(ə-)rō-ˌd(y)ü(ə)l\ *n* [LL *hierodulus*, fr. Gk *hierodoulos*, fr. *hier-* + *doulos* slave] **:** a slave in the service of a temple — **hi·ero·du·lic** \ˌhī-(ə-)rō-ˈd(y)ü-lik\ *adj*
hi·ero·glyph \ˈhī-(ə-)rə-ˌglif\ *n* [F *hiéroglyphe*, fr. MF, back-formation fr. *hieroglyphique*] **:** a character used in a system of hieroglyphic writing
¹**hi·ero·glyph·ic** \ˌhī-(ə-)rə-ˈglif-ik\ *adj* [MF *hieroglyphique*, fr. LL *hieroglyphicus*, fr. Gk *hieroglyphikos*, fr. *hier-* + *glyphein* to carve — more at CLEAVE] **1 :** written in, constituting, or belonging to a system of writing mainly in pictorial characters **2 :** inscribed with hieroglyphic **3 :** resembling hieroglyphic in difficulty of decipherment — **hi·ero·glyph·i·cal** *adj* — **hi·ero·glyph·i·cal·ly** \-i-k(ə-)lē\ *adv*
²**hieroglyphic** *n* **1 :** HIEROGLYPH **2 :** a system of hieroglyphic writing; *specif* **:** the picture script of the ancient Egyptian priesthood — often used in pl. but sing. or pl. in constr. **3 :** something that resembles a hieroglyphic esp. in difficulty of decipherment

Egyptian hieroglyphics

hi·ero·phant \ˈhī-(ə-)rə-ˌfant\ *n* [LL *hierophanta*, fr. Gk *hierophantēs*, fr. *hier-* + *phainein* to show] **1 :** a priest in ancient Greece; *specif* **:** the chief priest of the Eleusinian mysteries **2 a :** EXPOSITOR **b :** ADVOCATE — **hi·ero·phan·tic** \ˌhī-(ə-)rə-ˈfant-ik\ *adj*
hi–fi \ˈhī-ˈfī\ *n* **1 :** HIGH FIDELITY **2 :** equipment for reproduction of sound with high fidelity
hig·gle \ˈhig-əl\ *vi* **hig·gling** \-(ə-)liŋ\ [prob. alter. of *haggle*] **:** HAGGLE — **hig·gler** \-(ə-)lər\ *n*
hig·gle·dy–pig·gle·dy \ˌhig-əl-dē-ˈpig-əl-dē\ *adv* [origin unknown] **:** in confusion **:** TOPSY-TURVY — **higgledy–piggledy** *adj*
¹**high** \ˈhī\ *adj* [ME, fr. OE *hēah;* akin to OHG *hōh* high, L *cacumen* point, top] **1 a :** extending or raised up **:** ELEVATED **b :** having a specified elevation **:** TALL ⟨six feet ~⟩ **2 a :** advanced toward its fullness or culmination ⟨~ summer⟩ **b :** beginning to taint ⟨~ game⟩ **c :** long past **:** REMOTE ⟨~ antiquity⟩ **3 a :** SHRILL, SHARP ⟨~ note⟩ **b :** elevated in pitch ⟨a ~ tone⟩ **4 :** relatively far from the equator ⟨~ latitude⟩ **5 :** exalted in character **:** NOBLE **6 :** of greater degree, size, amount, or content than average or ordinary ⟨~ pressure⟩ **7 :** of relatively great importance: as **a :** foremost in rank, dignity, or standing **b :** SERIOUS, GRAVE ⟨~ crimes⟩ **8 :** FORCIBLE, STRONG ⟨~ winds⟩ **9 a :** BOASTFUL, ARROGANT **b :** showing elation or excitement **c :** INTOXICATED **10 :** COSTLY, DEAR **11 :** advanced in complexity, development, or elaboration ⟨~*er* mathematics⟩ **12 :** articulated with some part of the tongue close to the palate ⟨\ē\ is a ~ vowel⟩ — **high·ly** *adv*
syn TALL, LOFTY: HIGH implies marked extension upward, or placement at a conspicuous height above the ground or above some standard level; TALL applies to what grows or rises high by comparison with others of its kind and usu. implies relative narrowness; LOFTY implies great or imposing altitude. Figuratively HIGH implies excellence or distinction, or complexity in development, or arrogance of manner; TALL implies exaggeration; LOFTY suggests moral grandeur or dignity, or sometimes superciliousness
²**high** *adv* **1 :** at or to a high place, altitude, or degree **2 :** RICHLY, LUXURIOUSLY
³**high** *n* **1 :** an elevated place or region: as **a :** HILL, KNOLL **b :** SKY, HEAVEN **2 :** a region of high barometric pressure **:** ANTICYCLONE **3 a :** a high point or level **:** HEIGHT **b :** the transmission gear of an automotive vehicle giving the highest ratio of propeller-shaft to engine-shaft speed and consequently the highest speed of travel
high analysis *adj, of a fertilizer* **:** containing more than 20 percent of total plant nutrients
¹**high·ball** \ˈhī-ˌbȯl\ *n* **1 a :** a railroad signal for a train to proceed at full speed **b :** a fast train **2 :** a drink of alcoholic liquor and water or a carbonated beverage served in a tall glass
²**highball** *vi* **:** to go at full or high speed
high beam *n* **:** the long-range focus of a vehicle headlight
high·bind·er \-ˌbīn-dər\ *n* [the *Highbinders*, gang of vagabonds in New York City *ab*1806] **1 :** a professional killer operating in the Chinese quarter of an American city **2 :** a corrupt or scheming politician
high blood pressure *n* **:** HYPERTENSION
high·born \-ˈbȯ(ə)rn\ *adj* **:** of noble birth
high·boy \-ˌbȯi\ *n* **:** a high chest of drawers mounted on a base with long legs
high·bred \-ˈbred\ *adj* **:** coming from superior stock
high·brow \ˈhī-ˌbrau̇\ *n* **:** a person of superior learning or culture **:** INTELLECTUAL — **highbrow** *adj* — **high·browed** \-ˌbrau̇d\ *adj* — **high·brow·ism** \-ˌbrau̇-ˌiz-əm\ *n*
high·bush \-ˈbu̇sh\ *adj* **:** forming a notably tall or erect bush; *also* **:** borne on a highbush plant
high chair *n* **:** a child's chair with long legs, a feeding tray, and a footrest
High Church *adj* **:** tending toward or stressing sacerdotal, liturgical, ceremonial, traditional, and Catholic elements as appropriate to the life of the Christian church — **High Churchman** *n*
high command *n* **1 :** the supreme headquarters of a military force **2 :** the highest leaders in an organization
high commissioner *n* **:** a principal or a high-ranking commissioner; *esp* **:** an ambassadorial representative of the government of one country stationed in another
higher criticism *n* **:** study of biblical writings to determine their literary history and the purpose and meaning of the authors
higher fungus *n* **:** a fungus with hyphae well-developed and septate
high·er–up \ˌhī-(ə-)ˈrəp\ *n* **:** a superior officer or official
high explosive *n* **:** an explosive (as TNT) that generates gas with extreme rapidity and has a shattering effect
high·fa·lu·tin \ˌhī-fə-ˈlüt-ᵊn\ *adj* [perh. fr. ²*high* + alter. of *fluting*, prp. of *flute*] **1 :** PRETENTIOUS **2 :** expressed in or marked by the use of high-flown bombastic language **:** POMPOUS
high fidelity *n* **:** the reproduction of sound with a high degree of faithfulness to the original
high·fli·er *or* **high·fly·er** \ˈhī-ˈflī(-ə)r\ *n* **1 :** a high-flying person **2 :** an extremely orthodox or doctrinaire person
high–flown \-ˈflōn\ *adj* **1 :** EXALTED **2 :** BOMBASTIC, PRETENTIOUS

high–fly·ing \-'flī-iŋ\ *adj* **:** marked by extravagance, pretension, or excessive ambition

high frequency *n* **:** a radio frequency in the middle range of the radio spectrum — see RADIO FREQUENCY table

High German *n* **1 :** German as natively used in southern and central Germany **2 :** GERMAN 2b

high grade *n* **:** a grade animal that in conformation and economic qualities approximates the breed to which its known purebred ancestors belong

high–grown \'hī-'grōn\ *adj* **:** covered with tall vegetation

high–hand·ed \-'han-dəd\ *adj* **:** OVERBEARING, ARBITRARY — **high–hand·ed·ly** *adv* — **high–hand·ed·ness** *n*

high hat *n* **:** BEAVER 2

high–hat \'hī-'hat\ *adj* **:** SUPERCILIOUS, SNOBBISH — **high–hat** *vt*

High Holiday *n* **:** either of two important Jewish holidays: **a :** ROSH HASHANAH **b :** YOM KIPPUR

high horse *n* **:** an arrogant mood or attitude

high jump *n* **:** a jump for height in a track-and-field contest

1high·land \'hī-lənd\ *n* **:** elevated or mountainous land

2highland *adj* **1 :** of or relating to a highland **2** *cap* **:** of or relating to the Highlands of Scotland

high·land·er \-lən-dər\ *n* **1 :** an inhabitant of a highland **2** *cap* **:** an inhabitant of the Highlands of Scotland

Highland fling *n* **:** a lively Scottish folk dance

high–lev·el \'hī-'lev-əl\ *adj* **1 :** being of high importance or rank **2 :** occurring, done, or placed at a high level

1high·light \'hī-,līt\ *n* **1 :** the lightest spot or area (as in a painting) **:** any of several spots in a modeled drawing or painting that receives the greatest amount of illumination **2 :** an event or detail of major significance

2highlight *vt* **1 :** to throw a strong light upon **2 a :** to center attention upon **:** EMPHASIZE **b :** to constitute a highlight of

high–low–jack \,hī-,lō-'jak\ *n* **:** a card game in which scores are made by winning the highest trump, the lowest trump, the jack of trumps, and either the ten of trumps or the most points

high mass *n, often cap H&M* **:** a sung mass usu. with full ceremonials and incense and with the celebrant assisted by a deacon and subdeacon

high–mind·ed \'hī-'mīn-dəd\ *adj* **:** marked by elevated principles and feelings — **high–mind·ed·ly** *adv* — **high–mind·ed·ness** *n*

high–muck–a–muck \,hī-,mək-i-'mək\ *or* **high–muck·ety–muck** \,hī-,mək-ət-ē-'mək\ *n* [by folk etymology fr. Chinook Jargon *hiu muckamuck* plenty to eat] **:** an important and often arrogant person

high·ness \'hī-nəs\ *n* **1 :** the quality or state of being high **2 —** used as a title for a person of exalted rank (as a king or prince)

high–octane *adj* **:** having a high octane number and hence good antiknock properties ⟨~ gasoline⟩

high place *n* **:** a temple or altar used by the ancient Semites and built usu. on a hill or elevation

1high–pressure *adj* **1 a :** having or involving a high or comparatively high pressure esp. greatly exceeding that of the atmosphere **b :** having a high barometric pressure **2 :** using or involving aggressive and insistent sales techniques

2high–pressure *vt* **:** to sell or influence by high-pressure tactics

high priest *n* **1 :** a chief priest esp. of the ancient Jewish priesthood **2 :** a priest of the Melchizedek priesthood in the Mormon Church

high relief *n* **:** sculptural relief in which at least half of the circumference of the modeled form projects

high–rise \'hī-'rīz\ *adj* **:** being multistory and equipped with elevators ⟨~ apartments⟩

high·road \'hī-,rōd\ *n* **1** *chiefly Brit* **:** HIGHWAY **2 :** the easiest course

1high school *n* **:** a secondary school usu. comprising the 9th to 12th or 10th to 12th years of study

2high school *n* **:** a system of advanced exercises in horsemanship

high sea *n* **:** the open part of a sea or ocean esp. outside territorial waters — usu. used in pl.

high–sound·ing \'hī-'saun-diŋ\ *adj* **:** POMPOUS, IMPOSING

high–spir·it·ed \-'spir-ət-əd\ *adj* **:** characterized by a bold or lofty spirit — **high–spir·it·ed·ly** *adv* — **high–spir·it·ed·ness** *n*

high–strung \-'strəŋ\ *adj* **:** having an extremely nervous or sensitive temperament

hight \'hīt\ *adj* [ME, irreg. pp. of *hoten* to command, call, be called, fr. OE *hātan;* akin to OHG *heizzan* to command, call and prob. to L *ciēre* to move, Gk *kinein*] *archaic* **:** CALLED, NAMED

high·tail \'hī-,tāl\ *vi* **:** to retreat at full speed

high–tension *adj* **:** having a high voltage; *also* **:** relating to apparatus to be used at high voltage

high–test *adj* **:** passing a difficult test; *specif* **:** having a high volatility ⟨~ gasoline⟩

high tide *n* **1 :** the tide when the water is at its greatest elevation **2 :** culminating point **:** CLIMAX

high–toned \'hī-'tōnd\ *adj* **1 :** high in social, moral, or intellectual quality **2 :** PRETENTIOUS, POMPOUS

high treason *n* **:** TREASON 2

high–water *adj* **:** unusually short ⟨~ pants⟩

high·way \'hī-,wā\ *n* **:** a public way; *esp* **:** a main direct road

high·way·man \-mən\ *n* **:** a person who robs travelers on a road

high–wrought *adj* **:** extremely agitated

hi·jack *or* **high–jack** \'hī-,jak\ *vt* [origin unknown] **1 a :** to steal by stopping a vehicle on the highway **b :** to stop and steal from (a vehicle in transit) **2 a :** STEAL, ROB **b :** FORCE, COERCE — **hi·jack·er** *n*

1hike \'hīk\ *vb* [perh. akin to 1*hitch*] *vt* **1 a :** to move or raise with a sudden effort **b :** to raise in amount sharply or suddenly ⟨~ rents⟩ **2 :** to take on a hike ~ *vi* **1 a :** to go on a long walk esp. for pleasure or exercise **b :** to travel by any means **2 :** to rise up; *esp* **:** to work upward out of place ⟨skirt had *hiked* up in back⟩ — **hik·er** *n*

2hike *n* **1 :** a long walk esp. for pleasure or exercise **2 :** an upward movement **:** RISE

hi·lar \'hī-lər\ *adj* **:** of, relating to, or located near a hilum

hi·lar·i·ous \hil-'ar-ē-əs, hī-'lar-, hil-'er-, hī-'ler-\ *adj* [irreg. fr. L *hilarus, hilaris* cheerful, fr. Gk *hilaros*] **:** marked by or affording hilarity — **hi·lar·i·ous·ly** *adv* — **hi·lar·i·ous·ness** *n*

hi·lar·i·ty \-ət-ē\ *n* **:** boisterous merriment **syn** see MIRTH

hil·ding \'hil-diŋ\ *n* [*hilding,* adj. (base)] *archaic* **:** a base contemptible person

1hill \'hil\ *n* [ME, fr. OE *hyll;* akin to L *collis* hill, *culmen* top] **1 :** a usu. rounded natural elevation of land lower than a mountain **2 :** an artificial heap or mound (as of earth) **3 :** several seeds or plants planted in a group rather than a row

2hill *vt* **1 :** to form into a heap **2 :** to draw earth around the roots or base of — **hill·er** *n*

hill·bil·ly \'hil-,bil-ē\ *n* [1*hill* + *Billy,* nickname for *William*] **:** a person from a backwoods area

hillbilly music *n* **:** music deriving from or imitating the folk style of the southern U.S. or of the Western cowboy

hill myna *n* **:** a largely black Asiatic starling (*Gracula religiosa*) often tamed and taught to pronounce words

hill·ock \'hil-ək\ *n* **:** a small hill — **hill·ocky** \-ə-kē\ *adj*

hill·side \'hil-,sīd\ *n* **:** a part of a hill between the summit and the foot

hilly \'hil-ē\ *adj* **1 :** abounding in hills **2 :** STEEP

hilt \'hilt\ *n* [ME, fr. OE; akin to OE *healt* lame — more at HALT] **:** a handle esp. of a sword or dagger — **to the hilt :** COMPLETELY

hi·lum \'hī-ləm\ *n, pl* **hi·la** \-lə\ [NL, fr. L, trifle] **1 a :** a scar on a seed (as a bean) marking the point of attachment of the ovule **b :** the nucleus of a starch grain **2 :** a notch in or opening from a bodily part suggesting the hilum of a bean

him \im, (')him\ *pron, objective case of* HE

Hi·ma·la·yan \,him-ə-'lā-ən, him-'äl-(ə-)yən\ *n* [*Himalaya* mountains, Asia] **:** any of a breed of small white domesticated rabbits with black nose, feet, tail, and ear tips

hi·mat·i·on \him-'at-ē-,än\ *n* [Gk, fr. *hennynai* to clothe — more at WEAR] **:** a rectangular cloth draped over the left shoulder and about the body and worn as a garment in ancient Greece

him·self \(h)im-'self\ *pron* **1 :** that identical male one **:** that identical one whose sex is unknown or immaterial — compare 1HE; used reflexively, for emphasis, or in absolute constructions ⟨considers ~ lucky⟩ ⟨he ~ did it⟩ ⟨~ unhappy, he understood the situation⟩ **2 :** his normal, healthy, or sane condition or self **3** *Irish & Scot* **:** a man of consequence; *esp* **:** the master of the house

1Him·yar·ite \'him-yə-,rīt\ *n* [*Himyar,* legendary king in Yemen] **1 :** a member of an ancient people of southern Arabia **2 :** an Arab of a group of related ancient peoples of southern Arabia

2Himyarite *or* **Him·yar·it·ic** \,him-yə-'rit-ik\ *adj* **:** of or relating to the ancient Himyarites or their language

Himyaritic *or* **Himyarite** *n* **:** the language of the Himyarites recorded in inscriptions

hin \'hin\ *n* [Heb *hīn,* fr. Egypt *hnw*] **:** an ancient Hebrew unit of liquid measure equal to about a gallon and a half

Hi·na·ya·na \,hē-nə-'yän-ə\ *n* [Skt *hīnayāna,* lit., lesser vehicle] **:** a southern conservative branch of Buddhism adhering to the Pali scriptures and the nontheistic ideal of purification of the self to nirvana — **Hi·na·ya·nist** \-'yän-əst\ *n* — **Hi·na·ya·nis·tic** \,hē-nə-(,)yä-'nis-tik\ *adj*

1hind \'hīnd\ *n, pl* **hinds** *also* **hind** [ME, fr. OE; akin to OHG *hinta* hind, Gk *kemas* young deer] **1 :** a female of the red deer — compare HART **2 :** any of various typically spotted groupers

2hind *n* [ME *hine* servant, farmhand, fr. OE *hīna,* gen. of *hīwan,* pl., members of a household; akin to OE *hām* home — more at HOME] **1 :** a British farm assistant **2** *archaic* **:** RUSTIC

3hind *adj* [ME, prob. back-formation fr. OE *hinder,* adv., behind; akin to OHG *hintar,* prep., behind] **:** of or forming the part that follows or is behind **:** REAR

hind·brain \'hīn(d)-,brān\ *n* **1 a :** the posterior of the three primary divisions of the vertebrate brain or the parts developed from it including the cerebellum, pons, and medulla oblongata **b :** METENCEPHALON **c :** MYELENCEPHALON **2 :** the posterior segment of the brain of an invertebrate

1hin·der \'hin-dər\ *vb* **hin·der·ing** \-d(ə-)riŋ\ [ME *hindren,* fr. OE *hindrian;* akin to OE *hinder* behind] *vt* **1 :** to make slow or difficult the progress of **:** HAMPER **2 :** to hold back **:** CHECK ~ *vi* **:** to delay, impede, or prevent action — **hin·der·er** \-dər-ər\ *n*
syn IMPEDE, OBSTRUCT, BLOCK: HINDER stresses causing harmful or annoying delay or interference with progress; IMPEDE implies making forward progress difficult by clogging, hampering, or fettering; OBSTRUCT implies interfering with something in motion or in progress by the sometimes intentional placing of obstacles in the way; BLOCK implies complete obstruction to passage or progress

2hind·er \'hīn-dər\ *adj* [ME, fr. OE *hinder,* adv.] **:** situated behind or in the rear **:** POSTERIOR

hind·gut \'hīn(d)-,gət\ *n* **:** the posterior part of the alimentary canal

Hin·di \'hin-(,)dē\ *n* [Hindi *hindī,* fr. *Hind,* India, fr. Per] **1 :** a literary and official language of northern India **2 :** a complex of Indic dialects of northern India for which Hindi is the usual literary language — **Hindi** *adj*

hind·most \'hīn(d)-,mōst\ *adj* **:** farthest to the rear **:** LAST

hind·quar·ter \-,kwȯ(r)t-ər\ *n* **1 :** the back half of a side of beef, veal, mutton, or lamb including a leg and usu. one or more ribs **2** *pl* **:** the hind biped of a quadruped; *broadly* **:** all the structures of a quadruped that lie posterior to the attachment of the hind legs to the trunk

hin·drance \'hin-drən(t)s\ *n* **1 :** the state of being hindered **2 :** the action of hindering **3 :** IMPEDIMENT

hind·sight \'hīn(d)-,sīt\ *n* **1 :** a rear sight of a firearm **2 :** perception of the nature and demands of an event after it has happened

1Hin·du *also* **Hin·doo** \'hin-(,)dü\ *n* [Per *Hindū* inhabitant of India, fr. *Hind* India] **1 :** an adherent of Hinduism **2 :** a native or inhabitant of India

2Hindu *also* **Hindoo** *adj* **:** of, relating to, or characteristic of the Hindus or Hinduism

Hin·du·ism \-,iz-əm\ *n* **1 :** a body of social, cultural, and religious beliefs and practices native to the Indian subcontinent; *specif* **:** the dominant cultic religion of India marked by participation in one of the devotional sects **2 :** a religious philosophy based on Hinduism — compare KARMA

1Hin·du·stani *also* **Hin·do·stani** \,hin-dü-'stan-ē, -'stän-ē\ *n* [Hindi *Hindūstānī,* fr. Per *Hindūstān* India] **1 :** a group of Indic dialects of northern India of which literary Hindi and Urdu are

considered diverse written forms **2 :** a form of speech allied to Urdu but less divergent from Hindi used in some urban areas

2**Hindustani** *also* **Hindostani** *adj* **:** of or relating to Hindustan or its people or Hindustani

1**hinge** \'hinj\ *n* [ME *heng;* akin to MD *henge* hook, OE *hangian* to hang] **1 a :** a jointed or flexible device on which a door, lid, or other swinging part turns **b :** a flexible ligamentous joint **c :** a small piece of thin gummed paper used in fastening a postage stamp in an album **2 :** a determining factor **:** TURNING POINT

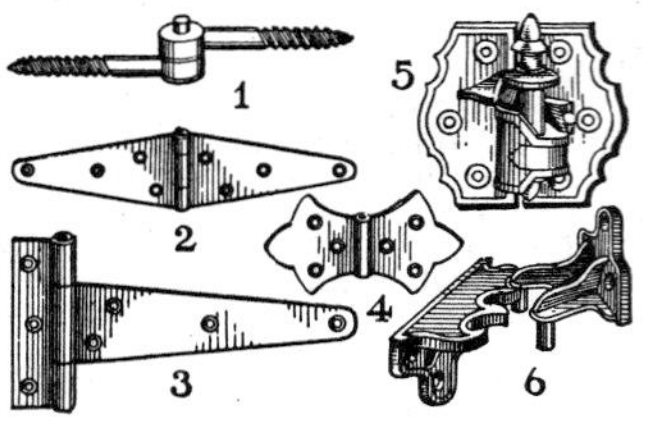

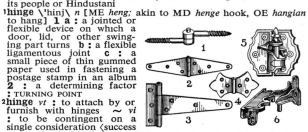

hinges 1: *1* hook-and-eye, *2* strap, *3* T, *4* flap, *5* blind, *6* gate

2**hinge** *vt* **:** to attach by or furnish with hinges **~** *vi* **:** to be contingent on a single consideration ⟨success ~*s* on the decision⟩

hinge joint *n* **:** a bodily joint that permits motion in one plane

hin•ny \'hin-ē\ *n* [L *hinnus*] **:** a hybrid between a stallion and a she ass — compare MULE

1**hint** \'hint\ *n* [prob. alter. of obs. *hent* act of seizing, fr. *hent* vb.] **1** *archaic* **:** OPPORTUNITY, TURN **2 a :** an indirect or summary suggestion **b :** a statement conveying by implication what it is preferred not to say explicitly **3 :** a slight indication **:** CLUE **4 :** a very small amount **:** TRACE

2**hint** *vt* **:** to convey by a hint **:** INTIMATE **~** *vi* **:** to give a hint **syn** see SUGGEST — **hint•er** *n*

hin•ter•land \'hint-ər-,land\ *n* [G, fr. *hinter* hinder + *land*] **1 :** a region behind a coast **2 :** a region that provides supplies **3 :** a region remote from cities and towns

1**hip** \'hip\ *n* [ME *hipe*, fr. OE *hēope;* akin to OHG *hiafo* hip] **:** the ripened false fruit of a rose that consists of a fleshy receptacle enclosing numerous achenes

2**hip** *n* [ME, fr. OE *hype;* akin to OHG *huf* hip, L *cubitus* elbow, *cubare* to lie, Gk *kybos* cube, die, OE *hēah* high — more at HIGH] **1 a :** the laterally projecting region of each side of the lower or posterior part of the mammalian trunk formed by the lateral parts of the pelvis and upper part of the femur together with the fleshy parts covering them **b :** HIP JOINT **2 :** the external angle formed by the meeting of two sloping sides of a roof that have their wall plates running in different directions

3**hip** *vt* **hipped; hip•ping :** to make (as a roof) with a hip

4**hip** *adj* [origin unknown] **1 :** characterized by a keen informed awareness of or interest in the newest developments **2 :** WISE, ALERT

hip and thigh *adv* **:** OVERWHELMINGLY, UNSPARINGLY

hip•bone \'hip-'bōn, -,bōn\ *n* **:** INNOMINATE BONE

hip joint *n* **:** the articulation between the femur and the innominate bone

hipp- *or* **hippo-** *comb form* [L, fr. Gk, fr. *hippos* — more at EQUINE] **:** horse ⟨*hippo*phagous⟩

1**hipped** \'hipt\ *adj* **:** having hips ⟨broad-*hipped*⟩

2**hipped** *adj* [*hip* (hypochondria)] **1 :** DEPRESSED **2 :** OBSESSED ⟨~ on philately⟩

hip•pie *or* **hip•py** \'hip-ē\ *n* [4*hip* + *-ie*] **:** a young person who rejects the mores of established society, dresses and behaves unconventionally, adheres to a nonviolent ethic, and prefers the use of psychedelic drugs or marijuana to alcohol — **hip•pie•dom** \-dəm\ *n* — **hip•pie•hood** \-,hu̇d\ *n*

hip•po \'hip-(,)ō\ *n* **:** HIPPOPOTAMUS

hip•po•cam•pal \,hip-ə-'kam-pəl\ *adj* **:** of or relating to the hippocampus

hip•po•cam•pus \-pəs\ *n, pl* **hip•po•cam•pi** \-,pī, -,pē\ [NL, fr. Gk *hippokampos* sea horse, fr. *hipp-* + *kampos* sea monster] **:** a curved elongated ridge extending over the floor of the descending horn of each lateral ventricle of the brain

hip•po•cras \'hip-ə-,kras\ *n* [ME *ypocras*, fr. *Ypocras* Hippocrates, its legendary inventor] **:** a highly spiced wine of medieval Europe

Hip•po•crat•ic \,hip-ə-'krat-ik\ *adj* **:** of or relating to Hippocrates or to the school of medicine that took his name

Hippocratic oath *n* **:** an oath embodying a code of medical ethics usu. taken by those about to begin medical practice

Hip•po•crene \'hip-ə-,krēn, ,hip-ə-'krē-nē\ *n* [L, fr. Gk *Hippokrēnē*] **:** a fountain on Mount Helicon sacred to the Muses and believed to be a source of poetic inspiration

hip•po•drome \'hip-ə-,drōm\ *n* [MF, fr. L *hippodromos*, fr. Gk, fr. *hipp-* + *dromos* racecourse — more at DROMEDARY] **1 :** an oval stadium for horse and chariot races in ancient Greece **2 :** an arena for equestrian performances

hip•po•griff \'hip-ə-,grif\ *n* [F *hippogriffe*, fr. It *ippogrifo*, fr. *ippo-* hipp- (fr. L *hipp-*) + *grifo* griffin, fr. L *gryphus*] **:** a legendary animal having the foreparts of a griffin and the body and hindquarters of a horse

Hip•pol•y•tus \hip-'äl-ət-əs\ *n* [L, fr. Gk *Hippolytos*] **:** a son of Theseus in Greek legend falsely accused by his stepmother Phaedra and in response to his father's plea killed through the agency of Poseidon

Hip•pom•e•nes \hip-'äm-ə-,nēz\ *n* [L, fr. Gk *Hippomenēs*] **:** the successful suitor of Atalanta in Greek legend

hip•po•pot•a•mus \,hip-ə-'pät-ə-məs\ *n, pl* **hip•po•pot•a•mus•es** *or* **hip•po•pot•a•mi** \-,mī, -(,)mē\ [L, fr. Gk *hippopotamos*, fr. *hipp-* + *potamos* river, fr. *petesthai* to fly, rush] **:** any of several large herbivorous 4-toed chiefly aquatic mammals (family Hippopotamidae and esp. genus *Hippopotamus*) with an extremely large head and mouth, bare and very thick skin, and short legs

-hip•pus \'hip-əs\ *n comb form* [NL, fr. Gk *hippos* — more at EQUINE] **:** horse — in generic names esp. in paleontology ⟨Eo*hippus*⟩

hip roof *n* **:** a roof having sloping ends and sloping sides

hip•ster \'hip-stər\ *n* [4*hip*] **:** one who is hip

1**hire** \'hī(ə)r\ *n* [ME, fr. OE *hȳr;* akin to MD *hūre* hire] **1 a :** payment for the temporary use of something **b :** payment for labor or personal services **:** WAGES **2 a :** the act of hiring **b :** the state of being hired **:** EMPLOYMENT **syn** see WAGE

2**hire** *vt* **1 a :** to engage the personal services of for a set sum ⟨~ on a new crew⟩ **b :** to engage the temporary use of for a fixed sum ⟨~ a hall⟩ **2 :** to grant the personal services of or temporary use of for a fixed sum ⟨~ themselves out⟩ **3 :** to get done for pay ⟨~ the mowing done⟩ **~** *vi* **:** to take employment ⟨~ out as a waitress during the tourist season⟩ — **hir•er** *n*

syn HIRE, LET, LEASE, RENT, CHARTER mean to engage or grant for use at a price. HIRE and LET are complementary terms, HIRE implying the act of engaging, and LET the act of granting, for use; LEASE strictly implies a contract but is often applied informally to hiring on a lease; RENT stresses the payment of money for the full use of property and may imply either hiring or letting; CHARTER implies the hiring of a ship or a public vehicle for exclusive use **syn** see in addition EMPLOY

hire•ling \'hī(ə)r-liŋ\ *n* **:** a person who serves for hire esp. for purely mercenary motives

hire purchase *n, chiefly Brit* **:** purchase on the installment plan

hiring hall *n* **:** a union-operated placement office where registered applicants are referred in rotation to jobs

hir•ple \'hir-pəl\ *vi* [ME (Sc) *hirplen*] *Scot* **:** LIMP, HOBBLE

hir•sute \'hər-,süt, 'hi(ə)r-, ,hər-', hi(ə)r-'\ *adj* [L *hirsutus;* akin to L *horrēre* to bristle — more at HORROR] **:** roughly hairy; *esp* **:** pubescent with coarse stiff hairs — **hir•sute•ness** *n*

hir•su•tu•lous \,hər-'sü-chə-ləs, hir-\ *adj* **:** minutely or slightly hirsute

hir•u•din \'hir-(y)əd-ən\ *n* [fr. *Hirudin*, a trademark] **:** an anticoagulant extracted from the buccal glands of a leech

1**his** \(h)iz, ,hiz\ *adj* [ME, fr. OE, gen. of *hē* he] **:** of or relating to him or himself esp. as possessor, agent, or object of an action ⟨~ house⟩ ⟨~ writings⟩ ⟨~ confirmation⟩ — compare 1HE

2**his** \'hiz\ *pron, sing or pl in constr* **:** his one **:** his ones — used without a following noun as a pronoun equivalent in meaning to the adjective *his*

His•pan•ic \his-'pan-ik\ *adj* [L *hispanicus*, fr. *Hispania* Iberian peninsula, Spain] **:** of or relating to the people, speech, or culture of Spain, Spain and Portugal, or Latin America — **His•pan•i•cism** \-'pan-ə-,siz-əm\ *n* — **His•pan•i•cist** \-'pan-ə-səst\ *n* — **His•pan•i•cize** \-,sīz\ *vt*

his•pa•nism \'his-pə-,niz-əm\ *n, often cap* **1 :** a movement to reassert the cultural unity of Spain and Latin America — called also *his•pa•ni•dad* \(,)ē-,spä-nē-'thä(th)\ **2 :** a linguistic feature of Spanish origin or influence

his•pid \'his-pəd\ *adj* [L *hispidus;* prob. akin to L *horrēre*] **:** rough or covered with bristles, stiff hairs, or minute spines ⟨~ leaf⟩ — **his•pid•i•ty** \his-'pid-ət-ē\ *n*

his•pid•u•lous \his-'pij-ə-ləs\ *adj* **:** minutely hispid

hiss \'his\ *vb* [ME *hissen*, of imit. origin] *vi* **:** to make a sharp sibilant sound often as an expression of disapproval **~** *vt* **1 :** to condemn by hissing **2 :** to utter with a hiss — **hiss** *n* — **hiss•er** *n*

1**hist** \s *often prolonged and usu with* p *preceding and* t *following; often read as* 'hist\ *interj* [origin unknown] — used to attract attention

2**hist** \'hīst\ *dial var of* HOIST

hist- *or* **histo-** *comb form* [F, fr. Gk *histos* mast, loom beam, web, fr. *histanai* to cause to stand] **:** tissue ⟨*histo*physiology⟩

his•ta•mi•nase \his-'tam-ə-,nās, 'his-tə-mə-, -,nāz\ *n* [ISV] **:** a widely occurring flavoprotein enzyme that oxidizes histamine and various diamines

his•ta•mine \'his-tə-,mēn, -mən\ *n* [ISV] **:** a compound $C_5H_9N_3$ found in ergot and many animal tissues or made synthetically and held responsible for the dilatation and increased permeability of blood vessels which play a major role in allergic reactions — **his•ta•min•ic** \,his-tə-'min-ik\ *adj*

his•ta•min•er•gic \,his-tə-mə-'nər-jik\ *adj* [ISV *hist*amine + Gk *ergon* work — more at WORK] *of autonomic nerve fibers* **:** liberating or activated by histamine

his•ti•dine \'his-tə-,dēn\ *n* [ISV] **:** a crystalline basic amino acid $C_6H_9N_3O_2$ formed in the splitting of most proteins

his•tio•cyte \'his-tē-ə-,sīt\ *n* [Gk *histion* web (dim. of *histos*), + ISV *-cyte*] **:** a phagocytic tissue cell that may be fixed or freely motile, is derived from the reticuloendothelial system, and resembles the monocyte with which it is sometimes identified — **his•tio•cyt•ic** \,his-tē-ə-'sit-ik\ *adj*

his•to•chem•i•cal \,his-(,)tō-'kem-i-kəl\ *adj* **:** of or relating to histochemistry — **his•to•chem•i•cal•ly** \-k(ə-)lē\ *adv*

his•to•chem•is•try \-'kem-ə-strē\ *n* [ISV] **:** a science dealing with the chemical makeup of cells and tissues

his•to•gen \'his-tə-jən\ *n* [ISV] **:** a zone or clearly delimited region of primary tissue in or from which the specific parts of a plant organ are believed to be produced

his•to•gen•e•sis \,his-tə-'jen-ə-səs\ *n* [NL] **:** the formation and differentiation of tissues — **his•to•ge•net•ic** \-jə-'net-ik\ *adj* — **his•to•ge•net•i•cal•ly** \-i-k(ə-)lē\ *adv*

his•to•gram \'his-tə-,gram\ *n* [*history* + *-gram*] **:** a representation of a frequency distribution by means of rectangles whose widths represent class intervals and whose heights represent corresponding frequencies

his•to•log•i•cal \,his-tə-'läj-i-kəl\ *or* **his•to•log•ic** \-ik\ *adj* **:** of or relating to histology — **his•to•log•i•cal•ly** \-i-k(ə-)lē\ *adv*

his•tol•o•gist \his-'täl-ə-jəst\ *n* **:** a specialist in histology

his•tol•o•gy \-jē\ *n* [F *histologie*, fr. *hist-* + *-logie* -logy] **1 :** a branch of anatomy that deals with the minute structure of animal and plant tissues as discernible with the microscope **2 :** a treatise on histology **3 :** tissue structure or organization

his•tol•y•sis \his-'täl-ə-səs\ *n* [NL, fr. *hist-* + *-lysis*] **:** the breakdown of bodily tissues — **his•to•lyt•ic** \,his-tə-'lit-ik\ *adj*

his•tone \'his-,tōn\ *n* [ISV] **:** any of various simple water-soluble proteins that yield a high proportion of basic amino acids on hydrolysis and are found esp. in glandular tissues (as thymus) combined with deoxyribonucleic acid

his•to•pa•thol•o•gy \,his-(,)tō-pə-'thäl-ə-jē, -(,)pa-\ *n* [ISV] **1 :** a branch of pathology concerned with the tissue changes characteristic of disease **2 :** the tissue changes that affect a part or accompany a disease

his•to•phys•i•ol•o•gy \-,fiz-ē-'äl-ə-jē\ *n* **1 :** a branch of physiology concerned with the function and activities of tissues **2 :** structural and functional tissue organization

his•to•plas•mo•sis \,his-tə-,plaz-'mō-səs\ *n* [NL, fr. *Histoplasma*, genus of fungi] **:** a disease caused by infection with a fungus (*Histoplasma capsulatum*) and marked by benign involvement of lymph nodes of the trachea and bronchi or by severe progressive

generalized involvement of the lymph nodes and the reticuloendothelial system
his·to·ri·an \his-ˈtōr-ē-ən, -ˈtȯr-\ *n* **1 :** a student or writer of history; *esp* **:** one that produces a scholarly synthesis **2 :** CHRONICLER
his·tor·ic \his-ˈtȯr-ik, -ˈtär-\ *adj* **:** HISTORICAL; *esp* **:** famous in history
his·tor·i·cal \-i-kəl\ *adj* **1 a :** of, relating to, or having the character of history **b :** based on history **c :** used only in historical presentations **2 :** famous in history **3 a :** SECONDARY 1c **b :** DIACHRONIC — **his·tor·i·cal·ly** \-i-k(ə-)lē\ *adv* — **his·tor·i·cal·ness** \-i-kəl-nəs\ *n*
historical materialism *n* **:** the Marxist theory of history and society that holds that ideas and social institutions develop only as the superstructure of a material economic base — compare DIALECTICAL MATERIALISM
historical present *n* **:** the present tense used to relate past events
historical school *n* **:** a school esp. in economics, legal philosophy, and ethnology emphasizing evolutionary developments and historical methods of research, analysis, and interpretation
his·tor·i·cism \his-ˈtȯr-ə-ˌsiz-əm, -ˈtär-\ *n* **:** a theory that emphasizes the importance of history as a standard of value or as a determinant of events — **his·tor·i·cist** \-səst\ *adj or n*
his·to·ric·i·ty \ˌhis-tə-ˈris-ət-ē\ *n* **:** historical actuality **:** FACT
his·tor·i·cize \his-ˈtȯr-ə-ˌsīz, -ˈtär-\ *vt* **:** to render historical ~ *vi* **:** to use historical material
his·to·ri·og·ra·pher \his-ˌtōr-ē-ˈäg-rə-fər, -ˌtȯr-\ *n* [MF *historiographeur*, fr. LL *historiographus*, fr. Gk *historiographos*, fr. *historia* + *graphein* to write — more at CARVE] **:** a usu. official writer of history **:** HISTORIAN — **his·to·rio·graph·ic** \-ē-ə-ˈgraf-ik\ *or* **his·to·rio·graph·i·cal** \-i-kəl\ *adj* — **his·to·rio·graph·i·cal·ly** \-i-k(ə-)lē\ *adv* — **his·to·ri·og·ra·phy** \-ē-ˈäg-rə-fē\ *n*
his·to·ry \ˈhis-t(ə-)rē\ *n* [L *historia*, fr. Gk, inquiry, history, fr. *histōr, istōr* knowing, learned; akin to Gk *eidenai* to know — more at WIT] **1 :** TALE, STORY **2 a :** a chronological record of significant events (as affecting a nation, institution) usu. including an explanation of their causes **b :** a treatise presenting systematically related natural phenomena **c :** an account of a sick person's medical background **3 :** a branch of knowledge that records and explains past events **4 a :** events that form the subject matter of a history **b :** past events **c :** previous treatment, handling, or experience (as of a metal)
his·tri·on·ic \ˌhis-trē-ˈän-ik\ *adj* [LL *histrionicus*, fr. L *histrion-*, *histrio* actor, alter. of *hister*, fr. Etruscan] **1 :** of or relating to actors, acting, or the theater **2 :** deliberately affected **:** THEATRICAL — **his·tri·on·i·cal·ly** \-i-k(ə-)lē\ *adv*
his·tri·on·ics \-iks\ *n pl but sing or pl in constr* **1 :** theatrical performances **2 :** deliberate display of emotion for effect
1**hit** \ˈhit\ *vb* **hit; hit·ting** [ME *hitten*, fr. ON *hitta* to meet with, hit] *vt* **1 a :** to reach with or as if with a blow **b :** to come in contact with **2 a :** to cause to come into contact **b :** to deliver (as a blow) by action **3 :** to affect to the detriment of **4 :** to make a request of **5 :** to discover or meet esp. by chance **6 a :** to accord with **:** SUIT **b :** REACH, ATTAIN **c** *of fish* **:** to bite at or on **d :** to drop or move onto ⟨~ the road⟩ **e :** to reflect accurately ⟨~ the right note⟩ **7 :** to indulge in excessively ⟨~ the bottle⟩ ~ *vi* **1 :** to strike a blow **2 a :** to come into contact with something **b :** ATTACK **c** *of a fish* **:** STRIKE *vi* 11b **d :** COME, HAPPEN **3 :** to succeed in attaining something **4** *obs* **:** to be in agreement **:** SUIT **5** *of an internal-combustion engine* **:** to fire the charge in the cylinders **syn** see STRIKE — **hit·ter** *n*
2**hit** *n* **1 a :** a blow striking an object aimed at **b :** COLLISION **2 a :** a stroke of luck **b :** something that is conspicuously successful **3 :** a telling remark **4 :** a stroke in an athletic contest; *esp* BASE HIT
hit-and-miss \ˌhit-ᵊn-ˈmis\ *adj* **:** sometimes hitting and sometimes not
hit-and-run \-ˈrən\ *adj* **1 :** being or relating to a baseball play in which a base runner starts for the next base as the pitcher starts to pitch and the batter attempts to hit the ball **2 :** being or involving a motor-vehicle driver who does not stop after being involved in an accident **3 :** involving or intended for quick specific action or results
1**hitch** \ˈhich\ *vb* [ME *hytchen*] *vt* **1 :** to move by jerks **2 a :** to catch or fasten by or as if by a hook or knot **:** make fast **b :** UNITE, YOKE **3 :** HITCHHIKE ~ *vi* **1 :** to move with halts and jerks **:** HOBBLE **2 :** to become entangled, made fast, or linked **3 :** HITCHHIKE — **hitch·er** *n*
2**hitch** *n* **1 :** a sudden movement or pull **:** JERK **2 :** LIMP **3 :** a sudden halt **:** STOPPAGE **4 :** the act or fact of catching hold **5 :** a connection between a vehicle or implement and a detachable source of power (as a tractor or horse) **6** *slang* **:** a period usu. of military service **7 :** any of various knots used to form a temporary noose in a line or to secure a line temporarily to an object **8 :** LIFT 5b
hitch·hike \-ˌhīk\ *vi* **:** to travel by securing free rides ~ *vt* **:** to solicit or obtain (a free ride) — **hitch·hik·er** *n*
hitch up *vi* **:** to harness and make fast a draft animal or team
1**hith·er** \ˈhith-ər\ *adv* [ME *hider, hither*, fr. OE *hider;* akin to Goth *hidre* hither, L *citra* on this side — more at HE] **:** to this place
2**hither** *adj* **:** being on the near or adjacent side
hith·er·most \-ˌmōst\ *adj* **:** nearest on this side
hith·er·to \-ˌtü, ˌhith-ər-ˈtü\ *adv* **:** up to this time
hith·er·ward \ˈhith-ə(r)-wərd\ *adv* **:** HITHER
Hit·le·ri·an \hit-ˈlir-ē-ən\ *adj* **:** of, relating to, or suggesting Adolf Hitler or his regime in Germany
Hit·ler·ism \ˈhit-lə-ˌriz-əm\ *n* **1 :** the nationalistic and totalitarian principles and policies associated with Hitler **2 :** the Hitlerian movement — **Hit·ler·ite** \-ˌrīt\ *n or adj*
hit off *vt* **:** to characterize precisely and usu. satirically ~ *vi* **:** HARMONIZE, AGREE
hit or miss *adv* **:** HAPHAZARDLY — **hit-or-miss** \ˌhit-ər-ˈmis\ *adj*
Hit·tite \ˈhi-ˌtīt\ *n* [Heb *Ḥittī*, fr. Hitt *Hatti*] **1 :** a member of a conquering people in Asia Minor and Syria with an empire in the 2d millennium B.C. **2 :** an Indo-European or Indo-Hittite language of the Hittite people known from cuneiform texts — **Hittite** *adj*
1**hive** \ˈhīv\ *n* [ME, fr. OE *hȳf;* akin to Gk *kypellon* cup, OE *hēah* high — more at HIGH] **1 :** a container for housing honeybees **2 :** a colony of bees **3 :** a place swarming with busy occupants — **hiveless** \-ləs\ *adj*

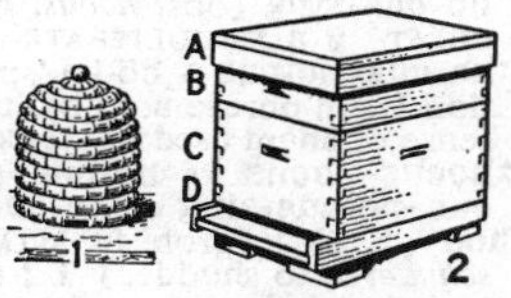

hives 1: *1* old-fashioned; *2* modern: *A* cover, *B* super, *C* brood chamber, *D* bottom

2**hive** *vt* **1 :** to collect into a hive **2 :** to store up in or as if in a hive ~ *vi* **1** *of bees* **:** to enter and take possession of a hive **2 :** to reside in close association
3**hive** *n* [back-formation fr. *hives*] **:** an urticarial wheal
hives \ˈhīvz\ *n pl but sing or pl in constr* [origin unknown] **:** URTICARIA
ho \ˈhō\ *interj* [ME] — used esp. to attract attention to something specified
1**hoar** \ˈhō(ə)r, ˈhȯ(ə)r\ *adj* [ME *hor*, fr. OE *hār;* akin to OHG *hēr* hoary, Gk *kirros* orange yellow] *archaic* **:** HOARY
2**hoar** *n* [ME, hoariness, fr. *hor*, adj.] **:** FROST 1c
hoard \ˈhō(ə)rd, ˈhȯ(ə)rd\ *n* [ME *hord* fr. OE; akin to Gk *kysthos* vulva, OE *hȳdan* to hide] **:** a hidden supply or fund stored up — **hoard** *vt* — **hoard·er** *n*
hoard·ing \ˈhōrd-iŋ, ˈhȯrd-\ *n* [*hourd, hoard* (hoarding)] **1 :** a temporary board fence put about a building being erected or repaired — called also *hoard* **2** *Brit* **:** BILLBOARD
hoar·frost \ˈhō(ə)r-ˌfrȯst, ˈhȯ(ə)r-\ *n* **:** FROST 1c
hoar·i·ness \ˈhōr-ē-nəs, ˈhȯr-\ *n* **:** the quality or state of being hoary
hoarse \ˈhō(ə)rs, ˈhȯ(ə)rs\ *adj* [ME *hos, hors*, fr. OE *hās;* akin to OE *hāt* hot — more at HOT] **1 :** rough and harsh in sound **:** GRATING ⟨~ voice⟩ **2 :** having a hoarse voice — **hoarse·ly** *adv* — **hoars·en** \ˈhōrs-ᵊn, ˈhȯrs-\ *vb* **hoars·en·ing** \ˈhōrs-niŋ, -ᵊn-iŋ\ — **hoarse·ness** \ˈhō(ə)r-snəs, ˈhȯ(ə)r-\ *n*
hoary \ˈhōr-ē, ˈhȯr-\ *adj* **1 a :** gray or white with age **b :** having grayish or whitish usu. pubescent leaves **2 :** ANCIENT, VENERABLE
hoa·tzin \wä(t)-ˈsēn\ *n* [AmerSp, fr. Nahuatl *uatzin*] **:** a peculiar crested So. American bird (*Opisthocomos cristatus* of the order Galliformes) smaller than a pheasant with olive-colored plumage marked with white above and claws on the first and second fingers of the wing
1**hoax** \ˈhōks\ *vt* [prob. contr. of *hocus*] **:** to trick into believing or accepting as genuine something false and often preposterous **syn** see DUPE — **hoax·er** *n*
2**hoax** *n* **1 :** an act intended to trick or dupe **:** IMPOSTURE **2 :** something accepted or established by fraud or fabrication
1**hob** \ˈhäb\ *n* [ME *hobbe*, fr. *Hobbe*, nickname for Robert] **1** *dial Eng* **:** HOBGOBLIN, ELF **2 :** MISCHIEF, TROUBLE ⟨raise ~⟩
2**hob** *n* [origin unknown] **1 :** a projection at the back or side of a fireplace on which something may be kept warm **2 :** a cutting tool used for cutting the teeth of worm wheels or gear wheels
3**hob** *vt* **hobbed; hob·bing 1 :** to furnish with hobnails **2 :** to cut with a hob
Hobbes·ian \ˈhäb-zē-ən\ *adj* **:** of or relating to Hobbes or Hobbism
Hob·bism \ˈhäb-ˌiz-əm\ *n* **:** the philosophical system of Hobbes; *esp* **:** the Hobbesian theory that absolutism in government is necessary to prevent the war of each against all to which natural selfishness inevitably leads mankind — **Hob·bist** \-əst\ *n or adj*
1**hob·ble** \ˈhäb-əl\ *vb* **hob·bling** \-(ə-)liŋ\ [ME *hoblen;* akin to MD *hobbelen* to turn, roll] *vi* **:** to move along unsteadily or with difficulty; *esp* **:** to limp along ~ *vt* **1 :** to cause to limp **:** make lame **:** CRIPPLE **2** [prob. alter. of *hopple* (to hobble)] **a :** to fasten together the legs of (as a horse) to prevent straying **:** FETTER **b :** HAMPER, IMPEDE — **hob·bler** \-(ə-)lər\ *n*
2**hobble** *n* **1 :** a hobbling movement **2** *archaic* **:** an awkward situation **3 :** something used to hobble an animal
hob·ble·de·hoy \ˈhäb-əl-di-ˌhȯi\ *n* [origin unknown] **:** an awkward gawky youth
hobble skirt *n* **:** a skirt constricted at the ankles by a band
1**hob·by** \ˈhäb-ē\ *n* [short for *hobbyhorse*] **:** a pursuit outside one's regular occupation engaged in for relaxation — **hob·by·ist** \-ē-əst\ *n*
2**hobby** *n* [ME *hoby*, fr. MF *hobé*] **:** a small Old World falcon (*Falco subbuteo*) formerly trained and flown at small birds
hob·by·horse \-ˌhȯ(ə)rs\ *n* [*hobby* (small light horse)] **1 a :** a figure of a horse fastened about the waist in the morris dance **b :** a dancer wearing this figure **2** *obs* **:** BUFFOON **3 a :** a stick having an imitation horse's head at one end that a child pretends to ride **b :** ROCKING HORSE **4 a :** a topic to which one constantly reverts **b :** 1HOBBY
hob·gob·lin \ˈhäb-ˌgäb-lən\ *n* **1 :** a mischievous goblin **2 :** BOGEY 2, BUGABOO
hob·nail \-ˌnāl\ *n* [2*hob*] **:** a short large-headed nail for studding shoe soles
hob·nob \-ˌnäb\ *vi* **hob·nobbed; hob·nob·bing** [fr. the obs phrase *drink hobnob* (to drink alternately to one another)] **1** *archaic* **:** to drink sociably **2 :** to associate familiarly — **hob·nob·ber** *n*
ho·bo \ˈhō-(ˌ)bō\ *n, pl* **hoboes** *also* **hobos** [perh. alter. of *ho, boy*] **1 :** a migratory worker **2 a :** a homeless and usu. penniless vagrant **:** TRAMP **b :** 4BUM 1 — **hobo** *vi* — **ho·bo·ism** \-ˌiz-əm\ *n*
Hob·son's choice \ˌhäb-sənz-\ *n* [Thomas *Hobson* †1631 E liveryman, who required every customer to take the horse nearest the door] **:** apparently free choice with no real alternative
1**hock** \ˈhäk\ *n* [ME *hoch, hough*, fr. OE *hōh* heel; akin to ON *hāsin* hock, Skt *kaṅkāla* skeleton] **:** the tarsal joint or region in the hind limb of a digitigrade quadruped (as the horse) corresponding to the ankle of man but elevated and bending backward; *also* **:** a corresponding joint of a fowl's leg
2**hock** *n, often cap* [modif. of G *hochheimer*, fr. *Hochheim*, Germany] *chiefly Brit* **:** RHINE WINE 1
3**hock** *n* [D *hok* pen, prison] **1 :** 1PAWN 2 **2** *slang* **:** PRISON
4**hock** *vt* **:** PAWN — **hock·er** *n*
hock·ey \ˈhäk-ē\ *n* [perh. fr. MF *hoquet* shepherd's crook, dim. of *hoc* hook, of Gmc origin; akin to OE *hōc* hook] **:** a game played on a field or on ice in which two sides try to drive a small object through opposite goals by hitting it with a curved or hooked stick

ho·cus \'hō-kəs\ *vt* **ho·cused** *or* **ho·cussed; ho·cus·ing** *or* **ho·cus·sing** [obs. *hocus,* n., short for *hocus-pocus*] **1 :** DECEIVE, CHEAT **2 a :** ADULTERATE **b :** DRUG

1**ho·cus–po·cus** \,hō-kə-'spō-kəs\ *n* [prob. fr. *hocus pocus,* imitation Latin phrase used by jugglers] **1 :** SLEIGHT OF HAND **2 :** nonsense or sham used to cloak deception

2**hocus–pocus** *vt* **ho·cus–po·cussed** *or* **ho·cus–po·cused; ho·cus–po·cus·sing** *or* **ho·cus–po·cus·ing :** to play tricks on

hod \'häd\ *n* [prob. fr. MD *hodde;* akin to MHG *hotte* cradle, ME *schuderen* to shudder] **1 :** a tray or trough that has a pole handle and that is borne on the shoulder for carrying mortar, brick, or similar loads **2 :** a coal scuttle

hod carrier *n* **:** a laborer employed in carrying supplies to bricklayers, stonemasons, cement finishers, or plasterers on the job

hodge·podge \'häj-,päj\ *n* [alter. of *hotchpotch*] **:** a heterogeneous mixture

hoe \'hō\ *n* [ME *howe,* fr. MF *houe,* of Gmc origin; akin to OHG *houwa* mattock, *houwan* to hew — more at HEW] **:** any of various implements; *esp* **:** an implement with a thin flat blade on a long handle used esp. for cultivating, weeding, or loosening the earth around plants — **hoe** *vb* — **ho·er** \'hō(-ə)r\ *n*

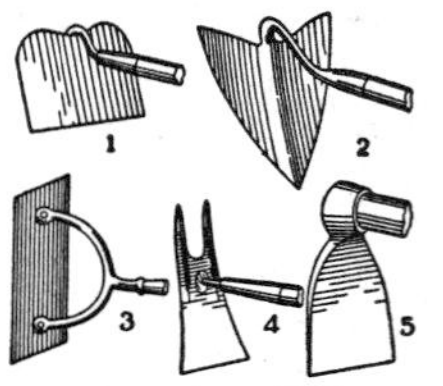

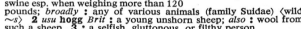

hoes: *1* garden, *2* Warren, *3* scuffle, *4* weeding, *5* grub

hoe·cake \'hō-,kāk\ *n* [fr. its being baked on the blade of a hoe] **:** a small cake made of cornmeal

hoe·down \-,dau̇n\ *n* **1 :** SQUARE DANCE **2 :** a gathering featuring hoedowns

1**hog** \'hȯg, 'häg\ *n, pl* **hogs** *also* **hog** [ME *hogge,* fr. OE *hogg*] **1 :** a domestic swine esp. when weighing more than 120 pounds; *broadly* **:** any of various animals (family Suidae) ⟨wild ~*s*⟩ **2** *usu* **hogg** *Brit* **:** a young unshorn sheep; *also* **:** wool from such a sheep **3 :** a selfish, gluttonous, or filthy person

2**hog** *vb* **hogged; hog·ging** *vt* **1 :** to cut (a horse's mane) short **:** ROACH **2 :** to cause to arch like the back of a hog **3 :** to take in excess of one's due ~ *vi* **:** to become curved upward in the middle like a hog's back — used of a ship's bottom or keel

ho·gan \'hō-,gän\ *n* [Navaho] **:** an earth-covered lodge of the Navaho Indian

hog·back \'hȯg-,bak, 'häg-\ *n* **:** a ridge of land formed by the outcropping edges of tilted strata; *broadly* **:** a ridge with a sharp summit and steeply sloping sides

hog cholera *n* **:** a highly infectious often fatal virus disease of swine characterized by fever, loss of appetite, diarrhea, and petechial hemorrhages esp. in the kidneys and lymph glands

hog·fish \'hȯg-,fish, 'häg-\ *n* **:** any of various fishes felt to resemble a hog: as **a :** a large West Indian and Florida wrasse (*Lachnolaimus maximus*) often used for food **b :** a pigfish (*Orthopristis chrysopterus*) **c :** a large red spiny-headed European marine scorpion fish (*Scorpaena scorfa*)

hog·gish \'hȯg-ish, 'häg-\ *adj* **:** grossly selfish, gluttonous, or filthy — **hog·gish·ly** *adv* — **hog·gish·ness** *n*

Hog·ma·nay \,häg-mə-'nā\ *n* [origin unknown] **1** *Scot* **:** the eve of New Year's Day **2** *Scot* **:** a gift solicited or given at Hogmanay

hog·nose snake \,hȯg-,nōz, ,häg-\ *n* **:** any of several rather small harmless stout-bodied No. American colubrid snakes (genus *Heterodon*) — called also *hog-nosed snake*

hogs·head \'hȯgz-,hed, 'hägz- *also* 'hȯg-zəd, 'häg-\ *n* **1 :** a large cask or barrel; *esp* **:** one containing from 63 to 140 gallons **2 :** any of various units of capacity; *esp* **:** a U.S. unit equal to 63 gallons

hog–tie \'hȯg-,tī, 'häg-\ *vt* **1 :** to tie together the feet of **2 :** to make helpless

hog·wash \-,wȯsh, -,wäsh\ *n* **1 :** SWILL 1a, SLOP 4a **2 :** worthless or nonsensical language

1**Ho·hen·stau·fen** \'hō-ən-,s(h)tau̇-fən\ *adj* **:** of or relating to a princely German family furnishing monarchs of the Holy Roman Empire from 1138–1254 and of Sicily from 1194–1266

2**Hohenstaufen** *n* **:** a member of the Hohenstaufen family; *esp* **:** a Hohenstaufen monarch

1**Ho·hen·zol·lern** \'hō-ən-,zäl-ərn\ *adj* **:** of or relating to a princely German family furnishing kings of Prussia from 1701–1918 and German emperors from 1871–1918

2**Hohenzollern** *n* **:** a member of the Hohenzollern family; *esp* **:** a Hohenzollern monarch

hoi pol·loi \,hȯi-pə-'lȯi\ *n pl* [Gk, the many] **:** the general populace **:** MASSES

hoise \'hȯiz\ *vt* **hoised** \'hȯizd\ *or* **hoist** \'hȯist\ **hois·ing** \'hȯi-ziŋ\ [origin unknown] **:** HOIST — **hoist with one's own petard :** blown up by one's own bomb

1**hoist** \'hȯist, *chiefly dial* 'hīst\ *vb* [alter. of E dial *hoise* (to hoist)] *vt* **:** to raise into position by or as if by means of tackle ~ *vi* **:** to become hoisted **:** RISE **syn** see LIFT — **hoist·er** *n*

2**hoist** *n* **1 :** an act of hoisting **:** LIFT **2 :** an apparatus for hoisting **3 :** the height of a flag when viewed flying

1**hoi·ty–toi·ty** \,hȯit-ē-'tȯit-ē, ,hīt-ē-'tīt-ē\ *n* [irreg. redupl. of E dial. *hoit* (to play the fool)] **:** thoughtless giddy behavior

2**hoity–toity** *adj* **1 :** GIDDY, FLIGHTY **2 :** HAUGHTY, PATRONIZING

ho·key·po·key \,hō-kē-'pō-kē\ *n* **1 :** HOCUS-POCUS **2 :** ice cream sold by street vendors

hok·ku \'hō-(,)kü\ *n, pl* **hokku** [Jap] **1 :** a fixed lyric form of Japanese origin consisting of three short unrhymed lines of five, seven, and five syllables that are typically epigrammatic or suggestive **2 :** a lyric in hokku form

ho·kum \'hō-kəm\ *n* [prob. fr. *hocus*-pocus + bun*kum*] **1 :** a device used (as by showmen) to evoke a desired response esp. of mirth or sentiment **2 :** HOCUS-POCUS, BUNKUM

hol- *or* **holo-** *comb form* [ME, fr. OF, fr. L, fr. Gk, fr. *holos* whole — more at SAFE] **1 :** complete **:** total ⟨*holo*hedral⟩ **2 :** completely **:** totally ⟨*hol*andric⟩

hol·an·dric \hä-'lan-drik, hō-\ *adj* [ISV] **1 :** inherited solely in the male line **2 :** transmitted by a gene in the nonhomologous portion of the Y chromosome — **ho·lan·dry** \'häl-,an-drē, 'hō-,lan-\ *n*

Hol·arc·tic \-'lärk-tik, -'lärt-ik\ *adj* **:** of, relating to, or being the biogeographic region including the northern parts of both hemispheres

1**hold** \'hōld\ *vb* **held** \'held\ **hold·ing** [ME *holden,* fr. OE *healdan;* akin to OHG *haltan* to hold, L *celer* rapid] *vt* **1 a :** to maintain possession of **:** POSSESS **b :** to retain by force **c :** to keep control of or authority over **d :** to keep as a threat or means of coercion **2 :** to impose restraint upon: as **a :** to refrain from producing **b** (1) **:** to keep back (2) **:** STAY, ARREST (3) **:** DELAY (4) **:** to stop the action of temporarily **c :** to keep from advancing or succeeding in attack **d :** to restrict or limit by acting to control or oppose **e :** to bind legally or morally **:** CONSTRAIN **f :** to tense muscles in order to brace (oneself) **3 a :** to have or keep in the grasp **b :** to cause to be or remain in a particular situation, position, or relation ⟨~ a ladder steady⟩ **c :** SUPPORT, SUSTAIN **d :** to keep in custody **e :** to have in one's keeping **:** STORE, RESERVE ⟨~ a room⟩ **4 :** BEAR, CARRY, COMPORT ⟨the soldierly way he ~*s* himself⟩ **5 a :** to maintain in being or action **:** keep up without interruption, diminution, or flagging ⟨~ silence⟩ **b :** to keep the uninterrupted interest, attention, or devotion of **6 a :** to receive and retain **:** CONTAIN, ACCOMMODATE **b :** to have in reserve ⟨what the future ~*s*⟩ **7 a :** HARBOR, ENTERTAIN ⟨~ a theory⟩ **b :** CONSIDER, REGARD, JUDGE ⟨truths *held* to be self-evident⟩ **c :** ESTEEM, VALUE **8 a :** to engage in with someone else or with others **:** do by concerted action ⟨~ a conversation⟩ **b :** CONVOKE, CONVENE ⟨~ a meeting of the council⟩ **9 a :** to have earned or been appointed, promoted, or elected to and now occupy (as an office) ⟨~*s* a captaincy in the navy⟩ **b :** to have earned or been awarded ⟨~*s* a Ph.D.⟩ **10 :** to handle so as to guide or manage (as reins or a gun) ~ *vi* **1 a :** to maintain position **:** not retreat **b** (1) **:** to continue in the same way or state **:** LAST ⟨hopes the weather will ~⟩ (2) **:** to endure a test or trial ⟨if his interest ~*s* up⟩ **2 :** to maintain a grasp on something **:** remain fastened to something ⟨the anchor *held* in the rough sea⟩ **3 :** to derive right or title **4 :** to bear or carry oneself ⟨asked him to ~ still⟩ **5 :** to be or remain valid **:** APPLY ⟨the rule ~*s* in most cases⟩ **6 :** to go ahead as one has been going ⟨*held* south for several miles⟩ **7 :** to forbear an intended or threatened action **:** HALT, PAUSE **syn** see CONTAIN, HAVE — **hold a candle to :** to qualify for comparison with — **hold forth :** to preach or harangue at length — **hold one's own :** to prove at least equal to opposition — **hold the bag 1 :** to be left empty-handed **2 :** to bear alone a responsibility that should have been shared by others — **hold water :** to stand up under criticism or analysis — **hold with :** to agree with or approve of

2**hold** *n* **1 :** STRONGHOLD **2 a :** CONFINEMENT, CUSTODY **b :** PRISON **3 a** (1) **:** the act or the manner of holding or grasping **:** GRIP (2) **:** a manner of grasping an opponent in wrestling **b :** a nonphysical bond that attaches, restrains, or constrains or by which something is affected, controlled, or dominated **c :** full comprehension **4 :** something that may be grasped as a support **5 a :** FERMATA **b :** the time between the onset and the release of a vocal articulation **6 :** a sudden motionless posture at the end of a dance **7 :** an order or indication that something is to be reserved or delayed

3**hold** *n* [alter. of *hole*] **1 :** the interior of a ship below decks; *esp* **:** the cargo deck of a ship **2 :** the cargo compartment of a plane

hold·all \'hōl-,dȯl\ *n* **:** a container for miscellaneous articles; *esp* **:** an often cloth traveling case or bag

hold·back \'hōl(d)-,bak\ *n* **1 :** a device that retains or restrains **2 a :** the act of holding back **b :** something held back

hold·en \'hōl-dən\ *archaic past part of* HOLD

hold·er \'hōl-dər\ *n* **1 :** a person that holds: **a** (1) **:** OWNER (2) **:** TENANT **b :** a person in possession of and legally entitled to receive payment of a bill, note, or check **2 :** a device that holds ⟨cigarette ~⟩

hold·fast \'hōl(d)-,fast\ *n* **1 a :** a part by which a plant clings to a flat surface **b :** an organ by which a parasitic animal attaches itself to its host **2 :** something to which something else may be secured firmly

hold·ing \'hōl-diŋ\ *n* **1 a :** land held esp. of a superior **b :** property (as bonds or stocks) owned **2 :** a ruling of a court esp. upon an issue of law raised in a case — compare DICTUM **3 :** something that holds

holding company *n* **:** a company that owns part or all of other companies to control them

hold out *vt* **1 :** OFFER, PROFFER **2 :** to represent to be ~ *vi* **1 :** to remain unsubdued or operative **:** LAST **2 :** to refuse to come to an agreement — **hold·out** \'hōl-,dau̇t\ *n*

hold over *vi* **:** to continue (as in office) beyond the normal term ~ *vt* **1 a :** POSTPONE **b :** to keep in one's possession **:** RETAIN **2 a :** to retain in an office **b :** to renew the engagement of

hold·over \'hōl-,dō-vər\ *n* **:** a person or thing that is held over (as a person who remains in office after his term)

hold up *vt* **1 :** DELAY, IMPEDE **2 :** to rob at gun point — **hold·up** \'hōl-,dəp\ *n*

hole \'hōl\ *n* [ME, fr. OE *hol* (fr. neut. of *hol,* adj., hollow) & *holh;* akin to OHG *hol,* adj., hollow, L *caulis* stalk, stem, Gk *kaulos*] **1 :** an opening into or through a thing **2 a :** a hollow place; *esp* **:** PIT, CAVE **b :** a deep place in a body of water **c :** a defect in a crystal (as of a semiconductor) due to an electron having left its normal position in one of the crystal bonds that is equivalent in many respects to a positively charged particle **3 :** an underground habitation **:** BURROW **4 :** FLAW, FAULT **5 :** the unit of play from the tee to the cup in golf **6 :** a mean or dingy place **7 :** an awkward position **:** FIX — **hole** *vb* — **hole·able** \'hō-lə-bəl\ *adj* — **hol·er** \-lər\ *n* — **hol·ey** \-lē\ *adj* — **in the hole :** having a score below zero

hol·i·day \'häl-ə-,dā\ *n* [ME, fr. OE *hāligdæg,* fr. *hālig* holy + *dæg* day] **1 :** HOLY DAY; *specif* **:** a day or series of days observed in Judaism with commemorative ceremonies and practices **2 :** a day on which one is exempt from work; *specif* **:** a day marked by a general suspension of work in commemoration of an event **3 :** a period of relaxation **:** VACATION — often used in pl. — **holiday** *vi* — **hol·i·day·er** *n*

hol·i·days \-,dāz\ *adv* **:** on holidays repeatedly **:** on any holiday ⟨runs ~⟩

ho·li·ly \'hō-lə-lē\ *adv* **:** in a holy manner

1**ho·li·ness** \'hō-lē-nəs\ *n* **1 :** the quality or state of being holy — used as a title for various high religious dignitaries ⟨His *Holiness* Pope Pius XII⟩ **2 :** SANCTIFICATION 2

2**holiness** *adj, often cap* **:** emphasizing the doctrine of the second blessing; *specif* **:** of or relating to a perfectionist movement arising in U.S. Protestantism in the late 19th century

ho·lism \'hō-,liz-əm\ *n* [*hol-* + *-ism*] **:** a theory that the determin-

ing factors esp. in living nature are irreducible wholes — **ho·list** \-ləst\ *n*

ho·lis·tic \hō-ˈlis-tik\ *adj* **1 :** of or relating to holism **2 :** emphasizing the organic or functional relation between parts and wholes ⟨~ rather than atomistic⟩ — **ho·lis·ti·cal·ly** \-ti-k(ə-)lē\ *adv*

hol·land \ˈhäl-ənd\ *n, often cap* [ME *holand,* fr. *Holand,* county in the Netherlands, fr. MD *Holland*] **1 :** a cotton or linen fabric in plain weave usu. heavily sized or glazed and used for window shades, bookbinding, and clothing **2 :** 2DUTCH 1b

hol·lan·daise \ˌhäl-ən-ˈdāz\ *n* [F (*sauce*) *hollandaise,* lit., Dutch sauce] **:** a sauce made of butter, yolks of eggs, and lemon juice or vinegar

Hol·lands \ˈhäl-ən(d)z\ *n* [D *hollandsch,* fr. *hollandsch genever* Dutch gin] **:** gin made in the Netherlands — called also *Holland gin*

1hol·ler \ˈhäl-ər\ *vb* **hol·ler·ing** \-(ə-)riŋ\ [alter. of *hollo* (to cry hollo)] *vi* **1 :** to cry out (as to attract attention or in pain) **:** SHOUT **2 :** GRIPE, COMPLAIN ~ *vt* **:** to call out (a word or phrase)

2holler *n* **1 :** SHOUT, CRY **2 :** COMPLAINT **3 :** a freely improvised American Negro work song

3holler *chiefly dial var of* HOLLOW

hol·lo \ˈhäl-(ˌ)ō, hä-ˈlō\ *or* **hol·la** \ˈhäl-ə\ *interj* [origin unknown] **1** — used to attract attention **2** — used as a call of encouragement or jubilation

hol·low \ˈhäl-(ˌ)ō, -ə(-w)\ *adj* [ME *holw, holh,* fr. *holh* hole, den, fr. OE *holh* hole, hollow — more at HOLE] **1 a :** CONCAVE, SUNKEN **b :** marked by sunken areas **2 a :** having a cavity within ⟨~ tree⟩ **b :** devoid of value or significance ⟨~ victory⟩ **3 :** reverberating like a sound made in or by beating on a large empty enclosure **:** MUFFLED **4 :** FALSE, DECEITFUL ⟨~ promises⟩ **syn** see VAIN — **hollow** *vb* — **hollow** *n* — **hollow** *adv* — **hol·low·ly** \ˈhäl-ō-lē, -ə-lē\ *adv* — **hol·low·ness** *n*

hollow organ *n* **:** a visceral organ (as the stomach or intestine) that is a hollow tube or pouch or that includes a cavity which subserves a vital function (as the heart or bladder)

hollow ware *n* **:** vessels usu. of pottery, glass, or metal (as bowls, cups, or vases) with a significant depth and volume

hol·ly \ˈhäl-ē\ *n* [ME *holin, holly,* fr. OE *holegn;* akin to OHG *hulis* holly, MIr *cuilenn*] **1 a :** any of a genus (*Ilex*) of trees and shrubs (family Aquifoliaceae, the holly family) having thick glossy spiny-margined leaves and usu. bright red berries **b :** the foliage or branches of the holly **2 :** any of various trees with foliage resembling that of a holly

hol·ly·hock \ˈhäl-ē-ˌhäk, -ˌhȯk\ *n* [ME *holihoc,* fr. *holi* holy + *hoc* mallow, fr. OE] **:** a tall widely cultivated perennial Chinese herb (*Althaea rosea*) of the mallow family with large coarse rounded leaves and tall spikes of showy flowers

Hol·ly·wood \ˈhäl-ē-ˌwu̇d\ *n, often attrib* [*Hollywood,* district of Los Angeles, Calif] **:** the American motion-picture industry — **Hol·ly·wood·ish** \-ish\ *adj*

Hollywood bed *n* **:** a mattress on a box spring supported by low legs sometimes with an upholstered headboard

holm \ˈhō(l)m\ *n* [ME, fr. OE, fr. ON *hōlmr;* akin to OE *hyll* hill] *Brit* **:** a small inland or inshore island; *also* **:** BOTTOMS

hol·mi·um \ˈhō(l)-mē-əm\ *n* [NL, fr. *Holmia* Stockholm, Sweden] **:** a trivalent metallic element of the rare-earth group that occurs with yttrium and forms highly magnetic compounds — see ELEMENT table

holo- — see HOL-

ho·lo·blas·tic \ˌhäl-ō-ˈblas-tik, ˌhō-lō-\ *adj* [ISV] *of an egg* **:** having cleavage planes that divide the whole egg into distinct and separate though coherent blastomeres — compare MEROBLASTIC — **ho·lo·blas·ti·cal·ly** \-ti-k(ə-)lē\ *adv*

ho·lo·caust \ˈhäl-ə-ˌkȯst, ˈhō-lə-\ *n* [ME, fr. OF *holocauste,* fr. LL *holocaustum,* fr. Gk *holokauston,* fr. neut. of *holokaustos* burnt whole, fr. *hol-* + *kaustos* burnt, fr. *kaiein* to burn — more at CAUSTIC] **1 :** a sacrifice consumed by fire **2 :** a thorough destruction esp. by fire

Ho·lo·cene \ˈhäl-ə-ˌsēn, ˈhō-lə-\ *adj* [ISV] **:** RECENT 2 — **Holocene** *n*

ho·lo·crine \-krən, -ˌkrīn, -ˌkrēn\ *adj* [ISV *hol-* + Gk *krinein* to separate — more at CERTAIN] **:** producing a secretion consisting of altered secretory cells; *also* **:** produced by a holocrine gland

ho·lo·en·zyme \ˌhäl-ō-ˈen-ˌzīm, ˌhō-lō-\ *n* [ISV] **:** a complete active enzyme consisting of an apoenzyme combined with its coenzyme

Hol·o·fer·nes \ˌhäl-ə-ˈfər-(ˌ)nēz\ *n* [LL, fr. Gk *Holophernēs*] **:** a general of Nebuchadnezzar slain by Judith

ho·log·a·mous \hə-ˈläg-ə-məs\ *adj* **:** having gametes of essentially the same size and structural features as vegetative cells — **ho·log·a·my** \-mē\ *n*

ho·lo·gram \ˈhäl-ə-ˌgram, ˈhō-lə-\ *n* [*hol-* + *-gram*] **:** a three-dimensional picture made without a camera on photographic film by the pattern of interference formed by light reflected from the object with the picture to be viewed by light passing through it — **ho·lo·graph·ic** \ˌhäl-ə-ˈgraf-ik, ˌhō-lə-\ *adj* — **ho·log·ra·phy** \hə-ˈläg-rə-fē\ *n*

ho·lo·graph \ˈhäl-ə-ˌgraf, ˈhō-lə-\ *n* [LL *holographus,* fr. LGk *holographos,* fr. Gk *hol-* + *graphein* to write — more at CARVE] **:** a document wholly in the handwriting of the purported author — **holograph** *or* **ho·lo·graph·ic** \ˌhäl-ə-ˈgraf-ik, ˌhō-lə-\ *adj*

ho·lo·gyn·ic \ˌhäl-ō-ˈjin-ik, ˌhō-lō-, -ˈgīn-\ *adj* **:** inherited solely in the female line presumably through transmission as a recessive factor in the nonhomologous portion of the X chromosome — **ho·log·y·ny** \hə-ˈläj-ə-nē\ *n*

ho·lo·he·dral \ˌhäl-ō-ˈhē-drəl, ˌhō-lō-\ *adj* [*hol-* + Gk *hedra* seat — more at SIT] *of a crystal* **:** having all the faces required by complete symmetry — compare HEMIHEDRAL, TETARTOHEDRAL

ho·lo·me·tab·o·lism \-mə-ˈtab-ə-ˌliz-əm\ *n* **:** development of insects involving complete metamorphosis — **ho·lo·me·tab·o·lous** \-ləs\ *adj*

ho·lo·my·ar·i·an \-ˌmī-ˈar-ē-ən, -ˈer-\ *adj* [deriv. of Gk *holos* whole + *mys* muscle — more at SAFE, MOUSE] *of a nematode worm* **:** having the muscle layer continuous or divided into two longitudinal zones without true muscle cells

ho·lo·phras·tic \ˌhäl-ə-ˈfras-tik, ˌhō-lə-\ *adj* [ISV *hol-* + *-phrastic* (fr. Gk *phrazein* to point out, declare)] **:** expressing a complex of ideas in a single word

ho·lo·phyt·ic \ˌhäl-ō-ˈfit-ik, ˌhō-lō-\ *adj* **:** obtaining food after the manner of a green plant

ho·lo·thu·ri·an \-ˈth(y)u̇r-ē-ən\ *n* [deriv. of Gk *holothourion* water polyp] **:** any of a class (Holothurioidea) of echinoderms having an elongate flexible tough muscular body **:** SEA CUCUMBER — **holothurian** *adj*

ho·lo·type \ˈhäl-ə-ˌtīp, ˈhō-lə-\ *n* **1 :** the single specimen designated by an author as the type of a species or lesser taxon at the time of establishing the group **2 :** the type of a species or lesser taxon designated at a date later than that of establishing a group or by another person than the author of the taxon — **ho·lo·typ·ic** \ˌhäl-ə-ˈtip-ik, ˌhō-lə-\ *adj*

ho·lo·zo·ic \ˌhäl-ə-ˈzō-ik, ˌhō-lə-\ *adj* **:** obtaining food after the manner of most animals by ingesting complex organic matter **:** HETEROTROPHIC

holp \ˈhō(l)p\ *chiefly dial past of* HELP

hol·pen \ˈhō(l)-pən\ *chiefly dial past part of* HELP

hol·stein-frie·sian \ˌhōl-ˌstēn-ˈfrē-zhən, -ˌstīn-\ *or* **hol·stein** \ˈhōl-\ *n* [*Holstein,* Germany, its later locality + *Friesian*] **:** any of a breed of large black-and-white dairy cattle orig. from northern Holland and Friesland that produce large quantities of comparatively low-fat milk

hol·ster \ˈhōl(t)-stər\ *n* [D; akin to OE *heolstor* cover, *helan* to conceal — more at HELL] **:** a usu. leather case for a pistol

holt \ˈhōlt\ *n* [ME, fr. OE; akin to OHG *holz* wood, Gk *klados* twig — more at GLADIATOR] *archaic* **:** a small woods **:** COPSE

ho·lus-bo·lus \ˌhō-ləs-ˈbō-ləs\ *adv* [prob. redupl. of *bolus*] **:** all at once **:** ALTOGETHER

ho·ly \ˈhō-lē\ *adj* [ME, fr. OE *hālig;* akin to OE *hāl* whole — more at WHOLE] **1 :** set apart to the service of God or a god **:** SACRED ⟨the ~ priesthood⟩ **2 a :** characterized by perfection and transcendence **:** commanding absolute adoration and reverence ⟨the ~ Lord God Almighty⟩ **b :** spiritually pure **:** GODLY **3 a :** evoking or meriting veneration or awe ⟨the ~ cross⟩ **b :** being awesome, frightening, or beyond belief ⟨a ~ terror⟩ **4 :** filled with superhuman and potentially fatal power

holy city *n* **:** a city that is the center of religious worship and traditions

Holy Communion *n* **:** COMMUNION 2

holy day *n* **:** a day observed as a religious feast or fast

holy day of obligation : a feast on which Roman Catholics are obliged to hear mass and abstain from physical or manual work

Holy Father *n* **:** POPE 1

Holy Ghost *n* **:** the third person of the Trinity **:** HOLY SPIRIT

Holy Grail *n* **:** GRAIL 1

Holy Hour *n* **:** an hour of prayer and meditation before the Blessed Sacrament esp. in memory of the Passion

Holy Innocents' Day *n* **:** December 28 observed in commemoration of the children slain by Herod

Holy Joe \ˌhō-lē-ˈjō\ *n, slang* **:** PARSON, CHAPLAIN

Holy Office *n* **:** a congregation and tribunal of the curia charged with protecting faith and morals

holy of holies : the innermost chamber of the Jewish tabernacle and temple

holy oil *n* **:** olive oil blessed by a bishop for use in a sacrament or sacramental

holy order *n, often cap H&O* **1 :** MAJOR ORDER **2** *pl* **:** the rite or sacrament of ordination

Holy Roller *n* **:** a member of one of the religious sects whose meetings are characterized by frenzied excitement — often taken to be offensive

Holy Roman Empire *n* **:** an empire consisting primarily of a loose confederation of German and Italian territories under the suzerainty of an emperor and existing from the 9th or 10th century to 1806

Holy Saturday *n* **:** the Saturday before Easter

Holy See *n* **:** the see of the pope

Holy Spirit *n* **:** the active presence of God in human life constituting the third person of the Trinity

ho·ly·stone \ˈhō-lē-ˌstōn\ *n* **:** a soft sandstone used to scrub a ship's decks — **holystone** *vb*

Holy Synod *n* **:** the governing body of a self-governing Eastern church

Holy Thursday *n* **1 :** ASCENSION DAY **2 :** MAUNDY THURSDAY

holy water *n* **:** water blessed by a priest and used as a purifying sacramental

Holy Week *n* **:** the week before Easter

Holy Writ *n* **:** BIBLE 1, 2

Holy Year *n* **:** a jubilee year

hom- *or* **homo-** *comb form* [L, fr. Gk, fr. *homos* — more at SAME] **:** one and the same **:** similar **:** alike ⟨*homo*graph⟩ ⟨*homo*sporous⟩

hom·age \ˈ(h)äm-ij\ *n* [ME, fr. OF *hommage,* fr. *homme* man, vassal, fr. L *homin-, homo* man; akin to OE *guma* man, L *humus* earth — more at HUMBLE] **1 a :** a ceremony by which a man acknowledges himself the vassal of a lord **b :** the relationship between a feudal lord and his man **c :** an act done or payment made in meeting the obligations of vassalage **2 a :** reverential regard **:** DEFERENCE **b :** flattering attention **:** TRIBUTE **syn** see HONOR

hom·ag·er \ˈ(h)äm-ij-ər\ *n* **:** VASSAL

homalographic *var of* HOMOLOGRAPHIC

hom·bre \ˈäm-brē, ˈəm-, -ˌbrā\ *n* [Sp, man, fr. L *homin-, homo*] **:** GUY, FELLOW

hom·burg \ˈhäm-ˌbərg\ *n* [*Homburg,* Germany] **:** a man's felt hat with a stiff curled brim and a high crown creased lengthwise

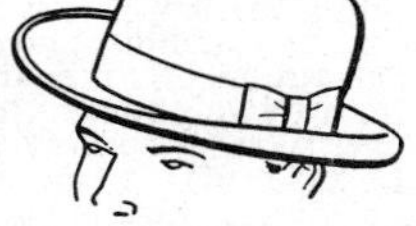

homburg

1home \ˈhōm\ *n, often attrib* [ME *hom,* fr. OE *hām* village, home; akin to Gk *kōmē* village, L *civis* citizen, Gk *koiman* to put to sleep — more at CEMETERY] **1 a :** a family's place of residence **:** DOMICILE **b :** HOUSE **2 :** the social unit formed by a family living together **3 a :** a congenial environment **b :** HABITAT **4 a :** a place of origin **b :** HEADQUARTERS **5 :** the objective in various games — **home·grown** \-ˈgrōn\ *adj* — **home·land** \-ˌland\ *n* — **home·less** \-ləs\ *adj*

2home *adv* **1 :** to or at home **2 :** to a final, closed, or standard

position ⟨drive a nail ~⟩ **3 :** to a successful or rewarding end **4 :** to a vital core ⟨the truth struck ~⟩

3**home** *vi* **1 a :** to go or return home **b** *of an animal* **:** to return accurately to its home or natal area from a distance **c :** to proceed to or toward a source of radiated energy used as a guide ⟨missiles ~ in on radar⟩ **2 :** to have a home ~ *vt* **:** to send to or provide with a home

home- *or* **homeo-** *also* **homoi-** *or* **homoio-** *comb form* [L&Gk; L *homoeo-*, fr. Gk *homoi-*, *homoio-*, fr. *homoios*, fr. *homos* same — more at SAME] **:** like **:** similar ⟨*homeo*stasis⟩ ⟨*homoio*thermic⟩

home·body \ˈhōm-ˌbäd-ē\ *n* **:** one whose life centers in the home

home·bred \-ˈbred\ *adj* **:** produced at home **:** INDIGENOUS

home brew *n* **:** an alcoholic beverage made at home

home·com·ing \ˈhōm-ˌkəm-iŋ\ *n* **1 :** a return home **2 :** the return of a group of people esp. on a special occasion to a place formerly frequented

home economics *n pl but sing or pl in constr* **:** the theory and practice of homemaking

home front *n* **:** the sphere of civilian activity in war

home·like \ˈhōm-ˌlīk\ *adj* **:** characteristic of a home: **a :** CHEERFUL, COZY **b :** SIMPLE, WHOLESOME

home·li·ness \-lē-nəs\ *n* **:** the quality or state of being homely

home·ly \ˈhōm-lē\ *adj* **1 :** HOMELIKE **2 :** COMMONPLACE, FAMILIAR **3 :** of a sympathetic character **:** KINDLY **4 a :** unaffectedly natural **:** SIMPLE **b :** PLAIN, UNADORNED **5 :** lacking beauty or proportion

home·made \ˈhō(m)-ˈmād\ *adj* **1 :** made in the home, on the premises, or by one's own efforts **2 :** of domestic manufacture

home·mak·er \ˈhōm-ˌmā-kər\ *n* **:** one who manages a household esp. as a wife and mother — **home·mak·ing** *n or adj*

ho·meo·chro·mat·ic \ˌhō-mē-ō-krə-ˈmat-ik, ˌhäm-ē-\ *adj* **:** of similar color

ho·meo·mor·phic \-ə-ˈmȯr-fik\ *adj* **:** characterized by homeomorphism

ho·meo·mor·phism \-ˌfiz-əm\ *n* [ISV] **1 :** a near similarity of crystalline forms between unlike chemical compounds **2 :** a one-to-one mapping in topology between two figures that is continuous in both directions

ho·meo·path \ˈhō-mē-ə-ˌpath, ˈhäm-ē-\ *n* **:** a practitioner or adherent of homeopathy

ho·meo·path·ic \ˌhō-mē-ə-ˈpath-ik, ˌhäm-ē-\ *adj* **:** of or relating to homeopathy — **ho·meo·path·i·cal·ly** \-i-k(ə-)lē\ *adv*

ho·me·op·a·thy \ˌhō-mē-ˈäp-ə-thē, ˌhäm-ē-\ *n* [G *homöopathie*, fr. *homöo-* home- + *-pathie* -pathy] **:** a system of medical practice that treats a disease esp. by the administration of minute doses of a remedy that would in healthy persons produce symptoms of the disease treated

ho·meo·sta·sis \ˌhō-mē-ō-ˈstā-səs, -ō-ˈstas-əs, -ˈäs-tə-səs, ˌhäm-ē-\ *n* [NL] **:** a relatively stable state of equilibrium or a tendency toward such a state between the different but interdependent elements or groups of elements of an organism or group — **ho·meo·stat·ic** \-ō-ˈstat-ik\ *adj*

ho·meo·typ·ic \ˌhō-mē-ō-ˈtip-ik, ˌhäm-ē-\ *adj* **:** being or relating to the second or equational meiotic division — **ho·meo·typ·i·cal** \-i-kəl\ *adj*

home plate *n* **:** a rubber slab at the apex of a baseball diamond that must be touched by a base runner in order to score

1**ho·mer** \ˈhō-mər\ *n* [Heb *ḥōmer*] **:** an ancient Hebrew unit of capacity equal to about 10½ or later 11½ bushels or 100 gallons

2**hom·er** \ˈhō-mər\ *n* **1 :** HOMING PIGEON **2 :** HOME RUN

home range *n* **:** the area to which an animal confines his activities

Ho·mer·ic \hō-ˈmer-ik\ *adj* **:** of, relating to, or characteristic of the Greek poet Homer, his age, or his writings — **Ho·mer·i·cal·ly** \-i-k(ə-)lē\ *adv*

home·room \ˈhōm-ˌrüm, -ˌru̇m\ *n* **:** a schoolroom where pupils of the same class report at the opening of school

home rule *n* **1 :** self-government in internal affairs by the people of a dependent political unit **2 :** limited autonomy in the organization and management of local affairs granted by a state to a county or municipality

home run *n* **:** a hit in baseball that enables the batter to make a complete circuit of the bases and score a run

home·sick \ˈhōm-ˌsik\ *adj* [back-formation fr. *homesickness*] **:** longing for home and family while absent from them — **home·sick·ness** *n*

1**home·spun** \-ˌspən\ *adj* **1 a :** spun or made at home **b :** made of homespun **2 :** SIMPLE, HOMELY

2**homespun** *n* **:** a loosely woven usu. woolen or linen fabric orig. made from homespun yarn

1**home·stead** \ˈhōm-ˌsted, -stəd\ *n* **1 a :** the home and adjoining land occupied by a family **b :** an ancestral home **c :** HOUSE **2 :** a tract of land acquired from U.S. public lands by filing a record and living on and cultivating the tract

2**home·stead** \-ˌsted\ *vt* **:** to acquire or occupy as a homestead ~ *vi* **:** to acquire or settle on land under a homestead law — **home·stead·er** \-ˌsted-ər\ *n*

homestead law *n* **1 :** a law exempting a homestead from attachment or sale under execution for general debts **2 :** any of several legislative acts authorizing the sale of public lands in homesteads to settlers

home·stretch \ˈhōm-ˈstrech\ *n* **1 :** the part of a racecourse between the last curve and the winning post **2 :** a final stage

1**home·ward** \-wərd\ *or* **home·wards** \-wərdz\ *adv* **:** toward home ⟨look ~, angel —John Milton⟩

2**homeward** *adj* **:** being or going in the direction of home

home·work \-ˌwərk\ *n* **1 :** piecework carried on at home for pay **2 :** an assignment given to a student to be completed outside of the classroom **3 :** preparatory reading or research (as for a discussion)

hom·ey *also* **homy** \ˈhō-mē\ *adj* **hom·i·er; hom·i·est :** HOMELIKE, INTIMATE — **hom·ey·ness** *or* **hom·i·ness** *n*

ho·mi·ci·dal \ˌhäm-ə-ˈsīd-ᵊl, ˌhō-mə-\ *adj* **:** of, relating to, or tending toward homicide — **ho·mi·ci·dal·ly** \-ᵊl-ē\ *adv*

ho·mi·cide \ˈhäm-ə-ˌsīd, ˈhō-mə-\ *n* [in sense 1, fr. ME, fr. MF, fr. L *homicida*, fr. *homo* man + *-cida* -cide; in sense 2, fr. ME, fr. MF, fr. L *homicidium*, fr. *homo* + *-cidium* -cide] **1 :** a person who kills another **2 :** a killing of one human being by another

hom·i·let·ic \ˌhäm-ə-ˈlet-ik\ *adj* [LL *homileticus*, fr. Gk *homilētikos* of conversation, fr. *homilein*] **1 :** of the nature of a homily **2 :** of or relating to homiletics — **hom·i·let·i·cal** \-i-kəl\ *adj* — **hom·i·let·i·cal·ly** \-i-k(ə-)lē\ *adv*

hom·i·let·ics \-iks\ *n pl but sing in constr* **:** the art of preaching

hom·i·ly \ˈhäm-ə-lē\ *n* [ME *omelie*, fr. MF, fr. LL *homilia*, fr. LGk, fr. Gk, conversation, discourse, fr. *homilein* to consort with, address, fr. *homilos* crowd, assembly] **1 :** a religious discourse usu. before a congregation; *specif* **:** an informal exposition of Scripture **2 :** a moral lecture

homing pigeon *n* **:** a racing pigeon trained to return home

hom·i·nid \ˈhäm-ə-nəd\ *also* **ho·min·i·an** \hō-ˈmin-ē-ən\ *n* [deriv. of L *homin-*, *homo* man] **:** any of a family (Hominidae) of bipedal primate mammals comprising recent man, his immediate ancestors, and related forms — **hominid** *also* **hominian** *adj*

hom·i·noid \ˈhäm-ə-ˌnȯid\ *adj* **:** resembling or related to man — **hominoid** *n*

hom·i·ny \ˈhäm-ə-nē\ *n* [prob. of Algonquian origin; akin to Natick *-minne* grain] **:** hulled corn with the germ removed

hominy grits *n pl but sing or pl in constr* **:** hominy in uniform granular particles

ho·mo \ˈhō-(ˌ)mō\ *n* [NL *Homin-*, *Homo*, genus name, fr. L, man] **:** any of a genus (*Homo*) of primate mammals that consists of mankind and is usu. held to include a single recent species (*H. sapiens*) comprising all surviving and various extinct men

homo- — see HOM-

ho·mo·cer·cal \ˌhō-mō-ˈsər-kəl, ˌhäm-ō-\ *adj* **1 :** having the upper and lower lobes approximately symmetrical and the vertebral column ending at or near the middle of the base — used of the tail fin of a fish **2 :** having or relating to a homocercal tail fin

ho·mo·chro·mat·ic \-krə-ˈmat-ik\ *adj* **:** of or relating to one color

ho·mo·chro·mo·some \-ˈkrō-mə-ˌsōm\ *n* **:** AUTOSOME

ho·moe·cious \hō-ˈmē-shəs, hä-\ *adj* [*hom-* + Gk *oikia* house; akin to Gk *oikos* house — more at VICINITY] **:** having the same host during the entire life cycle

ho·mo·erot·ic \ˌhō-mō-i-ˈrät-ik, ˌhäm-ō-\ *adj* **:** HOMOSEXUAL — **ho·mo·erot·i·cism** \-ˈrät-ə-ˌsiz-əm\ *n*

ho·mog·a·mous \hō-ˈmäg-ə-məs, hä-\ *or* **ho·mo·gam·ic** \ˌhō-mō-ˈgam-ik, ˌhäm-ō-\ *adj* **:** characterized by or relating to homogamy

ho·mog·a·my \hō-ˈmäg-ə-mē, hä-\ *n* [G *homogamie*, fr. *hom-* + *-gamie* -gamy] **1 a :** a state of having flowers alike throughout **b :** the maturing of stamens and pistils at the same period **2 :** reproduction within an isolated group perpetuating qualities by which it is differentiated from the larger group of which it is a part; *broadly* **:** the mating of like with like

ho·mog·e·nate \hō-ˈmäj-ə-ˌnāt, hə-\ *n* **:** a product of homogenizing

ho·mo·ge·ne·ity \ˌhō-mə-jə-ˈnē-ət-ē *also* ˌhäm-ə-\ *n* **:** the quality or state of being homogeneous

ho·mo·ge·neous \-ˈjē-nē-əs, -nyəs\ *adj* [ML *homogeneus*, *homogenus*, fr. Gk *homogenēs*, fr. *hom-* + *genos* kind — more at KIN] **1 :** of the same or a similar kind or nature **2 :** of uniform structure or composition throughout **3 :** of the same mathematical degree or dimensions ⟨~ equation⟩ **4 :** HOMOGENOUS 1 **syn** see SIMILAR — **ho·mo·ge·neous·ly** *adv* — **ho·mo·ge·neous·ness** *n*

ho·mo·gen·ic \-ˈjen-ik\ *adj* **1 :** HOMOGENOUS **2 :** having only one allele of a gene ⟨~ gamete⟩

ho·mog·e·ni·za·tion \hō-ˌmäj-ə-nə-ˈzā-shən, hə-\ *n* **1 :** the quality or state of being homogenized **2 :** the act or process of homogenizing

ho·mog·e·nize \hō-ˈmäj-ə-ˌnīz, hə-\ *vt* **1 a :** to blend into a smooth mixture **b :** to make homogeneous **2 a :** to reduce to small particles of uniform size and distribute evenly usu. in a liquid **b :** to reduce the particles of so that they are uniformly small and evenly distributed; *specif* **:** to break up the fat globules of (milk) into very fine particles esp. by forcing through minute openings ~ *vi* **:** to become homogenized — **ho·mog·e·niz·er** *n*

ho·mog·e·nous \-ˈmäj-ə-nəs\ *adj* **1 :** of, relating to, or exhibiting homogeny **2 :** HOMOPLASTIC 2 **3 :** HOMOGENEOUS

ho·mog·e·ny \-nē\ *n* **:** correspondence between parts or organs due to descent from the same ancestral type

ho·mog·o·nous \hō-ˈmäg-ə-nəs, hə-\ *adj* [*homogony*, fr. *hom-* + *-gony*] **:** having a single kind of perfect flower with androecium and gynoecium of uniform relative length — **ho·mog·o·nous·ly** *adv* — **ho·mog·o·ny** \-nē\ *n*

ho·mo·graft \ˈhō-mō-ˌgraft, ˈhäm-ō-\ *n* **:** a graft of tissue taken from a donor of the same species as the recipient

ho·mo·graph \ˈhäm-ə-ˌgraf, ˈhō-mə-\ *n* **:** one of two or more words spelled alike but differing in derivation, meaning, or pronunciation (as *fair* market and *fair* beautiful) — **ho·mo·graph·ic** \ˌhäm-ə-ˈgraf-ik, ˌhō-mə-\ *adj*

homoi- *or* **homoio-** — see HOME-

ho·moio·ther·mic \hō-ˌmȯi-ə-ˈthər-mik\ *or* **ho·moio·ther·mal** \-məl\ *adj* **:** WARM-BLOODED — **ho·moio·ther·my** \-ˈmȯi-ə-ˌthər-mē\ *n*

ho·moi·ou·si·an \hō-ˈmȯi-ˌü-zē-ən, hä-ˈmȯi-, -ˈü-sē-\ *n* [LGk *homoiousios* of like substance, fr. Gk *homoi-* home- + *ousia* essence, substance, fr. *ont-*, *ōn*, prp. of *einai* to be — more at IS] **:** an adherent of an ecclesiastical party of the 4th century holding that the Son is essentially like the Father but not of the same substance

ho·mo·lec·i·thal \ˌhō-mō-ˈles-ə-thəl, ˌhäm-ō-\ *adj* [*hom-* + Gk *lekithos* yolk] **:** having the yolk small in amount and nearly uniformly distributed

ho·mol·o·gate \hō-ˈmäl-ə-ˌgāt, hə-\ *vt* [ML *homologatus*, pp. of *homologare* to agree, fr. Gk *homologein*, fr. *homologos*] **:** SANCTION, ALLOW — **ho·mol·o·ga·tion** \-ˌmäl-ə-ˈgā-shən\ *n*

ho·mo·log·i·cal \ˌhō-mə-ˈläj-i-kəl, ˌhäm-ə-\ *adj* **:** HOMOLOGOUS — **ho·mo·log·i·cal·ly** \-i-k(ə-)lē\ *adv*

ho·mol·o·gize \hō-ˈmäl-ə-ˌjīz, hə-\ *vt* **1 :** to make homologous **2 :** to demonstrate the homology of — **ho·mol·o·giz·er** *n*

ho·mol·o·gous \hō-ˈmäl-ə-gəs, hə-\ *adj* [Gk *homologos* agreeing, fr. *hom-* + *legein* to say — more at LEGEND] **1 a :** having the same relative position, value, or structure **b** (1) **:** exhibiting biological homology (2) **:** of like genic constitution **c :** belonging to or consisting of a chemical series whose members exhibit homology **2 :** derived from or developed in response to organisms of the same species ⟨~ tissue graft⟩

hom·o·lo·graph·ic \ˌhäm-ə-lə-ˈgraf-ik\ *adj* [F *homalographique*, fr. Gk *homalos* even, level (akin to Gk *homos* same) + *graphein* to write — more at SAME, CARVE] **:** preserving the mutual relations of parts esp. as to size and form

ho·mo·logue *or* **ho·mo·log** \ˈhō-mə-ˌlȯg, ˈhäm-ə-, -ˌläg\ *n* **:** something that exhibits homology

ho·mol·o·gy \hō-ˈmäl-ə-jē, hə-\ *n* **1 :** a similarity often attributable

to common origin **2 a :** likeness in structure between parts of different organisms due to evolutionary differentiation from the same or a corresponding part of a remote ancestor — compare ANALOGY **b :** correspondence in structure between different parts of the same individual **3 a :** the relation existing between chemical compounds in a series whose successive members have in composition a regular difference esp. of one carbon and two hydrogen atoms CH_2 **b :** the relation existing among elements in the same group of the periodic table **4 :** a classification of configurations in topology into distinct types

ho·mol·o·sine projection \hō-'mäl-ə-,sīn-\ *n* [irreg. fr. Gk *homalos*] **:** an equal-area map projection that is interrupted over the oceans so that each continent is in the center of a projection

ho·mol·y·sis \hō-'mäl-ə-səs\ *n* [NL] **:** the decomposition of a chemical compound into two neutral atoms or radicals — **ho·mo·lyt·ic** \,hō-mə-'lit-ik, ,häm-ə-\ *adj*

ho·mo·mor·phic \,hō-mə-'mȯr-fik, ,häm-ə-\ *adj* **:** of, relating to, or characterized by homomorphism

ho·mo·mor·phism \-,fiz-əm\ *n* [ISV] **1 :** likeness in form: as **a :** HOMOMORPHY **b :** the having of perfect flowers of only one type **2 :** a mapping of one group on itself or another so that the results of the group operations correspond — **ho·mo·mor·phous** \-fəs\ *adj*

ho·mo·mor·phy \'hō-mə-,mȯr-fē, 'häm-ə-\ *n* [ISV] **:** similarity of form with different fundamental structure; *specif* **:** superficial resemblance between organisms of different groups due to convergence — compare HOMOLOGY 2a

hom·onym \'häm-ə-,nim, 'hō-mə-\ *n* [L *homonymum*, fr. Gk *homōnymon*, fr. neut. of *homōnymos*] **1 a :** HOMOPHONE **b :** HOMOGRAPH **c :** one of two or more words spelled and pronounced alike but different in meaning (as *pool* of water and *pool* the game) **2 :** NAMESAKE **3 :** a taxonomic designation rejected because the identical term has been used to designate another group of the same rank — compare SYNONYM — **hom·onym·ic** \,häm-ə-'nim-ik, ,hō-mə-\ *adj*

hom·on·y·mous \hō-'män-ə-məs\ *adj* [L *homonymus* having the same name, fr. Gk *homōnymos*, fr. *hom-* + *onyma*, *onoma* name — more at NAME] **1 :** AMBIGUOUS **2 :** having the same designation **3 :** HOMONYMIC — **hom·on·y·mous·ly** *adv* — **hom·on·y·my** \-mē\ *n*

ho·mo·ou·si·an \hō-'mō-,ü-zē-ən, hä-'mō-, -,ü-sē-\ *n* [LGk *homoousios* of the same substance, fr. Gk *hom-* + *ousia* substance — more at HOMOIOUSIAN] **:** an adherent of an ecclesiastical party of the 4th century holding to the doctrine of the Nicene Creed that the Son is of the same substance with the Father

ho·mo·phone \'häm-ə-,fōn, 'hō-mə-\ *n* [ISV] **1 :** one of two or more words pronounced alike but different in meaning or derivation or spelling (as *to*, *too*, and *two*) **2 :** a character or group of characters pronounced the same as another — **ho·moph·o·nous** \hō-'mäf-ə-nəs\ *adj*

ho·mo·phon·ic \,häm-ə-'fän-ik, ,hō-mə-\ *adj* [Gk *homophōnos* being in unison, fr. *hom-* + *phōnē* sound — more at BAN] **:** of, relating to, or being music consisting of a single accompanied melodic line — **ho·moph·o·ny** \hō-'mäf-ə-nē\ *n*

ho·mo·phy·ly \'hō-mə-,fī-lē, 'häm-ə-; hō-'mäf-ə-lē\ *n* [ISV *hom-* + *phyl-* + *-y*] **:** resemblance due to common ancestry — compare HOMOMORPHY

ho·mo·plas·tic \,hō-mə-'plas-tik, ,häm-ə-\ *adj* **1 :** of or relating to homoplasy **2 :** of, relating to, or derived from another individual of the same species — **ho·mo·plas·ti·cal·ly** \-ti-k(ə-)lē\ *adv*

ho·mo·pla·sy \'hō-mə-,plā-sē, 'häm-ə-, -,plas-ē; hō-'mäp-lə-sē\ *n* **:** correspondence between parts or organs acquired as the result of parallel evolution or convergence

ho·mop·ter·an \hō-'mäp-tə-rən\ *n* **:** a homopterous insect — **homopteran** *adj*

ho·mop·ter·ous \-rəs\ *adj* [deriv. of Gk *hom-* + *pteron* wing — more at FEATHER] **:** of or relating to a large order or suborder (Homoptera) of insects having sucking mouthparts and comprising the cicadas, aphids, scale insects, and related forms

Ho·mo sa·pi·ens \,hō-(,)mō-'sap-ē-ənz, -'sā-pē-, -,enz\ *n* [NL, species name, fr. *Homo*, genus name + *sapiens*, specific epithet, fr. L, wise, intelligent, — more at HOMO, SAPIENT] **:** MANKIND 1

ho·mo·sex·u·al \,hō-mə-'seksh-(ə-)wəl, -'sek-shəl\ *adj* **:** of, relating to, or exhibiting sexual desire toward a member of one's own sex — **homosexual** *n* — **ho·mo·sex·u·al·i·ty** \-,sek-shə-'wal-ət-ē\ *n*

ho·mo·spo·rous \,hō-mə-'spōr-əs, ,häm-ə-, -'spȯr-; hō-'mäs-pə-rəs\ *adj* **:** producing asexual spores of one kind only — **ho·mo·spo·ry** \'hō-mə-,spōr-ē, 'häm-ə-; hō-'mäs-pə-rē\ *n*

ho·mo·tax·i·al \,hō-mō-'tak-sē-əl, ,häm-ō-\ *adj* **:** of or relating to homotaxis

ho·mo·tax·is \-'tak-səs\ *n* [NL] **:** similarity in arrangement; *esp* **:** similarity in fossils and in order of arrangement of stratified deposits that are not necessarily contemporaneous

ho·mo·thal·lic \-'thal-ik\ *adj* [*hom-* + Gk *thallein* to sprout, grow — more at THALLUS] **1 :** having only one haploid phase producing genetically compatible gametes **2 :** MONOECIOUS — **ho·mo·thal·lism** \-'thal-,iz-əm\ *n*

ho·mo·trans·plant \,hō-mō-'tran(t)-,splant, ,häm-ō-\ *n* **:** HOMOGRAFT — **ho·mo·trans·plan·ta·tion** \-,tran(t)-,splan-'tā-shən\ *n*

ho·mo·zy·go·sis \-(,)zī-'gō-səs\ *n* [NL] **1 :** the union of gametes identical for one or more pairs of genes **2 :** the state of being a homozygote — **ho·mo·zy·gos·i·ty** \-'gäs-ət-ē\ *n* — **ho·mo·zy·got·ic** \-'gät-ik\ *adj*

ho·mo·zy·gote \-'zī-,gōt\ *n* [ISV] **:** an animal or plant containing either but not both members of at least one pair of allelomorphic characters — **ho·mo·zy·gous** \-gəs\ *adj* — **ho·mo·zy·gous·ly** *adv*

ho·mun·cu·lus \hō-'məŋ-kyə-ləs\ *n*, *pl* **ho·mun·cu·li** \-,lī, -,lē\ [L, dim. of *homin-*, *homo* man — more at HOMAGE] **:** a little man **:** MANIKIN

homy *var of* HOMEY

¹hone \'hōn\ *n* [ME, fr. OE *hān* stone; akin to ON *hein* whetstone, L *cot-*, *cos*, Gk *kōnos* cone] **1 :** a fine-grit stone for sharpening a cutting implement **2 :** a tool for enlarging holes to precise tolerances and controlling finishes by means of a mechanically rotated and expanded abrasive

²hone *vt* **1 :** to sharpen, enlarge, or smooth with a hone **2 :** to make more acute, intense, or effective **:** WHET — **hon·er** *n*

³hone *vi* [MF *hoigner* to grumble] **1** *dial* **:** GRUMBLE, MOAN **2** *dial* **:** YEARN

hon·est \'än-əst\ *adj* [ME, fr. OF *honeste*, fr. L *honestus* honorable, fr. *honos*, *honor* honor] **1 a :** free from deception **:** TRUTHFUL **b :** GENUINE, REAL **c :** HUMBLE, PLAIN **2 a :** REPUTABLE, RESPECTABLE **b** *chiefly Brit* **:** GOOD, WORTHY **3 :** CREDITABLE **4 a :** marked by integrity **:** UPRIGHT **b :** FRANK, SINCERE **c :** INNOCENT, SIMPLE

syn see UPRIGHT — **hon·est** *adv* — **hon·est·ly** *adv*

hon·es·ty \'än-ə-stē\ *n* **1** *obs* **:** CHASTITY **2 a :** fairness and straightforwardness of conduct **:** INTEGRITY **b :** adherence to the facts **:** SINCERITY **3 :** any of a genus (*Lunaria*) of European plants of the mustard family

syn HONESTY, HONOR, INTEGRITY, PROBITY mean uprightness of character or action. HONESTY implies a refusal to lie, steal, or deceive in any way; HONOR suggests an active or anxious regard for the standards of one's profession, calling, or position; INTEGRITY implies trustworthiness and incorruptibility to a degree that one is incapable of being false to a trust, responsibility, or pledge; PROBITY implies tried and proven honesty or integrity

¹hon·ey \'hən-ē\ *n* [ME *hony*, fr. OE *hunig*; akin to OHG *honag* honey, L *canicae* bran] **1 a :** a sweet viscid material elaborated out of the nectar of flowers in the honey sac of various bees **b :** a sweet fluid resembling honey that is collected or elaborated by various insects **2 a :** SWEETHEART, DEAR **b :** something superlative **3 :** SWEETNESS

²honey *vt* **hon·eyed** *also* **hon·ied; hon·ey·ing 1 :** to sweeten with or as if with honey **2 :** to speak ingratiatingly to **:** FLATTER ~ *vi* **:** to use blandishments or cajolery

³honey *adj* **1 :** of, relating to, or resembling honey **2** *archaic* **:** DEAR

hon·ey·bee \'hən-ē-,bē\ *n* **:** a social honey-producing bee (*Apis* or related genera); *esp* **:** a native European bee (*A. mellifera*) kept for its honey and wax

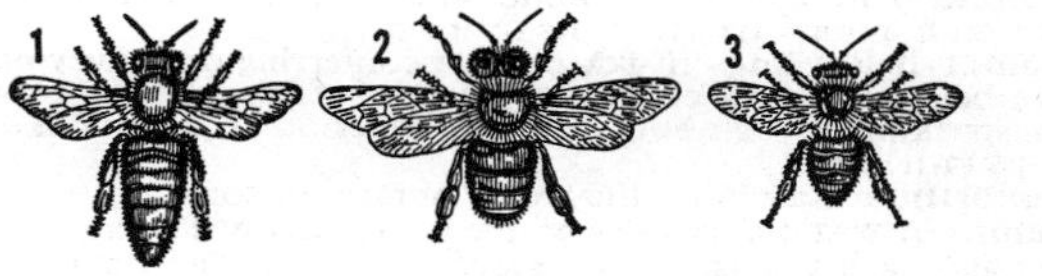

honeybees: *1* queen, *2* drone, *3* worker

¹hon·ey·comb \-,kōm\ *n* **1 :** a mass of hexagonal wax cells built by honeybees in their nest to contain brood and stores of honey **2 :** something that resembles a honeycomb in structure or appearance

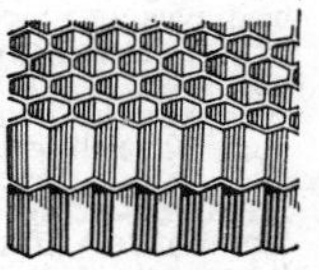

honeycomb 1

²honeycomb *vt* **1 :** to cause to be full of cavities like a honeycomb **2 :** SUBVERT, WEAKEN ~ *vi* **:** to become pitted, checked, or cellular

hon·ey·dew \-,d(y)ü\ *n* **:** a saccharine deposit secreted on the leaves of plants usu. by aphids or scales but sometimes by a fungus

honeydew melon *n* **:** a pale smooth-skinned muskmelon with greenish sweet flesh

honey eater *n* **:** any of several oscine birds (family Meliphagidae) mostly of the South Pacific with a long protrusible tongue adapted for extracting nectar and small insects from flowers

honey guide *n* **:** any of several small plainly colored nonpasserine birds (family Indicatoridae and esp. genera *Indicator* and *Prodotiscus*) that inhabit Africa, the Himalayas, and the East Indies and lead men or lower animals to the nests of bees

honey locust *n* **:** a tall usu. spiny No. American leguminous tree (*Gleditsia triacanthos*) with long twisted pods containing seeds resembling beans and separated by a sweet edible pulp and very hard durable wood

hon·ey·moon \'hən-ē-,mün\ *n*, *often attrib* [fr. the idea that the first month of marriage is the sweetest] **1 :** a trip or vacation taken by a newly married couple **2 :** a period of harmony immediately following marriage — **honeymoon** *vi* — **hon·ey·moon·er** *n*

hon·ey·suck·le \'hən-ē-,sək-əl\ *n* [ME *honysoukel*, alter. of *honysouke*, fr. OE *hunisūce*, fr. *hunig* honey + *sūcan* to suck] **:** any of a genus (*Lonicera*) of shrubs (family Caprifoliaceae, the honeysuckle family) with opposite leaves and often showy flowers rich in nectar; *broadly* **:** any of various plants (as a columbine or azalea) with tubular flowers rich in nectar

hong \'häŋ, 'hȯŋ\ *n* [Chin (Cant) *hōng*] **:** a commercial establishment or house of foreign trade in China

honk \'häŋk, 'hȯŋk\ *n* [imit.] **:** the cry of a goose or a similar sound — **honk** *vb* — **honk·er** *n*

hon·ky–tonk \'häŋ-kē-,täŋk, 'hȯŋ-kē-,tȯŋk\ *n* [origin unknown] **:** a cheap nightclub or dance hall **:** DIVE

¹hon·or *or chiefly Brit* **hon·our** \'än-ər\ *n* [ME, fr. OF *honor*, fr. L *honos*, *honor*] **1 a :** good name or public esteem **:** REPUTATION **b :** outward respect **:** RECOGNITION **2 :** PRIVILEGE **3 :** a person of superior standing ⟨if your *Honor* please⟩ — now used esp. as a title for a holder of high office **4 :** one whose worth brings respect or fame **:** CREDIT ⟨was an ~ to his profession⟩ **5 :** an evidence or symbol of distinction: as **a :** an exalted title or rank **b** (1) **:** BADGE, DECORATION (2) **:** a ceremonial rite or observance **c** *archaic* **:** a gesture of deference **:** BOW **d** *pl* **:** social courtesies or civilities extended by a host **e** *pl* (1) **:** an academic distinction conferred on a superior student (2) **:** a course of study for superior students supplementing or replacing a regular course **f :** an award in a contest or field of competition **6 :** CHASTITY, PURITY **7 a :** a keen sense of ethical conduct **:** INTEGRITY **b :** one's word given as a guarantee of performance **8 a** (1) **:** an ace, king, queen, jack, or ten (2) **:** the ace, king, queen, jack, or ten of the trump suit in bridge or any ace when the contract is no-trump (3) **:** the scoring value of honors held in bridge — usu. used in pl. **b :** the privilege of playing first from the tee in golf

syn HONOR, HOMAGE, REVERENCE, DEFERENCE, OBEISANCE mean respect and esteem shown to another. HONOR may apply to the recognition of one's title to great respect or to any expression of such recognition; HOMAGE adds the implication of accompanying praise; REVERENCE implies profound respect mingled with love, devotion, or awe; DEFERENCE implies a yielding or submitting to

another's judgment or preference out of respect or reverence; OBEISANCE implies a showing of honor or reverence by a gesture indicating humility or submission **syn** see in addition HONESTY

²**honor** *or chiefly Brit* **honour** *vt* **hon·or·ing** \-(ə-)riŋ\ **1 a :** to regard or treat with honor or respect **b :** to confer honor on **2 :** to live up to or fulfill the terms of; *specif* **:** to accept and pay when due ⟨~ a draft⟩ **3 :** to salute with a bow in square dancing — **hon·or·er** \'än-ər-ər\ *n*

¹**hon·or·able** *or chiefly Brit* **hon·our·able** \'än-(ə-)rə-bəl, 'än-ər-bəl\ *adj* **1 :** deserving of honor **2 :** performed or accompanied with marks of honor or respect **3 a :** of great renown **:** ILLUSTRIOUS **b :** entitled to honor — used as a title for the children of certain British noblemen and for various government officials **4 a :** doing credit to the possessor **b :** consistent with an untarnished reputation **5 :** characterized by integrity **:** ETHICAL **syn** see UPRIGHT — **hon·or·abil·i·ty** \,än-(ə-)rə-'bil-ət-ē\ *n* — **hon·or·able·ness** \'än-(ə-)rə-bəl-nəs, 'än-ər-bəl-\ *n* — **hon·or·ably** \-blē\ *adv*

²**honorable** *or chiefly Brit* **honourable** *n* **1 :** any of various members of British noble families **2 :** any of various officials to whom the title of Honorable is applied

hon·or·ar·i·ly \,än-ə-'rer-ə-lē\ *adv* **:** in an honorary manner

hon·o·rar·i·um \,än-ə-'rer-ē-əm\ *n, pl* **hon·o·rar·ia** \-ē-ə\ *also* **hon·o·rar·i·ums** [L, fr. neut. of *honorarius*] **:** a reward usu. for services on which custom or propriety forbids a price to be set

¹**hon·or·ary** \'än-ə-,rer-ē\ *adj* [L *honorarius*, fr. *honor*] **1 a :** having or conferring distinction **b :** COMMEMORATIVE **2 a :** conferred in recognition of achievement or service without the usual prerequisites or obligations **b :** UNPAID, VOLUNTARY **3 :** dependent on honor for fulfillment

²**honorary** *n* **1** *archaic* **:** HONORARIUM **2 :** an honorary society **3 :** an honorary degree or its recipient

¹**hon·or·if·ic** \,än-ə-'rif-ik\ *adj* **1 :** conferring or conveying honor **2 :** belonging to or constituting a class of grammatical forms used in speaking to or about a social superior — **hon·or·if·i·cal·ly** \-i-k(ə-)lē\ *adv*

²**honorific** *n* **:** an honorific word, phrase, or form

honors of war : courtesies granted a vanquished enemy

hooch \'hüch\ *n* [short for *hoochinoo* (a distilled liquor made by the Hoochinoo Indians)] *slang* **:** alcoholic liquor esp. when inferior or illicitly made or obtained

¹**hood** \'hu̇d\ *n* [ME, fr. OE *hōd;* akin to OHG *huot* head covering] **1 a** (1) **:** a flexible covering for the head and neck (2) **:** a protective covering for the head and face **b :** a covering for a hawk's head and eyes **c :** a covering for a horse's head; *also* **:** BLINDER **2 a :** an ornamental scarf worn over an academic gown that indicates by its color the wearer's college or university **b :** a color marking or crest on the head of an animal or an expansion of the head that suggests a hood **3 a :** something resembling a hood in form or use **b :** a cover for parts of mechanisms; *specif* **:** the movable metal covering over the engine of an automobile — **hood** *vt* — **hood·like** \-,līk\ *adj*

²**hood** \'hu̇d, 'hüd\ *n, slang* **:** HOODLUM

-hood \,hu̇d\ *n suffix* [ME *-hod*, fr. OE *-hād;* akin to OHG *-heit* state, condition, *heitar* bright, clear] **1 :** state **:** condition **:** quality **:** character ⟨boy*hood*⟩ ⟨hardi*hood*⟩ **2 :** instance of a (specified) state or quality ⟨false*hood*⟩ **3 :** individuals sharing a (specified) state or character ⟨brother*hood*⟩

hood·ed \'hu̇d-əd\ *adj* **1 :** having a hood **2 :** shaped like a hood ⟨~ spathes⟩ **3 a :** having the head conspicuously different in color from the rest of the body ⟨~ bird⟩ **b :** having a crest on the head that suggests a hood ⟨~ seals⟩ **c :** having the skin at each side of the neck capable of expansion by movements of the ribs ⟨~ cobra⟩ — **hood·ed·ness** *n*

hood·lum \'hüd-ləm, 'hu̇d-\ *n* [origin unknown] **1 :** THUG; *esp* **:** one who commits acts of violence **2 :** a young ruffian

hood·man–blind \,hu̇d-mən-'blīnd\ *n, archaic* **:** BLINDMAN'S BUFF

hoo·doo \'hüd-(,)ü\ *n* [of African origin; akin to Hausa *hu³'du³'ba¹* to arouse resentment] **1 :** VOODOO **2 :** something that brings bad luck **3 :** a natural column of rock in western No. America often in fantastic form — **hoodoo** *vt* — **hoo·doo·ism** \-,iz-əm\ *n*

hood·wink \'hu̇d-,wiŋk\ *vt* [¹*hood* + *wink*] **1** *archaic* **:** BLINDFOLD **2** *obs* **:** HIDE **3 :** to deceive by false appearance **:** impose upon — **hood·wink·er** *n*

hoo·ey \'hü-ē\ *n* [origin unknown] **:** NONSENSE

¹**hoof** \'hu̇f, 'hüf\ *n, pl* **hooves** \'hu̇vz, 'hüvz\ *or* **hoofs** [ME, fr. OE *hōf;* akin to OHG *huof* hoof, Skt *śapha*] **1 :** a curved covering of horn that protects the front of or encloses the ends of the digits of an ungulate mammal and that corresponds to a nail or claw **2 :** a hoofed foot esp. of a horse — **on the hoof** *of a meat animal* **:** LIVING

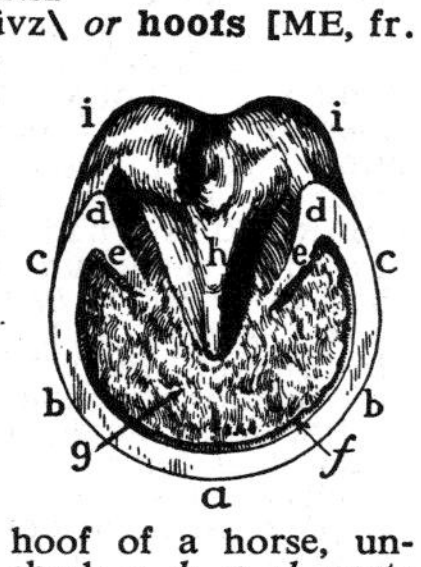

hoof of a horse, unshod: *a, b, c, d,* parts of wall (*a,* toe; *b, b,* side walls; *c, c,* quarters; *d, d,* buttresses); *e, e,* bars; *f,* white line; *g,* sole; *h,* frog; *i, i,* bulbs

²**hoof** *vt* **1 :** WALK **2 :** KICK, TRAMPLE ~ *vi* **:** to move on the feet; *specif* **:** DANCE

hoofed \'hu̇ft, 'hüft, 'hu̇vd, 'hüvd\ *adj* **:** furnished with hoofs **:** UNGULATE

hoof·er \'hu̇f-ər, 'hü-fər\ *n* **:** a professional dancer

¹**hook** \'hu̇k\ *n* [ME, fr. OE *hōc;* akin to MD *hoec* fishhook, corner, Lith *kengė* hook] **1 :** a curved or bent device for catching, holding, or pulling **2 :** something curved or bent like a hook **3 :** a flight of a ball that deviates from a straight course in a direction opposite to the dominant hand of the player propelling it **4 :** a short blow delivered with a circular motion by a boxer while the elbow remains bent and rigid — **by hook or by crook :** by any means — **off the hook :** out of trouble — **on one's own hook :** by oneself **:** INDEPENDENTLY

²**hook** *vt* **1 :** to form into a hook **:** CROOK **2 :** to seize, make fast, or connect by or as if by a hook **3 :** STEAL, PILFER **4 :** to strike or pierce as if with a hook **5 :** to make (as a rug) by drawing loops of yarn, thread, or cloth through a coarse fabric with a hook **6 :** to hit or throw (a ball) so that a hook results ~ *vi* **1 :** to form a hook **:** CURVE **2 :** to become hooked

hoo·kah \'hu̇k-ə, 'hü-kə\ *n* [Ar *ḥuqqah* bottle of a water pipe] **:** a pipe for smoking that has a long flexible tube whereby the smoke is cooled by passing through water

hook–bill \'hu̇k-,bil\ *n* **:** a bird of the parrot family

hooked \'hu̇kt, *1 is also* 'hu̇k-əd\ *adj* **1 :** having the form of a hook **2 :** provided with a hook **3 :** made by hooking **4** *slang* **:** addicted to narcotics — **hooked·ness** \'hu̇k(t)-nəs, 'hu̇k-əd-nəs\ *n*

¹**hook·er** \'hu̇k-ər\ *n* **:** one that hooks

²**hook·er** \'hu̇k-ər\ *n* [D *hoeker*, alter. of MD *hoecboot*, fr. *hoec* fishhook + *boot* boat] **1 :** a one-masted fishing boat used on the English and Irish coasts **2 :** an old, outmoded, or clumsy boat

hook·let \'hu̇k-lət\ *n* **:** a small hook

hook·up \'hu̇k-,əp\ *n* **1 :** an assemblage (as of circuits) used for a specific purpose (as radio transmission); *also* **:** the plan of such an assemblage **2 :** an arrangement of mechanical parts **3 :** connection often between antagonistic elements

hook·worm \'hu̇k-,wərm\ *n* **1 :** a parasitic nematode worm (family Ancylostomatidae) having strong buccal hooks or plates for attaching to the host's intestinal lining and including serious bloodsucking pests **2 :** ANCYLOSTOMIASIS

hooky *or* **hookey** \'hu̇k-ē\ *n* [prob. fr. slang *hook, hook it* (to make off)] **:** TRUANT — used chiefly in the phrase *play hooky*

hoo·li·gan \'hü-li-gən\ *n* [perh. fr. Patrick *Hooligan fl*1898 Irish hoodlum in Southwark, London] **:** RUFFIAN, HOODLUM — **hoo·li·gan·ism** \-gə-,niz-əm\ *n*

¹**hoop** \'hu̇p, 'hüp\ *n, often attrib* [ME, fr. OE *hōp;* akin to MD *hoep* ring, hoop, Lith *kabė* hook] **1 :** a circular strip used esp. for holding together the staves of containers or as a plaything **2 :** a circular figure or object **:** RING **3 :** a circle or series of circles of flexible material used to expand a woman's skirt

²**hoop** *vt* **:** to bind or fasten with or as if with a hoop — **hoop·er** *n*

hoop·la \'hü-,plä, 'hu̇p-,lä\ *n* [F *houp-là*, interj.] **1 :** often gay and excited commotion **:** TO-DO **2 :** utterances designed to bewilder

hoo·poe \'hü-(,)pü, -(,)pō\ *n* [alter. of obs. *hoop*, fr. MF *huppe*, fr. L *upupa*, of imit. origin] **:** any of several Old World nonpasserine birds (family Upupidae) having a slender decurved bill

hoop·skirt \'hu̇p-'skərt, 'hüp-\ *n* **:** a skirt stiffened with hoops

hoo·ray \hu̇-'rā\ *var of* HURRAH

hoose·gow \'hüs-,gau̇\ *n* [Sp *juzgado* panel of judges, courtroom, fr. pp. of *juzgar* to judge, fr. L *judicare*] *slang* **:** JAIL

Hoo·sier \'hü-zhər\ *n* [perh. alter. of E dial. *hoozer* anything large of its kind] **:** a native or resident of Indiana — used as a nickname — **Hoosier** *adj*

¹**hoot** \'hüt\ *vb* [ME *houten*, of imit. origin] *vi* **1 :** to utter a loud shout usu. in contempt **2 :** to make the natural throat noise of an owl or a similar cry **3 :** to make a loud clamorous mechanical sound ~ *vt* **1 :** to assail or drive out by hooting **2 :** to express in or by hoots — **hoot·er** *n*

²**hoot** *n* **1 :** a sound of hooting; *esp* **:** the cry of an owl **2 :** a very small amount

³**hoot** \'hüt\ *or* **hoots** \'hüts\ *interj* [origin unknown] *chiefly Scot* — used to express impatience, dissatisfaction, or objection

hoo·te·nan·ny \'hüt-ᵊn-,an-ē\ *n* [origin unknown] **1** *chiefly dial* **:** GADGET **2 :** a gathering at which folk singers entertain often with the audience joining in

¹**hop** \'häp\ *vb* **hopped; hop·ping** [ME *hoppen*, fr. OE *hoppian;* akin to OE *hype* hip] *vi* **1 :** to move by a quick springy leap or in a series of leaps; *esp* **:** to jump on one foot **2 :** to make a quick trip esp. by air ~ *vt* **1 :** to jump over **2 :** to ride upon esp. gratis

²**hop** *n* **1 a :** a short brisk leap esp. on one leg **b :** BOUNCE, REBOUND **2 :** DANCE, BALL **3 a :** a flight in an aircraft **b :** a short trip **c :** a free ride

³**hop** *n* [ME *hoppe*, fr. MD; akin to OHG *hopfo* hop, OE *scēaf* sheaf — more at SHEAF] **1 :** a twining vine (*Humulus lupulus*) of the mulberry family with 3-lobed or 5-lobed leaves and inconspicuous flowers of which the pistillate ones are in glandular cone-shaped catkins **2** *pl* **:** the ripe dried pistillate catkins of a hop used esp. to impart a bitter flavor to malt liquors **3** *slang* **:** a narcotic drug; *esp* **:** OPIUM

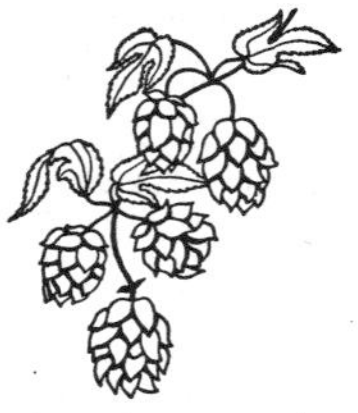
hop, leaves and strobiles

⁴**hop** *vt* **hopped; hop·ping 1 :** to impregnate with hops **2 :** DOPE **3 :** to increase the power of beyond an original rating

¹**hope** \'hōp\ *vb* [ME *hopen*, fr. OE *hopian;* akin to MHG *hoffen* to hope] *vi* **1 :** to desire with expectation of fulfillment **2** *archaic* **:** TRUST ~ *vt* **1 :** to long for with expectation of obtainment **2 :** to expect with desire **:** TRUST **syn** see EXPECT — **hop·er** *n*

²**hope** *n* **1 :** TRUST, RELIANCE **2 a :** desire accompanied by expectation of or belief in fulfillment **b :** someone or something on which hopes are centered **c :** something hoped for

hope chest *n* **:** a young woman's accumulation of clothes and domestic furnishings (as silver, linen) kept in anticipation of her marriage; *also* **:** a chest for such an accumulation

¹**hope·ful** \'hōp-fəl\ *adj* **1 :** full of or inclined to hope **2 :** having qualities which inspire hope — **hope·ful·ly** \-fə-lē\ *adv* — **hope·ful·ness** *n*

²**hopeful** *n* **:** a person who aspires hopefully ⟨political ~*s*⟩

hope·less \'hō-pləs\ *adj* **1 a :** having no expectation of good or success **:** DESPAIRING **b :** not susceptible of remedy or cure **:** INCURABLE **2 a :** giving no ground for hope **:** DESPERATE **b :** incapable of solution, management, or accomplishment **:** IMPOSSIBLE **syn** see DESPONDENT — **hope·less·ly** *adv* — **hope·less·ness** *n*

hop·head \'häp-,hed\ *n, slang* **:** a drug addict

Ho·pi \'hō-pē\ *n, pl* **Hopi** *also* **Hopis** [Hopi *Hópi*, lit., good, peaceful] **1 a :** a Shoshonean people of Pueblo Indians in northeastern Arizona **b :** a member of this people **2 :** the language of the Hopi people

hop·lite \'häp-,līt\ *n* [Gk *hoplitēs*, fr. *hoplon* tool, weapon, fr. *hepein* to care for, work at — more at SEPULCHER] **:** a heavily armed infantry soldier of ancient Greece

hop–o'–my–thumb \,häp-ə-mə-'thəm\ *n* **:** a very small person

hop·per \'häp-ər\ *n* **1 a :** one that hops **b :** a leaping insect; *specif* **:** an immature hopping form of an insect **2** [fr. the shaking motion of hoppers used to feed grain into a mill] **a :** a usu. funnel-shaped receptacle for delivering material (as grain or coal) **b :** a box in which a bill to be considered by a legislative body is dropped **c :** a tank holding liquid and having a device for releasing its contents through a pipe

hop·scotch \'häp-,skäch\ *n* **:** a child's game in which a player tosses a stone or similar object consecutively into areas of a figure

outlined on the ground and hops through the figure and back to regain the object

ho·ra also **ho·rah** \'hȯr-ə, 'hȯr-ə\ n [NHeb *hōrāh*, fr. Romanian *horă*] : a circle dance of Romania and Israel

Ho·rae \'hō-(ə)r-,ē, 'hȯ(ə)r-, -,ī\ n pl [L, fr. Gk *Hōrai*] : the goddesses of the seasons in Greek mythology

ho·ra·ry \'hōr-ə-rē, 'hȯr-, 'här-\ adj [ML *horarius*, fr. L *hora* hour — more at HOUR] : of or relating to an hour; also : HOURLY

Ho·ra·tian \hə-'rā-shən\ adj [L *Horatianus*, fr. *Horatius* Horace] : of, relating to, or characteristic of Horace or his poetry

Ho·ra·tius \hə-'rā-sh(ē-)əs\ n [L] : a hero in Roman legend noted for his defense of a bridge over the Tiber against the Etruscans

horde \'hō(ə)rd, 'hȯ(ə)rd\ n [MF, G & Pol; MF & G, fr. Pol *horda*, of Mongolic origin; akin to Mongolian *orda* camp, horde] **1 a** : a tribal group of Mongolian nomads **b** : a people or tribe of nomadic life **2** : THRONG, SWARM syn see CROWD

hore·hound \'hō(ə)r-,haùnd, 'hȯ(ə)r-\ n [ME *horhoune*, fr. OE *hārhūne*, fr. *hār* hoary + *hūne* horehound — more at HOAR] **1 a** : a bitter mint (*Marrubium vulgare*) with hoary downy leaves **b** : an extract or confection made from this plant **2** : any of several mints resembling the horehound

ho·ri·zon \hə-'rīz-ᵊn\ n [ME *orizon*, fr. LL *horizont-, horizon*, fr. Gk *horizont-, horizōn*, fr. prp. of *horizein* to bound, define, fr. *horos* boundary; akin to L *urvus* circumference of a city] **1 a** : the apparent junction of earth and sky — called also *apparent horizon, visible horizon* **b** (1) : the plane tangent to the earth's surface at an observer's position — called also *sensible horizon* (2) : the plane parallel to the sensible horizon but passing through the earth's center; also : the great circle formed by the intersection of this plane with the celestial sphere — called also *celestial horizon, rational horizon* **c** : a level mirror (as the surface of mercury in a shallow vessel or a plane reflector adjusted to the true level artificially) used esp. in observing altitudes **d** : range of perception or experience **2 a** : the geological deposit of a particular time usu. identified by distinctive fossils **b** : any of the reasonably distinct layers of soil or its underlying material in a vertical section of land **c** : a cultural area or level of development indicated by separated groups of artifacts — **ho·ri·zon·al** \-'rīz-nəl, -ᵊn-əl\ adj

hor·i·zon·tal \,hȯr-ə-'zänt-ᵊl, ,här-\ adj **1 a** : of, relating to, or situated near the horizon **b** : parallel to, in the plane of, or operating in a plane parallel to the horizon or to a base line : LEVEL 〈~ distance〉 〈~ engine〉 **2** : relating to or consisting of individuals of similar status in a hierarchy 〈~ labor unions〉 — **horizontal** n — **hor·i·zon·tal·ly** \-ᵊl-ē\ adv

hor·mon·al \hȯr-'mōn-ᵊl\ adj : of, relating to, or effected by hormones — **hor·mon·al·ly** \-ᵊl-ē\ adv

hor·mone \'hȯr-,mōn\ n [Gk *hormōn*, prp. of *horman* to stir up, fr. *hormē* impulse, assault — more at SERUM] **1** : a product of living cells that circulates in body fluids or sap and produces a specific effect on the activity of cells remote from its point of origin; esp : one exerting a stimulatory effect on a cellular activity **2** : a synthetic substance that acts like a hormone

hor·mo·noid \-mə-,nȯid\ adj : resembling a hormone

horn \'hȯ(ə)rn\ n, often attrib [ME, fr. OE; akin to OHG *horn*, L *cornu*, Gk *keras*] **1 a** (1) : one of the paired bony processes that arise from the upper part of the head of many ungulate mammals, that function chiefly as weapons, and that in cattle and related forms are usu. present in both sexes and are unbranched and permanent with a bony core anchored to the skull and a sheath of horn and in deer are solid deciduous bony outgrowths usu. branching and usu. present only in the male (2) : a part like an animal's horn attributed esp. to the devil **b** : a natural projection or excrescence from an animal resembling or suggestive of a horn **c** (1) : the tough fibrous material consisting chiefly of keratin that covers or forms the horns of cattle and related animals, hooves, or other horny parts (as claws or nails) (2) : a manufactured product (as a plastic) resembling horn **d** : a hollow horn used to hold something **2** : something resembling or suggestive of a horn: as **a** : one of the curved ends of a crescent **b** : a sharp mountain peak **c** : a beak-shaped part of an anvil **d** : a high pommel of a saddle **3 a** : an animal's horn used as a wind instrument **b** : a brass wind instrument; specif : FRENCH HORN **c** : a usu. electrical device that makes a noise like that of a horn **4** : a source of strength — **horn·less** \-ləs\ adj — **horn·less·ness** n — **horn·like** \-,līk\ adj

horn·beam \-,bēm\ n : any of a genus (*Carpinus*) of trees of the birch family having smooth gray bark and hard white wood

horn·bill \-,bil\ n : any of a family (Bucerotidae) of large nonpasserine Old World birds having enormous bills

horn·blende \-,blend\ n [G] : a mineral approximately Ca_2Na-$(Mg,Fe)_4(Al,Fe,Ti)_3Si_6O_{22}(O,OH)_2$ that is the common dark variety of aluminous amphibole; broadly : AMPHIBOLE — **horn·blend·ic** \-,blen-dik\ adj

horn·book \-,bùk\ n **1** : a child's primer consisting of a sheet of parchment or paper protected by a sheet of transparent horn **2** : a rudimentary treatise

horned \'hȯ(ə)rnd\ adj : having a horn — often used in combination — **horned·ness** \'hȯr-nəd-nəs, 'hȯ(ə)rn(d)-nəs\ n

horned pout n : a bullhead (genus *Ameiurus*); esp : a common bullhead (*A. nebulosus*) of the eastern U.S. that has been introduced into streams of the Pacific coast

horned toad n : any of several small harmless insectivorous lizards (genus *Phrynosoma*) of the western U.S. and Mexico having hornlike spines

hor·net \'hȯr-nət\ n [ME *hernet*, fr. OE *hyrnet*; akin to OHG *hornaz* hornet, L *crabro*] : any of the larger social wasps (family Vespidae) — compare YELLOW JACKET

horn in vi : to participate without invitation or consent : INTRUDE

hor·ni·to \(h)ȯr-'nēt-(,)ō\ n [Sp] : a low dome-shaped mound in volcanic regions that emits smoke and vapors

horn-mad \'hȯ(ə)rn-'mad\ adj : furiously enraged

horn of plenty : CORNUCOPIA

horn·pipe \'hȯ(ə)rn-,pīp\ n **1** : a single reed wind instrument consisting of a wooden or bone pipe with holes at intervals and a bell and mouthpiece usu. of horn **2** : a lively folk dance of the British Isles orig. accompanied by hornpipe playing

horn·stone \-,stōn\ n : a mineral that is a variety of quartz much like flint but more brittle

horn·swog·gle \-,swäg-əl\ vt **horn·swog·gling** \-(ə-)liŋ\ [origin unknown] slang : BAMBOOZLE, HOAX

horn·tail \-,tāl\ n : any of various hymenopterous insects (family Siricidae) related to the typical sawflies but having larvae that burrow in woody plants and on the females a stout hornlike ovipositor for depositing the egg

horn·worm \-,wərm\ n : a hawkmoth caterpillar having a hornlike tail process

horny \'hȯr-nē\ adj **1 a** : of or made of horn **b** : HARD, CALLOUS 〈*horny*-handed〉 **c** : compact and homogeneous with a dull luster — used of a mineral **2** : having horns

hor·o·loge \'hȯr-ə-,lōj, 'här-\ n [ME, fr. MF, fr. L *horologium*, fr. Gk *hōrologion*, fr. *hōra* hour + *legein* to gather — more at YEAR, LEGEND] : a timekeeping device

ho·rol·o·ger \hə-'räl-ə-jər\ n : HOROLOGIST

ho·ro·log·ic \,hȯr-ə-'läj-ik, ,här-\ adj : of or relating to a horologe or horology — **ho·ro·log·i·cal** \-i-kəl\ adj

ho·rol·o·gist \hə-'räl-ə-jəst\ n **1** : a person skilled in the practice or theory of horology **2** : a maker of clocks or watches

ho·rol·o·gy \-jē\ n [Gk *hōra* + E -*logy*] **1** : the science of measuring time **2** : the art of constructing instruments for indicating time

horo·scope \'hȯr-ə-,skōp, 'här-\ n [MF, fr. L *horoscopus*, fr. Gk *hōroskopos*, fr. *hōra* + *skopein* to look at — more at SPY] : a diagram of the relative positions of planets and signs of the zodiac at a specific time for use by astrologers in foretelling events of a person's life

hor·ren·dous \hȯ-'ren-dəs, hä-\ adj [L *horrendus*, fr. gerundive of *horrēre*] : DREADFUL, HORRIBLE — **hor·ren·dous·ly** adv

hor·rent \'hȯr-ənt, 'här-\ adj [L *horrent-, horrens*, prp. of *horrēre*] **1** archaic : BRISTLED **2** archaic : BRISTLING

hor·ri·ble \'hȯr-ə-bəl, 'här-\ adj **1** : marked by or conducive to horror **2** : extremely unpleasant or disagreeable — **horrible** n — **hor·ri·ble·ness** n — **hor·ri·bly** \-blē\ adv

hor·rid \'hȯr-əd, 'här-\ adj [L *horridus*, fr. *horrēre*] **1** archaic : ROUGH, BRISTLING **2 a** : HIDEOUS, SHOCKING **b** : REPULSIVE, OFFENSIVE — **hor·rid·ly** adv — **hor·rid·ness** n

hor·rif·ic \hȯ-'rif-ik, hä-\ adj : HORRIFYING, HORRIBLE

hor·ri·fy \'hȯr-ə-,fī, 'här-\ vt : to cause to feel horror syn see DISMAY

hor·ror \'hȯr-ər, 'här-\ n, often attrib [ME *horrour*, fr. MF *horror*, fr. L, action of trembling, fr. *horrēre* to tremble; akin to OE *gorst* gorse, Gk *chersos* dry land] **1 a** : painful and intense fear, dread, or dismay : CONSTERNATION **b** : intense aversion or repugnance **2 a** : the quality of inspiring horror **b** : something that inspires horror **3** pl : a state of extreme depression or apprehension

hors de com·bat \,ȯrd-ə-(,)kōⁿ-'bä\ adv (or adj) [F] : out of combat : DISABLED

hors d'oeuvre \ȯr-'dərv\ n, pl **hors d'oeuvres** also **hors d'oeuvre** \-'dərv(z)\ [F *hors-d'œuvre*, lit., outside of work] : any of various savory foods usu. served as appetizers

¹horse \'hȯ(ə)rs\ n, pl **hors·es** also **horse** [ME *hors*, fr. OE; akin

horse 1a: *1* mouth, *2* nose, *3* nostril, *4* face, *5* forehead, *6* forelock, *7* ear, *8* poll, *9* mane, *10* withers, *11* ribs, *12* flank, *13* loin, *14* haunch, *15* croup, *16* tail, *17* thigh, *18* buttock, *19, 19* fetlocks, *20, 20* hooves, *21, 21* coronets, *22, 22* pasterns, *23, 23* cannons, *24* hock, *25* gaskin, *26* stifle, *27* belly, *28* knee, *29* forearm, *30* elbow, *31* shoulder, *32* breast, *33* neck, *34* throatlatch, *35* lower jaw, *36* cheek

to OHG *hros* horse] **1 a** : a large solid-hoofed herbivorous mammal (*Equus caballus*, family Equidae, the horse family) domesticated by man since a prehistoric period and used as a beast of burden, a draft animal, or for riding — compare PONY **b** : a male horse : STALLION; also : a gelding as distinguished from an entire male **c** : a recent or extinct animal of the horse family **2 a** : JACKSTAY 1 **b** : a frame usu. with legs used for supporting something **c** : a gymnastic apparatus shaped something like the body of a small horse **3** horse pl : CAVALRY **4** : a mass of the same geological character as the wall rock occurring within a vein **5** : HORSEPOWER — **from the horse's mouth** : from the original source

²horse vt **1** : to provide with a horse **2** : to move by brute force ~ vi **1** : to be in heat **2** : to engage in horseplay

³horse adj **1 a** : of or relating to a horse **b** : worked by horsepower **2** : large or coarse of its kind **3** : mounted on horses

¹horse·back \'hȯrs-,bak\ n **1** : the back of a horse **2** : a natural ridge : HOGBACK

²horseback adv : on horseback

horse·car \-,kär\ n **1** : a streetcar drawn by horses **2** : a car fitted for transporting horses

horse chestnut n **1** : a large Asiatic tree (*Aesculus hippocastanum* of the family Hippocastanaceae, the horse-chestnut family) widely cultivated as an ornamental and shade tree and naturalized as an escape; also : BUCKEYE **2** : the large glossy brown seed of a horse chestnut

horse coper *n, Brit* : a horse dealer
horse·flesh \'hȯrs-ˌflesh\ *n* : horses for riding, driving, or racing
horse·fly \-ˌflī\ *n* : any of a family (Tabanidae) of swift usu. large two-winged flies with bloodsucking females
horse·hair \-ˌha(ə)r, -ˌhe(ə)r\ *n* **1** : the hair of a horse esp. from the mane or tail **2** : cloth made from horsehair
horse·hide \-ˌhīd\ *n* **1** : the dressed or raw hide of a horse **2** : the ball used in the game of baseball
horse latitudes *n pl* : either of two belts or regions in the neighborhood of 30° N and 30° S latitude characterized by high pressure, calms, and light baffling winds
horse·laugh \'hȯr-ˌslaf, -ˌslȧf\ *n* : a loud boisterous laugh : GUFFAW
horse·less carriage \ˌhȯr-slə-'skar-ij\ *n* : AUTOMOBILE
horse mackerel *n* **1** : any of several large scombroid fishes (as a bluefin tuna) **2** : any of various large fishes (family Carangidae); *esp* : a large Atlantic food fish (*Trachurus trachurus*)
horse·man \'hȯr-smən\ *n* **1 a** : a rider on horseback **b** : one skilled in managing horses **2** : a breeder or raiser of horses — **horse·man·ship** \-ˌship\ *n* — **horse·wom·an** \-ˌwu̇m-ən\ *n*
horse·mint \'hȯr-ˌsmint\ *n* : any of various coarse mints; *esp* : MONARDA
horse nettle *n* : a coarse prickly weed (*Solanum carolinense*) of the nightshade family with bright yellow fruit resembling berries
horse opera *n* : a motion picture or radio or television play usu. about western cowboys
horse·play \'hȯr-ˌsplā\ *n* : rough or boisterous play
horse·pow·er \'hȯr-ˌspau̇(-ə)r\ *n* : a unit of power equal in the U.S. to 746 watts and nearly equivalent to the English gravitational unit of the same name that equals 550 foot-pounds of work per second
horsepower–hour *n* : the work performed or energy consumed by working at the rate of one horsepower for one hour that is equal to 1,980,000 foot-pounds
horse·rad·ish \'hȯrs-ˌrad-ish, -ˌred-\ *n* : a tall coarse white-flowered herb (*Armoracia lapathifolia*) of the mustard family; *also* : its pungent root used as a condiment
horse sense *n* : COMMON SENSE
horse·shoe \'hȯrs(h)-ˌshü\ *n* **1** : a shoe for horses usu. consisting of a narrow plate of iron shaped to fit the rim of a horse's hoof **2** : something (as a valley) shaped like a horseshoe **3** *pl* : a game like quoits played with horseshoes or with horseshoe-shaped pieces of metal — **horseshoe** *vt* — **horse·sho·er** \-ˌshü-ər\ *n*

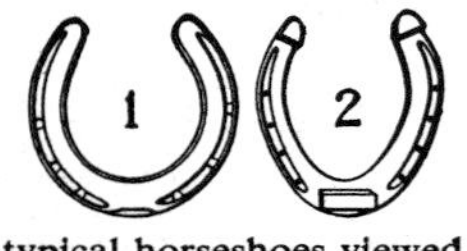

typical horseshoes viewed from below: *1* plain shoe, *2* shoe with toe and heel calks

horseshoe arch *n* — see ARCH illustration
horseshoe crab *n* : KING CRAB 1
horse·tail \'hȯr-ˌstāl\ *n* : any of a genus (*Equisetum*) of perennial flowerless plants related to the ferns — called also *scouring rush*
horse trade *n* : negotiation accompanied by shrewd bargaining and reciprocal concessions — **horse–trade** \'hȯr-ˌstrād\ *vi* — **horse trader** *n*
horse·weed \'hȯr-ˌswēd\ *n* **1** : a common No. American composite weed (*Erigeron canadense*) with linear leaves and small discoid heads of yellowish flowers **2** : a coarse annual ragweed (*Ambrosia trifida*) **3** : a wild lettuce
horse·whip \'hȯrs-ˌhwip, 'hȯr-ˌswip\ *vt* : to flog with or as if with a whip made to be used on a horse — **horse·whip·per** *n*
hors·ey *or* **horsy** \'hȯr-sē\ *adj* **hors·i·er**; **hors·i·est 1** : relating to, resembling, or suggestive of a horse **2 a** : having to do with horses or horse racing **b** : characteristic of horsemen — **hors·i·ly** \-sə-lē\ *adv* — **hors·i·ness** \-sē-nəs\ *n*
horst \'hȯ(ə)rst\ *n* [G] : a block of the earth's crust separated by faults from adjacent relatively depressed blocks
hor·ta·tive \'hȯrt-ət-iv\ *adj* [LL *hortativus*, fr. L *hortatus*, pp. of *hortari* to urge — more at YEARN] : giving exhortation : ADVISORY — **hor·ta·tive·ly** *adv*
hor·ta·to·ry \'hȯrt-ə-ˌtōr-ē, -ˌtȯr-\ *adj* : HORTATIVE, EXHORTATORY
hor·ti·cul·tur·al \ˌhȯrt-ə-'kəlch-(ə-)rəl\ *adj* : of, relating to, or produced by horticulture — **hor·ti·cul·tur·al·ly** \-ē\ *adv*
hor·ti·cul·ture \'hȯrt-ə-ˌkəl-chər\ *n* [L *hortus* garden + E *-i-* + *culture* — more at YARD] : the science and art of growing fruits, vegetables, flowers, or ornamental plants — **hor·ti·cul·tur·ist** \ˌhȯrt-ə-'kəlch-(ə-)rəst\ *n*
ho·san·na \hō-'zan-ə\ *interj* [ME *osanna*, fr. LL, fr. Gk *hōsanna*, fr. Heb *hōshī'āh-nnā* pray, save (us)!] — used as a cry of acclamation and adoration
¹hose \'hōz\ *n, pl* **hose** *or* **hos·es** [ME, fr. OE *hosa* stocking, husk; akin to OHG *hosa* leg covering, Gk *kystis* bladder, OE *hȳd* hide] **1** *pl* **hose a** (1) : a cloth leg covering that sometimes covers the foot (2) : STOCKING, SOCK **b** (1) : a close-fitting garment covering the legs and waist that is usu. attached to a doublet by points (2) : short breeches reaching to the knee **2** : a flexible tube for conveying fluids (as from a faucet or hydrant)
²hose *vt* : to spray, water, or wash with a hose
Ho·sea \hō-'zē-ə, -'zā-\ *n* [Heb *Hōshēa'*] : a Hebrew prophet of the 8th century B.C.
ho·sel \'hü-zəl\ *n* [¹*hose*] : a socket in the head of a golf club into which the shaft is inserted
ho·siery \'hōzh-(ə-)rē, 'hōz(-ə)-\ *n* **1** : HOSE 1a **2** *chiefly Brit* : KNITWEAR
hos·pice \'häs-pəs\ *n* [F, fr. L *hospitium*, fr. *hospit-, hospes*] : a lodging for travelers or for young persons or the underprivileged esp. when maintained by a religious order
hos·pi·ta·ble \hä-'spit-ə-bəl, 'häs-(ˌ)pit-\ *adj* **1 a** : given to generous and cordial reception of guests **b** : promising or suggesting generous and cordial welcome **c** : offering a pleasant or sustaining environment **2** : readily receptive : OPEN ⟨~ to new ideas⟩ — **hos·pi·ta·bly** \-blē\ *adv*
hos·pi·tal \'häs-ˌpit-ᵊl\ *n* [ME, fr. OF, fr. ML *hospitale*, fr. LL, hospice, fr. L, guest room, fr. neut. of *hospitalis* of a guest, fr. *hospit-, hospes*] **1** : a charitable institution for the needy, aged, infirm, or young **2** : an institution where the sick or injured are given medical or surgical care **3** : a repair shop for specified small objects ⟨clock ~⟩
Hos·pi·tal·er *or* **Hos·pi·tal·ler** \-ᵊl-ər\ *n* [ME *hospitalier*, fr. MF, fr. ML *hospitalarius*, fr. LL *hospitale*] : a member of a religious military order established in Jerusalem in the 12th century
hos·pi·tal·i·ty \ˌhäs-pə-'tal-ət-ē\ *n* : hospitable treatment, reception, or disposition
hos·pi·tal·iza·tion \ˌhäs-ˌpit-ᵊl-ə-'zā-shən\ *n* : the condition of being hospitalized; *also* : the period of such condition
hos·pi·tal·ize \'häs-ˌpit-ᵊl-ˌīz\ *vt* : to place in a hospital as a patient
¹host \'hōst\ *n* [ME, fr. OF, fr. LL *hostis*, fr. L, stranger, enemy — more at GUEST] **1** : ARMY **2** : a very large number : MULTITUDE
²host *n* [ME *hoste* host, guest, fr. OF, fr. L *hospit-, hospes*, fr. *hostis*] **1** : one who receives or entertains guests socially or commercially **2 a** : a living animal or plant affording subsistence or lodgment to a parasite **b** : the larger, stronger, or dominant member of a commensal or symbiotic pair — **host** *vt* — **host·al** \-ᵊl\ *adj*
³host *n, often cap* [ME *hoste*, fr. MF *hoiste*, fr. LL & L; LL *hostia* Eucharist, fr. L, sacrifice] : the eucharistic bread
hos·tage \'häs-tij\ *n* [ME, fr. OF, fr. *hoste*] : a person kept as a pledge pending the fulfillment of an agreement
hos·tel \'häst-ᵊl\ *n* [ME, fr. OF, fr. LL *hospitale* hospice] **1** : INN **2** : a supervised lodging for use by youth esp. on bicycling trips — called also *youth hostel*
hos·tel·er \'häs-tə-lər\ *n* **1** : one that lodges guests or strangers **2** : a young traveler who stops at hostels overnight
hos·tel·ry \'häst-ᵊl-rē\ *n* : INN, HOTEL
host·ess \'hō-stəs\ *n* : a female host
hos·tile \'häst-ᵊl, 'häs-ˌtīl\ *adj* [MF or L; MF, fr. L *hostilis*, fr. *hostis*] **1** : of or relating to an enemy **2** : marked by esp. overt antagonism **3** : not hospitable — **hostile** *n* — **hos·tile·ly** \-ᵊl-(l)ē, -ˌtīl-lē\ *adv*
hos·til·i·ty \hä-'stil-ət-ē\ *n* **1 a** : a hostile state **b** (1) : hostile action (2) *pl* : overt acts of warfare : WAR **2** : antagonism, opposition, or resistance in thought or principle **syn** see ENMITY
hos·tler \'(h)äs-lər\ *n* [ME, innkeeper, hostler, fr. *hostel*] **1** : one who takes care of horses or mules **2** : one who services a vehicle (as a locomotive or truck) or machine (as a crane)
¹hot \'hät\ *adj* **hot·ter**; **hot·test** [ME, fr. OE *hāt*; akin to OHG *heiz* hot, Lith *kaīsti* to get hot] **1 a** : having a relatively high temperature **b** : capable of giving a sensation of heat or of burning, searing, or scalding **c** : having heat in a degree exceeding normal body heat **2 a** : ARDENT, FIERY ⟨~ temper⟩ **b** : VIOLENT, RAGING **c** : LUSTFUL, LECHEROUS **d** : EAGER ⟨~ for reform⟩ **e** *of jazz* : ecstatic and emotionally exciting and marked by strong rhythms and free melodic improvisations **3** : having or causing the sensation of an uncomfortable degree of body heat **4** : newly made : FRESH ⟨~ scent⟩; *also* : close to something sought **5 a** : suggestive of heat or of burning or glowing objects **b** : PUNGENT, PEPPERY **6 a** : unusually lucky or favorable **b** : temporarily capable of unusual performance **c** : currently popular **d** (1) — used as a generalized term of approval (2) : ABSURD, UNBELIEVABLE **7 a** : electrically energized esp. with high voltage **b** : RADIOACTIVE; *also* : dealing with radioactive material **c** *of a vehicle* : FAST **8 a** : recently and illegally obtained **b** : wanted by the police; *also* : unsafe for a fugitive — **hot·ly** *adv* — **hot·ness** *n*
²hot *adv* : HOTLY
hot air *n* : empty talk
hot·bed \'hät-ˌbed\ *n* **1** : a bed of soil enclosed in glass, heated esp. by fermenting manure, and used for forcing or for raising seedlings **2** : an environment that favors rapid growth or development
hot·blood \-ˌbləd\ *n* : THOROUGHBRED 1
hot–blood·ed \-'bləd-əd\ *adj* **1** : EXCITABLE, ARDENT **2 a** *of a horse* : having Arab or Thoroughbred ancestors **b** *of livestock* : of pure or superior breeding — **hot–blood·ed·ness** *n*
hot·box \-ˌbäks\ *n* : a journal bearing (as of a railroad car) overheated by friction
hotch \'häch\ *vi* [prob. fr. MF *hocher* to shake, fr. OF *hochier*] *Scot* : WIGGLE, FIDGET
hotch·pot \-ˌpät\ *n* [AF *hochepot*, fr. OF, hotchpotch] : the combining of properties into a common lot to ensure equality of division among heirs
hotch·potch \-ˌpäch\ *n* [ME *hochepot*, fr. MF, fr. OF, fr. *hochier* to shake + *pot*] **1 a** : a stew of various ingredients **b** : HODGEPODGE **2** : HOTCHPOT
hot dog \'hät-ˌdȯg\ *n* : a cooked frankfurter usu. served in a long split roll
ho·tel \hō-'tel\ *n* [F *hôtel*, fr. OF *hostel*] : a house that provides lodging and usu. meals, entertainment, and various personal services for the public : INN
Hotel — a communications code word for the letter *h*
hot flash *n* : a sudden brief flushing and sensation of heat caused by dilation of skin capillaries usu. associated with menopausal endocrine imbalance
¹hot·foot \'hät-ˌfu̇t\ *adv* : in haste
²hotfoot *vi* : to go hotfoot : HURRY — used with *it*
³hotfoot *n, pl* **hotfoots** : the surreptitious insertion of a match into the side of a victim's shoe and lighting it
hot·head \'hät-ˌhed\ *n* : a hotheaded person
hot·head·ed \-'hed-əd\ *adj* : FIERY, HASTY, IMPETUOUS — **hot·head·ed·ly** *adv* — **hot·head·ed·ness** *n*
¹hot·house \'hät-ˌhau̇s\ *n* **1** *obs* : BROTHEL **2** : a greenhouse maintained at a high temperature esp. for the culture of tropical plants
²hothouse *adj* **1** : grown in a hothouse **2** : having the qualities of a plant raised in a hothouse; *esp* : DELICATE
hot pepper *n* **1** : an often thin-walled and small capsicum fruit of marked pungency **2** : a pepper plant bearing hot peppers
hot plate *n* **1** : a heated iron plate for cooking **2** : a simple portable appliance for heating or for cooking in limited spaces
hot rod *n* : an automobile rebuilt or modified for high speed and fast acceleration — **hot–rod·der** \'hät-'räd-ər\ *n*
hot seat *n, slang* : ELECTRIC CHAIR
hot·shot \'hät-ˌshät\ *n* **1** : a fast freight **2** : a showily skillful person
hot spring *n* : THERMAL SPRING; *esp* : a spring with water above 98° F
Hot·ten·tot \'hät-ᵊn-ˌtät\ *n* [Afrik] **1 a** : a people of southern Africa apparently akin to both the Bushmen and the Bantus **b** : a member of such people **2** : the language of the Hottentot people

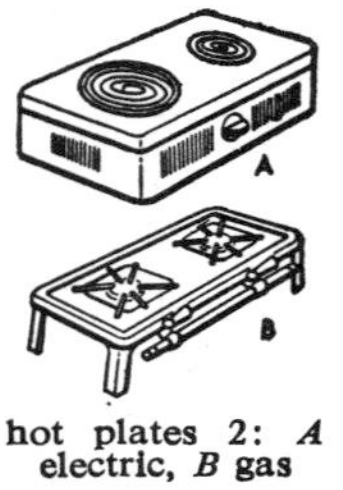

hot plates 2: *A* electric, *B* gas

hot war *n* : a conflict involving actual fighting
hot water *n* : a distressing predicament : DIFFICULTY
Hou·dan \'hü-,dan\ *n* [F, fr. *Houdan*, France] : any of a French breed of crested domestic fowls with black-and-white or white plumage and five toes
¹**hound** \'haůnd\ *n* [ME, fr. OE *hund*; akin to OHG *hunt* dog, L *canis*, Gk *kyōn*] **1 a :** DOG **b :** a dog of any of various hunting breeds typically having large drooping ears and a deep voice and following their prey by scent **2 :** a despicable person **3 :** DOGFISH **4 :** ADDICT, FAN
²**hound** *vt* : to pursue with or as if with hounds **syn** see BAIT — **hound·er** *n*
³**hound** *n* [ME *hune*, of Scand origin; akin to ON *hūnn* cube — more at CAVE] **1** *pl* **:** the framing at the masthead of a ship to support the heel of the topmast and the upper parts of the lower rigging **2 :** a side bar connecting and giving rigidity to parts of a wagon
hound's-tongue \'haůn(d)z-,təŋ\ *n* : any of various coarse plants (genus *Cynoglossum*, esp. *C. officinale*) of the borage family having tongue-shaped leaves and reddish flowers
hounds·tooth check *or* **hound's-tooth check** \,haůn(d)z-,tüth-\ *n* : a small broken-check textile pattern
hour \'aů(-ə)r\ *n* [ME, fr. OF *heure*, fr. LL & L; LL *hora*, fr. L, hour fr. Gk *hōra*] **1 :** a time or office for daily liturgical devotion; *esp* **:** CANONICAL HOUR **2 :** the 24th part of a day **3 a :** the time of day indicated by a timepiece **b :** the time reckoned from midnight to midnight ⟨attack at 0900 ~*s*⟩ **4 a :** a customary time **b :** a particular time **5 :** an angular unit of right ascension equal to 15 degrees measured along the equinoctial **6 :** the work done or distance traveled at normal rate in an hour **7 :** a class session
hour angle *n* : the angle between the celestial meridian of an observer and the hour circle of a celestial object measured westward from the meridian
hour circle *n* : a circle of the celestial sphere passing through the two poles
hour·glass \'aů(ə)r-,glas\ *n* : an instrument for measuring time consisting of a glass vessel having two compartments from the uppermost of which a quantity of sand, water, or mercury runs in an hour into the lower one — **hourglass** *adj*

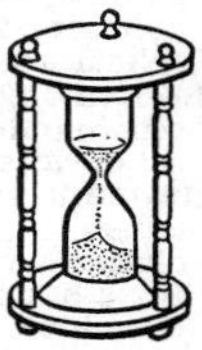
hourglass

hou·ri \'hů(ə)r-ē, 'hü-rē\ *n* [F, fr. Per *hūri*, fr. Ar *ḥūrīyah*] : one of the beautiful maidens among the pleasures of the Muslim paradise
¹**hour·ly** \'aů(ə)r-lē\ *adv* : at or during every hour; *also* : FREQUENTLY, CONTINUALLY
²**hourly** *adj* **1 a :** occurring hour by hour **b :** FREQUENT, CONTINUAL **2 :** computed in terms of an hour
¹**house** \'haůs\ *n, pl* **hous·es** \'haů-zəz\ [ME *hous*, fr. OE *hūs*; akin to OHG *hūs* house] **1 :** a building that serves as living quarters for one or a few families **2 a :** something that serves an animal for shelter or habitation **b :** a building in which something is housed ⟨carriage ~⟩ **3 a :** one of the 12 equal sectors in which the celestial sphere is divided in astrology **b :** a zodiacal sign that is the seat of a planet's greatest influence **4 a :** HOUSEHOLD **b :** a family including ancestors, descendants, and kindred **5 a :** a residence for a religious community or for students **b :** the community or students in residence **6 a :** a legislative, deliberative, or consultative assembly; *esp* **:** one constituting a division of a bicameral body **b :** the building or chamber where such an assembly meets **c :** a quorum of such an assembly **7 a :** a place of business or entertainment **b** (1) **:** a business organization (2) **:** the operator of a gambling establishment **c :** the audience in a theater or concert hall
²**house** \'haůz\ *vt* **1 a :** to provide with living quarters or shelter **b :** to store in a house **2 a :** to encase, enclose, or shelter as if by putting in a house **b :** to stow or secure in a safe place ⟨~ spars⟩ **3 :** to serve as shelter for **:** CONTAIN **~** *vi* **:** to take shelter **:** LODGE
house arrest *n* : confinement often under guard to one's house or quarters instead of in prison
house·boat \'haůs-,bōt\ *n* : a barge fitted for use as a dwelling or for leisurely cruising
house·break \-,brāk\ *vt* [back-formation fr. *housebroken*] : to make housebroken
house·break·er \-,brā-kər\ *n* : one that commits housebreaking
house·break·ing \-kiŋ\ *n* : an act of breaking open and entering with a felonious purpose the dwelling house of another
house·bro·ken \-,brō-kən\ *adj* **1 :** trained to excretory habits acceptable in indoor living **2 :** made tractable or polite
house·carl \-,kär(ə)l\ *n* [OE *hūscarl*, fr. ON *hūskarl*, fr. *hūs* house + *karl* man] : a member of the bodyguard of a Danish or early English king or noble
house·clean \'haůs-,klēn\ *vb* [back-formation fr. *housecleaning*] *vi* **1 :** to clean a house and its furniture **2 :** to get rid of unwanted or undesirable items or people **~** *vt* **1 :** to clean the surfaces and furnishings of **2 :** to improve or reform by ridding of undesirable people or practices — **house·clean·ing** *n*
house·coat \'haů-,skōt\ *n* : a woman's usu. long-skirted informal garment for wear around the house
house·fly \'haůs-,flī\ *n* : a cosmopolitan two-winged fly (*Musca domestica*) that is often about human habitations and acts as a mechanical vector of diseases (as typhoid fever); *also* : any of various flies of similar appearance or habitat
house·ful \-,fůl\ *n* : as much or as many as a house will accommodate
¹**house·hold** \'haůs-,hōld, 'haů-,sōld\ *n* : those who dwell under the same roof and compose a family
²**household** *adj* **1 :** of or relating to a household **:** DOMESTIC **2 :** FAMILIAR, COMMON
household art *n* : one of the techniques of use in maintenance and care of a household — usu. used in pl.
house·hold·er *n* : one who occupies a house or tenement alone or as the head of a household
household troops *n pl* : troops appointed to attend and guard a sovereign or his residence
house·keep \'haů-,skēp\ *vi* [back-formation fr. *housekeeper*] : to keep house
house·keep·er \-,skē-pər\ *n* : a woman employed to keep house
house·keep·ing \-piŋ\ *n* **1 :** the management of a house and home affairs **2 :** the care and management of property and the provision of equipment and services (as for an industrial organization)
hou·sel \'haů-zəl\ *n* [ME, fr. OE *hūsel* sacrifice, Eucharist; akin to Goth *hunsl* sacrifice] *archaic* : the Eucharist or the act of administering or receiving it — **housel** *vt, archaic*
house·leek \'haů-,slēk\ *n* : a pink-flowered European plant (*Sempervivum tectorum*) of the orpine family found on old walls and roofs; *broadly* : SEMPERVIVUM
house·less \'haů-sləs, 'haůz-ləs\ *adj* **1 :** HOMELESS **2 :** destitute of houses — **house·less·ness** *n*
house·lights \'haů-,slīts\ *n pl* : the lights that illuminate the parts of a theater occupied by the audience
house·line \'haůz-,līn, 'haů-,slīn\ *n* [prob. fr. ²*house*] : a light rope made of three strands and used for seizing
house·maid \'haů-,smād\ *n* : a female servant employed to do housework
housemaid's knee *n* [so called fr. its frequent occurrence among servant girls who work a great deal on their knees] : a swelling over the knee due to an enlargement of the bursa in the front of the patella
house·man \'haů-,smən\ *n* : a person who performs general work about a house — called also *house·boy* \'haůs-,bȯi\
house·moth·er \'haů-,sməth-ər\ *n* : a woman acting as hostess, chaperon, and often housekeeper in a residence for young people
house of assembly : HOUSE 6a; *esp* : the lower house of any of various legislatures
House of Burgesses : the colonial representative assembly of Virginia
House of Commons : the lower house of the British and Canadian parliaments
house of correction : an institution where persons are confined who have committed a minor offense and are considered capable of reformation
house of delegates : HOUSE 6a; *esp* : the lower house of the state legislature in Maryland, Virginia, and West Virginia
House of Lords : the upper house of the British Parliament composed of the peers temporal and spiritual
house of representatives : the lower house of the U.S. Congress, most state legislatures, and other legislative bodies
house organ *n* : a periodical distributed by a business concern among its employees, sales personnel, and customers
house party *n* : a party lasting over one or more nights at a home, fraternity house, or other residence
house physician *n* : a physician who is employed by and lives in a hospital
house-rais·ing \'haůs-,rā-ziŋ\ *n* : the joint erection of a house or its framework by a gathering of neighbors
house·room \-,rüm, -,rům\ *n* : space for accommodation in a house
house·top \'haů-,stäp\ *n* : ROOF
house·warm·ing \'haů-,swȯr-miŋ\ *n* : a party to celebrate the taking possession of a house or premises
house·wife \'haů-,swīf, *2 is often* 'həz-əf, 'həs-əf\ *n* **1 :** a married woman in charge of a household **2 :** a small container for small articles (as thread) — **house·wife·li·ness** \'haů-,swī-flē-nəs\ *n* — **house·wife·ly** \-flē\ *adj* — **house·wif·ery** \-f(ə-)rē\ *n*
house·work \'haů-,swərk\ *n* : the work of housekeeping
¹**hous·ing** \'haů-ziŋ\ *n* **1 a :** SHELTER, LODGING **b :** dwellings provided for people **2 a :** something that covers or protects **b :** a casing (as an enclosed bearing) in which a shaft revolves **c :** a frame or other support for mechanical parts **3 :** a portion of a mast that is beneath the deck or of a bowsprit that is inboard **4 a :** the space taken out of a structural member (as a timber) to admit the insertion of part of another **b :** a niche for a sculpture
²**housing** *n* **1 :** an ornamental cover for a saddle **2** *pl* **:** TRAPPINGS
Hou·yhn·hnm \hü-'in-əm, 'hwin-\ *n* : a member of a race of horses endowed with reason in Swift's *Gulliver's Travels*
hove *past of* HEAVE
hov·el \'həv-əl, 'häv-\ *n* [ME] **1 :** an open shed or shelter **2 :** TABERNACLE **3 :** a small mean house **:** HUT
hov·er \'həv-ər, 'häv-\ *vb* **hov·er·ing** \-(ə-)riŋ\ [ME *hoveren*, freq. of *hoven* to hover] *vi* **1 a :** to hang fluttering in the air or on the wing **b :** to remain suspended over a place or object **2 a :** to move to and fro near a place **b :** to be in a state of uncertainty, irresolution, or suspense **~** *vt* **:** to brood over ⟨hen ~*s* her chicks⟩ — **hover** *n* — **hov·er·er** \-ər-ər\ *n*
hov·er·craft \-ər-,kraft\ *n* [*hover* + *craft*] : a vehicle for traveling over land or water a short distance above the surface supported on a cushion of air produced by downwardly directed fans
¹**how** \(')haů\ *adv* [ME, fr. OE *hū*; akin to OHG *hwuo* how, OE *hwā* who — more at WHO] **1 a :** in what manner or way **b :** with what meaning **:** to what effect **c :** by what name or title **d :** for what reason **:** WHY **2 :** to what degree or extent **3 :** in what state or condition **4 :** at what price ⟨~ a score of ewes now —Shak.⟩ — **how about :** what do you say to or think of
²**how** *conj* **1 a** (1) **:** the way or manner in which ⟨remember ~ they fought⟩; *also* **:** the state or condition in which (2) **:** of the way or manner in which ⟨be careful ~ you talk⟩ **b :** THAT ⟨told them ~ he had a situation —Charles Dickens⟩ **2 :** in whatever way or manner **:** HOWEVER, AS ⟨a reader can shift his attention ~ he likes —William Empson⟩
³**how** \'haů\ *n* **1 :** a question about manner or method **2 :** MANNER, METHOD
¹**how·be·it** \haů-'bē-ət\ *adv* : NEVERTHELESS
²**howbeit** *conj* : ALTHOUGH
how·dah \'haůd-ə\ *n* [Hindi *hauda*] : a seat or covered pavilion on the back of an elephant or camel
howe \'haů, 'hō\ *n* [ME (northern) *how*, *holl*, fr. OE *hol*, fr. *hol*, adj., hollow — more at HOLE] *Scot* : HOLLOW, VALLEY
¹**how·ev·er** \haů-'ev-ər\ *conj* **1 :** in whatever manner or way ⟨can go ~ he likes⟩ **2** *archaic* **:** ALTHOUGH
²**however** *adv* **1 a :** to whatever degree or extent ⟨has done this for ~ many thousands of years —Emma Hawkridge⟩ **b :** in whatever manner or way ⟨shall serve you, sir, truly, ~ else —Shak.⟩ **2 :** in spite of that **:** on the other hand **:** BUT ⟨still seems possible, ~, that conditions will improve⟩ ⟨would like to go; ~, I think I'd better not⟩ **3 :** how in the world ⟨~ did you manage to do it⟩
howff *or* **howf** \'haůf, 'hōf\ *n* [D *hof* enclosure; akin to OE *hof* enclosure, *hȳf* hive] *Scot* : HAUNT, RESORT

how·it·zer \'haü-ət-sər\ *n* [D *houwitser*, deriv. of Czech *houfnice* ballista] **:** a short cannon used to fire projectiles at medium muzzle velocities and with relatively high trajectories

howl \'haü(ə)l\ *vb* [ME *houlen;* akin to MHG *hiulen* to howl, Gk *kōkyein* to shriek] *vi* **1 :** to emit a loud sustained doleful sound characteristic of dogs **2 :** to cry loudly and without restraint under strong impulse (as pain, grief) **3 :** to go on a spree ~ *vt* **1 :** to utter with unrestrained outcry **2 :** to affect, effect, or drive by adverse outcry — **howl** *n*

howl·er \'haü-lər\ *n* **1 :** one that howls **2 :** a stupid and ridiculous blunder

how·so·ev·er \,haü-sə-'wev-ər\ *adv* **1 :** in whatever manner **2 :** to whatever degree or extent

¹**hoy** \'hȯi\ *interj* [ME] — used in attracting attention or in driving animals

²**hoy** *n* [ME, fr. MD *hoei*] **1 :** a small usu. sloop-rigged coasting ship **2 :** a heavy barge for bulky cargo

hoy·den \'hȯid-ᵊn\ *n* [perh. fr. obs D *heiden* country lout, fr. MD, heathen; akin to OE *hǣthen* heathen] **:** a girl or woman of saucy, boisterous, or carefree behavior — **hoy·den·ish** \-ish\ *adj*

hoyle \'hȯi(ə)l\ *n, often cap* [Edmond *Hoyle* †1769 E writer on games] **:** an encyclopedia of the rules of card and other indoor games

Hr factor \ā-'chär-\ *n* **:** a substance present in Rh-negative blood and apparently reciprocally related to the Rh factor

hua·ra·che \wə-'räch-ē\ *n* [MexSp] **:** a low-heeled sandal having an upper made of interwoven leather thongs

hub \'həb\ *n* [prob. alter. of ²*hob*] **1 :** the central part of a wheel, propeller, or fan **2 :** a center of activity **3 :** a steel punch from which a working die for a coin or medal is made

hub·ble–bub·ble \'həb-əl-,bəb-əl\ *n* [redupl. of *bubble*] **1 :** WATER PIPE **2 :** a flurry of sound or activity **:** COMMOTION

hub·bub \'həb-,əb\ *n* [prob. of Celt origin; akin to ScGael *ub ub*, interj. of contempt] **1 :** a noisy confusion of sound **:** UPROAR **2 :** CONFUSION, TURMOIL

hu·bris \'hyü-brəs\ *n* [Gk *hybris* — more at OUT] **:** overweening pride or self-confidence **:** ARROGANCE

huck·a·back \'hək-ə-,bak\ *n* [origin unknown] **:** an absorbent durable fabric of cotton, linen, or both used chiefly for towels

huck·le·ber·ry \'hək-əl-,ber-ē\ *n* [perh. alter. of *hurtleberry* (huckleberry)] **1 :** any of a genus (*Gaylussacia*) of American shrubs of the heath family; *also* **:** the edible dark blue to black usu. acid berry (esp. of *G. baccata*) with 10 bony nutlets **2 :** BLUEBERRY

¹**huck·ster** \'hək-stər\ *n* [ME *hukster*, fr. MD *hokester*, fr. *hoeken* to peddle; akin to MLG *hōken* to peddle — more at HAWKER] **1 :** HAWKER, PEDDLER **2 :** one who produces advertising material for commercial clients esp. for radio or television

²**huckster** *vb* **huck·ster·ing** \-st(ə-)riŋ\ *vi* **:** HAGGLE ~ *vt* **1 :** to retail for profit **2 :** to promote by showmanship

¹**hud·dle** \'həd-ᵊl\ *vb* **hud·dling** \'həd-liŋ, -ᵊl-iŋ\ [prob. fr. or akin to ME *hoderen* to huddle] *vt* **1** *Brit* **:** to arrange carelessly or hurriedly **2 a :** to crowd together **b :** to draw (oneself) together **:** CROUCH **3** *archaic* **:** to herd into or out of a place in a disorderly mass ~ *vi* **1 a :** to gather in a group **b :** to curl up **:** CROUCH **2 :** to hold a consultation **:** CONFER; *specif* **:** to gather behind the scrimmage line in a football game and agree on team strategy — **hud·dler** \'həd-lər, -ᵊl-ər\ *n*

²**huddle** *n* **1 :** a close-packed group **:** BUNCH **2 a :** MEETING, CONFERENCE **b :** a strategy conference of football players behind the line of scrimmage

Hu·di·bras·tic \,hyüd-ə-'bras-tik\ *adj* [irreg. fr. *Hudibras*, satirical poem by Samuel Butler †1680] **1 :** written in humorous octosyllabic couplets **2 :** MOCK-HEROIC — **Hudibrastic** *n*

Hud·son seal \,həd-sən-\ *n* [*Hudson* bay, sea in Canada] **:** the fur of the muskrat dressed to simulate seal

hue \'hyü\ *n* [ME *hewe*, fr. OE *hīw;* akin to OE *hār* hoary — more at HOAR] **1 :** SHAPE, ASPECT **2 a :** gradation of color **b :** the attribute of colors that permits them to be classed as red, yellow, green, blue or an intermediate between any contiguous pair of these colors — compare LIGHTNESS, SATURATION **syn** see COLOR

hue and cry *n* [*hue* (outcry)] **1 a :** a loud outcry used in the pursuit of felons **b :** the pursuit of a felon **2 :** a clamor of pursuit or protest

hued \'hyüd\ *adj* **:** COLORED ⟨green-*hued*⟩

¹**huff** \'həf\ *vb* [imit.] *vi* **1 :** to emit puffs **2 a :** to make empty threats **:** BLUSTER **b :** to react or behave indignantly ~ *vt* **1 :** to puff up **:** INFLATE **2** *archaic* **:** to treat with contempt **:** BULLY **3 :** to make angry **:** PROVOKE

²**huff** *n* **:** a fit of anger or pique **syn** see OFFENSE

huff·ish \'həf-ish\ *adj* **:** ARROGANT, SULKY

huffy \'həf-ē\ *adj* **1 :** HAUGHTY, ARROGANT **2 a :** roused to indignation **:** IRRITATED **b :** easily offended **:** TOUCHY

hug \'həg\ *vt* **hugged; hug·ging** [perh. of Scand origin; akin to ON *hugga* to soothe] **1 :** to press tightly esp. in the arms **2 a :** CONGRATULATE **b :** to hold fast **:** CHERISH **3 :** to stay close to ⟨road ~*s* the river⟩ — **hug** *n*

huge \'hyüj, 'yüj\ *adj* [ME, fr. OF *ahuge*] **:** very large or extensive: as **a :** of great size or area **b :** of sizable scale or degree **c :** of limitless scope or character **syn** see ENORMOUS — **huge·ly** *adv* — **huge·ness** *n*

huge·ous \-əs\ *adj* **:** HUGE — **huge·ous·ly** *adv*

¹**hug·ger–mug·ger** \'həg-ər-,məg-ər\ *n* [origin unknown] **1 :** SECRECY **2 :** CONFUSION, MUDDLE

²**hugger–mugger** *adj* **1 :** SECRET **2 :** CONFUSED, JUMBLED

³**hugger–mugger** *vb* **hug·ger–mug·ger·ing** \-,məg-(ə-)riŋ\ *vt* **:** to keep secret ~ *vi* **:** to act stealthily

hug–me–tight \'həg-mē-,tīt\ *n* **:** a woman's short usu. knitted sleeveless close-fitting jacket

Hu·gue·not \'hyü-gə-,nät\ *n* [MF, French Protestant, fr. MF dial. *huguenot*, adherent of a Swiss political movement, alter. (influenced by Besançon *Hugues* †1532 Swiss political leader) of *eidgnot*, fr. G dial. *eidgnoss* confederate] **:** a member of the French Reformed communion — **Hu·gue·not·ic** \,hyü-gə-'nät-ik\ *adj* — **Hu·gue·not·ism** \'hyü-gə-,nät-,iz-əm\ *n*

hu·la \'hü-lə\ *or* **hu·la–hu·la** \,hü-lə-'hü-lə\ *n* [Hawaiian] **:** a sinuous mimetic Polynesian dance usu. accompanied by chants and rhythmic drumming

¹**hulk** \'həlk\ *n* [ME *hulke*, fr. OE *hulc*, fr. ML *holcas*, fr. Gk *holkas*, fr. *helkein* to pull — more at SULCUS] **1 :** a heavy clumsy ship **2 :** a bulky or unwieldy person or thing **3 a :** the body of an old ship unfit for service **b :** an abandoned wreck or shell **c :** a ship used as a prison — usu. used in pl.

²**hulk** *vi* **1** *dial Eng* **:** to move ponderously **2 :** to appear impressively large or massive **:** BULK

hulk·ing \'həl-kiŋ\ *adj* **:** ³HUSKY, MASSIVE

¹**hull** \'həl\ *n* [ME, fr. OE *hulu;* akin to OHG *hala* hull, OE *helan* to conceal — more at HELL] **1 a :** the outer covering of a fruit or seed **b :** the persistent calyx or involucre that subtends some fruits **2 a :** the frame or body of a ship exclusive of masts, yards, sails, and rigging **b (1) :** the portion of a flying boat which furnishes buoyancy when in contact with the water and to which the main supporting surfaces and other parts are attached **(2) :** the main structure of a rigid airship **3 :** COVERING, CASING — **hull–less** \'həl-ləs\ *adj*

²**hull** *vt* **1 :** to remove the hulls of — **hull·er** *n*

hul·la·ba·loo \'həl-ə-bə-,lü\ *n* [perh. irreg. fr. *hallo* + Sc *balloo*, interj. used to hush children] **:** a confused noise **:** UPROAR

hull down *adv (or adj), of a ship* **:** at such a distance that only the superstructure is visible

hul·lo \(,)hə-'lō\ *chiefly Brit var of* HELLO

hum \'həm\ *vb* **hummed; hum·ming** [ME *hummen;* akin to MHG *hummen* to hum, MD *hommel* bumblebee] *vi* **1 a :** to utter a sound like that of the speech sound \m\ prolonged **b :** to make the natural noise of an insect in motion or a similar sound **:** DRONE **c :** to give forth a low continuous blend of sound **2 :** to be busily active ~ *vt* **1 :** to sing with the lips closed and without articulation **2 :** to affect or express by humming — **hum** *n* — **hum·mer** *n*

hu·man \'hyü-mən, 'yü-\ *adj* [ME *humain*, fr. MF, fr. L *humanus;* akin to L *homo* man — more at HOMAGE] **1 :** of, relating to, or characteristic of man **2 a :** being a man **b :** consisting of men **3 :** having human form or attributes — **human** *n* — **hu·man·ness** \-mən-nəs\ *n*

hu·mane \hyü-'mān, yü-\ *adj* [ME *humain*] **1 :** marked by compassion, sympathy, or consideration for other human beings or animals **2 :** HUMANISTIC — **hu·mane·ly** *adv* — **hu·mane·ness** \-'mān-nəs\ *n*

human engineering *n* **1 :** management of human beings and affairs esp. in industry **2 :** a science that deals with the design of mechanical devices for efficient use by human beings

hu·man·ism \'hyü-mə-,niz-əm, 'yü-\ *n* **1 :** the revival of classical letters, individualistic and critical spirit, and emphasis on secular concerns characteristic of the Renaissance **2 :** HUMANITARIANISM **3 :** a doctrine, attitude, or way of life centered on human interests or values; *esp* **:** a philosophy that asserts the dignity and worth of man and his capacity for self-realization through reason and that often rejects supernaturalism — **hu·man·ist** \-nəst\ *n or adj* — **hu·man·is·tic** \,hyü-mə-'nis-tik, ,yü-\ *adj*

hu·man·i·tar·i·an \(,)hyü-,man-ə-'ter-ē-ən, (,)yü-\ *n* **:** a person promoting human welfare and social reform **:** PHILANTHROPIST — **humanitarian** *adj* — **hu·man·i·tar·i·an·ism** \-ē-ə-,niz-əm\ *n*

hu·man·i·ty \hyü-'man-ət-ē, yü-\ *n* **1 :** the quality or state of being humane **2 a :** the quality or state of being human **b** *pl* **:** human attributes or qualities **3** *pl* **:** the branches of learning having primarily a cultural character **4 :** MANKIND

hu·man·iza·tion \,hyü-mə-nə-'zā-shən, ,yü-\ *n* **1 :** the act or process of humanizing **2 :** the condition of being humanized

hu·man·ize \'hyü-mə-,nīz, 'yü-\ *vt* **1 a :** to represent as or endow with a human character **b :** to adapt to human nature or use **2 :** to make humane — **hu·man·iz·er** *n*

hu·man·kind \-mən-,kīnd\ *n sing but sing or pl in constr* **:** MANKIND

hu·man·ly *adv* **1 a :** from the viewpoint of man **b :** within the range of human capacity **2 :** in a human manner

hu·man·oid \'hyü-mə-,nȯid, 'yü-\ *adj* **:** having human characters esp. as opposed to anthropoid — **humanoid** *n*

hu·mate \'hyü-,māt\ *n* **:** a salt or ester of a humic acid

¹**hum·ble** \'həm-bəl, 'əm-\ *adj* **hum·bler** \-b(ə-)lər\ **hum·blest** \-b(ə-)ləst\ [ME, fr. OF, fr. L *humilis* low, humble, fr. *humus* earth; akin to Gk *chthōn* earth, *chamai* on the ground] **1 :** not proud or haughty **:** not arrogant or assertive **2 :** reflecting, expressing, or offered in a spirit of deference or submission ⟨~ apology⟩ **3 :** ranking low in some hierarchy or scale **:** INSIGNIFICANT, UNPRETENTIOUS — **hum·ble·ness** \-bəl-nəs\ *n* — **hum·bly** \-blē\ *adv*

syn MEEK, MODEST, LOWLY: HUMBLE and MEEK may suggest virtues, HUMBLE implying absence of vanity and arrogance, MEEK the absence of wrath or vindictiveness, but HUMBLE may also imply undue self-depreciation and MEEK may suggest lack of spirit or a timid submissiveness; MODEST implies a lack of boastfulness or conceit, without any implication of abjectness; LOWLY is close to HUMBLE and may stress lack of pretentiousness

²**humble** *vt* **hum·bling** \-b(ə-)liŋ\ **1 :** to make humble in spirit or manner **2 :** to destroy the power, independence, or prestige of — **hum·bler** \-b(ə-)lər\ *n*

hum·ble–bee \'həm-bəl-,bē\ *n* [ME *humbylbee*, fr. *humbyl-* (akin to MD *hommel* bumblebee) + *bee* — more at HUM] **:** BUMBLEBEE

¹**hum·bug** \'həm-,bəg\ *n* [origin unknown] **1 a :** something designed to deceive and mislead **b :** a person who passes himself off as something that he is not **2 :** an attitude or spirit of pretense and deception **3 :** DRIVEL, NONSENSE **syn** see IMPOSTURE — **hum·bug·gery** \-,bəg-(ə-)rē\ *n*

²**humbug** *vt* **:** DECEIVE, HOAX ~ *vi* **:** to engage in humbug

hum·ding·er \'həm-'diŋ-ər\ *n* [prob. alter. of *hummer* (humdinger)] **:** a person or thing of striking excellence

hum·drum \'həm-,drəm\ *adj* [irreg. redupl. of *hum*] **:** MONOTONOUS, DULL — **humdrum** *n*

hu·mec·tant \hyü-'mek-tənt\ *n* [L *humectant-*, *humectans*, prp. of *humectare* to moisten, fr. *humectus* moist, fr. *humēre* to be moist — more at HUMOR] **:** a substance that promotes retention of moisture — **humectant** *adj*

hu·mer·al \'hyüm-(ə-)rəl\ *adj* **1 :** of, relating to, or situated in the region of the humerus or shoulder **2 :** of, relating to, or being a body part analogous to the humerus or shoulder — **humeral** *n*

humeral veil *n* **:** an oblong vestment worn around the shoulders and over the hands by a priest or subdeacon holding a sacred vessel

hu·mer·us \'hyüm-(ə-)rəs\ *n, pl* **hu·meri** \'hyü-mə-,rī, -,rē\ [NL, fr. L, upper arm, shoulder; akin to Goth *ams* shoulder, Gk *ōmos*] **:** the long bone of the upper arm or forelimb extending from the shoulder to the elbow

hu·mic \'hyü-mik, 'yü-\ *adj* **:** of, relating to, or derived at least in part from humus

humic acid *n* **:** any of various organic acids obtained from humus

hu·mid \'hyü-məd, 'yü-\ *adj* [F or L; F *humide*, fr. L *humidus*, fr. *humēre*] **:** containing or characterized by perceptible moisture **:** DAMP **syn** see WET — **hu·mid·ly** *adv*

hu·mid·i·fi·ca·tion \hyü-ˌmid-ə-fə-'kā-shən, yü-\ *n* **:** the process of making humid

hu·mid·i·fi·er \-'mid-ə-ˌfī(-ə)r\ *n* **:** a device for supplying or maintaining humidity

hu·mid·i·fy \-ˌfī\ *vt* **:** to make humid **:** MOISTEN

hu·mid·i·stat \-ˌstat\ *n* **:** an instrument for regulating or maintaining the degree of humidity

hu·mid·i·ty \hyü-'mid-ət-ē, yü-\ *n* **:** a moderate degree of wetness esp. of the atmosphere **:** DAMPNESS — compare RELATIVE HUMIDITY

hu·mi·dor \'hyü-mə-ˌdȯ(ə)r, 'yü-\ *n* [*humid* + *-or* (as in *cuspidor*)] **:** a case usu. for storing cigars in which the air is kept properly humidified

hu·mi·fi·ca·tion \ˌhyü-mə-fə-'kā-shən, ˌyü-\ *n* **:** formation of or conversion into humus

hu·mi·fied \'hyü-mə-ˌfīd, 'yü-\ *adj* **:** converted into humus

hu·mil·i·ate \hyü-'mil-ē-ˌāt, yü-\ *vt* [LL *humiliatus*, pp. of *humiliare*, fr. L *humilis* low — more at HUMBLE] **:** to reduce to a lower position in one's own eyes or others' eyes **:** MORTIFY **syn** see ABASE — **hu·mil·i·a·tion** \hyü-ˌmil-ē-'ā-shən, yü-\ *n*

hu·mil·i·at·ing *adj* **:** HUMBLING, MORTIFYING

hu·mil·i·ty \-'mil-ət-ē\ *n* **:** the quality or state of being humble

hu·mi·ture \'hyü-mə-ˌchu̇(ə)r, 'yü-\ *n* [*humidity* + *temperature*] **:** a combined measurement of temperature and humidity computed in integers by adding the temperature in degrees Fahrenheit to the relative humidity

hum·ming·bird \'həm-iŋ-ˌbərd\ *n* **:** any of numerous tiny brightly colored nonpasserine birds (family Trochilidae) related to the swifts and like them having narrow wings with long primaries, a slender bill, and a very extensile tongue

hum·mock \'həm-ək\ *n* [alter. of 2*hammock*] **1 :** a rounded knoll or hillock **2 :** a ridge of ice **3 :** 2HAMMOCK 2 — **hum·mocky** \-ə-kē\ *adj*

1**hu·mor** *or chiefly Brit* **hu·mour** \'hyü-mər, 'yü-\ *n* [ME *humour*, fr. MF *humeur*, fr. ML & L; ML *humor*, fr. L, moisture; akin to ON *vǫkr* damp, L *humēre* to be moist, Gk *hygros* wet] **1 a :** a normal functioning fluid or semifluid of the body **b :** a secretion that is an excitant of activity **2 a** *in medieval physiology* **:** a fluid or juice of an animal or plant; *specif* **:** one of the four fluids entering into the constitution of the body and determining by their relative proportions a person's health and temperament **b :** HABIT, TEMPERAMENT **c :** temporary state of mind **d :** a sudden, unpredictable, or unreasoning inclination **:** WHIM **3 a :** that quality which appeals to a sense of the ludicrous or absurdly incongruous **b :** the mental faculty of discovering, expressing, or appreciating the ludicrous or absurdly incongruous **c :** something that is or is designed to be comical or amusing **syn** see MOOD, WIT — **out of humor :** out of sorts

2**humor** *or chiefly Brit* **humour** *vt* **hu·mor·ing** \'hyüm-(ə-)riŋ, 'yüm-\ **1 :** to soothe or content by indulgence **2 :** to adapt oneself to **syn** see INDULGE

hu·mor·al \'hyüm-(ə-)rəl, 'yüm-\ *adj* **:** of, relating to, proceeding from, or involving a bodily humor (as a hormone)

hu·mor·esque \ˌhyü-mə-'resk, ˌyü-\ *n* [G *humoreske*, fr. *humor*, fr. E] **:** a musical composition typically whimsical or fanciful in character **:** CAPRICCIO

hu·mor·ist \'hyüm-(ə-)rəst, 'yüm-\ *n* **1** *archaic* **:** a person subject to whims **2 :** a person specializing in or noted for humor

hu·mor·is·tic \ˌhyü-mə-'ris-tik, ˌyü-\ *adj* **:** HUMOROUS

hu·mor·less \'hyü-mər-ləs, 'yü-\ *adj* **1 :** lacking a sense of humor **2 :** lacking humorous characteristics — **hu·mor·less·ness** *n*

hu·mor·ous \'hyüm-(ə-)rəs, 'yüm-\ *adj* **1** *obs* **:** HUMID **2 a :** full of or characterized by humor **:** JOCULAR **b :** indicating or expressive of a sense of humor **syn** see WITTY — **hu·mor·ous·ly** *adv* — **hu·mor·ous·ness** *n*

1**hump** \'həmp\ *n* [akin to MLG *hump* bump, L *incumbere* to lie down, Gk *kymbē* bowl, OE *hype* hip] **1 :** a rounded protuberance: as **a :** HUMPBACK 1 **b :** a fleshy protuberance on the back of an animal **c** (1) **:** MOUND, HUMMOCK (2) **:** MOUNTAIN, RANGE ⟨Himalayan ~⟩ **2** *Brit* **:** a fit of depression or sulking **3 :** a difficult, trying, or critical phase — often used in the phrase *over the hump*

2**hump** *vt* **1 :** to exert (oneself) vigorously **2 :** to make humpbacked **:** HUNCH **3** *chiefly Brit* **:** to put or carry on the back; *also* **:** TRANSPORT ~ *vi* **1 :** to exert oneself **:** HUSTLE **2 :** to move swiftly **:** RACE

hump·back \-ˌbak\ *n* **1 :** a humped or crooked back; *also* **:** KYPHOSIS **2 :** HUNCHBACK 2 **3 :** a large whalebone whale (genus *Megaptera*) related to the rorquals but having very long flippers

hump·backed \-'bakt\ *adj* **1 :** having a humped back **2 :** convexly curved ⟨a ~ bridge⟩

humped \'həm(p)t\ *adj* **:** having a hump; *esp* **:** HUMPBACKED

humped cattle *n* **:** domestic cattle developed from an Indian species (*Bos indicus*) and characterized by a hump of fat and muscle above the shoulders

humph *a snort or* h *followed by* m *or nasalized* 'ə; *often read as* 'həm(p)f\ *interj* [imit. of a grunt] — used to express doubt or contempt

humpy \'həm-pē\ *adj* **1 :** full of humps **2 :** covered with humps

hu·mus \'hyü-məs, 'yü-\ *n* [NL, fr. L, earth] **:** a brown or black complex variable material resulting from partial decomposition of plant or animal matter and forming the organic portion of soil

Hun \'hən\ *n* [LL *Hunni*, pl.] **1 :** a member of a nomadic Mongolian people gaining control of a large part of central and eastern Europe under Attila about A.D. 450 **2 a** *often not cap* **:** a person who is wantonly destructive **:** VANDAL **b :** GERMAN; *esp* **:** a German soldier — usu. used disparagingly

1**hunch** \'hənch\ *vb* [origin unknown] *vi* **1 :** to thrust oneself forward **2 :** to assume a bent or crooked posture ~ *vt* **1 :** JOSTLE, SHOVE **2 :** to thrust into a hump

2**hunch** *n* **1 :** an act or instance of hunching **:** PUSH **2 a :** HUMP **b :** a thick piece **:** LUMP **3 :** a strong intuitive feeling concerning a future event or result

hunch·back \-ˌbak\ *n* **1 :** HUMPBACK 1 **2 :** a person with a humpback — **hunch·backed** \-'bakt\ *adj*

hun·dred \'hən-drəd, -dərd\ *n, pl* **hundreds** *or* **hundred** [ME, fr. OE; akin to ON *hundrath* hundred; both fr. a prehistoric WGmc-NGmc compound whose constituents were akin respectively to OE *hund* hundred and to Goth *garathjan* to count; akin to L *centum* hundred, Gk *hekaton*, Av *satəm*, OE *tīen* ten — more at TEN, REASON] **1** — see NUMBER table **2 :** the number occupying the position three to the left of the decimal point in the Arabic system of numerals **3 :** a hundred-dollar bill **4 :** a subdivision of some English and American counties **5 :** the numbers 100 to 999 — **hundred** *adj* — **hun·dredth** \-drədth, -drətth\ *adj or n* — **by the hundred** *or* **by the hundreds :** in great numbers

hun·dred–per·cent·er \ˌhən-drəd-pər-'sent-ər, -dərd-\ *n* [*hundred-percent* (*American*)] **:** a thoroughgoing nationalist — **hun·dred–per·cent·ism** \-'sent-ˌiz-əm\ *n*

hun·dred·weight \'hən-drə-ˌdwāt, -dər-ˌdwāt\ *n, pl* **hundred-weight** *or* **hundredweights 1 a :** a unit of weight equal to 100 pounds — called also *short hundredweight;* see MEASURE table **b** *Brit* **:** a unit of weight equal to 112 pounds — called also *long hundredweight* **2 :** METRIC HUNDREDWEIGHT

hung *past of* HANG

Hun·gar·i·an \ˌhəŋ-'ger-ē-ən, -'gar-\ *n* **1 a :** a native or inhabitant of Hungary **:** MAGYAR **b :** a person of Hungarian descent **2 :** MAGYAR 2 — **Hungarian** *adj*

1**hun·ger** \'həŋ-gər\ *n* [ME, fr. OE *hungor;* akin to OHG *hungar* hunger, Skt *kāṅksati* he desires] **1 a :** a craving or urgent need for food or a specific nutrient **b :** an uneasy sensation occasioned by the lack of food **c :** a weakened condition brought about by prolonged lack of food **2 :** a strong desire **:** CRAVING

2**hunger** *vb* **hun·ger·ing** \-g(ə-)riŋ\ *vi* **1 :** to feel or suffer hunger **2 :** to have an eager desire ~ *vt* **:** to make hungry **syn** see LONG

hunger strike *n* **:** refusal esp. by a prisoner to eat enough to sustain life

hung over *adj* **:** suffering from a hangover

hun·gri·ly \'həŋ-grə-lē\ *adv* **:** in a hungry manner

hun·gri·ness \-grē-nəs\ *n* **:** the quality or state of being hungry

hun·gry \'həŋ-grē\ *adj* **1 a :** feeling hunger **b :** characterized by or characteristic of hunger or appetite **2 :** EAGER, AVID **3 :** not rich or fertile **:** BARREN

hunk \'həŋk\ *n* [Flem *hunke*] **:** a large lump or piece

hun·ker \'həŋ-kər\ *vi* **hun·ker·ing** \-k(ə-)riŋ\ [perh. of Scand origin; akin to ON *hūka* to squat; akin to MLG *hōken* to squat — more at HAWKER] **:** CROUCH, SQUAT

hun·kers \'həŋ-kərz\ *n pl* **:** HAUNCHES

hunks \'həŋ(k)s\ *n pl but sing or pl in constr* [origin unknown] **:** a surly ill-natured person; *esp* **:** MISER

hun·ky–do·ry \ˌhəŋ-kē-'dōr-ē, -'dȯr-\ *adj* [obs. E dial. *hunk* (home base) + *-dory* (origin unknown)] **:** quite satisfactory **:** FINE

Hun·nish \'hən-ish\ *adj* **:** relating to or resembling the Huns **:** BARBAROUS

1**hunt** \'hənt\ *vb* [ME *hunten*, fr. OE *huntian;* akin to OHG *herihunda* battle spoils] *vt* **1 a :** to pursue for food or in sport ⟨~ buffalo⟩ **b :** to manage in the search for game ⟨~*s* a pack of dogs⟩ **2 a :** to pursue with intent to capture **b :** to search out **:** SEEK **3 :** to drive or chase esp. by harrying **4 :** to traverse in quest of prey ⟨~*s* the woods⟩ ~ *vi* **1 :** to take part in a hunt **2 :** to attempt to find something

2**hunt** *n* **1 :** the act, the practice, or an instance of hunting **2 :** an association of huntsmen; *esp* **:** persons with horses and dogs engaged in hunting or riding to hounds

hunt·er \'hənt-ər\ *n* **1 a :** a person who hunts game **b :** a dog used or trained for hunting **c :** a horse used or adapted for use in hunting; *esp* **:** a fast strong horse trained for cross-country work and jumping **2 :** a person who searches for something

hunt·ing *n* **1 :** the act of one that hunts; *specif* **:** the pursuit of game **2 :** a periodic variation in speed of a synchronous electrical machine from that of the true synchronous speed

hunt·ress \'hən-trəs\ *n* **:** a female hunter

hunts·man \'hən(t)-smən\ *n* **1 :** HUNTER 1a **2 :** a person who manages a hunt and looks after the hounds

hur·dies \'hərd-ēz\ *n pl* [origin unknown] *dial Brit* **:** BUTTOCKS, RUMP

1**hur·dle** \'hərd-ᵊl\ *n* [ME *hurdel*, fr. OE *hyrdel;* akin to OHG *hurd* hurdle, L *cratis* wickerwork, hurdle] **1 a :** a portable panel usu. of wattled withes and stakes used esp. for enclosing land or livestock **b :** a frame or sled formerly used in England for dragging traitors to execution **c :** an artificial barrier over which men or horses leap in a race **2 :** BARRIER, OBSTACLE

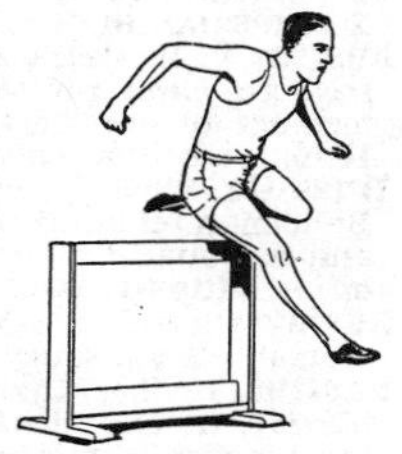
hurdle 1c

2**hurdle** *vt* **hur·dling** \'hərd-liŋ, -ᵊl-iŋ\ **1 :** to leap over while running **2 :** OVERCOME, SURMOUNT — **hur·dler** \'hərd-lər, -ᵊl-ər\ *n*

hur·dy–gur·dy \ˌhərd-ē-'gərd-ē\ *n* [prob. imit.] **:** a musical instrument in which the sound is produced by turning a crank; *esp* **:** BARREL ORGAN

hurl \'hər(-ə)l\ *vb* **hurl·ing** \'hər-liŋ\ [ME *hurlen*] *vi* **1 :** RUSH, HURTLE **2 :** PITCH 4 ~ *vt* **1 :** to impel with vigor **:** THRUST **2 :** to throw down with violence **3 a :** to throw forcefully **:** FLING **b :** PITCH 2a **syn** see THROW — **hurl** *n* — **hurl·er** \'hər-lər\ *n*

hur·ly \'hər-lē\ *n* [prob. short for *hurly-burly*] **:** UPROAR, TUMULT

hur·ly–bur·ly \ˌhər-lē-'bər-lē\ *n* [prob. alter. & redupl. of *hurling*] **:** UPROAR, TUMULT

Hu·ron \'hyu̇r-ən, 'hyu̇(ə)r-ˌän\ *n, pl* **Huron** *or* **Hurons** [F, lit., boor] **:** a member of an Iroquoian people orig. of the St. Lawrence valley and Ontario

1**hur·rah** \hu̇-'rȯ, -'rä\ *also* **hur·ray** \hu̇-'rā\ *interj* [perh. fr. G *hurra*] — used to express joy, approbation, or encouragement

2**hurrah** *n* **1 :** EXCITEMENT, FANFARE **2 :** FUSS, CONTROVERSY

hur·ri·cane \'hər-ə-ˌkān, -i-kən, 'hə-rə-, 'hə-ri-\ *n* [Sp *huracán*, fr. Taino *hurakán*] **:** a tropical cyclone with winds of 73 miles per hour or greater but rarely exceeding 150 miles per hour that is usu. accompanied by rain, thunder, and lightning

hurricane deck *n* **:** PROMENADE DECK

hurricane lamp *n* **:** a candlestick or an electric lamp equipped with a glass chimney

hur·ried \'hər-ēd, 'hə-rēd\ *adj* **1 :** going or working at speed **2 :** done in a hurry **:** HASTY — **hur·ried·ly** \-(r)ēd-lē, -(r)əd-\ *adv* — **hur·ried·ness** \-(r)ēd-nəs\ *n*

hur·ri·er \'hər-ē-ər, 'hə-rē-\ *n* **:** one that hurries

1**hur·ry** \'hər-ē, 'hə-rē\ *vb* [perh. fr. ME *horyen*] *vt* **1 a :** to carry or cause to go with haste ⟨~ him to the hospital⟩ **b :** to impel to rash or precipitate action **2 a :** to impel to greater speed **:** PROD ⟨used spurs to ~ the horse⟩ **b :** EXPEDITE; *specif* **:** to perform with undue haste ⟨~ a minuet⟩ ~ *vi* **:** to move or act with haste ⟨please ~ up⟩

2**hurry** *n* **1 :** DISTURBANCE, COMMOTION **2 :** a recurrent agitation of sound **3 a :** excessive haste **:** PRECIPITANCY **b :** a state of eagerness or urgency **syn** see HASTE

hur·ry–scur·ry *or* **hur·ry–skur·ry** \,hər-ē-'skər-ē, ,hə-rē-'skə-rē\ *n* [redupl. of 2*hurry*] **:** a confused rush **:** TURMOIL — **hurry–scurry** *adj or adv*

1**hurt** \'hərt\ *vb* **hurt; hurt; hurt·ing** [ME *hurten*] *vt* **1 a :** to inflict with physical pain **:** WOUND **b :** to do substantial or material harm to **:** DAMAGE **2 a :** to cause pain or anguish to **:** OFFEND **b :** to be detrimental to **:** HAMPER ~ *vi* **1 a :** to feel pain **:** SUFFER **b** *chiefly Midland* **:** to be in need **:** WANT **2 :** to cause damage or distress ⟨hit where it ~*s*⟩ **syn** see INJURE — **hurt·er** *n*

2**hurt** *n* **1 :** a wounding blow **:** cause of injury or damage **2 a :** a bodily injury or wound **b :** mental distress or anguish **:** SUFFERING **3 :** WRONG, HARM

hurt·ful \'hərt-fəl\ *adj* **:** causing injury or suffering **:** DAMAGING — **hurt·ful·ly** \-fə-lē\ *adv* — **hurt·ful·ness** *n*

hur·tle \'hərt-ᵊl\ *vb* **hur·tling** \'hərt-liŋ, -ᵊl-iŋ\ [ME *hurtlen* to collide, freq. of *hurten* to cause to strike, hurt] *vi* **:** to move with or as if with a rushing sound ~ *vt* **:** HURL, FLING

hurt·less \'hərt-ləs\ *adj, archaic* **:** HARMLESS

1**hus·band** \'həz-bənd\ *n* [ME *husbonde*, fr. OE *hūsbonda* master of a house, fr. ON *hūsbōndi*, fr. *hūs* house + *bōndi* householder] **1 :** a married man **2** *Brit* **:** MANAGER, STEWARD **3 :** a frugal manager

2**husband** *vt* **1 a :** to manage prudently and economically **b :** to use sparingly **:** CONSERVE **2** *archaic* **:** to find a husband for **:** MATE — **hus·band·er** *n*

hus·band·man \'həz-bən(d)-mən\ *n* **1 :** one that plows and cultivates land **:** FARMER **2 :** a specialist in a branch of farm husbandry

hus·band·ry \-bən-drē\ *n* **1** *obs* **:** the care of a household **2 :** the control or judicious use of resources **:** CONSERVATION **3 a :** the cultivation or production of plants and animals **:** AGRICULTURE **b :** the scientific control and management of a branch of farming and esp. of domestic animals

1**hush** \'həsh\ *vb* [back-formation fr. *husht* (hushed), fr. ME *hussht*, fr. *huissht*, interj.] *vt* **1 :** CALM, QUIET **2 :** to put at rest **:** QUELL **3 :** to keep from public knowledge **:** SUPPRESS ⟨~ the story up⟩ ~ *vi* **:** to become quiet

2**hush** *adj* **1** *archaic* **:** SILENT, STILL **2 :** intended to prevent the dissemination of certain information ⟨~ money⟩

3**hush** *n* **:** a silence or calm esp. following noise **:** QUIET

hush–hush \'həsh-,həsh\ *adj* **:** SECRET, CONFIDENTIAL

1**husk** \'həsk\ *n* [ME] **1 a :** a typically dry or membranous outer covering (as of hulls, bracts, or pod) of a seed or fruit; *also* **:** one of the constituent parts **b :** a carob pod **2 a :** an outer layer **:** SHELL **b :** a supporting framework

2**husk** *vt* **:** to strip the husk from — **husk·er** *n*

husk·i·ly \'həs-kə-lē\ *adv* **:** in a husky manner

husk·i·ness \-kē-nəs\ *n* **:** the quality or state of being husky

husk·ing *n* **:** a gathering of farm families to husk corn

husk–tomato *n* **:** GROUND-CHERRY

1**husky** \'həs-kē\ *adj* **:** resembling, containing, or full of husks

2**husky** *adj* [prob. fr. *husk* (huskiness), fr. obs. *husk* (to have a dry cough)] **:** hoarse with or as if with emotion

3**husky** *adj* [prob. fr. 1*husk*] **1 :** BURLY, ROBUST **2 :** LARGE

4**husky** *n* **:** one that is husky

5**hus·ky** \'həs-kē\ *n* [prob. by shortening & alter. fr. *Eskimo*] **1 :** a heavy-coated working dog of the New World arctic region **2 :** SIBERIAN HUSKY

hus·sar \(,)hə-'zär\ *n* [Hung *huszár* hussar, (obs.) highway robber, fr. Serb *husar* pirate, fr. ML *cursarius* — more at CORSAIR] **:** a member of any of various European units orig. modeled on the Hungarian light cavalry of the 15th century

Huss·ite \'həs-,īt, 'hùs-\ *n* [NL *Hussita*, fr. John Huss †1415 Bohemian religious reformer] **:** a member of the Bohemian religious and nationalist movement originating with John Huss — **Hussite** *adj* — **Huss·it·ism** \-,īt-,iz-əm\ *n*

hus·sy \'həz-ē, 'həs-\ *n* [alter. of *housewife*] **1 :** a lewd or brazen woman **2 :** a saucy or mischievous girl

hus·tings \'həs-tiŋz\ *n pl but sing or pl in constr* [ME, fr. OE *hūsting*, fr. ON *hūsthing*, fr. *hūs* house + *thing* assembly] **1 a :** a local court formerly held in various English municipalities and still held infrequently in London **b :** a local court in some cities in Virginia **2 a :** a raised platform used until 1872 for the nomination of candidates for the British Parliament and for election speeches **b :** an election platform **:** STUMP **c :** the proceedings of an election campaign

hus·tle \'həs-əl\ *vb* **hus·tling** \'həs-(ə-)liŋ\ [D *husselen* to shake, fr. MD *hutselen*, freq. of *hutsen;* akin to MD *hodde* hod] *vt* **1 a :** JOSTLE, SHOVE **b :** to convey forcibly or hurriedly **c :** to urge forward precipitately **2 a :** to obtain by energetic activity **b :** to sell something to or obtain something from by energetic and esp. underhanded activity ~ *vi* **1 :** SHOVE, PRESS **2 :** HASTEN, HURRY **3 :** to make strenuous efforts to secure often illicit money or business — **hustle** *n* — **hus·tler** \-(ə-)lər\ *n*

hut \'hət\ *n* [MF *hutte*, of Gmc origin; akin to OHG *hutta* hut; akin to OE *hӯd* skin, hide] **1 :** an often small and temporary dwelling of simple construction **:** SHACK **2 :** a simple shelter from the elements — **hut** *vb* **hut·ted; hut·ting**

hutch \'həch\ *n* [ME *huche*, fr. OF] **1 a :** a chest or compartment for storage **b :** a low cupboard usu. surmounted by open shelves **2 :** a pen or coop for an animal **3 :** SHACK, SHANTY

hut·ment \'hət-mənt\ *n* **1 :** a collection of huts **:** ENCAMPMENT **2 :** HUT

huz·zah *or* **huz·za** \(,)hə-'zä\ *interj* — used to express joy or approbation

hy·a·cinth \'hī-ə-(,)sin(t)th\ *n, pl* **hyacinths** \-(,)sin(t)s, -(,)sin(t)ths\ [L *hyacinthus*, a precious stone, a flowering plant, fr. Gk *hyakinthos*] **1 a :** a precious stone of the ancients sometimes held to be the sapphire **b :** a gem zircon or essonite **2 a :** a plant of the ancients held to be a lily, iris, larkspur, or gladiolus **b** (1) **:** any of a genus (*Hyacinthus*) of bulbous herbs of the lily family; *esp* **:** a common garden plant (*H. orientalis*) widely grown for the beauty and fragrance of its flowers (2) **:** any of several other plants of the lily family **3 :** a light violet to moderate purple — **hy·a·cin·thine** \,hī-ə-'sin(t)-thən\ *adj*

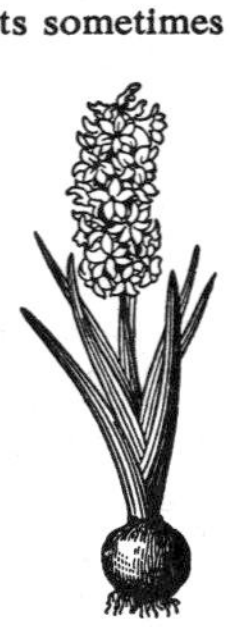
hyacinth 2b(1)

Hy·a·cin·thus \,hī-ə-'sin(t)-thəs\ *n* [L, fr. Gk *Hyakinthos*] **:** a youth loved and accidentally killed by Apollo who according to Greek mythology causes a hyacinth to grow from his blood

Hy·a·des \'hī-ə-,dēz\ *n pl* [L, fr. Gk] **:** a V-shaped cluster of stars in the head of the constellation Taurus supposed by the ancients to indicate rainy weather when they rise with the sun

hy·ae·na *var of* HYENA

hyal- *or* **hyalo-** *comb form* [LL, glass, fr. Gk, fr. *hyalos*] **:** glass **:** glassy **:** hyaline ⟨*hyal*escent⟩ ⟨*hyalo*gen⟩

1**hy·a·line** \'hī-ə-lən, -,līn\ *adj* [LL *hyalinus*, fr. Gk *hyalinos*, fr. *hyalos*] **1 :** of or relating to glass **2 a :** transparent or nearly so and usu. homogeneous **b** (1) **:** GLASSY (2) **:** lacking crystallinity **:** AMORPHOUS

2**hy·a·line** \'hī-ə-lən, -,līn, *in sense 2* -,lēn *or* -lən\ *n* **1 :** something (as the clear atmosphere) that is transparent **2** *or* **hy·a·lin** \-lən\ **:** any of several translucent nitrogenous substances related to chitin found esp. around cells and readily stained by eosin

hyaline cartilage *n* **:** translucent bluish white cartilage with the cells embedded in an apparently homogeneous matrix that is present in joints and respiratory passages and forms most of the fetal skeleton

hy·a·lite \'hī-ə-,līt\ *n* [G *hyalit*, fr. Gk *hyalos*] **:** a colorless opal that is clear as glass or sometimes translucent or whitish

hy·a·loid \'hī-ə-,lȯid\ *adj* [Gk *hyaloeidēs*, fr. *hyalos*] **:** GLASSY, TRANSPARENT

hy·a·lo·plasm \hī-'al-ə-,plaz-əm, 'hī-ə-lō-\ *n* [prob. fr. G *hyaloplasma*, fr. *hyal-* + *-plasma* -plasm] **:** the clear apparently homogeneous ground substance of cytoplasm that is essentially the continuous phase of a multiple-phase colloidal system

hy·al·uron·ic acid \,hī-əl-yù-,rän-ik-, ,hī-əl-yù-\ *n* [ISV] **:** a viscous mucopolysaccharide acid chiefly of connective tissues or their derivatives

hy·al·uron·i·dase \-'rän-ə-,dās, -,dāz\ *n* [ISV, irreg. fr. *hyaluronic* (*acid*) + *-ase*] **:** an enzyme that splits and lowers the viscosity of hyaluronic acid facilitating the spreading of fluids through tissues

hy·brid \'hī-brəd\ *n* [L *hybrida*] **1 :** an offspring of two animals or plants of different races, breeds, varieties, species, or genera **2 :** a person produced by the blending of two diverse cultures or traditions **3 a :** something heterogeneous in origin or composition **:** COMPOSITE **b :** a word composed of elements from different languages — **hybrid** *adj* — **hy·brid·ism** \-,iz-əm\ *n* — **hy·brid·i·ty** \hī-'brid-ət-ē\ *n*

hy·bri·da \'hī-brəd-ə\ *n, pl* **hy·bri·dae** \-brə-,dē\ [NL, fr. L] **:** an interspecific hybrid

hy·brid·iza·tion \,hī-brəd-ə-'zā-shən\ *n* **:** the act or process of hybridizing or the state of being hybridized

hy·brid·ize \'hī-brə-,dīz\ *vt* **:** to cause to produce hybrids **:** INTERBREED ~ *vi* **:** to produce hybrids — **hy·brid·iz·er** *n*

hybrid perpetual rose *n* **:** any of numerous vigorous hardy bush roses derived from the bourbon rose and grown esp. for their sometimes recurrent often fragrant bloom

hybrid tea rose *n* **:** any of numerous moderately hardy cultivated bush roses derived chiefly from tea roses and hybrid perpetual roses and grown esp. for their strongly recurrent bloom of large usu. scentless flowers

hy·bris \'hī-brəs\ *var of* HUBRIS

hy·da·thode \'hīd-ə-,thōd\ *n* [ISV, fr. Gk *hydat-*, *hydōr* water + *hodos* road — more at CEDE] **:** an epidermal structure in higher plants functioning in the exudation of water

hy·da·tid \'hīd-ə-təd\ *n* [Gk *hydatid-*, *hydatis* watery cyst, fr. *hydat-*, *hydōr*] **:** a larval tapeworm occurring as a fluid-filled sac containing daughter cysts and scolices or forming a proliferating spongy mass that actively invades and metastasizes in the host's tissues

hydr- *or* **hydro-** *comb form* [ME *ydr-*, *ydro-*, fr. OF, fr. L *hydr-*, *hydro-*, fr. Gk, fr. *hydōr* — more at WATER] **1 a :** water ⟨*hydr*ous⟩ ⟨*hydro*electricity⟩ **b :** liquid ⟨*hydro*kinetics⟩ **2 :** hydrogen **:** containing or combined with hydrogen ⟨*hydro*carbon⟩ ⟨*hydr*oxyl⟩ **3 :** hydroid ⟨*hydro*medusa⟩

Hy·dra \'hī-drə\ *n* [ME *Ydra*, fr. L *Hydra*, fr. Gk] **1 :** a 9-headed serpent or monster of Greek mythology slain by Hercules each head of which when cut off is replaced by two others unless the wound is cauterized **2** *not cap* **:** a multifarious evil not to be overcome by a single effort **3** [L (gen. *Hydrae*), fr. Gk] **:** a southern constellation of great length that lies south of Cancer, Sextans, Corvus, and Virgo and is represented on old maps by a serpent **4** *not cap* [NL, genus name, fr. L, Hydra] **:** any of numerous small tubular freshwater hydrozoan polyps (as of the genus *Hydra*)

hy·dran·gea \hī-'drān-jə\ *n* [NL, genus name, fr. *hydr-* + Gk *angeion* vessel — more at ANGI-] **:** any of a genus (*Hydrangea*) of shrubs and one woody vine of the saxifrage family with opposite leaves and showy corymbose clusters of usu. sterile white or tinted flowers

hy·drant \'hī-drənt\ *n* **1 :** a discharge pipe with a valve and spout at which water may be drawn from the mains of waterworks — called also *fireplug* **2 :** FAUCET

hy·dranth \'hī-,dran(t)th\ *n* [ISV *hydr-* + Gk *anthos* flower — more at ANTHOLOGY] **:** one of the nutritive zooids of a hydroid colony

hy·dras·tine \hī-'dras-,tēn, -tən\ *n* **:** a bitter crystalline alkaloid $C_{21}H_{21}NO_6$ that is an active constituent of hydrastis

hy·dras·tis \-təs\ *n* [NL, genus name] **:** the dried rhizome and roots of a goldenseal (*Hydrastis canadensis*) formerly used as a bitter tonic, hemostatic, and antiseptic

1**hy·drate** \'hī-,drāt\ *n* **1 :** a compound or complex ion formed by the union of water with some other substance **2 :** HYDROXIDE ⟨calcium ~⟩

²**hydrate** *vt* **:** to cause to take up or combine with water or the elements of water ~ *vi* **:** to become a hydrate — **hy·dra·tion** \hī-ˈdrā-shən\ *n* — **hy·dra·tor** \ˈhī-ˌdrāt-ər\ *n*

hy·drau·lic \hī-ˈdrȯ-lik\ *adj* [L *hydraulicus*, fr. Gk *hydraulikos*, fr. *hydraulis* hydraulic organ, fr. *hydr-* + *aulos* reed instrument — more at ALVEOLUS] **1 :** operated, moved, or effected by means of water **2 a :** of or relating to hydraulics ⟨~ engineer⟩ **b :** of or relating to water or other liquid in motion ⟨~ erosion⟩ **3 :** operated by the resistance offered or the pressure transmitted when a quantity of water, oil, or other liquid is forced through a comparatively small orifice or through a tube **4 :** hardening or setting under water ⟨~ cement⟩ — **hy·drau·li·cal·ly** \-li-k(ə-)lē\ *adv*

hydraulic ram *n* **:** a pump that forces running water to a higher level by utilizing the kinetic energy of flow

hy·drau·lics \hī-ˈdrȯ-liks\ *n pl but sing or pl in constr* **:** a branch of science that deals with practical applications (as the transmission of energy or the effects of flow) of water or other liquid in motion

hy·dra·zine \ˈhī-drə-ˌzēn\ *n* [ISV] **:** a colorless fuming corrosive strongly reducing liquid base NH_2NH_2 used esp. in fuels for rocket and jet engines; *also* **:** an organic base derived from this compound

hy·dra·zo·ic acid \ˌhī-drə-ˌzō-ik-\ *n* [*hydr-* + *azo-* + *-ic*] **:** a colorless volatile poisonous explosive liquid HN_3 that has a foul odor and yields explosive salts of heavy metals

hy·dric \ˈhī-drik\ *adj* **:** characterized by, relating to, or requiring an abundance of moisture — **hy·dri·cal·ly** \-dri-k(ə-)lē\ *adv*

-hy·dric \ˈhī-drik\ *adj suffix* **1 :** containing acid hydrogen ⟨mono*hydric*⟩ **2 :** containing hydroxyl ⟨hexa*hydric* alcohols⟩

hy·dride \ˈhī-ˌdrīd\ *n* **:** a compound of hydrogen usu. with a more electropositive element or radical

hy·dri·od·ic acid \ˌhī-drē-ˌäd-ik-\ *n* [ISV] **:** an aqueous solution of hydrogen iodide HI that is a strong liquid acid resembling hydrochloric acid chemically but is a strong reducing agent

¹**hy·dro** \ˈhī-(ˌ)drō\ *n* [short for *hydropathic establishment*] *Brit* **:** a hotel that caters to people taking a water cure or an establishment that furnishes water cures **:** SPA

²**hydro** *adj* **:** HYDROELECTRIC ⟨~ power⟩

hy·dro–air·plane \ˌhī-drō-ˈa(ə)r-ˌplān, -ˈe(ə)r-\ *n* **:** SEAPLANE

hy·dro·bomb \ˈhī-drō-ˌbäm\ *n* **:** an aerial torpedo propelled by a rocket engine after entering the water

hy·dro·bro·mic acid \ˌhī-drə-ˌbrō-mik-\ *n* [ISV] **:** an aqueous solution of hydrogen bromide HBr that is a strong liquid acid resembling hydrochloric acid chemically but is a weak reducing agent

hy·dro·car·bon \ˌhī-drə-ˈkär-bən\ *n* **:** an organic compound (as acetylene or benzene) containing only carbon and hydrogen and often occurring in petroleum, natural gas, coal, and bitumens — **hy·dro·car·bo·na·ceous** \-ˌkär-bə-ˈnā-shəs\ *or* **hy·dro·car·bon·ic** \-ˈbän-ik\ *or* **hy·dro·car·bon·ous** \-ˈkär-bə-nəs\ *adj*

hy·dro·cele \ˈhī-drə-ˌsēl\ *n* [L, fr. Gk *hydrokēlē*, fr. *hydr-* + *kēlē* tumor — more at -CELE] **:** an accumulation of serous fluid in a sacculated cavity (as the scrotum)

hy·dro·ce·phal·ic \ˌhī-drō-sə-ˈfal-ik\ *adj* **:** relating to, characterized by, or exhibiting hydrocephalus — **hydrocephalic** *n* — **hy·dro·ceph·a·lous** \-ˈsef-ə-ləs\ *adj*

hy·dro·ceph·a·lus \-ˈsef-ə-ləs\ *also* **hy·dro·ceph·a·ly** \-lē\ *n* [NL *hydrocephalus*, fr. LL, hydrocephalous, fr. Gk *hydrokephalos*, fr. *hydr-* + *kephalē* head — more at CEPHALIC] **:** an abnormal increase in the amount of cerebrospinal fluid within the cranial cavity, with expansion of the cerebral ventricles, enlargement of the skull esp. the forehead, and atrophy of the brain

hy·dro·chlo·ric acid \ˌhī-drə-ˌklōr-ik-, -ˌklȯr-\ *n* [ISV] **:** an aqueous solution of hydrogen chloride HCl that is a strong corrosive irritating liquid acid, is normally present in dilute form in gastric juice, and is widely used in industry and in the laboratory

hy·dro·chlo·ride \-ˈklō(ə)r-ˌīd, -ˈklȯ(ə)r-\ *n* **:** a compound of hydrochloric acid

hy·dro·col·loid \ˌhī-drə-ˈkäl-ˌȯid\ *n* **:** a substance that yields a gel with water — **hy·dro·col·loi·dal** \-kə-ˈlȯid-ᵊl, -kä-\ *adj*

hy·dro·cor·ti·sone \ˌhī-(ˌ)drō-ˈkȯrt-ə-ˌsōn, -ˌzōn\ *n* **:** a crystalline hormone $C_{21}H_{30}O_5$ of the adrenal cortex that is a derivative of cortisone and is used similarly

hy·dro·cy·an·ic acid \ˌhī-drō-(ˌ)sī-ˌan-ik-\ *n* [ISV] **:** an aqueous solution of hydrogen cyanide HCN that is a weak poisonous liquid acid and is used chiefly in fumigating and in organic synthesis

hy·dro·dy·nam·ic \-(ˌ)dī-ˈnam-ik\ *adj* [NL *hydrodynamicus*, fr. *hydr-* + *dynamicus* dynamic] **:** of or relating to hydrodynamics — **hy·dro·dy·nam·i·cal** \-i-kəl\ *adj* — **hy·dro·dy·nam·i·cal·ly** \-i-k(ə-)lē\ *adv*

hy·dro·dy·nam·ics \-iks\ *n pl but sing or pl in constr* **:** a branch of science that deals with the motion of fluids and the forces acting on solid bodies immersed in fluids and in motion relative to them — compare HYDROSTATICS

hy·dro·elec·tric \ˌhī-drō-i-ˈlek-trik\ *adj* [ISV] **:** of or relating to production of electricity by waterpower — **hy·dro·elec·tric·i·ty** \-ˌlek-ˈtris-ət-ē, -ˈtris-tē\ *n*

hy·dro·flu·or·ic acid \ˌhī-drō-flü-ˌȯr-ik, -ˌär-\ *n* [ISV] **:** an aqueous solution of hydrogen fluoride HF that is a weak poisonous liquid acid resembling hydrochloric acid chemically but attacking silica and silicates and is used esp. in polishing and etching glass

hy·dro·foil \ˈhī-drə-ˌfȯil\ *n* **1 :** a body similar to an airfoil but designed for action in or on water **2 :** a motorboat that has metal plates or fins attached by struts fore and aft for lifting the hull clear of the water as speed is attained

hy·dro·form·ing \-ˌfȯr-miŋ\ *n* [*hydr-* + *reforming*] **:** a process for producing high-octane gasoline from petroleum naphthas by catalytic dehydrogenation and aromatization in the presence of hydrogen

hy·dro·gen \ˈhī-drə-jən\ *n* [F *hydrogène*, fr. *hydr-* + *-gène* -gen; fr. the fact that water is generated by its combustion] **:** a nonmetallic univalent element that is the simplest and lightest of the elements, is normally a colorless odorless highly flammable diatomic gas, and is used esp. in the production of its economic compounds — compare DEUTERIUM, TRITIUM; see ELEMENT table — **hy·drog·e·nous** \hī-ˈdräj-ə-nəs\ *adj*

hy·dro·ge·nate \hī-ˈdräj-ə-ˌnāt, ˈhī-drə-jə-\ *vt* **:** to combine or treat with or expose to hydrogen; *esp* **:** to add hydrogen to the molecule of (an unsaturated organic compound) — **hy·dro·ge·na·tion** \(ˌ)hī-ˌdräj-ə-ˈnā-shən, ˌhī-drə-jə-\ *n*

hydrogen bomb *n* **:** a bomb whose violent explosive power is due to the sudden release of atomic energy resulting from the union of light nuclei (as of hydrogen atoms) at very high temperature and pressure to form helium nuclei

hydrogen ion *n* **1 :** the cation H^+ of acids consisting of a hydrogen atom whose electron has been transferred to the anion of the acid **2 :** HYDRONIUM

hydrogen peroxide *n* **:** an unstable compound H_2O_2 used esp. as an oxidizing and bleaching agent, an antiseptic, and a propellant

hydrogen sulfide *n* **:** a flammable poisonous gas H_2S of disagreeable odor found esp. in many mineral waters and in putrefying matter

hy·drog·ra·pher \hī-ˈdräg-rə-fər\ *n* **:** a specialist in hydrography

hy·dro·graph·ic \ˌhī-drə-ˈgraf-ik\ *adj* **:** of or relating to hydrography — **hy·dro·graph·i·cal·ly** \-i-k(ə-)lē\ *adv*

hy·drog·ra·phy \hī-ˈdräg-rə-fē\ *n* [MF *hydrographie*, fr. *hydr-* + *-graphie* -graphy] **1 :** the description and study of seas, lakes, rivers, and other waters: as **a :** the measurement of flow and investigation of the behavior of streams esp. with reference to the control of their waters **b :** the charting of bodies of water **2 :** bodies of water

¹**hy·droid** \ˈhī-ˌdrȯid\ *adj* [deriv. of NL *Hydra*] **:** of or relating to a hydrozoan; *esp* **:** resembling a typical hydra

²**hydroid** *n* **:** HYDROZOAN; *esp* **:** a hydrozoan polyp as distinguished from a medusa

hy·dro·ki·net·ic \ˌhī-drō-kə-ˈnet-ik, -(ˌ)kī-\ *adj* **:** of or relating to the motions of fluids or the forces which produce or affect such motions — compare HYDROSTATIC

hy·dro·log·ic \-drə-ˈläj-ik\ *adj* **:** of or relating to hydrology — **hy·dro·log·i·cal** \-i-kəl\ *adj* — **hy·dro·log·i·cal·ly** \-k(ə-)lē\ *adv*

hy·drol·o·gist \hī-ˈdräl-ə-jəst\ *n* **:** a specialist in hydrology

hy·drol·o·gy \-jē\ *n* [NL *hydrologia*, fr. L *hydr-* + *-logia* -logy] **:** a science dealing with the properties, distribution, and circulation of water on the surface of the land, in the soil and underlying rocks, and in the atmosphere

hy·drol·y·sate *also* **hy·drol·y·zate** \hī-ˈdräl-ə-ˌsāt, -ˌzāt\ *n* **:** a product of hydrolysis

hy·drol·y·sis \hī-ˈdräl-ə-səs\ *n* [NL] **:** a chemical process of decomposition involving splitting of a bond and addition of the elements of water — **hy·dro·lyte** \ˈhī-drə-ˌlīt\ *n* — **hy·dro·lyt·ic** \ˌhī-drə-ˈlit-ik\ *adj*

hy·dro·lyz·able \ˈhī-drə-ˌlī-zə-bəl\ *adj* **:** capable of hydrolyzing or being hydrolyzed

hy·dro·lyze \ˈhī-drə-ˌlīz\ *vb* [ISV, fr. NL *hydrolysis*] *vt* **:** to subject to hydrolysis ~ *vi* **:** to undergo hydrolysis

hy·dro·man·cer \-ˌman(t)-sər\ *n* **:** a diviner using hydromancy

hy·dro·man·cy \-sē\ *n* [ME *ydromancie*, fr. MF, fr. L *hydromantia*, fr. *hydr-* + *-mantia* -mancy] **:** divination by water or other liquid

hy·dro·me·du·sa \ˌhī-drō-mi-ˈd(y)ü-sə, -zə\ *n, pl* **hy·dro·me·du·sae** \-ˌsē, -ˌzē\ [NL] **:** a medusa produced as a bud from a hydroid (as of the orders Anthomedusae and Leptomedusae) — **hy·dro·me·du·san** \-ˈd(y)üs-ᵊn, -ˈd(y)üz-\ *adj or n* — **hy·dro·me·du·soid** \-ˈd(y)ü-ˌsȯid, -ˌzȯid\ *adj*

hy·dro·mel \ˈhī-drə-ˌmel\ *n* [ME *ydromel*, fr. MF & L; MF, fr. L *hydromeli*, fr. Gk, fr. *hydr-* + *meli* honey] **:** a liquor consisting of honey diluted in water which upon fermentation becomes mead

hy·dro·met·al·lur·gy \ˌhī-drō-ˈmet-ᵊl-ˌər-jē\ *n* [ISV] **:** the treatment of ores by wet processes (as leaching)

hy·dro·me·te·or \-ˈmēt-ē-ər, -ē-ˌȯ(ə)r\ *n* [ISV] **:** an occurrence of atmospheric water vapor in any of its forms — **hy·dro·me·te·o·rol·o·gy** \-ˌmēt-ē-ə-ˈräl-ə-jē\ *n*

hy·drom·e·ter \hī-ˈdräm-ət-ər\ *n* **:** a floating instrument for determining specific gravities of liquids and hence the strength (as of spirituous liquors, saline solutions) — **hy·dro·met·ric** \ˌhī-drə-ˈme-trik\ *or* **hy·dro·met·ri·cal** \-tri-kəl\ *adj* — **hy·drom·e·try** \hī-ˈdräm-ə-trē\ *n*

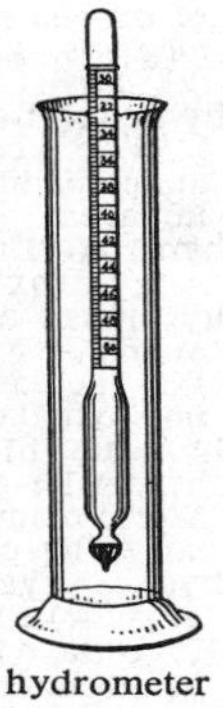

hydrometer

hy·dro·mor·phic \ˌhī-drə-ˈmȯr-fik\ *adj, of a soil* **:** developed in the presence of an excess of moisture which tends to suppress aerobic factors in soil-building

hy·dro·ni·um \hī-ˈdrō-nē-əm\ *n* **:** a hydrated hydrogen ion H_3O^+

hy·dro·path·ic \-ˈpath-ik\ *adj* **:** of or relating to hydropathy — **hy·dro·path·i·cal·ly** \-i-k(ə-)lē\ *adv*

hy·drop·a·thy \hī-ˈdräp-ə-thē\ *n* [ISV] **:** the empirical use of water in the treatment of disease — compare HYDROTHERAPY

hy·dro·phane \ˈhī-drə-ˌfān\ *n* **:** a semitranslucent opal that becomes translucent or transparent on immersion in water

hy·dro·phil·ic \ˌhī-drə-ˈfil-ik\ *or* **hy·dro·phile** \ˈhī-drə-ˌfīl\ *adj* [NL *hydrophilus*, fr. Gk *hydr-* + *-philos* -philous] **:** of, relating to, or having a strong affinity for water

hy·droph·i·lous \hī-ˈdräf-ə-ləs\ *adj* [NL *hydrophilus*] **1 :** pollinated by the agency of water **2 :** HYDROPHYTIC — **hy·droph·i·ly** \-lē\ *n*

hy·dro·pho·bia \ˌhī-drə-ˈfō-bē-ə\ *n* [LL, fr. Gk, fr. *hydr-* + *-phobia* fear of something] **1 :** a morbid dread of water **2 :** RABIES

hy·dro·pho·bic \-ˈfō-bik, -ˈfäb-ik\ *adj* **1 :** of, relating to, or suffering from hydrophobia **2 :** lacking affinity for water — **hy·dro·pho·bic·i·ty** \-fō-ˈbis-ət-ē\ *n*

hy·dro·phone \ˈhī-drə-ˌfōn\ *n* **:** an instrument for listening to sound transmitted through water

hy·dro·phyte \-ˌfīt\ *n* [ISV] **1 :** a perennial vascular aquatic plant having its overwintering buds under water **2 :** a plant growing in water or in soil too waterlogged for most plants to survive — **hy·dro·phyt·ic** \ˌhī-drə-ˈfit-ik\ *adj*

¹**hy·dro·plane** \ˈhī-drə-ˌplān\ *n* **1 :** HYDROFOIL **2 a :** a speedboat with hydrofoils or a stepped bottom so that the hull is raised wholly or partly out of the water **b :** a rudder on a horizontal axis on a submarine for steering it upward or downward **3 :** SEAPLANE

²**hydroplane** *vi* **1 :** to skim over the water with the hull more or less clear of the surface **2 :** to drive or ride in a hydroplane

hy·dro·pon·ic \ˌhī-drə-ˈpän-ik\ *adj* **:** of or relating to hydroponics — **hy·dro·pon·i·cal·ly** \-i-k(ə-)lē\ *adv*

hy·dro·pon·ics \-ˈpän-iks\ *n pl but sing or pl in constr* [*hydr-* +

-ponics (as in *geoponics*)] **:** the growing of plants in nutrient solutions with or without an inert medium to provide mechanical support
hy·dro·pow·er \'hī-drə-,pau̇(-ə)r\ *n* **:** hydroelectric power
hy·dro·qui·none \,hī-drō-kwin-'ōn, -'kwin-,ōn\ *n* [ISV] **:** a white crystalline strongly reducing phenol $C_6H_4(OH)_2$ made usu. by reduction of quinone and used esp. as a photographic developer and as an antioxidant and stabilizer
hy·dro·scope \'hī-drə-,skōp\ *n* [ISV] **:** a mirror device for enabling a person to see an object at considerable distance below the surface of water
hy·dro–ski \'hī-drō-,skē\ *n* **:** a hydrofoil attached below the fuselage of a seaplane to accelerate takeoffs
hy·dro·sol \'hī-drə-,säl, -,sȯl\ *n* [*hydr-* + *-sol* (fr. *solution*)] **:** a sol in which the liquid is water — **hy·dro·sol·ic** \,hī-drə-'säl-ik\ *adj*
hy·dro·sphere \'hī-drə-,sfi(ə)r\ *n* [ISV] **1 :** the aqueous vapor of the atmosphere **2 :** the aqueous envelope of the earth including bodies of water and aqueous vapor in the atmosphere
hy·dro·stat·ic \,hī-drə-'stat-ik\ *adj* [prob. fr. NL *hydrostaticus*, fr. *hydr-* + *staticus* static] **:** of or relating to liquids at rest or to the pressures they exert or transmit — compare HYDROKINETIC — **hy·dro·stat·i·cal** \-i-kəl\ *adj* — **hy·dro·stat·i·cal·ly** \-i-k(ə-)lē\ *adv*
hy·dro·stat·ics \-'stat-iks\ *n pl but sing or pl in constr* **:** a branch of physics that deals with the characteristics of liquids at rest and esp. with the pressure in a liquid or exerted by a liquid on an immersed body — compare HYDRODYNAMICS
hy·dro·sul·fide \,hī-drə-'səl-,fīd\ *n* [ISV] **:** a compound derived from hydrogen sulfide by the replacement of half its hydrogen by an element or radical
hy·dro·sul·fite \-,fīt\ *n* [ISV] **:** a salt of hydrosulfurous acid; *esp* **:** sodium hydrosulfite used as a reducing and bleaching agent
hy·dro·sul·fu·rous acid \,hī-drō-,səl-f(y)ə-rəs-, -,fyu̇r-əs-\ *n* [ISV] **:** an unstable acid $H_2S_2O_4$ known only in aqueous solution formed by reducing sulfurous acid
hy·dro·tac·tic \,hī-drō-'tak-tik\ *adj* **:** of or relating to hydrotaxis
hy·dro·tax·is \-'tak-səs\ *n* [NL] **:** a taxis in which moisture is the directive factor
hy·dro·ther·a·py \-'ther-ə-pē\ *n* [ISV] **:** the scientific use of water in the treatment of disease — compare HYDROPATHY
hy·dro·ther·mal \,hī-drō-'thər-məl\ *adj* [ISV] **:** of or relating to hot water — used esp. of the formation of minerals by hot solutions rising from a cooling magma
hy·dro·tho·rax \-'thō(ə)r-,aks, -'thȯ(ə)r-\ *n* [NL] **:** an excess of serous fluid in the pleural cavity
hy·dro·trop·ic \,hī-drə-'träp-ik\ *adj* **:** exhibiting or characterized by hydrotropism — **hy·dro·trop·i·cal·ly** \-i-k(ə-)lē\ *adv*
hy·drot·ro·pism \hī-'drä-trə-,piz-əm\ *n* [ISV] **:** a tropism (as in plant roots) in which water or water vapor is the orienting factor
hy·drous \'hī-drəs\ *adj* **:** containing water usu. chemically combined (as in hydrates)
hy·drox·ide \hī-'dräk-,sīd\ *n* [ISV] **1 :** a compound of hydroxyl with an element or radical **2 :** any of various hydrated oxides regarded as containing hydroxyl
hydroxide ion *n* **:** the anion OH^- of basic hydroxides — called also *hydroxyl ion*
hydroxy- *or* **hydrox-** *comb form* [ISV, fr. *hydroxyl*] **:** hydroxyl **:** containing hydroxyl esp. in place of hydrogen ⟨*hydroxy*acetic acid⟩ — **hy·droxy** \hī-'dräk-sē\ *adj*
hy·droxy·bu·tyr·ic acid \(,)hī-,dräk-sē-byu̇-,tir-ik-\ *n* **:** a hydroxy derivative $C_4H_8O_3$ of butyric acid
hy·drox·yl \hī-'dräk-səl\ *n* [*hydr-* + *ox-* + *-yl*] **:** the univalent group or radical OH consisting of one atom of hydrogen and one of oxygen that is characteristic esp. of hydroxides, oxygen acids, alcohols, glycols, and phenols — **hy·drox·yl·ic** \,hī-,dräk-'sil-ik\ *adj*
hy·drox·yl·amine \(,)hī-,dräk-sə-lə-'mēn, ,hī-,dräk-'sil-ə-,mēn\ *n* [ISV] **:** a colorless odorless nitrogenous base NH_2OH resembling ammonia in its reactions but less basic that is used esp. as a reducing agent
hy·drox·yl·ate \hī-'dräk-sə-,lāt\ *vt* **:** to introduce hydroxyl into — **hy·drox·yl·ation** \(,)hī-,dräk-sə-'lā-shən\ *n*
hy·dro·zo·an \,hī-drə-'zō-ən\ *n* [deriv. of Gk *hydr-* + *zōion* animal — more at ZO-] **:** any of a class (Hydrozoa) of coelenterates that includes simple and compound polyps and jellyfishes having no stomodaeum or gastric tentacles — **hydrozoan** *adj*
hy·e·na \hī-'ē-nə\ *n* [L *hyaena*, fr. Gk *hyaina*, fr. *hys* hog — more at SOW] **:** any of several large strong nocturnal carnivorous Old World mammals (family Hyaenidae) — **hy·e·nic** \-'ē-nik, -'en-ik\ *adj* — **hy·e·noid** \-'ē-,nȯid\ *adj*
hyet- *or* **hyeto-** *comb form* [Gk, fr. *hyetos*, fr. *hyein* to rain — more at SUCK] **:** rain ⟨*hyet*ology⟩
Hy·ge·ia \hī-'jē-(y)ə\ *n* [L, fr. Gk *Hygieia*] **:** the goddess of health in Greek mythology
hy·giene \'hī-,jēn\ *n* [F *hygiène* & NL *hygieina*, fr. Gk, neut. pl. of *hygieinos* healthful, fr. *hygiēs* healthy; akin to Skt *su* well and to L *vivus* living — more at QUICK] **1 :** a science of the establishment and maintenance of health **2 :** conditions or practices (as of cleanliness) conducive to health — **hy·gien·ic** \,hī-jē-'en-ik, hī-'jen-, hī-'jēn-\ *adj* — **hy·gien·i·cal·ly** \-i-k(ə-)lē\ *adv* — **hy·gien·ist** \hī-'jēn-əst, -'jen-, 'hī-,\ *n*
hy·gien·ics \,hī-jē-'en-iks, hī-'jen-, hī-'jēn-\ *n pl but sing in constr* **:** HYGIENE 1
hygr- *also* **hygro-** *comb form* [Gk, fr. *hygros* wet — more at HUMOR] **:** humidity **:** moisture ⟨*hygro*scope⟩
hy·gro·graph \'hī-grə-,graf\ *n* [ISV] **:** an instrument for automatic recording of variations in atmospheric humidity
hy·grom·e·ter \hī-'gräm-ət-ər\ *n* [prob. fr. F *hygromètre*, fr. *hygr-* + *-mètre* -meter] **:** any of several instruments for measuring the humidity of the atmosphere — **hy·gro·met·ric** \,hī-grə-'me-trik\ *adj* — **hy·grom·e·try** \hī-'gräm-ə-trē\ *n*
hy·gro·phyte \'hī-grə-,fīt\ *n* [ISV] **:** HYDROPHYTE — **hy·gro·phyt·ic** \,hī-grə-'fit-ik\ *adj*
hy·gro·scope \'hī-grə-,skōp\ *n* **:** an instrument that shows changes in humidity (as of the atmosphere)
hy·gro·scop·ic \,hī-grə-'skäp-ik\ *adj* [fr. the use of such materials in the hygroscope] **1 :** readily taking up and retaining moisture **2 :** involving or induced by the taking up of moisture — **hy·gro·scop·i·cal·ly** \-i-k(ə-)lē\ *adv* — **hy·gro·scop·ic·i·ty** \-(,)skäp-'is-ət-ē\ *n*
hy·gro·ther·mo·graph \,hī-grō-'thər-mə-,graf\ *n* **:** an instrument that records both humidity and temperature on the same chart
hying *pres part of* HIE
hyl- *or* **hylo-** *comb form* [Gk, fr. *hylē*, lit., wood] **:** matter **:** material ⟨*hylo*morphous⟩
hy·la \'hī-lə\ *n* [NL, fr. Gk *hylē* wood] **:** TREE TOAD
hy·lo·zo·ism \,hī-lə-'zō-,iz-əm\ *n* [Gk *hylē* + *zōos* alive, living; akin to Gk *zōē* life — more at QUICK] **:** a doctrine held esp. by early Greek philosophers that all matter is animated — **hy·lo·zo·ist** \-'zō-əst\ *n* — **hy·lo·zo·is·tic** \-zō-'is-tik\ *adj*
¹**hy·men** \'hī-mən\ *n* [L, fr. Gk *Hymēn*] **1** *cap* **:** the god of marriage in Greek mythology **2** *archaic* **:** MARRIAGE
²**hymen** *n* [LL, fr. Gk *hymēn* membrane] **:** a fold of mucous membrane partly closing the orifice of the vagina — **hy·men·al** \-mən-ᵊl\ *adj*
¹**hy·me·ne·al** \,hī-mə-'nē-əl\ *adj* [L *hymenaeus* wedding song, wedding, fr. Gk *hymenaios*, fr. *Hymēn*] **:** NUPTIAL — **hy·me·ne·al·ly** \-'nē-ə-lē\ *adv*
²**hymeneal** *n* **1** *pl, archaic* **:** NUPTIALS **2** *archaic* **:** a wedding hymn
hy·me·ni·um \hī-'mē-nē-əm\ *n, pl* **hy·me·nia** \-nē-ə\ *or* **hy·me·ni·ums** [NL, fr. Gk *hymēn* membrane] **:** a spore-bearing layer in fungi consisting of a group of asci or basidia often interspersed with sterile structures
hy·me·nop·ter·an \,hī-mə-'näp-tə-rən\ *adj* **:** HYMENOPTEROUS
hy·me·nop·ter·on \-tə-,rän, -rən\ *also* **hy·me·nop·ter·an** \-rən\ *n, pl* **hy·me·nop·tera** \-rə\ [NL *hymenopteron* fr. Gk, neut. of *hymenopteros* membrane-winged, fr. *hymēn* + *pteron* wing — more at FEATHER] **:** any of an order (Hymenoptera) of highly specialized insects with complete metamorphosis that include the bees, wasps, ants, ichneumon flies, sawflies, gall wasps, and related forms, often associate in large colonies with complex social organization, and have usu. four membranous wings and the abdomen generally borne on a slender pedicel — **hy·me·nop·ter·ous** \-rəs\ *adj*
¹**hymn** \'him\ *n* [ME *ymne*, fr. OF, fr. L *hymnus* song of praise, fr. Gk *hymnos*] **1 a :** a song of praise to God **b :** a metrical composition adapted for singing in a religious service **2 :** a song of praise or joy **3 :** something resembling a hymn **:** PAEAN
²**hymn** *vb* **hymn·ing** \'him-iŋ\ *vt* **:** to praise or worship in hymns; *also* **:** VOICE ~ *vi* **:** to sing a hymn
hym·nal \'him-nᵊl\ *n* [ME *hymnale*, fr. ML, fr. L *hymnus*] **:** a collection of church hymns
hym·na·ry \'him-nə-rē\ *n* **:** HYMNAL
hymn·book \'him-,bu̇k\ *n* **:** HYMNAL
hym·no·dy \'him-nəd-ē\ *n* [LL *hymnodia*, fr. Gk *hymnōidia*, fr. *hymnos* + *aeidein* to sing — more at ODE] **1 :** hymn singing **2 :** hymn writing **3 :** the hymns of a time, place, or church
hym·nol·o·gy \him-'näl-ə-jē\ *n* [Gk *hymnologia* singing of hymns, fr. *hymnos* + *-logia* -logy] **1 :** HYMNODY **2 :** the study of hymns
hy·oid \'hī-,ȯid\ *adj* [NL *hyoides* hyoid bone] **:** of or relating to the hyoid bone
hyoid bone *n* [NL *hyoides*, fr. Gk *hyoeidēs* shaped like the letter upsilon (Υ, υ), being the hyoid bone, fr. *y*, *hy* upsilon] **:** a bone or complex of bones situated at the base of the tongue and supporting the tongue and its muscles
hy·o·scine \'hī-ə-,sēn\ *n* [ISV *hyoscy*amine + *-ine*] **:** SCOPOLAMINE; *esp* **:** the levorotatory form of scopolamine
hy·o·scy·a·mine \,hī-ə-'sī-ə-,mēn\ *n* [G *hyoscyamin*, fr. NL *Hyoscyamus* genus of herbs, fr. L, henbane, fr. Gk *hyoskyamos*, lit., swine's bean, fr. *hyos* (gen. of *hys* swine) + *kyamos* bean — more at SOW] **:** a poisonous crystalline alkaloid $C_{17}H_{23}NO_3$; *esp* **:** its levorotatory form found in henbane and other plants of the nightshade family and used similarly to atropine
hyp \'hip\ *n, archaic* **:** HYPOCHONDRIA — often used in pl.
hyp- — see HYPO-
hyp·abys·sal \,hip-ə-'bis-əl, ,hī-pə-\ *adj* [ISV] **:** of or relating to a fine-grained igneous rock usu. formed at a moderate distance below the surface
hy·pae·thral \hip-'ē-thrəl, hī-'pē-\ *adj* [L *hypaethrus* exposed to the open air, fr. Gk *hypaithros*, fr. *hypo-* + *aithēr* ether, air — more at ETHER] **1 :** having a roofless central space ⟨~ temple⟩ **2 :** open to the sky **3 :** OUTDOOR
hy·pan·thi·al \hip-'an(t)-thē-əl, hī-'pan(t)-\ *adj* **:** of or relating to a hypanthium
hy·pan·thi·um \-thē-əm\ *n, pl* **hy·pan·thia** \-ə\ [NL] **:** an enlargement of the floral receptacle bearing on its rim the stamens, petals, and sepals and often enlarging and surrounding the fruits (as in the rose hip)
hype \'hīp\ *n* [by shortening & alter.] **1** *slang* **:** HYPODERMIC **2** *slang* **:** a narcotics addict
hyper- *prefix* [ME *iper-*, fr. L *hyper-*, fr. Gk, fr. *hyper* — more at OVER] **1 :** above **:** beyond **:** SUPER- ⟨*hyper*physical⟩ **2 a :** excessively ⟨*hyper*sensitive⟩ **b :** excessive ⟨*hyper*emia⟩ **3 :** that is or exists in a space of more than three dimensions ⟨*hyper*cube⟩ ⟨*hyper*space⟩
hy·per·ac·id \,hī-pə-'ras-əd\ *adj* **:** containing more than the normal amount of acid — **hy·per·acid·i·ty** \-rə-'sid-ət-ē\ *n*
hy·per·ac·tive \,hī-pə-'rak-tiv\ *adj* **:** excessively or pathologically active
hy·per·bo·la \hī-'pər-bə-lə\ *n, pl* **hyperbolas** *or* **hy·per·bo·lae** \-,lē\ [NL, fr. Gk *hyperbolē*] **:** a plane curve generated by a point so moving that the difference of the distances from two fixed points is a constant **:** a curve formed by the intersection of a double right circular cone with a plane that cuts both halves of the cone

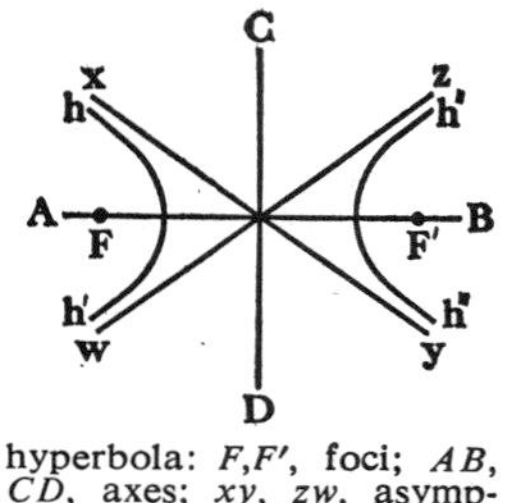

hyperbola: *F,F'*, foci; *AB*, *CD*, axes; *xy*, *zw*, asymptotes; *hh'*, *h''h'''*, hyperbolas

hy·per·bo·le \hī-'pər-bə-(,)lē\ *n* [L, fr. Gk *hyperbolē* excess, hyperbole, hyperbola, fr. *hyperballein* to exceed, fr. *hyper-* + *ballein* to throw — more at DEVIL] **:** extravagant exaggeration used as a figure of speech — **hy·per·bo·list** \-ləst\ *n*
¹**hy·per·bol·ic** \,hī-pər-'bäl-ik\ *adj* **:** of, characterized by, or given to hyperbole — **hy·per·bol·i·cal** \-i-kəl\ *adj* — **hy·per·bol·i·cal·ly** \-i-k(ə-)lē\ *adv*
²**hyperbolic** *adj* **1 :** of, relating to, or analogous to a hyperbola **2 :** of, relating to, or being a space in which more than one line

parallel to a given line passes through a point ⟨~ geometry⟩ **3 :** of, relating to, or being a function related to the hyperbola as a trigonometric function is related to a circle ⟨~ cosine⟩ — **hyper·bolical** *adj*

hy·per·bo·lize \hī-ˈpər-bə-ˌlīz\ *vi* **:** to indulge in hyperbole ~ *vt* **:** to exaggerate to a hyperbolic degree

hy·per·bo·re·an \ˌhī-pər-ˈbōr-ē-ən, -ˈbȯr-; -(ˌ)pər-bə-ˈrē-ən\ *adj* **1 :** of or relating to an extreme northern region **:** FROZEN **2 :** of or relating to any of the arctic peoples

Hyperborean *n* [L *Hyperborei* (pl.), fr. Gk *Hyperboreoi*, fr. *hyper-* + *Boreas*] **1 :** a member of a people held by the ancient Greeks to live beyond the north wind in a region of perpetual sunshine **2 :** an inhabitant of a cool northern climate

hy·per·cat·a·lec·tic \ˌhī-pər-ˌkat-ᵊl-ˈek-tik\ *adj* [LL *hypercatalecticus*, fr. Gk *hyperkatalēktos*, fr. *hyper-* + *katalēktos* catalectic] *of a verse* **:** having an additional syllable after the final complete foot or dipody — **hy·per·cat·a·lex·is** \-ˈek-səs\ *n*

hy·per·chro·mic anemia \ˌhī-pər-ˌkrō-mik-\ *n* [NL *hyperchromia*, fr. *hyper-* + Gk *chrōma* color — more at CHROMATIC] **:** an anemia with increase of hemoglobin in individual red blood cells and reduction in the number of red blood cells

hy·per·com·plex number \ˌhī-pər-ˌkäm-ˌpleks-, -kəm-\ *n* **:** an extension (as a quaternion) of the notion of complex number to an expression of the same type involving a finite number of units or components in which addition is by components and multiplication does not have all of the properties of real or complex numbers

hy·per·crit·ic \ˌhī-pər-ˈkrit-ik\ *n* [NL *hypercriticus*, fr. *hyper-* + L *criticus* critic] **:** a carping or unduly censorious critic — **hy·per·crit·i·cism** \-ˈkrit-ə-ˌsiz-əm\ *n*

hy·per·crit·i·cal \-ˈkrit-i-kəl\ *adj* **:** meticulously or excessively critical **:** CAPTIOUS **syn** see CRITICAL

hy·per·crit·i·cal·ly \-k(ə-)lē\ *adv* **:** in a hypercritical manner **:** CAPTIOUSLY

hy·per·emia \ˌhī-pə-ˈrē-mē-ə\ *n* [NL] **:** excess of blood in a body part **:** CONGESTION — **hy·per·emic** \-mik\ *adj*

hy·per·es·the·sia *or* **hy·per·aes·the·sia** \ˌhī-pə-res-ˈthē-zhə\ *n* [NL, fr. *hyper-* + *-esthesia* (as in *anesthesia*)] **:** unusual or pathological sensitivity of the skin or of a particular sense — **hy·per·es·thet·ic** \-ˈthet-ik\ *adj*

hy·per·eu·tec·tic \ˌhī-pər-yu̇-ˈtek-tik\ *adj* **:** containing the minor component in an amount in excess of that contained in the eutectic mixture

hy·per·eu·tec·toid \-ˌtȯid\ *adj* **:** containing the minor component in an amount in excess of that contained in the eutectoid

hy·per·fo·cal distance \ˌhī-pər-ˌfō-kəl-\ *n* [ISV] **:** the nearest distance upon which a photographic lens may be focused to produce satisfactory definition at infinity

hy·per·geo·met·ric \-ˌjē-ə-ˈme-trik\ *adj* **:** relating to or based on a mathematical series involving three arbitrary constants whose form covers as instances the geometric, the binomial, and other common series

hy·per·gly·ce·mia \-(ˌ)glī-ˈsē-mē-ə\ *n* [NL] **:** excess of sugar in the blood — **hy·per·gly·ce·mic** \-mik\ *adj*

hy·per·gol \ˈhī-pər-ˌgȯl, -ˌgōl\ *n* [G, fr. *hyper-* + *erg-* + *-ol*] **:** a hypergolic fluid propellant

hy·per·gol·ic \ˌhī-pər-ˈgäl-ik\ *adj* **:** igniting itself upon contact of components ⟨~ rocket propellant⟩

hy·per·in·su·lin·ism \ˌhī-pə-ˈrin(t)-s(ə-)lə-ˌniz-əm\ *n* [ISV] **:** the presence of excess insulin in the body resulting in hypoglycemia

Hy·pe·ri·on \hī-ˈpir-ē-ən\ *n* [L, fr. Gk *Hyperiōn*] **:** a Titan in Greek mythology who is the father of Helios

hy·per·ir·ri·ta·bil·i·ty \ˌhī-pə-ˌrir-ət-ə-ˈbil-ət-ē\ *n* **:** abnormally great or uninhibited response to stimuli — **hy·per·ir·ri·ta·ble** \-ˈrir-ət-ə-bəl\ *adj*

hy·per·ker·a·to·sis \ˌhī-pər-ˌker-ə-ˈtō-səs\ *n, pl* **hy·per·ker·a·to·ses** \-ˈtō-ˌsēz\ [NL] **:** hypertrophy of the corneous layer of the skin — **hy·per·ker·a·tot·ic** \-ˈtät-ik\ *adj*

hy·per·me·ter \hī-ˈpər-mət-ər\ *n* [LL *hypermetrus* hypercatalectic, fr. Gk *hypermetros* beyond measure, beyond the meter, fr. *hyper-* + *metron* measure, meter] **1 :** a hypercatalectic verse **2 :** a period comprising more than two or three cola — **hy·per·met·ric** \ˌhī-pər-ˈme-trik\ *or* **hy·per·met·ri·cal** \-tri-kəl\ *adj*

hy·per·me·tro·pia \ˌhī-pər-mi-ˈtrō-pē-ə\ *n* [NL, fr. Gk *hypermetros* + NL *-opia*] **:** HYPEROPIA — **hy·per·me·tro·pic** \-ˈtrōp-ik, -ˈträp-\ *adj* — **hy·per·me·tro·pi·cal** \-i-kəl\ *adj* — **hy·per·met·ro·py** \-ˈme-trə-pē\ *n*

hy·perm·ne·sia \ˌhī-(ˌ)pərm-ˈnē-zh(ē-)ə\ *n* [NL, fr. *hyper-* + *-mnesia* (as in *amnesia*)] **:** abnormally vivid or complete memory or recall of the past — **hy·perm·ne·sic** \-ˈnē-zik, -sik\ *adj*

hy·per·morph \ˈhī-pər-ˌmȯrf\ *n* **1 :** ECTOMORPH **2 :** a mutant gene having a similar but greater effect than the corresponding wild-type gene — **hy·per·mor·phic** \ˌhī-pər-ˈmȯr-fik\ *adj* — **hy·per·mor·phism** \-ˌfiz-əm\ *n*

hy·per·on \ˈhī-pə-ˌrän\ *n* [prob. fr. *hyper-* + *-on*] **:** any of various elementary particles greater in mass than the proton or neutron

hy·per·ope \ˈhī-pə-ˌrōp\ *n* [back-formation fr. *hyperopia*] **:** one affected with hyperopia

hy·per·opia \ˌhī-pə-ˈrō-pē-ə\ *n* [NL] **:** a condition in which visual images come to a focus behind the retina of the eye and vision is better for distant than for near objects — **hy·per·opic** \-ˈrōp-ik, -ˈräp-\ *adj*

hy·per·os·to·sis \ˌhī-pə-ˌräs-ˈtō-səs\ *n, pl* **hy·per·os·to·ses** \-ˈtō-ˌsēz\ [NL] **:** excessive growth or thickening of bone tissue — **hy·per·os·tot·ic** \-ˈtät-ik\ *adj*

hy·per·phys·i·cal \ˌhī-pər-ˈfiz-i-kəl\ *adj* **:** extending, lying beyond, or independent of the physical — **hy·per·phys·i·cal·ly** \-i-k(ə-)lē\ *adv*

hy·per·pi·tu·ita·rism \-pə-ˈt(y)ü-ə-tə-ˌriz-əm\ *n* [ISV] **:** excessive production of growth hormones by the pituitary body — **hy·per·pi·tu·itary** \-ˌter-ē\ *adj*

hy·per·pla·sia \ˌhī-pər-ˈplā-zh(ē-)ə\ *n* [NL] **:** an abnormal or unusual increase in the elements composing a part (as tissue cells) — **hy·per·plas·tic** \-ˈplas-tik\ *adj*

hy·per·ploid \ˈhī-pər-ˌplȯid\ *adj* [ISV] **:** having a chromosome number slightly greater than an exact multiple of the monoploid number — **hyperploid** *n* — **hy·per·ploi·dy** \-ˌplȯid-ē\ *n*

hy·per·pnea \ˌhī-pər-ˈnē-ə, -ˌpərp-ˈnē-\ *n* [NL] **:** abnormally rapid or deep breathing — **hy·per·pne·ic** \-ˈnē-ik\ *adj*

hy·per·py·ret·ic \ˌhī-pər-(ˌ)pī-ˈret-ik\ *adj* [ISV] **:** of or relating to hyperpyrexia

hy·per·py·rex·ia \-ˈrek-sē-ə\ *n* [NL] **:** exceptionally high fever (as for a particular disease)

hy·per·sen·si·tive \-ˈsen(t)-sət-iv, -ˈsen(t)-stiv\ *adj* **:** excessively or abnormally sensitive — **hy·per·sen·si·tive·ness** *n* — **hy·per·sen·si·tiv·i·ty** \-ˌsen(t)-sə-ˈtiv-ət-ē\ *n*

hy·per·son·ic \-ˈsän-ik\ *adj* [ISV] **1 :** of or relating to speed five or more times that of sound in air — compare SONIC **2 :** moving, capable of moving, or utilizing air currents that move at hypersonic speed ⟨~ wind tunnel⟩

hy·per·sthene \ˈhī-pərs-ˌthēn\ *n* [F *hypersthène*, fr. Gk *hyper-* + *sthenos* strength] **:** an orthorhombic grayish or greenish black or dark brown pyroxene $(MgFe)SiO_3$ — **hy·per·sthe·nic** \ˌhī-pərs-ˈthen-ik, -ˈthē-\ *adj*

hy·per·ten·sion \ˌhī-pər-ˈten-chən\ *n* [ISV] **:** abnormally high blood pressure and esp. arterial blood pressure; *also* **:** the systemic condition accompanying high blood pressure — **hy·per·ten·sive** \-ˈten(t)-siv\ *adj or n*

hy·per·thy·roid \-ˈthī-ˌrȯid\ *adj* [back-formation fr. *hyperthyroidism*] **:** of or relating to hyperthyroidism

hy·per·thy·roid·ism \-ˌrȯi-ˌdiz-əm\ *n* [ISV] **:** excessive functional activity of the thyroid gland; *also* **:** the resulting condition marked esp. by increased metabolic rate, enlargement of the thyroid gland, rapid heart rate, and high blood pressure

hy·per·ton·ic \-ˈtän-ik\ *adj* [ISV] **1 :** having excessive tone or tension **2 :** having a higher osmotic pressure than a fluid under comparison — **hy·per·to·nic·i·ty** \-tə-ˈnis-ət-ē\ *n*

hy·per·tro·phic \hī-ˈpər-trə-fik; ˌhī-pər-ˈträf-ik, -ˈtrōf-\ *adj* **:** of, relating to, or tending to hypertrophy

1**hy·per·tro·phy** \hī-ˈpər-trə-fē\ *n* [prob. fr. NL *hypertrophia*, fr. *hyper-* + *-trophia* -trophy] **1 :** excessive development of an organ or part; *specif* **:** increase in bulk (as by thickening of muscle fibers) without multiplication of parts **2 :** exaggerated growth or complexity **:** ELABORATION

2**hypertrophy** *vt* **:** to affect with hypertrophy ~ *vi* **:** to undergo hypertrophy

hy·per·vi·ta·min·osis \ˌhī-pər-ˌvīt-ə-mə-ˈnō-səs\ *n, pl* **hy·per·vi·ta·min·oses** \-ˈnō-ˌsēz\ [NL, fr. *hyper-* + ISV *vitamin* + NL *-osis*] **:** an abnormal state resulting from excessive intake of one or more vitamins

hy·pha \ˈhī-fə\ *n, pl* **hy·phae** \-(ˌ)fē\ [NL, fr. Gk *hyphē* web; akin to Gk *hyphos* web — more at WEAVE] **:** one of the threads that make up the mycelium of a fungus, increase by apical growth, and are coenocytic or transversely septate — **hy·phal** \-fəl\ *adj*

hy·phen \ˈhī-fən\ *n* [LL & Gk; LL, fr. Gk, fr. *hyph' hen* under one, fr. *hypo* under + *hen*, neut. of *heis* one — more at UP, SAME] **:** a punctuation mark - used to divide or to compound words or word elements — **hyphen** *vt* **hy·phen·ing** \ˈhīf-(ə-)niŋ\

hy·phen·ate \ˈhī-fə-ˌnāt\ *vt* **:** HYPHEN — **hy·phen·ation** \ˌhī-fə-ˈnā-shən\ *n*

hy·phen·at·ed *adj* [fr. the use of hyphenated words (as German-American) to designate foreign-born citizens of the U.S.] **:** of mixed origin ⟨~ citizens formerly suspected of having conflicting loyalties⟩

hy·phen·iza·tion \ˌhīf-(ə-)nə-ˈzā-shən\ *n* **:** the act of hyphenizing **:** the state of being hyphenized

hy·phen·ize \ˈhī-fə-ˌnīz\ *vt* **:** HYPHEN

hypn- *or* **hypno-** *comb form* [F, fr. LL, fr. Gk, fr. *hypnos* — more at SOMNOLENT] **1 :** sleep ⟨*hypno*phobia⟩ **2 :** hypnotism ⟨*hypno*genesis⟩

hyp·na·gog·ic *or* **hyp·no·gog·ic** \ˌhip-nə-ˈgäj-ik\ *adj* [F *hypnagogique*, fr. Gk *hypn-* + *-agōgos* leading, inducing, fr. *agein* to lead — more at AGENT] **:** of, relating to, or associated with the drowsiness preceding sleep

hyp·no·anal·y·sis \ˌhip-nō-ə-ˈnal-ə-səs\ *n* **:** the treatment of mental disease using hypnosis and psychoanalytical methods

hyp·no·gen·e·sis \-ˈjen-ə-səs\ *n* [NL] **:** the induction of a hypnotic state — **hyp·no·ge·net·ic** \-jə-ˈnet-ik\ *adj* — **hyp·no·ge·net·i·cal·ly** \-i-k(ə-)lē\ *adv*

hyp·noid \ˈhip-ˌnȯid\ *or* **hyp·noi·dal** \hip-ˈnȯid-ᵊl\ *adj* **:** of or relating to sleep or hypnosis

hyp·no·pom·pic \ˌhip-nə-ˈpäm-pik\ *adj* [*hypn-* + Gk *pompē* act of sending — more at POMP] **:** dispelling sleep or associated with the semiconsciousness preceding waking

hyp·no·sis \hip-ˈnō-səs\ *n, pl* **hyp·no·ses** \-ˈnō-ˌsēz\ [NL] **1 :** a state that resembles sleep but is induced by a hypnotizer whose suggestions are readily accepted by the subject **2 :** any of various conditions that resemble sleep **3 :** HYPNOTISM 1

hyp·no·ther·a·py \ˌhip-nō-ˈther-ə-pē\ *n* **1 :** the treatment of disease by hypnotism **2 :** psychotherapy that facilitates suggestion, reeducation, or analysis by means of hypnosis

1**hyp·not·ic** \hip-ˈnät-ik\ *adj* [F or LL; F *hypnotique*, fr. LL *hypnoticus*, fr. Gk *hypnōtikos*, fr. *hypnoun* to put to sleep, fr. *hypnos*] **1 :** tending to produce sleep **:** SOPORIFIC **2 :** of or relating to hypnosis or hypnotism — **hyp·not·i·cal·ly** \-i-k(ə-)lē\ *adv*

2**hypnotic** *n* **1 :** a sleep-inducing agent **:** SOPORIFIC **2 :** one that is or can be hypnotized

hyp·no·tism \ˈhip-nə-ˌtiz-əm\ *n* **1 :** the study or act of inducing hypnosis — compare MESMERISM **2 :** HYPNOSIS 1 — **hyp·no·tist** \-təst\ *n*

hyp·no·tiz·able \ˈhip-nə-ˌtī-zə-bəl\ *adj* **:** amenable to being hypnotized

hyp·no·ti·za·tion \ˌhip-nət-ə-ˈzā-shən\ *n* **:** the act of hypnotizing **:** the state of being hypnotized

hyp·no·tize \ˈhip-nə-ˌtīz\ *vt* **1 :** to induce hypnosis in **2 :** to dazzle or overcome by or as if by suggestion ⟨a voice that ~s its hearers⟩ ⟨drivers *hypnotized* by speed⟩ — **hyp·no·tiz·er** *n*

1**hy·po** \ˈhī-(ˌ)pō\ *n* **:** HYPOCHONDRIA

2**hypo** *n* [short for *hyposulfite*] **:** sodium thiosulfate used as a fixing agent in photography

3**hypo** *n* **1 :** HYPODERMIC SYRINGE **2 :** HYPODERMIC INJECTION **3 :** STIMULUS

4**hypo** *vt* **:** STIMULATE

hypo- *or* **hyp-** *prefix* [ME *ypo-*, fr. OF, fr. LL *hypo-*, *hyp-*, fr. Gk,

ə abut; ᵊ kitten; ər further; a back; ā bake; ä cot, cart; au̇ out; ch chin; e less; ē easy; g gift; i trip; ī life
j joke; ŋ sing; ō flow; ȯ flaw; ȯi coin; th thin; t͟h this; ü loot; u̇ foot; y yet; yü few; yu̇ furious; zh vision

fr. *hypo* — more at UP] **1 :** under **:** beneath **:** down ⟨*hypo*blast⟩ ⟨*hypo*dermic⟩ **2 :** less than normal or normally ⟨*hyp*esthesia⟩ ⟨*hypo*tension⟩ **3 :** in a lower state of oxidation **:** in a low usu. the lowest position in a series of compounds ⟨*hypo*nitrous acid⟩ ⟨*hypo*xanthine⟩

hy·po·blast \ˈhī-pə-ˌblast\ *n* **:** the endoderm of an embryo — **hy·po·blas·tic** \ˌhī-pə-ˈblas-tik\ *adj*

hy·po·bran·chi·al \ˌhī-pō-ˈbraŋ-kē-əl\ *adj* **:** situated below the gills; *specif* **:** of or relating to the ventral wall of the pharynx — **hypobranchial** *n*

hy·po·caust \ˈhī-pə-ˌkȯst\ *n* [L *hypocaustum*, fr. Gk *hypokauston*, fr. *hypokaiein* to light a fire under, fr. *hypo-* + *kaiein* to burn — more at CAUSTIC] **:** an ancient Roman central heating system with underground furnace and tile flues to distribute the heat

hy·po·cen·ter \ˌhī-pō-ˈsent-ər\ *n* **:** the point on the earth's surface directly below the center of a nuclear bomb explosion

hy·po·chlo·rite \ˌhī-pə-ˈklō(ə)r-ˌīt, -ˈklȯ(ə)r-\ *n* **:** a salt or ester of hypochlorous acid

hy·po·chlo·rous acid \ˌhī-pə-ˌklōr-əs-, -ˌklȯr-\ *n* [ISV] **:** an unstable strongly oxidizing but weak acid $HClO$ obtained in solution along with hydrochloric acid by reaction of chlorine with water and used esp. in the form of salts as an oxidizing agent, bleaching agent, disinfectant, and chlorinating agent

hy·po·chon·dria \ˌhī-pə-ˈkän-drē-ə\ *n* [NL, fr. LL, pl., upper abdomen (formerly regarded as the seat of hypochondria), fr. Gk, lit., the parts under the cartilage (of the breastbone), fr. *hypo-* + *chondros* cartilage — more at GRIND] **:** extreme depression of mind or spirits often centered on imaginary physical ailments; *specif* **:** HYPOCHONDRIASIS

1**hy·po·chon·dri·ac** \-drē-ˌak\ *adj* [F *hypochondriaque*, fr. Gk *hypochondriakos*, fr. *hypochondria*] **1 a :** situated below the costal cartilages **b :** of, relating to, or being the two regions of the abdomen lying on either side of the epigastric region and above the lumbar regions **2 :** affected or produced by hypochondria

2**hypochondriac** *n* **:** one affected by hypochondria

hy·po·chon·dri·a·cal \-kən-ˈdrī-ə-kəl, -ˌkän-\ *adj* **:** HYPOCHONDRIAC 2 — **hy·po·chon·dri·a·cal·ly** \-ə-k(ə-)lē\ *adv*

hy·po·chon·dri·a·sis \-ˈdrī-ə-səs\ *n, pl* **hy·po·chon·dri·a·ses** \-ə-ˌsēz\ [NL, fr. *hypochondria* + *-iasis*] **:** morbid concern about one's health esp. when accompanied by delusions of physical disease

hy·po·chro·mic anemia \ˌhī-pə-ˌkrō-mik-\ *n* **:** an anemia marked by deficient hemoglobin and usu. microcytic red blood cells

hy·po·co·rism \hī-ˈpäk-ə-ˌriz-əm; ˌhī-pə-ˈkō(ə)r-ˌiz-, -ˈkȯ(ə)r-\ *n* [LL *hypocorisma*, fr. Gk *hypokorisma*, fr. *hypokorizesthai* to call by pet names, fr. *hypo-* + *korizesthai* to caress, fr. *koros* boy, *korē* girl] **:** a pet name or the use of pet names; *also* **:** EUPHEMISM — **hy·po·co·ris·tic** \ˌhī-pə-kə-ˈris-tik\ *or* **hy·po·co·ris·ti·cal** \-ti-kəl\ *adj* — **hy·po·co·ris·ti·cal·ly** \-ti-k(ə-)lē\ *adv*

hy·po·cot·yl \ˈhī-pə-ˌkät-ᵊl\ *n* [ISV *hypo-* + *cotyl*edon] **:** the part of the axis of a plant embryo or seedling below the cotyledon

hy·poc·ri·sy \hip-ˈäk-rə-sē\ *n* [ME *ypocrisie*, fr. OF, fr. LL *hypocrisis*, fr. Gk *hypokrisis* act of playing a part on the stage, hypocrisy, fr. *hypokrinesthai* to answer, act on the stage, fr. *hypo-* + *krinein* to decide — more at CERTAIN] **:** a feigning to be what one is not or to believe what one does not; *esp* **:** the false assumption of an appearance of virtue or religion

hyp·o·crite \ˈhip-ə-ˌkrit\ *n* [ME *ypocrite*, fr. OF, fr. LL *hypocrita*, fr. Gk *hypokritēs* actor, hypocrite, fr. *hypokrinesthai*] **:** one who affects virtues or qualities he does not have **:** DISSEMBLER — **hypocrite** *adj* — **hyp·o·crit·i·cal** \ˌhip-ə-ˈkrit-i-kəl\ *adj* — **hyp·o·crit·i·cal·ly** \-i-k(ə-)lē\ *adv*

hy·po·derm \ˈhī-pə-ˌdərm\ *n* [NL *hypoderma*, fr. *hypo-* + *-derma*] **1 a :** HYPODERMIS 2b **b :** HYPOBLAST **2 :** HYPODERMIS 1

hy·po·der·mal \ˌhī-pə-ˈdər-məl\ *or* **hy·po·der·mous** \-məs\ *adj* **:** of or relating to a hypodermis; *also* **:** lying beneath an outer skin or epidermis

1**hy·po·der·mic** \-ˈdər-mik\ *adj* [ISV] **1 :** of or relating to the parts beneath the skin **2 :** adapted for use in or administered by injection beneath the skin **3 :** resembling a hypodermic injection in effect **:** STIMULATING — **hy·po·der·mi·cal·ly** \-mi-k(ə-)lē\ *adv*

2**hypodermic** *n* **1 :** HYPODERMIC INJECTION **2 :** HYPODERMIC SYRINGE

hypodermic injection *n* **:** an injection made into the subcutaneous tissues

hypodermic needle *n* **1 :** NEEDLE 1c(2) **2 :** a hypodermic syringe complete with needle

hypodermic syringe *n* **:** a small syringe used with a hollow needle for injection of material into or beneath the skin

hy·po·der·mis \ˌhī-pə-ˈdər-məs\ *n* [NL] **1 :** the tissue immediately beneath the epidermis of a plant esp. when modified to serve as a supporting and protecting layer **2 a :** HYPOBLAST **b :** the cellular layer that underlies and secretes the chitinous cuticle (as of an arthropod)

hy·po·eu·tec·tic \ˌhī-pō-yu̇-ˈtek-tik\ *adj* **:** containing the minor component in an amount less than in the eutectic mixture

hy·po·eu·tec·toid \-ˈtek-ˌtȯid\ *adj* **:** containing the minor component in an amount less than that contained in the eutectoid

hy·po·gas·tric \ˌhī-pə-ˈgas-trik\ *adj* [F *hypogastrique*, fr. *hypogastre* hypogastric region, fr. Gk *hypogastrion*, fr. *hypo-* + *gastr-*, *gastēr* belly — more at GASTRIC] **:** of or relating to the lower median region of the abdomen

hy·po·ge·al \ˌhī-pə-ˈjē-əl\ *or* **hy·po·ge·ous** \-ˈjē-əs\ *adj* [LL *hypogeus* subterranean, fr. Gk *hypogaios*, fr. *hypo-* + *gē* earth] **:** growing or living below the surface of the ground; *esp, of a cotyledon* **:** remaining below the ground while the epicotyl elongates — **hy·po·ge·al·ly** \-ˈjē-ə-lē\ *adv*

hy·po·gene \ˈhī-pə-ˌjēn\ *adj* [*hypo-* + Gk *-genēs* born, produced — more at -GEN] **:** formed, crystallized, or lying at depths below the earth's surface **:** PLUTONIC — used of various rocks

hy·pog·e·nous \hī-ˈpäj-ə-nəs\ *adj* [ISV] **:** growing on the lower side (as of a leaf) ⟨~ fungus⟩

hy·po·ge·um \ˌhī-pə-ˈjē-əm\ *n, pl* **hy·po·gea** \-ˈjē-ə\ [L, fr. Gk *hypogaion*, fr. neut. of *hypogaios*] **:** the subterranean part of an ancient building **:** CELLAR; *also* **:** an ancient underground burial chamber **:** CATACOMB

hy·po·glos·sal \ˌhī-pə-ˈgläs-əl\ *adj* **:** of, relating to, or being the 12th and final pair of cranial nerves which are motor nerves arising from the medulla oblongata and supplying muscles of the tongue in higher vertebrates — **hypoglossal** *n*

hy·po·gly·ce·mia \ˌhī-pə-(ˌ)glī-ˈsē-mē-ə\ *n* [NL] **:** abnormal decrease of sugar in the blood — **hy·po·gly·ce·mic** \-mik\ *adj*

hy·pog·na·thous \hī-ˈpäg-nə-thəs\ *adj* **:** having the lower jaw longer than the upper

hy·pog·y·nous \hī-ˈpäj-ə-nəs\ *adj* **1** *of a floral organ* **:** inserted upon the receptacle or axis below the gynoecium and free from it **2 :** having hypogynous floral organs — **hy·pog·y·ny** \-nē\ *n*

hy·po·ma·nia \ˌhī-pə-ˈmā-nē-ə, -nyə\ *n* [NL] **:** a mild mania — **hy·po·man·ic** \-ˈman-ik\ *adj*

hy·po·morph \ˈhī-pə-ˌmȯrf\ *n* **1 :** ENDOMORPH **2 :** a mutant gene having a similar but weaker effect than the corresponding wild-type gene — **hy·po·mor·phic** \ˌhī-pə-ˈmȯr-fik\ *adj*

hy·po·ni·trite \ˌhī-pō-ˈnī-ˌtrīt\ *n* **:** a salt or ester of hyponitrous acid

hy·po·ni·trous acid \ˌhī-pō-ˌnī-trəs-\ *n* **:** an explosive crystalline weak acid $H_2N_2O_2$ obtained usu. in the form of its salts by oxidation of hydroxylamine or by reduction of nitrites

hy·po·phar·ynx \ˌhī-pō-ˈfar-iŋ(k)s\ *n* [NL] **1 :** an appendage or thickened fold on the floor of the mouth of many insects that resembles a tongue **2 :** the pharyngeal end of the esophagus

hy·po·phos·phate \ˌhī-pə-ˈfäs-ˌfāt\ *n* [ISV, fr. *hypophosphoric acid*] **:** a salt or ester of hypophosphoric acid

hy·po·phos·phite \-ˌfīt\ *n* **:** a salt of hypophosphorous acid

hy·po·phos·pho·ric acid \ˌhī-pə-ˌfäs-ˌfȯr-ik-, -ˌfär-; -ˌfäs-f(ə-)rik-\ *n* [ISV] **:** an unstable tetrabasic acid $H_4P_2O_6$ usu. obtained in the form of its salts

hy·po·phos·pho·rous acid \-ˌfäs-f(ə-)rəs-; -ˌfäs-ˌfōr-əs-, -ˌfȯr-\ *n* **:** a crystalline strong monobasic acid H_3PO_2 usu. obtained by acidifying one of its salts and used as a reducing agent

hy·po·phy·se·al \(ˌ)hī-ˌpäf-ə-ˈsē-əl, -ˈzē-; ˌhī-pə-ˈfiz-ē-\ *adj* [irreg. fr. NL *hypophysis*] **:** of or relating to the hypophysis

hy·poph·y·sis \hī-ˈpäf-ə-səs\ *n, pl* **hy·poph·y·ses** \-ə-ˌsēz\ [NL, fr. Gk, attachment underneath, fr. *hypophyein* to grow beneath, fr. *hypo-* + *phyein* to grow, produce — more at BE] **:** PITUITARY BODY

hy·po·pi·tu·ita·rism \ˌhī-pō-pə-ˈt(y)ü-ət-ə-ˌriz-əm\ *n* [ISV] **:** deficient production of growth hormones by the pituitary body — **hy·po·pi·tu·itary** \-ˈt(y)ü-ə-ˌter-ē\ *adj*

hy·po·pla·sia \ˌhī-pə-ˈplā-zh(ē-)ə\ *n* [NL] **:** arrested development of an organ or part below normal size or in an immature state — **hy·po·plas·tic** \-ˈplas-tik\ *adj*

hy·po·ploid \ˈhī-pə-ˌplȯid\ *adj* **:** having a chromosome number slightly less than an exact multiple of the monoploid number — **hypoploid** *n* — **hy·po·ploi·dy** \-ˌplȯid-ē\ *n*

hy·po·sen·si·ti·za·tion \ˌhī-pō-ˌsen(t)-sət-ə-ˈzā-shən, -ˌsen(t)-stə-ˈzā-\ *n* **:** the state or process of being hyposensitized

hy·po·sen·si·tize \-ˈsen(t)-sə-ˌtīz\ *vt* **:** to reduce the sensitivity of esp. to an allergen **:** DESENSITIZE

hy·pos·ta·sis \hī-ˈpäs-tə-səs\ *n, pl* **hy·pos·ta·ses** \-tə-ˌsēz\ [LL, substance, sediment, fr. Gk, support, foundation, substance, sediment, fr. *hyphistasthai* to stand under, support, fr. *hypo-* + *histasthai* to be standing — more at STAND] **1 a :** something that settles at the bottom of a fluid **b :** the settling of blood in the dependent parts of an organ or body **2 :** PERSON 3 **3 a :** the substance or essential nature of an individual **b :** HYPOSTATIZATION **4** [NL, fr. LL] **:** failure of a gene to produce its usual effect when coupled with another gene that is epistatic toward it — **hy·po·stat·ic** \ˌhī-pə-ˈstat-ik\ *or* **hy·po·stat·i·cal** \-i-kəl\ *adj* — **hy·po·stat·i·cal·ly** \-i-k(ə-)lē\ *adv*

hy·pos·ta·ti·za·tion \hī-ˌpäs-tət-ə-ˈzā-shən\ *n* **:** an act or instance of hypostatizing **:** REIFICATION; *also* **:** something that is hypostatized

hy·pos·ta·tize \hī-ˈpäs-tə-ˌtīz\ *vt* [Gk *hypostatos* substantially existing, fr. *hyphistasthai*] **:** to construe (a conceptual entity) as a real existent **:** REIFY

hy·po·style \ˈhī-pə-ˌstīl\ *adj* [Gk *hypostylos*, fr. *hypo-* + *stylos* pillar — more at STEER] **:** having the roof resting on rows of columns — **hypostyle** *n*

hy·po·sul·fite \ˌhī-pō-ˈsəl-ˌfīt\ *n* [*hyposulfurous acid*] **1 :** THIOSULFATE — used chiefly in photography **2 :** HYDROSULFITE

hy·po·sul·fu·rous acid \ˌhī-pō-ˌsəl-f(y)ə-rəs-, -ˌfyu̇r-əs-\ *n* [ISV] **:** HYDROSULFUROUS ACID

hy·po·tac·tic \ˌhī-pə-ˈtak-tik\ *adj* [Gk *hypotaktikos*, fr. *hypotassein*] **:** of or relating to hypotaxis

hy·po·tax·is \-ˈtak-səs\ *n* [NL, fr. Gk, subjection, fr. *hypotassein* to arrange under, fr. *hypo-* + *tassein* to arrange — more at TACTICS] **:** syntactic subordination (as by a conjunction)

hy·po·ten·sion \ˌhī-pō-ˈten-chən\ *n* [ISV] **:** deficiency of tension; *specif* **:** abnormally low blood pressure — **hy·po·ten·sive** \-ˈten(t)-siv\ *adj or n*

hy·pot·e·nuse \hī-ˈpät-ᵊn-ˌ(y)üs, -ˌ(y)üz\ *also* **hy·poth·e·nuse** \-ˈpäth-ən-\ *n* [L *hypotenusa*, fr. Gk *hypoteinousa*, fr. fem. of *hypoteinōn*, prp. of *hypoteinein* to subtend, fr. *hypo-* + *teinein* to stretch — more at THIN] **:** the side of a right-angled triangle that is opposite the right angle

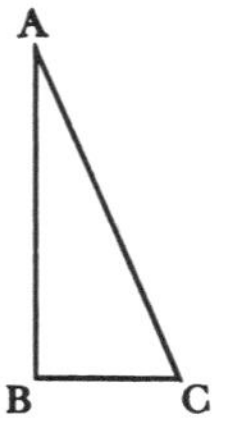

AC, hypotenuse

hy·po·tha·lam·ic \ˌhī-pō-thə-ˈlam-ik\ *adj* **1 :** located below the thalamus **2 :** of or relating to the hypothalamus

hy·po·thal·a·mus \-ˈthal-ə-məs\ *n* [NL] **:** a basal part of the diencephalon that lies beneath the thalamus on each side, forms the floor of the third ventricle, and is usu. considered to include vital autonomic regulatory centers

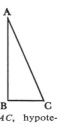

1**hy·poth·e·cate** \hip-ˈäth-ə-ˌkāt, hīp-\ *vt* [ML *hypothecare* to pledge, fr. LL *hypotheca* pledge, fr. Gk *hypothēkē*, fr. *hypotithenai* to put under, deposit as a pledge] **:** to pledge without delivery of title or possession; *specif* **:** to pledge (a ship) by a bottomry bond — **hy·poth·e·ca·tion** \-ˌäth-ə-ˈkā-shən\ *n* — **hy·poth·e·ca·tor** \-ˈäth-ə-ˌkāt-ər\ *n*

2**hy·poth·e·cate** \hī-ˈpäth-ə-ˌkāt\ *vt* **:** HYPOTHESIZE

hy·po·ther·mal \ˌhī-pō-ˈthər-məl\ *adj* **:** of or relating to a hydrothermal metalliferous ore vein deposited at high temperature

hy·poth·e·sis \hī-ˈpäth-ə-səs\ *n, pl* **hy·poth·e·ses** \-ə-ˌsēz\ [Gk, fr. *hypotithenai* to put under, suppose, fr. *hypo-* + *tithenai* to put — more at DO] **1 :** a tentative assumption made in order to draw out and test its logical or empirical consequences **2 a :** an assumption or concession made for the sake of argument **b :** an interpretation of a practical situation or condition taken as the ground for action

syn HYPOTHESIS, THEORY, LAW mean a formula derived by inference from scientific data that explains a principle operating in nature. HYPOTHESIS implies insufficiency of presently attainable evidence and therefore a tentative explanation; THEORY implies a greater range of evidence and greater likelihood of truth; LAW implies a statement of order and relation in nature that has been found to be invariable under the same conditions

hy·poth·e·size \-ə-ˌsīz\ vi : to make a hypothesis ~ vt : to adopt as a hypothesis

hy·po·thet·i·cal \ˌhī-pə-'thet-i-kəl\ adj 1 : involving logical hypothesis : not categorical : CONDITIONAL 2 : of or depending on supposition : CONJECTURAL — **hy·po·thet·i·cal·ly** \-i-k(ə-)lē\ adv

hy·po·thy·roid \ˌhī-pō-'thī-ˌróid\ adj : of, relating to, or affected by hypothyroidism

hy·po·thy·roid·ism \ˌhī-pō-'thī-ˌrói-ˌdiz-əm\ n [ISV] : deficient activity of the thyroid gland; also : a resultant lowered metabolic rate and loss of vigor

hy·po·ton·ic \ˌhī-pə-'tän-ik\ adj [ISV] 1 : having deficient tone or tension 2 : having a lower osmotic pressure than a fluid under comparison — **hy·po·to·nic·i·ty** \-tə-'nis-ət-ē\ n

hy·pot·ro·phy \hī-'pä-trə-fē\ n [ISV] : subnormal growth

hy·po·xan·thine \ˌhī-pō-'zan-ˌthēn\ n [ISV] : a purine base $C_5H_4N_4O$ found in plant and animal tissues that yields xanthine on oxidation

hyp·ox·ia \hip-'äk-sē-ə, hī-'päk-\ n [NL, fr. hypo- + ox-] : a deficiency of oxygen reaching the tissues of the body — **hyp·ox·ic** \-sik\ adj

hyps- or **hypso-** comb form [Gk, fr. hypsos height; akin to OE ūp up] : height ⟨hypsography⟩

hyp·sog·ra·phy \hip-'säg-rə-fē\ n [ISV] 1 : a branch of geography that deals with the measurement and mapping of the varying elevations of the earth's surface 2 : topographic relief or the devices (as color shadings) by which it is indicated on maps

hyp·som·e·ter \hip-'säm-ət-ər\ n [ISV] 1 : an apparatus for estimating elevations in mountainous regions from the boiling points of liquids 2 : any of various instruments for determining the height of trees by triangulation — **hyp·so·met·ric** \ˌhip-sə-'me-trik\ adj

hyp·som·e·try \hip-'säm-ə-trē\ n : the measurement of heights (as with reference to the sea level)

hy·rax \'hī-(ˌ)raks\ n, pl **hy·rax·es** \-ˌrak-səz\ also **hy·ra·ces** \'hī-rə-ˌsēz\ [Gk hyrak-, hyrax shrewmouse] : any of several small ungulate mammals (order Hyracoidea) characterized by thickset body with short legs and ears and rudimentary tail, feet with soft pads and broad nails, and teeth of which the molars resemble

those of the rhinoceros and the incisors those of rodents — called also coney

hy·son \'hīs-ᵊn\ n [Chin (Pek) hsiⁱ ch'unⁱ, lit., flourishing spring] : a Chinese green tea made from thinly rolled and twisted leaves

hys·sop \'his-əp\ n [ME ysop, fr. OE ysope, fr. L hyssopus, fr. Gk hyssōpos, of Sem origin; akin to Heb ēzōbh hyssop] 1 : a plant used in purificatory sprinkling rites by the ancient Hebrews 2 : a European mint (Hyssopus officinalis) that has highly aromatic and pungent leaves and is often cultivated as a remedy for bruises

hyster- or **hystero-** comb form [F or L; F hystér-, fr. L hyster-, fr. Gk, fr. hystera] 1 : womb ⟨hysterotomy⟩ 2 [NL, fr. hysteria] a : hysteria ⟨hysterogenic⟩ b : hysteria and ⟨hysteroneurasthenia⟩

hys·ter·ec·to·mize \ˌhis-tə-'rek-tə-ˌmīz\ vt : to remove the uterus of by surgery — **hys·ter·ec·to·my** \-mē\ n

hys·ter·e·sis \ˌhis-tə-'rē-səs\ n [NL, fr. Gk hysterēsis shortcoming, fr. hysterein to be late, fall short, fr. hysteros later — more at OUT] : a retardation of the effect when the forces acting upon a body are changed (as if from viscosity or internal friction); esp : a lagging in the values of resulting magnetization in a magnetic material (as iron) due to a changing magnetizing force — **hys·ter·et·ic** \ˌhis-tə-'ret-ik\ adj

hys·te·ria \his-'ter-ē-ə, -'tir-\ n [NL, fr. E hysteric, adj., fr. L hystericus of the womb, fr. Gk hysterikos, fr. hystera womb; fr. the former notion that hysteric women were suffering from disturbances of the womb] 1 : a psychoneurosis marked by emotional excitability and disturbances of the psychic, sensory, vasomotor, and visceral functions 2 : unmanageable fear or emotional excess — **hys·ter·ic** \-'ter-ik\ n — **hysteric** or **hys·ter·i·cal** \-'ter-i-kəl\ adj — **hys·ter·i·cal·ly** \-i-k(ə-)lē\ adv

hys·ter·ics \-'ter-iks\ n pl but sing or pl in constr : a fit of uncontrollable laughter or crying : HYSTERIA

hys·tero·gen·ic \ˌhis-tə-rō-'jen-ik\ adj : inducing hysteria

hys·ter·oid \'his-tə-ˌróid\ adj : resembling hysteria

hys·ter·on prot·er·on \ˌhis-tə-ˌrän-'prät-ə-ˌrän\ n [LL, fr. Gk, lit., (the) later earlier, (the) latter first] 1 : a figure of speech consisting of reversal of a natural or rational order (as in "then came the thunder and the lightning") 2 : a logical fallacy of assuming as a premise something that follows from what is to be proved

hys·tero·tely \'his-tə-rō-ˌtel-ē\ n [Gk hysteros later + telein to complete, perfect, fr. telos end — more at WHEEL] : relatively retarded differentiation of a structure usu. associated with an earlier stage of development

hys·ter·ot·o·my \ˌhis-tə-'rät-ə-mē\ n [NL hysterotomia, fr. hyster- + -tomia -tomy] : surgical incision of the uterus; esp : CESAREAN

---

¹i \'ī\ n, often cap, often attrib 1 a : the ninth letter of the English alphabet b : a graphic representation of this letter c : a speech counterpart of orthographic i 2 : ONE 3 : a graphic device for reproducing the letter i 4 : something designated i esp. as the ninth in order or class 5 : something shaped like the letter I 6 : a unit vector parallel to the x-axis

²I \(ˈ)ī, ə\ pron [ME, fr. OE ic; akin to OHG ih I, L ego, Gk egō] : the one who is speaking or writing ⟨~ feel fine⟩ ⟨it wasn't ~⟩ — compare ME, MINE, MY, WE

³I \'ī\ n, pl **I's** or **Is** \'īz\ 1 : someone aware of possessing a personal individuality : EGO 2 : an excessively egotistic person

-i- [ME, fr. OF, fr. L, stem vowel of most nouns and adjectives in combination] — used as a connective vowel to join word elements esp. of Latin origin ⟨raticide⟩

¹-ia n suffix [NL, fr. L & Gk, suffix forming feminine nouns] 1 : pathological condition ⟨hysteria⟩ 2 : genus of plants or animals ⟨Fuchsia⟩

²-ia n pl suffix [NL, fr. L (neut. pl. of -ius, adj. ending) & Gk, neut. pl. of -ios, adj. ending] 1 : higher taxon (as class, order) consisting of (such plants or animals) ⟨Sauria⟩ 2 : things derived from or relating to (something specified) ⟨tabloidia⟩

³-ia pl of -IUM

Ia·go \ē-'äg-(ˌ)ō\ n : the ensign of Othello and villain of Shakespeare's tragedy Othello

-ial adj suffix [ME, fr. MF, fr. L -ialis, fr. -i- + -alis -al] : ¹-AL ⟨gerundial⟩

iamb \'ī-ˌam(b)\ or **iam·bus** \ī-'am-bəs\ n, pl **iambs** \'ī-ˌamz\ or **iam·bus·es** also **iam·bi** \ī-'am-ˌbī\ [L iambus, fr. Gk iambos] : a metrical foot consisting of one short syllable followed by one long syllable or of one unstressed syllable followed by one stressed syllable (as in above) — compare TROCHEE — **iam·bic** \ī-'am-bik\ adj or n

-ian — see -AN

-iana — see -ANA

-i·a·sis \'ī-ə-səs\ n suffix, pl **-i·a·ses** \'ī-ə-ˌsēz\ [NL, fr. L, fr. Gk, suffix of action, fr. denominative verbs in -ian, -iazein] : disease having characteristics of or produced by (something specified) ⟨hypochondriasis⟩ ⟨ancylostomiasis⟩

iat·ric \ī-'a-trik\ adj [Gk iatrikos, fr. iatros healer, fr. iasthai to heal] : of or relating to a physician or medical treatment : MEDICAL — **iat·ri·cal** \-tri-kəl\ adj

-i·at·ric \ē-'a-trik\ also **-i·at·ri·cal** \-tri-kəl\ adj comb form [NL -iatria] : of or relating to (such) medical treatment or healing ⟨pediatric⟩

-i·at·rics \ē-'a-triks\ n pl comb form but sing or pl in constr : medical treatment ⟨pediatrics⟩

iat·ro·gen·ic \ī-ˌa-trə-'jen-ik\ adj [Gk iatros + E -genic] : induced by a physician — used chiefly of imagined ailments

-i·a·try \'ī-ə-trē, in a few words ē-ˌa-trē\ n comb form [F -iatrie, fr.

NL -iatria, fr. Gk iatreia art of healing, fr. iatros] : medical treatment : healing ⟨podiatry⟩

I beam n : an iron or steel beam

¹Ibe·ri·an \ī-'bir-ē-ən\ n [Iberia, ancient region of the Caucasus] : a member of one or more peoples anciently inhabiting the Caucasus in Asia between the Black and Caspian seas — **Iberian** adj

²Iberian n [Iberia, peninsula in Europe] 1 a : a member of one or more Caucasoid peoples anciently inhabiting the peninsula comprising Spain and Portugal and the Basque region about the Pyrenees, prob. related in origin to peoples of northern Africa and prob. the builders of neolithic stone structures (as cairns) found esp. in Spain and in northern Africa, France, and Great Britain b : a native or inhabitant of Spain or Portugal or the Basque region 2 : one or more of the languages of the ancient Iberians — **Iberian** adj

ibex \'ī-ˌbeks\ n, pl **ibex** or **ibex·es** [L] 1 : any of several wild goats living chiefly in high mountain areas of the Old World and having large recurved horns transversely ridged in front 2 : a wild goat (Capra aegagrus) found in Asia Minor and supposed to be the progenitor of the domestic goat

ibi·dem \'ib-ə-ˌdem, ib-'īd-əm\ adv [L] : in the same place

-ibil·i·ty \ə-'bil-ət-ē\ — see -ABILITY

ibis \'ī-bəs\ n, pl **ibis** or **ibis·es** [L, fr. Gk, fr. Egypt hby] : any of several wading birds (family Threskiornithidae) related to the herons but distinguished by a long slender downwardly curved bill

-ible \ə-bəl\ — see -ABLE

Ib·sen·ism \'ib-sə-ˌniz-əm, 'ip-\ n 1 : dramatic invention or construction characteristic of Ibsen 2 : championship of Ibsen's plays and ideas — **Ib·sen·ite** \-ˌnīt\ n or adj

¹-ic \ik\ adj suffix [ME, fr. OF & L; OF -ique, fr. L -icus — more at -Y] 1 : having the character or form of : being ⟨panoramic⟩ : consisting of ⟨runic⟩ 2 : of or relating to ⟨aldermanic⟩ b : related to, derived from, or containing ⟨alcoholic⟩ ⟨oleic⟩ 3 : in the manner of : like that of : characteristic of ⟨Byronic⟩ 4 : associated or dealing with ⟨Vedic⟩ : utilizing ⟨electronic⟩ 5 : characterized by : exhibiting ⟨nostalgic⟩ : affected with ⟨allergic⟩ 6 : caused by ⟨amoebic⟩ 7 : tending to produce ⟨analgesic⟩ 8 : having a valence relatively higher than in compounds or ions named with an adjective ending in -ous ⟨ferric iron⟩

²-ic n suffix : one having the character or nature of : one belonging to or associated with : one exhibiting or affected by : one that produces

-i·cal \i-kəl\ adj suffix [ME, fr. LL -icalis (as in clericalis clerical, radicalis radical)] : -IC ⟨symmetrical⟩ ⟨geological⟩ — sometimes differing from -ic in that adjectives formed with -ical have a wider or more transferred semantic range than corresponding adjectives in -ic

Icar·i·an \ik-'ar-ē-ən, -'er-; ī-'kar-, -'ker-\ adj : of, relating to, or characteristic of Icarus: a : soaring too high for safety b : inadequate for an ambitious project

Ic·a·rus \'ik-ə-rəs\ n [L, fr. Gk Ikaros] : the son of Daedalus who in escaping from imprisonment falls into the sea when the wax of his wings melts as he flies too near the sun

---

ə abut; ᵊ kitten; ər further; a back; ā bake; ä cot, cart; aú out; ch chin; e less; ē easy; g gift; i trip; ī life
j joke; ŋ sing; ō flow; ò flaw; ói coin; th thin; t͟h this; ü loot; ú foot; y yet; yü few; yú furious; zh vision

1ice \'īs\ *n, often attrib* [ME *is*, fr. OE *īs;* akin to OHG *īs* ice, Av *isu-* icy] **1 a :** frozen water **b :** a sheet or stretch of ice **2 :** a state of coldness (as from formality or reserve) **3 :** a substance resembling ice; *specif* **:** ICING **4 a :** a frozen dessert containing a fruit juice or other flavoring; *esp* **:** one containing no milk or cream **b** *Brit* **:** a serving of ice cream **5** *slang* **:** DIAMONDS; *broadly* **:** JEWELRY — **on ice 1 :** with every likelihood of being won or accomplished **2 :** in reserve or safekeeping — **on thin ice :** in a situation involving great risk

2ice *vt* **1 a :** to coat with or convert into ice **b :** to chill with ice **c :** to supply with ice **2 :** to cover with or as if with icing **3 :** to put on ice ~ *vi* **1 :** to become ice-cold **2 a :** to become covered with ice **b :** to have ice form inside

ice age *n* **1 :** a time of widespread glaciation **2** *cap I&A* **:** the Pleistocene glacial epoch

ice bag *n* **:** a waterproof bag to hold ice for local application of cold to the body

ice·berg \'īs-,bərg\ *n* [prob. part trans. of Dan or Norw *isberg*, fr. *is* ice + *berg* mountain] **1 :** a large floating mass of ice detached from a glacier **2 :** an emotionally cold person

ice·blink \-,bliŋk\ *n* **:** a glare in the sky over an ice field

ice·boat \-,bōt\ *n* **1 :** a skeleton boat or frame on runners propelled on ice usu. by sails **2 :** ICEBREAKER

ice·bound \-,baủnd\ *adj* **:** surrounded or obstructed by ice

ice·box \-,bäks\ *n* **:** REFRIGERATOR

ice·break·er \-,brā-kər\ *n* **1 :** a structure that protects a bridge pier from floating ice **2 :** a ship equipped to make and maintain a channel through ice **3 :** something that breaks the ice (as on a social occasion)

ice cap *n* **1 :** an ice bag shaped to the head **2 :** a cover of perennial ice and snow; *specif* **:** a glacier forming on an extensive area of relatively level land and flowing outward from its center — called also *ice sheet*

ice–cold \'ī-'skōld\ *adj* **:** extremely cold

ice cream \(')ī-'skrēm, 'ī-,\ *n* **:** a frozen food containing cream or butterfat, flavoring, sweetening, and usu. eggs

ice–cream *adj* **:** of a color similar to that of vanilla ice cream

ice·fall \'īs-,fȯl\ *n* **1 :** a frozen waterfall **2 :** the mass of usu. jagged blocks into which a glacier may break when it moves down a steep declivity

ice field *n* **1 :** an extensive sheet of sea ice **2 :** ICE CAP

ice floe *n* **:** a flat free mass of floating sea ice; *broadly* **:** a large floating fragment of sheet ice

ice foot *n* **:** a wall or belt of ice frozen to the shore in arctic regions having a base at or below the low-water mark

ice·house \'īs-,haủs, 'ī-,saủs\ *n* **:** a building for storing ice

1Ice·lan·dic \ī-'slan-dik\ *adj* **:** of, relating to, or characteristic of Iceland, the Icelanders, or Icelandic

2Icelandic *n* **:** the North Germanic language of the Icelandic people

Ice·land moss \,ī-slən(d)-, ,ī-,slan(d)-\ *n* **:** a lichen (*Cetraria islandica*) of arctic regions sometimes used medicinally or as food

Iceland poppy *n* **:** any of various perennial cultivated poppies prob. derived from two species (*Papaver nudicaule* and *P. alpinum*) and characterized by rather small single or double chiefly pastel flowers

Iceland spar *n* **:** a doubly refracting transparent calcite the best of which is obtained in Iceland

ice·man \'ī-,sman\ *n* **1 :** a man skilled in traveling on ice **2 :** one who sells or delivers ice

ice needle *n* **:** one of a number of slender ice particles that float in the air in clear cold weather — called also *ice crystal*

Ice·ni \ī-'sē-,nī\ *n pl* [L] **:** an ancient British people in revolt under its queen Boadicea against the Romans in A.D. 61 — **Ice·ni·an** \-'sē-nē-ən\ *or* **Ice·nic** \-'sē-nik, -'sen-ik\ *adj*

ice pack *n* **:** an expanse of pack ice

ice pick *n* **:** a hand tool ending in a spike for chipping ice

ice plant *n* **:** an Old World annual herb (*Mesembryanthemum crystallinum*) of the carpetweed family with fleshy foliage covered with glistening papillate dots or vesicles that is widely naturalized in warm regions; *broadly* **:** FIG MARIGOLD

ice–skate \'ī(s)-,skāt\ *vi* **:** to skate on ice — **ice skater** *n*

ice storm *n* **:** a storm in which falling rain freezes on contact

ice water *n* **:** chilled or iced water esp. for drinking

ichn- *or* **ichno-** *comb form* [Gk, fr. *ichnos*] **:** footprint **:** track ⟨*ichno*logy⟩

ich·neu·mon \ik-'n(y)ü-mən\ *n* [L, fr. Gk *ichneumōn*, lit., tracker, fr. *ichneuein* to track, fr. *ichnos*] **:** MONGOOSE

ichneumon fly *n* **:** any of a large superfamily (Ichneumonoidea) of hymenopterous insects whose larvae are usu. internal parasites of other insect larvae and esp. of caterpillars

ich·no·lite \'ik-nə-,līt\ *or* **ich·nite** \-,nīt\ *n* **:** a fossil footprint

ich·nol·o·gy \ik-'näl-ə-jē\ *n* **:** the study of fossil footprints

ichor \'ī-,kȯ(ə)r, -kər\ *n* [Gk *ichōr*] **1 :** an ethereal fluid taking the place of blood in the veins of the ancient Greek gods **2 :** a thin watery or blood-tinged discharge — **ichor·ous** \-kə-rəs\ *adj*

ichthy- *or* **ichthyo-** *comb form* [L, fr. Gk, fr. *ichthys;* akin to Arm *jukn* fish] **:** fish ⟨*ichthy*ic⟩

ich·thy·oid \'ik-thē-,ȯid\ *or* **ich·thy·oi·dal** \,ik-thē-'ȯid-ᵊl\ *adj* [Gk *ichthyoeidēs*, fr. *ichthys*] **:** resembling a fish — **ichthyoid** *n*

ich·thyo·log·i·cal \,ik-thē-ə-'läj-i-kəl\ *adj* **1 :** of or relating to ichthyology **2 :** PISCINE — **ich·thyo·log·i·cal·ly** \-k(ə-)lē\ *adv*

ich·thy·ol·o·gist \,ik-thē-'äl-ə-jəst\ *n* **:** a specialist in ichthyology

ich·thy·ol·o·gy \-jē\ *n* **1 :** a branch of zoology that deals with fishes **2 :** a treatise on fishes

ich·thy·oph·a·gous \,ik-thē-'äf-ə-gəs\ *adj* [Gk *ichthyophagos*, fr. *ichthy-* + *phagein* to eat — more at BAKSHEESH] **:** eating or subsisting on fish

ich·thy·or·nis \,ik-thē-'ȯr-nəs\ *n* [NL, genus name, fr. *ichthy-* + Gk *ornis* bird — more at ERNE] **:** any of a genus (*Ichthyornis*) of extinct toothed birds

ich·thyo·saur \'ik-thē-ə-,sȯ(ə)r\ *n* [deriv. of Gk *ichthy-* + *sauros* lizard — more at SAURIAN] **:** any of an order (Ichthyosauria) of extinct marine reptiles with fish-shaped body and elongated snout — **ich·thyo·sau·ri·an** \,ik-thē-ə-'sȯr-ē-ən\ *adj or n*

ich·thy·o·sis \,ik-thē-'ō-səs\ *n* **:** a congenital disease usu. of hereditary origin in which the skin is rough, thick, and scaly — **ich·thy·ot·ic** \-'ät-ik\ *adj*

-i·cian \'ish-ən\ *n suffix* [ME, fr. OF *-icien*, fr. L *-ica* (as in *rhetorica* rhetoric) + OF *-ien* -ian] **:** specialist **:** practitioner ⟨beaut*ician*⟩

ici·cle \'ī-,sik-əl\ *n* [ME *isikel*, fr. *is* ice + *ikel* icicle, fr. OE *gicel;* akin to OHG *ihilla* icicle, MIr *aig* ice] **1 :** a pendent mass of ice formed by the freezing of dripping water **2 :** an emotionally unresponsive person

ic·i·ly \'ī-sə-lē\ *adv* **:** in an icy manner

ic·i·ness \'ī-sē-nəs\ *n* **:** the quality or state of being icy

1ic·ing \'ī-siŋ\ *n* **:** a coating for baked goods usu. made from sugar and butter combined with water, milk, or egg white and flavoring

2icing *n* **:** an act by an ice-hockey player of shooting from within his defensive zone beyond the opponents' goal line

ick·er \'ik-ər\ *n* [deriv. of OE *ēar, eher* — more at EAR] *Scot* **:** a head of grain

icon \'ī-,kän\ *n* [L, fr. Gk *eikōn*, fr. *eikenai* to resemble] **1 :** a usu. pictorial representation **:** IMAGE **2** [LGk *eikōn*, fr. Gk] **:** a conventional religious image typically painted on a small wooden panel and venerated by Eastern Christians **3 :** an object of uncritical devotion **:** IDOL

icon- *or* **icono-** *comb form* [Gk *eikon-*, *eikono-*, fr. *eikon-*, *eikōn*] **:** image ⟨*icono*later⟩

icon·ic \ī-'kän-ik\ *adj* **1 :** of, relating to, or having the character of an icon **2 :** resembling an icon — **icon·i·cal·ly** \ī-'kän-i-k(ə-)lē\ *adv* — **ico·nic·i·ty** \,ī-kə-'nis-ət-ē\ *n*

icon·o·clasm \ī-'kän-ə-,klaz-əm\ *n* **:** the doctrine, practice, or attitude of an iconoclast

icon·o·clast \-,klast\ *n* [ML *iconoclastes*, fr. MGk *eikonoklastēs*, lit., image destroyer, fr. Gk *eikono-* + *klan* to break — more at GLADIATOR] **1 :** one who destroys religious images or opposes their veneration **2 :** one who attacks established beliefs or institutions — **icon·o·clas·tic** \(,)ī-,kän-ə-'klas-tik\ *adj* — **icon·o·clas·ti·cal·ly** \-ti-k(ə-)lē\ *adv*

ico·nog·ra·pher \,ī-kə-'näg-rə-fər\ *n* **:** a maker or designer of figures or drawings esp. of a conventional or mechanical type

icono·graph·ic \(,)ī-,kän-ə-'graf-ik\ *adj* **1 :** of or relating to iconography **2 :** representing something by pictures or diagrams — **icono·graph·i·cal** \-i-kəl\ *adj* — **icono·graph·i·cal·ly** \-i-k(ə-)lē\ *adv*

ico·nog·ra·phy \,ī-kə-'näg-rə-fē\ *n* [Gk *eikonographia* sketch, description, fr. *eikonographein* to describe, fr. *eikon-* + *graphein* to write — more at CARVE] **1 a :** illustration by pictures or other visual representations **b :** visual representations relating to a subject; *specif* **:** art representing religious or legendary subjects by conventional images and symbols **c** (1) **:** the imagery selected to convey the meaning of a work of art (2) **:** the conventions governing such imagery **2 :** ICONOLOGY

ico·nol·a·ter \,ī-kə-'näl-ət-ər\ *n* **:** a worshiper of images or icons — **ico·nol·a·try** \-'näl-ə-trē\ *n*

icono·log·i·cal \(,)ī-,kän-ᵊl-'äj-i-kəl\ *adj* **:** of or relating to iconology

ico·nol·o·gy \,ī-kə-'näl-ə-jē\ *n* [F *iconologie*, fr. *icono-* icon- + *-logie* -logy] **:** the study of icons or artistic symbolism

icono·scope \ī-'kän-ə-,skōp\ *n* [fr. *Iconoscope*, a trademark] **:** a camera tube containing an electron gun and a photoemissive mosaic screen each cell of which produces a charge proportional to the varying light intensity of the image focused on the screen

ico·nos·ta·sis \,ī-kə-'näs-tə-səs\ *n, pl* **ico·nos·ta·ses** \-tə-,sēz\ [MGk *eikonostasi*] **:** a screen or partition with doors and tiers of icons that separates the bema from the nave in Eastern churches

ico·sa·he·dral \(,)ī-,kō-sə-'hē-drəl\ *adj* **:** of or having the form of an icosahedron

ico·sa·he·dron \-drən\ *n, pl* **icosahedrons** *or* **ico·sa·he·dra** \-drə\ [Gk *eikosaedron*, fr. *eikosi* twenty + *-edron* -hedron — more at VIGESIMAL] **:** a polyhedron having 20 faces

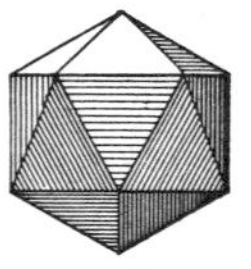
regular icosahedron

-ics \(,)iks\ *n pl suffix but sing or pl in constr* [*-ic* + *-s;* trans. of Gk *-ika*, fr. neut. pl. of *-ikos* -ic] **1 :** study **:** knowledge **:** skill **:** practice ⟨linguist*ics*⟩ ⟨electron*ics*⟩ **2 :** characteristic actions or activities ⟨acrobat*ics*⟩ **3 :** characteristic qualities, operations, or phenomena ⟨mechan*ics*⟩

ic·ter·ic \ik-'ter-ik\ *adj* **:** of, relating to, or affected with jaundice

ic·ter·us \'ik-tə-rəs\ *n* [NL, fr. Gk *ikteros;* akin to Gk *iktis*, a yellow bird] **:** JAUNDICE

ic·tus \'ik-təs\ *n* [L, fr. *ictus*, pp. of *icere* to strike; akin to Gk *aichmē* lance] **:** the recurring stress or beat in a rhythmic or metrical series of sounds

icy \'ī-sē\ *adj* **1 a :** covered with, abounding in, or consisting of ice **b :** intensely cold **2 :** characterized by coldness **:** FRIGID ⟨an ~ stare⟩

1id \'id\ *n* [NL, fr. L, it] **:** the undifferentiated source of the organism's energy from which both ego and libido are derived

2id *n* [*-id*, fr. F *-ide*, fr. L *-id-*, *-is*, fem. patronymic suffix] **:** an allergic skin rash that is secondary to a primary infection elsewhere in or on the body

1-id \əd, (,)id\ *n suffix* [in sense 1, fr. L *-ides*, masc. patronymic suffix, fr. Gk *-idēs;* in sense 2, fr. It *-ide*, fr. L *-id-*, *is*, fem. patronymic suffix, fr. Gk] **1 :** one belonging to a (specified) dynastic line ⟨Fatim*id*⟩ **2 :** meteor associated with or radiating from a (specified) constellation or comet ⟨Perse*id*⟩

2-id *n suffix* [prob. fr. L *-id-*, *-is*, fem. patronymic suffix, fr. Gk] **:** body **:** particle ⟨energ*id*⟩

I'd \(,)īd\ **:** I had **:** I should **:** I would

-i·dae \ə-,dē\ *n pl suffix* [NL, fr. L, fr. Gk *-idai*, pl. of *-idēs*] **:** members of the family of — in names of zoological families ⟨Fel*idae*⟩

-ide \,īd\ *also* **-id** \əd, (,)id\ *n suffix* [G & F; G *-id*, fr. F *-ide* (as in *oxide*)] **1 :** binary chemical compound — added to the contracted name of the nonmetallic or more electronegative element ⟨hydrogen sulf*ide*⟩ or radical ⟨cyan*ide*⟩ **2 :** chemical compound derived from or related to another (usu. specified) compound ⟨anhydr*ide*⟩ ⟨glucos*ide*⟩

idea \ī-'dē-ə, 'īd-(,)ē-ə, *esp South* 'īd-ē\ *n* [L, fr. Gk, fr. *idein* to see — more at WIT] **1 a :** a transcendent entity that is a real pattern of which existing things are imperfect representations **b :** a standard of perfection **:** IDEAL **c :** a plan for action **:** DESIGN **2** *archaic* **:** a visible representation of a conception **:** a replica of a pattern **3 a** *obs* **:** an image recalled by memory **b :** an indefinite or unformed conception **:** SUPPOSITION **c :** an entity (as a thought, concept, sensation, or image) actually or potentially present to consciousness **4 :** a formulated thought or opinion **5 :** whatever is known or supposed regarding an object **6 :** the central meaning

or chief end of a particular action or situation **7** *Christian Science* **:** an image in Mind — **idea·less** \ī-'dē-ə-ləs\ *adj*
syn CONCEPT, CONCEPTION, THOUGHT, NOTION, IMPRESSION: IDEA may apply to a mental image or formulation of something seen or known or imagined, or to a pure abstraction, or to something assumed or vaguely sensed; CONCEPT may apply to the idea formed by consideration of instances of a species or genus or, more broadly, to any idea of what a thing ought to be; CONCEPTION is often interchangeable with CONCEPT; it may stress the process of imagining or formulating rather than the result; THOUGHT is likely to suggest the result of reflecting, reasoning, or meditating rather than of imagining; NOTION suggests an idea not much resolved by analysis or reflection and may suggest the capricious or accidental; IMPRESSION applies to an idea or notion resulting immediately from some stimulation of the senses

[1]**ide·al** \ī-'dē(-ə)l\ *adj* [F or LL; F *idéal*, fr. LL *idealis*, fr. L *idea*] **1 a :** existing as a mere mental image or in fancy or imagination only; *broadly* **:** lacking practicality **b :** relating to or constituting mental images, ideas, or conceptions **2 :** of, relating to, or embodying an ideal **3 :** existing as an archetypal idea **4 :** IDEALISTIC

[2]**ideal** *n* **1 :** a standard of perfection, beauty, or excellence **2 :** one regarded as exemplifying an ideal and often taken as a model for imitation **3 :** an ultimate object or aim of endeavor **:** GOAL **syn** see MODEL — **ide·al·less** \ī-'dē-əl-ləs\ *adj*

ide·al·ism \-'dē-(ə-),liz-əm\ *n* **1 a** (1) **:** a theory that ultimate reality lies in a realm transcending phenomena (2) **:** a theory that the essential nature of reality lies in consciousness or reason **b** (1) **:** a theory that only the perceptible is real (2) **:** a theory that only mental states or entities are knowable **2 a :** the practice of forming ideals or living under their influence **b :** something that is idealized **3 :** literary or artistic theory or practice that values ideal or subjective types or aspects of beauty more than formal or sensible qualities or that affirms the preeminent value of imagination as compared with faithful copying of nature

[1]**ide·al·ist** \-(ə-)ləst\ *n* **1 a :** an adherent of a philosophical theory of idealism **b :** an artist or author who advocates or practices idealism in art or writing **2 :** one guided by ideals; *esp* **:** one that places ideals before practical considerations **:** DREAMER

[2]**idealist** *adj* **:** IDEALISTIC

ide·al·is·tic \(,)ī-,dē-(ə-)'lis-tik\ *adj* **:** of or relating to idealists or idealism — **ide·al·is·ti·cal·ly** \-ti-k(ə-)lē\ *adv*

ide·al·i·ty \,īd-ē-'al-ət-ē\ *n* **1 a :** the quality or state of being ideal **b :** existence only in idea **2 :** something imaginary or idealized

ide·al·iza·tion \(,)ī-,dē-(ə-)lə-'zā-shən\ *n* **:** an act or a product of idealizing

ide·al·ize \ī-'dē-(ə-),līz\ *vt* **1 :** to give an ideal form or value to **2 :** to treat idealistically ~ *vi* **1 :** to form ideals **2 :** to work idealistically — **ide·al·iz·er** *n*

ide·al·ly \ī-'dē-(ə-)lē, -'dē(-ə)l-lē\ *adv* **1 :** in idea or imagination **:** MENTALLY **2 :** in relation to an exemplar **3 a :** conformably to or in respect to an ideal **:** PERFECTLY **b :** in accordance with an ideal or typical standard **:** CLASSICALLY

ideal point *n* **:** a point added to the plane or to space to eliminate special cases; *specif* **:** the point at infinity added in projective geometry as the assumed intersection of two parallel lines

ide·ate \'īd-ē-,āt\ *vt* **:** to have ideas, thoughts, or impressions of esp. when not in the actual presence of ~ *vi* **:** to form an idea

ide·ation \,īd-ē-'ā-shən\ *n* **:** the capacity of the mind to form or entertain ideas

ide·ation·al \-shnəl, -shən-ᵊl\ *adj* **:** of, relating to, or produced by ideation; *broadly* **:** consisting of or referring to ideas or thoughts of objects not immediately present to the senses — **ide·ation·al·ly** \-ē\ *adv*

ide·ative \ī-'dē-ət-iv, 'īd-ē-,āt-\ *adj* **:** IDEATIONAL

idem \'īd-,em, 'ēd-, 'id-\ *pron* [L, same — more at IDENTITY] **:** something previously mentioned **:** SAME

iden·tic \ī-'dent-ik, ə-\ *adj* **:** IDENTICAL; *esp* **:** constituting a diplomatic action or expression in which two or more governments follow precisely the same course or employ an identical form

iden·ti·cal \-i-kəl\ *adj* [prob. fr. ML *identicus*, fr. LL *identitas*] **1 :** being the same ⟨the ~ place we stopped before⟩ **2 :** having such close resemblance as to be essentially the same ⟨~ hats⟩ **3 :** having the same cause or origin **syn** see SAME — **iden·ti·cal·ly** \-i-k(ə-)lē\ *adv* — **iden·ti·cal·ness** \-kəl-nəs\ *n*

identical equation *n* **:** an equation that is satisfied for all values of the symbols

iden·ti·fi·able \ī-'dent-ə-,fī-ə-bəl, ə-'dent-\ *adj* **:** capable of being identified — **iden·ti·fi·ably** \-blē\ *adv*

iden·ti·fi·ca·tion \-,dent-ə-fə-'kā-shən\ *n* **1 a :** an act of identifying **:** the state of being identified **b :** evidence of identity **2 :** orientation of the self in regard to something (as a person or group) with a resulting feeling of close emotional association

iden·ti·fi·er \ī-'dent-ə-,fī(-ə)r, ə-'dent-\ *n* **:** one that identifies

iden·ti·fy \-,fī\ *vt* **1 a :** to cause to be or become identical **b :** to conceive as united; *broadly* **:** to associate with some interest **2 a :** to establish the identity of **b :** to determine the taxonomic position of (a biological specimen) ~ *vi* **:** to be or become the same

iden·ti·ty \ī-'den(t)-ət-ē, ə-'den(t)-\ *n* [MF *identité*, fr. LL *identitat-, identitas*, irreg. fr. L *idem* same, fr. *is* that — more at ITERATE] **1 a :** sameness of essential or generic character in different instances **b :** sameness in all that constitutes the objective reality of a thing **:** ONENESS **2 :** unity and persistence of personality **3 :** the condition of being the same with something described or asserted **4 :** IDENTICAL EQUATION

ideo- *comb form* [F *idéo-*, fr. Gk *idea*] **:** idea ⟨*ideo*gram⟩

ideo·gram \'īd-ē-ə-,gram, 'id-\ *n* **1 :** a picture or symbol used in a system of writing to represent a thing or an idea but not a particular word or phrase for it; *esp* **:** one that represents not the object pictured but some thing or idea that the object pictured is supposed to suggest **2 :** LOGOGRAM a — **ideo·gram·ic** *or* **ideo·gram·mic** \,īd-ē-ə-'gram-ik, ,id-\ *adj*

ideo·graph \'īd-ē-ə-,graf, 'id-\ *n* **:** IDEOGRAM — **ideo·graph·ic** \,īd-ē-ə-'graf-ik, ,id-\ *adj* — **ideo·graph·i·cal·ly** \-i-k(ə-)lē\ *adv*

ide·og·ra·phy \,īd-ē-'äg-rə-fē, ,id-\ *n* **1 :** the use of ideograms **2 :** the representation of ideas by graphic symbols

ideo·log·i·cal \,īd-ē-ə-'läj-i-kəl, ,id-\ *also* **idea·log·i·cal** *adj* **1 :** of, relating to, or based on ideology **2 :** relating to or concerned with ideas — **ideo·log·i·cal·ly** \-'läj-i-k(ə-)lē\ *adv*

ide·ol·o·gist \,īd-ē-'äl-ə-jəst, ,id-\ *n* **1 :** an advocate or adherent of a particular system or doctrine of ideology **2 :** THEORIST, VISIONARY

ide·ol·o·gy \-'äl-ə-jē\ *also* **ide·al·o·gy** \-'äl-ə-jē, -'al-\ *n* [F *idéologie*, fr. *idéo-* ideo- + *-logie* -logy] **1 :** visionary theorizing **2 a :** a systematic body of concepts esp. about human life or culture **b :** a manner or the content of thinking characteristic of an individual, group, or culture **c :** the integrated assertions, theories, and aims that constitute a sociopolitical program

ideo·mo·tor \,īd-ē-ə-'mōt-ər, ,id-\ *adj* [ISV] **:** not reflex but resulting from the impingement of ideas on the system

ides \'īdz\ *n pl but sing or pl in constr* [MF, fr. L *idus*] **:** the 15th day of March, May, July, or October or the 13th day of any other month in the ancient Roman calendar; *broadly* **:** this day and the seven days preceding it

-i·din \əd-ən, -ᵊn\ *or* **-i·dine** \ə-,dēn\ *n suffix* [ISV *-ide* + *-in, -ine*] **:** chemical compound related in origin or structure to another compound ⟨tolu*idine*⟩ ⟨guan*idine*⟩

idio- *comb form* [Gk, fr. *idios* — more at IDIOT] **:** one's own **:** personal **:** separate **:** distinct ⟨*idio*blast⟩

id·io·blast \'id-ē-ə-,blast\ *n* [ISV] **1 :** an isolated plant cell that differs markedly from neighboring cells **2 :** a hypothetical structural unit of a living cell — **id·io·blas·tic** \,id-ē-ə-'blas-tik\ *adj*

id·i·o·cy \'id-ē-ə-sē\ *n* **1 :** extreme mental deficiency commonly due to incomplete or abnormal development of the brain **2 :** something notably stupid or foolish

id·io·graph·ic \,id-ē-ə-'graf-ik\ *adj* [ISV] **:** relating to or dealing with the concrete, individual, or unique

id·io·lect \'id-ē-ə-,lekt\ *n* [*idio-* + *-lect* (as in *dialect*)] **:** the language or speech pattern of one individual at a particular period of his life

id·i·om \'id-ē-əm\ *n* [MF & LL; MF *idiome*, fr. LL *idioma* individual peculiarity of language, fr. Gk *idiōmat-, idiōma*, fr. *idiousthai* to appropriate, fr. *idios*] **1 a :** the language peculiar to a people or to a district, community, or class **:** DIALECT **b :** the syntactical, grammatical, or structural form peculiar to a language **2 :** an expression in the usage of a language that is peculiar to itself either grammatically (as *no, it wasn't me*) or in having a meaning that cannot be derived from the conjoined meanings of its elements (as *Monday week* for "the Monday a week after next Monday") **3 :** a style or form of artistic expression that is characteristic of an individual, a period or movement, or a medium or instrument

id·i·om·at·ic \,id-ē-ə-'mat-ik\ *adj* **1 :** of, relating to, or conforming to idiom **2 :** peculiar to a particular group or individual — **id·i·om·at·i·cal·ly** \-i-k(ə-)lē\ *adv* — **id·i·om·at·ic·ness** \-ik-nəs\ *n*

id·io·mor·phic \,id-ē-ə-'mȯr-fik\ *adj* [Gk *idiomorphos*, fr. *idio-* + *-morphos* -morphous] **:** having the proper form or shape — used of minerals whose crystalline growth has not been interfered with — **id·io·mor·phi·cal·ly** \-fi-k(ə-)lē\ *adv*

id·io·path·ic \,id-ē-ə-'path-ik\ *adj* **1 :** peculiar to the individual **2 :** arising spontaneously or from an obscure or unknown cause **:** PRIMARY — **id·io·path·i·cal·ly** \-'path-i-k(ə-)lē\ *adv*

id·i·op·a·thy \,id-ē-'äp-ə-thē\ *n* [Gk *idiopatheia*, fr. *idio-* + *-patheia* -pathy] **:** an idiopathic anomaly or disease

id·io·phone \'id-ē-ə-,fōn\ *n* [G *idiophon*, fr. *idio-* + *-phon* -phone] **:** a musical instrument (as a gong) that sounds by the vibration of its constituent material — **id·io·phon·ic** \,id-ē-ə-'fän-ik\ *adj*

id·io·plasm \'id-ē-ə-,plaz-əm\ *n* [ISV] **:** the part of protoplasm held to function specif. in hereditary transmission and commonly equated with chromatin — compare TROPHOPLASM — **id·io·plas·mat·ic** \,id-ē-ə-,plaz-'mat-ik\ *or* **id·io·plas·mic** \-'plaz-mik\ *adj*

id·io·syn·cra·sy \,id-ē-ə-'siŋ-krə-sē\ *n* [Gk *idiosynkrasia*, fr. *idio-* + *synkerannynai* to blend, fr. *syn-* + *kerannynai* to mingle, mix — more at CRATER] **1 :** characteristic peculiarity of habit or structure **2 a :** a peculiarity of constitution or temperament **b :** individual hypersensitiveness (as to a drug or to food) **syn** see ECCENTRICITY — **id·io·syn·crat·ic** \,id-ē-ō-(,)sin-'krat-ik\ *adj* — **id·io·syn·crat·i·cal·ly** \-'krat-i-k(ə-)lē\ *adv*

id·i·ot \'id-ē-ət\ *n* [ME, fr. L *idiota* ignorant person, fr. Gk *idiōtēs* one in a private station, layman, ignorant person, fr. *idios* one's own, private; akin to L *sed, se* without, *sui* of oneself] **1 :** a person afflicted with idiocy; *esp* **:** a feebleminded person having a mental age not exceeding three years and requiring complete custodial care **2 :** a silly or foolish person **syn** see FOOL — **idiot** *adj*

id·i·ot·ic \,id-ē-'ät-ik\ *adj* **:** characterized by idiocy **:** FOOLISH — **id·i·ot·i·cal** \-i-kəl\ *adj* — **id·i·ot·i·cal·ly** \-i-k(ə-)lē\ *adv* — **id·i·ot·i·cal·ness** \-i-kəl-nəs\ *n*

id·i·o·tism *n* [in sense 1, fr. MF *idiotisme*, fr. L *idiotismus* common speech, fr. Gk *idiōtismos*, fr. *idiōtēs*; in sense 2, fr. *idiot*] **1** \'id-ē-ə-,tiz-əm\ **a** *obs* **:** IDIOM 1 **b :** IDIOM 2 **2** \-ē-ət-,iz-əm\ *archaic* **:** IDIOCY

-id·i·um \'id-ē-əm\ *n suffix, pl* **-id·i·ums** *or* **-id·ia** \-ē-ə\ [NL, fr. Gk *-idion*, dim. suffix] **:** small one ⟨anther*idium*⟩

[1]**idle** \'īd-ᵊl\ *adj* **idler** \'īd-lər, -ᵊl-ər\ **idlest** \'īd-ləst, -ᵊl-əst\ [ME *idel*, fr. OE *īdel*; akin to OHG *ītal* worthless] **1 :** lacking worth or basis **:** USELESS ⟨~ rumor⟩ **2 :** not occupied or employed: as **a :** having no employment **:** INACTIVE ⟨~ workmen⟩ **b :** not turned to appropriate use ⟨~ funds⟩ **3 a :** TRIFLING, LAZY ⟨~ fellows⟩ **b :** having no evident lawful means of support ⟨the charge of being an ~ person⟩ **syn** see INACTIVE, VAIN — **idle·ness** \'īd-ᵊl-nəs\ *n* — **idly** \'īd-lē\ *adv*

[2]**idle** *vb* **idling** \'īd-liŋ, -ᵊl-iŋ\ *vi* **1 a :** to spend time in idleness **b :** to move idly **2 :** to run disconnected so that power is not used for useful work ⟨the engine is *idling*⟩ ~ *vt* **1 :** to pass in idleness **2 :** to make idle **3 :** to cause to idle — **idler** \'īd-lər, -ᵊl-ər\ *n*

idler pulley *n* **:** a guide or tightening pulley for a belt or chain

idler wheel *n* **1 :** a wheel, gear, or roller used to transfer motion or to guide or support something **2 :** IDLER PULLEY

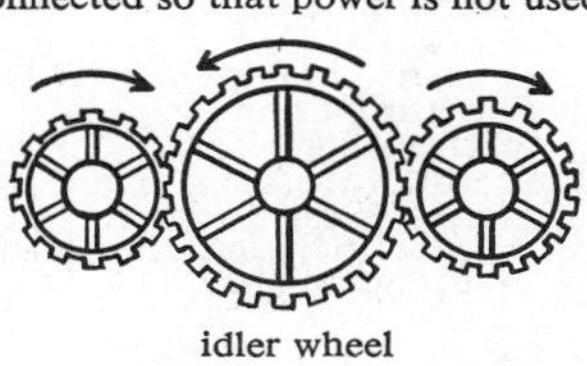

idler wheel

idlesse \ˈīd-ləs\ *n* [*idle* + ME *-esse* (as in *richesse* wealth) — more at RICHES] **:** IDLENESS
ido·crase \ˈīd-ə-ˌkrās, ˈid-, -ˌkrāz\ *n* [F, fr. Gk *eidos* + *krasis* mixture fr. *kerannynai* to mix — more at CRATER] **:** a mineral $Ca_{10}(Mg,Fe)_2Al_4Si_9O_{34}(OH)_4$ that is a complex silicate of calcium, magnesium, iron, and aluminum
idol \ˈīd-ᵊl\ *n* [ME, fr. OF *idole*, fr. LL *idolum*, fr. Gk *eidōlon* phantom, idol; akin to Gk *eidos* form — more at IDYLL] **1 :** a representation or symbol of a deity used as an object of worship; *broadly* **:** a false god **2 a :** any likeness of something **b** *obs* **:** PRETENDER, IMPOSTOR **3 :** a form or appearance visible but without substance **4 :** an object of passionate devotion **5 :** a false conception **:** FALLACY
idol·a·ter \ī-ˈdäl-ət-ər\ *n* [ME *idolatrer*, fr. MF *idolatre*, fr. LL *idololatres*, fr. Gk *eidōlolatrēs*, fr. *eidōlon* + *-latrēs* -later] **1 :** a worshiper of idols **2 :** a person that admires or loves intensely and often blindly
idol·a·trous \ī-ˈdäl-ə-trəs\ *adj* **1 :** of or relating to idolatry **2 :** having the character of idolatry **3 :** given to idolatry — **idol·a·trous·ly** *adv* — **idol·a·trous·ness** *n*
idol·a·try \-trē\ *n* **1 :** the worship of a physical object as a god **2 :** immoderate attachment or devotion to something
idol·iza·tion \ˌīd-ᵊl-ə-ˈzā-shən\ *n* **:** the act of idolizing **:** the state of being idolized
idol·ize \ˈīd-ᵊl-ˌīz\ *vt* **:** to worship idolatrously; *broadly* **:** to love or admire to excess ~ *vi* **:** to practice idolatry — **idol·iz·er** *n*
ido·ne·ous \ī-ˈdō-nē-əs\ *adj* [L *idoneus*] *archaic* **:** SUITABLE
idyll *or* **idyl** \ˈīd-ᵊl\ *n* [L *idyllium*, fr. Gk *eidyllion*, fr. dim. of *eidos* form; akin to Gk *idein* to see — more at WIT] **1 a :** a simple descriptive work either in poetry or prose that deals with rustic life or pastoral scenes or suggests a mood of peace and contentment **b :** a narrative poem treating an epic, romantic, or tragic theme **2 a :** a fit subject for an idyll **b :** a romantic interlude **3 :** a pastoral or romantic musical composition — **idyl·lic** \ī-ˈdil-ik\ *adj* — **idyl·li·cal·ly** \-i-k(ə-)lē\ *adv*
idyll·ist \ˈīd-ᵊl-əst\ *n* **:** a composer of idylls
-ie *also* **-y** \ē\ *n suffix, pl* **-ies** [ME] **1 :** little one **:** dear little one ⟨bird*ie*⟩ ⟨sonn*y*⟩ — sometimes in names of articles of apparel ⟨pant*ie*⟩ **2 :** one belonging to **:** one having to do with ⟨town*y*⟩ **3 :** one of (such) a kind or quality ⟨cut*ie*⟩ ⟨tough*ie*⟩
-ier — see -ER
1if \(ˌ)if, əf\ *conj* [ME, fr. OE *gif*; akin to OHG *ibu* if] **1 a :** in the event that **b :** allowing that **c :** on condition that **2 :** WHETHER ⟨asked ~ the mail had come⟩ **3** — used as a function word to introduce an exclamation expressing a wish ⟨~ it would only rain⟩ **4 :** even though ⟨an interesting ~ untenable argument⟩
2if \ˈif\ *n* **1 :** CONDITION, STIPULATION **2 :** SUPPOSITION
-if·er·ous \ˈif-(ə-)rəs\ *adj comb form* [ME, fr. L *-ifer*, fr. *-i-* + *-fer* -ferous] **:** -FEROUS
if·fy \ˈif-ē\ *adj* [*1if*] **:** abounding in contingencies or unknown qualities or conditions
-i·form \ə-ˌfȯrm\ *adj comb form* [MF & L; MF *-iforme*, fr. L *-iformis*, fr. *-i-* + *-formis* -form] **:** -FORM ⟨rami*form*⟩
-i·fy \ə-ˌfī\ *vb suffix* [ME *-ifien*, fr. OF *-ifier*, fr. L *-ificare*, fr. *-i-* + *-ficare* -fy] **:** -FY
ig·loo *also* **ig·lu** \ˈig-(ˌ)lü\ *n* [Eskimo *iglu*, *igdlu* house] **1 :** an Eskimo house or hut often made of snow blocks and in the shape of a dome **2 :** a building or structure shaped like a dome
ig·ne·ous \ˈig-nē-əs\ *adj* [L *igneus*, fr. *ignis* fire; akin to Skt *agni* fire] **1 :** of, relating to, or resembling fire **:** FIERY **2 a :** relating to, resulting from, or suggestive of the intrusion or extrusion of magma or the activity of volcanoes **b :** formed by solidification of molten magma ⟨~ rock⟩
ig·nes·cent \ig-ˈnes-ᵊnt\ *adj* **1 :** capable of emitting sparks **2 :** flaring up
igni- *comb form* [L, fr. *ignis*] **:** fire **:** burning ⟨*igni*tron⟩
ig·nis fat·u·us \ˌig-nəs-ˈfach-(ə-)wəs\ *n, pl* **ig·nes fat·ui** \-ˌnēz-ˈfach-ə-ˌwī\ [ML, lit., foolish fire] **1 :** a light that sometimes appears in the night over marshy ground and is often attributable to the combustion of gas from decomposed organic matter **2 :** a deceptive goal or hope
ig·nit·able *also* **ig·nit·ible** \ig-ˈnīt-ə-bəl\ *adj* **:** capable of being ignited
ig·nite \ig-ˈnīt\ *vb* [L *ignitus*, pp. of *ignire* to ignite, fr. *ignis*] *vt* **1 :** to subject to fire or intense heat; *specif* **:** to render luminous by heat **2 a :** to set afire; *also* **:** KINDLE **b :** to cause (a fuel mixture) to burn ~ *vi* **1 :** to catch fire **2 :** to begin to glow — **ig·nit·er** *or* **ig·ni·tor** \-ˈnīt-ər\ *n*
ig·ni·tion \ig-ˈnish-ən\ *n* **1 :** the act or action of igniting **:** KINDLING **2 :** the process or means (as an electric spark) of igniting a fuel mixture
ig·ni·tron \ig-ˈnī-ˌträn\ *n* **:** a mercury-containing rectifier tube in which the arc is struck again at the beginning of each cycle by a special electrode separately energized by an auxiliary circuit
ig·no·ble \ig-ˈnō-bəl\ *adj* [L *ignobilis*, fr. *in-* + *nobilis* noble] **1 :** of low birth or common origin **:** PLEBEIAN **2 :** characterized by baseness or meanness **syn** see MEAN — **ig·no·ble·ness** *n* — **ig·no·bly** \-blē *also* -bə-lē\ *adv*
ig·no·min·i·ous \ˌig-nə-ˈmin-ē-əs\ *adj* **1 :** marked with or characterized by disgrace or shame **:** DISHONORABLE **2 :** deserving of shame or infamy **:** DESPICABLE **3 :** HUMILIATING, DEGRADING — **ig·no·min·i·ous·ly** *adv* — **ig·no·min·i·ous·ness** *n*
ig·no·mi·ny \ˈig-nə-ˌmin-ē, -mə-nē; ig-ˈnäm-ə-nē\ *n* [MF or L; MF *ignominie*, fr. L *ignominia*, fr. *ig-* (as in *ignorare* to be ignorant of, ignore) + *nomin-*, *nomen* name, repute — more at NAME] **1 :** deep personal humiliation and disgrace **2 :** disgraceful or dishonorable conduct, quality, or action **syn** see DISGRACE
ig·no·ra·mus \ˌig-nə-ˈrā-məs\ *n* [*Ignoramus*, ignorant lawyer in *Ignoramus* (1615) play by George Ruggle] **:** an utterly ignorant person **:** DUNCE
ig·no·rance \ˈig-nə-rən(t)s\ *n* **:** the state of being ignorant
ig·no·rant \-rənt\ *adj* **1 a :** destitute of knowledge or education **:** UNLEARNED ⟨an ~ society⟩ **b :** resulting from or showing lack of knowledge or intelligence ⟨~ errors⟩ **2 :** UNAWARE, UNINFORMED — **ig·no·rant·ly** *adv* — **ig·no·rant·ness** *n*
syn IGNORANT, ILLITERATE, UNLETTERED, UNTUTORED, UNLEARNED mean not having knowledge; IGNORANT may imply a general condition or it may apply to lack of knowledge or awareness of a particular thing; ILLITERATE applies to either an absolute or a relative inability to read and write; UNLETTERED implies ignorance of the knowledge gained by reading; UNTUTORED may imply lack of schooling in the arts and ways of civilization; UNLEARNED suggests ignorance of advanced subjects
ig·no·ra·tio elen·chi \ˌig-nə-ˌrät-ē-ˌō-i-ˈleŋ-ˌkē\ *n* [L, lit., ignorance of proof] **:** a fallacy in logic of supposing a point proved or disproved by an argument proving or disproving something not at issue
ig·nore \ig-ˈnō(ə)r, -ˈnȯ(ə)r\ *vt* [F *ignorer*, fr. L *ignorare*, fr. *ignarus* ignorant, unknown, fr. *in-* + *gnoscere*, *noscere* to know — more at KNOW] **1 :** to refuse to take notice of **2 :** to reject (a bill of indictment) as ungrounded **syn** see NEGLECT — **ig·nor·er** *n*
Igo·rot \ˌē-gə-ˈrōt\ *n, pl* **Igorot** *or* **Igorots 1 :** a member of any of several related peoples of northwestern Luzon, Philippines **2 :** any of the Austronesian languages of the Igorot
Igraine \i-ˈgrān\ *n* **:** the wife of Uther and mother of Arthur in Arthurian legend
igua·na \i-ˈgwän-ə\ *n* [Sp, fr. Arawak *iwana*] **:** any of various large herbivorous typically dark-colored tropical American lizards (family Iguanidae) with a serrated dorsal crest that are important as human food in their native habitat; *broadly* **:** any of various large lizards
iguan·odont \i-ˈgwän-ə-ˌdänt\ *n* [NL *Iguanodont-*, *Iguanodon*, genus name] **:** any of a genus (*Iguanodon*) of gigantic herbivorous dinosaurs from the early Cretaceous of Belgium and England — **iguanodont** *adj*
IHS \ˌī-ˌā-ˈches\ [LL, part transliteration of Gk ΙΗΣ, abbreviation for ΙΗΣΟΥΣ *Iēsous* Jesus] — used as a Christian symbol and monogram for *Jesus*
ikon *var of* ICON
il- — see IN-
ilang–ilang \ˌē-ˌläŋ-ˈē-ˌläŋ\ *n* [Tag] **1 :** a tree (*Canangium odoratum*) of the custard-apple family of the Malay archipelago, the Philippines, and adjacent areas that has very fragrant greenish yellow flowers **2 :** a perfume distilled from the flowers of the ilang-ilang tree
ile- *also* **ileo-** *comb form* [NL *ileum*] **1 :** ileum ⟨*ile*itis⟩ **2 :** ileal and ⟨*ileo*cecal⟩
1-ile \əl, ᵊl, ˌīl, (ˌ)il\ *adj suffix* [ME, fr. MF, fr. L *-ilis*] **:** of, relating to, or capable of ⟨contract*ile*⟩
2-ile *n suffix* [prob. fr. *-ile* (as in *quartile*, n.)] **:** segment of a (specified) size in a frequency distribution ⟨dec*ile*⟩
il·e·al \ˈil-ē-əl\ *also* **il·e·ac** \-ē-ˌak\ *adj* **:** of, relating to, or involving the ileum
il·e·itis \ˌil-ē-ˈīt-əs\ *n* [NL] **:** inflammation of the ileum
il·e·um \ˈil-ē-əm\ *n, pl* **il·ea** \-ē-ə\ [NL, fr. L, groin, viscera] **:** the last division of the small intestine extending between the jejunum and large intestine
il·e·us \ˈil-ē-əs\ *n* [L, fr. Gk *eileos*, fr. *eilyein* to roll — more at VOLUBLE] **:** obstruction of the bowel; *specif* **:** a condition marked by painful distended abdomen, vomiting, toxemia, and dehydration and caused by failure of peristalsis
ilex \ˈī-ˌleks\ *n* [L] **1 :** a southern European evergreen oak (*Quercus ilex*) — called also *holm oak* **2 :** HOLLY
il·i·ac \ˈil-ē-ˌak\ *also* **il·i·al** \ˈil-ē-əl\ *adj* [LL *iliacus*, fr. L *ilium*] **:** of, relating to, or located near the ilium
Il·i·ad \ˈil-ē-əd, -ē-ˌad\ *n* [*Iliad*, ancient Greek epic poem attributed to Homer, fr. L *Iliad-*, *Ilias*, fr. Gk] **1 :** a long narrative; *esp* **:** an epic in the Homeric tradition **2 a :** a series of exploits regarded as suitable for an epic **b :** a series of miseries — **Il·i·ad·ic** \ˌil-ē-ˈad-ik\ *adj*
ilio- *comb form* [NL *ilium*] **:** iliac and ⟨*ilio*lumbar⟩
il·i·um \ˈil-ē-əm\ *n, pl* **il·ia** \-ē-ə\ [NL, fr. L *ilium*, *ileum*] **:** the dorsal and upper one of the three bones composing either lateral half of the pelvis
1ilk \ˈilk\ *pron* [ME, fr. OE *ilca*, fr. a prehistoric compound whose constituents are akin respectively to Goth *is* he (akin to L *is* he, that) and OE *gelīc* like — more at ITERATE, LIKE] *chiefly Scot* **:** SAME — used with *that* esp. in the names of landed families
2ilk *n* **:** SORT, KIND
3ilk *pron* [ME, adj. & pron., fr. OE *ylc*, *ǣlc*] *chiefly Scot* **:** EACH
il·ka \ˈil-kə\ *adj* [ME, fr. *ilk* + *a* (indef. art.)] *chiefly Scot* **:** EACH, EVERY
1ill \ˈil\ *adj* **worse** \ˈwərs\ **worst** \ˈwərst\ [ME, fr. ON *illr*] **1 a** *chiefly Scot* **:** IMMORAL, VICIOUS **b :** showing or implying evil intention ⟨~ deeds⟩ **2 a :** causing suffering or distress ⟨~ weather⟩ **b** (1) **:** not normal or sound ⟨~ health⟩ (2) **:** not in good health; *also* **:** NAUSEATED **3 a :** not suited to circumstances or not to one's advantage **:** UNLUCKY ⟨~ omen⟩ **b :** involving difficulty **:** HARD ⟨an ~ man to please⟩ **4 a :** not meeting an accepted standard ⟨~ manners⟩ **b** *archaic* **:** notably unskillful or inefficient **5 a :** UNFRIENDLY, HOSTILE ⟨~ feeling⟩ **b :** HARSH, CRUEL ⟨~ treatment⟩ **syn** see BAD, SICK
2ill *adv* **worse**; **worst 1 a :** with displeasure or hostility **b :** in a harsh manner **c :** so as to reflect unfavorably **2 :** in a reprehensible manner **3 :** HARDLY, SCARCELY **4 a :** BADLY, UNLUCKILY **b :** in a faulty or inefficient manner
3ill *n* **1 :** the reverse of good **:** EVIL **2 a :** MISFORTUNE, DISTRESS **b** (1) **:** AILMENT, SICKNESS (2) **:** something that disturbs or afflicts **:** TROUBLE **3 :** something that reflects unfavorably
I'll \(ˌ)ī(ə)l\ **:** I will **:** I shall
ill–ad·vised \ˌil-əd-ˈvīzd\ *adj* **:** resulting from or showing lack of wise and sufficient counsel or deliberation — **ill–ad·vised·ly** \-ˈvī-zəd-lē, -ˈvīz-dlē\ *adv*
il·la·tion \il-ˈā-shən\ *n* [LL *illation-*, *illatio*, fr. L, action of bringing in, fr. *illatus* (pp. of *inferre* to bring in), fr. *in-* + *latus*, pp. of *ferre* to carry — more at TOLERATE, BEAR] **1 :** the action of inferring **:** INFERENCE **2 :** a conclusion inferred
1il·la·tive \ˈil-ət-iv, il-ˈāt-\ *n* **1 :** a word (as *therefore*) or phrase (as *as a consequence*) introducing an inference **2 :** ILLATION 2
2illative *adj* **:** INFERENTIAL — **il·la·tive·ly** *adv*
il·laud·able \(ˈ)il-ˈ(l)ȯd-ə-bəl\ *adj* [L *illaudabilis*, fr. *in-* + *laudabilis* laudable] **:** deserving no praise — **il·laud·ably** \-blē\ *adv*
ill–be·ing \ˈil-ˈbē-iŋ\ *n* **:** the condition of being less than prosperous
ill–bod·ing \ˈil-ˈbōd-iŋ\ *adj* **:** boding evil **:** INAUSPICIOUS
ill–bred \-ˈbred\ *adj* **1 :** badly brought up **:** IMPOLITE **2 :** inferior by reason of being the offspring of badly matched parents
il·le·gal \(ˈ)il-ˈ(l)ē-gəl\ *adj* [F or ML; F *illégal*, fr. ML *illegalis*, fr. L *in-* + *legalis* legal] **:** not according to or authorized by law **:** UNLAWFUL; *also* **:** not sanctioned by official rules — **il·le·gal·i·ty** \ˌil-ē-ˈgal-ət-ē\ *n* — **il·le·gal·ly** \(ˈ)il-ˈ(l)ē-gə-lē\ *adv*

il·leg·i·bil·i·ty \(ˌ)il-ˌej-ə-ˈbil-ət-ē\ *n* **:** the quality or state of being illegible

il·leg·i·ble \(ˈ)il-ˈ(l)ej-ə-bəl\ *adj* **:** not legible **:** UNDECIPHERABLE — **il·leg·i·bly** \-blē\ *adv*

il·le·git·i·ma·cy \ˌil-i-ˈjit-ə-mə-sē\ *n* **1 :** the quality or state of being illegitimate **2 :** BASTARDY 2

il·le·git·i·mate \-ˈjit-ə-mət\ *adj* **1 :** not recognized as lawful offspring; *specif* **:** born of parents not married to each other **2 :** not rightly deduced or inferred **:** ILLOGICAL **3 :** departing from the regular **:** ERRATIC **4 a :** ILLEGAL **b :** not authorized by good usage **c** *of a taxon* **:** published either validly or invalidly but not according with the rules of the relevant international code — **il·le·git·i·mate·ly** *adv*

ill–fat·ed \ˈil-ˈfāt-əd\ *adj* **1 :** having an evil fate **2 :** that causes or marks the beginning of misfortune

ill–fa·vored \-ˈfā-vərd\ *adj* **1 :** unattractive in physical appearance; *esp* **:** having an ugly face **2 :** OFFENSIVE, OBJECTIONABLE

ill–got·ten \-ˈgät-ᵊn\ *adj* **:** acquired by evil means

ill–hu·mored \ˈil-ˈhyü-mərd, -ˈyü-\ *adj* **:** SURLY, IRRITABLE — **ill–hu·mored·ly** *adv*

il·lib·er·al \(ˈ)il-ˈ(l)ib-(ə-)rəl\ *adj* [MF or L; MF, fr. L *illiberalis* ignoble, stingy, fr. L *in-* + *liberalis* liberal] **:** not liberal: as **a** *archaic* (1) **:** lacking a liberal education (2) **:** lacking culture and refinement **b** *archaic* **:** not generous **:** STINGY **c** (1) **:** not broad-minded **:** BIGOTED (2) **:** opposed to liberalism — **il·lib·er·al·i·ty** \(ˌ)il-ˌib-ə-ˈral-ət-ē\ *n* — **il·lib·er·al·ly** \(ˈ)il-ˈ(l)ib-(ə-)rə-lē\ *adv* — **il·lib·er·al·ness** \-(ə-)rəl-nəs\ *n*

il·lic·it \(ˈ)il-ˈ(l)is-ət\ *adj* [L *illicitus*, fr. *in-* + *licitus* lawful — more at LICIT] **:** not permitted **:** UNLAWFUL — **il·lic·it·ly** *adv*

il·lim·it·abil·i·ty \(ˌ)il-ˌim-ət-ə-ˈbil-ət-ē\ *n* **:** ILLIMITABLENESS

il·lim·it·able \(ˈ)il-ˈ(l)im-ət-ə-bəl\ *adj* **:** incapable of being limited or bounded **:** MEASURELESS — **il·lim·it·able·ness** *n* — **il·lim·it·ably** \-blē\ *adv*

il·lin·i·um \il-ˈin-ē-əm\ *n* [NL, fr. *Illinois*] **:** PROMETHIUM

Il·li·nois \ˌil-ə-ˈnȯi *also* -ˈnȯiz\ *n, pl* **Illinois** [F, of Algonquian origin; akin to Shawnee *hilenawe* man] **1 :** a confederacy of Indian peoples of Illinois, Iowa, and Wisconsin **2 :** a member of one of the Illinois peoples

il·liq·uid \(ˈ)il-ˈ(l)ik-wəd\ *adj* **1 :** not being cash or readily convertible into cash **2 :** having no liquid assets — **il·li·quid·i·ty** \ˌil-(ˌ)ik-ˈwid-ət-ē\ *n*

il·lite \ˈil-ˌīt\ *n* [*Illinois*, U.S.A.] **:** a group of clay minerals having essentially the crystal structure of muscovite; *also* **:** one of these minerals — **il·lit·ic** \il-ˈit-ik\ *adj*

il·lit·er·a·cy \(ˈ)il-ˈ(l)it-ə-rə-sē, -ˈ(l)i-trə-sē\ *n* **1 :** the quality or state of being illiterate; *esp* **:** inability to read or write **2 :** a mistake or crudity made by or typical of one who is illiterate

il·lit·er·ate \-ˈ(l)it-ə-rət, -ˈ(l)i-trət\ *adj* [L *illiteratus*, fr. *in-* + *litteratus* literate] **1 :** having little or no education **:** UNLETTERED; *esp* **:** unable to read or write **2 a :** showing or marked by a lack of familiarity with language and literature **b :** violating approved patterns of speaking or writing **3 :** showing or marked by a lack of acquaintance with the fundamentals of a particular field of knowledge **syn** see IGNORANT — **illiterate** *n* — **il·lit·er·ate·ly** *adv* — **il·lit·er·ate·ness** *n*

ill–man·nered \ˈil-ˈman-ərd\ *adj* **:** marked by bad manners **:** RUDE

ill–na·tured \-ˈnā-chərd\ *adj* **1 :** MALEVOLENT, SPITEFUL **2 :** having a bad disposition **:** CROSS, SURLY — **ill–na·tured·ly** *adv*

ill·ness \ˈil-nəs\ *n* **1** *obs* **a :** WICKEDNESS **b :** UNPLEASANTNESS **2 :** an unhealthy condition of body or mind **:** SICKNESS

il·log·ic \(ˈ)il-ˈ(l)äj-ik\ *n* **:** the quality or state of being illogical

il·log·i·cal \-i-kəl\ *adj* **1 :** not observing the principles of logic **2 :** devoid of logic **:** SENSELESS — **il·log·i·cal·i·ty** \(ˌ)il-ˌäj-i-ˈkal-ət-ē\ *n* — **il·log·i·cal·ly** \(ˈ)il-ˈ(l)äj-i-k(ə-)lē\ *adv* — **il·log·i·cal·ness** \-kəl-nəs\ *n*

ill–sort·ed \ˈil-ˈsȯrt-əd\ *adj* **1 :** not well matched **2** *Scot* **:** DISPLEASED

ill–starred \-ˈstärd\ *adj* **:** ILL-FATED, UNLUCKY

ill–treat \-ˈtrēt\ *vt* **:** to treat cruelly or improperly **:** MALTREAT — **ill–treat·ment** \-mənt\ *n*

il·lume \il-ˈüm\ *vt* **:** ILLUMINATE

il·lu·mi·na·ble \il-ˈü-mə-nə-bəl\ *adj* **:** capable of being illuminated

il·lu·mi·nance \-mə-nən(t)s\ *n* **:** ILLUMINATION 2

il·lu·mi·nant \-nənt\ *n* **:** an illuminating device or substance

¹il·lu·mi·nate \il-ˈü-mə-nət\ *adj* **1** *archaic* **:** brightened with light **2** *archaic* **:** intellectually or spiritually enlightened

²il·lu·mi·nate \-ˌnāt\ *vt* [L *illuminatus*, pp. of *illuminare*, fr. *in-* + *luminare* to light up, fr. *lumin-*, *lumen* light — more at LUMINARY] **1 a** (1) **:** to supply or brighten with light (2) **:** to make luminous or shining **b :** ENLIGHTEN **c** *archaic* **:** to set alight **2 :** to make clear **:** ELUCIDATE **3 :** to make illustrious or resplendent **4 :** to decorate (as a manuscript) with gold or silver or brilliant colors or with often elaborate designs or miniature pictures — **il·lu·mi·na·tor** \il-ˈü-mə-ˌnāt-ər\ *n*

³il·lu·mi·nate \-nət\ *n, archaic* **:** one having or claiming unusual enlightenment

il·lu·mi·na·ti \il-ˌü-mə-ˈnät-ē\ *n pl* [It & NL; It, fr. NL, fr. L, pl. of *illuminatus*] **1** *cap* **:** any of various groups claiming special usu. religious enlightenment **2 :** persons who are or who claim to be unusually enlightened

il·lu·mi·na·tion \il-ˌü-mə-ˈnā-shən\ *n* **1 :** the action of illuminating or state of being illuminated: as **a :** spiritual or intellectual enlightenment **b** (1) **:** a lighting up (2) **:** decorative lighting or lighting effects **c :** decoration by the art of illuminating **2 :** the luminous flux per unit area on an intercepting surface at any given point **3 :** one of the decorative features used in the art of illuminating or in decorative lighting

il·lu·mi·na·tive \il-ˈü-mə-ˌnāt-iv\ *adj* **:** of, relating to, or producing illumination **:** ILLUMINATING

il·lu·mine \il-ˈü-mən\ *vt* **:** ILLUMINATE

il·lu·mi·nism \-mə-ˌniz-əm\ *n* **1 :** belief in or claim to a personal enlightenment not accessible to mankind in general **2** *cap* **:** beliefs or claims viewed as forming doctrine or principles of Illuminati — **il·lu·mi·nist** \-mə-nəst\ *n*

ill–us·age \ˈil-ˈyü-sij, -zij\ *n* **:** harsh, unkind, or abusive treatment

ill–use \-ˈyüz\ *vt* **:** MALTREAT, ABUSE

il·lu·sion \il-ˈü-zhən\ *n* [ME, fr. MF, fr. LL *illusion-*, *illusio*, fr. L, action of mocking, fr. *illusus*, pp. of *illudere* to mock at, fr. *in-* + *ludere* to play, mock — more at LUDICROUS] **1 a** *obs* **:** the action of deceiving **b** (1) **:** the state or fact of being intellectually deceived or misled **:** MISAPPREHENSION (2) **:** an instance of such deception **2 a** (1) **:** a misleading image presented to the vision (2) **:** something that deceives or misleads intellectually **b** (1) **:** perception of something objectively existing in such a way as to cause misinterpretation of its actual nature (2) **:** HALLUCINATION 1 (3) **:** a pattern capable of reversible perspective **3 :** a fine plain transparent bobbinet or tulle usu. made of silk and used for veils, trimmings, and dresses **syn** see DELUSION — **il·lu·sion·al** \-ˈüzh-nəl, -ən-ᵊl\ *adj* — **il·lu·sion·ary** \il-ˈü-zhə-ˌner-ē\ *adj*

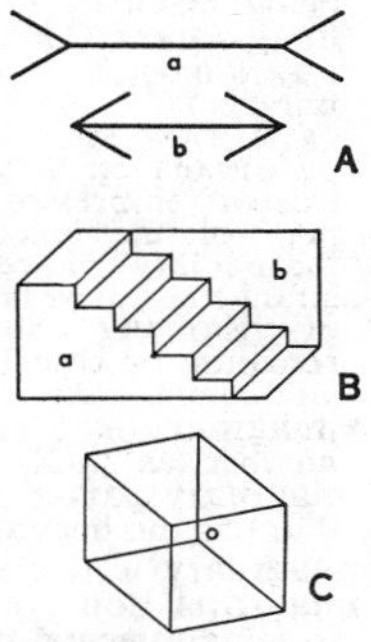

optical illusions: fig. *A*: *a* equals *b* in length; fig. *B*: either side *a* or side *b* may appear nearer the observer; fig. *C*: *o* may be regarded as either the near or the far corner of the block

il·lu·sion·ism \-ˈü-zhə-ˌniz-əm\ *n* **:** the use of often extreme illusionary effects esp. in art

il·lu·sion·ist \il-ˈüzh-(ə-)nəst\ *n* **:** one that produces illusions: as **a :** an artist whose work is marked by illusionism **b :** a ventriloquist or sleight-of-hand performer

il·lu·sive \il-ˈü-siv, -ˈü-ziv\ *adj* **:** ILLUSORY — **il·lu·sive·ly** *adv* — **il·lu·sive·ness** *n*

il·lu·so·ri·ly \il-ˈüs-(ə-)rə-lē, -ˈüz-\ *adv* **:** in an illusory manner

il·lu·so·ri·ness \-rē-nəs\ *n* **:** the quality or state of being illusory

il·lu·so·ry \il-ˈüs-(ə-)rē, -ˈüz-\ *adj* **:** based on or producing illusion **:** DECEPTIVE **syn** see APPARENT

il·lus·trate \ˈil-ə-ˌstrāt, il-ˈəs-ˌtrāt\ *vb* [L *illustratus*, pp. of *illustrare*, fr. *in-* + *lustrare* to purify, make bright — more at LUSTER] *vt* **1** *obs* **a :** ENLIGHTEN **b :** to light up **2 a** *archaic* **:** to make illustrious **b** *obs* (1) **:** to make bright (2) **:** ADORN **3 a :** to make clear **:** CLARIFY **b :** to make clear by giving or by serving as an example or instance **c** (1) **:** to provide with visual features intended to explain or decorate (2) **:** to serve to explain or decorate **4 :** to show clearly **:** DEMONSTRATE ~ *vi* **:** to give an example or instance — **il·lus·tra·tor** \ˈil-ə-ˌstrāt-ər, il-ˈəs-ˌtrāt-\ *n*

il·lus·tra·tion \ˌil-ə-ˈstrā-shən, il-ˌəs-\ *n* **1 a :** the action of illustrating **:** the condition of being illustrated **b** *archaic* **:** the action of making illustrious or honored or distinguished **2 :** something that serves to illustrate: as **a :** an example or instance that helps make something clear **b :** a picture or diagram that helps make something clear or attractive **syn** see INSTANCE

il·lus·tra·tive \il-ˈəs-trət-iv\ *adj* **:** serving, tending, or designed to illustrate — **il·lus·tra·tive·ly** *adv*

il·lus·tri·ous \il-ˈəs-trē-əs\ *adj* [L *illustris*, prob. back-formation fr. *illustrare*] **1 :** notably or brilliantly outstanding because of dignity or achievements or actions **:** EMINENT **2** *obs* **a :** shining brightly with light **b :** clearly evident **syn** see FAMOUS — **il·lus·tri·ous·ly** *adv* — **il·lus·tri·ous·ness** *n*

il·lu·vi·al \(ˈ)il-ˈü-vē-əl\ *adj* **:** of, relating to, or marked by illuviation or illuviated materials or areas

il·lu·vi·ate \-vē-ˌāt\ *vi* **:** to undergo illuviation

il·lu·vi·a·tion \(ˌ)il-ˌü-vē-ˈā-shən\ *n* [*in-* + *-luviation* (as in *eluviation*)] **:** accumulation of dissolved or suspended soil materials in one area or horizon as a result of eluviation from another

il·lu·vi·um \(ˈ)il-ˈü-vē-əm\ *n, pl* **il·lu·vi·ums** *or* **il·lu·via** \-vē-ə\ [NL, fr. *in-* + *-luvium* (as in *alluvium*)] **:** material leached from one soil horizon and deposited in another

ill will *n* **:** unfriendly feeling **syn** see MALICE

ill–wish·er \ˈil-ˈwish-ər\ *n* **:** one that wishes ill to another

il·ly \ˈil-(l)ē\ *adv* **:** BADLY, ILL ⟨~ chosen⟩

¹Il·lyr·i·an \il-ˈir-ē-ən\ *adj* **:** of, relating to, or characteristic of ancient Illyria, the Illyrians, or their languages

²Illyrian *n* **1 :** a native or inhabitant of ancient Illyria **2 :** the poorly attested Indo-European languages of the Illyrians

il·men·ite \ˈil-mə-ˌnīt\ *n* [G *ilmenit*, fr. *Ilmen* range, Ural Mts., U.S.S.R.] **:** a usu. massive iron-black mineral $FeTiO_3$ composed of iron, titanium, and oxygen

Ilo·ca·no *or* **Ilo·ka·no** \ˌē-lə-ˈkän-(ˌ)ō\ *n, pl* **Ilocano** *or* **Ilocanos** *or* **Ilokano** *or* **Ilokanos** **1 a :** a major people of northern Luzon in the Philippines **b :** a member of this people **2 :** the Austronesian language of the Ilocano people

im- — see IN-

I'm \(ˌ)īm\ **:** I am

¹im·age \ˈim-ij\ *n* [ME, fr. OF, short for *imagene*, fr. L *imagin-*, *imago*; akin to L *imitari* to imitate] **1 :** a reproduction or imitation of the form of a person or thing; *esp* **:** an imitation in solid form **2 a :** the optical counterpart of an object produced by a lens, mirror, or other optical system **b :** any likeness of an object produced on a photographic material **3 :** exact likeness **4 a :** a tangible or visible representation **:** INCARNATION **b** *archaic* **:** an illusory form **:** APPARITION **5 a** (1) **:** a mental picture of something not actually present **:** IMPRESSION (2) **:** a mental conception held in common by members of a group and symbolic of a basic attitude and orientation **b :** IDEA, CONCEPT **6 :** a vivid or graphic representation or description **7 a :** something introduced to represent something else that it strikingly resembles or suggests **b :** FIGURE OF SPEECH **8 :** a person strikingly like another person

²image *vt* **1 :** to describe or portray in language esp. vividly **2 :** to call up a mental picture of **:** IMAGINE **3 a :** REFLECT, MIRROR **b :** to make appear **:** PROJECT **4 a :** to create a representation of **b :** to represent symbolically

im·ag·ery \ˈim-ij-(ə-)rē\ *n* **1 :** the product of image makers **:** IMAGES; *also* **:** the art of making images **2 :** figurative language **3 :** mental images; *esp* **:** the products of imagination

imag·in·able \im-ˈaj-(ə-)nə-bəl\ *adj* **:** capable of being imagined **:** CONCEIVABLE — **imag·in·able·ness** *n* — **imag·in·ably** \-blē\ *adv*

¹imag·i·nal \im-ˈaj-ən-ᵊl\ *adj* [*imagine* + *-al*] **:** of or relating to imagination or to images or imagery

²ima·gi·nal \im-ˈā-gən-ᵊl, -ˈäg-ən-\ *adj* [NL *imagin-*, *imago*] **:** of or relating to the insect imago

imag·i·nar·i·ly \im-ˌaj-ə-ˈner-ə-lē\ *adv* : in an imaginary manner
imag·i·nar·i·ness \im-ˈaj-ə-ˌner-ē-nəs\ *n* : the quality or state of being imaginary
¹imag·i·nary \im-ˈaj-ə-ˌner-ē\ *adj* **1** : existing only in imagination : FANCIED **2** : containing or relating to the imaginary unit ⟨~ number⟩
syn FANCIFUL, VISIONARY, FANTASTIC, CHIMERICAL, QUIXOTIC: IMAGINARY stresses lack of actuality; it applies to what could be existent or present but in fact is not; FANCIFUL suggests the free play of the imagination; VISIONARY stresses impracticality or incapability of realization; FANTASTIC implies incredibility or strangeness beyond belief; CHIMERICAL combines the implication of VISIONARY and FANTASTIC; QUIXOTIC implies a devotion to romantic or chivalrous ideals unrestrained by ordinary prudence and common sense
²imaginary *n* **1** *obs* : a figment of imagination **2** : a complex number (as 2+3i) whose imaginary part is not zero
imaginary part *n* : the part of a complex number (as *3i* in *2+3i*) that has the imaginary unit as a factor
imaginary unit *n* : the positive square root of minus 1 : $+\sqrt{-1}$
imag·i·na·tion \im-ˌaj-ə-ˈnā-shən\ *n* **1** : the act or power of forming a mental image of something not present to the senses or never before wholly perceived in reality **2 a** : creative ability **b** : ability to confront and deal with a problem : RESOURCEFULNESS **3 a** : a creation of the mind; *esp* : an idealized or poetic creation **b** : fanciful or empty assumption **4** : popular or traditional belief or conception
syn IMAGINATION, FANCY, FANTASY mean the power to form mental images of things not before one. IMAGINATION is the most general term and the freest from derogatory connotation; it may apply to the representation either of what is remembered, or of what has never been experienced in its entirety, or of what is actually nonexistent; FANCY applies esp. to the power of inventing the novel and unreal by altering or recombining the elements of reality; FANTASY implies the unrestrained and often extravagant or delusive operation of the fancy
imag·i·na·tive \im-ˈaj-(ə-)nət-iv, -ˈaj-ə-ˌnāt-\ *adj* **1** : of, relating to, or characterized by imagination **2** : given to imagining : having a lively imagination **3** : of or relating to images; *esp* : showing a command of imagery — **imag·i·na·tive·ly** *adv* — **imag·i·na·tive·ness** *n*
imag·ine \im-ˈaj-ən\ *vt* **imag·in·ing** \-ˈaj-(ə-)niŋ\ [ME *imaginen*, fr. MF *imaginer*, fr. L *imaginari*, fr. *imagin-*, *imago* image] *vt* **1** : to form a mental image of (something not present) **2** : PLAN, SCHEME **3** : THINK, SUPPOSE, GUESS ⟨I ~ it will rain⟩ ~ *vi* **1** : to use the imagination **2** : SUPPOSE, THINK **syn** see THINK
im·ag·ism \ˈim-ij-ˌiz-əm\ *n* : a movement in poetry advocating free verse and the expression of ideas and emotions through clear precise images — **im·ag·ist** \-ij-əst\ *n* — **imagist** *or* **im·ag·is·tic** \ˌim-ij-ˈis-tik\ *adj* — **im·ag·is·ti·cal·ly** \-ti-k(ə-)lē\ *adv*
ima·go \im-ˈā-(ˌ)gō, -ˈäg-(ˌ)ō\ *n, pl* **imagoes** *or* **ima·gi·nes** \-ˈā-gə-ˌnēz, -ˈäg-ə-\ [NL, fr. L, image] **1** : an insect in its final adult sexually mature usu. winged state **2** : an idealized mental image of any person including the self
imam \i-ˈmäm, -ˈmam\ *n* [Ar *imām*] **1** : the prayer leader of a mosque **2** *cap* : a Muslim leader of the line of Ali held by Shiites to be the divinely appointed, sinless, infallible successors of Muhammad **3** : any of various rulers that claim descent from Muhammad and exercise spiritual and temporal leadership over a Muslim region
imam·ate \-ˌāt\ *n, often cap* **1** : the office of an imam **2** : the region or country ruled over by an imam
ima·ret \i-ˈmär-ət\ *n* [Turk] : an inn or hospice in Turkey
im·bal·ance \(ˈ)im-ˈbal-ən(t)s\ *n* : lack of balance: as **a** : lack of functional balance between body parts or its effect **b** : numerical disproportion between males and females in a population
im·be·cile \ˈim-bə-səl, -ˌsil\ *n* [F *imbécile*, fr. *imbécile* weak, weak-minded, fr. L *imbecillus*] **1** : a mentally deficient person; *esp* : a feebleminded person having a mental age of three to seven years and requiring supervision in the performance of routine daily tasks of caring for himself **2** : FOOL, IDIOT **syn** see FOOL — **imbecile** *or* **im·be·cil·ic** \ˌim-bə-ˈsil-ik\ *adj* — **im·be·cile·ly** \ˈim-bə-sə(l)-lē, -ˌsil-lē\ *adv*
im·be·cil·i·ty \ˌim-bə-ˈsil-ət-ē\ *n* **1** : the quality or state of being imbecile or an imbecile **2 a** : utter foolishness; *also* : FUTILITY **b** : something that is foolish or nonsensical
imbed *var of* EMBED
im·bibe \im-ˈbīb\ *vb* [in sense 1, fr. ME *enbiben*, fr. MF *embiber*, fr. L *imbibere* to drink in, conceive, fr. *in-* + *bibere* to drink; in other senses, fr. L *imbibere* — more at POTABLE] *vt* **1** *archaic* : SOAK, STEEP **2 a** : to receive into the mind and retain ⟨~ moral principles⟩ **b** : to assimilate or take into solution **3 a** : DRINK **b** : ABSORB ~ *vi* **1** : DRINK 2 **2 a** : to take in liquid **b** : to absorb or assimilate moisture, gas, light, or heat **syn** see ABSORB — **im·bib·er** *n*
im·bi·bi·tion \ˌim-bə-ˈbish-ən\ *n* : the act or action of imbibing; *esp* : the taking up of fluid by a colloidal system resulting in swelling — **im·bi·bi·tion·al** \-ˈbish-nəl, -ən-ᵊl\ *adj*
imbitter *var of* EMBITTER
imbosom *var of* EMBOSOM
¹im·bri·cate \ˈim-bri-kət\ *adj* [LL *imbricatus*, pp. of *imbricare* to cover with pantiles, fr. L *imbric-*, *imbrex* pantile, fr. *imbr-*, *imber* rain; akin to Gk *ombros* rain] : lying lapped over each other in regular order ⟨~ scales⟩ — **im·bri·cate·ly** *adv*
²im·bri·cate \ˈim-brə-ˌkāt\ *vb* : OVERLAP
im·bri·ca·tion \ˌim-brə-ˈkā-shən\ *n* **1** : an overlapping of edges (as of tiles) **2** : a decoration or pattern showing imbrication

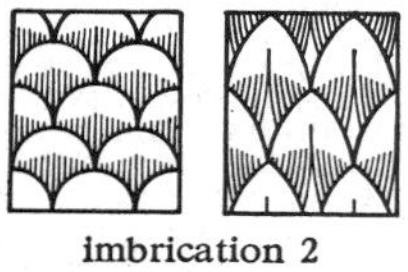
imbrication 2

im·bro·glio \im-ˈbrōl-(ˌ)yō\ *n* [It, fr. *imbrogliare* to entangle, fr. MF *embrouiller* — more at EMBROIL] **1** : a confused mass **2 a** : an intricate or complicated situation **b** : an acutely painful or embarrassing misunderstanding : EMBROILMENT
imbrown *var of* EMBROWN
im·brue \im-ˈbrü\ *vt* [ME *enbrewen*, prob. fr. MF *abrevrer*, *embevrer* to soak, drench, deriv. of L *bibere* to drink — more at POTABLE] : DRENCH, STAIN
im·brute \im-ˈbrüt\ *vi* : to sink to the level of a brute ~ *vt* : to degrade to the level of a brute
im·bue \im-ˈbyü\ *vt* [L *imbuere*] **1** : to tinge or dye deeply **2** : to cause to become penetrated : PERMEATE **syn** see INFUSE
im·burse \im-ˈbərs\ *vt* [ML *imbursare*, fr. L *in-* + ML *bursa* purse — more at PURSE] : to put into or as if into a purse
im·id·az·ole \ˌim-ə-ˈdaz-ˌōl\ *n* [ISV] : a white crystalline heterocyclic base $C_3H_4N_2$; *broadly* : any of various derivatives of this
im·ide \ˈim-ˌīd\ *n* [ISV, alter. of *amide*] : a compound derived from ammonia by replacement of two hydrogen atoms by a metal or an equivalent of acid radicals — compare AMIDE — **im·id·ic** \im-ˈid-ik\ *adj*
im·i·do \ˈim-ə-ˌdō\ *adj* : relating to or containing the group =NH or a substituted group =NR united to one or two radicals of acid character
im·ine \ˈim-ˌēn\ *n* [ISV, alter. of *amine*] : a compound derived from ammonia by replacement of two hydrogen atoms by a bivalent hydrocarbon radical or other nonacid organic radical
im·i·no \ˈim-ə-ˌnō\ *adj* : relating to or containing the group =NH or a substituted group =NR united to a radical other than an acid radical
im·i·ta·ble \ˈim-ət-ə-bəl\ *adj* : capable or worthy of being imitated or copied
im·i·tate \ˈim-ə-ˌtāt\ *vt* [L *imitatus*, pp. of *imitari* — more at IMAGE] **1** : to follow as a pattern, model, or example : COPY **2** : to produce a copy of : REPRODUCE **3** : to be or appear like : RESEMBLE **4** : MIMIC, COUNTERFEIT **syn** see COPY — **im·i·ta·tor** \-ˌtāt-ər\ *n*
im·i·ta·tion \ˌim-ə-ˈtā-shən\ *n* **1** : an act of imitating **2** : something produced as a copy : COUNTERFEIT **3** : a literary work designed to reproduce the style of another author **4** : the repetition in a voice part of the melodic theme, phrase, or motive previously found in another part **5** : participation by a sensible object in a transcendent idea **6 a** : the execution of an act supposedly as a direct response to the perception of another person performing the act **b** : the assumption of the modes of behavior observed in other individuals — **imitation** *adj* — **im·i·ta·tion·al** \-shnəl, -shən-ᵊl\ *adj*
im·i·ta·tive \ˈim-ə-ˌtāt-iv\ *adj* **1 a** : marked by imitation **b** : ONOMATOPOEIC **c** : exhibiting mimicry **2** : inclined to imitate **3** : imitating something superior : COUNTERFEIT — **im·i·ta·tive·ly** *adv* — **im·i·ta·tive·ness** *n*
im·mac·u·la·cy \im-ˈak-yə-lə-sē\ *n* : IMMACULATENESS
im·mac·u·late \im-ˈak-yə-lət\ *adj* [ME *immaculat*, fr. L *immaculatus*, fr. *in-* + *maculatus*, pp. of *maculare* to stain — more at MACULATE] **1** : having no stain or blemish : PURE **2** : containing no flaw or error **3 a** : spotlessly clean **b** : having no colored spots or marks ⟨petals ~⟩ — **im·mac·u·late·ly** *adv* — **im·mac·u·late·ness** *n*
Immaculate Conception *n* : a conception in which the offspring is preserved free from original sin by divine grace held in Roman Catholic dogma to be the manner of the conception of the Virgin Mary
im·mane \im-ˈān\ *adj* [L *immanis*, fr. *in-* + *manus* good — more at MATURE] *archaic* : HUGE; *also* : monstrous in character : INHUMAN
im·ma·nence \ˈim-ə-nən(t)s\ *or* **im·ma·nen·cy** \-nən-sē\ *n* : the state or quality of being immanent : INHERENCE
im·ma·nent \-nənt\ *adj* [LL *immanent-*, *immanens*, prp. of *immanēre* to remain in place, fr. L *in-* + *manēre* to remain — more at MANSION] **1** : remaining or operating within a domain of reality or realm of discourse : INHERENT **2** : confined to consciousness or to the mind : SUBJECTIVE — compare TRANSCENDENT — **im·ma·nent·ly** *adv*
im·ma·nent·ism \-ˌiz-əm\ *n* : any of several theories according to which God or an abstract mind or spirit is immanent in the world — **im·ma·nent·ist** \-nənt-əst, -ˌnent-\ *n* — **im·ma·nent·is·tic** \ˌim-ə-nənt-ˈis-tik\ *adj*
im·ma·te·ri·al \ˌim-ə-ˈtir-ē-əl\ *adj* [ME *immateriel*, fr. MF, fr. LL *immaterialis*, fr. L *in-* + LL *materialis* material] **1** : not consisting of matter : INCORPOREAL **2** : of no substantial consequence : UNIMPORTANT — **im·ma·te·ri·al·ly** \-ē-ə-lē\ *adv* — **im·ma·te·ri·al·ness** *n*
im·ma·te·ri·al·ism \-ē-ə-ˌliz-əm\ *n* : a theory that external bodies are in essence mental — **im·ma·te·ri·al·ist** \-ləst\ *n*
im·ma·te·ri·al·i·ty \ˌim-ə-ˌtir-ē-ˈal-ət-ē\ *n* **1** : the quality or state of being immaterial **2** : something immaterial
im·ma·te·ri·al·ize \-ˈtir-ē-ə-ˌlīz\ *vt* : to make immaterial or incorporeal
im·ma·ture \ˌim-ə-ˈt(y)u̇(ə)r *also* -ˈchu̇(ə)r\ *adj* [L *immaturus*, fr. *in-* + *maturus* mature] **1** *archaic* : PREMATURE **2 a** : lacking complete growth, differentiation, or development : UNRIPE **b** (1) : CRUDE, UNFINISHED (2) *of a topographic feature* : predictably due to undergo further changes — used esp. of valleys and drainages while most of the area is well above baselevel — **immature** *n* — **im·ma·ture·ly** *adv* — **im·ma·ture·ness** *n* — **im·ma·tur·ity** \-ˈt(y)u̇r-ət-ē *also* -ˈchu̇r-\ *n*
im·mea·sur·able \(ˈ)im-ˈ(m)ezh-(ə-)rə-bəl, -ˈ(m)ezh-ər-bəl, -ˈ(m)āzh-\ *adj* : incapable of being measured; *broadly* : indefinitely extensive — **im·mea·sur·able·ness** *n* — **im·mea·sur·ably** \-blē\ *adv*
im·me·di·a·cy \im-ˈēd-ē-ə-sē, *Brit often* -ˈē-jə-sē\ *n* **1** : the quality or state of being immediate; *esp* : freedom from an intervening medium **2** : something that is immediate — usu. used in pl. **3** : direct presence to cognition or perception; *specif* : SELF-EVIDENCE, INTUITIVENESS
im·me·di·ate \im-ˈēd-ē-ət, *Brit often* -ˈē-jit\ *adj* [LL *immediatus*, fr. L *in-* + LL *mediatus* intermediate — more at MEDIATE] **1 a** : acting or being without the intervention of another object, cause, or agency : DIRECT ⟨the ~ cause of death⟩ **b** : present to the mind independently of other states or factors ⟨~ awareness⟩ **2** : being next in line or relation ⟨~ parties to the quarrel⟩ **3 a** : made or done at once : INSTANT ⟨an ~ need⟩ **b** *of time* : near to or related to the present ⟨the ~ past⟩ **4** : existing without intervening space or substance ⟨~ contact⟩; *broadly* : being near at hand ⟨~ neighborhood⟩ **syn** see DIRECT
¹im·me·di·ate·ly *adv* **1** : without intermediary : CLOSELY **2** : without interval of time : STRAIGHTWAY
²immediately *conj* : as soon as
im·me·di·ate·ness *n* : IMMEDIACY
im·med·i·ca·ble \(ˈ)im-ˈ(m)ed-i-kə-bəl\ *adj* [L *immedicabilis*, fr. *in-* + *medicabilis* medicable] : INCURABLE — **im·med·i·ca·bly** \-blē\ *adv*
Im·mel·mann \ˈim-əl-mən\ *n* [Max *Immelmann* †1916 G aviator]

: a turn in which an airplane in flight is first made to complete half of a loop and is then rolled half of a complete turn

im·me·mo·ri·al \ˌim-ə-ˈmōr-ē-əl, -ˈmȯr-\ *adj* [prob. fr. F *immémorial*, fr. MF, fr. *in-* + *memorial*] : extending beyond the reach of memory, record, or tradition — **im·me·mo·ri·al·ly** \-ē-ə-lē\ *adv*

im·mense \im-ˈen(t)s\ *adj* [MF, fr. L *immensus* immeasurable, fr. *in-* + *mensus*, pp. of *metiri* to measure — more at MEASURE] **1** : marked by greatness esp. in size or degree : HUGE **2** : supremely good : EXCELLENT **syn** see ENORMOUS — **im·mense·ly** *adv* — **im·mense·ness** *n*

im·men·si·ty \im-ˈen(t)-sət-ē\ *n* **1** : the quality or state of being immense **2** : something immense

im·men·su·ra·ble \(ˈ)im-ˈ(m)en(t)s-(ə-)rə-bəl, -ˈ(m)ench-(ə-)rə-\ *adj* [LL *immensurabilis*, fr. L *in-* + LL *mensurabilis* measurable] : IMMEASURABLE

im·merge \im-ˈərj\ *vb* [L *immergere*] *vt, archaic* : IMMERSE ~ *vi* : to plunge into or immerse oneself in something — **im·mer·gence** \-ˈər-jən(t)s\ *n*

im·merse \im-ˈərs\ *vt* [L *immersus*, pp. of *immergere*, fr. *in-* + *mergere* to merge] **1** : to plunge into something that surrounds or covers; *esp* : to plunge or dip into a fluid **2** : to baptize by immersion **3** : ENGROSS, ABSORB

im·mersed *adj, of a plant* : growing wholly under water

im·mer·sion \im-ˈər-zhən, -shən\ *n* **1** : an act of immersing : a state of being immersed; *specif* : baptism by complete submersion of the person in water **2** : disappearance of a celestial body behind or into the shadow of another

im·mesh \im-ˈesh\ *var of* ENMESH

im·me·thod·i·cal \ˌim-ə-ˈthäd-i-kəl\ *adj* : not methodical — **im·me·thod·i·cal·ly** \-k(ə-)lē\ *adv*

im·mi·grant \ˈim-i-grənt\ *n* : one that immigrates: **a** : a person who comes to a country to take up permanent residence **b** : a plant or animal that becomes established in an area where it was previously unknown **syn** see EMIGRANT — **immigrant** *adj*

im·mi·grate \ˈim-ə-ˌgrāt\ *vb* [L *immigratus*, pp. of *immigrare* to remove, go in, fr. *in-* + *migrare* to migrate] *vi* : to enter and usu. become established; *esp* : to come into a country of which one is not a native for permanent residence ~ *vt* : to bring in or send as immigrants — **im·mi·gra·tion** \ˌim-ə-ˈgrā-shən\ *n*

im·mi·nence \ˈim-ə-nən(t)s\ *n* **1** *also* **im·mi·nen·cy** \-nən-sē\ : the quality or state of being imminent **2** : something imminent; *esp* : impending evil or danger

im·mi·nent \-nənt\ *adj* [L *imminent-*, *imminens*, prp. of *imminēre* to project, threaten, fr. *in-* + *-minēre* (akin to L *mont-*, *mons* mountain) — more at MOUNT] : ready to take place; *esp* : hanging threateningly over one's head **syn** see IMPENDING — **im·mi·nent·ly** *adv* — **im·mi·nent·ness** *n*

im·min·gle \im-ˈiŋ-gəl\ *vb* : BLEND, INTERMINGLE

im·mis·ci·bil·i·ty \(ˌ)im-ˌis-ə-ˈbil-ət-ē\ *n* : inability to mix

im·mis·ci·ble \(ˈ)im-ˈ(m)is-ə-bəl\ *adj* : incapable of mixing or attaining homogeneity — **im·mis·ci·bly** \-blē\ *adv*

im·mit·i·ga·ble \(ˈ)im-ˈ(m)it-i-gə-bəl\ *adj* [LL *immitigabilis*, fr. L *in-* + *mitigare* to mitigate] : not capable of being mitigated — **im·mit·i·ga·ble·ness** *n* — **im·mit·i·ga·bly** \-blē\ *adv*

im·mix \im-ˈiks\ *vt* [back-formation fr. *immixed* mixed in, fr. ME *immixte*, fr. L *immixtus*, pp. of *immiscēre*, fr. *in-* + *miscēre* to mix — more at MIX] : to mix intimately : COMMINGLE

im·mix·ture \im-ˈiks-chər\ *n* : the action of immixing : the state of being immixed

im·mo·bile \(ˈ)im-ˈ(m)ō-bəl, -ˌbēl, -ˌbīl\ *adj* [ME *in-mobill*, fr. L *immobilis*, fr. *in-* + *mobilis* mobile] **1** : incapable of being moved : FIXED **2** : not moving : MOTIONLESS — **im·mo·bil·i·ty** \ˌim-(ˌ)ō-ˈbil-ət-ē\ *n*

im·mo·bi·li·za·tion \im-ˌō-b(ə-)lə-ˈzā-shən\ *n* : the act of immobilizing : the state of being immobilized

im·mo·bi·lize \im-ˈō-bə-ˌlīz\ *vt* : to make immobile: as **a** : to prevent freedom of movement or effective use of **b**: to reduce or eliminate motion of (the body or a part) by mechanical means or by strict bed rest **c** (1) : to withhold (specie) from circulation to serve as security for other money (2) : to convert (circulating capital) into fixed capital — **im·mo·bi·liz·er** *n*

im·mod·er·a·cy \(ˈ)im-ˈ(m)äd-(ə-)rə-sē\ *n* : lack of moderation

im·mod·er·ate \-(ə-)rət\ *adj* [ME *immoderat*, fr. L *immoderatus*, fr. *in-* + *moderatus*, pp. of *moderare* to moderate] **1** : lacking in moderation **2** *obs* **a** : INTEMPERATE **b** : having no limits **syn** see EXCESSIVE — **im·mod·er·ate·ly** \-ˈ(m)äd-ərt-lē, -(ə-)rət-lē\ *adv* — **im·mod·er·ate·ness** \-(ə-)rət-nəs\ *n* — **im·mod·er·a·tion** \(ˌ)im-ˌäd-ə-ˈrā-shən\ *n*

im·mod·est \(ˈ)im-ˈ(m)äd-əst\ *adj* [L *immodestus*, fr. *in-* + *modestus* modest] : not modest; *specif* : INDECENT — **im·mod·est·ly** *adv* — **im·mod·es·ty** \-ə-stē\ *n*

im·mo·late \ˈim-ə-ˌlāt\ *vt* [L *immolatus*, pp. of *immolare*, fr. *in-* + *mola* spelt grits; fr. the custom of sprinkling victims with sacrificial meal; akin to L *molere* to grind — more at MILL] **1** : to offer in sacrifice; *esp* : to kill as a sacrificial victim **2** : KILL, DESTROY — **im·mo·la·tor** \ˈim-ə-ˌlāt-ər\ *n*

im·mo·la·tion \ˌim-ə-ˈlā-shən\ *n* **1** : the act of immolating : the state of being immolated **2** : something that is immolated

im·mor·al \(ˈ)im-ˈ(m)ȯr-əl, -ˈ(m)är-\ *adj* : inconsistent with purity or good morals — **im·mor·al·ly** \-ə-lē\ *adv*

im·mor·al·ist \-ə-ləst\ *n* : an advocate of immorality

im·mo·ral·i·ty \ˌim-ˌȯ-ˈral-ət-ē, ˌim-ə-ˈral-\ *n* **1** : the quality or state of being immoral : WICKEDNESS; *esp* : UNCHASTITY **2** : an immoral act or practice

1**im·mor·tal** \(ˈ)im-ˈȯrt-ᵊl\ *adj* [ME, fr. L *immortalis*, fr. *in-* + *mortalis* mortal] **1** : exempt from death **2** : connected with or relating to immortality **3** : exempt from oblivion : IMPERISHABLE — **im·mor·tal·ly** \-ᵊl-ē\ *adv*

2**immortal** *n* **1 a** : one exempt from death **b** *pl, often cap* : the gods of the Greek and Roman pantheon **2 a** : a person whose fame is lasting **b** *cap* : any of the 40 members of the Académie française

im·mor·tal·i·ty \ˌim-ˌȯr-ˈtal-ət-ē\ *n* : the quality or state of being immortal: **a** : unending existence **b** : lasting fame

im·mor·tal·ize \im-ˈȯrt-ᵊl-ˌīz\ *vt* : to make immortal — **im·mor·tal·iz·er** *n*

im·mor·telle \ˌim-ˌȯr-ˈtel\ *n* [F, fr. fem. of *immortel* immortal, fr. L *immortalis*] : EVERLASTING 3

im·mo·tile \(ˈ)im-ˈ(m)ōt-ᵊl, -ˈ(m)ō-ˌtīl\ *adj* : lacking motility — **im·mo·til·i·ty** \ˌim-ō-ˈtil-ət-ē\ *n*

im·mov·abil·i·ty \(ˌ)im-ˌü-və-ˈbil-ət-ē\ *n* : the quality or state of being immovable

1**im·mov·able** \(ˈ)im-ˈ(m)ü-və-bəl\ *adj* **1** : incapable of being moved; *broadly* : not moving or not intended to be moved **2 a** : STEADFAST, UNYIELDING **b** : not capable of being moved emotionally — **im·mov·able·ness** *n* — **im·mov·ably** \-blē\ *adv*

2**immovable** *n* **1** : one that cannot be moved **2** *pl* : real property

im·mune \im-ˈyün\ *adj* [L *immunis*, fr. *in-* + *munia* services, obligations; akin to L *munus* service] **1** : FREE, EXEMPT ⟨~ from taxation⟩ **2** : not susceptible or responsive ⟨~ to all pleas⟩; *esp* : having a high degree of resistance to a disease ⟨~ to diphtheria⟩ **3 a** : having or producing antibodies to a corresponding antigen ⟨an ~ serum⟩ **b** : produced in response to the presence of a corresponding antigen ⟨~ agglutinins⟩ — **immune** *n*

im·mu·ni·ty \im-ˈyü-nət-ē\ *n* : the quality or state of being immune; *specif* : a condition of being able to resist a particular disease esp. through preventing development of a pathogenic microorganism or by counteracting the effects of its products

im·mu·ni·za·tion \ˌim-yə-nə-ˈzā-shən, im-ˌyü-\ *n* : the quality or state of being immunized : the act of immunizing

im·mu·nize \ˈim-yə-ˌnīz\ *vt* : to make immune

immuno- *comb form* [ISV, fr. *immune*] : immunity ⟨*immuno*genetics⟩

im·mu·no·chem·is·try \ˌim-yə-nō-ˈkem-ə-strē\ *n* [ISV] : a branch of chemistry that deals with the chemical aspects of immunology

im·mu·no·ge·net·ic \-jə-ˈnet-ik\ *adj* : of or relating to immunogenetics — **im·mu·no·ge·net·i·cal** \-i-kəl\ *adj*

im·mu·no·ge·net·ics \-iks\ *n pl but sing in constr* **1** : a branch of immunology that deals with the interrelation of immunity to disease and genetic makeup **2** : a study of biological interrelationships by serological means

im·mu·no·gen·ic \-ˈjen-ik\ *adj* : producing immunity — **im·mu·no·gen·i·cal·ly** \-ˈjen-i-k(ə-)lē\ *adv* — **im·mu·no·ge·nic·i·ty** \-jə-ˈnis-ət-ē\ *n*

im·mu·no·log·ic \ˌim-yə-nə-ˈläj-ik\ *adj* : of or relating to immunology — **im·mu·no·log·i·cal** \-i-kəl\ *adj* — **im·mu·no·log·i·cal·ly** \-i-k(ə-)lē\ *adv*

im·mu·nol·o·gist \ˌim-yə-ˈnäl-ə-jəst\ *n* : a specialist in immunology

im·mu·nol·o·gy \-jē\ *n* [ISV] : a science that deals with the phenomena and causes of immunity

im·mu·no·ther·a·py \ˌim-yə-nō-ˈther-ə-pē\ *n* [ISV] : treatment of or prophylaxis against disease by means of antigens or antigenic preparations

im·mure \im-ˈyü(ə)r\ *vt* [ML *immurare*, fr. L *in-* + *murus* wall] **1 a** : to enclose within walls **b** : IMPRISON **2** : to build into a wall; *esp* : to entomb in a wall — **im·mure·ment** \-mənt\ *n*

im·mu·si·cal \(ˈ)im-ˈ(m)yü-zi-kəl\ *adj* : not musical

im·mu·ta·bil·i·ty \(ˌ)im-ˌyüt-ə-ˈbil-ət-ē\ *n* : the quality or state of being immutable

im·mu·ta·ble \(ˈ)im-ˈ(m)yüt-ə-bəl\ *adj* [ME, fr. L *immutabilis*, fr. *in-* + *mutabilis* mutable] : not capable or susceptible of change — **im·mu·ta·ble·ness** *n* — **im·mu·ta·bly** \-blē\ *adv*

1**imp** \ˈimp\ *n* [ME *impe*, fr. OE *impa*, fr. *impian* to imp] **1 a** *obs* : SHOOT, BUD; *also* : GRAFT **b** *archaic* : OFFSPRING, SCION **2 a** *archaic* : an evil creature **b** : a small demon : FIEND **c** : a mischievous child : URCHIN

2**imp** *vt* [ME *impen*, fr. OE *impian*; akin to OHG *impfōn* to graft; both fr. a prehistoric WGmc word borrowed fr. (assumed) VL *imputare*, fr. L *in-* + *putare* to prune — more at PAVE] **1** *archaic* **a** : to graft or repair (a wing, tail, or feather) with a feather to improve a falcon's flying capacity **b** : to equip with wings **2** *archaic* : to eke out : STRENGTHEN

1**im·pact** \im-ˈpakt\ *vt* [L *impactus*, pp. of *impingere* to push against — more at IMPINGE] **1 a** : to fix firmly by or as if by packing or wedging **b** : to press together **2** : to impinge upon

2**im·pact** \ˈim-ˌpakt\ *n* **1 a** : an impinging or striking (as of one body against another) **b** : a forceful contact, collision, or onset; *also* : the impetus communicated in or as if in a collision **2** : the force of impression or operation of one thing on another : EFFECT

im·pact·ed \im-ˈpak-təd\ *adj, of a tooth* : wedged between the jawbone and another tooth

im·pac·tion \im-ˈpak-shən\ *n* : the act of becoming or the state of being impacted; *esp* : lodgment of something (as feces) in a body passage or cavity

im·paint \im-ˈpānt\ *vt, obs* : PAINT, DEPICT

1**im·pair** \im-ˈpa(ə)r, -ˈpe(ə)r\ *vt* [ME *empeiren*, fr. MF *empeirer*, fr. (assumed) VL *impejorare*, fr. L *in-* + LL *pejorare* to make worse — more at PEJORATIVE] : to diminish in quantity, value, excellence, or strength : DAMAGE **syn** see INJURE — **im·pair·er** *n* — **im·pair·ment** \-mənt\ *n*

2**impair** *n, archaic* : IMPAIRMENT, DETERIORATION

im·pa·la \im-ˈpal-ə, -ˈpäl-\ *n* [Zulu] : a large brownish African antelope (*Aepyceros melampus*) that in the male has slender lyrate horns

im·pale \im-ˈpā(ə)l\ *vt* [MF & ML; MF *empaler*, fr. ML *impalare*, fr. L *in-* + *palus* stake — more at POLE] **1** *archaic* : to enclose with or as if with stakes or a palisade : SURROUND **2** : to pierce with or as if with something pointed; *esp* : to torture or kill by fixing on a sharp stake **3** : to join coats of arms on a heraldic shield divided vertically by a pale — **im·pale·ment** \-mənt\ *n*

im·pal·pa·bil·i·ty \(ˌ)im-ˌpal-pə-ˈbil-ət-ē\ *n* : the quality or state of being impalpable

im·pal·pa·ble \(ˈ)im-ˈpal-pə-bəl\ *adj* **1** : incapable of being felt by the touch : INTANGIBLE **2** : not readily discerned or apprehended — **im·pal·pa·bly** \-blē\ *adv*

im·pan·el \im-ˈpan-ᵊl\ *vt* : to enroll in or on a panel ⟨~ a jury⟩

im·par·a·dise \im-ˈpar-ə-ˌdīs, -ˌdīz\ *vt* : ENRAPTURE

im·par·i·ty \(ˈ)im-ˈpar-ət-ē\ *n* [LL *imparitas*, fr. L *impar* unequal, fr. *in-* + *par* equal] : INEQUALITY, DISPARITY

im·park \im-ˈpärk\ *vt* [ME *imparken*, fr. AF *emparker*, fr. OF *en-* + *parc* park] *archaic* : to enclose in or for a park : CONFINE

im·part \im-ˈpärt\ *vt* [MF & L; MF *impartir*, fr. L *impartire*, fr. *in-* + *partire* to divide, part] **1** : to give or grant from one's store or abundance : TRANSMIT **2** : to communicate the knowledge

of : DISCLOSE **syn** see COMMUNICATE — **im·part·able** \-ə-bəl\ *adj* — **im·par·ta·tion** \ˌim-ˌpär-ˈtā-shən\ *n* — **im·part·ment** \im-ˈpärt-mənt\ *n*

im·par·tial \(ˈ)im-ˈpär-shəl\ *adj* : not partial : UNBIASED **syn** see FAIR — **im·par·tial·i·ty** \(ˌ)im-ˌpär-shē-ˈal-ət-ē, -ˌpär-ˈshal-\ *n* — **im·par·tial·ly** \(ˈ)im-ˈpärsh-(ə-)lē\ *adv*

im·par·ti·ble \(ˈ)im-ˈpärt-ə-bəl\ *adj* [LL *impartibilis*, fr. L *in-* + LL *partibilis* divisible, fr. L *partire*] : not partible : not subject to partition — **im·par·ti·bly** \-blē\ *adv*

im·pass·abil·i·ty \(ˌ)im-ˌpas-ə-ˈbil-ət-ē\ *n* : the quality or state of being impassable

im·pass·able \(ˈ)im-ˈpas-ə-bəl\ *adj* : incapable of being passed, traversed, or circulated — **im·pass·able·ness** *n* — **im·pass·ably** \-blē\ *adv*

im·passe \ˈim-ˌpas, im-ˈ\ *n* [F, fr. *in-* + *passer* to pass] **1** : an impassable road or way : CUL-DE-SAC **2 a** : a predicament affording no obvious escape **b** : DEADLOCK

im·pas·si·bil·i·ty \(ˌ)im-ˌpas-ə-ˈbil-ət-ē\ *n* : the quality or state of being impassible

im·pas·si·ble \(ˈ)im-ˈpas-ə-bəl\ *adj* [ME, fr. MF or LL; MF, fr. LL *impassibilis*, fr. L *in-* + LL *passibilis* passible] **1 a** : incapable of suffering or of experiencing pain **b** : inaccessible to injury **2** : incapable of feeling : IMPASSIVE — **im·pas·si·bly** \-blē\ *adv*

im·pas·sion \im-ˈpash-ən\ *vt* **im·pas·sion·ing** \-(ə-)niŋ\ [prob. fr. It *impassionare*, fr. *in-* (fr. L) + *passione* passion, fr. LL *passion-, passio*] : to arouse the feelings or passions of

im·pas·sioned *adj* : filled with passion or zeal : showing great warmth or intensity of feeling

syn IMPASSIONED, PASSIONATE, ARDENT, FERVENT, FERVID, PERFERVID mean showing intense feeling. IMPASSIONED implies warmth and intensity without violence and flowing readily into verbal expression; PASSIONATE implies great vehemence and often violence and wasteful diffusion of emotion; ARDENT implies an intense degree of zeal, devotion, or enthusiasm; FERVENT stresses sincerity and steadiness of emotional warmth or zeal; FERVID suggests warmly and spontaneously and often feverishly expressed emotion; PERFERVID implies the expression of exaggerated or overwrought feelings

im·pas·sive \(ˈ)im-ˈpas-iv\ *adj* **1 a** *archaic* : unsusceptible to pain **b** : unsusceptible to physical feeling : INSENSIBLE **c** : unsusceptible to or destitute of emotion : APATHETIC **2** : giving no sign of feeling or emotion : EXPRESSIONLESS **3** : not moving in any way : MOTIONLESS — **im·pas·sive·ly** *adv* — **im·pas·sive·ness** *n* — **im·pas·siv·i·ty** \ˌim-ˌpas-ˈiv-ət-ē\ *n*

syn IMPASSIVE, STOIC, PHLEGMATIC, APATHETIC, STOLID mean unresponsive to something that might normally excite interest or emotion. IMPASSIVE stresses the absence of any external sign of emotion in action or facial expression; STOIC implies an apparent indifference to pleasure or esp. to pain often as a matter of principle or self-discipline; PHLEGMATIC implies a temperament or constitution hard to arouse; APATHETIC may imply a puzzling or deplorable indifference or inertness; STOLID implies an habitual absence of interest, responsiveness, or curiosity concerning anything outside of an accustomed routine

im·paste \im-ˈpāst\ *vt* [It *impastare*, fr. *in-* (fr. L) + *pasta* paste, fr. LL] **1** : to make into a paste **2** : to decorate by impasto

im·pas·to \im-ˈpas-(ˌ)tō, -ˈpäs-\ *n* [It, fr. *impastare*] : the thick application of a pigment to a canvas or panel in painting; *also* : the body of pigment so applied

im·pa·tience \(ˈ)im-ˈpā-shən(t)s\ *n* : the quality or state of being impatient: as **a** : restlessness of spirit (as under irritation, delay, or opposition) **b** : restless or eager desire or longing

im·pa·tiens \im-ˈpā-shənz, -shən(t)s\ *n* [NL, genus name, fr. L] : any of a widely distributed genus (*Impatiens*) of watery-juiced annual herbs (family Balsaminaceae, the jewelweed family) with irregular spurred or saccate flowers and dehiscent capsules

im·pa·tient \(ˈ)im-ˈpā-shənt\ *adj* [ME *impacient*, fr. MF, fr. L *impatient-, impatiens*, fr. *in-* + *patient-, patiens* patient] **1 a** : not patient : restless or short of temper esp. under irritation, delay, or opposition **b** : INTOLERANT ⟨~ of poverty⟩ **2** : prompted or marked by impatience **3** : eagerly desirous : ANXIOUS — **im·pa·tient·ly** *adv*

im·pav·id \(ˈ)im-ˈpav-əd\ *adj* [L *impavidus*, fr. *in-* + *pavidus* pavid] *archaic* : FEARLESS — **im·pav·id·ly** *adv*

im·pawn \im-ˈpȯn, -ˈpän\ *vt, archaic* : to put in pawn : PLEDGE

¹im·peach \im-ˈpēch\ *vt* [ME *empechen*, fr. MF *empeechier* to hinder, fr. LL *impedicare* to fetter, fr. L *in-* + *pedica* fetter, fr. *ped-, pes* foot — more at FOOT] **1 a** : to bring an accusation against **b** : to charge with a crime or misdemeanor; *specif* : to charge (a public official) before a competent tribunal with misconduct in office **2** : to call in question; *esp* : to challenge the credibility or validity of ⟨~ the testimony of a witness⟩ — **im·peach·able** \-ˈpē-chə-bəl\ *adj* — **im·peach·ment** \-ˈpēch-mənt\ *n*

²impeach *n, obs* : IMPEACHMENT

im·pearl \im-ˈpər(-ə)l\ *vt* [prob. fr. MF *emperler*, fr. *en-* + *perle* pearl] : to form into pearls; *also* : to form of or adorn with pearls

im·pec·ca·bil·i·ty \(ˌ)im-ˌpek-ə-ˈbil-ət-ē\ *n* : the quality or state of being impeccable

im·pec·ca·ble \(ˈ)im-ˈpek-ə-bəl\ *adj* [L *impeccabilis*, fr. *in-* + *peccare* to sin] **1** : not capable of sinning or liable to sin **2** : free from fault or blame : FLAWLESS — **im·pec·ca·bly** \-blē\ *adv*

im·pe·cu·ni·os·i·ty \ˌim-pi-ˌkyü-nē-ˈäs-ət-ē\ *n* : IMPECUNIOUSNESS

im·pe·cu·nious \ˌim-pi-ˈkyü-nyəs, -nē-əs\ *adj* [*in-* + obs. E *pecunious* (rich), fr. ME, fr. L *pecuniosus*, fr. *pecunia* money — more at FEE] : having very little or no money usu. habitually : PENNILESS — **im·pe·cu·nious·ly** *adv* — **im·pe·cu·nious·ness** *n*

im·ped·ance \im-ˈpēd-ᵊn(t)s\ *n* **1** : the apparent opposition in an electrical circuit to the flow of an alternating current that is analogous to the actual electrical resistance to a direct current and that is the ratio of effective electromotive force to the effective current **2** : the ratio of the pressure to the volume displacement at a given surface in a sound-transmitting medium

im·pede \im-ˈpēd\ *vt* [L *impedire*, fr. *in-* + *ped-, pes*] : to interfere with the progress of : BLOCK **syn** see HINDER — **im·ped·er** *n*

im·ped·i·ment \im-ˈped-ə-mənt\ *n* **1 a** : OBSTRUCTION **b** : something that impedes; *esp* : an organic obstruction to speech **2** : a bar or hindrance (as lack of sufficient age) to a lawful marriage

im·ped·i·men·ta \im-ˌped-ə-ˈment-ə\ *n pl* [L, pl. of *impedimentum* impediment, fr. *impedire*] : things (as baggage or supplies) that impede

im·pel \im-ˈpel\ *vt* **im·pelled**; **im·pel·ling** [L *impellere*, fr. *in-* + *pellere* to drive — more at FELT] **1** : to urge or drive forward or on through the exertion of strong moral pressure : FORCE **2** : PROPEL **syn** see MOVE

¹im·pel·lent \im-ˈpel-ənt\ *adj* [L *impellent-, impellens*, prp. of *impellere*] : IMPELLING

²impellent *n* : something that impels

im·pel·ler *also* **im·pel·lor** \im-ˈpel-ər\ *n* **1** : one that impels **2** : ROTOR; *also* : a blade of a rotor

im·pend \im-ˈpend\ *vi* [L *impendēre*, fr. *in-* + *pendēre* to hang — more at PENDANT] **1** *archaic* : to hang suspended **2 a** : to hover threateningly : MENACE **b** : to be about to occur

im·pen·dent \im-ˈpen-dənt\ *adj* : IMPENDING

im·pend·ing *adj* : threatening to occur soon : APPROACHING

syn IMPENDING, IMMINENT mean threatening to occur very soon. IMPENDING implies signs that keep one in suspense; IMMINENT emphasizes the shortness of time before happening

im·pen·e·tra·bil·i·ty \(ˌ)im-ˌpen-ə-trə-ˈbil-ət-ē\ *n* **1** : the quality or state of being impenetrable **2** : the inability of two portions of matter to occupy the same space at the same time

im·pen·e·tra·ble \(ˈ)im-ˈpen-ə-trə-bəl\ *adj* [ME *impenetrabel*, fr. MF *impenetrable*, fr. L *impenetrabilis*, fr. *in-* + *penetrabilis* penetrable] **1 a** : incapable of being penetrated or pierced **b** : inaccessible to knowledge, reason, or sympathy : IMPERVIOUS **2** : incapable of being comprehended : INSCRUTABLE **3** : having the property of impenetrability — **im·pen·e·tra·ble·ness** *n* — **im·pen·e·tra·bly** \-blē\ *adv*

im·pen·i·tence \(ˈ)im-ˈpen-ə-tən(t)s\ *n* : the quality or state of being impenitent

im·pen·i·tent \-tənt\ *adj* [LL *impaenitent-, impaenitens*, fr. L *in-* + *paenitent-, paenitens* penitent] : not penitent — **impenitent** *n* — **im·pen·i·tent·ly** *adv*

¹im·per·a·tive \im-ˈper-ət-iv\ *adj* [LL *imperativus*, fr. L *imperatus*, pp. of *imperare* to command — more at EMPEROR] **1 a** : of, relating to, or constituting the grammatical mood that expresses the will to influence the behavior of another **b** : expressive of a command, entreaty, or exhortation **c** : having power to restrain, control, and direct **2** : not to be avoided or evaded : URGENT **syn** see MASTERFUL — **im·per·a·tive·ly** *adv* — **im·per·a·tive·ness** *n*

²imperative *n* **1** : the imperative mood or a verb form or verbal phrase expressing it **2** : something that is imperative: as **a** : COMMAND, ORDER **b** : RULE, GUIDE **c** : an obligatory act or duty **d** : an imperative judgment or proposition

im·pe·ra·tor \ˌim-pə-ˈrät-ər, -ˈrä-ˌtȯ(ə)r\ *n* [L — more at EMPEROR] : a supreme leader esp. of the ancient Romans : EMPEROR — **im·per·a·to·ri·al** \(ˌ)im-ˌper-ə-ˈtōr-ē-əl, -ˈtȯr-\ *adj*

im·per·ceiv·able \ˌim-pər-ˈsē-və-bəl\ *adj, archaic* : IMPERCEPTIBLE

im·per·cep·ti·bil·i·ty \ˌim-pər-ˌsep-tə-ˈbil-ət-ē\ *n* : the quality or state of being imperceptible

im·per·cep·ti·ble \ˌim-pər-ˈsep-tə-bəl\ *adj* [MF, fr. ML *imperceptibilis*, fr. L *in-* + LL *perceptibilis* perceptible] : not perceptible by a sense or by the mind : extremely slight, gradual, or subtle — **im·per·cep·ti·bly** \-blē\ *adv*

im·per·cep·tive \ˌim-pər-ˈsep-tiv\ *adj* : not perceptive — **im·per·cep·tive·ness** *n*

im·per·cip·i·ent \ˌim-pər-ˈsip-ē-ənt\ *adj* : UNPERCEPTIVE

¹im·per·fect \(ˈ)im-ˈpər-fikt\ *adj* [ME *imperfit*, fr. MF *imparfait*, fr. L *imperfectus*, fr. *in-* + *perfectus* perfect] **1** : not perfect : DEFECTIVE **2** : of, relating to, or constituting a verb tense used to designate a continuing state or an incomplete action esp. in the past **3** : DIMINISHED **4** : not enforceable at law — **im·per·fect·ly** \-fik-(t)lē\ *adv* — **im·per·fect·ness** \-fik(t)-nəs\ *n*

²imperfect *n* : an imperfect tense; *also* : the verb form expressing it

imperfect flower *n* : a diclinous flower

imperfect fungus *n* : a fungus (order Fungi Imperfecti) of which only the conidial stage is known

im·per·fec·tion \ˌim-pər-ˈfek-shən\ *n* : the quality or state of being imperfect; *also* : FAULT, BLEMISH

im·per·fec·tive \ˌim-pər-ˈfek-tiv *also* (ˈ)im-ˈpər-fik-\ *adj, of a verb form or aspect* : expressing action as incomplete or without reference to completion or as reiterated — compare PERFECTIVE

im·per·fo·rate \(ˈ)im-ˈpər-f(ə-)rət, -fə-ˌrāt\ *adj* **1** : having no opening or aperture; *specif* : lacking the usual or normal opening **2** *of a stamp or a sheet of stamps* : lacking perforations or rouletting — **imperforate** *n*

¹im·pe·ri·al \im-ˈpir-ē-əl\ *adj* [ME, fr. MF, fr. LL *imperialis*, fr. L *imperium* command, empire] **1 a** : of, relating to, or befitting an empire or an emperor **b** (1) : of or relating to the United Kingdom as distinguished from the constituent parts (2) : of or relating to the British Commonwealth and Empire **2 a** *obs* : SOVEREIGN **b** : REGAL, IMPERIOUS **3** : of superior or unusual size or excellence **4** : belonging to the official British series of weights and measures — see MEASURE table — **im·pe·ri·al·ly** \-ə-lē\ *adv*

²imperial *n* **1** *cap* : an adherent or soldier of the Holy Roman emperor **2** : EMPEROR **3** : a size of paper usu. 23 x 31 inches **4** [fr. the beard worn by Napoleon III] : a pointed beard growing below the lower lip **5** : something of unusual size or excellence

im·pe·ri·al·ism \im-ˈpir-ē-ə-ˌliz-əm\ *n* **1** : imperial government, authority, or system **2** : the policy, practice, or advocacy of extending the power and dominion of a nation esp. by direct territorial acquisitions or by gaining indirect control over the political or economic life of other areas — **im·pe·ri·al·ist** \-ləst\ *n* — **imperialist** *or* **im·pe·ri·al·is·tic** \(ˌ)im-ˌpir-ē-ə-ˈlis-tik\ *adj* — **im·pe·ri·al·is·ti·cal·ly** \-ti-k(ə-)lē\ *adv*

imperial moth *n* : a large American moth (*Eacles imperialis*) marked with yellow, lilac, or purplish brown

im·per·il \im-ˈper-əl\ *vt* **im·per·iled** *or* **im·per·illed**; **im·per·il·ing** *or* **im·per·il·ling** : to bring into peril : ENDANGER — **im·per·il·ment** \-əl-mənt\ *n*

im·pe·ri·ous \im-ˈpir-ē-əs\ *adj* [L *imperiosus*, fr. *imperium*] **1** : COMMANDING, LORDLY **2** : ARROGANT, DOMINEERING **3** : IMPERATIVE, URGENT **syn** see MASTERFUL — **im·pe·ri·ous·ly** *adv* — **im·pe·ri·ous·ness** *n*

im·per·ish·abil·i·ty \(ˌ)im-ˌper-ish-ə-ˈbil-ət-ē\ *n* : the quality or state of being imperishable

im·per·ish·able \(ˈ)im-ˈper-ish-ə-bəl\ *adj* : not perishable or subject to decay : INDESTRUCTIBLE — **imperishable** *n* — **im·per·ish·able·ness** *n* — **im·per·ish·ably** \-blē\ *adv*

im·pe·ri·um \im-ˈpir-ē-əm\ *n* [L — more at EMPIRE] **1 a** : supreme

power or absolute dominion : CONTROL **b** : EMPIRE **2** : the right to command or to employ the force of the state : SOVEREIGNTY

im·per·ma·nence \(ˈ)im-ˈpərm-(ə-)nən(t)s\ *also* **im·per·ma·nen·cy** \-nən-sē\ *n* : the quality or state of being impermanent

im·per·ma·nent \-nənt\ *adj* : not permanent : TRANSIENT — **im·per·ma·nent·ly** *adv*

im·per·me·abil·i·ty \(ˌ)im-ˌpər-mē-ə-ˈbil-ət-ē\ *n* : the quality or state of being impermeable

im·per·me·able \(ˈ)im-ˈpər-mē-ə-bəl\ *adj* [LL *impermeabilis*, fr. L *in-* + LL *permeabilis* permeable] : not permitting passage (as of a fluid) through its substance : IMPERVIOUS — **im·per·me·able·ness** *n* — **im·per·me·ably** \-blē\ *adv*

im·per·mis·si·bil·i·ty \ˌim-pər-ˌmis-ə-ˈbil-ət-ē\ *n* : the quality or state of being impermissible

im·per·mis·si·ble \-ˈmis-ə-bəl\ *adj* : not permissible

im·per·son·al \(ˈ)im-ˈpərs-nəl, -ᵊn-əl\ *adj* [LL *impersonalis*, fr. L *in-* + LL *personalis* personal] **1 a** *of a verb* : denoting the action of an unspecified agent and hence used with no expressed subject (as *methinks*) or with a merely formal subject (as *rained* in *it rained*) **b** *of a pronoun* : INDEFINITE **2 a** : having no personal reference or connection ⟨~ criticism⟩ **b** : not engaging the human personality or emotions **c** : not existing as a person ⟨an ~ deity⟩ — **im·per·son·al·i·ty** \(ˌ)im-ˌpərs-ᵊn-ˈal-ət-ē\ *n* — **im·per·son·al·ize** \(ˈ)im-ˈpərs-nə-ˌlīz, -ᵊn-ə-ˌlīz\ *vt* — **im·per·son·al·ly** \-nə-lē, -ᵊn-ə-lē\ *adv*

im·per·son·ate \im-ˈpərs-ᵊn-ˌāt\ *vt* **1** *archaic* : EMBODY, EXEMPLIFY **2** : to assume or act the character of : PERSONATE — **im·per·son·ation** \(ˌ)im-ˌpərs-ᵊn-ˈā-shən\ *n* — **im·per·son·ator** \im-ˈpərs-ᵊn-ˌāt-ər\ *n*

im·per·ti·nence \(ˈ)im-ˈpərt-ᵊn-ən(t)s, -ˈpərt-nən(t)s\ *also* **im·per·ti·nen·cy** \-ˈpərt-ᵊn-ən-sē, -ˈpərt-nən-sē\ *n* **1** : the quality or state of being impertinent: as **a** : IRRELEVANCE, UNFITNESS **b** : INCIVILITY, INSOLENCE **2** : something impertinent

im·per·ti·nent \(ˈ)im-ˈpərt-ᵊn-ənt, -ˈpərt-nənt\ *adj* [ME, fr. MF, fr. LL *impertinent-*, *impertinens*, fr. L *in-* + *pertinent-*, *pertinens*, prp. of *pertinēre* to pertain] **1** : not pertinent : IRRELEVANT **2** : not restrained within due or proper bounds : INSOLENT — **im·per·ti·nent·ly** *adv*

syn OFFICIOUS, MEDDLESOME, INTRUSIVE, OBTRUSIVE: IMPERTINENT implies exceeding the bounds of propriety in showing interest or curiosity or in offering advice; OFFICIOUS implies the offering of services or attention that are unwelcome or annoying; MEDDLESOME stresses an annoying and usu. prying interference in others' affairs; INTRUSIVE implies a tactless or otherwise objectionable thrusting into others' affairs; OBTRUSIVE stresses improper or offensive conspicuousness of interfering actions

im·per·turb·abil·i·ty \ˌim-pər-ˌtər-bə-ˈbil-ət-ē\ *n* : the quality or state of being imperturbable

im·per·turb·able \ˌim-pər-ˈtər-bə-bəl\ *adj* [ME, fr. LL *imperturbabilis*, fr. L *in-* + *perturbare* to perturb] : marked by extreme calm, impassivity, and steadiness : SERENE **syn** see COOL — **im·per·turb·ably** \-blē\ *adv*

im·per·vi·ous \(ˈ)im-ˈpər-vē-əs\ *adj* [L *impervius*, fr. *in-* + *pervius* pervious] **1** : not allowing entrance or passage : IMPENETRABLE ⟨a coat ~ to rain⟩ **2** : not capable of being affected or disturbed ⟨~ to criticism⟩ — **im·per·vi·ous·ly** *adv* — **im·per·vi·ous·ness** *n*

im·pe·tig·i·nous \ˌim-pə-ˈtij-ə-nəs\ *adj* : of, relating to, or like impetigo

im·pe·ti·go \ˌim-pə-ˈtē-(ˌ)gō, -ˈtī-\ *n* [L, fr. *impetere*] : an acute contagious skin disease characterized by vesicles, pustules, and yellowish crusts

im·pe·trate \ˈim-pə-ˌtrāt\ *vt* [L *impetratus*, pp. of *impetrare*, fr. *in-* + *patrare* to accomplish — more at PERPETRATE] **1** : to obtain by request or entreaty **2** : ENTREAT — **im·pe·tra·tion** \ˌim-pə-ˈtrā-shən\ *n*

im·pet·u·os·i·ty \(ˌ)im-ˌpech-ə-ˈwäs-ət-ē\ *n* **1** : the quality or state of being impetuous **2** : an impetuous action or impulse

im·pet·u·ous \im-ˈpech-(ə-)wəs\ *adj* [ME, fr. MF *impetueux*, fr. LL *impetuosus*, fr. L *impetus*] **1** : marked by force and violence **2** : marked by impulsive vehemence **syn** see PRECIPITATE — **im·pet·u·ous·ly** *adv* — **im·pet·u·ous·ness** *n*

im·pe·tus \ˈim-pət-əs\ *n* [L, assault, impetus, fr. *impetere* to attack, fr. *in-* + *petere* to go to, seek — more at FEATHER] **1 a** : a driving force : IMPULSE **b** : INCENTIVE, STIMULUS **2** : the property possessed by a moving body in virtue of its mass and its motion — used of bodies moving suddenly or violently to indicate the origin and intensity of the motion

im·pi·ety \(ˈ)im-ˈpī-ət-ē\ *n* **1 a** : the quality or state of being impious **b** : UNDUTIFULNESS **2** : an impious act

im·pinge \im-ˈpinj\ *vb* [L *impingere*, fr. *in-* + *pangere* to fasten, drive in — more at PACT] *vi* **1** : to strike or dash esp. with a sharp collision **2** : to come into close contact **3** : ENCROACH, INFRINGE ~ *vt* : to cause (as a gas or a flame) to strike — **im·pinge·ment** \-mənt\ *n*

im·pi·ous \ˈim-pē-əs, (ˈ)im-ˈpī-\ *adj* [L *impius*, fr. *in-* + *pius* pious] : not pious: **a** : IRREVERENT, PROFANE **b** : UNDUTIFUL, UNFILIAL — **im·pi·ous·ly** *adv*

imp·ish \ˈim-pish\ *adj* : of, relating to, or befitting an imp; *esp* : MISCHIEVOUS — **imp·ish·ly** *adv* — **imp·ish·ness** *n*

im·pla·ca·bil·i·ty \(ˌ)im-ˌplak-ə-ˈbil-ət-ē, -ˌplā-kə-\ *n* : the quality or state of being implacable

im·pla·ca·ble \(ˈ)im-ˈplak-ə-bəl, -ˈplā-kə-\ *adj* [MF or L; MF, fr. L *implacabilis*, fr. *in-* + *placabilis* placable] **1** : not placable : not capable of being appeased, pacified, or mitigated **2** : UNALTERABLE — **im·pla·ca·ble·ness** *n* — **im·pla·ca·bly** \-blē\ *adv*

1**im·plant** \im-ˈplant\ *vt* **1 a** : to fix or set securely or deeply **b** : to set as permanent in the consciousness or habit patterns : INCULCATE **2** : to insert in a living site (as for growth or formation of an organic union) — **im·plan·ta·tion** \ˌim-ˌplan-ˈtā-shən\ *n* — **im·plant·er** *n*

syn IMPLANT, INCULCATE, INSTILL, INSEMINATE, INFIX mean to introduce into the mind. IMPLANT implies teaching that makes for permanence of what is taught; INCULCATE implies persistent or repeated efforts to impress on the mind; INSTILL stresses gradual, gentle imparting of knowledge over a long period of time; INSEMINATE applies to a sowing of ideas in many minds so that they spread through a class or nation; INFIX stresses firmly inculcating a habit of thought

2**im·plant** \ˈim-ˌplant\ *n* : something (as a graft or pellet) implanted in tissue

im·plau·si·bil·i·ty \(ˌ)im-ˌplȯ-zə-ˈbil-ət-ē\ *n* : the quality or state of being implausible

im·plau·si·ble \(ˈ)im-ˈplȯ-zə-bəl\ *adj* : not plausible — **im·plau·si·bly** \-blē\ *adv*

im·plead \im-ˈplēd\ *vt* [ME *empleden*, fr. MF *emplaider*, fr. OF *emplaidier*, fr. *en-* + *plaidier* to plead] **1 a** : to sue or prosecute at law **b** *archaic* : ACCUSE, IMPEACH **2** *archaic* : PLEAD

1**im·ple·ment** \ˈim-plə-mənt\ *n* [ME, fr. LL *implementum* action of filling up, fr. L *implēre* to fill up, fr. *in-* + *plēre* to fill — more at FULL] **1** : an article serving to equip **2** : TOOL, UTENSIL, INSTRUMENT **3** : one that serves as an instrument or tool

syn IMPLEMENT, TOOL, INSTRUMENT, APPLIANCE, UTENSIL apply to any relatively simple device for performing work. IMPLEMENT may apply to anything necessary to effect an end; TOOL suggests an implement adapted to facilitate a definite kind or stage of work and suggests the need of skill more strongly than IMPLEMENT; INSTRUMENT suggests a device capable of delicate or precise work; APPLIANCE refers to a tool or instrument utilizing a power source and suggests portability or temporary attachment; UTENSIL applies to a device used in domestic work or some routine unskilled activity

2**im·ple·ment** \-ˌment\ *vt* **1** : to carry out : FULFILL; *esp* : to give practical effect to and ensure of actual fulfillment by concrete measures **2** : to provide implements for **syn** see ENFORCE — **im·ple·men·tal** \ˌim-plə-ˈment-ᵊl\ *adj* — **im·ple·men·ta·tion** \ˌim-plə-mən-ˈtā-shən, -ˌmen-\ *n*

im·pli·cate \ˈim-plə-ˌkāt\ *vt* [L *implicatus*, pp. of *implicare* — more at EMPLOY] **1** *archaic* : to fold or twist together : ENTWINE **2** : IMPLY **3** : to bring into intimate or incriminating connection

im·pli·ca·tion \ˌim-plə-ˈkā-shən\ *n* **1 a** : the act of implicating or the state of being implicated **b** : close connection; *esp* : an incriminating involvement **2 a** : the act of implying or the state of being implied **b** (1) : a logical relation between two propositions that fails to hold only if the first is true and the second is false (2) : a logical relationship between two propositions in which if the first is true the second is true (3) : a statement exhibiting a relation of implication **3** : something implied — **im·pli·ca·tive** \ˈim-plə-ˌkāt-iv, im-ˈplik-ət-\ *adj* — **im·pli·ca·tive·ly** *adv* — **im·pli·ca·tive·ness** *n*

im·plic·it \im-ˈplis-ət\ *adj* [L *implicitus*, pp. of *implicare*] **1 a** : capable of being understood from something else though unexpressed : IMPLIED **b** : involved in the nature or essence of something though not revealed, expressed, or developed : POTENTIAL **2** : being without doubt or reserve : UNQUESTIONING, ABSOLUTE — **im·plic·it·ly** *adv* — **im·plic·it·ness** *n*

implicit function *n* : a mathematical function whose definition requires the solution of one or more equations

im·plode \im-ˈplōd\ *vi* [*in-* + *-plode* (as in *explode*)] : to burst inward

im·plore \im-ˈplō(ə)r, -ˈplȯ(ə)r\ *vt* [MF or L; MF *implorer*, fr. L *implorare*, fr. *in-* + *plorare* to cry out] **1** : to call upon in supplication : BESEECH **2** : to call or pray for earnestly : ENTREAT **syn** see BEG

im·plo·sion \im-ˈplō-zhən\ *n* [*in-* + *-plosion* (as in *explosion*)] **1** : the action of imploding **2** : the inrush of air in forming a suction stop — **im·plo·sive** \-ˈplō-siv, -ziv\ *adj or n*

im·ply \im-ˈplī\ *vt* [ME *emplien*, fr. MF *emplier*, fr. L *implicare*] **1** *obs* : ENFOLD, ENTWINE **2** : to involve or indicate by inference, association, or necessary consequence rather than by direct statement **3** : to contain potentially **4** : to express indirectly **syn** see INCLUDE, SUGGEST

im·po·lite \ˌim-pə-ˈlīt\ *adj* [L *impolitus*, fr. *in-* + *politus* polite] : not polite : RUDE — **im·po·lite·ly** *adv* — **im·po·lite·ness** *n*

im·pol·i·tic \(ˈ)im-ˈpäl-ə-ˌtik\ *adj* : not politic : UNWISE — **im·po·lit·i·cal** \ˌim-pə-ˈlit-i-kəl\ *adj* — **im·po·lit·i·cal·ly** \-ˈlit-i-k(ə-)lē\ *adv* — **im·pol·i·tic·ly** \(ˈ)im-ˈpäl-ə-ˌtik-lē\ *adv*

im·pon·der·a·bil·i·ty \(ˌ)im-ˌpän-d(ə-)rə-ˈbil-ət-ē\ *n* : the quality or state of being imponderable

im·pon·der·a·ble \(ˈ)im-ˈpän-d(ə-)rə-bəl\ *adj* [ML *imponderabilis*, fr. L *in-* + LL *ponderabilis* ponderable] : not ponderable : incapable of being weighed or evaluated with exactness — **imponderable** *n* — **im·pon·der·a·ble·ness** *n* — **im·pon·der·a·bly** \-blē\ *adv*

im·pone \im-ˈpōn\ *vt* [L *imponere* to put upon, fr. *in-* + *ponere* to put — more at POSITION] *obs* : STAKE, WAGER

1**im·port** \im-ˈpō(ə)rt, -ˈpȯ(ə)rt, ˈim-ˌ\ *vb* [ME *importen*, fr. L *importare* to bring into, fr. *in-* + *portare* to carry — more at FARE] *vt* **1 a** : to bear or convey as meaning or portent : SIGNIFY **b** *archaic* : EXPRESS, STATE **c** : IMPLY **2** : to bring from a foreign or external source; *esp* : to bring (as merchandise) into a place or country from another country **3** *archaic* : to be of importance to : CONCERN ~ *vi* : MATTER — **im·port·able** \-ə-bəl\ *adj* — **im·port·er** *n*

2**im·port** \ˈim-ˌpō(ə)rt, -ˌpȯ(ə)rt\ *n* **1** : PURPORT, SIGNIFICATION **2** : IMPORTANCE, SIGNIFICANCE **3** : something that is imported **4** : IMPORTATION **syn** see MEANING

im·por·tance \im-ˈpȯrt-ᵊn(t)s, *oftenest in South* -ən(t)s\ *n* **1 a** : the quality or state of being important : CONSEQUENCE **b** : an important aspect or bearing : SIGNIFICANCE **2** *obs* : IMPORT, MEANING **3** *obs* : IMPORTUNITY **4** *obs* : a weighty matter

syn CONSEQUENCE, MOMENT, WEIGHT, SIGNIFICANCE: IMPORTANCE implies the power of influencing or the quality of having evident value either generally or in a particular relation and often by merely existing; CONSEQUENCE may imply importance in social rank but more generally implies importance because of probable or possible effects; MOMENT implies conspicuous or self-evident consequence; WEIGHT implies a judgment of the immediate relative importance of something; SIGNIFICANCE implies a quality or character that should mark a thing as important but that is not self-evident and may or may not be recognized

im·por·tan·cy \-ᵊn-sē, -ən-\ *n*, *archaic* : IMPORTANCE

im·por·tant \im-ˈpȯrt-ᵊnt, -ənt\ *adj* [MF, fr. OIt *importante*, fr. L *important-*, *importans*, prp of *importare*] **1** : marked by or possessing weight or consequence **2** : marked by self-complacency, ostentation, or pompousness **3** *obs* : IMPORTUNATE, URGENT — **im·por·tant·ly** *adv*

im·por·ta·tion \ˌim-ˌpōr-ˈtā-shən, -ˌpȯr-, -pər-\ *n* **1** : the act or

practice of importing **2 :** something imported
im·por·tu·nate \im-'pȯrch-(ə-)nət\ *adj* **1 :** TROUBLESOME **2 :** troublesomely urgent **:** overly persistent in request or demand — **im·por·tu·nate·ly** *adv* — **im·por·tu·nate·ness** *n*
1im·por·tune \,im-pər-'t(y)ün, im-'pȯr-chən\ *adj* [ME, fr. MF & L; MF *importun*, fr. L *importunus*, fr. *in-* + *-portunus* (as in *opportunus* fit) — more at OPPORTUNE] **:** IMPORTUNATE — **im·portune·ly** *adv*
2importune *vt* **1 a :** to press or urge with troublesome persistence **b** *archaic* **:** to request or beg for urgently **2 :** ANNOY, TROUBLE ~ *vi* **:** to beg, urge, or solicit persistently or troublesomely **syn** see BEG — **im·por·tun·er** *n*
im·por·tu·ni·ty \,im-pər-'t(y)ü-nət-ē\ *n* **:** the quality or state of being importunate
im·pose \im-'pōz\ *vb* [MF *imposer*, fr. L *imponere*, lit., to put upon (perf. indic. *imposui*), fr. *in-* + *ponere* to put — more at POSITION] *vt* **1 a :** to establish or apply as compulsory **:** LEVY ⟨~ a tax⟩ **b :** to make prevail by force ⟨*imposed* himself as their leader⟩ **2 a** *archaic* **:** PLACE, SET **b :** to arrange (typeset or plated pages) in order for printing as a signature **3 :** to palm off ⟨~ fake antiques on the public⟩ **4 :** OBTRUDE ⟨~ oneself upon others⟩ ~ *vi* **1 :** to take unwarranted advantage of something ⟨*imposed* upon his good nature⟩ **2 :** to practice deception ⟨clever enough to ~ on the public⟩ — **im·pos·er** *n*
im·pos·ing \im-'pō-ziŋ\ *adj* **:** impressive because of size, bearing, dignity, or grandeur **:** COMMANDING **syn** see GRAND — **im·pos·ing·ly** \-ziŋ-lē\ *adv*
im·po·si·tion \,im-pə-'zish-ən\ *n* **1 :** the act of imposing **2 :** something imposed: as **a :** LEVY, TAX **b :** an excessive or uncalled-for requirement or burden **3 :** DECEPTION
im·pos·si·bil·i·ty \(,)im-,päs-ə-'bil-ət-ē\ *n* **1 :** the quality or state of being impossible **2 :** something impossible
im·pos·si·ble \(')im-'päs-ə-bəl\ *adj* [ME, fr. MF & L; MF, fr. L *impossibilis*, fr. *in-* + *possibilis* possible] **1 a :** incapable of being or of occurring **b :** felt to be incapable of being done, attained, or fulfilled **:** insuperably difficult **:** HOPELESS **2 a :** extremely undesirable **:** UNACCEPTABLE **b :** markedly difficult to deal with **:** OBJECTIONABLE — **im·pos·si·ble·ness** *n* — **im·pos·si·bly** \-blē\ *adv*
1im·post \'im-,pōst\ *n* [MF, fr. ML *impositum*, fr. L, neut. of *impositus*, pp. of *imponere*] **:** something imposed or levied **:** TAX, DUTY
2impost *n* [F *imposte*, deriv. of L *impositus*] **:** a block, capital, or molding from which an arch springs
im·pos·tor *or* **im·pos·ter** \im-'päs-tər\ *n* **:** one that assumes an identity or title not his own for the purpose of deception **:** PRETENDER
im·pos·tume \im-'päs-(,)chüm\ *or* **im·pos·thume** \-(,)th(y)üm\ *n* [ME *emposteme*, deriv. of Gk *apostēma*, fr. *aphistanai* to remove — more at APOSTASY] *archaic* **:** ABSCESS
im·pos·ture \im-'päs-chər\ *n* [LL *impostura*, fr. L *impositus*, *impostus*, pp. of *imponere*] **:** the act or conduct of an impostor **:** DECEPTION; *esp* **:** fraudulent impersonation
syn IMPOSTURE, FRAUD, SHAM, FAKE, HUMBUG, COUNTERFEIT mean a thing imposed on one by false pretenses. IMPOSTURE applies to any situation in which a spurious object or action is passed off as genuine; FRAUD usu. implies a deliberate perversion of the truth, but applied to a person it may suggest merely pretense and hypocrisy; SHAM applies to fraudulent imitation of a real thing or action; FAKE implies an imitation of or substitution for the genuine but does not necessarily imply dishonesty; HUMBUG suggests elaborate pretense usu. so flagrant as to be transparent; COUNTERFEIT applies esp. to the close imitation of something valuable
im·po·tence \'im-pət-ən(t)s\ *also* **im·po·ten·cy** \-ən-sē\ *n* **:** the quality or state of being impotent
im·po·tent \'im-pət-ənt\ *adj* [ME, fr. MF & L; MF, fr. L *impotent-*, *impotens*, fr. *in-* + *potent-*, *potens* potent] **1 a :** not potent **:** lacking in power, strength, or vigor **:** HELPLESS **b :** unable to copulate; *broadly* **:** STERILE — usu. used of males **2** *obs* **:** incapable of self-restraint **:** UNGOVERNABLE **syn** see STERILE — **impotent** *n* — **im·po·tent·ly** *adv*
im·pound \im-'paủnd\ *vt* **1 a :** to shut up in or as if in a pound **:** CONFINE **b :** to seize and hold in the custody of the law **2 :** to collect (water) in a reservoir
im·pound·ment \-'paủn(d)-mənt\ *n* **1 :** the act of impounding **:** the state of being impounded **2 :** a body of water formed by impounding
im·pov·er·ish \im-'päv-(ə-)rish\ *vt* [ME *enpoverisen*, fr. MF *empovriss-*, stem of *empovrir*, fr. *en-* + *povre* poor — more at POOR] **1 :** to make poor **2 :** to deprive of strength, richness, or fertility **syn** see DEPLETE — **im·pov·er·ish·er** *n* — **im·pov·er·ish·ment** \-mənt\ *n*
im·prac·ti·ca·bil·i·ty \(,)im-,prak-ti-kə-'bil-ət-ē\ *n* **:** IMPRACTICABLENESS
im·prac·ti·ca·ble \(')im-'prak-ti-kə-bəl\ *adj* **1 a :** not practicable **:** incapable of being put into practice or use **b :** IMPASSABLE ⟨an ~ road⟩ **2** *archaic* **:** UNMANAGEABLE, INTRACTABLE — **im·prac·ti·ca·ble·ness** *n* — **im·prac·ti·ca·bly** \-blē\ *adv*
im·prac·ti·cal \(')im-'prak-ti-kəl\ *adj* **:** not practical: as **a** (1) **:** not wise to put into or keep in practice or effect (2) **:** IDEALISTIC, THEORETICAL **b :** incapable of dealing sensibly or prudently with practical matters **c :** IMPRACTICABLE — **im·prac·ti·cal·i·ty** \(,)im-,prak-ti-'kal-ət-ē\ *n* — **im·prac·ti·cal·ness** *n*
im·pre·cate \'im-pri-,kāt\ *vb* [L *imprecatus*, pp. of *imprecari*, fr. *in-* + *precari* to pray — more at PRAY] *vt* **1 a** *archaic* **:** INVOKE **b :** to invoke evil upon **:** CURSE **2** *archaic* **:** to beg or pray for ~ *vi* **:** to utter curses
im·pre·ca·tion \,im-pri-'kā-shən\ *n* **1 :** the act of imprecating **2 :** CURSE — **im·pre·ca·to·ry** \'im-pri-kə-,tōr-ē, im-'prek-ə-, -,tȯr-\ *adj*
im·pre·cise \,im-pri-'sīs\ *adj* **:** not precise **:** INEXACT, VAGUE — **im·pre·cise·ly** *adv* — **im·pre·cise·ness** *n* — **im·pre·ci·sion** \-'sizh-ən\ *n*
im·preg·na·bil·i·ty \(,)im-,preg-nə-'bil-ət-ē\ *n* **:** the quality or state of being impregnable
1im·preg·na·ble \im-'preg-nə-bəl\ *adj* [ME *imprenable*, fr. MF, fr. *in-* + *prenable* vulnerable to capture, fr. *prendre* to take — more at PRIZE] **:** incapable of being taken by assault **:** UNCONQUERABLE; *also* **:** UNASSAILABLE — **im·preg·na·ble·ness** *n* — **im·preg·na·bly** \-blē\ *adv*
2impregnable *adj* **:** capable of being impregnated
im·preg·nant \im-'preg-nənt\ *n* **:** a substance used for impregnating another substance
1im·preg·nate \im-'preg-nət\ *adj* **:** IMPREGNATED
2im·preg·nate \im-'preg-,nāt\ *vt* [LL *impraegnatus*, pp. of *impraegnare*, fr. L *in-* + *praegnas* pregnant] **1 a** (1) **:** to make pregnant (2) **:** to introduce sperm cells into **b :** FERTILIZE **2 a :** to cause to be filled, imbued, permeated, or saturated **b :** INTERPENETRATE **syn** see SOAK — **im·preg·na·tion** \,im-,preg-'nā-shən\ *n* — **im·preg·na·tor** \im-'preg-,nāt-ər\ *n*
im·pre·sa \im-'prā-zə\ *n* [It, lit., undertaking] **:** a device with a motto used in the 16th and 17th centuries; *broadly* **:** EMBLEM
im·pre·sa·rio \,im-prə-'sär-ē-,ō, -'sar-, -'ser-\ *n* [It, fr. *impresa* undertaking, fr. *imprendere* to undertake, fr. (assumed) VL *imprehendere* — more at EMPRISE] **1 :** the projector, manager, or conductor of an opera or concert company **2 :** one who puts on or sponsors an entertainment **3 :** MANAGER, PRODUCER
im·pre·scrip·ti·ble \,im-pri-'skrip-tə-bəl\ *adj* [MF, fr. *in-* + *prescriptible*] **:** not subject to prescription **:** INALIENABLE — **im·pre·scrip·ti·bly** \-blē\ *adv*
1im·press \im-'pres\ *vb* [ME *impressen*, fr. L *impressus*, pp. of *imprimere*, fr. *in-* + *premere* to press — more at PRESS] *vt* **1 a :** to apply with pressure so as to imprint **b :** to produce (as a mark) by pressure **c :** to mark by or as if by pressure or stamping **2 a :** to produce a vivid impression of **b :** to affect esp. forcibly or deeply **:** INFLUENCE **3 a :** TRANSFER, TRANSMIT **b :** to apply (as an electromotive force) to a circuit from an outside source ~ *vi* **:** to produce an impression **syn** see AFFECT
2im·press \'im-,pres\ *n* **1 :** the act of impressing **2 a :** a mark made by pressure **:** IMPRINT **b :** an image of something formed by or as if by pressure; *esp* **:** SEAL **c :** a product of pressure or influence **3 :** a characteristic or distinctive mark **:** STAMP **4 :** IMPRESSION, EFFECT
3im·press \im-'pres\ *vt* [*in-* + *press*] **1 :** to levy or take by force for public service; *esp* **:** to force into naval service **2 a :** to procure or enlist by forcible persuasion **b :** FORCE
4im·press \'im-,pres\ *n* **:** IMPRESSMENT
im·press·ibil·i·ty \(,)im-,pres-ə-'bil-ət-ē\ *n* **:** the quality or state of being impressible
im·press·ible \im-'pres-ə-bəl\ *adj* **:** capable of being impressed **:** SENSITIVE — **im·press·ibly** \-blē\ *adv*
im·pres·sion \im-'presh-ən\ *n* **1 :** the act of impressing: as **a :** an affecting by stamping or pressing **b :** a communicating of a mold, trait, or character by an external force or influence **2 :** the effect produced by impressing: as **a :** a stamp, form, or figure resulting from physical contact **b :** an imprint of the teeth and adjacent portions **c :** an esp. marked influence or effect on feeling, sense, or mind **3 a :** a characteristic trait or feature resulting from influence **b :** an effect of alteration or improvement **c :** a telling image impressed on the senses or the mind **4 a :** the amount of pressure with which an inked printing surface deposits its ink on the paper **b :** one instance of the meeting of a printing surface and the material being printed; *also* **:** a single print or copy so made **c :** all the copies of a book or other publication printed in one continuous operation from a single makeready **5 :** a usu. indistinct or imprecise notion or remembrance **6 a :** the first coat of color in painting **b :** a coat of paint for ornament or preservation **7 :** an imitation or representation of salient features in an artistic or theatrical medium; *esp* **:** an imitation in caricature of a noted personality as a form of theatrical entertainment **syn** see IDEA — **im·pres·sion·al** \-'presh-nəl, -ən-ᵊl\ *adj*
im·pres·sion·abil·i·ty \(,)im-,presh-(ə-)nə-'bil-ət-ē\ *n* **:** the quality or state of being impressionable
im·pres·sion·able \im-'presh-(ə-)nə-bəl\ *adj* **:** capable of being easily impressed **:** easily molded or influenced **:** PLASTIC — **im·pres·sion·able·ness** *n* — **im·pres·sion·ably** \-blē\ *adv*
im·pres·sion·ism \im-'presh-ə-,niz-əm\ *n* **1** *often cap* **:** a theory or practice in painting esp. among French painters of about 1870 of depicting the natural appearances of objects by means of dabs or strokes of primary unmixed colors in order to simulate actual reflected light **2 a :** the depiction of scene, emotion, or character by details intended to achieve a vividness or effectiveness more by evoking subjective and sensory impressions than by recreating an objective reality **b :** a style of musical composition designed to create moods through rich and varied harmonies and timbres **3 :** a practice of presenting and elaborating one's subjective reactions to a work of art — **im·pres·sion·ist** \-'presh-(ə-)nəst\ *n or adj* — **im·pres·sion·is·tic** \(,)im-,presh-ə-'nis-tik\ *adj* — **im·pres·sion·is·ti·cal·ly** \-ti-k(ə-)lē\ *adv*
im·pres·sive \im-'pres-iv\ *adj* **:** making or tending to make a marked impression **:** stirring deep feeling esp. of awe or admiration **syn** see MOVING — **im·pres·sive·ly** *adv* — **im·pres·sive·ness** *n*
im·press·ment \im-'pres-mənt\ *n* **:** the act of seizing for public use or of impressing into public service
im·pres·sure \im-'presh-ər\ *n* **:** IMPRESSION
1im·prest \im-'prest\ *vt* [prob. fr. It *imprestare* to lend money, fr. *in-* (fr. L) + *prestare* to lend, fr. L *praestare* to pay — more at PREST] *archaic* **:** to make an advance or loan of (money)
2im·prest \'im-,prest\ *n* **:** a loan or advance of money; *esp* **:** an advance from government funds to enable a person to discharge his duties
im·pri·ma·tur \,im-prə-'mät-ər\ *n* [NL, let it be printed, fr. *imprimere* to print, fr. L, to imprint, impress — more at IMPRESS] **1 a :** a license to print or publish **b :** approval of a publication under circumstances of official censorship **2 :** SANCTION, APPROVAL
im·pri·mis \im-'prī-məs, -'prē-\ *adv* [ME *inprimis*, fr. L *in primis*] among the first (things)] **:** in the first place
1im·print \im-'print, 'im-,\ *vt* **1 :** to mark by or as if by pressure **:** IMPRESS **2** *archaic* **:** PRINT
2im·print \'im-,print\ *n* [MF *empreinte*, fr. fem. of *empreint*, pp. of *empreindre* to imprint, fr. L *imprimere*] **:** something imprinted or printed: as **a :** IMPRESS **b :** a publisher's name often with address and date of publication printed at the foot of a title page **c :** an indelible distinguishing effect or influence
im·pris·on \im-'priz-ᵊn\ *vt* [ME *imprisonen*, fr. OF *emprisoner*, fr. *en-* + *prison*] **:** to put in or as if in prison **:** CONFINE — **im·pris·on·ment** \-mənt\ *n*
im·prob·a·bil·i·ty \(,)im-,präb-ə-'bil-ət-ē\ *n* **1 :** the quality or state of being improbable **2 :** something improbable
im·prob·a·ble \(')im-'präb(-ə)-bəl\ *adj* [MF or L; MF, fr. L *improbabilis*, fr. *in-* + *probabilis* probable] **:** unlikely to be true or to

occur — **im·prob·a·ble·ness** *n* — **im·prob·a·bly** \-blē\ *adv*

im·pro·bi·ty \(ˈ)im-ˈprō-bət-ē, -ˈpräb-ət-\ *n* [MF or L; MF *improbité*, fr. L *improbitat-*, *improbitas*, fr. *improbus* dishonest, fr. *in-* + *probus* honest] **:** lack of probity or integrity **:** DISHONESTY

im·promp·tu \im-ˈpräm(p)-(ˌ)t(y)ü\ *adj* [F, fr. *impromptu* extemporaneously, fr. L *in promptu* in readiness] **1 :** made or done on or as if on the spur of the moment **:** IMPROVISED **2 :** composed or uttered without previous study or preparation — **impromptu** *adv or n*

im·prop·er \(ˈ)im-ˈpräp-ər\ *adj* [MF *impropre*, fr. L *improprius*, fr. *in-* + *proprius* proper] **:** not proper: as **a :** not accordant with fact or right procedure **:** INCORRECT ⟨~ inference⟩ **b :** not regularly or normally formed or not properly so called **c :** not suited to the circumstances, design, or end ⟨~ medicine⟩ **d :** not in accord with propriety, modesty, or good manners **e :** INDECENT ⟨~ language⟩ **syn** see INDECOROUS — **im·prop·er·ly** *adv* — **im·prop·er·ness** *n*

improper fraction *n* **:** a fraction whose numerator is larger or of higher degree than the denominator

im·pro·pri·ety \ˌim-p(r)ə-ˈprī-ət-ē\ *n* [F or LL; F *impropriété*, fr. LL *improprietat-*, *improprietas*, fr. L *improprius*] **1 :** the quality or state of being improper **2 :** an improper or indecorous act or remark; *specif* **:** an unacceptable use of a word or of language

im·prov·abil·i·ty \(ˌ)im-ˌprü-və-ˈbil-ət-ē\ *n* **:** capability of improving or of being improved

im·prov·able \im-ˈprü-və-bəl\ *adj* **:** capable of improvement

im·prove \im-ˈprüv\ *vb* [AF *emprouer* to invest profitably, fr. OF *en-* + *prou* advantage, fr. LL *prode* — more at PROUD] *vt* **1 :** to make greater in amount or degree **2 a :** to enhance in value or quality **:** make better **b :** to increase the value of (land or property) by betterment (as cultivation or the erection of buildings) **c :** to grade and drain (a road) and apply surfacing material other than pavement **3** *archaic* **:** EMPLOY, USE **4 :** to turn to good account ~ *vi* **1 a :** INCREASE **b :** to rise in value **2 :** to grow better **3 :** to make useful additions or amendments ⟨~ on the carburetor⟩ — **im·prov·er** *n*

syn IMPROVE, BETTER, HELP, AMELIORATE mean to make more acceptable or bring nearer some standard. IMPROVE and BETTER are general and interchangeable and apply to what is capable of being made better whether it is good or bad; HELP implies a bettering that still leaves room for improvement; AMELIORATE implies making more tolerable or acceptable conditions that are hard to endure

im·prove·ment \im-ˈprüv-mənt\ *n* **1 :** the act or process of improving **2 a :** the state of being improved; *esp* **:** enhanced value or excellence **b :** an instance of such improvement **:** something that improves in this way

im·prov·i·dence \(ˈ)im-ˈpräv-əd-ən(t)s, -ə-ˌden(t)s\ *n* **:** the quality or state of being improvident

im·prov·i·dent \-əd-ənt, -ə-ˌdent\ *adj* [LL *improvident-*, *improvidens*, fr. L *in-* + *provident-*, *providens* provident] **:** not provident **:** not providing for the future — **im·prov·i·dent·ly** *adv*

im·pro·vi·sa·tion \(ˌ)im-ˌpräv-ə-ˈzā-shən, ˌim-prə-və-\ *n* **1 :** the act or art of improvising **2 :** something improvised — **im·pro·vi·sa·tion·al** \-shnəl, -shən-ᵊl\ *adj*

im·prov·i·sa·tor \im-ˈpräv-ə-ˌzāt-ər\ *n* **:** IMPROVISER — **im·prov·i·sa·to·ri·al** \(ˌ)im-ˌpräv-ə-zə-ˈtōr-ē-əl, -ˈtȯr-\ *or* **im·pro·vi·sa·to·ry** \im-ˈpräv-ə-zə-ˌtōr-ē, ˌim-prə-ˈvī-zə-, -ˌtȯr-\ *adj*

im·pro·vise \ˌim-prə-ˈvīz\ *vb* [F *improviser*, fr. It *improvvisare*, fr. *improvviso* sudden, fr. L *improvisus*, lit., unforeseen, fr. *in-* + *provisus*, pp. of *providēre* to see ahead — more at PROVIDE] *vt* **1 :** to compose, recite, or sing on the spur of the moment**:** EXTEMPORIZE **2 :** to make, invent, or arrange offhand ~ *vi* **:** to improvise something — **im·pro·vis·er** *or* **im·pro·vi·sor** \-ˈvī-zər\ *n*

im·pru·dence \(ˈ)im-ˈprüd-ᵊn(t)s\ *n* **1 :** the quality or state of being imprudent **2 :** an imprudent act

im·pru·dent \-ᵊnt\ *adj* [ME, fr. L *imprudent-*, *imprudens*, fr. *in-* + *prudent-*, *prudens* prudent] **:** not prudent **:** lacking discretion — **im·pru·dent·ly** *adv*

im·pu·dence \ˈim-pyəd-ən(t)s\ *n* **:** the quality or state of being impudent

im·pu·dent \-ənt\ *adj* [ME, fr. L *impudent-*, *impudens*, fr. *in-* + *pudent-*, *pudens*, prp. of *pudēre* to feel shame] **1** *obs* **:** lacking modesty **2 :** marked by contemptuous or cocky boldness or disregard of others **:** INSOLENT — **im·pu·dent·ly** *adv*

im·pu·dic·i·ty \ˌim-pyu̇-ˈdis-ət-ē\ *n* **:** IMMODESTY, SHAMELESSNESS

im·pugn \im-ˈpyün\ *vt* [ME *impugnen*, fr. MF *impugner*, fr. L *inpugnare*, fr. *in-* + *pugnare* to fight — more at PUGNACIOUS] **1** *obs* **a :** ASSAIL **b :** RESIST **2 :** to assail by words or arguments **:** oppose or attack as false **syn** see DENY — **im·pugn·er** *n*

im·puis·sance \(ˈ)im-ˈpwis-ᵊn(t)s, (ˈ)im-ˈpyü-ə-sən(t)s; ˌim-pyü-ˈis-ᵊn(t)s\ *n* [MF, fr. *in-* + *puissance*] **:** POWERLESSNESS, WEAKNESS

1im·pulse \ˈim-ˌpəls\ *n* [L *impulsus*, fr. *impulsus*, pp. of *impellere* to impel] **1 a :** the act of driving onward with sudden force **:** IMPULSION **b :** motion produced by such an impulsion **:** IMPETUS **c :** a wave of excitation transmitted through tissues and esp. nerve fibers and muscles that results in physiological activity or inhibition **2 a :** a force so communicated as to produce motion suddenly **b :** INCENTIVE **c :** INSPIRATION, MOTIVATION **3 a :** a sudden spontaneous inclination or incitement to some usu. unpremeditated action **b :** a propensity or natural tendency usu. other than rational **4 a :** the product of the average value of a force and the time during which it acts being a quantity equal to the change in momentum produced by the force **b :** PULSE 4a **syn** see MOTIVE

2im·pulse \ˈim-ˌpəls, im-ˈ\ *vt* **:** to give an impulse to

im·pul·sion \im-ˈpəl-shən\ *n* **1 a :** the act of impelling **:** the state of being impelled **b :** the impelling force **c :** an onward tendency derived from an impulsion **:** IMPETUS **2 :** IMPULSE 3a **3 :** COMPULSION 2

im·pul·sive \im-ˈpəl-siv\ *adj* **1 :** having the power of or actually driving or impelling **2 :** actuated by or prone to act on impulse **3 :** acting momentarily **syn** see SPONTANEOUS — **im·pul·sive·ly** *adv* — **im·pul·sive·ness** *n*

im·pu·ni·ty \im-ˈpyü-nət-ē\ *n* [MF or L; MF *impunité*, fr. L *impunitat-*, *impunitas*, fr. *impune* without punishment, fr. *in-* + *poena* pain] **:** exemption or freedom from punishment, harm, or loss

im·pure \(ˈ)im-ˈpyu̇(ə)r\ *adj* [F & L; F, fr. L *impurus*, fr. *in-* + *purus* pure] **:** not pure: as **a :** UNCHASTE, OBSCENE ⟨~ language⟩ **b :** containing something unclean **:** FOUL ⟨~ water⟩ **c :** ritually unclean **d :** marked by an intermixture of foreign elements or by substandard, incongruous, or objectionable locutions **e :** ADULTERATED ⟨an ~ chemical⟩ **f :** MIXED, BASTARD ⟨an ~ style⟩ — **im·pure·ly** *adv* — **im·pure·ness** *n*

im·pu·ri·ty \(ˈ)im-ˈpyu̇r-ət-ē\ *n* **1 :** the quality or state of being impure **2 :** something that is impure or makes something else impure

im·put·abil·i·ty \(ˌ)im-ˌpyüt-ə-ˈbil-ət-ē\ *n* **:** the quality or state of being imputable

im·put·able \im-ˈpyüt-ə-bəl\ *adj* **:** capable of being imputed **:** ASCRIBABLE — **im·put·ably** \-blē\ *adv*

im·pu·ta·tion \ˌim-pyə-ˈtā-shən\ *n* **1 :** the act of imputing: as **a :** ASCRIPTION **b :** ACCUSATION **c :** INSINUATION **2 :** something imputed — **im·pu·ta·tive** \im-ˈpyüt-ət-iv\ *adj* — **im·pu·ta·tive·ly** *adv*

im·pute \im-ˈpyüt\ *vt* [ME *inputen*, fr. L *imputare*, fr. *in-* + *putare* to consider — more at PAVE] **1 a :** to lay the responsibility or blame for **:** CHARGE **b :** to credit to a person or a cause **:** ATTRIBUTE **2 :** to credit by transferal **syn** see ASCRIBE

1in \(ˈ)in, ən, ᵊn\ *prep* [ME, fr. OE; akin to OHG *in* in, L *in*, Gk *en*] **1 a** (1) — used as a function word to indicate spatial inclusion ⟨swimming ~ the lake⟩ (2) — used as a function word to indicate inclusion by something immaterial ⟨~ the summer⟩ **b :** INTO 1a ⟨went ~ the house⟩ **2** — used as a function word to indicate means or instrumentality ⟨written ~ pencil⟩ **3 a** — used as a function word to indicate a limitation or qualification ⟨alike ~ some respects⟩ ⟨left ~ a hurry⟩ **b :** INTO 2a ⟨broke ~ pieces⟩ **4** — used as a function word to indicate purpose ⟨said ~ reply⟩ **5** — used as a function word to indicate the larger member of a ratio ⟨one ~ six is eligible⟩

2in \ˈin\ *adv* **1 a** (1) **:** to or toward the inside esp. of a house or other building ⟨come ~⟩ (2) **:** to or toward some destination or particular place ⟨flew ~ on the first plane⟩ (3) **:** at close quarters **:** NEAR ⟨play close ~⟩ **b :** into the midst of something so as to form a part ⟨mix ~ the flour⟩ **c** (1) **:** to or at its proper place ⟨fit a piece ~⟩ (2) **:** into line ⟨fell ~ with our plans⟩ **2 a :** WITHIN **b :** in the position of participant, insider, or officeholder **c** (1) **:** on good terms (2) **:** in a specified relation ⟨~ bad with the boss⟩ (3) **:** in a position of assured or definitive success **d :** in vogue or season **e** *of an oil well* **:** in production **f** (1) **:** at hand (2) **:** in a completed or terminated state ⟨after harvests are ~⟩

3in \ˈin\ *adj* **1 a :** that is located inside or within ⟨the ~ part⟩ **b :** that is in position, operation, or power ⟨the ~ party⟩ **2 :** that is directed or bound inward **:** INCOMING ⟨the ~ train⟩ **3 a :** keenly aware of and responsive to what is new and smart ⟨the ~ crowd⟩ **b :** extremely fashionable ⟨the ~ thing to do⟩

4in \ˈin\ *n* **1 :** one who is in office or power or on the inside **2 :** INFLUENCE, PULL

1in- *or* **il-** *or* **im-** *or* **ir-** *prefix* [ME, fr. MF, fr. L; akin to OE *un-*] **:** not **:** NON-, UN- — usu. *il-* before *l* ⟨*il*logical⟩ and *im-* before *b*, *m*, or *p* ⟨*im*balance⟩ ⟨*im*moral⟩ ⟨*im*practical⟩ and *ir-* before *r* ⟨*ir*redeemable⟩ and *in-* before other sounds ⟨*in*conclusive⟩

2in- *or* **il-** *or* **im-** *or* **ir-** *prefix* [ME, fr. MF, fr. L, fr. *in* in, into] **1 :** in **:** within **:** into **:** toward **:** on ⟨*il*luviation⟩ ⟨*im*mingle⟩ ⟨*ir*radiance⟩ — usu. *il-* before *l*, *im-* before *b*, *m*, or *p*, *ir-* before *r*, and *in-* before other sounds **2 :** 1EN- ⟨*im*brute⟩ ⟨*im*peril⟩ ⟨*in*spirit⟩

-in \ən, ᵊn, ˌin\ *n suffix* [F *-ine*, fr. L *-īna*, fem. of *-īnus* of or belonging to — more at -EN] **1 a :** neutral chemical compound ⟨insul*in*⟩ **b :** enzyme ⟨pancreat*in*⟩ **c :** antibiotic ⟨penicill*in*⟩ **2 :** 2-INE 1a,1b ⟨epinephr*in*⟩ **3 :** pharmaceutical product ⟨niac*in*⟩

-i·na \ˈē-nə\ *n suffix* [prob. fr. It *-ina*, dim. suffix, fr. L *-īna*] **:** musical instrument ⟨concert*ina*⟩

in·abil·i·ty \ˌin-ə-ˈbil-ət-ē\ *n* [ME *inabilite*, fr. MF *inhabilité*, fr. *in-* + *habilité* ability] **:** the quality or state of being unable

in ab·sen·tia \ˌin-(ˌ)ab-ˈsen-ch(ē-)ə\ *adv* [L] **:** in absence

in·ac·ces·si·bil·i·ty \ˌin-ik-ˌses-ə-ˈbil-ət-ē, ˌin-(ˌ)ak-\ *n* **:** the quality or state of being inaccessible

in·ac·ces·si·ble \-ˈses-ə-bəl\ *adj* [MF or LL; MF, fr. LL *inaccessibilis*, fr. L *in-* + LL *accessibilis* accessible] **:** not accessible — **in·ac·ces·si·bly** \-blē\ *adv*

in·ac·cu·ra·cy \(ˈ)in-ˈak-yə-rə-sē\ *n* **1 :** the quality or state of being inaccurate **2 :** MISTAKE, ERROR

in·ac·cu·rate \(ˈ)in-ˈak-yə-rət\ *adj* **:** not accurate **:** FAULTY — **in·ac·cu·rate·ly** \-yə-rət-lē, -yart-\ *adv*

in·ac·tion \(ˈ)in-ˈak-shən\ *n* **:** lack of action or activity **:** IDLENESS

in·ac·ti·vate \(ˈ)in-ˈak-tə-ˌvāt\ *vt* **:** to make inactive — **in·ac·ti·va·tion** \(ˌ)in-ˌak-tə-ˈvā-shən\ *n*

in·ac·tive \(ˈ)in-ˈak-tiv\ *adj* **:** not active: as **a** (1) **:** SEDENTARY (2) **:** INDOLENT, SLUGGISH **b** (1) **:** being out of use (2) **:** relating to members of the armed forces who are not performing or available for military duties (3) *of a disease* **:** QUIESCENT **c** (1) **:** chemically inert (2) **:** optically neutral in polarized light **d :** biologically inert because of the loss of some quality — **in·ac·tive·ly** *adv* — **in·ac·tiv·i·ty** \ˌin-(ˌ)ak-ˈtiv-ət-ē\ *n*

syn IDLE, INERT, PASSIVE, SUPINE: INACTIVE applies to anyone or anything not in action or in operation or at work; IDLE applies to persons that are not busy or occupied or to their powers or their implements; INERT as applied to things implies powerlessness to move or to affect other things; as applied to persons it suggests an inherent or habitual indisposition to activity; PASSIVE implies immobility or lack of normally expected response to an external force or influence and often suggests deliberate submissiveness or self-control; SUPINE applies only to persons and commonly implies abjectness or indolence

in·ad·e·qua·cy \(ˈ)in-ˈad-i-kwə-sē\ *n* [irreg. fr. *inadequate*] **1 :** the quality or state of being inadequate **2 :** INSUFFICIENCY, DEFICIENCY, FAULT

in·ad·e·quate \-kwət\ *adj* **:** not adequate **:** INSUFFICIENT — **in·ad·e·quate·ly** *adv* — **in·ad·e·quate·ness** *n*

in·ad·mis·si·bil·i·ty \ˌin-əd-ˌmis-ə-ˈbil-ət-ē\ *n* **:** the quality or state of being inadmissible

in·ad·mis·si·ble \ˌin-əd-ˈmis-ə-bəl\ *adj* **:** not admissible — **in·ad·mis·si·bly** \-blē\ *adv*

in·ad·ver·tence \ˌin-əd-ˈvərt-ᵊn(t)s\ *n* [ML *inadvertentia*, fr. L *in-* + *advertent-*, *advertens*, prp. of *advertere* to advert] **1 :** the fact or action of being inadvertent **:** INATTENTION **2 :** a result of inattention **:** OVERSIGHT

in·ad·ver·ten·cy \-ᵊn-sē\ *n* **:** HEEDLESSNESS, INADVERTENCE

in·ad·ver·tent \-ᵊnt\ *adj* [back-formation of *inadvertence*] **1 :** not

turning the mind to a matter : INATTENTIVE **2** : UNINTENTIONAL — **in·ad·ver·tent·ly** *adv*

in·ad·vis·abil·i·ty \ˌin-əd-ˌvī-zə-'bil-ət-ē\ *n* : the quality or state of being inadvisable

in·ad·vis·able \-'vī-zə-bəl\ *adj* : not advisable

-i·nae \'ī-(ˌ)nē\ *n pl suffix* [NL *-inae*, fr. L, fem. pl. of *-inus*] : members of the subfamily of — in all names of zoological subfamilies in recent classifications ⟨Fel*inae*⟩

in·alien·abil·i·ty \(ˌ)in-ˌāl-yə-nə-'bil-ət-ē, -ˌā-lē-ə-nə-\ *n* : the quality or state of being inalienable

in·alien·able \(')in-'āl-yə-nə-bəl, -'ā-lē-ə-nə-\ *adj* [prob. fr. F *inaliénable*, fr. *in-* + *aliénable* alienable] : incapable of being alienated, surrendered, or transferred — **in·alien·ably** \-blē\ *adv*

in·al·ter·abil·i·ty \(ˌ)in-ˌȯl-t(ə-)rə-'bil-ət-ē\ *n* : the quality or state of being inalterable

in·al·ter·able \(')in-'ȯl-t(ə-)rə-bəl\ *adj* : not alterable : UNALTERABLE — **in·al·ter·able·ness** *n* — **in·al·ter·ably** \-blē\ *adv*

in·amo·ra·ta \(ˌ)in-ˌam-ə-'rät-ə\ *n* [It *innamorata*, fr. fem. of *innamorato*, pp. of *innamorare* to inspire with love, fr. *in-* (fr. L) + *amore* love, fr. L *amor* — more at AMOROUS] : a woman with whom one is in love or has intimate relations

in–and–in \ˌin-ən-'(d)in\ *adv* (*or adj*) : in repeated generations of the same or closely related stock

1**inane** \in-'ān\ *adj* [L *inanis*] **1** : EMPTY, INSUBSTANTIAL **2** : lacking significance, meaning, or point : SILLY **syn** see INSIPID — **inane·ly** *adv* — **inane·ness** \-'ān-nəs\ *n* — **inan·i·ty** \-'an-ət-ē\ *n*

2**inane** *n* : the emptiness of space

in·an·i·mate \(')in-'an-ə-mət\ *adj* [LL *inanimatus*, fr. L *in-* + *animatus*, pp. of *animare* to animate] **1** : not animate: **a** : not endowed with life or spirit **b** : lacking consciousness or power of motion **2** : not animated or lively : DULL — **in·an·i·mate·ly** *adv* — **in·an·i·mate·ness** *n*

in·a·ni·tion \ˌin-ə-'nish-ən\ *n* : EMPTINESS: **a** : the condition which results from lack of food and water **b** : lack of vitality or vigor : LETHARGY

inan·i·ty \in-'an-ət-ē\ *n* **1** : the quality or state of being inane: as **a** : EMPTINESS **b** : FATUOUSNESS **2** : something that is inane

in·ap·par·ent \ˌin-ə-'par-ənt, -'per-\ *adj* : not apparent

in·ap·peas·able \ˌin-ə-'pē-zə-bəl\ *adj* : UNAPPEASABLE

in·ap·pe·tence \(')in-'ap-ət-ən(t)s\ *n* : lack of appetite

in·ap·pli·ca·bil·i·ty \(ˌ)in-ˌap-li-kə-'bil-ət-ē *also* ˌin-ə-ˌplik-ə-\ *n* : the condition of being inapplicable

in·ap·pli·ca·ble \(')in-'ap-li-kə-bəl *also* ˌin-ə-'plik-ə-\ *adj* : not applicable : IRRELEVANT, UNSUITABLE — **in·ap·pli·ca·bly** \-blē\ *adv*

in·ap·po·site \(')in-'ap-ə-zət\ *adj* : not apposite — **in·ap·po·site·ly** *adv* — **in·ap·po·site·ness** *n*

in·ap·pre·cia·ble \ˌin-ə-'prē-shə-bəl\ *adj* [prob. fr. F *inappréciable*, fr. MF *inappreciable*, fr. *in-* + *appreciable*] **1** *archaic* : INVALUABLE **2** : too small to be perceived — **in·ap·pre·cia·bly** \-blē\ *adv*

in·ap·pre·cia·tive \ˌin-ə-'prē-shət-iv *also* -shē-ˌāt-\ *adj* : not appreciative — **in·ap·pre·cia·tive·ly** *adv* — **in·ap·pre·cia·tive·ness** *n*

in·ap·proach·able \ˌin-ə-'prō-chə-bəl\ *adj* : not approachable : INACCESSIBLE

in·ap·pro·pri·ate \ˌin-ə-'prō-prē-ət\ *adj* : not appropriate : UNSUITABLE — **in·ap·pro·pri·ate·ly** *adv* — **in·ap·pro·pri·ate·ness** *n*

in·apt \(')in-'apt\ *adj* : not apt: **a** : not suitable **b** : INEPT — **in·ap·ti·tude** \-'ap-tə-ˌt(y)üd\ *n* — **in·apt·ly** \-'ap-(t)lē\ *adv* — **in·apt·ness** \-'ap(t)-nəs\ *n*

in·ar·tic·u·late \ˌin-(ˌ)är-'tik-yə-lət\ *adj* [LL *inarticulatus*, fr. L *in-* + *articulatus*, pp. of *articulare* to utter distinctly — more at ARTICULATE] **1 a** *of a sound* : uttered or formed without the definite articulations of intelligible speech **b** (1) : incapable of speech esp. under stress of emotion : MUTE (2) : incapable of being expressed by speech (3) : UNSPOKEN **2** : incapable of giving coherent, clear, or effective expression to one's ideas or feelings **3** [NL *inarticulatus*, fr. L *in-* + NL *articulatus* articulate] **a** : having no distinct body segments **b** : lacking a hinge — used esp. of a brachiopod shell — **in·ar·tic·u·late·ly** *adv* — **in·ar·tic·u·late·ness** *n*

in·ar·tis·tic \ˌin-(ˌ)är-'tis-tik\ *adj* : not artistic — **in·ar·tis·ti·cal·ly** \-ti-k(ə-)lē\ *adv*

in·as·much as \ˌin-əz-ˌməch-əz\ *conj* **1** : in the degree that **2** : in view of the fact that : SINCE

in·at·ten·tion \ˌin-ə-'ten-chən\ *n* : failure to pay attention : DISREGARD

in·at·ten·tive \-'tent-iv\ *adj* : not attentive — **in·at·ten·tive·ly** *adv* — **in·at·ten·tive·ness** *n*

in·au·di·bil·i·ty \(ˌ)in-ˌȯd-ə-'bil-ət-ē\ *n* : the quality or state of being inaudible

in·au·di·ble \(')in-'ȯd-ə-bəl\ *adj* [LL *inaudibilis*, fr. L *in-* + LL *audibilis* audible] : not audible — **in·au·di·bly** \-blē\ *adv*

1**in·au·gu·ral** \in-'ȯ-gyə-rəl, -g(ə-)rəl\ *adj* **1** : of or relating to an inauguration **2** : marking a beginning : first in a projected series

2**inaugural** *n* **1** : an inaugural address **2** : INAUGURATION

in·au·gu·rate \in-'ȯ-g(y)ə-ˌrāt\ *vt* [L *inauguratus*, pp. of *inaugurare*, lit., to practice augury, fr. *in-* + *augurare* to augur; fr. the rites connected with augury] **1** : to induct into an office with suitable ceremonies **2 a** : to dedicate ceremoniously : observe formally the beginning of **b** : to bring about the beginning of **syn** see BEGIN — **in·au·gu·ra·tion** \-ˌȯ-g(y)ə-'rā-shən\ *n* — **in·au·gu·ra·tor** \-'ȯ-g(y)ə-ˌrāt-ər\ *n*

Inauguration Day *n* : January 20 following a presidential election on which the president of the U.S. is inaugurated

in·aus·pi·cious \ˌin-(ˌ)ȯ-'spish-əs\ *adj* : not auspicious — **in·aus·pi·cious·ly** *adv* — **in·aus·pi·cious·ness** *n*

in·board \'in-ˌbō(ə)rd, -ˌbȯ(ə)rd\ *adv* **1** : inside the line of a ship's bulwarks or hull : toward the center line of a ship **2** : toward the inside **3** : in a position closer or closest to the longitudinal axis of an aircraft — **inboard** *adj*

in·born \'in-'bȯ(ə)rn\ *adj* **1** : born in or with one : NATURAL **2** : INHERITED, HEREDITARY **syn** see INNATE

in·bound \'in-ˌbaund\ *adj* : inward bound

in·breathe \'in-'brēth\ *vt* : to breathe (something) in : INHALE

in·bred \'in-'bred\ *adj* **1 a** : INCULCATED **b** : produced by selective breeding **2** [fr. pp. of *inbreed*] : subjected to or produced by inbreeding **syn** see INNATE

in·breed \'in-'brēd\ *vt* : to subject to inbreeding

in·breed·ing \'in-ˌbrēd-iŋ\ *n* **1** : the interbreeding of closely related individuals esp. to preserve and fix desirable characters of and to eliminate unfavorable characters from a stock **2** : confinement to a narrow range or a local or limited field of choice

In·ca \'iŋ-kə\ *n* [Sp, fr. Quechua *inka* male of royal blood] **1** : a noble or a member of the ruling family of the Incaic Empire **2** : an Indian of a Quechuan people or group of peoples of the highlands of Peru maintaining an empire until the Spanish conquest — **In·ca·ic** \iŋ-'kā-ik, in-\ *adj* — **In·can** \'iŋ-kən\ *adj*

in·cal·cu·la·bil·i·ty \(ˌ)in-ˌkal-kyə-lə-'bil-ət-ē\ *n* : the quality or state of being incalculable

in·cal·cu·la·ble \(')in-'kal-kyə-lə-bəl\ *adj* : not capable of being calculated: as **a** : very great **b** : UNPREDICTABLE, UNCERTAIN — **in·cal·cu·la·bly** \-blē\ *adv*

in·ca·les·cence \ˌin-kə-'les-ᵊn(t)s, ˌiŋ-\ *n* [L *incalescere* to become warm, fr. *in-* + *calescere* to become warm, fr. *calēre* to be warm — more at LEE] : a growing warm or ardent — **in·ca·les·cent** \-ᵊnt\ *adj*

in·can·desce \ˌin-kən-'des\ *vb* [L *incandescere*] *vi* : to be or become incandescent ~ *vt* : to cause to become incandescent

in·can·des·cence \ˌin-kən-'des-ᵊn(t)s\ *n* : emission by a hot body of radiation that makes it visible

in·can·des·cent \-ᵊnt\ *adj* [prob. fr. F, fr. L *incandescent-*, *incandescens*, prp. of *incandescere* to become hot, fr. *in-* + *candescere* to become hot, fr. *candēre* to glow — more at CANDID] **1 a** : white, glowing, or luminous with intense heat **b** : strikingly bright, radiant, or clear **c** : BRILLIANT **2 a** : of, relating to, or being light produced by incandescence **b** : producing light by incandescence — **in·can·des·cent·ly** *adv*

incandescent lamp *n* : an electric lamp in which a filament gives off light when heated to incandescence by an electric current

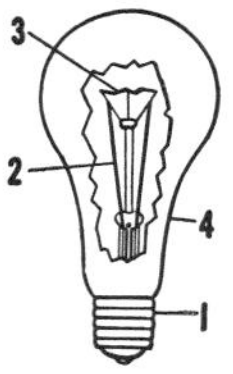

incandescent lamp: *1* base, *2* lead-in wire, *3* filament, *4* bulb

in·can·ta·tion \ˌin-ˌkan-'tā-shən\ *n* [ME *incantacioun*, fr. MF *incantation*, fr. LL *incantation-*, *incantatio*, fr. L *incantatus*, pp. of *incantare* to enchant] : a use of spells or verbal charms spoken or sung as a part of a ritual of magic; *also* : a formula of words chanted or recited in or as if in such a ritual — **in·can·ta·tion·al** \-shnəl, -shən-ᵊl\ *adj* — **in·can·ta·to·ry** \in-'kant-ə-ˌtōr-ē, -ˌtȯr-\ *adj*

in·ca·pa·bil·i·ty \(ˌ)in-ˌkā-pə-'bil-ət-ē\ *n* : the quality or state of being incapable

in·ca·pa·ble \(')in-'kā-pə-bəl\ *adj* [MF, fr. *in-* + *capable*] **1** : lacking capacity, ability, or qualification for the purpose or end in view: as **a** *obs* : not able to take in, hold, or keep **b** *obs* : INTOLERANT **c** *archaic* : not receptive **d** : not in a state or of a kind to admit : INSUSCEPTIBLE **e** : not able or fit for the doing or performance : INCOMPETENT **2** : lacking legal qualification or power : DISQUALIFIED — **in·ca·pa·ble·ness** *n* — **in·ca·pa·bly** \-blē\ *adv*

in·ca·pac·i·tate \ˌin-kə-'pas-ə-ˌtāt\ *vt* **1** : to deprive of capacity or natural power : DISABLE **2** : to make legally incapable or ineligible — **in·ca·pac·i·ta·tion** \-ˌpas-ə-'tā-shən\ *n*

in·ca·pac·i·ty \ˌin-kə-'pas-ət-ē\ *n* [F *incapacité*, fr. MF, fr. *in-* + *capacité* capacity] : the quality or state of being incapable

in·car·cer·ate \in-'kär-sə-ˌrāt\ *vt* [L *incarceratus*, pp. of *incarcerare*, fr. *in-* + *carcer* prison] **1** : to put in prison **2** : CONFINE — **in·car·cer·a·tion** \(ˌ)in-ˌkär-sə-'rā-shən\ *n*

1**in·car·na·dine** \in-'kär-nə-ˌdīn, -ˌdēn, -nəd-ən\ *adj* [MF *incarnadin*, fr. OIt *incarnadino*, fr. *incarnato* flesh-colored, fr. LL *incarnatus*] **1** : of the color flesh **2** : RED; *esp* : BLOODRED

2**incarnadine** *vt* : to make incarnadine : REDDEN

1**in·car·nate** \in-'kär-nət, -ˌnāt\ *adj* [ME *incarnat*, fr. LL *incarnatus*, pp. of *incarnare* to incarnate, fr. L *in-* + *carn-*, *caro* flesh — more at CARNAL] **1 a** : invested with bodily esp. human nature and form **b** : EMBODIED, PERSONIFIED ⟨a fiend ~⟩ **2** : INCARNADINE ⟨~ clover⟩

2**in·car·nate** \-ˌnāt\ *vt* : to make incarnate: as **a** : to give bodily form and substance to **b** : to give a concrete or actual form to : REALIZE, ACTUALIZE **c** : to constitute an embodiment or type of

in·car·na·tion \ˌin-ˌkär-'nā-shən\ *n* **1** : the act of incarnating : the state of being incarnate **2 a** (1) : the embodiment of a deity or spirit in some earthly form (2) *cap* : the union of divinity with humanity in Jesus Christ **b** : a concrete or actual form of a quality or concept; *esp* : a person showing a trait or typical character to a marked degree

incase *var of* ENCASE

in·cau·tion \(')in-'kȯ-shən\ *n* : lack of caution : HEEDLESSNESS

in·cau·tious \-shəs\ *adj* : lacking in caution : HEEDLESS, CARELESS — **in·cau·tious·ly** *adv* — **in·cau·tious·ness** *n*

in·cen·di·a·rism \in-'sen-dē-ə-ˌriz-əm\ *n* : incendiary action or behavior

1**in·cen·di·ary** \in-'sen-dē-ˌer-ē\ *n* [L *incendiarius*, fr. *incendium* conflagration, fr. *incendere*] **1 a** : a person who deliberately sets fire to a building or other property **b** : an incendiary agent (as a bomb) **2** : a person who excites factions, quarrels, or sedition : AGITATOR

2**incendiary** *adj* **1** : of, relating to, or involving a deliberate burning of property **2** : tending to excite or inflame : INFLAMMATORY **3 a** : igniting combustible materials spontaneously **b** : relating to, being, or involving the use of a missile containing chemicals that ignite on bursting or on contact

1**in·cense** \'in-ˌsen(t)s\ *n* [ME *encens*, fr. OF, fr. LL *incensum*, fr. L, neut. of *incensus*, pp. of *incendere* to set on fire, fr. *in-* + *-cendere* to burn; akin to L *candēre* to glow — more at CANDID] **1** : material used to produce a fragrant odor when burned **2** : the perfume exhaled from some spices and gums when burned; *broadly* : a pleasing scent **3** : pleasing attention : FLATTERY **syn** see FRAGRANCE

2**incense** *vt* **1** : to apply or offer incense to **2** : to perfume with incense

3**in·cense** \in-'sen(t)s\ *vt* [ME *encensen*, fr. MF *incenser*, fr. L *incensus*] **1** *obs* : to inflame with a passion or emotion **2** : to arouse the extreme anger or indignation of

in·cen·tive \in-'sent-iv\ *n* [ME, fr. LL *incentivum*, fr. neut. of *incentivus* stimulating, fr. L, setting the tune, fr. *incentus*, pp. of *incinere* to set the tune, fr. *in-* + *canere* to sing — more at CHANT] : something that incites or has a tendency to incite to determination or action **syn** see MOTIVE — **incentive** *adj*

in·cept \in-'sept\ *vi* [L *inceptus*, pp. of *incipere* to begin, fr. *in-* +

capere to take — more at HEAVE] **:** to enter upon a career — **in·cep·tor** \-'sep-tər\ *n*
in·cep·tion \in-'sep-shən\ *n* **:** an act, process, or instance of beginning or incepting **:** COMMENCEMENT **syn** see ORIGIN
1**in·cep·tive** \in-'sep-tiv\ *n* **:** INCHOATIVE
2**inceptive** *adj* **1 :** BEGINNING **2 :** INCHOATIVE 2 — **in·cep·tive·ly** *adv*
in·cer·ti·tude \(')in-'sərt-ə-,t(y)üd\ *n* [MF, fr. LL *incertitudo*, fr. L *in-* + LL *certitudo* certitude] **:** UNCERTAINTY: **a :** absence of assurance or confidence **:** DOUBT **b :** INSECURITY, INSTABILITY
in·ces·sant \(')in-'ses-ᵊnt\ *adj* [ME *incessaunt*, fr. LL *incessant-, incessans*, fr. L *in-* + *cessant-, cessans*, prp. of *cessare* to delay — more at CEASE] **:** continuing or following without interruption **:** UNCEASING **syn** see CONTINUAL — **in·ces·sant·ly** *adv*
in·cest \'in-,sest\ *n* [ME, fr. L *incestum* & *incestus; incestum* fr. neut. of *incestus*, fr. *incestus* impure, fr. *in-* + *castus* pure — more at CASTE] **:** sexual intercourse between persons so closely related that they are forbidden by law to marry; *also* **:** the statutory crime of such a relationship
in·ces·tu·ous \in-'ses(h)-chə-wəs\ *adj* **1 :** constituting or involving incest **2 :** guilty of incest — **in·ces·tu·ous·ly** *adv* — **in·ces·tu·ous·ness** *n*
1**inch** \'inch\ *n* [ME, fr. OE *ynce*, fr. L *uncia* — more at OUNCE] **1 :** a unit of length equal to 1/36 yard — see MEASURE table **2 :** a small amount, distance, or degree **3** *pl* **:** STATURE, HEIGHT **4 a :** a fall (as of rain or snow) sufficient to cover a surface or to fill a gauge to the depth of one inch **b :** a degree of atmospheric or other pressure sufficient to balance the weight of a column of liquid (as mercury) one inch high in a barometer or manometer **c :** WATER-INCH
2**inch** *vb* **:** to move by small degrees
3**inch** *n* [ME, fr. ScGael *innis*] *chiefly Scot* **:** ISLAND
inched \'incht\ *adj* **:** measuring a specified number of inches
inch·meal \'inch-,mēl\ *adv* [1*inch* + *-meal* (as in *piecemeal*)] **:** little by little **:** GRADUALLY
in·cho·ate \in-'kō-ət, 'in-kə-,wāt\ *adj* [L *inchoatus*, pp. of *inchoare*, lit., to hitch up, fr. *in-* + *cohum* strap fastening a plow beam to the yoke] **:** being recently begun **:** being only partly in existence or operation **:** imperfectly formed **:** INCIPIENT — **in·cho·ate·ly** *adv* — **in·cho·ate·ness** *n*
in·cho·ative \in-'kō-ət-iv\ *adj* **1 :** INITIAL, FORMATIVE **2 :** denoting the beginning of an action, state, or occurrence — used of verbs — **inchoative** *n* — **in·cho·ative·ly** *adv*
inch·worm \'inch-,wərm\ *n* **:** LOOPER 1
in·ci·dence \'in(t)-səd-ən(t)s, -sə-,den(t)s\ *n* **1 a :** an act or the fact or manner of falling upon or affecting **:** OCCURRENCE **b :** rate of occurrence or influence **2 a :** the arrival of something (as a projectile or a ray of light) at a surface **b :** ANGLE OF INCIDENCE
1**in·ci·dent** \'in(t)-səd-ənt, -sə-,dent\ *n* [ME, fr. MF, fr. ML *incident-, incidens*, fr. L, prp. of *incidere* to fall into, fr. *in-* + *cadere* to fall — more at CHANCE] **1 a :** an occurrence of an action or situation that is a separate unit of experience **:** HAPPENING **b :** an accompanying minor occurrence or condition **:** CONCOMITANT **2 :** an action likely to lead to grave consequences esp. in matters diplomatic **3 :** something dependent on or subordinate to something else of greater or principal importance **syn** see OCCURRENCE
2**incident** *adj* **1 :** occurring or likely to occur esp. as a minor consequence or accompaniment **2** *archaic* **:** occurring accidentally **:** INCIDENTAL **3 :** dependent on or relating to another thing **4 :** falling or striking on ⟨~ light rays⟩
1**in·ci·den·tal** \,in(t)-sə-'dent-ᵊl\ *adj* **1 a :** occurring merely by chance or without intention or calculation **b :** occurring as a minor concomitant **2 :** being likely to ensue as a chance or minor consequence **syn** see ACCIDENTAL — **in·ci·den·tal·ly** \-'dent-lē, -ᵊl-ē\ *adv*
2**incidental** *n* **1 :** something that is incidental **2** *pl* **:** minor items (as of expense) that are not particularized
in·cin·er·ate \in-'sin-ə-,rāt\ *vt* [ML *incineratus*, pp. of *incinerare*, fr. L *in-* + *ciner-, cinis* ashes; akin to Gk *konis* dust, ashes] **:** to cause to burn to ashes — **in·cin·er·a·tion** \(,)in-,sin-ə-'rā-shən\ *n*
in·cin·er·a·tor \in-'sin-ə-,rāt-ər\ *n* **:** one that incinerates; *esp* **:** a furnace or a container for incinerating waste materials
in·cip·i·en·cy \in-'sip-ē-ən-sē\ *also* **in·cip·i·ence** \-ən(t)s\ *n* **:** the state or fact of being incipient **:** BEGINNING
in·cip·i·ent \-ənt\ *adj* [L *incipient-, incipiens*, prp. of *incipere* to begin — more at INCEPT] **:** beginning to be or to be apparent **:** COMMENCING — **in·cip·i·ent·ly** *adv*
in·ci·pit \'in(t)-sə-pət, 'iŋ-kə-\ *n* [L, it begins, fr. *incipere*] **:** BEGINNING; *specif* **:** the opening words of a text of a medieval manuscript or early printed book
incircumspect *adj* [LL *incircumspectus*, fr. L *in-* + *circumspectus* circumspect] *obs* **:** IMPRUDENT, INDISCREET — **incircumspection** *n*, *obs* — **incircumspectly** *adv*, *obs*
in·cise \in-'sīz\ *vt* [MF or L; MF *inciser*, fr. L *incisus*, pp. of *incidere*, fr. *in-* + *caedere* to cut — more at CONCISE] **1 :** to cut into **2 a :** to carve figures, letters, or devices into **:** ENGRAVE **b :** to carve (as an inscription) into a surface
in·cised *adj* **1 a :** cut in **:** ENGRAVED; *esp* **:** decorated with incised figures **b** *of a wound* **:** made or as if made with a sharp knife **2 :** having a margin that is deeply and sharply notched ⟨an ~ leaf⟩
in·ci·sion \in-'sizh-ən\ *n* **1 a :** a marginal notch (as in a leaf) **b :** CUT, GASH; *specif* **:** an incised wound made esp. surgically into the body **2 :** an act of incising **3 :** INCISIVENESS
in·ci·sive \in-'sī-siv\ *adj* **1 :** CUTTING, PENETRATING **2 :** ACUTE, CLEAR-CUT — **in·ci·sive·ly** *adv* — **in·ci·sive·ness** *n*
syn TRENCHANT, CLEAR-CUT, CUTTING, BITING, CRISP: INCISIVE implies a power to impress the mind by directness and decisiveness; TRENCHANT implies an energetic cutting or probing deeply into a matter so as to reveal distinctions or to reach the center; CLEAR-CUT suggests the absence of any blurring, ambiguity, or uncertainty of statement or analysis; CUTTING implies a ruthless accuracy or directness wounding to the feelings; BITING adds a greater implication of harsh vehemence or ironic force; CRISP suggests both incisiveness and vigorous terseness
in·ci·sor \in-'sī-zər\ *n*, *often attrib* **:** a tooth adapted for cutting; *esp* **:** one of the cutting teeth in mammals in front of the canines
in·ci·ta·tion \,in-,sī-'tā-shən, ,in(t)-sə-\ *n* **1 :** an act of inciting **:** STIMULATION **2 :** INCITEMENT, INCENTIVE

in·cite \in-'sīt\ *vt* [MF *inciter*, fr. L *incitare*, fr. *in-* + *citare* to put in motion — more at CITE] **:** to move to action **:** stir up **:** spur on **:** urge on — **in·cite·ment** \-mənt\ *n* — **in·cit·er** *n*
syn INSTIGATE, ABET, FOMENT: INCITE stresses a stirring up and urging on, and may or may not imply initiating; INSTIGATE definitely implies responsibility for initiating another's action and often connotes underhandedness or evil intention; ABET implies both assisting and encouraging; FOMENT implies persistence in goading but usu. does not imply initiating
in·ci·vil·i·ty \,in(t)-sə-'vil-ət-ē\ *n* [MF *incivilité*, fr. LL *incivilitat-, incivilitas*, fr. *incivilis*, fr. L *in-* + *civilis* civil] **1 :** the quality or state of being uncivil **2 :** a rude or discourteous act
in·clem·en·cy \(')in-'klem-ən-sē\ *n* **:** the quality or state of being inclement
in·clem·ent \(')in-'klem-ənt\ *adj* [L *inclement-, inclemens*, fr. *in-* + *clement-, clemens* clement] **:** lacking clemency: as **a :** physically severe **:** STORMY ⟨~ weather⟩ **b :** severe in temper or action **:** UNMERCIFUL — **in·clem·ent·ly** *adv*
in·clin·able \in-'klī-nə-bəl\ *adj* **:** having a tendency or inclination **:** DISPOSED; *also* **:** FAVORABLE
in·cli·na·tion \,in-klə-'nā-shən, ,iŋ-\ *n* **1 :** an act or the action of bending or inclining: as **a :** BOW, NOD **b :** a tilting of something **2 a** *obs* **:** natural disposition **:** CHARACTER **b :** PROPENSITY, BENT; *esp* **:** LIKING **3 a :** a deviation from the true vertical or horizontal **:** SLANT; *also* **:** the degree of such deviation **b :** an inclined surface **:** SLOPE **c** (1) **:** the angle determined by two lines or planes (2) **:** the angle made by a line with the x-axis measured counterclockwise from the positive direction of that axis **4 :** a tendency to a particular aspect, state, character, or action — **in·cli·na·tion·al** \-shnəl, -shən-ᵊl\ *adj*
1**in·cline** \in-'klīn\ *vb* [ME *inclinen*, fr. MF *incliner*, fr. L *inclinare*, fr. *in-* + *clinare* to lean — more at LEAN] *vi* **1 :** to bend the head or body forward **:** BOW **2 :** to lean, tend, or become drawn toward an opinion or course of conduct **3 :** to deviate from a line, direction, or course **:** LEAN; *specif* **:** to deviate from the vertical or horizontal ~ *vt* **1 :** to cause to stoop or bow **:** BEND **2 :** to have influence on **:** PERSUADE **3 :** to give a bend or slant to — **in·clin·er** *n*
syn INCLINE, BIAS, DISPOSE, PREDISPOSE mean to influence one to have or take an attitude toward something. INCLINE implies a tendency to favor one of two alternative actions or conclusions; BIAS suggests a settled and predictable leaning in one direction and connotes unfair prejudice; DISPOSE suggests an affecting of one's mood or temper so as to incline one toward something; PREDISPOSE implies the operation of a disposing influence well in advance of the opportunity to reveal itself
2**in·cline** \'in-,klīn\ *n* **:** an inclined plane **:** GRADE, SLOPE
in·clined \in-'klīnd, *2 also* 'in-,\ *adj* **1 :** having inclination, disposition, or tendency **2 a :** having a leaning or slope **b :** making an angle with a line or plane
inclined plane *n* **:** a plane surface that makes an oblique angle with the plane of the horizon
in·clin·ing \in-'klī-niŋ\ *n* **1 :** INCLINATION **2** *archaic* **:** PARTY, FOLLOWING
in·cli·nom·e·ter \,in-klə-'näm-ət-ər, ,iŋ-\ *n* **1 :** an apparatus for determining the direction of the earth's magnetic field with reference to the plane of the horizon **2 :** a machinist's clinometer **3 :** an instrument for indicating the inclination to the horizontal of an axis of a ship or an airplane

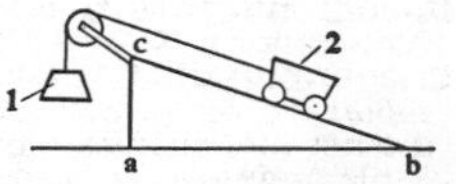

inclined plane: *ab* base, *ac* height, *cb* inclined plane, *1* force, *2* resistance

in·clip \in-'klip\ *vt*, *archaic* **:** CLASP, ENCLOSE
inclose, inclosure *var of* ENCLOSE, ENCLOSURE
in·clud·able *or* **in·clud·ible** \in-'klüd-ə-bəl\ *adj* **:** capable of being included
in·clude \in-'klüd\ *vt* [ME *includen*, fr. L *includere*, fr. *in-* + *claudere* to close — more at CLOSE] **1 :** to shut up **:** ENCLOSE **2 :** to take in or comprise as a part of a larger aggregate or principle
syn INCLUDE, COMPREHEND, EMBRACE, INVOLVE, IMPLY mean to contain within as part of the whole. INCLUDE suggests the containment of something as a constituent, component, or subordinate part of a larger whole; COMPREHEND implies that something comes within the range or scope of a statement or definition whether clearly mentioned or not; EMBRACE implies a gathering of separate items within a whole; INVOLVE suggests a rolling up or entangling in a whole as by being its consequence or a necessary element of its definition; IMPLY suggests that something can be inferred through a hint, or as a necessary cause or effect, or as something commonly associated in experience
in·clud·ed *adj* **:** ENCLOSED, EMBRACED; *specif* **:** not projecting beyond the mouth of the corolla — used of a stamen or pistil
in·clu·sion \in-'klü-zhən\ *n* [L *inclusion-, inclusio*, fr. *inclusus*, pp. of *includere*] **1 :** the act of including **:** the state of being included **2 :** something that is included: as **a :** a gaseous, liquid, or solid foreign body enclosed in the mass of a mineral **b :** a passive product of cell activity (as a starch grain) within the protoplasm
inclusion body *n* **:** a rounded or oval intracellular body that consists of elementary bodies in a matrix, is characteristic of some virus diseases, and is believed to represent a stage in the multiplication of the virus
in·clu·sive \in-'klü-siv, -ziv\ *adj* **1 :** ENCLOSING, ENCOMPASSING: as **a :** broad in orientation or scope **b :** covering or intended to cover all items, costs, or services **2 :** comprehending the stated limits or extremes — **in·clu·sive·ly** *adv* — **in·clu·sive·ness** *n*
in·co·erc·ible \,in-kō-'ər-sə-bəl\ *adj* **:** incapable of being controlled, checked, or confined
in·cog·i·tant \in-'käj-ət-ənt\ *adj* [L *incogitant-, incogitans*, fr. *in-* + *cogitant-, cogitans*, prp. of *cogitare* to cogitate] **:** THOUGHTLESS, INCONSIDERATE
in·cog·ni·ta \,in-,käg-'nēt-ə, in-'käg-nət-ə\ *adv* (*or adj*) [It, fem. of *incognito*] **:** INCOGNITO — used only of a woman — **incognita** *n*
1**in·cog·ni·to** \,in-,käg-'nēt-(,)ō, in-'käg-nə-,tō\ *adv* (*or adj*) [It, fr. L *incognitus* unknown, fr. *in-* + *cognitus*, pp. of *cognoscere* to know — more at COGNITION] **:** with one's identity concealed; *esp* **:** in a capacity other than one's official capacity or under a name or title not calling for special recognition
2**incognito** *n* **1 :** one appearing or living incognito **2 :** the state or disguise of an incognito or incognita

in·cog·ni·zant \'in-'käg-nə-zənt\ *adj* **:** lacking awareness or consciousness

in·co·her·ence \,in-kō-'hir-ən(t)s, -'her\ *n* **1 :** the quality or state of being incoherent **2 :** something that is incoherent

in·co·her·ent \-'hir-ənt, -'her-\ *adj* **:** lacking coherence: as **a :** lacking cohesion **:** LOOSE **b :** lacking orderly continuity or relevance **:** INCONSISTENT — **in·co·her·ent·ly** *adv*

in·com·bus·ti·ble \,in-kəm-'bəs-tə-bəl\ *adj or n* [ME, prob. fr. MF, fr. *in-* + *combustible*] **:** NONCOMBUSTIBLE

in·come \'in-,kəm\ *n, often attrib* **1** *archaic* **:** ENTRANCE, INFLUX **2 :** a gain or recurrent benefit usu. measured in money that derives from capital or labor; *also* **:** the amount of such gain received by an individual in a given period of time

income account *n* **:** a financial statement of a business showing the details of revenues, costs, expenses, losses, and profits for a given period — called also *income statement*

income tax \,in-(,)kəm-\ *n* **:** a tax on the net income of an individual or business concern

[1]**in·com·ing** \'in-,kəm-iŋ\ *n* **1 :** the act of coming in **:** ARRIVAL **2 :** INCOME — usu. used in pl.

[2]**incoming** *adj* **:** coming in: as **a :** taking a new place or position **b :** ACCRUING **c :** BEGINNING

in·com·men·su·ra·bil·i·ty \,in-kə-,men(t)s-(ə-)rə-'bil-ət-ē, -,mench-(ə-)rə-\ *n* **:** the quality or state of being incommensurable

in·com·men·su·ra·ble \,in-kə-'men(t)s-(ə-)rə-bəl, -'mench-(ə-)rə-\ *adj* **:** not commensurable; *broadly* **:** lacking a common basis of comparison in respect to a quality normally subject to comparison — **incommensurable** *n* — **in·com·men·su·ra·bly** \-blē\ *adv*

in·com·men·su·rate \-(ə-)rət\ *adj* **:** not commensurate: as **a :** INCOMMENSURABLE **b :** INADEQUATE **c :** DISPROPORTIONATE

in·com·mode \,in-kə-'mōd\ *vt* [MF *incommoder*, fr. L *incommodare*, fr. *incommodus* inconvenient, fr. *in-* + *commodus* convenient — more at COMMODE] **:** to give inconvenience or distress to **:** DISTURB

in·com·mo·di·ous \,in-kə-'mōd-ē-əs\ *adj* **:** not commodious **:** INCONVENIENT — **in·com·mo·di·ous·ly** *adv* — **in·com·mo·di·ous·ness** *n*

in·com·mod·i·ty \-'mäd-ət-ē\ *n* **:** INCONVENIENCE, DISADVANTAGE

in·com·mu·ni·ca·bil·i·ty \,in-kə-,myü-ni-kə-'bil-ət-ē\ *n* **:** the quality or state of being incommunicable

in·com·mu·ni·ca·ble \,in-kə-'myü-ni-kə-bəl\ *adj* [MF or LL; MF, fr. LL *incommunicabilis*, fr. L *in-* + LL *communicabilis* communicable] **:** not communicable: as **a :** incapable of being communicated or imparted **b :** UNCOMMUNICATIVE — **in·com·mu·ni·ca·bly** \-blē\ *adv*

in·com·mu·ni·ca·do \,in-kə-,myü-nə-'käd-(,)ō\ *adv (or adj)* [Sp *incomunicado*, fr. pp. of *incomunicar* to deprive of communication, fr. *in-* (fr. L) + *comunicar* to communicate, fr. L *communicare*] **:** without means of communication; *also* **:** in solitary confinement

in·com·mu·ni·ca·tive \,in-kə-'myü-nə-,kāt-iv, -ni-kət-\ *adj* **:** UNCOMMUNICATIVE

in·com·mut·able \,in-kə-'myüt-ə-bəl\ *adj* [ME, fr. L *incommutabilis*, fr. *in-* + *commutabilis* commutable] **:** not commutable: as **a :** not interchangeable **b :** UNCHANGEABLE — **in·com·mut·ably** \-blē\ *adv*

in·com·pa·ra·bil·i·ty \(,)in-,käm-p(ə-)rə-'bil-ət-ē\ *n* **:** the quality or state of being incomparable

in·com·pa·ra·ble \(')in-'käm-p(ə-)rə-bəl\ *adj* [ME, fr. MF, fr. L *incomparabilis*, fr. *in-* + *comparabilis* comparable] **1 :** eminent beyond comparison **:** MATCHLESS **2 :** not suitable for comparison — **in·com·pa·ra·bly** \-blē\ *adv*

in·com·pat·i·bil·i·ty \,in-kəm-,pat-ə-'bil-ət-ē\ *n* **1 :** the quality or state of being incompatible **2 :** lack of interfertility between two plants **3** *pl* **:** mutually antagonistic things or qualities

in·com·pat·i·ble \,in-kəm-'pat-ə-bəl\ *adj* [MF & ML; MF, fr. ML *incompatibilis*, fr. L *in-* + ML *compatibilis* compatible] **1 :** incapable of being held by one person at one time **2 a :** incapable of association because incongruous, discordant, or disagreeing ⟨~ colors⟩ **b :** unsuitable for use together because of undesirable chemical or physiological effects ⟨~ drugs⟩ **c :** not both true ⟨~ propositions⟩ **d :** not satisfiable by the same set of values for the unknowns ⟨~ equations⟩ **e :** incapable of blending into a stable homogeneous mixture — used of solids or solutions — **incompatible** *n* — **in·com·pat·i·bly** \-blē\ *adv*

in·com·pe·tence \(')in-'käm-pət-ən(t)s\ *also* **in·com·pe·ten·cy** \-ən-sē\ *n* **:** the state or fact of being incompetent

in·com·pe·tent \(')in-'käm-pət-ənt\ *adj* [MF *incompétent*, fr. *in-* + *compétent* competent] **1 :** lacking the qualities necessary to effective independent action **2 :** not legally qualified **3 :** inadequate to or unsuitable for a particular purpose expressed or implied — **incompetent** *n* — **in·com·pe·tent·ly** *adv*

in·com·plete \,in-kəm-'plēt\ *adj* [ME *incompleet*, fr. LL *incompletus*, fr. L *in-* + *completus* complete] **:** lacking a part: as **a :** lacking one or more sets of floral organs **b** *of a football pass* **:** not legally caught — **in·com·plete·ly** *adv* — **in·com·plete·ness** *n*

in·com·pli·ant \,in-kəm-'plī-ənt\ *adj* **:** not compliant or pliable **:** UNYIELDING

in·com·pre·hen·si·bil·i·ty \(,)in-,käm-pri-,hen(t)-sə-'bil-ət-ē\ *n* **:** the quality or state of being incomprehensible

in·com·pre·hen·si·ble \-'hen(t)-sə-bəl\ *adj* [ME, fr. L *incomprehensibilis*, fr. *in-* + *comprehensibilis* comprehensible] **1** *archaic* **:** having or subject to no limits **2 :** impossible to comprehend: **a :** UNINTELLIGIBLE **b :** UNFATHOMABLE — **in·com·pre·hen·si·ble·ness** *n* — **in·com·pre·hen·si·bly** \-blē\ *adv*

in·com·pre·hen·sion \-'hen-chən\ *n* **:** lack of comprehension or understanding

in·com·press·ibil·i·ty \,in-kəm-,pres-ə-'bil-ət-ē\ *n* **:** the quality or state of being incompressible

in·com·press·ible \-'pres-ə-bəl\ *adj* **:** incapable of or resistant to compression — **in·com·press·ibly** \-blē\ *adv*

in·com·put·able \,in-kəm-'pyüt-ə-bəl\ *adj* **:** not computable **:** very great — **in·com·put·ably** \-blē\ *adv*

in·con·ceiv·abil·i·ty \,in-kən-,sē-və-'bil-ət-ē\ *n* **:** the quality or state of being inconceivable

in·con·ceiv·able \,in-kən-'sē-və-bəl\ *adj* **:** not conceivable: as **a :** UNIMAGINABLE **b :** UNTHINKABLE **c :** UNBELIEVABLE — **in·con·ceiv·able·ness** *n* — **in·con·ceiv·ably** \-blē\ *adv*

in·con·cin·ni·ty \,in-kən-'sin-ət-ē\ *n* [L *inconcinnitas*, fr. *in-* + *concinnitas* concinnity] **:** lack of suitability or congruity **:** INELEGANCE

in·con·clu·sive \,in-kən-'klü-siv, -ziv\ *adj* **:** leading to no conclusion or definite result — **in·con·clu·sive·ly** *adv* — **in·con·clu·sive·ness** *n*

in·con·dens·able \,in-kən-'den(t)-sə-bəl\ *adj* **:** incapable of being condensed

in·con·dite \in-'kän-dət, -,dīt\ *adj* [L *inconditus*, fr. *in-* + *conditus*, pp. of *condere* to put together, fr. *com-* + *-dere* to put — more at DO] **:** badly put together **:** CRUDE

in·con·for·mi·ty \,in-kən-'fȯr-mət-ē\ *n* **:** NONCONFORMITY

in·con·gru·ence \,in-kən-'grü-ən(t)s, (')in-'käŋ-grə-wən(t)s\ *n* **:** INCONGRUITY

in·con·gru·ent \-ənt, -wənt\ *adj* [L *incongruent-*, *incongruens*, fr. *in-* + *congruent-*, *congruens* congruent] **:** not congruent ⟨~ triangles⟩ — **in·con·gru·ent·ly** *adv*

in·con·gru·ity \,in-kən-'grü-ət-ē, -,kän-\ *n* **1 :** the quality or state of being incongruous **2 :** something that is incongruous

in·con·gru·ous \(')in-'käŋ-grə-wəs\ *adj* [LL *incongruus*, fr. L *in-* + *congruus* congruous] **:** lacking congruity: as **a :** not harmonious **:** INCOMPATIBLE ⟨~ colors⟩ **b :** not conforming **:** DISAGREEING ⟨conduct ~ with avowed principles⟩ **c :** inconsistent within itself ⟨an ~ story⟩ **d :** lacking propriety **:** UNSUITABLE ⟨~ manners⟩ — **in·con·gru·ous·ly** *adv* — **in·con·gru·ous·ness** *n*

in·con·scient \(')in-'kän-chənt\ *adj* [prob. fr. F, fr. *in-* + *conscient* mindful, fr. L *conscient-*, *consciens*, prp. of *conscire* to be conscious — more at CONSCIENCE] **:** UNCONSCIOUS, MINDLESS

in·con·sec·u·tive \,in-kən-'sek-(y)ət-iv\ *adj* **:** not consecutive

in·con·se·quence \(')in-'kän(t)-sə-,kwen(t)s, -si-kwən(t)s\ *n* **:** the quality or state of being inconsequent

in·con·se·quent \-,kwent, -kwənt\ *adj* [LL *inconsequent-*, *inconsequens*, fr. L *in-* + *consequent-*, *consequens* consequent] **1 a :** lacking reasonable sequence **:** ILLOGICAL **b :** INCONSECUTIVE **2 :** IRRELEVANT **3 :** INCONSEQUENTIAL 2 — **in·con·se·quent·ly** *adv*

in·con·se·quen·tial \(,)in-,kän(t)-sə-'kwen-chəl\ *adj* **1 a :** ILLOGICAL **b :** IRRELEVANT **2 :** of no significance **:** UNIMPORTANT — **in·con·se·quen·ti·al·i·ty** \-,kwen-chē-'al-ət-ē\ *n* — **in·con·se·quen·tial·ly** \-'kwench-(ə-)lē\ *adv*

in·con·sid·er·able \,in-kən-'sid-ər-(ə-)bəl, -'sid-rə-bəl\ *adj* [MF, fr. *in-* + *considerable*, fr. ML *considerabilis* considerable] **:** not considerable **:** TRIVIAL — **in·con·sid·er·able·ness** *n* — **in·con·sid·er·ably** \-blē\ *adv*

in·con·sid·er·ate \,in-kən-'sid-(ə-)rət\ *adj* [L *inconsideratus*, fr. *in-* + *consideratus* considerate] **1 :** not adequately considered **:** ILL-ADVISED **2 a :** HEEDLESS, THOUGHTLESS **b :** failing in regard for the rights or feelings of others — **in·con·sid·er·ate·ly** *adv* — **in·con·sid·er·ate·ness** *n* — **in·con·sid·er·ation** \-,sid-ə-'rā-shən\ *n*

in·con·sis·ten·cy \,in-kən-'sis-tən-sē\ *also* **in·con·sis·tence** \-tən(t)s\ *n* **1 :** the quality or state of being inconsistent **2 :** an instance of being inconsistent

in·con·sis·tent \,in-kən-'sis-tənt\ *adj* **:** lacking consistency: as **a :** not compatible with another fact or claim ⟨~ statements⟩ **b :** containing incompatible elements ⟨an ~ argument⟩ **c :** incoherent or illogical in thought or actions **:** CHANGEABLE — **in·con·sis·tent·ly** *adv*

in·con·sol·able \,in-kən-'sō-lə-bəl\ *adj* [L *inconsolabilis*, fr. *in-* + *consolabilis* consolable] **:** incapable of being consoled **:** DISCONSOLATE — **in·con·sol·able·ness** *n* — **in·con·sol·ably** \-blē\ *adv*

in·con·so·nance \(')in-'kän(t)-s(ə-)nən(t)s\ *n* **:** lack of consonance or harmony **:** DISAGREEMENT

in·con·so·nant \-s(ə-)nənt\ *adj* **:** not consonant **:** DISCORDANT

in·con·spic·u·ous \,in-kən-'spik-yə-wəs\ *adj* [L *inconspicuus*, fr. *in-* + *conspicuus* conspicuous] **:** not readily noticeable — **in·con·spic·u·ous·ly** *adv* — **in·con·spic·u·ous·ness** *n*

in·con·stan·cy \(')in-'kän(t)-stən-sē\ *n* **:** the quality or state of being inconstant

in·con·stant \-stənt\ *adj* [ME, fr. MF, fr. L *inconstant-*, *inconstans*, fr. *in-* + *constant-*, *constans* constant] **:** likely to change frequently without apparent or cogent reason — **in·con·stant·ly** *adv*

syn FICKLE, CAPRICIOUS, MERCURIAL, UNSTABLE: INCONSTANT implies an incapacity for steadiness and an inherent tendency to change; FICKLE suggests unreliability because of perverse changeability and incapacity for steadfastness; CAPRICIOUS suggests motivation by sudden whim or fancy and stresses unpredictability; MERCURIAL implies a rapid changeability in mood esp. from depression to elation; UNSTABLE implies an incapacity for remaining in a fixed position or steady course and applies esp. to a lack of emotional balance

in·con·sum·able \,in-kən-'sü-mə-bəl\ *adj* **:** not capable of being consumed — **in·con·sum·ably** \-blē\ *adv*

in·con·test·abil·i·ty \,in-kən-,tes-tə-'bil-ət-ē\ *n* **:** the quality or state of being incontestable

in·con·test·able \-'tes-tə-bəl\ *adj* [F, fr. *in-* + *contestable*, fr. *contester* to contest] **:** not contestable **:** INDISPUTABLE — **in·con·test·ably** \-blē\ *adv*

in·con·ti·nence \(')in-'känt-ᵊn-ən(t)s\ *also* **in·con·ti·nen·cy** \-ᵊn-ən-sē\ *n* **:** the quality or state of being incontinent: as **a :** failure to restrain sexual appetite **:** UNCHASTITY **b :** inability of the body to control the evacuative functions

in·con·ti·nent \-ᵊn-ənt\ *adj* [ME, fr. MF or L; MF, fr. L *incontinent-*, *incontinens*, fr. *in-* + *continent-*, *continens* continent] **:** not continent: as **a :** lacking self-restraint **b :** unable to contain, keep, or restrain **c :** UNCONTROLLED

[1]**in·con·ti·nent·ly** *also* **incontinent** *adv* **:** without delay **:** IMMEDIATELY

[2]**incontinently** *adv* **:** in an incontinent or unrestrained manner: as **a :** LEWDLY **b :** UNCONTROLLABLY

in·con·trol·la·ble \,in-kən-'trō-lə-bəl\ *adj* **:** UNCONTROLLABLE

in·con·tro·vert·ible \(,)in-,kän-trə-'vərt-ə-bəl\ *adj* **:** not open to question **:** INDISPUTABLE ⟨~ evidence⟩ — **in·con·tro·vert·ibly** \-blē\ *adv*

[1]**in·con·ve·nience** \,in-kən-'vē-nyən(t)s\ *n* **1 :** the quality or state of being inconvenient **:** DISCOMFORT **2 :** something that is inconvenient

[2]**inconvenience** *vt* **:** to subject to inconvenience **:** INCOMMODE

in·con·ve·nien·cy \-nyən-sē\ *n* **:** INCONVENIENCE

in·con·ve·nient \,in-kən-'vē-nyənt\ *adj* [ME, fr. MF, fr. L *inconvenient-*, *inconveniens*, fr. *in-* + *convenient-*, *conveniens* convenient] **1 :** not suitable **:** UNFIT **2 :** not convenient esp. in giving trouble or annoyance **:** INOPPORTUNE — **in·con·ve·nient·ly** *adv*

in·con·vert·ibil·i·ty \ˌin-kən-ˌvərt-ə-ˈbil-ət-ē\ *n* **:** the quality or state of being inconvertible

in·con·vert·ible \-ˈvərt-ə-bəl\ *adj* [prob. fr. LL *inconvertibilis*, fr. L *in-* + *convertibilis* convertible] **:** not convertible: as **a** *of paper money* **:** not exchangeable on demand for specie **b** *of a currency* **:** not exchangeable for a foreign currency — **in·con·vert·ibly** \-blē\ *adv*

in·con·vinc·ible \ˌin-kən-ˈvin(t)-sə-bəl\ *adj* **:** incapable of being convinced

in·co·or·di·nate \ˌin-kō-ˈȯrd-nət, -ᵊn-ət, -ᵊn-ˌāt\ *also* **in·co·or·di·nat·ed** \-ˈȯrd-ᵊn-ˌāt-əd\ *adj* **:** not coordinate

in·co·or·di·na·tion \ˌin-kō-ˌȯrd-ᵊn-ˈā-shən\ *n* **:** lack of coordination esp. of muscular movements resulting from loss of voluntary control

in·cor·po·ra·ble \in-ˈkȯr-p(ə-)rə-bəl\ *adj* **:** capable of being incorporated

1**in·cor·po·rate** \in-ˈkȯr-pə-ˌrāt\ *vb* [ME *incorporaten*, fr. LL *incorporatus*, pp. of *incorporare*, fr. L *in-* + *corpor-*, *corpus* body — more at MIDRIFF] *vt* **1 a :** to unite thoroughly with or work indistinguishably into something already existent **b :** to admit to membership in a corporation **2 a :** to blend or combine thoroughly to form a consistent whole **b :** to form into a legal corporation **3 :** to give material form to **:** EMBODY ~ *vi* **1 :** to unite in or as one body **2 :** to form or become a corporation — **in·cor·po·ra·tion** \(ˌ)in-ˌkȯr-pə-ˈrā-shən\ *n* — **in·cor·po·ra·tive** \in-ˈkȯr-pə-ˌrāt-iv, -p(ə-)rət-\ *adj* — **in·cor·po·ra·tor** \-pə-ˌrāt-ər\ *n*

2**in·cor·po·rate** \in-ˈkȯr-p(ə-)rət\ *adj* **:** INCORPORATED

in·cor·po·rat·ed *adj* **1 :** united in one body **2 :** formed into a legal corporation

in·cor·po·re·al \ˌin-(ˌ)kȯr-ˈpōr-ē-əl, -ˈpȯr-\ *adj* [L *incorporeus*, fr. *in-* + *corporeus* corporeal] **1 :** not corporeal **:** having no material body or form **:** IMMATERIAL **2 :** of, relating to, or constituting a right that has no physical existence but that issues out of corporate property (as bonds or patents) — **in·cor·po·re·al·ly** \-ə-lē\ *adv*

in·cor·po·re·ity \ˌin-ˌkȯr-pə-ˈrē-ət-ē\ *n* **:** the quality or state of being incorporeal **:** IMMATERIALITY

in·cor·rect \ˌin-kə-ˈrekt\ *adj* [ME, fr. MF or L; MF, fr. L *incorrectus*, fr. *in-* + *correctus* correct] **1** *obs* **:** not corrected or chastened **2 a :** INACCURATE, FAULTY **b :** not true **:** WRONG **3 :** UNBECOMING, IMPROPER — **in·cor·rect·ly** \-ˈrek-(t)lē\ *adv* — **in·cor·rect·ness** \-ˈrek(t)-nəs\ *n*

in·cor·ri·gi·bil·i·ty \(ˌ)in-ˌkȯr-ə-jə-ˈbil-ət-ē, -ˌkär-\ *n* **:** the quality or state of being incorrigible

in·cor·ri·gi·ble \(ˈ)in-ˈkȯr-ə-jə-bəl, -ˈkär-\ *adj* [ME, fr. LL *incorrigibilis*, fr. L *in-* + *corrigere* to correct — more at CORRECT] **:** incapable of being corrected or amended: as **a** (1) **:** not reformable **:** DEPRAVED (2) **:** DELINQUENT **b** *archaic* **:** INCURABLE **c :** UNMANAGEABLE **d :** UNALTERABLE, DETERMINED — **incorrigible** *n* — **in·cor·ri·gi·ble·ness** *n* — **in·cor·ri·gi·bly** \-blē\ *adv*

in·cor·rupt \ˌin-kə-ˈrəpt\ *also* **in·cor·rupt·ed** \-ˈrəp-təd\ *adj* [ME, fr. L *incorruptus*, fr. *in-* + *corruptus* corrupt] **:** free from corruption: as **a** *obs* **:** not affected with decay **b :** not defiled or depraved **:** UPRIGHT **c :** free from error — **in·cor·rupt·ly** \-ˈrəp-(t)lē\ *adv* — **in·cor·rupt·ness** \-ˈrəp(t)-nəs\ *n*

in·cor·rupt·ibil·i·ty \ˌin-kə-ˌrəp-tə-ˈbil-ət-ē\ *n* **:** the quality or state of being incorruptible

1**in·cor·rupt·ible** \ˌin-kə-ˈrəp-tə-bəl\ *adj* **:** incapable of corruption: as **a :** not subject to decay or dissolution **b :** incapable of being bribed or morally corrupted — **in·cor·rupt·ibly** \-blē\ *adv*

2**incorruptible** *n* **:** something that is not subject to corruption; *esp* **:** something of spiritual nature

in·cor·rup·tion \ˌin-kə-ˈrəp-shən\ *n, archaic* **:** the quality or state of being free from physical decay

in·creas·able \in-ˈkrē-sə-bəl\ *adj* **:** capable of being increased

1**in·crease** \in-ˈkrēs, ˈin-ˌ\ *vb* [ME *encresen*, fr. MF *encreistre*, fr. L *increscere*, fr. *in-* + *crescere* to grow — more at CRESCENT] *vi* **1 :** to become greater **:** GROW **2 :** to multiply by the production of young ~ *vt* **1 :** to make greater **:** AUGMENT **2** *archaic* **:** ENRICH, PROMOTE — **in·creas·er** *n*

syn ENLARGE, AUGMENT, MULTIPLY: INCREASE used intransitively implies progressive growth in size, amount, intensity; used transitively it may imply simple not necessarily progressive addition; ENLARGE implies expansion or extension that makes greater in size or capacity; AUGMENT implies addition to what is already well grown or well developed; MULTIPLY implies increase in number by natural generation, or by splitting or folding, or by indefinite repetition of a process

2**in·crease** \ˈin-ˌkrēs, in-ˈ\ *n* **1 :** act of increasing: as **a :** addition or enlargement in size, extent, quantity **b** *obs* **:** PROPAGATION **2 :** something that is added to the original stock by augmentation or growth (as offspring, produce, profit)

in·creas·ing·ly \-ˈkrē-siŋ-lē, -ˌkrē-\ *adv* **:** to an increasing degree

in·cre·ate \ˌin-krē-ˈāt, in-ˈkrē-ət\ *adj* [ME *increat*, fr. LL *increatus*, fr. L *in-* + *creatus*, pp. of *creare* to create — more at CRESCENT] **:** not created — **in·cre·ate·ly** *adv*

in·cred·i·bil·i·ty \(ˌ)in-ˌkred-ə-ˈbil-ət-ē\ *n* **1 :** the quality or state of being incredible **2 :** something that is incredible

in·cred·i·ble \(ˈ)in-ˈkred-ə-bəl\ *adj* [ME, fr. L *incredibilis*, fr. *in-* + *credibilis* credible] **:** too extraordinary and improbable to admit of belief; *also* **:** hard to believe — **in·cred·i·ble·ness** *n* — **in·cred·i·bly** \-blē\ *adv*

in·cre·du·li·ty \ˌin-kri-ˈd(y)ü-lət-ē\ *n* **:** the quality or state of being incredulous **:** DISBELIEF **syn** see UNBELIEF

in·cred·u·lous \(ˈ)in-ˈkrej-ə-ləs\ *adj* [L *incredulus*, fr. *in-* + *credulus* credulous] **1 :** not credulous **:** SKEPTICAL **2 :** expressing incredulity **3** *obs* **:** INCREDIBLE — **in·cred·u·lous·ly** *adv*

in·cre·ment \ˈiŋ-krə-mənt, ˈin-\ *n* [ME, fr. L *incrementum*, fr. *increscere*] **1 :** an increase esp. in quantity or value **:** ENLARGEMENT; *also* **:** QUANTITY **2 a :** something gained or added **b :** one of a series of regular consecutive additions **c :** a minute increase in quantity **3 :** a positive or negative change in the value of one or more of a set of variables — **in·cre·men·tal** \ˌiŋ-krə-ˈment-ᵊl, ˌin-\ *adj*

in·cres·cent \in-ˈkres-ᵊnt\ *adj* [L *increscent-*, *increscens*, prp. of *increscere*] **:** INCREASING, WAXING ⟨the ~ moon⟩

in·cre·tion \in-ˈkrē-shən\ *n* [ISV *in-* + *secretion*] **:** internal secretion; *also* **:** a product of it **:** AUTACOID — **in·cre·tion·ary** \-shə-ˌner-ē\ *or* **in·cre·to·ry** \in-ˈkrēt-ə-rē\ *adj*

in·crim·i·nate \in-ˈkrim-ə-ˌnāt\ *vt* [LL *incriminatus*, pp. of *incriminare*, fr. L *in-* + *crimin-*, *crimen* crime] **:** to charge with or involve in a crime or fault — **in·crim·i·na·tion** \(ˌ)in-ˌkrim-ə-ˈnā-shən\ *n* — **in·crim·i·na·to·ry** \in-ˈkrim-(ə-)nə-ˌtōr-ē, -ˌtȯr-\ *adj*

in·cross \ˈin-ˌkrȯs\ *n* **:** an individual produced by crossing inbred lines of the same breed or strain

in·cross·bred \ˈin-ˈkrȯs-ˌbred\ *n* **:** an individual produced by crossing inbred lines of separate breeds or strains

incrust *var of* ENCRUST

in·crus·ta·tion \ˌin-ˌkrəs-ˈtā-shən\ *n* [L *incrustation-*, *incrustatio*, fr. *incrustatus*, pp. of *incrustare* to encrust] **1 :** the act of encrusting or state of being encrusted **2 a :** a crust or hard coating **b :** something resembling a crust **3 a :** OVERLAY **a b :** INLAY

in·cu·bate \ˈiŋ-kyə-ˌbāt, ˈin-\ *vb* [L *incubatus*, pp. of *incubare*, fr. *in-* + *cubare* to lie — more at HIP] *vt* **1 :** to sit upon (eggs) so as to hatch by the warmth of the body; *also* **:** to maintain (as an embryo or a chemically active system) under conditions favorable for hatching, development, or reaction **2 :** to cause to develop ~ *vi* **1 :** to sit on eggs **2 :** to undergo incubation — **in·cu·ba·tive** \-ˌbāt-iv\ *adj*

in·cu·ba·tion \ˌiŋ-kyə-ˈbā-shən, ˌin-\ *n* **1 :** the act or process of incubating **2 :** the period between the infection of an individual by a pathogen and the manifestation of the disease it causes — **in·cu·ba·tion·al** \-shnəl, -shən-ᵊl\ *adj*

in·cu·ba·tor \ˈiŋ-kyə-ˌbāt-ər, ˈin-\ *n* **:** one that incubates: as **a :** an apparatus by which eggs are hatched artificially **b :** an apparatus for the maintenance of controlled conditions esp. for the cultivation of microorganisms or the housing of premature or sick babies

in·cu·bus \ˈiŋ-kyə-bəs, ˈin-\ *n, pl* **in·cu·bi** \-ˌbī, -ˌbē\ *also* **in·cu·bus·es** [ME, fr. LL, fr. L *incubare*] **1 :** an evil spirit supposed to lie upon persons in their sleep and esp. to have sexual intercourse with women by night — compare SUCCUBUS **2 :** NIGHTMARE 2 **3 :** a person or thing that oppresses or burdens like a nightmare

in·cul·cate \in-ˈkəl-ˌkāt, ˈin-(ˌ)kəl-\ *vt* [L *inculcatus*, pp. of *inculcare*, lit., to tread on, fr. *in-* + *calcare* to trample, fr. *calc-*, *calx* heel — more at CALK] **:** to teach and impress by frequent repetitions or admonitions **syn** see IMPLANT — **in·cul·ca·tion** \ˌin-(ˌ)kəl-ˈkā-shən\ *n* — **in·cul·ca·tor** \in-ˈkəl-ˌkāt-ər, ˈin-(ˌ)kəl-\ *n*

in·cul·pa·ble \(ˈ)in-ˈkəl-pə-bəl\ *adj* **:** free from guilt **:** BLAMELESS

in·cul·pate \in-ˈkəl-ˌpāt, ˈin-(ˌ)kəl-\ *vt* [LL *inculpatus*, fr. L *in-* + *culpatus*, pp. of *culpare* to blame — more at CULPABLE] **:** INCRIMINATE — **in·cul·pa·tion** \ˌin-(ˌ)kəl-ˈpā-shən\ *n* — **in·cul·pa·to·ry** \in-ˈkəl-pə-ˌtōr-ē, -ˌtȯr-\ *adj*

in·cult \in-ˈkəlt\ *adj* [L *incultus*, fr. *in-* + *cultus*, pp. of *colere* to cultivate — more at WHEEL] **1** *archaic* **:** UNTILLED, WILD **2 :** UNCULTIVATED, UNPOLISHED

in·cum·ben·cy \in-ˈkəm-bən-sē\ *n* **1 :** the quality or state of being incumbent **2 :** something that is incumbent **3 :** the sphere of action or period of office of an incumbent

1**in·cum·bent** \in-ˈkəm-bənt\ *n* [ME, fr. L *incumbent-*, *incumbens*, prp. of *incumbere* to lie down on, fr. *in-* + *-cumbere* to lie down; akin to L *cubare* to lie — more at HIP] **:** the holder of an office or ecclesiastical benefice

2**incumbent** *adj* **1 a :** lying or resting on something else **b** *of a geologic stratum* **:** SUPERIMPOSED, OVERLYING **2 :** imposed as a duty **:** OBLIGATORY **3 :** occupying a specified office **4 a** *archaic* **:** bending over **:** OVERHANGING **b** *obs* **:** IMPENDING **c :** bent over so as to rest on or touch an underlying surface

incumber *var of* ENCUMBER

in·cu·nab·u·lum \ˌin-kyə-ˈnab-yə-ləm, ˌiŋ-\ *n, pl* **in·cu·nab·u·la** \-lə\ [NL, fr. L *incunabula*, pl., swaddling clothes, cradle, fr. *in-* + *cunae* cradle — more at CEMETERY] **:** a book printed before 1501; *also* **:** a work of art or of human industry of an early epoch

in·cur \in-ˈkər\ *vt* **in·curred; in·cur·ring** [L *incurrere*, lit., to run into, fr. *in* + *currere* to run — more at CURRENT] **1 :** to meet with (as an inconvenience) **2 :** to become liable or subject to **:** bring down upon oneself

syn INCUR, CONTRACT, CATCH mean to bring something upon oneself. INCUR may or may not imply foreknowledge but usu. implies responsibility for the act; CONTRACT implies more strongly effective acquirement but less often implies definite responsibility for the act of acquiring; CATCH is the popular term for transmitting infection and stresses involuntary acquiring through personal contact or association

in·cur·abil·i·ty \(ˌ)in-ˌkyu̇r-ə-ˈbil-ət-ē\ *n* **:** the quality or state of being incurable

in·cur·able \(ˈ)in-ˈkyu̇r-ə-bəl\ *adj* [ME, fr. MF or LL; MF, fr. LL *incurabilis*, fr. L *in-* + *curabilis* curable] **:** not curable — **incurable** *n* — **in·cur·able·ness** *n* — **in·cur·ably** \-blē\ *adv*

in·cu·ri·os·i·ty \ˌin-ˌkyu̇r-ē-ˈäs-ət-ē, -ˈäs-tē\ *n* **:** INCURIOUSNESS

in·cu·ri·ous \(ˈ)in-ˈkyu̇r-ē-əs\ *adj* [L *incuriosus*, fr. *in-* + *curiosus* curious] **:** not curious or inquisitive **:** UNINTERESTED **syn** see INDIFFERENT — **in·cu·ri·ous·ly** *adv* — **in·cu·ri·ous·ness** *n*

in·cur·rence \in-ˈkər-ən(t)s, -ˈkə-rən(t)s\ *n* **:** the act or process of incurring

in·cur·rent \-ənt, -rənt\ *adj* [L *incurrent-*, *incurrens*, prp. of *incurrere*] **:** giving passage to a current that flows inward

in·cur·sion \in-ˈkər-zhən\ *n* [ME, fr. MF or L; MF, fr. L *incursion-*, *incursio*, fr. *incursus*, pp. of *incurrere*] **1 :** a hostile entrance into a territory **:** RAID **2 :** a running, bringing, or entering in or into

in·cur·sive \in-ˈkər-siv\ *adj* **:** making incursions

in·cur·vate \ˈin-ˌkər-ˌvāt, (ˈ)in-ˈkər-\ *vt* **:** to cause to curve inward **:** BEND — **in·cur·vate** \ˈin-ˌkər-ˌvāt, (ˈ)in-ˈkər-vət\ *adj* — **in·cur·va·tion** \ˌin-ˌkər-ˈvā-shən\ *n* — **in·cur·va·ture** \(ˈ)in-ˈkər-və-ˌchu̇(ə)r, -chər, -ˌt(y)u̇(ə)r\ *n*

1**in·curve** \(ˈ)in-ˈkərv\ *vb* [L *incurvare*, fr. *in-* + *curvare* to curve, fr. *curvus* curved — more at CROWN] **:** to bend so as to curve inward

2**in·curve** \ˈin-ˌkərv\ *n* **:** a curving in

in·cus \ˈiŋ-kəs\ *n, pl* **in·cu·des** \iŋ-ˈkyüd-(ˌ)ēz\ [NL, fr. L, anvil, fr. *incudere*] **:** the middle of a chain of three small bones in the ear of mammals — called also *anvil*

in·cuse \in-ˈkyüz, -ˈkyüs\ *adj* [L *incusus*, pp. of *incudere* to stamp, strike, fr. *in-* + *cudere* to beat — more at HEW] **:** formed by stamp-

ing or punching in — used chiefly of old coins or features of their design — **incuse** *n*

Ind \'ind, 'īnd\ *n* **1** *archaic* **:** INDIA **2** *obs* **:** INDIES

ind- *or* **indi-** *or* **indo-** *comb form* [ISV, fr. L *indicum* — more at INDIGO] **1 :** indigo ⟨*ind*oxyl⟩ **2 :** resembling indigo (as in color) ⟨*indo*phenol⟩

Ind- *or* **Indo-** *comb form* [Gk, fr. *Indos* India] **1 :** India or the East Indies ⟨*Indo*phile⟩ ⟨*Indo*-Briton⟩ **2 :** Indo-European ⟨*Indo*-Hittite⟩

in·da·ba \in-'däb-ə\ *n* [Zulu *in-daba* affair] *southern Africa* **:** CONFERENCE, PARLEY

in·da·gate \'in-də-,gāt\ *vt* [L *indagatus*, pp. of *indagare*, fr. *indago* act of enclosing, investigation, fr. OL *indu* in + L *agere* to drive — more at INDIGENOUS, AGENT] *archaic* **:** to search into **:** INVESTIGATE — **in·da·ga·tion** \,in-də-'gā-shən\ *n, archaic* — **in·da·ga·tor** \'in-də-,gāt-ər\ *n, archaic*

in·da·mine \'in-də-,mēn\ *n* [ISV] **:** any of a series of organic bases of which the simplest has the formula $NH{=}C_6H_4{=}NC_6H_4\text{-}NH_2$ and which form salts that are unstable blue and green dyes

in·debt·ed \in-'det-əd\ *adj* [ME *indetted*, fr. OF *endeté*, pp. of *endeter* to involve in debt, fr. *en-* + *dete* debt] **1 :** owing money **2 :** owing gratitude or recognition to another **:** BEHOLDEN

in·debt·ed·ness *n* **1 :** the condition of being indebted **2 :** something that is owed

in·de·cen·cy \(')in-'dēs-ᵊn-sē\ *n* **1 :** the quality or state of being indecent **2 :** something (as a word or action) that is indecent

in·de·cent \-ᵊnt\ *adj* [MF or L; MF *indécent*, fr. L *indecent-*, *indecens*, fr. *in-* + *decent-*, *decens* decent] **:** not decent: **a :** UNBECOMING, UNSEEMLY **b :** morally offensive **syn** see INDECOROUS — **in·de·cent·ly** *adv*

in·de·ci·pher·able \,in-di-'sī-f(ə-)rə-bəl\ *adj* **:** that cannot be deciphered

in·de·ci·sion \,in-di-'sizh-ən\ *n* [F *indécision*, fr. *indécis* undecided, fr. LL *indecisus*, fr. L *in-* + *decisus*, pp. of *decidere* to decide] **:** a wavering between two or more possible courses of action **:** IRRESOLUTION

in·de·ci·sive \,in-di-'sī-siv\ *adj* **1 :** not decisive **:** INCONCLUSIVE **2 :** marked by or prone to indecision **:** IRRESOLUTE **3 :** not clearly marked out **:** INDEFINITE — **in·de·ci·sive·ly** *adv* — **in·de·ci·sive·ness** *n*

in·de·clin·able \,in-di-'klī-nə-bəl\ *adj* [MF, fr. LL *indeclinabilis*, fr. L *in-* + LL *declinabilis* capable of being inflected, fr. L *declinare* to inflect — more at DECLINE] **:** having no grammatical inflections

in·de·com·pos·able \,in-,dē-kəm-'pō-zə-bəl\ *adj* **:** not capable of being broken up into component parts

in·de·co·rous \(')in-'dek-(ə-)rəs; ,in-di-'kōr-əs, -'kȯr-\ *adj* [L *indecorus*, fr. *in-* + *decorus* decorous] **:** not decorous — **in·de·co·rous·ly** *adv* — **in·de·co·rous·ness** *n*

syn IMPROPER, UNSEEMLY, INDECENT, UNBECOMING, INDELICATE: INDECOROUS suggests a violation of accepted standards of good manners; IMPROPER applies to a broader range of transgressions of rules not only of social behavior but of ethical practice or logical procedure or prescribed method; UNSEEMLY adds a suggestion of special inappropriateness to a situation or an offensiveness to good taste; INDECENT implies great unseemliness or gross offensiveness esp. in referring to sexual matters; UNBECOMING suggests behavior or language that does not suit one's character or status; INDELICATE implies a lack of modesty or of tact or of refined perception of feeling

in·de·co·rum \,in-di-'kōr-əm, -'kȯr-\ *n* [L, neut. of *indecorus*] **1 :** something that is indecorous **2 :** lack of decorum **:** IMPROPRIETY

in·deed \in-'dēd\ *adv* **1 :** without any question **:** TRULY — often used interjectionally to express irony or disbelief or surprise **2 :** in reality **3 :** all things considered **4 :** ADMITTEDLY, UNDENIABLY

in·de·fat·i·ga·bil·i·ty \,in-di-,fat-i-gə-'bil-ət-ē\ *n* **:** the quality or state of being indefatigable

in·de·fat·i·ga·ble \-'fat-i-gə-bəl\ *adj* [MF, fr. L *indefatigabilis*, fr. *in-* + *defatigare* to fatigue, fr. *de* down + *fatigare* to fatigue — more at DE-] **:** incapable of being fatigued **:** UNTIRING — **in·de·fat·i·ga·ble·ness** *n* — **in·de·fat·i·ga·bly** \-blē\ *adv*

in·de·fea·si·bil·i·ty \,in-di-,fē-zə-'bil-ət-ē\ *n* **:** the quality or state of being indefeasible

in·de·fea·si·ble \-'fē-zə-bəl\ *adj* **:** not capable of being annulled or voided or undone ⟨an ~ right⟩ — **in·de·fea·si·bly** \-blē\ *adv*

in·de·fec·ti·bil·i·ty \,in-di-,fek-tə-'bil-ət-ē\ *n* **:** the quality or state of being indefectible

in·de·fec·ti·ble \-'fek-tə-bəl\ *adj* **1 :** not subject to failure or decay **:** LASTING **2 :** free of faults **:** FLAWLESS — **in·de·fec·ti·bly** \-blē\ *adv*

in·de·fen·si·bil·i·ty \,in-di-,fen(t)-sə-'bil-ət-ē\ *n* **:** the quality or state of being indefensible

in·de·fen·si·ble \-'fen(t)-sə-bəl\ *adj* **1 a :** incapable of being maintained as right or valid **:** UNTENABLE **b :** incapable of being justified or excused **:** INEXCUSABLE **2 :** incapable of being protected against physical attack — **in·de·fen·si·bly** \-blē\ *adv*

in·de·fin·abil·i·ty \,in-di-,fī-nə-'bil-ət-ē\ *n* **:** the quality or state of being indefinable

in·de·fin·able \-'fī-nə-bəl\ *adj* **:** incapable of being precisely described or analyzed — **indefinable** *n* — **in·de·fin·able·ness** *n* — **in·de·fin·ably** \-blē\ *adv*

in·def·i·nite \(')in-'def-(ə-)nət\ *adj* [L *indefinitus*, fr. *in-* + *definitus* definite] **:** not definite: as **a** *of a grammatical modifier* **:** typically designating an unidentified or not immediately identifiable person or thing ⟨the ~ article⟩ **b :** not precise **:** VAGUE **c :** having no exact limits — **indefinite** *n* — **in·def·i·nite·ly** *adv* — **in·def·i·nite·ness** *n*

indefinite integral *n* **:** a mathematical function which is a function of another function and whose derivative is the other function

in·de·his·cence \,in-di-'his-ᵊn(t)s\ *n* **:** the quality or state of being indehiscent

in·de·his·cent \-ᵊnt\ *adj* **:** remaining closed at maturity ⟨~ fruits⟩

in·del·i·bil·i·ty \(,)in-,del-ə-'bil-ət-ē\ *n* **:** the quality or state of being indelible

in·del·ible \in-'del-ə-bəl\ *adj* [ML *indelibilis*, alter. of L *indelebilis*, fr. *in-* + *delere* to delete] **1 :** that cannot be removed, washed away, or erased **2 :** making marks that cannot easily be removed ⟨an ~ pencil⟩ — **in·del·i·bly** \-blē\ *adv*

in·del·i·ca·cy \(')in-'del-i-kə-sē\ *n* **1 :** the quality or state of being indelicate **2 :** something that is indelicate

in·del·i·cate \(')in-'del-i-kət\ *adj* **:** not delicate: **a** (1) **:** lacking in or offending against propriety **:** IMPROPER (2) **:** verging on the indecent **:** COARSE **b :** marked by a lack of feeling for the sensibilities of others **:** TACTLESS **syn** see INDECOROUS — **in·del·i·cate·ly** *adv* — **in·del·i·cate·ness** *n*

in·dem·ni·fi·ca·tion \in-,dem-nə-fə-'kā-shən\ *n* **1 a :** the action of indemnifying **b :** the condition of being indemnified **2 :** INDEMNITY 2b

in·dem·ni·fi·er \in-'dem-nə-,fī(-ə)r\ *n* **:** one that indemnifies

in·dem·ni·fy \-,fī\ *vt* [L *indemnis* unharmed, fr. *in-* + *damnum* damage] **1 :** to secure against hurt, loss, or damage **2 :** to make compensation to for incurred hurt, loss, or damage **syn** see PAY

in·dem·ni·ty \in-'dem-nət-ē\ *n* **1 a :** security against hurt, loss, or damage **b :** exemption from incurred penalties or liabilities **2 a :** INDEMNIFICATION 1 **b :** something that indemnifies

in·de·mon·stra·ble \,in-di-'män(t)-strə-bəl, (')in-'dem-ən-strə-\ *adj* **:** incapable of being demonstrated **:** not subject to proof — **in·de·mon·stra·bly** \-blē\ *adv*

in·dene \'in-,dēn\ *n* [ISV, fr. *indole*] **:** a liquid hydrocarbon C_9H_8 obtained from coal tar by distillation

[1]**in·dent** \in-'dent\ *vb* [ME *indenten*, fr. MF *endenter*, fr. OF, fr. *en-* + *dent* tooth, fr. L *dent-*, *dens* — more at TOOTH] *vt* **1 a :** to cut or otherwise divide (a document carrying two or more copies) to produce sections with irregular edges that can be matched for authentication **b :** to draw up (as a deed) in two or more exactly corresponding copies **2 a :** to notch the edge of **:** make jagged **b :** to cut into for the purpose of mortising or dovetailing **3 :** INDENTURE **4 :** to set (as a line of a paragraph) in from the margin **5 :** to join together by or as if by mortises or dovetails **6** *chiefly Brit* **:** to order by an indent ~ *vi* **1** *obs* **:** to make a formal or express agreement **2 :** to form an indentation **3** *chiefly Brit* **:** to make out an indent for something — **in·dent·er** *n* — **indent on 1** *chiefly Brit* **:** to make a requisition on **2** *chiefly Brit* **:** to draw on

[2]**in·dent** \in-'dent, 'in-,\ *n* **1 a :** INDENTURE 1 **b :** a certificate issued by the U.S. at the close of the American Revolution for the principal or interest on the public debt **2** *chiefly Brit* **a :** an official requisition **b :** a purchase order for goods esp. when sent from a foreign country **3 :** INDENTION

[3]**in·dent** \in-'dent\ *vt* [ME *endenten*, fr. *en-* + *denten* to dent] **1 :** to force inward so as to form a depression **2 :** to form a dent in — **in·dent·er** *n*

[4]**in·dent** \in-'dent, 'in-,\ *n* **:** INDENTATION

in·den·ta·tion \,in-,den-'tā-shən\ *n* **1 a :** an angular cut in an edge **:** NOTCH **b :** a usu. deep recess (as in a coastline) **2 :** the action of indenting **:** the condition of being indented **3 :** DENT **4 :** INDENTION 2b

in·den·tion \in-'den-chən\ *n* **1** *archaic* **:** INDENTATION 1 **2 a :** the action of indenting **:** the condition of being indented **b :** the blank space produced by indenting

[1]**in·den·ture** \in-'den-chər\ *n* **1 a** (1) **:** a document or a section of a document that is indented (2) **:** a formal or official document usu. executed in two or more copies (3) **:** a contract binding one person to work for another for a given period of time — usu. used in pl. **b :** a formal certificate (as an inventory or voucher) prepared for purposes of control **2 :** INDENTATION 1 **3** [[3]*indent*] **:** DENT

[2]**indenture** *vt* **in·den·tur·ing** \-'dench-(ə-)riŋ\ **1 :** to bind (as an apprentice) by indentures **2** *archaic* **:** to make a dent in

in·de·pen·dence \,in-də-'pen-dən(t)s\ *n* **1 :** the quality or state of being independent **:** FREEDOM **2** *archaic* **:** COMPETENCE 1

Independence Day *n* **:** July 4 observed as a legal holiday in the U.S. in commemoration of the adoption of the Declaration of Independence in 1776

in·de·pen·den·cy \,in-də-'pen-dən-sē\ *n* **1 :** INDEPENDENCE 1 **2** *cap* **:** the Independent polity or movement **3 :** an independent political unit

[1]**in·de·pen·dent** \,in-də-'pen-dənt\ *adj* **1 :** not dependent: as **a** (1) **:** not subject to control by others **:** SELF-GOVERNING (2) **:** not affiliated with a larger controlling unit **b** (1) **:** not requiring or relying on something else **:** not contingent ⟨~ conclusion⟩ (2) **:** not looking to others for one's opinions or for the guidance of one's conduct (3) **:** not bound by or committed definitively to a political party **c** (1) **:** not requiring or relying on others ⟨~ of his parents⟩ (2) **:** making up a competence **d** (1) **:** refusing to accept help from or to be under obligation to others (2) **:** showing a desire for freedom and absence of constraint **2** *cap* **:** of or relating to the Independents **3 a :** MAIN 5 ⟨~ clause⟩ **b :** neither deducible from nor incompatible with another statement ⟨~ postulates⟩ **c :** varying without respect to other variables ⟨in $x=y^2+3$, y is the ~ variable⟩ **syn** see FREE — **in·de·pen·dent·ly** *adv*

[2]**independent** *n* **1** *cap* **:** a sectarian of an English religious movement for congregational autonomy originating in the late 16th century, giving rise to Congregationalists, Baptists, and Friends, and forming one of the major political groupings of the period of Cromwell **2 :** one that is independent; *esp* **:** one that is not bound by or definitively committed to a political party

in·de·scrib·able \,in-di-'skrī-bə-bəl\ *adj* **1 :** that cannot be described ⟨an ~ sensation⟩ **2 :** surpassing description ⟨~ joy⟩ — **in·de·scrib·able·ness** *n* — **in·de·scrib·ably** \-blē\ *adv*

in·de·struc·ti·bil·i·ty \,in-di-,strək-tə-'bil-ət-ē\ *n* **:** the quality or state of being indestructible

in·de·struc·ti·ble \-'strək-tə-bəl\ *adj* [prob. fr. LL *indestructibilis*, fr. L *in-* + *destructus*, pp. of *destruere* to tear down — more at DESTROY] **:** not destructible — **in·de·struc·ti·ble·ness** *n* — **in·de·struc·ti·bly** \-blē\ *adv*

in·de·ter·min·able \,in-di-'tərm-(ə-)nə-bəl\ *adj* **1 :** incapable of being definitely decided or settled **2 :** incapable of being definitely fixed or ascertained — **in·de·ter·min·able·ness** *n* — **in·de·ter·min·ably** \-blē\ *adv*

in·de·ter·mi·na·cy \-(ə-)nə-sē\ *n* **:** the quality or state of being indeterminate

indeterminacy principle *n* **:** UNCERTAINTY PRINCIPLE

in·de·ter·mi·nate \,in-di-'tərm-(ə-)nət\ *adj* [ME *indeterminat*, fr. LL *indeterminatus*, fr. L *in-* + *determinatus*, pp. of *determinare* to determine] **1 a :** not definitely or precisely determined or fixed **:** VAGUE **b :** not known in advance **c :** not leading to a definite end or result **2 a :** RACEMOSE **b :** having the parts of the perianth separate and not overlapping in the bud — **in·de·ter·mi·nate·ly** *adv* — **in·de·ter·mi·nate·ness** *n* — **in·de·ter·mi·na·tion** \-,tər-mə-'nā-shən\ *n*

in·de·ter·min·ism \-'tər-mə-,niz-əm\ *n* **1 :** a theory that the will is free and that deliberate choice and actions are not determined by or predictable from antecedent causes **2 :** the quality or state of being indeterminate; *esp* **:** UNPREDICTABILITY — **in·de·ter·min·ist** \-'tərm-(ə-)nəst\ *n* — **in·de·ter·min·is·tic** \-,tər-mə-'nis-tik\ *adj*
in·de·vout \,in-di-'vau̇t\ *adj* **:** not devout — **in·de·vout·ly** *adv*
[1]**in·dex** \'in-,deks\ *n, pl* **in·dex·es** *or* **in·di·ces** \-də-,sēz\ [L *indic-, index,* fr. *indicare* to indicate] **1 :** a guide (as a table, file, or series of notches cut in the fore edge of a book) for facilitating reference; *esp* **:** a usu. alphabetical list of items (as topics or names) treated in a printed work that gives with each item the page number where it may be found **2 :** something that serves as a pointer or indicator **3 :** something that indicates or discloses **:** TOKEN **4 :** a list of restricted or prohibited material; *specif, cap* **:** a list of books the reading of which is prohibited or restricted for Roman Catholics by the church authorities **5** *pl usu indices* **:** a number or symbol or expression (as an exponent) associated with another to indicate a mathematical operation or use or position in an arrangement or expansion **6 :** a character ☞ used to direct particular attention to a note or paragraph — called also *fist* **7 a :** a ratio or other number derived from a series of observations and used as an indicator or measure (as of a condition, property, or phenomenon); *specif* **:** INDEX NUMBER **b :** the ratio of one dimension of a thing (as an anatomical structure) to another dimension — **in·dex·i·cal** \in-'dek-si-kəl\ *adj*
[2]**index** *vt* **1 a :** to provide with an index **b :** to list in an index **2 :** to serve as an index of ~ *vi* **:** to index something — **in·dex·er** *n*
index finger *n* **:** FOREFINGER
index fossil *n* **:** a fossil usu. with a narrow time range and wide spatial distribution that is used in the identification of related geologic formations
index number *n* **:** a number used to indicate change in magnitude (as of cost or price) as compared with the magnitude at some specified time usu. taken as 100
index of refraction : the ratio of the velocity of light or other radiation in the first of two media to its velocity in the second as it passes from one into the other
indi- — see IND-
In·dia \'in-dē-ə\ — a communications code word for the letter *i*
india ink *n, often cap 1st I* **1 :** a solid black pigment (as specially prepared lampblack) used in drawing and lettering **2 :** a fluid ink consisting usu. of a fine suspension of india ink in a liquid
In·dia·man \'in-dē-ə-mən\ *n* **:** a merchant ship formerly used in trade with India; *esp* **:** a large sailing ship used in this trade
In·di·an \'in-dē-ən\ *n* **1 :** a native or inhabitant of the subcontinent of India or of the East Indies **2 a** [fr. the belief held by Columbus that the lands he discovered were part of Asia] **:** AMERICAN INDIAN **b :** one of the native languages of American Indians — **Indian** *adj*
Indian club *n* **:** a wooden club which is swung for gymnastic exercise

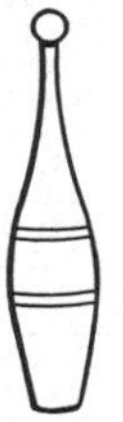
Indian club

Indian corn *n* **1 :** a tall widely cultivated American cereal grass (*Zea mays*) bearing seeds on elongated ears **2 :** the ears of Indian corn; *also* **:** its edible seeds
Indian file *n* **:** SINGLE FILE
Indian giver *n* **:** one who gives something to another and then takes it back or expects an equivalent in return — **Indian giving** *n*
Indian hemp *n* **1 :** an American dogbane (*Apocynum cannabinum*) with milky juice, tough fibrous bark, and an emetic and cathartic root **2 :** HEMP 1
Indian licorice *n* **:** an East Indian leguminous twining herb (*Abrus precatorius*) whose root is a substitute for licorice
Indian meal *n* **:** CORNMEAL
Indian paintbrush *n* **1 :** any of a genus (*Castilleja*) of the figwort family with brightly colored bracts—called also *painted cup* **2 :** a European hawkweed (*Hieracium aurantiacum*) with orange-red ray flowers that is a troublesome weed in parts of No. America — called also *orange hawkweed*
Indian pipe *n* **:** a waxy white leafless saprophytic herb (*Monotropa uniflora* of the family Monotropaceae, the Indian-pipe family) of Asia and the U.S.
Indian pudding *n* **:** a pudding made chiefly of cornmeal, milk, and molasses
Indian red *n* **1 a :** a yellowish red earth containing hematite and used as a pigment **b :** any of various light red to purplish brown pigments made by calcining iron salts **2 :** a strong or moderate reddish brown
Indian sign *n* **:** HEX, SPELL
Indian summer *n* **1 :** a period of warm or mild weather late in autumn or in early winter **2 :** a happy or flourishing period occurring toward the end of something
Indian tobacco *n* **1 :** an American wild lobelia (*Lobelia inflata*) with small blue flowers **2 :** a wild tobacco (*Nicotiana rustica*) **3 :** a common cat's-foot (*Antennaria plantaginifolia*) of eastern No. America
Indian turnip *n* **:** JACK-IN-THE-PULPIT; *also* **:** its acrid root
India paper *n* **1 :** a thin absorbent paper used esp. for proving inked intaglio surfaces (as steel engravings) **2 :** a thin tough opaque printing paper
india rubber *n, often cap I* **1 :** RUBBER **2 :** something made of rubber
In·dic \'in-dik\ *adj* **1 :** of or relating to the subcontinent of India **:** INDIAN **2 :** of, relating to, or constituting the Indian branch of the Indo-European languages — see INDO-EUROPEAN LANGUAGES table — **Indic** *n*
in·di·can \'in-də-,kan\ *n* [L *indicum* indigo — more at INDIGO] **1 :** a glucoside $C_{14}H_{17}NO_6$ occurring esp. in the indigo plant and being a source of natural indigo **2 :** An indigo-forming substance $C_8H_6NOSO_2OH$ found as a salt in urine and other animal fluids
in·di·cant \'in-di-kənt\ *n* **:** something that serves to indicate
in·di·cate \'in-də-,kāt\ *vt* [L *indicatus,* pp. of *indicare,* fr. *in-* + *dicare* to proclaim, dedicate — more at DICTION] **1 a :** to point out or point to with more or less exactness **b :** to be a sign, symptom, or index of **c :** to demonstrate or suggest the necessity or advisability of **2 :** to state or express briefly **:** SUGGEST
in·di·ca·tion \,in-də-'kā-shən\ *n* **1 :** the action of indicating **2 a :** something that serves to indicate **b :** something that is indicated as advisable or necessary **3 :** the degree indicated on a graduated instrument **:** READING
[1]**in·dic·a·tive** \in-'dik-ət-iv\ *adj* **1 :** of, relating to, or constituting a verb form or set of verb forms that represents the denoted act or state as an objective fact ⟨the ~ mood⟩ ⟨an ~ verb form⟩ **2 :** serving to indicate ⟨actions ~ of fear⟩ — **in·dic·a·tive·ly** *adv*
[2]**indicative** *n* **1 :** the indicative mood of a language **2 :** a form in the indicative mood
in·di·ca·tor \'in-də-,kāt-ər\ *n* **1 :** one that indicates: as **a :** an index hand (as on a dial) **:** POINTER **b** (1) **:** a pressure gauge (2) **:** an instrument for automatically making a diagram that indicates the pressure in and volume of the working fluid of an engine throughout the cycle **c :** a dial that registers (as the movement of an elevator) **2 a :** a substance used to show visually (as by change of color) the condition of a solution with respect to the presence of free acid, alkali, or other substance **b :** TRACER **3 :** an organism or ecological community so strictly associated with particular environmental conditions that its presence is indicative of the existence of these conditions — **in·dic·a·to·ry** \in-'dik-ə-,tōr-ē, -,tȯr-\ *adj*
indices *pl of* INDEX
in·di·cia \in-'dish-(ē-)ə\ *n pl* [L, pl. of *indicium* sign, fr. *indicare*] **1 :** distinctive marks **:** INDICATIONS **2 :** postal markings often imprinted on mail or on labels to be affixed to mail
in·dict \in-'dīt\ *vt* [alter. of earlier *indite,* fr. ME *inditen,* fr. AF *enditer,* fr. OF, to write down — more at INDITE] **1 :** to charge with some offense **:** ACCUSE **2 :** to charge with a crime by the finding or presentment of a jury (as a grand jury) in due form of law — **in·dict·able** \-ə-bəl\ *adj* — **in·dict·er** *or* **in·dict·or** \-ər\ *n*
in·dic·tion \in-'dik-shən\ *n* [ME *indiccioun,* fr. LL *indiction-, indictio,* fr. L, proclamation, fr. *indictus,* pp. of *indicere* to proclaim, fr. *in-* + *dicere* to say — more at DICTION] **:** a 15-year cycle used as a chronological unit in several ancient and medieval systems
in·dict·ment \in-'dīt-mənt\ *n* **1 a :** the action or the legal process of indicting **b :** the state of being indicted **2 :** a formal written statement framed by a prosecuting authority and found by a jury (as a grand jury) charging a person with an offense
in·dif·fer·ence \in-'dif-ərn(t)s, -'dif-(ə-)rən(t)s\ *n* **1 :** the quality, state, or fact of being indifferent **2 a** *archaic* **:** lack of difference or distinction between two or more things **b :** absence of compulsion to or toward one thing or another
in·dif·fer·en·cy \-ərn-sē, -rən-sē\ *n, archaic* **:** INDIFFERENCE
in·dif·fer·ent \in-'dif-ərnt, -'dif-(ə-)rənt\ *adj* [ME, fr. MF or L; MF, regarded as neither good nor bad, fr. L *indifferent-, indifferens,* fr. *in-* + *different-, differens,* prp. of *differre* to be different — more at DIFFERENT] **1 :** marked by impartiality **:** UNBIASED **2 a :** that does not matter one way or the other **b :** that has nothing that calls for sanction or condemnation in either observance or neglect **:** of no importance or value one way or the other **3 a :** marked by no special liking for or dislike of something **b :** marked by a lack of interest in or concern about something **:** APATHETIC **4 :** being neither excessive nor defective **5 a :** being neither good nor bad **:** MEDIOCRE **b :** being neither right nor wrong **6 :** characterized by lack of active quality **:** NEUTRAL **7 a :** UNDIFFERENTIATED **b :** capable of development in more than one direction; *esp* **:** not yet embryologically determined — **in·dif·fer·ent·ly** *adv*
syn INDIFFERENT, UNCONCERNED, INCURIOUS, ALOOF, DETACHED, DISINTERESTED mean not showing or feeling interest. INDIFFERENT implies neutrality of attitude from lack of inclination, preference, or prejudice; UNCONCERNED suggests a lack of sensitivity or regard for others' needs or troubles; INCURIOUS implies an inability to take a normal interest due to dullness of mind or to self-centeredness; ALOOF suggests a cool reserve arising from a sense of superiority or disdain for inferiors or from shyness; DETACHED implies an objective attitude achieved through absence of prejudice or selfishness; DISINTERESTED implies a circumstantial freedom from concern for personal or esp. financial advantage that enables one to judge or advise without bias
in·dif·fer·ent·ism \-ərnt-,iz-əm, -rənt-\ *n* **:** INDIFFERENCE; *specif* **:** belief that all religions are equally valid — **in·dif·fer·ent·ist** \-ərnt-əst, -rənt-\ *n*
in·di·gence \'in-di-jən(t)s\ *n* **:** NEEDINESS **syn** see POVERTY
in·di·gene \'in-də-,jēn\ *also* **in·di·gen** \-di-jən, -də-,jen\ *n* [L *indigena*] **:** NATIVE 2b
in·dig·e·nous \in-'dij-ə-nəs\ *adj* [LL *indigenus,* fr. L *indigena,* n., native, fr. OL *indu, endo* in, within (akin to L *in* and to L *de* down) + L *gignere* to beget] **1 :** produced, growing, or living naturally in a particular region or environment **2 :** INBORN, INNATE **syn** see NATIVE — **in·dig·e·nous·ly** *adv* — **in·dig·e·nous·ness** *n*
in·di·gent \'in-di-jənt\ *adj* [ME, fr. MF, fr. L *indigent-, indigens,* prp. of *indigēre* to need, fr. OL *indu* + L *egēre* to need; akin to OHG *ekrōdi* thin] **1 :** IMPOVERISHED, NEEDY **2 a** *archaic* **:** DEFICIENT **b** *archaic* **:** totally lacking in something specified
in·di·gest·ed \,in-(,)dī-'jes-təd, -də-\ *adj* **:** not carefully thought out or arranged **:** FORMLESS
in·di·gest·ibil·i·ty \-,jes-tə-'bil-ət-ē\ *n* **:** the quality of being indigestible
in·di·gest·ible \-'jes-tə-bəl\ *adj* [LL *indigestibilis,* fr. L *in-* + LL *digestibilis* digestible] **:** not digestible **:** not easily digested
in·di·ges·tion \-'jes(h)-chən\ *n* **1 :** inability to digest or difficulty in digesting something **2 :** a case or attack of indigestion — **in·di·ges·tive** \-'jes-tiv\ *adj*
in·dign \in-'dīn\ *adj* [ME *indigne,* fr. MF, fr. L *indignus*] **1** *archaic* **:** UNWORTHY, UNDESERVING **2** *obs* **:** UNBECOMING, DISGRACEFUL
in·dig·nant \in-'dig-nənt\ *adj* [L *indignant-, indignans,* prp. of *indignari* to be indignant, fr. *indignus* unworthy, fr. *in-* + *dignus* worthy — more at DECENT] **:** filled with or marked by indignation — **in·dig·nant·ly** *adv*
in·dig·na·tion \,in-(,)dig-'nā-shən\ *n* **:** anger aroused by something unjust, unworthy, or mean **syn** see ANGER
in·dig·ni·ty \in-'dig-nət-ē\ *n* [L *indignitat-, indignitas,* fr. *indignus*] **1** *obs* **:** lack or loss of dignity or honor **2 a :** an act that offends against a person's dignity or self-respect **:** INSULT **b :** humiliating treatment **syn** see AFFRONT
in·di·go \'in-di-,gō\ *n, pl* **indigos** *or* **indigoes** [It dial., fr. L *indicum,* fr. Gk *indikon,* fr. neut. of *indikos* Indic, fr. *Indos* India] **1 a :** a blue vat dye obtained from plants (as indigo plants) by alteration of the indican present **b :** the principal coloring matter

$C_{16}H_{10}N_2O_2$ of natural indigo usu. synthesized as a blue powder with a coppery luster from synthetic indoxyl **c :** any of several blue vat dyes derived from or closely related to indigo **2 :** a variable color averaging a dark grayish blue

indigo plant *n* **:** a plant that yields indigo; *esp* **:** any of a genus (*Indigofera*) of leguminous herbs

indigo snake *n* **:** a large harmless blue-black snake (*Drymarchon corais couperi*) of the southern U.S. — called also *gopher snake*

in·di·go·tin \in-ˈdig-ət-ən, ˌin-di-ˈgōt-ᵊn\ *n* [ISV *indigo* + connective *-t-* + *-in*] **:** INDIGO 1b

in·di·rect \ˌin-də-ˈrekt, -(ˌ)dī-\ *adj* [ME, fr. ML *indirectus*, fr. L *in-* + *directus* direct] **:** not direct: as **a** (1) **:** deviating from a direct line or course **:** ROUNDABOUT (2) **:** not going straight to the point ⟨an ~ accusation⟩ **b :** not straightforward and open **:** DECEITFUL **c :** not directly aimed at or achieved ⟨~ consequences⟩ **d :** stating what a real or supposed original speaker said with changes in wording that conform the statement grammatically to the sentence in which it is included ⟨~ discourse⟩ — **in·di·rect·ly** \-ˈrek-(t)lē\ *adv* — **in·di·rect·ness** \-ˈrek(t)-nəs\ *n*

in·di·rec·tion \-ˈrek-shən\ *n* **1 a :** lack of straightforwardness and openness **:** DECEITFULNESS **b :** something marked by lack of straightforwardness **2 a :** indirect action or procedure **b :** lack of direction **:** AIMLESSNESS

indirect lighting *n* **:** lighting in which the light emitted by a source is diffusely reflected (as by the ceiling)

indirect object *n* **:** a grammatical object representing the secondary goal of the action of its verb ⟨*borrower* in "I gave the borrower the book" is an *indirect object*⟩

indirect proof *n* **:** REDUCTIO AD ABSURDUM

indirect tax *n* **:** a tax exacted from a person other than the one on whom the ultimate burden of the tax is expected to fall

in·dis·cern·ible \ˌin-dis-ˈər-nə-bəl, -diz-\ *adj* **:** incapable of being discerned **:** not recognizable as distinct

in·dis·ci·pline \(ˈ)in-ˈdis-ə-plən, -(ˌ)plin\ *n* **:** lack of discipline

in·dis·cov·er·able \ˌin-dis-ˈkəv-(ə-)rə-bəl\ *adj* **:** UNDISCOVERABLE

in·dis·creet \ˌin-dis-ˈkrēt\ *adj* [ME *indiscrete*, fr. MF & LL; MF *indiscret*, fr. LL *indiscretus*, fr. L, indistinguishable, fr. *in-* + *discretus*, pp. of *discernere* to separate — more at DISCERN] **:** not discreet **:** IMPRUDENT — **in·dis·creet·ly** *adv* — **in·dis·creet·ness** *n*

in·dis·crete \ˌin-dis-ˈkrēt, (ˈ)in-ˈdis-ˌ\ *adj* [L *indiscretus*] **:** not separated into distinct parts ⟨an ~ mass⟩

in·dis·cre·tion \ˌin-dis-ˈkresh-ən\ *n* **1 :** lack of discretion **:** IMPRUDENCE **2 :** something marked by lack of discretion

in·dis·crim·i·nate \ˌin-dis-ˈkrim-(ə-)nət\ *adj* **1 a :** not marked by discrimination ⟨~ reading habits⟩ **b :** HAPHAZARD, RANDOM **2 a :** UNRESTRAINED, PROMISCUOUS **b :** CONFUSED, HETEROGENEOUS — **in·dis·crim·i·nate·ly** *adv* — **in·dis·crim·i·nate·ness** *n*
syn WHOLESALE, SWEEPING: INDISCRIMINATE implies lack of consideration of individual merits or deserts ⟨*indiscriminate* charity⟩ WHOLESALE may imply any result of dealing with things by the whole mass rather than one by one ⟨*wholesale* slaughter of a population⟩ SWEEPING suggests a reaching out so as to bring all or everything within its range ⟨*sweeping* generalization⟩

in·dis·crim·i·nat·ing \-ˈkrim-ə-ˌnāt-iŋ\ *adj* **:** UNDISCRIMINATING — **in·dis·crim·i·nat·ing·ly** \-iŋ-lē\ *adv*

in·dis·crim·i·na·tion \ˌin-dis-ˌkrim-ə-ˈnā-shən\ *n* **:** lack of discrimination

in·dis·pens·abil·i·ty \ˌin-dis-ˌpen(t)-sə-ˈbil-ət-ē\ *n* **:** the quality or state of being indispensable

in·dis·pens·able \-ˈpen(t)-sə-bəl\ *adj* **1 :** not subject to being set aside or neglected ⟨an ~ obligation⟩ **2 :** absolutely necessary **:** ESSENTIAL ⟨an ~ worker⟩ — **indispensable** *n* — **in·dis·pens·able·ness** *n* — **in·dis·pens·ably** \-blē\ *adv*

in·dis·pose \ˌin-dis-ˈpōz\ *vt* [prob. back-formation fr. *indisposed*] **1 a :** to make unfit **:** DISQUALIFY **b :** to make averse **:** DISINCLINE **2** *archaic* **:** to cause to be in poor physical health

in·dis·posed \-ˈpōzd\ *adj* **1 :** slightly ill **2 :** AVERSE

in·dis·po·si·tion \(ˌ)in-ˌdis-pə-ˈzish-ən\ *n* **:** the condition of being indisposed: **a :** DISINCLINATION **b :** a usu. slight illness

in·dis·pu·ta·ble \ˌin-dis-ˈpyüt-ə-bəl, (ˈ)in-ˈdis-pyət-\ *adj* [LL *indisputabilis*, fr. L *in-* + *disputabilis* disputable] **:** not disputable **:** UNQUESTIONABLE ⟨~ proof⟩ — **in·dis·pu·ta·ble·ness** *n* — **in·dis·pu·ta·bly** \-blē\ *adv*

in·dis·sol·u·bil·i·ty \ˌin-dis-ˌäl-yə-ˈbil-ət-ē\ *n* **:** the quality or state of being indissoluble

in·dis·sol·u·ble \-ˈäl-yə-bəl\ *adj* **:** not dissoluble: as **a :** incapable of being annulled, undone, or broken **:** PERMANENT ⟨an ~ contract⟩ **b :** incapable of being dissolved, decomposed, or disintegrated — **in·dis·sol·u·ble·ness** *n* — **in·dis·sol·u·bly** \-blē\ *adv*

in·dis·tinct \ˌin-dis-ˈtiŋ(k)t\ *adj* [L *indistinctus*, fr. *in-* + *distinctus* distinct] **:** not distinct: as **a :** not sharply outlined or separable **:** BLURRED **b :** FAINT, DIM **c :** not clearly recognizable or understandable **:** UNCERTAIN — **in·dis·tinct·ly** \-ˈtiŋ(k)-tlē, -ˈtiŋ-klē\ *adv* — **in·dis·tinct·ness** \-ˈtiŋt-nəs, -ˈtiŋk-nəs\ *n*

in·dis·tinc·tive \-ˈtiŋ(k)-tiv\ *adj* **:** lacking distinctive qualities

in·dis·tin·guish·able \ˌin-dis-ˈtiŋ-gwish-ə-bəl\ *adj* **:** not distinguishable: as **a :** indeterminate in shape or structure **b :** not clearly recognizable or understandable **c :** lacking identifying or individualizing qualities — **in·dis·tin·guish·able·ness** *n* — **in·dis·tin·guish·ably** \-blē\ *adv*

in·dite \in-ˈdīt\ *vt* [ME *enditen*, fr. OF *enditer* to write down, proclaim, fr. (assumed) VL *indictare* to proclaim, fr. L *indictus*, pp. of *indicere* to proclaim, fr. *in-* + *dicere* to say — more at DICTION] **1 a :** to make up **:** COMPOSE ⟨~ an epistle⟩ **b :** to give literary or formal expression to **c :** to put down in writing **2** *obs* **:** DICTATE — **in·dit·er** *n*

in·di·um \ˈin-dē-əm\ *n* [ISV [2]*ind-* + NL *-ium*] **:** a malleable fusible silvery metallic element that is chiefly trivalent, occurs esp. in sphalerite ores, and is used as a plating for bearings — see ELEMENT table

in·di·vert·ible \ˌin-də-ˈvərt-ə-bəl, -(ˌ)dī-\ *adj* **:** not to be diverted or turned aside — **in·di·vert·ibly** \-blē\ *adv*

[1]**in·di·vid·u·al** \ˌin-də-ˈvij-(ə-)wəl, -ˈvij-əl\ *adj* [ML *individualis*, fr. L *individuus* indivisible, fr. *in-* + *dividuus* divided, fr. *dividere* to divide] **1** *obs* **:** INSEPARABLE **2 a :** of, relating to, or used by an individual ⟨~ traits⟩ **b :** being an individual or existing as an indivisible whole **c :** intended for one person ⟨an ~ serving⟩ **3 :** existing as a distinct entity **:** SEPARATE **4 :** having marked individuality ⟨an ~ style⟩ **syn** see CHARACTERISTIC, SPECIAL — **in·di·vid·u·al·ly** \-ē\ *adv*

[2]**individual** *n* **1 a :** a particular being or thing as distinguished from a class, species, or collection: as (1) **:** a single human being as contrasted with a social group or institution (2) **:** a single organism as distinguished from a group **b :** a particular person **2 :** an indivisible entity **3 :** the reference of a name or variable of the lowest logical type in a calculus

in·di·vid·u·al·ism \-ˈvij-(ə-)wə-ˌliz-əm, -ˈvij-ə-ˌliz-\ *n* **1 a** (1) **:** a doctrine that the interests of the individual are or ought to be ethically paramount; *also* **:** conduct guided by such a doctrine (2) **:** the conception that all values, rights, and duties originate in individuals **b :** a theory maintaining the political and economic independence of the individual and stressing individual initiative, action, and interests; *also* **:** conduct or practice guided by such a theory **2 a :** INDIVIDUALITY **b :** an individual peculiarity **:** IDIOSYNCRASY

in·di·vid·u·al·ist \-ləst\ *n* **1 :** one who pursues a markedly independent course in thought or action **2 :** one who advocates or practices individualism — **individualist** *adj* — **in·di·vid·u·al·is·tic** \-ˌvij-(ə-)wə-ˈlis-tik, -ˌvij-ə-ˈlis-\ *adj* — **in·di·vid·u·al·is·ti·cal·ly** \-ˈlis-ti-k(ə-)lē\ *adv*

in·di·vid·u·al·i·ty \-ˌvij-ə-ˈwal-ət-ē\ *n* **1 a :** total character peculiar to and distinguishing an individual from others **b :** PERSONALITY **2** *archaic* **:** INDIVISIBILITY, INSEPARABILITY **3 :** INDIVIDUAL, PERSON **4 :** separate or distinct existence

in·di·vid·u·al·iza·tion \ˌin-də-ˌvij-(ə-)wə-lə-ˈzā-shən, -ˌvij-ə-lə-\ *n* **:** the act of individualizing **:** the state of being individualized

in·di·vid·u·al·ize \-ˈvij-(ə-)wə-ˌlīz, -ˈvij-ə-ˌlīz\ *vt* **1 :** to make individual in character **2 :** to treat or notice individually **:** PARTICULARIZE **3 :** to adapt to the needs or special circumstances of an individual

in·di·vid·u·ate \ˌin-də-ˈvij-ə-ˌwāt\ *vt* **1 :** to give individuality to **2 :** to form into a distinct entity

in·di·vid·u·a·tion \-ˌvij-ə-ˈwā-shən\ *n* **1 :** the act or process of individuating: as **a** (1) **:** the development of the individual from the universal (2) **:** the determination of the individual in the general **b :** the process by which individuals in society become differentiated from one another **c :** regional differentiation along a primary embryonic axis **2 :** the state of being individuated; *specif* **:** INDIVIDUALITY

in·di·vis·i·bil·i·ty \ˌin-də-ˌviz-ə-ˈbil-ət-ē\ *n* **:** the quality or state of being indivisible

in·di·vis·i·ble \ˌin-də-ˈviz-ə-bəl\ *adj* [ME, fr. LL *indivisibilis*, fr. L *in-* + LL *divisibilis* divisible] **:** not divisible — **indivisible** *n* — **in·di·vis·i·ble·ness** *n* — **in·di·vis·i·bly** \-blē\ *adv*

Indo- — see IND-

In·do–Ary·an \ˌin-ˌdō-ˈar-ē-ən, -ˈer-\ *n* **1 :** a member of one of the peoples of India of Aryan speech and physique **2 :** one of the early Indo-European invaders of Persia, Afghanistan, and India **3 :** the Indo-European languages of India and Pakistan as a group — **Indo–Aryan** *adj*

In·do–Chi·nese \-ˌchī-ˈnēz, -ˈnēs\ *n* **1 :** a native or inhabitant of Indochina **2 :** SINO-TIBETAN — **Indo–Chinese** *adj*

in·doc·ile \(ˈ)in-ˈdäs-əl\ *adj* [MF, fr. L *indocilis*, fr. *in-* + *docilis* docile] **:** unwilling or indisposed to be taught or disciplined **:** INTRACTABLE — **in·do·cil·i·ty** \ˌin-ˌdä-ˈsil-ət-ē, ˌin-dō-\ *n*

in·doc·tri·nate \in-ˈdäk-trə-ˌnāt\ *vt* [prob. fr. ME *endoctrinen*, fr. MF *endoctriner*, fr. OF, fr. *en-* + *doctrine*] **1 :** to instruct esp. in fundamentals or rudiments **:** TEACH **2 :** to imbue with a usu. partisan or sectarian opinion, point of view, or principle — **in·doc·tri·na·tion** \(ˌ)in-ˌdäk-trə-ˈnā-shən\ *n* — **in·doc·tri·na·tor** \in-ˈdäk-trə-ˌnāt-ər\ *n*

In·do–Eu·ro·pe·an \ˌin-(ˌ)dō-ˌyu̇r-ə-ˈpē-ən\ *adj* **:** of, relating to, or constituting the Indo-European languages — **Indo–European** *n*

Indo–European languages *n pl* **:** a family of languages comprising those spoken in most of Europe and in the parts of the world colonized by Europeans since 1500 and also in Persia, the subcontinent of India, and some other parts of Asia

In·do–Ger·man·ic \ˌin-(ˌ)dō-jər-ˈman-ik\ *n* **:** INDO-EUROPEAN — **Indo–Germanic** *adj*

In·do–Hit·tite \-ˈhi-ˌtīt\ *n, often attrib* **1 :** a language family including Indo-European and Anatolian **2 :** a hypothetical parent language of Indo-European and Anatolian

In·do–Ira·ni·an \-ir-ˈā-nē-ən\ *adj* **:** of, relating to, or constituting a subfamily of the Indo-European languages that consists of the Indic and the Iranian branches — **Indo–Iranian** *n*

in·dole \ˈin-ˌdōl\ *n* **:** a crystalline compound C_8H_7N that is a decomposition product of proteins containing tryptophan, often formed by reduction distillation of indigo, and used in perfumes; *also* **:** a derivative of indole

in·dole·ace·tic acid \ˌin-ˌdōl-ə-ˌsēt-ik-\ *n* **:** a crystalline plant hormone $C_{10}H_9NO_2$ that promotes growth and rooting of plants — called also *heteroauxin*

in·dole·bu·tyr·ic acid \-byü-ˌtir-ik-\ *n* **:** a crystalline acid $C_{12}H_{13}NO_2$ similar to indoleacetic acid in its effects on plants

in·do·lence \ˈin-də-lən(t)s\ *n* **1 :** a condition of causing little or no pain **2 :** indisposition to labor **:** SLOTH

in·do·lent \-lənt\ *adj* [LL *indolent-*, *indolens* insensitive to pain, fr. L *in-* + *dolent-*, *dolens*, prp. of *dolēre* to feel pain — more at CONDOLE] **1 a :** causing little or no pain **b :** slow to develop or heal **2 a :** indulging in ease **:** averse to exertion **b :** conducing to or encouraging laziness ⟨~ heat⟩ **c :** exhibiting indolence ⟨an ~ sigh⟩ **syn** see LAZY — **in·do·lent·ly** *adv*

in·dom·i·ta·bil·i·ty \(ˌ)in-ˌdäm-ət-ə-ˈbil-ət-ē\ *n* **:** the quality or state of being indomitable

in·dom·i·ta·ble \in-ˈdäm-ət-ə-bəl\ *adj* [LL *indomitabilis*, fr. L *in-* + *domitare* to tame — more at DAUNT] **:** incapable of being subdued **:** UNCONQUERABLE ⟨~ courage⟩ — **in·dom·i·ta·ble·ness** *n* — **in·dom·i·ta·bly** \-blē\ *adv*

In·do·ne·sian \ˌin-də-ˈnē-zhən, -shən\ *n* **1 :** a native or inhabitant of the Malay archipelago **2 a :** a native or inhabitant of the Republic of Indonesia **b :** the language based on Malay that is the national language of the Republic of Indonesia — **Indonesian** *adj*

in·door \ˌin-ˌdō(ə)r, -ˌdȯ(ə)r\ *adj* **1 :** of or relating to the interior of a building **2 :** done, living, or belonging within doors

in·doors \(ˈ)in-ˈdō(ə)rz, -ˈdȯ(ə)rz\ *adv* **:** in or into a building

in·do·phe·nol \ˌin-dō-ˈfē-ˌnōl, ˌin-(ˌ)dō-fi-ˈ\ *n* [ISV] **:** any of various blue or green dyes derived from quinone imines

indorse *var of* ENDORSE

in·dox·yl \in-ˈdäk-səl\ *n* [ISV [2]*ind-* + hydr*oxyl*] **:** a crystalline compound C_8H_7NO found in plants and animals or synthesized as a step in indigo manufacture

INDO-EUROPEAN LANGUAGES

| BRANCH | GROUP | LANGUAGES AND MAJOR DIALECTS[1] | | | PROVENIENCE |
		ANCIENT	MEDIEVAL	MODERN	
GERMANIC	East		*Gothic*		eastern Europe
	North		*Old Norse*	Icelandic	Iceland
				Faeroese	Faeroe islands
				Norwegian	Norway
				Swedish	Sweden
				Danish	Denmark
	West		*Old High German*	German	Germany, Switzerland, Austria
			Middle High German		
				Yiddish	Germany, eastern Europe
			Old Saxon	Low German	Northern Germany
			Middle Low German		
			Middle Dutch	Dutch	Netherlands
				Afrikaans	So. Africa
			Middle Flemish	Flemish	Belgium
			Old Frisian	Frisian	Netherlands, Germany
			Old English	English	England
			Middle English		
CELTIC	Continental	*Gaulish*			Gaul
	Brythonic		*Old Welsh*	Welsh	Wales
			Middle Welsh		
			Old Cornish	*Cornish*	Cornwall
			Middle Breton	Breton	Brittany
	Goidelic		*Old Irish*	Irish Gaelic	Ireland
			Middle Irish		
				Scottish Gaelic	Scotland
				Manx	Isle of Man
ITALIC	Osco-Umbrian	*Oscan, Sabellian*			ancient Italy
		Umbrian			
	Latinian or Romance[2]	*Venetic, Faliscan*			ancient Italy
		Lanuvian, Praenestine			
		Latin			
				Portuguese	Portugal
				Spanish	Spain
				Judeo-Spanish	Mediterranean lands
				Catalan	Spain (Catalonia)
			Old Provençal	Provençal	southern France
			Old French	French	France, Belgium, Switzerland
			Middle French		
				Haitian Creole	Haiti
				Italian	Italy, Switzerland
				Rhaeto-Romanic	Switzerland, Italy
				Sardinian	Sardinia
				Dalmatian	Adriatic coast
				Romanian	Romania, Balkans
Scantily recorded and of uncertain affinities within Indo-European		*Ligurian, Messapian*			ancient Italy
		Illyrian, Thracian			Balkans
		Phrygian			Asia Minor
Albanian				Albanian	Albania, southern Italy
Greek	Greek	Greek	Greek	Greek	Greece, the eastern Mediterranean
SLAVIC	Baltic		*Old Prussian*		East Prussia
				Lithuanian	Lithuania
				Latvian	Latvia
	South		Old Church Slavonic	Slovene	Yugoslavia
				Serbo-Croatian	Yugoslavia
				Macedonian	Macedonia
				Bulgarian	Bulgaria
	West		*Old Czech*	Czech, Slovak	Czechoslovakia
				Polish, Kashubian	Poland
				Wendish, *Polabian*	Germany
	East		*Old Russian*	Russian	Russia
				Ukrainian	Ukraine
				Belorussian	White Russia
Armenian			Armenian	Armenian	Asia Minor, Caucasus
IRANIAN	West	*Old Persian*	*Pahlavi*		Persia
			Persian	Persian	Persia (Iran)
				Kurdish	Persia, Iraq, Turkey
				Baluchi	West Pakistan
				Tajiki	central Asia
	East	Avestan			ancient Persia
			Sogdian		central Asia
			Khotanese		central Asia
				Pashto	Afghanistan, West Pakistan
				Ossetic	Caucasus
INDIC	Dard			Shina, Khowar, Kafiri	upper Indus valley
				Kashmiri	Kashmir
	Sanskritic	Sanskrit, Pali	*Prakrits*		India
		Prakrits			
				Lahnda	western Punjab
				Sindhi	Sind
				Panjabi	Punjab
				Rajasthani	Rajasthan
				Gujarati	Gujarat
				Marathi	western India
				Konkani	western India
				Oriya	Orissa
				Bengali	Bengal
				Assamese	Assam
				Bihari	Bihar
				Hindi	northern India
				Urdu	Pakistan, India
				Nepali	Nepal
				Sinhalese	Ceylon
				Romany	uncertain
Tocharian			*Tocharian A*		central Asia
			Tocharian B		

The following is sometimes considered as another branch of Indo-European, and sometimes as coordinate with Indo-European, the two together constituting Indo-Hittite

Anatolian		*Hittite, Lydian, Lycian*			ancient Asia Minor
		Luwian			
		Palaic			
		Hieroglyphic Hittite			

[1]Italics denote dead languages. Listing of a language only in the ancient or medieval column but in roman type indicates that it survives only in some special use, as in literary composition or liturgy
[2]Romance is normally applied only to medieval and modern languages; Latinian is normally applied only to ancient languages

in·draft \'in-ˌdraft, -ˌdrȧft\ *n* **1 :** a drawing or pulling in **2 :** an inward flow or current (as of air or water)

in·drawn \'in-ˌdrȯn\ *adj* **1 :** drawn in **2 :** ALOOF, RESERVED

in·du·bi·ta·bil·i·ty \(ˌ)in-ˌd(y)ü-bət-ə-'bil-ət-ē\ *n* **:** the quality or state of being unquestionable **:** CERTAINTY

in·du·bi·ta·ble \(')in-'d(y)ü-bət-ə-bəl\ *adj* [F or L; F, fr. L *indubitabilis*, fr. *in-* + *dubitabilis* dubitable] **:** too evident to be doubted **:** UNQUESTIONABLE — **in·du·bi·ta·ble·ness** *n* — **in·du·bi·ta·bly** \-blē\ *adv*

in·duce \in-'d(y)üs\ *vt* [ME *inducen*, fr. L *inducere*, fr. *in-* + *ducere* to lead — more at TOW] **1 a :** to lead on **:** move by persuasion or influence **b :** to call forth or bring about by influence or stimulation **2 a :** EFFECT, CAUSE **b :** to cause the formation of **c :** to produce (as an electric current) by induction **d :** to arouse by indirect stimulation ⟨~ a contrast color⟩ **3 :** to determine by induction; *specif* **:** infer from particulars — **in·duc·er** *n* — **in·duc·ible** \-'d(y)ü-sə-bəl\ *adj*

syn INDUCE, PERSUADE, PREVAIL (*on*), PREVAIL (*upon*) mean to move one to act or decide in a certain way. INDUCE implies influencing the reason or judgment; PERSUADE suggests appealing chiefly to the emotions; PREVAIL (*on*) or PREVAIL (*upon*) carries a strong implication of overcoming opposition or reluctance by sustained argument or entreaty

in·duce·ment \in-'d(y)ü-smənt\ *n* **1 :** the act or process of inducing **2 :** something that induces **:** MOTIVE **3 :** matter presented by way of introduction or background to explain the principal allegations of a legal cause, plea, or defense **syn** see MOTIVE

in·duct \in-'dəkt\ *vt* [ME *inducten*, fr. ML *inductus*, pp. of *inducere*, fr. L] **1 :** to put in formal possession (as of a benefice or office) **:** INSTALL **2 a :** to admit as a member **b :** INTRODUCE, INITIATE **c :** to enroll for military training or service (as under a selective-service act) **3 :** LEAD, CONDUCT — **in·duct·ee** \(ˌ)in-ˌdək-'tē, in-'dək-ˌtē\ *n*

in·duc·tance \in-'dək-tən(t)s\ *n* **1 :** a property of an electric circuit by which an electromotive force is induced in it by a variation of current either (1) in the circuit itself or (2) in a neighboring circuit **2 :** a circuit or a device possessing inductance

in·duc·tile \(')in-'dək-tᵊl\ *adj* **:** not ductile

in·duc·tion \in-'dək-shən\ *n* **1 a :** the act or process of inducting (as into office) **b :** an initial experience **:** INITIATION **c :** the formality by which a civilian is inducted into military service **2 a :** the act, process, or result or an instance of reasoning from a part to a whole, from particulars to generals, or from the individual to the universal **b :** mathematical demonstration of the validity of a law concerning all the positive integers by proving that it holds for the first integer and that if it holds for all the integers preceding a given integer it must hold for the next following integer **3 :** a preface, prologue, or introductory scene esp. of an early English play **4 a :** the act of bringing forward or adducing (as facts or particulars) **b :** the act of causing or bringing on or about **c :** the process by which an electrical conductor becomes electrified when near a charged body, by which a magnetizable body becomes magnetized when in a magnetic field or in the magnetic flux set up by a magnetomotive force, or by which an electromotive force is produced in a circuit by varying the magnetic field linked with the circuit **d :** the inspiration of the fuel-air charge from the carburetor into the combustion chamber of an internal-combustion engine **e :** the sum of the processes by which the fate of embryonic cells is determined and morphogenetic differentiation brought about

induction coil *n* **:** an apparatus for obtaining intermittent high voltage consisting of a primary coil through which the direct current flows, an interrupter, and a secondary coil of a larger number of turns in which the high voltage is induced

induction heating *n* **:** heating material by means of an electric current that is caused to flow through the material or its container by electromagnetic induction

in·duc·tive \in-'dək-tiv\ *adj* **1 :** leading on **:** INDUCING **2 :** of, relating to, or employing mathematical or logical induction **3 :** of or relating to inductance or electrical induction **4 :** INTRODUCTORY **5 :** involving the action of an embryological inductor **:** tending to produce induction — **in·duc·tive·ly** *adv* — **in·duc·tive·ness** *n*

in·duc·tor \in-'dək-tər\ *n* **1 :** one that inducts **2 a :** a part of an electrical apparatus that acts upon another or is itself acted upon by induction **b :** REACTOR **3 :** a factor capable of inducing a specific type of development in embryonic or other undifferentiated tissue

indue *var of* ENDUE

in·dulge \in-'dəlj\ *vb* [L *indulgēre* to grant as a favor] *vt* **1 a :** to give free rein to **b :** to take unrestrained pleasure in **:** GRATIFY **2 a :** to yield to the desire of **:** HUMOR **b :** to treat leniently or generously ~ *vi* **:** to indulge oneself — **in·dulg·er** *n*

syn INDULGE, PAMPER, HUMOR, SPOIL, BABY, MOLLYCODDLE mean to show undue favor to a person's desires and feelings. INDULGE implies excessive compliance and weakness in gratifying another's or one's own desires; PAMPER implies inordinate gratification of desire for luxury and comfort with consequent enervating effect; HUMOR stresses a yielding to a person's moods or whims; SPOIL stresses the injurious effects on character by indulging or pampering; BABY suggests excessive care, attention, or solicitude; MOLLYCODDLE suggests an absurd degree of care and attention to another's health or welfare and shielding from normal hazards

¹in·dul·gence \in-'dəl-jən(t)s\ *n* **1 :** remission of the temporal and esp. purgatorial punishment that according to Roman Catholicism is due for sins whose eternal punishment has been remitted and whose guilt has been pardoned by the reception of the sacrament of penance **2 :** the act of indulging **:** the state of being indulgent **3 a :** an indulgent act **b :** an extension of time for payment or performance granted as a favor **4 a :** the act of indulging in something **:** the thing indulged in **b :** SELF-INDULGENCE

²indulgence *vt* **:** to attach an indulgence to ⟨*indulgenced* prayers⟩

in·dul·gent \in-'dəl-jənt\ *adj* [L *indulgent-*, *indulgens*, prp. of *indulgēre*] **:** indulging or characterized by indulgence **:** LENIENT — **in·dul·gent·ly** *adv*

in·du·line \'in-d(y)ə-ˌlēn\ *n* [ISV *ind-* + *-ule* + *-ine*] **:** any of numerous blue or violet dyes related to the safranines

in·dult \'in-ˌdəlt, in-'\ *n* [ME (Sc), fr. ML *indultum*, fr. LL, grant, fr. L, neut. of *indultus*, pp. of *indulgēre*] **:** a temporary or personal privilege granted in the Roman Catholic Church

in·du·pli·cate \in-'d(y)ü-pli-kət\ *adj* [prob. fr. (assumed) NL *induplicatus*, fr. L *in-* + *duplicatus*, pp. of *duplicare* to double — more at DUPLICATE] **1 :** having the edges bent abruptly toward the axis — used of the parts of the calyx or corolla in a bud **2 :** having the edges rolled inward and then arranged about the axis without overlapping — used of leaves in a bud

¹in·du·rate \'in-d(y)ə-rət, in-'d(y)u̇r-ət\ *adj* **:** physically or morally hardened

²in·du·rate \'in-d(y)ə-ˌrāt\ *vb* [L *induratus*, pp. of *indurare*, fr. *in-* + *durare* to harden, fr. *durus* hard — more at DURING] *vt* **1 :** to make unfeeling, stubborn, or obdurate **2 :** to make hardy **:** INURE **3 a :** to make hard ⟨great heat ~*s* clay⟩ **b :** to increase the fibrous elements of ⟨*indurated* tissue⟩ **4 :** to establish firmly **:** CONFIRM ~ *vi* **1 :** to grow hard **:** HARDEN **2 :** to become established — **in·du·ra·tion** \ˌin-d(y)ə-'rā-shən\ *n* — **in·du·ra·tive** \'in-d(y)ə-ˌrāt-iv, in-'d(y)u̇r-ət-\ *adj*

in·du·si·um \in-'d(y)ü-z(h)ē-əm\ *n, pl* **in·du·sia** \-z(h)ē-ə\ [NL, fr. L, tunic] **:** an investing outgrowth or membrane: as **a :** an outgrowth of a fern frond that invests the sori **b :** the annulus of a fungus esp. when large and full **c :** AMNION

¹in·dus·tri·al \in-'dəs-trē-əl\ *adj* **1 :** of or relating to industry **2 :** characterized by highly developed industries ⟨an ~ nation⟩ **3 :** engaged in industry ⟨the ~ classes⟩ **4 :** derived from human industry **5 :** used in industry — **in·dus·tri·al·ly** \-trē-ə-lē\ *adv*

²industrial *n* **1 a :** one that is employed in industry **b :** a company engaged in industrial production or service **2 :** a stock or bond issued by an industrial corporation or enterprise

industrial arts *n pl but sing or pl in constr* **:** a subject taught in elementary and secondary schools that aims at developing manual skill and familiarity with tools and machines

in·dus·tri·al·ism \in-'dəs-trē-ə-ˌliz-əm\ *n* **:** social organization in which industries and esp. large-scale industries are dominant

in·dus·tri·al·ist \-ləst\ *n* **:** one owning or engaged in the management of an industry **:** MANUFACTURER

in·dus·tri·al·iza·tion \in-ˌdəs-trē-ə-lə-'zā-shən\ *n* **:** the act or process of industrializing **:** the state of being industrialized

in·dus·tri·al·ize \in-'dəs-trē-ə-ˌlīz\ *vt* **:** to make industrial ~ *vi* **:** to become industrial

industrial school *n* **:** a school specializing in the teaching of the industrial arts; *specif* **:** a public institution of this kind for juvenile delinquents

industrial union *n* **:** a labor union that admits to membership workmen in an industry irrespective of their occupation or craft — compare CRAFT UNION

in·dus·tri·ous \in-'dəs-trē-əs\ *adj* **1** *obs* **:** SKILLFUL, INGENIOUS **2 :** persistently active **:** ZEALOUS **3 :** constantly, regularly, or habitually occupied **:** DILIGENT **syn** see BUSY — **in·dus·tri·ous·ly** *adv* — **in·dus·tri·ous·ness** *n*

in·dus·try \'in-(ˌ)dəs-trē\ *n* [MF *industrie* skill, employment involving skill, fr. L *industria* diligence, fr. *industrius* diligent, fr. OL *indostruus*, fr. *indu* in + *-struus* (akin to L *struere* to build) — more at INDIGENOUS, STRUCTURE] **1 :** diligence in an employment or pursuit **2 a :** systematic labor esp. for the creation of value **b :** a department or branch of a craft, art, business, or manufacture; *esp* **:** one that employs a large personnel and capital esp. in manufacturing **c :** a distinct group of productive enterprises **d :** manufacturing activity as a whole **syn** see BUSINESS

in·dwell \(')in-'dwel\ *vi* **:** to exist as an inner activating spirit, force, or principle ~ *vt* **:** to exist within as an activating spirit, force, or principle — **in·dwell·er** *n*

¹-ine \ˌīn, ən, (ˌ)in, ˌēn\ *adj suffix* **1** [ME *-in*, *-ine*, fr. MF&L; MF *-in*, fr. L *-inus* — more at -EN] **:** of or relating to ⟨estuar*ine*⟩ **2** [ME *-in*, *-ine*, fr. MF&L; MF *-in*, fr. L *-īnus*, fr. Gk *-inos* — more at -EN] **:** made of **:** like ⟨opal*ine*⟩

²-ine \ˌēn, 'ēn, ən, (ˌ)in\ *n suffix* [ME *-ine*, *-in*, fr. MF&L; MF *-ine*, fr. L *-īna*, fr. fem. of *-īnus*, adj suffix] **1 :** chemical substance: as **a :** halogen element ⟨chlor*ine*⟩ **b :** basic or base-containing carbon compound ⟨quin*ine*⟩ ⟨cyst*ine*⟩ **c :** mixture of compounds (as of hydrocarbons) ⟨gasol*ine*⟩ **d :** hydride ⟨ars*ine*⟩ **2 :** -IN 1a **3 :** commercial product or material ⟨glass*ine*⟩

ine·bri·ant \in-'ē-brē-ənt\ *n* **:** INTOXICANT — **inebriant** *adj*

¹ine·bri·ate \-brē-ˌāt\ *vt* [L *inebriatus*, pp. of *inebriare*, fr. *in-* + *ebriare* to intoxicate, fr. *ebrius* drunk — more at SOBER] **1 :** to make drunk **:** INTOXICATE **2 :** to exhilarate or stupefy as if by liquor — **ine·bri·a·tion** \in-ˌē-brē-'ā-shən\ *n*

²ine·bri·ate \in-'ē-brē-ət\ *adj* **1 :** INTOXICATED, DRUNK **2 :** addicted to drinking to excess

³ine·bri·ate \-ət\ *n* **:** one who is drunk; *esp* **:** an habitual drunkard

ine·bri·at·ed *adj* **:** exhilarated or confused by or as if by alcohol **:** INTOXICATED **syn** see DRUNK

in·ebri·ety \ˌin-i-'brī-ət-ē\ *n* [prob. blend of *inebriation* and *ebriety* (drunkenness)] **:** INEBRIATION, DRUNKENNESS

in·ed·i·ble \(')in-'ed-ə-bəl\ *adj* **:** not fit for food

in·ed·it·ed \(')in-'ed-ət-əd\ *adj* [NL *ineditus*, fr. L, not made known, fr. *in-* + *editus*, pp. of *edere* to proclaim — more at EDITION] **:** not edited; *esp* **:** UNPUBLISHED

in·ed·u·ca·ble \(')in-'ej-ə-kə-bəl\ *adj* **:** incapable of being educated

in·ef·fa·bil·i·ty \(ˌ)in-ˌef-ə-'bil-ət-ē\ *n* **:** the quality or state of being ineffable

in·ef·fa·ble \(')in-'ef-ə-bəl\ *adj* [ME, fr. MF, fr. L *ineffabilis*, fr. *in-* + *effabilis* capable of being expressed, fr. *effari* to speak out, fr. *ex-* + *fari* to speak — more at BAN] **1 a :** incapable of being expressed in words **:** INDESCRIBABLE ⟨~ joy⟩ **b :** UNSPEAKABLE ⟨~ disgust⟩ **2 :** not to be uttered **:** TABOO ⟨the ~ name of Jehovah⟩ — **in·ef·fa·ble·ness** *n* — **in·ef·fa·bly** \-blē\ *adv*

in·ef·face·abil·i·ty \ˌin-ə-ˌfā-sə-'bil-ət-ē\ *n* **:** the quality or state of being ineffaceable

in·ef·face·able \-'fā-sə-bəl\ *adj* [prob. fr. F *ineffaçable*, fr. MF, fr. *in-* + *effaçable* effaceable] **:** not effaceable **:** INERADICABLE — **in·ef·face·ably** \-blē\ *adv*

in·ef·fec·tive \ˌin-ə-'fek-tiv\ *adj* **1 :** not producing an intended effect **:** INEFFECTUAL **2 :** not capable of performing efficiently **:** INCAPABLE — **in·ef·fec·tive·ly** *adv* — **in·ef·fec·tive·ness** *n*

in·ef·fec·tu·al \ˌin-ə-'fek-chə(-wə)l, -'feksh-wəl\ *adj* **:** not producing the proper or usual effect **:** FUTILE — **in·ef·fec·tu·al·i·ty** \-ˌfek-chə-'wal-ət-ē\ *n* — **in·ef·fec·tu·al·ly** \-'fek-chə-(wə-)lē, -'feksh-wə-\ *adv* — **in·ef·fec·tu·al·ness** *n*

in·ef·fi·ca·cious \(ˌ)in-ˌef-ə-'kā-shəs\ *adj* **:** lacking the power to produce a desired effect **:** INADEQUATE — **in·ef·fi·ca·cious·ly** *adv* — **in·ef·fi·ca·cious·ness** *n*

in·ef·fi·ca·cy \(ˈ)in-ˈef-i-kə-sē\ *n* [LL *inefficacia*, fr. L *inefficac-*, *inefficax* inefficacious, fr. *in-* + *efficac-*, *efficax* efficacious] **:** lack of power to produce a desired effect

in·ef·fi·cien·cy \ˌin-ə-ˈfish-ən-sē\ *n* **:** the quality, state, or fact of being inefficient

in·ef·fi·cient \-ˈfish-ənt\ *adj* **:** not efficient: **a :** not producing the effect intended or desired **:** INEFFICACIOUS **b :** wasteful of time or energy **c :** INCAPABLE, INCOMPETENT — **inefficient** *n* — **in·ef·fi·cient·ly** *adv*

in·elas·tic \ˌin-ə-ˈlas-tik\ *adj* **:** not elastic: **a :** slow to react or respond to changing conditions **b :** INFLEXIBLE, UNYIELDING — **in·elas·tic·i·ty** \ˌin-i-ˌlas-ˈtis-ət-ē, (ˌ)in-ˌē-ˌlas-, -ˈtis-tē\ *n*

in·el·e·gance \(ˈ)in-ˈel-i-gən(t)s\ *n* **:** lack of elegance

in·el·e·gant \-gənt\ *adj* [MF, fr. L *inelegant-*, *inelegans*, fr. *in-* + *elegant-*, *elegans* elegant] **:** lacking in refinement, grace, or good taste — **in·el·e·gant·ly** *adv*

in·el·i·gi·bil·i·ty \(ˌ)in-ˌel-ə-jə-ˈbil-ət-ē\ *n* **:** the condition or fact of being ineligible

in·el·i·gi·ble \(ˈ)in-ˈel-ə-jə-bəl\ *adj* [F *inéligible*, fr. *in-* + *éligible* eligible] **1 :** not qualified to be chosen for an office **2 :** not worthy to be chosen or preferred — **ineligible** *n*

in·el·o·quent \(ˈ)in-ˈel-ə-kwənt\ *adj* **:** not eloquent — **in·el·o·quent·ly** *adv*

in·eluc·ta·bil·i·ty \ˌin-i-ˌlək-tə-ˈbil-ət-ē\ *n* **:** the quality or state of being ineluctable

in·eluc·ta·ble \-ˈlək-tə-bəl\ *adj* [L *ineluctabilis*, fr. *in-* + *eluctari* to struggle out, fr. *ex-* + *luctari* to struggle — more at LOCK] **:** not to be avoided, changed, or resisted **:** INEVITABLE — **in·eluc·ta·bly** \-blē\ *adv*

in·elud·ible \ˌin-i-ˈlüd-ə-bəl\ *adj* **:** INESCAPABLE

in·enar·ra·ble \ˌin-i-ˈnar-ə-bəl\ *adj* [ME, fr. MF, fr. L *inenarrabilis*, fr. *in-* + *enarrare* to explain in detail, fr. *e-* + *narrare* to narrate] **:** incapable of being narrated **:** INDESCRIBABLE

in·ept \in-ˈept\ *adj* [F *inepte*, fr. L *ineptus*, fr. *in-* + *aptus* apt] **1 :** lacking in fitness or aptitude **:** UNFIT **2 :** out of place **:** INAPPROPRIATE **3 :** lacking sense or reason **:** FOOLISH **4 :** generally incompetent **:** BUNGLING **syn** see AWKWARD — **in·ep·ti·tude** \in-ˈep-tə-ˌt(y)üd\ *n* — **in·ept·ly** \-ˈep-(t)lē\ *adv* — **in·ept·ness** \-ˈep(t)-nəs\ *n*

in·equal·i·ty \ˌin-i-ˈkwäl-ət-ē\ *n* [MF *inequalité*, fr. L *inaequalitat-*, *inaequalitas*, fr. *inaequalis* unequal, fr. *in-* + *aequalis* equal] **1 :** the quality of being unequal or uneven: as **a :** UNEVENNESS **b :** social disparity **c :** disparity of distribution or opportunity **d :** VARIABLENESS, CHANGEABLENESS **2 :** an instance of being unequal **3 :** a formal statement of inequality between two quantities

in·eq·ui·ta·ble \(ˈ)in-ˈek-wət-ə-bəl\ *adj* **:** not equitable **:** UNFAIR — **in·eq·ui·ta·bly** \-blē\ *adv*

in·eq·ui·ty \-wət-ē\ *n* **1 :** INJUSTICE, UNFAIRNESS **2 :** an instance of injustice or unfairness

in·equi·valve \(ˈ)in-ˈē-kwə-ˌvalv\ *also* **in·equi·valved** \-ˌvalvd\ *adj, of a bivalve mollusk or its shell* **:** having the valves unequal in size and form

in·erad·i·ca·ble \ˌin-i-ˈrad-i-kə-bəl\ *adj* **:** incapable of being eradicated — **in·erad·i·ca·bly** \-blē\ *adv*

in·er·ran·cy \(ˈ)in-ˈer-ən-sē\ *n* **:** exemption from error **:** INFALLIBILITY

in·er·rant \-ənt\ *adj* [L *inerrant-*, *inerrans*, fr. *in-* + *errant-*, *errans*, prp. of *errare* to err] **:** free from error **:** INFALLIBLE

in·ert \in-ˈərt\ *adj* [L *inert-*, *iners* unskilled, idle, fr. *in-* + *art-*, *ars* skill — more at ARM] **1 :** not having the power to move itself **2 :** deficient in active properties; *esp* **:** lacking a usual or anticipated chemical or biological action **3 :** very slow to move or act **:** SLUGGISH **syn** see INACTIVE — **inert** *n* — **in·ert·ly** *adv* — **in·ert·ness** *n*

in·er·tia \in-ˈər-shə, -shē-ə\ *n* [NL, fr. L, lack of skill, fr. *inert-*, *iners*] **1 a :** a property of matter by which it remains at rest or in uniform motion in the same straight line unless acted upon by some external force **b :** an analogous property of other physical quantities (as electricity) **2 :** indisposition to motion, exertion, or change **:** INERTNESS — **in·er·tial** \-shəl\ *adj*

inertial guidance *n* **:** guidance (as of an aircraft) by means of self-contained automatically controlling devices that respond to inertial forces — called also *inertial navigation*

in·es·cap·able \ˌin-ə-ˈskā-pə-bəl\ *adj* **:** incapable of being escaped **:** INEVITABLE — **in·es·cap·ably** \-blē\ *adv*

in·es·sen·tial \ˌin-ə-ˈsen-chəl\ *adj* **1 :** having no essence **2 :** not essential **:** UNESSENTIAL

in·es·ti·ma·ble \(ˈ)in-ˈes-tə-mə-bəl\ *adj* [ME, fr. MF, fr. L *inaestimabilis*, fr. *in-* + *aestimabilis* estimable] **1 :** incapable of being estimated or computed **2 :** too valuable or excellent to be measured or appreciated — **in·es·ti·ma·bly** \-blē\ *adv*

in·ev·i·ta·bil·i·ty \in-ˌev-ət-ə-ˈbil-ət-ē\ *n* **:** the quality or state of being inevitable

in·ev·i·ta·ble \in-ˈev-ət-ə-bəl\ *adj* [ME, fr. L *inevitabilis*, fr. *in-* + *evitabilis* evitable] **:** incapable of being avoided or evaded — **in·ev·i·ta·ble·ness** *n* — **in·ev·i·ta·bly** \-blē\ *adv*

in·ex·act \ˌin-ig-ˈzakt\ *adj* [F, fr. *in-* + *exact*] **1 :** not precisely correct or true **:** INACCURATE **2 :** not rigorous and careful — **in·ex·ac·ti·tude** \-ˈzak-tə-ˌt(y)üd\ *n* — **in·ex·act·ly** \-ˈzak-(t)lē\ *adv* — **in·ex·act·ness** \-ˈzak(t)-nəs\ *n*

in·ex·cus·able \ˌin-ik-ˈskyü-zə-bəl\ *adj* [L *inexcusabilis*, fr. *in-* + *excusabilis* excusable] **:** being without excuse or justification — **in·ex·cus·able·ness** *n* — **in·ex·cus·ably** \-blē\ *adv*

in·ex·haust·ibil·i·ty \ˌin-ig-ˌzo-stə-ˈbil-ət-ē\ *n* **:** the quality or state of being inexhaustible

in·ex·haust·ible \-ˈzo-stə-bəl\ *adj* **:** not exhaustible: as **a :** incapable of being used up **b :** incapable of being wearied or worn out — **in·ex·haust·ible·ness** *n* — **in·ex·haust·ibly** \-blē\ *adv*

in·ex·is·tence \ˌin-ig-ˈzis-tən(t)s\ *n* **:** NONEXISTENCE

in·ex·is·tent \-tənt\ *adj* [LL *inexsistent-*, *inexsistens*, fr. L *in-* + *exsistent-*, *exsistens*, prp. of *exsistere* to exist] **:** not having being **:** NONEXISTENT

in·ex·o·ra·bil·i·ty \(ˌ)in-ˌeks-(ə-)rə-ˈbil-ət-ē, -ˌegz-ə-rə-\ *n* **:** the quality of being inexorable

in·ex·o·ra·ble \(ˈ)in-ˈeks-(ə-)rə-bəl, -ˈegz-ə-rə-\ *adj* [L *inexorabilis*, fr. *in-* + *exorabilis* pliant, fr. *exorare* to prevail upon, fr. *ex-* + *orare* to speak — more at ORATION] **:** not to be persuaded or moved by entreaty **:** RELENTLESS **syn** see INFLEXIBLE — **in·ex·o·ra·ble·ness** *n* — **in·ex·o·ra·bly** \-blē\ *adv*

in·ex·pe·di·en·cy \ˌin-ik-ˈspēd-ē-ən-sē\ *or* **in·ex·pe·di·ence** \-ən(t)s\ *n* **:** the quality or fact of being inexpedient

in·ex·pe·di·ent \-ənt\ *adj* **:** not expedient **:** INADVISABLE — **in·ex·pe·di·ent·ly** *adv*

in·ex·pen·sive \ˌin-ik-ˈspen(t)-siv\ *adj* **:** reasonable in price **:** CHEAP — **in·ex·pen·sive·ly** *adv* — **in·ex·pen·sive·ness** *n*

in·ex·pe·ri·ence \ˌin-ik-ˈspir-ē-ən(t)s\ *n* [MF, fr. LL *inexperientia*, fr. L *in-* + *experientia* experience] **1 :** lack of practical experience **2 :** lack of knowledge or proficiency gained by experience — **in·ex·pe·ri·enced** \-ən(t)st\ *adj*

in·ex·pert \(ˈ)in-ˈek-ˌspərt, ˌin-ik-ˈ\ *adj* [ME, fr. MF, fr. L *inexpertus*, fr. *in-* + *expertus* expert] **:** not expert **:** UNSKILLED — **in·ex·pert** \(ˈ)in-ˈek-ˌspərt\ *n* — **in·ex·pert·ly** \(ˈ)in-ˈek-ˌspərt-lē, ˌin-ik-ˈ\ *adv* — **in·ex·pert·ness** *n*

in·ex·pi·a·ble \(ˈ)in-ˈek-spē-ə-bəl\ *adj* [L *inexpiabilis*, fr. *in-* + *expiare* to expiate] **1 :** not capable of being atoned for **2** *obs* **:** IMPLACABLE, UNAPPEASABLE — **in·ex·pi·a·bly** \-blē\ *adv*

in·ex·plain·able \ˌin-ik-ˈsplā-nə-bəl\ *adj* **:** INEXPLICABLE

in·ex·pli·ca·bil·i·ty \ˌin-ik-ˌsplik-ə-ˈbil-ət-ē, (ˌ)in-ˌek-(ˌ)splik-\ *n* **:** the quality of being inexplicable

in·ex·pli·ca·ble \ˌin-ik-ˈsplik-ə-bəl, (ˈ)in-ˈek-(ˌ)splik-\ *adj* [MF, fr. L *inexplicabilis*, fr. *in-* + *explicabilis* explicable] **:** incapable of being explained, interpreted, or accounted for — **in·ex·pli·ca·ble·ness** *n* — **in·ex·pli·ca·bly** \-blē\ *adv*

in·ex·plic·it \ˌin-ik-ˈsplis-ət\ *adj* **:** not explicit

in·ex·press·ibil·i·ty \ˌin-ik-ˌspres-ə-ˈbil-ət-ē\ *n* **:** the quality of being inexpressible

in·ex·press·ible \-ˈspres-ə-bəl\ *adj* **:** not capable of being expressed **:** INDESCRIBABLE — **in·ex·press·ible·ness** *n* — **in·ex·press·ibly** \-blē\ *adv*

in·ex·pres·sive \-ˈspres-iv\ *adj* **1** *obs* **:** INEXPRESSIBLE **2 :** lacking expression or meaning — **in·ex·pres·sive·ly** *adv* — **in·ex·pres·sive·ness** *n*

in·ex·pug·na·ble \ˌin-ik-ˈspyü-nə-bəl, -ˈspəg-nə-\ *adj* [MF, fr. L *inexpugnabilis*, fr. *in-* + *expugnare* to take by storm, fr. *ex-* + *pugnare* to fight — more at PUNGENT] **:** incapable of being subdued or overthrown **:** IMPREGNABLE — **in·ex·pug·na·ble·ness** *n* — **in·ex·pug·na·bly** \-blē\ *adv*

in·ex·ten·si·ble \ˌin-ik-ˈsten(t)-sə-bəl\ *adj* **:** incapable of being stretched

in ex·ten·so \ˌin-ik-ˈsten(t)-(ˌ)sō\ *adv* [L] **:** at full length

in·ex·tin·guish·able \ˌin-ik-ˈstiŋ-gwish-ə-bəl\ *adj* **:** not extinguishable **:** UNQUENCHABLE — **in·ex·tin·guish·ably** \-blē\ *adv*

in ex·tre·mis \ˌin-ik-ˈstrā-məs, -ˌmēs\ *adv* [L] **:** in extreme circumstances; *esp* **:** at the point of death

in·ex·tri·ca·bil·i·ty \ˌin-ik-ˌstrik-ə-ˈbil-ət-ē, (ˌ)in-ˌek-(ˌ)strik-\ *n* **:** the quality or state of being inextricable

in·ex·tri·ca·ble \ˌin-ik-ˈstrik-ə-bəl, (ˈ)in-ˈek-(ˌ)strik-\ *adj* [MF or L; MF, fr. L *inextricabilis*, fr. *in-* + *extricabilis* extricable] **1 :** forming a maze or tangle from which it is impossible to get free **2 a :** incapable of being disentangled or untied **b :** UNSOLVABLE — **in·ex·tri·ca·bly** \-blē\ *adv*

in·fal·li·bil·i·ty \(ˌ)in-ˌfal-ə-ˈbil-ət-ē\ *n* **:** the quality or state of being infallible

in·fal·li·ble \(ˈ)in-ˈfal-ə-bəl\ *adj* [ML *infallibilis*, fr. L *in-* + LL *fallibilis* fallible] **1 :** incapable of error **:** UNERRING ⟨~ memory⟩ **2 :** SURE, CERTAIN ⟨~ remedy⟩ **3 :** incapable of error in defining doctrines touching faith or morals — **in·fal·li·bly** \-blē\ *adv*

in·fa·mous \ˈin-fə-məs\ *adj* [ME, fr. L *infamis*, fr. *in-* + *fama* fame] **1 :** having a reputation of the worst kind **2 :** causing or bringing infamy **:** DISGRACEFUL **3 :** convicted of an offense bringing infamy **syn** see VICIOUS — **in·fa·mous·ly** *adv*

in·fa·my \-mē\ *n* **1 :** evil reputation brought about by something grossly criminal, shocking, or brutal **2 a :** an extreme and publicly known criminal or evil act **b :** the state of being infamous **syn** see DISGRACE

in·fan·cy \ˈin-fən-sē\ *n* **1 :** early childhood **2 :** a beginning or early period of existence **3 :** the legal status of an infant

[1]in·fant \ˈin-fənt\ *n* [ME *enfaunt*, fr. MF *enfant*, fr. L *infant-*, *infans*, fr. *infant-*, *infans*, incapable of speech, young, fr. *in-* + *fant-*, *fans*, prp. of *fari* to speak — more at BAN] **1 :** a child in the first period of life **2 :** a person who is not of full age **:** MINOR; *specif* **:** a person under the age of 21

[2]infant *adj* **1 :** of, relating to, or being in infancy **2 :** being in an early stage of development **3 :** intended for young children

in·fan·ta \in-ˈfant-ə, -ˈfänt-\ *n* [Sp & Pg, fem. of *infante*] **:** a daughter of a Spanish or Portuguese monarch

in·fan·te \in-ˈfant-ē, -ˈfän-(ˌ)tā\ *n* [Sp & Pg, lit., infant, fr. L *infant-*, *infans*] **:** a younger son of a Spanish or Portuguese monarch

in·fan·ti·cide \in-ˈfant-ə-ˌsīd\ *n* [LL *infanticidium*, fr. L *infant-*, *infans* + *-i-* + *-cidium* -cide] **1 :** the killing of an infant **2 :** one who kills an infant

in·fan·tile \ˈin-fən-ˌtīl, -təl, -ˌtēl, -(ˌ)til\ *adj* **1 :** of or relating to infants or infancy **2 :** suitable to or characteristic of an infant **:** CHILDISH **3** *of topography* **:** being in a very early stage of development following an uplift or equivalent change — **in·fan·til·i·ty** \ˌin-fən-ˈtil-ət-ē\ *n*

infantile paralysis *n* **:** POLIOMYELITIS

in·fan·til·ism \ˈin-fən-ˌtīl-ˌiz-əm, -təl-, -ˌtēl-, -(ˌ)til-\ *n* **1 :** retention of childish physical, mental, or emotional qualities in adult life; *esp* **:** failure to attain sexual maturity **2 :** an act or expression characteristic of lack of maturity

in·fan·tine \ˈin-fən-ˌtīn, -ˌtēn\ *adj* **:** INFANTILE, CHILDISH

in·fan·try \ˈin-fən-trē\ *n* [MF & OIt; MF *infanterie*, fr. OIt *infanteria*, fr. *infante* boy, foot soldier, fr. L *infant-*, *infans*] **1 a :** soldiers trained, armed, and equipped to fight on foot **b :** a branch of an army composed of these soldiers **2 :** an infantry regiment — **in·fan·try·man** \-mən\ *n*

in·farct \ˈin-ˌfärkt\ *n* [L *infarctus*, pp. of *infarcire* to stuff, fr. *in-* + *farcire* to stuff — more at FARCE] **:** an area of necrosis in a tissue or organ resulting from obstruction of the local circulation by a thrombus or embolus — **in·farc·tion** \in-ˈfärk-shən\ *n*

in·fare \ˈin-ˌfa(ə)r, -ˌfe(ə)r\ *n* [ME *infer*, fr. OE *infær* entrance, fr. *in* + *fær* way, fr. *faran* to go — more at FARE] *chiefly dial* **:** a reception for a newly married couple

¹in·fat·u·ate \in-ˈfach-ə-wət\ *adj* **:** INFATUATED
²in·fat·u·ate \-ˌwāt\ *vt* [L *infatuatus*, pp. of *infatuare*, fr. *in-* + *fatuus* fatuous] **1 :** to make foolish **2 :** to inspire with a foolish or extravagant love or admiration — **in·fat·u·at·ed** *adj* — **in·fat·u·a·tion** \in-ˌfach-ə-ˈwā-shən\ *n*
in·fea·si·ble \(ˈ)in-ˈfē-zə-bəl\ *adj* **:** not feasible **:** IMPRACTICABLE
in·fect \in-ˈfekt\ *vt* [ME *infecten*, fr. L *infectus*, pp. of *inficere*, fr. *in-* + *facere* to make, do — more at DO] **1 :** to contaminate with a disease-producing substance, germs, or bacteria **2 a :** to communicate a pathogen or a disease to **b** *of a pathogenic organism* **:** to invade (an individual or organ) usu. by penetration **3 a :** CONTAMINATE, CORRUPT **b :** to work upon or seize upon so as to induce sympathy, belief, or support — **in·fec·tor** \-ˈfek-tər\ *n*
in·fec·tion \in-ˈfek-shən\ *n* **1 :** the act or result of affecting injuriously **2 :** an act or process of infecting; *also* **:** the establishment of a pathogen in its host after invasion **3 :** the state produced by the establishment of an infective agent in or on a suitable host; *also* **:** a contagious or infectious disease **4 :** an infective agent or material contaminated with an infective agent **5 :** the communication of emotions or qualities through example or contact
in·fec·tious \-shəs\ *adj* **1 a :** capable of causing infection **b :** communicable by infection — compare CONTAGIOUS **2 :** CORRUPTING, CONTAMINATING **3 :** capable of being easily diffused or spread — **in·fec·tious·ly** *adv* — **in·fec·tious·ness** *n*
infectious hepatitis *n* **:** an acute virus inflammation of the liver characterized by jaundice, fever, nausea, vomiting, and abdominal discomfort
infectious mononucleosis *n* **:** an acute infectious disease characterized by fever, swelling of lymph glands, and lymphocytosis
in·fec·tive \in-ˈfek-tiv\ *adj* **1 :** producing infection **:** able to produce infection **:** INFECTING **2 :** affecting others **:** INFECTIOUS — **in·fec·tiv·i·ty** \(ˌ)in-ˌfek-ˈtiv-ət-ē\ *n*
in·fe·lic·i·tous \ˌin-fi-ˈlis-ət-əs\ *adj* **:** not appropriate in application or expression — **in·fe·lic·i·tous·ly** *adv*
in·fe·lic·i·ty \-ət-ē\ *n* [ME *infelicite*, fr. L *infelicitas*, fr. *infelic-*, *infelix* unhappy, fr. *in-* + *felic-*, *felix* fruitful — more at FEMININE] **1 :** the quality or state of being infelicitous **2 :** something that is infelicitous
in·fer \in-ˈfər\ *vb* **in·ferred; in·fer·ring** [MF or L; MF *inferer*, fr. L *inferre*, lit., to carry or bring into, fr. *in-* + *ferre* to carry — more at BEAR] *vt* **1 :** to derive as a conclusion from facts or premises **2 :** GUESS, SURMISE **3 a :** to involve as a normal outcome of thought **b :** to point out **:** INDICATE — compare IMPLY **4 :** HINT, SUGGEST ~ *vi* **:** to draw inferences — **in·fer·able** *or* **in·fer·ri·ble** \in-ˈfər-ə-bəl\ *adj* — **in·fer·rer** \-ˈfər-ər\ *n*
syn DEDUCE, CONCLUDE, JUDGE, GATHER: INFER implies arriving at a conclusion by reasoning from evidence; if the evidence is slight the term comes close to *surmise;* DEDUCE adds to INFER the special implication of drawing a particular inference from a generalization; CONCLUDE implies arriving at a logically necessary inference at the end of a chain of reasoning; JUDGE stresses critical examination of the evidence on which a conclusion is based; GATHER suggests a direct or intuitive forming of a conclusion from hints or implications usu. in the absence of clear evidence or plain statement
in·fer·ence \ˈin-f(ə-)rən(t)s, -fərn(t)s\ *n* **1 :** the act or process of inferring; *specif* **:** the act of passing from one proposition, statement, or judgment considered as true to another whose truth is believed to follow from that of the former **2 :** something that is inferred; *esp* **:** a proposition arrived at by inference **3 :** the premises and conclusion of a process of inferring
in·fer·en·tial \ˌin-fə-ˈren-chəl\ *adj* [ML *inferentia*, fr. L *inferent-*, *inferens*, prp. of *inferre*] **:** deduced or deducible by inference — **in·fer·en·tial·ly** \-ˈrench-(ə-)lē\ *adv*
in·fe·ri·or \in-ˈfir-ē-ər\ *adj* [ME, fr. L, compar. of *inferus* — more at UNDER] **1 :** situated lower down **:** LOWER **2 :** of low or lower degree or rank **3 :** of little or less importance, value, or merit **4** *of an anatomical structure* **a :** situated below a similar superior part **b :** situated in a relatively low posterior or ventral position **c** (1) **:** situated below another organ (2) **:** ABAXIAL **5 :** SUBSCRIPT **6 a :** nearer the sun than the earth is ⟨~ planet⟩ **b :** nearer the earth than the sun is ⟨~ conjunction of Venus⟩ — **inferior** *n* — **in·fe·ri·or·i·ty** \(ˌ)in-ˌfir-ē-ˈór-ət-ē, -ˈär-\ *n* — **in·fe·ri·or·ly** \in-ˈfir-ē-ər-lē\ *adv*
inferiority complex *n* **:** an acute sense of personal inferiority resulting either in timidity or through overcompensation in exaggerated aggressiveness
in·fer·nal \in-ˈfərn-ᵊl\ *adj* [ME, fr. OF, fr. LL *infernalis*, fr. *infernus* hell, fr. L, lower; akin to L *inferus* inferior] **1 :** of or relating to a nether world of the dead **2 a :** of or relating to hell **b :** HELLISH, DIABOLICAL **3 :** DAMNABLE, DAMNED — **in·fer·nal·ly** \-ᵊl-ē\ *adv*
infernal machine *n* **:** a machine or apparatus maliciously designed to explode and destroy life or property
in·fer·no \in-ˈfər-(ˌ)nō\ *n* [It, hell, fr. LL *infernus*] **:** a place or a state that resembles or suggests hell
in·fero- \ˌin-fə-(ˌ)rō\ *comb form* [L *inferus*] **:** below and ⟨*inferolateral*⟩
in·fer·tile \(ˈ)in-ˈfərt-ᵊl\ *adj* [MF, fr. LL *infertilis*, fr. L *in-* + *fertilis* fertile] **:** not fertile or productive **:** BARREN **syn** see STERILE — **in·fer·til·i·ty** \ˌin-(ˌ)fər-ˈtil-ət-ē\ *n*
in·fest \in-ˈfest\ *vt* [MF *infester*, fr. L *infestare*, fr. *infestus* hostile] **1 :** to spread or swarm in or over in a troublesome manner **2 :** to live in or on as a parasite — **in·fes·tant** \-ˈfes-tənt\ *n* — **in·fes·ta·tion** \ˌin-ˌfes-ˈtā-shən\ *n* — **in·fest·er** \in-ˈfes-tər\ *n*
in·fi·del \ˈin-fəd-ᵊl, -fə-ˌdel\ *n* [MF *infidele*, fr. LL *infidelis* unbelieving, fr. L, unfaithful, fr. *in-* + *fidelis* faithful — more at FEAL] **1 :** one who is not a Christian or opposes Christianity **2 a :** an unbeliever in respect to a particular religion **b :** one who acknowledges no religious belief **3 :** a disbeliever in something specified or understood **syn** see ATHEIST — **infidel** *adj*
in·fi·del·i·ty \ˌin-fə-ˈdel-ət-ē, -(ˌ)fī-\ *n* **1 :** lack of belief in a religion **2 a :** unfaithfulness to a moral obligation **:** DISLOYALTY **b :** marital unfaithfulness or an instance of it
in·field \ˈin-ˌfēld\ *n* **1 :** a field near a farmhouse **2 a :** the area of a baseball or softball field enclosed by the three bases and home plate **b :** the defensive positions comprising first base, second base, shortstop, and third base **3 :** the area enclosed by a racetrack or running track
in·field·er \-ˌfēl-dər\ *n* **:** a baseball player who plays the infield
in·fight·er \ˈin-ˌfīt-ər\ *n* **:** one who practices infighting
in·fight·ing \-iŋ\ *n* **1 :** fighting or boxing at close quarters **2 :** rough-and-tumble fighting
in·fil·trate \in-ˈfil-ˌtrāt, ˈin-(ˌ)fil-\ *vt* **1 :** to cause something (as a liquid) to enter by penetrating the interstices of **2 :** to pass into or through by filtering or permeating **3 :** to pass (troops) singly or in small groups through gaps in the enemy line **4 :** to enter or become established in gradually or unobtrusively ~ *vi* **:** to enter, permeate, or pass through a substance or area by filtering — **in·fil·tra·tion** \ˌin-(ˌ)fil-ˈtrā-shən\ *n* — **in·fil·tra·tive** \ˈin-(ˌ)fil-ˌtrāt-iv, in-ˈfil-trət-\ *adj* — **in·fil·tra·tor** \-ˌtrāt-ər\ *n*
in·fi·nite \ˈin-fə-nət\ *adj* [ME *infinit*, fr. MF or L; MF, fr. L *infinitus*, fr. *in-* + *finitus* finite] **1 :** subject to no limitation or external determination **2 :** extending indefinitely **:** ENDLESS **3 :** immeasurably or inconceivably great or extensive **:** INEXHAUSTIBLE **4 a :** extending or lying beyond any preassigned value however large ⟨~ number of positive numbers⟩ **b :** extending to infinity ⟨~ plane surface⟩ **c :** capable of being put into one-to-one correspondence with a proper part of itself ⟨~ set⟩ — **infinite** *n* — **in·fi·nite·ly** *adv* — **in·fi·nite·ness** *n*
¹in·fin·i·tes·i·mal \(ˌ)in-ˌfin-ə-ˈtes-ə-məl, -ˈtez-\ *n* [NL *infinitesimus* infinite in rank, fr. L *infinitus*] **1 :** a function that can be made arbitrarily close to zero **2 :** an infinitesimal quantity
²infinitesimal *adj* **1 :** capable of being made arbitrarily close to zero **2 :** immeasurably or incalculably small — **in·fin·i·tes·i·mal·ly** \-mə-lē\ *adv*
infinitesimal calculus *n* **:** CALCULUS 3b
in·fin·i·ti·val \(ˌ)in-ˌfin-ə-ˈtī-vəl\ *adj* **:** relating to the infinitive
¹in·fin·i·tive \in-ˈfin-ət-iv\ *adj* [LL *infinitivus*, fr. L *infinitus*] **:** formed with the infinitive — **in·fin·i·tive·ly** *adv*
²infinitive *n* **:** a verb form normally identical in English with the first person singular that performs some functions of a noun and at the same time displays some characteristics of a verb and is used with *to* (as "I asked him *to go*") except with auxiliary and various other verbs (as "no one *saw* him *leave*")
in·fin·i·tude \in-ˈfin-ə-ˌt(y)üd\ *n* **1 :** the quality or state of being infinite **:** INFINITENESS **2 :** something that is infinite esp. in extent **3 :** an infinite number or quantity
in·fin·i·ty \in-ˈfin-ət-ē\ *n* **1 a :** the quality of being infinite **b :** unlimited extent of time, space, or quantity **:** BOUNDLESSNESS **2 :** an indefinitely great number or amount **3 a :** the limit of a function that can be made to become and remain numerically larger than any preassigned value **b :** a part of a geometric magnitude that lies beyond any part whose distance from a given reference position is finite **4 :** a distance so great that the rays of light from a point source at that distance may be regarded as parallel
in·firm \in-ˈfərm\ *adj* [ME, fr. L *infirmus*, fr. *in-* + *firmus* firm] **1 :** of poor or deteriorated vitality; *esp* **:** feeble from age **2 :** weak of mind, will, or character **:** IRRESOLUTE, VACILLATING **3 :** not solid or stable **:** INSECURE **syn** see WEAK — **in·firm·ly** *adv*
in·fir·ma·ry \in-ˈfərm-(ə-)rē\ *n* **:** a place where the infirm or sick are lodged for care and treatment
in·fir·mi·ty \in-ˈfər-mət-ē\ *n* **:** the quality or state of being infirm: as **a :** FEEBLENESS, FRAILTY **b :** DISEASE, MALADY **c :** a personal failing **:** FOIBLE
¹in·fix \ˈin-ˌfiks, in-ˈ\ *vt* [L *infixus*, pp. of *infigere*, fr. *in-* + *figere* to fasten — more at DIKE] **1 :** to fasten or fix by piercing or thrusting in **2 :** INSTILL, INCULCATE **3 :** to insert (a sound or letter) as an infix **syn** see IMPLANT
²in·fix \ˈin-ˌfiks\ *n* **:** a derivational or inflectional affix appearing in the body of a word (as Sanskrit *-n-* in *vindami* "I know" as contrasted with *vid* "to know"; English *stand* as contrasted with *stood*)
in·flame \in-ˈflām\ *vb* [ME *enflamen*, fr. MF *enflamer*, fr. L *inflammare*, fr. *in-* + *flamma* flame] *vt* **1 :** to set on fire **:** KINDLE **2 a :** to excite to excessive or unnatural action or feeling **b :** to make more heated or violent **:** INTENSIFY **3 :** to cause to redden or grow hot from anger or excitement **4 :** to cause inflammation in (bodily tissue) ~ *vi* **1 :** to burst into flame **2 :** to become excited or angered **3 :** to become affected with inflammation — **in·flam·er** *n*
in·flam·ma·bil·i·ty \in-ˌflam-ə-ˈbil-ət-ē\ *n* **:** the quality or state of being inflammable
in·flam·ma·ble \in-ˈflam-ə-bəl\ *adj* **1 :** FLAMMABLE **2 :** easily inflamed, excited, or angered **:** IRASCIBLE — **inflammable** *n* — **in·flam·ma·ble·ness** *n* — **in·flam·ma·bly** \-blē\ *adv*
in·flam·ma·tion \ˌin-flə-ˈmā-shən\ *n* **1 :** the act of inflaming **:** the state of being inflamed **2 :** a local response to cellular injury marked by capillary dilatation, leukocytic infiltration, redness, heat, and pain that serves as a mechanism initiating the elimination of noxious agents and of damaged tissue
in·flam·ma·to·ry \in-ˈflam-ə-ˌtōr-ē, -ˌtór-\ *adj* **1 :** tending to inflame or excite the senses **2 :** tending to excite anger, disorder, or tumult **:** SEDITIOUS **3 :** accompanied by or tending to cause inflammation
in·flat·able \in-ˈflāt-ə-bəl\ *adj* **:** capable of being inflated
in·flate \in-ˈflāt\ *vb* [L *inflatus*, pp. of *inflare*, fr. *in-* + *flare* to blow — more at BLOW] *vt* **1 :** to swell or distend with air or gas **2 :** to puff up **:** ELATE **3 :** to expand or increase abnormally ~ *vi* **:** to become inflated **syn** see EXPAND — **in·fla·tor** *or* **in·flat·er** \-ˈflāt-ər\ *n*
in·flat·ed *adj* **1 :** distended with air or gas **2 :** BOMBASTIC, EXAGGERATED **3 :** expanded to an abnormal or unjustifiable volume or level **4 a :** being hollow and distended **b :** open and swelled out or enlarged
syn INFLATED, FLATULENT, TUMID, TURGID mean distended by gas or fluid beyond normal size. INFLATED implies stretching to a point of tension with danger of speedy collapse; FLATULENT implies a distension of the belly by internally generated gases, and suggests figuratively something seemingly full but actually without substance; TUMID stresses morbid enlargement by swelling or bloating or figuratively verbosity and empty pretentiousness of style; TURGID may differ from TUMID in implying a normal fullness or distension; figuratively it suggests disorder and lack of emotional restraint in style
in·fla·tion \in-ˈflā-shən\ *n* **1 :** an act of inflating **:** a state of being inflated: as **a :** DISTENSION **b :** empty pretentiousness **:** POMPOSITY **2 :** an increase in the volume of money and credit relative to available goods resulting in a substantial and continuing rise in the general price level
in·fla·tion·ary \-shə-ˌner-ē\ *adj* **:** of, characterized by, or productive of inflation
inflationary spiral *n* **:** a continuous rise in prices that is sustained by the tendency of wage increases and cost increases to react on each other

in·fla·tion·ism \in-ˈflā-shə-ˌniz-əm\ *n* **:** the policy of economic inflation — **in·fla·tion·ist** \-sh(ə-)-nəst\ *n or adj*

in·flect \in-ˈflekt\ *vb* [ME *inflecten*, fr. L *inflectere*, fr. *in-* + *flectere* to bend] *vt* **1 :** to turn from a direct line or course **:** CURVE **2 :** to vary (a word) by inflection **:** DECLINE, CONJUGATE **3 :** to change or vary the pitch of (as the voice) **:** MODULATE ~ *vi* **:** to become modified by inflection — **in·flec·tive** \-ˈflek-tiv\ *adj*

in·flec·tion \in-ˈflek-shən\ *n* **1 :** the act or result of curving or bending **2 :** change in pitch or loudness of the voice **3 a :** the change of form that words undergo to mark such distinctions as those of case, gender, number, tense, person, mood, or voice **b :** a form, suffix, or element involved in such variation **c :** ACCIDENCE **4 a :** change of curvature with respect to a fixed line from concave to convex or conversely **b :** the point where such a change takes place

in·flec·tion·al \-shnəl, -shən-ᵊl\ *adj* **:** of, relating to, or characterized by inflection ⟨an ~ language⟩ — **in·flec·tion·al·ly** \-ē\ *adv*

in·flexed \ˈin-ˌflekst\ *adj* [L *inflexus*, pp. of *inflectere*] **:** bent or turned abruptly inward or downward or toward the axis ⟨~ petals⟩

in·flex·i·bil·i·ty \(ˌ)in-ˌflek-sə-ˈbil-ət-ē\ *n* **:** the quality or state of being inflexible

in·flex·i·ble \(ˈ)in-ˈflek-sə-bəl\ *adj* [ME, fr. L *inflexibilis*, fr. *in-* + *flexibilis* flexible] **1 :** not capable of being bent **:** RIGID **2 :** firm in will or purpose **:** UNYIELDING **3 :** incapable of change **:** UNALTERABLE — **in·flex·i·ble·ness** *n* — **in·flex·i·bly** \-blē\ *adv*

syn INEXORABLE, OBDURATE, ADAMANT: INFLEXIBLE implies rigid adherence or even slavish conformity to principle; INEXORABLE implies relentlessness of purpose or esp. when applied to things inevitableness; OBDURATE stresses hardness of heart and insensitivity to appeals for mercy or the influence of divine grace; ADAMANT implies utter immovability in the face of all temptation or entreaty **syn** see in addition STIFF

in·flex·ion *chiefly Brit var of* INFLECTION

in·flict \in-ˈflikt\ *vt* [L *inflictus*, pp. of *infligere*, fr. *in-* + *fligere* to strike] **1 a :** to give by striking **b :** to cause (something damaging or painful) to be endured **:** IMPOSE **2 :** AFFLICT — **in·flict·er** *or* **in·flic·tor** \-ˈflik-tər\ *n* — **in·flic·tive** \-tiv\ *adj*

in·flic·tion \in-ˈflik-shən\ *n* **1 :** the act of inflicting **2 :** something inflicted

in·flo·res·cence \ˌin-flə-ˈres-ᵊn(t)s\ *n* [NL *inflorescentia*, fr. LL

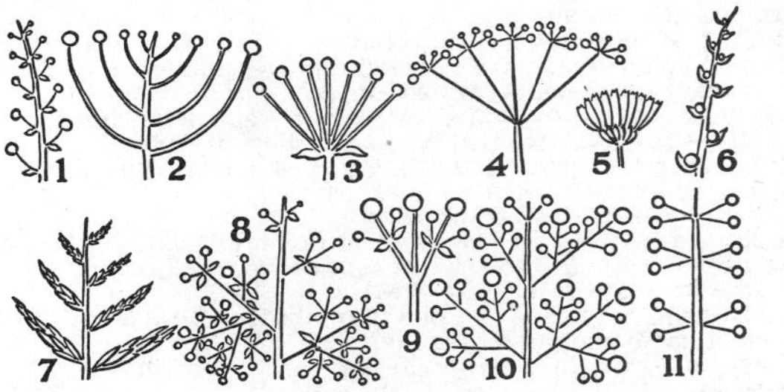

types of inflorescence: *1* raceme, *2* corymb, *3* umbel, *4* compound umbel, *5* capitulum, *6* spike, *7* compound spike, *8* panicle, *9* cyme, *10* thyrse, *11* verticillaster

inflorescent-, *inflorescens*, prp. of *inflorescere* to begin to bloom, fr. L *in-* + *florescere* to begin to bloom — more at FLORESCENCE] **1 a** (1) **:** the mode of development and arrangement of flowers on an axis (2) **:** a floral axis with its appendages; *also* **:** a flower cluster or sometimes a solitary flower **b :** a cluster of reproductive organs on a moss usu. subtended by a bract **2 :** the budding and unfolding of blossoms **:** FLOWERING — **in·flo·res·cent** \-ᵊnt\ *adj*

in·flow \ˈin-ˌflō\ *n* **:** INFLUX

1**in·flu·ence** \ˈin-ˌflü-ən(t)s\ *n* [ME, fr. MF, fr. ML *influentia*, fr. L *influent-*, *influens*, prp. of *influere* to flow in, fr. *in-* + *fluere* to flow — more at FLUID] **1 a :** an ethereal fluid thought to flow from the stars and to affect the actions of men **b :** an emanation of occult power held to derive from stars **2 :** an emanation of spiritual or moral force **3 a :** the act or power of producing an effect without apparent exertion of force or direct exercise of command **b :** corrupt interference with authority for personal gain **4 :** the power or capacity of causing an effect in indirect or intangible ways **:** SWAY **5 :** a person or thing that exerts influence **6 :** INDUCTION 4c

syn INFLUENCE, AUTHORITY, PRESTIGE, WEIGHT, CREDIT mean power exerted over the minds or behavior of others. INFLUENCE may apply to a force exercised and received unknowingly or to a conscious and deliberate affecting; AUTHORITY implies the power of winning devotion or allegiance or of compelling acceptance and belief; PRESTIGE implies the ascendancy given by conspicuous excellence or reputation for superiority; WEIGHT implies measurable or decisive influence in determining acts or choices; CREDIT suggests influence that arises from proven merit or favorable reputation

2**influence** *vt* **1 :** to affect or alter by indirect or intangible means **:** SWAY **2 :** to have an effect on the condition or development of **:** MODIFY **syn** see AFFECT — **in·flu·enc·er** *n*

1**in·flu·ent** \-ənt\ *adj* **:** flowing in

2**influent** *n* **:** a factor (as a kind of animal) modifying the balance and stability of an ecological community

in·flu·en·tial \ˌin-(ˌ)flü-ˈen-chəl\ *adj* **:** exerting or possessing influence — **in·flu·en·tial·ly** \-ˈench-(ə-)lē\ *adv*

in·flu·en·za \ˌin-(ˌ)flü-ˈen-zə\ *n* [It, lit., influence, fr. ML *influentia;* fr. the belief that epidemics were due to the influence of the stars] **1 :** an acute highly contagious virus disease characterized by sudden onset, fever, prostration, severe aches and pains, and progressive inflammation of the respiratory mucous membrane; *broadly* **:** a human respiratory infection of undetermined cause **2 :** any of numerous febrile usu. virus diseases of domestic animals marked by respiratory symptoms, inflammation of mucous membranes, and often systemic involvement

in·flux \ˈin-ˌfləks\ *n* [LL *influxus*, fr. L, pp. of *influere*] **1 :** a flowing in **:** INFLOW **2 :** the mouth of a river

in·fold \in-ˈfōld\ *vt* **:** ENFOLD ~ \ˈin-ˌ\ *vi* **:** to fold inward or toward one another

in·form \in-ˈfȯ(ə)rm\ *vb* [ME *informen*, fr. MF *enformer*, fr. L *informare*, fr. *in-* + *forma* form] *vt* **1** *obs* **a :** to give material form to **b :** ARRANGE **2 a :** to give character or essence to **b :** to be the characteristic quality of **:** ANIMATE **3** *obs* **:** TRAIN, DISCIPLINE **4** *obs* **:** GUIDE, DIRECT **5** *obs* **:** to make known **6 :** to communicate knowledge to ~ *vi* **1 :** to give information or knowledge **2 :** to act as an informer

syn INFORM, ACQUAINT, APPRISE, NOTIFY mean to make one aware of something. INFORM implies the imparting of knowledge esp. of facts or occurrences necessary for an understanding of a pertinent matter or as a basis for action; ACQUAINT lays stress on introducing to or familiarizing with; APPRISE implies communicating something of special interest or importance; NOTIFY implies sending notice of something requiring attention or demanding action

in·for·mal \(ˈ)in-ˈfȯr-məl\ *adj* **1 :** conducted or carried out without formality or ceremony **2 :** characteristic of or appropriate to ordinary, casual, or familiar use — **in·for·mal·i·ty** \ˌin-(ˌ)fȯr-ˈmal-ət-ē, -fər-\ *n* — **in·for·mal·ly** \(ˈ)in-ˈfȯr-mə-lē\ *adv*

in·for·mant \in-ˈfȯr-mənt\ *n* **:** one who gives information: as **a :** INFORMER **b :** one who supplies cultural or linguistic data in response to interrogation by an investigator

in for·ma pau·pe·ris \ˌin-ˌfȯr-mə-ˈpȯ-pə-rəs, -ˈpau̇-\ *adj* (*or adv*) [L, in the form of a pauper] **:** as a poor man

in·for·ma·tion \ˌin-fər-ˈmā-shən\ *n* **1 :** the communication or reception of knowledge or intelligence **2 a :** knowledge obtained from investigation, study, or instruction **b :** INTELLIGENCE, NEWS **c :** FACTS, DATA **d :** a signal (as one of the digits in dialing a telephone number) purposely impressed upon the input of a communication system or a calculating machine **3 :** the act of informing against a person **4 :** a formal accusation of a crime made by a prosecuting officer as distinguished from an indictment presented by a grand jury **5 :** a numerical quantity that measures the uncertainty in the outcome of an experiment to be performed — **in·for·ma·tion·al** \-shnəl, -shən-ᵊl\ *adj*

information theory *n* **:** a theory that deals statistically with the efficiency of processes of communication between men and machines (as in telecommunication or in computing machines)

in·for·ma·tive \in-ˈfȯr-mət-iv\ *adj* **:** imparting knowledge **:** INSTRUCTIVE — **in·for·ma·tive·ly** *adv* — **in·for·ma·tive·ness** *n*

in·for·ma·to·ry \-mə-ˌtōr-ē, -ˌtȯr-\ *adj* **:** conveying information

in·formed \in-ˈfȯ(ə)rmd\ *adj* **:** EDUCATED, INTELLIGENT

in·form·er *n* **1 :** one that imparts knowledge or news **2 :** one that informs against another; *specif* **:** one who makes a practice esp. for a financial reward of informing against others for violations of penal laws — called also *common informer*

in·fra \ˈin-frə, -ˌfrä\ *adv* [L] **1 :** BELOW **2 :** LATER

infra- *prefix* [L *infra* — more at UNDER] **1 :** below ⟨*infra*human⟩ ⟨*infra*sonic⟩ **2 :** within ⟨*infra*specific⟩ **3 :** below in a scale or series ⟨*infra*red⟩

in·fract \in-ˈfrakt\ *vt* [L *infractus*, pp. of *infringere* to break off — more at INFRINGE] **:** INFRINGE, VIOLATE — **in·frac·tor** \-ˈfrak-tər\ *n*

in·frac·tion \in-ˈfrak-shən\ *n* **:** the act of infringing **:** VIOLATION

in·fra dig \ˌin-frə-ˈdig\ *adj* [short for L *infra dignitatem*] **:** being beneath one's dignity **:** UNDIGNIFIED

in·fra·hu·man \ˌin-frə-ˈhyü-mən, -ˈyü-\ *adj* **:** less or lower than human; *specif* **:** ANTHROPOID — **infrahuman** *n*

in·fran·gi·bil·i·ty \(ˌ)in-ˌfran-jə-ˈbil-ət-ē\ *n* **:** INVIOLABILITY

in·fran·gi·ble \(ˈ)in-ˈfran-jə-bəl\ *adj* [MF, fr. LL *infrangibilis*, fr. L *in-* + *frangere* to break — more at BREAK] **1 :** not capable of being broken or separated into parts **2 :** not to be violated — **in·fran·gi·ble·ness** *n* — **in·fran·gi·bly** \-blē\ *adv*

in·fra·red \ˌin-frə-ˈred, -(ˌ)frä-\ *adj* **1 :** lying outside the visible spectrum at its red end — used of thermal radiation of wavelengths longer than those of visible light **2 :** relating to, producing, or employing infrared radiation **3 :** sensitive to infrared radiation — **infrared** *n*

in·fra·son·ic \-ˈsän-ik\ *adj* **1 :** having a frequency below the audibility range of the human ear **2 :** utilizing or produced by infrasonic waves or vibrations

in·fra·spe·cif·ic \-spi-ˈsif-ik\ *adj* **:** included within a species ⟨~ categories⟩

in·fra·struc·ture \ˈin-frə-ˌstrək-chər\ *n* **:** FOUNDATION; *esp* **:** the permanent installations required for military purposes

in·fre·quen·cy \(ˈ)in-ˈfrē-kwən-sē\ *or* **in·fre·quence** \-kwən(t)s\ *n* **:** the state of rarely occurring

in·fre·quent \(ˈ)in-ˈfrē-kwənt\ *adj* [L *infrequent-*, *infrequens*, fr. *in-* + *frequent-*, *frequens* frequent] **1 :** seldom happening or occurring **:** RARE **2 :** placed or occurring at considerable distances or intervals **:** OCCASIONAL — **in·fre·quent·ly** *adv*

syn INFREQUENT, UNCOMMON, SCARCE, RARE, SPORADIC mean not common or abundant. INFREQUENT implies occurrence at wide intervals in space or time; UNCOMMON suggests a frequency below normal expectation; SCARCE implies falling short of a standard or required abundance; RARE suggests extreme scarcity or infrequency and consequent high value; SPORADIC implies occurrence in scattered instances or isolated outbursts

in·fringe \in-ˈfrinj\ *vb* [L *infringere*, lit., to break off, fr. *in-* + *frangere* to break — more at BREAK] *vt* **1** *obs* **:** DEFEAT, FRUSTRATE **2 :** VIOLATE, TRANSGRESS ⟨~ a treaty⟩ ⟨~ a patent⟩ ~ *vi* **:** ENCROACH **syn** see TRESPASS — **in·fring·er** *n*

in·fringe·ment \-ˈfrinj-mənt\ *n* **1 :** the act of infringing **:** VIOLATION **2 :** an encroachment or trespass on a right or privilege

in·fun·dib·u·lar \ˌin-(ˌ)fən-ˈdib-yə-lər\ *or* **in·fun·dib·u·late** \-lət\ *adj* **1 :** INFUNDIBULIFORM **2 :** of, relating to, or having an infundibulum

in·fun·dib·u·li·form \-lə-ˌfȯrm\ *adj* [NL *infundibulum* + E *-iform*] **:** having the form of a funnel or cone

in·fun·dib·u·lum \ˌin-(ˌ)fən-ˈdib-yə-ləm\ *n, pl* **in·fun·dib·u·la** \-lə\ [NL, fr. L, funnel — more at FUNNEL] **:** any of various conical or dilated organs or parts: as **a :** the hollow conical process of gray matter by which the pituitary body is continuous with the brain **b :** any of the small spaces having walls beset with alveoli in which the bronchial tubes terminate in the lungs **c :** the enlarged process of the right ventricle from which the pulmonary artery arises **d :** the calyx of a kidney **e :** the abdominal opening of a fallopian tube

1**in·fu·ri·ate** \in-ˈfyu̇r-ē-ˌāt\ *vt* [ML *infuriatus*, pp. of *infuriare*, fr. L *in-* + *furia* fury] **:** to make furious **:** ENRAGE — **in·fu·ri·at·ing·ly**

\-iŋ-lē\ *adv* — **in·fu·ri·a·tion** \in-ˌfyu̇r-ē-ˈā-shən\ *n*

2in·fu·ri·ate \in-ˈfyu̇r-ē-ət\ *adj* **:** furiously angry — **in·fu·ri·ate·ly** *adv*

in·fuse \in-ˈfyüz\ *vt* [ME *infusen*, fr. MF & L; MF *infuser*, fr. L *infusus*, pp. of *infundere* to pour in, fr. *in-* + *fundere* to pour — more at FOUND] **1 a :** to instill a principle or quality in **b :** INTRODUCE, INSINUATE **2 :** INSPIRE, ANIMATE **3 :** to steep in water or other fluid without boiling for extracting useful qualities — **in·fus·er** *n*

syn INFUSE, SUFFUSE, IMBUE, INGRAIN, INOCULATE, LEAVEN mean to introduce one thing into another so as to affect it throughout. INFUSE implies a pouring in of something that gives new life or significance; SUFFUSE implies a spreading through of something that gives an unusual color or visual quality; IMBUE implies the introduction of a quality that fills and permeates the whole being; INGRAIN suggests the indelible stamping or deep implanting of a quality or trait; INOCULATE implies an imbuing or implanting with a germinal idea and often suggests surreptitiousness or subtlety; LEAVEN implies introducing something that enlivens, tempers, or markedly alters the total quality

in·fu·si·bil·i·ty \(ˌ)in-ˌfyü-zə-ˈbil-ət-ē\ *n* **:** the quality or state of being infusible

in·fu·si·ble \(ˈ)in-ˈfyü-zə-bəl\ *adj* **:** incapable or very difficult of fusion — **in·fu·si·ble·ness** *n*

in·fu·sion \in-ˈfyü-zhən\ *n* **1 :** the act or process of infusing: as **a :** the introducing of a solution into a vein **b :** the steeping or soaking usu. in water of a substance in order to extract its virtues **2 :** a product obtained by infusing

in·fu·so·ri·al \ˌin-fyü-ˈzōr-ē-əl, -ˈsōr-, -ˈzȯr-, -ˈsȯr-\ *adj* **:** of, relating to, or being infusorians

in·fu·so·ri·an \-ē-ən\ *n* [deriv. of L *infusus*] **:** any of a heterogeneous group of minute organisms found esp. in decomposing infusions of organic matter; *esp* **:** a ciliated protozoan — **infusorian** *adj*

1-ing \iŋ; *in some dialects usu., in other dialects informally,* ən, in, *or (in certain phonetic contexts)* ᵊn, ᵊm, ᵊŋ\ *vb suffix or adj suffix* [ME, alter. of *-ende*, fr. OE, fr. *-e-*, verb stem vowel + *-nde*, prp. suffix — more at -ANT] — used to form the present participle ⟨sail*ing*⟩ and sometimes to form an adjective resembling a present participle but not derived from a verb ⟨swashbuckl*ing*⟩

2-ing *n suffix* [ME, fr. OE; akin to OHG *-ing* one of a (specified) kind] **:** one of a (specified) kind ⟨sweet*ing*⟩

3-ing *n suffix* [ME, fr. OE, suffix forming nouns from verbs; akin to OHG *-ung*, suffix forming nouns from verbs] **1 :** action or process ⟨runn*ing*⟩ ⟨sleep*ing*⟩ **:** instance of an action or process ⟨a meet*ing*⟩ **2 a :** product or result of an action or process ⟨an engrav*ing*⟩ — often in pl. ⟨earn*ings*⟩ **b :** something used in an action or process ⟨a bed cover*ing*⟩ **3 :** action or process connected with (a specified thing) ⟨iceboat*ing*⟩ **4 :** something connected with, consisting of, or used in making (a specified thing) ⟨scaffold*ing*⟩ **5 :** something related to (a specified concept) ⟨off*ing*⟩

in·gath·er \ˈin-ˌgath-ər, -ˌgeth-\ *vt* **:** to gather in ~ *vi* **:** ASSEMBLE — **in·gath·er·ing** \-ˌgath-(ə-)riŋ, -ˌgeth-\ *n*

in·gem·i·nate \in-ˈjem-ə-ˌnāt\ *vt* [L *ingeminatus*, pp. of *ingeminare*, fr. *in-* + *geminare* to geminate] **:** REDOUBLE, REITERATE — **in·gem·i·na·tion** \(ˌ)in-ˌjem-ə-ˈnā-shən\ *n*

in·ge·nious \in-ˈjēn-yəs\ *adj* [MF *ingenieux*, fr. L *ingeniosus*, fr. *ingenium* natural capacity — more at ENGINE] **1** *obs* **a :** showing or calling for intelligence **b :** CONSCIOUS **2 :** marked by especial aptitude at discovering, inventing, or contriving **3 :** marked by originality, resourcefulness, and cleverness in conception or execution **syn** see CLEVER — **in·ge·nious·ly** *adv* — **in·ge·nious·ness** *n*

in·ge·nue *or* **in·gé·nue** \ˈan-jə-ˌnü, ˈa^{n}-zhə-, ˈä^{n}-zhə-\ *n* [F *ingénue*, fem. of *ingénu* ingenuous, fr. L *ingenuus*] **:** a naïve girl or young woman; *esp* **:** an actress representing such a person

in·ge·nu·ity \ˌin-jə-ˈn(y)ü-ət-ē\ *n* **1** *obs* **:** INGENUOUSNESS, CANDOR **2 a :** skill or cleverness in devising or combining **:** INVENTIVENESS **b :** cleverness or aptness of design or contrivance **3 :** an ingenious device or contrivance

in·gen·u·ous \in-ˈjen-yə-wəs\ *adj* [L *ingenuus* native, free born, fr. *in-* + *gignere* to beget — more at KIN] **1** *obs* **:** NOBLE, HONORABLE **2 a :** STRAIGHTFORWARD **b :** showing innocent or childlike simplicity **:** NAÏVE **3** [by alter.] *obs* **:** INGENIOUS **syn** see NATURAL — **in·gen·u·ous·ly** *adv* — **in·gen·u·ous·ness** *n*

in·gest \in-ˈjest\ *vt* [L *ingestus*, pp. of *ingerere* to carry in, fr. *in-* + *gerere* to bear — more at CAST] **:** to take in for or as if for digestion **:** ABSORB — **in·gest·ible** \-ˈjes-tə-bəl\ *adj* — **in·ges·tion** \-ˈjes(h)-chən\ *n* — **in·ges·tive** \-ˈjes-tiv\ *adj*

in·ges·ta \in-ˈjes-tə\ *n pl* [NL, fr. L, neut. pl. of *ingestus*] **:** material taken into the body by way of the digestive tract

in·gle \ˈiŋ-(g)əl\ *n* [ScGael *aingeal*] **1 :** FLAME, BLAZE **2 :** FIREPLACE

in·gle·nook \-ˌnu̇k\ *n* **:** a corner by the fire

in·glo·ri·ous \(ˈ)in-ˈglōr-ē-əs, -ˈglȯr-\ *adj* [L *inglorius*, fr. *in-* + *gloria* glory] **1 :** not glorious **:** lacking fame or honor **2 :** SHAMEFUL, IGNOMINIOUS — **in·glo·ri·ous·ly** *adv* — **in·glo·ri·ous·ness** *n*

in·got \ˈiŋ-gət\ *n* [ME, prob. modif. of MF *lingot* ingot of metal, incorrectly divided as *l'ingot*, as if fr. *le* the, fr. L *ille* that] **1 :** a mold in which metal is cast **2 :** a mass of metal cast into a convenient shape for storage or transportation to be later processed

ingot iron *n* **:** iron containing usu. less than 0.05 percent carbon and similarly small proportions of other impurities

ingraft *var of* ENGRAFT

1in·grain \(ˈ)in-ˈgrān\ *vt* **:** to work indelibly into the natural texture or mental or moral constitution **syn** see INFUSE

2in·grain \ˈin-ˌgrān\ *adj* **1 a :** made of fiber that is dyed before being spun into yarn **b :** made of yarn that is dyed before being woven or knitted **2 :** thoroughly worked in **:** INNATE

3in·grain \ˈin-ˌgrān\ *n* **1 :** an article made with ingrain yarns **2 :** innate quality or character

in·grained \ˈin-ˌgrānd, (ˈ)in-ˈ\ *adj* **:** worked into the grain or fiber **:** DEEP-SEATED — **in·grained·ly** \ˈin-ˌgrā-nəd-lē, ˈin-ˌgrān-dlē, (ˈ)in-ˈ\ *adv*

in·grate \ˈin-ˌgrāt\ *n* [L *ingratus* ungrateful, fr. *in-* + *gratus* grateful — more at GRACE] **:** an ungrateful person — **ingrate** *adj, archaic*

in·gra·ti·ate \in-ˈgrā-shē-ˌāt\ *vt* [*in-* + L *gratia* grace] **:** to gain favor or favorable acceptance for by deliberate effort — **in·gra·ti·a·tion** \-ˌgrā-shē-ˈā-shən\ *n* — **in·gra·tia·to·ry** \-ˈgrā-sh(ē-)ə-ˌtōr-ē, -ˌtȯr-\ *adj*

in·gra·ti·at·ing *adj* **1 :** capable of winning favor **:** PLEASING **2 :** intended or adopted in order to gain favor **:** FLATTERING — **in·gra·ti·at·ing·ly** \-iŋ-lē\ *adv*

in·grat·i·tude \(ˈ)in-ˈgrat-ə-ˌt(y)üd\ *n* [ME, fr. MF, fr. ML *ingratitudo*, fr. L *in-* + LL *gratitudo* gratitude] **:** forgetfulness of or poor return for kindness received **:** UNGRATEFULNESS

in·gre·di·ent \in-ˈgrēd-ē-ənt\ *n* [ME, fr. L *ingredient-*, *ingrediens*, prp. of *ingredi* to go into, fr. *in-* + *gradi* to go — more at GRADE] **:** something that enters into a compound or is a component part of any combination or mixture **:** CONSTITUENT **syn** see ELEMENT — **ingredient** *adj*

in·gress \ˈin-ˌgres\ *n* [ME, fr. L *ingressus*, fr. *ingressus*, pp. of *ingredi*] **1 :** the act of entering **:** ENTRANCE **2 :** the power or liberty of entrance or access

in·gres·sion \in-ˈgresh-ən\ *n* **:** INGRESS 1

in·gres·sive \in-ˈgres-iv\ *adj* **:** of or relating to ingress; *specif* **:** INCHOATIVE — **ingressive** *n* — **in·gres·sive·ness** *n*

in·group \ˈin-ˌgrüp\ *n* **:** a social group possessing a sense of solidarity or community of interests as opposed to other social groups

in·grow·ing \ˈin-ˌgrō-iŋ\ *adj* **:** growing or tending inward

in·grown \-ˌgrōn\ *adj* **:** grown in; *specif* **:** having the free tip or edge embedded in the flesh ⟨~ toenail⟩ — **in·grown·ness** \-ˈgrōn-nəs\ *n*

in·growth \ˈin-ˌgrōth\ *n* **1 :** a growing inward (as to fill a void) **2 :** something that grows in or into a space

in·gui·nal \ˈiŋ-gwən-ᵊl\ *adj* [L *inguinalis*, fr. *inguin-*, *inguen* groin — more at ADEN-] **:** of, relating to, or situated in the region of the groin or in either of the lowest lateral regions of the abdomen

in·gur·gi·tate \in-ˈgər-jə-ˌtāt\ *vt* [L *ingurgitatus*, pp. of *ingurgitare*, fr. *in-* + *gurgit-*, *gurges* whirlpool — more at VORACIOUS] **:** to swallow greedily or in large quantity **:** GUZZLE — **in·gur·gi·ta·tion** \(ˌ)in-ˌgər-jə-ˈtā-shən\ *n*

in·hab·it \in-ˈhab-ət\ *vb* [ME *enhabiten*, fr. MF & L; MF *enhabiter*, fr. L *inhabitare*, fr. *in-* + *habitare* to dwell, fr. *habitus*, pp. of *habēre* to have — more at GIVE] *vt* **:** to occupy as a place of settled residence or habitat **:** live in ~ *vi, archaic* **:** to have residence in a place **:** DWELL — **in·hab·it·able** \-ə-bəl\ *adj* — **in·hab·it·er** *n*

in·hab·i·tan·cy \-ət-ən-sē\ *n* **:** the act of inhabiting or the state of being inhabited **:** OCCUPANCY

in·hab·i·tant \in-ˈhab-ət-ənt\ *n* **:** a permanent resident in a place

in·hab·i·ta·tion \in-ˌhab-ə-ˈtā-shən\ *n* **:** the act of inhabiting **:** the state of being inhabited

in·hab·it·ed *adj* **:** having inhabitants

in·hal·ant \in-ˈhā-lənt\ *n* **:** something (as an allergen or medicated spray) that is inhaled — **inhalant** *adj*

in·ha·la·tion \ˌin-(h)ə-ˈlā-shən\ *n* **:** the act or an instance of inhaling — **in·ha·la·tion·al** \-shnəl, -shən-ᵊl\ *adj*

in·ha·la·tor \ˈin-(h)ə-ˌlāt-ər\ *n* **:** a device providing a mixture of oxygen and carbon dioxide for breathing that is used esp. in conjunction with artificial respiration

in·hale \in-ˈhā(ə)l\ *vb* [*in-* + *-hale* (as in *exhale*)] *vt* **1 :** to draw in by breathing **2 :** to take in esp. eagerly or greedily ~ *vi* **:** to breathe in — **in·hale** \in-ˈ, ˈin-ˌ\ *n*

in·hal·er \in-ˈhā-lər\ *n* **1 :** one that inhales **2 :** a device by means of which medicinal material is inhaled **3 :** SNIFTER

in·har·mon·ic \ˌin-(ˌ)här-ˈmän-ik\ *adj* **:** not harmonic **:** DISCORDANT

in·har·mo·ni·ous \-ˈmō-nē-əs\ *adj* **1 :** not harmonious **:** DISCORDANT **2 :** not fitting or congenial **:** CONFLICTING — **in·har·mo·ni·ous·ly** *adv* — **in·har·mo·ni·ous·ness** *n*

in·har·mo·ny \(ˈ)in-ˈhär-mə-nē\ *n* **:** DISCORD

in·haul \ˈin-ˌhȯl\ *n* **:** a rope used to draw in a ship's sail

in·here \in-ˈhi(ə)r\ *vi* [L *inhaerēre*, fr. *in-* + *haerēre* to adhere — more at HESITATE] **:** to be inherent **:** BELONG

in·her·ence \in-ˈhir-ən(t)s, -ˈher-\ *n* **:** the quality, state, or fact of inhering or of being inherent

in·her·ent \-ənt\ *adj* [L *inhaerent-*, *inhaerens*, prp. of *inhaerēre*] **:** involved in the constitution or essential character of something **:** INTRINSIC — **in·her·ent·ly** *adv*

in·her·it \in-ˈher-ət\ *vb* [ME *enheriten* to make heir, inherit, fr. MF *enheriter* to make heir, fr. LL *inhereditare*, fr. L *in-* + LL *hereditare* to inherit — more at HERITAGE] *vt* **1 :** to come into possession of **:** RECEIVE **2 :** to receive as a right or title descendible by law from an ancestor at his death **3 a :** to receive from ancestors by genetic transmission ⟨~ a strong constitution⟩ **b :** to have in turn or receive as if from an ancestor ⟨~*ed* the problem from his predecessor⟩ ~ *vi* **:** to take or hold a possession or rights by inheritance — **in·her·i·tor** \-ət-ər\ *n* — **in·her·i·tress** \-ə-trəs\ *or* **in·her·i·trix** \-ə-(ˌ)triks\ *n*

in·her·it·able \in-ˈher-ət-ə-bəl\ *adj* **1 :** capable of being inherited **:** TRANSMISSIBLE **2 :** capable of taking by inheritance — **in·her·it·able·ness** *n*

in·her·i·tance \-ət-ən(t)s\ *n* **1 a :** the act of inheriting property **b :** the reception of genetic qualities by transmission from parent to offspring **c :** the acquisition of a possession, condition, or trait from past generations **2 :** something that is or may be inherited **3 a :** TRADITION **b :** a valuable possession that is a common heritage from nature **4** *obs* **:** OWNERSHIP **syn** see HERITAGE

in·hib·it \in-ˈhib-ət\ *vb* [ME *inhibiten*, fr. L *inhibitus*, pp. of *inhibēre*, fr. *in-* + *habēre* to have — more at HABIT] *vt* **1 :** to prohibit from doing something **2 a :** to hold in check **:** RESTRAIN **b :** to discourage from free or spontaneous activity **:** REPRESS ~ *vi* **:** to cause inhibition **syn** see FORBID — **in·hib·i·tive** \-ət-iv\ *adj* — **in·hib·i·to·ry** \-ə-ˌtōr-ē, -ˌtȯr-\ *adj*

in·hi·bi·tion \ˌin-(h)ə-ˈbish-ən\ *n* **1 a :** the act of inhibiting **:** the state of being inhibited **b :** something that forbids or debars **2 :** an inner impediment to free activity, expression, or functioning: as **a :** a psychical activity imposing restraint upon another activity **b :** a restraining of the function of a bodily organ or an agent (as an enzyme)

in·hib·i·tor *or* **in·hib·it·er** \in-ˈhib-ət-ər\ *n* **:** one that inhibits; *esp* **:** an agent that slows or interferes with a chemical action

in·hos·pi·ta·ble \ˌin-ˌhäs-ˈpit-ə-bəl, (ˈ)in-ˈhäs-(ˌ)pit-\ *adj* **1 :** not showing hospitality **2 :** providing no shelter or sustenance **:** BARREN — **in·hos·pi·ta·ble·ness** *n* — **in·hos·pi·ta·bly** \-blē\ *adv*

in·hos·pi·tal·i·ty \(ˌ)in-ˌhäs-pə-ˈtal-ət-ē\ *n* **:** the quality or state of being inhospitable

in·hu·man \(ˈ)in-ˈhyü-mən, -ˈyü-\ *adj* [MF & L; MF *inhumain*, fr. L *inhumanus*, fr. *in-* + *humanus* human] **1 a :** lacking pity or kindness **:** SAVAGE **b :** COLD, IMPERSONAL **c :** not worthy of or con-

forming to the needs of human beings **2 :** of or suggesting a nonhuman class of beings — **in·hu·man·ly** *adv*

in·hu·mane \ˌin-(ˌ)hyü-ˈmān, -(ˌ)yü-\ *adj* [MF *inhumain* & L *inhumanus*] **:** not humane **:** INHUMAN 1 — **in·hu·mane·ly** *adv*

in·hu·man·i·ty \-ˈman-ət-ē\ *n* **1 :** the quality or state of being cruel or barbarous **2 :** a cruel or barbarous act

in·hu·ma·tion \ˌin-(ˌ)hyü-ˈmā-shən\ *n* **:** BURIAL, INTERMENT

in·hume \in-ˈhyüm\ *vt* [prob. fr. F *inhumer*, fr. L *inhumare*, fr. *in-* + *humus* earth — more at HUMBLE] **:** BURY, INTER

in·im·i·cal \in-ˈim-i-kəl\ *adj* [LL *inimicalis*, fr. L *inimicus* enemy — more at ENEMY] **1 a :** having the disposition of an enemy **:** HOSTILE **b :** reflecting or indicating hostility **:** UNFRIENDLY **2 :** HARMFUL, ADVERSE — **in·im·i·cal·ly** \-i-k(ə-)lē\ *adv*

in·im·i·ta·ble \(ˈ)in-ˈim-ət-ə-bəl\ *adj* [MF or L; MF, fr. L *inimitabilis*, fr. *in-* + *imitabilis* imitable] **:** not capable of being imitated **:** MATCHLESS — **in·im·i·ta·ble·ness** *n* — **in·im·i·ta·bly** \-blē\ *adv*

in·iq·ui·tous \in-ˈik-wət-əs\ *adj* **:** characterized by iniquity **syn** see VICIOUS — **in·iq·ui·tous·ly** *adv* — **in·iq·ui·tous·ness** *n*

in·iq·ui·ty \-wət-ē\ *n* [ME *iniquite*, fr. MF *iniquité*, fr. L *iniquitat-, iniquitas*, fr. *iniquus* uneven, fr. *in-* + *aequus* equal] **1 :** gross injustice **:** WICKEDNESS **2 :** an iniquitous act or thing **:** SIN

1**ini·tial** \in-ˈish-əl\ *adj* [MF & L; MF, fr. L *initialis*, fr. *initium* beginning, fr. *initus*, pp. of *inire* to go into, fr. *in-* + *ire* to go — more at ISSUE] **1 :** of or relating to the beginning **:** INCIPIENT **2 :** placed at the beginning **:** FIRST — **ini·tial·ly** \-ˈish-(ə-)lē\ *adv* — **ini·tial·ness** \-ˈish-əl-nəs\ *n*

2**initial** *n* **1 a :** the first letter of a name **b :** a large letter beginning a text or a division or paragraph **2 :** ANLAGE, PRECURSOR; *specif* **:** a meristematic cell

3**initial** *vt* **ini·tialed** *or* **ini·tialled; ini·tial·ing** *or* **ini·tial·ling** \-ˈish-(ə-)liŋ\ **:** to affix an initial to

initial teaching alphabet *n* **:** a 44-symbol alphabet designed esp. for use in the initial stages of teaching children to read English

1**ini·ti·ate** \in-ˈish-ē-ˌāt\ *vt* [LL *initiatus*, pp. of *initiare*, fr. L, to induct, fr. *initium*] **1 :** to set going **:** START **2 :** to instruct in the rudiments or principles of something **:** INTRODUCE **3 :** to induct into membership by or as if by special rites **syn** see BEGIN — **ini·ti·a·tor** \-ˌāt-ər\ *n*

2**ini·tiate** \in-ˈish-(ē-)ət\ *adj* **1 :** INITIATED **2** *obs* **:** relating to an initiate

3**ini·tiate** \in-ˈish-(ē-)ət\ *n* **1 :** a person who is undergoing or has passed an initiation **2 :** a person who is instructed or adept in some special field

ini·ti·a·tion \in-ˌish-ē-ˈā-shən\ *n* **1 a :** the act or an instance of initiating **b :** the process of being initiated **c :** the rites, ceremonies, ordeals, or instructions with which one is made a member of a sect or society or is invested with a particular function or status **2 :** the condition of being an initiate **:** KNOWLEDGEABLENESS

1**ini·tia·tive** \in-ˈish-ət-iv\ *adj* **:** of or relating to initiation **:** INTRODUCTORY, PRELIMINARY

2**initiative** *n* **1 :** an introductory step **2 :** energy or aptitude displayed in initiation of action **:** ENTERPRISE **3 a :** the right to initiate legislative action **b :** a procedure enabling a specified number of voters by petition to propose a law and secure its submission to the electorate or to the legislature for approval — compare REFERENDUM

ini·tia·to·ry \in-ˈish-(ē-)ə-ˌtōr-ē, -ˌtȯr-\ *adj* **1 :** constituting a beginning **2 :** tending or serving to initiate

in·ject \in-ˈjekt\ *vt* [L *injectus*, pp. of *inicere*, fr. *in-* + *jacere* to throw — more at JET] **1 a :** to throw, drive, or force into something **b :** to force a fluid into for medical purposes **2 :** to introduce as an element or factor in or into some situation or subject — **in·ject·able** \-ˈjek-tə-bəl\ *adj* — **in·jec·tor** \-ˈjek-tər\ *n*

in·jec·tion \in-ˈjek-shən\ *n* **1 :** an act or instance of injecting (as by a syringe or pump) **2 :** something (as a medication) that is injected

in·ju·di·cious \ˌin-jü-ˈdish-əs\ *adj* **:** not judicious **:** INDISCREET, UNWISE — **in·ju·di·cious·ly** *adv* — **in·ju·di·cious·ness** *n*

in·junc·tion \in-ˈjəŋ(k)-shən\ *n* [MF & LL; MF *injonction*, fr. LL *injunction-, injunctio*, fr. L *injunctus*, pp. of *injungere* to enjoin — more at ENJOIN] **1 :** the act or an instance of enjoining **:** ORDER, ADMONITION **2 :** a writ granted by a court of equity whereby one is required to do or to refrain from doing a specified act — **in·junc·tive** \-ˈjəŋ(k)-tiv\ *adj*

in·jure \ˈin-jər\ *vt* **in·jur·ing** \ˈinj-(ə-)riŋ\ [back-formation fr. *injury*] **1 a :** to do an injustice to **:** WRONG **b :** to harm, impair, or tarnish the standing of **c :** to give pain to ⟨~ a man's pride⟩ **2 a :** to inflict bodily hurt on **b :** to impair the soundness of **c :** to inflict material damage or loss on — **in·jur·er** \ˈin-jər-ər\ *n*

syn HARM, HURT, DAMAGE, IMPAIR, MAR: INJURE implies the inflicting of anything detrimental to one's looks, comfort, health, success; HARM often stresses the inflicting of pain, suffering, or loss; HURT implies inflicting a wound to the body or to the feelings; DAMAGE suggests injury that lowers value or impairs usefulness; IMPAIR suggests a making less complete or efficient by deterioration or diminution; MAR applies to injury that spoils perfection (as of a surface) or causes disfigurement

in·ju·ri·ous \in-ˈju̇r-ē-əs\ *adj* **1 :** inflicting or tending to inflict injury **:** DETRIMENTAL **2 :** ABUSIVE, DEFAMATORY — **in·ju·ri·ous·ly** *adv* — **in·ju·ri·ous·ness** *n*

in·ju·ry \ˈinj-(ə-)rē\ *n* [ME *injurie*, fr. L *injuria*, fr. *injurus* injurious, fr. *in-* + *jur-, jus* right — more at JUST] **1 a :** an act that damages or hurts **:** WRONG **b :** violation of another's rights for which the law allows an action to recover damages **2 :** hurt, damage, or loss sustained **syn** see INJUSTICE

in·jus·tice \(ˈ)in-ˈjəs-təs\ *n* [ME, fr. MF, fr. L *injustitia*, fr. *injustus* unjust, fr. *in-* + *justus* just] **1 :** absence of justice **:** violation of right or of the rights of another **:** UNFAIRNESS **2 :** an unjust act

syn INJURY, WRONG, GRIEVANCE: INJUSTICE is the general term applying to any act that involves unfairness to another or violation of his rights; INJURY applies in law specifically to an injustice for which one may sue to recover compensation; WRONG applies also in law to any act punishable according to the criminal code; it may apply more generally to any flagrant injustice; GRIEVANCE applies to any circumstance or condition that constitutes an injustice to the sufferer and gives him just ground for complaint

1**ink** \ˈiŋk\ *n, often attrib* [ME *enke*, fr. OF, fr. LL *encaustum*, fr. neut. of L *encaustus* burned in, fr. Gk *enkaustos*, verbal of *enkaiein* to burn in — more at ENCAUSTIC] **1 :** a usu. fluid colored material for writing and printing **2 :** the black protective secretion of a cephalopod — **ink·i·ness** \ˈiŋ-kē-nəs\ *n* — **inky** \ˈiŋ-kē\ *adj*

2**ink** *vt* **:** to put ink on — **ink·er** *n*

ink·ber·ry \ˈiŋk-ˌber-ē\ *n* **1 a :** a holly (*Ilex glabra*) of eastern No. America with evergreen oblong leathery leaves and small black berries **b :** POKEWEED **2 :** the fruit of an inkberry

ink·blot \ˈiŋk-ˌblät\ *n* **:** any of several plates showing blots of ink for use in psychological testing

1**ink·horn** \ˈiŋk-ˌhȯ(ə)rn\ *n* **:** a small portable bottle of horn or other material for holding ink

2**inkhorn** *adj* **:** ostentatiously learned **:** PEDANTIC ⟨~ terms⟩

in·kle \ˈiŋ-kəl\ *n* [origin unknown] **:** a colored linen tape or braid used for trimming; *also* **:** the thread used

in·kling \ˈiŋ-kliŋ\ *n* [ME *yngkiling*, prob. fr. *inclen* to hint at; akin to OE *inca* suspicion, Lith *ingis* sluggard] **1 :** HINT, INTIMATION **2 :** a slight knowledge or vague notion

ink·stand \ˈiŋk-ˌstand\ *n* **:** INKWELL; *also* **:** a pen and ink stand

ink·well \ˈiŋ-ˌkwel\ *n* **:** a container for writing ink

inky cap *n* **:** a mushroom (genus *Coprinus*, esp. *C. atramentarius*) whose pileus melts into an inky fluid after the spores have matured

in·laid \ˈin-ˈlād\ *adj* **:** set into a surface in a decorative design or decorated with such a design

1**in·land** \ˈin-ˌland, -lənd\ *n* **:** the interior part of a country

2**inland** *adj* **1** *chiefly Brit* **:** not foreign **:** DOMESTIC **2 :** of or relating to the interior of a country

3**inland** *adv* **:** into or toward the interior

in·land·er \ˈin-ˌlan-dər, -lən-\ *n* **:** one who lives inland

in–law \ˈin-ˌlȯ\ *n* [back-formation fr. *mother-in-law*, etc.] **:** a relative by marriage

1**in·lay** \(ˈ)in-ˈlā\ *vt* **1 a :** to set into a surface or ground material **b :** to adorn with insertions **c :** to insert (as a color plate) into a mat or other reinforcement **d :** to reinforce (silver-plated ware) at points of wear with additional silver **2 :** to rub, beat, or fuse (as wire) into an incision in metal, wood, or stone — **in·lay·er** *n*

2**in·lay** \ˈin-ˌlā\ *n* **1 :** inlaid work or a decorative inlaid pattern **2 :** a tooth filling shaped to fit a cavity and then cemented into place

in·let \ˈin-ˌlet, -lət\ *n, often attrib* **1 :** an act of letting in **2 a :** a bay or recess in a shore; *also* **:** CREEK **b :** an opening for intake **3 :** something inlaid

in·li·er \ˈin-ˌlī(-ə)r\ *n* [3*in* + *-lier* (as in *outlier*)] **1 :** a mass of rock whose outcrop is surrounded by rock of younger age **2 :** a distinct area or formation completely surrounded by another; *also* **:** ENCLAVE

in·ly \ˈin-lē\ *adv* **1 :** INWARDLY **2 :** INTIMATELY, THOROUGHLY

in·mate \ˈin-ˌmāt\ *n* **:** one of a group occupying a single residence; *esp* **:** a person confined in an asylum, prison, or poorhouse

in me·di·as res \in-ˌmād-ē-ˌäs-ˈrās\ *adv* [L, lit., into the midst of things] **:** in or into the middle of a narrative or plot

in me·mo·ri·am \ˌin-mə-ˈmōr-ē-əm, -ˈmȯr-\ *prep* [L] **:** in memory of — used esp. in epitaphs

in·most \ˈin-ˌmōst\ *adj* [ME, fr. OE *innemest*, superl. of *inne*, adv., in, within, fr. *in*, adv.] **:** deepest within

1**inn** \ˈin\ *n* [ME, fr. OE; akin to ON *inni* dwelling, inn, OE *in*, adv.] **1 a :** a public house for the lodging and entertaining of travelers **b :** TAVERN **2 :** a residence formerly provided for British students in London

2**inn** *vi* **:** to put up at an inn

in·nards \ˈin-ərdz\ *n pl* [alter. of *inwards*] **1 :** the internal organs of a man or animal; *esp* **:** VISCERA **2 :** the internal parts of a structure or mechanism

in·nate \in-ˈāt, ˈin-ˌ\ *adj* [ME *innat*, fr. L *innatus*, pp. of *innasci* to be born in, fr. *in-* + *nasci* to be born — more at NATION] **1 a :** existing in or belonging to an individual from birth **:** NATIVE **b :** belonging to the essential nature of something **:** INHERENT **c :** originating in or derived from the mind or the constitution of the intellect rather than from experience **2** *obs* **:** INTERNAL **3 a :** attached to the apex of the support — compare ADNATE **b :** ENDOGENOUS **c :** immersed or embedded in — **in·nate·ly** *adv* — **in·nate·ness** *n*

syn INNATE, INBORN, INBRED, CONGENITAL, HEREDITARY mean not acquired after birth. INNATE applies to qualities or characteristics that are part of one's inner essential nature; INBORN suggests a quality or tendency either actually present at birth or so marked and deep-seated as to seem so; INBRED suggests something acquired from parents either by heredity or early nurture but in any case deeply rooted and ingrained; CONGENITAL and HEREDITARY refer to something acquired before or at birth, CONGENITAL implying acquirement during fetal development, HEREDITARY implying transmission from an ancestor through the germ plasm

in·ner \ˈin-ər\ *adj* [ME, fr. OE *innera*, compar. of *inne* within — more at INMOST] **1 a :** situated farther in **b :** near a center esp. of influence **2 :** of or relating to the mind or spirit ⟨the ~ life of man⟩ — **inner** *n* — **in·ner·ly** *adv*

in·ner–di·rect·ed \ˌin-ər-də-ˈrek-təd, -(ˌ)dī-\ *adj* **:** directed in thought and action by one's own scale of values as opposed to external norms

inner light *n, often cap I & L* **:** a divine presence held (as in Quaker doctrine) to enlighten and guide the soul

1**in·ner·most** \ˈin-ər-ˌmōst\ *adj* **:** farthest inward **:** INMOST

2**innermost** *n* **:** the inmost part

in·ner·sole \ˌin-ər-ˈsōl\ *n* **:** INSOLE

inner tube *n* **:** TUBE 3

in·ner·vate \in-ˈər-ˌvāt, ˈin-(ˌ)ər-\ *vt* **:** to supply with nerves — **in·ner·va·tion** \ˌin-(ˌ)ər-ˈvā-shən, in-ˌər-\ *n* — **in·ner·va·tion·al** \-shnəl, -shən-ᵊl\ *adj*

in·nerve \in-ˈərv\ *vt* **:** to give nervous energy or power to

inn·hold·er \ˈin-ˌhōl-dər\ *n* **:** INNKEEPER

in·ning \ˈin-iŋ\ *n* [in sense 1, fr. E dial. *in* to reclaim; in other senses, fr. 2*in*] **1 :** the reclaiming of land esp. from the sea **2 a :** a baseball team's turn at bat ending with the 3d out; *also* **:** a division of a baseball game consisting of a turn at bat for each team **b** *pl but sing or pl in constr* **:** a division of a cricket match **3 :** a chance or turn for action or accomplishment

inn·keep·er \ˈin-ˌkē-pər\ *n* **:** the landlord of an inn

in·no·cence \ˈin-ə-sən(t)s\ *n* **1 a :** freedom from guilt or sin through being unacquainted with evil **:** BLAMELESSNESS **b :** freedom from legal guilt of a particular crime or offense **c :** GUILELESSNESS,

SIMPLICITY **d :** IGNORANCE **2 :** one that is innocent **3 a :** BLUET **b :** a small herb (*Collinsia verna* of the figwort family) of the central U.S. or a related California herb (*C. bicolor*)

in·no·cen·cy \-sən-sē\ *n* **:** INNOCENCE; *also* **:** an innocent action or quality

in·no·cent \ˈin-ə-sənt\ *adj* [ME, fr. MF, fr. L *innocent-, innocens,* fr. *in-* + *nocent-, nocens* wicked, fr. prp. of *nocēre* to harm — more at NOXIOUS] **1 a :** free from guilt or sin esp. through lack of knowledge of evil **:** BLAMELESS **b :** harmless in effect or intention; *also* **:** CANDID **c :** free from legal guilt or fault; *also* **:** LAWFUL **d :** lacking something **:** DESTITUTE **2 a :** ARTLESS, INGENUOUS **b :** IGNORANT — **innocent** *n* — **in·no·cent·ly** *adv*

in·noc·u·ous \in-ˈäk-yə-wəs\ *adj* [L *innocuus,* fr. *in-* + *nocēre*] **1 :** working no injury **:** HARMLESS **2 a :** not likely to arouse animus or give offense **b :** INOFFENSIVE, INSIPID — **in·noc·u·ous·ly** *adv* — **in·noc·u·ous·ness** *n*

Inn of Court 1 : one of four sets of buildings in London belonging to four societies of students and practitioners of the law **2 :** one of four societies that alone admit to practice at the English bar

in·nom·i·nate \in-ˈäm-ə-nət\ *adj* [LL *innominatus,* fr. L *in-* + *nominatus,* pp. of *nominare* to nominate] **:** having no name **:** UNNAMED; *also* **:** ANONYMOUS

innominate bone *n* **:** the large flaring bone that makes a lateral half of the pelvis in mammals and is composed of the ilium, ischium, and pubis which are consolidated into one bone in the adult

in·no·vate \ˈin-ə-ˌvāt\ *vb* [L *innovatus,* pp. of *innovare,* fr. *in-* + *novus* new — more at NEW] *vt* **:** to introduce as or as if new ~ *vi* **:** to make changes — **in·no·va·tive** \-ˌvāt-iv\ *adj* — **in·no·va·tor** \-ˌvāt-ər\ *n* — **in·no·va·to·ry** \ˈin-ə-və-ˌtōr-ē, in-ˈō-və-, -ˌtȯr-; ˈin-ə-ˌvāt-ə-rē\ *adj*

in·no·va·tion \ˌin-ə-ˈvā-shən\ *n* **1 :** the introduction of something new **2 :** a new idea, method, or device **:** NOVELTY

¹in·nu·en·do \ˌin-yə-ˈwen-(ˌ)dō\ *n, pl* **innuendos** *or* **innuendoes** [L, by hinting, fr. *innuere* to hint, fr. *in-* + *nuere* to nod — more at NUMEN] **1 :** an oblique allusion **:** HINT, INSINUATION; *esp* **:** a veiled or equivocal reflection on character or reputation **2 :** a parenthetical explanation introduced into the text of a legal document

²innuendo *vi* **:** to make an innuendo ~ *vt* **:** to insinuate by an innuendo

in·nu·mer·a·ble \in-ˈ(y)üm-(ə-)rə-bəl\ *adj* [ME, fr. L *innumerabilis,* fr. *in-* + *numerabilis* numerable] **:** too many to be numbered **:** COUNTLESS — **in·nu·mer·a·ble·ness** *n* — **in·nu·mer·a·bly** \-blē\ *adv*

in·nu·mer·ous \-(ə-)rəs\ *adj* [L *innumerus,* fr. *in-* + *numerus* number — more at NIMBLE] **:** INNUMERABLE

in·nu·tri·tion \ˌin-(n)(y)ü-ˈtrish-ən\ *n* **:** failure of nourishment

in·nu·tri·tious \-əs\ *adj* **:** not nutritious

in·ob·ser·vance \ˌin-əb-ˈzər-vən(t)s\ *n* [F & L; F, fr. L *inobservantia,* fr. *in-* + *observantia* observance] **1 :** lack of attention **:** HEEDLESSNESS **2 :** failure to fulfill **:** NONOBSERVANCE — **in·ob·ser·vant** \-vənt\ *adj*

in·oc·u·lant \in-ˈäk-yə-lənt\ *n* **:** INOCULUM

in·oc·u·late \-ˌlāt\ *vt* [ME *inoculaten* to insert a bud in a plant, fr. L *inoculatus,* pp. of *inoculare,* fr. *in-* + *oculus* eye, bud — more at EYE] **1 a :** to communicate a disease to by introducing its causative agent into the tissues **b :** to introduce (as an infective agent) into (as for growth) **c :** to treat (as seed) with bacteria usu. to stimulate nitrogen fixation **2 :** to introduce something into the mind of **syn** see INFUSE — **in·oc·u·la·tive** \-ˌlāt-iv\ *adj* — **in·oc·u·la·tor** \-ˌlāt-ər\ *n*

in·oc·u·la·tion \in-ˌäk-yə-ˈlā-shən\ *n* **1 :** the act or process or an instance of inoculating; *esp* **:** the introduction of a pathogen or antigen into a living organism to stimulate the production of antibodies **2 :** INOCULUM

in·oc·u·lum \in-ˈäk-yə-ləm\ *n, pl* **in·oc·u·la** \-lə\ [NL, fr. L *inoculare*] **:** material used for inoculation

in·of·fen·sive \ˌin-ə-ˈfen(t)-siv\ *adj* **1 :** causing no harm or injury **2 a :** giving no provocation **:** PEACEABLE **b :** unobjectionable to the senses — **in·of·fen·sive·ly** *adv* — **in·of·fen·sive·ness** *n*

in·op·er·a·ble \(ˈ)in-ˈäp-(ə-)rə-bəl\ *adj* [prob. fr. F *inopérable*] **1 :** not suitable for surgery **2 :** not operable

in·op·er·a·tive \-ˈäp-(ə-)rət-iv, -ˈäp-ə-ˌrāt-\ *adj* **:** not functioning — **in·op·er·a·tive·ness** *n*

in·oper·cu·late \ˌin-ō-ˈpər-kyə-lət\ *adj* **:** having no operculum — **inoperculate** *n*

in·op·por·tune \(ˌ)in-ˌäp-ər-ˈt(y)ün\ *adj* [L *inopportunus,* fr. *in-* + *opportunus* opportune] **:** INCONVENIENT, UNSEASONABLE — **in·op·por·tune·ly** *adv* — **in·op·por·tune·ness** \-ˈt(y)ün-nəs\ *n*

in order that *conj* **:** THAT

in·or·di·nate \in-ˈȯrd-ᵊn-ət, -ˈȯrd-nət\ *adj* [ME *inordinat,* fr. L *inordinatus,* fr. *in-* + *ordinatus,* pp. of *ordinare* to arrange — more at ORDAIN] **1 :** UNREGULATED, DISORDERLY **2 :** exceeding reasonable limits **:** IMMODERATE **syn** see EXCESSIVE — **in·or·di·nate·ly** *adv* — **in·or·di·nate·ness** *n*

in·or·gan·ic \ˌin-(ˌ)ȯr-ˈgan-ik\ *adj* **1 a (1) :** being or composed of matter other than plant or animal **:** MINERAL **(2) :** forming or belonging to the inanimate world **b :** of, relating to, or dealt with by a branch of chemistry concerned with substances not usu. classed as organic **2 :** not arising from natural growth **:** ARTIFICIAL; *also* **:** lacking structure, character, or vitality — **in·or·gan·i·cal·ly** \-i-k(ə-)lē\ *adv*

in·os·cu·late \in-ˈäs-kyə-ˌlāt\ *vb* **:** to unite by apposition or contact **:** BLEND — **in·os·cu·la·tion** \(ˌ)in-ˌäs-kyə-ˈlā-shən\ *n*

ino·si·tol \in-ˈō-sə-ˌtȯl, ī-ˈnō-, -ˌtōl\ *n* [ISV, fr. *inosite* inositol, fr. Gk *inos,* gen. of *is* sinew — more at WITHY] **:** any of nine crystalline stereoisomeric cyclic alcohols $C_6H_6(OH)_6$; *esp* **:** one that is a component of the vitamin B complex and a lipotropic agent and occurs widely in plant and animal tissues

in·pa·tient \ˈin-ˌpā-shənt\ *n* **:** a hospital patient who receives lodging and food as well as treatment

in per·so·nam \ˌin-pər-ˈsō-ˌnam, -ˌnäm\ *adv* (*or adj*) [LL] **1 :** against a particular person **2 :** against the person rather than a thing

in pet·to \in-ˈpet-(ˌ)ō\ *adv* (*or adj*) [It, lit., in the breast] **1 :** in private **:** SECRETLY **2 :** in miniature

in·phase \ˈin-ˌfāz\ *adj* [fr. the phrase *in phase*] **:** being of the same electrical phase

in·pour \(ˈ)in-ˈpō(ə)r, -ˈpȯ(ə)r\ *vb* **:** to pour in

in pro·pria per·so·na \in-ˌprō-prē-ə-pər-ˈsō-nə\ *adv* [ML] **:** in one's own person or character

in·put \ˈin-ˌpu̇t\ *n* **1 :** something that is put in; *esp* **:** an amount put in **:** power or energy put into a machine or system for storage or for conversion in kind or conversion of characteristics **2 :** the terminal for an electrical input **3 :** information fed into a computer or accounting machine **4 :** the act or process of putting in

in·quest \ˈin-ˌkwest\ *n* [ME *enqueste,* fr. OF *enqueste,* fr. (assumed) VL *inquaestus,* pp. of *inquaerere* to inquire] **1 a :** a judicial or official inquiry or examination esp. before a jury **b :** a body of men (as a jury) assembled to hold such an inquiry **c :** the finding of the jury upon such inquiry or the document recording it **2 :** INQUIRY, INVESTIGATION

in·qui·etude \(ˈ)in-ˈkwī-ə-ˌt(y)üd\ *n* [ME, fr. MF or LL; MF, fr. LL *inquietudo,* fr. L *inquietus* disturbed, fr. *in-* + *quietus* quiet] **:** DISQUIETUDE

in·qui·line \ˈin-kwə-ˌlīn, ˈiŋ-\ *n* [L *inquilinus* tenant, lodger, fr. *in-* + *colere* to cultivate, dwell — more at WHEEL] **:** an animal that lives habitually in the nest or abode of some other species — **inquiline** *adj* — **in·qui·lin·ism** \-lə-ˌniz-əm\ *n* — **in·qui·lin·i·ty** \ˌin-kwə-ˈlin-ət-ē, ˌiŋ-\ *n* — **in·qui·li·nous** \-ˈlī-nəs\ *adj*

in·quire \in-ˈkwī(ə)r\ *vb* [ME *enquiren,* fr. OF *enquerre,* fr. (assumed) VL *inquaerere,* alter. of L *inquirere,* fr. *in-* + *quaerere* to seek] *vt* **1 :** to ask about **2 :** to search into **:** INVESTIGATE ~ *vi* **1 :** to put a question **2 :** to make investigation or inquiry **syn** see ASK — **in·quir·er** *n* — **in·quir·ing·ly** \-iŋ-lē\ *adv* — **inquire after :** to ask about the health of

in·qui·ry \ˈin-ˌkwī(ə)r-ē, in-ˈ; ˈin-kwə-rē, ˈiŋ-\ *n* **1 :** a request for information **2 :** a systematic investigation of a matter of public interest

in·qui·si·tion \ˌin-kwə-ˈzish-ən\ *n* [ME *inquisicioun,* fr. MF *inquisition,* fr. L *inquisition-, inquisitio,* fr. *inquisitus,* pp. of *inquirere*] **1 :** the act of inquiring **2 :** a judicial or official inquiry or examination usu. before a jury; *also* **:** the finding of the jury **3 a** *cap* **:** a former Roman Catholic tribunal for the discovery and punishment of heresy **b :** an investigation conducted with little regard for individual rights **c :** a severe questioning — **in·qui·si·tion·al** \-ˈzish-nəl, -ən-ᵊl\ *adj*

in·quis·i·tive \in-ˈkwiz-ət-iv\ *adj* **1 :** given to examination or investigation **2 :** QUESTIONING; *esp* **:** PRYING **syn** see CURIOUS — **in·quis·i·tive·ly** *adv* — **in·quis·i·tive·ness** *n*

in·quis·i·tor \in-ˈkwiz-ət-ər\ *n* **:** one who inquires or makes inquisition — **in·quis·i·to·ri·al** \(ˌ)in-ˌkwiz-ə-ˈtōr-ē-əl, -ˈtȯr-\ *adj* — **in·quis·i·to·ri·al·ly** \-ē-ə-lē\ *adv*

in re \in-ˈrē, -ˈrā\ *prep* [L] **:** in the matter of **:** CONCERNING, RE

in rem \-ˈrem\ *adv* (*or adj*) [LL] **:** against a thing (as a right, status, property) — compare IN PERSONAM

in·road \ˈin-ˌrōd\ *n* **1 :** a sudden hostile incursion **:** RAID **2 :** a destructive encroachment

in·rush \ˈin-ˌrəsh\ *n* **:** a crowding or flooding in **:** INFLUX

in·sal·i·vate \in-ˈsal-ə-ˌvāt\ *vt* **:** to mix (food) with saliva by mastication — **in·sal·i·va·tion** \(ˌ)in-ˌsal-ə-ˈvā-shən\ *n*

in·sa·lu·bri·ous \ˌin(t)-sə-ˈlü-brē-əs\ *adj* [L *insalubris,* fr. *in-* + *salubris* healthful — more at SAFE] **:** UNWHOLESOME, NOXIOUS — **in·sa·lu·bri·ty** \-brət-ē\ *n*

in·sane \(ˈ)in-ˈsān\ *adj* [L *insanus,* fr. *in-* + *sanus* sane] **1 :** exhibiting insanity **:** MAD **2 :** used by, typical of, or intended for insane persons **3 :** FOOLISH, WILD — **in·sane·ly** *adv* — **in·sane·ness** \-ˈsān-nəs\ *n*

in·san·i·tary \(ˈ)in-ˈsan-ə-ˌter-ē\ *adj* **:** unclean enough to endanger health **:** CONTAMINATED

in·san·i·ty \in-ˈsan-ət-ē\ *n* **1 a :** unsoundness or derangement of the mind usu. occurring as a specific disorder (as schizophrenia) and usu. excluding such states as mental deficiency, psychoneurosis, and various character disorders **b :** a mental disorder **2 :** such unsoundness of mind or lack of understanding as prevents one from having the mental capacity required by law to enter into a particular relationship, status, or transaction or as excuses one from criminal or civil responsibility **3 a :** extreme folly or unreasonableness **b :** something utterly foolish or unreasonable

syn INSANITY, LUNACY, PSYCHOSIS, MANIA, DEMENTIA denote serious mental disorder. INSANITY implies unfitness to manage one's own affairs or safely enjoy liberty; LUNACY usu. implies periodic disorder or alternating madness and lucidity; PSYCHOSIS is the technical psychiatric term for a serious and prolonged behavioral disorder; MANIA implies insanity but is often used specifically of one of the spells of excitement that characterize some psychoses; DEMENTIA is a technical psychiatric term that denotes mental deterioration whether psychogenic in origin or resulting from damage to brain tissue

in·sa·tia·bil·i·ty \(ˌ)in-ˌsā-shə-ˈbil-ət-ē\ *n* **:** the quality or state of being insatiable

in·sa·tia·ble \(ˈ)in-ˈsā-shə-bəl\ *adj* [ME *insaciable,* fr. MF, fr. L *insatiabilis,* fr. *in-* + *satiare* to satisfy — more at SATIATE] **:** incapable of being satisfied **:** QUENCHLESS — **in·sa·tia·ble·ness** *n* — **in·sa·tia·bly** \-blē\ *adv*

in·sa·tiate \-ˈsā-sh(ē-)ət\ *adj* **:** not satiated or satisfied; *also* **:** INSATIABLE — **in·sa·tiate·ly** *adv* — **in·sa·tiate·ness** *n*

in·scribe \in-ˈskrīb\ *vt* [L *inscribere,* fr. *in-* + *scribere* to write — more at SCRIBE] **1 a :** to write, engrave, or print as a lasting record **b :** to enter on a list **:** ENROLL **c :** to write (letters or other characters) in a particular format in cryptography **2 a :** to write, engrave, or print characters upon **b :** to autograph or address as a gift **3 :** to dedicate to someone **4 :** to draw within a figure so as to touch in as many places as possible **5** *Brit* **:** to register the name of the holder of (a security) — **in·scrib·er** *n*

in·scrip·tion \in-ˈskrip-shən\ *n* [ME *inscripcioun,* fr. L *inscription-, inscriptio,* fr. *inscriptus,* pp. of *inscribere*] **1 a :** something that is inscribed; *also* **:** TITLE, SUPERSCRIPTION **b :** EPIGRAPH 2 **c :** the wording on a coin, medal, or seal **:** LEGEND **2 :** the dedication of a book or work of art **3 a :** the act of inscribing **b :** the entering of a name on or as if on a list **:** ENROLLMENT **4** *Brit* **a :** the act of inscribing securities **b** *pl* **:** inscribed securities — **in·scrip·tion·al** \-shnəl, -shən-ᵊl\ *adj*

in·scrip·tive \in-ˈskrip-tiv\ *adj* **:** relating to or constituting an inscription — **in·scrip·tive·ly** *adv*

in·scroll \in-ˈskrōl\ *vt* **:** to write on a scroll **:** RECORD

in·scru·ta·bil·i·ty \(ˌ)in-ˌskrüt-ə-ˈbil-ət-ē\ *n* **:** the quality or state of being inscrutable

in·scru·ta·ble \in-ˈskrüt-ə-bəl\ *adj* [ME, fr. LL *inscrutabilis,* fr. L *in-* + *scrutari* to search — more at SCRUTINY] **:** not readily understood **:** ENIGMATIC **syn** see MYSTERIOUS — **in·scru·ta·ble·ness** *n* — **in·scru·ta·bly** \-blē\ *adv*

in·sculp \in-ˈskəlp\ *vt* [ME *insculpen*, fr. L *insculpere*, fr. *in-* + *sculpere* to carve — more at SHELF] *archaic* : ENGRAVE, SCULPTURE

in·seam \ˈin-ˌsēm\ *n* : an inner seam of a garment or shoe

in·sect \ˈin-ˌsekt\ *n* [L *insectum*, fr. neut. of *insectus*, pp. of *insecare* to cut into, fr. *in-* + *secare* to cut — more at SAW] **1 a** : any of numerous small invertebrate animals (as spiders or centipedes) that are more or less obviously segmented **b** : any of a class (Insecta) of arthropods (as bugs or bees) with well-defined head, thorax, and abdomen, only three pairs of legs, and typically one or two pairs of wings **2** : any of various small animals (as earthworms or turtles) **3** : a trivial or contemptible person — **insect** *adj*

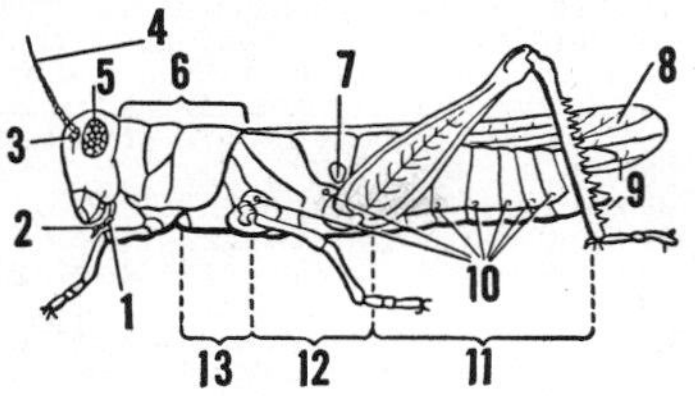

external parts of an insect: *1* labial palpus, *2* maxillary palpus, *3* simple eye, *4* antenna, *5* compound eye, *6* prothorax, *7* tympanum, *8* wing, *9* ovipositor, *10* spiracles, *11* abdomen, *12* metathorax, *13* mesothorax

in·sec·ta·ry \ˈin-ˌsek-tə-rē, in-ˈ\ *or* **in·sec·tar·i·um** \ˌin-ˌsek-ˈter-ē-əm\ *n, pl* **insectaries** *or* **in·sec·tar·ia** \ˌin-ˌsek-ˈter-ē-ə\ : a place for the keeping or rearing of living insects

in·sec·ti·ci·dal \(ˌ)in-ˌsek-tə-ˈsīd-ᵊl\ *adj* **1** : destroying or controlling insects **2** : of or relating to an insecticide — **in·sec·ti·ci·dal·ly** \-ᵊl-ē\ *adv*

in·sec·ti·cide \in-ˈsek-tə-ˌsīd\ *n* [ISV] : an agent that destroys insects

in·sec·ti·fuge \-tə-ˌfyüj\ *n* : an insect repellent

in·sec·tile \in-ˈsek-tᵊl, -ˌtīl\ *adj* : resembling or being an insect; *esp* : consisting of insects

in·sec·ti·vore \in-ˈsek-tə-ˌvō(ə)r, -ˌvȯ(ə)r\ *n* [deriv. of L *insectum* + *-vorus* -vorous] **1** : any of an order (Insectivora) of mammals comprising the moles, shrews, hedgehogs, and related forms that are mostly small, insectivorous, and nocturnal **2** : an insectivorous plant or animal

in·sec·tiv·o·rous \ˌin-ˌsek-ˈtiv-(ə-)rəs\ *adj* : depending on insects as food

in·se·cure \ˌin(t)-si-ˈkyu̇(ə)r\ *adj* [ML *insecurus*, fr. L *in-* + *securus* secure] **1** : UNCERTAIN, UNSURE **2** : UNPROTECTED, UNSAFE **3** : LOOSE, SHAKY **4** : lacking stability : INFIRM — **in·se·cure·ly** *adv* — **in·se·cure·ness** *n* — **in·se·cu·ri·ty** \-ˈkyu̇r-ət-ē\ *n*

in·sem·i·nate \in-ˈsem-ə-ˌnāt\ *vt* [L *inseminatus*, pp. of *inseminare*, fr. *in-* + *semin-*, *semen* seed — more at SEMEN] **1 a** : SOW **b** : to sow in **2** : to introduce semen into the genital tract of (a female) **syn** see IMPLANT — **in·sem·i·na·tion** \(ˌ)in-ˌsem-ə-ˈnā-shən\ *n*

in·sem·i·na·tor \in-ˈsem-ə-ˌnāt-ər\ *n* : one that inseminates cattle artificially

in·sen·sate \(ˈ)in-ˈsen-ˌsāt\ *adj* [LL *insensatus*, fr. L *in-* + LL *sensatus* having sense, fr. L *sensus* sense] **1** : lacking animate awareness or sensation **2** : lacking sense or understanding; *also* : FOOLISH **3** : BRUTAL, INHUMAN — **in·sen·sate·ly** *adv* — **in·sen·sate·ness** *n*

in·sen·si·bil·i·ty \(ˌ)in-ˌsen(t)-sə-ˈbil-ət-ē\ *n* : the quality or state of being insensible

in·sen·si·ble \(ˈ)in-ˈsen(t)-sə-bəl\ *adj* [ME, fr. MF & L; MF, fr. L *insensibilis*, fr. *in-* + *sensibilis* sensible] **1** : incapable or bereft of feeling or sensation: as **a** : INANIMATE, INSENTIENT ⟨~ earth⟩ **b** : UNCONSCIOUS **c** : lacking sensory perception ⟨~ to pain⟩; *also* : deprived of such perception or ability to react ⟨~ from cold⟩ **2** : IMPERCEPTIBLE; *broadly* : SLIGHT, GRADUAL ⟨~ motion⟩ **3** *archaic* : STUPID, SENSELESS **4** : APATHETIC, INDIFFERENT ⟨~ to fear⟩; *also* : UNAWARE ⟨~ of their danger⟩ **5** : not intelligible : MEANINGLESS **6** : lacking delicacy or refinement — **in·sen·si·ble·ness** *n* — **in·sen·si·bly** \-blē\ *adv*

in·sen·si·tive \(ˈ)in-ˈsen(t)-sət-iv, -ˈsen(t)-stiv\ *adj* : not sensitive; *esp* : lacking feeling — **in·sen·si·tive·ly** *adv* — **in·sen·si·tive·ness** *or* **in·sen·si·tiv·i·ty** \(ˌ)in-ˌsen(t)-sə-ˈtiv-ət-ē\ *n*

in·sen·tience \(ˈ)in-ˈsen-ch(ē-)ən(t)s\ *n* : the quality or state of being insentient

in·sen·tient \-ch(ē-)ənt\ *adj* : lacking perception, consciousness, or animation

in·sep·a·ra·bil·i·ty \(ˌ)in-ˌsep-(ə-)rə-ˈbil-ət-ē\ *n* : the quality or state of being inseparable

in·sep·a·ra·ble \(ˈ)in-ˈsep-(ə-)rə-bəl\ *adj* [ME, fr. L *inseparabilis*, fr. *in-* + *separabilis* separable] : incapable of being separated or disjoined — **inseparable** *n* — **in·sep·a·ra·ble·ness** *n* — **in·sep·a·ra·bly** \-blē\ *adv*

¹**in·sert** \in-ˈsərt\ *vb* [L *insertus*, pp. of *inserere*, fr. *in-* + *serere* to join — more at SERIES] *vt* **1** : to put or thrust in **2** : to put or introduce into the body of something : INTERPOLATE **3** : to set in and make fast; *esp* : to insert by sewing between two cut edges ~ *vi*, *of a muscle* : to be in attachment to the part to be moved **syn** see INTRODUCE — **in·sert·er** *n*

²**in·sert** \ˈin-ˌsərt\ *n* : something that is inserted or is for insertion; *esp* : written or printed material inserted (as between the leaves of a book)

in·ser·tion \in-ˈsər-shən\ *n* **1** : the act or process of inserting **2** : something that is inserted: as **a** : the part of a muscle that inserts **b** : the mode or place of attachment of an organ or part **c** : embroidery or needlework inserted as ornament between two pieces of fabric **d** : a single appearance of an advertisement — **in·ser·tion·al** \-shnəl, -shən-ᵊl\ *adj*

in·ses·so·ri·al \ˌin-ˌse-ˈsōr-ē-əl, -ˈsȯr-\ *adj* [L *insessus*, pp. of *insidēre* to sit on] : perching or adapted for perching

¹**in·set** \ˈin-ˌset\ *n* **1 a** : a place where something flows in : CHANNEL **b** : a setting or flowing in **2** : something that is inset: as **a** : a small graphic representation (as a map or picture) set within the compass of a larger one **b** : a piece of cloth set into a garment for decoration **c** : a part or section of a utensil that fits into an outer part

²**in·set** \ˈin-ˌset, in-ˈ\ *vt* **inset** *or* **in·set·ted**; **in·set·ting** : to set in : insert as an inset

¹**in·shore** \ˈin-ˈshō(ə)r, -ˈshȯ(ə)r\ *adj* **1** : situated or carried on near shore **2** : moving toward shore

²**inshore** *adv* : to or toward shore

¹**in·side** \(ˈ)in-ˈsīd, ˈin-ˌ\ *n* **1** : an inner side or surface **2 a** : an interior or internal part : the part within **b** : inward nature, thoughts, or feeling **c** : VISCERA, ENTRAILS — usu. used in pl. **3 a** : a position of power or confidence **b** *slang* : confidential information — **inside** *adj*

²**inside** *prep* **1 a** : in or into the interior of **b** : on the inner side of **2** : before the end of : WITHIN ⟨~ an hour⟩

³**inside** *adv* **1** : on the inner side **2** : in or into the interior

inside of *prep* : INSIDE

in·sid·er \(ˈ)in-ˈsīd-ər\ *n* : a person who is in a position of power or has access to confidential information

inside track *n* **1** : the inner side of a curved racecourse **2** : an advantageous competitive position

in·sid·i·ous \in-ˈsid-ē-əs\ *adj* [L *insidiosus*, fr. *insidiae* ambush, fr. *insidēre* to sit in, sit on, fr. *in-* + *sedēre* to sit — more at SIT] **1 a** : awaiting a chance to entrap : TREACHEROUS **b** : harmful but enticing : SEDUCTIVE **2 a** : having a gradual and cumulative effect : SUBTLE **b** *of a disease* : developing so gradually as to be well established before becoming apparent — **in·sid·i·ous·ly** *adv* — **in·sid·i·ous·ness** *n*

in·sight \ˈin-ˌsīt\ *n* **1** : the power or act of seeing into a situation : PENETRATION **2** : the act of apprehending the inner nature of things or of seeing intuitively **syn** see DISCERNMENT

in·sig·nia \in-ˈsig-nē-ə\ *or* **in·sig·ne** \-(ˌ)nē\ *n, pl* **in·sig·nia** *or* **in·sig·ni·as** [L *insignia*, pl. of *insigne* mark, badge, fr. neut. of *insignis* marked, distinguished, fr. *in-* + *signum* mark, sign] **1** : a badge of authority or honor : EMBLEM **2** : a distinguishing mark or sign

in·sig·nif·i·cance \ˌin(t)-sig-ˈnif-i-kən(t)s\ *n* : the quality or state of being insignificant

in·sig·nif·i·can·cy \-kən-sē\ *n* **1** : INSIGNIFICANCE **2** : an insignificant thing or person

in·sig·nif·i·cant \-kənt\ *adj* : not significant: as **a** : lacking meaning or import : INCONSEQUENTIAL **b** : INCONSIDERABLE, UNIMPORTANT **c** : lacking weight, position, or influence : CONTEMPTIBLE **d** : LITTLE, SMALL — **in·sig·nif·i·cant·ly** *adv*

in·sin·cere \ˌin(t)-sin-ˈsi(ə)r, -sən-\ *adj* [L *insincerus*, fr. *in-* + *sincerus* sincere] : not sincere : HYPOCRITICAL — **in·sin·cere·ly** *adv* — **in·sin·cer·i·ty** \-ˈser-ət-ē, -ˈsir-\ *n*

in·sin·u·ate \in-ˈsin-yə-ˌwāt\ *vb* [L *insinuatus*, pp. of *insinuare*, fr. *in-* + *sinuare* to bend, curve, fr. *sinus* curve] *vt* **1 a** : to introduce (as an idea) gradually or in a subtle, indirect, or covert way **b** : HINT, IMPLY **2** : to introduce (as oneself) by stealthy, smooth, or artful means ~ *vi* **1** *archaic* : to enter gently, slowly, or imperceptibly : CREEP **2** *archaic* : to ingratiate oneself **syn** see INTRODUCE, SUGGEST — **in·sin·u·a·tive** \-ˌwāt-iv\ *adj* — **in·sin·u·a·tor** \-ˌwāt-ər\ *n*

in·sin·u·at·ing *adj* **1** : tending gradually to cause doubt, distrust, or change of outlook ⟨~ remarks⟩ **2** : winning favor and confidence by imperceptible degrees ⟨~ voice⟩ : INGRATIATING — **in·sin·u·at·ing·ly** \-iŋ-lē\ *adv*

in·sin·u·a·tion \(ˌ)in-ˌsin-yə-ˈwā-shən\ *n* **1** : a subtly made suggestion : INNUENDO **2** : the artful pursuit of favor

in·sip·id \in-ˈsip-əd\ *adj* [F & LL; F *insipide*, fr. LL *insipidus*, fr. L *in-* + *sapidus* savory, fr. *sapere* to taste — more at SAGE] **1** : lacking taste or savor : TASTELESS **2** : lacking in qualities that interest, stimulate, or challenge : DULL, FLAT — **in·si·pid·i·ty** \ˌin(t)-sə-ˈpid-ət-ē\ *n* — **in·sip·id·ly** \in-ˈsip-əd-lē\ *adv*

syn VAPID, FLAT, JEJUNE, BANAL, INANE: INSIPID implies a lack of sufficient taste or savor to please or interest; VAPID suggests a want of liveliness, force, or spirit; FLAT implies extreme vapidness; JEJUNE suggests a lack of rewarding or satisfying substance; BANAL stresses the complete absence of freshness, novelty, or immediacy; INANE implies a want of significance or cogency

in·sip·i·ence \in-ˈsip-ē-ən(t)s\ *n* [ME, fr. OF, fr. L *insipientia* folly, fr. *insipient-*, *insipiens*, fr. *in-* + *sapient-*, *sapiens* sapient] *archaic* : lack of intelligence : STUPIDITY — **in·sip·i·ent** \-ənt\ *adj*

in·sist \in-ˈsist\ *vb* [MF or L; MF *insister*, fr. L *insistere* to stand upon, persist, fr. *in-* + *sistere* to stand; akin to L *stare* to stand — more at STAND] *vi* **1** : to take a resolute stand or course **2** : PERSIST ~ *vt* : to take a firm stand about ⟨~*ed* that we come in⟩

in·sis·tence \in-ˈsis-tən(t)s\ *also* **in·sis·ten·cy** \-tən-sē\ *n* : the act of insisting; *also* : an insistent attitude or quality : URGENCY

in·sis·tent \in-ˈsis-tənt\ *adj* [L *insistent-*, *insistens*, prp. of *insistere*] : disposed to insist : PERTINACIOUS — **in·sis·tent·ly** *adv*

in si·tu \in-ˈsī-(ˌ)tü, -ˈsi-; -ˈsich-(ˌ)ü\ *adv* (*or adj*) [L, in position] : in the natural or original position

in·so·cia·bil·i·ty \(ˌ)in-ˌsō-shə-ˈbil-ət-ē\ *n* : lack of sociability

in·so·cia·ble \(ˈ)in-ˈsō-shə-bəl\ *adj* [L *insociabilis*, fr. *in-* + *sociabilis* sociable] : not sociable — **in·so·cia·bly** \-blē\ *adv*

in·so·far \ˌin(t)-sə-ˈfär\ *adv* : to such extent or degree

insofar as \ˈin(t)-sə-ˌfär-əz\ *conj* : to the extent or degree that

in·so·late \ˈin(t)-(ˌ)sō-ˌlāt, in-ˈsō-\ *vt* [L *insolatus*, pp. of *insolare*, fr. *in-* + *sol* sun — more at SOLAR] : to expose to the sun's rays

in·so·la·tion \ˌin(t)-(ˌ)sō-ˈlā-shən, in-ˌsō-\ *n* **1** : the act or an instance of insolating **2** : SUNSTROKE **3 a** : solar radiation that has been received **b** : the rate of delivery of all direct solar energy per unit of horizontal surface

in·sole \ˈin-ˌsōl\ *n* **1** : an inside sole of a shoe **2** : a loose thin strip placed inside a shoe for warmth or comfort

in·so·lence \ˈin(t)-s(ə-)lən(t)s\ *n* : a haughty attitude or insulting act

in·so·lent \-lənt\ *adj* [ME, fr. L *insolent-*, *insolens*; akin to L *insolescere* to grow haughty] **1** : arrogant in speech or conduct : OVERBEARING **2** : exhibiting boldness or effrontery : IMPUDENT **syn** see PROUD — **insolent** *n* — **in·so·lent·ly** *adv*

in·sol·u·bil·i·ty \(ˌ)in-ˌsäl-yə-ˈbil-ət-ē\ *n* : the quality or state of being insoluble: as **a** : INDISSOLUBILITY **b** : INEXPLICABILITY

in·sol·u·ble \(ˈ)in-ˈsäl-yə-bəl\ *adj* [ME *insolible*, fr. L *insolubilis*, fr. *in-* + *solvere* to free, dissolve — more at SOLVE] : not soluble: as **a** *archaic* : INDISSOLUBLE **b** : having or admitting of no solution or explanation **c** : incapable of or only with difficulty being dissolved in a liquid — **insoluble** *n* — **in·sol·u·ble·ness** *n* — **in·sol·u·bly** \-blē\ *adv*

in·solv·able \(ˈ)in-ˈsäl-və-bəl, -ˈsȯl-\ *adj* **:** admitting no solution — **in·solv·ably** \-blē\ *adv*

in·sol·ven·cy \(ˈ)in-ˈsäl-vən-sē\ *n* **:** the state of being insolvent

in·sol·vent \-vənt\ *adj* **1 a :** unable or having ceased to pay debts as they fall due in the usual course of business; *specif* **:** having liabilities in excess of a reasonable market value of assets held **b :** insufficient to pay all debts ⟨an ~ estate⟩ **c :** IMPOVERISHED, DEFICIENT **2 :** relating to or for the relief of insolvents — **insolvent** *n*

in·som·nia \in-ˈsäm-nē-ə\ *n* [L, fr. *insomnis* sleepless, fr. *in-* + *somnus* sleep] **:** prolonged and usu. abnormal inability to obtain adequate sleep — **in·som·ni·ac** \-nē-ˌak\ *adj or n*

insomuch as \ˈin(t)-sə-ˌməch-əz\ *conj* **:** inasmuch as

insomuch that *conj* **:** so 1

in·sou·ci·ance \in-ˈsü-sē-ən(t)s, a^n-süs-yä^{n}s\ *n* [F] **:** a lighthearted unconcern **:** NONCHALANCE — **in·sou·ci·ant** \in-ˈsü-sē-ənt, a^n-süs-yä^n\ *adj* — **in·sou·ci·ant·ly** \in-ˈsü-sē-ənt-lē\ *adv*

insoul *var of* ENSOUL

in·span \in-ˈspan, ˈin-ˌ\ *vb* [Afrik, fr. D *inspannen*] *chiefly southern Africa* **:** YOKE, HARNESS

in·spect \in-ˈspekt\ *vb* [L *inspectus*, pp. of *inspicere*, fr. *in-* + *specere* to look — more at SPY] *vt* **1 :** to view closely in critical appraisal **:** look over **2 :** to examine officially ~ *vi* **:** to make an examination **syn** see SCRUTINIZE — **in·spec·tive** \-ˈspek-tiv\ *adj*

in·spec·tion \in-ˈspek-shən\ *n* **1 :** the act of inspecting **2 :** a checking or testing of an individual against established standards

in·spec·tor \in-ˈspek-tər\ *n* **1 :** a person employed to inspect something **2 a :** a police officer who is in charge of a number of precincts and ranks below a superintendent or deputy superintendent **b :** a person appointed to oversee a polling place — **in·spec·tor·ate** \-t(ə-)rət\ *n* — **in·spec·tor·ship** \-tər-ˌship\ *n*

inspector general *n* **:** an officer of a military corps of inspectors that investigates and reports on organizational matters

insphere *var of* ENSPHERE

in·spi·ra·tion \ˌin(t)-spə-ˈrā-shən, -(ˌ)spir-ˈā-shən\ *n* **1 :** a divine influence or manifestation that qualifies a person to receive and communicate sacred revelation **2 :** the act of inhaling or drawing in; *specif* **:** the drawing of air into the lungs **3 :** the act or power of moving the intellect or emotions **4 a :** the quality or state of being inspired **b :** something that is inspired **5 :** an inspiring agent or influence — **in·spi·ra·tion·al** \-shnəl, -shən-ᵊl\ *adj* — **in·spi·ra·tion·al·ly** \-ē\ *adv*

in·spi·ra·tor \ˈin(t)-spə-ˌrāt-ər\ *n* **:** one that inspires or inhales

in·spi·ra·to·ry \(ˈ)in-ˈspī-rə-ˌtōr-ē, -ˌtȯr-\ *adj* **:** relating to, used for, or associated with inspiration

in·spire \in-ˈspī(ə)r\ *vb* [ME *inspiren*, fr. MF & L; MF *inspirer*, fr. L *inspirare*, fr. *in-* + *spirare* to breathe — more at SPIRIT] *vt* **1 a** *archaic* **:** to breathe or blow into or upon **b** *archaic* **:** to infuse (as life) by breathing **2 :** INHALE 1 **3 a :** to influence, move, or guide by divine or supernatural inspiration **b :** to exert an animating, enlivening, or exalting influence upon **c :** AFFECT **4 a :** to communicate to an agent supernaturally **b :** CREATE, ELICIT **5 :** to bring about **:** OCCASION; *also* **:** INCITE **6 :** to spread (rumor) by indirect means or through the agency of another ~ *vi* **1 :** to impart inspiration **2 :** INHALE — **in·spir·er** *n*

in·spir·it \in-ˈspir-ət\ *vt* **:** ANIMATE, HEARTEN

[1]**in·spis·sate** \in-ˈspis-ət, ˈin(t)-spə-ˌsāt\ *or* **in·spis·sat·ed** \in-ˈspis-ˌāt-əd, ˈin(t)-spə-ˌsāt-\ *adj* [LL *inspissatus*, pp. of *inspissare*, fr. L *in-* + *spissus* thick; akin to Gk *spidios* extended, L *spatium* space — more at SPEED] **:** thickened in consistency; *broadly* **:** made thick, heavy, or intense

[2]**in·spis·sate** \in-ˈspis-ˌāt, ˈin(t)-spə-ˌsāt\ *vb* **:** CONDENSE, THICKEN — **in·spis·sa·tion** \ˌin(t)-spə-ˈsā-shən, (ˌ)in-ˌspis-ˈā-\ *n* — **in·spis·sa·tor** \in-ˈspis-ˌāt-ər, ˈin(t)-spə-ˌsāt-\ *n*

in·sta·bil·i·ty \ˌin(t)-stə-ˈbil-ət-ē\ *n* **:** the quality or state of being unstable

in·sta·ble \(ˈ)in-ˈstā-bəl\ *adj* [MF or L; MF, fr. L *instabilis*, fr. *in-* + *stabilis* stable] **:** UNSTABLE

in·stall *or* **in·stal** \in-ˈstȯl\ *vt* **in·stalled**; **in·stall·ing** [MF *installer*, fr. ML *installare*, fr. L *in-* + ML *stallum*, stall, fr. OHG *stal*] **1 a :** to place in office or dignity by seating in a stall or official seat **b :** to induct into an office, rank, or order **2 :** to establish in an indicated place, condition, or status **3 :** to set up for use or service — **in·stall·er** *n*

in·stal·la·tion \ˌin(t)-stə-ˈlā-shən\ *n* **1 :** the act of installing **:** the state of being installed **2 :** something that is installed for use **3 :** a military camp, fort, or base

[1]**in·stall·ment** *or* **in·stal·ment** \in-ˈstȯl-mənt\ *n* **:** INSTALLATION 1

[2]**installment** *also* **instalment** *n* [alter. of earlier *estallment* payment by installment, deriv. of OF *estaler* to place, fix, fr. *estal* place, of Gmc origin; akin to OHG *stal* place, stall] **1 :** one of the parts into which a debt is divided when payment is made at intervals **2 a :** one of several parts (as of a publication) presented at intervals **b :** one part of a serial story — **installment** *adj*

installment plan *n* **:** a system of paying for goods by installments

[1]**in·stance** \ˈin(t)-stən(t)s\ *n* **1 a** *archaic* **:** urgent or earnest solicitation **b :** INSTIGATION, REQUEST **2 a** *archaic* **:** EXCEPTION **b :** an illustrative case **c** *obs* **:** TOKEN, SIGN **d** *obs* **:** DETAIL, CIRCUMSTANCE **3 :** the institution and prosecution of a lawsuit **:** SUIT **4 :** an event that is part of a process or series

syn CASE, ILLUSTRATION, EXAMPLE, SAMPLE, SPECIMEN: INSTANCE applies to any individual person, act, or thing that may be offered in support or disproof of a general statement; CASE is used to direct attention to a real or assumed occurrence or situation that is to be considered, studied, or dealt with; ILLUSTRATION applies to an instance offered as a means of clarifying or illuminating a general statement; EXAMPLE applies to a typical, representative, or illustrative instance or case; SAMPLE implies a part or unit taken at random from a larger whole and so presumed to be typical of its qualities; SPECIMEN applies to any example or sample whether representative or merely existent and available
— **for instance :** as an example

[2]**instance** *vt* **1 :** to illustrate or demonstrate by an instance **2 :** to mention as a case or example **:** CITE

in·stan·cy \ˈin(t)-stən-sē\ *n* **1 :** URGENCY, INSISTENCE **2 :** NEARNESS, IMMINENCE **3 :** IMMEDIATENESS, INSTANTANEOUSNESS

[1]**in·stant** \ˈin(t)-stənt\ *n* [ME, fr. ML *instant-*, *instans*, fr. *instant-*, *instans*, adj., instant, fr. L] **1 :** an infinitesimal space of time **:** MOMENT **2 :** the present or current month

[2]**instant** *adj* [ME, fr. MF or L; MF, fr. L *instant-*, *instans*, fr. prp. of *instare* to stand upon, urge, fr. *in-* + *stare* to stand — more at STAND] **1 :** IMPORTUNATE, URGENT **2 a :** PRESENT, CURRENT **b :** of or occurring in the present month **3 :** IMMEDIATE, DIRECT **4 a :** premixed or precooked for easy final preparation **b :** immediately soluble in water — **in·stant·ness** *n*

in·stan·ta·neous \ˌin(t)-stən-ˈtā-nē-əs, -nyəs\ *adj* [ML *instantaneus*, fr. *instant-*, *instans* n.] **1 :** done, occurring, or acting without any perceptible duration of time **2 :** done without any delay being introduced purposely **3 :** occurring or present at a particular instant ⟨~ velocity⟩ — **in·stan·ta·neous·ly** *adv* — **in·stan·ta·neous·ness** *n*

in·stan·ter \in-ˈstant-ər\ *adv* [ML, fr. *instant-*, *instans*] **:** at once

in·stan·ti·ate \in-ˈstan-chē-ˌāt\ *vt* **:** to represent (an abstraction) by a concrete instance — **in·stan·ti·a·tion** \(ˌ)in-ˌstan-chē-ˈā-shən\ *n*

[1]**in·stant·ly** \ˈin(t)-stənt-lē\ *adv* **1 :** IMPORTUNATELY, URGENTLY **2 :** without the least delay **:** IMMEDIATELY

[2]**instantly** *conj* **:** as soon as

in·star \ˈin-ˌstär\ *n* [NL, fr. L, equivalent, figure; akin to L *instare* to stand upon] **:** a stage in the life of an insect or other arthropod between two successive molts; *also* **:** an individual in a specified instar

in·state \in-ˈstāt\ *vt* **1 :** to set or establish in a rank or office **:** INSTALL **2** *obs* **a :** INVEST, ENDOW **b :** BESTOW, CONFER

in sta·tu quo \in-ˌstā-(ˌ)tü-ˈkwō, -ˌsta-; -ˌstach-(ˌ)ü-\ [NL, lit., in the state in which] **:** in the former or same state

in·stau·ra·tion \ˌin-ˌstȯ-ˈrā-shən, ˌin(t)-stə-\ *n* [L *instauration-*, *instauratio*, fr. *instauratus*, pp. of *instaurare* to renew, restore — more at STORE] **1 :** restoration after decay, lapse, or dilapidation **2 :** an act of instituting or establishing something

in·stead \in-ˈsted\ *adv* **1 :** as a substitute or equivalent **2 :** as an alternative to something expressed or implied **:** RATHER

instead of \in-ˌsted-ə(v), -ˌstid-\ *prep* [ME *in sted of*] **:** as a substitute for or alternative to

in·step \ˈin-ˌstep\ *n* **1 :** the arched middle portion of the human foot in front of the ankle joint; *esp* **:** its upper surface **2 :** the part of the hind leg of the horse between the hock and the pastern joint **3 :** the part of a shoe or stocking over the instep

in·sti·gate \ˈin(t)-stə-ˌgāt\ *vt* [L *instigatus*, pp. of *instigare* — more at STICK] **:** to goad or urge forward **:** PROVOKE **syn** see INCITE — **in·sti·ga·tion** \ˌin(t)-stə-ˈgā-shən\ *n* — **in·sti·ga·tive** \ˈin(t)-stə-ˌgāt-iv\ *adj* — **in·sti·ga·tor** \-ˌgāt-ər\ *n*

in·still *also* **in·stil** \in-ˈstil\ *vt* **in·stilled**; **in·still·ing** [MF & L; MF *instiller*, fr. L *instillare*, fr. *in-* + *stillare* to drip — more at DISTILL] **1 :** to cause to enter drop by drop **2 :** to impart gradually **syn** see IMPLANT — **in·stil·la·tion** \ˌin(t)-stə-ˈlā-shən, -(ˌ)stil-ˈā-\ *n* — **in·still·er** \in-ˈstil-ər\ *n* — **in·still·ment** \-mənt\ *n*

[1]**in·stinct** \ˈin-ˌstiŋ(k)t\ *n* [ME, fr. L *instinctus* impulse, fr. *instinctus*, pp. of *instinguere* to incite; akin to L *instigare* to instigate] **1 :** a natural aptitude, impulse, or capacity **2 a :** complex and specific response by an organism to environmental stimuli that is largely hereditary and unalterable, does not involve reason, and has as its goal the removal of a somatic tension **b :** behavior that is mediated by reactions below the conscious level — **in·stinc·tu·al** \in-ˈstiŋ(k)-chə(-wə)l, -ˈstiŋ(k)sh-wəl\ *adj*

[2]**in·stinct** \in-ˈstiŋ(k)t, ˈin-ˌ\ *adj* **1** *obs* **:** impelled by an inner or animating or exciting agency **2 :** IMBUED, INFUSED

in·stinc·tive \in-ˈstiŋ(k)-tiv\ *adj* **:** of or relating to instinct or prompted by it **syn** see SPONTANEOUS — **in·stinc·tive·ly** *adv*

[1]**in·sti·tute** \ˈin(t)-stə-ˌt(y)üt\ *vt* [ME *instituten*, fr. L *institutus*, pp. of *instituere*, fr. *in-* + *statuere* to set up — more at STATUTE] **1 :** to establish in a position or office **2 a :** to originate and get established **:** ORGANIZE **b :** INAUGURATE, INITIATE — **in·sti·tut·er** *or* **in·sti·tu·tor** \-ˌt(y)üt-ər\ *n*

[2]**institute** *n* **1** *obs* **:** an act of instituting **2 :** something that is instituted: as **a** (1) **:** an elementary principle recognized as authoritative (2) *pl* **:** a collection of such principles and precepts; *esp* **:** a legal compendium **b :** an organization for the promotion of a cause **:** ASSOCIATION **c :** an educational institution **d :** a meeting for instruction or a brief course of such meetings

in·sti·tu·tion \ˌin(t)-stə-ˈt(y)ü-shən\ *n* **1 :** an act of instituting **:** ESTABLISHMENT **2 :** something that serves to instruct **3 a :** a significant practice, relationship, or organization in a society or culture **b :** an established society or corporation esp. of a public character — **in·sti·tu·tion·al** \-shnəl, -shən-ᵊl\ *adj* — **in·sti·tu·tion·al·ize** \-ˌīz\ *vt* — **in·sti·tu·tion·al·ly** \-ē\ *adv*

in·sti·tu·tion·al·ism \-shnəl-ˌiz-əm, -shən-ᵊl-ˌiz-\ *n* **1 :** emphasis on organization (as in religion) at the expense of other factors **2 :** public institutional care of defective, delinquent, or dependent persons **3 :** the doctrines and teachings of institutional economics — **in·sti·tu·tion·al·ist** \-shnəl-əst, -shən-ᵊl-əst\ *n*

in·struct \in-ˈstrəkt\ *vt* [ME *instructen*, fr. L *instructus*, pp. of *instruere*, fr. *in-* + *struere* to build — more at STRUCTURE] **1 :** to give knowledge to **:** TEACH **2 a :** to direct on the basis of law or technology **b :** ORDER **syn** see COMMAND, TEACH

in·struct·ed *adj* **1 :** TAUGHT, INFORMED **2 :** subject to specific instructions ⟨~ delegates⟩

in·struc·tion \in-ˈstrək-shən\ *n* **1 a :** LESSON, PRECEPT **b :** COMMAND, ORDER **c** *pl* **:** an outline or manual of technical procedure **:** DIRECTIONS **2 :** the action, practice, or profession of a teacher — **in·struc·tion·al** \-shnəl, -shən-ᵊl\ *adj*

in·struc·tive \in-ˈstrək-tiv\ *adj* **:** carrying a lesson **:** ENLIGHTENING — **in·struc·tive·ly** *adv* — **in·struc·tive·ness** *n*

in·struc·tor \in-ˈstrək-tər\ *n* **:** one that instructs **:** TEACHER; *specif* **:** a college teacher below professorial rank — **in·struc·tor·ship** \-ˌship\ *n* — **in·struc·tress** \-ˈstrək-trəs\ *n*

[1]**in·stru·ment** \ˈin(t)-strə-mənt\ *n* [ME, fr. L *instrumentum*, fr. *instruere* to arrange, instruct] **1 a :** a means whereby something is achieved, performed, or furthered **b :** DUPE, TOOL **2 :** UTENSIL, IMPLEMENT **3 :** a device used to produce music **4 :** a formal legal document (as a deed, bond, or agreement) **5 a :** a measuring device for determining the present value of a quantity under observation **b :** an electrical or mechanical device used in navigating an airplane; *specif* **:** such a device used as the sole means of navigating **syn** see IMPLEMENT, MEAN

[2]**in·stru·ment** \-ˌment\ *vt* **1 :** to address a legal instrument to **2 :** ORCHESTRATE **3 :** to equip with instruments

in·stru·men·tal \ˌin(t)-strə-ˈment-ᵊl\ *adj* **1 a :** serving as a means, agent, or tool **b :** of, relating to, or done with an instrument or tool **2 :** relating to, composed for, or performed on a musical instrument **3 :** of or relating to a grammatical case or form (as a suffix) expressing means or agency **4 :** of or relating to instrumen-

talism — **instrumental** *n* — **in·stru·men·tal·ly** \-ᵊl-ē\ *adv*
in·stru·men·tal·ism \-ᵊl-ˌiz-əm\ *n* **:** a doctrine that ideas are instruments of action and that their usefulness determines their truth
in·stru·men·tal·ist \-ᵊl-əst\ *n* **1 :** a player on a musical instrument **2 :** a student or exponent of instrumentalism — **instrumentalist** *adj*
in·stru·men·tal·i·ty \ˌin(t)-strə-mən-ˈtal-ət-ē, -ˌmen-\ *n* **1 :** the quality or state of being instrumental **2 :** MEANS, AGENCY
in·stru·men·ta·tion \ˌin(t)-strə-mən-ˈtā-shən, -ˌmen-\ *n* **1 a :** the use of instruments **b :** the application of instruments for observation, measurement, or control **2 :** the arrangement or composition of music for instruments esp. for a band or orchestra **3 a :** a science concerned with the development and manufacture of instruments **b :** instruments for a particular purpose
instrument flying *n* **:** navigation of an airplane by instruments only
instrument landing *n* **:** a landing made with little or no external visibility by means of instruments and by ground radio directive devices
instrument panel *n* **:** a panel on which instruments are mounted; *esp* **:** DASHBOARD 2 — called also *instrument board*
in·sub·or·di·nate \ˌin(t)-sə-ˈbȯrd-ᵊn-ət, -ˈbȯrd-nət\ *adj* **1 :** unwilling to submit to authority **:** REFRACTORY **2 :** not holding a lower or inferior position — **insubordinate** *n* — **in·sub·or·di·nate·ly** *adv* — **in·sub·or·di·na·tion** \ˌin(t)-sə-ˌbȯrd-ᵊn-ˈā-shən\ *n*
in·sub·stan·tial \ˌin(t)-səb-ˈstan-chəl\ *adj* [prob. fr. F *insubstantiel*, fr. LL *insubstantialis*, fr. L *in-* + LL *substantialis* substantial] **1 :** lacking substance or reality **:** IMAGINARY **2 :** lacking firmness or solidity — **in·sub·stan·ti·al·i·ty** \-ˌstan-chē-ˈal-ət-ē\ *n*
in·suf·fer·able \(ˈ)in-ˈsəf-(ə-)rə-bəl\ *adj* **:** incapable of being endured **:** INTOLERABLE ⟨~ bore⟩ — **in·suf·fer·able·ness** *n* — **in·suf·fer·ably** \-blē\ *adv*
in·suf·fi·cience \ˌin(t)-sə-ˈfish-ən(t)s\ *n* **:** INSUFFICIENCY
in·suf·fi·cien·cy \-ən-sē\ *n* **1 :** the quality or state of being insufficient: as **a :** lack of mental or moral fitness **b :** lack of adequate supply **c :** lack of physical power or capacity; *specif* **:** inability of an organ or body part to function normally **2 :** something insufficient
in·suf·fi·cient \ˌin(t)-sə-ˈfish-ənt\ *adj* [ME, fr. MF, fr. LL *insufficient-*, *insufficiens*, fr. L *in-* + *sufficient-*, *sufficiens* sufficient] **:** not sufficient; *also* **:** INCOMPETENT — **in·suf·fi·cient·ly** *adv*
in·suf·flate \ˈin(t)-sə-ˌflāt, in-ˈsəf-ˌlāt\ *vt* [LL *insufflatus*, pp. of *insufflare*, fr. L *in-* + *sufflare* to blow up, fr. *sub-* up + *flare* to blow] **1 :** to blow upon or into **2 :** to disseminate by blowing
in·suf·fla·tion \ˌin(t)-sə-ˈflā-shən, in-ˌsəf-ˈlā-\ *n* **:** an act or instance of insufflating; *also* **:** a Christian ceremonial rite of exorcism performed by breathing upon a person
in·suf·fla·tor \ˈin(t)-sə-ˌflāt-ər, in-ˈsəf-ˌlāt-\ *n* **:** a device for insufflating something
in·su·lant \ˈin(t)-sə-lənt\ *n* **:** an insulating material
in·su·lar \ˈin(t)s-(y)ə-lər, ˈin-shə-lər\ *adj* [LL *insularis*, fr. L *insula* island] **1 :** of, relating to, or forming an island **2 :** ISOLATED, DETACHED **3 :** of or relating to island people esp. when isolated and illiberal **:** NARROW **4 :** of or relating to an island of cells or tissue — **in·su·lar·ism** \-lə-ˌriz-əm\ *n* — **in·su·lar·i·ty** \ˌin(t)s-(y)ə-ˈlar-ət-ē, ˌin-shə-ˈlar-\ *n* — **in·su·lar·ly** *adv*
in·su·late \ˈin(t)-sə-ˌlāt\ *vt* [L *insula* island] **:** to place in a detached situation **:** ISOLATE; *specif* **:** to separate from conducting bodies by means of nonconductors so as to prevent transfer of electricity, heat, or sound
in·su·la·tion \ˌin(t)-sə-ˈlā-shən\ *n* **1 :** the act of insulating **:** the state of being insulated **2 :** material used in insulating
in·su·la·tor \ˈin(t)-sə-ˌlāt-ər\ *n* **:** one that insulates; *specif* **:** a material that is a poor conductor of electricity or a device made of such material and used for separating or supporting conductors to prevent undesired flow of electricity
in·su·lin \ˈin(t)-s(ə-)lən\ *n* [NL *insula* islet (of Langerhans), fr. L, island] **:** a protein pancreatic hormone secreted by the islets of Langerhans that is essential esp. for the metabolism of carbohydrates and is used in the treatment and control of diabetes mellitus

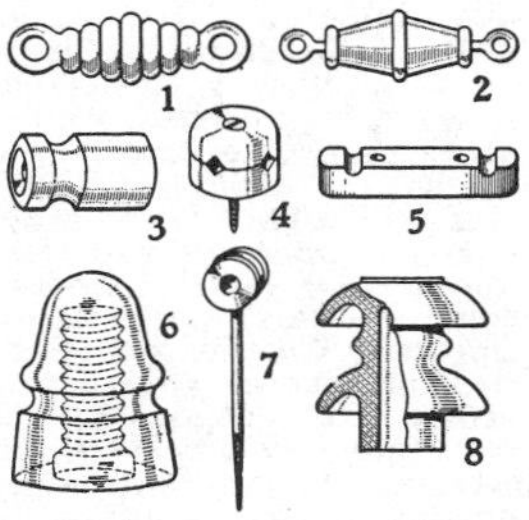

insulators: *1,2* used with antennas, *3* knob, *4* split-knob, *5* cleat, *6,8* petticoat, *7* standoff

insulin shock *n* **:** hypoglycemia associated with the presence of excessive insulin in the system and characterized by progressive development of coma
¹in·sult \in-ˈsəlt\ *vb* [MF or L; MF *insulter*, fr. L *insultare*, lit., to spring upon, fr. *in-* + *saltare* to leap — more at SALTATION] *vi*, *archaic* **:** to behave with pride or arrogance **:** VAUNT ~ *vt* **1 a :** to treat with insolence, indignity, or contempt **:** AFFRONT **b :** to make little of **2** *obs* **:** ASSAULT **syn** see OFFEND — **in·sult·er** *n*
²in·sult \ˈin-ˌsəlt\ *n* **1** *archaic* **:** an act of attacking **2 :** a gross indignity **:** INSOLENCE **3 :** injury to the body or one of its parts **syn** see AFFRONT
in·sul·ta·tion \ˌin-ˌsəl-ˈtā-shən\ *n*, *archaic* **:** INSULT
in·su·per·a·ble \(ˈ)in-ˈsü-p(ə-)rə-bəl\ *adj* [ME, fr. MF & L; MF, fr. L *insuperabilis*, fr. *in-* + *superare* to surmount, fr. *super* over — more at OVER] **:** incapable of being surmounted, overcome, or passed over — **in·su·per·a·bly** \-blē\ *adv*
in·sup·port·able \ˌin(t)-sə-ˈpōrt-ə-bəl, -ˈpȯrt-\ *adj* [MF or LL; MF, fr. LL *insupportabilis*, fr. L *in-* + *supportare* to support] **:** not supportable: **a :** UNENDURABLE **b :** UNJUSTIFIABLE — **in·sup·port·able·ness** *n* — **in·sup·port·ably** \-blē\ *adv*
in·sup·press·ible \ˌin(t)-sə-ˈpres-ə-bəl\ *adj* **:** IRREPRESSIBLE — **in·sup·press·ibly** \-blē\ *adv*
in·sur·abil·i·ty \in-ˌshu̇r-ə-ˈbil-ət-ē\ *n* **:** the quality or state of being insurable
in·sur·able \in-ˈshu̇r-ə-bəl\ *adj* **:** able or proper to be insured
in·sur·ance \in-ˈshu̇r-ən(t)s, *chiefly South* ˈin-ˌ\ *n* **1 a :** the action or process of insuring **:** the state of being insured **b :** means of insuring **2 a :** the business of insuring persons or property **b :** coverage by contract whereby one party undertakes to indemnify or guarantee another against loss by a specified contingency or peril **c :** the sum for which something is insured
in·sure \in-ˈshu̇(ə)r\ *vb* [ME *insuren*, prob. alter. of *assuren*] *vt* **1 :** to give, take, or procure an insurance on or for **2 :** to make certain **:** ENSURE ~ *vi* **:** to contract to give or take insurance; *specif* **:** UNDERWRITE **syn** see ENSURE
in·sured *n* **:** a person whose life or property is insured
in·sur·er \in-ˈshu̇r-ər\ *n* **:** one that insures; *specif* **:** an insurance underwriter
in·sur·gence \in-ˈsər-jən(t)s\ *n* **:** UPRISING, INSURRECTION
in·sur·gen·cy \-jən-sē\ *n* **1 :** the quality or state of being insurgent; *specif* **:** a condition of revolt against a government that is less than an organized revolution and is not recognized as belligerency **2 :** INSURGENCE
¹in·sur·gent \in-ˈsər-jənt\ *n* [L *insurgent-*, *insurgens*, prp. of *insurgere* to rise up, fr. *in-* + *surgere* to rise — more at SURGE] **1 :** a person who revolts against civil authority or an established government; *esp* **:** a rebel not recognized as a belligerent **2 :** one who acts contrary to the policies and decisions of his political party
²insurgent *adj* **:** rising in opposition to civil authority or an established government **:** REBELLIOUS — **in·sur·gent·ly** *adv*
in·sur·mount·able \ˌin(t)-sər-ˈmau̇nt-ə-bəl\ *adj* **:** incapable of being surmounted **:** INSUPERABLE — **in·sur·mount·ably** \-blē\ *adv*
in·sur·rec·tion \ˌin(t)-sə-ˈrek-shən\ *n* [ME, fr. MF, fr. LL *insurrection-*, *insurrectio*, fr. *insurrectus*, pp. of *insurgere*] **:** an act or instance of revolting against civil authority or an established government **syn** see REBELLION — **in·sur·rec·tion·al** \-shnəl, -shən-ᵊl\ *adj* — **in·sur·rec·tion·ary** \-shə-ˌner-ē\ *adj or n* — **in·sur·rec·tion·ist** \-sh(ə-)nəst\ *n*
in·sus·cep·ti·bil·i·ty \ˌin(t)-sə-ˌsep-tə-ˈbil-ət-ē\ *n* **:** the quality or state of being insusceptible
in·sus·cep·ti·ble \-ˈsep-tə-bəl\ *adj* **:** not susceptible — **in·sus·cep·ti·bly** \-blē\ *adv*
in·tact \in-ˈtakt\ *adj* [ME *intacte*, fr. L *intactus*, fr. *in-* + *tactus*, pp. of *tangere* to touch — more at TANGENT] **1 :** untouched esp. by anything that harms or diminishes **:** ENTIRE, UNINJURED **2** *of a living body or its parts* **:** having no relevant component removed or destroyed: **a :** physically virginal **b :** UNCASTRATED **syn** see PERFECT — **in·tact·ness** \-ˈtak(t)-nəs\ *n*
in·ta·glio \in-ˈtal-(ˌ)yō, -ˈtäl-; -ˈtag-lē-ˌō\ *n*, *often attrib* [It, fr. *intagliare* to engrave, cut, fr. ML *intaliare*, fr. L *in-* + LL *taliare* to cut — more at TAILOR] **1 a :** an engraving or incised figure in stone or other hard material depressed below the surface of the material so that an impression from the design yields an image in relief **b :** the art or process of executing intaglios **c :** printing (as in die stamping and gravure) done from a plate in which the image is sunk below the surface **2 :** something (as a gem) carved in intaglio
in·take \ˈin-ˌtāk\ *n* **1 :** an opening through which fluid enters an enclosure **2 a :** a taking in **b** (1) **:** the amount taken in (2) **:** energy taken in **:** INPUT
in·tan·gi·bil·i·ty \(ˌ)in-ˌtan-jə-ˈbil-ət-ē\ *n* **:** the quality or state of being intangible
¹in·tan·gi·ble \(ˈ)in-ˈtan-jə-bəl\ *adj* [F or ML; F, fr. ML *intangibilis*, fr. L *in-* + LL *tangibilis* tangible] **:** not tangible **:** IMPALPABLE — **in·tan·gi·ble·ness** *n* — **in·tan·gi·bly** \-blē\ *adv*
²intangible *n* **:** something intangible; *specif* **:** an asset (as goodwill) that is not corporeal
in·tar·sia \in-ˈtär-sē-ə\ *n* [G] **:** a mosaic usu. of wood fitted and glued into a wooden support popular in 15th century Italy for decoration; *also* **:** the art or process of making such work
in·te·ger \ˈint-i-jər\ *n* [L, adj., whole, entire — more at ENTIRE] **1 :** any of the natural numbers, the negatives of these numbers, or 0 **2 :** a complete entity
in·te·gra·ble \ˈint-i-grə-bəl\ *adj* **:** capable of being integrated
¹in·te·gral \ˈint-i-grəl (*usu so in mathematics*); in-ˈteg-rəl, -ˈtēg-\ *adj* **1 a :** essential to completeness **:** CONSTITUENT **b** (1) **:** being or relating to a mathematical integer (2) **:** relating to or concerned with mathematical integrals or integration **c :** formed as a unit with another part **2 :** composed of integral parts **:** INTEGRATED **3 :** lacking nothing essential **:** ENTIRE — **in·te·gral·i·ty** \ˌint-ə-ˈgral-ət-ē\ *n* — **in·te·gral·ly** \ˈint-i-grə-lē; in-ˈteg-rə-, -ˈtēg-\ *adv*
²integral *n* **:** the result of a mathematical integration — compare DEFINITE INTEGRAL, INDEFINITE INTEGRAL
integral calculus *n* **:** a branch of mathematics dealing with methods of finding indefinite integrals and applying them to the determination of lengths, areas, and volumes and to the solution of differential equations
in·te·grand \ˌint-ə-ˈgrand\ *n* [L *integrandus*, gerundive of *integrare*] **:** a mathematical expression to be integrated
in·te·grate \ˈint-ə-ˌgrāt\ *vb* [L *integratus*, pp. of *integrare*, fr. *integr-*, *integer*] *vt* **1 :** to form into a whole **:** UNITE **2 a :** to unite with something else **b :** to incorporate into a larger unit **3 :** to find the integral of (as a function or equation) **4 a :** to end the segregation of and bring into common and equal membership in society or an organization **b :** DESEGREGATE ⟨~ school districts⟩ ~ *vi* **:** to become integrated
integrated circuit *n* **:** a tiny complex of electronic components and their connections that is produced in or on a small slice of material (as silicon)
in·te·gra·tion \ˌint-ə-ˈgrā-shən\ *n* **1 :** the act or process or an instance of integrating: as **a :** incorporation as equals into society or an organization of individuals of different groups (as races) **b :** coordination of mental processes into a normal effective personality or with the individual's environment **2 a :** the operation of finding a function whose differential is known **b :** the operation of solving a differential equation
in·te·gra·tion·ist \-sh(ə-)nəst\ *n* **:** a person who believes in, advocates, or practices integration
in·te·gra·tor \ˈint-ə-ˌgrāt-ər\ *n* **:** one that integrates; *specif* **:** a device that totalizes variable quantities in a manner comparable to the mathematical solution of differential equations
in·teg·ri·ty \in-ˈteg-rət-ē\ *n* **1 :** an unimpaired condition **:** SOUNDNESS **2 :** adherence to a code of moral, artistic, or other values **3 :** the quality or state of being complete or undivided **:** COMPLETENESS **syn** see HONESTY, UNITY
in·teg·u·ment \in-ˈteg-yə-mənt\ *n* [L *integumentum*, fr. *integere* to cover, fr. *in-* + *tegere* to cover — more at THATCH] **:** something

that covers or encloses; *esp* **:** an enveloping layer (as a skin membrane or husk) of an organism or one of its parts — **in·teg·u·men·tal** \(ˌ)in-ˌteg-yə-'ment-ᵊl\ *adj*

in·tel·lect \'int-ᵊl-ˌekt\ *n* [ME, fr. MF or L; MF, fr L *intellectus*, fr. *intellectus*, pp. of *intellegere*] **1 a :** the power of knowing as distinguished from the power to feel and to will **:** the capacity for knowledge **b :** the capacity for rational or intelligent thought esp. when highly developed **2 :** a person of notable intellect

in·tel·lec·tion \ˌint-ᵊl-'ek-shən\ *n* **1 :** exercise of the intellect **:** REASONING **2 :** a specific act of the intellect **:** THOUGHT

in·tel·lec·tive \-'ek-tiv\ *adj* **:** having, relating to, or belonging to the intellect **:** RATIONAL — **in·tel·lec·tive·ly** *adv*

[1]**in·tel·lec·tu·al** \ˌint-ᵊl-'ek-chə(-wə)l, -'eksh-wəl\ *adj* **1 a :** of or relating to the intellect or its use **b :** developed or chiefly guided by the intellect rather than by emotion or experience **:** RATIONAL **c :** requiring use of the intellect **2 a :** given to study, reflection, and speculation **b :** engaged in activity requiring the creative use of the intellect — **in·tel·lec·tu·al·i·ty** \-ˌek-chə-'wal-ət-ē\ *n* — **in·tel·lec·tu·al·ly** \-'ek-chə(-wə)lē, -'eksh-wə-lē\ *adv* — **in·tel·lec·tu·al·ness** \-'ek-chə(-wə)l-nəs, -'eksh-wəl-\ *n*

[2]**intellectual** *n* **1** *pl, archaic* **:** intellectual powers **2 :** an intellectual person

in·tel·lec·tu·al·ism \ˌint-ᵊl-'ek-chə-(wə-)ˌliz-əm, -'eksh-wə-ˌliz-\ *n* **:** devotion to the exercise of intellect or to intellectual pursuits — **in·tel·lec·tu·al·ist** \-'ek-chə(-wə)-ləst, -'eksh(-wə)-\ *n* — **in·tel·lec·tu·al·is·tic** \-ˌek-chə(-wə)-'lis-tik, -ˌeksh-wə-\ *adj*

in·tel·lec·tu·al·ize \ˌint-ᵊl-'ek-chə-(wə-)ˌlīz, -'eksh-wə-ˌlīz\ *vt* **:** to give rational form or content to

in·tel·li·gence \in-'tel-ə-jən(t)s\ *n, often attrib* **1 a** (1) **:** the capacity to apprehend facts and propositions and their relations and to reason about them **:** REASON, INTELLECT; *also* **:** the use or exercise of the intellect esp. when carried on with considerable ability (2) *Christian Science* **:** the basic eternal quality of divine Mind **b :** mental acuteness **:** SHREWDNESS **2 :** an intelligent being; *esp* **:** ANGEL **3 :** the act of understanding **:** COMPREHENSION **4 a :** information communicated **:** NEWS **b :** information concerning an enemy or possible enemy or an area; *also* **:** an agency engaged in obtaining such information

intelligence quotient *n* **:** a number held to express the relative intelligence of a person determined by dividing his mental age by his chronological age and multiplying by 100

in·tel·li·genc·er \in-'tel-ə-jən-sər, -ˌjen(t)-sər\ *n* **1 :** a secret agent **:** SPY **2 :** a bringer of news **:** REPORTER

intelligence test *n* **:** a test designed to determine the relative mental capacity of a person

in·tel·li·gent \in-'tel-ə-jənt\ *adj* [L *intelligent-*, *intelligens*, prp. of *intelligere*, *intellegere* to understand, fr. *inter-* + *legere* to gather, select — more at LEGEND] **1 a :** possessing intelligence **b :** guided or directed by intellect **:** RATIONAL **2 a :** having or indicating a high or satisfactory degree of intelligence and mental capacity **b :** revealing or reflecting good judgment or sound thought **:** SKILLFUL — **in·tel·li·gen·tial** \(ˌ)in-ˌtel-ə-'jen-chəl\ *adj* — **in·tel·li·gent·ly** \in-'tel-ə-jənt-lē\ *adv*

syn CLEVER, ALERT, QUICK-WITTED, KNOWING: INTELLIGENT stresses success in coping with new situations and solving problems; CLEVER implies native ability or aptness and sometimes suggests a lack of more substantial qualities; ALERT stresses quickness in perceiving and understanding; QUICK-WITTED implies promptness in finding answers in debate or in devising expedients in moments of danger or challenge; KNOWING implies the possession of special knowledge; it may often connote sophistication, secretiveness, or cynicism

in·tel·li·gen·tsia \(ˌ)in-ˌtel-ə-'jen(t)-sē-ə, -'jen-ch(ē-)ə, -'gen(t)-sē-ə\ *n* [Russ *intelligentsiya*, fr. L *intelligentia* intelligence] **:** intellectuals who form an artistic, social, or political vanguard or elite

in·tel·li·gi·bil·i·ty \(ˌ)in-ˌtel-ə-jə-'bil-ət-ē\ *n* **:** the quality or state of being intelligible **:** CLARITY

in·tel·li·gi·ble \in-'tel-ə-jə-bəl\ *adj* [ME, fr. L *intelligibilis*; fr. *intelligere*] **1 :** capable of being understood or comprehended **2 :** apprehensible by the intellect only — **in·tel·li·gi·ble·ness** *n* — **in·tel·li·gi·bly** \-blē\ *adv*

in·tem·per·ance \(')in-'tem-p(ə-)rən(t)s\ *n* **:** lack of moderation esp. in satisfying an appetite or passion; *specif* **:** habitual or excessive drinking of intoxicants

in·tem·per·ate \-p(ə-)rət\ *adj* [ME *intemperat*, fr. L *intemperatus*, fr. *in-* + *temperatus*, pp. of *temperare* to temper] **:** not temperate; *specif* **:** given to excessive use of intoxicating liquors — **in·tem·per·ate·ly** *adv* — **in·tem·per·ate·ness** *n*

in·tend \in-'tend\ *vb* [ME *entenden*, *intenden*, fr. MF *entendre* to purpose, fr. L *intendere* to stretch out, to purpose, fr. *in-* + *tendere* to stretch — more at THIN] *vt* **1 a** [ME *entenden* to understand, fr. OF *entendre*, fr. LL *intendere*, fr. L, to purpose, have in mind] *archaic* **:** CONSTRUE, INTERPRET **b** (1) **:** SIGNIFY, MEAN (2) **:** to refer to **2 a :** to have in mind as a purpose or goal **:** PLAN **b :** to design for a specified use or future **3** *archaic* **:** to proceed on (a course) **4 :** to direct the mind on ~ *vi* **1 :** to have an aim or end in mind **2** *archaic* **:** to set out **:** START — **in·tend·er** *n*

in·ten·dance \in-'ten-dən(t)s\ *n* **1 :** MANAGEMENT, SUPERINTENDENCE **2 :** an administrative department

in·ten·dant \-dənt\ *n* **:** a governor or similar administrative official esp. under the French, Spanish, or Portuguese monarchies

[1]**in·tend·ed** *adj* **1 :** PROPOSED; *specif* **:** BETROTHED **2 :** INTENTIONAL — **in·tend·ed·ly** *adv* — **in·tend·ed·ness** *n*

[2]**intended** *n* **:** an affianced person **:** BETROTHED

in·tend·ment \in-'ten(d)-mənt\ *n* **:** the true meaning, understanding, or intention of something, esp. a law

in·ten·er·ate \in-'ten-ə-ˌrāt\ *vt* [[2]*in-* + L *tener* soft, tender — more at TENDER] **:** to make tender **:** SOFTEN — **in·ten·er·a·tion** \(ˌ)in-ˌten-ə-'rā-shən\ *n*

in·tense \in-'ten(t)s\ *adj* [ME, fr. MF, fr. L *intensus*, fr. pp. of *intendere* to stretch out] **1 a :** existing in an extreme degree **b :** having or showing a characteristic in extreme degree **c :** very large **:** CONSIDERABLE **2 :** strained or straining to the utmost **3 a :** feeling deeply esp. by nature or temperament **b :** deeply felt — **in·tense·ly** *adv* — **in·tense·ness** *n*

in·ten·si·fi·ca·tion \(ˌ)in-ˌten(t)-sə-fə-'kā-shən\ *n* **:** the act, process, or an instance of intensifying

in·ten·si·fi·er \in-'ten(t)-sə-ˌfī(-ə)r\ *n* **:** one that intensifies

in·ten·si·fy \in-'ten(t)-sə-ˌfī\ *vt* **1 :** to make intense or more intensive **:** STRENGTHEN **2 a :** to increase the density and contrast of (a photographic image) by chemical treatment **b :** to make more acute **:** SHARPEN ~ *vi* **:** to become intense or more intensive **:** grow stronger or more acute

syn INTENSIFY, AGGRAVATE, HEIGHTEN, ENHANCE mean to increase markedly in measure or degree. INTENSIFY implies a deepening or strengthening of a thing or of its characteristic quality; AGGRAVATE implies an increasing in gravity or seriousness, esp. the worsening of something already bad or undesirable; HEIGHTEN suggests a lifting above the ordinary or accustomed; ENHANCE implies a raising or strengthening above the normal in desirability, value, or attractiveness

in·ten·sion \in-'ten-chən\ *n* **1 :** INTENSITY **2 :** CONNOTATION 3 — **in·ten·sion·al** \-'tench-nəl, -'ten-chən-ᵊl\ *adj* — **in·ten·sion·al·ly** \-ē\ *adv*

in·ten·si·ty \in-'ten(t)-sət-ē\ *n* **1 :** the quality or state of being intense; *esp* **:** extreme degree of strength, force, or energy **2 :** the magnitude of force or energy per unit (as of surface, charge, or mass) **3 :** SATURATION 4a

[1]**in·ten·sive** \in-'ten(t)-siv\ *adj* **:** of, relating to, or marked by intensity or intensification: as **a :** CONCENTRATED **b :** INTENSIFYING; *esp* **:** tending to give force or emphasis ⟨~ adverb⟩ **c :** constituting or relating to a method of cultivation of land designed to increase the productivity of a given area by the expenditure of more capital and labor upon it — **in·ten·sive·ly** *adv* — **in·ten·sive·ness** *n*

[2]**intensive** *n* **:** an intensive linguistic element

[1]**in·tent** \in-'tent\ *n* [ME *entent*, fr. OF, fr. LL *intentus*, fr. L, act of stretching out, fr. *intentus*, pp. of *intendere*] **1 a :** the act or fact of intending **:** PURPOSE **b :** the state of mind with which an act is done **:** VOLITION **2 :** an end or object proposed **:** AIM **3 a :** MEANING, SIGNIFICANCE **b :** the connotation of a term **syn** see INTENTION

[2]**intent** *adj* [L *intentus*, fr. pp. of *intendere*] **1 :** directed with strained or eager attention **:** CONCENTRATED **2 a :** having the mind or attention fixedly directed on something **:** ENGROSSED **b :** having the mind or will concentrated on some end or purpose **:** DETERMINED — **in·tent·ly** *adv* — **in·tent·ness** *n*

in·ten·tion \in-'ten-chən\ *n* **1 :** a determination to act in a certain way **:** RESOLVE **2** *pl* **:** purpose with respect to marriage **3 :** an intended object **:** AIM; *specif* **:** the object for which a prayer, mass, or pious act is offered **4 :** IMPORT, SIGNIFICANCE **5 :** CONCEPT; *esp* **:** a concept considered as the product of attention directed to an object of knowledge **6 :** a process or manner of healing of incised wounds

syn INTENT, PURPOSE, DESIGN, AIM, END, OBJECT, OBJECTIVE, GOAL: INTENTION implies little more than what one has in mind to do or bring about; INTENT suggests clearer formulation or more deliberation; PURPOSE suggests a more settled determination; DESIGN implies a more carefully calculated plan; AIM adds to these implications of effort directed toward attaining or accomplishing; END stresses the intended effect of action often in distinction or contrast to the action or means as such; OBJECT may equal END but more often applies to a more individually determined wish or need and may nearly approach motive; OBJECTIVE implies something tangible and immediately attainable; GOAL suggests something attained only by prolonged effort and hardship

in·ten·tion·al \in-'tench-nəl, -'ten-chən-ᵊl\ *adj* **1 :** done by intention or design **:** INTENDED ⟨~ damage⟩ **2 a :** of or relating to logical intention **b :** having external reference **syn** see VOLUNTARY — **in·ten·tion·al·i·ty** \(ˌ)in-ˌten-chə-'nal-ət-ē\ *n* — **in·ten·tion·al·ly** \in-'tench-nə-lē, -'ten-chən-ᵊl-ē\ *adv*

in·ter \in-'tər\ *vt* **in·terred**; **in·ter·ring** [ME *enteren*, fr. OF *enterrer*, fr. (assumed) VL *interrare*, fr. *in-* + L *terra* earth — more at TERRACE] **:** to deposit (a dead body) in the earth or in a tomb **:** BURY

inter- *prefix* [ME *inter-*, *enter-*, fr. MF & L; MF *inter-*, *entre-*, fr. L *inter-*, fr. *inter*; akin to OHG *untar* between, among, Gk *enteron* intestine, OE *in* in] **1 :** between **:** among **:** in the midst ⟨*inter*crop⟩ ⟨*inter*penetrate⟩ ⟨*inter*stellar⟩ **2 :** reciprocal ⟨*inter*relation⟩ **:** reciprocally ⟨*inter*marry⟩ **3 :** located between ⟨*inter*face⟩ **4 :** carried on between ⟨*inter*national⟩ **5 :** occurring between **:** intervening ⟨*inter*glacial⟩ **6 :** shared by or derived from two or more ⟨*inter*faith⟩ **7 :** between the limits of **:** within ⟨*inter*tropical⟩

in·ter·act \ˌint-ə-'rakt\ *vi* **:** to act upon one another — **in·ter·ac·tive** \-'rak-tiv\ *adj*

in·ter·ac·tant \-'rak-tənt\ *n* **:** one that interacts; *specif* **:** a chemical reactant

in·ter·ac·tion \ˌint-ə-'rak-shən\ *n* **:** mutual or reciprocal action or influence — **in·ter·ac·tion·al** \-shnəl, -shən-ᵊl\ *adj*

in·ter alia \ˌint-ə-'rā-lē-ə, -'rä-\ *adv* [L] **:** among other things

in·ter ali·os \-lē-ˌōs\ *adv* [L] **:** among other persons

in·ter·brain \'int-ər-ˌbrān\ *n* **:** DIENCEPHALON

in·ter·breed \ˌint-ər-'brēd\ *vi* **:** to breed together: as **a :** CROSSBREED **b :** to breed within a closed population ~ *vt* **:** to cause to breed together

in·ter·ca·la·ry \in-'tər-kə-ˌler-ē, ˌint-ər-'kal-(ə-)rē\ *adj* [L *intercalarius*, fr. *intercalare*] **1 a** *of a day or month* **:** INTERCALATED **b** *of a year* **:** containing an intercalary period **2 :** INTERPOLATED

in·ter·ca·late \in-'tər-kə-ˌlāt\ *vt* [L *intercalatus*, pp. of *intercalare*, fr. *inter-* + *calare* to call, summon — more at LOW] **1 :** to insert (as a day) in a calendar **2 :** to insert between or among existing elements or layers **syn** see INTRODUCE — **in·ter·ca·la·tion** \in-ˌtər-kə-'lā-shən\ *n*

in·ter·cede \ˌint-ər-'sēd\ *vi* [L *intercedere*, fr. *inter-* + *cedere* to go — more at CEDE] **:** to act between parties with a view to reconciling differences **:** MEDIATE **syn** see INTERPOSE — **in·ter·ced·er** *n*

in·ter·cel·lu·lar \ˌint-ər-'sel-yə-lər\ *adj* **:** lying between cells ⟨~ spaces⟩

[1]**in·ter·cept** \ˌint-ər-'sept\ *vt* [L *interceptus*, pp. of *intercipere*, fr. *inter-* + *capere* to take, seize — more at HEAVE] **1 :** to stop or interrupt the progress or course of **2** *obs* **:** PREVENT, HINDER **3** *obs* **:** to interrupt communication or connection with **4 :** INTERSECT — **in·ter·cep·tion** \-'sep-shən\ *n* — **in·ter·cep·tive** \-'sep-tiv\ *adj*

[2]**in·ter·cept** \'int-ər-ˌsept\ *n* **:** the distance from the origin to a point where a graph crosses a coordinate axis

in·ter·cept·er \ˌint-ər-'sep-tər\ *n* **:** INTERCEPTOR

in·ter·cep·tor \-'sep-tər\ *n* **:** one that intercepts; *specif* **:** a light high-speed fast-climbing fighter plane designed for defense against raiding bombers

in·ter·ces·sion \ˌint-ər-ˈsesh-ən\ *n* [MF or L; MF, fr. L *intercession-, intercessio*, fr. *intercessus*, pp. of *intercedere*] **1 :** the act of interceding **2 :** prayer, petition, or entreaty in favor of another — **in·ter·ces·sion·al** \-ˈsesh-nəl, -ən-ᵊl\ *adj* — **in·ter·ces·sor** \-ˈses-ər\ *n* — **in·ter·ces·so·ry** \-ˈses-(ə-)rē\ *adj*

1in·ter·change \ˌint-ər-ˈchānj\ *vb* [ME *entrechaungen*, fr. MF *entrechangier*, fr. OF, fr. *entre-* inter- + *changier* to change] *vt* **1 :** to put each of (two things) in the place of the other **2 :** EXCHANGE ~ *vi* **:** to change places mutually — **in·ter·chang·er** *n*

2in·ter·change \ˈint-ər-ˌchānj\ *n* **1 :** the act, process, or an instance of interchanging **:** EXCHANGE **2 :** a junction of two or more highways by a system of separate levels that permit traffic to pass from one to another without the crossing of traffic streams

in·ter·change·abil·i·ty \ˌint-ər-ˌchān-jə-ˈbil-ət-ē\ *n* **:** the quality or state of being interchangeable

in·ter·change·able \ˌint-ər-ˈchān-jə-bəl\ *adj* **:** capable of being interchanged; *esp* **:** permitting mutual substitution ⟨~ parts⟩ — **in·ter·change·able·ness** *n* — **in·ter·change·ably** \-blē\ *adv*

in·ter·col·le·giate \ˌint-ər-kə-ˈlē-j(ē-)ət\ *adj* **:** existing, carried on, or participating in activities between colleges ⟨~ athletics⟩

in·ter·co·lum·ni·a·tion \ˌint-ər-kə-ˌləm-nē-ˈā-shən\ *n* [L *intercolumnium* space between two columns, fr. *inter-* + *columna* column] **1 :** the clear space between the columns of a series **2 :** the system of spacing of the columns of a colonnade

in·ter·com \ˈint-ər-ˌkäm\ *n* **:** INTERCOMMUNICATION SYSTEM

in·ter·com·mu·ni·cate \ˌint-ər-kə-ˈmyü-nə-ˌkāt\ *vi* **1 :** to exchange communication with one another **2 :** to afford passage from one to another — **in·ter·com·mu·ni·ca·tion** \-ˌmyü-nə-ˈkā-shən\ *n*

intercommunication system *n* **:** a two-way communication system with microphone and loudspeaker at each station for localized use

in·ter·com·mu·nion \ˌint-ər-kə-ˈmyü-nyən\ *n* **:** interdenominational participation in communion

in·ter·con·nect \ˌint-ər-kə-ˈnekt\ *vt* **:** to connect with one another — **in·ter·con·nec·tion** \-ˈnek-shən\ *n*

in·ter·con·ti·nen·tal \ˌint-ər-ˌkänt-ᵊn-ˈent-ᵊl\ *adj* **1 :** extending among continents or carried on between continents **2 :** capable of traveling between continents ⟨~ ballistic missile⟩

in·ter·con·ver·sion \ˌint-ər-kən-ˈvər-zhən, -shən\ *n* **:** mutual conversion ⟨~ of chemical compounds⟩ — **in·ter·con·vert** \-ˈvərt\ *vt* — **in·ter·con·vert·ible** \-ˈvərt-ə-bəl\ *adj*

in·ter·cool·er \ˌint-ər-ˈkü-lər\ *n* **:** a device for cooling a fluid between successive heat-generating processes

in·ter·cos·tal \ˌint-ər-ˈkäst-ᵊl\ *adj* [NL *intercostalis*, fr. L *inter-* + *costa* rib] **:** situated between the ribs; *also* **:** of or relating to an intercostal part — **intercostal** *n* — **in·ter·cos·tal·ly** \-ˈkäs-tə-lē\ *adv*

in·ter·course \ˈint-ər-ˌkō(ə)rs, -ˌkȯ(ə)rs\ *n* [ME *intercurse*, prob. fr. MF *entrecours*, fr. ML *intercursus*, fr. L, act of running between, fr. *intercursus*, pp. of *intercurrere* to run between, fr. *inter-* + *currere* to run — more at CURRENT] **1 :** connection between persons or groups **:** COMMUNICATION **2 :** COPULATION, COITUS

in·ter·crop \ˌint-ər-ˈkräp\ *vt* **:** to grow a crop in between elements (as rows) of (another) ~ *vi* **:** to grow two or more crops simultaneously (as in alternate rows) on the same plot

1in·ter·cross \ˌint-ər-ˈkrȯs\ *vb* **:** CROSS

2in·ter·cross \ˈint-ər-ˌkrȯs\ *n* **:** an instance or a product of crossbreeding

in·ter·cul·tur·al \ˌint-ər-ˈkəlch-(ə-)rəl\ *adj* **:** occurring between or relating to two or more cultures

in·ter·cur·rent \ˌint-ər-ˈkər-ənt, -ˈkə-rənt\ *adj* [L *intercurrent-, intercurrens*, prp. of *intercurrere*] **:** occurring in the midst of a process **:** INTERRUPTING — **in·ter·cur·rent·ly** *adv*

in·ter·de·nom·i·na·tion·al \ˌint-ər-di-ˌnäm-ə-ˈnā-shnəl, -shən-ᵊl\ *adj* **:** involving or occurring between different denominations — **in·ter·de·nom·i·na·tion·al·ism** \-ˌiz-əm\ *n*

in·ter·den·tal \ˌint-ər-ˈdent-ᵊl\ *adj* **1 :** situated between the teeth **2 :** formed with the tip of the tongue protruded between the upper and lower front teeth — **in·ter·den·tal·ly** \-ᵊl-ē\ *adv*

in·ter·de·part·men·tal \ˌint-ər-di-ˌpärt-ˈment-ᵊl, -ˌdē-\ *adj* **:** carried on between or involving departments esp. of an educational institution — **in·ter·de·part·men·tal·ly** \-ᵊl-ē\ *adv*

in·ter·de·pend \ˌint-ər-di-ˈpend\ *vi* **:** to depend upon one another — **in·ter·de·pen·dence** \-ˈpen-dən(t)s\ *n* — **in·ter·de·pen·den·cy** \-dən-sē\ *n* — **in·ter·de·pen·dent** \-dənt\ *adj* — **in·ter·de·pen·dent·ly** *adv*

1in·ter·dict \ˈint-ər-ˌdikt\ *n* [ME *entredit*, fr. OF, fr. L *interdictum* prohibition, praetorian interdict, fr. neut. of *interdictus*, pp. of *interdicere* to interpose, forbid, fr. *inter-* + *dicere* to say — more at DICTION] **1 :** a Roman Catholic ecclesiastical censure withdrawing most sacraments and Christian burial from a person or district **2 :** a prohibitory decree **:** PROHIBITION

2in·ter·dict \ˌint-ər-ˈdikt\ *vt* **1 :** to lay under or prohibit by an interdict **2 :** PROHIBIT, DEBAR **3 :** to destroy, cut, or damage (as an enemy line of supply) by firepower to stop or hamper an enemy **syn** see FORBID — **in·ter·dic·tion** \-ˈdik-shən\ *n* — **in·ter·dic·tive** \-ˈdik-tiv\ *adj* — **in·ter·dic·tor** \-tər\ *n* — **in·ter·dic·to·ry** \-t(ə-)rē\ *adj*

in·ter·dig·i·tate \ˌint-ər-ˈdij-ə-ˌtāt\ *vi* [*inter-* + L *digitus* finger — more at TOE] **:** to interlock like the fingers of folded hands — **in·ter·dig·i·ta·tion** \-ˌdij-ə-ˈtā-shən\ *n*

in·ter·dis·ci·plin·ary \ˌint-ər-ˈdis-ə-plə-ˌner-ē\ *adj* **:** involving two or more academic disciplines

1in·ter·est \ˈin-trəst; ˈint-ə-rəst, -ə-ˌrest, -ərst; ˈin-ˌtrest\ *n* [ME, prob. alter. of earlier *interesse*, fr. AF & ML; AF, fr. ML, fr. L, to be between, make a difference, concern, fr. *inter-* + *esse* to be — more at IS] **1 a (1) :** right, title, or legal share in something **(2) :** participation in advantage and responsibility **b :** a business in which one has an interest **2 :** WELFARE, BENEFIT; *specif* **:** SELF-INTEREST **3 a :** a charge for borrowed money generally a percentage of the amount borrowed **b :** an excess above what is due **4 :** a group financially interested in an industry or enterprise **5 a :** readiness to be concerned with or moved by an object or class of objects **b :** the quality in a thing that arouses interest

2interest *vt* **1 :** to involve the interest or welfare of **:** AFFECT, CONCERN **2 :** to induce or persuade to participate or engage **3 :** to engage the attention or arouse the interest of

interest group *n* **:** a group of persons having a common identifying interest that often provides a basis for action

in·ter·est·ing *adj* **:** holding the attention **:** arousing interest — **in·ter·est·ing·ly** *adv*

in·ter·face \ˈint-ər-ˌfās\ *n* **1 :** a surface forming a common boundary of two bodies, spaces, or phases **2 a :** the place at which independent systems meet and act upon or communicate with each other **b :** the means by which interaction or communication is effected at an interface — **in·ter·fa·cial** \ˌint-ər-ˈfā-shəl\ *adj*

in·ter·faith \ˌint-ər-ˈfāth\ *adj* **:** involving persons of different religious faiths

in·ter·fas·cic·u·lar \ˌint-ər-fə-ˈsik-yə-lər, -fa-\ *adj* **:** situated between fascicles

in·ter·fere \ˌint-ə(r)-ˈfi(ə)r\ *vi* [MF (*s'*)*entreferir* to strike one another, fr. OF, fr. *entre-* inter- + *ferir* to strike, fr. L *ferire* — more at BORE] **1 :** to strike one foot against the opposite foot or ankle in walking or running **2 :** to come in collision or be in opposition **:** CLASH **3 :** to enter into or take a part in the concerns of others **4 :** to act reciprocally so as to augment, diminish, or otherwise affect one another — used of waves **5 :** to claim substantially the same invention and thus question the priority of invention between the claimants **6** *football* **a :** to run ahead of and provide blocking for the ball carrier **b :** to hinder illegally an attempt of a player to catch a pass **syn** see INTERPOSE — **in·ter·fer·er** *n*

in·ter·fer·ence \ˌint-ə(r)-ˈfir-ən(t)s\ *n* **1 a :** the act or process of interfering **b :** something that interferes **:** OBSTRUCTION **2 :** the mutual effect on meeting of two wave trains of the same type so that such light waves produce lines, bands, or fringes either alternately light and dark or variously colored and sound waves produce silence, increased intensity, or beats **3 :** the act of hampering or blocking an opponent in football **4 a :** confusion of received radio signals due to strays or undesired signals **b :** something that produces such confusion — **in·ter·fer·en·tial** \-fə-ˈren-chəl, -ˌfir-ˈen-\ *adj*

in·ter·fer·o·gram \ˌint-ə(r)-ˈfir-ə-ˌgram\ *n* **:** a photographic record made by an apparatus for recording optical interference phenomena

in·ter·fer·om·e·ter \ˌint-ə(r)-fə-ˈräm-ət-ər, -ˌfir-ˈäm\ *n* [ISV] **:** an instrument that utilizes light interference phenomena for precise determinations of wavelength, spectral fine structure, indices of refraction, and very small linear displacements — **in·ter·fer·o·met·ric** \-ˌfir-ə-ˈme-trik\ *adj* — **in·ter·fer·om·e·try** \-fə-ˈräm-ə-trē, -ˌfir-ˈäm-\ *n*

in·ter·fer·tile \ˌint-ər-ˈfərt-ᵊl\ *adj* **:** capable of interbreeding — **in·ter·fer·til·i·ty** \-(ˌ)fər-ˈtil-ət-ē\ *n*

in·ter·fruit·ful \-ˈfrüt-fəl\ *adj* **:** capable of reciprocal cross-pollination — **in·ter·fruit·ful·ness** *n*

in·ter·fuse \ˌint-ər-ˈfyüz\ *vt* [L *interfusus*, pp. of *interfundere* to pour between, fr. *inter-* + *fundere* to pour — more at FOUND] **1 :** to combine by fusing **:** BLEND **2 :** to pass into or through others **:** INFUSE **3 :** PERVADE, PERMEATE — **in·ter·fu·sion** \-ˈfyü-zhən\ *n*

in·ter·ga·lac·tic \ˌint-ər-gə-ˈlak-tik\ *adj* **:** situated or occurring in the spaces between galaxies

in·ter·ge·ner·ic \-jə-ˈner-ik\ *adj* **:** existing or occurring between genera ⟨~ hybridization⟩

in·ter·gla·cial \-ˈglā-shəl\ *adj* **:** occurring or formed between glacial epochs

in·ter·gra·da·tion \-grā-ˈdā-shən, -grə-\ *n* **:** the condition of one that intergrades — **in·ter·gra·da·tion·al** \-shnəl, -shən-ᵊl\ *adj*

1in·ter·grade \ˌint-ər-ˈgrād\ *vi* **:** to merge gradually one with another through a continuous series of intermediate forms

2in·ter·grade \ˈint-ər-ˌgrād\ *n* **:** an intermediate or transitional form

in·ter·graft \ˌint-ər-ˈgraft\ *vi* **:** to be reciprocally capable of being grafted

in·ter·growth \ˈint-ər-ˌgrōth\ *n* **1 :** a growing between or together; *also* **:** the product of such growth **2 :** growth by intussusception

in·ter·im \ˈin-tə-rəm, -ˌrim\ *n* [L, adv., meanwhile, fr. *inter* between — more at INTER-] **:** a time intervening **:** INTERVAL — **interim** *adj*

1in·te·ri·or \in-ˈtir-ē-ər\ *adj* [MF & L; MF, fr. L, compar. of (assumed) OL *interus* inward, on the inside; akin to L *inter*] **1 :** lying, occurring, or functioning within the limits **:** INNER **2 :** remote from the border or shore **:** INLAND **3 :** ESSENTIAL **4 :** belonging to mental or spiritual life — **in·te·ri·or·ly** *adv*

2interior *n* **1 :** the internal or inner part of a thing **:** INSIDE **2 :** the inland part **3 :** internal nature **:** CHARACTER **4 :** the internal affairs of a state or nation **5 :** a representation of the interior of a building — **in·te·ri·or·i·ty** \(ˌ)in-ˌtir-ē-ˈȯr-ət-ē, -ˈär-\ *n*

interior decoration *n* **:** the art of planning the layout and furnishings of an architectural interior

in·ter·ject \ˌint-ər-ˈjekt\ *vt* [L *interjectus*, pp. of *intericere*, fr. *inter-* + *jacere* to throw — more at JET] **:** to throw in between or among other things **:** INTERPOLATE ⟨~ a remark⟩ **syn** see INTRODUCE — **in·ter·jec·tor** \-ˈjek-tər\ *n* — **in·ter·jec·to·ry** \-t(ə-)rē\ *adj*

in·ter·jec·tion \ˌint-ər-ˈjek-shən\ *n* **1 a :** the act of uttering exclamations **:** EJACULATION **b :** the act of putting in between **:** INTERPOSITION **2 :** something that interrupts **3 a :** an ejaculatory word (as *Wonderful*) or form of speech (as *ha ha*) **b :** a cry or inarticulate utterance (as *ouch*) expressing an emotion

in·ter·jec·tion·al \-shnəl, -shən-ᵊl\ *adj* **1 :** thrown in between other words **:** PARENTHETICAL **2 :** of, relating to, or constituting an interjection **:** EJACULATORY — **in·ter·jec·tion·al·ly** \-ē\ *adv*

in·ter·lace \ˌint-ər-ˈlās\ *vb* [ME *entrelacen*, fr. MF *entrelacer*, fr. OF *entrelacier*, fr. *entre-* inter- + *lacier* to lace] *vt* **1 :** to unite by or as if by lacing together **:** INTERWEAVE **2 :** to vary by alternation or intermixture **:** INTERSPERSE ~ *vi* **:** to cross one another as if woven together **:** INTERTWINE — **in·ter·lace·ment** \-ˈlā-smənt\ *n*

in·ter·lam·i·nate \ˌint-ər-ˈlam-ə-ˌnāt\ *vt* **1 :** to insert between laminae **2 :** to arrange in alternate laminae — **in·ter·lam·i·na·tion** \-ˌlam-ə-ˈnā-shən\ *n*

in·ter·lard \ˌint-ər-ˈlärd\ *vt* [MF *entrelarder*, fr. OF, fr. *entre* inter- + *larder* to lard, fr. *lard*, n.] **:** to introduce something foreign or irrelevant into ⟨text ~*ed* with photographs⟩

in·ter·lay·er \ˈint-ər-ˌlā-ər, -ˌle(-ə)r\ *n* **:** a layer placed between other layers

1in·ter·leaf \ˌint-ər-ˈlēf\ *vt* **:** INTERLEAVE

2in·ter·leaf \ˈint-ər-ˌlēf\ *n* **1 :** a usu. blank leaf inserted between two leaves of a book **2 :** SLIP SHEET

in·ter·leave \ˌint-ər-ˈlēv\ *vt* **1 a :** to equip with an interleaf **b :** SLIP-SHEET **2 :** INTERLAMINATE

1in·ter·line \ˌint-ər-ˈlīn\ *vt* [ME *enterlinen*, fr. ML *interlineare*, fr.

L *inter-* + *linea* line] **:** to insert between lines already written or printed; *also* **:** to insert something between the lines of ⟨~ a page⟩ — **in·ter·lin·ea·tion** \-ˌlin-ē-ˈā-shən\ *n*

2**interline** *vt* [ME *interlinen*, fr. *inter-* + *linen* to line] **:** to provide (a garment) with an interlining

in·ter·lin·ear \ˌint-ər-ˈlin-ē-ər\ *adj* [ME *interliniare*, fr. ML *interlinearis*, fr. L *inter-* + *linea* line] **1 :** inserted between lines already written or printed **2 :** written or printed in different languages or texts in alternate lines — **in·ter·lin·ear·ly** *adv*

in·ter·lin·ing \ˈint-ər-ˌlī-niŋ\ *n* **:** a lining sewn between the ordinary lining and the outside fabric

in·ter·link \ˌint-ər-ˈliŋk\ *vt* **:** to link together — **interlink** *n*

in·ter·lock \ˌint-ər-ˈläk\ *vi* **:** to become engaged or interrelated with one another ~ *vt* **1 :** to lock together **:** UNITE **2 :** to connect so that motion of any part is constrained by another; *esp* **:** to arrange the connections of (as railroad signals) to ensure movement in proper sequence — **in·ter·lock** \ˈint-ər-ˌläk\ *n* — **in·ter·lock·er** \ˌint-ər-ˈläk-ər\ *n*

in·ter·lo·cu·tion \ˌint-ər-lō-ˈkyü-shən\ *n* [L *interlocution-, interlocutio*, fr. *interlocutus*, pp. of *interloqui* to speak between, fr. *inter-* + *loqui* to speak] **:** interchange of speech **:** CONVERSATION

in·ter·loc·u·tor \ˌint-ər-ˈläk-yət-ər\ *n* **1 :** one who takes part in dialogue or conversation **2 :** a man in the middle of the line in a minstrel show who questions the end men

in·ter·loc·u·to·ry \ˌint-ər-ˈläk-yə-ˌtōr-ē, -ˌtȯr-\ *adj* **:** pronounced during the progress of a legal action and having only provisional force ⟨~ decree⟩

in·ter·lope \ˌint-ər-ˈlōp, ˈint-ər-ˌ\ *vi* [prob. back-formation fr. *interloper*, fr. *inter-* + *-loper* (akin to MD *lopen* to run, OE *hlēapan* to leap) — more at LEAP] **1 :** to encroach on the rights (as in trade) of others **2 :** INTRUDE, INTERMEDDLE — **in·ter·lop·er** *n*

in·ter·lude \ˈint-ər-ˌlüd\ *n* [ME *enterlude*, fr. ML *interludium*, fr. L *inter-* + *ludus* play — more at LUDICROUS] **1 a :** a light or farcical entertainment between the acts of a mystery or morality play or presented at a fete **b :** a farce or comedy derived from these entertainments **2 :** a performance or entertainment between the acts of a play **3 :** an intervening or interruptive period, space, or event **:** INTERVAL **4 :** a musical composition inserted between the parts of a longer composition, a drama, or a religious service

in·ter·lu·nar \ˌint-ər-ˈlü-nər\ *also* **in·ter·lu·na·ry** \-nə-rē\ *adj* [prob. fr. MF *interlunaire*, fr. L *interlunium* interlunary period, fr. *inter-* + *luna* moon — more at LUNAR] **:** relating to the interval between old and new moon when the moon is invisible

in·ter·mar·riage \ˌint-ər-ˈmar-ij\ *n* **1 :** marriage between members of different groups **2 :** ENDOGAMY 1

in·ter·mar·ry \-ˈmar-ē\ *vi* **1 a :** to marry each other **b :** to marry within a group **2 :** to become connected by marriage between members

in·ter·med·dle \ˌint-ər-ˈmed-ᵊl\ *vi* [ME *entermedlen*, fr. MF *entremedler*, fr. OF, fr. *entre-* inter- + *medler* to mix — more at MEDDLE] **:** MEDDLE, INTERFERE — **in·ter·med·dler** \-ˈmed-lər, -ᵊl-ər\ *n*

in·ter·me·di·a·cy \ˌint-ər-ˈmēd-ē-ə-sē\ *n* **:** INTERMEDIATENESS

1**in·ter·me·di·ary** \ˌint-ər-ˈmēd-ē-ˌer-ē\ *adj* **1 :** INTERMEDIATE **2 :** acting as a mediator

2**intermediary** *n* **1 a :** MEDIATOR, GO-BETWEEN **b :** MEDIUM, MEANS **2 :** an intermediate form or stage

1**in·ter·me·di·ate** \ˌint-ər-ˈmēd-ē-ət\ *adj* [ML *intermediatus*, fr. L *intermedius*, fr. *inter-* + *medius* mid, middle — more at MID] **:** being or occurring at the middle place or degree or between extremes — **in·ter·me·di·ate·ly** *adv* — **in·ter·me·di·ate·ness** *n*

2**intermediate** *n* **1 :** an intermediate term, object, or class **2 :** MEDIATOR, GO-BETWEEN **3 :** a chemical compound formed as an intermediate step between the starting material and the final product

intermediate host *n* **1 :** a host which is normally used by a parasite in the course of its life cycle and in which it may multiply asexually but not sexually **2 a :** RESERVOIR 3 **b :** VECTOR

in·ter·me·di·a·tion \ˌint-ər-ˌmēd-ē-ˈā-shən\ *n* **:** INTERVENTION, MEDIATION

in·ter·me·din \ˌint-ər-ˈmēd-ᵊn\ *n* **:** a hormone secreted by the intermediate part or anterior lobe of the pituitary body that induces expansion of vertebrate chromatophores

in·ter·ment \in-ˈtər-mənt\ *n* **:** the act or ceremony of interring

in·ter·mez·zo \ˌint-ər-ˈmet-(ˌ)sō, -ˈmed-(ˌ)zō\ *n, pl* **in·ter·mez·zi** \-(ˌ)sē, -(ˌ)zē\ *or* **intermezzos** [It, deriv. of L *intermedius* intermediate] **1 :** a short light entr'acte **2 a :** a movement coming between the major sections of a symphony or other extended work **b :** a short independent instrumental composition

in·ter·mi·na·ble \(ˈ)in-ˈtərm-(ə-)nə-bəl\ *adj* [ME, fr. LL *interminabilis*, fr. L *in-* + *terminare* to terminate] **:** ENDLESS; *esp* **:** wearisomely protracted — **in·ter·mi·na·ble·ness** *n* — **in·ter·mi·na·bly** \-blē\ *adv*

in·ter·min·gle \ˌint-ər-ˈmiŋ-gəl\ *vb* **:** INTERMIX

in·ter·mis·sion \ˌint-ər-ˈmish-ən\ *n* [L *intermission-, intermissio*, fr. *intermissus*, pp. of *intermittere*] **1 :** the act of intermitting **:** the state of being intermitted **2 :** a temporary halt esp. in a public performance **:** PAUSE

in·ter·mit \ˌint-ər-ˈmit\ *vb* **in·ter·mit·ted; in·ter·mit·ting** [L *intermittere*, fr. *inter-* + *mittere* to send — more at SMITE] *vt* **:** to cause to cease for a time or at intervals **:** DISCONTINUE ~ *vi* **:** to be intermittent **syn** see DEFER — **in·ter·mit·ter** *n*

in·ter·mit·tence \ˌint-ər-ˈmit-ᵊn(t)s\ *n* **:** the quality or state of being intermittent

in·ter·mit·tent \-ᵊnt\ *adj* [L *intermittent-, intermittens*, prp. of *intermittere*] **:** coming and going at intervals — **in·ter·mit·tent·ly** *adv*

syn INTERMITTENT, RECURRENT, PERIODIC, ALTERNATE mean occurring or appearing in interrupted sequence. INTERMITTENT stresses breaks in continuity; RECURRENT stresses repetition; PERIODIC implies recurrence at essentially regular intervals; ALTERNATE may apply to two contrasting things appearing repeatedly one after the other ⟨*alternate* hope and despair⟩ or to every second member of a series ⟨meet on *alternate* Tuesdays⟩

intermittent current *n* **:** an electric current that flows and ceases to flow at intervals but is not reversed

in·ter·mix \ˌint-ər-ˈmiks\ *vb* [back-formation fr. obs. *intermixt* (intermingled), fr. L *intermixtus*, pp. of *intermiscēre* to intermix, fr. *inter-* + *miscēre* to mix — more at MIX] **:** to mix together — **in·ter·mix·ture** \-ˈmiks-chər\ *n*

in·ter·mo·lec·u·lar \ˌint-ər-mə-ˈlek-yə-lər\ *adj* **:** existing or acting between molecules — **in·ter·mo·lec·u·lar·ly** *adv*

1**in·tern** *or* **in·terne** \in-ˈtərn, ˈin-ˌ\ *adj* [MF *interne*, fr. L *internus*] *archaic* **:** INTERNAL

2**in·tern** \ˈin-ˌtərn, in-ˈ\ *vt* **:** to confine or impound esp. during a war

3**in·tern** \ˈin-ˌtərn\ *n* **:** INTERNEE

4**in·tern** *or* **in·terne** \ˈin-ˌtərn\ *n* **:** an advanced student or graduate esp. in medicine gaining supervised practical experience (as in a hospital) — **in·tern·ship** \-ˌship\ *n*

5**in·tern** \ˈin-ˌtərn\ *vi* **:** to act as an intern

in·ter·nal \in-ˈtərn-ᵊl\ *adj* [L *internus*; akin to L *inter* between] **1 a :** existing or situated within the limits or surface of something **b** (1) **:** situated near the inside of the body (2) **:** situated on the side toward the median plane of the body **2 :** capable of being applied through the stomach by being swallowed **3 :** relating or belonging to or existing within the mind **4 :** INTRINSIC, INHERENT ⟨~ consistency⟩ **5 :** present or arising within an organism or one of its parts ⟨~ stimulus⟩ **6 :** of or relating to the domestic affairs of a state ⟨~ revenue⟩ — **in·ter·nal·i·ty** \ˌin-ˌtər-ˈnal-ət-ē\ *n* — **in·ter·nal·ly** \in-ˈtərn-ᵊl-ē\ *adv*

internal-combustion engine *n* **:** a heat engine in which the combustion that generates the heat takes place inside the engine proper instead of in a furnace

in·ter·nal·iza·tion \in-ˌtərn-ᵊl-ə-ˈzā-shən\ *n* **:** the act or process of internalizing

in·ter·nal·ize \in-ˈtərn-ᵊl-ˌīz\ *vt* **:** to give a subjective character to; *specif* **:** to incorporate within the self as guiding principles

internal medicine *n* **:** a branch of medicine that deals with the diagnosis and treatment of nonsurgical diseases

internal respiration *n* **:** exchange of gases between the cells of the body and the blood by way of the fluid bathing the cells

internal rhyme *n* **:** rhyme between a word within a line and another either at the end of the same line or within another line

internal secretion *n* **:** HORMONE

1**in·ter·na·tion·al** \ˌint-ər-ˈnash-nəl, -ən-ᵊl\ *adj* **1 :** affecting or involving two or more nations ⟨~ trade⟩ **2 :** of, relating to, or constituting a group or association having members in two or more nations ⟨~ movement⟩ — **in·ter·na·tion·al·i·ty** \-ˌnash-ə-ˈnal-ət-ē\ *n* — **in·ter·na·tion·al·ly** \-ˈnash-nə-lē, -ən-ᵊl-ē\ *adv*

2**in·ter·na·tion·al** \-ˈnash-nəl, -ən-ᵊl, *in sense a often* -ˌnash-ə-ˈnal, -ˈnäl\ *n* **:** an organized group that transcends national limits: as **a** *also* **in·ter·na·tio·nale** \-ˌnash-ə-ˈnal, -ˈnäl\ **:** one of several socialist or communist organizations of international scope **b :** a labor union having locals in more than one country

international date line *n* **:** DATE LINE

in·ter·na·tion·al·ism \-ˈnash-nəl-ˌiz-əm, -ˈnash-ən-ᵊl-\ *n* **1 :** international character, principles, interests, or outlook **2 a :** a policy of cooperation among nations and esp. of the development of close international political and economic relations **b :** an attitude or belief favoring such a policy — **in·ter·na·tion·al·ist** \-əst\ *n or adj*

in·ter·na·tion·al·iza·tion \-ˌnash-nəl-ə-ˈzā-shən, -ˌnash-ən-ᵊl-\ *n* **:** the act or the result of internationalizing

in·ter·na·tion·al·ize \-ˈnash-nəl-ˌīz, -ˈnash-ən-ᵊl-\ *vt* **:** to make international; *specif* **:** to place under international control

international law *n* **:** a body of rules that control or affect the rights of nations in their relations with each other

International Phonetic Alphabet *n* **:** an alphabet designed to provide a system of symbols for representing the speech sounds of a wide variety of languages

international pitch *n* **:** a tuning standard of 440 vibrations per second for A above middle C

international relations *n pl but sing in constr* **:** a branch of political science concerned with relations between nations and primarily with foreign policies

International Scientific Vocabulary *n* **:** a part of the vocabulary of the sciences and other specialized studies that consists of words or other linguistic forms current in two or more languages and differing from New Latin in being adapted to the structure of the individual languages in which they appear

international unit *n* **:** a quantity of a biological (as a vitamin) that produces a particular biological effect agreed upon as an international standard

in·ter·ne·cine \ˌint-ər-ˈnes-ˌēn, -ˈnē-ˌsīn; in-ˈtər-nə-ˌsēn, ˌint-ər-ni-ˈsēn\ *adj* [L *internecinus*, fr. *internecare* to destroy, kill, fr. *inter-* + *necare* to kill, fr. *nec-, nex* violent death — more at NOXIOUS] **1 :** marked by slaughter **:** DEADLY; *esp* **:** mutually destructive **2 :** of, relating to, or involving conflict within a group

in·tern·ee \ˌin-ˌtər-ˈnē\ *n* **:** an interned person

in·ter·neu·ron \ˌint-ər-ˈn(y)ü-ˌrän, -ˈn(y)u̇(ə)r-ˌän\ *n* **:** an internuncial neuron — **in·ter·neu·ro·nal** \-ˈn(y)u̇r-ən-ᵊl, -nyu̇-ˈrōn-\ *adj*

in·ter·nist \in-ˈtər-nəst\ *n* **:** a specialist in internal medicine esp. as distinguished from a surgeon

in·tern·ment \in-ˈtərn-mənt\ *n* **:** the act of interning **:** the state of being interned

in·ter·node \ˈint-ər-ˌnōd\ *n* [L *internodium*, fr. *inter-* + *nodus* knot] **:** an interval or part between two nodes (as of a stem)

in·ter·nun·ci·al \ˌint-ər-ˈnən(t)-sē-əl, -ˈnu̇n(t)-\ *adj* **1 :** of or relating to an internuncio **2 :** serving to link sensory and motor neurons — **in·ter·nun·ci·al·ly** \-ə-lē\ *adv*

in·ter·nun·cio \-ˈnən(t)-sē-ˌō, -ˈnu̇n(t)-\ *n* [It *internunzio*, fr. L *internuntius, internuncius*, fr. *inter-* + *nuntius, nuncius* messenger] **1 :** a messenger between two parties **:** GO-BETWEEN **2 :** a papal legate of lower rank than a nuncio

in·ter·nup·tial \ˌint-ər-ˈnəp-shəl, -chəl\ *adj* **1 :** relating to intermarriage **2 :** intervening between married states

in·tero·cep·tive \ˌint-ə-rō-ˈsep-tiv\ *adj* [*inter-* (as in *interior*) + *-o-* + *-ceptive* (as in *receptive*)] **:** of, relating to, or being stimuli arising within the body and esp. the viscera

in·tero·cep·tor \-tər\ *n* **:** a sensory receptor excited by interoceptive stimuli

in·ter·of·fice \ˌint-ə-ˈrȯf-əs, -ˈräf-əs\ *adj* **:** functioning or communicating between the offices of an organization

in·ter·pel·late \ˌint-ər-ˈpel-ˌāt, -pə-ˈlāt\ *vt* [L *interpellatus*, pp. of *interpellare* to interrupt, fr. *inter-* + *-pellare* (fr. *pellere* to drive)] **:** to question (as an executive officer) formally concerning an official action or policy or personal conduct — **in·ter·pel·la·tion** \-pə-ˈlā-shən\ *n* — **in·ter·pel·la·tor** \-ˈpel-ˌāt-ər, -pə-ˈlāt-\ *n*

in·ter·pen·e·trate \ˌint-ər-ˈpen-ə-ˌtrāt\ *vt* **:** to penetrate between, within, or throughout **:** PERMEATE ~ *vi* **:** to penetrate mutually — **in·ter·pen·e·tra·tion** \-ˌpen-ə-ˈtrā-shən\ *n*

in·ter·per·son·al \-ˈpərs-nəl, -ən-ᵊl\ *adj* **:** being, relating to, or involving relations between persons — **in·ter·per·son·al·ly** \-ē\ *adv*

in·ter·plan·e·tary \ˌint-ər-ˈplan-ə-ˌter-ē\ *adj* **:** existing, carried on, or operating between planets

in·ter·plant \-ˈplant\ *vt* **:** to plant a crop between (plants of another kind); *esp* **:** to set out young trees among (existing growth)

in·ter·play \ˈint-ər-ˌplā\ *n* **:** INTERACTION — **in·ter·play** \ˌint-ər-ˈ\ *vi*

in·ter·plead \ˌint-ər-ˈplēd\ *vi* [AF *enterpleder*, fr. *enter-* inter- + *pleder* to plead, fr. OF *plaidier* — more at PLEAD] **:** to go to trial with each other in order to determine a right on which the action of a third party depends

1**in·ter·plead·er** \-ər\ *n* [AF *enterpleder*, fr. *enterpleder*, v.] **:** a proceeding to enable a person to compel parties making the same claim against him to litigate the matter between themselves

2**interpleader** *n* **:** one that interpleads

in·ter·po·late \in-ˈtər-pə-ˌlāt\ *vb* [L *interpolatus*, pp. of *interpolare* to refurbish, alter, interpolate, fr. *inter-* + *-polare* (fr. *polire* to polish)] *vt* **1 a :** to alter or corrupt (as a text) by inserting new or foreign matter **b :** to insert (words) into a text or into a conversation **2 :** to insert between other things or parts **:** INTERCALATE **3 :** to estimate values of (a function) between two known values ~ *vi* **:** to make insertions **syn** see INTRODUCE — **in·ter·po·la·tion** \(ˌ)in-ˌtər-pə-ˈlā-shən\ *n* — **in·ter·po·la·tive** \in-ˈtər-pə-ˌlāt-iv\ *adj* — **in·ter·po·la·tor** \-ˌlāt-ər\ *n*

in·ter·pose \ˌint-ər-ˈpōz\ *vb* [MF *interposer*, fr. L *interponere* (perf. indic. *interposui*), fr. *inter-* + *ponere* to put — more at POSITION] *vt* **1 a :** to place in an intervening position **b :** to put (oneself) between **:** INTRUDE **2 :** to introduce or throw in between the parts of a conversation or argument ~ *vi* **1 :** to be or come between **2 :** to step in between parties at variance **:** INTERVENE **3 :** INTERRUPT — **in·ter·pos·er** *n*

syn INTERPOSE, INTERFERE, INTERVENE, MEDIATE, INTERCEDE mean to come or go between. INTERPOSE implies no more than this; INTERFERE implies a getting in the way or otherwise hindering movement, view, or free operation; INTERVENE may imply an occurring in space or time between two things or a stepping in to halt or settle a quarrel or conflict; MEDIATE implies intervening between hostile factions or conflicting ideas or principles; INTERCEDE implies acting in behalf of an offender in begging mercy or forgiveness **syn** see in addition INTRODUCE

in·ter·po·si·tion \-pə-ˈzish-ən\ *n* **1 a :** the act of interposing **b :** the action of a state whereby its sovereignty is placed between its citizens and the federal government **2 :** something interposed

in·ter·pret \in-ˈtər-prət, *rapid* -pət\ *vb* [ME *interpreten*, fr. MF&L; MF *interpreter*, fr. L *interpretari*, fr. *interpret-*, *interpres* agent, negotiator, interpreter] *vt* **1 :** to explain the meaning of **:** ELUCIDATE **2 :** to conceive in the light of individual belief, judgment, or circumstance **:** CONSTRUE **3 :** to represent by means of art **:** bring to realization by performance ⟨~s a role⟩ ~ *vi* **:** to act as an interpreter between speakers of different languages **syn** see EXPLAIN — **in·ter·pret·abil·i·ty** \in-ˌtər-prət-ə-ˈbil-ət-ē, *rapid* -pət-\ *n* — **in·ter·pret·able** \in-ˈtər-prət-ə-bəl, *rapid* -pət-\ *adj* — **in·ter·pret·er** \-ər\ *n* — **in·ter·pre·tive** \-iv\ *adj* — **in·ter·pre·tive·ly** *adv*

in·ter·pre·ta·tion \in-ˌtər-prə-ˈtā-shən, *rapid* -pə-\ *n* **1 :** the act or the result of interpreting **:** EXPLANATION **2 :** an instance of artistic interpretation in performance or adaptation — **in·ter·pre·ta·tion·al** \-shnəl, -shən-ᵊl\ *adj* — **in·ter·pre·ta·tive** \in-ˈtər-prə-ˌtāt-iv, *rapid* -pə-\ *adj* — **in·ter·pre·ta·tive·ly** *adv*

in·ter·pu·pil·lary \ˌint-ər-ˈpyü-pə-ˌler-ē\ *adj* **:** extending between the pupils of the eyes; *also* **:** extending between the centers of a pair of spectacle lenses ⟨~ distance⟩

in·ter·ra·cial \ˌint-ə(r)-ˈrā-shəl\ *or* **in·ter·race** \-ˈrās\ *adj* **:** of, involving, or designed for members of different races

in·ter·reg·num \ˌint-ə-ˈreg-nəm\ *n, pl* **interregnums** *or* **in·ter·reg·na** \-nə\ [L, fr. *inter-* + *regnum* reign — more at REIGN] **1 :** the time during which a throne is vacant between two successive reigns or regimes **2 :** a period during which the normal functions of government or control are suspended **3 :** a lapse or pause in a continuous series

in·ter·re·late \ˌint-ə(r)-ri-ˈlāt\ *vt* **:** to bring into mutual relation ~ *vi* **:** to have mutual relationship — **in·ter·re·la·tion** \-ˈlā-shən\ *n* — **in·ter·re·la·tion·ship** \-ˌship\ *n*

in·ter·ro·gate \in-ˈter-ə-ˌgāt\ *vt* [L *interrogatus*, pp. of *interrogare*, fr. *inter-* + *rogare* to ask — more at RIGHT] **:** to question formally and systematically **syn** see ASK — **in·ter·ro·ga·tion** \in-ˌter-ə-ˈgā-shən\ *n* — **in·ter·ro·ga·tion·al** \-shnəl, -shən-ᵊl\ *adj*

interrogation point *n* **:** QUESTION MARK

1**in·ter·rog·a·tive** \ˌint-ə-ˈräg-ət-iv\ *adj* **1 a :** having the form or force of a question **b :** used in a question **2 :** QUESTIONING, INQUISITIVE — **in·ter·rog·a·tive·ly** *adv*

2**interrogative** *n* **1 :** an interrogative utterance **2 :** a word (as *who, what, which*) or a particle (as Latin *-ne*) used in asking questions

in·ter·ro·ga·tor \in-ˈter-ə-ˌgāt-ər\ *n* **1 :** one that interrogates **2 :** a radio transmitter and receiver for sending out a signal that triggers a transponder and for receiving and displaying the reply

1**in·ter·rog·a·to·ry** \ˌint-ə-ˈräg-ə-ˌtōr-ē, -ˌtȯr-\ *n* **:** a formal question or inquiry

2**interrogatory** *adj* **:** INTERROGATIVE

in·ter·rupt \ˌint-ə-ˈrəpt\ *vb* [ME *interrupten*, fr. L *interruptus*, pp. of *interrumpere*, fr. *inter-* + *rumpere* to break — more at REAVE] *vt* **1 :** to stop or hinder by breaking in **2 :** to break the uniformity or continuity of ~ *vi* **:** to break in upon an action; *esp* **:** to break in with questions or remarks while another is speaking — **in·ter·rup·tion** \-ˈrəp-shən\ *n* — **in·ter·rup·tive** \-ˈrəp-tiv\ *adj*

in·ter·rupt·er *n* **:** one that interrupts; *specif* **:** a device for periodically and automatically interrupting an electric current

in·ter·scho·las·tic \ˌint-ər-skə-ˈlas-tik\ *adj* **:** existing or carried on between schools

in·ter se \ˌint-ər-ˈsā, -ˈsē\ *adv (or adj)* [L] **:** among or between themselves

in·ter·sect \ˌint-ər-ˈsekt\ *vb* [L *intersectus*, pp. of *intersecare*, fr. *inter-* + *secare* to cut — more at SAW] *vt* **:** to pierce or divide by passing through or across **:** CROSS ~ *vi* **1 :** to meet and cross at a point **2 :** to share a common area **:** OVERLAP

in·ter·sec·tion \ˌint-ər-ˈsek-shən, *esp in sense 2* ˈint-ər-ˌ\ *n* **1 :** the act or process of intersecting **2 :** a place or area where two or more things intersect **3 :** the set of elements common to two sets; *esp* **:** the set of points common to two geometric configurations

in·ter·sex \ˈint-ər-ˌseks\ *n* [ISV] **:** an intersexual individual

in·ter·sex·u·al \ˌint-ər-ˈseksh-(ə-)wəl, -ˈsek-shəl\ *adj* [ISV] **1 :** existing between sexes ⟨~ hostility⟩ **2 :** intermediate in sexual characters between a typical male and a typical female — **in·ter·sex·u·al·i·ty** \-ˌsek-shə-ˈwal-ət-ē\ *n* — **in·ter·sex·u·al·ly** \ˈseksh-(ə-)wə-lē, -ˈseksh-(ə-)lē\ *adv*

1**in·ter·space** \ˈint-ər-ˌspās\ *n* **:** an intervening space **:** INTERVAL

2**in·ter·space** \ˌint-ər-ˈspās\ *vt* **:** to separate by spaces

in·ter·spe·cif·ic \ˌint-ər-spi-ˈsif-ik\ *or* **in·ter·spe·cies** \-ˈspē-(ˌ)shēz, -(ˌ)sēz\ *adj* **:** existing or arising between species ⟨~ hybrid⟩

in·ter·sperse \ˌint-ər-ˈspərs\ *vt* [L *interspersus* interspersed, fr. *inter-* + *sparsus* pp. of *spargere* to scatter — more at SPARK] **1 :** to insert at intervals among other things **2 :** to place something at intervals in or among — **in·ter·sper·sion** \-ˈspər-zhən, -shən\ *n*

in·ter·sta·di·al \ˌint-ər-ˈstād-ē-əl\ *n* [ISV *inter-* + NL *stadium* stage, phase, fr. L, stadium] **:** a subdivision within a glacial stage marking a temporary retreat of the ice

in·ter·state \ˌint-ər-ˈstāt\ *adj* **:** of, connecting, or existing between two or more states esp. of the U.S.

in·ter·stel·lar \-ˈstel-ər\ *adj* **:** located or taking place among the stars

in·ter·ster·ile \-ˈster-əl\ *adj* **:** mutually incapable of fertilizing — **in·ter·ste·ril·i·ty** \-stə-ˈril-ət-ē\ *n*

in·ter·stice \in-ˈtər-stəs\ *n, pl* **in·ter·stic·es** \-stə-ˌsēz, -stə-səz\ [F, fr. LL *interstitium*, fr. L *interstitus*, pp. of *intersistere* to stand still in the middle, fr. *inter-* + *sistere* to come to a stand; akin to L *stare* to stand] **:** a space that intervenes between things **:** INTERVAL; *esp* **:** one between closely spaced things **syn** see APERTURE

in·ter·sti·tial \ˌint-ər-ˈstish-əl\ *adj* **1 :** relating to or situated in the interstices **2 a :** situated within but not restricted to or characteristic of a particular organ or tissue — used esp. of fibrous tissue **b :** affecting the interstitial tissues of an organ or part — **in·ter·sti·tial·ly** \-ə-lē\ *adv*

in·ter·sub·jec·tive \ˌint-ər-səb-ˈjek-tiv\ *adj* **1 :** interrelating two consciousnesses **2 :** accessible to two or more subjects **:** OBJECTIVE — **in·ter·sub·jec·tive·ly** *adv* — **in·ter·sub·jec·tiv·i·ty** \-(ˌ)səb-ˌjek-ˈtiv-ət-ē\ *n*

in·ter·tes·ta·men·tal \ˌint-ər-ˌtes-tə-ˈment-ᵊl\ *adj* **:** of, relating to, or forming the period of two centuries between the composition of the last of the Old Testament and the New Testament

in·ter·tid·al \-ˈtīd-ᵊl\ *adj* **:** of, relating to, or being the part of the littoral zone above low-tide mark

in·ter·till \-ˈtil\ *vt* **:** to cultivate between the rows of (a crop) — **in·ter·till·age** \-ˈtil-ij\ *n*

in·ter·trop·i·cal \-ˈträp-i-kəl\ *adj* **1 :** situated between or within the tropics **2 :** relating to regions within the tropics **:** TROPICAL

in·ter·twine \-ˈtwīn\ *vt* **:** to unite by twining one with another ~ *vi* **:** to twine about one another — **in·ter·twine·ment** \-mənt\ *n*

1**in·ter·twist** \-ˈtwist\ *vb* **:** INTERTWINE

2**in·ter·twist** \ˈint-ər-ˌtwist\ *n* **:** an act or instance of intertwisting **:** the state of being intertwisted

in·ter·ur·ban \ˌint-ər-ˈər-bən\ *adj* **:** connecting cities or towns

in·ter·val \ˈint-ər-vəl\ *n* [ME *intervalle*, fr. MF, fr. L *intervallum* space between ramparts, interval, fr. *inter-* + *vallum* rampart — more at WALL] **1 :** a space of time between events or states **:** PAUSE **2 a :** a space between objects, units, or states **b :** difference in pitch between tones **3 :** a set of real numbers between two numbers either including or excluding one or both of them; *also* **:** the set of real numbers greater or less than and including or excluding a real number

in·ter·vale \ˈint-ər-ˌvāl, -vəl\ *n* [obs. *intervale* interval] *chiefly NewEng* **:** BOTTOM 5

in·ter·val·om·e·ter \ˌint-ər-və-ˈläm-ət-ər\ *n* **:** a device that operates a control (as for a camera shutter) at regular intervals

in·ter·vene \ˌint-ər-ˈvēn\ *vi* [L *intervenire* to come between, fr. *inter-* + *venire* to come — more at COME] **1 :** to enter or appear as an irrelevant or extraneous feature or circumstance **2 :** to occur, fall, or come between points of time or events **3 :** to come in or between by way of hindrance or modification ⟨~ to settle a quarrel⟩ **4 :** to occur or lie between two things **5 a :** to become a third party to a legal proceeding begun by others for the protection of an alleged interest **b :** to interfere usu. by force or threat of force in another nation's internal affairs esp. to compel or prevent an action or to maintain or alter a condition **syn** see INTERPOSE — **in·ter·ve·nor** \-ˈvē-nər, -ˌnȯ(ə)r\ *also* **in·ter·ven·er** \-ˈvē-nər\ *n* — **in·ter·ven·tion** \-ˈven-chən\ *n*

in·ter·ven·tion·ism \-ˈven-chə-ˌniz-əm\ *n* **:** the theory or practice of intervening; *specif* **:** governmental interference in economic affairs at home or in political affairs of another country — **in·ter·ven·tion·ist** \-ˈvench-(ə-)nəst\ *n or adj*

in·ter·ver·te·bral \ˌint-ər-ˈvərt-ə-brəl\ *adj* **:** situated between vertebrae — **in·ter·ver·te·bral·ly** \-brə-lē\ *adv*

intervertebral disk *n* **:** one of the tough elastic disks that are interposed between the centra of adjoining vertebrae and that consist of an outer fibrous ring enclosing an inner pulpy nucleus

in·ter·view \ˈint-ər-ˌvyü\ *n* [MF *entrevue*, fr. (*s'*)*entrevoir* to see one another, meet, fr. *entre-* inter- + *voir* to see — more at VIEW] **1 :** a formal consultation usu. to evaluate the aptitude, training, or progress of a student or prospective employee **2 a :** a meeting at which a reporter obtains information from a person **b :** a report or reproduction of information so obtained — **interview** *vt* — **in·ter·view·er** *n*

in·ter vi·vos \ˌint-ər-ˈvē-ˌvōs, -ˈvī-\ *adv (or adj)* [LL] **:** between living persons ⟨transaction *inter vivos*⟩; *esp* **:** from one living person to another ⟨*inter vivos* gifts⟩ ⟨property transferred *inter vivos*⟩

in·ter·vo·cal·ic \ˌint-ər-vō-ˈkal-ik\ *adj* **:** immediately preceded and immediately followed by a vowel

in·ter·weave \ˌint-ər-ˈwēv\ *vt* **1 :** to weave together **2 :** to blend together ~ *vi* **:** INTERTWINE, INTERMINGLE — **in·ter·wo·ven** \-ˈwō-vən\ *adj*

in·tes·ta·cy \in-ˈtes-tə-sē\ *n* **:** the quality or state of being or dying intestate

1**in·tes·tate** \in-ˈtes-ˌtāt, -tət\ *adj* [ME, fr. L *intestatus*, fr. *in-* + *testatus* testate] **1 :** having made no valid will **2 :** not disposed of by will

[2]intestate *n* : one who dies intestate

in·tes·ti·nal \in-'tes-tən-ᵊl, -'tes(t)-nəl\ *adj* **1** : of, relating to, or being the intestine **2** : affecting or occurring in the intestine; *also* : living in the intestine — **in·tes·ti·nal·ly** \-ē\ *adv*

intestinal fortitude *n* [euphemism for *guts*] : COURAGE, STAMINA

[1]**in·tes·tine** \in-'tes-tən\ *adj* [MF or L; MF *intestin*, fr. L *intestinus*, fr. *intus* within — more at ENT-] : INTERNAL; *specif* : of or relating to the internal affairs of a state or country

[2]**intestine** *n* [MF *intestin*, fr. L *intestinum*, fr. neut. of *intestinus*] : the tubular part of the alimentary canal that extends from the stomach to the anus

in·ti·ma \'int-ə-mə\ *n, pl* **in·ti·mae** \-,mē, -,mī\ *or* **intimas** [NL, fr. L, fem. of *intimus*] : the innermost coat of an organ consisting usu. of an endothelial layer backed by connective tissue and elastic tissue — **in·ti·mal** \-məl\ *adj*

in·ti·ma·cy \'int-ə-mə-sē\ *n* **1** : the state of being intimate : FAMILIARITY **2** : an instance of esp. objectionable intimacy

[1]**in·ti·mate** \'int-ə-,māt\ *vt* [LL *intimatus*, pp. of *intimare* to put in, announce, fr. L *intimus* innermost, superl. of (assumed) OL *interus* inward — more at INTERIOR] **1** : ANNOUNCE, DECLARE **2** : to communicate indirectly : HINT **syn** see SUGGEST — **in·ti·mat·er** *n* — **in·ti·ma·tion** \,int-ə-'mā-shən\ *n*

[2]**in·ti·mate** \'int-ə-mət\ *adj* [alter. of obs. *intime*, fr. L *intimus*] **1 a** : INTRINSIC, ESSENTIAL **b** : belonging to or characterizing one's deepest nature **2** : marked by very close association, contact, or familiarity **3 a** : marked by a warm friendship developing through long association **b** : suggesting informal warmth or privacy ⟨~ clubs⟩ **4** : of a very personal or private nature **syn** see FAMILIAR — **in·ti·mate·ly** *adv* — **in·ti·mate·ness** *n*

[3]**in·ti·mate** \'int-ə-mət\ *n* : an intimate friend or confidant

in·tim·i·date \in-'tim-ə-,dāt\ *vt* [ML *intimidatus*, pp. of *intimidare*, fr. L *in-* + *timidus* timid] : to make timid or fearful : FRIGHTEN; *esp* : to compel or deter by or as if by threats — **in·tim·i·da·tion** \(,)in-,tim-ə-'dā-shən\ *n* — **in·tim·i·da·tor** \in-'tim-ə-,dāt-ər\ *n*

in·tinc·tion \in-'tiŋ(k)-shən\ *n* [LL *intinction-*, *intinctio* baptism, fr. L *intinctus*, pp. of *intingere* to dip in, fr. *in-* + *tingere* to dip, moisten — more at TINGE] : the administration of the sacrament of Communion by dipping the bread in the wine and giving both together to the communicant

in·tit·ule \in-'tich-(,)ü(ə)l, *Brit* -'tit-(,)yü(ə)l\ *vt* [MF *intituler*, fr. LL *intitulare*, fr. L *in-* + *titulus* title] *Brit* : to give a title or designation to — used chiefly of a legislative act

in·to \,in-tə(-w), 'in-(,)tü\ *prep* [ME, fr. OE *intō*, fr. [2]*in* + *tō* to] **1 a** : to the inside of ⟨came ~ the room⟩ **b** — used as a function word to indicate entry, introduction, insertion, or inclusion ⟨enter ~ an alliance⟩ **2 a** : to the state, condition, or form of ⟨got ~ trouble⟩ **b** : to the occupation, action, or possession of ⟨go ~ farming⟩ **3** — used as a function word to indicate a period of time or an extent of space part of which is passed or occupied ⟨far ~ the night⟩ **4** : in the direction of ⟨looking ~ the sun⟩ **5** : to a position of contact with : AGAINST ⟨ran ~ a wall⟩

in·tol·er·a·bil·i·ty \(,)in-,täl-(ə-)rə-'bil-ət-ē\ *n* : the quality or state of being intolerable

in·tol·er·a·ble \(')in-'täl-(ə-)rə-bəl, -'täl-ər-bəl\ *adj* [ME, fr. L *intolerabilis*, fr. *in-* + *tolerabilis* tolerable] **1** : not tolerable : UNBEARABLE **2** : EXCESSIVE — **in·tol·er·a·ble·ness** *n* — **in·tol·er·a·bly** \-blē\ *adv*

in·tol·er·ance \(')in-'täl-(ə-)rən(t)s\ *n* : the quality or state of being intolerant; *specif* : exceptional sensitivity (as to a drug)

in·tol·er·ant \-(ə-)rənt\ *adj* **1** : unable to endure **2 a** : unwilling to endure **b** : unwilling to grant equal freedom of expression esp. in religious matters or other social, political, or professional rights : BIGOTED — **in·tol·er·ant·ly** *adv* — **in·tol·er·ant·ness** *n*

in·to·nate \'in-tə-,nāt\ *vt* : INTONE, UTTER

in·to·na·tion \,in-tə-'nā-shən\ *n* **1** : the act of intoning and esp. of chanting **2** : something that is intoned; *specif* : the opening tones of a Gregorian chant **3** : the manner of singing, playing, or uttering tones **4** : the rise and fall in pitch of the voice in speech — **in·to·na·tion·al** \-shnəl, -shən-ᵊl\ *adj*

intonation pattern *n* : a combination of pitch and terminal juncture that contributes to the total meaning of an utterance ⟨one *intonation pattern* makes *Leave* a command, another makes it a question⟩

in·tone \in-'tōn\ *vb* [ME *entonen*, fr. MF *entoner*, fr. ML *intonare* fr. L *in-* + *tonus* tone] *vt* **1** : to utter in musical or prolonged tones **2** : to recite in singing tones or in a monotone ~ *vi* : to utter something in singing tones or in monotone — **in·ton·er** *n*

in·tor·sion *or* **in·tor·tion** \in-'tȯr-shən, 'in-,\ *n* [LL *intortion-*, *intortio* act of curling, fr. L *intortus*, pp. of *intorquēre* to curl, fr. *in-* + *torquēre* to twist — more at TORTURE] : a winding, bending, or twisting around (as of the stem of a plant); *specif* : inward rotation about an axis or a fixed point

in to·to \in-'tōt-(,)ō\ *adv* [L, on the whole] : TOTALLY, ENTIRELY

in·tox·i·cant \in-'täk-si-kənt\ *n* : something that intoxicates; *esp* : an alcoholic drink — **intoxicant** *adj*

[1]**in·tox·i·cate** \in-'täk-si-kət\ *adj, archaic* : INTOXICATED

[2]**in·tox·i·cate** \-sə-,kāt\ *vt* [ML *intoxicatus*, pp. of *intoxicare*, fr. L *in-* + *toxicum* poison — more at TOXIC] **1** : POISON **2 a** : to excite or stupefy by alcohol or a narcotic esp. to the point where physical and mental control is markedly diminished **b** : to excite or elate to the point of enthusiasm or frenzy

in·tox·i·cat·ed *adj* **1** : affected by alcohol **2** : emotionally excited, elated, or exhilarated **syn** see DRUNK

in·tox·i·ca·tion \(,)in-,täk-sə-'kā-shən\ *n* **1** : an abnormal state that is essentially a poisoning ⟨intestinal ~⟩ **2 a** : the condition of being drunk : INEBRIATION **b** : a strong excitement or elation

in·tra- \,in-trə *also but not shown at individual entries* ,in-,trä\ *prefix* [LL, fr. L *intra*, fr. (assumed) OL *interus*, adj. inward — more at INTERIOR] **1 a** : within ⟨*intra*mural⟩ **b** : during ⟨*intra*natal⟩ **c** : between layers of ⟨*intra*dermal⟩ **2** : INTRO- ⟨an *intra*muscular injection⟩

in·tra·cel·lu·lar \,in-trə-'sel-yə-lər\ *adj* : being or occurring within a protoplasmic cell

in·trac·ta·bil·i·ty \(,)in-,trak-tə-'bil-ət-ē\ *n* : the quality or state of being intractable

in·trac·ta·ble \(')in-'trak-tə-bəl\ *adj* [L *intractabilis*, fr. *in-* + *tractabilis* tractable] **1** : not easily governed, managed, or directed : OBSTINATE **2** : not easily manipulated or wrought ⟨~ metal⟩ **3** : not easily relieved or cured ⟨~ pain⟩ **syn** see UNRULY — **in·trac·ta·ble·ness** *n* — **in·trac·ta·bly** \-blē\ *adv*

in·tra·cu·ta·ne·ous test \,in-trə-kyü-,tā-nē-əs-\ *n* : a test for immunity or hypersensitivity made by injecting a minute amount of diluted antigen into the skin

in·tra·der·mal \,in-trə-'dər-məl\ *also* **in·tra·der·mic** \-mik\ *adj* : situated or done within or between the layers of the skin — **in·tra·der·mal·ly** \-mə-lē\ *also* **in·tra·der·mi·cal·ly** \-mi-k(ə-)lē\ *adv*

in·tra·dos \'in-trə-,däs, -,dō; in-'trā-,däs\ *n, pl* **in·tra·dos** \-,dōz, -,däs\ *or* **in·tra·dos·es** \-,däs-əz\ F, fr. L *intra* within + F *dos* back — more at DOSSIER] : the interior curve of an arch

in·tra·mo·lec·u·lar \,in-trə-mə-'lek-yə-lər\ *adj* [ISV] : existing or acting within the molecule; *also* : formed by reaction between different parts of the same molecule — **in·tra·mo·lec·u·lar·ly** *adv*

in·tra·mu·ral \,in-trə-'myu̇r-əl\ *adj* **1 a** : being or occurring within the limits usu. of a community or institution **b** : competitive only within the student body ⟨~ sports⟩ **2** : being or occurring within the substance of the walls of an organ — **in·tra·mu·ral·ly** \-ə-lē\ *adv*

in·tra·mus·cu·lar \-'məs-kyə-lər\ *adj* [ISV] : being within or going into a muscle — **in·tra·mus·cu·lar·ly** *adv*

in·tran·si·geance \in-'tran(t)s-ə-jən(t)s, -'tranz-\ *n* [F] : INTRANSIGENCE — **in·tran·si·geant** \-jənt\ *adj or n* — **in·tran·si·geant·ly** *adv*

in·tran·si·gence \-jən(t)s\ *n* : the quality or state of being intransigent

in·tran·si·gent \-jənt\ *adj* [Sp *intransigente*, fr. *in-* + *transigente*, prp. of *transigir* to compromise, fr. L *transigere* to transact — more at TRANSACT] **1 a** : refusing to compromise or to abandon an extreme position or attitude : UNCOMPROMISING **b** : IRRECONCILABLE **2** : characteristic of an intransigent person — **intransigent** *n* — **in·tran·si·gent·ly** *adv*

in·tran·si·tive \(')in-'tran(t)s-ət-iv, -'tranz-; -'tran(t)s-tiv\ *adj* [LL *intransitivus*, fr. L *in-* + LL *transitivus* transitive] : not transitive; *esp* : characterized by not having or containing a direct object ⟨an ~ verb⟩ — **in·tran·si·tive·ly** *adv* — **in·tran·si·tive·ness** *n*

in·trant \'in-trənt\ *n* [L *intrant-*, *intrans*, prp. of *intrare* to enter — more at ENTER] : ENTRANT; *esp* : one entering an educational institution or a holy order

in·tra·psy·chic \,in-trə-'sī-kik\ *adj* : being or occurring within the psyche, mind, or personality — **in·tra·psy·chi·cal** \-ki-kəl\ *adj* — **in·tra·psy·chi·cal·ly** \-ki-k(ə-)lē\ *adv*

in·tra·spe·cif·ic \,in-trə-spi-'sif-ik\ *also* **in·tra·spe·cies** \-'spē-(,)shēz, -(,)sēz\ *adj* : occurring within a species or involving members of one species

in·tra·state \,in-trə-'stāt\ *adj* : existing or occurring within a state

in·tra·uter·ine \-'yüt-ə-rən, -,rīn\ *adj* [ISV] : being or occurring within the uterus; *esp* : involving the part of development that takes place in the uterus

intrauterine device *n* : a device inserted and left in the uterus to prevent effective conception

in·tra·ve·nous \,in-trə-'vē-nəs\ *adj* [ISV] : being within or entering by way of the veins; *also* : used in intravenous procedures — **in·tra·ve·nous·ly** *adv*

in·tra·vi·tal \-'vīt-ᵊl\ *adj* [ISV] : INTRAVITAM

in·tra·vi·tam \-'vī-,tam, -'wē-,täm\ *adj* [NL *intra vitam* during life] **1** : performed upon or found in a living subject **2** *of a stain* : having the property of tinting living cells without killing them

in·tra·zon·al \,in-trə-'zōn-ᵊl\ *adj* : of, relating to, or being a soil or a major soil group marked by relatively well-developed characteristics that are determined primarily by essentially local factors (as the parent material) rather than climate and vegetation — compare AZONAL, ZONAL

intreat *archaic var of* ENTREAT

intrench *var of* ENTRENCH

in·trep·id \in-'trep-əd\ *adj* [L *intrepidus*, fr. *in-* + *trepidus* alarmed — more at TREPIDATION] : characterized by resolute fearlessness, fortitude, and endurance — **in·tre·pid·i·ty** \,in-trə-'pid-ət-ē\ *n* — **in·trep·id·ly** \in-'trep-əd-lē\ *adv* — **in·trep·id·ness** *n*

in·tri·ca·cy \'in-tri-kə-sē\ *n* **1** : the quality or state of being intricate **2** : something intricate

in·tri·cate \'in-tri-kət\ *adj* [ME, fr. L *intricatus*, pp. of *intricare* to entangle, fr. *in-* + *tricae* trifles, impediments] **1** : having many complexly interrelating parts or elements : COMPLICATED **2** : difficult to resolve or analyze **syn** see COMPLEX — **in·tri·cate·ly** *adv* — **in·tri·cate·ness** *n*

in·tri·gant *or* **in·tri·guant** \,in-trē-'gänt, ,an-\ *n* [F *intrigant*, fr. It *intrigante*, prp. of *intrigare*] : INTRIGUER — **in·tri·gante** *or* **in·tri·guante** \-'gänt\ *n*

[1]**in·trigue** \in-'trēg\ *vb* [F *intriguer*, fr. It *intrigare*, fr. L *intricare* to entangle, perplex] *vt* **1** : CHEAT, TRICK **2** : to accomplish by intrigue **3** *obs* : ENTANGLE **4** : to arouse the interest, desire, or curiosity of ~ *vi* : to carry on an intrigue; *esp* : PLOT, SCHEME — **in·trigu·er** *n*

[2]**in·trigue** \'in-,trēg, in-'\ *n* **1 a** : a covert and involved stratagem : MACHINATION **b** : the practice of engaging in intrigues **2** : a clandestine love affair **syn** see PLOT

in·trin·sic \in-'trin-zik, -'trin(t)-sik\ *adj* [MF *intrinsèque* internal, fr. LL *intrinsecus*, fr. L, adv., inwardly; akin to L *intra* within — more at INTRA-] **1** : belonging to the essential nature or constitution of a thing **2** : originating or situated within the body or part acted on — **in·trin·si·cal** \-zi-kəl, -si-\ *adj* — **in·trin·si·cal·ly** \-k(ə-)lē\ *adv* — **in·trin·si·cal·ness** \-kəl-nəs\ *n*

intrinsic factor *n* : a substance produced by normal gastrointestinal mucosa that facilitates absorption of vitamin B_{12}

intro- *prefix* [ME, fr. MF, fr. L, fr. *intro* inside, to the inside, fr. (assumed) OL *interus*, adj., inward] **1** : in : into ⟨*intro*jection⟩ **2** : inward : within ⟨*intro*vert⟩ — compare EXTRO-

in·tro·duce \,in-trə-'d(y)üs\ *vt* [L *introducere*, fr. *intro-* + *ducere* to lead — more at TOW] **1** : to lead or bring in esp. for the first time **2 a** : to bring into play **b** : to bring into practice or use : INSTITUTE **3** : to lead to or make known by a formal act, announcement, or recommendation: as **a** : to cause to be acquainted **b** : to present formally at court or into society **c** : to present or announce formally or officially or by an official reading **d** : to make preliminary explanatory or laudatory remarks about **e** : to bring (as an actor, singer) before the public for the first time **4 a** : to put or insert into **b** : to put (an atom or group of atoms) into a molecule **5** : to bring to a knowledge of — **in·tro·duc·er** *n*

syn INSERT, INSINUATE, INTERPOLATE, INTERCALATE, INTERPOSE, INTERJECT: INTRODUCE is a general term for bringing or placing a thing or person into a group or body already in existence; INSERT

implies putting into a fixed or open space between or among; INSINUATE implies introducing gradually or by gentle pressure; INTERPOLATE applies to the inserting of something extraneous or spurious; INTERCALATE suggests an intrusive inserting of something in an existing series or sequence; INTERPOSE suggests inserting an obstruction or cause of delay; INTERJECT implies the introduction of something that breaks in

in·tro·duc·tion \ˌin-trə-ˈdək-shən\ *n* [ME *introduccioun* act of introducing, fr. MF *introduction*, fr. L *introduction-*, *introductio*, fr. *introductus*, pp. of *introducere*] **1 :** something that introduces: as **a** (1) **:** a part of a book or treatise preliminary to the main portion (2) **:** a preliminary treatise or course of study **b :** a short introductory musical passage **2 :** the act or process of introducing or the state of being introduced **3 :** a putting in **:** INSERTION **4 :** something introduced; *specif* **:** a new or exotic plant or animal

in·tro·duc·to·ri·ly \-ˈdək-t(ə-)rə-lē\ *adv* **:** in an introductory manner

in·tro·duc·to·ry \ˌin-trə-ˈdək-t(ə-)rē\ *adj* **:** serving to introduce **:** PRELIMINARY

in·tro·gres·sion \ˌin-trə-ˈgresh-ən\ *n* [*intro-* + *-gression* (as in *regression*)] **:** the entry or introduction of a gene from one gene complex into another — **in·tro·gres·sive** \-ˈgres-iv\ *adj*

in·troit \ˈin-ˌtrō-ət, -ˌtrȯit, in-ˈ\ *n* [MF *introite*, fr. ML *introitus*, fr. L, entrance, fr. *introitus*, pp. of *introire* to go in, fr. *intro-* + *ire* to go — more at ISSUE] **1** *often cap* **:** the first part of the proper of the mass consisting of an antiphon, verse from a psalm, and the Gloria Patri **2 :** a piece of music sung or played at the beginning of a worship service

in·tro·ject \ˌin-trə-ˈjekt\ *vt* [*intro-* + *-ject* (as in *project*, v.)] **:** to incorporate (attitudes or ideas) into one's personality unconsciously — **in·tro·jec·tion** \-ˈjek-shən\ *n*

in·tro·mis·sion \ˌin-trə-ˈmish-ən\ *n* [F, fr. L *intromissus*, pp. of *intromittere*] **:** the act or process of intromitting

in·tro·mit \-ˈmit\ *vt* **in·tro·mit·ted; in·tro·mit·ting** [L *intromittere*, fr. *intro-* + *mittere* to send] **:** to send or put in **:** INSERT — **in·tro·mit·tent** \-ˈmit-ᵊnt\ *adj* — **in·tro·mit·ter** *n*

in·trorse \ˈin-ˌtrȯ(ə)rs\ *adj* [L *introrsus*, adv., inward, fr. *intro-* + *versus* toward, fr. pp. of *vertere* to turn — more at WORTH] **:** facing inward or toward the axis of growth — **in·trorse·ly** *adv*

in·tro·spect \ˌin-trə-ˈspekt\ *vb* [L *introspectus*, pp. of *introspicere* to look inside, fr. *intro-* + *specere* to look — more at SPY] *vt* **:** to examine (one's own mind or its contents) reflectively ~ *vi* **:** to engage in an examination of one's thought process and sensory experience — **in·tro·spec·tion** \-ˈspek-shən\ *n* — **in·tro·spec·tion·al** \-shnəl, -shən-ᵊl\ *adj* — **in·tro·spec·tion·ism** \-shə-ˌniz-əm\ *n* — **in·tro·spec·tion·ist** \-sh(ə-)nəst\ *n or adj* — **in·tro·spec·tive** \-ˈspek-tiv\ *adj* — **in·tro·spec·tive·ly** *adv* — **in·tro·spec·tive·ness** *n*

in·tro·ver·sion \ˌin-trə-ˈvər-zhən, -shən\ *n* [*intro-* + *-version* (as in *diversion*)] **1 :** the act of introverting **:** the state of being introverted **2 :** the state of or tendency toward being wholly or predominantly concerned with and interested in one's own mental life — **in·tro·ver·sive** \-ˈvər-siv, -ziv\ *adj* — **in·tro·ver·sive·ly** *adv*

1**in·tro·vert** \ˈin-trə-ˌvərt\ *vt* [*intro-* + *-vert* (as in *divert*)] **:** to turn inward or in upon itself: as **a :** to bend inward; *also* **:** to draw in (a tubular part) usu. by invagination **b :** to concentrate or direct upon oneself

2**introvert** *n* **1 :** something (as the eyestalk of a snail) that is or can be introverted **2 :** one whose personality is characterized by introversion

in·trude \in-ˈtrüd\ *vb* [L *intrudere* to thrust in, fr. *in-* + *trudere* to thrust — more at THREAT] *vi* **1 :** to thrust oneself in without invitation, permission, or welcome **2 :** to enter as if by force ~ *vt* **1 :** to thrust or force in or upon esp. without permission, welcome, or fitness **2 :** to cause to enter as if by force — **in·trud·er** *n*

in·tru·sion \in-ˈtrü-zhən\ *n* [ME, fr. MF, fr. ML *intrusion-*, *intrusio*, fr. L *intrusus*, pp. of *intrudere*] **1 :** the act of intruding or the state of being intruded; *specif* **:** the act of wrongfully entering upon, seizing, or taking possession of the property of another **2 :** the forcible entry of molten rock or magma into or between other rock formations; *also* **:** the intruded magma

in·tru·sive \in-ˈtrü-siv, -ziv\ *adj* **1 a :** characterized by intrusion **b :** intruding where one is not welcome or invited **2 a :** projecting inward **b** (1) *of a rock* **:** having been forced while in a plastic state into cavities or between layers (2) **:** PLUTONIC **3** *of a sound or letter* **:** having nothing that corresponds to it in orthography or etymon ⟨~ \t\ in \ˈmints\ for *mince*⟩ ⟨~ *d* in *thunder*⟩ **syn** see IMPERTINENT — **in·tru·sive·ly** *adv* — **in·tru·sive·ness** *n*

intrust *var of* ENTRUST

in·tu·bate \ˈin-ˌt(y)ü-ˌbāt, in-ˈ\ *vt* **:** to perform intubation on

in·tu·ba·tion \ˌin-ˌt(y)ü-ˈbā-shən\ *n* **:** the introduction of a tube into a hollow organ (as the trachea) to keep the latter open

in·tu·it \in-ˈt(y)ü-ət\ *vt* **:** to apprehend by intuition — **in·tu·it·able** \-ə-bəl\ *adj*

in·tu·ition \ˌin-t(y)ü-ˈish-ən\ *n* [LL *intuition-*, *intuitio* act of contemplating, fr. L *intuitus*, pp. of *intueri* to look at, contemplate, fr. *in-* + *tueri* to look at] **1 a :** immediate apprehension or cognition **b :** knowledge or conviction gained by intuition **c :** the power or faculty of attaining to direct knowledge or cognition without rational thought and inference **2 :** quick and ready insight — **in·tu·ition·al** \-ˈish-nəl, -ən-ᵊl\ *adj*

in·tu·ition·ism \-ˈish-ə-ˌniz-əm\ *n* **1 a :** a doctrine that there are basic truths intuitively known **b :** a doctrine that objects of perception are intuitively known to be real **2 :** a doctrine that right or wrong or fundamental principles about what is right and wrong can be intuited — **in·tu·ition·ist** \-ˈish-(ə-)nəst\ *adj or n*

in·tu·itive \in-ˈt(y)ü-ət-iv\ *adj* **1 :** knowing or perceiving by intuition **2 a :** known or perceived by intuition **:** directly apprehended **b :** knowable by intuition **3 :** possessing or given to intuition or insight — **in·tu·itive·ly** *adv* — **in·tu·itive·ness** *n*

in·tu·mesce \ˌin-t(y)ü-ˈmes\ *vi* [L *intumescere* to swell up, fr. *in-* + *tumescere*, incho. of *tumēre* to swell — more at THUMB] **:** ENLARGE, SWELL

in·tu·mes·cence \-ˈmes-ᵊn(t)s\ *n* **1 a :** an enlarging, swelling, or bubbling up (as under the action of heat) **b :** the state of being swollen **2 :** something swollen or enlarged

in·tu·mes·cent \-ᵊnt\ *adj* [L *intumescent-*, *intumescens*, prp. of *intumescere*] **1 :** marked by intumescence **2** *of paint* **:** swelling and charring when exposed to flame

in·tus·sus·cept \ˌint-ə-sə-ˈsept\ *vb* [prob. fr. (assumed) NL *intussusceptus*, pp. of *intussuscipere*, fr. L *intus* within + *suscipere* to take up — more at ENT-, SUSCEPTIBLE] *vt* **:** to take in by or cause to undergo intussusception; *esp* **:** INVAGINATE ~ *vi* **:** to undergo intussusception

in·tus·sus·cep·tion \-ˈsep-shən\ *n* **:** a drawing in of something from without: as **a :** INVAGINATION; *esp* **:** the slipping of a length of intestine into an adjacent portion usu. producing obstruction **b :** the assimilation of new material and its dispersal among preexistent matter — **in·tus·sus·cep·tive** \-ˈsep-tiv\ *adj*

in·u·lin \ˈin-yə-lən\ *n* [prob. fr. G *inulin*, fr. L *inula* elecampane] **:** a tasteless white polysaccharide found esp. dissolved in the sap of the roots and rhizomes of composite plants

in·unc·tion \in-ˈəŋ(k)-shən\ *n* [ME, fr. L *inunction-*, *inunctio*, fr. *inunctus*, pp. of *inunguere* to anoint — more at ANOINT] **:** an act of applying oil or ointment **:** ANOINTING

in·un·date \ˈin-ən-ˌdāt\ *vt* [L *inundatus*, pp. *inundare*, fr. *in-* + *unda* wave — more at WATER] **:** to cover with a flood **:** OVERFLOW — **in·un·da·tion** \ˌin-ən-ˈdā-shən\ *n* — **in·un·da·tor** \ˈin-ən-ˌdāt-ər\ *n* — **in·un·da·to·ry** \in-ˈən-də-ˌtōr-ē, -ˌtȯr-\ *adj*

in·ure \in-ˈ(y)u̇(ə)r\ *vb* [ME *enuren*, fr. *en-* + *ure*, n., use, custom, fr. MF *uevre* work, practice, fr. L *opera* work — more at OPERA] *vt* **:** to accustom to accept something undesirable **:** HABITUATE ~ *vi* **:** to become of advantage **:** ACCRUE — **in·ure·ment** \-mənt\ *n*

in·urn \in-ˈərn\ *vt* **1 :** to enclose in an urn **2 :** ENTOMB

in·utile \(ˈ)in-ˈyüt-ᵊl, -ˈyü-ˌtīl\ *adj* [ME, fr. MF, fr. L *inutilis*, fr. *in-* + *utilis* useful — more at UTILITY] **:** USELESS, UNUSABLE — **in·util·i·ty** \ˌin-yü-ˈtil-ət-ē\ *n*

in vac·uo \in-ˈvak-yə-ˌwō\ *adv* [NL] **:** in a vacuum

in·vade \in-ˈvād\ *vt* [ME *invaden*, fr. L *invadere*, fr. *in-* + *vadere* to go — more at WADE] **1 :** to enter for conquest or plunder **2 :** to encroach upon **:** INFRINGE **3 a** (1) **:** to spread over or into **:** PERMEATE (2) **:** to affect injuriously and progressively **b :** PENETRATE **c :** RAID, ASSAULT **syn** see TRESPASS — **in·vad·er** *n*

in·vag·i·nate \in-ˈvaj-ə-ˌnāt\ *vb* [ML *invaginatus*, pp. of *invaginare*, fr. L *in-* + *vagina* sheath] *vt* **1 :** ENCLOSE, SHEATHE **2 :** to fold in so that an outer becomes an inner surface ~ *vi* **:** to undergo invagination

in·vag·i·na·tion \(ˌ)in-ˌvaj-ə-ˈnā-shən\ *n* **1 :** an act or process of invaginating: as **a :** the formation of a gastrula by an infolding of part of the wall of the blastula **b :** intestinal intussusception **2 :** an invaginated part

1**in·val·id** \(ˈ)in-ˈval-əd\ *adj* [L *invalidus* weak, fr. *in-* + *validus* strong — more at VALID] **:** being without foundation or force in fact, truth, or law — **in·va·lid·i·ty** \ˌin-və-ˈlid-ət-ē\ *n* — **in·val·id·ly** \(ˈ)in-ˈval-əd-lē\ *adv* — **in·val·id·ness** *n*

2**in·va·lid** \ˈin-və-ləd, *Brit usu* -ˌlēd\ *adj* [L & F; F *invalide*, fr. L *invalidus*] **1 :** suffering from disease or disability **:** SICKLY **2 :** of, relating to, or suited to one that is sick

3**invalid** *like* 2\ *n* **:** one that is sickly or disabled

4**in·va·lid** \ˈin-və-ləd, -ˌlid, *Brit usu* ˌin-və-ˈlēd\ *vt* **1 :** to make sickly or disabled **2 :** to remove from active duty by reason of sickness or disability

in·val·i·date \(ˈ)in-ˈval-ə-ˌdāt\ *vt* **:** to make invalid; *esp* **:** to weaken or destroy the cogency of **syn** see NULLIFY — **in·val·i·da·tion** \(ˌ)in-ˌval-ə-ˈdā-shən\ *n* — **in·val·i·da·tor** \in-ˈval-ə-ˌdāt-ər\ *n*

in·va·lid·ism \ˈin-və-lə-ˌdiz-əm\ *n* **:** a chronic condition of being an invalid

in·valu·able \(ˈ)in-ˈval-yə-(wə-)bəl\ *adj* [1*in-* + *value*, v. + *-able*] **:** valuable beyond estimation **:** PRICELESS **syn** see COSTLY — **in·valu·able·ness** *n* — **in·valu·ably** \-blē\ *adv*

in·vari·abil·i·ty \(ˌ)in-ˌver-ē-ə-ˈbil-ət-ē, -ˌvar-\ *n* **:** the quality or state of being invariable

in·vari·able \(ˈ)in-ˈver-ē-ə-bəl, -ˈvar-\ *adj* **:** not changing or capable of change **:** CONSTANT — **invariable** *n* — **in·vari·able·ness** *n* — **in·vari·ably** \-blē\ *adv*

in·vari·ance \-ē-ən(t)s\ *n* **:** INVARIABILITY

in·vari·ant \-ē-ənt\ *adj* **:** CONSTANT, UNCHANGING; *specif* **:** unaffected by the group of mathematical operations under consideration ⟨~ factor⟩ — **invariant** *n*

in·va·sion \in-ˈvā-zhən\ *n* [ME *invasioune*, fr. MF *invasion*, fr. LL *invasion-*, *invasio*, fr. L *invasus*, pp. of *invadere*] **1 :** an act of invading; *esp* **:** incursion of an army for conquest or plunder **2 :** the incoming or spread of something usu. hurtful

in·va·sive \-siv, -ziv\ *adj* **1 :** of, relating to, or characterized by military aggression **2 :** tending to spread; *esp* **:** tending to invade healthy tissue ⟨~ cancer cells⟩ **3 :** tending to infringe — **in·va·sive·ness** *n*

1**in·vec·tive** \in-ˈvek-tiv\ *adj* [ME *invectif*, fr. MF, fr. L *invectivus*, fr. *invectus*, pp. of *invehere*] **:** of, relating to, or characterized by insult or abuse **:** DENUNCIATORY — **in·vec·tive·ly** *adv* — **in·vec·tive·ness** *n*

2**invective** *n* **1 :** an abusive expression or speech **2 :** insulting or abusive language **:** VITUPERATION **syn** see ABUSE

in·veigh \in-ˈvā\ *vi* [L *invehi* to attack, inveigh, pass. of *invehere* to carry in, fr. *in-* + *vehere* to carry — more at WAY] **:** to protest or complain bitterly or vehemently **:** RAIL — **in·veigh·er** *n*

in·vei·gle \in-ˈvā-gəl, -ˈvē-\ *vt* **in·vei·gling** \-g(ə-)liŋ\ [modif. of MF *aveugler* to blind, hoodwink, fr. OF *avogler*, fr. *avogle* blind, fr. ML *ab oculis*, lit., lacking eyes] **1 :** to win over by flattery **:** ENTICE **2 :** to acquire by ingenuity or flattery **syn** see LURE — **in·vei·gle·ment** \-gəl-mənt\ *n* — **in·vei·gler** \-g(ə-)lər\ *n*

in·vent \in-ˈvent\ *vt* [ME *inventen*, fr. L *inventus*, pp. of *invenire* to come upon, find, fr. *in-* + *venire* to come — more at COME] **1** *archaic* **:** FIND, DISCOVER **2 :** to think up or imagine **:** FABRICATE **3 :** to create or produce for the first time **:** DEVISE — **in·ven·tor** \-ˈvent-ər\ *n*

syn INVENT, CREATE, DISCOVER mean to bring something new into existence. INVENT implies fabricating something useful usu. as a result of ingenious thinking or experiment; CREATE implies an evoking of life out of nothing or producing a thing for the sake of its existence rather than its function or use; DISCOVER presupposes preexistence of something and implies a finding rather than a making

in·ven·tion \in-ˈven-chən\ *n* **1 :** DISCOVERY, FINDING **2 :** INVENTIVENESS **3 a :** something invented: as (1) **:** a product of the imag-

ination; *esp* : a false conception (2) : a device, contrivance, or process originated after study and experiment **b** : a short keyboard composition usu. in double counterpoint **4** : the act or process of inventing

in·ven·tive \in-ˈvent-iv\ *adj* **1** : adept or prolific at producing : CREATIVE **2** : characterized by invention — **in·ven·tive·ly** *adv* — **in·ven·tive·ness** *n*

in·ven·to·ri·al \ˌin-vən-ˈtōr-ē-əl, -ˈtȯr-\ *adj* : of or relating to an inventory — **in·ven·to·ri·al·ly** \-ə-lē\ *adv*

¹in·ven·to·ry \ˈin-vən-ˌtōr-ē, -ˌtȯr-\ *n* **1 a** : an itemized list of current assets: as (1) : a catalog of the property of an individual or estate (2) : a list of goods on hand **b** : a survey of natural resources **c** : a list of traits, preferences, attitudes, interests, or abilities used to evaluate personal characteristics or skills **2** : the quantity of goods or materials on hand : STOCK **3** : the act or process of taking an inventory

²inventory *vt* : to make an inventory of : CATALOG

in·ver·ness \ˌin-vər-ˈnes\ *n* [*Inverness*, Scotland] : a loose belted coat having a cape with a close round collar

in·verse \(ˈ)in-ˈvərs, ˈin-ˌ\ *adj* [L *inversus*, fr. pp. of *invertere*] **1** : opposite in order, nature, or effect **2** : being an inverse function — **inverse** *n* — **in·verse·ly** *adv*

inverse function *n* : the mathematical function that expresses the independent variable of another function in terms of its dependent variable

in·ver·sion \in-ˈvər-zhən, -shən\ *n* **1** : the act or process of inverting **2** : a reversal of position, order, or relationship: as **a** : a change in normal word order; *esp* : the placement of a verb before its subject **b** : the process or result of changing or reversing the relative positions of the elements of an interval, chord, or phrase (as by repeating a phrase with its intervals in the contrary order) **3** : HOMOSEXUALITY **4** : a conversion of a substance showing dextrorotation into one showing levorotation or vice versa **5** : a conversion of direct current into alternating current **6** : increase of temperature of the air with increasing altitude

in·ver·sive \-ˈvər-siv, -ziv\ *adj* : marked by inversion

¹in·vert \in-ˈvərt\ *vt* [L *invertere*, fr. *in-* + *vertere* to turn — more at WORTH] **1 a** : to turn inside out or upside down **b** : to turn inward **2 a** : to reverse in position, order, or relationship **b** : to subject to musical inversion **c** : to subject to chemical inversion **syn** see REVERSE — **in·vert·ible** \-ə-bəl\ *adj*

²in·vert \ˈin-ˌvərt\ *n* : one characterized by inversion: *specif* : HOMOSEXUAL

³in·vert \ˌin-ˌ, ˈin-ˌ\ *adj* : subjected to chemical inversion

in·ver·tase \in-ˈvərt-ˌās, -ˌāz; ˈin-vər-ˌtās, -ˌtāz\ *n* [ISV] : an enzyme capable of inverting sucrose

in·ver·te·brate \(ˈ)in-ˈvərt-ə-brət, -ˌbrāt\ *adj* [NL *invertebratus*, fr. L *in-* + NL *vertebratus* vertebrate] **1** : lacking a spinal column; *also* : of or relating to invertebrate animals **2** : lacking in strength or vitality : WEAK — **invertebrate** *n*

inverted comma *n* **1** : a comma in type turned to print upside down at the top of the line **2** *chiefly Brit* : QUOTATION MARK

in·vert·er \in-ˈvərt-ər\ *n* **1** : one that inverts **2** : a device for converting direct current into alternating current by mechanical or electronic means

invert sugar *n* : a mixture of dextrose and levulose found in fruits or produced artificially by the inversion of sucrose; *also* : dextrose obtained from starch

¹in·vest \in-ˈvest\ *vt* [L *investire* to clothe, surround, fr. *in-* + *vestis* garment — more at WEAR] **1** [ML *investire*, fr. L, to clothe] **a** : to array in the symbols of office or honor **b** : to furnish with power or authority **c** : to grant someone control or authority over : VEST **2** : to cover completely : ENVELOP **3** : CLOTHE, ADORN **4** [MF *investir*, fr. OIt *investire*, fr. L, to surround] : to surround with troops or ships so as to prevent escape or entry **5** : to endow with a quality or characteristic : INFUSE

²invest *vb* [It *investire* to clothe, invest money, fr. L, to clothe] *vt* **1** : to commit (money) in order to earn a financial return **2** : to make use of for future benefits or advantages ~ *vi* : to make an investment — **in·vest·able** \-ˈves-tə-bəl\ *adj* — **in·ves·tor** \-tər\ *n*

in·ves·ti·gate \in-ˈves-tə-ˌgāt\ *vt* [L *investigatus*, pp. of *investigare* to track, investigate, fr. *in-* + *vestigium* footprint, track] : to observe or study by close examination and systematic inquiry — **in·ves·ti·ga·tion** \in-ˌves-ti-ˈgā-shən\ *n* — **in·ves·ti·ga·tion·al** \-shnəl, -shən-ᵊl\ *adj* — **in·ves·ti·ga·tive** \in-ˈves-tə-ˌgāt-iv\ *adj* — **in·ves·ti·ga·tor** \-ˌgāt-ər\ *n* — **in·ves·ti·ga·to·ry** \-ti-gə-ˌtōr-ē, -ˌtȯr-\ *adj*

in·ves·ti·ture \in-ˈves-tə-ˌchu̇(ə)r, -chər, -ˌt(y)u̇(ə)r\ *n* [ME, fr. ML *investitura*, fr. *investitus*, pp. of *investire*] **1** : the act of ratifying or establishing in office : CONFIRMATION **2** : something that covers or adorns

¹in·vest·ment \in-ˈves(t)-mənt\ *n* **1 a** *archaic* : VESTMENT **b** : an outer layer : ENVELOPE **2** : INVESTITURE 1 **3** : BLOCKADE, SIEGE

²investment *n* : the outlay of money for income or profit; *also* : the sum invested or the property purchased

in·vet·er·a·cy \in-ˈvet-ə-rə-sē, -ˈve-trə-\ *n* : the quality or state of being inveterate

in·vet·er·ate \in-ˈvet-ə-rət, -ˈve-trət\ *adj* [L *inveteratus*, fr. pp. of *inveterare* to age (v.t.), fr. *in-* + *veter-*, *vetus* old — more at WETHER] **1** : firmly established by long persistence **2** : confirmed in a habit : HABITUAL — **in·vet·er·ate·ly** *adv*

syn INVETERATE, CONFIRMED, CHRONIC, DEEP-SEATED, DEEP-ROOTED mean firmly established. INVETERATE applies to a habit, attitude, feeling of such long existence as to be practically ineradicable or unalterable; CONFIRMED implies a growing stronger and firmer with time so as to resist change or reform; CHRONIC suggests what is persistent or endlessly recurrent and troublesome; DEEP-SEATED and DEEP-ROOTED apply to qualities or attitudes so deeply embedded as to become part of the core of character or of lasting endurance

in·vi·a·bil·i·ty \ˌin-ˌvī-ə-ˈbil-ət-ē\ *n* : inviable state

in·vi·a·ble \(ˈ)in-ˈvī-ə-bəl\ *adj* [ISV] : incapable of surviving esp. because of genetic constitution

in·vid·i·ous \in-ˈvid-ē-əs\ *adj* [L *invidiosus* envious, invidious, fr. *invidia* envy — more at ENVY] **1** : tending to cause discontent, animosity, or envy **2** : ENVIOUS **3** : INJURIOUS **syn** see REPUGNANT — **in·vid·i·ous·ly** *adv* — **in·vid·i·ous·ness** *n*

in·vig·o·rate \in-ˈvig-ə-ˌrāt\ *vt* [prob. fr. *in-* + *vigor*] : to give life and energy to : ANIMATE — **in·vig·o·ra·tion** \(ˌ)in-ˌvig-ə-ˈrā-shən\ *n* — **in·vig·o·ra·tor** \in-ˈvig-ə-ˌrāt-ər\ *n*

in·vin·ci·bil·i·ty \(ˌ)in-ˌvin(t)-sə-ˈbil-ət-ē\ *n* : the quality or state of being invincible

in·vin·ci·ble \(ˈ)in-ˈvin(t)-sə-bəl\ *adj* [ME, fr. MF, fr. LL *invincibilis*, fr. L *in-* + *vincere* to conquer — more at VICTOR] : incapable of being conquered, overcome, or subdued — **in·vin·ci·ble·ness** *n* — **in·vin·ci·bly** \-blē\ *adv*

in·vi·o·la·bil·i·ty \(ˌ)in-ˌvī-ə-lə-ˈbil-ət-ē\ *n* : the quality or state of being inviolable

in·vi·o·la·ble \(ˈ)in-ˈvī-ə-lə-bəl\ *adj* [MF or L; MF, fr. L *inviolabilis*, fr. *in-* + *violare* to violate] **1** : secure from violation or profanation : SACROSANCT **2** : secure from assault or trespass : UNASSAILABLE — **in·vi·o·la·ble·ness** *n* — **in·vi·o·la·bly** \-blē\ *adv*

in·vi·o·late \(ˈ)in-ˈvī-ə-lət\ *adj* : not violated; *esp* : PURE, UNPROFANED — **in·vi·o·late·ly** *adv* — **in·vi·o·late·ness** *n*

in·vis·cid \(ˈ)in-ˈvis-əd\ *adj* **1** : having zero viscosity **2** : of or relating to an inviscid fluid

in·vis·i·bil·i·ty \(ˌ)in-ˌviz-ə-ˈbil-ət-ē\ *n* : the quality or state of being invisible

in·vis·i·ble \(ˈ)in-ˈviz-ə-bəl\ *adj* [ME, fr. MF, fr. L *invisibilis*, fr. *in-* + *visibilis* visible] **1 a** : incapable by nature of being seen **b** : inaccessible to view : HIDDEN **2 a** : not appearing in published financial statements **b** : not reflected in statistics **3** : IMPERCEPTIBLE, INCONSPICUOUS — **invisible** *n* — **in·vis·i·ble·ness** *n* — **in·vis·i·bly** \-blē\ *adv*

in·vi·ta·tion \ˌin-və-ˈtā-shən\ *n* **1 a** : the act of inviting **b** : an esp. formal request to be present or participate **2** : INCENTIVE, INDUCEMENT — **in·vi·ta·tion·al** \-shnəl, -shən-ᵊl\ *adj*

¹in·vi·ta·to·ry \in-ˈvīt-ə-ˌtōr-ē, -ˌtȯr-\ *adj* : containing an invitation

²invitatory *n* : an invitatory psalm or antiphon

¹in·vite \in-ˈvīt\ *vt* [MF or L; MF *inviter*, fr. L *invitare*] **1 a** : to offer an incentive or inducement to : ENTICE **b** : to increase the likelihood of **2 a** : to request the presence or participation of **b** : to request formally **c** : to urge politely : WELCOME — **in·vit·er** *n*

syn SOLICIT, COURT: INVITE commonly implies a formal or courteous requesting of one's presence or participation, but may also apply to a tacit or unintended attracting or tempting; SOLICIT suggests urgency rather than courtesy in encouraging or asking; COURT suggests an endeavoring to win favor or gain love by suitable acts or words

²in·vite \ˈin-ˌvīt\ *n, chiefly dial* : INVITATION 1

in·vit·ing \in-ˈvīt-iŋ\ *adj* : ATTRACTIVE, TEMPTING

in vi·tro \in-ˈvē-(ˌ)trō\ *adv (or adj)* [NL, lit., in glass] : outside the living body and in an artificial environment

in vi·vo \in-ˈvē-(ˌ)vō\ *adv (or adj)* [NL, lit., in the living] : in the living body of a plant or animal

in·vo·cate \ˈin-və-ˌkāt\ *vt, archaic* : INVOKE — **in·voc·a·to·ry** \in-ˈväk-ə-ˌtōr-ē, -ˌtȯr-\ *adj*

in·vo·ca·tion \ˌin-və-ˈkā-shən\ *n* [ME *invocacioun*, fr. MF *invocation*, fr. L *invocation-*, *invocatio*, fr. *invocatus*, pp. of *invocare*] **1 a** : the act or process of petitioning for help or support : SUPPLICATION; *specif, often cap* : an invocatory prayer (as at the beginning of a service of worship) **b** : a calling upon for authority or justification **2** : a formula for conjuring : INCANTATION **3** : an act of legal or moral implementation : ENFORCEMENT — **in·vo·ca·tion·al** \-shnəl, -shən-ᵊl\ *adj*

¹in·voice \ˈin-ˌvȯis\ *n* [modif. of MF *envois*, pl. of *envoi* message — more at ENVOI] **1** : an itemized list of goods shipped usu. specifying the price and the terms of sale : BILL **2** : a consignment of merchandise

²invoice *vt* : to submit an invoice for : BILL ~ *vi* : to make or submit an invoice

in·voke \in-ˈvōk\ *vt* [ME *invoken*, fr. MF *invoquer*, fr. L *invocare*, fr. *in-* + *vocare* to call — more at VOICE] **1 a** : to petition for help or support **b** : to appeal to or cite as authority **2** : to call forth by incantation : CONJURE **3** : to make an earnest request for : SOLICIT ⟨*invoked* their forgiveness⟩ **4** : to put into effect or operation : IMPLEMENT **5** : to bring about : CAUSE — **in·vok·er** *n*

in·vo·lu·cel \in-ˈväl-yə-ˌsel\ *n* [NL *involucellum*, dim. of *involucrum*] : a secondary involucre (as in each secondary umbel of a compound umbel) — **in·vol·u·cel·late** \(ˌ)in-ˌväl-yə-ˈsel-ət\ *or* **in·vol·u·cel·lat·ed** \-ˈsel-ˌāt-əd\ *adj*

in·vo·lu·cral \ˌin-və-ˈlü-krəl\ *adj* : of, relating to, or resembling an involucre

in·vo·lu·crate \-krət\ *adj* : having an involucre

in·vo·lu·cre \ˈin-və-ˌlü-kər\ *n* [F, fr. NL *involucrum*] : one or more whorls of bracts situated below and close to a flower, flower cluster, or fruit — **in·vo·lu·cred** \-kərd\ *adj* — **in·vo·lu·cri·form** \ˌin-və-ˈlü-krə-ˌfȯrm\ *adj*

in·vo·lu·crum \ˌin-və-ˈlü-krəm\ *n, pl* **in·vo·lu·cra** \-krə\ [NL, sheath, involucre, fr. L, sheath, fr. *involvere* to wrap] : a surrounding envelope or sheath; *esp* : INVOLUCRE

in·vol·un·tar·i·ly \(ˌ)in-ˌväl-ən-ˈter-ə-lē\ *adv* : in an involuntary manner

in·vol·un·tar·i·ness \(ˈ)in-ˈväl-ən-ˌter-ē-nəs\ *n* : the quality or state of being involuntary

in·vol·un·tary \-ˌter-ē\ *adj* [LL *involuntarius*, fr. L *in-* + *voluntarius* voluntary] **1** : done contrary to or without choice **2** : COMPULSORY **3** : not subject to control of the will : REFLEX

¹in·vo·lute \ˈin-və-ˌlüt\ *adj* [L *involutus* involved, fr. pp. of *involvere*] **1 a** (1) : curled spirally (2) : having the whorls closely coiled ⟨~ shell⟩ **b** (1) : curled or curved inward (2) : having the edges rolled over the upper surface toward the midrib ⟨an ~ leaf⟩ **2** : INVOLVED, INTRICATE — **in·vo·lute·ly** *adv*

²involute *n* : a curve traced by a point on a thread kept taut as it is unwound from another curve

³in·vo·lute \ˌin-və-ˈlüt\ *vi* **1** : to become involute **2 a** : to return to a former condition **b** : to become cleared up : DISAPPEAR

in·vo·lu·tion \ˌin-və-ˈlü-shən\ *n* [L *involution-*, *involutio*, fr. *involutus*, pp. of *involvere*] **1 a** (1) : the act or an instance of enfolding or entangling : INVOLVEMENT (2) : an involved grammatical construction usu. characterized by the insertion of clauses between the subject and predicate **b** : COMPLEXITY, INTRICACY **2** : the act or process of raising a quantity to power **3 a** : an inward curvature or penetration **b** : the formation of a gastrula by ingrowth of cells formed at the dorsal lip **4** : a shrinking or return to a former size **5** : the regressive alterations of a body or its parts characteristic of the aging process; *specif* : decline marked by a decrease of bodily vigor and in women by the menopause — **in·vo·lu-**

tion·al \-shnəl, -shən-ᵊl\ *adj* — **in·vo·lu·tion·ary** \-shə-ˌner-ē\ *adj*

in·volve \in-'välv, -'vȯlv\ *vt* [ME *involven* to roll up, wrap, fr. L *involvere*, fr. *in-* + *volvere* to roll — more at VOLUBLE] **1** *archaic* **:** to enfold or envelop so as to encumber **2 a :** to draw in as a participant **:** ENGAGE **b :** to oblige to become associated **:** IMPLICATE **c :** to occupy absorbingly **3 :** to surround as if with a wrapping **:** ENVELOP **4 a** *archaic* **:** to wind, coil, or wreathe about **:** ENTWINE **b :** to relate closely **:** CONNECT **5 a :** to have within or as part of itself **:** INCLUDE **b :** to require as a necessary accompaniment **:** IMPLY **c :** to have an effect on **:** AFFECT **syn** see INCLUDE — **in·volve·ment** \-mənt\ *n* — **in·volv·er** *n*

in·volved \-'välvd, -'vȯlvd\ *adj* **1 :** TWISTED **2 a :** COMPLICATED, INTRICATE **b :** CONFUSED, TANGLED **3 :** AFFECTED, IMPLICATED **syn** see COMPLEX — **in·volved·ly** \-'välv-(ə-)dlē, -'vȯlv-\ *adv*

in·vul·ner·a·bil·i·ty \(ˌ)in-ˌvəln-(ə-)rə-'bil-ət-ē\ *n* **:** the quality or state of being invulnerable

in·vul·ner·a·ble \(')in-'vəln-(ə-)rə-bəl, -'vəl-nər-bəl\ *adj* [L *invulnerabilis*, fr. *in-* + *vulnerare* to wound — more at VULNERABLE] **1 :** incapable of being wounded, injured, or damaged **2 :** immune to or proof against attack **:** IMPREGNABLE — **in·vul·ner·a·ble·ness** *n* — **in·vul·ner·a·bly** \-blē\ *adv*

1**in·ward** \'in-wərd\ *adj* [ME, fr. OE *inweard;* akin to OHG *inwert* inward; both fr. a prehistoric WGmc compound whose constituents are represented by OE *in* & OE *-weard* -ward] **1 :** situated on the inside **:** INNER **2 a :** MENTAL **b :** SPIRITUAL **3 :** marked by close acquaintance **:** FAMILIAR **4 :** directed toward the interior

2**inward** *or* **in·wards** \-wərdz\ *adv* **1 :** toward the inside, center, or interior ⟨slope ~⟩ **2 :** toward the inner being

3**inward** *n* **1 :** something that is inward **2 in·wards** \'in-ərdz, -wərdz\ *pl* **:** INNARDS

Inward Light *n* **:** INNER LIGHT

in·ward·ly \'in-wərd-lē\ *adv* **1 :** MENTALLY, SPIRITUALLY **2 a :** INTERNALLY ⟨bled ~⟩ **b :** to oneself **:** PRIVATELY ⟨cursed ~⟩

in·ward·ness *n* **1 :** close acquaintance **:** FAMILIARITY **2 :** fundamental nature **:** ESSENCE **3 :** internal quality or substance **4 :** absorption in one's own mental or spiritual life

in·weave \(')in-'wēv\ *vt* **:** to weave in or together **:** INTERLACE

in·wrought \(')in-'rȯt\ *adj* **1 :** having a decorative element worked or woven in **:** ORNAMENTED **2** *archaic* **:** WORKED, EMBROIDERED

Io \'ī-(ˌ)ō\ *n* [L, fr. Gk *Iō*] **:** a maiden loved by Zeus and changed by him into a heifer to disguise her

iod- *or* **iodo-** *comb form* [F *iode*] **:** iodine ⟨*iod*ize⟩ ⟨*iodo*form⟩

1**io·date** \'ī-ə-ˌdāt, -əd-ət\ *n* [F, fr. *iode*] **:** a salt of iodic acid

2**io·date** \'ī-ə-ˌdāt\ *vt* [*iod-* + *-ate*] **:** to impregnate or treat with iodine — **io·da·tion** \ˌī-ə-'dā-shən\ *n*

iod·ic \ī-'äd-ik\ *adj* [F *iodique*, fr. *iode*] **:** of, relating to, or containing iodine; *esp* **:** containing iodine with a valence of five

iodic acid *n* **:** a crystalline oxidizing solid HIO_3 formed by oxidation of iodine

io·dide \'ī-ə-ˌdīd\ *n* [ISV] **:** a binary compound of iodine usu. with a more electropositive element or radical; *esp* **:** a salt or ester of hydriodic acid

io·din·ation \ˌī-ə-də-'nā-shən\ *n* **:** a treating or combining with iodine

io·dine *also* **io·din** \'ī-ə-ˌdīn, -əd-ᵊn, -ə-ˌdēn\ *n, often attrib* [F *iode*, fr. Gk *ioeidēs* violet colored, fr. *ion* violet] **:** a nonmetallic univalent and multivalent halogen element obtained usu. as heavy shining blackish gray crystals and used esp. in medicine, photography, and analysis — see ELEMENT table

io·dize \'ī-ə-ˌdīz\ *vt* **:** to treat with iodine or an iodide

io·do·form \ī-'ōd-ə-ˌfȯrm, -'äd-\ *n* [ISV *iod-* + *-form* (as in *chloroform*)] **:** a yellow crystalline volatile compound CHI_3 with a penetrating persistent odor that is used as an antiseptic dressing

io·do·pro·tein \ˌī-əd-ō-'prō-ˌtēn, -'prōt-ē-ən\ *n* **:** an iodine-containing protein

io·dop·sin \ˌī-ə-'däp-sən\ *n* [*iod-* (fr. Gk *ioeidēs* violet colored) + Gk *opsis* sight, vision + E *-in* — more at OPTIC] **:** a photosensitive violet pigment in the retinal cones that is similar to rhodopsin but more labile, is formed from vitamin A, and is important in daylight vision

io·dous \ī-'ōd-əs, 'ī-əd-\ *adj* [ISV] **:** relating to or containing iodine and esp. iodine with a valence of three

io moth \ˌī-(ˌ)ō-\ *n* [L *Io*] **:** a large yellowish American moth (*Automeris io*) having a large ocellated spot on each hind wing and a larva with stinging spines

ion \'ī-ən, 'ī-ˌän\ *n* [Gk, neut. of *iōn*, prp. of *ienai* to go — more at ISSUE] **1 :** an atom or group of atoms that carries a positive or negative electric charge as a result of having lost or gained one or more electrons **2 :** a free electron or other charged subatomic particle

-ion *n suffix* [ME *-ioun, -ion*, fr. OF *-ion*, fr. L *-ion-, -io*] **1 a :** act or process ⟨validat*ion*⟩ **b :** result of an act or process ⟨regulat*ion*⟩ **2 :** state or condition ⟨hydrat*ion*⟩

ion exchange *n* **:** a technique of separating materials by reversible interchange between ions of like charge — **ion–ex·chang·er** *n*

ion·ic \ī-'än-ik\ *adj* [ISV] **:** relating to, employing, or existing in the form of ions

1**Ion·ic** \ī-'än-ik\ *adj* [L & MF; MF *ionique*, fr. L *ionicus*, fr. Gk *iōnikos*, fr. *Iōnia* Ionia] **1 :** of or relating to Ionia or the Ionians **2 :** belonging to or resembling the Ionic order of architecture characterized esp. by the spiral volutes of its capital

2**Ionic** *n* **:** a dialect of ancient Greek used in Ionia that is the vehicle of an important body of literature

io·ni·um \ī-'ō-nē-əm\ *n* [*ion;* fr. its ionizing action] **:** a natural radioactive isotope of thorium having a mass number of 230

ion·iza·tion \ˌī-ə-nə-'zā-shən\ *n* [ISV] **:** the process of ionizing **:** the state of being ionized

ionization chamber *n* **:** a partially evacuated tube with electrodes so that its conductivity due to the ionization of the residual gas reveals the presence of ionizing radiation

ion·ize \'ī-ə-ˌnīz\ *vb* [ISV] *vt* **:** to convert wholly or partly into ions ~ *vi* **:** to become ionized — **ion·iz·er** *n*

Io·none \'ī-ə-ˌnōn\ *trademark* — used for either of two oily liquid isomeric ketones $C_{13}H_{20}O$ with a strong violet odor prepared from citral and used in perfume

iono·sphere \ī-'än-ə-ˌsfi(ə)r\ *n* **:** the part of the earth's atmosphere beginning at an altitude of about 25 miles and extending outward 250 miles or more, containing free electrically charged particles by means of which radio waves are transmitted to great distances around the earth, and consisting of several regions within which occur one or more layers that vary in height and ionization with time of day, season, and the solar cycle — **iono·spher·ic** \(ˌ)ī-ˌän-ə-'sfi(ə)r-ik, -'sfer-\ *adj*

io·ta \ī-'ōt-ə\ *n* [L, fr. Gk *iōta*, of Sem origin; akin to Heb *yōdh* yodh] **1 :** the 9th letter of the Greek alphabet — symbol Ι or ι **2 :** an infinitesimal amount **:** JOT

io·ta·cism \-ˌsiz-əm\ *n* [LL *iotacismus* repetition of iota, fr. Gk *iōtakismos*, fr. *iōta*] **:** excessive use of the letter iota or I or of its sound; *specif* **:** the use in modern Greek of the sound \ē\ of iota in speaking words written with other vowels or diphthongs (as *ē, u, ei, oi*)

IOU \ˌī-(ˌ)ō-'yü\ *n* [fr. the pronunciation of *I owe you*] **:** a paper that has on it the letters IOU, a stated sum, and a signature and that is given as an acknowledgment of debt

-ious *adj suffix* [ME, partly fr. OF *-ious, -ieux*, fr. L *-iosus*, fr. *-i-* (penultimate vowel of some noun stems) + *-osus* -ous; partly fr. L *-ius*, adj. suffix] **:** -OUS ⟨edac*ious*⟩

ip·e·cac \'ip-i-ˌkak\ *or* **ipe·ca·cu·a·nha** *Pg* ē-ˌpek-ə-kü-'a-nʸə\ *n* [Pg *ipecacuanha*, fr. Tupi *ipekaaguéne*] **1 :** a tropical So. American creeping plant (*Cephaelis ipecacuanha*) of the madder family with drooping flowers **2 :** the dried rhizome and roots of ipecac valued esp. as a source of emetine; *also* **:** any of several roots similarly used

Iph·i·ge·nia \ˌif-ə-jə-'nī-ə\ *n* [L, fr. Gk *Iphigeneia*] **:** a daughter of Agamemnon offered by her father as a sacrifice but saved and made a priestess of Artemis

ip·se dix·it \ˌip-sē-'dik-sət\ *n* [L, he himself said it] **:** an assertion made but not proved **:** DICTUM

ip·si·lat·er·al \ˌip-si-'lat-ə-rəl, -'la-trəl\ *adj* [ISV, fr. L *ipse* self, himself + *later-, latus* side] **:** situated or appearing on or affecting the same side of the body — **ip·si·lat·er·al·ly** \-ē\ *adv*

ip·sis·si·ma ver·ba \ip-ˌsis-ə-mə-'vər-bə\ *n pl* [NL, lit., the selfsame words] **:** the exact language used by someone quoted

ip·so fac·to \ˌip-(ˌ)sō-'fak-(ˌ)tō\ *adv* [NL, lit., by the fact itself] **:** by the very nature of the case

ir- — see IN-

Ira·ni·an \ir-'ā-nē-ən\ *n* **1 :** a native or inhabitant of Iran **2 :** a branch of the Indo-European family of languages that includes Persian — see INDO-EUROPEAN LANGUAGES table — **Iranian** *adj*

Iraqi \i-'räk-ē, -'rak-\ *n* [Ar *'irāqīy*, fr. *'Irāq* Iraq] **1 :** a native or inhabitant of Iraq **2 :** the dialect of Modern Arabic spoken in Iraq — **Iraqi** *adj*

iras·ci·bil·i·ty \ir-ˌas-ə-'bil-ət-ē, (ˌ)ī-ˌras-\ *n* **:** the quality or state of being irascible

iras·ci·ble \ir-'as-ə-bəl, ī-'ras-\ *adj* [MF, fr. LL *irascibilis*, fr. L *irasci* to become angry, be angry, fr. *ira*] **:** marked by hot temper and easily provoked anger — **iras·ci·ble·ness** *n* — **iras·ci·bly** \-blē\ *adv*

syn IRASCIBLE, CHOLERIC, SPLENETIC, TESTY, TOUCHY, CRANKY, CROSS mean easily angered. IRASCIBLE implies a tendency to be angered on slight provocation; CHOLERIC may suggest impatient excitability and unreasonableness in addition to hot temper; SPLENETIC suggests moroseness, and bad rather than hot temper; TESTY suggests irascibility over small annoyances; TOUCHY implies undue sensitiveness as from jealousy or bad conscience; CRANKY suggests an habitual fretful irritability; CROSS suggests a snappishness or grumpy irritability as from disappointment or discomfort

irate \ī-'rāt\ *adj* **1 :** roused to or given to ire **:** INCENSED **2 :** arising from anger — **irate·ly** *adv* — **irate·ness** *n*

ire \'ī(ə)r\ *n* [ME, fr. OF, fr. L *ira;* akin to OE *ofost* haste, zeal, Gk *hieros* holy, *oistros* gadfly, frenzy] **:** ANGER, WRATH **syn** see ANGER — **ire** *vt* — **ire·ful** \-fəl\ *adj*

ire·nic \ī-'ren-ik, -'rē-nik\ *adj* [Gk *eirēnikos*, fr. *eirēnē* peace] **:** conducive to or operating toward peace or conciliation — **ire·ni·cal·ly** \-'ren-i-k(ə-)lē, -'rē-ni-\ *adv*

irid \'ī-rəd\ *n* [NL *Irid-, Iris*] **:** a plant of the iris family

irid- *or* **irido-** *comb form* **1** [L *irid-, iris*] **:** rainbow ⟨*irid*escent⟩ **2** [NL *irid-, iris*] **:** iris of the eye ⟨*irid*ectomy⟩ **3** [NL *iridium*] **:** iridium ⟨*irid*ic⟩ **:** iridium and ⟨*irid*osmium⟩

iri·da·ceous \ˌir-ə-'dā-shəs, ˌī-rə-\ *adj* **:** of or relating to the iris family

ir·i·des·cence \ˌir-ə-'des-ᵊn(t)s\ *n* **:** a play of colors producing rainbow effects (as in a soap bubble)

ir·i·des·cent \-ᵊnt\ *adj* **:** having or exhibiting iridescence — **ir·i·des·cent·ly** *adv*

irid·ic \1 *usu* ir-'id-ik, 2 *usu* ī-'rid-\ *adj* **1 :** of or relating to iridium; *esp* **:** containing tetravalent iridium **2 :** of or relating to the iris of the eye

irid·i·um \ir-'id-ē-əm\ *n* [NL, fr. L *irid-, iris;* fr. the colors produced by its dissolving in hydrochloric acid] **:** a silver-white hard brittle very heavy chiefly trivalent and tetravalent metallic element of the platinum group — see ELEMENT table

ir·i·dos·mine \ˌir-ə-'däz-ˌmēn\ *n* [G, fr. *irid-* + NL *osmium*] **:** a mineral that is a native iridium osmium alloy usu. containing some rhodium and platinum

iris \'ī-rəs\ *n, pl* **iris·es** *or* **iri·des** \'ī-rə-ˌdēz, 'ir-ə-\ [ME, fr. L *irid-, iris* rainbow, iris plant, fr. Gk, rainbow, iris plant, iris of the eye — more at WIRE] **1 :** RAINBOW **2** [NL *irid-, iris*, fr. Gk] **:** the opaque contractile diaphragm perforated by the pupil and forming the colored portion of the eye **3** [NL *Irid-, Iris*, genus name, fr. L] **:** any of a large genus (*Iris* of the family Iridaceae, the iris family) of perennial herbaceous plants with linear usu. basal leaves and large showy flowers

Iris \'ī-rəs\ *n* [L, fr. Gk] **:** the goddess of the rainbow and messenger of the gods in Greek mythology

iris diaphragm *n* **:** an adjustable diaphragm of thin opaque plates that can be turned by a ring so as to change the diameter of a central opening usu. to regulate the aperture of a lens

Irish \'ī(ə)r-ish\ *n* **1** *pl in constr* **:** natives or inhabitants of Ireland or their immediate descendants esp. when of Celtic speech or culture **2 a :** the Celtic language of Ireland **:** IRISH GAELIC **b :** English spoken by the Irish — **Irish** *adj*

Irish bull *n* **:** an apparently congruous but actually incongruous

expression (as "it was hereditary in his family to have no children")
Irish coffee *n* **:** hot sugared coffee with Irish whiskey and whipped cream
Irish Gaelic *n* **:** the Celtic language of Ireland esp. as used since the end of the medieval period
Irish·ism \'ī-rish-ˌiz-əm\ *n* **:** a word, phrase, or expression characteristic of the Irish
Irish·man \'ī-rish-mən\ *n* **1 :** a native or inhabitant of Ireland **2 :** a man of Irish descent
Irish moss *n* **1 :** the dried and bleached plants of two red algae (*Chondrus crispus* and *Gigartina mamillosa*) used as an agent for thickening or emulsifying or as a demulcent **2 :** CARRAGEEN
Irish setter *n* **:** any of a breed of bird dogs generally comparable to English setters but with a chestnut-brown or mahogany-red coat
Irish terrier *n* **:** any of a breed of active medium-sized terriers developed in Ireland and characterized by a dense close usu. reddish wiry coat
Irish water spaniel *n* **:** any of a breed of large retrievers developed in Ireland and characterized by a heavy curly liver-colored coat and a nearly hairless tail
Irish wolfhound *n* **:** a very large tall hound that resembles the deerhound but is much larger and stronger
Irish·wom·an \'ī-rish-ˌwu̇m-ən\ *n* **:** a woman born in Ireland or of Irish descent
irk \'ərk\ *vt* [ME *irken*] **:** to make weary, irritated, or bored **syn** see ANNOY
irk·some \'ərk-səm\ *adj* **:** tending to irk **:** TEDIOUS — **irk·some·ly** *adv* — **irk·some·ness** *n*
¹**iron** \'ī(-ə)rn\ *n* [ME, fr. OE *īsern, īren;* akin to OHG *īsarn* iron]

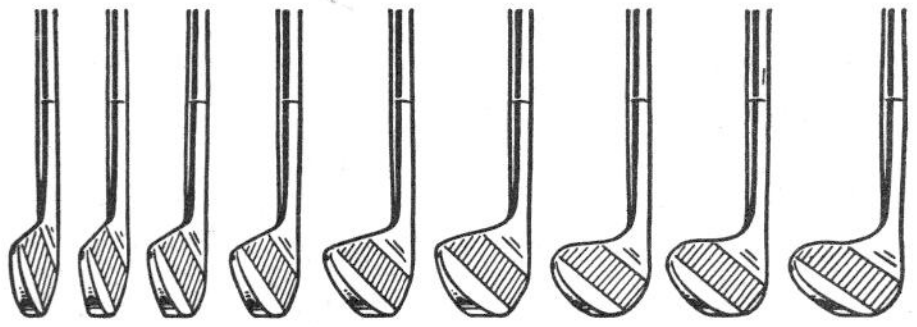

1 2 3 4 5 6 7 8 9
irons 2e

1 : a heavy malleable ductile magnetic chiefly bivalent and trivalent silver-white metallic element that readily rusts in moist air, occurs native in meteorites and combined in most igneous rocks, is the most used of metals, and is vital to biological processes — see ELEMENT table **2 :** something made of iron: as **a :** something (as handcuffs) used to bind or restrain — usu. used in pl. **b :** a heated metal implement used for branding or cauterizing **c :** HARPOON **d :** FLATIRON **e :** any of a series of numbered golf clubs having metal heads **3 :** STRENGTH, HARDNESS
²**iron** *adj* **1 :** of, relating to, or made of iron **2 :** resembling iron **3 a :** strong and healthy **:** ROBUST **b :** INFLEXIBLE, UNRELENTING **c :** holding or binding fast
³**iron** *vt* **1 :** to furnish or cover with iron **2 :** to shackle with irons **3 a :** to smooth with or as if with a heated flatiron **b :** to remove by ironing ⟨~ out wrinkles⟩ ~ *vi* **:** to smooth or press cloth or clothing with a heated flatiron
Iron Age *n* **1 :** the last and worst age of the world marked according to the ancients by toil, selfishness, and degeneracy **2 :** the period of human culture characterized by the smelting of iron and its use in industry beginning somewhat before 1000 B.C. in western Asia and Egypt
iron·bound \'ī(-ə)rn-'bau̇nd\ *adj* **:** bound with or as if with iron: as **a :** HARSH, RUGGED ⟨~ coast⟩ **b :** STERN, RIGOROUS
¹**iron·clad** \-'klad\ *adj* **1 :** sheathed in iron armor **2 :** RIGOROUS
²**iron·clad** \-ˌklad\ *n* **:** an armored naval vessel
iron curtain *n* **:** a political, military, and ideological barrier that cuts off and isolates an area; *specif* **:** one between an area under Soviet Russian control and other areas
iron·er \'ī(-ə)r-nər\ *n* **:** one that irons; *specif* **:** MANGLE
iron gray *n* **:** a nearly neutral very slightly greenish dark gray
iron horse *n* **:** a locomotive engine
iron·ic \ī-'rän-ik\ *adj* **1 :** relating to, containing, or constituting irony **2 :** given to irony — **iron·i·cal** \-i-kəl\ *adj* — **iron·i·cal·ly** \-k(ə-)lē\ *adv* — **iron·i·cal·ness** \-kəl-nəs\ *n*
iro·nist \'ī-rə-nəst\ *n* **:** a person given to irony
iron lung *n* **:** a device for artificial respiration in which rhythmic alternations in the air pressure in a chamber surrounding a patient's chest force air into and out of the lungs
iron·mas·ter \'ī(-ə)rn-ˌmas-tər\ *n* **:** a manufacturer of iron
iron·mon·ger \-ˌməŋ-gər, -ˌmäŋ-\ *n, Brit* **:** a dealer in iron and hardware — **iron·mon·gery** \-g(ə-)rē\ *n*
iron pyrites *n* **:** PYRITE — called also *iron pyrite*
iron·stone \'ī(-ə)rn-ˌstōn\ *n* **:** a hard sedimentary rock rich in iron; *esp* **:** a siderite in a coal region
iron·ware \-ˌwa(ə)r, -ˌwe(ə)r\ *n* **:** articles made of iron
iron·wood \-ˌwu̇d\ *n* **1 :** any of numerous trees and shrubs with exceptionally tough or hard wood **2 :** the wood of an ironwood
iron·work \-ˌwərk\ *n* **1 :** work in iron **2** *pl but sing or pl in constr* **:** a mill or building where iron or steel is smelted or heavy iron or steel products are made — **iron·work·er** \-ˌwər-kər\ *n*
iro·ny \'ī-rə-nē\ *n* [L *ironia*, fr. Gk *eirōnia*, fr. *eirōn* dissembler] **1 :** a pretense of ignorance and of willingness to learn from another assumed in order to make the other's false conceptions conspicuous by adroit questioning — called also *Socratic irony* **2 a :** the use of words to express something other than and esp. the opposite of the literal meaning **b :** a usu. humorous or sardonic literary style or form characterized by irony **c :** an ironic expression or utterance **3 a** (1) **:** incongruity between the actual result of a sequence of events and the normal or expected result (2) **:** an event or result marked by such incongruity **b :** incongruity between a situation developed in a drama and the accompanying words or actions that is understood by the audience but not by the characters in the play — called also *dramatic irony, tragic irony* **4 :** an attitude of detached awareness of incongruity typical of the depictor or observer of an ironic situation **syn** see WIT

Ir·o·quoi·an \ˌir-ə-'kwȯi-ən\ *n* **1 :** a language family of eastern No. America including Cayuga, Cherokee, Erie, Mohawk, Onondaga, Oneida, Seneca, Tuscarora **2 :** a member of any of the peoples constituting the Iroquois — **Iroquoian** *adj*
Ir·o·quois \'ir-ə-ˌkwȯi\ *n, pl* **Iroquois** \-ˌkwȯi(z)\ [F, fr. Algonquian *Irinakhoiw*] **1 :** an Indian confederacy that consisted orig. of the Cayuga, Mohawk, Oneida, Onondaga, and Seneca of central New York and later included the Tuscarora **2 :** a member of any of the Iroquois peoples
ir·ra·di·ance \ir-'ād-ē-ən(t)s\ *n* **1 :** something emitted like rays of light **2 :** radiant flux density on a given surface usu. expressed in watts per square centimeter or square meter
ir·ra·di·an·cy \-ən-sē\ *n* **:** the quality or state of being irradiant
ir·ra·di·ant \-ənt\ *adj* **:** emitting rays of light
ir·ra·di·ate \ir-'ād-ē-ˌāt\ *vb* [L *irradiatus*, pp. of *irradiare*, fr. *in-* + *radius* ray] *vt* **1 a :** to cast rays of light upon **:** ILLUMINATE **b :** to enlighten intellectually or spiritually **c :** to affect or treat by radiant energy (as heat); *specif* **:** to treat by exposure to radiation **2 :** to emit like rays of light **:** RADIATE ~ *vi, archaic* **:** to emit rays **:** SHINE — **ir·ra·di·a·tive** \-ˌāt-iv\ *adj*
ir·ra·di·a·tion \(ˌ)ir-ˌād-ē-'ā-shən\ *n* **1 :** emission of radiant energy (as heat or light) **2 :** exposure to X rays, radium rays, or other radiation **3 :** IRRADIANCE 2
ir·rad·i·ca·ble \(')ir-'(r)ad-i-kə-bəl\ *adj* [ML *irradicabilis*, fr. L *in-* + *radic-, radix* root — more at ROOT] **:** impossible to eradicate **:** DEEP-ROOTED — **ir·rad·i·ca·bly** \-blē\ *adv*
¹**ir·ra·tio·nal** \(')ir-'(r)ash-nəl, -ən-ᵊl\ *adj* [ME, fr. L *irrationalis*, fr. *in-* + *rationalis* rational] **:** not rational: as **a** (1) **:** not endowed with reason or understanding (2) **:** lacking usual or normal mental clarity or coherence **b :** not governed by or according to reason ⟨~ fears⟩ **c** *in ancient prosody* (1) *of a syllable* **:** having a quantity other than that required by the meter (2) *of a foot* **:** containing such a syllable — **ir·ra·tio·nal·i·ty** \(ˌ)ir-ˌ(r)ash-ə-'nal-ət-ē\ *n* — **ir·ra·tio·nal·ly** \(')ir-'(r)ash-nə-lē, -ən-ᵊl-ē\ *adv* — **ir·ra·tio·nal·ness** *n*
syn IRRATIONAL, UNREASONABLE mean not governed or guided by reason. IRRATIONAL may imply actual mental derangement but more often suggests words or actions directly in conflict with reason ⟨*irrational* beliefs⟩ UNREASONABLE suggests guidance by some force other than reason (as self-will, rage) that makes one deficient in good sense ⟨*unreasonable* extravagance⟩
²**irrational** *n* **1 :** an irrational being **2 :** a real number that is not expressible as the quotient of two integers
ir·ra·tio·nal·ism \(')ir-'(r)ash-nəl-ˌiz-əm, -ən-ᵊl-\ *n* **:** a system emphasizing intuition, instinct, feeling, or faith rather than reason or holding that the universe is governed by irrational forces — **ir·ra·tio·nal·ist** \-əst\ *n or adj* — **ir·ra·tio·nal·is·tic** \(ˌ)ir-ˌ(r)ash-nəl-'is-tik, -ən-ᵊl-\ *adj*
ir·re·claim·able \ˌir-i-'klā-mə-bəl\ *adj* **:** incapable of being reclaimed — **ir·re·claim·ably** \-blē\ *adv*
ir·rec·on·cil·abil·i·ty \(ˌ)ir-ˌ(r)ek-ən-ˌsī-lə-'bil-ət-ē\ *n* **:** the quality or state of being irreconcilable
¹**ir·rec·on·cil·able** \(ˌ)ir-ˌ(r)ek-ən-'sī-lə-bəl, (')ir-'(r)ek-ən-ˌ\ *adj* **:** impossible to reconcile — **ir·rec·on·cil·able·ness** *n* — **ir·rec·on·cil·ably** \-blē\ *adv*
²**irreconcilable** *n* **:** a person who opposes compromise or collaboration
ir·re·cov·er·able \ˌir-i-'kəv-(ə-)rə-bəl\ *adj* **:** not capable of being recovered or rectified **:** IRREPARABLE — **ir·re·cov·er·able·ness** *n* — **ir·re·cov·er·ably** \-blē\ *adv*
ir·re·cu·sa·ble \ˌir-i-'kyü-zə-bəl\ *adj* [LL *irrecusabilis*, fr. L *in-* + *recusare* to reject, refuse — more at RECUSANCY] **:** not subject to exception or rejection — **ir·re·cu·sa·bly** \-blē\ *adv*
ir·re·deem·able \ˌir-i-'dē-mə-bəl\ *adj* **1 :** not redeemable: as **a :** not terminable by payment of the principal ⟨~ bond⟩ **b :** INCONVERTIBLE **a 2 a :** admitting of no change **b :** insusceptible of redemption or reform — **ir·re·deem·ably** \-blē\ *adv*
ir·re·den·ta \ˌir-i-'dent-ə\ *n* [It *Italia irredenta* Italian-speaking territory not incorporated in Italy, lit., unredeemed Italy] **:** a territory historically or ethnically related to one political unit but presently subject to another
ir·re·den·tism \-'den-ˌtiz-əm\ *n* **:** a political principle or policy directed toward the incorporation of an irredenta within the boundaries of a political unit — **ir·re·den·tist** \-'dent-əst\ *n or adj*
ir·re·duc·ibil·i·ty \ˌir-i-ˌd(y)ü-sə-'bil-ət-ē\ *n* **:** the quality or state of being irreducible
ir·re·duc·ible \-'d(y)ü-sə-bəl\ *adj* **:** impossible to bring into a desired, normal, or simpler state ⟨~ equations⟩ — **ir·re·duc·ibly** \-blē\ *adv*
ir·re·flex·ive \ˌir-i-'flek-siv\ *adj* **:** not reflexive
ir·ref·ra·ga·bil·i·ty \(ˌ)ir-ˌ(r)ef-rə-gə-'bil-ət-ē\ *n* **:** the quality or state of being irrefragable
ir·ref·ra·ga·ble \(')ir-'(r)ef-rə-gə-bəl\ *adj* [LL *irrefragabilis*, fr. L *in-* + *refragari* to oppose, fr. *re-* + *-fragari* (as in *suffragari* to vote for); akin to L *suffragium* suffrage] **:** impossible to deny or refute **:** INVIOLABLE — **ir·ref·ra·ga·bly** \-blē\ *adv*
ir·re·fran·gi·ble \ˌir-i-'fran-jə-bəl\ *adj* **:** not capable of being refracted — used of visible light and other radiations
ir·re·fut·abil·i·ty \ˌir-i-ˌfyüt-ə-'bil-ət-ē, (ˌ)ir-ˌ(r)ef-yət-\ *n* **:** the quality or state of being irrefutable
ir·re·fut·able \ˌir-i-'fyüt-ə-bəl, (')ir-'(r)ef-yət-\ *adj* [LL *irrefutabilis*, fr. L *in-* + *refutare* to refute] **:** impossible to refute **:** INCONTROVERTIBLE — **ir·re·fut·ably** \-blē\ *adv*
ir·re·gard·less \ˌir-i-'gärd-ləs\ *adv* [prob. blend of *irrespective* and *regardless*] *nonstand* **:** REGARDLESS
¹**ir·reg·u·lar** \(')ir-'(r)eg-yə-lər\ *adj* [ME *irreguler*, fr. MF, fr. LL *irregularis* not in accordance with rule, fr. L *in-* + *regularis* regular] **1 a :** behaving without regard to established laws, customs, or moral principles **b :** not belonging to some particular group or organized body **2 a :** failing to accord with what is usual, proper, accepted, or right **b :** not conforming to the normal or usual manner of inflection ⟨*sell, cast, feed* are ~ verbs⟩; *specif* **:** STRONG **c** (1) **:** improper or inadequate because of failure to conform to a prescribed course (2) **:** celebrated without either proclamation of the banns or publication of intention to marry **:** CLANDESTINE ⟨~ marriage⟩ **d :** not belonging to the regular army organization but raised for a special purpose ⟨~ troops⟩ **3 :** lacking perfect symmetry or evenness; *specif* **:** ZYGOMORPHIC ⟨~ flowers⟩ **4 :** lacking continuity or regularity esp. of occurrence or activity — **ir·reg·u·lar·ly** *adv*
syn ANOMALOUS, UNNATURAL: IRREGULAR implies not conforming to a law or regulation imposed for the sake of uniformity in method,

practice, or conduct ⟨*irregular* behavior⟩ ANOMALOUS implies not conforming to what might be expected because of the class or type to which it belongs or the laws that govern its existence ⟨*anomalous* situation⟩ UNNATURAL suggests what is contrary to nature or to principles or standards felt to be essential to the well-being of civilized society ⟨*unnatural* cruelty⟩

²irregular *n* **:** one that is irregular: as **a :** a soldier who is not a member of a regular military force **b** *pl* **:** merchandise that has imperfections or that falls below the manufacturer's usual standard or specifications

ir·reg·u·lar·i·ty \(,)ir-,(r)eg-yə-'lar-ət-ē\ *n* **1 :** the quality or state of being irregular **2 :** something (as dishonest conduct) that is irregular

ir·rel·a·tive \(')ir-'(r)el-ət-iv\ *adj* **:** not relative: **a :** UNRELATED **b :** IRRELEVANT — **ir·rel·a·tive·ly** *adv*

ir·rel·e·vance \(')ir-'(r)el-ə-vən(t)s\ *or* **ir·rel·e·van·cy** \-vən-sē\ *n* **1 :** the quality or state of being irrelevant **2 :** something irrelevant

ir·rel·e·vant \-vənt\ *adj* **:** not relevant **:** INAPPLICABLE — **ir·rel·e·vant·ly** *adv*

ir·re·li·gion \,ir-i-'lij-ən\ *n* [MF or L; MF, fr. L *irreligion-, irreligio,* fr. *in-* + *religion-, religio* religion] **:** the quality or state of being irreligious — **ir·re·li·gion·ist** \-'lij-(ə-)nəst\ *n*

ir·re·li·gious \-'lij-əs\ *adj* **1 :** lacking religious emotions, doctrines, or practices **2 :** indicating lack of religion — **ir·re·li·gious·ly** *adv*

ir·re·me·able \(')ir-'(r)ē-mē-ə-bəl\ *adj* [L *irremeabilis,* fr. *in-* + *remeare* to go back, fr. *re-* + *meare* to go — more at PERMEATE] *archaic* **:** offering no possibility of return

ir·re·me·di·a·ble \,ir-i-'mēd-ē-ə-bəl\ *adj* [L *irremediabilis,* fr. *in-* + *remediabilis* remediable] **:** not remediable; *specif* **:** INCURABLE — **ir·re·me·di·a·ble·ness** *n* — **ir·re·me·di·a·bly** \-blē\ *adv*

ir·re·mov·abil·i·ty \,ir-i-,mü-və-'bil-ət-ē\ *n* **:** the quality or state of being irremovable

ir·re·mov·able \-'mü-və-bəl\ *adj* **:** not removable — **ir·re·mov·ably** \-blē\ *adv*

ir·rep·a·ra·ble \(')ir-'(r)ep-(ə-)rə-bəl\ *adj* [ME, fr. MF, fr. L *irreparabilis,* fr. *in-* + *reparabilis* reparable] **:** not reparable **:** IRRETRIEVABLE — **ir·rep·a·ra·ble·ness** *n* — **ir·rep·a·ra·bly** \-blē\ *adv*

ir·re·peal·able \,ir-i-'pē-lə-bəl\ *adj* **:** not repealable

ir·re·place·able \-'plā-sə-bəl\ *adj* **:** not replaceable

ir·re·press·ibil·i·ty \,ir-i-,pres-ə-'bil-ət-ē\ *n* **:** the quality or state of being irrepressible

ir·re·press·ible \-'pres-ə-bəl\ *adj* **:** impossible to repress, restrain, or control — **ir·re·press·ibly** \-blē\ *adv*

ir·re·proach·able \-'prō-chə-bəl\ *adj* **:** not reproachable **:** BLAMELESS — **ir·re·proach·able·ness** *n* — **ir·re·proach·ably** \-blē\ *adv*

ir·re·sist·ibil·i·ty \,ir-ə-,zis-tə-'bil-ət-ē\ *n* **:** the quality or state of being irresistible

ir·re·sist·ible \-'zis-tə-bəl\ *adj* **:** impossible to successfully resist — **ir·re·sist·ible·ness** *n* — **ir·re·sist·ibly** \-blē\ *adv*

ir·re·sol·u·ble \,ir-i-'zäl-yə-bəl\ *adj* [L *irresolubilis,* fr. *in-* + *resolvere* to resolve] **:** INSOLUBLE

ir·res·o·lute \(')ir-'(r)ez-ə-,lüt, -lət\ *adj* **:** uncertain how to act or proceed **:** VACILLATING — **ir·res·o·lute·ly** \-,lüt-lē, -lət-; (,)ir-,(r)ez-ə-'lüt-\ *adv* — **ir·res·o·lute·ness** \-,lüt-nəs, -lət-, -'lüt-\ *n* — **ir·res·o·lu·tion** \(,)ir-,(r)ez-ə-'lü-shən\ *n*

ir·re·solv·able \,ir-i-'zäl-və-bəl, -'zȯl-\ *adj* **:** incapable of being resolved; *esp* **:** not analyzable

ir·re·spec·tive \,ir-i-'spek-tiv\ *adj* **:** having no regard for persons, conditions, or consequences — **ir·re·spec·tive·ly** *adv*

irrespective of *prep* **:** without regard to **:** regardless of

ir·re·spi·rable \(')ir-'(r)es-p(ə-)rə-bəl, ,ir-i-'spī-rə-\ *adj* [F, fr. LL *irrespirabilis,* fr. L *in-* + *respirare* to breathe — more at RESPIRE] **:** unfit for breathing

ir·re·spon·si·bil·i·ty \,ir-i-,spän(t)-sə-'bil-ət-ē\ *n* **:** the quality or state of being irresponsible

ir·re·spon·si·ble \-'spän(t)-sə-bəl\ *adj* **:** not responsible: as **a :** not answerable to higher authority **b :** said or done with no sense of responsibility **c :** lacking a sense of responsibility **d :** unable esp. mentally or financially to bear responsibility — **ir·re·spon·si·ble·ness** *n* — **ir·re·spon·si·bly** \-blē\ *adv*

ir·re·spon·sive \-'spän(t)-siv\ *adj* **:** not responsive; *esp* **:** not able, ready, or inclined to respond — **ir·re·spon·sive·ness** *n*

ir·re·triev·able \,ir-i-'trē-və-bəl\ *adj* **:** not retrievable **:** IRRECOVERABLE — **ir·re·triev·ably** \-blē\ *adv*

ir·rev·er·ence \(')ir-'(r)ev-(ə-)rən(t)s, -'(r)ev-ərn(t)s\ *n* **1 :** lack of reverence **2 :** an irreverent act or utterance

ir·rev·er·ent \-'(r)ev-(ə-)rənt, -'(r)ev-ərnt\ *adj* [L *irreverent-, irreverens,* fr. *in-* + *reverent- reverens* reverent] **:** showing lack of reverence **:** DISRESPECTFUL — **ir·rev·er·ent·ly** *adv*

ir·re·vers·ibil·i·ty \,ir-i-,vər-sə-'bil-ət-ē\ *n* **:** the quality or state of being irreversible

ir·re·vers·ible \-'vər-sə-bəl\ *adj* **:** incapable of being reversed — **ir·re·vers·ibly** \-blē\ *adv*

ir·re·vo·ca·bil·i·ty \(,)ir-,(r)ev-ə-kə-'bil-ət-ē *also* ,ir-i-,vō-kə-\ *n* **:** the quality or state of being irrevocable

ir·re·vo·ca·ble \(')ir-'(r)ev-ə-kə-bəl *also* ,ir-i-'vō-kə-\ *adj* [ME, fr. L *irrevocabilis,* fr. *in-* + *revocabilis* revocable] **:** incapable of being revoked **:** UNALTERABLE — **ir·re·vo·ca·ble·ness** *n* — **ir·re·vo·ca·bly** \-blē\ *adv*

irridenta *var of* IRREDENTA

ir·ri·gate \'ir-ə-,gāt\ *vb* [L *irrigatus,* pp. of *irrigare,* fr. *in-* + *rigare* to water] *vt* **1 :** WET, MOISTEN; *esp* **:** to supply (as land) with water by artificial means **2 :** to refresh as if by watering ~ *vi* **:** to practice irrigation — **ir·ri·ga·tion** \,ir-ə-'gā-shən\ *n* — **ir·ri·ga·tor** \'ir-ə-,gāt-ər\ *n*

ir·ri·ta·bil·i·ty \,ir-ət-ə-'bil-ət-ē\ *n* **:** the quality or state of being irritable: as **a :** quick excitability to annoyance, impatience, or anger **:** PETULANCE **b :** abnormal or excessive excitability of an organ or part of the body **c :** the property of protoplasm and of living organisms that permits them to react to stimuli

ir·ri·ta·ble \'ir-ət-ə-bəl\ *adj* **:** capable of being irritated — **ir·ri·ta·ble·ness** *n* — **ir·ri·ta·bly** \-blē\ *adv*

¹ir·ri·tant \'ir-ə-tənt\ *adj* **:** IRRITATING; *specif* **:** tending to produce physical irritation

²irritant *n* **:** something that irritates or excites

ir·ri·tate \'ir-ə-,tāt\ *vb* [L *irritatus,* pp. of *irritare*] *vt* **1 :** to excite impatience, anger, or displeasure in **:** ANNOY **2 :** to induce irritability in or of ~ *vi* **:** to cause or induce displeasure or irritation **syn** EXASPERATE, NETTLE, PROVOKE, ROIL *or* RILE, PEEVE: IRRITATE implies an often gradual arousing of angry feelings that may range from impatience to rage; EXASPERATE suggests galling annoyance or vexation and the arousing of extreme impatience; NETTLE suggests a light stinging or piquing; PROVOKE implies an arousing of strong annoyance or vexation that may excite to action; ROIL *or* RILE implies inducing an angry or resentful agitation; PEEVE suggests arousing fretful often petty or querulous irritation

ir·ri·tat·ed *adj* **:** roughened, reddened, or inflamed by an irritant

ir·ri·ta·tion \,ir-ə-'tā-shən\ *n* **1 a :** the act of irritating **b :** something that irritates **c :** state of being irritated **:** ANNOYANCE **2 :** a condition of irritability, soreness, roughness, or inflammation of a bodily part

ir·ri·ta·tive \'ir-ə-,tāt-iv\ *adj* **1 :** serving to excite **:** IRRITATING **2 :** accompanied with or produced by irritation

ir·rupt \(')ir-'(r)əpt\ *vi* [L *irruptus,* pp. of *irrumpere,* lit., to break in, fr. *in-* + *rumpere* to break — more at RUPTURE] **1 :** to rush in forcibly or violently **2** *of a natural population* **:** to undergo a sudden upsurge in numbers esp. when natural ecological balances and checks are disturbed — **ir·rup·tion** \(')ir-'(r)əp-shən\ *n*

ir·rup·tive \(')ir-'(r)əp-tiv\ *adj* **1 :** irrupting or tending to irrupt **2** *of an igneous rock* **:** INTRUSIVE **3 :** marked by or undergoing irruption — **ir·rup·tive·ly** *adv*

is [ME, fr. OE; akin to OHG *ist* is (fr. *sīn* to be), L *est* (fr. *esse* to be), Gk *esti* (fr. *einai* to be)] *pres 3d sing of* BE, *dial pres 1st & 2d sing of* BE, *substand pres pl of* BE

is- *or* **iso-** *comb form* [LL, fr. Gk, fr. *isos* equal] **1 :** equal **:** homogeneous **:** uniform ⟨*is*acoustic⟩ **2 :** isomeric ⟨*iso*propyl⟩ **3 :** for or from different individuals of the same species ⟨*iso*agglutination⟩

Isaac \'ī-zik, -zək\ *n* [LL, fr. Heb *Yiṣḥāq*] **:** a Hebrew patriarch, son of Abraham and father of Jacob

Isa·iah \ī-'zā-ə, *chiefly Brit* -'zī-\ *or* **Isa·ias** \-əs\ *n* [Heb *Yĕsha'-yāhū*] **:** a major Hebrew prophet in Judah about 740 to 701 B.C.

is·al·lo·bar \(')ī-'sal-ə-,bär\ *n* [ISV *is-* + *all-* + *-bar* (as in *isobar*)] **:** an imaginary line or a line on a chart connecting the places of equal change of atmospheric pressure within a specified time — **is·al·lo·bar·ic** \,ī-,sal-ə-'bär-ik, -'bar-\ *adj*

isch·emia \is-'kē-mē-ə\ *n* [NL *ischaemia,* fr. *ischaemus* styptic, fr. Gk *ischaimos,* fr. *ischein* to restrain + *haima* blood; akin to Gk *echein* to hold — more at SCHEME] **:** localized tissue anemia due to obstruction of the inflow of arterial blood — **isch·emic** \-mik\ *adj*

is·chi·al \'is-kē-əl\ *adj* **:** of, relating to, or situated near the ischium

is·chi·um \-əm\ *n, pl* **is·chia** \-ə\ [L, hip joint, fr. Gk *ischion*] **:** the dorsal and posterior of the three principal bones composing either half of the pelvis

-ise \,īz\ *vb suffix, chiefly Brit* **:** -IZE

Iseult \i-'sült, -'zült\ *var of* ISOLDE

-ish \ish\ *adj suffix* [ME, fr. OE *-isc;* akin to OHG *-isc,* -ish, Gk *-iskos,* dim. suffix] **1 :** of, relating to, or being — chiefly in adjectives indicating nationality or ethnic group ⟨Finn*ish*⟩ **2 a :** characteristic of ⟨boy*ish*⟩ **:** having the undesirable qualities of ⟨mul*ish*⟩ **b (1) :** having a touch or trace of ⟨summer*ish*⟩ **:** somewhat ⟨purpl*ish*⟩ **(2) :** having the approximate age of ⟨forty*ish*⟩ **(3) :** being or occurring at the approximate time of ⟨eight*ish*⟩

Ish·ma·el \'ish-mē-əl\ *n* [Heb *Yishmā'ēl*] **1 :** the outcast son of Abraham and Hagar **2 :** a social outcast

Ish·ma·el·ite \-ə-,līt\ *n* **1 :** a descendant of Ishmael **2 :** ISHMAEL 2 — **Ish·ma·el·it·ish** \-,līt-ish\ *adj* — **Ish·ma·el·it·ism** \-,līt-,iz-əm\ *n*

isin·glass \'īz-ᵊn-,glas, 'ī-ziŋ-\ *n* [prob. by folk etymology fr. obs. D *huizenblas,* fr. MD *huusblase,* fr. *huus* sturgeon + *blase* bladder] **1 :** a semitransparent whitish very pure gelatin prepared from the air bladders of sturgeons and some other fishes and used esp. as a clarifying agent and in jellies and glue **2 :** MICA

Isis \'ī-səs\ *n* [L *Isid-, Isis,* fr. Gk, fr. Egypt *ist*] **:** the Egyptian goddess of motherhood and fertility and wife of Osiris

Is·lam \is-'läm, iz-, -'lam, 'is-, 'iz-,\ *n* [Ar *islām* submission (to the will of God)] **1 :** the religious faith of Muslims including belief in Allah as the sole deity and in Muhammad as his prophet **2 a :** the civilization erected upon Islamic faith **b :** the group of modern nations in which Islam is the dominant religion — **Is·lam·ic** \is-'läm-ik, iz-, -'lam-\ *adj* — **Is·lam·ics** \-iks\ *n pl but sing or pl in constr* — **Is·lam·ism** \-,iz-əm; 'iz-lə-,miz-\ *n* — **Is·lam·ize** \'iz-lə-,mīz; is-'läm-,īz, iz-'läm-, -'lam-\ *vt*

¹is·land \'ī-lənd\ *n* [alter. of earlier *iland,* fr. ME, fr. OE *īgland;* akin to ON *eyland* island; both fr. a prehistoric NGmc-WGmc compound whose first constituent is represented by OE *īg* island (akin to OE *ēa* river, L *aqua* water) and whose second constituent is represented by OE *land*] **1 :** a tract of land surrounded by water and smaller than a continent **2 :** something resembling an island in isolation **3 a :** SAFETY ISLAND **b :** SAFETY ZONE **4 :** a superstructure on the deck of an aircraft carrier or other ship **5 :** an isolated group or area; *specif* **:** an isolated ethnological group

²island *vt* **1 a :** to make into or as if into an island **b :** to dot with or as if with islands **2 :** ISOLATE

is·land·er \'ī-lən-dər\ *n* **:** a native or inhabitant of an island

island universe *n* **:** a galaxy other than the Milky Way

¹isle \'ī(ə)l\ *n* [ME, fr. OF, fr. L *insula*] **:** ISLAND; *esp* **:** a small island

²isle *vt* **1 :** to make an isle of **2 :** to place on or as if on an isle

is·let \'ī-lət\ *n* **:** a little island

islet of Lang·er·hans \-'läŋ-ər-,hän(t)s, -,hänz\ [Paul *Langerhans* †1888 G physician] **:** any of the groups of small slightly granular endocrine cells that form anastomosing trabeculae among the tubules and alveoli of the pancreas and secrete insulin

ism \'iz-əm\ *n* [*-ism*] **:** a distinctive doctrine, cause, or theory

-ism \,iz-əm; *see* m *in Guide*\ *n suffix* [ME *-isme,* fr. MF & L; MF, partly fr. L *-isma* (fr. Gk) & partly fr. L *-ismus,* fr. Gk *-ismos;* Gk *-isma* & *-ismos* fr. verbs in *-izein* -ize] **1 a :** act **:** practice **:** process ⟨critic*ism*⟩ ⟨plagiar*ism*⟩ **b :** manner of action or behavior characteristic of a (specified) person or thing ⟨animal*ism*⟩ **2 a :** state **:** condition **:** property ⟨barbarian*ism*⟩ **b :** abnormal state or con-

dition resulting from excess of a (specified) thing ⟨alcohol*ism*⟩ or marked by resemblance to (such) a person or thing ⟨mongol*ism*⟩ **3 a :** doctrine **:** theory **:** cult ⟨Buddh*ism*⟩ **b :** adherence to a system or a class of principles ⟨stoic*ism*⟩ **4 :** characteristic or peculiar feature or trait ⟨colloquial*ism*⟩

isn't \'iz-ᵊnt\ **:** is not

iso·ag·glu·ti·na·tion \ˌī-(ˌ)sō-ə-ˌglüt-ᵊn-'ā-shən\ *n* **:** agglutination of an agglutinogen of one individual by the serum of another of the same species — **iso·ag·glu·ti·na·tive** \-'glüt-ᵊn-ˌāt-iv\ *adj*

iso·ag·glu·ti·nin \-ᵊn-ən\ *n* **:** an agglutinin specific for the cells of another individual of the same species

iso·ag·glu·tin·o·gen \-ˌag-ˌlü-'tin-ə-jən\ *n* **:** a substance capable of provoking formation of or reacting with an isoagglutinin

iso·al·lox·a·zine \ˌī-(ˌ)sō-ə-'läk-sə-ˌzēn\ *n* **:** a yellow solid $C_{10}H_6N_4O_2$ that is the parent compound of riboflavin and other flavins

iso·an·ti·body \ˌī-(ˌ)sō-'ant-i-ˌbäd-ē\ *n* **:** an antibody against an antigen present in some members of a species that is produced by a member of the species lacking that antigen

iso·an·ti·gen \-'ant-i-jən\ *n* [ISV] **:** an antigen capable of inducing the production of an isoantibody — **iso·an·ti·gen·ic** \-ˌant-i-'jen-ik\ *adj*

iso·bar \'ī-sə-ˌbär\ *n* [ISV *is-* + *-bar* (fr. Gk *baros* weight); akin to Gk *barys* heavy — more at GRIEVE] **1 :** an imaginary line or a line on a map or chart connecting or marking places on the surface of the earth where the height of the barometer reduced to sea level is the same either at a given time or for a certain period **2 :** one of two or more atoms or elements having the same atomic weights or mass numbers but different atomic numbers — **iso·bar·ic** \ˌī-sə-'bär-ik, -'bar-\ *adj*

iso·bu·tyl·ene \ˌī-sō-'byüt-ᵊl-ˌēn\ *n* [ISV] **:** a gaseous butylene C_4H_8 used esp. in making butyl rubber and gasoline components

iso·chro·mat·ic \ˌī-sə-krō-'mat-ik\ *adj* [ISV] **:** ORTHOCHROMATIC

iso·chro·nal \ī-'säk-rən-ᵊl, ˌī-sə-'krōn-\ *adj* [Gk *isochronos*, fr. *is-* + *chronos* time] **:** uniform in time **:** having equal duration **:** recurring at regular intervals — **iso·chro·nal·ly** \-ᵊl-ē\ *adv* — **iso·chro·nism** \ī-'säk-rə-ˌniz-əm, ˌī-sə-'krō-\ *n*

iso·chro·nous \ī-'säk-rə-nəs, ˌī-sə-'krō-\ *adj* [Gk *isochronos*] **:** ISOCHRONAL — **iso·chro·nous·ly** *adv*

iso·chro·ous \ī-'säk-rə-wəs, ˌī-sə-'krō-əs\ *adj* [*is-* + Gk *chrōs* skin, color — more at CHROMATIC] **:** of the same color throughout

[1]**iso·cli·nal** \ˌī-sə-'klīn-ᵊl\ *adj* [ISV] **:** relating to, having, or indicating equality of inclination or dip — **iso·cli·nal·ly** \-ᵊl-ē\ *adv*

[2]**isoclinal** *n* **:** ISOCLINIC LINE

iso·cline \'ī-sə-ˌklīn\ *n* **:** an anticline or syncline so closely folded that the rock beds of the two sides have the same dip

iso·clin·ic \ˌī-sə-'klin-ik\ *adj* [ISV] **:** ISOCLINAL

isoclinic line *n* **:** a line on a map or chart joining points on the earth's surface at which a magnetic needle has the same inclination to the plumb line

iso·cy·a·nate \ˌī-sō-'sī-ə-ˌnāt, -nət\ *n* [ISV] **:** a salt or ester of isomeric cyanic acid HNCO used esp. in plastics and adhesives

iso·cy·clic \-'sī-klik, -'sik-lik\ *adj* [ISV] **:** having or being a ring composed of atoms of only one element

iso·di·a·met·ric \-ˌdī-ə-'me-trik\ *adj* [ISV] **:** having equal diameters

iso·di·mor·phism \-(ˌ)dī-'mȯr-ˌfiz-əm\ *n* [ISV] **:** isomorphism between the two forms severally of two dimorphous substances — **iso·di·mor·phous** \-fəs\ *adj*

iso·dose \'ī-sə-ˌdōs\ *adj* [ISV] **:** of or relating to points or zones in a medium that receive equal doses of radiation

iso·dy·nam·ic \ˌī-sō-(ˌ)dī-'nam-ik\ *adj* [ISV] **1 :** of or relating to equality of force **2 :** connecting points at which the magnetic intensity is the same ⟨~ line⟩

iso·elec·tric \ˌī-(ˌ)sō-i-'lek-trik\ *adj* [ISV] **1 :** having or representing zero difference of electric potential **2 :** being the pH at which the electrolyte will not migrate in an electrical field

iso·elec·tron·ic \-i-ˌlek-'trän-ik\ *adj* [ISV] **:** having the same number of electrons or valency electrons — **iso·elec·tron·i·cal·ly** \-i-k(ə-)lē\ *adv*

iso·ga·mete \ˌī-sō-gə-'mēt, -'gam-ˌēt\ *n* [ISV] **:** a gamete indistinguishable in form or size or behavior from another gamete with which it can unite to form a zygote — **iso·ga·met·ic** \-gə-'met-ik\ *adj*

isog·a·mous \ī-'säg-ə-məs\ *adj* [prob. fr. (assumed) NL *isogamus*, fr. *is-* + *-gamus* -gamous] **:** having or involving isogametes — **isog·a·my** \-mē\ *n*

iso·gloss \'ī-sə-ˌgläs, -ˌglȯs *also* 'ī-zə-\ *n* [ISV *is-* + Gk *glōssa* language — more at GLOSS] **1 a :** a boundary line between places or regions that differ in a particular linguistic feature **b :** a line on a map representing an isogloss **2 :** a linguistic feature shared by some but not all of the speakers of a dialect, language, or group of related languages — **iso·gloss·al** \ˌī-sə-'gläs-əl, -'glȯ-səl\ *adj*

[1]**iso·gon·ic** \ˌī-sə-'gän-ik\ *or* **iso·go·nal** \ī-'säg-ən-ᵊl, ˌī-sə-'gōn-\ *adj* [ISV *is-* + Gk *gōnia* angle — more at -GON] **:** of, relating to, or having equal angles

[2]**isogonic** *or* **isogonal** *n* **:** ISOGONIC LINE

[3]**isogonic** *adj* **:** of, relating to, or marked by isogony

isogonic line *n* **:** an imaginary line or a line on a map joining points on the earth's surface at which the magnetic declination is the same

isog·o·ny \ī-'säg-ə-nē\ *n* [*is-* + *-gony*] **:** equivalent relative growth of parts such that size relations remain constant

iso·gram \'ī-sə-ˌgram\ *n* **:** a line on a map or chart along which there is a constant value

iso·hel \'ī-sō-ˌhel\ *n* [*is-* + Gk *hēlios* sun — more at SOLAR] **:** a line drawn on a map or chart connecting places of equal duration of sunshine

iso·he·mol·y·sis \ˌī-(ˌ)sō-hi-'mäl-ə-səs\ *n* [NL] **:** lysis of the red blood cells of one individual by antibodies in the serum of another of the same species

iso·hy·et \ˌī-sō-'hī-ət\ *n* [ISV *is-* + Gk *hyetos* rain — more at HYET-] **:** an isohyetal line on a map or chart

iso·hy·e·tal \-'hī-ət-ᵊl\ *adj* **:** relating to or indicating equal rainfall

iso·late \'ī-sə-ˌlāt, 'is-ə-\ *vt* [back-formation fr. *isolated* set apart, fr. F *isolé*, fr. It *isolato*, fr. *isola* island, fr. L *insula*] **1 :** to set apart from others; *also* **:** QUARANTINE **2 :** to select from among others; *esp* **:** to separate from another substance so as to obtain pure or in a free state **3 :** INSULATE

iso·la·tion \ˌī-sə-'lā-shən, ˌis-ə-\ *n* **:** the action of isolating **:** the condition of being isolated **syn** see SOLITUDE

iso·la·tion·ism \-shə-ˌniz-əm\ *n* **:** a policy of national isolation by abstention from alliances and other international political and economic relations — **iso·la·tion·ist** \-sh(ə-)nəst\ *n or adj*

Isol·de \i-'zōl-də, -'zȯl-\ *n* [OF *Isolt*, *Iseut*] **1 :** an Irish princess married to King Mark of Cornwall and loved by Tristram **2 :** the daughter of the King of Brittany married to Tristram

iso·leu·cine \ˌī-sō-'lü-ˌsēn\ *n* [ISV] **:** a crystalline essential amino acid $C_6H_{13}NO_2$ isomeric with leucine

iso·line \'ī-(ˌ)sō-ˌlīn\ *n* **:** ISOGRAM

isol·o·gous \ī-'säl-ə-gəs\ *adj* [ISV *is-* + *-logous* (as in *homologous*)] **:** relating to or being any of two or more compounds of related structure and a characteristic difference of composition other than CH_2 — **iso·logue** *or* **iso·log** \'ī-sə-ˌlȯg, -ˌläg\ *n*

iso·mag·net·ic \ˌī-(ˌ)sō-mag-'net-ik\ *adj* [ISV] **1 :** of or relating to points of equal magnetic intensity or of equal value of a component of such intensity **2 :** connecting isomagnetic points ⟨~ line on a map⟩

iso·mer \'ī-sə-mər\ *n* [ISV, back-formation fr. *isomeric*] **:** a compound, radical, ion, or nuclide isomeric with one or more others

iso·mer·ic \ˌī-sə-'mer-ik\ *adj* [ISV, fr. Gk *isomerēs* equally divided, fr. *is-* + *meros* part — more at MERIT] **:** of, relating to, or exhibiting isomerism — **iso·mer·i·cal·ly** \-i-k(ə-)lē\ *adv*

isom·er·ism \ī-'säm-ə-ˌriz-əm\ *n* **1 :** the relation of two or more chemical compounds, radicals, or ions that contain the same numbers of atoms of the same elements but differ in structural arrangement and properties **2 :** the relation of two or more nuclides with the same mass numbers and atomic numbers but different energy states and rates of radioactive decay **3 :** the condition of being isomerous

isom·er·ous \-ə-rəs\ *adj* **:** having an equal number of parts (as ridges or markings); *specif* **:** having the members of each floral whorl equal in number

iso·met·ric \ˌī-sə-'me-trik\ *adj* **:** of, relating to, or characterized by equality of measure: as **a :** of, relating to, or being an isometric drawing or projection **b :** relating to or being a crystallographic system characterized by three equal axes at right angles — **iso·met·ri·cal** \-tri-kəl\ *adj* — **iso·met·ri·cal·ly** \-k(ə-)lē\ *adv*

isometric drawing *n* **:** the representation of an object in isometric projection but with lines parallel to the edges drawn in true length

isometric line *n* **1 :** a line drawn on a map and indicating a true constant value throughout its extent **2 :** a line representing changes of pressure or temperature under conditions of constant volume

isometric projection *n* **:** axonometric projection in which all three faces are equally inclined to the drawing surface so that all the edges are equally foreshortened

iso·met·rics \ˌī-sə-'me-triks\ *n pl but sing or pl in constr* **:** exercise or a system of exercises in which opposing muscles are so contracted that there is little shortening but great increase in tone of muscle fibers involved

iso·me·tro·pia \ˌī-sō-mi-'trō-pē-ə\ *n* [NL, fr. Gk *isometros* of equal measure (fr. *is-* + *metron* measure) + NL *-opia* — more at MEASURE] **:** equality in refraction in the two eyes

iso·morph \'ī-sə-ˌmȯrf\ *n* [ISV] **:** something identical with or similar to something else in form or structure: as **a :** one of two or more substances related by isomorphism **b :** an individual or group exhibiting isomorphism — **iso·mor·phic** \ˌī-sə-'mȯr-fik\ *adj*

iso·mor·phism \ˌī-sə-'mȯr-ˌfiz-əm\ *n* [ISV] **1 :** similarity in organisms of different ancestry resulting from convergence **2 a :** similarity of crystalline form between substances of similar composition **b :** HOMEOMORPHISM 1 **3 :** a one-to-one correspondence between two mathematical aggregates

iso·mor·phous \-fəs\ *adj* **:** ISOMORPHIC

iso·ni·a·zid \ˌī-sə-'nī-ə-zəd\ *n* [*iso*nicotinic acid hydr*azide*] **:** a crystalline compound $C_6H_7N_3O$ used in treating tuberculosis

ison·o·my \ī-'sän-ə-mē\ *n* [Gk *isonomia*, fr. *isonomos* characterized by isonomy, fr. *is-* + *nomos* right, law] **:** equality before the law

iso·oc·tane \ˌī-sō-'äk-ˌtān\ *n* [ISV] **:** an octane of branched-chain structure or a mixture of such octanes

iso·pi·es·tic \ˌī-sō-pē-'es-tik, -pī-\ *adj* [*is-* + Gk *piestos*, verbal of *piezein* to press] **:** of, relating to, or marked by equal pressure

iso·pleth \'ī-sə-ˌpleth\ *n* [ISV *is-* + Gk *plēthos* quantity; akin to Gk *plēthein* to be full — more at FULL] **1 :** an isogram on a graph showing the occurrence or frequency of a phenomenon as a function of two variables **2 :** a line on a map connecting points at which a given variable has a specified constant value

iso·pod \-ˌpäd\ *n* [deriv. of Gk *is-* + *pod-*, *pous* foot — more at FOOT] **:** any of a large order (Isopoda) of small sessile-eyed crustaceans in which the body is composed of seven free thoracic segments each bearing a pair of similar legs — **isopod** *adj* — **isop·o·dan** \ī-'säp-əd-ən\ *adj or n*

iso·prene \'ī-sə-ˌprēn\ *n* [prob. fr. *is-* + *propyl* + *-ene*] **:** a flammable liquid unsaturated hydrocarbon C_5H_8 used esp. in synthetic rubber — **iso·pre·noid** \ˌī-sə-'prē-ˌnȯid\ *adj or n*

iso·pro·pyl \-'prō-pəl\ *n* [ISV] **:** the alkyl radical $(CH_3)_2CH$— isomeric with normal propyl

isos·ce·les triangle \ī-ˌsäs-(ə-)ˌlēz-\ *n* [LL *isosceles* having two equal sides, fr. Gk *isoskelēs*, fr. *is-* + *skelos* leg — more at CYLINDER] **:** a triangle having two equal sides

iso·seis·mal \ˌī-sō-'sīz-məl\ *adj* **:** of, relating to, or marked by equal intensity of earthquake shock

is·os·mot·ic \ˌī-ˌsäs-'mät-ik, -ˌsäz-\ *adj* [ISV] **:** of, relating to, or exhibiting equal osmotic pressure

iso·spon·dy·lous \ˌī-sō-'spän-də-ləs\ *adj* [deriv. of Gk *isos* equal + Gk *spondylos* vertebra — more at SPONDYLITIS] **:** of or relating to an order (Isospondyli) of primitive soft-finned teleost fishes

iso·spo·rous \ˌī-sə-'spȯr-əs, -'spȯr-; ī-'säs-pə-rəs\ *adj* **:** producing sexual or asexual spores of but one kind — **iso·spo·ry** \'ī-sə-ˌspȯr-ē, -ˌspȯr-; ī-'säs-pə-rē\ *n*

isos·ta·sy \ī-'säs-tə-sē\ *n* [ISV *is-* + Gk *-stasia* condition of standing, fr. *histanai* to cause to stand — more at STAND] **1 :** the quality or state of being subjected to equal pressure from every side **2 :** general equilibrium in the earth's crust maintained by a yielding flow of rock material beneath the surface under gravitative stress — **iso·stat·ic** \ˌī-sə-'stat-ik\ *adj*

iso·therm \'ī-sə-ˌthərm\ *n* [F *isotherme*, adj.] **1 :** a line on a map or chart of the earth's surface connecting points having the same temperature at a given time or the same mean temperature

for a given period **2 :** a line on a chart representing changes of volume or pressure under conditions of constant temperature

iso·ther·mal \ˌī-sə-ˈthər-məl\ *adj* [F *isotherme,* fr. *is-* + Gk *thermos* hot — more at WARM] **1 :** of, relating to, or marked by equality of temperature **2 :** of, relating to, or marked by changes of volume or pressure under conditions of constant temperature

iso·ton·ic \ˌī-sə-ˈtän-ik\ *adj* [ISV] **1 :** of, relating to, or exhibiting equal tension **2 :** ISOSMOTIC — used of solutions — **iso·ton·i·cal·ly** \-i-k(ə-)lē\ *adv* — **iso·to·nic·i·ty** \ˌī-sə-tō-ˈnis-ət-ē\ *n*

iso·tope \ˈī-sə-ˌtōp *also* ˈī-zə-\ *n* [*is-* + Gk *topos* place — more at TOPIC] **1 :** any of two or more species of atoms of a chemical element with the same atomic number and position in the periodic table and nearly identical chemical behavior but with differing atomic mass or mass number and different behavior in the mass spectrograph, in radioactive transformations, and in physical properties **2 :** NUCLIDE — **iso·to·pic** \ˌī-sə-ˈtäp-ik, -ˈtō-pik *also* ˌī-zə-\ *adj* — **iso·to·pi·cal·ly** \-ˈtäp-i-k(ə-)lē, -ˈtō-pi-\ *adv* — **iso·to·py** \ˈī-sə-ˌtō-pē, -zə-; ī-ˈsät-ə-pē, -ˈzät-\ *n*

iso·trop·ic \ˌī-sə-ˈträp-ik\ *adj* [ISV] **:** exhibiting properties (as velocity of light transmission) with the same values when measured along axes in all directions ⟨an ~ crystal⟩ — **isot·ro·py** \ī-ˈsä-trə-pē\ *n*

Is·ra·el \ˈiz-rē-əl\ *n* [ME, fr. OE, fr. LL, fr. Gk *Israēl,* fr. Heb *Yiśrāʼēl*] **1 :** JACOB **2 :** the Jewish people **3 :** God's chosen people — **Israel** *adj*

1Is·rae·li \iz-ˈrā-lē\ *adj* [NHeb *yiśrĕʼēlī,* fr. Heb, Israelite, n. & adj., fr. *Yiśrāʼēl*] **:** of or relating to the republic of Israel

2Israeli *n, pl* **Israelis** *also* **Israeli :** a native or inhabitant of the republic of Israel

Is·ra·el·ite \ˈiz-rē-ə-ˌlīt\ *n* [ME, fr. LL *Israelita,* fr. Gk *Israēlitēs,* fr. *Israēl*] **:** a descendant of the Hebrew patriarch Jacob; *specif* **:** a native or inhabitant of the ancient northern kingdom of Israel — **Israelite** *or* **Is·ra·el·it·ish** \-ˌlīt-ish\ *adj*

Is·sa·char \ˈis-ə-ˌkär\ *n* [LL, fr. Gk, fr. Heb *Yiśśākhār*] **:** a son of Jacob and ancestor of one of the tribes of Israel

is·su·able \ˈish-ü-ə-bəl\ *adj* **1 :** open to contest, debate, or litigation **2 :** authorized for issue **3 :** possible as a result or consequence — **is·su·ably** \-blē\ *adv*

is·su·ance \ˈish-ü-ən(t)s\ *n* **:** ISSUE

is·su·ant \-ənt\ *adj* **1** *archaic* **:** coming forth **:** EMERGING **2** *of a heraldic animal* **:** rising with only the upper part visible

1is·sue \ˈish-(ˌ)ü, ˈish-ü, *chiefly Brit* ˈis-(ˌ)yü, -yü\ *n* [ME, exit, proceeds, fr. MF, fr. OF, fr. *issir* to come out, go out, fr. L *exire* to go out, fr. *ex-* + *ire* to go; akin to Goth *iddja* he went, Gk *ienai* to go, Skt *eti* he goes] **1** *pl* **:** proceeds from a source of revenue (as an estate) **2 :** the action of going, coming, or flowing out **:** EGRESS, EMERGENCE **3 :** a means or place of going out **:** EXIT, OUTLET **4 :** OFFSPRING, PROGENY **5 a :** final outcome **:** RESULT **b** *obs* **:** a final conclusion or decision about something arrived at after consideration **c** *archaic* **:** TERMINATION, END ⟨hope that his enterprise would have a prosperous ~ —T.B.Macaulay⟩ **6 a :** a matter that is in dispute between two or more parties **:** a point of debate or controversy **b :** the point at which an unsettled matter is ready for a decision ⟨brought the matter to an ~⟩ **7 :** a discharge (as of blood) from the body **8 a :** something coming forth from a specified source ⟨~s of a disordered imagination⟩ **b** *obs* **:** DEED **9 a :** the act of officially giving out or printing (as new currency, supplies, an order) **:** PUBLICATION **b :** the thing or the whole quantity of things given out at one time ⟨new ~ of stamps⟩ ⟨stock ~⟩ **syn** see EFFECT — **at issue 1 :** in a state of controversy **:** in disagreement **2** *also* **in issue :** under discussion or in dispute

2issue *vi* **1 a :** to go, come, or flow out **b :** to come forth **:** EMERGE **c :** to come to an issue of law or fact in pleading **2 :** ACCRUE **3 :** to descend from a specified parent or ancestor **4 :** to be a consequence or final outcome **:** EMANATE, RESULT **5 :** to appear or become available through being officially put forth or distributed **:** appear through issuance or publication **6 :** EVENTUATE, TERMINATE ~ *vt* **1 :** to cause to come forth **:** DISCHARGE, EMIT **2 a :** to put forth or distribute officially ⟨government *issued* a new airmail stamp⟩ ⟨~ orders to advance⟩ **b :** to send out for sale or circulation **:** PUBLISH **syn** see SPRING — **is·su·er** *n*

1-ist \əst\ *n suffix* [ME *-iste,* fr. OF & L; OF *-iste,* fr. L *-ista, -istes,* fr. Gk *-istēs,* fr. verbs in *-izein* -ize] **1 a :** one that performs a (specified) action ⟨cycl*ist*⟩ **:** one that makes or produces ⟨novel*ist*⟩ **b :** one that plays a (specified) musical instrument ⟨harp*ist*⟩ **c :** one that operates a (specified) mechanical instrument or contrivance ⟨automobil*ist*⟩ **2 :** one that specializes in a (specified) art or science or skill ⟨geolog*ist*⟩ ⟨ventriloqu*ist*⟩ **3 :** one that adheres to or advocates a (specified) doctrine or system or code of behavior ⟨social*ist*⟩ ⟨royal*ist*⟩ ⟨hedon*ist*⟩ or that of a (specified) individual ⟨Calvin*ist*⟩ ⟨Darwin*ist*⟩

2-ist *adj suffix* **:** of, relating to, or characteristic of ⟨dilettant*ist*⟩

1isth·mi·an \ˈis-mē-ən\ *n* **1 :** a native or inhabitant of an isthmus **2** *cap* **:** a native or inhabitant of the Isthmus of Panama

2isthmian *adj* **:** of, relating to, or situated in or near an isthmus: as **a** *often cap* **:** of or relating to the Isthmus of Corinth in Greece or the games anciently held there **b** *often cap* **:** of or relating to the Isthmus of Panama connecting the No. American and So. American continents

isth·mic \ˈis-mik\ *adj* **:** ISTHMIAN

isth·mus \ˈis-məs\ *n* [L, fr. Gk *isthmos*] **1 :** a narrow strip of land connecting two larger land areas **2 :** a contracted anatomical part or passage connecting two larger structures or cavities

-is·tic \ˈis-tik\ *also* **-is·ti·cal** \-ti-kəl\ *adj suffix* [MF & L & Gk; MF *-istique,* fr. L *-isticus,* fr. Gk *-istikos,* fr. *-istēs* -ist + *-ikos* -ic] **:** of, relating to, or characteristic of ⟨altru*istic*⟩

is·tle \ˈist-lē\ *n* [AmerSp *ixtle,* fr. Nahuatl *ichtli*] **:** a fiber obtained from any of various tropical American plants (as an epiphytic bromeliad [*Bromelia sylvestris*] or any of several Mexican agaves)

1it \(ˈ)it, ət\ *pron* [ME, fr. OE *hit* — more at HE] **1 :** that one — used as subject or direct object or indirect object of a verb or object of a preposition usu. in reference to a lifeless thing ⟨took a quick look at the house and noticed ~ was very old⟩, a plant ⟨there is a rosebush near the fence and ~ is now blooming⟩, a person or animal whose sex is unknown or disregarded ⟨don't know who ~ is⟩, a group of individuals or things, or an abstract entity ⟨beauty is everywhere and ~ is a source of joy⟩; compare HE, ITS, SHE, THEY **2** — used as subject of a verb that expresses a condition or action without reference to an agent ⟨~ is raining⟩ **3 a** — used as anticipatory subject or object of a verb ⟨~ is necessary to repeat the whole thing⟩; often used to shift emphasis to a part of a statement other than the subject ⟨~ was in this city that the treaty was signed⟩ **b** — used with many verbs as a direct object with little or no meaning ⟨footed ~ back to camp⟩ **4 :** the general state of affairs or circumstances ⟨how is ~ going⟩

2it \ˈit\ *n* **:** the player in a game who performs a function (as trying to catch others in a game of tag) essential to the nature of the game

it·a·col·u·mite \ˌit-ə-ˈkäl-(y)ə-ˌmīt\ *n* [*Itacolumi,* mountain in Brazil] **:** a quartzite resembling mica and flexible when split into thin slabs

it·a·con·ic acid \ˌit-ə-ˌkän-ik-\ *n* [ISV, anagram of *aconitic,* $C_3H_3(COOH)_3$] **:** a crystalline dicarboxylic acid $C_5H_6O_4$ obtained usu. by fermentation of sugars with molds (genus *Aspergillus*) and used as a monomer for vinyl-type polymers and polyesters

Ital·ian \ə-ˈtal-yən, i-\ *n* **1 a :** a native or inhabitant of Italy **b :** a person of Italian descent **2 :** the Romance language of the Italians — **Italian** *adj*

ital·ian·ate \-yə-ˌnāt\ *vt* **:** ITALIANIZE

Ital·ian·ate \-nət, -ˌnāt\ *adj* **:** Italian in quality or characteristics

Ital·ian·ism \-ˌniz-əm\ *n* **1 a :** a quality characteristic of Italy or the Italian people **b :** a pronunciation or idiom suggestive of the Italian language **2 a :** specialized interest in or emulation of Italian qualities or achievements **b :** promotion or love of Italian policies or ideals

Ital·ian·iza·tion \ə-ˌtal-yə-nə-ˈzā-shən, i-\ *n* **:** the act of italianizing **:** state of being italianized

ital·ian·ize \ə-ˈtal-yə-ˌnīz, i-\ *vi, often cap* **:** to act Italian; *specif* **:** to follow the style or technique of recognized Italian painters ~ *vt, often cap* **:** to make Italian in any respect

Italian sonnet *n* **:** a sonnet consisting of an octave rhyming *abba abba* and a sestet rhyming in any of various patterns (as *cde cde* or *cdc dcd*) — called also *Petrarchan sonnet*

1ital·ic \ə-ˈtal-ik, i-, ī-\ *adj* **1** *cap* **:** of or relating to ancient Italy, its peoples, or their Indo-European languages **2 :** of or relating to a type style with characters that slant upward to the right (as in "*these words are italic*")

2italic *n* **1 :** an italic character or type **2** *cap* **:** the Italic branch of the Indo-European language family — see INDO-EUROPEAN LANGUAGES table

Ital·i·cism \ə-ˈtal-ə-ˌsiz-əm, i-\ *n* **:** ITALIANISM 1b

ital·i·ci·za·tion \ə-ˌtal-ə-sə-ˈzā-shən, i-, ī-\ *n* **:** the use of italics or a single underscore in printing or writing

ital·i·cize \ə-ˈtal-ə-ˌsīz, i-, ī-\ *vt* **:** to print in italics or underscore with a single line

1itch \ˈich\ *vb* [ME *icchen,* fr. OE *giccan;* akin to OHG *jucchen* to itch] *vi* **1 a :** to have an itch **b :** to produce such a sensation **2 :** to have a restless desire or hankering for something ~ *vt* **1 :** to cause to itch **2 :** VEX, IRRITATE

2itch *n* **1 a :** an uneasy irritating sensation in the upper surface of the skin usu. held to result from mild stimulation of pain receptors **b :** a skin disorder accompanied by such a sensation; *esp* **:** a contagious eruption caused by a mite (*Sarcoptes scabiei*) that burrows in the skin and causes intense itching **2 a :** a restless usu. constant often compulsive desire **b :** LUST, PRURIENCE — **itch·i·ness** \ˈich-ē-nəs\ *n* — **itchy** \-ē\ *adj*

it'd \ˌit-əd\ **:** it had **:** it would

1-ite \ˌīt\ *n suffix* [ME, fr. OF & L; OF, fr. L *-ita, -ites,* fr. Gk *-itēs*] **1 a :** native **:** resident ⟨Brooklyn*ite*⟩ **b :** descendant ⟨Ephraim*ite*⟩ **c :** adherent **:** follower ⟨Jacob*ite*⟩ ⟨Pusey*ite*⟩ **2 a** (1) **:** product ⟨metabol*ite*⟩ (2) **:** commercially manufactured product ⟨ebon*ite*⟩ **b :** polyhydroxy alcohol usu. related to a sugar ⟨inos*ite*⟩ **3** [NL *-ites,* fr. L] **:** fossil ⟨ammon*ite*⟩ **4 :** mineral ⟨erythr*ite*⟩ **:** rock ⟨anorthos*ite*⟩ **5** [F, fr. L *-ita, -ites*] **:** segment or constituent part of a body or of a bodily part ⟨som*ite*⟩ ⟨dendr*ite*⟩

2-ite *n suffix* [F, alter. of *-ate* -ate, fr. NL *-atum*] **:** salt or ester of an acid with a name ending in *-ous*

1item \ˈī-ˌtem, ˈīt-əm\ *adv* [ME, fr. L, fr. *ita* thus] **:** and in addition **:** ALSO — used to introduce each article in a list or enumeration

2item \ˈīt-əm\ *n* **1** *obs* **:** WARNING, HINT **2 :** a separate particular in an enumeration, account, or series **:** ARTICLE **3 :** a separate piece of news or information ⟨column of local ~s⟩

syn ITEM, DETAIL, PARTICULAR mean one of the distinct parts of a whole. ITEM applies to each thing specified separately in a list or in a group of things that might be listed or enumerated; DETAIL applies to one of the small component parts of a larger whole such as a construction, building, painting, narration, process; PARTICULAR stresses the smallness, singleness, and esp. the concreteness of a detail or item

3item \ˈīt-əm\ *vt* **1** *archaic* **:** COMPUTE, RECKON **2** *archaic* **:** to set down the particular details of

item·iza·tion \ˌīt-ə-mə-ˈzā-shən\ *n* **:** the act of itemizing; *also* **:** an itemized list

item·ize \ˈīt-ə-ˌmīz\ *vt* **:** to set down in detail or by particulars **:** LIST

it·er·ance \ˈit-ə-rən(t)s\ *n* **:** REITERATION

it·er·ant \-rənt\ *adj* **:** ITERATING

it·er·ate \ˈit-ə-ˌrāt\ *vt* [L *iteratus,* pp. of *iterare,* fr. *iterum* again; akin to L *is* he, that, *ita* thus, Skt *itara* the other, *iti* thus] **:** REITERATE **syn** see REPEAT — **it·er·a·tion** \ˌit-ə-ˈrā-shən\ *n* — **it·er·a·tive** \ˈit-ə-ˌrāt-iv, -rət-\ *adj*

ithy·phal·lic \ˌith-i-ˈfal-ik\ *adj* [LL *ithyphallicus,* fr. Gk *ithyphallikos,* fr. *ithyphallos* erect phallus, fr. *ithys* straight + *phallos* phallus; akin to Skt *sādhati* he reaches the goal] **1 :** of or relating to the phallus carried in procession in ancient festivals of Bacchus **2 :** LEWD

itin·er·a·cy \ī-ˈtin-ə-rə-sē, ə-\ *n* [*itinerate,* adj. (itinerant)] **:** ITINERANCY

itin·er·an·cy \-rən-sē\ *n* **1 :** the act of itinerating **:** the state of being itinerant **2 :** a system (as in the Methodist Church) of rotating ministers who itinerate

itin·er·ant \-rənt\ *adj* [LL *itinerant-, itinerans,* prp. of *itinerari* to journey, fr. L *itiner-, iter* journey, way, fr. *ire* to go — more at ISSUE] **:** traveling from place to place; *esp* **:** covering a circuit ⟨~ preacher⟩ — **itinerant** *n* — **itin·er·ant·ly** *adv*

itin·er·ary \ī-ˈtin-ə-ˌrer-ē, ə- *also* -ˈtin-ə-rē\ *n* **1 :** the route of a

journey or the proposed outline of one **2 :** a travel diary **3 :** a traveler's guidebook — **itinerary** *adj*

itin·er·ate \ī-'tin-ə-,rāt, ə-\ *vi* **:** to travel a preaching or judicial circuit — **itin·er·a·tion** \(,)ī-,tin-ə-'rā-shən, ə-\ *n*

-i·tious \'ish-əs\ *adj suffix* [L *-icius, -itius*] **:** of, relating to, or having the characteristics of ⟨excrement*itious*⟩

-i·tis \'īt-əs *also but not shown at individual entries* 'ēt-\ *n suffix, pl* **-i·tis·es** *also* **-it·i·des** \'it-ə-,dēz\ *sometimes* **-i·tes** \'īt-(,)ēz, 'ēt-\ [NL, fr. L & Gk; L, fr. Gk, fr. fem. of *-itēs* -ite] **1 :** disease or inflammation ⟨bronch*itis*⟩ **2** *pl usu -itises* **a** (1) **:** malady arising from ⟨vacation*itis*⟩ (2) **:** forced endurance of ⟨television*itis*⟩ **b** (1) **:** marked proneness to ⟨accident*itis*⟩ (2) **:** infatuation with ⟨jazz*itis*⟩ (3) **:** excessive advocacy of or reliance on ⟨education*itis*⟩ **c :** excess of the qualities of ⟨big-business*itis*⟩

it'll \,it-ᵊl\ **:** it will **:** it shall

its \(,)its, əts\ *adj* **:** of or relating to it or itself esp. as possessor ⟨going to ~ kennel⟩, agent ⟨a child proud of ~ first drawings⟩, or object of an action ⟨~ final enactment into law⟩

it's \(,)its, əts\ **1 :** it is **2 :** it has

it·self \it-'self, ət-\ *pron* **1 :** that identical one — compare [1]IT 1; used reflexively ⟨watched the cat giving ~ a bath⟩, for emphasis ⟨the letter ~ was missing⟩, or in absolute constructions ⟨~ a splendid specimen of classic art, it is sure to be exhibited throughout the world⟩ **2 :** its normal, healthy, or sane condition or self

-ity \ət-ē\ *n suffix* [ME *-ite*, fr. OF or L; OF *-ité*, fr. L *-itat-, -itas*, fr. -i- (stem vowel of adjs.) + *-tat-, -tas* -ty; akin to Gk *-tēt-, -tēs* -ty] **:** quality **:** state **:** degree ⟨alkalin*ity*⟩

-ium *n suffix* **1** [NL, fr. L, ending of some neut. nouns] **a** (1) **:** a chemical element ⟨sod*ium*⟩ (2) **:** chemical radical ⟨ammon*ium*⟩ **b :** positive ion ⟨imidazol*ium* $[C_3H_4N_2H]^+$⟩ **2** *pl* **-iums** *or* **-ia** [NL, fr. L, fr. Gk *-ion*] **:** small one **:** mass — esp. in botanical terms ⟨pollin*ium*⟩

-ive \iv\ *adj suffix* [ME *-if, -ive*, fr. MF & L; MF *-if*, fr. L *-ivus*] **:** that performs or tends toward an (indicated) action ⟨amus*ive*⟩

I've \(,)īv\ **:** I have

ivied \'ī-vēd\ *adj* **:** overgrown with ivy

ivo·ry \'īv-(ə-)rē\ *n, often attrib* [ME *ivorie*, fr. OF *ivoire*, fr. L *eboreus* of ivory, fr. *ebor-, ebur* ivory, fr. Egypt *ꜣb, ꜣbw* elephant, ivory] **1 a :** the hard creamy-white modified dentine that composes the tusks of an elephant or sometimes another tusked mammal **b :** a tusk (as of an elephant) that yields ivory **2 :** a variable color averaging a pale yellow **3** *slang* **:** TOOTH **4 :** something (as dice or piano keys) made of ivory or of a similar substance

ivory black *n* **:** a fine black pigment made by calcining ivory

ivory nut *n* **:** the nutlike seed of a So. American palm (*Phytelephas macrocarpa*) containing a very hard endosperm used for carving and turning

ivory tower *n* **:** a secluded place for meditation **:** RETREAT

[1]**ivy** \'ī-vē\ *n* [ME, fr. OE *īfig;* akin to OHG *ebah* ivy] **1 :** a widely cultivated ornamental climbing or prostrate or sometimes shrubby Eurasian vine (*Hedera helix*) of the ginseng family with evergreen leaves, small yellowish flowers, and black berries **2 :** POISON IVY

[2]**ivy** *adj* [fr. the prevalence of ivy-covered buildings on the campuses of the older U.S. colleges] **:** ACADEMIC 1,4

Ivy League *adj* **:** of, relating to, or characteristic of a group of long-established eastern U.S. colleges widely regarded as high in scholastic and social prestige

iwis \ē-'wis, ī-\ *adv* [ME, fr. OE *gewis* certain; akin to OHG *giwisso* certainly, OE *witan* to know — more at WIT] *archaic* **:** CERTAINLY

Ix·i·on \ik-'sī-ən\ *n* [L, fr. Gk *Ixiōn*] **:** a Thessalian king punished by Zeus for aspiring to love Hera by being bound in Tartarus to an endlessly revolving wheel

ix·tle \'ist-lē\ *var of* ISTLE

Iyar \'ē-,yär\ *n* [Heb *Iyyār*] **:** the 8th month of the civil year or the 2d month of the ecclesiastical year in the Jewish calendar

-iza·tion \ə-'zā-shən *also esp when an unstressed syllable precedes but not shown at individual entries* (,)ī-'zā-\ *n suffix* **:** action **:** process **:** state ⟨social*ization*⟩

-ize \,īz\ *vb suffix* [ME *-isen*, fr. OF *-iser*, fr. LL *-izare*, fr. Gk *-izein*] **1 a** (1) **:** cause to be or conform to or resemble ⟨system*ize*⟩ ⟨american*ize*⟩ **:** cause to be formed into ⟨union*ize*⟩ (2) **:** subject to a (specified) action ⟨plagiar*ize*⟩ (3) **:** impregnate or treat or combine with ⟨albumin*ize*⟩ **b :** treat like ⟨idol*ize*⟩ **c :** treat according to the method of ⟨bowdler*ize*⟩ **2 a :** become **:** become like ⟨crystall*ize*⟩ **b :** be productive in or of ⟨hypothes*ize*⟩ **:** engage in a (specified) activity ⟨philosoph*ize*⟩ **c :** adopt or spread the manner of activity or the teaching of ⟨calvin*ize*⟩

iz·zard \'iz-ərd\ *n* [alter. of earlier *ezod, ezed*, prob. fr. MF *et zede* and Z] *chiefly dial* **:** the letter *z*

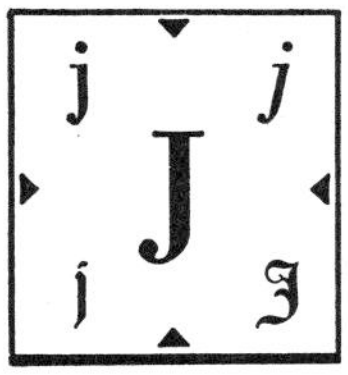

j \'jā\ *n, often cap, often attrib* **1 a :** the tenth letter of the English alphabet **b :** a graphic representation of this letter **c :** a speech counterpart of orthographic *j* **2 a :** a graphic device for reproducing the letter *j* **b :** ONE **c :** a unit vector parallel to the *y*-axis **3 :** one designated *j* esp. as the tenth in order or class **4 :** something shaped like the letter J

[1]**jab** \'jab\ *vb* **jabbed; jab·bing** [alter. of *job* (to strike)] *vt* **1 a :** to pierce with or as if with a sharp object **:** STAB **b :** to poke quickly or abruptly **:** THRUST **2 :** to strike with a short straight blow ~ *vi* **1 :** to make quick or abrupt thrusts with a sharp object **2 :** to strike a person with a short straight blow

[2]**jab** *n* **:** an act of jabbing; *specif* **:** a short straight boxing punch delivered with the leading hand

[1]**jab·ber** \'jab-ər\ *vb* **jab·ber·ing** \'jab-(ə-)riŋ\ [ME *jaberen*, of imit. origin] *vi* **:** to talk rapidly, indistinctly, or unintelligibly ~ *vt* **:** to speak rapidly or indistinctly — **jab·ber·er** \'jab-ər-ər\ *n*

[2]**jabber** *n* **:** GIBBERISH, CHATTER

jab·ber·wocky \'jab-ər-,wäk-ē\ *n* [*Jabberwocky*, nonsense poem by Lewis Carroll] **:** meaningless speech or writing

jab·i·ru \,jab-ə-'rü\ *n* [Pg, fr. Tupi & Guarani *jabirú*] **:** any of several large tropical storks

jab·o·ran·di \,jab-ə-,ran-'dē, -'ran-dē\ *n* [Pg, fr. Tupi *yaborandí*] **1 :** the dried leaves of two So. American shrubs (*Pilocarpus jaborandi* and *P. microphyllus*) of the rue family that are a source of pilocarpine **2 :** the root of a Brazilian pepper (*Piper jaborandi*) that is a source of pilocarpine

ja·bot \zha-'bō, ja-\ *n* [F] **1 :** a fall of lace or cloth attached to the front of a neckband and worn esp. by men in the 18th century **2 :** a pleated frill of cloth or lace attached down the center front of a woman's blouse or dress

ja·bo·ti·ca·ba \jə-,büt-i-'käb-ə\ *n* [Pg, fr. Tupi] **:** a tropical American shrubby tree (*Myrciaria cauiflora*) of the myrtle family cultivated in warm regions for its edible purplish fruit

ja·cal \hə-'käl\ *n, pl* **ja·ca·les** \-'käl-(,)ās\ *also* **ja·cals** [MexSp, fr. Nahuatl *xacalli*] **:** a hut in Mexico and southwestern U.S. with a thatched roof and walls made of upright poles or sticks covered and chinked with mud or clay

jac·a·mar \'jak-ə-,mär\ *n* [F, fr. Tupi *jacamá-ciri*] **:** any of several usu. iridescent green or bronze insectivorous birds (family Galbulidae) of American tropical forests

ja·ca·na \,yas-ᵊn-'äⁿ\ *n* [Pg *jaçanã*, fr. Tupi & Guarani] **:** any of several long-legged and long-toed wading birds (family Jacanidae) that frequent coastal freshwater marshes and ponds in warm regions

jac·a·ran·da \,jak-ə-,ran-'dä, -'ran-də\ *n* [NL, genus name, fr. Pg, a tree of this genus] **:** any of a genus (*Jacaranda*) of pinnate-leaved tropical American trees of the trumpet-creeper family with showy blue flowers in panicles

ja·cinth \'jās-ᵊn(t)th, 'jas-\ *n* [ME *iacinct*, fr. OF *jacinthe*, fr. L *hyacinthus*, a flowering plant, a gem] **1 :** HYACINTH **2 :** a gem more nearly orange in color than a hyacinth

ja·cinthe \'jäs-ᵊn(t)th, 'jas-; zhä-'sant\ *n* [F] **:** a moderate orange

[1]**jack** \'jak\ *n, often attrib* [ME *jacke*, fr. *Jacke*, nickname for *Johan* John] **1 a** *cap* **:** MAN; *esp* **:** one who is representative of the common people **b** *often cap* **:** SAILOR **c** (1) **:** LABORER, SERVANT (2) **:** LUMBERJACK **2 :** any of various mechanical devices: as **a :** a device for turning a spit **b :** any of various portable mechanisms for exerting pressure or lifting a heavy body a short distance **3 :** something that supports or holds in position: as **a :** a bar of iron at a topgallant masthead to support a royal mast and spread the royal shrouds **b :** a wooden brace fastened behind a scenic unit in a stage set to prop it up **4 a :** any of several fishes; *esp* **:** a young male salmon **b :** a male donkey **c :** any of several birds (as a jackdaw) **5 a :** something smaller than the usual of its kind — used in combination ⟨*jack*shaft⟩ **b :** a small white target ball in lawn bowling **c :** a small national flag flown by a ship **d** (1) *pl but sing in constr* **:** a game played with a set of small objects that are tossed, caught, and moved in various figures (2) **:** a small 6-pointed metal object used in the game of jacks **6 a :** a playing card carrying the figure of a soldier or servant and ranking usu. below the queen **b** [by shortening] **:** JACKPOT 1a (2) **7** *slang* **:** MONEY **8 :** a female fitting in an electric circuit used with a plug to make a connection with another circuit **9 a** [by shortening] **:** APPLEJACK **b :** BRANDY **10** [by shortening] **:** JACKKNIFE 2

[2]**jack** *vi* **:** to hunt or fish at night with a jacklight ~ *vt* **1 :** to hunt or fish for at night with a jacklight **2 a :** to move or lift by or as if by a jack **b** (1) **:** INCREASE (2) **:** to raise the level or quality of **c :** to take to task — **jack·er** *n*

jack·al \'jak-əl, -,ȯl\ *n* [Turk *çakal*, fr. Per *shagāl*, fr. Skt *sṛgāla*] **1 :** any of several Old World wild dogs smaller than the related wolves **2 a :** a person who performs routine or menial tasks for another **b :** a person who serves or collaborates with another esp. in the commission of base acts

Jack–a–Lent \'jak-ə-,lent\ *n* [[1]*jack* + *a* (of) + *Lent*] **1 :** a small stuffed puppet set up to be pelted as a sport in Lent **2 :** a simple or insignificant person

jack·a·napes \'jak-ə-,nāps\ *n* [ME *Jack Napis*, nickname for William de la Pole †1450 duke of Suffolk] **1 :** MONKEY, APE **2 a :** an impertinent or conceited fellow **b :** a pert or mischievous child

jack·ass \'jak-,as\ *n* **1 :** a male ass; *also* **:** DONKEY **2 :** a stupid person **:** FOOL

jack·ass·ery \'jak-,as-(ə-)rē\ *n* **:** a stupid or foolish act

jack bean *n* **:** a bushy annual tropical American legume (genus *Canavalia*); *esp* **:** a plant (*C. ensiformis*) grown esp. for forage

jack·boot \'jak-,büt\ *n* **:** a heavy military boot made of glossy black leather extending above the knee and worn esp. during the 17th and 18th centuries

jack·daw \'jak-,dȯ\ *n* **1 :** a common black and gray Eurasian bird (*Corvus monedula*) that is related to but smaller than the common crow **2 :** GRACKLE 2

[1]**jack·et** \'jak-ət\ *n* [ME *jaket*, fr. MF *jaquet*, dim. of *jaque* short jacket, fr. *jacque* peasant, fr. the name *Jacques* James] **1 a :** a garment for the upper body usu. having a front opening, collar, lapels, sleeves, and pockets **b :** something worn or fastened around the body but not for use as clothing **2 a** (1) **:** the natural covering of an animal (2) **:** the fur or wool of a mammal **b :** the skin of a potato **3 :** an outer covering or casing: as **a** (1) **:** a thermally nonconducting cover (2) **:** a covering that encloses an intermediate space through which a temperature-controlling fluid circulates (3) **:** a tough cold-worked metal casing that forms the outer shell of a built-up bullet **b** (1) **:** a wrapper or open envelope for a document (2) **:** an envelope for enclosing registered mail during delivery from one post office to another **c** (1) **:** a detachable protective wrapper for a book (2) **:** the cover of a paperback book (3) **:** the outside leaves for a booklet, pamphlet, or catalog that is to be stitched or wired through the saddle (4) **:** a paper or paperboard envelope for a phonograph record — **jack·et·ed** \-ət-əd\ *adj*

[2]**jacket** *vt* **:** to put a jacket on

Jack Frost *n* **:** frost or frosty weather personified

jack·fruit \'jak-,früt\ *n* [Pg *jaca* jackfruit + E *fruit*] **1 a :** a large

widely cultivated tropical tree (*Artocarpus heterophyllus*) related to the breadfruit that yields a fine-grained yellow wood and immense fruits which contain an edible pulp and nutritious seeds **b :** the fruit of this tree **2 :** DURIAN

jack·ham·mer \ˈjak-ˌham-ər\ *n* **1 :** a rock-drilling machine usu. held in the hands **2 :** a device in which a tool is worked by compressed air

jack–in–the–box \ˈjak-ən-t͟hə-ˌbäks\ *n, pl* **jack–in–the–box·es** *or* **jacks–in–the–box :** a small box out of which a figure (as of a clown's head) springs when the lid is raised

jack–in–the–pul·pit \ˌjak-ən-t͟hə-ˈpu̇l-ˌpit, -ˈpəl-, -pət\ *n, pl* **jack–in–the–pulpits** *or* **jacks–in–the–pulpit :** any of several plants (genus *Arisaema*) of the arum family; *esp* **:** an American spring-flowering woodland herb (*A. atrorubens*) having an upright club-shaped spadix arched over by a green and purple spathe

[1]jack·knife \ˈjak-ˌnīf\ *n* **1 :** a large strong clasp knife for the pocket **2 :** a dive executed headfirst in which the diver bends from the waist and touches his ankles while holding his knees unflexed before straightening out

[2]jackknife *vt* **1 :** to cut with a jackknife **2 :** to cause to jackknife ~ *vi* **1 :** to double up like a jackknife **2 :** to turn or rise and form an angle of 90 degrees or less with each other — used esp. of a pair of vehicles

jack·leg \ˈjak-ˌleg, -ˌlāg\ *adj* [[1]*jack* + *-leg* (as in *blackleg*)] **1 a :** lacking skill or training **:** AMATEUR ⟨~ carpenter⟩ **b :** characterized by unscrupulousness, dishonesty, or lack of professional standards ⟨~ lawyer⟩ **2 :** designed as a temporary expedient **:** MAKESHIFT — **jackleg** *n*

jack·light \-ˌlīt\ *n* **:** a light used esp. in hunting or fishing at night

jack mackerel *n* **:** a California market fish (*Trachurus symmetricus*) that is iridescent green or bluish above and silvery below; *also* **:** a closely related Australian fish (*T. novaezelandiae*)

jack–of–all–trades \ˌjak-ə-ˈvȯl-ˌtrādz\ *n, pl* **jacks–of–all–trades :** a person who can do passable work at various trades **:** HANDYMAN

jack–o'–lan·tern \ˈjak-ə-ˌlant-ərn\ *n* **1 a :** IGNIS FATUUS **b :** SAINT ELMO'S FIRE **2 :** a lantern made of a pumpkin cut to look like a human face

jack·pot \ˈjak-ˌpät\ *n* **1 a** (1) **:** a hand or game of draw poker in which a pair of jacks or better is required to open (2) **:** a large pot (as in poker) formed by the accumulation of stakes from previous play **b** (1) **:** a combination on a slot machine that wins a top prize or all the coins in the machine (2) **:** the sum so won **c :** a large fund of money or other reward formed by the accumulation of prizes **2 :** an impressive often unexpected success or reward **3** *chiefly West* **:** a tight spot **:** JAM

jack·rab·bit \ˈjak-ˌrab-ət\ *n* [[1]*jack* (jackass) + *rabbit;* fr. its long ears] **:** any of several large hares (genus *Lepus*) of western No. America having very long ears and long hind legs

jack salmon *n* **1 :** WALLEYED PIKE **2 :** GRILSE

jack·screw \ˈjak-ˌskrü\ *n* **:** a screw-operated jack for lifting or for exerting pressure

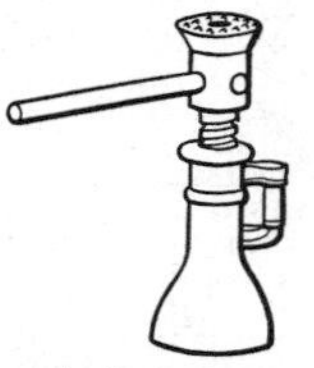

jackscrew

jack·shaft \-ˌshaft\ *n* **:** COUNTERSHAFT; *specif* **:** the intermediate driving shaft in an automobile

jack·smelt \-ˌsmelt\ *n* **:** a large silversides (*Atherinopsis californiensis*) of the Pacific coast of No. America that is the chief commercial smelt of the California markets

jack·snipe \-ˌsnīp\ *n* **:** an Old World true snipe (*Limnocryptes minima*) that is smaller and more highly colored than the common snipe

Jack·son Day \ˈjak-sən-\ *n* [Andrew *Jackson*, defender of New Orleans] **:** January 8 celebrated as a legal holiday in Louisiana commemorating the successful defense of New Orleans in 1815

Jack·so·ni·an \jak-ˈsō-nē-ən\ *adj* **:** of, relating to, or characteristic of Andrew Jackson or his political principles or policies — **Jacksonian** *n*

jack·stay \ˈjak-ˌstā\ *n* **1 a :** an iron rod, wooden bar, or wire rope stretching along a yard of a ship to which the sails are fastened **b :** a support of wood, iron, or rope running up and down a mast on which the parrel of a yard travels **2 :** a longitudinal rigging for maintaining the correct distance between the heads of various riggings on an airship

jack·straw \-ˌstrȯ\ *n* **1 :** one of the pieces used in the game jackstraws **2** *pl but sing in constr* **:** a game in which a set of straws or thin strips are let fall in a heap with each player in turn trying to remove them one at a time without disturbing the rest

jack–tar \-ˈtär\ *n, often cap* **:** SAILOR

Ja·cob \ˈjā-kəb\ *n* [LL, fr. Gk *Iacōb*, fr. Heb *Yaʻăqōbh*] **1 :** a Hebrew patriarch and son of Isaac and Rebekah **2 :** the ancient Hebrew nation

Jac·o·be·an \ˌjak-ə-ˈbē-ən\ *adj* [NL *Jacobaeus*, fr. *Jacobus* James] **:** of, relating to, or characteristic of James I of England or his age — **Jacobean** *n*

jacobean lily *n, often cap J* [LL *Jacobus* (St. James)] **:** a Mexican bulbous herb (*Sprekelia formosissima*) of the amaryllis family cultivated for its bright red solitary flower

Ja·co·bi·an \jə-ˈkō-bē-ən, yä-\ *n* [K. G. J. *Jacobi* †1851 G mathematician] **:** a determinant defined for a finite number of functions of the same number of variables in which each row consists of the first partial derivatives of the same function with respect to each of the variables

Jac·o·bin \ˈjak-ə-bən\ *n* [ME, fr. MF, fr. ML *Jacobinus*, fr. LL *Jacobus* (St. James); fr. the location of the first Dominican convent in the street of St. James, Paris] **1 :** DOMINICAN **2** [F, fr. *Jacobin* Dominican; fr. the group's founding in the Dominican convent in Paris] **:** a member of an extremist or radical political group; *esp* **:** a member of such a group advocating egalitarian democracy and engaging in terrorist activities during the French Revolution of 1789 — **Jac·o·bin·ic** \ˌjak-ə-ˈbin-ik\ *or* **Jac·o·bin·i·cal** \-i-kəl\ *adj* — **Jac·o·bin·ism** \ˈjak-ə-bə-ˌniz-əm\ *n* — **jac·o·bin·ize** \-ˌnīz\ *vt, often cap*

Jac·o·bite \ˈjak-ə-ˌbīt\ *n* [*Jacobus* (James II)] **:** a partisan of James II of England or of the Stuarts after the revolution of 1688 — **Jac·o·bit·i·cal** \ˌjak-ə-ˈbit-i-kəl\ *adj* — **Jac·o·bit·ism** \ˈjak-ə-ˌbīt-ˌiz-əm\ *n*

Jacob's ladder *n* **1 :** a ladder extending from earth to heaven seen by the patriarch Jacob in a dream **2 a :** a pinnate-leaved European perennial herb (*Polemonium caeruleum*) of the phlox family with bright blue or white flowers **b :** a related American herb **3 :** a marine ladder of rope or chain with wooden or iron rungs

Ja·co·bus \jə-ˈkō-bəs\ *n* [*Jacobus* (James I), during whose reign unites were coined] **:** UNITE

jac·o·net \ˈjak-ə-ˌnet\ *n* [modif. of Urdu *jagannāthī*] **:** a lightweight cotton cloth used for clothing and bandages

jac·quard \ˈjak-ˌärd\ *n, often cap* [Joseph *Jacquard* †1834 F inventor] **1 a :** a loom apparatus or head for weaving figured fabrics **b :** a loom having a jacquard **2 :** a fabric of intricate variegated weave or pattern

jac·que·rie \zhä-ˈkrē\ *n, often cap* [F, fr. the French peasant revolt in 1358, fr. MF, fr. *jacque* peasant — more at JACKET] **:** a peasants' revolt

jac·ta·tion \jak-ˈtā-shən\ *n* [L *jactation-, jactatio*, fr. *jactatus*, pp. of *jactare* to throw, boast — more at JET] **:** boastful declaration or display

jac·ti·ta·tion \ˌjak-tə-ˈtā-shən\ *n* [LL *jactitation-, jactitatio*, fr. *jactitatus*, pp. of *jactitare* to bring forward in public, freq. of *jactare*] **1 a** *archaic* **:** boastful public assertion **b :** false boasting or assertion made to the prejudice of another person **2 :** a tossing to and fro or jerking and twitching of the body

jac·u·late \ˈjak-yə-ˌlāt\ *vt* [L *jaculatus*, pp. of *jaculari* — more at EJACULATE] **:** to hurl forward **:** THROW — **jac·u·la·tion** \ˌjak-yə-ˈlā-shən\ *n*

[1]jade \ˈjād\ *n* [ME] **1 :** a broken-down, vicious, or worthless horse **2 a :** a disreputable woman **b :** a flirtatious girl

[2]jade *vt* **1 a :** to wear out by overwork or abuse **b :** to tire by severe or tedious tasks **2** *obs* **:** to make ridiculous ~ *vi* **:** to become weary **syn** see TIRE — **jad·ish** \ˈjād-ish\ *adj*

[3]jade *n* [F, fr. obs. Sp (*piedra de la*) *ijada*, lit., loin stone; fr. the belief that jade cures renal colic] **:** a tough compact usu. green gemstone that takes a high polish and is derived from jadeite or from nephrite

jad·ed *adj* **1 :** EXHAUSTED **2 :** SATIATED — **jad·ed·ly** *adv* — **jad·ed·ness** *n*

jade green *n* **:** a variable color averaging a light bluish green

jade·ite \ˈjā-ˌdīt\ *n* [F] **:** a monoclinic mineral that constitutes a valuable variety of jade

jade plant *n* **:** any of several stonecrops (genus *Crassula*) cultivated as foliage plants

jae·ger \ˈyā-gər\ *n* [G *jäger*] **1 a :** HUNTER, HUNTSMAN **b :** one attending a person of rank or wealth and wearing hunter's costume **2 :** any of several large dark-colored rapacious birds (family Stercorariidae) of northern seas

[1]jag \ˈjag\ *vb* **jagged; jag·ging** [ME *jaggen*] *vt* **1** *chiefly dial* **:** PRICK, STAB **2 a :** to slash or pink (a garment) for ornamentation **b :** to cut teeth or other indentations into **c :** to make (an edge) ragged by cutting or notching ~ *vi* **1 :** PRICK, THRUST **2 :** to move in jerks — **jag·ger** *n*

[2]jag *n* **:** a sharp projecting part **:** BARB

[3]jag *n* [origin unknown] **1 :** a small load **2 a :** a state or feeling of exhilaration or intoxication usu. induced by liquor **b :** SPREE

jag·ged \ˈjag-əd\ *adj* **1 :** having a sharply uneven edge or surface **2 :** having a harsh, rough, or irregular quality — **jag·ged·ly** *adv* — **jag·ged·ness** *n*

jag·gery \ˈjag-ə-rē\ *n* [Hindi *jāgrī*] **:** an unrefined brown sugar made from palm sap

jag·gy \ˈjag-ē\ *adj* **:** JAGGED, NOTCHED

jag·uar \ˈjag-ˌwär, -yə-ˌwär\ *n* [Sp *yaguar* & Pg *jaguar*, fr. Guarani *yaguara* & Tupi *jaguara*] **:** a large cat (*Felis onca*) of tropical America that is larger and stockier than the leopard and is brownish yellow or buff with black spots

jag·ua·run·di \ˌjag-wə-ˈrən-dē\ *n* [AmerSp & Pg, fr. Tupi *jaguarundi* & Guarani *yaguarundi*] **:** a slender long-tailed short-legged grayish wildcat (*Felis jaguarondi*) of Central and So. America

Jah·veh \ˈyä-(ˌ)vā\ *var of* YAHWEH

jai alai \ˈhī-ˌlī, ˌhī-ə-ˈlī\ *n* [Sp, fr. Basque, fr. *jai* festival + *alai* merry] **:** a court game somewhat like handball played by two or four players with a ball and a long curved wicker basket strapped to the right wrist

[1]jail \ˈjā(ə)l\ *n* [ME *jaiole*, fr. OF, fr. (assumed) VL *caveola*, dim. of L *cavea* cage — more at CAGE] **:** PRISON; *esp* **:** a building for the confinement of persons held in lawful custody

[2]jail *vt* **:** to confine in or as if in a jail

jail·bird \ˈjā(ə)l-ˌbərd\ *n* **:** a person confined in jail; *specif* **:** an habitual criminal

jail·break \-ˌbrāk\ *n* **:** a forcible escape from jail

jail delivery *n* **1 :** the clearing of a jail by bringing the prisoners to trial **2 :** the freeing of prisoners by force

jail·er *or* **jail·or** \ˈjā-lər\ *n* **1 :** a keeper of a jail **2 :** one that restricts another's liberty as if by imprisonment

Jain \ˈjīn\ *or* **Jai·na** \ˈjī-nə\ *n* [Hindi *Jain*, fr. Skt *Jaina*] **:** an adherent of Jainism

Jain·ism \ˈjī-ˌniz-əm\ *n* **:** a religion of India originating in the 6th century B.C. and teaching liberation of the soul by right knowledge, right faith, and right conduct

jake leg \ˈjā-ˌkleg, -ˌklāg\ *n* [*jake* (strong liquor)] **:** a paralysis caused by drinking strong liquor

jakes \ˈjāks\ *n pl but sing or pl in constr* [perh. fr. F *Jacques* James] *archaic* **:** PRIVY 2

jal·ap \ˈjal-əp, ˈjäl-\ *n* [F & Sp; F *jalap*, fr. Sp *jalapa*, fr. *Jalapa*, Mexico] **1 a :** the dried purgative tuberous root of a Mexican plant (*Exogonium purga*) or the powdered drug prepared from it that contains resinous glycosides and is the officinal jalap **b :** the root or derived drug of related plants **2 :** a plant yielding jalap

ja·lopy \jə-ˈläp-ē\ *n* [origin unknown] **:** a dilapidated old automobile or airplane

jal·ou·sie \ˈjal-ə-sē\ *n* [F, lit., jealousy, fr. OF *jelous* jealous] **1 :** a blind with adjustable horizontal slats for admitting light and air while excluding sun and rain **2 :** a window made of adjustable glass louvers that control ventilation

[1]jam \ˈjam\ *vb* **jammed; jam·ming** [perh. of imit. origin] *vt* **1 a :** to press into a close or tight position ⟨~ his hat on⟩ **b** (1) **:** to cause to become wedged so as to be unworkable ⟨~ the typewriter keys⟩ (2) **:** to make unworkable by such jamming **c :** to block passage of **:** OBSTRUCT **d :** to fill often to excess **:** PACK **2 :** to push

forcibly; *specif* **:** to apply (the brakes) suddenly with full force **3 :** CRUSH, BRUISE **4 a :** to make unintelligible by sending out interfering signals or messages **b :** to make (as a radar apparatus) ineffective by jamming signals or by causing reflection of radar waves **~** *vi* **1 a :** to become blocked or wedged **b :** to become unworkable through the jamming of a movable part **2 :** to force one's way into a restricted space **3 :** to take part in a jam session — **jam·mer** *n*

2jam *n* **1 a :** an act or instance of jamming **b :** a crowded mass that impedes or blocks **2 a :** the quality or state of being jammed **b :** the pressure or congestion of a crowd **:** CRUSH **3 :** a difficult state of affairs **syn** see PREDICAMENT

3jam *n* **:** a food made by boiling fruit and sugar to a thick consistency

Ja·mai·ca ginger \jə-ˌmā-kə-\ *n* [*Jamaica*, W. Indies] **1 :** an alcoholic extract of ginger used as a flavoring essence **2 :** the powdered root of ginger used as a medicinal infusion

Jamaica rum *n* **:** a heavy-bodied rum made by slow fermentation and marked by a pungent bouquet

jamb \ˈjam\ *n* [ME *jambe*, fr. MF, lit., leg, fr. LL *gamba* — more at GAMBIT] **1 :** an upright piece or surface forming the side of an opening **2 :** a projecting columnar part or mass

jam·ba·laya \ˌjəm-bə-ˈlī-ə\ *n* [LaF, fr. Prov *jambalaia*] **1 :** rice cooked with ham, sausage, chicken, shrimp, or oysters and seasoned with herbs **2 :** a mixture of diverse elements

jam·beau \ˈjam-(ˌ)bō\ *n, pl* **jam·beaux** \-(ˌ)bōz\ [ME, fr. (assumed) AF, fr. MF *jambe*] **:** a piece of medieval armor for the leg below the knee

jam·bo·ree \ˌjam-bə-ˈrē\ *n* [origin unknown] **1 :** a noisy or unrestrained carousal **2 a :** a large festive gathering **b :** a national or international camping assembly of boy scouts **3 :** a long mixed program of entertainment

James \ˈjāmz\ *n* [F, fr. LL *Jacobus*] **1 :** an apostle, son of Zebedee, and brother of the apostle John **2 :** an apostle and son of Alphaeus — called also *James the Less* **3 :** a brother of Jesus held to be the author of the New Testament Epistle of James

James·ian \ˈjām-zē-ən\ *adj* **1 :** of, relating to, or characteristic of William James or his teachings **2 :** of, relating to, or characteristic of Henry James or his writings

jam session *n* [*2jam*] **:** an impromptu performance engaged in by a group of jazz musicians and characterized by group improvisation

Jam·shid *or* **Jam·shyd** \jam-ˈshēd\ *n* [Per *Jamshīd*] **:** the king of the peris in Persian mythology

Jane Doe \ˈjān-ˈdō\ *n* **:** a female party to legal proceedings whose true name is unknown

1jan·gle \ˈjaŋ-gəl\ *vb* **jan·gling** \-g(ə-)liŋ\ [ME *janglen*, fr. OF *jangler*, of Gmc origin; akin to MD *jangelen* to grumble] *vi* **1** *archaic* **:** to talk idly **2 :** to quarrel verbally **3 :** to make a harsh or discordant sound **~** *vt* **1 :** to utter or sound in a discordant, babbling, or chattering way **2 a :** to cause to sound harshly or inharmoniously **b :** to excite to tense and discordant irritation — **jan·gler** \-g(ə-)lər\ *n*

2jangle *n* **1 :** idle talk **2 :** noisy quarreling **3 :** discordant sound

jan·is·sary *or* **jan·i·zary** \ˈjan-ə-ˌser-ē, -ˌzer-\ *n* [It *gianizzero*, fr. Turk *yeniçeri*] **1** *often cap* **:** a soldier of an elite corps of Turkish troops organized in the 14th century and abolished in 1826 **2 :** a member of a group of loyal or subservient troops, officials, or supporters

jan·i·tor \ˈjan-ət-ər\ *n* [L, fr. *janua* door, fr. *janus* arch, gate] **1 :** DOORKEEPER **2 :** one who keeps the premises of an apartment, office, or other building clean, tends the heating system, and makes minor repairs — **jan·i·to·ri·al** \ˌjan-ə-ˈtōr-ē-əl, -ˈtȯr-\ *adj* — **jan·i·tress** \ˈjan-ə-trəs\ *n*

Jan·sen·ism \ˈjan(t)-sə-ˌniz-əm\ *n* [F *jansénisme*, fr. Cornelis *Jansen* †1638 D theologian] **1 :** a theological doctrine maintaining that freedom of the will is nonexistent and that the redemption of mankind through the death of Jesus Christ is limited to only a part of mankind **2 :** a negative rigoristic moral attitude — **Jan·sen·ist** \-nəst\ *n* — **Jan·sen·is·tic** \ˌjan(t)-sə-ˈnis-tik\ *adj*

Jan·u·ary \ˈjan-yə-ˌwer-ē, ˈjen-\ *n* [ME *Januarie*, fr. L *Januarius*, first month of the ancient Roman year, fr. *Janus*] **:** the first month of the Gregorian calendar

Ja·nus \ˈjā-nəs\ *n* [L] **:** an ancient Roman god of gates and beginnings represented with two opposite faces — **Ja·nus-faced** \ˌjā-nəs-ˈfāst\ *adj* — **Ja·nus·like** \ˈjā-nə-ˌslīk\ *adj*

1ja·pan \jə-ˈpan, ji-, ja-\ *n* [*Japan*, country of Asia] **1 :** any of several varnishes; *esp* **:** one yielding a hard brilliant surface coating **2 a :** work varnished and figured in the Japanese manner **b :** Japanese china or silk

2japan *adj* **1 :** of, relating to, or characteristic of Japanese lacquered work **2 :** coated or treated with japan

3japan *vt* **ja·panned; ja·pan·ning 1 :** to cover with or as if with a coat of japan **2 :** to give a high gloss to

Japan allspice *n* **:** a Japanese shrub (*Chimonanthus praecox*) cultivated for its fragrant yellow flowers

Japan clover *n* **:** an annual lespedeza (*Lespedeza striata*) used as a forage, soil-improving, and pasture crop esp. in the southeastern U.S.

Jap·a·nese \ˌjap-ə-ˈnēz, -ˈnēs\ *n, pl* **Japanese 1 :** a native or inhabitant of Japan or one of his descendants **2 :** the language of the Japanese — **Japanese** *adj*

Japanese an·drom·e·da \-ˌan-ˈdräm-əd-ə\ *n* [NL *Andromeda* (genus of plants), fr. L *Andromeda*, Ethiopian princess, fr. Gk *Andromedē*] **:** a shrubby evergreen Asiatic heath (*Pieris japonica*) with glossy leaves and drooping clusters of whitish flowers

Japanese beetle *n* **:** a small metallic green and brown scarab beetle (*Popillia japonica*) introduced into America from Japan that as a grub feeds on the roots of grasses and decaying vegetation and as an adult eats foliage and fruits

Japanese iris *n* **:** any of various beardless garden irises with very large showy flowers

Japanese millet *n* **:** a coarse annual grass (*Echinochloa frumentacea*) cultivated esp. in Asia for its edible seeds

Japanese mink *n* **:** an Asiatic weasel (*Mustela sibirica*); *also* **:** its pale yellowish brown fur

Japanese persimmon *n* **:** an Asiatic persimmon (*Diospyros kaki*) widely cultivated for its large edible fruits

Japanese plum *n* **1 :** any of numerous large showy usu. yellow to light red cultivated plums **2 :** a tree that bears Japanese plums and is derived from a Chinese tree (*Prunus salicina*)

Japanese quince *n* **:** a hardy Chinese ornamental shrub (*Chaenomeles lagenaria*) of the rose family with scarlet flowers

Japanese spurge *n* **:** a low Japanese herb or subshrub (*Pachysandra terminales*) of the box family often used as a ground cover

ja·pa·niza·tion \ˌjap-ə-nə-ˈzā-shən; jə-ˌpan-ə-, ji-, ja-\ *n, often cap* **:** the act or process of japanizing

jap·a·nize \ˈjap-ə-ˌnīz\ *vt, often cap* **1 :** to make Japanese **2 :** to bring (an area) under the influence of Japan

Japan wax *n* **:** a yellowish fat obtained from the berries of several sumacs (as *Rhus verniciflua* and *R. succedanea*) and used chiefly in polishes

1jape \ˈjāp\ *vb* [ME *japen*] *vi* **:** to say or do something jokingly or mockingly **~** *vt* **:** to make mocking fun of — **jap·er** \ˈjā-pər\ *n* — **jap·ery** \ˈjā-p(ə-)rē\ *n*

2jape *n* **:** something designed to arouse amusement or laughter: as **a :** an amusing literary or dramatic production **b :** GIBE

Ja·pheth \ˈjā-fəth\ *n* [L *Japheth* or Gk *Iapheth*, fr. Heb *Yepheth*] **:** a son of Noah

ja·pon·i·ca \jə-ˈpän-i-kə, ji-, ja-\ *n* [NL, fr. fem. of *Japonicus* Japanese, fr. *Japonia* Japan] **:** JAPANESE QUINCE

1jar \ˈjär\ *vb* **jarred; jar·ring** [prob. of imit. origin] *vi* **1 a :** to make a harsh or discordant sound **b :** to be out of harmony; *specif* **:** BICKER **c :** to have a harshly disagreeable or disconcerting effect **2 :** to undergo severe vibration **~** *vt* **:** to cause to jar: as **a :** to affect disagreeably **b :** to make unstable **:** SHAKE

2jar *n* **1 a :** a harsh grating sound **b :** a state or manifestation of discord or conflict **2 a :** a sudden or unexpected shake **b :** an unsettling shock **c :** an unpleasant break or conflict in rhythm, flow, or transition

3jar *n* [MF *jarre*, fr. OProv *jarra*, fr. Ar *jarrah* earthen water vessel] **1 :** a wide-mouthed container made typically of earthenware or glass **2 :** JARFUL

4jar *n* [alter. of *char, chare*] *archaic* **:** TURN — usu. used in the phrase *on the jar*

jar·di·niere \ˌjärd-ᵊn-ˈi(ə)r, ˌzhärd-ᵊn-ˈ(y)e(ə)r\ *n* [F *jardinière*, lit., female gardener] **1 a :** an ornamental stand for plants or flowers **b :** a large ceramic flowerpot **2 :** a garnish for meat consisting of several cubed and cooked vegetables

jar·ful \ˈjär-ˌfu̇l\ *n* **:** the quantity held by a jar

1jar·gon \ˈjär-gən, -ˌgän\ *n* [ME, fr. MF] **1 a :** confused unintelligible language **b :** a strange, outlandish, or barbarous language or dialect **c :** a hybrid language or dialect simplified in vocabulary and grammar and used for communication between peoples of different speech **2 :** the technical terminology or characteristic idiom of a special activity or group **3 :** obscure and often pretentious language marked by circumlocutions and long words **syn** see DIALECT — **jar·gon·is·tic** \ˌjär-gə-ˈnis-tik\ *adj*

2jargon *vi* **1 :** TWITTER, WARBLE **2 :** JARGONIZE

jar·gon·ize \ˈjär-gə-ˌnīz\ *vi* **:** to speak or write jargon **~** *vt* **1 :** to express in jargon **2 :** to make into jargon

jar·goon \jär-ˈgün\ *or* **jar·gon** \-ˈgän\ *n* [F *jargon* — more at ZIRCON] **:** a colorless or pale yellow or smoky zircon

jarl \ˈyär(ə)l\ *n* [ON] **:** a Scandinavian noble ranking immediately below the king

ja·sey \ˈjā-zē\ *n* [prob. alter. of *jersey*] *Brit* **:** a wig made usu. of worsted

jas·mine \ˈjaz-mən\ *n* [F *jasmin*, fr. Ar *yāsamīn*, fr. Per] **1 a** (1) **:** any of numerous often climbing shrubs (genus *Jasminum*) of the olive family that usu. have extremely fragrant flowers (2) **:** a tall-climbing half-evergreen Asiatic shrub (*J. officinale*) with fragrant white flowers from which a perfume is extracted **b :** any of numerous other plants having sweet-scented flowers; *esp* **:** YELLOW JESSAMINE 2 **2 :** a light yellow

Ja·son \ˈjās-ᵊn\ *n* [L *Iason*, fr. Gk *Iasōn*] **:** a hero noted in Greek legend for his successful quest of the Golden Fleece

jas·per \ˈjas-pər\ *n* [ME *jaspre*, fr. MF, fr. L *jaspis*, fr. Gk *iaspis*, of Sem origin; akin to Heb *yāshĕpheh* jasper] **1 :** an opaque cryptocrystalline quartz of any of several colors; *esp* **:** green chalcedony **2 :** a stoneware often given delicate coloration with metallic stains while embossed designs are left white **3 :** a blackish green — **jas·pery** \-p(ə-)rē\ *adj*

jas·sid \ˈjas-əd\ *n* [deriv. of Gk *Iasos*, town in Asia Minor] **:** any of a large cosmopolitan family (Jassidae) of small leafhoppers that include many economically significant pests of cultivated plants; *broadly* **:** LEAFHOPPER

Jat \ˈjät\ *n* [Hindi *Jāṭ*] **:** a member of an Indo-Aryan people of the Punjab and Uttar Pradesh

ja·to unit \ˈjāt-(ˌ)ō-\ *n* [*j*et-*a*ssisted *t*ake*o*ff] **:** a unit for assisting the takeoff of an airplane consisting of one or more rocket engines

jauk \ˈjȯk\ *vi* [ME (Sc) *jaken*] *Scot* **:** DALLY, DAWDLE

jaunce \ˈjȯn(t)s, ˈjän(t)s\ *vi* [origin unknown] *archaic* **:** PRANCE

1jaun·dice \ˈjȯn-dəs, ˈjän-\ *n* [ME *jaundis*, fr. MF *jaunisse*, fr. *jaune* yellow, fr. L *galbinus* yellowish green, fr. *galbus* yellow] **1 :** yellowish pigmentation of the skin, tissues, and body fluids caused by the deposition of bile pigments **2 :** a disease or abnormal condition characterized by jaundice **3 :** a state or attitude characterized by satiety, distaste, or hostility

2jaundice *vt* **1 :** to affect with jaundice **2 :** PREJUDICE

1jaunt \ˈjȯnt, ˈjänt\ *vi* [origin unknown] **1** *archaic* **:** to trudge about **2 :** to make a short journey for pleasure

2jaunt *n* **1** *archaic* **:** a tiring trip **2 :** an excursion undertaken for pleasure

jaun·ti·ly \ˈjȯnt-ᵊl-ē, ˈjänt-\ *adv* **:** in a jaunty manner

jaun·ti·ness \ˈjȯnt-ē-nəs, ˈjänt-\ *n* **:** the quality or state of being jaunty

jaunting car *n* **:** a light two-wheeled open vehicle used esp. in Ireland with lengthwise seats placed face to face or back to back

jaun·ty \ˈjȯnt-ē, ˈjänt-\ *adj* [modif. of F *gentil*] **1** *archaic* **a :** GENTEEL **b :** STYLISH **2 :** sprightly in manner or appearance **:** LIVELY

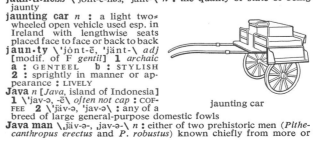

Java *n* [*Java*, island of Indonesia] **1** \ˈjav-ə, -ē\ *often not cap* **:** COFFEE **2** \ˈjäv-ə, ˈjav-ə\ **:** any of a breed of a large general-purpose domestic fowls

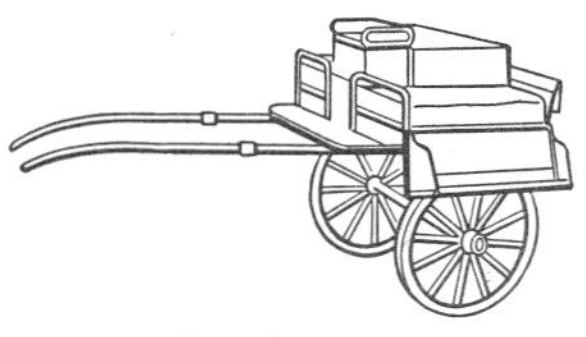

jaunting car

Java man \ˌjäv-ə-, ˌjav-ə-\ *n* **:** either of two prehistoric men (*Pithecanthropus erectus* and *P. robustus*) known chiefly from more or

less fragmentary skulls found in Trinil, Java

Ja·va·nese \ˌjav-ə-ˈnēz, ˌjäv-, -ˈnēs\ *n, pl* **Javanese** [*Java* + *-nese* (as in *Japanese*)] **1 a :** an Indonesian people inhabiting the island of Java **b :** a member of this people **2 :** an Austronesian language of the Javanese people — **Javanese** *adj*

Java sparrow *n* **:** a Javanese weaverbird (*Padda oryzivora*) that is glaucous gray and black above with pinkish underparts, white cheeks, and large pink bill and is a common cage bird

jav·e·lin \ˈjav-(ə-)lən\ *n* [MF *javeline,* alter. of *javelot,* of Celt origin; akin to OIr *gabul* forked stick] **1 :** a light spear thrown as a weapon of war or in hunting **2 :** a slender shaft of wood at least 260 centimeters long tipped with iron or steel and thrown for distance in an athletic field event

Ja·velle water \zha-ˈvel, zhə-\ *n* [*Javel,* former village in France] **:** an aqueous solution of sodium hypochlorite used as a disinfectant or a bleaching agent and in photography

1**jaw** \ˈjȯ\ *n* [ME] **1 a :** either of two complex cartilaginous or bony structures in most vertebrates that border the mouth, support the soft parts enclosing it, usu. bear teeth on their oral margin, and are an upper more or less firmly fused with the skull and a lower hinged, movable, and articulated with the temporal bone of either side **b :** the parts constituting the walls of the mouth and serving to open and close it — usu. used in pl. **c :** any of various organs of invertebrates that perform the function of the vertebrate jaws **2 :** something resembling the jaw of an animal: as **a :** one of the sides of a narrow pass or channel **b :** either of two or more movable opposing parts that open and close for holding or crushing something between them **3** *pl* **:** a threatening position or situation **4** *slang* **a :** impudent or offensive talk **b :** a friendly chat

2**jaw** *vt, slang* **:** to talk to in a scolding or boring manner ~ *vi* **:** to talk abusively, indignantly, or longwindedly

jaw·bone \ˈjȯ-ˈbōn, -ˌbōn\ *n* **:** JAW 1a; *esp* **:** MANDIBLE

jaw·break·er \-ˌbrā-kər\ *n* **1 :** a word difficult to pronounce **2 :** a round hard candy

jaw·line \-ˌlīn\ *n* **:** the outline of the lower jaw

1**jay** \ˈjā\ *n* [ME, fr. MF *jai,* fr. LL *gaius*] **1 a :** a predominantly fawn-colored Old World bird (*Garrulus glandarius*) of the crow family with a black-and-white crest and wings marked with black, white, and blue **b :** any of numerous crested largely blue birds that with the common Old World jay constitute a subfamily of the crow family, have roving habits and harsh voices, and are often destructive to the eggs and young of other birds **2 a :** an impertinent chatterer **b :** DANDY 1 **c :** GREENHORN **3 :** a moderate blue

2**jay** *n* **:** the letter *j*

jay·bird \ˈjā-ˌbərd\ *n, chiefly Midland* **:** JAY 1, 2

Jay·cee \ˈjā-ˈsē\ *n* [*junior chamber*] **:** a member of a junior chamber of commerce

jay·gee \ˈjā-ˈjē\ *n* [*junior grade*] **:** LIEUTENANT JUNIOR GRADE

jay·hawk·er \ˈjā-ˌhȯ-kər\ *n* [*jayhawk* (fictitious bird of Kansas)] **1 a** *often cap* **:** a member of a band of antislavery guerrillas in Kansas and Missouri before and during the Civil War **b :** PLUNDERER, PIRATE **2** *cap* **:** a native or resident of Kansas — used as a nickname

jay·vee \ˈjā-ˈvē\ *n* [*junior varsity*] **1 :** JUNIOR VARSITY **2 :** a member of a junior varsity team

jay·walk \ˈjā-ˌwȯk\ *vi* **:** to cross a street carelessly or in a dangerous or illegal direction so as to be endangered by traffic — **jay·walk·er** *n*

1**jazz** \ˈjaz\ *vb* [origin unknown] *vt* **1 a :** ENLIVEN — usu. used with *up* **b :** ACCELERATE **2 :** to play in the manner of jazz ~ *vi* **1 :** to go here and there **:** GAD ⟨~*ing* around⟩ **2 :** to dance to or play jazz

2**jazz** *n, often attrib* **1 a :** American music characterized by improvisation, syncopated rhythms, contrapuntal ensemble playing, and special melodic features peculiar to the individual interpretation of the player **b :** popular dance music influenced by jazz and played in a loud rhythmic manner **2 :** empty talk **:** STUFF, HUMBUG ⟨spouted all the scientific ~ — Pete Martin⟩ — **jazz·ist** \-əst\ *n* — **jazz·man** \-mən, -ˌman\ *n*

jazz·i·ly \ˈjaz-ə-lē\ *adv* **:** in a jazzy manner

jazz·i·ness \ˈjaz-ē-nəs\ *n* **:** the quality or state of being jazzy

jazzy \ˈjaz-ē\ *adj* **1 :** having the characteristics of jazz **2 :** marked by unrestraint, animation, or flashiness

jeal·ous \ˈjel-əs\ *adj* [ME *jelous,* fr. OF, fr. (assumed) VL *zelosus,* fr. LL *zelus* zeal — more at ZEAL] **1 a :** intolerant of rivalry or unfaithfulness **b :** disposed to suspect rivalry or unfaithfulness **:** apprehensive of the loss of another's exclusive devotion **2 :** hostile toward a rival or one believed to enjoy an advantage **3 :** vigilant in guarding a possession **4 :** distrustfully watchful **:** SUSPICIOUS **syn** see ENVIOUS — **jeal·ous·ly** *adv* — **jeal·ous·ness** *n*

jeal·ou·sy \ˈjel-ə-sē\ *n* **1 :** a jealous disposition, attitude, or feeling **2 :** zealous vigilance

jean \ˈjēn\ *n* [short for *jean fustian,* fr. ME *Gene* Genoa, Italy + *fustian*] **1 :** a durable twilled cotton cloth used esp. for sportswear and work clothes **2** *pl* **a :** pants made of jean or denim **b :** TROUSERS

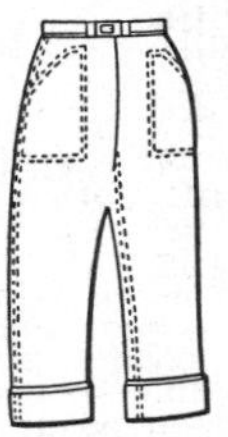
jeans 2a

jeep \ˈjēp\ *n* [alter. of *gee pee,* fr. *general-purpose*] **:** a small general-purpose motor vehicle with 80-inch wheelbase, ¼-ton capacity, and four-wheel drive used by the U.S. Army in World War II; *also* **:** a similar but larger and more powerful U.S. Army vehicle

1**jeer** \ˈji(ə)r\ *vb* [origin unknown] *vi* **:** to speak or cry out with derision or mockery ~ *vt* **:** DERIDE, RIDICULE **syn** see SCOFF — **jeer·er** *n* — **jeer·ing·ly** \-iŋ-lē\ *adv*

2**jeer** *n* **:** a jeering remark or sound **:** TAUNT

Jef·fer·son Da·vis's Birthday \ˌjef-ər-sən-ˈdā-vəs(-əz)-\ *n* **:** June 3 observed as a holiday in many southern states

Jefferson Day *n* **:** April 13 observed as a holiday in some states in commemoration of Thomas Jefferson's birthday

Jef·fer·so·nian \ˌjef-ər-ˈsō-nē-ən, -nyən\ *adj* **:** of, relating to, or characteristic of Thomas Jefferson or his political principles or policies — **Jeffersonian** *n* — **Jef·fer·so·nian·ism** \-nē-ə-ˌniz-əm, -nyə-ˌniz-\ *n*

Jef·frey pine \ˌjef-rē-\ *n* [John *Jeffrey,* 19th cent. Sc botanical explorer] **:** a pine (*Pinus jeffreyi*) of western No. America with long needles in groups of three

je·had *var of* JIHAD

Je·hosh·a·phat \ji-ˈhäs(h)-ə-ˌfat\ *n* [Heb *Yĕhōshāphāth*] **:** a king of Judah in the 9th century B.C.

Je·ho·vah \ji-ˈhō-və\ *n* [NL, false reading (as *Yĕhōwāh*) of Heb *Yahweh*] **:** GOD

Jehovah's Witnesses *n pl* **:** members of a group that witness by distributing literature and by personal evangelism to beliefs in the theocratic rule of God, the sinfulness of organized religions and governments, and an imminent millennium

je·hu \ˈjē-(ˌ)h(y)ü\ *n* [Heb *Yēhū*] **1** *cap* **:** a king of Israel in the 9th century B.C. **2 :** a driver of a coach or cab

jejun- *or* **jejuno-** *comb form* [L *jejunum*] **:** jejunum ⟨*jejun*ectomy⟩

je·ju·nal \ji-ˈjün-ᵊl\ *adj* **:** of or relating to the jejunum

je·june \ji-ˈjün\ *adj* [L *jejunus*] **1 :** lacking nutritive value ⟨~ diets⟩ **2 :** lacking interest or significance **:** DULL ⟨~ lectures⟩ **3 :** lacking maturity **:** PUERILE ⟨~ remarks on world affairs⟩ **syn** see INSIPID — **je·june·ly** *adv* — **je·june·ness** \-ˈjün-nəs\ *n*

je·ju·num \ji-ˈjü-nəm\ *n* [L, fr. neut. of *jejunus*] **:** the first two fifths of the small intestine beyond the duodenum

Je·kyll and Hyde \ˌjek-ə-lən-ˈhīd, ˌjē-kə-, ˌjā-kə-\ *n* [Dr. *Jekyll* & Mr. *Hyde,* representing the split personality of the protagonist in *The Strange Case of Dr. Jekyll and Mr. Hyde* (1886) by R. L. Stevenson] **:** a person having a split personality one side of which is good and the other evil

jell \ˈjel\ *vb* [back-formation fr. *jelly*] *vi* **1 :** to come to the consistency of jelly **2 :** to take shape **:** CRYSTALLIZE ~ *vt* **:** to cause to take form

jellied gasoline *n* **:** NAPALM

jel·li·fy \ˈjel-i-ˌfī\ *vt* **1 :** to make gelatinous **2 :** to make slack or weak ~ *vi* **:** to become gelatinous

Jell-O \ˈjel-(ˌ)ō\ *trademark* — used for a gelatin dessert often with the flavor and color of fruit

1**jel·ly** \ˈjel-ē\ *n* [ME *gelly,* fr. MF *gelee,* fr. fem. of *gelé,* pp. of *geler* to freeze, congeal, fr. L *gelare* — more at COLD] **1 :** a food preparation with a soft somewhat elastic consistency due usu. to the presence of gelatin or pectin; *esp* **:** a fruit product made by boiling sugar and the juice of fruit **2 :** a substance resembling jelly in consistency **3 :** a state of fear or irresolution **4 :** a shapeless structureless mass **:** PULP — **jel·ly·like** \-ˌlīk\ *adj*

2**jelly** *vi* **1 :** JELL **2 :** to make jelly ~ *vt* **:** to bring to the consistency of jelly

jelly bean *n* **1 :** a sugar-glazed bean-shaped candy **2 :** a weak, spineless, or effeminate person

jel·ly·fish \ˈjel-ē-ˌfish\ *n* **1 a :** a free-swimming marine coelenterate that is the sexually reproducing form of a hydrozoan or scyphozoan and has a nearly transparent saucer-shaped body and extensile marginal tentacles studded with stinging cells **b :** SIPHONOPHORE **c :** CTENOPHORE **2 :** a person lacking backbone or firmness

jelly roll *n* **:** a thin sheet of sponge cake spread with jelly and rolled up while hot

jel·u·tong \ˈjel-ə-ˌtȯŋ\ *n* [Malay *jĕlutong*] **1 :** any of several trees (genus *Dyera*) of the dogbane family **2 :** the resinous rubbery latex of a jelutong (esp. *Dyera costulata*) used esp. as a chicle substitute

je ne sais quoi \zhə-nə-ˌsā-ˈkwä\ *n* [F, lit., I know not what] **:** something that cannot be adequately described or expressed

jen·net \ˈjen-ət\ *n* [ME *genett,* fr. MF *genet,* fr. Catal, Zenete (member of a Berber people), horse] **1 :** a small Spanish horse **2 a :** a female donkey **b :** HINNY

jen·ny \ˈjen-ē\ *n* [fr. the name *Jenny*] **1 a :** a female bird ⟨~ wren⟩ **b :** a female donkey **2 :** SPINNING JENNY

jeop·ard \ˈjep-ərd\ *vt* [ME *jeoparden,* back-formation fr. *jeopardie*] **:** JEOPARDIZE

jeop·ar·dize \ˈjep-ər-ˌdīz\ *vt* **:** to expose to danger **:** IMPERIL

jeop·ar·dous \-ərd-əs\ *adj* **:** marked by risk or danger **:** PERILOUS

jeop·ar·dy \ˈjep-ərd-ē\ *n* [ME *jeopardie,* fr. AF *juparti,* fr. OF *jeu parti* alternative, lit., divided game] **1 :** exposure to or imminence of death, loss, or injury **:** DANGER **2 :** the danger that an accused person is subjected to when on trial for a criminal offense

je·quir·i·ty \jə-ˈkwir-ət-ē\ *n* [Pg *jequiriti*] **1 :** the scarlet and black seed of Indian licorice often used for beads **2 :** INDIAN LICORICE

jer·boa \jər-ˈbō-ə, jer-\ *n* [Ar *yarbū*ʻ] **:** any of several social nocturnal Old World jumping rodents (family Dipodidae) with long hind legs and long tail

jerboa mouse *n* **:** any of various leaping rodents usu. with elongated hind legs

jer·e·mi·ad \ˌjer-ə-ˈmī-əd, -ˌad\ *n* [F *jérémiade,* fr. *Jérémie* Jeremiah, fr. LL *Jeremias*] **:** a prolonged lamentation or complaint

Jer·e·mi·ah \-ˈmī-ə\ *n* [LL *Jeremias,* fr. Gk *Hieremias,* fr. Heb *Yirmĕyāh*] **1 :** a major Hebrew prophet of the 6th and 7th centuries B.C. **2 :** one who is pessimistic about the present and foresees a calamitous future

1**jerk** \ˈjərk\ *vb* [prob. alter. of *yerk*] *vt* **1 :** to give a quick suddenly arrested push, pull, or twist to **2 :** to throw with a quick suddenly arrested motion **3 :** to utter in an abrupt, snappy, or sharply broken manner **4 :** to mix and dispense (as sodas) behind a soda fountain ~ *vi* **1 :** to make a sudden spasmodic motion **2 :** to move in short abrupt motions or with frequent jolts **3 :** to throw an object with a jerk — **jerk·er** *n*

2**jerk** *n* **1 :** a single quick motion of short duration **2 a :** jolting, bouncing, or thrusting motions **b :** a tendency to produce spasmodic motions **3 a :** an involuntary spasmodic muscular movement due to reflex action **b** *pl* (1) **:** CHOREA (2) **:** involuntary twitchings due to nervous excitement **4 :** a stupid, foolish, or unconventional person **5 :** the pushing of a weight from shoulder height to a position overhead in weight lifting

3**jerk** *vt* [back-formation fr. 2*jerky*] **:** to cut (meat) into long slices or strips and dry in the sun

jerk·i·ly \ˈjər-kə-lē\ *adv* **:** in a jerky manner

jer·kin \ˈjər-kən\ *n* [origin unknown] **:** a close-fitting hip-length sleeveless jacket

jerk·i·ness \ˈjər-kē-nəs\ *n* **:** the quality or state of being jerky

jerk·wa·ter \ˈjər-ˌkwȯt-ər, -ˌkwät-\ *adj* [fr. *jerkwater* (rural train);

fr. the fact that it took on water carried in buckets from the source of supply] **1 :** remote and unimportant ⟨~ towns⟩ **2 :** PIDDLING

1**jerky** \'jər-kē\ *adj* **1 a :** moving along with or marked by fits and starts **b :** characterized by abrupt transitions **2 :** INANE, FOOLISH

2**jer·ky** \'jər-kē\ *n* [Sp *charqui*] **:** jerked meat

jer·o·bo·am \,jer-ə-'bō-əm\ *n* [*Jeroboam* I †*ab*912 B.C. king of the northern kingdom of Israel] **:** an oversize wine bottle holding about four 26-ounce quarts ⟨a ~ of champagne⟩

Jer·ry \'jer-ē\ *n* [by shortening & alter.] *chiefly Brit* **:** GERMAN

jer·ry–build \'jer-ē-,bild\ *vt* [back-formation fr. *jerry-built*] **:** to build cheaply and flimsily — **jer·ry–build·er** *n*

jer·ry–built \-,bilt\ *adj* [origin unknown] **1 :** built cheaply and unsubstantially **2 :** carelessly or hastily put together

jer·sey \'jər-zē\ *n* [*Jersey*, one of the Channel islands] **1 :** a plain weft-knitted fabric made of wool, cotton, nylon, rayon, or silk and used for clothing **2 :** any of various close-fitting usu. circular-knitted garments **3 :** any of a breed of small short-horned predominantly yellowish brown or fawn dairy cattle noted for their rich milk

Jersey giant *n* [*New Jersey*, state of U.S.] **:** any of a breed of large usu. black domestic fowls developed by interbreeding large Asiatic fowls with Langshans

Je·ru·sa·lem artichoke \jə-,rü-s(ə-)ləm-, -,rüz-(ə-)ləm-\ *n* [*Jerusalem* by folk etymology fr. It *girasole* girasol] **:** a perennial American sunflower (*Helianthus tuberosus*) widely cultivated for its tubers used as a vegetable, a livestock feed, and a source of levulose

Jerusalem cherry *n* [*Jerusalem*, Palestine] **:** either of two plants (*Solanum pseudo-capsicum* or *S. capsicastrum*) of the nightshade family cultivated as ornamental house plants for their orange to red berries

Jerusalem cricket *n* **:** a large-headed burrowing nocturnal insect (*Stenopelmatus fuscus*) of the southwestern U.S. related to the katydids

Jerusalem thorn *n* **1 :** CHRIST'S-THORN **2 :** a tropical American leguminous spiny shrub or shrubby tree (*Parkinsonia aculeata*) with pinnate leaves and showy racemose yellow flowers that is used for hedging and as emergency food for livestock

jess \'jes\ *n* [ME *ges*, fr. MF *gies*, fr. pl. of *jet* throw, fr. *jeter* to throw — more at JET] **:** a short strap secured on the leg of a hawk and usu. provided with a ring for attaching a leash — **jessed** \'jest\ *adj*

jes·sa·mine \'jes-(ə-)mən\ *var of* JASMINE

jes·se \'jes-ē\ *n* [prob. fr. *Jesse;* fr. "And there shall come forth a rod out of the stem of Jesse" (Isa 11:1—AV)] *chiefly dial* **:** a severe scolding or beating

Jes·se \'jes-ē\ *n* [Heb *Yishay*] **:** the father of David, king of Israel

1**jest** \'jest\ *n* [ME *geste*, fr. OF, fr. L *gesta* deeds, fr. neut. pl. of *gestus*, pp. of *gerere* to bear, wage — more at CAST] **1 a :** an act intended to provoke laughter **:** PRANK **b :** a comic incident **2 a :** JEER **b :** a witty remark **3 a :** a frivolous mood or manner ⟨spoken in ~⟩ **b :** gaiety and merriment **4 :** LAUGHINGSTOCK

syn JEST, JOKE, QUIP, WITTICISM, WISECRACK mean something said for the purpose of evoking laughter. JEST is chiefly literary and applies to any utterance not seriously intended whether sarcastic, ironic, witty, or merely playful; JOKE may apply to an act as well as an utterance and suggests no intent to hurt feelings; QUIP implies lightness and neatness of phrase more definitely than JEST; WITTICISM and WISECRACK both stress cleverness of phrasing and both may suggest flippancy or unfeelingness **syn** see in addition FUN

2**jest** *vi* **1 :** to utter taunts **:** GIBE **2 :** to speak or act without seriousness **3 :** to make a witty remark **:** JOKE ~ *vt* **:** to make fun of

jest·er \'jes-tər\ *n* **1 :** FOOL 2a **2 :** one given to jests

Je·su·it \'jezh-(ə-)wət, 'jez-\ *n* [NL *Jesuita*, fr. LL *Jesus*] **1 :** a member of a religious society for men founded by St. Ignatius Loyola in 1534 **2 :** one given to intrigue or equivocation — **je·su·it·ic** \,jez(h)-ə-'wit-ik\ *or* **je·su·it·i·cal** \-i-kəl\ *adj, often cap* — **je·su·it·i·cal·ly** \-i-k(ə-)lē\ *adv, often cap* — **je·su·it·ism** \'jezh-(ə-)wət-,iz-əm, 'jez-\ *or* **je·su·it·ry** \-wə-trē\ *n, often cap* — **je·su·it·ize** \-wət-,īz\ *vb, often cap*

Je·sus \'jē-zəs, -zəz, *in the Hail Mary also* -,zəs\ *n* [LL, fr. Gk *Iēsous*, fr. Heb *Yēshūa'*] **1 :** the founder of the Christian religion — called also *Jesus Christ* **2** *Christian Science* **:** the highest human corporeal concept of the divine idea rebuking and destroying error and bringing to light man's immortality

1**jet** \'jet\ *n* [ME, fr. MF *jaiet*, fr. L *gagates*, fr. Gk *gagatēs*, fr. *Gagas*, town and river in Asia Minor] **1 :** a compact velvet-black mineral similar to coal that takes a good polish and is often used for jewelry **2 :** a very dark black

2**jet** *vb* **jet·ted; jet·ting** [MF *jeter*, lit., to throw, fr. L *jactare* to throw, fr. *jactus*, pp. of *jacere* to throw; akin to Gk *hienai* to send] *vi* **:** to spout forth **:** GUSH ~ *vt* **:** to emit in a stream **:** SPOUT

3**jet** *n* **1 a :** a forceful rush of liquid, gas, or vapor through a narrow opening or a nozzle **b :** a nozzle for a jet of gas, water, or other fluid **2 :** something issuing in or as if in a jet

jet airplane *n* **:** an airplane powered by a jet engine that utilizes the surrounding air in the combustion of fuel or by a rocket-type jet engine that carries its fuel and all the oxygen needed for combustion

jet·bead \'jet-,bēd\ *n* **:** a shrub (*Rhodotypos scandens*) that has black shining fruit and is used as an ornamental

je·té \zhə-'tā\ *n* [F, fr. pp. of *jeter*] **:** a sharp leap in ballet with an outward thrust of the working leg

jet engine *n* **:** an engine that produces motion as a result of the rearward discharge of a jet of fluid; *specif* **:** an airplane engine having one or more exhaust nozzles for discharging rearwardly a jet of heated air and exhaust gases to produce forward propulsion

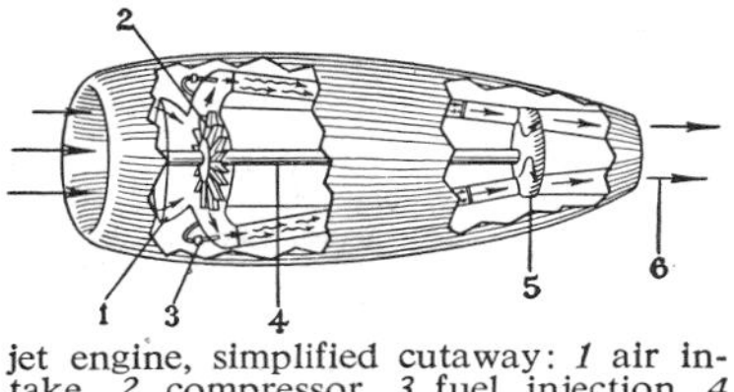

jet engine, simplified cutaway: *1* air intake, *2* compressor, *3* fuel injection, *4* drive shaft, *5* turbine, *6* exhaust

jet–pro·pelled \,jet-prə-'peld\ *adj* **1 :** propelled by a jet engine **2 :** suggestive of the speed and force of a jet airplane

jet propulsion *n* **:** propulsion of a body produced by the forwardly directed forces of the reaction resulting from the rearward discharge of a jet of fluid; *specif* **:** propulsion of an airplane by jet engines

jet·sam \'jet-səm\ *n* [alter. of *jettison*] **1 :** the part of a ship, its equipment, or cargo that is cast overboard to lighten the load in time of distress and that sinks or is washed ashore **2 :** FLOTSAM 2

jet set *n* **:** an international social group of wealthy individuals who frequent fashionable resorts

jet stream *n* **:** a long narrow meandering current of high-speed winds near the tropopause blowing from a generally westerly direction and often exceeding a speed of 250 miles per hour

1**jet·ti·son** \'jet-ə-sən, -ə-zən\ *n* [ME *jetteson*, fr. AF *getteson*, fr. OF *getaison* action of throwing, fr. L *jactation-*, *jactatio*, fr. *jactatus*, pp. of *jactare*] **1 :** a voluntary sacrifice of cargo to lighten a ship's load in time of distress **2 :** ABANDONMENT

2**jettison** *vt* **1 :** to make jettison of **2 :** to cast off as an encumbrance **:** DISCARD **3 :** to drop from an airplane in flight —**jet·ti·son·able** \-sə-nə-bəl, -zə-\ *adj*

1**jet·ty** \'jet-ē\ *n* [ME *jette*, fr. MF *jetee*, fr. fem. of *jeté*, pp. of *jeter* to throw — more at JET] **1 a :** a structure extended into a sea, lake, or river to influence the current or tide or to protect a harbor **b :** a protecting frame of a pier **2 :** a landing wharf **:** PIER

2**jetty** *vi* **:** PROJECT, JUT

3**jetty** *adj* **:** black as jet

jeu d'es·prit \zhœ̄-des-prē\ *n, pl* **jeux d'esprit** *same*\ [F, lit., play of the mind] **:** a witty comment or composition

jeune fille \zhœn-fē(y)\ *n, pl* **jeunes filles** *same*\ [F] **:** a young girl

jeu·nesse do·rée \zhœ-nes-dȯ-rā\ *n* [F, gilded youth] **:** young people of wealth and fashion

Jew \'jü\ *n* [ME, fr. OF *gyu*, fr. L *Judaeus*, fr. Gk *Ioudaios*, fr. Heb *Yĕhūdhī*, fr. *Yĕhūdhāh* Judah, Jewish kingdom] **1 a :** a member of the tribe of Judah **b :** ISRAELITE **2 :** a member of a nation existing in Palestine from the 6th century B.C. to the 1st century A.D. **3 :** one whose religion is Judaism

1**jew·el** \'jü(-ə)l, 'jü(-ə)l\ *n, often attrib* [ME *juel*, fr. OF, dim. of *jeu* game, play, fr. L *jocus* game, joke — more at JOKE] **1 :** an ornament of precious metal set with stones or finished with enamel and worn as an accessory of dress **2 :** one that is highly esteemed **3 :** a precious stone **:** GEM **4 :** a bearing for a pivot in a watch made of crystal, precious stone, or glass

2**jewel** *vt* **jew·eled** *or* **jew·elled; jew·el·ing** *or* **jew·el·ling** **1 :** to adorn or equip with jewels **2 :** to give beauty to as if with jewels

jew·el·er *or* **jew·el·ler** \'jü-(ə-)lər, 'jü(-ə)l-ər\ *n* **1 :** one who makes or repairs jewelry **2 :** one who deals in jewelry, precious stones, watches, and usu. silverware and china

jew·el·ly \'jü-(ə-)lē, 'jü(-ə)l-ē\ *adj* **1 :** having or wearing jewels **2 :** resembling a jewel

jew·el·ry \'jü(-ə)l-rē, 'jü(-ə)l-\ *n* **:** JEWELS; *esp* **:** objects of precious metal often set with gems and worn for personal adornment

jew·el·weed \-,wēd\ *n* **:** any of a genus (*Impatiens* of the family Balsaminaceae, the jewelweed family) of succulent often glaucous herbs with irregular often showy flowers

Jew·ess \'jü-əs\ *n* **:** a female Jew

jew·fish \'jü-,fish\ *n* **:** any of various large groupers that are usu. dusky green or blackish, thickheaded, and rough-scaled

1**Jew·ish** \'jü-ish\ *adj* **:** of, relating to, or characteristic of the Jews — **Jew·ish·ly** *adv* — **Jew·ish·ness** *n*

2**Jewish** *n* **:** YIDDISH

Jewish calendar *n* **:** a calendar in use among Jewish peoples that is reckoned from the year 3761 B.C. and dates in its present form from about A.D. 360 — see CALENDAR table

Jew·ry \'jù(ə)r-ē, 'jü-rē\ *n* **1 :** a district of a city inhabited by Jews **:** GHETTO **2 :** the Jewish people

Jew's harp *or* **Jews' harp** \'jüz-,härp, 'jüs-\ *n* **:** a small lyre-shaped instrument that when placed between the teeth gives tones from a metal tongue struck by the finger

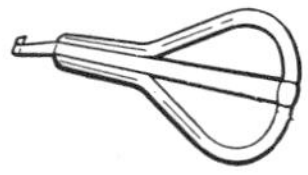
Jew's harp

Jez·e·bel \'jez-ə-,bel\ *n* [Heb *Īzebhel*] **1 :** the wife of Ahab noted for her wickedness **2** *often not cap* **:** an impudent, shameless, or abandoned woman

JHVH *var of* YHWH

1**jib** \'jib\ *n* [origin unknown] **:** a triangular sail set on a stay extending from the head of the foremast to the bowsprit or the jibboom

2**jib** *vb* **jibbed; jib·bing** *vt* **:** to cause (as a sail) to swing from one side of a ship to the other ~ *vi* **:** to shift across or swing round from one side of a ship to the other

3**jib** *n* [prob. by shortening & alter. fr. *gibbet*] **1 :** the projecting arm of a crane **2 :** a derrick boom

4**jib** *vi* **jibbed; jib·bing** [prob. fr. 2*jib*] **:** to refuse to go **:** BALK — **jib·ber** *n*

jib·boom \'jib-'(b)üm\ *n* [1*jib* + *boom*] **:** a spar that serves as an extension of the bowsprit

1**jibe** \'jīb\ *vb* [perh. modif. of D *gijben*] *vi* **1 :** to shift suddenly from one side to the other — used of a fore-and-aft sail **2 :** to change a ship's course so that the sail jibes ~ *vt* **:** to cause to jibe

2**jibe** *var of* GIBE

3**jibe** *vi* [origin unknown] **:** to be in accord **:** AGREE

jiff \'jif\ *n* [by shortening] **:** JIFFY

jif·fy \'jif-ē\ *n* [origin unknown] **:** MOMENT, INSTANT ⟨in a ~⟩

1**jig** \'jig\ *n* [prob. fr. MF *giguer* to dance, fr. *gigue* fiddle, of Gmc origin; akin to OHG *gīga* fiddle; akin to ON *geiga* to turn aside — more at GIG] **1 a :** any of several lively springy dances in triple rhythm **b :** music to which a jig may be danced **2 :** TRICK, GAME ⟨the ~ is up⟩ **3 a :** any of several fishing devices that are jerked up and down or drawn through the water **b :** a device used to maintain mechanically the correct positional relationship between a piece of work and the tool or between parts of work during assembly **c :** a device in which crushed ore is concentrated or coal is cleaned by agitating in water

2**jig** *vb* **jigged; jig·ging** *vt* **1 :** to dance in the rapid lively manner of a jig **2 :** to give a rapid jerky motion to **3 :** to catch (a fish) with a jig **4 :** to machine by means of a jig-controlled tool operation ~ *vi* **1 a :** to dance a jig **b :** to move with rapid jerky motions **2 :** to fish with a jig **3 :** to work with the aid of a jig

1**jig·ger** \'jig-ər\ *n* **1 :** one that jigs or operates a jig **2 :** a light general-purpose tackle used on shipboard **3 :** 1JIG 3a **4 a :** a small boat rigged like a yawl **b** (1) **:** a small mast stepped in the

stern (2) : the aftermost mast of a 4-masted ship **5 a :** a mechanical device; *esp* : one operating with a jerky reciprocating motion **b :** something too complex, tricky, or trivial to designate accurately : GADGET **6 :** a measure used in mixing drinks that usu. holds 1½ ounces

2**jigger** *n* [of African origin; akin to Wolof *jiga* insect] : CHIGGER

1**jig·gle** \'jig-əl\ *vb* **jig·gling** \'jig-(ə-)liŋ\ [freq. of 2*jig*] *vi* : to move with quick little jerks or oscillating motions ~ *vt* : to cause to jiggle

2**jiggle** *n* : a jiggling motion

jig·gly \'jig-(ə-)lē\ *adj* : UNSTEADY, JIGGLING

1**jig·saw** \'jig-,sȯ\ *n* **1 :** a machine saw with a narrow vertically reciprocating blade for cutting curved and irregular lines or ornamental patterns in openwork **2 :** SCROLL SAW

2**jigsaw** *vt* **1 :** to cut or form by or as if by a jigsaw **2 :** to arrange or place in an intricate or interlocking way

jigsaw puzzle *n* : a puzzle consisting of small irregularly cut pieces that are fitted together to form a picture

ji·had \ji-'häd, -'had\ *n* [Ar *jihād*] **1 :** a holy war waged on behalf of Islam as a religious duty **2 :** a crusade for a principle or belief

jil·lion \'jil-yən\ *n* [*j* + *-illion* (as in *million*)] : an indeterminately large number

1**jilt** \'jilt\ *n* [alter. of *jillet* (flirtatious girl)] : a woman who capriciously or unfeelingly casts aside a man previously accepted as a lover

2**jilt** *vt* : to cast aside (as a lover) capriciously or unfeelingly

jim crow \'jim-'krō\ *n, often cap J & C* [*Jim Crow*, stereotype Negro in a 19th cent. song-and-dance act] **1 :** NEGRO — usu. taken to be offensive **2 :** discrimination esp. against the Negro by legal enforcement or traditional sanctions — **jim crow·ism** \-,iz-əm\ *n, often cap J & C*

jim–dan·dy \'jim-'dan-dē\ *n* [fr. the name *Jim*] : something excellent of its kind

jim·jams \'jim-,jamz\ *n pl* [perh. alter. of *delirium tremens*] **1 :** DELIRIUM TREMENS **2 :** JITTERS

1**jim·my** \'jim-ē\ *n* [fr. the name *Jimmy*] : a short crowbar

2**jimmy** *vt* : to force open with or as if with a jimmy

jim·son·weed \'jim(p)-sən-,wēd\ *n, often cap* [*Jamestown*, Va.] : a poisonous tall coarse annual weed (*Datura stramonium*) of the nightshade family with rank-smelling foliage and large white or violet trumpet-shaped flowers

1**jin·gle** \'jiŋ-gəl\ *vb* **jin·gling** \-g(ə-)liŋ\ [ME *ginglen*, of imit. origin] *vi* **1 :** to make a light clinking or tinkling sound **2 :** to rhyme or sound in a catchy repetitious manner ~ *vt* : to cause to jingle — **jin·gler** \-g(ə-)lər\ *n*

2**jingle** *n* **1 a :** a light clinking or tinkling sound **b :** a catchy repetition of sounds in a poem **2 a :** something that jingles **b :** a short verse or song marked by catchy repetition **3 :** a 2-wheeled covered vehicle used esp. in Ireland and Australia — **jin·gly** \-g(ə-)lē\ *adj*

1**jin·go** \'jiŋ-(,)gō\ *interj* [prob. euphemism for *Jesus*] — used as a mild oath usu. in the phrase *by jingo*

2**jingo** *n* [fr. the fact that the phrase *by jingo* appeared in the refrain of a chauvinistic song] : one characterized by jingoism — **jin·go·ish** \-ish\ *adj*

jin·go·ism \'jiŋ-(,)gō-,iz-əm\ *n* : extreme chauvinism or nationalism marked esp. by a belligerent foreign policy — **jin·go·ist** \-əst\ *n* — **jin·go·is·tic** \,jiŋ-(,)gō-'is-tik\ *adj* — **jin·go·is·ti·cal·ly** \-'is-ti-k(ə-)lē\ *adv*

1**jink** \'jiŋk\ *n* [origin unknown] **1** *pl* : PRANKS, FROLICS ⟨high ~*s*⟩ **2 :** a quick evasive turn : SLIP

2**jink** *vi* : to make a quick or unexpected turn

jinn \'jin\ *or* **jin·ni** \jə-'nē, 'jin-ē\ *n, pl* **jinns** *or* **jinn** [Ar *jinnīy* demon] **1 :** one of a class of spirits held by the Muslims to inhabit the earth, to assume various forms, and to exercise supernatural power **2 :** a supernatural spirit that often takes human form and serves his summoner

jin·rik·i·sha \jin-'rik-,shȯ\ *n* [Jap] : a small covered 2-wheeled vehicle usu. for one passenger pulled by one man and used orig. in Japan

1**jinx** \'jiŋ(k)s\ *n* [prob. alter. of *jynx* (wryneck); fr. the use of wrynecks in witchcraft] : one that brings bad luck

2**jinx** *vt* : to foredoom to failure or misfortune

ji·pi·ja·pa \,hē-pē-'häp-ə\ *n* [Sp, fr. *Jipijapa*, Ecuador] **1 :** a Central and So. American plant (*Carludovica palmata*) resembling a palm **2 :** PANAMA

jit·ney \'jit-nē\ *n* [origin unknown] **1** *slang* : NICKEL 2a(1) **2** [fr. the 5 cent fare] : BUS 1; *esp* : a small bus that carries passengers over a regular route according to a flexible schedule

jit·ter \'jit-ər\ *vi* [origin unknown] : to be nervous or act in a nervous way

jit·ter·bug \'jit-ər-,bəg\ *n* **1 :** a dance in which couples two-step, balance, and twirl in standardized patterns or with vigorous acrobatics **2 :** one who dances the jitterbug — **jitterbug** *vi*

jit·ters \'jit-ərz\ *n pl* : extreme nervousness — **jit·tery** \-ə-rē\ *adj*

jiu·jit·su *or* **jiu·jut·su** *var of* JUJITSU

1**jive** \'jīv\ *n* [origin unknown] **1 :** swing music or the dancing performed to it **2 a** *slang* : glib, deceptive, or foolish talk **b :** the jargon of hipsters **c :** a special jargon of difficult or slang terms

2**jive** *vi* **1** *slang* : KID **2 :** to dance to or play jive ~ *vt* **1** *slang* : TEASE **2 :** SWING 5

jo \'jō\ *n* [alter. of *joy*] *chiefly Scot* : SWEETHEART, DEAR

1**job** \'jäb\ *n* [perh. fr. obs. E *job* (lump)] **1 a :** a piece of work; *specif* : a small miscellaneous piece of work undertaken on order at a stated rate **b :** the object or material on which work is being done **c :** something produced by or as if by work **2 a :** something done for private advantage **b :** a criminal enterprise; *specif* : ROBBERY **c** *slang* : a damaging piece of work ⟨did a ~ on him⟩ **3 a** (1) : something that has to be done : TASK (2) : an undertaking requiring unusual exertion **b :** a specific duty, role, or function **c :** a regular remunerative position **d :** state of affairs **4 :** the process of doing a piece of work **syn** see POSITION, TASK

2**job** *vb* **jobbed; job·bing** *vi* **1 :** to do odd or occasional pieces of work for hire **2 :** to carry on public business for private gain **3 :** to carry on the business of a middleman ~ *vt* **1 :** to buy and sell for profit : SPECULATE **2 :** to hire or let by the job or for a period of service **3 :** to get, deal with, or effect by jobbery **4 :** to do or cause to be done by separate portions or lots : SUBCONTRACT **5 :** SWINDLE, TRICK

3**job** *adj* **1** *Brit* : that is for hire for a given service or period **2 :** used in, engaged in, or done as job work

Job \'jōb\ *n* [L, fr. Gk *Iōb*, fr. Heb *Iyyōbh*] : the hero of an Old Testament book who endures afflictions with fortitude and faith

job·ber \'jäb-ər\ *n* : one that jobs: as **a** (1) : STOCKJOBBER (2) : WHOLESALER; *specif* : a wholesaler who operates on a small scale or who sells only to retailers and institutions **b :** one who works by the job or on job work

job·bery \'jäb-(ə-)rē\ *n* : the act or practice of jobbing; *esp* : corruption in public office

job·hold·er \'jäb-,hōl-dər\ *n* : one having a regular job; *specif* : a government employee

job·less \'jäb-ləs\ *adj* **1 :** having no job **2 :** of or relating to those having no job — **job·less·ness** *n*

job lot *n* **1 :** a miscellaneous collection of goods for sale as a lot usu. to a retailer **2 :** a miscellaneous and usu. inferior collection or group

Job's comforter \'jōbz-\ *n* [fr. the tone of the speeches made to Job by his friends] : one who discourages or depresses while seemingly giving comfort and consolation

Job's tears *n pl* **1 :** hard pearly white seeds often used as beads **2** *sing in constr* : an Asiatic grass (*Coix lacryma-jobi*) whose seeds are Job's tears

job work *n* : commercial printing of miscellaneous orders

Jo·cas·ta \jō-'kas-tə\ *n* [L, fr. Gk *Iokastē*] : a queen of Thebes and mother of Oedipus

1**jock** \'jäk\ *n* : JOCKEY 1

2**jock** *n* : JOCKSTRAP

1**jock·ey** \'jäk-ē\ *n* [*Jockey*, Sc nickname for *John*] **1 :** one who rides a horse esp. as a professional in a race **2 :** OPERATOR

2**jockey** *vt* **1 :** to deal shrewdly or fraudulently with **2 a :** to ride (a horse) as a jockey **b :** DRIVE, OPERATE **3 a :** to maneuver or manipulate by adroit or devious means **b :** to change the position of by a series of movements **c :** to bring by maneuvering ~ *vi* **1 :** to act as a jockey **2 :** to maneuver for advantage

jockey club *n* : an association for the promotion and regulation of horse racing

jock·strap \'jäk-,strap\ *n* [E slang *jock* (penis) + E *strap*] : a supporter for the genitals worn by men participating in sports or strenuous activities

jo·cose \jō-'kōs\ *adj* [L *jocosus*, fr. *jocus* joke] **1 :** given to joking : MERRY **2 :** characterized by joking : HUMOROUS **syn** see WITTY — **jo·cose·ly** *adv* — **jo·cose·ness** *n*

jo·cos·i·ty \jō-'käs-ət-ē\ *n* **1 :** the quality or state of being jocose **2 :** a jocose act or remark

joc·u·lar \'jäk-yə-lər\ *adj* [L *jocularis*, fr. *joculus*, dim. of *jocus*] **1 :** given to jesting : MIRTHFUL **2 :** characterized by jesting : PLAYFUL **syn** see WITTY — **joc·u·lar·ly** *adv*

joc·u·lar·i·ty \,jäk-yə-'lar-ət-ē\ *n* **1 :** the quality or state of being jocular **2 :** a jocular act or remark

jo·cund \'jäk-ənd *also* 'jōk-ənd\ *adj* [ME, fr. LL *jocundus*, alter. of L *jucundus*, fr. *juvare* to help] : marked by or suggestive of mirth or cheerfulness : GAY **syn** see MERRY — **jo·cund·ly** \-ən-(d)lē\ *adv*

jo·cun·di·ty \jō-'kən-dət-ē\ *n* **1 :** CHEERFULNESS **2 :** PLEASANTRY

jodh·pur \'jäd-pər\ *n* [*Jodhpur*, India] **1** *pl* : riding breeches cut full through the hips and close-fitting from knee to ankle **2 :** an ankle-high boot fastened with a strap that is buckled at the side

Jo·el \'jō-əl\ *n* [L, fr. Gk *Iōēl*, fr. Heb *Yō'ēl*] : a minor prophet of Old Testament times

joe–pye weed \'jō-'pī-\ *n* [origin unknown] : BONESET

1**jog** \'jäg\ *vb* **jogged; jog·ging** [prob. alter. of *shog*] *vt* **1 :** to give a slight shake or push to : NUDGE **2 :** to rouse to alertness **3 :** to cause to go at a jog ~ *vi* **1 :** to move up and down or about with a short heavy motion **2 a :** to run or ride at a slow trot **b :** to go at a slow, leisurely, or monotonous pace : TRUDGE — **jog·ger** *n*

2**jog** *n* **1 :** a slight shake : PUSH **2 a :** a jogging movement, pace, or trip **b :** a slow gait of a horse with marked beats

3**jog** *n* [prob. alter. of 2*jag*] **1 a :** a projecting or retreating part of a line or surface **b :** the space in the angle of a jog **2 :** a brief abrupt change in direction

4**jog** *vi* **jogged; jog·ging :** to make a jog

1**jog·gle** \'jäg-əl\ *vb* **jog·gling** \'jäg-(ə-)liŋ\ [freq. of 1*jog*] *vt* : to shake slightly ~ *vi* : to have or go with a shaking or jerking motion — **jog·gler** \-(ə-)lər\ *n*

2**joggle** *n* : 2JOG 2a

3**joggle** *n* [dim. of 3*jog*] **1 :** a notch or tooth in the joining surface of a piece of building material to prevent slipping **2 :** a dowel for joining two adjacent blocks of masonry

4**joggle** *vt* **jog·gling** \'jäg-(ə-)liŋ\ : to join by means of a joggle so as to prevent sliding apart

jog trot *n* **1 :** a slow regular jolting gait **2 :** a routine habit or course of action

jo·han·nes \jō-'han-əs\ *n, pl* **johannes** [*Johannes* John V †1750 king of Portugal] : a Portuguese gold coin of the 18th and 19th centuries equivalent to 6400 reis

Jo·han·nine \jō-'han-,īn, -ən\ *adj* [LL *Johannes*] : of, relating to, or characteristic of the apostle John or the New Testament books ascribed to him

john \'jän\ *n* [fr. the name *John*] : TOILET

John \'jän\ *n* [LL *Johannes*, fr. Gk *Iōannēs*, fr. Heb *Yōhānān*] **1 :** the baptizer of Jesus — called also *John the Baptist* **2 :** an apostle held to have written the fourth Gospel, three Epistles, and the Book of Revelation

John Barleycorn *n* : alcoholic liquor personified

john·boat \'jän-,bōt\ *n* [fr. the name *John*] : a narrow flat-bottomed square-ended boat propelled by a pole or paddle and used on inland waterways

John Bull \-'bu̇l\ *n* [*John Bull*, character typifying the English nation in *The History of John Bull* (1712) by John Arbuthnot] **1 :** the English nation personified : the English people **2 :** a typical Englishman — **John Bull·ish** \-ish\ *adj* — **John Bull·ish·ness** *n* — **John Bull·ism** \-,iz-əm\ *n*

John Doe \-'dō\ *n* **1 :** a party to legal proceedings whose true name is unknown **2 :** an average man

John Do·ry \-ˈdȯr-ē, -ˈdȯr-\ *n* **:** a common yellow to olive European food fish (*Zeus faber*) with an oval compressed body, long dorsal spines, and a dark spot on each side; *also* **:** a closely related and possibly identical fish widely distributed in southern seas
John Han·cock \-ˈhan-ˌkäk\ *n* [*John Hancock;* fr. the prominence of his signature on the Declaration of Independence] **:** an autograph signature
John Hen·ry \-ˈhen-rē\ *n* [fr. the name *John Henry*] **:** an autograph signature
john·ny \ˈjän-ē\ *n* [fr. the name *Johnny*] **1** *often cap* **:** FELLOW, GUY **2 :** a short-sleeved collarless gown with an opening in the back for wear by hospital bed patients
john·ny·cake \-ˌkāk\ *n* [prob. fr. the name *Johnny*] **:** a bread made with cornmeal, flour, eggs, and milk
John·ny–jump–up \ˌjän-ē-ˈjəm-ˌpəp\ *n* **1 :** WILD PANSY; *broadly* **:** any of various small-flowered cultivated pansies **2 :** any of various American violets
John·ny–on–the–spot \ˌjän-ē-ˌȯn-t͟hə-ˈspät, -ē-ˌän-\ *n* **:** one who is on hand and ready to perform a service or respond to an emergency
Johnny Reb \-ˈreb\ *n* [the name *Johnny* + *reb* (rebel)] **:** a Confederate soldier
John·son·ese \ˌjän(t)-sə-ˈnēz, -ˈnēs\ *n* [Samuel *Johnson* †1784 E lexicographer and writer] **:** a literary style characterized by balanced phraseology and Latinate diction
John·son grass \ˈjän(t)-sən-\ *n* [William *Johnson*, 19th cent. Am agriculturist] **:** a tall perennial sorghum (*Sorghum halepense*) naturalized as a hay and forage grass in warm regions
John·so·ni·an \jän-ˈsō-nē-ən\ *adj* **:** of, relating to, or characteristic of Samuel Johnson or his writings — **Johnsonian** *n*
joie de vi·vre \ˌzhwäd-ə-ˈvēvrᵊ\ *n* [F, lit., joy of living] **:** keen or buoyant enjoyment of life
¹join \ˈjȯin\ *vb* [ME *joinen*, fr. OF *joindre*, fr. L *jungere* — more at YOKE] *vt* **1 a :** to put or bring together so as to form a unit ⟨~ two blocks of wood with glue⟩ **b :** to connect (as points) by a line **c :** ADJOIN **2 :** to put or bring into close association or relationship ⟨~*ed* in marriage⟩ **3 :** to engage in (battle) **4 a :** to come into the company of ⟨~*ed* us for lunch⟩ **b :** to associate oneself with ⟨~*ed* the church⟩ ~ *vi* **1 a :** to come together so as to be connected ⟨nouns ~ to form compounds⟩ **b :** ADJOIN ⟨the two estates ~⟩ **2 :** to come into close association or relationship: as **a :** to form an alliance ⟨~*ed* to combat crime⟩ **b :** to become a member of a group **c :** to take part in a collective activity ⟨~ in singing⟩ — **join·able** \ˈjȯi-nə-bəl\ *adj*
syn JOIN, COMBINE, UNITE, CONNECT, LINK, ASSOCIATE, RELATE mean to bring or come together into some manner of union. JOIN implies a bringing into contact or conjunction of any degree of closeness; COMBINE implies some merging or mingling with corresponding loss of identity of each unit; UNITE implies somewhat greater loss of separate identity; CONNECT suggests a loose or external attachment with little or no loss of identity; LINK may imply strong connection or inseparability of elements still retaining identity; ASSOCIATE stresses the mere fact of frequent occurrence or existence together in space or in logical relation; RELATE suggests a connection based on some logical principle such as cause and effect or subordination ⟨*relate* one event to another⟩
²join *n* **:** JOINT
join·der \ˈjȯin-dər\ *n* [F *joindre* to join] **1 :** CONJUNCTION **2 a** (1) **:** a joining of parties as plaintiffs or defendants in a suit (2) **:** a joining of causes of action or defense **b :** acceptance of an issue tendered
join·er \ˈjȯi-nər\ *n* **:** one that joins: as **a :** a person whose occupation is to construct articles by joining pieces of wood **b :** a gregarious person who joins many organizations
join·ery \ˈjȯin-(ə-)rē\ *n* **1 :** the art or trade of a joiner **2 :** things made by a joiner
¹joint \ˈjȯint\ *n* [ME *jointe*, fr. OF, fr. *joindre*] **1 a** (1) **:** the point of contact between elements of an animal skeleton with the parts that surround and support it (2) **:** NODE 4b **b :** a part or space included between two articulations, knots, or nodes **c :** a large piece of meat for roasting **2 a :** a place where two things or parts are joined **b :** a space between the adjacent surfaces of two bodies joined and held together by cement, mortar, or other material **c :** a fracture or crack in rock not accompanied by dislocation **d :** the flexing part of a cover along either backbone edge of a book **e :** the junction of two or more members of a framed structure **f :** a union formed by two abutting rails in a track including the bars, bolts, and other elements necessary to hold the abutting rails together **g :** an area at which two ends, surfaces, or edges are attached **3 a :** a shabby or disreputable place of entertainment **b :** PLACE, ESTABLISHMENT — **joint·ed** \-əd\ *adj* — **joint·ed·ly** *adv* — **joint·ed·ness** *n* — **out of joint 1 a :** DISLOCATED **b :** at variance **2 a :** DISORDERED **b :** DISSATISFIED
²joint *adj* [ME, fr. MF, fr. pp. of *joindre*] **1 :** UNITED, COMBINED **2 :** common to two or more: as **a** (1) **:** involving the united activity of two or more (2) **:** constituting an activity, operation, or organization in which elements of more than one armed service participate (3) **:** constituting an action or expression of two or more governments **b :** shared by or affecting two or more **3 :** united, joined, or sharing with another
³joint *vb* [¹*joint*] *vt* **1 a :** to unite by a joint **b :** to provide with a joint **c :** to prepare (as a board) for joining by planing the edge **2 :** to separate the joints of ~ *vi* **1 :** to fit as if by joints **2 :** to form joints as a stage in growth
joint·er \ˈjȯint-ər\ *n* **:** one that joints; *esp* **:** any of various tools used in making joints
joint grass *n* **:** a coarse creeping grass (*Paspalum distichum*) used as fodder and as a soil binder
joint·ly *adv* **:** in a joint manner **:** TOGETHER
joint resolution *n* **:** a resolution passed by both houses of a legislative body that has the force of law when signed by or passed over the veto of the executive
join·tress \ˈjȯin-trəs\ *n* **:** a woman having a legal jointure
joint stock *n* **:** stock or capital held in company **:** capital held as a common stock or fund
joint–stock company *n* **:** a company or association consisting of individuals organized to conduct a business for gain and having a joint stock with the shares owned by a member being transferable without the consent of the rest
join·ture \ˈjȯin-chər\ *n* **1 a :** an act of joining **:** the state of being joined **b :** JOINT **2 a :** an estate settled on a wife to be taken by her in lieu of dower **b :** a settlement on the wife of a freehold estate for her lifetime
joint·worm \ˈjȯint-ˌwərm\ *n* **:** the larva of any of several small chalcid flies (genus *Harmolita*) that attack the stems of grain and cause swellings like galls at or just above the first joint
joist \ˈjȯist\ *n* [ME *giste*, fr. MF, fr. (assumed) VL *jacitum*, fr. L *jacēre* to lie — more at ADJACENT] **1 :** any of the small timbers or metal beams ranged parallel from wall to wall in a building to support the floor or ceiling **2 :** a stud or scantling about 3 by 4 inches in section

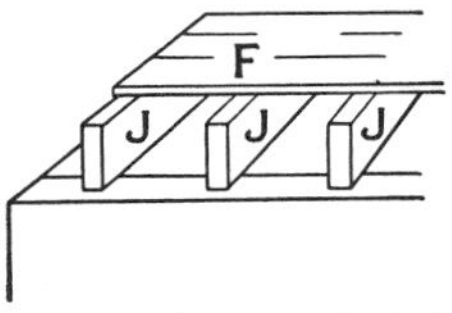

joists 1: *f*, floor; *j*, *j*, *j*, joists

¹joke \ˈjōk\ *n* [L *jocus;* akin to OHG *gehan* to say, Skt *yācati* he implores] **1 a :** something said or done to provoke laughter; *esp* **:** a brief oral narrative with a climactic humorous twist **b** (1) **:** the humorous or ridiculous element in something (2) **:** RAILLERY, KIDDING ⟨can't take a ~⟩ **c :** PRACTICAL JOKE **d :** LAUGHINGSTOCK **2 a :** something lacking substance, genuineness, or quality **b :** something presenting no difficulty **syn** see JEST
²joke *vi* **:** to make jokes **:** JEST ~ *vt* **1 :** to make the object of a joke **:** KID **2 :** to get by joking — **jok·ing·ly** \ˈjō-kiŋ-lē\ *adv*
jok·er \ˈjō-kər\ *n* **1 a :** a person given to joking **b :** FELLOW **2 a :** a playing card added to a pack as a wild card or as the highest-ranking card **b** (1) **:** an ambiguous or apparently immaterial clause inserted in a legislative bill to make it inoperative or uncertain in some respect (2) **:** an unsuspected, misleading, or misunderstood clause, phrase, or word in a document that nullifies or greatly alters it **c :** something held in reserve to gain an end or escape from a predicament **d :** an unsuspected or not readily apparent fact, factor, or condition that thwarts or nullifies a seeming advantage
jol·li·fi·ca·tion \ˌjäl-i-fə-ˈkā-shən\ *n* **:** a festive celebration **:** MERRYMAKING
jol·li·ty \ˈjäl-ət-ē\ *n* **1 :** the quality or state of being jolly **:** MERRIMENT **2** *Brit* **:** a festive gathering **syn** see MIRTH
¹jol·ly \ˈjäl-ē\ *adj* [ME *joli*, fr. OF] **1 a** (1) **:** full of high spirits **:** JOYOUS (2) **:** given to conviviality **:** JOVIAL **b :** expressing, suggesting, or inspiring gaiety **:** CHEERFUL **2 :** extremely pleasant or agreeable **:** SPLENDID **syn** see MERRY
²jolly *adv* **:** VERY — often used as an intensive
³jolly *vi* **:** to engage in good-natured banter ~ *vt* **:** to put in good humor esp. to gain an end
jol·ly boat \ˈjäl-ē-\ *n* [origin unknown] **:** a medium-sized ship's boat used for general rough or small work
Jol·ly Rog·er \ˌjäl-ē-ˈräj-ər\ *n* [prob. fr. ¹*jolly* + the name *Roger*] **:** a black flag with a white skull and crossbones
¹jolt \ˈjōlt\ *vb* [prob. blend of obs. *joll* (to strike) and *jot* (to bump)] *vt* **1 :** to cause to move with a sudden jerky motion **2 :** to give a knock or blow to; *specif* **:** to jar with a quick or hard blow in boxing **3 a :** to disturb the composure of **b :** to interfere with roughly, abruptly, and disconcertingly ~ *vi* **:** to move with a sudden jerky motion — **jolt·er** *n*
²jolt *n* **1 a :** an abrupt sharp jerky blow or movement **b :** a jarring blow in boxing **2 a** (1) **:** a sudden feeling of shock, surprise, or disappointment (2) **:** an event or development causing such a feeling **b :** a serious check or reverse **3 :** a small portion — **jolty** \ˈjōl-tē\ *adj*
jolt–wag·on \ˈjōlt-ˌwag-ən\ *n, Midland* **:** a farm wagon
Jo·nah \ˈjō-nə\ *n* [Heb *Yōnāh*] **1 :** an Old Testament prophet cast overboard during a storm sent by God because of his disobedience, swallowed by a great fish, and vomited up after three days in its belly **2 :** one believed to bring bad luck
Jonah crab *n* **:** a large reddish crab (*Cancer borealis*) of the eastern coast of No. America
Jon·a·than \ˈjän-ə-thən\ *n* [Heb *Yōnāthān*] **1 :** a son of Saul and friend of David **2 :** AMERICAN; *esp* **:** a New Englander
jon·gleur \zhōⁿ-ˈglər\ *n* [F, fr. OF *jogleour* — more at JUGGLER] **:** an itinerant medieval minstrel providing entertainment chiefly by song or recitation
jon·quil \ˈjän-kwəl, ˈjäŋ-\ *n* [F *jonquille*, fr. Sp *junquillo*, dim. of *junco* reed, fr. L *juncus;* akin to ON *einir* juniper, L *juniperus*] **:** a Mediterranean perennial bulbous herb (*Narcissus jonquilla*) of the amaryllis family with long linear leaves that is widely cultivated for its yellow or white fragrant short-tubed clustered flowers — compare DAFFODIL
Jon·so·ni·an \jän-ˈsō-nē-ən\ *adj* **:** of, relating to, or characteristic of Ben Jonson or his works
Jor·dan almond \ˌjȯrd-ᵊn-\ *n* [ME *jardin almande*, fr. MF *jardin* garden + ME *almande* almond] **1 :** an almond imported from Málaga and used extensively in confectionery **2 :** an almond coated with sugar of various colors
jo·rum \ˈjōr-əm, ˈjȯr-\ *n* [perh. fr. *Joram* in the Bible who "brought with him vessels of silver" (2 Sam 8:10—AV)] **:** a large drinking vessel or its contents
jo·seph \ˈjō-zəf *also* -səf\ *n* [L, fr. Gk *Iōsēph*, fr. Heb *Yōsēph*] **1** *cap* **a :** a son of Jacob sold into slavery by his brothers **b :** the husband of Mary the mother of Jesus **2 :** a long cloak worn esp. by women in the 18th century
Joseph of Ar·i·ma·thea \-ˌar-ə-mə-ˈthē-ə\ **:** a rich councilor believed to have placed the body of Jesus in the tomb and held in medieval legend to have taken the Holy Grail to England
Joseph's coat *n* [*Joseph;* fr. his coat of many colors] **:** any of several plants with variegated foliage; *esp* **:** COLEUS
¹josh \ˈjäsh\ *vb* [origin unknown] *vt* **:** to make fun of **:** TEASE ~ *vi* **:** to engage in banter **:** JOKE — **josh·er** *n*
²josh *n* **:** a good-humored joke **:** JEST
Josh·ua \ˈjäsh-(ə-)wə\ *n* [Heb *Yĕhōshūaʻ*] **:** an Old Testament hero, successor of Moses, and leader of the Israelites during their settlement in Canaan
Joshua tree *n* **:** a tall branched arborescent yucca (*Yucca brevifolia*) of the southwestern U.S. that has short leaves and clustered greenish white flowers
joss \ˈjäs, ˈjȯs\ *n* [pidgin E, fr. Pg *deus* god, fr. L — more at DEITY] **:** a Chinese idol or cult image
joss house *n* **:** a Chinese temple or shrine
¹jos·tle \ˈjäs-əl\ *vb* **jos·tling** \-(ə-)liŋ\ [alter. of *justle*, freq. of ¹*joust*] *vi* **1 a :** to come in contact or into collision **b :** to make

one's way by pushing and shoving **c** : to exist in close proximity **2** : to vie in gaining an objective : CONTEND ~ *vt* **1 a** : to come in contact or into collision with **b** : to force by pushing : ELBOW **c** : to stir up : AGITATE **d** : to exist in close proximity with **2** : to vie with in attaining an objective

2jostle *n* **1** : a jostling encounter or experience **2** : the state of being jostled together

1jot \'jät\ *n* [L *iota, jota* iota] : the least bit : IOTA

2jot *vt* **jot·ted; jot·ting** : to write briefly or hurriedly : set down in the form of a note ⟨~ this down⟩

jot·ting *n* : a brief note : MEMORANDUM

Jo·tunn \'yō-,tün\ *n* [ON *jötunn*] : a member of a race of giants in Norse mythology

Jo·tunn·heim \-,hām, 'yōt-ᵊn-\ *n* [ON *jötunheimar*, pl.] : the home of a race of giants in Norse mythology

joule \'jü(ə)l, 'jaù(ə)l\ *n* [James P. *Joule* †1889 E physicist] : the absolute mks unit of work or energy equal to 10^7 ergs or approximately 0.7375 foot-pounds

1jounce \'jaùn(t)s\ *vb* [ME *jouncen*] *vi* : to move in an up-and-down manner : BOUNCE ~ *vt* : to cause to jounce

2jounce *n* : JOLT — **jouncy** \'jaùn(t)-sē\ *adj*

jour·nal \'jərn-ᵊl\ *n* [ME, service book containing the day hours, fr. MF, fr. *journal* daily, fr. L *diurnalis*, fr. *diurnus* of the day, fr. *dies* day — more at DEITY] **1 a** : a record of current transactions: as (1) : DAYBOOK 2 (2) : a book of original entry in double-entry bookkeeping **b** : an account of day-to-day events **c** : a record of experiences, ideas, or reflections kept for private use **d** : a record of transactions kept by a deliberative or legislative body **e** : LOG 3, 4 **2 a** : a daily newspaper **b** : a periodical dealing esp. with matters of current interest **3** : the part of a rotating shaft, axle, roll, or spindle that turns in a bearing

journal box *n* : a metal housing to support and protect a journal bearing

jour·nal·ese \,jərn-ᵊl-'ēz, -'ēs\ *n* : a style of writing held to be characteristic of newspapers

jour·nal·ism \'jərn-ᵊl-,iz-əm\ *n* **1 a** : the collection and editing of material of current interest for presentation through news media **b** : the editorial or business management of an agency engaged in the collection and dissemination of news **c** : an academic study concerned with the collection and editing of news or the management of a news medium **2 a** : writing designed for publication in a newspaper or popular magazine **b** : writing characterized by a direct presentation of facts or description of events without an attempt at interpretation **c** : writing designed to appeal to current popular taste or public interest **3** : newspapers and magazines

jour·nal·ist \-əst\ *n* **1 a** : one engaged in journalism **b** : a writer who aims at a mass audience **2** : one who keeps a journal

jour·nal·is·tic \,jərn-ᵊl-'is-tik\ *adj* : of, relating to, or characteristic of journalism or journalists — **jour·nal·is·ti·cal·ly** \-ti-k(ə-)lē\ *adv*

jour·nal·ize \'jərn-ᵊl-,īz\ *vt* : to record in a journal ~ *vi* **1** : to keep a journal in accounting **2** : to keep a personal journal — **jour·nal·iz·er** *n*

1jour·ney \'jər-nē\ *n* [ME, fr. OF *journee*, fr. *jour* day, fr. LL *diurnum*, fr. L, neut. of *diurnus*] **1** : travel or passage from one place to another : TRIP **2** *chiefly dial* : a day's travel **3** : something suggesting travel or passage from one place to another

2journey *vi* : to go on a journey : TRAVEL ~ *vt* : to travel over or through : TRAVERSE — **jour·ney·er** *n*

jour·ney·man \-mən\ *n* [ME, fr. *journey* journey, a day's labor + *man*] **1** : a worker who has learned a trade and works for another person usu. by the day **2** : an experienced reliable workman in any field

jour·ney·work \-,wərk\ *n* **1** : work done by a journeyman **2** : HACKWORK

1joust \'jaùst *also* 'jəst\ *vi* [ME *jousten*, fr. OF *juster*, fr. (assumed) VL *juxtare*, fr. L *juxta* near; akin to L *jungere* to join — more at YOKE] **1 a** : to fight on horseback as a knight or man-at-arms **b** : to engage in combat with lances on horseback **2** : to engage in personal combat or competition — **joust·er** *n*

2joust *n* **1 a** : a combat on horseback between two knights with lances esp. as part of a tournament **b** *pl* : TOURNAMENT **2** : something resembling jousting : STRUGGLE

Jove \'jōv\ *n* [L *Jov-, Juppiter*] : JUPITER — often used interjectionally to express surprise or agreement esp. in the phrase *by Jove*

jo·vial \'jō-vē-əl, -vyəl\ *adj* **1** *cap* : of or relating to Jove **2** : marked by good humor : JOLLY **syn** see MERRY — **jo·vial·ly** \-ē\ *adv*

jo·vi·al·i·ty \,jō-vē-'al-ət-ē\ *n* : the quality or state of being jovial

Jo·vi·an \'jō-vē-ən\ *adj* : of, relating to, or characteristic of Jove

jow \'jaù\ *n* [E dial. *jow* (to strike, toll)] *chiefly Scot* : STROKE, TOLL

1jowl \'jaù(ə)l, 'jōl\ *n* [alter. of ME *chavel*, fr. OE *ceafl;* akin to MHG *kivel* jaw, Av *zafar-* mouth] **1 a** : JAW; *esp* : MANDIBLE **b** : one of the lateral halves of the mandible **2 a** : CHEEK 1 **b** : the cheek meat of a hog

2jowl *n* [ME *cholle*] : usu. slack flesh (as a dewlap, wattle, or the pendulous part of a double chin) associated with the lower jaw or throat — **jowly** \'jaù-lē, 'jō-lē\ *adj*

3jowl *n* [ME *choll*] : a cut of fish consisting of the head and usu. adjacent parts

1joy \'jòi\ *n* [ME, fr. OF *joie*, fr. L *gaudia*, pl. of *gaudium*, fr. *gaudēre* to rejoice; akin to Gk *gēthein* to rejoice] **1 a** : the emotion evoked by well-being, success, or good fortune or by the prospect of possessing what one desires : DELIGHT **b** : the expression or exhibition of such emotion : GAIETY **2** : a state of happiness or felicity : BLISS **3** : a source or cause of delight **syn** see PLEASURE

2joy *vi* : to experience great pleasure or delight : REJOICE ~ *vt* **1** *archaic* : GLADDEN **2** *archaic* : ENJOY

joy·ance \'jòi-ən(t)s\ *n* : DELIGHT, ENJOYMENT

Joyc·ean \'jòi-sē-ən\ *adj* : of, relating to, or characteristic of James Joyce or his writings — **Joycean** *n*

joy·ful \'jòi-fəl\ *adj* : experiencing, causing, or showing joy : HAPPY **syn** see GLAD — **joy·ful·ly** \-fə-lē\ *adv* — **joy·ful·ness** *n*

joy·less \-ləs\ *adj* : not feeling or causing joy : CHEERLESS — **joy·less·ly** *adv* — **joy·less·ness** *n*

joy·ous \'jòi-əs\ *adj* : JOYFUL **syn** see GLAD — **joy·ous·ly** *adv* — **joy·ous·ness** *n*

joy·ride \'jòi-,rīd\ *n* **1** : a ride taken for pleasure and often marked by reckless driving **2** : something resembling a joyride esp. in disregarding cost or consequences — **joy·rid·er** *n* — **joy·rid·ing** *n*

ju·ba \'jü-bə\ *n* [origin unknown] : a dance of Southern plantation Negroes accompanied by complexly rhythmic hand clapping and slapping of the knees and thighs

ju·bi·lant \'jü-bə-lənt\ *adj* : expressing great joy : EXULTANT — **ju·bi·lant·ly** *adv*

ju·bi·lar·i·an \,jü-bə-'ler-ē-ən, -'lar-\ *n* : one celebrating a jubilee

ju·bi·late \'jü-bə-,lāt\ *vi* [L *jubilatus*, pp. of *jubilare;* akin to MHG *jū* (exclamation of joy), Gk *iygē* shout] : REJOICE

Ju·bi·la·te \,yü-bə-'lä-,tā, ,jü-\ *n* [L, 2d pers. pl. imper. of *jubilare*] **1 a** : the 100th Psalm in the Authorized Version **b** *not cap* : a joyous song or outburst **2** : the 3d Sunday after Easter

ju·bi·la·tion \,jü-bə-'lā-shən\ *n* **1** : an act of rejoicing or the state of being jubilant **2** : an expression of great joy

ju·bi·lee \'jü-bə-,lē, ,jü-bə-'lē\ *n* [ME, fr. MF & LL; MF *jubilé*, fr. LL *jubilaeus*, modif. of LGk *iōbēlaios*, fr. Heb *yōbhēl* ram's horn, jubilee] **1** *often cap* : a year of emancipation and restoration provided by ancient Hebrew law to be kept every 50 years by the emancipation of Hebrew slaves, restoration of alienated lands to their former owners, and omission of all cultivation of the land **2 a** : a special anniversary; *esp* : a 50th anniversary **b** : a celebration of such an anniversary **3 a** : a period of time proclaimed by the Roman Catholic pope ordinarily every 25 years as a time of special solemnity **b** : a special plenary indulgence granted during a year of jubilee to Roman Catholics who perform certain specified works of repentance and piety **4 a** : JUBILATION **b** : a season of celebration **5** : a Negro folk song with references to a future happy time

Ju·dah \'jüd-ə\ *n* [Heb *Yĕhūdhāh*] : a son of Jacob and ancestor of one of the tribes of Israel

Ju·da·ic \jü-'dā-ik\ *adj* [L *judaicus*, fr. Gk *ioudaikos*, fr. *Ioudaios* Jew — more at JEW] : of, relating to, or characteristic of Jews or Judaism — **Ju·da·ical** \-'dā-ə-kəl\ *adj*

Ju·da·ism \'jüd-ə-,iz-əm, 'jüd-ē-\ *n* **1** : a religion developed among the ancient Hebrews and marked by belief in one God who is creator, ruler, and redeemer of the universe and by the moral and ceremonial laws of the Old Testament and the rabbinic tradition **2** : conformity to Jewish rites, ceremonies, and practices **3** : the cultural, social, and religious beliefs and practices of the Jews **4** : the whole body of Jews

Ju·da·ist \'jüd-ə-əst, 'jüd-ē-, jü-'dā-\ *n* : one that believes in or practices Judaism — **Ju·da·is·tic** \,jüd-ə-'is-tik, ,jüd-ē-\ *adj*

Ju·da·iza·tion \,jüd-ə-ə-'zā-shən, ,jüd-ē-ə-, (,)jü-,dā-ə-\ *n* : the act or process of Judaizing or being Judaized

Ju·da·ize \'jü-də-,īz, -dē-\ *vi* : to adopt the customs, beliefs, or character of a Jew ~ *vt* : to make Jewish — **Ju·da·iz·er** *n*

Ju·das \'jüd-əs\ *n* [LL, fr. Gk *Ioudas*, fr. Heb *Yĕhūdhāh*] **1 a** : an apostle and betrayer of Jesus — called also *Judas Is·car·i·ot* \is-'kar-ē-ət\ **b** : a son of James and one of the twelve apostles **2** : TRAITOR; *esp* : one who betrays under the guise of friendship **3** *not cap* : PEEPHOLE

Judas tree *n* [fr. the belief that Judas Iscariot hanged himself from a tree of this kind] : any of a genus (*Cercis*) of leguminous trees and shrubs often cultivated for their showy flowers; *esp* : a Eurasian tree (*C. siliquastrum*) with purplish rosy flowers

Jude \'jüd\ *n* [LL *Judas*] : the author of the New Testament Epistle of Jude

Ju·deo–Span·ish \jü-,dā-ō-'span-ish, ,jüd-ē-(,)ō-, jü-,dē-ō-\ *n* [L *Judaeus* Jew + E *Spanish* — more at JEW] : the Romance language of Sephardic Jews in the Balkans, Greece, and Asia Minor

1judge \'jəj\ *vb* [ME *juggen*, fr. OF *jugier*, fr. L *judicare*, fr. *judic-, judex* judge, fr. *jus* right, law + *dicere* to decide, say — more at JUST, DICTION] *vt* **1** : to form an authoritative opinion about **2** : to sit in judgment on : TRY **3** : to determine or pronounce after inquiry and deliberation **4** : GOVERN, RULE — used of a Hebrew tribal leader **5** : to form an estimate of **6** : THINK ~ *vi* **1** : to form an opinion **2** : to decide as a judge **syn** see INFER — **judg·er** *n*

2judge *n* [ME *juge*, fr. MF, fr. L *judex*] : one who judges: as **a** : a public official authorized to decide questions brought before a court **b** *often cap* : a tribal hero exercising authority over the Hebrews after the death of Joshua **c** : one appointed to decide in a contest or competition : UMPIRE **d** : one who gives an authoritative opinion **e** : CRITIC

judge advocate *n* **1** : an officer assigned to the judge advocate general's corps or department **2** : a staff officer serving as legal adviser to a military commander

judge advocate general *n* : the senior legal officer in an army, air force, or navy

judge·ship \'jəj-,ship\ *n* : the jurisdiction or office of a judge

judg·mat·ic \,jəj-'mat-ik\ *adj* [prob. irreg. fr. *judgment*] : JUDICIOUS — **judg·mat·i·cal** \-i-kəl\ *adj* — **judg·mat·i·cal·ly** \-i-k(ə-)lē\ *adv*

judg·ment *or* **judge·ment** \'jəj-mənt\ *n* **1 a** : a formal utterance of an authoritative opinion **b** : an opinion so pronounced **2 a** : a formal decision given by a court **b** (1) : an obligation (as a debt) created by the decree of a court (2) : a certificate evidencing such a decree **3 a** *cap* : the final judging of mankind by God **b** : a divine sentence or decision; *specif* : a calamity held to be sent by God **4 a** : the process of forming an opinion or evaluation by discerning and comparing **b** : an opinion or estimate so formed **5 a** : the capacity for judging : DISCERNMENT **b** : the exercise of this capacity **6** : a proposition stating something believed or asserted **syn** see SENSE — **judg·men·tal** \,jəj-'ment-ᵊl\ *adj*

judgment day *n* **1** *cap J&D* : the day of the Last Judgment **2** : a day of final judgment

ju·di·ca·ble \'jüd-i-kə-bəl\ *adj* : capable of being or liable to be judged

ju·di·ca·tive \'jüd-ə-,kāt-iv, 'jüd-i-kət-\ *adj* : having the power to judge : JUDICIAL

ju·di·ca·to·ry \'jüd-i-kə-,tōr-ē, -,tòr-\ *n* **1** : JUDICIARY 1a **2** : JUDICATURE 2

ju·di·ca·ture \'jüd-i-kə-,chù(ə)r, -chər, -,t(y)ù(ə)r\ *n* [MF, fr. ML *judicatura*, fr. L *judicatus*, pp. of *judicare*] **1** : the administration of

justice **2 :** a court of justice **3 :** JUDICIARY 1
ju·di·cial \jü-'dish-əl\ *adj* [ME, fr. L *judicialis*, fr. *judicium* judgment, fr. *judex*] **1 :** of or relating to a judgment, the function of judging, the administration of justice, or the judiciary **2 :** ordered or enforced by a court **3 :** of, characterized by, or expressing judgment **:** CRITICAL 1c **4 :** arising from a judgment of God **5 :** belonging or appropriate to a judge or the judiciary — **ju·di·cial·ly** \-'dish-(ə-)lē\ *adv*
1**ju·di·cia·ry** \-'dish-ē-,er-ē, -'dish-(ə-)rē\ *adj* **:** of or relating to the judiciary **:** JUDICIAL
2**judiciary** *n* **1 a :** a system of courts of law **b :** the judges of these courts **2 :** a branch of government in which judicial power is vested
ju·di·cious \jü-'dish-əs\ *adj* **:** having, exercising, or characterized by sound judgment **:** DISCREET **syn** see WISE — **ju·di·cious·ly** *adv* — **ju·di·cious·ness** *n*
Ju·dith \'jüd-əth\ *n* [L, fr. Gk *Ioudith*, fr. Heb *Yĕhūdhīth*] **:** the heroine of the Old Testament apocryphal book of Judith
ju·do \'jüd-(,)ō\ *n* [Jap *jūdō*] **:** a modern refined form of jujitsu that uses special applications of the principles of movement, balance, and leverage
1**jug** \'jəg\ *n* [perh. fr. *Jug*, nickname for *Joan*] **1 a** *chiefly Brit* **:** a small pitcher **b (1) :** a large deep earthenware or glass container with a narrow mouth and a handle **(2) :** the contents of such a container **2 :** JAIL
2**jug** *vt* **jugged; jug·ging 1 :** to stew (as a hare) in an earthenware vessel **2 :** IMPRISON
ju·gate \'jü-,gāt, -gət\ *adj* [NL *jugum*] **1 :** PAIRED **2 :** having a jugum
jug·ful \'jəg-,fu̇l\ *n, pl* **jugfuls** \-,fu̇lz\ *or* **jugs·ful** \'jəgz-,fu̇l\ **1 :** the quantity held by a jug **2 :** a great deal — used in the phrase *not by a jugful*
jug·ger·naut \'jəg-ər-,nȯt, -,nät\ *n* [Hindi *Jagannāth*, title of Vishnu, lit., lord of the world] **:** a massive inexorable force or object that crushes whatever is in its path
1**jug·gle** \'jəg-əl\ *vb* **jug·gling** \-(ə-)liŋ\ [ME *jogelen*, fr. MF *jogler* to joke, fr. L *joculari*, fr. *joculus*, dim. of *jocus* joke] *vi* **1 :** to perform the tricks of a juggler **2 :** to engage in manipulation esp. to achieve a desired end ~ *vt* **1 a :** to practice deceit or trickery on **:** BEGUILE **b :** to manipulate esp. to achieve a desired end **2 a :** to toss in the manner of a juggler **b :** to hold or balance insecurely
2**juggle** *n* **:** an act or instance of juggling: **a :** a trick of magic **b :** a show of manual dexterity **c :** an act of manipulation esp. to achieve a desired end
jug·gler \'jəg-(ə-)lər\ *n* [ME *jogelour*, fr. OE *geogelere*, fr. OF *jogleour*, fr. L *joculator*, fr. *joculatus*, pp. of *joculari*] **1 a :** one who performs tricks or acts of magic **b :** one skilled in keeping several objects in motion in the air at the same time by alternately tossing and catching them **2 :** one who manipulates esp. to achieve a desired end
jug·glery \'jəg-lə-rē\ *n* **1 :** the art or practice of a juggler **2 :** TRICKERY
jug·u·lar \'jəg-yə-lər\ *adj* [LL *jugularis*, fr. L *jugulum* collarbone, throat; akin to L *jungere* to join — more at YOKE] **1 a :** of or relating to the throat or neck **b :** of or relating to the jugular vein **2 a** *of a fish* **:** having the ventral fins on the throat anterior to the pectoral fins **b** *of a fin* **:** located on the throat
jugular vein *n* **:** any of several veins of each side of the neck that return blood from the head
jug·u·lum \'jəg-yə-ləm\ *n, pl* **jug·u·la** \-lə\ [NL, fr. L] **1 :** the part of the neck just above the breast of a bird **2 :** JUGUM 2
ju·gum \'jü-gəm\ *n, pl* **ju·ga** \-gə\ *or* **jugums** [NL, fr. L, yoke — more at YOKE] **1 :** a pair of the opposite leaflets of a pinnate leaf **2 :** the most posterior and basal region of an insect's wing modified in some lepidopterans into a lobe that couples the fore and hind wings during flight
1**juice** \'jüs\ *n* [ME *jus*, fr. OF, broth, juice, fr. L; akin to Skt *yūṣa* broth] **1 :** the extractable fluid contents of cells or tissues **2 a** *pl* **:** the natural fluids of an animal body **b :** the liquid or moisture contained in something **3 a :** the inherent quality of a thing **:** ESSENCE **b :** virile strength and vigor **4 :** a medium that supplies power — **juiced** \'jüst\ *adj* — **juice·less** \'jü-sləs\ *adj*
2**juice** *vt* **1 :** to extract the juice of **2 :** to add juice to
juic·er \'jü-sər\ *n* **:** an appliance for extracting juice from fruit or vegetables
juice up *vt* **:** to give life, energy, or spirit to
juic·i·ly \'jü-sə-lē\ *adv* **:** in a juicy manner
juic·i·ness \'jü-sē-nəs\ *n* **:** the quality or state of being juicy
juicy \'jü-sē\ *adj* **1 :** having much juice **:** SUCCULENT **2 :** financially rewarding **3 a :** rich in interest **:** COLORFUL **b :** PIQUANT, RACY **c :** full of vitality
ju·jit·su *or* **ju·jut·su** \jü-'jit-(,)sü\ *n* [Jap *jūjutsu*] **:** the Japanese art of defending oneself by grasping or striking an opponent so that his own strength and weight are used against him
ju·ju \'jü-(,)jü\ *n* [of W. African origin; akin to Hausa *djudju* fetish] **1 :** a fetish, charm, or amulet of West African tribes **2 :** the magic attributed to or associated with jujus
ju·jube \'jü-,jüb\ *n* [ME, fr. ML *jujuba*, alter. of L *zizyphum*, fr. Gk *zizyphon*] **1 a :** an edible drupaceous fruit of any of several trees (genus *Ziziphus*) of the buckthorn family **b :** a tree producing this fruit **2 :** a fruit-flavored gumdrop or lozenge
juke·box \'jük-,bäks\ *n* [Gullah *juke* disorderly, of W. African origin; akin to Bambara *dzugu* wicked] **:** a cabinet containing an automatic player of phonograph records that are played by inserting a coin in a slot
juke joint *n* **:** a small inexpensive establishment for eating, drinking, or dancing to the music of a jukebox
ju·lep \'jü-ləp\ *n* [ME, fr. MF, fr. Ar *julāb*, fr. Per *gulāb*, fr. *gul* rose + *āb* water] **1 :** a drink consisting of sweet syrup, flavoring, and water **2 :** a drink consisting of bourbon, sugar, and mint served in a frosted tumbler filled with crushed ice
Ju·lian calendar \,jül-yən-\ *n* [L *julianus*, fr. Gaius *Julius* Caesar †44 B.C. Roman general] **:** a calendar introduced in Rome in 46 B.C. establishing the 12-month year of 365 days with each 4th year having 366 days and the months each having 31 or 30 days except for February which has 28 or in leap years 29 days — compare GREGORIAN CALENDAR
1**ju·li·enne** \,jü-lē-'en, ,zhü-\ *n* [F] **:** a clear soup containing julienne vegetables
2**julienne** *adj* **:** cut in long thin strips ⟨~ potatoes⟩
Ju·liet \'jül-yət, -ē-,et, -ē-ət; ,jül-ē-'et, jül-'yet, 'jül-,yet\ *n* **:** a daughter of Capulet in love with Romeo in Shakespeare's *Romeo and Juliet*
Ju·li·ett \,jül-ē-'et\ [prob. irreg. fr. *Juliet*] — a communications code word for the letter *j*
Ju·ly \jü-'lī\ *n* [ME *Julie*, fr. OE *Julius*, fr. L, fr. Gaius *Julius* Caesar] **:** the 7th month of the Gregorian calendar
Ju·ma·da \jü-'mäd-ə\ *n* [Ar *Jumāda*] **:** either of two months of the Muhammadan year: **a :** the 5th month **b :** the 6th month
1**jum·ble** \'jəm-bəl\ *vb* **jum·bling** \-b(ə-)liŋ\ [perh. imit.] *vi* **:** to move or mingle in a confused or disordered manner ~ *vt* **:** to mix in a confused mass
2**jumble** *n* **1 a :** a mass of things mingled together without order or plan **b :** a state of confusion **2** *Brit* **a :** articles for a rummage sale **b :** RUMMAGE SALE
3**jumble** *n* [origin unknown] **:** a small thin usu. ring-shaped sugared cake
jum·bo \'jəm-(,)bō\ *n* [*Jumbo*, a huge elephant exhibited by P. T. Barnum] **:** a very large specimen of its kind
1**jump** \'jəmp\ *vb* [prob. akin to LG *gumpen* to jump] *vi* **1 a :** to spring into the air **:** LEAP; *esp* **:** to spring free from the ground or other base by the muscular action of feet and legs **b :** to give a sudden movement **:** START **c :** to move over a position occupied by an opponent's man in a board game **d :** SKIP ⟨his typewriter ~*s*⟩ **e :** to undergo a vertical or lateral displacement owing to improper alignment of the film on a projector mechanism **f :** to begin a forward movement — usu. used with *off* **g :** to move energetically **:** HUSTLE **2 :** COINCIDE, AGREE **3 a :** to move haphazardly or aimlessly ⟨~*ed* from job to job⟩ **b :** to change employment in violation of contract **c :** to rise suddenly in rank or status **d :** to undergo a sudden sharp increase ⟨prices ~*ed*⟩ **e :** to make a jump bid in bridge **f :** to make a hurried judgment ⟨~ to conclusions⟩ **g :** to show eagerness ⟨~*ed* at the chance⟩ **h :** to enter eagerly — usu. used with *in* or *into* **4 :** to make a sudden physical or verbal attack ⟨~*ed* on him for his criticism⟩ **5 :** to bustle with activity ~ *vt* **1 a :** to pass over by a leap ⟨~ a hurdle⟩ **b :** to move over (a man) in a board game **c :** BYPASS ⟨~ electrical connections⟩ **d :** ANTICIPATE ⟨~ the gun in starting a race⟩ **e :** to leap aboard ⟨~ a freight⟩ **2** *obs* **:** RISK, HAZARD **3 a :** to escape from **b :** to leave hastily or in violation of contract **c :** to depart from (a normal course) ⟨~ the track⟩ **4 a :** to make a sudden physical or verbal attack on **b :** to occupy illegally ⟨~ a mining claim⟩ **5 a (1) :** to cause to leap **(2) :** START, FLUSH **b :** to elevate in rank or status **c :** to raise (a bridge partner's bid) by more than one rank **d :** to increase suddenly and sharply
2**jump** *adv, obs* **:** EXACTLY, PAT
3**jump** *n* **1 a (1) :** an act of jumping **:** LEAP **(2) :** any of several sports competitions featuring a leap, spring, or bound **(3) :** a space cleared or covered by a leap **(4) :** an obstacle to be jumped over **b (1) :** a sudden involuntary movement **:** START **(2)** *pl* **:** FIDGETS **c :** a move made in a board game by jumping **2** *obs* **:** VENTURE **3 a :** a sharp sudden increase **b :** a sudden change **c (1) :** a quick short journey **(2) :** one in a series of moves from one place to another **4 :** an advantage at the start
jump bid *n* **:** a bridge bid of more tricks than are necessary to overcall the preceding bid
1**jump·er** \'jəm-pər\ *n* **1 :** a person who jumps **2 a :** any of various devices operating with a jumping motion **b :** any of several sleds **c :** a short wire used to close a break or cut out part of a circuit **3 :** any of several jumping animals; *esp* **:** a saddle horse trained to jump obstacles **4 :** one who will jump
2**jumper** *n* [prob. fr. E dial. *jump* (jumper)] **1 :** a loose blouse or jacket worn by workmen **2 :** a sleeveless one-piece dress worn usu. with a blouse **3 :** a child's one-piece coverall — usu. used in pl.
jump·i·ness \'jəm-pē-nəs\ *n* **:** NERVOUSNESS
jumping bean *n* **:** a seed of any of several Mexican shrubs (genera *Sebastiania* and *Sapium*) of the spurge family that tumbles about because of the movements of the larva of a small moth (*Carpocapsa saltitans*) inside it
jumping jack *n* **:** a toy figure of a man jointed and made to jump or dance by means of strings or a sliding stick
jumping mouse *n* **:** any of several small hibernating No. American rodents (family Zapodidae) with long hind legs and tail and no cheek pouches
jumping-off place \,jəm-piŋ-'ȯf-\ *n* **1 :** a remote or isolated place **2 :** a place from which an enterprise is launched
jumping plant louse *n* **:** any of numerous plant lice (family Psyllidae) with the femurs thickened and adapted for leaping
jump-off \'jəm-,pȯf\ *n* **:** the start of a race or an attack
jump pass *n* **:** a pass made by a player (as in football or basketball) while jumping
jump seat *n* **1 :** a movable carriage seat **2 :** a folding seat between the front and rear seats of a passenger automobile
jump shot *n* **:** a shot made by a basketball player at the peak of a jump
jumpy \'jəm-pē\ *adj* **1 :** characterized by jumps or sudden variations **2 :** NERVOUS, JITTERY
jun·co \'jəŋ-(,)kō\ *n, pl* **juncos** *or* **juncoes** [NL, genus name, fr. Sp, bird, reed — more at JONQUIL] **:** any of a genus (*Junco*) of small widely distributed American finches usu. having a pink bill, ashy gray head and back, and conspicuous white lateral tail feathers
junc·tion \'jəŋ(k)-shən\ *n* [L *junction-*, *junctio*, fr. *junctus*, pp. of *jungere* to join — more at YOKE] **1 :** an act of joining **:** the state of being joined **2 a :** a place or point of meeting **b :** an intersection of roads esp. where one terminates **3 :** something that joins — **junc·tion·al** \-shnəl, -shən-ᵊl\ *adj*
junc·tur·al \'jəŋ(k)-chə-rəl, 'jəŋ(k)sh-rəl\ *adj* **:** of or relating to grammatical juncture
junc·ture \'jəŋ(k)-chər\ *n* **1 :** an instance of joining **:** UNION **2 a :** JOINT, CONNECTION **b :** the manner of transition or mode of relationship between two consecutive sounds in speech **3 :** a point of time; *esp* **:** one made critical by a concurrence of circumstances
syn JUNCTURE, PASS, EXIGENCY, EMERGENCY, CONTINGENCY, PINCH, STRAITS, CRISIS mean a critical or crucial time or state of affairs. JUNCTURE stresses the significant concurrence or convergence of events; PASS implies a bad or distressing state or situation brought about by a combination of causes; EXIGENCY stresses the pressure of restrictions or urgency of demands created by a special situation; EMERGENCY applies to a sudden unforeseen situation requiring prompt action to avoid disaster; CONTINGENCY implies an emergency or exigency that is regarded as possible or even probable but uncer-

tain of occurrence; PINCH implies urgency or pressure for action to a less intense degree than EXIGENCY or EMERGENCY; STRAITS applies to a troublesome situation from which escape is extremely difficult; CRISIS applies to a juncture whose outcome will make a decisive difference

June \'jün\ *n* [ME, fr. MF & L; MF *Juin*, fr. L *Junius*] **:** the 6th month of the Gregorian calendar

june beetle *n, often cap J* **:** any of numerous rather large leaf-eating beetles (family Melolonthidae) that fly chiefly in late spring and have as larvae white grubs that live in soil and feed chiefly on the roots of grasses and other plants — called also *june bug*

June·ber·ry \'jün-,ber-ē\ *n* **:** any of various No. American trees and shrubs (genus *Amelanchier*) of the rose family sometimes cultivated for their showy white flowers or edible purple or red fruits

jun·gle \'jəŋ-gəl\ *n, often attrib* [Hindi *jaṅgal*] **1 a :** an impenetrable thicket or tangled mass of tropical vegetation **b :** a tract overgrown with thickets or masses of vegetation **2 :** a hobo camp **3 a** (1) **:** a confused or chaotic mass of objects **:** JUMBLE (2) **:** something that baffles or frustrates by its tangled or complex character **:** MAZE **b :** a place of ruthless struggle for survival — **jun·gly** \-g(ə-)lē\ *adj*

jungle fowl *n* **:** any of several Asiatic wild birds (genus *Gallus*); *esp* **:** a bird (*G. gallus*) of southeastern Asia from which domestic fowls are held to have descended

jungle gym *n* [fr. *Junglegym*, a trademark] **:** a structure of vertical and horizontal bars for use by children at play

[1]**ju·nior** \'jü-nyər\ *n* [L, n. & adj.] **1 a :** a person who is younger than another **b :** a clothing size for women and girls with slight figures **2 a :** a person holding a lower position in a hierarchy of ranks **b :** a student in his next-to-the-last year before graduating from an educational institution

[2]**junior** *adj* [L, compar. of *juvenis* young — more at YOUNG] **1 a :** YOUNGER — used chiefly to distinguish a son with the same given name as his father **b** (1) **:** YOUTHFUL (2) **:** designed esp. for adolescents **c** (1) **:** of more recent date (2) **:** of more recent date and therefore inferior or subordinate ⟨a ~ lien⟩ **2 :** lower in standing or rank ⟨~ partners⟩ **3 :** of or relating to juniors or the class containing juniors

ju·nior·ate \'jü-nyə-,rāt, -rət\ *n* **1 :** a course of high school or college study for candidates for the priesthood, brotherhood, or sisterhood; *specif* **:** one preparatory to the course in philosophy **2 :** a seminary for juniorate training

junior college *n* **:** an educational institution that offers two years of studies corresponding to those in the first two years of a four-year college and that often offers technical, vocational, and liberal studies to the adults of a community

junior high school *n* **:** a school usu. including the 7th and 8th grades and the 1st year of high school

Junior Leaguer *n* **:** a member of a league of young women organized for volunteer service to civic and social organizations

junior miss *n* **1 :** an adolescent girl **2 :** JUNIOR 1b

junior varsity *n* **:** the members of a varsity squad lacking the experience or class qualification for the first team

ju·ni·per \'jü-nə-pər\ *n* [ME *junipere*, fr. L *juniperus* — more at JONQUIL] **1 :** an evergreen shrub or tree (genus *Juniperus*) of the pine family; *esp* **:** one having a prostrate or shrubby habit **2 :** any of several coniferous trees resembling true junipers

juniper oil *n* **:** an acrid essential oil obtained from the fruit of the common juniper and used esp. in gin and liqueurs

[1]**junk** \'jəŋk\ *n, often attrib* [ME *jonke*] **1 :** pieces of old cable or cordage used esp. to make gaskets, mats, swabs, or oakum **2 :** hard salted beef for use on shipboard **3 a** (1) **:** old iron, glass, paper, or other waste that may be used again in some form (2) **:** secondhand, worn, or discarded articles of little value **b :** a shoddy product **:** TRASH **c :** something of little meaning or significance **4** *slang* **:** NARCOTICS; *esp* **:** HEROIN — **junk·man** \-,man\ *n* — **junky** \'jəŋ-kē\ *adj*

[2]**junk** *vt* **:** to get rid of as worthless **:** SCRAP **syn** see DISCARD

[3]**junk** *n* [Pg *junco*, fr. Jav *joṅ*] **:** any of various ships of Chinese waters with bluff lines, a high poop and overhanging stem, little or no keel, high pole masts, and a deep rudder

junk art *n* **:** three-dimensional art made from discarded material (as metal, mortar, glass, or wood) — **junk artist** *n*

Jun·ker \'yuŋ-kər\ *n* [G] **:** a member of the Prussian landed aristocracy — **Jun·ker·dom** \-kərd-əm\ *n* — **Jun·ker·ism** \-kə-,riz-əm\ *n*

[1]**jun·ket** \'jəŋ-kət\ *n* [ME *ioncate*, deriv. of (assumed) VL *juncata*, fr. L *juncus* rush] **1 a :** a cream cheese or a dish of curds and cream **b :** a dessert of sweetened flavored milk set in a jelly **2 a :** a festive social affair **b** (1) **:** a tour or journey usu. undertaken for pleasure (2) **:** a trip made by an official at public expense

[2]**junket** *vi* **1 :** FEAST, BANQUET **2 :** to go on a junket — **jun·ke·teer** \,jəŋ-kə-'ti(ə)r\ *or* **jun·ket·er** \'jəŋ-kət-ər\ *n*

junk·ie \'jəŋ-kē\ *n* **1 :** a junk dealer **2** *or* **junky** \-kē\ *slang* **:** a narcotics peddler or addict

Ju·no \'jü-(,)nō\ *n* [L] **:** the queen of heaven in Roman mythology

Ju·no·esque \,jü-(,)nō-'esk\ *adj* **:** marked by stately beauty

jun·ta \'hùn-tə, 'hün-tə, 'jənt-ə\ *n* [Sp, fr. fem. of *junto* joined, fr. L *junctus*, pp. of *jungere* to join — more at YOKE] **1 :** a council or committee for political or governmental purposes; *esp* **:** a group of persons controlling a government esp. after a revolutionary seizure of power **2 :** JUNTO

jun·to \'jənt-(,)ō\ *n* [prob. alter. of *junta*] **:** a group of persons joined for a common purpose

Ju·pi·ter \'jü-pət-ər\ *n* [L] **1 :** the chief god in Roman mythology and husband of Juno **2 :** the largest of the planets and fifth in order of distance from the sun — see PLANET table

Ju·ra \'jùr-ə\ *n* [prob. G, fr. the *Jura* mountain range] **:** the Jurassic geological period or the rocks belonging to it

jur·al \'jùr-əl\ *adj* [L *jur-, jus* law] **1 :** of or relating to law **2 :** of or relating to rights or obligations — **jur·al·ly** \-ə-lē\ *adv*

Ju·ras·sic \jù-'ras-ik\ *adj* [F *jurassique*, fr. *Jura* mountain range] **:** of, relating to, or being the period of the Mesozoic era between the Comanchean and the Triassic or the corresponding system of rocks marked by the presence of dinosaurs and the first appearance of birds — **Jurassic** *n*

ju·rat \'jù(ə)r-,at\ *n* [short for L *juratum* (*est*) it has been sworn, 3d sing. perf. pass. of *jurare* to swear] **:** a certificate added to an affidavit stating when, before whom, and where it was made

ju·ra·to·ry \'jùr-ə-,tōr-ē, -,tòr-\ *adj* **:** of, relating to, or expressed in an oath

ju·rel \hü-'rel\ *n* [Sp] **:** any of several food fishes (family Carangidae) of warm seas

ju·rid·i·cal \jù-'rid-i-kəl\ *or* **ju·rid·ic** \-ik\ *adj* [L *juridicus*, fr. *jur-, jus* + *dicere* to say — more at DICTION] **1 :** of or relating to the administration of justice or the office of a judge **2 :** of or relating to law in general or jurisprudence **:** LEGAL — **ju·rid·i·cal·ly** \-i-k(ə-)lē\ *adv*

ju·ris·con·sult \,jùr-ə-'skän-,səlt, -skən-'\ *n* [L *jurisconsultus*, fr. *juris* (gen. of *jus*) + *consultus*, pp. of *consulere* to consult] **:** JURIST

ju·ris·dic·tion \,jùr-əs-'dik-shən\ *n* [ME *jurisdiccioun*, fr. OF & L; OF *juridiction*, fr. L *jurisdiction-, jurisdictio*, fr. *juris* + *diction-, dictio* act of saying — more at DICTION] **1 :** the power, right, or authority to interpret and apply the law **2 :** the authority of a sovereign power to govern or legislate **3 :** the limits or territory within which authority may be exercised **:** CONTROL **syn** see POWER — **ju·ris·dic·tion·al** \-shnəl, -shən-ᵊl\ *adj* — **ju·ris·dic·tion·al·ly** \-ē\ *adv*

ju·ris·pru·dence \,jùr-ə-'sprüd-ᵊn(t)s\ *n* **1 a :** a system or body of law **b :** the course of court decisions **2 :** the science or philosophy of law **3 :** a department of law ⟨medical ~⟩ — **ju·ris·pru·den·tial** \-(,)sprü-'den-chəl\ *adj* — **ju·ris·pru·den·tial·ly** \-'dench-(ə-)lē\ *adv*

ju·ris·pru·dent \-'sprüd-ᵊnt\ *n* [LL *jurisprudent-, jurisprudens*, fr. L *juris* + *prudent-, prudens* skilled, prudent] **:** JURIST

ju·rist \'jù(ə)r-əst\ *n* [MF *juriste*, fr. ML *jurista*, fr. L *jur-, jus*] **:** one having a thorough knowledge of law: **a :** LAWYER **b :** JUDGE

ju·ris·tic \jù-'ris-tik\ *adj* **1 :** of or relating to a jurist or jurisprudence **2 :** of, relating to, or recognized in law — **ju·ris·ti·cal·ly** \-ti-k(ə-)lē\ *adv*

ju·ror \'jùr-ər, 'jù(ə)r-,ò(ə)r\ *n* **1 a :** a member of a jury **b :** a person summoned to serve on a jury **2 :** a person who takes an oath esp. of allegiance **3 :** a member of a jury for a contest or exhibition

[1]**ju·ry** \'jù(ə)r-ē\ *n* [ME *jure*, fr. AF *juree*, fr. OF *jurer* to swear, fr. L *jurare*, fr. *jur-, jus*] **1 :** a body of men sworn to give a verdict on some matter submitted to them; *esp* **:** a body of men legally selected and sworn to inquire into any matter of fact and to give their verdict according to the evidence **2 :** a committee for judging and awarding prizes at a contest or exhibition — **ju·ry·man** \-mən\ *n*

[2]**jury** *adj* [origin unknown] **:** improvised for temporary use esp. in an emergency **:** MAKESHIFT ⟨a ~ mast⟩

jus gen·ti·um \'yüs-'gent-ē-əm, -,ùm\ *n* [L, law of nations] **:** INTERNATIONAL LAW

jus san·gui·nis \-'säŋ-gwə-nəs\ *n* [L, right of blood] **:** a rule that a child's citizenship is determined by its parents' citizenship

jus·sive \'jəs-iv\ *n* [L *jussus*, pp. of *jubēre* to order; akin to Gk *hysminē* battle] **:** a word, form, case, or mood expressing command — **jussive** *adj*

jus so·li \'yüs-'sō-,lē\ *n* [L, right of the soil] **:** a rule that the citizenship of a child is determined by the place of its birth

[1]**just** \'jəst\ *var of* JOUST

[2]**just** \'jəst\ *adj* [ME, fr. MF & L; MF *juste*, fr. L *justus*, fr. *jus* right, law; akin to Skt *yos* welfare] **1 a :** having a basis in or conforming to fact or reason **:** REASONABLE ⟨a ~ comment⟩ **b** *archaic* **:** faithful to an original **c :** conforming to a standard of correctness **:** PROPER ⟨~ proportions⟩ **2 a** (1) **:** morally right or good **:** RIGHTEOUS ⟨a ~ war⟩ (2) **:** MERITED, DESERVED ⟨~ punishment⟩ **b :** legally right ⟨a ~ title⟩ **syn** see FAIR, UPRIGHT — **just·ly** *adv* — **just·ness** \'jəs(t)-nəs\ *n*

[3]**just** \(,)jəst, (,)jist, (,)jest\ *adv* **1 a :** EXACTLY, PRECISELY ⟨~ right⟩ **b :** very recently ⟨the bell ~ rang⟩ **2 a :** by a very small margin **:** BARELY ⟨~ too late⟩ **b :** IMMEDIATELY, DIRECTLY ⟨~ west of here⟩ **3 a :** ONLY, MERELY ⟨~ a note⟩ **b :** QUITE, VERY ⟨~ wonderful⟩

jus·tice \'jəs-təs\ *n, often attrib* [ME, fr. OF, fr. L *justitia*, fr. *justus*] **1 a :** the maintenance or administration of what is just esp. by the impartial adjustment of conflicting claims or the assignment of merited rewards or punishments **b :** JUDGE **c :** the administration of law; *esp* **:** the establishment or determination of rights according to the rules of law or equity **2 a :** the quality of being just, impartial, or fair **b** (1) **:** the principle or ideal of just dealing or right action (2) **:** conformity to this principle or ideal **:** RIGHTEOUSNESS **c :** the quality of conforming to law **3 :** conformity to truth, fact, or reason **:** CORRECTNESS — **do justice 1 a :** to act justly **b :** to treat fairly or adequately **c :** to show due appreciation for **2 :** to acquit in a way worthy of one's powers

justice of the peace : a local magistrate empowered chiefly to administer summary justice in minor cases, to commit for trial, and to administer oaths and perform marriages

jus·ti·cia·ble \,jəs-'tish-(ē-)ə-bəl\ *adj* **:** liable to trial in a court of justice

jus·ti·ci·ar \,jəs-'tish-ē-ər, -ē-,är\ *n* **:** the chief political and judicial officer of the Norman and later kings of England until the 13th century

jus·ti·fi·abil·i·ty \,jəs-tə-,fī-ə-'bil-ət-ē\ *n* **:** the quality or state of being justifiable

jus·ti·fi·able \'jəs-tə-,fī-ə-bəl\ *adj* **:** capable of being justified **:** EXCUSABLE — **jus·ti·fi·ably** \-blē\ *adv*

jus·ti·fi·ca·tion \,jəs-tə-fə-'kā-shən\ *n* **1 :** the act, process, or state of being justified by God **2 a :** the act or an instance of justifying **:** VINDICATION **b :** something that justifies — **jus·ti·fi·ca·tive** \'jəs-tə-fə-,kāt-iv\ *adj*

jus·ti·fi·ca·to·ry \,jəs-'tif-i-kə-,tōr-ē, 'jəst-(ə-)fə-, -,tòr-; 'jəs-tə-fə-,kāt-ə-rē\ *adj* **:** tending to justify **:** VINDICATORY

jus·ti·fi·er \'jəs-tə-,fī(-ə)r\ *n* **:** one that justifies

jus·ti·fy \'jəs-tə-,fī\ *vb* [ME *justifien*, fr. MF or LL; MF *justifier*, fr. LL *justificare*, fr. L *justus*] *vt* **1 a :** to prove or show to be just, right, or reasonable **:** VINDICATE **b** (1) **:** to show to have had a sufficient legal reason (2) **:** to qualify (oneself) as a surety by taking oath to the ownership of sufficient property **2 a** *archaic* **:** to administer justice to **b** *archaic* **:** ABSOLVE **c** (1) **:** to make righteous (2) **:** to release from the guilt of sin and accept as righteous **3 :** to adjust or arrange exactly; *specif* **:** to set (type) so as to fill a full line **~** *vi* **1 a :** to show a sufficient lawful reason

for an act done **b :** to qualify as bail or surety **2 :** to fit exactly; *specif* **:** to fill a full line **syn** see MAINTAIN
1jut \'jət\ *vb* **jut·ted; jut·ting** [perh. short for *2jutty*] *vi* **:** to shoot out, up, or forward **:** PROJECT ~ *vt* **:** to cause to project
2jut *n* **:** something that juts **:** PROJECTION
jute \'jüt\ *n, often attrib* [Hindi & Bengali *jūṭ*] **:** the glossy fiber of either of two East Indian plants (*Corchorus olitorius* and *C. capsularis*) of the linden family used chiefly for sacking, burlap, and twine; *also* **:** a plant producing jute
Jute \'jüt\ *n* [ME, fr. ML *Jutae* Jutes] **:** a member of a Low German people invading England from the Continent and settling in Kent in the 5th century — **Jut·ish** \'jüt-ish\ *adj*
1jut·ty \'jət-ē\ *n* [ME] **1** *archaic* **:** JETTY **2 :** a projecting part of a building
2jutty *vt, obs* **:** to project beyond
ju·ve·nal \'jü-vən-ᵊl\ *adj* **:** JUVENILE
ju·ve·nes·cence \,jü-və-'nes-ᵊn(t)s\ *n* **:** the state of growing young — **ju·ve·nes·cent** \-ᵊnt\ *adj*
1ju·ve·nile \'jü-və-,nīl, -vən-ᵊl\ *adj* [F or L; F *juvénile,* fr. L *juvenilis,* fr. *juvenis* young person — more at YOUNG] **1 :** physiologically immature or undeveloped **:** YOUNG **2 :** of, relating to, or characteristic of children or young people **3 :** reflecting psychological or intellectual immaturity **:** CHILDISH
2juvenile *n* **1 a :** a young person **:** YOUTH **b :** a book for young people **2 :** a young individual resembling an adult of its kind except in size and reproductive activity: as **a :** a fledged bird not yet in adult plumage **b :** a 2-year old racehorse **3 :** one who plays youthful parts
juvenile court *n* **:** a court having special jurisdiction over delinquent and dependent children usu. up to the age of 18
juvenile delinquency *n* **1 :** a status in a juvenile characterized by antisocial behavior that is beyond parental control and therefore subject to legal action **2 :** a violation of the law committed by a juvenile and not punishable by death or life imprisonment — **juvenile delinquent** *n*
juvenile officer *n* **:** a police officer charged with the detection, prosecution, and care of juvenile delinquents
ju·ve·nil·ia \,jü-və-'nil-ē-ə\ *n pl* [L, neut. pl. of *juvenilis*] **1 :** youthful writing or other artistic work **2 :** artistic or literary compositions for the young
ju·ve·nil·i·ty \,jü-və-'nil-ət-ē\ *n* **1 :** the quality or state of being juvenile **:** YOUTHFULNESS **2 :** an instance of being juvenile
jux·ta·pose \'jək-stə-,pōz\ *vt* [prob. back-formation fr. *juxtaposition*] **:** to place side by side
jux·ta·po·si·tion \,jək-stə-pə-'zish-ən\ *n* [L *juxta* near + E *position* — more at JOUST] **:** the act or an instance of placing two or more objects side by side; *also* **:** the state of being so placed — **jux·ta·po·si·tion·al** \-'zish-nəl, -ən-ᵊl\ *adj*

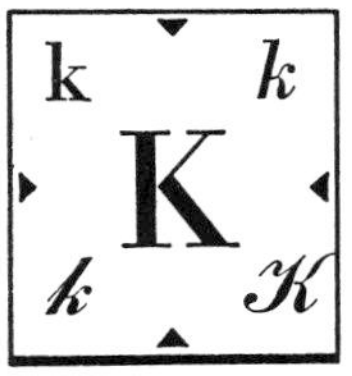

k \'kā\ *n, often cap, often attrib* **1 a :** the 11th letter of the English alphabet **b :** a graphic representation of this letter **c :** a speech counterpart of orthographic *k* **2 :** a graphic device for reproducing the letter *k* **3 :** one designated *k* esp. as the 10th or when j is used for the 10th the 11th in order or class **4 :** something shaped like the letter K **5 :** a unit vector parallel to the z-axis
Kaa·ba \'käb-ə\ *n* [Ar *ka'bah,* lit., square building] **:** a small stone building in the court of the Great Mosque at Mecca that contains a sacred black stone and is the goal of Islamic pilgrimage and the point toward which Muslims turn in praying
kabala *or* **kabbala** *or* **kabbalah** *var of* CABALA
ka·bob \'kā-,bäb, kə-'\ *n* [Per, Hindi, Ar & Turk; Per & Hindi *kabāb,* fr. Ar, fr. Turk *kebap*] **:** cubes of meat (as lamb) marinated and cooked with onions, tomatoes, or other vegetables usu. on a skewer
Ka·bu·ki \kə-'bü-kē, 'käb-ü-(,)kē\ *n* [Jap, lit., art of singing and dancing] **:** traditional Japanese popular drama with singing and dancing performed in a highly stylized manner
Ka·byle \kə-'bī(ə)l\ *n* [Ar *qabā'il,* pl. of *qabīlah* tribe] **1 :** a Berber of the mountainous coastal area east of Algiers **2 :** the Berber language of the Kabyles
kad·dish \'käd-ish\ *n, often cap* [Aram *qaddīsh* holy] **:** a Jewish prayer recited in the daily ritual of the synagogue and by mourners at public services after the death of a close relative
kaf·fee·klatsch \'kȯ-fē-,klach; 'käf-ē-,klach, -,kläch\ *n, often cap* [G, fr. *kaffee* coffee + *klatsch* gossip] **:** an informal social gathering for coffee and talk
Kaf·fir *or* **Kaf·ir** \'kaf-ər\ *n* [Ar *kāfir* infidel] **:** a member of a group of southern African Bantu-speaking peoples
kaf·ir \'kaf-ər\ *n* **:** a grain sorghum with stout short-jointed somewhat juicy stalks and erect heads
Kaf·ir \'kaf-ər\ *n* **:** a member of a people of the Hindu Kush in northeastern Afghanistan
Kaf·iri \'kaf-ə-rē\ *n* **:** the Dard language of the Kafir people
kail·yard school \,kā(ə)l-,yärd-\ *n, often cap K* [Sc *kailyard* (kitchen garden), fr. *kail, kale* + E *yard*] **:** a group of writers whose work is characterized by sentimental description of Scottish life and considerable use of Scots dialect
kai·nite \'kī-,nīt, 'kā-\ *also* **kai·nit** \kī-'nēt\ *n* [G *kainit,* fr. Gk *kainos* new — more at RECENT] **:** a natural salt $KMg(SO_4)Cl.3H_2O$ consisting of a hydrous sulfate and chloride of magnesium and potassium that is used as a fertilizer and as a source of potassium and magnesium compounds
kai·ser \'kī-zər\ *n* [ME, fr. ON *keisari;* akin to OHG *keisur* emperor; both fr. a prehistoric Gmc word borrowed fr. L *Caesar,* cognomen of the Emperor Augustus] **:** EMPEROR; *esp* **:** the ruler of Germany from 1871 to 1918 — **kai·ser·dom** \-zərd-əm\ *n* — **kai·ser·in** \-zə-rən\ *n* — **kai·ser·ism** \-zə-,riz-əm\ *n*
ka·ka \'käk-ə\ *n* [Maori] **:** an olive brown New Zealand parrot (*Nestor meridionalis*) with gray and red markings that talks and mimics well in captivity
ka·ka·po \,käk-ə-'pō\ *n* [Maori] **:** a chiefly nocturnal burrowing New Zealand parrot (*Strigops habroptilus*) with green and brown barred plumage
ka·ke·mo·no \,käk-i-'mō-(,)nō\ *n* [Jap] **:** a Japanese scroll picture or writing on silk or paper
kale \'kā(ə)l\ *n* [Sc, fr. ME (northern) *cal,* fr. OE *cāl* — more at COLE] **1 a :** COLE **b :** a hardy cabbage (*Brassica oleracea acephala*) with curled often finely incised leaves that do not form a dense head **2** *slang* **:** MONEY
ka·lei·do·scope \kə-'līd-ə-,skōp\ *n* [Gk *kalos* beautiful + *eidos* form + E *-scope* — more at CALLIGRAPHY, IDOL] **1 :** an instrument containing loose bits of colored glass between two flat plates and two plane mirrors so placed that changes of position of the bits of glass are reflected in an endless variety of patterns **2 :** a variegated changing pattern or scene — **ka·lei·do·scop·ic** \-,līd-ə-'skäp-ik\ *or* **ka·lei·do·scop·i·cal** \-i-kəl\ *adj* — **ka·lei·do·scop·i·cal·ly** \-k(ə-)lē\ *adv*
kalends *var of* CALENDS
Kal·muck *or* **Kal·muk** \'kal-,mək, kal-'\ *or* **Kal·myk** \kal-'mik\ *n* [Russ *Kalmyk,* fr. Kazan Tatar] **1 :** a member of a Buddhist Mongol people orig. of Dzungaria **2 :** the language of the Kalmucks
kalsomine *var of* CALCIMINE
kam·a·la \'kəm-ə-lə\ *n* [Skt] **1 :** an East Indian tree (*Mallotus philippinensis*) of the spurge family **2 :** an orange red powder from Kamala capsules used for dyeing silk and wool or as a vermifuge
kame \'kām\ *n* [Sc, kame, comb, fr. ME (northern) *camb* comb, fr. OE] **:** a short ridge, hill, or mound of stratified drift deposited by glacial meltwater
Ka·me·ha·me·ha Day \kə-,mā-ə-'mā-(,)hä-\ *n* **:** June 11 observed as a holiday in Hawaii in commemoration of the birthday of Kamehameha I
ka·mi·ka·ze \,käm-i-'käz-ē\ *n* [Jap, lit., divine wind] **1 :** a member of a Japanese air attack corps assigned to make a suicidal crash on a target **2 :** an airplane containing explosives to be flown in a suicide crash on a target
kam·pong \'käm-,pȯŋ\ *n* [Malay] **:** a native hamlet or village in a Malay-speaking country
Kan·a·rese \,kan-ə-'rēz, -'rēs\ *n, pl* **Kanarese** [*Kanara,* India] **1 a :** a Kannada-speaking people of Mysore, south India **b :** a member of this people **2 :** KANNADA
kan·ga·roo \,kaŋ-gə-'rü\ *n* [prob. native name in Australia] **:** any of various herbivorous leaping marsupial mammals (family Macropodidae) of Australia, New Guinea, and adjacent islands with a small head, large ears, long powerful hind legs, a long thick tail used as a support and in balancing, and rather small forelegs not used in progression
kangaroo court \,kaŋ-gə-,rü-\ *n* **1 :** a mock court in which the principles of law and justice are disregarded or perverted **2 :** a court characterized by irresponsible, unauthorized, or irregular status or procedures
Kan·na·da \'kän-əd-ə\ *n* [Kannada *kannaḍa*] **:** the major Dravidian language of Mysore, southern India
Kant·ian \'kant-ē-ən, 'känt-\ *adj* **:** of, relating to, or characteristic of Kant or his philosophy — **Kantian** *n* — **Kant·ian·ism** \-,iz-əm\ *n*
ka·olin *also* **ka·oline** \'kā-ə-lən\ *n* [F *kaolin,* fr. *Kao-ling,* hill in China] **:** a fine usu. white clay that is used in ceramics and refractories, as an adsorbent, and as a filler or extender
ka·olin·ite \-lə-,nīt\ *n* **:** a mineral $Al_2Si_2O_5(OH)_4$ consisting of a hydrous silicate of aluminum that constitutes the principal mineral in kaolin
ka·pell·mei·ster \kə-'pel-,mī-stər, kä-\ *n, often cap* [G, fr. *kapelle* choir + *meister* master] **:** the director of a choir or orchestra
kaph \'käf, 'kȯf\ *n* [Heb, lit., palm of the hand] **:** the 11th letter of the Hebrew alphabet — symbol כ or ך
ka·pok \'kā-,päk\ *n* [Malay] **:** a mass of silky fibers that clothe the seeds of the ceiba tree and are used esp. as a filling for mattresses, life preservers, and sleeping bags and as insulation
kap·pa \'kap-ə\ *n* [Gk, of Sem origin; akin to Heb *kaph*] **:** the 10th letter of the Greek alphabet — symbol K or κ
ka·put \kä-'pu̇t, kə-, -'püt\ *adj* [G, fr. F *capot* not having made a trick at piquet] **1 :** utterly defeated or destroyed **2 :** made useless or unable to function **3 :** hopelessly outmoded
karabiner *var of* CARABINER
Kara·ism \'kar-ə-,iz-əm\ *n* [LHeb *qĕrāīm* Karaites] **:** a Jewish doctrine originating in Baghdad in the 8th century that rejects rabbinism and talmudism and bases its tenets on interpretation of the Scriptures — **Kara·ite** \-,īt\ *n*
kar·a·kul \'kar-ə-kəl\ *n* [*Kara Kul,* lake in U.S.S.R.] **1 :** any of a breed of hardy fat-tailed sheep from Bukhara with a narrow body and coarse wiry brown fur **2 :** the tightly curled glossy black coat of the newborn lamb of a Karakul valued as fur
kar·at \'kar-ət\ *n* [prob. fr. MF *carat,* fr. ML *carratus* unit of weight for precious stones — more at CARAT] **:** a unit of fineness for gold equal to $\frac{1}{24}$ part of pure gold in an alloy
ka·ra·te \kə-'rät-ē\ *n* [Jap, lit., empty hand] **:** a Japanese system of self-defense without a weapon
Ka·re·lian \kə-'rē-lē-ən, -'rēl-yən\ *n* **1 :** a native or inhabitant of Karelia **2 :** the Finno-Ugric language of the Karelians — **Karelian** *adj*
Ka·ren \kə-'ren\ *n, pl* **Karen** *or* **Karens 1 a :** a group of peoples of eastern and southern Burma **b :** a member of any of these peoples **2 a :** a group of languages spoken by the Karen peoples **b :** a language of this group
kar·ma \'kär-mə, 'kər-\ *n, often cap* [Skt *karman* (nom. *karma*), lit., work] **:** the force generated by a person's actions held in Hinduism and Buddhism to perpetuate transmigration and in its ethical consequences to determine his destiny in his next existence — **kar·mic** \-mik\ *adj, often cap*

ka·ross \kə-'räs\ *n* [Afrik *karos*] **:** a simple garment or rug of skins used esp. by native tribesmen of southern Africa
kar·roo *or* **ka·roo** \kə-'rü\ *n* [Afrik *karo*] **:** a dry tableland of southern Africa
kary- *or* **karyo-** *also* **cary-** *or* **caryo-** *comb form* [NL, fr. Gk *karyon* nut — more at CAREEN] **1 :** nucleus of a cell ⟨*karyo*kinesis⟩ **2 :** nut **:** kernel ⟨*caryo*psis⟩
karyo·ki·ne·sis \,kar-ē-ō-kə-'nē-səs, -(,)kī-\ *n* [NL, fr. *kary-* + Gk *kinēsis* motion — more at KINESIOLOGY] **1 :** the nuclear phenomena characteristic of mitosis **2 :** the whole process of mitosis — **karyo·ki·net·ic** \-'net-ik\ *adj*
kary·ol·o·gy \,kar-ē-'äl-ə-jē\ *n* [ISV] **:** a branch of cytology that deals with the minute anatomy of cell nuclei and esp. the nature and structure of chromosomes
karyo·lymph \'kar-ē-ō-,lim(p)f\ *n* [ISV] **:** the clear homogeneous ground substance of a cell nucleus
karyo·plasm \-,plaz-əm\ *n* [ISV] **:** NUCLEOPLASM 1 — **karyo·plas·mic** \,kar-ē-ō-'plaz-mik\ *adj*
karyo·some \'kar-ē-ə-,sōm\ *n* [ISV] **:** a central body of a vesicular nucleus; *esp* **:** one that is a nucleolar mass of heterochromatin
karyo·sys·tem·at·ics \,kar-ē-ō-,sis-tə-'mat-iks\ *n pl but sing in constr* **:** a branch of systematics that seeks to determine natural relationships by the study of karyotypes
karyo·type \'kar-ē-ə-,tīp\ *n* [ISV] **:** the sum of the specific characteristics of a cell nucleus including chromosome number, form, size, and points of spindle attachment — **karyo·typ·ic** \,kar-ē-ə-'tip-ik\ *or* **karyo·typ·i·cal** \-i-kəl\ *adj*
Kasbah *var of* CASBAH
Kash·mir goat \,kash-,mi(ə)r-, ,kazh-\ *n* [*Kashmir*, region in India] **:** an Indian goat raised esp. for its undercoat of fine soft wool that constitutes the cashmere wool of commerce
Kash·miri \kash-'mi(ə)r-ē, kazh-\ *n, pl* **Kashmiris** *or* **Kashmiri 1 :** a native or inhabitant of Kashmir **2 :** the Indic language of Kashmir
kash·ruth *or* **kash·rut** \kä-'shrüt(h)\ *n* [Heb *kashrūth*, lit., fitness] **1 :** the state of being kosher **2 :** the Jewish dietary laws
Ka·shu·bi·an \kə-'shü-bē-ən\ *n* [*Kashube* (a member of a Slavic people)] **:** a West Slavic language spoken in the region of Danzig
Ka·tha·re·vu·sa \,käth-ə-'rev-ə-,sä\ *n* [NGk *kathareuousa*, fr. Gk, fem. of *kathareuōn*, prp. of *kathareuein* to be pure, fr. *katharos* pure] **:** modern Greek conforming to classic Greek usage
katharsis *var of* CATHARSIS
ka·ty·did \'kāt-ē-,did\ *n* [imit.] **:** any of several large green American long-horned grasshoppers having stridulating organs on the fore wings of the males that produce a loud shrill sound
kat·zen·jam·mer \'kat-sən-,jam-ər\ *n* [G, fr. *katzen* cats + *jammer* distress] **1 :** HANGOVER **2 :** DISTRESS, DEPRESSION **3 :** a discordant clamor
kau·ri \'kau̇(ə)r-ē\ *n* [Maori *kawri*] **1 :** any of various trees (genus *Agathis*) of the pine family; *esp* **:** a tall timber tree (*A. australis*) of New Zealand having fine white straight-grained wood **2 :** a light-colored to brown resin from the kauri tree found as a fossil in the ground or collected from living trees and used esp. in varnishes and linoleum
ka·va \'käv-ə\ *n* [Tongan & Marquesan, lit., bitter] **1 :** an Australasian shrubby pepper (*Piper methysticum*) from whose crushed root an intoxicating beverage is made **2 :** the beverage made from kava
kay \'kā\ *n* **:** the letter *k*
Kay \'kā\ *n* **:** a boastful malicious knight of the Round Table who is foster brother and seneschal of King Arthur
kay·ak \'kī-,ak\ *n* [Esk *qajaq*] **1 :** an Eskimo canoe made of a frame covered with skins except for a small opening in the center and propelled by a double-bladed paddle **2 :** a canvas-covered portable canoe used widely in the U.S. — **kay·ak·er** \-,ak-ər\ *n*

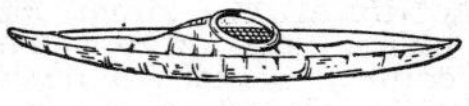
kayak 1

1kayo \kā-'ō, 'kā-(,)ō\ *n* [pronunciation of *KO*, abbr.] **:** KNOCKOUT
2kayo *vt* **kay·oed; kayo·ing :** to knock out
ka·zoo \kə-'zü\ *n* [imit.] **:** a toy musical instrument consisting of a tube with a membrane sealing one end and a side hole into which one sings or hums
kea \'kē-ə\ *n* [Maori] **:** a large predominantly green New Zealand parrot (*Nestor notabilis*) that is normally insectivorous but sometimes destroys sheep by slashing the back to feed on the kidney fat
ke·bab *or* **ke·bob** \'kā-,bäb, kə-'\ *var of* KABOB
keb·buck *or* **keb·bock** \'keb-ək\ *n* [ME (Sc dial.) *cabok*, fr. ScGael *ceapag*] *dial Brit* **:** a whole cheese
Ke·chu·ma·ran \,kech-ə-mə-'rän, kə-,chü-\ *n* [*Kechua* (Quechua) + *Aymaran*] **:** a language stock comprising Aymara and Quechua
1kedge \'kej\ *vt* [ME *caggen*] **:** to move (a ship) by means of a line attached to a kedge dropped at the distance and in the direction desired
2kedge *n* **:** a small anchor used esp. in kedging
1keek \'kēk\ *vi* [ME *kiken*] *chiefly Scot* **:** PEEP, LOOK
2keek *n, chiefly Scot* **:** PEEP, LOOK
1keel \'kē(ə)l\ *vb* [ME *kelen*, fr. OE *cēlan*, fr. *cōl* cool] *chiefly dial* **:** COOL
2keel *n* [ME *kele*, fr. MD *kiel;* akin to OE *cēol* ship, *cot* small house — more at COT] **1 a :** a flat-bottomed ship; *esp* **:** a barge used on the Tyne to carry coal **b :** a barge load of coal **2 :** a British unit of weight for coal equal to 21.2 long tons
3keel *n* [ME *kele*, fr. ON *kjölr;* akin to OE *ceole* throat, beak of a ship — more at GLUTTON] **1 a :** a longitudinal timber or plate extending along the center of the bottom of a ship and often projecting from the bottom **b :** SHIP **c :** the assembly of members at the bottom of the hull of a semirigid or rigid airship **2 :** a projection suggesting a keel; *specif* **:** CARINA
4keel *vt* **:** to cause to turn over **~** *vi* **1 :** to turn over **2 :** to fall in or as if in a faint — usu. used with *over*
5keel *n* [ME (Sc dial.) *keyle*] **1** *chiefly dial* **:** RUDDLE **2 :** a colored marking crayon used by engineers and surveyors
keel·boat \'kē(ə)l-,bōt\ *n* **:** a shallow covered riverboat with a keel that is usu. rowed, poled, or towed and used for freight — **keel·boat·man** \-mən\ *n*
keel·haul \-,hȯl\ *vt* [D *kielhalen*, fr. *kiel* keel + *halen* to haul] **1 :** to haul under the keel of a ship as punishment or torture **2 :** to rebuke severely
keel·son \'kel-sən, 'kē(ə)l-\ *n* [prob. of Scand origin; akin to Sw *kölsvin* keelson] **:** a longitudinal structure running above and fastened to the keel of a ship in order to stiffen and strengthen its framework
1keen \'kēn\ *adj* [ME *kene* brave, sharp, fr. OE *cēne* brave; akin to OHG *kuoni* brave, OE *cnāwan* to know — more at KNOW] **1 a :** having a fine edge or point **:** SHARP ⟨a ~ sword⟩ **b :** affecting one as if by cutting ⟨~ sarcasm⟩ **c :** pungent to the sense ⟨a ~ scent⟩ **2 a :** showing a quick and ardent responsiveness **:** ENTHUSIASTIC ⟨a ~ swimmer⟩ **b** *of emotion or feeling* **:** INTENSE **3 a :** ACUTE, ASTUTE ⟨~ mind⟩ **b :** sharply contested ⟨~ debate⟩ **c :** extremely sensitive in perception ⟨~ eyesight⟩ **4** *slang* **:** WONDERFUL, EXCELLENT **syn** see EAGER, SHARP — **keen·ly** *adv* — **keen·ness** \'kēn-nəs\ *n*
2keen *vb* [IrGael *caoinim* I lament] *vi* **1 a :** to lament with a keen **b :** to make a sound suggestive of a keen **2 :** to lament, mourn, or complain loudly **~** *vt* **:** to utter by keening — **keen·er** *n*
3keen *n* **:** a lamentation for the dead uttered in a loud wailing voice or sometimes in a wordless cry
1keep \'kēp\ *vb* **kept** \'kept\ **keep·ing** [ME *kepen*, fr. OE *cēpan;* akin to OHG *chapfēn* to look] *vt* **1 :** OBSERVE, FULFILL: as **a :** to be faithful to ⟨~ a promise⟩ **b :** to act fittingly in relation to ⟨~ the Sabbath⟩ **c :** to conform to in habits or conduct ⟨~ late hours⟩ **d :** to stay in accord with (a beat) ⟨~ time⟩ **2 :** PRESERVE, MAINTAIN: as **a :** to watch over and defend ⟨~ us from harm⟩ **b** (1) **:** to take care of **:** TEND ⟨~ a garden⟩ (2) **:** SUPPORT ⟨~ a wife⟩ (3) **:** to maintain in a good, fitting, or orderly condition ⟨~ house⟩ ⟨~*s* his car up⟩ **c :** to continue to maintain ⟨~ silence⟩ **d** (1) **:** to cause to remain in a given place, situation, or condition ⟨~ him waiting⟩ (2) **:** to preserve (food) in an unspoiled condition **e :** to have or maintain in one's service or at one's disposal ⟨~ a cook⟩ ⟨~ a mistress⟩ ⟨~ a horse⟩; *also* **:** to lodge or feed for pay ⟨~ boarders⟩ **f** (1) **:** to maintain a record in ⟨~ books⟩ (2) **:** to enter in a book ⟨~ records⟩ **g :** to have customarily in stock for sale **3 a :** to restrain from departure or removal **:** DETAIN ⟨~ children in after school⟩ **b :** to hold back ⟨~ him from going⟩ ⟨*kept* him back with difficulty⟩ ⟨*kept* her feelings in⟩ **c :** SAVE, RESERVE ⟨~ some for later⟩ ⟨*kept* some out for a friend⟩ **d :** to refrain from revealing ⟨~ a secret⟩ **4 a :** to retain in one's possession or power ⟨*kept* the money he found⟩ **b :** WITHHOLD ⟨*kept* the news back⟩ **c :** to have in control ⟨~ your temper⟩ **5 :** to confine oneself to ⟨~*s* her room⟩ **6 a :** to stay or continue in ⟨~ the path⟩ ⟨~ your seat⟩ **b :** to stay or remain on or in against opposition **:** HOLD ⟨~ the field under fire⟩ **7 :** to carry on **:** CONDUCT, MANAGE ⟨~ a tearoom⟩ **8 :** to associate with (company) **~** *vi* **1** *chiefly Brit* **:** LIVE, LODGE **2 a :** to maintain a course, direction, or progress ⟨~ right⟩ **b :** to continue usu. without interruption ⟨~ talking⟩ ⟨~ on smiling⟩ **c :** to persist in a practice ⟨*kept* bothering them⟩ ⟨*kept* on smoking in spite of warnings⟩ **3 :** STAY, REMAIN ⟨~ out of the way⟩ ⟨~ off the grass⟩: as **a :** to stay even ⟨try to ~ with the faster boys⟩ ⟨~ up with the Joneses⟩ **b :** to remain in good condition ⟨meat will ~ in the freezer⟩ **c :** to remain undivulged ⟨the secret would ~⟩ **d :** to call for no immediate action ⟨the matter will ~ until morning⟩ **4 :** ABSTAIN, REFRAIN ⟨can't ~ from talking⟩ **5 :** to be in session ⟨school ~*s* five days a week⟩
syn KEEP, RETAIN, DETAIN, WITHHOLD, RESERVE mean not to let go from one's possession or control. KEEP implies nothing more than this; RETAIN suggests continued keeping esp. against a threat to seize; DETAIN suggests a delay in letting go; WITHHOLD suggests delay or refusal to let go or give often for good reason; RESERVE stresses a keeping for anticipated future need
syn KEEP, OBSERVE, CELEBRATE, COMMEMORATE mean to notice or honor a day, occasion, or deed. KEEP stresses the idea of not neglecting or violating; OBSERVE implies punctilious performing of required acts or ceremonies; CELEBRATE suggests acknowledging an occasion by festivity or indulgence; COMMEMORATE implies observances that call to mind the day or event to be celebrated
— **keep an eye on :** WATCH — **keep at :** to persist in doing or concerning oneself with — **keep company :** to go together as frequent companions or in courtship — **keep one's hand in :** to keep in practice — **keep pace :** KEEP *vi* 3a — **keep step :** to keep in step — **keep to 1 a :** to stay in **b :** to limit oneself to **2 :** to abide by — **keep to oneself 1 :** to keep secret **2 :** to remain solitary or apart from other people
2keep *n* **1 a** *archaic* **:** CUSTODY, CHARGE **b :** MAINTENANCE **2 :** one that keeps or protects: as **a :** FORTRESS, CASTLE; *specif* **:** the strongest and securest part of a medieval castle **b :** KEEPER **c :** PRISON, JAIL **3 :** the means or provisions by which one is kept **4 :** a football play in which the quarterback keeps the ball and runs with it — **for keeps 1 a :** with the provision that one keep what he has won **b :** with deadly seriousness **2 :** PERMANENTLY **3 :** with the result of ending the matter
keep back *vi* **:** to refrain from approaching or advancing near something
keep down *vt* **1 :** to keep in control ⟨*keep* expenses *down*⟩ **2 :** to prevent from growing, advancing, or succeeding ⟨can't *keep* a good man *down*⟩
keep·er \'kē-pər\ *n* **1 :** one that keeps: as **a :** PROTECTOR **b :** GAMEKEEPER **c :** WARDEN **d :** CUSTODIAN **e :** CURATOR **2 :** any of various devices to keep something in position **3 :** one fit or suitable for keeping
keep·ing *n* **1 :** the act of one that keeps: as **a :** CUSTODY, MAINTENANCE **b :** OBSERVANCE **c :** a reserving or preserving for future use **2 a :** the means by which something is kept **:** SUPPORT, PROVISION **b :** the state of being kept or the condition in which something is kept **3 :** CONFORMITY ⟨in ~ with good taste⟩
keep off *vt* **1 :** to keep away **2 :** to ward off **~** *vi* **:** to keep back
keep·sake \'kēp-,sāk\ *n* [*1keep* + *-sake* (as in *namesake*)] **:** something kept or given to be kept as a memento
keep up *vt* **:** to persist or persevere in ⟨*kept* it *up* for a week⟩; *also* **:** MAINTAIN, SUSTAIN ⟨*keep* standards *up*⟩ **~** *vi* **1 :** to keep adequately informed ⟨*keep up* on international relations⟩ **2 :** to continue without interruption ⟨rain *kept up* all night⟩
keet \'kēt\ *n* [imit.] **:** GUINEA FOWL
kef \'kef, 'kāf\ *n* [Ar *kêf* pleasure] **1 :** a state of dreamy tranquillity **2 :** a smoking material (as Indian hemp) that produces kef

ə abut; ᵊ kitten; ər further; a back; ā bake; ä cot, cart; au̇ out; ch chin; e less; ē easy; g gift; i trip; ī life
j joke; ŋ sing; ō flow; ȯ flaw; ȯi coin; th thin; th this; ü loot; u̇ foot; y yet; yü few; yu̇ furious; zh vision

ke·fir \ke-'fi(ə)r\ *n* [Russ] **:** a slightly effervescent acidulous beverage made of fermented cow's milk

keg \'keg, 'kag, 'kāg\ *n* [ME *kag*, of Scand origin; akin to ON *kaggi* keg] **1 :** a small cask or barrel having a capacity of 30 gallons or less **2 :** the contents of a keg

keg·ler \'keg-lər, 'kā-glər\ *n* [G] **:** 1BOWLER

ke·loid \'kē-,lȯid\ *n* [F *kiloïde*, fr. Gk *chēlē* claw] **:** a thick scar resulting from excessive growth of fibrous tissue — **ke·loi·dal** \kē-'lȯid-ᵊl\ *adj*

kelp \'kelp\ *n* [ME *culp*] **1 a :** any of various large brown seaweeds (orders Laminariales and Fucales) **b :** a mass of large seaweeds **2 :** the ashes of seaweed used esp. as a source of iodine

1kel·pie \'kel-pē\ *n* [prob. of Celt origin; akin to ScGael *cailpeach* colt] **:** a water sprite held esp. in Scottish folklore to delight in or bring about the drowning of travelers

2kelpie *n* [*Kelpie*, a dog of this breed] **:** an Australian sheep dog of a breed developed by crossing the dingo with various British sheep dogs

Kelt \'kelt\ **Kelt·ic** \'kel-tik\ *var of* CELT, CELTIC

Kel·vin \'kel-vən\ *adj* [William Thomson, Lord *Kelvin* †1907 Brit physicist] **:** relating to, conforming to, or having a thermometric scale on which the unit of measurement equals the centigrade degree and according to which absolute zero is 0°, the equivalent of −273.16°C

kemp \'kemp\ *n* [ME *kempe*, fr. OE *cempa;* akin to OHG *kempho* warrior] *dial Brit* **:** CHAMPION

1ken \'ken\ *vb* **kenned; ken·ning** [ME *kennen*, fr. OE *cennan* to make known & ON *kenna* to perceive; both akin to OE *can* know — more at CAN] *vt* **1** *archaic* **:** SEE **2** *chiefly dial* **:** RECOGNIZE **3** *chiefly Scot* **:** KNOW **~** *vi, chiefly Scot* **:** KNOW

2ken *n* **1 a :** the range of vision **b :** SIGHT, VIEW **2 :** the range of perception, understanding, or knowledge

ke·naf \kə-'naf\ *n* [Per] **:** an East Indian hibiscus (*Hibiscus cannabinus*) widely cultivated for its fiber; *also* **:** the fiber used esp. for cordage

Ken·dal green \,ken-dᵊl-\ *n* [ME, fr. *Kendal*, England] **:** a green woolen cloth resembling homespun or tweed

1ken·nel \'ken-ᵊl\ *n* [ME *kenel*, deriv. of (assumed) VL *canile*, fr. L *canis* dog — more at HOUND] **1 a :** a shelter for a dog **b :** an establishment for the breeding or boarding of dogs **2 :** a pack of dogs

2kennel *vb* **ken·neled** *or* **ken·nelled; ken·nel·ing** *or* **ken·nel·ling** *vi* **:** to take shelter in or as if in a kennel **~** *vt* **:** to put or keep in or as if in a kennel

3kennel *n* [alter. of *cannel* (gutter)] **:** a gutter in a street

Ken·nel·ly–Heav·i·side layer \,ken-ᵊl-ē-,hev-ē-,sīd-\ *n* [Arthur *Kennelly* †1939 Am engineer and Oliver *Heaviside* †1925 E physicist] **:** IONOSPHERE

1ken·ning \'ken-iŋ\ *n, chiefly Scot* **:** a perceptible but small amount

2kenning *n* [ON, fr. *kenna*] **:** a metaphorical compound word or phrase used esp. in Old English and Old Norse poetry

Ken·ny method \'ken-ē-,\ *n* [Elizabeth *Kenny* †1952 Australian nurse] **:** a method of treating poliomyelitis consisting basically of application of hot fomentations and reeducation — called also *Kenny treatment* \,ken-ē-'\

ke·no \'kē-(,)nō\ *n* [F *quine*, set of five winning numbers in a lottery] **:** a game resembling lotto

ken·speck·le \'ken-,spek-əl\ *adj* [prob. of Scand origin; akin to Norw *kjennspak* quick to recognize] *chiefly Scot* **:** CONSPICUOUS

kent·ledge \'kent-lij\ *n* [origin unknown] **:** pig iron or scrap metal used as ballast

Ken·tucky coffee tree \kən-,tək-ē-\ *n* [*Kentucky*, state of the U.S.] **:** a tall No. American leguminous tree (*Gymnocladus dioica*) with bipinnate leaves and large woody brown pods whose seeds have been used as a substitute for coffee

ke·pi \'kā-pē, 'kep-ē\ *n* [F *képi*] **:** a military cap with a round flat top sloping toward the front and a visor

kerat- *or* **kerato-** — see CERAT-

ker·a·tin \'ker-ət-ᵊn\ *n* [ISV] **:** any of various sulfur-containing fibrous proteins that form the chemical basis of horny epidermal tissues — **ke·ra·ti·nous** \kə-'rat-ᵊn-əs, ,ker-ə-'tī-nəs\ *adj*

ker·a·to·sis \,ker-ə-'tō-səs\ *n* [NL] **:** an area of skin marked by overgrowth of horny tissue — **ker·a·tot·ic** \-'tät-ik\ *adj*

kerb \'kərb\ *n, Brit* **:** CURB 5

ker·chief \'kər-chəf, -,chēf\ *n, pl* **kerchiefs** \-chəfs\ *also* **kerchieves** \-,chēvz\ [ME *courchef*, fr. OF *cuevrechief*, fr. *covrir* to cover + *chief* head — more at CHIEF] **1 :** a square of cloth used by women as a head covering or worn as a scarf around the neck **2 :** HANDKERCHIEF 1

kerf \'kərf\ *n* [ME, fr. OE *cyrf* action of cutting; akin to OE *ceorfan* to carve — more at CARVE] **1 :** a slit or notch made by a saw or cutting torch **2 :** the width of cut made by a saw or cutting torch

Ker·man \kər-'män, ke(ə)r-\ *var of* KIRMAN

ker·mes \'kər-mēz\ *n* [F *kermès*, fr. Ar *qirmiz*] **:** the dried bodies of the females of various scale insects (genus *Kermes*) that are found on a Mediterranean oak (*Quercus coccinea*) and constitute a red dyestuff

ker·mis \'kər-məs\ *or* **ker·mess** \'kər-məs, (,)kər-'mes\ *n* [D *kermis*] **1 :** an outdoor festival of the Low Countries **2 :** a fair held usu. for charitable purposes

1kern *or* **kerne** \'kərn, 'ke(ə)rn\ *n* [ME *kerne*, fr. MIr *cethern* band of soldiers] **1 :** a light-armed foot soldier of medieval Ireland or Scotland **2 :** BOOR 3a

2kern \'kərn\ *n* [F *carne* corner, fr. L *cardin-*, *cardo* hinge — more at CARDINAL] **:** a part of the face of a type-cast letter that projects beyond the body

3kern *vt* **1 :** to form with a kern **2 :** to smooth (type) about the kern **~** *vi* **:** to become kerned

ker·nel \'kərn-ᵊl\ *n* [ME, fr. OE *cyrnel*, dim. of *corn*] **1** *chiefly dial* **:** a fruit seed **2 :** the inner softer part of a seed, fruit stone, or nut **3 :** a whole seed of a cereal **4 :** a central or essential part

kern·ite \'kər-,nīt\ *n* [*Kern* co., Calif.] **:** a mineral $Na_2B_4O_7.4H_2O$ that consists of a hydrous sodium borate and is an important source of borax

ker·o·gen \'ker-ə-jən\ *n* [Gk *kēros* wax + E *-gen* — more at CERUMEN] **:** bituminous material occurring in shale and yielding oil when heated

ker·o·sine *or* **ker·o·sene** \'ker-ə-,sēn, ,ker-ə-', 'kar-, ,kar-\ *n* [Gk *kēros* + E *-ene* (as in *camphene*)] **:** a flammable hydrocarbon oil usu. obtained by distillation of petroleum and used for a fuel and as a solvent

ker·ria \'ker-ē-ə\ *n* [NL, genus name, fr. William *Kerr* †1814 E gardener] **:** any of a genus (*Kerria*) of Chinese shrubs of the rose family with solitary yellow often double flowers

ker·ry \'ker-ē\ *n, often cap* [County *Kerry*, Ireland] **:** any of an Irish breed of small hardy long-lived black dairy cattle

Kerry blue terrier *n* **:** any of an Irish breed of medium-sized terriers with a long head, deep chest, and silky bluish coat

ker·sey \'kər-zē\ *n* [ME, fr. *Kersey*, England] **1 a :** a coarse ribbed woolen cloth for hose and work clothes **b :** a heavy wool or wool and cotton fabric used esp. for uniforms and coats **2 :** a garment of kersey

ker·sey·mere \-zē-,mi(ə)r\ *n* [alter. of *cassimere*] **:** a fine woolen fabric with a close nap made in fancy twill weaves

ke·ryg·ma \kə-'rig-mə\ *n* [Gk *kērygma*, fr. *kēryssein* to proclaim] **:** the apostolic preaching that Jesus is the Christ — **ker·yg·mat·ic** \,ker-ig-'mat-ik\ *adj*

kes·trel \'kes-trəl\ *n* [ME *castrel*, fr. MF *crecerelle*] **:** a small European falcon (*Falco tinnunculus*) that is noted for its habit of hovering in the air against a wind and is about a foot long, bluish gray above in the male, and reddish brown in the female; *broadly* **:** any of various small Old World falcons

ket- *or* **keto-** *comb form* [ISV] **:** ketone ⟨*ketosis*⟩

ketch \'kech\ *n* [ME *cache*] **:** a fore-and-aft rigged ship similar to a yawl but with a larger mizzen and with the mizzenmast stepped farther forward

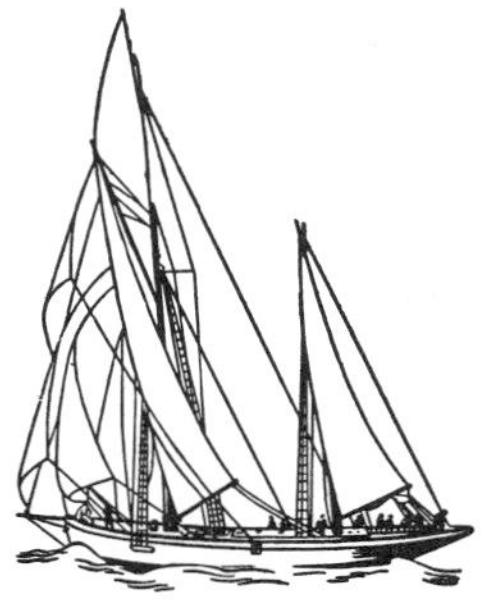

ketch

ketch·up *var of* CATSUP

ke·tene \'kē-,tēn\ *n* [ISV] **:** a colorless poisonous gas C_2H_2O of penetrating odor made by pyrolysis of acetic acid or acetone and used esp. as an acetylating agent

ke·to \'kēt-(,)ō\ *adj* [*ket-*] **:** of or relating to a ketone; *also* **:** containing a ketone group

ke·to·gen·e·sis \,kēt-ō-'jen-ə-səs\ *n* [NL] **:** the production of ketone bodies (as in diabetes) — **ke·to·gen·ic** \-'jen-ik\ *adj*

ke·tol \'kē-,tȯl, -,tōl\ *n* [ISV] **:** a compound that is both a ketone and an alcohol

ke·tone \'kē-,tōn\ *n* [G *keton*] **:** an organic compound with a carbonyl group attached to two carbon atoms or in a bivalent radical — **ke·ton·ic** \kē-'tän-ik\ *adj*

ketone body *n* **:** any of the three compounds acetoacetic acid, acetone, and beta-hydroxybutyric acid found in the blood and urine in abnormal amounts in conditions of impaired metabolism

ke·tose \'kē-,tōs, -,tōz\ *n* [ISV] **:** a sugar (as fructose) containing one ketone group per molecule

ke·to·sis \kē-'tō-səs\ *n* [NL] **:** an abnormal increase of ketone bodies in the body — **ke·tot·ic** \-'tät-ik\ *adj*

ke·to·ste·roid \,kēt-ō-'ster-,ȯid, -'sti(ə)r-\ *n* [ISV] **:** a steroid containing a ketone group

ket·tle \'ket-ᵊl\ *n* [ME *ketel*, fr. ON *ketill;* akin to OE *cietel* kettle; both fr. a prehistoric Gmc word borrowed fr. L *catillus*, dim. of *catinus* bowl] **1 :** a metallic vessel for boiling liquids; *esp* **:** TEAKETTLE **2** *obs* **:** KETTLEDRUM **3 a :** POTHOLE **b :** a steep-sided hollow without surface drainage esp. in a deposit of glacial drift

ket·tle·drum \-,drəm\ *n* **:** a percussion instrument that consists of a hollow brass or copper hemisphere with a parchment head whose controllable tension determines the pitch

kettle of fish *see* KETTLE\ **1 :** a bad state of affairs **:** MESS **2 :** something to be considered or reckoned with **:** MATTER

Kew·pie \'kyü-pē\ *trademark* — used for a small chubby doll with a topknot of hair

1key \'kē\ *n* [ME, fr. OE *cǣg;* akin to MLG *keige* spear] **1 a :** a usu. metal instrument by which the bolt of a lock is turned **b :** any of various devices having the form or function of such a key **2 :** a means of gaining or preventing entrance, possession, or control **3 a :** something that gives an explanation or provides a solution **b :** a list of words or phrases giving an explanation of symbols or abbreviations **c :** an arrangement of the salient characters of a group of plants or animals or of taxa designed to facilitate identification **d :** a map legend **4 a** (1) **:** COTTER PIN (2) **:** COTTER **b :** a keystone in an arch **c :** a wedge used to make a dovetail joint **d :** a small parallel-sided piece that fits into a groove and prevents relative motion between rotating parts; *also* **:** a wedge for drawing or holding parts together **5 a :** one of the levers of a keyboard musical instrument that actuates the mechanism and produces the tones **b :** a lever that controls a vent in the side of a woodwind instrument or a valve in a brass instrument **c :** a depressible digital that serves as one unit of a keyboard and that works usu. by lever action to set in motion a character or an escapement (as in some typesetting machines) **6 :** SAMARA **7 :** a leading individual or principle **8 :** a system of seven tones based on their relationship to a tonic; *specif* **:** the tonality of a scale **9 a :** characteristic style or tone **:** STRAIN **b :** the tone or pitch of a voice **c :** the predominant tone of a photograph with respect to its lightness or darkness **10 :** a decoration or charm resembling a key **11 :** a small switch for opening or closing an electric circuit

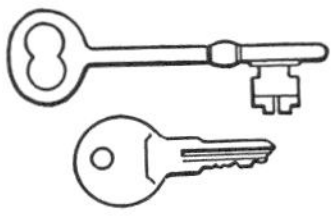

keys 1a

2key *vt* **1 :** to lock with a key: as **a :** to secure (as a pulley on a shaft) by a key **b :** to finish off (an arch) by inserting a keystone **2 :** to regulate the musical pitch of **3 :** to make conformable **:** ATTUNE **4 :** to identify (a biological specimen) by a key **5 :** to insert in (an advertisement) matter intended to identify answers **6 :** to make nervous or tense — usu. used with *up* **~** *vi* **:** to use a key

3key *adj* **:** of basic importance **:** FUNDAMENTAL

4key *n* [Sp *cayo*, fr. Lucayo] **:** a low island or reef; *specif* **:** one of the coral islets off the southern coast of Florida

1key·board \'kē-,bō(ə)rd, -,bȯ(ə)rd\ *n* **1 a :** a bank of keys on a musical instrument **b :** MANUAL **c :** a set of manuals **2 :** an assemblage of systematically arranged keys by which a machine is operated **3 :** a board on which keys for locks are hung

2keyboard *vi* **:** to operate a keyboard typesetting machine **~** *vt* **:** to

set by means of a keyboard typesetting machine — **key·board·er** *n*
key club *n* [so called because each member is provided with a key to the premises] **:** an informal private club serving liquor and providing entertainment
keyed \'kēd\ *adj* **1 :** furnished with keys **2 :** reinforced by a key or keystone **3 :** set to a key **4 :** ADJUSTED, ATTUNED
1**key·hole** \'kē-,hōl\ *n* **1 :** a hole for receiving a key **2 :** the free-throw area in basketball
2**keyhole** *adj* **1 :** revealingly intimate **2 :** intent on revealing intimate details
Keynes·ian \'kān-zē-ən\ *adj* **:** of, relating to, or characteristic of John M. Keynes or his economic theories and programs — **Keynesian** *n* — **Keynes·ian·ism** \-ə-,niz-əm\ *n*
1**key·note** \'kē-,nōt\ *n* **1 :** the first and harmonically fundamental tone of a scale **2 :** the fundamental or central fact, idea, or mood
2**keynote** *vt* **1 :** to set the keynote of **2 :** to deliver the keynote address at — **key·not·er** *n*
keynote address *n* **:** an address designed to present the issues of primary interest to an assembly and often to arouse unity and enthusiasm — called also *keynote speech*
key signature *n* **:** the sharps or flats placed after a clef in music to indicate the key
key·stone \'kē-,stōn\ *n* **1 :** the wedge-shaped piece at the crown of an arch that locks the other pieces in place **2 :** something on which associated things depend for support
key·way \'kē-,wā\ *n* **1 :** a groove or channel for a key **2 :** the aperture for the key in a lock having a flat metal key
key word *n* **:** a word that is a key; *specif* **:** a word exemplifying the meaning or value of a letter or symbol
khad·dar \'käd-ər\ *or* **kha·di** \'käd-ē\ *n* [Hindi *khādar, khādī*] **:** homespun cotton cloth of India
kha·ki \'kak-ē, 'käk-\ *n* [Hindi *k̲hākī* dust-colored, fr. *k̲hāk* dust, fr. Per] **1 a :** a khaki-colored cloth made usu. of cotton or wool and used esp. for military uniforms **b :** a garment of this cloth; *esp* **:** a military uniform **2 :** a light yellowish brown
Khal·kha \'kal-kə\ *n* **1 :** a member of a Mongol people of Outer Mongolia **2 :** the language of the Khalkha people used as the official language of the Mongolian People's Republic
kham·sin \kam-'sēn\ *n* [Ar *rīḥ al-khamsīn* the wind of the fifty (days between Easter and Pentecost)] **:** a hot southerly Egyptian wind coming from the Sahara
1**khan** \'kän, 'kan\ *n* [ME *caan*, fr. MF, of Turkic origin; akin to Turk *han* prince] **1 :** a medieval sovereign of China and ruler over the Turkish, Tatar, and Mongol tribes **2 :** a local chieftain or man of rank in some countries of central Asia — **khan·ate** \-,āt\ *n*
2**khan** *n* [Ar *khān*] **:** a caravansary or rest house in some Asian countries
khe·dive \kə-'dēv\ *n* [F *khédive*, fr. Turk *hidiv*] **:** a ruler of Egypt from 1867 to 1914 governing as a viceroy of the sultan of Turkey — **khe·div·ial** \-'dē-vē-əl\ *or* **khe·div·al** \-'dē-vəl\ *adj*
Khmer \kə-'me(ə)r\ *n, pl* **Khmer** *or* **Khmers 1 a :** an aboriginal people of Cambodia **b :** a member of this people **2 :** the Mon-Khmer language of the Khmer people that is the official language of Cambodia — **Khmer·ian** \-'mer-ē-ən\ *adj*
Kho·war \'kō-,wär\ *n* **:** a Dard language of northwest Pakistan
ki·ang \kē-'äŋ\ *n* [Tibetan *rkyaṅ*] **:** an Asiatic wild ass (*Equus hemionus*) usu. with reddish back and sides and white underparts, muzzle, and legs
kiaugh \'kyäk̲\ *n* [prob. fr. ScGael *cabhag*] *Scot* **:** TROUBLE, ANXIETY
kib·butz \kib-'ůts, -'üts\ *n, pl* **kib·but·zim** \-,ůt-'sēm, -,üt-\ [NHeb *qibbūṣ*] **:** a collective farm or settlement in Israel
kibe \'kīb\ *n* [ME] **:** an ulcerated chilblain esp. on the heel
ki·bitz \'kib-əts, kə-'bits\ *vb* [Yiddish *kibitsen*, fr. G *kiebitzen*, fr. *kiebitz*, lit., pewit] *vi* **:** to act as a kibitzer ~ *vt* **:** to observe as a kibitzer; *esp* **:** to be a kibitzer at ⟨~ a card game⟩
ki·bitz·er \'kib-ət-sər, kə-'bit-\ *n* **:** one who looks on and often offers unwanted advice or comment esp. at a card game
ki·bosh \'kī-,bäsh, ki-'; kib-'äsh\ *n* [origin unknown] **:** something that serves as a check or stop ⟨put the ~ on⟩ — **kibosh** *vt*
1**kick** \'kik\ *vb* [ME *kiken*] *vi* **1 a :** to strike out with the foot or feet **b :** to make a kick in football **2 :** to show opposition, resentment, or discontent **3** *of a firearm* **:** to recoil when fired **4 :** to go from one place to another as circumstance or whim dictates ~ *vt* **1 a :** to strike, thrust, or hit with the foot **b :** to strike suddenly and forcefully as if with the foot **2 :** to score by kicking a ball **3** *slang* **:** to free oneself of (a drug habit) **syn** see OBJECT — **kick·er** *n* — **kick over the traces :** to cast off restraint, authority, or control — **kick the bucket :** DIE — **kick up one's heels 1 :** to show sudden delight **2 :** to have a lively time — **kick upstairs :** to promote to a higher but less desirable position
2**kick** *n* **1 a :** a blow or sudden forceful thrust with the foot; *specif* **:** a sudden propelling of a ball with the foot **b :** the power to kick **c :** a rhythmic motion of the legs used in swimming **d :** a burst of speed in racing **2 :** a sudden forceful jolt or thrust suggesting a kick; *specif* **:** the recoil of a gun **3 a :** a feeling or expression of opposition or objection **b :** the grounds for objection **4 a :** a strongly stimulating effect **b :** a feeling of pleasure **:** THRILL **c** *pl, slang* **:** FUN **d** *slang* **:** SPREE **5 :** a sudden and striking surprise, revelation, or turn of events
kick around *vt* **1 :** to treat in an inconsiderate or high-handed fashion **2** *slang* **:** to consider, examine, or discuss from various angles
kick·back \'kik-,bak\ *n* **1 :** a sharp violent reaction **2 :** a return of a part of a sum received often because of confidential agreement or coercion
kick in *vt, slang* **:** CONTRIBUTE ~ *vi* **1** *slang* **:** DIE **2** *slang* **:** to make a contribution
kick off *vi* **1 :** to start or resume play in football by a place-kick **2 :** to begin proceedings **3** *slang* **:** DIE ~ *vt* **:** to mark the beginning of
kick·off \'kik-,ȯf\ *n* **1 :** a kick that puts the ball into play in a football or soccer game **2 :** COMMENCEMENT
kick out *vt* **:** to dismiss or eject forcefully or summarily
kick·shaw \'kik-,shȯ\ *n* [by folk etymology fr. F *quelque chose* something] **1 :** a fancy dish **:** DELICACY **2 :** BAUBLE, GEWGAW
kick turn *n* **:** a standing half turn in skiing made by swinging one ski high with a jerk and planting it in the desired direction and then lifting the other ski into a parallel position
kick·up \'kik-,əp\ *n* **:** a noisy quarrel **:** ROW
kick up *vt* **1 :** to cause to rise upward **2 :** PROVOKE ~ *vi* **:** to give evidence of disorder
1**kid** \'kid\ *n* [ME *kide*, of Scand origin; akin to ON *kith* kid] **1 a :** a young goat **b :** a young individual of various related animals **2 a :** the flesh, fur, or skin of a kid **b :** something made of kid **3 :** CHILD, YOUNGSTER — **kid·dish** \'kid-ish\ *adj*
2**kid** *vi* **kid·ded; kid·ding :** to bring forth young — used of a goat or an antelope
3**kid** *vb* **kid·ded; kid·ding** [prob. fr. 1*kid*] *vt* **1 :** to deceive as a joke **:** FOOL **2 :** to make fun of **:** TEASE ~ *vi* **:** to engage in good-humored fooling or teasing **:** JOKE — **kid·der** *n*
Kid·der·min·ster \'kid-ər-,min(t)-stər\ *n* [*Kidderminster*, England] **:** an ingrain carpet
kid·dush \'kid-,ůsh, kid-'üsh\ *n* [Heb *qiddūsh* sanctification] **:** a Jewish ceremony that proclaims the holiness of the incoming Sabbath or festival and consists of a benediction pronounced customarily before the evening meal
kid glove *n* **:** a dress glove made of or as if of kidskin — **kid-gloved** \'kid-'gləvd\ *adj* — **with kid gloves :** with special consideration
kid·nap \'kid-,nap\ *vt* **kid·napped** *or* **kid·naped** \-,napt\ **kid·nap·ping** *or* **kid·nap·ing** [prob. back-formation fr. *kidnapper*, fr. *kid* + obs. *napper* (thief)] **:** to seize and detain or carry away by unlawful force or fraud and often with a demand for ransom — **kid·nap·per** *or* **kid·nap·er** *n*
kid·ney \'kid-nē\ *n* [ME] **1 a :** one of a pair of vertebrate organs situated in the body cavity near the spinal column that excrete waste products of metabolism, in man are bean-shaped organs about 4½ inches long lying behind the peritoneum in a mass of fatty tissue, and consist chiefly of nephrons by which urine is secreted, collected, and discharged into a main cavity whence it is conveyed by the ureter to the bladder **b :** any of various excretory organs of invertebrate animals **2 :** the kidney of an animal eaten as food by man **3 a :** TEMPERAMENT, DISPOSITION **b :** KIND, SORT
kidney bean *n* **:** a bean (*Phaseolus vulgaris*) grown esp. for its nutritious seeds; *also* **:** a rather large dark red bean seed
kid·skin \'kid-,skin\ *n* **:** the skin of a young goat used in making leather goods
kier \'ki(ə)r\ *n* [prob. of Scand origin; akin to ON *ker* tub] **:** a large metal vat in which fibers, yarns, and fabrics are boiled, bleached, or dyed
kie·sel·guhr *or* **kie·sel·gur** \'kē-zəl-,gů(ə)r\ *n* [G *kieselgur*] **:** loose or porous diatomite
kie·ser·ite \'kē-zə-,rīt\ *n* [G *kieserit*, fr. Dietrich *Kieser* †1862 G physician] **:** a mineral $MgSO_4H_2O$ that is a white hydrous magnesium sulfate
kif \'kif, 'kīf\ *var of* KEF
kil·der·kin \'kil-dər-kən\ *n* [ME, fr. MD *kindekijn*, fr. ML *quintale* quintal] **1 :** CASK **2 :** an English unit of capacity equal to ½ barrel
1**kill** \'kil\ *vb* [ME *killen*] *vt* **1 a :** to deprive of life **b** (1) **:** to slaughter (as a hog) for food (2) **:** to convert a food animal into (as pork) by slaughtering **2 a :** to put an end to ⟨~ competition⟩ **b :** DEFEAT, VETO **c :** to mark for omission **3 a :** to destroy the vital or essential quality of **b :** to cause to stop ⟨~ the motor⟩ **c :** to check the flow of current through **4 :** to cause to elapse ⟨~ time⟩ **5 a :** to cause extreme pain to **b :** to tire almost to the point of collapse **6 :** to hit (a ball) so hard in a racket game that a return is impossible **7 :** to consume (as a drink) totally ~ *vi* **:** to deprive one of life

syn KILL, SLAY, MURDER, ASSASSINATE, DISPATCH, EXECUTE mean to deprive of life. KILL merely states the fact of death caused by an agency in any manner; SLAY is a chiefly literary term implying deliberateness and violence but not necessarily motive; MURDER specifically implies stealth and motive and premeditation and therefore full moral responsibility; ASSASSINATE applies to deliberate killing openly or secretly but for impersonal motives; DISPATCH implies nothing beside speed and directness in putting to death; EXECUTE applies to the carrying out of a sentence to death

2**kill** *n* **1 :** an act or instance of killing **2 :** something killed: as **a** (1) **:** an animal shot in a hunt (2) **:** animals killed in a hunt, season, or particular period of time **b :** an enemy airplane, submarine, or ship destroyed by military action **c :** a return shot in a racket game that is too hard for an opponent to handle
3**kill** *n, often cap* [D *kil*] **:** CHANNEL, CREEK — used chiefly in place names in Delaware and New York
kill·deer \'kil-,di(ə)r\ *n, pl* **killdeers** *or* **killdeer** [imit.] **:** a plover (*Charadrius vociferus* syn. *Oxyechus vociferus*) of temperate No. America characterized by a plaintive penetrating cry
kill·er \'kil-ər\ *n* **1 :** one that kills **2 :** a fierce carnivorous gregarious largely black whale (*Orcinus orca* syn. *Orca orca*) 20 to 30 feet long
kil·lick \'kil-ik\ *n* [origin unknown] **1 :** a small anchor **2 :** an anchor formed by a stone usu. enclosed by pieces of wood
kil·li·fish \'kil-ē-,fish\ *n* [*killie* (killifish) + *fish*] **1 :** any of numerous small oviparous fishes (family Cyprinodontidae) much used as bait and in mosquito control **2 :** TOPMINNOW
1**kill·ing** \'kil-iŋ\ *n* **1 :** the act of one that kills **2 :** KILL 2a **3 :** a sudden notable gain or profit
2**killing** *adj* **1 :** that kills or relates to killing **2 :** highly amusing
kill·joy \'kil-,jȯi\ *n* **:** one who spoils the pleasure of others
1**kiln** \'kiln, 'kil\ *n* [ME *kilne*, fr. OE *cyln*, fr. L *culina* kitchen, fr. *coquere* to cook — more at COOK] **:** an oven, furnace, or heated enclosure used for processing a substance by burning, firing, or drying
2**kiln** *vt* **:** to burn, fire, or dry in a kiln
ki·lo \'kē-(,)lō, 'kil-(,)ō\ *n* **1 :** KILOGRAM **2 :** KILOMETER
kilo- *comb form* [F, modif. of Gk *chilioi* — more at MILE] **:** thousand ⟨*kilo*ton⟩
Kilo — a communications code word for the letter *k*
kilo·cal·o·rie \'kil-ə-,kal-(ə-)rē\ *n* [ISV] **:** CALORIE 1b
kilo·cy·cle \'kil-ə-,sī-kəl\ *n* [ISV] **:** one thousand cycles; *esp* **:** one thousand cycles per second
kilo·gram \'kil-ə-,gram\ *n* [F *kilogramme*, fr. *kilo-* + *gramme* gram] **1 :** the basic metric unit of mass and weight equal to the mass

of a platinum-iridium cylinder kept at the International Bureau of Weights and Measures near Paris and nearly equal to 1000 cubic centimeters of water at the temperature of its maximum density — see METRIC SYSTEM table **2 :** a unit of force equal to the weight of a kilogram under standard gravity

kilogram–meter *n* **:** the mks gravitational unit of work and energy equal to the work done by a kilogram force acting through a distance of one meter in the direction of the force **:** about 7.235 foot-pounds

kilo·li·ter \'kil-ə-,lēt-ər\ *n* [F *kilolitre*, fr. *kilo-* + *litre* liter] — see METRIC SYSTEM table

ki·lo·me·ter \kil-'äm-ət-ər (*not parallel with other metric-system compounds*), 'kil-ə-,mēt-\ *n* [F *kilomètre*, fr. *kilo-* + *mètre* meter] — see METRIC SYSTEM table

kilo·par·sec \'kil-ə-,pär-,sek\ *n* **:** one thousand parsecs

kilo·ton \'kil-ə-,tən\ *n* **1 :** one thousand tons **2 :** an explosive force equivalent to that of one thousand tons of TNT

kilo·var \'kil-ə-,vär\ *n* [*kilo*volt + *a*mpere + *r*eactive] **:** the part of a kilovolt-ampere contributed by reactance

kilo·volt \'kil-ə-,vōlt\ *n* [ISV] **:** a unit of electromotive force equal to one thousand volts

kilo·volt·age \-,vōl-tij\ *n* **:** potential difference expressed in kilovolts

kilovolt–ampere *n* **:** a unit of apparent power in an electric circuit equal to 1000 volt-amperes

kilo·watt \'kil-ə-,wät\ *n* [ISV] **:** a unit of power equal to 1000 watts

kilowatt–hour *n* **:** a unit of work or energy equal to that expended by one kilowatt in one hour

1kilt \'kilt\ *vb* [ME *kilten*, of Scand origin; akin to ON *kjalta* fold of a gathered skirt] *vt* **1** *chiefly dial* **:** to tuck up (as a skirt) **2 :** to equip with a kilt ~ *vi* **:** to move nimbly

2kilt *n* **1 :** a knee-length pleated skirt usu. of tartan worn by men in Scotland and by Scottish regiments in the British armies **2 :** a garment that resembles a Scottish kilt

kil·ter \'kil-tər\ *n* [origin unknown] **:** proper condition **:** ORDER ⟨out of ~⟩

ki·mo·no \kə-'mō-nə\ *n* [Jap, clothes] **1 :** a loose robe with wide sleeves and a broad sash traditionally worn as an outer garment by the Japanese **2 :** a loose dressing gown worn chiefly by women

1kin \'kin\ *n* [ME, fr. OE *cyn;* akin to OHG *chunni* race, L *genus* birth, race, kind, Gk *genos*, L *gignere* to beget, Gk *gignesthai* to be born] **1 :** a group of persons of common ancestry **:** CLAN **2 a :** one's relatives **:** KINDRED **b :** KINSMAN **3** *archaic* **:** KINSHIP

2kin *adj* **:** KINDRED, RELATED

-kin \kən\ *also* **-kins** \kənz\ *n suffix* [ME, fr. MD *-kin;* akin to OHG *-chīn*, dim. suffix] **:** little ⟨cat*kin*⟩ ⟨baby*kins*⟩

ki·nase \'kīn-,ās, 'kin-, -,āz\ *n* [ISV, fr. *kinetic*] **:** a substance that converts a zymogen into an enzyme

1kind \'kīnd\ *n* [ME *kinde*, fr. OE *cynd;* akin to OE *cyn* kin] **1 a** *archaic* **:** NATURE **b :** a natural grouping **:** SPECIES **c** *archaic* **:** FAMILY, LINEAGE **2** *archaic* **:** MANNER **3 :** fundamental nature or quality **:** ESSENCE **4 a :** a group united by common traits or interests **:** CATEGORY **b :** SORT, TYPE **c :** a doubtful or barely admissible member of a category ⟨a ~ of gray⟩ **5 a :** goods or commodities as distinguished from money **b :** the equivalent of what has been offered or received **syn** see TYPE

2kind *adj* **1** *chiefly dial* **:** AFFECTIONATE **:** LOVING **2 a :** of a sympathetic nature **:** FRIENDLY **b :** of a forbearing nature **:** GENTLE **c :** arising from or characterized by sympathy or forbearance ⟨a ~ act⟩ **3 :** of a pleasant nature **:** AGREEABLE

syn KIND, KINDLY, BENIGN, BENIGNANT mean showing a gentle, considerate nature. KIND and KINDLY both imply sympathy and humaneness and interest in another's welfare, KIND stressing a disposition to be helpful ⟨a *kind* heart⟩ and KINDLY stressing more the expression of a sympathetic nature or impulse ⟨take a *kindly* interest⟩ BENIGN and BENIGNANT stress mildness and mercifulness and apply more often to gracious or patronizing acts or utterances of a superior rather than an equal

kin·der·gar·ten \'kin-dər-,gärt-ᵊn, -,gärd-\ *n* [G, fr. *kinder* children + *garten* garden] **:** a school or class for children of the 4 to 6 age group

kin·der·gart·ner \-,gärt-nər, -,gärd-\ *n* **1 :** a child attending kindergarten **2 :** a teacher at a kindergarten

kind·heart·ed \'kīnd-'härt-əd\ *adj* **:** marked by a sympathetic nature — **kind·heart·ed·ly** *adv* — **kind·heart·ed·ness** *n*

1kin·dle \'kin-dᵊl\ *vb* **kin·dling** \-(d)liŋ, -dᵊl-iŋ\ [ME *kindlen*, fr. ON *kynda;* akin to OHG *cuntesal* fire] *vt* **1 :** to start (a fire) burning **:** LIGHT **2 :** to stir up **:** AROUSE **3 :** to cause to glow **:** ILLUMINATE ~ *vi* **1 :** to catch fire **2 a :** to flare up **b :** to become animated **3 :** to become illuminated — **kin·dler** \-(d)lər, -dᵊl-ər\ *n*

2kindle *vb* [ME *kindlen*] *vt* **:** BEAR — used esp. of a rabbit ~ *vi* **:** to bring forth young — used esp. of a rabbit

kind·less \'kīn-(d)ləs\ *adj* **1** *obs* **:** INHUMAN **2 :** DISAGREEABLE, UNSYMPATHETIC — **kind·less·ly** *adv*

kind·li·ness \'kīn-(d)lē-nəs\ *n* **1 :** the quality or state of being kindly **2 :** a kindly deed

kin·dling \'kin-(d)liŋ, 'kin-lən\ *n* **:** easily combustible material for starting a fire

1kind·ly \'kīn-(d)lē\ *adj* **1 a** *obs* **:** NATURAL **b** *archaic* **:** LAWFUL **2 :** of an agreeable or beneficial nature **:** PLEASANT ⟨~ climate⟩ **3 :** of a sympathetic or generous nature **:** FRIENDLY ⟨~ men⟩ **syn** see KIND

2kindly *adv* **1 a :** NATURALLY **b :** READILY **2 a :** SYMPATHETICALLY **b :** as a gesture of good will **c :** COURTEOUSLY, OBLIGINGLY

kind·ness \'kīn(d)-nəs\ *n* **1 :** a kind deed **:** FAVOR **2 a :** the quality or state of being kind **b** *archaic* **:** AFFECTION

kind of \,kīn-də\ *adv* **:** to a moderate degree **:** SOMEWHAT

1kin·dred \'kin-drəd\ *n* [ME, fr. *kin* + OE *rǣden* condition, fr. *rǣdan* to advise, read] **1 a :** a group of related individuals **b :** one's relatives **2** *archaic* **:** family relationship **:** KINSHIP

2kindred *adj* **1 :** of a similar nature or character **:** LIKE **2** *archaic* **:** of the same ancestry **:** RELATED

kine \'kīn\ *archaic pl of* COW

kin·e·ma \'kin-ə-mə\ *Brit var of* CINEMA

ki·ne·mat·ic \,kin-ə-'mat-ik, ,kī-nə-\ *adj* **:** of or relating to kinematics — **ki·ne·mat·i·cal** \-i-kəl\ *adj*

ki·ne·mat·ics \-iks\ *n pl but sing in constr* [F *cinématique*, fr. Gk *kinēmat-*, *kinēma* motion — more at CINEMATOGRAPH] **:** a branch of dynamics that deals with aspects of motion apart from considerations of mass and force

1kin·e·scope \'kin-ə-,skōp\ *n* [fr. *Kinescope*, a trademark] **1 :** a cathode-ray tube having at one end a screen of luminescent material on which are produced visible images **2 :** a motion picture made from a television kinescope image

2kinescope *vt* **:** to make a kinescope of

ki·ne·si·ol·o·gy \kə-,nē-sē-'äl-ə-jē, (,)kī-, -zē-\ *n* [Gk *kinēsis* motion, fr. *kinein* to move; akin to L *ciēre* to move — more at HIGHT] **:** the study of the principles of mechanics and anatomy in relation to human movement

-ki·ne·sis \kə-'nē-səs, (,)kī-\ *n comb form, pl* **-ki·ne·ses** \-'nē-,sēz\ [NL, fr. Gk *kinēsis* motion, fr. *kinein* to move — more at HIGHT] **:** division ⟨karyo*kinesis*⟩

kin·es·the·sia \,kin-əs-'thē-zh(ē-)ə\ *or* **kin·es·the·sis** \-'thē-səs\ *n, pl* **kin·es·the·sias** *or* **kin·es·the·ses** \-'thē-,sēz\ [NL, fr. Gk *kinein* + *aisthēsis* perception — more at ANESTHESIA] **:** a sense mediated by end organs located in muscles, tendons, and joints and stimulated by bodily movements and tensions; *also* **:** sensory experience derived from this sense — **kin·es·thet·ic** \-'thet-ik\ *adj* — **kin·es·thet·i·cal·ly** \-i-k(ə-)lē\ *adv*

ki·net·ic \kə-'net-ik, kī-\ *adj* [Gk *kinētikos*, fr. *kinētos* moving, fr. *kinein*] **1 :** of or relating to the motion of material bodies and the forces and energy associated therewith **2 a :** ACTIVE, LIVELY **b :** ENERGIZING, DYNAMIC

kinetic energy *n* **:** energy associated with motion

ki·net·ics \kə-'net-iks, kī-\ *n pl but sing or pl in constr* **1 :** a branch of science that deals with the effects of forces upon the motions of material bodies or with changes in a physical or chemical system **2 :** the mechanism by which a physical or chemical change is effected

kinetic theory *n* **:** a theory in physics: the minute particles of a substance are in vigorous motion on the assumptions that (1) the particles of a gas move in straight lines with high average velocity, continually encounter one another and thus change their individual velocities and directions, and cause pressure by their impact against the walls of a container and that (2) the temperature of a substance increases with an increase in either the average kinetic energy of the particles or the average potential energy of separation (as in fusion) of the particles or in both when heat is added — called also respectively (1) *kinetic theory of gases*, (2) *kinetic theory of heat*

ki·neto·nu·cle·us \kə-,net-ō-'n(y)ü-klē-əs, kī-\ *n* [NL, fr. Gk *kinētos* + NL *nucleus*] **:** KINETOPLAST

ki·neto·plast \-'net-ə-,plast\ *n* [Gk *kinētos* + ISV *-plast*] **:** a complex cell structure found in association with the base of flagella and undulating membranes

Ki·neto·scope \-,skōp\ *trademark* — used for a device for viewing through a magnifying lens a sequence of pictures on an endless band of film moved continuously over a light source and a rapidly rotating shutter that creates an illusion of motion

kin·folk \'kin-,fōk\ *n* **:** RELATIVES

king \'kiŋ\ *n, often attrib* [ME, fr. OE *cyning;* akin to OHG *kuning* king, OE *cyn* kin] **1 a :** a male monarch of a major territorial unit; *esp* **:** one who inherits his position and rules for life **b :** a paramount chief **2** *cap* **:** GOD, CHRIST **3 :** one that holds a preeminent position; *esp* **:** a chief among competitors **4 :** the principal piece in a set of chessmen **5 :** a playing card that is marked with a stylized figure of a king **6 :** a checker that has been crowned

king·bird \-,bərd\ *n* **:** any of various American tyrant flycatchers

king·bolt \-,bōlt\ *n* **:** a vertical bolt by which the forward axle and wheels of a vehicle or the trucks of a railroad car are connected with the other parts

King Charles spaniel \kiŋ-,chärlz-\ *n* [*Charles* II †1685 king of England] **:** a dog of a black and tan variety of the English toy spaniel

king crab *n* **1 :** any of several closely related large marine arthropods (order Xiphosura and class Merostomata) with a broad crescentic cephalothorax **2 :** any of several very large crabs

king·craft \'kiŋ-,kraft\ *n* **:** the art of governing as a king

king·cup \-,kəp\ *n* **:** any of various buttercups

king·dom \'kiŋ-dəm\ *n* **1** *obs* **:** KINGSHIP **2 :** a politically organized community or major territorial unit having a monarchical form of government headed by a king or queen **3** *often cap* **a :** the eternal kingship of God **b :** the realm in which God's will is fulfilled **4 a :** a realm or region in which something is dominant **b :** an area or sphere in which one holds a preeminent position **5 :** one of the three primary divisions of lifeless material, plants, and animals into which natural objects are commonly classified — called also respectively *mineral kingdom, plant kingdom, animal kingdom*

king·fish \'kiŋ-,fish\ *n* **1 a :** any of several marine croakers (family Sciaenidae) **b :** any of various scombroid fishes; *esp* **:** CERO **c :** any of various marine percoid fishes (as of the family Carangidae) **2 :** an undisputed master in an area or group

king·fish·er \-,fish-ər\ *n* **:** any of numerous nonpasserine birds (family Alcedinidae) that are usu. crested and bright-colored with a short tail and a long stout sharp bill

King James Version \kiŋ-'jāmz-\ *n* [*James* I †1625 king of England] **:** AUTHORIZED VERSION

king·let \'kiŋ-lət\ *n* **1 :** a weak or petty king **2 :** any of several small birds (genus *Regulus*) that resemble warblers but have some of the habits of titmice

king·li·ness \'kiŋ-lē-nəs\ *n* **:** the quality or state of being kingly

king·ly \'kiŋ-lē\ *adj* **1 :** having royal rank **2 :** of, relating to, or befitting a king **3 :** MONARCHICAL — **kingly** *adv*

king·mak·er \'kiŋ-,mā-kər\ *n* **:** one having great influence over the choice of candidates for political office

king of arms : a heraldic officer of the highest rank

king·pin \'kiŋ-,pin\ *n* **1 :** any of several bowling pins: as **a :** HEADPIN **b :** the number 5 pin **2 :** the chief person in a group or undertaking **3 :** KINGBOLT

king post *n* **:** a vertical member connecting the apex of a triangular truss with the base

King's Birthday *n* **:** a legal holiday in parts of the British Commonwealth celebrating the birthday of the king

king's blue *n* **:** COBALT BLUE

King's Counsel *n* **:** a barrister selected to serve as counsel to the British crown

King's English *n* **:** standard, pure, or correct English speech or usage
king's evil *n, often cap K&E* [fr. the former belief that it could be healed by a king's touch] **:** SCROFULA
king·ship \'kiŋ-,ship\ *n* **1 :** the position, office, or dignity of a king **2 :** the personality of a king **:** MAJESTY **3 :** government by a king
king–size \'kiŋ-,sīz\ *or* **king–sized** \-,sīzd\ *adj* **1 :** longer than the regular or standard size **2 :** unusually large
king snake *n* **:** any of numerous brightly marked colubrid snakes (genus *Lampropeltis*) of the southern and central U. S. that are voracious consumers of rodents
king's yellow *n* **:** arsenic trisulfide used as a pigment
1kink \'kiŋk\ *n* [D; akin to MLG *kinke* kink] **1 :** a short tight twist or curl caused by a doubling or winding of something upon itself **2 a :** ECCENTRICITY, QUIRK **b :** WHIM **3 :** a clever unusual way of doing something **4 :** a cramp in some part of the body **5 :** an imperfection likely to cause difficulties in the operation of something

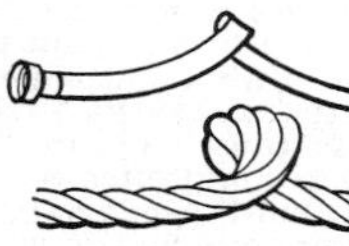
kinks 1

2kink *vi* **:** to form a kink ~ *vt* **:** to make a kink in
kin·ka·jou \'kiŋ-kə-,jü\ *n* [F, of Algonquian origin; akin to Ojibwa *qwíngwâage* wolverine] **:** a slender nocturnal arboreal carnivorous mammal (*Potos caudivolvulus*, family Procyonidae) of Mexico and Central and So. America that is about three feet long with a long prehensile tail, large lustrous eyes, and soft woolly yellowish brown fur
kinky \'kiŋ-kē\ *adj* [1*kink* + *-y*] **1 :** closely twisted or curled ⟨~ hair⟩ **2** *Brit* **:** FAR-OUT, OFFBEAT
kin·ni·kin·nick *also* **kin·ni·ki·nic** \,kin-i-kə-'nik\ *n* [of Algonquian origin; akin to Natick *kinukkinuk* mixture] **:** a mixture of dried leaves and bark and sometimes tobacco smoked by the Indians and pioneers esp. in the Ohio valley; *also* **:** a plant (as a sumac or dogwood) used in it
-kins — see -KIN
kins·folk \'kinz-,fōk\ *n* **:** RELATIVES
kin·ship \'kin-,ship\ *n* **:** the quality or state of being kin **:** RELATIONSHIP
kins·man \'kinz-mən\ *n* **:** RELATIVE; *specif* **:** a male relative
kins·wom·an \-,wu̇m-ən\ *n* **:** a female relative
ki·osk \'kē-,äsk, kē-'\ *n* [Turk *köşk*, fr. Per *kūshk* portico] **1 :** an open summerhouse or pavilion **2 :** a small light structure with one or more open sides used esp. as a newsstand or a telephone booth
1kip \'kip\ *n* [obs. D; akin to MLG *kip* bundle of hides] **:** a bundle of undressed hides of young or small animals; *also* **:** one of the hides
2kip *n* [*kilo* + *pound*] **:** a unit of weight equal to 1000 pounds used to express deadweight load
3kip *n, pl* **kip** *or* **kips** [Thai] — see MONEY table
1kip·per \'kip-ər\ *n* [ME *kypre*, fr. OE *cypera;* akin to OE *coper* copper] **1 :** a male salmon or sea trout during or after the spawning season **2 :** a kippered herring or salmon
2kipper *vt* **kip·per·ing** \-(ə-)riŋ\ **:** to cure by splitting, cleaning, salting, and smoking
Kir·ghiz \ki(ə)r-'gēz\ *n, pl* **Kirghiz** *or* **Kir·ghiz·es** [Kirghiz *Kyrghyz*] **1 a :** a people of Mongolian race prob. with some Caucasian intermixture inhabiting chiefly the Central Asian steppes **b :** a member of this people **2 :** the Turkic language of the Kirghiz
kirk \'ki(ə)rk, 'kərk\ *n* [ME (northern dial.), fr. ON *kirkja*, fr. OE *cirice* — more at CHURCH] **1** *chiefly Scot* **:** CHURCH **2** *cap* **:** the national church of Scotland as distinguished from the Church of England or the Episcopal Church in Scotland
Kir·man \kər-'män, ki(ə)r-\ *n* [*Kirman*, province in Iran] **:** a Persian carpet or rug characterized by elaborate fluid designs and soft colors
kir·mess \'kər-məs, (,)kər-'mes\ *var of* KERMIS
kirsch \'ki(ə)rsh\ *n* [G, short for *kirschwasser*, fr. *kirsche* cherry + *wasser* water] **:** a dry colorless brandy distilled from the fermented juice of the black morello cherry
kir·tle \'kərt-ᵊl\ *n* [ME *kirtel*, fr. OE *cyrtel*, fr. (assumed) OE *curt* short, fr. L *curtus* shortened] **1 :** a tunic or coat worn by men esp. in the Middle Ages **2 :** a long gown or dress worn by women
Kis·lev \'kis-ləf\ *n* [Heb *Kislēw*] **:** the 3d month of the civil year or the 9th month of the ecclesiastical year in the Jewish calendar
kis·met \'kiz-,met, -mət\ *n, often cap* [Turk, fr. Ar *qismah* portion, lot] **:** FATE 1, 2a
1kiss \'kis\ *vb* [ME *kissen*, fr. OE *cyssan;* akin to OHG *kussen* to kiss] *vt* **1 :** to touch with the lips esp. as a mark of affection or greeting **2 :** to touch gently or lightly ~ *vi* **1 :** to salute or caress one another with the lips **2 :** to come in gentle contact — **kiss·able** \-ə-bəl\ *adj* — **kiss good–bye 1 :** LEAVE **2 :** to resign oneself to the loss of
2kiss *n* **1 :** a caress with the lips **2 :** a gentle touch or contact **3 a :** a small meringue often with coconut **b :** a bite-size piece of candy often wrapped in paper or foil
kiss·er \'kis-ər\ *n* **1 :** one that kisses **2** *slang* **a :** MOUTH **b :** FACE
kissing bug *n* **:** CONENOSE
kist \'kist\ *n* [ME *kiste*, fr. ON *kista*] *chiefly dial* **:** CHEST
1kit \'kit\ *n* [ME] **1** *dial Brit* **:** a wooden tub **2 a** (1) **:** a collection of articles usu. for personal use ⟨a travel ~⟩ (2) **:** a set of tools or implements ⟨a carpenter's ~⟩ (3) **:** a set of parts to be assembled ⟨model-airplane ~⟩ (4) **:** a packaged collection of related material ⟨convention ~⟩ **b :** a container for any of such sets or collections **3 :** a group of persons or things — usu. used in the phrase *the whole kit and caboodle*
2kit *n* [origin unknown] **:** a small violin
3kit *n* **1 :** KITTEN **2 :** a young or undersized fur-bearing animal; *also* **:** its pelt
kitch·en \'kich-ən\ *n, often attrib* [ME *kichene*, fr. OE *cycene;* akin to OHG *chuhhina* kitchen; both fr. a prehistoric WGmc word borrowed fr. LL *coquina*, fr. L *coquere* to cook — more at COOK] **1 :** a room or other place with cooking facilities **2 :** the personnel that prepares, cooks, and serves food
kitchen cabinet *n* **1 :** a cupboard with drawers and shelves for use in a kitchen **2 :** an informal group of advisers to the head of a government
kitch·en·ette \,kich-ə-'net\ *n* **:** a small kitchen or an alcove containing cooking facilities
kitchen garden *n* **:** a garden in which vegetables are cultivated
kitchen midden *n* **:** a refuse heap; *specif* **:** a mound marking the site of a primitive human habitation
kitchen police *n* **1 :** enlisted men detailed to assist the cooks in a military mess **2 :** the work of kitchen police
kitch·en·ware \'kich-ən-,wa(ə)r, -,we(ə)r\ *n* **:** hardware for use in a kitchen
1kite \'kīt\ *n* [ME, fr. OE *cӯta;* akin to MHG *kūze* owl, Gk *goan* to lament] **1 :** any of various hawks (family Accipitridae) with long narrow wings, a deeply forked tail, and feet adapted for taking insects and small reptiles as prey **2 :** a person who preys on others **3 :** a light frame covered with paper or cloth, often provided with a balancing tail, and designed to be flown in the air at the end of a long string **4 a :** ACCOMMODATION PAPER **b :** a check drawn against uncollected funds in a bank account or fraudulently raised before cashing **5** *pl* **:** the lightest and usu. the loftiest sails carried only in a light breeze
2kite *vi* **1 :** to get money or credit by a kite **2 :** to go in a rapid, carefree, or flighty manner ~ *vt* **1 :** to use (a kite) to get money or credit **2 :** to cause to soar
kith \'kith\ *n* [ME, fr. OE *cӯthth*, fr. *cūth* known — more at UNCOUTH] **:** familiar friends, neighbors, or relatives ⟨~ and kin⟩
kithe \'kīth\ *vb* [ME *kithen*, fr. OE *cӯthan*, fr. *cūth*] *vt, chiefly Scot* **:** to make known ~ *vi, chiefly Scot* **:** to become known
kitsch \'kich\ *n* [G] **:** artistic or literary material of low quality
1kit·ten \'kit-ᵊn\ *n* [ME *kitoun*, fr. (assumed) ONF *caton*, dim. of *cat*, fr. LL *cattus*] **:** a young cat; *also* **:** an immature individual of various other small mammals
2kitten *vi* **kit·ten·ing** \'kit-niŋ, -ᵊn-iŋ\ **:** to give birth to kittens
kit·ten·ish \'kit-nish, -ᵊn-ish\ *adj* **:** resembling a kitten; *esp* **:** PLAYFUL — **kit·ten·ish·ly** *adv* — **kit·ten·ish·ness** *n*
kit·ti·wake \'kit-ē-,wāk\ *n* [imit.] **:** any of various gulls (genus *Rissa*) having the hind toe short or rudimentary
1kit·tle \'kit-ᵊl\ *vt* [ME (northern dial.) *kytyllen*] **1** *chiefly Scot* **:** TICKLE **2** *chiefly Scot* **:** PERPLEX
2kittle *adj* **1** *chiefly Scot* **a :** SKITTISH **b :** APT **c :** CAPRICIOUS **2** *chiefly Scot* **:** TICKLISH
1kit·ty \'kit-ē\ *n* **:** CAT 1a; *esp* **:** KITTEN
2kitty *n* [1*kit*] **1 :** a fund in a poker game made up of contributions from each pot **2 :** a sum of money or collection of goods made up of small contributions **:** POOL
kit·ty–cor·ner *or* **kit·ty–cor·nered** *var of* CATERCORNER
ki·va \'kē-və\ *n* [Hopi] **:** a Pueblo Indian ceremonial structure that is usu. round and partly underground
Ki·wa·ni·an \kə-'wän-ē-ən\ *n* [*Kiwanis* (*club*)] **:** a member of one of the major service clubs
ki·wi \'kē-(,)wē\ *n* [Maori, of imit. origin] **:** a flightless New Zealand bird (genus *Apteryx*) with rudimentary wings, stout legs, a long bill, and grayish brown hairlike plumage

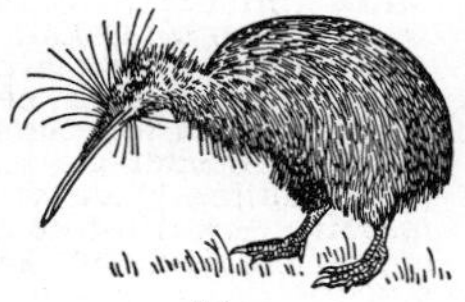
kiwi

Klan \'klan\ *n* [(*Ku Klux*) *Klan*] **:** an organization of Ku Kluxers; *also* **:** a subordinate unit of such an organization — **Klan·ism** \-,iz-əm\ *n* — **Klans·man** \'klanz-mən\ *n*
klatch *or* **klatsch** \'klach, 'kläch\ *n* [G *klatsch* gossip] **:** a gathering characterized by informal conversation
Klee·nex \'klē-,neks\ *trademark* — used for a cleansing tissue
klept- *or* **klepto-** *comb form* [Gk, fr. *kleptein* to steal; akin to Goth *hlifan* to steal, L *clepere*] **:** stealing **:** theft ⟨*klepto*mania⟩
klep·to·ma·nia \,klep-tə-'mā-nē-ə, -nyə\ *n* [NL] **:** a persistent neurotic impulse to steal esp. without economic motive
klep·to·ma·ni·ac \-nē-,ak\ *n* **:** a person evidencing kleptomania
klieg eyes *or* **kleig eyes** \'klē-'gīz\ *n pl* [*klieg* or *kleig* (*light*)] **:** a condition marked by conjunctivitis and watering of the eyes resulting from excessive exposure to intense light
klieg light *or* **kleig light** \-'glīt\ *n* [John H. *Kliegl* †1959 & Anton T. *Kliegl* †1927 German-born Amer. lighting experts] **:** a carbon arc lamp used in taking motion pictures
kloof \'klüf\ *n* [Afrik] *Africa* **:** a deep glen **:** RAVINE
kly·stron \'klī-,strän\ *n* [fr. *Klystron*, a trademark] **:** an electron tube in which bunching of electrons is produced by electric fields and which is used for the generation and amplification of ultrahigh-frequency current
knack \'nak\ *n* [ME *knak*] **1 a :** a task requiring adroitness and dexterity **b :** a clever way of doing something **c :** TRICK, STRATAGEM **2 :** a special ready capacity that is hard to analyze or teach **3** *archaic* **:** an ingenious device; *broadly* **:** TOY, KNICKKNACK **syn** see GIFT
knack·er \'nak-ər\ *n* [prob. fr. E dial., saddlemaker] **1** *Brit* **:** a buyer of worn-out domestic animals or their carcasses for use esp. as animal food or fertilizer **2** *Brit* **:** a buyer of old structures for their constituent materials — **knack·ery** \'nak-(ə-)rē\ *n*
1knap \'nap\ *n* [ME, fr. OE *cnæp;* akin to OE *cnotta* knot] **1** *chiefly dial* **:** a crest of a hill **:** SUMMIT **2** *chiefly dial* **:** a small hill
2knap *vt* **knapped; knap·ping** [ME *knappen*, of imit. origin] **1** *dial Brit* **:** RAP **2 :** to break with a quick blow; *esp* **:** to shape (as flints) by breaking off pieces **3** *dial Brit* **:** SNAP, CROP **4** *dial Brit* **:** CHATTER — **knap·per** *n*
knap·sack \'nap-,sak\ *n* [LG *knappsack* or D *knapzak*, fr. LG & D *knappen* to make a snapping noise, eat + LG *sack* or D *zak*] **:** a usu. canvas or leather bag or case strapped on the back and used esp. for carrying supplies while on a march or hike
knap·weed \-,wēd\ *n* [ME *knopwed*, fr. *knop* + *wed* weed] **:** any of various weedy composite plants (genus *Centaurea*); *esp* **:** a widely naturalized European perennial (*C. nigra*) with tough wiry stems and knobby heads of purple flowers
knave \'nāv\ *n* [ME, fr. OE *cnafa;* akin to OHG *knabo* boy] **1** *archaic* **a :** a boy servant **b :** a male servant **c :** a man of humble birth or position **2 :** a tricky deceitful fellow **:** ROGUE, RASCAL **3 :** JACK 6a

knav·ery \'nāv-(ə-)rē\ *n* **1 a :** the practices of a knave **:** RASCALITY **b :** a roguish or mischievous act **2** *obs* **:** roguish mischief

knav·ish \'nā-vish\ *adj* **:** of, relating to, or characteristic of a knave; *esp* **:** DISHONEST — **kna·vish·ly** *adv*

knead \'nēd\ *vt* [ME *kneden*, fr. OE *cnedan;* akin to OHG *knetan* to knead, OE *cnotta* knot] **1 :** to work and press into a mass with or as if with the hands **2 a :** to form or shape as if by kneading **b :** to treat as if by kneading — **knead·er** *n*

¹knee \'nē\ *n, often attrib* [ME, fr. OE *cnēow;* akin to OHG *kneo* knee, L *genu*, Gk *gony*] **1 a** (1) **:** a joint in the middle part of the human leg that is the articulation between the femur, tibia, and patella (2) **:** the part of the leg that includes this joint **b** (1) **:** the corresponding joint in the hind leg of a four-footed vertebrate (2) **:** the carpal joint of the foreleg of a four-footed vertebrate **c :** the tarsal joint of a bird **d :** the joint between the femur and tibia of an insect **2 a :** something resembling the human knee **b :** a rounded or conical process rising from the roots of various swamp-growing trees ⟨cypress ~⟩ **3 :** the part of a garment covering the knee **4 :** a blow with the bent knee — **kneed** \'nēd\ *adj*

²knee *vt* **kneed; knee·ing 1** *archaic* **:** to bend the knee to **2 :** to strike with the knee

knee action *n* **:** a front-wheel suspension of an automobile permitting independent vertical movement of each front wheel

knee·cap \'nē-,kap\ *n* **:** PATELLA

knee–deep \'nē-'dēp\ *adj* **1 :** KNEE-HIGH **2 a :** sunk to the knees **b :** deeply engaged or occupied

knee–high \'nē-'hī\ *adj* **:** rising or reaching upward to the knees

knee·hole \'nē-,hōl\ *n* **:** an open space for the knees

knee jerk *n* **:** an involuntary forward kick produced by a light blow on the tendon below the patella

kneel \'nē(ə)l\ *vi* **knelt** \'nelt\ *or* **kneeled; kneel·ing** [ME *knelen*, fr. OE *cnēowlian;* akin to OE *cnēow* knee] **:** to bend the knee **:** fall or rest on the knees — **kneel·er** *n*

knee·pan \'nē-,pan\ *n* **:** PATELLA

¹knell \'nel\ *vb* [ME *knellen*, fr. OE *cnyllan;* akin to MHG er*knellen* to toll] *vi* **1 :** to ring esp. for a death, funeral, or disaster **:** TOLL **2 :** to sound in an ominous manner or with an ominous effect ~ *vt* **:** to summon, announce, or proclaim by or as if by a knell

²knell *n* **1 :** a stroke or sound of a bell esp. when rung slowly for a death, funeral, or disaster **2 :** a sound or other indication of a death or of the end or failure of something

knew *past of* KNOW

knick·er·bock·er \'nik-ə(r)-,bäk-ər\ *n* [Diedrich *Knickerbocker*, fictitious author of *History of New York* (1809) by Washington Irving] **1** *cap* **:** a descendant of the early Dutch settlers of New York; *broadly* **:** a native or resident of the city or state of New York **2** *pl* **:** KNICKERS

knick·ers \'nik-ərz\ *n pl* [short for *knickerbockers*] **:** loose-fitting short pants gathered at the knee

knick·knack \'nik-,nak\ *n* [redupl. of *knack*] **:** a small trivial article intended for ornament

¹knife \'nīf\ *n, pl* **knives** \'nīvz\ *often attrib* [ME *knif*, fr. OE *cnīf;* akin to MLG *knīf* knife, OE *cnotta* knot] **1 a :** a cutting instrument consisting of a sharp blade fastened to a handle **b :** a weapon resembling a knife **2 :** a sharp cutting blade or tool in a machine — **knife·like** \'nī-,flīk\ *adj* — **under the knife :** in surgery

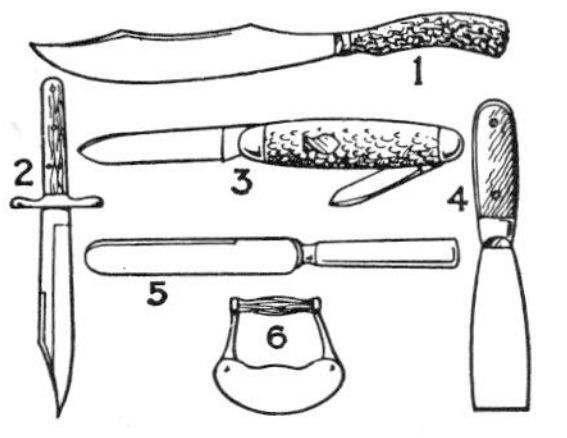

knives: *1* carving, *2* hunting, *3* pocket, *4* putty, *5* table, *6* chopping

²knife *vt* **1 :** to use a knife on; *specif* **:** to stab, slash, or wound with a knife **2 :** to cut, mark, or spread with a knife **3 :** to try to defeat by underhand means **4 :** to move like a knife in ~ *vi* **:** to cut a way with or as if with a knife blade

knife–edge \'nī-,fej\ *n* **1 :** a sharp narrow knifelike edge **2 :** a sharp wedge of steel or other hard material used as a fulcrum for a lever beam in a precision instrument

¹knight \'nīt\ *n* [ME, fr. OE *cniht;* akin to OHG *kneht* youth, military follower, OE *cnotta* knot] **1 a** (1) **:** a mounted man-at-arms serving a feudal superior; *esp* **:** a man ceremonially inducted into special military rank usu. after completing service as page and squire (2) **:** a man honored by a sovereign for merit and in Great Britain ranking below a baronet (3) **:** a person of antiquity equal to a knight in rank **b :** a man devoted to the service of a lady as her attendant or champion **c :** a member of an order or society **2 :** a chess piece that may cross occupied squares and that has an L-shaped move of three squares of which two are in a horizontal or vertical row and one is perpendicular to the row

²knight *vt* **:** to make a knight of

knight bachelor *n, pl* **knights bachelors** *or* **knights bachelor :** a knight of the most ancient and lowest order of English knights

knight–er·rant \'nīt-'er-ənt\ *n, pl* **knights–errant :** a knight traveling in search of adventures in which to exhibit military skill, prowess, and generosity

knight–er·rant·ry \'nīt-'er-ən-trē\ *n* **1 :** the practice or actions of a knight-errant **2 :** quixotic conduct

knight·hood \'nīt-,hu̇d\ *n* **1 :** the rank, dignity, or profession of a knight **2 :** the qualities befitting a knight **:** CHIVALRY **3 :** knights as a class or body

knight·li·ness \'nīt-lē-nəs\ *n* **:** the quality or state of being knightly

knight·ly \'nīt-lē\ *adj* **1 :** of, relating to, or characteristic of a knight **2 :** made up of knights — **knightly** *adv*

Knight of Co·lum·bus \-kə-'ləm-bəs\ *n, pl* **Knights of Columbus** [Christopher *Columbus* †1506 It explorer] **:** a member of a fraternal and benevolent society of Roman Catholic men

Knight Templar *n, pl* **Knights Templars** *or* **Knights Templar 1 :** TEMPLAR 1 **2 :** a member of an order of Freemasonry conferring three degrees in the York rite

knit \'nit\ *vb* **knit** *or* **knit·ted; knit·ting** [ME *knitten*, fr. OE *cnyttan;* akin to OE *cnotta* knot] *vt* **1** *chiefly dial* **:** to tie together **2 a :** to link firmly or closely **b :** to cause to grow together **c :** to contract into wrinkles **3 :** to form by interlacing yarn or thread in a series of connected loops with needles ~ *vi* **1 :** to make knitted fabrics or objects **2 a :** to become compact **b :** to grow together **c :** to become drawn together — **knit·ter** *n*

knit·ting *n* **1 :** the action or method of one that knits **2 :** work done or being done by one that knits

knit·wear \'nit-,wa(ə)r, -,we(ə)r\ *n* **:** knitted clothing

knob \'näb\ *n* [ME *knobbe;* akin to MLG *knubbe* knob, OE *-cnoppa* — more at KNOP] **1 a :** a rounded protuberance **:** LUMP **b :** a small rounded ornament or handle **2 :** a rounded usu. isolated hill or mountain — **knobbed** \'näbd\ *adj* — **knob·by** \'näb-ē\ *adj*

knob·ker·rie \'näb-,ker-ē\ *n* [Afrik *knopkierie*, fr. *knop* knob + *kierie* club] **:** a short wooden club with a knob at one end used as a missile or in close attack esp. by aborigines of southern Africa

¹knock \'näk\ *vb* [ME *knoken*, fr. OE *cnocian;* akin to MHG *knochen* to press] *vi* **1 :** to strike something with a sharp blow **2 :** to collide with something **3 a :** BUSTLE **b :** WANDER **4 a :** to make a pounding noise **b :** to have engine knock **5 :** to find fault ~ *vt* **1 a** (1) **:** to strike sharply (2) **:** to drive, force, or make by so striking **b :** to set forcibly in motion with a blow **2 :** to cause to collide **3 :** to find fault with

²knock *n* **1 a :** a sharp blow **b** (1) **:** a severe misfortune or hardship (2) **:** SETBACK, REVERSAL **2 a :** a pounding noise **b :** a sharp metallic noise caused by abnormal ignition in an automobile engine **3 :** a harsh and often petty criticism

¹knock·about \'näk-ə-,bau̇t\ *adj* **1 :** suitable for rough use **2 :** being noisy and rough **:** BOISTEROUS

²knockabout *n* **1 :** a performer or performance of knockabout comedy **2 :** a sloop with a simplified rig marked by absence of bowsprit and topmast **3 :** something suitable for rough use

knock down *vt* **1 :** to dispose of to a bidder at an auction sale **2 :** to take apart **:** DISASSEMBLE **3 :** to receive as income or salary **:** EARN **4 :** to make a reduction in

¹knock·down \'näk-,dau̇n\ *n* **1 :** the action of knocking down **2 :** something that strikes down or overwhelms **3 :** something easily assembled or disassembled

²knockdown *adj* **1 :** having such force as to strike down or overwhelm **2 :** that can easily be assembled or disassembled

knock·er \'näk-ər\ *n* **:** one that knocks; *specif* **:** a metal ring, bar, or hammer hinged to a door for use in knocking

knock–knee \'näk-'nē, -,nē\ *n* **:** a condition in which the legs curve inward at the knees — **knock–kneed** \-'nēd\ *adj*

knock off *vi* **:** to stop doing something ~ *vt* **1 :** to do hurriedly or routinely **2 :** DISCONTINUE, STOP **3 a :** KILL **b :** OVERCOME

knock out *vt* **1 :** to produce roughly or hastily **2 a :** to fell (a boxing opponent) by hitting with an immobilizing blow **b :** to make inoperative or useless **3 :** to tire out **:** EXHAUST **4 :** to drive (an opposing pitcher) from a baseball game by heavy hitting

knock·out \'näk-,au̇t\ *n* **1 a :** the act of knocking out **:** the condition of being knocked out **b :** a blow that knocks out an opponent **2 :** something sensationally striking or attractive — **knockout** *adj*

knock up *vt* **1** *Brit* **:** ROUSE, SUMMON **2** *slang* **:** to make pregnant

¹knoll \'nōl\ *n* [ME *knol*, fr. OE *cnoll;* akin to ON *knollr* mountaintop, OE *cnotta* knot] **:** a small round hill **:** MOUND

²knoll *vb* [ME *knollen*] *archaic* **:** KNELL

knop \'näp\ *n* [ME, fr. OE *-cnoppa* knob; akin to OE *cnotta*] **:** a usu. ornamental knob

¹knot \'nät\ *n* [ME, fr. OE *cnotta;* akin to OHG *knoto* knot, Lith *gniusti* to press] **1 a :** an interlacement of the parts of one or more flexible bodies forming a lump or knob **b :** the lump or knob so formed **2 :** something hard to solve **:** PROBLEM **3 :** a bond of union; *esp* **:** the marriage bond **4 a :** a protuberant lump or swelling in tissue **b :** the base of a woody branch enclosed in the stem from which it arises; *also* **:** its section in lumber **5 :** a cluster of persons or things **:** GROUP **6 :** an ornamental bow of ribbon **:** COCKADE **7 a :** a division of the log line serving to measure a ship's speed **b** (1) **:** one nautical mile per hour (2) **:** one nautical mile

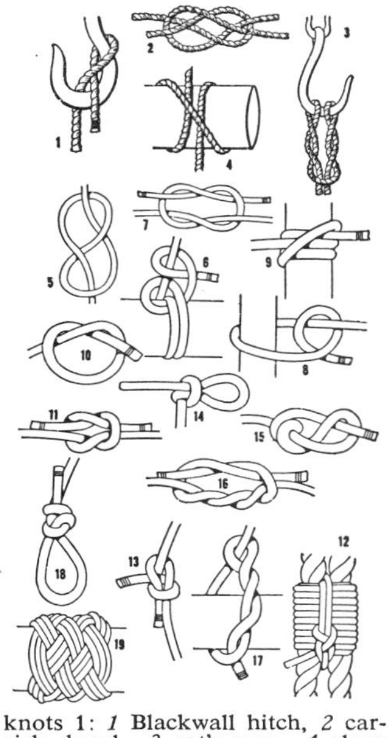

knots 1: *1* Blackwall hitch, *2* carrick bend, *3* cat's-paw, *4* clove hitch, *5* figure eight, *6* fisherman's bend, *7* granny knot, *8* half hitch, *9* magnus hitch, *10* overhand knot, *11* reef knot, *12* seizing, *13* sheet bend, *14* slipknot, *15* stevedore knot, *16* surgeon's knot, *17* timber hitch, *18* true lover's knot, *19* Turk's head

²knot *vb* **knot·ted; knot·ting** *vt* **1 :** to tie in or with a knot **:** form knots in **2 :** to unite closely or intricately **:** ENTANGLE ~ *vi* **1 :** to form knots **2 :** to knit knots for lace or trimming

³knot *n* [ME *knott*] **:** any of several sandpipers (genus *Calidris*) that breed in the Arctic and winter in temperate or warm parts of the New and Old World

knot·grass \'nät-,gras\ *n* **1 :** a cosmopolitan weed (*Polygonum aviculare*) of the buckwheat family with jointed stems, prominent sheathing stipules, and minute flowers; *broadly* **:** any of several congeneric plants **2 :** any of several grasses with geniculate stems

knot·hole \-,hōl\ *n* **:** a hole in a board or tree trunk where a knot or branch has come out

knot·ted *adj* **1 :** tied in or with a knot **2 :** full of knots **:** GNARLED **3 :** ENTANGLED **:** PUZZLING **4 :** ornamented with knots or knobs

knot·ter \'nät-ər\ *n* **1 :** one that makes knots **2 :** one that removes knots

knot·ty \'nät-ē\ *adj* **:** marked by or full of knots **syn** see COMPLEX

knotty pine *n* **:** pine wood with decorative distribution of knots used esp. for interior finish

¹knout \'nau̇t, 'nüt\ *n* [Russ *knut*, of Scand origin; akin to ON *knūtr* knot; akin to OE *cnotta*] **:** a whip for flogging criminals

2**knout** *vt* : to flog with a knout

1**know** \'nō\ *vb* **knew** \'n(y)ü\ **known** \'nōn\ **know·ing** [ME *knowen*, fr. OE *cnāwen;* akin to OHG bi*chnāan* to recognize, L *gnoscere, noscere* to come to know, Gk *gignōskein*] *vt* **1 a** (1) : to perceive directly : have direct cognition of (2) : to have understanding of ⟨importance of *~ing* oneself⟩ (3) : to recognize the nature of : DISCERN **b** (1) : to recognize as being the same as something previously known (2) : to be acquainted or familiar with (3) : to have experience of **2 a** : to be aware of the truth or factuality of : be convinced or certain of **b** : to have a practical understanding of ⟨*~s* how to write⟩ **3** *archaic* : to have sexual intercourse with ~ *vi* **1** : to have knowledge **2** : to be or become cognizant — **know·able** \'nō-ə-bəl\ *adj* — **know·er** \'nō(-ə)r\ *n*

2**know** *n* : KNOWLEDGE — **in the know** : in possession of confidential or otherwise exclusive knowledge or information

know-how \'nō-,hau̇\ *n* : knowledge of how to do something smoothly and efficiently

1**know·ing** *n* : ACQUAINTANCE, COGNIZANCE

2**knowing** *adj* **1** : having or reflecting knowledge, information, or intelligence **2** : shrewdly and keenly alert : ASTUTE **3** : COGNITIVE **4** : DELIBERATE **syn** see INTELLIGENT — **know·ing·ly** \-iŋ-lē\ *adv*

know-it-all \'nō-ət-,ȯl\ *n* : one claiming to know everything

knowl·edge \'näl-ij\ *n* [ME *knowlege*, fr. *knowlechen* to acknowledge, irreg. fr. *knowen*] **1** *obs* : COGNIZANCE **2 a** (1) : the fact or condition of knowing something with familiarity gained through experience or association (2) : acquaintance with or understanding of a science, art, or technique **b** (1) : the fact or condition of being aware of something (2) : the range of one's information or understanding **c** : the fact or condition of apprehending truth or fact : COGNITION **d** : the fact or condition of having information or of being learned **3** *archaic* : SEXUAL INTERCOURSE **4 a** : the sum of what is known : the body of truth, information, and principles acquired by mankind **b** *archaic* : a branch of learning

knowl·edge·able \'näl-i-jə-bəl\ *adj* : having or exhibiting knowledge or intelligence : KEEN — **knowl·edge·able·ness** *n* — **knowl·edge·ably** \-blē\ *adv*

know-noth·ing \'nō-,nəth-iŋ\ *n* **1 a** : IGNORAMUS **b** : AGNOSTIC **2** *cap K & N* : a member of a 19th century secret American political organization hostile to the political influence of recent immigrants and Roman Catholics

1**knuck·le** \'nək-əl\ *n* [ME *knokel;* akin to MHG *knöchel* knuckle, OE *cnotta*] **1 a** : the rounded prominence formed by the ends of the two adjacent bones at a joint — used esp. of those at the joints of the fingers **b** : the joint of a knuckle **2** : a cut of meat consisting of the tarsal or carpal joint with the adjoining flesh **3** : something resembling a knuckle: as **a** (1) : one of the joining parts of a hinge through which a pin or rivet passes (2) : KNUCKLE JOINT **b** : the meeting of two surfaces at a sharp angle (as in a roof) **4** *pl* : a set of metal finger rings or guards attached to a transverse piece and worn over the front of the doubled fist for use as a weapon

2**knuckle** *vb* **knuck·ling** \-(ə-)liŋ\ *vi* **1** : to place the knuckles on the ground in shooting a marble **2** : to give in : SUBMIT — usu. used with *under* **3** : to apply oneself earnestly — usu. used with *down* ~ *vt* : to press or rub with the knuckles

knuckle ball *n* : a baseball pitch in which the ball is gripped with the knuckles pressed against the top and thrown with little speed or spin — called also *knuckler*

knuck·le·bone \,nək-əl-'bōn, 'nək-əl-,\ *n* : the bone of a knuckle joint; *esp* : a metacarpal or metatarsal bone of a sheep formerly used in gaming or divination

knuck·le-dust·er \'nək-əl-,dəs-tər\ *n* : KNUCKLE 4

knuckle joint *n* : a hinge joint in which a projection with an eye on one piece enters a jaw between two corresponding projections with eyes on another piece and is retained by a pin or rivet

knur \'nər\ *n* [ME *knorre;* akin to OE *cnotta* knot] : a hard excrescence : GNARL

knurl \'nər(-ə)l\ *n* [prob. blend of *knur* and *gnarl*] **1** : a small protuberance, excrescence, or knob **2** : one of a series of small ridges or beads on a metal surface to aid in gripping — **knurled** \'nər(-ə)ld\ *adj* — **knurly** \'nər-lē\ *adj*

1**KO** \kā-'ō, 'kā-(,)ō\ *n* [knock out] : a knockout in boxing

2**KO** *vt* **KO'd** \kā-'ōd, 'kā-(,)ōd\ **KO'·ing** : to knock out in boxing

ko·ala \kō-'äl-ə, kə-'wäl-\ *n* [native name in Australia] : an Australian arboreal marsupial (*Phascolarctos cinereus*) about two feet long that has large hairy ears, gray fur, and sharp claws and feeds on eucalyptus leaves

ko·bold \'kō-,bȯld\ *n* [G — more at COBALT] **1** : a gnome that in German folklore inhabits underground places **2** : an often mischievous domestic spirit of German folklore

Ko·dak \'kō-,dak\ *trademark* — used for a small hand camera

Koh-i-noor \'kō-ə-,nu̇(ə)r\ *n* [Per *Kōh-i-nūr*, lit., mountain of light] : a large diamond discovered in India and made one of the British crown jewels

kohl \'kōl\ *n* [Ar *kuḥl*] : a preparation used by women esp. in Arabia and Egypt to darken the edges of the eyelids

kohl·ra·bi \kōl-'rab-ē, -'räb-\ *n, pl* **kohlrabies** [G, fr. It *cavolo rapa*, fr. *cavolo* cabbage + *rapa* turnip] : any of a race of cabbages having a greatly enlarged, fleshy, turnip-shaped edible stem

koi·ne \kȯi-'nā, 'kȯi-,; kē-'nē\ *n* [Gk *koinē*, fr. fem. of *koinos* common] **1** *cap* : the Greek language commonly spoken and written in eastern Mediterranean countries in the Hellenistic and Roman periods **2** : a dialect or language of a region that has become the common or standard language of a larger area

kok-sa·ghyz *or* **kok-sa·gyz** \,kōk-sə-'gēz, ,käk-, -'giz\ *n* [Russ *kok-sagyz*] : a perennial Asiatic dandelion (*Taraxacum kok-saghyz*) cultivated for its fleshy roots that have a high rubber content

kola *var of* COLA

ko·la nut \'kō-lə-\ *n* : the bitter caffeine-containing seed of a kola tree used esp. as a masticatory and in beverages

kola tree *n* : an African tree (genus *Cola*, esp. *C. nitida*) of the chocolate family cultivated in various tropical areas for its kola nuts

ko·lin·sky *or* **ko·lin·ski** \kə-'lin(t)-skē\ *n* [Russ *kolinskiĭ* of Kola, fr. *Kola*, town and peninsula in U.S.S.R.] **1** : any of several Asiatic minks (esp. *Mustela siberica*) **2** : the fur or pelt of a kolinsky

kol·khoz \käl-'kȯz, -'kȯs\ *n, pl* **kol·kho·zy** \-'kȯ-zē\ *or* **kol·khoz·es** [Russ, fr. *kol*lektivnoe *khoz*yaĭstvo collective farm] : a collective farm of the U.S.S.R.

Kol Ni·dre \kōl-'nid-(,)rā\ *n* [Aram *kol nidhrē* all the vows; fr. the opening phrase of the prayer] : an Aramaic prayer chanted in the synagogue on the eve of Yom Kippur

kom·man·da·tu·ra \kə-,man-də-'tu̇r-ə\ *n* [prob. fr. G *kommandantur* command post] : a military government headquarters

Kon·go \'käŋ-(,)gō\ *n, pl* **Kongo** *or* **Kongos** **1 a** : a Bantu people of the lower Congo river **b** : a member of this people **2** : the Bantu language of the Kongo people used as a trade language

Kon·ka·ni \'käŋ-kə-(,)nē\ *n* [Marathi *Koṅkaṇī*] : an Indic language of the west coast of India

koo·doo *or* **ku·du** \'küd-(,)ü\ *n* [Afrik *koedoe*] : a large grayish brown African antelope (*Strepsiceros strepsiceros*) with large annulated spirally twisted horns

kook \'kük\ *n* [by shortening and alter. fr. *cuckoo*] : one whose ideas or actions are eccentric, fantastic, or insane

kook·a·bur·ra \'ku̇k-ə-,bər-ə, -,bə-rə\ *n* [native name in Australia] : a kingfisher (*Dacelo gigas*) of Australia that is about the size of a crow and has a call resembling loud laughter

kooky \'kü-kē\ *adj* : having the characteristics of a kook

ko·peck *also* **ko·pek** \'kō-,pek\ *n* [Russ *kopeĭka*] — see *ruble* at MONEY table

koph *var of* QOPH

kop·je *or* **kop·pie** \'käp-ē\ *n* [Afrik *koppie*] : a small hill esp. on the African veld

kor \'kȯ(ə)r\ *n* [Heb *kōr*] : an ancient Hebrew and Phoenician unit of measure of capacity

Ko·ran \kə-'ran, -'rän; 'kō(ə)r-,an, 'kȯ(ə)r-\ *n* [Ar *qur'ān*] : the book composed of writings accepted by Muslims as revelations made to Muhammad by Allah — **Ko·ran·ic** \kə-'ran-ik\ *adj*

Ko·re·an \kə-'rē-ən, *esp South* (')kō-\ *n* **1** : a native or inhabitant of Korea **2** : the language of the Korean people — **Korean** *adj*

ko·ru·na \'kȯr-ə-,nä, 'kär-\ *n, pl* **ko·ru·ny** \-ə-nē\ *or* **korunas** [Czech, lit., crown, fr. L *corona*] — see MONEY table

1**ko·sher** \'kō-shər\ *adj* [Yiddish, fr. Heb *kāshēr* fit, proper] **1 a** : sanctioned by Jewish law; *esp* : ritually fit for use **b** : selling or serving food ritually fit according to Jewish law **2** : PROPER

2**kosher** *vt* **ko·sher·ing** \-sh(ə-)riŋ\ : to make kosher

kou·miss *or* **ku·miss** \kü-'mis, 'kü-məs\ *n* [Russ *kumys*] : a fermented beverage made orig. by the nomadic peoples of central Asia from mare's milk

1**kow·tow** \kau̇-'tau̇, 'kau̇-,\ *n* [Chin (Pek) *k'o*1 *t'ou*2, fr. *k'o*1 to bump + *t'ou*2 head] : an act of kowtowing

2**kowtow** *vi* **1** : to kneel and touch the forehead to the ground to show homage, worship, or deep respect **2** : to show obsequious deference

1**kraal** \'krȯl, 'kräl\ *n* [Afrik, fr. Pg *curral* pen for cattle, enclosure, fr. (assumed) VL *currale* enclosure for vehicles] **1 a** : a village of southern African natives **b** : the native village community **2** : an enclosure for domestic animals in southern Africa

2**kraal** *vt* : to pen in a kraal

kraft \'kraft\ *n* [G, lit., strength, fr. OHG — more at CRAFT] : a strong paper or board made from wood pulp derived from wood chips boiled in an alkaline solution containing sodium sulfate

krait \'krīt\ *n* [Hindi *karait*] : any of several brightly banded extremely venomous nocturnal elapid snakes (genus *Bungarus*) of eastern Asia and adjacent islands

kra·ken \'kräk-ən\ *n* [Norw dial.] : a fabulous Scandinavian sea monster

kra·ter \'krāt-ər, krä-'te(ə)r\ *n* [Gk *kratēr* — more at CRATER] : a jar or vase of classical antiquity with large round body, wide mouth, and small handles

K ration *n* [A. B. *Keys b*1904 Am physiologist] : a lightweight packaged ration of emergency foods developed for the U.S. armed forces in World War II

kraut \'krau̇t\ *n* [G — more at SAUERKRAUT] : SAUERKRAUT

Krebs cycle \'krebz-\ *n* [H. A. *Krebs* †1900 E biochemist] : a sequence of reactions in the living organism in which oxidation of acetic acid or acetyl equivalent provides energy for storage in phosphate bonds

krem·lin \'krem-lən\ *n* [prob. fr. obs. G *kremelin*, fr. Russ *kreml'*] **1** : the citadel of a Russian city **2** [the *Kremlin*, citadel of Moscow and governing center of the U.S.S.R.] *cap* : the Russian government

kreu·zer \'krȯit-sər\ *n* [G] : a small coin formerly used in Austria and Germany

krill \'kril\ *n* [Norw *kril* fry of fish] : planktonic crustaceans and larvae that constitute the principal food of whalebone whales

krim·mer \'krim-ər\ *n* [G, fr. *Krim* Crimea, U.S.S.R.] : a gray fur made from the pelts of young lambs of the Crimean peninsula region

kris \'krēs\ *n* [Malay *kĕris*] : a Malay or Indonesian dagger with a ridged serpentine blade

Krish·na·ism \'krish-nə-,iz-əm\ *n* [*Krishna*, eighth avatar of Vishnu, fr. Skt *Kṛṣṇa*] : a widespread form of Hindu worship

Kriss Krin·gle \'kris-'kriŋ-gəl\ *n* [G *Christkindl* Christ child, Christmas gift, dim. of *Christkind* Christ child] : SANTA CLAUS

1**kro·na** \'krō-nə\ *n, pl* **kro·nur** \-nər\ [Icel *krōna*, lit., crown] — see MONEY table

2**kro·na** \'krō-nə, 'krü-\ *n, pl* **kro·nor** \-,nȯ(ə)r\ [Sw, lit., crown] — see MONEY table

1**kro·ne** \'krō-nə\ *n, pl* **kro·nen** \-nən\ [G, lit., crown] **1** : the basic monetary unit of Austria from 1892 to 1925 **2** : a coin representing one krone

2**kro·ne** \'krō-nə, 'krü-\ *n, pl* **kro·ner** \-nər\ [Dan, lit., crown] — see MONEY table

kroon \'krün\ *n, pl* **kroo·ni** \'krü-nē\ *or* **kroons** [Estonian *kron*] **1** : the basic monetary unit of Estonia from 1928 to 1940 **2** : a coin or note representing one kroon

kryp·ton \'krip-,tän\ *n* [Gk, neut. of *kryptos* hidden — more at CRYPT] : a colorless inert gaseous element found in air at about one volume per million and used esp. in electric lamps — see ELEMENT table

Ksha·tri·ya \(kə-)'sha-trē-(y)ə, 'cha-\ *n* [Skt *kṣatriya*] : a Hindu of an upper caste traditionally assigned to governing and military occupations

Ku·che·an \kü-'chē-ən\ *n* [*Kuche, Kucha*, Sinkiang, China] : TOCHARIAN B

ə abut; ə kitten; ər further; a back; ā bake; ä cot, cart; au̇ out; ch chin; e less; ē easy; g gift; i trip; ī life
j joke; ŋ sing; ō flow; ȯ flaw; ȯi coin; th thin; th this; ü loot; u̇ foot; y yet; yü few; yu̇ furious; zh vision

ku·chen \'kü-kən, -k̲ən\ *n, pl* **kuchen** [G, cake, fr. OHG *kuocho* — more at CAKE] **:** any of various coffee cakes typically made from sweet yeast dough
ku·dos \'k(y)ü-ˌdäs, -ˌdōs\ *n, pl* **ku·dos** \-ˌdōz\ [Gk *kydos;* akin to Gk *akouein* to hear — more at HEAR] **:** fame and renown resulting from an act or achievement **:** GLORY
kud·zu \'kud-(ˌ)zü\ *n* [Jap *kuzu*] **:** a prostrate Asiatic leguminous vine (*Pueraria thunbergiana*) used widely for hay and forage and for erosion control
Ku Klux·er \'k(y)ü-ˌklək-sər *also* 'klü-\ *n* **:** a member of the Ku Klux Klan — **Ku Klux·ism** \-ˌklək-ˌsiz-əm\ *n*
Ku Klux Klan \ˌk(y)ü-ˌklək-'sklan *also* ˌklü-\ *n* **1 :** a post-Civil War secret society advocating white supremacy **2 :** a 20th-century secret fraternal group held to confine its membership to American-born Protestant whites
ku·lak \k(y)ü-'lak, -'läk, 'k(y)ü-ˌ\ *n* [Russ, lit., fist] **1 :** a prosperous or wealthy peasant farmer in 19th century Russia **2 :** a farmer characterized by Communists as having excessive wealth
kul·tur \kul-'tü(ə)r\ *n, often cap* [G, fr. L *cultura* culture] **1 :** CULTURE 5 **2 :** culture emphasizing practical efficiency and individual subordination to the state **3 :** German culture held to be superior esp. by militant Nazi and Hohenzollern expansionists
Kul·tur·kampf \-ˌkäm(p)f\ *n* [G, fr. *kultur* + *kampf* conflict] **:** conflict between civil government and religious authorities esp. over control of education and church appointments
küm·mel \'kim-əl\ *n* [G, lit., caraway seed, fr. OHG *kumīn* cumin] **:** a colorless aromatic liqueur flavored principally with caraway seeds
kum·quat \'kəm-ˌkwät\ *n* [Chin (Cant) *kam kwat,* fr. *kam* gold + *kwat* orange] **:** any of several small citrus fruits with sweet spongy rind and somewhat acid pulp that are used chiefly for preserves; *also* **:** a tree or shrub (genus *Fortunella*) of the rue family that bears kumquats
kunz·ite \'kun(t)-ˌsīt\ *n* [G. F. *Kunz* †1932 Am gem expert] **:** a spodumene that occurs in pinkish lilac crystals and is used as a gem
Kurd \'ku(ə)rd, 'kərd\ *n* **:** one of a numerous pastoral and agricultural people inhabiting a plateau region in adjoining parts of Turkey, Iran, Iraq, and Syria and in the Armenian and Azerbaidzhan sectors of the Soviet Caucasus — **Kurd·ish** \-ish\ *adj*
Kurdish *n* **:** the Iranian language of the Kurds
Kur·di·stan \ˌkurd-ə-'stan, ˌkərd-\ *n* [*Kurdistan,* region in Turkey, Iraq, and Iran] **:** one of the rugs of several varieties woven by the Kurds and noted for fine colors and durability
kur·ra·jong \'kər-ə-ˌjoŋ, 'kə-rə-, -ˌjäŋ\ *n* [native name in Australia] **:** any of several Australian trees or shrubs of the mallow or chocolate families having strong bast fiber used by Australian aborigines; *esp* **:** a widely planted shelter and forage tree (*Brachychiton populneum*)
Kur·rol's salt \ˌkər-əlz-, ˌkə-rəlz-, kə-ˌrōlz-\ *n* [origin unknown] **:** an insoluble sodium metaphosphate or potassium metaphosphate; *esp* **:** a fibrous crystalline sodium metaphosphate $NaPO_3$ formed by seeding a melt at 550°C
kur·to·sis \(ˌ)kər-'tō-səs\ *n* [Gk *kyrtōsis* convexity, fr. *kyrtos* convex; akin to L *curvus* curved — more at CROWN] **:** the peakedness or flatness of the graph of a frequency distribution
ku·rus \kə-'rüsh\ *n, pl* **kurus** [Turk *kuruş*] — see *pound* at MONEY table
kvass \kə-'väs, 'kfäs\ *n* [Russ *kvas*] **:** a beer of slight alcoholic content made in eastern Europe usu. by fermenting mixed cereals
kwa·cha \'kwäch-ə\ *n* [native name in Zambia, lit., dawn] — see MONEY table
ky·ack \'kī-ˌak\ *n* [origin unknown] **:** a packsack to be swung on either side of a packsaddle
ky·a·nite \'kī-ə-ˌnīt\ *n* [G *zyanit,* fr. Gk *kyanos* dark blue enamel, lapis lazuli] **:** an aluminum silicate Al_2SiO_5 occurring usu. in blue thin-bladed triclinic crystals and crystalline aggregates
ky·at \kē-'(y)ät\ *n* [Burmese] — see MONEY table
ky·mo·gram \'kī-mə-ˌgram\ *n* [ISV] **:** a record made by a kymograph
ky·mo·graph \-ˌgraf\ *n* [Gk *kyma* wave + ISV *-graph* — more at CYME] **:** a device which graphically records motion or pressure — **ky·mo·graph·ic** \ˌkī-mə-'graf-ik\ *adj*
Kymric *var of* CYMRIC
ky·pho·sis \kī-'fō-səs\ *n* [NL, fr. Gk *kyphōsis,* fr. *kyphos* humpbacked; akin to OE *hēah* high] **:** abnormal backward curvature of the spine — **ky·phot·ic** \-'fät-ik\ *adj*
ky·rie \'kir-ē-ˌā\ *n, often cap* [NL, fr. LL *kyrie eleison,* transliteration of Gk *kyrie eleēson* Lord, have mercy] **:** a short liturgical prayer that begins with or consists of the words "Lord, have mercy" — called also *kyrie elei·son* \ˌkir-ē-ˌā-ə-'lā-(ə-)ˌsän\
kyte \'kīt\ *n* [prob. fr. LG *küt* bowel] *chiefly Scot* **:** STOMACH, BELLY
kythe *var of* KITHE

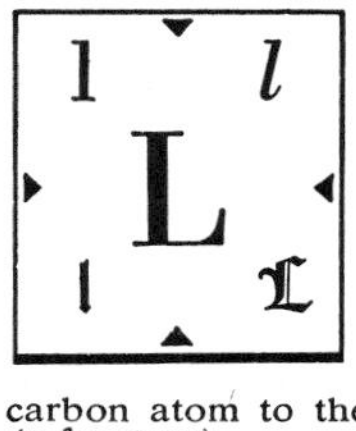

l \'el\ *n, often cap, often attrib* **1 a :** the 12th letter of the English alphabet **b :** a graphic representation of this letter **c :** a speech counterpart of orthographic *l* **2 :** fifty **3 :** a graphic device for reproducing the letter *l* **4 :** one designated *l* esp. as the 11th or when j is used for the 10th the 12th in order or class **5 :** something shaped like the letter L; *specif* **:** ELL **6 :** ELEVATED RAILROAD
l- *prefix* [ISV, fr. *lev-*] **1** \ˌlē-(ˌ)vō, ˌel, 'el\ **:** levorotatory ⟨*l*-tartaric acid⟩ **2** \ˌel, 'el\ **:** having a similar configuration at a selected carbon atom to the configuration of levorotatory glyceraldehyde ⟨L-fructose⟩
1**la** \'lä\ *n* [ME, fr. ML, fr. the syllable sung to this note in a medieval hymn to St. John the Baptist] **:** the sixth tone of the diatonic scale in solmization
2**la** \'lō, 'lä\ *interj* [ME (northern dial.), fr. OE *lā*] *chiefly dial* — used for emphasis or expressing surprise
laa·ger \'läg-ər\ *n* [obs. Afrik *lager* (now *laer*), fr. G] *Africa* **:** CAMP; *esp* **:** a usu. defensive encampment protected by a circle of wagons or armored vehicles — **laager** *vi* **laa·ger·ing** \-(ə-)riŋ\
lab \'lab\ *n* **:** LABORATORY
lab·a·rum \'lab-ə-rəm\ *n* [LL] **:** an imperial standard of the later Roman emperors resembling the vexillum; *esp* **:** the standard adopted by Constantine after his conversion to Christianity
lab·da·num \'lab-də-nəm\ *n* [ML *lapdanum*] **:** a soft dark fragrant bitter oleoresin derived from various rockroses (genus *Cistus*) and used in making perfumes
1**la·bel** \'lā-bəl\ *n* [ME, fr. MF] **1** *archaic* **:** BAND, FILLET; *specif* **:** one attached to a document to hold an appended seal **2 a :** a slip (as of paper or cloth) inscribed and affixed to something for identification or description **b :** written or printed matter accompanying an article to furnish identification or other information **c :** a descriptive or identifying word or phrase: as (1) **:** EPITHET (2) **:** a word or phrase used with a dictionary definition to provide additional information **3 :** a projecting molding by the sides and over the top of an opening **4 :** an adhesive stamp (as for postage or revenue) **5 a :** a brand of commercial recordings issued under a usu. trademarked name **b :** a recording so issued
2**label** *vt* **la·beled** *or* **la·belled; la·bel·ing** *or* **la·bel·ling** \'lā-b(ə-)liŋ\ **1 a :** to affix a label to **b :** to describe or designate with a label **2 a :** to distinguish (an element or atom) by using a radioactive isotope or an isotope of unusual mass for tracing through chemical reactions **b :** to distinguish (as a compound or molecule) by introducing a labeled atom — **la·bel·er** \-b(ə-)lər\ *n*
la·bel·late \lə-'bel-ət\ *adj* **:** having a labellum
la·bel·lum \lə-'bel-əm\ *n, pl* **la·bel·la** \-'bel-ə\ [NL, fr. L, dim. of *labrum* lip] **1 :** the median member of the corolla of an orchid **2 :** a terminal part of the labium or labrum of various insects
1**la·bi·al** \'lā-bē-əl\ *adj* **1 :** of or relating to the lips or labia **2 :** giving its tones from impact of an air current on a lip ⟨a ~ instrument⟩ **3 :** uttered with the participation of one or both lips ⟨the ~ sounds \f\, \p\, and \ü\⟩ — **la·bi·al·ly** \-ə-lē\ *adv*
2**labial** *n* **1 :** FLUE PIPE **2 :** a labial consonant
la·bi·al·iza·tion \ˌlā-bē-ə-lə-'zā-shən\ *n* **:** the action or result of labializing
la·bi·al·ize \'lā-bē-ə-ˌlīz\ *vt* **:** to make labial **:** ROUND
1**la·bi·ate** \'lā-bē-ət, -bē-ˌāt\ *adj* [NL *labiatus,* fr. L *labium*] **1 :** LIPPED: *esp* **:** having the limb of a tubular corolla or calyx divided into two unequal parts projecting one over the other like lips **2 :** of or relating to the mint family
2**labiate** *n* **:** a plant of the mint family
la·bile \'lā-ˌbīl, -bəl\ *adj* [F, fr. MF, prone to err, fr. LL *labilis,* fr. L *labi* to slip — more at SLEEP] **1 :** characterized by a ready capability for change **:** CHANGEABLE, ADAPTABLE **2 :** readily or continually undergoing chemical, physical, or biological change or breakdown **:** UNSTABLE ⟨a ~ mineral⟩ — **la·bil·i·ty** \lā-'bil-ət-ē\ *n*
labio- *comb form* [L *labium*] **:** labial and ⟨*labio*dental⟩
la·bio·den·tal \ˌlā-bē-ō-'dent-ᵊl\ *adj* **:** uttered with the participation of lip and teeth or lips and teeth ⟨the ~ sounds \f\ and \v\⟩ — **labiodental** *n*
la·bio·ve·lar \-'vē-lər\ *adj* [ISV] **:** both labial and velar ⟨the ~ sound \w\⟩ — **labiovelar** *n*
la·bi·um \'lā-bē-əm\ *n, pl* **la·bia** \-ə\ [NL, fr. L, lip — more at LIP] **1 :** any of the folds at the margin of the vulva **2 :** the lower lip of a labiate corolla **3 a :** the lower lip of an insect that is formed by the second pair of maxillae united in the middle line **b :** a liplike part of various invertebrates
1**la·bor** *or chiefly Brit* **la·bour** \'lā-bər\ *n* [ME, fr. OF, fr. L *labor*] **1 a :** expenditure of physical or mental effort esp. when difficult or compulsory **b** (1) **:** human activity that provides the goods or services in an economy (2) **:** the services performed by workers for wages as distinguished from those rendered by entrepreneurs for profits **c** (1) **:** the physical activities involved in parturition (2) **:** the period of such labor **2 :** an act or process requiring labor **:** TASK **3 :** a product of labor **4 a :** an economic group comprising those who do manual labor or work for wages **b :** workers employed in an establishment or available for employment **c :** the organizations or officials representing groups of workers **5** *usu Labour* **:** the Labour party of the United Kingdom or of another nation of the British Commonwealth **syn** see WORK
2**labor** *or chiefly Brit* **labour** *vb* **la·bor·ing** \-b(ə-)riŋ\ *vi* **1 :** to exert one's powers of body or mind esp. with painful or strenuous effort **:** WORK **2 :** to move with great effort **3 :** to be in the labor of giving birth **4 :** to suffer from some disadvantage or distress ⟨~ under a delusion⟩ **5** *of a ship* **:** to pitch or roll heavily ~ *vt* **1** *archaic* **a :** to spend labor on or produce by labor **b :** to strive to effect or achieve **2 :** to treat or work out in often laborious detail ⟨~ the obvious⟩ **3 :** BURDEN, DISTRESS **4 :** to cause to labor — **la·bor·er** \-bər-ər, -brər\ *n*
3**labor** *adj* **1 :** of or relating to labor **2** *cap* **:** of, relating to, or constituting a political party held to represent the interests of working-men or characterized by a membership in which organized labor groups predominate
lab·o·ra·to·ry \'lab-(ə-)rə-ˌtōr-ē, -ˌtȯr-, *Brit usu* lə-'bär-ə-t(ə-)rē\ *n, often attrib* [ML *laboratorium,* fr. L *laboratus,* pp. of *laborare* to labor, fr. *labor*] **1 :** a place equipped for experimental study in a science or for testing and analysis; *broadly* **:** a place providing opportunity for experimentation, observation, or practice in a field of study **2 :** an academic period set aside for laboratory work
labor camp *n* **1 :** a penal colony where forced labor is performed **2 :** a camp for migratory labor
Labor Day *n* **:** the first Monday in September observed in the U.S. and Canada as a legal holiday in recognition of the workingman
la·bored *adj* **1 :** produced or performed with labor **2 :** bearing marks of labor and effort; *esp* **:** lacking ease of expression
la·bo·ri·ous \lə-'bōr-ē-əs, -'bȯr-\ *adj* **1 :** devoted to labor **:** INDUSTRIOUS **2 :** involving or characterized by hard or toilsome effort **:** LABORED — **la·bo·ri·ous·ly** *adv* — **la·bo·ri·ous·ness** *n*
la·bor·ite \'lā-bə-ˌrīt\ *n* **1 :** a member of a group favoring the interests of labor **2** *cap* **a :** a member of a political party devoted

chiefly to the interests of labor **b** *usu* **La·bour·ite :** a member of the British Labour party
la·bor·sav·ing \'lā-bər-,sā-viŋ\ *adj* **:** adapted to replace or decrease human and esp. manual labor
labor union *n* **:** an organization of workers formed for the purpose of advancing its members' interests in respect to wages and working conditions
lab·ra·dor·ite \'lab-rə-,dȯ(ə)r-,īt\ *n* [*Labrador* peninsula, Canada] **:** a triclinic feldspar showing a play of several colors
Lab·ra·dor retriever \,lab-rə-,dȯr-(r)i-\ *n* [*Labrador*, Newfoundland] **:** a retriever largely developed in England from stock originating in Newfoundland and characterized by a short dense usu. black coat and notable breadth of head and chest
la·bret \'lā-brət\ *n* [L *labrum*] **:** an ornament worn in a perforation of the lip by some primitive peoples
la·brum \'lā-brəm\ *n* [NL, fr. L, lip, edge — more at LIP] **:** the upper or anterior lip of an arthropod consisting of a single median piece in front of or above the mandibles
la·bur·num \lə-'bər-nəm\ *n* [NL, genus name, fr. L, laburnum] **:** any of a small genus (*Laburnum*) of poisonous Eurasian leguminous shrubs and trees with pendulous racemes of bright yellow flowers; *esp* **:** an ornamental tree (*L. anagyroides*) often cultivated for Easter decoration
lab·y·rinth \'lab-ə-,rin(t)th, -rən(t)th\ *n* [ME *laborintus*, fr. L *labyrinthus*, fr. Gk *labyrinthos*] **1 a :** a place constructed of or full of intricate passageways and blind alleys **b :** a maze (as in a garden) formed by paths separated by high hedges **2 :** something extremely complex or tortuous in structure, arrangement, or character **:** INTRICACY, PERPLEXITY **3 :** a tortuous anatomical structure; *esp* **:** the internal ear or its bony or membranous part
lab·y·rin·thi·an \,lab-ə-'rin(t)-thē-ən\ *adj* **:** LABYRINTHINE
lab·y·rin·thine \-'rin(t)-thən; -'rin-,thīn, -,thēn\ *adj* **:** of, relating to, or resembling a labyrinth **:** INTRICATE, INVOLVED
[1]**lac** \'lak\ *n* [Per *lak* & Hindi *lākh*, fr. Skt *lākṣā*] **:** a resinous substance secreted by a scale insect (*Laccifer lacca*) and used chiefly in the form of shellac
[2]**lac** *var of* LAKH
lac·co·lith \'lak-ə-,lith\ *n* [Gk *lakkos* cistern + E *-lith*] **:** a mass of igneous rock that is intruded between sedimentary beds and produces a domical bulging of the overlying strata
[1]**lace** \'lās\ *n* [ME, fr. OF *laz*, fr. L *laqueus* snare — more at DELIGHT] **1 :** a cord or string used for drawing together two edges (as of a garment or a shoe) **2 :** an ornamental braid for trimming men's coats or uniforms **3 :** a fine openwork usu. figured fabric made of thread and used chiefly for household coverings or for ornament of dress — **laced** \'lāst\ *adj* — **lace·like** \'lā-,slīk\ *adj*
[2]**lace** *vb* [ME *lacen*, fr. OF *lacier*, fr. L *laqueare* to ensnare, fr. *laqueus*] *vt* **1 :** to draw together the edges of by or as if by a lace passed through eyelets **2 :** to draw or pass (as a lace) through something (as eyelets) **3 :** to confine or compress by tightening laces esp. of a corset **4 a :** to adorn with or as if with lace **b :** to mark with streaks of color **5 :** BEAT, LASH **6 a :** to add a dash of an alcoholic liquor to **b :** to give savor or zest to ~ *vi* **:** to admit of being tied or fastened with a lace — **lac·er** *n*
[1]**lac·er·ate** \'las-ə-rət, -,rāt\ *or* **lac·er·at·ed** \-,rāt-əd\ *adj* **1 a :** TORN, MANGLED **b :** HARROWED, DISTRACTED **2 :** having the edges deeply and irregularly cut ⟨a ~ petal⟩
[2]**lac·er·ate** \-,rāt\ *vt* [L *laceratus*, pp. of *lacerare* to tear; akin to L *lacer* mangled, Gk *lakis* rent] **1 :** to tear or rend roughly **2 :** to cause sharp mental or emotional pain to **:** DISTRESS — **lac·er·a·tive** \-,rāt-iv\ *adj*
lac·er·a·tion \,las-ə-'rā-shən\ *n* **1 :** the act of lacerating **2 :** a torn ragged wound
lac·er·til·ian \,las-ər-'til-ē-ən, -'til-yən\ *adj* [deriv. of L *lacerta* lizard — more at LIZARD] **:** of or relating to the lizards — **lacertilian** *n* — **lac·er·til·oid** \,las-ər-'til-,ȯid\ *adj*
lace·wing \'lā-,swiŋ\ *n* **:** any of various neuropterous insects (as of *Chrysopa*, *Hemerobius*, and related genera) having delicate lacelike wing venation, long antennae, and brilliant eyes
la·ches \'lach-əz, 'lā-chəz\ *n, pl* **laches** [ME *lachesse*, fr. MF *laschesse*] **:** negligence in the observance of duty or opportunity; *specif* **:** undue delay in asserting a legal right or privilege
Lach·e·sis \'lak-ə-səs\ *n* [L, fr. Gk] **:** the one of the three Fates in classical mythology who determines the length of the thread of life
lach·ry·mal *or* **lac·ri·mal** \'lak-rə-məl\ *adj* [MF or ML; MF *lachrymal*, fr. ML *lacrimalis*, fr. L *lacrima* tear — more at TEAR] **1** *usu lacrimal* **:** of, relating to, or constituting the glands that produce tears **2 :** of, relating to, or marked by tears
lach·ry·mose \-,mōs\ *adj* **1 :** given to tears or weeping **:** TEARFUL **2 :** tending to cause tears **:** MOURNFUL — **lach·ry·mose·ly** *adv*
lac·ing \'lā-siŋ\ *n* **1 :** the action of one that laces **2 :** something that laces **:** LACE **3 :** a contrasting marginal band of color (as on a feather) **4 a :** a dash of alcoholic liquor in a food or beverage **b :** a trace or sprinkling that adds spice or savor **5 :** BEATING, TROUNCING
la·cin·i·ate \lə-'sin-ē-ət, -,āt\ *or* **la·cin·i·at·ed** \-,āt-əd\ *adj* [L *lacinia* flap; akin to L *lacer*] **:** bordered with a fringe: **a :** cut into deep irregular usu. pointed lobes **b :** narrowly incised with divisions coarser than fimbriate — **la·cin·i·a·tion** \lə-,sin-ē-'ā-shən\ *n*
[1]**lack** \'lak\ *vb* [ME *laken*, fr. MD; akin to ON *leka* to leak] *vi* **1 :** to be wanting or missing **2 :** to be short or have need ~ *vt* **1 :** to be destitute of or deficient in **2 :** REQUIRE, NEED
syn LACK, WANT, NEED, REQUIRE mean to be without something essential or greatly desired. LACK may imply either an absence or a shortage in supply ⟨room *lacks* closets⟩ ⟨*lack* fuel for such a trip⟩ WANT adds to LACK the implication of desiring or needing urgently ⟨the house *wants* painting⟩ NEED clearly suggests urgent necessity ⟨he *needs* medicine⟩ REQUIRE suggests imperativeness of needing, desiring, or even craving
[2]**lack** *n* **1 :** the fact or state of being wanting or deficient **:** NEED **2 :** something that is lacking or is needed
lack·a·dai·si·cal \,lak-ə-'dā-zi-kəl\ *adj* [by folk etymology fr. *lackaday* + *-ical*] **:** lacking life, spirit, or zest **:** LANGUID — **lack·a·dai·si·cal·ly** \-k(ə-)lē\ *adv*
lack·a·day \'lak-ə-,dā\ *interj* [by alter. & shortening of *alack the day*] *archaic* — used to express regret or deprecation
[1]**lack·ey** \'lak-ē\ *n* [MF *laquais*] **1 :** a liveried retainer **:** FOOTMAN, FLUNKY **2 :** a servile follower **:** TOADY, HANGER-ON
[2]**lackey** *also* **lac·quey** \'lak-ē\ *vi, obs* **:** to play the lackey **:** TOADY ~ *vt* **:** to wait upon or serve obsequiously **:** ATTEND
lack·lus·ter \'lak-,ləs-tər\ *adj* **:** lacking in sheen, radiance, or vitality **:** DULL — **lackluster** *n*
la·con·ic \lə-'kän-ik\ *adj* [L *laconicus* Spartan, fr. Gk *lakōnikos*; fr. the Spartan reputation for terseness of speech] **:** sparing of words **:** TERSE **syn** see CONCISE — **la·con·i·cal·ly** \-i-k(ə-)lē\ *adv*
lac·o·nism \'lak-ə-,niz-əm\ *n* **:** brevity or terseness of expression or style
[1]**lac·quer** \'lak-ər\ *n* [Pg *lacré* sealing wax, fr. *laca* lac, fr. Ar *lakk*, fr. Per *lak*] **1 a :** a spirit varnish (as shellac) **b :** any of various durable natural varnishes; *esp* **:** a varnish obtained from an Asiatic sumac (*Rhus verniciflua*) — called also *Chinese lacquer*, *Japanese lacquer* **2 :** any of various clear or colored synthetic organic coatings that typically dry to form a film by evaporation of a volatile constituent
[2]**lacquer** *vt* **lac·quer·ing** \-(ə-)riŋ\ **1 :** to coat with lacquer **2 :** to give a smooth finish or appearance to — **lac·quer·er** \'lak-ər-ər\ *n*
lac·ri·ma·tion \,lak-rə-'mā-shən\ *n* **:** the secretion of tears esp. when abnormal or excessive
lac·ri·ma·tor *or* **lach·ry·ma·tor** \'lak-rə-,māt-ər\ *n* [L *lacrimatus*, pp. of *lacrimare* to weep, fr. *lacrima* tear — more at TEAR] **:** a tear-producing substance **:** TEAR GAS
la·crosse \lə-'krȯs\ *n* [CanF *la crosse*, lit., the crosier] **:** a game played on a turfed field in which the players use a long-handled racket to catch, carry, or throw the ball toward or into the opponents' goal
lact- *or* **lacti-** *or* **lacto-** *comb form* [F & L; F, fr. L, fr. *lact-*, *lac* — more at GALAXY] **1 :** milk ⟨*lacto*flavin⟩ **2 a :** lactic acid ⟨*lact*ate⟩ **b :** lactose ⟨*lact*ase⟩
lact·al·bu·min \,lak-,tal-'byü-mən\ *n* [ISV] **:** an albumin from whey similar to serum albumin
lac·tase \'lak-,tās, -,tāz\ *n* [ISV] **:** an enzyme that hydrolyzes lactose and other beta-galactosides and occurs esp. in the intestines of young mammals and in yeasts
[1]**lac·tate** \'lak-,tāt\ *n* **:** a salt or ester of lactic acid
[2]**lactate** *vi* [L *lactatus*, pp. of *lactare*, fr. *lact-*, *lac*] **:** to secrete milk — **lac·ta·tion** \lak-'tā-shən\ *n* — **lac·ta·tion·al** \-shnəl, -shən-ᵊl\ *adj* — **lac·ta·tion·al·ly** \-ē\ *adv*
[1]**lac·te·al** \'lak-tē-əl\ *adj* [L *lacteus* of milk, fr. *lact-*, *lac*] **1 :** consisting of, producing, or resembling milk **2 a :** conveying or containing a milky fluid **b :** of or relating to the lacteals
[2]**lacteal** *n* **:** one of the lymphatic vessels arising from the villi of the small intestine and conveying chyle to the thoracic duct
lac·tes·cent \lak-'tes-ᵊnt\ *adj* [L *lactescent-*, *lactescens*, prp. of *lactescere* to turn to milk, fr. *lact-*, *lac*] **1 :** becoming or appearing milky **2 a :** secreting milk **b :** yielding a milky juice — used of a plant
lac·tic \'lak-tik\ *adj* **1 a :** of or relating to milk **b :** obtained from sour milk or whey **2 :** involving the production of lactic acid
lactic acid *n* **:** a hygroscopic organic acid $C_3H_6O_3$ present normally in tissue, produced in carbohydrate matter usu. by bacterial fermentation, and used esp. in food and medicine and in industry
lac·tif·er·ous \lak-'tif-(ə-)rəs\ *adj* [F or LL; F *lactifère*, fr. LL *lactifer*, fr. L *lact-*, *lac* + *-fer*] **1 :** secreting or conveying milk **2 :** yielding a milky juice — **lac·tif·er·ous·ness** *n*
lac·to·ba·cil·lus \,lak-(,)tō-bə-'sil-əs\ *n* [NL] **:** any of a genus (*Lactobacillus*) of lactic-acid-forming bacteria
lac·to·gen·ic \,lak-tə-'jen-ik\ *adj* **:** inducing lactation
lac·tone \'lak-,tōn\ *n* [ISV] **:** any of various cyclic anhydrides of acids having one or more hydroxyl groups in addition to that in the acid group — **lac·ton·ic** \lak-'tän-ik\ *adj*
lac·tose \'lak-,tōs, -,tōz\ *n* [ISV] **:** a disaccharide sugar $C_{12}H_{22}O_{11}$ present in milk that on hydrolysis yields glucose and galactose and on fermentation yields esp. lactic acid
la·cu·na \lə-'k(y)ü-nə\ *n, pl* **la·cu·nae** \-'kyü-(,)nē, -'kü-,nī\ *or* **la·cu·nas** \-'k(y)ü-nəz\ [L, pit, pool — more at LAGOON] **1 :** a blank space or a missing part **:** GAP **2 :** a small cavity, pit, or discontinuity in an anatomical structure — **la·cu·nal** \-'k(y)ün-ᵊl\ *adj* — **la·cu·nar** \-'k(y)ü-nər\ *adj* — **la·cu·na·ry** \'lak-yə-,ner-ē, lə-'k(y)ü-nə-rē\ *adj* — **la·cu·nate** \lə-'k(y)ü-nət, -,nāt; 'lak-yə-,nāt\ *adj*
la·cu·nar \lə-'k(y)ü-nər\ *n* **1 :** a ceiling with recessed panels **2** *pl* **lac·u·nar·ia** \,lak-yə-'ner-ē-ə\ **:** a recessed panel in a patterned ceiling or soffit
la·cus·trine \lə-'kəs-trən\ *adj* [prob. fr. F or It *lacustre*, fr. L *lacus* lake] **:** of, relating to, or growing in lakes
lacy \'lā-sē\ *adj* **:** resembling or consisting of lace
lad \'lad\ *n* [ME *ladde*] **1 :** a male person of any age between early boyhood and maturity **:** BOY, YOUTH **2 :** FELLOW, CHAP
lad·a·num \'lad-ᵊn-əm, 'lad-nəm\ *var of* LABDANUM
lad·der \'lad-ər\ *n, often attrib* [ME, fr. OE *hlǣder*; akin to OHG *leitara* ladder, OE *hlinian* to lean — more at LEAN] **1 :** a structure for climbing up or down that consists of two long sidepieces joined at intervals by crosspieces on which one may step **2 :** something that resembles or suggests a ladder in form or use; *specif* **:** RUN 11a **3 :** a series of usu. ascending steps or stages **:** SCALE
lad·der-back \-,bak\ *adj, of furniture* **:** having a back consisting of two upright posts connected by horizontal slats
lad·die \'lad-ē\ *n* **:** a young lad
lade \'lād\ *vb* **lad·ed; laded** *or* **lad·en** \'lād-ᵊn\ **lad·ing** [ME *laden*, fr. OE *hladan*; akin to OHG *hladan* to load, OSlav *klasti*] *vt* **1 a :** to put a load or burden on or in **:** LOAD **b :** to put or place as a load esp. for shipment **:** SHIP **c :** to load heavily or oppressively **2 :** DIP, LADLE ~ *vi* **1 :** to take on cargo **:** LOAD **2 :** to take up or convey a liquid by dipping
[1]**lad·en** \'lād-ᵊn\ *vt* **lad·en·ing** \'lād-niŋ, -ᵊn-iŋ\ **:** LADE
[2]**laden** *adj* **:** LOADED, BURDENED
la–di–da \,läd-ē-'dä\ *adj* [perh. alter. of *lardy-dardy* (foppish)] **:** affectedly refined or polished **:** PRETENTIOUS, ELEGANT
ladies' man *also* **lady's man** *n* **:** a man who shows a marked fondness for the company of women or is esp. attentive to women
La·din \lə-'dēn\ *n* [Rhaeto-Romanic, fr. L *Latinum* Latin] **1 :** ROMANSH **2 :** one speaking Romansh as a mother tongue
lad·ing *n* **1 a :** LOADING 1 **b :** an act of bailing, dipping, or ladling **2 :** CARGO, FREIGHT

1la·di·no \lə-'dē-(,)nō\ *n* [Sp, fr. *ladino* cunning, learned, lit., Latin, fr. L *latinus*] **1 :** JUDEO-SPANISH **2** *often cap* [AmerSp] **:** a westernized Spanish-speaking Latin American; *esp* **:** MESTIZO **3** [AmerSp] *Southwest* **:** a cunningly vicious horse or steer

2la·di·no \lə-'dī-(,)nō, -nə\ *n* [prob. fr. It, of Graubünden, canton of Switzerland] **:** a large nutritious rapidly growing clover that is a variety of white clover and is widely planted for hay or silage

1la·dle \'lād-ᵊl\ *n* [ME *ladel*, fr. OE *hlædel*, fr. *hladan*] **1 :** a deep-bowled long-handled spoon used esp. for dipping up and conveying liquids **2 :** an instrument or device resembling a ladle in form or function

2ladle *vt* **la·dling** \'lād-liŋ, -ᵊl-iŋ\ **:** to take up and convey in or as if in a ladle

la·dy \'lād-ē\ *n, often attrib* [ME, fr. OE *hlǣfdīge*, fr. *hlāf* bread + *-dīge* (akin to *dǣge* kneader of bread) — more at LOAF, DAIRY] **1** *obs* **:** a female head of a household **:** MISTRESS **2 a :** a woman having proprietary rights or authority esp. as a feudal superior **b :** a woman receiving the homage or devotion of a knight or lover **3** *cap* **:** VIRGIN MARY — usu. used with *Our* **4 a :** a woman of superior social position **b :** a woman of refinement and gentle manners **c :** WOMAN, FEMALE **5 :** WIFE **6 a :** any of various titled women in Great Britain — used as the customary title of (1) a marchioness, countess, viscountess, or baroness and (2) the wife of a knight, baronet, member of the peerage, or one having the courtesy title of *lord* and used as a courtesy title for the daughter of a duke, marquess, or earl **b :** a female member of an order of knighthood — compare DAME **syn** see FEMALE

lady beetle *n* **:** LADYBUG

la·dy·bird \'lād-ē-,bərd\ *n* **:** LADYBUG

la·dy·bug \-,bəg\ *n* [Our *Lady*, the Virgin Mary] **:** any of numerous small nearly hemispherical often brightly colored beetles (family Coccinellidae) of temperate and tropical regions that usu. feed both as larvae and adults on other insects

lady chapel *n, often cap L&C* **:** a chapel dedicated to the Virgin Mary

Lady Day *n* **:** the feast of the Annunciation

la·dy·fin·ger \'lād-ē-,fiŋ-gər\ *n* **:** a small finger-shaped sponge cake

la·dy–in–wait·ing \,lād-ē-in-'wāt-iŋ\ *n, pl* **ladies–in–waiting :** a lady of a queen's or a princess's household appointed to wait upon or attend her

la·dy·kin \'lād-ē-kən\ *n* **:** a little lady

la·dy·like \-,līk\ *adj* **1 :** resembling a lady in appearance or manners **:** WELL-BRED **2 :** becoming or suitable to a lady **3 a :** feeling or showing too much concern about elegance or propriety **b :** lacking in strength, force, or virility **syn** see FEMININE

la·dy·love \'lād-ē-,ləv, ,lād-ē-'\ *n* **:** SWEETHEART, MISTRESS

la·dy's–ear·drop \,lād-ē-'zi(ə)r-,dräp\ *n* **:** any of several plants (as a fuchsia or bleeding heart) with flowers resembling eardrops — called also *ladies'-eardrops*

la·dy·ship \'lād-ē-,ship\ *n* **:** the condition of being a lady **:** rank of lady — used as a title for a woman having the rank of lady ⟨her *Ladyship* is not at home⟩ ⟨if your *Ladyship* please⟩

lady's slipper *or* **lady slipper** \'lād-ē(z)-,slip-ər\ *n* **:** any of several No. American temperate-zone orchids (as of the genus *Cypripedium*) having flowers whose shape suggests a slipper

la·dy's–smock \'lād-ē(z)-,smäk\ *n* **:** CUCKOOFLOWER 1

La·er·tes \lā-'ərt-ēz\ *n* [L, fr. Gk *Laertēs*] **1 :** the father of Odysseus in Greek legend **2 :** the son of Polonius and brother of Ophelia in Shakespeare's *Hamlet*

Lae·ta·re Sunday \lā-,tär-ē-, -,tar-ē-\ *n* [L *laetare*, sing. imper. of *laetari* to rejoice] **:** the fourth Sunday in Lent

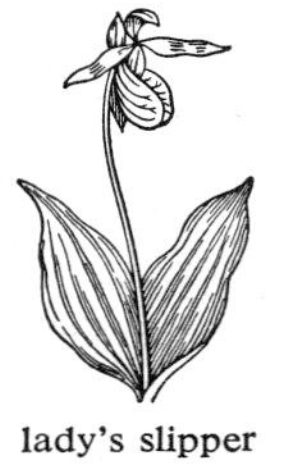

lady's slipper

1lag \'lag\ *vb* **lagged; lag·ging** [prob. of Scand origin; akin to Norw *lagga* to go slowly] *vi* **1 a :** to stay or fall behind **:** LINGER, LOITER **b :** to move, function, or develop with comparative slowness **c :** to become retarded in attaining maximum value **2 :** to slacken or weaken gradually **:** FLAG **3 :** to toss or roll a taw toward a line or a cue ball toward the head cushion to determine order of play ~ *vt* **1 :** to lag behind ⟨current that ~*s* the voltage⟩ **2 :** to pitch or shoot (as a coin or marble) at a mark **syn** see DELAY — **lag·ger** *n*

2lag *n* **1 :** one that lags or is last **2** *obs* **:** the lowest class **3 a :** the action or the condition of lagging **b :** comparative slowness or retardation **c** (1) **:** an amount of lagging or the time during which lagging continues (2) **:** a space of time esp. between related events or phenomena **:** INTERVAL **4 :** the action of lagging for opening shot (as in marbles or billiards)

3lag *adj* **:** LAST, HINDMOST

4lag *vt* **lagged; lag·ging** [origin unknown] **1** *slang* **:** to transport for crime or send to jail **2** *slang* **:** ARREST

5lag *n* **1** *slang* **a :** a person transported for crime **b :** CONVICT **c :** EX-CONVICT **2** *slang* **:** a jail sentence **:** STRETCH

6lag *n* [prob. of Scand origin; akin to ON *lögg* rim of a barrel] **1 :** a barrel stave **2 :** a stave or slat forming part of a covering for a cylindrical object

7lag *vt* **lagged; lag·ging :** to cover or provide with lags

lag·an \'lag-ən\ *also* **lag·end** \-ənd\ *n* [MF *lagan* or ML *laganum* debris washed up from the sea] **:** goods thrown into the sea with a buoy attached so that they may be found again

Lag b'Omer \'läg-'bō-mər, ,läg-bə-'ō-\ *n* [LHeb *LG bĕ 'ōmer*, lit., 33 in omer] **:** a Jewish holiday falling on the 33d day of the omer and commemorating the heroism of Bar Cocheba and Akiba

la·ger \'läg-ər\ *n* [G *lagerbier* beer made for storage, fr. *lager* storehouse + *bier* beer] **:** a beer brewed by slow fermentation and stored in refrigerated cellars for maturing

lag·gard \'lag-ərd\ *adj* **:** lagging or tending to lag **:** DILATORY — **laggard** *n* — **lag·gard·ly** *adv or adj* — **lag·gard·ness** *n*

lag·ging \'lag-iŋ\ *n* **:** a lag or material used for making lags: as **a :** material for thermal insulation esp. around a cylindrical object **b :** planking for preventing cave-ins in earthwork or for supporting an arch during construction

la·gniappe \'lan-,yap, lan-'\ *n* [AmerF, fr. AmerSp *la ñapa* the lagniappe] **:** a small gift given a customer by a merchant at the time of a purchase; *broadly* **:** something given or obtained gratuitously or by way of good measure

lago·morph \'lag-ə-,mȯrf\ *n* [deriv. of Gk *lagōs* hare + *morphē* form] **:** any of an order (Lagomorpha) of gnawing mammals having two pairs of upper incisors one behind the other and comprising the rabbits, hares, and pikas — **lago·mor·phic** \,lag-ə-'mȯr-fik\ *adj* — **lago·mor·phous** \-fəs\ *adj*

la·goon \lə-'gün\ *n* [F & It; F *lagune*, fr. It *laguna*, fr. L *lacuna* pit, pool, fr. *lacus* lake] **:** a shallow sound, channel, or pond near or communicating with a larger body of water — **la·goon·al** \-ᵊl\ *adj*

la·gu·na \lə-'gü-nə\ *n* [Sp, fr. L *lacuna*] **:** LAGOON, LAKE, POND

Lahn·da \'län-də\ *n* **:** an Indic language of West Punjab

la·ic \'lā-ik\ *adj* [LL *laicus*, n. & adj., fr. LGk *laïkos*, fr. Gk, of the people, fr. *laos* people] **:** of or relating to the laity **:** SECULAR — **laic** *n* — **la·ical** \-ə-kəl\ *adj* — **la·ical·ly** \-ə-k(ə-)lē\ *adv*

la·icism \'lā-ə-,siz-əm\ *n* **:** a political system characterized by the exclusion of ecclesiastical control and influence

la·ici·za·tion \,lā-ə-sə-'zā-shən\ *n* **:** the act or process of laicizing

la·icize \'lā-ə-,sīz\ *vt* **1 :** to reduce to lay status **2 :** to put under the direction of or open to laymen

laid *past of* LAY

laid paper \'lād-\ *n* **:** paper watermarked with fine lines running across the grain — compare WOVE PAPER

laigh \'lā\ *Scot var of* LOW

lain *past part of* LIE

1lair \'la(ə)r, 'le(ə)r\ *n* [ME, fr. OE *leger;* akin to OHG *legar* bed, OE *licgan* to lie — more at LIE] **1** *dial Brit* **:** a resting or sleeping place **:** BED **2 a :** the resting or living place of a wild animal **:** DEN **b :** a refuge or place for hiding

2lair *vb* [Sc *lair* (mire)] *vt, chiefly Scot* **:** to cause to sink in the mire ~ *vi, chiefly Scot* **:** WALLOW

laird \'la(ə)rd, 'le(ə)rd\ *n* [ME (northern dial.) *lord, lard* lord] *Scot* **:** a landed proprietor — **laird·ly** \-lē\ *adj*

lais·sez–faire *or chiefly Brit* **lais·ser–faire** \,le-,sā-'fa(ə)r, ,lā-, -,zā-, -'fe(ə)r\ *n* [F *laissez faire*, imper. of *laisser faire* to let (people) do (as they choose)] **1 :** a doctrine opposing governmental interference in economic affairs beyond the minimum necessary for the maintenance of peace and property rights **2 :** a philosophy or practice characterized by a usu. deliberate abstention from direction or interference esp. with individual freedom of choice and action — **laissez–faire** *adj*

lais·sez–pas·ser \-,pa-'sā\ *n* [F, fr. *laissez passer* let (someone) pass] **:** PERMIT, PASS

la·ity \'lā-ət-ē\ *n* [5*lay*] **1 :** the people of a religious faith as distinguished from its clergy **2 :** the mass of the people as distinguished from those of a particular profession or those specially skilled

La·ius \'lā-(y)əs, 'lī-əs\ *n* [Gk *Laïos*] **:** the father of Oedipus in Greek legend

1lake \'lāk\ *n, often attrib* [ME, fr. OF *lac* lake, fr. L *lacus;* akin to OE *lagu* sea, Gk *lakkos* pond] **1 :** a considerable inland body of standing water **2 :** a pool of other liquid

2lake *n* [F *laque* lac, fr. OProv *laca*, fr. Ar *lakk* — more at LACQUER] **1 a :** a purplish red pigment prepared from lac or cochineal **b :** any of numerous usu. bright translucent organic pigments composed essentially of a soluble dye adsorbed on or combined with an inorganic carrier **2 :** CARMINE 2 — **laky** \'lā-kē\ *adj*

3lake *vi, of blood* **:** to alter so that the hemoglobin is dissolved in the plasma ~ *vt* **:** to cause (blood) to lake

lake dweller *n* **:** one that lives in a lake dwelling

lake dwelling *n* **:** a dwelling built on piles in a lake; *specif* **:** one built in prehistoric times

lake herring *n* **:** a cisco (*Leucichthys artedi*) found from Lake Memphremagog to Lake Superior and northward and important as a commercial food fish; *broadly* **:** CISCO

Lake·land terrier \,lā-,klan(d)-, -klən(d)-\ *n* [*Lakeland*, England] **:** any of an English breed of rather small harsh-coated straight-legged terriers

lak·er \'lā-kər\ *n* **:** one associated with a lake; *esp* **:** a fish living in or taken from a lake

lakh \'läk, 'lak\ *n* [Hindi *lākh*] **1** *India* **:** one hundred thousand **2** *India* **:** a great number — **lakh** *adj*

-la·lia \'lā-lē-ə\ *n comb form* [NL, fr. Gk *lalia* chatter, fr. *lalein* to chat] **:** speech disorder (of a specified type) ⟨echo*lalia*⟩

lal·lan \'lal-ən\ *or* **lal·land** \-ən(d)\ *Scot var of* LOWLAND

Lal·lans \'lal-ənz\ *n* **:** Scots as spoken in the southern and eastern part of Scotland

Lal·ly \'lal-ē\ *trademark* — used for a concrete-filled cylindrical steel structural column

1lam \'lam\ *vb* **lammed; lam·ming** [of Scand origin; akin to ON *lemja* to thrash; akin to OE *lama* lame] *vt* **:** to beat soundly **:** THRASH ~ *vi* **1 :** STRIKE, THRASH **2 :** to flee hastily **:** SCRAM

2lam *n* **:** sudden or hurried flight esp. from the law ⟨on the ~⟩

la·ma \'läm-ə\ *n* [Tibetan *blama*] **:** a Lamaist monk

La·ma·ism \'läm-ə-,iz-əm\ *n* **:** the Mahayana Buddhism of Tibet and Mongolia marked by tantric and shamanistic ritual and a dominant hierarchical monasticism — **La·ma·ist** \-ə-əst\ *n or adj* — **La·ma·is·tic** \,läm-ə-'is-tik\ *adj*

La·marck·ian \lə-'mär-kē-ən\ *adj* **:** of or relating to Lamarckism

La·marck·ism \lə-'mär-,kiz-əm\ *n* [J. B. de Monet *Lamarck* †1829 F biologist] **:** a theory of organic evolution asserting that environmental changes cause structural changes in animals and plants that are transmitted to offspring

la·ma·sery \'läm-ə-,ser-ē\ *n* [F *lamaserie*, fr. *lama* + Per *sarāī* palace] **:** a monastery of lamas

1lamb \'lam\ *n, often attrib* [ME, fr. OE; akin to OHG *lamb* lamb, *elaho* elk — more at ELK] **1 a :** a young sheep esp. less than one year old or without permanent teeth **b :** the young of various other animals (as the smaller antelopes) **2 a :** a person

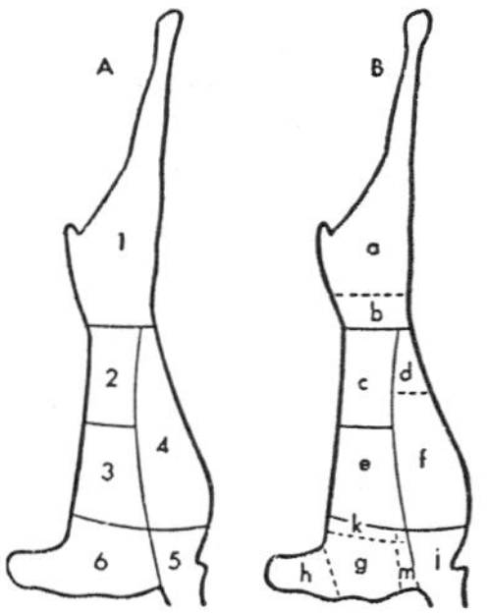

cuts of lamb: *A* wholesale cuts: *1* leg, *2* loin, *3* rack, *4* breast, *5* shank, *6* shoulder; *B* retail cuts: *a* leg, *b* sirloin chops and roast, *c* loin chops and rolled loin roast, *d* patties and chopped roast, *e* rib chops and crown roast, *f* riblets, stew, and stuffed or rolled breast, *g* square-cut shoulder roast, Saratoga chops, rolled shoulder, boneless shoulder chops, *h* neck slices, *i* shanks, *k* blade chops, *m* arm chops

as gentle or weak as a lamb **b :** DEAR, PET **c :** a person easily cheated or deceived esp. in trading securities **3 a :** the flesh of a lamb used as food **b :** LAMBSKIN

²**lamb** *vi* **:** to bring forth a lamb ~ *vt* **1 :** to bring forth (a lamb) **2 :** to tend (ewes) at lambing time — **lamb·er** \'lam-ər\ *n*

lam·baste *or* **lam·bast** \(')lam-'bāst, -'bast\ *vt* [prob. fr. ¹*lam* + *baste*] **1 :** to assault violently **:** BEAT, WHIP **2 :** to administer a verbal thrashing to **:** CENSURE

lamb·da \'lam-də\ *n* [Gk, of Sem origin; akin to Heb *lāmedh* lamed] **:** the 11th letter of the Greek alphabet — symbol Λ or λ

lam·ben·cy \'lam-bən-sē\ *n* **:** the quality, state, or an instance of being lambent

lam·bent \'lam-bənt\ *adj* [L *lambent-, lambens*, prp. of *lambere* to lick —more at LAP] **1 :** playing lightly on or over a surface **:** FLICKERING **2 :** softly bright or radiant **3 :** marked by lightness or brilliance esp. of expression — **lam·bent·ly** *adv*

lam·bert \'lam-bərt\ *n* [Johann H. *Lambert* †1777 G physicist] **:** the cgs unit of brightness equal to the brightness of a perfectly diffusing surface that radiates or reflects one lumen per square centimeter

lam·bre·quin \'lam-bər-kən, -bri-kən\ *n* [F] **1 :** a scarf used to cover a knight's helmet **2 a :** a short decorative drapery for a shelf edge or for the top of a window casing **:** VALANCE **b :** a scalloped color pattern used esp. on porcelain tableware

lamb·skin \'lam-,skin\ *n* **:** a lamb's skin or a small fine-grade sheepskin or the leather made from either; *specif* **:** such a skin dressed with the wool on and used esp. for winter clothing

lamb's–quar·ters \'lamz-,kwȯ(r)t-ərz\ *n pl but sing or pl in constr* **1 :** a goosefoot (*Chenopodium album*) with glaucous foliage that is sometimes used as a potherb **2 :** any of several oraches

¹**lame** \'lām\ *adj* [ME, fr. OE *lama;* akin to OHG *lam* lame, Lith *limti* to break down] **1 a :** physically disabled; *also* **:** having a part and esp. a limb so disabled as to impair freedom of movement **b :** halting in movement **:** LIMPING **2 :** lacking needful or desirable substance **:** WEAK ⟨a ~ excuse⟩ — **lame·ly** *adv* — **lame·ness** *n*

²**lame** *vt* **1 :** to make lame **:** CRIPPLE **2 :** to make weak or ineffective **:** DISABLE

³**lame** \'lām, 'lam\ *n* [MF, fr. L *lamina*] **1 :** a thin plate esp. of metal **:** LAMINA **2** *pl* **:** small overlapping steel plates joined to slide on one another (as in medieval armor)

⁴**la·mé** \lä-'mā, la-\ *n* [F] **:** a brocaded clothing fabric made from any of various fibers combined with tinsel filling threads often of gold or silver

la·med \'läm-,ed\ *n* [Heb *lāmedh*, lit., oxgoad] **:** the 12th letter of the Hebrew alphabet — symbol ל

lame duck *n* **1 :** an elected officer or group continuing to hold political office during a usu. brief interim between defeat for reelection and the inauguration of a successor **2 :** WEAKLING

lamell- *or* **lamelli-** *comb form* [NL, fr. *lamella*] **:** lamella ⟨*lamelli*rostral⟩ ⟨*lamell*ose⟩

la·mel·la \lə-'mel-ə\ *n, pl* **la·mel·lae** \-'mel-(,)ē, -,ī\ *also* **lamellas** [NL, fr. L, dim. of *lamina* thin plate] **:** a thin flat scale or part: as **a :** one of the thin plates composing the gills of a bivalve mollusk **b :** a gill of a mushroom — **la·mel·lar** \-'mel-ər\ *adj* — **la·mel·lar·ly** *adv*

la·mel·late \lə-'mel-ət, 'lam-ə-,lāt\ *or* **lam·el·lat·ed** \'lam-ə-,lāt-əd\ *adj* **1 :** composed of or furnished with lamellae **2 :** LAMELLIFORM — **la·mel·late·ly** *adv*

lam·el·la·tion \,lam-ə-'lā-shən\ *n* **1 :** formation or division into lamellae **2 :** LAMELLA

la·mel·li·branch \lə-'mel-ə-,braŋk\ *n* [NL *Lamellibranchia*, class-name, fr. *lamell-* + L *branchia* gill — more at BRANCHIA] **:** any of a class (Lamellibranchia) of bivalve mollusks (as clams, oysters, mussels) that have the body bilaterally symmetrical, compressed, and enclosed within the mantle and that build up a shell whose right and left parts are connected by a hinge over the animal's back — **lamellibranch** *adj* — **la·mel·li·bran·chi·ate** \lə-,mel-ə-'braŋ-kē-ət\ *adj or n*

la·mel·li·corn \lə-'mel-ə-,kȯ(ə)rn\ *adj* [deriv. of NL *lamella* + L *cornu* horn — more at HORN] **:** having or constituting antennae ending in flattened plates — **lamellicorn** *n*

la·mel·li·form \-,fȯrm\ *adj* **:** having the form of a thin plate

¹**la·ment** \lə-'ment\ *vi* **:** to mourn aloud **:** WAIL ~ *vt* **1 :** to express sorrow for **:** MOURN **2 :** to regret strongly **syn** see DEPLORE

²**lament** *n* [MF or L; MF, fr. L *lamentum;* akin to ON *lōmr* loon, L *latrare* to bark, Gk *lēros* nonsense] **1 :** a crying out in grief **:** WAILING **2 :** DIRGE, ELEGY

la·men·ta·ble \'lam-ən-tə-bəl, lə-'ment-ə-\ *adj* **1 :** that is to be regretted or lamented **:** DEPLORABLE **2 :** expressing grief **:** MOURNFUL — **la·men·ta·ble·ness** *n* — **la·men·ta·bly** \-blē\ *adv*

lam·en·ta·tion \,lam-ən-'tā-shən\ *n* **:** an act or instance of lamenting

la·ment·ed \lə-'ment-əd\ *adj* **:** mourned for — **la·ment·ed·ly** *adv*

la·mia \'lā-mē-ə\ *n* [ME, fr. L, fr. Gk, devouring monster — more at LEMUR] **:** a female demon **:** VAMPIRE

la·mi·a·ceous \,lā-mē-'ā-shəs\ *adj* [deriv. of Gk *lamia*] **:** LABIATE 2

lamin- *or* **lamini-** *or* **lamino-** *comb form* **:** lamina ⟨*lamin*ar⟩

lam·i·na \'lam-ə-nə\ *n, pl* **lam·i·nae** \-,nē, -,nī\ *or* **laminas** [L] **1 :** a thin plate or scale **2 :** the expanded part of a foliage leaf **3 :** one of the narrow thin parallel plates of soft vascular sensitive tissue that cover the flesh within the wall of a hoof

lam·i·nal \'lam-ən-ᵊl\ *adj* **:** LAMINAR

lam·i·nar \'lam-ə-nər\ *adj* **:** arranged in, consisting of, or resembling laminae

laminar flow *n* **:** streamline flow in a viscous fluid near a solid boundary — compare TURBULENT FLOW

lam·i·nar·ia \,lam-ə-'ner-ē-ə, -'nar-\ *n* [NL, genus name] **:** any of a genus (*Laminaria*) of large chiefly perennial kelps with an unbranched cylindrical or flattened stipe and a smooth or convoluted blade; *broadly* **:** any of various related kelps (order Laminariales) — **lam·i·nar·i·a·ceous** \-,ner-ē-'ā-shəs, -,nar-\ *adj* — **lam·i·nar·i·an** \-'ner-ē-ən, -'nar-\ *adj* — **lam·i·nar·i·oid** \-ē-,ȯid\ *adj*

¹**lam·i·nate** \'lam-ə-,nāt\ *vt* **1 :** to roll or compress into a thin plate **2 :** to separate into laminae **3 :** to make by uniting superposed layers of one or more materials ~ *vi* **:** to divide into laminae — **lam·i·na·tor** \-,nāt-ər\ *n*

²**lam·i·nate** \-nət, -,nāt\ *adj* **1 :** consisting of laminae **2 :** bearing or covered with laminae

³**lam·i·nate** \-nət, -,nāt\ *n* **:** a product made by laminating

lam·i·nat·ed \-,nāt-əd\ *adj* **1 :** LAMINATE 1 **2 :** composed of layers of firmly united material; *specif* **:** made by bonding or impregnating superposed layers of paper, wood, or fabric with resin and compressing under heat

lam·i·na·tion \,lam-ə-'nā-shən\ *n* **1 :** the process of laminating **2 :** the state of being laminated **3 :** a laminate structure **4 :** LAMINA

Lam·mas \'lam-əs\ *n* [ME *Lammasse*, fr. OE *hlāfmæsse*, fr. *hlāf* loaf + *mæsse* mass; fr. the consecration on this day of loaves made from the first ripe grain] **1 :** the first day of August — called also *Lammas Day* **2 :** the time of year around Lammas Day — called also *Lam·mas·tide* \'lam-ə-,stīd\

lam·mer·gei·er *or* **lam·mer·gey·er** \'lam-ər-,gī(-ə)r\ *n* [G *lämmergeier*] **:** the largest European bird of prey (*Gypaetus barbatus aureus*) occurring in mountain regions from the Pyrenees to northern China and resembling both the eagles and the vultures

lamp \'lamp\ *n* [ME, fr. OF *lampe*, fr. L *lampas*, fr. Gk, fr. *lampein* to shine; akin to ON *leiptr* lightning] **1 a :** a vessel with a wick for burning oil or other inflammable liquid to produce artificial light **b :** any of various devices for producing light or heat **2 :** a heavenly body **3 :** a source of intellectual or spiritual illumination

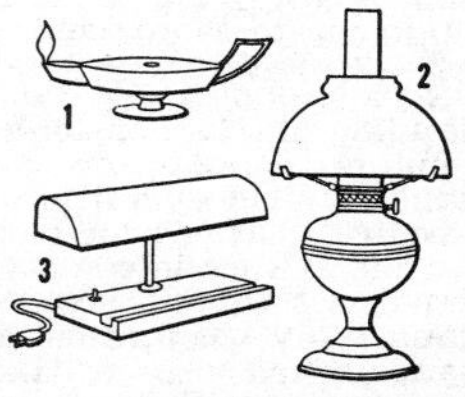

lamps: *1* ancient oil lamp, *2* kerosine lamp, *3* electric desk lamp

lamp·black \-,blak\ *n* **:** a fine bulky dull-black soot deposited in incomplete combustion of carbonaceous materials and used chiefly as a pigment (as in paints, enamels, printing inks)

lam·per eel \,lam-pər-\ *n* [alter. of *lamprey*] **1 :** LAMPREY **2 :** CONGO SNAKE

lamp·light·er \'lam-,plīt-ər\ *n* **:** one that lights a lamp

¹**lam·poon** \lam-'pün\ *n* [F *lampon*] **1 :** a harsh satire usu. directed against an individual **2 :** a light mocking satire

²**lampoon** *vt* **:** to make the subject of a lampoon **:** RIDICULE —**lam·poon·er** *n* — **lam·poon·ery** \-'pün-(ə-)rē\ *n*

lam·prey \'lam-prē\ *n* [ME, fr. OF *lampreie*, fr. ML *lampreda*] **:** any of an order (Hyperoartia) of aquatic vertebrates that are widely distributed in temperate and subarctic regions in both fresh and salt water and resemble eels but have a large suctorial mouth

lam·ster \'lam(p)-stər\ *or* **lam·is·ter** \'lam-ə-stər\ *n* **:** a fugitive esp. from the law

la·nai \lə-'nī, lä-\ *n* [Hawaiian] **:** PORCH, VERANDA

la·nate \'lā-,nāt, 'lan-,āt\ *adj* [L *lanatus*, fr. *lana* wool — more at WOOL] **:** covered with fine hair or filaments **:** WOOLLY

Lan·cas·tri·an \lan-'kas-trē-ən, laŋ-\ *adj* [John of Gaunt, duke of *Lancaster* †1399] **:** of, relating to, or supporting an English royal house furnishing sovereigns from 1399 to 1461 — **Lancastrian** *n*

¹**lance** \'lan(t)s\ *n* [ME, fr. OF, fr. L *lancea*] **1 :** a weapon of war consisting of a long shaft with a sharp steel head and carried by mounted knights or light cavalry **2 :** any of various sharp objects suggestive of a lance: as **a :** LANCET 1 **b :** a spear used for killing whales **3 :** LANCER 1b

²**lance** *vb* [ME *launcen*, fr. MF *lancer*, fr. LL *lanceare*, fr. L *lancea*] *vt* **1 a :** to pierce with a lance or similar weapon **b :** to open with or as if with a lancet **2 :** LAUNCH, HURL ~ *vi* **:** to move forward quickly

lance corporal *n* [*lance* (as in obs. *lancepesade* lance corporal, fr. MF *lancepessade*)] **:** an enlisted man in the marine corps ranking above a private first class and below a corporal

lance·let \'lan(t)-slət\ *n* **:** any of various small translucent marine animals (subphylum Cephalochordata) related to the vertebrates

Lan·ce·lot \'lan(t)-sə-,lät, 'län-, -s(ə-)lət\ *n* [F] **:** a knight of the Round Table and lover of Queen Guinevere in Arthurian legend

lan·ceo·late \'lan(t)-sē-ə-,lāt\ *also* **lan·ceo·lat·ed** \-,lāt-əd\ *adj* [LL *lanceolatus*, fr. L *lanceola*, dim. of *lancea*] **:** shaped like a lance head; *specif* **:** tapering to a point at the apex and sometimes at the base — **lan·ceo·late·ly** *adv*

lanc·er \'lan(t)-sər\ *n* **1 a :** one who carries a lance **b :** a member of a military unit formerly composed of light cavalry armed with lances **2** *pl but sing in constr* **a :** a set of five quadrilles each in a different meter **b :** the music for such dances

lan·cet \'lan(t)-sət\ *n* **:** a sharp-pointed and commonly two-edged surgical instrument used to make small incisions

lancet arch *n* — see ARCH illustration

lan·cet·ed \-sət-əd\ *adj* **:** having a lancet arch or lancet windows

lancet window *n* **:** a high narrow window with an acutely pointed head and without tracery

lance·wood \'lan(t)-,swu̇d\ *n* **:** a tough elastic wood used esp. for shafts, fishing rods, and bows; *also* **:** a tree (esp. *Oxandra lanceolata*) yielding this wood

lan·ci·nate \'lan(t)-sə-,nāt\ *vb* [L *lancinatus*, pp. of *lancinare;* akin to L *lacer* mangled — more at LACERATE] **:** PIERCE, STAB — **lan·ci·na·tion** \,lan(t)-sə-'nā-shən\ *n*

¹**land** \'land\ *n, often attrib* [ME, fr. OE; akin to OHG *lant* land, OIr *land* open space] **1 :** the solid part of the surface of the earth; *specif* **:** the surface of the earth and all its natural resources **2 a :** a portion of the earth's solid surface considered by itself **b :** the people of a country **c :** REALM, DOMAIN **3 a :** ground or soil of a specified nature or quality **b** *pl* **:** territorial possessions **4 :** ground owned privately or publicly **5 :** an area of a surface partly machined (as with grooves) that is left without such machining — **land·less** \'lan-dləs\ *adj*

²**land** *vt* **1 :** to set or put on shore from a ship **:** DISEMBARK **2 a :** to set down after conveying **b :** to cause to reach or come to rest in a particular place **c :** to bring (an airplane) to a landing **3 a :** to catch and bring in (as a fish) **b :** GAIN, SECURE ~ *vi* **1 a :** to go ashore from a ship **:** DISEMBARK **b** *of a ship or boat* **:** to touch at a place on shore **2 a :** to come to the end of a course or to a stage in a journey **:** ARRIVE **b :** to strike or meet the ground (as after a fall) **c** *of an airplane* **:** to alight on a surface

lan·dau \'lan-,dau̇, -(,)dȯ\ *n* [*Landau*, Bavaria, Germany] **1 :** a four-wheeled carriage with a top divided into two sections that can be let down, thrown back, or removed **2 :** a closed automobile

body with provision for opening or folding down the rear quarter top
lan·dau·let \ˌlan-dᵊl-'et\ *n* **1 :** a small landau **2 :** an automobile body with an open driver's seat and an enclosed rear section having one cross seat and a collapsible roof
land·ed \'lan-dəd\ *adj* **1 :** having an estate in land **2 :** consisting in or derived from land or real estate
land·fall \'lan(d)-ˌfȯl\ *n* **1 :** a sighting or making of land after a voyage or flight **2 :** the land first sighted on a voyage or flight
land·form \-ˌfȯrm\ *n* **:** a feature of the earth's surface attributable to natural causes
land grant *n* **:** a grant of land by the government esp. for roads, railroads, or agricultural colleges
land·grave \'lan(d)-ˌgrāv\ *n* [G *landgraf*] **1 :** a German count having a certain territorial jurisdiction — used also as a title by some German princes **2 :** a county nobleman in the Carolina colony ranking just below the proprietary
land·hold·er \'land-ˌhōl-dər\ *n* **:** a holder or owner of land — **land·hold·ing** \-diŋ\ *n*
land·ing *n* **1 :** an act or process of one that lands; *esp* **:** a going or bringing to shore, land, or other surface after a voyage or flight **2 :** a place for discharging and taking on passengers and cargo **3 :** a level part of a staircase (as at the end of a flight of stairs)
landing craft *n* **:** any of numerous naval craft specially designed for putting ashore troops and equipment
landing field *n* **:** a field where aircraft may land and take off
landing gear *n* **:** the undercarriage that supports the weight of an airplane when in contact with the land or water
landing strip *n* **:** AIRSTRIP
land·la·dy \'lan-ˌ(d)lād-ē\ *n* **:** a female landlord
land·locked \'lan-ˌ(d)läkt\ *adj* **1 :** enclosed or nearly enclosed by land **2 :** confined to fresh water by some barrier
land·lord \'lan-ˌ(d)lȯ(ə)rd\ *n* **1 :** the owner of land or other property which he leases or rents to another **2 :** the master of an inn or lodging house **:** INNKEEPER
land·lord·ism \-ˌiz-əm\ *n* **:** an economic system or practice by which ownership of land is vested in one who leases it to cultivators
land·lub·ber \'lan-ˌ(d)ləb-ər\ *n* **1 :** LANDSMAN 2 **2 :** one who is unacquainted with the sea or seamanship — **land·lub·ber·ly** *adj*
land·mark \'lan(d)-ˌmärk\ *n* **1 :** a mark for designating the boundary of land **2 a :** a conspicuous object on land that marks a locality **b :** an anatomical structure used as a point of orientation in locating other structures **3 :** an event or development that marks a turning point or a stage
land·mass \-ˌmas\ *n* **:** a large area of land
land office *n* **:** a government office in which entries upon and sales of public land are registered
land–office business *n* **:** extensive and rapid business
land·own·er \'lan-ˌdō-nər\ *n* **:** an owner of land
land plaster *n* **:** gypsum or gypsiferous rock ground fine for use as a fertilizer and soil amendment
land–poor \'lan(d)-ˌpu̇(ə)r\ *adj* **:** owning so much unprofitable or encumbered land as to lack funds to develop the land or pay the charges due thereon
Land·ra·ce \'län-ˌ(d)räs-ə\ *n* [Dan, fr. *land* + *race*] **1 :** any of several locally developed breeds of swine of northern Europe **2 :** any animal of a Landrace breed
land reform *n* **:** more equitable distribution of agricultural land esp. by governmental action
[1]**land·scape** \'lan(d)-ˌskāp\ *n, often attrib* [D *landschap*, fr. *land* + *-schap* -ship] **1 a :** a picture representing a view of natural inland scenery **b :** the art of depicting such scenery **2 a :** the landforms of a region in the aggregate **b :** a portion of land that the eye can comprehend in a single view **3 :** VISTA, PROSPECT
[2]**landscape** *vt* **:** to improve or ornament by landscape architecture or gardening ~ *vi* **:** to engage in the occupation of landscape gardening — **land·scap·er** *n*
landscape architect *n* **:** one whose profession is to arrange and modify the effects of natural scenery over a tract of land for aesthetic effect — **landscape architecture** *n*
landscape gardener *n* **:** one skilled in the development and decorative planting of gardens and grounds
land·side \'lan(d)-ˌsīd\ *n* **:** a sidepiece opposite the moldboard in a plow that guides the plow and takes the side pressure when the furrow is turned
land·slide \'lan(d)-ˌslīd\ *n* **1 :** the usu. rapid downward movement of a mass of rock, earth, or artificial fill on a slope; *also* **:** the mass that moves down **2 a :** a great majority of votes for one side **b :** an overwhelming victory
land·slip \-ˌslip\ *n* **:** LANDSLIDE 1
lands·man \'lan(d)z-mən\ *n* **1 :** a fellow countryman **2 :** one who lives on the land; *esp* **:** one who knows little or nothing of the sea
land·ward \'lan-(d)wərd\ *adj* **:** lying or being toward the land or on the side toward the land — **landward** *adv*
[1]**lane** \'lān\ *n* [ME, fr. OE *lanu;* akin to MD *lane* lane] **1 :** a narrow passageway between fences or hedges **2 :** a relatively narrow way or track: as **a :** an ocean route used by or prescribed for ships **b :** a strip of roadway for a single line of vehicles **c :** any of several parallel courses in which a competitor must stay during a race **d :** a bowling alley
[2]**lane** *Scot var of* LONE
lang·bein·ite \'laŋ-ˌbī-ˌnīt\ *n* [G *langbeinit*, fr. A. *Langbein*, 19th cent. G chemist] **:** a mineral $K_2Mg_2(SO_4)_3$ that is a double sulfate of potassium and magnesium much used in the fertilizer industry
lang·lauf \'läŋ-ˌlau̇f\ *n* [G, fr. *lang* long + *lauf* race] **:** cross-country running or racing on skis — **lang·lauf·er** *n*
lang·ley \'laŋ-lē\ *n* [Samuel P. *Langley* †1906 Am astronomer] **:** a unit of solar radiation equivalent to one gram calorie per square centimeter of irradiated surface
Lan·go·bard \'laŋ-gə-ˌbärd\ *n* [L *Langobardus*] **:** LOMBARD 1 — **Lan·go·bar·dic** \ˌlaŋ-gə-'bär-dik\ *adj*
lan·gouste \läⁿ-'güst\ *n* [F] **:** SPINY LOBSTER
Lang·shan \'laŋ-ˌshan\ *n* [*Langshan*, locality near Shanghai, China] **:** any of an Asiatic breed of large single-combed usu. black or white domestic fowls resembling the Cochin Chinas
lang syne \laŋ-'zīn, -'sīn\ *n* [ME (Sc), fr. *lang* long + *syne* since] *chiefly Scot* **:** times past — **lang syne** *adv or adj, chiefly Scot*
lan·guage \'laŋ-gwij\ *n, often attrib* [ME, fr. OF, fr. *langue* tongue, language, fr. L *lingua* — more at TONGUE] **1 a :** the words, their pronunciation, and the methods of combining them used and understood by a considerable community **b** (1) **:** a systematic means of communicating ideas or feelings by the use of conventionalized signs, gestures, marks, or esp. articulate vocal sound (2) **:** the suggestion by objects, actions, or conditions of associated ideas or feelings (3) **:** the means by which animals communicate (4) **:** a formal system of signs and symbols (as logical calculus) including rules for the formation and transformation of admissible expressions **2 a :** form or manner of verbal expression; *specif* **:** STYLE **b :** the vocabulary and phraseology belonging to an art or department of knowledge **c :** abusive epithets **:** PROFANITY **3 :** the study of language esp. as a school subject
langue d'oc \läⁿg-dȯk\ *n* [F, fr. OF, lit., language of *oc;* fr. the Provençal use of the word *oc* for "yes"] **:** PROVENÇAL
langue d'oïl \-dȯ-ēl\ *n* [F, fr. OF, lit., language of *oïl;* fr. the French use of the word *oïl* for "yes"] **:** FRENCH 1
lan·guet \'laŋ-gwət, laŋ-'gwet\ *n* [ME, fr. MF *languete*, dim. of *langue*] **:** something resembling the tongue in form or function
lan·guid \'laŋ-gwəd\ *adj* [MF *languide*, fr. L *languidus*, fr. *languēre* to languish — more at SLACK] **1 :** drooping or flagging from or as if from exhaustion **:** WEAK **2 :** sluggish in character or disposition **:** LISTLESS **3 :** lacking force or quickness of movement **:** SLOW — **lan·guid·ly** *adv* — **lan·guid·ness** *n*
lan·guish \'laŋ-gwish\ *vi* [ME *languishen*, fr. MF *languiss-*, stem of *languir*, fr. (assumed) VL *languire*, fr. L *languēre*] **1 a :** to be or become feeble, weak, or enervated **b :** to be or live in a state of depression or decreasing vitality **2 :** to become dispirited **:** PINE **3 :** to assume an expression of grief or emotion appealing for sympathy — **lan·guish·er** *n* — **lan·guish·ing** *adj* — **lan·guish·ing·ly** \-gwi-shiŋ-lē\ *adv* — **lan·guish·ment** \-gwish-mənt\ *n*
lan·guor \'laŋ-(g)ər\ *n* [ME, fr. OF, fr. L, fr. *languēre*] **1 :** a languid feeling **2 :** listless indolence **:** DREAMINESS **syn** see LETHARGY
lan·guor·ous \'laŋ-(g)ə-rəs, -grəs\ *adj* **1 :** full of or characterized by languor **2 :** producing or tending to produce languor — **lan·guor·ous·ly** *adv*
lan·gur \läŋ-'gu̇(ə)r\ *n* [Hindi *lãgūr*] **:** any of various Asiatic slender long-tailed monkeys (family Colobidae) with bushy eyebrows and a chin tuft
lank \'laŋk\ *adj* [(assumed) ME, fr. OE *hlanc;* akin to OHG *hlanca* loin, L *clingere* to girdle] **1 :** not well filled out **:** SLENDER, THIN ⟨~ cattle⟩ **2 :** SCANTY, MEAGRE ⟨~ grass⟩ **3 :** hanging straight and limp without spring or curl ⟨~ hair⟩ **syn** see LEAN — **lank·ly** *adv* — **lank·ness** *n*
lank·i·ly \'laŋ-kə-lē\ *adv* **:** in a lanky manner
lank·i·ness \-kē-nəs\ *n* **:** the quality or state of being lanky
lanky \'laŋ-kē\ *adj* **:** ungracefully tall and thin **syn** see LEAN
lan·ner \'lan-ər\ *n* [ME *laner*, fr. MF *lanier*] **:** a falcon (*Falco biarmicus*) of southern Europe, southwestern Asia, or Africa; *specif* **:** a female lanner
lan·ner·et \ˌlan-ə-'ret\ *n* **:** a male lanner
lan·o·lin \'lan-ᵊl-ən\ *n* [L *lana* wool + ISV *-ol* + *-in*] **:** wool grease esp. when refined for use in ointments and cosmetics
lan·ta·na \lan-'tän-ə\ *n* [NL, genus name, deriv. of It dial., viburnum] **:** any of a genus (*Lantana*) of tropical shrubs of the vervain family with showy heads of small bright flowers
lan·tern \'lant-ərn\ *n, often attrib* [ME *lanterne*, fr. MF, fr. L *lanterna*, fr. Gk *lamptēr*, fr. *lampein* to shine — more at LAMP] **1 :** a usu. portable protective case for a light with transparent openings **2 a** *obs* **:** LIGHTHOUSE **b :** the chamber in a lighthouse containing the light **c :** a structure with glazed or open sides above an opening in a roof for light or ventilation **d :** a small tower or cupola or one stage of a cupola **3 :** PROJECTOR 2b

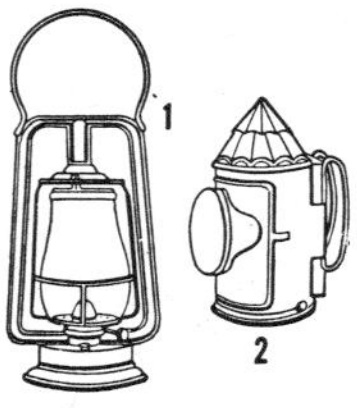

lanterns 1: *1* barn, *2* bull's-eye

lantern fly *n* **:** any of several large brightly marked insects (family Fulgoridae) having the front of the head prolonged into a hollow structure
lantern jaw *n* **:** an undershot jaw — **lan·tern–jawed** \ˌlant-ərn-'jȯd\ *adj*
lantern pinion *n* **:** a gear pinion having cylindrical bars instead of teeth
lan·tha·nide series \'lan(t)-thə-ˌnīd-\ *n* **:** the group of rare-earth metals often including lanthanum and sometimes yttrium — compare PERIODIC TABLE
lan·tha·num \'lan(t)-thə-nəm\ *n* [NL, fr. Gk *lanthanein* to escape notice] **:** a white soft malleable trivalent metallic element that occurs in rare-earth minerals and is usu. included in the rare-earth group — see ELEMENT table
lant·horn \'lant-ərn\ *n, chiefly Brit* **:** LANTERN
la·nu·gi·nous \lə-'n(y)ü-jə-nəs\ *also* **la·nu·gi·nose** \-ˌnōs\ *adj* [L *lanuginosus*, fr. *lanugin-, lanugo*] **:** covered with down or fine soft hair **:** DOWNY — **la·nu·gi·nous·ness** *n*
la·nu·go \lə-'n(y)ü-(ˌ)gō\ *n* [L, down — more at WOOL] **:** a dense cottony or downy growth; *specif* **:** the soft woolly hair that covers the human fetus and that of some other mammals
lan·yard \'lan-yərd\ *n* [ME *lanyer*, fr. MF *laniere*] **1 :** a piece of rope or line for fastening something in ships; *esp* **:** one of the pieces passing through deadeyes to extend shrouds or stays **2 a :** a cord worn around the neck to hold a knife or a whistle **b :** a cord worn as a symbol of a military citation **3 :** a strong cord with a hook at one end used in firing cannon
Lao \'lau̇\ *or* **Lao·tian** \lā-'ō-shən, 'lau̇-shən, lau̇-'ō-shən\ *n, pl* **Lao** *or* **Laos** *or* **Laotians 1 a :** a Buddhist people living in Laos and adjacent parts of northeastern Thailand and constituting an important branch of the Tai race **b :** a member of such people **2 :** the Thai language of the Lao people — **Lao** *or* **Laotian** *adj*
La·oc·o·ön \lā-'äk-ə-ˌwän\ *n* [L, fr. Gk *Laokoōn*] **:** a Trojan priest killed with his two sons by two sea serpents after warning the Trojans against the wooden horse
[1]**lap** \'lap\ *n* [ME *lappe*, fr. OE *læppa;* akin to OHG *lappa* flap, L *labi* to slide — more at SLEEP] **1 a :** a loose panel or hanging flap esp. of a garment **b** *archaic* **:** the skirt of a coat or dress **2 a** (1) **:** the clothing that lies on the knees, thighs, and lower part of the trunk when one sits (2) **:** the front part of the lower trunk and thighs of a seated person **b :** an environment of nurture ⟨the ~ of luxury⟩ **3 :** CHARGE, CONTROL ⟨in the ~ of the gods⟩
[2]**lap** *vb* **lapped; lap·ping** *vt* **1 a :** to fold over or around some-

thing : WIND **b** : to envelop entirely : SWATHE **2** : to fold over esp. into layers **3** : to hold protectively in or as if in the lap : CUDDLE **4 a** : to place over or next to so as to partially or wholly cover : OVERLAP **b** : to unite (as beams or timbers) so as to preserve the same breadth and depth throughout **5 a** : to smooth or polish to a high degree of refinement or accuracy **b** : to work two surfaces together with or without abrasives until a very close fit is produced **6 a** : to lead (an opponent) by one or more circuits of a racecourse **b** : to complete the circuit of (a racecourse) ~ *vi* **1** : FOLD, WIND **2 a** : to project beyond or spread over **b** : to lie partly over or alongside of something or of one another **3** : to traverse a course — **lap·per** *n*

3**lap** *n, often attrib* **1 a** : the amount by which one object overlaps or projects beyond another **b** : the part of an object that overlaps another **2** : a smoothing and polishing tool usu. comprising a piece of wood, leather, felt, or soft metal used with or without an embedded abrasive **3** : a doubling or layering of a flexible substance (as fibers or paper) **4 a** : one circuit around a racecourse **b** : one segment of a larger unit (as a journey) **c** : one complete turn

4**lap** *vb* [ME *lapen*, fr. OE *lapian*; akin to OHG *laffan* to lick, L *lambere*, Gk *laphyssein* to devour] *vi* **1** : to take in food or drink with the tongue **2 a** : to make a gentle intermittent splashing sound **b** : to move in little waves : WASH ~ *vt* **1** : to take in (food or drink) with the tongue **2** : to flow or splash against in little waves — **lap·per** *n*

5**lap** *n* **1 a** : an act or instance of lapping **b** : the amount that can be carried to the mouth by one lick or scoop of the tongue **2** : a thin or weak beverage or food **3** : a gentle splashing sound

lap·a·rot·o·my \ˌlap-ə-ˈrät-ə-mē\ *n* [Gk *lapara* flank + ISV *-tomy*] : surgical section of the abdominal wall

lap·board \ˈlap-ˌbō(ə)rd, -ˌbȯ(ə)rd\ *n* : a board used on the lap as a substitute for a table or desk

lap·dog \-ˌdȯg\ *n* : a small dog that may be held in the lap

la·pel \lə-ˈpel\ *n* [dim. of 1*lap*] : the part of a garment that is turned back; *specif* : the fold of the front of a coat that is usu. a continuation of the collar

lap·ful \ˈlap-ˌfu̇l\ *n, pl* **lapfuls** \-ˌfu̇lz\ *or* **laps·ful** \ˈlaps-ˌfu̇l\ : as much as the lap can hold or support

lap·i·dar·i·an \ˌlap-ə-ˈder-ē-ən\ *adj* **1** : sculptured in or inscribed on stone **2** : LAPIDARY 2

1**lap·i·dary** \ˈlap-ə-ˌder-ē\ *n* **1** : a cutter, polisher, or engraver of precious stones usu. other than diamonds **2** : the art of cutting gems

2**lapidary** *adj* [L *lapidarius* of stone, fr. *lapid-, lapis* stone; akin to Gk *lepas* crag] **1 a** : LAPIDARIAN 1 **b** : of or relating to precious stones or the art of cutting them **2** : having the elegance and precision associated with inscriptions on monumental stone

la·pil·lus \lə-ˈpil-əs\ *n, pl* **la·pil·li** \-ˌī, -(ˌ)ē\ [L, dim. of *lapis*] : a stony or glassy fragment of lava thrown out in a volcanic eruption

lap·in \ˈlap-ən\ *n* [F] **1** : RABBIT; *specif* : a castrated male rabbit **2** : rabbit fur usu. sheared and dyed

la·pis la·zu·li \ˌlap-ə-ˈslaz(h)-ə-lē\ *n* [ME, fr. ML, fr. L *lapis* + ML *lazuli*, gen. of *lazulum* lapis lazuli, fr. Ar *lāzaward* — more at AZURE] : a usu. rich azure blue semiprecious stone that is essentially a complex silicate often with spangles of iron pyrites

lap joint *n* : a joint made by overlapping two ends or edges and fastening them together — **lap–joint·ed** \ˈlap-ˈjȯint-əd\ *adj*

Lapp \ˈlap\ *n* [Sw] **1** : a member of a people of northern Scandinavia, Finland, and the Kola peninsula of northern Russia who are typically nomadic herders of reindeer, fishermen, and hunters of sea mammals **2** : any or all of the closely related Finno-Ugric languages of the Lapps

lap·pet \ˈlap-ət\ *n* **1** : a fold or flap on a garment or headdress **2** : a flat overlapping or hanging piece (as a roofing tile or the wattle of a bird)

1**lapse** \ˈlaps\ *n* [L *lapsus*, fr. *lapsus*, pp. of *labi* to slip — more at SLEEP] **1 a** : a slight error or slip **b** : a temporary deviation or fall esp. from a higher to a lower state **2 a** : DROP; *specif* : a decrease of temperature or pressure as the height increases **b** : LOWERING, DECLINE **3 a** (1) : the termination of a right or privilege through neglect to exercise it within some limit of time (2) : termination of coverage for nonpayment of premiums **b** : INTERRUPTION, DISCONTINUANCE **4** : an abandonment of religious faith : APOSTASY **5** : a passage of time; *also* : INTERVAL
syn see ERROR

2**lapse** *vi* **1 a** : to fall into error or folly; *specif* : BACKSLIDE, APOSTASIZE **b** : to sink or slip gradually : SUBSIDE **2** : to go out of existence : CEASE **3** : to pass from one proprietor to another by omission or negligence **4 a** *of time* : to run its course : PASS **b** : to glide past or along ~ *vt* : to let slip : FORFEIT — **laps·er** *n*

1**lap·strake** \ˈlap-ˌstrāk\ *also* **lap·streak** \-ˌstrēk\ *adj* : CLINKER-BUILT

2**lapstrake** *also* **lapstreak** *n* : a clinker-built boat

La·pu·tan \lə-ˈpyüt-ᵊn\ *n* : an inhabitant of a flying island in Swift's *Gulliver's Travels* characterized by a neglect of useful occupations and a devotion to visionary projects — **Laputan** *adj*

lap·wing \ˈlap-ˌwiŋ\ *n* [ME, by folk etymology fr. OE *hlēapewince*; akin to OE *hlēapan* to leap and to OE *wincian* to wink] : a crested Old World plover (*Vanellus vanellus*) noted for its slow irregular flapping flight and its shrill wailing cry; *also* : any of several related plovers

lar \ˈlär\ *n, pl* **lar·es** \ˈla(ə)r-(ˌ)ēz, ˈle(ə)r-\ [L — more at LARVA] *often cap* : a tutelary god or spirit of the ancient Romans

lar·board \ˈlär-bərd\ *n* [ME *ladeborde*] : PORT — **larboard** *adj*

lar·ce·ner \ˈlärs-nər, -ᵊn-ər\ *n* : LARCENIST

lar·ce·nist \-nəst, -ᵊn-əst\ *n* : one who commits larceny

lar·ce·nous \-nəs, -ᵊn-əs\ *adj* **1** : having the character of or constituting larceny **2** : committing larceny : THIEVISH — **lar·ce·nous·ly** *adv*

lar·ce·ny \ˈlärs-nē, -ᵊn-ē\ *n* [ME, fr. MF *larcin* theft, fr. L *latrocinium* robbery, fr. *latron-, latro* mercenary soldier; akin to OE *unlǣd* poor, Gk *latron* pay] **1** : the unlawful taking and carrying away of personal property with intent to deprive the rightful owner of his property permanently : THEFT **2** : any of various statutory offenses whereby property is obtained illegally

larch \ˈlärch\ *n* [prob. fr. G *lärche*, fr. L *laric-, larix*] **1** : any of a genus (*Larix*) of trees of the pine family with short fascicled deciduous leaves; *also* : any of several related trees (as of the genus *Abies*) **2** : the wood of a larch

1**lard** \ˈlärd\ *vt* **1 a** : to dress (meat) for cooking by inserting or covering with something (as strips of fat) **b** : to cover or soil with grease **2** : to decorate or intersperse with something : GARNISH **3** *obs* : to make rich with or as if with fat : ENRICH

2**lard** *n* [ME, fr. OF, fr. L *lardum*; akin to L *laetus* glad, *largus* abundant, Gk *larinos* fat] : a soft white solid or semisolid fat obtained by rendering fatty tissue of the hog — **lardy** \ˈlärd-ē\ *adj*

lar·der \ˈlärd-ər\ *n* [ME, fr. MF *lardier*, fr. OF, fr. *lard*] : a place where meat and other foods are kept

lar·doon \lär-ˈdün\ *or* **lar·don** \ˈlär-ˌdän\ *n* [F *lardon* piece of fat pork, fr. OF, fr. *lard*] : a strip (as of salt pork) with which meat is larded

lares and penates *see* LAR, PENATES\ *n pl* **1** : household gods **2** : personal or household effects

1**large** \ˈlärj\ *adj* [ME, fr. OF, fr. L *largus*] **1** *obs* : liberal in giving : LAVISH **2** *obs* **a** : AMPLE, ABUNDANT **b** : EXTENSIVE, BROAD **3** : having more than usual power, capacity, or scope : COMPREHENSIVE **4 a** : exceeding most other things of like kind in quantity or size : BIG **b** : dealing in great numbers or quantities **5** *obs* **a** *of language or expression* : COARSE, VULGAR **b** : lax in conduct : LOOSE **6** *of a wind* : FAVORABLE **7** : EXTRAVAGANT, BOASTFUL ⟨~ talk⟩ — **large·ly** *adv* — **large·ness** *n*
syn LARGE, BIG, GREAT mean above average in magnitude. LARGE is likely to be preferred when the dimensions, extent, capacity, or quantity is being considered ⟨*large* hall⟩ ⟨*large* allowance⟩ BIG suggests emphasis on bulk, weight, or volume ⟨*big* book⟩ ⟨*big* box⟩ GREAT may sometimes imply physical magnitude usu. with connotation of wonder, surprise, or awe, but more often implies magnitude in degree ⟨*great* kindness⟩ ⟨*great* haste⟩. Figuratively LARGE suggests breadth, comprehensiveness, generosity; BIG implies impressiveness rather than solidity; GREAT implies eminence, distinction, or supremacy

2**large** *adv* **1** *obs* : AMPLY, LIBERALLY **2** : with the wind abaft the beam

3**large** *n, obs* : LIBERALITY, GENEROSITY — **at large 1** : without restraint or confinement **2** : at length **3** : in a general way : at random **4** : as a whole ⟨society *at large*⟩ **5** : as the political representative of or to a whole area rather than of one of its subdivisions ⟨congressman-*at-large*⟩

large·heart·ed \ˈlärj-ˈhärt-əd\ *adj* : GENEROUS, SYMPATHETIC

large intestine *n* : the posterior division of the vertebrate intestine that is wider and shorter than the small intestine, typically divided into cecum, colon, and rectum, and concerned esp. with the dehydration of digestive residues into feces

large–mind·ed \ˈlärj-ˈmīn-dəd\ *adj* : generous or comprehensive in outlook, range, or capacity — **large–mind·ed·ly** *adv* — **large–mind·ed·ness** *n*

large–scale \-ˈskā(ə)l\ *adj* : larger than others of its kind: as **a** : involving great numbers or quantities : EXTENSIVE **b** *of a map* : having a scale that permits the plotting of much detail

lar·gess *or* **lar·gesse** \lär-ˈjes, ˈlär-ˌ\ *n* [ME *largesse*, fr. OF, fr. *large*] **1** : liberal giving to or as if to an inferior **2** : excessive or ostentatious gratuities **3** : an innate generosity of mind or spirit

large white *n* : any of a British breed of large long-bodied white swine

1**lar·ghet·to** \lär-ˈget-(ˌ)ō\ *adv* (*or adj*) [It, somewhat slow, fr. *largo*] : in a somewhat slow manner — used as a direction in music

2**larghetto** *n* : a larghetto movement

larg·ish \ˈlär-jish\ *adj* : rather large

1**lar·go** \ˈlär-(ˌ)gō\ *adv* (*or adj*) [It, slow, broad, fr. L *largus* abundant — more at LARD] : in a very slow and broad manner — used as a direction in music

2**largo** *n* : a largo movement

lar·i·at \ˈlar-ē-ət, ˈler-\ *n* [AmerSp *la reata* the lasso, fr. Sp *la* the (fem. of *el*, fr. L *ille* that; akin to L *uls* beyond) + AmerSp *reata* lasso, fr. Sp *reatar* to tie again, fr. *re-* + *atar* to tie, fr. L *aptare* to fit, — more at ALL, ADAPT] : a long light rope of hemp or leather used with a running noose to catch livestock or with or without the noose to picket grazing animals : LASSO

1**lark** \ˈlärk\ *n* [ME, fr. OE *lāwerce*; akin to OHG *lērihha* lark] **1** : any of numerous singing birds (family Alaudidae) mostly of Europe, Asia, and northern Africa; *esp* : SKYLARK **2** : any of various usu. ground-living birds ⟨meadow*lark*⟩ ⟨tit*lark*⟩ — **lark·er** \ˈlär-kər\ *n*

2**lark** *vi* [prob. alter. of *lake* (to frolic)] : FROLIC, SPORT

3**lark** *n* : FROLIC, ROMP; *also* : PRANK

lark·spur \ˈlärk-ˌspər\ *n* : any of a genus (*Delphinium*) of plants of the crowfoot family; *esp* : a cultivated annual delphinium grown for its showy irregular flowers with spurred calyxes

lar·ri·gan \ˈlar-i-gən\ *n* [origin unknown] : an oil-tanned moccasin with legs

lar·ri·kin \ˈlar-i-kən\ *n* [origin unknown] : HOODLUM, ROWDY — **larrikin** *adj*

1**lar·rup** \ˈlar-əp\ *vb* [perh. imit.] *vt* **1** *dial* : BEAT, WHIP **2** *dial* : DEFEAT, TROUNCE ~ *vi, dial* : to move indolently or clumsily : SLOUCH

2**larrup** *n, dial* : BLOW

lar·um \ˈlar-əm\ *n* [short for *alarum*] : ALARM

lar·va \ˈlär-və\ *n, pl* **lar·vae** \-(ˌ)vē, -ˌvī\ *also* **larvas** [NL, fr. L, specter, mask; akin to L *lar*] **1** : the immature, wingless, and often vermiform feeding form that hatches from the egg of many insects, alters chiefly in size while passing through several molts, and is finally transformed into a pupa or chrysalis from which the adult emerges **2** : the early form of any animal that at birth or hatching is fundamentally unlike its parent and must metamorphose before assuming the adult characters — **lar·val** \-vəl\ *adj*

larvi- *comb form* [NL, fr. *larva*] : larva ⟨*larvi*cide⟩

lar·vi·ci·dal \ˌlär-və-ˈsīd-ᵊl\ *adj* : of, relating to, or being a larvicide

lar·vi·cide \ˈlär-və-ˌsīd\ *n* : an agent for killing larval pests

laryng- *or* **laryngo-** *comb form* [NL, fr. Gk, fr. *laryng-, larynx*] **1** : larynx ⟨*laryng*itis⟩ **2** : laryngeal and ⟨*laryngo*pharyngeal⟩

1**la·ryn·geal** \lə-ˈrin-j(ē-)əl, ˌlar-ən-ˈjē-əl\ *adj* **1** : of, relating to, or used on the larynx **2** : produced by or with constriction of the larynx ⟨~ articulation of sounds⟩ — **la·ryn·geal·ly** \-ē\ *adv*

2laryngeal *n* **1 :** a laryngeal part **2 a :** a laryngeal sound **b :** any of a set of several (as three) phonemes reconstructed for Proto-Indo-European chiefly on indirect evidence

lar·yn·git·ic \\,lar-ən-'jit-ik\\ *adj* **:** of, relating to, or characteristic of laryngitis; *also* **:** affected with laryngitis — **laryngitic** *n*

lar·yn·gi·tis \\,lar-ən-'jīt-əs\\ *n* [NL] **:** inflammation of the larynx

lar·yn·gol·o·gy \\,lar-ən-'gäl-ə-jē\\ *n* [ISV] **:** a branch of medicine dealing with diseases of the larynx and nasopharynx

la·ryn·go·scope \\lə-'riŋ-gə-,skōp\\ *n* [ISV] **:** an instrument for examining the interior of the larynx — **la·ryn·go·scop·ic** \\lə-,riŋ-gə-'skäp-ik\\ *or* **la·ryn·go·scop·i·cal** \\-i-kəl\\ *adj* — **la·ryn·go·scop·i·cal·ly** \\-k(ə-)lē\\ *adv* — **lar·yn·gos·co·py** \\,lar-ən-'gäs-kə-pē\\ *n*

lar·ynx \\'lar-iŋ(k)s\\ *n, pl* **la·ryn·ges** \\lə-'rin-(,)jēz\\ *or* **lar·ynx·es** [NL *laryng-, larynx*, fr. Gk] **:** the modified upper part of the trachea of air-breathing vertebrates having in man, most other mammals, and a few lower forms a set of elastic vocal cords

las·car \\'las-kər\\ *n* [Hindi *lashkar* army] **:** an East Indian sailor, army servant, or native artilleryman

las·civ·i·ous \\lə-'siv-ē-əs\\ *adj* [L *lascivia* wantonness, fr. *lascivus* wanton — more at LUST] **:** LEWD, LUSTFUL — **las·civ·i·ous·ly** *adv* — **las·civ·i·ous·ness** *n*

la·ser \\'lā-zər\\ *n* [*l*ight *a*mplification by *s*timulated *e*mission of *r*adiation] **:** a device that utilizes the natural oscillations of atoms for amplifying or generating electromagnetic waves in the visible region of the spectrum

1lash \\'lash\\ *vb* [ME *lashen*] *vi* **1 :** to move violently or suddenly **:** DASH **2 :** to strike with or as if with a whip **3 :** to make a verbal attack or retort ~ *vt* **1 a :** WHIP, SCOURGE **b :** BEAT, FLAIL **2 a :** to assail with stinging words **b :** DRIVE, GOAD **c :** to cause to lash — **lash·er** *n*

2lash *n* **1 a** (1) **:** a stroke with a whip or with anything slender, pliant, and tough (2) **:** the flexible part of a whip; *also* **:** WHIP **b :** a sudden swinging blow **2 :** a verbal blow; *also* **:** SPUR **3 :** EYELASH

3lash *vt* [ME *lasschen* to lace, fr. MF *lacier* — more at LACE] **:** to bind with a rope, cord, or chain — **lash·er** *n*

lash·ing *n* **:** something used for binding, wrapping, or fastening

lash·ings \\'lash-iŋz, -ənz\\ *n pl* [fr. gerund of 1*lash*] *Brit* **:** a great plenty **:** ABUNDANCE

lash–up \\'lash-,əp\\ *n* [3*lash*] **1 :** something improvised **:** CONTRIVANCE **2 :** SETUP, LAYOUT

lass \\'las\\ *n* [ME *las*] **1 :** young woman **:** GIRL **2 :** SWEETHEART

lass·ie \\'las-ē\\ *n* **:** LASS, GIRL

las·si·tude \\'las-ə-,t(y)üd\\ *n* [MF, fr. L *lassitudo*, fr. *lassus* weary — more at LET] **1 :** WEARINESS, FATIGUE **2 :** LISTLESSNESS, LANGUOR **syn** see LETHARGY

1las·so \\'las-(,)ō, la-'sü\\ *n, pl* **lassos** *or* **lassoes** [Sp *lazo*, fr. L *laqueus* snare — more at DELIGHT] **:** a rope or long thong of leather with a running noose that is used esp. for catching horses and cattle **:** LARIAT

2lasso *vt* **:** to catch with or as if with a lasso **:** ROPE — **las·so·er** *n*

1last \\'last\\ *vb* [ME *lasten*, fr. OE *lǣstan* to last, follow; akin to OE *lāst* footprint] *vi* **1 :** to continue in time **:** go on **2 a :** to remain fresh or unimpaired **:** ENDURE **b :** to manage to continue (as in a course of action) ~ *vt* **:** SURVIVE, ENDURE **syn** see CONTINUE — **last·er** *n*

2last *adj* [ME, fr. OE *latost*, superl. of *læt* late] **1 a :** following all the rest ⟨~ one out⟩ **b :** being the only remaining ⟨his ~ dollar⟩ **2 a :** belonging to the final stage (as of life) **b :** administered to the dying ⟨~ sacraments⟩ **3 :** next before the present **:** LATEST **4 a :** lowest in rank or standing; *also* **:** WORST **b :** farthest from a specified quality, attitude, or likelihood ⟨he'd be the ~ to fall for flattery⟩ **5 a :** CONCLUSIVE, ULTIMATE **b :** highest in degree **:** SUPREME **c :** SINGLE — used as an intensive — **last·ly** *adv*

syn FINAL, TERMINAL, EVENTUAL, ULTIMATE: LAST applies to something that comes at the end of a series but does not always imply that the series is completed or stopped ⟨*last* page of a book⟩ ⟨*last* news we had of him⟩ FINAL applies to that which definitely closes a series, process, or progress ⟨*final* day of school⟩ TERMINAL may indicate a limit of extension, growth, or development ⟨*terminal* phase of a disease⟩ EVENTUAL applies to something that is bound to follow sooner or later as the final effect of causes already operating ⟨*eventual* defeat of the enemy⟩ ULTIMATE implies either the last element or stage of a long process or a stage beyond which further progress or change is impossible ⟨*ultimate* collapse of civilization⟩

3last *adv* **1 :** at the end **2 :** most lately **3 :** in conclusion

4last *n* **:** something that is last **:** END

5last *n* [ME, unit of weight, fr. OE *hlæst* load, akin to OHG *hlast* load, OE *hladan* to lade] **:** any of several greatly varying units of weight, capacity, or quantity

6last *n* [ME, fr. OE *lǣste*, fr. *lāst* footprint; akin to OHG *leist* shoemaker's last, L *lira* furrow — more at LEARN] **:** a wooden or metal form which is shaped like the human foot and over which a shoe is shaped or repaired

7last *vb* **:** to shape with a last — **last·er** *n*

Las·tex \\'las-,teks\\ *trademark* — used for an elastic yarn consisting of a core of latex thread wound with threads of cotton, rayon, nylon, or silk

1last·ing *adj* **:** existing or continuing a long while **:** ENDURING — **last·ing·ly** \\'las-tiŋ-lē\\ *adv* — **last·ing·ness** *n*

syn LASTING, PERMANENT, DURABLE, STABLE mean enduring for so long as to seem fixed or established. LASTING implies a capacity often surprising or unexpected to continue indefinitely ⟨*lasting* stain⟩ PERMANENT adds usu. the implication of being designed or planned to stand or continue indefinitely ⟨*permanent* arrangement⟩ DURABLE implies power to resist destructive agencies; STABLE implies lastingness because of resistance to being overturned or displaced

2lasting *n* **1** *archaic* **:** long life **2** [1*lasting*] **:** a sturdy cotton or worsted cloth used esp. in shoes and luggage

Last Supper *n* **:** the supper of Christ and his disciples on the night of his betrayal

last word *n* **1 :** the final remark in a verbal exchange **2 a :** the power of final decision **b :** a definitive statement or treatment **3 :** the most advanced, up-to-date, or fashionable exemplar of its kind

lat \\'lät, 'lat\\ *n, pl* **lats** *or* **lati** \\-ē\\ [Latvian *lats*] **1 :** the basic unit of monetary value of Latvia from 1922 to 1940 **2 :** a coin representing one lat

lat·a·kia \\,lat-ə-'kē-ə\\ *n* [*Latakia*, seaport in Syria] **:** a superior aromatic Turkish smoking tobacco

1latch \\'lach\\ *vi* [ME *lachen*, fr. OE *læccan;* akin to Gk *lambanein* to take, seize] **1 :** to catch or get hold — used with *on* or *onto* **2 :** to attach oneself ⟨~*ed* onto a rich widow⟩

2latch *n* **:** a device that holds something in place by entering a notch or cavity; *specif* **:** the catch which holds a door or gate when closed even if not bolted

3latch *vb* **:** CATCH, FASTEN

latch·et \\'lach-ət\\ *n* [ME *lachet*, fr. MF, shoestring, fr. *laz* snare, fr. L *laqueus* — more at DELIGHT] **:** a narrow leather strap, thong, or lace that fastens a shoe or sandal on the foot

latch·key \\'lach-,kē\\ *n* **1 :** a key used to lift or pull back a latch of a door **2 :** a front door key

latch·string \\-,(s)triŋ\\ *n* **:** a string on a latch that may be left hanging outside the door to permit the raising of the latch from the outside or drawn inside to prevent intrusion

1late \\'lāt\\ *adj* [ME, late, slow, fr. OE *læt;* akin to OHG *laz* slow, OE *lǣtan* to let] **1 a** (1) **:** coming or remaining after the due, usual, or proper time ⟨~ spring⟩ (2) **:** of, relating to, or imposed because of tardiness **b :** of or relating to an advanced stage in point of time or development ⟨~ Middle Ages⟩; *specif* **:** far advanced toward the close of the day or night ⟨~ hours⟩ **2 a :** living comparatively recently **b :** being something or holding some position or relationship recently but not now ⟨~ belligerents⟩ **c :** made, appearing, or happening just previous to the present time ⟨~ quarrel⟩ **syn** see DEAD — **late·ly** *adv* — **late·ness** *n*

2late *adv* **1 a :** after the usual or proper time **b :** at or to an advanced point in time **2 :** not long ago **:** RECENTLY — **of late :** LATELY, RECENTLY

lat·ed \\'lāt-əd\\ *adj* **:** BELATED

1la·teen \\lə-'tēn\\ *adj* [F (*voile*) *latine* lateen sail] **:** being or relating to a rig used esp. on the north coast of Africa and characterized by a triangular sail extended by a long spar slung to a low mast

2lateen *n* **1** *also* **la·teen·er** \\-'tē-nər\\ **:** a lateen-rigged ship **2 :** a lateen sail

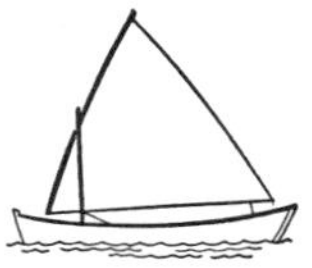

lateen 2

Late Greek *n* **:** the Greek language as used in the 3d to 6th centuries

Late Latin *n* **:** the Latin language used by writers in the 3d to 6th centuries

lat·en \\'lāt-ᵊn\\ *vb* **lat·en·ing** \\'lāt-niŋ, -ᵊn-iŋ\\ *vi* **:** to grow late ~ *vt* **:** to cause to grow late

la·ten·cy \\'lāt-ᵊn-sē\\ *n* **1 :** the quality or state of being latent **:** DORMANCY **2 :** something latent

La Tène \\lä-'ten, -'tān\\ *adj* [*Latène*, shallows of the Lake of Neuchâtel, Switzerland] **:** of or relating to the later period of the Iron Age in Europe assumed to date from 500 B.C. to A.D. 1

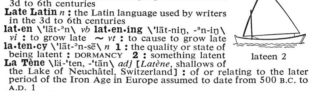

la·ten·si·fi·ca·tion \\lə-,ten(t)-sə-fə-'kā-shən, lə-\\ *n* [blend of 1*latent* and *intensification*] **:** intensification of a latent photographic image by chemical treatment or exposure to light of low intensity — **la·ten·si·fy** \\-'ten(t)-sə-,fī\\ *vt*

1la·tent \\'lāt-ᵊnt\\ *adj* [L *latent-, latens*, fr. prp. of *latēre* to lie hidden; akin to OHG *luog* den, Gk *lanthanein* to escape notice] **:** present but not visible or active ⟨~ fingerprint⟩ ⟨~ infection⟩ — **la·tent·ly** \\-ᵊn-tlē\\ *adv*

syn LATENT, DORMANT, QUIESCENT, POTENTIAL, ABEYANT mean not now showing its presence or existence. LATENT applies to a power or quality that has not yet come into sight or into action but may at any time; DORMANT suggests the inactivity of something (as a feeling, a power) as though sleeping; QUIESCENT suggests a usu. temporary cessation of activity; POTENTIAL applies to what does not yet have being or effect but is likely soon to have; ABEYANT applies to what is for the time being held off or suppressed

2latent *n* **:** a latent fingerprint

latent period *n* **1 :** the incubation period of a disease **2 :** the interval between stimulation and response

-l·a·ter \\l-ət-ər\\ *n comb form* [ME *-latrer*, fr. MF *-latre*, fr. LL *-latres*, fr. Gk *-latrēs;* akin to Gk *latron* pay — more at LARCENY] **:** worshiper ⟨icono*later*⟩

lat·er·ad \\'lat-ə-,rad\\ *adv* [L *later-, latus*] **:** toward the side

1lat·er·al \\'lat-ə-rəl, 'la-trəl\\ *adj* [L *lateralis*, fr. *later-, latus* side] **:** of or relating to the side **:** situated on, directed toward, or coming from the side — **lat·er·al·ly** \\-ē\\ *adv*

2lateral *n* **1 :** a side ditch or conduit (as in a water system) **2 :** a mining drift to one side of and parallel to a main drift

lateral pass *n* **:** a pass in football thrown parallel to the line of scrimmage or in a direction away from the opponent's goal

lat·er·ite \\'lat-ə-,rīt\\ *n* [L *later* brick] **:** a residual product of rock decay that is red in color and has a high content in the oxides of iron and hydroxide of aluminum

lat·er·i·za·tion \\,lat-ə-rə-'zā-shən\\ *n* **:** the process of conversion of rock to laterite

la·tex \\'lā-,teks\\ *n, pl* **lat·i·ces** \\'lat-ə-,sēz\\ *or* **la·tex·es** *often attrib* [NL *latic-, latex*, fr. L, fluid] **1 :** a milky usu. white fluid produced by cells of seed plants esp. of the milkweed family that yields rubber, gutta-percha, chicle, and balata as its chief commercial products **2 :** a water emulsion of a synthetic rubber or plastic obtained by polymerization and used esp. in coatings (as paint) and adhesives — **lat·i·cif·er·ous** \\,lat-ə-'sif-(ə-)rəs\\ *adj*

1lath \\'lath *also* 'la<u>th</u>\\ *n, pl* **laths** *or* **lath** [ME, fr. OE *lætt;* akin to OHG *latta* lath, W *llath* yard] **1 :** a thin narrow strip of wood nailed to rafters, joists, or studding as a groundwork for slates, tiles, or plaster **2 :** a building material in sheets used as a base for plaster **3 :** a quantity of laths

2lath *vt* **:** to cover or line with laths

1lathe \\'lā<u>th</u>\\ *n* [prob. fr. ME *lath* supporting stand] **:** a machine in which work is rotated about a horizontal axis and shaped by a fixed tool

2lathe *vt* **:** to cut or shape with a lathe

1lath·er \\'la<u>th</u>-ər\\ *n* [(assumed) ME, fr. OE *lēathor;* akin to OE *lēag* lye — more at LYE] **1 a :** a foam or froth formed when soap or some other detergent is agitated in water **b :** foam or froth from profuse sweating (as on a horse) **2 :** an agitated or overwrought state **:** DITHER — **lath·ery** \\'la<u>th</u>-(ə-)rē\\ *adj*

2lather *vb* **lath·er·ing** \\-(ə-)riŋ\\ *vt* **1 :** to spread lather over **2 :** to beat severely **:** FLOG ~ *vi* **:** to form a lather or a froth like lather — **lath·er·er** \\'la<u>th</u>-ər-ər\\ *n*

lath·ing *n* **1 :** the action or process of placing laths **2 :** a quantity or an installation of laths

lati·fun·di·um \ˌlat-ə-ˈfən-dē-əm\ *n, pl* **lati·fun·dia** \-dē-ə\ [L, fr. *latus* side + *fundus* piece of landed property — more at BOTTOM] **:** a great landed estate with primitive agriculture and often servile labor

lat·i·me·ria \ˌlat-ə-ˈmir-ē-ə\ *n* [NL, genus name, fr. Marjorie E. D. Courtenay-*Latimer* *b*1907 So. African museum director] **:** any of a genus (*Latimeria*) of living coelacanth fishes of deep seas off southern Africa

¹**Lat·in** \ˈlat-ᵊn\ *adj* [ME, fr. OE, fr. L *Latinus*, fr. *Latium*, ancient country of Italy] **1 :** of or relating to Latium or the Latins **2 a :** of, relating to, or composed in Latin **b :** ROMANCE **3 :** of or relating to the part of the Catholic Church that uses a Latin rite and forms the patriarchate of the pope **4 :** of or relating to the peoples or countries using Romance languages; *specif* **:** of or relating to the peoples or countries of Latin America

²**Latin** *n* **1 :** the Italic language of ancient Latium and of Rome and until modern times the dominant language of school, church, and state in western Europe **2 :** a member of the people of ancient Latium **3 :** a Catholic of the Latin rite **4 :** a member of one of the Latin peoples; *specif* **:** a native or inhabitant of Latin America **5 :** the Latin alphabet

Lat·in·ate \ˈlat-ᵊn-ˌāt\ *adj* **:** of, relating to, resembling, or derived from Latin

Latin cross *n* — see CROSS illustration

La·tin·i·an \la-ˈtin-ē-ən, lə-\ *n* **:** a division of the Italic languages that includes Latin

Lat·in·ism \ˈlat-ᵊn-ˌiz-əm\ *n* **1 :** a word, idiom, or mode of speech derived from or imitative of Latin **2 :** Latin quality, character, or mode of thought

Lat·in·ist \ˈlat-ᵊn-əst, ˈlat-nəst\ *n* **:** a specialist in the Latin language or Roman culture

la·tin·i·ty \la-ˈtin-ət-ē, lə-\ *n, often cap* **1 :** a manner of speaking or writing Latin **2 :** LATINISM

lat·in·iza·tion \ˌlat-ᵊn-ə-ˈzā-shən, ˌlat-nə-\ *n* **:** the act or result of latinizing

lat·in·ize \ˈlat-ᵊn-ˌīz\ *vt, often cap* **1 a** *obs* **:** to translate into Latin **b :** to give a Latin form to **c :** to introduce Latinisms into **d :** ROMANIZE 2 **2 :** to make Latin or Italian in doctrine, ideas, or traits; *specif* **:** to cause to resemble the Roman Catholic Church ~ *vi, often cap* **1 :** to use Latinisms **2 :** to exhibit the influence of the Romans or of the Roman Catholic Church

Latin Quarter *n* [F *Quartier Latin*] **:** a section of Paris south of the Seine frequented by students and artists

Latin square *n* **:** a square array in which the number of elements is the same as the number of columns and no element occurs twice in the same column or row and which is used for statistical investigations esp. in agriculture

lat·ish \ˈlāt-ish\ *adj (or adv)* **:** somewhat late

lat·i·tude \ˈlat-ə-ˌt(y)üd\ *n* [ME, fr. L *latitudin-*, *latitudo*, fr. *latus* wide; akin to Arm *lain* wide] **1** *archaic* **:** extent or distance from side to side **:** WIDTH **2 :** angular distance from some specified circle or plane of reference: as **a :** angular distance north or south from the earth's equator measured through 90 degrees **b :** angular distance of a celestial body from the ecliptic **c :** a region or locality as marked by its latitude **2 a** *archaic* **:** SCOPE, RANGE **b :** the range of exposures within which a film or plate will produce a negative or positive of satisfactory quality **3 :** freedom of action or choice — **lat·i·tu·di·nal** \ˌlat-ə-ˈt(y)üd-nəl, -ᵊn-əl\ *adj* — **lat·i·tu·di·nal·ly** \-ē\ *adv*

lat·i·tu·di·nar·i·an \ˌlat-ə-ˌt(y)üd-ᵊn-ˈer-ē-ən\ *n* **:** a person who is broad and liberal in his standards of religious belief and conduct — **latitudinarian** *adj* — **lat·i·tu·di·nar·i·an·ism** \-ē-ə-ˌniz-əm\ *n*

la·trine \lə-ˈtrēn\ *n* [F, fr. L *latrina*, contr. of *lavatrina*, fr. *lavere* to wash — more at LYE] **1 :** a receptacle (as a pit in the earth) for use as a toilet **2 :** TOILET

-la·try \l-ə-trē\ *n comb form* [ME *-latrie*, fr. OF, fr. LL *-latria*, fr. Gk, fr. *latreia*] **:** worship ⟨helio*latry*⟩

lat·ten *or* **lat·tin** \ˈlat-ᵊn\ *n* [ME *laton*, fr. MF] **1 :** an alloy of or resembling brass hammered into thin sheets formerly much used for church utensils **2 a :** iron plate covered with tin **b :** metal (as tin) in thin sheets

lat·ter \ˈlat-ər\ *adj* [ME, fr. OE *lætra*, compar. of *læt* late] **1 a :** more recent **:** LATER **b :** of or relating to the end **:** FINAL **c :** RECENT, PRESENT **2 :** of, relating to, or being the second of two things referred to — **lat·ter·ly** *adv*

lat·ter-day \ˌlat-ər-ˌdā\ *adj* **1 :** of a later or subsequent time **2 :** of present or recent times

Latter-Day Saint *n* **:** a member of a religious body tracing its origin to Joseph Smith in 1830 and accepting the Book of Mormon as divine revelation **:** MORMON

lat·tice \ˈlat-əs\ *n, often attrib* [ME *latis*, fr. MF *lattis*] **1 a :** a framework or structure of crossed wood or metal strips **b :** a window, door, or gate having a lattice **c** *obs* **:** a lattice used as the sign of an alehouse **2 :** a regular geometrical arrangement of points or objects over an area or in space: as **a :** SPACE LATTICE **b :** a geometrical arrangement of fissionable material in a nuclear reactor **c :** a mathematical set that has some elements ordered and that is such that for any two elements there exists a least element greater than both and a greatest element less than both — **lattice** *vt* — **lat·ticed** \-əst\ *adj*

lattice girder *n* **:** a girder with top and bottom flanges connected by a latticework web

lat·tice·work \ˈlat-ə-ˌswərk\ *n* **:** a lattice or work made of lattices

Lat·vi·an \ˈlat-vē-ən\ *n* **1 :** a native or inhabitant of Latvia **2 :** the Baltic language of the Latvian people — **Latvian** *adj*

¹**laud** \ˈlȯd\ *n* [ME *laudes*, pl., fr. MF or ML; MF, fr. ML, fr. L, pl. of *laud-*, *laus* praise; akin to OHG *liod* song] **1** *pl but sing or pl in constr, often cap* **:** an office of solemn praise to God forming with matins the first of the canonical hours **2 :** ACCLAIM, PRAISE

²**laud** *vt* **:** PRAISE, EXTOL

laud·abil·i·ty \ˌlȯd-ə-ˈbil-ət-ē\ *n* **:** the quality or state of being laudable

laud·able \ˈlȯd-ə-bəl\ *adj* **:** worthy of praise **:** COMMENDABLE — **laud·able·ness** *n* — **laud·ably** \-blē\ *adv*

lau·da·num \ˈlȯd-nəm, -ᵊn-əm\ *n* [NL] **1 :** any of various formerly used preparations of opium **2 :** a tincture of opium

lau·da·tion \lȯ-ˈdā-shən\ *n* **:** the act of praising **:** EULOGY

lau·da·tive \ˈlȯd-ət-iv\ *adj* **:** LAUDATORY

lau·da·to·ry \ˈlȯd-ə-ˌtōr-ē, -ˌtȯr-\ *adj* **:** of, relating to, or expressing praise

¹**laugh** \ˈlaf, ˈlȧf\ *vb* [ME *laughen*, fr. OE *hliehhan*; akin to OHG *lachēn* to laugh, OE *hlōwan* to moo — more at LOW] *vi* **1 a :** to show mirth, joy, or scorn with a smile and chuckle or explosive sound **b :** to find amusement or pleasure in something **c :** to become amused or derisive **2 a :** to produce the sound or appearance of laughter **b :** to be of a kind that inspires joy ~ *vt* **1 :** to influence or move by laughter **2 :** to utter with a laugh ⟨~*s* her consent⟩ — **laugh·er** *n* — **laugh·ing·ly** \-iŋ-lē\ *adv*

²**laugh** *n* **1 :** the act of laughing **2 a :** a cause for derision or merriment **:** JOKE **b :** an expression of scorn or mockery **:** JEER **3** *pl* **:** DIVERSION, SPORT

laugh·able \ˈlaf-ə-bəl, ˈlȧf-\ *adj* **:** fitted to provoke laughter or derision **:** RIDICULOUS — **laugh·able·ness** *n* — **laugh·ably** \-blē\ *adv*

syn LAUGHABLE, LUDICROUS, RIDICULOUS, COMIC, COMICAL, DROLL, FUNNY mean provoking laughter or mirth. LAUGHABLE applies to anything occasioning laughter intentionally or unintentionally; LUDICROUS suggests absurdity or preposterousness that excites both laughter and scorn or sometimes pity; RIDICULOUS suggests extreme absurdity, foolishness, or contemptibility; COMIC applies esp. to that which arouses thoughtful amusement; COMICAL applies to that which arouses unrestrained spontaneous hilarity; DROLL suggests laughable qualities arising from oddness or quaintness or from deliberate waggishness; FUNNY is a usual equivalent of DROLL or of COMICAL

laughing gas *n* **:** NITROUS OXIDE

laughing jackass *n* **:** KOOKABURRA

laugh·ing·stock \ˈlaf-iŋ-ˌstäk, ˈlȧf-\ *n* **:** an object of ridicule **:** BUTT

laugh·ter \ˈlaf-tər, ˈlȧf-\ *n* [ME, fr. OE *hleahtor*; akin to OE *hliehhan*] **1 :** a sound of or as if of laughing **2** *archaic* **:** a cause of merriment

launce \ˈlȯn(t)s, ˈlän(t)s\ *n* [prob. fr. ¹*lance*] **:** SAND LAUNCE

¹**launch** \ˈlȯnch, ˈlänch\ *vb* [ME *launchen*, fr. ONF *lancher*, fr. LL *lanceare* to wield a lance — more at LANCE] *vt* **1 a :** to throw forward **:** HURL **b :** to release, catapult, or send off (a self-propelled object) ⟨~ a rocket⟩ **c :** COMMENCE **2 a :** to set (a boat or ship) afloat **b :** to give (a person) a start **c** (1) **:** to originate or set in motion **:** INITIATE (2) **:** to get off to a good start ~ *vi* **1 a :** to spring forward or take off **b :** to throw oneself energetically **:** PLUNGE **2 a** *archaic* **:** to slide down the ways **b :** to make a start

²**launch** *n* **:** an act or instance of launching

³**launch** *n* [Sp or Pg; Sp *lancha*, fr. Pg] **1** *archaic* **:** a large ship's boat **2 :** a small open or half-decked motorboat

launch·er \ˈlȯn-chər, ˈlän-\ *n* **:** one that launches: as **a :** a device for firing a grenade from a rifle **b :** a device for launching a rocket or rocket shell **c :** CATAPULT

launching pad *n* **:** a nonflammable platform from which a rocket or guided missile can be launched

¹**laun·der** \ˈlȯn-dər, ˈlän-\ *n* [ME, launderer, fr. MF *lavandier*, fr. ML *lavandarius*, fr. L *lavandus*, gerundive of *lavare* to wash — more at LYE] **:** TROUGH; *specif* **:** a box conduit conveying middlings or tailings suspended in water in ore dressing

²**launder** *vb* **laun·der·ing** \-d(ə-)riŋ\ [ME *launder*, n.,] *vt* **1 :** to wash (as clothes) in water **2 :** to iron after washing ⟨a freshly ~*ed* shirt⟩ ~ *vi* **1 :** to wash or wash and iron clothing or household linens **2 :** to withstand washing and ironing — **laun·der·er** \-dər-ər, -drər\ *n* — **laun·dress** \-drəs\ *n*

laun·der·ette \ˌlȯn-də-ˈret, ˌlän-\ *n* [fr. *Launderette*, a service mark] **:** a self-service laundry

Laun·dro·mat \ˈlȯn-drə-ˌmat, ˈlän-\ *trademark* — used for an electric washing machine

laun·dry \ˈlȯn-drē, ˈlän-\ *n, often attrib* **1 :** clothes or linens that have been or are to be laundered **2 a :** a room for doing the family wash **b :** a commercial laundering establishment

laun·dry·man \-mən\ *n* **:** a male laundry worker — **laun·dry·wom·an** \-ˌwu̇m-ən\ *n*

lau·ra \ˈläv-rə\ *n* [LGk, fr. Gk, lane] **:** a monastery of the Eastern Church

¹**lau·re·ate** \ˈlȯr-ē-ət, ˈlär-\ *n* [L *laureatus* crowned with laurel, fr. *laurea* laurel wreath, fr. fem. of *laureus* of laurel, fr. *laurus*] **:** the recipient of honor for achievement in an art or science; *specif* **:** POET LAUREATE — **laureate** *adj* — **lau·re·ate·ship** \-ˌship\ *n*

²**lau·re·ate** \-ē-ˌāt\ *vt* **1 :** to crown with or as if with a laurel wreath for excellence or achievement **2 :** to appoint to the office of poet laureate — **lau·re·a·tion** \ˌlȯr-ē-ˈā-shən, ˌlär-\ *n*

¹**lau·rel** \ˈlȯr-əl, ˈlär-\ *n* [ME *lorel*, fr. OF *lorier*, fr. *lor* laurel, fr. L *laurus*] **1 :** any of a genus (*Laurus*) of trees or shrubs of a family (Lauraceae, the laurel family) including also the sassafras and cinnamon; *specif* **:** a tree (*L. nobilis*) of southern Europe with foliage used by the ancient Greeks to crown victors in the Pythian games **2 :** a tree or shrub (as a mountain laurel or cherry laurel) like the true laurel **3 :** a crown of laurel **:** HONOR — usu. used in pl.

²**laurel** *vt* **lau·reled** *or* **lau·relled**; **lau·rel·ing** *or* **lau·rel·ling :** to deck or crown with laurel

lau·ric acid \ˌlȯr-ik-, ˌlär-\ *n* [ISV, fr. L *laurus*] **:** a crystalline fatty acid $C_{12}H_{24}O_4$ found esp. in coconut oil and used in making soaps, esters, and lauryl alcohol

lau·ryl alcohol \ˌlȯr-əl-, ˌlär-\ *n* **:** a compound $C_{12}H_{26}O$; *also* **:** a liquid mixture of this and other alcohols used esp. in making anionic detergents

la·va \ˈläv-ə, ˈlav-\ *n* [It, fr. L *labes* fall; akin to L *labi* to slide — more at SLEEP] **:** fluid rock that issues from a volcano or from a fissure in the earth's surface; *also* **:** such rock solidified

la·va·bo \lə-ˈväb-(ˌ)ō\ *n* [L, I shall wash, fr. *lavare*] **1** *often cap* **:** a ceremony at Mass in which the celebrant washes his hands after offering the oblations and says Psalm 25:6–12 **2 a :** a washbasin and a tank with a spigot that are fastened to a wall **b :** this combination used as a planter

la·vage \lə-ˈväzh\ *n* [F, fr. MF, fr. *laver* to wash, fr. L *lavare*] **:** WASHING; *esp* **:** the therapeutic washing out of an organ

la·va·la·va \ˌläv-ə-ˈläv-ə\ *n* [Samoan, clothing] **:** a rectangular

cloth of cotton print worn like a kilt or skirt in Polynesia and esp. in Samoa

la·va·liere *or* **la·val·liere** \ˌläv-ə-ˈli(ə)r, ˌlav-\ *n* [F *lavallière* necktie with a large bow] **:** a pendant on a fine chain that is worn as a necklace

la·va·tion \lā-ˈvā-shən\ *n* [L *lavation-, lavatio,* fr. *lavatus*] **:** WASHING, CLEANSING — **la·va·tion·al** \-shnəl, -shən-ᵊl\ *adj*

lav·a·to·ry \ˈlav-ə-ˌtōr-ē, -ˌtȯr-\ *n* [ME *lavatorie,* fr. ML *lavatorium,* fr. L *lavatus,* pp. of *lavare* to wash — more at LYE] **1 :** a basin or other vessel for washing: as **a :** PISCINA **b :** a fixed bowl or basin with running water and drainpipe for washing **2 :** a room with conveniences for washing and usu. with one or more toilets **3 :** WATER CLOSET — **lavatory** *adj*

1lave \ˈlāv\ *n* [ME (northern dial.), fr. OE *lāf;* akin to OE *belīfan* to remain — more at LEAVE] *chiefly dial* **:** something that is left **:** RESIDUE

2lave *vb* [ME *laven,* fr. OE *lafian;* akin to OHG *labōn* to wash; both fr. a prehistoric WGmc word borrowed fr. L *lavare*] *vt* **1 a :** WASH, BATHE **b :** to flow along or against **2 :** POUR **3** *obs* **:** to dip or scoop up or out **:** BAIL ~ *vi, archaic* **:** to wash oneself **:** BATHE

la·veer \lə-ˈvi(ə)r\ *vi* [D *laveren*] **:** to beat against the wind in sailing **:** TACK

1lav·en·der \ˈlav-ən-dər\ *n* [ME *lavendre,* fr. AF, fr. ML *lavandula*] **1 a :** a Mediterranean mint (*Lavandula officinalis*) widely cultivated for its narrow aromatic leaves and spikes of lilac-purple flowers which are dried and used in sachets **b :** any of several other plants (genus *Lavandula*) used similarly to true lavender but often considered inferior **2 :** a variable color averaging a pale purple

2lavender *vt* **lav·en·der·ing** \-d(ə-)riŋ\ **:** to sprinkle or perfume with lavender

1la·ver \ˈlā-vər\ *n* [ME *lavour,* fr. MF *lavoir*] **1** *archaic* **:** a vessel, trough, or cistern for washing **2 :** a large basin used for ceremonial ablutions in ancient Judaism

2laver *n* [NL, fr. L, a water plant] **:** any of several mostly edible seaweeds; *specif* **:** SEA LETTUCE

lav·er·ock *or* **lav·rock** \ˈlav-(ə-)rək\ *n* [ME *laverok,* fr. OE *lāwerce*] *chiefly Scot* **:** LARK

1lav·ish \ˈlav-ish\ *adj* [ME *lavas* abundance, fr. MF *lavasse* downpour of rain, fr. *laver* to wash — more at LAVAGE] **1 :** expending or bestowing profusely **:** PRODIGAL **2 :** expended or produced in abundance **syn** see PROFUSE — **lav·ish·ly** *adj* — **lav·ish·ness** *n*

2lavish *vt* **:** to expend or bestow with profusion **:** SQUANDER

1law \ˈlȯ\ *n, often attrib* [ME, fr. OE *lagu,* of Scand origin; akin to ON *lög* law; akin to OE *licgan* to lie — more at LIE] **1 a (1) :** a binding custom or practice of a community **:** a rule of conduct or action prescribed or formally recognized as binding or enforced by a controlling authority **(2) :** the whole body of such customs, practices, or rules **(3) :** COMMON LAW **b (1) :** the control brought about by the existence or enforcement of such law **(2) :** the action of laws considered as a means of redressing wrongs; *also* **:** LITIGATION **(3) :** the agency of or an agent of established law **c :** a rule or order that it is advisable or obligatory to observe **d :** something compatible with or enforceable by established law **e :** CONTROL, AUTHORITY **2 a** *often cap* **:** the revelation of the will of God set forth in the Old Testament **b** *cap* **:** the first part of the Jewish scriptures **:** PENTATEUCH — compare HAGIOGRAPHA, PROPHETS **3 :** a rule of construction or procedure **4 :** the whole body of laws relating to one subject **5 a :** the legal profession **b :** law as a department of knowledge **:** JURISPRUDENCE **c :** legal knowledge **6** *obs* **:** MERCY, INDULGENCE **7 a :** a statement of an order or relation of phenomena that so far as is known is invariable under the given conditions **b :** a relation proved or assumed to hold between mathematical or logical expressions **c :** the observed regularity of nature

syn LAW, RULE, REGULATION, PRECEPT, STATUTE, ORDINANCE, CANON mean a principle governing action or procedure. LAW implies imposition by a sovereign authority and the obligation of obedience on the part of all subject to that authority; RULE applies to more restricted or specific situations, may include self-imposed principles of action, and implies much less inexorability; REGULATION often equals RULE but carries a stronger implication of prescription by authority in order to control an organization or system; PRECEPT commonly suggests something advisory and not obligatory communicated typically through teaching; STATUTE implies a law enacted by a legislative body; ORDINANCE applies to an order governing some detail of procedure or conduct enforced by a limited authority such as a municipality; CANON suggests in nonreligious use a principle or rule of behavior or procedure commonly accepted as a valid guide **syn** see in addition HYPOTHESIS

2law *vi* **:** to go to law ~ *vt, chiefly dial* **:** to sue or prosecute at law

law–abid·ing \ˈlȯ-ə-ˌbīd-iŋ\ *adj* **:** abiding by or obedient to the law — **law–abid·ing·ness** *n*

law·break·er \ˈlȯ-ˌbrā-kər\ *n* **:** one who violates the law

law·ful \ˈlȯ-fəl\ *adj* **1 a :** conformable to law **b :** constituted, authorized, or established by law **:** RIGHTFUL **2 :** LAW-ABIDING — **law·ful·ly** \-f(ə-)lē\ *adv* — **law·ful·ness** \-fəl-nəs\ *n*

syn LAWFUL, LEGAL, LEGITIMATE, LICIT mean being in accordance with law. LAWFUL may imply conformity with law of any sort (as divine, canon, or common); LEGAL implies reference to law as administered in the courts; LEGITIMATE implies a legal right (as applied to son, heir, successor) or one supported by tradition, custom, or accepted standards of authenticity; LICIT implies strict conformity to law specifically regulating the way something is performed or carried on

law·giv·er \ˈlȯ-ˌgiv-ər\ *n* **1 :** one who gives a code of laws to a people **2 :** LEGISLATOR

law–hand \-ˌhand\ *n* **:** a special style of handwriting used in engrossing old legal documents in England

law·less \ˈlȯ-ləs\ *adj* **1 :** not regulated by or based on law **2 :** not restrained or controlled by law **:** UNRULY; *also* **:** ILLEGAL — **law·less·ly** *adv* — **law·less·ness** *n*

law·mak·er \ˈlȯ-ˌmā-kər\ *n* **:** one that makes laws **:** LEGISLATOR — **law·mak·ing** \-kiŋ\ *n*

law merchant *n, pl* **laws merchant :** the legal rules formerly applied to cases arising in commercial transactions

1lawn \ˈlȯn, ˈlän\ *n* [ME, fr. *Laon,* France] **:** a fine sheer plain-woven linen or cotton fabric that is thinner than cambric — **lawny** \-ē\ *adj*

2lawn *n* [ME *launde,* fr. MF *lande* heath, of Celt origin; akin to OIr *land* open space — more at LAND] **1** *archaic* **:** an open space between woods **:** GLADE **2 :** ground covered with grass kept mowed around a house or in a garden or park — **lawn** *or* **lawny** \-ē\ *adj*

lawn bowling *n* **:** a bowling game played on a green with wooden balls which are rolled at a jack

lawn mower *n* **:** a machine for cutting grass on lawns

lawn tennis *n* **:** tennis played on a grass court

Law of Moses : PENTATEUCH

law of nations : INTERNATIONAL LAW

law·ren·ci·um \lȯ-ˈren(t)-sē-əm\ *n* [NL, fr. Ernest O. *Lawrence* †1958 Amer physicist] **:** a short-lived radioactive element produced from californium — see ELEMENT table

law·suit \ˈlȯ-ˌsüt\ *n* **:** a suit in law **:** a case before a court

law·yer \ˈlȯ-yər, ˈlȯi-ər\ *n* **:** one whose profession is to conduct lawsuits for clients or to advise as to legal rights and obligations in other matters

syn LAWYER, COUNSELOR, BARRISTER, COUNSEL, ATTORNEY, SOLICITOR mean one authorized to practice law. LAWYER applies to anyone in the profession; COUNSELOR applies to one who accepts court cases or gives advice on legal matters; BARRISTER is a British term corresponding to COUNSELOR but with the emphasis on pleading in open court which in English practice is permitted only to barristers; COUNSEL is equivalent to COUNSELOR or it may collectively designate a group acting for a legal cause in court; ATTORNEY is commonly nearly equivalent to LAWYER but strictly applies to one transacting legal business for a client; SOLICITOR is the British term corresponding to ATTORNEY

lax \ˈlaks\ *adj* [ME, fr. L *laxus* loose — more at SLACK] **1 a** *of the bowels* **:** LOOSE, OPEN **b :** having loose bowels **2 :** not strict or stringent **3 a :** not tense, firm, or rigid **:** SLACK **b :** having an open or loose texture **c :** having the constituents spread apart ⟨a ~ flower cluster⟩ **4** *of a speech sound* **:** produced with the muscles involved in a relatively relaxed state (as the vowels \i\ and \u̇\ in contrast with the vowels \ē\ and \ü\ **syn** see NEGLIGENT — **lax·a·tion** \lak-ˈsā-shən\ *n* — **lax·ly** *adv* — **lax·ness** *n*

1lax·a·tive \ˈlak-sət-iv\ *adj* [ME *laxatif,* fr. ML *laxativus,* fr. L *laxatus,* pp. of *laxare* to loosen, fr. *laxus*] **1 :** having a tendency to loosen or relax; *specif* **:** relieving constipation **2 :** having loose bowels **3 :** LOOSE, UNRESTRAINED ⟨a ~ tongue⟩ — **lax·a·tive·ly** *adv* — **lax·a·tive·ness** *n*

2laxative *n* **:** a usu. mild laxative drug

lax·ity \ˈlak-sət-ē\ *n* **:** the quality or state of being lax

1lay \ˈlā\ *vb* **laid** \ˈlād\ **lay·ing** [ME *leyen,* fr. OE *lecgan;* akin to OE *licgan* to lie — more at LIE] *vt* **1 :** to beat or strike down with force **2 a :** to put or set down **b :** to place for rest or sleep; *esp* **:** BURY **3 :** to bring forth and deposit (an egg) **4 :** CALM, ALLAY ⟨~ the dust⟩; **5 :** BET, WAGER **6 :** to press down smooth and even **7 a :** to dispose or spread over or on a surface ⟨~ track⟩ ⟨~ plaster⟩ **b :** to set in order or position ⟨~ a table for dinner⟩ ⟨~ brick⟩ **c :** to put (strands) in place and twist to form a rope, hawser, or cable; *also* **:** to make by so doing ⟨~ up rope⟩ **8 a :** to impose as a duty, burden, or punishment ⟨~ a tax⟩ **b :** to put as a burden of reproach ⟨*laid* the blame on him⟩ **c :** to advance as an accusation **:** IMPUTE **9 :** to place (something immaterial) on something ⟨~ stress on grammar⟩ **10 :** PREPARE, CONTRIVE ⟨a well-*laid* plan⟩ **11 a :** to put to **:** APPLY ⟨*laid* the watch to his ear⟩ **b :** to prepare or position for action or operation ⟨~ a fire⟩; *specif* **:** to adjust (a gun) to the proper direction and elevation **12 :** to bring to a specified condition ⟨~ waste the land⟩ **13 a :** ASSERT, ALLEGE ⟨~ claim to an estate⟩ **b :** to submit for examination and judgment ⟨*laid* his case before the commission⟩ ~ *vi* **1 :** to produce and deposit eggs **2** *nonstand* **:** 1LIE **3 :** WAGER, BET **4** *dial* **:** PLAN, PREPARE ⟨~ for a chance⟩ **5 a :** to apply oneself vigorously ⟨*laid* to his oars⟩ **b** *naut* **:** GO, COME ⟨~ aloft⟩ — **lay on the table 1 :** to remove (a parliamentary motion) from consideration indefinitely **2** *Brit* **:** to put (as legislation) on the agenda

2lay *n* **1 :** something (as a layer) that lies or is laid **2 :** COVERT, LAIR **3 a :** line of action **:** PLAN **b :** line of work **:** OCCUPATION **4 a :** terms of sale or employment **:** PRICE **b :** share of profit (as on a whaling voyage) paid in lieu of wages **5 a :** the amount of advance of any point in a rope strand for one turn **b :** the nature of a fiber rope as determined by the amount of twist, the angle of the strands, and the angle of the threads in the strands **6 :** the way in which a thing lies or is laid in relation to something else ⟨~ of the land⟩ **7 :** the state of one that lays eggs

3lay *past of* LIE

4lay *n* [ME, fr. OF *lai*] **1 :** a simple narrative poem **:** BALLAD **2 :** MELODY, SONG

5lay *adj* [ME, fr. OF *lai,* fr. LL *laicus,* fr. Gk *laikos* of the people, fr. *laos* people] **1 :** of or relating to the laity **:** not ecclesiastical **2 :** of or relating to members of a religious house occupied with domestic or manual work ⟨~ brother⟩ **3 :** not of or from a particular profession **:** UNPROFESSIONAL ⟨~ public⟩

lay away *vt* **:** to put aside for future use or delivery

lay by *vt* **1 :** to lay aside **:** DISCARD **2 :** to store for future use **:** SAVE **3** *South & Midland* **:** to cultivate (as corn) for the last time

lay day *n* **1 :** one of the days allowed by the charter for loading or unloading a vessel **2 :** a day of delay in port

lay down *vt* **1 :** to give up **:** SURRENDER ⟨*lay down* your arms⟩ **2 a :** ESTABLISH, PRESCRIBE ⟨*lays down* standards⟩ **b :** to assert or command dogmatically **3 :** STORE, PRESERVE

1lay·er \ˈlā-ər, ˈle(-ə)r\ *n* **1 :** one that lays (as a workman who lays brick or a hen that lays eggs) **2 a :** one thickness, course, or fold laid or lying over or under another **b :** STRATUM **c :** HORIZON 2 **3 a :** a branch or shoot of a plant treated to induce rooting while still attached to the parent plant **b :** a plant developed by layering — **lay·ered** \ˈlā-ərd, ˈle(-ə)rd\ *adj*

2layer *vt* **:** to propagate (a plant) by means of layers ~ *vi* **1 :** to separate into layers **2** *of a plant* **:** to form roots where a stem comes in contact with the ground

lay·er·age \ˈlā-ə-rij, ˈle-ə-\ *n* **:** the practice or art of layering plants

lay·ette \lā-ˈet\ *n* [F, fr. MF, dim. of *laye* box, fr. MD *lade;* akin to OE *hladan* to load — more at LADE] **:** a complete outfit of clothing and equipment for a newborn infant

lay figure \ˈlā-\ *n* [obs. E *layman* (lay figure), fr. D *leeman*] **1 :** a jointed model of the human body used by artists to show the disposition of drapery **2 :** a person likened to a dummy or puppet

lay in *vt* **:** to lay by **:** SAVE

lay·man \ˈlā-mən\ *n* **:** one of the laity; *also* **:** one not belonging to some particular profession

lay off *vt* **1 :** to mark or measure off **2 :** to cease to employ (a worker) usu. temporarily **3 a :** to let alone **b :** AVOID, QUIT ~ *vi* **:** to stop or rest from work

lay·off \'lā-,ȯf\ *n* **1 :** the act of laying off an employee or a work force; *also* **:** SHUTDOWN **2 :** a period of inactivity or idleness
lay on *vi* **:** ATTACK, BEAT
lay out *vt* **1 a :** to prepare (a corpse) for burial **b :** to knock flat or unconscious **2 :** to plan in detail ⟨*lay out* a campaign⟩ **3 :** to mark (work) for drilling, machining, or filing **4 :** ARRANGE, DESIGN **5 :** SPEND
lay·out \'lā-,au̇t\ *n* **1 a :** the act or process of laying out or planning in detail **b :** the plan or design or arrangement of something that is laid out: as (1) **:** DUMMY 6 (2) **:** final arrangement of matter to be reproduced esp. by printing (3) **:** the placing of men, machines, and materials in a manufacturing plant **2 :** something that is laid out **3 :** ESTABLISHMENT, PLACE **4 :** a set or outfit esp. of tools
lay over *vt* **:** POSTPONE
1lay·over \'lā-,ō-vər\ *n* **:** STOPOVER
2layover *n* [origin unknown] *dial* **:** something whose identity is intentionally concealed — used typically in the phrase *layovers to catch meddlers* as an evasive answer to a question from a child
lay reader *n* **:** an Anglican layman licensed to read sermons and conduct some religious services
lay to \-'tü\ *vt* **:** to bring (a ship) into the wind and hold stationary ~ *vi* **:** to lie to
lay up *vt* **1 :** to store up **:** lay by **2 :** to disable or confine with illness or injury **3 :** to take out of active service
lay–up \'lā-,əp\ *n* **:** the action of laying up or the condition of being laid up; *esp* **:** a jumping one-hand shot in basketball made off the backboard from close under the basket
lay·wom·an \'lā-,wu̇m-ən\ *n* **:** a woman who is a member of the laity
la·zar \'laz-ər, 'lā-zər\ *n* [ME, fr. ML *lazarus*, fr. LL *Lazarus*] **:** a person afflicted with a repulsive disease; *specif* **:** LEPER
laz·a·ret·to \,laz-ə-'ret-(,)ō\ *or* **laz·a·ret** \-'ret, -'rēt\ *n* [It dial. *lazareto*, alter. of *nazareto*, fr. *Santa Maria di Nazaret*, church in Venice that maintained a hospital] **1** *usu lazaretto* **:** a hospital for contagious diseases **2 :** a building or a ship used for detention in quarantine **3** *usu lazaret* **:** a space in a ship between decks used as a storeroom
Laz·a·rus \'laz-(ə-)rəs\ *n* [LL, fr. Gk *Lazaros*, fr. Heb *El'āzār*] **1 :** a brother of Mary and Martha raised by Jesus from the dead **2 :** the diseased beggar in the biblical parable of the rich man and the beggar
laze \'lāz\ *vb* [back-formation fr. *lazy*] *vi* **:** to act or lie lazily **:** IDLE ~ *vt* **:** to pass (time) in idleness or relaxation — **laze** *n*
la·zi·ly \'lā-zə-lē\ *adv* **:** in a lazy manner
la·zi·ness \-zē-nəs\ *n* **:** the quality or state of being lazy
lazuli *n* **:** LAPIS LAZULI — **la·zu·line** \'laz(h)-ə-,līn, -,lēn\ *adj*
la·zu·lite \'laz(h)-ə-,līt\ *n* [G *lazulith*, fr. ML *lazulum* lapis lazuli] **:** an often crystalline azure-blue mineral $(Mg,Fe)Al_2(PO_4)_2(OH)_2$ that is a hydrous phosphate of aluminum, iron, and magnesium — **la·zu·lit·ic** \,laz(h)-ə-'lit-ik\ *adj*
1la·zy \'lā-zē\ *adj* [perh. fr. MLG *lasich* feeble; akin to MHG *erleswen* to become weak] **1 a :** disliking activity or exertion **:** not energetic or vigorous **b :** encouraging inactivity or indolence **2 :** moving slowly **:** SLUGGISH **3 :** DROOPING, LAX **4 :** placed on its side ⟨~ E livestock brand⟩
syn LAZY, INDOLENT, SLOTHFUL mean not easily aroused to activity. LAZY suggests a disinclination to work or to take trouble; INDOLENT suggests a love of ease and a settled dislike of movement or activity; SLOTHFUL implies a temperamental inability to act promptly or speedily when action or speed is called for
2lazy *vi* **:** to move or lie lazily **:** LAZE
la·zy·bones \-,bōnz\ *n pl but sing or pl in constr* **:** a lazy person
la·zy·ish \'lā-zē-ish\ *adj* **:** somewhat lazy
lazy Su·san \,lā-zē-'süz-ᵊn\ *n* **:** a revolving tray placed on a dining table for serving food, condiments, or relishes

lazy Susan

lazy tongs *n pl* **:** a series of jointed and pivoted bars capable of great extension used orig. for picking up something at a distance
laz·za·ro·ne \,laz-ə-'rō-nē, ,läd-zə-\ *n*, *pl* **laz·za·ro·ni** \-(,)nē\ [It, aug. of *lazzaro* beggar, fr. ML *lazarus*] **:** one of the homeless idlers of Naples
lea *or* **ley** \'lē, 'lā\ *n* [ME *leye*, fr. OE *lēah;* akin to OHG *lōh* thicket, L *lucus* grove, *lux* light — more at LIGHT] **1 :** GRASSLAND, PASTURE **2** *usu ley* **:** arable land used temporarily for hay or grazing
1leach \'lēch\ *var of* LEECH
2leach *n* [prob. alter. of *letch* (muddy ditch)] **1 :** a perforated vessel to hold wood ashes through which water is passed to extract the lye **2** [3*leach*] **:** the process of leaching
3leach *vt* **1 :** to subject to the action of percolating water or other liquid in order to separate the soluble components **2 :** to dissolve out by the action of a percolating liquid ⟨~ out alkali from ashes⟩ ~ *vi* **:** to pass out or through by percolation — **leach·er** *n*
leach·abil·i·ty \,lē-chə-'bil-ət-ē\ *n* **:** the quality or state of being leachable
leach·able \'lē-chə-bəl\ *adj* **:** capable of being leached
leach·ing *n* **1 :** the process or an instance of leaching **2 :** a product of leaching
1lead \'lēd\ *vb* **led** \'led\ **lead·ing** [ME *leden*, fr. OE *lǣdan;* akin to OHG *leiten* to lead, OE *līthan* to go] *vt* **1 a :** to guide on a way esp. by going in advance **b :** to direct on a course or in a direction **c :** to serve as a channel for ⟨pipes ~ water into canals⟩ **2 :** to go through **:** LIVE ⟨~ a quiet life⟩ **3 a** (1) **:** to direct the operations, activity, or performance of ⟨~ an orchestra⟩ (2) **:** to have charge of ⟨~ a campaign⟩ **b** (1) **:** to go at the head of ⟨~ a parade⟩ (2) **:** to be first in or among ⟨~ the league⟩ (3) **:** to have a margin over ⟨*led* his opponent⟩ **4 :** to begin play with ⟨~ trumps⟩ **5 :** to aim in front of (a moving object) ⟨~ a duck⟩ **6 :** to direct (a blow) at an opponent in boxing ~ *vi* **1 a :** to guide someone or something along a way **b :** to lie, run, or open in a specified place or direction ⟨path ~*s* uphill⟩ **2 a :** to be first **b** (1) **:** BEGIN, OPEN ⟨~ off for the home team⟩ (2) **:** to play the first card **3 :** to tend toward a definite result ⟨study ~*ing* to a degree⟩ **syn** see GUIDE
2lead *n* **1 a** (1) **:** position at the front **:** VANGUARD (2) **:** INITIATIVE (3) **:** the act or privilege of leading in cards; *also* **:** the card or suit led **b** (1) **:** LEADERSHIP (2) **:** EXAMPLE, PRECEDENT **c :** a margin or measure of advantage or superiority or position in advance **2 :** one that leads: as **a** (1) **:** LODE 2b (2) **:** an auriferous gravel deposit in an old river bed; *esp* **:** one buried under lava **b :** a channel of water through a field of ice **c :** INDICATION, CLUE **d :** a principal role in a dramatic production; *also* **:** one who plays such a role **e :** LEASH 1 **f** (1) **:** an introductory section of a news story (2) **:** a news story of chief importance **3 :** an insulated electrical conductor **4 :** the length of a rope from end to end **5 :** a position taken by a base runner off a base toward the next
3lead *adj* **:** acting or serving as a leader ⟨~ article⟩
4lead \'led\ *n*, *often attrib* [ME *leed*, fr. OE *lēad;* akin to MHG *lōt* lead] **1 :** a heavy soft malleable ductile plastic but inelastic bivalent or tetravalent bluish white metallic element found mostly in combination and used esp. in pipes, cable sheaths, batteries, solder, type metal, and shields against radioactivity — see ELEMENT table **2 a :** a plummet for sounding at sea **b** *pl*, *Brit* **:** a usu. flat lead roof **c** *pl* **:** lead framing for panes in windows **d :** a thin strip of metal used to separate lines of type in printing **3 a :** a thin stick of marking substance in or for a pencil **b :** WHITE LEAD **4 :** BULLETS, PROJECTILES **5 :** TETRAETHYL LEAD
5lead \'led\ *vt* **1 :** to cover, line, or weight with lead **2 :** to fix (window glass) in position with leads **3 :** to place leads or other spacing material between the lines of (type matter) **4 :** to treat or mix with lead or a lead compound ⟨~*ed* gasoline⟩
lead acetate *n* **:** an acetate of lead; *esp* **:** a poisonous soluble salt $Pb(C_2H_3O_2)_2.3H_2O$
lead arsenate *n* **:** an arsenate of lead; *esp* **:** an acid salt $PbHAsO_4$ used as an insecticide
lead back *vt* **:** to lead (a card) from a suit that one's partner has orig. led
lead colic *n* **:** intestinal colic associated with obstinate constipation due to chronic lead poisoning
lead·en \'led-ᵊn\ *adj* **1 a :** made of lead **b :** of the color of lead **:** dull gray **2 :** low in quality **:** POOR **3 a :** oppressively heavy **b :** SLUGGISH **c :** lacking spirit or animation **:** DULL — **lead·en·ly** *adv* — **lead·en·ness** \-ᵊn-(n)əs\ *n*
lead·er \'lēd-ər\ *n* **1 :** something that leads: as **a :** a primary or terminal shoot of a plant **b :** TENDON, SINEW **c** *pl* **:** dots or hyphens (as in an index) used to lead the eye horizontally **:** ELLIPSIS 2 **d** *chiefly Brit* **:** a newspaper editorial **e** (1) **:** something for guiding fish into a trap (2) **:** a short length of material for attaching the end of a fishing line to a lure or hook **f :** a pipe for conducting fluid **g :** an article offered at an attractive special low price to stimulate business **h :** something that ranks first **2 :** a person that leads: as **a :** GUIDE, CONDUCTOR **b** (1) **:** a person who directs a military force or unit (2) **:** a person who has commanding authority or influence **c** (1) **:** the principal officer of a British political party (2) **:** a member chosen by his party to manage party activities in a legislative body (3) **:** such a member presiding over the whole legislative body when his party constitutes a majority (4) **:** one that exercises paramount but responsible authority over a state or local party organization (5) **:** the principal member of the party elite in a totalitarian system endowed by official ideology with a heroic or mystical character, exercising governmental power with a minimum of formal constitutional restraints, and characterized by extreme use of nationalist demagogy and claims to be above narrow class or group interests **d** (1) **:** CONDUCTOR c (2) **:** a first or principal performer of a group **3 :** a horse placed in advance of the other horses of a team **4 :** STRAW BOSS, FOREMAN — **lead·er·less** \-ləs\ *adj* — **lead·er·ship** \-,ship\ *n*
leader of the opposition : the principal member of the opposition party in a British legislative body who is given the status of a salaried government official and an important role in organizing the business of the house
lead glass *n* **:** glass of high refractive index containing lead oxide
lead–in \'lēd-,in\ *n* **:** something that leads in; *esp* **:** the part of a radio antenna that runs to the transmitting or receiving set — **lead–in** *adj*
lead·ing \'lēd-iŋ\ *adj* **1 :** coming or ranking first **:** FOREMOST **2 :** exercising leadership **3 :** GUIDING, DIRECTING ⟨~ question⟩ **4 :** given most prominent display ⟨~ story⟩
leading article \,lēd-\ *n* **1** *chiefly Brit* **:** EDITORIAL **2 :** the article given the most significant position or most prominent display in a periodical
leading lady *n* **:** an actress who plays the leading feminine role in a play or movie
leading man *n* **:** an actor who plays the leading male role in a play or movie
leading strings *n pl* **1 :** strings by which children are supported when beginning to walk **2 :** a state of dependence or tutelage **:** GUIDANCE — usu. used in the phrase *in leading strings*
leading tone *n* **:** the seventh musical degree of a major or minor scale — called also *subtonic*
lead·less \'led-ləs\ *adj* **:** being without lead
lead line \'led-\ *n* **:** SOUNDING LINE
lead off *vt* **:** to make a start on **:** OPEN
lead·off \'lēd-,ȯf\ *n* **1 :** a beginning or leading action **2 :** a player who leads off; *esp* **:** the player who heads the batting order or bats first in any inning in baseball
lead–off \'lē-,dȯf\ *adj* **:** leading off **:** OPENING
lead on *vt* **:** to entice or induce to proceed in a course esp. when unwise or mistaken
lead pencil \'led-\ *n* **:** a pencil using graphite as the marking material
lead poisoning *n* **:** chronic intoxication produced by the absorption of lead into the system
leads·man \'ledz-mən\ *n* **:** a man who uses a sounding lead to determine depth of water
lead up *vi* **1 :** to prepare the way **2 :** to make a gradual or indirect approach to a topic
lead–up \'lē-,dəp\ *n* **:** something that leads up to or prepares the way for something else
lead·work \'led-,wərk\ *n* **1 :** something made of lead **2 :** work that is done with lead
leady \'led-ē\ *adj* **:** containing or resembling lead

1leaf \'lēf\ *n, pl* **leaves** \'lēvz\ *often attrib* [ME *leef,* fr. OE *lēaf,*

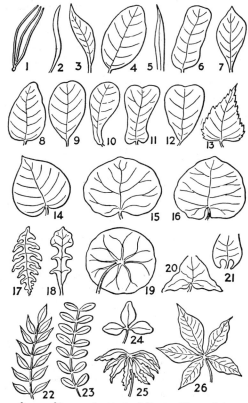

forms of leaves: *1* acerate; *2* linear; *3* lanceolate; *4* elliptic; *5* ensiform; *6* oblong; *7* oblanceolate, with acuminate tip; *8* ovate, with acute tip; *9* obovate; *10* spatulate; *11* pandurate; *12* cuneate; *13* deltoid; *14* cordate; *15* reniform; *16* orbiculate; *17* runcinate; *18* lyrate; *19* peltate; *20* hastate; *21* sagittate; *22* odd-pinnate; *23* abruptly pinnate; *24* palmate (trifoliolate); *25* palmate (pedate in form, with margin incised); *26* palmate (quinquefoliolate)

akin to OHG *loub* leaf, L *liber* bast, book] **1 a** (1) **:** a lateral outgrowth from a stem that constitutes a unit of the foliage of a plant and functions primarily in food manufacture by photosynthesis (2) **:** a modified leaf primarily engaged in functions other than food manufacture **b** (1) **:** FOLIAGE (2) **:** the leaves of a plant as an article of commerce **2 :** something suggestive of a leaf: as **a :** a part of a book or folded sheet containing a page on each side **b** (1) **:** a part (as of window shutters, folding doors, gates) that slides or is hinged (2) **:** the movable parts of a table top **c** (1) **:** a thin sheet or plate of any substance **:** LAMINA (2) **:** one of the plates of a leaf spring **d** *dial Brit* **:** a hat brim — **leaf·less** \'lē-fləs\ *adj*

2leaf *vi* **1 :** to shoot out or produce leaves **2 :** to turn over pages ⟨~ through a book⟩ ~ *vt* **:** to turn over the pages of

leaf·age \'lē-fij\ *n* **:** FOLIAGE

leaf bud *n* **:** a bud that develops into a leafy shoot and does not produce flowers

leafed \'lēft\ *adj* **:** having leaves usu. of a specified character or number

leaf fat *n* **:** the fat that lines the abdominal cavity and encloses the kidneys; *esp* **:** that of a hog used in the manufacture of lard

leaf·hop·per \'lēf-,häp-ər\ *n* **:** any of numerous small leaping homopterous insects (family Cicadellidae) that suck the juices of plants

leaf lard *n* **:** high quality lard made from leaf fat

leaf·let \'lē-flət\ *n* **1 a :** one of the divisions of a compound leaf **b :** a small or young foliage leaf **2 :** a leaflike organ or part **3 a :** a single printed sheet of paper unfolded or folded but not trimmed at the fold **b :** a sheet of small pages folded but not stitched

leaf·like \'lē-,flīk\ *adj* **:** resembling a leaf

leaf miner *n* **:** any of various small insects (as moths or two-winged flies) that in the larval stages burrow in and eat the parenchyma of leaves

leaf mold *n* **1 :** a compost or layer composed chiefly of decayed vegetable matter **2 :** a mold or mildew of foliage

leaf spring *n* **:** a spring made of superposed strips, plates, or leaves

leaf·stalk \'lēf-,stȯk\ *n* **:** PETIOLE

leafy \'lē-fē\ *adj* **1 a :** furnished with or abounding in leaves **b :** having broad-bladed leaves **c :** having leaves a major part **2 :** resembling a leaf; *specif* **:** LAMINATE

1league \'lēg\ *n* [ME *leuge, lege,* fr. LL *leuga*] **1 :** any of various units of distance from about 2.4 to 4.6 statute miles **2 :** a square league

2league *n* [ME (Sc) *ligg,* fr. MF *ligue,* fr. OIt *liga,* fr. *ligare* to bind, fr. L — more at LIGATURE] **1 a :** an association of nations or other political entities for a common purpose **b :** an association of persons or groups united by common interests or goals; *specif* **:** an association of ball clubs **c :** an informal alliance **2 :** CLASS, CATEGORY — **league** *vt*

1lea·guer \'lē-gər\ *n* [D *leger;* akin to OHG *legar* act of lying —

more at LAIR] **1 :** a military camp **2 :** SIEGE

2leaguer *vt, archaic* **:** BESIEGE, BELEAGUER

3leagu·er \'lē-gər\ *n* **:** a member of a league

1leak \'lēk\ *vb* [ME *leken,* fr. ON *leka;* akin to OE *leccan* to moisten, OIr *legaim* I melt] *vi* **1 a :** to enter or escape through an opening usu. by a fault or mistake ⟨fumes ~ in⟩ **b :** to let a substance or light in or out through an opening **2 :** to become known despite efforts at concealment ~ *vt* **1 :** to permit to enter or escape through or as if through a leak **2 :** to give out (information) surreptitiously

2leak *n* **1 a :** a crack or hole that usu. by mistake admits or lets escape **b :** something that permits the admission or escape of something else usu. with prejudicial effect **c :** a loss of electricity due to faulty insulation; *also* **:** the point or the path at which such loss occurs **2 :** the act, process, or an instance of leaking

leak·age \'lē-kij\ *n* **1 :** the act, process, or an instance of leaking **2 :** something or the amount that leaks

leaky \'lē-kē\ *adj* **:** permitting fluid to leak in or out

leal \'lē(ə)l\ *adj* [ME *leel, leel,* fr. *leial, leel* — more at LOYAL] *chiefly Scot* **:** LOYAL, TRUE — **leal·ly** \'lē(ə)l-lē\ *adv*

1lean \'lēn\ *vb* **leaned** \'lēnd, *chiefly Brit* 'lent\ **lean·ing** \'lē-niŋ\ [ME *lenen,* fr. OE *hleonian;* akin to OHG *hlinēn* to lean, Gk *klinein,* L *clinare*] *vi* **1 a :** to incline, deviate, or bend from a vertical position **b :** to cast one's weight to one side for support **2 :** to rely upon for support or inspiration **3 :** to incline in opinion, taste, or desire ~ *vt* **:** to cause to lean **:** INCLINE

2lean *n* **:** the act or an instance of leaning **:** INCLINATION

3lean *adj* [ME *lene,* fr. OE *hlæne*] **1 a :** lacking or deficient in flesh **b :** containing little or no fat **2 :** lacking richness, sufficiency, or productiveness **3 :** deficient in an essential or important quality or ingredient: as **a** *of ore* **:** containing little valuable mineral **b :** low in combustible component — used esp. of fuel mixtures **4 :** characterized by economy of style or expression — **lean·ly** *adv* — **lean·ness** \'lēn-nəs\ *n*

syn SPARE, LANK, LANKY, GAUNT, RAWBONED, SCRAWNY, SKINNY: LEAN stresses lack of fat and of curving contours; SPARE suggests leanness from abstemious living or constant exercise; LANK implies tallness as well as leanness; LANKY suggests awkwardness and loose-jointedness as well as thinness; GAUNT implies marked thinness or emaciation as from overwork or suffering; RAWBONED suggests a large ungainly build without implying undernourishment; SCRAWNY and SKINNY imply an extreme leanness that suggests deficient strength and vitality

4lean *vt* **:** to make lean

5lean *n* **:** the part of meat that consists principally of fat-free muscle

Le·an·der \lē-'an-dər\ *n* [L, fr. Gk *Leandros*] **:** a youth noted in Greek legend for swimming the Hellespont nightly to visit Hero

lean·ing \'lē-niŋ\ *n* **:** TENDENCY, INCLINATION

syn PROPENSITY, PROCLIVITY, PENCHANT, FLAIR: LEANING suggests a liking or attraction not strong enough to be decisive or uncontrollable; PROPENSITY implies a deeply ingrained and usu. irresistible longing; PROCLIVITY suggests a strong natural proneness usu. to something objectionable or evil; PENCHANT implies a strongly marked taste in the person or an irresistible attraction in the object; FLAIR suggests an instinctive or unaccountable power of discernment in certain matters, or it may describe a special and individual aptitude or knack

leant \'lent\ *chiefly Brit past of* LEAN

1lean-to \'lēn-,tü\ *n* **1 :** a wing or extension of a building having a lean-to roof **2 :** a rough shed or shelter with a lean-to roof

2lean-to *adj* **:** having only one slope or pitch ⟨~ roof⟩

1leap \'lēp\ *vb* **leaped** *or* **leapt** \'lēpt *also* 'lept\ **leap·ing** \'lē-piŋ\ [ME *lepen,* fr. OE *hlēapan;* akin to OHG *hlouffan* to run] *vi* **1 :** to spring free from or as if from the ground **:** JUMP ⟨~ over a fence⟩ ⟨fish ~s out of the water⟩ **2 a :** to pass abruptly from one state or topic to another **b :** to act precipitately ⟨~*ed* at the chance⟩ ~ *vt* **:** to pass over by a leap — **leap·er** \'lē-pər\ *n*

2leap *n* **1 a :** an act of leaping **:** SPRING, BOUND **b** (1) **:** a place leaped over or from (2) **:** the distance covered by a leap **2 :** a sudden transition

1leap·frog \'lēp-,frȯg, -,fräg\ *n* **:** a game in which one player bends down and another leaps over him

2leapfrog *vb* **leap·frogged; leap·frog·ging** *vi* **:** to leap or progress in or as if in leapfrog ~ *vt* **1 :** to go ahead of (each other) in turn; *specif* **:** to advance (two military units) by keeping one unit in action while moving the other unit past it to a position farther in front **2 :** to evade by or as if by a bypass

leap year *n* **1 :** a year in the Gregorian calendar containing 366 days with February 29 as the extra day **2 :** an intercalary year in any calendar

Lear \'li(ə)r\ *n* **:** a legendary king of Britain and hero of Shakespeare's tragedy *King Lear*

learn \'lərn\ *vb* **learned** \'lərnd, 'lərnt\ *also* **learnt** \'lərnt\ **learn·ing** \'lər-niŋ\ [ME *lernen,* fr. OE *leornian;* akin to OHG *lernēn* to learn, L *lira* furrow, track] *vt* **1 a** (1) **:** to gain knowledge or understanding of or skill in by study, instruction, or experience (2) **:** MEMORIZE ⟨~ the lines of a play⟩ **b :** to come to be able to **c :** to come to realize **2 a** *substand* **:** TEACH **b** *obs* **:** to inform of something **3 :** to find out **:** ASCERTAIN ~ *vi* **:** to acquire knowledge or skill syn see DISCOVER — **learn·able** \'lər-nə-bəl\ *adj* — **learn·er** *n*

learned *adj* **1** \'lər-nəd\ **:** characterized by or associated with learning **:** ERUDITE **2** \'lərnd, 'lərnt\ **:** acquired by learning — **learn·ed·ly** \'lər-nəd-lē\ *adv* — **learn·ed·ness** \'lər-nəd-nəs\ *n*

learn·ing *n* **1 :** the act or experience of one that learns **2 :** knowledge or skill acquired by instruction or study

1lease \'lēs\ *n* **1 :** a contract by which one conveys real estate for a term of years or at will usu. for a specified rent; *also* **:** the act of such conveyance or the term for which it is made **2 :** a piece of land or property that is leased

2lease *vt* [AF *lesser,* fr. OF *laissier* to let go, fr. L *laxare* to loosen, fr. *laxus* slack — more at SLACK] *vt* **1 :** to grant by lease **:** LET **2 :** to hold under a lease syn see HIRE

lease·hold \'lēs-,hōld\ *n* **1 :** a tenure by lease **2 :** land held by lease — **lease·hold·er** *n*

leash \'lēsh\ *n* [ME *lees, leshe,* fr. OF *laisse,* fr. *laissier*] **1 :** a line for leading or restraining an animal **2 a :** a set of three animals (as greyhounds, foxes, bucks, or hares) **b :** a set of three — **leash** *vt*

leas·ing \'lē-ziŋ, -siŋ\ *n* [ME *lesing,* fr. OE *lēasung,* fr. *lēasian* to

lie, fr. *lēas* false] *archaic* : the act of lying; *also* : LIE, FALSEHOOD

1**least** \'lēst\ *adj* [ME *leest*, fr. OE *lǣst* superl. of *lǣssa* less] **1** : lowest in importance or position **2 a** : smallest in size or degree **b** : being a member of a kind distinguished by diminutive size ⟨~ bittern⟩ **c** : smallest possible : SLIGHTEST

2**least** *n* : one that is least — **at least 1** : at the minimum **2** : in any case

3**least** *adv* : in the smallest or lowest degree

least squares *n pl* : a method of fitting a curve to a set of points representing statistical data in such a way that the sum of the squares of the distances of the points from the curve is a minimum

least•ways \'lēs-,twāz\ *adv, dial* : at least

least•wise \-,twīz\ *adv* : at least

1**leath•er** \'leth-ər\ *n* [ME *lether*, fr. OE *lether-;* akin to OHG *leder* leather] **1** : animal skin dressed for use **2** : the pendulous part of the ear of a dog **3** : something wholly or partly made of leather

2**leather** *vt* **leath•er•ing** \'leth-(ə-)riŋ\ **1** : to cover with leather **2** : to beat with a strap : THRASH

leath•er•back \'leth-ər-,bak\ *n* : the largest existing sea turtle (*Dermochelys coriacea*) distinguished by its flexible carapace composed of a mosaic of small bones embedded in a thick leathery skin

Leath•er•ette \,leth-ə-'ret\ *trademark* — used for a product colored, finished, and embossed in imitation of leather grains

leath•ern \'leth-ərn\ *adj* : made of, consisting of, or resembling leather

leath•er•neck \-ər-,nek\ *n* [fr. the leather neckband formerly part of the uniform] : MARINE

Leath•er•oid \-ə-,rȯid\ *trademark* — used for an artificial leather consisting of chemically treated paper combined with rubber and sandarac

leath•er•wood \'leth-ər-,wu̇d\ *n* : a small tree (*Dirca palustris*) of the mezereon family with pliant stems and yellow flowers

leath•ery \'leth-(ə-)rē\ *adj* : resembling leather in appearance or consistency : TOUGH

1**leave** \'lēv\ *vb* **left** \'left\ **leav•ing** [ME *leven*, fr. OE *lǣfan;* akin to OHG *verleiben* to leave, OE *belīfan* to be left over, Gk *lipos* fat] *vt* **1 a** : BEQUEATH **b** : to depart without removing (something caused or brought) ⟨wound ~*s* a scar⟩ ⟨mailman *left* a letter⟩ **c** : to fail to take or refrain from taking ⟨~ her at home⟩ **d** : to allow to remain in a specified state or undisturbed ⟨~ the door open⟩ **e** : to have as a remainder ⟨4 from 7 ~*s* 3⟩ **2 a** : to go away from : DEPART ⟨~ town⟩ **b** : DESERT, ABANDON ⟨*left* his wife⟩ **c** : to give up : RELINQUISH ⟨*left* business for research⟩ ~ *vi* : to set out : DEPART **syn** see GO — **leav•er** *n*

2**leave** *n* [ME *leve*, fr. OE *lēaf;* akin to MHG *loube* permission, OE *alȳfan* to allow — more at BELIEVE] **1 a** : PERMISSION **b** : authorized esp. extended absence from duty or employment **2** : an act of leaving : DEPARTURE

3**leave** *vi* [ME *leven*, fr. *leef* leaf] : LEAF

leaved \'lēvd\ *adj* : having leaves ⟨broad-*leaved*⟩

1**leav•en** \'lev-ən\ *n* [ME *levain*, fr. MF, fr. (assumed) VL *levamen*, fr. L *levare* to raise — more at LEVER] **1 a** : a substance (as yeast) used to produce fermentation in dough or a liquid; *esp* : SOURDOUGH **b** : a material (as baking powder) used to produce a gas that lightens dough or batter **2** : something that modifies or lightens a mass or aggregate

2**leaven** *vt* **leav•en•ing** \'lev-(ə-)niŋ\ **1** : to raise (as bread) with a leaven **2** : to mingle or permeate with some modifying, alleviating, or vivifying element **syn** see INFUSE

leav•en•ing *n* : a leavening agent : LEAVEN

leave off *vb* : STOP, CEASE

leaves *pl of* LEAF

leave–tak•ing \'lēv-,tā-kiŋ\ *n* : DEPARTURE, FAREWELL

leav•ings \'lē-viŋz\ *n pl* : REMNANT, RESIDUE

le•bens•raum \'lā-bənz-,rau̇m, -bən(t)s-\ *n, often cap* [G, fr. *leben* living, life + *raum* space] **1** : territory held esp. by Nazis to be necessary for national existence or economic self-sufficiency **2** : space required for life, growth, or activity

lech•er \'lech-ər\ *n* [ME *lechour*, fr. OF *lecheor*, fr. *lechier* to lick, live in debauchery, of Gmc origin; akin to OHG *leckōn* to lick — more at LICK] : a man who engages in lechery

lech•er•ous \'lech-(ə-)rəs\ *adj* : given to or suggestive of lechery — **lech•er•ous•ly** *adv* — **lech•er•ous•ness** *n*

lech•ery \'lech-(ə-)rē\ *n* : inordinate indulgence in sexual activity : LASCIVIOUSNESS

lec•i•thin \'les-ə-thən\ *n* [ISV, fr. Gk *lekithos* yolk of an egg] : any of several waxy hygroscopic phosphatides widely distributed in animals and plants that form colloidal solutions in water and have emulsifying, wetting, and antioxidant properties; *also* : a mixture of or substance rich in lecithins

lec•i•thin•ase \-thə-,nās, -,nāz\ *n* : any of several enzymes that hydrolyze lecithins or cephalins

lec•tern \'lek-tərn\ *n* [ME *lettorne*, fr. MF *letrun*, fr. ML *lectorinum*, fr. L *lector* reader, fr. *lectus*, pp. of *legere* to read — more at LEGEND] : READING DESK; *esp* : one from which scripture lessons are read in a church service

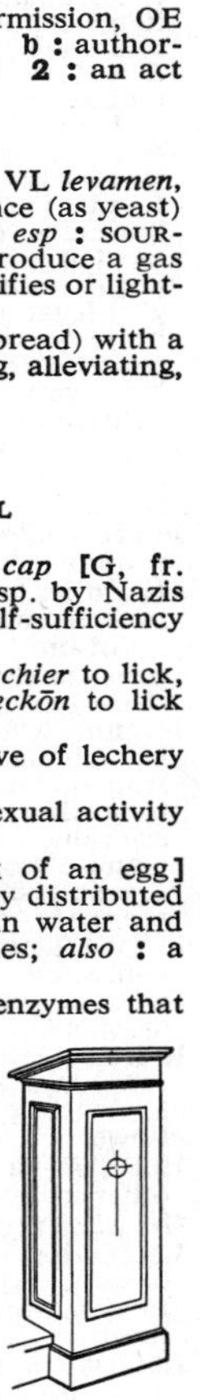
lectern

lec•tion \'lek-shən\ *n* [LL *lection-, lectio*, fr. L, act of reading — more at LESSON] **1** : a liturgical lesson for a particular day **2** [NL *lection-, lectio*, fr. L] : a variant reading of a text

lec•tion•ary \'lek-shə-,ner-ē\ *n* : a book or list of lections for the church year

lec•tor \'lek-tər, -,tȯ(ə)r\ *n* [LL, fr. L, reader] : one whose chief duty is to read the lessons in a church service

1**lec•ture** \'lek-chər\ *n* [ME, act of reading, fr. LL *lectura*, fr. L *lectus*, pp. of *legere* to read — more at LEGEND] **1** : a discourse given before an audience or class esp. for instruction **2** : a formal reproof : REPRIMAND — **lec•ture•ship** \-,ship\ *n*

2**lecture** *vb* **lec•tur•ing** \'lek-chə-riŋ, 'lek-shriŋ\ *vi* : to deliver a lecture or a course of lectures ~ *vt* **1** : to deliver a lecture to **2** : to reprove formally — **lec•tur•er** \-chər-ər, -shrər\ *n*

led *past of* LEAD

Le•da \'lēd-ə\ *n* [L, fr. Gk *Lēda*] : the mother of Clytemnestra and Castor by her husband Tyndareus, King of Sparta, and of Helen of Troy and Pollux by Zeus in the guise of a swan

le•der•ho•sen \'lād-ər-,hōz-ᵊn\ *n pl* [G, fr. MHG *lederhose*, fr. *leder* leather + *hose* trousers] : knee-length leather trousers worn esp. in Bavaria

ledge \'lej\ *n* [ME *legge* bar of a gate] **1** : a projecting ridge or raised edge along a surface : SHELF **2** : an underwater ridge or reef esp. near the shore **3** : a narrow flat surface or shelf; *esp* : one that projects (as from a wall of rock) **4** : LODE, VEIN

led•ger \'lej-ər\ *n* [ME *legger*, prob. fr. *leyen, leggen* to lay] **1** : a book containing accounts to which debits and credits are posted from books of original entry **2** : a horizontal timber secured to the uprights of scaffolding to support the putlog

ledger board *n* : a horizontal board forming the top rail of a simple fence or the handrail of a balustrade

ledger line *n* : a short line added above or below a musical staff to extend its range

1**lee** \'lē\ *n* [ME, fr. OE *hlēo;* akin to OHG *lāo* lukewarm, L *calēre* to be warm] **1** : protecting shelter **2** : the side (as of a ship) that is sheltered from the wind

2**lee** *adj* **1** : of or relating to the lee — compare WEATHER **2** : located on the side away from which an advancing glacier moves

lee•board \'lē-,bō(ə)rd, -,bȯ(ə)rd\ *n* : either of the wood or metal planes attached outside the hull of a sailboat to prevent leeway

1**leech** \'lēch\ *n* [ME *leche*, fr. OE *lǣce;* akin to OHG *lāhhi* physician] **1** *archaic* : PHYSICIAN, SURGEON **2** [fr. its former use by physicians for bleeding patients] : any of numerous carnivorous or bloodsucking usu. freshwater annelid worms (class Hirudinea) having typically a flattened lanceolate segmented body with a sucker at each end **3** : a hanger-on who seeks advantage or gain

2**leech** *vt* **1** : to bleed by the use of leeches **2** : to drain the substance of : EXHAUST ~ *vi* : to attach oneself to a person as a leech

3**leech** \'lēch\ *n* [ME *leche*, fr. MLG *līk* boltrope; akin to MHG *geleich* joint — more at LIGATURE] **1** : either vertical edge of a square sail **2** : the after edge of a fore-and-aft sail

leek \'lēk\ *n* [ME, fr. OE *lēac;* akin to OHG *louh* leek] : a biennial garden herb (*Allium porrum*) of the lily family grown for its mildly pungent succulent linear leaves and esp. its thick cylindrical stalk

1**leer** \'li(ə)r\ *vi* [prob. fr. obs. *leer* (cheek)] : to cast a sidelong glance; *esp* : to give a lascivious, knowing, or malicious look

2**leer** *n* : a knowing or wanton look

leery \'li(ə)r-ē\ *adj* : SUSPICIOUS, WARY

lees \'lēz\ *n pl* [ME *lie*, fr. MF, fr. ML *lia*] : the settlings of liquor during fermentation and aging : DREGS

Lee's Birthday \'lēz-\ *n* [General Robert E. *Lee* †1870 Am soldier] : January 19 observed as a legal holiday in several southern states

lee shore *n* : a shore lying off a ship's leeward side and constituting a severe danger in storm

1**lee•ward** \'lē-wərd, 'lü-ərd\ *adj* : situated away from the wind : DOWNWIND — compare WINDWARD

2**leeward** *n* : the lee side

lee•way \'lē-,wā\ *n* **1 a** : off-course lateral movement of a ship when under way **b** : the angle between the heading and the track of an airplane **2** : an allowable margin of freedom or variation : TOLERANCE

1**left** \'left\ *adj* [ME, fr. OE, weak; akin to MLG *lucht* left] **1 a** : relating to or being the weaker hand in most persons **b** : located nearer to the left hand than to the right: as (1) : located on the left when facing in the same direction as an observer (2) : located on the left when facing downstream **2** *often cap* : of, adhering to, or constituted by the left esp. in politics — **left** *adv*

2**left** *n* **1 a** : the left hand **b** : the location or direction of the left side **c** : the part on the left side **2** *often cap* **a** : the part of a legislative chamber located to the left of the presiding officer **b** : the members of a continental European legislative body occupying the left as a result of holding more radical political views than other members **3** *cap* **a** : those professing views usu. characterized by desire to reform or overthrow the established order esp. in politics and usu. advocating greater freedom or well-being of the common man **b** : a radical as distinguished from a conservative position

3**left** *past of* LEAVE

Left Bank *n* : the bohemian district of Paris situated on the left bank of the Seine river

left field *n* **1** : the part of the baseball outfield to the left looking out from the plate **2** : the position of the player defending left field — **left fielder** *n*

left–hand \'left-,hand, 'lef-,tand\ *adj* **1** : situated on the left **2** : LEFT-HANDED

left–hand•ed \-'han-dəd, -'tan-\ *adj* **1** : using the left hand habitually or more easily than the right **2** : relating to, designed for, or done with the left hand **3** : MORGANATIC **4** : CLUMSY, AWKWARD; *also* : INSINCERE, MALICIOUS **5 a** : having a direction contrary to that of the hands of a watch viewed from in front : COUNTERCLOCKWISE **b** : having a structure involving a counterclockwise direction — **left–handed** *adv* — **left–hand•ed•ly** *adv* — **left–hand•ed•ness** *n*

left–hand•er \-'han-dər, -'tan-\ *n* : a left-handed person : SOUTHPAW

left heart *n* : the half of the heart containing oxygenated blood and consisting of the left auricle and ventricle

left•ism \'lef-,tiz-əm\ *n* **1** : the principles and views of the Left; *also* : the movement embodying these principles **2** : advocacy of or adherence to the doctrines of the Left — **left•ist** \-təst\ *n or adj*

1**left•over** \'lef-,tō-vər\ *adj* : remaining as unused residue

2**leftover** *n* : an unused or unconsumed residue; *esp* : leftover food served at a later meal

left wing *n* **1** : the leftist division of a group **2** : LEFT 3a — **left–wing•er** \'lef-'twiŋ-ər\ *n*

1**leg** \'leg, 'lāg\ *n* [ME, fr. ON *leggr;* akin to OE *līra* muscle, calf, L *lacertus* muscle, upper arm] **1** : a limb of an animal used esp. for supporting the body and for walking: as **a** : the part of the vertebrate limb between the knee and foot **b** : the back half of a hindquarter of a meat animal **2 a** : a pole or bar serving as a support or prop **b** : a branch of a forked or jointed object **3** : the part of an article of clothing that covers the leg **4** : OBEISANCE, BOW — used chiefly in the phrase *to make a leg* **5** : either side of a triangle as distinguished from the base or hypotenuse **6** : BOOST

ə abut; ᵊ kitten; ər further; a back; ā bake; ä cot, cart; au̇ out; ch chin; e less; ē easy; g gift; i trip; ī life
j joke; ŋ sing; ō flow; ȯ flaw; ȯi coin; th thin; th this; ü loot; u̇ foot; y yet; yü few; yu̇ furious; zh vision

— called also *leg up* **7 a :** the course and distance sailed by a boat on a single tack **b :** a portion of a trip : STAGE **c :** one section of a relay race **8 :** a branch or part of an object or system — **leg·less** \-ləs\ *adj*

2leg *vt* **legged; leg·ging :** to use the legs in walking; *esp* : RUN

leg·a·cy \'leg-ə-sē\ *n* [ME *legacie* office of a legate, bequest, fr. MF or ML; MF, office of a legate, fr. ML *legatia*, fr. L *legatus*] **1 :** a gift by will esp. of money or other personal property : BEQUEST **2 :** something received from an ancestor or predecessor or from the past

1le·gal \'lē-gəl\ *adj* [ME, fr. MF, fr. L *legalis*, fr. *leg-*, *lex* law] **1 :** of or relating to law **2 a :** deriving authority from or founded on law : de jure **b :** having a formal status derived from law often without a basis in actual fact : TITULAR **c :** established by law; *esp* : STATUTORY **3 :** conforming to or permitted by law or established rules **4 :** recognized or made effective by a court of law as distinguished from a court of equity **5 :** of, relating to, or having the characteristics of the profession of law or of one of its members **6 :** created by the constructions of the law **syn** see LAWFUL — **le·gal·ly** \-gə-lē\ *adv*

2legal *n* **:** a class of securities in which trustees, savings banks, and other investors regulated by law may legally invest

legal cap *n* **:** a white often ruled writing paper for legal use usu. 8½ inches wide and 13 or 14 inches long

legal holiday *n* **:** a holiday established by legal authority and characterized by legal restrictions on work and transaction of official business

le·gal·ism \'lē-gə-,liz-əm\ *n* **:** strict, literal, or excessive conformity to the law or to a religious or moral code

le·gal·ist \-ləst\ *n* **1 :** an advocate or adherent of moral legalism **2 :** one that views things from a legal standpoint; *esp* : one that places primary emphasis on legal principles or on the formal structure of governmental institutions — **le·gal·is·tic** \,lē-gə-'lis-tik\ *adj* — **le·gal·is·ti·cal·ly** \-ti-k(ə-)lē\ *adv*

le·gal·i·ty \li-'gal-ət-ē\ *n* **1 :** attachment to or observance of law **2 :** the quality or state of being legal : LAWFULNESS **3** *pl* **:** obligations imposed by law

le·gal·iza·tion \,lē-gə-lə-'zā-shən\ *n* **1 :** the act of legalizing **2 :** the state of being or having been legalized

le·gal·ize \'lē-gə-,līz\ *vt* **:** to make legal; *esp* : to give legal validity or sanction to

legal reserve *n* **:** the minimum amount of bank deposits or life insurance company assets required by law to be kept as reserves

legal tender *n* **:** currency in such amounts and denominations as the law authorizes a debtor to tender and requires a creditor to receive in payment of money obligations

1leg·ate \'leg-ət\ *n* [ME, fr. OF & L; OF *legat*, fr. L *legatus* deputy, emissary, fr. pp. of *legare* to depute, send as emissary, bequeath, fr. *leg-*, *lex*] **:** a usu. official emissary — **leg·ate·ship** \-,ship\ *n*

2le·gate \li-'gāt\ *vt* [*legatus*, pp. of *legare* to bequeath] **:** BEQUEATH 1 — **le·ga·tor** \-'gāt-ər\ *n*

leg·a·tee \,leg-ə-'tē\ *n* **:** one to whom a legacy is bequeathed or a devise is given

leg·a·tine \'leg-ə-,tēn, -,tīn\ *adj* **:** of, headed by, or enacted under the authority of a legate

le·ga·tion \li-'gā-shən\ *n* **1 :** the sending forth of a legate **2 :** a body of deputies sent on a mission; *specif* : a diplomatic mission in a foreign country headed by a minister **3 :** the official residence and office of a diplomatic minister at the seat of a foreign government

le·ga·to \li-'gät-(,)ō\ *adv* (*or adj*) [It, lit., tied] **:** in a manner that is smooth and connected between successive tones — used as a direction in music

leg·end \'lej-ənd\ *n* [ME *legende*, fr. MF & ML; MF *legende*, fr. ML *legenda*, fr. L, fem. of *legendus*, gerundive of *legere* to gather, select, read; akin to Gk *legein* to gather, say, *logos* speech, word, reason] **1 a :** a story coming down from the past; *esp* : one popularly regarded as historical although not verifiable **b :** a body of such stories **c :** a popular myth of recent origin **d :** a person or thing that inspires legends **2 a :** an inscription or title on an object **b :** CAPTION 2b **c :** an explanatory list of the symbols on a map or chart

leg·end·ary \'lej-ən-,der-ē\ *adj* **:** of, relating to, or resembling a legend **syn** see FICTITIOUS

leg·end·ry \'lej-ən-drē\ *n* **:** LEGENDS

leg·er·de·main \,lej-ərd-ə-'mān\ *n* [ME, fr. MF *leger de main* light of hand] **:** SLEIGHT OF HAND

le·ger·i·ty \lə-'jer-ət-ē, le-\ *n* [MF *legereté*, fr. OF, lightness, fr. *leger* light, fr. (assumed) VL *leviarius*, fr. L *levis* — more at LIGHT] **:** AGILITY, NIMBLENESS **syn** see CELERITY

leges *pl of* LEX

legged \'leg-əd, 'lāg-, *Brit usu* 'legd\ *adj* **:** having legs ⟨one-*legged*⟩

leg·ging *or* **leg·gin** \'leg-ən, 'lāg-, -iŋ\ *n* **:** a covering for the leg usu. of leather or cloth — usu. used in pl.

leg·gy \'leg-ē, 'lāg-\ *adj* **1 :** having disproportionately long legs **2 :** having attractive legs **3 :** SPINDLY — used of a plant

leg·horn \'leg-,(h)ó(ə)rn, 'leg-ərn\ *n* [*Leghorn*, Italy] **1 a :** a fine plaited straw made from an Italian wheat **b :** a hat of this straw **2 :** any of a Mediterranean breed of small hardy fowls noted for their large production of white eggs

leg·i·bil·i·ty \,lej-ə-'bil-ət-ē\ *n* **:** the quality or state of being legible

leg·i·ble \'lej-ə-bəl\ *adj* [ME, fr. LL *legibilis*, fr. L *legere* to read] **:** capable of being read or deciphered : PLAIN — **leg·i·bly** \-blē\ *adv*

le·gion \'lē-jən\ *n* [ME, fr. OF, fr. L *legion-*, *legio*, fr. *legere* to gather] **1 :** the principal unit of the Roman army comprising 3000 to 6000 foot soldiers with cavalry **2 :** a large military force; *esp* : ARMY 1a **3 :** a very large number : MULTITUDE **4 :** a national association of ex-servicemen

1le·gion·ary \'lē-jə-,ner-ē\ *adj* [L *legionarius*, fr. *legion-*, *legio*] **:** of, relating to, or constituting a legion

2legionary *n* **:** LEGIONNAIRE

le·gion·naire \,lē-jə-'na(ə)r, -'ne(ə)r\ *n* [F *légionnaire*, fr. L *legionarius*] **:** a member of a legion

Legion of Honor : a French order conferred as a reward for civil or military merit

Legion of Merit : a U.S. military decoration awarded for exceptionally meritorious conduct in the performance of outstanding services

leg·is·late \'lej-ə-,slāt\ *vb* [back-formation fr. *legislator*] *vi* **:** to perform the function of legislation; *specif* : to make or enact laws ~ *vt* **:** to cause, create, or bring about by legislation

leg·is·la·tion \,ləj-ə-'slā-shən\ *n* **1 :** the action of legislating; *specif* : the exercise of the power and function of making laws and other rules having the force of authority by virtue of their promulgation by an official organ of a state or other organization **2 :** the enactments of a legislator or a legislative body **3 :** a matter of business for or under consideration by a legislative body

1leg·is·la·tive \'lej-ə-,slāt-iv\ *adj* **1 :** having the power or performing the function of legislating **2 a :** of or relating to a legislature ⟨~ committees⟩ ⟨~ immunity⟩ **b :** composed of members of a legislature **c :** created by a legislature esp. as distinguished from an executive or judicial body **d :** designed to assist a legislature or its members **3 :** of, concerned with, or created by legislation — **leg·is·la·tive·ly** *adv*

2legislative *n* **:** the body or department exercising the power and function of legislating : LEGISLATURE

legislative assembly *n, often cap L&A* **1 :** a bicameral legislature in an American state or territory **2 :** the lower house of a bicameral legislature **3 :** a unicameral legislature; *esp* : one in a Canadian province

legislative council *n, often cap L&C* **1 :** the upper house of a British bicameral legislature **2 :** a unicameral legislature in a British colony **3 :** the unicameral legislature of a U.S. territory **4 :** a permanent committee chosen from both houses that meets between sessions of a state legislature to study state problems and plan a legislative program

leg·is·la·tor \'lej-ə-,slāt-ər\ *n* [L *legis lator*, lit., proposer of law, fr. *legis*, gen. of *lex* law + *lator* proposer, fr. *latus* suppletive pp. of *ferre* to carry, propose — more at TOLERATE, BEAR] **:** one that makes laws esp. for a political unit; *esp* : a member of a legislative body — **leg·is·la·to·ri·al** \,lej-ə-slə-'tōr-ē-əl, -'tór-\ *adj* — **leg·is·la·tor·ship** \'lej-ə-,slāt-ər-,ship\ *n* — **leg·is·la·tress** \,lej-ə-'slā-trəs\ *n* — **leg·is·la·trix** \-triks\ *n*

leg·is·la·ture \'lej-ə-,slā-chər\ *n* **:** a body of persons having the power to legislate; *specif* : an organized body having the authority to make laws for a political unit and often exercising other functions

le·gist \'lē-jəst\ *n* [MF *legiste*, fr. ML *legista*, fr. L *leg-*, *lex*] **:** a specialist in law or a branch of law; *esp* : one learned in Roman or civil law

le·git \li-'jit\ *adj, slang* **:** LEGITIMATE

le·git·i·ma·cy \li-'jit-ə-mə-sē\ *n* **:** the quality or state of being legitimate

1le·git·i·mate \li-'jit-ə-mət\ *adj* [ML *legitimatus*, pp. of *legitimare* to legitimate, fr. L *legitimus* legitimate, fr. *leg-*, *lex* law] **1 a :** lawfully begotten; *specif* : born in wedlock **b :** having full filial rights and obligations by birth ⟨a ~ child⟩ **2 :** GENUINE ⟨~ grievance⟩ **3 a** (1) **:** accordant with law or with established legal forms and requirements ⟨a ~ government⟩ (2) **:** LAW-ABIDING **b :** ruling by or based upon the strict principle of hereditary right ⟨a ~ king⟩ **4 :** conforming to recognized principles or accepted rules and standards ⟨~ advertising expenditure⟩ ⟨~ inference⟩ **5 :** relating to plays acted by professional actors but not including revues, burlesque, or some forms of musical comedy ⟨~ theater⟩ **syn** see LAWFUL — **le·git·i·mate·ly** *adv*

2le·git·i·mate \-,māt\ *vt* **:** to make lawful or legal: **a** (1) **:** to give legal status or authorization to (2) **:** to show or affirm to be justified **b :** to put (a bastard) in the state of a legitimate child before the law by legal means — **le·git·i·ma·tion** \li-,jit-ə-'mā-shən\ *n*

le·git·i·ma·tize \li-'jit-ə-mə-,tīz\ *vt* **:** LEGITIMATE

le·git·i·mism \-,miz-əm\ *n, often cap* **:** adherence to the principles of political legitimacy or to a person claiming legitimacy — **le·git·i·mist** \-məst\ *n or adj*

le·git·i·mize \-,mīz\ *vt* **:** LEGITIMATE

leg·man \'leg-,man, 'lāg-\ *n* **1 :** a newspaperman assigned usu. to gather information **2 :** an assistant who gathers information, runs errands, and often performs other tasks

leg–of–mut·ton \,leg-ə(v)-'mət-ᵊn, ,lāg-\ *adj* **:** having the approximately triangular shape or outline of a leg of mutton ⟨~ sleeve⟩ ⟨~ sail⟩

le·gume \'leg-,yüm, li-'gyüm\ *n* [F *légume*, fr. L *legumin-*, *legumen* leguminous plant, fr. *legere* to gather — more at LEGEND] **1 a :** the fruit or seed of a leguminous plant (as peas or beans) used for food **b :** any vegetable used for food **2 :** a leguminous plant; *esp* : one (as clover, alfalfa, soybeans) grown as a forage or green-manure crop **3 :** a dry dehiscent one-celled fruit developed from a simple superior ovary and usu. dehiscing into two valves with the seeds attached to the ventral suture : POD

le·gu·mi·nous \li-'gyü-mə-nəs, le-\ *adj* **1 :** of, relating to, or consisting of dicotyledonous plants constituting a family (Leguminosae) characterized by fruits that are legumes **2 :** resembling a legume

le·hua \lā-'hü-ə\ *n* [Hawaiian] **:** a common very showy tree (*Metrosideros villosa*) of the myrtle family of the Pacific islands having bright red corymbose flowers and a hard wood; *also* : its flower

1lei \'lā, 'lā-,ē\ *n* [Hawaiian] **:** a wreath or necklace of flowers or other materials

2lei *pl of* LEU

Leices·ter \'les-tər\ *n* [*Leicester*, county in England] **:** any of a breed of white-faced long-wool mutton-type sheep originating in England and having white fleece finer than that of most long-wool sheep

Lei Day *n* **:** May Day in Hawaii celebrated with pageants and prizes for the most beautiful or distinctive leis

leish·ma·ni·a·sis \,lēsh-mə-'nī-ə-səs\ *n* [NL, fr. *Leishmania*, genus name, fr. Sir W. B. *Leishman* †1926 Brit medical officer] **:** infection with or disease caused by minute protozoans (genus *Leishmania*) that invade the tissues

leis·ter \'lē-stər\ *n* [of Scand origin; akin to ON *ljōstr* leister] **:** a spear armed with three or more barbed prongs for catching fish — **leister** *vt*

lei·sure \'lēzh-ər, 'lezh-, 'lāzh-\ *n* [ME *leiser*, fr. OF *leisir*, fr. *leisir* to be permitted, fr. L *licēre* — more at LICENSE] **1 :** freedom provided by the cessation of activities; *esp* : time free from work or duties **2 :** EASE, LEISURELINESS — **leisure** *adj*

lei·sure·li·ness \-lē-nəs\ *n* **:** the quality or state of being leisurely

lei·sure·ly \-lē\ *adj* **:** characterized by leisure **:** UNHURRIED — **leisurely** *adv*
leit·mo·tiv *or* **leit·mo·tif** \'līt-mō-,tēf\ *n* [G *leitmotiv,* fr. *leiten* to lead + *motiv* motive] **1 :** an associated melodic phrase or figure that accompanies the reappearance of an idea, person, or situation in a Wagnerian music drama **2 :** a dominant recurring theme
lek \'lek\ *n* [Alb] — see MONEY table
le·man \'lem-ən, 'lē-mən\ *n* [ME *lefman, leman,* fr. *lef* lief] *archaic* **:** SWEETHEART, LOVER; *esp* **:** MISTRESS
[1]**lem·ma** \'lem-ə\ *n, pl* **lemmas** *or* **lem·ma·ta** \'lem-ət-ə\ [L, fr. Gk *lēmma* thing taken, assumption, fr. *lambanein* to take — more at LATCH] **1 :** an auxiliary proposition accepted as true for use in the demonstration of another proposition **2 a :** the heading or theme of a comment or note on a text **b :** a glossed word or phrase
[2]**lemma** *n* [Gk, husk, fr. *lepein* to peel — more at LEPER] **:** the lower of the two bracts enclosing the flower in the spikelet of grasses
lem·ming \'lem-iŋ\ *n* [Norw; akin to ON *lōmr* guillemot, L *latrare* to bark — more at LAMENT] **:** any of several small short-tailed furry-footed rodents (genera *Lemmus* and *Dicrostonyx*) of circumpolar distribution that are notable for the recurrent mass migrations of a European form (*L. lemmus*) which often continue into the sea where vast numbers are drowned
lem·nis·cus \lem-'nis-kəs\ *n, pl* **lem·nis·ci** \-'nis-,(k)ī, -'nis-,kē\ [NL, fr. L, ribbon, fr. Gk *lēmniskos*] **:** a band of fibers and esp. nerve fibers
[1]**lem·on** \'lem-ən\ *n* [ME *lymon,* fr. MF *limon,* fr. ML *limon-, limo,* fr. Ar *laymūn*] **1 a :** an acid fruit that is botanically a many-seeded pale yellow oblong berry **b :** the stout thorny tree (*Citrus limon*) that bears this fruit **2 :** DUD, FAILURE
[2]**lemon** *adj* **1 a :** containing lemon **b :** having the flavor or scent of lemon **2 :** of the color lemon yellow
lem·on·ade \,lem-ə-'nād\ *n* **:** a beverage of sweetened lemon juice mixed with water
lemon balm *n* **:** a bushy perennial Old World mint (*Melissa officinalis*) often cultivated for its fragrant lemon-flavored leaves
lemon yellow *n* **:** a variable color averaging a brilliant greenish yellow
lem·pi·ra \lem-'pir-ə\ *n* [AmerSp, fr. *Lempira,* Indian chief] — see MONEY table
le·mur \'lē-mər\ *n* [L *lemures,* pl., ghosts; akin to Gk *lamia* devouring monster] **:** any of numerous arboreal chiefly nocturnal mammals formerly widespread but now largely confined to Madagascar that are related to the monkeys but usu. regarded as constituting a distinct superfamily (Lemuroidea) and usu. have a muzzle like a fox, large eyes, very soft woolly fur, and a long furry tail
le·mu·res \'lem-ə-,rās, 'lem-yə-,rēz\ *n pl* [L] **:** spirits of the dead exorcised from homes in early Roman religious observances
lend \'lend\ *vb* **lent** \'lent\ **lend·ing** [ME *lenen, lenden,* fr. OE *lǣnan,* fr. *lǣn* loan — more at LOAN] *vt* **1 a :** to give for temporary use on condition that the same or its equivalent be returned **b :** to let out (money) for temporary use on condition of repayment with interest **2 a :** AFFORD, FURNISH **b :** to adapt or apply (oneself) **:** ACCOMMODATE ~ *vi* **:** to make a loan — **lend·er** *n*
lend-lease \'len-'dlēs\ *n* [U.S. *Lend-Lease* Act (1941)] **:** the transfer of goods and services to an ally to aid in a common cause with payment being made by a return of the original items or their use in the common cause or by a similar transfer of other goods and services — **lend-lease** *vt*
length \'leŋ(k)th\ *n, pl* **lengths** \'leŋ(k)ths, 'leŋ(k)s\ [ME *lengthe,* fr. OE *lengthu,* fr. *lang* long] **1 a :** the longer or longest dimension of an object **b :** a measured distance or dimension ⟨10-inch ~⟩ — see MEASURE table, METRIC SYSTEM table **c :** the quality or state of being long **2 a :** duration or extent in time **b :** relative duration or stress of a sound **3 a :** distance or extent in space **b :** the length of something taken as a unit of measure ⟨horse led by a ~⟩ **4 :** the degree to which something is carried **5 a :** a long expanse or stretch **b :** a piece constituting or usable as part of a whole or of a connected series **:** SECTION **6 :** a vertical dimension of an article of clothing — **at length 1 :** COMPREHENSIVELY, FULLY **2 :** at last **:** FINALLY
length·en \'leŋ(k)-thən\ *vb* **length·en·ing** \'leŋ(k)th-(ə-)niŋ\ **:** to make longer ~ *vi* **:** to grow longer **syn** see EXTEND — **length·en·er** \'leŋ(k)th-(ə-)nər\ *n*
length·i·ly \'leŋ(k)-thə-lē\ *adv* **:** in a lengthy manner **:** at length
length·i·ness \'leŋ(k)-thē-nəs\ *n* **:** the quality or state of being lengthy
length·ways \'leŋ(k)th-,wāz\ *adv* **:** LENGTHWISE
length·wise \-,wīz\ *adv* **:** in the direction of the length **:** LONGITUDINALLY — **lengthwise** *adj*
lengthy \'leŋ(k)-thē\ *adj* **1 :** protracted excessively **:** OVERLONG **2 :** EXTENDED, LONG
le·nien·cy \'lē-nē-ən-sē, -nyən-sē\ *or* **le·nience** \-nē-ən(t)s, -nyən(t)s\ *n* **:** the quality or state of being lenient
le·nient \'lē-nē-ənt, -nyənt\ *adj* [L *lenient-, leniens,* prp. of *lenire* to soften, soothe, fr. *lenis* soft, mild — more at LET] **1** *archaic* **:** relieving pain or stress **2 :** of mild and tolerant disposition or effect; *esp* **:** INDULGENT **syn** see SOFT — **le·nient·ly** *adv*
Leni-Le·na·pe *or* **Len·ni-Le·na·pe** \,len-ē-lə-'näp-ē, ,len-ē-'len-ə-pē\ *n* [Delaware] **:** DELAWARE 1
Le·nin·ism \'len-ə-,niz-əm, 'lān-\ *n* **:** the political, economic, and social principles and policies advocated by Lenin; *esp* **:** the theory and practice of communism developed by or associated with Lenin — **Le·nin·ist** \-nəst\ *n or adj* — **Le·nin·ite** \-,nīt\ *n or adj*
le·nis \'lē-nəs, 'lā-\ *adj* [NL, fr. L, mild, smooth] **:** produced with relatively lax articulation and weak expiration ⟨\d\ in *doe* is ~, \t\ in *toe* is fortis⟩
len·i·tive \'len-ət-iv\ *adj* [MF *lenitif,* fr. ML *lenitivus,* fr. L *lenitus,* pp. of *lenire*] **:** alleviating pain or acrimony **:** MITIGATING — **lenitive** *n*
len·i·ty \'len-ət-ē\ *n* **:** MILDNESS, LENIENCY **syn** see MERCY
[1]**lens** \'lenz\ *n* [NL *lent-, lens,* fr. L, lentil; fr. its shape — more at LENTIL] **1 a :** a piece of glass or other transparent substance that has two opposite regular surfaces either both curved or one curved and the other plane and that is used either singly or combined in an optical instrument for forming an image by focusing rays of light **b :** a combination of two or more simple lenses **2 :** a device for directing or focusing radiation other than light (as sound waves, radio microwaves, electrons) **3 :** something shaped like a double-convex optical lens **4 :** a highly transparent biconvex lens-shaped or nearly spherical body in the eye that focuses light rays (as upon the retina)

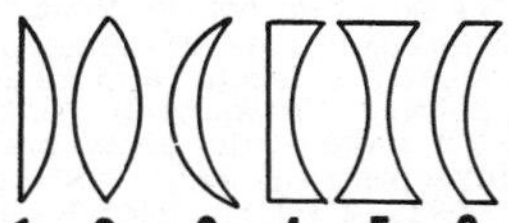

1 2 3 4 5 6

lens 1a: *1* plano-convex, *2* biconvex, *3* converging meniscus, *4* plano-concave, *5* biconcave, *6* diverging meniscus

[2]**lens** *vt* **:** PHOTOGRAPH; *esp* **:** to make a motion picture of
Lent \'lent\ *n* [ME *lente* springtime, Lent, fr. OE *lengten;* akin to OHG *lenzin* spring] **1 :** a period of penitence and fasting observed on the 40 weekdays from Ash Wednesday to Easter in the Roman Catholic and some other Christian churches **2 :** a period of religious fasting
len·ta·men·te \,lent-ə-'men-(,)tā\ *adv* (*or adj*) [It, fr. *lento* slow] **:** SLOWLY — used as a direction in music
len·tan·do \len-'tän-(,)dō\ *adv* (*or adj*) [It] **:** in a retarding manner — used as a direction in music
Lent·en \'lent-ᵊn\ *adj* **1 :** of or relating to Lent **2 :** suitable to Lent; *esp* **:** MEAGER, SOMBER
len·tic \'lent-ik\ *adj* [L *lentus* sluggish] **:** of, relating to, or living in still waters
len·ti·cel \'lent-ə-,sel\ *n* [NL *lenticella,* dim. of L *lent-, lens* lentil] **:** a pore in the stems of woody plants that is a path of exchange of gases between the atmosphere and the stem tissues — **len·ti·cel·late** \,lent-ə-'sel-ət\ *adj* — **len·tic·u·late** \len-'tik-yə-lət\ *adj*
len·tic·u·lar \len-'tik-yə-lər\ *adj* [L *lenticularis* lentil-shaped, fr. *lenticula* lentil] **1 :** having the shape of a double-convex lens **2 :** of or relating to a lens **3 a :** LENTICULATED **b :** utilizing lenticules
len·tic·u·late \len-'tik-yə-lət\ *vt* **:** to provide with lenticules (as by embossing, molding, or coating) ⟨*lenticulated* film⟩ — **len·tic·u·la·tion** \(,)len-,tik-yə-'lā-shən\ *n*
len·ti·cule \'lent-ə-,kyü(ə)l\ *n* [L *lenticula* lentil] **:** any of the minute lenses on the base side of a film used in stereoscopic or color photography
len·til \'lent-ᵊl\ *n* [ME, fr. OF *lentille,* fr. L *lenticula,* dim. of *lent-, lens;* akin to Gk *lathyros* vetch] **1 :** a widely cultivated Eurasian annual leguminous plant (*Lens culinaris*) with flattened edible seeds and leafy stalks used as fodder **2 :** the seed of the lentil
len·tis·si·mo \len-'tis-ə-,mō\ *adv* (*or adj*) [It, superl. of *lento*] **:** in a very slow manner — used as a direction in music
len·to \'len-(,)tō\ *adv* (*or adj*) [It, fr. *lento,* adj., slow, fr. L *lentus* pliant, sluggish, slow — more at LITHE] **:** in a slow manner — used as a direction in music
Leo \'lē-(,)ō\ *n* [L (gen. *Leonis*), lit., lion — more at LION] **1 :** a northern constellation east of Cancer **2 :** the 5th sign of the zodiac
Le·o·nar·desque \,lā-ə-,när-'desk\ *adj* [*Leonardo* da Vinci †1519 Florentine artist & scientist] **:** of, relating to, or suggesting Leonardo or his style of painting
le·one \lē'ōn\ *n* [*Sierra Leone*] — see MONEY table
Leo·nid \'lē-ə-nəd\ *n, pl* **Leonids** *or* **Le·on·i·des** \lē-'än-ə-,dēz\ [L *Leon-, Leo;* fr. their appearing to radiate from a point in Leo] **:** one of the shooting stars constituting the meteoric shower that recurs near the 14th of November
le·o·nine \'lē-ə-,nīn\ *adj* [ME, fr. L *leoninus,* fr. *leon-, leo*] **:** of, relating to, or resembling a lion
leop·ard \'lep-ərd\ *n* [ME, fr. OF *leupart,* fr. LL *leopardus,* fr. Gk *leopardos,* fr. *leōn* lion + *pardos* pard] **1 :** a large strong cat (*Felis pardus*) of southern Asia and Africa that is usu. tawny or buff with black spots arranged in broken rings or rosettes — called also *panther* **2 :** a heraldic representation of a lion walking forward with head to the front — **leop·ard·ess** \-ərd-əs\ *n*
le·o·tard \'lē-ə-,tärd\ *n* [Jules *Léotard,* 19th cent. F aerial gymnast] **1 :** a close-fitting garment usu. with long sleeves, a high neck, and ankle-length legs worn for practice or performance by dancers, acrobats, and aerialists **2 :** TIGHTS
lep·er \'lep-ər\ *n* [ME, fr. *lepre* leprosy, fr. OF, fr. LL *lepra,* fr. Gk, fr. *lepein* to peel; akin to OE *lǣfer* reed] **1 :** a person affected with leprosy **2 :** a person shunned for moral or social reasons
lepid- *or* **lepido-** *comb form* [NL, fr. Gk, fr. *lepid-, lepis* scale, fr *lepein*] **:** flake **:** scale ⟨*Lepido*ptera⟩
le·pid·o·lite \li-'pid-ᵊl-,īt\ *n* [G *lepidolith,* fr. *lepid-* + *-lith*] **:** a variable mineral typically $K(Li,Al)_3(Si,Al)_4O_{10}(F,OH)_2$ that consists of a mica containing lithium
lep·i·dop·ter \,lep-ə-'däp-tər\ *n* **:** LEPIDOPTERAN
lep·i·dop·ter·an \-tə-rən\ *n* [NL *Lepidoptera* order of insects, fr. *lepid-* + Gk *pteron* wing — more at FEATHER] **:** any of a large order (Lepidoptera) of insects comprising the butterflies and moths whose adults have four broad or lanceolate wings usu. covered with minute overlapping often brightly colored scales and whose larvae are caterpillars — **lep·i·dop·ter·al** \-tə-rəl\ *adj* — **lepidopteran** *adj* — **lep·i·dop·ter·id** \-rəd\ *n* — **lep·i·dop·ter·ous** \-rəs\ *adj*
lep·i·dop·ter·on \-rən, -,rän\ *n, pl* **lep·i·dop·tera** \-rə\ [NL, sing. of *Lepidoptera*] **:** LEPIDOPTERAN
lep·i·do·sis \,lep-ə-'dō-səs\ *n, pl* **lep·i·do·ses** \-'dō-,sēz\ [NL] **:** the arrangement and character of the scales or shields of an animal
lep·i·dote \'lep-ə-,dōt\ *adj* [Gk *lepidōtos* scaly, fr. *lepid-, lepis*] **:** covered with scurf or scurfy scales
lep·re·chaun \'lep-rə-,kän, -,kȯn\ *n* [IrGael *leipreachān*] **:** a mischievous elf of Irish folklore usu. believed to reveal the hiding place of treasure if caught
lep·rose \'lep-,rōs\ *adj* [LL *leprosus* leprous] **:** SCURFY, SCALY
lep·ro·sy \'lep-rə-sē\ *n* **1 :** a chronic disease caused by bacillus (*Mycobacterium leprae*) and characterized by the formation of nodules or of macules that enlarge and spread accompanied by loss of sensation with eventual paralysis, wasting of muscle, and production of deformities and mutilations **2 :** a harmful influence — **lep·rot·ic** \le-'prät-ik\ *adj*
lep·rous \'lep-rəs\ *adj* [ME, fr. LL *leprosus* leprous, fr. *lepra* leprosy] **1 a :** infected with leprosy **b :** of, relating to, or resembling leprosy or a leper **2 :** LEPROSE — **lep·rous·ly** *adv* — **lep·rous·ness** *n*

-lep·sy *n comb form* [MF *-lepsie*, fr. LL *-lepsia*, fr. Gk *-lēpsia*, fr. *lēpsis*, fr. *lambanein* to take, seize — more at LATCH] **:** taking **:** seizure ⟨nympho*lepsy*⟩

lep·to·ceph·a·lus \ˌlep-tə-ˈsef-ə-ləs\ *n, pl* **lep·to·ceph·a·li** \-ˌlī\ [NL, fr. Gk *leptos* + *kephalē* head — more at CEPHALIC] **:** a long thin small-headed transparent pelagic first larva of various eels

[1]**lep·ton** \ˈlep-ˌtän\ *n, pl* **lep·ta** \-tə\ [NGk, fr. Gk, a small coin, fr. neut. of *leptos* peeled, slender, small, fr. *lepein* to peel — more at LEPER] — see *drachma* at MONEY table

[2]**lepton** *n* [Gk *leptos* + E *-on*] **:** a charged or uncharged elementary particle (as a positron or a neutrino) of small mass

lep·to·some \ˈlep-tə-ˌsōm\ *adj* [G *leptosom*, fr. Gk *leptos* slender + *soma* body] **:** ASTHENIC 2, ECTOMORPHIC — **leptosome** *n*

lep·to·spi·ral \ˌlep-tə-ˈspī-rəl\ *adj* [NL *Leptospira*, genus of spirochetes, fr. Gk *leptos* + L *spira* coil] **:** of, relating to, or caused by slender aerobic spirochetes (genus *Leptospira*)

lep·tus \ˈlep-təs\ *n* [NL, fr. Gk *leptos* small] **:** any of several 6-legged larval mites — often used as if a generic name; compare CYSTICERCUS

[1]**les·bi·an** \ˈlez-bē-ən\ *adj, often cap* **1 :** of or relating to Lesbos **2** [fr. the reputed homosexual band associated with Sappho of Lesbos] **:** of or relating to homosexuality between females

[2]**lesbian** *n, often cap* **:** a female homosexual

les·bi·an·ism \-ə-ˌniz-əm\ *n* **:** female homosexuality

lese maj·es·ty *or* **lèse ma·jes·té** \ˈlēz-ˈmaj-ə-stē\ *n* [MF *lese majesté* fr. L *laesa majestas*, lit., injured majesty] **1 a :** a crime committed against a sovereign power **b :** an offense violating the dignity of a ruler as the representative of a sovereign power **2 :** a detraction from or affront to dignity or importance

le·sion \ˈlē-zhən\ *n* [ME, fr. MF, fr. L *laesion-*, *laesio*, fr. *laesus*, pp. of *laedere* to injure] **1 :** INJURY, HARM **2 :** an abnormal change in structure of an organ or part due to injury or disease; *esp* **:** one that is circumscribed and well defined

les·pe·de·za \ˌles-pə-ˈdē-zə\ *n* [NL, irreg. fr. V. M. de *Zespedes* *fl*1785 Sp governor of East Florida] **:** any of a genus (*Lespedeza*) of herbaceous or shrubby leguminous plants including some widely used for forage, soil improvement, and esp. hay

[1]**less** \ˈles\ *adj* [ME, partly fr. OE *lǣs*, adv. & n.; partly fr. *lǣssa*, adj.; akin to OFris *lēs* less, Gk *limos* hunger] **1 :** FEWER ⟨~ than three⟩ **2 :** of lower rank, degree, or importance ⟨no ~ a person than the president himself⟩ **3 a :** SMALLER, SLIGHTER **b :** more limited in quantity ⟨in ~ time⟩

[2]**less** *adv* **:** to a lesser extent or degree

[3]**less** *prep* **:** diminished by **:** MINUS

[4]**less** *n, pl* **less 1 :** a smaller portion or quantity **2 :** something of less importance

-less \ləs\ *adj suffix* [ME *-les*, *-lesse*, fr. OE *-lēas*, fr. *lēas* devoid, false; akin to OHG *lōs* loose, OE *losian* to get lost — more at LOSE] **1 :** destitute of **:** not having ⟨wit*less*⟩ ⟨child*less*⟩ **2 :** unable to be acted on or to act (in a specified way) ⟨daunt*less*⟩ ⟨fade*less*⟩

les·see \le-ˈsē\ *n* [ME, fr. AF, fr. *lessé*, pp. of *lesser* to lease — more at LEASE] **:** a tenant under a lease

less·en \ˈles-ᵊn\ *vb* **less·en·ing** \ˈles-niŋ, -ᵊn-iŋ\ *vi* **:** to shrink in size, number, or degree **:** DECREASE ~ *vt* **1 :** to reduce in size, extent, or degree **2 a** *archaic* **:** MINIMIZE **b** *obs* **:** to lower in status or dignity **:** DEGRADE **syn** see DECREASE

[1]**less·er** \ˈles-ər\ *adj* **1 :** LESS, SMALLER **2 :** INFERIOR

[2]**lesser** *adv* **:** LESS ⟨*lesser*-known⟩

Lesser Bear *n* **:** URSA MINOR

Lesser Dog *n* **:** CANIS MINOR

[1]**les·son** \ˈles-ᵊn\ *n* [ME, fr. OF *leçon*, fr. LL *lection-*, *lectio*, fr. L, act of reading, fr. *lectus*, pp. of *legere* to read — more at LEGEND] **1 :** a passage from sacred writings read in a service of worship **2 a :** a piece of instruction **:** TEACHING; *specif* **:** a reading or exercise to be studied by a pupil **b :** something learned by study or experience **3 a :** a division of a course of instruction **b :** an instructive example; *specif* **:** REPRIMAND

[2]**lesson** *vt* **les·son·ing** \ˈles-niŋ, -ᵊn-iŋ\ **1 :** to give a lesson to **:** INSTRUCT **2 :** LECTURE, REBUKE

les·sor \ˈles-ˌȯ(ə)r, le-ˈsȯ(ə)r\ *n* [ME *lessour*, fr. AF, fr. *lesser* to lease] **:** one that conveys by lease

lest \(ˌ)lest\ *conj* [ME *les the*, *leste*, fr. OE *thȳ lǣs the*, fr. *thȳ* (instrumental of *thæt* that) + *lǣs* + *the*, relative particle] **1 :** for fear that **2 :** THAT — used after an expression denoting fear or apprehension ⟨worried ~ he should be late⟩

[1]**let** \ˈlet\ *vt* **let·ted**; **letted** *or* **let**; **let·ting** [ME *letten*, fr. OE *lettan* to delay, hinder; akin to OHG *lezzen* to delay, hurt, OE *læt* late] *archaic* **:** HINDER, PREVENT

[2]**let** *n* **1 :** something that impedes **:** OBSTRUCTION **2 :** a stroke in racket games that does not count

[3]**let** *vb* **let**; **let·ting** [ME *leten*, fr. OE *lǣtan*; akin to OHG *lāzzan* to permit, L *lassus* weary, *lenis* soft, mild] *vt* **1 :** to cause to **:** MAKE ⟨~ it be known⟩ **2 a :** RENT, LEASE ⟨~ rooms⟩ **b :** to assign esp. after bids ⟨~ a contract⟩ **3 a :** to give opportunity to ⟨live and ~ live⟩ **b** — used in the imperative to introduce a request or proposal ⟨~ us pray⟩ **c** — used imperatively as an auxiliary to express a warning ⟨~ him try⟩ **4 :** to free from confinement **:** RELEASE ⟨~ the prisoner go⟩ **5 :** to permit to enter, pass, or leave ⟨~ them through⟩ ~ *vi* **1 :** to become rented or leased **2 :** to become awarded to a contractor

syn LET, ALLOW, PERMIT mean not to forbid or prevent. LET may imply a positive giving of permission but more often implies failure to prevent either through inadvertence and negligence or through lack of power or effective authority; ALLOW implies little more than a forbearing to prohibit; PERMIT implies willingness or acquiescence **syn** see in addition HIRE

-let \lət\ *n suffix* [ME, fr. MF *-elet*, fr. *-el*, dim. suffix (fr. L *-ellus*) + *-et*] **1 :** small one ⟨book*let*⟩ **2 :** article worn on ⟨wrist*let*⟩

let·down \ˈlet-ˌdau̇n\ *n* **1 a :** DISCOURAGEMENT, DISAPPOINTMENT **b :** a slackening of effort **:** RELAXATION **2 :** the descent of an airplane to the point at which a landing approach is begun

[1]**le·thal** \ˈlē-thəl\ *adj* [L *letalis*, *lethalis*, fr. *letum* death] **1 :** of, relating to, or causing death **2 :** capable of causing death **syn** see DEADLY — **le·thal·i·ty** \lē-ˈthal-ət-ē\ *n* — **le·thal·ly** \ˈlēth-(ə-)lē\ *adv*

[2]**lethal** *n* **1 :** an abnormality of genetic origin causing the death of the organism possessing it **2 :** LETHAL GENE

lethal gene *n* **:** a gene that in some (as homozygous) conditions may prevent development or cause the death of an organism or its germ cells — called also *lethal factor*

le·thar·gic \li-ˈthär-jik, le-\ *adj* **1 :** of, relating to, or characterized by lethargy **:** SLUGGISH **2 :** INDIFFERENT, APATHETIC — **le·thar·gi·cal·ly** \-ji-k(ə-)lē\ *adv*

leth·ar·gy \ˈleth-ər-jē\ *n* [ME *litargie*, fr. ML *litargia*, fr. LL *lethargia*, fr. Gk *lēthargia*, fr. *lēthargos* forgetful, lethargic, fr. *lēthē* + *argos* lazy — more at ARGON] **1 :** abnormal drowsiness **2 :** the quality or state of being lazy or indifferent

syn LETHARGY, LANGUOR, LASSITUDE, STUPOR, TORPOR mean physical or mental inertness. LETHARGY implies such drowsiness or aversion to activity as is induced by disease, injury, drugs; LANGUOR suggests inertia induced by an enervating climate or illness or amorous emotion; LASSITUDE stresses listlessness or indifference resulting from fatigue or poor health; STUPOR implies a deadening of the mind and senses by shock, by narcotics, or intoxicants; TORPOR implies a state of suspended animation as of hibernating animals but may suggest merely a lack of vigor or normal responsiveness

le·the \ˈlē-thē\ *n* [L, fr. Gk *Lēthē*, fr. *lēthē* forgetfulness; akin to Gk *lanthanein* to escape notice, *lanthanesthai* to forget — more at LATENT] **1** *cap* **:** a river of Hades whose water according to Greek mythology causes forgetfulness of the past in those who drink it **2 :** OBLIVION, FORGETFULNESS — **le·the·an** \ˈlē-thē-ən, li-ˈthē-\ *adj, often cap*

Le·to \ˈlē-ˌtō\ *n* [Gk *Lētō*] **:** the mother of Apollo and Artemis by Zeus

let's \(ˌ)lets, *rapid* (ˌ)les\ **:** let us

Lett \ˈlet\ *n* [G *Lette*, fr. Latvian *Latvi*] **:** a member of a people closely related to the Lithuanians and mainly inhabiting Latvia

[1]**let·ter** \ˈlet-ər\ *n* [ME, fr. OF *lettre*, fr. L *littera* letter of the alphabet, *litterae*, pl., epistle, literature] **1 :** a symbol usu. written or printed representing a speech sound and constituting a unit of an alphabet **2 a :** a direct or personal written or printed message addressed to a person or organization **b :** a written communication containing a grant — usu. used in pl. **3** *pl but sing or pl in constr* **a :** LITERATURE, BELLES LETTRES **b :** LEARNING **4 :** the strict or outward sense or significance **5 a :** a single piece of type **b :** a style of type **c :** TYPE; *esp* **:** a supply of type **6 :** the initial of a school awarded to a student for achievement usu. in athletics

[2]**letter** *vt* **1 :** to set down in letters **:** PRINT **2 :** to mark with letters **:** INSCRIBE — **let·ter·er** \-ər-ər\ *n*

[3]**let·ter** \ˈlet-ər\ *n* **:** one that rents or leases

letter carrier *n* **:** MAILMAN

let·tered \ˈlet-ərd\ *adj* **1 a :** LEARNED, EDUCATED **b :** of, relating to, or characterized by learning **:** CULTURED **2 :** inscribed with or as if with letters

let·ter·head \ˈlet-ər-ˌhed\ *n* **1 :** a sheet of stationery printed or engraved usu. with the name and address of an organization **2 :** the heading at the top of a letterhead

let·ter·ing *n* **:** letters used in an inscription

letter missive *n, pl* **letters missive :** a letter from a superior authority conveying a command, recommendation, permission, or invitation

letter of credence : a formal document furnished a diplomatic agent attesting to his power to act for his government — called also *letters of credence*

letter of credit 1 : a letter addressed by a banker to a correspondent certifying that a person named therein is entitled to draw on him or his credit up to a certain sum **2 :** a letter addressed by a banker to a person to whom credit is given authorizing him to draw on the issuing bank or on a bank in his country up to a certain sum and guaranteeing to accept the drafts if duly made

let·ter–per·fect \ˌlet-ər-ˈpər-fikt\ *adj* **:** correct to the smallest detail; *esp* **:** VERBATIM

let·ter·press \ˈlet-ər-ˌpres\ *n* **1 a :** the process of printing direct from an inked raised surface upon which the paper is impressed **b :** work done by this process **2 :** text that is distinct from pictorial illustrations

letter sheet *n* **:** a sheet of stationery that can be folded and sealed with the message inside to form its own envelope

letters of administration : a letter evidencing the right of an administrator to administer the goods or estate of a deceased person

letters of marque : written authority granted to a private person by a government to seize the subjects of a foreign state or their goods; *specif* **:** a license granted to a private person to fit out an armed ship to plunder the enemy

letters patent *n pl* **:** written grant from a government to a person in a form readily open for inspection by all

letters testamentary *n pl* **:** a written communication from a court or officer informing an executor of his appointment and authority to execute the will of the testator

[1]**Lett·ish** \ˈlet-ish\ *adj* **:** of or relating to the Latvians or their language

[2]**Lettish** *n* **:** LATVIAN 2

let·tre de ca·chet \ˌle-trə-də-ˌka-ˈshā\ *n, pl* **lettres de cachet** \-trə(z)-\ [F] **:** a letter bearing an official seal and usu. authorizing imprisonment without trial of a named person

let·tuce \ˈlet-əs\ *n* [ME *letuse*, fr. OF *laitues*, pl. of *laitue*, fr. L *lactuca*, fr. *lact-*, *lac* milk; fr. its milky juice — more at GALAXY] **:** any of a genus (*Lactuca*) of composite plants; *esp* **:** a common garden vegetable (*L. sativa*) the succulent leaves of which are used esp. in salads

let up *vi* **1 a :** to diminish or slow down **b :** CEASE, STOP **2 :** to become less severe — used with *on*

let·up \ˈlet-ˌəp\ *n* **:** a lessening of effort

leu \ˈleu̇\ *n, pl* **lei** \ˈlā\ [Romanian, lit., lion, fr. L *leo* — more at LION] — see MONEY table

leuc- *or* **leuco-** *also* **leuk-** *or* **leuko-** *comb form* [NL, fr. Gk *leuk-*, *leuko-*, fr. *leukos* — more at LIGHT] **1 :** white **:** colorless **:** weakly colored ⟨*leuko*cyte⟩ ⟨*leuko*rrhea⟩ **2 :** leukocyte ⟨*leuk*emia⟩ **3 :** white matter of the brain ⟨*leuco*tomy⟩

leu·cine \ˈlü-ˌsēn\ *n* [ISV] **:** a white crystalline essential amino acid $(CH_3)_2CHCH_2CH(NH_2)COOH$ obtained by the hydrolysis of most dietary proteins

leu·cite \ˈlü-ˌsīt\ *n* [G *leuzit*, fr. *leuz-* leuc-] **:** a white or gray mineral $KAlSi_2O_6$ consisting of a potassium aluminum silicate and occurring in igneous rocks — **leu·cit·ic** \lü-ˈsit-ik\ *adj*

leu·co·ma \lü-ˈkō-mə\ *n* [LL, fr. Gk *leukōma*, fr. *leukos* white] **:** a dense white opacity in the cornea of the eye

leu·co·maine \ˈlü-kə-ˌmān\ *n* [ISV *leuc-* + *-maine* (as in *ptomaine*)] **:** a basic substance normally produced in the body as a decomposition product of protein

leu·co·plast \-ˌplast\ *also* **leu·co·plas·tid** \ˌlü-kə-'plas-təd\ *n* [ISV] **:** a colorless plastid esp. in the cytoplasm of interior plant tissues that is potentially capable of developing into a chromoplast

leu·ke·mia \lü-'kē-mē-ə\ *n* [NL] **:** an acute or chronic disease of unknown cause in man and other warm-blooded animals characterized by an abnormal increase in the number of leukocytes in the tissues and often in the blood — **leu·ke·mic** \-mik\ *adj* — **leu·ke·moid** \-ˌmȯid\ *adj*

leukocyt- *or* **leukocyto-** *also* **leucocyt-** *or* **leucocyto-** *comb form* [ISV] **:** leukocyte ⟨*leukocyto*sis⟩

leu·ko·cyte \'lü-kə-ˌsīt\ *n* [ISV] **:** any of the white or colorless nucleated cells that occur in blood — **leu·ko·cyt·ic** \ˌlü-kə-'sit-ik\ *adj* — **leu·ko·cyt·oid** \-'sīt-ˌȯid\ *adj*

leu·ko·cy·to·blast \ˌlü-kə-'sīt-ə-ˌblast\ *n* **:** a cellular precursor of a leukocyte — **leu·ko·cy·to·blas·tic** \-ˌsīt-ə-'blas-tik\ *adj*

leu·ko·cy·to·sis \ˌlü-kə-ˌsī-'tō-səs\ *n* [NL] **:** an increase in the number of leukocytes in the circulating blood — **leu·ko·cy·tot·ic** \-'tät-ik\ *adj*

leu·kon \'lü-ˌkän\ *n* [NL, fr. Gk, neut. of *leukos*] **:** the white blood cells and their precursors

leu·ko·pe·nia \ˌlü-kə-'pē-nē-ə\ *n* [NL, fr. *leuc-* + Gk *penia* poverty, lack] **:** a condition in which the number of leukocytes circulating in the blood is abnormally low — **leu·ko·pe·nic** \-nik\ *adj*

leu·ko·poi·e·sis \-ˌpȯi-'ē-səs\ *n* [NL] **:** the formation of white blood cells — **leu·ko·poi·et·ic** \-'et-ik\ *adj*

leu·kor·rhea \ˌlü-kə-'rē-ə\ *n* [NL] **:** a whitish viscid discharge from the vagina resulting from inflammation or congestion of the mucous membrane — **leu·kor·rhe·al** \-'rē-əl\ *adj*

leu·ko·sis \lü-'kō-səs\ *n* [NL] **:** LEUKEMIA — **leu·kot·ic** \-'kät-ik\ *adj*

lev \'lef\ *n, pl* **le·va** \'lev-ə\ [Bulg, lit., lion] — see MONEY table

lev- *or* **levo-** *comb form* [F *lévo-*, fr. L *laevus* left; akin to Gk *laios* left] **1 :** levorotatory ⟨*lev*ulose⟩ **2 :** to the left ⟨*levo*rotatory⟩

Le·val·loi·si·an \ˌlev-ə-'lȯi-zē-ən\ *adj* [*Levallois*-Perret, suburb of Paris, France] **:** of or relating to a lower Paleolithic culture characterized by a technique of manufacturing tools by striking flakes from a flat flint nodule

le·vant \li-'vant\ *vi* [perh. fr. Sp *levantar* to break camp, deriv. of L *levare*] *chiefly Brit* **:** to run away from a debt

le·vant·er \-ər\ *n* **1** *cap* **:** a native or inhabitant of the Levant **2 :** a strong easterly Mediterranean wind

le·va·tor \li-'vāt-ər\ *n, pl* **lev·a·to·res** \ˌlev-ə-'tōr-(ˌ)ēz\ *or* **le·va·tors** \li-'vāt-ərz\ [NL, fr. L *levatus*, pp. of *levare* to raise — more at LEVER] **:** a muscle that serves to raise a body part — compare DEPRESSOR

[1]le·vee \'lev-ē; lə-'vē, -'vā\ *n* [F *lever*, fr. MF, act of arising, fr. (*se*) *lever* to rise] **1 :** a reception held by a person of distinction on rising from bed **2 :** an afternoon assembly at which the British king or his representative receives only men **3 :** a reception usu. in honor of a particular person

[2]lev·ee \'lev-ē\ *n* [F *levée*, fr. OF, act of raising, fr. *lever* to raise — more at LEVER] **1 a :** an embankment to prevent flooding **b :** a river landing place **:** PIER **2 :** a small continuous dike or ridge of earth for confining the irrigation checks of land to be flooded

[3]lev·ee \'lev-ē\ *vt* **lev·eed; lev·ee·ing :** to provide with a levee

[1]lev·el \'lev-əl\ *n* [ME, fr. MF *livel*, fr. (assumed) VL *libellum*, alter. of L *libella*, fr. dim. of *libra* weight, balance] **1 :** a device for establishing a horizontal line or plane by means of a bubble in a liquid that shows adjustment to the horizontal by movement to the center of a slightly bowed glass tube **2 :** a measurement of the difference of altitude of two points by means of a level **3 :** horizontal condition; *esp* **:** equilibrium of a fluid marked by a horizontal surface of even altitude ⟨water seeks its own ~⟩ **4 a :** an approximately horizontal line or surface taken as an index of altitude **b :** a practically horizontal surface or area **5 :** a position in any scale **:** RANK **6 a :** a line or surface that cuts perpendicularly all plumb lines that it meets and hence would everywhere coincide with a surface of still water **b :** the plane of the horizon or a line in it **7 :** a horizontal passage in a mine intended for regular working and transportation **8 :** a concentration of a constituent of the blood or other body fluid **9 :** the magnitude of a quantity considered in relation to an arbitrary reference value — **on the level :** bona fide **:** HONEST

[2]level *vb* **lev·eled** *or* **lev·elled; lev·el·ing** *or* **lev·el·ling** \'lev-(ə-)liŋ\ *vt* **1 :** to make (a line or surface) horizontal **:** make flat or level **2 a :** to bring to a horizontal aiming position **b :** AIM, DIRECT **3 :** to bring to a common level or plane **:** EQUALIZE **4 :** to lay level with the ground **:** RAZE **5 :** to make even, equal, or uniform **6 :** to find the heights of different points in (a piece of land) esp. with a surveyor's level ~ *vi* **1 :** to attain or come to a level **2 :** to aim a gun or other weapon horizontally **3 :** to bring persons or things to a level **4 :** to deal frankly and openly

[3]level *adj* **1 a :** having no part higher than another **:** conforming to the curvature of the liquid parts of the earth's surface **b :** parallel with the plane of the horizon **:** HORIZONTAL **2 a :** even or unvarying in height **b :** equal in advantage, progression, or standing **c :** proceeding monotonously or uneventfully **d** (1) **:** STEADY, UNWAVERING (2) **:** CALM, UNEXCITED **e :** contested on even terms **3 :** BALANCED ⟨a ~ head⟩ **4 :** distributed evenly ⟨~ stress⟩ **5 :** being a surface perpendicular to all lines of force in a field of force **:** EQUIPOTENTIAL **6 :** suited to a particular rank or plane of ability or achievement ⟨top-*level* thinking⟩ **7 :** bona fide **8 :** of or relating to the spreading out of a cost or charge in even payments over a period of time

syn LEVEL, FLAT, PLANE, EVEN, SMOOTH mean having a surface like that of a calm sea. LEVEL applies specifically to a horizontal surface conforming to the curvature of the earth or to the line from horizon to horizon; FLAT applies to a surface free of prominences or depressions; PLANE applies to any real or imaginary flat surface in which a straight line between any two points on it lies continuously in it; EVEN stresses lack of breaks or irregularities in a surface or line but does not imply the horizontal, the straight, or the plane; SMOOTH implies a relatively perfect evenness

— **level best :** very best

level crossing *n, Brit* **:** GRADE CROSSING

lev·el·er *or* **lev·el·ler** \'lev-(ə-)lər\ *n* **1 :** one that levels **2 a** *cap* **:** one of a group of radicals arising during the English Civil War and advocating equality before the law and religious toleration **b :** one favoring the removal of political, social, or economic social inequalities **c :** something that tends to reduce or eliminate differences among men

lev·el·head·ed \ˌlev-əl-'hed-əd\ *adj* **:** having sound judgment **:** SENSIBLE — **lev·el·head·ed·ness** *n*

leveling rod *n* **:** a graduated rod used in measuring the vertical distance between a point on the ground and the line of sight of a surveyor's level

lev·el·ly \'lev-ə(l)-lē\ *adv* **:** in a level manner

lev·el·ness \-əl-nəs\ *n* **:** the quality or state of being level

[1]le·ver \'lev-ər, 'lē-vər\ *n* [ME, fr. OF *levier*, fr. *lever* to raise, fr. L *levare;* akin to L *levis* light in weight — more at LIGHT] **1 a :** a bar used for prying or dislodging something **b :** an inducing or compelling force **:** TOOL **2 a :** a rigid piece that transmits and modifies force or motion when forces are applied at two points and it turns about a third; *specif* **:** a rigid bar used to exert a pressure or sustain a weight at one point of its length by the application of a force at a second and turning at a third on a fulcrum **b :** a projecting piece by which a mechanism is operated or adjusted

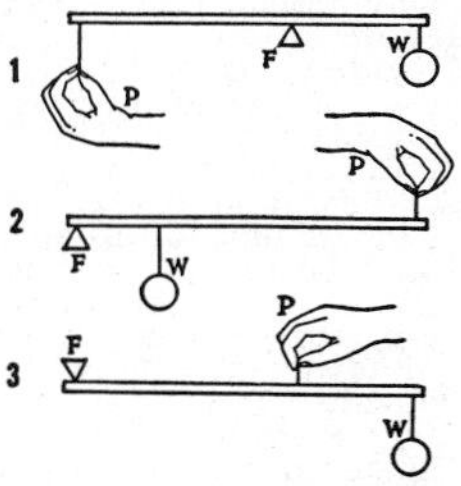

1, 2, 3, levers; *F* fulcrum, *P* power, *W* weight

[2]lever *vt* **le·ver·ing** \'lev-(ə-)riŋ, 'lēv-\ **1 :** to pry, raise, or move with or as if with a lever **2 :** to operate (a device) in the manner of a lever

le·ver·age \'lev-(ə-)rij, 'lēv-\ *n* **1 :** the action of a lever or the mechanical advantage gained by it **2 :** EFFECTIVENESS, POWER

lev·er·et \'lev-(ə-)rət\ *n* [ME, fr. (assumed) MF *levret*, fr. *levre* hare, fr. L *lepor-*, *lepus*] **:** a hare in its first year

Le·vi \'lē-ˌvī\ *n* [LL, fr. Gk *Leui*, fr. Heb *Lēwī*] **:** a son of Jacob and ancestor of one of the tribes of Israel

lev·i·able \'lev-ē-ə-bəl\ *adj* **:** capable of being levied or levied upon

le·vi·a·than \li-'vī-ə-thən\ *n* [ME, fr. LL, fr. Heb *liwyāthān*] **1 a** *often cap* **:** a sea monster often symbolizing evil in the Old Testament and Christian literature **b** (1) **:** a large sea animal (2) **:** a large oceangoing ship **2** *cap* **:** the political state; *esp* **:** a totalitarian state having a vast bureaucracy **3 :** something large or formidable — **leviathan** *adj*

lev·i·er \'lev-ē-ər\ *n* **:** one that levies

lev·i·gate \'lev-ə-ˌgāt\ *vt* [L *levigatus*, pp. of *levigare*, fr. *levis* smooth + *-igare* (akin to *agere* to drive) — more at LIME, AGENT] **1 :** POLISH, SMOOTH **2 a :** to grind to a fine smooth powder while in moist condition **b :** to separate (fine powder) from coarser material by suspending in a liquid — **lev·i·ga·tion** \ˌlev-ə-'gā-shən\ *n*

lev·in \'lev-ən\ *n* [ME *levene*] *archaic* **:** LIGHTNING

le·vi·rate \'lev-ə-rət, 'lē-və-\ *n* [L *levir* husband's brother; akin to OE *tācor* husband's brother, Gk *daēr*] **:** the sometimes compulsory marriage of a widow by the brother of her deceased husband — **le·vi·rat·ic** \ˌlev-ə-'rat-ik, ˌlē-və-\ *adj*

Le·vi's \'lē-ˌvīz\ *trademark* — used for close-fitting heavy blue denim pants reinforced at strain points with copper rivets

lev·i·tate \'lev-ə-ˌtāt\ *vb* [*levity*] *vi* **:** to rise or float in the air in seeming defiance of gravitation ~ *vt* **:** to cause to levitate — **lev·i·ta·tion** \ˌlev-ə-'tā-shən\ *n*

Le·vite \'lē-ˌvīt\ *n* **1 :** a member of the Hebrew tribe of Levi **2 :** a non-Aaronic descendant of Levi assigned to assist the Aaronic priests — **Le·vit·i·cal** \li-'vit-i-kəl\ *adj*

lev·i·ty \'lev-ət-ē\ *n* [L *levitat-*, *levitas*, fr. *levis* light in weight — more at LIGHT] **1 a :** excessive or unseemly frivolity **b :** lack of steadiness **:** CHANGEABLENESS **2 :** the quality or state of being light in weight **:** BUOYANCY **syn** see LIGHTNESS

le·vo \'lē-(ˌ)vō\ *adj* **:** LEVOROTATORY

levo- — see LEV-

le·vo·ro·ta·tion \ˌlē-və-rō-'tā-shən\ *n* **:** left-handed or counterclockwise rotation — used of the plane of polarization of light

le·vo·ro·ta·to·ry \-'rōt-ə-ˌtōr-ē, -ˌtȯr-\ *or* **le·vo·ro·ta·ry** \-'rōt-ə-rē\ *adj* **:** turning toward the left or counterclockwise; *esp* **:** rotating the plane of polarization of light to the left — compare DEXTROROTATORY

lev·u·lose \'lev-yə-ˌlōs, -ˌlōz\ *n* [ISV, irreg. fr. *lev-* + *-ose*] **:** FRUCTOSE 2

[1]levy \'lev-ē\ *n* [ME, fr. MF *levee*, fr. OF, act of raising — more at LEVEE] **1 a :** the imposition or collection of an assessment **b :** an amount levied **2 a :** the enlistment or conscription of men for military service **b :** troops raised by levy

[2]levy *vt* **1 a :** to impose or collect by legal authority **b :** to require by authority **2 :** to enlist or conscript for military service **3 :** to carry on (war) **:** WAGE **4 :** to arrange (a fine) in settlement of a suit to establish title to land ~ *vi* **:** to seize property

levy en masse *n* **:** the spontaneous act of the people of a territory of taking up arms for self-defense upon the approach of an enemy without having had time to organize in accordance with recognized rules of warfare

lewd \'lüd\ *adj* [ME *lewed* vulgar, fr. OE *lǣwede* laical, ignorant] **1** *obs* **:** EVIL, WICKED **2 a :** sexually unchaste or licentious **:** LASCIVIOUS **b :** OBSCENE, SALACIOUS — **lewd·ly** *adv* — **lewd·ness** *n*

lew·is \'lü-əs\ *n* [prob. fr. the name *Lewis*] **:** an iron dovetailed tenon that is made in sections, can be fitted into a dovetail mortise, and is used in hoisting large stones — called also *lewisson*

lew·is·ite \'lü-ə-ˌsīt\ *n* [Winford Lee *Lewis* †1943 Am chemist] **:** a colorless vesicant produced by a reaction of acetylene with arsenic trichloride and developed as a poison gas for war use

lex \'leks\ *n, pl* **le·ges** \'lā-(ˌ)gās\ [L *leg-*, *lex*] **:** LAW

lex·i·cal \'lek-si-kəl\ *adj* **1 :** of or relating to words or the vocabulary of a language as distinguished from its grammar and construction **2 :** of or relating to a lexicon or to lexicography — **lex·i·cal·i·ty** \ˌlek-sə-'kal-ət-ē\ *n* — **lex·i·cal·ly** \'lek-si-k(ə-)lē\ *adv*

lexical meaning *n* **:** the meaning of the base (as the word *play*) in a paradigm (as of the verb *play*) — compare GRAMMATICAL MEANING

lex·i·cog·ra·pher \ˌlek-sə-ˈkäg-rə-fər\ *n* [LGk *lexikographos*, fr *lexikon* + Gk *-graphos* -grapher] **:** an author or compiler of a dictionary

lex·i·co·graph·ic \ˌlek-sə-kō-ˈgraf-ik\ *adj* **:** of or relating to lexicography — **lex·i·co·graph·i·cal** \-i-kəl\ *adj* — **lex·i·co·graph·i·cal·ly** \-i-k(ə-)lē\ *adv*

lex·i·cog·ra·phy \ˌlek-sə-ˈkäg-rə-fē\ *n* **1 :** the editing or making of a dictionary **2 :** the principles and practices of dictionary making

lex·i·con \ˈlek-sə-ˌkän, -si-kən\ *n, pl* **lex·i·ca** \-si-kə\ *or* **lexicons** [LGk *lexikon*, fr. neut. of *lexikos* of words, fr. Gk *lexis* word, speech, fr. *legein* to say — more at LEGEND] **:** a book containing an alphabetical arrangement of the words in a language and their definitions **:** DICTIONARY

ley *var of* LEA

Ley·den jar \ˌlīd-ᵊn-\ *n* [*Leiden, Leyden*, Netherlands] **:** an electrical condenser consisting of a glass jar coated inside and outside with metal foil and having the inner coating connected to a conducting rod passed through the insulating stopper

li \ˈlē\ *n pl* **li** *also* **lis** \ˈlēz\ [Chin (Pek) *li*[3]] **:** any of various Chinese units of distance; *esp* **:** one equal to about $1/3$ mile

li·a·bil·i·ty \ˌlī-ə-ˈbil-ət-ē\ *n* **1 a :** the quality or state of being liable **b :** LIKELIHOOD **2 :** something for which one is liable; *esp, pl* **:** pecuniary obligations **:** DEBTS **3 :** one that works as a disadvantage **:** DRAWBACK

li·a·ble \ˈlī-ə-bəl, *esp in sense 2b also* ˈlī-bəl\ *adj* [(assumed) AF, fr. OF *lier* to bind, fr. L *ligare* — more at LIGATURE] **1 a :** obligated according to law or equity **:** RESPONSIBLE **b :** subject to appropriation or attachment **2 a :** SUSCEPTIBLE ⟨~ to diseases⟩ **b :** LIKELY, APT ⟨~ to fall⟩

syn OPEN, EXPOSED, SUBJECT, PRONE, SUSCEPTIBLE, SENSITIVE: LIABLE implies a possibility or probability of incurring something because of position, nature, or particular situation; OPEN stresses a lack of barriers preventing incurrence; EXPOSED suggests lack of protection or powers of resistance against something actually present or threatening; SUBJECT implies an openness for any reason to something that must be suffered or undergone; PRONE stresses natural tendency or propensity to incur something; SUSCEPTIBLE implies conditions existing in one's nature or individual constitution that make incurrence probable; SENSITIVE implies a readiness to respond to or be influenced by forces or stimuli ordinarily too slight to have effect **syn** see in addition RESPONSIBLE

li·aise \lē-ˈāz\ *vi* [back-formation fr. *liaison*] **:** to establish liaison with or act as a liaison officer toward

li·ai·son \ˈlē-ə-ˌzän, lē-ˈā-\ *n, often attrib* [F, fr. MF, fr. *lier*] **1 a :** a close bond or connection **:** INTERRELATIONSHIP **b :** an illicit sexual relationship **:** AFFAIR 3a **2 :** the pronunciation of an otherwise absent consonant sound at the end of the first of two consecutive words the second of which begins with a vowel sound and follows without pause **3 :** intercommunication esp. between parts of an armed force

li·a·na \lē-ˈän-ə, -ˈan-ə\ *or* **li·ane** \-ˈän, -ˈan\ *n* [F *liane*] **:** a climbing plant that roots in the ground and is characteristic when woody of tropical rain forests and when herbaceous of temperate regions — **li·a·noid** \-ˈän-ˌȯid, -ˈan-\ *adj*

li·ang \lē-ˈäŋ\ *n, pl* **liang** *also* **liangs** [Chin (Pek) *liang*[3]] **:** an old Chinese unit of weight equal to $1/16$ catty

li·ar \ˈlī(-ə)r\ *n* [ME, fr. OE *lēogere*, fr. *lēogan* to lie — more at LIE] **:** one that tells lies

Li·as \ˈlī-əs\ *adj* [*Lias*, division of the European Jurassic] **:** of or relating to a subdivision of the European Jurassic

li·ba·tion \lī-ˈbā-shən\ *n* [L *libation-, libatio*, fr. *libatus*, pp. of *libare* to pour as an offering; akin to Gk *leibein* to pour] **1 :** an act of pouring a liquid as a sacrifice (as to a deity) **2 a :** an act or instance of drinking **b :** BEVERAGE; *esp* **:** a drink containing alcohol — **li·ba·tion·ary** \-shə-ˌner-ē\ *adj*

li·bec·cio \li-ˈbech-(ˌ)ō, -ē-ˌō\ *or* **li·bec·chio** \-ˈbek-\ *n* [It] **:** a southwest wind

[1]**li·bel** \ˈlī-bəl\ *n* [ME, written declaration, fr. MF, fr. L *libellus*, dim. of *liber* book — more at LEAF] **1** *archaic* **:** a handbill esp. attacking or defaming someone **2 a :** a written or oral defamatory statement or representation that conveys an unjustly unfavorable impression **b** (1) **:** a statement or representation published without just cause and tending to expose another to public contempt (2) **:** defamation of a person by written or representational means (3) **:** the publication of blasphemous, treasonable, seditious, or obscene writings or pictures (4) **:** the act, tort, or crime of publishing such a libel

[2]**libel** *vb* **li·beled** *or* **li·belled; li·bel·ing** *or* **li·bel·ling** \-b(ə-)liŋ\ *vi* **:** to make libelous statements **~** *vt* **:** to make or publish a libel against — **li·bel·er** \-b(ə-)lər\ *n* — **li·bel·ist** \-bə-ləst\ *n*

li·bel·ant *or* **li·bel·lant** \ˈlī-bə-lənt\ *n* **:** one who makes or publishes a libel

li·bel·ee *or* **li·bel·lee** \ˌlī-bə-ˈlē\ *n* **:** one against whom a libel has been filed

li·bel·ous *or* **li·bel·lous** \ˈlī-b(ə-)ləs\ *adj* **:** constituting or including a libel **:** DEFAMATORY

Li·be·ra \ˈlē-bə-ˌrä\ *n* [L, lit., deliver, imper. of *liberare* to liberate; fr. the first word of the responsory] **:** a Roman Catholic funeral responsory

[1]**lib·er·al** \ˈlib(-ə)-rəl\ *adj* [ME, fr. MF, fr. L *liberalis* suitable for a freeman, generous, fr. *liber* free; akin to OE *lēodan* to grow, Gk *eleutheros* free] **1 a :** of, relating to, or based on the liberal arts ⟨~ education⟩ **b** *archaic* **:** of or befitting a man of free birth **2 a :** marked by generosity and openhandedness ⟨~ giver⟩ **b :** given in a generous and openhanded way ⟨~ amount⟩ **:** BOUNTIFUL **3** *obs* **:** lacking moral restraint **:** LICENTIOUS **4 :** not literal **:** LOOSE ⟨a ~ translation⟩ **5 :** BROAD-MINDED, TOLERANT; *esp* **:** not bound by authoritarianism, orthodoxy, or traditional forms **6 a :** of, favoring, or based upon the principles of liberalism **b** *cap* **:** of or constituting a political party advocating or associated with the principles of political liberalism; *esp* **:** of or constituting a political party in the United Kingdom associated with ideals of individual esp. economic freedom, greater individual participation in government, and constitutional, political, and administrative reforms designed to secure these objectives — **lib·er·al·ly** \-rə-lē\ *adv* — **lib·er·al·ness** *n*

syn LIBERAL, GENEROUS, BOUNTIFUL, MUNIFICENT mean giving freely and unstintingly. LIBERAL suggests openhandedness in the giver and largeness in the thing or amount given; GENEROUS stresses warmhearted readiness to give more than size or importance of the gift; BOUNTIFUL suggests lavish, unremitting giving or providing; MUNIFICENT suggests a scale of giving appropriate to lords or princes

[2]**liberal** *n* **:** one who is liberal: as **a :** one who is open-minded in the observance of orthodox or traditional forms **b** *cap* **:** a member or supporter of a Liberal party **c :** an advocate of liberalism esp. in individual rights

liberal arts *n pl* **1 :** the medieval studies comprising the trivium and quadrivium **2 :** the studies (as language, philosophy, history, literature, abstract science) in a college or university intended to provide chiefly general knowledge and to develop the general intellectual capacities

lib·er·al·ism \ˈlib(-ə)-rə-ˌliz-əm\ *n* **1 :** the quality or state of being liberal **2 a** *often cap* **:** a movement in modern Protestantism emphasizing intellectual liberty and the spiritual and ethical content of Christianity **b :** a theory in economics emphasizing individual freedom from restraint and usu. based upon free competition, the self-regulating market, and the gold standard **c :** a political philosophy based on belief in progress, the essential goodness of man, and the autonomy of the individual and standing for the protection of political and civil liberties **d** *cap* **:** the principles or policies of a Liberal party — **lib·er·al·ist** \-rə-ləst\ *n or adj* — **lib·er·al·is·tic** \ˌlib(-ə)-rə-ˈlis-tik\ *adj*

lib·er·al·i·ty \ˌlib-ə-ˈral-ət-ē\ *n* **1 :** the quality or state of being liberal: **a :** GENEROSITY **b :** BROAD-MINDEDNESS **2 :** a liberal gift **3 :** AMPLENESS, BROADNESS

lib·er·al·iza·tion \ˌlib-(ə-)rə-lə-ˈzā-shən\ *n* **:** an act of liberalizing or the state of being liberalized

lib·er·al·ize \ˈlib-(ə-)rə-ˌlīz\ *vt* **1 :** to make liberal **2 :** DECONTROL **~** *vi* **:** to become liberal — **lib·er·al·iz·er** *n*

lib·er·ate \ˈlib-ə-ˌrāt\ *vt* [L *liberatus*, pp. of *liberare*, fr. *liber*] **1 :** to set at liberty **:** RELEASE; *specif* **:** to free (as a country) from domination by a foreign power **2 :** to free from combination **syn** see FREE — **lib·er·a·tor** \-ˌrāt-ər\ *n*

lib·er·a·tion \ˌlib-ə-ˈrā-shən\ *n* **:** the act of liberating or the state of being liberated

lib·er·tar·i·an \ˌlib-ər-ˈter-ē-ən\ *n* **1 :** an advocate of the doctrine of free will **2 :** one who upholds the principles of liberty esp. of thought and action — **libertarian** *adj* — **lib·er·tar·i·an·ism** \-ē-ə-ˌniz-əm\ *n*

lib·er·tin·age \ˈlib-ər-ˌtē-nij\ *n* **:** LIBERTINISM

[1]**lib·er·tine** \ˈlib-ər-ˌtēn\ *n* [ME *libertyn*, fr. L *libertinus*, fr. *libertinus*, adj., of a freedman, fr. *libertus* freedman, fr. *liber*] **1 :** a manumitted Roman slave **2 :** a person who is unrestrained by convention or morality; *specif* **:** one leading a dissolute life — **lib·er·tin·ism** \-ˌtē-ˌniz-əm\ *n*

[2]**libertine** *adj* **:** of, relating to, or characteristic of a libertine

lib·er·ty \ˈlib-ərt-ē\ *n* [ME, fr. MF *liberté*, fr. L *libertat-, libertas*, fr. *liber* free — more at LIBERAL] **1 :** the quality or state of being free: **a :** the power to do as one pleases **b :** freedom from physical restraint **c :** freedom from arbitrary or despotic control **d :** the positive enjoyment of various social, political, or economic rights and privileges **e :** the power of choice **2 a :** a right or immunity enjoyed by prescription or by grant **:** PRIVILEGE **b :** permission esp. to go freely within specified limits **3 :** an action going beyond normal limits: as **a :** a breach of etiquette or propriety **:** FAMILIARITY **b :** RISK, CHANCE **c :** a violation of rules or standard practice **d :** a distortion of fact **4 :** a short authorized absence from naval duty usu. for less than 48 hours — **syn** see FREEDOM — **at liberty** **1 :** FREE **2 :** at leisure **:** UNOCCUPIED

liberty cap *n* **:** a close-fitting conical cap adopted by the French revolutionists and used as a symbol of liberty esp. in the U.S. before 1800

liberty pole *n* **:** a tall flagstaff surmounted by a liberty cap or the flag of a republic and set up as a symbol of liberty

li·bid·i·nal \lə-ˈbid-ᵊn-əl\ *adj* **:** of or relating to the libido — **li·bid·i·nal·ly** \-ə-lē\ *adv*

li·bid·i·nous \-ᵊn-əs\ *adj* [ME, fr. MF *libidineus*, fr. L *libidinosus*, fr. *libidin-, libido*] **1 :** having or marked by lustful desires **:** LASCIVIOUS **2 :** of or relating to the libido — **li·bid·i·nous·ly** *adv* — **li·bid·i·nous·ness** *n*

li·bi·do \lə-ˈbēd-(ˌ)ō, -ˈbīd-\ *n* [NL *libidin-, libido*, fr. L, desire, lust, fr. *libēre* to please — more at LOVE] **1 :** emotional or psychic energy derived from primitive biological urges and usu. goal-directed **2 :** sexual drive

li·bra *for 1 & 2a* ˈlī-brə *or* ˈlē-brə, *for 2b* ˈlē-brə *or* ˈlēv-rə\ *n* [ME, fr. L (gen. *Librae*), lit., scales, pound] **1** *cap* **a :** a southern zodiacal constellation between Virgo and Scorpio represented by a pair of scales **b :** the 7th sign of the zodiac **2 a** *pl* **li·brae** \ˈlī-ˌbrē, ˈlē-ˌbrī\ [L] **:** an ancient Roman unit of weight equal to 327.45 grams **b** [Sp & Pg, fr. L] **:** any of various Spanish, Portuguese, Colombian, or Venezuelan units of weight

li·brar·i·an \lī-ˈbrer-ē-ən\ *n* **:** a specialist in the care or management of a library — **li·brar·i·an·ship** \-ˌship\ *n*

li·brary \ˈlī-ˌbrer-ē\ *n, often attrib* [ME, fr. ML *librarium*, fr. L, neut. of *librarius* of books, fr. *libr-, liber* book — more at LEAF] **1 a :** a place in which books, manuscripts, musical scores, or other literary and artistic materials are kept for use but not for sale **b :** a collection of literary or artistic materials (as books or prints) **c :** an institution for the custody or administration of such a collection **2 a :** a series of related books issued by a publisher **b :** a specialized collection of reference material; *specif* **:** MORGUE 2

library paste *n* **:** a thick white adhesive made from starch

library science *n* **:** the study or the principles and practices of library care and administration

li·bra·tion \lī-ˈbrā-shən\ *n* [L *libration-, libratio*, fr. *libratus*, pp. of *librare* to balance, fr. *libra*] **:** an oscillation in the apparent aspect of a secondary body (as a planet or a satellite) as seen from the primary object around which it revolves — **li·bra·to·ry** \ˈlī-brə-ˌtōr-ē, -ˌtȯr-\ *adj*

li·bret·tist \lə-ˈbret-əst\ *n* **:** the writer of a libretto

li·bret·to \lə-ˈbret-(ˌ)ō\ *n, pl* **librettos** *or* **li·bret·ti** \-(ˌ)ē\ [It, dim. of *libro* book, fr. L *libr-, liber*] **1 :** the text of a work of musical theater (as an opera) **2 :** the book containing such a text

li·bri·form \ˈlī-brə-ˌfȯrm\ *adj* [L *libr-, liber* + ISV *-iform*] **:** resembling phloem fibers

Lib·y·an \ˈlib-ē-ən\ *n* **1 :** a native or inhabitant of Libya **2 :** a Berber language of ancient No. Africa — **Libyan** *adj*

lice *pl of* LOUSE

li·cens·able \ˈlīs-ᵊn-sə-bəl\ *adj* **:** capable of being licensed

1li·cense *or* **li·cence** \'līs-ᵊn(t)s\ *n* [ME, fr. MF *licence*, fr. L *licentia*, fr. *licent-, licens*, prp. of *licēre* to be permitted; akin to Latvian *līkt* to come to terms] **1 a :** permission to act **b :** freedom of action **2 a :** a permission granted by competent authority to engage in a business, occupation, or activity otherwise unlawful **b :** a document, plate, or tag evidencing a license granted **3 a :** freedom that allows or is used with irresponsibility **b :** LICENTIOUSNESS **4 :** deviation from fact, form, or rule by an artist or writer for the sake of the effect gained **syn** see FREEDOM

2license *also* **licence** *vt* **1 :** to issue a license to **2 :** to permit or authorize esp. by formal license — **li·cens·er** \-ᵊn-sər\ *or* **li·cen·sor** \-ᵊn-sər, ˌlīs-ᵊn-'sȯ(ə)r\ *n*

li·cens·ee \ˌlīs-ᵊn-'sē\ *n* **:** a licensed person

li·cen·sure \'līs-ᵊn-shər, -ˌshu̇(ə)r\ *n* **:** the granting of a license esp. to practice a profession

li·cen·ti·ate \lī-'sen-chē-ət, *esp in sense 2* li-\ *n* [ML *licentiatus*, fr. pp. of *licentiare* to allow, fr. L *licentia*] **1 :** one who has a license granted esp. by a university to practice a profession **2 :** an academic degree ranking below that of doctor given by some European universities

li·cen·tious \lī-'sen-chəs\ *adj* [L *licentiosus*, fr. *licentia*] **1 :** lacking legal or moral restraints; *esp* **:** disregarding sexual restraints **2 :** marked by disregard for rules — **li·cen·tious·ly** *adv* — **li·cen·tious·ness** *n*

li·chee *var of* LITCHI

1li·chen \'lī-kən\ *n* [L, fr. Gk *leichēn, lichēn*] **1 :** any of numerous complex thallophytic plants (group Lichenes) made up of an alga and a fungus growing in symbiotic association on a solid surface (as a rock) **2 :** any of several skin diseases characterized by a papular eruption — **li·chen·ous** \-kə-nəs\ *adj*

2lichen *vt* **:** to cover with lichens

lich–gate *var of* LYCH-GATE

licht \'likt\ *Scot var of* LIGHT

lic·it \'lis-ət\ *adj* [MF *licite*, fr. L *licitus*, fr. pp. of *licēre*] **:** LEGAL **syn** see LAWFUL — **lic·it·ly** *adv*

1lick \'lik\ *vb* [ME *licken*, fr. OE *liccian;* akin to OHG *leckōn* to lick, L *lingere*, Gk *leichein*] *vt* **1 a** (1) **:** to draw the tongue over (2) **:** to flicker over like a tongue **b :** to lap up **2 a :** to strike repeatedly **:** THRASH **b :** to get the better of **:** DEFEAT ∼ *vi* **1 :** to lap with or as if with the tongue **2 :** to move at top speed **syn** see CONQUER — **lick into shape :** to put into proper form or condition

2lick *n* **1 a :** an act or instance of licking **b :** a small amount**:** BIT; *specif* **:** an amount of something held on the tongue **c :** a hasty careless effort **2 a :** a sharp hit **:** BLOW **b :** OPPORTUNITY, TURN — usu. used in pl. **3 :** a place (as a spring) having a deposit of salt that animals regularly lick

lick·er·ish \'lik-(ə-)rish\ *adj* [alter. of *lickerous*, fr. ME *likerous*, fr. (assumed) ONF, fr. ONF *leckeur* lecher; akin to OF *lecheor* lecher] **1 a :** eager to taste or enjoy **b :** GREEDY, DESIROUS **2** *obs* **:** tempting to the appetite **3 :** LECHEROUS — **lick·er·ish·ly** *adv* — **lick·er·ish·ness** *n*

lick·e·ty–split \ˌlik-ət-ē-'split\ *adv* [prob. irreg. fr. 1*lick* + *split*] **:** at great speed

lick·ing *n* **1 :** an act of one that licks **2 a :** a sound thrashing **:** DRUBBING **b :** a severe setback **:** DEFEAT

lick·spit·tle \'lik-ˌspit-ᵊl\ *n* **:** a fawning subordinate **:** TOADY

lic·o·rice \'lik(-ə)-rish, -rəs\ *n* [ME *licorice*, fr. OF, fr. LL *liquiritia*, alter. of L *glycyrrhiza*, fr. Gk *glykyrrhiza*, fr. *glykys* sweet + *rhiza* root — more at ROOT] **1 :** a European leguminous plant (*Glycyrrhiza glabra*) with pinnate leaves and spikes of blue flowers **2 :** the dried root of licorice or an extract from it used esp. in medicine, brewing, and confectionery

lic·tor \'lik-tər\ *n* [L] **:** a Roman officer bearing the fasces as the insignia of his office with duties including attendance upon the chief magistrates in public appearances

1lid \'lid\ *n* [ME, fr. OE *hlid;* akin to OHG *hlit* cover, OE *hlinian* to lean — more at LEAN] **1 :** a movable cover for the opening of a hollow structure (as a box) **2 :** EYELID **3** *slang* **:** HAT **4 :** RESTRAINT, CURB

2lid *vt* **lid·ded; lid·ding :** to cover or supply with a lid

lid·less \'lid-ləs\ *adj* **1 :** having no lid **2 :** WATCHFUL

li·do \'lēd-(ˌ)ō\ *n* [*Lido*, Italy] **:** a fashionable beach resort

1lie \'lī\ *vi* **lay** \'lā\ **lain** \'lān\ **ly·ing** \'lī-iŋ\ [ME *lien*, fr. OE *licgan;* akin to OHG *ligen* to lie, L *lectus* bed, Gk *lechos*] **1 a :** to be or to stay at rest in a horizontal position **:** be prostrate **:** REST, RECLINE ⟨∼ motionless⟩ ⟨∼ asleep⟩ **b :** to assume a horizontal position — often used with *down* **c** *archaic* **:** to reside temporarily **:** stay for the night **:** LODGE **d** *archaic* **:** to have sexual intercourse — used with *with* **e :** to stay in concealment ⟨∼ in wait⟩ **2 :** to be in a helpless or defenseless state ⟨*lying* in prison⟩ **3** *of an inanimate thing* **:** to be or remain in a flat or horizontal position upon a broad support ⟨*lying* on the table⟩ **4 :** to have direction **:** EXTEND ⟨route *lay* to the west⟩ **5 a :** to occupy a certain relative place or position ⟨hills ∼ behind us⟩ **b :** to have a place in relation to something else ⟨real reason ∼*s* deeper⟩ **c :** to have an effect through mere presence, weight, or relative position ⟨remorse *lay* heavily on him⟩ **d :** to be sustainable or admissible **6 :** to remain at anchor or becalmed **7 :** to remain unused or uncared for ⟨∼ on the shelf⟩ — **li·er** \'lī(-ə)r\ *n* — **lie low 1 :** to lie prostrate, defeated, or disgraced **2 :** to stay in hiding **:** strive to avoid notice **3 :** to bide one's time **:** remain secretly ready for action

2lie *n* **1 :** the position or situation in which something lies **2** *chiefly Brit* **:** LAY 6 **3 :** the haunt of an animal (as a fish) **:** COVERT **4** *Brit* **:** an act or instance of lying or resting

3lie *vb* **lied; ly·ing** \'lī-iŋ\ [ME *lien*, fr. OE *lēogan;* akin to OHG *liogan* to lie, OSlav *lŭgati*] *vi* **1 :** to make an untrue statement with intent to deceive **2 :** to create a false or misleading impression ∼ *vt* **:** to affect by telling lies

syn LIE, PREVARICATE, EQUIVOCATE, PALTER, FIB mean to tell an untruth. LIE is the direct term, imputing dishonesty; PREVARICATE softens the bluntness of LIE by implying quibbling or confusing the issue; EQUIVOCATE implies using words having more than one sense so as to seem to say one thing but intend another; PALTER implies making unreliable statements of fact or intention or insincere promises; FIB applies to a telling of an untruth that is trivial in substance or significance

4lie *n* **1 a :** an assertion of something known or believed by the speaker to be untrue with intent to deceive **b :** an untrue or inaccurate statement that may or may not be believed true by the speaker **2 :** something that misleads or deceives **3 :** a charge of lying

lie by *vi* **:** to remain inactive **:** REST

lied \'lēt\ *n, pl* **lie·der** \'lēd-ər\ [G, song, fr. OHG *liod* — more at LAUD] **:** a German art song esp. of the 19th century

Lie·der·kranz \'lēd-ər-ˌkran(t)s, -ˌkrän(t)s\ *trademark* — used for a soft surface-ripened cheese with a fairly strong pungent flavor and odor

lie detector *n* **:** an instrument for detecting physical evidences of the tension that accompanies lying

lie down *vi* **1 :** to lie on a bed for a brief rest **2 :** to submit meekly or abjectly to defeat, disappointment, or insult **3 :** to fail to perform or to neglect one's part deliberately

1lief \'lēf, 'lēv\ *adj* [ME *lief, lef*, fr. OE *lēof;* akin to OE *lufu* love — more at LOVE] **1** *archaic* **:** DEAR, BELOVED **2** *archaic* **:** WILLING, GLAD

2lief \'lēv, 'lēf\ *adv* **:** GLADLY, WILLINGLY ⟨I had as ∼ go as not⟩

1liege \'lēj\ *adj* [ME, fr. OF, fr. LL *laeticus*, fr. *laetus* serf, of Gmc origin; akin to OFris *let* serf] **1 :** having the right to or obligated to render feudal allegiance and service **2 :** FAITHFUL, LOYAL

2liege *n* **1 a :** a vassal bound to feudal service and allegiance **b :** a loyal subject **2 :** a liege lord

liege man *n* **1 :** VASSAL **2 :** a devoted follower

lie in *vi* **:** to be in childbed

lien \'lēn, 'lē-ən\ *n* [MF, tie, band, fr. L *ligamen*, fr. *ligare* to bind — more at LIGATURE] **1 :** a charge upon real or personal property for the satisfaction of some debt or duty ordinarily arising by operation of law **2 a :** MORTGAGE **b :** the security interest created by a mortgage

li·enal \lī-'en-ᵊl, 'lī-ən-\ *adj* [ISV, fr. L *lien* spleen — more at SPLEEN] **:** SPLENIC

lie off *vi* **1 :** to keep a little away from the shore or another ship **2 :** to cease work for a time **3 :** to hold back in the early part of a race

lie over *vi* **:** to await attention at a later time

li·erne \lē-'ərn, -'e(ə)rn\ *n* [F] **:** a rib in Gothic vaulting that passes from one boss or intersection of the principal ribs to another

lie to \-'tü\ *vi, of a ship* **:** to stay stationary with head to windward

lieu \'lü\ *n* [MF, fr. L *locus* — more at STALL] *archaic* **:** PLACE, STEAD — **in lieu :** INSTEAD — **in lieu of :** in the place of **:** instead of

lie up *vi* **1 :** to stay in bed or at rest **2 :** to go into or remain in a dock

lieu·ten·an·cy \lü-'ten-ən-sē, *Brit* le(f)-'ten-\ *n* **:** the office, rank, or commission of a lieutenant

lieu·ten·ant \-'ten-ənt\ *n* [ME, fr. MF, fr. *lieu* + *tenant* holding, fr. *tenir* to hold, fr. L *tenēre* — more at THIN] **1 a :** an officer empowered to act for a higher official **b :** a representative of another in the performance of duty **2 a :** FIRST LIEUTENANT 1, SECOND LIEUTENANT **b :** a commissioned officer in the navy ranking above a lieutenant junior grade and below a lieutenant commander **c :** a fire or police department officer ranking below a captain

lieutenant colonel *n* **:** a commissioned officer in the army, air force, or marine corps ranking above a major and below a colonel

lieutenant commander *n* **:** a commissioned officer in the navy ranking above a lieutenant and below a commander

lieutenant general *n* **:** a commissioned officer in the army, air force, or marine corps ranking above a major general and below a general

lieutenant governor *n* **:** a deputy or subordinate governor**:** as **a :** an elected official serving as deputy to the governor of an American state **b :** the formal head of the government of a Canadian province appointed by the federal government as the representative of the crown

lieutenant junior grade *n, pl* **lieutenants junior grade :** a commissioned officer in the navy ranking above an ensign and below a lieutenant

1life \'līf\ *n, pl* **lives** \'līvz\ [ME *lif*, fr. OE *līf;* akin to OE *libban* to live — more at LIVE] **1 a :** the quality that distinguishes a vital and functional being from a dead body **b :** a principle or force held to underlie the distinctive quality of animate beings — compare VITALISM 1 **c :** an organismic state characterized by capacity for metabolism, growth, reaction to stimuli, and reproduction **2 a :** the sequence of physical and mental experiences that make up the existence of an individual **b :** one or more aspects of the process of living ⟨sex ∼⟩ **3 :** BIOGRAPHY 1 **4 :** spiritual existence transcending physical death **5 a :** the duration of an earthly existence **b :** a specific phase of earthly existence ⟨adult ∼⟩ **c :** a sentence of imprisonment for the remaining portion of a convict's existence **6 :** a way or manner of living **7 :** LIVELIHOOD **8 :** a vital or living being; *specif* **:** PERSON **9 :** an animating and shaping force or principle **10 :** ANIMATION, SPIRIT **11 :** the form or pattern of something existing in reality ⟨painted from ∼⟩ **12 :** the period of usefulness of something **13 :** the period of existence (as of a subatomic particle) — compare HALF-LIFE **14 :** a property of an inanimate substance or object resembling the animate quality of a living being ⟨∼ of a bow⟩ **15 :** living beings (as of a particular kind or environment) ⟨forest ∼⟩ **16 a :** human activities **b :** animate activity and movement ⟨stirrings of ∼⟩ **17 :** one providing interest and vigor ⟨∼ of the party⟩ **18 :** another chance given to one likely to lose **19** *cap, Christian Science* **:** 2GOD b

2life *adj* **1 :** of or relating to animate being **2 :** LIFELONG ⟨∼ tenure⟩ **3 :** using a living model ⟨a ∼ class⟩ **4 :** of, relating to, or provided by life insurance ⟨a ∼ policy⟩

life belt *n* **1 :** a life preserver in the form of a buoyant belt **2 :** SAFETY BELT

life·blood \'līf-'bləd\ *n* **1 :** blood regarded as the seat of vitality **2 :** a vital or life-giving force

life·boat \-ˌbōt\ *n* **1 :** a strong buoyant boat esp. designed for use in saving shipwrecked people **2 :** a boat carried by a ship for use in emergency

life buoy *n* **:** a float consisting of a ring of buoyant material to support a person who has fallen into the water

life cycle *n* **1 :** the series of stages in form and functional activity

through which an organism passes between successive recurrences of a specified primary stage **2 :** LIFE HISTORY 1a **3 :** a series of stages through which an individual, group, or culture passes during its lifetime

life expectancy *n* **:** an expected number of years of life based on statistical probability

life–force \ˈlīf-ˈfō(ə)rs, -ˈfȯ(ə)rs\ *n* **:** ÉLAN VITAL

life·ful \ˈlīf-fəl\ *adj* **:** full of or giving vitality

life–giv·ing \-ˌgiv-iŋ\ *adj* **:** giving life **:** INVIGORATING

life·guard \-ˌgärd\ *n* **:** a usu. expert swimmer employed to safeguard bathers

life history *n* **1 a :** a history of the changes through which an organism passes in its development from the primary stage to its natural death **b :** one series of these changes **2 :** the history of an individual's development in his social environment

life insurance *n* **:** insurance providing for payment of a stipulated sum to a designated beneficiary upon death of the insured

life·less \ˈlī-fləs\ *adj* **:** having no life: **a :** DEAD **b :** INANIMATE ⟨~ as marble⟩ **c :** lacking qualities expressive of life and vigor **:** DULL ⟨~ voice⟩ **d :** destitute of living beings — **life·less·ly** *adv* — **life·less·ness** *n*

life·like \ˈlī-ˌflīk\ *adj* **:** accurately representing or imitating real life — **life·like·ness** *n*

life·line \ˈlī-ˌflīn\ *n* **1 a :** a line to which persons may cling to save or protect their lives; *esp* **:** one stretched along the deck or from the yards of a ship **b :** a line attached to a diver's helmet by which he is lowered and raised **c :** a rope line for lowering a person to safety **2 :** something resembling a line used for the saving or protection of life **3 :** a land, sea, or air route regarded as indispensable to life

life·long \ˈlī-ˌflȯŋ\ *adj* **:** continuing through life

life·man·ship \ˈlīf-mən-ˌship\ *n* **:** the art of achieving superiority or an appearance of superiority over others by perplexing and demoralizing them

life net *n* **:** a strong net or sheet (as of canvas) held by firemen or others to catch persons jumping from burning buildings

life of Ri·ley \-ˈrī-lē\ **:** a carefree often luxurious way of living

life peer *n* **:** a British peer whose title is not hereditary — **life peerage** *n*

life preserver *n* **1 :** a device designed to save a person from drowning by buoying up the body while in the water **2 :** BLACKJACK 3

lif·er \ˈlī-fər\ *n* **:** a person sentenced to life imprisonment

life raft *n* **:** a raft usu. made of wood or an inflatable material and designed for use by people forced into the water

life·sav·er \ˈlīf-ˌsā-vər\ *n* **1 :** one trained to save lives of drowning persons **2 :** BOON 2

[1]**life·sav·ing** \-viŋ\ *n* **:** the skill or practice of saving or protecting the lives esp. of drowning persons

[2]**lifesaving** *adj* **:** designed for or used in saving lives

life–size \ˈlīf-ˈsīz\ *or* **life–sized** \-ˈsīzd\ *adj* **:** of natural size **:** of the size of the original

life·time \-ˌtīm\ *n* **1 :** the duration of an individual's existence **2 :** the duration of the existence of an ion or subatomic particle

life vest *n* **:** a life preserver designed as a vestlike garment of buoyant or inflatable material — called also *life jacket*

life·way \-ˌwā\ *n* **:** LIFE 6

life·work \-ˈwərk\ *n* **:** the entire or principal work of one's lifetime; *also* **:** a work extending over a lifetime

life zone *n* **:** a biogeographic zone

[1]**lift** \ˈlift\ *n* [ME, fr. OE *lyft*] *chiefly Scot* **:** HEAVENS, SKY

[2]**lift** *vb* [ME *liften*, fr. ON *lypta*; akin to OE *lyft* air — more at LOFT] *vt* **1 a :** to raise from a lower to a higher position **:** ELEVATE **b :** to raise in rank or condition **c :** to raise in rate or amount **2 :** to put an end to (a blockade or siege) by withdrawing investing forces **3 :** REVOKE, RESCIND **4 a :** STEAL **b :** PLAGIARIZE **c :** to take out of normal setting **5 :** to take up (as a root crop or transplants) from the ground **6 :** to pay off (an obligation) **7 a :** to shift (artillery fire) from one area to another **b :** to withhold (fire) from an area **8 :** to move from one place to another **:** TRANSPORT **9 :** to take up (a fingerprint) from a surface ~ *vi* **1 a :** ASCEND **b :** to appear elevated (as above surrounding objects) **2 a :** to disperse upward ⟨until the fog ~*s*⟩ **b :** to cease temporarily — **lift·er** *n*

syn LIFT, RAISE, REAR, ELEVATE, HOIST, HEAVE, BOOST mean to move from a lower to a higher place or position. LIFT usu. implies exerting effort to overcome resistance of weight or, figuratively, depression or sluggishness; RAISE carries a stronger implication of bringing up to the vertical or, figuratively, bringing into being; REAR may add an element of suddenness to RAISE; ELEVATE may replace LIFT or RAISE esp. when exalting or enhancing is implied; HOIST implies lifting something heavy esp. by mechanical means; HEAVE implies lifting with great effort or strain; BOOST suggests assisting to climb or advance by a push

[3]**lift** *n, often attrib* **1 :** the amount that may be lifted at one time **:** LOAD **2 a :** the action or an instance of lifting **b :** the action or an instance of rising **c :** elevated carriage **d :** the lifting up of a dancer by her partner **3 :** a device for lifting **4 :** an act of stealing **:** THEFT **5 a :** ASSISTANCE, HELP **b :** a ride along one's way **6 :** one of the layers forming the heel of a shoe **7 :** a rise or advance in position or condition **8 :** a slight rise or elevation **9 :** the distance or extent to which something rises **10 :** a set of pumps used in a mine **11 a** *chiefly Brit* **:** ELEVATOR 1 **b :** an apparatus for raising an automobile (as for repair) **c :** a conveyor for carrying people up or down a mountain slope **12 a :** an elevating influence **b :** an elevation of the spirits **13 :** the component of the total aerodynamic force acting on an airplane or airfoil that is perpendicular to the relative wind and that for an airplane constitutes the upward force that opposes the pull of gravity

lift·man \ˈlift-ˌman\ *n, Brit* **:** an elevator operator

lift–off \ˈlif-ˌtȯf\ *n* **:** a takeoff by an airplane or missile

lift truck *n* **:** a small truck equipped for lifting and transporting loads

lift van *n* **:** a large strong waterproof shipping case esp. for household goods

lig·a·ment \ˈlig-ə-mənt\ *n* [ME, fr. ML & L; ML *ligamentum*, fr. L, band, tie, fr. *ligare*] **1 :** a tough band of tissue connecting the articular extremities of bones or supporting an organ in place **2 :** a connecting or unifying bond — **lig·a·men·ta·ry** \ˌlig-ə-ˈment-ə-rē, -ˈmen-trē\ *or* **lig·a·men·tous** \-ˈment-əs\ *adj*

li·gan \ˈlī-gən\ *var of* LAGAN

li·gate \ˈlī-ˌgāt, lī-ˈ\ *vt* [L *ligatus*] **:** to tie with a ligature

li·ga·tion \lī-ˈgā-shən\ *n* **1 :** an act of ligating **2 :** LIGATURE

lig·a·ture \ˈlig-ə-ˌchu̇(ə)r, -chər, -ˌt(y)u̇(ə)r\ *n* [ME, fr. MF, fr. LL *ligatura*, fr. L *ligatus*, pp. of *ligare* to bind, tie; akin to MHG *geleich* joint, Alb *lith* I tie] **1 a :** something that is used to bind; *specif* **:** a filament (as a thread) used in surgery **b :** something that unites or connects **:** BOND **2 :** the action of binding or tying **3 :** a compound note in mensural notation indicating a group of musical notes to be sung to one syllable **4 :** a printed or written character consisting of two or more letters or characters united (as æ)

[1]**light** \ˈlīt\ *n* [ME, fr. OE *lēoht*; akin to OHG *lioht* light, L *luc-*, *lux* light, *lucēre* to shine, Gk *leukos* white] **1 a :** something that makes vision possible **b :** the sensation aroused by stimulation of the visual receptors **:** BRIGHTNESS **c :** an electromagnetic radiation in the wavelength range including infrared, visible, ultraviolet, and X rays and traveling in a vacuum with a speed of about 186,281 miles per second; *specif* **:** the part of this range that is visible to the human eye **2 a :** DAYLIGHT **b :** DAWN **3 :** a source of light: as **a :** a heavenly body **b :** CANDLE **c :** an electric light **4** *archaic* **:** EYESIGHT **5 a :** spiritual illumination **b :** INNER LIGHT **c :** ENLIGHTENMENT **d :** TRUTH **6 a :** public knowledge **b :** a particular aspect or appearance presented to view **7 :** a particular illumination **8 a :** WINDOW **b :** SKYLIGHT **9** *pl* **:** philosophy of life **:** STANDARDS **10 :** a noteworthy person in a particular place or field **:** LUMINARY **11 :** a particular expression of the eye **12 a :** LIGHTHOUSE, BEACON **b :** TRAFFIC SIGNAL **13 :** the representation of light in art **14 :** a flame for lighting something

[2]**light** *adj* **1 :** having light **:** BRIGHT **2 :** PALE

[3]**light** *vb* **light·ed** *or* **lit** \ˈlit\ **light·ing** *vi* **1 :** to become light **:** BRIGHTEN ⟨face *lit* up⟩ **2 :** to take fire **:** IGNITE ~ *vt* **1 :** to set fire to **2 a :** to conduct with a light **:** GUIDE **b :** ILLUMINATE ⟨rockets ~ up the sky⟩ **c :** ANIMATE, BRIGHTEN ⟨a smile *lit* up her face⟩

[4]**light** *adj* [ME, fr. OE *lēoht*; akin to OHG *līhti* light, L *levis*, Gk *elachys* small] **1 a :** having little weight **:** not heavy **b :** designed to carry a comparatively small load ⟨~ truck⟩ **c :** having relatively little weight in proportion to bulk ⟨aluminum is a ~ metal⟩ **d :** containing less than the legal, standard, or usual weight ⟨~ coin⟩ **2 a :** of little importance **:** TRIVIAL **b :** not abundant **:** SCANTY ⟨~ rain⟩ ⟨~ breakfast⟩ **3 a :** easily disturbed ⟨~ sleeper⟩ **b :** exerting a minimum of force or pressure **:** GENTLE **c :** resulting from a very slight pressure **:** FAINT **4 a :** easily endurable ⟨~ illness⟩ **b :** requiring little effort ⟨~ exercise⟩ **5 :** capable of moving swiftly or nimbly **6 a :** FRIVOLOUS ⟨~ conduct⟩ **b :** lacking in stability **:** CHANGEABLE ⟨~ opinions⟩ **c :** sexually promiscuous **7 :** free from care **:** CHEERFUL **8 :** intended chiefly to entertain ⟨~ reading⟩ **9 a :** having a comparatively low alcoholic content ⟨~ wines⟩ **b :** having a relatively mild flavor **10 a :** easily digested ⟨a ~ soup⟩ **b :** well leavened ⟨~ crust⟩ **11 :** lightly armed or equipped ⟨~ cavalry⟩ **12 :** coarse and sandy or easily pulverized ⟨~ soil⟩ **13 :** DIZZY, GIDDY **14 a :** carrying little or no cargo ⟨ship returned ~⟩ **b :** producing goods for direct consumption by the consumer ⟨~ industry⟩ **15 :** UNACCENTED ⟨~ syllable⟩ **16 :** having a clear soft quality ⟨~ voice⟩ **17 :** being in debt to the pot in a poker game ⟨three chips ~⟩ **syn** see EASY — **light·ish** \-ish\ *adj*

[5]**light** *adv* **1 :** LIGHTLY **2 :** with little baggage ⟨travel ~⟩

[6]**light** *vi* **light·ed** *or* **lit** \ˈlit\ **light·ing** [ME *lighten*, fr. OE *līhtan*; akin to OE *lēoht* light in weight] **1 :** DISMOUNT **2 :** SETTLE, ALIGHT ⟨a bird *lit* on the lawn⟩ **3 :** to fall unexpectedly **4 :** to arrive by chance **:** HAPPEN ⟨*lit* upon a solution⟩ — **light into :** to attack forcefully

light adaptation *n* **:** the phenomena including contraction of the pupil and decrease in visual purple by which the eye adapts to conditions of increased illumination

light air *n* **:** wind having a speed of 1 to 3 miles per hour

light bread \ˈlīt-ˌbred\ *n* [[4]*light*] *chiefly South & Midland* **:** wheat bread in loaves made from white flour leavened with yeast

light breeze *n* **:** wind having a speed of 4 to 7 miles per hour

[1]**light·en** \ˈlīt-ᵊn\ *vb* **light·en·ing** \ˈlīt-niŋ, -ᵊn-iŋ\ [ME *lightenen*, fr. *light*] *vt* **1 :** to make light or clear **:** ILLUMINATE **2** *archaic* **:** ENLIGHTEN **3 :** to make (as a color) lighter ~ *vi* **1 a :** to shine brightly **b :** to grow lighter **:** BRIGHTEN **2 :** to give out flashes of lightning — **light·en·er** \ˈlīt-nər, -ᵊn-ər\ *n*

[2]**lighten** *vb* **light·en·ing** \ˈlīt-niŋ, -ᵊn-iŋ\ *vt* **1 a :** to relieve of a burden in whole or in part ⟨~ the plane⟩ **b :** to reduce in weight or quantity **:** LESSEN ⟨~ his duties⟩ **2 :** CHEER, GLADDEN **3 :** to make less wearisome **:** ALLEVIATE ⟨~ his sorrow⟩ ~ *vi* **1 :** to become lighter or less burdensome **2 :** to become more cheerful ⟨his mood ~*ed*⟩ **syn** see RELIEVE — **light·en·er** \ˈlīt-nər, -ᵊn-ər\ *n*

[1]**ligh·ter** \ˈlīt-ər\ *n* [ME, fr. (assumed) MD *lichter*, fr. MD *lichten* to unload; akin to OE *lēoht* light in weight] **:** a large usu. flat-bottomed barge used esp. in unloading or loading ships

[2]**lighter** *vt* **:** to convey by a lighter

[3]**light·er** \ˈlīt-ər\ *n* **1 :** one that lights or sets a fire **2 :** a device for lighting a fire; *esp* **:** a mechanical or electrical device used for lighting cigarettes, cigars, or pipes

ligh·ter·age \ˈlīt-ə-rij\ *n* **1 :** a price paid for lightering **2 :** the loading, unloading, or transportation of goods by means of a lighter **3 :** the boats engaged in lightering

lighter–than–air *adj* **:** of less weight than the air displaced

light·face \ˈlīt-ˌfās\ *n* **:** a typeface or font of characters having comparatively light thin lines (as *this*) — **light·faced** \-ˈfāst\ *adj*

light·fast \-ˌfast\ *adj* **:** resistant to light and esp. to sunlight; *specif* **:** colorfast to light — **light·fast·ness** \-ˌfas(t)-nəs\ *n*

light–fin·gered \-ˈfiŋ-gərd\ *adj* **1 :** adroit in stealing esp. by picking pockets **2 :** having a light and dexterous touch **:** NIMBLE — **light–fin·gered·ness** *n*

light–foot·ed \-ˈfu̇t-əd\ *also* **light–foot** \-ˌfu̇t\ *adj* **1 :** having a light and springy step **2 :** moving gracefully and nimbly

light–hand·ed \-ˈhan-dəd\ *adj* **:** having a light or delicate touch **:** FACILE — **light–hand·ed·ness** *n*

light–head·ed \-ˈhed-əd\ *adj* **1 :** mentally disoriented **:** DIZZY **2 :** lacking in maturity or seriousness **:** FRIVOLOUS — **light–head·ed·ly** *adv* — **light–head·ed·ness** *n*

light·heart·ed \-ˈhärt-əd\ *adj* **1 :** free from care or anxiety **:** GAY **2 :** cheerfully optimistic and hopeful **:** EASYGOING **syn** see GLAD — **light·heart·ed·ly** *adv* — **light·heart·ed·ness** *n*

light heavyweight *n* **1 :** a boxer weighing more than 160 but not over 175 pounds — called also *light heavy* **2 :** a wrestler weighing more than 174 but not over 191 pounds

light·house \'līt-ˌhau̇s\ *n* **:** a tower or other structure with a powerful light that gives a continuous or intermittent signal for guiding navigators

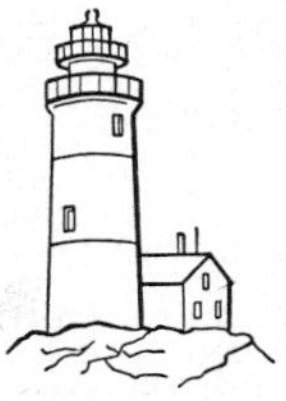
lighthouse

light housekeeping *n* **1 :** domestic work restricted to the less laborious duties **2 :** housekeeping in quarters with limited facilities for cooking
light·ing *n* **1 a :** ILLUMINATION **b :** IGNITION **2 :** an artificial supply of light or the apparatus providing it
light·less \'līt-ləs\ *adj* **1 :** receiving no light **:** DARK **2 :** giving no light
light·ly *adv* **1 :** with little weight or force **:** GENTLY **2 :** in a small degree or amount **3 :** with little difficulty **:** EASILY **4 :** NIMBLY, SWIFTLY **5 :** with indifference or carelessness **:** UNCONCERNEDLY **6 :** GAILY, FRIVOLOUSLY
light meter *n* **:** a small portable device for measuring illumination; *esp* **:** EXPOSURE METER
light–mind·ed \'līt-'mīn-dəd\ *adj* **:** lacking in seriousness **:** FRIVOLOUS — **light–mind·ed·ly** *adv* — **light–mind·ed·ness** *n*
1**light·ness** *n* **1 :** the quality or state of being illuminated **:** ILLUMINATION **2 :** the attribute of object colors by which the object appears to reflect or transmit more or less of the incident light
2**light·ness** *n* **1 :** the quality or state of being light in weight **2 :** LEVITY **3 a :** NIMBLENESS **b :** an ease and gaiety of style or manner **4 :** a lack of weightiness or force **:** DELICACY
syn LIGHTNESS, LEVITY, FRIVOLITY, FLIPPANCY, VOLATILITY, FLIGHTINESS mean gaiety or indifference when seriousness is expected. LIGHTNESS implies a lack of weight and seriousness in character, mood, or conduct; LEVITY suggests trifling or unseasonable gaiety; FRIVOLITY suggests irresponsible indulgence in gaieties or in idle speech or conduct; FLIPPANCY implies an unbecoming levity esp. in speaking of grave or sacred matters; VOLATILITY implies such fickleness of disposition as prevents long attention to any one thing; FLIGHTINESS implies extreme volatility that may approach loss of mental balance
1**light·ning** \'līt-niŋ\ *n* [ME, fr. gerund of *lightenen* to lighten] **1 :** the flashing of light produced by a discharge of atmospheric electricity from one cloud to another or from a cloud to the earth; *also* **:** the discharge itself **2 :** a sudden stroke of fortune
2**lightning** *adj* **:** moving with or having the speed and suddenness of lightning
3**lightning** *vi* **light·ninged; lightning :** to discharge a flash of lightning
lightning arrester *n* **:** a device for protecting an electrical apparatus or a radio set from injury by lightning
lightning bug *n* **:** FIREFLY
lightning rod *n* **:** a metallic rod set up on a building or mast and connected with the moist earth or water below to diminish the chances of destructive effect by lightning
light–o'–love \ˌlīt-ᵊl-'əv\ *n* **1 :** PROSTITUTE **2 :** LOVER, PARAMOUR
light opera *n* **:** OPERETTA
light out *vi* [6*light*] **:** to leave in a hurry
light pen *n* **:** a pen-shaped device for direct interaction with a computer through a cathode-ray tube display
light·plane \'līt-'plān\ *n* **:** a small and comparatively lightweight airplane; *esp* **:** a privately owned passenger airplane
light·proof \-'prüf\ *adj* **:** impenetrable by light
light quantum *n* **:** PHOTON; *esp* **:** one of luminous radiation
light red *n* **:** any of various pale red or reddish orange pigments; *esp* **:** a calcined yellow ocher
lights \'līts\ *n pl* [ME *lightes*, fr. *light* light in weight] **:** the lungs esp. of a slaughtered animal
light·ship \'līt-ˌship\ *n* **:** a ship equipped with a brilliant light and moored at a place dangerous to navigation
1**light·some** \'līt-səm\ *adj* **1 :** AIRY, NIMBLE **2 :** free from care **3 :** FRIVOLOUS, UNSTEADY — **light·some·ly** *adv* — **light·some·ness** *n*
2**lightsome** *adj* **1 :** giving light **:** LUMINOUS **2 :** well lighted **:** BRIGHT
lights–out \'līt-'sau̇t\ *n* **1 :** a command or signal for putting out lights **2 :** a prescribed bedtime for persons living under discipline
light–struck \'līt-ˌstrək\ *adj* **:** fogged by accidental exposure to light — used of a photographic material
light·tight \'līt-ˌtīt\ *adj* **:** LIGHTPROOF
light trap *n* **:** a device that allows movement of a sliding part or passage of a person (as into a darkroom) but excludes light
1**light·weight** \'līt-ˌwāt\ *n* **1 :** one of less than average weight: as **a :** a boxer weighing more than 126 but not over 135 pounds **b :** a wrestler weighing more than 134 but not over 145 pounds **2 :** one of little consequence
2**lightweight** *adj* **1 :** of, relating to, or characteristic of a lightweight **2 :** having less than average weight **3 :** INCONSEQUENTIAL
light·wood \'līt-ˌwu̇d, 'līt-əd\ *n, chiefly South* **:** wood used for kindling; *esp* **:** coniferous wood abounding in pitch
light–year \'līt-ˌyi(ə)r\ *n* **:** a unit of length in interstellar astronomy equal to the distance that light travels in one year in a vacuum or 5,878,000,000,000 miles
lign- *or* **ligni-** *or* **ligno-** *comb form* [L *lign-, ligni-*, fr. *lignum*] **:** wood ⟨*lignin*⟩ ⟨*lignocellulose*⟩
lig·ne·ous \'lig-nē-əs\ *adj* [L *ligneus*, fr. *lignum* wood, fr. *legere* to gather — more at LEGEND] **:** of or resembling wood **:** WOODY
lig·ni·fi·ca·tion \ˌlig-nə-fə-'kā-shən\ *n* **:** the process of becoming or the state of being lignified
lig·ni·fy \'lig-nə-ˌfī\ *vb* [F *lignifier*, fr. L *lignum*] *vt* **:** to convert into wood or woody tissue ~ *vi* **:** to become wood or woody
lig·nin \'lig-nən\ *n* **:** an amorphous polymeric substance related to cellulose that together with cellulose forms the woody cell walls of plants and the cementing material between them
lig·nite \'lig-ˌnīt\ *n* [F, fr. L *lignum*] **:** a usu. brownish black coal intermediate between peat and bituminous coal; *esp* **:** one in which the texture of the original wood is distinct — called also *brown coal* — **lig·nit·ic** \lig-'nit-ik\ *adj*
lig·no·cel·lu·lose \ˌlig-(ˌ)nō-'sel-yə-ˌlōs, -ˌlōz\ *n* [ISV] **:** any of several closely related substances constituting the essential part of woody cell walls and consisting of cellulose intimately associated with lignin — **lig·no·cel·lu·los·ic** \-ˌsel-yə-'lō-sik, -zik\ *adj*
lig·num vi·tae \ˌlig-nəm-'vīt-ē\ *n, pl* **lignum vitaes** [NL, lit., wood of life] **1 :** any of several tropical American trees (genus *Guaiacum*) of the bean-caper family **2 :** the very hard heavy wood of lignum vitae
lig·ro·in \'lig-rə-wən\ *n* [origin unknown] **:** any of several petroleum naphtha fractions boiling usu. in the range 20° to 135°C that are used esp. as solvents
lig·u·la \'lig-yə-lə\ *n, pl* **lig·u·lae** \-ˌlē, -ˌlī\ *also* **ligulas** [NL] **1 :** LIGULE **2 :** the distal lobed part of the labium of an insect
lig·u·late \'lig-yə-lət\ *also* **lig·u·lat·ed** \-ˌlāt-əd\ *adj* **1** [L *ligula*] **:** shaped like a strap ⟨~ corolla of a ray flower⟩ **2 :** furnished with ligules, ligulae, or ligulate corollas
lig·ule \'lig-(ˌ)yü(ə)l\ *n* [NL *ligula*, fr. L, small tongue, strap; akin to L *lingere* to lick — more at LICK] **:** a scalelike projection esp. on a plant: as **a :** a thin appendage of a foliage leaf **b :** a ligulate corolla of a ray floret in a composite head
lig·ure \'lig-ˌyu̇(ə)r\ *n* [LL *ligurius*, fr. Gk *ligyrion*] **:** a precious stone that is prob. the jacinth
lik·able *or* **like·able** \'lī-kə-bəl\ *adj* **:** having qualities that bring about a favorable regard **:** PLEASANT, AGREEABLE — **lik·able·ness** *n*
1**like** \'līk\ *vb* [ME *liken*, fr. OE *līcian*; akin to OE *gelīc* alike] *vt* **1** *chiefly dial* **:** to be suitable or agreeable to **2 a :** to feel attraction toward or take pleasure in **:** ENJOY ⟨~*s* baseball⟩ **b :** to feel toward **:** REGARD ⟨how would you ~ a change⟩ **3 :** to wish to have **:** WANT ⟨would ~ a drink⟩ ~ *vi* **1** *dial* **:** APPROVE **2 :** to feel inclined **:** CHOOSE **3 :** to find oneself attracted
2**like** *n* **:** a feeling of attraction **:** PREFERENCE
3**like** *adj* [ME, alter. of *ilich*, fr. OE *gelīc* like, alike; akin to OHG *gilīh* like, alike; both fr. a prehistoric Gmc compound whose first constituent is represented by OE *ge-* (associative prefix) and whose second constituent is represented by OE *līc* body; akin to Lith *lygus* like — more at CO-] **1 a :** the same or nearly the same (as in appearance, character, or quantity) ⟨suits of ~ design⟩ **b :** resembling or characteristic of ⟨bell-*like*⟩ **2 a :** LIKELY **b :** being about or as if about — used with an infinitive ⟨~ to die⟩
4**like** *prep* **1 a :** having the characteristics of **:** similar to ⟨his house is ~ a barn⟩ **b :** typical of ⟨was ~ him to do that⟩ **2 :** in the manner of **:** similarly to ⟨acts ~ a fool⟩ **3 :** inclined to ⟨looks ~ rain⟩ **4 :** such as ⟨a subject ~ physics⟩
5**like** *n* **:** one that is like another **:** COUNTERPART
6**like** *adv* **1** *archaic* **:** EQUALLY **2 :** LIKELY, PROBABLY ⟨~ enough, you will⟩ **3 :** to some extent **:** SEEMINGLY ⟨came in nonchalantly ~⟩
7**like** *conj* **1 :** in the same way that **:** AS ⟨they raven down scenery ~ children do sweetmeats —John Keats⟩ **2 :** as if ⟨looked ~ he was scared⟩
8**like** *or* **liked** \'līkt\ *verbal auxiliary, chiefly substand* **:** came near **:** was near ⟨had four quarrels and ~ to have fought one —Shak.⟩
like·li·hood \'lī-klē-ˌhu̇d\ *n* **1 :** PROBABILITY **2 :** appearance of probable success **:** PROMISE
1**like·ly** \'lī-klē\ *adj* [ME, fr. ON *glīkligr*, fr. *glīkr* like; akin to OE *gelīc*] **1 :** of such a nature or circumstance as to make something probable ⟨~ of success⟩ **2 a :** RELIABLE, CREDIBLE ⟨a ~ enough story⟩ **b :** fairly certain **:** PROBABLE ⟨it's ~ they'll win⟩ **3 :** apparently qualified **:** SUITABLE ⟨a ~ place⟩ **4 :** PROMISING ⟨a ~ subject⟩ **5 :** ATTRACTIVE ⟨a ~ child⟩ **syn** see PROBABLE
2**likely** *adv* **:** in all probability **:** PROBABLY
like–mind·ed \'līk-'mīn-dəd\ *adj* **:** of the same mind or habit of thought — **like–mind·ed·ly** *adv* — **like–mind·ed·ness** *n*
lik·en \'lī-kən\ *vt* **lik·en·ing** \'līk-(ə-)niŋ\ **:** COMPARE
like·ness *n* **1 :** the quality or state of being like **:** RESEMBLANCE **2 :** APPEARANCE, SEMBLANCE **3 :** COPY, PORTRAIT
syn SIMILARITY, RESEMBLANCE, SIMILITUDE, ANALOGY, AFFINITY: LIKENESS implies a closer correspondence than SIMILARITY which often implies that two things are merely somewhat alike; RESEMBLANCE implies similarity chiefly in appearance or external qualities; SIMILITUDE applies chiefly to the abstract idea of likeness; ANALOGY implies likeness or parallelism in relations rather than in appearance or qualities; AFFINITY suggests a cause such as kinship or experiences or influences in common accountable for the similarity
like·wise \'lī-ˌkwīz\ *adv* **1 :** in like manner **:** SIMILARLY **2 :** in addition **3 :** same here ⟨answered "~" to "Pleased to meet you"⟩
lik·ing \'lī-kiŋ\ *n* **:** favorable regard **:** FONDNESS, TASTE
li·ku·ta \li-'küt-ə\ *n, pl* **ma·ku·ta** \mä-\ [of Niger-Congo origin; prob. akin to obs. Nupe *kuta* stone] — see *zaire* at MONEY table
li·lac \'lī-lək, -ˌlak, -ˌläk\ *n* [obs. F, (now *lilas*), fr. Ar *līlak*, fr. Per *nīlak* bluish, fr. *nīl* blue, fr. Skt *nīla* dark blue] **1 :** any of a genus (*Syringa*) of the olive family; *esp* **:** a European shrub (*S. vulgaris*) that is often an escape in No. America and has cordate ovate leaves and large panicles of fragrant pink-purple flowers **2 :** a variable color averaging a moderate purple
lil·i·a·ceous \ˌlil-ē-'ā-shəs\ *adj* **:** of or relating to lilies or the lily family
lil·ied \'lil-ēd\ *adj* **1** *archaic* **:** resembling a lily in fairness **2 :** full of or covered with lilies
Lil·ith \'lil-əth\ *n* [Heb *Līlīth*] **1 :** a female evil spirit in Semitic mythology roaming in desolate places and attacking children **2 :** the first wife of Adam in Jewish folklore **3 :** a famous witch in medieval demonology
lil·li·put \'lil-i-(ˌ)pət\ *n, often cap* **:** LILLIPUTIAN 2
lil·li·pu·tian \ˌlil-ə-'pyü-shən\ *adj, often cap* **1 :** of, relating to, or characteristic of the Lilliputians or the island of Lilliput **2 a :** SMALL, MINIATURE **b :** PETTY
Lilliputian *n* **1 :** an inhabitant of an island in Swift's *Gulliver's Travels* who is six inches tall **2** *often not cap* **:** one resembling a Lilliputian; *esp* **:** an undersized individual
1**lilt** \'lilt\ *vb* [ME *lulten*] *vt* **:** to sing or play in a lively cheerful manner ~ *vi* **1 :** to sing or speak rhythmically and with fluctuating pitch **2 :** to move in a lively springy manner
2**lilt** *n* **1 :** a spirited and usu. gay song or tune **2 :** a rhythmical swing, flow, or cadence **3 :** a springy buoyant movement
lilt·ing \'lil-tiŋ\ *adj* **1 :** characterized by a rhythmical swing ⟨~ stride⟩ **2 :** CHEERFUL, BUOYANT ⟨~ comedy⟩ — **lilt·ing·ly** \-tiŋ-lē\ *adv* — **lilt·ing·ness** *n*
1**lily** \'lil-ē\ *n* [ME *lilie*, fr. OE, fr. L *lilium*] **1 :** any of numerous erect perennial leafy-stemmed bulbous herbs that constitute a genus (*Lilium*) of a large nearly cosmopolitan family (Liliaceae, the lily family), are native to the northern hemisphere, and are widely cultivated for their showy flowers; *broadly* **:** any of various plants of the

lily family or of the related amaryllis or iris families **2 :** any of various plants with showy flowers: as **a :** the scarlet anemone that grows wild in Palestine **b :** WATER LILY **c :** CALLA **3 :** IRIS 3

2lily *adj* **:** resembling a lily in fairness, purity, or fragility

lily–liv·ered \ˌlil-ē-ˈliv-ərd\ *adj* **:** lacking courage **:** COWARDLY

lily of the valley : a low perennial herb (*Convallaria majalis*) of the lily family having usu. two large oblong lanceolate leaves and a raceme of fragrant nodding bell-shaped usu. white flowers

lily pad *n* **:** a floating leaf of a water lily

1lily–white \ˌlil-ē-ˈhwīt, -ˈwīt\ *adj* **1 :** white as a lily **2 :** characterized by or favoring the exclusion of Negroes esp. from politics **3 :** IRREPROACHABLE, PURE

2lily–white *n* **:** a member of a lily-white political organization

Li·ma \ˈlē-mə\ — a communications code word for the letter *l*

li·ma bean \ˌlī-mə-\ *n* [*Lima*, Peru] **1 a :** any of various bush or tall-growing beans derived from a perennial tropical American bean (*Phaseolus limensis*) and widely cultivated for their flat edible usu. pale green or whitish seeds **b :** SIEVA BEAN **2 :** the seed of a lima bean

li·mac·i·form \lī-ˈmas-ə-ˌfȯrm\ *adj* [prob. fr. (assumed) NL *limaciformis*, fr. L *limac-*, *limax* slug + *-iformis* -iform] **:** resembling a slug ⟨~ insect larvae⟩

li·ma·cine \ˈlim-ə-ˌsīn, ˈlī-mə-\ *adj* [NL *limacinus*, fr. L *limac-*, *limax*] **:** of, relating to, or resembling a slug

li·man \li-ˈmän\ *n* [Russ] **:** a bay or estuary at the mouth of a river **:** LAGOON

1limb \ˈlim\ *n* [ME *lim*, fr. OE; akin to ON *limr* limb, L *limes* limit, *limen* threshold, Gk *leimōn* meadow] **1 :** one of the projecting paired appendages (as wings) of an animal body used esp. for movement and grasping but sometimes modified into sensory or sexual organs; *esp* **:** a leg or arm of a human being **2 :** a large primary branch of a tree **3 :** an active member or agent **4 :** EXTENSION, BRANCH **5 :** a mischievous child **syn** see SHOOT — **limbed** \ˈlimd\ *adj* — **limby** \ˈlim-ē\ *adj*

2limb *vt* **:** DISMEMBER; *esp* **:** to cut off the limbs of (a felled tree)

3limb *n* [L *limbus* border — more at LIMP] **1 :** the graduated margin of an arc or circle in an instrument for measuring angles **2 :** the outer edge of the apparent disk of a celestial body **3 :** the expanded portion of an organ or structure; *esp* **:** the spreading upper portion of a gamosepalous calyx or a gamopetalous corolla as distinguished from the lower tubular portion

lim·bate \ˈlim-ˌbāt\ *adj* [LL *limbatus* bordered, fr. L *limbus*] **:** having a part of one color surrounded by an edging of another color ⟨a ~ leaf⟩

lim·beck \ˈlim-ˌbek\ *n* [ME *lembike*, fr. ML *alembicum*] **:** ALEMBIC

1lim·ber \ˈlim-bər\ *n* [ME *lymour*] **:** a 2-wheeled vehicle to which a gun or caisson may be attached

2limber *adj* [origin unknown] **1 :** FLEXIBLE, SUPPLE ⟨~ mind⟩ **2 :** LITHE, NIMBLE — **lim·ber·ly** *adv* — **lim·ber·ness** *n*

3limber *vb* **lim·ber·ing** \-b(ə-)riŋ\ *vt* **:** to cause to become limber ⟨~ up his fingers⟩ **~** *vi* **:** to become limber ⟨~ up by running⟩

lim·bers \ˈlim-bərz\ *n pl* [modif. of F *lumière*, fr. OF, light, opening, fr. L *luminare* window — more at LUMINARY] **:** gutters or conduits on each side of the keelson of a ship that provide a passage for water to the pump well

limb·less \ˈlim-ləs\ *adj* **:** having no limbs

lim·bo \ˈlim-(ˌ)bō\ *n* [ME, fr. ML, abl. of *limbus* limbo, fr. L, border — more at LIMP] **1** *often cap* **:** an abode of souls (as of unbaptized infants) barred from heaven through no fault of their own **2 a :** a place or state of restraint or confinement **b :** a place or state of neglect or oblivion **c :** an intermediate or transitional place or state

Lim·burg·er \ˈlim-ˌbər-gər\ *n* [Flem, one from Limburg, fr. *Limburg*, Belgium] **:** a semisoft surface-ripened cheese with a rind of pungent odor and a creamy-textured body

lim·bus \ˈlim-bəs\ *n* [L, border] **:** a border distinguished by color or structure

1lime \ˈlīm\ *n* [ME, fr. OE *līm;* akin to OHG *līm* birdlime, L *linere* to smear, *levis* smooth, Gk *leios*] **1 :** BIRDLIME **2 a :** a caustic highly infusible solid that consists of calcium oxide often together with magnesia and is obtained by calcining limestone, shells, or other forms of calcium carbonate — called also *caustic lime* **b :** hydrated lime **c :** CALCIUM

2lime *vt* **1 :** to smear with a sticky substance (as birdlime) **2 :** to entangle with or as if with birdlime **3 :** to treat or cover with lime

3lime *adj* **:** of, relating to, or containing lime or limestone

4lime *n* [alter. of ME *lind*, fr. OE; akin to OHG *linta* linden] **:** LINDEN 1a

5lime *n* [F, fr. Prov *limo*, fr. Ar *līm*] **:** a spiny tropical citrus tree (*Citrus aurantifolia*) with elliptic oblong narrowly winged leaves; *also* **:** its small globose greenish yellow fruit with an acid juicy pulp used as a flavoring agent and as a source of ascorbic acid

lime·ade \lī-ˈmād\ *n* **:** a beverage of lime juice sweetened and mixed with plain or carbonated water

lime glass *n* **:** glass containing a substantial proportion of lime

lime–juic·er \ˈlīm-ˌjü-sər\ *n* [fr. the use of lime juice on British ships as a beverage to prevent scurvy] **1** *slang* **a :** a British ship **b :** a British sailor **2** *slang* **:** ENGLISHMAN

lime·kiln \-ˌkil(n)\ *n* **:** a kiln or furnace for reducing limestone or shells to lime by burning

1lime·light \-ˌlīt\ *n* **1 a :** a stage lighting instrument producing illumination by means of an oxyhydrogen flame directed on a cylinder of lime and usu. equipped with a lens to concentrate the light in a beam **b :** the white light produced by such an instrument **c** *Brit* **:** SPOTLIGHT **2 :** the center of public attention

2limelight *vt* **:** to center attention on **:** SPOTLIGHT — **lime·light·er** *n*

li·men \ˈlī-mən\ *n* [L *limin-*, *limen* — more at LIMB] **:** THRESHOLD 3

lim·er·ick \ˈlim-(ə-)rik\ *n* [*Limerick*, Ireland] **:** a light or humorous verse form of 5 chiefly anapestic verses of which lines 1, 2, and 5 are of 3 feet and lines 3 and 4 are of 2 feet with a rhyme scheme of *aabba*

lime·stone \ˈlīm-ˌstōn\ *n* **:** a rock that is formed chiefly by accumulation of organic remains (as shells or coral), consists mainly of calcium carbonate, is extensively used in building, and yields lime when burned

lime sulfur *n* **:** a fungicide and insecticide containing calcium polysulfides usu. obtained by boiling sulfur with lime and water

lime–twig \ˈlīm-ˌtwig\ *n* **1 :** a twig covered with birdlime to catch birds **2 :** SNARE

lime·wa·ter \ˈlīm-ˌwȯt-ər, -ˌwät-\ *n* **1 :** an alkaline water solution of calcium hydroxide used as an antacid **2 :** natural water containing calcium carbonate or calcium sulfate in solution

lim·ey \ˈlī-mē\ *n, often cap* [*lime*-juicer + *-y*] **1** *slang* **:** an English sailor **2** *slang* **:** ENGLISHMAN

li·mic·o·line \lī-ˈmik-ə-ˌlīn, -ə-lən\ *adj* [deriv. of L *limus* mud + *colere* to inhabit; akin to L *linere* to smear — more at LIME, WHEEL] **:** shore-inhabiting; *also* **:** of or relating to a suborder (Charadrii) of shore birds including plovers, snipes, and sandpipers

li·mi·nal \ˈlim-ən-ᵊl, ˈlī-mən-\ *adj* **:** of, relating to, or situated at the limen

1lim·it \ˈlim-ət\ *n* [ME, fr. MF *limite*, fr. L *limit-*, *limes* boundary — more at LIMB] **1 a :** a geographical or political boundary **b** *pl* **:** the place enclosed within a boundary **:** BOUNDS **2 a :** something that bounds, restrains, or confines **b :** the utmost extent **3 :** LIMITATION **4 :** a determining feature or differentia in logic **5 :** a prescribed maximum or minimum amount, quantity, or number: as **a :** the maximum quantity of game or fish that may be taken legally in a specified period **b :** a maximum established for a gambling bet, raise, or payoff **6 :** a number that for an infinite sequence of numbers is such that ultimately the terms of the sequence differ from this number by less than any given amount **7 :** something that is exasperating or intolerable

2limit *vt* **1 :** to fix or appoint definitely **:** PRESCRIBE **2 a :** to set bounds or limits to **:** CONFINE **b :** to curtail or reduce in quantity or extent — **lim·it·able** \-ət-ə-bəl\ *adj* — **lim·it·er** *n*

syn LIMIT, RESTRICT, CIRCUMSCRIBE, CONFINE mean to set bounds for. LIMIT implies setting a point or line in time or space, or a speed or degree beyond which something cannot or is not permitted to go; RESTRICT usu. connotes a narrowing or tightening within boundaries; CIRCUMSCRIBE stresses a restricting in every direction and by clearly marked limits; CONFINE may imply limiting, restricting, or circumscribing but carries stronger implications of cramping, hampering, bottling up, or otherwise positively reducing freedom of action

lim·i·tary \ˈlim-ə-ˌter-ē\ *adj* **1** *archaic* **:** subject to limits **2 a** *archaic* **:** of or relating to a boundary **b :** ENCLOSING, LIMITING

lim·i·ta·tion \ˌlim-ə-ˈtā-shən\ *n* **1 :** an act or instance of limiting **2 :** the quality or state of being limited **3 :** something that limits **:** RESTRAINT **4 :** a certain period limited by statute after which actions, suits, or prosecutions cannot be brought in the courts — **lim·i·ta·tion·al** \-shnəl, -shən-ᵊl\ *adj*

lim·i·ta·tive \ˈlim-ə-ˌtāt-iv\ *adj* **:** serving to limit or restrict **:** LIMITING

lim·it·ed *adj* **1 a :** confined within limits **:** RESTRICTED **b** *of a train* (1) **:** having a limited number of cars and making a limited number of stops (2) **:** offering superior and faster service and transportation **2 :** characterized by enforceable limitations prescribed (as by a constitution) upon the scope or exercise of powers ⟨~ monarchy⟩ **3 :** narrow and unimaginative — **lim·it·ed·ly** *adv* — **lim·it·ed·ness** *n*

limited war *n* **:** a war with an objective less than the total defeat of the enemy

lim·it·ing *adj* **1 :** functioning as a limit **:** RESTRICTIVE ⟨~ value⟩ **2 :** serving to specify the application of the modified noun ⟨*this* in *this book* is a ~ word⟩

lim·it·less \ˈlim-ət-ləs\ *adj* **:** having no limits — **lim·it·less·ly** *adv* — **lim·it·less·ness** *n*

lim·i·trophe \ˈlim-ə-ˌtrōf\ *adj* [F] **:** situated on a border or frontier **:** ADJACENT

li·miv·o·rous \lī-ˈmiv-ə-rəs\ *adj* [prob. fr. (assumed) NL *limivorus*, fr. L *limus* + *-vorus* -vorous] **:** swallowing mud for the organic matter contained in it

lim·mer \ˈlim-ər\ *n* [ME (Sc)] **1** *chiefly Scot* **:** SCOUNDREL **2** *chiefly Scot* **:** PROSTITUTE

limn \ˈlim\ *vt* **limn·ing** \ˈlim-(n)iŋ\ [ME *luminen*, *limnen* to illuminate (a manuscript), fr. MF *enluminer*, fr. L *illuminare* to illuminate] **1 a** (1) **:** DRAW (2) **:** PAINT **b :** to outline in clear sharp detail **:** DELINEATE **2 :** DESCRIBE — **limn·er** \ˈlim-(n)ər\ *n*

lim·net·ic \lim-ˈnet-ik\ *also* **lim·nic** \ˈlim-nik\ *adj* [ISV, fr. Gk *limnē* pool, marshy lake; akin to L *limen* threshold — more at LIMB] **:** of, relating to, or inhabiting the pelagic part of a body of fresh water ⟨~ worms⟩

lim·no·log·i·cal \ˌlim-nə-ˈläj-i-kəl\ *adj* **:** of or relating to limnology — **lim·no·log·i·cal·ly** \-k(ə-)lē\ *adv*

lim·nol·o·gist \lim-ˈnäl-ə-jəst\ *n* **:** a specialist in limnology

lim·nol·o·gy \-jē\ *n* [Gk *limnē* + ISV *-logy*] **:** the scientific study of physical, chemical, meteorological, and biological conditions in fresh waters

lim·o·nene \ˈlim-ə-ˌnēn\ *n* [ISV, fr. F *limon* lemon] **:** a widely distributed terpene hydrocarbon $C_{10}H_{16}$ occurring in essential oils and having a lemon odor

li·mo·nite \ˈlī-mə-ˌnīt\ *n* [G *limonit*, fr. Gk *leimōn* meadow — more at LIMB] **:** a native hydrous ferric oxide of variable composition that is a major ore of iron — **li·mo·nit·ic** \ˌlī-mə-ˈnit-ik\ *adj*

lim·ou·sine \ˈlim-ə-ˌzēn, ˌlim-ə-ˈ\ *n* [F, lit., cloak, fr. *Limousin*, France] **:** any of various passenger vehicles; *specif* **:** a large luxurious often chauffeur-driven sedan

1limp \ˈlimp\ *vi* [prob. fr. ME *lympen* to fall short; akin to OE *limpan* to happen, L *limbus* border, *labi* to slide — more at SLEEP] **1 a :** to walk lamely; *esp* **:** to walk favoring one leg **b :** to go unsteadily **:** FALTER **2 :** to proceed slowly or with difficulty ⟨~*ed* into harbor⟩ — **limp·er** *n*

2limp *n* **:** a limping movement or gait

3limp *adj* [akin to 1*limp*] **1 a :** having no defined shape **:** SLACK **b :** not stiff or rigid ⟨~ bookbinding⟩ **2 a :** DROOPING, EXHAUSTED **b :** lacking in strength or firmness **:** SPIRITLESS — **limp·ly** *adv* — **limp·ness** *n*

syn LIMP, LOPPY, FLACCID, FLABBY, FLIMSY, SLEAZY mean wanting firmness in texture or substance. LIMP implies a lack or loss of stiffness and a tendency to droop; LOPPY applies to something hanging limply or sagging; FLACCID implies a loss of power to keep or return to shape; FLABBY implies hanging or sagging by its own weight as through loss of muscular tone; FLIMSY suggests such looseness or lightness of structure as to be without value; SLEAZY implies a flimsiness suggesting cheap or careless workmanship or fraudulent manufacture

lim·pet \ˈlim-pət\ *n* [ME *lempet*, fr. OE *lempedu*, fr. ML *lampreda*] **1 :** a marine gastropod mollusk with a low conical shell broadly open beneath that browses over rocks or timbers in the littoral area and adheres very tightly when disturbed **2 :** a person who clings

tenaciously to someone or something **3 :** an explosive designed to cling to the hull of a ship

lim·pid \'lim-pəd\ *adj* [F or L; F *limpide*, fr. L *limpidus*, fr. *lympha*, *limpa* water — more at LYMPH] **1 a :** marked by transparency **:** PELLUCID **b :** readily intelligible **:** CLEAR **2 :** absolutely serene and untroubled **syn** see CLEAR — **lim·pid·i·ty** \lim-'pid-ət-ē\ *n* — **lim·pid·ly** \'lim-pəd-lē\ *adv* — **lim·pid·ness** *n*

limp·kin \'lim(p)-kən\ *n* [¹*limp*] **:** a large brown wading bird (*Aramus pictus*) that resembles a bittern but has a longer slightly curved bill, longer neck and legs, and white stripes on head and neck

limp·sy \'lim(p)-sē\ *adj* [³*limp* + *-sy* (as in *tipsy*)] *dial* **:** limp esp. from weakness

lim·u·lus \'lim-yə-ləs\ *n, pl* **lim·u·li** \-,lī, -,lē\ [NL, genus name, fr. L *limus* sidelong] **:** KING CRAB 1

limy \'lī-mē\ *adj* **1 :** smeared with or consisting of lime **:** VISCOUS **2 :** containing lime or limestone **3 :** resembling or having the qualities of lime

lin·age \'lī-nij\ *n* **1 :** the number of lines of printed or written matter **2 :** payment for literary matter at so much a line

lin·alo·ol \lī-'nal-ə-,wȯl, -,wōl\ *n* [ISV, fr. MexSp *lináloe*, tree yielding perfume, fr. ML *lignum aloes*, lit., wood of the aloe] **:** a fragrant liquid unsaturated tertiary alcohol $C_{10}H_{17}OH$ that occurs both free and in the form of esters in many essential oils and is used in perfumes, soaps, and flavoring materials

linch·pin \'linch-,pin\ *n* [ME *lynspin*, fr. *lyns*, linchpin (fr. OE *lynis*) + *pin*; akin to OE *eln* ell] **1 :** a locking pin inserted crosswise (as through the end of an axle or shaft) **2 :** something that serves to hold together the elements of a situation

Lin·coln \'liŋ-kən\ *n* [*Lincoln* county, England] **:** any of an English breed of long-wool mutton-type sheep similar to but heavier than the Leicester

Lin·coln·esque \,liŋ-kə-'nesk\ *adj* **:** resembling Abraham Lincoln

Lin·coln·i·an \liŋ-'kō-nē-ən\ *adj* **:** of or relating to Abraham Lincoln

Lin·coln·i·a·na \(,)liŋ-,kō-nē-'an-ə, -'än-ə, -'ā-nə\ *n pl* **:** matter relating to Abraham Lincoln

Lincoln's Birthday *n* [Abraham *Lincoln*] **:** February 12 observed as a legal holiday in many of the states of the U.S.

lin·dane \'lin-,dān\ *n* [T. van der *Lind*en, 20th cent. D chemist] **:** an insecticide consisting of not less than 99 percent of the gamma isomer of benzene hexachloride

lin·den \'lin-dən\ *n* [ME, made of linden wood, fr. OE, fr. *lind* linden tree] **1 :** any of a genus (*Tilia*) of trees (family Tiliaceae, the linden family) with large cordate leaves and cymose yellowish flowers rich in nectar: as **a :** a European tree (*T. europaea*) much used for ornamental planting **b :** a tall No. American forest tree (*T. americana*) — called also *basswood* **2 :** the light fine-grained white wood of a linden; *esp* **:** BASSWOOD

lin·dy \'lin-dē\ *n* [prob. fr. *Lindy*, nickname of Charles A. Lindbergh *b*1902 Am aviator] **:** a jitterbug dance originating in Harlem and later developing many local variants

¹**line** \'līn\ *vt* [ME *linen*, fr. *line* flax, fr. OE *līn* — more at LINEN] **1 :** to cover the inner surface of ⟨~ cloak with silk⟩ **2 :** to put something in the inside of **:** SUPPLY **3 :** to serve as the lining of ⟨tapestries *lined* the walls⟩ **4** *obs* **:** FORTIFY — **line one's pockets :** to take money freely esp. from questionable sources

²**line** *n, often attrib* [ME; partly fr. OF *ligne*, fr. L *linea*, fr. fem. of *lineus* made of flax, fr. *linum* flax; partly fr. OE *līne*; akin to OE *līn*] **1 a :** THREAD, STRING, CORD, ROPE: as (1) **:** a comparatively strong slender cord (2) **:** CLOTHESLINE (3) **:** a rope used on shipboard **b** (1) **:** a device for catching fish consisting of a cord with hooks and other appurtenances (2) **:** scope for activity **c :** a length of material used in measuring and leveling **d :** piping for conveying a fluid (as steam) **e** (1) **:** a wire or pair of wires connecting one telegraph or telephone station with another or a whole system of such wires (2) **:** the principal circuits of an electric power system **2 a :** a horizontal row of written or printed characters **b :** a unit in the rhythmic structure of verse formed by the grouping of a number of the smallest units of the rhythm (as metrical feet) **c :** a short letter **:** NOTE **d :** a certificate of marriage **e :** the words making up a part in a drama — usu. used in pl. **3 a :** something (as a ridge or seam) that is distinct, elongated, and narrow **b :** a narrow crease (as on the face) **:** WRINKLE **c :** the course or direction of something in motion **:** ROUTE **d** (1) **:** a real or imaginary straight line oriented in terms of stable points of reference (2) **:** a state of agreement **e :** a boundary esp. of a plot of ground — usu. used in pl. **f :** the track and roadbed of a railway **4 a :** a course of conduct, action, or thought **b :** a field of activity or interest **c :** a glib often persuasive way of talking **5 a :** LIMIT, RESTRAINT **b** *archaic* **:** position in life: LOT **6 a** (1) **:** FAMILY, LINEAGE (2) **:** a strain produced and maintained by selective breeding (3) **:** a chronological series **b :** dispositions made to cover extended military positions and presenting a front to the enemy — usu. used in pl. **c :** a military formation in which the different elements are abreast of each other **d :** naval ships arranged in a regular order **e** (1) **:** the combatant forces of an army distinguished from the staff corps and supply services (2) **:** the force of a regular navy **f** (1) **:** officers of the navy eligible for command at sea distinguished from officers of the staff (2) **:** officers of the army belonging to a combatant branch **g :** a rank of objects of one kind **h :** a group of public conveyances plying regularly under one management over a route; *broadly* **:** a system of transportation or the company owning or operating it **i :** a succession of musical notes esp. considered in melodic phrases **j :** an arrangement of operations in manufacturing permitting sequential occurrence on various stages of production **k** (1) **:** the 7 players including center, 2 guards, 2 tackles, and 2 ends who in offensive football play line up on or within one foot of the line of scrimmage (2) **:** the players who in defensive play line up within one yard of the line of scrimmage **7 :** a narrow elongated mark drawn or projected: as **a** (1) **:** a circle of latitude or longitude on a map (2) **:** EQUATOR **b :** a mark (as on a map) recording a boundary, division, or contour **c :** any of the horizontal parallel strokes on a music staff **d :** a mark (as by pencil) that forms part of the formal design of a picture distinguished from the shading or color **e :** a division on a bridge score dividing the honors from the tricks **f** (1) **:** a demarcation of a limit with reference to which the playing of some game or sport is regulated — usu. used in combination (2) **:** LINE OF SCRIMMAGE **8 :** a straight or curved geometric element that is generated by a moving point and that has extension only along the path of the point **:** CURVE **9 a :** a defining outline **:** CONTOUR **b :** a general plan **:** MODEL — usu. used in pl. **10 a** *chiefly Brit* **:** PICA — used to indicate the size of large type **b :** the unit of fineness of halftones expressed as the number of screen lines to the linear inch **11 :** a stock of goods on hand of the same general class of articles **12 :** a source of information **:** INSIGHT **13 :** a complete game of 10 frames in bowling — called also *string* — **liny** *also* **lin·ey** \'lī-nē\ *adj* — **down the line :** all the way **:** FULLY — **in line for :** due or in a position to receive — **on the line 1 :** in full view and at hazard **2 :** on the border between two categories **3 :** IMMEDIATELY

³**line** *vt* **1 :** to mark or cover with a line or lines **2 :** to depict with lines **:** DRAW **3 :** to place or form a line along ⟨pedestrians ~ the walks⟩ **4 a :** to form into a line or lines **:** ALIGN ⟨~ up troops⟩ **b :** ORGANIZE ⟨~ up votes⟩ **5 :** to throw or hit (as a baseball) so as to cause to travel swiftly and not far above the ground ~ *vi* **1 :** to form a line — often used with *up* **2 :** to hit a line drive in baseball **3 :** ALIGN

syn LINE, ALIGN, RANGE, ARRAY mean to arrange in a line or lines. LINE implies a setting in single file or in parallel rows; ALIGN implies a bringing of points or parts into a straight line; RANGE implies a forming in parallel lines but may connote a separation into groups or classes; ARRAY applies esp. to a setting in battle order and therefore suggests readiness for action or use as well as impressive aspect

¹**lin·eage** \'lin-ē-ij\ *n* **1 a :** descent in a line from a common progenitor **b :** DERIVATION **2 :** a group of persons tracing descent from a common ancestor regarded as its founder **syn** see ANCESTRY

²**line·age** \'lī-nij\ *var of* LINAGE

lin·eal \'lin-ē-əl\ *adj* **1 :** LINEAR **2 :** composed of or arranged in lines **3 a :** consisting of or being in a direct male or female line of ancestry **b :** relating to or derived from ancestors **:** HEREDITARY **c :** descended in a direct line **4 a :** belonging to one lineage **b :** of, relating to, or dealing with a lineage **5 :** of or relating to the line or officers of the line in an army or navy — **lin·eal·i·ty** \,lin-ē-'al-ət-ē\ *n* — **lin·eal·ly** \'lin-ē-ə-lē\ *adv*

lin·ea·ment \'lin-ē-ə-mənt\ *n* [ME, fr. L *lineamentum*, fr. *linea*] **1 :** an outline, feature, or contour of a body or figure and esp. of a face — usu. used in pl. **2 :** a distinguishing or characteristic feature — usu. used in pl. — **lin·ea·men·tal** \,lin-ē-ə-'ment-ᵊl\ *adj*

lin·ear \'lin-ē-ər\ *adj* **1 a** (1) **:** relating to, consisting of, or resembling a line **:** STRAIGHT (2) **:** involving a single dimension **b** (1) **:** of the first degree in any number of variables ⟨~ equation⟩ (2) **:** based on or involving linear equations **c :** characterized by an emphasis on line ⟨~ art⟩ **2 :** elongated with nearly parallel sides ⟨~ leaf⟩ **3 :** involving or expressed by a linear equation; *esp* **:** having or being a response or output that is directly proportional to the input — **lin·ear·i·ty** \,lin-ē-'ar-ət-ē\ *n* — **lin·ear·ly** \'lin-ē-ər-lē\ *adv*

linear accelerator *n* **:** a device in which charged particles are accelerated in a straight line by successive impulses from a series of electric fields

lin·ear·ize \'lin-ē-ə-,rīz\ *vt* **:** to give a linear form to; *also* **:** to project in linear form

linear measure *n* **1 :** a measure of length **2 :** a system of measures of length

linear perspective *n* **:** perspective projection in which an object is represented upon a surface by means of lines from points of the object through the drawing surface to a common point of intersection

linear programming *n* **:** planning of industrial and military operations in terms of maximized linear functions of many variables subject to constraints

lin·ea·tion \,lin-ē-'ā-shən\ *n* [ME *lineacion* outline, fr. L *lineation-*, *lineatio*, fr. *lineatus*, pp. of *lineare* to make straight, fr. *linea*] **1 a :** the action of marking with lines **:** DELINEATION **b :** OUTLINE **2 :** an arrangement of lines

line·back·er \'līn-,bak-ər\ *n* **:** a defensive football player who lines up immediately behind the line of scrimmage and acts either as a lineman or as a pass defender

line·breed \'līn-'brēd\ *vi* **:** to practice linebreeding ~ *vt* **:** to interbreed (animals) in linebreeding; *also* **:** to produce by linebreeding

line·breed·ing *n* **:** the interbreeding of individuals within a particular line of descent usu. to perpetuate desirable characters

line chief *n* **:** an air force noncommissioned officer who supervises flight-line upkeep

line·cut \'līn-,kət\ *n* **:** a letterpress printing plate photoengraved from a line drawing — called also *line block*, *line engraving*

line drawing *n* **:** a drawing made in solid lines as copy for a linecut

line drive *n* **:** a batted baseball whose flight is almost straight and not far above the ground

line engraving *n* **1 a :** a metal plate for use in intaglio printing made by hand-engraving lines of different widths and closeness **b :** a process involving such plates or a print made with them **2 :** LINECUT

line gauge *n* **:** a printer's ruler showing point sizes

line-haul \'līn-,hȯl\ *n* **:** the transporting of items between terminals

line·man \'līn-mən\ *n* **1 :** one who sets up or repairs electric wire communication or power lines — called also *linesman* **2 :** a player in the line in football

¹**lin·en** \'lin-ən\ *adj* [ME, fr. OE *līnen*, fr. *līn* flax; akin to OHG *līn* flax; both fr. a prehistoric Gmc word borrowed fr. L *linum* flax] **1 :** made of flax **2 :** made of or resembling linen

²**linen** *n* **1 a :** cloth made of flax and noted for its strength, coolness, and luster **b :** thread or yarn spun from flax **2 :** clothing or household articles made of linen cloth or similar fabric **3 :** paper made from linen fibers or with a linen finish

line of duty : all that is authorized, required, or normally associated with some field of responsibility

line officer *n* **:** a commissioned officer assigned to the line of the army or navy

line of force : a line in a field of force (as a magnetic or electric field) whose tangent at any point gives the direction of the field at that point

line of scrimmage : an imaginary line in football parallel to the

goal lines and tangent to the nose of the ball laid on the ground preparatory to a scrimmage

line of sight 1 : a line from an observer's eye to a distant point toward which he is looking 2 : LINE OF VISION 3 : the straight path between a radio transmitting antenna and receiving antenna when unobstructed by the horizon

line of vision : a straight line joining the fovea of the eye with the fixation point

lin·eo·late \'lin-ē-ə-ˌlāt\ *or* **lin·eo·lat·ed** \-ˌlāt-əd\ *adj* [NL *lineolatus*, fr. *lineola*, dim. of *linea* line — more at LINE] : marked with fine lines

line out *vt* 1 a : to mark with lines indicating material to be removed b : to indicate with or as if with lines : OUTLINE ⟨*line out* a route⟩ 2 a : to plant (young nursery stock) in rows for growing on b : to arrange in an extended line 3 : BELT ⟨*line out* a song⟩ ~ *vi* 1 : to move rapidly ⟨*lined out* for home⟩ 2 : to make an out by hitting a baseball in a line drive that is caught

[1]**lin·er** \'lī-nər\ *n* 1 : one that makes, draws, or uses lines 2 : something with which lines are made 3 a : a ship belonging to a regular line of ships b : an airplane belonging to an airline 4 : LINE DRIVE

[2]**liner** *n* : one that lines or is used to line or back something

lines·man \'līnz-mən\ *n* 1 : LINEMAN 1 2 : an official who assists a referee in various games; *specif* : a football official whose duties include marking the distances gained or lost and the points where the ball goes out-of-bounds and noting violations of the scrimmage formation

line squall *n* : a squall or thunderstorm occurring along a cold front

line storm *n, chiefly NewEng* : an equinoctial storm

line up *vi* : to assume an orderly linear arrangement ⟨*line up* for inspection⟩ ~ *vt* : to put into alignment

line·up \'lī-ˌnəp\ *n* 1 : a line of persons arranged esp. for inspection or identification by police 2 a (1) : a list of players taking part in a game (as of baseball) (2) : the players on such a list b : an alignment of persons or things having a common purpose or interest

[1]**ling** \'liŋ\ *n* [ME; akin to D *leng* ling, OE *lang* long] 1 : any of various fishes (as a hake or burbot) of the cod family (Gadidae) 2 : LINGCOD

[2]**ling** *n* [ME, fr. ON *lyng*; akin to OE [2]*-ling*] : a heath plant; *esp* : a common Old World heather (*Calluna vulgaris*)

[1]**-ling** \liŋ\ *n suffix* [ME, fr. OE; akin to OE *-ing*] 1 : one connected with or having the quality of ⟨hire*ling*⟩ 2 : young, small, or inferior one ⟨duck*ling*⟩

[2]**-ling** \liŋ\ *or* **-lings** \liŋz\ *adv suffix* [ME *-ling*, *-linges* (fr. *-ling* + *-es* -s); akin to OHG *-lingūn* -ling, Lith *lenkti* to bend] : in (such) a direction or manner ⟨side*ling*⟩ ⟨flat*lings*⟩

Lin·ga·la \liŋ-'gäl-ə\ *n* : a Bantu language widely used in trade and public affairs in the Congo

lin·gam \'liŋ-gəm\ *or* **lin·ga** \-gə\ *n* [Skt *liṅga* (nom. *liṅgam*), lit., characteristic] 1 : a stylized phallic symbol of the masculine cosmic principle and of the Hindu god Siva 2 : a symbol conjoining the lingam and yoni

Lin·ga·yat \liŋ-'gä-yət\ *n* [Kannada *liṅgāyata*] : a member of a Saiva sect of southern India characterized by wearing of the lingam and denial of caste distinctions

ling·cod \'liŋ-ˌkäd\ *n* : a large greenish-fleshed fish (*Ophiodon elongatus*) of the Pacific coast of No. America that is an important food fish closely related to the typical greenlings

lin·ger \'liŋ-gər\ *vb* **lin·ger·ing** \-g(ə-)riŋ\ [ME (northern dial.) *lengeren* to dwell, freq. of *lengen* to prolong, fr. OE *lengan*; akin to OE *lang* long] *vi* 1 : to be slow in leaving : TARRY 2 : to remain alive although waning or gradually dying 3 : to be slow to act : PROCRASTINATE 4 : to move slowly : SAUNTER ~ *vt* 1 *obs* : DELAY 2 : to pass (as a period of time) slowly **syn** see STAY — **lin·ger·er** \-gər-ər, -grər\ *n* — **lin·ger·ing·ly** \-g(ə-)riŋ-lē\ *adv*

lin·ge·rie \ˌlän-jə-'rā, ˌlaⁿ-zhə-, ˌlan-jə-, -'rē\ *n* [F, fr. MF, fr. *linge* linen, fr. L *lineus* made of linen — more at LINE] 1 *archaic* : linen articles or garments 2 : women's intimate apparel — **lingerie** *adj*

lin·go \'liŋ-(ˌ)gō\ *n, pl* **lingoes** [prob. fr. Prov, tongue, fr. L *lingua* — more at TONGUE] : strange or incomprehensible language or speech: as a : a foreign language b : the special vocabulary of a particular field of interest c : language characteristic of an individual **syn** see DIALECT

lingu- *or* **lingui-** *or* **linguo-** *comb form* [L *lingu-*, fr. *lingua*] 1 : language ⟨*lingui*st⟩ 2 : tongue ⟨*lingui*form⟩

lin·gua \'liŋ-gwə\ *n, pl* **lin·guae** \-ˌgwē, -ˌgwī\ [L] : a tongue or an organ resembling a tongue

lin·gua fran·ca \ˌliŋ-gwə-'fraŋ-kə\ *n, pl* **lingua francas** *or* **lin·guae fran·cae** \-ˌgwī-'fraŋ-ˌkī\ [It, lit., Frankish language] 1 : a common language that consists of Italian mixed with French, Spanish, Greek, and Arabic and is spoken in Mediterranean ports 2 : any of various languages used as common or commercial tongues among peoples of diverse speech 3 : something resembling a common language

lin·gual \'liŋ-gwəl\ *adj* 1 a : of, relating to, or resembling the tongue b : lying near or next to the tongue c : produced by the tongue 2 : LINGUISTIC — **lin·gual·ly** \-gwə-lē\ *adv*

lin·guist \'liŋ-gwəst\ *n* 1 : a person accomplished in languages; *esp* : one who speaks several languages 2 : one who specializes in linguistics

lin·guis·tic \liŋ-'gwis-tik\ *adj* : of or relating to language or linguistics — **lin·guis·ti·cal** \-ti-kəl\ *adj* — **lin·guis·ti·cal·ly** \-ti-k(ə-)lē\ *adv*

linguistic atlas *n* : a publication containing a set of maps on which speech variations are recorded — called also *dialect atlas*

linguistic form *n* : a meaningful unit of speech (as a morpheme, word, or sentence) — called also *speech form*

linguistic geographer *n* : a specialist in linguistic geography

linguistic geography *n* : local or regional variations of a language or dialect studied as a field of knowledge — called also *dialect geography*

lin·guis·ti·cian \ˌliŋ-(ˌ)gwis-'tish-ən\ *n* : LINGUIST 2

lin·guis·tics \liŋ-'gwis-tiks\ *n pl but sing or pl in constr* : the study of human speech including the units, nature, structure, and modification of language, languages, or a language — compare PHILOLOGY

lin·gu·late \'liŋ-gyə-lət\ *adj* [L *lingulatus*, fr. *lingula*, dim. of *lingua*] : shaped like a tongue or strap : LIGULATE

lin·i·ment \'lin-ə-mənt\ *n* [ME, fr. LL *linimentum*, fr. L *linere* to smear — more at LIME] : a preparation of a consistency thinner than an ointment for application to the skin as an anodyne or a counterirritant

li·nin \'lī-nən\ *n* [ISV, fr. L *linum* flax] : the feebly-staining portion of the reticulum of the nucleus of a resting cell in which chromatin granules appear to be embedded

lin·ing *n* 1 : material used to line esp. the inner surface of something (as a garment) 2 : the act or process of providing something with a lining

[1]**link** \'liŋk\ *n* [ME, of Scand origin; akin to ON *hlekkr* chain; akin to OE *hlanc* lank] 1 : a connecting structure: as a (1) : a single ring or division of a chain (2) : one of the standardized divisions of a surveyor's chain that is 7.92 inches long and serves as a measure of length b : a usu. ornamental device for fastening a cuff c : BOND 3c d : an intermediate rod or piece for transmitting force or motion; *esp* : a short connecting rod with a hole or pin at each end e : the fusible member of an electrical fuse 2 : something analogous to a link of chain: as a : a segment of sausage in a chain b : a connecting element c : a unit in a communication system 3 *pl, dial* : a winding of a river or watercourse; *also* : the ground along such a winding — **link·er** *n*

[2]**link** *vt* : to couple or connect by a link ~ *vi* : to become connected by a link **syn** see JOIN

[3]**link** *n* [perh. modif. of ML *linchinus* candle, alter. of L *lychnus*, fr. Gk *lychnos*; akin to Gk *leukos* white — more at LIGHT] : a torch formerly used to light a person on his way through the streets

[4]**link** *vi* [origin unknown] *Scot* : to trip or skip smartly along

link·age \'liŋ-kij\ *n* 1 : the manner or style of being united: as a : the manner in which atoms or radicals are linked in a molecule b : BOND 3c 2 : the quality or state of being linked; *esp* : a relationship between genes that causes them to be manifested together in inheritance and that is usu. considered to result from the location of such genes on the same chromosome 3 a : a system of links; *specif* : a system of links or bars which are jointed together and more or less constrained by having a link or links fixed and by means of which straight or nearly straight lines or other point paths may by traced b : the product of the magnetic flux through an electrical coil by its number of turns with the magnetic flux and the coil being connected like two links of a chain

link·boy \'liŋk-ˌbȯi\ *n* : an attendant formerly employed to bear a torch or other light for a person abroad at night

linked *adj* : exhibiting genetic linkage ⟨~ genes⟩

linking verb *n* : a verb (as *be, become, seem, feel, grow*) that connects a predicate with a subject : copulative verb

link·man \'liŋk-mən\ *n* : LINKBOY

links \'liŋ(k)s\ *n pl* [ME, fr. OE *hlincas*, pl. of *hlinc* ridge; akin to OE *hlanc*] 1 *Scot* : sand hills esp. along the seashore 2 : COURSE 2d

links·man \'liŋ(k)-smən\ *n* : GOLFER

link·up \'liŋ-ˌkəp\ *n* 1 : MEETING 2 : something that serves as a linking device or factor

link·work \'liŋ-ˌkwərk\ *n* 1 : something consisting of interlocking links 2 : LINKAGE 3a

linn \'lin\ *n* [ScGael *linne* pool] 1 *chiefly Scot* : WATERFALL 2 *chiefly Scot* : PRECIPICE

Lin·nae·an *or* **Lin·ne·an** \lə-'nē-ən, 'lin-ē-\ *adj* [NL Carolus *Linnaeus* (Carl von Linné)] : of, relating to, or following the method of the Swedish botanist Linné who established the system of binomial nomenclature

lin·net \'lin-ət\ *n* [MF *linette*, fr. *lin* flax, fr. L *linum*] : a common small Old World finch (*Carduelis cannabina*) having plumage that varies greatly according to age, sex, and season

li·no \'lī-(ˌ)nō\ *n, chiefly Brit* : LINOLEUM

li·no·cut \-ˌkət\ *n* : a print made by cutting a design on a mounted piece of linoleum

li·no·le·ate \lə-'nō-lē-ˌāt\ *n* : a salt or ester of linoleic acid

lin·ole·ic acid \ˌlin-ə-ˌlē-ik-, -ˌlā-\ *n* [Gk *linon* flax + ISV *oleic* (*acid*)] : a liquid unsaturated fatty acid $C_{18}H_{32}O_2$ found in drying and semidrying oils and held to be essential in animal nutrition

lin·ole·nate \-'lē-ˌnāt, -'lā-\ *n* : a salt or ester of linolenic acid

lin·ole·nic acid \-ˌlē-nik-, -ˌlā-\ *n* [ISV, irreg. fr. *linoleic*] : a liquid unsaturated fatty acid $C_{18}H_{30}O_2$ found esp. in drying oils and held to be essential in animal nutrition

li·no·leum \lə-'nō-lē-əm, -'nōl-yəm\ *n, often attrib* [L *linum* flax + *oleum* oil — more at OIL] 1 : a floor covering made by laying on a burlap or canvas backing a mixture of solidified linseed oil with gums, cork dust or wood flour or both, and usu. pigments 2 : a material similar to linoleum

Li·no·type \'lī-nə-ˌtīp\ *trademark* 1 — used for a keyboard-operated typesetting machine that uses circulating matrices and produces each line of type in the form of a solid metal slug 2 : matter produced by a Linotype machine or printing done from such matter

lin·sang \'lin-ˌsaŋ\ *n* [Malay] : any of various Asiatic viverrine mammals (*Prionodon* and related genera) that resemble long-tailed cats and are related to the civets and genets

lin·seed \'lin-ˌsēd\ *n* [ME, fr. OE *līnsǣd*, fr. *līn* flax + *sǣd* seed — more at LINEN] : FLAXSEED

linseed oil *n* : a yellowish drying oil obtained from flaxseed and used esp. in paint, varnish, printing ink, and linoleum

lin·sey–wool·sey \ˌlin-zē-'wu̇l-zē\ *n* [ME *lynsy wolsye*] : a coarse sturdy fabric of wool and linen or cotton

lin·stock \'lin-ˌstäk\ *n* [D *lontstok*, fr. *lont* match + *stok* stick] : a pointed forked staff shod with iron at the foot formerly used to hold a lighted match for firing cannon

lint \'lint\ *n* [ME] 1 a : a soft fleecy material made from linen usu. by scraping b : fuzz consisting esp. of fine ravelings and short fibers of yarn and fabric 2 : a fibrous coat of thick convoluted hairs borne by cotton seeds that yields the cotton staple — **linty** \-ē\ *adj*

lin·tel \'lint-ᵊl\ *n* [ME, fr. MF, fr. LL *limitaris* threshold, fr. L, constituting a boundary, fr. *limit-*, *limes* boundary — more at LIMB] : a horizontal architectural member spanning and usu. carrying the load above an opening

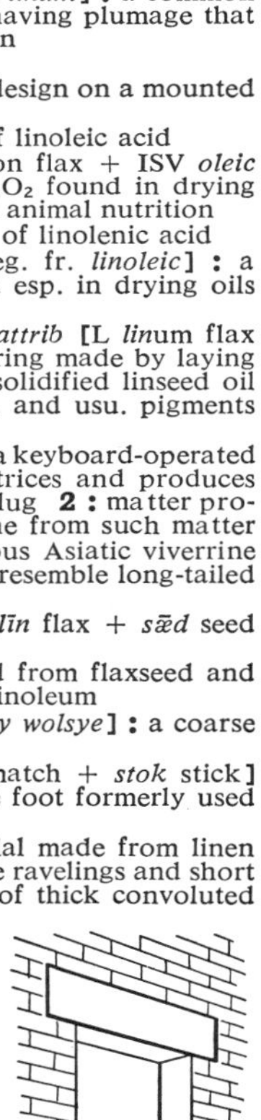
lintel

lint·er \'lint-ər\ *n* 1 : a machine for removing linters 2 *pl* : the fuzz of short fibers that adheres to cottonseed after ginning

lint·white \-ˌhwīt, -ˌwīt\ *n* [ME *lynkwhyt*, by folk etymology fr. OE *linetwige*] : LINNET

li·num \'lī-nəm\ *n* [NL, genus name, fr. L,

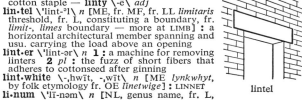

flax] : any of a genus (*Linum*) of herbaceous small-leaved plants of the flax family; *esp* : one growing wild or cultivated for ornament

li·on \'lī-ən\ *n, pl* **lions** [ME, fr. OF, fr. L *leon-*, *leo*, fr. Gk *leōn*] **1 a** *or pl* **lion** : a large carnivorous chiefly nocturnal cat (*Felis leo*) of open or rocky areas of Africa and esp. formerly southern Asia that has a tawny body with a tufted tail and a shaggy blackish or dark brown mane in the male **b** : any of several large wildcats; *esp* : COUGAR **2 a** : a person felt to resemble a lion (as in courage or ferocity) **b** : a person of outstanding interest or importance **3** *cap* : a member of one of the major service clubs — **li·on·ess** \'lī-ə-nəs\ *n* — **li·on·like** \'lī-ən-,līk\ *adj*

li·on·heart·ed \,lī-ən-'härt-əd\ *adj* : having a courageous heart : BRAVE

li·on·iza·tion \,lī-ə-nə-'zā-shən\ *n* : an act of lionizing

li·on·ize \'lī-ə-,nīz\ *vt* **1** : to treat as an object of great interest or importance **2** *Brit* : to show the sights of a place to — **li·on·iz·er** *n*

¹lip \'lip\ *n* [ME, fr. OE *lippa;* akin to OHG *leffur* lip and prob. to L *labium*, *labrum* lip] **1** : either of two fleshy folds that surround the mouth in man and many other vertebrates and in man are organs of speech **2** *slang* : BACK TALK **3 a** : a fleshy edge or margin (as of a wound) **b** : LABIUM 2 **c** : LABELLUM 1 **4 a** : the edge of a hollow vessel or cavity **b** : a projecting edge: as (1) : the slanted upper edge of the mouth of an organ flue pipe (2) : the sharp cutting edge on the end of an auger or similar tool (3) : a short spout (as on a pitcher) **5** : EMBOUCHURE 1 — **lip·less** \-ləs\ *adj* — **lip·like** \-,līk\ *adj* — **lipped** \'lipt\ *adj*

²lip *adj* **1** : spoken with the lips only : INSINCERE ⟨~ praise⟩ **2** : produced with the participation of the lips : LABIAL ⟨~ consonants⟩

³lip *vt* **lipped; lip·ping 1** : to touch with the lips; *specif* : KISS **2** : UTTER **3** : to lap against : LICK **4** : to strike a golf ball so that it hits the edge of (the cup) but fails to drop in

lip- *or* **lipo-** *comb form* [NL, fr. Gk, fr. *lipos* — more at LEAVE] : fat : fatty tissue : fatty ⟨lipoid⟩ ⟨*lipo*protein⟩

li·pase \'līp-,ās, 'lip-, -,āz\ *n* [ISV] : an enzyme that accelerates the hydrolysis or synthesis of fats or the breakdown of lipoproteins

lip·ide \'lip-,īd\ *or* **lip·id** \-əd\ *n* [ISV] : any of various substances including fats, waxes, phosphatides, cerebrosides, and related and derived compounds that with proteins and carbohydrates constitute the principal structural components of living cells

li·poid \'lip-,ȯid, 'līp-\ *or* **li·poi·dal** \lip-'ȯid-ᵊl, lī-'pȯid-\ *adj* [ISV] : resembling fat — **lipoid** *n*

li·pol·y·sis \lip-'äl-ə-səs, lī-'päl-\ *n* [NL] : the hydrolysis of fat — **li·po·lyt·ic** \,lip-ə-'lit-ik, ,līp-\ *adj*

li·po·ma \lip-'ō-mə, lī-'pō-\ *n, pl* **lipomas** *or* **li·po·ma·ta** \-mət-ə\ [NL] : a tumor of fatty tissue — **li·po·ma·tous** \lip-'äm-ət-əs, lī-'päm-, lip-'ōm-, lī-'pōm-\ *adj*

li·po·phil·ic \,lip-ə-'fil-ik, ,līp-\ *adj* : having an affinity for fats or other lipides

li·po·pro·tein \-'prō-,tēn, -'prōt-ē-ən\ *n* : a protein containing a lipide group

li·po·trop·ic \-'träp-ik\ *adj* [ISV] : promoting the physiologic utilization of fat — **li·pot·ro·pism** \lip-'ä-trə-,piz-əm, lī-'pä-\ *n*

lip·pen \'lip-ən\ *vb* [ME *lipnien*] *vi, chiefly Scot* : TRUST, RELY ~ *vt, chiefly Scot* : ENTRUST

lip·ping \'lip-iŋ\ *n* **1** : outgrowth of bone in liplike form at a joint margin **2** : a piece of wood set in an archer's bow where a flaw has been cut out **3** : EMBOUCHURE 1

lip·py \'lip-ē\ *adj* : given to back talk : IMPUDENT

lip–read \'lip-,rēd\ *vt* : to understand by lipreading ~ *vi* : to use lipreading — **lip–read·er** *n*

lip·read·ing *n* : the interpreting of a speaker's words without hearing his voice by watching his lip and facial movements

lip service *n* : avowal of allegiance that goes no further than expression in words

lip·stick \'lip-,stik\ *n* : a waxy solid colored cosmetic in stick form for the lips; *also* : a stick of such cosmetic with its case

li·quate \'lī-,kwāt\ *vt* [L *liquatus*, pp. of *liquare;* akin to L *liquēre*] : to cause (a substance that is more fusible than a substance with which it is combined) to separate out by the application of heat — **li·qua·tion** \lī-'kwā-shən\ *n*

liq·ue·fa·cient \,lik-wə-'fā-shənt\ *n* [L *liquefacient-*, *liquefaciens*, prp. of *liquefacere*, fr. *liquēre* + *facere* to make — more at DO] : something serving to liquefy or to promote liquefaction

liq·ue·fac·tion \-'fak-shən\ *n* [ME, fr. LL *liquefaction-*, *liquefactio*, fr. L *liquefactus*, pp. of *liquefacere*] **1** : the process of making or becoming liquid **2** : the state of being liquid

liq·ue·fi·able \'lik-wə-,fī-ə-bəl\ *adj* : capable of being liquefied

liquefied petroleum gas *n* : a compressed gas consisting of flammable light hydrocarbons and used esp. as fuel or as raw material for chemical synthesis

liq·ue·fi·er \'lik-wə-,fī(-ə)r\ *n* : one that liquefies

liq·ue·fy \-,fī\ *also* **liq·ui·fy** \-wə-,fī\ *vb* [MF *liquefier*, fr. L *liquefacere*] *vt* : to reduce to a liquid state ~ *vi* : to become liquid

li·ques·cence \lik-'wes-ᵊn(t)s\ *n* : the quality or state of being liquescent

li·ques·cent \-ᵊnt\ *adj* [L *liquescent-*, *liquescens*, prp. of *liquescere* to become fluid, incho. of *liquēre*] : being or tending to become liquid : MELTING

li·queur \li-'kər, -'k(y)u̇(ə)r\ *n* [F, fr. OF *licour* liquid — more at LIQUOR] : an alcoholic beverage flavored with aromatic substances and usu. sweetened

¹liq·uid \'lik-wəd\ *adj* [ME, fr. MF *liquide*, fr. L *liquidus*, fr. *liquēre* to be fluid; akin to L *lixa* water, lye, OIr *fliuch* damp] **1** : flowing freely like water **2** : neither solid nor gaseous : characterized by free movement of the constituent molecules among themselves but without the tendency to separate characteristic of gases ⟨~ mercury⟩ **3 a** : shining clear ⟨large ~ eyes⟩ **b** : being musical and free of harshness in sound **c** : smooth and unconstrained in movement **d** : that is without friction and like a vowel ⟨~ consonant⟩ **4** : consisting of or capable of ready conversion into cash ⟨~ assets⟩ — **li·quid·i·ty** \lik-'wid-ət-ē\ *n* — **liq·uid·ly** \'lik-wəd-lē\ *adv* — **liq·uid·ness** *n*

syn FLUID: LIQUID implies the flow characteristic of water and suggests a substance that has definite volume but that more or less readily takes the shape of its container; FLUID implies flowing of any kind and is applied to liquids, gases, and melted or viscous substances; figuratively LIQUID suggests drinking, connotes clearness and brightness, and is opposed to *fixed;* FLUID is opposed to *rigid* or *stiff* and may stress extreme susceptibility to change of form or pattern

²liquid *n* **1** : a liquid substance **2** : a liquid consonant

liquid air *n* : air in the liquid state that is prepared by subjecting it to great pressure and then cooling it by its own expansion to a temperature below the boiling point of its chief constituents and that is used chiefly as a refrigerant

liq·uid·am·bar \,lik-wə-'dam-bər\ *n* [NL, genus name, fr. L *liquidus* + ML *ambar* amber] **1** : any of a genus (*Liquidambar*) of trees of the witch hazel family with monoecious flowers and a globose fruit of many woody carpels **2** : an American storax from the sweet gum (*Liquidambar styraciflua*)

liq·ui·date \'lik-wə-,dāt\ *vb* [LL *liquidatus*, pp. of *liquidare* to melt, fr. L *liquidus*] *vt* **1 a** (1) : to determine by agreement or by litigation the precise amount of (indebtedness, damages, accounts) (2) : to determine the liabilities and apportion assets toward discharging the indebtedness of **b** : to settle (a debt) by payment or other settlement **2** : to get rid of; *specif* : KILL **3** *archaic* : to make clear **4** : to convert (assets) into cash ~ *vi* **1** : to liquidate debts or damages or accounts **2** : to determine liabilities and apportion assets toward discharging indebtedness — **liq·ui·da·tion** \,lik-wə-'dā-shən\ *n*

liq·ui·da·tor \'lik-wə-,dāt-ər\ *n* : one that liquidates; *esp* : an individual appointed by law to liquidate assets

liquid crystal *n* : a liquid having certain physical esp. optical properties shown by crystalline solids but not by ordinary liquids

liq·uid·ize \'lik-wə-,dīz\ *vt* : to cause to be liquid

liquid measure *n* **1** : a unit or series of units for measuring liquid capacity — see MEASURE table, METRIC SYSTEM table **2** : a measure for liquids

¹li·quor \'lik-ər\ *n* [ME *licour*, fr. OF, fr. L *liquor*, fr. *liquēre*] : a liquid substance: as **a** : a distilled alcoholic beverage rather than a fermented one **b** : a watery solution of a drug **c** : BATH 2b(1)

²liquor *vt* **li·quor·ing** \'lik-(ə-)riŋ\ **1 a** : to treat with a liquid substance **b** : to cover or dress with oil or grease **2** : to make drunk with alcoholic liquor — usu. used with *up* ~ *vi* : to drink alcoholic liquor esp. to excess — usu. used with *up*

li·quo·rice *chiefly Brit var of* LICORICE

li·ra \'lir-ə, 'lē-rə\ *n* [It, fr. L *libra* unit of weight] **1** *pl* **li·re** \'lē-(,)rā\ *also* **liras** — see MONEY table **2** [Turk, fr. It] *pl* **liras** *also* **lire** : a Turkish or Syrian pound **3** *pl* **li·roth** *or* **li·rot** \'lē-,rōt(h)\ [NHeb, fr. It] : the Israeli pound

lir·i·pipe \'lir-ə-,pīp\ *n* [ML *liripipium*] : a pendent part of a tippet; *also* : TIPPET, SCARF

lisle \'lī(ə)l\ *n* [*Lisle* Lille, France] : a smooth tightly twisted thread usu. made of long-staple cotton

¹lisp \'lisp\ *vb* [ME *lispen*, fr. OE *-wlyspian;* akin to OHG *lispen* to lisp] *vi* **1** : to pronounce the sibilants *s* and *z* imperfectly esp. by giving them the sound of *th* **2** : to speak falteringly, childishly, or with a lisp ~ *vt* : to utter falteringly or with a lisp — **lisp·er** *n*

²lisp *n* **1** : a speech defect or affectation characterized by lisping **2** : a sound resembling a lisp

lis pen·dens \'lis-'pen-,denz\ *n* [L] : a pending lawsuit

lis·some *also* **lis·som** \'lis-əm\ *adj* [alter. of *lithesome*] **1** : easily flexed : LITHE **2** : NIMBLE — **lis·some·ly** *adv* — **lis·some·ness** *n*

¹list \'list\ *vb* [ME *lysten*, fr. OE *lystan;* akin to OE *lust*] *vt* : PLEASE, SUIT ~ *vi* : WISH, CHOOSE

²list *n* [ME, prob. fr. *lysten*] *archaic* : INCLINATION, CRAVING

³list *vb* [ME *listen*, fr. OE *hlystan*, fr. *hlyst* hearing, fr. *hlysnan*] *vi* : LISTEN ~ *vt, archaic* : to listen to : HEAR

⁴list *n* [ME, fr. OE *līste;* akin to OHG *līsta* edge, Alb *leth*] **1 a** *obs* : a strip of cloth **b** : LISTEL **c** : SELVAGE **d** : a band or strip of any material; *esp* : a narrow strip of wood cut from the edge of a plank or board **2** *pl but sing or pl in constr* **a** : an arena for jousting **b** : an arena for combat **c** : a field of competition or controversy **3** *obs* : LIMIT, BOUNDARY **4** : STRIPE

⁵list *vt* **1** : to cut away a narrow strip (as sapwood) from the edge of **2** : to prepare or plant (land) in ridges and furrows with a lister

⁶list *n* [F *liste*, fr. It *lista*, of Gmc origin; akin to OHG *līsta*] **1** : ROLL, ROSTER **2** : INDEX, CATALOG

⁷list *vt* **1 a** : to make a list of : ENUMERATE **b** : to include on a list : REGISTER **2** : to put (oneself) down **3** *archaic* : RECRUIT ~ *vi* **1** *archaic* : ENLIST **2** : to become entered in a catalog with a selling price

⁸list *vb* [origin unknown] *vi* : to lean to one side : TILT ~ *vt* : to cause to list

⁹list *n* : a deviation from the vertical : TILT

lis·tel \'list-ᵊl, lis-'tel\ *n* [F, fr. It *listello*, dim. of *lista* fillet, roster] : a narrow band in architecture : FILLET

¹lis·ten \'lis-ᵊn\ *vb* **lis·ten·ing** \'lis-niŋ, -ᵊn-iŋ\ [ME *listnen*, fr. OE *hlysnan;* akin to Skt *śroṣati* he hears, OE *hlūd* loud] *vt, archaic* : to give ear to : HEAR ~ *vi* **1** : to pay attention to sound ⟨~ to music⟩ **2** : to hear with thoughtful attention : HEED ⟨~ to a plea⟩ **3** : to be alert to catch an expected sound ⟨~ for his step⟩ — **lis·ten·er** \'lis-nər, -ᵊn-ər\ *n*

²listen *n* : an act of listening

listen in *vi* **1** : to tune in to or monitor a broadcast **2** : to give ear to a conversation without participating in it; *esp* : EAVESDROP — **lis·ten·er–in** \,lis-nə-'rin, ,lis-ᵊn-ə-\ *n*

¹list·er \'lis-tər\ *n* : one that lists or catalogs

²lister *n* **1** : a double-moldboard plow often equipped with a subsoiling attachment and used mainly where rainfall is limited **2** : a lister plow with an attachment for dropping seeds into the furrow

list·ing *n* **1** : an act or instance of making or including in a list **2** : something that is listed

list·less \'list-ləs\ *adj* : characterized by lack of inclination or impetus to exertion : LANGUID — **list·less·ly** *adv* — **list·less·ness** *n*

list price *n* : the basic price of an item as published in a catalog, price list, or advertisement but subject to trade, quantity, and other discounts

lit *past of* LIGHT

lit·a·ny \'lit-ᵊn-ē, 'lit-nē\ *n* [ME *letanie*, fr. OF, fr. LL *litania*, fr. LGk *litaneia*, fr. Gk, entreaty, fr. *litanos* entreating; akin to OE *līm* lime] **1 :** a prayer consisting of a series of invocations and supplications by the leader with alternate responses by the congregation **2 :** a resonant or repetitive recital or chant

li·tchi \'lī-(,)chē, 'lē-\ *n* [Chin (Pek) li^4 $chih^1$] **:** the oval fruit of a tree (*Litchi chinensis*) of the soapberry family having a hard scaly outer covering, small hard seed, and flesh surrounding the seed that when dried is firm, sweetish, and black and constitutes the edible part of the fruit; *also* **:** the tree bearing this fruit

-lite \,līt\ *n comb form* [F, alter. of *-lithe*, fr. Gk *lithos* stone] **:** mineral ⟨rhodo*lite*⟩ **:** rock ⟨aero*lite*⟩ **:** fossil ⟨ichno*lite*⟩

li·ter \'lēt-ər\ *n* [F *litre*, fr. ML *litra*, a measure, fr. Gk, a weight] **:** a metric unit of capacity equal to the volume of one kilogram of water at 4°C and at standard atmospheric pressure of 760 millimeters of mercury — see METRIC SYSTEM table

lit·er·a·cy \'lit-ə-rə-sē, 'li-trə-\ *n* **:** the quality or state of being literate

lit·er·al \'lit-ə-rəl, 'li-trəl\ *adj* [ME, fr. MF, fr. ML *litteralis*, fr. L, of a letter, fr. *littera* letter] **1 a :** according with the letter of the scriptures **b :** adhering to fact or to the ordinary construction or primary meaning of a term or expression **c :** PLAIN, UNADORNED **d :** characterized by a concern mainly with facts **:** PROSAIC **2 :** of, relating to, or expressed in letters **3 :** reproduced word for word **:** EXACT, VERBATIM — **lit·er·al·ly** \'lit-ər-(ə-)lē, 'li-trə-lē\ *adv* — **lit·er·al·ness** \'lit-ə-rəl-nəs, 'li-trəl-\ *n*

lit·er·al·ism \'lit-ə-rə-,liz-əm, 'li-trə-\ *n* **1 :** adherence to the explicit substance of an idea or expression **2 :** fidelity to observable fact **:** REALISM — **lit·er·al·ist** \-ləst\ *n* — **lit·er·al·is·tic** \,lit-ə-rə-'lis-tik, ,li-trə-\ *adj*

lit·er·al·i·ty \,lit-ə-'ral-ət-ē\ *n* **:** the quality or state of being literal **:** LITERALNESS

lit·er·al·ize \'lit-ə-rə-,līz, 'li-trə-\ *vt* **:** to make literal

lit·er·ar·i·ly \,lit-ə-'rer-ə-lē\ *adv* **:** in a literary manner

lit·er·ar·i·ness \'lit-ə-,rer-ē-nəs\ *n* **:** the quality or state of being literary

lit·er·ary \'lit-ə-,rer-ē\ *adj* **1 a :** of, relating to, or having the characteristics of letters, humane learning, or literature **b :** BOOKISH 2 **c :** of or relating to books **2 a :** WELL-READ **b :** of or relating to men of letters or writing as a profession

1lit·er·ate \'lit-ə-rət, 'li-trət\ *adj* [ME *literat*, fr. L *litteratus* marked with letters, literate, fr. *litterae* letters, literature, fr. pl. of *littera*] **1 a :** EDUCATED, CULTURED **b :** able to read and write **2 a :** versed in literature or creative writing **:** LITERARY **b :** POLISHED, LUCID — **lit·er·ate·ly** *adv*

2literate *n* **1 :** an educated person **2 :** one who can read and write

li·te·ra·ti \,lit-ə-'rät-(,)ē\ *n pl* [It, fr. L *litterati*, pl. of *litteratus*] **1 :** the educated class **:** INTELLIGENTSIA **2 :** men of letters

lit·er·a·tim \,lit-ə-'rät-əm, -'rät-\ *adv (or adj)* [ML, fr. L *littera*] **:** letter for letter

lit·er·a·tion \,lit-ə-'rā-shən\ *n* [L *littera* + E *-ation*] **:** the representation of sound or words by letters

lit·er·a·tor \'lit-ə-,rāt-ər, ,lit-ə-'rät-\ *n* **:** LITTERATEUR

lit·er·a·ture \'lit-ə-rə-,chu̇(ə)r, 'li-trə-,chu̇(ə)r, 'lit-ə(r)-,chu̇(ə)r, -chər, -,t(y)u̇(ə)r\ *n, often attrib* **1** *archaic* **:** literary culture **2 :** the production of literary work esp. as an occupation **3 a :** writings in prose or verse; *esp* **:** writings having excellence of form or expression and expressing ideas of permanent or universal interest **b :** the body of writings on a particular subject **c :** printed matter (as leaflets or circulars) **4 :** the aggregate of musical compositions

lith- *or* **litho-** *comb form* [L, fr. Gk, fr. *lithos*] **1 :** stone ⟨*litho*logy⟩ **2** [NL *lithium*] **:** lithium ⟨*lith*ic⟩

-lith \,lith\ *n comb form* [NL *-lithus* & F *-lithe*, fr. Gk *lithos*] **1 a :** structure or implement of stone ⟨mega*lith*⟩ ⟨eo*lith*⟩ **b :** artificial stone ⟨grano*lith*⟩ **2 :** calculus ⟨uro*lith*⟩ **3 :** -LITE ⟨lacco*lith*⟩

li·tharge \'lith-,ärj, lith-'\ *n* [ME, fr. MF, fr. L *lithargyrus*, fr. Gk *lithargyros*, fr. *lithos* + *argyros* silver — more at ARGENT] **:** a fused lead monoxide; *broadly* **:** lead monoxide

lithe \'līth, 'līth\ *adj* [ME, fr. OE *līthe* gentle; akin to OHG *lindi* gentle, L *lentus* slow] **1 :** lissomely agile **:** easily flexed **:** SUPPLE, RESILIENT **2 :** characterized by effortless grace — **lithe·ly** *adv* — **lithe·ness** *n*

lithe·some \'līth-səm, 'līth-\ *adj* **:** LISSOME

lith·ia \'lith-ē-ə\ *n* [NL, fr. Gk *lithos*] **:** lithium oxide Li_2O obtained as a white crystalline substance

li·thi·a·sis \lith-'ī-ə-səs\ *n* [NL, fr. Gk, fr. *lithos*] **:** the formation of stony concretions in the body (as in the gall bladder)

lithia water *n* **:** a mineral water containing lithium salts

lith·ic \'lith-ik\ *adj* [Gk *lithikos*, fr. *lithos*] **1 :** of, relating to, or made of stone **2 :** of or relating to lithium — **lith·i·cal·ly** \-i-k(ə-)lē\ *adv*

-lith·ic \'lith-ik\ *adj comb form* [*lithic*] **:** relating to or characteristic of a (specified) stage in man's use of stone as a cultural tool ⟨Neo*lithic*⟩

lith·i·um \'lith-ē-əm\ *n* [NL, fr. *lithia*] **:** a soft silver-white univalent element of the alkali metal group that is the lightest metal known and that is used esp. in nuclear reactions and metallurgy — see ELEMENT table

1litho·graph \'lith-ə-,graf\ *vt* **:** to produce, copy, or portray by lithography — **li·tho·gra·pher** \lith-'äg-rə-fər, 'lith-ə-,graf-ər\ *n*

2lithograph *n* **:** a print made by lithography — **litho·graph·ic** \,lith-ə-'graf-ik\ *adj* — **litho·graph·i·cal·ly** \-i-k(ə-)lē\ *adv*

li·thog·ra·phy \lith-'äg-rə-fē\ *n* [G *lithographie*, fr. *lith-* + *-graphie* -graphy] **1 :** the process of printing from a plane surface (as a smooth stone or metal plate) on which the image to be printed is ink-receptive and the blank area ink-repellent **2 :** PLANOGRAPHY

litho·log·ic \,lith-ə-'läj-ik\ *adj* **:** of or relating to lithology — **litho·log·i·cal** \-i-kəl\ *adj* — **litho·log·i·cal·ly** \-i-k(ə-)lē\ *adv*

li·thol·o·gy \lith-'äl-ə-jē\ *n* **1 :** the study of rocks **2 :** the character of a rock formation

litho·marge \'lith-ə-,märj\ *n* [*lith-* + L *marga* marl] **:** a smooth compact common kaolin

litho·phyte \'lith-ə-,fīt\ *n* [F, fr. *lith-* + *-phyte*] **1 :** an organism (as a coral) having a hard stony structure or skeleton **2 :** a plant that grows on rock — **litho·phyt·ic** \,lith-ə-'fit-ik\ *adj*

litho·pone \'lith-ə-,pōn\ *n* [ISV *lith-* + Gk *ponos* work] **:** a white pigment consisting essentially of a precipitated zinc sulfide and barium sulfate

litho·print \'lith-ə-,print\ *vt* **:** to print by offset or photo-offset

litho·sol \'lith-ə-,säl, -,sȯl\ *n* [*lith-* + L *solum* soil] **:** an azonal shallow soil consisting of imperfectly weathered rock fragments

litho·sphere \'lith-ə-,sfi(ə)r\ *n* [ISV] **:** the solid part of the earth

li·thot·o·my \lith-'ät-ə-mē\ *n* [LL *lithotomia*, fr. Gk, fr. *lithotomein* to perform a lithotomy, fr. *lith-* + *temnein* to cut — more at TOME] **:** surgical incision of the urinary bladder for removal of a stone

Lith·u·a·nian \,lith-(y)ə-'wā-nē-ən, -nyən\ *n* **1 :** a native or inhabitant of Lithuania **2 :** the Baltic language of the Lithuanian people — **Lithuanian** *adj*

lit·i·ga·ble \'lit-i-gə-bəl\ *adj* **:** capable of being litigated

lit·i·gant \'lit-i-gənt\ *n* **:** one engaged in a lawsuit — **litigant** *adj*

lit·i·gate \'lit-ə-,gāt\ *vb* [L *litigatus*, pp. of *litigare*, fr. *lit-*, *lis* lawsuit + *agere* to drive — more at AGENT] *vi* **:** to carry on a legal contest by judicial process ~ *vt* **1** *archaic* **:** DISPUTE **2 :** to contest in law — **lit·i·ga·tion** \,lit-ə-'gā-shən\ *n*

li·ti·gious \lə-'tij-əs, li-\ *adj* [ME, fr. MF *litigieux*, fr. L *litigiosus*, fr. *litigium* dispute, fr. *litigare*] **1 a :** DISPUTATIOUS, CONTENTIOUS **b :** prone to engage in lawsuits **2 a** *obs* **:** DISPUTABLE **b :** subject to litigation **3 :** of, relating to, or marked by litigation — **li·ti·gious·ly** *adv* — **li·ti·gious·ness** *n*

lit·mus \'lit-məs\ *n* [of Scand origin; akin to ON *litmosi* herbs used in dyeing, fr. *litr* color + *mosi* moss; akin to OHG ant*lizzi* face, L *vultus*, and to OE *mōs* moss] **:** a coloring matter from lichens that turns red in acid solutions and blue in alkaline solutions and is used as an acid-base indicator

litmus paper *n* **:** unsized paper colored with litmus

li·to·tes \'līt-ə-,tēz, 'lit-\ *n, pl* **litotes** [Gk *litotēs*, fr. *litos* simple; akin to Gk *leios* smooth — more at LIME] **:** understatement in which an affirmative is expressed by the negative of the contrary (as in "not a bad singer")

li·tre \'lēt-ər\ *var of* LITER

lit·ten \'lit-ᵊn\ *adj* [alter. of *lit*, pp. of *light*] *archaic* **:** LIGHTED

1lit·ter \'lit-ər\ *n* [ME, fr. OF *litiere*, fr. *lit* bed, fr. L *lectus* — more at LIE] **1 a :** a covered and curtained couch provided with shafts and used for carrying a single passenger **b :** a device (as a stretcher) for carrying a sick or injured person **2 a :** material used as bedding for animals **b :** the uppermost slightly decayed layer of organic matter on the forest floor **3 :** the offspring at one birth of a multiparous animal **4 :** an untidy accumulation of objects lying about **:** RUBBISH — **lit·tery** \-ə-rē\ *adj*

2litter *vt* **1 :** BED 1a **2 :** to give birth to (young) **3 a :** to strew with scattered articles **b :** to scatter about in disorder ~ *vi* **1 :** to give birth to a litter **2 :** to strew litter

lit·te·rae hu·ma·ni·o·res \'lit-ə-,rī-hü-,män-ē-'ō(ə)r-,ās, -'ȯ(ə)r-\ *n pl* [ML, lit., more humane letters] **:** HUMANITIES

lit·ter·a·teur \,lit-ə-rə-'tər, ,li-trə-\ *n* [F *littérateur*, fr. L *litterator* critic, fr. *litteratus* literate] **:** a literary man; *esp* **:** a professional writer

lit·ter·bug \'lit-ər-,bəg\ *n* **:** one who litters a public area

1lit·tle \'lit-ᵊl\ *adj* **lit·tler** \'lit-ᵊl-ər, 'lit-lər\ *or* **less** \'les\ *or* **less·er** \'les-ər\ **lit·tlest** \'lit-ᵊl-əst, 'lit-ləst\ *or* **least** \'lēst\ [ME *littel*, fr. OE *lӯtel*; akin to OHG *luzzil* little, Lith *liusti* to be sad] **1 :** not big: as **a :** small in size or extent **:** TINY ⟨has ~ feet⟩ **b** *of a plant or animal* **:** small in comparison with related forms **c :** small in number **d :** small in condition, distinction, or scope **e :** NARROW, MEAN **f :** pleasingly small **2 :** not much: as **a :** existing only in a small amount or to a slight degree **b :** short in duration **:** BRIEF **3 :** small in importance or interest **:** TRIVIAL **syn** see SMALL — **lit·tle·ness** \'lit-ᵊl-nəs\ *n*

2little *adv* **less** \'les\ **least** \'lēst\ **1 a :** in only a small quantity or degree **:** SLIGHTLY **b :** not at all **2 :** INFREQUENTLY, RARELY

3little *n* **1 :** a small amount or quantity **2 a :** a short time **b :** a short distance — **in little :** on a small scale; *esp* **:** in miniature

Little Bear *n* **:** URSA MINOR

Little Hours *n pl* **:** the offices of prime, terce, sext, and none

little leaf \'lit-ᵊl-,(l)ēf\ *n* **:** a plant disorder characterized by small and often chlorotic and distorted foliage: as **a :** a zinc-deficiency disease of deciduous woody plants (as grape, peach, pecan) **b** *usu* **little-leaf disease :** a destructive disease of southern pines (as *Pinus echinata*) of unknown cause

lit·tle·neck clam \,lit-ᵊl-,nek-\ *n* [*Littleneck* Bay, Long Island, N.Y.] **:** a young quahog suitable to be eaten raw

Little Office *n* **:** an office in honor of the Virgin Mary like but shorter than the Divine Office

little slam *n* **:** the winning of all tricks except one in bridge

little theater *n* **:** a small theater for low-cost experimental drama designed for a relatively limited audience

1lit·to·ral \'lit-ə-rəl; ,lit-ə-'ral, -'räl\ *adj* [L *litoralis*, fr. *litor-*, *litus* seashore] **:** of, relating to, or situated or growing on or near a shore esp. of the sea

2littoral *n* **:** a coastal region

li·tur·gi·cal \lə-'tər-ji-kəl, li-\ *adj* **1 a :** of, relating to, or having the characteristics of liturgy **b :** prescribed by the rubrics **2 :** using or favoring the use of liturgy — **li·tur·gi·cal·ly** \-k(ə-)lē\ *adv*

li·tur·gics \-jiks\ *n pl but sing or pl in constr* **:** the study of formal public worship

li·tur·gi·ol·o·gist \-,tər-jē-'äl-ə-jəst\ *n* **:** LITURGIST 2

li·tur·gi·ol·o·gy \-'äl-ə-jē\ *n* **:** LITURGICS

lit·ur·gist \'lit-ər-jəst\ *n* **1 :** one who adheres to, compiles, or leads a liturgy **2 :** a specialist in liturgics

lit·ur·gy \'lit-ər-jē\ *n* [LL *liturgia*, fr. Gk *leitourgia*, fr. (assumed) Gk (Attic) *leïtos* public (fr. Gk *laos* — Attic *leōs* — people) + *-ourgia* -urgy] **1 :** a rite or body of rites prescribed for public worship **2** *often cap* **:** a eucharistic rite

liv·abil·i·ty \,liv-ə-'bil-ət-ē\ *n* **1 :** survival expectancy **:** VIABILITY — used esp. of poultry and livestock **2 :** suitability for human living

liv·able *also* **live·able** \'liv-ə-bəl\ *adj* **1 :** suitable for living in or with **2 :** ENDURABLE — **liv·able·ness** *n*

1live \'liv\ *vb* [ME *liven*, fr. OE *libban*; akin to OHG *lebēn* to live, L cae*lebs* unmarried] *vi* **1 :** to be alive **:** have the life of an animal or plant **2 :** to continue alive **3 :** to maintain oneself **:** SUBSIST **4 :** to conduct or pass one's life ⟨*lived* up to his principles⟩ **5 :** DWELL, RESIDE **6 :** to attain eternal life **7 :** to remain in human memory or record **8 :** to have a life rich in experience **9 :** COHABIT ~ *vt* **1 :** to pass through or spend the duration of **2 :** ENACT, PRACTICE **3 :** to exhibit vigor, gusto, or enthusiasm in

2live \'līv\ *adj* [short for *alive*] **1 :** having life **:** LIVING **2 :** abounding with life **:** VIVID **3 :** exerting force or containing energy: as

a : AFIRE, GLOWING ⟨~ cigar⟩ b : connected to electric power c : charged with explosives and containing shot or a bullet ⟨~ ammunition⟩; *also* : UNEXPLODED ⟨~ bomb⟩ d : imparting or driven by power e : charged with fissionable material 4 : of continuing or current interest : UNCLOSED ⟨~ issue⟩ 5 : being in a pure native state 6 : of bright vivid color 7 : being in play ⟨a ~ ball⟩ 8 a : not yet printed from or plated ⟨~ type⟩ b : not yet typeset ⟨~ copy⟩ 9 a : of or involving the actual presence of real people ⟨~ audience⟩ b : broadcast directly at the time of production instead of from recorded or filmed material ⟨a ~ radio program⟩

live–bear·ing \'līv-'ba(ə)r-iŋ, -'be(ə)r-\ *adj* : VIVIPAROUS

live–box \-ˌbäks\ *n* : a box or pen suspended in water to keep aquatic animals alive

lived \'līvd, 'livd\ *adj* [ME, fr. *lif* life] : having a life of a specified kind or length ⟨long-*lived*⟩

live down *vt* : to live so as to wipe out the memory or effects of

live–for·ev·er \'liv-fə-ˌrev-ər\ *n* : SEDUM

live·li·hood \'līv-lē-ˌhu̇d\ *n* [ME *livelode* course of life, fr. OE *līflād*, fr. *līf* + *lād* course — more at LODE] 1 : means of support or subsistence 2 *obs* : LIVELINESS

live·li·ly \'līv-lə-lē\ *adv* : in a lively manner

live·li·ness \'līv-lē-nəs\ *n* : the quality or state of being lively

live·long \ˌliv-ˌlȯŋ\ *adj* [ME *lef long*, fr. *lef* dear + *long* — more at LIEF] : WHOLE, ENTIRE ⟨the ~ day⟩

live·ly \'līv-lē\ *adj* [ME, fr. OE *līflīc*, fr. *līf* life] 1 *obs* : LIVING 2 : ANIMATED, VIGOROUS 3 : ACTIVE, INTENSE 4 : BRILLIANT, FRESH ⟨a ~, flashing wit⟩ 5 : ENLIVENING, SPARKLING 6 : quick to rebound : RESILIENT 7 : responding readily to the helm ⟨a ~ boat⟩ 8 : full of life, movement, or incident — **lively** *adv*

syn ANIMATED, VIVACIOUS, SPRIGHTLY, GAY: LIVELY suggests briskness, alertness, or energy; ANIMATED applies to what is spirited, active, and sparkling; VIVACIOUS suggests an activeness of gesture and wit, often playful or alluring; SPRIGHTLY suggests lightness and spirited vigor of manner or of wit; GAY stresses complete freedom from care and overflowing spirits

liv·en \'lī-vən\ *vb* **liv·en·ing** \'līv-(ə-)niŋ\ *vt* : ENLIVEN ~ *vi* : to become lively

live oak \'lī-ˌvōk\ *n* : any of several American evergreen oaks

[1]**liv·er** \'liv-ər\ *n* [ME, fr. OE *lifer*; akin to OHG *lebra* liver] 1 a : a large very vascular glandular organ of vertebrates that secretes bile and causes important changes in many of the substances contained in the blood (as by converting sugars into glycogen which it stores up until required and in forming urea) b : any of various large compound glands associated with the digestive tract of invertebrate animals and prob. concerned with the secretion of digestive enzymes 2 *archaic* : a determinant of the quality or temper of a man 3 : the tissue of the liver (as of a calf or pig) eaten as food — **liv·ered** \-ərd\ *adj*

[2]**liv·er** \'liv-ər\ *n* 1 : one that lives esp. in a specified way ⟨a fast ~⟩ 2 : RESIDENT

liver fluke *n* : any of various trematode worms (as *Fasciola hepatica*) that invade the mammalian liver

liv·er·ied \'liv-(ə-)rēd\ *adj* : wearing a livery

liv·er·ish \'liv-(ə-)rish\ *adj* 1 : resembling liver esp. in color 2 a : suffering from liver disorder : BILIOUS b : CRABBED, MELANCHOLY — **liv·er·ish·ness** *n*

liver sausage *n* : a sausage containing cooked ground liver and lean pork trimmings — called also *liver pudding*

liv·er·wort \'liv-ər-ˌwərt, -ˌwȯ(ə)rt\ *n* 1 : a bryophyte of a class (Hepaticae) related to and resembling the mosses but differing in reproduction, development, and in the structure of the gametophyte 2 : HEPATICA

liv·er·wurst \'liv-ə(r)-ˌwərst, -ˌwu̇(ə)rst; 'liv-ər-ˌwu̇st\ *n* [part trans. of G *leberwurst*, fr. *leber* liver + *wurst* sausage] : LIVER SAUSAGE

[1]**liv·ery** \'liv-(ə-)rē\ *n, often attrib* [ME, fr. OF *livree*, lit., delivery, fr. *livrer* to deliver, fr. L *liberare* to free — more at LIBERATE] 1 *archaic* : the apportioning of provisions esp. to servants : ALLOWANCE 2 a : the distinctive clothing or badge formerly worn by the retainers of a person of rank b : a servant's uniform c : distinctive dress : GARB 3 *archaic* a : one's retainers or retinue b : the members of a British livery company 4 a : the feeding, stabling, and care of horses for pay b : a stable keeping horses and usu. carriages for hire c : a concern offering vehicles of any of various kinds for rent 5 : the act of delivering legal possession of property

[2]**livery** *adj* 1 : resembling liver 2 : suggesting liver disorder : LIVERISH

livery company *n* : any of various London craft or trade associations that are descended from medieval guilds

liv·ery·man \'liv-(ə-)rē-mən\ *n* 1 *archaic* : a liveried retainer 2 : a freeman of the city of London entitled to wear the livery of the company to which he belongs 3 : the keeper of a vehicle-rental service

livery stable *n* : a stable where horses and vehicles are kept for hire and where stabling is provided

lives *pl of* LIFE

live steam *n* : steam direct from a boiler and under full pressure

live·stock \'līv-ˌstäk\ *n* : animals kept or raised for use or pleasure; *esp* : farm animals kept for use and profit

live wire *n* : an alert, active, aggressive person

liv·id \'liv-əd\ *adj* [F *livide*, fr. L *lividus*, fr. *livēre* to be blue; akin to OE *slāh* sloe, Russ *sliva* plum] 1 : discolored by bruising : BLACK-AND-BLUE 2 : ASHEN, PALLID — **li·vid·i·ty** \liv-'id-ət-ē\ *n* — **liv·id·ness** \'liv-əd-nəs\ *n*

[1]**liv·ing** \'liv-iŋ\ *adj* 1 a : having life b : ACTIVE, FUNCTIONING 2 a : exhibiting the life or motion of nature : NATURAL b : [2]LIVE 3 a : full of life or vigor ⟨made mathematics a ~ subject⟩ b : true to life : VIVID c : suited for living ⟨the ~ area⟩ 4 : involving living persons 5 : VERY — used as an intensive — **liv·ing·ness** *n*

syn LIVING, ALIVE, ANIMATE, ANIMATED, VITAL mean having or showing life. LIVING and ALIVE apply to organic bodies having life as opposed to those from which life has gone; ANIMATE is used chiefly in direct opposition to *inanimate* to denote things capable of life; ANIMATED is applied to that which comes alive and active or is given motion simulating life; VITAL often suggests the opposite of *mechanical* in implying the energy and esp. the power to grow and reproduce characteristic of life

[2]**living** *n* 1 : the condition of being alive 2 : conduct or manner of life 3 a : means of subsistence : LIVELIHOOD b *archaic* : ESTATE, PROPERTY c *Brit* : BENEFICE 1

living death *n* : life emptied of joys and satisfactions

living room *n* 1 : a room in a residence used for the common social activities of the occupants 2 : LEBENSRAUM — called also *living space*

living wage *n* 1 : a subsistence wage 2 : a wage sufficient to provide the necessities and comforts held to comprise an acceptable standard of living

lix·iv·i·ate \lik-'siv-ē-ˌāt\ *vt* [LL *lixivium* lye, fr. L *lixivius* made of lye, fr. *lixa* lye — more at LIQUID] : to extract a soluble constituent from (a solid mixture) by washing or percolation — **lix·iv·i·a·tion** \(ˌ)lik-ˌsiv-ē-'ā-shən\ *n*

liz·ard \'liz-ərd\ *n* [ME *liserd*, fr. MF *laisarde*, fr. L *lacerta*; akin to L *lacertus* muscle — more at LEG] : any of a suborder (Lacertilia) of reptiles distinguished from the snakes by a fused inseparable lower jaw, a single temporal opening, two pairs of well differentiated functional limbs which may be lacking in burrowing forms, external ears, and eyes with movable lids; *broadly* : any relatively long-bodied reptile (as a crocodile or dinosaur) with legs and tapering tail

typical lizard

'll \l, əl, ᵊl\ *vb* : WILL ⟨you'*ll* be late⟩

lla·ma \'läm-ə\ *n* [Sp, fr. Quechua] : any of several wild and domesticated So. American ruminants related to the camels but smaller and without a hump; *esp* : the domesticated guanaco used in the Andes as a beast of burden and a source of wool

Lloyd's \'lȯidz\ *n* : an association of individual underwriters in London specializing in marine insurance and shipping news and insuring for losses of almost every conceivable kind

lo \'lō\ *interj* [ME, fr. OE *lā*] — used to call attention or to express wonder or surprise

loach \'lōch\ *n* [ME *loche*, fr. MF] : any of a family (Cobitidae) of small Old World freshwater fishes related to the carps

[1]**load** \'lōd\ *n* [ME *lod*, fr. OE *lād* support, carrying — more at LODE] 1 a : whatever is put on a man or pack animal to be carried : PACK b : whatever is put in a ship or vehicle or airplane for conveyance : CARGO; *specif* : a quantity of material assembled or packed as a shipping unit c : the quantity that can be carried at one time by a specified means; *specif* : a measured quantity of a commodity fixed for each type of carrier — often used in combination ⟨a boat-*load* of tourists⟩ 2 a : a mass or weight supported by something b : the forces to which a structure is subjected due to superposed weight or to wind pressure on the vertical surfaces 3 a : something that weighs down the mind or spirits ⟨a ~ of care⟩ b : a burdensome or laborious responsibility 4 *slang* : an intoxicating amount of liquor drunk 5 : a large quantity : LOT — usu. used in pl. 6 a : a charge for a firearm b : the quantity of material loaded into a device at one time 7 : external resistance overcome by a machine or prime mover 8 a : power output (as of a power plant) b : a device to which power is delivered 9 a (1) : the amount of work that a person carries or is expected to carry (2) : the amount of authorized work to be performed by a machine, a group, a department, or a factory b : the demand upon the operating resources of a system (as a telephone exchange or a refrigerating apparatus) 10 *slang* : EYEFUL; *also* : EARFUL — used in the phrase *get a load of*

[2]**load** *vt* 1 a : to put a load in or on b : to place in or on a means of conveyance 2 a : to encumber or oppress with something heavy, laborious, or disheartening : BURDEN b : to place as a burden or obligation ⟨~ more work on him⟩ 3 a : to increase the weight of by adding something heavy b : to add a conditioning substance (as a mineral salt) to for body; *esp* : to add filler to (paper) c : to weight (dice) to fall unfairly d : BIAS e : to weight (as a test) with factors influencing validity or outcome 4 : to supply in abundance or excess : HEAP 5 a : to put a load or charge in ⟨~ a gun⟩ b : to place or insert as a load ⟨~ film in a camera⟩ 6 : to alter by adding an adulterant or drug 7 a : to add loading to (an insurance premium) b : to add a sum to after profits and expenses are accounted for ⟨~*ed* prices⟩ ~ *vi* 1 : to receive a load 2 : to put a load on or in a carrier, device, or container; *specif* : to insert the charge or cartridge in the chamber of a firearm

load·ed *adj* 1 *slang* : DRUNK 2 : having a large amount of money

load·er \'lōd-ər\ *n* : one that loads

load·ing *n* 1 : a cargo, weight, or stress placed on something 2 : an amount added (as to the net premium in insurance) to represent business expenses, future contingencies, or profit 3 : material used to load something : FILLER

load line *n* : the line on a ship indicating the depth to which it sinks in the water when properly loaded

load·star *var of* LODESTAR

load·stone *var of* LODESTONE

[1]**loaf** \'lōf\ *n, pl* **loaves** \'lōvz\ [ME *lof*, fr. OE *hlāf*; akin to OHG *hleib* loaf] 1 : a shaped or molded mass of bread 2 : a regularly molded often rectangular mass: as a : a conical mass of sugar b : a dish (as of seasoned meat or fish) baked in the form of a loaf

[2]**loaf** *vi* [prob. back-formation fr. *loafer*] : to spend time in idleness

loaf·er \'lō-fər\ *n* [perh. short for *landloafer*, fr. G *landläufer* tramp, fr. *land* + *läufer* runner] : one that loafs : IDLER

loam \'lōm, 'lüm\ *n* [ME *lom*, fr. OE *lām*; akin to OE *līm* lime] 1 : a mixture composed chiefly of moistened clay 2 : SOIL; *specif* : a soil consisting of a friable mixture of varying proportions of clay, silt, and sand — **loamy** \'lō-mē, 'lü-\ *adj*

[1]**loan** \'lōn\ *n* [ME *lon*, fr. ON *lān*; akin to OE *lǣn* loan, *lēon* to lend, L *linquere* to leave, Gk *leipein*] 1 a : money lent at interest b : something lent for the borrower's temporary use 2 : the grant of temporary use 3 : LOANWORD

[2]**loan** *vt* : LEND

loan·ing \'lō-niŋ\ *n* 1 *dial Brit* : LANE 2 *dial Brit* : a milking yard

loan translation *n* : a compound, derivative, or phrase introduced into a language through translation of the constituent parts of a term in another language (as *reason of state* from French *raison d'état*)

loan·word \'lōn-ˌwərd\ *n* : a word taken from another language and at least partly naturalized

loath \'lōth, 'lōt͟h\ *adj* [ME *loth* loathsome, fr. OE *lāth*; akin to

OHG *leid* loathsome, OIr *liuss* aversion] **:** unwilling to do something contrary to one's likes, sympathies, or ways of thinking **:** RELUCTANT **syn** see DISINCLINED — **loath·ness** *n*
loathe \'lōt͟h\ *vt* [ME *lothen*, fr. OE *lāthian*, fr. *lāth*] **:** to dislike greatly **:** DETEST **syn** see HATE
loath·ing \'lō-t͟hiŋ\ *n* **:** extreme disgust **:** DETESTATION
1**loath·ly** \'lōt͟h-lē, 'lōth-\ *adj* **:** LOATHSOME, REPULSIVE
2**loath·ly** \'lōth-lē, 'lōt͟h-\ *adv* **:** UNWILLINGLY
loath·some \'lōth-səm, 'lōt͟h-\ *adj* [ME *lothsum*, fr. *loth* evil, fr. OE *lāth*, fr. *lāth*, adj.] **:** exciting loathing — **loath·some·ly** *adv* — **loath·some·ness** *n*
loathy \'lō-t͟hē, -thē\ *adj* **:** LOATHSOME
1**lob** \'läb\ *n* [prob. of LG origin; akin to LG *lubbe* coarse person] *dial Brit* **:** a dull heavy person **:** LOUT
2**lob** *vb* **lobbed; lob·bing** [*lob* (a loosely hanging object)] *vt* **1** *archaic* **:** to let hang heavily **:** DROOP **2 :** to throw, hit, or propel slowly in or as if in a high arc ~ *vi* **1 :** to move slowly and heavily **2 :** to hit a tennis ball easily in a high arc
3**lob** *n* **1 :** a cricket ball bowled or thrown underhand usu. slowly **2 :** a tennis ball hit slowly in a high arc
lob- *or* **lobo-** *comb form* [*lobe*] **:** lobe ⟨*lob*ar⟩ ⟨*lobo*tomy⟩
lo·bar \'lō-bər, -,bär\ *adj* **:** of or relating to a lobe
lo·bate \'lō-,bāt\ *also* **lo·bat·ed** \-,bāt-əd\ *adj* [NL *lobatus*, fr. LL *lobus*] **1 :** having lobes **2 :** resembling a lobe — **lo·bate·ly** *adv*
lo·ba·tion \lō-'bā-shən\ *n* **1 a :** the quality or state of being lobed **b :** the formation of lobes or lobules **2 a :** LOBE **b :** LOBULE

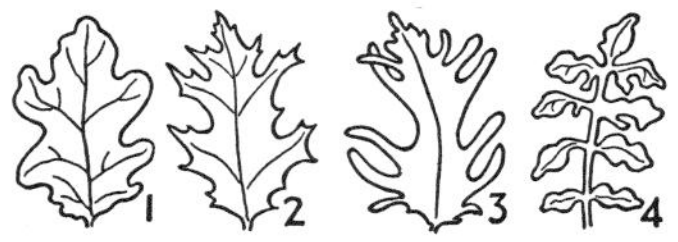

lobation: *1* lobed, *2* cleft, *3* parted, *4* divided

1**lob·by** \'läb-ē\ *n* [ML *lobium* gallery, of Gmc origin; akin to OHG *louba* porch] **1 :** a corridor or hall connected with a larger room or series of rooms and used as a passageway or waiting room: as **a :** an anteroom of a legislative chamber; *esp* **:** one of two anterooms of a British parliamentary chamber to which members go to vote during a division **b :** a large hall serving as a foyer (as of a hotel or theater) **2 :** a group of persons engaged in lobbying esp. as representatives of a particular interest group
2**lobby** *vi* **:** to conduct activities aimed at influencing public officials and esp. members of a legislative body on legislation and other policy decisions ~ *vt* **:** to promote (as a project) or secure the passage of (as legislation) by influencing public officials — **lob·by·er** *n* — **lob·by·ism** \-ē-,iz-əm\ *n* — **lob·by·ist** \-ē-əst\ *n*
lobe \'lōb\ *n* [MF, fr. LL *lobus*, fr. Gk *lobos* — more at SLEEP] **:** a curved or rounded projection or division; *specif* **:** a usu. somewhat rounded projection or division of a bodily organ or part
lo·bec·to·my \lō-'bek-tə-mē\ *n* [ISV] **:** surgical removal of a lobe of an organ (as a lung) or gland
lobed \'lōbd\ *adj* **:** LOBATE 1
lo·be·lia \lō-'bēl-yə, -'bē-lē-ə\ *n* [NL, genus name, fr. Matthias de *Lobel* †1616 Flem botanist] **:** any of a genus (*Lobelia* of the family Lobeliaceae, the lobelia family) of widely distributed and often cultivated herbaceous plants
lob·lol·ly \'läb-,läl-ē\ *n* [prob. fr. E dial. *lob* (to boil) + obs. E dial. *lolly* broth] **1** *dial* **a :** a thick gruel **b :** a miry mess **2** *dial* **:** LOUT
lo·bo \'lō-(,)bō\ *n* [Sp, wolf, fr. L *lupus* — more at WOLF] **:** a wolf (*Canis lupus lycaon*) formerly common over much of No. America — called also *timber wolf*
lo·bot·o·my \lō-'bät-ə-mē\ *n* [ISV] **:** incision into the brain (as into the frontal lobes) to sever nerve fibers for the relief of some mental disorders and tensions
lob·scouse \'läb-,skau̇s\ *n* [origin unknown] **:** a sailor's dish prepared by stewing or baking bits of meat with vegetables and hardtack
lob·ster \'läb-stər\ *n* [ME, fr. OE *loppestre*, fr. *loppe* spider; akin to ME *sloberen* to slobber] **1 a :** a large marine decapod crustacean (family Homaridae) commonly used for food; *esp* **:** one of a genus (*Homarus*) including the American lobster (*H. americanus*) and the European lobster (*H. vulgaris*) of the Atlantic coasts and the very small Cape lobster (*H. capensis*) of southern Africa **b :** SPINY LOBSTER **2 :** a stupid or awkward person **:** LUMMOX

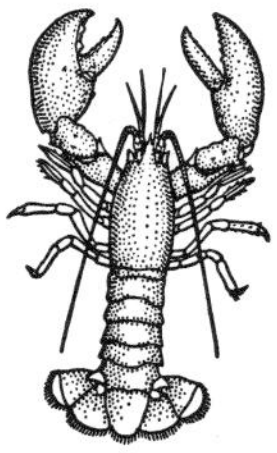
American lobster

lobster New·burg *or* **lobster New·burgh** \,läb-stər-'n(y)ü-,bərg\ *n* [origin unknown] **:** cooked lobster meat heated usu. in a chafing dish in a sauce of cream, egg yolk, and sherry
lobster pot *n* **:** an oblong case with slat sides and a funnel-shaped net used as a trap for catching lobsters
lobster ther·mi·dor \,läb-stər-'thər-mə-,dȯ(ə)r\ *n* **:** a mixture of cooked lobster meat, mushrooms, cream, egg yolks, and sherry stuffed into a lobster shell and browned
lob·u·lar \'läb-yə-lər\ *adj* **:** of, relating to, or resembling a lobule — **lob·u·lar·ly** *adv*
lob·u·late \'läb-yə-lāt\ *also* **lob·u·lat·ed** \-,lāt-əd\ *adj* **:** made up of or provided with lobules — **lob·u·la·tion** \,läb-yə-'lā-shən\ *n*
lob·ule \'läb-(,)yü(ə)l\ *n* **:** a small lobe; *also* **:** a subdivision of a lobe — **lob·u·lose** \'läb-yə-,lōs\ *adj*
1**lo·cal** \'lō-kəl\ *adj* [ME *localle*, fr. MF *local*, fr. LL *localis*, fr. L *locus* place — more at STALL] **1 :** characterized by or relating to position in space **2 :** characterized by, relating to, or occupying a particular place **3 :** not broad or general **4 a :** primarily serving the needs of a particular limited district **b** *of a public conveyance* **:** making all the stops on its run **5 :** involving or affecting only a restricted part of the organism **:** TOPICAL — **lo·cal·ly** \-kə-lē\ *adv*
2**local** *n* **:** a local person or thing: as **a :** a local train, elevator, or other public conveyance **b :** a local or particular branch, lodge, or chapter of an organization
local color *n* **:** color in writing derived from the presentation of the features and peculiarities of a particular locality and its inhabitants
lo·cale \lō-'kal\ *n* [modif. of F *local*, fr. *local*, adj.] **1 :** a place or locality esp. when viewed in relation to a particular event or characteristic **2 :** SITE, SCENE
local government *n* **:** the government of a specific local area constituting a subdivision of a nation, state, or other major political unit; *also* **:** the body of persons constituting such a government
lo·cal·ism \'lō-kə-,liz-əm\ *n* **1 :** affection or partiality for a particular place **:** SECTIONALISM **2 :** a local idiom or peculiarity of speaking or acting
lo·cal·i·ty \lō-'kal-ət-ē\ *n* **1 :** the fact or condition of having a location in space or time **2 :** a particular spot, situation, or location
lo·cal·iza·tion \,lō-kə-lə-'zā-shən\ *n* **:** an act of localizing **:** the state of being localized
lo·cal·ize \'lō-kə-,līz\ *vt* **:** to make local ~ *vi* **:** to collect in a specific or limited area
local option *n* **:** the power granted by a legislature to a political subdivision to determine by popular vote the local applicability of a law on a controversial issue
lo·cate \'lō-,kāt, lō-'\ *vb* [L *locatus*, pp. of *locare* to place, fr. *locus*] *vi* **:** to establish oneself or one's business **:** SETTLE ~ *vt* **1 :** to determine or indicate the place, site, or limits of **2 :** to set or establish in a particular spot **:** STATION **3 :** to determine the location of **4 :** to find or fix the place of in a sequence — **lo·cat·er** *n*
lo·ca·tion \lō-'kā-shən\ *n* **1 :** the act or process of locating **2 a :** a position or site occupied or available for occupancy or marked by some distinguishing feature **:** SITUATION **b :** a tract of land designated for a purpose **c :** a place outside a motion-picture studio where a picture or part of it is filmed — **lo·ca·tion·al** \-shnəl, -shən-ᵊl\ *adj* — **lo·ca·tion·al·ly** \-ē\ *adv*
1**loc·a·tive** \'läk-ət-iv\ *n* [L *locus* + E *-ative* (as in *vocative*)] **:** the locative case or a word in that case
2**locative** *adj* **:** of or being a grammatical case that denotes place or the place where or wherein
lo·ca·tor \'lō-,kāt-ər, lō-'\ *n* **:** one that locates; *specif* **:** one that locates land or a mining claim
loch \'läk, 'läk̲\ *n* [ME (Sc) *louch*, fr. ScGael *loch*; akin to L *lacus* lake] **1** *Scot* **:** LAKE **2** *Scot* **:** a bay or arm of the sea esp. when nearly landlocked
loci *pl of* LOCUS
1**lock** \'läk\ *n* [ME *lok*, fr. OE *locc*; akin to OHG *loc* lock, L *luctari* to struggle, *luxus* dislocated] **1 a :** a tuft, tress, or ringlet of hair **b** *pl* **:** the hair of the head **2 :** a cohering bunch (as of wool, cotton, flax) **:** TUFT
2**lock** *n* [ME *lok*, fr. OE *loc*; akin to OHG *loh* enclosure, OE *locc* lock of hair] **1 a :** a fastening (as for a door) operated by a key or a combination **b :** the mechanism for exploding the charge or cartridge of a firearm **2 a :** an enclosure (as in a canal) with gates at each end used in raising or lowering boats as they pass from level to level **b :** AIR LOCK **3 a :** a locking or fastening together **b :** an intricate mass of objects impeding each other (as in a traffic jam) **c :** a hold in wrestling secured on one part of the body
3**lock** *vt* **1 a :** to fasten the lock of **b :** to make fast with or as if with a lock ⟨~ up the house⟩ **2 a :** to make secure or inaccessible by means of locks **:** CONFINE **b :** to hold fast or inactive **:** FIX **3 a :** to make fast by the interlacing or interlocking of parts **b :** to hold in a close embrace; *also* **:** to grapple in combat **c :** to fasten (imposed letterpress matter) securely in a chase or on the bed of a press by tightening the quoins; *also* **:** to attach (a curved plate) to the plate cylinder of a rotary press **4 :** to invest (capital) without assurance of easy convertibility into money **5 a :** to move or permit to pass by raising or lowering in a lock **b :** to provide with locks **c :** to divide off by a lock ~ *vi* **1 :** to become locked **2 :** INTERLACE, INTERLOCK **3 a :** to build locks to facilitate navigation **b :** to go or pass by means of a lock (as in a canal)
lock·age \'läk-ij\ *n* **1 :** an act or the process of passing a ship through a lock **2 :** a system of locks **3 :** toll paid for passing through a lock
lock·er \'läk-ər\ *n* **1 a :** a drawer, cupboard, or compartment that may be closed with a lock; *esp* **:** one for individual storage use **b :** a chest or compartment on shipboard for compact stowage of articles **c :** a compartment for storing quick-frozen foods for long periods usu. at or below 0° F and at 80% relative humidity **2 :** one that locks
locker paper *n* **:** a flexible protective paper for wrapping food for quick-freezing and storage
locker room *n* **:** a room devoted to storage lockers; *esp* **:** one in which participants in a sport have individual lockers for their clothes and special equipment and change into and out of sports costume
lock·et \'läk-ət\ *n* [MF *loquet* latch, fr. MD *loke*; akin to OE *loc*] **:** a small case usu. of precious metal for a memento that is worn typically suspended from a chain or necklace
lock·jaw \'läk-,jȯ\ *n* **:** an early symptom of tetanus characterized by spasm of the jaw muscles and inability to open the jaws; *also* **:** TETANUS
lock·nut \'läk-,nət, -'nət\ *n* **1 :** a nut screwed down hard on another to prevent it from slacking back **2 :** a nut so constructed that it locks itself when screwed up tight
lock on *vt* **:** to sight and follow (a target) automatically by means of a radar beam
lock out *vt* **:** to subject (a body of employees) to a lockout
lock·out \'läk-,au̇t\ *n* **:** the withholding of employment by an employer and the whole or partial closing of his business establishment in order to gain concessions from employees
lock·ram \'läk-rəm\ *n* [ME *lokerham*, fr. *Locronan*, town in Brittany] **:** a coarse plain-woven linen formerly used in England
lock·smith \'läk-,smith\ *n* **:** one who makes or repairs locks
lock·step \-,step, -'step\ *n* **:** a mode of marching in step by a body of men going one after another as closely as possible
lock·stitch \-,stich\ *n* **:** a sewing machine stitch formed by the looping together of two threads one on each side of the material being sewn — **lock·stitch** \-'stich\ *vb*
lock, stock, and barrel *adv* [fr. the principal parts of a flintlock] **:** WHOLLY, COMPLETELY
lock·up \'läk-,əp\ *n* **1 :** an act of locking **:** the state of being locked **2 :** JAIL; *esp* **:** a local jail where persons are detained prior to court hearing
1**lo·co** \'lō-(,)kō\ *n*, *pl* **locos** *or* **locoes** [MexSp, fr. Sp, crazy] **1 :** LOCOWEED **2 :** LOCOISM
2**loco** *vt* **1 :** to poison with locoweed **2 :** to make frenzied or crazy
3**loco** *adj* [Sp] *slang* **:** out of one's mind **:** CRAZY
lo·co·fo·co \,lō-kə-'fō-(,)kō\ *n*, *pl* **locofocos** [prob. fr. 1*loco*motive + It *fuoco*, *foco* fire, fr. L *focus* hearth] **1 :** a match or cigar capable of being ignited by friction on any hard dry rough surface **2** *cap*

a : a member of a radical group of New York Democrats organized in 1835 in opposition to the regular party organization **b** : DEMOCRAT 2

lo·co·ism \'lō-(,)kō-,iz-əm\ *n* : a disease of horses, cattle, and sheep caused by chronic poisoning with locoweeds

lo·co·mo·tion \,lō-kə-'mō-shən\ *n* [L *locus* + E *motion*] **1** : an act or the power of moving from place to place **2** : TRAVEL

¹**lo·co·mo·tive** \,lō-kə-'mōt-iv\ *adj* **1 a** : of, relating to, or functioning in locomotion **b** : having the ability to move independently from place to place **2** : of or relating to travel **3** : of, relating to, or being a machine that moves about by operation of its own mechanism — **lo·co·mo·tive·ness** *n*

²**locomotive** *n* **1** : a self-propelled vehicle that runs on rails, utilizes any of several forms of energy for producing motion, and is used for moving railroad cars **2** : a school or college cheer characterized by a slow beginning and a progressive increase in speed

lo·co·mo·tor \,lō-kə-'mōt-ər\ *also* **lo·co·mo·to·ry** \-ə-rē\ *adj* **1** : LOCOMOTIVE 1 **2** : affecting or involving the locomotive organs

locomotor ataxia *n* : a syphilitic disorder of the nervous system marked esp. by disturbances of gait and difficulty in coordinating voluntary movements

lo·co·weed \'lō-(,)kō-,wēd\ *n* : any of several leguminous plants (genera *Astragalus* and *Oxytropis*) of western No. America that cause locoism in livestock

loc·u·lar \'läk-yə-lər\ *adj* : having or composed of loculi

loc·u·late \'läk-yə-lət, -,lāt\ *or* **loc·u·lat·ed** \-,lāt-əd\ *adj* : having or divided into loculi — **loc·u·la·tion** \,läk-yə-'lā-shən\ *n*

loc·ule \'läk-(,)yü(ə)l\ *n* [F, fr. L *loculus*] : LOCULUS *esp* : any of the cells of a compound ovary of a plant—**loc·uled** \-(,)yü(ə)ld\ *adj*

loc·u·li·ci·dal \,läk-yə-lə-'sīd-ᵊl\ *adj* [NL *loculus* + L *-cidere* to cut, fr. *caedere* — more at CONCISE] : dehiscent longitudinally so as to bisect each loculus ⟨~ fruit⟩ — **loc·u·li·ci·dal·ly** \-ᵊl-ē\ *adv*

loc·u·lus \'läk-yə-ləs\ *n, pl* **loc·u·li** \-,lī, -,lē\ [NL, fr. L, dim. of *locus*] : a small chamber or cavity esp. in a plant or animal body

lo·cum te·nens \,lō-kəm-'tē-,nenz, -nənz\ *n, pl* **locum te·nen·tes** \-tə-'nen-,tēz\ [ML, lit., one holding an office] : one filling an office for a time or temporarily taking the place of another — used esp. of a doctor or clergyman

lo·cus \'lō-kəs\ *n, pl* **lo·ci** \'lō-,sī, -,kī, -,kē\ [L — more at STALL] **1** : PLACE, LOCALITY **2** : the set of all points whose location is determined by stated conditions

lo·cus clas·si·cus \,lō-kəs-'klas-i-kəs\ *n, pl* **lo·ci clas·si·ci** \-,sī-'klas-ə-,sī, -,kī-'klas-ə-kī, -,kē-'klas-ə-,kē\ [L] : a standard passage important for the elucidation of a word or subject

lo·cust \'lō-kəst\ *n* [ME, fr. L *locusta*] **1** : SHORT-HORNED GRASSHOPPER; *esp* : a migratory grasshopper often traveling in vast swarms and stripping the areas passed of all vegetation **2** : CICADA **3 a** : any of various hard-wooded leguminous trees: as (1) : CAROB 1 (2) : HONEY LOCUST **b** : the wood of a locust tree

lo·cu·tion \lō-'kyü-shən\ *n* [ME *locucioun*, fr. L *locution-, locutio*, fr. *locutus*, pp. of *loqui* to speak] **1** : a particular form of expression or a peculiarity of phrasing **2** : style of discourse : PHRASEOLOGY

lode \'lōd\ *n* [ME, fr. OE *lād* course, support; akin to OE *līthan* to go — more at LEAD] **1** *dial Eng* : WATERWAY **2 a** : a mineral deposit that fills a fissure **b** : an ore deposit occurring in place within definite boundaries separating it from the adjoining rocks **3** : something that resembles a lode : an abundant store

lode·star \'lōd-,stär\ *n* **1** : a star that leads or guides; *esp* : NORTH STAR **2** : something that serves as a guiding star

lode·stone \'lōd-,stōn\ *n* **1** : magnetite possessing polarity **2** : something that strongly attracts : MAGNET

¹**lodge** \'läj\ *vt* **1 a** : to provide temporary quarters for **b** : to establish or settle in a place **c** : to rent lodgings to **2** : to serve as a receptacle for : CONTAIN **3** : to beat (as a crop) to the ground **4** : to bring to an intended or a fixed position (as by throwing or thrusting) **5** : to deposit for safeguard or preservation **6** : to place or vest esp. in a source, means, or agent **7** : to lay (as a complaint) before a proper authority : FILE ~ *vi* **1 a** : to occupy a place temporarily : SLEEP **b** (1) : to have a residence : DWELL (2) : to be a lodger **2** : to come to a rest **3** : to fall or lie down — used esp. of hay or grain crops

²**lodge** *n* [ME *loge*, fr. OF, of Gmc origin; akin to OHG *louba* porch] **1** *chiefly dial* : a rude shelter or abode **2 a** : the meeting place of a branch (as of a fraternal organization) **b** : the body of members of such a branch **3 a** : a house set apart for residence in the hunting or other special season **b** : an inn or resort hotel **4 a** : a house on an estate orig. for the use of a gamekeeper, caretaker, or porter **b** : a shelter for an employee (as a gatekeeper of an institution) **5** : a den or lair esp. of gregarious animals **6 a** : WIGWAM **b** : a family of No. American Indians

lodg·er \'läj-ər\ *n* : one that lodges; *esp* : one that occupies a rented room in another's house

lodg·ing *n* **1 a** : a place to live : DWELLING **b** : LODGMENT 3b **2 a** (1) : sleeping accommodations (2) : a temporary place to stay **b** : a room in the house of another used as a place of residence — usu. used in pl. **3** : the act of lodging

lodging house *n* : a house where lodgings are provided and let

lodg·ment *or* **lodge·ment** \'läj-mənt\ *n* **1 a** : a lodging place : SHELTER **b** : ACCOMMODATIONS, LODGINGS **2 a** : the act, fact, or manner of lodging **b** : a placing, depositing, or coming to rest **3 a** : an accumulation or collection deposited in a place or remaining at rest **b** : a place of rest or deposit

lod·i·cule \'läd-i-,kyü(ə)l\ *n* [L *lodicula*, dim. of *lodic-, lodix* cover] : one of usu. two delicate membranous hyaline scales at the base of the ovary of a grass that by their swelling assist in anthesis

loess \'les, 'lə(r)s, 'lō-əs\ *n* [G *löss*] : an unstratified usu. buff to yellowish brown loamy deposit found in No. America, Europe, and Asia and believed to be chiefly deposited by the wind — **loess·ial** \'les-ē-əl, 'lə(r)s-, lō-'es-\ *adj*

¹**loft** \'lȯft\ *n* [ME, fr. OE, fr. ON *lopt* air; akin to OHG *luft* air] **1** : a room or floor above another : ATTIC **2 a** : a gallery in a church or hall **b** : one of the upper floors of a warehouse or business building esp. when not partitioned **c** : HAYLOFT **3 a** : the backward slant of the face of a golf-club head **b** : the act of lofting

²**loft** *vt* **1** : to place, house, or store in a loft **2** : to cause (a ball) to rise high into the air **3** : to lay out a full sized working drawing of the lines of ~ *vi* : to propel a ball high into the air

loft·i·ly \'lȯf-tə-lē\ *adv* : in a lofty manner

loft·i·ness \-tē-nəs\ *n* : the quality or state of being lofty

lofty \'lȯf-tē\ *adj* **1** : having a haughty overbearing manner : SUPERCILIOUS **2 a** : elevated in character and spirit : NOBLE **b** : elevated in position : SUPERIOR **3 a** : rising high in the air : TOWERING **b** : REMOTE, ESOTERIC **syn** see HIGH

¹**log** \'lȯg, 'läg\ *n, often attrib* [ME *logge*, prob. of Scand origin; akin to ON *lāg* fallen tree; akin to OE *licgan* to lie — more at LIE] **1** : a usu. bulky piece or length of unshaped timber; *esp* : a length of a tree trunk ready for sawing and over six feet long **2** : an apparatus for measuring the rate of a ship's motion through the water consisting of a block fastened to a line and run out from a reel **3 a** : the record of the rate of a ship's speed or of her daily progress; *also* : the full nautical record of a ship's voyage **b** : the full record of a flight by an aircraft **4** : any record of performance

²**log** *vb* **logged; log·ging** *vt* **1** : to cut (trees) for lumber or to clear (land) of trees in lumbering **2** : to enter details of or about in a log **3 a** : to move (an indicated distance) or attain (an indicated speed) as noted in a log **b** (1) : to sail a ship or fly an airplane for (an indicated distance) (2) : to have (an indicated record) to one's credit ~ *vi* : LUMBER 1

³**log** *n* : LOGARITHM

log- *or* **logo-** *comb form* [Gk, fr. *logos* — more at LEGEND] : word : thought : speech : discourse ⟨*logo*gram⟩ ⟨*logo*rrhea⟩

lo·gan·ber·ry \'lō-gən-,ber-ē\ *n* [James H. *Logan* †1928 Am lawyer + E *berry*] : a red-fruited upright-growing dewberry regarded as a variety (*Rubus ursinus loganobaccus*) of the western dewberry or as a hybrid of the western dewberry and the red raspberry; *also* : its berry

log·a·oe·dic \,läg-ə-'ēd-ik\ *adj* [LL *logaoedicus*, fr. LGk *logaoidikos*, fr. Gk *log-* + *aeidein* to sing — more at ODE] : marked by the mixture of several meters; *specif* : having a rhythm that uses both dactyls and trochees or anapests and iambs — **logaoedic** *n*

log·a·rithm \'lȯg-ə-,rit͟h-əm, 'läg-\ *n* [NL *logarithmus*, fr. *log-* + Gk *arithmos* number — more at ARITHMETIC] : the exponent that indicates the power to which a number is raised to produce a given number ⟨the ~ of 100 to the base 10 is 2⟩

log·a·rith·mic \,lȯg-ə-'rit͟h-mik, ,läg-\ *adj* : relating to, based on, or characteristic of logarithms

log·book \'lȯg-,bu̇k, 'läg-\ *n* : LOG 3, 4

loge \'lōzh\ *n* [F — more at LODGE] **1 a** : a small compartment : BOOTH **b** : a box in a theater **2 a** : a small partitioned area **b** : the forward section of a theater mezzanine

logged \'lȯgd, 'lägd\ *adj* **1** : made heavy or sluggish so that movement is impossible or difficult **2** : sodden esp. with water

log·ger \'lȯg-ər, 'läg-\ *n* : one engaged in logging

log·ger·head \'lȯg-ər-,hed, 'läg-\ *n* [prob. fr. E dial. *logger* (block of wood) + *head*] **1** *chiefly dial* **a** : BLOCKHEAD **b** : HEAD; *esp* : a large cumbrous head **2 a** : any of various very large marine turtles (family Cheloniidae); *esp* : a carnivorous turtle (*Caretta caretta*) of the warmer parts of the western Atlantic **b** : ALLIGATOR SNAPPER **c** : a snapping turtle (*Chelydra serpentina*) **3** : an iron tool consisting of a long handle terminating in a ball or bulb that is heated and used to melt tar or to heat liquids — **at loggerheads** : in or into a state of quarrelsome disagreement

log·gets *or* **log·gats** \-əts\ *n pl but sing or pl in constr* [prob. fr. ¹*log* + *-et*] : a game formerly played in England in which players throw pieces of wood at a stake

log·gia \'läj-(ē-)ə, 'lȯ-,jä\ *n, pl* **loggias** \'läj-(ē-)əz, 'lȯ-,jäz\ *also* **log·gie** \'lȯ-,jā\ [It, fr. F *loge*] : a roofed open gallery in the side of a building esp. at an upper story overlooking an open court

log·ic \'läj-ik\ *n* [ME *logik*, fr. MF *logique*, fr. L *logica*, fr. Gk *logikē*, fr. fem. of *logikos* of reason, fr. *logos* reason — more at LEGEND] **1 a** (1) : a science that deals with the canons and criteria of validity of inference and demonstration : the science of the normative formal principles of reasoning (2) : a branch of semiotic; *esp* : SYNTACTICS (3) : the formal principles of a branch of knowledge **b** : a particular mode of reasoning **c** : interrelation or sequence of facts or events when seen as inevitable or predictable **d** : the fundamental principles and the connection of circuit elements for arithmetical computation in a computer **2** : something that forces a decision apart from or in opposition to reason ⟨the ~ of war⟩ — **lo·gi·cian** \lō-'jish-ən\ *n*

log·i·cal \'läj-i-kəl\ *adj* **1 a** : relating to, in accordance with, or skilled in logic **b** : formally true or valid : ANALYTIC, DEDUCTIVE **2** : that is in accordance with inferences reasonably drawn from events or circumstances — **log·i·cal·i·ty** \,läj-ə-'kal-ət-ē\ *n* — **log·i·cal·ly** \'läj-i-k(ə-)lē\ *adv* — **log·i·cal·ness** \-i-kəl-nəs\ *n*

logical positivism *or* **logical empiricism** *n* : a 20th century philosophical movement that holds characteristically that all meaningful statements are either analytic or conclusively verifiable or at least confirmable by observation and experiment and that metaphysical theories are therefore strictly meaningless — **logical positivist** *or* **logical empiricist** *n*

lo·gi·on \'lō-gē-,än\ *n, pl* **lo·gia** \-gē-,ä\ *or* **logions** [Gk, dim. of *logos*] : SAYING; *esp* : one of the agrapha

¹**lo·gis·tic** \lō-'jis-tik, lə-\ *adj* **1 a** : of or relating to symbolic logic **b** : of or relating to the philosophical attempt to reduce mathematics to logic **2** : of or relating to logistics — **lo·gis·ti·cal** \-ti-kəl\ *adj* — **lo·gis·ti·cal·ly** \-k(ə-)lē\ *adv*

²**logistic** *n* : SYMBOLIC LOGIC

logistic curve *n* : a curve representing a function expressed in terms of the exponential function and shaped like the letter S

lo·gis·ti·cian \(,)lō-,jis-'tish-ən\ *n* : a specialist in logistics

lo·gis·tics \lō-'jis-tiks, lə-\ *n pl but sing or pl in constr* [F *logistique* art of calculating, logistics, fr. Gk *logistikē* art of calculating, fr. fem. of *logistikos* of calculation, fr. *logizein* to calculate, fr. *logos* reason] : the procurement, maintenance, and transportation of military matériel, facilities, and personnel

log·jam \'lȯg-,jam, 'läg-\ *n* **1** : a deadlocked jumble of logs in a watercourse **2** : DEADLOCK, BLOCKAGE

logo·gram \'lȯg-ə-,gram, 'läg-\ *n* : a letter, symbol, or sign used to represent an entire word — **logo·gram·mat·ic** \,lȯg-ə-grə-'mat-ik, ,läg-\ *adj*

logo·graph \'lȯg-ə-,graf, 'läg-\ *n* : LOGOGRAM — **logo·graph·ic** \,lȯg-ə-'graf-ik, ,läg-\ *adj* — **logo·graph·i·cal·ly** \-i-k(ə-)lē\ *adv*

logo·griph \'lòg-ə-,grif, 'läg-\ *n* [log- + Gk *griphos* reed basket, riddle — more at CRIB] **:** a word puzzle
lo·gom·a·chy \lō-'gäm-ə-kē\ *n* [Gk *logomachia*, fr. *log-* + *machesthai* to fight] **:** a dispute over or about words; *esp* **:** a controversy marked by verbiage
log·or·rhea \,lòg-ə-'rē-ə, ,läg-\ *n* [NL] **:** excessive and often incoherent talkativeness — **log·or·rhe·ic** \-'rē-ik\ *adj*
Lo·gos \'lō-,gäs, -,gōs\ *n, pl* **Lo·goi** \-,gòi\ [Gk, speech, word, reason — more at LEGEND] **1 :** reason that in ancient Greek philosophy is the controlling principle in the universe **2 :** the divine wisdom manifest in the creation, government, and redemption of the world and often identified with the second person of the Trinity
logo·type \'lòg-ə-,tīp, 'läg-\ *n* **:** a single piece of type or a single plate faced with a term (as the name of a newspaper or a trademark)
log·roll \'lòg-,rōl, 'läg-\ *vb* [back-formation fr. *logrolling*] *vi* **:** to take part in logrolling ~ *vt* **:** to promote passage of by logrolling — **log·roll·er** *n*
log·roll·ing \-,rō-liŋ\ *n* **1 :** the rolling of logs in water by treading; *also* **:** a sport in which men treading logs try to dislodge one another **2 :** the exchanging of assistance or favors; *specif* **:** the trading of votes by legislators to secure favorable action on projects of interest to each one
-logue *or* **-log** \,lòg, ,läg\ *n comb form* [ME *-logue*, fr. OF, fr. L *-logus*, fr. Gk *-logos*, fr. *legein* to speak — more at LEGEND] **1 :** discourse **:** talk ⟨duo*logue*⟩ **2 :** student **:** specialist ⟨sino*logue*⟩
log·wood \'lòg-,wu̇d, 'läg-\ *n* **:** a Central American and West Indian leguminous tree (*Haematoxylon campechianum*); *also* **:** its very hard brown or brownish red heartwood used in dyeing or an extract of this
lo·gy \'lō-gē\ *also* **log·gy** \'lòg-ē, 'läg-\ *adj* [perh. fr. D *log* heavy; akin to MLG *luggish* lazy] **:** marked by sluggishness and lack of vitality
-lo·gy \l-ə-jē\ *n comb form* [ME *-logie*, fr. OF, fr. L *-logia*, fr. Gk, fr. *logos* word] **1 :** oral or written expression ⟨phraseo*logy*⟩ **2 :** doctrine **:** theory **:** science ⟨ethno*logy*⟩
Lo·hen·grin \'lō-ən-,grin\ *n* [G] **:** a son of Parsifal and knight of the Holy Grail in German legend
loin \'lòin\ *n* [ME *loyne*, fr. MF *loigne*, fr. (assumed) VL *lumbea* fr. L *lumbus;* akin to OE *lendenu* loins, OSlav *lędvĭję*] **1 a :** the part of a human being or quadruped on each side of the spinal column between the hipbone and the false ribs **b :** a cut of meat comprising this part of one or both sides of a carcass with the adjoining half of the vertebrae included but without the flank **2** *pl* **a :** the upper and lower abdominal regions and the region about the hips **b** (1) **:** the pubic region (2) **:** the generative organs
loin·cloth \-,klòth\ *n* **:** a cloth worn about the loins often as the sole article of clothing in warm climates
loi·ter \'lòit-ər\ *vi* [ME *loiteren*] **1 :** to delay an activity with aimless idle stops and pauses **:** LINGER **2 a :** to hang around **b :** to lag behind **syn** see DELAY — **loi·ter·er** \-ər-ər\ *n*
Lo·ki \'lō-kē\ *n* [ON] **:** a Norse god who contrives discord and mischief
1**loll** \'läl\ *vb* [ME *lollen*] *vi* **1 :** to hang loosely or laxly **:** DROOP **2 :** to recline, lean, or move in a lax, lazy, or indolent manner **:** LOUNGE ~ *vt* **:** to let droop or dangle
2**loll** *n, archaic* **:** the act or posture of lolling
Lol·lard \'läl-ərd\ *n* [ME, fr. MD *lollaert*] **:** a follower of Wycliffe in the 14th and 15th centuries — **Lol·lard·ism** \-ər-,diz-əm\ *n* — **Lol·lardy** \-ərd-ē\ *n*
lol·li·pop *or* **lol·ly·pop** \'läl-ē-,päp\ *n* [prob. fr. 1*loll* + *-i-* + *pop*] **:** a lump of hard candy on the end of a stick
lol·lop \'läl-əp\ *vi* [2*loll* + *-op* (as in *gallop*)] **1** *dial Eng* **:** LOLL **2 :** to proceed with a bounding or bobbing motion
lol·ly \'läl-ē\ *n* [short for *lollipop*] *Brit* **:** a piece of candy; *esp* **:** hard candy
Lom·bard \'läm-,bärd, -bərd\ *n, often attrib* [ME *Lumbarde*, fr. MF *lombard*, fr. OIt *lombardo*, fr. L *Langobardus*] **1 a :** a member of a Teutonic people invading Italy in A.D. 568, settling in the Po valley, and establishing a kingdom **b :** a native of the part of Italy settled by the Lombards **2** [fr. the prominence of Lombards as moneylenders] **:** BANKER, MONEYLENDER — **Lom·bar·dic** \läm-'bärd-ik\ *adj*
Lombard Street *n* **:** the money market of London
lo·ment \'lō-,ment, -mənt\ *n* [NL *lomentum*, fr. L, wash made fr. bean meal, fr. *lotus*, pp. of *lavare* to wash — more at LYE] **:** a dry indehiscent one-celled fruit that is produced from a single superior ovary and breaks transversely into numerous segments at maturity
lone \'lōn\ *adj* [ME, short for *alone*] **1 a :** having no company **:** SOLITARY **b :** preferring solitude **2 :** ONLY, SOLE **3 :** situated by itself **:** ISOLATED — **lone·ness** \'lōn-nəs\ *n*
lone·li·ly \'lōn-lə-lē\ *adv* **:** in a lonely manner
lone·li·ness \'lōn-lē-nəs\ *n* **:** the quality or state of being lonely
lone·ly \'lōn-lē\ *adj* **1 a :** being without company **:** LONE **b :** cut off from others **:** SOLITARY **2 :** not frequented by human beings **:** DESOLATE **3 :** sad from being alone **:** LONESOME **4 :** producing a feeling of bleakness or desolation **syn** see ALONE
1**lone·some** \'lōn(t)-səm\ *adj* **1 a :** sad or dejected as a result of lack of companionship or separation from others **b :** causing a feeling of loneliness **2 a :** REMOTE, UNFREQUENTED **b :** LONE **syn** see ALONE — **lone·some·ly** *adv* — **lone·some·ness** *n*
2**lonesome** *n* **:** SELF ⟨sat all by his ~⟩
1**long** \'lòŋ\ *adj* **lon·ger** \'lòŋ-gər\ **lon·gest** \'lòŋ-gəst\ [ME *long, lang*, fr. OE; akin to OHG *lang* long, L *longus*, Gk *dolichos*] **1 a :** extending for a considerable distance **b :** having greater length than usual **c :** having greater height than usual **:** TALL **d :** having a greater length than breadth **:** ELONGATED **e :** having a greater length than desirable or necessary **2 a :** having a specified length **b :** forming the chief linear dimension **3 a :** extending over a considerable time **b :** having a specified duration **c :** prolonged beyond the usual time **:** TEDIOUS **4 a :** containing many items in a series **b :** having a specified number of units **c :** consisting of a greater number or amount than usual **:** LARGE **5 a** *of a speech sound* **:** having a relatively long duration **b :** being the member of a pair of similarly spelled vowel or vowel-containing sounds that is descended from a vowel long in duration ⟨~ *a* in *fate*⟩ ⟨~ *i* in *sign*⟩ **c** *of a syllable in prosody* (1) **:** of relatively extended duration (2) **:** STRESSED **6 :** having the capacity to reach or extend a considerable distance **7 :** larger or longer than the standard **8 a :** extending far into the future **b :** extending beyond what is known **c :** payable after a considerable period **9 :** strong in or well furnished with **10 a :** of an unusual degree of difference between the amounts wagered on each side **b :** of or relating to the larger amount wagered **11 :** subject to great odds **12 :** holding securities or goods in anticipation of an advance in prices — **at long last :** after a long wait **:** FINALLY — **long in the tooth :** past one's best days **:** OLD
2**long** *adv* **1 :** for or during a long time **2 :** at or to a long distance **:** FAR ⟨*long*-traveled⟩ **3 :** for the duration of a specified period **4 :** at a point of time far before or after a specified moment or event **5 :** after or beyond a specified time — **as long as** *or* **so long as 1 :** seeing that **:** SINCE **2 :** PROVIDING, IF — **so long :** GOOD-BYE
3**long** *n* **1 :** a long period of time **2 :** a long syllable **3 :** one who purchases or operates on the long side of the market **4 a** *pl* **:** long trousers **b :** a size in clothing for tall men — **the long and short** *or* **the long and the short :** the sum and substance **:** GIST
4**long** *vi* **long·ing** \'lòŋ-iŋ\ [ME *longen*, fr. OE *langian;* akin to OHG *langēn* to long, OE *lang* long] **:** to feel a strong desire or craving **:** YEARN
syn LONG, YEARN, HANKER, PINE, HUNGER, THIRST mean to have a strong desire for something. LONG implies a wishing with one's whole heart and often a striving to attain; YEARN suggests an eager, restless, or painful longing; HANKER suggests the uneasy promptings of unsatisfied appetite or desire; PINE implies a languishing or a fruitless longing for what is impossible; HUNGER and THIRST imply an insistent or impatient craving or a compelling need
5**long** *vi* [ME *longen*, fr. *along* (*on*) because (of)] *archaic* **:** to be suitable or fitting
lon·ga·nim·i·ty \,lòŋ-gə-'nim-ət-ē\ *n* [LL *longanimitas*, fr. *longanimis* patient, fr. L *longus* long + *animus* soul — more at ANIMATE] **:** a disposition to bear injuries patiently **:** FORBEARANCE
long·boat \'lòŋ-,bōt\ *n* **:** the largest boat carried by a merchant sailing ship
long bone *n* **:** one of the elongated bones supporting a vertebrate limb and consisting of an essentially cylindrical shaft that contains marrow and ends in enlarged heads for articulation with other bones
long·bow \'lòŋ-,bō\ *n* **:** a wooden bow drawn by hand and usu. 5½ to 6 feet long
1**long–dis·tance** \-'dis-tən(t)s\ *adj* **1 a :** situated a long distance away **b :** covering a long distance **2 :** of or relating to telephone communication with a distant point
2**long–distance** *adv* **:** by long-distance telephone
long distance *n* **1 :** communication by long-distance telephone **2 :** a telephone operator or exchange that gives long-distance connections
long division *n* **:** arithmetical division in which the several steps corresponding to the division of parts of the dividend by the divisor are indicated in detail
long dozen *n* **:** one more than a dozen **:** THIRTEEN
lon·ge·ron \'län-jə-,rän\ *n* [F] **:** a fore-and-aft framing member of an airplane fuselage
lon·gev·i·ty \län-'jev-ət-ē, lòn-\ *n* [LL *longaevitas*, fr. L *longaevus* long-lived, fr. *longus* long + *aevum* age — more at AYE] **1 a :** a long duration of individual life **b :** length of life **2 :** long continuance **:** SENIORITY
lon·ge·vous \-'jē-vəs\ *adj* **:** LONG-LIVED
long green *n, slang* **:** paper money **:** CASH
long·hair \'lòŋ-,ha(ə)r, -,he(ə)r\ *n* [back-formation fr. *long-haired*] **1 :** a person of artistic gifts or interests; *esp* **:** a lover of classical music **2 :** an impractical intellectual — **long–hair** *or* **long–haired** *adj*
long·hand \'lòŋ-,hand\ *n* **:** the characters used in ordinary writing **:** HANDWRITING
long·head *n* **1** \-'hed\ **:** a head with a low cephalic index **2** \-,hed\ **:** a dolichocephalic person
long·head·ed \-'hed-əd\ *adj* **1 :** having unusual foresight or wisdom **2 :** DOLICHOCEPHALIC — **long·head·ed·ness** *n*
long·horn \'lòŋ-,hò(ə)rn\ *n* **:** any of the long-horned cattle of Spanish derivation formerly common in southwestern U.S.
long–horned beetle \,lòŋ-,hòrn(d)-\ *also* **long·horn beetle** \,lòŋ-,hòrn-\ *n* **:** any of various beetles (family Cerambycidae) usu. distinguished by their very long antennae
long–horned grasshopper *n* **:** any of various grasshoppers (family Tettigoniidae) distinguished by their very long antennae
long·house \'lòŋ-,hau̇s, -'hau̇s\ *n* **:** a communal dwelling esp. of the Iroquois
longi- *comb form* [ME, fr. L, fr. *longus*] **:** long ⟨*longi*pennate⟩
lon·gi·corn \'län-jə-,kò(ə)rn\ *adj* [deriv. of *longi-* + L *cornu* horn — more at HORN] **1 :** of or relating to long-horned beetles **2 :** having long antennae — **longicorn** *n*
long·ing \'lòŋ-iŋ\ *n* **:** an eager desire esp. for something unattainable **:** CRAVING — **long·ing·ly** \-iŋ-lē\ *adv*
long·ish \'lòŋ-ish\ *adj* **:** somewhat long
lon·gi·tude \'län-jə-,t(y)üd\ *n* [ME, fr. L *longitudin-, longitudo*, fr. *longus*] **1 a :** LENGTH **b** *archaic* **:** long duration **2 a :** angular distance measured on a great circle of reference from the intersection of the adopted zero meridian with this reference circle to the similar intersection of the meridian passing through the object **b :** the arc or portion of the earth's equator intersected between the meridian of a given place and the prime meridian (as from Greenwich, England) and expressed either in degrees or in time
lon·gi·tu·di·nal \,län-jə-'t(y)üd-nəl, -ᵊn-əl\ *adj* **1 :** of or relating to length or the lengthwise dimension **2 :** placed or running lengthwise — **lon·gi·tu·di·nal·ly** \-ē\ *adv*
long jump *n, Brit* **:** BROAD JUMP
long·leaf pine \,lòŋ-,lēf-\ *also* **long–leaved pine** \-,lēvd-\ *n* **:** a large pine (*Pinus palustris*) of the southern U.S. with green leaves and long cones that is a major timber tree; *also* **:** its tough coarse-grained reddish orange wood
long–lived \'lòŋ-'līvd, -'livd\ *adj* **1 :** having or characterized by a long life **2 :** lasting long — **long–lived·ness** \-'līv(d)-nəs, -'liv(d)-\ *n*
Lon·go·bard \'lòŋ-gə-,bärd, 'läŋ-\ *n, pl* **Longobards** *or* **Lon·go·bar·di** \,lòŋ-gə-'bär-,dī, ,läŋ-, -'bärd-ē\ [L *Langobardus, Longobardus*] **:** LOMBARD — **Lon·go·bar·dic** \,lòŋ-gə-'bärd-ik, ,läŋ-\ *adj*
long pig *n* **:** a human victim of a cannibal feast

long play *n* : a long-playing record
long-play·ing \'lȯŋ-'plā-iŋ\ *adj* : having a diameter of 10 or 12 inches and turning at 33⅓ revolutions per minute — used of a microgroove record
long-range \-'rānj\ *adj* **1** : involving or taking into account a long period of time **2** : relating to or fit for long distances
long·shore·man \'lȯŋ-'shōr-mən, -'shȯr-\ *n* [*longshore*, short for *alongshore*] : one who is employed at a seaport to work at the loading and unloading of ships
long shot \'lȯŋ-,shät\ *n* **1** : an entry (as in a horse race) given little chance of winning **2** : a bet in which the chances of winning are slight but the possible winnings great **3** : a venture involving great risk but promising a great reward if successful — **by a long shot** : by a great deal
long·sight·ed \-'sīt-əd\ *adj* : FARSIGHTED — **long·sight·ed·ness** *n*
long·some \'lȯŋ(k)-səm\ *adj* : tediously long — **long·some·ly** *adv* — **long·some·ness** *n*
long·spur \'lȯŋ-,spər\ *n* : any of several long-clawed finches (esp. genus *Calcarius*) of the arctic regions and the Great Plains of No. America
long-suf·fer·ing \'lȯŋ-'səf-(ə-)riŋ\ *or* **long-suf·fer·ance** \-(ə-)rən(t)s\ *n* : long and patient endurance of offense — **long-suffering** *adj* — **long-suf·fer·ing·ly** \-(ə-)riŋ-lē\ *adv*
long suit *n* **1** : a holding of more than the average number of cards in a suit **2** : the activity or quality in which a person excels
long-term \'lȯŋ-'tərm\ *adj* **1** : occurring over or involving a relatively long period of time **2 a** : of, relating to, or constituting a financial operation or obligation based on a term usu. of more than 10 years **b** : of or relating to capital assets held for more than six months
Long Tom \-'täm\ *n* [fr. the name *Tom*] **1** : a long pivot gun formerly carried on the deck of a warship **2** : a large gun having a long range used on land
lon·gueur \lōⁿ-gœr\ *n*, *pl* **longueurs** \-gœr(z)\ [F, lit., length] : a dull and tedious passage or section
long-wind·ed \'lȯŋ-'win-dəd\ *adj* **1** : not easily subject to loss of breath **2** : tediously long in speaking or writing — **long-wind·ed·ly** *adv* — **long-wind·ed·ness** *n*
¹**loo** \'lü\ *n* [short for obs. E *lanterloo*, fr. F *lanturelu* piffle] **1** : an old card game **2** : money staked at loo
²**loo** *vt* : to obligate to contribute to a new pool at loo for failing to win a trick
loo·by \'lü-bē\ *n* [ME *loby*] : an awkward clumsy fellow : LUBBER
¹**look** \'lu̇k\ *vb* [ME *looken*, fr. OE *lōcian*; akin to OS *lōcōn* to look] *vt* **1** : to make sure or take care (that something is done) **2** : to ascertain by the use of one's eyes **3 a** : to exercise the power of vision upon : EXAMINE **b** *archaic* : to search for **4** : EXPECT **5** *archaic* : to bring into a place or condition by the exercise of the power of vision **6** : to express by the eyes or facial expression **7** : to have an appearance that befits or accords with ~ *vi* **1 a** : to exercise the power of vision : SEE **b** : to direct one's attention **c** : to direct the eyes **2** : to have the appearance of being : SEEM **3** : to have a specified outlook ⟨the house ~*ed* east⟩ **4** : to gaze in wonder or surprise : STARE **5** : to show a tendency ⟨the evidence ~*s* to acquittal⟩ **syn** see EXPECT, SEE — **look after** : to take care of — **look for 1** : to await with hope or anticipation **2** : to search for
²**look** *n* **1 a** : the act of looking **b** : GLANCE **2 a** : the expression of the countenance **b** : physical appearance; *esp* : attractive physical appearance — usu. used in pl. **3** : the state or form in which something appears : ASPECT
look·er \'lu̇k-ər\ *n* **1** : one that looks **2** : one having an appearance of a specified kind
look·er-on \,lu̇k-ə-'rȯn, -'rän\ *n*, *pl* **lookers-on** : ONLOOKER
looking glass *n* : MIRROR
look·out \'lu̇k-,au̇t\ *n*, *often attrib* **1** : one engaged in keeping watch : WATCHMAN **2** : an elevated place or structure affording a wide view for observation **3** : a careful looking or watching **4** : VIEW, OUTLOOK **5** : a matter of care or concern
¹**loom** \'lüm\ *n* [ME *lome* tool, loom, fr. OE *gelōma* tool; akin to MD al*lame* tool] **1** : a frame or machine for interlacing at right angles two or more sets of threads or yarns to form a cloth **2** [prob. of Scand origin; akin to ON *hlummr* handle of an oar] : the part of an oar that is inboard from the oarlock
²**loom** *vi* [origin unknown] **1** : to come into sight in enlarged or distorted and indistinct form often as a result of atmospheric conditions **2 a** : to appear in an impressively great or exaggerated form **b** : to take shape as an impending occurrence
³**loom** *n* : the indistinct and exaggerated appearance of something seen on the horizon or through fog or darkness; *also* : a looming shadow or reflection
¹**loon** \'lün\ *n* [ME *loun*] **1** : IDLER, LOUT **2** *chiefly Scot* **a** : MISTRESS, HARLOT **b** : BOY **3 a** : a crazy person **b** : SIMPLETON
²**loon** *n* [of Scand origin; akin to ON *lōmr* loon — more at LAMENT] : any of several large fish-eating diving birds (genus *Gavia*) of the northern part of the northern hemisphere
loo·ny *or* **loo·ney** \'lü-nē\ *adj* **loo·ni·er**; **loo·ni·est** [by shortening & alter. fr. *lunatic*] : CRAZY, FOOLISH — **loony** *n*
¹**loop** \'lüp\ *n* [ME *loupe*] *archaic* : LOOPHOLE 1a
²**loop** *n*, *often attrib* [ME *loupe*, of unknown origin] **1 a** : a fold or doubling of a line leaving an aperture between the parts through which another line can be passed or into which a hook may be hooked **b** : such a fold of cord or ribbon serving as an ornament **2 a** : something shaped like a loop **b** : a maneuver in which an airplane starting from straight and level flight passes successively through a climb, inverted flight, a dive, and then returns to normal flight **3** : a ring or curved piece used to form a fastening or a handle **4 a** : the portion of a vibrating body between two nodes **b** : the middle point of such a portion **5** : a closed electric circuit — **loopy** \'lü-pē\ *adj* — **for a loop** : into a state of amazement, confusion, or distress
³**loop** *vi* **1** : to make or form a loop **2** : to execute a loop in an airplane ~ *vt* **1 a** : to make a loop in, on, or about **b** : to fasten with a loop **2** : to join (two courses of loops) in knitting **3** : to connect (electric conductors) so as to complete a loop
loop·er \'lü-pər\ *n* **1** : any of the usu. rather small hairless caterpillars that are mostly larvae of moths (family Geometridae) and move with a looping movement in which the anterior and posterior prolegs are alternately made fast and released **2** : one that loops
¹**loop·hole** \'lüp-,hōl\ *n* **1 a** : a small opening through which small firearms may be discharged **b** : a similar opening to admit light and air or to permit observation **2** : a means of escape; *esp* : an ambiguity or omission in the text through which the intent of a statute, contract, or obligation may be evaded
²**loophole** *vt* : to make loopholes in
¹**loose** \'lüs\ *adj* [ME *lous*, fr. ON *lauss*; akin to OHG *lōs* loose — more at -LESS] **1 a** : not rigidly fastened or securely attached **b** (1) : having worked partly free from attachments (2) : having relative freedom of movement **c** : produced freely and accompanied by raising of mucus ⟨a ~ cough⟩ **d** : not fast ⟨a ~ dye⟩ **e** : not tight-fitting **2 a** : free from a state of confinement, restraint, or obligation **b** : not brought together in a bundle, container, or binding **c** *archaic* : DISCONNECTED, DETACHED **3** : not dense, close, or compact in structure or arrangement **4 a** : lacking in restraint or power of restraint **b** : LEWD, UNCHASTE **5 a** : not tightly drawn or stretched : SLACK **b** : having a flexible or relaxed character **6 a** : lacking in precision, exactness, or care **b** : permitting freedom of interpretation — **loose·ly** *adv* — **loose·ness** *n*
²**loose** *vt* **1 a** : to let loose : RELEASE **b** : to free from restraint **2 a** : to make loose : UNTIE ⟨~ a knot⟩ **b** *archaic* : DISSOLVE **3** : to cast loose : DETACH **4** : to let fly : DISCHARGE **5** : to make less rigid, tight, or strict : RELAX, SLACKEN ~ *vi* : to let fly a missile (as an arrow) : FIRE
³**loose** *adv* : LOOSELY
loose end *n* **1** : something left hanging loose **2** : a fragment of unfinished business
loose-joint·ed \'lüs-'jȯint-əd\ *adj* **1** : having joints apparently not closely articulated **2** : characterized by unusually free movements — **loose-joint·ed·ness** *n*
loos·en \'lüs-ᵊn\ *vb* **loos·en·ing** \'lüs-niŋ, -ᵊn-iŋ\ *vt* **1** : to release from restraint **2** : to make looser **3** : to relieve (the bowels) of constipation **4** : to cause or permit to become less strict ~ *vi* : to become loose or looser
loose sentence *n* : a sentence in which the principal clause comes first and the latter part contains subordinate modifiers or trailing elements
loose smut *n* : a smut disease of grains in which the entire head is transformed into a dusty mass of spores
loose·strife \'lü(s)-,strīf\ *n* [intended as trans. of Gk *lysimacheios* loosestrife (as if fr. *lysis* act of loosing + *machesthai* to fight) — more at LYS-] **1** : any of a genus (*Lysimachia*) of plants of the primrose family with leafy stems and yellow or white flowers **2** : any of a genus (*Lythrum*, family Lythraceae, the loosestrife family) of herbs including some with showy spikes of purple flowers
¹**loot** \'lüt\ *n* [Hindi *lūṭ*, fr. Skt *luṇṭati* he robs] **1** : goods usu. of considerable value taken in war : SPOILS **2** : something held to resemble goods of value seized in war: as **a** : anything taken by force or violence **b** : illicit gains by public officials **c** : MONEY **3** : the action of looting **syn** see SPOIL
²**loot** *vt* **1 a** : to plunder or sack in war **b** : to rob esp. on a large scale and usu. by violence or corruption **2** : to seize and carry away by force esp. in war ~ *vi* : to engage in robbing or plundering esp. in war — **loot·er** *n*
¹**lop** \'läp\ *n* [ME *loppe*] : material cut away from a tree; *esp* : parts discarded in lumbering
²**lop** *vt* **lopped**; **lop·ping** **1 a** (1) : to cut off branches or twigs from (2) : to sever from a woody plant **b** (1) *archaic* : to cut off the head or limbs of (2) : to cut from a person **2 a** : to remove superfluous parts from **b** : to eliminate as unnecessary or undesirable — usu. used with *off* — **lop·per** *n*
³**lop** *vi* **lopped**; **lop·ping** [perh. imit.] : to hang downward; *also* : to flop or sway loosely
¹**lope** \'lōp\ *n* [ME *loup*, *lope* leap, fr. ON *hlaup*; akin to OE *hlēapan* to leap — more at LEAP] **1** : an easy natural gait of a horse resembling a canter **2** : an easy bounding gait capable of being sustained for a long time
²**lope** *vi* : to go, move, or ride at a lope — **lop·er** *n*
lop-eared \'läp-'i(ə)rd\ *adj* : having ears that droop
lop·py \'läp-ē\ *adj* : hanging loose : LIMP **syn** see LIMP
lop·sid·ed \'läp-'sīd-əd\ *adj* **1** : leaning to one side **2** : lacking in balance, symmetry, or proportion — **lop·sid·ed·ly** *adv* — **lop·sid·ed·ness** *n*
lo·qua·cious \lō-'kwā-shəs\ *adj* [L *loquac-*, *loquax*, fr. *loqui* to speak] : given to excessive talking : GARRULOUS **syn** see TALKATIVE — **lo·qua·cious·ly** *adv* — **lo·qua·cious·ness** *n* — **lo·quac·i·ty** \-'kwas-ət-ē\ *n*
lo·quat \'lō-,kwät\ *n* [Chin (Cant) *lō-kwat*] : an Asiatic evergreen tree (*Eriobotrya japonica*) of the rose family often cultivated for its fruit; *also* : its yellow edible fruit used esp. for preserves
lor·al \'lōr-əl, 'lȯr-\ *adj* : of or relating to a lore
lo·ran \'lō(ə)r-,an, 'lȯ(ə)r-\ *n* [*lo*ng-*ra*nge *n*avigation] : a system of long-range navigation in which pulsed signals sent out by two pairs of radio stations are used by a navigator to determine the geographical position of a ship or an airplane
¹**lord** \'lȯ(ə)rd\ *n* [ME *loverd*, *lord*, fr. OE *hlāford*, fr. *hlāf* loaf + *weard* keeper — more at LOAF, WARD] **1** : one having power and authority over others: **a** : a ruler by hereditary right or preeminence to whom service and obedience are due **b** : one of whom a fee or estate is held in feudal tenure **c** : an owner of land or other real property **d** *obs* : the male head of a household **e** : HUSBAND **f** : one who has achieved mastery or who exercises leadership or great power in some area ⟨vice ~*s*⟩ **2** *cap* **a** : ²GOD **b** : CHRIST **3** : a man of rank or high position: as **a** : a feudal tenant holding directly of the king **b** : a British nobleman: as (1) : BARON 2a (2) : an hereditary peer of the rank of marquess, earl, or viscount (3) : the son of a duke or a marquess or the eldest son of an earl (4) : a bishop of the Church of England **c** *pl, cap* : HOUSE OF LORDS **4** — used as a British title: as **a** — used as part of an official title ⟨*Lord* Advocate⟩ **b** — used informally in place of the full title for a marquess, earl, or viscount **c** — used for a baron **d** — used by courtesy before the name and surname of a younger son of a duke or a marquess **5** : a person chosen to preside over a festival
²**lord** *vi* : to play the lord : DOMINEER — used with *it*
lord chancellor *n*, *pl* **lords chancellor** : a British officer of state who presides over the House of Lords in both its legislative and

judicial capacities, serves as the head of the British judiciary, and is usu. a leading member of the cabinet
lord·ing \'lȯrd-iŋ\ *n* **1** *archaic* **:** LORD **2** *obs* **:** LORDLING
lord·li·ness \'lȯrd-lē-nəs\ *n* **1 :** the quality or state of being a lord **2 a :** the manner and behavior suitable to a lord **:** DIGNITY **b :** an attitude of superiority toward inferiors **:** HAUGHTINESS
lord·ling \'lȯ(ə)rd-liŋ\ *n* **:** a little or insignificant lord
lord·ly \-lē\ *adj* **1 a :** of, relating to, or having the characteristics of a lord **:** DIGNIFIED **b :** GRAND, NOBLE **2 :** exhibiting pride or superiority **:** HAUGHTY **syn** see PROUD — **lordly** *adv*
lord of misrule : a master of Christmas revels in England esp. in the 15th and 16th centuries
lor·do·sis \lȯr-'dō-səs\ *n* [NL, fr. Gk *lordōsis*, fr. *lordos* curving forward; akin to OE *belyrtan* to deceive] **:** abnormal curvature of the spine forward — **lor·dot·ic** \-'dät-ik\ *adj*
Lord's day *n, often cap D* [fr. the Christian belief that Christ arose from the dead on Sunday] **:** SUNDAY
lord·ship \'lȯ(ə)rd-,ship\ *n* **1 a :** the rank or dignity of a lord — used as a title ⟨his *Lordship* is not at home⟩ **b :** the authority or power of a lord **:** DOMINION **2 :** the territory under the jurisdiction of a lord **:** SEIGNIORY
Lord's Prayer *n* **:** the prayer in Matthew 6:9–13 that Christ taught his disciples
Lord's Supper *n* [ME *Lordis sopere*, trans. of LL *dominica cena*, trans. of Gk *kyriakon deipnon*] **:** COMMUNION 2a
Lord's table *n, often cap T* **:** ALTAR 2
1**lore** \'lō(ə)r, 'lȯ(ə)r\ *n* [ME, fr. OE *lār;* akin to OHG *lēra* doctrine, OE *leornian* to learn] **1** *archaic* **:** something that is taught **:** LESSON **2 :** something that is learned: **a :** knowledge gained through study or experience **b :** traditional knowledge or belief **3 :** a particular body of knowledge or tradition
2**lore** *n* [NL *lorum*, fr. L, thong, rein; akin to Gk *eulēra* reins] **:** the space between the eye and bill in a bird or the corresponding region in a reptile or fish — **lo·re·al** \'lōr-ē-əl, 'lȯr-\ *adj*
Lo·re·lei \'lōr-ə-,lī, 'lȯr-\ *n* [G] **:** a siren in German legend whose singing lures sailors to destruction on a reef in the Rhine
lor·gnette \lȯrn-'yet\ *n* [F, fr. *lorgner* to take a sidelong look at, fr. MF, fr. *lorgne* cross-eyed] **:** a pair of eyeglasses or opera glasses with a handle

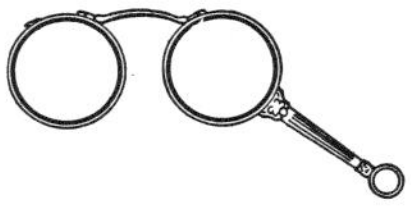
lorgnette

lor·gnon \-'yōⁿ\ *n* [F, fr. *lorgner*] **:** LORGNETTE
lo·ri·ca \lə-'rī-kə\ *n, pl* **lo·ri·cae** \-,kē, -,sē\ [L, fr. *lorum*] **1 :** a Roman cuirass of leather or metal **2** [NL, fr. L] **:** a hard protective case or shell (as of a rotifer) — **lor·i·cate** \'lȯr-i-kət, 'lȯr-ə-,kāt, 'lär-\ *or* **lor·i·cat·ed** \-ə-,kāt-əd\ *adj* — **loricate** *n*
lor·i·keet \'lȯr-ə-,kēt, 'lär-\ *n* [*lory* + *-keet* (as in *parrakeet*)] **:** any of numerous small arboreal usu. brush-tongued parrots mostly of Australasia
lo·ris \'lōr-əs, 'lȯr-\ *n* [F] **:** either of two small nocturnal slow-moving lemurs: **a :** a slim-bodied lemur (*Loris gracilis*) of southern India and Ceylon **b :** a stockier heavier-limbed lemur (*Bradicebus tardigradus*) of India and the East Indies — **lo·ris·i·form** \lə-'ris-ə-,fȯrm\ *adj*
lorn \'lȯ(ə)rn\ *adj* [ME, fr. *loren*, pp. of *lesen* to lose, fr. OE *lēosan* — more at LOSE] **1** *archaic* **:** LOST, RUINED **2 :** FORSAKEN, DESOLATE — **lorn·ness** \'lȯ(ə)rn-nəs\ *n*
Lor·raine cross \lə-,rān-, lȯ-\ *n* **:** CROSS OF LORRAINE
lor·ry \'lȯr-ē, 'lär-\ *n* [origin unknown] **1 a :** a large low horse-drawn wagon without sides **b** *Brit* **:** a motor truck esp. if open **2 :** any of various trucks running on rails
lo·ry \'lōr-ē, 'lȯr-\ *n* [Malay *nuri, luri*] **:** any of numerous parrots (esp. of the genera *Domicella*, *Trichoglossus*, *Chalcopsitta*, and *Eos*) of Australia, New Guinea, and adjacent islands usu. having the tongue papillose at the tip and the mandibles less toothed than other parrots
los·able \'lü-zə-bəl\ *adj* **:** capable of being lost — **los·able·ness** *n*
lose \'lüz\ *vb* **lost** \'lȯst\ **los·ing** [ME *losen*, fr. OE *losian* to perish, lose, fr. *los* destruction; akin to OE *lēosan* to lose; akin to ON *losa* to loosen, L *luere* to release, atone for, Gk *lyein* to loosen, dissolve, destroy] *vt* **1 :** to bring to destruction — used chiefly in passive constructions ⟨ship was *lost* on the reef⟩; *specif* **:** DAMN ⟨if he shall gain the whole world and ~ his own soul —Mt 16:26 (AV)⟩ **2 :** to miss from one's possession or customary or supposed place **3 :** to suffer deprivation of **:** part with esp. in an unforeseen or accidental manner **4 a :** to suffer loss through the death or removal of or final separation from (a person) **b :** to fail to keep control of or allegiance of ⟨~ votes⟩ **5 a :** to fail to use **:** let slip by **:** WASTE ⟨~ the tide⟩ **b :** to fail to win, gain, or obtain ⟨~ a prize⟩ ⟨~ a contest⟩ **:** undergo defeat in ⟨*lost* every battle⟩ **c :** to fail to catch with the senses or the mind ⟨*lost* part of what he said⟩ **6 :** to cause the loss of ⟨one careless statement *lost* him the election⟩ **7 :** to fail to keep, sustain, or maintain ⟨*lost* his balance⟩ **8 a :** to cause to miss one's way or bearings ⟨*lost* himself in the maze of streets⟩ **b :** to make (oneself) withdrawn from immediate reality ⟨*lost* himself in daydreaming⟩ **9 a :** to wander or go astray from ⟨*lost* his way⟩ **b :** to draw away from **:** OUTSTRIP ⟨*lost* his pursuers⟩ **10 :** to fail to keep in sight or in mind **11 :** to free oneself from **:** get rid of ⟨dieting to ~ some weight⟩ ~ *vi* **1 :** to undergo deprivation of something of value **2 :** to undergo defeat ⟨~ with good grace⟩ **3** *of a timepiece* **:** to run slow — **lose ground :** to suffer loss or disadvantage **:** fail to advance or improve — **lose one's heart :** to fall in love
lo·sel \'lō-zəl\ *n* [ME, fr. *losen* (pp. of *lesen* to lose), alter. of *loren*] **:** a worthless person — **losel** *adj* — **lo·sel·ry** \-rē\ *n*
lose out *vi* **:** to fail to win in competition **:** fail to receive an expected reward or gain
los·er \'lü-zər\ *n* **:** one that loses
loss \'lȯs\ *n* [ME *los*, prob. back-formation fr. *lost*, pp. of *losen* to lose] **1 a :** the act of losing **b :** the harm or privation resulting from loss or separation **c :** an instance of losing **2 :** a person or thing or an amount that is lost: as **a** *pl* **:** killed, wounded, or captured soldiers **b :** the power diminution of a circuit element corresponding to conversion of electric power into heat by resistance **3 :** failure to gain, win, obtain, or utilize; *specif* **:** an amount by which the cost of an article or service exceeds the selling price **4 :** decrease in amount, magnitude, or degree **5 :** DESTRUCTION, RUIN **6 :** the amount of an insured's financial detriment by death or damage that the insurer becomes liable for — **at a loss :** PUZZLED, UNCERTAIN — **for a loss :** into a state of distress
loss leader *n* **:** an article sold at a loss in order to draw customers
loss ratio *n* **:** the ratio between insurance losses incurred and premiums earned during a given period
lost \'lȯst\ *adj* [pp. of *lose*] **1 :** not made use of, won, or claimed **2 a :** unable to find the way **b :** no longer visible **c :** lacking assurance or self-confidence **:** HELPLESS **3 :** ruined or destroyed physically or morally **:** DESPERATE **4 a :** no longer possessed **b :** no longer known **5 a :** taken away or beyond reach or attainment **:** DENIED ⟨regions ~ to the faith⟩ **b :** HARDENED, INSENSIBLE ⟨~ to shame⟩ **6 :** ABSORBED, RAPT ⟨~ in reverie⟩ — **lost·ness** \'lȯs(t)-nəs\ *n*
1**lot** \'lät\ *n* [ME, fr. OE *hlot;* akin to OHG *hlōz* lot, Lith *kliudyti* to hook on] **1 :** an object used as a counter in determining a question by chance **2 a :** the use of lots as a means of deciding something **b :** the resulting choice **3 a :** something that comes to one upon whom a lot has fallen **:** SHARE **b :** one's way of life or worldly fate **:** FORTUNE **4** *obs* **:** a customs fee **:** DUTY **5 a :** a portion of land **b :** a measured parcel of land having fixed boundaries and designated on a plot or survey **c :** a motion-picture studio and its adjoining property **6 :** a number of units of an article or a parcel of articles offered as one item (as in an auction sale) **7 a :** a number of associated persons **:** SET **b :** KIND, SORT **8 :** a considerable quantity **syn** see FATE
2**lot** *vb* **lot·ted; lot·ting** *vi* **:** to cast or draw lots ~ *vt* **1 :** to form or divide into lots **2 :** ALLOT, APPORTION **3** *obs* **:** to draw lots for
Lot \'lät\ *n* [Heb *Lōṭ*] **:** a nephew of Abraham whose wife is turned into a pillar of salt for looking back during their flight from Sodom
lo·ta *or* **lo·tah** \'lōt-ə\ *n* [Hindi *loṭā*] **:** a small usu. spherical water vessel of brass or copper used in India
loth *var of* LOATH
lo·thar·io \lō-'thar-ē-,ō, -'ther-, -'thär-\ *n, often cap* [*Lothario*, seducer in the play *The Fair Penitent* (1703) by Nicholas Rowe] **:** SEDUCER
lo·tic \'lōt-ik\ *adj* [L *lotus*, pp.] **:** of, relating to, or living in actively moving water
lo·tion \'lō-shən\ *n* [L *lotion-*, *lotio*, fr. *lotus*, pp. of *lavere* to wash — more at LYE] **1 :** the act of washing **:** ABLUTION **2 :** a liquid preparation for cosmetic and external medicinal use
lots \'läts\ *adv* [pl. of 1*lot*] **:** MUCH
lot·tery \'lät-ə-rē, 'lä-trē\ *n, often attrib* [MF *loterie*, fr. MD, fr. *lot* lot; akin to OE *hlot* lot] **1 :** a drawing of lots in which prizes are distributed to the winners among persons buying a chance **2 :** an event or affair whose outcome is or seems to be determined by chance
lot·to \'lät-(,)ō\ *n* [It, lottery, fr. F *lot* lot, of Gmc origin; akin to OE *hlot*] **:** a game of chance played with cards having numbered squares corresponding with numbered balls drawn at random and won by covering five such squares in a row
lo·tus *or* **lo·tos** \'lōt-əs\ *n* [L & Gk; L *lotus*, fr. Gk *lōtos*, fr. Heb *lōṭ* myrrh] **1 :** a fruit eaten by the lotus-eaters and held to cause indolence and dreamy contentment; *also* **:** a tree (as *Zizyphus lotus* of the buckthorn family) reputed to bear this fruit **2 :** any of various water lilies including several represented in ancient Egyptian and Hindu art and religious symbolism **3** [NL, genus name, fr. L] **a :** any of a genus (*Lotus*) of widely distributed upright leguminous herbs or subshrubs **b :** SWEET CLOVER
lo·tus–eat·er *or* **lo·tos–eat·er** \'lōt-ə-,sēt-ər\ *n* **:** one of a people described in the Odyssey of Homer as subsisting on the lotus and living in the dreamy indolence it induced
loud \'lau̇d\ *adj* [ME, fr. OE *hlūd;* akin to OHG *hlūt* loud, L *inclutus* famous, Gk *klytos*, Skt *śṛṇoti* he hears] **1 a :** marked by intensity or volume of sound **b :** producing a loud sound **2 :** CLAMOROUS, NOISY **3 :** obtrusive or offensive in appearance or smell **:** OBNOXIOUS — **loud** *adv* — **loud·ly** *adv* — **loud·ness** *n*
loud·en \'lau̇d-ᵊn\ *vb* **loud·en·ing** \'lau̇d-niŋ, -ᵊn-iŋ\ **:** to make or become loud
loud·mouthed \'lau̇d-'mau̇thd, -'mau̇tht\ *adj* **:** given to loud offensive talk
loud·speak·er \'lau̇d-'spē-kər\ *n* **:** a device similar to a telephone receiver in operation but amplifying sound
lough \'läk\ *n* [ME, of Celt origin; akin to OIr *loch* lake; akin to L *lacus* lake] **1** *chiefly Irish* **:** LAKE **2** *chiefly Irish* **:** a bay or inlet of the sea
lou·is d'or \,lü-ē-'dȯ(ə)r\ *n, pl* **louis d'or** [F, fr. *Louis* XIII †1643 king of France + *d'or* of gold] **1 :** a French gold coin first struck in 1640 and issued up to the Revolution **2 :** the French 20-franc gold piece issued after the Revolution
Lou·is Qua·torze \,lü-ē-kə-'tȯ(ə)rz\ *adj* [F, Louis XIV] **:** of, relating to, or characteristic of the architecture or furniture of the reign of Louis XIV of France
Louis Quinze \-'kaⁿz\ *adj* [F, Louis XV] **:** of, relating to, or characteristic of the architecture or furniture of the reign of Louis XV of France
Louis Seize \-'sāz, -'sez\ *adj* [F, Louis XVI] **:** of, relating to, or characteristic of the architecture or furniture of the reign of Louis XVI of France
Louis Treize \-'trāz, -'trez\ *adj* [F, Louis XIII] **:** of, relating to, or characteristic of the furniture or architecture of the reign of Louis XIII of France
1**lounge** \'lau̇nj\ *vb* [origin unknown] *vi* **:** to act or move idly or lazily **:** LOAF ~ *vt* **:** to pass (time) idly ⟨~ away the afternoon⟩ — **loung·er** *n*
2**lounge** *n* **1 :** a place for lounging: as **a :** a room in a private home or public building for leisure occupations **:** LIVING ROOM; *also* **:** LOBBY **b :** a room in a public building or vehicle often combining lounging, smoking, and toilet facilities **2** *archaic* **:** a lounging gait or posture **3 :** a long couch
lounge car *n* **:** a railroad passenger car with seats for lounging and facilities for serving refreshments
loup \'lōp\ *vb* [ME *loupen*, fr. ON *hlaupa;* akin to OE *hlēapan* to leap — more at LEAP] *chiefly Scot* **:** LEAP, FLEE — **loup** *n*
loupe \'lüp\ *n* [F, gem of imperfect brilliancy, loupe] **:** a small magnifying glass used esp. by jewelers and watchmakers
loup–ga·rou \,lü-gə-'rü\ *n, pl* **loups–garous** \,lü-gə-'rü(z)\ [MF] **:** WEREWOLF
lour \'lau̇(-ə)r\ **loury** \'lau̇(ə)r-ē\ *var of* LOWER, LOWERY
1**louse** \'lau̇s\ *n* [ME *lous*, fr. OE *lūs;* akin to OHG *lūs* louse, W *llau* lice] **1** *pl* **lice** \'līs\ **a :** any of various small wingless usu. flattened insects (orders Anoplura and Mallophaga) parasitic on

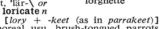

warm-blooded animals; *broadly* **:** a small usu. sluggish arthropod that lives on other animals or on plants and sucks their blood or juices **b :** any of several small arthropods that are not parasitic **2** *pl* **lous·es :** a contemptible person **:** HEEL

2**louse** \'laüs, 'laüz\ *vt* **:** to pick lice from **:** DELOUSE

louse up \'laü-'səp\ *vt* **:** to foul up **:** SNARL ~ *vi* **:** to make a mess

louse·wort \'laü-,swərt, -,swȯ(ə)rt\ *n* **:** any of a genus (*Pedicularis*) of plants of the figwort family formerly reputed to cause sheep feeding upon them to be subject to vermin

lous·i·ly \'laü-zə-lē\ *adv* **:** in a lousy manner **:** CONTEMPTIBLY

lous·i·ness \-zē-nəs\ *n* **1 :** PEDICULOSIS **2 :** VILENESS **3 :** a fuzziness of silk fabric caused by splitting of the fiber

lousy \'laü-zē\ *adj* **1 :** infested with lice **2 a :** totally repulsive **:** CONTEMPTIBLE **b :** miserably poor or inferior **c :** amply supplied **:** REPLETE ⟨~ with money⟩ **3** *of silk* **:** fuzzy and specked because of splitting of the fiber

1**lout** \'laüt\ *vi* [ME *louten*, fr. OE *lūtan;* akin to ON *lūta* to bow down, OE *lȳtel* little] **1 :** to bow in courtesy or respect **2 :** to bend in submission **:** YIELD

2**lout** *n* [perh. fr. ON *lūtr* bent down, fr. *lūta*] **:** an awkward clownish fellow **:** OAF

3**lout** *vt* **:** to treat as a lout **:** SCORN

lout·ish \'laüt-ish\ *adj* **:** CLOWNISH, RUDE **syn** see BOORISH — **lout·ish·ly** *adv* — **lout·ish·ness** *n*

lou·ver *or* **lou·vre** \'lü-vər\ *n* [ME *lover*, fr. MF *lovier*] **1 :** a roof lantern or turret often with slatted apertures for escape of smoke or admission of light in a medieval building **2 a :** an opening provided with one or more slanted fixed or movable fins to allow flow of air but to exclude rain or sun or to provide privacy **b :** a finned or vaned device for controlling a flow of air or the radiation of light **c :** a fin or shutter of a louver — **lou·vered** \-vərd\ *adj*

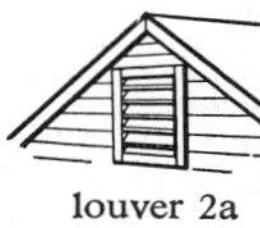
louver 2a

lov·able *also* **love·able** \'ləv-ə-bəl\ *adj* **:** having qualities that attract affection — **lov·able·ness** *n* — **lov·ably** \-blē\ *adv*

lov·age \'ləv-ij\ *n* [ME *lovache*, fr. AF, fr. LL *levisticum*, alter. of L *ligusticum*, fr. neut. of *ligusticus* Ligurian, fr. *Ligur-*, *Ligus*, n., Ligurian] **:** any of several aromatic perennial herbs of the carrot family; *esp* **:** a European herb (*Levisticum officinale*) sometimes cultivated as a domestic remedy, flavoring agent, or potherb

1**love** \'ləv\ *n* [ME, fr. OE *lufu;* akin to OHG *lupa* love, OE *lēof* dear, L *lubēre, libēre* to please] **1 a :** affection based on admiration or benevolence **b :** an assurance of love **2 a :** warm attachment, enthusiasm, or devotion ⟨~ of the sea⟩ **b :** the object of such attachment or devotion **3 a :** unselfish concern that freely accepts another in loyalty and seeks his good: (1) **:** the fatherly concern of God for man (2) **:** brotherly concern for others **b :** man's adoration of God **4 a :** the attraction based on sexual desire **:** the affection and tenderness felt by lovers **b :** a god or personification of love **c :** an amorous episode **:** LOVE AFFAIR **d :** the sexual embrace **:** COPULATION **5 :** a beloved person **:** DARLING **6 :** a score of zero in tennis **7** *cap*, *Christian Science* **:** GOD

2**love** *vt* **1 :** to hold dear **:** CHERISH **2 a :** to feel a lover's passion, devotion, or tenderness for **b :** CARESS **3 :** to like or desire actively **:** take pleasure in ⟨*loved* to play the violin⟩ **4 :** to thrive in ⟨the rose ~*s* sunlight⟩ ~ *vi* **:** to feel affection or experience desire

love affair *n* **1 :** a romantic attachment or episode between lovers **2 :** a lively enthusiasm

love·bird \'ləv-,bərd\ *n* **:** any of various small usu. gray or green parrots (as of the genera *Agapornis* of Africa, *Loriculus* of Asia, and *Psittacula* of So. America) that show great affection for their mates

love feast *n* **1 :** a meal eaten in common by a Christian congregation in token of brotherly love **2 :** a banquet or celebration held to reconcile differences and promote good feeling or show someone affectionate honor

love game *n* **:** a game (as in tennis) won without loss of a point

love-in-a-mist \'ləv-ən-ə-,mist\ *n* **:** a European garden plant (*Nigella damascena*) of the crowfoot family having the flowers enveloped in numerous finely dissected bracts

love knot *n* **:** a stylized knot sometimes used as an emblem of love

love·less \'ləv-ləs\ *adj* **1 :** UNLOVING **2 :** UNLOVED — **love·less·ly** *adv* — **love·less·ness** *n*

love·li·ly \'ləv-lə-lē\ *adv* **:** in a lovely manner

love·li·ness \'ləv-lē-nəs\ *n* **:** the quality or state of being lovely **:** BEAUTY

love·lock \'ləv-,läk\ *n* **:** a long lock of hair worn over the shoulder by men in the 17th and 18th centuries

love·lorn \-,lȯ(ə)rn\ *adj* **:** bereft of love or of a lover — **love·lorn·ness** \-,lȯrn-nəs\ *n*

1**love·ly** \'ləv-lē\ *adj* **1** *obs* **:** LOVING; *also* **:** LOVABLE **2 :** eliciting love by moral or ideal worth **3 :** delightful for beauty, harmony, or grace **:** ATTRACTIVE **4 :** GRAND, SWELL **syn** see BEAUTIFUL — **lovely** *adv*

2**lovely** *n* **1 :** one that is lovely; *specif* **:** a professional beauty **2 :** a lovely object

love·mak·ing \'ləv-,mā-kiŋ\ *n* **1 :** COURTSHIP **2 :** sexual activity between lovers

lov·er \'ləv-ər\ *n* **1 a :** a person in love; *esp* **:** a man in love with a girl or woman **b** *pl* **:** two persons in love with each other **2 :** an affectionate or benevolent friend **3 :** DEVOTEE **4 :** PARAMOUR

lov·er·ly \-lē\ *adj* (*or adv*) **:** resembling or as a lover

love seat *n* **:** a double chair, sofa, or settee for two persons

love set *n* **:** a set in tennis won without loss of a game

love-sick \'ləv-,sik\ *adj* **1 :** languishing with love **:** YEARNING **2 :** expressing a lover's longing — **love·sick·ness** *n*

love·some \'ləv-səm\ *adj* **1 :** WINSOME, LOVELY **2 :** AFFECTIONATE, AMOROUS

lov·ing \'ləv-iŋ\ *adj* **:** AFFECTIONATE — **lov·ing·ly** \-iŋ-lē\ *adv* — **lov·ing·ness** *n*

loving cup *n* [fr. its former use in ceremonial drinking] **1 :** a large ornamental drinking vessel with two or more handles **2 :** a loving cup given as a token or trophy

lov·ing-kind·ness \,ləv-iŋ-'kīn(d)-nəs\ *n* **:** tender and benevolent affection

1**low** \'lō\ *vi* [ME *loowen*, vb., fr. OE *hlōwan;* akin to OHG *hluoen* to moo, L *calare* to call, summon, Gk *kalein*] **:** MOO — **low** *n*

2**low** *adj* **low·er** \'lō(-ə)r\ **low·est** \'lō-əst\ [ME *lah, low*, fr. ON *lāgr;* akin to MHG *læge* low, flat] **1 a :** having a small upward extension or elevation ⟨~ wall⟩ **b :** situated or passing little above a reference line, point, or plane ⟨~ bridge⟩ **c :** DÉCOLLETÉ **2 a :** situated or passing below the normal level, surface, or base of measurement, or the mean elevation ⟨~ ground⟩ **b :** marking a nadir or bottom ⟨~ point of his career⟩ **3 a :** DEAD **b :** PROSTRATE ⟨laid ~⟩ **4 a :** not loud **:** SOFT; *also* **:** FLAT **b :** located in the contraoctave ⟨~ G⟩ **c :** depressed in pitch ⟨a ~ tone⟩ **5 :** being near the equator ⟨~ northern latitudes⟩ **6 :** humble in character or status ⟨~ birth⟩ **7 a :** lacking strength, health, or vitality **:** WEAK **b :** lacking spirit or vivacity **:** DEPRESSED **8 a :** of lesser degree, size, or amount than average or ordinary ⟨~ pressure⟩ **b** (1) **:** small in number or amount (2) **:** INADEQUATE ⟨~ level of employment⟩ (3) **:** CHEAP ⟨~ price⟩ (4) **:** DEPLETED, SHORT ⟨~ supply⟩ **9 :** falling short of some standard: as **a :** lacking dignity or elevation ⟨~ style of writing⟩ **b :** morally reprehensible **:** BASE ⟨~ trick⟩ **c :** COARSE, VULGAR ⟨~ language⟩ **10 a :** not advanced in complexity, development, or elaboration ⟨~ organisms⟩ **b** *often cap* **:** Low Church **11 :** UNFAVORABLE, DISPARAGING ⟨~ opinion of him⟩ **12 :** articulated with a wide opening between the relatively flat tongue and the palate **:** OPEN ⟨the sounds \ä\, \à\, \a\ are ~⟩ **syn** see BASE — **low** *adv* — **low·ness** *n*

3**low** *n* **1 :** something that is low: as **a :** DEPTH **b :** a region of low barometric pressure **2 :** the transmission gear of an automotive vehicle giving the lowest ratio of propeller-shaft to engine-shaft speed and the highest amplification of torque

4**low** *or* **lowe** \'lō\ *n* [ME, fr. ON *logi, log;* akin to OE *lēoht* light — more at LIGHT] *chiefly Scot* **:** FLAME, BLAZE

5**low** *or* **lowe** *vb, Scot* **:** FLAME, BLAZE

low beam *n* **:** the short-range focus of a vehicle headlight

low blood pressure *n* **:** HYPOTENSION

low·born \'lō-'bȯ(ə)rn\ *adj* **:** born in a low condition or rank

low·boy \-,bȯi\ *n* **:** a dressing table about three feet high with drawers

low·bred \-'bred\ *adj* **:** RUDE, VULGAR

low·brow \'lō-,braü\ *n* **:** an uncultivated person — **lowbrow** *adj*

Low Church *adj* **:** tending to minimize the priesthood, sacraments, and formal rites and often to emphasize evangelical principles — **Low Churchman** *n*

low comedy *n* **:** comedy bordering on farce and employing burlesque, horseplay, or the representation of low life

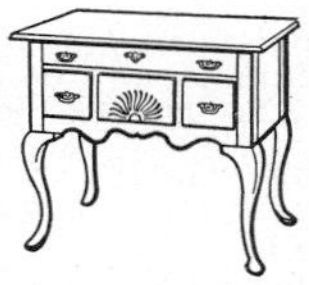
lowboy

low-down \'lō-'daün\ *adj* **:** CONTEMPTIBLE, BASE

low·down \-,daün\ *n* **:** the inside facts **:** DOPE

1**low·er** \'laü(-ə)r\ *vi* [ME *louren;* akin to MHG *lūren* to lie in wait] **1 :** to look sullen **:** FROWN **2 :** to become dark, gloomy, and threatening ⟨~*ing* clouds⟩ **syn** see FROWN

2**lower** *n* **:** a lowering look **:** FROWN; *also* **:** a gloomy sky or aspect of weather

3**low·er** \'lō(-ə)r\ *adj* **1 :** relatively low in position, rank, or order **2 :** constituting the popular and often the larger and more representative branch of a bicameral legislative body **3 a :** situated or held to be situated beneath the earth's surface **b** *cap* **:** of, relating to, or constituting an earlier geologic period or formation **4 :** SOUTHERN ⟨~ New York State⟩

4**low·er** \'lō(-ə)r\ *vi* **:** to move down **:** DROP; *also* **:** DIMINISH ~ *vt* **1 a :** to let descend by its own weight **b :** to depress as to direction **c :** to reduce the height of **2 a :** to reduce in value or amount ⟨~ the price⟩ **b** (1) **:** to bring down **:** DEGRADE (2) **:** ABASE, HUMBLE **c :** to reduce the objective of

1**low·er·case** \,lō(-ə)r-'kās\ *adj* [fr. the compositor's practice of keeping such types in the lower of a pair of type cases] *of a letter* **:** having as its typical form a f g or *b n i* rather than A F G or *B N I* — **lowercase** *n*

2**lowercase** *vt* **:** to print or set in lowercase letters

lower class *n* **:** a social class occupying a position below the middle class and having the lowest status in a society

low·er·class·man \,lō(-ə)r-'klas-mən\ *n* **:** UNDERCLASSMAN

lower criticism *n* **:** textual criticism of the Bible

lower fungus *n* **:** a fungus with hyphae absent or rudimentary and nonseptate

low·er·most \'lō(-ə)r-,mōst\ *adj* **:** LOWEST

low·ery \'laü-(ə-)rē\ *adj* **:** GLOOMY, LOWERING

lowest common multiple *n* **1 :** the smallest common multiple of two or more numbers **2 :** the common multiple of lowest degree of two or more polynomials

low frequency *n* **:** a radio frequency in the next to lowest range of the radio spectrum — see RADIO FREQUENCY table

Low German *n* **1 :** the German dialects of northern Germany esp. as used since the end of the medieval period **:** PLATTDEUTSCH **2 :** the West Germanic languages other than High German

low-key \'lō-'kē\ *adj* **1 :** of low intensity **:** RESTRAINED **2 :** having or producing dark tones only with little contrast

low·land \-lənd, -,land\ *n* **:** low or level country — **lowland** *adj*

low·land·er \-lən-dər, -,lan-\ *n* **1 :** a native or inhabitant of a lowland region **2** *cap* **:** an inhabitant of the Lowlands of Scotland

Low Latin *n* **:** postclassical Latin in its later stages

low-lev·el \'lō-'lev-əl\ *adj* **1 :** being of low importance or rank **2 :** occurring, done, or placed at a low level

low·li·head \'lō-lē-,hed\ *n* [ME *lowliheed*, fr. *lowly* + *-hed* -hood; akin to ME *-hod* -hood] *archaic* **:** lowly state

low·li·ness \-lē-nəs\ *n* **:** the quality or state of being lowly

low-low \'lō-'lō\ *adj* **:** slower than ordinary low gear and thereby adapted to heavy loads or steep grades — **low-low** *n*

1**low·ly** \'lō-lē\ *adv* **1 :** HUMBLY, MEEKLY **2 :** in a low position, manner, or degree **3 :** not loudly

2**lowly** *adj* **1 :** MODEST, MEEK **2 :** of or relating to a low social or economic rank **3 :** low in the scale of biological or cultural evolution **4 :** ranking low in some hierarchy **5 :** not lofty or sublime **:** PROSAIC **syn** see HUMBLE

low mass *n, often cap L&M* **:** a mass that is not sung but said in the simplest ceremonial form

low–mind·ed \'lō-'mīn-dəd\ *adj* **:** inclined to low or unworthy things — **low–mind·ed·ly** *adv* — **low–mind·ed·ness** *n*

lown \'laün, 'lün\ *adj* [ME (Sc) *lowne*] *dial* **:** CALM, QUIET

low–necked \'lō-'nekt\ *or* **low–neck** \-,nek\ *adj* **:** DÉCOLLETÉ 2

low–pres·sure \'lō-'presh-ər\ *adj* **1 :** having, exerting, or operating under a relatively small pressure **2 :** EASYGOING

low relief *n* **:** BAS-RELIEF

low–spir·it·ed \'lō-'spir-ət-əd\ *adj* **:** DEJECTED, DEPRESSED — **low–spir·it·ed·ly** *adv* — **low–spir·it·ed·ness** *n*

Low Sunday *n* **:** the Sunday following Easter

low–ten·sion \'lō-'ten-chən\ *adj* **1 :** having a low potential or voltage **2 :** constructed to be used at low voltage

low–test \-'test\ *adj* **:** having a low volatility ⟨~ gasoline⟩

low tide *n* **:** the farthest ebb of the tide

low water *n* **:** a low stage of the water in a river or lake; *also* **:** LOW TIDE

1**lox** \'läks\ *n* [*l*iquid *ox*ygen] **:** liquid oxygen

2**lox** *n, pl* **lox** *or* **lox·es** [Yiddish *laks,* fr. MHG *lahs* salmon] **:** smoked salmon

loxo·drome \'läk-sə-,drōm\ *n* [ISV, back-formation fr. *loxodromic*] **:** RHUMB LINE

loxo·drom·ic \,läk-sə-'dräm-ik\ *adj* [prob. fr. (assumed) NL *loxodromicus,* fr. Gk *loxos* oblique + *dromos* course; akin to L *ulna* elbow] **:** relating to a rhumb line or to sailing on rhumb lines — **loxo·drom·i·cal·ly** \-i-k(ə-)lē\ *adv*

loy·al \'lȯi(-ə)l\ *adj* [MF, fr. OF *leial, leel,* fr. L *legalis* legal] **1 a :** faithful in allegiance to one's lawful government **b :** faithful to a private person to whom fidelity is held to be due **2 :** showing loyalty **3 :** faithful to a cause, ideal, or custom **4** *obs* **:** LAWFUL, LEGITIMATE **syn** see FAITHFUL — **loy·al·ly** \'lȯi-ə-lē\ *adv*

loy·al·ist \'lȯi-ə-ləst\ *n* **:** one who is or remains loyal to a political cause, party, government, or sovereign; *esp* **:** TORY 4

loy·al·ty \'lȯi(-ə)l-tē\ *n, often attrib* [ME *loyaltee,* fr. MF *loialté,* fr. OF *leialté,* fr. *leial*] **:** the quality or state of being loyal **syn** see FIDELITY

loz·enge \'läz-ᵊnj\ *n* [ME *losenge,* fr. MF *losange*] **1 :** a figure with four equal sides and two acute and two obtuse angles **:** DIAMOND **2 :** something shaped like a lozenge; *specif* **:** a small often medicated candy

LP \'el-'pē\ *trademark* — used for a microgroove phonograph record turning at 33⅓ revolutions per minute

LSD \,el-,es-'dē\ *n* [*lys*ergic acid *d*iethylamide] **:** a complex organic compound that induces psychotic symptoms similar to those of schizophrenia — called also *lysergic acid diethylamide*

lu·au \'lü-,aü\ *n* [Hawaiian *lu'au*] **:** a Hawaiian feast

lub·ber \'ləb-ər\ *n* [ME *lobre, lobur*] **1 :** a big clumsy fellow **2 :** a clumsy seaman — **lubber** *adj* — **lub·ber·li·ness** \-lē-nəs\ *n* — **lub·ber·ly** \-lē\ *adj or adv*

lubber line *n* **:** a fixed line on the compass of a ship or airplane that is aligned with the longitudinal axis

lubber's hole *n* **:** a hole in a ship's top near the mast through which one may go farther aloft without going over the rim by the futtock shrouds

lube \'lüb\ *n* [short for *lubricating oil*] **:** LUBRICANT

lu·bric \'lü-brik\ *adj* [MF *lubrique,* fr. ML *lubricus*] *archaic* **:** LUBRICIOUS — **lu·bri·cal** \-bri-kəl\ *adj*

lu·bri·cant \'lü-bri-kənt\ *n* **1 :** a substance capable of reducing friction, heat, and wear when introduced as a film between solid surfaces **2 :** something that lessens or prevents friction or difficulty — **lubricant** *adj*

lu·bri·cate \'lü-brə-,kāt\ *vb* [L *lubricatus,* pp. of *lubricare* fr. *lubricus* slippery — more at SLEEVE] *vt* **1 :** to make smooth or slippery **2 :** to apply a lubricant to ~ *vi* **:** to act as a lubricant — **lu·bri·ca·tion** \,lü-brə-'kā-shən\ *n* — **lu·bri·ca·tive** \'lü-brə-,kāt-iv\ *adj* — **lu·bri·ca·tor** \-,kāt-ər\ *n*

lu·bri·cious \lü-'brish-əs\ *or* **lu·bri·cous** \'lü-bri-kəs\ *adj* [ML *lubricus,* fr. L, slippery, easily led astray] **1 :** marked by wantonness **:** LECHEROUS; *also* **:** SALACIOUS **2** [L *lubricus*] **a :** having a smooth or slippery quality ⟨a ~ skin⟩ **b :** marked by uncertainty or instability **:** SHIFTY — **lu·bri·cious·ly** *adv* — **lu·bric·i·ty** \lü-'bris-ət-ē\ *n*

lu·bri·to·ri·um \,lü-brə-'tōr-ē-əm, -'tȯr-\ *n* [*lubri*cate + *-torium* (as in *sanatorium*)] **:** a station for lubricating motor vehicles

Lu·can \'lü-kən\ *adj* [LL *lucanus,* fr. *Lucas* Luke, fr. Gk *Loukas*] **:** of or relating to Luke or the Gospel ascribed to him

lu·carne \lü-'kärn\ *n* [F] **:** DORMER

lu·cen·cy \'lüs-ᵊn-sē\ *n* **:** the quality or state of being lucent

lu·cent \-ᵊnt\ *adj* [L *lucent-, lucens,* prp. of *lucēre* to shine — more at LIGHT] **1 :** glowing with light **:** LUMINOUS **2 :** marked by clarity or translucence **:** CLEAR — **lu·cent·ly** *adv*

lu·cern \lü-'sərn\ *n* [prob. modif. of G *lüchsern* of a lynx, fr. *luchs* lynx] *obs* **:** LYNX

lu·cerne *also* **lu·cern** \lü-'sərn\ *n* [F *luzerne,* fr. Prov *luserno*] *chiefly Brit* **:** ALFALFA

lu·cid \'lü-səd\ *adj* [L *lucidus;* akin to L *lucēre*] **1 a :** suffused with light **:** LUMINOUS **b :** TRANSLUCENT **2 :** having full use of one's faculties **:** SANE **3 :** clear to the understanding **:** INTELLIGIBLE **syn** see CLEAR — **lu·cid·ly** *adv* — **lu·cid·ness** *n*

lu·cid·i·ty \lü-'sid-ət-ē\ *n* **1 :** clearness of thought or style **2 :** a presumed capacity to perceive the truth directly and instantaneously **:** CLAIRVOYANCE

Lu·ci·fer \'lü-sə-fər\ *n* [ME, the morning star, a fallen rebel archangel, the Devil, fr. OE, fr. L, the morning star, fr. *lucifer* light-bearing, fr. *luc-, lux* light + *-fer* -ferous — more at LIGHT] **1 :** DEVIL **2 :** the planet Venus when appearing as the morning star **3** *not cap* **:** a friction match having as active substances antimony sulfide and potassium chlorate

lu·cif·er·ase \lü-'sif-ə-,rās, -,rāz\ *n* [ISV, fr. *luciferin*] **:** an enzyme that catalyzes the oxidation of luciferin

lu·cif·er·in \-(ə-)rən\ *n* [ISV, fr. L *lucifer* light-bearing] **:** a pigment in luminescent organisms that furnishes practically heatless light in undergoing oxidation

lu·cif·er·ous \lü-'sif-(ə-)rəs\ *adj* [L *lucifer*] *archaic* **:** bringing light or insight **:** ILLUMINATING

Lu·ci·na \lü-'sī-nə\ *n* [L, Roman goddess of childbirth] *archaic* **:** MIDWIFE

Lu·cite \'lü-,sīt\ *trademark* — used for an acrylic resin or plastic consisting essentially of polymerized methyl methacrylate

luck \'lək\ *n* [ME *lucke,* fr. MD *luc;* akin to MHG *gelücke* luck] **1 a :** a force that brings good fortune or adversity **b :** the events or circumstances that operate for or against an individual **2 :** favoring chance; *also* **:** SUCCESS — **luck·less** \-ləs\ *adj*

luck·i·ly \'lək-ə-lē\ *adv* **:** in a lucky manner **:** FORTUNATELY

luck·i·ness \'lək-ē-nəs\ *n* **:** the quality or state of being lucky

lucky \'lək-ē\ *adj* **1 :** having good luck **2 :** happening by chance **:** FORTUITOUS **3 :** producing or resulting in good by chance **:** FAVORABLE **4 :** seeming to bring good luck

syn LUCKY, FORTUNATE, HAPPY, PROVIDENTIAL mean meeting with unforeseen success. LUCKY stresses the agency of chance in bringing about a favorable result; FORTUNATE suggests being rewarded beyond one's deserts; HAPPY combines the implications of LUCKY and FORTUNATE with stress on being blessed; PROVIDENTIAL more definitely implies the help or intervention of a higher power

lu·cra·tive \'lü-krət-iv\ *adj* [ME *lucratif,* fr. MF, fr. L *lucrativus,* fr. *lucratus* pp. of *lucrari* to gain, fr. *lucrum*] **:** producing wealth **:** PROFITABLE — **lu·cra·tive·ly** *adv* — **lu·cra·tive·ness** *n*

lu·cre \'lü-kər\ *n* [ME, fr. L *lucrum;* akin to OE *lēan* reward, OHG *lōn,* Gk *leia* booty] **:** monetary gain **:** PROFIT; *also* **:** MONEY

lu·cu·brate \'lü-k(y)ə-,brāt\ *vi* [back-formation fr. *lucubration*] **:** to write learnedly **:** EXPATIATE — **lu·cu·bra·tor** \-,brāt-ər\ *n*

lu·cu·bra·tion \,lü-k(y)ə-'brā-shən\ *n* [L *lucubration-, lucubratio* study by night, work produced at night, fr. *lucubratus,* pp. of *lucubrare* to work by lamplight; akin to L *luc-* *lux*] **1 :** laborious study **:** MEDITATION **2 :** studied or pretentious expression in speech or writing

lu·cu·lent \'lü-kyə-lənt\ *adj* [ME, fr. L *luculentus,* fr. *luc-, lux* light] **:** clear in thought or expression **:** LUCID — **lu·cu·lent·ly** *adv*

Lu·cul·lan \lü-'kəl-ən\ *or* **Lu·cul·li·an** \-'kəl-ē-ən\ *adj* **1 :** of or relating to Lucullus **2 :** LAVISH, LUXURIOUS ⟨a ~ feast⟩

Ludd·ite \'ləd-,īt\ *n* [Ned *Ludd fl* 1779 half-witted Leicestershire workman] **:** one of a group of early 19th century English workmen destroying laborsaving machinery as a protest

lu·di·crous \'lüd-ə-krəs\ *adj* [L *ludicrus,* fr. *ludus* play, sport; akin to L *ludere* to play, Gk *loidoros* abusive] **1 :** amusing or laughable through obvious absurdity, incongruity, exaggeration, or eccentricity **2 :** meriting derisive laughter or scorn as absurdly inept, false, or foolish **syn** see LAUGHABLE — **lu·di·crous·ly** *adv* — **lu·di·crous·ness** *n*

lu·es \'lü-(,)ēz\ *n, pl* **lues** [NL, fr. L, plague; akin to Gk *lyein* to loosen, destroy — more at LOSE] **:** SYPHILIS — **lu·et·ic** \lü-'et-ik\ *adj* — **lu·et·i·cal·ly** \-i-k(ə-)lē\ *adv*

Luf·bery circle \,ləf-,ber-ē-, -bə-rē-\ *n* [Raoul *Lufbery* †1918 Am aviator] **:** a military flying formation or maneuver in which two or more airplanes follow each other closely in circular line or ascending spiral

1**luff** \'ləf\ *n* [ME, weather side of a ship, luff, fr. MF *lof* weather side of ship] **1 a :** the act of sailing a ship closer to the wind **b :** the forward edge of a fore-and-aft sail **2 :** a radial or in-and-out movement of the load being carried by a crane produced by raising or lowering the jib

2**luff** *vi* **1 :** to sail nearer the wind **2 :** to move the jib of a crane in and out

1**lug** \'ləg\ *vb* **lugged; lug·ging** [ME *luggen* to pull by the hair or ear, drag, prob. of Scand origin; akin to Norw *lugga* to pull by the hair] *vt* **1 :** DRAG, PULL **2 :** to carry laboriously **3 :** to introduce in a forced manner ⟨~ a story into the conversation⟩ ~ *vi* **1 :** to pull with effort **:** TUG **2 :** to move heavily or by jerks

2**lug** *n* **1** *archaic* **a :** an act of lugging **b :** something that is lugged **2** *pl* **:** superior airs or affectations ⟨put on ~*s*⟩ **3 :** LUGSAIL **4** *slang* **:** an exaction of money — used in the phrase *put the lug on*

3**lug** *n* [ME (Sc) *lugge,* perh. fr. ME *luggen*] **1** *chiefly dial* **:** EAR **2 :** something (as a handle) that projects like an ear **3 :** a leather loop on a harness saddle through which the shaft passes **4 :** a fitting of copper or brass to which electrical wires are soldered or connected **5 :** BLOCKHEAD, LOUT

lug·gage \'ləg-ij\ *n* **:** something that is lugged; *esp* **:** suitcases or traveling bags containing a traveler's belongings **:** BAGGAGE

lug·ger \'ləg-ər\ *n* [*lugsail*] **:** a small fishing or coasting boat that carries one or more lugsails

lug·gie \'ləg-ē\ *n* [3*lug*] *chiefly Scot* **:** a small wooden pail or dish with a handle

lug·sail \'ləg-,sāl, -səl\ *n* [perh. fr. 3*lug*] **:** a four-sided sail bent to a yard that hangs obliquely on a mast and is hoisted and lowered with the sail

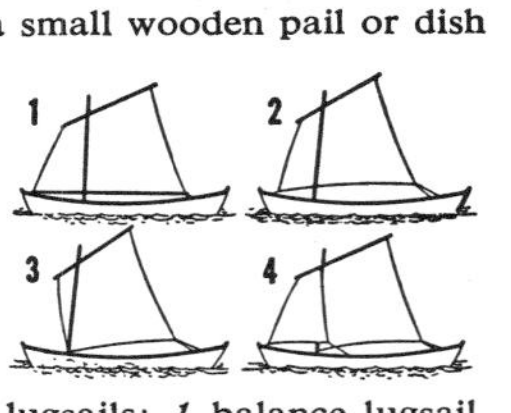

lugsails: *1* balance lugsail, *2* dipping lug, *3* standing lug, *4* split lug

lu·gu·bri·ous \lü-'gü-brē-əs *also* -'gyü-\ *adj* [L *lugubris,* fr. *lugēre* to mourn; akin to Gk *lygros* mournful] **:** MOURNFUL; *esp* **:** exaggeratedly or affectedly mournful — **lu·gu·bri·ous·ly** *adv* — **lu·gu·bri·ous·ness** *n*

lug·worm \'ləg-,wərm\ *n* [origin unknown] **:** any of a genus (*Arenicola*) of marine polychaete worms that have a row of tufted gills along each side of the back and are used for bait

Lukan *var of* LUCAN

Luke \'lük\ *n* [L *Lucas,* fr. Gk *Loukas*] **:** a physician and companion of the apostle Paul believed to be the author of the third Gospel in the New Testament and of the Book of Acts

luke·warm \'lü-'kwȯ(ə)rm\ *adj* [ME, fr. *luke* lukewarm + *warm;* akin to OHG *lāo* lukewarm — more at LEE] **1 :** moderately warm **:** TEPID **2 :** lacking conviction **:** HALFHEARTED — **luke·warm·ly** *adv* — **luke·warm·ness** *n*

1**lull** \'ləl\ *vt* [ME *lullen;* prob. of imit. origin] **1 :** to cause to sleep or rest **:** SOOTHE **2 :** to cause to relax vigilance

2**lull** *n* **1** *archaic* **:** something that lulls; *esp* **:** LULLABY **2 :** a temporary calm before or during a storm **3 :** a temporary drop in activity

1**lul·la·by** \'ləl-ə-,bī\ *n* [obs. E *lulla,* interj. used to lull a child (fr. ME) + *bye,* interj. used to lull a child, fr. ME *by*] **:** a song to quiet children or lull them to sleep

2**lullaby** *vt* **:** to quiet with a lullaby

lu·lu \'lü-(,)lü\ *n* [prob. fr. *Lulu,* nickname fr. *Louise*] *slang* **:** one that is remarkable or wonderful

lum \'ləm\ *n* [origin unknown] *chiefly Scot* **:** CHIMNEY

lumb- *or* **lumbo-** *comb form* [L *lumbus* loin — more at LOIN] **:** lumbar and ⟨*lumbo*sacral⟩
lum·ba·go \ˌləm-ˈbā-(ˌ)gō\ *n* [L, fr. *lumbus*] **:** usu. painful muscular rheumatism involving the lumbar region
lum·bar \ˈləm-bər, -ˌbär\ *adj* [NL *lumbaris*, fr. L *lumbus*] **:** of, relating to, or constituting the loins or the vertebrae between the thoracic vertebrae and sacrum
¹**lum·ber** \ˈləm-bər\ *vi* **lum·ber·ing** \-b(ə-)riŋ\ [ME *lomeren*] **:** to move heavily or clumsily; *also* **:** RUMBLE
²**lumber** *n* [perh. fr. *Lombard;* fr. the use of pawnshops as storehouses of disused property] **1 :** surplus or disused articles (as furniture) that are stored away **2 a :** timber or logs esp. when dressed for use **b :** any of various structural materials prepared in a form similar to lumber — **lumber** *adj*
³**lumber** *vb* **lum·ber·ing** \-b(ə-)riŋ\ *vt* **1 :** to clutter with or as if with lumber **:** ENCUMBER **2 :** to heap together in disorder **3 :** to log and saw the timber of ~ *vi* **1 :** to cut logs for lumber **2 :** to saw logs into lumber for the market — **lum·ber·er** \-bər-ər\ *n* — **lum·ber·man** \-bər-mən\ *n*
lum·ber·jack \ˈləm-bər-ˌjak\ *n* **:** LOGGER
lum·ber·yard \-ˌyärd\ *n* **:** a yard where a stock of lumber is kept for sale
lum·bri·coid \ˈləm-bri-ˌkȯid\ *n* [L *lumbricus* earthworm] **:** a creature (as an ascarid) that resembles an earthworm
lu·men \ˈlü-mən\ *n, pl* **lu·mi·na** \-mə-nə\ *or* **lumens** [NL *lumin-, lumen*, fr. L, light, airshaft, opening] **1 :** the cavity of a tubular organ ⟨the ~ of a blood vessel⟩ **2 :** the bore of a tube (as of a hollow needle or catheter) **3 :** a unit of luminous flux equal to the light emitted in a unit solid angle by a uniform point source of one candle — **lu·mi·nal** *also* **lu·men·al** \-mən-ᵊl\ *adj*
lumin- *or* **lumini-** *or* **lumino-** *comb form* [ME *lumin-*, fr. L *lumin-, lumen*] **:** light ⟨*lumini*ferous⟩
lu·mi·naire \ˌlü-mə-ˈna(ə)r, -ˈne(ə)r\ *n* [F, lamp, lighting] **:** a complete lighting unit
Lu·mi·nal \ˈlü-mə-ˌnal, -ˌnȯl\ *trademark* — used for phenobarbital
lu·mi·nance \ˈlü-mə-nən(t)s\ *n* **1 :** the quality or state of being luminous **2 :** the luminous intensity of a surface in a given direction per unit of projected area
lu·mi·nary \ˈlü-mə-ˌner-ē\ *n* [ME *luminarye*, fr. MF & LL; MF *luminaire* lamp, fr. LL *luminaria*, pl. of *luminare* lamp, heavenly body, fr. L, window, fr. *lumin-, lumen* light; akin to L *lucēre* to shine — more at LIGHT] **1 :** one who is notable in his chosen field **2 :** an artificial light **3 :** a body that gives light; *esp* **:** one of the heavenly bodies — **luminary** *adj*
lu·mine \ˈlü-mən\ *vt* [ME *luminen* to illuminate (a manuscript) — more at LIMN] **:** ILLUMINE
lu·mi·nesce \ˌlü-mə-ˈnes\ *vi* [back-formation fr. *luminescent*] **:** to exhibit luminescence
lu·mi·nes·cence \ˌlü-mə-ˈnes-ᵊn(t)s\ *n* **1 :** an emission of light that is not ascribable directly to incandescence and therefore occurs at low temperatures and that is produced by physiological processes (as in the firefly), by chemical action, by friction, or by electrical action **2 :** the light produced by luminescence
lu·mi·nes·cent \-ᵊnt\ *adj* **:** relating to, exhibiting, or adapted for the production of luminescence
lu·mi·nif·er·ous \ˌlü-mə-ˈnif-(ə-)rəs\ *adj* **:** transmitting, producing, or yielding light
lu·mi·nist \ˈlü-mə-nəst\ *n* [F *luministe*, fr. L *lumin-, lumen*] **:** a painter who makes a specialty of the effects of light on colored objects
lu·mi·nos·i·ty \ˌlü-mə-ˈnäs-ət-ē\ *n* **1 a :** the quality or state of being luminous **b :** something luminous **2 a :** the relative quantity of light **b :** BRIGHTNESS **3 :** the luminous efficiency of radiant energy
lu·mi·nous \ˈlü-mə-nəs\ *adj* [ME, fr. L *luminosus*, fr. *lumin-, lumen*] **1 :** emitting light **:** SHINING **2 :** LIGHTED ⟨a public square ~ with sunlight⟩ **3 :** ENLIGHTENED, INTELLIGENT; *also* **:** CLEAR, INTELLIGIBLE **syn** see BRIGHT — **lu·mi·nous·ly** *adv* — **lu·mi·nous·ness** *n*
luminous energy *n* **:** energy transferred in the form of visible radiation
luminous flux *n* **:** radiant flux in the visible-wavelength range usu. expressed in lumens instead of watts
luminous paint *n* **:** a paint containing a phosphor (as zinc sulfide activated with copper) and so able to glow in the dark
lum·mox \ˈləm-əks\ *n* [origin unknown] **:** a clumsy person
¹**lump** \ˈləmp\ *n* [ME] **1 :** a piece or mass of indefinite size and shape **2 a :** AGGREGATE, TOTALITY ⟨taken in the ~⟩ **b :** MAJORITY **3 :** PROTUBERANCE; *esp* **:** an abnormal swelling **4 :** a thickset heavy person; *specif* **:** one who is stupid or dull **5** *pl* **a :** BEATINGS ⟨on the back waterways the single small craft takes its ~*s* —A.W. Baum⟩ **b :** COMEUPPANCE
²**lump** *vt* **1 :** to group without discrimination **2 :** to make into lumps; *also* **:** to make lumps on or in **3 :** to move noisily and clumsily ~ *vi* **1 :** to become formed into lumps **2 :** to move oneself noisily and clumsily
³**lump** *vt* [origin unknown] **:** to put up with ⟨like it or ~ it⟩
lum·pen \ˈlüm-pən\ *adj* [G *lumpenproletariat* degraded and contemptible section of the proletariat, fr. *lump* contemptible person + *proletariat*] **:** of or relating to dispossessed and uprooted individuals cut off from the economic and social class with which they might normally be identified ⟨~ proletariat⟩ ⟨~ intellectuals⟩
lump·er \ˈləm-pər\ *n* **:** a laborer employed to handle freight or cargo
lump·i·ly \ˈləm-pə-lē\ *adv* **:** in a lumpy manner
lump·i·ness \-pē-nəs\ *n* **:** the quality or state of being lumpy
lump·ish \-pish\ *adj* **1 :** DULL, SLUGGISH **2** *obs* **:** low in spirits **:** DEJECTED **3 :** HEAVY, AWKWARD **4 :** LUMPY 1 **5 a :** sounding dull or heavy **b :** TEDIOUS, PEDANTIC — **lump·ish·ly** *adv* — **lump·ish·ness** *n*
lumpy \-pē\ *adj* **1 a :** filled or covered with lumps **b :** characterized by choppy waves **2 :** having a thickset clumsy appearance **3 :** uneven and often crude in style
lumpy jaw *n* **:** ACTINOMYCOSIS; *esp* **:** actinomycosis of the head in cattle
lu·na \ˈlü-nə\ *n* [ME, fr. ML, fr. L, moon] **:** SILVER — used in alchemy
lu·na·cy \ˈlü-nə-sē\ *n* [*lunatic*] **1 a :** insanity interrupted by lucid intervals **b :** any of various forms of insanity **c :** insanity amounting to lack of capacity or of responsibility in the eyes of the law **2 :** wild foolishness **:** extravagant folly **syn** see INSANITY
lu·na moth \ˌlü-nə-\ *n* [NL *luna* (specific epithet of *Actias luna*), fr. L, moon] **:** a large mostly pale green American moth (*Actias luna*) with long tails to the hind wings
lu·nar \ˈlü-nər\ *adj* [L *lunaris*, fr. *luna* moon; akin to L *lucēre* to shine — more at LIGHT] **1 a :** of or relating to the moon **b :** ORBED, CRESCENT **c :** measured by the moon's revolution ⟨~ month⟩ **2** [*luna*] **:** relating to or containing silver
lunar caustic *n* **:** silver nitrate fused and molded into sticks for use as a caustic
lunar eclipse *n* **:** an eclipse in which the moon near the full phase passes partially or wholly through the umbra of the earth's shadow
lu·nate \ˈlü-ˌnāt\ *adj* [L *lunatus*, pp. of *lunare* to bend in a crescent, fr. *luna*] **:** shaped like a crescent — **lu·nate·ly** *adv*
lu·na·tic \ˈlü-nə-ˌtik\ *adj* [ME *lunatik*, fr. OF or LL; OF *lunatique*, fr. LL *lunaticus*, fr. L *luna;* fr. the belief that lunacy fluctuated with the phases of the moon] **1 a :** affected with lunacy **:** INSANE **b :** designed for the care of insane persons ⟨~ asylum⟩ **2 :** wildly foolish **:** GIDDY — **lunatic** *n*
lunatic fringe *n* **:** an extreme or wild group on the periphery of a larger group; *esp* **:** the members of a political or social movement espousing extreme, eccentric, or fanatical views
lu·na·tion \lü-ˈnā-shən\ *n* [ME *lunacioun*, fr. ML *lunation-, lunatio*, fr. L *luna*] **:** the period of time averaging 29 days, 12 hours, 44 minutes, and 2.8 seconds elapsing between two successive new moons
¹**lunch** \ˈlənch\ *n* [prob. short for *luncheon*] **1 :** a light meal; *esp* **:** one taken in the middle of the day **2 :** the food prepared for a lunch
²**lunch** *vi* **:** to eat lunch ~ *vt* **:** to provide lunch for — **lunch·er** *n*
lun·cheon \ˈlən-chən\ *n* [perh. alter. of *nuncheon* (light snack)] **1** *archaic* **:** a piece of food **:** CHUNK **2 a :** a light meal at midday **:** LUNCH **b :** a light meal eaten in company
lun·cheon·ette \ˌlən-chə-ˈnet\ *n* **:** a place where light lunches are sold
lunch·room \ˈlənch-ˌrüm, -ˌrům\ *n* **:** a small restaurant specializing in food ready to serve or quickly prepared
lunes \ˈlünz\ *n pl* [F, pl. of *lune* crazy whim, fr. MF, moon, crazy whim, fr. L *luna*] **:** fits of lunacy
lu·nette \lü-ˈnet\ *n* [F, fr. OF *lunete* small object shaped like the moon, fr. *lune* moon] **1 a :** an opening in a vault esp. for a window **b :** the surface at the upper part of a wall that is partly surrounded by a vault which the wall intersects and that is often filled by windows or by mural painting **2 :** a temporary fortification consisting of two faces forming a salient angle and two parallel flanks **3 :** the figure or shape of a crescent moon
lung \ˈləŋ\ *n* [ME *lunge*, fr. OE *lungen;* akin to OHG *lungun* lung, *līhti* light in weight — more at LIGHT] **1 a :** one of the usu. paired compound saccular thoracic organs that constitute the basic respiratory organ of air-breathing vertebrates **b :** any of various respiratory organs of invertebrates **2 a :** a device enabling individuals abandoning a submarine to rise to the surface **b :** a mechanical device for regularly introducing fresh air into and withdrawing stale air from the lung **:** RESPIRATOR
¹**lunge** \ˈlənj\ *vb* [by shortening & alter. fr. obs. *allonge* (to make a thrust with a sword)] *vt* **:** to thrust or push with a lunge ~ *vi* **:** to make a thrust or a forceful forward movement
²**lunge** *n* **1 :** a sudden thrust or pass (as with a sword or foil) **2 :** the act of plunging forward
lunged \ˈləŋd\ *adj* **1 :** having lungs **:** PULMONATE **2 :** having such or so many lungs ⟨one-*lunged*⟩
¹**lung·er** \ˈlən-jər\ *n* **:** one that lunges
²**lung·er** \ˈləŋ-ər\ *n* **:** one suffering from a chronic disease of the lungs; *esp* **:** one that is tubercular
lung·fish \ˈləŋ-ˌfish\ *n* **:** any of various fishes (order Dipneusti or Cladistia) that breathe by a modified air bladder as well as gills
lung·wort \ˈləŋ-ˌwərt, -ˌwȯ(ə)rt\ *n* **:** any of several plants (as a mullein or black hellebore) formerly used in the treatment of respiratory disorders; *esp* **:** a European herb (*Pulmonaria officinalis*) of the borage family with hispid leaves and bluish flowers
lu·ni·so·lar \ˌlü-ni-ˈsō-lər\ *adj* [L *luna* moon + E *-i-* + *solar*] **:** relating or attributed to the moon and the sun
lu·ni·tid·al \-ˈtīd-ᵊl\ *adj* [L *luna* + E *-i-* + *tidal*] **:** relating to tidal movements dependent on the moon
lunitidal interval *n* **:** the interval between the transit of the moon and the time of the lunar high tide next following
lun·ker \ˈləŋ-kər\ *n* [origin unknown] **:** something large of its kind — used esp. of a fish
lunk·head \ˈləŋk-ˌhed\ *n* [prob. alter. of *lump* + *head*] **:** a dull-witted person **:** DOLT — **lunk·head·ed** \-ˈhed-əd\ *adj*
lunt \ˈlənt\ *n* [D *lont*] **1** *chiefly Scot* **:** SLOW MATCH; *also* **:** TORCH **2** *chiefly Scot* **:** SMOKE; *also* **:** hot vapor
lu·nu·late \ˈlü-nyə-ˌlāt\ *adj* **:** resembling a small crescent; *also* **:** having crescent-shaped markings
lu·nule \ˈlü-(ˌ)nyü(ə)l\ *n* [NL *lunula*, fr. L, crescent-shaped ornament, fr. dim. of *luna* moon] **:** a crescent-shaped body part or marking (as the whitish mark at the base of a fingernail)
lu·ny \ˈlü-nē\ *var of* LOONY
lu·pa·nar \lü-ˈpā-nər, -ˈpän-ər\ *n* [L, fr. *lupa* prostitute, lit., she-wolf, fem. of *lupus*] **:** BROTHEL
Lu·per·ca·lia \ˌlü-pər-ˈkā-lē-ə, -ˈkāl-yə\ *n* [L, pl., fr. *Lupercus*, god of flocks] **:** an ancient Roman festival celebrated February 15 to ensure fertility for the people, fields, and flocks — **Lu·per·ca·lian** \-ˈkā-lē-ən, -ˈkāl-yən\ *adj*
¹**lu·pine** \ˈlü-pən\ *n* [ME, fr. L *lupinus, lupinum*, fr. *lupinus*, adj.] **:** any of a genus (*Lupinus*) of leguminous herbs some of which are poisonous and others cultivated for green manure, fodder, or their edible seeds; *also* **:** an edible lupine seed (as of the European *L. albus*)
²**lu·pine** \-ˌpīn\ *adj* [L *lupinus*, fr. *lupus* wolf — more at WOLF] **:** WOLFISH
lu·pu·lin \ˈlü-pyə-lən\ *n* [NL *lupulus* (specific epithet of the hop plant *Humulus lupulus*), fr. dim. of L *lupus* wolf, hop] **:** a fine

yellow resinous powder on the strobiles of hops having the characteristic hop flavor and odor

lu·pus \'lü-pəs\ *n* [ML, fr. L, wolf] **:** any of several diseases characterized by skin lesions; *esp* **:** LUPUS VULGARIS

lupus vul·gar·is \,lü-pəs-,vəl-'gar-əs, -'ger-\ *n* [NL, lit., common lupus] **:** tuberculous disease of the skin marked by formation of soft brownish nodules with ulceration and scarring

1**lurch** \'lərch\ *vb* [ME *lorchen*, prob. alter. of *lurken* to lurk] *vi, dial chiefly Eng* **:** to loiter about a place furtively **:** PROWL ~ *vt* **1** *obs* **:** to obtain by fraud or stealth **:** STEAL **2** *archaic* **:** to do out of something **:** CHEAT

2**lurch** *n, archaic* **:** an act of lurching **:** a state of watchful readiness

3**lurch** *n* [MF *lourche*, adj., defeated by a lurch, deceived] **1** *obs* **:** an act or instance of discomfiture **:** SETBACK **2 :** a decisive defeat in which an opponent wins a game by more than double the defeated player's score esp. in cribbage — **in the lurch :** in a vulnerable and unsupported position

4**lurch** *vt* **1 :** to defeat by a lurch (as in cribbage) **2** *archaic* **:** to leave in the lurch

5**lurch** *n* [origin unknown] **1 :** a sudden roll of a ship to one side **2 :** an act or instance of swaying or tipping; *esp* **:** a staggering gait

6**lurch** *vi* **:** to roll or tip abruptly **:** PITCH; *also* **:** STAGGER

lurch·er \'lər-chər\ *n* [1*lurch*] **1** *archaic* **:** a petty thief **:** PILFERER **2** *archaic* **:** LURKER, SPY **3** *Brit* **:** a mongrel dog; *esp* **:** one used by poachers

lur·dane \'lərd-ᵊn\ *n* [ME *lurdan*, fr. MF *lourdin* dullard, fr. *lourd* dull, stupid, fr. L *luridus* lurid] *archaic* **:** a lazy stupid person — **lurdane** *adj*

1**lure** \'lü(ə)r\ *n* [ME, fr. MF *loire*, of Gmc origin; akin to MHG *luoder* bait; akin to OE *lathian* to invite, OHG *ladōn*] **1 :** a bunch of feathers attached to a long cord and used by a falconer to recall a hawk **2 a :** an inducement to pleasure or gain **:** ENTICEMENT **b :** APPEAL, ATTRACTION **3 :** a decoy for attracting animals to capture; *esp* **:** artificial bait used for catching fish

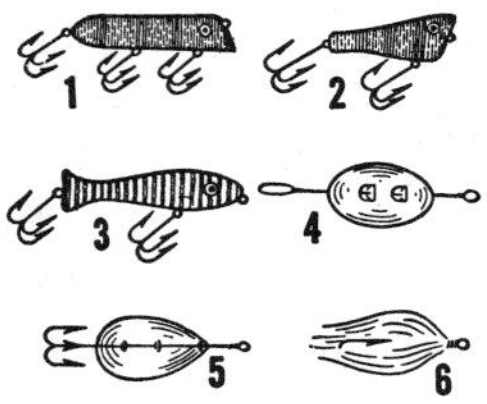

lures for fishing: *1* wiggler, *2* plunker, *3* minnow, *4* spinner, *5* spoon, *6* bucktail

2**lure** *vt* **1 :** to recall (a hawk) by means of a lure **2 :** to tempt with a promise of pleasure or gain **:** ENTICE — **lur·er** *n*

syn ENTICE, INVEIGLE, DECOY, TEMPT, SEDUCE: LURE implies a drawing into danger, evil, or difficulty through attracting and deceiving; ENTICE suggests drawing by artful or adroit means; INVEIGLE implies enticing by cajoling or flattering; DECOY implies a luring into entrapment by artifice; TEMPT implies the presenting of an attraction so strong that it overcomes the restraints of conscience or better judgment; SEDUCE implies a leading astray by persuasion or false promises

lu·rid \'lür-əd\ *adj* [L *luridus* pale yellow, sallow] **1 a :** wan and ghastly pale in appearance **:** LIVID **b :** of any of several light or medium grayish colors ranging in hue from yellow to orange **2 :** shining with the red glow of fire seen through smoke or cloud **3 a :** causing horror or revulsion **:** GRUESOME **b :** highly colored **:** SENSATIONAL **syn** see GHASTLY — **lu·rid·ly** *adv* — **lu·rid·ness** *n*

lurk \'lərk\ *vi* [ME *lurken;* akin to MHG *lūren* to lie in wait — more at LOWER] **1 a :** to lie in ambush **:** SKULK **b :** to move furtively or inconspicuously **:** SNEAK **c :** to persist in staying **2 a :** to be concealed but capable of being discovered; *specif* **:** to constitute a latent threat **b :** to lie hidden — **lurk·er** *n*

syn LURK, SKULK, SLINK, SNEAK mean to behave so as to escape attention. LURK implies a lying in wait in a place of concealment and suggests a readiness to attack; SKULK suggests more strongly cowardice or fear or sinister intent; SLINK implies moving stealthily often merely to escape attention; SNEAK may add an implication of entering or leaving a place or evading a difficulty by furtive, indirect, or underhanded methods

lus·cious \'ləsh-əs\ *adj* [ME *lucius*, perh. alter. of *licius*, short for *delicious*] **1 a :** having a delicious taste or smell **:** SWEET **b** *archaic* **:** excessively sweet **:** CLOYING **2 :** having sensual appeal **:** SEDUCTIVE **3 :** richly luxurious or appealing to the senses; *also* **:** FLORID — **lus·cious·ly** *adv* — **lus·cious·ness** *n*

1**lush** \'ləsh\ *adj* [ME *lusch* soft, tender] **1 a :** producing luxuriant foliage ⟨~ grass⟩ **b :** GREEN, FERTILE ⟨~ pastures⟩ **2 a :** THRIVING **b :** characterized by abundance **:** PLENTIFUL **c :** PROSPEROUS, PROFITABLE **3 a :** SAVORY, DELICIOUS **b :** SENSUOUS, VOLUPTUOUS **c :** OPULENT, SUMPTUOUS **syn** see PROFUSE — **lush·ly** *adv* — **lush·ness** *n*

2**lush** *n* [origin unknown] **1** *slang* **:** intoxicating liquor **:** DRINK **2 :** an habitual heavy drinker **:** DRUNKARD

3**lush** *vb, slang* **:** DRINK

1**lust** \'ləst\ *n* [ME, fr. OE; akin to OHG *lust* pleasure, L *lascivus* wanton] **1** *obs* **a :** PLEASURE, DELIGHT **b :** personal inclination **:** WISH **2 :** usu. intense sexual desire **:** LASCIVIOUSNESS **3 a :** an intense longing **:** CRAVING **b :** EAGERNESS, ENTHUSIASM

2**lust** *vi* **:** to have an intense desire or need **:** CRAVE; *specif* **:** to have a sexual urge

1**lus·ter** *or* **lus·tre** \'ləs-tər\ *n* [ME *lustre*, fr. L *lustrum*] **:** a period of five years **:** LUSTRUM 2

2**luster** *or* **lustre** *n* [MF *lustre*, fr. OIt *lustro*, fr. *lustrare* to brighten, fr. L; akin to L *lucēre* to shine — more at LIGHT] **1 :** a glow of reflected light **:** SHEEN; *specif* **:** the appearance of the surface of a mineral as to its reflecting qualities **2 a :** a glow of light from within **:** LUMINOSITY **b :** an inner beauty **:** RADIANCE **3 :** BRILLIANCE, DISTINCTION **4 a :** a glass pendant used esp. to ornament a candlestick or chandelier **b :** a decorative object (as a chandelier) hung with glass pendants **5** *chiefly Brit* **:** a fabric with cotton warp and a filling of wool, mohair, or alpaca **6 :** LUSTERWARE — **lus·ter·less** \-tər-ləs\ *adj*

3**luster** *or* **lustre** *vb* **lus·ter·ing** *or* **lus·tring** \-t(ə-)riŋ\ *vi* **:** to have luster **:** GLEAM ~ *vt* **1 :** to give luster or distinction to **2 :** to coat or treat with a substance that imparts luster

lus·ter·ware \'ləs-tər-,wa(ə)r, -,we(ə)r\ *n* **:** pottery decorated by applying to the glaze metallic compounds which become iridescent metallic films in the process of firing

lust·ful \'ləst-fəl\ *adj* **1 :** excited by lust **:** LECHEROUS **2** *archaic* **:** full of vigor or enthusiasm **:** LUSTY — **lust·ful·ly** \-fə-lē\ *adv* — **lust·ful·ness** *n*

lust·i·hood \'ləs-tē-,hüd\ *n* **1 :** vigor of body or spirit **:** ROBUSTNESS **2 :** sexual inclination or capacity

lust·i·ly \'ləs-tə-lē\ *adv* **:** in a lusty manner

lust·i·ness \-tē-nəs\ *n* **:** the quality or state of being lusty

lus·tral \'ləs-trəl\ *adj* [L *lustralis*, fr. *lustrum*] **1 :** PURIFICATORY **2** *archaic* **:** of or relating to a lustrum **:** QUINQUENNIAL

lus·trate \'ləs-,trāt\ *vt* [L *lustratus*, pp. of *lustrare* to brighten, purify] **:** to purify ceremonially — **lus·tra·tion** \,ləs-'trā-shən\ *n*

1**lus·tring** \'ləs-triŋ\ *n* [modif. of It *lustrino*] **:** LUTESTRING

2**lus·tring** \-t(ə-)riŋ\ *n* **:** a finishing process (as calendering) for giving a gloss to yarns and cloth

lus·trous \'ləs-trəs\ *adj* **1 :** having a gloss **:** SHINING **2 :** radiant in character or reputation **:** ILLUSTRIOUS **syn** see BRIGHT — **lus·trous·ly** *adv* — **lus·trous·ness** *n*

lus·trum \'ləs-trəm\ *n, pl* **lustrums** *or* **lus·tra** \-trə\ [L; akin to L *lustrare* to brighten, purify] **1 a :** a purification of the whole Roman people made in ancient times after the census every five years **b :** the Roman census **2 :** a period of five years **:** QUINQUENNIUM

lusty \'ləs-tē\ *adj* **1** *archaic* **:** MERRY, JOYOUS **2 :** LUSTFUL ⟨~ passion⟩ **3 :** full of vitality **:** ROBUST **4 :** full of strength **:** POWERFUL **syn** see VIGOROUS

lu·sus na·tu·rae \,lü-sə-snə-'t(y)ù(ə)r-(,)ē, -'tù(ə)r-,ī\ *n* [NL, lit., play of nature] **:** a sport or freak of nature

lu·ta·nist *or* **lu·te·nist** \'lüt-ᵊn-əst, 'lüt-nəst\ *n* [ML *lutanista*, fr. *lutana* lute, prob. fr. MF *lut*] **:** a lute player

1**lute** \'lüt\ *n* [ME, fr. MF *lut*, fr. OProv *laut*, fr. Ar *al-'ūd*, lit., the wood] **:** a stringed musical instrument with a large pear-shaped body, a neck with a fretted fingerboard, and a head with pegs for tuning

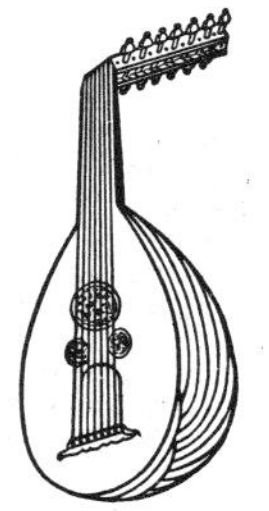
lute

2**lute** *vi* **:** to play a lute ~ *vt* **:** to play on a lute

3**lute** *n* [ME, fr. L *lutum* mud — more at POLLUTE] **:** a substance (as cement or clay) for packing a joint or coating a porous surface to make it impervious to gas or liquid

4**lute** *vt* **:** to seal or cover with lute

lute- *or* **luteo-** *comb form* [NL (*corpus*) *luteum*] **:** corpus luteum ⟨*luteal*⟩

lu·te·al \'lüt-ē-əl\ *adj* **:** of, relating to, or involving the corpus luteum

lu·tein \'lüt-ē-ən, 'lü-,tēn\ *n* [fr. its occurrence in corpus luteum] **1 :** an orange xanthophyll $C_{40}H_{54}(OH)_2$ occurring esp. in plants usu. with carotenes and chlorophylls **2 :** a preparation (as a hormone) from corpus luteum

lu·tein·ize \-,īz\ *vt* **:** to cause the production of corpora lutea in ~ *vi* **:** to undergo transformation into corpus luteum

luteinizing hormone *n* **:** a hormone from the anterior lobe of the pituitary body that in the female stimulates esp. the development of corpora lutea and in the male the development of interstitial tissue

lu·te·ous \'lüt-ē-əs\ *adj* [L *luteus* yellowish, fr. *lutum*, a plant used for dyeing yellow] **:** yellow tinged with green or brown

lu·teo·vi·res·cent \,lüt-ē-(,)ō-və-'res-ᵊnt, -(,)vī-\ *adj* [L *luteus* + E *-o-* + *virescent*] **:** greenish yellow

lute·string \'lüt-(,)striŋ\ *n* [by folk etymology fr. It *lustrino* glossy fabric, fr. *lustro* luster] **:** a plain glossy silk formerly much used for women's dresses and ribbons

lu·te·tium *or* **lu·te·cium** \lü-'tē-sh(ē-)əm\ *n* [NL, fr. L *Lutetia*, ancient name of Paris] **:** a trivalent metallic element of the rare-earth group — see ELEMENT table

1**Lu·ther·an** \'lü-th(ə-)rən\ *n* **:** a member of a Lutheran church

2**Lutheran** *adj* [Martin *Luther* †1546 G religious reformer] **1 :** of or relating to Luther or his religious doctrines (as justification by faith alone) **2 :** of or relating to the Protestant churches adhering to Lutheran doctrines, liturgy, or polity — **Lu·ther·an·ism** \-,iz-əm\ *n*

lut·ing \'lüt-iŋ\ *n* **:** 3LUTE

lut·ist \'lüt-əst\ *n* **1 :** a lute player **2 :** a maker of lutes

lux \'ləks\ *n, pl* **lux** *or* **lux·es** [L, light — more at LIGHT] **:** a unit of illumination equal to the direct illumination on a surface that is everywhere one meter from a uniform point source of one candle or equal to one lumen per square meter

lux·ate \'lək-,sāt\ *vt* [L *luxatus*, pp. of *luxare*, fr. *luxus* dislocated — more at LOCK] **:** to throw out of place or out of joint **:** DISLOCATE — **lux·a·tion** \,lək-'sā-shən\ *n*

luxe \'lüks, 'ləks, 'lüks\ *n* [F, fr. L *luxus* — more at LUXURY] **:** the quality or state of being sumptuous **:** LUXURY

lux·u·ri·ance \(,)ləg-'zhür-ē-ən(t)s, (,)lək-'shür-\ *n* **:** the quality or state of being luxuriant

lux·u·ri·an·cy \-ē-ən-sē\ *n, archaic* **:** LUXURIANCE

lux·u·ri·ant \-ē-ənt\ *adj* **1 a :** yielding abundantly **:** PRODUCTIVE **b :** characterized by abundant growth **:** LUSH **2 a :** exuberantly rich and varied **:** PROLIFIC **b :** excessively elaborate **:** FLORID **3 :** characterized by luxury **:** LUXURIOUS **syn** see PROFUSE — **lux·u·ri·ant·ly** *adv*

lux·u·ri·ate \-ē-,āt\ *vi* [L *luxuriatus*, pp. of *luxuriare* fr. *luxuria*] **1 a :** to grow profusely **:** THRIVE **b :** to develop extensively **:** PROLIFERATE **2 :** to indulge oneself luxuriously **:** REVEL

lux·u·ri·ous \(,)ləg-'zhür-ē-əs, (,)lək-'shür-\ *adj* **1 :** of or relating to unrestrained gratification of the senses **:** VOLUPTUOUS **2 a :** fond of luxury or self-indulgence **:** SYBARITIC **b :** characterized by opulence or rich abundance; *specif* **:** excessively ornate — **lux·u·ri·ous·ly** *adv* — **lux·u·ri·ous·ness** *n*

syn LUXURIOUS, SUMPTUOUS, OPULENT mean ostentatiously rich or magnificent. LUXURIOUS applies to what is choice and costly and suggests gratification of the senses and desire for comfort; SUMPTUOUS applies to what is extravagantly rich, splendid, or luxurious; OPULENT suggests a flaunting of luxuriousness, luxuriance, or costliness **syn** see in addition SENSUOUS

lux·u·ry \'ləksh-(ə-)rē, 'ləgzh-\ *n* [ME *luxurie*, fr. MF, fr. L *luxuria* rankness, luxury, excess; akin to L *luxus* luxury, excess] **1** *archaic* **:** LECHERY, LUST **2 :** sumptuous living or equipment **:** great ease or comfort **:** rich surroundings ⟨lived in ~⟩ **3 a :** something desirable but costly or hard to get ⟨a ~ few can afford⟩ **b :** something adding to pleasure or comfort but not absolutely necessary — **luxury** *adj*

1**-ly** \lē\ *adj suffix* [ME, fr. OE *-līc, -lic;* akin to OHG *-līh;* both

fr. a prehistoric Gmc noun represented by OE *līc* body — more at LIKE] **1 :** like in appearance, manner, or nature **:** having the characteristics of ⟨queen*ly*⟩ ⟨father*ly*⟩ **2 :** characterized by regular recurrence in (specified) units of time **:** every ⟨hour*ly*⟩

²-ly *adv suffix* [ME, fr. OE *-līce, -lice,* fr. *-līc,* adj. suffix] **1 :** in a (specified) manner ⟨slow*ly*⟩ **:** in the manner of a ⟨part*ly*⟩ **2 :** from a (specified) point of view ⟨eschatological*ly*⟩

ly·am–hound \ˈlī-əm-ˌhau̇nd\ *or* **lyme–hound** \ˈlīm-ˌhau̇nd\ *n* [obs. *lyam* (leash)] *archaic* **:** BLOODHOUND

ly·art \ˈlī-ərt\ *adj* [ME, fr. MF *liart*] *chiefly Scot* **:** streaked with gray **:** GRAY

ly·can·thrope \ˈlī-kən-ˌthrōp, lī-ˈkan-\ *n* [NL *lycanthropus,* fr. Gk *lykanthrōpos* werewolf, fr. *lykos* wolf + *anthrōpos* man — more at WOLF] **1 :** a person displaying lycanthropy **2 :** WEREWOLF

ly·can·throp·ic \ˌlī-kən-ˈthräp-ik\ *adj* **:** of or relating to lycanthropy

ly·can·thro·py \lī-ˈkan(t)-thrə-pē\ *n* **1 :** a delusion that one has become a wolf **2 :** the assumption of the form and characteristics of a wolf held to be possible by witchcraft or magic

ly·cée \lē-ˈsā\ *n* [F, fr. MF, lyceum, fr. L *Lyceum*] **:** a French public secondary school that prepares for the university

ly·ce·um \lī-ˈsē-əm, ˈlī-sē-\ *n* [L *Lyceum,* gymnasium near Athens where Aristotle taught, fr. Gk *Lykeion,* fr. neut. of *lykeios,* epithet of Apollo] **1 :** a hall for public lectures or discussions **2 :** an association providing public lectures, concerts, and entertainments **3 :** LYCÉE

ly·chee *var of* LITCHI

lych–gate \ˈlich-ˌgāt\ *n* [ME *lycheyate,* fr. *lich* body, corpse, (fr. OE *līc*) + *gate, yate* gate] **:** a roofed gate in a churchyard under which a bier rests during the initial part of the burial service

lych·nis \ˈlik-nəs\ *n* [NL, genus name, fr. L, a red flower, fr. Gk; akin to Gk *lychnos* lamp, L *lux* light — more at LIGHT] **:** any of a genus (*Lychnis*) of herbs of the pink family with terminal cymes of showy mostly red or white flowers

ly·co·pod \ˈlī-kə-ˌpäd\ *n* [NL *Lycopodium*] **:** LYCOPODIUM 1; *broadly* **:** CLUB MOSS

ly·co·po·di·um \ˌlī-kə-ˈpōd-ē-əm\ *n* [NL, genus name, fr. Gk *lykos* wolf + *podion,* dim. of *pod-, pous* foot — more at FOOT] **1 :** any of a large genus (*Lycopodium*) of erect or creeping club mosses with evergreen one-nerved leaves in four to many ranks **2 :** a fine yellowish flammable powder composed of lycopodium spores and used in pharmacy and as a component of fireworks and flashlight powders

lydd·ite \ˈlid-ˌīt\ *n* [*Lydd,* England] **:** a high explosive composed chiefly of picric acid

lye \ˈlī\ *n* [ME, fr. OE *lēag,* akin to OHG *louga* lye, L *lavare, lavere* to wash, Gk *louein*] **1 :** a strong alkaline liquor rich in potassium carbonate leached from wood ashes and used esp. in making soap and washing; *broadly* **:** a strong alkaline solution (as of sodium hydroxide or potassium hydroxide) **2 :** a solid caustic

ly·gus bug \ˈlī-gəs-\ *n* [NL *Lygus,* genus name] **:** any of various small sucking bugs (genus *Lygus*) including some vectors of virus diseases of plants

ly·ing \ˈlī-iŋ\ *adj* [prp. of ³*lie*] **:** UNTRUTHFUL, FALSE **syn** see DISHONEST

ly·ing–in \ˌlī-iŋ-ˈin\ *n, pl* **lyings–in** *or* **lying–ins :** the state attending and consequent to childbirth **:** CONFINEMENT

lymph \ˈlim(p)f\ *n, pl* **lymphs** \ˈlim(p)fs, ˈlim(p)s\ [L *lympha,* water goddess, water, fr. Gk *nymphē* nymph — more at NUPTIAL] **1** *archaic* **:** a spring or stream of water; *also* **:** pure clear water **2** *archaic* **:** the sap of plants **3** [NL *lympha,* fr. L, water] **:** a pale coagulable fluid that consists of a liquid portion resembling blood plasma and containing white blood cells

lymph– *or* **lympho–** *comb form* [NL *lympha*] **:** lymph **:** lymphatic tissue ⟨*lympho*granuloma⟩

lymph·ad·e·ni·tis \ˌlim-ˌfad-ᵊn-ˈīt-əs\ *n* [NL, fr. *lymphaden* lymph gland, fr. *lymph-* + Gk *adēn* gland — more at ADEN-] **:** inflammation of lymph glands

¹lym·phat·ic \lim-ˈfat-ik\ *adj* **1 a :** of, relating to, or produced by lymph, lymphoid tissue, or lymphocytes **b :** conveying lymph **2 :** lacking physical or mental energy **:** SLUGGISH — **lym·phat·i·cal·ly** \-i-k(ə-)lē\ *adv*

²lymphatic *n* **:** a vessel that contains or conveys lymph

lymph cell *n* **:** a cell in lymph; *specif* **:** LYMPHOCYTE

lymph gland *n* **:** one of the rounded masses of lymphoid tissue surrounded by a capsule of connective tissue that occur in the course of the lymphatic vessels and that consist of a reticulum of connective tissue fibers in the meshes of which are contained numerous small round cells each having a large round deeply staining nucleus and when carried off by the lymph flowing through the gland becoming a lymphocyte — called also *lymph follicle, lymph node*

lymph nodule *n* **:** a small simple lymph gland — called also *lymph follicle*

lym·pho·blast \ˈlim(p)-fə-ˌblast\ *n* [ISV] **:** a cell giving rise to lymphocytes — **lym·pho·blas·tic** \ˌlim(p)-fə-ˈblas-tik\ *adj*

lym·pho·cyte \ˈlim(p)-fə-ˌsīt\ *n* [ISV] **:** a colorless weakly motile cell produced in lymphoid tissue that is the typical cellular element of lymph and constitutes 20 to 30 percent of the leukocytes of normal human blood — **lym·pho·cyt·ic** \ˌlim(p)-fə-ˈsit-ik\ *adj*

lym·pho·cy·to·sis \ˌlim(p)-fə-ˌsī-ˈtō-səs\ *n* [NL, fr. ISV *lymphocyte*] **:** an increase in the number of lymphocytes in the blood usu. associated with chronic infections or inflammations — **lym·pho·cy·tot·ic** \-ˈtät-ik\ *adj*

lym·pho·gran·u·lo·ma \ˌlim(p)-fō-ˌgran-yə-ˈlō-mə\ *n, pl* **lymphogranulomas** *or* **lym·pho·gran·u·lo·ma·ta** \-mət-ə\ [NL] **1 :** a nodular swelling of a lymph node **2 :** a contagious venereal virus disease marked by swelling and ulceration of lymphatic tissues in the iliac and inguinal regions — **lym·pho·gran·u·lo·ma·to·sis** \-ˌlō-mə-ˈtō-səs\ *n*

lym·phoid \ˈlim-ˌfȯid\ *adj* **1 :** of, relating to, or resembling lymph **2 :** of, relating to, or constituting the tissue characteristic of the lymph glands

lym·pho·ma \lim-ˈfō-mə\ *n, pl* **lymphomas** *or* **lym·pho·ma·ta** \-mət-ə\ [NL] **:** a tumor of lymphoid tissue — **lym·pho·ma·toid** \-mə-ˌtȯid\ *adj* — **lym·pho·ma·to·sis** \(ˌ)lim-ˌfō-mə-ˈtō-səs\ *n* — **lym·pho·ma·tous** \lim-ˈfäm-ət-əs, -ˈfō-mət-\ *adj*

lym·pho·poi·e·sis \ˌlim(p)-fə-ˌpȯi-ˈē-səs\ *n, pl* **lym·pho·poi·e·ses** \-ˈē-ˌsēz\ [NL] **:** the formation of lymphocytes or lymphatic tissue — **lym·pho·poi·et·ic** \-ˌpȯi-ˈet-ik\ *adj*

lyn·ce·an \lin-ˈsē-ən, ˈlin(t)-sē-\ *adj* [L *lynceus,* fr. Gk *lynkeios,* lit., of Lynceus, Argonaut famous for his sharpness of sight, fr. *Lynkeus* Lynceus] **:** SHARP-SIGHTED

lynch \ˈlinch\ *vt* [*lynch law*] **:** to put to death by mob action without legal sanction — **lynch·er** *n*

lynch law *n* [prob. fr. Charles *Lynch* †1796 Am justice of the peace; fr. his presiding over an extralegal court to suppress Tory activity] **:** the punishment of presumed crimes or offenses usu. by death without due process of law

lynx \ˈliŋ(k)s\ *n, pl* **lynx** *or* **lynx·es** [L, fr. Gk; akin to OE *lox* lynx, Gk *leukos* white — more at LIGHT] **:** any of various wildcats with relatively long legs, a short stubby tail, mottled coat, and often tufted ears: as **a :** the common lynx (*Lynx lynx*) of northern Europe and Asia **b :** BOBCAT **c :** a No. American lynx (*L. canadensis*) with soft fur and large padded feet — called also *Canada lynx*

lynx–eyed \ˈliŋ(k)-ˈsīd\ *adj* **:** SHARP-SIGHTED

lyo– *comb form* [prob. fr. NL, fr. Gk *lyein* to loosen, dissolve — more at LOSE] **:** dispersed state **:** dispersion ⟨*lyo*philic⟩

ly·on·naise \ˌlī-ə-ˈnāz\ *adj* [F (*à la*) *lyonnaise* in the manner of Lyons, fr. fem. of *lyonnais* of Lyons, fr. *Lyon* Lyons, France] **:** prepared with onions

Ly·on·nesse \ˌlī-ə-ˈnes\ *n* **:** a country held in Arthurian legend to have been contiguous to Cornwall before sinking beneath the sea

lyo·phile \ˈlī-ə-ˌfīl\ *adj* [ISV] **1 :** LYOPHILIC **2 a :** of or relating to lyophilization **b** *or* **lyo·philed** \-ˌfīld\ **:** obtained by lyophilization

lyo·phil·ic \ˌlī-ə-ˈfil-ik\ *adj* **:** marked by strong affinity between a dispersed phase and the liquid in which it is dispersed ⟨a ~ colloid⟩

ly·oph·i·li·za·tion \(ˌ)lī-ˌäf-ə-lə-ˈzā-shən\ *n* **:** the process of lyophilizing or the state of being lyophilized

ly·oph·i·lize \lī-ˈäf-ə-ˌlīz\ *vt* **:** FREEZE-DRY

lyo·pho·bic \ˌlī-ə-ˈfō-bik\ *adj* **:** marked by lack of strong affinity between a dispersed phase and the liquid in which it is dispersed ⟨a ~ colloid⟩

Ly·ra \ˈlī-rə\ *n* [L (gen. *Lyrae*), lit., lyre] **:** a northern constellation representing the lyre of Orpheus or Mercury and containing Vega

ly·rate \ˈlī(ə)r-ˌāt\ *or* **ly·rat·ed** \-ˌāt-əd\ *adj* **:** having or suggesting the shape of a lyre — **ly·rate·ly** *adv*

lyre \ˈlī(ə)r\ *n* [ME *lire,* fr. OF, fr. L *lyra,* fr. Gk] **1 :** a stringed musical instrument of the harp class used by the ancient Greeks esp. to accompany song and recitation **2** *cap* **:** LYRA

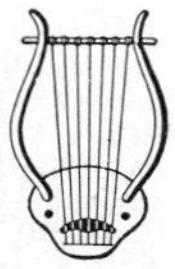
lyre

lyre·bird \ˈlī(ə)r-ˌbərd\ *n* **:** either of two Australian passerine birds (genus *Menura*) distinguished in the male by very long tail feathers displayed during courtship in the shape of a lyre

¹lyr·ic \ˈlir-ik\ *adj* **1 :** of or relating to a lyre or harp **2 :** suitable to sing to the lyre or for being set to music and sung **3 a :** expressing direct usu. intense personal emotion **b :** EXUBERANT, RHAPSODIC

²lyric *n* **1 :** a lyric composition; *specif* **:** a lyric poem **2** *pl* **:** the words of a popular song or musical-comedy number

lyr·i·cal \ˈlir-i-kəl\ *adj* **:** LYRIC — **lyr·i·cal·ly** \-i-k(ə-)lē\ *adv* — **lyr·i·cal·ness** \-kəl-nəs\ *n*

lyr·i·cism \ˈlir-ə-ˌsiz-əm\ *n* **1 a :** the quality or state of being lyric **:** SONGFULNESS **b :** a personal direct intense style or quality in poetry or the other arts **2 :** exuberance of style or feeling

lyr·i·cist \-ə-səst\ *n* **:** a writer of lyrics

lyr·ism \ˈli(ə)r-ˌiz-əm\ *n* **:** LYRICISM

lyr·ist *n* **1** \ˈlī(ə)r-əst\ **:** a player on the lyre **2** \ˈlir-əst\ **:** LYRICIST

lys– *or* **lysi–** *or* **lyso–** *comb form* [NL, fr. Gk *lys-, lysi-* loosening, fr. *lysis*] **:** lysis ⟨*lys*in⟩

ly·sate \ˈlī-ˌsāt\ *n* **:** a product of lysis

lyse \ˈlīs, ˈlīz\ *vb* [back-formation fr. NL *lysis*] *vt* **:** to cause to undergo lysis ~ *vi* **:** to undergo lysis

Ly·sen·ko·ism \lə-ˈseŋ-(ˌ)kō-ˌiz-əm\ *n* [Trofim *Lysenko* b1898 Russ geneticist] **:** a biological doctrine asserting the fundamental influence of somatic and environmental factors on heredity in contradiction of orthodox genetics

ly·ser·gic acid \lə-ˌsər-jik-, (ˌ)lī-\ *n* [*lys-* + *ergot*] **:** a crystalline acid $C_{16}H_{16}N_2O_2$ from ergotic alkaloids

ly·sin \ˈlīs-ᵊn\ *n* **:** a substance capable of causing lysis; *esp* **:** an antibody capable of causing disintegration of red blood cells or microorganisms

ly·sine \ˈlī-ˌsēn\ *n* **:** a crystalline basic amino acid $C_6H_{14}N_2O_2$ that is essential to animal nutrition

ly·sis \ˈlī-səs\ *n, pl* **ly·ses** \ˈlī-ˌsēz\ [NL, fr. Gk, act of loosening, dissolution, remission of fever, fr. *lyein* to loosen — more at LOSE] **1 :** the gradual decline of a disease process (as fever) **2 :** a process of disintegration or dissolution (as of cells)

-l·y·sis \l-ə-səs\ *n comb form, pl* **-l·y·ses** \l-ə-ˌsēz\ [NL, fr. L & Gk; L, loosening, fr. Gk, fr. *lysis*] **1 :** decomposition ⟨electro*lysis*⟩ **2 :** disintegration **:** breaking down ⟨auto*lysis*⟩

ly·so·gen·e·sis \ˌlī-sə-ˈjen-ə-səs\ *n* [NL] **:** the production of lysins or of the phenomenon of lysis — **ly·so·ge·net·ic** \-jə-ˈnet-ik\ *adj*

ly·so·some \ˈlī-sə-ˌsōm\ *n* [ISV *lys-* + ³*-some*] **:** a cellular organelle held to be the seat of various hydrolytic enzymes — **ly·so·som·al** \ˌlī-sə-ˈsō-məl\ *adj*

ly·so·zyme \ˈlī-sə-ˌzīm\ *n* **:** a basic bacteriolytic protein present in egg white and in secretions that functions as a mucinolytic enzyme

-lyte \ˌlīt\ *n comb form* [Gk *lytos* that may be untied, soluble, fr. *lyein*] **:** substance capable of undergoing (such) decomposition ⟨hydro*lyte*⟩

lyt·ic \ˈlit-ik\ *adj* [Gk *lytikos* able to loose, fr. *lyein*] **:** of or relating to lysis or a lysin; *also* **:** productive of or effecting lysis (as of cells)

-lyt·ic \ˈlit-ik\ *adj suffix* [Gk *lytikos*] **:** of, relating to, or effecting (such) decomposition ⟨hydro*lytic*⟩

lyt·ta \ˈlit-ə\ *n, pl* **lyt·tae** \ˈlit-ˌē, -ˌī\ [L, fr. Gk, lit., madness, rabies; fr. the belief that it might cause rabies unless removed] **:** a fibrous and cartilaginous rod lying within the longitudinal axis of the tongue in many carnivorous mammals (as the dog)

-lyze \ˌlīz\ *vb comb form* [ISV, prob. irreg. fr. NL *-lysis*] **:** produce or undergo lysis (sense 2) ⟨electro*lyze*⟩

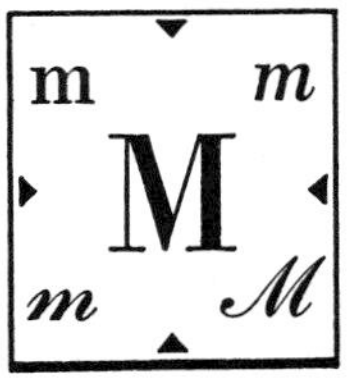

m \'em\ *n, often cap, often attrib* **1 a :** the 13th letter of the English alphabet **b :** a graphic representation of this letter **c :** a speech counterpart of orthographic *m* **2 :** one thousand **3 :** a graphic device for reproducing the letter *m* **4 :** one designated *m* esp. as the 12th or when j is used for the 10th the 13th in order or class **5 :** something shaped like the letter M **6 a :** EM 2 **b :** PICA

'm \m\ *vb* **:** AM ⟨I'*m* going⟩

ma \'mä, 'mȯ\ *n* [short for *mama*] **:** MOTHER

ma'am \'mam, *after "yes" often* əm\ *n* **:** MADAM

Mab \'mab\ *n* **:** a fairy queen held to govern men's dreams

mac \'mak\ *n, Brit* **:** MACKINTOSH

ma·ca·bre \mə-'käbrᵊ\ *adj* [F, fr. (*danse*) *macabre* dance of death, fr. MF (*danse de*) *Macabré*] **1 :** having death as a subject **:** comprising or including a personalized representation of death **2 :** dwelling on the gruesome **3 :** tending to produce horror in a beholder **syn** see GHASTLY — **ma·ca·bre·ly** \-'käb-rə-lē\ *adv*

mac·ad·am \mə-'kad-əm\ *n* [John L. *McAdam* †1836 Brit engineer] **1 :** macadamized roadway or pavement esp. with a bituminous binder **2 :** the broken stone used in macadamizing

mac·a·da·mia nut \,mak-ə-'dā-mē-ə-\ *n* [NL *Macadamia*, genus of evergreens, fr. John *Macadam* †1865 Australian chemist] **:** a hard-shelled nut somewhat resembling a filbert and produced by an Australian evergreen tree (*Macadamia ternifolia*) of the protea family

mac·ad·am·ize \mə-'kad-ə-,mīz\ *vt* **:** to construct or finish (a road) by compacting into a solid mass a layer of small broken stone on a convex well-drained roadbed

ma·caque \mə-'kak, -'käk\ *n* [F, fr. Pg *macaco*] **:** any of numerous short-tailed Old World monkeys (*Macaca* and related genera) chiefly of southern Asia and the East Indies; *esp* **:** RHESUS MONKEY

mac·a·ro·ni \,mak-ə-'rō-nē\ *n* [It *maccheroni*, pl. of *maccherone*, fr. It dial. *maccarone* dumpling, macaroni] **1 :** a paste composed chiefly of semolina dried in the form of slender tubes for use as food **2** *pl* **macaronis** *or* **macaronies a :** a member of a class of traveled young Englishmen of the late 18th and early 19th centuries who affected foreign ways **b :** an affected young man **:** FOP

mac·a·ron·ic \-'rän-ik\ *adj* [NL *macaronicus*, fr. It dial. *maccarone* macaroni] **1** *archaic* **:** being a jumble or medley **:** MIXED **2 a :** characterized by a mixture of vernacular words with Latin words or with non-Latin words having Latin endings **b :** characterized by a mixture of two languages — **macaronic** *n* — **mac·a·ron·i·cal·ly** \-i-k(ə-)lē\ *adv*

mac·a·roon \,mak-ə-'rün\ *n* [F *macaron*, fr. It dial. *maccarone*] **:** a small cake composed chiefly of the white of eggs, sugar, and ground almonds or coconut

ma·caw \mə-'kȯ\ *n* [Pg *macau*] **:** any of numerous parrots (esp. genus *Ara*) of South and Central America including some of the largest and showiest of parrots

Mac·beth \mək-'beth, mak-\ *n* **:** a Scottish general who is the protagonist of Shakespeare's tragedy *Macbeth*

Mac·ca·be·an \,mak-ə-'bē-ən\ *adj* **:** of or relating to the Maccabees

Mac·ca·bees \'mak-ə-,bēz\ *n pl* [Gk *Makkabaioi*, fr. pl. of *Makkabaios*, surname of Judas Maccabaeus 2d cent. B.C. Jewish patriot] **:** a priestly family leading a Jewish revolt begun in 168 B.C. against Hellenism and Syrian rule and reigning over Palestine from 142 B.C. to 63 B.C.

mac·ca·boy \'mak-ə-,bȯi\ *n* [F *macouba*, fr. *Macouba*, district in Martinique] **:** a snuff from Martinique

Mc·Car·thy·ism \mə-'kär-thē-,iz-əm *also* -'kärt-ē-\ *n* [Joseph R. *McCarthy* †1957 U.S. senator] **:** a mid-twentieth-century political attitude characterized chiefly by opposition to elements held to be subversive and by the use of tactics involving personal attacks on individuals by means of widely publicized indiscriminate allegations esp. on the basis of unsubstantiated charges — **Mc·Car·thy·ite** \-,īt\ *n*

Mac·cles·field \'mak-əlz-,fēld\ *n* [*Macclesfield*, England] **:** a silk with small allover patterns used esp. for neckties

Mc·Coy \mə-'kȯi\ *n* [alter. of *Mackay* (in the phrase *the real Mackay* the true chief of the Mackay clan, a position often disputed)] **:** something that is neither imitation nor substitute

¹mace \'mās\ *n* [ME, fr. MF, fr. (assumed) VL *mattia;* akin to OHG *medela* plow, L *mateola* mallet] **1 a :** a heavy often spiked staff or club used esp. in the Middle Ages for breaking armor **b :** a club used as a weapon **2 a :** an ornamental staff borne as a symbol of authority before a public official or a legislative body **b :** one who carries a mace **3 a :** a rod with a flat wooden head formerly used in billiards instead of a cue **b :** a similar rod in bagatelle

²mace *n* [ME, fr. MF *macis*, fr. L *macir*, an East Indian spice, fr. Gk *makir*] **:** an aromatic spice consisting of the dried external fibrous covering of a nutmeg

ma·cé·doine \,mas-ə-'dwän\ *n* [F, fr. *Macédoine* Macedonia; perh. fr. the mixture of races in Macedonia] **1 :** a mixture of fruits or vegetables served as a salad or cocktail or in a jellied dessert or used in a sauce or as a garnish **2 :** a confused mixture **:** MEDLEY

Mac·e·do·nian \,mas-ə-'dō-nyən, -nē-ən\ *n* **1 :** a native or inhabitant of ancient or modern Macedonia **2 :** the Slavic language of modern Macedonia **3 :** the probably Indo-European language of ancient Macedonia

mac·er·ate \'mas-ə-,rāt\ *vb* [L *maceratus*, pp. of *macerare* to soften, steep] *vt* **1 :** to cause to waste away by or as if by excessive fasting **2 :** to cause to become soft or separated into constituent elements by or as if by steeping in fluid ~ *vi* **:** to soften and wear away esp. as a result of being wetted or steeped — **mac·er·a·tion** \,mas-ə-'rā-shən\ *n* — **mac·er·a·tor** \'mas-ə-,rāt-ər\ *n*

ma·chete \mə-'shet-ē, -'chet-\ *n* [Sp] **1 :** a large heavy knife used for cutting sugarcane and underbrush and as a weapon **2 :** a small four-stringed Portuguese guitar

Ma·chi·a·vel·lian \,mak-ē-ə-'vel-ē-ən, -'vel-yən\ *adj* **1 :** of or relating to Machiavelli or Machiavellianism **2 :** suggesting the principles of conduct laid down by Machiavelli; *specif* **:** characterized by cunning, duplicity, or bad faith — **Machiavellian** *n*

Ma·chi·a·vel·lian·ism \-,iz-əm\ *n* **:** the political theory of Machiavelli; *esp* **:** the view that politics is amoral and that any means however unscrupulous can justifiably be used in achieving political power

ma·chic·o·late \mə-'chik-ə-,lāt\ *vt* [ML *machicolatus*, pp. of *machicolare*, fr. OF *machicoller*, fr. *machicoleis* machicolation, fr. *macher* to crush + *col* neck, fr. L *collum* — more at COLLAR] **:** to furnish with machicolations

ma·chic·o·la·tion \mə-,chik-ə-'lā-shən\ *n* **1 a :** an opening between the corbels of a projecting parapet or in the floor of a gallery or roof of a portal for discharging missiles upon assailants below **b :** a gallery or parapet containing such openings **2 :** construction imitating medieval machicolation

ma·chin·abil·i·ty \mə-,shē-nə-'bil-ət-ē\ *n* **:** the quality or state of being machinable

ma·chin·able *also* **ma·chine·able** \mə-'shē-nə-bəl\ *adj* **:** capable of or suitable for being machined

mach·i·nate \'mak-ə-,nāt, 'mash-ə-\ *vb* [L *machinatus*, pp. of *machinari*, fr. *machina* machine, contrivance] *vi* **:** to plan or plot esp. to do harm ~ *vt* **:** to scheme or contrive to bring about **:** PLOT

mach·i·na·tion \,mak-ə-'nā-shən, ,mash-ə-\ *n* **1 :** an act of machinating **2 :** a scheming or crafty action or artful design intended to accomplish some usu. evil end **syn** see PLOT

mach·i·na·tor \'mak-ə-,nāt-ər, 'mash-ə-\ *n* **:** one that machinates **:** a plotter or artful schemer

¹ma·chine \mə-'shēn\ *n, often attrib* [MF, fr. L *machina*, fr. Gk *mēchanē* (Dor dial. *machana*), fr. *mēchos* means, expedient — more at MAY] **1 a** *archaic* **:** a constructed thing whether material or immaterial **b :** CONVEYANCE, VEHICLE; *specif* **:** AUTOMOBILE **c** *archaic* **:** a military engine **d :** any of various apparatus formerly used to produce stage effects **e** (1) **:** an assemblage of parts that transmit forces, motion, and energy one to another in a predetermined manner (2) **:** an instrument (as a lever) designed to transmit or modify the application of power, force, or motion **2 a :** a living organism or one of its functional systems **b :** a person or organization that acts like a machine **c** (1) **:** a combination of persons acting together for a common end together with the agencies they use (2) **:** a highly organized political group under the leadership of a boss or small clique **3 :** a literary device or contrivance introduced for dramatic effect

²machine *vt* **:** to turn, shape, plane, mill, or otherwise reduce or finish by machine-operated tools

machine gun *n* **:** an automatic gun using small-arms ammunition for rapid continuous firing — **ma·chine–gun** \mə-'shēn-,gən\ *vb* — **machine gun·ner** \-,gən-ər\ *n*

ma·chine·like \mə-'shēn-,līk\ *adj* **:** resembling a machine esp. in regularity of action or stereotyped uniformity of product

ma·chin·ery \mə-'shēn-(ə-)rē\ *n* **1 a :** machines in general or as a functioning unit: as (1) **:** apparatus for producing stage effects (2) **:** literary devices used esp. for dramatic effect **b :** the working parts of a machine **2 :** the means by which something is kept in action or a desired result is obtained

machine shop *n* **:** a workshop in which work is machined to size and assembled

machine tool *n* **:** a usu. power-driven machine designed for shaping solid work

ma·chin·ist \mə-'shē-nəst\ *n* **1 a :** a worker who fabricates, assembles, or repairs machinery **b :** a craftsman skilled in the use of machine tools **c :** one who operates a machine **2** *archaic* **:** a person in charge of the mechanical aspects of a theatrical production **3 :** a warrant officer who supervises machinery and engine operation

machinist's mate *n* **:** a navy petty officer who operates engine-room equipment

Mach number \'mäk-\ *n* [Ernst *Mach* †1916 Austrian physicist] **:** a number representing the ratio of the speed of a body to the speed of sound in the surrounding atmosphere

mack *var of* MAC

mack·er·el \'mak-(ə-)rəl\ *n, pl* **mackerel** *or* **mackerels** [ME *makerel*, fr. OF] **1 :** a fish (*Scomber scombrus*) of the No. Atlantic that is green above with dark blue bars and silvery below, reaches a length of about 18 inches, and is one of the most important food fishes **2 :** a fish of the suborder (Scombroidea) to which the common mackerel belongs; *esp* **:** a comparatively small member of this group as distinguished from a bonito or tuna

mackerel sky *n* **:** a sky covered with rows of altocumulus or cirrocumulus clouds resembling the patterns on a mackerel's back

mack·i·naw \'mak-ə-,nȯ\ *n* [*Mackinaw* City, Michigan, formerly an Indian trading post] **1 :** a flat-bottomed boat with pointed prow and square stern formerly much used on the upper Great Lakes **2 :** a heavy woolen blanket formerly distributed by the U.S. government to the Indians **3 a :** a heavy cloth of wool or wool and other fibers often with a plaid design and usu. heavily napped and felted **b :** a short coat of mackinaw or similar heavy fabric

mack·in·tosh *also* **mac·in·tosh** \'mak-ən-,täsh\ *n* [Charles *Macintosh* †1843 Sc chemist & inventor] **1** *chiefly Brit* **:** RAINCOAT **2 :** a lightweight waterproof fabric orig. of rubberized cotton

¹mack·le \'mak-əl\ *n* [F *macule* spot, mackle, fr. L *macula* spot, stain] **:** a blur or a double impression on a printed sheet

²mackle *vb* **mack·ling** \-(ə-)liŋ\ **:** BLUR

ma·cle \'mak-əl\ *n* [F, wide-meshed net, lozenge voided, macle, fr. OF, mesh, lozenge voided, of Gmc origin; akin to OHG *masca* mesh — more at MESH] **1 a :** a twin crystal **b :** a flat often triangular diamond that is usu. a twin crystal **2 :** a dark or discolored spot (as in a mineral) — **ma·cled** \'mak-əld\ *adj*

macr- *or* **macro-** *comb form* [F & L, fr. Gk *makr-*, *makro-* long, fr. *makros* — more at MEAGER] **1 :** long ⟨*macro*diagonal⟩ **2 :** large ⟨*macro*spore⟩

mac·ra·me \,mak-rə-'mā\ *n* [F or It; F *macramé*, fr. It *macramè*, fr. Turk *makrama* napkin, towel, fr. Ar *migramah* embroidered veil] **:** a coarse lace or fringe made by knotting threads or cords in a geometrical pattern

macrame knot *n* **:** an ornate knot used in making macrame

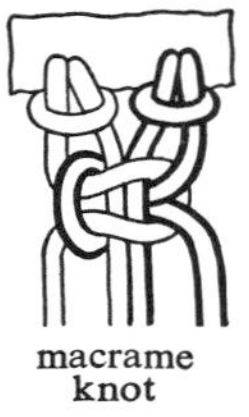
macrame knot

mac·ro \'mak-(,)rō\ *adj* [*macr-*] **1 :** excessively developed **:** LARGE, THICK **2 :** of or involving large quantities **3 :** GROSS 1c

mac·ro·ceph·a·lous \,mak-rō-'sef-ə-ləs\ *or* **mac·ro·ce·phal·ic** \-sə-'fal-ik\ *adj* [F *macrocéphale*, fr. Gk *makrokephalos* having a long head, fr. *makr-* + *kephalē* head — more at CEPHALIC] **:** having or being an exceptionally large head or cranium ⟨a ~ idiot⟩ — **mac·ro·ceph·a·ly** \-'sef-ə-lē\ *n*

mac·ro·cosm \'mak-rə-ˌkäz-əm\ *n* [F *macrocosme*, fr. ML *macrocosmos*, fr. L *macr-* + Gk *kosmos* order, universe] **1 :** the great world **:** UNIVERSE **2 :** a complex that is a large-scale reproduction of one of its constituents — **mac·ro·cos·mic** \ˌmak-rə-'käz-mik\ *adj* — **mac·ro·cos·mi·cal·ly** \-mi-k(ə-)lē\ *adv*

mac·ro·cyte \'mak-rō-ˌsīt\ *n* [ISV] **:** an exceptionally large red blood cell occurring chiefly in anemias — **mac·ro·cyt·ic** \ˌmak-rō-'sit-ik\ *adj* — **mac·ro·cy·to·sis** \ˌmak-rō-ˌsī-'tō-səs\ *n*

mac·ro·evo·lu·tion \ˌmak-(ˌ)rō-ˌev-ə-'lü-shən *also* -ˌē-və-\ *n* **:** evolutionary change involving relatively large and complex steps — **mac·ro·evo·lu·tion·ary** \-shə-ˌner-ē\ *adj*

mac·ro·ga·mete \ˌmak-(ˌ)rō-gə-'mēt, ˌmak-rō-'gam-ˌēt\ *n* [ISV] **:** the larger and usu. female gamete of a heterogamous organism

mac·ro·mere \'mak-rō-ˌmi(ə)r\ *n* **:** a large blastomere

ma·cron \'māk-ˌrän, 'mak-, -rən\ *n* [Gk *makron*, neut. of *makros* long] **:** a mark ¯ placed over a vowel to indicate that the vowel is long or placed over a syllable or used alone to indicate a stressed or long syllable in a metrical foot

mac·ro·nu·cle·us \ˌmak-(ˌ)rō-'n(y)ü-klē-əs\ *n* [NL] **:** a relatively large densely staining nucleus that is believed to exert a controlling influence over the trophic activities of most ciliated protozoans

mac·ro·nu·tri·ent \-'n(y)ü-trē-ənt\ *n* **:** a chemical element of which relatively large quantities are essential to the growth and welfare of a plant

mac·ro·phage \'mak-rə-ˌfāj, -ˌfäzh\ *n* [F, fr. *macr-* + *-phage*] **:** a large phagocyte; *specif* **:** HISTIOCYTE — **mac·ro·phag·ic** \ˌmak-rə-'faj-ik\ *adj*

mac·rop·ter·ous \ma-'kräp-tə-rəs\ *adj* [Gk *makropteros*, fr. *makr-* + *pteron* wing — more at FEATHER] **:** having long or large wings or fins

mac·ro·scop·ic \ˌmak-rə-'skäp-ik\ *adj* [ISV *macr-* + *-scopic* (as in *microscopic*)] **1 :** large enough to be observed by the naked eye **2 :** considered in terms of large units or elements — **mac·ro·scop·i·cal** \-i-kəl\ *adj* — **mac·ro·scop·i·cal·ly** \-k(ə-)lē\ *adv*

ma·cru·ral \mə-'krür(ə)r-əl\ *adj* [deriv. of Gk *makros* long + *oura* tail — more at MEAGER, SQUIRREL] **:** of or relating to a suborder (Macrura) of decapod crustaceans with well-developed abdomens — **ma·cru·ran** \-ən\ *adj or n* — **ma·cru·roid** \-ˌȯid\ *adj*

ma·cru·rous \-əs\ *adj* **1 :** having a long tail **2 :** MACRURAL

mac·u·la \'mak-yə-lə\ *n, pl* **mac·u·lae** \-ˌlē, -ˌlī\ *also* **maculas** [L] **1 :** BLOTCH, SPOT; *esp* **:** MACULE **2 :** an anatomical structure having the form of a spot differentiated from surrounding tissues — **mac·u·lar** \-lər\ *adj*

¹**mac·u·late** \-ˌlāt\ *vt* [ME *maculaten*, fr. L *maculatus*, pp. of *maculare*, fr. *macula*] **1** *archaic* **:** SPOT, SPECKLE **2** *archaic* **:** BESMIRCH, DEFILE

²**mac·u·late** \-lət\ *or* **mac·u·lat·ed** \-ˌlāt-əd\ *adj* **1 :** marked with spots **:** BLOTCHED **2 :** BESMIRCHED, IMPURE

mac·u·la·tion \ˌmak-yə-'lā-shən\ *n* **1** *archaic* **:** the act of spotting **:** the state of being spotted **2 a :** SPOT, BLEMISH **b :** the arrangement of spots and markings on an animal or plant

mac·ule \'mak-(ˌ)yü(ə)l\ *n* [F, fr. L *macula*] **:** a patch of skin altered in color but usu. not elevated that is a characteristic feature of various diseases (as smallpox)

¹**mad** \'mad\ *adj* **mad·der; mad·dest** [ME *medd, madd*, fr. OE *gemǣd*, pp. of (assumed) *gemǣdan* to madden, fr. *gemād* silly, mad; akin to OHG *gimeit* foolish, crazy, Skt *methati* he hurts] **1 :** disordered in mind **:** INSANE **2 a :** completely unrestrained by reason and judgment **:** SENSELESS **b :** incapable of being explained or accounted for **:** ILLOGICAL **3 a :** carried away by intense anger **:** FURIOUS **b :** keenly displeased **:** ANGRY **4 :** carried away by enthusiasm or desire **5 :** affected with rabies **:** RABID **6 :** marked by wild gaiety and merriment **:** HILARIOUS **7 :** intensely excited **:** DISTRAUGHT, FRANTIC **8 :** marked by intense and often chaotic activity **:** WILD

²**mad** *vb* **mad·ded; mad·ding :** MADDEN

³**mad** *n* **1 :** ANGER, FURY **2 :** a fit or mood of bad temper

mad·am \'mad-əm\ *n, pl* **madams** [ME, fr. OF *ma dame*, lit., my lady] **1** *pl* **mes·dames** \mā-'däm, -'dam\ **:** LADY — used without a name as a form of respectful or polite address to a woman **2 :** MISTRESS 1 — used as a title formerly with the given name but now with the surname as an equivalent of *Madame* or esp. with a designation of rank or office ⟨*Madam* Chairman⟩ ⟨*Madam* President⟩ **3 :** the female head of a house of prostitution **4 :** the female head of a household **:** WIFE

ma·dame \mə-'dam, ma-', *before a surname also* ˌmad-əm\ *n* [F, fr. OF *ma dame*] **1** *pl* **mes·dames** \mā-'däm, -'dam\ **:** MISTRESS — used as a title equivalent to *Mrs.* for a married woman not of English-speaking nationality and as a title of distinction for a professional woman **2** *pl* **madames :** MADAM 3

mad–brained \'mad-'brānd\ *adj* **:** HOTHEADED, RASH

mad·cap \'mad-ˌkap\ *adj* **:** marked by impulsiveness or recklessness — **madcap** *n*

mad·den \'mad-ᵊn\ *vb* **mad·den·ing** \'mad-niŋ, -ᵊn-iŋ\ *vi* **:** to become or act as if mad ~ *vt* **1 :** to drive mad **:** CRAZE **2 :** to make intensely angry **:** ENRAGE

mad·den·ing *adj* **1 :** tending to craze **2 a :** tending to infuriate **b :** tending to vex **:** IRRITATING — **mad·den·ing·ly** \'mad-niŋ-lē, -ᵊn-iŋ-\ *adv*

mad·der \'mad-ər\ *n* [ME, fr. OE *mædere;* akin to OHG *matara* madder] **1 :** a Eurasian herb (*Rubia tinctorum* of the family Rubiaceae, the madder family) with verticillate leaves and small yellowish panicled flowers succeeded by berries; *broadly* **:** any of several related herbs (genus *Rubia*) **2 a :** the root of the Eurasian madder used formerly in dyeing; *also* **:** an alizarin dye prepared from it **b :** a moderate to strong red

mad·der·wort \-ˌwərt, -ˌwȯ(ə)rt\ *n* **:** a plant of the madder family

mad·ding \'mad-iŋ\ *adj* **1 :** acting as if mad **:** FRENZIED **2 :** MADDENING

mad·dish \'mad-ish\ *adj* **:** somewhat mad

made \'mād\ *adj* [ME, fr. pp. of *maken* to make] **1 a :** artificially produced ⟨~ ground⟩ **b :** INVENTED, FICTITIOUS ⟨a ~ excuse⟩ **c :** put together of various ingredients ⟨a ~ dish⟩ **2 :** assured of success ⟨a ~ man⟩

Ma·dei·ra \mə-'dir-ə, -'der-\ *n* [Pg, fr. *Madeira* islands] **:** an amber-colored dessert wine of Madeira; *also* **:** a similar wine made elsewhere

ma·de·moi·selle \ˌmad-(ə-)m(w)ə-'zel, mam-'zel\ *n, pl* **ma·de·moi·selles** \-'zelz\ *or* **mes·de·moi·selles** \ˌmād-(ə-)m(w)ə-'zel\ [F, fr. OF *ma damoisele*, lit., my (young) lady] **1 :** an unmarried French girl or woman — used as a title equivalent to *Miss* for an unmarried woman not of English-speaking nationality **2 :** a French governess

made–up \'mā-'dəp\ *adj* **1 :** marked by the use of makeup **2 :** fancifully conceived or falsely devised **3 :** fully manufactured

mad·house \'mad-ˌhau̇s\ *n* **1 :** a place where insane persons are detained and treated **2 :** a place of bewildering uproar or confusion

mad·ly \'mad-lē\ *adv* **:** in a mad manner or to a degree suggestive of madness

mad·man \'mad-ˌman, -mən\ *n* **:** a man who is or acts as if insane **:** LUNATIC — **mad·wom·an** \-ˌwu̇m-ən\ *n*

mad·ness \'mad-nəs\ *n* **1 :** the quality or state of being mad: as **a :** INSANITY **b :** extreme folly **c :** RAGE **d :** ECSTASY, ENTHUSIASM **2 :** any of several ailments of animals marked by frenzied behavior; *specif* **:** RABIES

Ma·don·na \mə-'dän-ə\ *n* [It, fr. OIt *ma donna*, lit., my lady] **1** *archaic* **:** LADY — used as a form of respectful address **2** *obs* **:** an Italian lady **3 :** VIRGIN MARY

Madonna lily *n* **:** a white lily (*Lilium candidum*) with bell-shaped to broad funnel-shaped flowers formerly extensively forced for spring blooming

ma·dras \mə-'dras, -'dräs; 'mad-rəs\ *n* [*Madras*, India] **1 a :** a fine plain-woven shirting and dress fabric usu. of cotton with small designs in bright colors or in white **b :** a light open usu. cotton fabric with a heavy design used for curtains **2 :** a large silk or cotton kerchief usu. of bright colors that is often worn as a turban

mad·re·pore \'mad-rə-ˌpō(ə)r, -ˌpȯ(ə)r\ *n* [F *madrépore*, fr. It *madrepora*, fr. *madre* mother (fr. L *mater*) + *poro* pore (fr. L *porus*) — more at MOTHER] **:** any of various stony reef-building corals (order Madreporaria) of tropical seas that assume a variety of branching, encrusting, or massive forms — **mad·re·po·ri·an** \ˌmad-rə-'pōr-ē-ən, -'pȯr-\ *adj or n* — **mad·re·por·ic** \-'pōr-ik, -'pȯr-\ *adj*

mad·ri·gal \'mad-ri-gəl\ *n* [It *madrigale*, fr. ML *matricale*, fr. neut. of (assumed) *matricalis* simple, fr. LL, of the womb, fr. L *matric-*, *matrix* womb] **1 :** a medieval short lyrical poem in a strict poetic form **2 a :** a complex polyphonic unaccompanied vocal piece on a secular text flourishing in the 16th and 17th centuries **b :** PART-SONG; *esp* **:** GLEE — **mad·ri·gal·ist** \-gə-ləst\ *n*

ma·dri·lene \ˌmad-rə-'len, -'lān\ *n* [F (*consommé*) *madrilène*, lit., Madrid consommé] **:** a consommé flavored with tomato

ma·dro·na *or* **ma·dro·ne** *or* **ma·dro·no** \mə-'drō-nə\ *n* [Sp *madroño*] **:** an evergreen tree or shrub (*Arbutus menziesii*) of the heath family of the Pacific coast of No. America with smooth bark, thick shining leaves, and edible red berries

ma·du·ro \mə-'dü(ə)r-(ˌ)ō\ *n* [Sp, fr. *maduro* ripe, fr. L *maturus* — more at MATURE] **:** a dark-colored relatively strong cigar

mad·wort \'mad-ˌwərt, -ˌwȯ(ə)rt\ *n* **1 :** ALYSSUM 1 **2 :** GOLD OF PLEASURE

mae \'mā\ *Scot var of* MORE

Mae·ce·nas \mi-'sē-nəs\ *n* [L, fr. Gaius *Maecenas* †8 B.C. Roman statesman & patron of literature] **:** a generous patron esp. of literature or art

mael·strom \'mā(ə)l-strəm, -ˌsträm\ *n* [obs. D (now *maalstroom*), fr. *malen* to grind + *strom* stream; akin to OHG *malan* to grind and to OHG *stroum* stream — more at MEAL, STREAM] **1 :** a powerful often violent whirlpool sucking in objects within a given radius **2 :** something resembling a maelstrom in turbulence **:** TURMOIL

mae·nad \'mē-ˌnad\ *n* [L *maenad-*, *maenas*, fr. Gk *mainad-*, *mainas*, fr. *mainesthai* to be mad; akin to Gk *menos* spirit — more at MIND] **1 :** a woman participant in orgiastic Dionysian rites **:** BACCHANTE **2 :** an unnaturally excited or distraught woman — **mae·nad·ic** \mē-'nad-ik\ *adj*

mae·sto·so \mī-'stō-(ˌ)sō, -(ˌ)zō\ *adj (or adv)* [It, fr. *maestà* majesty, fr. L *majestas*] **:** so as to be majestic and stately — used as a direction in music

mae·stro \'mī-(ˌ)strō\ *n, pl* **maestros** *or* **mae·stri** \-ˌstrē\ [It, lit., master, fr. L *magister* — more at MASTER] **:** a master in an art; *esp* **:** an eminent composer, conductor, or teacher of music

Mae West \'mā-'west\ *n* [*Mae West* b1892 Am actress noted for her full figure] **:** an inflatable life jacket

maf·fick \'maf-ik\ *vi* [back-formation fr. *Mafeking night*, English celebration of the lifting of the siege of Mafeking, So. Africa, May 17, 1900] **:** to celebrate with boisterous rejoicing and hilarious behavior

Ma·fia \'mäf-ē-ə, 'maf-\ *n* [*Mafia*, *Maffia*, a Sicilian secret criminal society, fr. It] **1 :** a secret society of political terrorists **2 :** a secret organization composed chiefly of criminal elements and usu. held to control racketeering, peddling of narcotics, gambling, and other illicit activities throughout the world

mag \'mag\ *n, slang* **:** MAGAZINE

mag·a·zine \'mag-ə-ˌzēn, ˌmag-ə-'\ *n* [MF, fr. OProv, fr. Ar *makhāzin*, pl. of *makhzan* storehouse] **1 :** a place where goods or supplies are stored **:** WAREHOUSE **2 :** a room in which powder and other explosives are kept in a fort or a ship **3 :** the contents of a magazine: as **a :** an accumulation of munitions of war **b :** a stock of provisions or goods **4 a :** a periodical containing miscellaneous pieces (as articles, stories, poems) often illustrated **b :** a similar section of a newspaper usu. appearing on Sunday **5 :** a supply chamber: as **a :** a holder in or on a gun for cartridges to be fed into the gun chamber automatically **b :** a lighttight chamber for films or plates on a camera or for film on a motion-picture projector

mag·a·zin·ist \-əst\ *n* **:** one who writes for or edits a magazine

mag·da·len \'mag-də-lən\ *or* **mag·da·lene** \-ˌlēn\ *n, often cap* [Mary *Magdalen* or *Magdalene* woman healed by Jesus of evil spirits (Lk 8:2), considered identical with a reformed prostitute (Lk 7:36–50)] **1 :** a reformed prostitute **2 :** a house of refuge or reformatory for prostitutes

Mag·da·le·ni·an \ˌmag-də-'lē-nē-ən\ *adj* [F *magdalénien*, fr. *La Madeleine*, rock shelter in southwest France] **:** of or relating to an Upper Paleolithic culture characterized by flint, bone, and ivory implements, carving, and paintings

Mag·el·lan·ic Cloud \ˌmaj-ə-ˌlan-ik-, *chiefly Brit* ˌmag-\ *n* [Ferdinand *Magellan* †1521 Pg navigator] **:** either of the two nearest galaxies to the Milky Way system located within 25 degrees of the south celestial pole and appearing as conspicuous patches of light

Ma·gen Da·vid \ˌmȯ-gən-ˈdȯ-vəd\ *n* [Heb *māghēn Dāwīdh,* lit., shield of David] **:** a hexagram used as a symbol of Judaism

ma·gen·ta \mə-ˈjent-ə\ *n* [*Magenta,* Italy] **1 :** FUCHSINE **2 :** a deep purplish red

mag·got \ˈmag-ət\ *n* [ME *mathek, magotte,* of Scand origin; akin to ON *mathkr* maggot; akin to OE *matha* maggot] **1 :** a soft-bodied legless grub that is the larva of a dipterous insect (as the housefly) **2 :** a fantastic or eccentric idea **:** WHIM — **mag·goty** \-ē\ *adj*

magi *pl of* MAGUS

1**Ma·gi·an** \ˈmā-jē-ən\ *n* **:** MAGUS

2**Ma·gi·an** \-jē-ən, -ˌjī-\ *adj* **:** of or relating to the Magi — **Ma·gi·an·ism** \-ə-ˌniz-əm\ *n*

1**mag·ic** \ˈmaj-ik\ *n* [ME *magik,* fr. MF *magique,* fr. L *magice,* fr. Gk *magikē,* fem. of *magikos* Magian, magical, fr. *magos* magus, sorcerer, of Iranian origin; akin to OPer *mogush* sorcerer] **1 a :** the use of means (as charms, spells) believed to have supernatural power over natural forces **b :** magic rites or incantations **2 a :** an extraordinary power or influence seemingly from a supernatural source **b :** something that seems to cast a spell **:** ENCHANTMENT **3 :** the art of producing illusions by legerdemain

2**magic** *adj* **1 :** of or relating to magic **2 a :** having seemingly supernatural qualities or powers **b :** ENCHANTING — **mag·i·cal** \ˈmaj-i-kəl\ *adj* — **mag·i·cal·ly** \-k(ə-)lē\ *adv*

ma·gi·cian \mə-ˈjish-ən\ *n* **1 :** one skilled in magic; *esp* **:** SORCERER **2 :** one who performs tricks of illusion and sleight of hand

magic lantern *n* **:** an early form of optical projector of still pictures using a transparent slide

Ma·gi·not Line \ˌmazh-ə-ˌnō-, ˌmaj-\ *n* [André *Maginot* †1932 Fr minister of war] **:** a line of defensive fortifications built before World War II to protect the eastern border of France but easily outflanked by German invaders

mag·is·te·ri·al \ˌmaj-ə-ˈstir-ē-əl\ *adj* [LL *magisterialis* of authority, fr. *magisterium* office of a master, fr. *magister*] **1 a** (1) **:** of, relating to, or having the characteristics of a master or teacher **:** AUTHORITATIVE (2) **:** marked by a dignified, sedate, or pompous manner or aspect **b :** of, relating to, or required for a master's degree **2 :** of or relating to a magistrate, his office, or his duties **syn** see DICTATORIAL — **mag·is·te·ri·al·ly** \-ē-ə-lē\ *adv*

mag·is·tra·cy \ˈmaj-ə-strə-sē\ *n* **1 :** the state of being a magistrate **2 :** the office, power, or dignity of a magistrate **3 :** a body of magistrates **4 :** the district under a magistrate

ma·gis·tral \ˈmaj-ə-strəl, mə-ˈjis-trəl\ *adj* [LL *magistralis,* fr. L *magistr-, magister*] **:** of, relating to, or characteristic of a master **:** MAGISTERIAL 1a — **ma·gis·tral·ly** \-ē\ *adv*

mag·is·trate \ˈmaj-ə-ˌstrāt, -strət\ *n* [ME *magistrat,* fr. L *magistratus* magistracy, magistrate, fr. *magistr-, magister* master, political superior — more at MASTER] **:** an official entrusted with administration of the laws: as **a :** a principal official exercising governmental powers over a major political unit (as a nation) **b :** a local official exercising administrative and often judicial functions **c :** a local judiciary official having limited original jurisdiction esp. in criminal cases — **mag·is·trat·i·cal** \ˌmaj-ə-ˈstrat-i-kəl, -ˈstrāt-\ *adj* — **mag·is·trat·i·cal·ly** \-k(ə-)lē\ *adv*

mag·is·tra·ture \ˈmaj-ə-ˌstrā-chər, -strə-ˌchu̇(ə)r\ *n* **:** MAGISTRACY

mag·ma \ˈmag-mə\ *n* [L *magmat-, magma,* fr. Gk, thick unguent, fr. *massein* to knead — more at MINGLE] **1** *archaic* **:** DREGS, SEDIMENT **2 :** a thin pasty suspension (as of a precipitate in water) **3 :** molten rock material within the earth from which an igneous rock results by cooling — **mag·mat·ic** \mag-ˈmat-ik\ *adj*

Mag·na Char·ta *or* **Mag·na Car·ta** \ˌmag-nə-ˈkärt-ə\ *n* [ML, lit., great charter] **1 :** a charter of liberties to which the English barons forced King John to give his assent in June 1215 at Runnymede **2 :** a document constituting a fundamental guarantee of rights and privileges

mag·na cum lau·de \ˌmäg-nə-(ˌ)ku̇m-ˈlau̇d-ə, -ˈlau̇d-ē; ˌmag-nə-ˌkəm-ˈlȯd-ē\ *adv (or adj)* [L] **:** with great distinction — used as a mark of academic achievement

mag·na·nim·i·ty \ˌmag-nə-ˈnim-ət-ē\ *n* **1 :** the quality of being magnanimous **:** loftiness of spirit enabling one to bear trouble calmly, to disdain meanness and revenge, and to make sacrifices for worthy ends **2 :** a magnanimous act

mag·nan·i·mous \mag-ˈnan-ə-məs\ *adj* [L *magnanimus,* fr. *magnus* great + *animus* spirit — more at MUCH, ANIMATE] **1 :** showing or suggesting a lofty and courageous spirit **2 :** showing or suggesting nobility of feeling and generosity of mind **:** FORGIVING — **mag·nan·i·mous·ly** *adv* — **mag·nan·i·mous·ness** *n*

mag·nate \ˈmag-ˌnāt, -nət\ *n* [ME *magnates,* pl., fr. LL, fr. L *magnus*] **:** a person of rank, power, influence, or distinction often in a specified area

mag·ne·sia \mag-ˈnē-shə, -ˈnē-zhə\ *n* [NL, fr. *magnes carneus,* a white earth, lit., flesh magnet] **1 :** a white highly infusible magnesium oxide used esp. in refractories, in cements, insulation, fertilizers, and rubber, and in medicine as an antacid and mild laxative **2 :** MAGNESIUM — **mag·ne·sian** \-shən, -zhən\ *adj*

mag·ne·site \ˈmag-nə-ˌsīt\ *n* **:** native magnesium carbonate $MgCO_3$ used esp. in making refractories and magnesia

mag·ne·sium \mag-ˈnē-zē-əm, -zhəm\ *n* [NL, fr. *magnesia*] **:** a silver-white light malleable ductile bivalent metallic element that occurs abundantly in nature and is used in metallurgical and chemical processes, in photography, signaling, and pyrotechny because of the intense white light it produces on burning, and structurally esp. in the form of light alloys — see ELEMENT table

mag·net \ˈmag-nət\ *n* [ME *magnete,* fr. MF, fr. L *magnet-, magnes,* fr. Gk *magnēs* (*lithos*), lit., stone of Magnesia, ancient city in Asia Minor] **1 a :** LODESTONE **b :** a body having the property of attracting iron and producing a magnetic field external to itself; *specif* **:** a mass of iron, steel, or alloy that has this property artificially imparted **2 :** something that attracts

magnet- *or* **magneto-** *comb form* [L *magnet-, magnes*] **1 :** magnetic force ⟨*magneto*meter⟩ **2 :** magnetism **:** magnetic ⟨*magneto*electric⟩ ⟨*magnet*on⟩ **3 :** magnetoelectric ⟨*magneto*generator⟩

mag·net·ic \mag-ˈnet-ik\ *adj* **1 a :** of or relating to a magnet or to magnetism **b :** of, relating to, or characterized by the earth's magnetism **c :** magnetized or capable of being magnetized **d :** actuated by magnetic attraction **2 :** possessing an extraordinary power or ability to attract ⟨a ~ personality⟩ — **mag·net·i·cal·ly** \-i-k(ə-)lē\ *adv*

magnetic deviation *n* **:** DECLINATION 6

magnetic equator *n* **:** ACLINIC LINE

magnetic field *n* **:** the portion of space near a magnetic body or a body carrying a current in which the forces due to the body or current can be detected

magnetic flux *n* **:** the total amount of magnetic induction across or through a given surface

magnetic moment *n* **:** the product of the distance between the poles of a magnet and the strength of either pole

magnetic needle *n* **:** a slender bar of magnetized steel that when suspended so as to be free to turn indicates the direction of a magnetic field in which it is placed and that constitutes the essential part of a compass

magnetic north *n* **:** the northerly direction in the earth's magnetic field indicated by the north-seeking pole of the horizontal magnetic needle

magnetic pole *n* **1 :** either of the poles of a magnet **2 :** either of two small nonstationary regions which are located respectively in the polar areas of the northern and southern hemispheres and toward which the compass needle points from any direction throughout adjacent regions

magnetic recording *n* **:** the process of recording sound, data (as for a computer), or a television program by producing varying local magnetization of a moving tape, wire, or disc

magnetic storm *n* **:** a marked temporary disturbance of the earth's magnetic field held to be related to sunspots

magnetic tape *n* **:** a ribbon of thin paper or plastic coated for use in magnetic recording

magnetic wire *n* **:** a thin wire used in magnetic recording

mag·ne·tism \ˈmag-nə-ˌtiz-əm\ *n* **1 a :** a class of physical phenomena that include the attraction for iron observed in lodestone and a magnet, are believed to be inseparably associated with moving electricity, are exhibited by both magnets and electric currents, and are characterized by fields of force **b :** a science that deals with magnetic phenomena **2 :** an ability to attract or charm

mag·ne·tite \ˈmag-nə-ˌtīt\ *n* **:** a black isometric mineral (Fe_3O_4) of the spinel group that is an oxide of iron and an important iron ore — **mag·ne·tit·ic** \ˌmag-nə-ˈtit-ik\ *adj*

mag·ne·tiz·able \ˈmag-nə-ˌtī-zə-bəl\ *adj* **:** capable of being magnetized

mag·ne·tiza·tion \ˌmag-nət-ə-ˈzā-shən\ *n* **:** a magnetizing or state of being magnetized; *also* **:** degree to which a body is magnetized

mag·ne·tize \ˈmag-nə-ˌtīz\ *vt* **1 :** to attract like a magnet **:** CHARM **2 :** to communicate magnetic properties to — **mag·ne·tiz·er** *n*

mag·ne·to \mag-ˈnēt-(ˌ)ō\ *n, pl* **magnetos :** a magnetoelectric machine; *esp* **:** an alternator with permanent magnets used to generate current for the ignition in an internal-combustion engine

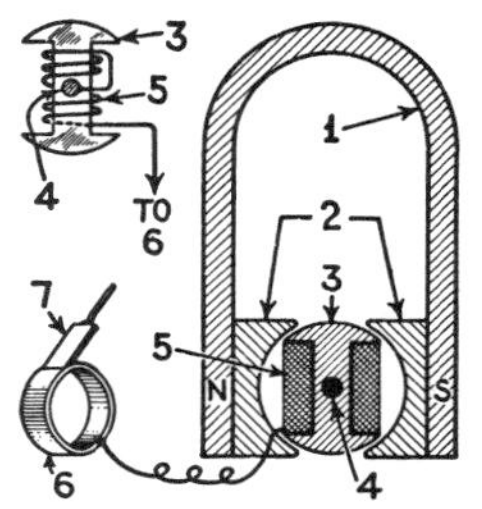

magneto: *1* permanent magnet, *2* pole pieces, *3* armature core, *4* armature shaft, *5* armature winding, *6* slip ring, *7* collector brush

mag·ne·to·elec·tric \-ˌnēt-(ˌ)ō-ə-ˈlek-trik\ *adj* **:** relating to or characterized by electromotive forces developed by magnetic means ⟨~ induction⟩

mag·ne·to·hy·dro·dy·nam·ic \-ˌhī-drə-(ˌ)dī-ˈnam-ik\ *adj* **:** of or relating to phenomena arising from the motion of electrically conducting fluids in the presence of electric and magnetic fields — **mag·ne·to·hy·dro·dy·nam·ics** \-iks\ *n pl but sing or pl in constr*

mag·ne·tom·e·ter \ˌmag-nə-ˈtäm-ət-ər\ *n* **:** an instrument for measuring magnetic intensity esp. of the earth's magnetic field — **mag·ne·to·met·ric** \mag-ˌnēt-ə-ˈme-trik\ *adj* — **mag·ne·tom·e·try** \ˌmag-nə-ˈtäm-ə-trē\ *n*

mag·ne·to·mo·tive force \mag-ˌnēt-ə-ˌmōt-iv-\ *n* **:** a force that is the cause of a flux of magnetic induction

mag·ne·ton \ˈmag-nə-ˌtän\ *n* [ISV] **:** a unit of the quantized magnetic moment of a particle (as an atom)

mag·ne·to·stric·tion \mag-ˈnēt-ō-ˌstrik-shən\ *n* [ISV *magnet-* + *-striction* (as in *constriction*)] **:** the change in the dimensions of a ferromagnetic body caused by a change in its state of magnetization — **mag·ne·to·stric·tive** \-ˌnēt-ō-ˈstrik-tiv\ *adj*

mag·ne·tron \ˈmag-nə-ˌträn\ *n* [blend of *magnet* and *-tron*] **:** a diode vacuum tube in which the flow of electrons is controlled by an externally applied magnetic field to generate power at microwave frequencies

mag·nif·ic \mag-ˈnif-ik\ *adj* [MF *magnifique,* fr. L *magnificus*] **1 :** MAGNIFICENT 2 **2 :** imposing in size or dignity **3 a :** EXALTED, SUBLIME **b :** GRANDILOQUENT, POMPOUS — **mag·nif·i·cal** \-i-kəl\ *adj* — **mag·nif·i·cal·ly** \-k(ə-)lē\ *adv*

mag·nif·i·cat \mag-ˈnif-i-ˌkat, män-ˈyif-i-ˌkät\ *n* [ME, fr. L, magnifies, fr. *magnificare* to magnify; fr. the first word of the canticle] **1** *cap* **:** the canticle of the Virgin Mary in Luke 1:46–55 **2 :** a song or hymn of praise

mag·ni·fi·ca·tion \ˌmag-nə-fə-ˈkā-shən\ *n* **1 :** the act of magnifying **2 a :** the state of being magnified **b :** the apparent enlargement of an object by an optical instrument

mag·nif·i·cence \mag-ˈnif-ə-sən(t)s\ *n* [ME, fr. MF, fr. L *magnificentia,* fr. *magnificus* noble in character, magnificent, fr. *magnus* great — more at MUCH] **1 :** the quality or state of being magnificent **2 :** splendor of surroundings

mag·nif·i·cent \-sənt\ *adj* **1 :** great in deed or place — used only of former famous rulers ⟨Lorenzo the *Magnificent*⟩ **2 :** characterized by splendor or grandeur **3 :** strikingly beautiful or impressive ⟨a ~ physique⟩ **4 :** EXALTED, SUBLIME ⟨~ prose⟩ **5 :** exceptionally fine ⟨a ~ day⟩ **syn** see GRAND — **mag·nif·i·cent·ly** *adv*

mag·nif·i·co \mag-ˈnif-i-ˌkō\ *n, pl* **magnificoes** *or* **magnificos** [It, fr. *magnifico,* adj., magnificent, fr. L *magnificus*] **1 :** a nobleman of Venice **2 :** a person of high position or distinguished appearance and manner

mag·ni·fi·er \ˈmag-nə-ˌfī(-ə)r\ *n* **:** one that magnifies

mag·ni·fy \ˈmag-nə-ˌfī\ *vb* [ME *magnifien,* fr. MF *magnifier,* fr. L *magnificare,* fr. *magnificus*] *vt* **1 a :** EXTOL, LAUD **b :** to cause to be held in greater esteem or respect **2 a :** to increase in significance **:** INTENSIFY **b :** EXAGGERATE **3 :** to enlarge in fact or in appearance

~ *vi* : to have the power of causing objects to appear larger than they are

mag·nil·o·quence \mag-'nil-ə-kwən(t)s\ *n* [L *magniloquentia*, fr. *magniloquus* magniloquent, fr. *magnus* + *loqui* to speak] : the quality or state of being magniloquent

mag·nil·o·quent \-kwənt\ *adj* [back-formation fr. *magniloquence*] : speaking in or characterized by a high-flown often bombastic style or manner : GRANDILOQUENT — **mag·nil·o·quent·ly** *adv*

mag·ni·tude \'mag-nə-,t(y)üd\ *n* [ME, fr. L *magnitudo*, fr. *magnus*] **1** *obs* : greatness of character or position **2 a** : great size or extent **b** (1) : spatial quality : SIZE (2) : QUANTITY, NUMBER (3) : volume of sound : LOUDNESS **3** : the importance, quality, or caliber of something **4** : a number representing the intrinsic or apparent brightness of a celestial body on a logarithmic scale in which a difference of one unit corresponds to the multiplication or division of the brightness of light by 2.512+ **5** : a numerical quantitative measure expressed usu. as a multiple of a standard unit

mag·no·lia \mag-'nōl-yə\ *n* [NL, genus name, fr. Pierre *Magnol* †1715 Fr. botanist] : any of a genus (*Magnolia* of the family Magnoliaceae, the magnolia family) of No. American and Asian shrubs and trees with entire evergreen or deciduous leaves and usu. showy white, yellow, rose, or purple flowers appearing in early spring

mag·num \'mag-nəm\ *n* [L, neut. of *magnus* great] : a large wine bottle holding about 2/5 of a gallon

mag·num opus \,mag-nə-'mō-pəs\ *n* [L] : a great work; *esp* : the greatest achievement of an artist or writer

mag·nus hitch \,mag-nəs-\ *n* [origin unknown] : a rolling hitch similar in form to a clove hitch

mag·pie \'mag-,pī\ *n* [*Mag* (nickname for *Margaret*) + *pie*] **1** : any of numerous birds (esp. of the genus *Pica*) related to the jays but having a long graduated tail and black-and-white plumage **2** : a person who chatters noisily

ma·guey \mə-'gā\ *n* [Sp, fr. Taino] **1 a** : any of various fleshy-leaved agaves **b** : a plant of a closely related genus (*Furcraea*) **2** : any of several hard fibers derived from magueys; *esp* : CANTALA

ma·gus \'mā-gəs\ *n, pl* **ma·gi** \'mā-,jī\ [ME, fr. L, fr. Gk *magos* — more at MAGIC] **1** : a member of a hereditary priestly class among the ancient Medes and Persians; *specif, often cap* : one of the traditionally three wise men from the East paying homage to the infant Jesus **2** : MAGICIAN, SORCERER

Mag·yar \'mag-,yär, 'mäg-; 'mäj-,är\ *n* [Hung] **1** : a member of the dominant people of Hungary **2** : the Finno-Ugric language of the Magyars — **Magyar** *adj*

ma·ha·ra·ja *or* **ma·ha·ra·jah** \,mä-hə-'räj-ə, -'räzh-ə\ *n* [Skt *mahārāja*, fr. *mahat* great + *rājan* raja; akin to Gk *megas* great — more at MUCH] : a Hindu prince ranking above a raja

ma·ha·ra·ni *or* **ma·ha·ra·nee** \-'rän-ē\ *n* [Hindi *mahārānī*, fr. *mahā* great (fr. Skt *mahat*) + *rānī* rani] **1** : the wife of a maharaja **2** : a Hindu princess ranking above a rani

ma·hat·ma \mə-'hät-mə, -'hat-\ *n* [Skt *mahātman*, fr. *mahātman* great-souled, fr. *mahat* + *ātman* soul — more at ATMAN] **1** : a person to be revered for high-mindedness, wisdom, and selflessness **2** : a person of great prestige in some field of endeavor

Ma·ha·ya·na \,mä-hə-'yän-ə\ *n* [Skt *mahāyāna*, lit. great vehicle] : a theistic branch of Buddhism comprising sects chiefly in Tibet, China, and Japan, assimilating native language and culture, and teaching compassion and universal salvation

Mah·di \'mäd-ē\ *n* [Ar *mahdīy*, lit., one rightly guided] : the expected messiah of Muslim tradition — **Mah·dism** \'mäd-,iz-əm\ *n* — **Mah·dist** \'mäd-əst\ *n*

Ma·hi·can \mə-'hē-kən\ *n, pl* **Mahican** *or* **Mahicans** [Mahican] **1** : an Indian people of the upper Hudson river valley **2** : a member of the Mahican people

Mah–Jongg \(')mäzh-'äŋ, (')mäj-, -'ȯŋ, 'mäzh-,, 'mäj-,\ *trademark* — used for a game of Chinese origin usu. played by 4 persons with 144 tiles that are drawn and discarded until one player secures a winning hand

mahl·stick \'mȯl-\ *var of* MAULSTICK

ma·hog·a·ny \mə-'häg-ə-nē\ *n* [origin unknown] **1** : the wood of any of various chiefly tropical trees (family Meliaceae, the mahogany family): **a** (1) : the durable yellowish brown to reddish brown usu. moderately hard and heavy wood of a West Indian tree (*Swietenia mahogani*) that is widely used for cabinetwork and fine finish work (2) : the similar wood of another tree of the same genus **b** (1) : the rather hard heavy usu. odorless wood of African trees (genus *Khaya*) (2) : the rather lightweight cedar-scented wood of African trees (genus *Entandrophragma*) that varies in color from pinkish to deep reddish brown **2** : any of various woods resembling or substituted for mahogany obtained from trees of the mahogany family **3** : a tree that yields mahogany **4** : a moderate reddish brown

ma·ho·nia \mə-'hō-nē-ə\ *n* [NL, genus name, fr. Bernard Mc*Mahon* †1816 Am botanist] : any of a genus (*Mahonia*) of No. American and Asiatic shrubs of the barberry family

Ma·hound \mə-'haůnd, -'hünd\ *n* [ME *Mahun, Mahoun*, fr. OF *Mahom, Mahun*, short for *Mahomet*] **1** *archaic* : Muhammad **2** *Scot* : DEVIL

ma·hout \mə-'haůt\ *n* [Hindi *mahāwat, mahāut*] : a keeper and driver of an elephant

mah·rat·ta *var of* MARATHA

maid \'mād\ *n* [ME *maide*, short for *maiden*] **1** : an unmarried girl or woman esp. when young : VIRGIN **2** : a female servant

¹maid·en \'mād-ᵊn\ *n* [ME, fr. OE *mægden, mæden*, dim. of *mægeth*; akin to OHG *magad* maiden, OIr *mug* serf, *macc* son] **1** : an unmarried girl or woman : MAID **2** : a former Scottish beheading device resembling the guillotine **3** : a horse that has never won a race

²maiden *adj* **1 a** (1) : UNMARRIED ⟨~ aunt⟩ (2) : VIRGIN **b** *of a female animal* (1) : never yet mated (2) : never having borne young **2** : of, relating to, or befitting a maiden **3** : FIRST, EARLIEST ⟨~ voyage⟩ **4** : INTACT, FRESH

maid·en·hair \-,ha(ə)r, -,he(ə)r\ *n* : any of a genus (*Adiantum*) of ferns with delicate palmately branched fronds

maid·en·head \-,hed\ *n* [ME *maidenhed*, fr. *maiden* + *-hed* -hood; akin to ME *-hod* -hood] **1** : the quality or state of being a maiden : VIRGINITY **2** : HYMEN

maid·en·hood \-,hu̇d\ *n* : the quality, state, or time of being a maiden

maid·en·li·ness \-lē-nəs\ *n* : conduct or traits befitting a maiden

maid·en·ly \-lē\ *adj* : of, resembling, or suitable to a maiden

maiden name *n* : the surname of a woman before she is married

maid·hood \'mād-,hu̇d\ *n* : MAIDENHOOD

maid–in–wait·ing \,mād-ᵊn-'wāt-iŋ\ *n, pl* **maids–in–wait·ing** \,mād-zən-\ : a young woman of a queen's or princess's household appointed to attend her

maid of honor 1 : an unmarried lady usu. of noble birth whose duty it is to attend a queen or a princess **2** : a bride's principal unmarried wedding attendant

maid·ser·vant \'mād-,sər-vənt\ *n* : a female servant

ma·ieu·tic \mā-'yüt-ik, mī-\ *adj* [Gk *maieutikos* of midwifery] : relating to or resembling the Socratic method

¹mail \'mā(ə)l\ *n* [ME *male, maille*, fr. OE *māl* agreement, pay, fr. ON *māl* speech, agreement; akin to OE *mǣl* speech, *mōt* meeting — more at MEET] *chiefly Scot* : PAYMENT, RENT

²mail *n, often attrib* [ME *male*, fr. OF, of Gmc origin; akin to OHG *malaha* bag] **1** *chiefly Scot* : BAG, WALLET **2 a** : the bags of letters and the other postal matter conveyed under public authority from one post office to another **b** : the postal matter consigned at one time to or from one person or one post office or conveyed by a particular train, airplane, or ship **c** : a conveyance that transports mail **3 a** : a nation's postal system **b** : postal matter

³mail *vt* : to send by mail : POST

⁴mail *n* [ME *maille*, fr. MF, fr. L *macula* spot, mesh] **1** : armor made of metal links or plates **2** : the hard enclosing covering of various animals (as of a tortoise)

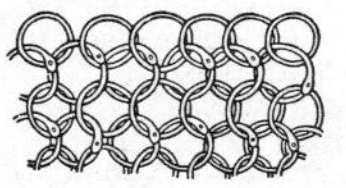

mail 1

⁵mail *vt* : to arm with mail

mail·abil·i·ty \,mā-lə-'bil-ət-ē\ *n* : the quality or state of being mailable

mail·able \'mā-lə-bəl\ *adj* : adapted for mailing : legally admissible as mail

mail·bag \'mā(ə)l-,bag\ *n* **1** : a letter carrier's shoulder bag **2** : a pouch used in the shipment of mail

mail·box \-,bäks\ *n* **1** : a public box for deposit of outgoing mail **2** : a box at or near a dwelling for the occupants' mail

mail drop *n* **1** : a receptacle or a slot for deposit of mail **2** : an address used in transmitting secret communications

mailed \'mā(ə)ld\ *adj* **1** : protected or armed with mail **2** : protected by an outer covering (as of scales or plates)

mailed fist *n* : a threat of armed force

mail·er \'mā-lər\ *n* **1** : one that mails **2** : a machine for addressing mail matter **3** : a container for mailing something in

mail·ing \'mā-liŋ\ *n* [ME *mailling*, fr. *maille* rent] **1** *Scot* : a rented farm **2** *Scot* : the rent paid for a farm

mail·lot \mī-'ō\ *n* [F] **1** : tights for dancers or gymnasts **2** : JERSEY 2 **3** : a woman's one-piece bathing suit

mail·man \'mā(ə)l-,man\ *n* : a man who delivers mail — called also *postman*

mail order *n* : an order for goods that is received and filled by mail

mail–order house *n* : a retail establishment whose business is conducted by mail

¹maim \'mām\ *vt* [ME *maynhen, maymen*, fr. OF *maynier*] **1** : to commit mayhem upon **2** : to mutilate, disfigure, or wound seriously : CRIPPLE — **maim·er** *n*

²maim *n* **1** *obs* : serious physical injury; *esp* : loss of a member of the body **2** *obs* : a serious loss

¹main \'mān\ *n* [in sense 1, fr. ME, fr. OE *maegen*; akin to OHG *magan* strength, OE *magan* to be able; in other senses, fr. ²*main* or by shortening — more at MAY] **1** : physical strength : FORCE — used in the phrase *with might and main* **2 a** : MAINLAND **b** : HIGH SEA **3** : the chief part : essential point **4** : a pipe, duct, or circuit to or from which lead tributary branches of a utility system and which carries their combined flow **5 a** : MAINMAST **b** : MAINSAIL

²main *adj* [ME, fr. OE *maegen-*, fr. *maegen* strength] **1 a** : OUTSTANDING, CONSPICUOUS **b** : CHIEF, PRINCIPAL **2** : fully exerted : SHEER ⟨~ force⟩ ⟨by ~ strength⟩ **3** *obs* : of or relating to a broad expanse (as of sea) **4** : connected with or located near the mainmast or mainsail **5** : expressing the chief predication in a complex sentence ⟨the ~ clause⟩

³main *n* [prob. fr. ²*main*] **1** : a number exceeding four and not exceeding nine called by the caster in the game of hazard before throwing **2** : a cockfight series consisting of an odd number of matches

main·land \-,land, -lənd\ *n* : a continuous body of land constituting the chief part of a country or continent — **main·land·er** \-ər\ *n*

main·ly \'mān-lē\ *adv* **1** *obs* : FORCEFULLY **2** : for the most part : CHIEFLY

main·mast \'mān-,mast, -məst\ *n* : a sailing ship's principal mast usu. second from the bow

mains \'mānz\ *n pl but sing in constr* [short for *domains*] *dial Brit* : the home farm of a manor

main·sail \'mān-,sāl, 'mān(t)-səl\ *n* : the principal sail on the mainmast

main·sheet \'mān-,shēt\ *n* : a rope by which the mainsail is trimmed and secured

main·spring \-,spriŋ\ *n* **1** : the chief spring in a mechanism esp. of a watch or clock **2** : the chief or most powerful motive, agent, or cause

main·stay \-,stā\ *n* **1** : a ship's stay extending from the maintop forward usu. to the foot of the foremast **2** : a chief support

main stem *n* : a main trunk or channel: as **a** : the main course of a stream **b** : the main line of a railroad **c** : the main street of a city or town

main·stream \'mān-,strēm\ *n* : a prevailing current or direction of activity or influence

Main Street *n* **1** : the principal street of a small town **2 a** : the sections of a country centering about its small towns **b** : any place or environment characterized by materialistic self-complacent provincialism — **Main Street·er** \'mān-,strēt-ər\ *n*

main·tain \mān-'tān, mən-\ *vt* [ME *mainteinen*, fr. OF *maintenir*, fr. ML *manutenēre*, fr. L *manu tenēre* to hold in the hand] **1** : to keep in an existing state (as of repair, efficiency, or validity) : preserve from failure or decline ⟨~ one's health⟩ ⟨~ machinery⟩ **2** : to sustain against opposition or danger : uphold and defend ⟨~ a position⟩ **3** : to continue or persevere in : carry on : keep up

⟨couldn't ~ his composure⟩ **4 a :** to support or provide for **:** bear the expense of ⟨has a family to ~⟩ **b :** SUSTAIN ⟨enough food to ~ life⟩ **5 :** to affirm in or as if in argument **:** ASSERT ⟨~*ed* that all men are not equal⟩ — **main·tain·able** \-ˈtā-nə-bəl\ *adj* — **main·tain·er** *n*

syn MAINTAIN, ASSERT, DEFEND, VINDICATE, JUSTIFY mean to uphold as true, right, just or reasonable. MAINTAIN stresses firmness of conviction; ASSERT suggests determination to make others accept what one puts forward; DEFEND implies maintaining in the face of attack or criticism; VINDICATE implies successfully defending; JUSTIFY implies showing to be true, just, or valid by appeal to a standard or to precedent

main·te·nance \ˈmānt-nən(t)s, -ᵊn-ən(t)s\ *n* [ME, fr. MF, fr. OF, fr. *maintenir*] **1 :** the act of maintaining **:** the state of being maintained **:** SUPPORT **2 :** something that maintains **3 :** the upkeep of property or equipment **4 :** an officious or unlawful intermeddling in a legal suit by assisting either party with means to carry it on

main·top \ˈmān-ˌtäp\ *n* **:** a platform about the head of the mainmast of a square-rigged ship

main–top·mast \mān-ˈtäp-ˌmast, -məst\ *n* **:** a mast next above the mainmast

main yard *n* **:** the yard of a mainsail

mair \ˈmār\ *chiefly Scot var of* MORE

mai·son·ette \ˌmāz-ᵊn-ˈet\ *n* [F *maisonnette*, fr. OF, dim. of *maison* house, fr. L *mansion-*, *mansio* dwelling place — more at MANSION] **1 :** a small house **2 :** an apartment often of two stories

maî·tre d' \ˌmāt-ər-ˈdē\ *n*, *pl* **maî·tre d's** \-ˈdēz\ **:** MAÎTRE D'HÔTEL

maî·tre d'hô·tel \ˌmā-trə-(ˌ)dō-ˈtel, ˌmāt-dō-\ *n*, *pl* **maîtres d'hôtel** *same*\ [F, lit. master of house] **1 a :** MAJORDOMO **b :** HEADWAITER **2 :** a sauce of melted butter, chopped parsley, salt, pepper, and lemon juice

maize \ˈmāz\ *n* [Sp *maíz*, fr. Taino *mahiz*] **:** INDIAN CORN

ma·jes·tic \mə-ˈjes-tik\ *adj* **:** having or exhibiting majesty **:** STATELY **syn** see GRAND — **ma·jes·ti·cal** \-ti-kəl\ *adj* — **ma·jes·ti·cal·ly** \-k(ə-)lē\ *adv*

maj·es·ty \ˈmaj-ə-stē\ *n* [ME *maieste*, fr. OF *majesté*, fr. L *majestat-*, *majestas;* akin to L *major* greater] **1 :** sovereign power, authority, or dignity; *also* **:** the person of a sovereign — used as a title for a king, queen, emperor, or empress ⟨if your *Majesty* please⟩ ⟨Her Britannic *Majesty's* Consulate General⟩ **2 a :** royal bearing or aspect **:** GRANDEUR **b :** greatness or splendor of quality or character

ma·jol·i·ca \mə-ˈjäl-i-kə\ *also* **ma·iol·i·ca** \-ˈyäl-\ *n* [It *maiolica*, fr. ML *Majolica* Majorca, fr. LL *Majorca*] **:** a Renaissance Italian pottery glazed, richly colored, and ornamented; *also* **:** a modern imitation of it

1ma·jor \ˈmā-jər\ *adj* [ME *maiour*, fr. L *major*, compar. of *magnus* great, large — more at MUCH] **1 :** greater in dignity, rank, importance, or interest **2 :** greater in number, quantity, or extent **3 :** having attained majority **4 :** notable or conspicuous in effect or scope **5 :** SERIOUS ⟨a ~ illness⟩ **6 a :** of or relating to a subject of academic study chosen as a field of specialization **b :** of or relating to a secondary-school course requiring a maximum of classroom hours **7 a :** having half steps between the third and fourth and the seventh and eighth degrees ⟨~ scale⟩ **b :** based on a major scale ⟨~ key⟩ **c :** equivalent to the distance between the keynote and another tone (except the fourth and fifth) of a major scale ⟨~ interval⟩ **d :** containing a major third ⟨~ triad⟩

2major *n* **1 :** a person having attained majority **2 a :** one that is superior in rank, importance, station, or performance **b :** a major musical interval, scale, key, or mode **3 :** a commissioned officer in the army, air force, or marine corps ranking above a captain and below a lieutenant colonel **4 a :** a subject of academic study chosen as a field of specialization **b :** a student specializing in such field

3major *vi* **ma·jor·ing** \ˈmāj-(ə-)riŋ\ **:** to pursue an academic major

ma·jor·do·mo \ˌmā-jər-ˈdō-(ˌ)mō\ *n*, *pl* **majordomos** [Sp *mayordomo* or obs. It *maiordomo*, fr. ML *major domus*, lit., chief of the house] **1 :** a man having charge of a great household **:** a head steward **2 :** BUTLER, STEWARD

majorette *n* **:** DRUM MAJORETTE

major form class *n* **:** any one of the parts of speech of traditional grammar (as noun, verb, or preposition)

major general *n* [F *major général*, fr. *major*, n. + *général*, adj., general] **:** a commissioned officer in the army, air force, or marine corps ranking above a brigadier general and below a lieutenant general

ma·jor·i·ty \mə-ˈjȯr-ət-ē, -ˈjär-\ *n*, *often attrib* **1** *obs* **:** the quality or state of being greater **:** SUPERIORITY **2 a :** the age at which full civil rights are accorded; *esp* **:** the age of 21 **b :** the status of one who has attained this age **3 a :** a number greater than half of a total **b :** the excess of such a greater number over the remainder of the total **:** MARGIN **c :** the preponderant quantity or share **4 :** the group or party whose votes preponderate **5 :** the military office, rank, or commission of a major

majority rule *n* **:** a political principle providing that a majority usu. constituted by fifty percent plus one of an organized group shall have the power to make decisions binding upon the whole

major league *n* **:** a league of highest classification in U.S. professional baseball; *also* **:** a league of major importance in any of various other sports

major order *n* **1 :** the order of priest, deacon, or subdeacon in the Roman Catholic Church **2 :** the order of bishop, priest, or deacon in the Eastern, Anglican, or Episcopal Church

major party *n* **:** a political party having electoral strength sufficient to permit it to win control of a government usu. with comparative regularity and when defeated to constitute the principal opposition to the party in power

major premise *n* **:** the premise of a syllogism containing the major term

major seminary *n* **:** a Roman Catholic seminary giving usu. the entire six years of senior college and theological training

major suit *n* **:** either of two bridge suits of superior scoring value: **a :** SPADES **b :** HEARTS

major term *n* **:** the term of a syllogism constituting the predicate of the conclusion

ma·jus·cu·lar \mə-ˈjəs-kyə-lər\ *adj* **:** of, relating to, or resembling a majuscule

ma·jus·cule \ˈmaj-əs-ˌkyü(ə)l, mə-ˈjəs-\ *n* [F, fr. L *majusculus* rather large, dim. of *major*] **:** a large letter (as a capital) — **majuscule** *adj*

mak·able \ˈmā-kə-bəl\ *adj* **:** capable of being made

mak·ar \ˈmāk-ər, ˈmak-\ *n* [ME *maker*] *chiefly Scot* **:** POET

ma·ka·tea \ˌmäk-ə-ˈtā-ə\ *n* [Tuamotu] **:** a broad uplifted coral reef surrounding an island in the south Pacific

1make \ˈmāk\ *vb* **made** \ˈmād\ **mak·ing** [ME *maken*, fr. OE *macian;* akin to OHG *mahhōn* to prepare, make, OSlav *mazati* to anoint] *vt* **1 a** *obs* **:** BEHAVE, ACT **b :** to seem to begin (an action) **2 a :** to cause to happen to or be experienced by someone **b :** to cause to exist, occur, or appear **:** CREATE ⟨~ a disturbance⟩ **c :** to favor the growth or occurrence of ⟨haste ~*s* waste⟩ **d :** to fit, intend, or destine by or as if by creating ⟨was *made* to be an actor⟩ **3 a :** to bring into being by forming, shaping, or altering material **:** FASHION ⟨~ a dress⟩ **b :** COMPOSE, WRITE **c :** to lay out and construct ⟨~ a road⟩ **4 :** to frame or formulate in the mind ⟨~ plans⟩ **5 :** to put together from components **:** CONSTITUTE ⟨house *made* of stone⟩ **6 a :** to compute or estimate to be **b :** to form and hold in the mind ⟨~ no doubt of it⟩ **7 a :** to put together and set alight (a fire) **b :** to set in order **:** PREPARE **c :** to shuffle (a deck of cards) in preparation for dealing **8 :** to cut (hay) and spread for drying **9 a :** to cause to be or become ⟨*made* himself useful⟩ **b :** APPOINT **10 a :** ENACT, ESTABLISH **b :** to execute in an appropriate manner ⟨~ a will⟩ **c :** SET, NAME ⟨~ a price⟩ **11 a** *chiefly dial* **:** to make fast **:** SHUT **b :** to cause (an electric circuit) to be completed **12 a :** to conclude as to the nature or meaning of ⟨what to ~ of his actions⟩ **b :** to regard as being ⟨not the fool some ~ him⟩ **13 a :** to carry out (an indicated action) ⟨~ war⟩ **b :** to perform with a bodily movement ⟨~ a bow⟩ **c :** to achieve by traversing ⟨~ a detour⟩ ⟨mailman *making* his rounds⟩ **14 a :** to produce as a result of action, effort, or behavior with respect to something ⟨~ a mess of the job⟩ ⟨tried to ~ a thorough job of it⟩ **b :** EAT ⟨*made* a good breakfast⟩ **c** *archaic* **:** to turn into another language by translation **15 :** to cause to act in a certain way **:** COMPEL ⟨~ him return⟩ **16 :** to cause or assure the success or prosperity of ⟨anyone he takes a liking to is *made*⟩ **17 a :** to amount to in significance ⟨~*s* a great difference⟩ **b :** to form the essential being of ⟨clothes ~ the man⟩ **c :** to form by an assembling of individuals ⟨~ a quorum⟩ **d :** to count as ⟨~ a fourth at bridge⟩ **18 a :** to be or be capable of being changed or fashioned into ⟨rags ~ the best paper⟩ **b :** to develop into ⟨she will ~ a fine wife⟩ **c :** FORM 5b **19 a :** REACH, ATTAIN — often used with *it* ⟨you'll never ~ it that far⟩ **b :** to gain the rank of ⟨~ major⟩ **c :** to gain a place on ⟨~ the team⟩ **20 :** to gain (as money) by working, trading, or dealing **21 a :** to act so as to win or acquire **b :** to score (points) in a game or sport **22 a :** to fulfill (a contract) in a card game **b :** to win a trick with (a card) **23 a :** to include in a route or itinerary **b :** CATCH ⟨time to ~ the train⟩ **24 :** to persuade to consent to sexual intercourse ~ *vi* **1** *archaic* **:** to compose poetry **2 a :** BEHAVE, ACT **b :** to begin or seem to begin a certain action ⟨*made* as though to hand it to me⟩ **c :** to act so as to be or to seem to be ⟨~ merry⟩ **d** *slang* **:** to play a part ⟨~ like a bird⟩ **3 :** to set out **:** HEAD ⟨*made* after the fox⟩ **4 :** to increase in height or size ⟨the tide is *making* now⟩ **5 :** to reach or extend in a certain direction **6 :** to have weight or effect **:** TELL ⟨courtesy ~*s* for safer driving⟩ **7 :** to undergo manufacture or processing ⟨hay ~*s* better in small heaps⟩

syn MAKE, FORM, SHAPE, FASHION, FABRICATE, MANUFACTURE, FORGE mean to cause to come into being. MAKE may imply any such action of producing or creating whether by an intelligent agency or blind forces and resulting in either material or immaterial existence; FORM implies a definite outline, structure, or design in the thing produced; SHAPE suggests impressing a form upon some material; FASHION suggests the use of inventive power or ingenuity; FABRICATE suggests a making of many parts into a whole and often implies an ingenious inventing of elaborate falsehood; MANUFACTURE implies making repeatedly by a fixed process and usu. by machinery; FORGE implies a making or effecting by great physical or mental effort

— **make a face :** to distort one's features **:** GRIMACE — **make away with 1 :** to carry off **2 :** SPEND, DISSIPATE **3 :** DESTROY, KILL **4 :** CONSUME, EAT — **make believe :** PRETEND, FEIGN — **make bold :** VENTURE, DARE — **make bones :** to show hesitation, uncertainty, or scruple ⟨*makes* no *bones* about his dislike⟩ — **make book :** to accept bets at calculated odds on all the entrants in a race or contest — **make eyes :** OGLE — **make good :** to make valid or complete ⟨*made good* his escape⟩: as **a :** to make up for (a deficiency) **b :** INDEMNIFY ⟨*make good* the loss⟩ **c :** to carry out (a promise or prediction) **:** FULFILL **d :** PROVE ⟨*make good* a charge⟩ **e :** SUCCEED — **make hay :** to make use of offered opportunity esp. in gaining an early advantage — **make head 1 :** to make progress esp. against resistance **2 :** to rise in armed revolt **3 :** to build up pressure (as in a steam boiler) — **make love 1 :** WOO, COURT **2 a :** NECK, PET **b :** to engage in sexual intercourse — **make public :** DISCLOSE — **make sail 1 :** to raise or spread sail **2 :** to set out on a voyage — **make time 1 :** to travel fast **2 :** to gain time **3 :** to make progress toward winning favor ⟨trying to *make time* with the waitress⟩ — **make tracks 1 :** to proceed at a walk or run **2 :** to go in a hurry **:** run away **:** FLEE — **make water 1** *of a boat* **:** LEAK **2 :** URINATE — **make way 1 :** to open or give room for passing or entering **:** fall back or move aside **2 :** to make progress — **make with** *slang* **:** PRODUCE, PERFORM — usu. used with *the* and in place of the idiomatic verb ⟨start *making with* the answers⟩ ⟨*making with* the tears⟩

2make *n* **1 a :** the manner or style in which a thing is constructed **b :** the origin of a manufactured article **2 :** the physical, mental, or moral constitution of a person **3 a :** the action of producing or manufacturing **b :** the actual yield or amount produced over a specified period **:** OUTPUT **4 :** the declaration of trumps in an early form of bridge **5 :** the closing or completing of an electric circuit **6 :** the act of shuffling cards; *also* **:** turn to shuffle — **on the make 1 :** in the process of forming, growing, or improving **2 :** in quest of a higher social or financial status **3 :** in search of sexual adventure

make·bate \ˈmāk-ˌbāt\ *n* [1*make* + obs. *bate* (strife)] *archaic* **:** one that excites contentions and quarrels

1make–be·lieve \ˈmāk-bə-ˌlēv\ *n* **1 :** a pretending to believe **:** PRETENSE **2 :** one who makes believe or pretends

2make–believe *adj* **:** FEIGNED ⟨a private *make-believe* world⟩ **:** INSINCERE

make–do \ˈmāk-ˌdü\ *adj* **:** MAKESHIFT — **make–do** *n*

make·fast \-ˌfast\ *n* **:** something to which a boat is fastened

make off *vi* **:** to leave suddenly or in haste
make out *vt* **1 :** to draw up or prepare in writing **2 :** to find or grasp the meaning of **3 a :** DEMONSTRATE, ESTABLISH **b :** CONCLUDE ⟨how do you *make* that *out*⟩ **4 :** to represent as being **5 :** to represent or delineate in detail **6 :** DISCERN **~** *vi* **:** to get along
make over *vt* **1 :** to transfer the title of **2 :** REMAKE, REMODEL
mak·er \ˈmā-kər\ *n* **:** one that makes: as **a** *cap* **:** ²GOD **b** *archaic* **:** POET **c :** a person who makes a promissory note **d :** a declarer in bridge
make·ready \ˈmā-ˌkred-ē\ *n* **:** final preparation (as of a form on a printing press) for running; *also* **:** material used in this preparation
make·shift \ˈmāk-ˌshift\ *n* **:** a temporary expedient **syn** see RESOURCE — **makeshift** *adj*
make up *vt* **1 a :** COMPILE **b :** INVENT, IMPROVISE **c :** to set (an account) in order **:** BALANCE **2 a :** to form by fitting together or assembling **b :** to arrange type matter into (columns or pages) for printing **c :** to put together from ingredients **3 :** to wrap or fasten up **4 a :** to set in order **:** ARRANGE **b :** to shuffle (a deck) for dealing **5 :** to make good (a deficiency) **6 a** *of parts or quantities* **:** to combine to produce (a whole) **b :** CONSTITUTE, COMPOSE **7 :** SETTLE, DECIDE **8 a :** to prepare in physical appearance for a role **b :** to apply cosmetics to **~** *vi* **1 :** to become reconciled **2 a :** to act ingratiatingly or flatteringly **b :** to make love **3 :** COMPENSATE, PAY **4 :** to apply cosmetics
make·up \ˈmā-ˌkəp\ *n* **1 a :** the way in which the parts or ingredients of something are put together **:** COMPOSITION **b :** physical, mental, and moral constitution **2 :** the operation of making up (as of matter for printing); *also* **:** the arrangement of such matter **3 a :** cosmetics used to color and beautify the face; *also* **:** a cosmetic applied to other parts of the body **b :** the total of cosmetics, wigs, and other items
make·weight \ˈmā-ˌkwāt\ *n* **1 a :** something thrown into a scale to bring the weight to a desired value **b :** something of little independent value thrown in to fill a gap **2 :** COUNTERWEIGHT, COUNTERPOISE
mak·ing \ˈmā-kiŋ\ *n* **1 :** the act or process of forming, causing, doing, or coming into being **2 :** a process or means of advancement or success **3 :** something made; *esp* **:** a quantity produced at one time **:** BATCH **4 a :** POTENTIALITY — often used in pl. **b** *pl* **:** the material from which something is to be made; *specif* *usu* ˈmā-kənz\ **:** paper and tobacco for cigarettes
makuta *pl of* LIKUTA
mal- *comb form* [ME, fr. MF, fr. OF, fr. *mal* bad (fr. L *malus*) & *mal* badly, fr. L *male*, fr. *malus* — more at SMALL] **1 a :** bad ⟨*mal*practice⟩ **b :** badly ⟨*mal*odorous⟩ **2 a :** abnormal ⟨*mal*formation⟩ **b :** abnormally ⟨*mal*formed⟩ **3 a :** inadequate ⟨*mal*adjustment⟩ **b :** inadequately ⟨*mal*nourished⟩
malac- *or* **malaco-** *comb form* [L, fr. Gk *malak-*, *malako-*, fr. *malakos;* akin to L *molere* to grind] **:** soft ⟨*malaco*pterygii⟩
ma·lac·ca cane \mə-ˌlak-ə-\ *n* [*Malacca*, Malaya] **:** an often mottled cane from an Asiatic rattan palm (*Calamus rotang*)
Mal·a·chi \ˈmal-ə-ˌkī\ *or* **Mal·a·chi·as** \ˌmal-ə-ˈkī-əs\ *n* [Heb *Mal'ākhī*] **:** a minor Hebrew prophet of the 5th century B.C.
mal·a·chite \ˈmal-ə-ˌkīt\ *n* [ME *melochites*, fr. L *molochites*, fr. Gk *molochitēs*, fr. *molochē* mallow] **:** a mineral $Cu_2CO_3(OH)_2$ that is a green basic carbonate of copper used as an ore and for making ornamental objects
mal·a·col·o·gy \ˌmal-ə-ˈkäl-ə-jē\ *n* [F *malacologie*, contr. of *malacozoologie*, fr. NL *Malacozoa*, zoological group including soft-bodied animals (fr. *malac-* + *-zoa*) + F *-logie* -logy] **:** a branch of zoology dealing with mollusks
mal·a·cos·tra·can \ˌmal-ə-ˈkäs-tri-kən\ *n* [deriv. of Gk *malakostrakos* soft-shelled, fr. *malak-* + *ostrakon* shell — more at OYSTER] **:** any of a major subclass (Malacostraca) of crustaceans including most of the well-known marine, freshwater, and terrestrial members of the group (as crabs, sow bugs) — **malacostracan** *adj* — **mal·a·cos·tra·cous** \-tri-kəs\ *adj*
mal·ad·ap·ta·tion \ˌmal-ˌad-ˌap-ˈtā-shən\ *n* **:** poor or inadequate adaptation
mal·adapt·ed \ˌmal-ə-ˈdap-təd\ *adj* **:** unsuited or poorly suited (as to a particular use, purpose, or situation)
mal·adap·tive \-tiv\ *adj* **1 :** marked by poor or inadequate adaptation **2 :** not conducive to adaptation
mal·ad·just·ed \ˌmal-ə-ˈjəs-təd\ *adj* **:** poorly or inadequately adjusted; *specif* **:** lacking harmony with one's environment from failure to adjust one's desires to the conditions of one's life
mal·ad·jus·tive \-ˈjəs-tiv\ *adj* **:** not conducive to adjustment
mal·ad·just·ment \ˌmal-ə-ˈjəs(t)-mənt\ *n* **:** poor or inadequate adjustment
mal·ad·min·is·ter \ˌmal-əd-ˈmin-ə-stər\ *vt* **:** to administer badly — **mal·ad·min·is·tra·tion** \ˌmal-əd-ˌmin-ə-ˈstrā-shən\ *n*
mal·adroit \ˌmal-ə-ˈdrȯit\ *adj* [F, fr. MF, fr. *mal-* + *adroit*] **:** lacking adroitness **:** INEPT **syn** see AWKWARD — **mal·adroit·ly** *adv* — **mal·adroit·ness** *n*
mal·a·dy \ˈmal-əd-ē\ *n* [ME *maladie*, fr. OF, fr. *malade* sick, fr. L *male habitus* in bad condition] **1 :** a disease or disorder of the animal body **2 :** an unwholesome condition
ma·la fi·de \ˌmal-ə-ˈfīd-ē, -ˈfīd-ə\ *adv* (*or adj*) [LL] **:** with or in bad faith
Ma·la·ga \ˈmal-ə-gə\ *n* **:** any of several usu. sweet dessert wines of Málaga, Spain; *also* **:** a similar wine made elsewhere
Mal·a·gasy \ˌmal-ə-ˈgas-ē\ *n, pl* **Malagasy** *also* **Mal·a·gas·ies** **1 :** a native or inhabitant of Madagascar or of the Malagasy Republic **2 :** the Austronesian language of the Malagasy people — **Malagasy** *adj*
ma·la·gue·na \ˌmal-ə-ˈgān-yə, ˌmäl-\ *n* [Sp *malagueña*, fr. fem. of *malagueño* of Málaga, fr. *Málaga*] **1 :** a folk tune native to Málaga that is similar to a fandango **2 :** a Spanish dance similar to a fandango
mal·aise \ma-ˈlāz\ *or* **mal·ease** \-ˈlēz\ *n* [F *malaise*, fr. OF, fr. *mal-* + *aise* comfort — more at EASE] **1 :** an indefinite feeling of debility or lack of health often indicative of or accompanying the onset of an illness **2 :** a vague sense of mental or moral ill-being
mal·a·mute *or* **mal·e·mute** \ˈmal-ə-ˌmyüt\ *n* [*Malemute*, an Alaskan Eskimo people] **:** a sled dog of northern No. America; *esp* **:** ALASKAN MALAMUTE
mal·apert \ˌmal-ə-ˈpərt\ *adj* [ME, fr. MF unskillful, fr. *mal-* + *apert* skillful, modif. of L *expertus* expert] **:** impudently bold **:** SAUCY — **mal·apert·ly** *adv* — **mal·apert·ness** *n*
mal·a·prop \ˈmal-ə-ˌpräp\ *or* **mal·a·prop·ian** \ˌmal-ə-ˈpräp-ē-ən\ *adj* [Mrs. *Malaprop*] **:** using or marked by the use of malapropisms
mal·a·prop·ism \ˈmal-ə-ˌpräp-ˌiz-əm\ *n* [Mrs. *Malaprop*, character noted for her misuse of words in R. B. Sheridan's comedy *The Rivals* (1775)] **1 :** a usu. humorous misapplication of a word; *specif* **:** use of a word sounding somewhat like the one intended but ludicrously wrong in the context **2 :** an example of malapropism (as in "an allegory on the banks of the Nile")
mal·ap·ro·pos \ˌmal-ˌap-rə-ˈpō, (ˈ)mal-ˈap-rə-ˌ\ *adv* [F *mal à propos*] **:** in an inappropriate or inopportune way — **malapropos** *adj*
ma·lar \ˈmā-lər\ *adj* [NL *malaris*, fr. L *mala* jawbone, cheek] **:** of or relating to the cheek or the side of the head
ma·lar·ia \mə-ˈler-ē-ə\ *n* [It, fr. *mala aria* bad air] **1** *archaic* **:** air infected with a noxious substance capable of causing disease; *esp* **:** MIASMA **2 a :** a human disease caused by sporozoan parasites (genus *Plasmodium*) in the red blood cells, transmitted by the bite of anopheline mosquitoes, and characterized by periodic attacks of chills and fever **b :** any of various diseases of birds and mammals caused by blood protozoans — **ma·lar·i·al** \-əl\ *also* **ma·lar·i·an** \-ən\ *adj* — **ma·lar·i·ous** \-əs\ *adj*
ma·lar·key \mə-ˈlär-kē\ *n* [origin unknown] **:** insincere or foolish talk **:** BUNKUM
ma·late \ˈmal-ˌāt, ˈmā-ˌlāt\ *n* **:** a salt or ester of malic acid
Mal·a·thi·on \ˌmal-ə-ˈthī-ˌän\ *trademark* — used for a thiophosphate insecticide $C_{10}H_{19}O_6PS_2$ with a lower mammalian toxicity than parathion
Ma·lay \mə-ˈlā, ˈmā-(ˌ)lā\ *n* [obs. D *Malayo* (now *Maleier*), fr. Malay *Mĕlayu*] **1 :** a member of a people of the Malay peninsula, eastern Sumatra, parts of Borneo, and some adjacent islands **2 :** the Austronesian language of the Malays — **Malay** *adj* — **Ma·lay·an** \mə-ˈlā-ən, ˈmā-ˌlā-\ *n or adj*
Mal·a·ya·lam \ˌmal-ə-ˈyäl-əm\ *n* **:** the Dravidian language of Kerala, southwest India, closely related to Tamil
Ma·layo- \mə-ˌlā-(ˌ)ō-, mā-\ *comb form* **:** Malayan and ⟨*Malayo*-Indonesian⟩
mal·con·tent \ˌmal-kən-ˈtent\ *adj* [MF, fr. OF, fr. *mal-* + *content*] **:** marked by a restless, moody, or bitter dissatisfaction with the existing state of affairs **:** DISCONTENTED; *specif* **:** disaffected with an established order or government — **malcontent** *n*
mal de mer \ˌmal-də-ˈme(ə)r\ *n* [F] **:** SEASICKNESS
¹male \ˈmā(ə)l\ *adj* [ME, fr. MF *masle*, *male*, adj. & n., fr. L *masculus*, dim. of *mar-*, *mas* male] **1 a** (1) **:** of, relating to, or being the sex that begets young by performing the fertilizing function in generation and produces relatively small usu. motile gametes (as sperms, spermatozoids, spermatozoa) by which the eggs of a female are made fertile ⟨~ organs⟩ (2) **:** STAMINATE; *esp* **:** having only staminate flowers and not producing fruit or seeds ⟨a ~ holly⟩ **b** (1) **:** of, relating to, or characteristic of the male sex ⟨a deep ~ voice⟩ (2) **:** made up of male individuals and esp. men ⟨a ~ choir⟩ **2 :** MASCULINE 3a **3 :** designed for fitting into a corresponding hollow part — **male·ness** \-nəs\ *n*
syn MASCULINE, MANLY, MANLIKE, MANNISH, MANFUL, VIRILE: MALE applies to animals and plants as well as to human beings and always indicates sex; MASCULINE suggests qualities distinguishing men from women; MANLY suggests the admirable qualities of a mature man and applies esp. to youth; MANLIKE suggests the characteristic qualities of men and particularly applies to masculine foibles; MANNISH applies chiefly to women having or affecting manlike qualities; MANFUL is somewhat narrower in scope than MANLY in stressing courage and resolution; VIRILE differs from MANLY in stressing driving energy, aggressiveness, or male sexuality
²male *n* **:** a plant or animal that is male
male alto *n* **:** COUNTERTENOR
¹male·dict \ˌmal-ə-ˈdikt\ *adj* [LL *maledictus*] *archaic* **:** ACCURSED
²maledict *vt, archaic* **:** EXECRATE, CURSE
male·dic·tion \ˌmal-ə-ˈdik-shən\ *n* [ME *malediccioun*, fr. LL *malediction-*, *maledictio*, fr. *maledictus*, pp. of *maledicere* to curse, fr. L, to speak evil of, fr. *male* badly + *dicere* to speak, say — more at MAL-, DICTION] **:** CURSE, EXECRATION — **male·dic·to·ry** \-ˈdik-t(ə-)rē\ *adj*
male·fac·tion \ˌmal-ə-ˈfak-shən\ *n* **:** an evil deed **:** CRIME
male·fac·tor \ˈmal-ə-ˌfak-tər\ *n* [ME, fr. L, fr. *malefactus*, pp. of *malefacere* to do evil, fr. *male* + *facere* to do — more at DO] **1 :** one who commits an offense against the law; *esp* **:** FELON **2 :** EVILDOER
male fern *n* **:** a fern (*Dryopteris filix-mas*) producing an oleoresin used in expelling tapeworms
ma·lef·ic \mə-ˈlef-ik\ *adj* [L *maleficus* wicked, mischievous, fr. *male*] **1 :** having malignant influence **:** BALEFUL **2 :** MALICIOUS
ma·lef·i·cence \mə-ˈlef-ə-sən(t)s\ *n* **1 a :** EVILDOING **b :** an evil deed **2 :** the quality or state of being maleficent
ma·lef·i·cent \-sənt\ *adj* [back-formation fr. *maleficence*] **:** working or productive of harm or evil **:** BALEFUL
ma·le·ic hydrazide \mə-ˌlē-ik-, -ˌlā-\ *n* [*maleic acid* (malic acid)] **:** a crystalline cyclic hydrazide $C_4H_4N_2O_2$ used to retard plant growth
mal·en·ten·du \mȧ-lä̃ⁿ-tä̃ⁿ-dü̅\ *n* [F, fr. *mal entendu* misunderstood] **:** MISUNDERSTANDING
male–ster·ile \ˈmā(ə)l-ˈster-əl\ *adj* **:** having male gametes lacking or nonfunctional
ma·lev·o·lence \mə-ˈlev-ə-lən(t)s\ *n* **1 :** the quality or state of being malevolent **2 :** malevolent behavior **syn** see MALICE
ma·lev·o·lent \-lənt\ *adj* [L *malevolent-*, *malevolens*, fr. *male* badly + *volent-*, *volens*, prp. of *velle* to wish — more at MAL-, WILL] **:** having, showing, or arising from intense often vicious ill will, spite, or hatred — **ma·lev·o·lent·ly** *adv*
mal·fea·sance \(ˈ)mal-ˈfēz-ᵊn(t)s\ *n* [*mal-* + obs. *feasance* (doing, execution)] **:** wrongful conduct esp. by a public official
mal·for·ma·tion \ˌmal-fȯr-ˈmā-shən, -fər-\ *n* **:** irregular, anomalous, abnormal, or faulty formation or structure
mal·formed \(ˈ)mal-ˈfȯ(ə)rmd\ *adj* **:** characterized by malformation **:** badly or imperfectly formed **:** MISSHAPEN
mal·func·tion \(ˈ)mal-ˈfəŋ(k)-shən\ *vi* **:** to fail to operate in the

normal or usual manner — **malfunction** *n*

mal·gré \mal-ˈgrā, ˈmal-ˌ\ *prep* [F, fr. OF *maugré* — more at MAUGRE] **:** DESPITE

ma·lic acid \ˌmal-ik-, ˌmā-lik-\ *n* [F *acide malique*, fr. L *malum* apple, fr. Gk *mēlon, malon*] **:** a crystalline hydroxy dicarboxylic acid $C_4H_6O_5$ found esp. in various plant juices

mal·ice \ˈmal-əs\ *n* [ME, fr. OF, fr. L *malitia*, fr. *malus* bad — more at SMALL] **:** ILL WILL; *specif* **:** intent to commit an unlawful act or cause harm without legal justification or excuse

syn MALEVOLENCE, ILL WILL, SPITE, MALIGNITY, SPLEEN, GRUDGE: MALICE may imply a deep-seated and often unreasonable dislike and a desire to see one suffer or it may suggest a causeless passing mischievous impulse; MALEVOLENCE implies a deep and lasting hatred; ILL WILL may suggest a briefer feeling of antipathy and resentment often with cause; SPITE implies active malevolence together with envy or meanness of spirit; MALIGNITY stresses the intensity and driving force of malevolence; SPLEEN implies ill will together with hot temper; GRUDGE implies a cherished feeling of resentment or ill will that seeks satisfaction

ma·li·cious \mə-ˈlish-əs\ *adj* **:** given to, marked by, or arising from malice — **ma·li·cious·ly** *adv* — **ma·li·cious·ness** *n*

malicious mischief *n* **:** willful, wanton, or reckless damage to or destruction of another's property

1**ma·lign** \mə-ˈlīn\ *adj* [ME *maligne*, fr. MF, fr. L *malignus*, fr. *male* badly + *gignere* to beget — more at MAL-, KIN] **1 a :** evil in nature, influence, or effect **:** INJURIOUS **b :** MALIGNANT, VIRULENT **2 :** having or showing intense often vicious ill will **:** MALEVOLENT **syn** see SINISTER

2**malign** *vt* [ME *malignen*, fr. MF *maligner* to act maliciously, fr. LL *malignari*, fr. L *malignus*] **:** to utter injuriously misleading or false reports about **:** speak evil of

syn MALIGN, TRADUCE, ASPERSE, VILIFY, CALUMNIATE, DEFAME, SLANDER mean to injure by speaking ill of regardless of truth. MALIGN suggests specific and often subtle misrepresentation but may not always imply deliberate lying; TRADUCE stresses the resulting ignominy and distress to the victim; ASPERSE implies continued attack on a reputation often by indirect or insinuated detraction; VILIFY implies attempting to destroy a reputation by open and direct abuse; CALUMNIATE imputes malice to the speaker and falsity to his assertions; DEFAME and SLANDER stress the effects, DEFAME suggesting actual loss of or injury to one's good name, SLANDER the suffering of the victim

ma·lig·nance \mə-ˈlig-nən(t)s\ *n* **:** MALIGNANCY

ma·lig·nan·cy \-nən-sē\ *n* **1 :** the quality or state of being malignant **2 a :** exhibition (as by a tumor) of malignant qualities **:** VIRULENCE **b :** a malignant tumor

1**ma·lig·nant** \mə-ˈlig-nənt\ *adj* [LL *malignant-, malignans*, prp. of *malignari*] **1 a** *obs* **:** DISAFFECTED, MALCONTENT **b :** evil in nature, influence, or effect **:** INJURIOUS **c :** extremely malevolent or malicious **2 :** tending to produce death or deterioration ⟨~ malaria⟩; *esp* **:** tending to infiltrate, metastasize, and terminate fatally ⟨~ tumor⟩ — **ma·lig·nant·ly** *adv*

2**malignant** *n, archaic* **:** MALCONTENT

ma·lig·ni·ty \mə-ˈlig-nət-ē\ *n* **1 :** MALIGNANCY, MALEVOLENCE **2 :** an instance of malignant or malicious behavior or nature **syn** see MALICE

ma·li·hi·ni \ˌmäl-ē-ˈhē-nē\ *n* [Hawaiian] **:** a newcomer or stranger among the people of Hawaii

ma·lines \mə-ˈlēn\ *n, pl* **ma·lines** \-ˈlēn(z)\ [F, fr. *Malines* (Mechelen), Belgium] **1 :** MECHLIN **2** *also* **ma·line :** a fine stiff net with a hexagonal mesh

ma·lin·ger \mə-ˈliŋ-gər\ *vi* **ma·lin·ger·ing** \-g(ə-)riŋ\ [F *malingre* sickly] **:** to pretend to be ill or otherwise incapacitated so as to avoid duty or work — **ma·lin·ger·er** \-gər-ər\ *n*

Ma·lin·ke \mə-ˈliŋ-kē\ *n, pl* **Malinke** *or* **Malinkes 1 a :** a people of Mandingo affiliation widespread in the western part of Africa **b :** a member of such people **2 :** the language of the Malinke people

mal·i·son \ˈmal-ə-sən, -zən\ *n* [ME, fr. OF *maleïçon*, fr. LL *malediction-, maledictio*] **:** MALEDICTION, CURSE

mal·kin \ˈmȯ-kən\ *n* [ME *malkyn*, fr. *Malkyn*, fem. name] **1** *dial chiefly Brit* **:** an untidy woman **:** SLATTERN **2 a :** CAT **b :** HARE

1**mall** \ˈmȯl\ *var of* MAUL

2**mall** \ˈmȯl, ˈmal\ *n* [short for obs. *pall-mall* (mallet used in pall-mall)] **1 a :** the mallet used in pall-mall **b :** the game of pall-mall **c :** an alley used for pall-mall **2** [The *Mall*, promenade in London, orig. a pall-mall alley] **a :** a usu. public area often set with shade trees and designed as a promenade or as a pedestrian walk **b :** a usu. paved or grassy strip between two roadways

mal·lard \ˈmal-ərd\ *n, pl* **mallard** *or* **mallards** [ME, fr. MF *mallart*] **:** a common and widely distributed wild duck (*Anas platyrhynchos*) of the northern hemisphere that is the source of the domestic ducks

mal·lea·bil·i·ty \ˌmal-ē-ə-ˈbil-ət-ē, ˌmal-(y)ə-ˈbil-\ *n* **:** the quality or state of being malleable

mal·lea·ble \ˈmal-ē-ə-bəl, ˈmal-(y)ə-bəl\ *adj* [ME *malliable*, fr. MF or ML; MF *malleable*, fr. ML *malleabilis*, fr. *malleare* to hammer, fr. L *malleus* hammer — more at MAUL] **1 :** capable of being extended or shaped by beating with a hammer or by the pressure of rollers **2 :** susceptible of being fashioned into a different form or shape **syn** see PLASTIC — **mal·lea·ble·ness** *n*

mal·lee \ˈmal-ē\ *n* [native name in Australia] **1 :** any of several low-growing shrubby Australian eucalypts (as *Eucalyptus dumosa* and *E. oleosa*) **2 :** a dense thicket or growth of mallees; *also* **:** land covered by such growth

mal·le·muck \ˈmal-i-ˌmək\ *n* [D *mallemuk*, fr. *mal* silly + *mok* gull] **:** any of several large oceanic birds (as the fulmar or petrel)

mal·let \ˈmal-ət\ *n* [ME *maillet*, fr. MF, fr. OF, dim. of *mail* maul — more at MAUL] **:** a hammer with typically a barrel-shaped head of wood: as **a :** a tool with a large head for driving another tool or for striking a surface without marring it **b :** an implement for striking a ball (as in polo)

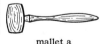

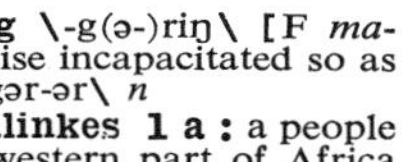
mallet a

mal·le·us \ˈmal-ē-əs\ *n, pl* **mal·lei** \-ē-ˌī, -ē-ˌē\ [NL, fr. L, hammer] **:** the outermost of the three small bones of the mammalian ear

mal·low \ˈmal-(ˌ)ō, -ə(-w)\ *n* [ME *malwe*, fr. OE *mealwe*, fr. L *malva*] **:** any of a genus (*Malva*) of herbs (family Malvaceae, the mallow family) with palmately lobed or dissected leaves and usu. showy flowers

malm \ˈmäm, ˈmälm\ *n* [ME *malme*, fr. OE *mealm-*; akin to OE *melu* meal — more at MEAL] **1 :** a soft friable chalky limestone **2 :** an artificial mixture of clay and chalk used in the manufacture of bricks

malm·sey \ˈmäm-zē, ˈmälm-\ *n, often cap* [ME *malmesey*, fr. ML *Malmasia* Monemvasia, Greece] **1 :** a sweet aromatic wine produced around Monemvasia and later throughout the Mediterranean **2 :** the sweetest variety of Madeira wine

mal·nour·ished \(ˈ)mal-ˈnər-isht, -ˈnə-risht\ *adj* **:** UNDERNOURISHED

mal·nu·tri·tion \ˌmal-n(y)u̇-ˈtrish-ən\ *n* **:** faulty or inadequate nutrition

mal·oc·clu·sion \ˌmal-ə-ˈklü-zhən\ *n* **:** improper occlusion; *esp* **:** abnormality in the coming together of teeth

mal·odor \(ˈ)mal-ˈōd-ər\ *n* **:** an offensive odor

mal·odor·ous \-ˈōd-ə-rəs\ *adj* **:** ill-smelling — **mal·odor·ous·ly** *adv* — **mal·odor·ous·ness** *n*

syn MALODOROUS, STINKING, FETID, NOISOME, PUTRID, RANK, FUSTY, MUSTY mean bad-smelling. MALODOROUS may range from the unpleasant to the strongly offensive; STINKING and FETID suggest the foul or disgusting; NOISOME adds a suggestion of being harmful or unwholesome as well as offensive; PUTRID implies particularly the sickening odor of decaying flesh; RANK suggests a strong smell that is not necessarily bad in quality; FUSTY and MUSTY suggest lack of fresh air and sunlight, FUSTY also implying prolonged uncleanliness, MUSTY stressing the effects of dampness, mildew, or age

Mal·pi·ghi·an \mal-ˈpig-ē-ən, -ˈpē-gē-\ *adj* **:** of, relating to, or discovered by Marcello Malpighi

malpighian corpuscle *n, often cap M* **:** the part of a nephron that consists of a glomerulus and its membrane

Malpighian layer *n* **:** the deeper part of the epidermis consisting of cells whose protoplasm has not yet changed into horny material

Malpighian tube *n* **:** any of a group of long blind vessels opening into the posterior part of the alimentary canal in most insects and some other arthropods and functioning primarily as excretory organs

mal·po·si·tion \ˌmal-pə-ˈzish-ən\ *n* **:** wrong or faulty position

mal·prac·tice \(ˈ)mal-ˈprak-təs\ *n* **1 :** a dereliction from professional duty or a failure of professional skill or learning that results in injury, loss, or damage **2 :** an injurious, negligent, or improper practice **:** MALFEASANCE — **mal·prac·ti·tion·er** \ˌmal-ˌprak-ˈtish-(ə-)nər\ *n*

1**malt** \ˈmȯlt\ *n, often attrib* [ME, fr. OE *mealt;* akin to OHG *malz* malt, OE *meltan* to melt] **1 :** grain softened by steeping in water, allowed to germinate, and used esp. in brewing and distilling **2 :** liquor made with malt **3 :** MALTED MILK — **malty** \ˈmȯl-tē\ *adj*

2**malt** *vt* **1 :** to convert into malt **2 :** to make or treat with malt or malt extract ~ *vi* **1 :** to become malt **2 :** to make grain into malt

Mal·ta fever \ˌmȯl-tə-\ *n* [*Malta*, Brit island] **:** typical human brucellosis

malt·ase \ˈmȯl-ˌtās, -ˌtāz\ *n* **:** an enzyme that accelerates the hydrolysis of maltose and other alpha-glucosides to glucose

malted milk *n* **1 :** a soluble powder prepared from dried milk and malted cereals **2 :** a beverage made by dissolving malted milk in milk or other liquid

Mal·tese \mȯl-ˈtēz, -ˈtēs\ *n, pl* **Maltese 1 :** a native or inhabitant of Malta **2 :** the Semitic language of the Maltese people — **Maltese** *adj*

Maltese cat *n* **:** a bluish gray domestic short-haired cat

Maltese cross *n* **1** — see CROSS illustration **2 :** a Eurasian perennial (*Lychnis chalcedonica*) having scarlet or rarely white flowers in dense terminal heads

mal·tha \ˈmal-thə\ *also* **mal·thite** \-ˌthīt\ *n* [L *maltha*] **:** a black viscid substance intermediate between petroleum and asphalt

Mal·thu·sian \mal-ˈth(y)ü-zhən, mȯl-\ *adj* [Thomas R. *Malthus* †1834 E economist] **:** of or relating to Malthus or to his theory that population tends to increase at a faster rate than its means of subsistence and that unless it is checked by moral restraint or by disease, famine, war, or other disaster widespread poverty and degradation inevitably result — **Malthusian** *n* — **Mal·thu·sian·ism** \-zhə-ˌniz-əm\ *n*

malt liquor *n* **:** a fermented liquor (as beer) made with malt

malt·ose \ˈmȯl-ˌtōs, -ˌtōz\ *n* [F, fr. E 1*malt*] **:** a crystalline dextrorotatory fermentable reducing sugar $C_{12}H_{22}O_{11}$ formed esp. from starch by amylase

mal·treat \(ˈ)mal-ˈtrēt\ *vt* [F *maltraiter*, fr. MF, fr. *mal-* + *traiter* to treat, fr. OF *traitier* — more at TREAT] **:** to treat cruelly or roughly **:** ABUSE — **mal·treat·ment** \-mənt\ *n*

malt·ster \ˈmȯlt-stər\ *n* **:** a maker of malt

mal·va·sia \ˌmal-və-ˈzē-ə\ *n* [It, fr. *Monemvasia*, Greece] **:** MALMSEY — **mal·va·si·an** \-ən\ *adj*

mal·ver·sa·tion \ˌmal-vər-ˈsā-shən\ *n* [MF, fr. *malverser* to be corrupt, fr. *mal* + *verser* to turn, handle, fr. L *versare*, fr. *versus*, pp. of *vertere* to turn — more at WORTH] **1 :** misbehavior and esp. corruption in an office, trust, or commission **2 :** corrupt administration

mal·voi·sie \ˌmalv-wə-ˈzē\ *n* [F, fr. MF *malvesie*, fr. *Malvesie* Monemvasia] **:** MALMSEY

mam·ba \ˈmäm-bə, ˈmam-\ *n* [Zulu *im-amba*] **:** any of several tropical and southern African venomous snakes (genus *Dendraspis*) related to the cobras but with no hood

mam·bo \ˈmäm-(ˌ)bō\ *n* [AmerSp] **:** a complex staccato usu. fast dance related to the rumba and of Haitian origin; *also* **:** the style of music for this dance — **mambo** *vi*

Mam·luk \ˈmam-ˌlük\ *or* **Mam·e·luke** \ˈmam-ə-ˌlük\ *n* [Ar *mamlūk*, lit., slave] **1 :** a member of a politically powerful Egyptian military class occupying the sultanate from 1250 to 1517 **2** *usu mameluke, often not cap* **a :** a white or yellow slave in Muslim countries **b :** a member of a body of slave soldiers

1**mam·ma** *or* **ma·ma** \ˈmäm-ə, *chiefly Brit* mə-ˈmä\ *n* [baby talk] **:** MOTHER

2**mam·ma** \ˈmam-ə\ *n, pl* **mam·mae** \ˈmam-ˌē, -ˌī\ [L, mother, breast, of baby-talk origin] **:** a mammary gland and its accessory parts — **mam·mate** \ˈmam-ˌāt\ *adj*

mam·mal \ˈmam-əl\ *n* [deriv. of LL *mammalis* of the breast, fr. L *mamma* breast] **:** any of a class (Mammalia) of higher vertebrates comprising man and all other animals that nourish their young with milk secreted by mammary glands and have the skin usu. more or less covered with hair — **mam·ma·lian** \mə-ˈmā-lē-ən, ma-ˈmā-, -ˈmāl-yən\ *adj or n*

mam·mal·o·gy \mə-ˈmal-ə-jē, ma-ˈmal-, -ˈmäl-\ *n* [ISV, blend of

mammal and *-logy*] : a branch of zoology dealing with mammals

mam·ma·ry \'mam-ə-rē\ *adj* : of, relating to, or being one of the large compound modified sebaceous glands that in female mammals are modified to secrete milk, are situated ventrally in pairs, and usu. terminate in a nipple

mam·ma·to·cu·mu·lus \ma-,māt-ō-'kyü-myə-ləs\ *n* [NL, fr. L *mammatus* having breasts, (fr. *mamma*) + NL *cumulus*] : a cumulus or cumulostratus storm cloud having breast-shaped protuberances below

mam·mer \'mam-ər\ *vi* [ME *mameren* to stammer, of imit. origin] *obs* : WAVER, HESITATE

mam·mi·form \'mam-ə-,fȯrm\ *adj* : MAMMILLARY

mam·mil·la·ry \'mam-ə-,ler-ē, ma-'mil-ə-rē\ *adj* [L *mammilla* breast, nipple, dim. of *mamma*] **1** : of, relating to, or resembling the breasts **2** : studded with breast-shaped protuberances

mam·mil·late \'mam-ə-,lāt, ma-'mil-,āt\ *or* **mam·mil·lat·ed** \-əd\ *adj* [LL *mammillatus*, fr. L *mammilla*] **1** : having nipples or small protuberances **2** : having the form of a bluntly rounded protuberance — **mam·mil·la·tion** \,mam-ə-'lā-shən\ *n*

[1]mam·mock \'mam-ək\ *n* [origin unknown] *chiefly dial* : a broken piece : SCRAP

[2]mammock *vt, chiefly dial* : to tear into fragments : MANGLE

mam·mon \'mam-ən\ *n, often cap* [LL *mammona*, fr. Gk *mamōna*, fr. Aram *māmōnā* riches] : material wealth or possessions esp. having a debasing influence — **mam·mon·ish** \-ə-nish\ *adj* — **mam·mon·ism** \-ə-,niz-əm\ *n* — **mam·mon·ist** \-ə-nəst\ *or* **mam·mon·ite** \-ə-,nīt\ *n*

[1]mam·moth \'mam-əth\ *n* [Russ *mamont, mamot*] **1** : any of numerous extinct Pleistocene elephants distinguished from recent elephants by molars with cementum filling the spaces between the ridges of enamel and by large size, very long upcurved tusks, and well-developed body hair **2** : something immense of its kind : GIANT

[2]mammoth *adj* : of very great size : GIGANTIC **syn** see ENORMOUS

mam·my \'mam-ē\ *n* **1** : MAMMA **2** : a Negro woman serving as a nurse to white children esp. formerly in the Southern states

[1]man \'man, *in compounds* ,man *or* mən\ *n, pl* **men** \'men, *in compounds* ,men *or* mən\ [ME, fr. OE; akin to OHG *man* man, Skt *manu*] **1 a** (1) : a human being; *esp* : an adult male human (2) : HUSBAND **b** : the human race : MANKIND **c** : a bipedal primate mammal (*Homo sapiens*) that is anatomically related to the great apes but distinguished esp. by notable development of the brain with a resultant capacity for articulate speech and abstract reasoning, is usu. held to form a variable number of freely interbreeding races, and is the sole recent representative of a natural family (Hominidae); *broadly* : any living or extinct member of this family **d** (1) : one possessing in high degree the qualities considered distinctive of manhood (2) *obs* : MANLINESS **e** : FELLOW, CHAP — used as a mode of familiar address **2 a** : a feudal tenant : VASSAL **b** : an adult male servant **c** *pl* : the working force as distinguished from the employer and usu. the management **3 a** : INDIVIDUAL, PERSON **b** : ANYONE **4** : one of the pieces with which various games (as chess) are played **5** *Christian Science* : the compound idea of infinite Spirit : the spiritual image and likeness of God : the full representation of Mind — **as one man** : UNANIMOUSLY — **to a man** : without exception

[2]man *vt* **manned**; **man·ning** **1 a** : to supply with men ⟨~ a fleet⟩ **b** : to station members of a ship's crew at ⟨~ the capstan⟩ **c** : to serve in the force or complement of ⟨~ the production lines⟩ **2** : to furnish with strength or powers of resistance : BRACE

ma·na \'män-ə\ *n* [of Melanesian & Polynesian origin; akin to Hawaiian & Maori *mana*] **1** : the power of the elemental forces of nature embodied in an object or person **2** : moral authority : PRESTIGE

man-about-town \,man-ə-,baůt-'taůn\ *n* : a worldly and socially active man

[1]man·a·cle \'man-i-kəl\ *n* [ME *manicle*, fr. MF, fr. L *manicula*, dim. of *manus* hand — more at MANUAL] **1** : a shackle for the hand or wrist : HANDCUFF **2** : something used as a restraint — usu. used in pl.

[2]manacle *vt* **man·a·cling** \-k(ə-)liŋ\ **1** : to confine (the hands) with manacles **2** : to make fast or secure : BIND; *broadly* : RESTRAIN **syn** see HAMPER

[1]man·age \'man-ij\ *vb* [It *maneggiare*, fr. *mano* hand, fr. L *manus*] *vt* **1** : HANDLE, CONTROL **2** : to make and keep submissive **3** : to treat with care : HUSBAND **4** : to alter by manipulation **5** : to succeed in accomplishing : CONTRIVE ~ *vi* **1 a** : to direct or carry on business or affairs **b** : to admit of being carried on **2** : to achieve one's purpose **syn** see CONDUCT

[2]manage *n* [It *maneggio* management, training of a horse, fr. *maneggiare*] **1 a** *archaic* : the action and paces of a trained riding horse **b** : the schooling or handling of a horse **c** : a riding school : MANEGE **2** *obs* : MANAGEMENT

man·age·abil·i·ty \,man-ij-ə-'bil-ət-ē\ *n* : the quality or state of being manageable

man·age·able \'man-ij-ə-bəl\ *adj* : capable of being managed : TRACTABLE — **man·age·able·ness** *n* — **man·age·ably** \-blē\ *adv*

man·age·ment \'man-ij-mənt\ *n* **1** : the act or art of managing : CONTROL, DIRECTION **2** : judicious use of means to accomplish an end **3** : capacity for managing : executive skill **4** : the collective body of those who manage or direct an enterprise

man·ag·er \'man-ij-ər\ *n* : one that manages: as **a** : one who conducts business or household affairs with economy and care **b** : a person whose work or profession is management **c** : a person who directs a team or athlete — **man·ag·er·ess** \-ə-rəs\ *n* — **man·ag·er·ship** \-ər-,ship\ *n*

man·a·ge·ri·al \,man-ə-'jir-ē-əl\ *adj* : of or relating to a manager — **man·a·ge·ri·al·ly** \-ē-ə-lē\ *adv*

[1]ma·ña·na \mən-'yän-ə\ *adv* [Sp, lit., tomorrow, fr. earlier *cras mañana* early tomorrow, fr. *cras* tomorrow (fr. L) + *mañana* early, fr. L *mane* early in the morning] : at an indefinite time in the future

[2]mañana *n* : an indefinite time in the future

man ape *n* **1** : GREAT APE **2** : any of various fossil primates intermediate in characters between recent man and the great apes

Ma·nas·seh \mə-'nas-ə\ *n* [Heb *Mĕnashsheh*] **1** : a son of Joseph and ancestor of one of the tribes of Israel **2** : a king of Judah in the 7th century B.C.

man-at-arms \,man-ət-'ärmz\ *n, pl* **men-at-arms** : SOLDIER; *esp* : a heavily armed and usu. mounted soldier

man·a·tee \'man-ə-,tē\ *n* [Sp *manatí*] : any of several chiefly tropical aquatic herbivorous mammals (genus *Trichechus*) that differ from the related dugong esp. in having the tail broad and rounded

man·chet \'man-chət\ *n* [ME] *chiefly dial* : a loaf or roll of fine wheat bread

man·chi·neel \,man-chə-'nē(ə)l\ *n* [F *mancenille*, fr. Sp *manzanilla*, fr. dim. of *manzana* apple] : a poisonous tropical American tree (*Hippomane mancinella*) of the spurge family having a blistering milky juice and apple-shaped fruit

Man·chu \'man-(,)chü, man-'\ *n, pl* **Manchu** *or* **Manchus** **1** : a member of the native Mongolian race of Manchuria that is related to the Tungus, was orig. nomad but conquered China and established a dynasty there in 1644, and has largely assimilated Chinese culture **2** : the Tungusic language of the Manchu people — **Manchu** *adj*

man·ci·ple \'man(t)-sə-pəl\ *n* [ME, fr. ML *mancipium* office of steward, fr. L, act of purchase, fr. *mancip-, manceps* purchaser — more at EMANCIPATE] : a steward or purveyor esp. for a college or monastery

-man·cy \,man(t)-sē\ *n comb form* [ME *-mancie*, fr. OF, fr. L *-mantia*, fr. Gk *-manteia*, fr. *manteia*, fr. *mantis* diviner, prophet — more at MANTIS] : divination ⟨oneiro*mancy*⟩

Man·dae·an \man-'dē-ən\ *n* [Mandaean *mandayyā* having knowledge] **1** : a member of a Gnostic sect of the lower Tigris and Euphrates **2** : a form of Aramaic found in documents written by Mandaeans — **Mandaean** *adj*

man·da·la \'mən-də-lə\ *n* [Skt *maṇḍala* circle] : a Hindu or Buddhist graphic symbol of the universe; *specif* : a circle enclosing a square with a deity on each side

man·da·mus \man-'dā-məs\ *n* [L, we enjoin, fr. *mandare*] : a writ issued by a superior court commanding the performance of a specified official act or duty

[1]man·da·rin \'man-d(ə-)rən\ *n* [Pg *mandarim*, fr. Malay *mĕntĕri*, fr. Skt *mantrin* counselor, fr. *mantra* counsel — more at MANTRA] **1** : a public official under the Chinese Empire of any of nine superior grades **2** *cap* **a** : the primarily northern dialect of Chinese used by the court and the official classes under the Empire **b** : the chief dialect of China that is spoken in about four fifths of the country and has a standard variety centering about Peking **3** [F *mandarine*, fr. Sp *mandarina*, prob. fr. *mandarin* mandarin, fr. Pg *mandarim*; prob. fr. the color of a mandarin's robes] **a** : a small spiny Chinese orange tree (*Citrus reticulata*) with yellow to reddish orange loose-skinned fruits; *also* : a cultivated selection or hybrid of the Chinese mandarin **b** : the fruit of a mandarin — **man·da·rin·ate** \-,āt\ *n* — **man·da·rin·ism** \-,iz-əm\ *n*

[2]mandarin *adj* **1** : of, relating to, or typical of a mandarin ⟨~ graces⟩ **2** : marked by polished ornate complexity of language ⟨~ style⟩

man·da·tary \'man-də-,ter-ē\ *n* : MANDATORY

[1]man·date \'man-,dāt\ *n* [MF & L; MF *mandat*, fr. L *mandatum*, fr. neut. of *mandatus*, pp. of *mandare* to entrust, enjoin, prob. irreg. fr. *manus* band + *-dere* to put — more at MANUAL, DO] **1** : an authoritative command; *esp* : a formal order from a superior court or official to an inferior one **2** : an authorization to act given to a representative **3 a** : an order or commission granted by the League of Nations to a member nation for the establishment of a responsible government over a former German colony or other conquered territory **b** : a mandated territory

[2]mandate *vt* : to administer or assign under a mandate

man·da·tor \'man-,dāt-ər\ *n* : one that gives a mandate

[1]man·da·to·ry \'man-də-,tōr-ē, -,tȯr-\ *adj* **1** : containing or constituting a command : OBLIGATORY **2** : of, relating to, or holding a League of Nations mandate

[2]mandatory *n* : one given a mandate; *esp* : a nation holding a mandate from the League of Nations

man·di·ble \'man-də-bəl\ *n* [MF, fr. LL *mandibula*, fr. L *mandere* to chew — more at MOUTH] **1 a** : JAW 1a; *esp* : a lower jaw consisting of a single bone or completely fused bones **b** : the lower jaw with its investing soft parts **c** : either the upper or lower segment of the bill of a bird **2** : any of various invertebrate mouthparts serving to hold or bite food materials; *esp* : either member of the anterior pair of mouth appendages of an arthropod often forming strong biting jaws — **man·dib·u·lar** \man-'dib-yə-lər\ *adj* — **man·dib·u·lary** \-,ler-ē\ *adj* — **man·dib·u·late** \-lət\ *adj or n*

Man·din·go \man-'diŋ-(,)gō\ *n, pl* **Mandingo** *or* **Mandingoes** *or* **Mandingos** **1 a** : a people widely spread over West Africa centering in the upper Niger valley **b** : a member of this people **2** : the language of the Mandingo people

man·do·lin \,man-də-'lin, 'man-dᵊl-ən\ *also* **man·do·line** \,man-də-'lēn, 'man-dᵊl-ən\ *n* [It *mandolino*, deriv. of Gk *pandoura* three-stringed lute] : a musical instrument of the lute family that has a pear-shaped body and fretted neck and four to six pairs of strings — **man·do·lin·ist** \,man-də-'lin-əst\ *n*

man·drag·o·ra \man-'drag-ə-rə\ *n* [ME] : MANDRAKE 1

man·drake \'man-,drāk\ *n* [ME, prob. alter. of *mandragora*, fr. OE, fr. L *mandragoras*, fr. Gk] **1 a** : a Mediterranean herb (*Mandragora officinarum*) of the nightshade family with ovate leaves, whitish or purple flowers, and a large forked root superstitiously credited with human attributes **b** : the root of this plant formerly used esp. to promote conception, as a cathartic, or as a narcotic and soporific **2** : MAYAPPLE

mandrake 1

man·drel *also* **man·dril** \'man-drəl\ *n* [prob. modif. of F *mandrin*] **1 a** : a usu. tapered or cylindrical axle, spindle, or arbor inserted into a hole in a piece of work to support it during machining **b** : a metal bar that serves as a core around which metal or other material may be cast, molded, forged, bent, or otherwise shaped **2** : the shaft and bearings on which a tool is mounted

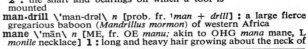

man·drill \'man-drəl\ *n* [prob. fr. [1]*man* + *drill*] : a large fierce gregarious baboon (*Mandrillus mormon*) of western Africa

mane \'mān\ *n* [ME, fr. OE *manu*; akin to OHG *mana* mane, L *monile* necklace] **1** : long and heavy hair growing about the neck of

some mammals **2 :** long heavy hair on a person's head — **maned** \'mānd\ *adj*

man–eat·er \'man-,ēt-ər\ *n* **:** one that has or is thought to have an appetite for human flesh: as **a :** CANNIBAL 1 **b :** a large voracious shark (*Carcharodon carcharias*) known to attack and devour human beings **c :** a lion or tiger that has acquired the habit of feeding on human flesh — **man–eat·ing** \-,ēt-iŋ\ *adj*

ma·nege *also* **ma·nège** \ma-'nezh, mə-, -'nāzh\ *n* [F *manège*, fr. It *maneggio* training of a horse — more at MANAGE] **1 :** a school for teaching horsemanship and for training horses **2 :** the art of horsemanship or of training horses **3 :** the movements or paces of a trained horse

ma·nes \'män-,ās, 'mā-,nēz\ *n pl* [L] **1** *often cap* **:** the spirits of the dead and gods of the lower world in ancient Roman belief **2** *sing or pl in constr* **:** the venerated or appeased spirit of a dead person

1**ma·neu·ver** \mə-'n(y)ü-vər\ *n* [F *manœuvre*, fr. OF *maneuvre* work done by hand, fr. ML *manuopera*, fr. L *manu operare* to work by hand] **1 a :** a military or naval evolution **b :** an armed forces training exercise; *esp* **:** an extended and large-scale training exercise involving military and naval units separately or in combination — often used in pl. **2 :** a procedure usu. involving expert physical management **3 a :** evasive movement or shift of tactics **b :** an intended and controlled variation from a straight and level flight path in the operation of an airplane **4 :** an action taken to gain a tactical end **syn** see TRICK

2**maneuver** *vb* **ma·neu·ver·ing** \-'n(y)üv-(ə-)riŋ\ *vi* **1 a :** to perform a movement in military or naval tactics in order to secure an advantage in attack or defense **b :** to make a series of changes in direction and position for a specific purpose **2 :** to use stratagems **:** SCHEME ~ *vt* **1 :** to cause to execute tactical movements **2 :** to manage into or out of a position or condition **:** MANIPULATE **3 a :** to guide with adroitness and design **b :** to bring about or secure as a result of skillful management — **ma·neu·ver·abil·i·ty** \-,n(y)üv-(ə-)rə-'bil-ət-ē\ *n* — **ma·neu·ver·able** \-'n(y)üv-(ə-)rə-bəl\ *adj* — **ma·neu·ver·er** \-'n(y)ü-vər-ər, -'n(y)üv-rər\ *n*

man Fri·day \'man-'frīd-ē\ *n* [*Friday* native servant in *Robinson Crusoe* (1719), novel by Daniel Defoe] **:** a valued efficient aide or employee **:** a right-hand man

man·ful \'man-fəl\ *adj* **:** having or showing courage and resolution **syn** see MALE — **man·ful·ly** \-fə-lē\ *adv* — **man·ful·ness** *n*

mangan- *or* **mangano-** *comb form* [G *mangan*, fr. F *manganèse*] **:** manganese ⟨*manganous*⟩

man·ga·nate \'maŋ-gə-,nāt\ *n* **1 :** a salt of manganic acid **2 :** MANGANITE

man·ga·nese \'maŋ-gə-,nēz, -,nēs\ *n* [F *manganèse*, fr. It *manganese* magnesia, manganese, fr. ML *magnesia*] **:** a grayish white usu. hard and brittle polyvalent metallic element that resembles iron but is not magnetic — see ELEMENT table — **man·ga·ne·sian** \,maŋ-gə-'nē-zhən, -shən\ *adj*

manganese spar *n* **:** RHODONITE

man·gan·ic \man-'gan-ik, maŋ-\ *adj* **:** of, relating to, or derived from manganese; *esp* **:** containing this element with a valence of three or six

manganic acid *n* **:** an acid H_2MnO_4 known only in solution and esp. in the form of its salts

man·ga·nite \'maŋ-gə-,nīt\ *n* **1 :** an ore of manganese MnO(OH) consisting of manganic hydroxide usu. in brilliant steel-gray or iron-black crystals **2 :** any of various unstable salts made by reaction of manganese dioxide with a base

man·ga·nous \-nəs\ *adj* **:** of, relating to, or derived from manganese; *esp* **:** containing this element in bivalent form

mange \'mānj\ *n* [ME *manjewe*, fr. MF *mangene* itching, fr. *mangier* to eat] **:** any of various persistent contagious skin diseases marked esp. by eczematous inflammation and loss of hair that affect domestic animals or sometimes man; *esp* **:** one caused by a minute parasitic mite

man·gel–wur·zel \'maŋ-gəl-,wər-zəl\ *n* [G *mangoldwurzel*, *mangelwurzel*, fr. *mangold* beet + *wurzel* root] **:** a large coarse yellow to reddish orange beet extensively grown as food for cattle

man·ger \'mān-jər\ *n* [ME *mangeour*, *manger*, fr. MF *maingeure*, fr. *mangier* to eat, fr. L *manducare* to chew, devour, fr. *manducus* glutton, fr. *mandere* to chew — more at MOUTH] **:** a trough or box holding feed or fodder for livestock

mang·i·ly \'mān-jə-lē\ *adv* **:** in a mangy manner

mang·i·ness \-jē-nəs\ *n* **:** the quality or state of being mangy

1**man·gle** \'maŋ-gəl\ *vt* **man·gling** \-g(ə-)liŋ\ [ME *manglen*, fr. AF *mangler*, freq. of OF *maynier* to maim] **1 :** to cut, bruise, or hack with repeated blows or strokes **2 :** to spoil or injure in making or performing — **man·gler** \-g(ə-)lər\ *n*

2**mangle** *n* [D *mangel*, fr. G, fr. MHG, dim. of *mange* mangonel, mangle, fr. L *manganum*] **:** a machine for ironing laundry by passing it between heated rollers

3**mangle** *vt* **man·gling** \-g(ə-)liŋ\ **:** to press or smooth (as damp linen) with a mangle — **man·gler** \-g(ə-)lər\ *n*

man·go \'maŋ-(,)gō\ *n, pl* **mangoes** *or* **mangos** [Pg *manga*, fr. Tamil *mān-kāy*] **1 :** a yellowish red tropical fruit with a firm skin, hard central stone, and juicy aromatic subacid pulp; *also* **:** the evergreen tree (*Mangifera indica*) of the sumac family that bears this fruit **2 :** SWEET PEPPER

man·go·nel \'maŋ-gə-,nel\ *n* [ME, fr. MF, prob. fr. ML *manganellus*, dim. of LL *manganum* philter, mangonel, fr. Gk *manganon;* akin to MIr *meng* deception] **:** a military engine formerly used to throw missiles

man·go·steen \'maŋ-gə-,stēn\ *n* [Malay *mangustan*] **:** a dark reddish brown East Indian fruit with thick rind and juicy flesh having a flavor suggestive of both peach and pineapple; *also* **:** a tree (*Garcinia mangostana*, family Guttiferae) that bears this fruit

man·grove \'man-,grōv, 'maŋ-\ *n* [prob. fr. Pg *mangue* (fr. Sp *mangle*, fr. Taino) + E *grove*] **1 :** any of a genus (*Rhizophora*, esp. *R. mangle*) of tropical maritime trees or shrubs that throw out many prop roots and form dense masses important in coastal land building **2 :** a tree (genus *Avicennia*) of the verbena family with growth habits like those of the true mangroves

mangy \'mān-jē\ *adj* **1 :** affected with or resulting from mange **2 :** SEEDY, SHABBY

man·han·dle \'man-,han-dᵊl\ *vt* **1 :** to move or manage by human force **2 :** to handle roughly

man·hat·tan \man-'hat-ᵊn, mən-\ *n, often cap* [*Manhattan*, borough of New York city] **:** a cocktail consisting of sweet vermouth, rye or bourbon whiskey, and sometimes a dash of bitters

man·hole \'man-,hōl\ *n* **:** a hole through which a man may go esp. to gain access to an underground or enclosed structure

man·hood \'man-,hu̇d\ *n* **1 :** the condition of being a human being **2 :** manly qualities **:** COURAGE **3 :** the condition of being an adult male as distinguished from a child or female **4 :** adult males **:** MEN

man–hour *n* **:** a unit of one hour's work by one man used esp. as a basis for cost accounting and wages

man·hunt \'man-,hənt\ *n* **:** an organized and usu. intensive hunt for a man esp. if charged with a crime

ma·nia \'mā-nē-ə *also* -nyə\ *n* [ME, fr. LL, fr. Gk *mainesthai* to be mad; akin to Gk *menos* spirit — more at MIND] **1 :** excitement manifested by mental and physical hyperactivity, disorganization of behavior, and elevation of mood; *specif* **:** the manic phase of manic-depressive psychosis **2 :** excessive or unreasonable enthusiasm **:** CRAZE **syn** see INSANITY

1**ma·ni·ac** \'mā-nē-,ak\ *adj* [LL *maniacus*, fr. Gk *maniakos*, fr. *mania*] **1 :** affected with or suggestive of madness **2 :** characterized by ungovernable excitement or frenzy **:** FRANTIC — **ma·ni·a·cal** \mə-'nī-ə-kəl\ *adj* — **ma·ni·a·cal·ly** \mə-'nī-ə-k(ə-)lē\ *adv*

2**maniac** *n* **1 :** LUNATIC, MADMAN **2 :** a person characterized by an inordinate or ungovernable enthusiasm for something

man·ic \'man-ik\ *adj* **:** affected with, relating to, or resembling mania — **manic** *n*

man·ic–de·pres·sive \,man-ik-di-'pres-iv\ *adj* **:** characterized either by mania or psychotic depression or by alternating mania and depression — **manic–depressive** *n*

Man·i·chae·an *or* **Man·i·che·an** \,man-ə-'kē-ən\ *or* **Man·i·chee** \'man-ə-,kē\ *n* [LL *manichaeus*, fr. LGk *manichaios*, fr. *Manichaios* Manes †*ab*276 A.D. Pers founder of the sect] **1 :** a believer in a syncretistic religious dualism originating in Persia in the 3d century A.D. and teaching the release of the spirit from matter through asceticism **2 :** a believer in religious or philosophical dualism — **Manichaean** *adj* — **Man·i·chae·an·ism** \,man-ə-'kē-ə-,niz-əm\ *n* — **Man·i·chae·ism** \'man-ə-(,)kē-,iz-əm\ *n*

1**mani·cure** \'man-ə-,kyu̇(ə)r\ *n* [F, fr. L *manus* hand + F *-icure* (as in *pédicure* pedicure) — more at MANUAL] **1 :** MANICURIST **2 :** a treatment for the care of the hands and nails

2**manicure** *vt* **1 :** to do manicure work on; *esp* **:** to trim and polish the fingernails of **2 :** to trim closely and evenly

mani·cur·ist \-,kyu̇(ə)r-əst\ *n* **:** a person who gives manicure treatments

1**man·i·fest** \'man-ə-,fest\ *adj* [ME, fr. MF or L; MF *manifeste*, fr. L *manifestus*, lit., hit by the hand, fr. *manus* + *-festus* (akin to L in*festus* hostile) — more at DARE] **1 :** readily perceived by the senses and esp. by the sight **2 :** easily understood or recognized by the mind **:** OBVIOUS **syn** see EVIDENT — **man·i·fes·ta·tive** \,man-ə-'fes-tət-iv\ *adj* — **man·i·fes·ta·tive·ly** *adv* — **man·i·fest·ly** \'man-ə-,fest-lē\ *adv*

2**manifest** *vt* **:** to make evident or certain by showing or displaying **syn** see SHOW — **man·i·fest·er** *n*

3**manifest** *n* **1 :** MANIFESTATION, INDICATION **2 :** MANIFESTO **3 :** a list (as of passengers) or an invoice of cargo for a ship or plane

man·i·fes·tant \,man-ə-'fes-tənt\ *n* **:** one who makes or participates in a manifestation

man·i·fes·ta·tion \,man-ə-fə-'stā-shən, -,fes-'tā-\ *n* **1 a :** the act, process, or an instance of manifesting **b :** something that manifests **c :** one of the forms in which an individual is manifested **d :** an occult phenomenon; *specif* **:** MATERIALIZATION **2 :** a public demonstration of power and purpose

manifest destiny *n, often cap M&D* **:** an ordering of human history that is obviously inevitable and apparent and that leads a people or race to expand to geographic limits held to be natural or to extend sovereignty over a usu. indefinite area

1**man·i·fes·to** \,man-ə-'fes-(,)tō\ *n, pl* **manifestos** *or* **manifestoes** [It, denunciation, manifest, fr. *manifestare* to manifest, fr. L, fr. *manifestus*] **:** a public declaration of intentions, motives, or views

2**manifesto** *vi* **:** to issue a manifesto

1**man·i·fold** \'man-ə-,fōld\ *adj* [ME, fr. OE *manigfeald*, fr. *manig* many + *-feald* -fold] **1 :** marked by diversity or variety **2 :** comprehending or uniting various features **:** MULTIFARIOUS **3 :** rightfully so-called for many reasons ⟨a ~ liar⟩ **4 :** consisting of or operating many of one kind combined ⟨a ~ bell pull⟩ — **man·i·fold·ly** \-,fōl-(d)lē\ *adv* — **man·i·fold·ness** \-,fōl(d)-nəs\ *n*

2**manifold** *n* **:** something that is manifold: as **a :** a whole uniting or consisting of many diverse elements **b :** a pipe fitting with several lateral outlets for connecting one pipe with others **c :** SET 17; *specif* **:** a space topologically equivalent to a sphere in a euclidean space **d :** an abstract generalization of a surface; *specif* **:** a set of elements having properties common to various elementary configurations

manifold b

3**manifold** *vt* **1 :** to make many or several copies of **2 :** to make manifold **:** MULTIPLY ~ *vi* **:** to make several or many copies

man·i·kin *or* **man·ni·kin** \'man-i-kən\ *n* [D *mannekijn* little man, fr. MD, dim. of *man;* akin to OE *man*] **1 :** MANNEQUIN **2 :** a little man **:** DWARF, PYGMY

ma·nila *also* **ma·nil·la** \mə-'nil-ə\ *adj* **1 :** made of manila paper **2** *cap* **:** made from Manila hemp — **manila** *n*

Manila hemp *n* [*Manila*, Philippine islands] **:** ABACA

manila paper *n, often cap M* **:** a strong and durable paper of a brownish or buff color and smooth finish made orig. from Manila hemp

ma·nille \mə-'nil\ *n* [modif. of Sp *malilla*] **:** the second highest trump in various card games

man in the street : an average or ordinary man

man·i·oc \'man-ē-,äk\ *or* **man·i·o·ca** \,man-ē-'ō-kə\ *n* [F *manioc* & Sp & Pg *mandioca*, of Tupian origin; akin to Tupi *manioca* cassava] **:** CASSAVA

man·i·ple \'man-ə-pəl\ *n* [ML *manipulus*, fr. L, handful, fr. *manus* hand + *-pulus* (akin to L *plēre* to fill); fr. its having been originally held in the hand — more at MANUAL, FULL] **1 :** a long narrow band worn at mass over the left arm by ministers of or above the order of subdeacon **2** [L *manipulus*, fr. *manipulus* handful; fr. the custom of using a handful of hay on the end of a pole as a military standard] **:** a subdivision of the Roman legion consisting of either 120 or 60 men

ma·nip·u·la·bil·i·ty \mə-ˌnip-yə-lə-ˈbil-ət-ē\ *n* **:** the quality or state of being manipulable
ma·nip·u·la·ble \mə-ˈnip-yə-lə-bəl\ *adj* **:** MANIPULATABLE
ma·nip·u·lar \-lər\ *adj* **1 :** of or relating to the ancient Roman maniple **2 :** MANIPULATORY
ma·nip·u·lat·able \-ˌlāt-ə-bəl\ *adj* **:** capable of being manipulated
ma·nip·u·late \mə-ˈnip-yə-ˌlāt\ *vt* [back-formation fr. *manipulation*] **1 :** to treat or operate with the hands or by mechanical means esp. with skill **2 a :** to manage or utilize skillfully **b :** to control or play upon by artful, unfair, or insidious means esp. to one's own advantage **3 :** to change by artful or unfair means so as to serve one's purpose **:** DOCTOR **syn** see HANDLE — **ma·nip·u·la·tive** \-ˌlāt-iv\ *adj* — **ma·nip·u·la·tor** \-ˌlāt-ər\ *n* — **ma·nip·u·la·to·ry** \-lə-ˌtōr-ē, -ˌtȯr-\ *adj*
ma·nip·u·la·tion \mə-ˌnip-yə-ˈlā-shən\ *n* [F, fr. *manipule* handful of herbs, fr. L *manipulus*] **1 :** the act, process, or an instance of manipulating **2 :** the condition of being manipulated
man·i·tou *or* **man·i·tu** \ˈman-ə-ˌtü\ *also* **man·i·to** \-ˌtō\ *n* [of Algonquian origin; akin to Ojibwa *manito* spirit, god] **:** one of the Algonquian deities or spirits dominating the forces of nature
man jack \ˈman-ˌjak, -ˈjak\ *n* **:** individual man ⟨every *man jack*⟩
man·kind *n sing but sing or pl in constr* **1** \ˈman-ˈkīnd, -ˌkīnd\ **:** the human race **:** the totality of human beings **2** \-ˌkīnd\ **:** men as distinguished from women
man·like \ˈman-ˌlīk\ *adj* **:** resembling, relating to, or characteristic of a man **syn** see MALE
man·li·ness \ˈman-lē-nəs\ *n* **:** the quality or state of being manly
1**man·ly** \ˈman-lē\ *adj* **1 :** having qualities appropriate to a man **:** BOLD, RESOLUTE **2 :** appropriate in character to a man **syn** see MALE
2**manly** *adv* **:** in a manly manner
man-made \ˈman-ˈmād\ *adj* **:** manufactured, created, or constructed by man; *specif* **:** SYNTHETIC
mann- *or* **manno-** *comb form* [ISV, fr. *manna*] **:** manna ⟨*mannose*⟩
man·na \ˈman-ə\ *n* [ME, fr. OE, fr. LL, fr. Gk, fr. Heb *mān*] **1 a :** food miraculously supplied to the Israelites in their journey through the wilderness **b :** divinely supplied spiritual nourishment **c :** something likened to the biblical manna **2 :** sweetish dried exudate esp. of a European ash that contains mannitol and has been used as a laxative and demulcent
manned \ˈmand\ *adj* **:** carrying or performed by a man ⟨~ space flight⟩
man·ne·quin \ˈman-i-kən\ *n* [F, fr. D *mannekijn* little man — more at MANIKIN] **1 :** an artist's, tailor's, or dressmaker's lay figure; *also* **:** a form representing the human figure used esp. for displaying clothes **2 :** a woman who models clothing **:** MODEL
man·ner \ˈman-ər\ *n* [ME *manere*, fr. OF *maniere* way of acting, fr. (assumed) VL *manuaria*, fr. L, fem. of *manuarius* of the hand, fr. *manus* hand — more at MANUAL] **1 :** KIND, SORT **2 a** (1) **:** a characteristic or customary mode of acting **:** CUSTOM (2) **:** a mode of procedure or way of acting **:** FASHION (3) **:** method of artistic execution or mode of presentation **:** STYLE **b** *pl* **:** social conduct or rules of conduct as shown in the prevalent customs **c :** BEARING, MIEN **d** (1) *pl* **:** habitual conduct or deportment **:** BEHAVIOR (2) *pl* **:** good manners **e :** a distinguished or stylish air **syn** see BEARING, METHOD
man·nered \ˈman-ərd\ *adj* **1 :** having manners of a specified kind ⟨well-*mannered*⟩ **2 a :** having or displaying a particular manner **b :** having an artificial or stilted character
man·ner·ism \ˈman-ə-ˌriz-əm\ *n* **1 a :** exaggerated or affected adherence to a particular style or manner **:** ARTIFICIALITY, PRECIOSITY **b** *often cap* **:** an art style in late 16th century Europe characterized by spatial incongruity and excessive elongation of the human figures **2 :** a characteristic mode or peculiarity of action, bearing, or treatment **syn** see POSE — **man·ner·ist** \-rəst\ *n* — **man·ner·is·tic** \ˌman-ə-ˈris-tik\ *adj*
man·ner·less \ˈman-ər-ləs\ *adj* **:** destitute of manners
man·ner·li·ness \-lē-nəs\ *n* **:** the quality or state of being mannerly
man·ner·ly \-lē\ *adj* **:** showing good manners — **mannerly** *adv*
man·nish \ˈman-ish\ *adj* **1 :** resembling or suggesting a man rather than a woman **2 :** suitable to or characteristic of a man rather than a woman ⟨her ~ clothes⟩ **syn** see MALE — **man·nish·ly** *adv* — **man·nish·ness** *n*
man·nite \ˈman-ˌīt\ *n* [F, fr. *manna*, fr. LL] **:** MANNITOL — **man·nit·ic** \ma-ˈnit-ik\ *adj*
man·ni·tol \ˈman-ə-ˌtȯl, -ˌtōl\ *n* [ISV] **:** a slightly sweet crystalline alcohol $C_6H_8(OH)_6$ found in many plants and used esp. in testing kidney function
man·nose \ˈman-ˌōs, -ˌōz\ *n* [ISV] **:** an aldose sugar $C_6H_{12}O_6$ obtained by oxidation of mannitol
ma·noeu·vre \mə-ˈn(y)ü-vər\ *var of* MANEUVER
man-of-war \ˌman-ə(v)-ˈwȯ(ə)r\ *n, pl* **men-of-war :** a combatant warship of a recognized navy
ma·nom·e·ter \mə-ˈnäm-ət-ər\ *n* [F *manomètre*, fr. Gk *manos* sparse, loose, rare + F *-mètre* — more at MONK] **1 :** an instrument for measuring the pressure of gases and vapors **:** PRESSURE GAUGE **2 :** SPHYGMOMANOMETER — **mano·met·ric** \ˌman-ə-ˈme-trik\ *adj* — **mano·met·ri·cal** \-tri-kəl\ *adj* — **mano·met·ri·cal·ly** \-k(ə-)lē\ *adv*
man·or \ˈman-ər\ *n* [ME *maner*, fr. OF *manoir*, fr. *manoir* to sojourn, dwell, fr. L *manēre*] **1 a :** the house or hall of an estate **:** MANSION **b :** a landed estate **2 a :** a unit of English rural territorial organization; *esp* **:** such a unit in the Middle Ages consisting of an estate under a lord enjoying a variety of rights over land and tenants including the right to hold court **b :** a tract of land in No. America occupied by tenants who pay a fixed rent in money or kind to the proprietor — **ma·no·ri·al** \mə-ˈnōr-ē-əl, -ˈnȯr-\ *adj* — **ma·no·ri·al·ism** \-ə-ˌliz-əm\ *n*
manor house *n* **:** the house of the lord of a manor
man power *n* **1 :** power available from or supplied by the physical effort of man **2** *usu* **manpower :** the available persons constituting total strength (as of a nation); *specif* **:** the persons available for the military service of a nation
man·qué \mä^{n}-ˈkā\ *adj* [F, fr. pp. of *manquer* to lack] **:** short of or frustrated in the fulfillment of one's aspirations or talents ⟨a poet ~⟩
man·rope \ˈman-ˌrōp\ *n* **:** a side rope (as to a ship's gangway or ladder) used as a handrail
man·sard \ˈman-ˌsärd\ *n* [F *mansarde*, fr. François *Mansart* †1666 F architect] **:** a roof having two slopes on all sides with the lower slope steeper than the upper one
manse \ˈman(t)s\ *n* [ME *manss*, fr. ML *mansa*, *mansus*, *mansum*, fr. L *mansus*, pp. of *manēre*] **1** *archaic* **:** the dwelling of a householder **2 :** the residence of a clergyman; *esp* **:** the house of a Presbyterian clergyman
man·ser·vant \ˈman-ˌsər-vənt\ *n, pl* **men·ser·vants** \ˈmen-ˌsər-vən(t)s\ **:** a male servant
-man·ship \-mən-ˌship\ *n suffix* [*sportsmanship*] **:** skill in maneuvering to gain a tactical advantage ⟨games*manship*⟩
man·sion \ˈman-chən\ *n* [ME, fr. MF, fr. L *mansion-*, *mansio*, fr. *mansus*, pp. of *manēre* to remain, dwell; akin to Gk *menein* to remain] **1 a** *obs* **:** the act of remaining or dwelling **:** STAY **b** *archaic* **:** ABODE **2 a** (1) **:** the house of the lord of a manor (2) **:** a large imposing residence **b :** a separate apartment or lodging in a large structure **3 a :** HOUSE 3b **b :** one of the 28 parts into which the moon's monthly course through the heavens is divided
man-size \ˈman-ˌsīz\ *or* **man-sized** \-ˌsīzd\ *adj* **:** suitable for or requiring a man
man·slaugh·ter \ˈman-ˌslȯt-ər\ *n* **:** the unlawful killing of a human being without express or implied malice
man·slay·er \ˈman-ˌslā-ər\ *n* **:** one who slays a man
man·sue·tude \ˈman(t)-swi-ˌt(y)üd, man-ˈsü-ə-\ *n* [ME, fr. L *mansuetudo*, fr. *mansuetus* tame, mild, fr. pp. of *mansuescere* to tame, fr. *manus* hand + *suescere* to accustom; akin to Gk *ēthos* custom] **:** the quality or state of being gentle **:** MEEKNESS, TAMENESS
man·ta \ˈmant-ə\ *n* [Sp] **1 :** a square piece of cloth or blanket used in southwestern U.S. and Latin America usu. as a cloak or shawl **2** [AmerSp, fr. Sp] **:** DEVILFISH 1
man·teau \man-ˈtō, ˈman-ˌ\ *n* [F, fr. OF *mantel*] **:** a loose cloak, coat, or robe
man·tel \ˈmant-ᵊl\ *n* [MF, fr. OF, mantle] **1 a :** a beam, stone, or arch serving as a lintel to support the masonry above a fireplace **b :** the finish around a fireplace **2 :** a shelf above a fireplace
man·telet \ˈmant-lət, -ᵊl-ət, ˌmant-ᵊl-ˈet\ *n* **1 :** a very short cape or cloak **2** *or* **mantlet** \ˈmant-lət\ **:** a movable shelter formerly used by besiegers as a protection when attacking
man·tel·let·ta \ˌmant-ᵊl-ˈet-ə\ *n* [It] **:** a knee-length mantle worn by a high prelate (as a cardinal) of the Roman Catholic Church
man·tel·piece \ˈmant-ᵊl-ˌpēs\ *n* **1 :** a mantel with its side elements **2 :** the shelf of a mantel
man·tic \ˈmant-ik\ *adj* [Gk *mantikos*, fr. *mantis*] **:** of or relating to the faculty of divination **:** PROPHETIC
man·ti·core \ˈmant-i-ˌkō(ə)r, -ˌkȯ(ə)r\ *n* [ME, fr. L *mantichora*, fr. Gk *mantichōras*] **:** a legendary animal with the head of a man, the body of a lion, and the tail of a dragon or scorpion
man·til·la \man-ˈtē-(y)ə, -ˈtil-ə\ *n* [Sp, dim. of *manta*] **1 :** a light scarf worn over the head and shoulders esp. by Spanish and Latin American women **2 :** a short light cape or cloak
man·tis \ˈmant-əs\ *n, pl* **man·tis·es** *or* **man·tes** \ˈman-ˌtēz\ [NL, fr. Gk, lit., diviner, prophet; akin to Gk *mainesthai* to be mad — more at MANIA] **:** an insect (order Manteodea and esp. genus *Mantis*) that feeds upon other insects and clasps its prey in forelimbs held up as if in prayer
man·tis·sa \man-ˈtis-ə\ *n* [L *mantisa*, *mantissa* makeweight, fr. Etruscan] **:** the decimal part of a logarithm
1**man·tle** \ˈmant-ᵊl\ *n* [ME *mantel*, fr. OF, fr. L *mantellum*] **1 :** a loose sleeveless garment worn over other clothes **:** CLOAK **2 a :** something that covers, enfolds, or envelops **b** (1) **:** a fold or lobe or pair of lobes of the body wall of a mollusk or brachiopod lining the shell in shell-bearing forms and bearing shell-secreting glands (2) **:** the soft external body wall that lines the test or shell of a tunicate or barnacle **c :** the outer wall and casing of a blast furnace above the hearth **3 :** the back, scapulars, and wings of a bird **4 :** a lacy hood or sheath of some refractory material that gives light by incandescence when placed over a flame **5 a :** MANTLEROCK **b :** the part of the earth's interior beneath the lithosphere and above the central core **6 :** MANTEL
2**mantle** *vb* **man·tling** \ˈmant-liŋ, -ᵊl-iŋ\ *vt* **:** to cover with or as if with a mantle **:** CLOAK ~ *vi* **1 :** to become covered with a coating **2 :** to spread over a surface **3 :** BLUSH
man·tle·rock \ˈmant-ᵊl-ˌräk\ *n* **:** unconsolidated residual or transported material that overlies the earth's solid rock in place
Man·toux test \ˌman-ˌtü-, ˌmä^{n}-\ *n* [Charles *Mantoux* †1947 F physician] **:** an intracutaneous test for hypersensitivity to tuberculin and thus for past or present infection with tubercle bacilli
man·tra \ˈman-trə\ *n* [Skt, sacred counsel, formula, fr. *manyate* he thinks; akin to L *mens* mind — more at MIND] **:** a mystical formula of invocation or incantation in Hinduism and Mahayana Buddhism
man·trap \ˈman-ˌtrap\ *n* **:** a trap for catching men **:** SNARE
man·tua \ˈmanch-(ə-)wə, ˈmant-ə-wə\ *n* [modif. of F *manteau*] **:** a usu. loose-fitting gown worn esp. in the 17th and 18th centuries
1**man·u·al** \ˈman-yə(-wə)l\ *adj* [ME *manuel*, fr. MF, fr. L *manualis*, fr. *manus* hand; akin to OE *mund* hand, Gk *marē*] **1 a :** of, relating to, or involving the hands ⟨~ dexterity⟩ **b :** worked by hand ⟨~ choke⟩ **2 :** requiring or using physical skill and energy ⟨~ labor⟩ ⟨~ workers⟩ — **man·u·al·ly** \-ē\ *adv*
2**manual** *n* **1 :** a book capable of being conveniently handled; *esp* **:** HANDBOOK **2 :** the prescribed movements in the handling of a weapon or other military item during a drill or ceremony **3 :** a keyboard for the hands; *specif* **:** one of the several keyboards of a pipe-organ console that controls a separate division of the instrument
manual alphabet *n* **:** an alphabet for deaf-mutes in which the letters are represented by finger positions
manual training *n* **:** a course of training to develop skill in using the hands and to teach practical arts
ma·nu·bri·um \mə-ˈn(y)ü-brē-əm\ *n, pl* **ma·nu·bria** \-brē-ə\ *also* **manubriums** [NL, fr. L, handle, fr. *manus*] **:** an anatomical process or part shaped like a handle; *esp* **:** the cephalic segment of the sternum of man and many other mammals
man·u·fac·to·ry \ˌman-(y)ə-ˈfak-t(ə-)rē\ *n* **:** FACTORY 2

1man·u·fac·ture \ˌman-(y)ə-ˈfak-chər\ *n* [MF, fr. L *manu factus* made by hand] **1 :** something made from raw materials **2 a :** the process of making wares by hand or by machinery esp. when carried on systematically with division of labor **b :** a productive industry using mechanical power and machinery **3 :** the act or process of producing something

2manufacture *vb* **man·u·fac·tur·ing** \-ˈfak-chə-riŋ, -ˈfak-shriŋ\ *vt* **1 :** to make into a product suitable for use **2 a :** to make from raw materials by hand or by machinery **b :** to produce according to an organized plan and with division of labor **3 :** INVENT, FABRICATE **4 :** to produce as if by manufacturing **:** CREATE ~ *vi* **:** to engage in manufacture **syn** see MAKE — **man·u·fac·tur·ing** *n*

manufactured gas *n* **:** a combustible gaseous mixture made from coal, coke, or petroleum products

man·u·fac·tur·er \-ˈfak-chər-ər, -ˈfak-shrər\ *n* **:** one that manufactures; *specif* **:** an employer of workers in manufacturing

man·u·mis·sion \ˌman-yə-ˈmish-ən\ *n* [ME, fr. MF, fr. L *manumission-, manumissio,* fr. *manumissus,* pp. of *manumittere*] **:** the act or process of manumitting; *esp* **:** formal emancipation from slavery

man·u·mit \ˌman-yə-ˈmit\ *vt* **man·u·mit·ted; man·u·mit·ting** [ME *manumitten,* fr. MF *manumitter,* fr. L *manumittere,* fr. *manus* hand + *mittere* to let go, send — more at SMITE] **:** to release from slavery **syn** see FREE

1ma·nure \mə-ˈn(y)u̇(ə)r\ *vt* [ME *manouren,* fr. MF *manouvrer,* lit., to do work by hand, fr. L *manu operare*] **1** *obs* **:** CULTIVATE **2 :** to enrich (land) by the application of manure — **ma·nur·er** *n*

2manure *n* **:** material that fertilizes land; *esp* **:** refuse of stables and barnyards consisting of livestock excreta with or without litter — **ma·nu·ri·al** \-ˈn(y)u̇r-ē-əl\ *adj*

ma·nus \ˈmā-nəs, ˈmä-\ *n, pl* **ma·nus** \-nəs, -ˌnüs\ [NL, fr. L, hand] **:** the distal segment of the vertebrate forelimb including the carpus and forefoot or hand

1manu·script \ˈman-yə-ˌskript\ *adj* [L *manu scriptus*] **:** written by hand or typed

2manuscript *n* **1 :** a written or typewritten composition or document as distinguished from a printed copy **2 :** writing as opposed to print

1man·ward \ˈman-wərd\ *adv* **:** toward man

2manward *adj* **:** directed toward man

man·wise \ˈman-ˌwīz\ *adv* **:** in the manner of men

1Manx \ˈmaŋ(k)s\ *adj* [alter. of earlier *Maniske,* fr. (assumed) ON *manskr,* fr. *Mana* Isle of Man] **:** of, relating to, or characteristic of the Isle of Man, its people, or the Manx language

2Manx *n* **1** *pl in constr* **:** the people of the Isle of Man **2 :** the Celtic language of the Manx people almost completely displaced by English

Manx cat *n* **:** a short-haired domestic cat with no external tail

1many \ˈmen-ē\ *adj* **more** \ˈmō(ə)r, ˈmȯ(ə)r\ **most** \ˈmōst\ [ME, fr. OE *manig;* akin to OHG *manag* many, OSlav *mŭnogŭ* much] **1 :** consisting of or amounting to a large but indefinite number ⟨worked for ~ years⟩ **2 :** being one of a large but indefinite number ⟨~ a man⟩ ⟨~ another student⟩ — **as many :** the same in number ⟨saw three plays in *as many* days⟩

2many *pron, pl in constr* **:** a large number of persons or things ⟨~ of them⟩

3many *n, pl in constr* **1 :** a large but indefinite number ⟨a good ~ of them⟩ **2 :** the great majority of people ⟨the ~⟩

many·fold \ˌmen-ē-ˈfōld\ *adv* **:** by many times

many–sid·ed \ˌmen-ē-ˈsīd-əd\ *adj* **1 :** having many sides or aspects **2 :** having many interests or aptitudes **:** VERSATILE **syn** see VERSATILE — **many·sid·ed·ness** *n*

many–val·ued \ˌmen-ē-ˈval-(ˌ)yüd\ *adj* **:** possessing more than the customary two truth-values of truth and falsehood

man·za·ni·ta \ˌman-zə-ˈnēt-ə\ *n* [AmerSp, dim. of Sp *manzana* apple] **:** any of various western No. American evergreen shrubs (genus *Arctostaphylos*) of the heath family

Mao·ism \ˈmau̇-ˌiz-əm\ *n* **:** the theory and practice of Marxism-Leninism developed in China chiefly by Mao Tse-tung — **Mao·ist** \ˈmau̇-əst\ *n or adj*

Mao·ri \ˈmau̇(ə)r-ē\ *n, pl* **Maori** *or* **Maoris 1 a :** a Polynesian people native to New Zealand **b :** a member of this people **2 :** the Austronesian language of the Maori

1map \ˈmap\ *n* [ML *mappa,* fr. L, napkin, towel] **1 a :** a representation usu. on a flat surface of the whole or a part of an area **b :** a representation of the celestial sphere or part of it **2 :** something that represents with a clarity suggestive of a map

2map *vt* **mapped; map·ping 1 a :** to make a map of **b :** to delineate as if on a map **c :** to make a survey of for the purpose of making a map **d :** to assign to every element of (a mathematical set) an element of the same or another set **2 :** to plan in detail ⟨~ out a program⟩ — **map·per** *n* — **map·ping** *n*

ma·ple \ˈmā-pəl\ *n* [ME, fr. OE *mapul-;* akin to ON *möpurr* maple] **:** any of a genus (*Acer*) of trees or shrubs of a family (Aceraceae, the maple family) with opposite leaves and a fruit of two united samaras; *also* **:** the hard light-colored close-grained wood of a maple used esp. for flooring and furniture

maple sugar *n* **:** sugar made by boiling maple syrup

maple syrup *n* **:** syrup made by concentrating the sap of the sugar maple or various other maples

ma·quette \ma-ˈket\ *n* [F] **:** a usu. small preliminary model

ma·quil·lage \ˌmak-ē-ˈ(y)äzh\ *n* [F] **:** MAKEUP 3

ma·quis \ma-ˈkē, mä-\ *n, pl* **ma·quis** \-ˈkē(z)\ [F] **1 a :** thick scrubby underbrush of Mediterranean shores and esp. of the island of Corsica **b :** an area of such underbrush **2** *often cap* **a :** a guerrilla fighter in the French underground during World War II **b :** a band of maquis

mar \ˈmär\ *vt* **marred; mar·ring** [ME *marren,* fr. OE *mierran* to obstruct, waste; akin to OHG *merren* to obstruct] **1 :** to detract from the perfection or wholeness of **:** SPOIL **2 a** *archaic* **:** to inflict serious bodily harm on **b** *obs* **:** DESTROY **syn** see INJURE

mar·a·bou *or* **mar·a·bout** \ˈmar-ə-ˌbü\ *n* [F *marabout,* lit., marabout] **1 a :** a large stork (genus *Leptoptilos*) **b :** a soft feathery fluffy material prepared from the long coverts of marabous or usu. from turkey feathers and used esp. for trimming **2 a :** a thrown silk usu. dyed in the gum **b :** a fabric made of this silk

mar·a·bout \ˈmar-ə-ˌbü\ *n, often cap* [F, fr. Pg *marabuto,* fr. Ar *murābiṭ*] **:** a dervish in Muslim Africa credited with supernatural power

ma·ra·ca \mə-ˈräk-ə, -ˈrak-\ *n* [Pg *maracá*] **:** a dried gourd or a rattle like a gourd that contains dried seeds or pebbles and is used as a percussion instrument

mar·a·schi·no \ˌmar-ə-ˈskē-(ˌ)nō, -ˈshē-\ *n, often cap* [It, fr. *marasca* bitter wild cherry] **1 :** a sweet liqueur distilled from the fermented juice of a bitter wild cherry **2 :** a usu. large cherry preserved in true or imitation maraschino

ma·ras·mus \mə-ˈraz-məs\ *n* [LL, fr. Gk *marasmos,* fr. *marainein* to waste away — more at SMART] **:** progressive emaciation esp. in the young associated usu. with faulty assimilation and utilization of food

Ma·ra·tha \mə-ˈrät-ə\ *n* [Marathi *Marāṭhā* & Hindi *Marhaṭṭā,* fr. Skt *Mahārāṣṭra* Maharashtra] **1 :** a people of the south central part of the subcontinent of India **2 :** a member of the Maratha people

Ma·ra·thi \mə-ˈrät-ē\ *n* [Marathi *marāṭhī*] **:** the chief Indic language of the state of Maharashtra in India

mar·a·thon \ˈmar-ə-ˌthän\ *n* [*Marathon,* Greece, site of a victory of Greeks over Persians in 490 B.C. the news of which was carried to Athens by a long-distance runner] **1 :** a long-distance race: **a :** a footrace run on an open course of usu. 26 miles 385 yards **b :** a race other than a footrace marked by esp. great length **2 :** an endurance contest — **marathon** *adj*

ma·raud \mə-ˈrȯd\ *vb* [F *marauder*] *vi* **:** to roam about and raid in search of plunder ~ *vt* **:** RAID, PILLAGE — **ma·raud·er** *n*

mar·a·ve·di \ˌmar-ə-və-ˈdē\ *n* [Sp *maravedí,* fr. Ar *Murābiṭīn* 11th & 12th cent. Muslim dynasty in No. Africa & Spain] **:** a medieval Spanish copper coin unit worth 1/34 real

1mar·ble \ˈmär-bəl\ *n* [ME, fr. OF *marbre,* fr. L *marmor,* fr. Gk *marmaros*] **1 a :** limestone that is more or less crystallized by metamorphism, that ranges from granular to compact in texture, that is capable of taking a high polish, and that is used in architecture and sculpture **b :** something composed of or made from marble; *esp* **:** a piece of sculpture **c :** something suggesting marble **2 a :** a little ball made of a hard substance (as glass) and used in various games **b** *pl but sing in constr* **:** a children's game played with these little balls **3 :** MARBLING

2marble *vt* **mar·bling** \-b(ə-)liŋ\ **:** to stain or vein like marble

3marble *adj* **:** resembling or suggestive of marble

marble cake *n* **:** a cake made with light and dark batter so as to have a mottled appearance

mar·ble·ize \ˈmär-bə-ˌlīz\ *vt* **:** MARBLE

mar·bling *n* **1 :** coloration or markings resembling or suggestive of marble **2 :** an intermixture of fat and lean in a cut of meat esp. when evenly distributed

mar·bly \ˈmär-b(ə-)lē\ *adj* **:** MARBLE

marc \ˈmärk\ *n* [F, fr. MF, fr. *marchier* to trample] **1 :** the residue remaining after a fruit has been pressed **2 :** brandy made from the residue of grapes or apples after pressing

mar·ca·site \ˈmär-kə-ˌsīt, -ˌzīt; ˌmär-kə-ˈzēt\ *n* [ME *marchasite,* fr. ML *marcasita,* fr. Ar *marqashītha*] **1 a :** crystallized iron pyrites **b :** a mineral of the same composition and appearance as iron pyrites but of different crystalline organization and lower specific gravity **2 :** a piece of marcasite used for ornaments — **mar·ca·sit·i·cal** \ˌmär-kə-ˈsit-i-kəl, -ˈzit-\ *adj*

1mar·cel \mär-ˈsel\ *n* [*Marcel* Grateau †1936 F hairdresser] **:** a deep soft wave made in the hair by the use of a heated curling iron

2marcel *vb* **mar·celled; mar·cel·ling** *vt* **:** to make a marcel in ~ *vi* **:** to make a marcel

1march \ˈmärch\ *n* [ME *marche,* fr. OF, of Gmc origin; akin to OHG *marha* boundary — more at MARK] **1 :** a border region **:** FRONTIER **2** *pl* **:** the borderlands between England and Scotland and England and Wales

2march *vi* **:** to have common borders or frontiers

3march *vb* [MF *marchier* to trample, march, fr. OF, to trample, prob. of Gmc origin; akin to OHG *marcōn* to mark] *vi* **1 :** to move along steadily with a regular measured stride esp. rhythmically and in step with others **2 a :** to move in a direct purposeful manner **:** PROCEED **b :** to make steady progress **:** ADVANCE ~ *vt* **1 :** to cause to march **2 :** to cover by marching **:** TRAVERSE

4march *n* **1 a** (1) **:** the action of marching (2) **:** the distance covered within a specific period of time by marching (3) **:** a regular measured stride or rhythmic step used in marching **b :** forward movement **:** PROGRESS **2 :** an instrumental or vocal composition that is in duple rhythm (as 4/4 time) or triply compound rhythm (as 6/8 time) with a strongly accentuated beat and that is designed or suitable to accompany marching

March \ˈmärch\ *n* [ME, fr. OF, fr. L *martius,* fr. *martius* of Mars, fr. *Mart-, Mars*] **:** the 3d month of the Gregorian calendar

mär·chen \ˈme(ə)r-k̲ən\ *n, pl* **märchen** [G] **:** TALE; *esp* **:** FOLKTALE

1march·er \ˈmär-chər\ *n* **:** one who inhabits a border region

2marcher *n* **:** one that marches

mar·che·sa \mär-ˈkā-zə\ *n, pl* **mar·che·se** \-(ˌ)zā\ [It, fem. of *marchese*] **:** an Italian woman holding the rank of a marchese **:** MARCHIONESS

mar·che·se \-(ˌ)zā\ *n, pl* **mar·che·si** \-(ˌ)zē\ [It, fr. ML *marcensis,* fr. *marca* border region, of Gmc origin; akin to OHG *marha*] **:** an Italian nobleman next in rank above a count **:** MARQUIS

mar·chio·ness \ˈmär-sh(ə-)nəs\ *n* [ML *marchionissa,* fr. *marchion-, marchio* marquess, fr. *marca*] **1 :** the wife or widow of a marquess **2 :** a woman who holds the rank of marquess in her own right

march·pane \ˈmärch-ˌpān\ *n* [It *marzapane*] **:** MARZIPAN

march–past \ˈmärch-ˌpast\ *n* **:** a filing by **:** PROCESSION

Mar·cio·nism \ˈmär-shə-ˌniz-əm, -s(h)ē-ə-\ *n* [*Marcion* 2d cent. A.D. Christian Gnostic] **:** a Christian Gnostic movement of the 2d and 3d centuries A.D. rejecting the Creator God and the Old Testament — **Mar·cio·nite** \-ˌnīt\ *n*

Mar·co·ni \mär-ˈkō-nē\ *adj* **:** of or relating to the system of wireless telegraphy invented by Marconi

mar·co·ni·gram \-ˌgram\ *n* [Guglielmo *Marconi*] **:** RADIOGRAM

Marconi rig *n* **:** BERMUDA RIG

Mar·di Gras \ˌmärd-ē-ˈgrä\ *n* [F, lit., fat Tuesday] **1 a :** Shrove Tuesday often observed (as in New Orleans) with parades and merrymaking **b :** a carnival period climaxing on Shrove Tuesday **2 :** a festive occasion resembling a pre-Lenten Mardi Gras

1mare *n* [ME, fr. OE; akin to OHG *mara* incubus, Croatian *mora*] *obs* **:** an evil preternatural being causing nightmare

2mare \ˈma(ə)r, ˈme(ə)r\ *n* [ME, fr. OE *mere;* akin to OHG *merha* mare, OE *mearh* horse, W *march*] **:** a female horse or other equine animal esp. when fully mature or of breeding age

3ma·re \ˈmä-(ˌ)rē, ˈmä-(ˌ)ā\ *n, pl* **ma·ria** \ˈmä-rē-ə, ˈmär-ē-ə\ [NL, fr. L, sea — more at MARINE] **:** one of several dark areas of

considerable extent on the surface of the moon or Mars

ma·re clau·sum \ˌmä-(ˌ)rē-ˈklȯ-səm, -zəm; ˌmär-(ˌ)ā-ˈklau̇-ˌsu̇m\ *n* [NL, lit., closed sea] **:** a sea or other navigable body of water that is under the jurisdiction of one nation and that is closed to other nations

ma·re li·be·rum \-(ˌ)rē-ˈlib-ə-rəm, -(ˌ)rā-ˈlē-bə-ˌru̇m\ *n* [NL, lit., free sea] **1 :** a sea or other navigable body of water that is open to all nations **2 :** FREEDOM OF THE SEAS

ma·re nos·trum \-(ˌ)rē-ˈnäs-trəm; -(ˌ)rā-ˈnō-ˌstru̇m, -ˈnȯ-\ *n* [L, our sea] **:** a sea that belongs to a single nation or is mutually shared by two or more nations

mare's nest *n* **1 :** a false discovery, illusion, or deliberate hoax **2 :** a place, condition, or situation of great disorder or confusion

mare's tail *n* **1 :** a cirrus cloud that has a long slender flowing appearance **2 a :** a common aquatic plant (*Hippuris vulgaris*) with elongated shoots clothed with dense whorls of subulate leaves **b :** HORSETAIL

mar·gar·ic acid \ˌmär-ˌgar-ik-\ *n* [F *margarique*, fr. *margarine*] **:** a crystalline synthetic fatty acid $C_{17}H_{34}O_2$ intermediate between palmitic acid and stearic acid

mar·ga·rine \ˈmärj-(ə-)rən, -ə-ˌrēn\ *n* [F, fr. Gk *margaron* pearl] **:** a food product made from usu. vegetable oils churned with ripened skim milk to a plastic consistency, often fortified with vitamins A and D, and used as a spread and as a cooking fat

mar·ga·rite \ˈmär-gə-ˌrīt\ *n* [ME, fr. MF, fr. L *margarita*, fr. Gk *margaritēs*, fr. *margaron*] *archaic* **:** PEARL

mar·gay \ˈmär-ˌgā, mär-ˈ\ *n* [F, fr. Tupi *maracaja*] **:** a small American spotted cat (*Felis tigrina*) resembling the ocelot and ranging from southernmost Texas to Brazil

marge \ˈmärj\ *n* [MF, fr. L *margo*] *archaic* **:** MARGIN

mar·gent \ˈmär-jənt\ *n*, *archaic* **:** MARGIN

1mar·gin \ˈmär-jən\ *n* [ME, fr. L *margin-*, *margo* border — more at MARK] **1 :** the part of a page outside the main body of printed or written matter **2 :** the outside limit and adjoining surface of something **:** EDGE **3 a :** a spare amount or measure or degree allowed or given for contingencies or special situations **b :** the limit below which economic activity cannot be continued under normal conditions **4 a :** the difference which exists between net sales and the cost of merchandise sold and from which expenses are usu. met or profit derived **b :** the excess market value of collateral over the face of a loan **c** (1) **:** cash or collateral which is deposited with a broker to secure him from loss on a contract (2) **:** a customer's equity if his account is terminated at prevailing market prices (3) **:** a speculative transaction in which the broker does part of the financing (4) **:** an allowance above or below a certain figure within which a purchase or sale is to be made **5 :** measure or degree of difference **syn** see BORDER — **mar·gined** \-jənd\ *adj*

2margin *vt* **1 :** to enter or summarize in the margin of (a page or sheet) **2 a :** to provide with an edging or border **b :** to form a margin to **:** BORDER **3 :** to deposit a margin upon (as stock); *specif* **:** to hold or keep secured by depositing or adding to a margin

mar·gin·al \ˈmärj-nəl, -ən-ᵊl\ *adj* [ML *marginalis*, fr. L *margin-*, *margo*] **1 :** written or printed in the margin of a page or sheet ⟨~ notes⟩ **2 a :** of, relating to, or situated at a margin or border **b** (1) **:** occupying the borderland of a relatively stable territorial or cultural area ⟨~ tribes⟩ (2) **:** characterized by the incorporation of habits and values from two divergent cultures and by incomplete assimilation in either ⟨the ~ cultural habits of new immigrant groups⟩ **3 :** located at the fringe of consciousness ⟨~ sensations⟩ **4 a :** close to the lower limit of qualification or acceptability ⟨~ ability⟩ **b** (1) **:** having a character or capacity fitted to yield a supply of goods which when marketed at existing price levels will barely cover the cost of production ⟨~ land⟩ (2) **:** of, relating to, or derived from goods produced and marketed with such result ⟨~ profits⟩ — **mar·gin·al·i·ty** \ˌmär-jə-ˈnal-ət-ē\ *n* — **mar·gin·al·ly** \ˈmärj-nə-lē, -ən-ᵊl-ē\ *adv*

mar·gi·na·lia \ˌmär-jə-ˈnā-lē-ə\ *n pl* [NL, fr. ML, neut. pl. of *marginalis*] **:** marginal notes

marginal utility *n* **:** the amount of additional utility provided by an additional unit of an economic good or service

1mar·gin·ate \ˈmär-jə-ˌnāt\ *vt* **:** MARGIN — **mar·gin·ation** \ˌmär-jə-ˈnā-shən\ *n*

2mar·gin·ate \ˈmär-jə-nət, -ˌnāt\ *or* **mar·gin·at·ed** \-ˌnāt-əd\ *adj* **:** having a margin distinct in appearance or structure

mar·gra·vate \ˈmär-grə-ˌvāt\ *or* **mar·gra·vi·ate** \mär-ˈgrā-vē-ət, -ˌāt\ *n* **:** the territory of a margrave

mar·grave \ˈmär-ˌgrāv\ *n* [D *markgraaf*, fr. MD *marcgrave*; akin to OHG *marcgrāvo*; both fr. a prehistoric D-G compound whose constituents are akin to OHG *marha* boundary and to OHG *grāvo* count — more at MARK] **1 :** the military governor esp. of a German border province **2 :** a member of the German nobility corresponding in rank to a British marquess — **mar·gra·vi·al** \mär-ˈgrā-vē-əl\ *adj*

mar·gra·vine \ˈmär-grə-ˌvēn, ˌmär-grə-ˈ\ *n* **:** the wife of a margrave

mar·gue·rite \ˌmär-g(y)ə-ˈrēt\ *n* [F, fr. MF *margarite* pearl, daisy, — more at MARGARITE] **1 :** DAISY 1a **2 :** any of various single-flowered chrysanthemums; *esp* **:** a chrysanthemum (*Chrysanthemum frutescens*) of the Canary islands **3 :** any of several cultivated chamomiles (genus *Anthemis*)

ma·ri·a·chi \ˌmär-ē-ˈäch-ē\ *n* [MexSp] **:** a Mexican street band; *also* **:** a musician belonging to such a band

Mar·i·an \ˈmer-ē-ən, ˈmar-ē-, ˈmā-rē-\ *adj* **1 :** of or relating to Mary Tudor or her reign (1553-58) **2 :** of or relating to the Virgin Mary

Mar·i·an·ist \-ə-nəst\ *n* **:** a priest or brother of the Roman Catholic Society of Mary of Paris devoted esp. to education

Ma·ria The·re·sa dollar \mə-ˌrē-ə-tə-ˌrē-sə-, -ˌrā-sə-, -ˌrā-zə\ *n* [*Maria Theresa* †1780 Archduchess of Austria] **:** a silver coin with the image of Maria Theresa and the date 1780 used as a trade coin in the Middle East

mari·gold \ˈmar-ə-ˌgōld, ˈmer-\ *n* [ME, fr. *Mary*, mother of Jesus + ME *gold*] **1 :** POT MARIGOLD **2 :** any of a genus (*Tagetes*) of herbaceous composite plants with showy yellow or red and yellow flower heads

mar·i·jua·na *or* **mar·i·hua·na** \ˌmar-ə-ˈ(h)wän-ə\ *n* [MexSp *mariguana*, *marihuana*] **1 :** a wild tobacco (*Nicotiana glauca*) **2 a :** HEMP 1 **b :** the dried leaves and flowering tops of the pistillate hemp plant that yield cannabin and are sometimes smoked in cigarettes for their intoxicating effect

ma·rim·ba \mə-ˈrim-bə\ *n* [of African origin; akin to Kimbundu *marimba* xylophone] **:** a primitive xylophone of southern Africa and Central America with resonators beneath each bar; *also* **:** a modern improved form of this instrument

ma·ri·na \mə-ˈrē-nə\ *n* [It & Sp, seashore, fr. fem. of *marino*, adj. marine, fr. L *marinus*] **:** a dock or basin providing secure moorings for motorboats and yachts and often offering supply, repair, and other facilities

1mar·i·nade \ˌmar-ə-ˈnād\ *vt* **:** MARINATE

2marinade *n* **:** a brine or pickle in which meat or fish is soaked to enrich its flavor

mar·i·nate \ˈmar-ə-ˌnāt\ *vt* [prob. fr. It *marinato*, pp. of *marinare* to marinate, fr. *marino*] **:** to steep (as meat or fish) in a marinade

1ma·rine \mə-ˈrēn\ *adj* [ME, fr. L *marinus*, fr. *mare* sea; akin to OE *mere* sea, pool, OHG *meri* sea, OSlav *morje*] **1 a :** of or relating to the sea ⟨~ life⟩ **b :** of or relating to the navigation of the sea **:** NAUTICAL ⟨~ chart⟩ **c :** of or relating to the commerce of the sea **:** MARITIME ⟨~ law⟩ **2 :** of or relating to marines ⟨~ barracks⟩

2marine *n* **1 a :** the mercantile and naval shipping of a country **b :** seagoing ships esp. in relation to nationality or class **2 :** one of a class of soldiers serving on shipboard or in close association with a naval force; *specif* **:** a member of the U.S. Marine Corps **3 :** an executive department (as in France) having charge of naval affairs **4 :** a marine picture

marine glue *n* **:** a water-insoluble adhesive

mar·i·ner \ˈmar-ə-nər\ *n* **:** one who navigates or assists in navigating a ship **:** SEAMAN, SAILOR

mariner's compass *n* **:** a compass used in navigation consisting of parallel magnetic needles or bundles of needles permanently attached to a card marked to indicate directions and degrees of a circle

Mar·i·ol·a·try \ˌmer-ē-ˈäl-ə-trē, ˌmar-ē-, ˌmā-rē-\ *n* **:** excessive veneration of the Virgin Mary

Mar·i·ol·o·gy \-ˈäl-ə-jē\ *n* **:** study or doctrine relating to the Virgin Mary

mar·i·o·nette \ˌmar-ē-ə-ˈnet, ˌmer-\ *n* [F *marionnette*, fr. MF *maryonete*, fr. *Marion* dim. of *Marie* Mary] **:** a puppet moved by strings or by hand

mar·i·po·sa lily \ˌmar-ə-ˌpō-zə-, -sə-\ *n* [prob. fr. AmSp *mariposa*, fr. Sp, butterfly] **:** any of a genus (*Calochortus*) of western No. American plants of the lily family usu. with showily blotched flowers — called also *mariposa tulip*

mar·ish \ˈmar-ish\ *n*, *archaic* **:** MARSH

Mar·ist \ˈmar-əst, ˈmer-\ *n* [F *mariste*, fr. *Marie* Mary] **:** a priest of the Roman Catholic Society of Mary founded in France in 1816 and devoted to education

mar·i·tal \ˈmar-ət-ᵊl, *Brit also* mə-ˈrīt-\ *adj* [L *maritalis*, fr. *maritus* married] **1 :** of or relating to marriage or the married state **:** CONJUGAL **2** *archaic* **:** of or relating to a husband **syn** see MATRIMONIAL — **mar·i·tal·ly** \-ᵊl-ē\ *adv*

mar·i·time \ˈmar-ə-ˌtīm\ *adj* [L *maritimus*, fr. *mare*] **1 :** of or relating to navigation or commerce on the sea **2 :** of, relating to, or bordering on the sea **3 :** having the characteristics of a mariner

mar·jo·ram \ˈmärj-(ə-)rəm\ *n* [alter. of ME *majorane*, fr. MF, fr. ML *majorana*] **:** any of various usu. fragrant and aromatic mints (genera *Origanum* and *Majorana*) sometimes used in cookery

1mark \ˈmärk\ *n* [ME, fr. OE *mearc* boundary, march, sign; akin to OHG *marha* boundary, L *margo*] **1 :** a boundary land **2 a :** a conspicuous object serving as a guide for travelers **b :** one of the bits of leather or colored bunting placed on a sounding line at intervals **c :** TARGET **d :** the starting line or position in a track event **e** (1) **:** GOAL, OBJECT (2) **:** an object of attack, ridicule, or abuse; *specif* **:** a victim of a swindle (3) **:** the point under discussion **f :** a standard of performance, quality, or condition **:** NORM **3 a** (1) **:** SIGN, INDICATION (2) **:** an impression (as a scratch, scar, or stain) made on something (3) **:** a distinguishing trait or quality **:** CHARACTERISTIC **b :** a symbol used for identification or indication of ownership **c :** a cross made in place of a signature **d :** TRADEMARK **e :** POSTMARK **f :** a symbol used by a teacher to represent his estimate of a student's work or conduct; *esp* **:** GRADE **g :** RECORD **4 a :** ATTENTION, NOTICE **b :** IMPORTANCE, DISTINCTION **c :** a lasting or strong impression **d :** an assessment of merits **syn** see SIGN

2mark *vb* [ME *marken*, fr. OE *mearcian*; akin to OHG *marcōn* to determine the boundaries of, OE *mearc* boundary] *vt* **1 a** (1) **:** to fix or trace out the bounds or limits of (2) **:** to plot the course of **:** CHART **b :** to set apart by a line or boundary — usu. used with *off* **2 a** (1) **:** to designate as if by a mark ⟨~*ed* for greatness⟩ (2) **:** to make a mark on (3) **:** to furnish with natural marks (4) **:** to label to indicate price or quality (5) **:** to make notations in or on **b** (1) **:** to make note of in writing **:** JOT (2) **:** to indicate by a mark or symbol; *also* **:** REGISTER, RECORD (3) **:** to determine the value of by means of marks or symbols **:** GRADE **c** (1) **:** CHARACTERIZE, DISTINGUISH (2) **:** SIGNALIZE **3 :** to take notice of **:** OBSERVE **~** *vi* **:** to notice or observe critically **:** NOTE — **mark time 1 :** to keep the time of a marching step by moving the feet alternately without advancing **2 :** to function or operate in a listless or unproductive manner

3mark *n* [ME, fr. OE *marc*, prob. of Scand origin; akin to ON *mörk* mark; akin to OE *mearc* sign] **1 :** any of various old European units of weight used esp. for gold and silver; *esp* **:** a unit equal to about 8 ounces **2 :** a unit of value: **a :** an old English unit equal to 13*s* 4*d* **b :** any one of various old Scandinavian or German units of value; *specif* **:** a unit and corresponding silver coin of the 16th century worth ½ taler **c** — see MONEY table **d :** MARKKA

Mark \ˈmärk\ *n* [L *Marcus*] **1 :** an evangelist believed to be the author of the second Gospel in the New Testament **2 :** a king of Cornwall, uncle of Tristram, and husband of Isolde

mark down *vt* **:** to put a lower price on

mark·down \ˈmärk-ˌdau̇n\ *n* **1 :** a lowering of price **2 :** the amount by which an original selling price is reduced

marked \ˈmärkt\ *adj* **1 :** having an identifying mark **2 :** having a distinctive or emphasized character **:** NOTICEABLE **3 a :** enjoying fame or notoriety **b :** being an object of attack, suspicion, or vengeance **4 :** overtly signaled by a linguistic feature — **mark·ed·ly** \ˈmär-kəd-lē\ *adv*

mark·er \ˈmär-kər\ *n* **1 :** one that marks **2 :** something used for marking

1mar·ket \ˈmär-kət\ *n* [ME, fr. ONF, fr. L *mercatus* trade, market-

place, fr. *mercatus*, pp. of *mercari* to trade, fr. *merc-*, *merx* merchandise; akin to Oscan *amiricadut* without remuneration] **1 a** (1) **:** a meeting together of people for the purpose of trade by private purchase and sale and usu. not by auction (2) **:** the people assembled at such a meeting **b** (1) **:** a public place where a market is held; *specif* **:** a place where provisions are sold at wholesale (2) **:** a retail establishment usu. of a specified kind **2** *archaic* **:** the act or an instance of buying and selling **3 :** the rate or price offered for a commodity or security **4 a :** a geographical area of demand for commodities **b :** the course of commercial activity by which the exchange of commodities is effected **c :** a formal organized coming together of buyers and sellers of goods ⟨the stock ~⟩

2**market** *vi* **:** to deal in a market ~ *vt* **1 :** to expose for sale in a market **2 :** SELL — **mar·ke·teer** \ˌmär-kə-ˈti(ə)r\ *or* **mar·ket·er** \ˈmär-kət-ər\ *n*

mar·ket·abil·i·ty \ˌmär-kət-ə-ˈbil-ət-ē\ *n* **:** the quality or state of being marketable

mar·ket·able \ˈmär-kət-ə-bəl\ *adj* **1 :** fit to be offered for sale in a market **2 :** of or relating to buying or selling **3 :** wanted by purchasers **:** SALABLE

market garden *n* **:** a plot in which vegetables are raised for market — **market gardener** *n* — **market gardening** *n*

mar·ket·ing *n* **:** the act or process of selling or purchasing in a market

market order *n* **:** an order to buy or sell securities or commodities at the best price obtainable in the market when the order is executed

mar·ket·place \ˈmär-kət-ˌplās\ *n* **1 a :** an open square or place in a town where markets or public sales are held **b :** MARKET **2 :** the world of trade or economic activity

market price *n* **:** a price actually given in current market dealings

market research *n* **:** the gathering of factual information as to consumer preferences for goods and services

market value *n* **:** a price at which both buyers and sellers are willing to do business

mark·ing *n* **1 :** the act, process, or an instance of making or giving a mark **2 a :** a mark made **b :** arrangement, pattern, or disposition of marks

mark·ka \ˈmär-ˌkä\ *n*, *pl* **mark·kaa** \ˈmär-ˌkä\ *or* **markkas** \-ˌkäz\ [Finn, fr. Sw *mark*, a unit of value; akin to ON *mörk*] — see MONEY table

marks·man \ˈmärk-smən\ *n* **:** one that shoots at a mark; *esp* **:** a person skillful or practiced at hitting a mark or target — **marks·man·ship** \-ˌship\ *n*

mark up *vt* **:** to set a higher price on

mark·up \ˈmär-ˌkəp\ *n* [*mark up*] **1 :** a raise in the price of an article **2 :** an amount added to the cost price to determine the selling price

1**marl** \ˈmär(ə)l\ *n* [ME, fr. MF *marle*, fr. ML *margila*, dim. of L *marga* marl, fr. Gaulish] **:** a loose or crumbling earthy deposit (as of sand, silt, or clay) that contains a substantial amount of calcium carbonate — **marly** \ˈmär-lē\ *adj*

2**marl** *vt* **:** to dress (land) with marl

3**marl** *vt* [D *marlen*, back-formation fr. *marling*] **:** to cover or fasten with marline

mar·lin \ˈmär-lən\ *n* [short for *marlinspike*; fr. the appearance of its beak] **1 :** any of several large oceanic sport fishes (genus *Makaira*) related to sailfishes and spearfishes **2 :** SPEARFISH

mar·line *also* **mar·lin** \ˈmär-lən\ *n* [D *marlijn*, alter. of *marling*, fr. *meren*, *marren* to tie, moor, fr. MD *meren*, *maren* — more at MOOR] **:** a small usu. tarred line of two strands twisted loosely left-handed that is used for seizing and as a covering for wire rope

mar·line·spike *also* **mar·lin·spike** \ˈmär-lən-ˌspīk\ *n* **:** an iron tool that tapers to a point and is used to separate strands of rope or wire (as in splicing)

marlinespike

marl·ite \ˈmär(ə)l-ˌīt\ *n* **:** a marl resistant to the action of air — **mar·lit·ic** \mär-ˈlit-ik\ *adj*

mar·ma·lade \ˈmär-mə-ˌlād\ *n* [Pg *marmelada* quince conserve, fr. *marmelo* quince, fr. L *melimelum*, a sweet apple, fr. Gk *melimēlon*, fr. *meli* honey + *mēlon* apple — more at MELLIFLUOUS] **:** a clear jelly holding in suspension pieces of fruit and fruit rind

mar·mo·re·al \mär-ˈmōr-ē-əl, -ˈmȯr-\ *or* **mar·mo·re·an** \-ē-ən\ *adj* [L *marmoreus*, fr. *marmor* marble, fr. Gk *marmaros*] **:** of, relating to, or resembling marble or a marble statue — **mar·mo·re·al·ly** \-ē-ə-lē\ *adv*

mar·mo·set \ˈmär-mə-ˌset, -ˌzet\ *n* [ME *marmusette*, fr. MF *marmoset* grotesque figure, fr. *marmouser* to mumble, of imit. origin] **:** any of numerous soft-furred So. and Central American monkeys (family Callithricidae) with claws instead of nails on all the digits except the great toe

mar·mot \ˈmär-mət\ *n* [F *marmotte*] **:** a stout-bodied short-legged burrowing rodent (genus *Marmota*) with coarse fur, a short bushy tail, and very small ears

Mar·o·nite \ˈmar-ə-ˌnīt\ *n* [ML *maronita*, fr. *Maron-*, *Maro* 5th cent. A.D. Syrian monk] **:** a member of a Uniate church chiefly in Lebanon having a Syriac liturgy and married clergy

1**ma·roon** \mə-ˈrün\ *n* [modif. of AmerSp *cimarrón*, fr. *cimarrón* wild, savage] **1** *cap* **:** a fugitive Negro slave of the West Indies and Guiana in the 17th and 18th centuries **:** a descendant of such a slave **2 :** a person who is marooned

2**maroon** *vt* **1 :** to put ashore on a desolate island or coast and leave to one's fate **2 :** to place or leave in isolation or without hope of escape

3**maroon** *n* [F *marron* Spanish chestnut] **:** a variable color averaging a dark red

mar·plot \ˈmär-ˌplät\ *n* **:** one who frustrates or ruins a plan or undertaking by his meddling

1**marque** \ˈmärk\ *n* [ME, fr. MF, fr. OProv *marca*, fr. *marcar* to mark, seize as pledge, of Gmc origin; akin to OHG *marcōn* to mark] *obs* **:** REPRISAL, RETALIATION

2**marque** *n* [F, mark, brand, fr. MF, fr. *marquer* to mark, of Gmc origin; akin to OHG *marcōn* to mark] **:** a brand or make of a product (as a sports car)

mar·quee \mär-ˈkē\ *n* [modif. of F *marquise*, lit., marchioness] **1 :** a large field tent set up for an outdoor party, reception, or exhibition **2 :** a permanent canopy usu. of metal and glass projecting over an entrance (as of a hotel or theater)

Mar·que·san \mär-ˈkāz-ᵊn, -ˈkās-\ *n* **1 :** a Polynesian of the Marquesas islands **2 :** the Austronesian language of the Marquesans — **Marquesan** *adj*

mar·quess \ˈmär-kwəs\ *or* **mar·quis** \ˈmär-kwəs, mär-ˈkē\ *n*, *pl* **mar·quess·es** *or* **mar·quis·es** \-kwə-səz\ *or* **mar·quis** \-ˈkē(z)\ [ME *marquis*, *markis*, fr. MF *marquis*, alter. of *marchis*, fr. *marche* march] **:** a nobleman of hereditary rank in Europe and Japan; *specif* **:** a member of the second grade of the peerage in Great Britain ranking below a duke and above an earl — **mar·quess·ate** \ˈmär-kwə-sət\ *or* **mar·quis·ate** \ˈmär-kwə-zət, -sət\ *n*

mar·que·try *also* **mar·que·terie** \ˈmär-kə-trē\ *n* [MF *marqueterie*, fr. *marqueter* to checker, inlay, fr. *marque* mark] **1 :** a decorative process in which elaborate patterns are formed by the insertion of pieces of wood, shell, or ivory into a wood veneer that is then applied to a piece of furniture **2 :** an object decorated in marquetry

mar·quise \mär-ˈkēz\ *n*, *pl* **mar·quises** \-ˈkēz(-əz)\ [F, fem. of *marquis*] **1 :** MARCHIONESS **2 :** MARQUEE **3 :** a gem or a ring setting or bezel usu. elliptical in shape but with pointed ends

mar·qui·sette \ˌmär-k(w)ə-ˈzet\ *n* **:** a sheer meshed fabric used for clothing, curtains, and mosquito nets

Mar·ra·no \mə-ˈrän-(ˌ)ō\ *n* [Sp, lit., pig] **:** a Christianized Jew or Moor of medieval Spain

mar·riage \ˈmar-ij\ *n* **1 a :** the state of being married **b :** the mutual relation of husband and wife **:** WEDLOCK **c :** the institution whereby men and women are joined in a special kind of social and legal dependence for the purpose of founding and maintaining a family **2 :** an act of marrying or the rite by which the married status is effected; *esp* **:** the wedding ceremony and attendant festivities or formalities **3 :** an intimate or close union — **mar·riage·able** \-i-jə-bəl\ *adj*

marriage of convenience : a marriage contracted for social, political, or economic advantage

1**mar·ried** *adj* **1 a :** being in the state of matrimony **:** WEDDED **b :** of or relating to marriage **:** CONNUBIAL **2 :** UNITED, JOINED

2**married** *n* **:** a married person

mar·ron \ma-ˈrōⁿ\ *n* [F] **1 :** a large Mediterranean chestnut (*Castanea sativa*) or its sweet edible nut — called also *Spanish chestnut* **2 mar·rons** \-ˈrōⁿ(z)\ *pl* **:** chestnuts preserved in syrup flavored with vanilla — called also *mar·rons gla·cés* \(ˌ)ma-ˌrōⁿ-ˌgla-ˈsā\

Mar·ron \ma-ˈrōⁿ\ *n* [F, fr. AmerSp *cimarrón*] **:** MAROON 1

1**mar·row** \ˈmar-(ˌ)ō, -ə(-w)\ *n* [ME *marowe*, fr. OE *mearg*; akin to OHG *marag* marrow, Skt *majjan*] **1 a :** a soft highly vascular modified connective tissue that occupies the cavities and cancellous part of most bones **b :** the substance of the spinal cord **2 :** the choicest part: as **a :** the choicest of food **b :** the seat of animal vigor **c :** the inmost, best, or essential part **3** *chiefly Brit* **:** VEGETABLE MARROW — **mar·row·less** \-ō-ləs, -ə-ləs\ *adj* — **mar·rowy** \ˈmar-ə-wē\ *adj*

2**marrow** *n* [ME *marwe*, *marrow*] *chiefly Scot* **:** one of a pair **:** MATCH, EQUAL

marrow bean *n* **:** any of several garden beans grown primarily as field beans for their large white seeds

mar·row·bone \ˈmar-ə-ˌbōn, -ō-ˌbōn\ *n* **1 :** a bone containing marrow **2** *pl* **:** KNEES

mar·row·fat \-ō-ˌfat, -ə-ˌfat\ *n* **:** any of several wrinkled-seeded garden peas

1**mar·ry** \ˈmar-ē\ *vb* [ME *marien*, fr. OF *marier*, fr. L *maritare*, fr. *maritus* married] *vt* **1 a :** to join as husband and wife according to law or custom ⟨were *married* yesterday⟩ **b :** to give in marriage **c :** to take as spouse **:** WED ⟨*married* the girl next door⟩ **d :** to perform the ceremony of marriage for ⟨*married* the couple⟩ **2 :** to unite in close and usu. permanent relation ~ *vi* **1 :** to take a spouse **:** WED **2 :** to enter into a close or intimate union

2**marry** *interj* [ME *marie*, fr. *Marie*, the Virgin Mary] *archaic* — used to express agreement or surprise esp. in answer to a question

Mars \ˈmärz\ *n* [L *Mart-*, *Mars*] **1 :** the god of war in Roman mythology **2 :** the planet fourth in order from the sun conspicuous for the redness of its light — see PLANET table

Mar·seilles \mär-ˈsā(ə)lz\ *n* [*Marseilles*, France] **:** a firm cotton fabric that is similar to piqué

marsh \ˈmärsh\ *n*, *often attrib* [ME *mersh*, fr. OE *merisc*, *mersc*; akin to MD *mersch* marsh, OE *mere* sea, pool — more at MARINE] **:** a tract of soft wet land usu. characterized by monocotyledons (as grasses or cattails)

1**mar·shal** \ˈmär-shəl\ *n* [ME, fr. OF *mareschal*, of Gmc origin; akin to OHG *marahscalc* marshal, fr. *marah* horse + *scalc* servant] **1 a :** a high official in the household of a medieval king, prince, or noble orig. having charge of the cavalry but later usu. in command of the military forces **b :** a person who arranges and directs the ceremonial aspects of any gathering **2 a :** FIELD MARSHAL **b :** a general officer of the highest military rank **c :** an officer (as of the British Royal Air Force) equivalent in rank to an army field marshal **3 a :** an officer having charge of prisoners **b** (1) **:** a ministerial officer appointed for a judicial district (as of the U.S.) to execute the process of the courts and perform various duties similar to those of a sheriff (2) **:** a city law officer entrusted with particular duties **c :** the administrative head of a city police department or fire department — **mar·shal·cy** \-sē\ *n* — **mar·shal·ship** \-ˌship\ *n*

2**marshal** *vb* **mar·shaled** *or* **mar·shalled**; **mar·shal·ing** *or* **mar·shal·ling** \ˈmärsh-(ə-)liŋ\ *vt* **1 :** to place in proper rank or position ⟨~*ing* the troops⟩ **2 a :** to arrange in order ⟨~*ing* his arguments⟩ **b :** to assemble and dispatch (the elements of a railway train) **3 :** to lead with ceremony **:** USHER ~ *vi* **:** to take form or order **syn** see ORDER

marsh elder *n* **1 :** GUELDER ROSE **2 :** any of various coarse shrubby composite plants (genus *Iva*) of moist areas in eastern and central No. America

marsh gas *n* **:** METHANE

marsh hen *n* **:** any of various American birds (family Rallidae)

marsh·i·ness \ˈmär-shē-nəs\ *n* **:** the quality or state of being marshy

marsh·mal·low \ˈmärsh-ˌmel-ō, -ˌmel-ə(-w), -ˌmal-\ *n* **1 :** a pink-flowered European perennial herb (*Althaea officinalis*) of the mallow family that is naturalized in the eastern U.S. and has a mucilaginous root sometimes used in confectionery and in medicine **2 a :** a sweetened pasty confection made from the root of the marshmallow **b :** a confection made from corn syrup, sugar, albumen, and gelatin beaten to a light creamy consistency

marsh marigold *n* **:** a swamp herb (*Caltha palustris*) of the crowfoot family occurring in Europe and No. America and having

bright yellow flowers resembling buttercups — called also *cowslip*

marshy \'mär-shē\ *adj* **1 :** resembling or constituting a marsh **:** BOGGY **2 :** relating to or occurring in marshes

1mar·su·pi·al \mär-'sü-pē-əl\ *adj* **1 :** of, relating to, or being a marsupial **2 :** of, relating to, or forming a marsupium

2marsupial *n* [deriv. of NL *marsupium*] **:** any of an order (Marsupialia) of lowly mammals comprising kangaroos, wombats, bandicoots, opossums, and related animals that with few exceptions develop no placenta and have a pouch on the abdomen of the female containing the teats and serving to carry the young

mar·su·pi·um \-pē-əm\ *n, pl* **mar·su·pia** \-pē-ə\ [NL, fr. L, purse, pouch, fr. Gk *marsypion*] **1 :** an abdominal pouch formed by a fold of the skin and enclosing the mammary glands of most marsupials **2 :** any analogous structure in lower animals for enclosing or carrying eggs or young

1mart \'märt\ *n* [ME, fr. MD *marct, mart,* prob. fr. ONF *market*] **1** *archaic* **:** a coming together of people to buy and sell **:** FAIR 1 **2** *obs* **:** the activity of buying and selling; *also* **:** BARGAIN **3 :** MARKET

2mart *vt, archaic* **:** to deal in **:** SELL

mar·tel·lo tower \mär-'tel-ō-\ *n, often cap M* [Cape *Mortella,* Corsica] **:** a circular masonry fort or blockhouse

mar·ten \'märt-ᵊn\ *n, pl* **marten** *or* **martens** [ME *martryn,* fr. MF *martrine* marten fur, fr. OF, fr. *martre* marten, of Gmc origin; akin to OE *mearth* marten] **1 :** any of several semiarboreal slender-bodied carnivorous mammals (genus *Martes*) larger than the related weasels **2 :** the fur or pelt of a marten

mar·tens·ite \'märt-ᵊn-,zīt\ *n* [Adolf *Martens* †1914 G metallurgist] **:** the hard constituent of which quenched steel is chiefly composed — **mar·tens·it·ic** \,märt-ᵊn-'zit-ik\ *adj*

Mar·tha \'mär-thə\ *n* [LL, fr. Gk] **:** a sister of Lazarus and Mary and friend of Jesus

mar·tial \'mär-shəl\ *adj* [ME, fr. L *martialis* of Mars, fr. *Mart-, Mars*] **1 :** of, relating to, or suited for war or a warrior **2 :** relating to an army or to military life **3 :** experienced in or inclined to war **:** WARLIKE — **mar·tial·ly** \-shə-lē\ *adv*

syn MARTIAL, WARLIKE, MILITARY mean of or characteristic of war. MARTIAL suggests esp. the pomp and circumstance of war; WARLIKE implies esp. the feeling or temper that leads to or accompanies war; MILITARY applies to what pertains to a soldier or to the art or conduct of war esp. on land

martial law *n* **1 :** the law applied in occupied territory by the military authority of the occupying power **2 :** the law administered by military forces that is invoked by a government in an emergency when the civilian law enforcement agencies are unable to maintain public order and safety

Mar·tian \'mär-shən\ *adj* **:** of or relating to the planet Mars or its hypothetical inhabitants — **Martian** *n*

mar·tin \'märt-ᵊn\ *n* [MF, fr. St. *Martin;* prob. fr. the migration of martins around Martinmas] **:** a small European swallow (*Delichon urbica*) with a forked tail, bluish black head and back, and white rump and underparts; *broadly* **:** any of various swallows and flycatchers

mar·ti·net \,märt-ᵊn-'et\ *n* [Jean *Martinet,* 17th cent. F army officer] **:** a strict disciplinarian

mar·tin·gale \'märt-ᵊn-,gāl, -iŋ-\ *n* [MF] **1 :** a device for steadying a horse's head or checking its upward movement that typically consists of a strap fastened to the girth, passing between the forelegs, and bifurcating to end in two rings through which the reins pass **2 a :** a lower stay of rope or chain for the jib boom or flying jibboom used to sustain the strain of the forestays and fastened to or rove through the dolphin striker **b :** DOLPHIN STRIKER **3 :** any of several systems of betting in which a player increases his stake usu. by doubling each time he loses a bet

mar·ti·ni \mär-'tē-nē\ *n* [prob. fr. the name *Martini*] **:** a cocktail consisting of gin and dry vermouth

Mar·tin·mas \'märt-ᵊn-məs, -,mas\ *n* [ME *martinmasse,* fr. St. *Martin* + ME *masse* mass] **:** the feast of St. Martin on November 11

mart·let \'märt-lət\ *n* [MF, prob. alter. of *martinet,* dim. of *martin*] **:** the common European martin

1mar·tyr \'märt-ər\ *n* [ME, fr. OE, fr. LL, fr. Gk *martyr-,martys,* lit., witness; akin to L *memor* mindful] **1 :** one who voluntarily suffers death as the penalty of witnessing to and refusing to renounce his religion **2 :** one who sacrifices his life or something of great value for the sake of principle **3 :** a great or constant sufferer — **mar·tyr·iza·tion** \,märt-ə-rə-'zā-shən\ *n* — **mar·tyr·ize** \'märt-ə-,rīz\ *vb*

2martyr *vt* **1 :** to put to death for adhering to a belief, faith, or profession **2 :** to inflict agonizing pain upon **:** TORTURE

mar·tyr·dom \'märt-ərd-əm\ *n* **1 :** the suffering of death on account of adherence to one's religious faith or to any cause **2 :** AFFLICTION, TORTURE

mar·tyr·ol·o·gist \,märt-ə-'räl-ə-jəst\ *n* **:** a writer of or a specialist in martyrology

mar·tyr·ol·o·gy \-jē\ *n* **1 :** a catalog of Roman Catholic martyrs and saints arranged by the dates of their feasts **2 :** ecclesiastical history treating the lives and sufferings of martyrs

mar·tyry \'märt-ə-rē\ *n* [LL *martyrium,* fr. LGk *martyrion,* fr. Gk *martyr-, martys*] **:** a shrine erected in honor of a martyr

1mar·vel \'mär-vəl\ *n* [ME *mervel,* fr. OF *merveille,* fr. LL *mirabilia* marvels, fr. L, neut. pl. of *mirabilis* wonderful, fr. *mirari* to wonder — more at SMILE] **1 :** something that causes wonder or astonishment **2 :** intense surprise or interest **:** ASTONISHMENT

2marvel *vb* **mar·veled** *or* **mar·velled; mar·vel·ing** *or* **mar·vel·ling** \'märv-(ə-)liŋ\ *vi* **:** to become filled with surprise, wonder, or amazed curiosity ⟨~*ed* at his dexterity⟩ ~ *vt* **:** to feel astonishment or perplexity at or about ⟨~*ed* that they had escaped⟩

mar·vel·ous *or* **mar·vel·lous** \'märv-(ə-)ləs\ *adj* **1 :** causing wonder **:** ASTONISHING **2 :** having the characteristics of a miracle **3 :** of the highest kind or quality **:** SPLENDID — **mar·vel·ous·ly** *adv* — **mar·vel·ous·ness** *n*

Marx·ian \'märk-sē-ən, -shən\ *adj* [Karl *Marx* †1883 G political philosopher] **:** of, developed by, or influenced by the doctrines of Marx ⟨~ socialism⟩

Marx·ism \'märk-,siz-əm\ *n* **:** the political, economic, and social principles and policies advocated by Marx; *esp* **:** a theory and practice of socialism including the labor theory of value, dialectical materialism, the class struggle, and dictatorship of the proletariat until the establishment of a classless society — **Marx·ist** \-səst\ *n or adj*

Marx·ism–Le·nin·ism \'märk-,siz-əm-'len-ə-,niz-əm, -'lān-\ *n* **:** a theory and practice of communism developed by Lenin from the doctrines of Marx

Mary \'me(ə)r-ē, 'ma(ə)r-ē, 'mā-rē\ *n* [LL *Maria,* fr. Gk *Mariam, Maria* fr. Heb *Miryām*] **1 :** the mother of Jesus **2 :** a sister of Lazarus and Martha

Mary·knoll \-,nōl\ *adj* [*Maryknoll,* N. Y.] **:** of or relating to one of the institutes of priests, brothers, and sisters of the Catholic Foreign Mission Society of America organized in 1911

Mary Mag·da·lene \-'mag-də-,lēn, -,mag-də-'lē-nē\ *n* [LL *Magdalene,* fr. Gk *Magdalēnē*] **:** a woman healed of evil spirits by Jesus — called also *the Magdalene*

mar·zi·pan \'märt-sə-,pän, -,pan; 'mär-zə-,pan\ *n* [G, fr. It *marzapane,* a medieval coin, marzipan, fr. Ar *mawthabān,* a medieval coin] **:** a confection of crushed almonds or almond paste, sugar, and whites of eggs that is often shaped into various forms

Ma·sai \mä-'sī\ *n, pl* **Masai** *or* **Masais** **1 :** a pastoral and hunting people of Kenya and Tanganyika **2 :** a member of this people

mas·cara \ma-'skar-ə\ *n* [It *maschera* mask] **:** a cosmetic for coloring the eyelashes and eyebrows

mas·cot \'mas-,kät, -kət\ *n* [F *mascotte,* fr. Prov *mascoto,* fr. *masco* witch, fr. ML *masca*] **:** a person, animal, or object supposed to bring good luck

1mas·cu·line \'mas-kyə-lən\ *adj* [ME *masculin,* fr. MF, fr. L *masculinus,* fr. *masculus,* n., male, dim. of *mas* male] **1 a :** MALE **b :** MANLY **2 :** of, relating to, or constituting the gender that ordinarily includes most words or grammatical forms referring to males **3 a :** having or occurring in a stressed final syllable **b :** having the final chord occurring on a strong beat **4 :** of or forming the formal, active, or generative principle of the cosmos **syn** see MALE — **mas·cu·line·ly** *adv* — **mas·cu·line·ness** \-lən-nəs\ *n* — **mas·cu·lin·i·ty** \,mas-kyə-'lin-ət-ē\ *n*

2masculine *n* **1 :** a male person **2 :** a noun, pronoun, adjective, or inflectional form or class of the masculine gender **3 :** the masculine gender

mas·cu·lin·ize \'mas-kyə-lə-,nīz\ *vt* **:** to give a preponderantly masculine character to; *esp* **:** to cause (a female) to take on male characters

ma·ser \'mā-zər\ *n* [*m*icrowave *a*mplification by *s*timulated *e*mission of *r*adiation] **:** a device that utilizes the natural oscillations of atoms or molecules for amplifying or generating electromagnetic waves in the microwave region of the spectrum

1mash \'mash\ *n* [ME, fr. OE *māx-;* akin to MHG *meisch* mash] **1 :** crushed malt or grain meal steeped and stirred in hot water to produce wort **2 :** a mixture of ground feeds for livestock **3 :** a soft pulpy mass

2mash *vt* **1 a :** to reduce to a soft pulpy state by beating or pressure **b :** CRUSH, SMASH ⟨~ a finger⟩ **2 :** to subject (as crushed malt) to the action of water with heating and stirring in preparing wort

3mash *vt* [prob. fr. *2mash*] **:** to make amorous or flirtatious advances to

4mash *n* **:** CRUSH 4

1mash·er \'mash-ər\ *n* **:** one that mashes

2masher *n* **:** a man who makes amorous advances

mash·ie \'mash-ē\ *n* [perh. fr. F *massue* club, fr. (assumed) VL *mattiuca,* fr. *mattia* mace — more at MACE] **:** an iron golf club with a rather wide blade well laid back — called also *number five iron*

1mask \'mask\ *n* [MF *masque,* fr. OIt *maschera*] **1 a** (1) **:** a cover or partial cover for the face used for disguise (2) **:** a person wearing a mask **:** MASKER (3) **:** MASQUE **b** (1) **:** a figure of a head worn on the stage in antiquity to identify the character and project the voice (2) **:** a grotesque false face worn at carnivals or in rituals **c :** an often grotesque carved head or face used as an ornament (as on a keystone) **d :** a sculptured face or a copy of a face made by means of a mold **2 a :** something that serves to conceal or disguise **:** PRETENSE, CLOAK, POSE **b :** something that conceals from view **c :** a translucent or opaque screen to cover part of the sensitive surface in taking or printing a photograph **3 a :** a protective covering for the face **b :** GAS MASK **c :** a device covering the mouth and nose to facilitate inhalation **d :** a comparable device to prevent exhalation of infective material **e :** a cosmetic preparation for the skin of the face that produces a tightening effect as it dries **4 :** the face of an animal (as a fox or dog)

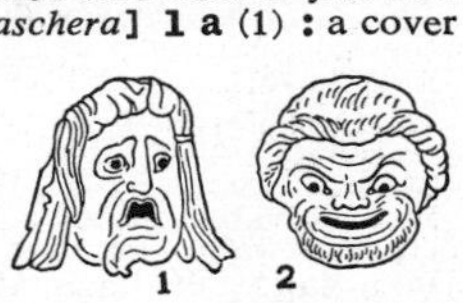

ancient Greek masks: *1* tragedy, *2* comedy

2mask *vi* **1 :** to take part in a masquerade **2 a :** to assume a mask **b :** to disguise one's true character or intentions ~ *vt* **1 a :** to conceal from view ⟨~ a gun battery⟩ **b :** to make indistinct or imperceptible ⟨~*s* undesirable flavors⟩ **c :** to cover up ⟨~*ed* his real purpose⟩ **2 a :** to cover for protection **b :** to modify the size or shape of (as a photograph) by means of an opaque border **c :** FLAVOR ⟨~ a drug⟩ **syn** see DISGUISE

masked \'maskt\ *adj* **1 a :** having its true character concealed **b :** screened from view **c :** failing to present or produce the usual symptoms **:** LATENT ⟨~ fever⟩ ⟨a ~ virus⟩ **2 a :** wearing a mask **b :** marked by the use of masks ⟨~ ball⟩

mask·er \'mas-kər\ *n* **:** a person who wears a mask

mas·och·ism \'mas-ə-,kiz-əm, 'maz-\ *n* [ISV, fr. Leopold von Sacher-*Masoch* †1895 G novelist] **:** abnormal sexual passion characterized by pleasure in being abused by one's associate; *broadly* **:** any pleasure in being abused or dominated — **mas·och·ist** \-kəst\ *n* — **mas·och·is·tic** \,mas-ə-'kis-tik, ,maz-\ *adj*

1ma·son \'mās-ᵊn\ *n* [ME, fr. OF *maçon*] **1 :** a skilled workman who builds with stone or similar material **2** *cap* **:** FREEMASON

2mason *vt* **ma·son·ing** \'mās-niŋ, -ᵊn-iŋ\ **1 :** to construct of or repair with masonry **2 :** to build stonework or brickwork about, under, in, or over

mason bee *n* **:** any of numerous solitary bees that construct nests of hardened mud and sand

Ma·son–Dix·on line \,mās-ᵊn-'dik-sən-\ *n* [Charles *Mason* †1787 E astronomer and Jeremiah *Dixon,* 18th cent. E surveyor] **:** the

southern boundary line of Pennsylvania; *also* **:** the boundary line between the northern and southern states — called also *Mason and Dixon's line*

Ma·son·ic \mə-'sän-ik\ *adj* **:** of, relating to, or characteristic of Freemasons or Freemasonry

Ma·son·ite \'mās-ᵊn-,īt\ *trademark* — used for fiberboard made from steam-exploded wood fiber

ma·son jar \,mās-ᵊn-\ *n* [John L. *Mason*, 19th cent. Am inventor] **:** a widemouthed jar used for home canning

ma·son·ry \'mās-ᵊn-rē\ *n* **1 a :** something constructed of materials used by masons **b :** the art, trade, or occupation of a mason **c :** work done by a mason **2** *cap* **:** FREEMASONRY

mason wasp *n* **:** any of various solitary wasps that construct nests of hardened mud

Ma·so·ra *or* **Ma·so·rah** \mə-'sōr-ə, -'sȯr-\ *n* [NHeb *mĕsōrāh*, fr. LHeb *māsōreth* tradition, fr. Heb, bond] **:** a body of notes on the textual traditions of the Hebrew Old Testament compiled by scribes between the 6th and 10th centuries A.D.

Mas·o·rete *or* **Mas·so·rete** \'mas-ə-,rēt\ *n* [MF *massoreth*, fr. LHeb *māsōreth*] **:** one of the scribes who wrote down the Masorah — **Mas·o·ret·ic** \,mas-ə-'ret-ik\ *adj*

masque \'mask\ *n* [MF *masque*, fr. OIt *maschera* mask] **1 :** MASQUERADE **2 :** a short allegorical dramatic entertainment of the 16th and 17th centuries performed by masked actors

masqu·er \'mas-kər\ *n* **:** MASKER

[1]**mas·quer·ade** \,mas-kə-'rād\ *n* [MF, fr. OIt dial. *mascarada*, fr. OIt *maschera*] **1 a :** a social gathering of persons wearing masks and often fantastic costumes **b :** a costume for wear at such a gathering **2 :** an action or appearance that is mere disguise or outward show

[2]**masquerade** *vi* **1 a :** to disguise oneself; *also* **:** to go about disguised **b :** to take part in a masquerade **2 :** to pass oneself off as something one is not **:** POSE — **mas·quer·ad·er** *n*

[1]**mass** \'mas\ *n* [ME, fr. OE *mæsse*, modif. of (assumed) VL *messa*, lit., dismissal at the end of a religious service, fr. LL *missa*, fr. L, fem. of *missus*, pp. of *mittere* to send — more at SMITE] **1** *cap* **:** a sequence of prayers and ceremonies forming the eucharistic office esp. of the Latin rite **2** *often cap* **:** a celebration of the Eucharist **3 :** a musical setting for the ordinary of the Mass

[2]**mass** *n* [ME *masse*, fr. MF, fr. L *massa*, fr. Gk *maza*; akin to Gk *massein* to knead — more at MINGLE] **1 a :** a quantity or aggregate of matter usu. of considerable size **b** (1) **:** EXPANSE, BULK (2) **:** MASSIVENESS (3) **:** the principal part or main body (4) **:** AGGREGATE, WHOLE ⟨men in the ~⟩ **c :** the property of a body that is a measure of its inertia, that is commonly taken as a measure of the amount of material it contains, that causes a body to have weight in a gravitational field, and that along with length and time constitutes one of the fundamental quantities on which all physical measurements are based **2 :** a large quantity, amount, or number ⟨a great ~ of material⟩ **3 a :** a large body of persons in a compact group **:** a body of persons regarded as an aggregate **b :** the body of people as contrasted with the elite — usu. used in pl. **syn** see BULK

[3]**mass** *vb* **:** to form or collect into a mass

[4]**mass** *adj* **1 a :** of or relating to the mass of the people ⟨~ market⟩ ⟨~ education⟩ **b :** participated in by or affecting a large number of individuals ⟨~ destruction⟩ ⟨~ demonstrations⟩ **c :** LARGE-SCALE, WHOLESALE ⟨~ production⟩ **2 :** viewed as a whole **:** TOTAL

Mas·sa·chu·set \,mas-(ə-)'chü-sət, -zət\ *or* **Mas·sa·chu·setts** \-səts, -zəts\ *n, pl* **Massachuset** *or* **Massachusets** *or* **Massachusetts** [Massachuset *Massa-adchu-es-et*, a locality, lit., about the big hill] **1 a :** an Indian people of the region of Massachusetts Bay **b :** a member of this people **2 :** the Algonquian language of the Massachuset people

[1]**mas·sa·cre** \'mas-i-kər, *substand* 'mas-ə-,krē\ *vt* **mas·sa·cring** \-i-k(ə-)riŋ, *substand* -ə-,krē-iŋ\ **:** to kill by massacre **:** SLAUGHTER — **mas·sa·crer** \-i-kər-ər, -i-krər, *substand* -ə-,krē-ər\ *n*

[2]**massacre** *n* [MF] **1 :** the act or an instance of killing a number of human beings under circumstances of atrocity or cruelty **2 :** a cruel or wanton murder **3 :** a wholesale slaughter of animals

[1]**mas·sage** \mə-'säzh, -'säj\ *n* [F, fr. *masser* to massage, fr. Ar *massa* to stroke] **:** manipulation of tissues for remedial or hygienic purposes (as by rubbing, stroking, kneading, or tapping) with the hand or an instrument

[2]**massage** *vt* **:** to subject to massage — **mas·sag·er** *n*

mas·sa·sau·ga \,mas-ə-'sȯ-gə\ *n* [*Missisauga* river, Ontario, Canada] **:** any of several small rattlesnakes (genus *Sistrurus*)

mass card *n* **:** a card notifying the recipient of a mass to be offered for a special intention (as for a deceased relative)

mass defect *n* **:** the difference between the mass of an isotope and its mass number

mass–energy equation *n* **:** an equation for the interconversion of mass and energy: $E=MC^2$ where *E* is energy in ergs, *M* is mass in grams, and *C* is the velocity of light in centimeters per second

mas·se·ter \mə-'sēt-ər, ma-\ *n* [NL, fr. Gk *masētēr*, fr. *masasthai* to chew] **:** a large muscle that raises the lower jaw and assists in mastication — **mas·se·ter·ic** \,mas-ə-'ter-ik\ *adj*

mas·seur \ma-'sər, mə-\ *n* [F, fr. *masser*] **:** a man who practices massage and physiotherapy

mas·seuse \-'sə(r)z, -'süz\ *n* [F, fem. of *masseur*] **:** a female masseur

mas·si·cot \'mas-ə-,kät, -,kō(t)\ *n* [ME *masticot*, fr. MF, fr. OIt *massicotto* pottery glaze] **:** unfused lead monoxide PbO

mas·sif \ma-'sēf\ *n* [F, fr. *massif*, adj.] **1 :** a principal mountain mass **2 :** a block of the earth's crust bounded by faults or flexures and displaced as a unit without internal change

mas·sive \'mas-iv\ *adj* [ME *massiffe*, fr. MF *massif*, fr. *masse* mass] **1 :** forming or consisting of a large mass: **a :** BULKY **b :** WEIGHTY, HEAVY ⟨~ walls⟩ ⟨a ~ volume⟩ **c :** impressively large or ponderous **d :** having no regular form but not necessarily lacking crystalline structure ⟨~ sandstone⟩ **2 a :** large, solid, or heavy in structure ⟨~ jaw⟩ **b :** large in scope or degree ⟨~ effect⟩ ⟨~ retaliation⟩ **c** (1) **:** large in comparison to what is typical ⟨~ dose of penicillin⟩ (2) **:** being extensive and severe ⟨~ hemorrhage⟩ ⟨~ collapse of a lung⟩ (3) **:** imposing in excellence or grandeur **:** MONUMENTAL ⟨~ simplicity⟩ — **mas·sive·ly** *adv* — **mas·sive·ness** *n*

mass noun *n* **:** a noun that characteristically denotes in many languages a homogeneous substance or a concept without subdivisions and that in English is preceded in indefinite singular constructions by *some* rather than *a* or *an*

mass number *n* **:** an integer that expresses the mass of an isotope and designates the number of nucleons in the nucleus

Mass of the Presanctified : a Roman Catholic service for Good Friday including communion with previously consecrated elements

mass–pro·duce \,mas-prə-'d(y)üs\ *vt* [back formation fr. *mass production*] **:** to produce in quantity usu. by machinery — **mass production** *n*

mass spectrograph *n* **:** an apparatus that separates a stream of charged particles into a spectrum according to the masses of the particles by means of electric and magnetic fields and that is used for measuring atomic masses and determining the relative abundance of isotopes in an element

massy \'mas-ē\ *adj* **:** having bulk and weight or substance **:** MASSIVE

[1]**mast** \'mast\ *n* [ME, fr. OE *mæst*; akin to OHG *mast*, L *malus*] **1 :** a long pole or spar rising from the keel or deck of a ship and supporting the yards, booms, and rigging **2 :** a vertical or nearly vertical pole (as an upright post in various cranes) **3 :** a disciplinary proceeding at which the commanding officer of a naval unit hears and disposes of cases against his enlisted men — called also *captain's mast* — **mast·ed** \'mas-təd\ *adj* — **before the mast 1 :** forward of the foremast **2 :** as a common sailor

[2]**mast** *vt* **:** to furnish with a mast

[3]**mast** *n* [ME, fr. OE *mæst*; akin to OE *mete* food — more at MEAT] **:** nuts (as beechnuts and acorns) accumulated on the forest floor and often serving as food for hogs or other animals

mast- *or* **masto-** *comb form* [NL, fr. Gk, fr. *mastos* — more at MEAT] **:** breast **:** nipple **:** mammary gland ⟨*mast*itis⟩

mas·ta·ba \'mas-tə-bə\ *n* [Ar *maṣṭabah* stone bench] **:** an Egyptian tomb of the time of the Memphite dynasties that is oblong in shape with sloping sides and is connected with a mummy chamber in the rock beneath

mas·tec·to·my \ma-'stek-tə-mē\ *n* **:** excision or amputation of the breast

[1]**mas·ter** \'mas-tər\ *n* [ME, fr. OE *magister* & OF *maistre*, both fr. L *magister*; akin to L *magnus* great — more at MUCH] **1 a** (1) **:** a male teacher (2) **:** a person holding an academic degree higher than a bachelor's but lower than a doctor's **b** *often cap* **:** a revered religious leader **c :** a workman qualified to teach apprentices **d :** an artist or performer of consummate skill **2 a :** one having authority over another **:** RULER, GOVERNOR **b :** VICTOR, SUPERIOR **c :** a person licensed to command a merchant ship **d** (1) **:** one having control (2) **:** an owner esp. of a slave or animal **e :** EMPLOYER **f** (1) *dial* **:** HUSBAND (2) **:** the male head of a household **3 a** (1) *archaic* **:** MISTER (2) **:** a youth or boy too young to be called *mister* — used as a title **b :** the eldest son of a Scottish viscount or baron **4 a :** a presiding officer in an institution or society (as a college) **b :** any of several officers of court appointed to assist (as by hearing and reporting) a judge **5 a :** a master mechanism or device **b :** a master phonograph record

[2]**master** *vt* **mas·ter·ing** \-t(ə-)riŋ\ **1 :** to become master of **:** OVERCOME **2 a :** to become skilled or proficient in the use of **b :** to gain a thorough understanding of

[3]**master** *adj* **:** being or relating to a master: as **a :** DOMINANT **b :** SKILLED, PROFICIENT **c :** PRINCIPAL, PREDOMINANT **d :** SUPERLATIVE **e :** being a device or mechanism that controls the operation of another mechanism or that establishes a standard (as a dimension or weight) **f :** being a phonograph disc record from which duplicates are made

master–at–arms *n, pl* **masters–at–arms :** a petty officer charged with maintaining discipline aboard ship

master chief petty officer *n* **:** a petty officer of the highest enlisted rating in the navy

mas·ter·ful \'mas-tər-fəl\ *adj* **1 :** IMPERIOUS, DOMINEERING **2 :** having or reflecting the technical or artistic skill of a master ⟨~ drawings⟩ — **mas·ter·ful·ly** \-fə-lē\ *adv* — **mas·ter·ful·ness** *n*

syn DOMINEERING, IMPERIOUS, PEREMPTORY, IMPERATIVE: MASTERFUL implies a strong virile personality and ability to deal authoritatively with affairs; DOMINEERING suggests an overbearing or tyrannical manner and an obstinate attempt to enforce one's will; IMPERIOUS implies more arrogance than MASTERFUL but less insolence than DOMINEERING; PEREMPTORY stresses insistence on an immediate response to one's commands; IMPERATIVE implies peremptoriness arising more from the urgency of the situation than from one's temperament

master gunnery sergeant *n* **:** a sergeant major in the marine corps

master key *n* **:** a key designed to open several different locks

mas·ter·li·ness \'mas-tər-lē-nəs\ *n* **:** the quality or state of being masterly

mas·ter·ly \-lē\ *adj* **:** suitable to or resembling that of a master; *esp* **:** indicating thorough knowledge or superior skill and power ⟨~ performance⟩ — **masterly** *adv*

mas·ter·mind \'mas-tər-,mīnd, ,mas-tər-'\ *n* **:** a person who supplies the directing or creative intelligence for a project — **mastermind** *vt*

master of ceremonies : a person who determines the forms to be observed on a public occasion or acts as host at a formal event

mas·ter·piece \'mas-tər-,pēs\ *n* **1 :** a piece of work presented to a guild as evidence of qualification for the rank of master **2 :** a work done with extraordinary skill; *esp* **:** a supreme intellectual or artistic achievement

master race *n* **:** a people held to be racially preeminent and hence fitted to rule or enslave other peoples

master sergeant *n* **:** a noncommissioned officer ranking in the army above a sergeant first class and below a sergeant major, in the air force above a technical sergeant and below a senior master sergeant, and in the marine corps above a gunnery sergeant and below a sergeant major

mas·ter·ship \'mas-tər-,ship\ *n* **1 :** the authority or control of a master **2 :** the status, office, or function of a master **3 :** the proficiency of a master

mas·ter·sing·er \-,siŋ-ər\ *n* **:** MEISTERSINGER

mas·ter·stroke \-,strōk\ *n* **:** a masterly performance or move

mas·ter·work \-,wərk\ *n* **:** MASTERPIECE

mas·tery \'mas-t(ə-)rē\ *n* [ME *maistrie*, fr. OF, fr. *maistre* master] **1 a :** MASTERSHIP, DOMINION **b :** SUPERIORITY, ASCENDANCY **2 a :** possession or display of great skill or technique **b :** skill or knowledge that makes one master of a subject **:** COMMAND

mast·head \'mast-,hed\ *n* **1 :** the top of a mast **2 a :** the printed matter in a newspaper or periodical that gives the title and pertinent details of ownership, advertising rates, and subscription rates **b :** the name of a newspaper displayed on the top of the first page

mas·tic \ˈmas-tik\ *n* [ME *mastik*, fr. L *mastiche*, fr. Gk *mastichē*; akin to Gk *mastichan*] **1 :** an aromatic resinous exudate from mastic trees used chiefly in varnishes **2 :** any of various pasty materials used as protective coatings or cements

mas·ti·cate \ˈmas-tə-ˌkāt\ *vb* [LL *masticatus*, pp. of *masticare*, fr. Gk *mastichan* to gnash the teeth; akin to Gk *masasthai* to chew — more at MOUTH] *vt* **1 :** to grind or crush (food) with or as if with the teeth in preparation for swallowing **:** CHEW **2 :** to soften or reduce to pulp by crushing or kneading ~ *vi* **:** CHEW — **mas·ti·ca·tion** \ˌmas-tə-ˈkā-shən\ *n* — **mas·ti·ca·tor** \ˈmas-tə-ˌkāt-ər\ *n*

1mas·ti·ca·to·ry \ˈmas-ti-kə-ˌtōr-ē, -ˌtȯr-\ *adj* **1 :** used for or adapted to chewing ⟨~ limbs of an arthropod⟩ **2 :** of, relating to, or involving the organs of mastication ⟨~ paralysis⟩

2masticatory *n* **:** a substance chewed to increase saliva

mastic tree *n* **:** a small southern European tree (*Pistacia lentiscus*) of the sumac family that yields mastic

mas·tiff \ˈmas-təf\ *n* [ME *mastif*, modif. of MF *mastin*, fr. (assumed) VL *mansuetinus*, fr. L *mansuetus* tame — more at MANSUETUDE] **:** a very large powerful deep-chested smooth-coated dog of an old breed used chiefly as a watchdog and guard dog

mas·ti·goph·o·ran \ˌmas-tə-ˈgäf-ə-rən\ *n* [deriv. of Gk *mastig-*, *mastix* whip + *pherein* to carry — more at BEAR] **:** any of a class (Mastigophora) of protozoans comprising forms with flagella and including many often treated as algae — **mastigophoran** *adj* — **mas·ti·goph·o·rous** \-rəs\ *adj*

mas·ti·gote \ˈmas-tə-ˌgōt\ *adj* [irreg. fr. Gk *mastig-*, *mastix*] **:** having a flagellum

mas·ti·tis \ma-ˈstīt-əs\ *n* [NL] **:** inflammation of the breast or udder usu. caused by infection

mast·odon \ˈmas-tə-ˌdän, -dən\ *n* [NL *mastodont-*, *mastodon*, fr. Gk *mast-* + *odont-*, *odōn*, *odous* tooth — more at TOOTH] **1 :** any of numerous extinct mammals (esp. genus *Mammut*) that differ from the related mammoths and existing elephants chiefly in the form of the molar teeth **2 :** something of unusually large size **:** GIANT — **mast·odon·ic** \ˌmas-tə-ˈdän-ik\ *adj* — **mast·odont** \ˈmas-tə-ˌdänt\ *adj or n*

1mas·toid \ˈmas-ˌtȯid\ *adj* [NL *mastoides*, fr. Gk *mastoeidēs*, fr. *mastos* breast — more at MEAT] **1 :** resembling a nipple or breast **2 a :** being a process of the temporal bone behind the ear **b :** of, relating to, or occurring in the region of this process

2mastoid *n* **1 :** a mastoid bone or process **2 a :** MASTOIDITIS **b :** an operation for the relief of mastoiditis

mastoid cell *n* **:** one of the small cavities in the mastoid process that develop after birth and are filled with air

mas·toid·ec·to·my \ˌmas-ˌtȯi-ˈdek-tə-mē\ *n* [ISV] **:** surgical removal of the mastoid cells or of the mastoid process

mas·toid·itis \ˌmas-ˌtȯi-ˈdīt-əs\ *n* [NL] **:** inflammation of the mastoid and esp. of the mastoid cells

mas·tur·bate \ˈmas-tər-ˌbāt\ *vb* [L *masturbatus*, pp. of *masturbari*] *vi* **:** to practice masturbation ~ *vt* **:** to practice masturbation on

mas·tur·ba·tion \ˌmas-tər-ˈbā-shən\ *n* **:** stimulation of the genital organs to orgasm achieved by manual or other bodily contact exclusive of sexual intercourse — **mas·tur·ba·tion·al** \-shnəl, -shən-ᵊl\ *adj*

ma·su·ri·um \mə-ˈzu̇r-ē-əm, -ˈsu̇r-\ *n* [NL, fr. *Masuria*, region in Poland] **:** TECHNETIUM

1mat \ˈmat\ *n* [ME, fr. OE *meatte*, fr. LL *matta*, of Sem origin; akin to Heb *miṭṭāh* bed] **1 a** (1) **:** a piece of coarse woven or plaited fabric used as a floor covering or support (2) **:** a piece of material placed at a door for cleaning shoes **b :** a decorative piece of material used as a support for a dish or other small item **c :** a large thick pad or cushion used as a surface for wrestling, tumbling, and gymnastics **2 :** something made up of many intertwined or tangled strands

2mat *vb* **mat·ted; mat·ting** *vt* **1 :** to provide with a mat or matting **2 :** to form into a tangled mass ~ *vi* **:** to become matted

3mat *vt* **mat·ted; mat·ting 1 :** to make (as a metal, glass, or color) mat **2 :** to provide (a picture) with a mat

4mat *adj* [F, fr. OF, defeated, fr. L *mattus* drunk; akin to L *madēre* to be wet — more at MEAT] **:** lacking or deprived of luster or gloss: as **a :** having a usu. smooth even surface free from shine or highlights ⟨~ metals⟩ ⟨a ~ white face⟩ **b** *usu* **matte** \ˈmat\ **:** having a rough or granular surface ⟨a *matte* bacterial colony⟩

5mat *n* **1 :** a border going around a picture between picture and frame or serving as the frame **2 :** a dead or dull finish or a roughened surface (as in gilding or painting) **3** [by shortening] **:** MATRIX 4a

mat·a·dor \ˈmat-ə-ˌdȯ(ə)r\ *n* [Sp, fr. *matar* to kill] **1 :** a bullfighter who has the principal role and who kills the bull in a bullfight **2 :** a principal trump in some card games

Ma·ta·ra \mə-ˈtär-ə\ *trademark* — used for a natural brown or a dyed brown sealskin

1match \ˈmach\ *n* [ME *macche*, fr. OE *mæcca*; akin to OE *macian* to make — more at MAKE] **1 a :** a person or thing equal or similar to another **b :** one able to cope with another **c :** an exact counterpart **2 :** a pair suitably associated ⟨carpet and curtains are a ~⟩ **3 :** a process of matching; *esp* **:** a contest between two or more parties **4 a :** a marriage union **b :** a prospective partner in marriage

2match *vt* **1 a :** to encounter successfully as an antagonist **b** (1) **:** to set in competition with or opposition to ⟨~*ing* his strength against his enemy's⟩ (2) **:** to provide with a worthy competitor **c :** to set in comparison with **2 :** to join or give in marriage **3 a** (1) **:** to put in a set possessing equal or harmonizing attributes (2) **:** to cause to correspond **:** SUIT **b** (1) **:** to be the counterpart of (2) **:** to harmonize with **c :** to provide with a counterpart **4 :** to fit together or make suitable for fitting together **5 a :** to flip or toss (coins) and compare exposed faces **b :** to toss coins with ~ *vi* **:** to be a counterpart — **match·er** *n*

3match *n* [ME *macche*, fr. MF *meiche*] **1 :** a chemically prepared wick or cord formerly used in firing firearms or powder **2 :** a short slender piece of wood or other flammable material tipped with a combustible mixture that bursts into flame through friction (as by being scratched against a rough surface)

match·able \ˈmach-ə-bəl\ *adj* **:** capable of being matched

match·board \ˈmach-ˌbō(ə)rd, -ˌbȯ(ə)rd\ *or* **matched board** \ˈmach(t)-ˈ\ *n* **:** a board with a groove cut along one edge and a tongue along the other so as to fit snugly with the edges of similarly cut boards

matchboards

match·book \ˈmach-ˌbu̇k\ *n* **:** a small folder containing rows of paper matches

matched order *n* **:** an order to buy stock to be sold at once at the same price through another broker; *also* **:** the order to sell such stock

match·less \ˈmach-ləs\ *adj* **:** having no equal **:** PEERLESS — **match·less·ly** *adv*

match·lock \-ˌläk\ *n* **1 :** a slow-burning cord lowered over a hole in the breech of a musket to ignite the charge **2 :** a musket equipped with a matchlock

match·mak·er \-ˌmā-kər\ *n* **:** one that arranges a match; *esp* **:** one that arranges marriages — **match·mak·ing** \-kiŋ\ *n*

match play *n* **:** golf competition in which the winner is the person or team winning the greater number of holes

match point *n* **:** the last point needed to win a match

match·wood \ˈmach-ˌwu̇d\ *n* **:** small pieces of wood **:** SPLINTERS

1mate \ˈmāt\ *vt* [ME *maten*, fr. MF *mater*, fr. OF *mat*, n., checkmate, fr. Ar *māt* (in *shāh māt*)] **:** CHECKMATE 2

2mate *n* **:** CHECKMATE 1

3mate *n* [ME, prob. fr. MLG *māt*; akin to OE *gemetta* guest at one's table, *mete* food — more at MEAT] **1 a** (1) **:** ASSOCIATE, COMPANION (2) **:** an assistant to a more skilled workman **:** HELPER ⟨plumber's ~⟩ **b** *archaic* **:** MATCH, PEER **2 :** a deck officer on a merchant ship ranking below the captain **3 :** one of a pair; *esp* **:** one of a married pair

4mate *vt* **1** *archaic* **:** EQUAL, MATCH **2 :** to join or fit together **:** COUPLE **3 a :** to join together as mates **b :** to provide a mate for ~ *vi* **:** to become mated ⟨gears that ~ well⟩

5ma·té *or* **ma·te** \ˈmä-ˌtā\ *n* [F & AmerSp; F *maté*, fr. AmerSp *mate*, fr. Quechua] **1 :** an aromatic beverage used chiefly in So. America **2 :** a So. American holly (*Ilex paraguayensis*) whose leaves and shoots are used in making maté; *also* **:** these leaves and shoots

ma·te·lote \ˌmat-ᵊl-ˈōt, mat-ˈlōt\ *n* [F] **:** fish stewed in a sauce of wine, onions, seasonings, and fish stock

ma·ter \ˈmāt-ər\ *n* [L] *chiefly Brit* **:** MOTHER

ma·ter·fa·mil·i·as \ˌmāt-ər-fə-ˈmil-ē-əs, ˌmät-\ *n* [L, fr. *mater* + *familias*, archaic gen. of *familia* household — more at FAMILY] **:** a woman who is head of a household

1ma·te·ri·al \mə-ˈtir-ē-əl\ *adj* [ME *materiel*, fr. MF & LL; MF, fr. LL *materialis*, fr. L *materia* matter — more at MATTER] **1 a** (1) **:** relating to, derived from, or consisting of matter; *esp* **:** PHYSICAL ⟨~ world⟩ (2) **:** BODILY ⟨~ needs⟩ **b** (1) **:** of or relating to matter rather than form ⟨~ cause⟩ (2) **:** of or relating to the subject matter of reasoning; *esp* **:** EMPIRICAL ⟨~ knowledge⟩ **2 a :** having real importance or great consequence **b** (1) **:** ESSENTIAL (2) **:** RELEVANT, PERTINENT **3 a :** being of a physical or worldly nature **b :** relating to or concerned with physical rather than spiritual or intellectual things ⟨~ progress⟩ **4 :** of or relating to the production and distribution of economic goods and the social relationships of owners and laborers — **ma·te·ri·al·ly** \-ē-ə-lē\ *adv* — **ma·te·ri·al·ness** *n*

syn MATERIAL, PHYSICAL, CORPOREAL, PHENOMENAL, SENSIBLE, OBJECTIVE mean of or belonging to actuality. MATERIAL implies formation out of tangible matter; used in contrast with *spiritual* or *ideal* it may connote the mundane, crass, or grasping; PHYSICAL applies to what is perceived directly by the senses and may contrast with *mental*, *spiritual*, or *imaginary*; CORPOREAL implies having the tangible qualities of a body such as shape, size, or resistance to force; PHENOMENAL applies to what is known or perceived through the senses rather than by intuition or rational deduction; SENSIBLE stresses the capability of readily or forcibly impressing the senses; OBJECTIVE may stress material or independent existence apart from a subject perceiving it **syn** see in addition RELEVANT

2material *n* **1 a :** the elements, constituents, or substances of which something is composed or can be made **b :** data that may be worked into a more finished form **c :** MATTER 3b **2 a :** apparatus necessary for doing or making something ⟨writing ~*s*⟩ **b :** MATÉRIEL

ma·te·ri·al·ism \mə-ˈtir-ē-ə-ˌliz-əm\ *n* **1 a :** a theory that physical matter is the only reality and that all being and processes and phenomena can be explained as manifestations or results of matter **b :** a doctrine that the only or the highest values or objectives lie in material well-being and in the furtherance of material progress **c :** a doctrine that economic or social change is materially caused — compare HISTORICAL MATERIALISM **2 :** a preoccupation with or stress upon material rather than intellectual or spiritual things — **ma·te·ri·al·ist** \-ləst\ *n or adj* — **ma·te·ri·al·is·tic** \-ˌtir-ē-ə-ˈlis-tik\ *adj* — **ma·te·ri·al·is·ti·cal·ly** \-ti-k(ə-)lē\ *adv*

ma·te·ri·al·i·ty \mə-ˌtir-ē-ˈal-ət-ē\ *n* **1 :** something that is material **2 :** the quality or state of being material ⟨questioned the ~ of the evidence⟩

ma·te·ri·al·iza·tion \mə-ˌtir-ē-ə-lə-ˈzā-shən\ *n* **1 :** the action of materializing or of becoming materialized **2 :** something that has been materialized; *esp* **:** APPARITION

ma·te·ri·al·ize \mə-ˈtir-ē-ə-ˌlīz\ *vt* **1 a :** to make material **:** OBJECTIFY ⟨~*ing* an idea in words⟩ **b :** to cause to appear in bodily form ⟨~ the spirits of the dead⟩ **2 :** to cause to be materialistic ~ *vi* **1 :** to assume bodily form **2 a :** to come into existence **b :** to put in an appearance; *esp* **:** to appear suddenly — **ma·te·ri·al·iz·er** *n*

ma·te·ria med·i·ca \mə-ˌtir-ē-ə-ˈmed-i-kə\ *n* [NL, lit., medical matter] **1 :** material or substance used in the composition of medical remedies **2 a :** a branch of medical science that treats of the sources, nature, properties, and preparation of drugs **b :** a treatise on this subject

ma·té·ri·el *or* **ma·te·ri·el** \mə-ˌtir-ē-ˈel\ *n* [F *matériel*, fr. *matériel*, adj.] **:** equipment, apparatus, and supplies used by an organization or institution

ma·ter·nal \mə-ˈtərn-ᵊl\ *adj* [ME, fr. MF *maternel*, fr. L *maternus*, fr. *mater* mother — more at MOTHER] **1 :** of, relating to, or characteristic of a mother **:** MOTHERLY **2 a :** related through a mother **b :** inherited or derived from a mother — **ma·ter·nal·ly** \-ᵊl-ē\ *adv*

ma·ter·ni·ty \mə-ˈtər-nət-ē\ *n, often attrib* **1 a :** the quality or state of being a mother **:** MOTHERHOOD **b :** the qualities of a mother **:** MOTHERLINESS **2 :** a hospital facility designed for the care of women before and during childbirth and for the care of newborn babies

mat·ey \ˈmāt-ē\ *adj, chiefly Brit* **:** COMPANIONABLE

math \ˈmath\ *n* **:** MATHEMATICS

math·e·mat·i·cal \ˌmath-ə-ˈmat-i-kəl\ *adj* [L *mathematicus,* fr. Gk *mathēmatikos,* fr. *mathēmat-, mathēma* mathematics, fr. *manthanein* to learn; akin to Goth *mundon* to pay attention, Skt *medhā* intelligence] **1 :** of, relating to, or according with mathematics **2 a :** rigorously exact **:** PRECISE **b :** CERTAIN **3 :** possible but highly improbable ⟨only a ~ chance⟩ — **math·e·mat·i·cal·ly** \-i-k(ə-)lē\ *adv*

mathematical logic *n* **:** SYMBOLIC LOGIC

math·e·ma·ti·cian \ˌmath-(ə-)mə-ˈtish-ən\ *n* **:** a specialist or expert in mathematics

math·e·mat·ics \ˌmath-ə-ˈmat-iks\ *n pl but usu sing in constr* **1 :** the science of numbers and their operations, interrelations, combinations, generalizations, and abstractions and of space configurations and their structure, measurement, transformations, and generalizations **2 :** a branch of, operation in, or use of mathematics ⟨~ of physical chemistry⟩

mat·in \ˈmat-ᵊn\ *adj* **:** of or relating to matins or to early morning

mat·in·al \ˈmat-ᵊn-əl\ *adj* **1 :** of or relating to matins **2 :** EARLY

mat·i·nee *or* **mat·i·née** \ˌmat-ᵊn-ˈā\ *n* [F *matinée,* lit., morning, fr. OF, fr. *matin* morning, fr. L *matutinum,* fr. neut. of *matutinus* of the morning, fr. *Matuta,* goddess of morning; akin to L *maturus* ripe — more at MATURE] **:** a musical or dramatic performance or social or public event held in the daytime and esp. the afternoon

mat·ins \ˈmat-ᵊnz\ *n pl but sing or pl in constr, often cap* [ME *matines,* fr. OF, fr. LL *matutinae,* fr. L, fem. pl. of *matutinus*] **1 :** the night office forming with lauds the first of the canonical hours **2 :** MORNING PRAYER

matr- *or* **matri-** *or* **matro-** *comb form* [L *matr-, matri-,* fr. *matr-, mater*] **:** mother ⟨*matri*arch⟩ ⟨*matro*nymic⟩

ma·tri·arch \ˈmā-trē-ˌärk\ *n* **:** a woman who rules a family, group, or state; *specif* **:** a mother who is head and ruler of her family and descendants — **ma·tri·ar·chal** \ˌmā-trē-ˈär-kəl\ *adj*

ma·tri·ar·chate \ˈmā-trē-ˌär-kət, -ˌkāt\ *n* **1 :** a family, group, or state governed by a matriarch **2 :** a theoretical stage or state in primitive society in which matriarchs hold the chief authority

ma·tri·ar·chy \ˈmā-trē-ˌär-kē\ *n* **1 :** MATRIARCHATE **2 :** a system of social organization in which descent and inheritance are traced through the female line

ma·tri·ci·dal \ˌma-trə-ˈsīd-ᵊl, ˌmā-\ *adj* **:** of or relating to a matricide

ma·tri·cide \ˈma-trə-ˌsīd, ˈmā-\ *n* **1** [L *matricidium,* fr. *matr-* + *-cidium* -cide] **:** murder of a mother by her son or daughter **2** [L *matricida,* fr. *matr-* + *-cida* -cide] **:** one that murders his mother

ma·tric·u·lant \mə-ˈtrik-yə-lənt\ *n* **:** one that is matriculating

ma·tric·u·late \-ˌlāt\ *vb* [ML *matriculatus,* pp. of *matriculare,* fr. LL *matricula* public roll, dim. of *matric-, matrix* list, fr. L, womb] *vt* **:** to enroll as a member of a body and esp. of a college or university ~ *vi* **:** to become matriculated — **ma·tric·u·la·tion** \mə-ˌtrik-yə-ˈlā-shən\ *n*

ma·tri·lin·eal \ˌma-trə-ˈlin-ē-əl, ˌmā-\ *adj* **:** relating to, based on, or tracing descent through the maternal line ⟨~ society⟩ — **ma·tri·lin·eal·ly** \-ē-ə-lē\ *adv*

mat·ri·mo·nial \ˌma-trə-ˈmō-nē-əl, -nyəl\ *adj* **:** of or relating to matrimony — **mat·ri·mo·nial·ly** \-ē\ *adv*

syn MARITAL, CONJUGAL, CONNUBIAL, NUPTIAL: MATRIMONIAL applies to whatever has to do with the married state or married persons; MARITAL may imply reference particularly to the husband and his part in marriage but is often equal to MATRIMONIAL; CONJUGAL and CONNUBIAL are often interchanged but CONJUGAL refers rather to persons who are married, CONNUBIAL to the married state; NUPTIAL refers to the rites and ceremonies attending marriage

mat·ri·mo·ny \ˈma-trə-ˌmō-nē\ *n* [ME, fr. MF *matremoine,* fr. L *matrimonium,* fr. *matr-, mater* mother, matron — more at MOTHER] **1 :** the union of man and woman as husband and wife **:** MARRIAGE **2 a :** a card game in which bets are placed on combinations of cards **b :** a combination of king and queen in this game

matrimony vine *n* **:** a shrub or vine (genus *Lycium*) of the nightshade family with often showy flowers and bright berries

ma·trix \ˈmā-triks\ *n, pl* **ma·tri·ces** \ˈmā-trə-ˌsēz, ˈma-\ *or* **ma·trix·es** \ˈmā-trik-səz\ [L, womb, fr. *matr-, mater*] **1 a :** the intercellular substance of a tissue (as cartilage) **b :** the thickened epithelium at the base of a fingernail or toenail from which new nail substance develops **2 :** something within which something else originates or develops **3 :** the natural material in which a fossil, metal, gem, crystal, or pebble is embedded **4 a :** a mold from which a relief surface (as a stereotype) is made by pouring or pressing **b :** DIE 5a(1) **c :** an engraved or inscribed die or stamp **d :** an electroformed impression of a phonograph record used for mass-producing duplicates of the original **5 :** a rectangular array of mathematical elements (as the coefficients of simultaneous linear equations) that is subject to special algebraic laws ⟨a ~ combines with numbers and other *matrices*⟩

ma·tron \ˈmā-trən\ *n* [ME *matrone,* fr. MF, fr. L *matrona,* fr. *matr-, mater*] **1 a :** a married woman usu. marked by dignified maturity or social distinction **b :** a woman that supervises women or children (as in a school or police station) **c :** the chief officer in a women's organization **2 :** a brood female

ma·tron·ize \-trə-ˌnīz\ *vt* **1 :** to make matronly **2 :** to superintend as a matron **:** CHAPERONE

ma·tron·ly \ˈmā-trən-lē\ *adj* **:** having the character of or suitable to a matron

matron of honor : a bride's principal married wedding attendant

mat·ro·nym·ic \ˌma-trə-ˈnim-ik\ *n* [*matr-* + *-onymic* (as in *patronymic*)] **:** a name derived from that of the mother or a maternal ancestor

matt *or* **matte** \ˈmat\ *var of* MAT

matte \ˈmat\ *n* [F] **:** a crude mixture of sulfides formed in smelting sulfide ores of metals (as copper, lead, or nickel)

[1]**mat·ter** \ˈmat-ər\ *n* [ME *matere,* fr. OF, fr. L *materia* matter, physical substance, fr. *mater*] **1 a :** a subject under consideration **b :** a subject of disagreement or litigation **c** *pl* **:** the events or circumstances of a particular situation **d :** the elements that constitute material for treatment in thought, discourse, or writing **e :** an element of a field of knowledge, inquiry, or specialization ⟨~*s* of faith⟩ **f :** something to be proved in law **g** *obs* **:** sensible or serious material as distinguished from nonsense or drollery **h** (1) *obs* **:** REASON, CAUSE (2) **:** a source esp. of feeling or emotion **i :** a condition affecting a person or thing usu. unfavorably ⟨what's the ~⟩ **2 a :** the substance of which a physical object is composed **b :** a substance that constitutes the observable universe and together with energy forms the basis of objective phenomena **c :** a material substance of a particular kind or for a particular purpose **d** (1) **:** material (as feces or urine) discharged from the living body (2) **:** material discharged by suppuration **:** PUS **3 a :** the indeterminate subject of reality; *esp* **:** the element in the universe that undergoes formation and alteration **b :** the formless substratum of all things which exists only potentially and upon which form acts to produce realities **4 :** a more or less definite amount or quantity ⟨a ~ of 10 years⟩ **5 a :** something written or printed **b** (1) **:** set type (2) **:** text material esp. as distinguished from illustrations **6 :** MAIL **7** *Christian Science* **:** the illusion that the objects perceived by the physical senses have the reality of substance

[2]**matter** *vi* **1 :** to be of importance **:** SIGNIFY **2 :** to form or discharge pus **:** SUPPURATE ⟨~*ing* wound⟩

matter of course : something that is to be expected as a natural or logical consequence

mat·ter-of-fact \ˌmat-ə-rə-ˈfakt\ *adj* **:** adhering to or concerned with fact; *esp* **:** not fanciful or imaginative **:** PRACTICAL — **mat·ter-of-fact·ly** \-ˈfak-(t)lē\ *adv* — **mat·ter-of-fact·ness** \-ˈfak(t)-nəs\ *n*

mat·tery \ˈmat-ə-rē\ *adj* **:** producing or containing pus or material resembling pus ⟨eyes all ~⟩

Mat·the·an *or* **Mat·thae·an** \ma-ˈthē-ən, mə-\ *adj* [LL *Matthaeus*] **:** of, relating to, or characteristic of the evangelist Matthew or the gospel ascribed to him

Mat·thew \ˈmath-(ˌ)yü *also* ˈmath-(ˌ)ü\ *n* [F *Mathieu,* fr. LL *Matthaeus,* fr. Gk *Matthaios,* fr. Heb *Mattithyāh*] **:** a customs collector chosen as one of the twelve apostles and believed to be the author of the first Gospel in the New Testament

[1]**mat·ting** \ˈmat-iŋ\ *n* **1 :** material for mats **2 :** MATS

[2]**matting** *n* [fr. gerund of [3]*mat*] **:** a dull lusterless surface (as on gilding, metalwork, or satin)

mat·tins *often cap, chiefly Brit var of* MATINS

mat·tock \ˈmat-ək\ *n* [ME *mattok,* fr. OE *mattuc*] **:** a digging and grubbing implement with features of an adz, ax, and pick

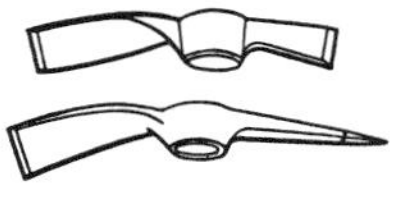

mattocks: *1* cutter, *2* pick

mat·tress \ˈma-trəs\ *n* [ME *materas,* fr. OF, fr. Ar *maṭraḥ* place where something is thrown] **1 a :** a fabric case filled with resilient material used either alone as a bed or on a bedstead **b :** an inflatable airtight sack for use as a mattress **2 :** a mass of interwoven brush and poles to protect a bank from erosion; *also* **:** a similar mass serving as a foundation in soft ground

mat·u·rate \ˈmach-ə-ˌrāt\ *vb* **:** MATURE

mat·u·ra·tion \ˌmach-ə-ˈrā-shən\ *n* **1 a :** the process of becoming mature **b :** the emergence of personal characteristics and behavioral phenomena through growth processes **c :** the final stages of differentiation of cells, tissues, or organs **2 a :** the entire process by which diploid gonocytes are transformed into haploid gametes involving meiosis accompanied in the female or followed in the male by physiological and structural changes fitting the gamete for its future role **b :** SPERMIOGENESIS 1 — **mat·u·ra·tion·al** \-shnəl, -shən-ᵊl\ *adj* — **ma·tur·a·tive** \mə-ˈt(y)u̇r-ət-iv\ *adj*

[1]**ma·ture** \mə-ˈt(y)u̇(ə)r *also* -ˈchu̇(ə)r\ *adj* [ME, fr. L *maturus* ripe; akin to L *mane* in the morning, *manus* good] **1 :** based on slow careful consideration **2 a** (1) **:** having completed natural growth and development **:** RIPE (2) **:** having undergone maturation **b :** having attained a final or desired state ⟨~ wine⟩ **3 a :** of or relating to a condition of full development **b :** characteristic of or suitable to a mature individual ⟨~ outlook⟩ **4 :** due for payment ⟨~ loan⟩ **5 a :** well dissected by the erosion of running water so that slopes predominate greatly over flats **b :** belonging to the middle portion of a cycle of erosion — **ma·ture·ly** *adv* — **ma·ture·ness** *n*

[2]**mature** *vt* **:** to bring to maturity or completion ~ *vi* **1 :** to become fully developed or ripe **2 :** to become due

ma·tu·ri·ty \mə-ˈt(y)u̇r-ət-ē *also* -ˈchu̇r-\ *n* **1 :** the quality or state of being mature; *esp* **:** full development **2 :** termination of the period that an obligation has to run **3 :** the second of the three principal stages in a cycle of erosion or of other geologic change

ma·tu·ti·nal \ˌmach-ü-ˈtīn-ᵊl; mə-ˈt(y)üt-nəl, -ᵊn-əl\ *adj* [LL *matutinalis,* fr. L *matutinus* — more at MATINEE] **:** of, relating to, or occurring in the morning **:** EARLY — **ma·tu·ti·nal·ly** \-ē\ *adv*

mat·zo \ˈmät-sə, -(ˌ)sō\ *n, pl* **mat·zoth** \-ˌsōt(h), -ˌsōs\ *or* **mat·zos** \-səz, -səs, -ˌsōz\ [Yiddish *matse,* fr. Heb *maṣṣāh*] **1 :** unleavened bread eaten at the Passover **2 :** a wafer of matzo

maud·lin \ˈmȯd-lən\ *adj* [alter. of Mary *Magdalene;* fr. the practice of depicting her as a weeping, penitent sinner] **1 :** weakly and effusively sentimental **2 :** drunk enough to be emotionally silly **:** FUDDLED

mau·gre \ˌmȯ-gər\ *prep* [ME, fr. OF *maugré,* fr. *maugré* displeasure, fr. *mau, mal* evil + *gré* pleasure] *archaic* **:** in spite of

[1]**maul** \ˈmȯl\ *n* [ME *malle,* fr. OF *mail,* fr. L *malleus;* akin to L *molere* to grind — more at MEAL] **:** a heavy hammer often with a wooden head used esp. for driving wedges or piles

[2]**maul** *vt* **1 a :** BEAT, BRUISE **b :** to injure by beating **:** MANGLE **c :** to handle roughly **2 :** to split (wood) with a maul and wedges — **maul·er** *n*

maul·stick \ˈmȯl-ˌstik\ *n* [part trans. of D *maalstok,* fr. obs. D *malen* to paint + D *stok* stick] **:** a stick used by painters as a rest for the hand while working

maun \(ˈ)män, mən\ *verbal auxiliary* [ME *man,* fr. ON] *chiefly Scot* **:** MUST

maund \ˈmȯnd\ *n* [Hindi *man*] **:** any of various Indian units of weight; *esp* **:** a unit equal to 82.28 pounds

maun·der \ˈmȯn-dər, ˈmän-\ *vi* **maun·der·ing** \-d(ə-)riŋ\ [prob. imit.] **1** *dial Brit* **:** GRUMBLE **2 :** to wander slowly and idly **3 :** to speak indistinctly or disconnectedly — **maun·der·er** \-dər-ər\ *n*

Maun·dy Thursday \ˌmȯn-dē-, ˌmän-\ *n* [ME *maunde* ceremony of washing the feet of the poor on Maundy Thursday, fr. OF

mandé, fr. L *mandatum* command; fr. Jesus's words in John 13:34 — more at MANDATE] **:** Thursday in Holy Week observed in commemoration of the institution of the Eucharist

mau·so·le·um \ˌmȯ-sə-ˈlē-əm, ˌmȯ-zə-\ *n, pl* **mausoleums** *or* **mau·so·lea** \-ˈlē-ə\ [L, fr. Gk *mausōleion*, fr. *Mausōlos* Mausolus †*ab* 353 B.C. ruler of Caria] **1 :** a large tomb; *esp* **:** a usu. stone building with places for entombment of the dead above ground **2 :** a large gloomy building or room

mauve \ˈmōv, ˈmȯv\ *n* [F, mallow, fr. L *malva*] **1 :** a moderate purple, violet, or lilac color **2 :** a strong purple

mav·er·ick \ˈmav-(ə-)rik\ *n* [Samuel A. *Maverick* †1870 Am pioneer who did not brand his calves] **1 :** an unbranded range animal; *esp* **:** a motherless calf **2 :** an independent individual who refuses to conform with his group

ma·vis \ˈmā-vəs\ *n* [ME, fr. MF *mauvis*] **1 :** an Old World thrush (*Turdus ericetorum*) largely brown above and white below — called also *song thrush, throstle* **2 :** a European thrush (*Turdus viscivorus*) with spotted underparts that feeds on mistletoe berries — called also *mistle thrush*

ma·vour·neen *also* **ma·vour·nin** \mə-ˈvu̇(ə)r-ˌnēn\ *n* [IrGael *mo muirnīn*] *Irish* **:** my darling

maw \ˈmȯ\ *n* [ME, fr. OE *maga;* akin to OHG *mago* stomach, Lith *makas* purse] **1 :** the receptacle into which food is taken by swallowing: **a :** STOMACH **b :** CROP **2 :** the throat, gullet, or jaws esp. of a voracious carnivore

mawk·ish \ˈmȯ-kish\ *adj* [ME *mawke* maggot, fr. ON *mathkr* — more at MAGGOT] **1 :** having an insipid often unpleasant taste **2 :** sickly or puerilely sentimental — **mawk·ish·ly** *adv* — **mawk·ish·ness** *n*

max·il·la \mak-ˈsil-ə\ *n, pl* **max·il·lae** \-ˈsil-(ˌ)ē, -ˌī\ *or* **maxillas** [L, dim. of *mala* jaw] **1 a :** JAW 1a **b** (1) **:** an upper jaw esp. of man or other mammals in which the bony elements are closely fused (2) **:** either of two membrane bone elements of the upper jaw lying lateral to the premaxillae and in higher vertebrates and man bearing most of the teeth **2 :** one of the first or second pair of mouthparts posterior to the mandibles in insects, myriopods, crustaceans, and closely related arthropods — **max·il·lary** \ˈmak-sə-ˌler-ē, *chiefly Brit* mak-ˈsil-ə-rē\ *also* **max·il·lar** \ˈmak-sə-lər, mak-ˈsil-ər\ *adj* — **maxillary** *n*

max·il·li·ped \mak-ˈsil-ə-ˌped\ *or* **max·il·li·pede** \-ˌpēd\ *n* [ISV] **:** one of the three pairs of appendages of crustaceans situated next behind the maxillae — **max·il·li·ped·ary** \(ˌ)mak-ˌsil-ə-ˈped-ə-rē, -ˈpēd-\ *adj*

max·il·lo- \mak-ˌsil-(ˌ)ō, ˌmak-sə-(ˌ)lō\ *comb form* [L *maxilla*] **:** maxillary and ⟨*maxillo*facial⟩

max·im \ˈmak-səm\ *n* [ME *maxime*, fr. MF, fr. ML *maxima*, fr. L, fem. of *maximus*, superl. of *magnus* great — more at MUCH] **1 :** a general truth, fundamental principle, or rule of conduct **2 :** a saying of proverbial nature

max·i·mal \ˈmak-s(ə-)məl\ *adj* **1 :** most comprehensive **:** COMPLETE **2 :** being an upper limit **:** HIGHEST — **max·i·mal·ly** \-ē\ *adv*

max·i·mal·ist \-s(ə-)mə-ləst\ *n* **:** one who advocates immediate and direct action to secure the whole of a program; *specif* **:** a socialist advocating the immediate seizure of power by revolutionary means

max·i·mize \ˈmak-sə-ˌmīz\ *vt* **1 :** to increase to a maximum **2 :** to assign maximum importance to **3 :** to find a maximum value of ~ *vi* **:** to interpret something in the broadest sense — **max·i·miz·er** *n*

max·i·mum \ˈmak-s(ə-)məm\ *n, pl* **maximums** *or* **max·i·ma** \-sə-mə\ [L, neut. of *maximus*] **1 a :** the greatest quantity or value attainable or attained **b :** the period of highest, greatest, or utmost development **2 :** an upper limit allowed by authority (as law) **3 :** the largest of a set of numbers; *specif* **:** the largest value assumed by a real-valued continuous function defined on a closed interval — **maximum** *adj*

ma·xixe \mə-ˈshēsh(-ə)\ *n, pl* **ma·xi·xes** \-ˈshē-shəz\ [Pg] **:** a ballroom dance of Brazilian origin roughly like the two-step

max·well \ˈmak-ˌswel, -swəl\ *n* [James Clerk *Maxwell* †1879 Sc physicist] **:** the cgs electromagnetic unit of magnetic flux equal to the flux per square centimeter of normal cross section in a region where the magnetic induction is one gauss

1may \(ˈ)mā\ *vb, past* **might** \(ˈ)mīt\; *pres sing & pl* **may** [ME (1st & 3d sing. pres. indic.), fr. OE *mæg;* akin to OHG *mag* (1st & 3d sing. pres. indic.) have power, am able (infin. *magan*), Gk *mēchos* means, expedient] *vi, obs* **:** to be able ~ *verbal auxiliary* **1** *archaic* **:** have the ability to **:** CAN **2 a :** have permission to ⟨you ~ go now⟩ **:** have liberty to — used nearly interchangeably with *can* **b :** be in some degree likely to ⟨you ~ be right⟩ **3** — used in auxiliary function to express a wish or desire esp. in prayer, imprecation, or benediction ⟨long ~ he reign⟩ **4** — used in auxiliary function expressing purpose or expectation ⟨I laugh that I ~ not weep⟩ or contingency ⟨he'll do his duty come what ~⟩ or concession ⟨he ~ be slow but he is thorough⟩ **5 :** SHALL, MUST — used in law where the sense, purpose, or policy requires this interpretation

2may \ˈmā\ *n* [ME, fr. OE *mæg* kinsman, kinswoman, maiden] *archaic* **:** MAIDEN

May \ˈmā\ *n* [ME, fr. OF & L; OF *mai*, fr. L *maius*, fr. *Maia*, Roman goddess] **1 :** the 5th month of the Gregorian calendar **2** *often not cap* **:** the vigorous blooming time of human life **3 :** the merrymaking of May Day **4** *not cap* **a :** green or flowering branches (as of hawthorn) used for May Day decorations **b :** a plant that yields may: as (1) **:** HAWTHORN (2) **:** a spring-flowering spirea

ma·ya \ˈmä-yə, ˈmī-ə\ *n* [Skt *māyā*] **:** the sense-world of manifold phenomena held in Vedanta to conceal the unity of absolute being; *broadly* **:** ILLUSION

Ma·ya \ˈmī-ə\ *n, pl* **Maya** *or* **Mayas** [Sp] **1 a :** a group of people of Yucatán, British Honduras, northern Guatemala, and the state of Tabasco, Mexico whose languages are Mayan **b :** a member of this people **2 a :** a Mayan language of the ancient Maya peoples recorded in inscriptions **b :** YUCATEC; *esp* **:** the older form of that language known from documents of the Spanish period

Ma·yan \-ən\ *n* **1 :** an extensive language stock of Central America and Mexico including Yucatec **2 a :** the peoples speaking Mayan languages **b :** a member of these peoples — **Mayan** *adj*

may·ap·ple \ˈmā-ˌap-əl\ *n* **:** a No. American herb (*Podophyllum peltatum*) of the barberry family with a poisonous rootstock, one or two large-lobed peltate leaves, and a single large white flower followed by a yellow egg-shaped edible but often insipid fruit; *also* **:** the fruit

may·be \ˈmā-bē, ˈmeb-ē\ *adv* **:** PERHAPS

May Day \ˈmā-ˌdā\ *n* **:** May 1 celebrated as a springtime festival and in some countries as Labor Day

May·day \mā-ˈdā\ [F *m'aider* help me] — an international radiotelephone signal word used as a distress call

may·est *or* **mayst** \ˈmā-əst, (ˈ)māst\ *archaic pres 2d sing of* MAY

may·flow·er \ˈmā-ˌflau̇(-ə)r\ *n* **:** any of various spring-blooming plants: as **a :** an arbutus (*Epigaea repens*) **b :** HEPATICA **c :** any of several No. American anemones **d :** MAYAPPLE

May-flowering tulip *n* **:** COTTAGE TULIP

may·fly \ˈmā-ˌflī\ *n* **:** a slender fragile-winged short-lived imago insect (order Plectophora)

may·hap \ˈmā-ˌhap, mā-ˈ\ *adv* [fr. the phrase *may hap*] **:** PERHAPS

may·hem \ˈmā-ˌhem, ˈmā-əm\ *n* [ME *mayme*, fr. AF *mahaim*, fr. OF, loss of a limb, fr. *maynier* to maim] **1 a :** willful and permanent deprivation of a bodily member resulting in the impairment of a person's fighting ability **b :** willful and permanent crippling, mutilation, or disfigurement of any part of the body **2 :** needless or willful damage

may·ing \ˈmā-iŋ\ *n, often cap* **:** the celebrating of May Day

mayn't \ˈmā-ənt, (ˈ)mānt\ **:** may not

may·on·naise \ˈmā-ə-ˌnāz, ˌmā-ə-ˈ\ *n* [F] **:** a dressing of raw eggs or egg yolks, vegetable oil, and vinegar or lemon juice usu. with salt and condiments

may·or \ˈmā-ər, ˈme(-)ər, *esp before names* (ˌ)mer\ *n* [ME *maire*, fr. OF, fr. L *major* greater — more at MAJOR] **:** an official elected to act as chief executive or nominal head of a city or borough — **may·or·al** \ˈmā-ə-rəl, ˈme-ə-\ *adj*

may·or·al·ty \ˈmā-ə-rəl-tē, ˈme-; ˈmār-əl-tē, ˈmer-\ *n* [ME *mairaltee*, fr. MF *mairalté*, fr. OF, fr. *maire*] **:** the office or term of office of a mayor

may·or·ess \ˈmā-ə-rəs, ˈme-\ *n* **1 :** the wife of a mayor **2 :** a woman holding the office of mayor

may·pole \ˈmā-ˌpōl\ *n, often cap* **:** a tall flower-wreathed pole forming a center for May Day sports and dances

may·pop \ˈmā-ˌpäp\ *n* [modif. of *maracock* (in some Algonquian language of Virginia)] **:** a climbing perennial passionflower (*Passiflora incarnata*) of the southern U.S. with a large ovoid yellow edible but insipid berry; *also* **:** its fruit

May queen *n* **:** a girl chosen queen of a May Day festival

May·tide \ˈmā-ˌtīd\ *or* **May·time** \-ˌtīm\ *n* **:** the month of May

maz·ard \ˈmaz-ərd\ *n* [obs. E *mazard* mazer, alter. of E *mazer*] *chiefly dial* **:** HEAD, FACE

1maze \ˈmāz\ *vt* [ME *mazen*] **1** *chiefly dial* **:** STUPEFY, DAZE **2 :** BEWILDER, PERPLEX

2maze *n* **1 :** a confusing intricate network of passages **2** *chiefly dial* **:** a state of bewilderment

ma·zer \ˈmā-zər\ *n* [ME, fr. OF *mazere*, of Gmc origin; akin to OHG *masar* gnarled excrescence on a tree] **:** a large drinking bowl orig. of a hard wood

ma·zur·ka \mə-ˈzər-kə, -ˈzu̇(ə)r-\ *n* [Russ, fr. Pol *mazurek*] **1 :** a Polish dance in moderate triple measure **2 :** music for the mazurka or in its rhythm usu. in moderate 3/4 or 3/8 time

mazy \ˈmā-zē\ *adj* **:** resembling a maze in confusing turns and windings

maz·zard \ˈmaz-ərd\ *n* [origin unknown] **:** SWEET CHERRY; *esp* **:** wild or seedling sweet cherry used as a rootstock for grafting

M-day \ˈem-ˌdā\ *n* [*mobilization day*] **:** a day on which a military mobilization is to begin

me \(ˈ)mē\ *pron* [ME, fr. OE *mē;* akin to OHG *mīh* me, L *me*, Gk *me*, Skt *mā*] *objective case of* I

1mead \ˈmēd\ *n* [ME *mede*, fr. OE *medu;* akin to OHG *metu* mead, Gk *methy* wine] **:** a fermented drink made of water and honey, malt, and yeast

2mead *n* [ME *mede*, fr. OE *mǣd*] *archaic* **:** MEADOW

mead·ow \ˈmed-(ˌ)ō, -ə(-w)\ *n, often attrib* [ME *medwe*, fr. OE *mǣdwe*, oblique case form of *mǣd;* akin to OE *māwan* to mow — more at MOW] **:** land in or predominantly in grass; *esp* **:** a tract of moist low-lying usu. level grassland

meadow beauty *n* **:** any of a genus (*Rhexia*) of low perennial American herbs (family Melastomaceae, the meadow-beauty family) with showy cymose flowers

meadow fescue *n* **:** a tall vigorous perennial European fescue grass (*Festuca elatior*) with broad flat leaves widely cultivated for permanent pasture and hay

meadow grass *n* **:** any of various grasses (as of the genus *Poa*) that thrive in the presence of abundant moisture; *esp* **:** Kentucky bluegrass

mead·ow·lark \ˈmed-ō-ˌlärk, -ə-ˌlärk\ *n* **:** any of several No. American songbirds (genus *Sturnella*) largely brown and buff above with a yellow breast marked with a back crescent

meadow mouse *n* **:** any of various mice (esp. genus *Microtus*) that frequent open fields

meadow mushroom *n* **:** a common edible agaric (*Agaricus campestris*) occurring naturally in moist open organically rich soil and being the cultivated edible mushroom of commerce

meadow nematode *n* **:** any of numerous plant-parasitic nematode worms (esp. genus *Pratylenchus*) formerly held to be a single variable species (*P. pratensis*) that destructively invade the roots of plants

meadow rue *n* **:** any of a genus (*Thalictrum*) of plants of the crowfoot family with leaves resembling those of rue

meadow saffron *n* **:** COLCHICUM 1

mead·ow·sweet \ˈmed-ō-ˌswēt, -ə-ˌswēt\ *n* **1 :** SPIREA 1; *esp* **:** a No. American native or naturalized spirea (as *Spiraea alba* or *S. tomentosa*) **2 :** a plant of a genus (*Filipendula*) closely related to the spireas

mea·ger *or* **mea·gre** \ˈmē-gər\ *adj* [ME *megre*, fr. MF *maigre*, fr. L *macr-*, *macer* lean; akin to OE *mæger* lean, Gk *makros* long] **1 :** having little flesh **:** THIN **2 :** lacking richness, strength, or comparable qualities — **mea·ger·ly** *adv* — **mea·ger·ness** *n*

syn SCANTY, SCANT, EXIGUOUS, SPARE, SPARSE: MEAGER implies lack of fullness, richness, or plenty; SCANTY implies insufficiency in quantity, degree, or extent; SCANT suggests a deficiency in amount

or quantity of something desired or desirable often in consequence of deliberate withholding; EXIGUOUS implies a marked deficiency in number or measure; SPARE may suggest a slight falling short of adequacy or merely an absence of superfluity; SPARSE implies a thin scattering of units esp. where density or plenty is desirable

1**meal** \'mē(ə)l\ *n* [ME *meel* appointed time, meal, fr. OE *mǣl;* akin to OHG *māl* time, L *metiri* to measure — more at MEASURE] **1 :** the portion of food taken at one time to satisfy appetite **2 :** an act or the time of eating a meal

2**meal** *n* [ME *mele,* fr. OE *melu;* akin to OHG *melo* meal, L *molere* to grind, Gk *mylē* mill] **1 :** the usu. coarsely ground and unbolted seeds of a cereal grass or pulse; *esp* **:** CORNMEAL **2 :** a product resembling seed meal esp. in particle size or texture

-meal \ˌmēl, 'mē(ə)l\ *adv comb form* [ME *-mele,* fr. OE *-mǣlum,* fr. *mǣlum,* dat. pl. of *mǣl*] **:** by a (specified) portion or measure at a time ⟨piece*meal*⟩

mea·lie \'mē-lē\ *n* [Afrik *mielie*] **1** *Africa* **:** INDIAN CORN **2** *Africa* **:** an ear of Indian corn

meal·time \'mē(ə)l-ˌtīm\ *n* **:** the usual time at which a meal is served

meal·worm \-ˌwərm\ *n* **:** the larva of various beetles (family Tenebrionidae) that infests and pollutes grain products but is often raised as food for insectivorous animals, for laboratory use, or as bait for fishing

mealy \'mē-lē\ *adj* **1 :** soft, dry, and friable **2 :** containing meal **:** FARINACEOUS **3 a :** covered with meal or with fine granules **b :** flecked with another color **c :** SPOTTY **d :** PALLID, BLANCHED **4 :** MEALYMOUTHED

mealy·bug \-ˌbəg\ *n* **:** any of numerous scale insects (family Pseudococcidae) having a white powdery covering and being destructive pests esp. of fruit trees

mealy·mouthed \ˌmē-lē-'mau̇thd, -'mau̇tht\ *adj* **:** being smooth, plausible, and insincere ⟨~ orator⟩

1**mean** \'mēn\ *adj* [ME *mene,* fr. *imene,* fr. OE *gemǣne;* akin to OHG *gimeini* common, L *communis* common, *munus* service, gift] **1 :** lacking distinction or eminence **:** HUMBLE **2 :** lacking power or acumen **:** ORDINARY **3 :** SHABBY, CONTEMPTIBLE **4 :** IGNOBLE, BASE **5 :** PENURIOUS, STINGY **6 a :** characterized by petty selfishness or malice **b :** HARASSING, VEXATIOUS **c** *slang* **:** EXCELLENT, EFFECTIVE **7 a :** ASHAMED **b :** UNWELL, INDISPOSED

syn IGNOBLE, ABJECT, SORDID: MEAN suggests having repellent characteristics (as small-mindedness, ill temper, or cupidity); IGNOBLE suggests a loss or lack of some essential high quality of mind or spirit; ABJECT may imply degradation, debasement, or servility; SORDID is stronger than all of these in stressing physical or spiritual degradation and abjectness

2**mean** \'mēn\ *vb* **meant** \'ment\ **mean·ing** \'mē-niŋ\ [ME *menen* fr. OE *mǣnan;* akin to OHG *meinen* to have in mind, OSlav *mĕniti* to mention] *vt* **1 :** to have in the mind as a purpose **:** INTEND **2 :** to serve to convey, show, or indicate **:** SIGNIFY **3 :** to direct to a particular individual **~** *vi* **1 :** to have an intended purpose ⟨he ~*s* well⟩ **2 :** to be of a specified degree of importance ⟨health ~*s* everything⟩ — **mean business :** to be in earnest

3**mean** \'mēn\ *n* **1 a** (1) **:** something intervening or intermediate (2) **:** a middle point between extremes **b** (1) **:** a value that lies within a range of values, that is computed from the range according to a prescribed law, and that represents the range; *specif* **:** ARITHMETIC MEAN (2) **:** the arithmetic mean of the two extremes of a range of values (3) **:** either of the middle two terms of a proportion **2** *pl but sing or pl in constr* **:** something useful or helpful to a desired end **3** *pl* **:** resources available for disposal; *esp* **:** material resources affording a secure life

syn MEAN (or MEANS), INSTRUMENT, AGENT, AGENCY, MEDIUM mean something or someone necessary or useful in effecting an end. MEAN or usu. MEANS is very general and may be abstract in applying to a person or thing of any sort; INSTRUMENT suggests a degree of applicability or adaptability for achieving a definite purpose; applied to a person it often suggests one acting at another's will without full moral responsibility; AGENT applies to a person acting to achieve an end conceived by another or to a thing producing an immediate effect or definite result; AGENCY applies to the activity or operation of a means or agent; MEDIUM implies a usu. intangible means of conveying, transmitting, or communicating **syn** see in addition AVERAGE

4**mean** \'mēn\ *adj* [ME *mene,* fr. MF *meien,* fr. L *medianus* — more at MEDIAN] **1 :** occupying a middle position **:** intermediate in space, order, time, kind, or degree **2 :** occupying a position about midway between extremes: as **a :** being near the average **b :** of a moderate degree of excellence **:** MIDDLING **c :** being the mean of a set of values **:** AVERAGE ⟨~ temperature⟩ **3 :** serving as a means **:** INTERMEDIARY

1**me·an·der** \mē-'an-dər\ *n* [L *maeander,* fr. Gk *maiandros,* fr. *Maiandros* (now *Menderes*), river in Asia Minor] **1 :** a turn or winding of a stream **2 :** a winding path or course **:** LABYRINTH — **me·an·drous** \-'an-drəs\ *adj*

2**meander** *vi* **me·an·der·ing** \-d(ə-)riŋ\ **1 :** to follow a winding or intricate course **2 :** to wander aimlessly or casually without urgent destination **:** RAMBLE

mean deviation *n* **:** the arithmetic mean of the absolute values of the deviations from the arithmetic mean of a statistical distribution

mean distance *n* **:** the arithmetical mean of the maximum and minimum distances of a planet, satellite, or secondary star from its primary

mean·er \'mē-nər\ *n* **:** one that means

mean·ing \'mē-niŋ\ *n* **1 a :** the thing one intends to convey esp. by language **:** PURPORT **b :** the thing that is conveyed esp. by language **:** IMPORT **2 :** INTENT, PURPOSE **3 :** SIGNIFICANCE **4 a :** CONNOTATION **b :** DENOTATION — **meaning** *adj*

syn MEANING, SENSE, ACCEPTATION, SIGNIFICATION, SIGNIFICANCE, IMPORT denote the idea conveyed to the mind. MEANING is the general term used of anything (as a word, sign, poem, or action) requiring or allowing of interpretation; SENSE denotes the meaning or more often a particular meaning of a word or phrase; ACCEPTATION is used of a sense of a word or phrase as regularly understood by a large number of speakers and writers; SIGNIFICATION denotes the established meaning of a term, symbol, or character; SIGNIFICANCE applies specifically to a covert as distinguished from the ostensible meaning of an utterance, act, or work of art; IMPORT suggests the meaning a speaker tries to convey esp. through language

mean·ing·ful \-fəl\ *adj* **1 :** having a meaning or purpose ⟨~ work⟩ ⟨a ~ experience⟩ **2 :** having an assigned function in a language system ⟨~ propositions⟩ — **mean·ing·ful·ly** \-fə-lē\ *adv* — **mean·ing·ful·ness** *n*

mean·ing·less \'mē-niŋ-ləs\ *adj* **1 :** having no meaning **2 :** having no assigned function in a language system ⟨~ metaphysical statement⟩ — **mean·ing·less·ly** *adv* — **mean·ing·less·ness** *n*

1**mean·ly** \'mēn-lē\ *adv, archaic* **:** MODERATELY

2**meanly** *adv* **:** in a mean manner: as **a :** POORLY, HUMBLY **b :** in an inferior manner **:** BADLY **c :** UNGENEROUSLY, STINGILY

mean·ness \'mēn-nəs\ *n* **:** the quality or state of being mean

mean solar time *n* **:** time that is based on the motion of the mean sun and that has the mean solar second as its unit — called also *mean time*

mean square *n* **:** the arithmetic mean of the squares of a set of values

mean square deviation *n* **1 :** VARIANCE 5 **2 :** STANDARD DEVIATION

means test *n* **:** a test made in Great Britain of an unemployed person's means when his unemployment insurance payments are exhausted to determine his eligibility to receive further payments from other funds

mean sun *n* **:** a fictitious sun that moves uniformly along the celestial equator and completes crossings of the vernal equinox at intervals of a tropical year

1**mean·time** \'mēn-ˌtīm\ *n* **:** the intervening time

2**meantime** *adv* **:** MEANWHILE

1**mean·while** \'mēn-ˌhwīl, -ˌwīl\ *n* **:** MEANTIME

2**meanwhile** *adv* **:** during the intervening time

mea·sle \'mē-zəl\ *n* [sing. of *measles*] **:** a tapeworm cysticercus larva; *specif* **:** one found in the muscles of a domesticated mammal — **mea·sled** \-zəld\ *adj*

mea·sles \'mē-zəlz\ *n pl but sing or pl in constr* [ME *meseles,* pl. of *mesel* measles, spot characteristic of measles; akin to MD *masel* spot characteristic of measles] **1 a :** an acute contagious viral disease marked by an eruption of distinct red circular spots **b :** any of various eruptive diseases **2** [ME *mesel* infested with tapeworms, lit., leprous, fr. OF, fr. ML *misellus* leper, fr. L, wretch, fr. *misellus,* dim. of *miser* miserable] **:** infestation with or disease caused by larval tapeworms in the muscles and tissues

mea·sly \'mēz-(ə-)lē\ *adj* **1 :** infected with measles **2 a :** containing larval tapeworms **b :** TRICHINIZED **3 :** contemptibly small

mea·sur·abil·i·ty \ˌmezh-(ə-)rə-'bil-ət-ē, ˌmāzh-\ *n* **:** the quality or state of being measurable

mea·sur·able \'mezh-(ə-)rə-bəl, 'mezh-ər-bəl, 'māzh-\ *adj* **:** capable of being measured — **mea·sur·able·ness** *n* — **mea·sur·ably** \-blē\ *adv*

1**mea·sure** \'mezh-ər, 'māzh-\ *n* [ME *mesure,* fr. OF, fr. L *mensura,* fr. *mensus,* pp. of *metiri* to measure; akin to OE *mǣth* measure, Gk *metron*] **1 a** (1) **:** an adequate or due portion (2) **:** a moderate degree; *also* **:** MODERATION, TEMPERANCE (3) **:** a fixed or suitable limit **:** BOUNDS **b :** the dimensions, capacity, or amount of something ascertained by measuring **c** (1) **:** a measured quantity (2) **:** AMOUNT, DEGREE **2 a :** an instrument or utensil for measuring **b** (1) **:** a standard or unit of measurement (2) **:** a system of standard units of measure ⟨metric ~⟩ **3 :** the act or process of measuring **4 a** (1) **:** MELODY, TUNE (2) **:** DANCE; *esp* **:** a slow and stately dance **b :** rhythmic structure or movement **:** CADENCE: as (1) **:** poetic rhythm measured by temporal quantity or accent; *specif* **:** METER (2) **:** musical time **c** (1) **:** a grouping of musical beats made by the regular recurrence of primary accents and located on the staff immediately following a vertical bar (2) **:** a metrical unit **:** FOOT **5 :** an exact divisor of a number **6 :** a basis or standard of comparison **:** CRITERION **7 :** a step planned or taken as a means to an end; *specif* **:** a proposed legislative act

2**measure** *vb* **mea·sur·ing** \-(ə-)riŋ\ *vt* **1 a :** to choose or control with cautious restraint **:** REGULATE ⟨~ his acts⟩ **b :** to regulate by a standard **:** GOVERN **2 :** to allot or apportion in measured amounts ⟨~ out 3 cups⟩ **3 :** to lay off by making measurements **4 :** to ascertain the measurements of **5 :** to estimate or appraise by a criterion ⟨~*s* his skill against his rival⟩ **6** *archaic* **:** to travel over **:** TRAVERSE **7 :** to serve as a measure of ⟨thermometer ~*s* temperature⟩ **~** *vi* **1 :** to take or make a measurement **2 :** to have a specified measurement — **mea·sur·er** \-ər-ər\ *n*

mea·sured \'mezh-ərd, 'māzh-\ *adj* **1 :** marked by due proportion **2 :** RHYTHMICAL, METRICAL **3 :** DELIBERATE, CALCULATED

mea·sure·less \-ər-ləs\ *adj* **:** without measure **:** IMMEASURABLE

mea·sure·ment \'mezh-ər-mənt, 'māzh-\ *n* **1 :** the act or process of measuring **2 :** a figure, extent, or amount obtained by measuring **:** DIMENSION **3 :** MEASURE 2b(2)

measure up *vi* **1 :** to have necessary or fitting qualifications **2 :** to be the equal (as in ability) — used with *to*

measuring worm *n* **:** LOOPER 1

meat \'mēt\ *n* [ME *mete,* fr. OE; akin to OHG *maz* food, L *madēre* to be wet, Gk *madaros* wet, *mastos* breast] **1 a :** FOOD; *esp* **:** solid food as distinguished from drink **b :** the edible part of something as distinguished from the husk, shell, or other covering **2 :** animal tissue used as food: **a :** FLESH 2b **b :** FLESH 1a; *specif* **:** flesh of domesticated animals **3** *archaic* **:** MEAL 2; *esp* **:** DINNER

meat·ball \-ˌbȯl\ *n* **:** a small ball of chopped or ground meat

meat by-product *n* **:** a usable product other than flesh obtained from slaughter animals

meat·i·ness \'mēt-ē-nəs\ *n* **:** the quality or state of being meaty

meat·man \'mēt-ˌman\ *n* **:** a vendor of meat **:** BUTCHER

me·atus \mē-'āt-əs\ *n, pl* **me·atus·es** *or* **me·atus** \-'āt-əs, -'ā-ˌtüs\ [LL, fr. L, going, passage, fr. *meatus,* pp. of *meare* to go — more at PERMEATE] **:** a natural body passage

meaty \'mēt-ē\ *adj* **1 :** full of meat **2 :** rich in matter for thought

mec·ca \'mek-ə\ *n, often cap* [*Mecca* Saudi Arabia, birthplace of Muhammad and holy city of Islam] **:** a place sought as a goal by numerous people, practitioners, or connoisseurs

mechan- *or* **mechano-** *comb form* [ME *mechan-,* fr. MF or L, fr. Gk *mēchan-,* fr. *mēchanē* machine — more at MACHINE] **:** machine ⟨*mechano*morphic⟩ **:** mechanical ⟨*mechan*ize⟩

1**me·chan·ic** \mi-'kan-ik\ *adj* [prob. fr. MF *mechanique,* adj. & n., fr. L *mechanicus,* fr. Gk *mēchanikos,* fr. *mēchanē* machine — more at MACHINE] **1 :** of or relating to manual work or skill **2 :** of the nature of or resembling a machine esp. in routine or automatic performance

2**mechanic** *n* **1 :** a manual worker **:** ARTISAN **2 :** MACHINIST; *esp* **:** a repairer of machines

me·chan·i·cal \mi-'kan-i-kəl\ *adj* **1 a** (1) **:** of or relating to machinery or tools (2) **:** produced or operated by a machine or tool

MEASURES AND WEIGHTS

UNIT	ABBR. OR SYMBOL	EQUIVALENTS IN OTHER UNITS OF SAME SYSTEM	METRIC EQUIVALENT
		length	
mile	mi	5280 feet, 320 rods, 1760 yards	1.609 kilometers
rod	rd	5.50 yards, 16.5 feet	5.029 meters
yard	yd	3 feet, 36 inches	0.914 meters
foot	ft *or* '	12 inches, 0.333 yards	30.480 centimeters
inch	in *or* "	0.083 feet, 0.027 yards	2.540 centimeters
		area	
square mile	sq mi *or* m²	640 acres, 102,400 square rods	2.590 square kilometers
acre	a *or* ac (seldom used)	4840 square yards, 43,560 square feet	0.405 hectares, 4047 square meters
square rod	sq rd *or* rd²	30.25 square yards, 0.006 acres	25.293 square meters
square yard	sq yd *or* yd²	1296 square inches, 9 square feet	0.836 square meters
square foot	sq ft *or* ft²	144 square inches, 0.111 square yards	0.093 square meters
square inch	sq in *or* in²	0.007 square feet, 0.00077 square yards	6.451 square centimeters
		volume	
cubic yard	cu yd *or* yd³	27 cubic feet, 46,656 cubic inches	0.765 cubic meters
cubic foot	cu ft *or* ft³	1728 cubic inches, 0.0370 cubic yards	0.028 cubic meters
cubic inch	cu in *or* in³	0.00058 cubic feet, 0.000021 cubic yards	16.387 cubic centimeters
		weight	
		avoirdupois	
ton	tn (seldom used)		
short ton		20 short hundredweight, 2000 pounds	0.907 metric tons
long ton		20 long hundredweight, 2240 pounds	1.016 metric tons
hundredweight	cwt		
short hundredweight		100 pounds, 0.05 short tons	45.359 kilograms
long hundredweight		112 pounds, 0.05 long tons	50.802 kilograms
pound	lb *or* lb av *also* ℔	16 ounces, 7000 grains	0.453 kilograms
ounce	oz *or* oz av	16 drams, 437.5 grains	28.349 grams
dram	dr *or* dr av	27.343 grains, 0.0625 ounces	1.771 grams
grain	gr	0.036 drams, 0.002285 ounces	0.0648 grams
		troy	
pound	lb t	12 ounces, 240 pennyweight, 5760 grains	0.373 kilograms
ounce	oz t	20 pennyweight, 480 grains	31.103 grams
pennyweight	dwt *also* pwt	24 grains, 0.05 ounces	1.555 grams
grain	gr	0.042 pennyweight, 0.002083 ounces	0.0648 grams
		apothecaries'	
pound	lb ap	12 ounces, 5760 grains	0.373 kilograms
ounce	oz ap *or* ℥	8 drams, 480 grains	31.103 grams
dram	dr ap *or* ʒ	3 scruples, 60 grains	3.887 grams
scruple	s ap *or* ℈	20 grains, 0.333 drams	1.295 grams
grain	gr	0.05 scruples, 0.002083 ounces, 0.0166 drams	0.0648 grams
		capacity	
		U.S. liquid measure	
gallon	gal	4 quarts (231 cubic inches)	3.785 liters
quart	qt	2 pints (57.75 cubic inches)	0.946 liters
pint	pt	4 gills (28.875 cubic inches)	0.473 liters
gill	gi	4 fluidounces (7.218 cubic inches)	118.291 milliliters
fluidounce	fl oz *or* f ℥	8 fluidrams (1.804 cubic inches)	29.573 milliliters
fluidram	fl dr *or* f ʒ	60 minims (0.225 cubic inches)	3.696 milliliters
minim	min *or* ♏	¹⁄₆₀ fluidram (0.003759 cubic inches)	0.061610 milliliters
		U.S. dry measure	
bushel	bu	4 pecks (2150.42 cubic inches)	35.238 liters
peck	pk	8 quarts (537.605 cubic inches)	8.809 liters
quart	qt	2 pints (67.200 cubic inches)	1.101 liters
pint	pt	½ quart (33.600 cubic inches)	0.550 liters
		British imperial liquid and dry measure	
bushel	bu	4 pecks (2219.36 cubic inches)	0.036 cubic meters
peck	pk	2 gallons (554.84 cubic inches)	0.009 cubic meters
gallon	gal	4 quarts (277.420 cubic inches)	4.545 liters
quart	qt	2 pints (69.355 cubic inches)	1.136 liters
pint	pt	4 gills (34.678 cubic inches)	568.26 cubic centimeters
gill	gi	5 fluidounces (8.669 cubic inches)	142.066 cubic centimeters
fluidounce	fl oz *or* f ℥	8 fluidrams (1.7339 cubic inches)	28.416 cubic centimeters
fluidram	fl dr *or* f ʒ	60 minims (0.216734 cubic inches)	3.5516 cubic centimeters
minim	min *or* ♏	¹⁄₆₀ fluidram (0.003612 cubic inches)	0.059194 cubic centimeters

b : of or relating to manual operations **2 :** of or relating to artisans or machinists **3 :** done as if by a machine : AUTOMATIC ⟨~ singing⟩ **4 a :** relating to, governed by, or in accordance with the principles of mechanics **b :** relating to the quantitative relations of force and matter **5 :** caused by, resulting from, or relating to a process that involves a purely physical change **syn** see SPONTANEOUS — **me·chan·i·cal·ly** \-i-k(ə-)lē\ *adv*

mechanical advantage *n* **:** the advantage gained by the use of a mechanism in transmitting force; *specif* **:** the ratio of the force that performs the useful work of a machine to the force that is applied to the machine

mechanical drawing *n* **1 :** drawing done with the aid of instruments **2 :** a drawing made with instruments

mechanical tissue *n* **:** plant tissue serving as a supporting framework

mech·a·ni·cian \ˌmek-ə-'nish-ən\ *n* **:** MECHANIC, MACHINIST

me·chan·ics \mi-'kan-iks\ *n pl but sing or pl in constr* **1 : a :** a branch of physical science that deals with energy and forces and their effect on bodies **2 :** the practical application of mechanics to the design, construction, or operation of machines **3 :** mechanical or functional details

mech·a·nism \'mek-ə-ˌniz-əm\ *n* **1 a :** a piece of machinery **b :** a process or technique for achieving a result **2 :** mechanical operation or action **3 :** a doctrine that holds natural processes (as of life) to be mechanically determined and capable of complete explanation by the laws of physics and chemistry **4 :** the fundamental physical or chemical processes involved in or responsible for an action, reaction, or other natural phenomenon

mech·a·nist \-nəst\ *n* **1** *archaic* **:** MECHANIC **2 :** an adherent of the doctrine of mechanism

mech·a·nis·tic \ˌmek-ə-'nis-tik\ *adj* **1 :** mechanically determined ⟨~ universe⟩ **2 :** of or relating to the doctrine of mechanism **3 :** MECHANICAL — **mech·a·nis·ti·cal·ly** \-ti-k(ə-)lē\ *adv*

mech·a·ni·za·tion \ˌmek-ə-nə-'zā-shən\ *n* **:** the act or process of mechanizing **:** the state of being mechanized

mech·a·nize \'mek-ə-ˌnīz\ *vt* **1 :** to make mechanical; *esp* **:** to make automatic or routine **2 a :** to equip with machinery esp.

to replace human or animal labor **b :** to equip with armed and armored motor vehicles **c :** to provide with mechanical power **3 :** to produce by or as if by machine — **mech·a·niz·er** *n*

Mech·lin \'mek-lən\ *n* [*Mechlin*, Belgium] **:** a delicate bobbin lace used for dresses and millinery

me·co·ni·um \mi-'kō-nē-əm\ *n* [L, lit., poppy juice, fr. Gk *mēkōnion*, fr. *mēkōn* poppy; akin to OHG *mago* poppy] **:** a dark greenish mass that accumulates in the bowel during fetal life and is discharged shortly after birth

me·cop·ter·an \mi-'käp-tə-rən\ *n* [deriv. of Gk *mēkos* length + *pteron* wing; akin to Gk *makros* long — more at MEAGER, FEATHER] **:** any of an order (Mecoptera) of primitive carnivorous insects usu. with membranous wings and a long beak with biting mouthparts at the tip — **me·cop·ter·ous** \-tə-rəs\ *adj*

med·al \'med-ᵊl\ *n* [MF *medaille*, fr. OIt *medaglia* coin worth half a denarius, medal, fr. (assumed) VL *medalis* half, fr. LL *medialis* middle, fr. L *medius* — more at MID] **1 :** a metal disk bearing a religious emblem or picture **2 :** a piece of metal (as a coin) issued to commemorate a person or event or awarded for excellence or achievement

Medal for Merit : a U.S. decoration awarded to civilians for exceptionally meritorious conduct in the performance of outstanding services

med·al·ist *or* **med·al·list** \'med-ᵊl-əst\ *n* **1 :** a designer, engraver, or maker of medals **2 :** a recipient of a medal as an award

me·dal·lion \mə-'dal-yən\ *n* [F *médaillon*, fr. It *medaglione*, aug. of *medaglia*] **1 :** a large medal **2 :** something resembling a large medal; *esp* **:** a tablet or panel in a wall or window bearing a figure in relief, a portrait, or an ornament

Medal of Freedom : a U.S. decoration awarded to civilians for the performance of a meritorious act or service in prosecuting a war against an enemy or in furthering the interests of the security of the U.S.

Medal of Honor : a U.S. military decoration awarded in the name of the Congress for conspicuous gallantry and intrepidity at the risk of life above and beyond the call of duty in action with an enemy

ə abut; ᵊ kitten; ər further; a back; ā bake; ä cot, cart; au̇ out; ch chin; e less; ē easy; g gift; i trip; ī life
j joke; ŋ sing; ō flow; ȯ flaw; ȯi coin; th thin; t͟h this; ü loot; u̇ foot; y yet; yü few; yu̇ furious; zh vision

medal play *n* **:** golf competition scored by total strokes

med·dle \'med-ᵊl\ *vb* **med·dling** \'med-liŋ, -ᵊl-iŋ\ [ME *medlen*, fr. OF *mesler, medler*, fr. (assumed) VL *misculare*, fr. L *miscēre* to mix — more at MIX] *vt, obs* **:** MIX, MINGLE ~ *vi* **:** to interfere without right or propriety — **med·dler** \-lər, -ᵊl-ər\ *n*

med·dle·some \'med-ᵊl-səm\ *adj* **:** given to meddling in the affairs of others **syn** see IMPERTINENT — **med·dle·some·ness** *n*

Mede \'mēd\ *n* [ME, fr. L *Medus*, fr. Gk *Mēdos*] **:** a native or inhabitant of ancient Media in Persia

Me·dea \mi-'dē-ə\ *n* [L, fr. Gk *Mēdeia*] **:** an enchantress noted in Greek legend for helping Jason to win the Golden Fleece and for killing her children, setting fire to the palace, and fleeing on his deserting her

medi- *or* **medio-** *comb form* [L, fr. *medius*] **:** middle ⟨*medi*eval⟩

1**media** *pl of* MEDIUM

2**me·dia** \'mēd-ē-ə\ *n, pl* **me·di·ae** \-ē-,ē\ **1** [LL, fr. L, fem. of *medius*; fr. the voiced stops' being regarded as intermediate between the tenues and the aspirates] **:** a voiced stop **2** [NL, fr. L, fem. of *medius*] **:** the middle coat of the wall of a blood or lymph vessel consisting chiefly of circular muscle fibers

me·di·a·cy \'mēd-ē-ə-sē\ *n* **:** the quality or state of being mediate

me·di·ad \'mēd-ē-,ad\ *adv* **:** toward the median line or plane of a body or part

me·di·al \'mēd-ē-əl\ *adj* **1 a :** being or occurring in the middle **:** MEDIAN **b :** extending toward the middle **2 :** situated between the extremes of initial and final in a word or morpheme **3 :** MEAN, AVERAGE — **medial** *n* — **me·di·al·ly** \-ə-lē\ *adv*

1**me·di·an** \'mēd-ē-ən\ *n* **1 :** a medial part **2 :** a value in an ordered set of values below and above which there are an equal number of values **3 a :** a line from a vertex of a triangle to the midpoint of the opposite side **b :** a line joining the midpoints of the nonparallel sides of a trapezoid **syn** see AVERAGE

2**median** *adj* [MF or L; MF, fr. L *medianus*, fr. *medius* middle — more at MID] **1 :** being in the middle or in an intermediate position **:** MEDIAL **2 :** equivalent in lightness to median gray **3 :** relating to or constituting a statistical median **4 :** lying in the plane dividing a bilateral animal into right and left halves **5 :** produced without occlusion along the lengthwise middle line of the tongue — **me·di·an·ly** *adv*

me·di·ant \'mēd-ē-ənt\ *n* [It *mediante*, fr. LL *mediant-, medians*, prp. of *mediare*] **:** the third musical degree of a scale midway between the tonic and the dominant

me·di·as·ti·nal \,mēd-ē-ə-'stīn-ᵊl, -ē-(,)a-'\ *adj* **:** of or relating to a mediastinum

me·di·as·ti·num \-'stī-nəm\ *n, pl* **me·di·as·ti·na** \-nə\ [NL, fr. L, neut. of *mediastinus* medial, fr. *medius*] **:** an irregular median septum of the thoracic cavity formed of the opposing medial walls of the parietal pleura that encloses the thoracic viscera except the lungs

1**me·di·ate** \'mēd-ē-ət\ *adj* [ME, fr. LL *mediatus* intermediate, fr. pp. of *mediare*] **1 :** occupying a middle position **2 a :** acting through an intervening agency **b :** exhibiting indirect causation, connection, or relation — **me·di·ate·ly** *adv* — **me·di·ate·ness** *n*

2**me·di·ate** \'mēd-ē-,āt\ *vb* [ML *mediatus*, pp. of *mediare*, fr. LL, to be in the middle, fr. L *medius* middle — more at MID] *vi* **1 :** to interpose between parties in order to reconcile them **2 :** to reconcile differences ~ *vt* **1 a :** to effect by action as an intermediary **b :** to bring accord out of by action as an intermediary **2 a :** to act as intermediary agent in bringing, effecting, or communicating **:** CONVEY **b :** to transmit as intermediate mechanism or agency **syn** see INTERPOSE

me·di·a·tion \,mēd-ē-'ā-shən\ *n* **:** the act or process of mediating; *esp* **:** intervention between conflicting parties to promote reconciliation, settlement, or compromise

me·di·a·tive \'mēd-ē-,āt-iv\ *adj* **:** of or relating to mediation

me·di·a·tor \'mēd-ē-,āt-ər\ *n* **1 :** one that mediates; *esp* **:** one that mediates between parties at variance **2 :** a mediating agent in a chemical or biological process — **me·di·a·tress** \-,ā-trəs\ *n*

me·di·a·to·ry \'mēd-ē-ə-,tōr-ē, -,tȯr-\ *adj* **:** of, relating to, or directed toward mediation

me·di·a·trice \,mēd-ē-'ā-trəs\ *n* [ME, fr. MF, fr. LL *mediatric-, mediatrix*, fem. of *mediator*, fr. *mediatus*, pp.] **:** MEDIATRESS

me·di·a·trix \-'ā-triks\ *n* [ME, fr. LL] **:** MEDIATRESS

1**med·ic** \'med-ik\ *n* [ME *medike*, fr. L *medica*, fr. Gk *mēdikē*, fr. fem. of *mēdikos* of Media, fr. *Mēdia* Media, ancient country in southern Asia] **:** any of a genus (*Medicago*) of leguminous herbs (as alfalfa)

2**medic** *n* [L *medicus*] **:** one engaged in medical work

med·i·ca·ble \'med-i-kə-bəl\ *adj* **:** CURABLE, REMEDIABLE — **med·i·ca·bly** \-blē\ *adv*

med·ic·aid \'med-i-,kād\ *n* [*medical aid*] **:** a program of medical aid designed for those unable to afford regular medical service and financed jointly by the state and federal governments

med·i·cal \'med-i-kəl\ *adj* [F or LL; F *médical*, fr. LL *medicalis*, fr. L *medicus* physician, fr. *mederi* to heal; akin to Av vī-*mad*- healer, L *meditari* to meditate] **1 :** of, relating to, or concerned with physicians or the practice of medicine **2 :** requiring or devoted to medical treatment — **med·i·cal·ly** \-k(ə-)lē\ *adv*

medical examiner *n* **:** a public officer who makes postmortem examinations of bodies to find the cause of death

me·dic·a·ment \mi-'dik-ə-mənt, 'med-i-kə-\ *n* **:** a substance used in therapy — **me·di·ca·men·tous** \mi-,dik-ə-'ment-əs, ,med-i-kə-\ *adj*

medi·care \'med-i-,ke(ə)r, -ka(ə)r\ *n* [blend of *medical* and *care*] **:** a government program of medical care esp. for the aged

med·i·cate \'med-ə-,kāt\ *vt* [L *medicatus*, pp. of *medicare* to heal, fr. *medicus*] **1 :** to treat medicinally **2 :** to impregnate with a medicinal substance

med·i·ca·tion \,med-ə-'kā-shən\ *n* **1 :** the act or process of medicating **2 :** a medicinal substance **:** MEDICAMENT

Med·i·ce·an \,med-ə-'chē-ən, -'sē-\ *adj* **:** of or relating to the Medici family of Renaissance Florence

me·dic·i·na·ble \mi-'dis-nə-bəl, -ᵊn-ə-; *archaic or Brit* 'med-sə-nə-\ *adj* **:** MEDICINAL

me·dic·i·nal \mə-'dis-nəl, -ᵊn-əl\ *adj* **1 :** tending or used to cure disease or relieve pain **2 :** SALUTARY — **medicinal** *n* — **me·dic·i·nal·ly** \-ē\ *adv*

medicinal leech *n* **:** a large European freshwater leech (*Hirudo medicinalis*) formerly used by physicians for bleeding patients

med·i·cine \'med-ə-sən, *Brit usu* 'med-sən\ *n* [ME, fr. OF, fr. L *medicina*, fr. fem. of *medicinus* of a physician, fr. *medicus*] **1 a :** a substance or preparation used in treating disease **b :** something that affects well-being **2 :** the science and art of preventing, alleviating, or curing disease; *esp* **:** the branch of this field concerned with the nonsurgical treatment of disease **3 :** a drug or similar substance used other than to treat disease **4 :** an object held by the No. American Indians to give control over natural or magical forces; *also* **:** magical power or a magical rite — **medicine** *vt*

medicine ball *n* **:** a large stuffed leather-covered ball used for conditioning exercises

medicine man *n* **:** a priestly healer or sorcerer esp. among Amerindian peoples **:** SHAMAN

medicine show *n* **:** a traveling show using entertainers to attract a crowd among which remedies or nostrums are sold

med·i·co \'med-i-,kō\ *n, pl* **medicos** [It *medico* or Sp *médico*, both fr. L *medicus*] **:** a medical practitioner; *also* **:** a medical student

medico- *comb form* [NL, fr. L *medicus*] **1 :** medical ⟨*medico*psychology⟩ **2 :** medical and ⟨*medico*legal⟩

me·di·eval *or* **me·di·ae·val** \,mēd-ē-'ē-vəl, ,med-, ,mid-; mē-'dē-vəl\ *adj* [*medi-* + L *aevum* age — more at AYE] **:** of, relating to, or characteristic of the Middle Ages — **me·di·eval·ly** \-ē\ *adv*

me·di·eval·ism \-,iz-əm\ *n* **1 :** medieval quality, character, or state **2 :** devotion to the institutions, arts, and practices of the Middle Ages

me·di·eval·ist \-'ēv-(ə-)ləst, -'dēv-\ *n* **1 :** a specialist in medieval history and culture **2 :** a connoisseur or devotee of medieval arts and culture

Medieval Latin *n* **:** the Latin used esp. for liturgical and literary purposes from the 7th to the 15th centuries inclusive

medio- — see MEDI-

me·di·o·cre \,mēd-ē-'ō-kər\ *adj* [MF, fr. L *mediocris*, lit., halfway up a mountain, fr. *medi-* + *ocris* stony mountain; akin to L *acer* sharp — more at EDGE] **:** of moderate or low quality **:** ORDINARY

me·di·oc·ri·ty \,mēd-ē-'äk-rət-ē\ *n* **1 a :** the quality or state of being mediocre **b :** moderate ability or value **2 :** a mediocre person

med·i·tate \'med-ə-,tāt\ *vb* [L *meditatus*, pp. of *meditari* — more at METE] *vt* **1 :** to reflect on or muse over **:** CONTEMPLATE **2 :** INTEND, PURPOSE ~ *vi* **:** to engage in contemplation or reflection **syn** see PONDER — **med·i·ta·tor** \-,tāt-ər\ *n*

med·i·ta·tion \,med-ə-'tā-shən\ *n* **1 :** a discourse intended to express its author's reflections or to guide others in contemplation **2 :** the act or process of meditating

med·i·ta·tive \'med-ə-,tāt-iv\ *adj* **:** disposed or given to meditation — **med·i·ta·tive·ly** *adv* — **med·i·ta·tive·ness** *n*

Med·i·ter·ra·nean \,med-ə-tə-'rā-nē-ən, -nyən\ *adj* **1** *not cap* [L *mediterraneus*, fr. *medi-* + *terra* land — more at TERRACE] **:** enclosed or nearly enclosed with land **2 :** of or relating to the Mediterranean sea **3 :** of or relating to a group or physical type of the Caucasian race characterized by medium or short stature, slender build, dolichocephaly, and dark complexion

Mediterranean flour moth *n* **:** a small largely gray and black nearly cosmopolitan moth (*Anagasta kuehniella*) having a larva that destroys processed grain products

Mediterranean fruit fly *n* **:** a widely distributed two-winged fly (*Ceratitis capitata*) with black and white markings having a larva that lives and feeds in ripening fruit

1**me·di·um** \'mēd-ē-əm\ *n, pl* **mediums** *or* **me·dia** \-ē-ə\ [L, fr. neuter of *medius* middle — more at MID] **1 a :** something in a middle position **b :** a middle condition or degree **:** MEAN **2 :** a means of effecting or conveying something: as **a** (1) **:** a substance regarded as the means of transmission of a force or effect (2) **:** a surrounding or enveloping substance **b** (1) **:** a channel of communication (2) *media pl but sometimes sing in constr* **:** a publication or broadcast that carries advertising **c :** GO-BETWEEN, INTERMEDIARY **d :** an individual held to be a channel of communication between the earthly world and a world of spirits **e :** material or technical means of artistic expression **3 a :** a condition in which something may function or flourish **b** (1) **:** a nutrient system for the artificial cultivation of bacteria or other organisms or cells (2) **:** a fluid or solid in which organic structures are placed (as for preservation or mounting) **c :** a liquid with which pigment is mixed by a painter **4 :** a size of paper usu. 23 x 18 inches **syn** see MEAN

2**medium** *adj* **:** intermediate in amount, quality, position, or degree

medium frequency *n* **:** a radio frequency between low and high frequencies — see RADIO FREQUENCY table

me·di·um·is·tic \,mēd-ē-ə-'mis-tik\ *adj* **:** of, relating to, or having the qualities of a spiritualistic medium

medium of exchange : something commonly accepted in exchange for goods and services and recognized as representing a standard of value

med·lar \'med-lər\ *n* [ME *medeler*, fr. MF *medlier*, fr. *medle* medlar fruit, fr. L *mespilum*, fr. Gk *mespilon*] **:** a small Eurasian tree (*Mespilus germanica*) of the rose family; *also* **:** its fruit that resembles a crab apple and is used in preserves

1**med·ley** \'med-lē\ *n* [ME *medle*, fr. MF *medlee*, fr. fem. of *medlé*, pp. of *medler* to mix — more at MEDDLE] **1** *archaic* **:** MELEE **2 :** MIXTURE; *esp* **:** HODGEPODGE **3 :** a musical composition made up of a series of songs or other musical pieces

2**medley** *adj* **:** MIXED, MOTLEY

me·dul·la \mə-'dəl-ə\ *n, pl* **medullas** *or* **me·dul·lae** \-'dəl-(,)ē, -,ī\ [L] **1** *pl medullae* **:** MARROW 1 **2 a :** the inner or deep part of an animal or plant structure **b :** MEDULLARY SHEATH

medulla ob·lon·ga·ta \-,äb-,lȯŋ-'gät-ə\ *n, pl* **medulla oblongatas** *or* **medullae ob·lon·ga·tae** \-'gät-ē, -'gä-,tī\ [NL, lit., oblong medulla] **:** the somewhat pyramidal last part of the vertebrate brain continuous posteriorly with the spinal cord

med·ul·lary \'med-ᵊl-,er-ē, 'mej-ə-,ler-; mə-'dəl-ə-rē\ *adj* **1 :** of or relating to a medulla and esp. the medulla oblongata **2 :** of or relating to the pith of a plant

medullary ray *n* **1 :** a ray in the stele of various cryptogamous and dicotyledonous vascular plants that extends outward from the medulla often separating the vascular bundles **2 :** VASCULAR RAY

medullary sheath *n* **:** the layer of myelin surrounding a medullated nerve fiber

med·ul·lat·ed \'med-ᵊl-,āt-əd, 'mej-ə-,lāt-\ *adj* **1** *of a nerve fiber* **:** having a medullary sheath **2** *of other fibers* **:** having a medulla

me·du·sa \mi-'d(y)ü-sə, -zə\ *n* **1** *cap* [L, fr. Gk *Medousa*] **:** a Gorgon slain by Perseus **2** *pl* **me·du·sae** \-,sē, -,zē\ [NL, fr. L]

: JELLYFISH; *esp* : a small hydrozoan jellyfish — **me·du·sal** \-səl, -zəl\ *adj* — **me·du·san** \-'d(y)üs-ᵊn, -'d(y)üz-\ *adj or n* — **me·du·soid** \-'d(y)ü-ˌsȯid, -ˌzȯid\ *adj or n*

meed \'mēd\ *n* [ME, fr. OE *mēd;* akin to OHG *miata* reward, Gk *misthos*] **1** *archaic* : a reward or wage earned **2** : a fitting return

meek \'mēk\ *adj* [ME, of Scand origin; akin to ON *mjūkr* gentle; akin to L *mucus*] **1** : enduring injury with patience and without resentment : MILD **2** : deficient in spirit and courage : SUBMISSIVE **3** : not violent or strong : MODERATE **syn** see HUMBLE — **meek·ly** *adv* — **meek·ness** *n*

meer·schaum \'mi(ə)r-shəm, -ˌshȯm\ *n* [G, fr. *meer* sea + *schaum* foam] **1** : a fine light white clayey mineral that is a hydrous magnesium silicate $H_4Mg_2Si_3O_{10}$ found chiefly in Asia Minor and used esp. for tobacco pipes **2** : a tobacco pipe of meerschaum

1**meet** \'mēt\ *vb* **met** \'met\ **meet·ing** [ME *meten,* fr. OE *mētan;* akin to OHG *muoz* meeting, Arm *matčim* I approach] *vt* **1 a** : to come into the presence of : FIND **b** : to approach from another direction **c** : to come into contact or conjunction with : JOIN **d** : to appear to the perception of **2** : to encounter as antagonist or foe : OPPOSE **3** : to join in discussion or intercourse **4** : to conform to **5** : to pay fully : SETTLE **6** : to cope with : MATCH **7** : to provide for **8** : to become acquainted with ~ *vi* **1 a** : to come together from different directions **b** : to come together for a common purpose : ASSEMBLE **2** : to come into intercourse or conflict **3** : to become joined into one : UNITE — **meet·er** *n*

2**meet** *n* **1** : an assembling for a hunt or for competitive sports **2** : a meeting usu. for competition or a specific activity

3**meet** *adj* [ME *mete,* fr. OE *gemǣte;* akin to OE *metan* to mete] : SUITABLE, PROPER **syn** see FIT — **meet·ly** *adv*

meet·ing \'mēt-iŋ\ *n* **1** : an act or process of coming together: as **a** : an assembly for worship or other common purpose **b** : a session of horse or dog racing **2** : a permanent organizational unit of the Society of Friends **3** : INTERSECTION, JUNCTION

meet·ing·house \-ˌhau̇s\ *n* : a building used for public assembly and esp. for Protestant worship

mega- *or* **meg-** *comb form* [Gk, fr. *megas* large — more at MUCH] **1 a** : great : large ⟨*mega*spore⟩ **b** : having a (specified) part of large size ⟨*mega*cephalic⟩ **2** : million : multiplied by one million ⟨*meg*ohm⟩ ⟨*mega*cycle⟩

mega·ce·phal·ic \ˌmeg-ə-sə-'fal-ik\ *also* **mega·ceph·a·lous** \-'sef-ə-ləs\ *adj* [*mega-* + Gk *kephalē* head — more at CEPHALIC] : large-headed; *specif* : having a cranial capacity in excess of the mean — **mega·ceph·a·ly** \-'sef-ə-lē\ *n*

mega·cy·cle \'meg-ə-ˌsī-kəl\ *n* : one million cycles; *esp* : one million cycles per second

mega·death \'meg-ə-ˌdeth\ *n* : one million deaths — used as a unit in reference to atomic warfare

mega·ga·mete \ˌmeg-ə-gə-'mēt, -'gam-ˌēt\ *n* : MACROGAMETE

megal- *or* **megalo-** *comb form* [NL, fr. Gk, fr. *megal-, megas* — more at MUCH] : large : of giant size ⟨*megalo*polis⟩ : grandiose ⟨*megalo*mania⟩

mega·lith \'meg-ə-ˌlith\ *n* : one of the huge undressed stones used in various prehistoric monuments — **mega·lith·ic** \ˌmeg-ə-'lith-ik\ *adj*

meg·a·lo·ma·nia \ˌmeg-ə-lō-'mā-nē-ə, -nyə\ *n* [NL] **1** : a mania for great or grandiose performance **2** : infantile feelings of omnipotence esp. when retained in later life — **meg·a·lo·ma·ni·ac** \-'mā-nē-ˌak\ *adj or n* — **meg·a·lo·ma·ni·a·cal** \-ə-(ˌ)lō-mə-'nī-ə-kəl\ *or* **meg·a·lo·man·ic** \-ə-lō-'man-ik\ *adj*

meg·a·lop·o·lis \ˌmeg-ə-'läp-ə-ləs\ *n* : a very large urban unit — **meg·a·lo·pol·i·tan** \-ə-lō-'päl-ət-ᵊn\ *n or adj* — **meg·a·lo·pol·i·tan·ism** \-ˌiz-əm\ *n*

1**mega·phone** \'meg-ə-ˌfōn\ *n* : a cone-shaped device used to intensify or direct the voice — **mega·phon·ic** \ˌmeg-ə-'fän-ik\ *adj*

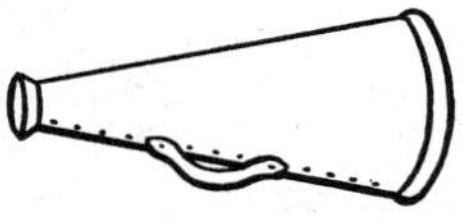

megaphone

2**megaphone** *vb* : to speak through or as if through a megaphone

mega·scop·ic \ˌmeg-ə-'skäp-ik\ *adj* [*mega-* + *-scopic* (as in *microscopic*)] **1** : ENLARGED, MAGNIFIED **2 a** : visible to the unaided eye **b** : based on or relating to observations made with the unaided eye — **mega·scop·i·cal·ly** \-i-k(ə-)lē\ *adv*

mega·spo·ran·gi·um \ˌmeg-ə-spə-'ran-jē-əm\ *n* [NL] : a sporangium that develops only megaspores

mega·spore \'meg-ə-ˌspō(ə)r, -ˌspȯ(ə)r\ *n* [ISV] : one of the spores in heterosporous plants that give rise to female gametophytes and are generally larger than the microspores — **mega·spor·ic** \ˌmeg-ə-'spōr-ik, -'spȯr-\ *adj* — **mega·spor·o·gen·e·sis** \-ˌspōr-ə-'jen-ə-səs, -ˌspȯr-\ *n*

mega·spo·ro·phyll \ˌmeg-ə-'spōr-ə-ˌfil, -'spȯr-\ *n* : a sporophyll that develops only megasporangia

mega·there \'meg-ə-ˌthi(ə)r\ *n* [NL *Megatherium,* genus name, fr. *mega-* + *-therium*] : any of a genus (*Megatherium*) of Pliocene and Pleistocene ground sloths related to the sloths and anteaters and often of gigantic size — **mega·the·ri·an** \ˌmeg-ə-'thir-ē-ən\ *n*

mega·ton \'meg-ə-ˌtən\ *n* : an explosive force equivalent to that of a million tons of TNT

mega·watt \-ˌwät\ *n* [ISV] : one million watts

me·gilp \mi-'gilp\ *n* [origin unknown] : a gelatinous preparation commonly of linseed oil and mastic varnish used by artists as a vehicle for oil colors

meg·ohm \'meg-ˌōm\ *n* [ISV] : one million ohms

1**me·grim** \'mē-grəm\ *n* [ME *migreime,* fr. MF *migraine*] **1 a** : MIGRAINE **b** : VERTIGO, DIZZINESS **2 a** : FANCY **b** *pl* : low spirits

2**megrim** *n* [origin unknown] : any of several small flatfishes; *esp* : a European flounder (*Arnoglossus laterna*)

Mei·ji \'mā-(ˌ)jē\ *n* [Jap, lit., enlightened rule] : the period of the reign (1868–1912) of Emperor Mutsuhito of Japan

mei·kle \'mē-kəl\ *var of* MICKLE

mei·ny \'mā-nē\ *n* [ME *meynie* — more at MENIAL] **1** *archaic* : RETINUE, COMPANY **2** *chiefly Scot* : MULTITUDE

mei·o·sis \mī-'ō-səs\ *n* [NL, fr. Gk *meiōsis* diminution, fr. *meioun* to diminish, fr. *meiōn* less — more at MINOR] : the sequence of complex nuclear changes resulting in the production of cells (as gametes) with half the number of chromosomes present in the original cell and typically involving first an actual reduction division in which the chromosomes without undergoing prior splitting separate so that of each pair a chromosome from one parent only enters each daughter nucleus and secondly a mitotic division — **mei·ot·ic** \mī-'ät-ik\ *adj* — **mei·ot·i·cal·ly** \-i-k(ə-)lē\ *adv*

Mei·ster·sing·er \'mī-stər-ˌsiŋ-ər, -ˌziŋ-\ *n, pl* **Meistersinger** *or* **Meistersingers** [G, fr. MHG, fr. *meister* master + *singer*] : a member of any of various German guilds formed chiefly in the 15th and 16th centuries by workingmen and craftsmen for the cultivation of poetry and music

mel·a·mine \'mel-ə-ˌmēn\ *n* [G *melamin*] **1** : a white crystalline high-melting organic base $C_3H_6N_6$ that is a cyclic trimer of cyanamide usu. made from calcium cyanamide and used esp. in melamine resins **2** : a melamine resin or a plastic made from such a resin

melamine resin *n* : a thermosetting resin made from melamine and an aldehyde and used esp. in molded or laminated products, adhesives, and coatings

melan- *or* **melano-** *comb form* [ME, fr. MF, fr. LL, fr. Gk, fr. *melan-, melas* — more at MULLET] **1** : black : dark ⟨*melan*ic⟩ **2** : melanin ⟨*melan*oid⟩

mel·an·cho·lia \ˌmel-ən-'kō-lē-ə\ *n* [NL, fr. LL, melancholy] : a mental condition characterized by extreme depression, bodily complaints, and often hallucinations and delusions; *esp* : a manic-depressive psychosis **syn** see SADNESS — **mel·an·cho·li·ac** \-lē-ˌak\ *n*

mel·an·chol·ic \ˌmel-ən-'käl-ik\ *adj* **1** : of, relating to, or subject to melancholy : DEPRESSED **2** : of or relating to melancholia **3** : DEPRESSING, SADDENING — **melancholic** *n* — **mel·an·chol·i·cal·ly** \-i-k(ə-)lē\ *adv*

mel·an·choly \'mel-ən-ˌkäl-ē\ *n* [ME *malencolie,* fr. MF *melancolie,* fr. LL *melancholia,* fr. Gk, fr. *melan-* + *cholē* bile — more at GALL] **1 a** : an abnormal state attributed to an excess of black bile and characterized by irascibility or depression **b** : BLACK BILE **c** : MELANCHOLIA **2 a** : depression of spirits : DEJECTION **b** : a pensive mood **syn** see SADNESS — **melancholy** *adj*

Mel·a·ne·sian \ˌmel-ə-'nē-zhən, -shən\ *n* **1** : a member of the dominant native group of Melanesia characterized by dark skin, thick beards, and frizzy hair **2** : a language group consisting of the Austronesian languages of Melanesia — **Melanesian** *adj*

mé·lange \mā-'läⁿzh, -'länj\ *n* [F, fr. MF, fr. *mesler, meler* to mix — more at MEDDLE] : a mixture esp. of incongruous elements

me·lan·ic \mə-'lan-ik\ *adj* **1** : MELANOTIC **2** : MELANISTIC

mel·a·nin \'mel-ə-nən\ *n* : a dark brown or black animal or plant pigment

mel·a·nism \'mel-ə-ˌniz-əm\ *n* **1** : an unusual development of black or nearly black color in the skin, plumage, or pelage whether characteristic of a variety or an individual variation **2** : high pigmentation in man in skin, eyes, and hair — **mel·a·nist** \-nəst\ *n* — **mel·a·nis·tic** \ˌmel-ə-'nis-tik\ *adj*

mel·a·nite \'mel-ə-ˌnīt\ *n* [G *melanit,* fr. *melan-*] : a black andradite garnet — **mel·a·nit·ic** \ˌmel-ə-'nit-ik\ *adj*

mel·a·nize \'mel-ə-ˌnīz\ *vt* **1** : to convert into or infiltrate with melanin **2** : to make dark or black

mel·a·noch·roi \ˌmel-ə-'näk-rə-ˌwī, -'näk-ˌrȯi\ *n pl* [NL, irreg. fr. *melan-* + Gk *ōchros* yellow, pale] : Caucasians having dark hair and pale complexion — **mel·a·no·chro·ic** \ˌmel-ə-nō-'krō-ik\ *adj*

mel·a·noid \'mel-ə-ˌnȯid\ *adj* [ISV] **1** : characterized or darkened by melanins **2** : relating to or occurring in melanosis — **melanoid** *n*

mel·a·no·ma \ˌmel-ə-'nō-mə\ *n, pl* **melanomas** *also* **mel·a·no·ma·ta** \-mət-ə\ [NL] : a usu. malignant tumor containing dark pigment

mel·a·no·sis \ˌmel-ə-'nō-səs\ *n* [NL] : a condition characterized by abnormal deposition of melanins or sometimes other pigments in the tissues of the body

mel·a·not·ic \-'nät-ik\ *adj* : having or characterized by black pigmentation

mel·a·nous \'mel-ə-nəs\ *adj* : having black hair and dark brown or blackish skin

mela·phyre \'mel-ə-ˌfī(ə)r\ *n* [F *mélaphyre,* fr. Gk *melas* black + F *-phyre* — more at MULLET] : a porphyritic igneous rock with dark-colored aphanitic groundmass and phenocrysts of various kinds

mel·ba toast \ˌmel-bə-\ *n* [Nellie *Melba* †1931 Austral soprano] : very thin bread toasted till crisp

Mel·chite *or* **Mel·kite** \'mel-ˌkīt\ *n* [ML *Melchita,* fr. MGk *Melchitēs,* lit., royalist, fr. Syr *malkā* king] **1** : an Eastern Christian adhering to Chalcedonian orthodoxy **2** : a member of a Uniate body derived from the Melchites

1**Mel·chiz·e·dek** \mel-'kiz-ə-ˌdek\ *n* [Gk *Melchisedek,* fr. Heb *Malkī-ṣedheq*] : a priest-king paid tithes by Abraham

2**Melchizedek** *adj* : of or forming the higher order of the Mormon priesthood

1**meld** \'meld\ *vb* [G *melden* to announce, fr. OHG *meldōn;* akin to OE *meldian* to announce, OSlav *moliti* to ask for] : to declare or announce for a score in a card game

2**meld** *n* : a card or combination of cards that is or can be melded in a card game

3**meld** *vb* [blend of *melt* and *weld*] : MERGE

Mele·ager \'mel-ē-ˌā-jər, ˌmel-ē-'\ *n* [L, fr. Gk *Meleagros*] : an Argonaut and slayer of the Calydonian boar

me·lee \'mā-ˌlā, mā-'\ *n* [F *mêlée,* fr. OF *meslee,* fr. *mesler* to mix — more at MEDDLE] : a confused struggle

mel·ic \'mel-ik\ *adj* [L *melicus,* fr. Gk *melikos,* fr. *melos* song — more at MELODY] : of or relating to song : LYRIC; *esp* : of or relating to Greek lyric poetry of the 7th and 6th centuries B.C.

mel·i·lot \'mel-ə-ˌlät\ *n* [ME *mellilot,* fr. MF *melilot,* fr. L *melilotos,* fr. Gk *melilōtos,* fr. *meli* + *lōtos* clover, lotus] : SWEET CLOVER; *esp* : a yellow-flowered sweet clover (*Melilotus officinalis*)

me·lio·rate \'mēl-yə-ˌrāt, 'mē-lē-ə-\ *vb* [LL *melioratus,* pp. of *meliorare,* fr. L *melior* better; akin to L *multus* much, Gk *mala* very] : to make or become better : IMPROVE — **me·lio·ra·tion** \ˌmēl-yə-'rā-shən, ˌmē-lē-ə-\ *n* — **me·lio·ra·tive** \'mēl-yə-ˌrāt-iv, 'mē-lē-ə-\ *adj* — **me·lio·ra·tor** \-ˌrāt-ər\ *n*

me·lio·rism \'mēl-yə-ˌriz-əm, 'mē-lē-ə-\ *n* : the belief that the world tends to become better and that man can aid its betterment —

me·lio·rist \-rəst\ *adj or n* — **me·lio·ris·tic** \ˌmēl-yə-ˈris-tik, ˌmē-lē-ə-\ *adj*

mell \ˈmel\ *vb* [ME *mellen*, fr. MF *mesler*] *dial Brit* : MIX

mel·lif·er·ous \me-ˈlif-(ə-)rəs\ *adj* [L *mellifer*, fr. *mell-*, *mel* + *-fer* -ferous] : producing or yielding honey

mel·lif·lu·ent \me-ˈlif-lə-wənt\ *adj* [LL *mellifluent-*, *mellifluens*, fr. L *mell-*, *mel* + *fluent-*, *fluens*, prp. of *fluere*] *archaic* : MELLIFLUOUS — **mel·lif·lu·ent·ly** *adv*

mel·lif·lu·ous \me-ˈlif-lə-wəs, mə-\ *adj* [LL *mellifluus*, fr. L *mell-*, *mel* honey + *fluere* to flow; akin to Goth *milith* honey, Gk *melit-*, *meli*] **1** : flowing or sweetened with or as if with honey **2** : sweetly flowing — **mel·lif·lu·ous·ly** *adv* — **mel·lif·lu·ous·ness** *n*

mel·lo·phone \ˈmel-ə-ˌfōn\ *n* [*mellow* + *-phone*] : an althorn in circular form sometimes used as a substitute for the French horn

mel·low \ˈmel-(ˌ)ō, -ə(-w)\ *adj* [ME *melowe*] **1 a** *of a fruit* : tender and sweet because of ripeness **b** *of a wine* : well aged and pleasingly mild **2** : made gentle by age or experience **3** *of soil* : of soft and loamy consistency **4** : rich and full but free from garishness or stridency **5** : warmed and relaxed by liquor — **mellow** *vb* — **mel·low·ly** *adv* — **mel·low·ness** *n*

me·lo·de·on \mə-ˈlōd-ē-ən\ *n* [G *melodion*, fr. *melodie* melody, fr. OF] : a small reed organ in which a suction bellows draws air inward through the reeds

me·lod·ic \mə-ˈläd-ik\ *adj* : of or relating to melody : MELODIOUS — **me·lod·i·cal·ly** \-i-k(ə-)lē\ *adv*

me·lo·di·ous \mə-ˈlōd-ē-əs\ *adj* **1** : agreeable to the ear because of a succession of sweet sounds **2** : of, relating to, or producing melody — **me·lo·di·ous·ly** *adv* — **me·lo·di·ous·ness** *n*

mel·o·dist \ˈmel-əd-əst\ *n* **1** : SINGER **2** : a composer of melodies

mel·o·dize \ˈmel-ə-ˌdīz\ *vt* **1** : to make melodious : set to melody ~ *vi* : to compose a melody — **mel·o·diz·er** *n*

melo·dra·ma \ˈmel-ə-ˌdräm-ə, -ˌdram-\ *n* [modif. of F *mélodrame*, fr. Gk *melos* + F *drame* drama, fr. LL *drama*] **1 a** : an extravagantly theatrical play in which action and plot predominate over characterization **b** : the genre of dramatic literature constituted by such plays **2** : melodramatic events or behavior — **melo·dra·ma·tist** \ˌmel-ə-ˈdram-ət-əst, -ˈdräm-\ *n*

melo·dra·mat·ic \ˌmel-ə-drə-ˈmat-ik\ *adj* **1** : of, relating to, or characteristic of melodrama **2** : sensational in situation or action **syn** see DRAMATIC — **melo·dra·mat·i·cal·ly** \-i-k(ə-)lē\ *adv*

melo·dra·mat·ics \-ˈmat-iks\ *n pl but sing or pl in constr* : melodramatic conduct

mel·o·dy \ˈmel-əd-ē\ *n* [ME *melodie*, fr. OF, fr. LL *melodia*, fr. Gk *melōidia* chanting, music, fr. *melos* limb, musical phrase, song + *aeidein* to sing; akin to Bret *mell* joint — more at ODE] **1** : a sweet or agreeable succession or arrangement of sounds : TUNEFULNESS **2 a** : a rhythmic succession of single tones organized as an aesthetic whole **b** : a musical line as it appears on the staff when viewed horizontally **c** : the chief part in a harmonic composition

mel·oid \ˈmel-ˌȯid, ˈmel-ə-wəd\ *adj* [deriv. of NL *Meloe*, genus of beetles] : of or relating to the oil beetles — **meloid** *n*

mel·o·lon·thid \ˌmel-ə-ˈlän(t)-thəd\ *n* [deriv. of Gk *mēlolonthē*] : COCKCHAFER

mel·on \ˈmel-ən\ *n, often attrib* [ME, fr. MF, fr. LL *melon-*, *melo*, short for L *melopepon-*, *melopepo*, fr. Gk *mēlopepōn*, fr. *mēlon* apple + *pepōn*, an edible gourd — more at PUMPKIN] **1** : any of various gourds (as a muskmelon or watermelon) usu. eaten raw as fruits **2** : something rounded like a melon; *also* : an abdomen that protrudes **3 a** : a surplus of profits available for distribution to stockholders **b** : a financial windfall

Mel·pom·e·ne \mel-ˈpäm-ə-(ˌ)nē\ *n* [L, fr. Gk *Melpomenē*] : the Greek Muse of tragedy

[1]**melt** \ˈmelt\ *vb* **melt·ed; melted** *also* **mol·ten** \ˈmōlt-ᵊn\ **melt·ing** [ME *melten*, fr. OE *meltan*; akin to L *mollis* soft, *molere* to grind — more at MEAL] *vi* **1** : to become altered from a solid to a liquid state usu. by heat **2 a** : DISSOLVE, DISINTEGRATE **b** : to disappear as if dissolving **3** *obs* : to become subdued or crushed **4** : to become mild, tender, or gentle **5** : to lose distinct outline : BLEND ~ *vt* **1** : to reduce from a solid to a liquid state usu. by heat **2** : to cause to disappear or disperse **3** : to make tender or gentle : SOFTEN — **melt·abil·i·ty** \ˌmel-tə-ˈbil-ət-ē\ *n* — **melt·able** \ˈmel-tə-bəl\ *adj* — **melt·er** *n*

[2]**melt** *n* **1 a** : a melted substance **b** : the mass melted at a single operation or the quantity melted during a specified period **2** : an act of melting : the condition of being melted

[3]**melt** *n* [ME *milte*, fr. OE; akin to OHG *miltzi* spleen] : SPLEEN

melting point *n* : the temperature at which a solid melts

melting pot *n* **1** : a vessel for melting something : CRUCIBLE **2** : a place exhibiting racial amalgamation and assimilation

mel·ton \ˈmelt-ᵊn\ *n* [*Melton* Mowbray, England] : a heavy smooth woolen fabric with short nap

melt·wa·ter \ˈmelt-ˌwȯt-ər, -ˌwät-\ *n* : water derived from the melting of ice and snow

mem \ˈmem\ *n* [Heb *mēm*, lit., water] : the 13th letter of the Hebrew alphabet — symbol מ or ם

mem·ber \ˈmem-bər\ *n* [ME *membre*, fr. OF, fr. L *membrum*; akin to Goth *mimz* flesh, Gk *mēros* thigh, *mēninx* membrane] **1** : a body part or organ: as **a** : LIMB **b** : PENIS **c** : a unit of structure in a plant body **2** : one of the individuals composing a group **3** : a person baptized or enrolled in a church **4** : a constituent part of a whole: as **a** : a syntactic or rhythmic unit of a sentence : CLAUSE **b** : one of the propositions of a syllogism **c** : one of the elements of a mathematical set **d** : one of the components of a logical class **e** : either of the equated elements in a mathematical equation **syn** see PART — **mem·bered** \-bərd\ *adj*

mem·ber·ship \ˈmem-bər-ˌship\ *n* **1** : the state or status of being a member **2** : the body of members **3** : the relation between a member of a class and the class

mem·bra·na·ceous \ˌmem-brə-ˈnā-shəs\ *adj* : MEMBRANOUS — **mem·bra·na·ceous·ly** *adv*

mem·brane \ˈmem-ˌbrān\ *n* [L *membrana* skin, parchment, fr. *membrum*] **1** : a thin soft pliable sheet or layer esp. of animal or plant origin **2** : a piece of parchment forming part of a roll — **mem·braned** \-ˌbrānd\ *adj*

membrane bone *n* : a bone that ossifies directly in connective tissue without previous existence as cartilage

mem·bra·nous \ˈmem-brə-nəs, mem-ˈbrā-\ *adj* **1** : of, relating to, or resembling membrane **2** : thin, pliable, and often somewhat transparent **3** : characterized or accompanied by the formation of a membrane or membranous layer — **mem·bra·nous·ly** *adv*

membranous labyrinth *n* : the sensory structures of the inner ear

me·men·to \mi-ˈment-(ˌ)ō\ *n, pl* **mementos** *or* **mementoes** [ME, fr. L, remember, fr. *meminisse* to remember; akin to L *ment-*, *mens* mind] : something that serves to warn or remind; *also* : SOUVENIR

me·men·to mo·ri \mi-ˌment-ō-ˈmōr-ē, -ˈmō(ə)r-ˌī, -ˈmȯ(ə)r-\ *n, pl* **memento mori** [L, remember that you must die] : a death's head or other reminder of mortality

Mem·non \ˈmem-ˌnän\ *n* [L, fr. Gk *Memnōn*] : an Ethiopian king killed by Achilles in the Trojan War and made immortal by Zeus

memo \ˈmem-(ˌ)ō\ *n* : MEMORANDUM

mem·oir \ˈmem-ˌwär, -ˌwȯ(ə)r\ *n* [F *mémoire*, lit., memory, fr. L *memoria*] **1** : an official note or report **2 a** : a narrative composed from personal experience **b** : AUTOBIOGRAPHY — usu. used in pl. **c** : BIOGRAPHY **3 a** : an account of something noteworthy : REPORT **b** *pl* : the record of the proceedings of a learned society

mem·o·ra·bil·ia \ˌmem-ə-rə-ˈbil-ē-ə, -ˈbil-yə\ *n pl* [L, fr. neut. pl. of *memorabilis*] : things remarkable and worthy of remembrance; *also* : a record of such things

mem·o·ra·ble \ˈmem-(ə-)rə-bəl, ˈmem-ər-bəl\ *adj* [ME, fr. L *memorabilis*, fr. *memorare* to remind, mention, fr. *memor* mindful] : worth remembering : NOTABLE — **mem·o·ra·ble·ness** *n* — **mem·o·ra·bly** \-(ə-)rə-blē\ *adv*

mem·o·ran·dum \ˌmem-ə-ˈran-dəm\ *n, pl* **memorandums** *or* **mem·o·ran·da** \-də\ [ME, fr. L, neut. of *memorandus* to be remembered, gerundive of *memorare*] **1** : an informal record; *also* : a written reminder **2** : an informal written note of a transaction or proposed instrument **3** : an informal diplomatic communication

[1]**me·mo·ri·al** \mə-ˈmōr-ē-əl, -ˈmȯr-\ *adj* **1** : serving to preserve remembrance : COMMEMORATIVE **2** : of or relating to memory — **me·mo·ri·al·ly** \-ə-lē\ *adv*

[2]**memorial** *n* **1 a** : something that keeps remembrance alive; *esp* : MONUMENT **b** : COMMEMORATION 2 **c** : MEMENTO **2 a** : RECORD, MEMOIR **b** : MEMORANDUM, NOTE; *specif* : a legal abstract **c** : a statement of facts addressed to a government often accompanied with a petition or remonstrance

Memorial Day *n* **1** : May 30 observed as a legal holiday in most states of the U.S. in commemoration of dead servicemen **2** : CONFEDERATE MEMORIAL DAY

me·mo·ri·al·ist \-ē-ə-ləst\ *n* **1** : a person who writes or signs a memorial **2** : the writer of a commemorative memoir

me·mo·ri·al·ize \-ē-ə-ˌlīz\ *vt* **1** : to address or petition by a memorial **2** : COMMEMORATE

memorial park *n* : CEMETERY

me·mo·ri·ter \mə-ˈmȯr-ə-ˌte(ə)r, -ˈmär-\ *adv* (*or adj*) [L, fr. *memor*] : by or from memory : by heart

mem·o·ri·za·tion \ˌmem-(ə-)rə-ˈzā-shən\ *n* : the act of memorizing

mem·o·rize \ˈmem-ə-ˌrīz\ *vt* : to commit to memory : learn by heart — **mem·o·riz·er** *n*

mem·o·ry \ˈmem-(ə-)rē\ *n* [ME *memorie*, fr. MF *memoire*, fr. L *memoria*, fr. *memor* mindful; akin to OE *mimorian* to remember, L *mora* delay, Gk *mermēra* care, Skt *smarati* he remembers] **1 a** : the power or process of reproducing or recalling what has been learned and retained esp. through associative mechanisms **b** : persistent modification of structure or behavior resulting from an organism's activity or experience **c** : the store of things learned and retained as evidenced by recall and recognition **2 a** : commemorative remembrance **b** : the fact or condition of being remembered **3 a** : a particular act of recall or recollection **b** : an image or impression of someone or something remembered **c** : the time within which past events can be or are remembered **4** : a component in an electronic computing machine into which information can be inserted, stored, and extracted when needed

syn REMEMBRANCE, RECOLLECTION, REMINISCENCE: MEMORY applies both to the power of remembering and to what is remembered; REMEMBRANCE applies to the act of remembering or the fact of being remembered; RECOLLECTION adds an implication of consciously bringing back to mind often with some effort; REMINISCENCE suggests the recalling of incidents, experience, or feelings from a remote past

mem·sa·hib \ˈmem-ˌsä-(h)ib, -ˌsäb\ *n* [Hindi *memsāhib*, fr. E *ma'am* + Hindi *sāhib* sahib] : a white foreign woman of some social status living in India; *esp* : the wife of a British official

men *pl of* MAN

men- *or* **meno-** *comb form* [NL, fr. Gk *mēn* month — more at MOON] : menstruation ⟨*menorrhagia*⟩

[1]**men·ace** \ˈmen-əs\ *n* [ME, fr. MF, fr. L *minacia*, fr. *minac-*, *minax* threatening, fr. *minari* to threaten — more at MOUNT] **1** : a show of intention to inflict harm : THREAT **2 a** : someone or something that represents a threat : DANGER **b** : a person who causes annoyance

[2]**menace** *vt* **1** : to make a show of intention to harm **2** : ENDANGER ~ *vi* : to act in a threatening manner **syn** see THREATEN — **men·ac·ing·ly** \-ə-siŋ-lē\ *adv*

me·nad *var of* MAENAD

men·a·di·one \ˌmen-ə-ˈdī-ˌōn\ *n* [*me*thyl + *na*phthoquinone + *di-* + ket*one*] : a yellow crystalline compound $C_{11}H_8O_2$ with the biological activity of natural vitamin K

mé·nage \mā-ˈnäzh\ *n* [F, fr. OF *mesnage* dwelling, fr. (assumed) VL *mansionaticum*, fr. L *mansion-*, *mansio* mansion] : a domestic establishment : HOUSEHOLD; *also* : HOUSEKEEPING

me·nag·er·ie \mə-ˈnaj-(ə-)rē, -ˈnazh-\ *n* [F *ménagerie*, fr. MF, management of a household or farm, fr. *menage*] **1** : a place where animals are kept and trained esp. for exhibition **2** : a collection of wild or foreign animals kept esp. for exhibition

men·ar·che \mə-ˈnär-kē\ *n* [NL, fr. *men-* + Gk *archē* beginning] : the initiation of menstruation — **men·ar·che·al** \-kē-əl\ *adj*

[1]**mend** \ˈmend\ *vb* [ME *menden*, short for *amenden* — more at AMEND] *vt* **1 a** : to improve in manners or morals : REFORM **b** : to set right : CORRECT **c** : to put into good shape or working order again : patch up : REPAIR **d** : to restore to health : CURE **2** : to make amends or atonement for ⟨least said, soonest ~*ed*⟩ ~ *vi* **1** : to improve morally : REFORM **2** : to become corrected or improved **3** : to improve in health; *also* : HEAL — **mend·er** *n*

syn REPAIR, PATCH, REBUILD, REMODEL: MEND implies making whole or sound something broken, torn, or injured; REPAIR applies to the mending of more extensive damage or dilapidation; PATCH implies an often temporary mending of a rent or breach with new material; REBUILD suggests making like new without completely replacing; REMODEL implies making considerable change in structure or design

[2]**mend** *n* **1** : an act of mending : REPAIR **2** : a mended place — **on the mend** : IMPROVING

men·da·cious \men-ˈdā-shəs\ *adj* [L *mendac-*, *mendax* — more at AMEND] **1** : given to deception or falsehood **2** : LYING **syn** see

DISHONEST — **men·da·cious·ly** *adv* — **men·da·cious·ness** *n*
men·dac·i·ty \men-ˈdas-ət-ē\ *n* **:** the quality or state of being mendacious; *also* **:** LIE
men·de·le·vi·um \ˌmen-də-ˈlē-vē-əm, -ˈlā-\ *n* [NL, fr. Dmitri *Mendeleev* †1907 Russ chemist] **:** a radioactive element artificially produced — see ELEMENT table
Men·de·lian \men-ˈdē-lē-ən, -ˈdēl-yən\ *adj* **:** of, relating to, or according with Mendel's laws or Mendelism — **Mendelian** *n* — **Men·de·lian·ist** \-əst\ *n*
Men·del·ism \ˈmen-dᵊl-ˌiz-əm\ *n* **:** the principles or the operations of Mendel's laws; *also* **:** PARTICULATE INHERITANCE — **Men·del·ist** \-dᵊl-əst\ *adj or n*
Men·del's law \ˌmen-dᵊlz-\ *n* [Gregor *Mendel* †1884 Austrian botanist] **1 :** a principle in genetics: paired hereditary units representing alternate characters separate during gamete formation so that every gamete receives but one member of a pair **2 :** a principle in genetics limited and modified by the subsequent discovery of the phenomenon of linkage: the corresponding hereditary units in a pair of gametes unite in the zygote to form new combinations according to the laws of chance **3 :** a principle in genetics proved subsequently to be subject to many limitations: because one of each pair of hereditary units dominates the other in expression, characters are inherited alternatively on an all or nothing basis
men·di·can·cy \ˈmen-di-kən-sē\ *n* **1 :** a beggar's state **2 :** the practice of begging
men·di·cant \ˈmen-di-kənt\ *n* [L *mendicant-, mendicans*, prp. of *mendicare* to beg, fr. *mendicus* beggar] **1 :** BEGGAR 1 **2** *often cap* **:** a member of a religious order (as the Franciscans) combining monastic life and outside religious activity and orig. owning neither personal nor community property **:** FRIAR — **mendicant** *adj*
men·dic·i·ty \men-ˈdis-ət-ē\ *n* [ME *mendicite*, fr. MF *mendicité*, fr. L *mendicitat-, mendicitas*, fr. *mendicus*] **:** MENDICANCY
Men·e·la·us \ˌmen-ᵊl-ˈā-əs\ *n* [L, fr. Gk *Menelaos*] **:** a king of Sparta, brother of Agamemnon, and husband of Helen of Troy
men·folk \ˈmen-ˌfōk\ *or* **men·folks** \-ˌfōks\ *n pl* **1 :** men in general **2 :** the men of a family or community
men·ha·den \men-ˈhād-ᵊn, mən-\ *n, pl* **menhaden** *also* **menhadens** [of Algonquian origin; prob. akin to Narraganset *munnawhatteaûg* menhaden] **:** a marine fish (*Brevoortia tyrannus*) of the herring family abundant along the Atlantic coast of the U.S. where it is used for bait or converted into oil and fertilizer
men·hir \ˈmen-ˌhi(ə)r\ *n* [F, fr. Bret, fr. *men* stone + *hir* long] **:** a single upright rude monolith usu. of prehistoric origin
¹me·nial \ˈmē-nē-əl, -nyəl\ *adj* [ME *meynial*, fr. *meynie* household, retinue, fr. OF *mesnie*, fr. (assumed) VL *mansionata*, fr. L *mansion-, mansio* dwelling] **1 :** of or relating to servants **:** LOW **2 :** HUMBLE; *also* **:** SERVILE **syn** see SUBSERVIENT — **me·nial·ly** \-ē\ *adv*
²menial *n* **:** a domestic servant or retainer
mening- *or* **meningo-** *also* **meningi-** *comb form* [NL, fr. *mening-, meninx*] **:** meninges ⟨*meningo*coccus⟩ ⟨*mening*itis⟩
me·nin·geal \mə-ˈnin-j(ē-)əl, ˌmen-ən-ˈjē-əl\ *adj* **:** of, relating to, or affecting the meninges
men·in·git·ic \ˌmen-ən-ˈjit-ik\ *adj* **:** of or relating to meningitis
men·in·gi·tis \-ˈjīt-əs\ *n* [NL] **1 :** inflammation of the meninges and esp. of the pia mater and the arachnoid **2 :** a usu. bacterial disease in which inflammation of the meninges occurs
me·nin·go·coc·cic \mə-ˌniŋ-gō-ˈkäk-(s)ik, -ˌnin-\ *or* **me·nin·go·coc·cal** \-ˈkäk-əl\ *adj* **:** of or caused by meningococci
me·nin·go·coc·cus \-ˈkäk-əs\ *n, pl* **me·nin·go·coc·ci** \-ˈkäk-ˌ(s)ī, -(ˌ)(s)ē\ [NL] **:** the bacterium (*Neisseria meningitidis*) that causes cerebrospinal meningitis
me·ninx \ˈmēn-(ˌ)iŋ(k)s, ˈmen-\ *n, pl* **me·nin·ges** \mə-ˈnin-(ˌ)jēz\ [NL, fr. Gk *mēning-, mēninx* membrane; akin to L *membrana* membrane] **:** any of the three membranes that envelop the brain and spinal cord
me·nis·cus \mə-ˈnis-kəs\ *n, pl* **me·nis·ci** \-ˈnis-ˌ(k)ī, -ˌkē\ *also* **me·nis·cus·es** [NL, fr. Gk *mēniskos*, fr. dim. of *mēn* moon, crescent — more at MOON] **1 :** a crescent or crescent-shaped body **2 :** a fibrous cartilage within a joint esp. of the knee **3 :** a concavo-convex lens **4 :** the curved upper surface of a liquid column that is concave when the containing walls are wetted by the liquid and convex when not

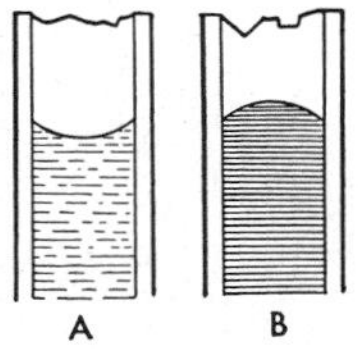

meniscus 4: *A* concave meniscus of water, *B* convex meniscus of mercury

Men·no·nite \ˈmen-ə-ˌnīt\ *n* [G *Mennonit*, fr. *Menno* Simons †1559 Frisian religious reformer] **:** a member of one of the Christian groups derived from the Anabaptist movement in Holland and noted for simplicity of life and rejection of oaths, public office, and military service
me·no mos·so \ˌmā-nō-ˈmȯ(s)-(ˌ)sō\ *adv* [It] **:** less rapid — used as a direction in music
meno·paus·al \ˌmen-ə-ˈpȯ-zəl\ *adj* **:** of, relating to, or undergoing menopause
meno·pause \ˈmen-ə-ˌpȯz\ *n* [F *ménopause*, fr. *méno-* men- + *pause*] **:** the period of natural cessation of menstruation occurring usu. between the ages of 45 and 50
me·no·rah \mə-ˈnōr-ə, -ˈnȯr-\ *n* [Heb *mĕnōrāh* candlestick] **:** a candelabrum used in Jewish worship
men·or·rha·gia \ˌmen-ə-ˈrā-j(ē-)ə\ *n* [NL] **:** abnormally profuse menstrual flow — **men·or·rhag·ic** \-ˈraj-ik\ *adj*
men·sal \ˈmen(t)-səl\ *adj* [LL *mensalis*, fr. L *mensa* table] **:** belonging to, used, or done at the table
¹mense \ˈmen(t)s\ *n* [ME *menske*, fr. ON *mennska* humanity] *Scot* **:** PROPRIETY — **mense·ful** \-fəl\ *adj* — **mense·less** \-ləs\ *adj*
²mense *vt, dial Brit* **:** to do honor to **:** GRACE
men·ses \ˈmen-ˌsēz\ *n pl but sing or pl in constr* [L, lit., months, pl. of *mensis* month — more at MOON] **:** the menstrual flow
Men·she·vik \ˈmen-chə-ˌvik, -shə-, -ˌvēk\ *n, pl* **Mensheviks** *or* **Men·she·vi·ki** \ˌmen-chə-ˈvik-ē, -shə-, -ˈvē-kē\ [Russ *men'shevik*, fr. *men'she* less; fr. their forming the minority group of the party] **:** a member of a wing of the Russian Social Democratic party before and during the Russian Revolution believing in the gradual achievement of socialism by parliamentary methods in opposition to the Bolsheviks — **Men·she·vism** \ˈmen-chə-ˌviz-əm, -shə-\ *n* — **Men·she·vist** \-vəst\ *n or adj*
men·stru·al \ˈmen(t)-strə(-wə)l\ *adj* **1 :** of or relating to menstruation **2 :** occurring once a month **:** MONTHLY
men·stru·ate \ˈmen(t)-strə-ˌwāt, ˈmen-ˌstrāt\ *vi* [LL *menstruatus*, pp. of *menstruari*, fr. L *menstrua* menses, fr. neut. pl. of *menstruus* monthly, fr. *mensis*] **:** to undergo menstruation
men·stru·a·tion \ˌmen(t)-strə-ˈwā-shən, men-ˈstrā-\ *n* **:** a discharging of blood, secretions, and tissue debris from the uterus that recurs in nonpregnant breeding-age primate females at approximately monthly intervals and that is usu. held to represent a readjustment of the uterus to the nonpregnant state following proliferative changes accompanying the preceding ovulation; *also* **:** PERIOD 6c
men·stru·ous \ˈmen(t)-strə(-wə)s\ *adj* [L *menstruus*] **:** of, relating to, or undergoing menstruation
men·stru·um \ˈmen(t)-strə(-wə)m\ *n, pl* **menstruums** *or* **men·strua** \-str(ə-w)ə\ [ML, lit., menses, alter. of L *menstrua*] **:** a substance that dissolves a solid or holds it in suspension **:** SOLVENT
men·su·ra·bil·i·ty \ˌmen(t)s-(ə-)rə-ˈbil-ət-ē, ˌmench-(ə-)rə-\ *n* **:** the quality or state of being mensurable
men·su·ra·ble \ˈmen(t)s-(ə-)rə-bəl, ˈmench-(ə-)rə-\ *adj* [LL *mensurabilis*, fr. *mensurare* to measure, fr. *mensura* measure — more at MEASURE] **1 :** capable of being measured **:** MEASURABLE **2 :** MENSURAL 1 — **men·su·ra·ble·ness** *n*
men·su·ral \ˈmen(t)s-(ə-)rəl, ˈmench-(ə-)rəl\ *adj* [LL *mensuralis*, fr. L *mensura*] **1 :** relating to mensural music **2 :** of or relating to measure
mensural music *or* **mensurable music** *n* **:** polyphonic music originating in the 13th century with each note having a definite and exact time value
men·su·ra·tion \ˌmen(t)-sə-ˈrā-shən; ˌmen-chə-, -shə-\ *n* **1 :** the act of measuring **:** MEASUREMENT **2 :** geometry applied to the computation of lengths, areas, or volumes from given dimensions or angles
-ment \mənt; *homographic verbs are* ˌment *also* mənt, *the latter less often before a syllable-increasing suffix*\ *n suffix* [ME, fr. OF, fr. L *-mentum*; akin to L *-men*, suffix denoting concrete result, Gk *-mat-, -ma*] **1 a :** concrete result, object, or agent of a (specified) action ⟨embank*ment*⟩ ⟨entangle*ment*⟩ **b :** concrete means or instrument of a (specified) action ⟨entertain*ment*⟩ **2 a :** action **:** process ⟨encircle*ment*⟩ ⟨develop*ment*⟩ **b :** place of a (specified) action ⟨encamp*ment*⟩ **3 :** state **:** condition ⟨amaze*ment*⟩
¹men·tal \ˈment-ᵊl\ *adj* [ME, fr. MF, fr. LL *mentalis*, fr. L *ment-, mens* mind — more at MIND] **1 a :** of or relating to mind; *specif* **:** relating to the total emotional and intellectual response of an individual to environment **b :** of or relating to intellectual as contrasted with emotional activity **c :** of, relating to, or being intellectual as contrasted with overt physical activity **d :** occurring or experienced in the mind **:** INNER **e :** relating to mind, its activity, or its products as an object of study **:** IDEOLOGICAL **f :** relating to spirit or idea as opposed to matter **2 a :** of, relating to, or affected by a psychiatric disorder ⟨a ~ patient⟩ **b :** intended for the care or treatment of persons affected by psychiatric disorders **3 :** relating to telepathic, mind-reading, or other occult powers — **men·tal·ly** \-ᵊl-ē\ *adv*
²mental *adj* [L *mentum* chin; akin to L *mont-, mons* mountain — more at MOUNT] **:** of or relating to the chin **:** GENIAL
mental deficiency *n* **:** failure in intellectual development that results in social incompetence and is held to be caused by defect in the central nervous system and to be incurable **:** FEEBLEMINDEDNESS
men·tal·i·ty \men-ˈtal-ət-ē, mən-\ *n* **1 :** mental power or capacity **:** INTELLIGENCE **2 :** mode or way of thought **:** OUTLOOK
men·thene \ˈmen-ˌthēn\ *n* [ISV *menthol* + *-ene*] **:** an oily unsaturated hydrocarbon $C_{10}H_{18}$ obtained from menthol by dehydration
men·thol \ˈmen-ˌthȯl, -ˌthōl\ *n* [G, deriv. of L *mentha* mint] **:** a crystalline alcohol $C_{10}H_{19}OH$ that occurs esp. in mint oils and is used esp. as a local anodyne
men·tho·lat·ed \ˈmen(t)-thə-ˌlāt-əd\ *adj* **:** containing or impregnated with menthol
¹men·tion \ˈmen-chən\ *n* [ME *mencioun*, fr. OF *mention*, fr. L *mention-, mentio*, fr. *ment-, mens*] **1 :** the act or an instance of citing or calling attention to someone or something esp. in a casual or incidental manner **2 :** formal citation for outstanding achievement
²mention *vt* **men·tion·ing** \ˈmench-(ə-)niŋ\ **:** to refer to **:** CITE; *also* **:** to cite for outstanding achievement — **men·tion·able** \ˈmench-(ə-)nə-bəl\ *adj* — **men·tion·er** \-(ə-)nər\ *n*
men·tor \ˈmen-ˌtȯ(ə)r, ˈment-ər\ *n* [L, fr. Gk *Mentōr*] **1** *cap* **:** a friend of Odysseus entrusted with the education of Telemachus **2 :** a trusted counselor or guide **3 :** TUTOR, COACH
menu \ˈmen-(ˌ)yü, ˈmān-\ *n, pl* **menus** [F, fr. *menu* small, detailed, fr. L *minutus* minute (adj.)] **1 :** a list of the dishes (as in a restaurant) that are to be served at a meal **2 :** the dishes served at a meal or the meal itself
me·ow \mē-ˈau̇\ *n* [imit.] **1 :** the cry of a cat **2 :** a spiteful or malicious remark — **meow** *vb*
me·per·i·dine \mə-ˈper-ə-ˌdēn\ *n* [*me*thyl + pi*peridine*] **:** a synthetic narcotic drug $C_{15}H_{21}NO_2$ used in the form of its hydrochloride as an analgesic, sedative, and antispasmodic
Meph·is·toph·e·les \ˌmef-ə-ˈstäf-ə-ˌlēz\ *n* [G] **:** one of the seven chief devils in medieval demonology known esp. as the cold scoffing relentless fiend in the Faust legend — **Me·phis·to·phe·lian** \ˌmef-ə-stə-ˈfēl-yən, mə-ˌfis-tə-, -ˈfē-lē-ən\ *or* **Me·phis·to·phe·lean** *same, or* ˌmef-ə-ˌstäf-ə-ˈlē-ən\ *adj*
me·phit·ic \mə-ˈfit-ik\ *adj* **:** of, relating to, or resembling mephitis **:** foul-smelling
me·phi·tis \mə-ˈfīt-əs\ *n* [L, fr. Oscan] **:** a noxious, pestilential, or foul exhalation from the earth; *also* **:** STENCH
me·pro·ba·mate \mə-ˈprō-bə-ˌmāt\ *n* [*me*thyl + *pro*pyl + dicar*bamate*] **:** a bitter carbamate $C_9H_{18}N_2O_4$ used as a tranquilizer
mer- *comb form* [ME, fr. *mere*, fr. OE] **:** sea ⟨*mer*maid⟩
-mer \mər\ *n comb form* [ISV, fr. Gk *meros* part — more at MERIT] **:** member of (such) a class ⟨mono*mer*⟩
mer·bro·min \ˌmər-ˈbrō-mən\ *n* [*mer*curic acetate + di*brom-* + fluorescein] **:** a green crystalline mercurial compound $C_{20}H_8Br_2HgNa_2O_6$ used as a local antiseptic and germicide in the form of its red solution
mer·can·tile \ˈmər-kən-ˌtēl, -ˌtīl\ *adj* [F, fr. It, fr. *mercante* mer-

chant, fr. L *mercant-, mercans,* fr. prp. of *mercari* to trade — more at MERCHANT] **1 :** of or relating to merchants or trading **2 :** of, relating to, or having the characteristics of mercantilism ⟨~ system⟩

mer·can·til·ism \-,tē(ə)l-,iz-əm, -,tī(ə)l-\ *n* **1 :** the theory or practice of mercantile pursuits **:** COMMERCIALISM **2 :** an economic system developing during the decay of feudalism to unify and increase the power and esp. the monetary wealth of a nation by a strict governmental regulation of the entire national economy usu. through policies designed to secure an accumulation of bullion, a favorable balance of trade, the development of agriculture and manufactures, and the establishment of foreign trading monopolies — **mer·can·til·ist** \-,tē-ləst, -,tī-\ *n or adj* — **mer·can·til·is·tic** \,mər-kən-,tē-'lis-tik, -,tī-\ *adj*

mer·cap·tan \(,)mər-'kap-,tan\ *n* [G, fr. Dan, fr. ML *mercurium captans,* lit., seizing mercury] **:** any of various compounds with the general formula RSH that are analogous to the alcohols and phenols but contain sulfur in place of oxygen and often have disagreeable odors

Mer·ca·tor projection \(,)mər-,kāt-ər-\ *n* [Gerhardus *Mercator* †1594 Flemish geographer] **:** a map projection in which the meridians are drawn parallel to each other and the parallels of latitude are straight lines whose distance from each other increases with their distance from the equator

mer·ce·nar·i·ly \,mərs-ᵊn-'er-ə-lē\ *adv* **:** in a mercenary manner

mer·ce·nar·i·ness \'mərs-ᵊn-,er-ē-nəs\ *n* **:** the quality or state of being mercenary

¹**mer·ce·nary** \'mərs-ᵊn-,er-ē\ *n* [ME, fr. L *mercenarius,* fr. *merced-, merces* wages — more at MERCY] **:** one that serves merely for wages; *esp* **:** a soldier hired into foreign service

²**mercenary** *adj* **1 :** serving merely for pay or sordid advantage **:** VENAL; *also* **:** GREEDY **2 :** hired for service in the army of a foreign country

mer·cer \'mər-sər\ *n* [ME, fr. OF *mercier* merchant, fr. *mers* merchandise, fr. L *merc-, merx*] *Brit* **:** a dealer in textile fabrics

mer·cer·ize \'mər-sə-,rīz\ *vt* [John *Mercer* †1866 E calico printer] **:** to give (cotton yarn or cloth) luster, strength, and receptiveness to dyes by treatment under tension with caustic soda

mer·cery \'mərs-(ə-)rē\ *n, Brit* **:** a mercer's wares, shop, or occupation

¹**mer·chan·dise** \'mər-chən-,dīz, -,dīs\ *n* [ME *marchaundise,* fr. OF *marcheandise,* fr. *marcheant*] **1 :** the commodities or goods that are bought and sold in business **:** WARES **2** *archaic* **:** the occupation of a merchant **:** TRADE

²**mer·chan·dise** \-,dīz\ *vi* **:** to carry on commerce **:** TRADE ~ *vt* **1 :** to buy and sell in business **2 :** to promote the sale of — **mer·chan·dis·er** \-,dī-zər\ *n*

¹**mer·chant** \'mər-chənt\ *n* [ME *marchant,* fr. OF *marcheant,* fr. (assumed) VL *mercatant-, mercatans,* fr. prp. of *mercatare* to trade, fr. L *mercatus,* pp. of *mercari,* fr. *merc-, merx* merchandise] **1 :** a buyer and seller of commodities for profit **:** TRADER **2 :** the operator of a retail business **:** STOREKEEPER — **merchant** *adj*

²**merchant** *vi, archaic* **:** to deal or trade as a merchant ~ *vt* **:** to deal or trade in — **mer·chant·able** \-ə-bəl\ *adj*

mer·chant·man \-mən\ *n* **1** *archaic* **:** MERCHANT **2 :** a ship used in commerce

merchant marine *n* **1 :** the privately or publicly owned commercial ships of a nation **2 :** the personnel of a merchant marine

Mer·cian \'mər-sh(ē-)ən\ *n* **1 :** a native or inhabitant of Mercia **2 :** the Old English dialect of Mercia — **Mercian** *adj*

mer·ci·ful \'mər-si-fəl\ *adj* **:** full of mercy **:** COMPASSIONATE — **mer·ci·ful·ly** \-f(ə-)lē\ *adv* — **mer·ci·ful·ness** \-fəl-nəs\ *n*

mer·ci·less \'mər-si-ləs\ *adj* **:** having no mercy **:** PITILESS — **mer·ci·less·ly** *adv* — **mer·ci·less·ness** *n*

mercur- *or* **mercuro-** *comb form* [ISV, fr. *mercury*] **:** mercury ⟨*mercurous*⟩

mer·cu·rate \'mər-kyə-,rāt\ *vt* **:** to combine or treat with mercury or a mercury salt — **mer·cu·ra·tion** \,mər-kyə-'rā-shən\ *n*

¹**mer·cu·ri·al** \(,)mər-'kyu̇r-ē-əl\ *adj* **1 :** of, relating to, or born under the planet Mercury **2 :** having qualities of eloquence, ingenuity, or thievishness attributed to the god Mercury or to the influence of the planet Mercury **3 :** characterized by rapid and unpredictable changeableness of mood **4** [*mercury* + *-al*] **:** of, relating to, containing, or caused by mercury **syn** see INCONSTANT — **mer·cu·ri·al·ly** \-ē-ə-lē\ *adv* — **mer·cu·ri·al·ness** *n*

²**mercurial** *n* **:** a pharmaceutical or chemical containing mercury

mer·cu·ric \(,)mər-'kyu̇(ə)r-ik\ *adj* **:** of, relating to, or containing mercury; *esp* **:** containing bivalent mercury

Mer·cu·ro·chrome \mər-'kyu̇r-ə-,krōm\ *trademark* — used for merbromin

mer·cu·rous \(,)mər-'kyu̇r-əs, 'mər-kyə-rəs\ *adj* **:** of, relating to, or containing mercury; *esp* **:** containing univalent mercury

mer·cu·ry \'mər-kyə-rē, -k(ə-)rē\ *n, often attrib* [L *Mercurius,* Roman god and the planet] **1 a** *cap* **:** a Roman god who serves as herald and messenger of the other gods and presides over commerce, eloquence, cunning, and theft **b** *often cap, archaic* **:** a bearer of messages or news or a conductor of travelers **2** [ME *mercurie,* fr. ML *mercurius,* fr. L, the god] **a :** a heavy silver-white univalent and bivalent poisonous metallic element that is liquid at ordinary temperatures — see ELEMENT table **b :** the mercury in a thermometer or barometer **3** *cap* **:** the planet nearest the sun — see PLANET table **4 :** a poisonous European plant (*Mercurialis perennis*) of the spurge family

mercury chloride *n* **:** a chloride of mercury: as **a :** CALOMEL — called also *mercurous chloride* **b :** a heavy crystalline poisonous compound $HgCl_2$ used as a disinfectant and fungicide and in photography — called also *mercuric chloride*

mercury–vapor lamp *n* **:** an electric lamp in which the discharge takes place through mercury vapor

mer·cy \'mər-sē\ *n* [ME, fr. OF *merci,* fr. ML *merced-, merces,* fr. L, price paid, wages, fr. *merc-, merx* merchandise — more at MARKET] **1 a :** compassion or forbearance shown to an offender or subject **:** CLEMENCY **b :** imprisonment rather than death imposed as penalty for first-degree murder **2 a :** a blessing that is an act of divine favor or compassion **b :** a fortunate circumstance **3 :** relief of distress **:** compassion shown to victims of misfortune — **mercy** *adj*

syn CHARITY, CLEMENCY, GRACE, LENITY: MERCY implies compassion that forbears punishing even when justice demands it; CHARITY stresses benevolence and goodwill shown in broad understanding and tolerance of others and generous forgiving or overlooking of their faults or failures; CLEMENCY implies a mild or merciful disposition in one having the power or duty of punishing; GRACE may combine the implications of CHARITY and CLEMENCY; LENITY implies lack of severity in punishing

mercy seat *n* **1 :** the gold plate resting on the ancient Jewish ark **2 :** the throne of God

¹**mere** \'mi(ə)r\ *n* [ME, fr. OE — more at MARINE] **:** a sheet of standing water **:** POOL

²**mere** *n* [ME, fr. OE *mǣre* — more at MUNITION] *archaic* **:** BOUNDARY, LANDMARK

³**mere** *adj* [ME, fr. L *merus* pure, unmixed — more at MORN] **1** *obs* **:** ABSOLUTE, UNDIMINISHED **2 :** apart from anything else **:** BARE **3 :** having no admixture **:** PURE — **mere·ly** *adv*

-mere \,mi(ə)r\ *n comb form* [F *-mère,* fr. Gk *meros* part — more at MERIT] **:** part **:** segment ⟨arthro*mere*⟩

mer·e·tri·cious \,mer-ə-'trish-əs\ *adj* [L *meretricius,* fr. *meretric-, meretrix* prostitute, fr. *merēre* to earn — more at MERIT] **1 :** of or relating to a prostitute **2 a :** tawdrily attractive ⟨~ glamour⟩ **b :** based on pretense or insincerity **:** SPECIOUS ⟨~ argument⟩ **syn** see GAUDY — **mer·e·tri·cious·ly** *adv* — **mer·e·tri·cious·ness** *n*

mer·gan·ser \(,)mər-'gan(t)-sər\ *n* [NL, fr. L *mergus,* a waterfowl (fr. *mergere*) + *anser* goose — more at GOOSE] **:** any of various fish-eating diving ducks (esp. genus *Mergus*) with a slender bill hooked at the end and serrated along the margins and usu. a crested head

merge \'mərj\ *vb* [L *mergere;* akin to Skt *majjati* he dives] *vt* **1** *obs* **:** to plunge or engulf in something **:** IMMERSE **2 :** to cause to combine, unite, or coalesce **3 :** to blend gradually by stages that blur the distinctness of ~ *vi* **:** to become combined into one **syn** see MIX — **mer·gence** \'mər-jən(t)s\ *n*

merg·er \'mər-jər\ *n* [*merge* + *-er* (as in *waiver*)] **1** *law* **:** the absorption of an estate, a contract, or an interest in another, of a minor offense in a greater, or of an obligation into a judgment **2 :** absorption by a corporation of one or more others; *also* **:** any of various methods of combining two or more business concerns or other organizations

me·rid·i·an \mə-'rid-ē-ən\ *n* [ME, fr. MF *meridien,* fr. *meridien* of noon, fr. L *meridianus,* fr. *meridies* noon, south, irreg. fr. *medius* mid + *dies* day — more at MID, DEITY] **1** *obs* **:** the hour of noon **:** MIDDAY **2 :** a great circle of the celestial sphere passing through its poles and the zenith of a given place **3 :** a high point **4 a** (1) **:** a great circle on the surface of the earth passing through the poles and any given place (2) **:** the half of such a circle included between the poles **b :** a representation of such a circle or half circle numbered for longitude on a map or globe **syn** see SUMMIT — **meridian** *adj*

¹**me·rid·i·o·nal** \mə-'rid-ē-ən-ᵊl\ *adj* [ME, fr. MF *meridionel,* fr. LL *meridionalis,* irreg. fr. L *meridies* noon, south] **1 :** of, relating to, or situated in the south **:** SOUTHERN **2 :** of, relating to, or characteristic of people living in the south esp. of France **3 :** of or relating to a meridian — **me·rid·i·o·nal·ly** \-ᵊl-ē\ *adv*

²**meridional** *n* **:** an inhabitant of southern Europe and esp. southern France

me·ringue \mə-'raŋ\ *n* [F] **1 :** a dessert topping baked from a mixture of beaten egg whites and powdered sugar **2 :** a shell made of meringue and filled with fruit or ice cream

me·ri·no \mə-'rē-(,)nō\ *n* [Sp] **1 :** any of a breed of fine-wooled white sheep originating in Spain and producing a heavy fleece of exceptional quality **2 :** a soft wool or wool and cotton clothing fabric resembling cashmere **3 :** a fine wool and cotton yarn used for hosiery and knitwear — **merino** *adj*

-m·er·ism \m-ə-,riz-əm\ *n comb form* [ISV, fr. Gk *meros* part — more at MERIT] **1 :** possession of (such) an arrangement of or relation among constituent chemical units ⟨tauto*merism*⟩ **2 :** possession of (such or so many) parts ⟨penta*merism*⟩

mer·i·stem \'mer-ə-,stem\ *n* [Gk *meristos* divided (fr. *merizein* to divide fr. *meros*) + E *-em* (as in *system*)] **:** a formative plant tissue usu. made up of small cells capable of dividing indefinitely and giving rise to similar cells or to cells that differentiate to produce the definitive tissues and organs — **mer·i·ste·mat·ic** \,mer-ə-stə-'mat-ik\ *adj* — **mer·i·ste·mat·i·cal·ly** \-i-k(ə-)lē\ *adv*

me·ris·tic \mə-'ris-tik\ *adj* [Gk *meristos*] **1 :** SEGMENTAL **2 :** involving modification in number or in geometrical relation of body parts — **me·ris·ti·cal·ly** \-ti-k(ə-)lē\ *adv*

¹**mer·it** \'mer-ət\ *n* [ME, fr. OF *merite,* fr. L *meritum,* fr. neut. of *meritus,* pp. of *merēre* to deserve, earn; akin to Gk *meros* part, L *memor* mindful — more at MEMORY] **1 a** *obs* **:** reward or punishment due **b :** the qualities or actions that constitute the basis of one's deserts **c :** a praiseworthy quality **:** VIRTUE **d :** character or conduct deserving reward, honor, or esteem **2 :** spiritual credit held to be earned by performance of righteous acts and to ensure future benefits **3 a** *pl* **:** the intrinsic rights and wrongs of a legal case as determined by substance rather than form **b :** legal significance, standing, or importance

²**merit** *vt* **:** to be worthy of or entitled or liable to **:** EARN ~ *vi* **1** *obs* **:** to be entitled to reward or honor **2 :** DESERVE

mer·i·to·ri·ous \,mer-ə-'tōr-ē-əs, -'tȯr-\ *adj* **:** deserving of reward or honor — **mer·i·to·ri·ous·ly** *adv* — **mer·i·to·ri·ous·ness** *n*

merit system *n* **:** a system by which appointments and promotions in the civil service are based on competence rather than political favoritism

merl *or* **merle** \'mər(-ə)l\ *n* [MF *merle,* fr. L *merulus;* akin to OE *ōsle* blackbird, OHG *amsla*] **:** BLACKBIRD a

mer·lin \'mər-lən\ *n* [ME *meriloun,* fr. AF *merilun,* fr. OF *esmerillon,* aug. of *esmeril,* of Gmc origin; akin to OHG *smiril* merlin] **1 :** a small European falcon (*Falco aesalon*) related to the American pigeon hawk **2 :** a pigeon hawk (*Falco columbarius*)

Mer·lin \'mər-lən\ *n* [ML *Merlinus,* fr. W *Myrddin*] **:** a prophet and magician in Arthurian legend

mer·lon \'mər-lən\ *n* [F, fr. It *merlone,* aug. of *merlo* battlement, fr. ML *merulus,* fr. L, merl] **:** one of the solid intervals between crenels of a battlemented parapet

mer·maid \'mər-,mād\ *n* **:** a fabled marine creature usu. represented with a woman's body and a fish's tail

mer·man \-,man, -mən\ *n* **:** a fabled marine male creature usu. represented with a man's body and a fish's tail

mero·blas·tic \,mer-ə-'blas-tik\ *adj* [Gk *meros* part + ISV *-blastic*] *of an egg* **:** undergoing incomplete cleavage as a result of the presence of an impeding mass of yolk material — compare HOLOBLASTIC — **mero·blas·ti·cal·ly** \-ti-k(ə-)lē\ *adv*

mero·crine \'mer-ə-krən, -,krīn, -,krēn\ *adj* [ISV fr. Gk *meros* + *krinein* to separate — more at CERTAIN] **:** producing a secretion

that is discharged without major damage to the secreting cells; *also* : produced by a merocrine gland

mero·mor·phic function \ˌmer-ə-ˌmȯr-fik-\ *n* [Gk *meros* + E *-morphic*] : a function of a complex variable that is regular in a region except for a finite number of points at which it has infinity as limit

-m·er·ous \m-ə-rəs\ *adj comb form* [NL *-merus*, fr. Gk *-merēs*, fr. *meros* — more at MERIT] : having (such or so many) parts ⟨*dimerous*⟩ ⟨*polymerous*⟩

Mer·o·vin·gian \ˌmer-ə-ˈvin-j(ē-)ən\ *adj* [F *mérovingien*, fr. ML *Merovingi* Merovingians, fr. *Merovaeus* Merowig †458 Frankish founder of the dynasty] : of or relating to the first Frankish dynasty reigning from about A.D. 500 to 751 — **Merovingian** *n*

mer·ri·ly \ˈmer-ə-lē\ *adv* : in a merry manner : GAILY

mer·ri·ment \ˈmer-i-mənt\ *n* **1** : lighthearted gaiety or fun-making : HILARITY **2** : a gay celebration or party : FESTIVITY

mer·ry \ˈmer-ē\ *adj* [ME *mery*, fr. OE *myrge, merge;* akin to OHG *murg* short — more at BRIEF] **1** *archaic* : giving pleasure : DELIGHTFUL **2** : full of gaiety or high spirits : MIRTHFUL **3** : marked by festivity or gaiety **4** : BRISK, INTENSE ⟨a ~ pace⟩

syn BLITHE, JOCUND, JOVIAL, JOLLY: MERRY suggests cheerful, joyous, uninhibited enjoyment of frolic or festivity; BLITHE suggests freshness and lightheartedness as shown by singing, skipping, dancing; JOCUND stresses elation and exhilaration of spirits; JOVIAL suggests the stimulation of conviviality and good fellowship; JOLLY suggests high spirits expressed in laughing, bantering, and jesting

mer·ry–an·drew \ˌmer-ē-ˈan-(ˌ)drü\ *n, often cap M&A* [*merry* + *Andrew*, proper name] : one that clowns publicly : BUFFOON

mer·ry–go–round \ˈmer-ē-gō-ˌrau̇nd, -gə-\ *n* **1** : an amusement park ride with seats often in the form of animals (as horses) revolving about a fixed center **2** : a busy rapid round : WHIRL

mer·ry·mak·er \ˈmer-ē-ˌmā-kər\ *n* : one that shares in festivity or gaiety : REVELER

mer·ry·mak·ing \-kiŋ\ *n* **1** : gay or festive activity : CONVIVIALITY **2** : a convivial occasion : FESTIVITY

mer·ry·thought \-ˌthȯt\ *n, chiefly Brit* : WISHBONE

Mer·thi·o·late \(ˌ)mər-ˈthī-ə-ˌlāt, -lət\ *trademark* — used for thimerosal

mes- *or* **meso-** *comb form* [L, fr. Gk, fr. *mesos* — more at MID] **1** : mid : in the middle ⟨*meso*carp⟩ **2** : intermediate (as in size or type) ⟨*meso*morph⟩ ⟨*meson*⟩

me·sa \ˈmā-sə\ *n* [Sp, lit., table, fr. L *mensa*] : a usu. isolated hill having steeply sloping sides and a level top; *also* : a broad terrace with an abrupt slope on one side : BENCH

més·al·liance \ˌmā-ˌzal-ˈyäⁿs, ˌmā-zə-ˈlī-ən(t)s\ *n, pl* **més·al·liances** \-ˈyäⁿs(-əz), -ˈlī-ən-səz\ [F, fr. *més-* mis- + *alliance*] : a marriage with a person of inferior social position

mes·arch \ˈmez-ˌärk, ˈmes-\ *adj* : originating in a mesic habitat — used of an ecological succession

mes·cal \me-ˈskal, mə-\ *n* [Sp *mezcal*, fr. Nahuatl *mexcalli* mescal liquor] **1** : a small cactus (*Lophophora williamsii*) with rounded stems covered with jointed tubercles that are used as a stimulant and antispasmodic esp. among the Mexican Indians **2 a** : a usu. colorless Mexican liquor distilled esp. from the central leaves of maguey plants **b** : a plant from which mescal is produced; *esp* : MAGUEY

mescal button *n* : one of the dried discoid tops of the mescal

mes·ca·line \ˈmes-kə-ˌlēn\ *n* : a hallucinatory crystalline alkaloid $C_{11}H_{17}NO_3$ that is the chief active principle in mescal buttons

mesdames *pl of* MADAM *or of* MADAME

mesdemoiselles *pl of* MADEMOISELLE

me·seems \mi-ˈsēmz\ *vb impersonal, past* **me·seemed** \-ˈsēmd\ *archaic* : seems to me

me·sem·bry·an·the·mum \mə-ˌzem-brē-ˈan(t)-thə-məm\ *n* [NL, genus name, fr. Gk *mesēmbria* midday (fr. *mes-* + *hēmera* day) + *anthemon* flower, fr. *anthos* — more at HEMERA, ANTHOLOGY] : any of a genus (*Mesembryanthemum*) of chiefly southern African fleshy-leaved herbs or subshrubs of the carpetweed family

mes·en·ce·phal·ic \ˌmez-ˌen(t)-sə-ˈfal-ik, ˌmes-\ *adj* : of or relating to the midbrain

mes·en·ceph·a·lon \ˌmez-ˌen-ˈsef-ə-ˌlän, ˌmez-ᵊn-, ˌmes-, -lən\ *n* [NL] : the middle division of the brain : MIDBRAIN

mes·en·chy·mal \məz-ˈeŋ-kə-məl, məs-, -ˈen-; ˌmez-ᵊn-ˈkī-məl, ˌmes-\ *or* **mes·en·chym·a·tous** \ˌmez-ᵊn-ˈkim-ət-əs, ˌmes-\ *adj* [ISV] : of, resembling, or being mesenchyme

mes·en·chyme \ˈmez-ᵊn-ˌkīm, ˈmes-\ *n* [G *mesenchym*, fr. *mes-* + NL *-enchyma*] : a loosely organized mesodermal connective tissue comprising all the mesoblast except the mesothelium and giving rise to such structures as connective tissues, blood, lymphatics, bone, and cartilage

mes·en·ter·ic \ˌmes-ᵊn-ˈter-ik, ˌmez-\ *adj* : of, relating to, or located in or near a mesentery

mes·en·ter·on \(ˈ)mez-ˈent-ə-ˌrän, (ˈ)mes-, -rən\ *n, pl* **mes·en·tera** \-ə-rə\ [NL] : the part of the alimentary canal that is developed from the archenteron and is lined with hypoblast — **mes·en·ter·on·ic** \ˌmez-ˌent-ə-ˈrän-ik, ˌmes-\ *adj*

mes·en·tery \ˈmes-ᵊn-ˌter-ē, ˈmez-\ *n* [NL *mesenterium*, fr. MF & Gk; MF *mesentere*, fr. Gk *mesenterion*, fr. *mes-* + *enteron* intestine — more at INTER-] **1 a** : the vertebrate membranes or one of the membranes that consist of a double fold of the peritoneum and invest the intestines and their appendages and connect them with the dorsal wall of the abdominal cavity **b** : a comparable fold of membrane supporting a viscus that is not a part of the digestive tract **2** : a support or partition in an invertebrate like the vertebrate mesentery

¹mesh \ˈmesh\ *n* [prob. fr. obs. D *maesche;* akin to OHG *masca* mesh, Lith *mazgos* knot] **1** : one of the openings between the threads or cords of a net; *also* : one of the similar spaces in a network — often used to designate screen size as the number of openings per linear inch **2 a** : the fabric of a net **b** : a woven, knit, or knotted fabric of open texture with evenly spaced small holes **c** : an arrangement of interlocking metal links used esp. for jewelry **3 a** : an interlocking or intertwining arrangement or construction : NETWORK **b** : WEB, SNARE — usu. used in pl. **4** : working contact (as of the teeth of gears) ⟨in ~⟩

²mesh *vt* **1 a** : to catch in the openings of a net **b** : ENMESH, ENTANGLE **2 a** : to provide with a mesh **b** : to cause to resemble network **3 a** : to cause to engage **b** : to coordinate closely : INTERLOCK ~ *vi* **1** : to become entangled in or as if in meshes **2** : to be in or come into mesh — used esp. of gears **3** : to fit together properly : COORDINATE

mesh·work \ˈmesh-ˌwərk\ *n* : MESHES, NETWORK

me·sial \ˈmez-ē-əl, ˈmē-, ˈmes-, ˈmēs-; ˈmē-zhəl, -shəl\ *adj* : MIDDLE; *esp* : dividing an animal into right and left halves — **me·sial·ly** \-ē\ *adv*

me·sic \ˈmez-ik, ˈmēz-, ˈmes-, ˈmēs-\ *adj, of a habitat* : moderately moist — **me·si·cal·ly** \-i-k(ə-)lē\ *adv*

me·sit·y·lene \mə-ˈsit-ᵊl-ˌēn\ *n* [*mesityl* (the radical C_3H_5)] : an oily hydrocarbon C_9H_{12} that is found in coal tar and petroleum or made synthetically and is a powerful solvent

mes·mer·ic \mez-ˈmer-ik, me-ˈsmer-\ *adj* **1** : of, relating to, or induced by mesmerism **2** : FASCINATING, IRRESISTIBLE — **mes·mer·i·cal·ly** \-i-k(ə-)lē\ *adv*

mes·mer·ism \ˈmez-mə-ˌriz-əm, ˈmes-\ *n* [F. A. *Mesmer* †1815 Austrian physician] **1** : hypnotic induction held to involve animal magnetism; *broadly* : HYPNOTISM **2** : hypnotic appeal — **mes·mer·ist** \-rəst\ *n*

mes·mer·ize \ˈmez-mə-ˌrīz, ˈmes-\ *vt* **1** : to subject to mesmerism **2** : SPELLBIND, FASCINATE — **mes·mer·iz·er** *n*

mesne \ˈmēn\ *adj* [AF, alter. of MF *meien* — more at MEAN] : MIDDLE, INTERVENING; *specif* : intermediate in time of occurrence or performance

mesne lord *n* : a feudal lord who holds land as tenant of a superior but is lord to his own tenant

meso·blast \ˈmez-ə-ˌblast, ˈmes-\ *n* : the middle germ layer of an embryo — **meso·blas·tic** \ˌmez-ə-ˈblas-tik, ˌmes-\ *adj*

meso·carp \ˈmez-ə-ˌkärp, ˈmes-\ *n* : the middle layer of a pericarp — **meso·car·pic** \ˌmez-ə-ˈkär-pik, ˌmes-\ *adj*

meso·derm \ˈmez-ə-ˌdərm, ˈmes-\ *n* [ISV] : MESOBLAST; *broadly* : tissue derived from this germ layer — **meso·der·mal** \ˌmez-ə-ˈdər-məl, ˌmes-\ *or* **meso·der·mic** \-mik\ *adj*

meso·glea *or* **meso·gloea** \ˌmez-ə-ˈglē-ə, ˌmes-\ *n* [NL, fr. *mes-* + LGk *gloia, glia* glue — more at CLAY] : a gelatinous substance between the endoderm and ectoderm of sponges or coelenterates — **meso·gloe·al** \-ˈglē-əl\ *adj*

Meso·lith·ic \-ˈlith-ik\ *adj* [ISV] : of or relating to a transitional period of the Stone Age between the Paleolithic and the Neolithic

meso·mere \ˈmez-ə-ˌmi(ə)r, ˈmes-\ *n* **1** : a primitive segment of an embryo **2** : a blastomere of medium size

me·som·er·ism \mə-ˈzäm-ə-ˌriz-əm, -ˈsäm-\ *n* : RESONANCE 4

meso·morph \ˈmez-ə-ˌmȯrf, ˈmes-\ *n* : an intermediate or average type of human body

meso·mor·phic \ˌmez-ə-ˈmȯr-fik, ˌmes-\ *adj* : characterized by predominance of the structures developed from the mesodermal layer of the embryo : of the muscular or athletic type of body-build — **meso·mor·phism** \-ˌfiz-əm\ *n* — **meso·mor·phy** \ˈmez-ə-ˌmȯr-fē, ˈmes-\ *n*

me·son \ˈmez-ˌän, ˈmēz-, ˈmes-, ˈmēs-\ *n* [ISV *mes-* + *-on*] : an unstable nuclear particle first observed in cosmic rays that has a mass typically between that of the electron and the proton, that is either positively or negatively charged or neutral, and that occurs in more than one variety — **me·son·ic** \me-ˈzän-ik, mē-, -ˈsän-\ *adj*

meso·neph·ric \ˌmez-ə-ˈnef-rik, ˌmes-\ *adj* : of or relating to the mesonephros

meso·neph·ros \-ˈnef-rəs, -ˌräs\ *n, pl* **meso·neph·roi** \-ˌrȯi\ [NL, fr. *mes-* + Gk *nephros* kidney — more at NEPHRITIS] : one of the middle of the three pairs of embryonic renal organs of higher vertebrates

meso·phyll \ˈmez-ə-ˌfil, ˈmes-\ *n* [NL *mesophyllum*, fr. *mes-* + Gk *phyllon* leaf — more at BLADE] : the parenchyma between the epidermal layers of a foliage leaf — **meso·phyl·lic** \ˌmez-ə-ˈfil-ik, ˌmes-\ *adj* — **meso·phyl·lous** \-ˈfil-əs\ *adj*

meso·phyte \ˈmez-ə-ˌfīt, ˈmes-\ *n* [ISV] : a plant that grows under medium conditions of moisture — **meso·phyt·ic** \ˌmez-ə-ˈfit-ik, ˌmes-\ *adj*

meso·sphere \ˈmez-ə-ˌsfi(ə)r, ˈmes-\ *n* : a layer of the atmosphere extending from the top of the stratosphere to an altitude of about 50 miles — **meso·spher·ic** \ˌmez-ə-ˈsfi(ə)r-ik, ˌmes-, -ˈsfer-\ *adj*

meso·the·li·al \ˌmez-ə-ˈthē-lē-əl, ˌmes-\ *adj* : of, relating to, or being mesothelium

meso·the·li·um \-lē-əm\ *n, pl* **meso·the·lia** \-lē-ə\ [NL, fr. *mes-* + *epithelium*] : epithelium derived from mesoderm that lines the body cavity of a vertebrate embryo and gives rise to epithelia (as of the peritoneum, pericardium, and pleurae), striated and heart muscle, and several minor structures

meso·tho·rax \ˌmez-ə-ˈthō(ə)r-ˌaks, -ˈthȯ(ə)r-\ *n* [NL] : the middle of the three segments of the thorax of an insect

meso·tho·ri·um \-ˈthōr-ē-əm, -ˈthȯr-\ *n* [NL] : either of two radioactive products intermediate between thorium and radiothorium **a** : an isotope of radium — called also *mesothorium 1* **b** : an isotope of actinium — called also *mesothorium 2*

meso·tron \ˈmez-ə-ˌträn, ˈmes-\ *n* [*mes-* + *electron*] : MESON — **meso·tron·ic** \ˌmez-ə-ˈträn-ik, ˌmes-\ *adj*

Meso·zo·ic \ˌmez-ə-ˈzō-ik, ˌmes-\ *adj* : of, relating to, or being an era of geological history including the interval between the Permian and the Tertiary and marked by the dinosaurs, marine and flying reptiles, ganoid fishes, cycads, and evergreen trees; *also* : relating to the system of rocks formed in this era — **Mesozoic** *n*

mes·quite \mə-ˈskēt, me-\ *n* [Sp, fr. Nahuatl *mizquitl*] : a spiny deep-rooted leguminous tree or shrub (*Prosopis juliflora*) of the southwestern U.S. and Mexico bearing pods rich in sugar and important as a livestock feed and forming extensive thickets

¹mess \ˈmes\ *n* [ME *mes*, fr. OF, fr. LL *missus* course at a meal, fr. *missus*, pp. of *mittere* to put, fr. L, to send — more at SMITE] **1** : a quantity of food: **a** *archaic* : food set on a table at one time **b** : a prepared dish of soft food; *also* : a mixture of ingredients cooked or eaten together **c** : enough food of a specified kind for a dish or a meal **2** : a group of persons who regularly take their meals together; *also* : a meal so taken **3** : a confused, dirty, or offensive state or condition : JUMBLE

²mess *vt* **1 a** : to assign to a mess **b** : to supply with meals **2** : to make dirty or untidy : DISARRANGE; *also* : BUNGLE **3** : to interfere

with **4 :** to rough up **:** MANHANDLE **~** *vi* **1 :** to prepare food for and serve messes **2 :** to take meals with a mess **3 :** to make a mess **4 a :** PUTTER, TRIFLE **b :** INTERFERE, MEDDLE

¹mes·sage \'mes-ij\ *n* [ME, fr. OF, fr. ML *missaticum*, fr. L *missus*, pp. of *mittere*] **1 :** a communication in writing, in speech, or by signals **2 :** a messenger's errand or function

²message *vt* **1 :** to send as a message or by messenger **2 :** to order or instruct by message **~** *vi* **:** to communicate by message

mes·sa·line \,mes-ə-'lēn\ *n* [F] **:** a lightweight silk dress fabric with a warp satin weave

mes·san \'mes-ᵊn\ *n* [ScGael *measan*] *chiefly Scot* **:** LAPDOG

mes·sen·ger \'mes-ᵊn-jər\ *n* [ME *messangere*, fr. OF *messagier*, fr. *message*] **1 :** one who bears a message or does an errand: as **a** *obs* **:** FORERUNNER, HERALD **b :** a dispatch bearer in government or military service **c :** an employee who carries messages **2 :** a light line used in hauling a heavier line (as between ships)

mes·si·ah \mə-'sī-ə\ *n* [Heb *māshīaḥ* & Aram *mĕshīḥā*, lit., anointed] **1** *cap* **a :** the expected king and deliverer of the Jews **b :** JESUS 1 **2 :** a professed or accepted leader of some hope or cause — **mes·si·ah·ship** \-,ship\ *n* — **mes·si·an·ic** \,mes-ē-'an-ik\ *adj* — **mes·si·a·nism** \mə-'sī-ə-,niz-əm\ *n*

Mes·si·as \mə-'sī-əs\ *n* [ME, fr. LL, fr. Gk, fr. Aram *mĕshīḥā*] **:** MESSIAH 1

messieurs *pl of* MONSIEUR

mess·i·ly \'mes-ə-lē\ *adv* **:** in a messy manner

mess·i·ness \'mes-ē-nəs\ *n* **:** the quality or state of being messy

mess jacket *n* **:** a man's short tight jacket

mess kit *n* **:** a kit consisting of a metal dish and eating utensils for use by soldiers and campers

Messrs \,mes-ərz\ — used as a plural for the title *Mister* ⟨~ Jones, Brown, and Robinson⟩

mes·suage \'mes-wij\ *n* [ME, fr. AF, prob. alter. of OF *mesnage* — more at MENAGE] **:** a dwelling house with the adjacent buildings and curtilage and the adjoining lands used in connection with the household

messy \'mes-ē\ *adj* **:** marked by confusion, disorder, or dirt **:** UNTIDY

mes·ti·za \me-'stē-zə, mə-\ *n* [Sp, fem. of *mestizo*] **:** a female mestizo

mes·ti·zo \-(,)zō\ *n* [Sp, fr. *mestizo* mixed, fr. LL *mixticius*, fr. L *mixtus*, pp. of *miscēre* to mix — more at MIX] **:** a person of mixed blood; *specif* **:** a person of mixed European and American Indian ancestry

met *past of* MEET

meta- *or* **met-** *comb form* [NL & ML, fr. L or Gk; L, change, fr. Gk, among, with, after, change, fr. *meta* among, with, after; akin to OE *mid*, *mith* with, OHG *mit*] **1 a :** occurring later than or in succession to **:** after ⟨*met*estrus⟩ **b :** situated behind or beyond ⟨*met*encephalon⟩ ⟨*meta*carpus⟩ **c :** later or more highly organized or specialized form of ⟨*Meta*zoa⟩ **2 :** change **:** transformation **3 :** more comprehensive **:** transcending ⟨*meta*psychology⟩ — used with the name of a discipline to designate a new but related discipline designed to deal critically with the original one ⟨*meta*language⟩ **4 a :** isomeric with or otherwise closely related to ⟨*met*aldehyde⟩ **b :** involving substitution at or characterized by two positions in the benzene ring that are separated by one carbon atom **c :** derived from by loss of water ⟨*meta*phosphoric acid⟩

met·a·bol·ic \,met-ə-'bäl-ik\ *adj* **1 :** of, relating to, or based on metabolism **2 a :** undergoing metamorphosis **b :** VEGETATIVE 1a — **met·a·bol·i·cal** \-i-kəl\ *adj* — **met·a·bol·i·cal·ly** \-i-k(ə-)lē\ *adv*

me·tab·o·lism \mə-'tab-ə-,liz-əm\ *n* [ISV, fr. Gk *metabolē* change, fr. *metaballein* to change, fr. *meta-* + *ballein* to throw — more at DEVIL] **1 a :** the sum of the processes in the building up and destruction of protoplasm incidental to life; *specif* **:** the chemical changes in living cells by which energy is provided for vital processes and activities and new material is assimilated to repair the waste **b :** the sum of the processes by which a particular substance is handled in the living body **2 :** METAMORPHOSIS 2

me·tab·o·lite \-,līt\ *n* **:** a product of metabolism

me·tab·o·lize \-,līz\ *vt* **:** to subject to metabolism **~** *vi* **:** to perform metabolism

¹meta·car·pal \,met-ə-'kär-pəl\ *adj* **:** of or relating to the metacarpus

²metacarpal *n* **:** a metacarpal bone

meta·car·pus \,met-ə-'kär-pəs\ *n* [NL] **:** the part of the hand or forefoot between the carpus and the phalanges

meta·cen·ter \'met-ə-,sent-ər\ *n* [F *métacentre*, fr. *méta-* meta- + *centre* center] **:** the point of intersection of the vertical through the center of buoyancy of a floating body with the vertical through the new center of buoyancy when the body is displaced

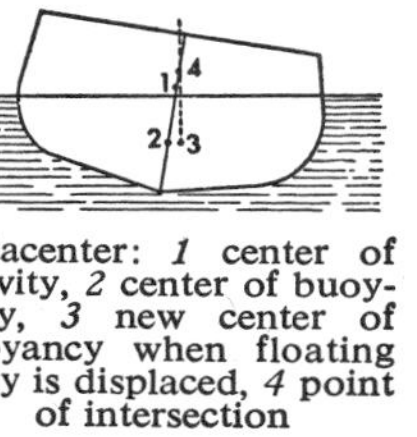

metacenter: *1* center of gravity, *2* center of buoyancy, *3* new center of buoyancy when floating body is displaced, *4* point of intersection

meta·cer·car·ia \,met-ə-(,)sər-'kar-ē-ə, -'ker-\ *n* [NL] **:** a tailless encysted late larva of a digenetic trematode that is usu. the form which is infective for the definitive host

meta·ga·lac·tic \-gə-'lak-tik\ *adj* [ISV] **:** of or relating to the metagalaxy

meta·gal·axy \-'gal-ək-sē\ *n* [ISV] **:** the entire system of galaxies external to our own galaxy **:** UNIVERSE

meta·gen·e·sis \-'jen-ə-səs\ *n* [NL] **:** alternation of generations esp. of a sexual and an asexual generation — **meta·ge·net·ic** \-jə-'net-ik\ *adj* — **meta·ge·net·i·cal·ly** \-i-k(ə-)lē\ *adv*

¹met·al \'met-ᵊl\ *n, often attrib* [ME, fr. OF, fr. L *metallum* mine, metal, fr. Gk *metallon*] **1 :** any of various opaque, fusible, ductile, and typically lustrous substances; *esp* **:** one that is a chemical element as distinguished from an alloy **2 a :** METTLE **b :** the material or substance out of which a person or thing is made **3 :** glass in its molten state **4 a :** printing type metal **b :** set type matter — **met·al·ware** \'met-ᵊl-,wa(ə)r, -,we(ə)r\ *n*

²metal *vt* **met·aled** *or* **met·alled**; **met·al·ing** *or* **met·al·ling** **:** to cover or furnish with metal

me·tal·lic \mə-'tal-ik\ *adj* **1 a :** of, relating to, or being a metal **b :** made of or containing a metal **c :** having properties of a metal **2 :** yielding metal **3 :** resembling metal **4 :** HARSH, GRATING — **me·tal·li·cal·ly** \-i-k(ə-)lē\ *adv*

met·al·lif·er·ous \,met-ᵊl-'if-(ə-)rəs\ *adj* [L *metallifer*, fr. *metallum* + *-fer* -ferous] **:** yielding or containing metal

met·al·lize *also* **met·al·ize** \'met-ᵊl-,īz\ *vt* **1 :** to treat or combine with a metal **2 :** MINERALIZE

met·al·log·ra·pher \,met-ᵊl-'äg-rə-fər\ *n* **:** a specialist in metallography

me·tal·lo·graph·ic \mə-,tal-ə-'graf-ik\ *adj* **:** of, relating to, or produced by means of metallography — **me·tal·lo·graph·i·cal·ly** \-i-k(ə-)lē\ *adv*

met·al·log·ra·phy \,met-ᵊl-'äg-rə-fē\ *n* [F *métallographie*, fr. L *metallum* + F *-graphie* -graphy] **:** a study of the structure of metals esp. with the microscope

¹met·al·loid \'met-ᵊl-,ȯid\ *n* [L *metallum*] **1 :** NONMETAL; *esp* **:** one that can combine with a metal to form an alloy **2 :** an element intermediate in properties between the typical metals and nonmetals

²metalloid *also* **met·al·loi·dal** \,met-ᵊl-'ȯid-ᵊl\ *adj* **1 :** resembling a metal **2 :** of, relating to, or being a metalloid

met·al·lur·gi·cal \,met-ᵊl-'ər-ji-kəl\ *adj* **:** of or relating to metallurgy — **met·al·lur·gi·cal·ly** \-ji-k(ə-)lē\ *adv*

met·al·lur·gist \'met-ᵊl-,ər-jəst\ *n* **:** a specialist in the science or application of metallurgy

met·al·lur·gy \-jē\ *n* [NL *metallurgia*, fr. Gk *metallon* + NL *-urgia* -urgy] **:** the science and technology of metals

met·al·work \'met-ᵊl-,wərk\ *n* **:** the product of metalworking — **met·al·work·er** \-,wər-kər\ *n*

met·al·work·ing \-,wər-kiŋ\ *n* **:** the act or process of shaping things out of metal

meta·mere \'met-ə-,mi(ə)r\ *n* [ISV] **:** any of a linear series of primitively similar segments into which the body of a higher invertebrate or vertebrate is divisible — **meta·mer·ic** \,met-ə-'mer-ik, -'mi(ə)r-\ *adj* — **meta·mer·i·cal·ly** \-i-k(ə-)lē\ *adv* — **me·tam·er·ism** \mə-'tam-ə-,riz-əm\ *n*

meta·mor·phic \,met-ə-'mȯr-fik\ *adj* **1 :** of or relating to metamorphosis **2** *of a rock* **:** of, relating to, or produced by metamorphism

meta·mor·phism \-'mȯr-,fiz-əm\ *n* **1 :** METAMORPHOSIS **2 :** a change in the constitution of rock; *specif* **:** a pronounced change effected by pressure, heat, and water that results in a more compact and more highly crystalline condition

meta·mor·phose \-,fōz, -,fōs\ *vb* [prob. fr. MF *metamorphoser*, fr. *metamorphose* metamorphosis, fr. L *metamorphosis*] *vt* **1 a :** to change into a different physical form esp. by supernatural means **b :** to change strikingly the appearance or character of **:** TRANSFORM **2 :** to cause (rock) to undergo metamorphism **~** *vi* **:** to undergo metamorphosis **syn** see TRANSFORM

meta·mor·pho·sis \-'mȯr-fə-səs\ *n* [L, fr. Gk *metamorphōsis*, fr. *metamorphoun* to transform, fr. *meta-* + *morphē* form] **1 a :** change of physical form, structure, or substance esp. by supernatural means **b :** a striking alteration in appearance, character, or circumstances **2 :** a marked and more or less abrupt change in the form or structure of an animal occurring subsequent to birth or hatching

meta·neph·ric \-'nef-rik\ *adj* **:** of or relating to the metanephros

meta·neph·ros \-'nef-rəs, -,räs\ *n, pl* **meta·neph·roi** \-,rȯi\ [NL, fr. *meta-* + Gk *nephros* kidney — more at NEPHRITIS] **:** one of the posterior of the three pairs of embryonic renal organs of higher vertebrates persisting as the definitive kidney

meta·phase \'met-ə-,fāz\ *n* [ISV] **:** the stage of mitosis preceding the anaphase

met·a·phor \'met-ə-,fȯ(ə)r, -fər\ *n* [MF or L; MF, *metaphore*, fr. L *metaphora*, fr. Gk, fr. *metapherein* to transfer, fr. *meta-* + *pherein* to bear — more at BEAR] **:** a figure of speech in which a word or phrase literally denoting one kind of object or idea is used in place of another to suggest a likeness or analogy between them (as in *the ship plows the sea*); *broadly* **:** figurative language — **met·a·phor·i·cal** \,met-ə-'fȯr-i-kəl, -'fär-\ *adj* — **met·a·phor·i·cal·ly** \-i-k(ə-)lē\ *adv*

meta·phos·phate \,met-ə-'fäs-,fāt\ *n* [ISV] **:** a salt or ester of a metaphosphoric acid

meta·phos·pho·ric acid \-,fäs-,fȯr-ik-, -,fär-; -,fäs-f(ə-)rik-\ *n* **:** a glassy solid acid HPO_3 or $(HPO_3)_n$ formed by heating orthophosphoric acid

meta·phys·ic \,met-ə-'fiz-ik\ *n* [ME *metaphesyk*, fr. ML *Metaphysica*] **1 a :** METAPHYSICS **b :** a particular system of metaphysics **2 :** the system of principles underlying a particular study or subject — **metaphysic** *adj*

meta·phys·i·cal \,met-ə-'fiz-i-kəl\ *adj* **1 :** of or relating to metaphysics **2 a :** of or relating to the transcendent or supersensible **b :** SUPERNATURAL **3 :** highly abstract or abstruse **4 :** of or relating to poetry esp. of the early 17th century that is marked by elaborate subtleties of thought and expression — **meta·phys·i·cal·ly** \-i-k(ə-)lē\ *adv*

meta·phy·si·cian \-fə-'zish-ən\ *n* **:** a student of or specialist in metaphysics

meta·phys·ics \,met-ə-'fiz-iks\ *n pl but sing or pl in constr* [ML *Metaphysica*, title of Aristotle's treatise on the subject, fr. Gk (*ta*) *meta* (*ta*) *physika*, lit., the (works) after the physical (works); fr. its position in his collected works] **1 a** (1) **:** a division of philosophy that includes ontology and cosmology (2) **:** philosophy made up of ontology and epistemology (3) **:** ONTOLOGY **b :** the more abstruse philosophical sciences **2 :** METAPHYSIC 2

meta·pla·sia \,met-ə-'plā-zh(ē-)ə\ *n* [NL] **1 :** transformation of one tissue into another **2 :** abnormal replacement of cells of one type by cells of another — **meta·plas·tic** \-'plas-tik\ *adj*

meta·plasm \'met-ə-,plaz-əm\ *n* **1** [L *metaplasmus*, lit., transformation, fr. Gk *metaplasmos*, fr. *metaplassein* to remold, fr. *meta-* + *plassein* to mold — more at PLASTER] **:** alteration of regular structure usu. by transposition of the letters or syllables of a word or of the words in a sentence **2** [ISV] **:** material consisting of lifeless derivatives of protoplasm — **meta·plas·mic** \,met-ə-'plaz-mik\ *adj*

meta·pro·tein \,met-ə-'prō-,tēn, -'prōt-ē-ən\ *n* **:** any of various products derived from proteins through the action of acids or alkalies by which the solubility and sometimes the composition of the proteins is changed

meta·psy·cho·log·i·cal \,met-ə-,sī-kə-'läj-i-kəl\ *adj* **:** of or relating to metapsychology

meta·psy·chol·o·gy \-,sī-'käl-ə-jē\ *n* [ISV] **:** a theory that aims to supplement the facts and empirical laws of psychology by specu-

lations on the connection of mental and physical processes or on the place of mind in the universe

meta·se·quoia \-si-ˈkwȯi-ə\ *n* [NL, genus name, fr. *meta-* + *Sequoia*] **:** any of a genus (*Metasequoia*) of fossil and living deciduous coniferous trees of the pine family

meta·so·mat·ic \-sō-ˈmat-ik\ *adj* **:** of or relating to metasomatism

meta·so·ma·tism \-ˈsō-mə-ˌtiz-əm\ *n* [*meta-* + Gk *sōmat-*, *sōma* body — more at SOMAT-] **:** metamorphism that involves changes in the chemical composition as well as in the texture of rock

meta·sta·ble \ˌmet-ə-ˈstā-bəl\ *adj* [ISV] **:** marked by only a slight margin of stability ⟨a ~ compound⟩

me·tas·ta·sis \mə-ˈtas-tə-səs\ *n, pl* **me·tas·ta·ses** \-tə-ˌsēz\ [NL, fr. LL, transition, fr. Gk, fr. *methistanai* to change, fr. *meta-* + *histanai* to set — more at STAND] **:** change of position, state, or form: as **a :** transfer of a disease-producing agency from the site of disease to another part of the body **b :** a secondary metastatic growth of a malignant tumor — **met·a·stat·ic** \ˌmet-ə-ˈstat-ik\ *adj* — **met·a·stat·i·cal·ly** \-i-k(ə-)lē\ *adv*

me·tas·ta·size \mə-ˈtas-tə-ˌsīz\ *vi* **:** to spread by metastasis

1**meta·tar·sal** \ˌmet-ə-ˈtär-səl\ *adj* **:** of or relating to the metatarsus — **meta·tar·sal·ly** \-sə-lē\ *adv*

2**metatarsal** *n* **:** a metatarsal bone

meta·tar·sus \ˌmet-ə-ˈtär-səs\ *n* [NL] **:** the part of the foot in man or of the hind foot in quadrupeds between the tarsus and phalanges

me·tath·e·sis \mə-ˈtath-ə-səs\ *n, pl* **me·tath·e·ses** \-ə-ˌsēz\ [Gk, fr. *metatithenai* to transpose, fr. *meta-* + *tithenai* to place — more at DO] **:** a change of place or condition; *specif* **:** transposition of two phonemes in a word (as in Old English *wæsp, wæps*) — **met·a·thet·i·cal** \ˌmet-ə-ˈthet-i-kəl\ *or* **met·a·thet·ic** \-ik\ *adj* — **met·a·thet·i·cal·ly** \-i-k(ə-)lē\ *adv*

meta·tho·rax \ˌmet-ə-ˈthō(ə)r-ˌaks, -ˈthȯ(ə)r-\ *n* [NL] **:** the posterior segment of the thorax of an insect

meta·zo·al \ˌmet-ə-ˈzō-əl\ *adj* [NL *Metazoa*] **:** METAZOAN

meta·zo·an \-ˈzō-ən\ *n* [NL *Metazoa*, group name, fr. *meta-* + *-zoa*] **:** any of a group (*Metazoa*) that comprises all animals having the body composed of cells differentiated into tissues and organs and usu. a digestive cavity lined with specialized cells — **metazoan** *adj*

1**mete** \ˈmēt\ *vt* [ME *meten*, fr. OE *metan*; akin to OHG *mezzan* to measure, L *modus* measure, *meditari* to meditate] **1** *archaic* **:** MEASURE **2 :** to assign by measure **:** ALLOT

2**mete** *n* [AF, fr. L *meta*] **:** BOUNDARY ⟨~*s* and bounds⟩

me·tem·psy·cho·sis \mə-ˌtem(p)-si-ˈkō-səs, ˌmet-əm-ˌsī-\ *n* [LL, fr. Gk *metempsychōsis*, fr. *metempsychousthai* to undergo metempsychosis, fr. *meta-* + *empsychos* animate, fr. *en-* + *psychē* soul — more at PSYCHE] **:** the passing of the soul at death into another body either human or animal

met·en·ce·phal·ic \ˌmet-ˌen(t)-sə-ˈfal-ik\ *adj* **:** of or relating to the metencephalon

met·en·ceph·a·lon \ˌmet-ˌen-ˈsef-ə-ˌlän, -lən\ *n* [NL] **1 :** the anterior segment of the rhombencephalon **2 :** the cerebellum and pons that evolve from this segment

me·te·or \ˈmēt-ē-ər, -ē-ˌȯ(ə)r\ *n* [ME, fr. MF *meteore*, fr. ML *meteorum*, fr. Gk *meteōron* phenomenon in the sky, fr. neut. of *meteōros* high in air, fr. *meta-* + *-eōros* (akin to Gk *aeirein* to lift)] **1 :** a phenomenon or appearance in the atmosphere (as lightning, a rainbow, or a snowfall) **2 a :** one of the small particles of matter in the solar system observable directly only when it falls into the earth's atmosphere where friction may cause its temporary incandescence **b :** the streak of light produced by the passage of a meteor

me·te·or·ic \ˌmēt-ē-ˈȯr-ik, -ˈär-\ *adj* **1 :** of, relating to, or derived from the earth's atmosphere **2 :** of, relating to, or resembling a meteor — **me·te·or·i·cal·ly** \-i-k(ə-)lē\ *adv*

me·te·or·ite \ˈmēt-ē-ə-ˌrīt\ *n* **:** a meteor that reaches the surface of the earth without being completely vaporized — **me·te·or·it·ic** \ˌmēt-ē-ə-ˈrit-ik\ *adj* — **me·te·or·it·i·cal** \-i-kəl\ *adj*

me·te·or·it·ics \ˌmēt-ē-ə-ˈrit-iks\ *n pl but sing in constr* **:** a science that deals with meteors

me·te·or·o·graph \-ˈȯr-ə-ˌgraf, -ˈär-\ *n* **:** an autographic apparatus for recording simultaneously several meteorologic elements — **me·te·or·o·graph·ic** \-ˌȯr-ə-ˈgraf-ik, -ˌär-\ *adj*

me·te·or·oid \ˈmēt-ē-ə-ˌrȯid\ *n* **1 :** a meteor revolving around the sun **2 :** a meteor particle itself without relation to the phenomena it produces when entering the earth's atmosphere

me·te·o·ro·log·i·cal \ˌmēt-ē-ˌȯr-ə-ˈläj-i-kəl, -ˌär-ə-, -ə-rə-\ *also* **me·te·o·ro·log·ic** \-ˈläj-ik\ *adj* **:** of or relating to meteorology — **me·te·o·ro·log·i·cal·ly** \-i-k(ə-)lē\ *adv*

me·te·o·rol·o·gist \ˌmēt-ē-ə-ˈräl-ə-jəst\ *n* **:** a specialist in meteorology

me·te·o·rol·o·gy \-jē\ *n* [F or Gk; F *météorologie*, fr. MF, fr. Gk *meteōrologia*, fr. *meteōron* + *-logia* -logy] **1 :** a science that deals with the atmosphere and its phenomena and esp. with weather and weather forecasting **2 :** the atmospheric phenomena and weather of a region

meteor shower *also* **meteoric shower** *n* **:** the phenomenon observed when members of a group of meteors encounter the earth's atmosphere and their luminous paths appear to diverge from a single point

1**me·ter** *or chiefly Brit* **me·tre** \ˈmēt-ər\ *n* [ME, fr. OE & MF; OE *mēter*, fr. L *metrum*, fr. Gk *metron* measure, meter; MF *metre*, fr. OF, fr. L *metrum* — more at MEASURE] **1 a :** systematically arranged and measured rhythm in verse: (1) **:** rhythm that continuously repeats a single basic pattern ⟨iambic ~⟩ (2) **:** rhythm characterized by regular recurrence in larger figures ⟨ballad ~⟩ **b :** a measure or unit of metrical verse — usu. used in combination and pronounced \m-ət-ər\ ⟨penta*meter*⟩; compare FOOT **c :** a fixed metrical pattern **:** verse form **2 :** the basic recurrent rhythmical pattern of note values, accents, and beats per measure in music

2**met·er** \ˈmēt-ər\ *n* [ME, fr. *meten* to mete] **:** one that measures; *esp* **:** an official measurer of commodities

3**me·ter** *or chiefly Brit* **me·tre** \ˈmēt-ər\ *n* [F *mètre*, fr. Gk *metron* measure] **:** the basic metric unit of length — see METRIC SYSTEM table

4**me·ter** *n* [*-meter*] **1 :** an instrument for measuring and sometimes recording the amount of something **2 :** a philatelic cover bearing an impression of a postage meter

5**me·ter** *vt* **1 :** to measure by means of a meter **2 :** to supply in a measured or regulated amount **3 :** to print postal indicia on by means of a postage meter

-me·ter \m-ət-ər, *in some words* ˌmēt-\ *n comb form* [F *-mètre*, fr. Gk *metron* measure] **:** instrument or means for measuring ⟨baro*meter*⟩

meter-kilogram-second *adj* **:** of, relating to, or being a system of units based on the meter as the unit of length, the kilogram as the unit of mass, and the mean solar second as the unit of time

met·es·trus \(ˈ)met-ˈes-trəs\ *n* [NL] **:** the period of regression that follows estrus

meth- *or* **metho-** *comb form* [ISV, fr. *methyl*] **:** methyl ⟨*meth*acrylic⟩

meth·ac·ry·late \(ˈ)meth-ˈak-rə-ˌlāt\ *n* [ISV] **1 :** a salt or ester of methacrylic acid **2 :** an acrylic resin or plastic made from a derivative of methacrylic acid

meth·acryl·ic acid \ˌmeth-ə-ˌkril-ik-\ *n* [ISV] **:** an unsaturated acid $C_4H_6O_2$ usu. obtained by reaction of acetone cyanohydrin and sulfuric acid and used in making acrylic resins or plastics

meth·a·done \ˈmeth-ə-ˌdōn\ *or* **meth·a·don** \-ˌdän\ *n* [6-di*methyl*amino-4, 4-diphenyl-3-heptan*one*] **:** a synthetic addictive narcotic drug $C_{21}H_{27}NO$ used esp. in the form of its hydrochloride for the relief of pain

meth·ane \ˈmeth-ˌān\ *n* [ISV] **:** a colorless odorless flammable gaseous hydrocarbon CH_4 that is a product of decomposition of organic matter in marshes and mines or of the carbonization of coal and is used as a fuel and as a raw material in chemical synthesis

methane series *n* **:** a homologous series of saturated open-chain hydrocarbons C_nH_{2n+2} of which methane is the first and lowest member

meth·a·nol \ˈmeth-ə-ˌnȯl, -ˌnōl\ *n* [ISV] **:** a light volatile flammable poisonous liquid alcohol CH_3OH formed in the destructive distillation of wood or made synthetically and used esp. as a solvent, antifreeze, or denaturant for ethyl alcohol and in the synthesis of other chemicals — **meth·a·no·lic** \ˌmeth-ə-ˈnō-lik\ *adj*

me·theg·lin \mə-ˈtheg-lən\ *n* [W *meddyglyn*] **:** a beverage usu. made of fermented honey and water **:** MEAD

met·he·mo·glo·bin \(ˈ)met-ˈhē-mə-ˌglō-bən, -ˈhem-ə-; ˌmet-ˌhē-mə-ˈ, -ˌhem-ə-ˈ\ *n* [ISV] **:** a soluble brown crystalline basic blood pigment that differs from hemoglobin in containing ferric iron and in being unable to combine reversibly with molecular oxygen

me·the·na·mine \mə-ˈthē-nə-ˌmēn, -mən\ *n* [*methene* (methylene) + *amine*] **:** hexamethylenetetramine used as a urinary antiseptic

me·thinks \mi-ˈthiŋ(k)s\ *vb impersonal, past* **me·thought** \-ˈthȯt\ [ME *me thinketh*, fr. OE *mē thincth*, fr. *mē* (dat. of *ic* I) + *thincth* seems, fr. *thyncan* to seem — more at I, THINK] *archaic* **:** seems to me

me·thi·o·nine \mə-ˈthī-ə-ˌnēn\ *n* [ISV, fr. *methyl* + *thion-* + *-ine*] **:** a crystalline sulfur-containing essential amino acid $C_5H_{11}NO_2S$

meth·od \ˈmeth-əd\ *n* [MF or L; MF *methode*, fr. L *methodus*, fr. Gk *methodos*, fr. *meta-* + *hodos* way — more at CEDE] **1 :** a procedure or process for attaining an object: as **a** (1) **:** a discipline that deals with the principles and techniques of scientific inquiry (2) **:** a systematic procedure, technique, or mode of inquiry employed by or proper to a particular discipline or art (3) **:** a systematic plan followed in presenting material for instruction **b** (1) **:** a way, technique, or process of or for doing something (2) **:** a body of skills or techniques **2 a :** orderly arrangement, development, or classification **:** PLAN **b :** the habitual practice of orderliness and regularity

syn METHOD, MODE, MANNER, WAY, FASHION, SYSTEM denote the means taken or procedure followed in achieving an end. METHOD implies an orderly logical effective arrangement usu. in steps; MODE implies an order or course followed by custom, tradition, or personal preference; MANNER is close to MODE but may imply a procedure or method that is individual or distinctive; WAY may be used for any of the preceding words with more expressive or intimate effect; FASHION may be a less formal equivalent to MODE or it may connote something more superficial or ephemeral than WAY; SYSTEM suggests a fully developed or carefully formulated method often emphasizing the idea of rational orderliness

me·thod·ic \mə-ˈthäd-ik\ *adj* **:** METHODICAL, SYSTEMATIC

me·thod·i·cal \-i-kəl\ *adj* **1 :** arranged, characterized by, or performed with method or order **2 :** habitually proceeding according to method **:** SYSTEMATIC — **me·thod·i·cal·ly** \-i-k(ə-)lē\ *adv* — **me·thod·i·cal·ness** \-kəl-nəs\ *n*

meth·od·ism \ˈmeth-ə-ˌdiz-əm\ *n* **1** *cap* **a :** the doctrines and practice of Methodists **b :** the Methodist churches **2 :** methodical procedure

meth·od·ist \-əd-əst\ *n* **1 :** a person devoted to or laying great stress on method **2** *cap* **:** a member of one of the denominations deriving from the Wesleyan revival in the Church of England, having Arminian doctrine and in the U.S. modified episcopal polity, and stressing personal and social morality — **methodist** *adj* — **meth·od·is·tic** \ˌmeth-ə-ˈdis-tik\ *adj*

meth·od·ize \ˈmeth-ə-ˌdīz\ *vt* **:** to reduce to method **:** SYSTEMATIZE
syn see ORDER

meth·od·olog·i·cal \ˌmeth-əd-ᵊl-ˈäj-i-kəl\ *adj* **:** of or relating to method or methodology — **meth·od·olog·i·cal·ly** \-i-k(ə-)lē\ *adv*

meth·od·ol·o·gist \-ə-ˈdäl-ə-jəst\ *n* **:** a student of methodology

meth·od·ol·o·gy \-jē\ *n* [NL *methodologia*, fr. L *methodus* + *-logia* -logy] **1 :** a body of methods, rules, and postulates employed by a discipline **:** a particular procedure or set of procedures **2 :** the analysis of the principles or procedures of inquiry in a particular field

meth·ox·ide \me-ˈthäk-ˌsīd\ *n* **:** a base formed from methanol by replacement of the hydroxyl hydrogen with a metal

me·thoxy·chlor \me-ˈthäk-si-ˌklō(ə)r, -ˌklȯ(ə)r\ *n* [*meth-* + *oxy-* + tri*chlor*ethane] **:** a crystalline insecticide $C_{16}Cl_3H_{15}O_2$ said to be faster acting and less toxic to warm-blooded animals than DDT

Me·thu·se·lah \mə-ˈth(y)üz-(ə-)lə\ *n* [Heb *Mĕthūshā'ēl*] **:** a biblical patriarch held to have lived 969 years

meth·yl \ˈmeth-əl\ *n* [ISV, back-formation fr. *methylene*] **:** an alkyl radical CH_3 derived from methane by removal of one hydrogen atom — **me·thyl·ic** \mə-ˈthil-ik\ *adj*

meth·yl·al \ˈmeth-ə-ˌlal\ *n* [ISV] **:** a volatile flammable liquid

acetal $CH_2(OCH_3)_2$ of pleasant ethereal odor made by partial oxidation of methanol and used esp. as a solvent and in organic synthesis

methyl alcohol *n* : METHANOL

me·thyl·amine \ˌmeth-ə-lə-'mēn, -'lam-ən; mə-'thil-ə-ˌmēn\ *n* [ISV] : a flammable explosive gas CH_3NH_2 with a strong ammoniacal odor that is usu. made from methanol and ammonia and used esp. in organic synthesis

¹**meth·yl·ate** \'meth-ə-ˌlāt\ *n* : METHOXIDE

²**methylate** *vt* **1** : to impregnate or mix with methanol **2** : to introduce the methyl group into — **meth·yl·a·tion** \ˌmeth-ə-'lā-shən\ *n* — **meth·yl·ator** \'meth-ə-ˌlāt-ər\ *n*

methyl bromide *n* : a poisonous gaseous compound CH_3Br used chiefly as a fumigant against rodents, worms, and insects

meth·y·lene \'meth-ə-ˌlēn\ *n* [F *méthylène*, fr. Gk *methy* wine + *hylē* wood — more at MEAD] : a bivalent hydrocarbon radical $CH_2=$ or $--CH_2--$ derived from methane by removal of two hydrogen atoms

methylene blue *n* : a basic Thiazine dye used esp. as a biological stain, an antidote in cyanide poisoning, and an oxidation-reduction indicator

me·tic·u·los·i·ty \mə-ˌtik-yə-'läs-ət-ē\ *n* : the quality or state of being meticulous : METICULOUSNESS

me·tic·u·lous \mə-'tik-yə-ləs\ *adj* [L *meticulosus*, fr. *metus* fear] **1** *obs* : TIMID, FEARFUL **2** : marked by extreme or excessive care in the consideration or treatment of details **syn** see CAREFUL — **me·tic·u·lous·ly** *adv* — **me·tic·u·lous·ness** *n*

mé·tier \mā-'tyā\ *n* [F, fr. (assumed) VL *misterium*, alter. of L *ministerium* work, ministry] **1** : VOCATION, TRADE **2** : an area of activity in which one is expert or successful : FORTE **syn** see WORK

mé·tis \mā-'tē(s)\ *n, pl* **mé·tis** \-'tē(s), -'tēz\ [F, fr. LL *mixticius* mixed — more at MESTIZO] : one of mixed blood: **a** : HALF-BREED **b** : a crossbred animal

Me·tol \'mē-ˌtól, -ˌtōl\ *trademark* — used for a photographic developer

met·onym \'met-ə-ˌnim\ *n* [back-formation fr. *metonymy*] : a word used in metonymy

met·onym·ic \ˌmet-ə-'nim-ik\ *adj* : of or relating to metonymy : used in metonymy — **met·onym·i·cal** \-i-kəl\ *adj* — **met·onym·i·cal·ly** \-i-k(ə-)lē\ *adv*

met·on·y·my \mə-'tän-ə-mē\ *n* [L *metonymia*, fr. Gk *metōnymia*, fr. *meta-* + *-ōnymia* -onymy] : a figure of speech consisting of the use of the name of one thing for that of another of which it is an attribute or with which it is associated (as in "lands belonging to the *crown*")

me-too \'mē-'tü\ *adj* : marked by similarity to or acceptance of the successful or persuasive policies or practices of a political rival — **me-too·er** \-ər\ *n* — **me-too·ism** \-ˌiz-əm\ *n*

met·ope \'met-ˌōp, 'met-ə-(ˌ)pē\ *n* [Gk *metopē*, fr. *meta-* + *opē* opening; akin to Gk *ōps* eye, face — more at EYE] : the space between two triglyphs of a Doric frieze often adorned with carved work

met·o·pon \'met-ə-ˌpän\ *n* [*m*ethyldihydromor*phinone*] : a narcotic drug $C_{18}H_{21}NO_3$ derived from morphine

metr- or **metro-** *comb form* [NL, fr. Gk *mētr-*, fr. *mētra*, fr. *mētr-*, *mētēr* mother — more at MOTHER] : uterus ⟨*metritis*⟩ ⟨*metr*orrhagia⟩

Met·ra·zol \'me-trə-ˌzól, -ˌzōl\ *trademark* — used for pentylene-tetrazol

me·tre \'mēt-ər\ *chiefly Brit var of* METER

¹**met·ric** \'me-trik\ *n* **1** *pl* : a part of prosody that deals with metrical structure **2** : a standard of measurement

²**metric** or **met·ri·cal** \-tri-kəl\ *adj* : of, relating to, or based on the meter as a standard of measurement — **met·ri·cal·ly** \-tri-k(ə-)lē\ *adv*

-met·ric \'me-trik\ or **-met·ri·cal** \-tri-kəl\ *adj comb form* **1** : of, employing, or obtained by (such) a meter ⟨galvano*metric*⟩ **2** : of or relating to (such) an art, process, or science of measuring ⟨chrono*metric*⟩ ⟨gravi*metrical*⟩

met·ri·cal \'me-tri-kəl\ or **met·ric** \-trik\ *adj* **1** : of, relating to, or composed in meter **2** : of or relating to measurement — **met·ri·cal·ly** \-tri-k(ə-)lē\ *adv*

metric hundredweight *n* : a unit of weight equal to 50 kilograms

metric system *n* : a decimal system of weights and measures based on the meter and on the kilogram

metric ton *n* — see METRIC SYSTEM table

me·trist \'me-trəst, 'mē-\ *n* **1** : a maker of verses **2** : one skillful in handling meter

me·tro \'me-(ˌ)trō\ *n* [F *métro*, short for (*chemin de fer*) *métropolitain* metropolitan railroad] : SUBWAY

met·ro·log·i·cal \ˌme-trə-'läj-i-kəl\ *adj* : of or relating to metrology — **met·ro·log·i·cal·ly** \-i-k(ə-)lē\ *adv* — **me·trol·o·gist** \me-'träl-ə-jəst\ *n*

me·trol·o·gy \me-'träl-ə-jē\ *n* [F *métrologie*, fr. Gk *metrologia* theory of ratios, fr. *metron* measure — more at MEASURE] **1** : the science of weights and measures or of measurement **2** : a system of weights and measures

met·ro·nome \'me-trə-ˌnōm\ *n* [Gk *metron* + *-nomos* controlling, fr. *nomos* law — more at NIMBLE] : an instrument designed to mark exact time by a regularly repeated tick — **met·ro·nom·ic** \ˌme-trə-'näm-ik\ *adj* — **met·ro·nom·i·cal·ly** \-i-k(ə-)lē\ *adv*

metronome

me·trop·o·lis \mə-'träp-(ə-)ləs\ *n* [LL, fr. Gk *metropolis*, fr. *mētr-*, *mētēr* mother + *polis* city — more at MOTHER, POLICE] **1** : the mother city or state of a colony esp. in ancient Greece **2** : the chief or capital city of a country, state, or region **3** : a principal seat or center of an activity

¹**me·tro·pol·i·tan** \ˌme-trə-'päl-ət-ᵊn\ *n* **1** : the primate of an ecclesiastical province **2** : one who lives in a metropolis or evinces metropolitan manners or customs

²**metropolitan** *adj* [LL *metropolitanus* of the see of a metropolitan, fr. *metropolita*, n., metropolitan, fr. LGk *metropolitēs*, fr. *metropolis* see of a metropolitan, fr. Gk, capital] **1** : of or constituting a metropolitan or his see **2** : of, relating to, or characteristic of a metropolis **3** : of, relating to, or constituting a mother country

me·tror·rha·gia \ˌmē-trə-'rā-j(ē-)ə\ *n* [NL] : profuse bleeding from the uterus esp. between menstrual periods — **me·tror·rhag·ic** \-'raj-ik\ *adj*

-me·try \m-ə-trē\ *n comb form* [ME *-metrie*, fr. MF, fr. L *-metria*, fr. Gk, fr. *metrein* to measure, fr. *metron* — more at MEASURE] : art, process, or science of measuring (something specified) ⟨chrono*metry*⟩ ⟨photo*metry*⟩

met·tle \'met-ᵊl\ *n* [alter. of *metal*] **1** : quality of temperament or disposition **2 a** : SPIRIT, ARDOR **b** : STAMINA **syn** see COURAGE — **met·tled** \-ᵊld\ *adj* — **met·tle·some** \-ᵊl-səm\ *adj* — **on one's mettle** : aroused to do one's best

¹**mew** \'myü\ *n* [ME, fr. OE *mǣw*; akin to ON *mār* gull] : GULL; *esp* : the common European gull (*Larus canus*)

²**mew** *vb* [ME *mewen*, of imit. origin] *vi* : to utter a mew or similar sound ⟨gulls ~ed over the bay⟩ ~ *vt* : to utter by mewing : MEOW

³**mew** *n* : MEOW

⁴**mew** *n* [ME *mewe*, fr. MF *mue*, fr. *muer* to molt, fr. L *mutare* to

METRIC SYSTEM

LENGTH

unit	abbreviation	number of meters	approximate U.S. equivalent
myriameter	mym	10,000	6.2 miles
kilometer	km	1,000	0.62 mile
hectometer	hm	100	109.36 yards
decameter	dkm	10	32.81 feet
meter	m	1	39.37 inches
decimeter	dm	0.1	3.94 inches
centimeter	cm	0.01	0.39 inch
millimeter	mm	0.001	0.04 inch

AREA

unit	abbreviation	number of square meters	approximate U.S. equivalent
square kilometer	sq km *or* km²	1,000,000	0.3861 square mile
hectare	ha	10,000	2.47 acres
are	a	100	119.60 square yards
centare	ca	1	10.76 square feet
square centimeter	sq cm *or* cm²	0.0001	0.155 square inch

VOLUME

unit	abbreviation	number of cubic meters	approximate U.S. equivalent
decastere	dks	10	13.10 cubic yards
stere	s	1	1.31 cubic yards
decistere	ds	0.10	3.53 cubic feet
cubic centimeter	cu cm *or* cm³ *also* cc	0.000001	0.061 cubic inch

CAPACITY

unit	abbreviation	number of liters	cubic	dry	liquid
			approximate U.S. equivalent		
kiloliter	kl	1,000	1.31 cubic yards		
hectoliter	hl	100	3.53 cubic feet	2.84 bushels	
decaliter	dkl	10	0.35 cubic foot	1.14 pecks	2.64 gallons
liter	l	1	61.02 cubic inches	0.908 quart	1.057 quarts
deciliter	dl	0.10	6.1 cubic inches	0.18 pint	0.21 pint
centiliter	cl	0.01	0.6 cubic inch		0.338 fluidounce
milliliter	ml	0.001	0.06 cubic inch		0.27 fluidram

MASS AND WEIGHT

unit	abbreviation	number of grams	approximate U.S. equivalent
metric ton	MT *or* t	1,000,000	1.1 tons
quintal	q	100,000	220.46 pounds
kilogram	kg	1,000	2.2046 pounds
hectogram	hg	100	3.527 ounces
decagram	dkg	10	0.353 ounce
gram	g *or* gm	1	0.035 ounce
decigram	dg	0.10	1.543 grains
centigram	cg	0.01	0.154 grain
milligram	mg	0.001	0.015 grain

change — more at MISS] **1** *archaic* **:** a cage for hawks esp. while molting **2 :** a place for hiding or retirement **3** *pl but sing or pl in constr, chiefly Brit* **a :** stables usu. with living quarters built around a court **b :** back street **:** ALLEY

⁵mew *vt* **:** to shut up **:** CONFINE

mewl \'myü(ə)l\ *vi* [imit.] **:** to cry weakly like a child **:** WHIMPER

Mex·i·can \'mek-si-kən\ *n* **1 a :** a native or inhabitant of Mexico **b :** a person of Mexican descent **c** *Southwest* **:** a person of mixed Spanish and Indian descent **2 :** NAHUATL 2 — **Mexican** *adj*

Mexican bean beetle *n* **:** a spotted ladybug (*Epilachna varivestis*) that feeds on the leaves of beans

Mexican hairless *n* **:** any of an old breed of small nearly hairless dogs found in Mexico

Mexican Spanish *n* **:** the Spanish used in Mexico

me·ze·re·on \mə-'zir-ē-ən\ *n* [ME *mizerion*, fr. ML *mezereon*, fr. Ar *māzariyūn*, fr. Per] **:** a small European shrub (*Daphne mezereum* of the family Thymelaeaceae, the mezereon family) with fragrant lilac purple flowers and an acrid bark used in medicine

me·zu·zah *or* **me·zu·za** \mə-'zu̇z-ə\ *n* [Heb *mĕzūzāh* doorpost] **:** a small parchment scroll inscribed with Deut 6:4–9 and 11:13–21 and the name Shaddai and placed in a case fixed to the doorpost by some Jewish families as a sign and reminder of their faith

mez·za·nine \'mez-ᵊn-,ēn, ,mez-ᵊn-'\ *n* [F, fr. It *mezzanino*, fr. *mezzano* middle, fr. L *medianus* middle, median] **1 :** a low-ceilinged story between two main stories of a building; *esp* **:** an intermediate story that projects in the form of a balcony **2 a :** the lowest balcony in a theater **b :** the first few rows of such a balcony

mez·zo for·te \,met-(,)sō-'fȯr-,tā, ,me(d)z-(,)ō-, -'fȯrt-ē\ *adj* (*or adv*) [It] **:** moderately loud — used as a direction in music

mez·zo–re·lie·vo \-ri-'lē-(,)vō, -rēl-'yā-(,)vō\ *n, pl* **mezzo–relievos** [It *mezzorilievo*, fr. *mezzo* half + *rilievo* relief] **:** sculptural relief intermediate between bas-relief and high relief

mez·zo–so·pra·no \-sə-'pran-(,)ō, -'prän-\ *n* [It *mezzosoprano*, fr. *mezzo* + *soprano*] **:** a woman's voice of a full deep quality between that of the soprano and contralto; *also* **:** a singer having such a voice

mez·zo·tint \'met-sō-,tint, 'me(d)z-ō-\ *n* [modif. of It *mezzatinta*, fr. *mezza* (fem. of *mezzo*) + *tinta* tint] **1 :** a manner of engraving on copper or steel by scraping or burnishing a roughened surface to produce light and shade **2 :** an engraving produced by mezzotint

mho \'mō\ *n* [backward spelling of *ohm*] **:** the practical unit of conductance equal to the reciprocal of the ohm

mi \'mē\ *n* [ML, fr. the syllable sung to this note in a medieval hymn to St. John the Baptist] **:** the 3d tone of the diatonic scale in solmization

mi- *or* **mio-** *comb form* [prob. fr. NL *meio-*, fr. Gk, fr. *meiōn* — more at MINOR] **:** less ⟨*Mio*cene⟩

Mi·ami \mī-'am-ē, -'am-ə\ *n, pl* **Mi·ami** *or* **Mi·am·is 1 :** an Indian people of northern Indiana **2 :** a member of the Miami people

mi·aow \mē-'au̇\ *var of* MEOW

mi·as·ma \mī-'az-mə, mē-\ *n, pl* **miasmas** *or* **mi·as·ma·ta** \-'az-mət-ə\ [NL, fr. Gk, defilement, fr. *miainein* to pollute] **1 :** a vaporous exhalation formerly believed to cause disease; *broadly* **:** a heavy vaporous emanation **2 :** a noxious influence or atmosphere — **mi·as·mal** \-məl\ *adj* — **mi·as·mat·ic** \,mī-əz-'mat-ik\ *adj* — **mi·as·mic** \mī-'az-mik, mē-\ *adj*

mi·ca \'mī-kə\ *n, often attrib* [NL, fr. L, grain, crumb; akin to Gk *mikros* small] **:** any of various colored or transparent mineral silicates crystallizing in monoclinic forms that readily separate into very thin leaves — **mi·ca·ceous** \mī-'kā-shəs\ *adj*

Mi·cah \'mī-kə\ *n* [Heb *Mīkhāh*] **:** a Hebrew prophet of the 8th century B.C.

mice *pl of* MOUSE

mi·cel·lar \mī-'sel-ər\ *adj* [ISV] **:** of, relating to, or characterized by micelles — **mi·cel·lar·ly** *adv*

mi·celle \mī-'sel\ *n* [NL *micella*, fr. L *mica*] **:** a unit of structure (as a colloidal particle) built up from polymeric molecules or ions

Mi·chael \'mī-kəl\ *n* [Heb *Mīkhā'ēl*] **:** one of the archangels

Mich·ael·mas \'mik-əl-məs\ *n* [ME *mychelmesse*, fr. OE *Michaeles mæsse* Michael's mass] **:** the feast of St. Michael the Archangel on September 29 and one of the four quarter days in England

Michaelmas daisy *n* **:** a wild aster; *esp* **:** one blooming about Michaelmas

Mick·ey Finn \,mik-ē-'fin\ *n* [prob. fr. the name *Mickey Finn*] **:** a drink of liquor doctored with a purgative or a drug

mick·le \'mik-əl\ *adj* [ME *mikel*, fr. OE *micel* — more at MUCH] *chiefly Scot* **:** GREAT, MUCH — **mickle** *adv, chiefly Scot*

Mic·mac \'mik-,mak\ *n, pl* **Micmac** *or* **Micmacs** [Micmac *Migmac*, lit., allies] **1 a :** an Indian people of the Maritime Provinces and Newfoundland, Canada **b :** a member of this people **2 :** the Algonquian language of the Micmac people

micr- *or* **micro-** *comb form* [ME *micro-*, fr. L, fr. Gk *mikr-*, *mikro-*, fr. *mikros*, *smikros* small, short; akin to OE *smēalīc* careful, exquisite] **1 a :** small **:** minute ⟨*micro*film⟩ **b :** enlarging **:** magnifying or amplifying ⟨*micro*phone⟩ ⟨*micro*scope⟩ **c :** used for or involving minute quantities or variations ⟨*micro*barograph⟩ **d :** minutely ⟨*micro*level⟩ **2 :** one millionth part of a (specified) unit ⟨*micro*gram⟩ ⟨*micro*ohm⟩ **3 a :** using microscopy ⟨*micro*dissection⟩ **:** used in microscopy **b :** revealed by or having its structure discernible only by microscopical examination ⟨*micro*organism⟩ **4 :** abnormally small ⟨*micro*cyte⟩ **5 :** of or relating to a small area ⟨*micro*climate⟩ **6 :** employed in or connected with microphotographing or microfilming ⟨*micro*copy⟩

mi·cro \'mī-(,)krō\ *adj* [*micr-*] **:** MICROSCOPIC

mi·cro·baro·graph \,mī-krō-'bar-ə-,graf\ *n* [ISV] **:** a barograph for recording small and rapid changes

mi·crobe \'mī-,krōb\ *n* [ISV *micr-* + Gk *bios* life — more at QUICK] **:** MICROORGANISM, GERM — **mi·cro·bi·al** \mī-'krō-bē-əl\ *or* **mi·cro·bic** \-bik\ *adj*

mi·cro·bi·o·log·i·cal \,mī-krō-,bī-ə-'läj-i-kəl\ *also* **mi·cro·bi·o·log·ic** \-ik\ *adj* **:** of or relating to microbiology — **mi·cro·bi·o·log·i·cal·ly** \-i-k(ə-)lē\ *adv* — **mi·cro·bi·ol·o·gist** \-(,)bī-'äl-ə-jəst\ *n*

mi·cro·bi·ol·o·gy \-(,)bī-'äl-ə-jē\ *n* [ISV] **:** a branch of biology dealing esp. with microscopic forms of life

Mi·cro·card \'mī-krō-,kärd\ *trademark* — used for a sensitized card approximately 3 in. x 5 in. on which printed matter is reproduced photographically in greatly reduced form

mi·cro·cli·mate \-,klī-mət\ *n* [ISV] **:** the essentially uniform local climate of a usu. small site or habitat — **mi·cro·cli·mat·ic** \,mī-krō-(,)klī-'mat-ik\ *adj* — **mi·cro·cli·ma·to·log·i·cal** \-,klī-mət-ᵊl-'äj-i-kəl\ *adj* — **mi·cro·cli·ma·tol·o·gy** \-,klī-mə-'täl-ə-jē\ *n*

mi·cro·cline \'mī-krō-,klīn\ *n* [G *mikroklin*, fr. *mikr-* micr- + Gk *klinein* to lean — more at LEAN] **:** a triclinic white to pale yellow, red, or green mineral $KAlSi_3O_8$ of the feldspar group that is like orthoclase in composition

mi·cro·coc·cus \,mī-krō-'käk-əs\ *n* [NL, genus name] **:** a small spherical bacterium; *esp* **:** one of a genus (*Micrococcus*) in which growth forms irregular groups

mi·cro·copy \'mī-krō-,käp-ē\ *n* [ISV] **:** a photographic copy in which graphic matter is reduced in size — **microcopy** *vb*

mi·cro·cosm \'mī-krə-,käz-əm\ *n* [ME, fr. ML *microcosmus*, modif. of Gk *mikros kosmos*] **1 :** a little world; *esp* **:** man or human nature that is an epitome of the world or the universe **2 :** a community or other unity that is an epitome of a larger unity — **mi·cro·cos·mic** \,mī-krə-'käz-mik\ *adj* — **mi·cro·cos·mi·cal·ly** \-'käz-mi-k(ə-)lē\ *adv*

microcosmic salt *n* **:** a white crystalline salt $NaNH_5PO_4.4H_2O$ used as a flux in testing for metallic oxides and salts

mi·cro·crys·tal·line \,mī-krō-'kris-tə-lən\ *adj* [ISV] **:** having the constituent crystalline grains visible only by microscope — **mi·cro·crys·tal·lin·i·ty** \-,kris-tə-'lin-ət-ē\ *n*

mi·cro·cyte \'mī-krə-,sīt\ *n* [ISV] **:** a small red blood cell present esp. in some anemias — **mi·cro·cyt·ic** \,mī-krə-'sit-ik\ *adj*

mi·cro·el·e·ment \,mī-krō-'el-ə-mənt\ *n* **:** TRACE ELEMENT

mi·cro·evo·lu·tion \,mī-krō-,ev-ə-'lü-shən *also* -,ē-və-\ *n* **:** evolutionary change resulting from selective accumulation of minute variations — **mi·cro·evo·lu·tion·ary** \-shə-,ner-ē\ *adj*

mi·cro·fiche \'mī-krō-,fēsh\ *n* [F, fr. *micr-* + *fiche* peg, tag, slide, fr. OF, fr. *ficher* to stick in — more at FICHU] **:** a sheet of microfilm

mi·cro·fi·lar·ia \,mī-krō-fə-'lar-ē-ə, -'ler-\ *n* [NL] **:** a minute larval filaria

mi·cro·film \'mī-krə-,film\ *n* [ISV] **:** a film bearing a photographic record on a reduced scale of printed or other graphic matter — **microfilm** *vb* — **mi·cro·film·er** *n*

mi·cro·form \-,fȯrm\ *n* [*micr-* + *form*] **1 :** a process for reproducing printed matter in a much reduced size ⟨documents in ~⟩ **2 :** matter reproduced by microform

mi·cro·ga·mete \,mī-krō-gə-'mēt, -'gam-,ēt\ *n* [ISV] **:** the smaller and usu. male gamete of a heterogamous organism

mi·cro·gram \'mī-krə-,gram\ *n* **1** [ISV] **:** one millionth of a gram **2 :** MICROGRAPH 2

mi·cro·graph \-,graf\ *n* [ISV] **1 :** an instrument for executing minute writing or engraving **2 :** a graphic reproduction of the image of an object formed by a microscope **3 :** an instrument for measuring minute movements by the magnified record of movements of a diaphragm

mi·cro·graph·ic \,mī-krə-'graf-ik\ *adj* [ISV] **:** of, relating to, or disclosed by micrography — **mi·cro·graph·i·cal·ly** \-i-k(ə-)lē\ *adv*

mi·crog·ra·phy \mī-'kräg-rə-fē\ *n* **1 :** examination with the microscope **2 :** the art or process of producing micrographs

mi·cro·groove \'mī-krō-,grüv\ *n* **:** a minute closely spaced V-shaped groove used on long-playing phonograph records

mi·cro·mere \-,mi(ə)r\ *n* [ISV] **:** a small blastomere

mi·cro·me·te·or·ite \,mī-krō-'mēt-ē-ə-,rīt\ *n* **:** a meteorite so small that it can pass through the earth's atmosphere without becoming intensely heated

mi·crom·e·ter \mī-'kräm-ət-ər\ *n* [F *micromètre*, fr. *micr-* + *-mètre* -meter] **:** an instrument used with a telescope or microscope for measuring minute distances

micrometer caliper *n* **:** a caliper having a spindle moved by a finely threaded screw for making precise measurements

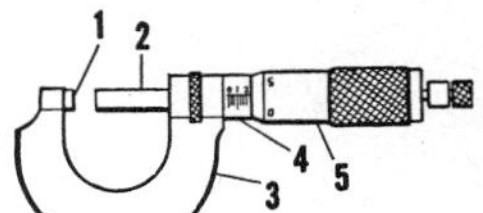

micrometer caliper: *1* anvil, *2* spindle, *3* frame, *4* sleeve, *5* thimble

mi·crom·e·try \mī-'kräm-ə-trē\ *n* [ISV] **:** measurement with a micrometer

mi·cro·mi·cron \,mī-krō-'mī-,krän\ *n* **:** one millionth of a micron

mi·cron \'mī-,krän\ *n* [NL, fr. Gk *mikron*, neut. of *mikros* small — more at MICR-] **:** a unit of length equal to one thousandth of a millimeter

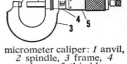

Mi·cro·ne·sian \,mī-krə-'nē-zhən, -shən\ *n* **1 :** a native or inhabitant of Micronesia **2 :** a group of Austronesian languages spoken in the Micronesian islands — **Micronesian** *adj*

mi·cron·ize \'mī-krə-,nīz\ *vt* **:** to pulverize esp. into particles a few microns in diameter

mi·cro·nu·cle·us \,mī-krō-'n(y)ü-klē-əs\ *n* [NL] **:** a minute nucleus; *specif* **:** one regarded as primarily concerned with reproductive and genetic functions in most ciliated protozoans

mi·cro·nu·tri·ent \-'n(y)ü-trē-ənt\ *n* **1 :** TRACE ELEMENT **2 :** an organic compound (as a vitamin) essential in minute amounts to the growth and welfare of an animal

mi·cro·or·ga·nism \-'ȯr-gə-,niz-əm\ *n* [ISV] **:** an organism of microscopic or ultramicroscopic size

mi·cro·pa·le·on·tol·o·gy \-,pā-lē-(,)än-'täl-ə-jē, -ən-, *esp Brit* -,pal-ē-\ *n* [ISV] **:** the study of microscopic fossils

mi·cro·par·a·site \-'par-ə-,sīt\ *n* **:** a parasitic microorganism — **mi·cro·par·a·sit·ic** \-,par-ə-'sit-ik\ *adj*

mi·cro·phage \'mī-krə-,fāj, -,fäzh\ *n* [ISV] **:** a small phagocyte

mi·cro·phone \'mī-krə-,fōn\ *n* [ISV] **:** an instrument whereby sound waves are caused to generate or modulate an electric current usu. for the purpose of transmitting or recording speech or music — **mi·cro·phon·ic** \,mī-krə-'fän-ik\ *adj*

mi·cro·phon·ics \,mī-krə-'fän-iks\ *n pl* **:** noises in a loudspeaker resulting from mechanical movement of tubes or other parts

mi·cro·pho·to·graph \,mī-krə-'fōt-ə-,graf\ *n* [ISV] **1 :** a small photograph that is normally magnified for viewing **:** MICROCOPY

2 : PHOTOMICROGRAPH — **microphotograph** *vt* — **mi·cro·pho·to·graph·ic** \-ˌfōt-ə-ˈgraf-ik\ *adj* — **mi·cro·pho·tog·ra·phy** \-fə-ˈtäg-rə-fē\ *n*

mi·cro·print \ˈmī-krō-ˌprint\ *n* **:** a photographic or photomechanical copy of graphic matter in reduced size — **microprint** *vt*

mi·cro·pro·jec·tor \ˌmī-krō-prə-ˈjek-tər\ *n* **:** a projector utilizing a compound microscope for projecting on a screen a greatly enlarged image of a microscopic object

mi·cro·py·lar \ˌmī-krə-ˈpī-lər\ *adj* [ISV] **:** of, relating to, or adjacent to a micropyle

mi·cro·pyle \ˈmī-krə-ˌpīl\ *n* [ISV *micr-* + Gk *pylē* gate] **1 :** a differentiated area of surface in an egg through which a sperm enters **2 :** a minute opening in the integument of an ovule of a seed plant through which the pollen tube penetrates to the embryo sac

mi·cro·ra·dio·graph \ˌmī-krō-ˈrād-ē-ə-ˌgraf\ *n* **:** an X-ray photograph showing minute internal structure — **mi·cro·ra·dio·graph·ic** \-ˌrād-ē-ə-ˈgraf-ik\ *adj* — **mi·cro·ra·di·og·ra·phy** \-ē-ˈäg-rə-fē\ *n*

mi·cro·read·er \ˈmī-krō-ˌrēd-ər\ *n* **:** an apparatus that gives an enlarged image of a microphotograph esp. for reading

mi·cro·scope \ˈmī-krə-ˌskōp\ *n* [NL *microscopium*, fr. *micr-* + *-scopium* -scope] **1 :** an optical instrument consisting of a lens or combination of lenses for making enlarged images of minute objects; *esp* **:** COMPOUND MICROSCOPE **2 :** an instrument using radiations other than light for making enlarged images of minute objects

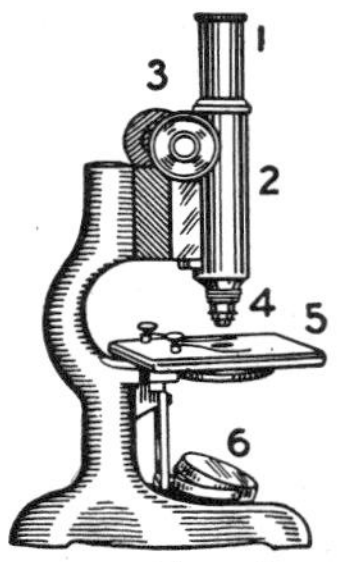

compound microscope: *1* eyepiece, *2* tube, *3* adjusting screw, *4* objective lens, *5* table or stage, *6* illuminating mirror

mi·cro·scop·ic \ˌmī-krə-ˈskäp-ik\ *or* **mi·cro·scop·i·cal** \-i-kəl\ *adj* **1** *usu microscopical* **:** of, relating to, or conducted with the microscope or microscopy **2 :** resembling a microscope esp. in perception **3 a :** invisible or indistinguishable without the use of a microscope **b :** very small or fine — **mi·cro·scop·i·cal·ly** \-i-k(ə-)lē\ *adv*

mi·cros·co·py \mī-ˈkräs-kə-pē\ *n* **:** the use of or investigation with the microscope

mi·cro·sec·ond \ˌmī-krō-ˈsek-ənd, -ənt\ *n* [ISV] **:** one millionth of a second

mi·cro·seism \ˈmī-krə-ˌsī-zəm\ *n* [ISV] **:** a feeble rhythmically recurring earth tremor — **mi·cro·seis·mic** \ˌmī-krə-ˈsīz-mik, -ˈsīs-\ *adj*

mi·cro·some \ˈmī-krə-ˌsōm\ *n* [G *mikrosom*, fr. *mikr-* micr- + *-som* -some] **:** a minute protoplasmic granule held to be a seat of protein formation — **mi·cro·so·mi·al** \ˌmī-krə-ˈsō-mē-əl\ *or* **mi·cro·so·mic** \-ˈsō-mik\ *adj*

mi·cro·spo·ran·gi·um \ˌmī-krō-spə-ˈran-jē-əm\ *n* [NL] **:** a sporangium that develops only microspores

mi·cro·spore \ˈmī-krə-ˌspō(ə)r, -ˌspȯ(ə)r\ *n* [ISV] **:** one of the spores in heterosporous plants that give rise to male gametophytes and are generally smaller than the megaspore — **mi·cro·spor·ic** \ˌmī-krə-ˈspōr-ik, -ˈspȯr-\ *or* **mi·cro·spo·rous** \-ˈspōr-əs, -ˈspȯr-; mī-ˈkräs-pə-rəs\ *adj* — **mi·cro·spor·o·gen·e·sis** \ˌmī-krə-ˌspōr-ə-ˈjen-ə-səs, -ˌspȯr-\ *n*

mi·cro·spor·o·phyll \ˌmī-krə-ˈspōr-ə-ˌfil, -ˈspȯr-\ *n* **:** a sporophyll that develops only microsporangia

mi·cro·struc·ture \ˈmī-krō-ˌstrək-chər\ *n* [ISV] **:** the microscopic structure of a material

mi·cro·wave \ˈmī-krə-ˌwāv\ *n* **:** a very short electromagnetic wave; *esp* **:** one between 100 centimeters and 1 centimeter in wavelength

mic·tu·rate \ˈmik-chə-ˌrāt, ˈmik-tə-\ *vi* [L *micturire*, fr. *mictus*, pp. of *mingere*; akin to OE *mīgan* to urinate, Gk *omeichein*] **:** URINATE — **mic·tu·ri·tion** \ˌmik-chə-ˈrish-ən, ˌmik-tə-\ *n*

mid \ˈmid\ *adj* [ME, fr. OE *midde*; akin to OHG *mitti* middle, L *medius*, Gk *mesos*] **1 :** being the part in the middle or midst ⟨in ~ ocean⟩ ⟨*mid*-August⟩ **2 :** occupying a middle position ⟨the ~ finger⟩ **3** *of a vowel* **:** articulated with the arch of the tongue midway between its highest and its lowest elevation — **mid** *adv or prep*

Mi·das \ˈmīd-əs\ *n* [L, fr. Gk] **:** a legendary king of Phrygia having the power to turn into gold everything he touched

mid·brain \ˈmid-ˌbrān\ *n* **:** the middle division of the embryonic vertebrate brain; *also* **:** the parts of the definitive brain developed from this region

mid·day \ˈmid-ˌdā, -ˈdā\ *n, often attrib* **:** the middle part of the day **:** NOON

mid·den \ˈmid-ᵊn\ *n* [ME *midding*, of Scand origin; akin to ON *myki* dung & ON *dyngja* manure pile — more at MUCUS, DUNG] **1 :** DUNGHILL **2 :** a refuse heap; *esp* **:** KITCHEN MIDDEN

1**mid·dle** \ˈmid-ᵊl\ *adj* [ME *middel*, fr. OE; akin to L *medius*] **1 :** equally distant from the extremes **:** MEDIAL, CENTRAL ⟨the ~ house in the row⟩ **2 :** being at neither extreme **:** INTERMEDIATE **3** *cap* **a :** constituting a division intermediate between those prior and later or upper and lower ⟨*Middle* Paleozoic⟩ **b :** constituting a period of a language or literature intermediate between one called *Old* and one called *New* or *Modern* ⟨*Middle* Dutch⟩ **4** *of a verb form or voice* **:** typically asserting that a person or thing both performs and is affected by the action represented

2**middle** *n* **1 :** a middle part, point, or position **2 :** the central portion of the human body **:** WAIST **3 :** the position of being among or in the midst of something **4 :** something intermediate between extremes **:** MEAN

middle age *n* **:** the period of life from about 40 to about 60 — **mid·dle-aged** \ˌmid-ᵊl-ˈājd\ *adj*

Middle Ages *n pl* **:** the period of European history from about A.D. 500 to about 1500

mid·dle·brow \ˈmid-ᵊl-ˌbrau̇\ *n* **:** a person who is moderately but not highly cultivated — **middlebrow** *adj*

mid·dle·bust·er \-ˌbəs-tər\ *n* **:** LISTER 1

middle C *n* **:** the note designated by the first ledger line below the treble staff and the first above the bass staff

middle class *n* **:** a class occupying a position between the upper class and the lower class; *esp* **:** a fluid heterogeneous socioeconomic grouping composed principally of business and professional people, bureaucrats, and some farmers and skilled workers sharing common social characteristics and values

middle distance *n* **1 :** a part of a pictorial representation or scene between the foreground and the background **2 :** any footrace distance from 400 meters and 440 yards to 1500 meters and one mile

middle ear *n* **:** a small membrane-lined cavity that is separated from the outer ear by the eardrum and that transmits sound waves from the eardrum to the partition between the middle and inner ears through a chain of tiny bones

Middle English *n* **:** the English in manuscripts of the 12th to 15th centuries

Middle French *n* **:** the French in manuscripts of the 14th to 16th centuries

Middle Greek *n* **:** the Greek language used in the 7th to 15th centuries

Middle High German *n* **:** the High German in use from about 1100 to 1500

Middle Irish *n* **:** the Irish in use between the 11th and 15th centuries

Middle Low German *n* **:** the Low German in use from about 1100 to 1500

mid·dle·man \ˈmid-ᵊl-ˌman\ *n* **:** an intermediary or agent between two parties; *esp* **:** a dealer or agent intermediate between the producer of goods and the retailer or consumer

Middle Scots *n* **:** the Scots language in use between the latter half of the 15th and the early decades of the 17th centuries

middle term *n* **:** the term of a syllogism that occurs in both premises

mid·dle·weight \ˈmid-ᵊl-ˌwāt\ *n* **:** one of average weight: as **a :** a boxer weighing more than 147 but not over 160 pounds **b :** a wrestler weighing more than 158 but not over 174 pounds

Middle Welsh *n* **:** the Welsh in use from about 1150 to 1500

1**mid·dling** \ˈmid-liŋ, -lən\ *adj* **1 :** of middle, medium, or moderate size, degree, or quality **2 :** MEDIOCRE, SECOND-RATE — **mid·dling** *adv* — **mid·dling·ly** \-liŋ-lē, -lən-\ *adv*

2**middling** *n* **1 :** any of various commodities of intermediate size, quality, or position **2** *pl but sing or pl in constr* **:** a granular product of grain milling; *esp* **:** a wheat milling by-product used in animal feeds

mid·dor·sal \ˈmid-ˈdȯr-səl\ *adj* **:** situated in the middle part or median line of the back

mid·dy \ˈmid-ē\ *n* [by shortening & alter.] **1 :** MIDSHIPMAN **2 :** a loosely fitting blouse with a sailor collar worn by women and children

Mid·gard \ˈmid-ˌgärd\ *n* [ON *mithgarthr*] **:** the abode of human beings in Norse mythology

midge \ˈmij\ *n* [ME *migge*, fr. OE *mycg*; akin to OHG *mucka* midge, Gk *myia* fly, L *musca*] **:** a tiny two-winged fly (as of the family Chironomidae)

midg·et \ˈmij-ət\ *n* [*midge*] **1 :** a very small person **:** DWARF **2 :** a creature or thing much smaller than usual — **midget** *adj*

mid·gut \ˈmid-ˌgət\ *n* **:** the middle part of the alimentary canal

Mid·i·an·ite \ˈmid-ē-ə-ˌnīt\ *n* [*Midian*, son of Abraham] **:** a member of an ancient northern Arabian people

mid·iron \ˈmid-ˌī(-ə)rn\ *n* **:** an iron golf club with more loft than a driving iron and less than a mashie — called also *number two iron*

mid·land \-lənd, -ˌland\ *n* **1 :** the interior or central region of a country **2** *cap* **a :** the dialect of English spoken in the midland counties of England **b :** the dialect of English spoken in parts of New Jersey and Delaware, northern Maryland, central and southern Pennsylvania, Ohio, Indiana, Illinois, the Appalachian Mountain area, West Virginia, Kentucky, and most of Tennessee — **midland** *adj, often cap*

mid·line \-ˌlīn, -ˈlīn\ *n* **:** a median line

mid·most \-ˌmōst\ *adj* **1 :** being in the exact middle **2 :** the middle of **3 :** most intimate **:** INNERMOST — **midmost** *adv or n*

mid·night \-ˌnīt\ *n* **1 :** the middle of the night; *specif* **:** 12 o'clock at night **2 :** deep or extended darkness or gloom — **midnight** *adj* — **mid·night·ly** *adv or adj*

midnight sun *n* **:** the sun above the horizon at midnight in the arctic or antarctic summer

mid·point \ˈmid-ˌpȯint, -ˈpȯint\ *n* **:** a point at or near the center or middle

mid·rash \ˈmid-ˌräsh\ *n, pl* **mid·rash·im** \mid-ˈräsh-əm\ [Heb *midhrāsh* exposition, explanation] **1 :** a haggadic or halakic exposition of the underlying significance of a Bible text **2 :** a collection of midrashim **3** *cap* **:** the midrashic literature written between the 4th century B.C. and 11th century A.D. — **mid·rash·ic** \mid-ˈräsh-ik\ *adj, often cap*

mid·rib \ˈmid-ˌrib\ *n* **:** the central vein of a leaf

mid·riff \ˈmid-ˌrif\ *n* [ME *midrif*, fr. OE *midhrif*, fr. *midde* mid + *hrif* belly; akin to OHG *href* body, L *corpus*] **1 :** DIAPHRAGM 1 **2 :** the mid-region of the human torso **3 a :** a section of a woman's garment that covers the midriff **b :** a woman's garment that exposes the midriff

mid·sec·tion \ˈmid-ˌsek-shən\ *n* **:** a section midway between the extremes; *esp* **:** MIDRIFF 2

mid·ship·man \ˈmid-ˌship-mən, (ˈ)mid-ˈ\ *n* **:** a student naval officer ranking above a master chief petty officer and below a warrant officer

mid·ships \ˈmid-ˌships\ *adv* **:** AMIDSHIPS

midst \ˈmidst, ˈmitst\ *n* [ME *middest*, alter. of *middes*, back-formation fr. *amiddes* amid] **1 :** the interior or central part or point **:** MIDDLE, INTERIOR ⟨in the ~ of the forest⟩ **2 :** a position of proximity to the members of a group or company ⟨a visitor in our ~⟩ **3 :** the condition of being surrounded or beset ⟨in the ~ of his troubles⟩ **4 :** a period of time about the middle of a continuing act or condition ⟨in the ~ of a long reign⟩ — **midst** *prep*

mid·sum·mer \ˈmid-ˈsəm-ər, -ˌsəm-\ *n* **1 :** the middle of summer **2:** the summer solstice

Midsummer Day *n* **:** the feast of the nativity of John the Baptist on June 24 and one of the four quarter days in England

1**mid·way** \ˈmid-ˌwā\ *n* [*Midway* (*Plaisance*), Chicago, site of the amusement section of the Columbian Exposition 1893] **:** an avenue at a fair, carnival, or amusement park for concessions and light amusements

2**mid·way** \-ˌwā, -ˈwā\ *adv* (*or adj*) **:** in the middle of the way or distance **:** HALFWAY

mid·week \-ˌwēk\ *n* **:** the middle of the week — **midweek** *adj* — **mid·week·ly** \-ˌwē-klē, -ˈwē-\ *adj or adv*

mid·wife \ˈmid-ˌwīf\ *n* [ME *midwif*, fr. *mid* with (fr. OE) + *wif* woman] **:** a woman who assists other women in childbirth

mid·wife·ry \-ˌwī-f(ə-)rē\ *n* **:** the art or act of assisting at childbirth; *also* **:** OBSTETRICS

mid·win·ter \ˈmid-ˈwint-ər, -ˌwint-\ *n* **1 :** the middle of winter **2 :** the winter solstice

mid·year \-ˌyi(ə)r\ *n* **1 a :** the middle or middle portion of a calendar year **b :** the middle of an academic year **2 a :** a midyear examination **b** *pl* **:** the set of examinations at midyear; *also* **:** the period of midyear examinations — **midyear** *adj*

mien \'mēn\ *n* [by shortening & alter. fr. [2]*demean*] **1 :** air or bearing esp. as expressive of mood or personality **:** DEMEANOR **2 :** APPEARANCE, ASPECT **syn** see BEARING

[1]**miff** \'mif\ *n* [origin unknown] **1 :** a fit of ill humor **2 :** a trivial quarrel

[2]**miff** *vt* **:** to put into an ill humor **:** OFFEND

[1]**might** \(')mīt\ [ME, fr. OE *meahte, mihte;* akin to OHG *mahta, mohta* could] *past of* MAY — used in auxiliary function to express permission, liberty, probability, possibility in the past ⟨the king ~ do nothing without parliament's consent⟩ or a present condition contrary to fact ⟨if he were older he ~ understand⟩ or less probability or possibility than *may* ⟨~ get there before it rains⟩ or as a polite alternative to *may* ⟨~ I ask who is calling⟩ or to *ought* or *should* ⟨you ~ at least apologize⟩

[2]**might** \'mīt\ *n* [ME, fr. OE *miht;* akin to OHG *maht* might, *magan* to be able — more at MAY] **1 a :** the power, authority, or resources wielded by an individual, group, or other entity **b** (1) **:** bodily strength (2) **:** the power, energy, or intensity of which one is capable ⟨striving with ~ and main⟩ **2** *dial* **:** a great deal **syn** see POWER

might·i·ly \'mīt-ᵊl-ē\ *adv* **1 :** in a mighty manner **:** VIGOROUSLY **2 :** very much

might·i·ness \'mīt-ē-nəs\ *n* **:** the quality or state of being mighty

mighty \'mīt-ē\ *adj* **1 :** possessing might **:** POTENT **2 :** accomplished or characterized by might **3 :** great or imposing in size or extent **:** EXTRAORDINARY — **mighty** *adv*

mi·gnon·ette \ˌmin-yə-'net\ *n* [F *mignonnette,* fr. obs. F, fem. of *mignonnet* dainty, fr. MF, fr. *mignon* darling] **:** any of a genus (*Reseda* of the family Resedaceae, the mignonette family) of herbs; *esp* **:** a garden annual (*R. odorata*) bearing racemes of fragrant greenish yellow flowers

mi·graine \'mī-ˌgrān\ *n* [F, fr. LL *hemicrania* pain in one side of the head, fr. Gk *hēmikrania,* fr. *hēmi-* hemi- + *kranion* cranium] **:** a condition marked by recurrent severe headache often with nausea and vomiting — **mi·grain·oid** \-ˌgrā-ˌnȯid\ *adj* — **mi·grain·ous** \-nəs\ *adj*

mi·grant \'mī-grənt\ *n* **:** one that migrates: as **a :** a person who moves in order to find work esp. in harvesting crops **b :** an animal that shifts from one habitat to another — **migrant** *adj*

mi·grate \'mī-ˌgrāt\ *vi* [L *migratus,* pp. of *migrare;* akin to Gk *ameibein* to change] **1 :** to move from one country, place, or locality to another **2 :** to pass usu. periodically from one region or climate to another for feeding or breeding **3 :** to change position in an organism or substance — **mi·gra·tion** \mī-'grā-shən\ *n* — **mi·gra·tion·al** \-shnəl, -shən-ᵊl\ *adj* — **mi·gra·tor** \'mī-ˌgrāt-ər\ *n*

mi·gra·to·ry \'mī-grə-ˌtōr-ē, -ˌtȯr-\ *adj* **1 :** of, relating to, or characterized by migration **2 :** ROVING, WANDERING

mi·ka·do \mə-'käd-(ˌ)ō\ *n* [Jap] **:** an emperor of Japan

mike \'mīk\ *n* [by shortening & alter.] **:** MICROPHONE

Mike \'mīk\ — a communications code word for the letter *m*

mil \'mil\ *n* [L *mille*] **1 :** a unit of length equal to $\frac{1}{1000}$ inch used esp. for the diameter of wire **2 :** a unit of angular measurement used in artillery and equal to $\frac{1}{6400}$ of 360 degrees **3** — see *pound* at MONEY table

mi·la·dy \mil-'ād-ē, *US also* mī-'lād-\ *n* [F, fr. E *my lady*] **1 :** an Englishwoman of noble or gentle birth **2 :** a woman of fashion

milch \'milk, 'milch, 'milks\ *adj* [ME *milche,* fr. OE *-milce;* akin to OE *melcan* to milk — more at EMULSION] **:** giving milk; *specif* **:** bred or suitable primarily for milk production

mild \'mī(ə)ld\ *adj* [ME, fr. OE *milde;* akin to Gk *malthakos* soft, OE *melu* meal — more at MEAL] **1 :** gentle in nature or behavior **2 :** moderate in action or effect **3 :** TEMPERATE **4 :** SOFT, MALLEABLE ⟨~ steel⟩ **syn** see SOFT — **mild·ly** \'mī(ə)l-(d)lē\ *adv* — **mild·ness** \'mī(ə)l(d)-nəs\ *n*

[1]**mil·dew** \'mil-ˌd(y)ü\ *n* [ME, fr. OE *meledēaw;* akin to OHG *militou* honeydew] **1 a :** a superficial usu. whitish growth produced on organic matter or living plants by fungi (as of the families Erysiphaceae and Peronosporaceae) **b :** a fungus producing mildew **2 :** a discoloration caused by fungi — **mil·dewy** \-ē\ *adj*

[2]**mildew** *vt* **:** to affect with mildew ~ *vi* **:** to become affected with mildew

mile \'mī(ə)l\ *n* [ME, fr. OE *mīl;* akin to OHG *mīla* mile; both fr. a prehistoric WGmc word borrowed fr. L *milia* miles, fr. *milia passuum,* lit., thousands of paces, fr. *milia,* pl. of *mille* thousand, perh. fr. a prehistoric compound whose constituents are akin to Gk *mia* (fem. of *heis* one) and to Gk *chilioi* thousand, Skt *sahasra* — more at SAME] **:** any of various units of distance: as **a :** a unit equal to 5280 feet — see MEASURE table **b :** NAUTICAL MILE

mile·age \'mī-lij\ *n* **1 :** an allowance for traveling expenses at a certain rate per mile **2 :** aggregate length or distance in miles: as **a :** the total miles traveled in a day or other period of time **b :** the amount of service that something will yield expressed in terms of miles of travel

mile·post \'mī(ə)l-ˌpōst\ *n* **:** a post indicating the distance in miles from a given point; *also* **:** a post placed a mile from a similar post

mil·er \'mī-lər\ *n* **:** a man or a horse that competes in mile races

mi·les glo·ri·o·sus \'mē-ˌlās-ˌglōr-ē-'ō-səs, -ˌglȯr-\ *n, pl* **mi·li·tes glo·ri·o·si** \'mē-lə-ˌtās-ˌglōr-ē-'ō-(ˌ)sē, -ˌglȯr-\ [L] **:** a boastful soldier; *esp* **:** a stock character of this type in comedy

mile·stone \'mī(ə)l-ˌstōn\ *n* **1 :** a stone serving as a milepost **2 :** a significant point in development

mil·foil \'mil-ˌfȯil\ *n* [ME, fr. OF, fr. L *millefolium,* fr. *mille* + *folium* leaf — more at BLADE] **1 :** YARROW **2 :** WATER MILFOIL

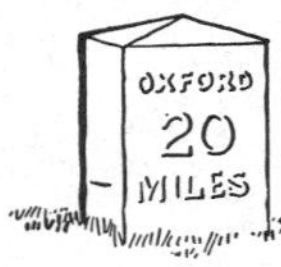

milestone

mil·i·ar·ia \ˌmil-ē-'ar-ē-ə, -'er-\ *n* [NL, fr. L, fem. of *miliarius*] **:** an inflammatory disorder of the skin characterized by redness, eruption, burning or itching, and excessive sweating; *esp* **:** PRICKLY HEAT

mil·i·ary \'mil-ē-ˌer-ē\ *adj* [L *miliarius* of millet, fr. *milium* millet — more at MILLET] **:** having or made up of many small projections or lesions

mi·lieu \mēl-'yə(r), -'yü; mē-lyœ̄\ *n* [F, fr. OF, midst, fr. *mi* middle (fr. L *medius*) + *lieu* place, fr. L *locus*] **:** ENVIRONMENT, SETTING

mil·i·tan·cy \'mil-ə-tən-sē\ *n* **:** the quality or state of being militant

mil·i·tant \'mil-ə-tənt\ *adj* **1 :** engaged in warfare **:** FIGHTING **2 :** aggressively active **:** COMBATIVE **syn** see AGGRESSIVE — **militant** *n* — **mil·i·tant·ly** *adv* — **mil·i·tant·ness** *n*

mil·i·tar·i·ly \ˌmil-ə-'ter-ə-lē\ *adv* **1 :** in a military manner **2 :** from a military standpoint

mil·i·ta·rism \'mil-ə-tə-ˌriz-əm\ *n* **1 a :** predominance of the military class or its ideals **b :** exaltation of military virtues and ideals **2 :** a policy of aggressive military preparedness — **mil·i·ta·rist** \-rəst\ *n* — **mil·i·ta·ris·tic** \ˌmil-ə-tə-'ris-tik\ *adj* — **mil·i·ta·ris·ti·cal·ly** \-ti-k(ə-)lē\ *adv*

mil·i·ta·ri·za·tion \ˌmil-ə-t(ə-)rə-'zā-shən, ˌmil-ə-ˌter-ə-\ *n* **:** the act or process of militarizing

mil·i·ta·rize \'mil-ə-tə-ˌrīz\ *vt* **1 :** to equip with military forces and defenses **2 :** to give a military character to

[1]**mil·i·tary** \'mil-ə-ˌter-ē\ *adj* [MF *militaire,* fr. L *militaris,* fr. *milit-, miles*] **1 :** of or relating to soldiers, arms, or war **2 a :** performed or made by armed forces **b :** supported by armed force **3 :** of or relating to the army **syn** see MARTIAL

[2]**military** *n, pl* **military** *also* **mil·i·tar·ies** **1 :** ARMED FORCES **2 :** military persons; *esp* **:** army officers

military police *n* **:** a branch of an army that exercises guard and police functions

mil·i·tate \'mil-ə-ˌtāt\ *vi* [L *militatus,* pp. of *militare* to engage in warfare, fr. *milit-, miles* soldier] **:** to have weight or effect

mi·li·tia \mə-'lish-ə\ *n* [L, military service, fr. *milit-, miles*] **1 :** a part of the organized armed forces of a country liable to call only in emergency **2 :** the whole body of able-bodied male citizens declared by law as being subject to call to military service — **mi·li·tia·man** \-mən\ *n*

mil·i·um \'mil-ē-əm\ *n, pl* **mil·ia** \-ē-ə\ [NL, fr. L, millet — more at MILLET] **:** a small whitish lump in the skin due to retention of secretion in an oil gland duct

[1]**milk** \'milk\ *n* [ME, fr. OE *meolc, milc;* akin to OHG *miluh* milk] **1 :** a fluid secreted by the mammary glands of females for the nourishment of their young **2 :** a liquid like milk in appearance

[2]**milk** *vt* **1 a** (1) **:** to draw milk from the breasts or udder of (2) *obs* **:** SUCKLE 2 **b :** to draw (milk) from the breast or udder **c :** SUCKLE 1 — used of lower mammals **2 :** to draw something from as if by milking ~ *vi* **:** to draw or yield milk — **milk·er** *n*

milk–and–wa·ter \ˌmil-kən-'(d)wȯt-ər, -'(d)wät-\ *adj* **:** WEAK, INSIPID

milk·i·ness \'mil-kē-nəs\ *n* **:** the quality or state of being milky

milk leg *n* **:** a painful swelling of the leg at childbirth caused by inflammation and clotting in the veins

milk–liv·ered \'mil-'kliv-ərd\ *adj* **:** COWARDLY, TIMOROUS

milk·maid \'milk-ˌmād\ *n* **:** DAIRYMAID

milk·man \-ˌman, -mən\ *n* **:** a man who sells or delivers milk

milk of magnesia : a milk-white suspension of magnesium hydroxide in water used as an antacid and laxative

milk punch *n* **:** a mixed drink of alcoholic liquor, milk, and sugar

milk shake *n* **:** milk and a flavoring syrup sometimes with ice cream shaken or blended thoroughly

milk sickness *n* **1 :** an acute disease characterized by weakness, vomiting, and constipation and caused by eating dairy products or meat from cattle poisoned by various plants **2 :** TREMBLE 3

milk snake *n* **:** KING SNAKE; *esp* **:** a common harmless grayish or tan snake (*Lampropeltis triangulum*) with black-bordered brown blotches and an arrow-shaped occipital spot

milk·sop \'milk-ˌsäp\ *n* **:** an unmanly man **:** MOLLYCODDLE

milk sugar *n* **:** LACTOSE

milk tooth *n* **:** a temporary deciduous tooth of a mammal; *esp* **:** one of man's set consisting of four incisors, two canines, and four molars in each jaw

milk vetch *n* **:** a yellow-flowered perennial Old World leguminous herb (*Astragalus glycyphyllous*) popularly supposed to increase the milk yield of goats; *also* **:** any of various related plants

milk·weed \'mil-ˌkwēd\ *n* **:** any of various plants that secrete latex; *esp* **:** any of a genus (*Asclepias* of the family Asclepiadaceae, the milkweed family) of erect perennial herbs with milky juice and umbellate flowers

milk·wort \'mil-ˌkwərt, -ˌkwȯ(ə)rt\ *n* **:** any herb of a genus (*Polygala* of the family Polygalaceae, the milkwort family)

milky \'mil-kē\ *adj* **1 :** resembling milk in color or consistency **2 :** MILD, TIMOROUS **3 a :** consisting of, containing, or abounding in milk **b :** yielding milk; *specif* **:** having the characteristics of a good milk producer

milky disease *n* **:** a destructive bacterial disease of Japanese beetle larvae and other scarabaeid grubs

milky way *n* **1** *cap M&W* **:** a broad luminous irregular band of light that stretches completely around the celestial sphere and is caused by the light of myriads of faint stars; *specif* **:** MILKY WAY GALAXY **2 :** GALAXY

Milky Way galaxy *n* **:** the galaxy of which the sun and the solar system are a part and which contains the myriads of stars that comprise the Milky Way together with all the individual stars, clusters, and bright and dark nebulosities in the sky

[1]**mill** \'mil\ *n* [ME *mille,* fr. OE *mylen;* akin to OHG *muli* mill; both fr. a prehistoric NGmc-WGmc word borrowed fr. LL *molina, molinum,* fr. fem. and neut. of *molinus* of a mill, of a millstone, fr. L *mola* mill, millstone; akin to L *molere* to grind — more at MEAL] **1 :** a building provided with machinery for grinding grain into flour **2 a :** a machine for grinding grain **:** QUERN **b :** a machine for crushing or comminuting **3 :** a machine that manufactures by the continuous repetition of some simple action **4 :** a building or collection of buildings with machinery for manufacturing **5 a :** a machine for stamping coins **b :** a machine for expelling juice from vegetable tissues by pressure or grinding **c :** a machine for polishing **6 :** MILLING MACHINE, MILLING CUTTER

[2]**mill** *vt* **1 :** to subject to an operation or process in a mill: as **a :** to grind into flour, meal, or powder **b :** to shape or dress by means of a rotary cutter **c :** to mix and condition (as rubber) by passing between rotating rolls **2 :** to give a raised rim or a ridged or corrugated edge to (a coin) ~ *vi* **1 :** to hit out with the fists **2 :** to move in a circle or in an eddying mass **3 :** to undergo milling

3mill *n* [L *mille* thousand — more at MILE] **:** a unit of monetary value equal to 1/1000 U.S. dollar
mill·board \'mil-,bō(ə)rd, -,bȯ(ə)rd\ *n* [alter. of *milled board*] **:** strong heavy hard paperboard suitable for lining book covers and for paneling in furniture
mill·dam \-,dam\ *n* **:** a dam to make a millpond; *also* **:** MILLPOND
mil·le·nar·i·an \,mil-ə-'ner-ē-ən\ *adj* **1 :** of or relating to 1000 years **2 :** of or relating to belief in the millennium — **millenarian** *n* — **mil·le·nar·i·an·ism** \-ē-ə-,niz-əm\ *n*
1mil·le·na·ry \'mil-ə-,ner-ē, mə-'len-ə-rē\ *n* [LL *millenarium*, fr. neut. of *millenarius* of a thousand, fr. L *milleni* one thousand each, fr. *mille*] **1 a :** a group of 1000 units or things **b :** 1000 years **:** MILLENNIUM **2 :** MILLENARIAN
2millenary *adj* [L *millenarius*] **1 :** relating to or consisting of 1000 **2 :** MILLENNIAL
mil·len·ni·al \mə-'len-ē-əl\ *adj* **:** of or relating to a millennium
mil·len·ni·al·ism \-ē-ə-,liz-əm\ *n* **:** MILLENARIANISM — **mil·len·ni·al·ist** \-ləst\ *n*
mil·len·ni·um \mə-'len-ē-əm\ *n, pl* **mil·len·nia** \-ē-ə\ *or* **mil·len·ni·ums** [NL, fr. L *mille* thousand + NL *-ennium* (as in *biennium*)] **1 a :** a period of 1000 years **b :** a 1000th anniversary or its celebration **2 a :** the thousand years mentioned in Revelation 20 during which holiness is to prevail and Christ is to reign on earth **b :** a period of great happiness or human perfection
mil·le·pore \'mil-ə-,pō(ə)r, -,pȯ(ə)r\ *n* [deriv. of L *mille* thousand + *porus* pore] **:** any of an order (Milleporina) of often large stony hydrozoan reef-building corals of encrusting, branching, or massive form
mill·er \'mil-ər\ *n* **1 :** one that operates a mill; *specif* **:** one that grinds grain into flour **2 :** any of various moths having powdery wings **3 a :** MILLING MACHINE **b :** a tool for use in a milling machine
mil·ler·ite \'mil-ə-,rīt\ *n* [G *millerit*, fr. William H. *Miller* †1880 E mineralogist] **:** sulfide of nickel NiS usu. occurring as a mineral in capillary yellow crystals
mill·er's–thumb \,mil-ərz-'thəm\ *n* **:** any of several small freshwater spiny-finned sculpins (genus *Cottus*) of Europe and No. America
mil·les·i·mal \mə-'les-ə-məl\ *n* [L *millesimus*, adj., thousandth, fr. *mille*] **:** THOUSANDTH — **millesimal** *adj* — **mil·les·i·mal·ly** \-mə-lē\ *adv*
mil·let \'mil-ət\ *n* [ME *milet*, fr. MF, dim. of *mil*, fr. L *milium*; akin to Gk *melinē* millet] **1 :** any of various small-seeded annual cereal and forage grasses: **a :** a grass (*Panicum miliaceum*) cultivated for its grain which is used for food **b :** any of several grasses related to common millet **2 :** the seed of a millet
milli- *comb form* [F, fr. L *milli-* thousand, fr. *mille* — more at MILE] **:** thousandth ⟨*milli*ampere⟩
mil·li·am·pere \,mil-ē-'am-,pi(ə)r\ *n* [ISV] **:** one thousandth of an ampere
mil·liard \'mil-ē-,ärd, 'mil-,yärd\ *n* [F, fr. MF *miliart*, fr. *mili-*, (fr. *milion* million)] *Brit* **:** a thousand millions — see NUMBER table
mil·li·ary \'mil-ē-,er-ē\ *adj* [L *milliarius*, *miliarius* consisting of a thousand, one mile long, fr. *mille* thousand, mile] **:** marking the distance of a Roman mile
mil·li·bar \'mil-ə-,bär\ *n* [ISV] **:** a unit of atmospheric pressure equal to 1/1000 bar or 1000 dynes per square centimeter
mil·li·cu·rie \,mil-ə-'kyu̇(ə)r-(,)ē, -kyu̇-'rē\ *n* [ISV] **:** one thousandth of a curie
mil·lieme \mē(l)-'yem\ *n, pl* **milliemes** \-'yem(z)\ [F *millième* thousandth, fr. MF, fr. *mille* thousand, fr. L] — see *dinar*, *pound* at MONEY table
mil·li·far·ad \,mil-ə-'far-,ad, -əd\ *n* **:** one thousandth of a farad
mil·li·gal \'mil-ə-,gal\ *n* [ISV] **:** a unit of acceleration equivalent to 1/1000 gal
mil·li·gram \-,gram\ *n* [F *milligramme*, fr. *milli-* + *gramme* gram] — see METRIC SYSTEM table
mil·li·hen·ry \-,hen-rē\ *n* [ISV] **:** one thousandth of a henry
mil·li·lam·bert \,mil-ə-'lam-bərt\ *n* **:** one thousandth of a lambert
mil·li·li·ter \'mil-ə-,lēt-ər\ *n* [F *millilitre*, fr. *milli-* + *litre* liter] — see METRIC SYSTEM table
mil·lime \mə-'lēm\ *n* [modif. of Ar *mallīm*, fr. F *millième*] — see *dinar* at MONEY table
mil·li·me·ter \'mil-ə-,mēt-ər\ *n* [F *millimètre*, fr. *milli-* + *mètre* meter] — see METRIC SYSTEM table
mil·li·mi·cron \,mil-ə-'mī-,krän\ *n* [ISV] **:** a unit of length equal to one thousandth of a micron or one millionth of a millimeter
mil·line \'mil-'līn\ *n* [blend of *million* and *line*] **:** a unit of space and circulation equivalent to one agate line appearing in one million copies of a publication
mil·li·ner \'mil-ə-nər\ *n* [irreg. fr. *Milan*, Italy; fr. the importation of women's finery from Italy in the 16th century] **:** one who designs, makes, trims, or sells women's hats
mil·li·nery \'mil-ə-,ner-ē\ *n* **1 :** women's apparel for the head **2 :** the business or work of a milliner
mill·ing \'mil-iŋ\ *n* **:** a corrugated edge on a coin
milling cutter *n* **:** a rotary tool-steel cutter used in a milling machine for shaping and dressing metal surfaces
milling machine *n* **:** a machine tool on which work usu. of metal secured to a carriage is shaped by being fed against rotating milling cutters
mil·lion \'mil-yən\ *n, pl* **millions** *or* **million** [ME *milioun*, fr. MF *milion*, fr. OIt *milione*, aug. of *mille* thousand, fr. L — more at MILE] **1** — see NUMBER table **2 :** a very large or indefinitely great number ⟨~*s* of mosquitoes⟩ **3 :** the mass of people — **million** *adj* — **mil·lionth** \-yən(t)th\ *adj* — **millionth** *n, pl* **millionths** \-yən(t)s, -yən(t)ths\
mil·lion·aire \,mil-yə-'na(ə)r, -'ne(ə)r, 'mil-yə-,\ *n* [F *millionnaire*, fr. *million*, fr. MF *milion*] **:** one whose wealth is estimated at a million or more (as of dollars)
mil·li·pede \'mil-ə-,pēd\ *n* [L *millepeda* a small crawling animal, fr. *mille* thousand + *ped-*, *pes* foot — more at FOOT] **:** any of numerous myriopods (class Diplopoda) having usu. a cylindrical segmented body covered with hard integument, two pairs of legs on most apparent segments, and no poison fangs
mil·li·roent·gen \,mil-ə-'rent-gən, -'rənt-, -jən; -'ren-chən, -'rən-\ *n* **:** one thousandth of a roentgen
mil·li·sec·ond \'mil-ə-,sek-ənd, -ənt\ *n* [ISV] **:** one thousandth of a second
mil·li·volt \-,vōlt\ *n* [ISV] **:** one thousandth of a volt
mill·pond \'mil-,pänd\ *n* **:** a pond produced by damming a stream to produce a head of water for operating a mill
mill·race \-,rās\ *n* **:** a canal in which water flows to and from a mill wheel; *also* **:** the current that drives the wheel
mill run *n* **1 :** the salable lumber output of a sawmill **2 :** the common run of an article passing through a mill
mill·stone \'mil-,stōn\ *n* **1 :** either of two circular stones used for grinding grain or other substance **2 a :** something that grinds or crushes **b :** a heavy burden
mill·stream \-,strēm\ *n* **1 :** a stream whose flow is utilized to run a mill **2 :** MILLRACE
mill wheel *n* **:** a waterwheel that drives a mill
mill·wright \'mil-,rīt\ *n* **:** one whose occupation is planning and building mills or setting up their machinery
mi·lo \'mī-(,)lō\ *n* [Sotho *maili*] **:** a small usu. early and drought-resistant grain sorghum with compact bearded heads of large yellow or whitish seeds
mi·lord \mil-'ȯ(ə)r, -'ȯ(ə)rd\ *n* [F, fr. E *my lord*] **:** an Englishman of noble or gentle birth
mil·reis \mil-'rās(h)\ *n, pl* **mil·reis** \-'rās(h), -'rāz(h)\ [Pg *mil-réis*] **1 :** a Portuguese unit of value equal before 1911 to 1000 reis **2 :** the basic monetary unit of Brazil until 1942 **3 :** a coin representing one milreis
milt \'milt\ *n* [prob. fr. MD *milte* milt of fish, spleen; akin to OE *milte* spleen — more at MELT] **:** the male reproductive glands of fishes when filled with secretion; *also* **:** the secretion itself — **milt·er** \'mil-tər\ *n* — **milty** \-tē\ *adj*
Mil·ton·ic \mil-'tän-ik\ *or* **Mil·to·ni·an** \-'tō-nē-ən\ *adj* **:** of, relating to, or characteristic of John Milton or his writings
mim \'mim\ *adj* [imit. of the act of pursing the lips] *dial* **:** affectedly shy or modest
1mime \'mīm, 'mēm\ *n* [L *mimus*, fr. Gk *mimos*; akin to Gk *mimeisthai* to imitate] **1 a :** an actor in a mime **b :** one that practices mime **2 :** MIMIC **3 :** an ancient dramatic entertainment representing scenes from life usu. in a ridiculous manner **4 a :** the art of portraying a character or of narration by body movement **b :** a performance of mime
2mime *vi* **:** to act a part with mimic gesture and action usu. without words ~ *vt* **1 :** MIMIC **2 :** to act out in the manner of a mime — **mim·er** *n*
mim·eo·graph \'mim-ē-ə-,graf\ *n* [fr. *Mimeograph*, a trademark] **:** a duplicator for making many copies that utilizes a stencil through which ink is pressed — **mimeograph** *vt*
mi·me·sis \mə-'mē-səs, mī-\ *n* [LL, fr. Gk *mimēsis*, fr. *mimeisthai*] **:** IMITATION, MIMICRY
mi·met·ic \-'met-ik\ *adj* [LL *mimeticus*, fr. Gk *mimētikos*, fr. *mimeisthai*] **1 :** IMITATIVE **2 :** relating to, characterized by, or exhibiting mimicry ⟨~ coloring of a butterfly⟩ — **mi·met·i·cal·ly** \-i-k(ə-)lē\ *adv*
1mim·ic \'mim-ik\ *n* **1 :** MIME 1 **2 :** one that mimics
2mimic *adj* [L *mimicus*, fr. Gk *mimikos*, fr. *mimos* mime] **1 a :** IMITATIVE **b :** IMITATION, MOCK ⟨~ battle⟩ **2 :** of or relating to mime or mimicry — **mim·i·cal** \-i-kəl\ *adj*
3mimic *vt* **mim·icked** \-ikt\ **mim·ick·ing 1 :** to imitate closely **:** APE **2 :** to ridicule by imitation **3 :** SIMULATE **4 :** to resemble by biological mimicry **syn** see COPY
mim·ic·ry \'mim-i-krē\ *n* **1 a :** an instance of mimicking **b :** the action, practice, or art of mimicking **2 :** a superficial resemblance of one organism to another or to natural objects among which it lives that secures it concealment, protection, or other advantage
Mi·mir \'mē-,mi(ə)r\ *n* [ON *Mīmir*] **:** a giant in Norse mythology who lives by the well at the root of Yggdrasil and who knows the past and future
mi·mo·sa \mə-'mō-sə, mī-, -zə\ *n* [NL, genus name, fr. L *mimus* mime] **:** any of a genus (*Mimosa*) of leguminous trees, shrubs, and herbs of tropical and warm regions with usu. bipinnate often prickly leaves and globular heads of small white or pink flowers
mi·na \'mī-nə\ *n* [L, fr. Gk *mna*, of Sem origin; akin to Heb *māneh* mina] **:** an ancient unit of weight and value equal to 1/60 talent
min·able *or* **mine·able** \'mī-nə-bəl\ *adj* **:** capable of being mined
min·a·ret \,min-ə-'ret\ *n* [F, fr. Turk *minare*, fr. Ar *manārah* lighthouse] **:** a slender lofty tower attached to a mosque and surrounded by one or more projecting balconies from which the summons to prayer is cried by the muezzin
mi·na·to·ry \'min-ə-,tōr-ē, 'mī-nə-, -,tȯr-\ *adj* [LL *minatorius*, fr. L *minatus*, pp. of *minari* to threaten — more at MOUNT] **:** THREATENING, MENACING
1mince \'min(t)s\ *vb* [ME *mincen*, fr. MF *mincer*, fr. (assumed) VL *minutiare*, fr. L *minutia* smallness — more at MINUTIA] *vt* **1 a :** to cut or chop into very small pieces **b :** to subdivide minutely; *esp* **:** to damage by cutting up **2 :** to utter or pronounce with affectation **3 a** *archaic* **:** to diminish the force of **:** MINIMIZE **b :** to restrain (words) within the bounds of decorum ~ *vi* **:** to walk with short steps in a prim affected manner — **minc·er** *n*
2mince *n* **:** small chopped bits; *specif* **:** MINCEMEAT
mince·meat \'min(t)-,smēt\ *n* **1 :** minced meat **2 :** a finely chopped mixture of raisins, apples, spices, and other ingredients with or without meat
mince pie *n* **:** a pie made of mincemeat
minc·ing \'min(t)-siŋ\ *adj* **:** affectedly dainty or delicate — **minc·ing·ly** \-siŋ-lē\ *adv*
1mind \'mīnd\ *n* [ME, fr. OE *gemynd*; akin to OHG *gimunt* memory; both fr. a prehistoric EGmc-WGmc compound whose first constituent is represented by OE *ge-* (perfective prefix) and whose second constituent is akin to L *ment-*, *mens* mind, *monēre* to remind, warn, Gk *menos* spirit, *mnasthai*, *mimnēskesthai* to remember — more at CO-] **1 :** RECOLLECTION, MEMORY **2 a :** the element or complex of elements in an individual that feels, perceives, thinks, wills, and esp. reasons **b :** the conscious events and capabilities in an organism **c :** the organized conscious and unconscious adaptive activity of an organism **3 :** INTENTION, DESIRE **4 :** the normal or healthy condition of the mental faculties **5 :** OPINION, VIEW **6 :** DISPOSITION, MOOD **7 a :** a person or group embodying mental qualities ⟨the public ~⟩ **b :** intellectual ability **8** *cap*, *Christian Science* **:** 2GOD b **9 :** a conscious substratum or factor in the universe
2mind *vt* **1** *chiefly dial* **:** REMIND **2** *chiefly dial* **:** REMEMBER **3 :** to attend to closely **4 a :** to become aware of **:** NOTICE **b** *chiefly*

dial : INTEND, PURPOSE **5 a :** to give heed to **b :** OBEY **6 a :** to be concerned about **b :** DISLIKE **7 a :** to be careful : SEE ⟨~ you finish it⟩ **b :** to be cautious about ⟨~ the broken rung⟩ **8 :** to take charge of : TEND ~ *vi* **1 :** to be attentive or wary **2 :** to become concerned : CARE **3 :** to pay heed; *esp* : OBEY — **mind·er** *n*

mind·ed \'mīn-dəd\ *adj* **1 :** having a mind of a specified character **2 :** DISPOSED, INCLINED

mind·ful \'mīn(d)-fəl\ *adj* **1 :** bearing in mind : AWARE **2 :** inclined to be aware — **mind·ful·ly** \-fə-lē\ *adv* — **mind·ful·ness** *n*

mind·less \'mīn-(d)ləs\ *adj* **1 :** destitute of mind or consciousness; *esp* : UNINTELLIGENT **2 :** INATTENTIVE, HEEDLESS — **mind·less·ly** *adv* — **mind·less·ness** *n*

mind reader *n* **:** one that professes or is held to be able to perceive another's thought without normal means of communication — **mind reading** *n*

mind's eye *n* **:** the mental faculty of conceiving imaginary or recollected scenes

1**mine** \(')mīn\ *adj* [ME *min* — more at MY] *archaic* : MY — used before a word beginning with a vowel or *h* ⟨~ own true love⟩ ⟨~ host⟩ or sometimes as a modifier of a preceding noun ⟨mother ~⟩

2**mine** \'mīn\ *pron, sing or pl in constr* **:** my one : my ones — used without a following noun as a pronoun equivalent in meaning to the adjective *my*

3**mine** \'mīn\ *n* [ME, fr. MF] **1 a :** a pit or excavation in the earth from which mineral substances are taken **b :** an ore deposit **2 :** a subterranean passage under an enemy position **3 :** an encased explosive designed to destroy enemy personnel **4 :** a rich source of supply **5 :** a pyrotechnic piece comprising various small fireworks that are scattered into the air with a loud report

4**mine** \'mīn\ *vi* **:** to dig a mine ~ *vt* **1 a :** to dig under to gain access or cause the collapse of (an enemy position) **b :** UNDERMINE **2 :** to get (as ore) from the earth **3 :** to burrow beneath the surface of ⟨larva that ~*s* leaves⟩ **4 :** to place military mines in, on, or under **5 a :** to dig into for ore or metal **b :** to process for obtaining a natural constituent ⟨~ the air for nitrogen⟩ — **min·er** *n*

mine·lay·er \'mīn-,lā-ər, -,le(-ə)r\ *n* **:** a naval vessel for laying underwater mines

1**min·er·al** \'min-(ə-)rəl\ *n* [ME, fr. ML *minerale*, fr. neut. of *mineralis*] **1 a :** a solid homogeneous crystalline chemical element or compound that results from the inorganic processes of nature; *broadly* **:** any of various naturally occurring homogeneous substances (as stone, coal, salt, sulfur, sand, petroleum, water, or natural gas) obtained for man's use usu. from the ground **b :** a synthetic substance having the chemical composition and crystalline form and properties of a naturally occurring mineral **2** *obs* : MINE **3 :** something neither animal nor vegetable **4 :** ORE **5 :** an inorganic substance **6** *pl, Brit* : MINERAL WATER

2**mineral** *adj* [ME, fr. ML *mineralis*, fr. *minera* mine, ore, fr. OF *miniere*, fr. *mine*] **1 :** of or relating to minerals : INORGANIC **2 :** impregnated with mineral substances

min·er·al·iza·tion \,min-(ə-)rə-lə-'zā-shən\ *n* **1 :** the action of mineralizing **2 :** the state of being mineralized

min·er·al·ize \'min-(ə-)rə-,līz\ *vt* **1 :** to transform (a metal) into an ore **2 a :** to impregnate or supply with minerals or an inorganic compound **b :** to convert into mineral or inorganic form **3 :** PETRIFY — **min·er·al·iz·er** *n*

min·er·al·og·i·cal \,min-(ə-)rə-'läj-i-kəl\ *adj* **:** of or relating to mineralogy

min·er·al·o·gist \,min-ə-'räl-ə-jəst, -'ral-\ *n* **:** a specialist in mineralogy

min·er·al·o·gy \-jē\ *n, often attrib* [prob. fr. (assumed) NL *mineralogia*, irreg. fr. ML *minerale* + L *-logia* -logy] **1 :** a science dealing with minerals, their crystallography, physical and chemical properties, classification, and the ways of distinguishing them **2 :** the materials of mineralogy **3 :** a treatise on mineralogy

mineral oil *n* **:** an oil of mineral origin; *esp* **:** a refined petroleum oil used as a laxative

mineral pitch *n* **:** ASPHALT 1

mineral tar *n* **:** MALTHA

mineral water *n* **:** water naturally or artificially impregnated with mineral salts or gases (as carbon dioxide)

mineral wax *n* **:** a wax of mineral origin; *esp* **:** OZOKERITE

mineral wool *n* **:** any of various lightweight vitreous fibrous materials used esp. in heat and sound insulation

Mi·ner·va \mə-'nər-və\ *n* [L] **:** the Roman goddess of wisdom

min·e·stro·ne \,min-ə-'strō-nē, -'strōn\ *n* [It, aug. of *minestra*, fr. *minestrare* to serve, dish up, fr. L *ministrare*, fr. *minister* servant — more at MINISTER] **:** a rich thick vegetable soup with dried beans, macaroni, vermicelli, or similar ingredients

mine·sweep·er \'mīn-,swē-pər\ *n* **:** a warship designed for removing or neutralizing mines by dragging — **mine·sweep·ing** *n*

Ming \'miŋ\ *n* [Chin (Pek) *ming*2 luminous] **:** a Chinese dynasty dated 1368–1644 and marked by restoration of earlier traditions and in the arts by perfection of established techniques

min·gle \'miŋ-gəl\ *vb* **min·gling** \-g(ə-)liŋ\ [ME *menglen*, freq. of *mengen* to mix, fr. OE *mengan*; akin to MHG *mengen* to mix, Gk *massein* to knead] *vt* **1 :** to bring or combine together or with something else : INTERMIX **2 :** to prepare by mixing : CONCOCT ~ *vi* **:** to become mingled **syn** see MIX

ming tree \'miŋ-\ *n* [perh. fr. *Ming* (Chinese dynasty, 1368–1644)] **1 a :** a dwarfed evergreen conifer grown in a container or pot **b :** BONSAI **2 :** an artificial plant made by attaching flattened pads of alpine buckwheat (*Eriogonum ovalifolium*) left natural gray or colored to one or more twiggy branches usu. of manzanita

mini- *comb form* [*miniature*] **:** miniature **:** of small dimensions

1**min·ia·ture** \'min-ē-ə-,chu̇(ə)r, 'min-i-,chu̇(ə)r, 'min-yə-, -chər, -,t(y)u̇(ə)r\ *n* [It *miniatura* art of illuminating a manuscript, fr. ML, fr. L *miniatus*, pp. of *miniare* to color with red lead, fr. *minium* red lead, of Iberian origin; akin to Basque *arminéa* cinnabar] **1 :** a copy on a much reduced scale **2 :** a painting in an illuminated book or manuscript **3 :** the art of painting miniatures **4 :** a very small portrait or other painting (as on ivory or metal) — **min·ia·tur·ist** \-,chu̇r-əst, -chər-, -,t(y)u̇r-\ *n*

2**miniature** *adj* **1 :** being or represented on a small scale **2 :** of or relating to still photography using film 35 mm. wide or smaller **syn** see SMALL

min·ia·tur·iza·tion \,min-ē-ə-,chu̇r-ə-'zā-shən, ,min-i-, ,min-yə-, -chər-, -,t(y)u̇r-\ *n* **:** the act or process of miniaturizing

min·ia·tur·ize \'min-ē-ə-,chu̇(ə)r-,īz, 'min-i-, 'min-yə-, -chər-, -,t(y)u̇(ə)r-\ *vt* **:** to design or construct in small size

mini·cab \'min-ē-,kab\ *n* **:** a very small car used as a taxicab

mini·cam \-,kam\ *also* **mini·cam·era** \-,kam-(ə-)rə\ *n* **:** a miniature camera

min·ié ball \'min-ē-,bȯl, ,min-ē-,ā-'bȯl\ *n* [Claude Étienne *Minié* †1879 F army officer] **:** a rifle bullet with a conical head used in the middle of the 19th century

min·i·fy \'min-ə-,fī\ *vt* [L *mini*mus smallest + E *-fy*] **:** LESSEN

min·i·kin \'min-i-kən\ *n* [obs. D *minneken* darling] *archaic* **:** a small or dainty creature — **minikin** *adj*

min·im \'min-əm\ *n* [L *minimus* least] **1 :** HALF NOTE **2 :** something very minute **3** — see MEASURE table — **minim** *adj*

min·i·mal \'min-ə-məl\ *adj* **:** relating to or being a minimum **:** LEAST — **min·i·mal·ly** \-mə-lē\ *adv*

min·i·mal·ist \-mə-ləst\ *n* **:** one who favors restricting the functions and powers of a political organization or the achievement of a set of goals to a minimum

min·i·mi·za·tion \,min-ə-mə-'zā-shən\ *n* **:** the act or process of minimizing

min·i·mize \'min-ə-,mīz\ *vt* **1 :** to reduce to a minimum **2 a :** to estimate at a minimum **b :** BELITTLE **syn** see DECRY — **min·i·miz·er** *n*

min·i·mum \'min-ə-məm\ *n, pl* **min·i·ma** \-ə-mə\ *or* **minimums** [L, neuter of *minimus* smallest; akin to L *minor* smaller] **1 :** the least quantity assignable, admissible, or possible **2 :** the least of a set of numbers; *specif* **:** the smallest value assumed by a continuous function defined on a closed interval **3 :** the lowest degree or amount of variation reached or recorded — **mini·mum** *adj*

minimum wage *n* **1 :** LIVING WAGE **2 :** a wage fixed by legal authority or by contract as the least that will provide the minimum standard of living necessary for employee health, efficiency, and well-being

min·ing \'mī-niŋ\ *n* **:** the process or business of working mines

min·ion \'min-yən\ *n* [MF *mignon* darling] **1 :** a servile dependent **2 :** one highly favored : IDOL **3 :** a subordinate official

min·is·cule \'min-əs-,kyü(ə)l\ *var of* MINUSCULE

mini·skirt \'min-ē-,skərt\ *n* **:** a woman's short skirt with the hemline several inches above the knee

1**min·is·ter** \'min-ə-stər\ *n* [ME *ministre*, fr. OF, fr. L *minister* servant; akin to L *minor* smaller] **1 :** AGENT **2 a :** one officiating or assisting at the administration of a sacrament **b :** a Protestant clergyman **c :** a person exercising clerical functions **3** *or* **minister-general :** the superior of one of several religious orders **4 :** a high officer of state entrusted with the management of a division of governmental activities **5 a :** a diplomatic representative (as an ambassador) accredited to the court or seat of government of a foreign state **b :** a diplomatic representative ranking below an ambassador and usu. accredited to states of less importance

2**minister** *vi* **min·is·ter·ing** \-st(ə-)riŋ\ **1 :** to perform the functions of a minister of religion **2 :** to give aid : SERVE ⟨~ to the sick⟩

min·is·te·ri·al \,min-ə-'stir-ē-əl\ *adj* **1 :** of or relating to a minister or the ministry **2 a :** being or having the characteristics of an act or duty prescribed by law as part of the duties of an administrative office **b :** relating to or being an act done after ascertaining the existence of a specified state of facts in obedience to a legal order without exercise of personal judgment or discretion **3 :** acting or active as an agent : INSTRUMENTAL — **min·is·te·ri·al·ly** \-ē-ə-lē\ *adv*

minister plenipotentiary *n, pl* **ministers plenipotentiary :** a diplomatic agent ranking below an ambassador but possessing full power and authority

minister resident *n, pl* **ministers resident :** a diplomatic agent resident at a foreign court or seat of government and ranking below a minister plenipotentiary

min·is·trant \'min-ə-strənt\ *adj* **:** performing service as a minister — **ministrant** *n*

min·is·tra·tion \,min-ə-'strā-shən\ *n* **:** the act or process of ministering

min·is·try \'min-ə-strē\ *n* **1 :** MINISTRATION **2 :** the office, duties, or functions of a minister **3 :** the body of ministers of religion **:** CLERGY **4 :** AGENCY 2, INSTRUMENTALITY **5 :** the period of service or office of a minister or ministry **6** *often cap* **a :** the body of ministers governing a nation or state from which a smaller cabinet is sometimes selected **b :** the group of ministers constituting a cabinet **7 a :** a government department presided over by a minister **b :** the building in which the business of a ministry is transacted

mini·track \'min-ē-,trak\ *n* **:** an electronic system for tracking an earth satellite or rocket by radio waves transmitted from it to a chain of ground stations

min·i·um \'min-ē-əm\ *n* [ME, fr. L, cinnabar, red lead, of Iberian origin; akin to Basque *arminéa* cinnabar] **:** RED LEAD

min·i·ver \'min-ə-vər\ *n* [ME *meniver*, fr. OF *menu vair* small vair] **:** a white fur worn orig. by medieval nobles and used chiefly for robes of state

mink \'miŋk\ *n, pl* **mink** *or* **minks** [ME] **1 :** soft fur or pelt of the mink varying in color from white to dark brown **2 :** any of several slender-bodied semiaquatic carnivorous mammals (genus *Mustela*) that resemble and are closely related to the weasels and have partially webbed feet, a rather short bushy tail, and a soft thick coat

min·ne·sing·er \'min-i-,siŋ-ər, 'min-ə-,ziŋ-\ *n* [G, fr. MHG, fr. *minne* love + *singer*] **:** one of a class of German lyric poets and musicians of the 12th to the 14th centuries

min·now \'min-(,)ō, -ə(-w)\ *n, pl* **minnows** *also* **minnow** [ME *menawe*; akin to OE *myne* minnow, Russ *men'* eelpout] **1 :** any of various small fishes; *esp* **:** a small European cyprinid fish (*Phoxinus phoxinus*) common in gravelly streams and attaining a length of about three inches **2 :** a live or artificial minnow used as bait

1**Mi·no·an** \mə-'nō-ən, mī-\ *adj* [L *minous* of Minos, fr. Gk *minōios*, fr. *Minōs* Minos] **:** of or relating to a Bronze Age culture of Crete (3000 B.C.–1100 B.C.)

2**Minoan** *n* **:** a native or inhabitant of ancient Crete

1**mi·nor** \'mī-nər\ *n* **1 :** a person who has not attained majority

2 : a minor musical interval, scale, key, or mode 3 : a minor academic subject

[2]**minor** *adj* [ME, fr. L, smaller, inferior; akin to OHG *minniro* smaller, L *minuere* to lessen, Gk *meiōn* less] **1 :** inferior in importance, size, or degree **:** comparatively unimportant **2 :** not having reached majority **3 a :** having the third, sixth, and sometimes the seventh degrees lowered a semitone ⟨~ scale⟩ **b :** based on a minor scale ⟨~ key⟩ **c :** less by a semitone than the corresponding major interval ⟨~ third⟩ **d :** containing a minor third ⟨~ triad⟩ **4 :** not serious or involving risk to life ⟨~ illness⟩ **5 :** of or relating to an academic subject requiring fewer courses than a major

[3]**minor** *vi* **:** to take courses in a minor subject

mi·nor·ca \mə-ˈnȯr-kə\ *n* [*Minorca*, one of the Balearic islands] **:** any of a breed of domestic fowls of the Mediterranean class resembling leghorns but larger

Mi·nor·ite \ˈmī-nə-ˌrīt\ *n* [fr. *Friar Minor* (Franciscan)] **:** FRANCISCAN

mi·nor·i·ty \mə-ˈnȯr-ət-ē, mī-, -ˈnär-\ *n, often attrib* **1 a :** the period before attainment of majority **b :** the state of being a legal minor **2 :** the smaller in number of two groups constituting a whole; *specif* **:** a group having less than the number of votes necessary for control **3 :** a part of a population differing from others in some characteristics and often subjected to differential treatment

minor league *n* **:** a league of professional clubs in a sport other than the recognized major leagues

minor order *n* **:** one of the four lower clerical orders; *esp* **:** one conferred on candidates for the Roman Catholic priesthood for nominal service as a doorkeeper, lector, exorcist, or acolyte

minor party *n* **:** a political party whose electoral strength is so small as to prevent its gaining control of a government except in rare and exceptional circumstances

minor premise *n* **:** the premise of a syllogism that contains the minor term

minor seminary *n* **:** a Roman Catholic seminary giving all or part of high school and junior college training

minor suit *n* **:** clubs or diamonds in bridge

minor term *n* **:** the term of a syllogism that forms the subject of the conclusion

Mi·nos \ˈmī-nəs, -ˌnäs\ *n* [L, fr. Gk *Minōs*] **:** a king and lawgiver of Crete, son of Zeus and Europa, and after death a judge in Hades

Mi·no·taur \ˈmin-ə-ˌtȯ(ə)r, ˈmī-nə-\ *n* [ME, fr. MF, fr. L *Minotaurus*, fr. Gk *Minōtauros*, fr. *Minōs* + *tauros* a bull] **:** a monster shaped half like a man and half like a bull, confined in the labyrinth built by Daedalus for Minos, and given a periodical tribute of seven youths and seven maidens until slain by Theseus

min·ster \ˈmin(t)-stər\ *n* [ME, monastery, minster, fr. OE *mynster*, fr. LL *monasterium* monastery] **1 :** a church attached to a monastery **2 :** a large or important church

min·strel \ˈmin(t)-strəl\ *n* [ME *menestrel*, fr. OF, official, servant, minstrel, fr. LL *ministerialis* imperial household officer, fr. L *ministerium* service, fr. *minister* servant — more at MINISTER] **1 :** one of a class of medieval musical entertainers; *esp* **:** a singer of verses to the accompaniment of a harp **2 a :** MUSICIAN **b :** POET **3 a :** one of a troupe of performers typically giving a program of Negro melodies, jokes, and impersonations and usu. blacked in imitation of Negroes **b :** a performance by a troupe of minstrels

min·strel·sy \-sē\ *n* [ME *minstralcie*, fr. MF *menestralsie*, fr. *menestrel*] **1 :** the singing and playing of a minstrel **2 :** a body of minstrels **3 :** a group of songs or verse

[1]**mint** \ˈmint\ *n* [ME *mynt* coin, money, fr. OE *mynet*; akin to OHG *munizza* coin; both fr. a prehistoric WGmc word borrowed fr. L *moneta* mint, coin, fr. *Moneta*, epithet of Juno; fr. the fact that the Romans coined money in the temple of Juno Moneta] **1 :** a place where coins are made **2 :** a place where something is manufactured **3 :** a vast sum or amount

[2]**mint** *vt* **1 :** to make (money) out of metal **:** COIN **2 :** FABRICATE, INVENT — **mint·er** *n*

[3]**mint** *adj* **:** unmarred as if fresh from a mint ⟨~ coins⟩

[4]**mint** *n* [ME *minte*, fr. OE; akin to OHG *minza*; both fr. a prehistoric WGmc word borrowed fr. L *mentha* mint] **1 :** any of various aromatic plants constituting a family (Labiatae, the mint family); *esp* **:** one of a genus (*Mentha*) used in flavoring and cookery **2 :** a confection flavored with mint

mint·age \ˈmint-ij\ *n* **1 :** the action or process of minting coins **2 :** an impression placed upon a coin **3 :** coins produced by minting **4 :** the cost of manufacturing coins

mint julep *n* **:** JULEP 2

min·u·end \ˈmin-yə-ˌwend\ *n* [L *minuendum*, neut. of *minuendus*, gerundive of *minuere* to lessen — more at MINOR] **:** a number from which the subtrahend is to be subtracted

min·u·et \ˌmin-yə-ˈwet\ *n* [F *menuet*, fr. obs. F, tiny, fr. OF, fr. *menu* small, fr. L *minutus*] **1 :** a slow graceful dance consisting of forward balancing, bowing, and toe pointing **2 :** music for or in the rhythm of a minuet

[1]**mi·nus** \ˈmī-nəs\ *prep* [ME, fr. L *minus*, adv., less, fr. neut. of *minor* smaller — more at MINOR] **1 :** diminished by **:** LESS ⟨seven ~ four is three⟩ **2 :** deprived of **:** WITHOUT ⟨~ his hat⟩

[2]**minus** *n* **1 :** a negative quantity **2** DEFICIENCY, DEFECT

[3]**minus** *adj* **1 :** algebraically negative ⟨~ quantity⟩ **2 :** having negative qualities

[1]**mi·nus·cule** \ˈmin-əs-ˌkyü(ə)l, min-ˈəs-, ˈmin-yəs-, mī-ˈnəs-\ *n* [F, fr. L *minusculus* rather small, dim. of *minor* smaller] **1 a :** one of several ancient and medieval writing styles developed from cursive and having simplified and small forms **b :** a letter in this style **2 :** a lowercase letter

[2]**minuscule** *adj* **1 :** written in or in the size or style of minuscules **2 :** very small

minus sign *n* **:** a sign — used in mathematics to indicate subtraction (as in $8-6=2$) or a negative quantity (as in $-10°$)

[1]**min·ute** \ˈmin-ət\ *n* [ME, fr. MF, fr. LL *minuta*, fr. L *minutus* small, fr. pp. of *minuere* to lessen — more at MINOR] **1 :** the 60th part of an hour of time or of a degree **2 :** the distance one can traverse in a minute **3 :** a short space of time **:** MOMENT **4 a :** MEMORANDUM, DRAFT **b** *pl* **:** the official record of the proceedings of a meeting

[2]**minute** *vt* **:** to make notes or a brief summary of

[3]**mi·nute** \mī-ˈn(y)üt, mə-\ *adj* [L *minutus*] **1 :** very small **:** INFINITESIMAL **2 :** of small importance **:** TRIFLING **3 :** marked by close attention to details **syn** see CIRCUMSTANTIAL, SMALL — **mi·nute·ness** *n*

minute hand *n* **:** the long hand that marks the minutes on the face of a watch or clock

[1]**mi·nute·ly** \mī-ˈn(y)üt-lē, mə-\ *adv* **1 :** into very small pieces **2 :** in a minute manner or degree

[2]**min·ute·ly** \ˈmin-ət-lē\ *adv* **:** every minute — **minutely** *adj*

min·ute·man \ˈmin-ət-ˌman\ *n* **:** a member of a group of armed men pledged to take the field at a minute's notice during and immediately before the American Revolution

min·ute steak \ˌmin-ət-\ *n* **:** a small thin steak that can be quickly cooked

mi·nu·tia \mə-ˈn(y)ü-sh(ē-)ə, mī-\ *n, pl* **mi·nu·ti·ae** \-shē-ˌē, -ˌī\ [L *minutiae* trifles, details, fr. pl. of *minutia* smallness, fr. *minutus*] **:** a minute or minor detail — usu. used in pl.

minx \ˈmiŋ(k)s\ *n* [origin unknown] **1 :** a pert girl **2** *obs* **:** a wanton woman

mio- — see MI-

Mio·cene \ˈmī-ə-ˌsēn\ *adj* **:** of, relating to, or being an epoch of the Tertiary between the Pliocene and the Oligocene or the corresponding system of rocks — **Miocene** *n*

mi·que·let \ˌmik-ə-ˈlet\ *n* [Sp *miquelete*] **1 :** a Spanish or French irregular soldier during the Peninsular War **2 :** a member of various Spanish local infantry regiments

mir \ˈmi(ə)r\ *n* [Russ] **:** a village community in czarist Russia characterized by joint ownership of the land and cultivation by individual families

mi·ra·bi·le dic·tu \mə-ˌräb-ə-lē-ˈdik-(ˌ)tü\ [L] **:** wonderful to relate

mir·a·cle \ˈmir-i-kəl\ *n* [ME, fr. OF, fr. L *miraculum*, fr. *mirari* to wonder at — more at SMILE] **1 :** an extraordinary event manifesting a supernatural work of God **2 :** an extremely outstanding or unusual event, thing, or accomplishment **3** *Christian Science* **:** a divinely natural occurrence that must be learned humanly

miracle play *n* **:** a medieval dramatic representation of episodes from the life of a miracle-working saint or martyr

mi·rac·u·lous \mə-ˈrak-yə-ləs\ *adj* [MF *miraculeux*, fr. ML *miraculosus*, fr. L *miraculum*] **1 :** of the nature of a miracle **:** SUPERNATURAL **2 :** resembling a miracle **:** MARVELOUS **3 :** working or able to work miracles — **mi·rac·u·lous·ly** *adv* — **mi·rac·u·lous·ness** *n*

mir·a·dor \ˈmir-ə-ˌdō(ə)r, ˌmir-ə-ˈ\ *n* [Sp, fr. Catal, fr. *mirar* to look at, fr. L *mirari*] **:** a turret, window, or balcony designed to command an extensive outlook

mi·rage \mə-ˈräzh\ *n* [F, fr. *mirer* to look at, fr. L *mirari*] **1 a :** an optical phenomenon produced by a layer of heated air of varying density across which are seen usu. inverted reflections of distant objects **b :** an atmospheric phenomenon in which the air appears to move in ascending waves **2 :** something illusory and unattainable like a mirage **syn** see DELUSION

[1]**mire** \ˈmī(ə)r\ *n* [ME, fr. ON *mȳrr*; akin to OE *mōs* marsh — more at MOSS] **1 :** MARSH, BOG **2 :** heavy often deep mud, slush, or dirt — **miry** \ˈmī(ə)r-ē\ *adj*

[2]**mire** *vt* **1 a :** to cause to stick fast in or as if in mire **b :** ENTANGLE, INVOLVE **2 :** to soil with mud, slush, or dirt **~** *vi* **:** to stick or sink in mire

mirk, mirky *var of* MURK, MURKY

[1]**mir·ror** \ˈmir-ər\ *n* [ME *mirour*, fr. OF, fr. *mirer* to look at, fr. L *mirari* to wonder at — more at SMILE] **1 :** a polished or smooth substance (as of glass) that forms images by reflection **2 a :** something that gives a true representation **b :** an exemplary model

[2]**mirror** *vt* **:** to reflect in or as if in a mirror

mirth \ˈmərth\ *n* [ME, fr. OE *myrgth*, fr. *myrge* merry — more at MERRY] **:** gladness or gaiety as shown by or accompanied with laughter — **mirth·ful** \-fəl\ *adj* — **mirth·ful·ly** \-fə-lē\ *adv* — **mirth·ful·ness** *n*

syn GLEE, JOLLITY, HILARITY: MIRTH implies generally lightness of heart and love of gaiety and specif. denotes laughter; GLEE stresses exultation shown in laughter, cries of joy, or sometimes malicious delight; JOLLITY suggests exuberance or lack of restraint in mirth or glee; HILARITY suggests loud or irrepressible laughter or high-spirited boisterousness

[1]**mis-** *prefix* [partly fr. ME, fr. OE; partly fr. ME *mes-*, *mis-*, fr. OF *mes-*, of Gmc origin; akin to OE *mis-*; akin to OE *missan* to miss] **1 a :** badly **:** wrongly ⟨*mis*judge⟩ **b :** unfavorably ⟨*mis*esteem⟩ **c :** in a suspicious manner ⟨*mis*doubt⟩ **2 :** bad **:** wrong ⟨*mis*deed⟩ **3 :** opposite or lack of ⟨*mis*trust⟩ **4 :** not ⟨*mis*know⟩

[2]**mis-** *or* **miso-** *comb form* [Gk, fr. *misein* to hate] **:** hatred ⟨*miso*gamy⟩

mis·ad·ven·ture \ˌmis-əd-ˈven-chər\ *n* [ME *mesaventure*, fr. OF, fr. *mesavenir* to chance badly, fr. *mis-* + *avenir* to chance, happen, fr. L *advenire* — more at ADVENTURE] **:** MISFORTUNE, MISHAP; *esp* **:** a minor sometimes ridiculous mishap

mis·al·li·ance \ˌmis-ə-ˈlī-ən(t)s\ *n* [modif. of F *mésalliance*] **:** an improper alliance; *esp* **:** a marriage between persons unsuited to each other

mis·an·thrope \ˈmis-ᵊn-ˌthrōp\ *n* [Gk *misanthrōpos* hating mankind, fr. *mis-* + *anthrōpos* man] **:** one who hates mankind

mis·an·throp·ic \ˌmis-ᵊn-ˈthräp-ik\ *adj* **1 :** of, relating to, or characteristic of a misanthrope **2 :** marked by a hatred or contempt for mankind — **mis·an·throp·i·cal·ly** \-i-k(ə-)lē\ *adv*

mis·an·thro·py \mis-ˈan(t)-thrə-pē\ *n* **:** a hatred or distrust of mankind

mis·ap·pli·ca·tion \ˌmis-ˌap-lə-ˈkā-shən\ *n* **:** the action of misapplying

mis·ap·ply \ˌmis-ə-ˈplī\ *vt* **:** to apply wrongly

mis·ap·pre·hend \ˌmis-ˌap-ri-ˈhend\ *vt* **:** to apprehend wrongly **:** MISUNDERSTAND — **mis·ap·pre·hen·sion** \-ˈhen-chən\ *n*

mis·ap·pro·pri·ate \ˌmis-ə-ˈprō-prē-ˌāt\ *vt* **:** to appropriate wrongly — **mis·ap·pro·pri·a·tion** \-ˌprō-prē-ˈā-shən\ *n*

mis·be·come \ˌmis-bi-ˈkəm\ *vt* **:** to be inappropriate or unbecoming to

mis·be·got·ten \-ˈgät-ᵊn\ *adj* **1 :** unlawfully conceived **2 :** of improper origin

mis·be·have \ˌmis-bi-ˈhāv\ *vi* **:** to behave improperly — **mis·be·hav·er** *n* — **mis·be·hav·ior** \-ˈhā-vyər\ *n*

mis·be·lief \ˌmis-bə-ˈlēf\ *n* **:** erroneous or false belief

mis·be·lieve \-ˈlēv\ *vi, obs* **:** to hold a false or unorthodox belief — **mis·be·liev·er** *n*

mis·brand \(')mis-'brand\ *vt* **:** to brand falsely or in a misleading way
mis·cal·cu·late \(')mis-'kal-kyə-,lāt\ *vt* **:** to calculate wrongly ~ *vi* **:** to make a mistake in calculation — **mis·cal·cu·la·tion** \,mis-,kal-kyə-'lā-shən\ *n*
mis·call \(')mis-'kȯl\ *vt* **:** to call by a wrong name **:** MISNAME
mis·car·riage \mis-'kar-ij\ *n* **1 :** MISMANAGEMENT; *esp* **:** a failure in the administration of justice **2 a :** expulsion of a human fetus before it is viable and esp. between the 12th and 28th weeks of gestation **b :** ABORTION
mis·car·ry \(')mis-'kar-ē\ *vi* **1** *obs* **:** to come to harm **2 :** to suffer miscarriage of a fetus **3 :** to fail of an effect or in one's intention
mis·cast \(')mis-'kast\ *vt* **:** to give an unsuitable role to
mis·ce·ge·na·tion \(,)mis-,ej-ə-'nā-shən, ,mis-i-jə-'nā-\ *n* [L *miscēre* to mix + *genus* race — more at MIX, KIN] **:** a mixture of races; *esp* **:** marriage or cohabitation between a white person and a member of another race
mis·cel·la·nea \,mis-ə-'lā-nē-ə, -nyə\ *n pl* [L, fr. neut. pl. of *miscellaneus*] **:** a collection of miscellaneous objects or writings
mis·cel·la·neous \,mis-ə-'lā-nē-əs, -nyəs\ *adj* [L *miscellaneus*, fr. *miscellus* mixed, prob. fr. *miscēre*] **1 :** consisting of diverse things or members **:** HETEROGENEOUS **2 :** having various traits **3 :** dealing with or interested in diverse subjects — **mis·cel·la·neous·ly** *adv* — **mis·cel·la·neous·ness** *n*
mis·cel·la·nist \'mis-ə-,lā-nəst, *chiefly Brit* mis-'el-ə-nist\ *n* **:** a writer of miscellanies
mis·cel·la·ny \-nē\ *n* [prob. modif. of F *miscellanées*, pl., fr. L *miscellanea*] **1 :** a mixture of various things **2 a** *pl* **:** separate writings collected in one volume **b :** a collection of writings on various subjects
mis·chance \(')mis(h)-'chan(t)s\ *n* [ME *mischaunce*, fr. OF *meschance*, fr. *mis-* + *chance*] **1 :** bad luck **2 :** a piece of bad luck **:** MISHAP **syn** see MISFORTUNE
mis·chief \'mis(h)-chəf\ *n* [ME *meschief*, fr. OF, calamity, fr. *mes-* + *chief* head, end — more at CHIEF] **1 :** injury or damage caused by a human agency **2 :** a cause or source of harm, evil, or irritation; *esp* **:** a person who causes mischief **3 a :** action that annoys or irritates **b :** MISCHIEVOUSNESS
mis·chie·vous \'mis(h)-chə-vəs\ *adj* **1 :** HARMFUL, INJURIOUS **2 a :** able or tending to cause annoyance, trouble, or minor injury **b :** irresponsibly playful — **mis·chie·vous·ly** *adv* — **mis·chie·vous·ness** *n*
mis·ci·bil·i·ty \,mis-ə-'bil-ət-ē\ *n* **:** the property of being miscible
mis·ci·ble \'mis-ə-bəl\ *adj* [ML *miscibilis*, fr. L *miscēre* to mix — more at MIX] **:** capable of being mixed; *specif* **:** capable of mixing in any ratio without separation of two phases ⟨~ liquids⟩
mis·con·ceive \,mis-kən-'sēv\ *vt* **:** to interpret incorrectly **:** MISJUDGE — **mis·con·ceiv·er** *n* — **mis·con·cep·tion** \-'sep-shən\ *n*
mis·con·duct \(')mis-'kän-(,)dəkt\ *n* **1 :** mismanagement esp. of governmental or military responsibilities **2 :** intentional wrongdoing; *specif* **:** deliberate violation of a law or standard esp. by a government official **:** MALFEASANCE **3 :** improper behavior; *esp* **:** ADULTERY — **mis·con·duct** \,mis-kən-'dəkt\ *vt*
mis·con·struc·tion \,mis-kən-'strək-shən\ *n* **:** the act, the process, or an instance of misconstruing
mis·con·strue \,mis-kən-'strü\ *vt* **:** to construe wrongly **:** MISINTERPRET
mis·count \(')mis-'kau̇nt\ *vb* [ME *misconten*, fr. MF *mesconter*, fr. *mes-* + *conter* to count] *vt* **:** to count wrongly **:** MISCALCULATE ~ *vi* **:** to make a wrong count — **miscount** *n*
[1]**mis·cre·ant** \'mis-krē-ənt\ *adj* [ME *miscreaunt*, fr. MF *mescreant*, prp. of *mescroire* to disbelieve, fr. *mes-* [1]mis + *croire* to believe, fr. L *credere* — more at CREED] **1 :** UNBELIEVING, HERETICAL **2 :** DEPRAVED, VILLAINOUS
[2]**miscreant** *n* **1 :** INFIDEL, HERETIC **2 :** one who behaves criminally or viciously
mis·cre·ate \,mis-krē-'āt\ *vt* **:** to create misshapen or amiss — **mis·cre·ate** \'mis-krē-ət, ,mis-krē-'āt\ *adj* — **mis·cre·ation** \,mis-krē-'ā-shən\ *n*
[1]**mis·cue** \(')mis-'kyü\ *n* **1 :** a faulty stroke in billiards in which the cue slips **2 :** MISTAKE, SLIP
[2]**miscue** *vi* **1 :** to make a miscue **2 a :** to miss a stage cue **b :** to answer a wrong cue
mis·deal \(')mis-'dē(ə)l\ *vi* **:** to deal cards incorrectly ~ *vt* **:** to deal incorrectly — **misdeal** *n*
mis·deed \(')mis-'dēd\ *n* **:** a wrong deed **:** OFFENSE
mis·deem \-'dēm\ *vt* **:** MISJUDGE
mis·de·mean·ant \,mis-də-'mē-nənt\ *n* **:** a person convicted of a misdemeanor
mis·de·mea·nor \,mis-di-'mē-nər\ *n* **1 :** a crime less serious than a felony **2 :** MISDEED
mis·di·rect \,mis-də-'rekt, -(,)dī-\ *vt* **:** to give a wrong direction to — **mis·di·rec·tion** \-'rek-shən\ *n*
mis·do \(')mis-'dü\ *vt* **:** to do wrongly or improperly — **mis·do·er** *n* — **mis·do·ing** *n*
mis·doubt \(')mis-'dau̇t\ *vt* **1 :** to doubt the reality or truth of **2 :** SUSPECT, FEAR — **misdoubt** *n*
mise-en-scène \,mē-,zäⁿ-'sen, -'säⁿ\ *n, pl* **mise-en-scènes** \-'sen(z), -'säⁿ(z)\ [F *mise en scène*] **1 a :** the process of arranging actors and scenery on a stage for a theatrical production **b :** stage setting **2 a :** the physical setting of an action **b :** ENVIRONMENT, MILIEU
mi·ser \'mī-zər\ *n* [L *miser* miserable] **:** a mean grasping person; *esp* **:** one who lives miserably in order to hoard his wealth
mis·er·a·ble \'miz-ər-bəl, 'miz-(ə-)rə-bəl\ *adj* [ME, fr. MF, fr. L *miserabilis* wretched, pitiable, fr. *miserari* to pity, fr. *miser*] **1 a :** wretchedly deficient or meager ⟨a ~ hovel⟩ **b :** causing extreme discomfort or unhappiness **2 :** extremely poor or unhappy **:** WRETCHED **3 :** SHAMEFUL, DISCREDITABLE — **miserable** *n* — **mis·er·a·ble·ness** *n* — **mis·er·a·bly** \-blē\ *adv*
mi·se·re·re \,miz-ə-'ri(ə)r-ē, -'re(ə)r-; ,mē-zə-'rā-(,)rā\ *n* [L, be merciful, fr. *misereri* to be merciful, fr. *miser* wretched; fr. the first word of the Psalm] **1** *cap* **a :** the 50th Psalm in the Vulgate **b :** a musical setting of this Psalm **2 :** MISERICORD
mi·seri·cord *or* **mi·seri·corde** \mə-'zer-ə-,kȯ(ə)rd, -'ser-\ *n* [ML *misercordia* seat in church, fr. L, mercy, fr. *misericord-*, *misericors* merciful, fr. *misereri* + *cord-*, *cor* heart — more at HEART] **:** a small projection on the bottom of a hinged church seat that gives support to a standing worshiper when the seat is turned up
mi·ser·li·ness \'mī-zər-lē-nəs\ *n* **:** the quality or state of being miserly
mi·ser·ly \-lē\ *adj* **:** of, relating to, or characteristic of a miser **:** GRASPING **syn** see STINGY
mis·ery \'miz-(ə-)rē\ *n* **1 :** a state of suffering and want that is the result of poverty or affliction **2 :** a circumstance, thing, or place that causes suffering or discomfort **3 :** a state of great unhappiness and emotional distress **syn** see DISTRESS
mis·es·teem \,mis-ə-'stēm\ *vt* **:** to esteem wrongly and esp. too low
mis·es·ti·mate \(')mis-'es-tə-,māt\ *vt* **:** to estimate falsely — **mis·es·ti·ma·tion** \,mis-,es-tə-'mā-shən\ *n*
mis·fea·sance \mis-'fēz-ᵊn(t)s\ *n* [MF *mesfaisance*, fr. *mesfaire* to do wrong, fr. *mes-* [1]mis- + *faire* to make, do, fr. L *facere* — more at DO] **:** TRESPASS; *specif* **:** the performance of a lawful action in an illegal or improper manner — **mis·fea·sor** \-'fē-zər, -,zȯ(ə)r\ *n*
mis·file \(')mis-'fī(ə)l\ *vt* **:** to file in an inappropriate place
mis·fire \(')mis-'fī(ə)r\ *vi* **1 :** to have the explosive or propulsive charge fail to ignite at the proper time ⟨the engine *misfired*⟩ **2 :** to fail to fire ⟨the gun *misfired*⟩ **3 :** to miss an intended effect — **misfire** *n*
mis·fit \'mis-,fit, (')mis 'fit\ *n* **1 :** something that fits badly **2 :** a person poorly adjusted to his environment
mis·for·tune \(')mis-'fȯr-chən\ *n* **1 :** bad fortune **:** ADVERSITY **2 :** an instance of bad luck **:** MISHAP
syn MISCHANCE, ADVERSITY: MISFORTUNE and MISCHANCE may both refer to an incident or conjunction of events that involves a change of fortune, but MISFORTUNE emphasizes the resulting mental or physical distress, MISCHANCE the practical inconvenience or disruption of plans; ADVERSITY cannot refer to an instance; it implies serious and continued misfortune
mis·give \(')mis-'giv\ *vt* **:** to suggest doubt or fear to ⟨his mind *misgave* him⟩ ~ *vi* **:** to be fearful or apprehensive
mis·giv·ing \-'giv-iŋ\ *n* **:** a feeling of doubt or suspicion esp. concerning a future event
mis·gov·ern \(')mis-'gəv-ərn\ *vt* **:** to govern badly — **mis·gov·ern·ment** \-'gəv-ər(n)-mənt, -'gəv-ᵊm-ənt\ *n*
mis·guid·ance \(')mis-'gīd-ᵊn(t)s\ *n* **:** MISDIRECTION
mis·guide \-'gīd\ *vt* **:** to lead astray **:** MISDIRECT — **mis·guid·er** *n*
mis·han·dle \(')mis-'han-dᵊl\ *vt* **1 :** to treat roughly **:** MALTREAT **2 :** to manage wrongly
mi·shan·ter \mə-'shant-ər\ *n* [ME *misaunter*, alter. of *mesaventure*] *chiefly Scot* **:** MISADVENTURE
mis·hap \'mis-,hap, mis-'\ *n* **1** *archaic* **:** bad luck **:** MISFORTUNE **2 :** an unfortunate accident
mish·mash \'mish-,mash, -,mäsh\ *n* [redupl. of [1]*mash*] **:** HODGEPODGE, JUMBLE
Mish·nah *or* **Mish·na** \'mish-nə\ *n* [Heb *mishnāh* instruction, oral law] **:** the collection of Jewish halakic traditions compiled about A.D. 200 and made the basic half of the Talmud — **Mish·na·ic** \mish-'nā-ik\ *adj*
mis·in·form \,mis-ᵊn-'fȯ(ə)rm\ *vt* **:** to give untrue or misleading information to — **mis·in·for·ma·tion** \,mis-,in-fər-'mā-shən\ *n*
mis·in·ter·pret \,mis-ᵊn-'tər-prət, *rapid* -pət\ *vt* **1 :** to understand wrongly **2 :** to explain wrongly — **mis·in·ter·pre·ta·tion** \-,tər-prə-'tā-shən, *rapid* -pə-\ *n*
mis·join·der \(')mis-'jȯin-dər\ *n* **:** an improper union of parties or of causes of action in a single legal proceeding
mis·judge \(')mis-'jəj\ *vt* **1 :** to estimate wrongly **2 :** to have an unjust opinion of ~ *vi* **:** to be mistaken in judgment — **mis·judg·ment** \-'jəj-mənt\ *n*
mis·know \(')mis-'nō\ *vt* **:** MISUNDERSTAND — **mis·knowl·edge** \-'näl-ij\ *n*
mis·lay \(')mis-'lā\ *vt* **:** to put in an unremembered place **:** LOSE
mis·lead \(')mis-'lēd\ *vt* **:** to lead in a wrong direction or into a mistaken action or belief **syn** see DECEIVE
mis·leared \(')mis-'li(ə)rd\ *adj, chiefly Scot* [[1]*mis-* + *lear* (to learn)] **:** UNMANNERLY, ILL-BRED
mis·like \(')mis-'līk\ *vt* **1** *archaic* **:** DISPLEASE **2 :** DISLIKE — **mis·like** *n*
mis·man·age \(')mis-'man-ij\ *vt* **:** to manage wrongly or incompetently — **mis·man·age·ment** \-mənt\ *n*
mis·mar·riage \-'mar-ij\ *n* **:** an unsuitable marriage
mis·match \-'mach\ *vt* **:** to match wrongly or unsuitably — **mis·match** *n*
mis·mate \-'māt\ *vt* **:** to mate unsuitably
mis·name \(')mis-'nām\ *vt* **:** to name incorrectly **:** MISCALL
mis·no·mer \(')mis-'nō-mər\ *n* [ME *misnoumer*, fr. MF *mesnommer* to misname, fr. *mes-* [1]mis- + *nommer* to name, fr. L *nominare* — more at NOMINATE] **1 :** the misnaming of a person in a legal instrument **2 a :** a use of a wrong name **b :** a wrong name or designation
miso- — see MIS-
mi·sog·a·mist \mə-'säg-ə-məst\ *n* [*misogamy*] **:** one who hates marriage — **mi·sog·a·my** \-ə-mē\ *n*
miso·gy·nic \,mis-ə-'jin-ik, -'gī-nik\ *adj* [*misogyny*, fr. Gk *misogynia*, fr. *mis-* + *gynē* woman — more at QUEEN] **:** having or showing a hatred and distrust of women **syn** see CYNICAL — **mi·sog·y·nist** \mə-'säj-ə-nəst\ *n* — **mi·sog·y·ny** \-ə-nē\ *n*
mi·sol·o·gy \mə-'säl-ə-jē\ *n* [Gk *misologia*, fr. *mis-* + *-logia* -logy] **:** a hatred of argument, reasoning, or enlightenment
miso·ne·ism \,mis-ə-'nē-,iz-əm\ *n* [It *misoneismo*, fr. *mis-* + Gk *neos* new + It *-ismo* -ism — more at NEW] **:** a hatred or intolerance of something new or changed
mis·place \(')mis-'plās\ *vt* **1 a :** to put in a wrong place **b :** MISLAY **2 :** to set on a wrong object ⟨~ trust⟩ — **mis·place·ment** \-'plā-smənt\ *n*
mis·play \(')mis-'plā\ *n* **:** a wrong or unskillful play — **misplay** *vt*
mis·print \(')mis-'print\ *vt* **:** to print incorrectly — **mis·print** \'mis-,print, (')mis-'\ *n*
[1]**mis·pri·sion** \mis-'prizh-ən\ *n* [ME, fr. MF *mesprison* error, wrongdoing, fr. OF, fr. *mespris*, pp. of *mesprendre* to make a mistake, fr. *mes-* mis- + *prendre* to take, fr. L *prehendere* to seize — more at PREHENSILE] **1 a :** neglect or wrong performance of official duty **b :** concealment of treason or felony by one not guilty

c : seditious conduct against the government or the courts 2 : MISUNDERSTANDING, MISTAKE
²**misprision** *n* [*misprize*] : CONTEMPT, SCORN
mis·prize \(ˈ)mis-ˈprīz\ *vt* [MF *mesprisier*, fr. *mes-* mis- + *prisier* to appraise — more at PRIZE] 1 : to hold in contempt : DESPISE 2 : UNDERVALUE
mis·pro·nounce \ˌmis-prə-ˈnaun(t)s\ *vt* : to pronounce incorrectly or in a way regarded as incorrect — **mis·pro·nun·ci·a·tion** \ˌmis-prə-ˌnən(t)-sē-ˈā-shən\ *n*
mis·quo·ta·tion \ˌmis-kwō-ˈtā-shən *also* -kō-\ *n* : the act or an instance of misquoting
mis·quote \(ˈ)mis-ˈkwōt *also* -ˈkōt\ *vt* : to quote incorrectly
mis·read \(ˈ)mis-ˈrēd\ *vt* 1 : to read incorrectly 2 : to misinterpret in or as if in reading
mis·reck·on \-ˈrek-ən\ *vb* : MISCALCULATE, MISCOUNT
mis·re·mem·ber \ˌmis-ri-ˈmem-bər\ *vt* : to remember incorrectly or inadequately; *esp, chiefly dial* : FORGET
mis·re·port \ˌmis-ri-ˈpō(ə)rt, -ˈpȯ(ə)rt\ *vt* : to report falsely — **misreport** *n*
mis·rep·re·sent \ˌmis-ˌrep-ri-ˈzent\ *vt* 1 : to give a false or misleading representation of 2 : to serve badly or improperly as a representative of — **mis·rep·re·sen·ta·tion** \(ˌ)mis-ˌrep-ri-ˌzen-ˈtā-shən, -zən-\ *n*
¹**mis·rule** \(ˈ)mis-ˈrül\ *vt* : to rule badly : MISGOVERN
²**misrule** *n* 1 : the action of misruling : the condition of being misruled 2 : DISORDER, ANARCHY
¹**miss** \ˈmis\ *vb* [ME *missen*, fr. OE *missan*; akin to OHG *missan* to miss, L *mutare* to change] *vt* 1 : to fail to hit, reach, or contact 2 : to discover or feel the absence of 3 : to fail to obtain 4 : ESCAPE, AVOID 5 : to leave out : OMIT 6 : to fail to comprehend, sense, or experience 7 : to fail to perform or attend ~ *vi* 1 *archaic* : to fail to get, reach, or do something 2 : to fail to hit something 3 a : to be unsuccessful b : MISFIRE ⟨the engine ~*ed*⟩
²**miss** *n* 1 *chiefly dial* : disadvantage or regret resulting from loss 2 a : a failure to hit b : a failure to attain a result 3 : MISFIRE
³**miss** *n* [short for *mistress*] 1 a — used as a title prefixed to the name of an unmarried woman or girl b — used before the name of a place or of a line of activity or before some epithet to form a title for a usu. young unmarried female who is representative of the thing indicated ⟨*Miss* America⟩ 2 : young lady — used without a name as a conventional term of address to a young woman 3 : a young unmarried woman or girl
mis·sa can·ta·ta \ˌmis-ə-kən-ˈtät-ə\ *n* [NL] : sung mass
mis·sal \ˈmis-əl\ *n* [ME *messel*, fr. MF & ML; MF, fr. ML *missale*, fr. neut. of *missalis* of the mass, fr. LL *missa* mass — more at MASS] : a book containing all that is said or sung at mass during the entire year
mis·send \(ˈ)mis-ˈsend\ *vt* : to send incorrectly ⟨*missent* mail⟩
mis·shape \(ˈ)mis(h)-ˈshāp\ *vt* : to shape badly : DEFORM — **mis·shap·en** \-ˈshā-pən\ *adj*
¹**mis·sile** \ˈmis-əl, *chiefly Brit* -ˌīl\ *adj* [L *missilis*, fr. *missus*, pp. of *mittere* to throw, send — more at SMITE] 1 : capable of being thrown or projected to strike a distant object 2 : adapted for throwing or hurling missiles
²**missile** *n* 1 : a weapon or other object thrown or projected 2 : a self-propelled unmanned weapon (as a rocket)
mis·sil·eer \ˌmis-ə-ˈli(ə)r\ *n* : MISSILEMAN
mis·sile·man \ˈmis-əl-mən\ *n* : one who helps to design, build, or operate guided missiles
mis·sile·ry *also* **mis·sil·ry** \ˈmis-əl-rē\ *n* 1 : MISSILES; *esp* : GUIDED MISSILES 2 : the science dealing with the design, manufacture, and use of guided missiles
miss·ing \ˈmis-iŋ\ *adj* : ABSENT; *also* : LOST
missing link *n* 1 : an absent member needed to complete a series 2 : a hypothetical intermediate form between man and his presumed simian progenitors
¹**mis·sion** \ˈmish-ən\ *n* [NL, ML, & L; NL *mission-, missio* religious mission, fr. ML, task assigned, fr. L, act of sending, fr. *missus*, pp. of *mittere*] 1 *obs* : the act or an instance of sending 2 a : a ministry commissioned by a religious organization to propagate its faith or carry on humanitarian work b : assignment to or work in a field of missionary enterprise c (1) : a mission establishment (2) : a local church or parish dependent on a larger religious organization for direction or financial support d *pl* : organized missionary work e : a course of sermons and services given to convert to or quicken Christian faith 3 : a body of persons sent to perform a service or carry on an activity: as a : a group sent to a foreign country to conduct diplomatic or political negotiations b : a permanent embassy or legation c : a team of specialists or cultural leaders sent to a foreign country 4 : a task or function assigned or undertaken
²**mission** *vt* **mis·sion·ing** \ˈmish-(ə-)niŋ\ 1 : to send on or entrust with a mission 2 : to carry on a religious mission among or in
³**mission** *adj* : of or relating to a style used in the early Spanish missions of the southwestern U.S. ⟨~ architecture⟩
¹**mis·sion·ary** \ˈmish-ə-ˌner-ē\ *adj* 1 : relating to, engaged in, or devoted to missions 2 : characteristic of a missionary
²**missionary** *n* : a person undertaking a mission and esp. a religious mission
mis·sion·er \ˈmish-(ə-)nər\ *n* : MISSIONARY
Mis·sis·sip·pi·an \ˌmis-(ə-)ˈsip-ē-ən\ *adj* [*Mississippi* river] 1 : of or relating to Mississippi, its people, or the Mississippi river 2 : of, relating to, or being the period of the Paleozoic era in No. America following the Devonian and preceding the Pennsylvanian or the corresponding system of rocks
mis·sive \ˈmis-iv\ *n* [MF *lettre missive*, lit., letter intended to be sent] : a written communication : LETTER
mis·spell \(ˈ)mis-ˈspel\ *vt* : to spell incorrectly
mis·spell·ing \-iŋ\ *n* : an incorrect spelling
mis·spend \(ˈ)mis-ˈspend\ *vt* : to spend wrongly : SQUANDER
mis·state \(ˈ)mis-ˈstāt\ *vt* : to state incorrectly — **mis·state·ment** \-mənt\ *n*
mis·step \(ˈ)mis-ˈstep\ *n* 1 : a wrong step 2 : a mistake in judgment or action : BLUNDER
mis·sus *or* **mis·sis** \ˈmis-əz, -əs, *esp South* ˈmiz-\ *n* [alter. of *mistress*] 1 : WIFE 2 *dial* : MISTRESS 1a, 1b
missy \ˈmis-ē\ *n* : a young girl : MISS
¹**mist** \ˈmist\ *n* [ME, fr. OE; akin to MD *mist* mist, Gk *omichlē*] 1 : water in the form of particles floating or falling in the atmosphere at or near the surface of the earth and approaching the form of rain 2 : something that dims or obscures 3 : a film before the eyes 4 : a cloud of small particles or objects suggestive of a mist **syn** see HAZE
²**mist** *vi* 1 : to be or become misty 2 : to become dim or blurred ~ *vt* : to cover with mist
mis·tak·able \mə-ˈstā-kə-bəl\ *adj* : capable of being misunderstood or mistaken
¹**mis·take** \mə-ˈstāk\ *vb* **mis·took** \-ˈstu̇k\ **mis·tak·en** \-ˈstā-kən\ **mis·tak·ing** [ME *mistaken*, fr. ON *mistaka* to take by mistake, fr. *mis-* + *taka* to take — more at TAKE] *vt* 1 : to choose wrongly 2 a : to misunderstand the meaning or intention of : MISINTERPRET b : to make a wrong judgment of the character or ability of 3 : to identify wrongly ~ *vi* : to be wrong ⟨you *mistook* when you thought I laughed at you —Thomas Hardy⟩ — **mis·tak·er** *n*
²**mistake** *n* 1 : a misunderstanding of the meaning or implication of something 2 : a wrong action or statement proceeding from faulty judgment, inadequate knowledge, or inattention **syn** see ERROR
mis·ter \ˈmis-tər\ *n* [alter. of *master*] 1 a — used as a title prefixed to the name of a man or to a designation of occupation or office and usu. written *Mr.* or in the plural *Messrs.* b — used before the name of a place or of a line of activity or before some epithet to form a title for a male viewed as representative of the thing indicated ⟨*Mr.* Baseball⟩ 2 : SIR — used without a name as a conventional term of address to a man 3 : a man not entitled to a title of rank or an honorific or professional title ⟨just a plain ~⟩ 4 : HUSBAND
mis·think \(ˈ)mis-ˈthiŋk\ *vi, archaic* : to think mistakenly or unfavorably ~ *vt, archaic* : to think badly or unfavorably of
mist·i·ly \ˈmis-tə-lē\ *adv* : in a misty manner
mis·time \(ˈ)mis-ˈtīm\ *vt* : to time wrongly
mist·i·ness \ˈmis-tē-nəs\ *n* : the quality or state of being misty
mis·tle·toe \ˈmis-əl-ˌtō, *chiefly Brit* ˈmiz-\ *n* [ME *mistilto* basil, fr. OE *misteltān*, fr. *mistel* mistletoe, basil, + *tān* twig; akin to OHG & OS *mistil* mistletoe and to OHG *zein* twig] : a European semiparasitic green shrub (*Viscum album* of the family Loranthaceae, the mistletoe family) with thick leaves, small yellowish flowers, and waxy-white glutinous berries; *broadly* : any of various plants of the mistletoe family (as of an American genus *Phoradendron*) resembling the true mistletoe
mis·tral \ˈmis-trəl, mi-ˈsträl\ *n* [F, fr. Prov, fr. *mistral* masterful, fr. L *magistralis* — more at MAGISTRAL] : a violent cold dry northerly wind of the Mediterranean provinces of France
mis·treat \(ˈ)mis-ˈtrēt\ *vt* [ME *mistreten*, prob. fr. MF *mestraitier*, fr. OF, fr. *mis-* + *traitier* to treat — more at TREAT] : to treat badly : ABUSE — **mis·treat·ment** \-mənt\ *n*
mis·tress \ˈmis-trəs; *as an abbreviated title* ˌmis-əz, -əs, *esp South* ˌmiz-əz, -əs, (ˌ)miz, *or before given names* (ˌ)mis\ *n* [ME *maistresse*, fr. MF, fr. OF, fem. of *maistre* master — more at MASTER] 1 : a woman who has power, authority, or ownership: as a : the female head of a household b : a woman who employs or supervises servants c : a woman who possesses or controls something d : a woman who is in charge of a school or other establishment e : a woman of the Scottish nobility having a status comparable to that of a master 2 a *chiefly Brit* : a female teacher or tutor b : a woman who has achieved mastery in some field 3 : a country or state having supremacy over others 4 : something personified as female that rules or directs 5 a : a woman with whom a man habitually cohabits without being married to her b *archaic* : SWEETHEART 6 — used archaically as a title prefixed to the name of a married or unmarried woman and now superseded by the contracted forms *Mrs.*, or in the plural *Mesdames*, for a married woman and *Miss* for an unmarried woman
mis·tri·al \(ˈ)mis-ˈtrī(-ə)l\ *n* : a trial that has no legal effect by reason of some error or serious prejudicial misconduct in the proceedings
¹**mis·trust** \(ˈ)mis-ˈtrəst\ *n* : a lack of confidence : DISTRUST **syn** see UNCERTAINTY — **mis·trust·ful** \-fəl\ *adj* — **mis·trust·ful·ly** \-fə-lē\ *adv* — **mis·trust·ful·ness** *n*
²**mistrust** *vt* 1 : to have no trust or confidence in : SUSPECT 2 : to doubt the truth, validity, or effectiveness of 3 : SURMISE ~ *vi* : to be suspicious
misty \ˈmis-tē\ *adj* 1 a : obscured by mist b : consisting of or marked by mist 2 a : INDISTINCT b : VAGUE, CONFUSED
mis·un·der·stand \(ˌ)mis-ˌən-dər-ˈstand\ *vt* 1 : to fail to understand 2 : to interpret incorrectly
mis·un·der·stand·ing \-ˈstan-diŋ\ *n* 1 : a mistake of meaning : MISINTERPRETATION 2 : DISAGREEMENT, QUARREL
mis·us·age \mish-ˈü-sij, (ˈ)mis(h)-ˈyü-, -zij\ *n* [MF *mesusage*, fr. *mis-* + *usage*] 1 : bad treatment : ABUSE 2 : wrong or improper use
¹**mis·use** \mish-ˈüz, (ˈ)mis(h)-ˈyüz\ *vt* [ME *misusen*, partly fr. *mis-* + *usen* to use; partly fr. MF *mesuser* to abuse, fr. OF, fr. *mis-* + *user* to use] 1 : to use incorrectly : MISAPPLY 2 : ABUSE, MISTREAT
²**mis·use** \mish-ˈüs, (ˈ)mis(h)-ˈyüs\ *n* : incorrect or improper use : MISAPPLICATION
mis·val·ue \(ˈ)mis-ˈval-(ˌ)yü, -yə-w\ *vt* : UNDERVALUE
mis·ven·ture \(ˈ)mis-ˈven-chər\ *n* : MISADVENTURE
mis·write \(ˈ)mis-ˈrīt\ *vt* : to write incorrectly
mite \ˈmīt\ *n* [ME, fr. OE *mīte*; akin to MD *mite* mite, small copper coin, OHG *meizan* to cut, OE *gemād* silly — more at MAD] 1 : any of numerous small to very minute arachnids (order Acarina) often infesting animals, plants, and stored foods and including important disease vectors 2 [ME, fr. MF or MD; MF, small Flemish copper coin, fr. MD] : a small coin or sum of money 3 a : a very little : BIT b : a very small object or creature
¹**mi·ter** *or* **mi·tre** \ˈmīt-ər\ *n* [ME *mitre*, fr. MF, fr. L *mitra* headband, turban, fr. Gk; akin to Skt *mitra* friend] 1 : a liturgical headdress worn by bishops and abbots 2 a : a surface forming the beveled end or edge of a piece where a joint is made by cutting two pieces at an angle and fitting them together b : MITER SQUARE
²**miter** *or* **mitre** *vt* **mi·tered** *or* **mi·tred**; **mi·ter·ing** *or* **mi·tring** \ˈmīt-ə-riŋ\ 1 : to confer a miter on 2 a : to match or fit together in a miter joint b : to bevel the ends of for making a miter joint — **mi·ter·er** \ˈmīt-ər-ər\ *n*
miter box *n* : a device for guiding a handsaw at the proper angle in making a miter joint in wood

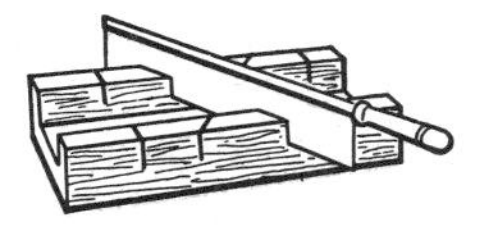
miter box, with saw

miter gear *n* : one of a pair of inter-

changeable bevel gears with axes at right angles

miter square *n* **:** a bevel with an immovable arm at an angle of 45 degrees for striking miter lines; *also* **:** a square with an arm adjustable to any angle

Mith·ra·ic \mith-'rā-ik\ *adj* [LGk *mithraikos* of Mithras, ancient Per god of light, fr. Gk *Mithras*, fr. OPer *Mithra*] **:** of or relating to an oriental mystery cult for men flourishing in the late Roman empire — **Mith·ra·ism** \'mith-rə-,iz-əm, -(,)rā-\ *n* — **Mith·ra·ist** \mith-'rā-əst, 'mith-, ; 'mith-rā-,ist, -rə-\ *n or adj*

mith·ri·date \'mith-rə-,dāt\ *n* [ML *mithridatum*, fr. LL *mithridatium*, fr. L, dogtooth violet (used as an antidote), fr. Gk *mithridation*, fr. *Mithradatēs*] **:** an antidote against poison; *esp* **:** an electuary held to be effective against poison

mith·ri·da·tism \,mith-rə-'dāt-,iz-əm\ *n* [*Mithridates* VI †63 B.C. king of Pontus, fr. L *Mithridates*, fr. Gk *Mithridatēs*; fr. the fact that he reputedly produced this condition in himself] **:** tolerance to a poison acquired by taking gradually increased doses of it

mi·ti·cide \'mīt-ə-,sīd\ *n* [*mite*] **:** an agent used to kill mites

mit·i·ga·ble \'mit-i-gə-bəl\ *adj* **:** capable of being mitigated

mit·i·gate \'mit-ə-,gāt\ *vt* [ME *mitigaten*, fr. L *mitigatus*, pp. of *mitigare* to soften, fr. *mitis* soft + *-igare* (akin to L *agere* to drive); akin to OIr *mōith* soft — more at AGENT] **1 :** to cause to become less harsh or hostile **:** MOLLIFY **2 :** to make less severe or painful **:** ALLEVIATE — **mit·i·ga·tion** \,mit-ə-'gā-shən\ *n* — **mit·i·ga·tive** \'mit-ə-,gāt-iv\ *adj* — **mit·i·ga·tor** \-,gāt-ər\ *n* — **mit·i·ga·to·ry** \'mit-i-gə-,tōr-ē, -,tȯr-\ *adj*

mi·to·chon·dri·al \,mīt-ə-'kän-drē-əl\ *adj* **:** of, relating to, or being mitochondria

mi·to·chon·dri·on \-drē-ən\ *n, pl* **mi·to·chon·dria** \-drē-ə\ [NL, fr. Gk *mitos* thread + *chondrion*, dim. of *chondros* grain — more at GRIND] **:** any of various round or long bodies found in cells that are rich in fats, proteins, and enzymes and are held to be centers of cellular respiration

mi·to·sis \mī-'tō-səs\ *n, pl* **mi·to·ses** \-'tō-,sēz\ [NL, fr. Gk *mitos* thread] **1 :** cell division in which complex nuclear division usu. involving halving of chromosomes precedes cytoplasmic fission and which involves typically a series of steps consisting of prophase, metaphase, anaphase, and telophase **2 :** KARYOKINESIS 1 — **mi·tot·ic** \-'tät-ik\ *adj* — **mi·tot·i·cal·ly** \-i-k(ə-)lē\ *adv*

mi·trail·leuse \,mē-trə-'yə(r)z\ *n* [F] **1 :** a breech-loading machine gun with a number of barrels **2 :** MACHINE GUN

mi·tral \'mī-trəl\ *adj* **1 :** resembling a miter **2 :** relating to, being, or adjoining a mitral valve or orifice

mitral valve *n* **:** a cardiac valve guarding the orifice between the left auricle and ventricle and preventing the return of blood to the auricle

mitt \'mit\ *n* [short for *mitten*] **1 a :** a woman's glove that leaves the fingers uncovered **b :** MITTEN 1 **c :** a baseball catcher's or first baseman's glove **2** *slang* **:** HAND

mit·ten \'mit-ᵊn\ *n* [ME *mitain*, fr. MF *mitaine*, fr. OF, fr. *mite* mitten] **1 :** a covering for the hand and wrist having a separate section for the thumb only **2 :** MITT 1a

mit·ti·mus \'mit-ə-məs\ *n* [L, we send, fr. *mittere* to send — more at SMITE] **:** a warrant of commitment to prison

mitz·vah \'mits-və\ *n, pl* **mitz·voth** \-,vōt(h), -,vōs\ *or* **mitz·vahs** [Heb *miṣwāh*] **1 :** a commandment of the Jewish law **2 :** a meritorious act

1mix \'miks\ *vb* [ME *mixen*, back-formation fr. *mixte* mixed, fr. MF, fr. L *mixtus*, pp. of *miscēre* to mix; akin to Gk *mignynai* to mix] *vt* **1 a** (1) **:** to combine or blend into one mass (2) **:** to combine with another **b :** to bring into close association **2 :** to form by mixing components **3 :** CONFUSE ~ *vi* **1 a :** to become mixed **b :** to be capable of mixing **2 :** to enter into relations **:** ASSOCIATE **3 :** CROSSBREED **4 :** to become involved **:** PARTICIPATE — **mix·able** \'mik-sə-bəl\ *adj* — **mix·er** *n*

syn MINGLE, COMMINGLE, BLEND, MERGE, COALESCE, AMALGAMATE, FUSE: MIX may or may not imply loss of each element's identity; MINGLE usu. suggests that the elements are still somewhat distinguishable or separately active; COMMINGLE implies a closer or more thorough mingling; BLEND implies that the elements as such disappear in enhancing the resulting mixture; MERGE suggests a combining in which one or more elements are lost in the whole; COALESCE implies an affinity in the merging elements and usu. a resulting organic unity; AMALGAMATE implies the forming of a close union without complete loss of individual identities; FUSE stresses oneness and indissolubility of the resulting product

2mix *n* **1 :** an act or process of mixing **2 :** a product of mixing; *specif* **:** a commercially prepared mixture of food ingredients

mixed \'mikst\ *adj* [ME *mixte*] **1 :** combining characteristics of more than one kind; *specif* **:** combining features of two or more systems of government ⟨a ~ constitution⟩ **2 :** made up of or involving individuals or items of more than one kind: as **a :** made up of or involving persons differing in race, national origin, religion, or class **b :** made up of or involving individuals of both sexes ⟨~ company⟩ **3 :** including or accompanied by inconsistent or incompatible elements **4 :** deriving from two or more races or breeds

mixed bud *n* **:** a bud that produces a branch and leaves as well as flowers

mixed farming *n* **:** the growing of food or cash crops, feed crops, and livestock on the same farm

mixed media *n* **1 :** a work of art executed in more than one medium; *also* **:** a commercial production (as a motion picture) combining disparate techniques or art forms **2 :** a presentation (as in a theater) in which several media are employed simultaneously

mixed number *n* **:** a number (as $5\frac{2}{3}$) composed of an integer and a fraction

mix·ture \'miks-chər\ *n* [MF, fr. OF *misture*, fr. L *mixtura*, fr. *mixtus*] **1 a :** the act, the process, or an instance of mixing **b** (1) **:** the state of being mixed (2) **:** the relative proportions of constituents; *specif* **:** the proportion of fuel to air produced in a carburetor **2 :** a product of mixing **:** COMBINATION: as **a :** a portion of matter consisting of two or more components that do not bear a fixed proportion to one another and that however thoroughly commingled are regarded as retaining a separate existence **b :** a fabric woven of variously colored threads **c :** a combination of several different kinds

mix-up \'mik-,səp\ *n* **1 :** a state or instance of confusion **2 :** MIXTURE **3 :** CONFLICT, FIGHT

Mi·zar \'mī-,zär\ *n* [Ar *Mi'zar*, lit., veil, cloak] **:** a star of the second magnitude in the handle of the Big Dipper

1miz·zen *or* **miz·en** \'miz-ᵊn\ *n* [ME *meson*, prob. fr. MF *misaine*, deriv. of Ar *mazzān* mast] **1 :** a fore-and-aft sail set on the mizzenmast **2 :** MIZZENMAST

2mizzen *or* **mizen** *adj* **:** of or relating to the mizzenmast ⟨~ shrouds⟩

miz·zen·mast \-,mast, -məst\ *n* **:** the mast aft or next aft of the mainmast in a ship

1miz·zle \'miz-əl\ *vi* **miz·zling** \-(ə-)liŋ\ [ME *misellen*; akin to Flem *mizzelen* to drizzle, MD *mist* fog, mist] *chiefly dial* **:** to rain in very fine drops **:** DRIZZLE — **mizzle** *n* — **miz·zly** \-(ə-)lē\ *adj*

2mizzle *vi* [origin unknown] *slang chiefly Brit* **:** to depart suddenly

mne·mon·ic \ni-'män-ik\ *adj* [Gk *mnēmonikos*, fr. *mnēmōn* mindful, fr *mimnēskesthai* to remember — more at MIND] **1 :** assisting or intended to assist memory; *also* **:** of or relating to mnemonics **2 :** of or relating to memory — **mne·mon·i·cal·ly** \-i-k(ə-)lē\ *adv*

mne·mon·ics \-iks\ *n pl but sing in constr* **:** a technique of improving the memory

Mne·mos·y·ne \ni-'mäs-ᵊn-ē, -'mäz-\ *n* [L, fr. Gk *Mnēmosynē*] **:** the goddess of memory in Greek mythology and mother of the Muses by Zeus

-mo \(,)mō\ *n suffix* [duodecim*o*] — after numerals or their names to indicate the number of leaves made by folding a sheet of paper ⟨sixteen*mo*⟩ ⟨16*mo*⟩

moa \'mō-ə\ *n* [Maori] **:** any of various usu. very large extinct flightless ratite birds of New Zealand (family Dinornithidae) including one (*Dinornis giganteus*) about 12 feet in height

Mo·ab·ite \'mō-ə-,bīt\ *n* [ME, fr. LL *Moabita*, *Moabites*, fr. Gk *Mōabitēs*, fr. *Mōab* Moab, ancient kingdom in Syria] **:** a member of an ancient Semitic people related to the Hebrews — **Moabite** *or* **Mo·ab·it·ish** \-,bīt-ish\ *adj* — **Mo·ab·it·ess** \-,bīt-əs\ *n*

1moan \'mōn\ *n* [ME *mone*, fr. (assumed) OE *mān*] **1 :** LAMENTATION, COMPLAINT **2 :** a low prolonged sound of pain or of grief

2moan *vt* **1 :** to bewail audibly **:** LAMENT **2 :** to utter with moans ~*vi* **1 :** LAMENT, COMPLAIN **2 :** to make a moan **:** GROAN

1moat \'mōt\ *n* [ME *mote*] **:** a deep and wide trench around the rampart of a fortified place (as a castle) that is usu. filled with water

2moat *vt* **:** to surround with or as if with a moat

1mob \'mäb\ *n* [L *mobile vulgus* vacillating crowd] **1 :** MASSES, RABBLE **2 :** a large disorderly crowd **3 :** a criminal set **:** GANG **syn** see CROWD — **mob·bish** \-ish\ *adj*

2mob *vt* **mobbed; mob·bing :** to crowd about and attack or annoy

mob·cap \'mäb-,kap\ *n* [*mob* (woman's cap) + *cap*] **:** a woman's fancy indoor cap made with a high full crown and often tied under the chin

1mo·bile \'mō-bəl, -,bēl, -,bīl\ *adj* [MF, fr. L *mobilis*, fr. *movēre* to move] **1 :** capable of moving or being moved **:** MOVABLE **2 a :** changeable in appearance, mood, or purpose **b :** ADAPTABLE, VERSATILE **3 :** MIGRATORY **4 :** characterized by the mixing of social groups **5 :** using vehicles for transportation ⟨~ warfare⟩ **6 :** of or relating to a mobile — **mo·bil·i·ty** \mō-'bil-ət-ē\ *n*

2mo·bile \'mō-,bēl\ *n* **:** a construction or sculpture frequently of wire and sheet metal shapes with parts that can be set in motion by air currents; *also* **:** a similar structure suspended so that it moves in a current of air

mobile home *n* **:** TRAILER 3b

mo·bi·li·za·tion \,mō-b(ə-)lə-'zā-shən\ *n* **:** the act of mobilizing **:** the state of being mobilized

mo·bi·lize \'mō-bə-,līz\ *vt* **1 :** to put into movement or circulation **2 a :** to assemble and make ready for war duty **b :** to marshal (as resources) for action ~ *vi* **:** to undergo mobilization

mob·oc·ra·cy \mä-'bäk-rə-sē\ *n* **1 :** rule by the mob **2 :** the mob as a ruling class — **mob·ocrat** \'mäb-ə-,krat\ *n* — **mob·ocrat·ic** \,mäb-ə-'krat-ik\ *adj*

mob·ster \'mäb-stər\ *n* **:** a member of a criminal gang

moc·ca·sin \'mäk-ə-sən\ *n* [of Algonquian origin; akin to Natick *mokkussin* shoe] **1 :** a soft leather heelless shoe or boot with the sole brought up the sides of the foot and over the toes where it is joined with a puckered seam to a U-shaped piece lying on top of the foot **2 a :** WATER MOCCASIN **b :** a snake (as of the genus *Natrix*) resembling a moccasin

moccasin flower *n* **:** any of several lady's slippers (genus *Cypripedium*); *esp* **:** a once common woodland orchid (*C. acaule*) of eastern No. America with pink or white moccasin-shaped flowers

mo·cha \'mō-kə\ *n* [*Mocha*, seaport in Arabia] **1 a** (1) **:** superior arabica coffee with small green or yellowish beans grown in Arabia (2) **:** a coffee of superior quality **b :** a flavoring made of a strong coffee infusion or of a mixture of cocoa or chocolate with coffee **2 :** a pliable suede-finished glove leather from African sheepskins

1mock \'mäk, 'mȯk\ *vb* [ME *mocken*, fr. MF *mocquer*] *vt* **1 :** to treat with contempt or ridicule **:** DERIDE **2 :** to disappoint the hopes of **:** DELUDE **3 :** DEFY, CHALLENGE **4 a :** IMITATE, MIMIC **b :** to mimic in sport or derision ~ *vi* **:** JEER, SCOFF **syn** see COPY, RIDICULE — **mock·er** *n* — **mock·ing·ly** \-iŋ-lē\ *adv*

2mock *n* **1 :** an act of ridicule or derision **:** JEER **2 :** one that is an object of derision or scorn **3 :** MOCKERY **4 a :** an act of imitation **b :** something made as an imitation — **mock** *adj*

3mock *adv* **:** in an insincere or counterfeit manner — usu. used in combination ⟨*mock*-serious⟩

mock·ery \'mäk-(ə-)rē, 'mȯk-\ *n* **1 :** insulting or contemptuous action or speech **:** DERISION **2 :** a subject of laughter, derision, or sport **3 a :** a counterfeit appearance **:** IMITATION **b :** an insincere, contemptible, or impertinent imitation **4 :** something ridiculously or impudently unsuitable

mock-he·ro·ic \,mäk-hi-'rō-ik, ,mȯk-\ *adj* **:** ridiculing or burlesquing heroic style, character, or action ⟨a ~ poem⟩ — **mock-he·ro·ical·ly** \-i-k(ə-)lē\ *adv*

mock·ing·bird \'mäk-iŋ-,bərd, 'mȯk-\ *n* **:** a common bird (*Mimus polyglottos*) of the southern U.S. remarkable for its exact imitations of the notes of other birds

mock orange *n* **:** a usu. shrubby plant held to resemble the orange; *esp* **:** PHILADELPHUS

mock turtle soup *n* **:** a soup made of calf's head, veal, or other meat with condiments in imitation of green turtle soup

mock-up \'mäk-,əp, 'mȯk-\ *n* **:** a full-sized structural model built accurately to scale chiefly for study, testing, or display

mod \'mäd\ *adj* **:** MODERN; *esp* **:** bold, free, and unconventional in style, behavior, or dress
mod·acryl·ic fiber \ˌmäd-ə-ˌkril-ik-\ *n* [*mod*ified *acrylic*] **:** any of various synthetic textile fibers that are long-chain polymers composed of 35 to 85 percent by weight of acrylonitrile units
mod·al \'mōd-ᵊl\ *adj* [ML *modalis*, fr. L *modus*] **1 :** of or relating to modality in logic **2 :** containing provisions as to the mode of procedure or the manner of taking effect — used of a contract or legacy **3 :** of or relating to a musical mode **4 :** of or relating to structure as opposed to substance **5 :** of, relating to, or constituting a grammatical form or category characteristically indicating predication of an action or state in some manner other than as a simple fact **6 :** of or relating to a statistical mode — **mod·al·ly** \-ᵊl-ē\ *adv*
modal auxiliary *n* **:** a verb that is characteristically used with a verb of predication and expresses a modal modification (as *can, must, might, may*) and that in English differs formally from other verbs in lacking *-s* and *-ing* forms
mo·dal·i·ty \mō-'dal-ət-ē\ *n* **1 a :** the quality or state of being modal **b :** a modal quality or attribute **:** FORM **2 :** the classification of logical propositions according to their asserting or denying the possibility, impossibility, contingency, or necessity of their content **3 :** a therapeutic agency used esp. in physical therapy
1mode \'mōd\ *n* [ME *moede*, fr. L *modus* measure, manner, musical mode — more at METE] **1 a :** an arrangement of the eight diatonic notes or tones of an octave according to one of several fixed schemes of their intervals **b :** a rhythmical scheme (as in 13th and 14th century music) **2 :** 2MOOD 2 **3** [LL *modus*, fr. L] **a :** 2MOOD 1 **b :** the modal form of the assertion or denial of a logical proposition **4 a :** a particular form or variety of something **b :** a form or manner of expression **:** STYLE **5 :** a manner of doing something **6 :** a manifestation, form, or arrangement of being; *specif* **:** a particular form or manifestation of an underlying substance **7 :** the most frequent value in a frequency distribution **8 :** the vibration pattern of electromagnetic waves; *also* **:** the state of a vibrating system that corresponds to a particular pattern **9 :** the actual mineral composition of a rock **syn** see METHOD
2mode *n* [F, fr. L *modus*] **:** a prevailing fashion or style of dress or behavior **syn** see FASHION
1mod·el \'mäd-ᵊl\ *n* [MF *modelle*, fr. OIt *modello*, fr. (assumed) VL *modellus*, fr. L *modulus* small measure, fr. *modus*] **1** *obs* **:** a set of plans for a building **2** *dial Brit* **:** COPY, IMAGE **3 :** structural design **4 :** a miniature representation of something; *also* **:** a pattern of something to be made **5 :** an example for imitation or emulation **6 :** a person or thing that serves as a pattern for an artist; *esp* **:** one who poses for an artist **7 :** ARCHETYPE **8 :** one who is employed to display clothes or other merchandise **:** MANNEQUIN **9 a :** a type or design of clothing **b :** a type or design of product (as a car or airplane) **10 :** a description or analogy used to help visualize something (as an atom) that cannot be directly observed **11 :** a system of postulates, data, and inferences presented as a mathematical description of an entity or state of affairs — **model** *adj*
syn EXAMPLE, PATTERN, EXEMPLAR, IDEAL: MODEL applies to something taken or proposed as worthy of imitation; EXAMPLE applies to a person to be imitated or in some contexts on no account to be imitated but to be regarded as a warning; PATTERN suggests a clear and detailed archetype or prototype; EXEMPLAR suggests either a faultless example to be emulated or a perfect typification; IDEAL implies the best possible exemplification either in reality or in conception
2model *vb* **mod·eled** *or* **mod·elled; mod·el·ing** *or* **mod·el·ling** \'mäd-liŋ, -ᵊl-iŋ\ *vt* **1 :** to plan or form after a pattern **:** SHAPE **2** *archaic* **:** to make into an organization (as an army, government, or parish) **3 :** to shape or fashion in a plastic material **4 :** to construct or fashion in imitation of a particular model ⟨*~ed* its constitution on that of the U.S.⟩ **5 :** to display by wearing, using, or posing with ⟨*~ed* gowns⟩ **~** *vi* **1 :** to design or imitate forms **:** make a pattern ⟨enjoys *~ing* in clay⟩ **2 :** to work or act as a fashion model — **mod·el·er** \-lər, -ᵊl-ər\ *n*
1mod·er·ate \'mäd-(ə-)rət\ *adj* [ME, fr. L *moderatus*, fr. pp. of *moderare* to moderate; akin to L *modus* measure] **1 a :** avoiding extremes of behavior or expression **:** observing reasonable limits **b :** CALM, TEMPERATE **2 a :** tending toward the mean or average amount or dimension **b :** having average or less than average quality **:** MEDIOCRE **3 :** avoiding extreme political or social measures **4 :** limited in scope or effect **5 :** not expensive **:** reasonable or low in price **6** *of a color* **:** of medium lightness and medium chroma — **moderate** *n* — **mod·er·ate·ly** \'mäd-ərt-lē, 'mäd-(ə-)rət-\ *adv* — **mod·er·ate·ness** \'mäd-(ə-)rət-nəs\ *n*
syn MODERATE, TEMPERATE mean neither too much nor too little. MODERATE implies absence or avoidance of excess; TEMPERATE suggests the effect of restraint or restriction
2mod·er·ate \'mäd-ə-ˌrāt\ *vt* **1 :** to lessen the intensity or extremeness of **:** TEMPER **2 :** to preside over or act as chairman of **~** *vi* **1 :** to act as a moderator **2 :** to become less violent, severe, or intense — **mod·er·a·tion** \ˌmäd-ə-'rā-shən\ *n*
moderate breeze *n* **:** wind having a speed of 13 to 18 miles per hour
moderate gale *n* **:** wind having a speed of 32 to 38 miles per hour
mod·er·a·to \ˌmäd-ə-'rät-(ˌ)ō\ *adv (or adj)* [It, fr. L *moderatus*] **:** MODERATE — used as a direction in music to indicate tempo
mod·er·a·tor \'mäd-ə-ˌrāt-ər\ *n* **1 :** one who arbitrates **:** MEDIATOR **2 :** one who presides over an assembly, meeting, or discussion: as **a :** the presiding officer of a Presbyterian governing body **b :** the nonpartisan presiding officer of a town meeting **c :** the chairman of a discussion group **3 :** a substance used for slowing down neutrons in a nuclear reactor — **mod·er·a·tor·ship** \-ˌship\ *n*
1mod·ern \'mäd-ərn, *nonstand* 'mäd-(ə-)rən\ *adj* [LL *modernus*, fr. L *modo* just now, fr. *modus* measure — more at METE] **1 :** of, relating to, or characteristic of the present or the immediate past **:** CONTEMPORARY **2** *cap* **:** of, relating to, or having the characteristics of the present or most recent period of development of a language **syn** see NEW — **mo·der·ni·ty** \mə-'dər-nət-ē, mä-\ *n* — **mod·ern·ly** \'mäd-ərn-lē\ *adv* — **mod·ern·ness** \-ərn-nəs\ *n*
2modern *n* **1 :** a person of modern times or views **2 :** a style of printing type distinguished by regularity of shape, precise curves, straight hairline serifs, and heavy downstrokes
Modern Hebrew *n* **:** Hebrew as used in present-day Israel
mod·ern·ism \'mäd-ər-ˌniz-əm\ *n* **1 :** a practice, usage, or expression peculiar to modern times **2 a** *often cap* **:** a movement in Protestant Christianity that seeks to establish the meaning and validity of the Christian faith for present human experience **b** *cap* **:** a position taken by some Anglicans asserting that all knowledge by which religion can be affected necessarily reaffirms the fundamental Christian truths **c** *often cap* **:** a position according to which the only vital element in religion is its power to communicate the best religious experience of the race **3 :** the philosophy and practices of modern art; *esp* **:** a self-conscious break with the past and a search for new forms of expression — **mod·ern·ist** \-nəst\ *n or adj* — **mod·ern·is·tic** \ˌmäd-ər-'nis-tik\ *adj*
mod·ern·iza·tion \ˌmäd-ər-nə-'zā-shən\ *n* **:** the act of modernizing **:** the state of being modernized; *also* **:** something modernized
mod·ern·ize \'mäd-ər-ˌnīz\ *vt* **:** to make modern in taste, style, or usage **~** *vi* **:** to adopt modern ways — **mod·ern·iz·er** *n*
mod·est \'mäd-əst\ *adj* [L *modestus* moderate; akin to L *modus* measure] **1 :** placing a moderate estimate on one's abilities or worth; *also* **:** DIFFIDENT **2 :** observing the proprieties of dress and behavior **:** DECENT **3 :** limited in size, amount, or aim **:** UNPRETENTIOUS **syn** see CHASTE, HUMBLE, SHY — **mod·est·ly** *adv*
mod·es·ty \'mäd-ə-stē\ *n* **1 :** freedom from conceit or vanity **2 :** propriety in dress, speech, or conduct
mod·i·cum \'mäd-i-kəm, 'mōd-\ *n* [ME, fr. L, neut. of *modicus* moderate, fr. *modus* measure] **:** a small portion
mod·i·fi·able \'mäd-ə-ˌfī-ə-bəl\ *adj* **:** capable of being modified — **mod·i·fi·able·ness** *n*
mod·i·fi·ca·tion \ˌmäd-ə-fə-'kā-shən\ *n* **1 :** the limiting of a statement **:** QUALIFICATION **2 :** 1MODE 6 **3 a :** the making of a limited change in something **b :** a change in an organism caused by environmental factors
mod·i·fi·er \'mäd-ə-ˌfī(-ə)r\ *n* **1 :** one that modifies **2 :** a grammatical qualifier
mod·i·fy \'mäd-ə-ˌfī\ *vb* [ME *modifien*, fr. MF *modifier*, fr. L *modificare* to measure, moderate, fr. *modus*] *vt* **1 :** to make less extreme **:** MODERATE **2 a :** to limit or restrict the meaning of esp. in a grammatical construction **:** QUALIFY **b :** to change (a vowel) by umlaut **3 a :** to make minor changes in **b :** to make a basic or important change in **~** *vi* **:** to undergo change **syn** see CHANGE
mo·dil·lion \mō-'dil-yən\ *n* [It *modiglione*] **:** an ornamental block or bracket under the corona of the cornice in the Corinthian and other orders
mod·ish \'mōd-ish\ *adj* **:** FASHIONABLE, STYLISH — **mod·ish·ly** *adv* — **mod·ish·ness** *n*
mo·diste \mō-'dēst\ *n* [F, fr. *mode* style, mode] **:** a fashionable dressmaker
Mo·dred \'mō-drəd, 'mäd-rəd\ *n* **:** a knight of the Round Table and rebellious nephew of King Arthur
mod·u·la·bil·i·ty \ˌmäj-ə-lə-'bil-ət-ē\ *n* **:** the capability of being modulated
mod·u·lar \'mäj-ə-lər\ *adj* **1 :** of, relating to, or based on a module or a modulus **2 :** constructed with standardized units or dimensions for flexibility and variety in use
mod·u·late \'mäj-ə-ˌlāt\ *vb* [L *modulatus*, pp. of *modulari* to play, sing, fr. *modulus* small measure, rhythm, dim. of *modus* measure — more at METE] *vt* **1 :** to tune to a key or pitch **2 :** to adjust to or keep in proper measure or proportion **:** TEMPER **3 :** to vary the amplitude, frequency, or phase of (a carrier wave or signal) in telephony, telegraphy, radio, or television **~** *vi* **1 :** to play or sing with modulation **2 :** to pass by regular chord or melodic progression from one musical key or tonality into another — **mod·u·la·tor** \-ˌlāt-ər\ *n* — **mod·u·la·to·ry** \'mäj-ə-lə-ˌtōr-ē, -ˌtȯr-\ *adj*
mod·u·la·tion \ˌmäj-ə-'lā-shən\ *n* **1 :** a regulating according to measure or proportion **:** TEMPERING **2 :** an inflection of the tone or pitch of the voice; *specif* **:** the use of stress or pitch to convey meaning **3 :** a changing from one tonality to another by regular melodic or chord succession **4 :** the variation of the amplitude, frequency, or phase of a carrier or signal in telegraphy, telephony, radio, or television
mod·ule \'mäj-(ˌ)ü(ə)l\ *n* [L *modulus*] **1 :** a standard or unit of measurement **2 :** the size of some one part taken as a unit of measure by which the proportions of an architectural composition are regulated **3 a :** any in a series of standardized units for use together **b :** a usu. packaged functional assembly of electronic components for use with other such assemblies **4 :** an independent unit that is a part of the total structure of a space vehicle
mod·u·lo \'mäj-ə-ˌlō\ *prep* [NL, abl. of *modulus*] **:** with respect to a modulus of ⟨19 and 54 are congruent ~ 7⟩
mod·u·lus \'mäj-ə-ləs\ *n, pl* **mod·u·li** \-ə-ˌlī, -ˌlē\ [NL, fr. L, small measure] **1 :** a constant or coefficient that expresses numerically the degree in which a property is possessed by a substance or body **2 a :** ABSOLUTE VALUE 2 **b :** a number (as a positive integer) or other mathematical entity (as a polynomial) that in a congruence divides the difference of the two congruent members without leaving a remainder — compare RESIDUE b **c :** the factor by which a logarithm of a number to one base is multiplied to obtain the logarithm of the number to a new base
mo·dus ope·ran·di \ˌmōd-ə-ˌsäp-ə-'ran-dē, -ˌdī\ *n, pl* **mo·di operandi** \'mō-ˌdē-ˌäp-, 'mō-ˌdī-\ [NL] **:** a method of procedure
mo·dus vi·ven·di \ˌmōd-əs-vi-'ven-dē, -ˌdī\ *n, pl* **mo·di vivendi** \'mō-ˌdē-vi-, 'mō-ˌdī-\ [NL, manner of living] **:** a feasible arrangement or practical compromise; *esp* **:** one that bypasses difficulties
mo·fette *or* **mof·fette** \mō-'fet, mä-\ *n* [F *mofette* gaseous exhalation] **:** a vent in the earth from which carbon dioxide and some nitrogen and oxygen issue
mog \'mäg, 'mȯg\ *vi* **mogged; mog·ging** [origin unknown] *dial* **:** to move away; *also* **:** JOG
mo·gul \'mō-(ˌ)gəl, mō-'\ *n* [Per *Mughul*, fr. Mongolian *Mongol*] **1** *or* **mo·ghul** *cap* **:** an Indian Muslim of or descended from one of several conquering groups of Mongol, Turkish, and Persian origin **2 :** a great personage **:** MAGNATE **3 :** a bump in a ski run — **mogul** *adj, often cap*
mo·hair \'mō-ˌha(ə)r, -ˌhe(ə)r\ *n* [modif. of obs. It *mocaiarro*, fr. Ar *mukhayyar*, lit., choice] **:** a fabric or yarn made wholly or in part of the long silky hair of the Angora goat; *also* **:** this hair
Mo·ham·med·an *var of* MUHAMMADAN
Mo·hawk \'mō-ˌhȯk\ *n, pl* **Mohawk** *or* **Mohawks** [of Algonquian origin; akin to Narraganset *Mohowaúuck*] **1 a :** an Iroquoian people of the Mohawk river valley, New York **b :** a member of this people **2 :** the language of the Mohawk people
Mo·he·gan \mō-'hē-gən, mə-\ *or* **Mo·hi·can** \-'hē-kən\ *n, pl*

Mohegan *or* **Mohegans** *or* **Mohican** *or* **Mohicans** **1 :** an Indian people of southeastern Connecticut **2 :** a member of the Mohegan people

Mo·hi·can \mō-'hē-kən, mə-\ *var of* MAHICAN

Moh·ism \'mo-ˌiz-əm\ *n* [*Mo* Ti *fl* 400 B.C. Chin philosopher] **:** the teachings of Mo Ti characterized by an emphasis on egalitarian universal love and opposition to traditionalism and Confucianism — **Moh·ist** \'mo-əst\ *n or adj*

Mo·ho \'mō-ˌhō\ *or* **Mo·ho·ro·vi·cic discontinuity** \ˌmō-hə-'rō-və-ˌchich-\ *n* [Andrija *Mohorovičić fl* 1908 Yugoslav geologist] **:** a point ranging from about three miles beneath the ocean basin floor to about 25 miles beneath the continental surface at which seismological studies indicate a transition in earth materials from those of the earth's crust to those of the subjacent mantle

Mo·hock \'mō-ˌhäk\ *n* [alter. of *mohawk*] **:** one of a gang of aristocratic ruffians who assaulted and otherwise maltreated people in London streets in the early 18th century — **Mo·hock·ism** \-ˌiz-əm\ *n*

Mohs' scale \'mōz-, 'mōs-, ˌmō-səz-\ *n* [Friedrich *Mohs* †1839 G mineralogist] **1 :** a scale of hardness for minerals in which 1 represents the hardness of talc; 2, gypsum; 3, calcite; 4, fluorite; 5, apatite; 6, orthoclase; 7, quartz; 8, topaz; 9, corundum; and 10, diamond **2 :** a revised and expanded version of the original Mohs' scale in which 1 represents the hardness of talc; 2, gypsum; 3, calcite; 4, fluorite; 5, apatite; 6, orthoclase; 7, vitreous pure silica; 8, quartz; 9, topaz; 10, garnet; 11, fused zirconia; 12, fused alumina; 13, silicon carbide; 14, boron carbide; and 15, diamond

mo·hur \'mō(-ə)r, mə-'hu̇(ə)r\ *n* [Hindi *muhr* gold coin, seal, fr. Per; akin to Skt *mudrā* seal] **:** a former gold coin of India and Persia equal to 15 rupees

moi·dore \mȯi-'dō(ə)r, -'dȯ(ə)r, 'mȯi-ˌ\ *n* [modif. of Pg *moeda de ouro*, lit., coin of gold] **:** a former Portuguese gold coin

moi·ety \'mȯi-ət-ē\ *n* [ME *moite*, fr. MF *moité*, fr. LL *medietat-, medietas*, fr. L *medius* middle — more at MID] **1 a :** one of two equal parts **:** HALF **b :** one of two approximately equal parts **2 :** one of two basic complementary tribal subdivisions

[1]**moil** \'mȯi(ə)l\ *vb* [ME *moillen*, fr. MF *moillier*, fr. (assumed) VL *molliare*, fr. L *mollis* soft — more at MELT] *vt, chiefly dial* **:** to make wet or dirty ~ *vi* **:** to work hard **:** DRUDGE — **moil·er** *n*

[2]**moil** *n* **1 :** hard work **:** DRUDGERY **2 :** CONFUSION, TURMOIL

moil·ing \'mȯi-liŋ\ *adj* **1 a :** requiring hard work **b :** INDUSTRIOUS **2 :** violently agitated **:** TURBULENT — **moil·ing·ly** \-liŋ-lē\ *adv*

[1]**moire** \'mȯi(-ə)r, 'mō(ə)r, 'mwär\ *n* [F, fr. E *mohair*] *archaic* **:** a watered mohair

[2]**moi·ré** \mȯ-'rā, mwä-\ *or* **moire** *same, or* 'mȯi(-ə)r, 'mō(ə)r, 'mwär\ *n* [F *moiré*, fr. *moiré* like moire, fr. *moire*] **1 a :** an irregular wavy finish on a fabric **b :** a ripple pattern on a stamp **2 :** a fabric having a wavy watered appearance — **moiré** *adj*

moist \'mȯist\ *adj* [ME *moiste*, fr. MF, fr. (assumed) VL *muscidus*, alter. of L *mucidus* slimy, fr. *mucus*] **:** slightly or moderately wet **:** DAMP; *also* **:** TEARFUL **syn** see WET — **moist·ly** *adv* — **moist·ness** \'mȯis(t)-nəs\ *n*

moist·en \'mȯis-ᵊn\ *vb* **moist·en·ing** \'mȯis-niŋ, -ᵊn-iŋ\ *vt* **:** to make moist ~ *vi* **:** to become moist — **moist·en·er** \'mȯis-nər, -ᵊn-ər\ *n*

mois·ture \'mȯis(h)-chər\ *n* [ME, modif. of MF *moistour*, fr. *moiste*] **:** liquid diffused or condensed in relatively small quantity

moke \'mōk\ *n* [origin unknown] **1** *slang Brit* **:** DONKEY **2** *slang Austral* **:** NAG

mo·la \'mō-lə\ *n, pl* **mola** *or* **molas** [NL, fr. L, millstone] **:** OCEAN SUNFISH

mol·al \'mō-ləl\ *adj* **:** of, relating to, or containing a mole and esp. one mole of solute per 1000 grams of solvent — **mo·lal·i·ty** \mō-'lal-ət-ē\ *n*

[1]**mo·lar** \'mō-lər\ *n* [L *molaris*, fr. *molaris* of a mill, fr. *mola* millstone — more at MILL] **:** a tooth with a rounded or flattened surface adapted for grinding; *specif* **:** one of tne cheek teeth in mammals behind the incisors and canines

[2]**molar** *adj* **1 :** pulverizing by friction **:** GRINDING **2 :** of, relating to, or located near the molar teeth

[3]**molar** *adj* **1** [L *moles* mass — more at MOLE] **:** of or relating to a mass of matter as distinguished from the properties or motions of molecules or atoms **2** [[5]*mole*] **:** of, relating to, or containing a mole or molecules and esp. one mole of solute in 1000 milliliters of solution — **mo·lar·i·ty** \mō-'lar-ət-ē\ *n*

mo·las·ses \mə-'las-əz\ *n, often attrib* [Pg *melaço*, fr. LL *mellaceum* grape juice, fr. L *mell-, mel* honey — more at MELLIFLUOUS] **:** the thick dark to light brown viscid syrup that is separated from raw sugar in sugar manufacture

[1]**mold** \'mōld\ *n* [ME, fr. OE *molde;* akin to OHG *molta* soil, L *molere* to grind — more at MEAL] **1 :** crumbling soft friable earth suited to plant growth **:** SOIL; *esp* **:** soil rich in humus — compare LEAF MOLD **2** *dial Brit* **a :** the surface of the earth **:** GROUND **b :** the earth of the burying ground **3** *archaic* **:** earth that is the substance of the human body

[2]**mold** *n* [ME, fr. OF *modle*, fr. L *modulus*, dim. of *modus* measure — more at METE] **1 :** distinctive nature or character **:** TYPE **2 :** the frame on or around which an object is constructed **3 a :** a cavity in which a substance is shaped: as **(1) :** a matrix for casting metal **(2) :** a form for a jelly or other food **b :** a molded object **4 :** MOLDING **5 a** *obs* **:** an example to be followed **b :** PROTOTYPE **c :** a fixed pattern or contour

[3]**mold** *vt* **1** *archaic* **:** to knead (dough) into a desired consistency or shape **2 a :** to shape in a mold **b :** to exert influence on **3 :** to fit the contours of **4 :** to ornament with molding or carving — **mold·able** \'mōl-də-bəl\ *adj* — **mold·er** *n*

[4]**mold** *n* [ME *mowlde*] **1 :** a superficial often woolly growth produced on damp or decaying organic matter or on living organisms **2 :** a fungus (as of the order Mucorales) that produces mold

[5]**mold** *vi* **:** to become moldy

mold·board \'mōl(d)-ˌbō(ə)rd, -ˌbȯ(ə)rd\ *n* **1 a :** a curved iron plate attached above a plowshare to lift and turn the soil **b :** the flat or curved blade (as of a bulldozer) that pushes material to one side as the machine advances **2 :** one of the boards forming a mold for concrete

mold·er \'mōl-dər\ *vi* **mold·er·ing** \-d(ə-)riŋ\ **:** to crumble into particles

mold·i·ness \'mōl-dē-nəs\ *n* **:** the quality or state of being moldy

mold·ing \'mōl-diŋ\ *n* **1 a :** an act or process of molding **b :** an object produced by molding **c :** the art or occupation of a molder **2 a :** a decorative recessed or relieved surface **b :** a decorative plane or curved strip used for ornamentation or finishing

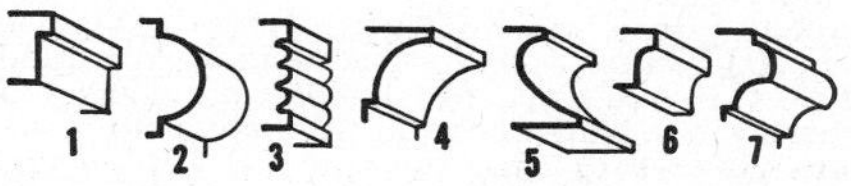

moldings 2a: *1* fillet and fascia, *2* torus, *3* reeding, *4* cavetto, *5* scotia, *6* congé, *7* beak

moldy \'mōl-dē\ *adj* **1 :** of, resembling, or covered with a mold-producing fungus **2 a :** being old and moldering **:** CRUMBLING **b :** ANTIQUATED, FUSTY

[1]**mole** \'mōl\ *n* [ME, fr. OE *māl;* akin to OHG *meil* spot] **:** a congenital spot, mark, or small permanent protuberance on the human body; *esp* **:** a pigmented nevus

[2]**mole** *n* [ME; akin to MLG *mol*] **1 :** any of numerous burrowing insectivores (esp. family Talpidae) with minute eyes, concealed ears, and soft fur **2 :** one who works in the dark

[3]**mole** *n* [MF, fr. OIt *molo*, fr. LGk *mōlos*, fr. L *moles*, lit., mass, exertion; akin to OHG *muodi* weary, Gk *mōlos* exertion] **1 :** a massive work formed of masonry and large stones or earth laid in the sea as a pier or breakwater **2 :** the harbor formed by a mole

[4]**mole** *n* [F *môle*, fr. L *mola* mole, lit., mill, millstone — more at MILL] **:** an abnormal mass in the uterus esp. when containing fetal tissues

[5]**mole** *also* **mol** \'mōl\ *n* [G *mol*, short for *molekulargewicht* molecular weight, fr. *molekular* molecular + *gewicht* weight] **:** GRAM MOLECULE

mo·lec·u·lar \mə-'lek-yə-lər\ *adj* **1 :** of, relating to, or produced by molecules ⟨~ oxygen⟩ **2 a :** of or relating to simple or elementary organization **b (1) :** INDIVIDUAL **(2) :** ATOMISTIC, DIVISIVE — **mo·lec·u·lar·i·ty** \mə-ˌlek-yə-'lar-ət-ē\ *n* — **mo·lec·u·lar·ly** \mə-'lek-yə-lər-lē\ *adv*

molecular formula *n* **:** a chemical formula based on both analysis and molecular weight

mol·e·cule \'mäl-i-ˌkyü(ə)l\ *n* [F *molécule*, fr. NL *molecula*, dim. of L *moles* mass] **1 a :** the smallest particle of an element or compound capable of retaining chemical identity with the substance in mass **b :** a quantity proportional to the molecular weight; *esp* **:** GRAM MOLECULE **2 :** a tiny bit **:** PARTICLE

mole·hill \'mōl-ˌhil\ *n* **:** a little ridge of earth thrown up by a mole

mole·skin \-ˌskin\ *n* **1 :** the skin of the mole used as fur **2 a :** a heavy durable cotton fabric with a short thick velvety nap on one side **b :** a garment made of moleskin — usu. used in pl.

mo·lest \mə-'lest\ *vt* [ME *molesten*, fr. MF *molester*, fr. L *molestare*, fr. *molestus* burdensome, annoying, fr. *moles* mass] **1 :** ANNOY, DISTURB **2 :** to make indecent advances to — **mo·les·ta·tion** \ˌmō-ˌles-'tā-shən, ˌmōl-əs-, ˌmäl-\ *n* — **mo·lest·er** \mə-'les-tər\ *n*

mo·line \mə-'līn\ *adj* [(assumed) AF *moliné*, fr. OF *molin* mill, fr. LL *molinum* — more at MILL] *of a heraldic cross* **:** having the end of each arm forked and recurved — see CROSS illustration

moll \'mäl, 'mȯl\ *n* [prob. fr. *Moll*, nickname for Mary] **1 :** PROSTITUTE **2 a :** DOLL 2 **b :** a gangster's girl friend

mol·lie *also* **molly** \'mäl-ē\ *n* **:** MOLLIENISIA

mol·lie·ni·sia \ˌmäl-i-'nizh-(ē-)ə\ *n* [NL, genus name, fr. Comte François N. *Mollien* †1850 F statesman] **:** any of a genus (*Mollienisia*) of brightly colored topminnows (family Poeciliidae) highly valued as aquarium fishes

mol·li·fi·ca·tion \ˌmäl-ə-fə-'kā-shən\ *n* **:** the act of mollifying **:** the state of being mollified

mol·li·fy \'mäl-ə-ˌfī\ *vb* [ME *mollifien*, fr. MF *mollifier*, fr. LL *mollificare*, fr. L *mollis* soft — more at MELT] *vt* **1 :** to soothe in temper or disposition **:** APPEASE **2 :** to reduce the rigidity of **:** SOFTEN **3 :** ASSUAGE ~ *vi, archaic* **:** SOFTEN, RELENT **syn** see PACIFY

mol·lus·can *also* **mol·lusk·an** \mə-'ləs-kən\ *adj* **:** of or relating to the mollusks

mol·lus·coid \-'ləs-ˌkȯid\ *n* **:** any of various aquatic invertebrates (as a brachiopod or bryozoan) distinguished by a tentacular organ about the mouth and sometimes grouped in a phylum (Molluscoidea) — **molluscoid** *adj* — **mol·lus·coi·de·an** \ˌmäl-(ˌ)əs-'kȯid-ē-ən\ *adj or n*

mol·lusk *or* **mol·lusc** \'mäl-əsk\ *n* [F *mollusque*, fr. NL *Mollusca*, phylum name, fr. L, neut. pl. of *molluscus* soft, fr. *mollis*] **:** any of a large phylum (Mollusca) of invertebrate animals (as snails or clams) with a soft unsegmented body usu. enclosed in a calcareous shell; *broadly* **:** SHELLFISH

Moll·wei·de projection \ˌmȯl-ˌvīd-ə-, ˌmōl-ˌwīd-ə-\ *n* [Karl B. *Mollweide* †1825 G mathematician and astronomer] **:** an equal-area map projection capable of showing the entire surface of the earth in the form of an ellipse with all parallels as straight lines more widely spaced at the equator than at the poles, with the central meridian as one half the length of the equator, and with all other meridians as ellipses equally spaced

[1]**mol·ly·cod·dle** \'mäl-ē-ˌkäd-ᵊl\ *n* [*Molly*, nickname for Mary] **1 :** a pampered weakling; *specif* **:** an effeminate man **2 :** GOODY-GOODY

[2]**mollycoddle** *vt* **mol·ly·cod·dling** \-ˌkäd-liŋ, -ᵊl-iŋ\ **:** CODDLE, PAMPER **syn** see INDULGE — **mol·ly·cod·dler** \-ˌkäd-lər, -ᵊl-ər\ *n*

Mo·loch \'mäl-ək, 'mō-ˌläk\ *or* **Mo·lech** \'mäl-ək, 'mō-ˌlek\ *n* [LL & Heb; LL *Moloch*, fr. Gk, fr. Heb *Mōlekh*] **:** a Semitic deity worshiped through the sacrifice of children

Mo·lo·tov cocktail \ˌmäl-ə-ˌtȯf-, ˌmȯl-, ˌmōl-\ *n* [Vyacheslav M. *Molotov b*1890 Russ statesman] **:** a crude hand grenade made of a bottle filled with a flammable liquid (as gasoline) and fitted with a wick or saturated rag taped to the bottom and ignited at the moment of hurling

[1]**molt** \'mōlt\ *vb* [alter. of ME *mouten*, fr. (assumed) OE *-mūtian* to change, fr. L *mutare* — more at MISS] *vi* **:** to shed hair, feathers, shell, horns, or an outer layer periodically ~ *vt* **:** to cast off (an outer covering) periodically; *specif* **:** to throw off (the old cuticle) — used of arthropods — **molt·er** *n*

[2]**molt** *n* **:** the act or process of molting

mol·ten \'mōlt-ᵊn\ *adj* [ME, fr. pp. of *melten* to melt] **1 :** fused or

liquefied by heat : MELTED; *also* : GLOWING **2** : made by melting and casting
mol·to \'mōl-(,)tō, 'mȯl-\ *adv* [It, fr. L *multum*, fr. neut. of *multus* much] : MUCH, VERY — used in music directions ⟨~ sostenuto⟩
mo·ly \'mō-lē\ *n* [L, fr. Gk *mōly;* akin to Skt *mūla* root] : a mythical herb with a black root and milk-white blossoms and magical powers
mo·lyb·de·nite \mə-'lib-də-,nīt\ *n* [NL *molybdena*] : a blue usu. foliated mineral MoS_2 that is molybdenum disulfide and a source of molybdenum
mo·lyb·de·num \-nəm\ *n* [NL, fr. *molybdena*, a lead ore, molybdenite, molybdenum, fr. L *molybdaena* galena, fr. Gk *molybdaina*, fr. *molybdos* lead] : a polyvalent metallic element that resembles chromium and tungsten in many properties and is used in strengthening and hardening steel — see ELEMENT table
mo·lyb·dic \mə-'lib-dik\ *adj* [NL *molybdenum*] : of, relating to, or containing molybdenum esp. with one of its higher valences
mo·lyb·dous \-dəs\ *adj* [NL *molybdenum*] : of, relating to, or containing molybdenum esp. with one of its lower valences
mome \'mōm\ *n, archaic* [origin unknown] : BLOCKHEAD, FOOL
mo·ment \'mō-mənt\ *n* [ME, fr. MF, fr. L *momentum* movement, particle sufficient to turn the scales, moment, fr. *movēre* to move] **1** : a minute portion or point of time : INSTANT **2** : a time of excellence or conspicuousness ⟨he has his ~*s*⟩ **3** : importance in influence or effect : CONSEQUENCE **4** *obs* : a cause or motive of action **5** : a stage in historical or logical development **6 a** : tendency or measure of tendency to produce motion esp. about a point or axis **b** : the product of quantity (as a force) and the distance to a particular axis or point **7** : the sum of all products formed by multiplying a power of the deviation of a value of a statistical variable from a specified point by its frequency at the value **syn** see IMPORTANCE
mo·men·tar·i·ly \,mō-mən-'ter-ə-lē\ *adv* **1** : for a moment **2** : INSTANTLY **3** : at any moment
mo·men·tar·i·ness \'mō-mən-,ter-ē-nəs\ *n* : the quality or state of being momentary
mo·men·tary \'mō-mən-,ter-ē\ *adj* **1 a** : continuing only a moment : TRANSITORY **b** : having a very brief life : EPHEMERAL **2** : operative or recurring at every moment **syn** see TRANSIENT
mo·ment·ly \'mō-mənt-lē\ *adv* **1** : from moment to moment **2** : at any moment **3** : for a moment
mo·men·to \mə-'ment-(,)ō\ *var of* MEMENTO
moment of truth **1** : the final sword thrust in a bullfight **2** : a moment of crisis on whose outcome much or everything depends
mo·men·tous \mō-'ment-əs, mə-'ment-\ *adj* : IMPORTANT, CONSEQUENTIAL — **mo·men·tous·ly** *adv* — **mo·men·tous·ness** *n*
mo·men·tum \mō-'ment-əm, mə-'ment-\ *n, pl* **mo·men·ta** \-'ment-ə\ *or* **momentums** [NL, fr. L, movement] : a property of a moving body that determines the length of time required to bring it to rest when under the action of a constant force or moment; *broadly* : IMPETUS
Mo·mus \'mō-məs\ *n* [L, fr. Gk *Mōmos*] **1** : the Greek god of censure and mockery **2** : a carping critic
mon \'män\ *dial chiefly Brit var of* MAN
Mon \'mōn\ *n, pl* **Mon** *or* **Mons** **1 a** : the dominant native people of Pegu in Burma **b** : a member of this people **2** : the Mon-Khmer language of the Mon people
mon- *or* **mono-** *comb form* [ME, fr. MF & L; MF, fr. L, fr. Gk, fr. *monos* alone, single — more at MONK] **1** : one : single : alone ⟨*mono*plane⟩ ⟨*mono*drama⟩ ⟨*mono*phobia⟩ **2 a** : containing one (usu. specified) atom, radical, or group ⟨*mono*hydrate⟩ ⟨*mon*oxide⟩ **b** : monomolecular ⟨*mono*film⟩ ⟨*mono*layer⟩
mon·a·chal \'män-i-kəl\ *adj* [MF or LL; MF, fr. LL *monachalis*, fr. *monachus* monk — more at MONK] : MONASTIC
mon·a·chism \'män-ə-,kiz-əm\ *n* : MONASTICISM
mo·nad \'mō-,nad\ *n* [LL *monad-, monas*, fr. Gk, fr. *monos*] **1 a** : UNIT, ONE **b** : ATOM 1 **c** : an elementary unextended individual spiritual substance from which material properties are derived **2** : a minute simple organism or organic unit **3** : a univalent element, atom, or radical — **mo·nad·ic** \mō-'nad-ik, mə-\ *adj* — **mo·nad·ism** \'mō-,nad-,iz-əm\ *n*
mon·adel·phous \,män-ə-'del-fəs, ,mō-nə-\ *adj, of stamens* : united by the filaments into one group usu. forming a tube around the gynoecium
mo·nad·nock \mə-'nad-,näk\ *n* [Mt. *Monadnock*, N.H.] : a hill or mountain of resistant rock surmounting a peneplain
mon·an·drous \mə-'nan-drəs, (')mä-, (')mō-\ *adj* **1** : having a single stamen or flowers with a single stamen **2** [Gk *monandros*, fr. *mon-* + *-andros* having (so many) men — more at -ANDROUS] : of, relating to, or characterized by monandry
mo·nan·dry \'män-,an-drē, 'mō-,nan-\ *n* **1** [*monandrous*] : a marriage form or custom in which a woman has only one husband at a time **2** : a monandrous condition of a plant or flower
mon·arch \'män-ərk, -,ärk\ *n* [LL *monarcha*, fr. Gk *monarchos*, fr. *mon-* + *-archos* -arch] **1** : a person who reigns over a kingdom or empire: as **a** : a sovereign ruler **b** : a constitutional king or queen **2** : someone or something holding preeminent position or power **3** : a large migratory American butterfly (*Danaus plexippus*) having orange-brown wings with black veins and borders and larvae that feed on milkweed — **mo·nar·chal** \mə-'när-kəl, mä-\ *or* **mo·nar·chi·al** \-kē-əl\ *adj*
Mo·nar·chi·an \mə-'när-kē-ən, mä-\ *n* : an adherent of one of two anti-Trinitarian groups of the 2d and 3d centuries A.D. teaching that God is one person as well as one being — **Mo·nar·chi·an·ism** \-,iz-əm\ *n*
mo·nar·chi·cal \mə-'när-ki-kəl, mä-\ *or* **mo·nar·chic** \-kik\ *adj* : of, relating to, or characteristic of a monarch or monarchy — **mo·nar·chi·cal·ly** \-ki-k(ə-)lē\ *adv*
mon·ar·chism \'män-ər-,kiz-əm, -,är-\ *n* : monarchical government or principles — **mon·ar·chist** \-kəst\ *n or adj*
mon·ar·chy \'män-ər-kē *also* -,är-\ *n* **1** : undivided rule or absolute sovereignty by a single person **2** : a nation or state having a monarchical government **3** : a government having a hereditary chief of state with life tenure and powers varying from nominal to absolute
mo·nar·da \mə-'närd-ə\ *n* [NL, genus name, fr. Nicolas *Monardes* †1588 Sp botanist] : any of a genus (*Monarda*) of coarse No. American mints with whorls of showy flowers
mon·as·te·ri·al \,män-ə-'stir-ē-əl, -'ster-\ *adj* : of or relating to monasteries or monastic life
mon·as·tery \'män-ə-,ster-ē\ *n* [ME *monasterie*, fr. LL *monasterium*, fr. LGk *monastērion*, fr. Gk, hermit's cell, fr. *monazein* to live alone, fr. *monos* single — more at MONK] : a house for persons under religious vows; *esp* : an establishment for monks **syn** see CLOISTER
mo·nas·tic \mə-'nas-tik\ *adj* : of or relating to monasteries or to monks or nuns — **monastic** *n* — **mo·nas·ti·cal·ly** \-ti-k(ə-)lē\ *adv* — **mo·nas·ti·cism** \-tə-,siz-əm\ *n*
mon·atom·ic \,män-ə-'täm-ik, ,mō-nə-\ *adj* **1 a** : consisting of one atom; *esp* : having but one atom in the molecule **b** : having a thickness equal to the diameter of a constituent atom **2** : UNIVALENT **3** : having one replaceable atom or radical
mon·au·ral \(')mä-'nȯr-əl, (')mō-\ *adj* : MONOPHONIC 2 — **mon·au·ral·ly** \-ə-lē\ *adv*
mon·ax·i·al \(')mä-'nak-sē-əl, (')mō-\ *adj* : having or based on a single axis : UNIAXIAL ⟨~ symmetry⟩
mon·a·zite \'män-ə-,zīt\ *n* [G *monazit*, fr. Gk *monazein*] : a mineral $(Ce,La,Md,Pr,Th)PO_4$ that is a yellow, red, or brown phosphate of the cerium metals and thorium found often in sand and gravel deposits
Mon·day \'mən-dē\ *n* [ME, fr. OE *mōnandæg;* akin to OHG *mānatag* Monday; both fr. a prehistoric WGmc compound whose components are represented by OE *mōna* moon and by OE *dæg* day] : the second day of the week — **Mon·days** \-dēz\ *adv*
M-1 \'em-'wən\ *n, pl* **M-1's** \-'wənz\ : GARAND RIFLE
mon·ecious *var of* MONOECIOUS
mon·es·trous \(')mä-'nes-trəs, (')mō-\ *adj* : experiencing estrus once each year
mon·e·tar·i·ly \,män-ə-'ter-ə-lē, ,mən-\ *adv* : with respect to money
mon·e·tary \'män-ə-,ter-ē, 'mən-\ *adj* [LL *monetarius* of a mint, of money, fr. L *moneta*] **1** : of or relating to coinage or currency **2** : PECUNIARY **syn** see FINANCIAL
monetary unit *n* : the standard unit of value of a currency
mon·e·ti·za·tion \,män-ət-ə-'zā-shən, ,mən-\ *n* : the act or process of monetizing
mon·e·tize \'män-ə-,tīz, 'mən-\ *vt* [L *moneta*] : to coin into money; *also* : to establish as legal tender
mon·ey \'mən-ē\ *n, pl* **moneys** *or* **mon·ies** \'mən-ēz\ [ME *moneye*, fr. MF *moneie*, fr. L *moneta* mint, money — more at MINT] **1** : something generally accepted as a medium of exchange, a measure of value, or a means of payment: as **a** : officially coined or stamped metal currency **b** : MONEY OF ACCOUNT **c** : PAPER MONEY **2** : wealth reckoned in terms of money **3** : a form or denomination of coin or paper money **4 a** : the first, second, and third place winners in a horse or dog race **b** : prize money ⟨his horse took third ~⟩ **5** : persons or interests possessing or controlling great wealth — **mon·ey·lend·er** \'mən-ē-,len-dər\ *n*

MONEY

NAME	SYMBOL	SUBDIVISIONS	COUNTRY
afghani	Af	100 puls	Afghanistan
baht	Bht *or* B	100 satang	Thailand
balboa	B/	100 centesimos	Panama
bolivar	B	100 centimos	Venezuela
cedi	¢	100 pesewas	Ghana
colon	C *or* ¢	100 centimos	Costa Rica
colon	C *or* ¢	100 centavos	El Salvador
cordoba	C$	100 centavos	Nicaragua
cruzeiro	Cr$	100 centavos	Brazil
deutsche mark	DM	100 pfennigs	West Germany
dinar	DA	100 centimes	Algeria
dinar	ID	1000 fils	Iraq
dinar	JD	1000 fils	Jordan
dinar	KD	1000 fils	Kuwait
dinar	£SY	1000 fils	Southern Yemen
dinar	D	1000 millimes	Tunisia
dinar	Din	100 para	Yugoslavia
dirham	Dh	100 francs	Morocco
dollar	$	100 cents	United States
dollar	$	100 cents	Canada
dollar	$	100 cents	Australia
dollar	$	100 cents	Bahamas
dollar	$	100 cents	Barbados
dollar	$	100 cents	Bermuda
dollar	$Eth	100 cents	Ethiopia
dollar	$G	100 cents	Guyana
dollar	HK$	100 cents	Hong Kong
dollar	$	100 cents	Jamaica
dollar	$	100 cents	Liberia
dollar	M$ *or* Mal$	100 cents	Malaysia
dollar	$	100 cents	New Zealand
dollar	S$	100 cents	Singapore
dollar	TT$	100 cents	Trinidad and Tobago
drachma	Dr	100 lepta	Greece
escudo	E *or* E°	100 centesimos	Chile
escudo	$ *or* Esc	100 centavos	Portugal
forint	F *or* Ft	100 filler	Hungary
franc	Fr *or* F	100 centimes	France
franc	Fr *or* F	100 centimes	Belgium
franc	Fr *or* F	100 centimes	Burundi
franc	Fr *or* F	100 centimes	Luxembourg
franc	Fr *or* F	100 centimes	Switzerland
franc	Fr *or* F	100 centimes	Cameroon
franc	Fr *or* F	100 centimes	Cen. African R.
franc	Fr *or* F	100 centimes	Chad
franc	Fr *or* F	100 centimes	Congo (Brazzaville)
franc	Fr *or* F	100 centimes	Dahomey
franc	Fr *or* F	100 centimes	Gabon
franc	Fr *or* F	100 centimes	Guinea
franc	Fr *or* F	100 centimes	Ivory Coast
franc	Fr *or* F	100 centimes	Malagasy Rep.
franc	Fr *or* F	100 centimes	Mali
franc	Fr *or* F	100 centimes	Mauritania
franc	Fr *or* F	100 centimes	Niger
franc	Fr *or* F	100 centimes	Rwanda
franc	Fr *or* F	100 centimes	Senegal
franc	Fr *or* F	100 centimes	Togo
franc	Fr *or* F	100 centimes	Upper Volta
gourde	G *or* Gde	100 centimes	Haiti
guarani	₲ *or* G	100 centimos	Paraguay
gulden	G	100 cents	Netherlands
kip	K	100 at	Laos
koruna	Kč	100 halers	Czechoslovakia
krona	Kr	100 aurar	Iceland

NAME	SYMBOL	SUBDIVISIONS	COUNTRY
krona	Kr	100 öre	Sweden
krone	Kr	100 öre	Denmark
krone	Kr	100 öre	Norway
kwacha	K	100 ngwee	Zambia
kyat	K	100 pyas	Burma
lek	L	100 qintar	Albania
lempira	L	100 centavos	Honduras
leone	Le	100 cents	Sierra Leone
leu	L	100 bani	Romania
lev	Lv	100 stotinki	Bulgaria
lira	L	100 centesimi	Italy
markka	M or Mk	100 pennia	Finland
peseta	Pta or P	100 centimos	Spain
peso	$	100 centavos	Argentina
peso	$B	100 centavos	Bolivia
peso	$	100 centavos	Colombia
peso	$	100 centavos	Cuba
peso	$	100 centavos	Dominican Rep.
peso	$	100 centavos	Mexico
peso	P	100 centavos	Philippines
peso	$	100 centesimos	Uruguay
piaster	VN$ or Pr	100 cents	So. Vietnam
pound	£	20 shillings / 240 pence	United Kingdom
pound	£	1000 mils	Cyprus
pound	£	20 shillings / 240 pence	Gambia
pound	£	20 shillings / 240 pence	Ireland
pound	I£	100 agorot	Israel
pound	£L	100 piasters	Lebanon
pound	£L	1000 milliemes	Libya
pound	£	20 shillings / 240 pence	Malawi
pound	£	20 shillings / 240 pence	Nigeria
pound	£S	10 rials / 100 piasters	Sudan
pound	£S	100 piasters	Syria
pound	£T	100 piasters (kurus)	Turkey
pound	£E	100 piasters / 1000 milliemes	United Arab Republic
quetzal	Q	100 centavos	Guatemala
rand	R	100 cents	Botswana
rand	R	100 cents	Lesotho
rand	R	100 cents	So. Africa
rand	R	100 cents	Swaziland
rial	R	100 dinars	Iran
riel	J or CR	100 sen	Cambodia
riyal or rial	YR	40 buqshas	Yemen
riyal or rial	R	20 qursh	Saudi Arabia
ruble	R or Rub	100 kopecks	U.S.S.R.
rupee	R or Re	100 cents	Ceylon
rupee	R or Re	100 paise	India
rupee	R or Re	100 cents	Mauritius
rupee	R or Re	100 paisa	Pakistan
rupiah	Rp	100 sen	Indonesia
schilling	S	100 groschen	Austria
shilling	Sh	100 cents	Kenya
shilling	Sh	100 cents	Tanzania
shilling	Sh	100 cents	Uganda
sol	$ or S/	100 centavos	Peru
Somali shilling	Som Sh	100 cents	Somalia
sucre	S/	100 centavos	Ecuador
won	W	100 chon	So. Korea
yen	Y or Y	100 sen	Japan
yuan	$	10 chiao	China
zaire	Z	100 makuta (sing. likuta)	Congo (Kinshasa)
zloty	Zl or Z	100 groszy	Poland

mon·ey·bags \'mən-ē-ˌbagz\ *n pl but sing or pl in constr* **1** : WEALTH **2** : a wealthy person

money changer *n* **1** : one whose occupation is the exchanging of kinds or denominations of currency **2** : a device for holding and dispensing sorted change

mon·eyed *or* **mon·ied** \'mən-ēd\ *adj* **1** : having money : WEALTHY **2** : consisting in or derived from money

mon·ey·er \'mən-ē-ər\ *n* [ME, fr. OF *monier*, fr. LL *monetarius* master of a mint, coiner, fr. *monetarius* of a mint] : an authorized coiner of money : MINTER

mon·ey·mak·er \'mən-ē-ˌmā-kər\ *n* **1** : one that accumulates wealth **2** : a plan or product that produces profit — **mon·ey·mak·ing** \-kiŋ\ *adj or n*

money of account : a denominator of value or basis of exchange which is used in keeping accounts and for which there may or may not be an equivalent coin or denomination of paper money

money order *n* : an order issued by a post office, bank, or telegraph office for payment of a specified sum of money at another office

mon·ey·wort \'mən-ē-ˌwərt, -ˌwȯ(ə)rt\ *n* : a trailing perennial herb (*Lysimachia nummularia*) with rounded opposite leaves and solitary yellow flowers in their axils

¹mon·ger \'məŋ-gər\ *n* [ME *mongere*, fr. OE *mangere*, fr. L *mangon-*, *mango*, of Gk origin; akin to Gk *manganon* charm, philter — more at MANGONEL] **1** : BROKER, DEALER

²monger *vt* **mon·ger·ing** \-g(ə-)riŋ\ : to deal in : PEDDLE

Mon·gol \'mäŋ-gəl, 'män-ˌgōl, 'mäŋ-\ *n* [Mongolian *Moṅgol*] **1** : a member of one of the chiefly pastoral Mongoloid peoples of Mongolia **2** : MONGOLIAN 2 **3** : MONGOLOID — **Mongol** *adj*

¹Mon·go·lian \män-'gōl-yən, mäŋ-, -'gō-lē-ən\ *adj* **1** : of, relating to, or constituting Mongolia, the Mongolian People's Republic, the Mongols, or Mongolian **2** : MONGOLOID **3** *not cap* : of, relating to, or afflicted with mongolism

²Mongolian *n* **1 a** : MONGOL 1 **b** : MONGOLOID **c** : a native or inhabitant of the Mongolian People's Republic **2** : the Mongolic language of the Mongol people

¹Mon·gol·ic \män-'gäl-ik, mäŋ-\ *adj* : MONGOLOID

²Mongolic *n* : a group of Altaic languages including Mongolian and Kalmuck

mon·gol·ism \'mäŋ-gə-ˌliz-əm\ *or* **mon·go·lian·ism** \män-'gōl-yə-,niz-əm, mäŋ-, -'gō-lē-ə-,niz-\ *n* : a congenital idiocy of unknown ultimate cause in which a child is born with slanting eyes, a broad short skull, and broad hands with short fingers

Mon·gol·oid \'mäŋ-gə-ˌlȯid\ *adj* **1** : of, constituting, or characteristic of a major racial stock native to Asia including peoples of northern and eastern Asia, Malaysians, Eskimos, and often American Indians **2** *not cap* : MONGOLIAN **3** — **Mongoloid** *n*

mon·goose \'män-ˌgüs, 'mäŋ-\ *n, pl* **mon·goos·es** [Hindi *māgūs*, fr. Prakrit *maṅguso*] : an agile grizzled ferret-sized viverrine mammal (*Herpestes nyula*) of India that feeds on snakes and rodents; *broadly* : any of various related Asian and African mammals

mon·grel \'məŋ-grəl, 'mäŋ-, -'män-\ *n* [prob. fr. ME *mong* mixture, short for *ymong*, fr. OE *gemong* crowd — more at AMONG] **1** : an individual resulting from the interbreeding of diverse breeds or strains; *esp* : one of unknown ancestry **2** : a cross between types of persons or things — **mongrel** *or* **mon·grel·ly** \-grə-lē\ *adj* — **mon·grel·ism** \-grə-ˌliz-əm\ *n* — **mon·grel·ize** \-ˌlīz\ *vt*

monies *pl of* MONEY

mon·i·ker *or* **mon·ick·er** \'män-i-kər\ *n* [origin unknown] *slang* : NAME, NICKNAME

mo·nil·i·form \mə-'nil-ə-ˌfȯrm\ *adj* [L *monile* necklace — more at MANE] : jointed or constricted at regular intervals so as to resemble a string of beads — **mo·nil·i·form·ly** *adv*

mon·ish \'män-ish\ *vt* [ME *monesen*, alter. of *monesten*, fr. OF *monester*, fr. (assumed) VL *monestare*, fr. L *monēre* to warn] : WARN

mo·nism \'mō-ˌniz-əm, 'män-ˌiz-\ *n* [G *monismus*, fr. *mono-* + *-ismus* -ism] **1 a** : a view that there is only one kind of ultimate substance **b** : the view that reality is one unitary organic whole with no independent parts **2** : MONOGENESIS — **mo·nist** \'mō-nəst, 'män-əst\ *n* — **mo·nis·tic** \mō-'nis-tik, mä-\ *or* **mo·nis·ti·cal** \-ti-kəl\ *adj*

mo·ni·tion \mō-'nish-ən, mə-\ *n* [ME *monicioun*, fr. MF *monition*, fr. L *monition-*, *monitio*, fr. *monitus*, pp. of *monēre*] **1** : WARNING, CAUTION **2** : an intimation or presentiment esp. of danger **3** : a legal summons or citation to appear and answer a default

¹mon·i·tor \'män-ət-ər\ *n* [L, one that warns, overseer, fr. *monitus*, pp. of *monēre* to warn — more at MIND] **1 a** : a student appointed to assist a teacher **b** : a person or thing that warns or instructs **c** : one that monitors or is used in monitoring; *specif* : a receiver used to view the picture being picked up by a television camera **2** : any of various large tropical Old World pleurodont lizards (genus *Varanus* and family Varanidae) closely related to the iguanas **3** [*Monitor*, first ship of the type] **a** : a heavily armored warship formerly used in coastal operations having a very low freeboard and one or more revolving gun turrets **b** : a small modern warship with shallow draft for coastal bombardment — **mon·i·to·ri·al** \ˌmän-ə-'tōr-ē-əl, -'tȯr-\ *adj* — **mon·i·tor·ship** \'män-ət-ər-ˌship\ *n* — **mon·i·tress** \'män-ə-trəs\ *n*

²monitor *vt* **mon·i·tor·ing** \'män-ət-ə-riŋ, 'män-ə-triŋ\ **1** : to check (as a radio or television signal or program) by means of a receiver for quality or fidelity to a band or for military, political, or criminal significance **2** : to test for intensity of radiations esp. if due to radioactivity **3** : to watch, observe, or check esp. for a special purpose **4** : to keep track of, regulate, or control **5** : to check or regulate the volume or quality of (sound) in recording

¹mon·i·to·ry \'män-ə-ˌtōr-ē, -ˌtȯr-\ *adj* [L *monitorius*, fr. *monitus*] : ADMONISHING, WARNING

²monitory *n* : a letter containing an admonition or warning

monk \'məŋk\ *n* [ME, fr. OE *munuc*, fr. LL *monachus*, fr. L Gk *monachos*, fr. Gk, adj., single, fr. *monos* single, alone; akin to OHG *mengen* to lack, Gk *manos* sparse] : a man who is a member of a religious order and lives in a monastery; *also* : a solitary ascetic or cenobite *syn* see RELIGIOUS — **monk·ish** \'məŋ-kish\ *adj* — **monk·ish·ly** *adv* — **monk·ish·ness** *n*

monk·ery \'məŋ-kə-rē\ *n* **1** : MONASTICISM **2** : MONASTERY

¹mon·key \'məŋ-kē\ *n* [prob. of LG origin; akin to *Moneke*, name of an ape, prob. of Romance origin; akin to OSp *mona* monkey] **1** : a primate mammal other than man and usu. also the lemurs and tarsiers; *esp* : any of the smaller longer-tailed primates as contrasted with the apes **2 a** : a person resembling a monkey **b** : a ludicrous figure : DUPE **3** : any of various machines, implements, or vessels; *esp* : the falling weight of a pile driver

²monkey *vi* **1** : to act in a grotesque or mischievous manner **2 a** : FOOL, TRIFLE **b** : TAMPER ~ *vt* : MIMIC, MOCK

monkey jacket *n* : MESS JACKET

mon·key·shine \'məŋ-kē-ˌshīn\ *n* : PRANK — usu. used in pl.

monkey wrench *n* **1** : a wrench with one fixed and one adjustable jaw at right angles to a straight handle **2** : something that disrupts ⟨threw a *monkey wrench* into the peace negotiations⟩

Mon-Khmer \ˌmōn-kə-'me(ə)r\ *n* : a language family containing Mon, Khmer, and several other languages of southeast Asia

monk·hood \'məŋk-ˌhud\ *n* **1** : the character, condition, or profession of a monk : MONASTICISM **2** : monks as a class

monk's cloth *n* : a coarse heavy fabric in basket weave made orig. of worsted and used for monk's habits but now chiefly of cotton or linen and used for draperies

monks·hood \'məŋ(k)s-ˌhud\ *n* **1** : ACONITUM 1; *esp* : a poisonous Eurasian herb (*Aconitum napellus*) often cultivated for its showy terminal racemes of white or purplish flowers

mo·no \'män-(ˌ)ō, 'mō-(ˌ)nō\ *n* : INFECTIOUS MONONUCLEOSIS

mono- — see MON-

¹mono·ac·id \ˌmän-ō-(ˌ)ō-'as-əd, ˌmō-(ˌ)nō-\ *adj* **1** : having a single hydroxyl group and able to react with only one molecule of a monobasic acid to form a salt or ester — used of bases and alcohols **2** : having one acid hydrogen atom

²monoacid *n* : an acid having only one acid hydrogen atom

mo·no·ba·sic \ˌmän-ə-'bā-sik, ˌmō-nə-\ *adj* [ISV] **1** : having only one acid hydrogen atom **2** : containing only one atom of a univalent metal or its equivalent **3** : having a single basic hydroxyl group and able to react with only one molecule of a monobasic acid — used of bases and basic salts — **mo·no·ba·sic·i·ty** \-bā-'sis-ət-ē\ *n*

mo·no·car·box·yl·ic \-ˌkär-(ˌ)bäk-'sil-ik\ *adj* : containing one carboxyl group

mo·no·car·pel·lary \-'kär-pə-,ler-ē\ *adj* **:** consisting of a single carpel

mo·no·car·pic \-'kär-pik\ *adj* [prob. fr. (assumed) NL *monocarpicus*, fr. NL *mon-* + *-carpicus* -carpic] **:** bearing fruit but once and dying

mo·no·cha·si·um \-'kā-z(h)ē-əm\ *n, pl* **mo·no·cha·sia** \-z(h)ē-ə\ [NL, fr. *mon-* + *-chasium* (as in *dichasium*)] **:** a cymose inflorescence that produces only one main axis

mo·no·chla·myd·e·ous \-klə-'mid-ē-əs\ *adj* [deriv. of Gk *mon-* + *chlamyd-, chlamys* cloak] **:** lacking petals or sepals but not both; *also* **:** having monochlamydeous flowers

mo·no·chord \'män-ə-,kó(ə)rd, 'mō-nə-\ *n* [ME *monocorde*, fr. MF, fr. ML *monochordum*, fr. Gk *monochordon*, fr. *mon-* + *chordē* string — more at YARN] **:** an instrument of ancient origin for measuring and demonstrating the mathematical relations of musical tones that consists of a single string stretched over a sounding board and a movable bridge set on a graduated scale

mo·no·chro·mat \'män-ə-krō-,mat, 'mō-nə-, ,män-ə-', ,mō-nə-'\ *n* [*mon-* + Gk *chrōmat-, chrōma*] **:** a completely color-blind individual

mo·no·chro·mat·ic \,män-ə-krō-'mat-ik, ,mō-nə-\ *adj* [L *monochromatos*, fr. Gk *monochrōmatos*, fr. *mon-* + *chrōmat-, chrōma* color — more at CHROMATIC] **1 :** having or consisting of one color or hue **2 :** consisting of radiation of a single wavelength or of a very small range of wavelengths **3 :** of, relating to, or exhibiting monochromatism — **mo·no·chro·mat·i·cal·ly** \-i-k(ə-)lē\ *adv* — **mo·no·chro·ma·tic·i·ty** \-,krō-mə-'tis-ət-ē\ *n*

mo·no·chro·ma·tism \-'krō-mə-,tiz-əm\ *n* **:** complete color blindness in which all colors appear as shades of gray

¹mono·chrome \'män-ə-,krōm\ *n* [ML *monochroma*, fr. L, fem. of *monochromos* of one color, fr. Gk *monochrōmos*, fr. *mon-* + *-chrōmos* -chrome] **:** a painting, drawing, or photograph in a single hue — **mono·chro·mic** \,män-ə-'krō-mik\ *adj* — **mono·chrom·ist** \'män-ə-,krō-məst\ *n*

²monochrome *adj* **:** of, relating to, or made with a single color or hue; *also* **:** characterized by the reproduction of visual images in tones of gray

mon·o·cle \'män-i-kəl\ *n* [F, fr. LL *monoculus* having one eye, fr. L *mon-* + *oculus* eye — more at EYE] **:** an eyeglass for one eye — **mon·o·cled** \-kəld\ *adj*

mo·no·cli·nal \,män-ə-'klīn-ᵊl, ,mō-nə-\ *adj* **:** having or relating to a single oblique inclination ⟨~ fold⟩ — **monoclinal** *n*

mo·no·cline \'män-ə-,klīn, 'mō-nə-\ *n* **:** a monoclinal geologic fold

mo·no·clin·ic \,män-ə-'klin-ik, ,mō-nə-\ *adj* [ISV] **:** having one oblique intersection of the crystallographic axes

monoclinic system *n* **:** a crystal system characterized by three unequal axes with one oblique intersection

mo·no·cli·nous \-'klī-nəs\ *adj* [NL *monoclinus*, fr. *mon-* + *-clinus* -clinous] **:** having both stamens and pistils in the same flower

mo·no·coque \'män-ə-,kōk, 'mō-nə-, -,käk\ *n* [F, fr. *mon-* + *coque* shell, fr. L *coccum* excrescence on a tree, fr. Gk *kokkos* berry] **1 :** an aircraft structure in which the outer covering skin carries all or a major part of the stresses **2 :** the structure of a vehicle in which the body is integral with the chassis

mo·no·cot \-,kät\ *or* **mo·no·cot·yl** \-,kät-ᵊl\ *n* **:** MONOCOTYLEDON

mo·no·cot·y·le·don \,män-ə-,kät-ᵊl-'ēd-ᵊn, ,mō-nə-\ *n* [deriv. of NL *mon-* + *cotyledon*] **:** any of a subclass (Monocotyledoneae) of seed plants having an embryo with a single cotyledon and usu. parallel-veined leaves — **mo·no·cot·y·le·don·ous** \-ᵊn-əs\ *adj*

mo·noc·ra·cy \mä-'näk-rə-sē, mō-, mə-\ *n* **:** government by a single person — **mo·no·crat** \'män-ə-,krat, 'mō-nə-\ *n* — **mo·no·crat·ic** \,män-ə-'krat-ik, ,mō-nə-\ *adj*

mon·oc·u·lar \mä-'näk-yə-lər, mō-, mə-\ *adj* [LL *monoculus* having one eye] **:** suitable for use with only one eye

mo·no·cul·ture \'män-ə-,kəl-chər, 'mō-nə-\ *n* **:** the cultivation of a single product to the exclusion of other uses of land

mo·no·cy·cle \-,sī-kəl\ *n* [*mon-* + *-cycle* (as in *bicycle*)] **:** UNICYCLE

mo·no·cy·clic \,män-ə-'sī-klik, ,mō-nə-, -'sik-lik\ *adj* [ISV *mon-* + *cyclic*] **1 :** arranged in or consisting of one whorl or circle **2 :** containing one ring in the molecular structure — **mo·no·cy·cly** \'män-ə-,sī-klē, 'mō-nə-\ *n*

mo·no·cyte \'män-ə-,sīt, 'mō-nə-\ *n* [ISV] **:** a large phagocytic leukocyte with basophilic cytoplasm containing faint eosinophil granulations — **mo·no·cyt·ic** \,män-ə-'sit-ik, ,mō-nə-\ *adj* — **mo·no·cyt·oid** \-'sīt-,óid\ *adj*

mo·nod·ic \mə-'näd-ik\ *adj* **:** of or relating to monody — **mo·nod·i·cal** \-i-kəl\ *adj* — **mo·nod·i·cal·ly** \-k(ə-)lē\ *adv*

mon·o·dist \'män-əd-əst\ *n* **:** a writer, singer, or composer of monody

mo·no·dra·ma \'män-ə-,dräm-ə, 'mō-nə-, -,dram-\ *n* **:** a drama acted or designed to be acted by a single person — **mo·no·dra·mat·ic** \,män-ə-drə-'mat-ik, ,mō-nə-\ *adj*

mon·o·dy \'män-əd-ē\ *n* [ML *monodia*, fr. Gk *monōidia*, fr. *monōidos* singing alone, fr. *mon-* + *aidein* to sing — more at ODE] **1 :** an ode sung by one voice (as in a Greek tragedy) **2 :** ELEGY, DIRGE **3 a :** a monophonic vocal piece **b :** the monophonic style of 17th century opera

mon·oe·cious \mə-'nē-shəs, (')mä-, (')mō-\ *adj* [deriv. of Gk *mon-* + *oikos* house — more at VICINITY] **1 :** having male and female sex organs in the same individual **:** HERMAPHRODITIC **2 :** having pistillate and staminate flowers on the same plant — **mon·oe·cious·ly** *adv* — **mon·oe·cism** \-'nē-,siz-əm\ *or* **mon·oe·cy** \'män-,ē-sē, 'mō-,nē-\ *n*

mo·no·fil \'män-ə-,fil, 'mō-nə-\ *n* **:** MONOFILAMENT

mo·no·fil·a·ment \,män-ə-'fil-ə-mənt, ,mō-nə-\ *n* **:** a single untwisted synthetic filament

mo·no·fu·el \'män-ō-,fyü(-ə)l, 'mō-nō-, -,fyü(-ə)l\ *n* **:** MONOPROPELLANT

mo·no·gam·ic \,män-ə-'gam-ik, ,mō-nə-\ *adj* **:** MONOGAMOUS

mo·nog·a·mist \mə-'näg-ə-məst\ *n* **:** one who practices or upholds monogamy

mo·nog·a·mous \-məs\ *adj* **:** of, relating to, or practicing monogamy — **mo·nog·a·mous·ly** *adv* — **mo·nog·a·mous·ness** *n*

mo·nog·a·my \-mē\ *n* [F *monogamie*, fr. LL *monogamia*, fr. Gk, fr. *monogamos* monogamous, fr. *mon-* + *gamos* marriage — more at BIGAMY] **:** single marriage: **a :** one marriage only during life **b :** marriage with but one person at a time

mo·no·gen·e·sis \,män-ə-'jen-ə-səs, ,mō-nə-\ *n* [NL] **:** unity of origin; *specif* **:** the presumed origin of all life from one original entity or cell — **mo·no·ge·net·ic** \-jə-'net-ik\ *adj*

mo·no·gen·ic \-'jen-ik\ *adj* [ISV] **:** of, relating to, or controlled by a single gene and esp. by either of an allelic pair — **mo·no·gen·i·cal·ly** \-i-k(ə-)lē\ *adv*

¹mono·gram \'män-ə-,gram\ *n* [LL *monogramma*, fr. Gk *mon-* + *gramma* letter] **:** a sign of identity usu. formed of the combined initials of a name — **mono·gram·mat·ic** \,män-ə-grə-'mat-ik\ *adj*

²monogram *vt* **mono·grammed**; **mono·gram·ming :** to mark with a monogram

¹mono·graph \'män-ə-,graf\ *n* **:** a learned treatise on a small area of learning; *also* **:** a written account of a single thing — **mono·graph·ic** \,män-ə-'graf-ik\ *adj*

²monograph *vt* **:** to write a monograph on

mo·nog·y·nous \mə-'näj-ə-nəs, mä-, mō-\ *adj* **1 :** having one pistil or flowers with one pistil **2 :** of, relating to, or living in monogyny

mo·nog·y·ny \-nē\ *n* [ISV] **:** the state or custom of having only one wife at a time

mo·no·hy·dric \,män-ə-'hī-drik, ,mō-nə-\ *adj* **1 :** containing one atom of acid hydrogen **2 :** MONOHYDROXY

mo·no·hy·droxy \-(,)hī-'dräk-sē\ *adj* [ISV *monohydroxy-*, fr. *mon-* + *hydroxy-*] **:** containing one hydroxyl group in the molecule

mo·no·lay·er \'män-ə-,lā-ər, 'mō-nə-, -,le(-ə)r\ *n* **:** a layer or film one molecule in thickness ⟨a ~ of stearic acid⟩

mo·no·lin·gual \,män-ə-'liŋ-gwəl, ,mō-nə-\ *adj* **:** expressed in or knowing or using only one language — **monolingual** *n*

mo·no·lith \'män-ᵊl-,ith, 'mōn-\ *n* [F *monolithe*, fr. *monolithe* consisting of a single stone, fr. L *monolithus*, fr. Gk *monolithos*, fr. *mon-* + *lithos* stone] **:** a single great stone often in the form of an obelisk or column

mo·no·lith·ic \,män-ᵊl-'ith-ik, ,mōn-\ *adj* **1 :** of or relating to a monolith **2 :** exhibiting massive uniformity **:** UNDIFFERENTIATED

mono·logue *also* **mono·log** \'män-ᵊl-,óg, -,äg\ *n* [F *monologue*, fr. *mon-* + *-logue* (as in *dialogue*)] **1 :** a dramatic soliloquy; *also* **:** a dramatic sketch performed by one actor **2 :** a literary soliloquy **3 :** a long speech monopolizing conversation — **mono·logu·ist** \-,óg-əst, -,äg-\ *or* **mo·no·lo·gist** \mə-'näl-ə-jəst; 'män-ᵊl-,óg-əst, -,äg-\ *n*

mo·no·ma·nia \,män-ə-'mā-nē-ə, ,mō-nə-, -'mā-nyə\ *n* [NL] **1 :** mental derangement restricted to one idea or group of ideas **2 :** excessive concentration on a single object or idea — **mo·no·ma·ni·ac** \-'mā-nē-,ak\ *n or adj*

mo·no·mer \'män-ə-mər, 'mō-nə-\ *n* [ISV] **:** the simple unpolymerized form of a chemical compound — **mo·no·mer·ic** \,män-ə-'mer-ik, ,mō-nə-\ *adj*

mo·no·me·tal·lic \,män-ō-mə-'tal-ik, ,mō-nō-\ *adj* **1 :** consisting of or employing one metal **2 :** of or relating to monometallism

mo·no·met·al·lism \-'met-ᵊl-,iz-əm\ *n* [ISV *mon-* + *-metallism* (as in *bimetallism*)] **:** the adoption of one metal only in a currency — **mo·no·met·al·list** \-ᵊl-əst\ *n*

mo·nom·e·ter \mə-'näm-ət-ər\ *n* [LL, fr. Gk *monometros*, fr. *mon-* + *metron* measure — more at MEASURE] **:** a verse consisting of a single foot or dipody

mo·no·mi·al \mä-'nō-mē-əl, mə-, mō-\ *n* [blend of *mon-* + *-nomial* (as in *binomial*)] **:** a mathematical expression consisting of a single term; *also* **:** a taxonomic name consisting of a single word or term — **monomial** *adj*

mo·no·mo·lec·u·lar \,män-ō-mə-'lek-yə-lər, ,mō-nō-\ *adj* **:** being only one molecule thick ⟨a ~ film⟩ — **mo·no·mo·lec·u·lar·ly** *adv*

mo·no·mor·phe·mic \-(,)mór-'fē-mik\ *adj* **:** consisting of only one morpheme ⟨*raise* is ~ but *rays* is not⟩

mo·no·mor·phic \-'mór-fik\ *or* **mo·no·mor·phous** \-fəs\ *adj* **:** having but a single form or structural pattern — **mo·no·mor·phism** \-,fiz-əm\ *n*

mo·no·nu·cle·ar \,män-ō-'n(y)ü-klē-ər, ,mō-nō-\ *adj* [ISV] **1 :** having only one nucleus **2 :** MONOCYCLIC 2 — **mononuclear** *n*

mo·no·nu·cle·o·sis \-,n(y)ü-klē-'ō-səs\ *n* [NL, fr. ISV *mononuclear* + NL *-osis*] **:** an abnormal increase of agranulocytes in the blood — see INFECTIOUS MONONUCLEOSIS

mo·noph·a·gous \mə-'näf-ə-gəs\ *adj* **:** feeding on or utilizing a single kind of food; *esp* **:** feeding on a single kind of plant or animal — **mo·noph·a·gy** \-ə-jē\ *n*

mo·no·phon·ic \,män-ə-'fän-ik, ,mō-nə-\ *adj* **1 :** having a single melodic line with little or no accompaniment **2 :** of or relating to sound transmission, recording, or reproduction involving a single transmission path

mo·noph·o·ny \mə-'näf-ə-nē\ *n* **:** monophonic music

mon·oph·thong \'män-ə(f)-,thóŋ\ *n* [LGk *monophthongos* single vowel, fr. Gk *mon-* + *phthongos* sound] **:** a vowel sound that throughout its duration has a single constant articulatory position — **mon·oph·thon·gal** \,män-ə(f)-'thóŋ-(g)əl\ *adj*

mo·no·phy·let·ic \,män-ō-(,)fī-'let-ik, ,mō-nō-\ *adj* [ISV] **:** of or relating to a single stock; *specif* **:** developed from a single common parent form — **mo·no·phy·le·tism** \-'fī-lə-,tiz-əm\ *or* **mo·no·phy·le·ty** \-lət-ē\ *n*

Mo·noph·y·site \mə-'näf-ə-,sīt\ *n* [ML *Monophysita*, fr. MGk *Monophysitēs*, fr. Gk *mon-* + *physis* nature — more at PHYSICS] **:** one holding the anti-Chalcedonian doctrine that the human and divine in Christ constitute only one nature — **Monophysite** *or* **Mo·noph·y·sit·ic** \-,näf-ə-'sit-ik\ *adj* — **Mo·noph·y·sit·ism** \-'näf-ə-,sīt-,iz-əm\ *n*

mono·plane \'män-ə-,plān\ *n* **:** an airplane with only one main supporting surface

mo·no·ploid \'män-ə-,plóid, 'mō-nə-\ *adj* [ISV] **:** having or being a chromosome set comprising a single genome — **monoploid** *n*

mo·no·po·di·al \,män-ə-'pōd-ē-əl, ,mō-nə-\ *adj* [NL *monopodium*, fr. *mon-* + *-podium*] **:** having or involving the formation of offshoots from a main axis — **mo·no·po·di·al·ly** \-ē-ə-lē\ *adv*

mo·nop·o·list \mə-'näp-ə-ləst\ *n* **:** one who monopolizes — **mo·nop·o·lis·tic** \-,näp-ə-'lis-tik\ *adj* — **mo·nop·o·lis·ti·cal·ly** \-ti-k(ə-)lē\ *adv*

mo·nop·o·li·za·tion \mə-,näp-(ə-)lə-'zā-shən\ *n* **:** the act of monopolizing **:** the state of being monopolized

mo·nop·o·lize \mə-'näp-ə-,līz\ *vt* **:** to get a monopoly of — **mo·nop·o·liz·er** *n*

mo·nop·o·ly \mə-'näp-(ə-)lē\ *n* [L *monopolium*, fr. Gk *monopōlion*, fr. *mon-* + *pōlein* to sell] **1 :** exclusive ownership through legal privilege, command of supply, or concerted action **2 :** exclusive possession **3 :** a commodity controlled by one party **4 :** a person or group having a monopoly

syn CORNER, POOL, SYNDICATE, TRUST, CARTEL: MONOPOLY implies

exclusive control of a public service or of exclusive power to buy or sell a commodity in a specified market; CORNER implies a temporary complete control of something sold on an exchange so that buyers are compelled to pay the price asked; POOL applies to a joint undertaking by competing companies to regulate output and manipulate prices; SYNDICATE may apply to a group of financiers organized in order to profit by a monopoly but more often in order to carry out a temporary enterprise (as marketing a bond issue or purchasing a large property); TRUST applies to a merger of corporations by which control is given to trustees and the individual owners are compensated by shares of stock; CARTEL commonly implies an international combination of firms for controlling production and sale of their products

mo•no•pro•pel•lant \ˌmän-ō-prə-ˈpel-ənt, ˌmō-nō-\ *n* **:** a rocket propellant containing both the fuel and the oxidizer in a single substance

mo•nop•so•ny \mə-ˈnäp-sə-nē\ *n* [*mon-* + *-opsony* (as in *oligopsony*)] **:** an oligopsony limited to one buyer

mo•no•rail \ˈmän-ə-ˌrāl, ˈmō-nə-\ *n* **:** a single rail serving as a track for a wheeled conveyance

mo•no•sac•cha•ride \ˌmän-ə-ˈsak-ə-ˌrīd, ˌmō-nə-\ *n* [ISV] **:** a sugar not decomposable to simpler sugars by hydrolysis

mono•so•di•um glu•ta•mate \ˌmän-ə-ˌsōd-ē-əm-ˈglüt-ə-ˌmāt\ *n* **:** a crystalline salt $C_5H_8O_4NaN$ used for seasoning foods

mono•some \ˈmän-ə-ˌsōm\ *n* **:** a chromosome lacking a synaptic mate; *esp* **:** an unpaired X chromosome

mono•so•mic \ˌmän-ə-ˈsō-mik\ *adj* **:** having one less than the diploid number of chromosomes — **monosomic** *n*

mo•no•stele \ˈmän-ə-ˌstēl, ˈmō-nə-; ˌmän-ə-ˈstē-lē, ˌmō-nə-\ *n* **:** PROTOSTELE — **mo•no•ste•lic** \ˌmän-ə-ˈstē-lik, ˌmō-nə-\ *adj* — **mo•no•ste•ly** \ˈmän-ə-ˌstē-lē, ˈmō-nə-\ *n*

mo•no•sty•lous \ˌmän-ə-ˈstī-ləs, ˌmō-nə-\ *adj* **:** having a single style ⟨a ~ flower⟩

mono•syl•lab•ic \ˌmän-ə-sə-ˈlab-ik\ *adj* [prob. fr. F *monosyllabique*, fr. *monosyllabe*] **1 :** consisting of one syllable or of monosyllables **2 a :** using or speaking only monosyllables **b :** conspicuously brief in answering or commenting **:** TERSE — **mono•syl•lab•i•cal•ly** \-i-k(ə-)lē\ *adv* — **mono•syl•la•bic•i•ty** \-ˌsil-ə-ˈbis-ət-ē\ *n*

mono•syl•la•ble \ˈmän-ə-ˌsil-ə-bəl, ˌmän-ə-ˈ\ *n* [modif. of MF or LL; MF *monosyllabe*, fr. LL *monosyllabon*, fr. Gk, fr. neut. of *monosyllabos* having one syllable, fr. *mon-* + *syllabē* syllable] **:** a word of one syllable

mo•no•sym•met•ric \ˌmän-ə-sə-ˈme-trik, ˌmō-nə-\ *adj* **1 :** MONOCLINIC **2 :** symmetrical bilaterally with reference to a single plane **:** ZYGOMORPHIC — **mo•no•sym•met•ri•cal** \-tri-kəl\ *adj* — **mo•no•sym•met•ri•cal•ly** \-k(ə-)lē\ *adv* — **mo•no•sym•me•try** \-ˈsim-ə-trē\ *n*

mo•no•the•ism \ˈmän-ə-(ˌ)thē-ˌiz-əm, ˈmō-nə-\ *n* **:** the doctrine or belief that there is but one God — **mo•no•the•ist** \-ˌthē-əst\ *n* — **mo•no•the•is•tic** \ˌmän-ə-thē-ˈis-tik, ˌmō-nə-\ *or* **mo•no•the•is•ti•cal** \-ti-kəl\ *adj* — **mo•no•the•is•ti•cal•ly** \-k(ə-)lē\ *adv*

mono•tint \ˈmän-ə-ˌtint\ *n* **:** MONOCHROME

mono•tone \ˈmän-ə-ˌtōn\ *n* [Gk *monotonos* monotonous] **1 :** a succession of syllables, words, or sentences in one unvaried key or pitch **2 :** a single unvaried musical tone **3 :** a tedious sameness or reiteration **4 :** a person unable to produce musical intervals properly with the voice — **monotone** *adj* — **mono•ton•ic** \ˌmän-ə-ˈtän-ik\ *adj* — **mono•ton•i•cal•ly** \-i-k(ə-)lē\ *adv*

mo•not•o•nous \mə-ˈnät-ᵊn-əs, -ˈnät-nəs\ *adj* [Gk *monotonos*, fr. *mon-* + *tonos* tone] **1 :** uttered or sounded in one unvarying tone **2 :** tediously uniform or unvarying — **mo•not•o•nous•ly** *adv* — **mo•not•o•nous•ness** *n*

mo•not•o•ny \mə-ˈnät-ᵊn-ē, -ˈnät-nē\ *n* **1 :** tedious sameness **2 :** sameness of tone or sound

mo•no•tre•ma•tous \ˌmän-ə-ˈtrem-ət-əs, ˌmō-nə-, -ˈtrē-mət-\ *adj* [deriv. of Gk *mon-* + *trēmat-*, *trēma* hole, fr. *tetrainein* to bore — more at THROW] **:** of or relating to an order (Monotremata) of lowly mammals comprising the duckbills and echidnas — **mo•no•treme** \ˈmän-ə-ˌtrēm, ˈmō-nə-\ *n*

mo•not•ri•chous \mə-ˈnä-tri-kəs\ *adj* **:** having a single flagellum at one pole — used of bacteria

mono•type \ˈmän-ə-ˌtīp\ *n* **:** an impression on paper of a design painted usu. with the finger or a brush on a surface (as glass)

Monotype *trademark* **1** — used for a keyboard typesetting machine that casts and sets type in separate characters **2 :** matter produced by a Monotype machine or printing done from such matter

mono•typ•ic \ˌmän-ə-ˈtip-ik\ *adj* [*mon-* + *type*] **:** including a single representative — used esp. of a genus with only one species

mo•no•va•lence \ˌmän-ə-ˈvā-lən(t)s, ˌmō-nə-\ *or* **mo•no•va•len•cy** \-lən-sē\ *n* **:** the quality or state of being monovalent

mo•no•va•lent \-lənt\ *adj* [ISV] **1 :** UNIVALENT **2 :** containing antibodies specific for or antigens of a single strain of an organism

mon•ovu•lar \(ˈ)mä-ˈnō-vyə-lər, (ˈ)mō-\ *adj* **:** derived from a single ovum ⟨~ twins⟩

mon•ox•ide \mə-ˈnäk-ˌsīd\ *n* [ISV] **:** an oxide containing one atom of oxygen in the molecule

Mon•roe Doctrine \mən-ˌrō-, ˌmən-, ˌmän-\ *n* [James *Monroe* †1831, 5th U.S. president] **:** a statement of U.S. foreign policy expressing opposition to extension of European control or influence in the western hemisphere

mon•sei•gneur \ˌmōⁿ-ˌsān-ˈyər\ *n, pl* **mes•sei•gneurs** \ˌmā-ˌsān-ˈyər(z)\ [F, lit., my lord] **:** a French dignitary (as a prince or prelate) — used as a title preceding a title of office or rank

mon•sieur \məs(h)-ˈyə(r), mə-ˈsi(ə)r\ *n, pl* **mes•sieurs** \məs(h)-ˈyə(r)(z), mə-ˈsi(ə)r(z)\ [MF, lit., my lord] **:** a Frenchman of high rank or station — used as a title equivalent to *Mister* and prefixed to the name of a Frenchman

mon•si•gnor \män-ˈsē-nyər, mə(n)-\ *n, pl* **monsignors** *or* **mon•si•gno•ri** \ˌmän-ˌsēn-ˈyōr-ē, -ˈyȯr-\ [It *monsignore*, fr. F *monseigneur*] **:** a Roman Catholic prelate with the office or titular distinction of chamberlain, domestic prelate, or prothonotary apostolic — used as a title prefixed to the surname or to the given name and surname — **mon•si•gno•ri•al** \ˌmän-ˌsēn-ˈyōr-ē-əl, -ˈyȯr-\ *adj*

mon•soon \män-ˈsün\ *n* [obs. D *monssoen*, fr. Pg *monção*, fr. Ar *mawsim* time, season] **:** a periodic wind esp. in the Indian ocean and southern Asia; *also* **:** the season of the southwest monsoon in India and adjacent countries — **mon•soon•al** \-ᵊl\ *adj*

mon•ster \ˈmän(t)-stər\ *n* [ME *monstre*, fr. MF, fr. L *monstrum* evil omen, monster] **1** *obs* **:** PRODIGY **2 a :** an animal or plant of abnormal form or structure **b :** one who deviates from normal behavior or character **3 :** a threatening force **4 a :** an animal of strange or terrifying shape **b :** one unusually large for its kind **5 :** something monstrous; *esp* **:** a person of unnatural or extreme ugliness, deformity, wickedness, or cruelty

mon•strance \ˈmän(t)-strən(t)s\ *n* [MF, fr. ML *monstrantia*, fr. L *monstrant-*, *monstrans*, prp. of *monstrare* to show — more at MUSTER] **:** a vessel in which the consecrated Host is exposed for the adoration of the faithful

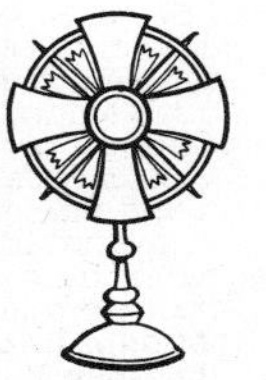
monstrance

mon•stros•i•ty \män-ˈsträs-ət-ē\ *n* **1 a :** a malformation of a plant or animal **b :** something deviating from the normal **:** FREAK **2 :** the quality or state of being monstrous **3 a :** an object of terrifying size or force or complexity **b :** an excessively bad or shocking example

mon•strous \ˈmän(t)-strəs\ *adj* **1** *obs* **:** STRANGE, UNNATURAL **2 :** having extraordinary often overwhelming size **:** GIGANTIC **3 a :** having the qualities or appearance of a monster **b** *obs* **:** teeming with monsters **4 a :** extraordinarily ugly or vicious **:** HORRIBLE **b :** shockingly wrong or ridiculous **5 :** deviating greatly from the natural form or character **:** ABNORMAL **6 :** very great — used as an intensive — **mon•strous•ly** *adv* — **mon•strous•ness** *n*

syn MONSTROUS, PRODIGIOUS, TREMENDOUS, STUPENDOUS mean extremely impressive esp. in size. MONSTROUS further implies ugliness, deformity, or fabulousness; PRODIGIOUS suggests a marvelousness exceeding belief; TREMENDOUS may imply a power to terrify or inspire awe; STUPENDOUS a power to stun or astound **syn** see in addition OUTRAGEOUS

mons ve•ne•ris \ˌmänz-ˈven-ə-rəs\ *n, pl* **mon•tes veneris** \ˌmän-ˌtēz-ˈven-\ [NL, lit., eminence of Venus or of venery] **:** a rounded eminence of fatty tissue upon the pubic symphysis of the human female

mon•ta•dale \ˈmänt-ə-ˌdāl\ *n* [*Monta*na state + *dale*] **:** any of an American breed of white-faced hornless sheep noted for its heavy fleece and good meat conformation

[1]**mon•tage** \män-ˈtäzh\ *n* [F, fr. *monter* to mount] **1 :** a composite picture made by combining several separate pictures **2 :** a literary, musical, or artistic composite of juxtaposed more or less heterogeneous elements **3 :** the production of a rapid succession of images in a motion picture to illustrate an association of ideas

[2]**montage** *vt* **:** to combine into or depict in a montage

Mon•ta•gue \ˈmänt-ə-ˌgyü\ *n* **:** the family of Romeo in Shakespeare's *Romeo and Juliet*

mon•tan wax \ˈmänt-ᵊn-\ *n* [L *montanus* of a mountain — more at MOUNTAIN] **:** a hard brittle mineral wax obtained usu. from lignites by extraction and used esp. in polishes, carbon paper, and insulating compositions

mont–de–pié•té \mōⁿd-pyā-tā\ *n, pl* **monts–de–piété** *same*\ [F, fr. It *monte di pietà*, lit., bank of pity] **:** a public pawnbroker's office for lending money at reasonable rates

mon•te \ˈmänt-ē\ *n* [Sp, lit., bank, fr. It, mountain, heap, bank, fr. L *mont-*, *mons* mountain] **1 :** a card game in which players select any two of four cards faced in a layout and bet that one of them will be matched before the other as cards are dealt one at a time from the pack — called also *monte bank* **2 :** THREE-CARD MONTE

mon•teith \män-ˈtēth\ *n* [*Monteith*, 17th cent. Sc eccentric who wore a cloak with a scalloped hem] **:** a large silver punch bowl with scalloped rim

mon•te•ro \män-ˈte(ə)r-(ˌ)ō\ *n* [Sp, hunter, fr. *monte* mountain] **:** a round cap with a flap worn by huntsmen

Mon•tes•so•ri•an \ˌmänt-ə-ˈsōr-ē-ən, -ˈsȯr-\ *adj* [Maria *Montessori* †1952 It physician and educator] **:** of or relating to a system of teaching young children by individual guidance rather than strict control

mont•gol•fi•er \mänt-ˈgäl-fē-ər, -fē-ˌā\ *n* [Joseph M. *Montgolfier* †1810 and Jacques E. *Montgolfier* †1799 F inventors] **:** a balloon raised by the buoyancy of air heated by a fire in the lower part

month \ˈmən(t)th\ *n, pl* **months** \ˈmən(t)s, ˈmən(t)ths\ [ME, fr. OE *mōnath*; akin to OHG *mānōd* month, OE *mōna* moon] **:** a measure of time corresponding nearly to the period of the moon's revolution and amounting to approximately 4 weeks or 30 days or 1/12 of a year — see CALENDAR table

[1]**month•ly** \ˈmən(t)th-lē\ *adv* **:** once a month **:** by the month

[2]**monthly** *adj* **1 a :** of or relating to a month **b :** payable or reckoned by the month **2 :** lasting a month **3 :** occurring every month

[3]**monthly** *n* **1 :** a monthly periodical **2** *pl* **:** a menstrual period

Monthly Meeting *n* **:** a district unit of the Society of Friends

month's mind *n* **:** a Roman Catholic requiem mass for a person a month after his death

mon•ti•cule \ˈmänt-i-ˌkyü(ə)l\ *n* [F, fr. LL *monticulus*, dim. of L *mont-*, *mons* mountain — more at MOUNT] **:** a little mount; *specif* **:** a subordinate cone of a volcano

mont•mo•ril•lon•ite \ˌmänt-mə-ˈril-ə-ˌnīt\ *n* [F, fr. *Montmorillon*, France] **:** a soft clayey mineral that is a hydrous aluminum silicate with considerable capacity for exchanging part of the aluminum for magnesium, alkalies, and other bases — **mont•mo•ril•lon•it•ic** \-ˌril-ə-ˈnit-ik\ *adj*

mon•u•ment \ˈmän-yə-mənt\ *n* [ME, fr. L *monumentum*, lit., memorial, fr. *monēre* to remind — more at MIND] **1** *obs* **:** a burial vault **:** SEPULCHER **2** *archaic* **:** a written legal document or record **:** TREATISE **3 a :** a lasting evidence or reminder of someone or something notable **b :** a memorial stone or a building erected in remembrance of a person or event **4** *archaic* **:** an identifying mark **:** EVIDENCE; *also* **:** PORTENT, SIGN **5** *obs* **:** a carved statue **:** EFFIGY **6 :** a boundary marker (as a stone) **7 :** a mountain, canyon, or area reserved by the government as public property **8 :** a written tribute

mon•u•men•tal \ˌmän-yə-ˈment-ᵊl\ *adj* **1 :** serving as or resembling a monument **:** MASSIVE; *also* **:** OUTSTANDING **2 :** of or relating to a monument **3 :** very great — **mon•u•men•tal•ly** \-ᵊl-ē\ *adv*

mon•u•men•tal•ize \-ᵊl-ˌīz\ *vt* **:** to record or memorialize lastingly by a monument

mon·zo·nite \män-'zō-,nīt\ *n* [F, fr. Mt. *Monzoni*, Italy] **:** a granular igneous rock composed of plagioclase and orthoclase in about equal quantities together with augite and a little biotite — **mon·zo·nit·ic** \,män-zə-'nit-ik\ *adj*

moo \'mü\ *vi* [imit.] **:** to make the throat noise of a cow — **moo** *n*

mooch \'müch\ *vb* [prob. fr. F dial. *muchier* to hide, lurk] *vi* **1 :** to wander aimlessly **:** AMBLE; *also* **:** SNEAK **2 :** SPONGE, CADGE ~ *vt* **1 :** to take surreptitiously **:** STEAL **2 :** CADGE, BEG — **moocher** *n*

¹**mood** \'müd\ *n* [ME, fr. OE *mōd;* akin to OHG *muot* mood, L *mos* will, custom] **1 :** a conscious state of mind or predominant emotion **:** FEELING **2** *archaic* **:** a fit of anger **:** RAGE **3 :** a prevailing attitude **:** DISPOSITION

syn MOOD, HUMOR, TEMPER, VEIN mean a state of mind in which an emotion or set of emotions gains ascendancy. MOOD implies pervasiveness and compelling quality of the emotion; HUMOR implies a mood that results from one's special temperament or one's physical or mental condition at the moment; TEMPER suggests a mood dominated by a single strong emotion such as anger; VEIN suggests a transitory mood or humor

²**mood** *n* [alter. of ¹*mode*] **1 :** the form of a syllogism according to the quantity and quality of the constituent propositions **2 :** distinction of form or a particular set of inflectional forms of a verb to express whether the action or state it denotes is conceived as fact or in some other manner (as command, possibility, or wish) **3 :** MODE 1b

mood·i·ly \'müd-ᵊl-ē\ *adv* **:** in a moody manner **:** GLOOMILY

mood·i·ness \'müd-ē-nəs\ *n* **:** the quality or state of being moody

moody \'müd-ē\ *adj* **1 :** subject to depression **:** GLOOMY **2 :** subject to moods **:** TEMPERAMENTAL

mool \'mül\ *n* **1** *dial Brit* **:** ¹MOLD 1 **2** *dial Brit* **:** ¹MOLD 2b

moo·la *or* **moo·lah** \'mü-lə\ *n* [origin unknown] *slang* **:** MONEY

¹**moon** \'mün\ *n* [ME *mone*, fr. OE *mōna;* akin to OHG *māno* moon, L *mensis* month, Gk *mēn* month, *mēnē* moon] **1 a :** the earth's only known natural satellite shining by the sun's reflected light, revolving about the earth from west to east in about 29½ days with reference to the sun or about 27⅓ days with reference to the stars and having a diameter of 2160 miles and a mean distance from the earth of about 238,857 miles, a mass about one eightieth that of the earth, and a volume about one forty-ninth **b :** one complete moon cycle consisting of four phases **c :** SATELLITE **2 :** a synodic month **3 :** MOONLIGHT **4 :** something that resembles a moon

²**moon** *vt* **:** to spend in idle reverie **:** DREAM — used with *away* ~ *vi* **:** to behave abstractedly **:** DREAM

moon·beam \-,bēm\ *n* **:** a ray of light from the moon

moon–blind \-,blīnd\ *adj* **:** afflicted with moon blindness

moon blindness *n* **1 :** a recurrent inflammation of the eye of the horse **2 :** NIGHT BLINDNESS

moon·calf \'mün-,kaf, -,käf\ *n* **1 :** MONSTER 2a **2 :** a foolish or absentminded person **:** SIMPLETON

moon–eyed \'mü-'nīd\ *adj* **:** having the eyes wide open

moon·fish \'mün-,fish\ *n, pl* **moonfish** *or* **moon·fish·es :** any of various compressed often short deep-bodied silvery or yellowish marine fishes

moon·flow·er \-,flau̇(-ə)r\ *n* **:** a tropical American morning glory (*Calonyction aculeatum*) with fragrant flowers; *also* **:** any of several related plants

moon·ish \'mü-nish\ *adj* **:** influenced by the moon; *also* **:** CAPRICIOUS — **moon·ish·ly** *adv*

moon·let \'mün-lət\ *n* **:** a small natural or artificial satellite

moon·light \-,līt\ *n* **:** the light of the moon

moon·light·er \-,līt-ər\ *n* **:** a person holding two jobs at the same time — **moon·light·ing** \-iŋ\ *n*

moon·lit \'mün-,lit\ *adj* **:** lighted by the moon

moon·rise \-,rīz\ *n* **1 :** the rising of the moon above the horizon **2 :** the time of the moon's rising

moon·scape \-,skāp\ *n* **:** the surface of the moon as seen or as depicted

moon·seed \-,sēd\ *n* **:** any of a genus (*Menispermum* of the family Menispermaceae, the moonseed family) of twining plants with crescent-shaped seeds and black fruits

moon·set \-,set\ *n* **1 :** the descent of the moon below the horizon **2 :** the time of the moon's setting

moon·shine \-,shīn\ *n, often attrib* **1 :** MOONLIGHT **2 :** empty talk **:** NONSENSE **3 :** intoxicating liquor; *esp* **:** illegally distilled corn whiskey

moon·shin·er \-,shī-nər\ *n* **:** a maker or seller of illicit whiskey

moon shot *or* **moon shoot** *n* **:** the launching of an unmanned vehicle to the moon or its vicinity

moon·stone \-,stōn\ *n* **:** a transparent or translucent feldspar of pearly or opaline luster used as a gem

moon·struck \-,strək\ *adj* **:** affected by or as if by the moon: as **a :** mentally unbalanced **b :** romantically sentimental **c :** BEMUSED

moony \'mü-nē\ *adj* **1 :** of or relating to the moon **2 a :** crescent shaped **b :** resembling the full moon **:** ROUND **3 :** MOONLIT **4 :** DREAMY, MOONSTRUCK

¹**moor** \'mu̇(ə)r\ *n* [ME *mor*, fr. OE *mōr;* akin to OHG *meri* sea — more at MARINE] **1** *chiefly Brit* **:** an expanse of open rolling infertile land **2 :** a boggy area of wasteland usu. peaty and dominated by grasses and sedges

²**moor** *vb* [ME *moren;* akin to MD *meren, maren* to tie, moor] *vt* **:** to make fast with cables, lines, or anchors ~ *vi* **1 :** to secure a boat by mooring **:** ANCHOR **2 :** to be made fast

Moor \'mu̇(ə)r\ *n* [ME *More*, fr. MF, fr. L *Maurus*] **1 a :** one of the mixed Arab and Berber conquerors of Spain in the 8th century A.D. **b :** BERBER **2 :** MUSLIM — **Moor·ish** \-ish\ *adj*

moor·age \'mu̇(ə)r-ij\ *n* **1 :** an act of mooring **2 :** a place to moor

moor·hen \-,hen\ *n* **:** GALLINULE

moor·ing \-iŋ\ *n* **1 :** an act of making fast a boat or aircraft with lines or anchors **2 a :** a place where or an object to which a craft can be made fast **b :** a chain, line, or other device by which an object is secured in place **3 :** moral or spiritual resources **:** ANCHORAGE 2 — usu. used in pl.

moose \'müs\ *n, pl* **moose** [of Algonquian origin; akin to Natick *moos* moose] **1 :** a large ruminant mammal (*Alces americana*) of the deer family inhabiting forested parts of Canada and the northern U. S. **2 :** ELK 1a

¹**moot** \'müt\ *n* [ME, fr. OE *mōt;* akin to OE *mētan* to meet — more at MEET] **1 :** a deliberative assembly primarily for the administration of justice; *esp* **:** one held by the freemen of an Anglo-Saxon community **2** *obs* **:** ARGUMENT, DISCUSSION

²**moot** *vt* **1** *archaic* **:** to discuss from a legal standpoint **:** ARGUE **2 a :** to bring up for discussion **:** BROACH **b :** DEBATE

³**moot** *adj* **1 a :** open to question **:** DEBATABLE **b :** subjected to discussion **:** DISPUTED **2 :** deprived of practical significance **:** made abstract or purely academic

moot court *n* **:** a mock court in which students of law argue hypothetical cases for practice

mop \'mäp\ *n* [ME *mappe*] **1 :** an implement made of absorbent material fastened to a handle and used esp. for cleaning floors **2 :** something that resembles a mop; *esp* **:** a thick mass of hair — **mop** *vt* **mopped; mop·ping** — **mop·per** *n*

mop·board \'mäp-,bō(ə)rd, -,bȯ(ə)rd\ *n* **:** BASEBOARD

¹**mope** \'mōp\ *vb* [prob. fr. obs. *mop, mope* fool] *vi* **1** *archaic* **:** to act in a dazed or stupid manner **2 :** to give oneself up to dull or dejected brooding **3 :** to move slowly or aimlessly **:** DAWDLE ~ *vt* **1 :** to make dull, dejected, or listless **2 :** to pass in a dull, dejected, or listless state — **mop·er** *n*

²**mope** *n* **1 :** one that mopes **2** *pl* **:** BLUES

mop·pet \'mäp-ət\ *n* [obs. E *mop* fool, child] **1** *archaic* **:** BABY, DARLING **2 :** CHILD

mop up *vt* **:** to clean, remove, or take by or as if by mopping: as **a :** to consume eagerly **b :** to beat decisively **c :** to clear of remaining troops ~ *vi* **:** to finish a task

mop–up \'mäp-,əp\ *n* **:** a concluding action

mo·quette \mō-'ket\ *n* [F] **:** a carpet or upholstery fabric having a velvety pile

mor \'mȯ(ə)r\ *n* [Dan] **:** forest humus with a layer of largely organic matter abruptly distinct from the mineral soil beneath

mo·ra \'mōr-ə, 'mȯr-\ *n, pl* **mo·rae** \'mō(ə)r-(,)ē, 'mȯ(ə)r-, -,ī\ *or* **moras** [L, delay — more at MEMORY] **:** the minimal unit of measure in quantitative verse equivalent to the time of an average short syllable

mo·rain·al \mə-'rān-ᵊl\ *adj* **:** of or relating to a moraine

mo·raine \mə-'rān\ *n* [F] **:** an accumulation of earth and stones carried and finally deposited by a glacier — **mo·rain·ic** \-'rā-nik\ *adj*

¹**mor·al** \'mȯr-əl, 'mär-\ *adj* [ME, fr. MF, fr. L *moralis*, fr. *mor-, mos* custom — more at MOOD] **1 a :** of or relating to principles of right and wrong in behavior **:** ETHICAL ⟨~ philosophy⟩ **b :** expressing or teaching a conception of right behavior ⟨a ~ poem⟩ **c :** conforming to a standard of right behavior **d :** sanctioned by or operative on one's conscience or ethical judgment ⟨a ~ obligation⟩ **e :** capable of right and wrong action ⟨a ~ agent⟩ **2 :** probable though not proved **:** VIRTUAL ⟨a ~ certainty⟩ **3 :** of, relating to, or acting on the mind, character, or will ⟨a ~ victory⟩ — **mor·al·ly** \-ə-lē\ *adv*

syn ETHICAL, VIRTUOUS, RIGHTEOUS, NOBLE: MORAL may be opposed to *immoral* in implying conformity to a standard of what is good and right, or it may contrast with *intellectual* or *aesthetic* as being concerned with character or conduct rather than achievement, beauty, success, logical perfection; ETHICAL may suggest the involvement of more difficult or subtle questions of rightness, fairness, or equity; VIRTUOUS implies the possession or manifestation of moral excellence in character; RIGHTEOUS stresses guiltlessness or blamelessness and often suggests the sanctimonious; NOBLE implies moral eminence and freedom from anything petty, mean, or dubious in conduct and character

²**moral** \'mȯr-əl, 'mär-; *3 is* mə-'ral\ *n* **1 a :** the moral significance or practical lesson (as of a story) **b :** a passage pointing out usu. in conclusion the lesson to be drawn from a story **2** *pl* **a :** moral practices or teachings **b :** ETHICS **3 :** MORALE

mo·rale \mə-'ral\ *n* [in sense 1, fr. F, fr. fem. of *moral*, adj.; in other senses, modif. of F *moral* morale, fr. *moral*, adj.] **1 :** moral principles, teachings, or conduct **2 a :** the mental and emotional attitudes of an individual to the function or tasks expected of him by his group and loyalty to it **b :** a sense of common purpose with respect to a group **:** ESPRIT DE CORPS **3 :** a state of individual psychological well-being based on such factors as a sense of purpose and confidence in the future

moral hazard *n* **:** the possibility of loss to an insurance company arising from the character or circumstances of the insured

mor·al·ism \'mȯr-ə-,liz-əm, 'mär-\ *n* **1 a :** the habit or practice of moralizing **b :** an instance of moralizing **2 :** the practice of morality as distinct from religion

mor·al·ist \-ləst\ *n* **1 :** one who leads a moral life **2 :** a teacher or student of morals **3 :** one concerned with regulating the morals of others

mor·al·is·tic \,mȯr-ə-'lis-tik, ,mär-\ *adj* **1 :** characterized by or expressive of a concern with morality **2 :** characterized by or expressive of a narrow and conventional moral attitude — **mor·al·is·ti·cal·ly** \-ti-k(ə-)lē\ *adv*

mo·ral·i·ty \mə-'ral-ət-ē, mȯ-\ *n* **1 a :** a moral discourse, statement, or lesson **b :** a literary or other imaginative work teaching a moral lesson **2 a :** a doctrine or system of morals **b** *pl* **:** particular moral principles or rules of conduct **3 :** conformity to ideals of right human conduct **4 :** moral conduct **:** VIRTUE

morality play *n* **:** an allegorical play popular esp. in the 15th and 16th centuries in which the characters personify moral qualities or abstractions

mor·al·iza·tion \,mȯr-ə-lə-'zā-shən, ,mär-\ *n* **:** an act, process, or instance of moralizing

mor·al·ize \'mȯr-ə-,līz, 'mär-\ *vt* **1 :** to explain or interpret morally **2 a :** to give a moral quality or direction to **b :** to improve the morals of ~ *vi* **:** to make moral reflections — **mor·al·iz·er** *n*

moral philosophy *n* **:** ETHICS

mo·rass \mə-'ras, mȯ-\ *n* [D *moeras*, modif. of OF *maresc*, of Gmc origin; akin to OE *mersc* marsh — more at MARSH] **1 :** MARSH, SWAMP **2 :** something that traps, confuses, or impedes — **mo·rassy** \-'ras-ē\ *adj*

mor·a·to·ri·um \,mȯr-ə-'tōr-ē-əm, ,mär-, -'tȯr-\ *n, pl* **moratoriums** *or* **mor·a·to·ria** \-ē-ə\ [NL, fr. LL, neut. of *moratorius*] **1 a :** a legally authorized period of delay in the performance of a legal obligation or the payment of a debt **b :** a waiting period set by an authority **2 :** a suspension of activity

mor·a·to·ry \'mȯr-ə-,tōr-ē, 'mär-, -,tȯr-\ *adj* [F *moratoire*, fr. LL *moratorius* dilatory, fr. L *moratus*, pp. of *morari* to delay, fr. *mora* delay — more at MEMORY] **:** of, relating to, or authorizing delay in payment of an obligation

Mo·ra·vi·an \mə-'rā-vē-ən\ n 1 : a member of a Christian denomination that traces its history back through the evangelical movement in Moravia and Bohemia to the doctrines of John Huss 2 a : a native or inhabitant of Moravia b : the group of Czech dialects spoken by the Moravian people and transitional between Slovak and Bohemian — **Moravian** adj

mo·ray \mə-'rā, 'mȯr-,(,)ā\ n [Pg moréia, fr. L muraena, fr. Gk myraina] : any of numerous often brightly colored savage voracious eels (family Muraenidae) occurring in warm seas and including a Mediterranean eel (Muraena helena) valued for food

mor·bid \'mȯr-bəd\ adj [L morbidus diseased, fr. morbus disease; akin to Gk marainein to waste away — more at SMART] 1 a : of, relating to, or characteristic of disease ⟨~ anatomy⟩ b : affected with or induced by disease ⟨~ condition⟩ c : productive of disease ⟨~ substances⟩ 2 : abnormally susceptible to or characterized by gloomy or unwholesome feelings 3 : GRISLY, GRUESOME ⟨~ details⟩ ⟨~ curiosity⟩ — **mor·bid·ly** adv — **mor·bid·ness** n

mor·bid·i·ty \mȯr-'bid-ət-ē\ n 1 : the quality or state of being morbid 2 : the relative incidence of disease

mor·da·cious \mȯr-'dā-shəs\ adj [L mordac-, mordax biting, fr. mordēre to bite — more at SMART] 1 : biting or sharp in style or manner : CAUSTIC 2 : given to biting : BITING — **mor·dac·i·ty** \-'das-ət-ē\ n

mor·dan·cy \'mȯrd-ᵊn-sē\ n 1 : a biting and caustic quality of style : INCISIVENESS 2 : a sharply critical or bitter quality of thought or feeling : HARSHNESS

¹mor·dant \'mȯrd-ᵊnt\ adj [MF, prp. of mordre to bite, fr. L mordēre] 1 : biting and caustic in thought, manner, or style : INCISIVE 2 : acting as a mordant 3 : BURNING, PUNGENT — **mor·dant·ly** adv

²mordant n 1 : a chemical that fixes a dye in or on a substance by combining with the dye to form an insoluble compound 2 : a corroding substance used in etching

³mordant vt : to treat with a mordant

Mor·de·cai \'mȯrd-i-,kī\ n [Heb Mordĕkhai] : a cousin of Esther who saves the Jews from the destruction planned by Haman

mor·dent \'mȯrd-ᵊnt, mȯr-'dent\ n [It mordente, fr. L mordent-, mordens, prp. of mordēre] : a musical ornament made by a quick alternation of a principal tone with the tone below

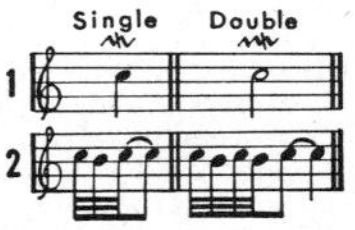

¹more \'mō(ə)r, 'mȯ(ə)r\ adj [ME, fr. OE māra; akin to OE mā, adv., more, OHG mēr, OIr mōr large] 1 : GREATER 2 : ADDITIONAL, FURTHER

²more adv 1 a : in addition b : MOREOVER 2 : to a greater or higher degree — often used with an adjective or adverb to form the comparative

³more n 1 : a greater quantity, amount, or number 2 a : something additional : an additional amount b : additional persons or things 3 obs : persons of higher rank

mo·reen \mə-'rēn, mȯ-\ n [prob. irregular fr. ¹moire] : a strong fabric of wool, wool and cotton, or cotton with a plain glossy or moiré finish

mo·rel \mə-'rel, mȯ-\ n [F morille, of Gmc origin; akin to OHG morhila morel] : a large pitted edible fungus (genus Morchella, esp. M. esculenta)

mo·rel·lo \mə-'rel-(,)ō\ n [prob. modif. of Flem amarelle, marelle, fr. ML amarellum amarelle] : a cultivated cherry derived from the sour cherry and distinguished from an amarelle by the dark-colored skin and juice

more·over \mȯr-'ō-vər, mȯr-, 'mȯr-,, 'mȯr-\ adv : in addition to what has been said : BESIDES

mo·res \'mō(ə)r-,āz, 'mō(ə)r-, -(,)ēz\ n pl [L, pl. of mor-, mos custom — more at MOOD] 1 : the fixed morally binding customs of a particular group 2 : moral attitudes 3 : HABITS, MANNERS

¹mo·resque \mȯ-'resk, mə-\ adj, often cap [F, fr. Sp morisco, fr. Moro Moor, fr. L Maurus] : having the characteristics of Moorish art or architecture

²moresque n, often cap : an ornament or decorative motif in Moorish style

Mor·gan \'mȯr-gən\ n [Justin Morgan †1798 Am teacher] : any of an American breed of light horses originated in Vermont from the progeny of one prepotent stallion of uncertain ancestry

mor·ga·nat·ic \,mȯr-gə-'nat-ik\ adj [NL matrimonium ad morganaticam, lit., marriage with morning gift] : of or relating to a marriage contracted by a member of a European royal or noble family with a person of inferior rank on the understanding that the rank of the inferior partner remains unchanged and that the children of the marriage do not succeed to the titles, fiefs, or entailed property of the parent of higher rank — **mor·ga·nat·i·cal·ly** \-i-k(ə-)lē\ adv

mor·gan·ite \'mȯr-gə-,nīt\ n [J. P. Morgan †1913 Am financier] : a rose-colored gem variety of beryl

Mor·gan le Fay \,mȯr-gən-lə-'fā\ n [OF Morgain la fée Morgan the fairy] : a fairy and sister of King Arthur

mor·gen \'mȯr-gə(n)\ n, pl **morgen** [D, lit., morning] : a Dutch and southern African unit of land area equal to 2.116 acres

morgue \'mȯ(ə)rg\ n [F] 1 : a place where the bodies of persons found dead are kept until released for burial 2 : a collection of reference works and files of reference material in a newspaper or news periodical office

mor·i·bund \'mȯr-ə-(,)bənd, 'mär-\ adj [L moribundus, fr. mori to die — more at MURDER] : being in a dying state — **mor·i·bun·di·ty** \,mȯr-ə-'bən-dət-ē, ,mär-\ n

¹mo·ri·on \'mōr-ē-,än, 'mȯr-\ n [MF] : a high-crested helmet with no visor

²morion n [modif. of L mormorion] : a nearly black variety of smoky quartz

Mo·ris·co \mə-'ris-(,)kō\ n, pl **Moriscos** or **Moriscoes** [Sp, fr. Morisco, adj., fr. Moro Moor] : MOOR; esp : a Spanish Moor — **Morisco** adj

Mor·mon \'mȯr-mən\ n 1 : the narrator and prophet of the Book of Mormon published by Joseph Smith in 1830 2 : LATTER-DAY SAINT; esp : a member of the Church of Jesus Christ of Latter-Day Saints — **Mor·mon·ism** \-mə-,niz-əm\ n

morn \'mȯ(ə)rn\ n [ME, fr. OE morgen; akin to OHG morgan

morning, L merus pure, unmixed] 1 : DAWN 2 : MORNING

morn·ing \'mȯr-niŋ\ n [ME, fr. morn + -ing (as in evening)] 1 a : DAWN b : the time from sunrise to noon c : the time from midnight to noon 2 : a period of first development : BEGINNING

morning glory n : any of various usu. twining plants (genus Ipomoea of the family Convolvulaceae, the morning-glory family) with showy trumpet-shaped flowers; broadly : a plant of the morning-glory family including herbs, vines, shrubs, or trees with alternate leaves and regular pentamerous flowers

Morning Prayer n : a morning service of liturgical prayer in churches of the Anglican communion

morn·ings \'mȯr-niŋz\ adv : in the morning repeatedly : on any morning ⟨goes to the office ~⟩

morning sickness n : nausea and vomiting on rising in the morning occurring esp. during the earlier months of pregnancy

morning star n : a bright planet (as Venus) seen in the eastern sky before or at sunrise

Mo·ro \'mō(ə)r-(,)ō, 'mȯ(ə)r-\ n [Sp, lit., Moor, fr. L Maurus] 1 : a member of any of several Muslim peoples of the southern Philippines 2 : any of the Austronesian languages of the Moro peoples

mo·roc·co \mə-'räk-(,)ō\ n [Morocco, kingdom in Africa] : a fine leather from goatskin tanned with sumac

mo·ron \'mō(ə)r-,än, 'mȯ(ə)r-\ n [irreg. fr. Gk mōros foolish, stupid; akin to Skt mūra foolish] 1 : a feebleminded person or mental defective with a potential mental age of between eight and twelve years who is capable of doing routine work under supervision 2 : a very stupid person syn see FOOL — **mo·ron·ic** \mə-'rän-ik, mȯ-\ adj — **mo·ron·i·cal·ly** \-i-k(ə-)lē\ adv — **mo·ron·ism** \'mōr-,än-,iz-əm, 'mȯr-\ n — **mo·ron·i·ty** \mə-'rän-ət-ē, mȯ-\ n

mo·rose \mə-'rōs, mȯ-\ adj [L morosus, lit., capricious, fr. mor-, mos will — more at MOOD] 1 : having a sullen and gloomy disposition 2 : marked by or expressive of gloom syn see SULLEN — **mo·rose·ly** adv — **mo·rose·ness** n — **mo·ros·i·ty** \-'räs-ət-ē\ n

morph \'mȯrf\ n [back-formation fr. morpheme] 1 : ²ALLOMORPH 2 : a phoneme or sequence of phonemes that is presumably an allomorph but that is not considered as assigned to any particular morpheme

morph- or **morpho-** comb form [G, fr. Gk, fr. morphē] : form ⟨morphogenesis⟩

-morph \,mȯrf\ n comb form [ISV, fr. -morphous] : one having (such) a form ⟨isomorph⟩

morph·al·lax·is \,mȯr-fə-'lak-səs\ n, pl **morph·al·lax·es** \-'lak-,sēz\ [NL, fr. morph- + Gk allaxis exchange, fr. allassein to change, exchange, fr. allos other — more at ELSE] : regeneration of a part or organism from a fragment by reorganization without cell proliferation

mor·pheme \'mȯr-,fēm\ n [F morphème, fr. Gk morphē form] : a meaningful linguistic unit whether a free form (as pin) or a bound form (as the -s of pins) that contains no smaller meaningful parts — **mor·phe·mic** \mȯr-'fē-mik\ adj — **mor·phe·mi·cal·ly** \-i-k(ə-)lē\ adv

mor·phe·mics \mȯr-'fē-miks\ n pl but sing in constr 1 : a branch of linguistic analysis that consists of the study of morphemes 2 : the structure of a language in terms of morphemes

Mor·pheus \'mȯr-fē-əs, -,fyüs\ n [L, fr. Gk] : the god of dreams in Greek mythology

mor·phia \'mȯr-fē-ə\ n [NL, fr. Morpheus] : MORPHINE

-mor·phic \'mȯr-fik\ adj comb form [prob. fr. F -morphique, fr. Gk morphē] : having (such) a form ⟨dolichomorphic⟩

mor·phine \'mȯr-,fēn\ n [F, fr. Morpheus] : a bitter crystalline addictive narcotic base $C_{17}H_{19}NO_3$ that is the principal alkaloid of opium and is used as an analgesic and sedative — **mor·phin·ic** \mȯr-'fē-nik, -'fin-ik\ adj

mor·phin·ism \'mȯr-,fē-,niz-əm, -fə-\ n : a disordered condition produced by habitual use of morphine

-mor·phism \'mȯr-,fiz-əm\ n comb form [LL -morphus -morphous fr. Gk -morphos] 1 : quality or state of having (such) a form ⟨heteromorphism⟩ 2 : conceptualization in (such) a form ⟨zoomorphism⟩

mor·pho·gen·e·sis \,mȯr-fə-'jen-ə-səs\ n [NL] 1 : BIOGENESIS 2 2 : ORGANOGENESIS — **mor·pho·ge·net·ic** \-jə-'net-ik\ adj — **mor·pho·gen·ic** \-'jen-ik\ adj

mor·pho·log·i·cal \,mȯr-fə-'läj-i-kəl\ adj : of or relating to morphology — **mor·pho·log·i·cal·ly** \-i-k(ə-)lē\ adv

mor·phol·o·gist \mȯr-'fäl-ə-jəst\ n : a specialist in morphology

mor·phol·o·gy \-jē\ n [G morphologie, fr. morph- + logie -logy] 1 a : a branch of biology that deals with the form and structure of animals and plants b : the features comprised in the form and structure of an organism or any of its parts 2 a : a study and description of word formation in a language including inflection, derivation, and compounding b : the system of word-forming elements and processes in a language 3 a : a study of structure or form b : STRUCTURE, FORM 4 : the external structure of rocks in relation to the development of erosional forms or topographic features

mor·pho·pho·ne·mics \,mȯr-(,)fō-fə-'nē-miks\ n pl but sing in constr [morpheme + -o- + phonemics] 1 : a study of the phonemic differences between allomorphs of the same morpheme 2 : the distribution of allomorphs in one morpheme 3 : the structure of a language in terms of morphophonemics

-mor·pho·sis \'mȯr-fə-səs, also (,)mȯr-'fō-\ n comb form, pl **-mor·pho·ses** \-,sēz\ [L, fr. Gk morphōsis process of forming, fr. morphoun to form, fr. morphē form] : development or change of form of a (specified) thing or in a (specified) manner ⟨geronto-morphosis⟩

-mor·phous \'mȯr-fəs\ adj comb form [Gk -morphos, fr. morphē form] : having (such) a form ⟨isomorphous⟩

-mor·phy \,mȯr-fē\ n comb form [ISV, fr. -morphous] : quality or state of having (such) a form ⟨homomorphy⟩

mor·ris \'mȯr-əs, 'mär-\ n [ME moreys daunce, fr. moreys, Moorish (fr. More Moor) + daunce dance] : a vigorous English dance performed by men wearing costumes and bells

mor·ris chair \,mȯr-əs-, ,mär-\ n [William Morris †1896 E poet and artist] : an easy chair with adjustable back and removable cushions

---

ə abut; ᵊ kitten; ər further; a back; ā bake; ä cot, cart; au̇ out; ch chin; e less; ē easy; g gift; i trip; ī life
j joke; ŋ sing; ō flow; ȯ flaw; ȯi coin; th thin; th this; ü loot; u̇ foot; y yet; yü few; yu̇ furious; zh vision

mor·row \'mär-(,)ō, 'mȯr-, -ə(-w)\ *n* [ME *morn, morwen* morn] **1** *archaic* **:** MORNING **2 :** the next following day

Morse code \'mȯrs-\ *n* [Samuel F. B. *Morse* †1872 Am inventor] **:** either of two codes consisting of dots and dashes or long and short sounds used for transmitting messages by audible or visual signals

MORSE CODE

AMERICAN MORSE CODE[1]

A •–	K –•–	U ••–	5 –––
B –•••	L —	V •••–	6 ••••••
C •• •	M ––	W •––	7 ––••
D –••	N –•	X •–••	8 –••••
E •	O • •	Y •• ••	9 –••–
F •–•	P •••••	Z ••• •	0 —
G ––•	Q ••–•	1 •––•	, (comma) •–•–
H ••••	R • ••	2 ••–••	. ••––••
I ••	S •••	3 •••–•	& • •••
J –•–•	T –	4 ••••–	

INTERNATIONAL CODE[2]

A •–	N –•	Á •––•–	8 –––••
B –•••	O –––	Ä •–•–	9 ––––•
C –•–•	P •––•	É ••–••	0 –––––
D –••	Q ––•–	Ñ ––•––	, (comma) ––••––
E •	R •–•	Ö –––•	. •–•–•–
F ••–•	S •••	Ü ••––	? ••––••
G ––•	T –	1 •––––	; –•–•–•
H ••••	U ••–	2 ••–––	: –––•••
I ••	V •••–	3 •••––	' (apostrophe) •––––•
J •–––	W •––	4 ••••–	- (hyphen) –••••–
K –•–	X –••–	5 •••••	/ –••–•
L •–••	Y –•––	6 –••••	parenthesis –•––•–
M ––	Z ––••	7 ––•••	underline ••––•–

[1]Formerly used on overland telegraph lines in the U.S. and Canada but now largely out of use

[2]Often called the continental code; a modification of this code, with dots only, is used on ocean cables

[1]**mor·sel** \'mȯr-səl\ *n* [ME, fr. OF, dim. of *mors* bite, fr. L *morsus*, fr. *morsus*, pp. of *mordēre* to bite — more at SMART] **1 :** a small piece of food **:** BITE **2 :** a small quantity **:** FRAGMENT **3 a :** a tasty dish **b :** something delectable **4 :** a negligible person

[2]**morsel** *vt* **mor·seled** *or* **mor·selled; mor·sel·ing** *or* **mor·sel·ling :** to divide into or distribute in small pieces

[1]**mort** \'mȯ(ə)rt\ *n* [prob. alter. of ME *mot* horn note, fr. MF word, horn note — more at MOT] **1 :** a note sounded on a hunting horn when a deer is killed **2 :** KILLING

[2]**mort** *n* [prob. back-formation fr. [1]*mortal*] **:** a great quantity or number

[1]**mor·tal** \'mȯrt-ᵊl\ *adj* [ME, fr. MF, fr. L *mortalis*, fr. *mort-, mors* death — more at MURDER] **1 :** causing or capable of causing death **:** FATAL **2 a :** subject to death ⟨~ man⟩ **b :** CONCEIVABLE, EARTHLY ⟨every ~ thing⟩ **c :** very tedious or prolonged ⟨three ~ hours⟩ **3 :** marked by unrelenting hostility **:** IMPLACABLE ⟨a ~ enemy⟩ **4 a :** committed in a grave matter with awareness of guilt and full consent and held in Roman Catholicism to bring death to the soul ⟨~ sin⟩ — compare VENIAL **b :** marked by great intensity or severity **:** EXTREME ⟨~ fear⟩ **c :** very great **:** AWFUL ⟨a ~ shame⟩ **5 :** HUMAN ⟨~ limitations⟩ **6 :** of, relating to, or connected with death ⟨~ agony⟩ **syn** see DEADLY — **mor·tal·ly** \-ᵊl-ē\ *adv*

[2]**mortal** *adv, chiefly dial* **:** MORTALLY

[3]**mortal** *n* **:** a human being

mor·tal·i·ty \mȯr-'tal-ət-ē\ *n* **1 :** the quality or state of being mortal **2 :** the death of large numbers **3** *archaic* **:** DEATH **4 :** the human race **:** MANKIND **5 a :** the number of deaths in a given time or place **b :** the proportion of deaths to population **c :** the number lost or the rate of loss or failure

mortality table *n* **:** an actuarial table based on mortality statistics over a number of years

mortal mind *n, Christian Science* **:** a belief that life, substance, and intelligence are in and of matter **:** ILLUSION

[1]**mor·tar** \'mȯrt-ər\ *n* [ME *morter*, fr. OE *mortere* & MF *mortier*, fr. L *mortarium;* akin to Gk *marainein* to waste away — more at SMART] **1 a :** a strong vessel in which substances are pounded or rubbed with a pestle **b :** a large cast-iron receptacle in which ore is crushed in a stamp mill **2** [MF *mortier*] **a :** a muzzle-loading cannon having a tube short in relation to its caliber that is used to throw projectiles with low muzzle velocities at high angles **b :** any of several similar firing devices

[2]**mortar** *n* **:** a plastic building material (as a mixture of cement, lime, or gypsum plaster with sand and water) that hardens and is used in masonry or plastering

[3]**mortar** *vt* **:** to plaster or make fast with mortar

mor·tar·board \'mȯrt-ər-,bō(ə)rd, -,bȯ(ə)rd\ *n* **1 a :** HAWK 2 **b :** a board or platform about 3 feet square for holding mortar **2 :** an academic cap consisting of a closely fitting headpiece with a broad flat projecting square top

mortarboard 2

[1]**mort·gage** \'mȯr-gij\ *n* [ME *morgage*, fr. MF, fr. OF, fr. *mort* dead (fr. L *mortuus*, fr. pp. of *mori* to die) + *gage* — more at MURDER] **1 :** a conveyance of property on condition that it becomes void on payment or performance according to stipulated terms **2 a :** the instrument by which a mortgage conveyance is made **b :** the state of the property so conveyed **c :** the interest of the mortgagee in such property

[2]**mortgage** *vt* **1 :** to grant or convey by a mortgage **2 :** to subject to a claim or obligation **:** PLEDGE

mort·gag·ee \,mȯr-gi-'jē\ *n* **:** a person to whom property is mortgaged

mort·ga·gor \,mȯr-gi-'jȯ(ə)r\ *also* **mort·gag·er** \'mȯr-gi-jər\ *n* **:** a person who mortgages his property

mor·ti·cian \mȯr-'tish-ən\ *n* [L *mort-, mors* death] **:** UNDERTAKER 2

mor·ti·fi·ca·tion \,mȯrt-ə-fə-'kā-shən\ *n* **1 :** the subjection and denial of bodily passions and appetites by abstinence or self-inflicted pain or discomfort **2 :** NECROSIS, GANGRENE **3 a :** a sense of humiliation and shame caused by something that wounds one's pride or self-respect **b :** the cause of such humiliation or shame

mor·ti·fy \'mȯrt-ə-,fī\ *vb* [ME *mortifien*, fr. MF *mortifier*, fr. LL *mortificare*, fr. L *mort-, mors*] *vt* **1** *obs* **:** to destroy the strength, vitality, or functioning of **2 :** to subdue or deaden (as the body or bodily appetites) esp. by abstinence or self-inflicted pain or discomfort **3 :** to subject to humiliation or shame **~** *vi* **1 :** to practice mortification **2 :** to become necrotic or gangrenous

[1]**mor·tise** *also* **mor·tice** \'mȯrt-əs\ *n* [ME *mortays*, fr. MF *mortaise*] **:** a hole, groove, or slot into or through which some other part of any arrangement of parts fits or passes; *specif* **:** a usu. rectangular cavity cut into a piece of timber or other material to receive a tenon

[2]**mortise** *also* **mortice** *vt* **1 :** to join or fasten securely; *specif* **:** to join or fasten by a tenon and mortise **2 :** to cut or make a mortise in

mort·main \'mȯrt-,mān\ *n* [ME *morte-mayne*, fr. MF *mortemain*, fr. OF, fr. *morte* (fem. of *mort* dead) + *main* hand, fr. L *manus* — more at MANUAL] **1 a :** an inalienable possession of lands or buildings by an ecclesiastical or other corporation **b :** the condition of property or other gifts left to a corporation in perpetuity esp. for religious, charitable, or public purposes **2 :** the influence of the past regarded as controlling the present

[1]**mor·tu·ary** \'mȯr-chə-,wer-ē\ *n* [ME *mortuarie*, fr. ML *mortuarium*, fr. L, neut. of *mortuarius* of the dead, fr. *mortuus*, pp.] **:** a place in which dead bodies are kept until burial; *esp* **:** FUNERAL HOME

[2]**mortuary** *adj* **1 :** of or relating to the burial of the dead **2 :** of, relating to, or characteristic of death

mor·u·la \'mȯr-(y)ə-lə, 'mär-\ *n, pl* **mor·u·lae** \-,lē, -,lī\ [NL, fr. L *morum* mulberry] **:** a globular solid mass of blastomeres formed by cleavage of a zygote that typically precedes the blastula — **mor·u·lar** \-lər\ *adj* — **mor·u·la·tion** \,mȯr-(y)ə-'lā-shən, ,mär-\ *n*

[1]**mo·sa·ic** \mō-'zā-ik\ *n* [ME *musycke*, fr. MF *mosaique*, fr. OIt *mosaico*, fr. ML *musaicum*, alter. of LL *musivum*, fr. neut. of *musivus* of a muse, artistic, fr. L *Musa* muse] **1 :** a surface decoration made by inlaying small pieces of variously colored material to form pictures or patterns; *also* **:** the process of making it **2 :** a picture or design made in mosaic **3 :** something resembling a mosaic **4 a :** CHIMERA 3 **b :** a virus disease of plants characterized by diffuse light and dark green or yellow and green mottling of the foliage **5 :** a composite map made of aerial photographs **6 :** the part of a television camera tube consisting of many minute photoelectric particles that convert light to an electric charge — **mosaic** *adj* — **mo·sa·i·cal·ly** \-i-k(ə-)lē\ *adv*

[2]**mosaic** *vt* **mo·sa·icked** \-ikt\ **mo·sa·ick·ing 1 :** to decorate with mosaics **2 :** to form into a mosaic

Mo·sa·ic \mō-'zā-ik\ *adj* [NL *Mosaicus*, fr. *Moses*] **:** of or relating to Moses or the institutions or writings attributed to him

mosaic gold *n* **1 :** a yellow scaly crystalline pigment consisting essentially of stannic sulfide **2 :** ORMOLU

mo·sa·icism \mō-'zā-ə-,siz-əm\ *n* **:** a condition in which patches of tissue of unlike genetic constitution are mingled in an organism

mo·sa·icist \-səst\ *n* **1 a :** a designer of mosaics **b :** a workman who makes mosaics **2 :** a dealer in mosaics

Mos·an \'mōs-ᵊn\ *n* [*mōs* four (in various Mosan languages)] **:** an American Indian language phylum of British Columbia and Washington including the Salishan stock

Mo·selle \mō-'zel\ *n* [G *moselwein*, fr. *Mosel*, Moselle, river in Germany + G *wein* wine] **:** a white table wine made in the valley of the Moselle; *also* **:** a similar wine made elsewhere

Mo·ses \'mō-zəz *also* -zəs\ *n* [L, fr. Gk *Mōsēs*, fr. Heb *Mōsheh*] **:** a Hebrew prophet and lawgiver and liberator of the Israelites from Egypt

mo·sey \'mō-zē\ *vi* [origin unknown] **1 :** to hurry away **2 :** to move in a leisurely or aimless manner **:** SAUNTER

Mos·lem \'mäz-ləm *also* 'mäs-\ *var of* MUSLIM

mosque \'mäsk\ *n* [MF *mosquee*, fr. OIt *moschea*, fr. OSp *mezquita*, fr. Ar *masjid* temple, fr. *sajada* to prostrate oneself] **:** a building used for public worship by Muslims

mos·qui·to \mə-'skēt-(,)ō, -ə(-w)\ *n, pl* **mosquitoes** *also* **mosquitos** [Sp, fr. *mosca* fly, fr. L *musca* — more at MIDGE] **:** any of numerous two-winged flies (family Culicidae) with females having a set of slender organs in the proboscis adapted to puncture the skin of animals to suck the blood and being in some cases vectors of serious diseases — **mos·qui·to·ey** \-'skēt-ə-wē\ *adj*

mosquito hawk *n* **:** DRAGONFLY

mosquito net *n* **:** a net or screen for keeping out mosquitoes

[1]**moss** \'mȯs\ *n* [ME, fr. OE *mōs;* akin to OHG *mos* moss, L *muscus*] **1** *chiefly Scot* **:** BOG, SWAMP; *esp* **:** a peat bog **2 a :** any of a class (Musci) of bryophytic plants having a small leafy often tufted stem bearing sex organs at its tip; *also* **:** a clump or sward of these plants **b :** any of various plants that form a mossy growth **3 :** a mossy covering — **moss·like** \'mȯ-,slīk\ *adj*

[2]**moss** *vt* **:** to cover or overgrow with moss

moss agate *n* **:** an agate mineral containing brown, black, or green mosslike or dendritic markings

moss·back \'mȯs-,bak\ *n* **1 a :** an old turtle with a mossy growth on its back **b :** a large sluggish fish **c :** a wild old range steer or cow **2 :** an extremely conservative person **:** FOGY

moss–grown \-,grōn\ *adj* **1 :** overgrown with moss **2 :** ANTIQUATED

moss pink *n* **:** a low tufted perennial phlox (*Phlox subulata*) widely cultivated for its abundant usu. pink or white flowers

moss–troop·er \'mȯ-'strü-pər\ *n* **1 :** one of a class of 17th century raiders in the marshy border country between England and Scotland **2 :** FREEBOOTER — **moss–troop·ing** \-piŋ\ *adj*

mossy \'mȯ-sē\ *adj* **1 :** covered with moss or something like moss **2 :** resembling moss

[1]**most** \'mōst\ *adj* [ME, fr. OE *mǣst;* akin to OHG *meist* most, OE *māra* more — more at MORE] **1 :** the majority of ⟨~ men⟩ **2 :** greatest in quantity, extent, or degree ⟨the ~ ability⟩

[2]**most** *adv* **1 :** to the greatest or highest degree — often used with

an adjective or adverb to form the superlative **2 :** to a very great degree
³most *n* **1 :** the greatest amount **2 :** the greatest number or part
⁴most *adv* **:** ALMOST
-most \ˌmōst\ *adj suffix* [ME, alter. of *-mest* (as in *formest* foremost)] **:** most ⟨inner*most*⟩ **:** most toward ⟨head*most*⟩
most·ly \ˈmōst-lē\ *adv* **:** for the greatest part **:** MAINLY
Most Reverend — used as a title for an archbishop or a Roman Catholic bishop
mot \ˈmō\ *n, pl* **mots** \ˈmō(z)\ [F, word, saying, fr. L *muttum* grunt — more at MOTTO] **:** a pithy or witty saying
¹mote \(ˈ)mōt\ *verbal auxiliary* [ME *moten*, fr. OE *mōtan* to be allowed to — more at MUST] *archaic* **:** MAY
²mote \ˈmōt\ *n* [ME *mot*, fr. OE; akin to MD & Fris *mot* sand] **:** a small particle
mo·tel \mō-ˈtel\ *n* [blend of *motor* and *hotel*] **:** a building or group of buildings used as a hotel in which the rooms are directly accessible from an outdoor parking area
mo·tet \mō-ˈtet\ *n* [ME, fr. MF, dim. of *mot*] **:** a polyphonic choral composition on a sacred text usu. without instrumental accompaniment
moth \ˈmȯth\ *n, pl* **moths** \ˈmȯthz, ˈmȯths\ [ME *mothe*, fr. OE *moththe;* akin to MHG *motte* moth] **1 :** CLOTHES MOTH **2 :** a usu. nocturnal insect (order Lepidoptera) with mostly feathery antennae and a stouter body, less brilliant coloring, and proportionately smaller wings than the butterflies and with larvae that are plant-eating caterpillars
moth·ball \ˈmȯth-ˌbȯl\ *n* **1 :** a ball made formerly of camphor but now of naphthalene and used to keep moths from clothing **2** *pl* **:** the condition of being put into protective storage
moth–eat·en \ˈmȯ-ˌthēt-ᵊn\ *adj* **1 :** eaten into by moths **2 :** resembling or suggestive of cloth eaten into by moths
¹moth·er \ˈməth-ər\ *n* [ME *moder*, fr. OE *mōdor;* akin to OHG *muoter* mother, L *mater*, Gk *mētēr*, Skt *mātṛ*] **1 a :** a female parent **b** (1) **:** a woman in authority; *specif* **:** the superior of a religious community of women (2) **:** an old or elderly woman **2 :** SOURCE, ORIGIN **3 :** maternal tenderness or affection — **moth·er·less** \-ləs\ *adj* — **moth·er·less·ness** *n*
²mother *adj* **1 a :** of, relating to, or being a mother **b :** bearing the relation of a mother **2 :** derived from or as if from one's mother **3 :** acting as or providing parental stock — used without reference to sex
³mother *vt* **moth·er·ing** \ˈməth-(ə-)riŋ\ **1 a :** to give birth to **b :** to give rise to **:** PRODUCE **2 a :** to attribute to a particular person the maternity or origin of **b :** to acknowledge that one is the mother or author of **3 :** to care for or protect like a mother
⁴mother *n* [akin to MD *modder*, mud, lees, dregs, MLG *mudde* mud] **:** a slimy membrane composed of yeast and bacterial cells that develops on the surface of alcoholic liquids undergoing acetous fermentation and is added to wine or cider to produce vinegar
Mother Car·ey's chicken \ˌməth-ər-ˌkar-ēz-, -ˌker-\ *n* [origin unknown] **:** any of several small petrels; *esp* **:** STORM PETREL
Mother Goose *n* **:** the legendary author of a collection of nursery rhymes first published in London about 1760
moth·er·hood \ˈməth-ər-ˌhu̇d\ *n* **:** the state of being a mother
moth·er·house \ˈməth-ər-ˌhau̇s\ *n* **1 :** the convent in which the superior of a religious community resides **2 :** the original convent of a religious community
Mother Hub·bard \ˌməth-ər-ˈhəb-ərd\ *n* [prob. fr. *Mother Hubbard*, character in a nursery rhyme] **:** a loose usu. shapeless dress
moth·er–in–law \ˈməth-(ə-)rən-ˌlȯ, ˈməth-ərn-ˌlȯ\ *n, pl* **mothers–in–law** \ˈməth-ər-zən-\ **1 :** the mother of one's spouse **2 :** STEPMOTHER
moth·er·land \ˈməth-ər-ˌland\ *n* **1 :** a country regarded as a place of origin **2 :** FATHERLAND
moth·er·li·ness \-lē-nəs\ *n* **:** the quality or state of being motherly
moth·er·ly \-lē\ *adj* **1 :** of, proper to, or characteristic of a mother **2 :** resembling a mother **:** MATERNAL
moth·er–of–pearl \ˌməth-ə-rə(v)-ˈpər(-ə)l\ *n* **:** the hard pearly iridescent substance forming the inner layer of a mollusk shell
Mother's Day *n* **:** the 2d Sunday in May appointed for the honoring of mothers
mother tongue *n* **1 :** one's native language **2 :** a language from which another language derives
mother wit *n* **:** natural wit or intelligence
mo·tif \mō-ˈtēf\ *n* [F, motive, motif] **1 a :** a usu. recurring salient thematic element esp. in a work of art; *esp* **:** a dominant idea or central theme **b :** a single or repeated design or color **2 :** an influence or stimulus prompting to action
¹mo·tile \ˈmōt-ᵊl, ˈmō-ˌtīl\ *adj* [L *motus*, pp.] **:** exhibiting or capable of movement — **mo·til·i·ty** \mō-ˈtil-ət-ē\ *n*
²motile *n* **:** a person whose prevailing mental imagery takes the form of inner feelings of action
¹mo·tion \ˈmō-shən\ *n* [ME *mocioun*, fr. MF *motion*, fr. L *motion-*, *motio* movement, fr. *motus*, pp. of *movēre* to move] **1 a :** a proposal for action; *esp* **:** a formal proposal made in a deliberative assembly **b :** an application made to a court or judge to obtain an order, ruling, or direction **2 :** an act, process, or instance of changing place **:** MOVEMENT **3 :** an impulse or inclination of the mind or will **4** *obs* **a :** a puppet show **b :** PUPPET **5 :** MACHINE 1e(2) **6** *pl* **:** ACTIVITIES, MOVEMENTS **7 :** melodic change of pitch — **mo·tion·al** \ˈmō-shnəl, -shən-ᵊl\ *adj* — **mo·tion·less** \ˈmō-shən-ləs\ *adj* — **mo·tion·less·ly** *adv* — **mo·tion·less·ness** *n*
²motion *vb* **mo·tion·ing** \ˈmō-sh(ə-)niŋ\ *vt* **:** to direct by a motion ∼ *vi* **:** to signal by a movement or gesture
motion picture *n* **1 :** a series of pictures projected on a screen in rapid succession with objects shown in successive positions slightly changed so as to produce the optical effect of a continuous picture in which the objects move **2 :** a representation of a story or other subject matter by means of motion pictures
motion sickness *n* **:** sickness induced by motion (as in travel by air, car, or ship) and characterized by nausea
mo·ti·vate \ˈmōt-ə-ˌvāt\ *vt* **:** to provide with a motive — **mo·ti·va·tion** \ˌmōt-ə-ˈvā-shən\ *n* — **mo·ti·va·tion·al** \-shnəl, -shən-ᵊl\ *adj* — **mo·ti·va·tive** \ˈmōt-ə-ˌvāt-iv\ *adj*
¹mo·tive \ˈmōt-iv, *2 is also* mō-ˈtēv\ *n* [ME, fr. MF *motif*, fr. *motif*, adj., moving] **1 :** something (as a need or desire) that causes a person to act **2 :** a recurrent thematic fragment usu. treated developmentally in a musical composition — **mo·tive·less** \-ləs\ *adj*
syn MOTIVE, SPRING, IMPULSE, INCENTIVE, INDUCEMENT, SPUR, GOAD mean a stimulus to action. MOTIVE implies an emotion or desire operating on the will and causing it to act; SPRING, usu. in the plural, suggests a basic motive, often one not fully recognized; IMPULSE suggests a driving power arising from personal temperament or constitution; INCENTIVE applies to an external influence (as an expected reward) inciting to action; INDUCEMENT suggests a motive prompted by the deliberate enticements or allurements of another; SPUR applies to a motive that stimulates the faculties or increases energy or ardor; GOAD suggests a motive that keeps one going against one's will or desire
²mo·tive \ˈmōt-iv\ *adj* [MF or ML; MF *motif*, fr. ML *motivus*, fr. L *motus*, pp.] **1 :** moving or tending to move to action **2 :** of or relating to motion or the causing of motion ⟨∼ energy⟩
³mo·tive \ˈmōt-iv\ *vt* **:** MOTIVATE
motive power *n* **:** an agency (as water or steam) used to impart motion to machinery
mo·tiv·i·ty \mō-ˈtiv-ət-ē\ *n* **1 :** the power of moving or producing motion **2 :** available energy
mot juste \mō-zhüest\ *n, pl* **mots justes** *same*\ [F] **:** the exactly right word
¹mot·ley \ˈmät-lē\ *adj* [ME, perh. fr. *mot* mote, speck] **1 :** variegated in color **2 :** composed of diverse often incongruous elements
²motley *n* [ME, prob. fr. ¹*motley*] **1 :** a woolen fabric of mixed colors made in England between the 14th and 17th centuries **2 :** a garment made of motley; *esp* **:** the characteristic dress of the professional fool **3 :** JESTER, FOOL **4 :** a mixture esp. of incongruous elements
mot·mot \ˈmät-ˌmät\ *n* [AmerSp *mot-mot*, of imit. origin] **:** any of numerous long-tailed mostly green nonpasserine birds (family Momotidae) of tropical forests from Mexico to Brazil
mo·to·neu·ron \ˌmōt-ə-ˈn(y)ü-ˌrän, -ˈn(y)u̇(ə)r-ˌän\ *n* [*motor* + *neuron*] **:** a motor nerve cell with its processes
¹mo·tor \ˈmōt-ər\ *n* [L, fr. *motus*, pp. of *movēre* to move] **1 :** one that imparts motion **2 a :** PRIME MOVER **b :** a small compact engine **c :** INTERNAL-COMBUSTION ENGINE; *esp* **:** a gasoline engine **3 :** MOTOR VEHICLE; *esp* **:** AUTOMOBILE **4 :** a rotating machine that transforms electrical energy into mechanical energy
²motor *adj* **1 a :** causing or imparting motion **b :** of, relating to, or being a nerve or nerve fiber that passes from the central nervous system or a ganglion to a muscle and conducts an impulse that causes movement **c :** of, relating to, or involving muscular movement **2 a :** equipped with or driven by a motor **b :** of, in, or relating to an automobile **c :** designed for motor vehicles or motorists
³motor *vi* **:** to travel by automobile **:** DRIVE ∼ *vt* **:** to transport by automobile
mo·tor·boat \ˈmōt-ər-ˌbōt\ *n* **:** a boat propelled by an internal-combustion engine or an electric motor
motor bus *n* **:** BUS 1a — called also *motor coach*
mo·tor·cade \ˈmōt-ər-ˌkād\ *n* **:** a procession of motor vehicles
mo·tor·car \-ˌkär\ *n* **1 :** AUTOMOBILE **2** *usu* **motor car :** a railroad car containing motors for propulsion
motor court *n* **:** MOTEL
mo·tor·cy·cle \ˈmōt-ər-ˌsī-kəl\ *n* [*motor* bi*cycle*] **:** a 2-wheeled automotive vehicle having 1 or 2 saddles and sometimes a 3d wheel for support of a sidecar — **motorcycle** *vi* — **mo·tor·cy·cling** \-ˌsī-k(ə-)liŋ\ *n* — **mo·tor·cy·clist** \-ˌsī-k(ə-)ləst\ *n*
mo·tor·drome \ˈmōt-ər-ˌdrōm\ *n* **:** a track or course with seats for spectators at races or tests of automobiles or motorcycles
mo·tor·ist \ˈmōt-ə-rəst\ *n* **:** a person who travels by automobile
mo·tor·iza·tion \ˌmōt-ə-rə-ˈzā-shən\ *n* **:** an act or process of motorizing
mo·tor·ize \ˈmōt-ə-ˌrīz\ *vt* **:** to equip with a motor: as **a :** to equip with motor-driven vehicles in substitution for others **b :** to equip with motor-driven vehicles for transportation **c :** to equip with automobiles
mo·tor·man \ˈmōt-ər-mən\ *n* **:** an operator of a motor-driven vehicle (as a streetcar or subway train)
motor pool *n* **:** a group of motor vehicles controlled by a single governmental agency and dispatched for use as needed
motor scooter *n* **:** a low 2- or 3-wheeled automotive vehicle resembling a child's scooter and having a seat so that the rider does not straddle the engine
motor torpedo boat *n* **:** a high-speed 60 to 100 foot motorboat usu. equipped with torpedo tubes, machine guns, and depth charges — called also *mosquito boat*
mo·tor·truck \ˈmōt-ər-ˌtrək\ *n* **:** an automotive truck for transporting freight
motor vehicle *n* **:** an automotive vehicle not operated on rails; *esp* **:** one with rubber tires for use on highways
¹mot·tle \ˈmät-ᵊl\ *n* [prob. back-formation fr. *motley*] **1 :** a colored spot **2 :** an appearance like that of a surface having colored spots or blotches
²mottle *vt* **mot·tling** \ˈmät-liŋ, -ᵊl-iŋ\ **:** to mark with spots or blotches of different color or shades of color as if stained — **mot·tler** \-lər, -ᵊl-ər\ *n*
mottled enamel *n* **:** spotted tooth enamel caused by drinking water containing excessive fluorides during the time the teeth are calcifying
mot·to \ˈmät-(ˌ)ō\ *n, pl* **mottoes** *also* **mottos** [It, fr. L *muttum* grunt, fr. *muttire* to mutter] **1 :** a sentence, phrase, or word inscribed on something as appropriate to or indicative of its character or use **2 :** a short expression of a guiding principle
moue \ˈmü\ *n* [F — more at MOW] **:** a little grimace **:** POUT
mou·flon *or* **mouf·flon** \mü-ˈflōⁿ\ *n* [F *mouflon*, fr. It dial. *movrone*, fr. LL *mufron-*, *mufro*] **:** a wild sheep (*Ovis musimon*) of the mountains of Sardinia and Corsica with large curling horns in the male; *broadly* **:** a wild sheep with large horns
mouil·lé \mü-ˈyā\ *adj* [F] **:** pronounced palatally
mou·jik \mü-ˈzhēk, -ˈzhik\ *var of* MUZHIK
mou·lage \mü-ˈläzh\ *n* [F, molding, fr. MF, fr. *mouler* to mold, fr. OF *modle* mold — more at MOLD] **1 :** the taking of an impression for use as evidence in a criminal investigation **2 :** an impression or cast made for use as evidence in a criminal investigation

mould \'mōld\ *var of* MOLD
mou·lin \mü-'laⁿ\ *n* [F, fr. LL *molinum* — more at MILL] **:** a nearly cylindrical vertical shaft in a glacier scoured out by water from melting snow and ice and rock debris
moult \'mōlt\ *var of* MOLT
moult·en \'mōlt-ᵊn\ *adj, obs* **:** having lost plumage **:** MOLTED
¹mound \'maùnd\ *vt* [origin unknown] **1** *archaic* **:** to enclose or fortify with a fence or a ridge of earth **2 :** to form into a mound
²mound *n, often attrib* [origin unknown] **1** *archaic* **:** HEDGE, FENCE **2 a** (1) **:** an artificial bank or hill of earth or stones (2) **:** the slightly elevated ground on which the pitcher stands in baseball **b :** KNOLL, HILL **3 :** HEAP, PILE
Mound Builder *n* **:** a member of a prehistoric Indian people of central No. America whose extensive earthworks are found esp. around the Great Lakes and in the Mississippi valley region
¹mount \'maùnt\ *n* [ME, fr. OE *munt* & OF *mont*, fr. L *mont-, mons;* akin to ON *mœna* to project, L *minari* to project, threaten] **1 :** a high hill **:** MOUNTAIN — used esp. before its name ⟨*Mount* Everest⟩ **2** *archaic* **:** a protective earthwork **3 :** MOUND 2a(1) **4** *cap* **:** a small area of raised flesh on the palm of the hand esp. at the base of a finger that is held by palmists to indicate temperament or traits of character
²mount *vb* [ME *mounten*, fr. MF *monter*, fr. (assumed) VL *montare*, fr. L *mont-, mons*] *vi* **1 :** to increase in amount or extent **2 :** RISE, ASCEND **3 :** to get up on something above the level of the ground; *esp* **:** to seat oneself (as on a horse) for riding ~ *vt* **1 a :** to go up **:** CLIMB **b** (1) **:** to seat or place oneself on (2) **:** COVER 6a **2 a :** to lift up **:** RAISE **b** (1) **:** to put or have (as artillery) in position (2) **:** to have as equipment **3 :** to set on something that elevates **4 a :** to cause to get on a means of conveyance **b :** to furnish with animals for riding **5 :** to post or set up for defense or observation **6 a :** to attach to a support **b :** to arrange or assemble for use or display **7 a :** to prepare (as a specimen) for examination or display **b :** to prepare and supply with the materials necessary for performance or execution **syn** see ASCEND — **mount·er** *n*
³mount *n* **1 :** an act or instance of mounting; *specif* **:** an opportunity to ride a horse in a race **2 :** FRAME, SUPPORT: as **a :** the cardboard or similar material on which a picture is mounted **b :** a jewelry setting **c :** an undercarriage or part that fits a device for use or attaches an accessory **d :** a hinge, card, or acetate envelope for mounting a stamp **e :** a glass slide with its accessories on which objects are placed for examination with a microscope **3 :** a means of conveyance; *specif* **:** SADDLE HORSE — **mount·able** \'maùnt-ə-bəl\ *adj*
moun·tain \'maùnt-ᵊn\ *n, often attrib* [ME, fr. OF *montaigne*, fr. (assumed) VL *montanea*, fr. fem. of *montaneus* of a mountain, alter. of L *montanus*, fr. *mont-, mons*] **1 :** a land mass that projects conspicuously above its surroundings and is higher than a hill **2 a :** a great mass **b :** a vast number or quantity
mountain ash *n* **:** any of various trees (genus *Sorbus*) of the rose family with pinnate leaves and red fruits
mountain cranberry *n* **:** a low evergreen shrub (*Vaccinium vitis-idaea*) of north temperate uplands with dark red edible berries
mountain dew *n* **:** MOONSHINE 3
moun·tain·eer \,maùnt-ᵊn-'i(ə)r\ *n* **1 :** a native or inhabitant of a mountainous region **2 :** one who climbs mountains for sport — **mountaineer** *vi*
mountain goat *n* **:** a mammal (*Oreamnos montanus*) of mountainous northwestern No. America related to the Old World chamois
mountain laurel *n* **:** a No. American evergreen shrub (*Kalmia latifolia*) of the heath family with glossy leaves and umbels of rose-colored or white flowers
mountain lion *n* **:** COUGAR
mountain mahogany *n* **:** any of several western No. American shrubs or small shrubby trees (genus *Cercocarpus*) of the rose family often important as browse or forage plants
moun·tain·ous \'maùnt-ᵊn-əs, 'maùnt-nəs\ *adj* **1 :** containing many mountains **2 :** resembling a mountain **:** HUGE — **moun·tain·ous·ly** *adv* — **moun·tain·ous·ness** *n*
mountain sickness *n* **:** altitude sickness experienced esp. above 10,000 feet and caused by insufficient oxygen in the air
moun·tain·side \'maùnt-ᵊn-,sīd\ *n* **:** the side of a mountain
mountain time *n, often cap M* **:** the time of the 7th time zone west of Greenwich that includes the west central U.S.
moun·tain·top \'maùnt-ᵊn-,täp\ *n* **:** the summit of a mountain
moun·tainy \'maùnt-ᵊn-ē, 'maùnt-nē\ *adj* **1 :** MOUNTAINOUS **2 :** of, relating to, or living in mountains
moun·tant \'maùnt-ᵊnt\ *n* **:** an adhesive for fastening a print or drawing to a mount
moun·te·bank \'maùnt-i-,baŋk\ *n* [It *montimbanco*, fr. *montare* to mount (fr.—assumed—VL) + *in* in, on (fr. L) + *banco, banca* bench — more at BANK] **1 :** a person who sells quack medicines from a platform **2 :** a boastful unscrupulous pretender **:** CHARLATAN — **mountebank** *vi* — **moun·te·bank·ery** \-,baŋ-k(ə-)rē\ *n*
Mount·ie \'maùnt-ē\ *n* [*mount*ed policeman] **:** a member of the Royal Canadian Mounted Police
mount·ing \'maùnt-iŋ\ *n* **:** ³MOUNT 2
mourn \'mō(ə)rn, 'mȯ(ə)rn\ *vb* [ME *mournen*, fr. OE *murnan;* akin to OHG *mornēn* to mourn, Gk *mermēra* care — more at MEMORY] *vi* **1 :** to feel or express grief or sorrow **2 :** to show the customary signs of grief for a death; *esp* **:** to wear mourning **3 :** to murmur mournfully — used esp. of doves ~ *vt* **1 :** to feel or express grief or sorrow for **2 :** to utter mournfully — **mourn·er** *n* — **mourn·ing·ly** \'mōr-niŋ-lē, 'mȯr-\ *adv*
mourn·ful \'mō(ə)rn-fəl, 'mȯ(ə)rn-\ *adj* **1 :** expressing sorrow **:** SORROWFUL **2 :** full of sorrow **:** SAD **3 :** causing sorrow **:** SADDENING — **mourn·ful·ly** \-fə-lē\ *adv* — **mourn·ful·ness** *n*
mourn·ing \'mōr-niŋ, 'mȯr-\ *n* **1 a :** the customary exhibition of grief for a person's death **b :** the period of such an exhibition **2 :** the black clothing or other symbols of grief for a person's death
mourning cloak *n* **:** a blackish brown butterfly (*Nymphalis antiopa*) with a broad yellow border on the wings found in Europe and No. America
mourning dove *n* **:** a wild dove (*Zenaidura macroura carolinensis*) of the U.S. with a mournful call
¹mouse \'maùs\ *n, pl* **mice** \'mīs\ [ME, fr. OE *mūs;* akin to OHG *mūs* mouse, L *mus*, Gk *mys* mouse, muscle] **1 :** any of numerous small rodents (as of the genus *Mus*) with pointed snout, rather small ears, elongated body, and slender tail **2 a** *slang* **:** WOMAN **b :** a timid person **3 :** a dark-colored swelling caused by a blow; *specif* **:** a black eye
²mouse \'maùz\ *vi* **1 :** to hunt for mice **2 :** to search or move slyly ~ *vt* **1** *obs* **a :** BITE, GNAW **b :** to toy with roughly **2 :** to search for carefully
mouse–ear \'maù-,si(ə)r\ *n* **:** any of several plants with soft, hairy, and usu. small leaves
mouse–ear chickweed *n* **:** any of several hairy chickweeds (esp. *Cerastium vulgatum* and *C. viscosum*)
mous·er \'maù-zər\ *n* **:** a catcher of mice and rats; *esp* **:** a cat or other animal proficient at mousing
mous·ing \'maù-ziŋ\ *n* [gerund of *mouse* (to apply a mousing)] **:** a turn or lashing used by seamen esp. across the open end of a hook to prevent the load carried from slipping off
Mous·que·taire \,mü-skə-'ta(ə)r, -'te(ə)r\ *n* [F — more at MUSKETEER] **:** a French musketeer; *esp* **:** one of the royal musketeers of the 17th and 18th centuries conspicuous for their daring and their dandified dress
mousse \'müs\ *n* [F, lit., froth, fr. LL *mulsa* hydromel; akin to L *mel* honey — more at MELLIFLUOUS] **:** a light spongy food usu. containing cream or gelatin; *esp* **:** a dessert made with sweetened and flavored whipped cream or thin cream and gelatin and frozen without stirring
mous·se·line \,müs-(ə-)'lēn\ *n* [F, lit., muslin — more at MUSLIN] **:** a fine sheer fabric (as of rayon) that resembles muslin
mousseline de soie \,müs-(ə-),lēn-də-'swä\ *n, pl* **mousselines de soie** *same*\ [F, lit., silk muslin] **:** a silk muslin resembling chiffon but having a crisp finish
mous·tache \'məs-,tash, (,)məs-'\ *n* [MF, fr. OIt *mustaccio*, fr. MGk *moustaki*, dim. of Gk *mystak-, mystax* upper lip, moustache] **1 :** the hair growing on the human upper lip **2 :** hair or bristles about the mouth of a mammal
mous·ta·chio *var of* MUSTACHIO
Mous·te·ri·an \mü-'stir-ē-ən\ *adj* [F *moustérien*, fr. Le *Moustier*, cave in Dordogne, France] **:** of or relating to a lower Paleolithic culture
mousy *or* **mous·ey** \'maù-sē, -zē\ *adj* **mous·i·er; mous·i·est** **:** of or resembling a mouse: as **a :** QUIET **b :** TIMID, COLORLESS
¹mouth \'maùth\ *n, pl* **mouths** \'maù*th*z, 'maùths; *in synecdochic compounds like "blabbermouths"* ths *more frequently*\ *often attrib* [ME, fr. OE *mūth;* akin to OHG *mund* mouth, L *mandere* to chew, Gk *masasthai* to chew, *mastax* mouth, jaws] **1 a** (1) **:** the opening through which food passes into the body of an animal (2) **:** the cavity bounded externally by the lips and internally by the pharynx that encloses in the typical vertebrate the tongue, gums, and teeth **b :** GRIMACE **2 a :** VOICE, SPEECH **b :** MOUTHPIECE 3a **3 :** something that resembles a mouth esp. in affording entrance or exit: as **a :** the place where a stream enters a larger body of water **b :** the surface opening of an underground cavity **c :** the opening of a container **d :** an opening in the side of an organ flue pipe — **mouthed** \'maù*th*d, 'maùtht\ *adj* — **mouth·like** \'maùth-,līk\ *adj*
²mouth \'maù*th*\ *vt* **1 a :** SPEAK, PRONOUNCE **b :** to utter bombastically **:** DECLAIM **c :** to repeat without comprehension or sincerity **d :** to utter indistinctly **:** MUMBLE **2 :** to take into the mouth ~ *vi* **1 :** to talk pompously **:** RANT **2 :** to move the mouth esp. so as to make faces — **mouth·er** *n*
mouth·breed·er \'maùth-,brēd-ər\ *n* **:** any of several fishes that carry their eggs and young in the mouth; *esp* **:** a No. African percoid fish (*Haplochromes multicolor*) often kept in aquariums
mouth·ful \-,fùl\ *n* **1 a :** as much as a mouth will hold **b :** the quantity usu. taken into the mouth at one time **2 :** a small quantity **3 :** a very long word or phrase
mouth organ *n* **1 :** PANPIPE **2 :** HARMONICA 2
mouth·part \'maùth-,pärt\ *n* **:** a structure or appendage near the mouth
mouth·piece \-,pēs\ *n* **1 :** something placed at or forming a mouth **2 :** a part that goes in the mouth or to which the mouth is applied **3 a :** one that expresses or interprets another's views **:** SPOKESMAN **b** *slang* **:** a criminal lawyer
mouthy \'maù-*th*ē, -thē\ *adj* **1 :** excessively talkative **:** GARRULOUS **2 :** BOMBASTIC
mou·ton \'mü-,tän, mü-'\ *n* [F, sheep, sheepskin, fr. MF, ram — more at MUTTON] **:** processed sheepskin that has been sheared and dyed to resemble beaver or seal
moutonnée *n* **:** ROCHE MOUTONNÉE
mov·abil·i·ty *or* **move·abil·i·ty** \,mü-və-'bil-ət-ē\ *n* **:** the quality or state of being movable
¹mov·able *or* **move·able** \'mü-və-bəl\ *adj* **1 :** capable of being moved **2 :** changing date from year to year ⟨~ holidays⟩ — **mov·able·ness** *n* — **mov·ably** \-blē\ *adv*
²movable *or* **moveable** *n* **:** something that can be removed or displaced
¹move \'müv\ *vb* [ME *moven*, fr. MF *movoir*, fr. L *movēre*] *vi* **1 a :** to go continuously from one point to another **:** PROCEED **b :** to start away from some point or place **:** DEPART **c :** to change one's residence or location **d :** to change hands by being sold or rented **2 a** (1) **:** to change position or posture **:** STIR (2) **:** to begin operating or functioning or working in a usual way **b :** to show marked activity **:** HUM **3 :** to live one's life in a specified environment **4 :** to take action **:** ACT **5 :** to make a formal request or application or appeal **6** *of the bowels* **:** EVACUATE ~ *vt* **1 a** (1) **:** to change the place or position of (2) **:** to dislodge or displace from a fixed position **:** BUDGE **b :** to transfer (as a piece in chess) from one position to another **c :** to cause to change hands through sale or rent **2 a** (1) **:** to cause to go continuously from one point to another ⟨*moved* the flag slowly up and down⟩ (2) **:** to cause to advance **b :** to activate into operating or functioning or working in a usual way **:** ACTUATE **c :** to put into activity or rouse up from inactivity **3 :** to cause to change position or posture **4 :** to prompt or rouse to the doing of something **:** PERSUADE **5 :** to stir the emotions, feelings, or passions of **6 a** *obs* **:** BEG **b :** to make a formal application to **7 :** to propose formally in a deliberative assembly **8 :** to cause (the bowels) to void
syn MOVE, ACTUATE, DRIVE, IMPEL mean to set or keep in motion. MOVE is very general and implies no more than the fact of changing position; ACTUATE stresses the communication of power to work or set in motion; DRIVE implies imparting forward and continuous motion and often stresses the effect rather than the impetus; IMPEL suggests the working of a greater impetus producing more headlong action

2move *n* **1 a :** the act of moving a piece (as in chess) **b :** the turn of a player to move **2 a :** a step taken so as to gain an objective **:** MANEUVER **b :** the action of moving from a motionless position **c :** a change of residence or location — **on the move 1 :** in a state of moving about from place to place **2 :** in a state of moving ahead or making progress

move·less \'müv-ləs\ *adj* **:** MOTIONLESS, FIXED — **move·less·ly** *adv* — **move·less·ness** *n*

move·ment \'müv-mənt\ *n* **1 a** (1) **:** the act or process of moving; *esp* **:** change of place or position or posture (2) **:** a particular instance or manner of moving **b** (1) **:** a tactical or strategic shifting of a military unit **:** MANEUVER (2) **:** the advance of a military unit **c :** ACTION, ACTIVITY **d :** a change in the price of a commodity or stock **2 a :** TENDENCY, TREND **b :** a series of organized activities working toward an objective **3 :** the moving parts of a mechanism that transmit a definite motion **4 a :** MOTION 7 **b :** the rhythmic character or quality of a musical composition **c :** TIME 7 **d :** TEMPO **e :** a distinct structural unit or division forming part of an extended musical composition **f :** particular rhythmic flow of language **:** CADENCE **5 a :** a quality in a work of art of representing or suggesting motion **b :** the quality in literature of having a quickly moving plot or an abundance of incident **6 a :** an act of voiding the bowels **b :** matter expelled from the bowels at one passage **:** STOOL

mov·er \'mü-vər\ *n* **:** one that moves or sets something into motion

mov·ie \'mü-vē\ *n* [*moving picture*] **1 :** MOTION PICTURE **2** *pl* **a :** a showing of a motion picture **b :** the motion-picture industry

mov·ing *adj* **1 :** marked by or capable of movement **2 a :** producing or transferring motion or action **b :** arousing or affecting the emotions or sensibilities — **mov·ing·ly** \'mü-viŋ-lē\ *adv*

syn IMPRESSIVE, POIGNANT, AFFECTING, TOUCHING, PATHETIC: MOVING may apply to any strong emotional effect including thrilling, agitating, saddening, calling forth pity or sympathy; IMPRESSIVE implies compelling attention, admiration, wonder, or conviction; POIGNANT applies to what keenly or sharply affects one's sensitivities esp. in compelling pity or inducing nostalgia; AFFECTING is close to MOVING but most often suggests pathos; TOUCHING implies arousing tenderness or compassion; PATHETIC implies moving to pity or sometimes contempt

moving picture *n* **:** MOTION PICTURE

moving staircase *n* **:** ESCALATOR — called also *moving stairway*

1mow \'mau̇\ *n* [ME, heap, stack fr. OE *mūga;* akin to ON *mūgi* heap, Gk *mykōn*] **:** the part of a barn where hay or straw is stored

2mow \'mō\ *vb* **mowed; mowed** *or* **mown** \'mōn\ **mow·ing** [ME *mowen,* fr. OE *māwan;* akin to OHG *māen* to mow, L *metere* to reap, mow, Gk *aman*] *vt* **1 a :** to cut down with a scythe or sickle or machine **b :** to cut the standing herbage (as grass) of **2 a** (1) **:** to kill or destroy in great numbers or without mercy or concern (2) **:** to cause to fall **b :** to overcome swiftly and decisively **:** ROUT ~ *vi* **:** to cut down standing herbage (as grass) — **mow·er** \'mō(-ə)r\ *n*

3mow \'mau̇, 'mō\ *n* [ME *mowe,* fr. MF *moue,* of Gmc origin; akin to MD *mouwe* protruding lip] **:** GRIMACE

4mow \'mau̇, 'mō\ *vi* **:** to make grimaces

mox·ie \'mäk-sē\ *n* [fr. *Moxie,* a trademark for a soft drink] **1** *slang* **:** ENERGY **2** *slang* **:** COURAGE

moyen–âge \mwȧ-ye-näzh\ *adj* [F *moyen âge* middle ages] **:** of or relating to medieval times

moz·zet·ta \mōt-'set-ə\ *n* [It] **:** a short cape with a small ornamental hood worn over the rochet by the pope and privileged dignitaries

Mrs. Grun·dy \-'grən-dē\ *n* [fr. a character alluded to in Thomas Morton's *Speed the Plough* (1798)] **:** one marked by prudish conventionality in personal conduct

mu \'myü, 'mü\ *n* [Gk *my*] **:** the 12th letter of the Greek alphabet — symbol M or μ

muc- *or* **muci-** *or* **muco-** *comb form* [L *muc-,* fr. *mucus*] **1 :** mucus ⟨*muco*protein⟩ **2 :** mucous and ⟨*muco*purulent⟩

1much \'məch\ *adj* **more** \'mō(ə)r, 'mȯ(ə)r\ **most** \'mōst\ [ME *muche* large, much, fr. *michel, muchel,* fr. OE *micel, mycel;* akin to OHG *mihhil* great, large, L *magnus,* Gk *megas*] **1 a :** great in quantity, amount, extent, or degree **b :** existing or present in a relative quantity or amount or to a relative extent or degree ⟨taken too ~ time⟩ **2** *obs* **:** many in number

2much *adv* **more; most 1 a** (1) **:** to a great degree or extent **:** CONSIDERABLY ⟨~ happier⟩ (2) **:** VERY **b** (1) **:** FREQUENTLY, OFTEN (2) **:** LONG **2 :** APPROXIMATELY, NEARLY

3much *n* **1 :** a great quantity, amount, extent, or degree ⟨gave away ~⟩ **2 :** something considerable or impressive ⟨was not ~ to look at⟩

much as *conj* **:** however much **:** even though

much·ness \'məch-nəs\ *n* **:** GREATNESS

mu·cic acid \,myü-sik-\ *n* [ISV *muc-*] **:** an optically inactive crystalline acid $C_6H_{10}O_8$ obtained from galactose or lactose by oxidation with nitric acid

mu·cif·er·ous \myü-'sif-(ə-)rəs\ *adj* **:** producing or filled with mucus ⟨~ ducts⟩

mu·ci·lage \'myü-s(ə-)lij\ *n* [ME *muscilage,* fr. LL *mucilago* mucus, musty juice, fr. L *mucus*] **1 :** a gelatinous substance esp. from seaweeds that contains protein and polysaccharides and is similar to plant gums **2 :** an aqueous usu. viscid solution of a gum or similar substance used esp. as an adhesive

mu·ci·lag·i·nous \,myü-sə-'laj-ə-nəs\ *adj* [LL *mucilaginosus,* fr. *mucilagin-, mucilago*] **1 :** being moist and viscid **2 :** of, relating to, or secreting mucilage — **mu·ci·lag·i·nous·ly** *adv*

mu·cin \'myüs-ᵊn\ *n* [ISV *muc-*] **:** any of various proteins originating from mucous membranes — **mu·cin·oid** \'myüs-ᵊn-,ȯid\ *adj* — **mu·cin·ous** \-ᵊn-əs, 'myü-snəs\ *adj*

mu·cin·o·gen \myü-'sin-ə-jən\ *n* [ISV] **:** a substance easily converted into a mucin

mu·ci·no·lyt·ic \,myüs-ᵊn-ō-'lit-ik\ *adj* **:** tending to break down or lower the viscosity of mucin-containing body secretions or components

1muck \'mək\ *n* [ME *muk,* perh. fr. OE *-moc;* akin to ON *myki* dung — more at MUCUS] **1 :** soft moist farmyard manure **2 :** slimy dirt or filth **3 :** defamatory remarks or writings **4 a** (1) **:** dark highly organic soil (2) **:** MIRE, MUD **b :** something resembling muck **5 :** material removed in the process of excavating or mining — **mucky** \'mək-ē\ *adj*

2muck *vt* **1 a :** to clean up; *esp* **:** to clear of manure or filth **b :** to clear of muck **2 :** to dress with muck **3 :** to dirty with muck **:** SOIL — **muck·er** *n*

muck·luck *var of* MUKLUK

muck·rake \'mək-,rāk\ *vi* [obs. *muckrake,* n. (rake for dung)] **:** to search out and expose publicly real or apparent misconduct of prominent individuals — **muck·rak·er** *n*

mu·co·cu·ta·ne·ous \,myü-(,)kō-kyù-'tā-nē-əs\ *adj* **:** made up of or involving both typical skin and mucous membrane

1mu·coid \'myü-,kȯid\ *adj* [ISV *muc-*] **:** resembling mucus

2mucoid *n* [ISV] **:** any of a group of complex proteins similar to mucins or mucoproteins but occurring esp. in connective tissue and in cysts

mu·coi·tin·sul·fu·ric acid \myü-'kō-ət-ᵊn-,səl-,fyu̇r-ik-, -'kȯit-ᵊn-\ *n* [ISV *mucoitin* (a mucopolysaccharide acid)] **:** an acidic mucopolysaccharide found esp in the cornea of the eye and in gastric mucosa

mu·co·poly·sac·cha·ride \'myü-(,)kō-,päl-i-'sak-ə-,rīd\ *n* [ISV] **:** any of various polysaccharides derived from a hexosamine that are constituents of mucoproteins, glycoproteins, and blood-group substances

mu·co·pro·tein \-'prō-,tēn, -'prōt-ē-ən\ *n* **:** any of various complex compounds (as mucins) containing polysaccharides and occurring in body fluids and tissues

mu·co·sa \myü-'kō-sə, -'kō-zə\ *n, pl* **mu·co·sae** \-(,)sē, -(,)zē, -,sī, -,zī\ *or* **mucosas** [NL, fr. L, fem. of *mucosus* mucous] **:** MUCOUS MEMBRANE — **mu·co·sal** \-səl, -zəl\ *adj*

mu·co·se·rous \,myü-(,)kō-'sir-əs\ *adj* **:** containing or producing both mucous and serous material

mu·cous \'myü-kəs\ *adj* [L *mucosus,* fr. *mucus*] **1 :** covered with or as if with mucus **:** SLIMY **2 :** of, relating to, or resembling mucus **3 :** secreting or containing mucus

mucous membrane *n* **:** a membrane rich in mucous glands; *specif* **:** one that lines body passages and cavities which communicate directly or indirectly with the exterior

mu·cro \'myü-,krō\ *n, pl* **mu·cro·nes** \myü-'krō-(,)nēz\ [NL *mucron-, mucro,* fr. L, point, edge; akin to Gk *amyssein* to scratch, sting] **:** an abrupt sharp terminal point or tip or process (as of a leaf) — **mu·cro·nate** \'myü-krə-,nāt\ *adj* — **mu·cro·na·tion** \,myü-krə-'nā-shən\ *n*

mu·cus \'myü-kəs\ *n* [L, nasal mucus; akin to ON *myki* dung, Gk *myxa* mucus] **:** a viscid slippery secretion usu. rich in mucins produced by mucous membranes which it moistens and protects

1mud \'məd\ *n* [ME *mudde,* prob. fr. MLG; akin to OE *mōs* bog — more at MOSS] **1 :** a slimy sticky mixture of solid material with water; *esp* **:** soft wet earth **2 :** abusive and malicious remarks or charges

2mud *vt* **mud·ded; mud·ding :** to make muddy or turbid

mud dauber *n* **:** any of various wasps (esp. family Sphecidae) that construct mud cells in which the female places an egg with spiders or insects paralyzed by a sting to serve as food for the larva

mud·di·ly \'məd-ᵊl-ē\ *adv* **:** in a muddy manner

mud·di·ness \'məd-ē-nəs\ *n* **:** the quality or state of being muddy

1mud·dle \'məd-ᵊl\ *vb* **mud·dling** \'məd-liŋ, -ᵊl-iŋ\ [prob. fr. obs. D *moddelen,* fr. MD, fr. *modde* mud; akin to MLG *mudde*] *vt* **1 :** to make turbid or muddy **2 :** to befog or stupefy esp. with liquor **3 :** to mix confusedly **4 :** to make a mess of **:** BUNGLE ~ *vi* **:** to think or act in a confused aimless way — **mud·dler** \-lər, -ᵊl-ər\ *n*

2muddle *n* **1 :** a state of esp. mental confusion **2 :** a confused mess

mud·dle·head·ed \,məd-ᵊl-'hed-əd\ *adj* **1 :** mentally confused **2 :** BUNGLING, INEPT — **mud·dle·head·ed·ness** *n*

1mud·dy \'məd-ē\ *adj* **1 :** morally impure **:** BASE **2 a :** full of or covered with mud **b :** turbid with sediment **3 :** CLOUDY, DULL **4 :** MUDDLED, CONFUSED **syn** see TURBID

2muddy *vt* **1 :** to soil or stain with or as if with mud **2 :** to make turbid **3 :** to make cloudy or dull **4 :** CONFUSE

mud·guard \'məd-,gärd\ *n* **1 :** FENDER d **2 :** a strip of material applied to a shoe upper just above the sole for protection against dampness or as an ornament

mud puppy *n* **:** any of various mostly large American salamanders; *esp* **:** HELLBENDER

mud·sill \'məd-,sil\ *n* **:** the lowest sill of a structure usu. embedded in soil

mud·sling·er \-,sliŋ-ər\ *n* **:** one that uses offensive epithets and invective esp. against a political opponent — **mud·sling·ing** \-,sliŋ-iŋ\ *n*

mud·stone \'məd-,stōn\ *n* **:** an indurated shale produced by the consolidation of mud

mud turtle *n* **:** a bottom-dwelling freshwater turtle: as **a :** a musk turtle (genus *Kinosternon*) **b :** SOFT SHELLED TURTLE

Muen·ster \'mən(t)-stər, 'm(y)ün(t)-, 'mu̇n(t)-, 'min(t)-\ *n* [*Münster, Munster,* France] **:** a semisoft cheese of bland or sharp flavor

mu·ez·zin \m(y)ü-'ez-ᵊn, 'mwez-ᵊn\ *n* [Ar *mu'adhdhin*] **:** a Muslim crier who calls the hour of daily prayers

1muff \'məf\ *n* [D *mof,* fr. MF *moufle* mitten, fr. ML *muffula*] **1 :** a warm tubular covering for the hands **2 :** a cluster of feathers on the side of the face of some domestic fowls

2muff *n* **:** a bungling performance; *specif* **:** a failure to hold a ball in attempting a catch — **muff** *vb*

muf·fin \'məf-ən\ *n* [prob. fr. LG *muffen,* pl. of *muffe* cake] **:** a quick bread made of batter containing egg and baked in a small cup-shaped pan; *also* **:** a similarly shaped biscuit made from yeast dough

1muf·fle \'məf-əl\ *vt* **muf·fling** \'məf-(ə-)liŋ\ [ME *muflen*] **1 :** to wrap up so as to conceal or protect **:** ENVELOP **2 :** BLINDFOLD **3 a :** to wrap or pad with something to dull the sound of **b :** to deaden the sound of **4 :** to keep down **:** SUPPRESS

2muffle *n* [F *mufle*] **:** the end of the muzzle of a mammal

muf·fler \'məf-lər\ *n* **1 a :** a scarf worn around the neck **b :** something that hides or disguises **2 :** a device to deaden noise

1muf·ti \'məf-tē, 'mu̇f-\ *n* [Ar *muftī*] **:** a professional jurist who interprets Muslim law

2muf·ti \'məf-tē\ *n* [prob. fr. 1*mufti*] **:** civilian clothes

ə abut; ᵊ kitten; ər further; a back; ā bake; ä cot, cart; au̇ out; ch chin; e less; ē easy; g gift; i trip; ī life
j joke; ŋ sing; ō flow; ȯ flaw; ȯi coin; th thin; t͟h this; ü loot; u̇ foot; y yet; yü few; yu̇ furious; zh vision

[1]**mug** \'məg\ *n* [origin unknown] **1 :** a usu. metal or earthenware cylindrical drinking cup **2 a :** the face or mouth of a person **b :** GRIMACE **c :** a photograph of a suspect's face **3 :** PUNK, THUG

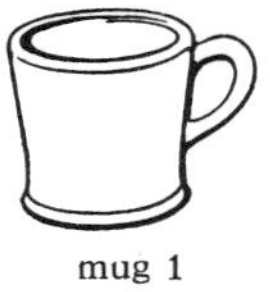

mug 1

[2]**mug** *vb* **mugged; mug·ging** *vi* **:** to make faces esp. to attract the attention of an audience ~ *vt* **:** PHOTOGRAPH

[3]**mug** *vb* **mugged; mug·ging** [back-formation fr. [2]*mugger*] **:** to assault esp. by garroting usu. with intent to rob

[1]**mug·ger** \'məg-ər\ *n* [Hindi *magar*, fr. Skt *makara* water monster] **:** a common usu. harmless freshwater crocodile (*Crocodylus palustris*) of southeastern Asia

[2]**mugger** *n* [prob. fr. obs. *mug* (to punch in the face)] **:** one who attacks usu. from behind with intent to rob

[3]**mugger** *n* [[2]*mug*] **:** one that grimaces esp. before an audience

mug·gi·ly \'məg-ə-lē\ *adv* **:** in a muggy manner

mug·gi·ness \'məg-ē-nəs\ *n* **:** tne quality or state of being muggy

mug·gy \'məg-ē\ *adj* [E dial. *mug* (drizzle)] **:** being warm, damp, and close

mu·gho pine \,m(y)ü-(,)gō-\ *n* [prob. fr. F *mugho* mugho pine, fr. It *mugo*] **:** a shrubby spreading pine (*Pinus mugo mughus*) widely cultivated as an ornamental

mug·wump \'məg-,wəmp\ *n* [obs. slang *mugwump* (kingpin), fr. Natick *mugwomp* captain] **1 :** a bolter from the Republican party in 1884 **2 :** an independent in politics

Mu·ham·mad·an \mō-'ham-əd-ən, -'häm- *also* mü-\ *adj* **:** of or relating to Muhammad or Islam — **Muhammadan** *n* — **Mu·ham·mad·an·ism** \-əd-ə-,niz-əm\ *n*

Muhammadan calendar *n* **:** a lunar calendar reckoned from the Hegira in A.D. 622 and organized in cycles of 30 years — see CALENDAR table

Mu·har·ram \mü-'har-əm\ *n* [Ar *Muḥarram*] **1 :** the first month of the Muhammadan year **2 :** a Muslim festival held during Muharram

mu·jik \mü-'zhēk, -'zhik\ *var of* MUZHIK

muk·luk \'mək-,lək\ *n* [Esk *muklok* large seal] **1 :** a sealskin or reindeer-skin boot worn by Eskimos **2 :** a boot often of duck with a soft leather sole and worn over several pairs of socks

mu·lat·to \m(y)ü-'lat-(,)ō, -ə(-w)\ *n, pl* **mulattoes** *or* **mulattos** [Sp *mulato*, fr. *mulo* mule, fr. L *mulus*] **1 :** the first-generation offspring of a Negro and a white **2 :** a person of mixed Caucasian and Negro ancestry

mul·ber·ry \'məl-,ber-ē, -b(ə-)rē\ *n* [ME *murberie, mulberie*, fr. OF *moure* mulberry (fr. L *morum*, fr. Gk *moron*) + ME *berie* berry] **1 :** any of a genus (*Morus* of the family Moraceae, the mulberry family) of trees with edible usu. purple berrylike fruit; *also* **:** the fruit **2 :** a dark purple or purplish black

mulch \'məlch\ *n* [perh. irreg. fr. E dial. *melch* (soft, mild)] **:** a protective covering (as of sawdust, compost, or paper) used on the ground esp. to reduce evaporation, prevent erosion, control weeds, or enrich the soil **:** LITTER — **mulch** *vt*

[1]**mulct** \'məlkt\ *n* [L *multa, mulcta*] **:** FINE, PENALTY

[2]**mulct** *vt* **1 :** to punish by a fine **2 a :** to defraud esp. of money **:** SWINDLE **b :** to obtain by fraud, duress, or theft

[1]**mule** \'myü(ə)l\ *n* [ME, fr. OF *mul*, fr. L *mulus*] **1 a :** a hybrid between a horse and an ass; *esp* **:** the offspring of a male ass and a mare **b :** a self-sterile plant whether hybrid or not **c :** a usu. sterile hybrid **2 :** a very stubborn person **3 :** a machine for simultaneously drawing and twisting fiber into yarn or thread and winding it into cops

[2]**mule** *n* [MF, a kind of slipper, fr. L *mulleus* shoe worn by magistrates] **:** a slipper without quarter and usu. without counter

mule–foot \-,fu̇t\ *or* **mule–foot·ed** \-'fu̇t-əd\ *adj* **:** having a solid rather than a cleft hoof

mule skinner *n* **:** MULETEER

mu·le·teer \,myü-lə-'ti(ə)r\ *n* [F *muletier*, fr. *mulet*, fr. OF, dim. of *mul* mule] **:** one who drives mules

mu·ley *also* **mul·ley** \'myü-lē, 'mu̇l-ē, 'mü-lē\ *adj* [of Celtic origin; akin to IrGael & ScGael *maol* bald, hornless, W *moel*] **:** POLLED, HORNLESS; *esp* **:** naturally hornless

mu·li·eb·ri·ty \,myü-lē-'eb-rət-ē\ *n* [LL *muliebritat-, muliebritas*, fr. L *muliebris* of a woman, fr. *mulier* woman] **1 :** WOMANHOOD **2 :** FEMININITY

mul·ish \'myü-lish\ *adj* [[1]*mule*] **:** STUBBORN, INFLEXIBLE **syn** see OBSTINATE — **mul·ish·ly** *adv* — **mul·ish·ness** *n*

[1]**mull** \'məl\ *vb* [ME *mullen*, fr. *mul, mol* dust, prob. fr. MD; akin to OE *melu* meal — more at MEAL] *vt* **1 :** to grind or mix thoroughly **:** PULVERIZE **2 :** to consider at length **:** PONDER ~ *vi* **:** MEDITATE, PONDER

[2]**mull** *vt* [origin unknown] **:** to sweeten, spice, and heat esp. with a hot poker ⟨~*ed* wine⟩

[3]**mull** *n* [by shortening & alter. fr. *mulmul* (muslin)] **:** a soft fine sheer fabric of cotton, silk, or rayon

[4]**mull** *n* [G, fr. Dan *muld*, fr. ON *mold* dust, soil; akin to OHG *molta* dust, soil — more at MOLD] **:** granular forest humus with a layer of mixed organic matter and mineral soil merging gradually into the mineral soil beneath

mul·lah \'məl-ə, 'mu̇l-ə\ *n* [Turk *molla* & Per & Hindi *mulla*, fr. Ar *mawlā*] **:** a Muslim of a quasi-clerical class trained in traditional law and doctrine; *esp* **:** one who is head of a mosque — **mul·lah·ism** \-,iz-əm\ *n*

mul·lein *also* **mul·len** \'məl-ən\ *n* [ME *moleyne*, fr. AF *moleine*] **:** any of a genus (*Verbascum*) of usu. woolly-leaved herbs of the figwort family

mullein pink *n* **:** a European herb (*Lychnis coronaria*) cultivated for its white woolly herbage and showy crimson flowers

mull·er \'məl-ər\ *n* [alter. of ME *molour*, prob. fr. *mullen* to grind] **:** a stone or piece of wood, metal, or glass used as a pestle

mul·let \'məl-ət\ *n, pl* **mullet** *or* **mullets** [ME *molet*, fr. MF *mulet*, fr. L *mullus* red mullet, fr. Gk *myllos*; akin to Gk *melas* black, Skt *malina* dirty,black] **1 :** any of a family (Mugilidae) of valuable food fishes — called also *gray mullet* **2 :** any of a family (Mullidae) of moderate-sized usu. red or golden fishes with two barbels on the chin

mul·li·gan \'məl-i-gən\ *n* [prob. fr. the name *Mulligan*] **:** a stew basically of vegetables and meat or fish

mul·li·ga·taw·ny \,məl-i-gə-'tȯ-nē, -'tän-ē\ *n* [Tamil *miḷakutaṇṇi*, fr. *miḷaku* pepper + *taṇṇi* water] **:** a soup usu. of chicken stock seasoned with curry

mul·lion \'məl-yən\ *n* [prob. alter. of *monial* (mullion)] **:** a slender vertical pier between lights of windows, doors, or screens — **mullion** *vt*

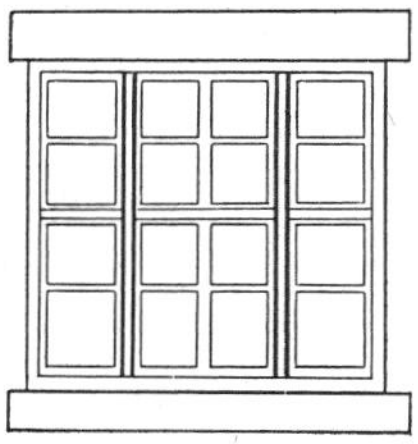

mullions

mull·ite \'məl-,īt\ *n* [*Mull*, island of the Inner Hebrides] **:** a mineral $Al_6Si_2O_{13}$ or $3Al_2O_3.2SiO_2$ that is an orthorhombic silicate of aluminum resistant to corrosion and heat and used as a refractory

multi- *comb form* [ME, fr. MF or L; MF, fr. L, fr. *multus* much, many — more at MELIORATE] **1 a :** many **:** multiple **:** much ⟨*multi*valent⟩ **b :** more than two ⟨*multi*lateral⟩ **c :** more than one ⟨*multi*para⟩ **2 :** many times over ⟨*multi*millionaire⟩

mul·ti·cel·lu·lar \,məl-ti-'sel-yə-lər, -,tī-\ *adj* [ISV] **:** having or consisting of many cells

mul·ti·col·ored \,məl-ti-'kəl-ərd\ *adj* **:** of various colors **:** PARTICOLORED

mul·ti·di·men·sion·al \,məl-tid-ə-'mench-nəl, -ti-(,)dī-, -ən-ᵊl; ,məl-,tīd-ə-'mench-\ *adj* **:** of, relating to, or marked by several dimensions

mul·ti·far·i·ous \,məl-tə-'far-ē-əs, -'fer-\ *adj* [L *multifarius*, fr. *multi-* + *-farius* (akin to *facere* to make, do)] **:** having great variety **:** DIVERSE — **mul·ti·far·i·ous·ly** *adv* — **mul·ti·far·i·ous·ness** *n*

mul·ti·fid \'məl-ti-,fid\ *adj* [L *multifidus*, fr. *multi-* + *-fidus* -fid] **:** cleft into several parts ⟨a ~ leaf⟩ — **mul·ti·fid·ly** *adv*

mul·ti·flo·ra rose \,məl-tə-,flōr-ə-, -,flȯr-\ *n* [NL *multiflora*, specific epithet, lit., having many flowers] **:** a vigorous thorny rose (*Rosa multiflora*) with clusters of small flowers

mul·ti·fold \'məl-ti-,fōld\ *adj* **:** MANIFOLD

mul·ti·form \'məl-ti-,fȯrm\ *adj* [F *multiforme*, fr. L *multiformis*, fr. *multi-* + *-formis* -form] **:** having many forms or appearances — **multiform** *n* — **mul·ti·for·mi·ty** \,məl-ti-'fȯr-mət-ē\ *n*

mul·ti·lat·er·al \,məl-ti-'lat-ə-rəl, -,tī-, -'la-trəl\ *adj* **1 :** having many sides **2 :** participated in by more than two states or parties — **mul·ti·lat·er·al·ly** \-ē\ *adv*

mul·ti·me·dia \-'mēd-ē-ə\ *adj* **:** using, involving, or encompassing several media ⟨a ~ approach to learning⟩ ⟨a ~ exhibition⟩

mul·ti·mil·lion·aire \-,mil-yə-'na(ə)r, -'ne(ə)r, -'mil-yə-,\ *n* **:** one worth many millions

mul·ti·nu·cle·ate \,məl-ti-'n(y)ü-klē-ət, -,tī-\ *or* **mul·ti·nu·cle·ar** \-klē-ər\ *adj* [ISV] **:** having more than two nuclei

mul·tip·a·rous \,məl-'tip-ə-rəs\ *adj* [NL *multiparus*, fr. *multi-* + L *-parus* -parous] **1 :** producing many or more than one at a birth **2 :** having experienced one or more previous parturitions **3 :** producing several lateral axes ⟨a ~ cyme⟩

mul·ti·par·tite \,məl-ti-'pär-,tīt\ *adj* [L *multipartitus*, fr. *multi-* + *partitus*, pp. of *partire* to divide, fr. *part-, pars* part] **1 :** divided into several or many parts **2 :** having numerous members or signatories

mul·ti·ped \'məl-ti-,ped\ *n* [L *multipeda*, fr. *multi-* + *ped-, pes* foot] **:** an animal with more than four feet — **multiped** *adj*

mul·ti·phase \'məl-ti-,fāz\ *adj* **:** having many phases; *specif* **:** POLYPHASE — **mul·ti·pha·sic** \,məl-ti-'fā-zik, -,tī-\ *adj*

[1]**mul·ti·ple** \'məl-tə-pəl\ *adj* [F, fr. L *multiplex*, fr. *multi-* + *-plex* -fold — more at SIMPLE] **1 :** consisting of, including, or involving more than one **2 :** MANY, MANIFOLD **3 :** shared by many **4 :** VARIOUS, COMPLEX **5 a :** being a circuit with a number of conductors in parallel **b :** being a group of terminals which make a circuit available at a number of points **6 :** formed by coalescence of the ripening ovaries of several flowers

[2]**multiple** *n* **1 a :** the product of a quantity by an integer ⟨35 is a ~ of 7⟩ **b :** an assemblage with respect to any of its divisions or parts ⟨lay mines in ~⟩ **2 :** PARALLEL 4b

mul·ti·ple–choice \,məl-tə-pəl-'chȯis\ *adj* **:** having several answers given from which the correct one is to be chosen

multiple factor *n* **:** one of a group of nonallelic genes that according to the multiple-factor hypothesis control various quantitative hereditary characters

multiple sclerosis *n* **:** a diseased condition marked by patches of hardened tissue in the brain or the spinal cord and associated esp. with partial or complete paralysis and jerking muscle tremor

multiple star *n* **:** several stars in close proximity that appear to form a single system

mul·ti·plet \'məl-tə-plət\ *n* **:** a spectrum line having several components

multiple voting *n* **1 :** voting by the same individual at the same election in various places in each of which he possesses the legal qualifications **2 :** illegal voting by one person in two or more constituencies

[1]**mul·ti·plex** \'məl-tə-,pleks\ *adj* [L] **1 :** MANIFOLD, MULTIPLE **2 :** being or relating to a system of transmitting several messages simultaneously on the same circuit or channel

[2]**multiplex** *vt* **:** to send (several messages or signals) by a multiplex system ~ *vi* **:** to multiplex messages or signals

mul·ti·pli·able \'məl-tə-,plī-ə-bəl\ *adj* **:** capable of being multiplied

mul·ti·plic·a·ble \,məl-tə-'plik-ə-bəl\ *adj* **:** MULTIPLIABLE

mul·ti·pli·cand \,məl-tə-pli-'kand\ *n* [L *multiplicandus*, gerundive of *multiplicare*] **:** the number that is to be multiplied by another

mul·tip·li·cate \,məl-'tip-li-kət\ *adj* [ME, fr. L *multiplicatus*, pp.] **1 :** MULTIPLE **2 :** having many folds

mul·ti·pli·ca·tion \,məl-tə-plə-'kā-shən\ *n* [ME *multiplicacioun*, fr. MF *multiplication*, fr. L *multiplication-, multiplicatio*, fr. *multiplicatus*, pp. of *multiplicare* to multiply] **1 a :** the act or process of multiplying **b :** the state of being multiplied **2 :** a mathematical operation that at its simplest is an abbreviated process of adding an integer to itself a specified number of times and that is extended to other numbers in accordance with laws that are valid for integers

mul·ti·pli·ca·tive \,məl-tə-'plik-ət-iv, 'məl-tə-plə-,kāt-\ *adj* **:** tending or having the power to multiply numbers — **mul·ti·pli·ca·tive·ly** *adv*

mul·ti·plic·i·ty \,məl-tə-'plis-ət-ē\ *n* [MF *multiplicité*, fr. LL *multiplicitat-, multiplicitas*, fr. L *multiplic-, multiplex*] **1 :** the quality or state of being multiple or various **2 :** a great number

mul·ti·pli·er \'məl-tə-,plī(-ə)r\ *n* **:** one that multiplies: as **a :** a number by which another number is multiplied **b :** an instrument

or device for multiplying or intensifying some effect **c :** a key-operated machine or mechanism or circuit on a machine that multiplies figures and records the products **d :** the ratio between the ultimate increase of income arising from an increment of investment and the initial new investment itself

1mul·ti·ply \ˈməl-tə-ˌplī\ *vb* [ME *multiplien*, fr. OF *multiplier*, fr. L *multiplicare*, fr. *multiplic-*, *multiplex* multiple] *vt* **1 :** to increase in number esp. greatly or in multiples **:** AUGMENT **2 a :** to combine by multiplication ⟨~ 7 and 8⟩ **b :** to combine with (another number) by multiplication ⟨7 *multiplied* by 8 is 56⟩ ~ *vi* **1 a :** to become greater in number **:** SPREAD **b :** BREED, PROPAGATE **2 :** to perform multiplication **syn** see INCREASE

2mul·ti·ply \-plē\ *adv* **:** in a multiple manner

mul·ti–ply \ˌməl-ti-ˌplī\ *adj* **:** composed of several plies

mul·ti·po·lar \ˌməl-ti-ˈpō-lər, -ˌtī-\ *adj* [ISV] **:** having several poles

mul·ti·ra·cial \-ˈrā-shəl\ *adj* **:** composed of, relating to, or representing various races

mul·ti·stage \ˌməl-ti-ˌstāj\ *adj* **1 :** functioning by stages **2 :** conducted by stages

mul·ti·sto·ry \ˌməl-ti-ˌstōr-ē, -ˌstȯr-\ *adj* **:** having several stories

mul·ti·tude \ˈməl-tə-ˌt(y)üd\ *n* [ME, fr. MF or L; MF, fr. L *multitudin-*, *multitudo*, fr. *multus* much] **1 :** the state of being many **2 :** a great number **:** HOST **3 :** CROWD **4 :** POPULACE, PUBLIC

mul·ti·tu·di·nous \ˌməl-tə-ˈt(y)üd-nəs, -ᵊn-əs\ *adj* **1 :** including a multitude of individuals **:** POPULOUS **2 :** existing in a great multitude **3 :** existing in or consisting of innumerable elements or aspects — **mul·ti·tu·di·nous·ly** *adv* — **mul·ti·tu·di·nous·ness** *n*

mul·tiv·a·lence \ˌməl-ˈtiv-ə-lən(t)s\ *n* **:** the quality or state of having many values, meanings, or appeals

mul·ti·va·lent \ˌməl-ti-ˈvā-lənt, -ˌtī-, *esp in sense 3* ˌməl-ˈtiv-ə-\ *adj* [ISV] **1 :** POLYVALENT **2 :** represented more than twice in the somatic chromosome number ⟨~ chromosomes⟩ **3 :** having many values, meanings, or appeals — **multivalent** *n*

mul·ti·ver·si·ty \ˌməl-ti-ˈvər-sət-ē, -stē\ *n* [*multi-* + *-versity* (as in *university*)] **:** a large university with many component schools, colleges, or divisions, with widely diverse functions (as the teaching of freshmen and the carrying on of advanced research), and with a large staff engaged in activities other than instruction

mul·ti·vol·ume \ˌməl-ti-ˈväl-yəm, -ˌtī-, -(ˌ)yüm\ *or* **mul·ti·vol·umed** \-yəmd, -(ˌ)yümd\ *adj* **:** comprising several volumes

mul·ture \ˈməl-chər, *Scot usu* ˈmüt-ər\ *n* [ME *multyr*, fr. OF *molture*, lit., grinding, fr. (assumed) VL *molitura*, fr. L *molitus*, pp. of *molere* to grind] *chiefly Scot* **:** a fee for grinding grain at a mill

1mum \ˈməm\ *adj* [prob. imit. of a sound made with closed lips] **:** SILENT ⟨keep ~⟩ — often used interjectionally

2mum *vi* **mummed; mum·ming** [ME *mommen*, fr. MF *momer* to go masked] **1 :** to act or play usu. in mask or disguise **2 :** to go about merrymaking in disguise during festivals

3mum *n* [G *mumme*] **:** a strong ale or beer

4mum *n* **:** CHRYSANTHEMUM

mum·ble \ˈməm-bəl\ *vb* **mum·bling** \-b(ə-)liŋ\ [ME *momelen*, of imit. origin] *vi* **:** to utter words in a low confused indistinct manner **:** MUTTER ~ *vt* **1 :** to utter with a low inarticulate voice **2 :** to chew or bite with or as if with toothless gums — **mumble** *n* — **mum·bler** \-b(ə-)lər\ *n*

mum·ble·ty–peg *or* **mum·ble–the–peg** \ˈməm-bəl-ˌpeg, -(b)lē-ˌ, -(b)ə-lē-ˌ, -(b)əl-tē-ˌ, -(b)əl-dē-ˌ, -(b)əl-t͟hə-ˌ, ˈməm-əl-ˌ, ˈməm-lən-ˌ\ *n* [fr. the phrase *mumble the peg*; fr. the loser's originally having to pull out with his teeth a peg driven into the ground] **:** a game in which the players try to flip a knife from various positions so that the blade will stick into the ground

mum·bo jum·bo \ˌməm-(ˌ)bō-ˈjəm-(ˌ)bō\ *n* [*Mumbo Jumbo*, an idol or deity held to have been worshiped in Africa] **1 :** an object of superstitious homage and fear **2 a :** a complicated often ritualistic observance with elaborate trappings **b :** complicated activity intended to obscure and confuse **3 :** unnecessarily involved and incomprehensible language **:** GIBBERISH

mum·mer \ˈməm-ər\ *n* [MF *momeur*, fr. *momer* to go masked] **1 :** an actor in a pantomime; *broadly* **:** ACTOR **2 :** one who goes merrymaking in disguise during festivals

mum·mery \ˈməm-ə-rē\ *n* **1 :** a performance by mummers **2 :** a ridiculous, hypocritical, or pretentious ceremony or performance

mum·mi·fi·ca·tion \ˌməm-i-fə-ˈkā-shən\ *n* **:** the process of mummifying **:** the state of being mummified

mum·mi·fy \ˈməm-i-ˌfī\ *vt* **1 :** to embalm and dry as or as if a mummy **2 a :** to make into or like a mummy **b :** to cause to dry up and shrivel ~ *vi* **:** to dry up and shrivel like a mummy

mum·my \ˈməm-ē\ *n* [ME *mummie* powdered parts of a mummified body used as a drug, fr. MF *momie*, fr. ML *mumia* mummy, powdered mummy, fr. Ar *mūmiyah* bitumen, mummy, fr. Per *mūm* wax] **1 a :** a body embalmed or treated for burial with preservatives after the manner of the ancient Egyptians **b :** a body unusually well preserved **2 :** one resembling a mummy — **mummy** *vb*

1mump \ˈməmp\ *vb* [prob. imit.] *vt*, *chiefly dial* **:** MUMBLE ~ *vi* **1** *dial Eng* **:** GRIN **2 :** to be sulky

2mump *vi* [obs. D *mompen*] *dial Eng* **:** BEG, SPONGE — **mump·er** *n*

mumps \ˈməm(p)s\ *n pl but sing or pl in constr* [fr. pl. of obs. *mump* (grimace)] **:** an acute contagious viral disease marked by fever and by swelling esp. of the parotid gland

munch \ˈmənch\ *vb* [ME *monchen*, prob. of imit. origin] **:** to chew with a crunching sound — **munch·er** *n*

mun·dane \ˌmən-ˈdān, ˈmən-ˌ\ *adj* [ME *mondeyne*, fr. MF *mondain*, fr. LL *mundanus*, fr. L *mundus* world] **1 :** of, relating to, or characteristic of the world **2 :** characterized by the practical, transitory, and ordinary **syn** see EARTHLY — **mun·dane·ly** *adv*

mun·dun·gus \ˌmən-ˈdəŋ-(g)əs\ *n* [modif. of Sp *mondongo* tripe] *archaic* **:** foul-smelling tobacco

mun·go \ˈməŋ-(ˌ)gō\ *n, pl* **mungos** [origin unknown] **:** reclaimed wool of poor quality and very short staple

mu·nic·i·pal \myu̇-ˈnis-(ə-)pəl, *nonstand* ˌmyü-nə-ˈsip-əl\ *adj* [L *municipalis* of a municipality, fr. *municip-*, *municeps* inhabitant of a municipality, lit., undertaker of duties, fr. *munus* duty, service + *capere* to take — more at MEAN, HEAVE] **1 :** of or relating to the internal affairs of a nation or other major political unit **2 a :** of, relating to, or characteristic of a municipality **b :** having local self-government **3 :** restricted to one locality

mu·nic·i·pal·i·ty \myu̇-ˌnis-ə-ˈpal-ət-ē\ *n* **1 :** a primarily urban political unit having corporate status and usu. powers of self-government **2 :** the governing body of a municipality

mu·nic·i·pal·iza·tion \myu̇-ˌnis-(ə-)pə-lə-ˈzā-shən\ *n* **:** the action or result of municipalizing

mu·nic·i·pal·ize \myu̇-ˈnis-ə-pə-ˌlīz\ *vt* **:** to bring under municipal ownership or supervision

mu·nic·i·pal·ly \myu̇-ˈnis-ə-p(ə-)lē\ *adv* **:** by or in terms of a municipality

mu·nif·i·cence \myu̇-ˈnif-(ə-)sən(t)s\ *n* [MF, fr. L *munificentia*, fr. *munificus* generous, fr. *munus* service, gift] **:** the quality or state of being munificent

mu·nif·i·cent \-sənt\ *adj* [back-formation fr. *munificence*] **1 :** very liberal in giving or bestowing **:** LAVISH **2 :** characterized by great liberality or generosity **syn** see LIBERAL — **mu·nif·i·cent·ly** *adv*

mu·ni·ment \ˈmyü-nə-mənt\ *n* [AF, fr. MF, defense, fr. L *munimentum*, fr. *munire* to fortify] **1** *pl* **:** the evidences or writings that enable one to defend the title to an estate or a claim to rights and privileges **2** *archaic* **:** a means of defense

mu·ni·tion \myu̇-ˈnish-ən\ *n* [MF, fr. L *munition-*, *munitio*, fr. *munitus*, pp. of *munire* to fortify, fr. *moenia* walls; akin to OE *mǣre* boundary, L *murus* wall] **1** *archaic* **:** RAMPART, DEFENSE **2 :** ARMAMENT, AMMUNITION — **munition** *vt* **mu·ni·tion·ing** \-(ə-)niŋ\

mun·tin \ˈmənt-ᵊn\ *or* **mun·ting** \-ᵊn, -iŋ\ *n* [alter. of *montant* vertical dividing bar, fr. F, fr. prp. of *monter* to rise — more at MOUNT] **:** a strip separating panes of glass in a sash

munt·jac *also* **munt·jak** \ˈmən(t)-ˌjak, ˈmən-ˌchak\ *n* [prob. modif. of Jav *mindjangan* deer] **:** any of several small deer (genus *Muntiacus*) of southeastern Asia and the East Indies

1mu·ral \ˈmyu̇r-əl\ *adj* [L *muralis*, fr. *murus* wall] **1 :** of, relating to, or resembling a wall **2 :** applied to and made integral with a wall surface

2mural *n* **:** a mural painting — **mu·ral·ist** \-ə-ləst\ *n*

1mur·der \ˈmərd-ər\ *n* [partly fr. ME *murther*, fr. OE *morthor*; partly fr. ME *murdre*, fr. OF, of Gmc origin; akin to OE *morthor*; akin to OHG *mord* murder, L *mort-*, *mors* death, *mori* to die, Gk *brotos* mortal] **1 :** the crime of unlawfully killing a person esp. with malice aforethought **2 :** something very difficult or dangerous

2murder *vb* **mur·der·ing** \-(ə-)riŋ\ *vt* **1 :** to kill (a human being) unlawfully and with premeditated malice **2 :** to slaughter in a brutal manner **3 a :** to put an end to **b :** TEASE, TORMENT **c :** MUTILATE, MANGLE ⟨~s French⟩ ~ *vi* **:** to commit murder **syn** see KILL — **mur·der·er** \-ər-ər\ *n* — **mur·der·ess** \-ə-rəs\ *n*

mur·der·ous \ˈmərd-(ə-)rəs\ *adj* **1 a :** having the purpose or capability of murder **b :** characterized by or causing murder or bloodshed **2 :** OVERWHELMING, DEVASTATING — **mur·der·ous·ly** *adv* — **mur·der·ous·ness** *n*

mure \ˈmyu̇(ə)r\ *vt* [ME *muren*, fr. MF *murer*, fr. LL *murare* fr. L *murus* wall — more at MUNITION] **:** IMMURE

mu·rex \ˈmyu̇(ə)r-ˌeks\ *n, pl* **mu·ri·ces** \ˈmyu̇r-ə-ˌsēz\ *or* **mu·rex·es** [NL, genus name, fr. L, purple shell; akin to Gk *myak-*, *myax* sea-mussel] **:** any of a genus (*Murex*) of marine gastropod mollusks having a rough and often spinose shell, abounding in tropical seas, and yielding a purple dye

mu·ri·ate \ˈmyu̇r-ē-ˌāt\ *n* [F, back-formation fr. (*acide*) *muriatique* muriatic acid] **:** CHLORIDE

mu·ri·at·ic acid \ˌmyu̇r-ē-ˌat-ik-\ *n* [F *muriatique*, fr. L *muriaticus* pickled in brine, fr. *muria* brine; akin to OHG *mos* moss] **:** HYDROCHLORIC ACID

mu·ri·cate \ˈmyu̇r-ə-ˌkāt\ *also* **mu·ri·cat·ed** \-ˌkāt-əd\ *adj* [L *muricatus* spinose like a murex shell, fr. *muric-*, *murex*] **:** roughened with sharp hard points

mu·rid \ˈmyu̇r-əd\ *adj* [deriv. of L *mur-*, *mus* mouse — more at MOUSE] **:** of or relating to a family (Muridae) comprising the typical mice and rats — **murid** *n*

mu·rine \ˈmyu̇(ə)r-ˌīn, ˈmyü-ˌrīn\ *adj* [deriv. of L *mur-*, *mus*] **:** of or relating to a genus (*Mus*) or the subfamily to which it belongs and which includes the common household rats and mice; *also* **:** of, relating to, or involving these rodents and esp. the house mouse ⟨~ typhus⟩ — **murine** *n*

murk \ˈmərk\ *n* [ME *mirke*] **:** DARKNESS, GLOOM; *also* **:** FOG — **murk** *adj*, *archaic*

murk·i·ly \ˈmər-kə-lē\ *adv* **:** in a murky manner **:** DARKLY

murk·i·ness \ˈmər-kē-nəs\ *n* **:** the quality or state of being murky

murky \ˈmər-kē\ *adj* **1 :** characterized by intense darkness or gloominess **2 :** characterized by thickness and heaviness of air **:** FOGGY, MISTY **syn** see DARK

mur·mur \ˈmər-mər\ *n* [ME *murmure*, fr. MF, fr. L *murmur* murmur, roar, of imit. origin] **1 :** a half-suppressed or muttered complaint **:** GRUMBLING **2 a :** a low indistinct but often continuous sound **b :** a soft or gentle utterance **3 :** an atypical sound of the heart indicating a functional or structural abnormality — **murmur** *vb* **mur·mur·ing** \ˈmərm-(ə-)riŋ\ — **mur·mur·er** \ˈmər-mər-ər\ *n*

mur·mur·ous \ˈmərm-(ə-)rəs\ *adj* **:** filled with or characterized by murmurs **:** low and indistinct — **mur·mur·ous·ly** *adv*

mur·phy \ˈmər-fē\ *n* [*Murphy*, a common Irish surname] **:** POTATO

Murphy bed \ˌmər-fē-\ *n* [William L. *Murphy*, 20th cent. Am inventor] **:** a bed that may be folded or swung into a closet

mur·rain \ˈmər-ən, ˈmə-rən\ *n* [ME *moreyne*, fr. MF *morine*, fr. *morir* to die, fr. L *mori* — more at MURDER] **:** a pestilence or plague affecting domestic animals or plants

murre \ˈmər\ *n* [origin unknown] **1 :** any of several guillemots (genus *Uria*); *esp* **:** a common bird (*U. aalge*) of southern seas **2 :** RAZORBILL

mur·rey \ˈmər-ē, ˈmə-rē\ *n* [ME, fr. MF *moré*, fr. ML *moratum*, fr. neut. of *moratus* mulberry colored, fr. L *morum* mulberry — more at MULBERRY] **:** a purplish black **:** MULBERRY

mur·ther \ˈmər-t͟hər\ *chiefly dial var of* MURDER

mus·ca·dine \ˈməs-kə-ˌdīn\ *n* [prob. alter. of *muscatel*] **:** a grape (*Vitis rotundifolia*) of the southern U.S. with musky fruits in small clusters

mus·cae vo·li·tan·tes \ˈməs-ˌ(k)ē-ˌväl-ə-ˈtan-ˌtēz\ *n pl* [NL, lit., flying flies] **:** spots before the eyes due to cells and cell fragments in the vitreous humor and lens

mus·cari \(ˌ)məs-ˈka(ə)r-ē, -ˈke(ə)r-\ *n, pl* **muscari** or **mus·car·is** [deriv. of Gk *moschos* musk —more at MUSK] **:** GRAPE HYACINTH

mus·ca·rine \ˈməs-kə-ˌrēn\ *n* [G *muskarin*, fr. NL *muscaria*, specific epithet of *Amanita muscaria* fly agaric] **:** a quaternary

ammonium base $C_8H_{19}NO_3$ chemically related to choline that is the toxic principle of fly agaric and acts directly on smooth muscle — **mus·ca·rin·ic** \ˌməs-kə-ˈrin-ik\ *adj*

mus·cat \ˈməs-ˌkat, -kət\ *n* [F, fr. Prov, fr. *muscat* musky, fr. *musc* musk, fr. LL *muscus*] **1 :** any of several cultivated grapes used in making wine and raisins **2 :** MUSCATEL

mus·ca·tel \ˌməs-kə-ˈtel\ *n* [ME *muskadelle*, fr. MF *muscadel*, fr. OProv, fr. *muscadel* resembling musk, fr. *muscat*] **1 :** a sweet dessert wine from muscat grapes **2 :** a raisin from muscat grapes

1**mus·cle** \ˈməs-əl\ *n, often attrib* [MF, fr. L *musculus*, fr. dim. of *mus* mouse — more at MOUSE] **1 a :** a tissue that functions to produce motion and is made up of elongated cells capable of contracting when stimulated **b :** an organ that contracts to produce, enhance, or check a particular movement and is made up of muscle tissue and firmly attached at either end to a fixed point **2 a :** muscular strength **:** BRAWN **b :** effective strength **:** POWER

2**muscle** *vi* **mus·cling** \-(ə-)liŋ\ **:** to make one's way by brute strength or by force

mus·cle–bound \ˈməs-əl-ˌbau̇nd\ *adj* **1 :** having some of the muscles tense and enlarged and of impaired elasticity sometimes as a result of excessive exercise **2 :** lacking in flexibility **:** RIGID

muscle sense *n* **:** a positional sense whose end organs lie in the muscles

mus·co·va·do \ˌməs-kə-ˈväd-(ˌ)ō\ *n* [Sp or Pg; Sp (*azúcar*) *mascabado*, lit., separated sugar, fr. Pg (*açúcar*) *mascavado*] **:** unrefined sugar obtained from the juice of the sugarcane by evaporation and draining off the molasses

mus·co·vite \ˈməs-kə-ˌvīt\ *n* [ML or NL *Muscovia, Moscovia* Moscow] **1** *cap* **a :** a native or resident of the ancient principality of Moscow or of the city of Moscow **b :** RUSSIAN **2** [*muscovy* (*glass*)] **:** a mineral essentially $KAl_3Si_3O_{10}(OH)_2$ that is a colorless to pale brown potassium mica — **Muscovite** *adj*

Mus·co·vy duck \ˌməs-ˌkō-vē-\ *n* [*Muscovy*, principality of Moscow, Russia] **:** a large crested duck (*Cairina moschata*) native from Mexico to southern Brazil but widely kept in domestication

muscul- *or* **musculo-** *comb form* [LL *muscul-*, fr. L *musculus*] **:** muscle ⟨*muscul*ar⟩

mus·cu·lar \ˈməs-kyə-lər\ *adj* **1 a :** of, relating to, or constituting muscle **b :** of, relating to, or performed by the muscles **2 :** having well-developed musculature **3 a :** of or relating to physical strength **:** BRAWNY **b :** having strength of expression or character **:** VIGOROUS — **mus·cu·lar·i·ty** \ˌməs-kyə-ˈlar-ət-ē\ *n* — **mus·cu·lar·ly** *adv*

muscular dystrophy *n* **:** a hereditary disease characterized by progressive wasting of muscles

mus·cu·la·ture \ˈməs-kyə-lə-ˌchu̇(ə)r, -chər, -ˌt(y)u̇(ə)r\ *n* [F, fr. L *musculus*] **:** the muscles of an animal or of any part of it as a structural and functional system

mus·cu·lo·skel·e·tal \ˌməs-kyə-(ˌ)lō-ˈskel-ət-ᵊl\ *adj* **:** of, relating to, or involving both musculature and skeleton

1**muse** \ˈmyüz\ *vb* [ME *musen*, fr. MF *muser* to gape, idle, muse, fr. *muse* mouth of an animal, fr. ML *musus*] *vi* **1 :** to become absorbed in thought **:** MEDITATE **2** *archaic* **:** WONDER, MARVEL ~ *vt* **:** to think or say reflectively **syn** see PONDER — **mus·er** *n* — **mus·ing·ly** \ˈmyü-ziŋ-lē\ *adv*

2**muse** *n* **:** a state of deep thought or dreamy abstraction **:** BROWN STUDY

3**muse** *n* [ME, fr. MF, fr. L *Musa*, fr. Gk *Mousa*] **1** *cap* **:** any of the nine sister goddesses in Greek mythology presiding over song and poetry and the arts and sciences **2 :** a source of inspiration; *esp* **:** a guiding genius **3 :** POET

mu·sette \myü-ˈzet\ *n* [F, fr. MF, dim. of *muse* bagpipe, fr. *muser* to muse, play the bagpipe] **1 :** a small bagpipe having a soft sweet tone **2 :** a small knapsack with a shoulder strap used esp. by soldiers for carrying provisions and personal belongings — called also *musette bag*

mu·se·um \myü-ˈzē-əm, ˈmyü-ˌ\ *n* [L *Museum* place for learned occupation, fr. Gk *Mouseion*, fr. neut. of *Mouseios* of the Muses, fr. *Mousa*] **:** an institution devoted to the procurement, care, and display of objects of lasting interest or value; *also* **:** a place where objects are exhibited

1**mush** \ˈməsh\ *n* [prob. alter. of *mash*] **1 :** cornmeal boiled in water **2 :** something soft and spongy or shapeless **3 a :** weak sentimentality **:** DRIVEL **b :** mawkish amorousness

2**mush** *vt, chiefly dial* **:** to reduce to mush **:** CRUMBLE ~ *vi, of an airplane* **:** to fly in a partly stalled condition with controls ineffective; *also* **:** to fail to gain altitude — **mush·er** *n*

3**mush** *vi* [prob. fr. AmerF *moucher* to go fast, fr. F *mouche* fly, fr. L *musca* — more at MIDGE] **:** to travel esp. over snow with a sled drawn by dogs — often used as a command to a dog team

4**mush** *n* **:** a trip esp. across snow with a dog team

mush·i·ly \ˈməsh-ə-lē\ *adv* **:** in a mushy manner

mush·i·ness \ˈməsh-ē-nəs\ *n* **:** the quality or state of being mushy

1**mush·room** \ˈməsh-ˌrüm, -ˌru̇m\ *n, often attrib* [ME *musseroun*, fr. MF *mousseron*, fr. LL *mussirion-, mussirio*] **1 a :** an enlarged complex aerial fleshy fruiting body of a fungus (as of the class Basidiomycetes) that consists typically of a stem bearing a flattened cap; *esp* **:** one that is edible **b :** FUNGUS 1 **2** *archaic* **:** UPSTART **3 :** something resembling a mushroom

2**mushroom** *vi* **1 :** to spring up suddenly or multiply rapidly **2 a** *of a bullet* **:** to flatten at the end at impact **b :** to well up and spread out laterally from a central source

mushy \ˈməsh-ē\ *adj* **1 :** having the consistency of mush **:** SOFT **2 :** excessively tender or emotional; *esp* **:** mawkishly amorous

mu·sic \ˈmyü-zik\ *n, often attrib* [ME *musik*, fr. OF *musique*, fr. L *musica*, fr. Gk *mousikē* any art presided over by the Muses, fr. fem. of *mousikos* of the Muses, fr. *Mousa* Muse] **1 a :** the science or art of incorporating intelligible combinations of tones into a composition having structure and continuity **b :** vocal or instrumental sounds having rhythm, melody, or harmony **2 :** an agreeable sound **:** EUPHONY **3 :** punishment for a misdeed **4 :** a musical accompaniment **5 :** a musical ensemble **6 :** the score of a musical composition set down on paper

1**mu·si·cal** \ˈmyü-zi-kəl\ *adj* **1 a :** of or relating to music **b :** having the pleasing harmonious qualities of music **:** MELODIOUS **2 :** having an interest in or talent for music **3 :** set to or accompanied by music **4 :** of or relating to musicians or music lovers — **mu·si·cal·ly** \-k(ə-)lē\ *adv*

2**musical** *n* **1** *archaic* **:** MUSICALE **2 :** a film or theatrical production consisting of musical numbers and dialogue based upon a unifying plot — called also *musical comedy*

musical chairs *n pl but sing in constr* **:** a game in which players march to music around a row of chairs numbering one less than the players and scramble for seats when the music stops

mu·si·cale \ˌmyü-zi-ˈkal\ *n* [F *soirée musicale*, lit., musical evening] **:** a social entertainment with music as the leading feature

mu·si·cal·i·ty \ˌmyü-zi-ˈkal-ət-ē\ *n* **1 :** the quality or state of being musical **:** MELODIOUSNESS **2 :** sensitivity to, knowledge of, or talent for music

musical saw *n* **:** a handsaw played by sounding the flexed blade with a hammer or violin bow

music box *n* **:** a container enclosing an apparatus that reproduces music mechanically when activated by clockwork

music drama *n* **:** an opera in which the action is not interrupted by formal song divisions (as recitatives or arias) and the music is determined solely by dramatic appropriateness

music hall *n* **:** a vaudeville theater

mu·si·cian \myu̇-ˈzish-ən\ *n* **:** one skilled in music; *esp* **:** a composer or professional performer of music — **mu·si·cian·ly** \-lē\ *adj* — **mu·si·cian·ship** \-ˌship\ *n*

music of the spheres : an ethereal harmony thought by the Pythagoreans to be produced by the vibration of the celestial spheres

mu·si·co·log·i·cal \ˌmyü-zi-kə-ˈläj-i-kəl\ *adj* **:** of or relating to musicology

mu·si·col·o·gist \ˌmyü-zi-ˈkäl-ə-jəst\ *n* **:** a specialist in musicology

mu·si·col·o·gy \-jē\ *n* [It *musicologia*, fr. L *musica* music + *-logia* -logy] **:** a study of music as a branch of knowledge or field of research; *esp* **:** the historical and theoretical investigation and analysis of specific types of music

1**mus·ing** *n* **:** MEDITATION

2**musing** *adj* **:** thoughtfully abstracted **:** MEDITATIVE — **mus·ing·ly** \ˈmyü-ziŋ-lē\ *adv*

musk \ˈməsk\ *n* [ME *muske*, fr. MF *musc*, fr. LL *muscus*, fr. Gk *moschos*, fr. Per *mushk*, fr. Skt *muṣka* testicle, fr. dim. of *mūṣ* mouse; akin to OE *mūs* mouse] **1 a :** a substance with a penetrating persistent odor obtained from a sac beneath the abdominal skin of the male musk deer and used as a perfume fixative; *also* **:** a similar substance from another animal or a synthetic substitute **b :** the odor of musk; *also* **:** an odor resembling musk esp. in heaviness or persistence **2 :** any of various plants with musky odors; *esp* **:** MUSK PLANT

musk deer *n* **:** a small heavy-limbed deer (*Moschus moschiferus*) of central Asiatic uplands valued for the musk of the male

mus·keg \ˈməs-ˌkeg, -ˌkāg\ *n* [of Algonquian origin; akin to Ojibwa *mūskeg* grassy bog] **1 :** BOG; *esp* **:** a sphagnum bog of northern No. America often with tussocks **2 :** a usu. thick deposit of partially decayed vegetable matter of wet boreal regions

mus·kel·lunge \ˈməs-kə-ˌlənj\ *n, pl* **muskellunge** [of Algonquian origin; akin to Cree *maskinonge* muskellunge] **:** a large No. American pike (*Esox masquinongy*) that may weigh 60 to 80 pounds and is prized as a sport fish

mus·ket \ˈməs-kət\ *n* [MF *mousquet*, fr. OIt *moschetto* arrow for a crossbow, musket, fr. dim. of *mosca* fly, fr. L *musca* — more at MIDGE] **:** a heavy large-caliber shoulder firearm; *broadly* **:** a shoulder gun carried by infantry

mus·ke·teer \ˌməs-kə-ˈti(ə)r\ *n* [modif. of MF *mousquetaire*, fr. *mousquet*] **:** a soldier armed with a musket

mus·ket·ry \ˈməs-kə-trē\ *n* **1 :** MUSKETS **2 :** MUSKETEERS **3 a :** musket fire **b :** the art or science of using small arms esp. in battle

musk·i·ness \ˈməs-kē-nəs\ *n* **:** the quality or state of being musky

musk·mel·on \ˈməsk-ˌmel-ən\ *n* **:** a usu. sweet musky-odored edible melon that is the fruit of a trailing or climbing Asiatic herbaceous vine (*Cucumis melo*): as **a :** any of various melons of small or moderate size with netted skin that include most of the muskmelons cultivated in No. America **b :** CANTALOUPE 1 **c :** WINTER MELON

Mus·ko·ge·an *or* **Mus·kho·ge·an** \(ˌ)məs-ˈkō-gē-ən\ *n* **:** a language family of southeastern U.S. that includes Muskogee

Mus·ko·gee \-ˈkō-gē\ *n, pl* **Muskogee** *or* **Muskogees** **1 :** a member of a people of Georgia and eastern Alabama constituting the nucleus of the Creek Confederacy **2 :** the language of the Muskogees and of some of the Seminoles

musk–ox \ˈməs-ˌkäks\ *n* **:** a heavy-set shaggy-coated wild ox (*Ovibos moschatus*) now confined to Greenland and the barren northern lands of No. America

musk plant *n* **:** a yellow-flowered No. American herb (*Mimulus moschatus*) of the figwort family with hairy foliage formerly of musky odor

musk·rat \ˈməs-ˌkrat\ *n, pl* **muskrat** *or* **muskrats** [prob. by folk etymology fr. a word of Algonquian origin; akin to Natick *musquash* muskrat] **:** an aquatic rodent (*Ondatra zibethica*) of the U.S. and Canada with a long scaly laterally compressed tail, webbed hind feet, and dark glossy brown fur; *also* **:** its fur or pelt

musk rose *n* **:** a rose (*Rosa moschata*) of the Mediterranean region with flowers having a musky odor

musk turtle *n* **:** a small American freshwater turtle (genera *Sternotherus* and *Kinosternon*); *esp* **:** a turtle (*S. odoratus*) having a strong musky odor

musky \ˈməs-kē\ *adj* **:** having an odor of or resembling musk

Mus·lim \ˈməz-ləm, ˈmu̇s-, ˈmu̇z-\ *n* [Ar *muslim*, lit., one who surrenders (to God)] **:** an adherent of Islam — **Muslim** *adj*

mus·lin \ˈməz-lən\ *n, often attrib* [F *mousseline*, fr. It *mussolina*, fr. Ar *mawṣilīy* of Mosul, fr. al-*Mawṣil* Mosul, Iraq] **:** a plain-woven sheer to coarse cotton fabric

mus·quash \ˈməs-ˌkwäsh, -ˌkwȯsh\ *n* [of Algonquian origin; akin to Natick *musquash* muskrat] **:** MUSKRAT

1**muss** \ˈməs\ *n* [origin unknown] **1** *obs* **a :** a game in which players scramble for small objects thrown to the ground **b :** SCRAMBLE **2** *slang* **:** a confused conflict **:** ROW **3 :** a state of disorder

2**muss** *vt* **:** to make untidy **:** DISARRANGE

mus·sel \ˈməs-əl\ *n, often attrib* [ME *muscle*, fr. OE *muscelle*; akin to OHG *muscula* mussel; both fr. a prehistoric WGmc word borrowed fr. (assumed) VL *muscula*, fr. L *musculus* muscle, mussel] **1 :** a marine bivalve mollusk (esp. genus *Mytilus*) usu. having a dark elongated shell **2 :** a freshwater bivalve mollusk (as of *Unio, Anodonta*, or related genera) that is esp. abundant in rivers of the central U.S. and has a shell with a lustrous nacreous lining

muss·i·ly \ˈməs-ə-lē\ *adv* **:** in a mussy manner

muss·i·ness \'məs-ē-nəs\ *n* **:** the quality or state of being mussy

Mus·sul·man *also* **Mus·sal·man** \'məs-əl-mən\ *n, pl* **Mussulmen** *or* **Mussulmans** [Turk *müslüman* & Per *musulmān*, modif. of Ar *muslim*] **:** MUSLIM

mussy \'məs-ē\ *adj* **:** characterized by clutter or muss **:** MESSY

¹must \məs(t), 'məst\ *vb, pres & past all persons* **must** [ME *moste*, fr. OE *mōste*, past indic. & subj. of *mōtan* to be allowed to, have to; akin to OHG *muozan* to be allowed to, have to, OE *metan* to measure — more at METE] *verbal auxiliary* **1 a :** is commanded or requested to ⟨you ~ stop⟩ **b :** is urged to **:** ought by all means to ⟨you ~ read that book⟩ **2 :** is compelled by physical necessity to ⟨man ~ eat to live⟩ **:** is required by immediate or future need or purpose to ⟨we ~ hurry if we want to catch the bus⟩ **3 a :** is obliged to **:** is compelled by social considerations to ⟨I ~ say you're looking much better⟩ **b :** is required by law, custom, or moral conscience to ⟨we ~ obey the rules⟩ **c :** is determined to ⟨if you ~ go at least wait till the storm is over⟩ **d :** is unreasonably or perversely compelled to ⟨why ~ you be so stubborn⟩ **4 :** is logically inferred or supposed to ⟨it ~ be time⟩ **5 :** is compelled by fate or by natural law to ⟨what ~ be will be⟩ **6 :** was presumably certain to **:** was bound to ⟨if he had really been there I ~ have seen him⟩ **7** *dial* **:** MAY, SHALL — used chiefly in questions **~** *vi, archaic* **:** ought to go **:** is obliged to go ⟨I ~ to Coventry —Shak.⟩

²must \'məst\ *n, often attrib* **1 :** an imperative need or duty **:** REQUIREMENT **2 :** an indispensable item **:** ESSENTIAL

³must *n* [ME, fr. OE, fr. L *mustum*] **:** the expressed juice of grapes or other fruit before and during fermentation

⁴must *n* [MF, alter. of *musc* musk] **1 :** MUSK **2 :** MUSTINESS, MOLD

mustache *var of* MOUSTACHE

mus·ta·chio \(,)mə-'stash-(,)ō, -'stäsh-, -ē-,ō\ *n* [Sp & It; Sp *mostacho*, fr. It *mustaccio*] **:** MOUSTACHE; *esp* **:** a large moustache — **mus·ta·chioed** \-(,)ōd, -ē-,ōd\ *adj*

mus·tang \'məs-,taŋ\ *n* [MexSp *mestengo*, fr. Sp, stray, fr. *mesteño* strayed, fr. *mesta* annual roundup of cattle that disposed of strays, fr. ML (*animalia*) *mixta* mixed animals] **:** the small hardy naturalized horse of the western plains directly descended from horses brought in by the Spaniards; *also* **:** BRONCO

mus·tard \'məs-tərd\ *n, often attrib* [ME, fr. OF *mostarde*, fr. *moust* must, fr. L *mustum*] **1 a :** a pungent yellow powder of the seeds of a common mustard used as a condiment or in medicine as a stimulant and diuretic, an emetic, or a counterirritant **b** *slang* **:** ZEST **2 :** any of several herbs (genus *Brassica* of the family Cruciferae, the mustard family) with lyrately lobed leaves, yellow flowers, and linear beaked pods **3 a :** MUSTARD GAS **b :** NITROGEN MUSTARD

mustard gas *n* **:** an irritant vesicant oily liquid $(ClCH_2CH_2)_2S$ used as a war gas

mustard plaster *n* **:** a counterirritant and rubefacient plaster containing powdered mustard

¹mus·ter \'məs-tər\ *vb* **mus·ter·ing** \-t(ə-)riŋ\ [ME *mustren* to show, muster, fr. OF *monstrer*, fr. L *monstrare* to show, fr. *monstrum* evil omen, monster — more at MONSTER] *vt* **1 a :** ENLIST **b :** to cause to gather **:** CONVENE **c :** to call the roll of **2 a :** to bring together **:** COLLECT **b :** to call forth **:** ROUSE **3 :** to amount to **:** COMPRISE **~** *vi* **:** to come together **:** CONGREGATE **syn** see SUMMON

²muster *n* **1 :** a representative specimen **:** SAMPLE **2 a :** an act of assembling; *specif* **:** formal military inspection **b :** critical examination **c :** an assembled group **:** COLLECTION **d :** INVENTORY

muster out *vt* **:** to discharge from service

muster roll *n* **:** INVENTORY, ROSTER; *specif* **:** a register of all the officers and men in a military unit or ship's company

musth *or* **must** \'məst\ *n* [Hindi *mast* intoxicated, fr. Per; akin to OE *mete* meat] **:** a periodic state of frenzy of the bull elephant usu. connected with the rutting season

must·i·ly \'məs-tə-lē\ *adv* **:** in a musty manner

must·i·ness \'məs-tē-nəs\ *n* **:** the quality or state of being musty

mustn't \'məs-ᵊnt\ **:** must not

musty \'məs-tē\ *adj* **1 a :** impaired by damp or mildew **:** MOLDY **b :** tasting of mold **c :** smelling of damp and decay **:** FUSTY **2 a :** TRITE, STALE **b :** ANTIQUATED, SUPERANNUATED **syn** see MALODOROUS

mu·ta·bil·i·ty \,myüt-ə-'bil-ət-ē\ *n* **:** the quality or state of being mutable or of being capable of mutation

mu·ta·ble \'myüt-ə-bəl\ *adj* [L *mutabilis*, fr. *mutare* to change — more at MISS] **1 :** prone to change **:** INCONSTANT **2 a :** capable of change or of being changed in form, quality, or nature **b :** capable of or liable to mutation — **mu·ta·ble·ness** *n* — **mu·ta·bly** \-blē\ *adv*

mu·ta·fa·cient \,myüt-ə-'fā-shənt\ *adj* [*mutation* + L *facient-, faciens*, prp. of *facere* to make, do — more at DO] **:** capable of inducing biological mutation

mu·ta·gen·ic \,myüt-ə-'jen-ik\ *adj* [*mutation* + *-genic*] **:** capable of inducing mutation — **mu·ta·gen·i·cal·ly** \-i-k(ə-)lē\ *adv*

mu·tant \'myüt-ᵊnt\ *adj* [L *mutant-, mutans*, prp. of *mutare*] **:** of, relating to, or produced by mutation — **mutant** *n*

mu·tate \'myü-,tāt, myü-'\ *vb* [L *mutatus*, pp. of *mutare*] *vt* **:** to cause to undergo mutation **~** *vi* **:** to undergo mutation

mu·ta·tion \myü-'tā-shən\ *n* **1 :** a significant and basic alteration **:** CHANGE **2 :** UMLAUT **3 a :** a hypothetical sudden fundamental change in heredity producing new individuals basically unlike their parents **b :** a relatively permanent change in hereditary material involving either a physical change in chromosome relations or a fundamental change in genes and occurring either in germ cells or in somatic cells but with only those in germ cells being capable of perpetuation by sexual reproduction **c** (1) **:** an individual or strain resulting from mutation (2) **:** an animal of a domesticated strain that differs esp. in coat color from the wild type **syn** see CHANGE — **mu·ta·tion·al** \-shnəl, -shən-ᵊl\ *adj* — **mu·ta·tion·al·ly** \-ē\ *adv* — **mu·ta·tive** \'myü-,tāt-iv, 'myüt-ət-\ *adj*

mu·ta·tis mu·tan·dis \mü-,tät-ə-smü-'tän-dəs, -,tät-(,)ē-smü-'tän-,dēs\ *adv* [L] **:** with the necessary changes having been made

mutch·kin \'məch-kən\ *n* [ME (Sc) *muchekyn*] **:** a Scotch unit of liquid capacity equal to 0.90 pint

¹mute \'myüt\ *adj* [ME *muet*, fr. MF, fr. OF *mu*, fr. L *mutus*; akin to OHG *māwen* to cry out, Gk *mytēs* mute] **1 :** unable to speak **:** DUMB **2 a :** characterized by absence of speech **b :** refusing to plead directly or stand trial ⟨the prisoner stands ~⟩ **3 a :** contributing nothing to the pronunciation of a word ⟨the *b* in *plumb* is ~⟩ **b :** contributing to the pronunciation of a word but not representing the nucleus of a syllable ⟨the *e* in *mate* is ~⟩ — **mute·ly** *adv* — **mute·ness** *n* — **mut·ism** \'myüt-,iz-əm\ *n*

²mute *n* **1 :** a person who cannot or does not speak **2 :** STOP 9 **3 :** a device on a musical instrument serving to reduce, soften, or muffle its tone

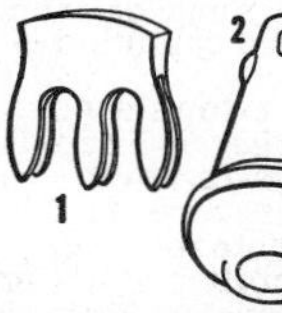

mutes 3: *1* for violin, *2* for trumpet

³mute *vt* **1 :** to muffle or reduce the sound of **2 :** to tone down (a color)

⁴mute *vi* [ME *muten*, fr. MF *meutir*] *of a bird* **:** VOID

mu·ti·cate \'myüt-ə-,kāt\ *or* **mu·ti·cous** \'myüt-i-kəs\ *adj* [L *muticus*] **:** lacking an awn or point

mu·ti·late \'myüt-ᵊl-,āt\ *vt* [L *mutilatus*, pp. of *mutilare*, fr. *mutilus* mutilated; akin to L *muticus* docked, OIr *mut* short] **1 :** to cut off or permanently destroy a limb or essential part of **:** CRIPPLE **2 :** to cut up or alter radically so as to make imperfect — **mu·ti·la·tion** \,myüt-ᵊl-'ā-shən\ *n* — **mu·ti·la·tor** \'myüt-ᵊl-,āt-ər\ *n*

mu·tine \'myüt-ᵊn\ *vi* [MF (*se*) *mutiner*] *obs* **:** REBEL, MUTINY

mu·ti·neer \,myüt-ᵊn-'i(ə)r\ *n* **:** one that mutinies

mu·ti·nous \'myüt-ᵊn-əs, 'myüt-nəs\ *adj* **1 a :** disposed to or in a state of mutiny **:** REBELLIOUS **b :** TURBULENT, UNRULY **2 :** of, relating to, or constituting mutiny — **mu·ti·nous·ly** *adv* — **mu·ti·nous·ness** *n*

mu·ti·ny \'myüt-ᵊn-ē, 'myüt-nē\ *n* [*mutine* to rebel, fr. MF (*se*) *mutiner*, fr. *mutin* mutinous, fr. *meute* revolt, fr. (assumed) VL *movita*, fr. fem. of *movitus*, alter. of L *motus*, pp. of *movēre* to move] **1** *obs* **:** TUMULT **2 :** willful refusal to obey constituted authority; *specif* **:** revolt against a superior officer **syn** see REBELLION — **mutiny** *vi*

mutt \'mət\ *n* [short for *muttonhead* (dull-witted person)] **1 :** a stupid or commonplace person **2 :** a mongrel dog **:** CUR

mut·ter \'mət-ər\ *vb* [ME *muteren*; akin to L *muttire* to mutter, *mutus* mute] *vi* **1 :** to utter indistinctly or with a low voice and lips partly closed **2 :** to murmur complainingly or angrily **:** GRUMBLE **~** *vt* **:** to utter esp. in a low or imperfectly articulated manner — **mutter** *n* — **mut·ter·er** \-ər-ər\ *n*

mut·ton \'mət-ᵊn\ *n* [ME *motoun*, fr. OF *moton* ram, wether, of Celt origin; akin to MBret *mout* wether] **:** the flesh of a mature sheep — **mut·tony** \'mət-ᵊn-ē, -nē\ *adj*

mut·ton·chops \'mət-ᵊn-,chäps\ *n pl* **:** side-whiskers that are narrow at the temple and broad and round by the lower jaws

mu·tu·al \'myüch-(ə-)wəl, 'myü-chəl\ *adj* [ME, fr. MF *mutuel*, fr. L *mutuus* lent, borrowed, mutual; akin to L *mutare* to change — more at MISS] **1 a :** given and received in equal amount **b :** having the same feelings one for the other **c :** COMMON **d :** JOINT **2 :** characterized by intimacy **3 :** of or relating to a plan whereby the members of an organization share in the profits and expenses; *specif* **:** of, relating to, or taking the form of an insurance method in which the policyholders constitute the members of the insuring company **syn** see RECIPROCAL — **mu·tu·al·ly** \-ē\ *adv*

mutual fund *n* **:** an open-end investment company that invests money of its shareholders in a usu. diversified group of securities of other corporations

mu·tu·al·ism \'myüch-(ə-)wə-,liz-əm, 'myü-chə-,liz-\ *n* **1 :** the doctrine or practice of mutual dependence as the condition of individual and social welfare **2 :** mutually beneficial association between different kinds of organisms — **mu·tu·al·ist** \-ləst\ *n* — **mu·tu·al·is·tic** \,myüch-(ə-)wə-'lis-tik, ,myü-chə-'lis-\ *adj*

mu·tu·al·i·ty \,myü-chə-'wal-ət-ē\ *n* **1 :** the quality or state of being mutual **2 :** a sharing of sentiments **:** INTIMACY

mu·tu·al·iza·tion \,myüch-(ə-)wə-lə-'zā-shən, ,myü-chə-lə-\ *n* **:** the act or action of making or becoming mutual

mu·tu·al·ize \'myüch-(ə-)wə-,līz, 'myü-chə-,līz\ *vt* **1 :** to make mutual **2 :** to convert (a corporation) into a mutual plan by purchase and retirement of its stocks

mutuel *n* **:** PARI-MUTUEL

mu·zhik \mü-'zhēk, -'zhik\ *n* [Russ] **:** a Russian peasant

muz·zi·ly \'məz-ə-lē\ *adv* **:** in a muzzy manner

muz·zi·ness \'məz-ē-nəs\ *n* **:** the quality or state of being muzzy

¹muz·zle \'məz-əl\ *n* [ME *musell*, fr. MF *musel*, fr. dim. of *muse* mouth of an animal, fr. ML *musus*] **1 :** the projecting jaws and nose of an animal **:** SNOUT **2 a :** a fastening or covering for the mouth of an animal used to prevent eating or biting **b :** something that restrains normal expression **3 :** the open end or mouth of an implement; *esp* **:** the discharging end of a weapon

²muzzle *vt* **muz·zling** \-(ə-)liŋ\ **1 :** to fit with a muzzle **2 :** to restrain from expression **:** GAG — **muz·zler** \-(ə-)lər\ *n*

muz·zy \'məz-ē\ *adj* [perh. blend of *muddled* and *fuzzy*] **1 :** muddled or confused in mind **:** DULL **2 :** BLURRED

my \(')mī, mə\ *adj* [ME, fr. OE *mīn*, fr. *mīn*, suppletive gen. of *ic* I; akin to OE *mē* me] **1 :** of or relating to me or myself esp. as possessor ⟨~ head⟩, agent ⟨kept ~ promise⟩, or object of an action ⟨~ injuries⟩ **2** — used interjectionally to express surprise and sometimes reduplicated ⟨~ oh ~⟩; used also interjectionally with names of various parts of the body to express doubt or disapproval ⟨~ foot⟩

my- *or* **myo-** *comb form* [NL, fr. Gk, fr. *mys* mouse, muscle — more at MOUSE] **:** muscle ⟨*myo*graph⟩

my·al·gia \mī-'al-j(ē-)ə\ *n* [NL] **:** pain in one or more muscles — **my·al·gic** \-jik\ *adj*

my·as·the·nia \,mī-əs-'thē-nē-ə\ *n* [NL] **:** muscular debility — **my·as·then·ic** \-'then-ik\ *adj*

myc- *or* **myco-** *comb form* [NL, fr. Gk *mykēt-, mykēs* fungus; akin to Gk *myxa* nasal mucus] **:** fungus ⟨*myc*ology⟩ ⟨*myc*osis⟩

my·ce·li·al \mī-'sē-lē-əl\ *adj* **:** of, relating to, or characterized by mycelium

my·ce·li·um \-lē-əm\ *n, pl* **my·ce·lia** \-lē-ə\ [NL, fr. *myc-* + Gk *hēlos* nail, wart, callus] **:** the mass of interwoven filamentous hyphae that forms esp. the vegetative portion of the thallus of a fungus; *also* **:** a similar mass of filaments formed by a higher bacterium

My·ce·nae·an \ˌmī-sə-ˈnē-ən\ *also* **My·ce·ni·an** \mī-ˈsē-nē-ən\ *adj* **:** of, relating to, or characteristic of Mycenae, its people, the period (1400 to 1100 B.C.) of Mycenae's political ascendancy, or the Bronze Age Mycenaean culture of the eastern Mediterranean area

my·ce·to·ma \ˌmī-sə-ˈtō-mə\ *n* [NL, fr. Gk *mykēt-, mykēs*] **:** a condition marked by invasion of the deep subcutaneous tissues with fungi or actinomycetes; *also* **:** a tumorous mass occurring in such a condition — **my·ce·to·ma·tous** \ˌmī-sə-ˈtäm-ət-əs, -ˈtōm-\ *adj*

my·ce·toph·a·gous \ˌmī-sə-ˈtäf-ə-gəs\ *adj* [Gk *mykēt-, mykēs* + E *-phagous*] **:** feeding on fungi

my·ce·to·zo·an \ˌmī-ˌsēt-ə-ˈzō-ən\ *n* [NL *Mycetozoa*, order of protozoans, fr. Gk *mykēt-, mykēs* + NL *-zoa*] **:** SLIME MOLD — **mycetozoan** *adj*

my·co·bac·te·ri·um \ˌmī-kō-(ˌ)bak-ˈtir-ē-əm\ *n* [NL, genus name, fr. *myc-* + *Bacterium*] **:** any of a genus (*Mycobacterium*) of nonmotile aerobic bacteria that are difficult to stain and include numerous saprophytes and the organisms causing tuberculosis and leprosy

my·co·log·ic \ˌmī-kə-ˈläj-ik\ *adj* **:** of or relating to mycology — **my·co·log·i·cal** \-i-kəl\ *adj* — **my·co·log·i·cal·ly** \-i-k(ə-)lē\ *adv*

my·col·o·gist \mī-ˈkäl-ə-jəst\ *n* **:** a specialist in mycology

my·col·o·gy \-jē\ *n* [NL *mycologia*, fr. *myc-* + L *-logia* -logy] **1 :** a branch of botany dealing with fungi **2 :** fungal life

my·coph·a·gist \mī-ˈkäf-ə-jəst\ *n* [*mycophagy*, fr. *myc-* + *-phagy*] **:** one that eats fungi (as mushrooms) — **my·coph·a·gous** \-ə-gəs\ *adj* — **my·coph·a·gy** \-ə-jē\ *n*

my·cor·rhi·za \ˌmī-kə-ˈrī-zə\ *n, pl* **my·cor·rhi·zae** \-ˈrī-ˌzē\ *or* **mycorrhizas** [NL, fr. *myc-* + Gk *rhiza* root — more at ROOT] **:** the symbiotic association of the mycelium of a fungus with the roots of a seed plant — **my·cor·rhi·zal** \-zəl\ *adj*

my·co·sis \mī-ˈkō-səs\ *n* [NL] **:** infection with or disease caused by a fungus — **my·cot·ic** \-ˈkät-ik\ *adj*

my·dri·a·sis \mə-ˈdrī-ə-səs\ *n* [L, fr. Gk] **:** a long-continued or excessive dilatation of the pupil of the eye — **myd·ri·at·ic** \ˌmid-rē-ˈat-ik\ *adj or n*

myel- *or* **myelo-** *comb form* [NL, fr. Gk, fr. *myelos*, fr. *mys* mouse, muscle — more at MOUSE] **:** marrow **:** spinal cord ⟨*myel*encephalon⟩

my·el·en·ce·phal·ic \ˌmī-ə-ˌlen(t)-sə-ˈfal-ik\ *adj* **:** of or relating to the myelencephalon

my·el·en·ceph·a·lon \ˌmī-ə-(ˌ)len-ˈsef-ə-ˌlän, -lən\ *n* [NL] **:** the posterior portion of the rhombencephalon: **a :** MEDULLA OBLONGATA **b :** the posterior part of the medulla oblongata that is continuous with the spinal cord

my·elin \ˈmī-ə-lən\ *also* **my·eline** \-lən, -ˌlēn\ *n* [ISV] **:** a soft white somewhat fatty material that forms a thick medullary sheath about the axis cylinder of medullated nerve fibers — **my·elin·ic** \ˌmī-ə-ˈlin-ik\ *adj*

myelin sheath *n* **:** MEDULLARY SHEATH

my·eli·tis \ˌmī-ə-ˈlīt-əs\ *n* [NL] **:** inflammation of the spinal cord or of the bone marrow

my·elog·e·nous \ˌmī-ə-ˈläj-ə-nəs\ *also* **my·elo·gen·ic** \ˌmī-ə-lō-ˈjen-ik\ *adj* [ISV] **:** of, relating to, originating in, or produced by the bone marrow ⟨~ sarcoma⟩

my·eloid \ˈmī-ə-ˌlȯid\ *adj* [ISV] **1 :** of or relating to the spinal cord **2 :** of, relating to, or resembling bone marrow

my·elo·ma \ˌmī-ə-ˈlō-mə\ *n* [NL] **:** a primary tumor of the bone marrow — **my·elo·ma·tous** \-ˈläm-ət-əs, -ˈlōm-\ *adj*

my·ia·sis \mī-ˈī-ə-səs, mē-\ *n* [NL, fr. Gk *myia* fly — more at MIDGE] **:** infestation with fly maggots

my·na *or* **my·nah** \ˈmī-nə\ *n* [Hindi *mainā*, fr. Skt *madana*] **:** any of various Asiatic starlings (esp. genera *Acridotheres, Gracula*, and *Sturnus*); *esp* **:** a dark brown slightly crested bird (*A. tristis*) of southeastern Asia

myn·heer \mə-ˈne(ə)r\ *n* [D *mijnheer*, fr. *mijn* my + *heer* master, sir] **:** a male Netherlander — used as a title equivalent to *Mister*

myo·car·di·al \ˌmī-ə-ˈkärd-ē-əl\ *adj* **:** of, relating to, or involving the myocardium

myo·car·dio·graph \ˌmī-ə-ˈkärd-ē-ə-ˌgraf\ *n* **:** a recording instrument for making a tracing of the action of the heart

myo·car·di·tis \ˌmī-ə-(ˌ)kär-ˈdīt-əs\ *n* [NL] **:** inflammation of the myocardium

myo·car·di·um \ˌmī-ə-ˈkärd-ē-əm\ *n* [NL, fr. *my-* + Gk *kardia* heart — more at HEART] **:** the middle muscular layer of the heart wall

myo·gen·ic \ˌmī-ə-ˈjen-ik\ *adj* [ISV] **:** originating in muscle

myo·glo·bin \-ˈglō-bən, ˈmī-ə-ˌ\ *n* [ISV] **:** a red iron-containing protein pigment in muscles that is similar to hemoglobin

myo·log·ic \ˌmī-ə-ˈläj-ik\ *adj* **:** of or relating to myology — **myo·log·i·cal** \-i-kəl\ *adj*

my·ol·o·gy \mī-ˈäl-ə-jē\ *n* [F or NL; F *myologie*, fr. NL *myologia*, fr. *my-* + L *-logia* -logy] **:** a scientific study of muscles

my·o·ma \mī-ˈō-mə\ *n, pl* **myomas** *or* **my·o·ma·ta** \-ˈō-mət-ə\ [NL] **:** a tumor consisting of muscle tissue — **my·o·ma·tous** \mī-ˈäm-ət-əs, -ˈōm-\ *adj*

myo·neu·ral \ˌmī-ō-ˈn(y)u̇r-əl\ *adj* **:** of or relating to both muscle and nerve

my·ope \ˈmī-ˌōp\ *n* [F, fr. LL *myops* myopic, fr. Gk *myōps*, fr. *myein* to be closed + *ōps* eye, face — more at MYSTERY, EYE] **:** a myopic person

my·o·pia \mī-ˈō-pē-ə\ *n* [NL, fr. Gk *myōpia*, fr. *myōp-, myōps*] **1 :** a condition in which the visual images come to a focus in front of the retina of the eye resulting esp. in defective vision of distant objects **2 :** deficiency of foresight or discernment — **my·o·pic** \-ˈō-pik, -ˈäp-ik\ *adj* — **my·o·pi·cal·ly** \-(ə-)lē\ *adv*

my·o·sin \ˈmī-ə-sən\ *n* [ISV, fr. Gk *myos*, gen. of *mys* mouse muscle — more at MOUSE] **:** either of two proteins of muscle thought to constitute the chief components of the contractile mechanism: **a :** ACTOMYOSIN **b :** a fibrous globulin that interreacts with actin and adenosine triphosphate

my·os·otis \ˌmī-ə-ˈsōt-əs\ *n* [NL, genus name, fr. L, mouse-ear, fr. Gk *myosōtis*, fr. *myos* (gen. of *mys* mouse) + *ōt-, ous* ear — more at MOUSE, EAR] **:** any of a genus (*Myosotis*) of herbs of the borage family including the common forget-me-not (*M. palustris*)

myo·tome \ˈmī-ə-ˌtōm\ *n* [ISV] **1 :** the portion of an embryonic somite from which skeletal musculature is produced **2 :** the muscles of a metamere esp. in a segmented invertebrate

myo·to·nia \ˌmī-ə-ˈtō-nē-ə\ *n* [NL] **:** tonic spasm of one or more muscles; *also* **:** a condition characterized by such spasms — **myo·ton·ic** \-ˈtän-ik\ *adj*

[1]myr·i·ad \ˈmir-ē-əd\ *n* [Gk *myriad-, myrias*, fr. *myrioi* countless, ten thousand] **1 :** ten thousand **2 :** an immense number

[2]myriad *adj* **1 :** INNUMERABLE, MULTITUDINOUS **2 :** having innumerable aspects or elements

myr·ia·me·ter \ˈmir-ē-ə-ˌmēt-ər\ *n* [F *myriamètre*, fr. Gk *myrioi* + F *-mètre* -meter] — see METRIC SYSTEM table

myr·ia·pod \-ˌpäd\ *adj or n* **:** MYRIOPOD

myr·io·pod \ˈmir-ē-ə-ˌpäd\ *n* [deriv. of Gk *myrioi* + NL *-poda*] **:** any of a former group (Myriopoda) of arthropods having the body made up of numerous similar segments nearly all of which bear true jointed legs and including the millipedes and centipedes — **myriopod** *adj*

my·ris·tate \mə-ˈris-ˌtāt, mī-\ *n* [ISV] **:** a salt or ester of myristic acid

my·ris·tic acid \mə-ˌris-tik-, (ˌ)mī-\ *n* [ISV, fr. NL *Myristica*, genus of trees] **:** a crystalline fatty acid $C_{14}H_{28}O_2$ occurring esp. in the form of glycerides in most fats

myrmec- *or* **myrmeco-** *comb form* [Gk *myrmēk-, myrmēko-*, fr. *myrmēk-, myrmēx* — more at PISMIRE] **:** ant ⟨*myrmeco*phagous⟩

myr·me·co·cho·rous \ˌmər-mi-kə-ˈkōr-əs, -ˈkȯr-\ *adj* **:** dispersed by ants — **myr·me·co·cho·ry** \ˈmər-mi-kə-ˌkōr-ē, -ˌkȯr-\ *n*

myr·me·col·o·gy \ˌmər-mə-ˈkäl-ə-jē\ *n* [ISV] **:** the scientific study of ants

myr·me·coph·a·gous \-ˈkäf-ə-gəs\ *adj* **:** feeding on ants

myr·meco·phile \ˈmər-mi-kə-ˌfīl; (ˌ)mər-ˈmek-ə-, -ˈmē-kə-\ *n* [ISV] **:** an organism that habitually shares an ant nest — **myr·me·coph·i·lous** \ˌmər-mə-ˈkäf-ə-ləs\ *adj* — **myr·me·coph·i·ly** \-lē\ *n*

myr·mi·don \ˈmər-mə-ˌdän, -məd-ən\ *n* [L *Myrmidon-, Myrmido*, fr. Gk *Myrmidōn*] **1** *cap* **:** a member of a Thessalian people accompanying their king Achilles to the Trojan War **2 :** a loyal follower; *esp* **:** a subordinate who executes orders unquestioningly or pitilessly

my·rob·a·lan \mī-ˈräb-ə-lən, mə-\ *n* [MF *mirobolan*, fr. L *myrobalanus*, fr. Gk *myrobalanos*, fr. *myron* unguent + *balanos* acorn — more at SMEAR, GLAND] **1 :** the dried astringent fruit of an East Indian tree (genus *Terminalia*) used chiefly in tanning and in inks **2 :** CHERRY PLUM

myrrh \ˈmər\ *n* [ME *myrre*, fr. OE, fr. L *myrrha*, fr. Gk, of Sem origin; akin to Ar *murr* myrrh] **:** a yellowish brown to reddish brown aromatic gum resin with a bitter slightly pungent taste obtained from a tree (esp. *Commiphora abyssinica*) of east Africa and Arabia; *also* **:** a mixture of myrrh and labdanum

myr·tle \ˈmərt-ᵊl\ *n, often attrib* [ME *mirtille*, fr. MF, fr. ML *myrtillus*, fr. L *myrtus*, fr. Gk *myrtos*] **1 :** any of various plants (family Myrtaceae, the myrtle family) including producers of gums and timber and of spices; *esp* **:** a European shrub (*Myrtus communis*) having ovate or lanceolate evergreen leaves and solitary white or rosy flowers followed by black berries **2 a :** a periwinkle (*Vinca minor*) **b :** CALIFORNIA LAUREL **c :** MONEYWORT

my·self \mī-ˈself, mə-\ *pron* **1 :** that identical one that is I — used reflexively ⟨I'm going to get ~ a new suit⟩, for emphasis ⟨I ~ will go⟩, or in absolute constructions ⟨~ a tourist, I nevertheless avoided other tourists⟩ **2 :** my normal, healthy, or sane condition or self ⟨didn't feel ~ yesterday⟩

myst·agogue \ˈmis-tə-ˌgäg\ *n* [L *mystagogus*, fr. Gk *mystagōgos*, fr. *mystēs* initiate + *agein* to lead — more at AGENT] **1 :** one who initiates into a mystery cult **2 :** a disseminator of mystical doctrines — **myst·ago·gy** \-ˌgäj-ē, -ˌgō-jē\ *n*

mys·te·ri·ous \mis-ˈtir-ē-əs\ *adj* **1 :** of, relating to, or implying a mystery **:** OBSCURE **2 :** stirred by or attracted to the inexplicable — **mys·te·ri·ous·ly** *adv* — **mys·te·ri·ous·ness** *n*

syn MYSTERIOUS, INSCRUTABLE mean beyond one's power to discover or explain. MYSTERIOUS applies to what excites wonder, curiosity, or surprise while baffling or eluding efforts to explain or understand; INSCRUTABLE applies to what defies all efforts to understand and leaves one with a feeling of hopelessness or defeat or exasperation

[1]mys·tery \ˈmis-t(ə-)rē\ *n* [ME *mysterie*, fr. L *mysterium*, fr. Gk *mystērion*, fr. (assumed) *mystos* keeping silence, fr. Gk *myein* to be closed (of eyes or lips)] **1 a :** a religious truth that man can know by revelation alone and cannot fully understand **b** *cap* **:** a Christian sacrament; *specif* **:** EUCHARIST **c** (1) **:** a secret religious rite believed (as in Eleusinian and Mithraic cults) to impart enduring bliss to the initiate (2) **:** a cult devoted to such rites **2 a :** something not understood or beyond understanding **:** ENIGMA **b** *obs* **:** a private secret **c :** the secret or specialized practices or ritual peculiar to an occupation or a body of people **d :** a piece of fiction dealing usu. with the solution of a mysterious crime **3 :** profound, inexplicable, or secretive quality or character

syn PROBLEM, ENIGMA, RIDDLE, PUZZLE, CONUNDRUM: MYSTERY applies to what cannot be fully understood by human reason or less strictly to whatever attracts curiosity and speculation but resists or defies explanation; PROBLEM applies to any question or difficulty calling for a solution or causing concern; ENIGMA applies to utterance or behavior that is very difficult to interpret; RIDDLE suggests an enigma or problem involving paradox or apparent contradiction; PUZZLE applies to an enigma or problem that challenges ingenuity for its solution; CONUNDRUM applies to a question whose answer involves a pun or less often to a problem whose solution can only be speculative

[2]mystery *n* [LL *misterium, mysterium*, alter. of *ministerium* service, occupation, fr. *minister* servant — more at MINISTER] **1** *archaic* **:** TRADE, CRAFT **2** *archaic* **:** a body of persons engaged in a particular trade, business, or profession **:** GUILD **3 :** one of a class of medieval religious dramas based on scriptural incidents and usu. centering in the life, death, and resurrection of Christ — called also *mystery play*

[1]mys·tic \ˈmis-tik\ *adj* [ME *mistik*, fr. L *mysticus* of mysteries, fr. Gk *mystikos*, fr. (assumed) *mystos*] **1 :** MYSTICAL 1 **2 :** of or relating to mysteries or esoteric rites **:** OCCULT **3 :** of or relating to mysticism or mystics **4 a :** MYSTERIOUS **b :** ENIGMATIC, OBSCURE **c :** inducing a feeling of awe or wonder **d :** having magical properties

[2]mystic *n* **:** a follower or an expounder of a mystical way of life

mys·ti·cal \-ti-kəl\ *adj* **1 :** having a spiritual meaning or reality that is neither apparent to the senses nor obvious to the intelligence **2 a :** of, relating to, or resulting from an individual's direct communion with God or ultimate reality **b :** based upon intuition,

insight, or similar subjective experience **3** : UNINTELLIGIBLE, CRYPTIC **4** : MYSTIC 2 — **mys·ti·cal·ly** \-k(ə-)lē\ adv

mys·ti·cism \'mis-tə-,siz-əm\ n **1** : the experience of mystical union or direct communion with ultimate reality reported by mystics **2 a** : religion based on mystical communion **b** : a theory of mystical knowledge **3 a** : obscure or irrational speculation **b** : a theory postulating the possibility of direct and intuitive acquisition of ineffable knowledge or power

mys·ti·fi·ca·tion \,mis-tə-fə-'kā-shən\ n **1** : an act or instance of mystifying **2** : the quality or state of being mystified **3** : something designed to mystify

mys·ti·fy \'mis-tə-,fī\ vt [F mistifier, fr. mystère mystery, fr. L mysterium] **1** : to perplex the mind of : BEWILDER **2** : to make mysterious or obscure

mys·tique \mi-'stēk\ n [F, fr. mystique, adj., mystic, fr. L mysticus] **1** : a complex of transcendental or somewhat mystical beliefs and attitudes developing around an object **2** : the special esoteric skill essential in a calling or activity

myth \'mith\ n [Gk mythos] **1** : a usu. traditional story of ostensibly historical events that serves to unfold part of the world view of a people or explain a practice, belief, or natural phenomenon **2** : PARABLE, ALLEGORY **3 a** : a person or thing having only an imaginary or unverifiable existence **b** : an ill-founded belief held uncritically esp. by an interested group **4** : the whole body of myths

myth·i·cal \'mith-i-kəl\ adj **1** : based on or described in a myth esp. as contrasted with factual history : IMAGINARY **2 a** : fabricated, invented, or imagined in an arbitrary way or in defiance of facts **b** : having qualities suitable to myth syn see FICTITIOUS — **myth·i·cal·ly** \-k(ə-)lē\ adv

myth·i·cize \'mith-ə-,sīz\ vt **1** : to turn into or envelop in myth **2** : to treat as myth — **myth·i·ciz·er** n

my·thog·ra·pher \mith-'äg-rə-fər\ n [Gk mythographos, fr. mythos + graphein to write — more at CARVE] : a compiler of or writer about myths

my·thol·o·ger \mith-'äl-ə-jər\ n : MYTHOLOGIST

mytho·log·i·cal \,mith-ə-'läj-i-kəl\ also **mytho·log·ic** \-ik\ adj **1** : of, relating to, or dealt with in mythology or myths **2** : MYTHI-

CAL, FABULOUS — **mytho·log·i·cal·ly** \-i-k(ə-)lē\ adv

my·thol·o·gist \mith-'äl-ə-jəst\ n : a student of mythology or myths

my·thol·o·gize \-,jīz\ vt **1** obs : to explain the mythological significance of **2** : to build a myth round : MYTHICIZE ~ vi : to relate, classify, and explain myths — **my·thol·o·giz·er** n

my·thol·o·gy \mith-'äl-ə-jē\ n [F or LL; F mythologie, fr. LL mythologia interpretation of myths, fr. Gk, legend, myth, fr. mythologein to relate myths, fr. mythos + logos speech — more at LEGEND] **1 a** : an allegorical narrative **b** : a body of myths; esp : the myths dealing with the gods, demigods, and legendary heroes of a particular people and usu. involving supernatural elements **2** : a branch of knowledge that deals with myth

mytho·ma·nia \,mith-ə-'mā-nē-ə, -nyə\ n [NL, fr. Gk mythos + LL mania] : an excessive or abnormal propensity for lying and exaggerating — **mytho·ma·ni·ac** \-nē-,ak\ n or adj

mytho·poe·ia \,mith-ə-'pē-(y)ə\ n [LL, fr. Gk mythopoiia, fr. mythopoiein to make a myth, fr. mythos + poiein to make — more at POEM] : a creating of myth : a giving rise to myths — **mytho·poe·ic** \-'pē-ik\ adj — **mytho·po·et·ic** \-pō-'et-ik\ or **mytho·po·et·i·cal** \-i-kəl\ adj

my·thos \'mī-,thäs, 'mith-,äs\ n [Gk] **1 a** : MYTH 1 **b** : MYTHOLOGY 1b **2** : a pattern of beliefs expressing often symbolically the characteristic or prevalent attitudes in a group or culture **3** : THEME, PLOT

myx·ede·ma \,mik-sə-'dē-mə\ n [NL, fr. Gk myxa lampwick, nasal mucus + NL edema — more at MUCUS] : severe hypothyroidism characterized by firm inelastic edema, dry skin and hair, and loss of mental and physical vigor — **myx·ede·ma·tous** \-'dem-ət-əs, -'dē-mət-\ adj

myx·o·ma \mik-'sō-mə\ n, pl myxomas or **myx·o·ma·ta** \-mət-ə\ [NL, fr. Gk myxa] : a soft tumor made up of gelatinous connective tissue resembling that found in the umbilical cord — **myx·o·ma·to·sis** \(,)mik-,sō-mə-'tō-səs\ n — **myx·o·ma·tous** \mik-'säm-ət-əs, -'sō-mət-\ adj

myxo·my·cete \,mik-sō-'mī-,sēt, ,mik-sō-(,)mī-'\ n [deriv. of Gk myxa + mykēt-, mykēs — more at MYC-] : SLIME MOLD — **myxo·my·ce·tous** \-(,)mī-'sēt-əs\ adj

---

n \'en\ n, often cap, often attrib **1 a** : the 14th letter of the English alphabet **b** : a graphic representation of this letter **c** : a speech counterpart of orthographic n **2** : a graphic device for reproducing the letter n **3 a** : one designated n esp. as the 13th or when j is used for the 10th the 14th in order or class **b** : an unspecified constant **4** : something shaped like the letter N **5** : EN 2

-n — see -EN

nab \'nab\ vt nabbed; nab·bing [perh. alter. of E dial. nap] **1** : to catch or seize in arrest : APPREHEND **2** : to seize suddenly

na·bob \'nā-,bäb\ n [Hindi nawwāb, fr. Ar nuwwāb, pl. of nā'ib governor] **1** : a provincial governor of the Mogul empire in India **2** : a man of great wealth or prominence — **na·bob·ess** \-əs\ n

Na·both \'nā-,bäth\ n [Heb Nābhōth] : the owner of a vineyard coveted and seized by Ahab king of Israel

na·celle \nə-'sel\ n [F, lit., small boat, fr. LL navicella, dim. of L navis ship — more at NAVE] : an enclosed shelter on an aircraft for an engine or sometimes for the crew

na·cre \'nā-kər\ n [F, fr. OIt naccara drum, nacre, fr. Ar naqqārah drum] : MOTHER-OF-PEARL — **na·cred** \-kərd\ adj — **na·cre·ous** \-krē-əs, -k(ə-)rəs\ adj

Na–de·ne also **Na–dé·né** \nä-'dā-nē\ n [na- (fr. an Athapaskan word stem akin to Haida na to dwell) + Déné] : a group of related American Indian languages spoken in parts of western No. America from Alaska to northern Mexico

na·dir \'nā-,di(ə)r, 'nād-ər\ n [ME, fr. MF, fr. Ar naẓīr opposite] **1** : the point of the celestial sphere that is directly opposite the zenith and vertically downward from the observer **2** : the lowest point

¹nag \'nag\ n [ME nagge; akin to D negge small horse] : HORSE; esp : one that is old or in poor condition

²nag vb nagged; nag·ging [prob. of Scand origin; akin to ON gnaga to gnaw; akin to OE gnagan to gnaw] vi **1** : to find fault incessantly : COMPLAIN **2** : to be a continuing source of annoyance ~ vt **1** : to irritate by constant scolding or urging **2** : BADGER, WORRY — **nag·ger** n — **nag·ging** adj — **nag·ging·ly** \-iŋ-lē\ adv

Na·huatl \'nä-,wät-ᵊl\ n, pl **Nahuatl** or **Nahuatls** [Sp, fr. Nahuatl] **1** : a group of peoples of southern Mexico and Central America **2** : the Uto-Aztecan language of the Nahuatl people — **Na·huat·lan** \-,wät-lən\ adj or n

Na·hum \'nā-(h)əm\ n [Heb Naḥūm] : a Hebrew prophet of the 7th century B.C.

na·iad \'nā-əd, 'nī-, -,ad\ n, pl na·iads or na·ia·des \-ə-,dēz\ [F or L; F naïade, fr. L naiad-, naias, fr. Gk, fr. naein to flow — more at NOURISH] **1** : one of the nymphs in ancient mythology living in and giving life to lakes, rivers, springs, and fountains **2** : the aquatic young of a mayfly, dragonfly, damselfly, or stone fly **3** : MUSSEL 2

na·if \nä-'ēf\ adj [F] : NAÏVE

¹nail \'nā(ə)l\ n, often attrib [ME, fr. OE nægl; akin to OHG nagal nail, fingernail, L unguis fingernail, toenail, claw, Gk onyx] **1** : a horny sheath protecting the upper end of each finger and toe of man and most other primates **b** : a corresponding structure (as a claw) terminating a digit **2** : a slender usu. pointed and headed fastener designed to be pounded in **3** : an English unit of ¹⁄₁₆ yard

²nail vt **1** : to fasten with or as if with a nail **2** : to fix in steady attention ⟨~ed his eye on the crack⟩ **3** : CATCH, TRAP; esp : to detect and expose so as to discredit **4 a** : STRIKE, HIT **b** : to put out (a runner) in baseball — **nail·er** n

nail down vt : to settle or establish clearly and unmistakably

nain·sook \'nān-,sùk\ n [Hindi nainsukh, fr. nain eye + sukh delight] : a soft lightweight muslin

na·ive also **na·ïve** \nä-'ēv\ adj [F naïve, fem. of naïf, fr. OF, inborn, natural, fr. L nativus native] **1** : marked by unaffected simplicity : ARTLESS, INGENUOUS **2** : showing lack of informed judgment; esp : CREDULOUS syn see NATURAL — **na·ive·ly** adv — **na·ive·ness** n

na·ive·té also **na·ive·te** \(,)nä-,ē-və-'tā, nä-'ē-və-,; ,nä-,ēv-'tā\ n [F naïveté, fr. OF, inborn character, fr. naif] **1** : the quality or state of being naïve **2** : a naïve remark or action

na·ive·ty also **na·ive·ty** \nä-'ē-vət-ē, -'ēv-tē\ n : NAÏVETÉ

na·ked \'nā-kəd, esp South 'nek-əd\ adj [ME, fr. OE nacod; akin to OHG nackot naked, L nudus, Gk gymnos] **1** : not covered by clothing : NUDE **2** : devoid of customary or natural covering : BARE as **a** : UNSHEATHED **b** : unprovided with a shade **c** of a plant or one of its parts : lacking pubescence or enveloping or subtending parts **d** : lacking foliage or vegetation **e** of an animal or one of its parts : lacking an external covering (as of hair, feathers, or shell) **3 a** : scantily supplied or furnished **b** : lacking embellishment : UNADORNED **4** : UNARMED, DEFENSELESS **5** : lacking confirmation or support **6** : devoid of concealment or disguise **7** : unaided by any optical device or instrument ⟨visible to the ~ eye⟩ syn see BARE — **na·ked·ly** adv — **na·ked·ness** n

nam·by–pam·by \,nam-bē-'pam-bē\ adj [Namby Pamby, nickname given to Ambrose Philips] **1** : lacking in character or substance : INSIPID **2** : WEAK, INDECISIVE — **namby–pamby** n

¹name \'nām\ n [ME, fr. OE nama; akin to OHG namo name, L nomen, Gk onoma, onyma] **1 a** : a word constituting the distinctive designation of a person or thing **b** (1) : a word or symbol that can serve as the subject of a sentence or expression in logic (2) : a designating expression **2** : a descriptive often disparaging epithet ⟨call someone ~s⟩ **3 a** : REPUTATION; esp : an illustrious record **b** : a name as the embodiment of a reputation **c** : a famous person **4** : FAMILY, CLAN **5** : semblance as opposed to reality ⟨a friend in ~ only⟩ **6** : spiritual nature or essence ⟨praise his holy ~⟩

²name vt **1** : to give a name to : CALL **2 a** : to mention or identify by name **b** : to accuse by name **3** : to nominate for office : APPOINT **4** : to decide upon : CHOOSE **5** : to speak about : MENTION ⟨~ a price⟩ — **nam·er** n

³name adj **1** : of, relating to, or bearing a name **2** : appearing in the name of a literary or theatrical production : TITLE **3 a** : having an established reputation **b** : featuring celebrities

name·able also **nam·able** \'nā-mə-bəl\ adj **1** : capable of being named : IDENTIFIABLE **2** : worthy of being named : MEMORABLE

name day n : the day of the saint whose name one bears

name·less \'nām-ləs\ adj **1** : UNDISTINGUISHED, OBSCURE **2** : not known by name : ANONYMOUS **3** : having no legal right to a name : ILLEGITIMATE **4** : not having been given a name : UNNAMED **5** : not marked with a name ⟨a ~ grave⟩ **6 a** : incapable of precise description : INDEFINABLE **b** : too repulsive or distressing to describe — **name·less·ly** adv — **name·less·ness** n

name·ly \'nām-lē\ adv : that is to say : AS

name·plate \-,plāt\ n : a plate or plaque bearing a name (as of a resident)

name·sake \'nām-,sāk\ n [prob. fr. name's sake] : one that has the same name as another; esp : one named after another

nan·keen \nan-'kēn\ also **nan·kin** \-'kēn, -'kin\ n [Nanking, China] **1** : a durable brownish yellow cotton fabric orig. loomed by hand in China **2** pl : trousers made of nankeen **3** cap : Chinese porcelain painted in blue on white

---

nan·ny goat \'nan-ē-\ *n* [*Nanny*, nickname for *Anne*] : a female domestic goat

nano- \'nan-(,)ō, -ə\ *comb form* [ISV, fr. Gk *nanos* dwarf] : one billionth (10^{-9}) part of ⟨*nano*second⟩

Na·o·mi \nā-'ō-mē\ *n* [Heb *Nā'ŏmī*] : the mother-in-law of the Old Testament heroine Ruth

1nap \'nap\ *vi* **napped; nap·ping** [ME *nappen*, fr. OE *hnappian;* akin to OHG *hnaffezen* to doze] **1** : to sleep briefly esp. during the day : DOZE **2** : to be off guard

2nap *n* : a short sleep esp. during the day : SNOOZE

3nap *n* [ME *noppe*, fr. MD, flock of wool, nap; akin to OE *hnoppian* to pluck, Gk *konis* ashes] : a hairy or downy surface on a woven fabric — **nap·less** \-ləs\ *adj* — **napped** \'napt\ *adj*

4nap *vt* **napped; nap·ping** : to raise a nap on (fabric or leather)

na·palm \'nā-,päm, -,pälm\ *n* [*na*phthene + *palm*itate] **1** : a thickener consisting of a mixture of aluminum soaps used in jelling gasoline **2** : fuel jelled with napalm

nape \'nāp, 'nap\ *n* [ME] : the back of the neck

na·pery \'nā-p(ə-)rē\ *n* [ME, fr. MF *naperie*, fr. *nappe*, *nape* tablecloth — more at NAPKIN] : household linen; *esp* : TABLE LINEN

Naph·ta·li \'naf-tə-,lī\ *n* [Heb *Naphtālī*] : a son of Jacob and ancestor of one of the tribes of Israel

naphth- *or* **naphtho-** *comb form* [ISV, fr. *naphtha* & *naphthalene*] **1** : naphtha ⟨*naphth*ene⟩ **2** : naphthalene ⟨*naphth*ol⟩

naph·tha \'naf-thə, 'nap-\ *n* [L, fr. Gk, of Iranian origin; akin to Per *neft* naphtha] **1** : PETROLEUM **2** : any of various volatile often flammable liquid hydrocarbon mixtures used chiefly as solvents and diluents

naph·tha·lene \-,lēn\ *n* [alter. of earlier *naphthaline*, irreg. fr. *naphtha*] : a crystalline aromatic hydrocarbon $C_{10}H_8$ usu. obtained by distillation of coal tar — **naph·tha·len·ic** \,naf-thə-'lēn-ik, ,nap-, -'len-\ *adj*

naph·thene \'naf-,thēn, 'nap-\ *n* [ISV] : any of various saturated cyclic hydrocarbons of the general formula C_nH_{2n}; *esp* : one that occurs in shale or tar oil and yields aromatic hydrocarbons on dehydrogenation — **naph·then·ic** \naf-'thēn-ik, nap-, -'then-\ *adj*

naph·thol \'naf-,thōl, 'nap-, -,thōl\ *n* [ISV] **1** : either of two white crystalline hydroxyl derivatives $C_{10}H_7OH$ of napththalene found in coal tar or made synthetically and used as antiseptics and in manufacture of dyes **2** : any of various hydroxy derivatives containing the naphthalene nucleus

Na·pier·ian logarithm \nə-,pir-ē-ən-, nā-\ *n* [John *Napier* †1617 Sc mathematician] : NATURAL LOGARITHM

na·pi·form \'nā-pə-,fȯrm\ *adj* [L *napus* turnip (fr. Gk *napy* mustard) + ISV *-iform;* akin to Gk *sinapy* mustard] *of a root* : globular at the top and tapering off abruptly

nap·kin \'nap-kən\ *n* [ME *nappekin*, fr. *nappe* tablecloth, fr. MF, fr. L *mappa* napkin] **1** : a piece of material (as cloth or paper) used at table to wipe the lips or fingers and protect the clothes **2** : a small cloth or towel: as **a** *dial Brit* : HANDKERCHIEF **b** *chiefly Scot* : KERCHIEF **c** *chiefly Brit* : DIAPER 2

na·po·leon \nə-'pōl-yən, -'pō-lē-ən\ *n* [*Napoleon* I †1821 F emperor] **1** [F *napoléon*, fr. *Napoléon* Napoleon I] : a French 20-franc gold coin **2 a** : a card game resembling euchre; *also* : a bid to win all five tricks in this game **b** : any of various forms of solitaire **3** : an oblong pastry consisting of layers of puff paste with a filling of cream, custard, or jelly

Na·po·le·on·ic \nə-,pō-lē-'än-ik\ *adj* : of, relating to, or characteristic of Napoleon I — **Na·po·le·on·i·cal·ly** \-i-k(ə-)lē\ *adv*

1nap·per \'nap-ər\ *n* : one that takes naps

2napper *n* : one that naps cloth

1nap·py \'nap-ē\ *n* [obs. *nappy*, adj. (foaming)] *chiefly Scot* : LIQUOR; *specif* : ALE

2nappy *n* [E dial. *nap* bowl, fr. ME, fr. OE *hnæpp;* akin to OHG *hnapf* bowl] : a shallow open serving dish

nap·ra·path \'nap-rə-,path\ *n* : a practitioner of naprapathy

na·prap·a·thy \nə-'prap-ə-thē\ *n* [Czech *náprava* + E *-pathy*] : a therapeutic system of treatment by manipulation and without use of drugs

nar·cism \'när-,siz-əm\ *n* [G *narcismus*, fr. L *Narcissus*] : NARCISSISM

nar·cis·sism \'när-sə-,siz-əm\ *n* [G *narzissismus*, fr. *Narziss* Narcissus, fr. L *Narcissus*] **1** : EGOISM, EGOCENTRISM **2** : love of one's own body — **nar·cis·sist** \'när-sə-səst\ *n or adj* — **nar·cis·sis·tic** \,när-sə-'sis-tik\ *adj*

nar·cis·sus \när-'sis-əs\ *n* [L, fr. Gk *Narkissos*] **1** *cap* : a beautiful youth in Greek legend caused to pine away for love of his own image and transformed into the narcissus **2** *pl* **narcissus** *or* **nar·cis·sus·es** \-'sis-ə-səz\ *or* **nar·cis·si** \-'sis-,ī, -(,)ē\ [NL, genus name, fr. L, narcissus, fr. Gk *narkissos*] : DAFFODIL; *esp* : one whose flowers have a short corona and are usu. borne separately

nar·cist \'när-səst\ *n* : NARCISSIST

nar·co·lep·sy \'när-kə-,lep-sē\ *n* [ISV, fr. Gk *narkē*] : a condition characterized by brief attacks of deep sleep — **nar·co·lep·tic** \,när-kə-'lep-tik\ *adj or n*

nar·co·sis \när-'kō-səs\ *n*, *pl* **nar·co·ses** \-'kō-,sēz\ [NL, fr. Gk *narkōsis*, action of benumbing, fr. *narkoun*] : a state of stupor, unconsciousness, or arrested activity produced by the influence of narcotics or other chemicals

1nar·cot·ic \när-'kät-ik\ *n* [ME *narkotik*, fr. MF *narcotique*, fr. *narcotique*, adj., fr. ML *narcoticus*, fr. Gk *narkōtikos*, fr. *narkoun* to benumb, fr. *narkē* numbness, — more at SNARE] **1** : a drug (as opium) that in moderate doses dulls the senses, relieves pain, and induces profound sleep but in excessive doses causes stupor, coma, or convulsions **2** : something that soothes, relieves, or lulls

2narcotic *adj* **1 a** : having the properties of or yielding a narcotic **b** : inducing mental lethargy : SOPORIFEROUS **2** : of, induced by, or concerned with narcotics **3** : of, involving, or intended for narcotic addicts — **nar·cot·i·cal·ly** \-i-k(ə-)lē\ *adv*

nar·co·tize \'när-kə-,tīz\ *vt* [ISV] **1 a** : to treat with or subject to a narcotic **b** : to put into a state of narcosis **2** : to soothe to unconsciousness or unawareness ~ *vi* : to act as a narcotizing agent

nard \'närd\ *n* [ME *narde*, fr. MF or L; MF, fr. L *nardus*, fr. Gk *nardos*, of Sem origin; akin to Heb *nērd* nard] : SPIKENARD 1b

na·ris \'nar-əs, 'ner-\ *n*, *pl* **na·res** \'na(ə)r-(,)ēz, 'ne(ə)r-\ [L; akin to L *nasus* nose — more at NOSE] : the opening of the nose or nasal cavity of a vertebrate

nark \'närk\ *n* [perh. fr. Romany *nak* nose] *Brit* : a spy employed by the police : STOOL PIGEON

nar·rate \'na(ə)r-,āt, na-'rāt\ *vt* [L *narratus*, pp. of *narrare*, fr. L *gnarus* knowing; akin to L *gnoscere*, *noscere* to know — more at KNOW] : to recite the details of (a story) : RELATE — **nar·ra·tor** \'na(ə)r-,āt-ər; na-'rāt-, nə-; 'nar-ət-\ *n*

nar·ra·tion \na-'rā-shən, nə-\ *n* **1** : the act or process or an instance of narrating **2** : STORY, NARRATIVE — **nar·ra·tion·al** \-shnəl, -shən-ᵊl\ *adj*

nar·ra·tive \'nar-ət-iv\ *n* **1** : something that is narrated : STORY **2** : the art or practice of narration — **narrative** *adj* — **nar·ra·tive·ly** *adv*

1nar·row \'nar-(,)ō, -ə(-w)\ *adj* [ME *narowe*, fr. OE *nearu;* akin to OHG *narwa* scar, *snuor* cord, Gk *narnax* box] **1 a** : of slender width **b** : of less than standard width **c** *of a textile* : woven in widths less than 18 inches **2** : limited in size or scope : RESTRICTED **3 a** : illiberal in views or disposition : PREJUDICED **b** *chiefly dial* : STINGY, NIGGARDLY **4 a** : barely sufficient : CLOSE **b** : barely successful **5** : minutely precise : METICULOUS **6** *of a ration* : relatively rich in protein as compared with carbohydrate and fat **7** : TENSE 3 — **nar·row·ly** *adv* — **nar·row·ness** *n*

2narrow *n* : a narrow part or passage; *specif* : a strait connecting two bodies of water — usu. used in pl. but sing. or pl. in constr.

3narrow *vb* : to lessen in width or extent : CONTRACT

nar·row–mind·ed \,nar-ō-'mīn-dəd\ *adj* : lacking in tolerance or breadth of vision : PETTY — **nar·row–mind·ed·ly** *adv* — **nar·row–mind·ed·ness** *n*

nar·thex \'när-,theks\ *n* [LGk *narthēx*, fr. Gk, giant fennel, cane, casket] **1** : the portico of an ancient church **2** : a vestibule leading to the nave of a church

nar·whal *also* **nar·wal** \'när-,(h)wäl, -wəl\ *or* **nar·whale** \-,(h)wāl\ *n* [Norw & Dan *narhval* & Sw *narval*, prob. modif. of Icel *náhvalr*, fr. ON *nāhvalr*, fr. *nār* corpse + *hvalr* whale; fr. its color] : an arctic cetacean (*Monodon monoceros*) about 20 feet long with the male having a long twisted ivory tusk of commercial value

nary \'na(ə)r-ē, 'ne(ə)r-\ *adj* [alter. of *ne'er a*] *dial* : not one

nas- *or* **naso-** *also* **nasi-** *comb form* [L *nasus* nose — more at NOSE] **1** : nose : nasal ⟨*naso*scope⟩ ⟨*naso*sinusitis⟩ **2** : nasal and ⟨*naso*labial⟩

1na·sal \'nā-zəl\ *n* [MF, fr. OF, fr. *nes* nose, fr. L *nasus*] **1** : the nosepiece of a helmet **2** : a nasal part **3** : a nasal consonant or vowel

2nasal *adj* **1** : of or relating to the nose **2 a** : uttered through the nose with the mouth passage occluded (as *m*, *n*, *ng*) **b** : uttered with the mouth open, the soft palate lowered, and the nose passage producing a phonemically essential resonance (as of a vowel in French) or a phonemically nonessential resonance (as of a vowel or consonant in English) **c** : characterized by resonance produced through the nose **3** *of a musical tone* : SHARP, PENETRATING — **na·sal·i·ty** \nā-'zal-ət-ē\ *n* — **na·sal·ly** \'nāz-(ə-)lē\ *adv*

na·sal·iza·tion \,nāz-(ə-)lə-'zā-shən\ *n* : the act or process of making, being, or becoming nasal

na·sal·ize \'nā-zə-,līz\ *vt* : to make nasal ~ *vi* : to speak in a nasal manner

na·scence \'nas-ᵊn(t)s, 'nās-\ *also* **na·scen·cy** \-ᵊn-sē\ *n* : BIRTH, ORIGIN

na·scent \'nas-ᵊnt, 'nās-\ *adj* [L *nascent-*, *nascens*, prp. of *nasci* to be born — more at NATION] : coming into existence : beginning to develop

na·so·pha·ryn·geal \,nā-(,)zō-fə-'rin-j(ē-)əl, -,far-ən-'jē-əl\ *adj* : of or relating to the nose and pharynx or the nasopharynx

na·so·phar·ynx \-'far-iŋ(k)s\ *n* [NL] : the upper part of the pharynx continuous with the nasal passages

nas·tic \'nas-tik\ *adj* [Gk *nastos* close-pressed, fr. *nassein* to press] : of, relating to, or constituting a movement of a plant part caused by disproportionate growth or increase of turgor in one surface

nas·ti·ly \'nas-tə-lē\ *adv* : in a nasty manner

nas·ti·ness \-tē-nəs\ *n* : the quality or state of being nasty

nas·tur·tium \nə-'stər-shəm, na-\ *n* [L, a cress] : any of a genus (*Tropaeolum* of the family Tropaeolaceae, the nasturtium family) of herbs bearing showy spurred flowers and having pungent seeds; *esp* : either of two widely cultivated ornamentals (*T. majus* and *T. minus*)

nas·ty \'nas-tē\ *adj* [ME] **1 a** : disgustingly filthy **b** : physically repugnant **2** : INDECENT, OBSCENE **3** : MEAN, TAWDRY **4 a** : extremely hazardous or harmful **b** : full of problems : KNOTTY **c** : sharply unpleasant ⟨~ shock⟩ **5** : lacking in courtesy or sportsmanship : SPITEFUL **syn** see DIRTY

-nas·ty \,nas-tē\ *n comb form* [G *-nastie*, fr. Gk *nastos*] : nastic movement of a plant part ⟨epi*nasty*⟩

na·tal \'nāt-ᵊl\ *adj* [ME, fr. L *natalis*, fr. *natus*, pp. of *nasci* to be born — more at NATION] **1** : NATIVE **2** : of, relating to, or present at birth ⟨~ day⟩; *esp* : associated with one's birth ⟨~ star⟩

na·tal·i·ty \nā-'tal-ət-ē, nə-\ *n* : BIRTHRATE

na·tant \'nāt-ᵊnt\ *adj* [L *natant-*, *natans*, prp. of *natare* to swim; akin to L *nare* to swim — more at NOURISH] : swimming or floating in water

na·ta·tion \nā-'tā-shən, na-\ *n* : the action or art of swimming

na·ta·to·ri·al \,nāt-ə-'tōr-ē-əl, ,nat-, -'tȯr-\ *or* **na·ta·to·ry** \'nāt-ə-,tōr-ē, 'nat-, -,tȯr-\ *adj* **1** : of or relating to swimming **2** : adapted to or characterized by swimming

na·ta·to·ri·um \,nāt-ə-'tōr-ē-əm, ,nat-, -'tȯr-\ *n* [LL, fr. L *natatus*, pp. of *natare*] : a place for swimming; *esp* : an indoor swimming pool

na·tes \'nā-,tēz\ *n pl* [L, pl. of *natis* buttock; akin to Gk *nōtos*, *nōton* back] : BUTTOCKS

nathe·less \'nāth-ləs\ *or* **nath·less** \'nath-\ *adv* [ME, fr. OE *nā thē lǣs* not the less] *archaic* : NEVERTHELESS, NOTWITHSTANDING

na·tion \'nā-shən\ *n* [ME *nacioun*, fr. MF *nation*, fr. L *nation-*, *natio* birth, race, nation, fr. *natus*, pp. of *nasci* to be born; akin to L *gignere* to beget — more at KIN] **1 a** (1) : NATIONALITY 5a (2) : a politically organized nationality **b** : a community of people composed of one or more nationalities and possessing a more or less defined territory and government **c** : a territorial division containing a body of people of one or more nationalities and usu. characterized by relatively large size and independent status **2** *archaic* : GROUP, AGGREGATION **3** : a tribe or federation of tribes (as of American Indians) — **na·tion·hood** \-,hu̇d\ *n*

1na·tion·al \'nash-nəl, -ən-ᵊl\ *adj* **1** : of or relating to a nation **2** : NATIONALIST **3** : comprising or characteristic of a nationality **4** : belonging to or maintained by the federal government **5** : of,

relating to, or being a coalition government formed by most or all major political parties usu. in a crisis — **na·tion·al·ly** \-ē\ *adv*

2national *n* **1 :** one that owes allegiance to or is under the protection of a nation without regard to the more formal status of citizen or subject **2 :** a competition that is national in scope — usu. used in pl. **syn** see CITIZEN

national bank *n* **1 :** a bank associated with the finances of a nation **2 :** a bank operating under federal charter and supervision

National Guard *n* **:** a militia force recruited by each state, equipped by the federal government, and jointly maintained subject to the call of either

national income *n* **:** the aggregate of earnings from a nation's current production including compensation of employees, interest, rental income, and profits of business after taxes

na·tion·al·ism \'nash-nəl-,iz-əm, -ən-ᵊl-\ *n* **:** loyalty and devotion to a nation; *esp* **:** a sense of national consciousness exalting one nation above all others and placing primary emphasis on promotion of its culture and interests as opposed to those of other nations or supranational groups

1na·tion·al·ist \-əst\ *n* **1 :** an advocate of or believer in nationalism **2** *cap* **:** a member of a political party or group advocating national independence or strong national government

2nationalist *adj* **1 :** of, relating to, or advocating nationalism **2** *cap* **:** of, relating to, or being a political group advocating or associated with nationalism

na·tion·al·is·tic \,nash-nəl-'is-tik, -ən-ᵊl-\ *adj* **1 :** of, favoring, or characterized by nationalism ⟨~ election speeches⟩ **2 :** NATIONAL 1 — **na·tion·al·is·ti·cal·ly** \-ti-k(ə-)lē\ *adv*

na·tion·al·i·ty \,nash-(ə-)'nal-ət-ē\ *n* **1 :** national character **2 :** NATIONALISM **3 a :** national status; *specif* **:** a legal relationship involving allegiance on the part of an individual and usu. protection on the part of the state **b :** membership in a particular nation **4 :** political independence or existence as a separate nation **5 a :** a people having a common origin, tradition, and language and capable of forming or actually constituting a nation-state **b :** an ethnic group constituting one element of a larger unit (as a nation)

na·tion·al·iza·tion \,nash-nəl-ə-'zā-shən, -ən-ᵊl-\ *n* **1 :** the action or process of nationalizing **2 :** the state of being nationalized

na·tion·al·ize \'nash-nəl-,īz, -ən-ᵊl-\ *vt* **1 :** to give a national character to **2 :** to invest control or ownership of in the national government — **na·tion·al·iz·er** *n*

national park *n* **:** an area of special scenic, historical, or scientific importance set aside and maintained by a national government esp. for recreation or study

national product *n* **:** the value of the goods and services produced in a nation during a year

national socialism *n* **:** NAZISM — **national socialist** *adj*

na·tion–state \'nā-shən-'stāt, -,stāt\ *n* **:** a form of political organization under which a relatively homogeneous people inhabits a sovereign state; *esp* **:** a state containing one as opposed to several nationalities

na·tion·wide \,nā-shən-'wīd\ *adj* **:** extending throughout a nation

1na·tive \'nāt-iv\ *adj* [ME *natif*, fr. MF, fr. L *nativus*, fr. *natus*, pp. of *nasci* to be born — more at NATION] **1 :** INBORN, INNATE **2 :** belonging to a particular place by birth **3** *archaic* **:** closely related **4 :** belonging to or associated with one by birth **5 :** NATURAL, NORMAL **6 a :** grown, produced, or originating in a particular place or in the vicinity **:** LOCAL **b :** INDIGENOUS **7 :** SIMPLE, UNAFFECTED **8 a :** constituting the original substance or source **b :** found in nature esp. in an unadulterated form **9** *chiefly Austral* **:** having a usu. superficial resemblance to a specified English plant or animal — **na·tive·ly** *adv* — **na·tive·ness** *n*

syn NATIVE, INDIGENOUS, ENDEMIC, ABORIGINAL mean belonging to a locality. NATIVE implies birth or origin in a place or region and may suggest compatibility with it; INDIGENOUS applies to species or races and adds to NATIVE the implication of not having been introduced from elsewhere; ENDEMIC implies being peculiar to a region; ABORIGINAL implies having no known race preceding in occupancy of the region

2native *n* **1 :** one born or reared in a particular place **2 a :** an original or indigenous inhabitant **b :** something indigenous to a particular locality **3 :** a local resident; *esp* **:** a person who has lived all his life in a place as distinguished from a visitor or a temporary resident

na·tiv·ism \'nāt-iv-,iz-əm\ *n* **1 :** a policy of favoring native inhabitants as opposed to immigrants **2 :** the revival or perpetuation of an indigenous culture esp. in opposition to acculturation — **na·tiv·ist** \-əst\ *n or adj* — **na·tiv·is·tic** \,nāt-iv-'is-tik\ *adj*

na·tiv·i·ty \nə-'tiv-ət-ē, nā-\ *n* [ME *nativite*, fr. MF *nativité*, fr. ML *nativitat-, nativitas*, fr. LL, birth, fr. L *nativus*] **1** *cap* **:** the birth of Christ **2** *cap* **:** CHRISTMAS 1 **3 :** the process or circumstances of being born **:** BIRTH **4 :** a horoscope at or of the time of one's birth **5 :** the place of origin

na·tro·lite \'na-trə-,līt\ *n* [G *natrolith*, fr. *natron* (fr. F) + *-lith* -lite] **:** a hydrous sodium aluminum silicate $Na_2Al_2Si_3O_{10}.2H_2O$ related to zeolite

na·tron \'nā-,trän, -trən\ *n* [F, fr. Sp *natrón*, fr. Ar *naṭrūn*, fr. Gk *nitron*] **:** a hydrated native sodium carbonate $Na_2CO_3.10H_2O$

nat·ti·ly \'nat-ᵊl-ē\ *adv* **:** in a natty manner **:** SMARTLY

nat·ti·ness \'nat-ē-nəs\ *n* **:** the quality or state of being natty

nat·ty \'nat-ē\ *adj* [perh. alter. of earlier *netty*, fr. obs. *net* neat, clean] **:** trimly neat and tidy **:** SMART

1nat·u·ral \'nach-(ə-)rəl\ *adj* [ME, fr. MF, fr. L *naturalis* of nature, fr. *natura* nature] **1 :** based on an inherent sense of right and wrong ⟨~ justice⟩ **2 a :** being in accordance with or determined by nature **b :** having or constituting a classification based on features existing in nature **3 a** *chiefly dial* (1) **:** begotten as distinguished from adopted; *esp* **:** LEGITIMATE (2) **:** being a relation by actual consanguinity as distinguished from adoption ⟨~ parents⟩ **b :** ILLEGITIMATE ⟨~ child⟩ **4 :** consonant with the nature or character of someone or something **5 :** INBORN, INNATE **6 :** of or relating to nature as an object of study and research **7 :** having a specified character by nature **8 a :** occurring in conformity with the ordinary course of nature ⟨~ causes⟩ **b :** inferred from nature rather than revelation ⟨~ theology⟩ **c :** having a normal or usual character **9 :** characterized by qualities held to be part of the nature of man **10 a :** growing as a native and without cultivation **b :** existing in or produced by nature **11 a :** being in a state of nature without spiritual enlightenment **:** UNREGENERATE **b :** living in or as if in a state of nature untouched by the influences of civilization and society **12 a :** having a physical or real existence as contrasted with one that is spiritual, intellectual, or mental **b :** of, relating to, or operating in the physical as opposed to the spiritual world **13 a :** closely resembling the object imitated **b :** free from artificiality, affectation, or constraint **c :** having a form or appearance found in nature **14 a :** having neither flats nor sharps ⟨the ~ scale of C major⟩ **b :** being neither sharp nor flat **c :** having the pitch modified by the natural sign — **nat·u·ral·ly** \'nach-(ə-)rə-lē, 'nach-ər-lē\ *adv* — **nat·u·ral·ness** \-(ə-)rəl-nəs\ *n*

syn INGENUOUS, NAÏVE, UNSOPHISTICATED, ARTLESS: NATURAL implies lacking artificiality and self-consciousness and having a spontaneousness suggesting the natural rather than the man-made world; INGENUOUS implies inability to disguise or conceal one's feelings or intentions; NAÏVE suggests lack of worldly wisdom often connoting credulousness and unchecked innocence; UNSOPHISTICATED implies a lack of experience and training necessary for social ease and adroitness; ARTLESS suggests a naturalness resulting from unawareness of the effect one is producing on others **syn** see in addition REGULAR

2natural *n* **1 :** one born without the usual powers of reason and understanding **:** IDIOT **2 a :** the character or sign ♮ placed on any degree of the musical staff to nullify the effect of a preceding sharp or flat **b :** a note or tone affected by the natural sign **3 :** a result or combination that immediately wins the stake in a game; *specif* **:** a throw of 7 or 11 on the first cast in craps **4 a :** one having natural skills, talents, or abilities **b :** something that is likely to become an immediate success **c :** one that is obviously suitable for a specific purpose **syn** see FOOL

natural gas *n* **:** gas issuing from the earth's crust through natural openings or bored wells; *esp* **:** a combustible mixture of methane and higher hydrocarbons used chiefly as a fuel and raw material

natural history *n* **1 :** a treatise on some aspect of nature **2 :** the study of natural objects esp. from an amateur or popular point of view

nat·u·ral·ism \'nach-(ə-)rə-,liz-əm\ *n* **1 :** action, inclination, or thought based only on natural desires and instincts **2 :** a theory denying that an event or object has a supernatural significance; *specif* **:** the doctrine that scientific laws are adequate to account for all phenomena **3 :** realism in art or literature; *specif* **:** a theory in literature emphasizing scientific observation of life without idealization or the avoidance of the ugly

1nat·u·ral·ist \-ləst\ *n* **1 :** one that advocates or practices naturalism **2 :** a student of natural history; *esp* **:** a field biologist

2naturalist *or* **nat·u·ral·is·tic** \,nach-(ə-)rə-'lis-tik\ *adj* **:** of, characterized by, or according with naturalism — **nat·u·ral·is·ti·cal·ly** \-ti-k(ə-)lē\ *adv*

nat·u·ral·iza·tion \,nach-(ə-)rə-lə-'zā-shən\ *n* **:** the act or process of naturalizing

nat·u·ral·ize \'nach-(ə-)rə-,līz\ *vt* **1 a :** to introduce into common use or into the vernacular **b :** to cause (as a plant) to become established as if native **2 :** to bring into conformity with nature **3 :** to confer the rights of a national on; *esp* **:** to admit to citizenship ~ *vi* **:** to become established as if native

natural law *n* **:** a body of law or a specific principle held to be derived from nature and binding upon human society in the absence of or in addition to positive law

natural logarithm *n* **:** a logarithm with *e* as a base

natural number *n* **:** the number 1 or any number (as 3, 12, 432) obtained by repeatedly adding 1 to this number

natural philosophy *n* **:** NATURAL SCIENCE; *specif* **:** PHYSICAL SCIENCE

natural resources *n pl* **:** industrial materials and capacities (as mineral deposits, waterpower) supplied by nature

natural science *n* **:** any of the sciences (as physics, chemistry, biology) that deal with matter, energy, and their interrelations and transformations or with objectively measurable phenomena

natural selection *n* **:** a natural process tending to cause the survival of individuals or groups best adjusted to the conditions under which they live and being equally important for the perpetuation of desirable genetic qualities and for the elimination of undesirable as these are brought forward by recombination or mutation of genes

natural theology *n* **:** theology deriving its knowledge of God from the study of nature independent of special revelation

na·ture \'nā-chər\ *n* [ME, fr. MF, fr. L *natura*, fr. *natus*, pp. of *nasci* to be born — more at NATION] **1 a :** the inherent character or basic constitution of a person or thing **:** ESSENCE **b :** DISPOSITION, TEMPERAMENT **2 a :** a creative and controlling force in the universe **b :** an inner force or the sum of such forces in an individual **3 :** general character **:** KIND ⟨acts of a ceremonial ~⟩ **4 :** the physical constitution or drives of an organism **5 :** a spontaneous attitude (as of generosity) **6 :** the external world in its entirety **7 a :** man's original or natural condition **b :** a simplified mode of life resembling this condition **8 :** natural scenery **syn** see TYPE

na·tur·o·path \'nā-chə-rə-,path, nə-'t(y)u̇r-ə-\ *n* [back-formation fr. *naturopathy*] **:** a practitioner of naturopathy

na·tur·o·path·ic \,nā-chə-rə-'path-ik, nə-,t(y)u̇r-ə-\ *adj* **:** of, relating to, or effected by naturopathy

na·tur·op·a·thy \,nā-chə-'räp-ə-thē\ *n* [*nature* + *-o-* + *-pathy*] **:** a system of treatment of disease emphasizing assistance to nature and including the use of natural medicinal substances and physical means (as manipulation and electrical treatment)

1naught \'nȯt, 'nät\ *pron* [ME, fr. OE *nāwiht*, fr. *nā* no + *wiht* creature, thing — more at NO, WIGHT] **:** NOTHING

2naught *n* **1 a :** NOTHING **b :** NOTHINGNESS, NONEXISTENCE **2 :** the arithmetical symbol 0 **:** ZERO, CIPHER

3naught *adj* **:** of no importance **:** INSIGNIFICANT

naugh·ti·ly \'nȯt-ᵊl-ē, 'nät-\ *adv* **:** in a naughty manner

naugh·ti·ness \'nȯt-ē-nəs, 'nät-\ *n* **:** the quality or state of being naughty

naughty \'nȯt-ē, 'nät-\ *adj* [2*naught*] **1 a** *archaic* **:** vicious in moral character **:** WICKED **b :** guilty of disobedience or misbehavior **2 :** lacking in taste or propriety **syn** see BAD

nau·ma·chia \nȯ-'mā-kē-ə, -'mak-ē-\ *n, pl* **nau·ma·chi·ae** \-'mā-kē-,ē; -'mak-ē-,ī, -,ē\ *or* **nau·ma·chi·as** [L, fr. Gk, naval battle, fr. *naus* ship + *machesthai* to fight — more at NAVE] **1 :** an ancient Roman spectacle representing a naval battle **2 :** a place for naumachiae

nau·pli·us \'nȯ-plē-əs\ *n, pl* **nau·plii** \-plē-,ī, -,ē\ [NL, fr. L, a shellfish, fr. Gk *nauplios*] **:** a crustacean larva in usu. the first stage after leaving the egg and with three pairs of appendages, a median eye, and little or no segmentation

nau·sea \'nȯ-zē-ə, -shə, -sē-ə, -zhə\ *n* [L, seasickness, nausea, fr. Gk *nautia, nausia,* fr. *nautēs* sailor] **1 :** a stomach distress with loathing for food and an urge to vomit **2 :** extreme disgust — **nau·se·ant** \-z(h)ē-ənt, -s(h)ē-\ *n or adj*

nau·se·ate \'nȯ-z(h)ē-,āt, -s(h)ē-\ *vi* **1 :** to become affected with nausea **2 :** to feel disgust ~ *vt* **:** to affect with nausea or disgust — **nau·se·at·ing** \-,āt-iŋ\ *adj* — **nau·se·at·ing·ly** \-iŋ-lē\ *adv*

nau·seous \'nȯ-shəs, 'nȯ-zē-əs\ *adj* **1 :** NAUSEATED **2 :** causing nausea **:** SICKENING — **nau·seous·ly** *adv* — **nau·seous·ness** *n*

nautch \'nȯch\ *n* [Hindi *nāc,* fr. Skt *nṛtya,* fr. *nṛtyati* he dances] **:** an entertainment in India consisting chiefly of dancing by professional dancing girls

nau·ti·cal \'nȯt-i-kəl, 'nät-\ *adj* [L *nauticus,* fr. Gk *nautikos,* fr. *nautēs* sailor, fr. *naus* ship — more at NAVE] **:** of, relating to, or associated with seamen, navigation, or ships — **nau·ti·cal·ly** \-k(ə-)lē\ *adv*

nautical mile *n* **:** any of various units of distance used for sea and air navigation based on the length of a minute of arc of a great circle of the earth and differing because the earth is not a perfect sphere: as **a :** a British unit equal to 6080 ft. or 1853.2 meters — called also *Admiralty mile* **b :** a U.S. unit no longer in official use equal to 6080.20 ft. or 1853.248 meters **c :** an international unit equal to 6076.115 ft. or 1852 meters used officially in the U.S. since July 1, 1959

nau·ti·loid \'nȯt-ᵊl-,ȯid, 'nät-\ *n* **:** any of an ancient group (Nautiloidea) of cephalopods represented in the recent fauna by the nautiluses — **nautiloid** *adj*

nau·ti·lus \'nȯt-ᵊl-əs, 'nät-\ *n, pl* **nau·ti·lus·es** *or* **nau·ti·li** \-ᵊl-,ī, -,ē\ [NL, genus name, fr. L, paper nautilus, fr. Gk *nautilos,* lit., sailor, fr. *naus* ship] **1 :** any of a genus (*Nautilus*) of cephalopod mollusks of the So. Pacific and Indian oceans having a spiral chambered shell pearly on the inside **2 :** a cephalopod (genus *Argonauta*) whose female has a delicate papery shell — called also *paper nautilus*

Na·va·ho *or* **Na·va·jo** \'nav-ə-,hō, 'näv-\ *n, pl* **Navaho** *or* **Navahos** *or* **Navajo** *or* **Navajos** [Sp (*Apache de*) *Navajó,* lit., Apache of Navajó, fr. *Navajó,* a pueblo] **1 a :** an Athapaskan people of northern New Mexico and Arizona **b :** a member of this people **2 :** the language of the Navaho people

na·val \'nā-vəl\ *adj* [L *navalis,* fr. *navis*] **1** *obs* **:** of or relating to ships or shipping **2 a :** of or relating to a navy **b :** consisting of or involving warships

1**nave** \'nāv\ *n* [ME, fr. OE *nafu;* akin to OE *nafela* navel] **:** the hub of a wheel

2**nave** *n* [ML *navis,* fr. L, ship; akin to OE *nōwend* sailor, Gk *naus* ship, Skt *nau*] **:** the main part of the interior of a church; *esp* **:** the long narrow central hall in a cruciform church that rises higher than the aisles flanking it to form a clerestory

na·vel \'nā-vəl\ *n* [ME, fr. OE *nafela;* akin to OHG *nabalo* navel, L *umbilicus,* Gk *omphalos*] **1 :** a depression in the middle of the abdomen marking the point of attachment of the umbilical cord or yolk stalk **2 :** the central point **:** MIDDLE

navel orange *n* **:** a seedless orange having a pit at the apex where the fruit encloses a small secondary fruit

1**na·vic·u·lar** \nə-'vik-yə-lər\ *adj* [L *navicula* boat, dim. of *navis*] **:** shaped like a boat ⟨a ~ bone⟩

2**navicular** *also* **na·vic·u·la·re** \nə-,vik-yə-'la(ə)r-ē, -'le(ə)r-, -'lär-\ *n* [NL (*os*) *naviculare* navicular bone] **:** a navicular bone esp. of the carpus

nav·i·ga·bil·i·ty \,nav-i-gə-'bil-ət-ē\ *n* **:** the quality or state of being navigable

nav·i·ga·ble \'nav-i-gə-bəl\ *adj* **1 :** deep enough and wide enough to afford passage to ships **2 :** capable of being steered — **nav·i·ga·ble·ness** *n* — **nav·i·ga·bly** \-blē\ *adv*

nav·i·gate \'nav-ə-,gāt\ *vb* [L *navigatus,* pp. of *navigare,* fr. *navis* ship + *-igare* (fr. *agere* to drive) — more at AGENT] *vi* **1 :** to travel by water **:** SAIL **2 :** to steer a course through any medium; *specif* **:** to operate an airplane **3 :** to get about **:** WALK ⟨well enough to ~ under his own power⟩ ~ *vt* **1 a :** to sail over, on, or through **b :** to make one's way over or through **:** TRAVERSE **2 a :** to steer or manage (a boat) in sailing **b :** to operate or control the course of (as an airplane)

nav·i·ga·tion \,nav-ə-'gā-shən\ *n* **1 :** the act or practice of navigating **2 :** the science of getting ships or airplanes from place to place; *esp* **:** the method of determining position, course, and distance traveled **3 :** ship traffic or commerce — **nav·i·ga·tion·al** \-shnəl, -shən-ᵊl\ *adj* — **nav·i·ga·tion·al·ly** \-ē\ *adv*

nav·i·ga·tor \'nav-ə-,gāt-ər\ *n* **:** one that navigates or is qualified to navigate; *esp* **:** one who explores by ship

nav·vy \'nav-ē\ *n* [by shortening & alter. fr. *navigator* (construction worker on a canal, navvy)] *Brit* **:** an unskilled laborer

na·vy \'nā-vē\ *n* [ME *navie,* fr. MF, fr. L *navigia* ships, fr. *navigare*] **1 :** a group of ships **:** FLEET **2 :** a nation's ships of war and of logistic support **3** *often cap* **:** the complete naval establishment of a nation including yards, stations, ships, and personnel **4 :** a variable color averaging a grayish purplish blue

navy bean *n* **:** a white-seeded kidney bean grown esp. for its nutritious seeds

Navy Cross *n* **:** a U.S. decoration awarded for extraordinary heroism in operations against an armed enemy

navy yard *n* **:** a yard where naval vessels are built or repaired

1**nay** \'nā\ *adv* [ME, fr. ON *nei,* fr. *ne* not + *ei* ever — more at AYE] **1 :** NO **2 :** not merely this but also **:** not only so but ⟨the letter made him happy, ~, ecstatic⟩

2**nay** *n* **1 :** DENIAL, REFUSAL **2 a :** a negative reply or vote **b :** one who votes no

Naz·a·rene \,naz-ə-'rēn\ *n* [ME *Nazaren,* fr. LL *Nazarenus,* fr. Gk *Nazarēnos,* fr. *Nazareth,* town in Palestine] **1 :** a native or resident of Nazareth **2 a :** CHRISTIAN 1a **b :** a member of the Church of the Nazarene that is a Protestant denomination deriving from the merging of three holiness groups and following Wesleyan doctrines and polity

na·zi \'nät-sē, 'nat-\ *n* [G, by shortening & alter. fr. *nationalsozialist,* fr. *national* + *sozialist* socialist] **1** *cap* **:** a member of a German fascist party controlling Germany from 1933 to 1945 under Adolf Hitler **2** *often cap* **:** one held to resemble a German Nazi — **nazi** *adj, often cap* — **na·zi·fi·ca·tion** \,nät-si-fə-'kā-shən, ,nat-\ *n, often cap* — **na·zi·fy** \'nät-si-,fī, 'nat-\ *vt, often cap* — **Na·zism** \'nät-,siz-əm, 'nat-\ *or* **Na·zi·ism** \-sē-,iz-əm\ *n*

Naz·i·rite *or* **Naz·a·rite** \'naz-ə-,rīt\ *n* [LL *nazaraeus,* fr. Gk *naziraios, nazaraios,* fr. Heb *nāzīr,* lit., consecrated] **:** a Jew of biblical times consecrated to God by a vow esp. to avoid drinking wine, cutting the hair, and being defiled by a corpse — **Naz·i·rit·ism** \-,rīt-,iz-əm\ *n*

ne- *or* **neo-** *comb form* [Gk, fr. *neos* new — more at NEW] **1 a :** new **:** recent ⟨*Neo*cene⟩ **b :** new and different period or form of ⟨*Neo*platonism⟩ **:** in a new and different form or manner ⟨*Neo*platonic⟩ **c :** New World ⟨*Neo*tropical⟩ **d :** new and abnormal ⟨*neo*plasm⟩ **2 :** new chemical compound isomeric with or otherwise related to (such) a compound ⟨*neo*arsphenamine⟩

Ne·an·der·thal \nē-'an-dər-,t(h)ȯl, nā-'än-dər-,täl\ *adj* **1 :** being, relating to, or resembling Neanderthal man **2 :** suggesting a caveman in appearance or behavior — **Neanderthal** *n*

Neanderthal man *n* [*Neanderthal,* valley in western Germany] **:** a Middle Paleolithic man (*Homo neanderthalensis*) known from skeletal remains in Europe, northern Africa, and western Asia — **Ne·an·der·thal·oid** \-,ȯid\ *adj or n*

neap \'nēp\ *adj* [ME *neep,* fr. OE *nēp* being at the stage of neap tide] **:** of, relating to, or constituting a neap tide

Ne·a·pol·i·tan ice cream \,nē-ə-,päl-ət-ᵊn-\ *n* [*Neapolitan* (of Naples), fr. L *neapolitanus,* fr. Gk *neapolitēs* citizen of Naples, fr. *Neapolis* Naples] **:** a brick of from two to four layers of ice cream of different flavors usu. including an ice

neap tide *n* **:** a tide of minimum range occurring at the first and the third quarters of the moon

1**near** \'ni(ə)r\ *adv* [ME *ner,* partly fr. *ner* nearer, fr. OE *nēar,* comparative of *nēah* nigh; partly fr. ON *nær* nearer, compar. of *nā-* nigh — more at NIGH] **1 :** at, within, or to a short distance or time **2 :** ALMOST, NEARLY ⟨~ dead⟩ **3 :** CLOSELY, INTIMATELY ⟨~ related⟩ **4** *archaic* **:** FRUGALLY

2**near** \(')ni(ə)r\ *prep* **:** close to

3**near** \'ni(ə)r\ *adj* **1 :** closely related or intimately associated **2 a :** not far distant in time, place, or degree **b :** barely avoided **c :** CLOSE, NARROW ⟨a ~ miss⟩ **3 a :** being the closer of two ⟨~ side⟩ **b :** being the left-hand one of a pair ⟨~ wheel of a cart⟩ **4 :** DIRECT, SHORT ⟨~*est* road⟩ **5 :** CLOSEFISTED, STINGY **6 a :** closely resembling a prototype **b :** approximating the genuine ⟨~ silk⟩ — **near·ly** *adv* — **near·ness** *n*

4**near** \'ni(ə)r\ *vb* **:** APPROACH

near·by \ni(ə)r-'bī, 'ni(ə)r-,\ *adv* (*or adj*) **:** close at hand

Ne·arc·tic \(')nē-'ärk-tik, -'ärt-ik\ *adj* **:** of, relating to, or being the biogeographic subregion that includes Greenland, arctic America, and the northern and mountainous parts of No. America

near point *n* **:** the point nearest the eye at which an object is accurately focused on the retina at full accommodation

near·sight·ed \'ni(ə)r-'sīt-əd\ *adj* **:** seeing distinctly at short distances only — **near·sight·ed·ly** *adv* — **near·sight·ed·ness** *n*

1**neat** \'nēt\ *n, pl* **neat** [ME *neet,* fr. OE *nēat;* akin to OHG *nōz* head of cattle, OE *nēotan* to make use of] **:** the common domestic bovine (*Bos taurus*)

2**neat** *adj* [MF *net,* fr. L *nitidus* bright, neat, fr. *nitēre* to shine; akin to OPer *naiba-* beautiful] **1 a :** free from admixture or dilution **:** STRAIGHT ⟨~ brandy⟩ **b :** free from irregularity **:** SMOOTH ⟨~ silk⟩ **2 :** marked by tasteful simplicity ⟨a ~ outfit⟩ **3 a :** PRECISE, SYSTEMATIC **b :** marked by skill or ingenuity **:** ADROIT **4 :** being orderly and clean **:** TIDY **5 :** CLEAR, NET ⟨~ profit⟩ **6** *slang* **:** FINE, ADMIRABLE — **neat·ly** *adv* — **neat·ness** *n*

syn TIDY, TRIM, TRIG: NEAT stresses cleanness, orderliness, and freedom from clutter, jumble, or raggedness; TIDY suggests pleasing neatness and order diligently maintained; TRIM suggests neat smartness, clean lines, and good proportions; TRIG suggests compactness and jaunty neatness

neath \(')nēth\ *prep, dial* **:** BENEATH

neat·herd \'nēt-,hərd\ *n* **:** HERDSMAN

neat's-foot oil \'nēts-,fu̇t-\ *n* **:** a pale yellow fatty oil made esp. from the bones of cattle and used chiefly as a leather dressing

neb \'neb\ *n* [ME, fr. OE; akin to ON *nef* beak] **1 a :** the beak of a bird or tortoise **:** BILL **b** *chiefly dial* **:** a person's mouth **c :** NOSE 1, SNOUT **2 :** NIB, TIP

Neb·u·chad·nez·zar \,neb-(y)ə-kəd-'nez-ər, -,kad-\ *also* **Neb·u·chad·rez·zar** \-'rez-\ *n* [Heb *Nĕbhūkhadhnĕṣṣar,* modif. of Bab *Nabû-kudurri-uṣur*] **:** king of Babylon from 605 to 562 B.C. and conqueror of Jerusalem

neb·u·la \'neb-yə-lə\ *n, pl* **nebulas** *or* **neb·u·lae** \-,lē, -,lī\ [NL, fr. L, mist, cloud; akin to OHG *nebul* fog, Gk *nephelē, nephos* cloud] **1 :** a slight cloudy opacity of the cornea **2 a :** any of many immense bodies of highly rarefied gas or dust in interstellar space **b :** GALAXY; *specif* **:** a galaxy outside the Milky Way galaxy — **neb·u·lar** \-lər\ *adj*

nebular hypothesis *n* **:** a hypothesis in astronomy: the solar system has evolved from a hot gaseous nebula

neb·u·lize \'neb-yə-,līz\ *vt* [L *nebula*] **:** to reduce to a fine spray — **neb·u·liz·er** *n*

neb·u·los·i·ty \,neb-yə-'läs-ət-ē\ *n* **1 :** the quality or state of being nebulous **2 :** nebulous matter **:** NEBULA

neb·u·lous \'neb-yə-ləs\ *adj* [L *nebulosus,* fr. *nebula*] **1 a** *archaic* **:** CLOUDY, FOGGY **b :** HAZY, INDISTINCT **2 :** of, relating to, or resembling a nebula **:** NEBULAR — **neb·u·lous·ly** *adv* — **neb·u·lous·ness** *n*

nec·es·sar·i·ly \,nes-ə-'ser-ə-lē\ *adv* **:** of necessity **:** UNAVOIDABLY

1**nec·es·sary** \'nes-ə-,ser-ē\ *n* **1 :** an indispensable item **:** ESSENTIAL; *specif* **:** MONEY **2** *chiefly New Eng* **:** PRIVY 2

2**necessary** *adj* [ME *necessarie,* fr. L *necessarius,* fr. *necesse* necessary, fr. *ne-* not + *cedere* to withdraw — more at NO, CEDE] **1 a :** of an inevitable nature **:** INESCAPABLE **b** (1) **:** logically unavoidable (2) **:** that cannot be denied without contradiction **c :** PREDETERMINED **d :** COMPULSORY **2 :** absolutely needed **:** REQUIRED

necessary condition *n* **:** a proposition whose invalidity is sufficient evidence that a second is invalid

ne·ces·si·tar·i·an \ni-,ses-ə-'ter-ē-ən\ *n* **:** one who accepts or advocates necessitarianism — **necessitarian** *adj*

ne·ces·si·tar·i·an·ism \-,iz-əm\ *n* **:** the theory that results follow by invariable sequence from causes

ne·ces·si·tate \ni-'ses-ə-,tāt\ *vt* **1 :** to cause to be a necessary concomitant, result, or consequence **2 :** FORCE, COMPEL — **ne·ces·si·ta·tion** \-,ses-ə-'tā-shən\ *n*

ne·ces·si·tous \ni-'ses-ət-əs\ *adj* **1 a :** NEEDY, IMPOVERISHED

b : STRAITENED **2** : URGENT, PRESSING **3** : NECESSARY — **ne·ces·si·tous·ly** *adv* — **ne·ces·si·tous·ness** *n*

ne·ces·si·ty \ni-'ses-ət-ē, -'ses-tē\ *n* [ME *necessite*, fr. MF *necessité*, fr. L *necessitat-, necessitas*, fr *necesse*] **1** : the quality or state of being necessary : INDISPENSABILITY **2 a** : pressure of circumstance **b** : natural compulsion ⟨physical ~⟩ **c** : impossibility of a contrary order or condition **3** : the quality or state of being in need; *esp* : POVERTY **4 a** : something that is necessary : REQUIREMENT **b** : an urgent need or desire **syn** see NEED

1**neck** \'nek\ *n* [ME *nekke*, fr. OE *hnecca;* akin to OHG *hnac* nape, OE *hnutu* nut — more at NUT] **1 a** : the part of an animal that connects the head with the body **b** : the part of a garment that covers or is next to the neck **2** : a relatively narrow part suggestive of a neck: as **a** (1) : the constricted end of a bottle (2) : the slender proximal end of a fruit **b** : CERVIX 2 **c** : the part of a stringed musical instrument extending from the body and supporting the fingerboard and strings **d** : a narrow stretch of land **e** : STRAIT 1b **f** : a column of solidified magma of a volcanic pipe or laccolith **3** : a narrow margin **4** : REGION, PART ⟨~ of the woods⟩ — **neck·cloth** \'nek-,klȯth\ *n* — **necked** \'nekt\ *adj* — **neck·line** \'nek-,līn\ *n*

2**neck** *vt* **1** : to reduce in diameter; *esp* : GROOVE **2** : to kiss and caress amorously ~ *vi* **1** : to engage in amorous kissing and caressing **2** : to become constricted : NARROW

neck·er·chief \'nek-ər-chəf, -(,)chif, -,chēf\ *n, pl* **neckerchiefs** *also* **neck·er·chieves** *see* HANDKERCHIEF *pl*\ [ME *nekkerchef*, fr. *nekke* + *kerchef* kerchief] : a kerchief for the neck

neck·ing \'nek-iŋ\ *n* **1** : a small molding near the top of a column or pilaster **2** : the act or practice of kissing and caressing amorously

neck·lace \'nek-ləs\ *n* : an ornament (as a string of beads) worn around the neck

neck–rein \'nek-,rān\ *vi, of a saddle horse* : to respond to the pressure of a rein on one side of the neck by turning in the opposite direction ~ *vt* : to guide or direct (a horse) by pressures of the rein on the neck

neck·tie \-,tī\ *n* : a narrow length of material worn about the neck and tied in front; *esp* : FOUR-IN-HAND

necr- *or* **necro-** *comb form* [LL, fr. Gk *nekr-, nekro-*, fr. *nekros* dead body — more at NOXIOUS] **1 a** : those that are dead ⟨*necro*philia⟩ **b** : one that is dead ⟨*necro*psy⟩ **2** : conversion to dead tissue ⟨*necro*biosis⟩

nec·ro·log·i·cal \,nek-rə-'läj-i-kəl\ *also* **nec·ro·log·ic** \-ik\ *adj* : of or relating to necrology — **nec·ro·log·i·cal·ly** \-i-k(ə-)lē\ *adv*

ne·crol·o·gist \nə-'kräl-ə-jəst, ne-\ *n* : one that writes or compiles a necrology

ne·crol·o·gy \-jē\ *n* [NL *necrologium*, fr. *necr-* + *-logium* (as in ML *eulogium* eulogy)] **1** : a list of the recently dead **2** : OBITUARY

nec·ro·man·cer \'nek-rə-,man(t)-sər\ *n* : one that practices necromancy

nec·ro·man·cy \-sē\ *n* [alter. of ME *nigromancie*, fr. MF, fr. ML *nigromantia*, by folk etymology fr. LL *necromantia*, fr. LGk *nekromanteia*, fr. Gk *nekr-* + *-manteia* -mancy] **1** : conjuration of the spirits of the dead for purposes of magically revealing the future or influencing the course of events **2** : MAGIC, SORCERY — **nec·ro·man·tic** \,nek-rə-'mant-ik\ *adj* — **nec·ro·man·ti·cal·ly** \-i-k(ə-)lē\ *adv*

nec·ro·pha·gia \,nek-rə-'fā-j(ē-)ə\ *n* [NL] : the act or practice of eating corpses or carrion — **ne·croph·a·gous** \nə-'kräf-ə-gəs, ne-\ *adj*

ne·crop·o·lis \nə-'kräp-ə-ləs, ne-\ *n, pl* **ne·crop·o·lis·es** *or* **ne·crop·o·les** \-ə-,lēz\ *also* **ne·crop·o·leis** \-,lās\ *or* **ne·crop·o·li** \-,lī, -,lē\ [LL, city of the dead, fr. Gk *nekropolis*, fr. *nekr-* + *-polis*] : CEMETERY; *esp* : a large elaborate cemetery of an ancient city

nec·rop·sy \'nek-,räp-sē\ *n* : POSTMORTEM EXAMINATION

ne·cro·sis \nə-'krō-səs, ne-\ *n, pl* **ne·cro·ses** \-'krō-,sēz\ [LL, fr. Gk *nekrōsis*, fr. *nekroun* to make dead, fr. *nekros* — more at NOXIOUS] : usu. localized death of living tissue — **ne·crot·ic** \-'krät-ik\ *adj*

nec·ro·tize \'nek-rə-,tīz\ *vi* [Gk *nekrōtikos* necrotic, fr. *nekroun*] : to undergo necrosis

nec·tar \'nek-tər\ *n* [L, fr. Gk *nektar*] **1 a** : the drink of the Greek and Roman gods **b** : any delicious drink **2** : a sweet liquid that is secreted by the nectaries of a plant and is the chief raw material of honey — **nec·tar·ous** \-t(ə-)rəs\ *adj*

nec·tar·ine \,nek-tə-'rēn\ *n* [obs. *nectarine*, adj. (like nectar)] : a peach with a smooth-skinned fruit that is a frequent somatic mutation of the normal peach; *also* : its fruit

nec·tary \'nek-t(ə-)rē\ *n* [NL *nectarium*, irreg. fr. L *nectar* + *-arium* -ary] : a plant gland that secretes nectar

née *or* **nee** \'nā\ *adj* [F *née*, fem. of *né*, lit., born, pp. of *naître* to be born, fr. L *nasci* — more at NATION] — used to identify a woman by her maiden family name

1**need** \'nēd\ *n* [ME *ned*, fr. OE *nīed, nēd;* akin to OHG *nōt* distress, need] **1** : necessary duty : OBLIGATION **2** : a lack of something requisite, desirable, or useful **3** : a condition requiring supply or relief : EXIGENCY **4** : want of the means of subsistence : POVERTY

syn NEED, NECESSITY, EXIGENCY mean a pressing lack of something essential. NEED implies urgency and may suggest distress; NECESSITY carries less emotional connotation but may stress imperative demand or compelling cause; EXIGENCY adds the implication of unusual difficulty or restriction imposed by special circumstances

2**need** *vi* **1** : to be in want **2** : to be needful or necessary ~ *vt* : to be in need of : REQUIRE ~ *verbal auxiliary* : be under necessity or obligation to ⟨he ~ not answer⟩ **syn** see LACK

1**need·ful** \'nēd-fəl\ *adj* : NECESSARY, REQUISITE — **need·ful·ly** \-fə-lē\ *adv* — **need·ful·ness** *n*

2**needful** *n* : something needed; *esp* : MONEY

need·i·ness \'nēd-ē-nəs\ *n* : the quality or state of being needy

1**nee·dle** \'nēd-ᵊl\ *n, often attrib* [ME *nedle*, fr. OE *nǣdl;* akin to OHG *nādala* needle, *nājan* to sew, L *nēre* to spin, Gk *nēn*] **1 a** : a small slender usu. steel instrument with an eye for thread at one end used for sewing **b** : any of various devices for carrying thread and making stitches in crocheting, knitting, netting, or hooking **c** (1) : a needle designed to carry sutures when sewing tissues in surgery (2) : a slender hollow instrument for introducing material into or removing material from the body parenterally (3) : a hollow device designed to contain radioactive material **2** : a slender usu. sharp-pointed indicator on a dial; *specif* : MAGNETIC NEEDLE **3 a** : a slender pointed object resembling a needle: as (1) : a pointed crystal (2) : a sharp rock (3) : OBELISK **b** : a needle-shaped leaf (as of a conifer) **c** : a slender piece of jewel, steel, wood, or fiber with a rounded tip used in a phonograph to transmit vibrations from the record **d** : a slender pointed rod controlling a fine inlet or outlet (as in a valve) — **nee·dle·like** \'nēd-ᵊl-,(l)īk\ *adj*

2**needle** *vb* **nee·dling** \'nēd-liŋ, -ᵊl-iŋ\ *vt* **1** : to sew or pierce with or as if with a needle **2** : PROD, GOAD; *esp* : to incite to action by repeated gibes **3** : to strengthen (a beverage) by adding raw alcohol ~ *vi* : SEW, EMBROIDER — **nee·dler** \-lər, -ᵊl-ər\ *n* — **nee·dling** *n*

nee·dle·fish \'nēd-ᵊl-,fish\ *n* **1** : any of a family (Belonidae) of voracious elongate teleost fishes resembling but not related to the freshwater gars **2** : PIPEFISH

nee·dle·point \-,pȯint\ *n* **1** : lace worked with a needle in buttonhole stitch over a paper pattern **2** : embroidery done on canvas usu. in simple even stitches across counted threads — **needlepoint** *adj*

need·less \'nēd-ləs\ *adj* : UNNECESSARY — **need·less·ly** *adv* — **need·less·ness** *n*

nee·dle·wom·an \'nēd-ᵊl-,wu̇m-ən\ *n* : a woman who does needlework; *esp* : SEAMSTRESS

nee·dle·work \-,wərk\ *n* **1** : work done with a needle; *specif* : work (as embroidery) other than plain sewing **2** : the occupation of one who does needlework — **nee·dle·work·er** \-,wər-kər\ *n*

needn't \'nēd-ᵊnt\ : need not

needs \'nēdz\ *adv* [ME *nedes*, fr. OE *nēdes*, fr. gen. of *nēd* need] : of necessity : NECESSARILY ⟨must ~ be recognized⟩

needy \'nēd-ē\ *adj* : being in want : POVERTY-STRICKEN

ne'er \(')ne(ə)r, (')na(ə)r\ *adv* : NEVER

ne'er–do–well \'ne(ə)rd-ü-,wel, 'na(ə)rd-\ *n* : an idle worthless person — **ne'er–do–well** *adj*

ne·far·i·ous \ni-'far-ē-əs, -'fer-\ *adj* [L *nefarius*, fr. *nefas* crime, fr. *ne-* not + *fas* right, divine law; akin to L *fari* to speak] : flagrantly wicked or impious : EVIL **syn** see VICIOUS — **ne·far·i·ous·ly** *adv* — **ne·far·i·ous·ness** *n*

ne·gate \ni-'gāt\ *vt* [L *negatus*, pp. of *negare* to say no, deny, fr. *neg-* no, not (akin to *ne-* not) — more at NO] **1** : to deny the existence or truth of **2** : to cause to be ineffective or invalid **syn** see NULLIFY — **negate** *n* — **ne·ga·tor** *or* **ne·gat·er** \-'gāt-ər\ *n*

ne·ga·tion \ni-'gā-shən\ *n* **1 a** : the action of negating : DENIAL **b** : a negative doctrine or statement **2 a** : something that is the absence of something actual : NONENTITY **b** : something that is the negative opposite of something positive — **ne·ga·tion·al** \-shnəl, -shən-ᵊl\ *adj*

1**neg·a·tive** \'neg-ət-iv\ *adj* **1 a** : marked by denial, prohibition, or refusal **b** (1) : denying a predicate of a subject or a part of a subject ⟨"no A is B" is a ~ proposition⟩ (2) : denoting the absence or the contradictory of something ⟨*nonwhite* is a ~ term⟩ **2 a** : lacking positive qualities : DISAGREEABLE **b** : marked by features opposing constructive treatment or development **3 a** : less than zero and opposite in sign to a positive number that when added to the given number yields zero ⟨−2 is a ~ number⟩ **b** : that is or is generated in a direction opposite to an arbitrarily chosen regular direction or position ⟨~ angle⟩ **4 a** : being, relating to, or charged with electricity of which the electron is the elementary unit **b** : gaining electrons **c** (1) : having lower electric potential and constituting the part toward which the current flows from the external circuit ⟨the ~ pole⟩ (2) : constituting an electrode through which a stream of electrons enters the space between electrodes in an electron tube **5 a** : not affirming the presence of the organism or condition in question ⟨~ diagnosis⟩ **b** : directed or moving away from a source of stimulation ⟨~ tropism⟩ **c** : less than the pressure of the atmosphere ⟨~ pressure⟩ **6** : having the light and dark parts in approximately inverse order to those of the original photographic subject — **neg·a·tive·ly** *adv* — **neg·a·tive·ness** *n* — **neg·a·tiv·i·ty** \,neg-ə-'tiv-ət-ē\ *n*

2**negative** *n* **1 a** : a proposition by which something is denied or contradicted **b** (1) : a reply that indicates the withholding of assent : REFUSAL (2) *archaic* : a right of veto (3) *obs* : an adverse vote : VETO **2** : something that is the opposite or negation of something else **3 a** : an expression (as the word *no*) of negation or denial **b** : a negative number **4** : the side that upholds the contradictory proposition in a debate **5** : the plate of a voltaic or electrolytic cell that is at the lower potential **6** : a negative photographic image on transparent material used for printing positive pictures; *also* : the material that carries such an image **7** : a reverse impression taken from a piece of sculpture or ceramics

3**negative** *vt* **1 a** : to refuse assent to **b** (1) : to reject by or as if by a vote (2) : VETO **2** : to demonstrate the falsity of : DISPROVE **3** : DENY, CONTRADICT **4** : NEUTRALIZE, COUNTERACT **syn** see DENY

neg·a·tiv·ism \'neg-ət-iv-,iz-əm\ *n* **1** : an attitude of mind marked by skepticism about nearly everything affirmed by others **2** : a tendency to refuse to do, do the opposite of, or do something at variance with what is asked — **neg·a·tiv·ist** \-əst\ *n* — **neg·a·tiv·is·tic** \,neg-ət-iv-'is-tik\ *adj*

neg·a·tron \'neg-ə-,trän\ *also* **neg·a·ton** \-,tän\ *n* [*negatron* fr. *nega*tive + elec*tron;* *negaton* fr. *nega*tive + *-on*] : ELECTRON

1**ne·glect** \ni-'glekt\ *vt* [L *neglectus*, pp. of *neglegere, neclegere*, fr. *nec-* not (akin to *ne-* not) + *legere* to gather — more at NO, LEGEND] **1** : to give little attention or respect to : DISREGARD **2** : to leave undone or unattended to esp. through carelessness — **ne·glect·er** *n*

syn NEGLECT, OMIT, DISREGARD, IGNORE, OVERLOOK, SLIGHT, FORGET mean to pass over without giving due attention. NEGLECT implies giving insufficient attention to something that has a claim to one's attention; OMIT implies absence of all attention; DISREGARD suggests voluntary inattention; IGNORE implies a failure to regard something obvious; OVERLOOK suggests disregarding or ignoring through haste or lack of care; SLIGHT implies contemptuous or disdainful disregarding or omitting; FORGET may suggest a willful ignoring or failure to impress on one's mind

2**neglect** *n* **1** : an act or instance of neglecting something **2** : the condition of being neglected

ne·glect·ful \ni-'glek(t)-fəl\ *adj* : given to neglecting : CARELESS,

HEEDLESS **syn** see NEGLIGENT — **ne·glect·ful·ly** \-fə-lē\ *adv* — **ne·glect·ful·ness** *n*

neg·li·gee *also* **neg·li·gé** \ˌneg-lə-ˈzhā\ *n* [F *négligé*, fr. pp. of *négliger* to neglect, fr. L *neglegere*] **1 :** a woman's long flowing dressing gown **2 :** carelessly informal or incomplete attire

neg·li·gence \ˈneg-li-jən(t)s\ *n* **1 a :** the quality or state of being negligent **b :** failure to exercise the care that a prudent person usu. exercises **2 :** an act or instance of negligence

neg·li·gent \-jənt\ *adj* [ME, fr. MF & L; MF, fr. L *neglegent-*, *neglegens*, prp. of *neglegere*] **1 :** marked by or given to neglect **2 :** marked by a carelessly easy manner — **neg·li·gent·ly** *adv*

syn NEGLECTFUL, LAX, SLACK, REMISS: NEGLIGENT implies inattention to one's duty or business; NEGLECTFUL adds a more censorious implication of laziness or callousness; LAX implies want of strictness, severity, or precision; SLACK implies want of due or necessary diligence or care; REMISS implies blameworthy carelessness shown in slackness, forgetfulness, or neglect

neg·li·gi·bil·i·ty \ˌneg-li-jə-ˈbil-ət-ē\ *n* **:** the quality or state of being negligible

neg·li·gi·ble \ˈneg-li-jə-bəl\ *adj* [L *neglegere*, *negligere*] **:** fit to be neglected or disregarded **:** TRIFLING — **neg·li·gi·bly** \-blē\ *adv*

ne·go·tia·bil·i·ty \ni-ˌgō-sh(ē-)ə-ˈbil-ət-ē\ *n* **:** the quality or state of being negotiable

ne·go·tia·ble \ni-ˈgō-sh(ē-)ə-bəl\ *adj* **:** capable of being negotiated; *esp* **:** transferable from one person to another in return for equivalent value by being delivered with or without endorsement so that the title passes to the transferee

ne·go·tiant \-sh(ē-)ənt\ *n* **:** NEGOTIATOR

ne·go·ti·ate \ni-ˈgō-shē-ˌāt\ *vb* [L *negotiatus*, pp. of *negotiari* to carry on business, fr. *negotium* business, fr. *neg-* not + *otium* leisure — more at NEGATE] *vi* **:** to confer with another so as to arrive at the settlement of some matter ~ *vt* **1 a :** to deal with **:** MANAGE **b :** to arrange for or bring about by negotiation **2 a :** to transfer (as a bill of exchange) to another by delivery or endorsement in return for equivalent value **b :** to convert into cash or the equivalent value ⟨~ securities⟩ **3 a :** to travel along or over successfully ⟨~ a turn⟩ **b :** COMPLETE, ACCOMPLISH ⟨~ the trip⟩ — **ne·go·ti·a·tor** \-ˌāt-ər\ *n*

ne·go·ti·a·tion \ni-ˌgō-s(h)ē-ˈā-shən\ *n* **:** the action or process of negotiating or being negotiated; *esp* **:** PARLEY 1 — **ne·go·tia·to·ry** \ni-ˈgō-sh(ē-)ə-ˌtōr-ē, -ˌtȯr-\ *adj*

Ne·gress \ˈnē-grəs\ *n* **:** a female Negro — usu. taken to be offensive

Ne·gril·lo \ni-ˈgril-(ˌ)ō, -ˈgrē-(ˌ)(y)ō\ *n, pl* **Negrillos** *or* **Negrilloes** [Sp, dim. of *negro*] **:** a member of a people (as Pygmies) belonging to a group of negroid peoples of small stature found in Africa

Ne·gri·to \nə-ˈgrēt-(ˌ)ō\ *n, pl* **Negritos** *or* **Negritoes** [Sp, dim. of *negro*] **:** a member of a people (as the Andamanese) belonging to a group of negroid peoples of small stature found in Oceania and the southeastern part of Asia

ne·gri·tude \ˈnē-grə-ˌtüd, ˈneg-rə-, -ˌtyüd\ *n* [F *négritude*, fr. *nègre* Negro + *-i-* + *-tude*] **:** a consciousness of and pride in the sum total of values that constitute the African heritage

Ne·gro \ˈnē-(ˌ)grō, *esp South* ˈnig-(ˌ)rō, -rə\ *n, pl* **Negroes** [Sp or Pg, fr. *negro* black, fr. L *nigr-*, *niger*] **1 :** a member of the black race of mankind distinguished by classification according to physical features but without regard to language or culture from members of other races; *esp* **:** a member of a people belonging to the African branch of the black race **2 :** a person of Negro ancestry — **Negro** *adj* — **ne·groid** \ˈnē-ˌgrȯid\ *n or adj, often cap*

ne·gro·phile \ˈnē-grō-ˌfīl\ *n, often cap* **:** one who is esp. friendly to Negroes and their interests — **ne·gro·phi·lism** \-ˌfī(ə)l-ˌiz-əm, ni-ˈgräf-ə-ˌliz-\ *n, often cap*

ne·gro·phobe \ˈnē-grə-ˌfōb\ *n, often cap* **:** one who strongly dislikes or fears Negroes — **ne·gro·pho·bia** \ˌnē-grə-ˈfō-bē-ə\ *n, often cap*

¹**ne·gus** \ˈnē-gəs, ni-ˈgüs\ *n* [Amharic *negūs*, fr. Eth *nĕgūša nagašt* king of kings] **:** KING — used as a title of the sovereign of Ethiopia

²**ne·gus** \ˈnē-gəs\ *n* [Francis *Negus* †1732 E colonel] **:** a beverage of wine, hot water, sugar, lemon juice, and nutmeg

Ne·he·mi·ah \ˌnē-(h)ə-ˈmī-ə\ *or* **Ne·he·mi·as** \-ˈmī-əs\ *n* [Heb *Nĕḥemyāh*] **:** a Jewish leader of the 5th century B.C.

neigh \ˈnā\ *vi* [ME *neyen*, fr. OE *hnǣgan*; akin to MHG *nēgen* to neigh] **:** to make the loud prolonged cry of a horse — **neigh** *n*

¹**neigh·bor** \ˈnā-bər\ *n* [ME, fr. OE *nēahgebūr*; akin to OHG *nāhgibūr* neighbor; both fr. a prehistoric WGmc compound represented by OE *nēah* near and by OE *gebūr* dweller — more at NIGH, BOOR] **1 :** one living or located near another **2 :** FELLOWMAN — often used as a term of address

²**neighbor** *adj* **:** NEIGHBORING

³**neighbor** *vb* **neigh·bor·ing** \-b(ə-)riŋ\ *vt* **1 a :** to be near to **b :** to border on **2 :** to provide with neighbors ~ *vi* **1 :** to live or be located as a neighbor **2 :** to associate in a neighborly way

neigh·bor·hood \ˈnā-bər-ˌhu̇d\ *n* **1 :** neighborly relationship, **2 :** the quality or state of being neighbors **:** PROXIMITY **3 a :** a place or region near **:** VICINITY **b :** an approximate amount, extent, or degree ⟨cost in the ~ of $10⟩ **4 a :** the people living near one another **b :** a section lived in by neighbors and usu. having distinguishing characteristics **5 :** the set of all points whose distances from a given point are not greater than a given positive number

neigh·bor·li·ness \-lē-nəs\ *n* **:** the quality or state of being neighborly

neigh·bor·ly \ˈnā-bər-lē\ *adj* **:** of, relating to, or characteristic of congenial neighbors; *esp* **:** FRIENDLY **syn** see AMICABLE

neighbour *chiefly Brit var of* NEIGHBOR

¹**nei·ther** \ˈnē-t͟hər *also* ˈnī-\ *pron* [ME, alter. of *nauther*, *nother*, fr. OE *nāhwæther*, *nōther*, fr. *nā*, *nō* not + *hwæther* which of two, whether] **:** not the one or the other of two or more

²**neither** *conj* **1 :** not either ⟨~ black nor white⟩ **2 :** also not ⟨~ did I⟩

³**neither** *adj* **:** not either ⟨~ hand⟩

⁴**neither** *adv* **1** *chiefly dial* **:** EITHER ⟨are not to be understood ~ —Earl of Chesterfield⟩ **2 :** similarly not **:** also not ⟨just as the serf was not permitted to leave the land, so ~ was his offspring —G.G. Coulton⟩

nek·ton \ˈnek-tən, -ˌtän\ *n* [G *nekton*, fr. Gk *nēkton*, neut. of *nēktos* swimming, fr. *nēchein* to swim; akin to L *nare* to swim] **:** free-swimming aquatic animals essentially independent of wave and current action — **nek·ton·ic** \nek-ˈtän-ik\ *adj*

nel·son \ˈnel-sən\ *n* [prob. fr. the name *Nelson*] **:** a wrestling hold marked by the application of leverage against an opponent's arm, neck, and head

ne·ma \ˈnē-mə\ *n* [by shortening] **:** NEMATODE

nemat- *or* **nemato-** *comb form* [NL, fr. Gk *nēmat-*, *nēmat-*, *nēma*, fr. *nēn* to spin — more at NEEDLE] **1 :** thread ⟨*Nemat*helminthes⟩ **2 :** nematode ⟨*nemato*logy⟩

ne·ma·thel·minth \ˌnem-ə-ˈthel-ˌmin(t)th, ˌnē-mə-\ *n* [deriv. of Gk *nēma* + *helmis* worm — more at HELMINTH] **:** any of a phylum (Nemathelminthes) of wormlike animals with a cylindrical unsegmented body covered by an unciliated ectoderm that secretes an external cuticle

ne·ma·to·ci·dal \ˌnem-ət-ə-ˈsīd-ᵊl, nə-ˌmat-ə-\ *adj* **:** capable of destroying nematodes — **ne·ma·to·cide** \ˈnem-ət-ə-ˌsīd, nə-ˈmat-ə-\ *n*

ne·ma·to·cyst \ˈnem-ət-ə-ˌsist, nə-ˈmat-ə-\ *n* [ISV] **:** one of the minute stinging organs of various coelenterates — **ne·ma·to·cys·tic** \ˌnem-ət-ə-ˈsis-tik, nə-ˌmat-ə-\ *adj*

nem·a·tode \ˈnem-ə-ˌtōd\ *n, often attrib* [deriv. of Gk *nēmat-*, *nēma*] **:** any of a class or phylum (Nematoda) of elongated cylindrical worms parasitic in animals or plants or free-living in soil or water

nem·a·tol·o·gy \ˌnem-ə-ˈtäl-ə-jē\ *n* **:** a branch of zoology that deals with nematodes

Nem·bu·tal \ˈnem-byə-ˌtȯl\ *trademark* — used for the sodium salt of pentobarbital

ne·mer·te·an \ni-ˈmərt-ē-ən\ *n* [deriv. of Gk *Nēmertēs* Nemertes, one of the Nereids] **:** any of a class (Nemertea) of often vividly colored marine worms most of which burrow in the mud or sand along seacoasts — **nemertean** *adj* — **nem·er·tine** \ˈnem-ər-ˌtīn\ *or* **nem·er·tin·e·an** \ˌnem-ər-ˈtin-ē-ən\ *adj or n*

nem·e·sis \ˈnem-ə-səs\ *n* [L, fr. Gk] **1** *cap* **:** the Greek goddess of retributive justice **2** *pl* **nem·e·ses** \-ə-ˌsēz\ **a :** one that inflicts retribution or vengeance **b :** a formidable and usu. victorious rival **3** *pl* **nemeses a :** an act or effect of retribution **b :** BANE 2, CURSE

ne·moph·i·la \ni-ˈmäf-ə-lə\ *n* [NL, genus name, fr. Gk *nemos* wooded pasture + *philos* loving] **:** any of a genus (*Nemophila*) of American annual herbs of the waterleaf family cultivated for their showy blue usu. spotted flowers

neo- — see NE-

neo·an·throp·ic \ˌnē-(ˌ)ō-an-ˈthräp-ik\ *adj* **:** belonging to the same species (*Homo sapiens*) as recent man **:** modern in anatomy or type

neo·ars·phen·a·mine \ˌnē-(ˌ)ō-ärs-ˈfen-ə-ˌmēn\ *n* **:** a yellow powder $C_{13}H_{13}As_2N_2NaO_4S$ similar to arsphenamine in structure and use

Neo·cene \ˈnē-ə-ˌsēn\ *adj* **:** relating to or being the later portion of the Tertiary including both the Miocene and Pliocene — **Neocene** *n*

neo·clas·sic \ˌnē-ō-ˈklas-ik\ *adj* **:** of or relating to a revival or adaptation of the classical style esp. in literature, art, or music — **neo·clas·si·cal** \-i-kəl\ *adj* — **neo·clas·si·cism** \-ˈklas-ə-ˌsiz-əm\ *n*

neo·co·lo·nial \ˌnē-(ˌ)ō-kə-ˈlō-nyəl, -ˈlō-nē-əl\ *adj* **:** of or relating to the policies by which a great power indirectly maintains or extends its influence over other areas or peoples — **neo·co·lo·nial·ism** *n*

neo–Dar·win·ian \ˌnē-(ˌ)ō-där-ˈwin-ē-ən\ *adj, often cap N* **:** of or relating to neo-Darwinism

neo–Dar·win·ism \-ˈdär-wə-ˌniz-əm\ *n, often cap N* **:** a theory that holds natural selection to be the chief factor in evolution and specif. denies the possibility of inheriting acquired characters — **neo–Dar·win·ist** \-nəst\ *n, often cap N*

neo·dym·i·um \ˌnē-ō-ˈdim-ē-əm\ *n* [NL, fr. *ne-* + *-dymium* (fr. *didymium*)] **:** a trivalent metallic element of the rare-earth group — see ELEMENT table

neo·gen·e·sis \ˌnē-ō-ˈjen-ə-səs\ *n* [NL] **:** new formation **:** REGENERATION — **neo·ge·net·ic** \ˌnē-(ˌ)ō-jə-ˈnet-ik\ *adj*

neo–im·pres·sion·ism \ˌnē-(ˌ)ō-im-ˈpresh-ə-ˌniz-əm\ *n, often cap N&I* [F *néo-impressionisme*, fr. *né-* ne- + *impressionisme* impressionism] **:** a late 19th century French art theory and practice characterized by an attempt to make impressionism more precise in form and the use of a pointillist painting technique — **neo–im·pres·sion·ist** \-ˈpresh-(ə-)nəst\ *adj or n, often cap N&I*

neo–La·marck·ism \ˌnē-(ˌ)ō-lə-ˈmär-ˌkiz-əm\ *n, often cap N* **:** a modern theory of evolution based on Lamarckism and retaining the fundamental concept that acquired characters are inherited and a major factor in evolution

Neo–Lat·in \ˌnē-ō-ˈlat-ᵊn\ *n* [ISV] **1 :** NEW LATIN **2 :** ROMANCE

neo·lith \ˈnē-ə-ˌlith\ *n* [back-formation fr. *neolithic*] **:** a Neolithic stone implement

neo·lith·ic \ˌnē-ə-ˈlith-ik\ *adj* **1** *cap* **:** of or relating to the latest period of the Stone Age characterized by polished stone implements **2 :** belonging to an earlier age and now outmoded

neo·log·i·cal \ˌnē-ə-ˈläj-i-kəl\ *adj* **:** of, relating to, or characterized by neology

ne·ol·o·gism \nē-ˈäl-ə-ˌjiz-əm\ *n* **1 :** a new word, usage, or expression **2 :** a meaningless word coined by a psychotic — **ne·ol·o·gist** \-jəst\ *n* — **ne·ol·o·gis·tic** \(ˌ)nē-ˌäl-ə-ˈjis-tik\ *adj*

ne·ol·o·gy \nē-ˈäl-ə-jē\ *n* [F *néologie*, fr. *né-* ne- + *-logie* -logy] **:** the use of a new word or expression or of an established word in a new or different sense

neo·my·cin \ˌnē-ə-ˈmīs-ᵊn\ *n* [*ne-* + *myc-* + *-in*] **:** a broad-spectrum antibiotic or mixture of antibiotics produced by a soil actinomycete (*Streptomyces fradiae*)

ne·on \ˈnē-ˌän\ *n, often attrib* [Gk, neut. of *neos* new — more at NEW] **1 :** a colorless odorless inert gaseous element found in minute amounts in air and used in electric lamps — see ELEMENT table **2 a :** a discharge lamp in which the gas contains a large amount of neon **b :** a sign composed of such lamps

neo·na·tal \ˌnē-ō-ˈnāt-ᵊl\ *adj* **:** of, relating to, or affecting the newborn and esp. the human infant during the first month after birth — **neo·na·tal·ly** \-ᵊl-ē\ *adv* — **neo·nate** \ˈnē-ə-ˌnāt\ *n*

neo·or·tho·dox \ˌnē-ō-ˈȯr-thə-ˌdäks\ *adj* **:** of or relating to a 20th century movement in Protestant theology characterized by a reaction against liberalism and emphasis on various Reformation doctrines — **neo·or·tho·doxy** \-ˌdäk-sē\ *n*

neo·phyte \ˈnē-ə-ˌfīt\ *n* [LL *neophytus*, fr. Gk *neophytos*, fr. *neophytos* newly planted, newly converted, fr. *ne-* + *phyein* to bring forth — more at BE] **1 :** a new convert **:** PROSELYTE **2 a :** a newly ordained Roman Catholic priest **b :** a novice in a convent **3 :** TYRO, BEGINNER

neo·pla·sia \ˌnē-ə-ˈplā-zh(ē-)ə\ *n* [NL] **1 :** the formation of tumors **2 :** a tumorous condition
neo·plasm \ˈnē-ə-ˌplaz-əm\ *n* [ISV] **:** a new growth of tissue serving no physiologic function **:** TUMOR
neo·plas·tic \ˌnē-ə-ˈplas-tik\ *adj* [ISV] **1 :** of, relating to, or constituting a neoplasm **2 :** of or relating to neoplasticism
neo·plas·ti·cism \-ˈplas-tə-ˌsiz-əm\ *n* [*ne-* + *plasticism*] **:** the de Stijl art principle in painting — **neo·plas·ti·cist** \-tə-səst\ *n*
Neo·pla·ton·ic \ˌnē-(ˌ)ō-plə-ˈtän-ik, -plā-\ *adj* **:** of or relating to Neoplatonism or Neoplatonists
Neo·pla·to·nism \ˌnē-ō-ˈplāt-ᵊn-ˌiz-əm\ *n* [ISV] **1 :** Platonism modified in later antiquity to accord with Aristotelian, post-Aristotelian, and oriental conceptions that conceives of the world as an emanation from the One with whom the soul is capable of being reunited in trance or ecstasy **2 :** doctrines similar to ancient Neoplatonism — **Neo·pla·to·nist** \-ᵊn-əst\ *n*
neo·prene \ˈnē-ə-ˌprēn\ *n* [*ne-* + chloro*prene*] **:** a synthetic rubber made by the polymerization of chloroprene and characterized by superior resistance (as to oils)
neo-scho·las·ti·cism \-skə-ˈlas-tə-ˌsiz-əm\ *n* **:** a contemporary movement among Catholic scholars aiming to restate the methods and teachings of medieval Scholasticism in a manner suited to the intellectual needs of the present
neo·te·nic \ˌnē-ə-ˈtē-nik, -ˈten-ik\ *adj* [ISV] **:** of, relating to, or exhibiting neoteny
neo·te·ny \ˈnē-ə-ˌtē-nē\ *n* [NL *neotenia*, fr. *ne-* + Gk *teinein* to stretch — more at THIN] **1 :** attainment of sexual maturity during the larval stage **2 :** retention of some larval or immature characters in adulthood
ne·o·ter·ic \ˌnē-ə-ˈter-ik\ *adj* [LL *neotericus*, fr. L Gk *neōterikos* fr. Gk, youthful, fr. *neōteros* compar. of *neos* new, young — more at NEW] **:** recent in origin **:** MODERN
Neo·zo·ic \-ˈzō-ik\ *adj* **:** of, relating to, or constituting the entire period from the end of the Mesozoic to the present time
Ne·pali \nə-ˈpȯl-ē, -ˈpäl-, -ˈpal-\ *n, pl* **Nepali** *also* **Nepalis** [Hindi *naipālī* of Nepal, fr. Skt *naipālīya*, fr. *Nepāla* Nepal] **1 :** the Indic language of Nepal **2 :** a native or inhabitant of Nepal — **Nepali** *adj*
ne·pen·the \nə-ˈpen(t)-thē\ *n* [L *nepenthes*, fr. Gk *nēpenthes*, neut. of *nēpenthēs* banishing pain and sorrow, fr. *nē-* not + *penthos* grief, sorrow; akin to Gk *pathos* suffering — more at NO, PATHOS] **1 :** a potion used by the ancients to dull pain and sorrow **2 :** something capable of causing oblivion of suffering — **ne·pen·the·an** \-thē-ən\ *adj*
neph·e·line \ˈnef-ə-ˌlēn\ *or* **neph·e·lite** \-ˌlīt\ *n* [F *néphéline*, fr. Gk *nephelē* cloud — more at NEBULA] **:** a hexagonal mineral $KNa_3Al_4Si_4O_{16}$ that is a usu. glassy crystalline silicate of sodium, potassium, and aluminum common in igneous rocks — **neph·e·lin·ic** \ˌnef-ə-ˈlin-ik\ *adj*
neph·e·lin·ite \ˈnef-ə-lə-ˌnīt\ *n* [ISV] **:** a silica-deficient igneous rock having nepheline as the predominant mineral
neph·e·lom·e·ter \ˌnef-ə-ˈläm-ət-ər\ *n* [Gk *nephelē* cloud + ISV *-meter*] **:** an instrument for measuring cloudiness; *specif* **:** an instrument for determining the concentration or particle size of suspensions by means of transmitted or reflected light — **neph·e·lo·met·ric** \ˌnef-ə-lō-ˈme-trik\ *adj* — **neph·e·lom·e·try** \-ˈläm-ə-trē\ *n*
neph·ew \ˈnef-(ˌ)yü, *chiefly Brit* ˈnev-\ *n* [ME *nevew*, fr. OF *neveu*, fr. L *nepot-*, *nepos* grandson, nephew; akin to OE *nefa* grandson, nephew, Skt *napāt* grandson] **1 a :** a son of one's brother or sister or of one's brother-in-law or sister-in-law **b :** an illegitimate son of an ecclesiastic **2** *obs* **:** a lineal descendant; *esp* **:** GRANDSON
nepho·scope \ˈnef-ə-ˌskōp\ *n* [Gk *nephos* cloud + ISV *-scope* — more at NEBULA] **:** an instrument for observing the direction and velocity of clouds
nephr- *or* **nephro-** *comb form* [NL, fr. Gk, fr. *nephros* — more at NEPHRITIS] **:** kidney ⟨*nephr*ic⟩ ⟨*nephro*logy⟩
ne·phrid·i·al \ni-ˈfrid-ē-əl\ *adj* **:** of or relating to a nephridium
ne·phrid·i·um \-ē-əm\ *n, pl* **ne·phrid·ia** \-ē-ə\ [NL] **1 :** a tubular glandular excretory organ characteristic of various coelomate invertebrates **2 :** a primarily excretory structure; *esp* **:** NEPHRON
neph·rite \ˈnef-ˌrīt\ *n* [G *nephrit*, fr. Gk *nephros*] **:** a compact tremolite or actinolite that is the less valuable kind of jade formerly worn as a remedy for kidney diseases
ne·phrit·ic \ni-ˈfrit-ik\ *adj* **1 :** RENAL **2 :** of, relating to, or affected with nephritis
ne·phri·tis \ni-ˈfrīt-əs\ *n* [LL, fr. Gk, fr. *nephros* kidney; akin to ME *nere* kidney, Lanuvian *nebrundines* testicles] **:** acute or chronic inflammation of the kidney caused by infection, degenerative process, or vascular disease
neph·ro·gen·ic \ˌnef-rə-ˈjen-ik\ *adj* **1 :** originating in the kidney **2 :** developing into or producing kidney tissue
neph·ron \ˈnef-ˌrän\ *n* [G, fr. Gk *nephros*] **:** a single excretory unit esp. of the vertebrate kidney
ne·phro·sis \ni-ˈfrō-səs\ *n* [NL] **:** degeneration of the kidneys chiefly affecting the renal tubules — **ne·phrot·ic** \-ˈfrät-ik\ *adj or n*
ne plus ul·tra \ˌnē-ˌpləs-ˈəl-trə, ˌnā-ˌplüs-ˈu̇l-\ *n* [NL, no further] **1 :** the highest point capable of being attained **:** ACME **2 :** the most profound degree of a quality or state
nep·o·tism \ˈnep-ə-ˌtiz-əm\ *n* [F *népotisme*, fr. It *nepotismo*, fr. *nepote* nephew, fr. L *nepot-*, *nepos* grandson, nephew — more at NEPHEW] **:** favoritism shown to a relative (as by giving an appointive job) on a basis of relationship
Nep·tune \ˈnep-ˌt(y)ün\ *n* [L *Neptunus*] **1 a :** the god of the sea in Roman mythology **b :** OCEAN **2 :** the planet eighth in order from the sun — see PLANET table — **Nep·tu·ni·an** \nep-ˈt(y)ü-nē-ən\ *adj*
nep·tu·ni·um \nep-ˈt(y)ü-nē-əm\ *n* [NL, fr. ISV *Neptune*] **:** a radioactive metallic element that is chemically similar to uranium and is obtained in nuclear reactors as a by-product in the production of plutonium — see ELEMENT table
Ne·re·id \ˈnir-ē-əd\ *n* [L *Nereid-*, *Nereis*, fr. Gk *Nēreid-*, *Nēreis*, fr. *Nēreus* Nereus] **:** any of the sea nymphs held in Greek mythology to be the daughters of the sea-god Nereus
ne·re·is \ˈnir-ē-əs\ *n, pl* **ne·re·ides** \nə-ˈrē-ə-ˌdēz\ [NL, genus name, fr. L, Nereid] **:** any of a genus (*Nereis*) of usu. large often dimorphic and greenish marine polychaete worms
ne·rit·ic \nə-ˈrit-ik\ *adj* [perh. fr. NL *Nerita*, genus of marine snails] **:** of, relating to, or constituting the belt or region of shallow water adjoining the seacoast
ner·o·li oil \ˈner-ə-lē-\ *n* [F *néroli*, fr. It *neroli*, fr. Anna Maria de La Trémoille, princess of *Nerole fl* 1670] **:** a fragrant pale yellow essential oil obtained from orange flowers and used esp. in cologne and as a flavoring
Ne·ro·ni·an \ni-ˈrō-nē-ən\ *or* **Ne·ron·ic** \-ˈrän-ik\ *adj* [L *neronianus*, fr. *Neron-*, *Nero* Nero †A.D. 68 Rom emperor] **:** of, relating to, or characteristic of Nero or his times
nerts \ˈnərts\ *n pl, slang* **:** NUTS 5
nerv- *or* **nervi-** *or* **nervo-** *comb form* [ME *nerv-*, fr. L, fr. *nervus-*] **:** NEUR- ⟨*nerv*ine⟩
ner·va·tion \ˌnər-ˈvā-shən\ *n* **:** an arrangement or system of nerves *also* **:** VENATION
¹**nerve** \ˈnərv\ *n* [L *nervus* sinew, nerve; akin to Gk *neuron* sinew, nerve, *nēn* to spin — more at NEEDLE] **1 :** SINEW, TENDON ⟨strain every ~⟩ **2 :** one of the filamentous bands of nervous tissue connecting parts of the nervous system with the other organs and conducting nervous impulses **3 a :** NERVE CENTER 2 **b :** power of endurance or control **:** FORTITUDE, STRENGTH **c** (1) **:** BOLDNESS, DARING (2) **:** BRASS, GALL **4 a :** a sore or sensitive point **b** *pl* **:** nervous disorganization or collapse **:** HYSTERIA **5 :** VEIN 3 **6 :** the sensitive pulp of a tooth **syn** see TEMERITY — **nerved** \ˈnərvd\ *adj*
²**nerve** *vt* **:** to give strength or courage to
nerve cell *n* **:** NEURON; *also* **:** a nerve cell body exclusive of its processes
nerve center *n* **1 :** CENTER 2b **2 :** a source of leadership, control, or energy
nerve fiber *n* **:** AXON, DENDRITE
nerve gas *n* **:** a war gas damaging esp. to the nervous and respiratory systems
nerve impulse *n* **:** the progressive alteration in the protoplasm of a nerve fiber that follows stimulation and serves to transmit a record of sensation from a receptor or an instruction to act to an effector
nerve·less \ˈnərv-ləs\ *adj* **1 :** destitute of strength or courage **:** FEEBLE **2 :** exhibiting control or balance **:** POISED — **nerve·less·ly** *adv* — **nerve·less·ness** *n*
nerve-rack·ing *or* **nerve-wrack·ing** \ˈnərv-ˌrak-iŋ\ *adj* **:** extremely trying on the nerves
nerv·i·ness \ˈnər-vē-nəs\ *n* **:** the quality or state of being nervy
ner·vous \ˈnər-vəs\ *adj* **1** *archaic* **:** SINEWY, STRONG **2 :** marked by strength of thought, feeling, or style **:** SPIRITED **3 :** of, relating to, or composed of neurons **4 a :** of or relating to the nerves; *also* **:** originating in or affected by the nerves **b :** easily excited or irritated **:** JUMPY **c :** TIMID, APPREHENSIVE ⟨~ smile⟩ **5 a :** UNEASY, DISTURBING ⟨~ moment⟩ **b :** ERRATIC, UNSTEADY ⟨~ canoe⟩ **syn** see VIGOROUS — **ner·vous·ly** *adv* — **ner·vous·ness** *n*
nervous breakdown *n* **1 :** NEURASTHENIA **2 :** a case of neurasthenia
nervous Nel·lie \ˌnər-və-ˈsnel-ē\ *n* [fr. the name *Nellie*] **:** a timid or ineffectual person
nervous system *n* **:** the bodily system that in vertebrates is made up of brain and spinal cord, nerves, ganglia, and parts of the receptor organs and that receives and interprets stimuli and transmits impulses to the effector organs
ner·vure \ˈnər-vyər\ *n* [F, fr. *nerf* sinew, fr. L *nervus*] **:** VEIN 3
nervy \ˈnər-vē\ *adj* **1** *archaic* **:** SINEWY, STRONG **2 a :** showing calm courage **:** BOLD **b :** marked by effrontery or presumption **:** BRASH **3 :** EXCITABLE, NERVOUS
ne·science \ˈnesh-(ē-)ən(t)s, ˈnēsh-; ˈnes-ē-ən(t)s, ˈnēs-\ *n* [LL *nescientia*, fr. L *nescient-*, *nesciens*, prp. of *nescire* not to know, fr. *ne-* not + *scire* to know — more at NO, SCIENCE] **:** lack of knowledge or awareness **:** IGNORANCE — **ne·scient** \-(ē-)ənt\ *adj*
ness \ˈnes\ *n* [ME *nasse*, fr. OE *næss*; akin to OE *nasu* nose — more at NOSE] **:** CAPE, PROMONTORY
-ness \nəs\ *n suffix* [ME *-nes*, fr. OE; akin to OHG *-nissa* -ness] **:** state **:** condition **:** quality **:** degree ⟨good*ness*⟩
Nes·sel·rode \ˈnes-əl-ˌrōd\ *n* [Count Karl R. *Nesselrode* †1862 Russ statesman] **:** a mixture of candied fruits, nuts, and maraschino used in puddings, pies, and ice cream
Nes·sus \ˈnes-əs\ *n* [L, fr. Gk *Nessos*] **:** a centaur shot by Hercules with a poisoned arrow for attempting to carry away his wife
¹**nest** \ˈnest\ *n* [ME, fr. OE; akin to OHG *nest* nest, L *nidus*] **1 a :** a bed or receptacle prepared by a bird for its eggs and young **b :** a place where eggs are laid and hatched **c :** a receptacle resembling a bird's nest **2 a :** a place of rest, retreat, or lodging **b :** DEN, HANGOUT **3 :** the occupants or frequenters of a nest **4 a :** a group of similar things **:** AGGREGATION **b :** HOTBED 2 **5 :** a group of objects made to fit close together or one within another
²**nest** *vi* **1 :** to build or occupy a nest **2 :** to fit compactly together or within one another ~ *vt* **1 :** to form a nest for **2 :** to pack compactly together
nest egg *n* **1 :** a natural or artificial egg left in a nest to induce a fowl to continue to lay there **2 :** a fund of money accumulated as a reserve
nest·er \ˈnes-tər\ *n* **1 :** one that nests **2** *West* **:** a homesteader or squatter who takes up open range for a farm
nes·tle \ˈnes-əl\ *vb* **nes·tling** \-(ə-)liŋ\ [ME *nestlen*, fr. OE *nestlian*, fr. *nest*] *vi* **1** *archaic* **:** NEST 1 **2 :** to settle snugly or comfortably **3 :** to lie in an inconspicuous or sheltered manner ~ *vt* **1 :** to settle, shelter, or house in or as if in a nest **2 :** to press closely and affectionately — **nes·tler** \-(ə-)lər\ *n*
nest·ling \ˈnest-liŋ\ *n* **:** a young bird that has not abandoned the nest
Nes·tor \ˈnes-tər, -ˌtȯ(ə)r\ *n* [L, fr. Gk *Nestōr*] **1 :** an aged and wise counselor of the Greeks in the Trojan War **2** *often not cap* **:** one who is a patriarch or leader in his field
Nes·to·ri·an \ne-ˈstōr-ē-ən, -ˈstȯr-\ *adj* **1 :** of or relating to the doctrine ascribed to Nestorius and ecclesiastically condemned in 431 that divine and human persons remained separate in the incarnate Christ **2 :** of or relating to a church separating from Byzantine Christianity after 431, centering in Persia, and surviving among Assyrians — **Nestorian** *n* — **Nes·to·ri·an·ism** \-ˌiz-əm\ *n*
¹**net** \ˈnet\ *n* [ME *nett*, fr. OE; akin to OHG *nezzi* net, L *nodus* knot] **1 a :** a meshed fabric twisted, knotted, or woven together at regular

ə abut; ᵊ kitten; ər further; a back; ā bake; ä cot, cart; au̇ out; ch chin; e less; ē easy; g gift; i trip; ī life
j joke; ŋ sing; ō flow; ȯ flaw; ȯi coin; th thin; t͟h this; ü loot; u̇ foot; y yet; yü few; yu̇ furious; zh vision

intervals **b :** something made of net; *esp* **:** a device for catching fish, birds, or insects **2 :** an entrapping situation **3 :** a network of lines, fibers, or figures **4 :** a ball hit into the net in a racket game **5 a :** a group of communications stations operating under unified control **b :** NETWORK 4 — **net·like** \-ˌlīk\ *adj* — **net·ty** \-ē\ *adj*

[2]net *vt* **net·ted; net·ting 1 :** to cover or enclose with or as if with a net **2 :** to catch in or as if in a net **3 :** to cover with a network **4 :** to hit (a ball) into the net for the loss of a point in a racket game — **net·ter** *n*

[3]net *adj* [ME, clean, bright, fr. MF] **1 :** free from all charges or deductions: as **a :** remaining after the deduction of all charges, outlay, or loss **b :** excluding all tare **2 :** FINAL ⟨~ result⟩

[4]net *vt* **net·ted; net·ting 1 a :** to make by way of profit **:** CLEAR **b :** to produce by way of profit **:** YIELD **2 :** to get possession **:** GAIN

[5]net *n* **1 :** a net amount, profit, weight, or price **2 :** the score of a golfer in a handicap match after deducting his handicap from his gross **3 :** ESSENCE, GIST

neth·er \'neth-ər\ *adj* [ME, fr. OE *nithera*, fr. *nither* down; akin to OHG *nidar* down, Skt *ni*, Gk *en*, *eni* in — more at IN] **1 :** situated down or below **:** LOWER **2 :** situated or believed to be situated beneath the earth's surface

neth·er·most \-ˌmōst\ *adj* **:** LOWEST

neth·er·world \-ˌwərld\ *n* **1 :** the world of the dead **2 :** UNDERWORLD 4

net·su·ke \'net-skē\ *n* [Jap] **:** a small toggle of wood, ivory, or metal used to fasten a small pouch or purse to a kimono sash

nett *Brit var of* NET

net·ting \'net-iŋ\ *n* **1 :** NETWORK **2 :** the act or process of making a net or network **3 :** the act, process, or right of fishing with a net

[1]net·tle \'net-ᵊl\ *n* [ME, fr. OE *netel;* akin to OHG *nazza* nettle, Gk *adikē*] **:** any of a genus (*Urtica* of the family Urticaceae, the nettle family) of chiefly coarse herbs armed with stinging hairs; *also* **:** any of many other prickly or stinging plants

[2]nettle *vt* **net·tling** \'net-liŋ, -ᵊl-iŋ\ **1 :** to strike or sting with or as if with nettles **2 :** PROVOKE, VEX **syn** see IRRITATE

nettle rash *n* **:** an eruption on the skin caused by or resembling the condition produced by stinging with nettles **:** URTICARIA

net·tle·some \'net-ᵊl-səm\ *adj* **:** causing vexation **:** IRRITATING

net–winged \'net-'wiŋd\ *adj* **:** having wings with a fine network of veins

net·work \'net-ˌwərk\ *n, often attrib* **1 :** a fabric or structure of cords or wires that cross at regular intervals and are knotted or secured at the crossings **2 :** a system of lines or channels resembling a network **3 :** an interconnected or interrelated chain, group, or system **4 a :** a group of radio or television stations linked by wire or radio relay **b :** a radio or television company that produces programs for broadcast over such a network

Neuf·châ·tel cheese \ˌn(y)ü-shə-ˌtel-, ˌnə(r)sh-ə-\ *n* [F *neufchâtel*, fr. *Neufchâtel*, France] **:** a soft unripened cheese made from whole or skim milk

neu·mat·ic \n(y)ü-'mat-ik\ *adj* **:** of or relating to neumes

neume \'n(y)üm\ *n* [F, fr. ML *pneuma*, *neuma*, fr. Gk *pneuma* breath — more at PNEUMATIC] **:** any of various symbols used in the notation of Gregorian chant

neur- *or* **neuro-** *comb form* [NL, fr. Gk, nerve, sinew, fr. *neuron*— more at NERVE] **:** nerve ⟨*neur*al⟩ ⟨*neuro*logy⟩

neu·ral \'n(y)ür-əl\ *adj* **1 :** of, relating to, or affecting a nerve or the nervous system **2 :** situated in the region of or on the same side of the body as the brain and spinal cord **:** DORSAL — **neu·ral·ly** \-ə-lē\ *adv*

neural arch *n* **:** the cartilaginous or bony arch enclosing the spinal cord on the dorsal side of a vertebra

neu·ral·gia \n(y)ü-'ral-jə\ *n* [NL] **:** acute paroxysmal pain radiating along the course of one or more nerves usu. without demonstrable changes in the nerve structure — **neu·ral·gic** \-jik\ *adj*

neural tube *n* **:** the hollow longitudinal tube formed by infolding and subsequent fusion of the opposite ectodermal folds in the vertebrate embryo

neur·as·the·nia \ˌn(y)ür-əs-'thē-nē-ə\ *n* [NL] **:** a condition marked by fatigue, worry, inadequacy, and lack of zest and often by headache, undue sensitiveness to light and noise, and by disturbances of digestion and circulation — **neur·as·then·ic** \-'then-ik\ *adj* — **neur·as·then·i·cal·ly** \-i-k(ə-)lē\ *adv*

neu·ri·lem·ma \ˌn(y)ür-ə-'lem-ə\ *n* [NL, fr. *neur-* + Gk *eilēma* covering, coil, fr. *eilein* to wind; akin to Gk *eilyein* to wrap — more at VOLUBLE] **1 :** the delicate nucleated outer sheath of a nerve fiber **2 :** PERINEURIUM — **neu·ri·lem·mal** \-'lem-əl\ *adj* — **neu·ri·lem·mat·ic** \-le-'mat-ik\ *adj* — **neu·ri·lem·ma·tous** \-'lem-ət-əs\ *adj*

neu·rit·ic \n(y)ü-'rit-ik\ *adj* **:** of, relating to, or affected by neuritis — **neuritic** *n*

neu·ri·tis \n(y)ü-'rīt-əs\ *n* [NL] **:** an inflammatory or degenerative lesion of a nerve marked esp. by pain, sensory disturbances, and impaired or lost reflexes

neu·ro·cir·cu·la·to·ry \ˌn(y)ür-ō-'sər-kyə-lə-ˌtōr-ē, -ˌtȯr-\ *adj* **:** of or relating to the nervous and circulatory systems

neu·ro·crine \'n(y)ür-ə-krən, -ˌkrīn, -ˌkrēn\ *adj* [*neur-* + *endocrine*] **:** of, relating to, or being a hormonal substance that influences the activity of the nerves — **neu·ro·crin·ism** \-ˌiz-əm\ *n*

neu·ro·ep·i·the·li·al \ˌn(y)ü(ə)r-(ˌ)ō-ˌep-ə-'thē-lē-əl\ *adj* **:** having qualities of both neural and epithelial cells

neu·ro·fi·bril \ˌn(y)ür-ō-'fīb-rəl, -'fib-rəl\ *n* [NL *neurofibrilla*, fr. *neur-* + *fibrilla* fibril] **:** one of a system of many minute fibrils in a neuron believed by some to be conducting elements — **neu·ro·fi·bril·lary** \-ˌer-ē\ *adj*

neu·ro·gen·ic \ˌn(y)ür-ə-'jen-ik\ *adj* **1 :** originating in nervous tissue **2 :** induced, controlled, or modified by nervous factors; *esp* **:** disordered because of abnormally altered neural relations — **neu·ro·gen·i·cal·ly** \-i-k(ə-)lē\ *adv*

neu·ro·glia \n(y)ü-'räg-lē-ə, ˌn(y)ür-ə-'glī-ə\ *n* [NL, fr. *neur-* + MGk *glia* glue] **:** supporting tissue intermingled with the essential elements of nervous tissue esp. in the brain, spinal cord, and ganglia — **neu·ro·gli·al** \-əl\ *or* **neu·ro·gli·ar** \-ər\ *adj*

neu·ro·hu·mor \ˌn(y)ür-ō-'hyü-mər, -'yü-\ *n* **:** a substance liberated at a nerve ending that participates in the transmission of a nerve impulse — **neu·ro·hu·mor·al** \-'(h)yüm-(ə-)rəl\ *adj*

neu·ro·log·i·cal \ˌn(y)ür-ə-'läj-i-kəl\ *or* **neu·ro·log·ic** \-ik\ *adj* **:** of or relating to neurology

neu·rol·o·gist \n(y)ü-'räl-ə-jəst\ *n* **:** one specializing in neurology; *esp* **:** a physician skilled in the diagnosis and treatment of disease of the nervous system

neu·rol·o·gy \-jē\ *n* [NL *neurologia*, fr. *neur-* + *-logia* -logy] **:** the scientific study of the nervous system

neu·ro·ma \n(y)ü-'rō-mə\ *n, pl* **neuromas** *or* **neu·ro·ma·ta** \-mət-ə\ [NL] **:** a tumor or mass growing from a nerve and usu. consisting of nerve fibers

neu·ro·mo·tor \ˌn(y)ür-ə-'mōt-ər\ *adj* **:** relating to efferent nervous impulses

neu·ro·mus·cu·lar \ˌn(y)ür-ō-'məs-kyə-lər\ *adj* [ISV] **:** of or relating to nerves and muscles or nervous and muscular tissue

neu·ron \'n(y)ü-ˌrän, 'n(y)ü(ə)r-ˌän\ *also* **neu·rone** \-ˌrōn, -ˌōn\ *n* [NL *neuron*, fr. Gk, nerve, sinew — more at NERVE] **:** a grayish or reddish granular cell with specialized processes that is the fundamental functional unit of nervous tissue — **neu·ro·nal** \'n(y)ür-ən-ᵊl, n(y)ü-'rōn-ᵊl\ *or* **neu·ron·ic** \n(y)ü-'rän-ik\ *adj*

neu·ro·path·ic \ˌn(y)ür-ə-'path-ik\ *adj* **:** of or relating to neuropathy; *also* **:** being or having nervous disease — **neu·ro·path·i·cal·ly** \-i-k(ə-)lē\ *adv*

neu·rop·a·thy \n(y)ü-'räp-ə-thē\ *n* [ISV] **:** an abnormal and usu. degenerative state of the nervous system or nerves; *also* **:** a systemic condition that stems from a neuropathy

neu·rop·ter·an \n(y)ü-'räp-tə-rən\ *n* [deriv. of Gk *neur-* + *pteron* wing — more at FEATHER] **:** any of an order (Neuroptera) of usu. net-winged insects that include the lacewings and ant lions — **neuropteran** *adj* — **neu·rop·ter·ous** \-rəs\ *adj*

neu·ro·sis \n(y)ü-'rō-səs\ *n, pl* **neu·ro·ses** \-'rō-ˌsēz\ [NL] **:** a functional nervous disorder without demonstrable physical lesion

[1]neu·rot·ic \n(y)ü-'rät-ik\ *adj* **:** of, relating to, constituting, or affected with neurosis — **neu·rot·i·cal·ly** \-i-k(ə-)lē\ *adv*

[2]neurotic *n* **:** an emotionally unstable individual or one affected with a neurosis

neu·ro·tox·ic \ˌn(y)ür-ə-'täk-sik\ *adj* **:** toxic to the nerves or nervous tissue — **neu·ro·tox·ic·i·ty** \-ˌtäk-'sis-ət-ē\ *n*

neu·ro·trop·ic \-'träp-ik\ *adj* [ISV] **:** having an affinity for or localizing selectively in nerve tissue

[1]neu·ter \'n(y)üt-ər\ *adj* [ME *neutre*, fr. MF & L; MF *neutre*, fr. L *neuter*, fr. *ne-* not + *uter* which of two — more at NO, WHETHER] **1 a :** of, relating to, or constituting the gender that ordinarily includes most words or grammatical forms referring to things classed as neither masculine nor feminine **b :** neither active nor passive **:** INTRANSITIVE **2 :** taking no side **:** NEUTRAL **3 :** lacking or having imperfectly developed or nonfunctional generative organs ⟨the worker bee is ~⟩

[2]neuter *n* **1 a :** a noun, pronoun, adjective, or inflectional form or class of the neuter gender **b :** the neuter gender **2 :** one that is neutral **3 a :** WORKER 2 **b :** a spayed or castrated animal

[3]neuter *vt* **:** CASTRATE, ALTER

[1]neu·tral \'n(y)ü-trəl\ *adj* [MF, fr. (assumed) ML *neutralis*, fr. L, of neuter gender, fr. *neutr-*, *neuter*] **1 :** not engaged on either side; *specif* **:** not aligned with a political or ideological grouping **2 :** of or relating to a neutral state or power **3 a :** neither one thing nor the other **:** MIDDLING **b** (1) **:** ACHROMATIC (2) **:** not decided in color **:** nearly achromatic **c** (1) **:** NEUTER 3 (2) **:** lacking stamens or pistils **d :** neither acid nor basic **e :** not electrically charged **4 :** produced with the tongue in the position it has when at rest ⟨the ~ vowels of \ə-'bəv\ *above*⟩ — **neu·tral·ly** \-trə-lē\ *adv* — **neu·tral·ness** *n*

[2]neutral *n* **1 :** one that is neutral **2 :** a neutral color **3 :** a position of disengagement (as of gears)

neu·tral·ism \'n(y)ü-trə-ˌliz-əm\ *n* **1 :** NEUTRALITY **2 :** a policy or the advocacy of neutrality esp. in international affairs — **neu·tral·ist** \-ləst\ *n* — **neu·tral·is·tic** \ˌn(y)ü-trə-'lis-tik\ *adj*

neu·tral·i·ty \n(y)ü-'tral-ət-ē\ *n* **:** the quality or state of being neutral; *esp* **:** immunity from invasion or use by belligerents

neu·tral·iza·tion \ˌn(y)ü-trə-lə-'zā-shən\ *n* **1 :** an act or process of neutralizing **2 :** the quality or state of being neutralized

neu·tral·ize \'n(y)ü-trə-ˌlīz\ *vt* **1 :** to make chemically neutral **2 :** to destroy the effectiveness of **:** NULLIFY **3 :** to make electrically inert by combining equal positive and negative quantities **4 :** to invest with conventional or obligatory neutrality conferring inviolability under international law by belligerents **5 :** to make neutral by blending with the complementary color **~** *vi* **:** to undergo neutralization — **neu·tral·iz·er** *n*

neutral red *n* **:** a basic phenazine dye used chiefly as a biological stain and acid-base indicator

neutral spirits *n pl but sing or pl in constr* **:** ethyl alcohol of 190 or higher proof used esp. for blending other alcoholic liquors

neu·tri·no \n(y)ü-'trē-(ˌ)nō\ *n* [It, dim. of *neutrone* neutron] **:** an uncharged elementary particle with zero rest mass

neu·tron \'n(y)ü-ˌträn\ *n* [prob. fr. *neutral*] **:** an uncharged elementary particle that has a mass nearly equal to that of the proton and is present in all known atomic nuclei except the hydrogen nucleus

neu·tro·phil \'n(y)ü-trə-ˌfil\ *or* **neu·tro·phile** \-ˌfīl\ *n* [L *neutr-*, *neuter* + E *-phil;* fr. its staining indifferently with acid or basic dyes] **:** a finely granular cell that is the chief phagocytic leukocyte of the blood

né·vé \nā-'vā\ *n* [F (Swiss dial.), fr. L *niv-*, *nix* snow — more at SNOW] **:** the partially compacted granular snow that forms the surface part of the upper end of a glacier; *broadly* **:** a field of granular snow

nev·er \'nev-ər\ *adv* [ME, fr. OE *nǣfre*, fr. *ne* not + *ǣfre* ever — — more at NO] **1 :** not ever **:** at no time **2 :** not in any degree, way, or condition

nev·er·more \ˌnev-ər-'mō(ə)r, -'mȯ(ə)r\ *adv* **:** never again

nev·er–nev·er land \ˌnev-ər-'nev-ər-\ *n* **:** an ideal or imaginary place

nev·er·the·less \ˌnev-ər-thə-'les\ *adv* **:** not the less **:** in spite of that **:** HOWEVER

ne·vus \'nē-vəs\ *n, pl* **ne·vi** \-ˌvī\ [NL, fr. L *naevus*] **:** a congenital pigmented area on the skin **:** BIRTHMARK

[1]new \'n(y)ü, *before a stress in geographical names also* n(y)ü *or* n(y)ə(-w)\ *adj* [ME, fr. OE *nīwe;* akin to OHG *niuwi* new, L *novus*, Gk *neos*] **1 :** having existed or having been made but a short time **:** RECENT **2 a** (1) **:** recently manifested, recognized, or experienced **:** NOVEL (2) **:** UNFAMILIAR ⟨visit ~ places⟩ **b :** being other than the former or old ⟨~ model⟩ **3 :** UNACCUSTOMED ⟨~ to the job⟩ **4 a :** beginning as the resumption or repetition of a previous act or thing ⟨~ day⟩ **b :** REFRESHED, REGENERATED ⟨awoke a ~ man⟩ **5 :** different from one of the same that has existed previously ⟨~ realism⟩ **6 :** of dissimilar origin and usu. of superior quality

⟨introducing ~ blood⟩ **7** *cap, of a language* **:** MODERN; *esp* **:** having been in use after medieval times — **new·ish** \'n(y)ü-ish\ *adj* — **new·ness** *n*

syn NEW, NOVEL, MODERN, ORIGINAL, FRESH mean having recently come into existence or use. NEW may apply to what is freshly made and unused ⟨*new* brick⟩ or has not been known before ⟨*new* design⟩ or not experienced before ⟨starts his *new* job⟩ NOVEL applies to what is not only new but strange or unprecedented; MODERN applies to what belongs to or is characteristic of the present time or the present era; ORIGINAL applies to what is the first of its kind to exist; FRESH applies to what has not lost its qualities of newness such as liveliness, energy, brightness

²**new** \'n(y)ü\ *adv* **:** NEWLY, RECENTLY

new·born \-'bȯ(ə)rn\ *adj* **1 :** recently born **2 :** born anew

New·burg *or* **New·burgh** \'n(y)ü-,bərg\ *adj* [prob. fr. *lobster Newburg*] **:** served with a sauce made of cream, butter, wine, and egg yolks

New·cas·tle disease \'n(y)ü-,kas-əl-, n(y)ü-'\ *n* [*Newcastle* upon Tyne, England] **:** a destructive virus disease of domestic fowl and other birds involving respiratory and nervous symptoms

New Catholic Edition *n* **:** an American revision of the Douay Version of the Bible published in 1949

New Church *adj* **:** of or relating to the Church of the New Jerusalem deriving from the Swedenborgian teachings

new·com·er \'n(y)ü-,kəm-ər\ *n* **1 :** one recently arrived **2 :** BEGINNER

New Criticism *n* **:** an analytic literary criticism marked by concentration on language, imagery, and emotional or intellectual tensions

new deal *n* [fr. the supposed resemblance to the situation of freshness and equality of opportunity afforded by a fresh deal in a card game] **1** *cap N&D* **a :** the legislative and administrative program of President F. D. Roosevelt designed to promote economic recovery and social reform during the 1930's **b :** the period of this program **2 :** a governmental program resembling the Roosevelt New Deal in objectives or techniques — **new deal·er** \-'dē-lər\ *n, often cap N&D* — **new deal·ish** \-'dē-lish\ *adj, often cap N&D* — **new deal·ism** \-'dē(ə)l-,iz-əm\ *n, often cap N&D*

new·el \'n(y)ü-əl\ *n* [ME *nowell,* fr. MF *nouel* stone of a fruit, fr. LL *nucalis* like a nut, fr. L *nuc-, nux* nut — more at NUT] **1 :** an upright post about which the steps of a circular staircase wind **2 :** a post at the foot of a straight stairway or one at a landing

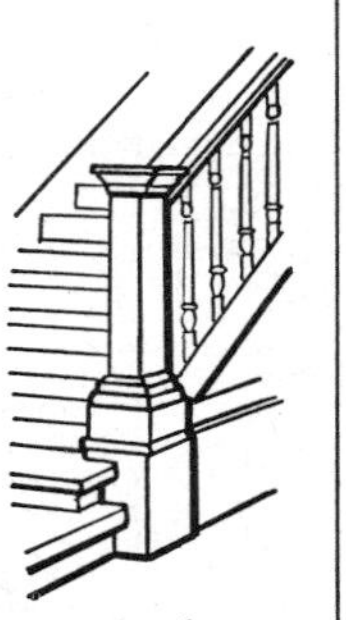
newel

New English Bible *n* **:** a translation of the Bible by a British interdenominational committee having the New Testament published in 1961

new·fan·gled \'n(y)ü-'fan-gəld\ *adj* [ME, fr. *newefangel,* fr. *new* + OE *fangen,* pp. of *fōn* to take, seize — more at PACT] **1 :** attracted to novelty **2 :** of the newest style **:** NOVEL

new–fash·ioned \-'fash-ənd\ *adj* **1 :** made in a new fashion or form **2 :** UP-TO-DATE

new·found \-'faůnd\ *adj* **:** newly found

New·found·land \'n(y)ü-fən-(d)lənd, -,(d)land, n(y)ü-'faůn-(d)lənd\ *n* [*Newfoundland,* province in Canada] **:** any of a breed of very large heavy highly intelligent usu. black dogs developed in Newfoundland

New·gate \'n(y)ü-,gāt, -gət\ *n* **:** a London prison razed in 1902

New Greek *n* **:** Greek as used by the Greeks since the end of the medieval period

New Hamp·shire \n(y)ů-'ham(p)-shər, -,shi(ə)r\ *n* [*New Hampshire,* U.S.A.] **:** any of a breed of single-combed general purpose domestic fowls developed chiefly in New Hampshire and noted for heavy winter egg production

New Hebrew *n* **:** the Hebrew language in use in present-day Israel

New Latin *n* **:** Latin as used since the end of the medieval period esp. in scientific description and classification

new·ly \'n(y)ü-lē\ *adv* **1 :** LATELY, RECENTLY **2 :** ANEW, AFRESH **3 :** in a new way

new·ly·wed \-,wed\ *n* **:** one recently married

new·mar·ket \'n(y)ü-,mär-kət\ *n* [*Newmarket,* England] **:** a long close-fitting coat worn in the 19th century

new moon *n* **1 :** the moon's phase when it is in conjunction with the sun so that its dark side is toward the earth; *also* **:** the thin crescent moon seen shortly after sunset a few days after the actual occurrence of the new moon phase **2 :** the first day of the Jewish month marked by a special liturgy

news \'n(y)üz\ *n pl but sing in constr, often attrib* **1 :** a report of recent events **2 a :** material reported in a newspaper or news periodical or on a newscast **b :** newsworthy matter **3 :** NEWSCAST

news agency *n* **:** an organization that supplies news to subscribing newspapers, periodicals, and newscasters

news·boy \-,bȯi\ *n* **:** a person who delivers or sells newspapers

news·break \-,brāk\ *n* **:** a newsworthy event

news·cast \-,kast\ *n* [*news* + broad*cast*] **:** a radio or television broadcast of news — **news·cast·er** \-,kas-tər\ *n*

news conference *n* **:** PRESS CONFERENCE

news·let·ter \'n(y)üz-,let-ər\ *n* **:** a newspaper containing news or information of interest chiefly to a special group

news·man \-mən, -,man\ *n* **:** one who gathers, reports, or comments on the news **:** REPORTER, CORRESPONDENT

news·mon·ger \-,məŋ-gər, -,mäŋ-\ *n* **:** GOSSIP

¹**news·pa·per** \'n(y)üz-,pā-pər\ *n, often attrib* **1 :** a paper that is printed and distributed usu. daily or weekly and contains news, articles of opinion, features, and advertising **2 :** an organization publishing a newspaper **3 :** newsprint or the paper making up a newspaper

²**newspaper** *vi* **:** to do newspaper work

news·pa·per·man \-,man\ *n* **:** one who owns or is employed by a newspaper; *esp* **:** one who writes or edits news or prepares advertising copy for a newspaper

news·print \'n(y)üz-,print\ *n* **:** cheap machine-finished paper made chiefly from wood pulp and used mostly for newspapers

news·reel \-,rēl\ *n* **:** a short movie dealing with current events

news·stand \'n(y)üz-,stand\ *n* **:** a place (as an outdoor stall) where newspapers and periodicals are sold

New Style *adj* **:** using or according to the Gregorian calendar

news·wor·thy \'n(y)üz-,wər-thē\ *adj* **:** sufficiently interesting to the general public to warrant reporting (as in a newspaper)

newsy \'n(y)ü-zē\ *adj* **:** filled with news; *esp* **:** GOSSIPY

newt \'n(y)üt\ *n* [ME, alter. (resulting from incorrect division of *an ewte*) of *ewte* — more at EFT] **:** any of various small semiaquatic salamanders (as of the genus *Triturus*)

New Testament *n* **:** the second part of the Christian Bible comprising the books relating to God's covenant with man in the gospel of Jesus Christ

New Thought *n* **:** a mental healing movement embracing small groups devoted to spiritual healing and the creative power of constructive thinking

new·ton \'n(y)üt-ᵊn\ *n* [Sir Isaac *Newton* †1727 E physicist] **:** the unit of force in the mks system of physical units that is of such size that under its influence a body whose mass is one kilogram would experience an acceleration of one meter per second per second

New·to·ni·an \n(y)ü-'tō-nē-ən\ *adj* **:** of, relating to, or following Sir Isaac Newton, his discoveries, or his doctrines — **Newtonian** *n*

New World *n* **:** the western hemisphere; *esp* **:** the continental landmass of No. and So. America

New Year *n* **1 :** NEW YEAR'S DAY; *also* **:** the first days of the year **2 :** ROSH HASHANAH

New Year's Day *n* **:** January 1 observed as a legal holiday in many countries

¹**next** \'nekst\ *adj* [ME, fr. OE *nīehst,* superl. of *nēah* nigh — more at NIGH] **:** immediately preceding or following **:** NEAREST

²**next** *adv* **1 :** in the time, place, or order nearest or immediately succeeding **2 :** on the first occasion to come

³**next** \(')nekst\ *prep* **:** nearest or adjacent to

next friend *n* **:** a person admitted to or appointed by a court to act for the benefit of an infant, a married woman, or a person not sui juris

next of kin : one or more persons in the nearest degree of relationship to another person

¹**next to** *prep* **:** immediately following or adjacent to

²**next to** *adv* **:** very nearly **:** ALMOST

nex·us \'nek-səs\ *n, pl* **nex·us·es** \-sə-səz\ *or* **nex·us** \-səs, -,süs\ [L, fr. *nexus,* pp. of *nectere* to bind] **1 :** CONNECTION, LINK **2 :** a connected group or series

Nez Percé \'nez-'pərs, *F* nā-per-sā\ *n* [F, lit., pierced nose] **1 :** a member of a Shahaptian people of central Idaho and adjacent parts of Washington and Oregon **2 :** a language of the Nez Percé people

ngwee \en-'gwē\ *n, pl* **ngwee** [native name in Zambia, lit., bright] — see *kwacha* at MONEY table

ni·a·cin \'nī-ə-sən\ *n* [*ni*cotinic *ac*id + *-in*] **:** NICOTINIC ACID

Ni·ag·a·ra \nī-'ag-(ə-)rə\ *n* [*Niagara* Falls, waterfall of the Niagara river] **:** an overwhelming flood **:** TORRENT

nib \'nib\ *n* [prob. alter. of *neb*] **1 :** BILL, BEAK **2 a :** the sharpened point of a quill pen **b :** a pen point **3 :** a small pointed or projecting part

¹**nib·ble** \'nib-əl\ *vb* **nib·bling** \-(ə-)liŋ\ [origin unknown] *vt* **1 a :** to bite gently **b :** to eat or chew in small bits **2 :** to take away bit by bit ~ *vi* **1 :** to take gentle, small, or cautious bites **2 :** to deal with something cautiously — **nib·bler** \-(ə-)lər\ *n*

²**nibble** *n* **1 :** an act of nibbling **2 :** a very small quantity

Ni·be·lung \'nē-bə-,lůŋ\ *n* [G] **1 :** a member of a race of dwarfs in Germanic legend owning a hoard and ring taken from them by Siegfried **2 :** any of the followers of Siegfried **3 :** any of the Burgundian kings in the medieval German *Nibelungenlied*

nib·lick \'nib-lik\ *n* [origin unknown] **:** an iron golf club with a wide deeply slanted face — called also *number nine iron*

nibs \'nibz\ *n pl but sing or pl in constr* [origin unknown] **:** an important or self-important person — usu. used in the phrase *his nibs*

nic·co·lite \'nik-ə-,līt\ *n* [NL *niccolum* nickel, prob. fr. Sw *nickel*] **:** a pale copper-red usu. massive mineral NiAs of metallic luster that is essentially a nickel arsenide

nice \'nīs\ *adj* [ME, foolish, wanton, fr. OF, fr. L *nescius* ignorant, fr. *nescire* not to know — more at NESCIENCE] **1** *obs* **a :** WANTON, DISSOLUTE **b :** COY, RETICENT **2 a :** showing fastidious or finicky tastes **:** REFINED **b :** SCRUPULOUS **3 :** marked by or demanding delicate discrimination or treatment ⟨~ distinction⟩ **4** *obs* **:** TRIVIAL **5 a :** PLEASING, AGREEABLE ⟨~ time⟩ ⟨~ person⟩ **b :** well-executed ⟨~ shot⟩ **6 :** most inappropriate **:** BAD ⟨a ~ one to talk⟩ **7 a :** socially acceptable **:** WELL-BRED **b :** VIRTUOUS, RESPECTABLE — **nice** *adv* — **nice·ly** *adv* — **nice·ness** *n*

syn DAINTY, FASTIDIOUS, FINICAL, PARTICULAR, SQUEAMISH: NICE implies fine discrimination in perception and evaluation; DAINTY suggests a tendency to reject what does not satisfy one's delicate taste or sensibility; FASTIDIOUS implies having very high and often capricious ethical, artistic, or social standards; FINICAL implies an affected often exasperating fastidiousness; PARTICULAR implies an insistence that one's exacting standards be met; SQUEAMISH suggests an oversensitive or prudish readiness to be nauseated, disgusted, or offended **syn** see in addition CORRECT

Ni·cene \'nī-,sēn, nī-'\ *adj* [ME, fr. LL *nicaenus,* fr. L *Nicaea* Nicaea] **:** of or relating to a church council held in Nicaea in A.D. 325 or to the Nicene Creed

Nicene Creed *n* **:** a Christian creed issued by the first Nicene Council and later expanded that begins "I believe in one God"

nice–nel·ly \'nī-'snel-ē\ *adj, often cap 2d N* [fr. the name *Nelly*] **1 :** PRUDISH **2 :** EUPHEMISTIC — **nice nelly** *n, often cap 2d N* — **nice–nel·ly·ism** \-,iz-əm\ *n, often cap 2d N*

nice·ty \'nī-sət-ē, -stē\ *n* [ME *nicete,* fr. MF *niceté* foolishness, fr. *nice,* adj.] **1 :** the quality or state of being nice **2 :** an elegant or civilized feature **3 :** a fine point or distinction **:** SUBTLETY **4 :** delicate exactness **:** PRECISION **5 :** FASTIDIOUSNESS

¹**niche** \'nich\ *n* [F, fr. MF, fr. *nicher* to nest, fr. (assumed) VL *nidicare,* fr. L *nidus* nest — more at NEST] **1 a :** a recess in a wall esp. for a statue **b :** something that resembles a niche **2 a :** a place, employment, or activity for which a person

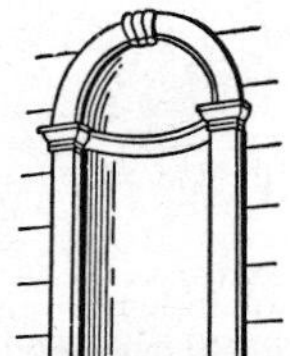
niche 1a

is best fitted **b :** a habitat supplying the factors necessary for the existence of an organism or species

2niche *vt* **:** to place in a niche

1nick \ˈnik\ *n* [ME *nyke*, prob. alter. of *nocke* nock] **1 :** NOTCH, SLIT; *specif* **:** a notch on the belly of a printing type **2 :** a final critical moment ⟨in the ~ of time⟩

2nick *vt* **1 :** to make a nick in **:** NOTCH, CHIP **2 :** to jot down **:** RECORD **3 :** to cut short **4 :** to catch at the right point or time **5 :** CHEAT, OVERCHARGE ~ *vi* **1 :** to make petty attacks **:** SNIPE **2 :** to complement one another genetically and produce superior offspring

1nick·el \ˈnik-əl\ *n, often attrib* [prob. fr. Sw, fr. G *kupfernickel* niccolite, prob. fr. *kupfer* copper + *nickel* goblin; fr. the deceptive copper color of niccolite] **1 :** a nearly silver-white hard malleable ductile metallic element capable of a high polish and resistant to corrosion used chiefly in alloys and as a catalyst — see ELEMENT table **2 a** (1) *also* **nick·le :** the U.S. 5-cent piece regularly containing 25 percent nickel and 75 percent copper (2) **:** the Canadian 5-cent piece **b :** five cents

2nick·el *vt* **nick·eled** *or* **nick·elled; nick·el·ing** *or* **nick·el·ling** \ˈnik-(ə-)liŋ\ **:** to plate with nickel

nic·kel·ic \nik-ˈel-ik\ *adj* **:** of, relating to, or containing nickel esp. with a higher valence than two

nick·el·if·er·ous \ˌnik-ə-ˈlif-(ə-)rəs\ *adj* **:** containing nickel

nick·el·ode·on \ˌnik-ə-ˈlōd-ē-ən\ *n* [prob. fr. 1*nickel* + *-odeon* (as in *melodeon* music hall)] **1 :** a theater presenting entertainment for an admission price of five cents **2 :** JUKEBOX

nick·el·ous \ˈnik-ə-ləs\ *adj* **:** of, relating to, or containing nickel esp. when bivalent

nickel silver *n* **:** a silver-white alloy of copper, zinc, and nickel

nick·er \ˈnik-ər\ *vi* **nick·er·ing** \-(ə-)riŋ\ [perh. alter. of *neigh*] **:** NEIGH, WHINNY — **nicker** *n*

nicknack *var of* KNICKKNACK

1nick·name \ˈnik-ˌnām\ *n* [ME *nekename* additional name, alter. (resulting from incorrect division of *an ekename*) of *ekename*, fr. *eke* + *name*] **1 :** a usu. descriptive name given instead of or in addition to the one belonging to an individual **2 :** a familiar form of a proper name

2nickname *vt* **1 :** MISNAME, MISCALL **2 :** to give (an individual) a nickname — **nick·nam·er** *n*

ni·co·ti·ana \nik-ˌō-shē-ˈan-ə, -ˈän-ə, -ˈā-nə\ *n* [NL, fr. *herba nicotiana*, lit., Nicot's herb, fr. Jean *Nicot* †1600 F diplomat and scholar] **:** any of several tobaccos (as *Nicotiana alata*) with showy flowers

nic·o·tin·amide \ˌnik-ə-ˈtē-nə-ˌmīd\ *n* [ISV] **:** a compound $C_6H_6N_2O$ of the vitamin B complex found esp. as a constituent of coenzymes and used similarly to nicotinic acid

nic·o·tine \ˈnik-ə-ˌtēn\ *n* [F, fr. NL *nicotiana*] **:** a poisonous alkaloid $C_{10}H_{14}N_2$ that is the chief active principle of tobacco and is used as an insecticide

nic·o·tin·ic \ˌnik-ə-ˈtē-nik, -ˈtin-ik\ *adj* [ISV] **:** of or relating to nicotine or nicotinic acid

nicotinic acid *n* **:** an acid $C_6H_5NO_2$ of the vitamin B complex found widely in animals and plants and used esp. against pellagra

nic·ti·tate \ˈnik-tə-ˌtāt\ *vi* [alter. of *nictate* (to wink), fr. L *nictatus*, pp. of *nictare* — more at CONNIVE] **:** WINK — **nic·ti·ta·tion** \ˌnik-tə-ˈtā-shən\ *n*

nictitating membrane *n* **:** a thin membrane found in many animals at the inner angle or beneath the lower lid of the eye and capable of extending across the eyeball

nid·get \ˈnij-ət\ *n* [alter. of earlier *nidiot*, alter. (resulting from incorrect division of *an idiot*) of *idiot*] *archaic* **:** IDIOT, FOOL

ni·dic·o·lous \nī-ˈdik-ə-ləs\ *adj* [L *nidus* nest + E *-colous*] **1 :** reared for a time in a nest **2 :** sharing the nest of another kind of animal

ni·di·fi·ca·tion \ˌnid-ə-fə-ˈkā-shən, ˌnīd-\ *n* [ML *nidification-*, *nidificatio*, fr. L *nidificatus*, pp. of *nidificare* to build a nest, fr. *nidus* nest] **:** the act, process, or technique of building a nest

ni·dif·u·gous \nī-ˈdif-yə-gəs, -ˈdif-i-gəs\ *adj* [L *nidus* nest + *fugere* to flee — more at FUGITIVE] **:** leaving the nest soon after hatching

ni·dus \ˈnīd-əs\ *n, pl* **ni·di** \ˈnī-ˌdī\ *or* **ni·dus·es** [NL, fr. L] **1 :** a nest or breeding place; *esp* **:** a place or substance in an animal or plant where bacteria or other organisms lodge and multiply **2 :** a place where something originates, develops, or is located

niece \ˈnēs\ *n* [ME *nece*, granddaughter, niece, fr. OF *niece*, fr. LL *neptia*, fr. L *neptis*; akin to L *nepot-*, *nepos* grandson, nephew — more at NEPHEW] **:** a daughter of one's brother or sister or of one's brother-in-law or sister-in-law

1ni·el·lo \nē-ˈel-(ˌ)ō\ *n, pl* **ni·el·li** \-ˈel-(ˌ)ē\ *or* **niellos** [It, fr. ML *nigellum*, fr. neut. of L *nigellus* blackish, dim. of *niger* black] **1 :** any of several metallic alloys of sulfur with silver, copper, or lead and a deep black color **2 :** the art or process of decorating metal with incised designs filled with niello **3 :** a piece of metal or other object decorated with niello

2niello *vt* **:** to inlay or ornament with niello

Ni·fl·heim \ˈniv-əl-ˌhām\ *n* [ON *Niflheimr*] **:** the northern region of cold and darkness in Norse mythology

nif·ty \ˈnif-tē\ *adj* [origin unknown] **:** FINE, SWELL — **nifty** *n*

1nig·gard \ˈnig-ərd\ *n* [ME, of Scand origin; akin to ON *hnøggr* niggardly; akin to L *cinis* ashes — more at INCINERATE] **:** a meanly covetous and stingy person **:** MISER — **niggard** *adj*

2niggard *vi, obs* **:** to act niggardly ~ *vt, obs* **:** to treat in a niggardly manner

nig·gard·li·ness \ˈnig-ərd-lē-nəs\ *n* **:** the quality or state of being niggardly

nig·gard·ly \-lē\ *adj* **1 :** grudgingly reluctant to spend or grant **:** STINGY **2 :** characteristic of a niggard **:** SCANTY **syn** see STINGY — **niggardly** *adv*

nig·ger \ˈnig-ər\ *n* [alter. of earlier *neger*, fr. MF *negre*, fr. Sp or Pg *negro*, fr. *negro* black, fr. L *niger*] **1 :** NEGRO — usu. taken to be offensive **2 :** a member of any darkskinned race — usu. taken to be offensive

nig·gle \ˈnig-əl\ *vb* **nig·gling** \-(ə-)liŋ\ [origin unknown] *vi* **1 a :** TRIFLE **b :** to spend too much effort on minor details **2 :** to find fault constantly in a petty way **:** CARP **3 :** GNAW ~ *vt* **:** to give stingily or in tiny portions — **nig·gler** \-(ə-)lər\ *n*

nig·gling \ˈnig-(ə-)liŋ\ *adj* **1 :** PETTY **2 a :** demanding meticulous care **b :** overly elaborate or feeble in execution — **niggling** *n* — **nig·gling·ly** \-(ə-)liŋ-lē\ *adv*

1nigh \ˈnī\ *adv* [ME, fr. OE *nēah*; akin to OHG *nāh*, adv., nigh, prep., nigh, after, ON *nā-* nigh] **1 :** near in place, time, or relationship **2 :** NEARLY, ALMOST

2nigh *adj* **1 :** CLOSE, NEAR **2** *chiefly dial* **:** DIRECT, SHORT **3 :** being on the left side ⟨the ~ horse⟩

3nigh \(ˌ)nī\ *prep* **:** NEAR

4nigh \ˈnī\ *vt* **:** to draw or come near to **:** APPROACH ~ *vi* **:** to draw near

night \ˈnīt\ *n* [ME, fr. OE *niht*; akin to OHG *naht* night, L *noct-*, *nox*, Gk *nykt-*, *nyx*] **1 :** the time from dusk to dawn when no light of the sun is visible **2 a :** an evening or night taken as an occasion or point of time **b :** an evening set aside for a particular purpose **3 a :** DARKNESS **b :** a condition or period felt to resemble the darkness of night; as (1) **:** a period of dreary inactivity or affliction (2) **:** mental or moral darkness **c :** the beginning of darkness **:** NIGHTFALL — **night** *adj*

night–blind \-ˌblīnd\ *adj* [back-formation fr. *night blindness*] **:** afflicted with night blindness

night blindness *n* **:** reduced visual capacity in faint light (as at night)

night–blooming cereus *n* **:** any of several night-blooming cacti; *esp* **:** a slender sprawling or climbing cactus (*Selenicereus grandiflorus*) often cultivated for its large showy fragrant white flowers

night·cap \ˈnīt-ˌkap\ *n* **1 :** a cloth cap worn with nightclothes **2 :** a usu. alcoholic drink taken at bedtime **3 :** the final race or contest of a day's sports; *esp* **:** the final game of a baseball doubleheader

night·clothes \-ˌklō(th)z\ *n pl* **:** garments worn in bed

night·club \-ˌkləb\ *n* **:** a place of entertainment open at night usu. serving food and liquor, having a floor show, and providing music and space for dancing

night crawler *n* **:** EARTHWORM; *esp* **:** a large earthworm found on the soil surface at night

night·dress \ˈnīt-ˌdres\ *n* **1 :** NIGHTGOWN **2 :** NIGHTCLOTHES

night·fall \-ˌfȯl\ *n* **:** the close of the day **:** DUSK

night·gown \-ˌgau̇n\ *n* **1** *archaic* **:** DRESSING GOWN **2 :** a long loose garment worn in bed

night·hawk \-ˌhȯk\ *n* **1 a :** any of several No. American goatsuckers (genus *Chordeiles*) related to the whippoorwill **b :** the European nightjar **2 :** a person who habitually stays up or goes about late at night

night heron *n* **:** any of various widely distributed nocturnal or crepuscular herons (as of the genus *Nycticorax*)

night·in·gale \ˈnīt-ᵊn-ˌgāl, -iŋ-\ *n* [ME, fr. OE *nihtegale*, fr. *niht* + *galan* to sing — more at YELL] **:** any of several Old World thrushes (genus *Luscinia*) noted for the sweet usu. nocturnal song of the male; *also* **:** any of various birds that sing at night

night·jar \ˈnīt-ˌjär\ *n* [fr. its harsh sound] **:** a common grayish brown European goatsucker (*Caprimulgus europaeus*); *broadly* **:** GOATSUCKER

night latch *n* **:** a door lock having a spring bolt operated from the outside by a key and from the inside by a knob

night letter *n* **:** a telegram sent at night at a reduced rate per word for delivery the following morning

1night·long \ˈnīt-ˌlȯŋ\ *adj* **:** lasting the whole night

2night·long \-ˈlȯŋ\ *adv* **:** through the whole night

1night·ly \ˈnīt-lē\ *adj* **1 :** of or relating to the night or every night **2 :** happening, done, or used by night or every night

2nightly *adv* **:** every night; *also* **:** at or by night

night·mare \ˈnīt-ˌma(ə)r, -ˌme(ə)r\ *n* **1 :** an evil spirit formerly thought to oppress people during sleep **2 :** a frightening dream accompanied by a sense of oppression or suffocation that usu. awakens the sleeper **3 :** an experience, situation, or object having the monstrous character of a nightmare or producing a feeling of anxiety or terror — **night·mar·ish** \-ish\ *adj*

night owl *n* **:** a person who keeps late hours at night **:** NIGHTHAWK

night rail \-ˌrāl\ *n* [*night* + *rail* (garment)] *archaic* **:** NIGHTGOWN

night raven *n* **:** a bird that cries at night

night rider *n* **:** a member of a secret band who ride masked at night doing acts of violence for the purpose of punishing or terrorizing

night–robe \ˈnīt-ˌrōb\ *n* **:** NIGHTGOWN

nights \ˈnīts\ *adv* **:** in the nighttime repeatedly **:** on any night ⟨works ~⟩

night·shade \ˈnīt-ˌshād\ *n* **1 :** any of a genus (*Solanum* of the family Solanaceae, the nightshade family) of herbs, shrubs, and trees with alternate leaves, cymose flowers, and fruits that are berries including poisonous weeds, various ornamentals, and important crop plants (as the potato and eggplant) **2 :** BELLADONNA **3 :** HENBANE

night·shirt \-ˌshərt\ *n* **:** a nightgown resembling a shirt

night soil *n* **:** human excrement collected for fertilizing the soil

night·stick \ˈnīt-ˌstik\ *n* **:** a policeman's club

night·tide \ˈnīt-ˌtīd\ *n* **:** NIGHTTIME

night·time \-ˌtīm\ *n* **:** the time from dusk to dawn

night·walk·er \-ˌwȯ-kər\ *n* **:** a person who roves about at night esp. with criminal or immoral intent

ni·gres·cence \nī-ˈgres-ᵊn(t)s\ *n* **:** a process of becoming black or dark

ni·gres·cent \-ᵊnt\ *adj* [L *nigrescent-*, *nigrescens*, prp. of *nigrescere* to become black, fr. *nigr-*, *niger* black] **:** BLACKISH

ni·gri·tude \ˈnī-grə-ˌt(y)üd\ *n* [L *nigritudo*, fr. *nigr-*, *niger*] **:** intense darkness **:** BLACKNESS

ni·gro·sine \ˈnī-grə-ˌsēn, -sən\ *also* **ni·gro·sin** \-sən\ *n, often cap* [L *nigr-*, *niger*] **:** any of several azine dyes closely related to the indulines

ni·hil·ism \ˈnī-əl-ˌiz-əm, ˈni-ˌhil-, ˈnī-ˌhil-, ˈnē-\ *n* [G *nihilismus*, fr. L *nihil* nothing — more at NIL] **1 a :** a viewpoint that traditional values and beliefs are unfounded and that existence is senseless and useless **b :** a doctrine that denies any objective ground of truth and esp. of moral truths **2 a** (1) **:** a doctrine or belief that conditions in the social organization are so bad as to make destruction desirable for its own sake independent of any constructive program or possibility (2) *usu cap* **:** the program of a 19th century Russian party advocating revolutionary reform and using terrorism and assassination **b :** TERRORISM — **ni·hil·ist** \-əst\ *n* — **nihilist** *or* **ni·hil·is·tic** \ˌnī-əl-ˈis-tik, ˌni-ˌhil-, ˌnī-ˌhil-, ˌnē-\ *adj*

ni·hil·i·ty \nī-ˈhil-ət-ē, ni-\ *n* **:** NOTHINGNESS

ni·hil ob·stat \ˌnī-ˌhil-ˈäb-ˌstät, ˌnik-ˌil-\ *n* [L, nothing hinders] **1 :** the certification by an official censor of the Roman Catholic

Church that a book has been examined and found to contain nothing opposed to faith and morals **2 :** authoritative or official approval

Ni·ke \ˈnī-kē\ *n* [Gk *Nikē*] **:** the Greek goddess of victory usu. represented as winged and as carrying a wreath and a palm branch

nil \ˈnil\ *n* [L, nothing, contr. of *nihil*, fr. OL *nihilum*, fr. *ne-* not + *hilum* trifle — more at NO] **:** NOTHING, ZERO — **nil** *adj*

nile green \ˈnī(ə)l-\ *n, often cap N* [*Nile* river, Africa] **:** a variable color averaging a pale yellow green

nill \ˈnil\ *vb* [ME *nilen*, fr. OE *nyllan*, fr. *ne* not + *wyllan* to wish — more at NO, WILL] *vi, archaic* **:** to be unwilling ~ *vt, archaic* **:** not to will **:** REFUSE

Ni·lot·ic \nī-ˈlät-ik\ *adj* [L *Niloticus*, fr. Gk *Neilōtēs*, fr. *Neilos* Nile] **:** of or relating to the Nile or the peoples of the Nile basin

nim \ˈnim\ *vb* **nimmed; nim·ming** [ME *nimen* to take, fr. OE *niman*] *vt, archaic* **:** STEAL, FILCH ~ *vi, archaic* **:** THIEVE

nim·ble \ˈnim-bəl\ *adj* **nim·bler** \-b(ə-)lər\ **nim·blest** \-b(ə-)ləst\ [ME *nimel*, fr. OE *numol* holding much, fr. *niman* to take; akin to OHG *neman* to take, L *numerus* number, Gk *nemein* to distribute, manage, *nomos* pasture, *nomos* usage, custom, law] **1 :** marked by quick light movement **:** LIVELY ⟨~ fingers⟩ **2 a :** marked by quick, alert, clever conception, comprehension, or resourcefulness ⟨~ mind⟩ **b :** SENSITIVE, RESPONSIVE ⟨a ~ listener⟩ **syn** see AGILE — **nim·ble·ness** \-bəl-nəs\ *n* — **nim·bly** \-blē\ *adv*

nim·bo·stra·tus \ˌnim-(ˌ)bō-ˈstrāt-əs, -ˈstrat-\ *n* [NL, fr. L *nimbus* + NL *stratus*] **:** a low dark gray rainy cloud layer

nim·bus \ˈnim-bəs\ *n, pl* **nim·bi** \-ˌbī, -ˌbē\ *or* **nim·bus·es** [L, rainstorm, cloud; akin to Pahlavi *namb* mist] **1 a :** a luminous vapor, cloud, or atmosphere about a god or goddess when on earth **b :** a cloud or atmosphere (as of romance) about a person or thing **2 :** an indication (as a circle) of radiant light or glory about the head of a drawn or sculptured divinity, saint, or sovereign **3 a :** the rain cloud that is of uniform grayness and extends over the entire sky **b :** a cloud from which rain is falling

ni·mi·ety \nim-ˈī-ət-ē\ *n* [LL *nimietas*, fr. L *nimius* too much, adj., fr. *nimis*, adv.] **:** EXCESS, REDUNDANCY

nim·i·ny–pim·i·ny \ˌnim-ə-nē-ˈpim-ə-nē\ *adj* [prob. alter. of *namby-pamby*] **:** MINCING, EFFEMINATE

Nim·rod \ˈnim-ˌräd\ *n* [Heb *Nimrōdh*] **1 :** a mighty hunter and great-grandson of Noah **2** *often not cap* **:** HUNTER

nin·com·poop \ˈnin-kəm-ˌpüp, ˈniŋ-\ *n* [origin unknown] **:** FOOL, SIMPLETON

nine \ˈnīn\ *n* [ME, fr. *nyne*, adj., fr. OE *nigon*; akin to OHG *niun* nine, L *novem*, Gk *ennea*] **1** — see NUMBER table **2 :** the ninth in a set or series ⟨the ~ of hearts⟩ **3 :** something having nine units or members: as **a** *cap* **:** the nine Muses **b :** a baseball team **c :** the first or last nine holes of an 18-hole golf course — **nine** *adj or pron* — **to the nines :** to the highest degree

nine days' wonder *n* **:** something that creates a short-lived sensation

nine·pence \ˈnīn-pən(t)s, *US also* -ˌpen(t)s\ *n* **:** the sum of nine usu. British pennies

nine·pin \ˈnīn-ˌpin\ *n* **1 :** a pin used in ninepins **2** *pl but sing in constr* **:** tenpins played without the headpin

nine·teen \(ˈ)nīn(t)-ˈtēn\ *n* [ME *nynetene*, adj., fr. OE *nigontēne*; akin to OE *tīen* ten] — see NUMBER table — **nineteen** *adj or pron* — **nine·teenth** \-ˈtēn(t)th\ *adj* — **nineteenth** *n, pl* **nine·teenths** \-ˈtēn(t)s, -ˈtēn(t)ths\

nine·ti·eth \ˈnīnt-ē-əth\ *n* — see NUMBER table — **ninetieth** *adj*

nine·ty \ˈnīnt-ē\ *n* [ME *ninety*, adj., fr. OE *nigontig*, short for *hundnigontig*, fr. *hundnigontig*, n., group of 90, fr. *hund* hundred + *nigon* nine + *-tig* group of 10 — more at HUNDRED, EIGHTY] **1** — see NUMBER table **2** *pl* **:** the numbers 90 to 99 — **ninety** *adj or pron*

nin·ny \ˈnin-ē\ *n* [perh. by shortening and alter. fr. *an innocent*] **:** FOOL, SIMPLETON

nin·ny·ham·mer \-ˌham-ər\ *n* **:** NINNY

ni·non \ˈnē-ˌnän\ *n* [prob. fr. F *Ninon*, nickname for *Anne*] **:** a smooth sheer fabric

ninth \ˈnīn(t)th\ *n, pl* **ninths** \ˈnīn(t)s, ˈnīn(t)ths\ **1** — see NUMBER table **2 a :** a musical interval embracing an octave and a second **b :** a chord containing a ninth — **ninth** *adj*

ninth cranial nerve *n* **:** GLOSSOPHARYNGEAL NERVE

Ni·o·be \ˈnī-ə-bē\ *n* [L, fr. Gk *Niobē*] **:** a daughter of Tantalus and wife of Amphion held in Greek legend to have been turned into stone while weeping for her slain children and to continue weeping her loss

ni·o·bic \nī-ˈō-bik\ *adj* **:** of, relating to, or containing niobium esp. when pentavalent

ni·o·bi·um \nī-ˈō-bē-əm\ *n* [NL, fr. L *Niobe*; fr. its occurrence in tantalite] **:** a lustrous platinum-gray ductile chiefly pentavalent metallic element that resembles tantalum chemically and is used in alloys — see ELEMENT table

ni·o·bous \nī-ˈō-bəs\ *adj* **:** of, relating to, or containing niobium esp. with a lower valence than in niobic compounds

¹nip \ˈnip\ *vb* **nipped; nip·ping** [ME *nippen*; akin to ON *hnippa* to prod, Gk *konis* ashes — more at INCINERATE] *vt* **1 :** to catch hold of and squeeze tightly between two surfaces, edges, or points **:** PINCH **2 a :** to sever by or as if by pinching sharply **b :** to destroy the growth, progress, maturing, or fulfillment of ⟨*nipped* in the bud⟩ **c :** to check sharply **3 :** to injure or make numb with cold **:** CHILL **4 :** SNATCH, STEAL ~ *vi, chiefly Brit* **:** to move briskly, nimbly, or quickly

²nip *n* **1 :** something that nips: as **a :** a sharp biting comment **b :** a sharp stinging cold **c :** a biting or pungent flavor **:** TANG **2 :** the act of nipping **:** PINCH, BITE **3 :** a small portion **:** BIT

³nip *n* [prob. fr. *nipperkin* (a liquor container)] **:** a small quantity of liquor **:** SIP

⁴nip *vi* **nipped; nip·ping :** to take liquor in nips **:** TIPPLE

ni·pa \ˈnē-pə\ *n* [prob. fr. It, fr. Malay *nipah* nipa palm] **1 :** an alcoholic drink made from the juice of an Australasian creeping palm (*Nipa fruticans*); *also* **:** this palm **2 :** thatch made of nipa leaves

nip and tuck \ˌnip-ən-ˈtək\ *adj (or adv)* **:** so close that the lead or advantage shifts rapidly from one contestant to another

nip·per \ˈnip-ər\ *n* **1 :** any of various devices for nipping (as pincers) **2 a :** an incisor of a horse **b :** CHELA **3** *chiefly Brit* **a :** a boy employed as a helper (as of a carter or hawker) **b :** CHILD

nip·ping \ˈnip-iŋ\ *adj* **:** that nips — **nip·ping·ly** \-iŋ-lē\ *adv*

nip·ple \ˈnip-əl\ *n* [earlier *neble*, *nible*, prob. dim. of *neb*, *nib*] **1 :** the protuberance of a mammary gland upon which the ducts open and from which milk is drawn **2 a :** an artificial teat through which a bottle-fed infant nurses **b :** a device with an orifice through which the discharge of a liquid can be regulated **3 a :** a protuberance resembling or suggesting the nipple of a breast **b :** a small projection through which oil or grease is injected into machinery **4 :** a pipe coupling consisting of a short piece of threaded tubing

Nip·pon·ese \ˌnip-ə-ˈnēz, -ˈnēs\ *adj* [*Nippon* (Japan)] **:** JAPANESE — **Nipponese** *n*

nip·py \ˈnip-ē\ *adj* **1 :** marked by a tendency to nip **2 :** brisk, quick, or nimble in movement **:** SNAPPY **3 :** PUNGENT, SHARP **4 :** CHILLY, CHILLING ⟨a ~ day⟩

nip–up \ˈnip-ˌəp\ *n* **:** a spring to a standing position from a supine position

nir·va·na \ni(ə)r-ˈvän-ə, nər-\ *n, often cap* [Skt *nirvāṇa*, lit., act of extinguishing, fr. *nis-* out + *vāti* it blows — more at WIND] **1 :** the final beatitude that transcends suffering, karma, and samsara and is sought esp. in Buddhism through the extinction of desire and individual consciousness **2 :** a place or state of oblivion to care, pain, or external reality

Ni·san \ˈnis-ᵊn, nē-ˈsän\ *n* [Heb *Nīsān*] **:** the 7th month of the civil year or the 1st month of the ecclesiastical year in the Jewish calendar

ni·sei \(ˈ)nē-ˈsā, ˈnē-ˌ\ *n, pl* **nisei** *also* **niseis** [Jap, lit., second generation, fr. *ni* second + *sei* generation] **:** a son or daughter of immigrant Japanese parents who is born and educated in America and esp. in the U.S.

ni·si \ˈnī-ˌsī\ *adj* [L, unless, fr. *ne-* not + *si* if] **:** taking effect at a specified time unless previously modified or avoided by cause shown, further proceedings, or a condition fulfilled ⟨decree ~⟩

Nis·sen hut \ˌnis-ᵊn-\ *n* [Peter N. *Nissen* †1930 Brit. mining engineer] **:** a barrel-shaped prefabricated shelter of corrugated iron with cement floor

ni·sus \ˈnī-səs\ *n, pl* **ni·sus** \-səs, -ˌsüs\ [L, fr. *nisus*, pp. of *niti* to bear down, strive; akin to L con*nivēre* to close the eyes — more at CONNIVE] **:** a conative state or condition **:** STRIVING

nit \ˈnit\ *n* [ME *nite*, fr. OE *hnitu*; akin to OHG *hniz* nit, Gk *konid-*, *konis*] **:** the egg of a louse or other parasitic insect; *also* **:** the insect itself when young

ni·ter *also* **ni·tre** \ˈnīt-ər\ *n* [ME *nitre* natron, fr. MF, fr. L *nitrum*, fr. Gk *nitron*, fr. Egypt *nṯry*] **1 :** POTASSIUM NITRATE **2 :** SODIUM NITRATE

nit·id \ˈnit-əd\ *adj* [L *nitidus* — more at NEAT] **:** BRIGHT, LUSTROUS

nit–pick·ing \ˈnit-ˌpik-iŋ\ *n* **:** minute and usu. unjustified criticism

nitr- *or* **nitro-** *comb form* [*niter*] **1 :** niter **:** nitrate ⟨*nitro*bacteria⟩ **2 a :** nitrogen ⟨*nitr*ide⟩ ⟨*nitro*meter⟩ **b** *usu* **nitro- :** containing the univalent group $-NO_2$ composed of one nitrogen and two oxygen atoms ⟨*nitro*benzene⟩

¹ni·trate \ˈnī-ˌtrāt, -trət\ *n* [F, fr. *nitrique*] **1 :** a salt or ester of nitric acid **2 :** sodium nitrate or potassium nitrate used as a fertilizer

²ni·trate \-ˌtrāt\ *vt* **:** to treat or combine with nitric acid or a nitrate; *esp* **:** to convert (an organic compound) into a nitro compound or a nitrate — **ni·tra·tion** \nī-ˈtrā-shən\ *n* — **ni·tra·tor** \ˈnī-ˌtrāt-ər\ *n*

ni·tric \ˈnī-trik\ *adj* [F *nitrique*, fr. *nitr-*] **:** of, relating to, or containing nitrogen esp. with a higher valence than in corresponding nitrous compounds

nitric acid *n* **:** a corrosive liquid inorganic acid HNO_3 used esp. as an oxidizing agent, in nitrations, and in making fertilizers, explosives, dyes, and other organic compounds

nitric bacterium *n* **:** a bacterium (as of the genus *Nitrobacter*) that oxidizes nitrites to nitrates

nitric oxide *n* **:** a colorless poisonous gas NO obtained by oxidation of nitrogen or ammonia

ni·tride \ˈnī-ˌtrīd\ *n* [ISV] **:** a binary compound of nitrogen with a more electropositive element

ni·tri·fi·ca·tion \ˌnī-trə-fə-ˈkā-shən\ *n* **:** the process of nitrifying; *specif* **:** the oxidation (as by bacteria) of ammonium salts to nitrites and the further oxidation of nitrites to nitrates

ni·tri·fy \ˈnī-trə-ˌfī\ *vt* [F *nitrifier*, fr. *nitr-*] **1 :** to combine or impregnate with nitrogen or a nitrogen compound **2 :** to subject to or produce by nitrification

ni·trile \ˈnī-trəl\ *n* [ISV] **:** an organic cyanide characterized by the univalent group CN which on hydrolysis yields an acid with elimination of ammonia

ni·trite \ˈnī-ˌtrīt\ *n* **:** a salt or ester of nitrous acid

¹ni·tro \ˈnī-(ˌ)trō\ *adj* [*nitr-*] **:** containing or being the univalent group $-NO_2$ united through nitrogen

²nitro *n* **:** any of various nitrated products; *esp* **:** NITROGLYCERIN

ni·tro·bac·te·ria \ˌnī-(ˌ)trō-bak-ˈtir-ē-ə\ *n pl* [NL] **:** soil bacteria concerned in nitrification; *esp* **:** NITRIC BACTERIA

ni·tro·ben·zene \ˌnī-trō-ˈben-ˌzēn, -ˌben-ˈ\ *n* [ISV] **:** a poisonous insoluble oil $C_6H_5NO_2$ made by nitration of benzene and used as a solvent, mild oxidizing agent, and starting material in making aniline and other dye intermediates

ni·tro·cel·lu·lose \-ˈsel-yə-ˌlōs, -ˌlōz\ *n* [ISV] **:** nitrated cellulose — **ni·tro·cel·lu·los·ic** \-ˌsel-yə-ˈlō-sik, -zik\ *adj*

ni·tro·fu·ran \ˌnī-trō-ˈfyù(ə)r-ˌan, -fyù-ˈran\ *n* **:** a derivative of furan with a nitro group used as a bacteria-inhibiting agent

ni·tro·gen \ˈnī-trə-jən\ *n, often attrib* [F *nitrogène*, fr. *nitr-* + *-gène* -gen] **:** a colorless tasteless odorless gaseous element that constitutes 78 percent of the atmosphere by volume and is a constituent of all living tissues — see ELEMENT table — **ni·trog·e·nous** \nī-ˈträj-ə-nəs\ *adj*

nitrogen balance *n* **:** the difference between nitrogen intake and nitrogen loss in the body or the soil

nitrogen cycle *n* **:** a continuous series of natural processes by which nitrogen passes through successive stations in air, soil, and organisms involving principally decay, nitrogen fixation, nitrification, and denitrification

nitrogen fixation *n* **1 :** the industrial conversion of free nitrogen into combined forms useful esp. as starting materials for fertilizers or explosives **2 :** the metabolic assimilation of atmospheric nitrogen by soil microorganisms and esp. rhizobia and its release for plant use by nitrification in the soil on the death of the microorganisms

nitrogen–fixing *adj* : capable of nitrogen fixation ⟨~ bacteria⟩
ni·tro·ge·nize \nī-'träj-ə-ˌnīz, 'nī-trə-jə-\ *vt* : to combine or impregnate with nitrogen or its compounds
nitrogen mustard *n* : any of various toxic blistering compounds analogous to mustard gas but with nitrogen replacing sulfur
ni·tro·glyc·er·in *or* **ni·tro·glyc·er·ine** \ˌnī-trō-'glis-(ə-)rən\ *n* [ISV] : a heavy oily explosive poisonous liquid $C_3H_5(ONO_2)_3$ obtained by nitrating glycerol and used chiefly in making dynamites and in medicine as a vasodilator
ni·tro·par·af·fin \-'par-ə-fən\ *n* [ISV] : a nitro derivative of any member of the methane series
nitros- *or* **nitroso-** *comb form* [NL *nitrosus* nitrous] : containing the univalent group —NO composed of one nitrogen and one oxygen atom ⟨*nitroso*benzene C_6H_5NO⟩ ⟨*nitros*amines⟩
ni·tro·sa·mine \nī-'trō-sə-ˌmēn\ *n* : any of various neutral compounds characterized by the grouping >NNO
ni·tro·so·bac·te·ri·um \nī-ˌtrō-sō-(ˌ)bak-'tir-ē-əm\ *n* [NL, fr. *nitrosus* + *-o-* + *bacterium*] : a bacterium that oxidizes ammonia to nitrites
ni·trous \'nī-trəs\ *adj* [NL *nitrosus*, fr. L, full of natron, fr. *nitrum* natron — more at NITER] **1** : of, relating to, or containing niter **2** : of, relating to, or containing nitrogen esp. with a lower valence than in corresponding nitric compounds
nitrous acid *n* : an unstable acid HNO_2 known only in solution or in the form of its salts
nitrous bacterium *n* : NITROSOBACTERIUM
nitrous oxide *n* : a colorless gas N_2O that when inhaled produces loss of sensibility to pain preceded by exhilaration and sometimes laughter and is used esp. as an anesthetic in dentistry — called also *laughing gas*
nit·ty–grit·ty \'nit-ē-ˌgrit-ē\ *n* [origin unknown] : the actual state of things : what is ultimately essential and true
nit·wit \'nit-ˌwit\ *n* [prob. fr. G dial. *nit* not + E *wit*] : a scatterbrained or stupid person
1**nix** \'niks\ *n* [G, fr. OHG *nihhus;* akin to OE *nicor* water monster, Gk *nizein* to wash] : a water sprite of Germanic folklore usu. having the form of a woman or a half human and half fish — called also *nixie*
2**nix** *n* [G *nichts* nothing] *slang* : NOTHING : no one
3**nix** *adv, slang* : NO — used to express disagreement or the withholding of permission
4**nix** *vt, slang* : VETO, FORBID
ni·zam \ni-'zäm, 'nī-ˌzam, nī-'\ *n* **1** [Hindi *nizām* order, governor, fr. Ar *niẓām*] : one of a line of sovereigns of Hyderabad, India, reigning from 1713 to 1950 **2** [Turk, fr. Ar *niẓām*] : a Turkish soldier — **ni·zam·ate** \ni-'zäm-ˌāt, nī-'zam-\ *n*
1**no** \(')nō\ *adv* [ME, fr. OE *nā*, fr. *ne* not + *ā* always; akin to ON & OHG *ne* not, L *ne-*, Gk *nē-* — more at AYE] **1 a** *chiefly Scot* : NOT **b** — used as a function word to express the negative of an alternative choice or possibility **2** : in no respect or degree — used in comparisons **3** : not so — used to express negation, dissent, denial, or refusal **4** — used with a following adjective to imply a meaning expressed by the opposite positive statement ⟨~ uncertain terms⟩ **5** — used as a function word to emphasize a following negative or to introduce a more emphatic, explicit, or comprehensive statement **6** — used as an interjection to express surprise, doubt, or incredulity
2**no** *adj* **1 a** : not any ⟨~ parking⟩ **b** : hardly any : very little ⟨finished in ~ time⟩ **2** : not a : quite other than a ⟨he's ~ expert⟩
3**no** \'nō\ *n, pl* **noes** *or* **nos** \'nōz\ **1** : an act or instance of refusing or denying by the use of the word *no* : DENIAL **2 a** : a negative vote or decision **b** *pl* : persons voting in the negative
4**no** \'nō\ *n, pl* **no** *often cap* [Jap *nō*, lit., talent] : classic Japanese dance-drama that is heroic in subject and in the use of measured chants and movements
No·a·chi·an \nō-'ā-kē-ən\ *adj* [Heb *Nōaḥ* Noah] **1** : of or relating to the patriarch Noah or his time **2** : ANCIENT, ANTIQUATED
No·ah \'nō-ə\ *n* [Heb *Nōaḥ*] : an Old Testament patriarch and builder of the ark in which he, his family, and living creatures of every kind survived the flood
1**nob** \'näb\ *n* [prob. alter. of *knob*] **1** *slang* : HEAD 1 **2** : a jack of the same suit as the starter in cribbage that scores one point for the holder
2**nob** *n* [perh. fr. 1*nob*] *chiefly Brit* : one in a superior position in life
nob·ble \'näb-əl\ *vt* **nob·bling** \-(ə-)liŋ\ [perh. irreg. freq. of *nab*] **1** *Brit* : to incapacitate (a racehorse) esp. by drugging **2** *slang Brit* **a** : to win over to one's side **b** : STEAL **c** : SWINDLE, CHEAT — **nob·bler** \-(ə-)lər\ *n*
nob·by \'näb-ē\ *adj* : of the first quality or style : SMART
no·bel·i·um \nō-'bel-ē-əm\ *n* [NL, fr. Alfred B. *Nobel*] : a radioactive element produced artificially — see ELEMENT table
No·bel prize \(ˌ)nō-ˌbel-\ *n* [Alfred B. *Nobel* †1896 Sw philanthropist] : any of various annual prizes (as in peace, literature, medicine) established by the will of Alfred Nobel for the encouragement of persons who work for the interests of humanity
no·bil·ia·ry \nō-'bil-ē-ˌer-ē, -'bil-yə-rē\ *adj* : of or relating to the nobility
no·bil·i·ty \nō-'bil-ət-ē\ *n* [ME *nobilite*, fr. MF *nobilité*, fr. L *nobilitat-*, *nobilitas*, fr. *nobilis*] **1** : the quality or state of being noble in character, quality, or rank **2** : the body of persons forming the noble class in a country or state : ARISTOCRACY
1**no·ble** \'nō-bəl\ *adj* **no·bler** \-b(ə-)lər\ **no·blest** \-b(ə-)ləst\ [ME, fr. OF, fr. L *nobilis* knowable, well known, noble, fr. *noscere* to come to know — more at KNOW] **1 a** : possessing outstanding qualities : ILLUSTRIOUS **b** : FAMOUS, NOTABLE ⟨~ deed⟩ **2** : of high birth or exalted rank : ARISTOCRATIC **3 a** : possessing very high or excellent qualities or properties ⟨~ hawk⟩ **b** : very good or excellent **4** : grand or impressive esp. in appearance ⟨~ edifice⟩ **5** : possessing, characterized by, or arising from superiority of mind or character : MAGNANIMOUS ⟨~ nature⟩ **6** : chemically inert or inactive esp. toward oxygen ⟨~ metal⟩ **syn** see MORAL — **no·ble·ness** \-bəl-nəs\ *n* — **no·bly** \-blē *also* -bə-lē\ *adv*
2**no·ble** \'nō-bəl\ *n* **1** : a person of noble rank or birth **2** : an old English gold coin equivalent to 6*s* 8*d* **3** *slang* : a captain of strikebreakers or an overseer in charge of strikebreaking operations
no·ble·man \-mən\ *n* : one belonging to the nobility — **no·ble·wom·an** \-ˌwu̇m-ən\ *n*
no·blesse \nō-'bles\ *n* [ME, fr. OF *noblesce*, fr. *noble*] **1** : noble birth or condition : NOBILITY **2** : the members esp. of the French nobility
no·blesse oblige \nō-ˌbles-ə-'blēzh\ *n* [F, lit., nobility obligates] : the obligation of honorable, generous, and responsible behavior associated with high rank or birth
1**no·body** \'nō-ˌbäd-ē, -bəd-ē\ *pron* : no person : not anybody
2**nobody** *n* : a person of no influence, importance, or worth
no·cent \'nōs-ᵊnt\ *adj* [ME, fr. L *nocent-*, *nocens*, fr. prp. of *nocēre* to harm, hurt] **1** : HARMFUL **2** *archaic* : GUILTY, CRIMINAL
no·ci·cep·tive \ˌnō-si-'sep-tiv\ *adj* [L *nocēre* + E *-i-* + *receptive*] **1** *of a stimulus* : PAINFUL, INJURIOUS **2** : of, induced by, or responding to a nociceptive stimulus — used esp. of receptors or protective reflexes
1**nock** \'näk\ *n* [ME *nocke* notched tip on the end of a bow; akin to MD *nocke* summit, tip, L *nux* nut — more at NUT] **1** : one of the notches cut in either of two tips of horn fastened on the ends of a bow or in the bow itself for holding the string **2 a** : the part of an arrow having a notch for the bowstring **b** : the notch itself
2**nock** *vt* : to make a notch in or fit into or by means of a notch
noct- *or* **nocti-** *or* **nocto-** *comb form* [L *noct-*, *nocti-*, fr. *noct-*, *nox* — more at NIGHT] : night ⟨*noct*ambulation⟩
noct·am·bu·la·tion \(ˌ)näk-ˌtam-byə-'lā-shən\ *or* **noct·am·bu·lism** \näk-'tam-byə-ˌliz-əm\ *n* [*noct-* + *-ambulation*, *-ambulism* (as in *somnambulation*, *somnambulism*)] : SOMNAMBULISM — **noct·am·bu·list** \näk-'tam-byə-ləst\ *n*
noc·ti·lu·ca \ˌnäk-tə-'lü-kə\ *n* [NL, genus name, fr. L, something that shines by night, fr. *noct-* + *lucēre* to shine — more at LIGHT] : any of a genus (*Noctiluca*) of marine bioluminescent flagellates (order Dinoflagellata) that often cause phosphorescence of the sea
noc·turn \'näk-ˌtərn\ *n* [ME *nocturne*, fr. MF, fr. ML *nocturna*, fr. L, fem. of *nocturnus*] : a principal division of the office of matins
noc·tur·nal \näk-'tərn-ᵊl\ *adj* [MF or LL; MF fr. LL *nocturnalis*, fr. L *nocturnus* of night, nocturnal, fr. *noct-*, *nox* night] **1** : of, relating to, or occurring in the night ⟨a ~ journey⟩ **2** : active at night ⟨a ~ predator⟩ — **noc·tur·nal·ly** \-ᵊl-ē\ *adv*
noc·turne \'näk-ˌtərn\ *n* [F, adj., nocturnal, fr. L *nocturnus*] : a work of art dealing with night; *esp* : a dreamy pensive composition for the piano
noc·u·ous \'näk-yə-wəs\ *adj* [L *nocuus*, fr. *nocēre* to harm — more at NOXIOUS] : likely to cause injury : HARMFUL — **noc·u·ous·ly** *adv*
1**nod** \'näd\ *vb* **nod·ded**; **nod·ding** [ME *nodden;* akin to OHG *hnotōn* to shake, L *cinis* ashes — more at INCINERATE] *vi* **1** : to make a quick downward motion of the head whether as a sign of assent, salutation, or command or involuntarily from drowsiness **2** : to incline or sway from the vertical as though ready to fall **3** : to bend or sway the upper part gently downward or forward **4** : to make a slip or error in a moment of abstraction ~ *vt* **1** : to incline (as the head) downward or forward **2** : to bring, invite, or send by a nod **3** : to signify by a nod — **nod·der** *n*
2**nod** *n* : the act of one who nods
nod·al \'nōd-ᵊl\ *adj* : being, relating to, or located at or near a node — **no·dal·i·ty** \nō-'dal-ət-ē\ *n* — **nod·al·ly** \'nōd-ᵊl-ē\ *adv*
nod·dle \'näd-ᵊl\ *n* [ME *nodle* back of the head or neck] : HEAD, PATE
nod·dy \'näd-ē\ *n* [prob. short for obs. *noddypoll*, alter. of *hoddypoll* (fumbling inept person)] **1** : a stupid person **2** : any of several stout-bodied terns (genera *Anous* and *Micranous*) of warm seas
node \'nōd\ *n* [L *nodus* knot, node — more at NET] **1** : an entangling complication : PREDICAMENT **2 a** : a thickened or swollen enlargement (as of a rheumatic joint) **b** : a discrete mass of one kind of tissue enclosed in tissue of a different kind **3** : either of the two points where the orbit of a planet or comet intersects the ecliptic **4 a** : a point at which subsidiary parts originate or center **b** : a point on a stem at which a leaf or leaves are inserted **5** : a point, line, or surface of a vibrating body that is free or relatively free from vibratory motion
no·di·cal \'nōd-i-kəl, 'näd-\ *adj* : of or relating to astronomical nodes
no·dose \'nō-ˌdōs\ *adj* [L *nodosus*, fr. *nodus*] : having numerous or conspicuous protuberances — **no·dos·i·ty** \nō-'däs-ət-ē\ *n*
nod·u·lar \'näj-(ə-)lər\ *adj* : of, relating to, characterized by, or occurring in the form of nodules
nod·ule \'näj-(ˌ)ü(ə)l\ *n* [L *nodulus*, dim. of *nodus*] : a small mass of rounded or irregular shape: as **a** : a small rounded lump of a mineral or mineral aggregate **b** : a swelling on a leguminous root that contains symbiotic bacteria
nod·u·lose \'näj-ə-ˌlōs\ *also* **nod·u·lous** \-(ə-)ləs\ *adj* : having minute nodules : finely knobby
no·dus \'nōd-əs\ *n, pl* **no·di** \'nō-ˌdī, -ˌdē\ [L, knot, node] : COMPLICATION, DIFFICULTY
no·el \nō-'el\ *n* [F *noël* Christmas, carol, fr. L *natalis* birthday, fr. *natalis* natal] **1** : a Christmas carol **2** *cap* : the Christmas season
noes *pl of* NO
no·et·ic \nō-'et-ik\ *adj* [Gk *noētikos* intellectual, fr. *noein* to think, fr. *nous* mind] : of, relating to, or based on purely intellectual apprehension
1**nog** \'näg\ *n* [origin unknown] : a wooden peg, pin, or block of the size of a brick; *esp* : one built into a wall as a hold for nails
2**nog** *n* [origin unknown] **1** : a strong ale formerly brewed in Norfolk, England **2** [by shortening] : EGGNOG **3** : an often alcoholic drink containing beaten egg, milk, or both
nog·gin \'näg-ən\ *n* [origin unknown] **1** : a small mug or cup **2** : a small quantity (as a gill) of drink **3** : a person's head
nog·ging \'näg-ən, -iŋ\ *n* [1*nog*] : rough brick masonry used to fill in the open spaces of a wooden frame
noh *var of* NO
no·how \'nō-ˌhau̇\ *adv, dial* : not at all
noil \'nȯi(ə)l\ *n* [origin unknown] : short fiber removed during the combing of a textile fiber spun into yarn for cloth
1**noise** \'nȯiz\ *n* [ME, fr. OF, strife, quarrel, noise, fr. L *nausea* nausea] **1** : loud, confused, or senseless shouting or outcry **2 a** : SOUND; *esp* : one that lacks agreeable musical quality or is noticeably unpleasant **b** : an unwanted signal in an electronic communication system **3** *obs* : common talk : RUMOR; *esp* : SLANDER
2**noise** *vt* : to spread by rumor or report ~ *vi* **1** : to talk much or loudly **2** : to make a noise
noise·less \-ləs\ *adj* : making or causing no noise — **noise·less·ly** *adv* — **noise·less·ness** *n*
noise·mak·er \-ˌmā-kər\ *n* : one that makes noise; *specif* : a device used to make noise at parties
nois·i·ly \'nȯi-zə-lē\ *adv* : in a noisy manner
nois·i·ness \-zē-nəs\ *n* : the quality or state of being noisy

noi·some \'nȯi-səm\ *adj* [ME *noysome*, fr. *noy* annoyance, fr. OF *enui, anoi* — more at ENNUI] **1 :** NOXIOUS, UNWHOLESOME **2 :** offensive to the smell or other senses : DISGUSTING **syn** see MALODOROUS — **noi·some·ly** *adv* — **noi·some·ness** *n*

noisy \'nȯi-zē\ *adj* **1 :** making noise **2 :** full of or characterized by noise

no·li me tan·ge·re \,nō-lē-(,)mē-'tan-jə-rē, -,lī-mē-\ *n* [L, do not touch me] **:** a warning against touching or interference

nol·le pro·se·qui \,näl-ē-'präs-ə-,kwī\ *n* [L, to be unwilling to pursue] **:** an entry on the record of a legal action denoting that the prosecutor or plaintiff will proceed no further in his action or suit either as a whole or as to some count or as to one or more of several defendants

no·lo \'nō-(,)lō\ *n* **:** NOLO CONTENDERE

no·lo con·ten·de·re \,nō-(,)lō-kən-'ten-də-rē\ *n* [L, I do not wish to contend] **:** a plea by the defendant in a criminal prosecution that without admitting guilt subjects him to conviction but does not preclude him from denying the truth of the charges in a collateral proceeding

nol–pros \'näl-'präs\ *vt* **nol–prossed; nol–pros·sing** [*nol*le *prosequi*] **:** to discontinue by entering a nolle prosequi

no·ma \'nō-mə\ *n* [NL, fr. Gk *nomē*, fr. *nemein* to spread (of an ulcer), lit., to graze, pasture — more at NIMBLE] **:** a spreading gangrene of the lining of cheek and lips occurring usu. in severely debilitated persons

no·mad \'nō-,mad, *Brit also* 'näm-əd\ *n* [L *nomad-, nomas* member of a wandering pastoral people, fr. Gk, fr. *nemein* to pasture — more at NIMBLE] **1 :** a member of a people that has no fixed residence but wanders from place to place **2 :** an individual who roams about aimlessly — **nomad** *or* **no·mad·ic** \nō-'mad-ik\ *adj* — **no·mad·ism** \'nō-,mad-,iz-əm\ *n*

no–man's–land \'nō-,manz-,land\ *n* **1 a :** an area of unowned, unclaimed, or uninhabited land **b :** an unoccupied area between opposing armies **2 :** an area of anomalous, ambiguous, or indefinite character

nom·bril \'näm-brəl\ *n* [MF, lit., navel, deriv. of L *umbilicus*] **:** the center point of the lower half of an armorial escutcheon

nom de guerre \,näm-di-'ge(ə)r\ *n, pl* **noms de guerre** \,näm(z)-di-\ [F, lit., war name] **:** PSEUDONYM

nom de plume \,näm-di-'plüm\ *n, pl* **noms de plume** \,näm(z)-di-\ [F *nom* name + *de* of + *plume* pen] **:** PSEUDONYM, PEN NAME

nome \'nōm\ *n* [Gk *nomos* district — more at NIMBLE] **:** a province of ancient Egypt

no·men \'nō-mən\ *n, pl* **no·mi·na** \'näm-ə-nə, 'nō-mə-\ [L *nomin-, nomen* name — more at NAME] **:** the second of the three usual names of an ancient Roman

no·men·cla·tor \'nō-mən-,klāt-ər\ *n* [L, slave whose duty was to tell his master the names of persons he met when campaigning for office, fr. *nomen* + *calatus*, pp. of *calare* to call — more at LOW] **1 :** a book containing collections or lists of words **2** *archaic* **:** one who announces the names of guests or of persons generally **3 :** one who gives names to or invents names for things — **no·men·cla·to·ri·al** \(,)nō-,men-klə-'tōr-ē-əl, -'tȯr-\ *adj*

no·men·cla·tur·al \,nō-mən-'klāch-(ə-)rəl\ *adj* **:** relating to nomenclature

no·men·cla·ture \'nō-mən-,klā-chər *also* nō-'men-klə-,chü(ə)r, -'meŋ-, -klə-chər, -klə-,t(y)ü(ə)r\ *n* [L *nomenclatura* calling by name, list of names, fr. *nomen* + *calatus*, pp.] **1 :** NAME, DESIGNATION **2 :** the act or process or an instance of naming **3 a :** a system or set of terms or symbols **b :** a system of terms used in a particular science, discipline, or art; *esp* **:** the standardized New Latin names used in biology

nom·i·nal \'näm-ən-ᵊl, 'näm-nəl\ *adj* [ME *nominalle*, fr. ML *nominalis*, fr. L, of a name, fr. *nomin-, nomen* name] **1 :** of, relating to, or being a noun or a word or expression taking a noun construction **2 a :** of, relating to, or constituting a name **b :** bearing the name of a person **3 a :** existing or being something in name or form only ⟨~ head of his party⟩ **b :** TRIFLING, INSIGNIFICANT **4 :** being according to plan **:** SATISFACTORY ⟨everything was ~ during the spacecraft launch⟩ — **nom·i·nal·ly** \-ē\ *adv*

nom·i·nal·ism \-,iz-əm\ *n* **:** a theory that there are no universal essences in reality and that the mind can frame no single concept or image corresponding to any universal or general term — **nom·i·nal·ist** \-əst\ *n* — **nominalist** *or* **nom·i·nal·is·tic** \,näm-ən-ᵊl-'is-tik, ,näm-nəl-\ *adj*

nominal value *n* **:** PAR 1b

nominal wages *n pl* **:** wages measured in money as distinct from actual purchasing power

nom·i·nate \'näm-ə-,nāt\ *vt* [L *nominatus*, pp. of *nominare*, fr. *nomin-, nomen* name] **1 :** DESIGNATE, NAME **2 a :** to appoint or propose for appointment to an office or place **b :** to propose as a candidate for election to office **c :** to propose for some honor **3 :** to enter (a horse) in a race — **nom·i·na·tor** \-,nāt-ər\ *n*

nom·i·na·tion \,näm-ə-'nā-shən\ *n* **1 :** the act, process, or an instance of nominating **2 :** the state of being nominated

nom·i·na·tive \'näm-(ə-)nət-iv; *2 & 3 are also* 'näm-ə-,nāt-\ *adj* [fr. the traditional use of the nominative form in naming a noun] **1 a :** marking typically the subject of a verb esp. in languages that have relatively full inflection ⟨~ case⟩ **b :** of or relating to the nominative case ⟨a ~ ending⟩ **2 :** nominated or appointed by nomination **3 :** bearing a person's name — **nominative** *n*

nom·i·nee \,näm-ə-'nē\ *n* [*nominate*] **:** a person who has been nominated

no·mo·gram \'näm-ə-,gram, 'nō-mə-\ *or* **no·mo·graph** \-,graf\ *n* [Gk *nomos* law + ISV *-gram* or *-graph* — more at NIMBLE] **:** a graph that enables one by the aid of a straightedge to read off the value of a dependent variable when the values of two or more independent variables are given — **no·mog·ra·phy** \nə-'mäg-rə-fē, nō-\ *n*

no·mo·log·i·cal \,näm-ə-'läj-i-kəl, ,nō-mə-\ *adj* [*nomology* (science of physical and logical laws)] **:** relating to or expressing physical laws or rules of reasoning ⟨~ statements⟩

-n·o·my \n-ə-mē\ *n comb form* [ME *-nomie*, fr. OF, fr. L *-nomia*, fr. Gk, fr. *nemein* to distribute] **:** system of laws governing or sum of knowledge regarding a (specified) field ⟨agro*nomy*⟩

non- \(')nän *also* ,nən *or* 'nən *before* '*-stressed syllable,* ,nän *also* ,nən *before* ,*-stressed or unstressed syllable; the variant with* ə *is also to be understood at pronounced entries, where it is not shown*\ *prefix* [ME, fr. MF, fr. L *non* not, fr. OL *noenum*, fr. *ne-* not + *oinom*, neut. of *oinos* one — more at NO, ONE] **:** not **:** reverse of **:** absence of

non·age \'nän-ij, 'nō-nij\ *n* [ME, fr. MF, fr. *non-* + *age*] **1 :** MINORITY 1 **2 a :** a period of youth **b :** IMMATURITY

no·na·ge·nar·i·an \,nō-nə-jə-'ner-ē-ən, ,nän-ə-\ *n* [L *nonagenarius* containing ninety, fr. *nonageni* ninety each, fr. *nonaginta* ninety, fr. *nona-* (akin to *novem* nine) + *-ginta* (akin to *viginti* twenty)] **:** a person who is in his nineties — **nonagenarian** *adj*

no·na·gon \'nō-nə-,gän, 'nän-ə-\ *n* [L *nonus* ninth + E *-gon* — more at NOON] **:** a polygon of nine angles and nine sides

non·aligned \,nän-ᵊl-'īnd\ *adj* **:** UNALIGNED — **non·align·ment** \-'īn-mənt\ *n*

non·al·le·lic \,nän-ᵊl-'ē-lik, -'el-ik\ *adj, of genes* **:** not behaving as alleles toward one another

[1]**nonce** \'nän(t)s\ *n* [ME *nanes*, alter. (fr. incorrect division of *then anes* in such phrases as *to then anes* for the one purpose) of *anes* one purpose, irreg. fr. *an* one, fr. OE *ān*] **:** the one, particular, or present occasion, purpose, or use ⟨for the ~⟩

[2]**nonce** *adj* **:** occurring, used, or made only once or for a special occasion ⟨~ word⟩

non·cha·lance \,nän-shə-'län(t)s, -chə-\ *n* **:** the state of being nonchalant

non·cha·lant \-'länt\ *adj* [F, fr. OF, fr. prp. of *nonchaloir* to disregard, fr. *non-* + *chaloir* to concern, fr. L *calēre* to be warm — more at LEE] **:** apparently unconcerned or indifferent **syn** see COOL — **non·cha·lant·ly** *adv*

non·com \'nän-,käm\ *n* **:** NONCOMMISSIONED OFFICER

non·com·ba·tant \,nän-kəm-'bat-ᵊnt, (')nän-'käm-bət-ənt\ *n* **:** a member (as a chaplain) of the armed forces whose duties do not include fighting; *also* **:** CIVILIAN — **noncombatant** *adj*

non·com·mis·sioned officer \,nän-kə-,mish-ənd-\ *n* **:** a subordinate officer in a branch of the armed forces appointed from enlisted personnel and holding one of various grades (as staff sergeant)

non·com·mit·tal \,nän-kə-'mit-ᵊl\ *adj* **1 :** giving no clear indication of attitude or feeling **2 :** having no clear or distinctive character — **non·com·mit·tal·ly** \-ᵊl-ē\ *adv*

non com·pos men·tis \,nän-,käm-pə-'sment-əs, ,nōn-\ *adj* [L, lit., not having mastery of one's mind] **:** not of sound mind

non·con·duc·tor \,nän-kən-'dək-tər\ *n* **:** a substance that conducts heat, electricity, or sound only in very small degree

non·con·form·ist \-'fȯr-məst\ *n* **1** *often cap* **:** a person who does not conform to an established church esp. the Church of England **2 :** a person who does not conform to a generally accepted pattern of thought or action — **nonconformist** *adj, often cap*

non·con·for·mi·ty \-mət-ē\ *n* **1 a :** failure or refusal to conform to an established church **b** *often cap* **:** the movement or principles of English Protestant dissent **c** *often cap* **:** the body of English Nonconformists **2 :** refusal to conform to an established or conventional creed, rule, or practice **3 :** absence of agreement or correspondence

non·co·op·er·a·tion \,nän-kō-,äp-ə-'rā-shən\ *n* **:** failure or refusal to cooperate; *specif* **:** refusal through civil disobedience of a people to cooperate with the government of a country — **non·co·op·er·a·tion·ist** \-sh(ə-)nəst\ *n* — **non·co·op·er·a·tive** \-'äp-(ə-)rət-iv, -ə-,rāt-\ *adj* — **non·co·op·er·a·tor** \-'äp-ə-,rāt-ər\ *n*

See *non-* and second element
nonabrasive
nonabsorbent
nonabstainer
nonacademic
nonacceptance
nonacid
nonactinic
nonactive
nonadaptive
nonadherence
nonadhesive
nonadjacent
nonadjustable
nonadministrative
nonadmission
nonaggression
nonaggressive
nonagreement
nonagricultural
nonalcoholic
nonalphabetic
nonanalytic
nonappearance
nonaquatic
nonaqueous
nonaspirated
nonassessable
nonassimilable
nonassimilation
nonathletic
nonattendance
nonattributive
nonauthoritative
nonautomatic
nonautomotive
nonbasic
nonbearing
nonbeing
nonbeliever
nonbelieving
nonbelligerency
nonbelligerent
nonbiting
nonbreakable
nonbureaucratic
nonbusiness
noncaking
noncalcareous
noncanonical
noncarbohydrate
noncarnivorous
noncash
noncellular
nonchargeable
noncitizen
nonclassical
nonclerical
nonclinical
nonclotting
noncoagulable
noncoercive
noncognitive
noncoital
noncollapsible
noncollectible
noncollegiate
noncolloid
noncombat
noncombining
noncombustible
noncommercial
noncommunicable
noncommunicant
noncommunication
noncommunist
noncompensating
noncompetent
noncompeting
noncompetitive
noncomplementary
noncompliance
noncomplying
noncompound
noncompressible
nonconclusive
nonconcur
nonconcurrence
nonconcurrent
noncondensable
noncondensing
nonconditioned
nonconductibility
nonconducting
nonconductive
nonconfidence
nonconflicting
nonconform
nonconformance
nonconformer
nonconforming
noncongenital
nonconscious
nonconstitutional
nonconstructive
nonconsumable
noncontact
noncontagious
noncontemporary
noncontentious
noncontiguous
noncontinuous
noncontraband
noncontradiction
noncontradictory
noncontributing
noncontributory
noncontrollable
noncontrolled
noncontrolling
noncontroversial
nonconvertible
noncorporate
noncorrodible
noncorroding
noncorrosive
noncovered
noncreative
noncriminal
noncritical
noncrystalline
noncultivated
noncultivation
noncumulative
noncurrent
noncyclic
noncyclical
nondeductibility
nondeductible
nondeferrable
nondefining
nondegenerate
nondelegable
nondelivery
nondemocratic
nondenominational
nondenominationalism
nondepartmental
nondeposition

non·de·script \ˌnän-di-ˈskript\ *adj* [*non-* + L *descriptus*, pp. of *describere* to describe] **:** belonging or appearing to belong to no particular class or kind **:** not easily described — **nondescript** *n*
non·dis·junc·tion \ˌnän-dis-ˈjəŋ(k)-shən\ *n* [ISV] **:** the failure of two homologous chromosomes to separate during reduction division — **non·dis·junc·tion·al** \-shnəl, -shən-ᵊl\ *adj*
non·dis·tinc·tive \-ˈtiŋ(k)-tiv\ *adj, of a speech sound* **:** having no signaling value
¹none \ˈnən\ *pron, sing or pl in constr* [ME, fr. OE *nān*, fr. *ne* not + *ān* one — more at NO, ONE] **1 :** not any **2 :** not one **:** NOBODY **3 :** not any such thing or person **4 :** no part **:** NOTHING
²none *adj, archaic* **:** not any **:** NO
³none *adv* **1 :** by no means **:** not at all **2 :** in no way **:** to no extent
⁴none \ˈnōn\ *n, often cap* [LL *nona*, fr. L, 9th hour of the day from sunrise — more at NOON] **:** the fifth of the canonical hours
non·en·ti·ty \nä-ˈnen(t)-ət-ē\ *n* **1 :** something that does not exist or exists only in the imagination **2 :** NONEXISTENCE **3 :** one of no consequence or significance
nones \ˈnōnz\ *n pl but sing or pl in constr* [ME *nonys*, fr. L *nonae*, fr. fem. pl. of *nonus* ninth] **1 :** the 9th day before the ides according to ancient Roman reckoning **2** *often cap* **:** ⁴NONE
none·such \ˈnən-ˌsəch\ *n* **:** a person or thing without an equal — **nonesuch** *adj*
none·the·less \ˌnən-thə-ˈles\ *adv* **:** NEVERTHELESS
non–eu·clid·e·an \ˌnän-yü-ˈklid-ē-ən\ *adj, often cap E* **:** not assuming or in accordance with all the postulates of Euclid's *Elements* ⟨~ geometry⟩
non·fea·sance \(ˈ)nän-ˈfēz-ᵊn(t)s\ *n* [*non-* + obs. E *feasance* (doing, execution)] **:** omission to do esp. what ought to be done
non·fer·rous \(ˈ)nän-ˈfer-əs\ *adj* **1 :** not containing, including, or relating to iron **2 :** relating to metals other than iron
no·nil·lion \nō-ˈnil-yən\ *n, often attrib* [F, fr. L *nonus* ninth + F *-illion* (as in *million*) — more at NOON] — see NUMBER table
non·in·duc·tive \ˌnän-in-ˈdək-tiv\ *adj* **:** having negligible inductance
non·in·ter·ven·tion \ˌnän-ˌint-ər-ˈven-chən\ *n* **:** the state or habit of not intervening **:** refusal or failure to intervene — **non·in·ter·ven·tion·ist** \-ˈvench-(ə-)nəst\ *n or adj*
non·ion·ic detergent \ˌnän-(ˌ)ī-ˌän-ik-\ *n* **:** a synthetic detergent that produces electrically neutral colloidal particles in solution
non·join·der \(ˈ)nän-ˈjȯin-dər\ *n* **:** the omission of a necessary party, plaintiff, or defendant to a suit at law or in equity
non·jur·ing \(ˈ)nän-ˈjü(ə)r-iŋ\ *adj* [*non-* + L *jur*are to swear — more at JURY] **:** not swearing allegiance
non·ju·ror \(ˈ)nän-ˈjür-ər, -ˈjü(ə)r-ˌȯ(ə)r\ *n* **:** a person refusing to take an oath esp. of allegiance, supremacy, or abjuration; *specif* **:** one of the beneficed clergy in England and Scotland refusing to take an oath of allegiance to William and Mary or to their successors after the revolution of 1688
non·met·al \(ˈ)nän-ˈmet-ᵊl\ *n* **:** a chemical element (as boron, carbon, or nitrogen) that lacks typical metallic properties and is able to form anions, acidic oxides and acids, and stable compounds with hydrogen
non·me·tal·lic \ˌnän-mə-ˈtal-ik\ *adj* **1 :** not metallic **2 :** of, relating to, or being a nonmetal
non·ob·jec·tive \ˌnän-əb-ˈjek-tiv\ *adj* **:** representing or intended to represent no concrete object of nature or natural appearance **:** ABSTRACT — **non·ob·jec·tiv·ism** \-tiv-ˌiz-əm\ *n* — **non·ob·jec·tiv·ist** \-əst\ *n* — **non·ob·jec·tiv·i·ty** \ˌnän-ˌäb-ˌjek-ˈtiv-ət-ē, ˌnän-əb-\ *n*
non ob·stan·te \ˌnän-əb-ˈstant-ē, ˌnōn-\ *prep* [L] **:** NOTWITHSTANDING
¹non·pa·reil \ˌnän-pə-ˈrel\ *adj* [MF, fr. *non-* + *pareil* equal, fr. (assumed) VL *pariculus*, fr. L *par* equal] **:** having no equal
²non·pa·reil \ˌnän-pə-ˈrel, *Brit also* ˈnän-prəl, ˈnäm- *for 2*\ *n* **1 :** an individual of unequaled excellence **:** PARAGON **2** [F *nonpareille*, fr. fem. of *nonpareil*, adj.] **:** 6-point interlinear space in printing **3 a :** a small flat disk of chocolate covered with white sugar pellets **b :** small sugar pellets of various colors
non·par·ti·san \(ˈ)nän-ˈpärt-ə-zən *also* -sən\ *adj* **:** not partisan, *esp.* **:** free from party affiliation, bias, or designation ⟨~ ballot⟩ ⟨a ~ board⟩ — **non·par·ti·san·ship** \-ˌship\ *n*
non·pas·ser·ine \(ˈ)nän-ˈpas-ə-ˌrīn\ *adj* **:** not passerine; *esp* **:** CORACIIFORM
non pla·cet \ˈnän-ˈplā-sət, ˈnōn-, -ˌset\ *n* [L, it does not please] **:** a negative vote
¹non·plus \(ˈ)nän-ˈpləs\ *n, pl* **non·plus·es** *or* **non·plus·ses** [L *non plus* no more] **:** a state of bafflement or perplexity **:** QUANDARY
²nonplus *vt* **non·plussed** *also* **non·plused; non·plus·sing** *also* **non·plus·ing :** to cause to be at a loss as to what to say, think, or do **:** PERPLEX **syn** see PUZZLE
non pos·su·mus \ˈnän-ˈpäs-ə-məs, ˈnōn-\ *n* [L, we cannot] **:** a statement expressing inability to do something
non·pro·duc·tive \ˌnän-prə-ˈdək-tiv\ *adj* **1 :** failing to produce or yield **:** UNPRODUCTIVE ⟨a ~ oil well⟩ **2 :** not directly productive ⟨~ labor⟩ **3** *of a cough* **:** DRY — **non·pro·duc·tive·ness** *n*
non·pros \ˈnän-ˈpräs\ *vt* **non·prossed; non·pros·sing** [*non prosequitur*] **:** to enter a non prosequitur against
non pro·se·qui·tur \ˌnän-prə-ˈsek-wət-ər, ˌnōn-\ *n* [LL, he does not prosecute] **:** a judgment entered against the plaintiff in a suit in which he does not appear to prosecute
non·rep·re·sen·ta·tion·al \ˌnän-ˌrep-ri-ˌzen-ˈtā-shnəl, -zən-, -shən-ᵊl\ *adj* **:** not representing an object of nature **:** ABSTRACT — **non·rep·re·sen·ta·tion·al·ism** \-ˌiz-əm\ *n*
non·res·i·dence \(ˈ)nän-ˈrez-əd-ən(t)s, -ˈrez-dən(t)s, -ˈrez-ə-ˌden(t)s\ *also* **non·res·i·den·cy** \-ˈrez-əd-ən-sē, -ˈrez-dən-, -ˈrez-ə-ˌden(t)-\ *n* **:** the state or fact of not residing in a particular place — **non·res·i·dent** \-ˈrez-əd-ənt, -ˈrez-dənt, -ə-ˌdent\ *adj or n*
non·re·sis·tance \ˌnän-ri-ˈzis-tən(t)s\ *n* **:** the principles or practice of passive submission to constituted authority even when unjust or oppressive; *also* **:** the principle or practice of not resisting violence by force — **non·re·sis·tant** \-tənt\ *adj or n*
non·re·stric·tive \-ˈstrik-tiv\ *adj* **:** not restrictive; *specif* **:** not limiting the reference of a modified word or phrase
nonrestrictive clause *n* **:** a descriptive clause that is not essential to the definiteness of the meaning of its antecedent (as in "the aldermen, *who were present*, assented")
non·rig·id \(ˈ)nän-ˈrij-əd\ *adj* **:** maintaining form by pressure of contained gas ⟨a ~ airship⟩
non·sched·uled \(ˈ)nän-ˈskej-(ˌ)ü(ə)ld, -ˈskej-əld\ *adj* **:** licensed to carry passengers or freight by air without a regular schedule ⟨~ airline⟩
non·sec·tar·i·an \ˌnän-(ˌ)sek-ˈter-ē-ən\ *adj* **:** not having a sectarian character
¹non·sense \ˈnän-ˌsen(t)s, ˈnän(t)-sən(t)s\ *n* **1 a :** words or language having no meaning or conveying no intelligible ideas **b :** language or conduct that is absurd or contrary to good sense **2 a :** things of no importance or value **:** TRIFLES **b :** foolish, affected, or impudent conduct or manner **:** HUMBUG — **non·sen·si·cal** \(ˈ)nän-ˈsen(t)-si-kəl\ *adj* — **non·sen·si·cal·ly** \-k(ə-)lē\ *adv* — **non·sen·si·cal·ness** \-kəl-nəs\ *n*
²nonsense *adj* **:** being a simulated unit of speech fabricated by arbitrary grouping of speech sounds or symbols ⟨\ˈshkrȯg-ˌthī-əmpth\ is a ~ word⟩ ⟨~ syllable⟩
non se·qui·tur \(ˈ)nän-ˈsek-wət-ər, (ˈ)nōn-\ *n* [L, it does not follow] **:** an inference that does not follow from the premises; *specif* **:** a fallacy resulting from a simple conversion of a universal affirmative proposition or from the transposition of a condition and its consequent
non·sig·nif·i·cant \ˌnän(t)-sig-ˈnif-i-kənt\ *adj* **:** not significant: as **a :** INSIGNIFICANT **b :** MEANINGLESS
non·sked \ˈnän-ˈsked\ *n* [by shortening & alter. fr. *nonscheduled*] **:** a nonscheduled airline or transport plane
non·skid \ˈnän-ˈskid\ *adj* **:** having the tread corrugated or otherwise specially constructed to resist skidding — **nonskid** *n*

---

nonderivative
nondestructive
nondeteriorative
nondetonating
nondevelopable
nondevelopment
nondifferentiation
nondiffusible
nondigestible
nondirectional
nondirective
nondisclosure
nondiscrimination
nondiscriminatory
nondiscursive
nondisqualifying
nondistribution
nondivided
nondocumentary
nondollar
nondomesticated
nondramatic
nondrying
nondurable
nondynastic
nonecclesiastical
noneconomic
noneffective
noneffervescent
nonelastic
nonelect
nonelection
nonelective
nonelectric
nonelectrical
nonelectrolyte
noneligible
nonemotional
nonempirical
nonenforceability
nonenforceable
nonenforcement
nonentanglement
nonepiscopal
noneruptive
nonessential
nonexclusive
nonexempt
nonexistence
nonexistent
nonexpendable
nonexplosive
nonexportation
nonextant
nonfarm
nonfat
nonfatal
nonfattening
nonfebrile
nonfederal
nonfederated
nonfeeding
nonfiction
nonfictional
nonfigurative
nonfilamentous
nonfilterable
nonfinancial
nonfissionable
nonflagellated
nonflammable
nonflowering
nonfluency
nonflying
nonforfeiture
nonfraternal
nonfreezing
nonfulfillment
nonfunctional
nongame
nongaseous
nongenetic
nongovernmental
nongregarious
nonhardy
nonharmonic
nonhereditary
nonhistorical
nonhomogeneous
nonhomologous
nonhuman
nonidentical
nonidentity
nonimmigrant
nonimmune
nonimportation
nonindustrial
noninfectious
noninflammable
noninflammatory
noninstitutional
noninstructional
nonintegrated
nonintellectual
nonintercourse
noninterference
nonintersecting
nonintoxicant
nonintoxicating
noninvolvement
nonionic
nonirrigated
nonlegal
nonlegato
nonlethal
nonlexical
nonlife
nonlinear
nonliquid
nonliterary
nonliterate
nonliturgical
nonliving
nonlocal
nonlogical
nonluminous
nonmagnetic
nonmailable
nonmalignant
nonmalleable
nonman
nonmarketable
nonmaterial
nonmechanical
nonmechanistic
nonmember
nonmembership
nonmetameric
nonmetered
nonmetrical
nonmilitary
nonmoney
nonmoral
nonmotile
nonmutant
nonnational
nonnative
nonnatural
nonnaturalism
nonnaturalist
nonnecessity
nonnegotiable
nonnitrogenous
nonnormative
nonobligatory
nonobservance
nonoccurrence
nonofficial
nonoperating
nonorganic
nonorthodox
nonpalatal
nonpalatalization
nonparallel
nonparalytic
nonparasitic
nonparticipant
nonparticipating
nonparticipation
nonparty
nonpaternity
nonpathogenic
nonpaying
nonpayment
nonpecuniary
nonperformance
nonperishable
nonpermanent
nonpersistent
nonpersonal
nonphonemic
nonphonetic
nonphysical
nonpoisonous
nonpolar
nonpolitical
nonporous
nonpossession
nonpractical
nonpredicative
nonpregnant
nonprinting
nonproducer
nonprofessional
nonprofit
nonprogressive
nonproprietary
nonprotein
nonproven
nonpublic
nonpungent
nonquota
nonrabbinic
nonracial
nonradical
nonradioactive
nonrandom
nonrated
nonrational
nonreactive
nonreader
nonrealistic
nonreciprocal
nonrecognition
nonrecourse
nonrecoverable
nonrecurrent
nonrecurring
nonreducing
nonrefillable
nonregistered
nonregulation
nonreligious
nonremovable
nonrenewable
nonrepayable
nonrepresentative
nonresidential
nonresonant
nonrestraint
nonrestricted
nonretractile
nonretroactive
nonreturnable
nonrevenue
nonreversible
nonrhetorical
nonrotating
nonruminant
nonsalable
nonscientific
nonscientist
nonseasonal
nonsecret
nonsecretory
nonsegregated
nonsegregation
nonselective
non-self-governing
nonsensitive
nonsensuous
nonseptate
nonsexual
nonshrinkable
nonsinkable
nonslaveholding
nonsmoker
nonsmoking

non·sport·ing \(ˈ)nän-ˈspōrt-iŋ, -ˈspȯrt-\ *adj* **1 :** lacking the qualities characteristic of a hunting dog **2 :** not subject to frequent mutation

non·stan·dard \(ˈ)nän-ˈstan-dərd\ *adj* **1 :** not standard **2** *of language* **:** not conforming in pronunciation, grammatical construction, idiom, or choice of word to the usage generally characteristic of educated native speakers of the language — compare SUBSTANDARD

non·stop \(ˈ)nän-ˈstäp\ *adj* **:** done or made without a stop — **nonstop** *adv*

non·such \ˈnən-ˌsəch, ˈnän-\ *var of* NONESUCH

non·suit \(ˈ)nän-ˈsüt\ *n* [ME, fr. AF *nounsuyte*, fr. *noun-* [1]non- + OF *siute* following, pursuit — more at SUIT] **:** a judgment against a plaintiff for his failure to prosecute his case or inability to establish a prima facie case — **nonsuit** *vt*

non·sup·port \ˌnän(t)-sə-ˈpō(ə)rt, -ˈpȯ(ə)rt\ *n* **:** failure to support; *specif* **:** failure of one under obligation to provide maintenance

non·syl·lab·ic \ˌnän(t)-sə-ˈlab-ik\ *adj* **:** not constituting a syllable or the nucleus of a syllable: **a** *of a consonant* **:** accompanied in the same syllable by a vowel ⟨\n\ is syllabic in \ˈbät-ᵊn-ē\ *botany*, ~ in \ˈbät-nē\⟩ **b** *of a vowel* **:** having vowel quality less prominent than that of another vowel in the syllable ⟨the second vowel of a falling diphthong is ~ (as \i\ in \ȯi\)⟩

non trop·po \(ˈ)nän-ˈtrō-(ˌ)pō, ˈnōn-\ *adv (or adj)* [It, lit., not too much] **:** without excess — used to qualify a direction in music

non·union \(ˈ)nän-ˈyü-nyən\ *adj* **1 :** not belonging to or affiliated with a trade union **2 :** not recognizing or favoring trade unions or their members

non·use \(ˈ)nän-ˈyüs\ *n* **1 :** failure to use **2 :** the fact or condition of not being used — **non·us·er** \-ˈyü-zər\ *n*

non·ver·bal \(ˈ)nän-ˈvər-bəl\ *adj* **:** not verbal: as **a :** being other than verbal **b :** involving minimal use of language ⟨~ tests⟩ **c :** ranking low in verbal skill

non·vi·a·ble \(ˈ)nän-ˈvī-ə-bəl\ *adj* **:** not capable of living, growing, or developing and functioning successfully

non·vi·o·lence \(ˈ)nän-ˈvī-ə-lən(t)s\ *n* **:** abstention on principle from violence; *also* **:** the principle of such abstention — **non·vi·o·lent** \-lənt\ *adj*

non·vol·a·tile \(ˈ)nän-ˈväl-ət-ᵊl\ *adj* **:** not volatile **:** not volatilizing readily

[1]**noo·dle** \ˈnüd-ᵊl\ *n* [perh. alter. of *noddle*] **1 :** a stupid person **:** SIMPLETON **2 :** HEAD

[2]**noodle** *n* [G *nudel*] **:** a food paste shaped typically in ribbon form and made with egg

nook \ˈnu̇k\ *n* [ME *noke, nok*] **1** *chiefly Scot* **:** a rectangular corner **2 a :** an interior angle formed by two meeting walls **:** RECESS **b :** a secluded or sheltered place or part

noon \ˈnün\ *n, often attrib* [ME, fr. OE *nōn* ninth hour from sunrise, fr. L *nona*, fr. fem. of *nonus* ninth; akin to L *novem* nine — more at NINE] **1 :** the middle of the day **:** MIDDAY **2 :** MIDNIGHT — used chiefly in the phrase *noon of night* **3 :** the highest point

noon·day \-ˌdā\ *n* **:** MIDDAY

no one *pron* **:** no person **:** NOBODY

noon·ing \ˈnü-niŋ, -nən\ *n* **1** *chiefly dial* **:** a meal eaten at noon **2** *chiefly dial* **:** a period at noon for eating or resting

noon·tide \ˈnün-ˌtīd\ *n* **1 :** the time of noon **:** MIDDAY **2 :** the highest or culminating point

noon·time \-ˌtīm\ *n* **:** NOONTIDE

[1]**noose** \ˈnüs\ *n* [prob. fr. Prov *nous* knot, fr. L *nodus* — more at NET] **1 :** a loop with a running knot that binds closer the more it is drawn **2 :** BOND, SNARE

[2]**noose** *vt* **1 :** to secure by a noose **2 :** to make a noose in or of

no·pal \nō-ˈpäl, -ˈpal; ˈnō-pəl\ *n* [Sp, fr. Nahuatl *nopalli*] **:** any of a genus (*Nopalea*) of cacti; *broadly* **:** PRICKLY PEAR

no-par *or* **no-par-val·ue** *adj* **:** having no nominal value ⟨~ share⟩

nope \ˈnōp, *or* ˈnō *followed by glottal stop*\ *adv* [by alter.] **:** NO — not often in formal use

[1]**nor** \nər, (ˈ)nȯ(ə)r\ *conj* [ME, contr. of *nother* neither, nor, fr. *nother*, pron. & adj., neither — more at NEITHER] **1** — used as a function word to introduce the second or last member or the second and each following member of a series of two or more items each of which is negated ⟨neither here ~ there⟩ ⟨not be done by you ~ by me ~ by anyone⟩ **2** — used as a function word to introduce and negate a clause or phrase following an affirmative that is equivalent to or implies a negative ⟨the book is too long; ~ is the style easy⟩ **3** *archaic* **:** NEITHER

[2]**nor** *conj* [ME, perh. fr. [1]*nor*] *dial* **:** THAN

[1]**Nor·dic** \ˈnȯrd-ik\ *adj* [F *nordique*, fr. *nord* north, fr. OE *north*] **1 :** of or relating to the Germanic peoples of northern Europe and esp. of Scandinavia **2 :** of or relating to a physical type characterized by tall stature, long head, light skin and hair, and blue eyes

[2]**Nordic** *n* **1 :** a native of northern Europe **2 :** a person of Nordic physical type or of a hypothetical Nordic division of the Caucasian race **3 :** a member of the peoples of Scandinavia

nor·epi·neph·rine \ˈnȯ(ə)r-ˌep-ə-ˈnef-ˌrēn, -rən\ *n* [*nor*mal + *epinephrine*] **:** a crystalline compound $C_8H_{11}NO_3$ occurring with epinephrine, having a strong vasoconstrictor action, and mediating transmission of sympathetic nerve impulses

Nor·folk jacket \ˌnȯr-fək-, -ˌfȯk-\ *n* [*Norfolk*, county in England] **:** a loose-fitting single-breasted jacket

no·ria \ˈnōr-ē-ə, ˈnȯr-\ *n* [Sp, fr. Ar *nāʿūrah*] **:** an undershot water-wheel of the bucket type

nor·land \ˈnȯ(ə)r-lənd\ *n, chiefly dial* **:** NORTHLAND

norm \ˈnȯ(ə)rm\ *n* [L *norma*, lit., carpenter's square] **1 :** an authoritative standard **:** MODEL **2 :** a principle of right action binding upon the members of a group and serving to guide, control, or regulate proper and acceptable behavior **3 :** AVERAGE: as **a :** a set standard of development or achievement usu. derived from the average or median achievement of a large group **b :** a pattern or trait taken to be typical in the behavior of a social group **syn** see AVERAGE

[1]**nor·mal** \ˈnȯr-məl\ *adj* [L *normalis*, fr. *norma* carpenter's square] **1 :** PERPENDICULAR; *esp* **:** perpendicular to a tangent at a point of tangency **2 :** according to, constituting, or not deviating from a norm, rule, or principle **:** REGULAR **3 :** occurring naturally ⟨~ immunity⟩ **4 a :** of, relating to, or characterized by average intelligence or development **b :** free from mental disorder **:** SANE **5 a** *of a solution* **:** having a concentration of one gram equivalent of solute per liter **b :** containing neither basic hydroxyl nor acid hydrogen ⟨~ silver phosphate Ag_3PO_4⟩ **c :** not associated ⟨~ molecules⟩ **d :** having a straight-chain structure ⟨~ pentane⟩ ⟨~ butyl alcohol⟩ **syn** see REGULAR — **nor·mal·i·ty** \nȯr-ˈmal-ət-ē\ *n* — **nor·mal·ly** \ˈnȯr-mə-lē\ *adv*

[2]**normal** *n* **1 a :** a normal line **b :** the portion of a normal line to a plane curve between the curve and the x-axis **2 :** one that is normal **3 :** a form or state regarded as the norm **:** STANDARD

nor·mal·cy \ˈnȯr-məl-sē\ *n* **:** NORMALITY

normal distribution *n* **:** a frequency distribution whose graph is bell-shaped, symmetrical, and of infinite extent

nor·mal·iza·tion \ˌnȯr-mə-lə-ˈzā-shən\ *n* **:** the act or process of making normal

nor·mal·ize \ˈnȯr-mə-ˌlīz\ *vt* **:** to make conform to or reduce to a norm or standard — **nor·mal·iz·er** *n*

normal school *n* [trans. of F *école normale;* fr. the fact that the first French school so named was intended to serve as a model] **:** a usu. two-year school for training chiefly elementary teachers

Nor·man \ˈnȯ(ə)r-mən\ *n* [ME, fr. OF *Normant*, fr. ON *Northmann-, Northmathr* Norseman, fr. *northr* north + *mann-, mathr* man; akin to OE *north* and to OE *man*] **1 :** a native or inhabitant of Normandy: **a :** one of the Scandinavian conquerors of Normandy in the 10th century **b :** one of the Norman-French conquerors of England in 1066 **2 :** NORMAN-FRENCH — **Norman** *adj*

Norman architecture *n* **:** a Romanesque style first appearing in and near Normandy about A.D. 950; *also* **:** architecture resembling or imitating this style

Norman-French *n* **1 :** the French language of the medieval Normans **2 :** the modern dialect of Normandy

nor·ma·tive \ˈnȯr-mət-iv\ *adj* [F *normatif*, fr. *norme* norm, fr. L *norma*] **:** of, relating to, or prescribing norms — **nor·ma·tive·ly** *adv* — **nor·ma·tive·ness** *n*

Norn \ˈnȯ(ə)rn\ *n* [ON] **:** any of the three Norse goddesses of fate

[1]**Norse** \ˈnȯ(ə)rs\ *n, pl* **Norse** [prob. fr. obs. D *noorsch*, adj., Norwegian, Scandinavian, alter. of obs. D *noordsch* northern, fr. D *noord* north; akin to OE *north*] **1** *pl* **a :** SCANDINAVIANS **b :** NORWEGIANS **2 a :** NORWEGIAN 2 **b :** any of the western Scandinavian dialects or languages **c :** the Scandinavian group of Germanic languages

[2]**Norse** *adj* **1 :** of or relating to ancient Scandinavia or the language of its inhabitants **2 :** NORWEGIAN

Norse·man \ˈnȯr-smən\ *n* **:** one of the ancient Scandinavians

[1]**north** \ˈnȯ(ə)rth\ *adv* [ME, fr. OE; akin to OHG *nord* north, Gk *nerteros* lower, infernal] **:** to, toward, or in the north **:** NORTHWARD

[2]**north** *adj* **1 :** situated toward or at the north **2 :** coming from the north

[3]**north** *n* **1 a :** the direction of the north terrestrial pole **:** the direction to the left of one facing east **b :** the cardinal point directly opposite to south **2** *cap* **:** regions or countries lying to the north of a specified or implied point of orientation

north·bound \ˈnȯrth-ˌbau̇nd\ *adj* **:** traveling or headed north

north by east : a compass point that is one point east of due north **:** N 11° 15′ E

north by west : a compass point that is one point west of due north **:** N 11° 15′ W

[1]**north·east** \nȯr-ˈthēst, *naut* nȯ-ˈrēst\ *adv* **:** to, toward, or in the northeast

[2]**northeast** *n* **1 a :** the general direction between north and east **b :** the point midway between the cardinal points north and east **2** *cap* **:** regions or countries lying to the northeast of a specified or implied point of orientation

[3]**northeast** *adj* **1 :** coming from the northeast ⟨~ wind⟩ **2 :** situated toward or at the northeast ⟨~ corner⟩

northeast by east : a compass point that is one point east of due northeast **:** N 56° 15′ E

northeast by north : a compass point that is one point north of due northeast **:** N 33° 45′ E

north·east·er \nȯr-ˈthē-stər, nȯ-ˈrē-\ *n* **:** a storm, strong wind, or gale coming from the northeast

north·east·er·ly \-stər-lē\ *adv (or adj)* [[2]*northeast* + *-erly* (as in *easterly*)] **1 :** from the northeast **2 :** toward the northeast

north·east·ern \-stərn\ *adj* [[2]*northeast* + *-ern* (as in *eastern*)] **1** *often cap* **:** of, relating to, or characteristic of a region conventionally designated Northeast **2 :** lying toward or coming from the northeast — **north·east·ern·most** \-stərn-ˌmōst\ *adj*

North·east·ern·er \-stə(r)-nər\ *n* **:** a native or inhabitant of a northeastern region (as of the U.S.)

[1]**north·east·ward** \nȯr-ˈthēs-twərd, nȯ-ˈrēs-\ *adv (or adj)* **:** toward the northeast

[2]**northeastward** *n* **:** NORTHEAST

nonsocial
nonsolid
nonspatial
nonspeaking
nonspecialist
nonspecialized
nonspecific
nonspectacular
nonspectral
nonspeculative
nonstaining
nonstarter
nonstationary
nonstatistical
nonstellar
nonstrategic
nonstriated
nonstriker
nonstriking
nonstructural
nonsubscriber
nonsuccess
nonsurgical
nonsymbiotic
nonsymbolic
nonsymmetrical
nonsynchronous
nonsyntactical
nontarnishable
nontaxable
nontechnical
nonteleological
nontemporal
nonterritorial
nontheatrical
nontheistic
nonthermal
nontidal
nontoxic
nontraditional
nontransferable
nontransparency
nontransparent
nontransposing
nontropical
nontrump
nontuberculous
nontypical
nonunderstandable
nonuniform
nonuniformity
nonutilitarian
nonvariant
nonvascular
nonvegetative
nonvenomous
nonvibratory
nonvintage
nonviolation
nonviscous
nonvisual
nonvocal
nonvocational
nonvoluntary
nonvoter
nonvoting
nonwhite
nonworker
nonworking
nonwoven
nonzero

ə abut; ᵊ kitten; ər further; a back; ā bake; ä cot, cart; au̇ out; ch chin; e less; ē easy; g gift; i trip; ī life
j joke; ŋ sing; ō flow; ȯ flaw; ȯi coin; th thin; t͟h this; ü loot; u̇ foot; y yet; yü few; yu̇ furious; zh vision

north·east·wards \-twərdz\ *adv* : NORTHEASTWARD

north·er \'nȯr-thər\ *n* : a northerly wind; *esp* : a sudden strong north wind over the Great Plains or such a wind in Texas and on the Gulf of Mexico and western Caribbean sea

1**north·er·ly** \-lē\ *adv* (*or adj*) [3*north* + *-erly* (as in *easterly*)] **1** : from the north **2** : toward the north

2**northerly** *n* : a wind from the north

1**north·ern** \'nȯr-thə(r)n\ *adj* [ME *northerne*, fr. OE; akin to OHG *nordrōni* northern, OE *north* north] **1** *often cap* **a** : of, relating to, or characteristic of a region conventionally designated North **b** : of, relating to, or constituting the northern dialect **2 a** : lying toward the north **b** : coming from the north — **north·ern·most** \-,mōst\ *adj*

2**northern** *n* : the dialect of English spoken in the part of the U.S. north of a line running northwest from central New Jersey across the northern tier of counties in Pennsylvania and through northern Ohio, Indiana, and Illinois

Northern Cross *n* : a cross formed by six stars in Cygnus

Northern Crown *n* : CORONA BOREALIS

North·ern·er \'nȯr-thə(r)-nər\ *n* : a native or inhabitant of the North; *esp* : a native or resident of the northern part of the U.S.

northern lights *n pl* : AURORA BOREALIS

North Germanic *n* : a subdivision of the Germanic languages including Icelandic, Norwegian, Swedish, and Danish

north·ing \'nȯr-thiŋ, -thiŋ\ *n* **1** : difference in latitude to the north from the last preceding point of reckoning **2** : northerly progress

north·land \'nȯrth-,land, -lənd\ *n*, *often cap* : land in the north : the north of a country

North·man \-mən\ *n* : NORSEMAN

north–north·east \'nȯrth-,nȯr-'thēst, -,nȯ-'rēst\ *n* — see COMPASS CARD

north–north·west \'nȯrth-,nȯr(th)-'west\ *n* — see COMPASS CARD

north pole *n* **1 a** *often cap N&P* : the northernmost point of the earth **b** : the zenith of the heavens as viewed from the north terrestrial pole **2** *of a magnet* : the pole that points toward the north

North Star *n* : the star of the northern hemisphere toward which the axis of the earth points — called also *polestar*

1**North·um·bri·an** \nȯr-'thəm-brē-ən\ *adj* **1** : of, relating to, or characteristic of ancient Northumbria, its people, or its language **2** : of, relating to, or characteristic of Northumberland, its people, or its language

2**Northumbrian** *n* **1** : a native or inhabitant of ancient Northumbria **2** : a native or inhabitant of Northumberland **3 a** : the Old English dialect of Northumbria **b** : the Modern English dialect of Northumberland

1**north·ward** \'nȯrth-wərd\ *adv* (*or adj*) : toward the north

2**northward** *n* : northward direction or part

north·wards \-wərdz\ *adv* : NORTHWARD

1**north·west** \nȯrth-'west, *naut* nȯr-'west\ *adv* : to, toward, or in the northwest

2**northwest** *n* **1 a** : the general direction between north and west **b** : the point midway between the cardinal points north and west **2** *cap* : regions or countries lying to the northwest of a specified or implied point of orientation

3**northwest** *adj* **1** : coming from the northwest **2** : situated toward or at the northwest

northwest by north : a compass point that is one point north of due northwest : N 33° 45′ W

northwest by west : a compass point that is one point west of due northwest : N 56° 15′ W

north·west·er \nȯr(th)-'wes-tər\ *n* : a storm, strong wind, or gale from the northwest

north·west·er·ly \-lē\ *adv* (*or adj*) [2*northwest* + *-erly* (as in *westerly*)] **1** : from the northwest **2** : toward the northwest

north·west·ern \-'wes-tərn\ *adj* [2*northwest* + *-ern* (as in *western*)] **1** *often cap* : of, relating to, or characteristic of a region conventionally designated Northwest **2** : lying toward or coming from the northwest

North·west·ern·er \-tə(r)-nər\ *n* : a native or inhabitant of the Northwest and esp. of the northwestern part of the U.S.

1**north·west·ward** \-'wes-twərd\ *adv* (*or adj*) : toward the northwest

2**northwestward** *n* : NORTHWEST

north·west·wards \-twərdz\ *adv* : NORTHWESTWARD

Nor·we·gian \nȯr-'wē-jən\ *n* [ML *Norwegia* Norway] **1 a** : a native or inhabitant of Norway **b** : a person of Norwegian descent **2** : the Germanic language of the Norwegian people — **Norwegian** *adj*

Norwegian elkhound *n* : any of a Norwegian breed of medium-sized compact short-bodied dogs with a very heavy gray coat tipped with black

nos- *or* **noso-** *comb form* [Gk, fr. *nosos*] : disease ⟨*noso*logy⟩

1**nose** \'nōz\ *n* [ME, fr. OE *nosu*; akin to OHG *nasa* nose, L *nasus*] **1** : the part of the face that bears the nostrils and covers the anterior part of the nasal cavity; *broadly* : this part together with the nasal cavity **2** : the sense of smell : OLFACTION **3** : the vertebrate olfactory organ **4 a** : the forward end or projection of something **b** : the projecting or working end of a tool **5** : the stem of a boat or its protective metal covering

2**nose** *vt* **1** : to detect by or as if by smell : SCENT **2 a** : to push or move with the nose **b** : to advance the nose into **3** : to touch or rub with the nose : NUZZLE **4** : to defeat by a narrow margin in a sport or contest ~ *vi* **1** : to use the nose in examining, smelling, or showing affection **2** : to search impertinently : PRY **3** : to move ahead slowly or cautiously

nose·band \-,band\ *n* : the part of a headstall that passes over a horse's nose

nose·bleed \-,blēd\ *n* **1** : bleeding from the nose **2** : an attack of nosebleed

nose cone *n* : a protective cone constituting the forward end of a rocket or missile

nose dive *n* **1** : the downward nose-first plunge of a flying object (as an airplane) **2** : a sudden extreme drop — **nose-dive** \'nōz-,dīv\ *vi*

nose·gay \-,gā\ *n* [1*nose* + E dial. *gay* (ornament)] : a small bunch of flowers : POSY

nose·piece \-,pēs\ *n* **1** : a piece of armor for protecting the nose **2** : NOSEBAND **3** : the end piece of a microscope body to which an objective is attached **4** : the bridge of a pair of eyeglasses

no–show \nō-'shō\ *n* [1*no* + *show*, v. (as in *show up*)] : a person who reserves space on a train, ship, or airplane but neither uses nor cancels the reservation

nos·i·ly \'nō-zə-lē\ *adv* : in a nosy manner

nos·i·ness \-zē-nəs\ *n* : the quality or state of being nosy

nos·ing \'nō-ziŋ\ *n* : the usu. rounded edge of a stair tread that projects over the riser; *also* : any of various similar rounded projections

no·so·log·ic \,nōs-ə-'läj-ik, ,nōz-, ,näs-\ *adj* : relating to nosology — **no·so·log·i·cal** \-i-kəl\ *adj* — **no·so·log·i·cal·ly** \-k(ə-)lē\ *adv*

no·sol·o·gy \nō-'säl-ə-jē, -'zäl-\ *n* [prob. fr. NL *nosologia*, fr. *nos-* + *-logia* -logy] **1** : a branch of medical science that deals with classification of diseases **2** : a classification or list of diseases

nos·tal·gia \nä-'stal-jə, nə-; nə-'stäl-; *also* nȯ-'stal-, nō-'stal-, -jē-ə\ *n* [NL, fr. Gk *nostos* return home + NL *-algia*; akin to OE *genesan* to survive, Skt *nasate* he approaches] **1** : HOMESICKNESS **2** : a wistful or excessively sentimental sometimes abnormal yearning for return to or of some past period or irrecoverable condition — **nos·tal·gic** \-jik\ *adj* — **nos·tal·gi·cal·ly** \-ji-k(ə-)lē\ *adv*

nos·tril \'näs-trəl\ *n* [ME *nosethirl*, fr. OE *nosthyrl*, fr. *nosu* nose + *thyrel* hole; akin to OE *thurh* through] **1** : an external naris; *broadly* : a naris with the adjoining passage on the same side of the nasal septum **2** : the fleshy lateral wall of the nose

nos·trum \'näs-trəm\ *n* [L, neut. of *noster* our, ours, fr. *nos* we — more at US] **1** : a medicine of secret composition recommended by its preparer but usu. lacking general repute **2** : a questionable remedy or scheme : PANACEA

nosy *or* **nos·ey** \'nō-zē\ *adj* **nos·i·er**; **nos·i·est** [1*nose*] : of prying or inquisitive disposition or quality : INTRUSIVE

not \(')nät\ *adv* [ME, alter. of *nought*, fr. *nought*, pron. — more at NAUGHT] **1** — used as a function word to make negative a group of words or a word **2** — used as a function word to stand for the negative of a preceding group of words ⟨is sometimes hard to see and sometimes ~⟩

not- *or* **noto-** *comb form* [NL, fr. Gk *nōt-*, *nōto-*, fr. *nōton*, *nōtos* back — more at NATES] : back : back part ⟨*noto*chord⟩

nota *pl of* NOTUM

no·ta be·ne \,nōt-ə-'ben-ē, -'bē-nē\ [L, mark well] — used to call attention to something important

no·ta·bil·i·ty \,nōt-ə-'bil-ət-ē\ *n* : a notable or prominent person

1**no·ta·ble** \'nōt-ə-bəl, *2 is also* 'nät-\ *adj* **1 a** : worthy of note : REMARKABLE **b** : DISTINGUISHED, PROMINENT **2** *archaic* : efficient or capable in performance of housewifely duties — **no·ta·ble·ness** *n* — **no·ta·bly** \-blē\ *adv*

2**no·ta·ble** \'nōt-ə-bəl\ *n* **1** : a person of note : NOTABILITY **2** *pl*, *often cap* : a group of persons summoned esp. in monarchical France to act as a deliberative body

no·tar·i·al \nō-'ter-ē-əl\ *adj* **1** : of, relating to, or characteristic of a notary **2** : done or executed by a notary — **no·tar·i·al·ly** \-ə-lē\ *adv*

no·ta·ri·za·tion \,nōt-ə-rə-'zā-shən\ *n* **1** : the act, process, or an instance of notarizing **2** : the notarial certificate appended to a document

no·ta·rize \'nōt-ə-,rīz\ *vt* : to acknowledge or attest as a notary public

no·ta·ry public \,nōt-ə-rē-\ *n*, *pl* **notaries public** *or* **notary publics** [ME *notary* clerk, notary public, fr. L *notarius* clerk, secretary, fr. *notarius* of shorthand, fr. *nota* note, shorthand character] : a public officer who attests or certifies writings (as a deed) to make them authentic and takes affidavits, depositions, and protests of negotiable paper

no·tate \'nō-,tāt\ *vt* [back-formation fr. *notation*] : to put into notation

no·ta·tion \nō-'tā-shən\ *n* [L *notation-*, *notatio*, fr. *notatus*, pp. of *notare* to note] **1** : ANNOTATION, NOTE **2 a** : the act, process, method, or an instance of representing by a system or set of marks, signs, figures, or characters **b** : a system of characters, symbols, or abbreviated expressions used in an art or science to express technical facts, quantities, or other data — **no·ta·tion·al** \-shnəl, -shən-ᵊl\ *adj*

1**notch** \'näch\ *n* [perh. alter. (fr. incorrect division of *an otch*) of (assumed) *otch*, fr. MF *oche*] **1 a** : a V-shaped indentation **b** : a slit made to serve as a record **2** : a deep close pass : GAP **3** : DEGREE, STEP — **notched** \'nächt\ *adj*

2**notch** *vt* **1** : to cut or make a notch in **2 a** : to mark or record by a notch **b** : SCORE, ACHIEVE

1**note** \'nōt\ *vt* [ME *noten*, fr. OF *noter*, fr. L *notare* to mark, note, fr. *nota*] **1 a** : to notice or observe with care **b** : to record or preserve in writing **2 a** : to make special mention of : REMARK **b** : INDICATE, SHOW — **not·er** *n*

2**note** *n* [L *nota* mark, character, written note] **1 a** (1) : MELODY, SONG (2) : a musical tone (3) : CALL, SOUND (4) : the musical call of a bird (5) : an expressive tone of voice **b** : a character used to indicate duration by its shape and musical pitch by its position on the staff **2 a** : a characteristic feature **b** : MOOD, QUALITY **3 a** (1) : MEMORANDUM (2) : a condensed or informal record **b** (1) : a brief comment or explanation (2) : a printed comment or reference set apart from the text **c** (1) : a written promise to pay a debt (2) : a piece of paper money **d** (1) : a short informal letter (2) : a formal diplomatic communication **e** : a scholarly or technical essay shorter than an article and restricted in scope **4 a** : DIS-

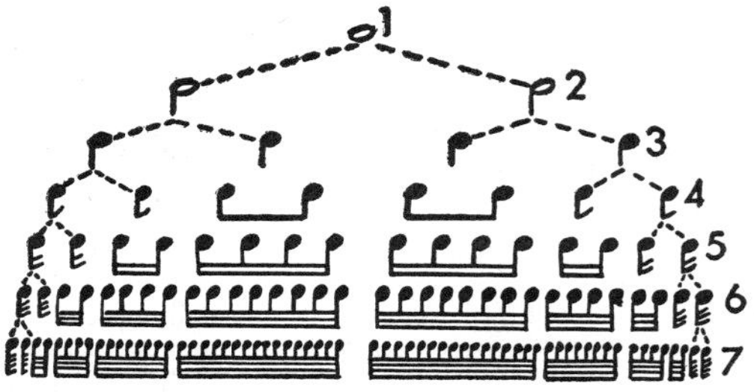

relative duration of notes 1b: *1* whole, *2* half, *3* quarter, *4* eighth, *5* sixteenth, *6* thirty-second, *7* sixty-fourth

TINCTION, REPUTATION **b :** OBSERVATION, NOTICE **c :** KNOWLEDGE, INFORMATION **syn** see SIGN

note·book \'nōt-ˌbu̇k\ *n* **:** a book for notes or memoranda

note·case \-ˌkās\ *n, Brit* **:** WALLET

not·ed \'nōt-əd\ *adj* **:** well-known by reputation **:** EMINENT **syn** see FAMOUS — **not·ed·ly** *adv* — **not·ed·ness** *n*

note·less \'nōt-ləs\ *adj* **1 :** not noticed **:** UNDISTINGUISHED **2 :** UNMUSICAL, VOICELESS

note of hand : PROMISSORY NOTE

note·wor·thi·ly \'nōt-ˌwər-t͟hə-lē\ *adv* **:** in a noteworthy manner

note·wor·thi·ness \-t͟hē-nəs\ *n* **:** the quality or state of being noteworthy

note·wor·thy \-t͟hē\ *adj* **:** worthy of note **:** REMARKABLE

1noth·ing \'nəth-iŋ\ *pron* [ME, fr. OE *nān thing, nāthing,* fr. *nān* no + *thing* — more at NONE] **1 :** not any thing **:** no thing **2 :** no part **3 :** one of no interest, value, or consequence — **nothing doing :** by no means **:** definitely no

2nothing *adv* **:** not at all **:** in no degree

3nothing *n* **1 a :** something that does not exist **b :** NOTHINGNESS 3b **2 :** an object, person, event, or remark of no or slight value

noth·ing·ness \-nəs\ *n* **1 :** the quality or state of being nothing: as **a :** NONEXISTENCE **b :** utter insignificance **c :** DEATH **2 :** something insignificant or valueless **3 a :** EMPTINESS, VOID **b :** a metaphysical entity opposed to and devoid of being and regarded by some existentialists as the ground of anxiety

1no·tice \'nōt-əs\ *n* [ME, fr. MF, acquaintance, fr. L *notitia* knowledge, acquaintance, fr. *notus* known, fr. pp. of *noscere* to come to know — more at KNOW] **1 a** (1) **:** warning or intimation of something **:** ANNOUNCEMENT (2) **:** notification by one of the parties to an agreement or relation of intention of terminating it at a specified time (3) **:** the condition of being warned or notified **b :** INFORMATION, INTELLIGENCE **2 a :** ATTENTION, HEED **b :** polite or favorable attention **:** CIVILITY **3 :** a written or printed announcement **4 :** a short critical account or examination

2notice *vt* **1 :** to give notice of **2 a :** to comment upon **:** NOTE **b :** REVIEW **3 a :** to treat with attention or civility **b :** to take notice of **:** MARK **4 :** to give a formal notice to

no·tice·able \'nōt-ə-sə-bəl\ *adj* **1 :** worthy of notice **2 :** capable of being noticed — **no·tice·ably** \-blē\ *adv*

syn NOTICEABLE, REMARKABLE, PROMINENT, OUTSTANDING, CONSPICUOUS, SALIENT, SIGNAL, STRIKING mean attracting notice or attention. NOTICEABLE implies an inability to escape attention; REMARKABLE applies to what demands attention; PROMINENT implies commanding notice as standing out from a background or surroundings; OUTSTANDING heightens the notion of rising above or excelling others of the kind; CONSPICUOUS implies an obviousness to the sight or mind; SALIENT suggests an emphatic quality that thrusts itself into attention; SIGNAL applies to what deserves attention as being unusually significant; STRIKING implies a character that impresses itself vividly or deeply on the sight or judgment

no·ti·fi·ca·tion \ˌnōt-ə-fə-'kā-shən\ *n* **1 :** the act or an instance of notifying **:** NOTICE **2 :** a written or printed matter that gives notice

no·ti·fi·er \'nōt-ə-ˌfī(-ə)r\ *n* **:** one that notifies

no·ti·fy \'nōt-ə-ˌfī\ *vt* [ME *notifien,* fr. MF *notifier* to make known, fr. LL *notificare,* fr. L *notus* known] **1** *obs* **:** to point out **2 :** to give notice of or report the occurrence of **3 :** to give formal notice to **syn** see INFORM

no·tion \'nō-shən\ *n* [L *notion-, notio,* fr. *notus,* pp. of *noscere*] **1 a** (1) **:** an inclusive general concept (2) **:** an individual's conception or impression of something known, experienced, or imagined (3) **:** a theory or belief held by a person or group **b :** INCLINATION, WHIM **2** *obs* **:** MIND, INTELLECT **3 a :** an ingenious device **:** KNICKKNACK **b** *pl* **:** small personal and clothing items (as ribbons) **syn** see IDEA

no·tion·al \'nō-shnəl, -shən-ᵊl\ *adj* **1 :** SPECULATIVE, THEORETICAL **2 :** existing in the mind only **:** IMAGINARY **3 :** given to foolish or fanciful moods or ideas **4 a :** of, relating to, or being a notion or idea **b** (1) **:** presenting an idea of a thing, action, or quality ⟨*has* is ~ in *he has luck,* relational in *he has gone*⟩ (2) **:** of or representing what exists or occurs in the world of things — **no·tion·al·i·ty** \ˌnō-shə-'nal-ət-ē\ *n* — **no·tion·al·ly** \'nō-shnə-lē, -shən-ᵊl-ē\ *adv*

noto- — see NOT-

no·to·chord \'nōt-ə-ˌkȯ(ə)rd\ *n* [*not-* + L *chorda* cord — more at CORD] **:** a longitudinal flexible rod of cells that in the lowest chordates (as amphioxus and the lampreys) and in the embryos of the higher vertebrates forms the supporting axis of the body — **no·to·chord·al** \ˌnōt-ə-'kȯrd-ᵊl\ *adj*

no·to·ri·ety \ˌnōt-ə-'rī-ət-ē\ *n* [MF or ML; MF *notorieté,* fr. ML *notorietat-, notorietas,* fr. *notorius*] **1 :** the quality or state of being notorious **2 :** a notorious person

no·to·ri·ous \nō-'tōr-ē-əs, nə-, -'tȯr-\ *adj* [ML *notorius,* fr. LL *notorium* information, indictment, fr. neut. of (assumed) LL *notorius* making known, fr. L *notus,* pp. of *noscere* to come to know — more at KNOW] **:** generally known and talked of; *esp* **:** widely and unfavorably known — **syn** see FAMOUS — **no·to·ri·ous·ly** *adv* — **no·to·ri·ous·ness** *n*

not·or·nis \nō-'tȯr-nəs, nōt-'ȯr-\ *n, pl* **notornis** [NL, genus name, fr. Gk *notos* south + *ornis* bird; akin to Gk *noteros* damp — more at NOURISH, ERNE] **:** any of a genus (*Notornis*) of flightless New Zealand birds related to the gallinules

no–trump \'nō-'trəmp\ *adj* **:** being a bid, contract, or hand suitable to play without any suit being trumps — **no–trump** *n*

no·tum \'nōt-əm\ *n, pl* **no·ta** \'nōt-ə\ [NL, fr. Gk *nōton* back — more at NATES] **:** a back part or surface of an animal

1not·with·stand·ing \ˌnät-with-'stan-diŋ, -wit͟h-\ *prep* [ME *notwithstonding,* fr. *not* + *withstonding,* prp. of *withstonden* to withstand] **:** in spite of

2notwithstanding *adv* **:** NEVERTHELESS, HOWEVER

3notwithstanding *conj* **:** ALTHOUGH

nou·gat \'nü-gət, *esp Brit* -ˌgä\ *n* [F, fr. Prov, fr. OProv *nogat,* fr. *noga* nut, fr. L *nuc-, nux* — more at NUT] **:** a confection of nuts or fruit pieces in a sugar paste

nought \'nȯt, 'nät\ *var of* NAUGHT

nou·me·nal \'nü-mən-ᵊl\ *adj* **:** of or relating to the noumena

nou·me·non \'nü-mə-ˌnän\ *n, pl* **nou·me·na** \-nə, -ˌnä\ [G, fr. Gk *nooumenon* thing thought, fr. neut. of pres. pass. part. of *noein* to think, fr. *nous* mind] **:** a ground of phenomena that is unknowable by the senses but is conceivable by reason

noun \'nau̇n\ *n, often attrib* [ME *nowne,* fr. AF *noun* name, noun, fr. OF *nom,* fr. L *nomen* — more at NAME] **1 :** a word that is the name of a subject of discourse (as a person, animal, plant, place, thing, substance, quality, idea, action, or state) and that in languages with grammatical number, case, and gender is inflected for number and case but has inherent gender **2 :** a word except a pronoun used in a sentence as subject or object of a verb, as object of a preposition, as the predicate after a copula, or as a name in an absolute construction

nour·ish \'nər-ish, 'nə-rish\ *vt* [ME *nurishen,* fr. OF *noriss-,* stem of *norrir,* fr. L *nutrire* to suckle, nourish; akin to Gk *nan* to flow, *noteros* damp, L *nare* to swim, Gk *nein*] **1 :** NURTURE, REAR **2 :** to promote the growth of **3 a :** to furnish or sustain with nutriment **:** FEED **b :** MAINTAIN, SUPPORT — **nour·ish·er** *n*

nour·ish·ing *adj* **:** giving nourishment **:** NUTRITIOUS

nour·ish·ment \'nər-ish-mənt, 'nə-rish-\ *n* **1 :** FOOD, NUTRIMENT **2 :** the act of nourishing or the state of being nourished

nous \'nüs\ *n* [Gk *noos, nous* mind] **:** MIND, REASON: as **a :** an intelligent purposive principle of the world **b :** the divine reason regarded in Neoplatonism as the first emanation of God

nou·veau riche \ˌnü-ˌvō-'rēsh\ *n, pl* **nou·veaux riches** *same*\ [F, lit., new rich] **:** a person newly rich **:** PARVENU

no·va \'nō-və\ *n, pl* **novas** *or* **no·vae** \-(ˌ)vē, -ˌvī\ [NL, fem. of L *novus* new] **:** a star that suddenly increases its light output tremendously and then fades away to its former obscurity in a few months or years

no·vac·u·lite \nō-'vak-yə-ˌlīt\ *n* [L *novacula* razor] **:** a very hard fine-grained siliceous rock used for whetstones and believed to be of sedimentary origin

no·va·tion \nō-'vā-shən\ *n* [LL *novation-, novatio* renewal, legal novation, fr. L *novatus,* pp. of *novare* to make new, fr. *novus*] **:** the substitution of a new legal obligation for an old one

1nov·el \'näv-əl\ *adj* [ME, fr. MF, new, fr. L *novellus,* fr. dim. of *novus* new — more at NEW] **1 :** having no precedent **:** NEW **2 :** STRANGE, UNUSUAL **syn** see NEW

2novel *n* [It *novella*] **1 :** an invented prose narrative that is usu. long and complex and deals with human experience through a connected sequence of events **2 :** the literary type constituted by novels — **nov·el·is·tic** \ˌnäv-ə-'lis-tik\ *adj*

nov·el·ette \ˌnäv-ə-'let\ *n* **1 :** a brief novel **2 :** a long short story

nov·el·ist \'näv-(ə-)ləst\ *n* **:** a writer of novels

nov·el·iza·tion \ˌnäv-(ə-)lə-'zā-shən\ *n* **:** the act or process of novelizing

nov·el·ize \'näv-ə-ˌlīz\ *vt* **:** to convert into the form of a novel

no·vel·la \nō-'vel-ə\ *n, pl* **novellas** \-əz\ *or* **no·vel·le** \-'vel-ē\ [It, fr. fem. of *novello* new, fr. L *novellus*] **1** *pl* **novelle :** a story with a compact and pointed plot **2** *pl usu* **novellas :** NOVELETTE

nov·el·ty \'näv-əl-tē\ *n* [ME *novelte,* fr. MF *noveleté,* fr. *novel*] **1 :** something new or unusual **2 :** the quality or state of being novel **:** NEWNESS **3 :** a small manufactured article intended mainly for personal or household adornment — usu. used in pl.

1No·vem·ber \nō-'vem-bər, nə-\ *n* [ME *Novembre,* fr. OF, fr. L *November* (ninth month), fr. *novem* nine — more at NINE] **:** the 11th month of the Gregorian calendar

2November — a communications code word for the letter *n*

no·vem·de·cil·lion \ˌnō-ˌvem-di-'sil-yən\ *n, often attrib* [L *novemdecim* nineteen (fr. *novem* + *decem* ten) + E *-illion* (as in *million*) — more at TEN] — see NUMBER table

no·ve·na \nō-'vē-nə\ *n* [ML, fr. L, fem. of *novenus* nine each, fr. *novem*] **:** a Roman Catholic nine days' devotion

nov·ice \'näv-əs\ *n* [ME, fr. MF, fr. ML *novicius,* fr. L, new, inexperienced, fr. *novus* — more at NEW] **1 :** a person admitted to probationary membership in a religious community **2 :** BEGINNER, TYRO

no·vi·tiate \nō-'vish-ət, nə-\ *n* [F *noviciat,* fr. ML *noviciatus,* fr. *novicius*] **1 :** the period or state of being a novice **2 :** NOVICE **3 :** a house where novices are trained

No·vo·cain \'nō-və-ˌkān\ *trademark* — used for a preparation containing procaine hydrochloride

1now \(')nau̇\ *adv* [ME, fr. OE *nū;* akin to OHG *nū* now, L *nunc,* Gk *nyn*] **1 a :** at the present time or moment **b :** in the time immediately before the present **c :** in the time immediately to follow **:** FORTHWITH **2** — used with the sense of present time weakened or lost to express command, request, or admonition ⟨~ hear this⟩ **3** — used with the sense of present time weakened or lost to introduce an important point or indicate a transition **4 :** SOMETIMES ⟨~ one and ~ another⟩ **5 :** under the present circumstances **6 :** at the time referred to ⟨~ the trouble began⟩

2now *conj* **:** in view of the fact that **:** SINCE ⟨~ that we are here⟩

3now \'nau̇\ *n* **:** the present time or moment **:** PRESENT

4now \'nau̇\ *adj* **:** of or relating to the present time **:** EXISTING ⟨the ~ president⟩

now·a·days \'nau̇-(ə-)ˌdāz\ *adv* [ME *now a dayes,* fr. *1now* + *a dayes* during the day] **:** at the present time

no·way \'nō-ˌwā\ *or* **no·ways** \-ˌwāz\ *adv* **:** NOWISE

no·where \'nō-ˌ(h)we(ə)r, -ˌ(h)wa(ə)r, -(h)wər\ *adv* **1 :** not in or at any place **2 :** to no place — **nowhere** *n*

nowhere near *adv* **:** not nearly

no·wheres \'nō-ˌ(h)we(ə)rz, -ˌ(h)wa(ə)rz, -(h)wərz\ *adv, chiefly dial* **:** NOWHERE

no·whith·er \nō-'(h)wit͟h-ər, 'nō-ˌ\ *adv* **:** to or toward no place

no·wise \'nō-ˌwīz\ *adv* **:** not at all

Nox \'näks\ *n* [L] **:** the Roman goddess of night

nox·ious \'näk-shəs\ *adj* [L *noxius,* fr. *noxa* harm; akin to L *nocēre* to harm, *nec-, nex* violent death, Gk *nekros* dead body] **1 :** HARMFUL, DESTRUCTIVE **2 :** morally corrupting **:** PERNICIOUS ⟨a ~ doctrine⟩ **3 :** DISTASTEFUL, OBNOXIOUS **syn** see PERNICIOUS — **nox·ious·ly** *adv* — **nox·ious·ness** *n*

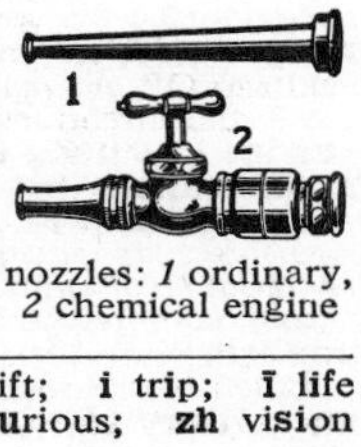

nozzles: *1* ordinary, *2* chemical engine

noz·zle \'näz-əl\ *n* [dim. of *nose*] **1 a :** a projecting vent of something **b :** a small spout (as of a pipe) **2** *slang* **:** NOSE

-n't \(ᵊ)nt\ *adv comb form* **:** not ⟨isn't⟩

ə abut; ᵊ kitten; ər further; a back; ā bake; ä cot, cart; au̇ out; ch chin; e less; ē easy; g gift; i trip; ī life
j joke; ŋ sing; ō flow; ȯ flaw; ȯi coin; th thin; t͟h this; ü loot; u̇ foot; y yet; yü few; yu̇ furious; zh vision

nth \'en(t)th\ *adj* [*n* + *-th*] **1 :** numbered with an unspecified or indefinitely large ordinal number **2 :** EXTREME, UTMOST ⟨to the ~ degree⟩

nu \'n(y)ü\ *n* [Gk *ny*, of Sem origin; akin to Heb *nūn* nun] **:** the 13th letter of the Greek alphabet — symbol N or *ν*

nu·ance \'n(y)ü-,än(t)s, -,äⁿs, n(y)ü-'\ *n* [F, fr. MF, shade of color, fr. *nuer* to make shades of color, fr. *nue* cloud, fr. L *nubes*; akin to Gk *nythos* dark] **1 :** a subtle distinction or variation **2 :** a subtle quality **:** NICETY

nub \'nəb\ *n* **1** [alter. of *knub*] **:** KNOB, LUMP **2 :** NUBBIN **3 :** GIST, POINT

nub·bin \'nəb-ən\ *n* [perh. dim. of *nub*] **:** a small or imperfect ear of Indian corn; *broadly* **:** something small, stunted, or imperfect

nub·ble \'nəb-əl\ *n* [dim. of *nub*] **:** a small knob or lump — **nub·bly** \-(ə-)lē\ *adj*

Nu·bi·an \'n(y)ü-bē-ən\ *n* **1 :** one of the people of Nubia; *esp* **:** a member of one of the group of negroid tribes forming a powerful empire between Egypt and Ethiopia from the 6th to the 14th centuries **2 :** any of several languages spoken in central and northern Sudan — **Nubian** *adj*

nu·bile \'n(y)ü-bəl, -,bīl\ *adj* [F, fr. L *nubilis*, fr. *nubere* to marry — more at NUPTIAL] **:** of marriageable condition or age ⟨~ girls⟩ — **nu·bil·i·ty** \n(y)ü-'bil-ət-ē\ *n*

nu·cel·lar \n(y)ü-'sel-ər\ *adj* **:** of or relating to a nucellus

nu·cel·lus \n(y)ü-'sel-əs\ *n*, *pl* **nu·cel·li** \-'sel-,ī\ [NL, fr. L *nucella* small nut, fr. *nuc-*, *nux* nut — more at NUT] **:** the central and chief part of an ovule containing the embryo sac

nu·chal \'n(y)ü-kəl\ *adj* [ML *nucha* nape, fr. Ar *nukhā'* spinal marrow] **:** of, relating to, or lying in the region of the nape — **nuchal** *n*

nucle- *or* **nucleo-** *comb form* [F *nuclé-*, *nucléo-*, fr. NL *nucleus*] **1 :** nucleus ⟨*nucleon*⟩ **2 :** nucleic acid ⟨*nucleoprotein*⟩

nu·cle·ar \'n(y)ü-klē-ər, *nonstand* -kyə-lər\ *adj* **1 :** of, relating to, or constituting a nucleus **2 :** of, relating to, or utilizing the atomic nucleus, atomic energy, the atom bomb, or atomic power

nu·cle·ase \'n(y)ü-klē-,ās, -,āz\ *n* **:** any of various enzymes that promote hydrolysis of nucleic acids

1nu·cle·ate \'n(y)ü-klē-,āt\ *vb* [LL *nucleatus*, pp. of *nucleare* to become stony, fr. L *nucleus*] *vt* **1 :** to form into a nucleus **:** CLUSTER **2 :** to act as a nucleus for **3 :** to supply nuclei to ~ *vi* **1 :** to form a nucleus **:** CLUSTER **2 :** to act as a nucleus — **nu·cle·ation** \,n(y)ü-klē-'ā-shən\ *n*

2nu·cle·ate \'n(y)ü-klē-ət\ *adj* [L *nucleatus*, fr. *nucleus* kernel] **:** having a nucleus or nuclei ⟨~ cells⟩

nu·cle·ic acid \n(y)ü-,klē-ik-, ,n(y)ü-, -,klā-\ *n* **:** any of various acids composed of a sugar or derivative of a sugar, phosphoric acid, and a base and found esp. in cell nuclei

nu·cle·in \'n(y)ü-klē-ən\ *n* **:** any of various substances obtained from cell nuclei

nu·cle·o·lar \n(y)ü-'klē-ə-lər, ,n(y)ü-klē-'ō-\ *adj* **:** of, relating to, or constituting a nucleolus

nu·cle·o·lus \n(y)ü-'klē-ə-ləs\ *n*, *pl* **nu·cle·o·li** \-,lī\ [NL, fr. L, dim. of *nucleus*] **:** a predominantly protein body of the metabolic nucleus usu. held to be a center of synthetic activity or storage; *broadly* **:** a differentiated nuclear body other than a chromosome

nu·cle·on \'n(y)ü-klē-,än\ *n* [ISV] **:** a proton or neutron esp. in the atomic nucleus — **nu·cle·on·ic** \,n(y)ü-klē-'än-ik\ *adj*

nu·cle·on·ics \,n(y)ü-klē-'än-iks\ *n pl but sing or pl in constr* **:** a branch of physical science that deals with nucleons or with all phenomena of the atomic nucleus

nu·cleo·plasm \'n(y)ü-klē-ə-,plaz-əm\ *n* [ISV] **1 :** the protoplasm of a nucleus **2 :** KARYOLYMPH — **nu·cleo·plas·mat·ic** \,n(y)ü-klē-(,)ō-,plaz-'mat-ik\ *or* **nu·cleo·plas·mic** \-klē-ə-'plaz-mik\ *adj*

nu·cleo·pro·tein \,n(y)ü-klē-(,)ō-'prō-,tēn, -'prōt-ē-ən\ *n* [ISV] **:** any of the proteins conjugated with nucleic acid that occur esp. in the nuclei of living cells and are an essential constituent of genes and viruses

nu·cle·o·side \'n(y)ü-klē-ə-,sīd\ *n* [ISV *nucle-* + *-ose* + *-ide*] **:** a glycoside that is formed by partial hydrolysis of a nucleic acid or a nucleotide and contains a purine or pyrimidine base

nu·cle·o·tide \-,tīd\ *n* [ISV, irreg. fr. *nucle-* + *-ide*] **:** a phosphoric ester of a nucleoside

nu·cle·us \'n(y)ü-klē-əs\ *n*, *pl* **nu·clei** \-klē-,ī\ *also* **nu·cle·us·es** [NL, fr. L, kernel, dim. of *nuc-*, *nux* nut — more at NUT] **1 :** the small, brighter, and denser portion of a galaxy or of the head of a comet **2 :** a central point, group, or mass about which gathering, concentration, or accretion takes place: as **a :** a portion of cell protoplasm held to be essential to vital phenomena and heredity, made up of a network rich in nucleoproteins from which chromosomes and nucleoli arise and a hyaline ground substance, and enclosed by a definite membrane **b :** a mass of gray matter or group of nerve cells in the central nervous system **c :** a characteristic and stable complex of atoms or groups in a molecule **d :** the positively charged central portion of an atom that comprises nearly all of the atomic mass and that consists of protons and neutrons except in hydrogen which consists of one proton only

nu·clide \'n(y)ü-,klīd\ *n* [*nucleus* + *-ide*, irreg. fr. Gk *eidos* form — more at IDOL] **:** a species of atom characterized by the constitution of its nucleus and hence by the number of protons, the number of neutrons, and the energy content — **nu·clid·ic** \n(y)ü-'klid-ik\ *adj*

1nude \'n(y)üd\ *adj* [L *nudus* naked — more at NAKED] **1 :** lacking an essential particular **2 :** devoid of covering **:** NAKED; *esp* **:** UNCLOTHED **syn** see BARE — **nude·ly** *adv* — **nude·ness** *n* — **nu·di·ty** \'n(y)üd-ət-ē\ *n*

2nude *n* **1 a :** a representation of a nude human figure **b :** a nude person **2 :** the condition of being nude ⟨in the ~⟩

nudge \'nəj\ *vt* [perh. of Scand origin; akin to ON *gnaga* to gnaw; akin to OE *gnagan* to gnaw] **1 :** to touch or push gently; *esp* **:** to seek the attention of by a push of the elbow **2 :** APPROACH — **nudge** *n* — **nudg·er** *n*

nu·di·branch \'n(y)üd-ə-,braŋk\ *n* [deriv. of L *nudus* + *branchia* gill — more at BRANCHIA] **:** any of a suborder (Nudibranchia) of marine gastropod mollusks without a shell in the adult state and without true gills — **nudibranch** *adj* — **nu·di·bran·chi·ate** \,n(y)üd-ə-'braŋ-kē-ət\ *adj or n*

nud·ism \'n(y)ü-,diz-əm\ *n* **:** the cult or practice of living unclothed for reasons of health — **nud·ist** \'n(y)üd-əst\ *n*

nu·ga·to·ry \'n(y)ü-gə-,tōr-ē, -,tȯr-\ *adj* [L *nugatorius*, fr. *nugatus*, pp. of *nugari* to trifle, fr. *nugae* trifles] **1 :** INCONSEQUENTIAL, WORTHLESS **2 :** having no force **:** INOPERATIVE **syn** see VAIN

nug·get \'nəg-ət\ *n* [origin unknown] **:** a solid lump; *esp* **:** a native lump of precious metal

nui·sance \'n(y)üs-ᵊn(t)s\ *n* [ME *nusaunce*, fr. AF, fr. OF *nuisir* to harm, fr. L *nocēre* — more at NOXIOUS] **1 :** HARM, INJURY **2 :** an annoying, unpleasant, or obnoxious thing or practice **3 :** PEST, ANNOYANCE

nuisance tax *n* **:** an excise tax collected in small amounts directly from the consumer

1null \'nəl\ *adj* [MF *nul*, lit., not any, fr. L *nullus*, fr. *ne-* not + *ullus* any; akin to L *unus* one — more at NO, ONE] **1 :** having no legal or binding force **:** INVALID **2 :** amounting to nothing **:** NIL **3 :** having no value **:** INSIGNIFICANT **4 :** having no members ⟨~ sequence⟩ **5 :** indicating usu. by a zero reading on a scale when current or voltage is zero **6 :** of, being, or relating to zero

2null *n* **1 :** ZERO 2a(1) **2 :** a condition of a radio receiver when minimum or zero signal is received

nul·lah \'nəl-ə\ *n* [Hindi *nālā*] **:** GULLY, RAVINE

null and void *adj* **:** having no force, binding power, or validity

nul·li·fi·ca·tion \,nəl-ə-fə-'kā-shən\ *n* **1 :** the act of nullifying **:** the state of being nullified **2 :** the action of a state impeding or attempting to prevent the operation and enforcement within its territory of a law of the U.S. — **nul·li·fi·ca·tion·ist** \-sh(ə-)nəst\ *n*

nul·li·fi·er \'nəl-ə-,fī(-ə)r\ *n* **:** one that nullifies; *specif* **:** one maintaining the right of nullification against the U.S. government

nul·li·fy \'nəl-ə-,fī\ *vt* [LL *nullificare*, fr. L *nullus*] **1 :** to make null; *specif* **:** ANNUL **2 :** to make of no value or consequence

syn NULLIFY, NEGATE, ANNUL, ABROGATE, INVALIDATE mean to deprive of effective or continued existence. NULLIFY implies counteracting completely the force, effectiveness, or value of something; NEGATE implies the destruction or canceling out of each of two things by the other; ANNUL suggests making ineffective or nonexistent often by legal or official action; ABROGATE is like ANNUL but more definitely implies a legal or official purposeful act; INVALIDATE implies making something powerless or unacceptable by declaration of its logical or moral or legal unsoundness

nul·li·ty \'nəl-ət-ē\ *n* **1 :** the quality or state of being null; *esp* **:** legal invalidity **2 :** something that is null; *specif* **:** an act void of legal effect

numb \'nəm\ *adj* [ME *nomen*, fr. pp. of *nimen* to take — more at NIM] **1 a :** devoid of sensation esp. from cold **b :** devoid of emotion **:** INDIFFERENT **2 :** characterized by numbness — **numb** *vt* — **numb·ly** *adv* — **numb·ness** *n*

1num·ber \'nəm-bər\ *n* [ME *nombre*, fr. OF, fr. L *numerus* — more at NIMBLE] **1 a** (1) **:** a sum of units **:** TOTAL (2) **:** COMPLEMENT 1b (3) **:** an indefinite usu. large total (4) *pl* **:** a numerous group **:** MANY; *also* **:** a numerical preponderance **b** (1) **:** the characteristic of an individual by which it is treated as a unit or of a collection by which it is treated in terms of a determinate unit of units (2) **:** a unit belonging to an abstract mathematical system and subject to specified laws of succession, addition, and multiplication; *also* **:** an element (as *π*) of any of many mathematical systems obtained by extension of or analogy with the natural number system (3) *pl* **:** ARITHMETIC **2 :** a distinction of word form to denote reference to one or more than one; *also* **:** a form or group of forms so distinguished **3** *pl* **a** (1) **:** metrical structure **:** METER (2) **:** metrical lines **:** VERSES **b** *archaic* **:** musical sounds **:** NOTES **4 a :** a word, symbol, letter, or combination of symbols representing a number **b :** a numeral or combination of numerals or other symbols used to identify or designate **c** (1) **:** a member of a sequence or collection designated by esp. consecutive numbers; *also* **:** an individual singled out from a group (2) **:** a position in a numbered sequence **5 :** insight into a person's ability or character ⟨had his ~⟩ **6** *pl but sing or pl in constr* **a :** a form of lottery in which bets are placed on numbers regularly published in newspapers for other purposes — called also *number pool*, *numbers game* **b :** 2POLICY 2a **syn** see SUM — **by the numbers 1 :** in unison to a specific count or cadence **2 :** in a systematic, routine, or mechanical manner

2number *vb* **num·ber·ing** \'nəm-b(ə-)riŋ\ *vt* **1 :** COUNT, ENUMERATE **2 :** to claim as part of a total **:** INCLUDE **3 :** to restrict to a definite number **4 :** to assign a number to **5 :** to comprise in number **:** TOTAL ~ *vi* **1 :** to comprise a total number **2 :** to call off numbers in sequence — **num·ber·able** \'nəm-b(ə-)rə-bəl\ *adj* — **num·ber·er** \-bər-ər\ *n*

num·ber·less \'nəm-bər-ləs\ *adj* **:** INNUMERABLE, COUNTLESS

numb·fish \'nəm-,fish\ *n* **:** ELECTRIC RAY

numb·ing *adj* **:** causing numbness — **numb·ing·ly** \-iŋ-lē\ *adv*

numb·skull \'nəm-,skəl\ *var of* NUMSKULL

nu·men \'n(y)ü-mən\ *n*, *pl* **nu·mi·na** \-mə-nə\ [L, nod, divine will, numen; akin to L *nuere* to nod, Gk *neuein*] **:** a spirit believed to inhabit a natural object, phenomenon, or locality

nu·mer·a·ble \'n(y)üm-(ə-)rə-bəl\ *adj* **:** capable of being counted

1nu·mer·al \'n(y)üm-(ə-)rəl\ *adj* [MF, fr. LL *numeralis*, fr. L *numerus*] **1 :** of, relating to, or expressing numbers **2 :** consisting of numbers or numerals — **nu·mer·al·ly** \-ē\ *adv*

2numeral *n* **1 :** a conventional symbol representing a number **2** *pl* **:** numbers designating by year a school or college class awarded for distinction in an extracurricular activity

nu·mer·ate \'n(y)ü-mə-,rāt\ *vt* [L *numeratus*, pp. of *numerare* to count, fr. *numerus*] **:** ENUMERATE

nu·mer·a·tion \,n(y)ü-mə-'rā-shən\ *n* **1 a :** the act or process or a system or instance of enumeration **b :** an act or instance of designating by a number **2 :** the art of reading in words numbers expressed by numerals

nu·mer·a·tor \'n(y)ü-mə-,rāt-ər\ *n* **1 :** the part of a fraction that is above the line and signifies the number of parts of the denominator taken **2 :** one that numbers

nu·mer·i·cal \n(y)ù-'mer-i-kəl\ *adj* [L *numerus*] **:** relating to, denoting, or denoted by a number — **nu·mer·i·cal·ly** \-k(ə-)lē\ *adv*

nu·mer·ol·o·gy \,n(y)ü-mə-'räl-ə-jē\ *n* [L *numerus* + E *-o-* + *-logy*] **:** the study of the occult significance of numbers

nu·mer·ous \'n(y)üm-(ə-)rəs\ *adj* [MF *numereux*, fr. L *numerosus*, fr. *numerus*] **:** consisting of great numbers of units or individuals — **nu·mer·ous·ly** *adv* — **nu·mer·ous·ness** *n*

nu·mi·nous \'n(y)ü-mə-nəs\ *adj* [L *numin-*, *numen*] **1 :** SUPERNATURAL, MYSTERIOUS **2 :** filled with a sense of the presence of divinity **:** HOLY **3 :** appealing to the higher emotions or to the aesthetic sense **:** SPIRITUAL

TABLE OF NUMBERS

CARDINAL NUMBERS[1]			ORDINAL NUMBERS[4]	
NAME[2]	SYMBOL		NAME[5]	SYMBOL[6]
	arabic	*roman*[3]		
naught *or* zero *or* cipher	0		first	1st
one	1	I	second	2d *or* 2nd
two	2	II	third	3d *or* 3rd
three	3	III	fourth	4th
four	4	IV	fifth	5th
five	5	V	sixth	6th
six	6	VI	seventh	7th
seven	7	VII	eighth	8th
eight	8	VIII	ninth	9th
nine	9	IX	tenth	10th
ten	10	X	eleventh	11th
eleven	11	XI	twelfth	12th
twelve	12	XII	thirteenth	13th
thirteen	13	XIII	fourteenth	14th
fourteen	14	XIV	fifteenth	15th
fifteen	15	XV	sixteenth	16th
sixteen	16	XVI	seventeenth	17th
seventeen	17	XVII	eighteenth	18th
eighteen	18	XVIII	nineteenth	19th
nineteen	19	XIX	twentieth	20th
twenty	20	XX	twenty-first	21st
twenty-one	21	XXI	twenty-second	22d *or* 22nd
twenty-two	22	XXII	twenty-third	23d *or* 23rd
twenty-three	23	XXIII	twenty-fourth	24th
twenty-four	24	XXIV	twenty-fifth	25th
twenty-five	25	XXV	twenty-sixth	26th
twenty-six	26	XXVI	twenty-seventh	27th
twenty-seven	27	XXVII	twenty-eighth	28th
twenty-eight	28	XXVIII	twenty-ninth	29th
twenty-nine	29	XXIX	thirtieth	30th
thirty	30	XXX	thirty-first	31st
thirty-one	31	XXXI	thirty-second *etc*	32d *or* 32nd
thirty-two *etc*	32	XXXII	fortieth	40th
forty	40	XL	forty-first	41st
forty-one *etc*	41	XLI	forty-second *etc*	42d *or* 42nd
fifty	50	L	fiftieth	50th
sixty	60	LX	sixtieth	60th
seventy	70	LXX	seventieth	70th
eighty	80	LXXX	eightieth	80th
ninety	90	XC	ninetieth	90th
one hundred	100	C	hundredth *or* one hundredth	100th
one hundred and one *or* one hundred one	101	CI	hundred and first *or* one hundred and first	101st
one hundred and two *etc*	102	CII	hundred and second *etc*	102d *or* 102nd
two hundred	200	CC	two hundredth	200th
three hundred	300	CCC	three hundredth	300th
four hundred	400	CD	four hundredth	400th
five hundred	500	D	five hundredth	500th
six hundred	600	DC	six hundredth	600th
seven hundred	700	DCC	seven hundredth	700th
eight hundred	800	DCCC	eight hundredth	800th
nine hundred	900	CM	nine hundredth	900th
one thousand *or* ten hundred *etc*	1,000	M	thousandth *or* one thousandth	1,000th
two thousand *etc*	2,000	MM	two thousandth *etc*	2,000th
five thousand	5,000	$\overline{\text{V}}$	ten thousandth	10,000th
ten thousand	10,000	$\overline{\text{X}}$	hundred thousandth *or* one hundred thousandth	100,000th
one hundred thousand	100,000	$\overline{\text{C}}$	millionth *or* one millionth	1,000,000th
one million	1,000,000	$\overline{\text{M}}$		

[1]The cardinal numbers are used in simple counting or in answer to "how many?" The words for these numbers may be used as nouns (he counted to *twelve*), as pronouns (*twelve* were found), or as adjectives (*twelve* boys).
[2]In formal contexts the numbers one to one hundred and in less formal contexts the numbers one to nine are commonly written out, while larger numbers are given in numerals. In nearly all contexts a number occurring at the beginning of a sentence is usually written out. Except in very formal contexts numerals are invariably used for dates. Arabic numerals from 1,000 to 9,999 are often written without commas (1000, 9999). Year numbers are always written without commas (1783).
[3]The roman numerals are written either in capitals or in lowercase letters.
[4]The ordinal numbers are used to show the order or succession in which such items as names, objects, and periods of time are considered (the *twelfth* month; the *fourth* row of seats; the *18th* century).
[5]Each of the terms for the ordinal numbers excepting *first* and *second* is used in designating one of a number of parts into which a whole may be divided (a *fourth*; a *sixth*; a *tenth*) and as the denominator in fractions designating the number of such parts constituting a certain portion of a whole (*one fourth*; *three fifths*). When used as nouns the fractions are usually written as two words, although they are regularly hyphenated as adjectives (a *two-thirds* majority). When fractions are written in numerals, the cardinal symbols are used (¼, ⅗, ⅚).
[6]The arabic symbols for the cardinal numbers may be read as ordinals in certain contexts (January 1=January first; 2 Samuel=Second Samuel). The roman numerals are sometimes read as ordinals (Henry IV=Henry the Fourth); sometimes they are written with the ordinal suffixes (XIXth Dynasty).

DENOMINATIONS ABOVE ONE MILLION

American system[1]				*British system*[1]			
NAME	VALUE IN POWERS OF TEN	NUMBER OF ZEROS[2]	NUMBER OF GROUPS OF THREE 0's AFTER 1,000	NAME	VALUE IN POWERS OF TEN	NUMBER OF ZEROS[2]	POWERS OF 1,000,000
billion	10^9	9	2	milliard	10^9	9	—
trillion	10^{12}	12	3	billion	10^{12}	12	2
quadrillion	10^{15}	15	4	trillion	10^{18}	18	3
quintillion	10^{18}	18	5	quadrillion	10^{24}	24	4
sextillion	10^{21}	21	6	quintillion	10^{30}	30	5
septillion	10^{24}	24	7	sextillion	10^{36}	36	6
octillion	10^{27}	27	8	septillion	10^{42}	42	7
nonillion	10^{30}	30	9	octillion	10^{48}	48	8
decillion	10^{33}	33	10	nonillion	10^{54}	54	9
undecillion	10^{36}	36	11	decillion	10^{60}	60	10
duodecillion	10^{39}	39	12	undecillion	10^{66}	66	11
tredecillion	10^{42}	42	13	duodecillion	10^{72}	72	12
quattuordecillion	10^{45}	45	14	tredecillion	10^{78}	78	13
quindecillion	10^{48}	48	15	quattuordecillion	10^{84}	84	14
sexdecillion	10^{51}	51	16	quindecillion	10^{90}	90	15
septendecillion	10^{54}	54	17	sexdecillion	10^{96}	96	16
octodecillion	10^{57}	57	18	septendecillion	10^{102}	102	17
novemdecillion	10^{60}	60	19	octodecillion	10^{108}	108	18
vigintillion	10^{63}	63	20	novemdecillion	10^{114}	114	19
centillion	10^{303}	303	100	vigintillion	10^{120}	120	20
				centillion	10^{600}	600	100

[1]The American system of numeration for denominations above one million is the same as the French system, and the British system corresponds to the German. In the American system each of the denominations above 1,000 millions (the American *billion*) is 1,000 times the one preceding (one trillion=1,000 billions; one quadrillion=1,000 trillions). In the British system the first denomination above 1,000 millions (the British *milliard*) is 1,000 times the preceding one, but each of the denominations above 1,000 milliards (the British *billion*) is 1,000,000 times the preceding one (one trillion=1,000,000 billions; one quadrillion=1,000,000 trillions).
[2]For convenience in reading large numerals the thousands, millions, etc., are usually separated by commas (21,530; 1,155,465) or by half spaces (1 155 465). Serial numbers (as a social security number or the engine number of a car) are often written with hyphens (583-695-20).

nu·mis·mat·ic \ˌn(y)ü-məz-ˈmat-ik, -mə-ˈsmat-\ *adj* [F *numismatique*, fr. L *nomismat-*, *nomisma* coin, fr. Gk, custom, coin; akin to Gk *nomos* custom, law — more at NIMBLE] **1 :** of or relating to numismatics **2 :** of or relating to currency **:** MONETARY — **nu·mis·mat·i·cal·ly** \-i-k(ə-)lē\ *adv*

nu·mis·mat·ics \-iks\ *n pl but sing in constr* **:** the study or collection of coins, tokens, medals, paper money, and similar objects — **nu·mis·ma·tist** \n(y)ü-ˈmiz-mət-əst\ *n*

num·mu·lar \ˈnəm-yə-lər\ *adj* [F *nummulaire*, fr. L *nummulus*, dim. of *nummus* coin, fr. Gk *nomimos* customary; akin to Gk *nomos*] **:** circular or oval in shape ⟨~ lesions⟩

num·mu·lit·ic limestone \ˌnəm-yə-ˌlit-ik-\ *n* [NL *Nummulites*, genus of foraminifers, fr. L *nummulus*] **:** the most widely distributed and distinctive formation of the Eocene in Europe, Asia, and northern Africa

num·skull \ˈnəm-ˌskəl\ *n* [*numb* + *skull*] **1 :** a dull or stupid person **:** DUNCE **2 :** a thick or muddled head

[1]**nun** \ˈnən\ *n* [ME, fr. OE *nunne*, fr. LL *nonna*] **:** a woman belonging to a religious order; *esp* **:** one under solemn vows of poverty, chastity, and obedience **syn** see RELIGIOUS

[2]**nun** \ˈnün\ *n* [Heb *nūn*] **:** the 14th letter of the Hebrew alphabet — symbol נ or ן

Nunc Di·mit·tis \ˌnəŋk-də-ˈmit-əs, -dī-; ˌnu̇ŋk-də-\ *n* [L, now lettest thou depart; fr. the first words of the canticle] **:** the prayer of Simeon in Luke 2:29–32 used as a canticle

nun·ci·a·ture \ˈnən(t)-sē-ə-ˌchu̇(ə)r, ˈnu̇n(t)-, -chər, -ˌt(y)u̇(ə)r\ *n* [It *nunciatura*, fr. *nuncio*] **1 :** the office or period of office of a nuncio **2 :** a papal delegation headed by a nuncio

nun·cio \ˈnən(t)-sē-ˌō, ˈnu̇n(t)-\ *n* [It, fr. L *nuntius* messenger, message] **:** a papal legate of the highest rank permanently accredited to a civil government

nun·cle \ˈnəŋ-kəl\ *n* [by alter. (resulting fr. incorrect division of *an uncle*)] *chiefly dial* **:** UNCLE

nun·cu·pa·tive \ˈnən-kyü-ˌpāt-iv, ˈnəŋ-; ˌnən-ˈkyü-pət-\ *adj* [ML *nuncupativus*, fr. LL, so-called, fr. L *nuncupatus*, pp. of *nuncupare* to name, contr. of *nomen capere*, fr. *nomen* name + *capere* to take — more at NAME, HEAVE] **:** not written **:** ORAL ⟨a ~ will⟩

nun·nery \ˈnən-(ə-)rē\ *n* **1 :** a convent of nuns **2 :** an order of nuns **:** SISTERHOOD **syn** see CLOISTER

[1]**nup·tial** \ˈnəp-shəl, -chəl, *nonstand* -chə-wəl\ *adj* [L *nuptialis*, fr. *nuptiae*, pl., wedding, fr. *nuptus*, pp. of *nubere* to marry; akin to Gk *nymphē* bride, nymph] **1 :** of or relating to marriage or the marriage ceremony **2 :** characteristic of the breeding season **syn** see MATRIMONIAL

[2]**nuptial** *n* **:** MARRIAGE, WEDDING — usu. used in pl.

[1]**nurse** \ˈnərs\ *n* [ME, fr. OF *nurice*, fr. LL *nutricia*, fr. L, fem. of *nutricius* nourishing — more at NUTRITIOUS] **1 a :** a woman who suckles an infant not her own **b :** a woman who takes care of a young child **2 :** one that looks after, fosters, or advises **3 :** one skilled or trained in caring for the sick or infirm esp. under the supervision of a physician **4 a :** a worker of a social insect that cares for the young **b :** a female mammal used to suckle the young of another

[2]**nurse** *vb* [ME *nurshen* to nourish, contr. of *nurishen*] *vt* **1 a :** to nourish at the breast **:** SUCKLE **b :** to take nourishment from the breast of **2 :** REAR, EDUCATE **3 a :** to promote the development or progress of **b :** to manage with care or economy **c :** to take charge of and watch over **4 a :** to care for and wait on (as a sick person) **b :** to attempt to cure by care and treatment **5 :** to hold in one's memory or consideration **6 a :** to use, handle, or operate carefully so as to conserve energy or avoid injury or pain **b :** to use sparingly ~ *vi* **1 a :** to give suck **b :** to feed at the breast **:** SUCK **2 :** to act or serve as a nurse — **nurs·er** *n*

nurse·maid \ˈnər-ˌsmād\ *n* **:** one who is regularly employed to look after children

nur·sery \ˈnərs-(ə-)rē\ *n* **1** *obs* **:** attentive care **:** FOSTERAGE **2 a :** a child's bedroom **b :** a place where children are temporarily cared for in their parents' absence **c :** DAY NURSERY **3 a :** something that fosters, develops, or promotes **b :** a place in which persons are trained or educated **4 :** an area where plants (as trees and shrubs) are grown for transplanting, for use as stocks for budding and grafting, or for sale

nur·sery·maid \-ˌmād\ *n* **:** NURSEMAID

nur·sery·man \-mən\ *n* **:** one whose occupation is the cultivation of plants (as trees and shrubs)

nursery rhyme *n* **:** a tale in rhymed verse for children

nursery school *n* **:** a school for children usu. under five years

nursing bottle *n* **:** a bottle with a rubber nipple used in supplying food to infants

nurs·ling \ˈnər-sliŋ\ *n* **1 :** one that is solicitously cared for **2 :** a nursing child

[1]**nur·ture** \ˈnər-chər\ *n* [ME, fr. MF *norriture*, fr. LL *nutritura* act of nursing, fr. L *nutritus*, pp. of *nutrire* to suckle, nourish — more at NOURISH] **1 :** TRAINING, UPBRINGING **2 :** something that nourishes **:** FOOD **3 :** the sum of the influences modifying the expression of the genetic potentialities of an organism

[2]**nurture** *vt* **nur·tur·ing** \ˈnərch-(ə-)riŋ\ **1 :** to supply with nourishment **2 :** EDUCATE **3 :** to further the development of **:** FOSTER — **nur·tur·er** \ˈnər-chər-ər\ *n*

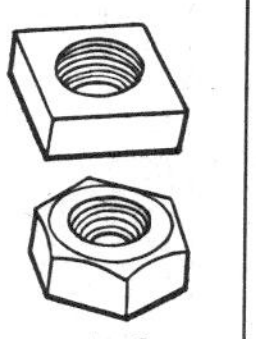

nuts 3

[1]**nut** \ˈnət\ *n* [ME *nute*, *note*, fr. OE *hnutu;* akin to OHG *nuz* nut, L *nux*] **1 a** (1) **:** a hard-shelled dry fruit or seed with a separable rind or shell and interior kernel (2) **:** the kernel of a nut **b :** a dry indehiscent one-seeded fruit with a woody pericarp **2 :** something resembling a nut in the difficulty it presents; *esp* **:** a hard problem or undertaking **3 :** a perforated block usu. of metal that has an internal screw thread and is used on a bolt or screw for tightening or holding something **4 :** the ridge in a stringed musical instrument over which the strings pass on the upper end of the fingerboard **5** *pl* **:** NONSENSE — often used interjectionally **6** *slang* **:** a person's head **7 a :** a foolish, eccentric, or crazy person **b :** ENTHUSIAST **8 :** EN 2 — **nut·like** \-ˌlīk\ *adj*

[2]**nut** *vi* **nut·ted; nut·ting :** to gather or seek nuts

nu·tant \ˈn(y)üt-ᵊnt\ *adj* [L *nutant-*, *nutans*, prp. of *nutare*] **:** DROOPING, NODDING

nu·ta·tion \n(y)ü-ˈtā-shən\ *n* [L *nutation-*, *nutatio*, fr. *nutatus*, pp. of *nutare* to nod, rock, freq. of *nuere* to nod — more at NUMEN] **1 :** the act of nodding the head **2 :** a libratory motion of the earth's axis like the nodding of a top **3 :** a spontaneous usu. spiral movement of a growing plant part — **nu·ta·tion·al** \-shnəl, -shən-ᵊl\ *adj*

nut–brown \ˈnət-ˈbrau̇n\ *adj* **:** of the color of a brown nut

nut·crack·er \-ˌkrak-ər\ *n* **:** an implement for cracking nuts

nut·hatch \ˈnət-ˌhach\ *n* [ME *notehache*, fr. *note* nut + *hache* ax, fr. OF, battle-ax — more at HASH] **:** any of various birds (family Sittidae) intermediate in character and habits between the titmice and creepers

nut·let \ˈnət-lət\ *n* **1 a :** a small nut **b :** a small fruit similar to a nut **2 :** the stone of a drupelet

nut·meg \ˈnət-ˌmeg, -ˌmāg\ *n* [ME *notemuge*, deriv. of OProv. *noz muscada*, fr. *noz* nut (fr. L *nuc-*, *nux*) + *muscada*, fem. of *muscat* musky — more at MUSCAT] **:** an aromatic seed used as a spice; *also* **:** a tree (*Myristica fragrans* of the family Myristicaceae, the nutmeg family) native to the Moluccas that produces it

nut·pick \ˈnət-ˌpik\ *n* **:** a small sharp-pointed table implement for extracting the kernels from nuts

nu·tria \ˈn(y)ü-trē-ə\ *n* [Sp, modif. of L *lutra* otter; akin to OE *oter* otter] **1 :** COYPU 1 **2 :** the durable usu. light brown fur of the coypu

[1]**nu·tri·ent** \ˈn(y)ü-trē-ənt\ *adj* [L *nutrient-*, *nutriens*, prp. of *nutrire* to nourish — more at NOURISH] **:** furnishing nourishment

[2]**nutrient** *n* **:** a nutritive substance or ingredient

nu·tri·ment \ˈn(y)ü-trə-mənt\ *n* [L *nutrimentum*, fr. *nutrire*] **:** something that nourishes or promotes growth and repairs the natural wastage of organic life

nu·tri·tion \n(y)u̇-ˈtrish-ən\ *n* [MF, fr. LL *nutrition-*, *nutritio*, fr. L *nutritus*, pp. of *nutrire*] **:** the act or process of nourishing or being nourished; *specif* **:** the sum of the processes by which an animal or plant takes in and utilizes food substances — **nu·tri·tion·al** \-ˈtrish-nəl, -ən-ᵊl\ *adj* — **nu·tri·tion·al·ly** \-ē\ *adv*

nu·tri·tion·ist \-ˈtrish-(ə-)nəst\ *n* **:** a specialist in the study of nutrition

nu·tri·tious \n(y)u̇-ˈtrish-əs\ *adj* [L *nutricius*, fr. *nutric-*, *nutrix* nurse; akin to L *nutrire* to nourish — more at NOURISH] **:** NOURISHING — **nu·tri·tious·ly** *adv* — **nu·tri·tious·ness** *n*

nu·tri·tive \ˈn(y)ü-trət-iv\ *adj* **1 :** of or relating to nutrition **2 :** NUTRITIOUS — **nu·tri·tive·ly** *adv*

nutritive ratio *n* **:** the ratio of digestible protein to other digestible nutrients in a foodstuff or ration

nuts \ˈnəts\ *adj* **1 :** ENTHUSIASTIC, KEEN **2 :** CRAZY, DEMENTED

nut·shell \ˈnət-ˌshel\ *n* **1 :** the hard external covering in which the kernel of a nut is enclosed **2 :** something of small size, amount, or scope — **in a nutshell :** in a small compass

nut·ti·ness \ˈnət-ē-nəs\ *n* **:** the quality or state of being nutty

nut·ty \ˈnət-ē\ *adj* **1 :** having or producing nuts **2 :** CRACKBRAINED, ECCENTRIC; *also* **:** mentally unbalanced **3 :** having a flavor like that of nuts

nux vom·i·ca \ˌnəks-ˈväm-i-kə\ *n, pl* **nux vomica** [NL, lit., emetic nut] **:** the poisonous seed of an Asiatic tree (*Strychnos nux-vomica* of the family Loganiaceae) that contains several alkaloids but chiefly strychnine and brucine; *also* **:** the tree yielding nux vomica

nuz·zle \ˈnəz-əl\ *vb* **nuz·zling** \-(ə-)liŋ\ [ME *noselen*, to bring the nose towards the ground, fr. *nose*] *vi* **1 :** to work with or as if with the nose; *esp* **:** to root, rub, or snuff something **2 :** to lie close or snug **:** NESTLE ~ *vt* **:** to root, rub, or touch with or as if with the nose **:** NUDGE

nyc·ta·lo·pia \ˌnik-tə-ˈlō-pē-ə\ *n* [LL] **:** NIGHT BLINDNESS — **nyc·ta·lo·pic** \-ˈlō-pik, -ˈläp-ik\ *adj*

ny·lon \ˈnī-ˌlän\ *n, often attrib* [coined word] **1 :** any of numerous strong tough elastic synthetic materials made usu. from a dicarboxylic acid and a diamine, fashioned into fibers, filaments, bristles, or sheets, and used esp. in textiles and plastics **2** *pl* **:** stockings made of nylon

nymph \ˈnim(p)f\ *n, pl* **nymphs** \ˈnim(p)fs, ˈnim(p)s\ [ME *nimphe*, fr. MF, fr. L *nympha* bride, nymph, fr. Gk *nymphē* — more at NUPTIAL] **1 :** one of the minor divinities of nature in ancient mythology represented as beautiful maidens dwelling in the mountains, forests, meadows, and waters **2 :** GIRL **3 :** any of various immature insects; *esp* **:** a larva of an insect with incomplete metamorphosis that differs chiefly in size and degree of differentiation from the imago — **nymph·al** \ˈnim(p)-fəl\ *adj*

nym·pho·lep·sy \ˈnim(p)-fə-ˌlep-sē\ *n* [*nympholept*, fr. Gk *nympholēptos* frenzied, lit., caught by nymphs, fr. *nymphē* + *lambanein* to seize — more at CATCH] **1 :** a demoniac enthusiasm held by the ancients to seize one bewitched by a nymph **2 :** a frenzy of emotion — **nym·pho·lept** \-ˌlept\ *n* — **nym·pho·lep·tic** \ˌnim(p)-fə-ˈlep-tik\ *adj*

nym·pho·ma·nia \ˌnim(p)-fə-ˈmā-nē-ə, -nyə\ *n* [NL, fr. *nymphae* inner lips of the vulva (fr. L, pl. of *nympha*) + LL *mania*] **:** excessive sexual desire by a female — **nym·pho·ma·ni·ac** \-nē-ˌak\ *n or adj*

nys·tag·mic \nis-ˈtag-mik\ *adj* [NL] **:** of or constituting nystagmus

nys·tag·mus \-məs\ *n* [NL, fr. Gk *nystagmos* drowsiness, fr. *nystazein* to doze; akin to Lith *snusti* to doze] **:** a rapid involuntary oscillation of the eyeballs (as from dizziness)

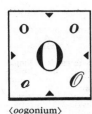

O o O o

1o \ˈō\ *n, often cap, often attrib* **1 a :** the 15th letter of the English alphabet **b :** a graphic representation of this letter **c :** a speech counterpart of orthographic *o* **2 :** a graphic device for reproducing the letter *o* **3 :** one designated *o* esp. as the 14th or when j is used for the 10th the 15th in order or class **4 :** something shaped like the letter O; *esp* **:** ZERO

2O *var of* OH

o- *or* **oo-** *comb form* [Gk ōi-, ōio-, fr. ōion — more at EGG] **:** egg ⟨*oology*⟩; *specif* **:** ovum ⟨*oogonium*⟩

1-o \(ˌ)ō\ *n suffix* [perh. fr. 1*oh*] **:** one that is, has the qualities of, or is associated with ⟨buck*o*⟩

2-o \(ˌ)ō, ˈō\ *interj suffix* [prob. fr. 1*oh*] — in interjections formed from other parts of speech ⟨cheeri*o*⟩ ⟨right*o*⟩

-o- [ME, fr. OF, fr. L, fr. Gk, thematic vowel of many nouns and adjectives in combination] — used as a connective vowel orig. to join word elements of Greek origin and now also to join word elements of Latin or other origin ⟨drunk*o*meter⟩ ⟨elast*o*mer⟩

o' *also* **o** \ə\ *prep* [ME *o, o-,* contr. of *on & of*] **1** *chiefly dial* **:** ON **2 :** OF ⟨one *o'*clock⟩

oaf \ˈōf\ *n* [of Scand origin; akin to ON *alfr* elf — more at ELF] **1 :** a stupid person **:** BOOB **2 :** a big clumsy slow-witted person **:** LUMMOX — **oaf·ish** \ˈō-fish\ *adj* — **oaf·ish·ly** *adv* — **oaf·ish·ness** *n*

oak \ˈōk\ *n, pl* **oaks** *or* **oak** *often attrib* [ME *ook,* fr. OE *āc;* akin to OHG *eih* oak, Gk *aigilōps,* a kind of oak] **1 :** a tree or shrub (genera *Quercus* or *Lithocarpus*) of the beech family **2 a :** the tough hard durable wood of an oak tree **b :** the leaves of an oak used as decoration

oak apple *n* **:** an oak gall produced by a gall wasp (esp. *Amphibolips concluentus* or *Andricus californicus*)

oak·en \ˈō-kən\ *adj* **:** of or relating to oak

oak–leaf cluster \ˈō-ˌklēf-\ *n* **:** a bronze or silver cluster of oak leaves and acorns added to various military decorations to signify a second or subsequent award of the basic decoration

oa·kum \ˈō-kəm\ *n* [ME *okum,* fr. OE *ācumba* tow, fr. *ā-* (separative & perfective prefix) + *-cumba* (akin to OE *camb* comb) — more at ABIDE] **:** loosely twisted hemp or jute fiber impregnated with tar or a tar derivative and used in caulking seams and packing joints

oak wilt *n* **:** a destructive disease of oak trees caused by a fungus (*Chalara quercina*) and characterized by wilting, discoloration, and defoliation

1oar \ˈō(ə)r, ˈȯ(ə)r\ *n* [ME *oor,* fr. OE *ār;* akin to ON *ār* oar] **1 :** a long pole with a broad blade at one end used for propelling or steering a boat **2 :** OARSMAN — **oared** \ˈō(ə)rd, ˈȯ(ə)rd\ *adj*

2oar *vt* **:** to propel with or as if with oars **:** ROW ~ *vi* **:** to progress by or as if by using oars

oar·fish \ˈō(ə)r-ˌfish, ˈȯ(ə)r-\ *n* **:** any of several sea fishes (genus *Regalecus*) with narrow soft bodies from 20 to 30 feet long, a dorsal fin running the entire length of the body, and red-tipped anterior rays rising above the head

oar·lock \-ˌläk\ *n* **:** a U-shaped device for holding an oar in place

oars·man \ˈō(ə)rz-mən, ˈȯ(ə)rz-\ *n* **:** one who rows esp. in a racing crew

oa·sis \ō-ˈā-səs\ *n, pl* **oa·ses** \-ˈā-ˌsēz\ [LL, fr. Gk] **1 :** a fertile or green area in an arid region **2 :** something providing relief from the usual **:** REFUGE

oat \ˈōt\ *n, often attrib* [ME *ote,* fr. OE *āte*] **1 a** (1) **:** any of several grasses (genus *Avena*); *esp* **:** a widely cultivated cereal grass (*Avena sativa*) (2) *usu pl but sing or pl in constr* **:** a crop or plot of the oat **b** *usu pl but sing or pl in constr* **:** oat seed **2** *archaic* **:** a reed instrument made of an oat straw

oat·cake \-ˌkāk\ *n* **:** a thin flat oatmeal cake

oat·en \ˈōt-ᵊn\ *adj* **:** of or relating to oats, oat straw, or oatmeal

oat grass *n* **:** WILD OAT 1a; *broadly* **:** one of several grasses resembling the oat

oath \ˈōth\ *n, pl* **oaths** \ˈōt͟hz, ˈōths\ [ME *ooth,* fr. OE *āth;* akin to OHG *eid* oath] **1 a** (1) **:** a solemn usu. formal calling upon God or a god to witness to the truth of what one says or to witness that one sincerely intends to do what one says (2) **:** a solemn attestation of the truth or inviolability of one's words **b :** something corroborated by an oath **c :** a form of expression used in taking an oath **2 :** an irreverent or careless use of a sacred name; *broadly* **:** SWEARWORD

oat·meal \ˈōt-ˌmēl, ōt-ˈmē(ə)l\ *n* **1 a :** meal made from oats **b :** rolled oats **2 :** porridge made from ground or rolled oats

ob- *prefix* [NL, fr. L, in the way, against, towards, fr. *ob* in the way of, on account of — more at EPI-] **:** inversely ⟨*ob*ovate⟩ ⟨*ob*cordate⟩

Oba·di·ah \ˌō-bə-ˈdī-ə\ *n* [Heb *ʻŌbhadhyāh*] **:** a minor Hebrew prophet

1ob·bli·ga·to \ˌäb-lə-ˈgät-(ˌ)ō\ *adj* [It, obligatory, fr. pp. of *obbligare* to oblige, fr. L *obligare*] **:** not to be omitted **:** OBLIGATORY — used as a direction in music

2obbligato *n, pl* **obbligatos** *also* **ob·bli·ga·ti** \-ˈgät-ē\ **1 :** a subordinate part to a solo in music **2 :** a persistent background motif

ob·con·ic \(ˈ)äb-ˈkän-ik\ *adj* **:** conical with the apex below or forming the point of attachment

ob·cor·date \-ˈkȯ(ə)r-ˌdāt\ *adj* **:** heart-shaped with the notch apical ⟨~ leaf⟩

ob·du·ra·cy \ˈäb-d(y)ə-rə-sē; äb-ˈd(y)u̇r-ə-, əb-\ *n* **:** the quality or state of being obdurate

ob·du·rate \ˈäb-d(y)ə-rət; äb-ˈd(y)u̇r-ət, əb-, ˈäb-,\ *adj* [ME, fr. L *obduratus,* pp. of *obdurare* to harden, fr. *ob-* against + *durus* hard — more at DURING] **1 a :** hardened in feelings **b :** stubbornly persistent in wrongdoing **2 :** resistant to persuasion or softening influences **:** UNYIELDING **syn** see INFLEXIBLE — **ob·du·rate·ly** *adv* — **ob·du·rate·ness** *n*

obe·ah \ˈō-bē-ə\ *also* **obi** \ˈō-bē\ *n, often cap* [of African origin; akin to Twi *ᵃ¹bi²ᵃ³,* a creeper used in making charms] **:** a system of belief among Negroes chiefly of the British West Indies, the Guianas, and the southeastern U.S. that is characterized by the use of sorcery and magic ritual

obe·di·ence \ō-ˈbēd-ē-ən(t)s, ə-\ *n* **1 a :** an act or instance of obeying **b :** the quality or state of being obedient **2 :** a sphere of jurisdiction; *esp* **:** an ecclesiastical or sometimes secular dominion **3 :** a usu. written injunction from a religious superior to one of the congregation

obe·di·ent \-ənt\ *adj* [ME, fr. OF, fr. L *oboedient-, oboediens,* fr. prp. of *oboedire* to obey — more at OBEY] **:** submissive to the restraint or command of authority — **obe·di·ent·ly** *adv*

syn DOCILE, TRACTABLE, AMENABLE: OBEDIENT implies compliance with the demands or requests of one in authority; DOCILE implies a predisposition to submit to control or guidance; TRACTABLE suggests having a character that permits easy handling or managing; AMENABLE suggests a willingness to yield to demands, advice, or contrary suggestion

obei·sance \ō-ˈbās-ᵊn(t)s, ə-, -ˈbēs-\ *n* [ME *obeisaunce* obedience, obeisance, fr. MF *obeissance,* fr. *obeissant,* prp. of *obeir* to obey] **1 :** a movement of the body made in token of respect or submission **:** BOW **2 :** DEFERENCE, HOMAGE **syn** see HONOR — **obei·sant** \-ᵊnt\ *adj*

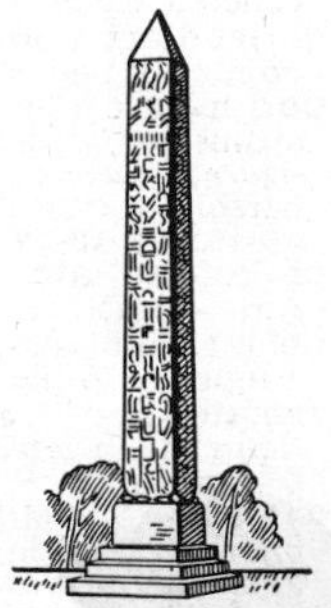

obelisk

ob·e·lisk \ˈäb-ə-ˌlisk, -lәsk\ *n* [MF *obelisque,* fr. L *obeliscus,* fr. Gk *obeliskos,* fr. dim. of *obelos*] **1 :** an upright 4-sided usu. monolithic pillar that gradually tapers as it rises and terminates in a pyramid **2 a :** OBELUS **b :** DAGGER 2b

ob·e·lize \-ˌlīz\ *vt* **:** to designate or annotate with an obelus

ob·e·lus \-ləs\ *n, pl* **ob·e·li** \-ˌlī, -ˌlē\ [LL, fr. Gk *obelos* spit, pointed pillar, obelus] **:** a symbol — or ÷ used in ancient manuscripts to mark a suspected passage

Ober·on \ˈō-bə-ˌrän, -rən\ *n* [F, fr. OF *Auberon*] **:** king of the fairies in medieval folklore

obese \ō-ˈbēs\ *adj* [L *obesus,* fr. pp. of *obedere* to eat up, fr. *ob-* against + *edere* to eat — more at OB-, EAT] **:** excessively fat **:** CORPULENT — **obe·si·ty** \ō-ˈbē-sət-ē\ *n*

obey \ō-ˈbā, ə-\ *vb* [ME *obeien,* fr. OF *obeir,* fr. L *oboedire,* fr. *ob-* towards + *-oedire* (akin to *audire* to hear) — more at OB-, AUDIBLE] *vt* **1 :** to follow the commands or guidance of **2 :** to comply with **:** EXECUTE ⟨~ an order⟩ ~ *vi* **:** to behave obediently — **obey·er** *n*

ob·fus·cate \ˈäb-fə-ˌskāt; äb-ˈfəs-ˌkāt, əb-\ *vt* [LL *obfuscatus,* pp. of *obfuscare,* fr. L *ob-* in the way + *fuscus* dark brown — more at OB-, DUSK] **1 a :** DARKEN **b :** to make obscure **2 :** CONFUSE — **ob·fus·ca·tion** \ˌäb-(ˌ)fəs-ˈkā-shən\ *n* — **ob·fus·ca·to·ry** \äb-ˈfəs-kə-ˌtōr-ē, əb-, -ˌtȯr-\ *adj*

obi \ˈō-bē\ *n* [Jap] **:** a broad sash worn with a Japanese kimono

obit \ō-ˈbit, ˈō-bət, *esp Brit* ˈäb-it\ *n* [ME, fr. MF, fr. L *obitus* decease, fr. *obitus,* pp. of *obire* to go to meet, die, fr. *ob-* in the way + *ire* to go — more at ISSUE] **:** OBITUARY

obi·ter dic·tum \ˌō-bət-ər-ˈdik-təm\ *n, pl* **obiter dic·ta** \-tə\ [LL, lit., something said in passing] **1 :** an incidental and collateral opinion that is uttered by a judge but is not binding **2 :** an incidental remark or observation

obit·u·ary \ə-ˈbich-ə-ˌwer-ē, ō-, -ˈbich-ə-rē\ *n* [ML *obituarium,* fr. L *obitus* decease] **:** a notice of a person's death usu. with a short biographical account — **obituary** *adj*

1ob·ject \ˈäb-jikt\ *n* [ME, fr. ML *objectum,* fr. L, neut. of *obicere* to throw in the way, present, hinder, fr. *ob-* in the way + *jacere* to throw — more at OB-, JET] **1 a :** something that is or is capable of being seen, touched, or otherwise sensed **b :** something physical or mental of which a subject is cognitively aware **2 :** something that arouses an emotion in an observer **3 :** END, GOAL; *also* **:** MOTIVE, PURPOSE **4 :** a thing that forms an element of or constitutes the subject matter of an investigation or science **5 a :** a noun or noun equivalent denoting in verb constructions that on or toward which the action of a verb is directed **b :** a noun or noun equivalent in a prepositional phrase **syn** see INTENTION — **ob·ject·less** \-jik-tləs\ *adj*

2ob·ject \əb-ˈjekt\ *vb* [ME *objecten,* fr. L *objectus,* pp. of *obicere* to throw in the way, object] *vt* **:** to offer in opposition **:** cite as an objection ~ *vi* **1 :** to oppose something **2 :** to feel distaste for something **:** DISAPPROVE — **ob·jec·tor** \-ˈjek-tər\ *n*

syn OBJECT, PROTEST, REMONSTRATE, EXPOSTULATE, KICK mean to oppose by arguing against. OBJECT stresses dislike or aversion; PROTEST suggests an orderly presentation of objections in speech or writing; REMONSTRATE implies an attempt to convince by warning or reproving; EXPOSTULATE suggests an earnest explanation of one's objection and firm insistence on change; KICK suggests more informally a strenuous protesting or complaining

object ball \ˈäb-jik(t)-\ *n* **:** the ball first struck by the cue ball in pool or billiards; *also* **:** a ball hit by the cue ball

object glass \ˈäb-jik(t)-\ *n* **:** OBJECTIVE 5

ob·jec·ti·fi·ca·tion \əb-ˌjek-tə-fə-ˈkā-shən\ *n* **1 :** an act or instance of making objective **2 :** the state of being objectified

ob·jec·ti·fy \əb-ˈjek-tə-ˌfī\ *vt* **1 a :** to cause to become an object **b :** to make objective **2 :** EXTERNALIZE 2

ob·jec·tion \əb-ˈjek-shən\ *n* **1 :** an act of objecting **2 a :** a reason or argument presented in opposition **b :** a feeling of disapproval

ob·jec·tion·able \-sh(ə-)nə-bəl\ *adj* **:** arousing objection **:** OFFENSIVE — **ob·jec·tion·able·ness** *n* — **ob·jec·tion·ably** \-blē\ *adv*

1ob·jec·tive \əb-ˈjek-tiv, äb-\ *adj* **1 a :** of or relating to an object of action or feeling **b :** having the status of or constituting an object: as (1) **:** existing only in relation to a knowing subject or willing agent (2) **:** existing independent of mind (3) **:** belonging to the sensible world and being intersubjectively observable or verifiable esp. by scientific methods (4) *of a symptom of disease* **:** perceptible to persons other than an affected individual **c :** emphasizing or expressing the nature of reality as it is apart from personal reflections or feelings **d :** expressing or involving the use of facts without distortion by personal feelings or prejudices **2 :** derived from sense perception **3 :** belonging or relating to an object to be delineated **4 :** relating to, designating, or constituting the case that follows a preposition or a transitive verb **syn** see FAIR, MATERIAL — **ob·jec·tive·ly** *adv* — **ob·jec·tive·ness** *n*

2objective *n* **1 :** something toward which effort is directed **:** an aim or end of action **:** GOAL, OBJECT **2 :** something that is objective;

O P

specif **:** something external to the mind **3 a :** the objective case **b :** a word in the objective case **4 :** a strategic position to be attained or purpose to be achieved by a military or naval operation **5 :** a lens or system of lenses that forms an image of an object **syn** see INTENTION

objective complement *n* **:** a noun, adjective, or pronoun used in the predicate as complement to a verb and as qualifier of its direct object

ob·jec·tiv·ism \əb-ˈjek-tiv-ˌiz-əm, äb-\ *n* **1 :** any of various theories stressing objective reality esp. as distinguished from subjective experience or appearance **2 :** an ethical theory that moral good is objectively real **3 :** the theory or practice of objective art or literature — **ob·jec·tiv·ist** \-əst\ *n* — **ob·jec·tiv·is·tic** \əb-ˌjek-tiv-ˈis-tik, (ˌ)äb-\ *adj*

ob·jec·tiv·i·ty \ˌäb-ˌjek-ˈtiv-ət-ē, əb-\ *n* **:** the quality or state of being objective

object lesson \ˈäb-jik-ˌtles-ᵊn\ *n* **1 :** a lesson having a material object as the basis of instruction **2 :** something that teaches by a concrete example

ob·jet d'art \ˌȯb-ˌzhā-ˈdär\ *n, pl* **ob·jets d'art** *same*\ [F, lit., art object] **1 :** an article of some artistic value **2 :** CURIO

ob·jur·gate \ˈäb-jər-ˌgāt\ *vt* [L *objurgatus*, pp. of *objurgare*, fr. *ob-* against + *jurgare* to quarrel, lit., to take to law, fr. *jur-*, *jus* law + *-igare* (fr. *agere* to lead) — more at OB-, JUST, AGENT] **:** to denounce harshly **:** CASTIGATE — **ob·jur·ga·tion** \ˌäb-jər-ˈgā-shən\ *n* — **ob·jur·ga·to·ry** \əb-ˈjər-gə-ˌtōr-ē, -ˌtȯr-\ *adj*

ob·lan·ceo·late \(ˈ)äb-ˈlan(t)-sē-ə-ˌlāt\ *adj* **:** inversely lanceolate ⟨an ~ leaf⟩

oblast \ˈō-bləst, -ˌbläst\ *n* [Russ *oblast'*] **:** a political subdivision of a republic in the U.S.S.R.

1oblate \äb-ˈlāt, əb-, ōb-, ˈäb-ˌ\ *adj* [prob. fr. NL *oblatus*, fr. *ob-* + *-latus* (as in *prolatus* prolate)] **:** flattened or depressed at the poles ⟨~ spheroid⟩ — **oblate·ness** *n*

2ob·late \ˈäb-ˌlāt\ *n* [ML *oblatus*, lit., one offered up, fr. L, pp. of *offerre*] **1 :** a layman living in a monastery under a modified rule and without vows **2** *cap* **:** a member of one of several Roman Catholic communities of men or women

obla·tion \ə-ˈblā-shən, ō-\ *n* [ME *oblacioun*, fr. MF *oblation*, fr. LL *oblation-*, *oblatio*, fr. L *oblatus*, pp. of *offerre* to offer] **1 a :** a religious offering of something inanimate **b** *cap* **:** the act of offering the eucharistic elements to God **2 :** something offered in worship

1ob·li·gate \ˈäb-li-gət, -lə-ˌgāt\ *adj* **1 :** restricted to a particular mode of life ⟨an ~ parasite⟩ **2 :** ESSENTIAL, NECESSARY — **ob·li·gate·ly** *adv*

2ob·li·gate \ˈäb-lə-ˌgāt\ *vt* [L *obligatus*, pp. of *obligare*] **1 a :** to bind legally or morally **:** CONSTRAIN **b :** OBLIGE 2a **2 :** to commit (as funds) to meet an obligation

ob·li·ga·tion \ˌäb-lə-ˈgā-shən\ *n* **1 :** an act of obligating oneself to a course of action **2 a** (1) **:** an obligating factor that binds one to a course of action (2) **:** the power in such a factor **b :** a bond with a condition annexed and a penalty for nonfulfillment; *broadly* **:** a formal and binding agreement or acknowledgment of a liability **c :** an investment security **3 :** something that one is bound to do **:** DUTY **4 :** INDEBTEDNESS **5 :** money committed to a particular purpose **:** LIABILITY

syn OBLIGATION, DUTY mean something that one is bound as a responsible person to do or refrain from doing. OBLIGATION implies an immediate constraint imposed by circumstances; DUTY suggests a more general but greater impulsion on moral or ethical grounds

oblig·a·to·ri·ly \ə-ˌblig-ə-ˈtōr-ə-lē, ä-, -ˈtȯr-; ˌäb-li-gə-\ *adv* **:** in an obligatory manner

oblig·a·to·ry \ə-ˈblig-ə-ˌtōr-ē, ä-, -ˌtȯr-; ˈäb-li-gə-\ *adj* **1 :** binding in law or conscience **2 :** relating to or enforcing an obligation ⟨a writ ~⟩ **3 :** REQUIRED, MANDATORY **4 :** OBLIGATE 1

oblige \ə-ˈblīj\ *vb* [ME *obligen*, fr. OF *obliger*, fr. L *obligare*, lit., to bind to, fr. *ob-* towards + *ligare* to bind — more at LIGATURE] *vt* **1 :** FORCE, COMPEL **2 a :** to bind by a favor or service **b :** to do a favor for ~ *vi* **:** to do something as a favor **syn** see FORCE — **oblig·er** *n*

ob·li·gee \ˌäb-lə-ˈjē\ *n* **1 :** one to whom another is obligated **2 :** one who is obliged

oblig·ing \ə-ˈblī-jiŋ\ *adj* **:** willing to do favors **:** ACCOMMODATING **syn** see AMIABLE — **oblig·ing·ly** \-jiŋ-lē\ *adv* — **oblig·ing·ness** *n*

ob·li·gor \ˌäb-lə-ˈgȯ(ə)r, -ˈjȯ(ə)r\ *n* **:** one that places himself under a legal obligation

1oblique \ō-ˈblēk, ə-, -ˈblīk; *military usu* ī\ *adj* [ME *oblike*, fr. L *obliquus*, fr. *ob-* towards + *-liquus* (akin to *ulna* elbow) — more at ELL] **1 a :** neither perpendicular nor parallel **:** INCLINED **b :** having the axis not perpendicular to the base ⟨~ cone⟩ **2 a :** not straightforward **:** INDIRECT **b :** DEVIOUS, UNDERHAND **3 :** situated obliquely and having one end not inserted on bone ⟨~ muscles⟩ **4 :** taken from an airplane with the camera directed horizontally or diagonally downward ⟨~ photograph⟩ **syn** see CROOKED — **oblique·ly** *adv* — **oblique·ness** *n*

2oblique *n* **1 :** something that is oblique **2 :** any of several oblique muscles; *esp* **:** one of the thin flat muscles forming the middle and outer layers of the lateral walls of the abdomen

3oblique *adv* **:** at a 45 degree angle ⟨to the right ~, march⟩

oblique angle *n* **:** an acute or obtuse angle

oblique case *n* **:** a grammatical case other than the nominative or vocative

obliq·ui·ty \ō-ˈblik-wət-ē, ə-\ *n* **1 :** DISHONESTY, PERVERSITY **2 a** (1) **:** deviation from parallelism or perpendicularity (2) **:** the amount of such deviation **:** DIVERGENCE **b :** the angle between the planes of the earth's equator and orbit having a mean value of 23°26′40″.16 in 1960 and diminishing 0″.47 per year ⟨~ of the ecliptic⟩ **3 a :** indirectness or deliberate obscurity of speech or conduct **b :** an obscure or confusing statement

oblit·er·ate \ə-ˈblit-ə-ˌrāt, ō-\ *vt* [L *oblitteratus*, pp. of *oblitterare*, fr. *ob* in the way of + *littera* letter — more at EPI-] **1 :** to make undecipherable or imperceptible by obscuring or wearing away **2 a :** to remove utterly from recognition or memory **b :** to destroy utterly all trace, indication, or significance of **c :** to cause to disappear **:** REMOVE **3 :** CANCEL **syn** see ERASE — **oblit·er·a·tion** \-ˌblit-ə-ˈrā-shən\ *n* — **oblit·er·a·tive** \-ˈblit-ə-ˌrāt-iv, -rət-\ *adj*

obliv·i·on \ə-ˈbliv-ē-ən, ō-, ä-\ *n* [ME, fr. MF, fr. L *oblivion-*, *oblivio*, fr. *oblivisci* to forget, perh. fr. *ob-* in the way + *levis* smooth — more at OB-, LIME] **1 :** an act or instance of forgetting **:** FORGETFULNESS **2 :** the quality or state of being forgotten **3 :** official ignoring of offenses **:** PARDON

obliv·i·ous \-ē-əs\ *adj* **1 :** lacking remembrance, memory, or mindful attention **2 :** lacking active conscious knowledge **:** UNAWARE **syn** see FORGETFUL — **obliv·i·ous·ly** *adv* — **obliv·i·ous·ness** *n*

ob·long \ˈäb-ˌlȯŋ\ *adj* [ME, fr. L *oblongus*, fr. *ob-* towards + *longus* long] **:** deviating from a square or circular form through elongation: **a :** rectangular with adjacent sides unequal **b :** rectangular with the normally horizontal dimension the greater — **oblong** *n*

ob·lo·quy \ˈäb-lə-kwē\ *n* [LL *obloquium*, fr. *obloqui* to speak against, fr. *ob-* against + *loqui* to speak — more at OB-] **1 :** strongly condemnatory utterance or language **2 :** the condition of one that is spoken ill of **:** bad repute **syn** see ABUSE

ob·nox·ious \äb-ˈnäk-shəs, əb-\ *adj* [L *obnoxius*, fr. *ob* in the way of, exposed to + *noxa* harm — more at EPI-, NOXIOUS] **1 :** liable esp. to a hurtful influence — used with *to* **2** *archaic* **:** deserving of censure **3 :** OFFENSIVE, REPUGNANT **syn** see REPUGNANT — **ob·nox·ious·ly** *adv* — **ob·nox·ious·ness** *n*

ob·nu·bi·late \äb-ˈn(y)ü-bə-ˌlāt\ *vt* [L *obnubilatus*, pp. of *obnubilare*, fr. *ob-* in the way + *nubilare* to be cloudy, fr. *nubilus* cloudy, fr. *nubes* cloud — more at OB-, NUANCE] **:** BECLOUD — **ob·nu·bi·la·tion** \(ˌ)äb-ˌn(y)ü-bə-ˈlā-shən\ *n*

oboe \ˈō-(ˌ)bō\ *n* [It, fr. F *hautbois* — more at HAUTBOIS] **1 :** a nontransposing woodwind instrument having a conical body, a double reed mouthpiece, and a nasal and penetrating tone quality **2 :** an organ reed stop with a tone resembling an oboe's

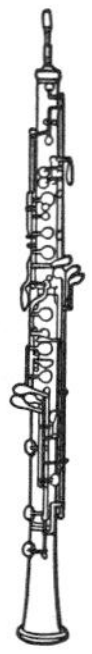
oboe

obo·ist \ˈō-ˌbō-əst, -bə-wəst\ *n* **:** an oboe player

obol \ˈäb-əl, ˈō-bəl\ *n* [L *obolus*, fr. Gk *obolos*; akin to Gk *obelos* spit] **:** an ancient Greek coin or weight equal to ⅙ drachma

ob·ovate \(ˈ)äb-ˈō-ˌvāt\ *adj* **:** ovate with the narrower end basal

ob·ovoid \-ˌvȯid\ *adj* **:** ovoid with the broad end toward the apex ⟨an ~ fruit⟩

ob·scene \äb-ˈsēn, əb-\ *adj* [MF, fr. L *obscenus*, *obscaenus*] **1 :** disgusting to the senses **:** REPULSIVE **2 :** abhorrent to morality or virtue; *specif* **:** designed to incite to lust or depravity **syn** see COARSE — **ob·scene·ly** *adv*

ob·scen·i·ty \-ˈsen-ət-ē\ *n* **1 :** the quality or state of being obscene **2 :** something that is obscene

ob·scur·ant \äb-ˈskyůr-ənt, əb-\ *or* **ob·scu·ran·tic** \ˌäb-skyə-ˈrant-ik\ *adj* **:** tending to make obscure — **ob·scurant** *n* — **ob·scu·ra·tion** \ˌäb-skyə-ˈrā-shən\ *n*

ob·scu·ran·tism \äb-ˈskyůr-ən-ˌtiz-əm, əb-; ˌäb-skyů-ˈran-\ *n* **1 :** opposition to the spread of knowledge **2 a :** deliberate vagueness or abstruseness **b :** an act or instance of obscurantism — **ob·scu·ran·tist** \-ən-təst, -ˈrant-əst\ *n or adj*

1ob·scure \äb-ˈskyů(ə)r, əb-\ *adj* [ME, fr. MF *obscur*, fr. L *obscurus*, fr. *ob-* in the way + *-scurus* (akin to Gk *keuthein* to conceal) — more at HIDE] **1 :** lacking or inadequately supplied with light **:** DARK, DUSKY **2 a :** withdrawn from the centers of human activity **:** REMOTE ⟨~ country village⟩ **b :** not readily understood or not clearly expressed **:** ABSTRUSE **c :** lacking showiness or prominence **:** INCONSPICUOUS, HUMBLE ⟨an ~ Roman poet⟩ **d :** not distinct **:** FAINT **3 :** constituting the unstressed vowel \ə\ or having unstressed \ə\ as its value — **ob·scure·ly** *adv* — **ob·scure·ness** *n*

syn OBSCURE, DARK, VAGUE, ENIGMATIC, CRYPTIC, AMBIGUOUS, EQUIVOCAL mean not clearly understandable. OBSCURE implies a hiding or veiling of meaning through some defect of expression or withholding of full knowledge; DARK implies an imperfect or clouded revelation often with ominous or sinister suggestion; VAGUE implies a lack of clear formulation because imperfectly conceived or thought out; ENIGMATIC stresses a puzzling, mystifying quality; CRYPTIC implies a purposely concealed meaning; AMBIGUOUS and EQUIVOCAL both imply the use of the same word in different senses, AMBIGUOUS usu. suggesting inadvertence and EQUIVOCAL an attempt to confuse or evade

2obscure *vt* **1 :** to make dark, dim, or indistinct **2 :** to conceal or hide by covering or intervening **3 :** to reduce (a vowel) to the value \ə\

3obscure *n* **:** OBSCURITY

ob·scu·ri·ty \-ˈskyůr-ət-ē\ *n* **1 :** the quality or state of being obscure **2 :** one that is obscure

ob·se·qui·ous \əb-ˈsē-kwē-əs, äb-\ *adj* [ME, fr. L *obsequiosus* compliant, fr. *obsequium* compliance, fr. *obsequi* to comply, fr. *ob-* toward + *sequi* to follow — more at OB-, SUE] **:** exhibiting a servile attentiveness or complaisance **:** SYCOPHANTIC **syn** see SUBSERVIENT — **ob·se·qui·ous·ly** *adv* — **ob·se·qui·ous·ness** *n*

ob·se·quy \ˈäb-sə-kwē\ *n* [ME *obsequie*, fr. MF, fr. ML *obsequiae* (pl.), alter. of L *exsequiae* — more at EXEQUY] **:** a funeral or burial rite — usu. used in pl.

ob·serv·able \əb-ˈzər-və-bəl\ *adj* **1 :** NOTEWORTHY **2 :** capable of being observed **:** DISCERNIBLE — **observable** *n* — **ob·serv·ably** \-blē\ *adv*

ob·ser·vance \-vən(t)s\ *n* **1 a :** a customary practice or ceremony **b :** a rule governing members of a religious order **2 :** an act or instance of following a custom, rule, or law **3 :** an act or instance of watching **:** OBSERVATION

1ob·ser·vant \əb-ˈzər-vənt\ *n, obs* **:** an assiduous or obsequious servant or attendant

2observant *adj* **1 :** paying strict attention **:** WATCHFUL **2 :** careful in observing **:** MINDFUL **3 :** quick to observe **:** KEEN — **ob·ser·vant·ly** *adv*

ob·ser·va·tion \ˌäb-sər-ˈvā-shən, -zər-\ *n* [MF, fr. L *observation-*, *observatio*, fr. *observatus*, pp. of *observare*] **1 :** an act or the faculty of observing **2 a :** an act of recognizing and noting a fact or occurrence often involving measurement with instruments **b :** a record so obtained **3 :** a judgment on or inference from what one has observed; *broadly* **:** REMARK, STATEMENT **4** *obs* **:** HEED **5 :** the condition of one that is observed — **observation** *adj* — **ob·ser·va·tion·al** \-shnəl, -shən-ᵊl\ *adj*

ob·ser·va·to·ry \əb-ˈzər-və-ˌtōr-ē, -ˌtȯr-\ *n* [prob. fr. NL *observatorium*, fr. L *observatus*] **1 :** a building or place given over to or equipped for observation of natural phenomena (as in astronomy); *also* **:** an institution whose primary purpose is making such observations **2 :** a situation or structure commanding a wide view **:** LOOKOUT

ob·serve \əb-ˈzərv\ *vb* [ME *observen*, fr. MF *observer*, fr. L *ob-*

servare to guard, watch, observe, fr. *ob-* in the way, toward + *servare* to keep — more at CONSERVE] *vt* **1 :** to conform one's action or practice to ⟨~ rules⟩ **2 :** to inspect or take note of as an augury, omen, or presage **3 :** to celebrate or solemnize (as a ceremony or festival) after a customary or accepted form **4 :** to see or sense esp. through directed careful analytic attention **5 :** to come to realize or know esp. through consideration of noted facts **6 :** to utter as a remark **7 :** to make a scientific observation on or of ~ *vi* **1 a :** to take notice **b :** to make observations **:** WATCH **2 :** REMARK, COMMENT **syn** see KEEP — **ob·serv·ing·ly** \-ˈzər-viŋ-lē\ *adv*

ob·serv·er \əb-ˈzər-vər\ *n* **:** one that observes: as **a :** a representative sent to observe but not participate officially in a gathering **b :** one who accompanies the pilot of an airplane to make observations

ob·sess \əb-ˈses, äb-\ *vt* [L *obsessus*, pp. of *obsidēre* to besiege, beset, fr. *ob-* against + *sedēre* to sit — more at OB-, SIT] **1** *archaic* **:** HARASS, BESET **2 :** to preoccupy intensely or abnormally

ob·ses·sion \äb-ˈsesh-ən, əb-\ *n* **1 :** a persistent disturbing preoccupation with an often unreasonable idea or feeling **2 :** an emotion or idea causing such a preoccupation — **ob·ses·sion·al** \-ˈsesh-nəl, -ən-ᵊl\ *adj* — **ob·ses·sion·al·ly** \-ē\ *adv*

ob·ses·sive \äb-ˈses-iv, əb-\ *adj* **1 a :** tending to cause obsession **b :** excessive often to an abnormal degree **2 :** of, relating to, or characterized by obsession — **obsessive** *n* — **ob·ses·sive·ly** *adv*

ob·sid·i·an \əb-ˈsid-ē-ən\ *n* [NL *obsidianus*, fr. L *obsidianus lapis* false MS reading for *obsianus lapis*, lit., stone of Obsius, fr. *Obsius*, its supposed discoverer] **:** volcanic glass that is generally black, banded, or spherulitic and has a marked conchoidal fracture and a composition similar to rhyolite

ob·so·lesce \ˌäb-sə-ˈles\ *vi* [L *obsolescere*] **:** to be or become obsolescent

ob·so·les·cence \-ˈles-ᵊn(t)s\ *n* **:** the process or condition of becoming obsolete

ob·so·les·cent \-ᵊnt\ *adj* **:** going out of use **:** becoming obsolete — **ob·so·les·cent·ly** *adv*

ob·so·lete \ˌäb-sə-ˈlēt, ˈäb-sə-ˌ\ *adj* [L *obsoletus*, fr. pp. of *obsolescere* to grow old, become disused] **1 a :** no longer in use **:** DISUSED **b :** of a kind or style no longer current **:** OUTMODED **2** *of a plant or animal part* **:** indistinct or imperfect as compared with a corresponding part in related organisms **:** VESTIGIAL — **ob·so·lete·ly** *adv* — **ob·so·lete·ness** *n*

ob·sta·cle \ˈäb-sti-kəl, -ˌstik-əl\ *n, often attrib* [ME, fr. MF, fr. L *obstaculum*, fr. *obstare* to stand in the way, fr. *ob-* in the way + *stare* to stand — more at OB-, STAND] **:** something that stands in the way or opposes **:** OBSTRUCTION

ob·stet·ric \əb-ˈste-trik, äb-\ *adj* [prob. fr. (assumed) NL *obstetricus*, fr. L *obstetric-*, *obstetrix* midwife, fr. *obstare* to stand in the way, stand in front of] **:** of or relating to childbirth or obstetrics — **ob·stet·ri·cal** \-tri-kəl\ *adj* — **ob·stet·ri·cal·ly** \-k(ə-)lē\ *adv*

ob·ste·tri·cian \ˌäb-stə-ˈtrish-ən\ *n* **:** a physician specializing in obstetrics

ob·stet·rics \əb-ˈste-triks, äb-\ *n pl but sing or pl in constr* **:** a branch of medical science that deals with birth and with its antecedents and sequels

ob·sti·na·cy \ˈäb-stə-nə-sē\ *n* **1 a :** the quality or state of being obstinate **:** STUBBORNNESS **b :** the quality or state of being difficult to remedy, relieve, or subdue **2 :** an instance of being obstinate

ob·sti·nate \ˈäb-stə-nət\ *adj* [ME, fr. L *obstinatus*, pp. of *obstinare* to be resolved, fr. *ob-* in the way + *-stinare* (akin to *stare* to stand)] **1 :** pertinaciously adhering to an opinion, purpose, or course in spite of reason, arguments, or persuasion **2 :** not easily subdued, remedied, or removed ⟨~ fever⟩ — **ob·sti·nate·ly** *adv* — **ob·sti·nate·ness** *n*

syn OBSTINATE, DOGGED, STUBBORN, PERTINACIOUS, MULISH mean fixed and unyielding in course or purpose. OBSTINATE implies usu. a perverse or unreasonable persistence; DOGGED suggests a tenacious frequently sullen persistence; STUBBORN implies sturdiness in resisting attempts to change or abandon a course or opinion; PERTINACIOUS suggests an annoying or irksome persistence; MULISH implies a thoroughly unreasonable obstinacy

ob·strep·er·ous \əb-ˈstrep-(ə-)rəs, äb-\ *adj* [L *obstreperus*, fr. *obstrepere* to clamor against, fr. *ob-* against + *strepere* to make a noise; akin to OE *thræft* discord — more at OB-] **1 :** uncontrollably noisy **:** CLAMOROUS **2 :** stubbornly defiant **:** UNRULY **syn** see VOCIFEROUS — **ob·strep·er·ous·ly** *adv* — **ob·strep·er·ous·ness** *n*

ob·struct \əb-ˈstrəkt, äb-\ *vt* [L *obstructus*, pp. of *obstruere*, fr. *ob-* in the way + *struere* to build — more at OB-, STRUCTURE] **1 :** to block or close up by an obstacle **2 :** to hinder from passage, action, or operation **:** IMPEDE **3 :** to cut off from sight ⟨a wall ~*s* the view⟩ **syn** see HINDER — **ob·struc·tive** \-ˈstrək-tiv\ *adj or n* — **ob·struc·tor** \-tər\ *n*

ob·struc·tion \əb-ˈstrək-shən, äb-\ *n* **1 :** an act of obstructing **:** the state of being obstructed: as **a :** a condition of being clogged or blocked **b :** a delay or attempted delay of business in a deliberative body **2 :** something that obstructs **:** HINDRANCE

ob·struc·tion·ism \-shə-ˌniz-əm\ *n* **:** deliberate interference with the progress or business esp. of a legislative body — **ob·struc·tion·ist** \-sh(ə-)nəst\ *n* — **ob·struc·tion·is·tic** \-ˌstrək-shə-ˈnis-tik\ *adj*

ob·tain \əb-ˈtān, äb-\ *vb* [ME *obteinen*, fr. MF & L; MF *obtenir*, fr. L *obtinēre* to hold on to, possess, obtain, fr. *ob-* in the way + *tenēre* to hold — more at THIN] *vt* **:** to gain or attain usu. by planning ~ *vi* **1** *archaic* **:** SUCCEED **2 :** to be generally recognized or established **:** PREVAIL **syn** see GET — **ob·tain·able** \-ˈtā-nə-bəl\ *adj* — **ob·tain·er** *n* — **ob·tain·ment** \-ˈtān-mənt\ *n*

ob·tect \əb-ˈtekt, äb-\ *also* **ob·tect·ed** \-ˈtek-təd\ *adj* [L *obtectus*, pp. of *obtegere* to cover over, fr. *ob-* in the way + *tegere* to cover more at THATCH] **:** enclosed in or characterized by enclosure in a firm chitinous case or covering ⟨an ~ pupa⟩

ob·test \äb-ˈtest\ *vb* [MF *obtester*, fr. L *obtestari* to call to witness, beseech, fr. *ob-* toward + *testis* witness — more at OB-, TESTAMENT] **:** BESEECH, SUPPLICATE — **ob·tes·ta·tion** \ˌäb-ˌtes-ˈtā-shən\ *n*

ob·trude \əb-ˈtrüd, äb-\ *vb* [L *obtrudere* to thrust at, fr. *ob-* in the way + *trudere* to thrust — more at OB-, THREAT] *vt* **1 :** to thrust out **:** EXTRUDE **2 :** to thrust forward or call to notice without warrant or request ~ *vi* **:** to thrust oneself upon attention **:** INTRUDE — **ob·trud·er** *n* — **ob·tru·sion** \-ˈtrü-zhən\ *n*

ob·tru·sive \-ˈtrü-siv, -ziv\ *adj* [L *obtrusus*, pp. of *obtrudere*] **1 :** thrust out **:** PROTRUDING **2 a :** FORWARD, PUSHING ⟨~ behavior⟩ **b :** undesirably noticeable or showy **syn** see IMPERTINENT — **ob·tru·sive·ly** *adv* — **ob·tru·sive·ness** *n*

ob·tu·rate \ˈäb-t(y)ə-ˌrāt\ *vt* [L *obturatus*, pp. of *obturare*, fr. *ob-* in the way + *-turare* (akin to *tumēre* to swell) — more at THUMB] **:** OBSTRUCT, CLOSE — **ob·tu·ra·tion** \ˌäb-t(y)ə-ˈrā-shən\ *n* — **ob·tu·ra·tor** \ˈäb-t(y)ə-ˌrāt-ər\ *n*

ob·tuse \äb-ˈt(y)üs, əb-, ˈäb-ˌ\ *adj* [L *obtusus* blunt, dull, fr. pp. of *obtundere* to beat against, blunt, fr. *ob-* against + *tundere* to beat — more at OB-, STUTTER] **1 :** lacking sharpness or quickness of sensibility **:** INSENSITIVE **2 a** (1) *of an angle* **:** exceeding 90 degrees but less than 180 degrees (2) **:** having an obtuse angle **b :** not pointed or acute **:** BLUNT **c** *of a leaf* **:** rounded at the free end **syn** see DULL — **ob·tuse·ly** *adv* — **ob·tuse·ness** *n*

1**ob·verse** \äb-ˈvərs, əb-, ˈäb-ˌ\ *adj* [L *obversus*, fr. pp. of *obvertere* to turn toward, fr. *ob-* toward + *vertere* to turn — more at OB-, WORTH] **1 :** facing the observer or opponent **2 :** having the base narrower than the top — **ob·verse·ly** *adv*

2**ob·verse** \ˈäb-ˌvərs, äb-ˈ, əb-ˈ\ *n* **1 a :** the side of a coin or currency note that bears the principal device and lettering **b :** a front or principal surface **2 a :** a counterpart necessarily involved in or answering to a fact or truth **b :** a proposition inferred immediately from another by denying the opposite of that which the given proposition affirms ⟨the ~ of "all *A* is *B*" is "no *A* is not *B*"⟩

ob·vert \äb-ˈvərt, əb-\ *vt* [L *obvertere* to turn toward] **:** to turn so as to present a different surface to view

ob·vi·ate \ˈäb-vē-ˌāt\ *vt* [LL *obviatus*, pp. of *obviare* to meet, withstand, fr. L *obviam* in the way] **:** to see beforehand and dispose of **:** make unnecessary **syn** see PREVENT — **ob·vi·a·tion** \ˌäb-vē-ˈā-shən\ *n*

ob·vi·ous \ˈäb-vē-əs, *rapid* ˈäv-ē-\ *adj* [L *obvius*, fr. *obviam* in the way, fr. *ob* in the way of + *viam*, acc. of *via* way — more at EPI-, VIA] **1** *archaic* **:** being in the way or in front **:** OPPOSITE **2 :** easily discovered, seen, or understood **:** PLAIN **syn** see EVIDENT — **ob·vi·ous·ly** *adv* — **ob·vi·ous·ness** *n*

ob·vo·lute \ˈäb-və-ˌlüt, ˌäb-və-ˈ\ *adj* [L *obvolutus*, pp. of *obvolvere* to wrap around, muffle, fr. *ob-* in the way + *volvere* to roll — more at OB-, VOLUBLE] **:** OVERLAPPING, CONVOLUTE

oc·a·ri·na \ˌäk-ə-ˈrē-nə\ *n* [It, fr. *oca* goose, fr. LL *auca*, deriv. of L *avis* bird — more at AVIARY] **:** a simple wind instrument usu. of terra-cotta having a mouthpiece and finger holes

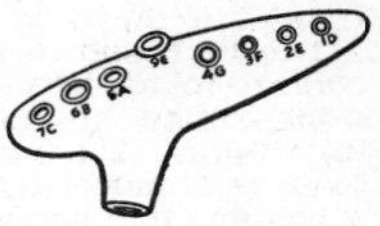

ocarina

1**oc·ca·sion** \ə-ˈkā-zhən\ *n* [ME, fr. MF or L; MF, fr. L *occasion-*, *occasio*, fr. *occasus*, pp. of *occidere* to fall, fall down, fr. *ob-* toward + *cadere* to fall — more at OB-, CHANCE] **1 :** a favorable opportunity or circumstance **2 :** a state of affairs that provides a ground or reason **3 :** an occurrence or condition that brings something about; *esp* **:** the immediate inciting circumstance as distinguished from fundamental cause **4 a :** HAPPENING, INCIDENT **b :** a time at which something happens **5 a :** a need arising from a particular circumstance **:** EXIGENCY **b** *archaic* **:** a personal want or need — usu. used in pl. **6** *pl* **:** AFFAIRS, BUSINESS **7 :** a special event or ceremony **:** CELEBRATION **syn** see CAUSE

2**occasion** *vt* **oc·ca·sion·ing** \-ˈkāzh-(ə-)niŋ\ **:** to give occasion to **:** CAUSE

oc·ca·sion·al \-ˈkāzh-nəl, -ən-ᵊl\ *adj* **1 :** occurring or operating on a particular occasion **2 :** acting as the occasion or contributing cause of something **3 :** composed for a particular occasion ⟨~ verse⟩ **4 :** met with, appearing, or occurring at irregular or rare intervals **5 :** acting in a specified capacity from time to time **6 :** designed or constructed to be used as the occasion demands — **oc·ca·sion·al·ly** \-ē\ *adv*

Oc·ci·dent \ˈäk-səd-ənt, -sə-ˌdent\ *n* [ME, fr. MF, fr. L *occident-*, *occidens*, fr. prp. of *occidere* to fall, set (of the sun)] **:** WEST 2

oc·ci·den·tal \ˌäk-sə-ˈdent-ᵊl\ *adj, often cap* **1 :** of, relating to, or situated in the Occident **:** WESTERN **2 :** of or relating to Occidentals — **oc·ci·den·tal·ly** \-ᵊl-ē\ *adv*

Occidental *n* **:** a member of one of the indigenous peoples of the Occident

Oc·ci·den·tal·ism \-ᵊl-ˌiz-əm\ *n* **:** the characteristic features of occidental peoples or culture — **Oc·ci·den·tal·ist** \-ᵊl-əst\ *n*

oc·ci·den·tal·ize \-ᵊl-ˌīz\ *vt, often cap* **:** to make occidental in standards or culture

oc·cip·i·tal \äk-ˈsip-ət-ᵊl\ *adj* **:** of or relating to the occiput or the occipital bone — **occipital** *n* — **oc·cip·i·tal·ly** \-ᵊl-ē\ *adv*

occipital bone *n* **:** a compound bone that forms the posterior part of the skull and articulates with the atlas

oc·ci·put \ˈäk-sə-(ˌ)pət\ *n, pl* **occiputs** *or* **oc·cip·i·ta** \äk-ˈsip-ət-ə\ [L *occipit-*, *occiput*, fr. *ob-* against + *capit-*, *caput* head — more at OB-, HEAD] **:** the back part of the head or skull

oc·clude \ə-ˈklüd, ä-\ *vb* [L *occludere*, fr. *ob-* in the way + *claudere* to shut, close — more at CLOSE] *vt* **1 :** to stop up **:** OBSTRUCT **2 :** to shut in or out **3 :** SORB **4 :** to cut off from contact with the surface of the earth and force aloft by the convergence of a cold front upon a warm front ⟨*occluded* warm air⟩ ~ *vi* **1 :** to close with the cusps fitting together ⟨his teeth do not ~ properly⟩ **2 :** to become occluded — **oc·clud·ent** \-ˈklüd-ᵊnt\ *adj* — **oc·clu·sive** \-ˈklü-siv, -ziv\ *adj*

occluded front *n* **:** OCCLUSION 2

oc·clu·sion \ə-ˈklü-zhən\ *n* [prob. fr. (assumed) NL *occlusion-*, *occlusio*, fr. L *occlusus*, pp. of *occludere*] **1 :** the act of occluding or the state of being occluded: as **a :** the complete obstruction of the breath passage in the articulation of a speech sound **b :** the bringing of the opposing surfaces of the teeth of the two jaws into contact; *also* **:** the relation between the surfaces when in contact **2 :** the front formed by a cold front overtaking a warm front and lifting the warm air above the earth's surface

1**oc·cult** \ə-ˈkəlt, ä-\ *vb* [L *occultare*, fr. *occultus*, pp.] *vt* **1 :** to hide from sight **:** CONCEAL **2 :** to conceal by occultation ~ *vi* **:** to become concealed or extinguished — **oc·cult·er** *n*

2**oc·cult** \ə-ˈkəlt, ä-; ˈäk-ˌəlt\ *adj* [L *occultus*, fr. pp. of *occulere* to cover up, fr. *ob-* in the way + *-culere* (akin to *celare* to conceal) — more at OB-, HELL] **1 :** not revealed **:** SECRET **2 :** ABSTRUSE, MYSTERIOUS **3 :** not able to be seen or detected **:** CONCEALED **4 :** of or relating to supernatural agencies, their effects, and knowledge of them — **oc·cult·ly** *adv*

³occult *like* ²\ *n* **:** occult matters

oc·cul·ta·tion \,äk-(,)əl-'tā-shən\ *n* **1 :** the state of being hidden from view or lost to notice **2 :** the shutting off of the light of one celestial body by the intervention of another; *esp* **:** an eclipse of a star or planet by the moon

oc·cult·ism \ə-'kəl-,tiz-əm, ä-; 'äk-,əl-\ *n* **:** a belief in or study of supernatural powers and the possibility of subjecting them to human control — **oc·cult·ist** \-təst\ *n*

oc·cu·pan·cy \'äk-yə-pən-sē\ *n* **1 :** the act of taking and holding possession **2 a :** the act of becoming or the state of being an occupant **b :** the condition of being occupied **3 :** the use to which property is put **4 :** an occupied building or part of a building (as an apartment or office)

oc·cu·pant \-pənt\ *n* **1 :** one who acquires title by occupancy **2 :** one who occupies; *esp* **:** TENANT, RESIDENT

oc·cu·pa·tion \,äk-yə-'pā-shən\ *n* [ME *occupacioun*, fr. MF *occupation*, fr. L *occupation-*, *occupatio*, fr. *occupatus*, pp. of *occupare*] **1 a :** an activity in which one engages **b :** the principal business of one's life **:** VOCATION **2 a :** the possession, use, or settlement of land **:** OCCUPANCY **b :** the holding of an office or position **3 :** the act or process of taking possession of a place or area **4 a :** the holding and control of an area by a foreign military force **b :** the military force occupying a country or the policies carried out by it **syn** see WORK

oc·cu·pa·tion·al \-shnəl, -shən-ᵊl\ *adj* **1 :** relating to or resulting from a particular occupation ⟨~ disease⟩ **2 :** of or relating to a military occupation — **oc·cu·pa·tion·al·ly** \-ē\ *adv*

occupational therapy *n* **:** therapy by means of activity; *specif* **:** creative activity prescribed for its effect in promoting recovery or rehabilitation

oc·cu·pi·er \'äk-yə-,pī(-ə)r\ *n* **:** one that occupies

oc·cu·py \'äk-yə-,pī\ *vt* [ME *occupien* to take possession of, occupy, modif. of MF *occuper*, fr. L *occupare*, fr. *ob-* toward + *-cupare* (akin to *capere* to seize) — more at OB-, HEAVE] **1 :** to engage the attention or energies of **2 :** to fill up (an extent in space or time) **3 :** to take or hold possession of **4 :** to reside in as an owner or tenant

oc·cur \ə-'kər\ *vi* **oc·curred; oc·cur·ring** \-'kər-iŋ\ [L *occurrere*, fr. *ob-* in the way + *currere* to run — more at OB-, CURRENT] **1 :** to be found or met with **:** APPEAR **2 :** to take place **3 :** to come to mind **syn** see HAPPEN

oc·cur·rence \ə-'kər-ən(t)s, -'kə-rən(t)s\ *n* **1 :** APPEARANCE, HAPPENING **2 :** INCIDENT, EVENT; *esp* **:** an unexpected happening
syn OCCURRENCE, EVENT, INCIDENT, EPISODE, CIRCUMSTANCE mean something that happens or takes place. OCCURRENCE may apply to a happening without intent, volition, or plan; EVENT usu. implies an occurrence of some importance and frequently one having antecedent cause; INCIDENT suggests either an occurrence of subordinate character or a small but unusual or consequential happening; EPISODE stresses the distinctiveness or apartness of an incident; CIRCUMSTANCE implies a specific detail attending an action or event as part of its setting or background

oc·cur·rent \-'kər-ənt, -'kə-rənt\ *adj* [MF, fr. L *occurrent-*, *occurrens*, prp. of *occurrere*] **1 :** occurring at present **:** CURRENT **2 :** INCIDENTAL — **occurrent** *n*

ocean \'ō-shən\ *n* [ME *occean*, fr. L *oceanus*, fr. Gk *Ōkeanos*, a river thought of as encircling the earth, ocean] **1 :** the whole body of salt water that covers nearly three fourths of the surface of the globe **2 :** one of the large bodies of water into which the great ocean is divided **3 :** an unlimited space or quantity

ocean·ar·i·um \,ō-shə-'nar-ē-əm, -'ner-\ *n* **:** a large marine aquarium

ocean·go·ing \'ō-shən-,gō-iŋ\ *adj* **:** of, relating to, or suitable for travel on the ocean

oce·an·ic \,ō-shē-'an-ik\ *adj* **1 :** of, relating to, produced by, or frequenting the ocean and esp. the open sea as distinguished from littoral or neritic waters **2 :** VAST, GREAT

Oce·a·nid \ō-'sē-ə-nəd\ *n* [Gk *ōkeanid-*, *ōkeanis*, fr. *Ōkeanos* Oceanus] **:** any of the ocean nymphs held in Greek mythology to be the daughters of Oceanus and Tethys

ocean·og·ra·pher \,ō-shə-'näg-rə-fər\ *n* **:** a specialist in oceanography

ocean·o·graph·ic \,ō-shə-nə-'graf-ik\ *adj* **:** of or relating to oceanography — **ocean·o·graph·i·cal** \-i-kəl\ *adj* — **ocean·o·graph·i·cal·ly** \-k(ə-)lē\ *adv*

ocean·og·ra·phy \,ō-shə-'näg-rə-fē\ *n* [ISV] **:** a science that deals with the ocean and its phenomena

ocean sunfish *n* **:** a large deep-bodied truncated marine fish (*Mola mola*) of warm and temperate seas

Oce·a·nus \ō-'sē-ə-nəs\ *n* [L, fr. Gk *Ōkeanos*] **:** the god of the great outer sea held in Greek mythology to encircle the earth

ocel·lar \ō-'sel-ər\ *adj* **:** of, relating to, or connecting with an ocellus

ocel·lat·ed \'ō-sə-,lāt-əd, 'äs-ə-; ō-'sel-,āt-\ *adj* **1 :** having ocelli **2 :** resembling an ocellus — **ocel·la·tion** \,ō-sə-'lā-shən, ,äs-ə-\ *n*

ocel·lus \ō-'sel-əs\ *n, pl* **ocel·li** \-'sel-,ī, -(,)ē\ [NL, fr. L, dim. of *oculus* eye — more at EYE] **1 :** a minute simple eye or eyespot of an invertebrate **2 :** a spot of color encircled by a band of another color

oce·lot \'äs-ə-,lät, 'ō-sə-\ *n* [F, fr. Nahuatl *ocelotl* jaguar] **:** a medium-sized American wildcat (*Felis pardalis*) ranging from Texas to Patagonia and having a tawny yellow or grayish coat that is dotted and striped with black

ocher *or* **ochre** \'ō-kər\ *n* [ME *oker*, fr. MF *ocre*, fr. L *ochra*, fr. Gk *ōchra*, fr. fem. of *ōchros* yellow] **:** an earthy usu. red or yellow and often impure iron ore used as a pigment **2 :** the color of ocher and esp. of yellow ocher — **ocher·ous** \'ō-k(ə-)rəs\ *or* **ochre·ous** \'ō-k(ə-)rəs, -krē-əs\ *adj*

och·loc·ra·cy \äk-'läk-rə-sē\ *n* [Gk & MF; MF *ochlocratie*, fr. Gk *ochlokratia*, fr. *ochlos* mob + *-kratia* -cracy] **:** government by the mob — **och·lo·crat** \'äk-lə-,krat\ *n* — **ochlocrat** *or* **och·lo·crat·i·cal** \,äk-lə-'krat-i-kəl\ *adj*

ochone \,ə-'kōn\ *interj* [ScGael & IrGael *ochōn*] *Irish & Scot* — used as an exclamation of regret or grief

-ock \ək, ik, ,äk\ *n suffix* [ME *-oc*, fr. OE] **:** small one ⟨hill*ock*⟩

o'clock \ə-'kläk\ *adv* [contr. of *of the clock*] **1 :** according to the clock ⟨the time is three ~⟩ **2 :** on a clock dial imagined in a horizontal position with the observer at the center facing the numeral 12 or in a vertical position in front of and facing the observer with the numeral 12 at the top — used for indicating position or direction ⟨an airplane approaching at eleven ~⟩

oco·ti·llo \,ō-kə-'tē-(,)(y)ō\ *n* [MexSp] **:** a thorny scarlet-flowered candlewood (*Fouquieria splendens*) of the southwestern U.S. and Mexico

oc·rea \'äk-rē-ə\ *n, pl* **oc·re·ae** \-rē-,ē, -,ī\ [NL, fr. L, greave] **:** a tubular sheath around the base of a leafstalk — **oc·re·ate** \-rē-,āt\ *adj*

octa- *or* **octo-** *also* **oct-** *comb form* [Gk *okta-*, *oktō-*, *okt-* (fr. *oktō*) & L *octo-*, *oct-*, fr. *octo* — more at EIGHT] **:** eight ⟨*octa*merous⟩ ⟨*octa*ne⟩ ⟨*octo*roon⟩

oc·ta·gon \'äk-tə-,gän\ *n* [L *octagonum*, fr. Gk *oktagōnon*, fr. *okta-* + *-gōnon* -gon] **:** a polygon of eight angles and eight sides — **oc·tag·o·nal** \äk-'tag-ən-ᵊl\ *adj* — **oc·tag·o·nal·ly** \-ᵊl-ē\ *adv*

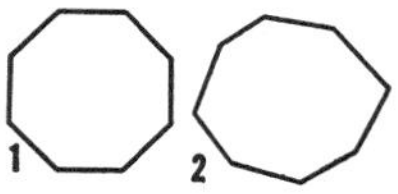
octagons: *1* regular, *2* irregular

oc·ta·he·dral \,äk-tə-'hē-drəl\ *adj* **1 :** having eight plane faces **2 :** of, relating to, or formed in octahedrons

oc·ta·he·dron \-drən\ *n, pl* **octahedrons** *or* **oc·ta·he·dra** \-drə\ [Gk *oktaedron*, fr *okta-* + *-edron* -hedron] **:** a solid bounded by eight plane faces

oc·tam·er·ous \äk-'tam-ə-rəs\ *or* **oc·tom·er·ous** \-'täm-\ *adj* [*octa-* + Gk *meros* part — more at MERIT] **:** having eight parts or having organs arranged in eights ⟨an ~ flower⟩

oc·tam·e·ter \äk-'tam-ət-ər\ *n* [LL, having eight feet, fr. LGk *oktametros*, fr. *okta-* + *metron* measure — more at MEASURE] **:** a verse consisting of eight feet

oct·an·dri·ous \äk-'tan-drē-əs\ *adj* [deriv. of NL *octa-* + *andr-*] **:** having eight stamens or flowers with eight stamens

oc·tane \'äk-,tān, äk-'\ *n* [ISV] **:** any of several isomeric liquid paraffin hydrocarbons C_8H_{18}

octane number *n* **:** a number that is used to measure the antiknock properties of a liquid motor fuel and that represents the percentage by volume of isooctane in a reference fuel consisting of a mixture of isooctane and normal heptane and matching in knocking properties the fuel being tested — called also *octane rating*

oc·ta·nol \'äk-tə-,nȯl, -,nōl\ *n* **:** any of four liquid alcohols $C_8H_{17}OH$ derived from normal octane

oc·tant \'äk-tənt\ *n* [L *octant-*, *octans* eighth of a circle, fr. *octo*] **1 a :** the position or aspect of a celestial body when distant from another body by 45 degrees **b :** an instrument for observing altitudes of a celestial body from a moving ship or aircraft **2 :** any of the eight parts into which a space is divided by three coordinate planes

oc·tar·i·us \äk-'ter-ē-əs, -'tar-\ *n* [NL, fr. L *octo* eight — more at EIGHT] **:** PINT

oc·tave \'äk-tiv, -təv, -,tāv\ *n* [ME, fr. ML *octava*, fr. L, fem. of *octavus* eighth, fr. *octo* eight — more at EIGHT] **1 :** an eight day period of observances beginning with the festival day **2 a :** a stanza of eight lines **:** OTTAVA RIMA **b :** the first two quatrains or first eight verses of a sonnet **3 a :** a musical interval embracing eight diatonic degrees **b :** a tone or note at this interval **c :** the harmonic combination of two tones an octave apart **d :** the whole series of notes, tones, or digitals comprised within this interval and forming the unit of the modern scale **e :** an organ stop giving tones an octave above those corresponding to the digitals **4 :** the eighth of the eight defensive positions in fencing **5 :** a group of eight

oc·ta·vo \äk-'tā-(,)vō, -'täv-(,)ō\ *n* [L, abl. of *octavus* eighth] **:** the size of a piece of paper cut eight from a sheet; *also* **:** a book, a page, or paper of this size

oc·tet \äk-'tet\ *n* **1 :** a musical composition for eight instruments or voices **2 :** a group or set of eight: as **a :** the musicians that perform an octet **b :** OCTAVE 2b

oc·til·lion \äk-'til-yən\ *n, often attrib* [F, fr. MF, fr. *oct-* octa- + *-illion* (as in *million*)] — see NUMBER table

Oc·to·ber \äk-'tō-bər\ *n* [ME *Octobre*, fr. OF, fr. L *October* (eighth month), fr. *octo*] **1 :** the 10th month of the Gregorian calendar **2** *Brit* **:** ale made in October

oc·to·de·cil·lion \,äk-tō-di-'sil-yən\ *n, often attrib* [L *octodecim* eighteen + E *-illion* (as in *million*)] — see NUMBER table

oc·to·dec·i·mo \,äk-tə-'des-ə-,mō\ *n* [L, abl. of *octodecimus* eighteenth, fr. *octodecim* eighteen, fr. *octo* eight + *decem* ten — more at TEN] **:** EIGHTEENMO

oc·to·ge·nar·i·an \,äk-tə-jə-'ner-ē-ən\ *n* [L *octogenarius* containing eighty, fr. *octogeni* eighty each, fr. *octoginta* eighty, fr. *octo* eight + *-ginta* (akin to *viginti* twenty) — more at VIGESIMAL] **:** a person who is in his eighties — **octogenarian** *adj*

oc·to·ploid \'äk-tə-,plȯid\ *adj* [ISV] **:** having eight parts or aspects; *specif* **:** having a chromosome number eight times the basic chromosome number — **octoploid** *n* — **oc·to·ploi·dy** \-ē\ *n*

oc·to·pod \'äk-tə-,päd\ *n* [deriv. of Gk *oktōpod-*, *oktōpous* scorpion, fr. *oktō* octa- + *pod-*, *pous* foot — more at FOOT] **:** any of an order (Octopoda) of cephalopod mollusks comprising the octopuses, argonauts, and related 8-armed mollusks — **octopod** *adj* — **oc·top·o·dan** \äk-'täp-əd-ən\ *adj or n* — **oc·top·o·dous** \-əd-əs\ *adj*

oc·to·pus \'äk-tə-pəs *also* -,pu̇s\ *n* [NL *Octopod-*, *Octopus*, genus name, fr. Gk *oktōpous*] **1 :** any of a genus (*Octopus*) including all of the common octopuses or restricted to a few typical forms; *broadly* **:** any octopod excepting the paper nautilus **2 :** something that resembles an octopus esp. in having many branches centrally directed

oc·to·roon \,äk-tə-'rün\ *n* [*octa-* + *-roon* (as in *quadroon*)] **:** a person of one-eighth Negro ancestry

oc·to·syl·lab·ic \,äk-tə-sə-'lab-ik, -(,)tō-\ *adj* [LL *octosyllabus*, fr. Gk *oktasyllabos*, fr. *okta-* + *syllabē* syllable] **:** consisting of eight syllables or composed of verses of eight syllables — **octosyllabic** *n* — **oc·to·syl·la·ble** \'äk-tə-,sil-ə-bəl, ,äk-tə-'\ *n*

oc·troi \,äk-trə-'wä, äk-'trwä, 'äk-,trȯi\ *n* [F] **:** a tax on commodities brought into a town

ocul- *or* **oculo-** *comb form* [L *ocul-*, fr. *oculus* — more at EYE] **:** eye ⟨*oculo*motor⟩

¹oc·u·lar \'äk-yə-lər\ *adj* [LL *ocularis* of eyes, fr. L *oculus* eye] **1 a :** done or perceived by the eye **b :** based on what has been seen ⟨~ testimony⟩ **2 a :** of or relating to the eye **b :** resembling or suggesting an eye in form or function

²ocular *n* **:** EYEPIECE

oc·u·list \'äk-yə-ləst\ *n* [F *oculiste*, fr. L *oculus*] **1 :** OPHTHALMOLOGIST **2 :** OPTOMETRIST

oc·u·lo·mo·tor \,äk-yə-lə-'mōt-ər\ *adj* **1 :** moving or tending to move the eyeball **2 :** of or relating to the oculomotor nerve

oculomotor nerve *n* **:** either of a pair of chiefly motor cranial nerves that arise from the midbrain and supply most muscles of the eye

od *or* **odd** \ˈäd\ *interj, often cap* [euphemism for *God*] — a mild oath

oda·lisque \ˈōd-ᵊl-ˌisk\ *n* [F, fr. Turk *odalık*] **:** a female slave or concubine in a harem

odd \ˈäd\ *adj* [ME *odde,* fr. ON *oddi* point of land, triangle, odd number; akin to OE *ord* point of a weapon] **1 a :** being without a corresponding mate ⟨an ~ shoe⟩ **b** (1) **:** left over after others are paired or grouped (2) **:** separated from a set or series **2 a :** somewhat more than the indicated approximate quantity, extent, or degree **b** (1) **:** left over as a remainder (2) **:** constituting a small amount **3 a :** being one of the sequence of natural numbers beginning with one and counting by twos that are not divisible by two **b :** marked by an odd number **4 :** apart from what is regular, expected, or planned **5 :** having an out-of-the-way location **:** REMOTE **6 :** differing markedly from the usual or ordinary or accepted **:** PECULIAR **syn** see STRANGE — **odd·ly** *adv* — **odd·ness** *n*

odd·ball \ˈäd-ˌbȯl\ *n* **:** one whose behavior is eccentric — **oddball** *adj*

Odd Fellow *n* **:** a member of one of the major benevolent and fraternal orders

odd·i·ty \ˈäd-ət-ē\ *n* **1 :** an odd person, thing, event, or trait **:** ECCENTRICITY **2 :** the quality or state of being odd

odd·ment \ˈäd-mənt\ *n* **1 :** something left over **:** REMNANT **2 :** something odd **:** ODDITY

odds \ˈädz\ *n pl but sing or pl in constr* **1 a** *archaic* **:** INEQUALITIES **b** *obs* **:** degree of unlikeness **2 a :** amount by which one thing exceeds or falls short of another **b** (1) **:** difference favoring one of two opposed things (2) **:** ADVANTAGE, BENEFIT **c** (1) **:** the probability that one thing is so or will happen rather than another **:** CHANCES (2) **:** the ratio of probability that one thing is so or will happen rather than another **3 :** DISAGREEMENT, VARIANCE — usu. used with *at* **4 a :** special favor **:** PARTIALITY **b :** an allowance granted by one making a bet to one accepting the bet designed to equalize the chances favoring one of the bettors

odds and ends *n pl* **1 :** miscellaneous articles or matters of business **2 :** miscellaneous remnants or leftovers

odds–on \(ˈ)äd-ˈzȯn, -ˈzän\ *adj* **:** having or viewed as having a better than even chance to win

ode \ˈōd\ *n* [MF or LL; MF, fr. LL, fr. Gk *ōidē*, lit., song, fr. *aeidein, aidein* to sing; akin to Gk *audē* voice, OHG far*wāzan* to deny] **:** a lyric poem usu. marked by exaltation of feeling and style, varying length of line, and complexity of stanza forms

-ode \ˌōd\ *n comb form* [Gk *-odos,* fr. *hodos* — more at CEDE] **1 :** way **:** path ⟨electr*ode*⟩ **2 :** electrode ⟨di*ode*⟩

ode·um \ō-ˈdē-əm, ˈōd-ē-\ *n* [L & Gk; L, fr. Gk *ōideion,* fr. *ōidē* song] **1 :** a small roofed theater of ancient Greece and Rome used chiefly for competitions in music and poetry **2 :** a theater or concert hall

od·ic \ˈōd-ik\ *adj* **:** relating to or forming an ode

Odin \ˈōd-ᵊn\ *n* [Dan, fr. ON *Ōthinn;* akin to OE *Wōden* Odin] **:** the chief god in Germanic mythology

odi·ous \ˈōd-ē-əs\ *adj* [ME, fr. MF *odieus,* fr. L *odiosus,* fr. *odium*] **:** exciting or deserving hatred or repugnance **syn** see HATEFUL — **odi·ous·ly** *adv* — **odi·ous·ness** *n*

odi·um \ˈōd-ē-əm\ *n* [L, hatred, fr. *odisse* to hate; akin to OE *atol* terrible, Gk *odyssasthai* to be angry] **1 a :** the state or fact of being subjected to hatred and contempt as a result of a despicable act or blameworthy situation **b :** hatred and condemnation marked by loathing or contempt **:** DETESTATION **2 a :** a mark of disgrace or reproach **:** STIGMA **b :** disrepute or infamy attached to something **:** OPPROBRIUM

odo·graph \ˈōd-ə-ˌgraf, ˈäd-\ *n* [*odo-* (as in *odometer*) + *-graph*] **1 :** an instrument for automatically plotting the course and distance traveled by a vehicle **2 :** a device for recording the length and rapidity of stride and the number of steps taken by a walker

odom·e·ter \ō-ˈdäm-ət-ər\ *n* [F *odomètre,* fr. Gk *hodometron,* fr. *hodos* way, road + *metron* measure — more at CEDE, MEASURE] **:** an instrument for measuring the distance traversed (as by a vehicle)

odon·ate \ˈōd-ᵊn-ˌāt, ō-ˈdän-\ *n* [irreg. deriv. of Gk *odous, odōn* tooth] **:** any of an order (Odonata) of predacious insects comprising the dragonflies and damselflies — **odonate** *adj*

odont- *or* **odonto-** *comb form* [F, fr. Gk, fr. *odont-, odous* — more at TOOTH] **:** tooth ⟨*odont*itis⟩ ⟨*odonto*blast⟩

-odont \ə-ˌdänt\ *adj comb form* [Gk *odont-, odous* tooth] **:** having teeth of a (specified) nature ⟨mes*odont*⟩

-odon·tia \ə-ˈdän-ch(ē-)ə\ *n comb form* [NL, fr. Gk *odont-, odous*] **:** form, condition, or mode of treatment of the teeth ⟨orth*odontia*⟩

odon·to·blast \ō-ˈdänt-ə-ˌblast\ *n* [ISV] **:** one of the elongated radially arranged outer cells of the dental pulp that secrete dentin — **odon·to·blas·tic** \-ˌdänt-ə-ˈblas-tik\ *adj*

odon·to·glos·sum \ō-ˌdänt-ə-ˈgläs-əm\ *n* [NL, genus name, fr. *odont-* + Gk *glōssa* tongue — more at GLOSS] **:** any of a genus (*Odontoglossum*) of widely cultivated tropical American epiphytic orchids

odon·toid \ō-ˈdän-ˌtȯid\ *adj* [Gk *odontoeidēs,* fr. *odont-, odous* tooth] **1 :** having the form of a tooth **2 :** of or relating to the odontoid process — **odontoid** *n*

odontoid process *n* **:** a toothlike process projecting from the anterior end of the centrum of the axis vertebra on which the atlas vertebra rotates

odon·tol·o·gist \(ˌ)ō-ˌdän-ˈtäl-ə-jəst\ *n* **:** a specialist in odontology

odon·tol·o·gy \-jē\ *n* [F *odontologie,* fr. *odont-* + *-logie* -logy] **:** a science dealing with the teeth, their structure and development, and their diseases

odor *or chiefly Brit* **odour** \ˈōd-ər\ *n* [ME *odour,* fr. OF, fr. L *odor;* akin to L *olēre* to smell, Gk *ozein* to smell, *osmē* smell, odor] **1 a :** a quality of something that stimulates the olfactory organ **:** SCENT **b :** a sensation resulting from adequate stimulation of the olfactory organ **:** SMELL **2 a :** a predominant quality **:** FLAVOR ⟨~ of sanctity⟩ **b :** REPUTE, ESTIMATION ⟨in bad ~⟩ **3** *archaic* **:** something that emits a sweet or pleasing scent **:** PERFUME **syn** see SMELL — **odored** \ˈōd-ərd\ *adj*

odor·ant \ˈōd-ə-rənt\ *n* **:** an odorous substance

odor·if·er·ous \ˌōd-ə-ˈrif-(ə-)rəs\ *adj* **1 :** yielding an odor **:** ODOROUS **2 :** morally offensive — **odor·if·er·ous·ly** *adv* — **odor·if·er·ous·ness** *n*

odor·ize \ˈōd-ə-ˌrīz\ *vt* **:** to make odorous **:** SCENT

odor·less \ˈōd-ər-ləs\ *adj* **:** free of odor

odor·ous \ˈōd-ə-rəs\ *adj* **:** having an odor **:** SCENTED: as **a :** FRAGRANT **b :** MALODOROUS — **odor·ous·ly** *adv* — **odor·ous·ness** *n*

Odys·seus \ō-ˈdish-ˌüs, -ˈdis-ˌyüs, -ˈdis-ē-əs\ *n* [Gk] **:** a king of Ithaca and Greek leader in the Trojan War whose ten-year wanderings after the war are recounted in Homer's *Odyssey*

od·ys·sey \ˈäd-ə-sē\ *n* [the *Odyssey,* epic poem attributed to Homer recounting the long wanderings of Odysseus] **:** a long wandering usu. marked by many changes of fortune

oe·cu·men·i·cal *esp Brit* ˌēk-\ *var of* ECUMENICAL

oe·de·ma *var of* EDEMA

oe·di·pal \ˈed-ə-pəl, ˈēd-\ *adj, often cap* **:** of or relating to the Oedipus complex

Oe·di·pus \-pəs\ *n* [L, fr. Gk *Oidipous*] **:** a son of Laius and Jocasta who kills his father and marries his mother as foretold by an oracle at his birth

Oedipus complex *n* **:** the positive libidinal feelings that a child develops toward the parent of the opposite sex and that when unresolved are conceived as a source of adult personality disorder

oeil–de–boeuf \ˌə(r)d-ə-ˈbəf, ˌəid-\ *n, pl* **oeils–de–boeuf** *same*\ [F, lit., ox's eye] **:** a circular or oval window

oeil·lade \ˌə(r)-ˈyäd, əi-\ *n* [F, fr. MF, fr. *oeil* eye, fr. L *oculus* — more at EYE] **:** a glance of the eye; *esp* **:** OGLE

oe·nol·o·gy *var of* ENOLOGY

oe·no·mel \ˈē-nə-ˌmel\ *n* [LL *oenomeli,* fr. Gk *oinomeli,* fr. *oinos* wine + *meli* honey — more at WINE, MELLIFLUOUS] **1 :** an ancient Greek beverage of wine and honey **2 :** a strong sweet draft (as of inspiration)

Oe·no·ne \ē-ˈnō-nē\ *n* [L, fr. Gk *Oinōnē*] **:** a nymph of Mount Ida and wife of Paris who abandons her for Helen of Troy

1o'er \ˈō(ə)r, ˈȯ(ə)r\ *adv* **:** OVER

2o'er \(ˈ)ō(ə)r, (ˈ)ȯ(ə)r\ *prep* **:** OVER

Oer·li·kon \ˈər-li-ˌkän\ *n* [*Oerlikon,* Switzerland] **:** any of several 20 mm. automatic aircraft or antiaircraft cannon

oer·sted \ˈər-stəd\ *n* [Hans Christian *Oersted* †1851 Dan physicist] **:** the cgs electromagnetic unit of magnetic intensity equal to the intensity of a magnetic field in a vacuum in which a unit magnetic pole experiences a mechanical force of one dyne in the direction of the field

oe·soph·a·gus *var of* ESOPHAGUS

oestradiol, oestrin, oestriol, oestrone *var of* ESTRADIOL, ESTRIN, ESTRIOL, ESTRONE

oestrogen *var of* ESTROGEN

oestrous, oestrus *var of* ESTROUS, ESTRUS

oeu·vre \œvrᵊ\ *n, pl* **oeuvres** *same*\ [F *œuvre,* lit., work, fr. L *opera* — more at OPERA] **:** a substantial body of work constituting the lifework of a writer, an artist, or a composer

of \əv, *before consonants also* ə; ˈəv, ˈäv\ *prep* [ME, off, of, fr. OE, adv. & prep.; akin to OHG *aba* off, away, L *ab* from, away, Gk *apo*] **1** — used as a function word to indicate a point of reckoning ⟨north ~ the lake⟩ **2 a** — used as a function word to indicate origin or derivation ⟨a man ~ noble birth⟩ **b** — used as a function word to indicate the cause, motive, or reason ⟨died ~ flu⟩ **c :** BY ⟨plays ~ Shakespeare⟩ **d :** on the part of ⟨very kind ~ him⟩ **3** — used as a function word to indicate the component material, parts, or elements or the contents ⟨throne ~ gold⟩ ⟨cup ~ water⟩ **4 a** — used as a function word to indicate the whole that includes the part denoted by the preceding word ⟨most ~ the army⟩ **b** — used as a function word to indicate a whole or quantity from which a part is removed or expended ⟨gave ~ his time⟩ **5 a :** relating to **:** ABOUT ⟨stories ~ his travels⟩ **b :** in respect to ⟨slow ~ speech⟩ **6** — used as a function word to indicate belonging or a possessive relationship ⟨king ~ England⟩ **7** — used as a function word to indicate separation ⟨eased ~ pain⟩ **8 a** — used as a function word to indicate a particular example belonging to the class denoted by the preceding noun ⟨the city ~ Rome⟩ **b** — used as a function word to indicate apposition ⟨that fool ~ a husband⟩ **9 a** — used as a function word to indicate the object of an action denoted or implied by the preceding noun ⟨love ~ nature⟩ **b** — used as a function word to indicate the application of a verb ⟨cheats him ~ a dollar⟩ or of an adjective ⟨fond ~ candy⟩ **10** — used as a function word to indicate a characteristic or distinctive quality or possession ⟨a man ~ courage⟩ **11 a** — used as a function word to indicate the position in time of an action or occurrence ⟨died ~ a Monday⟩ **b :** BEFORE ⟨quarter ~ ten⟩ **12** *archaic* **:** ON ⟨a plague ~ all cowards —Shak.⟩

ofay \ō-ˈfā\ *n* [origin unknown] *slang* **:** a white person

1off \ˈȯf\ *adv* [ME *of,* fr. OE — more at OF] **1 a :** from a place or position ⟨march ~⟩; *specif* **:** away from land ⟨ship stood ~ to sea⟩ **b :** so as to prevent close approach ⟨drove the dogs ~⟩ **c :** from a course **:** ASIDE ⟨turned ~ into a bypath⟩; *specif* **:** away from the wind **d :** into an unconscious state ⟨dozed ~⟩ **2 a :** so as not to be supported ⟨rolled to the edge of the table and ~⟩ or covering or enclosing ⟨blew the lid ~⟩ or attached ⟨the handle came ~⟩ **b :** so as to be divided ⟨surface marked ~ into squares⟩ **3 :** to a state of discontinuance ⟨shut ~ an engine⟩ or exhaustion ⟨drink ~ a glass⟩ or completion ⟨coat of paint to finish it ~⟩ **4 :** in absence from or suspension of regular work or service ⟨take time ~ for lunch⟩ **5 :** at a distance in space or time ⟨stood ten paces ~⟩ **6 :** OFFSTAGE

2off \(ˈ)ȯf\ *prep* **1** — used as a function word to indicate a supporting surface or a position of rest, attachment, or union from which separation is made ⟨take it ~ the table⟩ **2 a :** FROM ⟨borrowed a dollar ~ him⟩ **b :** at the expense of ⟨lived ~ his sister⟩ **c :** so as to consume ⟨dined ~ oysters⟩ **3 :** to seaward of ⟨two miles ~ shore⟩ **4 a** (1) — used as a function word to indicate a usual occupation in which one is not now engaged ⟨~ duty⟩ (2) **:** abstaining from ⟨~ liquor⟩ **b :** below the usual standard or level of ⟨~ his game⟩ ⟨a dollar ~ the list price⟩ **5 a :** diverging or opening from ⟨a path ~ the main walk⟩ **b :** being or occurring away or apart from ⟨a shop just ~ the main street⟩

3off \(ˈ)ȯf\ *adj* **1 a :** more removed or distant ⟨the ~ side of the building⟩ **b :** SEAWARD **c :** RIGHT **d :** of or relating to the side of the cricket field opposite to that on which the batsman stands **2 a :** started on the way ⟨~ on a spree⟩ **b :** CANCELED **c :** not operating **d :** not placed so as to permit operation **3 a :** not corresponding to fact **:** INCORRECT ⟨~ in his reckoning⟩ **b :** POOR,

SUBNORMAL **c :** not entirely sane **:** ECCENTRIC **d :** REMOTE, SLIGHT ⟨an ~ chance⟩ **4 a :** spent off duty ⟨reading on his ~ days⟩ **b :** SLACK ⟨~ season⟩ **5 a :** OFF-COLOR **b :** INFERIOR ⟨~ grade of oil⟩; *also* **:** TAINTED **c :** DOWN ⟨stocks were ~⟩ **6 :** CIRCUMSTANCED ⟨well ~⟩

4**off** \'ȯf\ *vi* **:** to go away **:** DEPART — used chiefly as an imperative

of·fal \'ȯ-fəl, 'äf-əl\ *n* [ME, fr. *of* off + *fall*] **1 :** the waste or by-product of a process: as **a :** trimmings of a hide **b :** the by-products of milling used esp. for stock feeds **c :** the viscera and trimmings of a butchered animal removed in dressing **2 :** RUBBISH

off and on *adv* **:** with interruptions **:** INTERMITTENTLY

1**off·beat** \'ȯf-,bēt\ *n* **:** the unaccented part of a musical measure

2**offbeat** *adj* **:** ECCENTRIC, UNCONVENTIONAL

off·cast \'ȯf-,kast\ *adj* **:** cast off **:** DISCARDED — **offcast** *n*

off–col·or \'ȯf-'kəl-ər\ *or* **off–col·ored** \-ərd\ *adj* **1 a :** not having the right or standard color **b :** being out of sorts **2 a :** of doubtful propriety **:** DUBIOUS **b :** RISQUÉ

of·fend \ə-'fend\ *vb* [ME *offenden*, fr. MF *offendre*, fr. L *offendere* to strike against, offend, fr. *ob-* against + *-fendere* to strike — more at OB-, DEFEND] *vi* **1 a :** to transgress the moral or divine law **:** SIN **b :** to violate a law or rule **:** do wrong ⟨~ against the law⟩ **2 a :** to cause difficulty or discomfort or injury **b :** to cause dislike, anger, or vexation ~ *vt* **1 a :** VIOLATE, TRANSGRESS **b :** to cause pain to **:** HURT **2** *obs* **:** to cause to sin or fall **3 :** to cause to feel vexed or resentful — **of·fend·er** *n*

syn OFFEND, OUTRAGE, AFFRONT, INSULT mean to cause hurt feelings or deep resentment. OFFEND may not imply intent; it may suggest a violation of the victim's sense of what is proper or fitting; OUTRAGE implies offending beyond endurance and calling forth extreme feelings; AFFRONT implies treating with deliberate rudeness or contemptuous indifference to courtesy; INSULT suggests deliberately causing humiliation, hurt pride, or shame

of·fense *or* **of·fence** \ə-'fen(t)s, 'äf-,en(t)s\ *n* [ME, fr. MF, fr. L *offensa*, fr. *offensus*, pp. of *offendere*] **1 a** *obs* **:** an act of stumbling **b** *archaic* **:** a cause or occasion of sin **:** STUMBLING BLOCK **2 :** something that outrages the moral or physical senses **:** NUISANCE **3 a :** the act of attacking **:** ASSAULT **b (1) :** the state of being on the attack and trying to score (as in football or hockey) **(2) :** an offensive team **c :** scoring ability **4 a :** the act of displeasing or affronting **b :** the state of being insulted or morally outraged **5 a :** SIN, MISDEED **b :** an infraction of law **:** CRIME — **of·fense·less** \-ləs\ *adj*

syn OFFENSE, RESENTMENT, UMBRAGE, PIQUE, DUDGEON, HUFF mean an emotional response to a slight or indignity. OFFENSE implies hurt displeasure; RESENTMENT suggests a longer lasting indignation or smoldering ill will; UMBRAGE implies a feeling of being snubbed or ignored; PIQUE applies to a transient feeling of wounded vanity; DUDGEON suggests an angry fit of indignation; HUFF implies a peevish short-lived spell of anger usu. at a petty cause

syn OFFENSE, SIN, VICE, CRIME, SCANDAL mean a transgression of law. OFFENSE is a general term applying to the infraction of any law, rule, or code; SIN implies an offense against the moral law; VICE applies to a habit or practice that degrades or corrupts; CRIME implies a serious offense punishable by the law of the state; SCANDAL applies to an offense that outrages the public conscience or damages the integrity of an organization or group

1**of·fen·sive** \ə-'fen(t)-siv, 'äf-,en(t)-\ *adj* **1 a :** making attack **:** AGGRESSIVE **b :** of, relating to, or designed for attack ⟨~ weapons⟩ **c :** being on offense ⟨a good ~ player⟩ **2 :** giving painful or unpleasant sensations **:** NAUSEOUS, OBNOXIOUS **3 :** INSULTING, AFFRONTING — **of·fen·sive·ly** *adv* — **of·fen·sive·ness** *n*

2**offensive** *n* **1 :** the act of an attacking party **2 :** ATTACK

1**of·fer** \'ȯf-ər, 'äf-\ *vb* **of·fer·ing** \-(ə-)riŋ\ [ME *offren*, in sense 1, fr. OE *offrian*, fr. LL *offerre*, fr. L, to present, tender, fr. *ob-* toward + *ferre* to carry; in other senses, fr. OF *offrir*, fr. L *offerre* — more at OB-, BEAR] *vt* **1 a :** to present as an act of worship or devotion **:** SACRIFICE **b :** to utter in devotion **2 a :** to present for acceptance or rejection **:** TENDER **b :** to present in order to satisfy a requirement **3 a :** PROPOSE, SUGGEST **b :** to declare one's readiness or willingness ⟨~*ed* to help me⟩ **4 a :** to put up ⟨~*ed* stubborn resistance⟩ **b :** THREATEN ⟨~*ed* to strike him with his cane⟩ **5 :** to make available **:** AFFORD; *esp* **:** to place (merchandise) on sale **6 :** to present in performance or exhibition **7 :** to propose as payment **:** BID ~ *vi* **1 :** to present something as an act of worship or devotion **:** SACRIFICE **2** *archaic* **:** to make an attempt **3 :** to present itself **4 :** to make a proposal (as of marriage)

2**offer** *n* **1 a :** PROPOSAL; *specif* **:** a proposal of marriage **b :** an undertaking to do an act or give something on condition that the party to whom the proposal is made do some specified act or make a return promise **2** *obs* **:** OFFERING **3 :** a price named by one proposing to buy **:** BID **4 a :** ATTEMPT, TRY **b :** an action or movement indicating a purpose or intention

of·fer·ing *n* **1 a :** the act of one who offers **b :** something offered; *esp* **:** a sacrifice ceremonially offered to God **c :** a contribution to the support of a church **2 :** something offered for sale **3 :** a course of instruction or study

of·fer·to·ry \'ȯf-ə(r)-,tōr-ē, 'äf-, -,tȯr-\ *n* [ML *offertorium*, fr. *offertus*, pp. of LL *offerre*] **1** *often cap* **a :** the eucharistic offering of bread and wine to God before they are consecrated at Communion **b :** a verse from a Psalm said or sung at the beginning of the offertory **2 a :** the presentation of the offerings of the congregation at public worship **b :** the musical accompaniment played or sung during an offertory

off·hand \'ȯf-'hand\ *adv* (*or adj*) **1 :** without premeditation or preparation **:** EXTEMPORE **2 :** from a standing position without a support or rest ⟨~ shooting⟩

off·hand·ed \-'han-dəd\ *adj* **:** OFFHAND — **off·hand·ed·ly** *adv* — **off·hand·ed·ness** *n*

of·fice \'ȯf-əs, 'äf-\ *n* [ME, fr. OF, fr. L *officium* service, duty, office, fr. *opus* work + *facere* to make, do — more at OPERATE, DO] **1 a :** a special duty, charge, or position conferred by an exercise of governmental authority and for a public purpose **:** a position of authority to exercise a public function and to receive whatever emoluments may belong to it ⟨hold public ~⟩ **b :** a position of responsibility or some degree of executive authority **2** [ME, fr. OF, fr. LL *officium*, fr. L] **:** a prescribed form or service of worship; *specif, cap* **:** DIVINE OFFICE **3 :** a religious or social ceremonial observance **:** RITE **4 a :** something that one ought to do or must do **:** an assigned or assumed duty, task, or role **b :** the proper or customary action of something **:** FUNCTION **5 :** a place where a particular kind of business is transacted or a service is supplied: as **a :** a place in which the functions (as consulting, record keeping, clerical work) of a public officer are performed **b :** the directing headquarters of an enterprise or organization **c :** the place in which a professional man (as a physician or lawyer) conducts his professional business **6** *pl, chiefly Brit* **:** the apartments, attached buildings, or outhouses in which the activities attached to the service of a house are carried on **7 a :** a major administrative unit in some governments ⟨British Foreign *Office*⟩ **b :** a subdivision of some government departments ⟨Patent *Office*⟩ **syn** see FUNCTION, POSITION

office boy *n* **:** a boy employed for odd jobs in a business office

of·fice·hold·er \-,hōl-dər\ *n* **:** one holding a public office esp. in the civil service

1**of·fi·cer** \'ȯf-ə-sər, 'äf-, *rapid* 'ȯf-sər, 'äf-\ *n* [ME, fr. MF *officier*, fr. ML *officiarius*, fr. L *officium*] **1 a** *obs* **:** AGENT **b :** one charged with police duties **2 :** one who holds an office of trust, authority, or command **3 a :** one who holds a position of authority or command in the armed forces; *specif* **:** one who holds a commission **b :** the master or any of the mates of a merchant or passenger ship

2**officer** *vt* **1 :** to furnish with officers **2 :** to command or direct as an officer

1**of·fi·cial** \ə-'fish-əl\ *n* **:** one who holds or is invested with an office and esp. a subordinate one **:** OFFICER

2**official** *adj* **1 :** of or relating to an office, position, or trust **2 :** holding an office **3 a :** AUTHORIZED, AUTHORITATIVE **b :** prescribed or recognized as authorized; *specif* **:** described by the U.S. Pharmacopeia or the National Formulary **4 :** befitting or characteristic of a person in office **:** FORMAL — **of·fi·cial·ly** \-'fish-(ə-)lē\ *adv*

of·fi·cial·dom \ə-'fish-əl-dəm\ *n* **:** officials as a class

of·fi·cial·ism \-'fish-ə-,liz-əm\ *n* **:** lack of flexibility and initiative combined with excessive adherence to regulations in the behavior of usu. government officials

of·fi·ci·ant \ə-'fish-ē-ənt\ *n* **:** an officiating priest or minister

1**of·fi·ci·ary** \ə-'fish-ē-,er-ē, ȯ-, ä-\ *n* [ML *officiarius*] **1 :** OFFICER, OFFICIAL **2 :** a body of officers or officials

2**officiary** *adj* **:** connected with, derived from, or having a title or rank by virtue of holding an office ⟨~ earl⟩

of·fi·ci·ate \ə-'fish-ē-,āt\ *vi* **1 :** to perform a ceremony, function, or duty **2 :** to act in an official capacity ~ *vt* **1 :** to carry out (an official duty or function) **2 :** to serve as a leader or celebrant of (a ceremony) **3 :** to administer the rules of (a game or sport) esp. as a referee or umpire — **of·fi·ci·a·tion** \-,fish-ē-'ā-shən\ *n*

of·fi·ci·nal \ə-'fis-ᵊn-əl, ȯ-, ä-; ,ȯf-ə-'sīn-ᵊl, ,äf-\ *adj* [ML *officinalis* of a storeroom, fr. *officina* storeroom, fr. L, workshop, fr. *opific-, opifex* workman, fr. *opus* work + *facere* to do] **1 :** available without special preparation or compounding ⟨~ medicine⟩; *also* **:** OFFICIAL 3b **2 :** MEDICINAL ⟨~ herbs⟩ — **officinal** *n* — **of·fi·ci·nal·ly** \-ē\ *adv*

of·fi·cious \ə-'fish-əs\ *adj* [L *officiosus*, fr. *officium* service, office] **1** *obs* **a :** KIND, OBLIGING **b :** DUTIFUL **2 :** volunteering one's services where they are neither asked nor needed **:** MEDDLESOME **3 :** INFORMAL, UNOFFICIAL **syn** see IMPERTINENT — **of·fi·cious·ly** *adv* — **of·fi·cious·ness** *n*

off·ing \'ȯf-iŋ, 'äf-\ *n* [1*off*] **1 :** the part of the deep sea seen from the shore **2 :** the near or foreseeable future or the near distance

off·ish \'ȯf-ish\ *adj* [1*off*] **:** inclined to stand aloof — **off·ish·ly** *adv* — **off·ish·ness** *n*

off of *prep* **:** OFF

off·print \'ȯf-,print\ *n* **:** a separately printed excerpt — **offprint** *vt*

off·scour·ing \-,skau̇(ə)r-iŋ\ *n* **1 :** something that is scoured off **:** REFUSE **2 :** someone rejected by society **:** OUTCAST

1**off·set** \-,set\ *n* **1 a** *archaic* **:** OUTSET, START **b :** CESSATION **2 a :** a short prostrate lateral shoot arising from the base of a plant **b :** a lateral or collateral branch (as of a family or race) **:** OFFSHOOT **c :** a spur from a range of hills **3 a :** a horizontal ledge on the face of a wall formed by a diminution of its thickness above **b :** an abrupt change in the dimension or profile of an object or the part set off by such change **4 :** something that sets off to advantage or embellishes something else **:** FOIL **5 :** an abrupt bend in an object by which one part is turned aside out of line **6 :** something that serves to counterbalance or to compensate for something else; *specif* **:** either of two balancing ledger items **7 a :** unintentional transfer of ink (as from a freshly printed sheet) **b :** a printing process in which an inked impression from a planographic surface is first made on a rubber-blanketed cylinder and then transferred to the paper being printed — **offset** *adj*

2**off·set** \'ȯf-,set, *vt senses are also* ȯf-'\ *vt* **1 a :** to place over against **:** BALANCE **b :** to compensate for **:** COUNTERBALANCE **2 :** to form an offset in ~ *vi* **:** to become marked by offset **syn** see COMPENSATE

off·shoot \'ȯf-,shüt\ *n* **1 :** a branch of a main stem **2 a :** a lateral branch (as of a mountain range) **b :** a collateral or derived branch, descendant, or member

1**off·shore** \'ȯf-'shō(ə)r, -'shȯ(ə)r\ *adv* **:** from the shore **:** at a distance from the shore

2**off·shore** \'ȯf-,\ *adj* **1 :** coming or moving away from the shore **2 a :** situated off the shore within a zone extending three miles from low-water line **b :** distant from the shore

off side *adv* (*or adj*) **:** illegally in advance of the ball or puck

off·spring \'ȯf-,spriŋ\ *n, pl* **offspring** *also* **offsprings** [ME *ofspring*, fr. OE, fr. *of* off + *springan* to spring] **1 :** the progeny of an animal or plant **:** YOUNG **2 :** PRODUCT, RESULT

off·stage \'ȯf-'stāj, -,stāj\ *adv* (*or adj*) **1 :** off or away from the stage **2 :** out of the public view

off–the–rec·ord \,ȯf-t͟hə-'rek-ərd *also* -'rek-,ȯ(ə)rd\ *adj* **:** given or made in confidence and not for publication

off–white \'ȯf-'hwīt, -'wīt\ *n* **:** a yellowish or grayish white

off year *n* **1 :** a year in which no major election is held **2 :** a year of diminished activity or production

oft \'ȯft\ *adv* [ME, fr. OE; akin to OHG *ofto* often] **:** OFTEN

of·ten \'ȯ-fən *also* 'ȯf-tən\ *adv* [ME, alter. of *oft*] **:** many times

of·ten·times \-,tīmz\ *or* **oft·times** \'ȯf(t)-,tīmz\ *adv* **:** OFTEN

O gauge \'ō-\ *n* [2*oh*] **:** a gauge of track in model railroading in which the rails are approximately 1¼ inches apart

ogee *also* **OG** \'ō-,jē\ *n* [obs. E *ogee* (ogive); fr. the use of such moldings in ogives] **1 :** a molding with an S-shaped profile

2 : a pointed arch having on each side a reversed curve near the apex

ogham *or* **ogam** \'äg-əm, 'ō(-ə)m\ *n* [IrGael *ogham*, fr. MIr *ogom, ogum*] **:** the alphabetic system of 5th and 6th century Old Irish in which an alphabet of 20 letters is represented by notches for vowels and lines for consonants cut on the edges of rough standing tombstones — **ogham·ic** \ä-'gam-ik, 'ō-(ə-)mik\ *adj* — **ogham·ist** \'äg-ə-məst, 'ō-(ə-)məst\ *n*

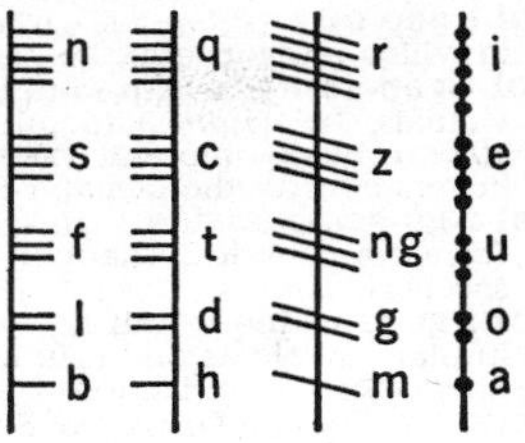

ogham

ogi·val \ō-'jī-vəl\ *adj* **:** of, relating to, or having the form of an ogive or an ogee

ogive \'ō-,jīv\ *n* [F] **1 a :** a diagonal arch or rib across a Gothic vault **b :** a pointed arch **2 :** a graph each of whose ordinates represents the sum of all the frequencies up to and including a corresponding frequency in a frequency distribution **3 :** OGEE 1

1ogle \'ō-gəl *also* 'äg-\ *vb* **ogling** \-(ə-)liŋ\ [prob. fr. LG *oegeln*, fr. *oog* eye; akin to OHG *ouga* eye — more at EYE] *vi* **:** to glance with amorous invitation or challenge ~ *vt* **:** to eye amorously or provocatively — **ogler** \-(ə-)lər\ *n*

2ogle *n* **:** an amorous or coquettish glance

ogre \'ō-gər\ *n* [F] **1 :** a hideous giant of fairy tales and folklore that feeds on human beings **:** MONSTER **2 :** a dreaded person or object — **ogre·ish** \'ō-g(ə-)rish\ *adj* — **ogress** \'ō-g(ə-)rəs\ *n*

1oh \(')ō\ *interj* [ME *o*] **1** — used to express various emotions (as astonishment, pain, or desire) **2** — used in direct address ⟨*Oh*, porter! Will you come here, please?⟩

2oh \'ō\ *n* [*o*; fr. the similarity of the symbol for zero (0) to the letter *O*] **:** ZERO

ohm \'ōm\ *n* [Georg Simon *Ohm* †1854 G physicist] **:** the practical mks unit of electric resistance equal to the resistance of a circuit in which a potential difference of one volt produces a current of one ampere — **ohm·ic** \'ō-mik\ *adj*

ohm·age \'ō-mij\ *n* **:** the ohmic resistance of a conductor

ohm·me·ter \'ō(m)-,mēt-ər\ *n* [ISV] **:** an instrument for indicating resistance in ohms directly

-o·ic \'ō-ik\ *adj suffix* [*-o-* + *-ic*] **:** containing carboxyl or a derivative ⟨decano*ic* acid⟩

1-oid \,ȯid\ *n suffix* **:** something resembling a (specified) object or having a (specified) quality ⟨glob*oid*⟩

2-oid *adj suffix* [MF & L; MF *-oïde*, fr. L *-oïdes*, fr. Gk *-oeidēs*, fr. *-o-* + *eidos* appearance, form — more at WISE] **:** resembling **:** having the form or appearance of ⟨petal*oid*⟩

1oil \'ȯi(ə)l\ *n* [ME *oile*, fr. OF, fr. L *oleum* olive oil, fr. Gk *elaion*, fr. *elaia* olive] **1 a :** any of numerous unctuous combustible substances that are liquid or at least easily liquefiable on warming, are soluble in ether but not in water, and leave a greasy stain on paper or cloth **b :** PETROLEUM **2 :** a substance of oily consistency **3 a :** an oil color used by an artist **b :** a painting done in oil colors **4 :** unctuous or flattering speech — **oil** *adj*

2oil *vt* **:** to smear, rub over, furnish, or lubricate with oil ~ *vi* **:** to take on fuel oil

oil beetle *n* **:** a blister beetle (*Meloe* or a related genus) emitting a yellowish liquid from the leg joints when disturbed

oil cake *n* **:** the solid residue after extracting the oil from seeds (as of cotton)

oil·cloth \'ȯi(ə)l-,klȯth\ *n* **:** cloth treated with oil or paint and used for table and shelf coverings

oil color *n* **1 :** a pigment used for oil paint **2 :** OIL PAINT

oil·er \'ȯi-lər\ *n* **1 :** one that oils **2 :** a receptacle or device for applying oil **3 :** a producing oil well **4 a :** a ship using oil as fuel **b :** an oil-cargo ship **5** *pl* **:** OILSKINS

oil field *n* **:** a region rich in petroleum deposits

oil·i·ly \'ȯi-lə-lē\ *adv* **:** in an oily manner **:** UNCTUOUSLY

oil·i·ness \-lē-nəs\ *n* **:** the quality or state of being oily

oil of vitriol : concentrated sulfuric acid

oil paint *n* **:** paint in which a drying oil is the vehicle

oil painting *n* **1 a :** the act or art of painting in oil colors **b :** a picture painted in oils **2 :** painting that uses pigments orig. ground in oil

oil palm *n* **:** an African pinnate-leaved palm (*Elaeis guineensis*) cultivated for its clustered fruit of which both the flesh and seeds yield palm oil

oil pan *n* **:** the lower section of the crankcase used as a lubricating-oil reservoir on an internal-combustion engine

oil·seed \'ȯi(ə)l-,sēd\ *n* **:** a seed or crop (as linseed) grown largely for oil

oil·skin \-,skin\ *n* **1 :** an oiled waterproof cloth used for coverings and garments **2 :** an oilskin raincoat **3** *pl* **:** an oilskin suit of coat and trousers

oil slick *n* **:** a film of oil floating on water

oil·stone \'ȯi(ə)l-,stōn\ *n* **:** a whetstone for use with oil

oil well *n* **:** a well from which petroleum is obtained

oily \'ȯi-lē\ *adj* **1 :** of, relating to, or consisting of oil **2 :** covered or impregnated with oil **:** GREASY ⟨~ rags⟩ **3 :** UNCTUOUS, INGRATIATING ⟨an ~ press agent⟩

oint·ment \'ȯint-mənt\ *n* [ME, alter. of *oignement*, fr. OF, modif. of L *unguentum*, fr. *unguere* to anoint; akin to OHG *ancho* butter, Skt *añjati* he salves] **:** a salve or unguent for application to the skin

oi·ti·ci·ca \,ȯit-ə-'sē-kə\ *n* [Pg, fr. Tupi] **:** any of several So. American trees; *esp* **:** a Brazilian tree (*Licania rigida*) whose seeds yield an oil similar to tung oil

Ojib·wa *or* **Ojib·way** \ō-'jib-(,)wā\ *n* [Ojibwa *ojib-ubway*, a kind of moccasin worn by the Ojibwas] **1 a :** an Indian people of the region around Lake Superior **b :** a member of this people **2 :** an Algonquian language of the Ojibwa people

1OK *or* **okay** \ō-'kā, *in assenting or agreeing also* 'ō-,kā *or* 'ō-,kā\ *adv (or adj)* [abbr. of *oll korrect*, alter. of *all correct*] **:** all right

2OK *or* **okay** \ō-'kā\ *vt* **OK'd** *or* **okayed; OK'·ing** *or* **okay·ing :** APPROVE, AUTHORIZE

3OK *or* **okay** \ō-'kā\ *n* **:** APPROVAL, ENDORSEMENT

oka·pi \ō-'käp-ē\ *n* [native name in Africa] **:** an African mammal (*Okapia johnstoni*) closely related to the giraffe but lacking the elongated neck

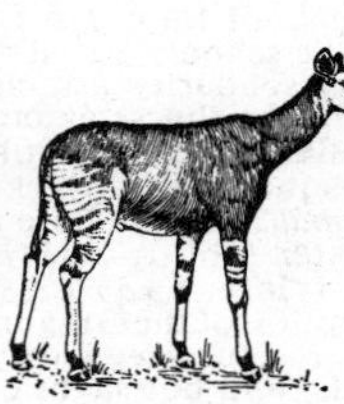
okapi

oke \'ōk\ *or* **oka** \ō-'kä\ *n* [F, NGk & Turk; F *oque*, fr. NGk & Turk; NGk *oka*, fr. Turk *okka*, fr. Ar *ūqiyah*] **:** any of three units of weight varying around 2.8 pounds and used respectively in Greece, Turkey, and Egypt

Okie \'ō-kē\ *n* [*Ok*lahoma + *-ie*] **:** a migrant agricultural worker; *esp* **:** such a worker from Oklahoma

okra \'ō-krə, *South also* -krē\ *n* [of African origin; akin to Twi ŋ^{1}ku^{1}rũ^{1}mã^3 okra] **1 :** a tall annual (*Hibiscus esculentus*) of the mallow family cultivated for its mucilaginous green pods used esp. in soups or stews; *also* **:** the pods of this plant **2 :** GUMBO 2

1-ol \,ȯl, ,ōl\ *n suffix* [ISV, fr. *alcohol*] **:** chemical compound (as an alcohol or phenol) containing hydroxyl ⟨glycer*ol*⟩ ⟨creos*ol*⟩

2-ol — see -OLE

3-ol *n comb form* [ISV, fr. L *oleum* oil — more at OIL] **:** hydrocarbon chemically related to benzene ⟨xyl*ol*⟩

1old \'ōld\ *adj* [ME, fr. OE *eald;* akin to OHG *alt* old, L *alere* to nourish, *alescere* to grow, *altus* high, deep] **1 a :** dating from the remote past **:** ANCIENT ⟨~ traditions⟩ **b :** persisting from an earlier time **:** CHRONIC ⟨an ~ ailment⟩ **c :** of long standing ⟨an ~ friend⟩ **2 a :** distinguished from an object of the same kind by being of an earlier date **b** *cap* **:** belonging to an early period in the development of a language or literature ⟨*Old* Irish⟩ **3 :** having existed for a specified period of time ⟨a girl three years ~⟩ **4 :** of, relating to, or originating in a past era **:** ANTIQUE ⟨the ~ chronicles⟩ **5 a :** advanced in years or age ⟨an ~ man⟩ **b :** showing the characteristics of age ⟨looked ~ at 20⟩ **6 :** EXPERIENCED ⟨an ~ offender⟩ **7 :** FORMER ⟨his ~ students⟩ **8 a :** showing the effects of time or use **:** WORN, AGED ⟨~ shoes⟩ **b :** well advanced toward reduction to baselevel — used of topographic features **c :** no longer in use **:** DISCARDED ⟨~ rags⟩ **d :** of a grayish or dusty tone color ⟨~ mauve⟩ **9 a :** long familiar ⟨same ~ story⟩ ⟨good ~ Joe⟩ **b** — used as an intensive ⟨a high ~ time⟩ ⟨any ~ time⟩

syn ANCIENT, VENERABLE, ANTIQUE, ANTIQUATED, ARCHAIC, OBSOLETE: OLD may imply either actual or merely relative length of existence; ANCIENT implies occurrence, existence, or use in the distant past; VENERABLE stresses the hoariness and dignity of great age; ANTIQUE suggests a surviving in knowledge or use from at least a fairly remote past; ANTIQUATED implies being discredited or outmoded or otherwise inappropriate to the present time; ARCHAIC implies having the character or characteristics of a much earlier period; OBSOLETE implies having gone out of currency or habitual practice

2old *n* **1 :** old or earlier time **2 :** one of a specified age ⟨a 3-year-*old*⟩

Old Bulgarian *n* **:** OLD CHURCH SLAVONIC

Old Catholic *n* **:** a member of one of various hierarchical and liturgical churches separating from the Roman Catholic Church since the 18th century

Old Christmas *n, chiefly Midland* **:** EPIPHANY 1

Old Church Slavonic *n* **:** the Slavic language used in the Bible translation of Cyril and Methodius and as the liturgical language of several Eastern churches — called also *Old Church Slavic*

old country *n* **:** an emigrant's country of origin; *esp* **:** EUROPE

old·en \'ōl-dən\ *adj* **:** of or relating to a bygone era **:** ANCIENT

Old English *n* **1 a :** the language of the English people from the time of the earliest documents in the 7th century to about 1100 **b :** English of any period before Modern English **2 :** BLACK LETTER

Old English sheepdog *n* **:** any of an English breed of medium-sized sheep and cattle dogs with a profuse, shaggy, blue-gray and white coat that hangs almost to the ground

old·fan·gled \'ōl(d)-'faŋ-gəld\ *adj* [*old* + *-fangled* (as in *newfangled*)] **:** OLD-FASHIONED

old-fash·ioned \-'fash-ənd\ *adj* **1 :** of, relating to, or characteristic of a past era **2 :** adhering to customs of a past era

Old French *n* **:** the French language from the 9th to the 16th century; *esp* **:** French from the 9th to the 13th century

Old Glory *n* **:** the flag of the U.S.

old gold *n* **:** a variable color averaging a dark yellow

old guard *n, often cap O & G* **:** the conservative members (as of a political party) who are unwilling to accept new ideas, practices, or conditions

old hand *n* **:** VETERAN

Old High German *n* **:** High German exemplified in documents prior to the 12th century

Old Ionic *n* **:** the Greek dialect of the Homeric epics

old·ish \'ōl-dish\ *adj* **:** somewhat old or elderly

old-line \'ōl-'(d)līn\ *adj* **1 :** having a reputation or authority based on seniority **:** ESTABLISHED **2 :** adhering to old policies or practices **:** CONSERVATIVE

old maid *n* **1 :** SPINSTER 3 **2 :** a prim nervous fussy person **3 :** a simple card game in which the player holding the odd queen at the end is an "old maid" — **old-maid·ish** \'ōl(d)-'mād-ish\ *adj*

old man *n* **1 a :** HUSBAND **b :** FATHER **2** *cap* **:** one in authority; *esp* **:** COMMANDING OFFICER

old master *n* **1 :** a superior artist or craftsman of established reputation; *esp* **:** a distinguished painter of the 16th, 17th, or early 18th century **2 :** a work by an old master

Old Nick \'ōl(d)-'nik\ *n* **:** DEVIL, SATAN

Old Norse *n* **:** the North Germanic language of the Scandinavian peoples prior to about 1350

Old North French *n* **:** the northern dialects of Old French including esp. those of Normandy and Picardy

Old Prussian *n* **:** a Baltic language used in East Prussia until the 17th century

old rose *n* **:** a variable color averaging a grayish red

Old Saxon *n* **:** the language of the Saxons of northwest Germany until about the 12th century

old school *n* **:** adherents to the policies and practices of the past

old school tie *n* **1 a :** a necktie displaying the colors of an English public school **b :** an attitude of conservatism, aplomb, and upper-class solidarity associated with English public school graduates **2 :** clannishness among members of an established clique
old sledge *n* **:** SEVEN-UP
old–squaw \'ōl(d)-'skwȯ\ *n* **:** a common sea duck (*Clangula hyemalis*) of the more northern parts of the northern hemisphere
old·ster \'ōl(d)-stər\ *n* **:** an old or elderly person
old style *n* **1** *cap O&S* **:** a style of reckoning time used before the adoption of the Gregorian calendar **2 :** a style of type distinguished by graceful irregularity among individual letters, slanted ascender serifs, and but slight contrast between light and heavy strokes
Old Style *adj* **:** using or according to the Julian calendar
Old Testament *n* **:** the first part of the Christian Bible containing the books relating to God's covenant with the Hebrews
old–time \'ōl(d)-,tīm\ *adj* **:** of, relating to, or characteristic of an earlier period
old–tim·er \-'tī-mər\ *n* **1 a :** VETERAN **b :** OLDSTER **2 :** something that is old-fashioned **:** ANTIQUE
Old Welsh *n* **:** the Welsh language exemplified in documents prior to about 1150
old·wife \'ōl-,(d)wīf\ *n* **1 :** any of several marine fishes (as an alewife, menhaden, or triggerfish) **2 :** OLD-SQUAW
old wives' tale *n* **:** a traditional tale or bit of lore
Old World *n* **:** EASTERN HEMISPHERE; *specif* **:** Europe
old–world \'ōl-'(d)wər(-ə)ld\ *adj* **:** OLD-FASHIONED, PICTURESQUE
ole- *or* **oleo-** *comb form* [F *olé-, oléo-*, fr. L *ole-*, fr. *oleum* — more at OIL] **:** oil ⟨*ole*ic⟩ ⟨*oleo*graph⟩
-ole \,ōl\ *also* **-ol** \,ȯl, ,ōl\ *n comb form* [ISV, fr. L *oleum*] **1 :** chemical compound containing a five-membered usu. heterocyclic ring ⟨diaz*ole*⟩ ⟨pyrr*ole*⟩ **2 :** chemical compound not containing hydroxyl ⟨eucalypt*ol*⟩ — esp. in names of ethers ⟨phenet*ole*⟩
ole·ag·i·nous \,ō-lē-'aj-ə-nəs\ *adj* [MF *oleagineux*, fr. L *oleagineus* of an olive tree, fr. *olea* olive tree, fr. Gk *elaia*] **1 :** resembling or having the properties of oil; *also* **:** containing or producing oil **2 :** UNCTUOUS — **ole·ag·i·nous·ly** *adv* — **ole·ag·i·nous·ness** *n*
ole·an·der \'ō-lē-,an-dər, ,ō-lē-'\ *n* [ML] **:** a poisonous evergreen shrub (*Nerium oleander*) of the dogbane family with fragrant white to red flowers
ole·as·ter \'ō-lē-,as-tər, ,ō-lē-'\ *n* [L, fr. *olea*] **:** any of several plants (genus *Elaeagnus* of the family Elaeagnaceae, the oleaster family); *esp* **:** RUSSIAN OLIVE
ole·ate \'ō-lē-,āt\ *n* **:** a salt or ester of oleic acid
ole·cra·non \,ō-lə-'krā-,nän\ *n* [NL, fr. Gk *ōlekranon*, fr. *ōlenē* elbow + *kranion* skull — more at ELL, CRANIUM] **:** the process of the ulna projecting behind the elbow joint
ole·fin \'ō-lə-fən\ *n* [ISV, fr. F (*gaz*) *oléfiant* ethylene, fr. L *oleum*] **:** an unsaturated open-chain hydrocarbon containing at least one double bond — **ole·fin·ic** \,ō-lə-'fin-ik\ *adj*
ole·ic \ō-'lē-ik, -'lā-\ *adj* **1 :** relating to, derived from, or contained in oil **2 :** of or relating to oleic acid
oleic acid *n* **:** an unsaturated fatty acid $C_{18}H_{34}O_2$ found as glycerides in natural fats and oils
ole·in \'ō-lē-ən\ *n* [F *oléine*, fr. L *oleum*] **1 :** an ester of glycerol and oleic acid **2** *also* **ole·ine** \-ən, -,ēn\ **:** the liquid portion of a fat
oleo \'ō-lē-,ō\ *n* **1** [short for *oleomargarine*] **:** MARGARINE **2 :** OLEOGRAPH
oleo·graph \'ō-lē-ə-,graf\ *n* [ISV *ole-* + *-graph*] **:** a chromolithograph printed on canvas or other cloth to imitate an oil painting — **oleo·graph·ic** \,ō-lē-ə-'graf-ik\ *adj* — **ole·og·ra·phy** \,ō-lē-'äg-rə-fē\ *n*
oleo·mar·ga·rine \,ō-lē-ō-'märj-(ə-)rən, -'märj-ə-,rēn\ *n* [F *oléomargarine*, fr. *olé-* + *margarine*] **:** MARGARINE
oleo·res·in \-'rez-ᵊn\ *n* [ISV] **1 :** a plant product (as copaiba) containing chiefly essential oil and resin; *esp* **:** TURPENTINE 1b **2 :** a preparation consisting essentially of oil holding resin in solution — **oleo·res·in·ous** \-'rez-ᵊn-əs, -'rez-nəs\ *adj*
oleri·cul·ture \ə-'ler-ə-,kəl-chər, ä-'ler-ə-, 'äl-ə-ri-\ *n* [L *holer-, holus* vegetables + E *-i-* + *culture*; akin to L *helvus* light bay — more at YELLOW] **:** a branch of horticulture that deals with the production, storage, processing, and marketing of vegetables
ole·um \'ō-lē-əm\ *n* [L — more at OIL] **1** *pl* **olea** \-lē-ə\ **:** OIL **2** *pl* **oleums :** a heavy oily strongly corrosive solution of sulfur trioxide in anhydrous sulfuric acid
ol·fac·tion \äl-'fak-shən, ōl-', 'äl-,, 'ōl-,\ *n* **:** the sense of smell **:** the act or process of smelling
ol·fac·to·ry \äl-'fak-t(ə-)rē, ōl-\ *adj* [L *olfactorius*, fr. *olfactus*, pp. of *olfacere* to smell, fr. *olēre* to smell + *facere* to do — more at ODOR, DO] **:** of, relating to, or connected with the sense of smell
olfactory nerve *n* **:** either of a pair of sensory cranial nerves that arise in the olfactory organ, pass to the anterior part of the cerebrum, and conduct stimuli from the olfactory organ to the brain — called also *first cranial nerve*
olfactory organ *n* **:** a membranous organ of chemical sense in the nasal cavity that receives stimuli interpreted as odors from volatile and soluble substances in low dilution
olib·a·num \ō-'lib-ə-nəm, ä-\ *n* [ME, fr. ML, fr. Ar *al-lubān* the frankincense] **:** FRANKINCENSE
olig- *or* **oligo-** *comb form* [ML, fr. Gk, fr. *oligos*; akin to Arm *alkat* scant] **:** few ⟨*oligo*phagous⟩
ol·i·garch \'äl-ə-,gärk\ *n* [Gk *oligarchēs*, fr. *olig-* + *-archēs* -arch] **:** a member or supporter of an oligarchy
ol·i·gar·chic \,äl-ə-'gär-kik\ *adj* **:** of, relating to, or based on an oligarchy — **ol·i·gar·chi·cal** \-ki-kəl\ *adj*
ol·i·gar·chy \'äl-ə-,gär-kē\ *n* **1 :** government by the few **2 :** a government in which a small group exercises control esp. for corrupt and selfish purposes **3 :** an organization under oligarchic control; *also* **:** a group exercising such control
Ol·i·go·cene \'äl-i-gō-,sēn\ *adj* [ISV] **:** of, relating to, or being an epoch of the Tertiary between the Eocene and Miocene or the corresponding system of rocks — **Oligocene** *n*
ol·i·go·chaete \'äl-i-gō-,kēt\ *n* [deriv. of Gk *olig-* + *chaitē* long hair — more at CHAETA] **:** any of a class or order (Oligochaeta) of hermaphroditic terrestrial or aquatic annelids lacking a specialized head and including the earthworms — **oligochaete** *or* **ol·i·go·chae·tous** \,äl-i-gō-'kēt-əs\ *adj*
ol·i·go·clase \'äl-i-gō-,klās, -,klāz\ *n* [G *oligoklas*, fr. *olig-* + Gk *klasis* breaking, fr. *klan* to break — more at HALT] **:** a mineral of the plagioclase series
ol·i·goph·a·gous \,äl-i-'gäf-ə-gəs\ *adj* **:** eating only a few specific kinds of food — **ol·i·goph·a·gy** \-'gäf-ə-jē\ *n*
ol·i·gop·o·ly \-'gäp-ə-lē\ *n* [*olig-* + mono*poly*] **:** a market situation in which a few producers control the demand from many buyers
ol·i·gop·so·ny \-'gäp-sə-nē\ *n* [*olig-* + Gk *opsōnia* purchase of victuals, fr. *opsōnein* to purchase victuals, fr. *opson* food + *ōneisthai* to buy — more at VENAL] **:** a market situation in which a few buyers control the demand from a large number of sellers
ol·i·go·sac·cha·ride \,äl-i-gō-'sak-ə-,rīd\ *n* [ISV] **:** a saccharide (as a disaccharide) that contains a known small number of monosaccharide units
ol·i·go·tro·phic \-'träf-ik, -'trō-fik\ *adj* [ISV] *of a lake* **:** deficient in plant nutrients and usu. having abundant dissolved oxygen with no marked stratification
olio \'ō-lē-,ō\ *n* [modif. of Sp *olla*] **1 :** OLLA PODRIDA 1 **2 :** a miscellaneous mixture or collection **:** HODGEPODGE, MEDLEY
ol·i·va·ceous \,äl-i-'vā-shəs\ *adj* **:** of the color olive or olive green
1ol·ive \'äl-iv, -əv\ *n* [ME, fr. OF, fr. L *oliva*, fr. Gk *elaia*] **1 a :** a tree (*Olea europaea* of the family Oleaceae, the olive family) cultivated for its drupaceous fruit that is an important food and source of oil; *also* **:** the fruit **b :** any of various shrubs and trees resembling the olive **2 :** any of several colors resembling that of the unripe fruit of the olive tree that are yellow to olive green in hue, of medium to low lightness, and of moderate to low saturation
2olive *adj* **1 :** of the color olive or olive green **2 :** approaching olive in color or complexion
olive drab *n* **1 :** a variable color averaging a grayish olive **2 a :** a wool or cotton fabric of an olive drab color **b :** a uniform of this fabric
olive gray *n* **:** a variable color averaging a grayish yellow green
olive green *n* **:** a variable color that is greener, lighter, and stronger than average olive color
oliv·enite \ō-'liv-ə-,nīt\ *n* [G *olivenit*, fr. L *oliva*] **:** a mineral $Cu_2(AsO_4)(OH)$ that is a basic olive green, dull brown, or yellowish arsenate of copper
Ol·i·ver \'äl-ə-vər\ *n* [F *Olivier*] **:** one of the twelve peers of Charlemagne and companion-in-arms of Roland
ol·iv·ine \'äl-i-,vēn, ,äl-i-'\ *n* [G *olivin*, fr. L *oliva*] **1 :** a mineral $(Mg,Fe)_2SiO_4$ that is a complex silicate of magnesium and iron used esp. in refractories **2 :** DEMANTOID — **ol·iv·in·ic** \,äl-i-'vin-ik\ *or* **ol·iv·in·it·ic** \,äl-i-və-'nit-ik\ *adj*
ol·la \'äl-ə; 'ȯ(l)-yə, 'ō(l)-\ *n* [Sp, fr. L, pot — more at OVEN] **1** *chiefly Southwest* **:** a large bulging widemouthed earthenware jar with looped handles used esp. as a pot for stewing or as a container for water **2** *chiefly Southwest* **:** OLLA PODRIDA 1
ol·la po·dri·da \,äl-ə-pə-'drēd-ə; ,ȯ(l)-yə-, ,ō(l)-\ *n, pl* **ol·la po·dri·das** \-'drēd-əz\ *also* **ol·las podridas** \-ə(z)-pə-drēd-əz, -yə(z)-pə-\ [Sp, lit., rotten pot] **1 :** a highly seasoned stew made of one or more meats and several vegetables cooked in an olla **2 :** OLIO 2
olym·pi·ad \ō-'lim-pē-,ad, ō-\ *n, often cap* [MF *Olympiade*, fr. L *Olympiad-, Olympias*, fr. Gk, fr. *Olympia*, site of ancient Olympian games] **1 :** one of the four-year intervals between Olympian games by which time was reckoned in ancient Greece **2 :** a quadrennial celebration of the modern Olympic Games
1Olym·pi·an \ə-'lim-pē-ən, ō-\ *adj* **1 :** of or relating to the ancient Greek region of Olympia **2 :** of, relating to, or constituting the Olympian games
2Olympian *n* **:** a participant in Olympic Games
3Olympian *adj* **1 :** of or relating to Mount Olympus in Thessaly **2 :** befitting or characteristic of the gods of Olympus **:** LOFTY
4Olympian *n* **1 :** one of the Greek deities dwelling on Olympus **2 :** a being of lofty detachment or superior attainments
Olympian games *n pl* **:** an ancient Panhellenic festival held every 4th year and made up of contests in sports, music, and literature with the victor's prize a crown of wild olive
Olym·pic \ə-'lim-pik, ō-\ *adj* **:** 3OLYMPIAN
Olympic Games *n pl* **1 :** OLYMPIAN GAMES **2 :** a modified revival of the Olympian games held once every four years and made up of international athletic contests — called also *Olympics*
Olym·pus \ə-'lim-pəs, ō-\ *n* [L, fr. Gk *Olympos*] **:** a mountain in Thessaly held to be the abode of the Greek gods
-o·ma \'ō-mə\ *n suffix, pl* **-o·mas** \-məz\ *or* **-o·ma·ta** \-mət-ə\ [L *-omat-, -oma*, fr. Gk *-ōmat-, -ōma*, fr. *-ō-* (stem of causative verbs in *-oun*) + *-mat-, -ma*, suffix denoting result — more at -MENT] **:** tumor ⟨aden*oma*⟩ ⟨fibr*oma*⟩
Oma·ha \'ō-mə-,hȯ, -,hä\ *n, pl* **Omaha** *or* **Omahas** [Omaha, lit., those going upstream or against the wind] **1 :** a Siouan people of northeastern Nebraska **2 :** a member of the Omaha people
oma·sum \ō-'mā-səm\ *n, pl* **oma·sa** \-sə\ [NL, fr. L, tripe of a bullock] **:** the division between the reticulum and the abomasum in the stomach of a ruminant
om·bre \'äm-bər; 'äm-brē, 'əm-, -,brā\ *n* [F or Sp; F *hombre*, fr. Sp, lit., man] **:** an old 3-handed card game; *also* **:** the player in this game who elects to name the trump and oppose the other 2 players
om·buds·man \'ȯm-bədz-,man\ *n, pl* **om·buds·men** \-,men\ [Sw, lit., representative, fr. *ombud* charge, commission + *man* man] **:** a government official (as in Sweden or New Zealand) appointed to receive and investigate complaints made by individuals against abuses or capricious acts of public officials
-ome \,ōm\ *n suffix* [NL *-oma*, fr. L, -oma] **:** mass ⟨phyll*ome*⟩
ome·ga \ō-'meg-ə, -'mē-gə\ *n* [Gk *ō mega*, lit., large o] **1 :** the 24th letter of the Greek alphabet — symbol Ω or ω **2 :** LAST, ENDING **3 :** the ordinal number of the ordered sequence of natural numbers — symbol ω
om·elet *also* **om·elette** \'äm-(ə-)lət\ *n* [F *omelette*, alter. of MF *alumelle*, lit., knife blade, modif. of L *lamella*, dim. of *lamina* thin plate] **:** eggs beaten to a froth, cooked without stirring until set, and served in a half-round form by folding one half over the other
omen \'ō-mən\ *n* [L *omin-, omen*] **:** an occurrence or phenomenon believed to portend a future event **:** AUGURY
omen·tal \ō-'ment-ᵊl\ *adj* **:** of, relating to, or formed from an omentum
omen·tum \ō-'ment-əm\ *n, pl* **omen·ta** \-ə\ *or* **omentums** [L, fr. *o-* (akin to *-uere* to put on) — more at EXUVIAE] **:** a free fold of peritoneum or one connecting or supporting viscera or other abdominal structures
omer \'ō-mər\ *n* [Heb *'ōmer*] **1 :** an ancient Hebrew unit of dry capacity equal to 1/10 ephah **2** *often cap* **:** a seven-week period in the Jewish year between Passover and Shabuoth

om·i·cron \'äm-ə-ˌkrän, *Brit* ō-'mī-krən\ *n* [Gk *o mikron*, lit., small o] **:** the 15th letter of the Greek alphabet — symbol O or *o*

om·i·nous \'äm-ə-nəs\ *adj* **:** being or exhibiting an omen **:** PORTENTOUS; *esp* **:** foreboding or foreshadowing evil **:** INAUSPICIOUS — **om·i·nous·ly** *adv* — **om·i·nous·ness** *n*

syn PORTENTOUS, FATEFUL: OMINOUS implies having a menacing, alarming character foreshadowing evil or disaster; PORTENTOUS suggests being frighteningly big or impressive but now seldom definitely connotes forewarning of calamity **:** FATEFUL suggests being of momentous or decisive importance

omis·si·ble \ō-'mis-ə-bəl\ *adj* **:** that may be omitted

omis·sion \ō-'mish-ən, ə-\ *n* [ME *omissioun*, fr. LL *omission-, omissio*, fr. L *omissus*, pp. of *omittere*] **1 a :** apathy toward or neglect of duty **b :** something neglected or left undone **2 :** the act of omitting **:** the state of being omitted

omis·sive \ō-'mis-iv\ *adj* **:** failing or neglecting to do **:** OMITTING — **omis·sive·ly** *adv*

omit \ō-'mit, ə-\ *vt* **omit·ted; omit·ting** [ME *omitten*, fr. L *omittere*, fr. *ob-* toward + *mittere* to let go, send — more at OB-, SMITE] **1 :** to leave out or leave unmentioned **2 :** to fail to perform or make use of **:** FORBEAR **3** *obs* **:** DISREGARD **4** *obs* **:** to give up **syn** see NEGLECT

om·ma·tid·i·al \ˌäm-ə-'tid-ē-əl\ *adj* **:** of, relating to, or having ommatidia

om·ma·tid·i·um \-ē-əm\ *n, pl* **om·ma·tid·ia** \-ē-ə\ [NL, fr. Gk *ommat-, omma* eye] **:** one of the elements corresponding to a small simple eye that make up the compound eye of an arthropod

1**om·ni·bus** \'äm-ni-(ˌ)bəs\ *n* [F, fr. L, for all, dat. pl. of *omnis* all] **1 :** a usu. automotive public vehicle designed to carry a comparatively large number of passengers **:** BUS **2 :** a book containing reprints of a number of works

2**omnibus** *adj* **:** of, relating to, or providing for many things or classes at once ⟨an ~ bill⟩

om·ni·di·rec·tion·al \ˌäm-ni-də-'rek-shnəl, -ˌnī-də-, -ni-(ˌ)dī-, -shən-ᵊl\ *adj* [L *omnis* + ISV *directional*] **:** receiving or sending radiations equally well in all directions ⟨~ antenna⟩

om·ni·far·i·ous \ˌäm-nə-'far-ē-əs, -'fer-\ *adj* [LL *omnifarius*, fr. L *omnis* + *-farius* (as in *multifarius* having great diversity) — more at MULTIFARIOUS] **:** of all varieties, forms, or kinds

om·nif·i·cent \äm-'nif-ə-sənt\ *adj* [L *omnis* + E *-ficent* (as in *magnificent*)] **:** unlimited in creative power

om·nip·o·tence \äm-'nip-ət-ən(t)s\ *n* **:** the quality or state of being omnipotent; *also* **:** an agency or force of unlimited power

1**om·nip·o·tent** \-ət-ənt\ *adj* [ME, fr. MF, fr. L *omnipotent-, omnipotens*, fr. *omnis* + *potent-, potens* potent] **1** *often cap* **:** ALMIGHTY 1 **2 a :** having virtually unlimited authority or influence **b** *obs* **:** ARRANT — **om·nip·o·tent·ly** *adv*

2**omnipotent** *n* **1 :** one who is omnipotent **2** *cap* **:** ALMIGHTY

om·ni·pres·ence \ˌäm-ni-'prez-ᵊn(t)s\ *n* **:** the quality or state of being omnipresent **:** UBIQUITY

om·ni·pres·ent \-ᵊnt\ *adj* [ML *omnipraesent-, omnipraesens*, fr. L *omnis* + *praesent-, praesens* present] **:** present in all places at all times

syn OMNIPRESENT, UBIQUITOUS mean present or existent everywhere. OMNIPRESENT in its strict sense is a divine attribute equivalent to *immanent;* more commonly it implies never being absent ⟨poverty is *omnipresent*⟩ UBIQUITOUS implies being so active or so numerous as to seem to be found everywhere ⟨*ubiquitous* tourist⟩

om·ni·range \'äm-ni-ˌrānj\ *n* [L *omnis* + E *range*] **:** a system of radio navigation in which any bearing relative to a special radio transmitter on the ground may be chosen and flown by an airplane pilot — called also *omnidirectional range*

om·ni·science \äm-'nish-ən(t)s\ *n* [ML *omniscientia*, fr. L *omnis* + *scientia* science] **:** the quality or state of being omniscient

om·ni·scient \-ənt\ *adj* [NL *omniscient-, omnisciens*, back-formation fr. ML *omniscientia*] **1 :** having infinite awareness, understanding, and insight **2 :** possessed of universal or complete knowledge — **om·ni·scient·ly** *adv*

om·ni·um-gath·er·um \ˌäm-nē-əm-'gath-ə-rəm\ *n* [L *omnium* (gen. pl. of *omnis*) + E *gather* + L *-um*, noun ending] **:** a miscellaneous collection of a variety of things or persons **:** HODGEPODGE

om·niv·o·ra \äm-'niv-ə-rə\ *n pl* [NL, fr. L, neut. pl. of *omnivorus*] **:** omnivorous animals

om·ni·vore \'äm-ni-ˌvō(ə)r, -ˌvȯ(ə)r\ *n* [NL *omnivora*] **:** one that is omnivorous

om·niv·o·rous \äm-'niv-(ə-)rəs\ *adj* [L *omnivorus*, fr. *omnis* all + *-vorus* -vorous] **1 :** feeding on both animal and vegetable substances **2 :** avidly taking in everything as if devouring or consuming — **om·niv·o·rous·ly** *adv* — **om·niv·o·rous·ness** *n*

1**on** \(')ȯn, (')än\ *prep* [ME *an, on*, prep. & adv., fr. OE; akin to OHG *ana* on, Gk *ana* up, on] **1 a** (1) **:** over and in contact with ⟨the book is ~ the table⟩ (2) **:** in contact or juxtaposition with ⟨a fly ~ the ceiling⟩ (3) — used as a function word to indicate a means of conveyance ⟨left ~ the early train⟩ (4) — used as a function word to indicate a part (as of the body) that supports and is in contact with something underneath ⟨stand ~ one foot⟩ (5) **:** in the direction or area of ⟨~ the right⟩ **b** (1) **:** to a position over and in contact with ⟨jumped ~ the horse⟩ (2) **:** into contact with ⟨put the notice ~ the bulletin board⟩ **2 a** — used as a function word to indicate the object of actual or implied action directed against or toward the object ⟨crept up ~ him⟩ ⟨smiled ~ her⟩ **b :** to the disadvantage of ⟨have some evidence ~ him⟩ **3** — used as a function word to indicate the basis or source (as of an action, opinion, or computation) ⟨know it ~ good authority⟩ ⟨ten cents ~ the dollar⟩ **4 a :** with regard or respect to **:** ABOUT ⟨agreed ~ a price⟩ ⟨a monopoly ~ wheat⟩ ⟨a satire ~ society⟩ **b** *archaic* **:** OF **5 a :** in connection, association, or activity with or with regard to ⟨~ a committee⟩ ⟨~ tour⟩ **b :** in a state or process of ⟨~ fire⟩ ⟨~ the increase⟩ **6 a** — used as a function word to indicate occurrence within the limits of a specified day or at a set time ⟨came ~ Monday⟩ ⟨every hour ~ the hour⟩ **b :** at or soon after the time of ⟨cash ~ delivery⟩ **7 :** through the means or agency of ⟨cut ~ a knife⟩ ⟨talking ~ the telephone⟩ **8** — used as a function word to indicate reduplication or succession in a series ⟨loss ~ loss⟩

2**on** \'ȯn, 'än\ *adv* **1 a :** in or into a position of contact with an upper surface ⟨put the plates ~⟩ **b :** in or into a position of being attached to or covering a surface ⟨has new shoes ~⟩ **2 a :** forward in space, time, or action **:** ONWARD ⟨went ~ home⟩ **b :** in continuance or succession ⟨and so ~⟩ **3 :** into operation or a position permitting operation ⟨turn the light ~⟩

3**on** \'ȯn, 'än\ *adj* **1 :** engaged in an activity or function (as a dramatic role) **2 a** (1) **:** OPERATING ⟨the radio is ~⟩ (2) **:** placed so as to permit operation ⟨the switch is ~⟩ **b :** taking place ⟨the game is ~⟩ **3 :** PLANNED ⟨has nothing ~ for tonight⟩

1**-on** \ˌän, ən\ *n suffix* [ISV, alter. of *-one*] **:** chemical compound not a ketone or other oxo compound ⟨parathi*on*⟩

2**-on** \ˌän\ *n suffix* [fr. *-on* (in *ion*)] **1 :** elementary particle ⟨nucle*on*⟩ **2 :** unit **:** quantum ⟨phot*on*⟩

3**-on** \ˌän\ *n suffix* [NL, fr. *-on* (in *argon*)] **:** inert gas ⟨rad*on*⟩

on·a·ger \'än-i-jər\ *n* [ME, wild ass, fr. L, fr. Gk *onagros*, fr. *onos* ass + *agros* field — more at ACRE] **1 :** a small pale-colored kiang with a broad dorsal stripe **2** [LL, fr. L] **:** an ancient and medieval heavy catapult

onan·ism \'ō-nə-ˌniz-əm\ *n* [prob. fr. NL *onanismus*, fr. *Onan*, son of Judah (Gen 38:9)] **1 :** uncompleted coitus **2 :** MASTURBATION — **onan·is·tic** \ˌō-nə-'nis-tik\ *adj*

1**once** \'wən(t)s\ *adv* [ME *ones*, fr. gen. of *on* one] **1 :** one time and no more **2 :** at any one time **:** under any circumstances **:** EVER **3 :** at some indefinite time in the past **:** FORMERLY **4 :** by one degree of relationship

2**once** *adj* **:** that once was **:** FORMER

3**once** *n* **:** one single time **:** one time at least — **at once 1 :** at the same time **:** SIMULTANEOUSLY **2 :** IMMEDIATELY

4**once** *also* **once that** *conj* **:** when once **:** if once **:** at the moment when **:** as soon as

once–over \'wən(t)-ˌsō-vər\ *n* **:** a swift examination or survey

on·cid·i·um \än-'sid-ē-əm, äŋ-'kid-\ *n* [NL, genus name, fr. Gk *onkos* barbed hook — more at ANGLE] **:** any of a genus (*Oncidium*) of showy tropical American epiphytic or terrestrial orchids

on·co·log·ic \ˌäŋ-kə-'läj-ik\ *adj* **:** of or relating to oncology

on·col·o·gy \än-'käl-ə-jē, äŋ-\ *n* [Gk *onkos* mass + ISV *-logy;* akin to Gk *enenkein* to carry — more at ENOUGH] **:** the study of tumors

on·com·ing \'ȯn-ˌkəm-iŋ, 'än-\ *adj* **1 a :** APPROACHING **b :** FUTURE **2 :** RISING, EMERGENT

1**one** \'wən, ˌwən\ *adj* [ME *on*, fr. OE *ān;* akin to OHG *ein* one, L *unus* (OL *oinos*), Skt *eka*] **1 :** being a single unit or thing ⟨~ man is going⟩ — see NUMBER table **2 a :** being one in particular ⟨early ~ morning⟩ **b :** being preeminently what is indicated ⟨~ fine person⟩ **3 a :** being the same in kind or quality ⟨both of ~ race⟩ **b** (1) **:** constituting a unified entity of two or more components ⟨the combined elements form ~ substance⟩ (2) **:** UNITED **4 :** existing or occurring as something not definitely fixed or placed ⟨will see you again ~ day⟩ **5 :** being the only individual of an indicated or implied kind ⟨the ~ person she wanted to marry⟩

2**one** *pron* **1 :** a certain indefinitely indicated person or thing ⟨saw ~ of his classmates⟩ **2 :** any individual of a vaguely indicated group ⟨~ wouldn't like to see that happen⟩ — sometimes used as a 3d person substitute for a pronoun of the first person ⟨~ supposes you will come⟩

3**one** \'wən\ *n* **1 :** the number denoting unity **2 :** the first in a set or series ⟨wears a ~⟩ **3 :** a single person or thing ⟨by ~s and twos⟩ **4 :** a one-dollar bill

-one \ˌōn\ *n suffix* [ISV, alter. of *-ene*] **:** ketone or related or analogous compound or class of compounds ⟨lact*one*⟩ ⟨quin*one*⟩ ⟨silic*one*⟩ ⟨sulf*one*⟩

one another *pron* **:** EACH OTHER

one–base hit \ˌwən-ˌbās-\ *n* **:** a base hit that enables a batter to reach first base safely — called also *one-bag·ger* \'wən-'bag-ər\

one–egg \ˌwən-ˌeg, -ˌāg\ *adj* **:** MONOVULAR

one–horse \ˌwən-ˌhȯrs\ *adj* **1 :** drawn or operated by one horse **2 :** small in scope or importance ⟨~ town⟩

Onei·da \ō-'nīd-ə\ *n, pl* **Oneida** *or* **Oneidas** [Iroquois *Onęyóde'*, lit., standing rock] **1 a :** an Iroquoian people orig. living near Oneida Lake in New York **b :** a member of this people **2 :** the language of the Oneida people

onei·ric \ō-'nī(ə)r-ik\ *adj* [Gk *oneiros* dream; akin to Arm *anurj* dream] **:** of or relating to dreams **:** DREAMY

onei·ro·crit·i·cal \ō-ˌnī-rō-'krit-i-kəl\ *adj* [Gk *oneirokritikos*, fr. *oneiros* + *kritikos* able to discern — more at CRITIC] **:** of, relating to, or specializing in the interpretation of dreams — **onei·ro·crit·i·cal·ly** \-k(ə-)lē\ *adv*

onei·ro·man·cy \ō-'nī-rə-ˌman(t)-sē\ *n* [Gk *oneiros* + E *-mancy*] **:** divination by means of dreams

one·ness \'wən-nəs\ *n* **:** the quality or state or fact of being one: as **a :** SINGLENESS **b :** WHOLENESS, INTEGRITY **c :** HARMONY **d :** SAMENESS, IDENTITY **e :** UNITY, UNION

oner·ous \'än-ə-rəs, 'ō-nə-\ *adj* [ME, fr. MF *onereus*, fr. L *onerosus*, fr. *oner-, onus* burden; akin to Skt *anas* cart] **1 :** involving, imposing, or constituting a burden **:** TROUBLESOME ⟨an ~ task⟩ **2 :** having legal obligations that outweigh the advantages ⟨~ contract⟩ — **oner·ous·ly** *adv* — **oner·ous·ness** *n*

syn ONEROUS, BURDENSOME, OPPRESSIVE, EXACTING mean imposing hardship. ONEROUS stresses being laborious and heavy esp. because distasteful; BURDENSOME suggests causing mental as well as physical strain; OPPRESSIVE implies extreme harshness or severity in what is imposed; EXACTING implies rigor or sternness rather than tyranny or injustice in the demands made or in the one demanding

one·self \(ˌ)wən-'self\ *also* **one's self** \(ˌ)wən-, ˌwənz-\ *pron* **1 :** a person's self **:** one's own self — used reflexively as object of a preposition or verb or for emphasis in various constructions **2 :** one's normal, healthy, or sane condition or self

one–shot \'wən-ˌshät\ *adj* **1 :** that is complete or effective through being done or used or applied only once **2 :** that is not followed by something else of the same kind

one–sid·ed \-'sīd-əd\ *adj* **1 a** (1) **:** having or occurring on one side only (2) **:** having one side prominent or more developed **b :** limited to one side **:** PARTIAL **2 :** UNILATERAL — **one–sid·ed·ly** *adv* — **one–sid·ed·ness** *n*

one–step \'wən-ˌstep\ *n* **1 :** a ballroom dance marked by quick walking steps backward and forward in 2/4 time **2 :** music used for the one-step — **one–step** *vi*

1**one·time** \-ˌtīm\ *adj* **:** FORMER, SOMETIME

2**onetime** *adv* **:** FORMERLY

one–to–one \ˌwən-tə-ˈwən, -də-\ *adj* **:** pairing each element of a class uniquely with an element of another class
one–track \ˈwən-ˌtrak\ *adj* **1 a :** able to handle only one thing at a time **:** INFLEXIBLE **b :** obsessed with one thing only **:** NARROW **2 :** lacking variety **:** UNDIVERSIFIED
one–up·man·ship \ˌwən-ˈəp-mən-ˌship\ *n* **:** the art or practice of going a friend or competitor one better or keeping one jump ahead of him
one–way \ˈwən-ˈwā\ *adj* **1 :** that moves in, allows movement in, or functions in only one direction ⟨~ traffic⟩ **2 :** ONE-SIDED, UNILATERAL
on·go·ing \ˈȯn-ˌgō-iŋ, ˈän-, -ˌgȯ(-)iŋ\ *adj* **:** continuously moving forward **:** GROWING — **ongoing** *n*
on·ion \ˈən-yən\ *n, often attrib* [ME, fr. MF *oignon*, fr. L *union-, unio*] **1 :** a widely cultivated Asiatic herb (*Allium cepa*) of the lily family with pungent edible bulbs; *also* **:** its bulb **2 :** any of various plants of the same genus as the onion
on·ion·skin \-ˌskin\ *n* **:** a thin strong translucent paper of very light weight
-o·ni·um \ˈō-nē-əm\ *n suffix* [NL, fr. *ammonium*] **:** an ion having a positive charge ⟨ox*onium*⟩ ⟨phosph*onium*⟩ — compare -IUM 1b
on·look·er \ˈȯn-ˌlu̇k-ər, ˈän-\ *n* **:** one that looks on; *esp* **:** a passive spectator — **on·look·ing** \-iŋ\ *adj*
1**on·ly** \ˈōn-lē\ *adj* [ME, fr. OE *ānlīc*, fr. *ān* one — more at ONE] **1 :** unquestionably the best **:** PEERLESS **2 :** alone in its class or kind **:** SOLE
2**only** *adv* **1 a :** as a single fact or instance and nothing more or different **:** MERELY ⟨worked ~ in the mornings⟩ **b :** EXCLUSIVELY, SOLELY ⟨known ~ to him⟩ **2 :** at the very least ⟨it was ~ too true⟩ **3 a :** in the final outcome ⟨will ~ make you sick⟩ **b :** with nevertheless the final result ⟨won the battles, ~ to lose the war⟩ **4 :** as recently as ⟨~ last week⟩ **:** in the immediate past ⟨~ just talked to her⟩
3**only** *conj* **1 a :** with the restriction that **:** BUT ⟨you may go, ~ come back early⟩ **b :** and yet **:** HOWEVER ⟨they look very nice, ~ we can't use them⟩ **2 :** were it not that **:** EXCEPT
on·o·mas·tic \ˌän-ə-ˈmas-tik\ *adj* [Gk *onomastikos*, fr. *onomazein* to name, fr. *onoma* name — more at NAME] **1 :** of, relating to, or consisting of a name or names **2** *of a signature* **:** written in the handwriting of the author of a letter or document
on·o·mas·tics \-tiks\ *n pl but sing or pl in constr* **1 a :** the science or study of the origins and forms of words esp. as used in a specialized field **b :** the science or study of the origin and forms of proper names of persons or places **2 :** the system underlying the formation and use of words esp. for proper names or of words used in a specialized field
on·o·mato·poe·ia \ˌän-ə-ˌmat-ə-ˈpē-(y)ə\ *n* [LL, fr. Gk *onomatopoiia*, fr. *onomat-, onoma* + *poiein* to make — more at POET] **1 :** the naming of a thing or action by a vocal imitation of the sound associated with it (as *buzz, hiss*) **2 :** the use of words whose sound suggests the sense — **on·o·mato·poe·ic** \-ˈpē-ik\ *or* **on·o·mato·po·et·ic** \-pō-ˈet-ik\ *adj* — **on·o·mato·poe·i·cal·ly** \-ˈpē-ə-k(ə-)lē\ *or* **on·o·mato·po·et·i·cal·ly** \-pō-ˈet-i-k(ə-)lē\ *adv*
On·on·da·ga \ˌän-ə(n)-ˈdȯ-gə\ *n, pl* **Onondaga** *or* **Onondagas** [Iroquois *Onõtáge*, village of the Onondaga people] **1 a :** an Iroquoian people of central New York **b :** a member of this people **2 :** the language of the Onondaga people
on·rush \ˈȯn-ˌrəsh, ˈän-\ *n* **1 :** a rushing forward or onward **2 :** ONSET — **on·rush·ing** \-iŋ\ *adj*
on·set \-ˌset\ *n* **1 :** ATTACK, ASSAULT **2 :** BEGINNING, COMMENCEMENT **3 :** ELECTRONOGRAPHY
on·shore \ˈȯn-ˌshō(ə)r, ˈän-, -ˌshȯ(ə)r\ *adj* **1 :** coming or moving toward or onto the shore **2 a :** situated on or near the shore **b :** DOMESTIC — **on·shore** \ˈȯn-ˈ, ˈän-ˈ\ *adv*
on side *adv* (*or adj*) **:** not off side **:** in a position legally to play or receive the ball or puck
on·slaught \ˈän-ˌslȯt, ˈȯn-\ *n* [modif. of D *aanslag* act of striking; akin to OE *an* on and to OE *slēan* to strike — more at SLAY] **:** an esp. fierce attack
on–stream \ˈȯn-ˈstrēm, ˈän-\ *adv* **:** in or into operation ⟨a new plant will go ~⟩
ont- *or* **onto-** *comb form* [NL, fr. LGk, fr. Gk *ont-, ōn*, prp. of *einai* to be — more at IS] **1 :** being **:** existence ⟨*onto*logy⟩ **2 :** organism ⟨*onto*geny⟩
-ont \ˌänt\ *n comb form* [Gk *ont-, ōn*, prp.] **:** cell **:** organism ⟨dipl*ont*⟩
on·tic \ˈänt-ik\ *adj* **:** of, relating to, or having real being — **on·ti·cal·ly** \-i-k(ə-)lē\ *adv*
on·to \ˌȯn-tə(-w), ˌän-; ˈȯn-(ˌ)tü, ˈän-\ *prep* **1 :** to a position on **2 :** in or into a state of awareness about ⟨is ~ your methods⟩
on·to·ge·net·ic \ˌän-tə-jə-ˈnet-ik\ *adj* [ISV, fr. NL *ontogenesis* ontogeny, fr. *ont-* + L *genesis*] **1 :** of, relating to, or appearing in the course of ontogeny **2 :** based on visible morphological characters — **on·to·ge·net·i·cal·ly** \-i-k(ə-)lē\ *adv*
on·tog·e·ny \än-ˈtäj-ə-nē\ *n* [ISV] **:** the development or course of development of an individual organism
on·to·log·i·cal \ˌänt-ᵊl-ˈäj-i-kəl\ *adj* **1 :** of or relating to ontology **2 :** relating to or based upon being or existence — **on·to·log·i·cal·ly** \-k(ə-)lē\ *adv*
on·tol·o·gist \än-ˈtäl-ə-jəst\ *n* **:** a specialist in ontology
on·tol·o·gy \-jē\ *n* [NL *ontologia*, fr. *ont-* + *-logia* -logy] **1 :** a branch of metaphysics relating to the nature and relations of being **2 :** a particular theory about the nature of being or the kinds of existence
onus \ˈō-nəs\ *n* **1** [L — more at ONEROUS] **a :** BURDEN **b :** a disagreeable necessity **:** OBLIGATION **c :** BLAME **d :** STIGMA **2** [NL] **:** BURDEN OF PROOF
1**on·ward** \ˈȯn-wərd, ˈän-\ *also* **on·wards** \-wərdz\ *adv* **:** toward or at a point lying ahead in space or time **:** FORWARD
2**onward** *adj* **:** directed or moving onward **:** FORWARD
-onym \ə-ˌnim\ *n comb form* [Gk *onomos, onymos* name — more at NAME] **:** name **:** word ⟨ant*onym*⟩
on·yx \ˈän-iks\ *n* [ME *onix*, fr. OF & L; OF, fr. L *onych-, onyx*, fr. Gk, lit., toenail or fingernail — more at NAIL] **:** chalcedony in parallel layers of different shades of color
oo- — see O-
oo·cyte \ˈō-ə-ˌsīt\ *n* [ISV] **:** an egg before maturation
oo·dles \ˈüd-ᵊlz\ *also* **ood·lins** \ˈüd-lənz\ *n pl but sing or pl in constr* [perh. alter. of 2*huddle*] **:** a great quantity **:** LOT
oo·ga·mete \ˌō-ə-gə-ˈmēt, -ˈgam-ˌēt\ *n* **:** a female gamete; *specif* **:** a relatively large nonmotile gamete containing reserve material
oog·a·mous \ō-ˈäg-ə-məs\ *adj* **1** *of sexual reproduction* **:** having a small motile male gamete and a large immobile female gamete **2 :** having oogamous reproduction — **oog·a·my** \-mē\ *n*
O O gauge \ˌdəb-ə-ˈlō-\ *n* **:** a gauge of track in model railroading in which the rails are approximately ¾ inch apart
oo·gen·e·sis \ˌō-ə-ˈjen-ə-səs\ *n* [NL] **:** formation and maturation of the egg — **oo·ge·net·ic** \-jə-ˈnet-ik\ *adj*
oo·go·ni·um \ˌō-ə-ˈgō-nē-əm\ *n* [NL] **1 :** a female sexual organ in various algae and fungi that corresponds to the archegonium of ferns and mosses **2 :** a descendant of a primordial germ cell that gives rise to oocytes
oo·lite \ˈō-ə-ˌlīt\ *n* [prob. fr. F *oolithe*, fr. *o-* + *-lithe* -lite] **:** a rock consisting of small round grains usu. of calcium carbonate cemented together — **oo·lit·ic** \ˌō-ə-ˈlit-ik\ *adj*
oo·log·i·cal \ˌō-ə-ˈläj-i-kəl\ *also* **oo·log·ic** \-ik\ *adj* **:** of or relating to oology — **oo·log·i·cal·ly** \-i-k(ə-)lē\ *adv*
ool·o·gist \ō-ˈäl-ə-jəst\ *n* **1 :** one specializing in oology **2 :** a collector of birds' eggs
ool·o·gy \-jē\ *n* **:** a branch of ornithology dealing with birds' eggs
oo·long \ˈü-ˌlȯŋ\ *n* [Chin (Pek) *wu1 lung2*, lit., black dragon] **:** a tea partially fermented before drying that combines characteristics of black and green teas
oo·mi·ak *also* **oo·mi·ack** *var of* UMIAK
oomph \ˈu̇m(p)f\ *n* [prob. imit. of an appreciative *mm* uttered by a man at the sight of an attractive woman] **1 :** personal charm or magnetism **:** GLAMOUR **2 :** SEX APPEAL **3 :** VITALITY, ENTHUSIASM
oo·phyte \ˈō-ə-ˌfīt\ *n* **:** the sexual generation in the life cycle of an archegoniate plant in which sexual organs are developed — **oo·phyt·ic** \ˌō-ə-ˈfit-ik\ *adj*
oo·sperm \ˈō-ə-ˌspərm\ *n* **:** ZYGOTE, OOSPORE
oo·sphere \-ˌsfi(ə)r\ *n* [ISV] **:** OVUM — used esp. of lower plants
oo·spore \-ˌspō(ə)r, -ˌspȯ(ə)r\ *n* [ISV] **:** ZYGOTE; *esp* **:** a spore produced by heterogamous fertilization that yields a sporophyte — **oo·spor·ic** \ˌō-ə-ˈspōr-ik, -ˈspȯr-\ *adj* — **oo·spo·rous** \ˌō-ə-ˈspōr-əs, -ˈspȯr-; ō-ˈäs-pə-rəs\ *adj*
oo·the·ca \ˌō-ə-ˈthē-kə\ *n, pl* **oo·the·cae** \-ˈthē-(ˌ)kē, -(ˌ)sē\ [NL] **:** a firm-walled and distinctive egg case (as of a cockroach) — **oo·the·cal** \-ˈthē-kəl\ *adj*
oo·tid \ˈō-ə-ˌtid\ *n* [irreg. fr. *o-* + *-id*] **:** an egg cell after meiosis
1**ooze** \ˈüz\ *n* [ME *wose*, fr. OE *wāse* mire; akin to L *virus* slime — more at VIRUS] **1 :** a soft deposit (as of mud, slime, or shells) on the bottom of a body of water **2 :** a piece of soft wet plastic ground (as a marsh or bog)
2**ooze** *n* [ME *wose* sap, juice, fr. OE *wōs*; akin to OHG *waso* damp, Gk *hearon* ewer] **1 :** a decoction of vegetable material used for tanning leather **2 :** the action of oozing **3 :** something that oozes
3**ooze** *vi* **1 :** to pass or flow slowly through or as if through small openings or interstices **2 :** to move slowly or imperceptibly **3 a :** to exude moisture **b :** to exude something in a way suggestive of the emitting of moisture **4 :** to escape slowly and quietly ~ *vt* **1 :** to emit or give out slowly **2 :** to exude or give off in a way suggestive of the emitting of moisture
ooze leather *n* **:** leather usu. made from calfskins by a vegetable tanning process and having a soft suede finish on the flesh side
oozy \ˈü-zē\ *adj* **1 :** containing or composed of ooze **2 :** exuding moisture **:** SLIMY
op \ˈäp\ *or* **op art** *n* **:** OPTICAL ART — **op artist** *n*
opac·i·ty \ō-ˈpas-ət-ē\ *n* [F *opacité* shadiness, fr. L *opacitat-, opacitas*, fr. *opacus* shaded, dark] **1 a :** the quality or state of a body that makes it impervious to the rays of light **:** OPAQUENESS **b :** the capacity of matter to obstruct the transmission of forms of radiant energy in addition to light **2 a :** obscurity of sense **:** UNINTELLIGIBLENESS **b :** mental obtuseness **3 :** an opaque spot on a normally transparent structure
opah \ˈō-pə, -ˌpä\ *n* [Ibo *úbà*] **:** a large elliptical marine fish (*Lampris regius*) with brilliant colors and rich oily red flesh
opal \ˈō-pəl\ *n, often attrib* [L *opalus*, fr. Skt *upala* stone, jewel] **:** a mineral $SiO_2.nH_2O$ that is a hydrated amorphous silica softer and less dense than quartz and typically with definite and often marked iridescent play of colors
opal·es·cence \ˌō-pə-ˈles-ᵊn(t)s\ *n* **:** the quality or state of being opalescent
opal·es·cent \-ᵊnt\ *adj* **:** reflecting an iridescent light
opal·ine \ˈō-pə-ˌlīn, -ˌlēn\ *adj* **:** resembling opal esp. in appearance
1**opaque** \ō-ˈpāk\ *adj* [L *opacus*] **1 :** neither reflecting nor emitting light **2 a :** not transparent or translucent **b :** impervious to forms of radiant energy other than visible light **3 a :** hard to understand or explain **:** UNINTELLIGIBLE **b :** OBTUSE, STUPID — **opaque·ly** *adv* — **opaque·ness** *n*
2**opaque** *n* **:** something that is opaque; *specif* **:** an opaque paint for blocking out portions of a photographic negative or print
ope \ˈōp\ *vb* **:** OPEN
1**open** \ˈō-pən, ˈōp-ᵊm\ *adj* **open·er** \ˈōp-(ə-)nər\ **open·est** \-(ə-)nəst\ [ME, fr. OE; akin to OHG *offan* open; both fr. a prehistoric NGmc-WGmc word akin to OE *ūp* up] **1 :** so arranged as to permit ingress, egress, or passage: as **a :** having no enclosing or confining barrier **b :** not shut or fast ⟨~ door⟩ **c** (1) **:** not stopped by a finger ⟨~ string of a violin⟩ (2) **:** having clarity and resonance unimpaired by undue tension or constriction of the throat ⟨~ vocal tone⟩ **2 a :** exposed to general knowledge ⟨~ ballot⟩ **b :** free from reserve ⟨~ manner⟩ **3 a :** having no roof, lid, or other covering **b :** having no protective or concealing cover **:** BARE **c :** SUBJECT ⟨~ to infection⟩ **4 a :** requiring no special status, identification, or permit for entry or participation ⟨~ meeting⟩ **b :** enterable by both amateur and professional contestants ⟨~ tournament⟩ **5 :** presenting no obstacle to passage or view **6 :** not drawn together, folded, or contracted **7 a :** LOW 12 **b :** formed with the tongue in a lower position ⟨Italian has an ~ and a close *e*⟩ **c :** ending in a vowel ⟨~ syllable⟩ **8 a :** ACCESSIBLE, USABLE ⟨keep an hour ~ on Friday⟩ **b :** available for consideration or decision ⟨~ verdict⟩ **c :** kept available for future custom ⟨an ~ pattern⟩ **d :** not terminated or liquidated **:** OPERATIVE **e :** legally available for hunting or fishing ⟨~ season⟩ **f :** unoccupied and undefended by military forces and divested of any military installation and so immune under international law from enemy bombardment ⟨~ city⟩ **9 :** characterized by ready accessibility and cooperative attitude: as **a :** generous in giving **b :** willing to hear and consider or to accept and deal with **:** RESPONSIVE **c :** accessible to the influx of new factors ⟨~ market⟩ **10 :** having openings, inter-

ruptions, or spaces: as **a :** porous and friable ⟨~ soil⟩ **b :** sparsely distributed **:** SCATTERED ⟨~ population⟩ **c** (1) **:** having relatively wide spacing between words or lines ⟨~ type⟩ (2) *of a compound* **:** having components separated by a space in writing or printing **11 :** ready to operate **:** ACTIVE ⟨the store is ~ from 9 to 5⟩ **12 a** (1) **:** characterized by lack of effective regulation of various commercial enterprises ⟨an ~ town⟩ (2) **:** not repressed by legal controls ⟨~ gambling⟩ **b :** free from checking or hampering restraints ⟨~ economy⟩ **c :** relatively unguarded by opponents ⟨~ court⟩ **13 :** having been opened by a first ante, bet, or bid ⟨the bidding is ~⟩ **14** *of punctuation* **:** characterized by sparing use esp. of the comma **syn** see FRANK, LIABLE — **open** *adv* — **open·ly** \'ō-pən-lē\ *adv* — **open·ness** \-pən-nəs\ *n*

²**open** \'ō-pən, 'ōp-ᵊm\ *vb* **opened** \'ō-pənd, 'ōp-ᵊmd\ **open·ing** \'ōp-(ə-)niŋ\ **opens** \'ō-pənz, 'ōp-ᵊmz\ *vt* **1 a :** to move (as a door) from closed position **b :** to make available for entry or passage by turning back, removing, or clearing away **2 a :** to make available for or active in a regular function ⟨~ a new store⟩ **b :** to make accessible for a particular purpose **3 a :** to disclose or expose to view **:** REVEAL **b :** to make more discerning or responsive **:** ENLIGHTEN **c :** to bring into view or come in sight of by changing position **4 a :** to make one or more openings in ⟨~*ed* the boil⟩ **b :** to loosen and make less compact ⟨~ the soil⟩ **5 :** to spread out **:** UNFOLD ⟨~*ed* the book⟩ **6 a :** to enter upon **:** BEGIN **b :** to commence action in a card game by making (a first bid), putting a first bet in (the pot), or playing (a card or suit) as first lead **7 :** to restore or recall (as an order) from a finally determined state to a state in which the parties are free to prosecute or oppose ~ *vi* **1 :** to become open **:** UNCLOSE **2 a :** to spread out **:** EXPAND ⟨the wound ~*ed* under the strain⟩ **b :** to become disclosed **3 :** to become enlightened or responsive **4 :** to give access ⟨the rooms ~ onto a hall⟩ **5 :** to speak out **6 a :** to begin a course or activity **b :** to make a bet, bid, or lead in commencing a round or hand of a card game

³**open** *n* **1 :** OPENING **2 :** open and unobstructed space; *also* **:** open water **3 :** an open contest, competition, or tournament

open air *n* **:** the space where air is unconfined; *esp* **:** OUT-OF-DOORS

open–air \,ō-pə-'na(ə)r, -'ne(ə)r\ *adj* **:** OUTDOOR

open–and–shut \,ō-pə-(ə-)nən-'shət, ,ōp-mən-, ,ōp-ᵊm-ən-\ *adj* **:** perfectly simple **:** OBVIOUS

open chain *n* **:** an arrangement of atoms represented in a structural formula by a chain whose ends are not joined so as to form a ring

open door *n* **1 :** a recognized right of admittance **:** freedom of access **2 :** a policy giving opportunity for commercial intercourse with a country to all nations on equal terms

open–end \,ō-pə-'nend\ *adj* **:** organized to allow for contingencies: as **a :** permitting additional debt to be incurred under the original indenture subject to specified conditions ⟨an ~ mortgage⟩ **b :** offering for sale or having issued outstanding capital shares redeemable on demand ⟨an ~ investment company⟩

open·er \'ōp-(ə-)nər\ *n* **:** one that opens: as **a** *obs* **:** APERIENT **b** *pl* **:** cards of sufficient value for a player to open the betting in a poker game **c :** the first item of a series

open–eyed \,ō-pə-'nīd\ *adj* **1 :** having the eyes open **2 :** WATCHFUL, DISCERNING

open·hand·ed \,ō-pən-'han-dəd, ,ōp-ᵊm-\ *adj* **:** generous in giving **:** MUNIFICENT — **open·hand·ed·ly** *adv* — **open·hand·ed·ness** *n*

open·heart·ed \-'härt-əd\ *adj* **:** candidly straightforward **:** FRANK — **open·heart·ed·ly** *adv* — **open·heart·ed·ness** *n*

open–hearth \,ō-pən-,härth, ,ōp-ᵊm-\ *adj* **:** of, relating to, involving, or produced by an open hearth ⟨~ steel⟩

open–hearth process *n* **:** a process of making steel in a furnace of the regenerative reverberatory type from pig iron

open house *n* **:** ready and usu. informal hospitality or entertainment for all comers

open·ing \'ōp-(ə-)niŋ\ *n* **1 a :** an act or instance of making or becoming open **b :** an act or instance of beginning **:** COMMENCEMENT; *esp* **:** a formal and usu. public event by which something new is put officially into operation **2 :** something that is open: as **a** (1) **:** BREACH, APERTURE (2) **:** an open width **:** SPAN **b :** an area without trees or with scattered usu. mature trees that occurs as a break in a forest **c :** two pages that face one another in a book **3 :** something that constitutes a beginning: as **a :** a planned series of moves made at the beginning of a game of chess or checkers **b :** a first performance **4 a :** OCCASION, CHANCE **b :** an opportunity for employment ⟨~*s* for skilled machinists⟩

open letter *n* **:** a letter of protest or appeal intended for the general public and printed in a newspaper or periodical

open–mind·ed \,ō-pən-'mīn-dəd, ,ōp-ᵊm-'(m)īn-\ *adj* **:** receptive of arguments or ideas **:** UNPREJUDICED — **open–mind·ed·ly** *adv* — **open–mind·ed·ness** *n*

open·mouthed \,ō-pən-'mau̇thd, -'mau̇tht; ,ōp-ᵊm-'(m)au̇t͟hd, -'(m)au̇tht\ *adj* **1 :** having the mouth widely open **2 :** struck with amazement or wonder **3 :** CLAMOROUS, VOCIFEROUS — **open-mouthed·ly** \-'(m)au̇-t͟həd-lē; -'(m)au̇th-tlē, -əd-lē\ *adv* — **open-mouthed·ness** \-'(m)au̇-t͟həd-nəs, -'(m)au̇th(t)-nəs\ *n*

open order *n* **:** a military formation in which the units are separated by considerable intervals

open–pol·li·nat·ed \,ō-pən-'päl-ə-,nāt-əd, ,ōp-ᵊm-\ *adj* **:** pollinated by natural agencies without human intervention

open ses·a·me \-'ses-ə-mē\ *n* [fr. *open sesame*, the magical command used by Ali Baba to open the door of the robbers' den in *Ali Baba and the Forty Thieves*] **:** something that unfailingly brings about a desired end

open shop *n* **:** an establishment in which eligibility for employment and retention on the payroll are not determined by membership or nonmembership in a labor union though there may be an agreement by which a union is recognized as sole bargaining agent

open sight *n* **:** a firearm rear sight having an open notch instead of a peephole or a telescope

open syllable *n* **:** a syllable ended by a vowel or diphthong

open up *vi* **1 :** to commence firing **2 :** to become communicative **3 :** to spread out or come into view **4 :** to launch an offensive ~ *vt* **1 :** to open by cutting into **2 :** to make plain or visible **:** DISCLOSE **3 :** to make available

open·work \'ō-pən-,wərk, 'ōp-ᵊm-\ *n, often attrib* **:** work so constructed or manufactured as to show openings through its substance — **open–worked** \-,wərkt\ *adj*

¹**opera** *pl of* OPUS

²**op·era** \'äp-(ə-)rə\ *n* [It, work, opera, fr. L, work, pains; akin to L *oper-*, *opus*] **1 :** a drama set to music and made up of vocal pieces with orchestral accompaniment and orchestral overtures and interludes **2 :** the score of a musical drama **3 :** the performance of an opera or a house where operas are performed

op·er·a·ble \'äp-(ə-)rə-bəl\ *adj* **1 :** fit, possible, or desirable to use **:** PRACTICABLE **2 :** suitable for surgical treatment ⟨an ~ cancer⟩ — **op·er·a·bly** \-blē\ *adv*

opé·ra bouffe \,äp-(ə-)rə-'büf\ *n* [F] **:** farcical comic opera

opé·ra co·mique \,äp-(ə-)rə-(,)käm-'ēk, -kō-'mēk\ *n* [F] **:** an opera characterized by spoken dialogue interspersed between the set arias and ensemble numbers

opera glass *n* **:** a small binocular optical instrument similar to the field glass and adapted for use at the opera — often used in pl.

opera hat *n* **:** a man's collapsible top hat consisting usu. of a dull silky fabric stretched over a steel frame

opera house *n* **:** a theater devoted principally to the performance of operas; *broadly* **:** THEATER

¹**op·er·ant** \'äp-ə-rənt\ *adj* **1 :** EFFECTIVE **2 :** of or relating to the observable or measurable

²**operant** *n* **:** one that operates

op·er·ate \'äp-(ə-),rāt\ *vb* [L *operatus*, pp. of *operari* to work, fr. *oper-*, *opus* work; akin to OE *efnan* to perform, Skt *apas* work] *vi* **1 :** to perform a work or labor **:** FUNCTION **2 :** to produce an appropriate effect **3 a :** to perform an operation or series of operations **b :** to perform surgery **c :** to carry on a military or naval action or mission ~ *vt* **1 :** to bring about **:** EFFECT **2 a :** to cause to function **:** WORK **b :** to put or keep in operation **:** MANAGE **3 :** to perform surgery on

op·er·at·ic \,äp-ə-'rat-ik\ *adj* [irreg. fr. *opera*] **:** of, relating to, resembling, or suitable to opera — **op·er·at·i·cal·ly** \-i-k(ə-)lē\ *adv*

op·er·a·tion \,äp-ə-'rā-shən\ *n* **1 :** a doing or performing of a practical work or of something involving practical application of principles or processes **2 a :** an exertion of power or influence **:** FUNCTIONING **b :** the quality or state of being functional or operative **c :** method or manner of functioning **3 :** EFFICACY, POTENCY **4 :** a procedure on a living body usu. with instruments for the repair of damage or the restoration of health **5 :** any of various mathematical or logical processes of deriving one expression from others according to a rule **6 a :** a military or naval action, mission, or maneuver including its planning and execution **b** *pl* **:** the office on the flight line of an airfield where pilots file clearances for flights and which controls flying from the field **7 :** a business transaction esp. when speculative

op·er·a·tion·al \-shnəl, -shən-ᵊl\ *adj* **1 :** of, relating to, or based on operations ⟨~ definition⟩ **2 a :** of, engaged in, or connected with execution of military or naval operations in campaign or battle **b :** ready for or in condition to undertake a destined function

op·er·a·tion·al·ism \-,iz-əm\ *also* **op·er·a·tion·ism** \-shən-,iz-əm\ *n* **:** a view that the concepts or terms used in nonanalytic scientific statements must be definable in terms of identifiable and repeatable operations — **op·er·a·tion·al·ist** \-shnəl-əst, -shən-ᵊl-\ *n* — **op·er·a·tion·al·is·tic** \-,rā-shnəl-'is-tik, -shən-ᵊl-\ *adj*

operations research *n* **:** the application of scientific and esp. mathematical methods to the study and analysis of complex overall problems

¹**op·er·a·tive** \'äp-(ə-)rət-iv, 'äp-ə-,rāt-\ *adj* **1 :** producing an appropriate effect **:** EFFICACIOUS **2 :** exerting force or influence **:** OPERATING **3 a :** having to do with physical operations **b :** WORKING ⟨an ~ craftsman⟩ **4 :** based upon or consisting of an operation — **op·er·a·tive·ly** *adv* — **op·er·a·tive·ness** *n*

²**operative** *n* **:** OPERATOR: as **a :** ARTISAN, MECHANIC **b :** a secret agent **:** private detective

op·er·a·tor \'äp-(ə-),rāt-ər\ *n* **1 :** one that operates: as **a :** one that operates a machine or device **b :** one that operates a business **c :** one that performs surgical operations **d :** one that deals in stocks or commodities **2 a :** MOUNTEBANK, FRAUD **b :** a shrewd and skillful person who knows how to circumvent restrictions or difficulties **3 :** a mathematical or logical symbol denoting an operation to be performed

oper·cu·lar \ō-'pər-kyə-lər\ *adj* **:** of, relating to, or constituting an operculum — **opercular** *n*

oper·cu·late \-lət\ *also* **oper·cu·lat·ed** \-,lāt-əd\ *adj* **:** having an operculum

oper·cu·lum \ō-'pər-kyə-ləm\ *n, pl* **oper·cu·la** \-lə\ *also* **oper·cu·lums** [NL, fr. L, cover, fr. *operire* to shut, cover — more at WEIR] **1 :** a lid or covering flap (as of a moss capsule or a pyxidium in a seed plant) **2 :** a body process or part that suggests a lid: as **a :** a horny or shelly plate on the posterior dorsal surface of the foot in many gastropod mollusks that closes the shell when the animal is retracted **b :** the covering of the gills of a fish

op·er·et·ta \,äp-ə-'ret-ə\ *n* [It, dim. of *opera*] **:** a light musical-dramatic production having usu. a romantic plot and containing spoken dialogue and dancing scenes — **op·er·et·tist** \-'ret-əst\ *n*

op·er·ose \'äp-ə-,rōs\ *adj* [L *operosus*, fr. *oper-*, *opus* work — more at OPERATE] **:** LABORIOUS, DILIGENT — **op·er·ose·ly** *adv* — **op·er·ose·ness** *n*

Ophe·lia \ō-'fēl-yə\ *n* **:** the daughter of Polonius in Shakespeare's *Hamlet*

ophi·cleide \'äf-ə-,klīd, 'ō-fə-\ *n* [F *ophicléide*, fr. Gk *ophis* snake + *kleid-*, *kleis* key — more at CLAVICLE] **:** a deep-toned brass wind instrument consisting of a large tapering tube bent double

ophid·i·an \ō-'fid-ē-ən\ *adj* [deriv. of Gk *ophis*] **:** of, relating to, or resembling snakes — **ophidian** *n*

ophi·ol·o·gy \,äf-ē-'äl-ə-jē, ,ō-fē-\ *n* [Gk *ophis* + E *-logy*] **:** a branch of herpetology dealing with snakes

ophi·oph·a·gous \,ō-fē-'äf-ə-gəs, ,äf-ē-\ *adj* [Gk *ophiophagos*, fr. *ophis* + *-phagos* -phagous] **:** feeding on snakes

Ophir \'ō-fər\ *n* [Heb *Ōphīr*] **:** a Biblical land rich in gold

ophite \'äf-,īt, 'ō-,fīt\ *n* [L, fr. Gk *ophitēs* (lithos), lit., serpentine (stone), fr. *ophitēs* snakelike, fr. *ophis* snake; akin to L *anguis* snake, *anguilla* eel, Gk *enchelys* eel, *echidna* viper, *echinos* hedgehog, OE *igil*] **:** any of various usu. green and often mottled or blotched rocks

ophit·ic \ä-'fit-ik, ō-\ *adj* **:** having or being a rock fabric in which

lath-shaped plagioclase crystals are enclosed in later formed augite

ophthalm- *or* **ophthalmo-** *comb form* [Gk, fr. *ophthalmos*] **:** eye ⟨*ophthalmo*logy⟩ **:** eyeball ⟨*ophthalm*itis⟩

oph·thal·mia \äf-ˈthal-mē-ə, äp-\ *n* [ME *obtalmia*, fr. LL *ophthalmia*, fr. Gk, fr. *ophthalmos* eye; akin to Gk *ōps* eye — more at EYE] **:** inflammation of the conjunctiva or eyeball

oph·thal·mic \-mik\ *adj* **:** of, relating to, or situated near the eye

oph·thal·mo·log·ic \(ˌ)äf-ˌthal-mə-ˈläj-ik, (ˌ)äp-\ *adj* **:** of or relating to ophthalmology — **oph·thal·mo·log·i·cal** \-i-kəl\ *adj* — **oph·thal·mo·log·i·cal·ly** \-i-k(ə-)lē\ *adv*

oph·thal·mol·o·gist \ˌäf-ˌthal-ˈmäl-ə-jəst, ˌäp-, -thə(l)-ˈmäl-\ *n* **:** a physician that specializes in ophthalmology — compare OPTICIAN, OPTOMETRIST

oph·thal·mol·o·gy \-jē\ *n* **:** a branch of medical science dealing with the structure, functions, and diseases of the eye

oph·thal·mo·scope \äf-ˈthal-mə-ˌskōp, äp-\ *n* [ISV] **:** an instrument with a mirror centrally perforated for viewing the interior of the eye and esp. the retina — **oph·thal·mo·scop·ic** \(ˌ)äf-ˌthal-mə-ˈskäp-ik, (ˌ)äp-\ *or* **oph·thal·mo·scop·i·cal** \-i-kəl\ *adj* — **oph·thal·mos·co·py** \ˌäf-ˌthal-ˈmäs-kə-pē, ˌäp-\ *n*

-opia \ˈō-pē-ə\ *n comb form* [NL, fr. Gk *-ōpia*, fr. *ōps*] **1 :** condition of having (such) vision ⟨dipl*opia*⟩ **2 :** condition of having (such) a visual defect ⟨hyper*opia*⟩

1opi·ate \ˈō-pē-ət, -ˌāt\ *adj* **1 :** containing or mixed with opium **2 a :** inducing sleep **:** NARCOTIC **b :** causing dullness or inaction

2opiate *n* **1 :** a preparation or derivative of opium; *broadly* **:** NARCOTIC 1 **2 :** something that induces rest or inaction or quiets uneasiness

opine \ō-ˈpīn\ *vb* [MF *opiner*, fr. L *opinari* to have an opinion] *vt* **:** to state as an opinion ∼ *vi* **:** to express opinions

opin·ion \ə-ˈpin-yən\ *n* [ME, fr. MF, fr. L *opinion-, opinio*; akin to L *opinari*] **1 a :** a view, judgment, or appraisal formed in the mind about a particular matter **b :** APPROVAL, ESTEEM **2 a :** belief stronger than impression and less strong than positive knowledge **b :** a generally held view **3 a :** a formal expression by an expert of his judgment or advice **b :** the formal expression of the legal reasons and principles upon which a legal decision is based

syn OPINION, VIEW, BELIEF, CONVICTION, PERSUASION, SENTIMENT mean a judgment one holds as true. OPINION implies a conclusion thought out yet open to dispute; VIEW suggests an opinion more or less colored by bias; BELIEF implies often deliberate acceptance and intellectual assent; CONVICTION applies to a firmly and seriously held belief; PERSUASION suggests a belief grounded on assurance (as by evidence) of its truth; SENTIMENT suggests an opinion more or less settled because rooted in individual character

opin·ion·at·ed \-yə-ˌnāt-əd\ *adj* **:** unduly adhering to one's own opinion or to preconceived notions — **opin·ion·at·ed·ly** *adv* — **opin·ion·at·ed·ness** *n*

opin·ion·ative \-ˌnāt-iv\ *adj* **1 :** of, relating to, or consisting of opinion **:** DOCTRINAL **2 :** OPINIONATED

op·is·thog·na·thous \ˌäp-əs-ˈthäg-nə-thəs\ *adj* [Gk *opisthen* behind + E *-gnathous*; akin to Gk *epi-* on — more at EPI-] **:** having retreating jaws

opi·um \ˈō-pē-əm\ *n, often attrib* [ME, fr. L, fr. Gk *opion*, fr. dim. of *opos* sap] **1 :** a bitter brownish addictive narcotic drug that consists of the dried juice of the opium poppy **2 :** something having an effect like that of opium **:** STUPEFIER

opium poppy *n* **:** an annual Eurasian poppy (*Papaver somniferum*) cultivated since antiquity as the source of opium, for its edible oily seeds, or for ornament

opos·sum \(ə-)ˈpäs-əm\ *n, pl* **opossums** *also* **opossum** *often attrib* [fr. *âpäsûm*, lit., white animal (in some Algonquian language of Virginia)] **1 :** any of various American marsupials (family Didelphidae); *esp* **:** a common omnivorous largely nocturnal and arboreal mammal (*Didelphis virginiana*) of the eastern U.S. **2 :** any of several Australian phalangers

1op·po·nent \ə-ˈpō-nənt\ *n* [L *opponent-, opponens*, prp. of *opponere*] **1 :** one that opposes **:** ADVERSARY **2 :** a muscle that opposes or counteracts and limits the action of another

syn ANTAGONIST, ADVERSARY: OPPONENT implies little more than position on the other side as in a debate, election, contest, or conflict; ANTAGONIST implies sharper opposition in a struggle for supremacy; ADVERSARY may carry an additional implication of active hostility

2opponent *adj* **1 :** OPPOSING, ANTAGONISTIC **2 :** situated in front

op·por·tune \ˌäp-ər-ˈt(y)ün\ *adj* [ME, fr. MF *opportun*, fr. L *opportunus*, fr. *ob-* toward + *portus* port, harbor — more at OB-] **1 :** suitable or convenient for a particular occurrence ⟨an ∼ moment⟩ **2 :** TIMELY **syn** see SEASONABLE — **op·por·tune·ly** *adv* — **op·por·tune·ness** \-ˈt(y)ün-nəs\ *n*

op·por·tun·ism \-ˈt(y)ü-ˌniz-əm\ *n* **:** the art, policy, or practice of taking advantage of opportunities or circumstances esp. with little regard for principles or consequences — **op·por·tun·ist** \-nəst\ *n or adj* — **op·por·tu·nis·tic** \-(ˌ)t(y)ü-ˈnis-tik\ *adj*

op·por·tu·ni·ty \ˌäp-ər-ˈt(y)ü-nət-ē\ *n* **1 :** a favorable juncture of circumstances **2 :** a good chance for advancement or progress

op·pos·abil·i·ty \ə-ˌpō-zə-ˈbil-ət-ē\ *n* **:** the quality or state of being opposable

op·pos·able \ə-ˈpō-zə-bəl\ *adj* **1 :** capable of being opposed or resisted **2 :** capable of being placed opposite something else

op·pose \ə-ˈpōz\ *vt* [F *opposer*, fr. L *opponere* (perf. indic. *opposui*), fr. *ob-* against + *ponere* to place — more at OB-, POSITION] **1 :** to place opposite or against something **2 :** to place over against something so as to provide resistance, counterbalance, or contrast **3 :** to offer resistance to — **op·pos·er** *n*

syn COMBAT, RESIST, WITHSTAND, ANTAGONIZE: OPPOSE may apply to a range extending from mere objection to bitter hostility or warfare; COMBAT stresses the actual conflict with what one actively opposes; RESIST and WITHSTAND imply answering an offensive action with counter force, WITHSTAND usu. adding a suggestion of successful outcome; ANTAGONIZE implies an arousing of resistance or hostility in another

op·pose·less \ə-ˈpōz-ləs\ *adj* **:** IRRESISTIBLE

1op·po·site \ˈäp-ə-zət, ˈäp-sət\ *n* **1 :** something that is opposed or contrary **2 :** ANTONYM

2opposite *adj* [ME, fr. MF, fr. L *oppositus*, pp. of *opponere*] **1 a :** set over against something that is at the other end or side of an intervening line or space ⟨∼ interior angles⟩ ⟨∼ ends of a diameter⟩ **b** (1) **:** situated in pairs on an axis each being separated from the other by half the circumference of the axis ⟨∼ leaves⟩ (2) *of floral parts* **:** SUPERPOSED **2 a :** OPPOSED, HOSTILE ⟨∼ sides of the question⟩ **b :** diametrically different (as in nature or character) ⟨∼ meanings⟩ **3 :** contrary to one another or to a thing specified **:** REVERSE ⟨∼ directions⟩ **4 :** being the other of a matching or contrasting pair **:** COMPLEMENTARY ⟨members of the ∼ sex⟩ — **op·po·site·ly** *adv* — **op·po·site·ness** *n*

syn CONTRADICTORY, CONTRARY, ANTITHETICAL: OPPOSITE applies to things in sharp contrast or in conflict; CONTRADICTORY applies to two things that completely negate each other so that if one is true or valid the other must be untrue or invalid; CONTRARY implies extreme divergence or diametrical opposition; ANTITHETICAL stresses clear and unequivocal diametrical opposition

3opposite *adv* **:** on opposite sides

4opposite *prep* **1 :** across from and usu. facing or on the same level with **2 :** in a role complementary to

opposite number *n* **:** a member of a system or class who holds relatively the same position as a particular member in a corresponding system or class

op·po·si·tion \ˌäp-ə-ˈzish-ən\ *n* **1 :** a configuration in which one celestial body is opposite another in the sky or in which the elongation is near or equal to 180 degrees **2 :** the relation between two propositions having the same subject and predicate but differing in quantity or quality or both **3 :** an act of setting opposite or over against **:** the condition of being so set **4 :** hostile or contrary action or condition **5 a :** something that opposes; *specif* **:** a body of persons opposing something **b** *often cap* **:** a political party opposing and prepared to replace the party in power — **op·po·si·tion·al** \-ˈzish-nəl, -ən-ᵊl\ *adj*

op·press \ə-ˈpres\ *vt* [ME *oppressen*, fr. MF *oppresser*, fr. L *oppressus*, pp. of *opprimere*, fr. *ob-* against + *premere* to press — more at OB-, PRESS] **1 a** *archaic* **:** SUPPRESS **b :** to crush or burden by abuse of power or authority **2 :** to burden spiritually or mentally as if by pressure **:** weigh down **syn** see DEPRESS, WRONG — **op·pres·sor** \-ˈpres-ər\ *n*

op·pres·sion \ə-ˈpresh-ən\ *n* **1 a :** unjust or cruel exercise of authority or power **b :** something that so oppresses **2 :** a sense of heaviness or obstruction in the body or mind **:** DEPRESSION

op·pres·sive \-ˈpres-iv\ *adj* **1 :** unreasonably burdensome or severe ⟨∼ legislation⟩ **2 :** TYRANNICAL **3 :** overpowering or depressing to the spirit or senses **syn** see ONEROUS — **op·pres·sive·ly** *adv* — **op·pres·sive·ness** *n*

op·pro·bri·ous \ə-ˈprō-brē-əs\ *adj* **1 :** expressive of opprobrium **:** SCURRILOUS ⟨∼ language⟩ **2 :** deserving of opprobrium — **op·pro·bri·ous·ly** *adv* — **op·pro·bri·ous·ness** *n*

op·pro·bri·um \-brē-əm\ *n* [L, fr. *opprobrare* to reproach, fr. *ob* in the way of + *probrum* reproach; akin to L *pro* forward and to L *ferre* to carry, bring — more at EPI-, FOR, BEAR] **1 :** something that brings disgrace **2 a :** public disgrace or ill fame that follows from conduct considered grossly wrong or vicious **:** INFAMY **b :** CONTEMPT, REPROACH **syn** see DISGRACE

op·pugn \ə-ˈpyün, ä-\ *vt* [ME *oppugnen*, fr. L *oppugnare*, fr. *ob-* against + *pugnare* to fight — more at OB-, PUNGENT] **1 :** to fight against **:** ASSAIL **2 :** to call in question — **op·pugn·er** *n*

Ops \ˈäps\ *n* [L] **:** the wife of Saturn and goddess of the harvest

-op·sis \ˈäp-səs\ *n comb form, pl* **-op·ses** \ˈäp-ˌsēz\ *or* **-op·si·des** \ˈäp-sə-ˌdēz\ [NL, fr. Gk, fr. *opsis* appearance, vision] **:** structure resembling a (specified) thing ⟨cary*opsis*⟩

op·son·ic \äp-ˈsän-ik\ *adj* **:** of, relating to, or involving opsonin

op·so·nin \ˈäp-sə-nən\ *n* [L *opsonium* relish, fr. Gk *opsōnion* victuals, fr. *opsōnein* to purchase victuals — more at OLIGOPSONY] **:** a constituent of blood serum that makes foreign cells more susceptible to the action of the phagocytes

-op·sy \ˌäp-sē, əp-\ *n comb form* [Gk *-opsia*, fr. *opsis*] **:** examination ⟨necr*opsy*⟩

opt \ˈäpt\ *vi* [F *opter*, fr. L *optare*] **:** to make a choice

op·ta·tive \ˈäp-tət-iv\ *adj* **1 a :** of, relating to, or constituting a mood of verbs that is expressive of wish or desire **b :** of, relating to, or constituting a sentence that is expressive of wish or hope **2 :** expressing desire or wish — **optative** *n* — **op·ta·tive·ly** *adv*

1op·tic \ˈäp-tik\ *adj* [MF *optique*, fr. ML *opticus*, fr. Gk *optikos*, fr. *opsesthai* to be going to see; akin to Gk *opsis* appearance, *ōps* eye — more at EYE] **1 :** of or relating to vision or the eye **2 :** dependent chiefly on vision for orientation

2optic *n* **1 :** EYE **2 :** any of the lenses, prisms, or mirrors of an optical instrument

op·ti·cal \ˈäp-ti-kəl\ *adj* **1 :** relating to the science of optics **2 :** relating to vision — **op·ti·cal·ly** \-k(ə-)lē\ *adv*

optical art *n* **:** nonobjective art characterized by the use of straight or curved lines or geometric patterns often for an illusory effect (as of perspective or motion)

optically active *adj* **:** capable of rotating the plane of polarization of light to the right or left

optically inactive *adj* **:** INACTIVE c (2)

optic axis *n* **:** a line in a doubly refracting medium that is parallel to the direction in which all components of plane-polarized light travel with the same speed

optic disk *n* **:** the nearly circular light-colored area at the back of the retina where the optic nerve enters the eyeball

op·ti·cian \äp-ˈtish-ən\ *n* **1 :** a maker of or dealer in optical items and instruments **2 :** one that grinds spectacle lenses to prescription and dispenses spectacles — compare OCULIST, OPTOMETRIST

optic nerve *n* **:** either of a pair of sensory cranial nerves that arise from the ventral part of the diencephalon, supply the retina, and conduct visual stimuli to the brain — called also *second cranial nerve*

op·tics \ˈäp-tiks\ *n pl but sing or pl in constr* **:** a science that deals with light, its genesis and propagation, the effects that it undergoes and produces, and other phenomena closely associated with it

optic thalamus *n* **:** either of two masses of nerve tissue in the floor of the diencephalon from which the optic nerves arise

op·ti·mal \ˈäp-tə-məl\ *adj* **:** most desirable or satisfactory **:** OPTIMUM — **op·ti·mal·ly** \-mə-lē\ *adv*

op·ti·mism \ˈäp-tə-ˌmiz-əm\ *n* [F *optimisme*, fr. L *optimum*, n., best, fr. neut. of *optimus* best; akin to L *ops* power — more at OPULENT] **1 :** a doctrine that this world is the best possible world **2 :** an inclination to put the most favorable construction upon actions and happenings or to anticipate the best possible outcome — **op·ti·mist** \-məst\ *n* — **optimist** *adj* — **op·ti·mis·tic** \ˌäp-tə-ˈmis-tik\ *adj* — **op·ti·mis·ti·cal** \-ti-kəl\ *adj* — **op·ti·mis·ti·cal·ly** \-k(ə-)lē\ *adv*

op·ti·mize \ˈäp-tə-ˌmīz\ *vt* **:** to make as perfect, effective, or functional as possible

op·ti·mum \ˈäp-tə-məm\ *n, pl* **op·ti·ma** \-mə\ *also* **optimums** [L] **1 :** the amount or degree of something that is most favorable to some end; *esp* **:** the most favorable condition for the growth and reproduction of an organism **2 :** greatest degree attained under implied or specified conditions — **optimum** *adj*

op·tion \ˈäp-shən\ *n* [F, fr. L *option-, optio* free choice; akin to L *optare* to choose, Gk *epiopsesthai* to be going to choose] **1 :** an act of choosing **2 a :** the power or right to choose **:** freedom of choice **b :** a privilege of demanding fulfillment of a contract on any day within a specified time **c :** a right to buy or sell designated securities or commodities at a specified price during the period of the contract **d :** a right of an insured person to choose the form in which payments due him on a policy shall be made or applied **syn** see CHOICE

op·tion·al \ˈäp-shnəl, -shən-ᵊl\ *adj* **:** involving an option **:** not compulsory — **op·tion·al·ly** \-ē\ *adv*

op·to·met·ric \ˌäp-tə-ˈme-trik\ *adj* **:** of or relating to optometry — **op·to·met·ri·cal** \-tri-kəl\ *adj*

op·tom·e·trist \äp-ˈtäm-ə-trəst\ *n* **:** a specialist in optometry — compare OPTICIAN

op·tom·e·try \-trē\ *n* [Gk *optos* (verbal of *opsesthai* to be going to see) + ISV *-metry* — more at OPTIC] **:** the art or profession of examining the eye for defects and faults of refraction and prescribing correctional lenses or exercises but not drugs or surgery

op·u·lence \ˈäp-yə-lən(t)s\ *n* **1 :** WEALTH, AFFLUENCE **2 :** PLENTY, PROFUSION

op·u·lent \-lənt\ *adj* [L *opulentus,* fr. *ops* power, help; akin to L *opus* work] **:** exhibiting or characterized by opulence: as **a :** having a large estate or property **b :** amply or plentifully provided or fashioned **syn** see LUXURIOUS, RICH — **op·u·lent·ly** *adv*

opun·tia \ō-ˈpən-ch(ē-)ə\ *n* [L, a plant, fr. fem. of *opuntius* of Opus, fr. *Opunt-, Opus* Opus, ancient city in Greece] **:** PRICKLY PEAR

opus \ˈō-pəs\ *n, pl* **opera** \ˈō-pə-rə, ˈäp-ə-\ *also* **opus·es** \ˈō-pə-səz\ [L *oper-, opus*] **:** WORK; *esp* **:** a musical composition or set of compositions

opus·cule \ō-ˈpəs-(ˌ)kyü(ə)l\ *n* [F, fr. L *opusculum,* dim. of *opus*] **:** a small or petty work **:** OPUSCULUM

opus·cu·lum \ō-ˈpəs-kyə-ləm\ *n, pl* **opus·cu·la** \-lə\ [L] **:** a minor work — usu. used in pl.

¹**or** \ər, (ˌ)ȯ(ə)r\ *conj* [ME *other, or,* fr. OE *oththe;* akin to OHG *eddo* or] **1** — used as a function word to indicate an alternative ⟨coffee ~ tea⟩ ⟨sink ~ swim⟩ **2** *archaic* **:** EITHER **3** *archaic* **:** WHETHER

²**or** *prep* [ME, fr. *or,* adv., early, before, fr. ON *ār;* akin to OE *ǣr* early — more at ERE] *archaic* **:** BEFORE

³**or** *conj, archaic* **:** BEFORE

⁴**or** \ˈȯ(ə)r\ *n* [MF, gold, fr. L *aurum* — more at ORIOLE] **:** the heraldic color gold or yellow

¹**-or** \ər, ˌȯ(ə)r, ˈȯ(ə)r\ *n suffix* [ME, fr. OF *-eur, -eor* & L *-or;* OF *-eur,* fr. L *-or;* OF *-eor,* fr. L *-ator* -or, fr. *-atus,* pp. suffix + *-or* — more at -ATE] **:** one that does a (specified) thing ⟨grant*or*⟩ ⟨elevat*or*⟩

²**-or** \ər\ *n suffix* [ME, fr. OF *-eur,* fr. L *-or*] **:** condition **:** activity ⟨demean*or*⟩

ora *pl of* OS

or·ache *or* **or·ach** \ˈȯr-ich, ˈär-\ *n* [ME *orage,* fr. MF *arrache,* fr. (assumed) VL *atrapic-, atrapex,* fr. Gk *atraphaxys*] **:** any of a genus (*Atriplex*) of herbs of the goosefoot family

or·a·cle \ˈȯr-ə-kəl, ˈär-\ *n* [ME, fr. MF, fr. L *oraculum,* fr. *orare* to speak — more at ORATION] **1 a :** a person (as a priestess of ancient Greece) through whom a deity is believed to speak **b :** a shrine in which a deity so reveals hidden knowledge or the divine purpose **c :** an answer or decision given by an oracle **2 a :** a person giving wise or authoritative decisions or opinions **b :** an authoritative or wise expression or answer

orac·u·lar \ȯ-ˈrak-yə-lər, ə-\ *adj* [L *oraculum*] **1 :** of, relating to, or being an oracle **2 :** resembling an oracle in wisdom, solemnity, or obscurity **syn** see DICTATORIAL — **orac·u·lar·i·ty** \-ˌrak-yə-ˈlar-ət-ē\ *n* — **orac·u·lar·ly** \-ˈrak-yə-lər-lē\ *adv*

oral \ˈōr-əl, ˈȯr-, ˈär-\ *adj* [L *or-, os* mouth; akin to OE *ōra* border, L *ora*] **1 a :** uttered by the mouth or in words **:** SPOKEN **b :** using speech or the lips esp. in teaching the deaf **2 a :** of, given through, or affecting the mouth **b :** being on or relating to the same surface as the mouth — **oral·ly** \-ə-lē\ *adv*

syn VERBAL: ORAL usu. applies to what is spoken rather than written; VERBAL applies to the use of words whether in speech or in writing often in contrast with other ways of communicating

¹**or·ange** \ˈȯr-inj, ˈär-, -ənj\ *n* [ME, fr. MF, fr. OProv *auranja,* fr. Ar *nāranj,* fr. Per *nārang,* fr. Skt *nāraṅga* orange tree, of Dravidian origin; akin to Tamil *naṟu* fragrant] **1 a :** a globose berry with a reddish yellow rind and a sweet edible pulp **b :** any of various rather small evergreen trees (genus *Citrus*) with ovate unifoliate leaves, hard yellow wood, fragrant white flowers, and fruits that are oranges **2 :** any of several trees or fruits resembling the orange **3 :** any of a group of colors that lie midway between red and yellow in hue and are of medium lightness and moderate to high saturation

²**orange** *adj* **1 :** of or relating to the orange **2 :** of the color orange

Orange *adj* [William III †1702 king of England and prince of *Orange*] **:** of, relating to, or sympathizing with Orangemen — **Or·ange·ism** \-ˌiz-əm\ *n*

or·ange·ade \ˌȯr-in-ˈjād, ˌär-, -ən-\ *n* [F, fr. *orange* + *-ade*] **:** a beverage of orange juice sweetened and mixed with plain or carbonated water

orange hawkweed *n* **:** INDIAN PAINTBRUSH 2

Or·ange·man \ˈȯr-inj-mən, ˈär-, -ənj-\ *n* **1 :** a member of a secret society organized in the north of Ireland in 1795 to defend the British sovereign and to support the Protestant religion **2 :** a Protestant Irishman esp. of Ulster

orange pekoe *n* **:** a tea formerly made from the tiny leaf and end bud of the spray; *broadly* **:** India or Ceylon tea of good quality

or·ange·ry \ˈȯr-inj-(ə-)rē, ˈär-, -ənj-\ *n* **:** a greenhouse or other protected place for raising oranges in cool climates

or·ange·wood \ˈȯr-inj-ˌwu̇d, ˈär-, -ənj-\ *n* **:** the wood of the orange tree used esp. in turnery and carving

orang·utan *or* **orang·ou·tan** \ə-ˈraŋ-ə-ˌtaŋ, -ˌtan\ *n* [Malay *orang hutan,* fr. *orang* man + *hutan* forest] **:** a largely herbivorous arboreal anthropoid ape (*Pongo pygmaeus*) of Borneo and Sumatra about two thirds as large as the gorilla

orate \ȯ-ˈrāt\ *vi* [back-formation fr. *oration*] **:** to speak in a declamatory or grandiloquent manner **:** HARANGUE

ora·tion \ə-ˈrā-shən, ȯ-\ *n* [L *oration-, oratio* speech, oration, fr. *oratus,* pp. of *orare* to plead, speak, pray; akin to Russ *orat'* to yell] **:** an elaborate discourse delivered in a formal and dignified manner usu. on some special occasion

or·a·tor \ˈȯr-ət-ər, ˈär-\ *n* **1 :** PETITIONER, PLAINTIFF **2 :** one who delivers an oration; *esp* **:** one distinguished for his skill and power as a public speaker

Or·a·to·ri·an \ˌȯr-ə-ˈtōr-ē-ən, ˌär-, -ˈtȯr-\ *n* **:** a member of the Congregation of the Oratory of St. Philip Neri originating in Rome in 1564 and comprising independent communities of secular priests under obedience but without vows — **Oratorian** *adj*

or·a·tor·i·cal \ˌȯr-ə-ˈtȯr-i-kəl, ˌär-ə-ˈtär-\ *adj* **:** of, relating to, or characteristic of an orator or oratory — **or·a·tor·i·cal·ly** \-k(ə-)lē\ *adv*

or·a·to·rio \ˌȯr-ə-ˈtōr-ē-ˌō, ˌär-, -ˈtȯr-\ *n* [It, fr. the *Oratorio* di San Filippo Neri (Oratory of St. Philip Neri) in Rome] **:** a choral work on a usu. scriptural subject consisting chiefly of recitatives, arias, and choruses without action or scenery

¹**or·a·to·ry** \ˈȯr-ə-ˌtōr-ē, ˈär-, -ˌtȯr-\ *n* [ME *oratorie,* fr. LL *oratorium,* fr. L *oratus,* pp.] **1 :** a place of prayer; *esp* **:** a private or institutional chapel **2 :** an Oratorian congregation, house, or church

²**oratory** *n* [L *oratoria,* fr. fem. of *oratorius* oratorical, fr. *oratus,* pp.] **1 :** the art of an orator **2 :** ORATION

¹**orb** \ˈȯ(ə)rb\ *n* [MF *orbe,* fr. L *orbis* circle, disk, orb; akin to L *orbita* track, rut] **1 :** any of the concentric spheres in old astronomy surrounding the earth and carrying the heavenly bodies in their revolutions **2** *archaic* **:** something circular **:** CIRCLE, ORBIT **3 :** a spherical body; *esp* **:** a celestial sphere **4 :** EYE **5 :** a sphere surmounted by a cross symbolizing kingly power and justice

²**orb** *vt* **1 :** to form into a disk or circle **2** *archaic* **:** ENCIRCLE, SURROUND, ENCLOSE ~ *vi, archaic* **:** to move in an orbit

or·bic·u·lar \ȯr-ˈbik-yə-lər\ *adj* [ME *orbiculer,* fr. MF or LL; MF *orbiculaire,* fr. LL *orbicularis,* fr. L *orbiculus,* dim. of *orbis*] **1 :** SPHERICAL, CIRCULAR **2 :** COMPLETE, ROUNDED — **or·bic·u·lar·i·ty** \(ˌ)ȯr-ˌbik-yə-ˈlar-ət-ē\ *n* — **or·bic·u·lar·ly** \ȯr-ˈbik-yə-lər-lē\ *adv*

or·bic·u·late \ȯr-ˈbik-yə-lət\ *adj* **:** ORBICULAR ⟨an ~ leaf⟩

¹**or·bit** \ˈȯr-bət\ *n* [L *orbita*] **1** [ML *orbita,* fr. L] **:** the bony socket of the eye **2 :** a path described by one body in its revolution about another (as by the earth about the sun or by an electron about an atomic nucleus); *also* **:** one complete revolution of a body describing such a path **3 :** range or sphere of activity — **or·bit·al** \-ᵊl\ *adj*

²**orbit** *vt* **1 :** to revolve in an orbit around **:** CIRCLE **2 :** to send up and make revolve in an orbit ⟨~ a satellite⟩ ~ *vi* **:** to travel in circles — **or·bit·er** *n*

orc \ˈȯ(ə)rk\ *n* [MF *orque,* fr. L *orca,* a whale] **:** GRAMPUS **:** a sea animal similar to the grampus; *also* **:** a sea monster

or·chard \ˈȯr-chərd\ *n* [ME, fr. OE *ortgeard,* fr. L *hortus* garden + OE *geard* yard — more at YARD] **:** a planting of fruit trees or nut trees; *also* **:** the trees of such a planting

or·chard·ist \-əst\ *or* **or·chard·man** \-mən, -ˌman\ *n* **:** an owner or supervisor of orchards

or·ches·tra \ˈȯr-kə-strə, -ˌkes-trə\ *n* [L, fr. Gk *orchēstra,* fr. *orcheisthai* to dance; akin to Skt *ṛghāyati* he raves] **1 a :** the circular space used by the chorus in front of the proscenium in an ancient Greek theater **b :** a corresponding semicircular space in a Roman theater used for seating important persons **2 a :** a group of instrumentalists including esp. string players organized to perform ensemble music **b (1) :** the space in front of the stage in a modern theater that is used by an orchestra **(2) :** the forward section of seats on the main floor of a theater

or·ches·tral \ȯr-ˈkes-trəl\ *adj* **1 :** of, relating to, or composed for an orchestra **2 :** suggestive of an orchestra or its musical qualities ⟨a poem of ~ sweep⟩ — **or·ches·tral·ly** \-trə-lē\ *adv*

or·ches·trate \ˈȯr-kə-ˌstrāt\ *vt* **1 a :** to compose or arrange (music) for an orchestra **b :** to provide with orchestration ⟨~ a ballet⟩ **2 :** to arrange or combine so as to achieve a maximum effect ⟨~s the elements of his art⟩ — **or·ches·tra·tion** \ˌȯr-kə-ˈstrā-shən\ *n* — **or·ches·tra·tor** *also* **or·ches·trat·er** \ˈȯr-kə-ˌstrāt-ər\ *n*

or·chid \ˈȯr-kəd\ *n* [irreg. fr. NL *Orchis*] **1 :** a plant or flower of a large family (Orchidaceae, the orchid family) of perennial epiphytic or terrestrial plants having usu. showy flowers with a corolla of three petals of which one differs greatly from the others **2 :** a variable color averaging a light purple

or·chis \ˈȯr-kəs\ *n* [NL, genus name, fr. L, orchid, fr. Gk, testicle, orchid; akin to MIr *uirgge* testicle] **:** ORCHID; *esp* **:** one of a genus (*Orchis*) with fleshy roots and a spurred lip

or·dain \ȯr-ˈdān\ *vb* [ME *ordeinen,* fr. OF *ordener,* fr. LL *ordinare,* fr. L, to put in order, appoint, fr. *ordin-, ordo* order] *vt* **1 :** to invest officially (as by the laying on of hands) with ministerial or sacerdotal authority **2 :** to establish or order by appointment, decree, or law **:** ENACT, DECREE; *specif* **:** DESTINE, PREDESTINE ~ *vi* **:** to issue an order — **or·dain·er** *n* — **or·dain·ment** \-ˈdān-mənt\ *n*

or·deal \ȯr-ˈdē(-ə)l, ˈȯr-ˌ\ *n* [ME *ordal,* fr. OE *ordāl;* akin to OHG *urteil* judgment; both fr. a prehistoric WGmc compound derived fr. a compound verb represented by OHG *irteilen* to judge, distribute, fr. *ir-,* perfective prefix + *teilen* to divide, render a verdict; akin to OHG *teil* part — more at ABIDE, DEAL] **1 :** a primitive means used to determine guilt or innocence by submitting the accused to dangerous or painful tests believed to be under supernatural control ⟨~ by fire⟩ **2 :** a severe trial or experience

¹**or·der** \ˈȯrd-ər\ *n* [MF *ordre,* fr. ML & L; ML *ordin-, ordo* ecclesiastical order, fr. L, arrangement, group, class; akin to L *ordiri* to lay the warp, begin] **1 a :** a group of people united (as by living under the same religious rules or by having won the same distinction) in some formal way **b :** a badge or medal of such a society; *also* **:** a military decoration **2 a :** any of the several grades of the Christian ministry **b** *pl* **:** the office of a person in the Christian ministry **c** *pl* **:** ORDINATION **3 a :** a rank, class, or special group in a community or society **b :** a class of persons

or things grouped according to quality, value, or natural characteristics; *specif* **:** a category of taxonomic classification ranking above the family and below the class **4 a :** the arrangement or sequence of objects in position or of events in time **b :** DEGREE 11 **c :** a transitive arrangement of mathematical elements **d :** the number of columns or rows in a determinant **5 a :** the prevailing mode or arrangement of things ⟨the old ~⟩ **b :** regular or harmonious arrangement ⟨the ~ of nature⟩; *also* **:** a condition characterized by such an arrangement **6 a :** the customary mode of procedure esp. in debate or other business ⟨point of ~⟩ **b :** a prescribed form of a religious service **:** RITE **7 a :** the rule of law or proper authority ⟨~ was restored⟩ **b :** a specific rule, regulation, or authoritative direction **:** COMMAND **8 a :** a style of building **b :** a type of column and entablature forming the unit of a style **9 :** state or condition esp. with regard to functioning or repair ⟨out of ~⟩ **10 a :** a written direction to pay money to someone **b :** a commission to purchase, sell, or supply goods or to perform work **c :** goods or items bought or sold — **in order to :** for the purpose of

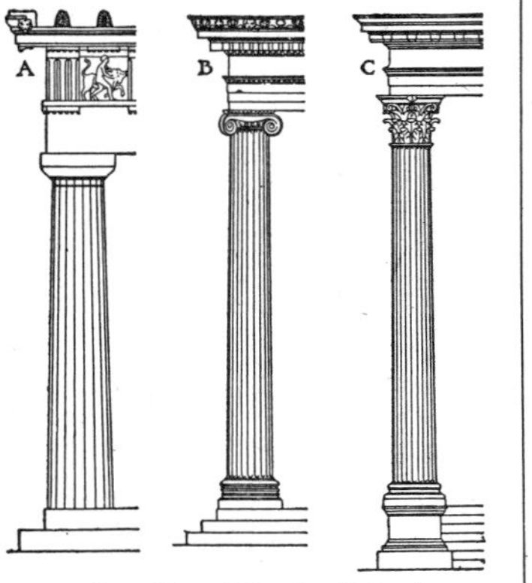

orders 8b: *A* Doric, *B* Ionic, *C* Corinthian

²**order** *vb* **or·der·ing** \'ȯrd-(ə-)riŋ\ *vt* **1 :** to put in order **:** ARRANGE **2 a :** to give an order to **:** COMMAND **b :** DESTINE, ORDAIN **c :** to command to go or come to a specified place **d :** to give an order for ~ *vi* **1 :** to bring about order **:** REGULATE **2 a :** to issue orders **:** COMMAND **b :** to give or place an order — **or·der·er** \-ər-ər\ *n*
syn ORDER, ARRANGE, MARSHAL, ORGANIZE, SYSTEMATIZE, METHODIZE mean to put persons or things into their proper places in relation to each other. ORDER suggests a straightening out so as to eliminate confusion; ARRANGE implies a setting in sequence, relationship, or adjustment; MARSHAL suggests gathering and arranging in preparation for a particular operation or effective use; ORGANIZE implies arranging so that the whole aggregate works as a unit with each element having a proper function; SYSTEMATIZE implies arranging according to a predetermined scheme; METHODIZE suggests imposing an orderly procedure rather than a fixed scheme **syn** see in addition COMMAND

or·dered \'ȯrd-ərd\ *adj* **:** characterized by order: as **a :** marked by system, regularity, or discipline **b :** marked by a regular or harmonious arrangement or disposition **c** (1) **:** having elements succeeding according to rule ⟨~ sequence⟩ (2) **:** having a specified first element ⟨~ pair⟩

or·der·li·ness \'ȯrd-ər-lē-nəs, 'ȯrd-ᵊl-ē-\ *n* **:** the quality or state of being orderly

¹**or·der·ly** \'ȯrd-ər-lē, 'ȯrd-ᵊl-ē\ *adj* **1 a** (1) **:** arranged or disposed in some order or pattern **:** REGULAR (2) **:** not marked by disorder **:** TIDY **b :** governed by law or system **:** REGULATED ⟨an ~ universe⟩ **c :** METHODICAL ⟨an ~ mind⟩ **2 :** well behaved **:** PEACEFUL ⟨an ~ crowd⟩ **3 :** relating to or charged with the transmission of military orders ⟨the ~ room⟩ — **orderly** *adv*

²**orderly** *n* **1 :** a soldier who attends a superior officer to convey messages and perform various services **2 :** a hospital attendant who does general work

¹**or·di·nal** \'ȯrd-nəl, -ᵊn-əl\ *n* **1** [ME, fr. ML *ordinale*, fr. LL, neut. of *ordinalis*] *cap* **:** a collection of forms to be used in ordination **2** [LL *ordinalis*, fr. *ordinalis*, adj.] **:** ORDINAL NUMBER

²**ordinal** *adj* [LL *ordinalis*, fr. L *ordin-*, *ordo*] **1 :** of a specified order or rank (as sixth) in a series **2 :** of or relating to an order (as of fishes)

ordinal number *n* **1 :** a number designating the place (as first, second, third) occupied by an item in an ordered sequence — see NUMBER table **2 :** a number that designates both the order of the elements of an ordered set and the cardinal number of the set

or·di·nance \'ȯrd-nən(t)s, 'ȯrd-ᵊn-ən(t)s\ *n* [ME, fr. MF & ML; MF *ordenance*, lit., act of arranging, fr. ML *ordinantia*, fr. L *ordinant-*, *ordinans*, prp. of *ordinare* to put in order — more at ORDAIN] **1 a :** an authoritative decree or direction **:** ORDER **b :** a law set forth by governmental authority; *specif* **:** a municipal regulation **2 :** something ordained or decreed by fate or a deity **3 :** a prescribed usage, practice, or ceremony **syn** see LAW

or·di·nand \,ȯrd-ᵊn-'and\ *n* [LL *ordinandus*, gerundive of *ordinare*] **:** a person being ordained

or·di·nar·i·ly \,ȯrd-ᵊn-'er-ə-lē\ *adv* **:** in an ordinary manner **:** to an ordinary degree

or·di·nar·i·ness \'ȯrd-ᵊn-,er-ē-nəs\ *n* **:** the quality or state of being ordinary

¹**or·di·nary** \'ȯrd-ᵊn-,er-ē\ *n* [ME *ordinarie*, fr. AF & ML; AF, fr. ML *ordinarius*, fr. L *ordinarius*, adj.] **1 a** (1) **:** a prelate exercising original jurisdiction over a specified territory or group (2) **:** a clergyman appointed formerly in England to attend condemned criminals **b :** a judge of probate in some states of the U.S. **2** *often cap* **:** the parts of the mass that do not vary from day to day **3 :** regular or customary condition or course of things ⟨nothing out of the ~⟩ **4 a** *Brit* **:** a meal served to all comers at a fixed price **b** *chiefly Brit* **:** a tavern or eating house serving regular meals **5 :** a common heraldic charge (as the bend or chevron) of simple form

²**ordinary** *adj* [ME *ordinarie*, fr. L *ordinarius*, fr. *ordin-*, *ordo* order] **1 :** to be expected **:** ROUTINE, NORMAL **2 :** having or constituting immediate or original jurisdiction; *also* **:** belonging to such jurisdiction **3 a :** of common quality, rank, or ability **b :** POOR, INFERIOR **c :** lacking in refinement **syn** see COMMON

or·di·nate \'ȯrd-nət, -ᵊn-ət, -ᵊn-,āt\ *n* [NL (*linea*) *ordinate* (*applicata*), lit., line applied in an orderly manner] **:** the Cartesian coordinate obtained by measuring parallel to the y-axis

or·di·na·tion \,ȯrd-ᵊn-'ā-shən\ *n* **:** the act of ordaining **:** the state of being ordained

ord·nance \'ȯrd-nən(t)s\ *n* [ME *ordinaunce*, fr. MF *ordenance*, lit., act of arranging] **1 a :** military supplies including weapons, ammunition, combat vehicles, and the necessary maintenance tools and equipment **b :** a service of the army charged with the procuring, distributing, and safekeeping of ordnance **2 :** CANNON, ARTILLERY

or·do \'ȯ(ə)rd-(,)ō\ *n* [ML, fr. L, order] **:** a list of offices and feasts of the Roman Catholic Church for each day of the year

or·don·nance \,ȯrd-ᵊn-'äⁿs\ *n* [F, alter. of MF *ordenance*] **1 :** disposition of the parts of a composition with regard to one another and the whole **:** ARRANGEMENT **2 :** DECREE, ORDER

Or·do·vi·cian \,ȯrd-ə-'vish-ən\ *adj* [L *Ordovices*, ancient people in northern Wales] **:** of, relating to, or being the period between the Cambrian and the Silurian or the corresponding system of rocks — **Ordovician** *n*

or·dure \'ȯr-jər\ *n* [ME, fr. MF, fr. *ord* filthy, fr. L *horridus* horrid] **1 :** EXCREMENT **2 :** something morally degrading or depraving

¹**ore** \'ō(ə)r, 'ȯ(ə)r\ *n, often attrib* [ME *or*, fr. OE *ār;* akin to OHG *ēr* bronze, L *aes* copper, bronze] **1 :** a mineral containing a valuable metallic or other constituent for which it is mined and worked **2 :** a source from which valuable matter is extracted

²**öre** \'ər-ə\ *n, pl* **öre** [Sw *öre* & Dan & Norw *øre*] — see *krona*, *krone* at MONEY table

ore·ad \'ōr-ē-,ad, 'ȯr-, -ē-əd\ *n* [L *oread-*, *oreas*, fr. Gk *oreiad-*, *oreias*, fr. *oreios* of a mountain, fr. *oros* mountain — more at RISE] **:** one of the nymphs of mountains and hills

ore dressing *n* **:** mechanical treatment of ore (as by crushing)

oreg·a·no \ə-'reg-ə-,nō, ȯ-'reg-\ *n* [Sp *orégano*, fr. L *origanum*] **:** a bushy perennial mint (*Oreganum vulgare*) used as a seasoning and a source of aromatic oil — called also *wild marjoram*

Or·e·gon grape \,ȯr-i-gən-, ,är-, -,gän-\ *n* [*Oregon*, U.S.A.] **:** an evergreen shrub (*Mahonia aquifolia*) of the barberry family native to the Pacific coast with yellow flowers and bluish black berries — called also *hol·ly·grape* \'häl-ē-,grāp\

Ores·tes \ȯ-'res-(,)tēz, ə-\ *n* [L, fr. Gk *Orestēs*] **:** a son of Agamemnon and Clytemnestra who avenges his father's murder by slaying his mother and Aegisthus

or·gan \'ȯr-gən\ *n* [ME, partly fr. OE *organa*, fr. L *organum*, fr. Gk *organon*, lit., tool, instrument; partly fr. OF *organe*, fr. L *organum;* akin to Gk *ergon* work — more at WORK] **1 a** *archaic* **:** any of various musical instruments; *esp* **:** WIND INSTRUMENT **b** (1) **:** a wind instrument consisting of sets of pipes made to sound by compressed air and controlled by keyboards and producing a variety of musical effects — called also *pipe organ* (2) **:** REED ORGAN (3) **:** an instrument in which the sound and resources of the pipe organ are approximated by means of electronic devices (4) **:** any of various similar cruder instruments **2 a :** a differentiated structure (as a heart, kidney, leaf, or stem) consisting of cells and tissues and performing some specific function **b :** bodily parts performing a function or cooperating in an activity ⟨the eyes and related structures that make up the visual ~*s*⟩ **3 :** an instrumentality exercising some function or accomplishing some end; *specif* **:** a governmental body **4 :** PERIODICAL

organ- *or* **organo-** *comb form* [ME, fr. ML, fr. L *organum*] **1 :** organ ⟨*organo*genesis⟩ **2 :** organic ⟨*organo*mercurial⟩

or·gan·dy *also* **or·gan·die** \'ȯr-gən-dē\ *n* [F *organdi*] **:** a very fine transparent muslin with a stiff finish

or·gan·elle \,ȯr-gə-'nel\ *n* [NL *organella*, fr. L *organum*] **:** a specialized part of a cell analogous to an organ

or·gan–grind·er \'ȯr-gən-,grīn-dər\ *n* **:** one that cranks a hand organ; *esp* **:** an itinerant street musician who grinds a barrel organ

or·gan·ic \ȯr-'gan-ik\ *adj* **1** *archaic* **:** INSTRUMENTAL **2 a :** of, relating to, or arising in a bodily organ **b :** affecting the structure of the organism **3 a :** of, relating to, or derived from living organisms **b** (1) **:** of, relating to, or containing carbon compounds (2) **:** of, relating to, or dealt with by a branch of chemistry concerned with the carbon compounds of living beings and most other carbon compounds **4 a :** forming an integral element of a whole **:** CONSTITUTIONAL **b :** having systematic coordination of parts **:** ORGANIZED ⟨an ~ whole⟩ **c :** developing in the manner of a living plant or animal ⟨society is ~⟩ **5 :** of, relating to, or constituting the law by which a government or organization exists — **or·gan·i·cal·ly** \-i-k(ə-)lē\ *adv*

or·gan·i·cism \ȯr-'gan-ə-,siz-əm\ *n* **:** a theory that life and living processes are the manifestation of an activity possible only because of the autonomous organization of the system rather than because of its individual components

or·gan·ism \'ȯr-gə-,niz-əm\ *n* **1 :** a complex structure of interdependent and subordinate elements whose relations and properties are largely determined by their function in the whole **2 :** an individual constituted to carry on the activities of life by means of organs separate in function but mutually dependent — **or·gan·is·mic** \,ȯr-gə-'niz-mik\ *adj* — **or·gan·is·mi·cal·ly** \-mi-k(ə-)lē\ *adv*

or·gan·ist \'ȯr-gə-nəst\ *n* **:** one who plays an organ

or·ga·niz·able \'ȯr-gə-,nī-zə-bəl\ *adj* **:** capable of being organized

or·ga·ni·za·tion \,ȯrg-(ə-)nə-'zā-shən\ *n* **1 :** the act or process of organizing or of being organized **2 :** the condition or manner of being organized **3 a :** ASSOCIATION, SOCIETY **b :** an administrative and functional structure; *also* **:** the personnel of such a structure — **or·ga·ni·za·tion·al** \-shnəl, -shən-ᵊl\ *adj* — **or·ga·ni·za·tion·al·ly** \-ē\ *adv*

or·ga·nize \'ȯr-gə-,nīz\ *vt* **1 :** to cause to develop an organic structure **2 :** to arrange or form into a coherent unity or functioning whole **:** INTEGRATE **3 :** to set up an administrative structure for; *specif* **:** to persuade to associate in an organization **:** UNIONIZE **4 :** to arrange by systematic planning and united effort ~ *vi* **1 :** to undergo physical or organic organization **2 :** to arrange elements into a whole of interdependent parts **3 :** to form an organization; *specif* **:** to form or persuade workers to join a union **syn** see ORDER

or·ga·niz·er \-,nī-zər\ *n* **1 :** one that organizes **2 :** INDUCTOR 3

or·gan·o·gen·e·sis \,ȯr-gə-nō-'jen-ə-səs, ȯr-,gan-ə-\ *n* [NL] **:** the origin and development of bodily organs — **or·gan·o·ge·net·ic** \-jə-'net-ik\ *adj* — **or·gan·o·ge·net·i·cal·ly** \-i-k(ə-)lē\ *adv*

or·gan·og·ra·phy \,ȯr-gə-'näg-rə-fē\ *n* **:** a descriptive study of bodily organs

or·gan·o·lep·tic \,ȯr-gə-nō-'lep-tik, ȯr-,gan-ə-\ *adj* [F *organoleptique*, fr. *organ-* + Gk *lēptikos* disposed to take, fr. *lambanein* to take — more at LATCH] **:** affecting or employing one or more of the organs of special sense; *also* **:** determined by organoleptic examination — **or·gan·o·lep·ti·cal·ly** \-ti-k(ə-)lē\ *adv*

or·gan·o·log·ic \ˌȯr-gə-nə-ˈläj-ik, ȯr-ˌgan-ᵊl-ˈäj-\ *adj* **:** of or relating to organology — **or·gan·o·log·i·cal** \-i-kəl\ *adj*
or·gan·ol·o·gy \ˌȯr-gə-ˈnäl-ə-jē\ *n* [ISV] **:** the study of bodily organs
or·ga·no·mer·cu·ri·al \ˌȯr-gə-(ˌ)nō-(ˌ)mər-ˈkyu̇r-ē-əl, ȯr-ˌgan-ō-\ *n* **:** an organic compound or a pharmaceutical preparation containing mercury
or·ga·non \ˈȯr-gə-ˌnän\ *n* [Gk, lit., tool — more at ORGAN] **:** an instrument for acquiring knowledge; *specif* **:** a body of principles of scientific or philosophic investigation
or·gan·o·ther·a·py \ˌȯr-gə-nō-ˈther-ə-pē, ȯr-ˌgan-ə-\ *n* [ISV] **:** treatment of disease by the use of animal organs or their extracts
or·gan·o·trop·ic \-ˈträp-ik\ *adj* **:** localizing in or entering the body by way of the visceral organs or occas. the somatic tissue — **or·gan·o·trop·i·cal·ly** \-i-k(ə-)lē\ *adv* — **or·gan·ot·ro·pism** \ˌȯr-gə-ˈnä-trə-ˌpiz-əm\ *n* — **or·gan·ot·ro·py** \-trə-pē\ *n*
or·ga·num \ˈȯr-gə-nəm\ *n* [ML, fr. L, organ] **1 :** ORGANON **2 :** early polyphony of the late Middle Ages; *also* **:** a composition in this style
or·gan·za \ȯr-ˈgan-zə\ *n* [prob. alter. of *Lorganza*, a trademark] **:** a sheer dress fabric resembling organdy and usu. made of silk, rayon, or nylon
or·gan·zine \ˈȯr-gən-ˌzēn\ *n* [F or It; F *organsin*, fr. It *organzino*] **:** a raw silk yarn used for warp threads in fine fabrics
or·gasm \ˈȯr-ˌgaz-əm\ *n* [NL *orgasmus*, fr. Gk *orgasmos*, fr. *organ* to grow ripe, be lustful; akin to Skt *ūrjā* sap, strength] **1 :** intense or paroxysmal emotional excitement; *esp* **:** the climax of sexual excitement typically occurring toward the end of coitus **2 :** an instance of orgasm — **or·gas·mic** \ȯr-ˈgaz-mik\ *or* **or·gas·tic** \-ˈgas-tik\ *adj*
or·geat \ˈȯ(ə)r-ˌzhä\ *n* [F, fr. MF, fr. *orge* barley, fr. L *hordeum;* akin to OHG *gersta* barley, Gk *kri*] **:** a sweet almond-flavored nonalcoholic syrup used as a cocktail ingredient or food flavoring
or·gi·as·tic \ˌȯr-jē-ˈas-tik\ *adj* [Gk *orgiastikos*, fr. *orgiazein* to celebrate orgies, fr. *orgia*] **:** of, relating to, or marked by orgies or esp. unrestrained emotion — **or·gi·as·ti·cal·ly** \-ti-k(ə-)lē\ *adv*
or·gu·lous \ˈȯr-g(y)ə-ləs\ *adj* [ME, fr. OF *orgueilleus*, fr. *orgueil* pride, of Gmc origin; akin to OHG *urguol* distinguished] **:** PROUD, HAUGHTY
or·gy \ˈȯr-jē\ *n* [MF *orgie*, fr. L *orgia*, pl., fr. Gk; akin to Gk *ergon* work — more at WORK] **1 :** secret ceremonial rites held in honor of an ancient Greek or Roman deity and usu. characterized by ecstatic singing and dancing **2 :** drunken revelry **3 :** an excessive indulgence in an activity
-oria *pl of* -ORIUM
-o·ri·al \ˈōr-ē-əl, ˈȯr-\ *adj suffix* [ME, fr. L *-orius* -ory + ME *-al*] **:** of, belonging to, or connected with ⟨gress*orial*⟩
ori·el \ˈōr-ē-əl, ˈȯr-\ *n* [ME, porch, oriel, fr. MF *oriol* porch] **:** a large bay window projecting from a wall and supported by a corbel or bracket

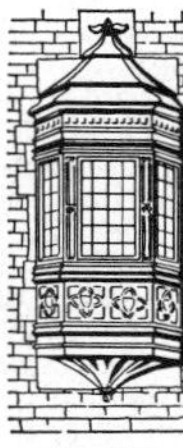

oriel

1ori·ent \ˈōr-ē-ənt, ˈȯr-, -ē-ˌent\ *n* [ME, fr. MF, fr. L *orient-, oriens*, fr. prp. of *oriri* to rise — more at RISE] **1** *archaic* **:** EAST 1b **2** *cap* **:** EAST 2 **3 a :** a pearl of great luster **b :** the luster or sheen of a pearl
2orient *adj* **1** *archaic* **:** ORIENTAL 1 **2 a :** LUSTROUS, SPARKLING ⟨~ gems⟩ **b** *archaic* **:** GLOWING, RADIANT **3** *archaic* **:** RISING
3ori·ent \-ˌent\ *vt* [F *orienter*, fr. MF, fr. *orient*] **1 a :** to cause to face or point toward the east; *specif* **:** to build (as a church) with the longitudinal axis pointing eastward and the chief altar at the eastern end **b :** to set or arrange in any determinate position esp. in relation to the points of the compass **c :** to ascertain the bearings of **2 a :** to set right by adjusting to facts or principles **b :** to acquaint with the existing situation or environment **3 :** to cause the axes of the molecules of to assume the same direction
ori·en·tal \ˌōr-ē-ˈent-ᵊl, ˌȯr-\ *adj* **1** *often cap* **:** of, relating to, or situated in the Orient **2 a :** of superior grade, luster, or value **b :** being corundum or sapphire but simulating another gem in color **3** *often cap* **:** of, relating to, or having the characteristics of Orientals **4** *cap* **:** of, relating to, or constituting the biogeographic region that includes Asia south and southeast of the Himalayas and part of the Malay archipelago — **ori·en·tal·ly** \-ᵊl-ē\ *adv*
Oriental *n* **:** a member of one of the indigenous peoples of the Orient
ori·en·tal·ism \-ᵊl-ˌiz-əm\ *n, often cap* **1 :** a trait, custom, or habit of expression characteristic of oriental peoples **2 :** learning in oriental subjects — **ori·en·tal·ist** \-ᵊl-əst\ *n, often cap*
ori·en·tal·ize \-ᵊl-ˌīz\ *vt, often cap* **:** to make oriental ~ *vi, often cap* **:** to become oriental
Oriental poppy *n* **:** an Asiatic perennial poppy (*Papaver orientale*) commonly cultivated for its large showy flowers
Oriental rug *n* **:** a handwoven or hand-knotted one-piece rug or carpet made in the Orient — called also *Oriental carpet*
ori·en·tate \ˈōr-ē-ən-ˌtāt, ˈȯr-, -ˌen-\ *vt* **:** ORIENT ~ *vi* **:** to face or turn to the east
ori·en·ta·tion \ˌōr-ē-ən-ˈtā-shən, ˌȯr-, -ˌen-\ *n* **1 :** the act or process of orienting or of being oriented **2 :** change of position by some protoplasmic bodies in response to external stimulus — **ori·en·ta·tion·al** \-shnəl, -shən-ᵊl\ *adj*
or·i·fice \ˈȯr-ə-fəs, ˈär-\ *n* [MF, fr. LL *orificium*, fr. L *or-, os* mouth — more at ORAL] **:** a mouth or similar opening **:** HOLE **syn** see APERTURE — **or·i·fi·cial** \ˌȯr-ə-ˈfish-əl, ˌär-\ *adj*
ori·flamme \ˈȯr-ə-ˌflam, ˈär-\ *n* [ME *oriflamble*, fr. MF, fr. ML *aurea flamma*, lit., golden flame] **1 :** a banner, symbol, or ideal inspiring devotion or courage **2 :** something suggestive of a brightly colored banner
ori·ga·mi \ˌȯr-ə-ˈgäm-ē\ *n* [Jap] **:** the art or process of Japanese paper folding
orig·a·num \ə-ˈrig-ə-nəm\ *n* [ME, fr. L, wild marjoram, fr. Gk *origanon*] **:** any of various fragrant aromatic plants of the mint or vervain families used as seasonings
or·i·gin \ˈȯr-ə-jən, ˈär-\ *n* [ME *origine*, prob. fr. MF, fr. L *origin-, origo*, fr. *oriri* to rise — more at RISE] **1 :** ANCESTRY, PARENTAGE **2 a :** rise, beginning, or derivation from a source **b :** primary source or cause **3 :** the more fixed, central, or larger attachment of a muscle **4 :** the intersection of coordinate axes
syn ORIGIN, SOURCE, INCEPTION, ROOT mean the point at which something begins its course or existence. ORIGIN applies to the things or persons from which something is ultimately derived and often to the causes operating before the thing itself comes in being; SOURCE applies more often to the point where something springs into being; INCEPTION stresses the beginning of the actual or material existence of something without implication concerning causes; ROOT suggests a first, ultimate, or fundamental source often not easily discerned
1orig·i·nal \ə-ˈrij-ən-ᵊl, -ˈrij-nəl\ *n* **1** *archaic* **:** the source or cause from which something arises; *specif* **:** ORIGINATOR **2 a :** that from which a copy, reproduction, or translation is made **:** PROTOTYPE **b :** a work composed firsthand **3 a :** a person of fresh initiative or inventive capacity **b** *archaic* **:** ECCENTRIC 2
2original *adj* **1 :** of, relating to, or constituting a rise or beginning **:** INITIAL **2 a :** having spontaneous origin **:** FRESH **b :** constituting that from which a copy, reproduction, or translation is made **3 :** independent and creative in thought or action **:** INVENTIVE **syn** see NEW — **orig·i·nal·ly** \-ē\ *adv*
orig·i·nal·i·ty \ə-ˌrij-ə-ˈnal-ət-ē\ *n* **1 :** the quality or state of being original **2 :** freshness of aspect, design, or style **3 :** the power of independent thought or constructive imagination
original sin *n* **:** radical sin often held in Christian theology to be inherited by each person as a consequence of the original sinful choice made by Adam
orig·i·nate \ə-ˈrij-ə-ˌnāt\ *vt* **:** to give rise to **:** INITIATE ~ *vi* **:** to take or have origin **:** BEGIN **syn** see SPRING — **orig·i·na·tion** \ə-ˌrij-ə-ˈnā-shən\ *n* — **orig·i·na·tor** \ə-ˈrij-ə-ˌnāt-ər\ *n*
orig·i·na·tive \ə-ˈrij-ə-ˌnāt-iv\ *adj* **:** having ability to originate **:** CREATIVE — **orig·i·na·tive·ly** *adv*
ori·ole \ˈōr-ē-ˌōl, ˈȯr-, -ē-əl\ *n* [F *oriol*, fr. L *aureolus*, dim. of *aureus* golden, fr. *aurum* gold; akin to Lith *auksas* gold] **1 :** any of a family (Oriolidae) of usu. brightly colored Old World passerine birds related to the crows **2 :** any of a family (Icteridae) of New World passerine birds of which the males are usu. bright black and yellow or orange and the females are chiefly greenish or yellowish
Ori·on \ə-ˈrī-ən, ō-\ *n* [L (gen. *Orionis*), fr. Gk *Ōriōn*] **:** a constellation on the equator east of Taurus represented on charts by the figure of a hunter with belt and sword
or·i·son \ˈȯr-ə-sən, ˈär-, -zən\ *n* [ME, fr. OF, fr. LL *oration-, oratio*, fr. L, oration] **:** PRAYER
-o·ri·um \ˈōr-ē-əm, ˈȯr-\ *n suffix, pl* **-oriums** *or* **-o·ria** \-ē-ə\ [L, fr. neut. of *-orius* -ory] **:** 1-ORY ⟨haust*orium*⟩
Ori·ya \ȯ-ˈrē-(y)ə\ *n* **:** the Indic language of Orissa, India
Or·lean·ist \ˈȯr-lē-ə-nəst, ȯr-ˈlē-(ə-)nəst\ *n* **:** a supporter of the Orleans family in its claim to the throne of France by descent from a younger brother of Louis XIV
Or·lon \ˈȯr-ˌlän\ *trademark* **1** — used for an acrylic fiber typically of high bulk and soft warm hand **2 :** a yarn or fabric made of Orlon fiber
or·lop deck \ˌȯr-ˌläp-\ *n* [ME *overlop* deck of a single decker, fr. MLG *overlōp*, lit., something that overleaps] **:** the deck below the lower deck
or·mo·lu \ˈȯr-mə-ˌlü\ *n, often attrib* [F *or moulu*, lit., ground gold] **:** a brass made to imitate gold and used for decorative purposes
1or·na·ment \ˈȯr-nə-mənt\ *n* [ME, fr. OF *ornement*, fr. L *ornamentum*, fr. *ornare*] **1** *archaic* **:** a useful accessory **2 a :** something that lends grace or beauty **b :** a manner or quality that adorns **3 :** one whose virtues or graces add luster to his place or society **4 :** the act of adorning or being adorned **5 :** an embellishing note not belonging to the essential harmony or melody
2or·na·ment \-ˌment\ *vt* **:** to provide with ornament **:** EMBELLISH **syn** see ADORN
1or·na·men·tal \ˌȯr-nə-ˈment-ᵊl\ *adj* **:** of, relating to, or serving as ornament; *specif* **:** grown as an ornamental — **or·na·men·tal·ly** \-ᵊl-ē\ *adv*
2ornamental *n* **:** a decorative object; *esp* **:** a plant cultivated for its beauty rather than for use
or·na·men·ta·tion \ˌȯr-nə-mən-ˈtā-shən, -ˌmen-\ *n* **1 :** the act or process of ornamenting **:** the state of being ornamented **2 :** a decorative device **:** EMBELLISHMENT
or·nate \ȯr-ˈnāt\ *adj* [ME *ornat*, fr. L *ornatus*, pp. of *ornare* to furnish, embellish; akin to L *ordinare* to order — more at ORDAIN] **1 :** marked by elaborate rhetoric or florid style **2 :** elaborately or excessively decorated — **or·nate·ly** *adv* — **or·nate·ness** *n*
or·neri·ness \ˈȯrn-(ə-)rē-nəs, ˈän-\ *n* **:** the quality or state of being ornery
or·nery \ˈȯrn-(ə-)rē, ˈän-\ *adj* [alter. of *ordinary*] **:** having an irritable disposition **:** CANTANKEROUS
ornith- *or* **ornitho-** *comb form* [L, fr. Gk, fr. *ornith-, ornis* — more at ERNE] **:** bird ⟨*ornitho*logy⟩
or·nith·ic \ȯr-ˈnith-ik\ *adj* [Gk *ornithikos*, fr. *ornith-, ornis*] **:** of, relating to, or characteristic of birds
or·ni·tho·log·i·cal \(ˌ)ȯr-ˌnith-ə-ˈläj-i-kəl, ˌȯr-nə-thə-\ *or* **or·ni·tho·log·ic** \-ik\ *adj* **:** of or relating to ornithology — **or·ni·tho·log·i·cal·ly** \-i-k(ə-)lē\ *adv*
or·ni·thol·o·gist \ˌȯr-nə-ˈthäl-ə-jəst\ *n* **:** a specialist in ornithology
or·ni·thol·o·gy \-jē\ *n* [NL *ornithologia*, fr. *ornith-* + *-logia* -logy] **1 :** a branch of zoology dealing with birds **2 :** a treatise on ornithology
or·ni·thop·ter \ˈȯr-nə-ˌthäp-tər\ *n* [ISV *ornith-* + *-pter* (as in *helicopter*)] **:** an airplane deriving its chief support and propulsion from flapping wings
or·ni·tho·sis \ˌȯr-nə-ˈthō-səs\ *n, pl* **or·ni·tho·ses** \-ˈthō-ˌsēz\ [NL] **:** PSITTACOSIS — **or·ni·thot·ic** \-ˈthät-ik\ *adj*
1oro- *comb form* [Gk *oros* — more at RISE] **:** mountain ⟨*oro*logy⟩
2oro- *comb form* [L *or-, os* — more at ORAL] **:** mouth ⟨*oro*pharynx⟩ **:** oral and ⟨*oro*facial⟩
oro·gen·ic \ˌōr-ə-ˈjen-ik, ˌȯr-\ *also* **oro·ge·net·ic** \-jə-ˈnet-ik\ *adj* **:** of or relating to orogeny
orog·e·ny \ȯ-ˈräj-ə-nē\ *also* **oro·gen·e·sis** \ˌōr-ə-ˈjen-ə-səs, ˌȯr-\ *n* [ISV] **:** the process of mountain formation esp. by folding of the earth's crust
oro·graph·ic \ˌōr-ə-ˈgraf-ik, ˌȯr-\ *adj* **:** of or relating to mountains — **oro·graph·i·cal** \-i-kəl\ *adj* — **oro·graph·i·cal·ly** \-k(ə-)lē\ *adv*

orog·ra·phy \ȯ-ˈräg-rə-fē\ *n* [ISV] **:** a branch of physical geography that deals with mountains

oro·ide \ˈōr-ə-ˌwīd, ˈȯr-\ *n* [F *oréide*] **:** an alloy that resembles gold and is used in cheap jewelry

oro·tund \ˈȯr-ə-ˌtənd, ˈär-, ˈōr-\ *adj* [modif. of L *ore rotundo*, lit., with round mouth] **1 :** marked by fullness, strength, and clarity of sound **:** SONOROUS **2 :** POMPOUS, BOMBASTIC — **oro·tun·di·ty** \ˌȯr-ə-ˈtən-dət-ē, ˌär-, ˌōr-\ *n*

[1]**or·phan** \ˈȯr-fən\ *n* [LL *orphanus*, fr. Gk *orphanos;* akin to OHG *erbi* inheritance, L *orbus* orphaned] **1 :** a child deprived by death of one or usu. both parents **2 :** a young animal that has lost its mother — **orphan** *adj* — **or·phan·hood** \-ˌhu̇d\ *n*

[2]**orphan** *vt* **or·phan·ing** \ˈȯrf-(ə-)niŋ\ **:** to cause to become an orphan

or·phan·age \ˈȯrf-(ə-)nij\ *n* **1 :** the state of being an orphan **2 :** an institution for the care of orphans

Or·phe·us \ˈȯr-fē-əs, -ˌfyüs\ *n* [L, fr. Gk] **:** a musician held in Greek legend to have descended to Hades after the death of his wife Eurydice and by his music to have obtained her release on condition that he not look back at her until reaching the upper world

or·phic \ˈȯr-fik\ *adj* **1** *cap* **:** of or relating to Orpheus or the rites or doctrines ascribed to him **2 :** MYSTIC, ORACULAR **3 :** ENTRANCING — **or·phi·cal·ly** \-fi-k(ə-)lē\ *adv*

Or·phism \ˈȯr-ˌfiz-əm\ *n* **:** a mystic Greek religion offering initiates purification of the soul from innate evil and release from the cycle of reincarnation

or·phrey \ˈȯr-frē\ *n* [ME *orfrey*, fr. MF *orfreis*, fr. ML *aurifrigium*, fr. L *aurum* gold + *Phrygius* Phrygian — more at ORIOLE] **1 a :** elaborate embroidery **b :** a piece of such embroidery **2 :** an ornamental border or band esp. on an ecclesiastical vestment

or·pi·ment \ˈȯr-pə-mənt\ *n* [ME, fr. MF, fr. L *auripigmentum*, fr. *aurum* + *pigmentum* pigment] **:** orange to lemon yellow arsenic trisulfide As_2S_3 found as a mineral or produced artificially and used as a pigment

or·pine \ˈȯr-pən\ *n* [ME *orpin*, fr. MF, fr. *orpiment*] **:** an herb (*Sedum telephium* of the family Crassulaceae, the orpine family) with fleshy leaves and pink or purple flowers used in folk medicine; *broadly* **:** SEDUM

Or·ping·ton \ˈȯr-piŋ-tən\ *n* [*Orpington*, Kent, England] **:** any of an English breed of large deep-chested domestic fowls

or·rery \ˈȯr-ər-ē, ˈär-\ *n* [Charles Boyle †1731 4th Earl of *Orrery*] **:** an apparatus showing the relative positions and motions of bodies in the solar system by balls moved by wheelwork

or·ris \ˈȯr-əs, ˈär-\ *n* [prob. alter. of ME *ireos*, fr. OIt, modif. of L *iris*] **:** a European iris (*Iris florentina*); *also* **:** its fragrant rootstock used esp. in perfume and sachet powder

or·ris·root \-ˌrüt, -ˌru̇t\ *n* **:** the fragrant rootstock of any of several European irises used esp. in perfumery

ort \ˈȯ(ə)rt\ *n* [ME] **:** a morsel left at a meal **:** SCRAP

orth- *or* **ortho-** *comb form* [ME, fr. MF, straight, right, true, fr. L, fr. Gk, fr. *orthos* — more at ARDUOUS] **1 :** straight **:** upright **:** vertical ⟨*ortho*tropic⟩ **2 :** correct **:** corrective ⟨*orth*odontia⟩ **3 a :** hydrated or hydroxylated to the highest degree ⟨*ortho*phosphoric acid⟩ **b :** involving substitution at or characterized by two neighboring positions in the benzene ring ⟨*ortho*-xylene⟩

or·thi·con \ˈȯr-thi-ˌkän\ *n* [ISV *orth-* + *iconoscope*] **:** a camera tube in which the charges are swept over by a low-velocity beam to eliminate the secondary emission

[1]**or·tho** \ˈȯr-(ˌ)thō\ *adj* [*orth-*] **1 :** derived from or being an acid **2 :** relating to or having an ortho-relation in the benzene ring

[2]**ortho** *adj* **:** ORTHOCHROMATIC

or·tho·ce·phal·ic \ˌȯr-thə-sə-ˈfal-ik\ *or* **or·tho·ceph·a·lous** \-ˈsef-ə-ləs\ *adj* [NL *orthocephalus* orthocephalic person, fr. *orth-* + Gk *kephalē* head — more at CEPHALIC] **:** having a medium ratio of the height to the length or breadth of the skull — **or·tho·ceph·a·ly** \-ˈsef-ə-lē\ *n*

or·tho·chro·mat·ic \ˌȯr-thə-krō-ˈmat-ik\ *adj* [ISV] **1 :** of, relating to, or producing tone values of light and shade in a photograph that correspond to the tones in nature **2 :** sensitive to all colors except red

or·tho·clase \ˈȯr-thə-ˌklās, -ˌklāz\ *n* [G *orthoklas*, fr. *orth-* + Gk *klasis* breaking, fr. *klan* to break — more at HALT] **:** a mineral $KAlSi_3O_8$ consisting of a monoclinic polymorph of common potassium feldspar often with sodium in place of some of the potassium

or·tho·clas·tic \ˌȯr-thə-ˈklas-tik\ *adj* [G *orthoklastisch*, fr. *orth-* + Gk *klastos* broken — more at CLASTIC] **:** cleaving in directions at right angles to each other

orth·odon·tia \ˌȯr-thə-ˈdän-ch(ē-)ə\ *n* [NL] **:** ORTHODONTICS

orth·odon·tic \-ˈdänt-ik\ *adj* **:** of, relating to, or involving orthodontics

orth·odon·tics \-iks\ *n pl but sing or pl in constr* **:** a branch of dentistry dealing with irregularities of the teeth and their correction — **orth·odon·tist** \-ˈdänt-əst\ *n*

or·tho·dox \ˈȯr-thə-ˌdäks\ *adj* [MF or LL; MF *orthodoxe*, fr. LL *orthodoxus*, fr. LGk *orthodoxos*, fr. Gk *orth-* + *doxa* opinion — more at DOXOLOGY] **1 a :** conforming to established doctrine esp. in religion **b :** CONVENTIONAL **2** *cap* **:** of, relating to, or constituting any of various conservative religious or political groups; *esp* **:** Eastern Orthodox — **orthodox** *n* — **or·tho·dox·ly** *adv*

Orthodox Judaism *n* **:** Judaism that adheres to biblical law as interpreted in the authoritative rabbinic tradition and seeks to observe all the practices commanded in it

or·tho·doxy \ˈȯr-thə-ˌdäk-sē\ *n* **1 :** the quality or state of being orthodox **2 :** an orthodox belief or practice

or·tho·ep·ic \ˌȯr-thə-ˈwep-ik\ *adj* **:** of or relating to orthoepy — **or·tho·ep·i·cal** \-i-kəl\ *adj* — **or·tho·ep·i·cal·ly** \-k(ə-)lē\ *adv*

or·tho·epist \ˈȯr-thə-ˌwep-əst, ȯr-ˈthō-ə-pəst\ *n* **:** a person who is skilled in orthoepy

or·tho·epy \ˈȯr-thə-ˌwep-ē, ȯr-ˈthō-ə-pē\ *n* [NL *orthoepia*, fr. Gk *orthoepeia*, fr. *orth-* + *epos* word — more at VOICE] **1 :** the customary pronunciation of a language **2 :** the study of the pronunciation of a language

or·tho·gen·e·sis \ˌȯr-thə-ˈjen-ə-səs\ *n* [NL] **1 :** variation of organisms in successive generations along some predestined line resulting in progressive evolutionary trends independent of external factors **2 :** the theory that social evolution takes place in the same direction and through the same stages in every culture despite differing external conditions — **or·tho·ge·net·ic** \-jə-ˈnet-ik\ *adj* — **or·tho·ge·net·i·cal·ly** \-i-k(ə-)lē\ *adv*

or·tho·gen·ic \-ˈjen-ik\ *adj* **1 :** ORTHOGENETIC **2** [*orth-* + *-genic*] **:** of, relating to, or devoted to the rehabilitation of emotionally disturbed or mentally retarded children

or·thog·na·thous \ȯr-ˈthäg-nə-thəs\ *adj* [ISV] **:** having straight jaws **:** not having the lower parts of the face projecting — **or·thog·na·thy** \-thē\ *or* **or·thog·na·thism** \-ˌthiz-əm\ *n*

or·thog·o·nal \ȯr-ˈthäg-ən-ᵊl\ *adj* [MF, fr. L *orthogonius*, fr. Gk *orthogōnios*, fr. *orth-* + *gōnia* angle — more at -GON] **1 :** mutually perpendicular **2 :** statistically independent — **or·thog·o·nal·i·ty** \(ˌ)ȯr-ˌthäg-ə-ˈnal-ət-ē\ *n* — **or·thog·o·nal·ly** \ȯr-ˈthäg-nə-lē, -ən-ᵊl-ē\ *adv*

or·tho·grade \ˈȯr-thə-ˌgrād\ *adj* **:** walking with the body upright or vertical

or·tho·graph·ic \ˌȯr-thə-ˈgraf-ik\ *adj* **1 :** ORTHOGONAL **2 a :** of or relating to orthography **b :** correct in spelling — **or·tho·graph·i·cal** \-i-kəl\ *adj* — **or·tho·graph·i·cal·ly** \-k(ə-)lē\ *adv*

orthographic projection *n* **1 :** projection of a single view of an object in which the view is projected along lines perpendicular to both the view and the drawing surface **2 :** the representation of related views of an object as if they were all in the same plane and projected by orthographic projection

or·thog·ra·phy \ȯr-ˈthäg-rə-fē\ *n* [ME *ortografie*, fr. MF, fr. L *orthographia*, fr. Gk, fr. *orth-* + *graphein* to write — more at CARVE] **1 a :** the art of writing words with the proper letters according to standard usage **b :** the representation of the sounds of a language by written or printed symbols **2 :** a part of language study that deals with letters and spelling

or·tho·pe·dic *also* **or·tho·pae·dic** \ˌȯr-thə-ˈpēd-ik\ *adj* [F *orthopédique*, fr. *orthopédie* orthopedics, fr. *orth-* + Gk *paid-*, *pais* child — more at FEW] **1 :** of, relating to, or employed in orthopedics **2 :** marked by deformities or crippling — **or·tho·pe·di·cal·ly** \-i-k(ə-)lē\ *adv*

or·tho·pe·dics *also* **or·tho·pae·dics** \-ˈpēd-iks\ *n pl but sing or pl in constr* **:** the correction or prevention of skeletal deformities — **or·tho·pe·dist** \-ˈpēd-əst\ *n*

or·tho·phos·phate \ˌȯr-thə-ˈfäs-ˌfāt\ *n* **:** a salt or ester of orthophosphoric acid

or·tho·phos·pho·ric acid \ˌȯr-thə-ˌfäs-ˌfȯr-ik-, -ˌfär-; -ˌfäs-f(ə-)rik-\ *n* [ISV] **:** a syrupy or deliquescent crystalline acid H_3PO_4 obtained by oxidation of phosphorus or decomposition of phosphates that forms two soluble acid phosphates used in fertilizers

or·tho·psy·chi·at·ric \ˌȯr-thə-ˌsī-kē-ˈa-trik\ *adj* **:** of or relating to orthopsychiatry — **or·tho·psy·chi·a·trist** \-sə-ˈkī-ə-trəst, -(ˌ)sī-\ *n*

or·tho·psy·chi·a·try \-sə-ˈkī-ə-trē, -(ˌ)sī-\ *n* **:** prophylactic psychiatry concerned esp. with incipient mental and behavioral disorders in youth

or·thop·ter·an \ȯr-ˈthäp-tə-rən\ *n* [deriv. of Gk *orth-* + *pteron* wing — more at FEATHER] **:** any of an order (Orthoptera) comprising insects with biting mouthparts, two pairs of wings or none, and an incomplete metamorphosis and usu. including the grasshoppers, mantises, and crickets — **orthopteran** *or* **or·thop·ter·al** \-rəl\ *or* **or·thop·ter·ous** \-rəs\ *adj* — **or·thop·ter·oid** \-ˌrȯid\ *n or adj* — **or·thop·ter·on** \-ˌrän\ *n*

or·tho·rhom·bic \ˌȯr-thə-ˈräm-bik\ *adj* [ISV] **:** of, relating to, or constituting a system of crystallization characterized by three unequal axes at right angles to each other

or·tho·scop·ic \-ˈskäp-ik\ *adj* [ISV *orth-* + *-scopic* (as in *microscopic*)] **1 :** giving an image in correct and normal proportions **2 :** giving a flat field of view

or·tho·trop·ic \-ˈträp-ik\ *adj* **:** having the longer axis more or less vertical — **or·tho·trop·i·cal·ly** \-i-k(ə-)lē\ *adv* — **or·thot·ro·pism** \ȯr-ˈthä-trə-ˌpiz-əm\ *n*

or·thot·ro·pous \ȯr-ˈthä-trə-pəs\ *adj* [ISV] **:** having the ovule straight

or·to·lan \ˈȯrt-ᵊl-ən\ *n* [F or It; F, fr. It *ortolano*, lit., gardener, fr. L *hortulanus*, fr. *hortulus*, dim. of *hortus* garden — more at YARD] **1 :** a European bunting (*Emberiza hortulana*) about six inches long that is valued as a table delicacy **2 a :** SORA **b :** BOBOLINK

[1]**-o·ry** \ˌōr-ē, ˌȯr-ē, (ə-)rē\ *n suffix* [ME *-orie*, fr. L *-orium*, fr. neut. of *-orius*, adj. suffix] **1 :** place of or for ⟨observat*ory*⟩ **2 :** something that serves for ⟨cremat*ory*⟩

[2]**-ory** *adj suffix* [ME *-orie*, fr. MF & L; MF, fr. L *-orius*] **1 :** of, relating to, or characterized by ⟨gustat*ory*⟩ **2 :** serving for, producing, or maintaining ⟨justificat*ory*⟩

oryx \ˈōr-iks, ˈȯr-, ˈär-\ *n, pl* **oryx** *or* **oryx·es** [NL, genus name, fr. L, a gazelle, fr. Gk, pickax, antelope, fr. *oryssein* to dig — more at ROUGH] **:** any of a genus (*Oryx*) of large straight-horned African antelopes

[1]**os** \ˈäs\ *n, pl* **os·sa** \ˈäs-ə\ [L *oss-*, *os* — more at OSSEOUS] **:** BONE

[2]**os** \ˈōs\ *n, pl* **ora** \ˈōr-ə, ˈȯr-ə\ [L *or-*, *os* — more at ORAL] **:** MOUTH, ORIFICE

[3]**os** \ˈōs\ *n, pl* **osar** \ˈō-ˌsär\ [Sw *ås* mountain ridge, fr. ON *āss;* akin to Gk *ōmos* shoulder — more at HUMERUS] **:** ESKER

Osage \ō-ˈsāj\ *n, pl* **Osage** *or* **Osag·es** [Osage *Wazhazhe*] **1 a :** a Siouan people of Missouri **b :** a member of this people **2 :** the language of the Osage people

Osage orange *n* **:** an ornamental American tree (*Maclura pomifera*) of the mulberry family having hard bright orange wood; *also* **:** its yellowish fruit

Os·can \ˈäs-kən\ *n* [L *Oscus*] **1 :** one of a people of ancient Italy occupying Campania **2 :** the language of the Oscan people

[1]**Os·car** \ˈäs-kər\ *n* [*Oscar* Pierce, 20th cent. Am wheat grower] **:** a golden statuette awarded for achievement in motion pictures; *also* **:** any similar award

[2]**Oscar** [fr. the name *Oscar*] — a communications code word for the letter *o*

os·cil·late \ˈäs-ə-ˌlāt\ *vi* [L *oscillatus*, pp. of *oscillare* to swing, fr. *oscillum* swing] **1 a :** to swing backward and forward like a pendulum **:** VIBRATE **b :** to move or travel back and forth between two points **2 :** to vary between opposing beliefs, feelings, or theories **:** FLUCTUATE **3 :** to vary above and below a mean value **syn** see SWING — **os·cil·la·to·ry** \ä-ˈsil-ə-ˌtōr-ē, -ˌtȯr-\ *adj*

os·cil·la·tion \ˌäs-ə-ˈlā-shən\ *n* **1 :** the act or fact of oscillating **:** VIBRATION **2 :** VARIATION, FLUCTUATION **3 :** a flow of electricity changing periodically from a maximum to a minimum; *esp* **:** a

flow periodically changing direction **4** : a single swing (as of an oscillating body) from one extreme limit to the other — **os·cil·la·tion·al** \-shnəl, -shən-ᵊl\ *adj*

os·cil·la·tor \'äs-ə-ˌlāt-ər\ *n* **1** : one that oscillates **2** : a device for producing alternating current; *specif* : a radio-frequency or audio-frequency generator

os·cil·lo·gram \ä-'sil-ə-ˌgram, ə-\ *n* [L *oscillare* + ISV *-gram*] : a record made by an oscillograph or oscilloscope

os·cil·lo·graph \-ˌgraf\ *n* [F *oscillographe*, fr. L *oscillare* + F *-graphe* -graph] : an instrument for recording alternating current wave forms or other electrical oscillations — **os·cil·lo·graph·ic** \-ˌsil-ə-'graf-ik\ *adj* — **os·cil·log·ra·phy** \ˌäs-ə-'läg-rə-fē\ *n*

os·cil·lo·scope \ä-'sil-ə-ˌskōp, ə-\ *n* [L *oscillare* + ISV *-scope*] : an instrument in which the variations in a fluctuating electrical quantity appear temporarily as a visible wave form on the fluorescent screen of a cathode-ray tube; *broadly* : OSCILLOGRAPH — **os·cil·lo·scop·ic** \-ˌsil-ə-'skäp-ik\ *adj*

os·cine \'äs-ˌīn\ *adj* [deriv. of L *oscin-, oscen* bird used in divination, fr. *obs-* in front of + *canere* to sing — more at OSTENSIBLE, CHANT] : PASSERINE 2 — **oscine** *n*

Os·co-Um·bri·an \ˌäs-(ˌ)kō-'əm-brē-ən\ *n* [L *Oscus* + E *Umbrian*] : a subdivision of the Italic branch of the Indo-European language family containing Oscan and Umbrian

os·cu·late \'äs-kyə-ˌlāt\ *vt* [L *osculatus*, pp. of *osculari*, fr. *osculum* kiss, fr. dim. of *os* mouth — more at ORAL] : KISS

os·cu·la·tion \ˌäs-kyə-'lā-shən\ *n* : the act of kissing; *also* : KISS — **os·cu·la·to·ry** \'äs-kyə-lə-ˌtōr-ē, -ˌtor-\ *adj*

¹-ose \ˌōs, 'ōs *sometimes* ˌōz, 'ōz\ *adj suffix* [ME, fr. L *-osus*] : full of : having : possessing the qualities of ⟨cym*ose*⟩

²-ose \ˌōs, ōz\ *n suffix* [F, fr. L *glucose*] **1** : carbohydrate ⟨amyl*ose*⟩; *esp* : sugar ⟨pent*ose*⟩ **2** : primary hydrolysis product ⟨prote*ose*⟩

osier \'ō-zhər\ *n, often attrib* [ME, fr. MF, fr. ML *auseria* osier bed] **1** : any of various willows (esp. *Salix viminalis*) whose pliable twigs are used for furniture and basketry **2** : a willow rod used in basketry **3** : any of several American dogwoods

Osi·ris \ō-'sī-rəs\ *n* [L, fr. Gk, fr. Egypt *Ws'r*] : the Egyptian god of the underworld and judge of the dead

-o·sis \'ō-səs\ *n suffix, pl* **-o·ses** \'ō-ˌsēz\ *or* **-o·sis·es** [ME, fr. L, fr. Gk *-ōsis*, fr. *-ō-* (stem of causative verbs in *-oun*) + *-sis*] **1 a** : action : process : condition ⟨hypn*osis*⟩ **b** : abnormal or diseased condition ⟨leuk*osis*⟩ **2** : increase : formation ⟨leukocyt*osis*⟩

Os·man·li \äz-'man-lē\ *n* [Turk *osmanlı*, fr. *Osman*, Othman †1326 founder of the Ottoman Empire] **1** : a Turk of the western branch of the Turkish peoples **2** : TURKISH

os·mat·ic \äz-'mat-ik\ *adj* [Gk *osmē* odor + E *-atic* (as in *aquatic*) — more at ODOR] : depending chiefly on the sense of smell for orientation

os·mic \'äz-mik\ *adj* [ISV] : of, relating to, or derived from osmium esp. with a relatively high valence

os·mi·rid·i·um \ˌäz-mə-'rid-ē-əm\ *n* [Gk *osmē* + NL *iridium*] : IRIDOSMINE

os·mi·um \'äz-mē-əm\ *n* [NL, fr. Gk *osmē* odor] : a hard brittle blue-gray or blue-black polyvalent metallic element of the platinum group with a high melting point that is the heaviest metal known and that is used esp. as a catalyst and in hard alloys — see ELEMENT table

os·mose \'äs-ˌmōs, 'äz-\ *vb* [back-formation fr. *osmosis*] *vt* : to subject to osmosis : DIALYZE ∼ *vi* : to diffuse by osmosis

os·mo·sis \ä-'smō-səs, äz-'mō-\ *n* [NL, short for *endosmosis*] **1** : a diffusion through a semipermeable membrane typically separating a solvent and a solution that tends to equalize their concentrations; *esp* : the passage of solvent in distinction from the passage of solute **2** : a process of absorption or diffusion suggestive of the flow of osmotic action — **os·mot·ic** \ä-'smät-ik, äz-'mät-\ *adj* — **os·mot·i·cal·ly** \-i-k(ə-)lē\ *adv*

os·mous \'äz-məs\ *adj* : of, relating to, or derived from osmium esp. with a relatively low valence

os·mun·da \äz-'mən-də\ *n* [NL, genus name, fr. ML, osmunda, fr. OF *osmonde*] : any of a genus (*Osmunda*) of rather large ferns with fibrous creeping rhizomes

os·prey \'äs-prē, -ˌprā\ *n* [ME *ospray*, fr. (assumed) MF *osfraie*, fr. L *ossifraga*] **1** : a large brown and white hawk (*Pandion haliaetus*) that feeds on fish **2** : a feather trimming used for millinery

os·se·in \'äs-ē-ən\ *n* [ISV, fr. L *oss-, os*] : the collagen of bones

os·se·ous \'äs-ē-əs\ *adj* [L *osseus*, fr. *oss-, os* bone; akin to Gk *osteon* bone] : BONY **1** — **os·se·ous·ly** *adv*

Os·set \'äs-ət, -ˌet; ä-'set\ *or* **Os·sete** \'äs-ət, -ˌēt; ä-'sēt\ *n* [Russ *Osetin*] : one of an Aryan people of central Caucasia — **Os·se·tian** \ä-'sē-shən\ *adj or n*

Os·set·ic \ä-'set-ik\ *n* : the Iranian language of the Ossets

Os·si·an·ic \ˌäs(h)-ē-'an-ik\ *adj* : of, relating to, or resembling the legendary Irish bard Ossian, the poems ascribed to him, or the rhythmic prose style used by James Macpherson in his alleged translations

os·si·cle \'äs-i-kəl\ *n* [L *ossiculum*, dim. of *oss-, os*] : a small bone or calcareous body part — **os·sic·u·lar** \ä-'sik-yə-lər\ *adj* — **os·sic·u·late** \-lət\ *adj*

os·si·fi·ca·tion \ˌäs-(ə-)fə-'kā-shən\ *n* **1 a** : the natural process of bone formation **b** : the hardening (as of muscular tissue) into a bony substance **2** : a mass or particle of ossified tissue **3** : a tendency toward or state of being callous or conventional in outlook — **os·si·fi·ca·to·ry** \ä-'sif-i-kə-ˌtōr-ē, ˌäs-(ə-)fi-, -ˌtor-\ *adj*

os·si·frage \'äs-ə-frij, -ˌfrāj\ *n* [L *ossifraga* sea eagle, fr. fem. of *ossifragus* bone-breaking, fr. *oss-, os* + *frangere* to break — more at BREAK] **1** : LAMMERGEIER **2** : OSPREY

os·si·fy \'äs-ə-ˌfī\ *vb* [prob. fr. (assumed) NL *ossificare*, fr. L *oss-, os*] *vi* **1** : to change into bone **2** : to become callous or conventional ∼ *vt* **1** : to change (as cartilage) into bone **2** : to make callous or rigid

os·su·ary \'äsh-ə-ˌwer-ē, 'äs-(y)ə-\ *n* [LL *ossuarium*, fr. L, neut. of *ossuarius* of bones, fr. OL *ossua*, pl. of *oss-, os*] : a depository for the bones of the dead

oste- *or* **osteo-** *comb form* [NL, fr. Gk, fr. *osteon* — more at OSSEOUS] : bone ⟨*oste*al⟩ ⟨*osteo*myelitis⟩

os·te·al \'äs-tē-əl\ *adj* [ISV] : of, relating to, or resembling bone;

also : affecting or involving bone or the skeleton

os·te·itis \ˌäs-tē-'īt-əs\ *n* [NL] : inflammation of bone

os·ten·si·ble \ä-'sten(t)-sə-bəl, ə-\ *adj* [F, fr. L *ostensus*, pp. of *ostendere* to show, fr. *obs-* in front of (akin to *ob-* in the way) + *tendere* to stretch — more at OB-, THIN] **1** : intended for display : open to view **2** : ALLEGED syn see APPARENT — **os·ten·si·bly** \-blē\ *adv*

os·ten·sive \ä-'sten(t)-siv\ *adj* **1** : obviously or directly demonstrative **2** : OSTENSIBLE 2 — **os·ten·sive·ly** *adv*

os·ten·so·ri·um \ˌäs-tən-'sōr-ē-əm, -ˌten-, -'sor-\ *n* [ML, fr. L *ostensus*] : MONSTRANCE

os·ten·ta·tion \ˌäs-tən-'tā-shən\ *n* [ME *ostentacion*, fr. MF *ostentation*, fr. L *ostentation-, ostentatio*, fr. *ostentatus*, pp. of *ostentare* to display ostentatiously, fr. *ostentus*, pp. of *ostendere*] **1** : excessive display : PRETENTIOUSNESS **2** *archaic* : an act of displaying : SHOW

os·ten·ta·tious \-shəs\ *adj* : marked by or tending toward ostentation : PRETENTIOUS syn see SHOWY — **os·ten·ta·tious·ly** *adv* — **os·ten·ta·tious·ness** *n*

os·teo·ar·thri·tis \ˌäs-tē-(ˌ)ō-ˌär-'thrīt-əs\ *n* [NL] : degenerative arthritis

os·teo·blast \'äs-tē-ə-ˌblast\ *n* [ISV] : a bone-forming cell — **os·teo·blas·tic** \ˌäs-tē-ə-'blas-tik\ *adj*

os·teo·clast \'äs-tē-ə-ˌklast\ *n* [ISV *osteo-* + Gk *klastos* broken — more at CLASTIC] : one of the large multinucleate cells in developing bone held to function in the dissolution of unwanted bone — **os·teo·clas·tic** \ˌäs-tē-ə-'klas-tik\ *adj*

os·teo·cra·ni·um \ˌäs-tē-ə-'krā-nē-əm\ *n* [NL] : the bony cranium; *esp* : the parts of the cranium that arise in membrane bone

os·te·oid \'äs-tē-ˌóid\ *adj* [ISV] : resembling bone

os·teo·log·ic \ˌäs-tē-ə-'läj-ik\ *adj* : of or relating to osteology — **os·teo·log·i·cal** \-i-kəl\ *adj* — **os·teo·log·i·cal·ly** \-k(ə-)lē\ *adv*

os·te·ol·o·gist \ˌäs-tē-'äl-ə-jəst\ *n* : a specialist in osteology

os·te·ol·o·gy \-jē\ *n* [NL *osteologia*, fr. Gk, description of bones, fr. *oste-* + *-logia* -logy] **1** : a branch of anatomy dealing with the bones **2** : the bony structure of an organism

os·te·o·ma \ˌäs-tē-'ō-mə\ *n, pl* **osteomas** *or* **os·te·o·ma·ta** \-mət-ə\ : a benign tumor composed of bone tissue

os·te·o·ma·la·cia \ˌäs-tē-(ˌ)ō-mə-'lā-sh(ē-)ə\ *n* [NL] : a disease characterized by softening of the bones in the adult and equivalent to rickets in the immature

os·teo·my·eli·tis \ˌäs-tē-(ˌ)ō-ˌmī-ə-'līt-əs\ *n* [NL] : an infectious inflammatory disease of bone marked by local death and separation of tissue

os·teo·path \'äs-tē-ə-ˌpath\ *n* : a practitioner of osteopathy

os·teo·path·ic \ˌäs-tē-ə-'path-ik\ *adj* : of, relating to, or employing osteopathy — **os·teo·path·i·cal·ly** \-i-k(ə-)lē\ *adv*

os·te·op·a·thy \ˌäs-tē-'äp-ə-thē\ *n* [NL *osteopathia*, fr. *oste-* + *-pathia* -pathy] : a system of medical practice based on a theory that diseases are due chiefly to loss of structural integrity which can be restored by manipulation of the parts supplemented by therapeutic measures (as use of medicine or surgery)

os·teo·phyte \'äs-tē-ə-ˌfīt\ *n* [ISV] : a pathological bony outgrowth — **os·teo·phyt·ic** \ˌäs-tē-ə-'fit-ik\ *adj*

os·teo·plas·tic \ˌäs-tē-ə-'plas-tik\ *adj* : of or relating to the surgical replacement of bone — **os·teo·plas·ty** \'äs-tē-ə-ˌplas-tē\ *n*

os·te·ot·o·my \ˌäs-tē-'ät-ə-mē\ *n* [prob. fr. (assumed) NL *osteotomia*, fr. NL *oste-* + *-tomia* -tomy] : a surgical operation in which a bone is divided or a piece cut out of it

os·ti·ary \'äs-tē-ˌer-ē, 'äs-chē-\ *n* [L *ostiarius*, fr. *ostium*] **1** : DOORKEEPER **2** : a member of the lowest of the Roman Catholic minor orders

os·ti·na·to \ˌäs-tə-'nät-(ˌ)ō, ˌó-stə-\ *n* [It, obstinate, fr. L *obstinatus*] : a persistently repeated musical figure

os·ti·ole \'äs-tē-ˌōl\ *n* [NL *ostiolum*, fr. L, dim. of *ostium*] : a small aperture, orifice, or pore

os·ti·um \'äs-tē-əm\ *n, pl* **os·tia** \-tē-ə\ [NL, fr. L, door, mouth of a river; akin to L *os* mouth — more at ORAL] : a mouthlike entrance or other opening

ostler *var of* HOSTLER

-os·to·sis \()ˌäs-'tō-səs\ *n comb form, pl* **-os·to·ses** \-'tō-ˌsēz\ *or* **-os·to·sis·es** \-'tō-sə-səz\ [NL, fr. Gk *-ostōsis*, fr. *osteon* bone — more at OSSEOUS] : ossification of a (specified) part or to a (specified) degree ⟨hyper*ostosis*⟩ ⟨ect*ostosis*⟩

os·tra·cism \'äs-trə-ˌsiz-əm\ *n* **1** : a method of temporary banishment by popular vote without trial or special accusation practiced in ancient Greece **2** : exclusion by general consent from common privileges or social acceptance

os·tra·cize \-ˌsīz\ *vt* [Gk *ostrakizein* to banish by voting with potsherds, fr. *ostrakon* shell, potsherd — more at OYSTER] **1** : to exile by ostracism **2** : to exclude from a group by common consent

os·tra·cod \'äs-trə-ˌkäd\ *n* [deriv. of Gk *ostrakon*] : any of a subclass (*Ostracoda*) of small active mostly freshwater crustaceans — **os·tra·co·dan** \ˌäs-trə-'kōd-ᵊn\ *adj* — **os·tra·co·dous** \-'kōd-əs\ *adj*

os·trich \'äs-trich, 'ós- *also* -trij\ *n* [ME, fr. OF *ostrusce*, fr. (assumed) VL *avis struthio*, fr. L *avis* bird + LL *struthio* ostrich — more at STRUTHIOUS] **1 a** : a swift-footed two-toed flightless ratite bird (genus *Struthio*, esp. *S. camelus* of northern Africa) with valuable wing and tail plumes that is the largest of existing birds and often weighs 300 pounds **b** : RHEA **2** : one who attempts to avoid danger by refusing to face it

Os·tro·goth \'äs-trə-ˌgäth\ *n* [LL *Ostrogothi*, pl.] : one of the East Goths — **Os·tro·goth·ic** \ˌäs-trə-'gäth-ik\ *adj*

Os·we·go tea \ä-ˌswē-gō-\ *n* [*Oswego* river, N.Y.] : a No. American mint (*Monarda didyma*) with showy bright scarlet irregular flowers

ot- *or* **oto-** *comb form* [Gk *ōt-, ōto-*, fr. *ōt-, ous* — more at EAR] : ear ⟨*ot*itis⟩ : ear and ⟨*oto*laryngology⟩

Othel·lo \ə-'thel-(ˌ)ō\ *n* : a Moor in the military service of Venice, husband of Desdemona, and protagonist of Shakespeare's tragedy *Othello*

¹oth·er \'əth-ər\ *adj* [ME, fr. OE *ōther*; akin to OHG *andar* other, Skt *antara*] **1 a** : being the one (as of two or more) left **b** : being the ones distinct from those first mentioned **2** : SECOND ⟨every ∼

day⟩ **2 :** not the same **:** DIFFERENT **3 :** ADDITIONAL **4 a :** recently past ⟨the ~ evening⟩ **b :** FORMER ⟨in ~ times⟩

2other *n* **1 a :** one that remains of two or more **b :** a thing opposite to or excluded by something else **2 :** a different or additional one

3other *pron, sometimes pl in constr* **1** *obs* **a :** one of two that remains **b :** each preceding one **2 :** a different or additional one ⟨something or ~⟩

4other *adv* **:** OTHERWISE

oth·er·guess \-ˌges\ *adj* [alter. of E dial. *othergates*] *archaic* **:** DIFFERENT

oth·er·ness \-nəs\ *n* **1 :** the quality or state of being other or different **2 :** something that is other or different

oth·er·where \-ˌhwe(ə)r, -ˌhwa(ə)r, -ˌwe(ə)r, -ˌwa(ə)r\ *adv* **:** in or to some other place **:** ELSEWHERE

oth·er·while \-ˌhwīl, -ˌwīl\ *also* **oth·er·whiles** \-ˌhwīlz, -ˌwīlz\ *adv* **1** *chiefly dial* **:** at another time **2** *chiefly dial* **:** SOMETIMES

1oth·er·wise \-ˌwīz\ *adv* [ME, fr. OE (*on*) *ōthre wīsan* in another manner] **1 :** in a different way or manner **:** DIFFERENTLY **2 :** in different circumstances **3 :** in other respects

2otherwise *adj* **:** DIFFERENT

oth·er·world \ˈəth-ər-ˌwərld\ *n* **:** a world beyond death or beyond present reality

oth·er·world·li·ness \ˈəth-ər-ˌwərl-(d)lē-nəs\ *n* **1 :** the quality or state of being otherworldly **2 :** an otherworldly characteristic

oth·er·world·ly \-(d)lē\ *adj* **1 a :** of or relating to a world other than the actual world **:** TRANSCENDENTAL **b :** devoted to preparing for a world to come **2 :** devoted to intellectual or imaginative pursuits

otic \ˈōt-ik\ *adj* [Gk *ōtikos*, fr. *ōt-*, *ous* ear — more at EAR] **:** of, relating to, or located in the region of the ear

1-ot·ic \ˈät-ik\ *adj suffix* [Gk *-ōtikos*, fr. *-ōtos*, ending of verbals, fr. *-o-* (stem of causative verbs in *-oun*) + *-tos*, suffix forming verbals — more at -ED] **1 a :** of, relating to, or characterized by a (specified) action, process, or condition ⟨symbi*otic*⟩ **b :** having an abnormal or diseased condition of a (specified) kind ⟨epizo*otic*⟩ **2 :** showing an increase or a formation of ⟨leukocyt*otic*⟩

2-otic \ˈōt-ik\ *adj comb form* [Gk *ōtikos*] **:** having (such) a relationship to the ear ⟨peri*otic*⟩

oti·ose \ˈō-shē-ˌōs, ˈōt-ē-\ *adj* [L *otiosus*, fr. *otium* leisure] **1 :** being at leisure **:** IDLE **2 :** STERILE, FUTILE **3 :** lacking use or effect **:** FUNCTIONLESS **syn** see VAIN — **oti·ose·ly** *adv* — **oti·ose·ness** *n* — **oti·os·i·ty** \ˌō-shē-ˈäs-ət-ē, ˌōt-ē-\ *n*

oti·tis \ō-ˈtīt-əs\ *n* [NL] **:** inflammation of the ear

oto·cyst \ˈōt-ə-ˌsist\ *n* [ISV] **:** one of the supposed auditory organs of many invertebrates that contains a fluid and otoliths **:** STATOCYST — **oto·cys·tic** \ˌōt-ə-ˈsis-tik\ *adj*

oto·lar·yn·gol·o·gy \ˌōt-(ˌ)ō-ˌlar-ən-ˈgäl-ə-jē\ *n* **:** a branch of medicine dealing with the ear, nose, and throat

oto·lith \ˈōt-ə-ˌlith\ *n* [F *otolithe*, fr. *ot-* + *-lithe* -lith] **:** a calcareous concretion in the internal ear of a vertebrate or in the otocyst of an invertebrate — **oto·lith·ic** \ˌōt-ə-ˈlith-ik\ *adj*

ot·ta·va \ō-ˈtäv-ə\ *adv* (*or adj*) [It, octave, fr. ML *octava*] **:** at an octave higher or lower than written — used as a direction in music

ot·ta·va ri·ma \ō-ˌtäv-ə-ˈrē-mə\ *n, pl* **ottava rimas** [It, lit., eighth rhyme] **:** a stanza of eight lines of heroic verse with a rhyme scheme of *abababcc*

Ot·ta·wa \ˈät-ə-wə, -ˌwä, -ˌwȯ\ *n, pl* **Ottawa** *or* **Ottawas** [F *Outouan*, of Algonquian origin; akin to Cree *atâweu* trader] **1 :** an Algonquian people of southern Ontario, Canada, and Michigan **2 :** a member of the Ottawa people

ot·ter \ˈät-ər\ *n, pl* **otters** *also* **otter** [ME *oter*, fr. OE *otor*; akin to OHG *ottar* otter, Gk *hydōr* water] **1 :** any of several aquatic fish-eating mammals (genus *Lutra*) related to the weasels and minks that have webbed and clawed feet and dark brown fur **2 :** the fur or pelt of an otter

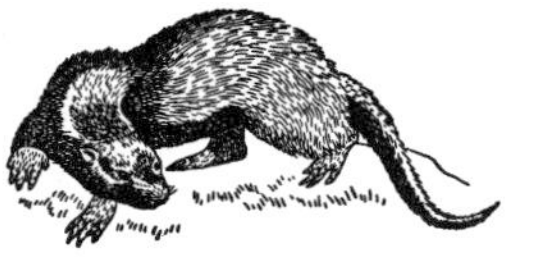
otter

ot·to \ˈät-(ˌ)ō\ *var of* ATTAR

ot·to·man \ˈät-ə-mən\ *n* **1** *cap* **:** TURK **2** [F *ottomane*, fr. fem. of *ottoman*, adj.] **a :** an upholstered often overstuffed seat or couch usu. without a back **b :** an overstuffed footstool

Ot·to·man \ˈät-ə-mən\ *adj* [F, adj. & n., prob. fr. It *ottomano*, fr. Ar *ʿothmānī*, fr. *ʿOthmān* Othman †1326 founder of the Ottoman Empire] **:** of or relating to the Turks or Turkey **:** TURKISH

oua·ba·in \wä-ˈbä-ən\ *n* [ISV, fr. F *ouabaïo*, an African tree, fr. Somali *waba yo*] **:** a poisonous glycoside $C_{29}H_{44}O_{12}$ obtained from several African shrubs or trees of the dogbane family and used medically like digitalis and in Africa as an arrow poison

ou·bli·ette \ˌü-blē-ˈet\ *n* [F, fr. MF, fr. *oublier* to forget, fr. L *oblitus*, pp. of *oblivisci* — more at OBLIVION] **:** a dungeon with an opening only at the top

1ouch \ˈau̇ch\ *n* [ME, alter. (resulting fr. incorrect division of *a nouche*) of *nouche*, fr. MF, of Gmc origin; akin to OHG *nusca* clasp; akin to OE *net*] **1** *obs* **:** CLASP, BROOCH **2 a :** a setting for a precious stone **b :** JEWEL, ORNAMENT; *esp* **:** a buckle or brooch set with precious stones

2ouch *interj* [origin unknown] — used to express sudden pain or displeasure

1ought \ˈȯt\ *verbal auxiliary* [ME *oughte* (1st & 3d sing. pres. indic.), fr. *oughte*, 1st & 3d sing. past indic. & subj. of *owen* to own, owe — more at OWE] — used to express moral obligation ⟨~ to pay our debts⟩, advisability ⟨~ to take care of yourself⟩, natural expectation ⟨~ to be here by now⟩, or logical consequence ⟨the result ~ to be infinity⟩

2ought \ˈȯ(k)t\ *vt* [ME *oughte*, 1st & 3d sing. past indic. of *owen*] **1** *chiefly Scot* **:** OWE **2** *chiefly Scot* **:** POSSESS

3ought \ˈȯt\ *n* **:** moral obligation **:** DUTY

4ought \ˈȯt, ˈät\ *var of* AUGHT

oughtn't \ˈȯt-ᵊnt\ **:** ought not

Oui·ja \ˈwē-jə, -jē\ *trademark* — used for a board with the alphabet and other signs on it that is used with a planchette to seek spiritualistic or telepathic messages

1ounce \ˈau̇n(t)s\ *n* [ME, fr. MF *unce*, fr. L *uncia* twelfth part, ounce, fr. *unus* one — more at ONE] **1 a :** any of various units of weight based on the ancient Roman unit equal to 1/12 Roman pound — see MEASURE table **b :** a small portion **2 :** FLUIDOUNCE

2ounce *n* [ME *once*, fr. OF, alter. (by incorrect division, as if *l'once* the ounce) of *lonce*, fr. (assumed) VL *lyncea*, fr. L *lync-*, *lynx* lynx] **:** SNOW LEOPARD

ouph *or* **ouphe** \ˈau̇f\ *n* [prob. alter. of *auf*, prob. fr. ON *alfr*] **:** ELF

our \är, (ˈ)au̇(ə)r\ *adj* [ME *oure*, fr. OE *ūre*; akin to OHG *unsēr* our, OE *ūs* us] **:** of or relating to us or ourselves or ourself esp. as possessors or possessor ⟨~ throne⟩, agents or agent ⟨~ actions⟩, or objects or object of an action ⟨~ being chosen⟩

Our Father *n* **:** LORD'S PRAYER

ours \(ˈ)au̇(ə)rz, ärz\ *pron, sing or pl in constr* **:** our one **:** our ones — used without a following noun as a pronoun equivalent in meaning to the adjective *our*

our·self \är-ˈself, au̇(ə)r-\ *pron* **:** MYSELF — used to refer to the single-person subject when *we* is used instead of *I* (as by a sovereign or writer) ⟨will keep ~ till supper time alone —Shak.⟩

our·selves \-ˈselvz\ *pron pl* **1 :** those identical ones that are we — compare WE 1; used reflexively ⟨we're doing it solely for ~⟩, for emphasis ⟨we ~ will never go⟩ ⟨our children and ~ will be glad to come⟩, or in absolute constructions ⟨~ no longer young, we can sympathize with those who are old⟩ **2 :** our normal, healthy, or sane condition or selves

-ous \əs\ *adj suffix* [ME, partly fr. OF *-ous*, *-eus*, *-eux*, fr. L *-osus*; partly fr. L *-us*, nom. sing. masc. ending of many adjectives] **1 :** full of **:** abounding in **:** having **:** possessing the qualities of ⟨clamor*ous*⟩ ⟨poison*ous*⟩ **2 :** having a valence lower than in compounds or ions named with an adjective ending in *-ic* ⟨mercur*ous*⟩

oust \ˈau̇st\ *vt* [AF *ouster*, fr. OF *oster*, fr. LL *obstare* to ward off, fr. L, to stand against, fr. *ob-* against + *stare* to stand — more at OB-, STAND] **1 a :** to eject from or deprive of property or position **:** DISPOSSESS **b :** BAR, REMOVE **2 :** SUPPLANT **syn** see EJECT

oust·er \ˈau̇s-tər\ *n* [AF, to oust] **1 a :** a wrongful dispossession **b :** a judgment removing an officer or depriving a corporation of a franchise **2 :** EXPULSION

1out \ˈau̇t\ *adv* [ME, fr. OE *ūt*; akin to OHG *ūz* out, Gk *hysteros* later, *hybris* arrogance, Skt *ud* up, out] **1 a :** in a direction away from the inside or center ⟨went ~ into the garden⟩ **b :** from among others ⟨picked ~ a hat⟩ **c :** away from the shore **d :** away from home or business ⟨~ to lunch⟩ **2 a :** out of the usual or proper place ⟨left a word ~⟩ **b :** beyond possession, control, or occupation ⟨lent ~ money⟩ **c :** into a state of loss or deprivation ⟨voted him ~⟩ **d :** into a state of vexation or disagreement ⟨put ~ by the delay⟩ ⟨friends fall ~⟩ **e :** into portions, shares, or allotments ⟨parceled ~ the farm⟩ **3 a :** beyond the limits of existence, continuance, or supply ⟨the food ran ~⟩ **b :** to extinction, exhaustion, or completion ⟨burn ~⟩ **c :** to the fullest degree ⟨all decked ~⟩ **4 a :** in or into the open ⟨the sun came ~⟩ ⟨let the secret ~⟩ **b :** ALOUD ⟨cried ~⟩ **5 a :** so as to retire a batter, batsman, or base runner **b :** so as to be retired **6** — used on a two-way radio circuit to indicate that a message is complete and no reply is expected

2out *vt* **:** to put out **:** EJECT **~** *vi* **:** to become public

3out *adj* **1 :** situated outside **:** EXTERNAL **2 :** situated at a distance **:** OUTLYING **3 a :** not being in power **b :** not successful in reaching base ⟨the batter was ~⟩ **4 :** directed outward or serving to direct something outward **:** OUTGOING

4out \(ˈ)au̇t\ *prep* **1 :** out through ⟨ran ~ the door⟩ **2 :** outward along or on ⟨drive ~ the old road⟩

5out \ˈau̇t\ *n* **1 :** OUTSIDE ⟨the width of the building from ~ to ~⟩ **2 :** one who is out of power ⟨the ~*s* are apt to be loud⟩ **3 :** copy matter inadvertently omitted in typesetting **4 a :** the retiring of a batter or base runner in baseball **b :** a player so retired **5** *pl, Brit* **:** money paid out esp. in taxes **6 :** a ball hit out-of-bounds in tennis or squash **7 :** an item that is out of stock **8 a :** a way of escaping from an embarrassing situation **b :** a way out of a difficulty **:** SOLUTION

out- *prefix* [¹out] **:** in a manner that goes beyond, surpasses, or excels ⟨*out*maneuver⟩

out·age \ˈau̇t-ij\ *n* **1 :** a quantity or bulk of something lost in transportation or storage **2 :** a failure or interruption in use or functioning **3 :** a period of interruption of electric current

out-and-out \ˌau̇t-ᵊn-ˈ(d)au̇t\ *adj* (*or adv*) **1 :** OPEN, UNDISGUISED **2 :** COMPLETE, THOROUGHGOING

out-and-out·er \-ər\ *n* **:** EXTREMIST

out·bal·ance \(ˈ)au̇t-ˈbal-ən(t)s\ *vt* **:** OUTWEIGH

out·bid \-ˈbid\ *vt* **:** to make a higher bid than

1out·board \ˈau̇t-ˌbō(ə)rd, -ˌbȯ(ə)rd\ *adj* **1 :** situated outboard **2 :** being a machine bearing, center, or other support used in conjunction with and outside of a main bearing **3 :** having, using, or limited to the use of an outboard motor

2outboard *adv* **1 :** outside a ship's bulwarks **:** in a lateral direction from the hull **2 :** in a position closer or closest to either of the wing tips of an airplane

outboard motor *n* **:** a small internal-combustion engine with propeller integrally attached for mounting at the stern of a small boat

out·bound \ˈau̇t-ˌbau̇nd\ *adj* **:** outward bound ⟨~ traffic⟩

out·brave \(ˈ)au̇t-ˈbrāv\ *vt* **1 :** to face or resist defiantly **2 :** to exceed in courage

out·break \ˈau̇t-ˌbrāk\ *n* **1 :** a sudden or violent increase in activity or currency ⟨the ~ of war⟩ **2 :** INSURRECTION, REVOLT

out·breed *vt* **1** \ˈau̇t-ˌbrēd\ **:** to subject to outbreeding **2** \(ˈ)au̇t-ˈ\ **:** to breed faster than

out·breed·ing \ˈau̇t-ˌbrēd-iŋ\ *n* **:** the interbreeding of relatively unrelated individuals; *esp* **:** a system of breeding of animals based on individual excellence and avoidance of close relationships

out·build·ing \ˈau̇t-ˌbil-diŋ\ *n* **:** a building separate from but accessory to a main house

out·burst \-ˌbərst\ *n* **1 :** a violent expression of feeling **2 :** a surge of activity or growth **3 :** ERUPTION

out·bye *or* **out·by** \ˈüt-ˌbī\ *adv* [ME (Sc) *out-by*, fr. *out* + *by*] *chiefly Scot* **:** a short distance away **:** OUTDOORS

out·cast \ˈau̇t-ˌkast\ *n* **1 :** one who is cast out by society **:** PARIAH **2** [Sc *cast out* to quarrel] *Scot* **:** QUARREL — **outcast** *adj*

out·caste \-ˌkast\ *n* **1 :** a Hindu who has been ejected from his caste for violation of its customs or rules **2 :** one who has no caste

out·class \(ˈ)au̇t-ˈklas\ *vt* **:** to excel or surpass so decisively as to appear of a higher class

out·come \ˈau̇t-ˌkəm\ n : final consequence : RESULT **syn** see EFFECT

¹out·crop \-ˌkräp\ n 1 a : a coming out of bedrock or of an unconsolidated deposit to the surface of the ground b : the part of a rock formation that appears at the surface of the ground 2 : ERUPTION, OUTBREAK

²out·crop \ˈau̇t-ˈkräp\ vi 1 : to come out to the surface of the ground ⟨rocks ~⟩ 2 : to come to the surface : APPEAR

out·cross \ˈau̇t-ˌkrȯs\ vt : to subject to outcrossing — **outcross** n

out·cross·ing \ˈau̇t-ˌkrȯ-siŋ\ n : a mating of individuals of different strains but usu. of the same breed

out·cry \ˈau̇t-ˌkrī\ n 1 a : a loud cry : CLAMOR b : a vehement protest 2 : AUCTION

out·curve \-ˌkərv\ n : a curve in baseball in which the ball breaks away from the batter

out·dat·ed \(ˈ)au̇t-ˈdāt-əd\ adj : OBSOLETE

out·dis·tance \(ˈ)au̇t-ˈdis-tən(t)s\ vt : to go far ahead of (as in a race) : OUTSTRIP

out·do \-ˈdü\ vt 1 : EXCEL, SURPASS 2 : DEFEAT, OVERCOME **syn** see EXCEED

out·door \ˌau̇t-ˌdō(ə)r, -ˌdȯ(ə)r\ also **out·doors** \-ˌdō(ə)rz, ˌdȯ(ə)rz\ adj [out (of) door, out (of) doors] 1 : of or relating to the outdoors 2 : performed outdoors 3 : not enclosed : having no roof

¹out·doors \(ˈ)au̇t-ˈdō(ə)rz, -ˈdȯ(ə)rz\ adv : outside a building : in or into the open air

²outdoors n pl but sing in constr 1 : the open air 2 : the world away from human habitations

out·er \ˈau̇t-ər\ adj [ME, fr. ³out + -er, compar. suffix] 1 : EXTERNAL, OBJECTIVE 2 a : situated farther out b : being away from a center

out·er-di·rect·ed \ˌau̇t-ər-də-ˈrek-təd, -(ˌ)dī-\ adj : conforming to the values and standards of society — **out·er-di·rec·tion** \-ˈrek-shən\ n

out·er·most \ˈau̇t-ər-ˌmōst\ adj : farthest out

outer space n 1 : space immediately outside the earth's atmosphere 2 : interplanetary or interstellar space

out·face \(ˈ)au̇t-ˈfās\ vt 1 : to stare down 2 : to confront unflinchingly : DEFY

out·fall \ˈau̇t-ˌfȯl\ n : the outlet of a river, stream, lake, drain, or sewer

out·field \-ˌfēld\ n 1 : the part of a baseball field beyond the infield and between the foul lines 2 : the baseball defensive positions comprising right field, center field, and left field — **out·field·er** \-ˌfēl-dər\ n

out·fight \au̇t-ˈfīt\ vt : to surpass in fighting : DEFEAT

out·fight·ing \ˈau̇t-ˌfīt-iŋ\ n : fighting at long range

¹out·fit \ˈau̇t-ˌfit\ n 1 : the act of fitting out or equipping 2 a : the tools or equipment for the practice of a trade b : wearing apparel with accessories for a special occasion c : physical, mental, or moral equipment 3 a : GROUP, TEAM b : RANCH

²outfit vt out·fit·ted; out·fit·ting 1 : to furnish with an outfit 2 : SUPPLY ~ vi : to acquire an outfit **syn** see FURNISH

out·fit·ter \-ˌfit-ər\ n : one who outfits: as a : HABERDASHER b : a dealer in equipment and supplies for expeditions or camping trips

out·flank \(ˈ)au̇t-ˈflaŋk\ vt : to get around the flank of (an opposing force) — **out·flank·er** n

out·flow \ˈau̇t-ˌflō\ n 1 : a flowing out 2 : something that flows out

out·foot \(ˈ)au̇t-ˈfu̇t\ vt : to outdo in speed : OUTSTRIP

out·fox \-ˈfäks\ vt : OUTSMART

out·gas \-ˈgas\ vt : to remove occluded gases from usu. by heating

out·gen·er·al \(ˈ)au̇t-ˈjen-(ə-)rəl\ vt : to surpass in generalship : OUTMANEUVER

¹out·go \(ˈ)au̇t-ˈgō\ vt : to go beyond : OUTDO

²out·go \ˈau̇t-ˌgō\ n 1 : something that goes out; specif : EXPENDITURE 2 a : the act of going out b : DEPARTURE 3 : OUTLET

out·go·ing \ˈau̇t-ˌgō-iŋ, -ˌgȯ(-)iŋ\ adj 1 a : going away : DEPARTING b : retiring or withdrawing from a place or position 2 : FRIENDLY, RESPONSIVE

out·grow \(ˈ)au̇t-ˈgrō\ vt 1 : to grow faster than 2 : to grow too large or too mature for

out·growth \ˈau̇t-ˌgrōth\ n 1 : a process or product of growing out 2 : CONSEQUENCE, BY-PRODUCT

out·guess \(ˈ)au̇t-ˈges\ vt : ANTICIPATE, OUTWIT

out·haul \ˈau̇t-ˌhȯl\ n : a rope used to haul a sail taut along a spar

out-Her·od \(ˈ)au̇t-ˈher-əd\ vt [out- + Herod Antipas †ab A.D. 40, depicted in medieval mystery plays as a blustering tyrant] : to exceed in violence or extravagance

out·house \ˈau̇t-ˌhau̇s\ n : OUTBUILDING; esp : PRIVY

out·ing \ˈau̇t-iŋ\ n : an excursion usu. with a picnic

outing flannel n : a flannelette sometimes having an admixture of wool

out·land \ˈau̇t-ˌland, -lənd\ n 1 : a foreign land 2 pl : the outlying regions of a country : PROVINCES — **outland** adj — **out·land·er** \-ˌlan-dər, -lən-\ n

out·land·ish \(ˈ)au̇t-ˈlan-dish\ adj 1 : of or relating to another country : FOREIGN 2 : foreign looking : BIZARRE 3 : remote from civilization **syn** see STRANGE — **out·land·ish·ly** adv — **out·land·ish·ness** n

out·last \(ˈ)au̇t-ˈlast\ vt : to last longer than : SURVIVE **syn** see OUTLIVE

¹out·law \ˈau̇t-ˌlȯ\ n [ME outlawe, fr. OE ūtlaga, fr. ON ūtlagi, fr. ūt out (akin to OE ūt out) + -lag-, lǫg law — more at OUT, LAW] 1 : a person excluded from the benefit or protection of the law 2 a : a lawless person or a fugitive from the law b : a person or organization under a ban or disability — **outlaw** adj

²outlaw vt 1 a : to deprive of the benefit and protection of law b : to make illegal 2 : to place under a ban or disability 3 : to remove from legal jurisdiction or enforcement — **out·law·ry** \ˈau̇t-ˌlȯ(ə)r-ē\ n

¹out·lay \(ˈ)au̇t-ˈlā\ vt : to lay out (money) : EXPEND

²outlay n 1 : the act of laying out or spending 2 : EXPENDITURE, PAYMENT

out·let \ˈau̇t-ˌlet, -lət\ n [¹out + let, v.] 1 a : a means of exit

: VENT b : a means of release or satisfaction for an emotion or impulse 2 : a stream flowing out of a lake or pond 3 : a market for a commodity 4 : a box at which electric wiring terminates for connection to electric appliances

out·li·er \-ˌlī(-ə)r\ n 1 : one that does not live where his office, business, or estate is 2 : something that lies, dwells, or is situated or classed away from a main or related body

¹out·line \ˈau̇t-ˌlīn\ n 1 a : a line that marks the outer limits of an object or figure : BOUNDARY b : CONTOUR, SHAPE 2 a : a style of drawing in which contours are marked without shading b : a sketch in outline 3 a : a summary of a written work b : SYNOPSIS 4 : a preliminary account of a project : PLAN 5 : a fishing line set out overnight : TROTLINE

syn CONTOUR, PROFILE, SILHOUETTE: OUTLINE applies to a line marking the outer limits or edges of a body or mass; CONTOUR stresses the quality of an outline or a bounding surface as being smooth, jagged, curving, or sharply angled; PROFILE suggests a varied and sharply defined outline against a lighter background; SILHOUETTE suggests a shape esp. of a head or figure with all detail blacked out in shadow leaving only the outline clearly defined

²outline vt 1 : to draw the outline of 2 : to indicate the principal features or different parts of

out·live \(ˈ)au̇t-ˈliv\ vt 1 : to live longer than 2 : to survive the effects of

syn OUTLAST, SURVIVE: OUTLIVE stresses the fact of enduring longer than another or of surmounting difficulty; OUTLAST is likely to stress capacity for endurance in relation to some other comparable or competing thing; SURVIVE implies a continuing to exist after a threatening event or circumstance

out·look \ˈau̇t-ˌlu̇k\ n 1 a : a place offering a view b : a view from a particular place 2 : POINT OF VIEW 3 : the act of looking out : LOOKOUT 4 : the prospect for the future **syn** see PROSPECT

out·ly·ing \ˈau̇t-ˌlī-iŋ\ adj : remote from a center or main body

out·ma·neu·ver \ˌau̇t-mə-ˈn(y)ü-vər\ vt 1 : to defeat by more skillful maneuvering 2 : to surpass in maneuverability

out·match \ˈau̇t-ˈmach\ vt 1 : to prove superior to : OUTDO

out·mode \-ˈmōd\ vt [out (of) mode] : to make unfashionable or obsolete

out·mod·ed \-ˈmōd-əd\ adj 1 : not in style 2 : no longer acceptable or usable

out·most \ˈau̇t-ˌmōst\ adj : farthest out : OUTERMOST

out·num·ber \(ˈ)au̇t-ˈnəm-bər\ vt : to exceed in number

out of prep 1 a (1) : from within to the outside of ⟨walked out of the room⟩ (2) — used as a function word to indicate a change in quality, state, or form ⟨woke up out of a deep sleep⟩ b (1) : beyond the range, limits, or sphere of ⟨out of sight⟩ (2) — used as a function word to indicate a position or state away from the usual or expected ⟨out of practice⟩ (3) — used as a function word to indicate origin or birth ⟨a colt out of an ordinary mare⟩ (4) : from among ⟨one out of four survived⟩ 2 : in or into a state of loss or not having ⟨cheated him out of his savings⟩ 3 : because of : FROM ⟨came out of curiosity⟩ 4 — used as a function word to indicate the constituent material, basis, or source ⟨built out of old lumber⟩

out-of-date \ˌau̇t-ə(v)-ˈdāt\ adj : OUTMODED, UNFASHIONABLE, OBSOLETE — **out-of-date·ness** n

out-of-door \ˌau̇t-ə(v)-ˈdō(ə)r, -ˈdȯ(ə)r\ or **out-of-doors** \-ˈdō(ə)rz, -ˈdȯ(ə)rz\ adj : OUTDOOR

out-of-doors n pl but sing in constr : OUTDOORS

out-of-the-way \ˌau̇t-ə(v)-thə-ˈwā\ adj : off the beaten track : UNUSUAL

out·pa·tient \ˈau̇t-ˌpā-shənt\ n : a patient who is not an inmate of a hospital but who receives diagnosis or treatment in a clinic or dispensary connected with it

out·play \(ˈ)au̇t-ˈplā\ vt : to excel or defeat in a game

out·point \-ˈpȯint\ vt 1 : to sail closer to the wind than 2 : to win more points than

out·post \ˈau̇t-ˌpōst\ n 1 a : a security detachment thrown out by a main body of troops to protect it from enemy surprise b : a military base established by treaty or agreement in another country 2 : an outlying or frontier settlement

out·pour \au̇t-ˈpō(ə)r, -ˈpȯ(ə)r\ vt : to pour out — **out·pour** \ˈau̇t-ˌ\ n

out·pour·ing \ˈau̇t-ˌpōr-iŋ, -ˌpȯr-\ n 1 : the act of pouring out 2 : something that pours out or is poured out : OUTFLOW

out·put \ˈau̇t-ˌpu̇t\ n 1 : something produced: as a : mineral, agricultural, or industrial production b : mental or artistic production c : the amount produced by a person in a given time d (1) : power or energy delivered by a machine or system for storage or for conversion in kind or in characteristics (2) : the terminal for the output on an electrical device e : the information fed out by a computer or accounting machine 2 : the act or process of producing

¹out·rage \ˈau̇t-ˌrāj\ n [ME, fr. OF, excess, outrage, fr. outre beyond, in excess, fr. L ultra — more at ULTRA-] 1 : an act of violence or brutality 2 : INJURY, INSULT 3 : the anger and resentment aroused by injury or insult

²outrage vt 1 a : RAPE b : to subject to injury or insult 2 : to arouse anger or resentment in **syn** see OFFEND

out·ra·geous \au̇t-ˈrā-jəs\ adj 1 a : EXCESSIVE, EXTRAVAGANT b : FANCIFUL, FANTASTIC 2 : VIOLENT, UNRESTRAINED 3 a : doing grave insult or injury : ATROCIOUS b : extremely offensive : RUDE — **out·ra·geous·ly** adv — **out·ra·geous·ness** n

syn OUTRAGEOUS, MONSTROUS, HEINOUS, ATROCIOUS mean enormously bad or horrible. OUTRAGEOUS implies exceeding the limits of what is bearable or endurable; MONSTROUS applies to what is abnormally or fantastically wrong, absurd, or horrible; HEINOUS implies being so flagrantly evil as to excite hatred or horror; ATROCIOUS implies merciless cruelty, savagery, or contempt of ordinary values

ou·trance \ü-ˈträⁿs\ n [ME, fr. MF, fr. outrer to pass beyond, carry to excess, fr. outre] : the last extremity

out·range \(ˈ)au̇t-ˈrānj\ vt : to surpass in range

ou·tré \ü-ˈtrā\ adj [F, fr. pp. of outrer to carry to excess] : violating convention or propriety : BIZARRE

¹out·reach \(ˈ)au̇t-ˈrēch\ vt 1 : to surpass in reach : EXCEED 2 : to get the better of by trickery : OVERREACH ~ vi 1 : to go too far 2 : to reach out

2**out·reach** \'au̇t-,rēch\ *n* **1 :** the act of reaching out **2 :** the extent or limit of reach

1**out·ride** \(')au̇t-'rīd\ *vt* **1 :** to ride better, faster, or farther than **:** OUTSTRIP **2 :** to ride out (a storm)

2**out·ride** \'au̇t-,rīd\ *n* **:** an unstressed syllable or group of syllables added to a foot in sprung rhythm but not counted in the scansion

out·rid·er \-,rīd-ər\ *n* **1 :** a mounted attendant **2 :** FORERUNNER, HARBINGER

out·rig·ger \'au̇t-,rig-ər\ *n* **1 a :** a projecting spar with a shaped log at the end attached to a canoe to prevent upsetting **b :** a spar or projecting beam run out from a ship's side to help secure the masts or from a mast to extend a rope or sail **c :** a projecting support for an oarlock; *also* **:** a boat so equipped **2 :** a projecting member run out from a main structure to provide additional stability or to support an extension; *esp* **:** a projecting frame to support the elevator or tail planes of an airplane or the rotor of a helicopter

1**out·right** \(')au̇t-'rīt\ *adv* **1** *archaic* **:** straight ahead **:** DIRECTLY **2 :** in entirety **:** COMPLETELY **3 :** on the spot **:** INSTANTANEOUSLY **4 :** without lien or encumbrance

2**out·right** \'au̇t-,\ *adj* **1 a :** UNQUALIFIED, THOROUGHGOING **b :** given without reservation **c :** made without encumbrance or lien ⟨~ sale⟩ **2** *archaic* **:** proceeding directly onward **3 :** COMPLETE, ENTIRE

out·run \(')au̇t-'rən\ *vt* **:** to run faster than; *also* **:** EXCEED

out·sell \-'sel\ *vt* **1** *archaic* **:** to sell for a higher price than **2 :** to exceed in number of items sold **3 :** to surpass in selling or salesmanship

out·sert \'au̇t-,sərt\ *n* [3*out* + *-sert* (as in *insert*)] **:** a usu. 4-page section so imposed and printed that it can be placed outside another signature

out·set \'au̇t-,set\ *n* **:** BEGINNING, START

out·shine \(')au̇t-'shīn\ *vt* **1 a :** to shine brighter than **b :** to excel in splendor or showiness **2 :** OUTDO, SURPASS **~** *vi* **:** to shine out

1**out·shoot** \-'shüt\ *vt* **1 :** to surpass in shooting or making shots **2 :** to shoot or go beyond

2**out·shoot** \'au̇t-,shüt\ *n* **:** something that shoots out

1**out·side** \(')au̇t-'sīd, 'au̇t-,\ *n* **1 :** a place or region beyond an enclosure or boundary **2 :** an outer side or surface **3 :** an outer manifestation **4 :** the extreme limit of a guess

2**outside** *adj* **1 a :** of, relating to, or being on or toward the outer side or surface ⟨the ~ edge⟩ **b :** of, relating to, or being on or toward the outer side of a curve or turn **2 a :** situated or performed outside a particular place **b :** connected with or giving access to the outside ⟨~ telephone line⟩ **3 :** MAXIMUM **4 a :** not included or originating in a particular group or organization **b :** not belonging to one's regular occupation or duties **5 :** barely possible **:** REMOTE ⟨an ~ chance⟩

3**outside** *adv* **:** on or to the outside **:** OUTDOORS

4**outside** *prep* **1 :** on the outer side of **2 :** beyond the limits of ⟨~ the law⟩ **3 :** to the outside of **4 :** EXCEPT 1

outside of *prep* **:** OUTSIDE

out·sid·er \(')au̇t-'sīd-ər\ *n* **1 :** a person not a member of some group **2 :** a contender not favored to win

out·sit \(')au̇t-'sit\ *vt* **:** to remain sitting or in session longer than or beyond the time of

1**out·size** \'au̇t-,sīz\ *n* **:** an unusual size; *esp* **:** a size larger than the standard

2**outsize** *also* **out·sized** \-,sīzd\ *adj* **1 :** unusually large or heavy **2 :** too large

out·skirt \'au̇t-,skərt\ *n* **:** a part remote from the center **:** BORDER — usu. used in pl.

out·smart \(')au̇t-'smärt\ *vt* **:** to get the better of; *esp* **:** OUTWIT

out·soar \-'sō(ə)r, -'sȯ(ə)r\ *vt* **:** to soar beyond or above

out·sole \'au̇t-,sōl\ *n* **:** the outside sole of a boot or shoe

out·speak \(')au̇t-'spēk\ *vt* **1 :** to excel in speaking **2 :** to declare openly or boldly

out·spent \-'spent\ *adj* **:** EXHAUSTED

out·spo·ken \au̇t-'spō-kən\ *adj* **:** direct and open in speech or expression **:** FRANK — **out·spo·ken·ly** *adv* — **out·spo·ken·ness** \-kən-nəs\ *n*

1**out·spread** \au̇t-'spred\ *vt* **:** to spread out **:** EXTEND

2**out·spread** \'au̇t-,\ *adj* **:** spread out **:** EXTENDED

out·stand \(')au̇t-'stand\ *vt* **1** *dial chiefly Eng* **:** to resist stubbornly **2 :** to endure beyond ⟨I have *outstood* my time —Shak.⟩ **~** *vi* **:** to stand out

out·stand·ing \'au̇t-,stan-diŋ\ *adj* **1 :** standing out **:** PROJECTING **2 a :** UNPAID **b :** CONTINUING, UNRESOLVED **c** *of stocks and bonds* **:** publicly issued and sold **3 a :** standing out from a group **:** CONSPICUOUS **b :** DISTINGUISHED, EMINENT **syn** see NOTICEABLE — **out·stand·ing·ly** \au̇t-'stan-diŋ-lē\ *adv*

out·sta·tion \'au̇t-,stā-shən\ *n* **:** a remote or outlying station

out·stay \(')au̇t-'stā\ *vt* **1 a :** to stay beyond **b :** to stay longer than **2 :** to surpass in staying power

out·stretch \au̇t-'strech\ *vt* **:** to stretch out **:** EXTEND

out·strip \au̇t-'strip\ *vt* [*out-* + obs. *strip* (to move fast)] **1 :** to go faster or farther than **2 :** EXCEL **syn** see EXCEED

out·turn \'au̇t-,tərn\ *n* **:** a quantity produced **:** OUTPUT

1**out·ward** \'au̇t-wərd\ *adj* **1 :** moving, directed, or turned toward the outside or away from a center **2 :** situated on the outside **:** EXTERIOR **3 :** of or relating to the body or to appearances rather than to the mind or the inner life **4 :** EXTERNAL, MANIFEST ⟨~ patterns⟩ **5** *dial Eng* **:** inclined to drink **:** DISSIPATED

2**outward** *or* **out·wards** \-wərdz\ *adv* **1 :** toward the outside **2** *obs* **:** on the outside **:** EXTERNALLY

3**outward** *n* **:** external form, appearance, or reality

out·ward·ly \'au̇t-wərd-lē\ *adv* **1 a :** on the outside **:** EXTERNALLY **b :** toward the outside **2 :** in outward state, behavior, or appearance

out·ward·ness \-nəs\ *n* **1 :** the quality or state of being existent or external **2 :** concern with or responsiveness to outward things

out·wear \(')au̇t-'wa(ə)r, -'we(ə)r\ *vt* **1 :** to wear out **:** EXHAUST **2 :** to last longer than

out·weigh \-'wā\ *vt* **:** to exceed in weight, value, or importance

out·wind \-'wind\ *vt* **:** to exhaust the breath of

out·wit \au̇t-'wit\ *vt* **1 :** to get the better of by superior cleverness **:** OUTSMART **2** *archaic* **:** to surpass in wisdom **syn** see FRUSTRATE

1**out·work** *vt* **1** \au̇t-'wərk\ **:** to work out **:** COMPLETE **2** \(')au̇t-\ **:** to outdo in working

2**out·work** \'au̇t-,wərk\ *n* **:** a minor defensive position constructed outside a fortified area

ou·zel *also* **ou·sel** \'ü-zəl\ *n* [ME *ousel*, fr. OE *ōsle* — more at MERL] **:** a European blackbird (*Turdus merula*)

ov- *or* **ovi-** *or* **ovo-** *comb form* [L *ov-*, *ovi-*, fr. *ovum* — more at EGG] **:** egg ⟨*ovi*form⟩ **:** ovum ⟨*ov*iduct⟩ ⟨*ovo*cyte⟩ ⟨*ovo*genesis⟩

ova *pl of* OVUM

1**oval** \'ō-vəl\ *adj* [ML *ovalis*, fr. LL, of an egg, fr. L *ovum*] **:** having the shape of an egg; *also* **:** broadly elliptical — **oval·ly** \-və-lē\ *adv*

2**oval** *n* **:** an oval figure or object

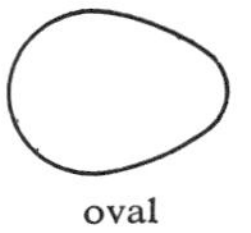
oval

ovar·i·an \ō-'var-ē-ən, -'ver-\ *also* **ovar·i·al** \-ē-əl\ *adj* **:** of, relating to, or involving an ovary

ovari·ec·to·my \ō-,var-ē-'ek-tə-mē, -,ver-\ *n* **:** the surgical removal of an ovary

ovar·i·ot·o·my \-'ät-ə-mē\ *n* **1 :** surgical incision of an ovary **2 :** OVARIECTOMY

ova·ri·tis \,ō-və-'rīt-əs\ *n* [NL, fr. *ovarium*] **:** inflammation of an ovary

ova·ry \'ōv-(ə-)rē\ *n* [NL *ovarium*, fr. L *ovum* egg] **1 :** the typically paired essential female reproductive organ that produces eggs and in vertebrates female sex hormones **2 :** the enlarged rounded usu. basal portion of the pistil or gynoecium of an angiospermous plant that bears the ovules and consists of one or more carpels

ovate \'ō-,vāt\ *adj* **1 :** shaped like an egg **2 :** having an outline like a longitudinal section of an egg with the basal end broader ⟨~ leaves⟩

ova·tion \ō-'vā-shən\ *n* [L *ovation-*, *ovatio*, fr. *ovatus*, pp. of *ovare* to exult; akin to Gk *euoi*, interjection used in bacchic revels] **1 :** a ceremony attending the entering of Rome by a general who had won a victory of less importance than that for which a triumph was granted **2 :** public homage or tribute **:** APPLAUSE

ov·en \'əv-ən\ *n* [ME, fr. OE *ofen;* akin to OHG *ofan* oven, Gk *ipnos*, L *aulla*, *olla* pot] **:** a chamber used for baking, heating, or drying

oven·bird \-,bərd\ *n* [fr. the shape of its nest] **1 :** any of various So. American passerine birds (genus *Furnarius*) **2 :** an American warbler (*Seiurus aurocapillus*) that builds a dome-shaped nest on the ground

1**over** \'ō-vər\ *adv* [ME, adv. & prep., fr. OE *ofer;* akin to OHG *ubar* (prep.) above, beyond, over, L *super*, Gk *hyper*] **1 a :** across a barrier or intervening space **b :** down or forward and down ⟨fell ~⟩ **c :** across the brim ⟨soup boiled ~⟩ **d :** so as to bring the underside up **e :** from a vertical to a prone or inclined position ⟨knocked him ~⟩ **f :** from one person or side to another ⟨hand it ~⟩ **g :** ACROSS ⟨got his point ~⟩ **h :** to agreement or concord ⟨won them ~⟩ **2 a :** beyond some quantity, limit, or norm often by a specified amount or to a specified degree ⟨show ran a minute ~⟩ **b :** till a later time **3 a :** ABOVE **b :** so as to cover the whole surface ⟨windows boarded ~⟩ **4 a :** at an end ⟨the day is ~⟩ **b** — used on a two-way radio circuit to indicate that a message is complete and a reply is expected **5 a :** THROUGH ⟨read it ~⟩; *also* **:** THOROUGHLY **b :** once more **:** AGAIN ⟨do it ~⟩

2**over** \,ō-vər, 'ō-\ *prep* **1 a** — used as a function word to indicate position higher than or above another ⟨towered ~ his mother⟩ **b :** beyond the comprehension of ⟨talked ~ their heads⟩ **2 a** — used as a function word to indicate the possession of authority, power, or jurisdiction in regard to some thing or person ⟨respected those ~ him⟩ **b** — used as a function word to indicate superiority, advantage, or preference ⟨a big lead ~ the others⟩ **3 :** more than ⟨cost ~ five dollars⟩ **4 a :** upon or down upon so as to cover or conceal ⟨laid a blanket ~ the child⟩ **b :** ON, UPON ⟨hit him ~ the head⟩ **c :** throughout a specified area **d :** along the length of ⟨~ the road⟩ **e** — used as a function word to indicate a particular medium or channel of communication ⟨~ the radio⟩ **f :** all through ⟨showed me ~ the house⟩ **g** — used as a function word to indicate study, review, or examination of something ⟨went ~ his notes⟩ **5 a** — used as a function word to indicate motion above something on the way to the other side or beyond ⟨fly ~ a lake⟩ **b** — used as a function word to indicate position on the other side or beyond ⟨lives ~ the way⟩ **6 a :** THROUGHOUT, DURING ⟨~ the past 25 years⟩ **b :** until the end of ⟨stay ~ Sunday⟩ **7 a** — used as a function word to indicate an object of solicitude, interest, consideration, or reference ⟨the Lord watches ~ his own⟩ **b** — used as a function word to indicate occupation or activity ⟨an hour ~ cards⟩ **c :** on account of ⟨trouble ~ money⟩

3**over** \'ō-vər, ,ō-\ *adj* **1 a :** UPPER, HIGHER **b :** COVERING, OUTER **c :** EXCESSIVE **2 :** REMAINING

4**over** \'ō-vər\ *vt* **over·ing** \'ōv-(ə-)riŋ\ **:** to leap over **:** CLEAR

over·abun·dance \,ō-və-rə-'bən-dən(t)s\ *n* **:** EXCESS, SURFEIT — **over·abun·dant** \-dənt\ *adj*

over·act \,ō-və-'rakt\ *vt* **:** to exaggerate in acting **~** *vi* **1 :** to act more than is necessary **2 :** to overact a part — **over·ac·tion** \-'rak-shən\ *n*

over·ac·tive \-'rak-tiv\ *adj* **:** excessively or abnormally active

over against *prep* **:** as opposed to **:** in contrast with

1**over·age** \,ō-və-'rāj\ *adj* [2*over* + *age*] **1 :** too old to be useful **2 :** older than is normal for one's position, function, or grade

2**over·age** \'ōv-(ə-)rij\ *n* [3*over* + *-age*] **:** SURPLUS, EXCESS

1**over·all** \,ō-və-'rȯl\ *adv* **1 :** as a whole **:** GENERALLY **2 :** from the extreme forward point to the extreme after point of a ship's deck including overhangs

2**over·all** \'ō-və-,rȯl\ *n* **1** *pl* **a** *archaic* **:** loose protective trousers worn over regular clothes **b :** trousers of strong material usu. with a bib and shoulder straps **2** *chiefly Brit* **:** a loose-fitting protective smock worn over regular clothing

3**over·all** \,ō-və-'rȯl, 'ō-və-,\ *adj* **:** including everything

over·arm \'ō-və-,rärm\ *adj* **:** done with the arm raised above the shoulder ⟨~ pitching⟩

over·awe \,ō-və-'rȯ\ *vt* **:** to restrain or subdue by awe

1**over·bal·ance** \,ō-vər-'bal-ən(t)s\ *vt* **1 :** OUTWEIGH **2 :** to cause to lose balance

2**overbalance** \'ō-vər-,\ *n* **:** something more than an equivalent

over·bear \,ō-vər-'ba(ə)r, -'be(ə)r\ *vt* **1 :** to bring down by superior weight or force **:** OVERWHELM **2 a :** to domineer over **b :** to surpass in importance or cogency **:** OUTWEIGH **~** *vi* **:** to bear fruit or offspring to excess

over·bear·ing \-iŋ\ *adj* **1 a :** OVERPOWERING, OVERWHELMING **b :** decisively important **:** DOMINANT **2 :** ARROGANT, DOMINEERING **syn** see PROUD — **over·bear·ing·ly** \-iŋ-lē\ *adv*

over·bid \,ō-vər-'bid\ *vi* **1 :** to bid in excess of value **2 a :** to bid

more than the scoring capacity of a hand at cards **b** *Brit* **:** to make a higher bid than the preceding one ~ *vt* **:** to bid beyond or in excess of; *specif* **:** to bid more than the value of (one's hand at cards) — **overbid** \'ō-vər-,\ *n*
1over·blown \,ō-vər-'blōn\ *adj* **1 :** excessively large of girth **:** PORTLY **2 :** INFLATED, PRETENTIOUS
2overblown *adj* **:** past the prime of bloom ⟨~ roses⟩
over·board \'ō-vər-,bō(ə)rd, -,bȯ(ə)rd\ *adv* **1 :** over the side of a ship or boat into the water **2 :** to extremes of enthusiasm **3 :** into discard **:** ASIDE
over·build \,ō-vər-'bild\ *vb* **:** to build beyond the actual demand
1over·bur·den \-'bərd-ᵊn\ *vt* **:** to place an excessive burden on
2overburden \'ō-vər-,\ *n* **:** material overlying a deposit of useful geological materials
over·buy \,ō-vər-'bī\ *vb* **:** to buy beyond need or ability to pay
over·call \-'kȯl\ *vt* **:** to make a higher card bid than (the previous bid or player) ~ *vi* **:** to bid over an opponent's bid in bridge when one's partner has not bid or doubled — **overcall** \'ō-vər-,\ *n*
over·cap·i·tal·iza·tion \,ō-vər-,kap-ət-ᵊl-ə-'zā-shən, -,kap-tᵊl-\ *n* **1 :** the act of overcapitalizing **2 :** the state of being overcapitalized
over·cap·i·tal·ize \-'kap-ət-ᵊl-,īz, -'kap-tᵊl-\ *vt* **1 :** to put a nominal value on the capital of (a corporation) higher than actual cost or fair market value **2 :** to capitalize beyond what the business or the profit-making prospects warrant
1over·cast *vt* **1** \,ō-vər-'kast, 'ō-vər-,\ **:** DARKEN, OVERSHADOW **2** \'ō-vər-,\ **:** to sew (raw edges of a seam) with long slanting widely spaced stitches to prevent raveling
2overcast \'ō-vər-,, ,ō-vər-'\ *adj* **:** clouded over ⟨an ~ night⟩
3overcast \'ō-vər-,\ *n* **:** COVERING; *esp* **:** a covering of clouds over the sky
over·cast·ing \'ō-vər-,kas-tiŋ\ *n* **:** the act of stitching raw edges of fabric to prevent raveling; *also* **:** the stitching so done

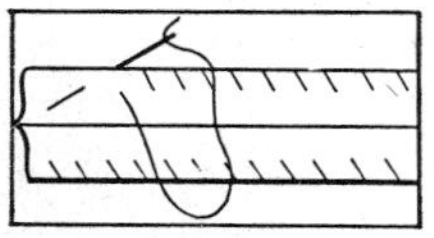
overcasting

overcast stitch *n* **:** a small close embroidery stitch sometimes done over a foundation thread and used to form outlines
over·cau·tious \,ō-vər-'kȯ-shəs\ *adj* **:** too cautious
over·cer·ti·fy \-'sərt-ə-,fī\ *vt* **:** to certify (a check) for more than the drawer's balance
over·charge \-'chärj\ *vb* **1 :** to charge too much **2 :** to fill too full **3 :** EXAGGERATE, OVERDRAW — **overcharge** \'ō-vər-,\ *n*
over·clothes \'ō-vər-,klō(th)z\ *n pl* **:** outer garments
over·cloud \,ō-vər-'klau̇d\ *vt* **:** to overspread with clouds **:** DARKEN
over·coat \'ō-vər-,kōt\ *n* **:** a warm coat worn over indoor clothing
over·come \,ō-vər-'kəm\ *vb* [ME *overcomen*, fr. OE *ofercuman*, fr. *ofer* over + *cuman* to come] *vt* **1 :** to get the better of **2 :** OVERPOWER, OVERWHELM ~ *vi* **:** to gain the superiority **:** WIN **syn** see CONQUER — **over·com·er** *n*
over·com·pen·sa·tion \-,käm-pən-'sā-shən, -,pen-\ *n* **:** excessive compensation; *specif* **:** excessive reaction to a feeling of inferiority, guilt, or inadequacy leading to an exaggerated attempt to overcome the feeling — **over·com·pen·sa·to·ry** \-kəm-'pen(t)-sə-,tōr-ē, -,tȯr-\ *adj*
over·con·fi·dence \-'kän-fəd-ən(t)s, -fə-,den(t)s\ *n* **:** excess of confidence — **over·con·fi·dent** \-fəd-ənt, -fə-,dent\ *adj*
over·crowd \,ō-vər-'krau̇d\ *vb* **:** to crowd to congestion
over·de·vel·op \,ō-vərd-i-'vel-əp\ *vt* **:** to develop excessively; *specif* **:** to subject (exposed photographic material) to a developing solution for excessive time or at excessive temperature, agitation, or concentration — **over·de·vel·op·ment** \-mənt\ *n*
over·do \,ō-vər-'dü\ *vt* **1 a :** to do to excess **b :** to use to excess **c :** EXAGGERATE **2 :** to cook too much **3 :** EXHAUST ~ *vi* **:** to go to extremes
1over·dose \'ō-vər-,dōs\ *n* **:** too great a dose
2overdose \,ō-vər-'\ *vt* **:** to give an overdose or too many doses to
over·draft \'ō-vər-,draft\ *n* **1 :** an act of overdrawing at a bank **:** the state of being overdrawn; *also* **:** the sum overdrawn **2 :** a draft or current of air passing over a fire in a furnace
over·draw \,ō-vər-'drȯ\ *vt* **1 :** to draw checks on (a bank account) for more than the balance **2 :** EXAGGERATE, OVERSTATE ~ *vi* **:** to make an overdraft
over·dress \'ō-vər-,dres\ *n* **:** a dress worn over another
over·drive \'ō-vər-,drīv\ *n* **:** an automotive transmission gear that transmits to the propeller shaft a speed greater than engine speed
over·due \,ō-vər-'d(y)ü\ *adj* **1 a :** unpaid when due **b :** delayed beyond an appointed time **2 :** too great **:** EXCESSIVE **3 :** more than ready
over·em·pha·sis \,ō-və-'rem(p)-fə-səs\ *n* **:** excessive emphasis — **over·em·pha·size** \-fə-,sīz\ *vb*
over·es·ti·mate \,ō-və-'res-tə-,māt\ *vt* **:** to estimate too highly — **over·es·ti·mate** \-mət\ *n* — **over·es·ti·ma·tion** \-,res-tə-'mā-shən\ *n*
over·ex·pose \,ō-və-rik-'spōz\ *vt* **:** to expose excessively; *specif* **:** to subject too long to the action of light or other radiation — **over·ex·po·sure** \-'spō-zhər\ *n*
over·ex·tend \,ō-və-rik-'stend\ *vt* **:** to extend or expand beyond a safe or reasonable point
over·fill \,ō-vər-'fil\ *vb* **:** to fill to overflowing
over·flight \'ō-vər-,flīt\ *n* **:** a passage over an area in an airplane — **over·fly** \,ō-vər-'flī\ *vt*
1over·flow \,ō-vər-'flō\ *vt* **1 :** to cover with or as if with water **:** INUNDATE **2 :** to flow over the brim of **3 :** to cause to overflow ~ *vi* **:** to flow over bounds
2overflow \'ō-vər-,\ *n* **1 :** a flowing over **:** INUNDATION **2 :** something that flows over **:** SURPLUS **3 :** an outlet or receptacle for surplus liquid
over·gar·ment \'ō-vər-,gär-mənt\ *n* **:** an outer garment
over·glaze \-,glāz\ *n* **:** a glaze applied over another
over·grow \,ō-vər-'grō\ *vt* **1 :** to grow over so as to cover with herbage **2 :** to grow beyond or rise above **:** OUTGROW ~ *vi* **1 :** to grow excessively **2 :** to become grown over — **over·growth** \'ō-vər-,grōth\ *n*
1over·hand \'ō-vər-,hand\ *adj* **1 :** made with the hand brought down from above **2 :** played with the hand downward or inward toward the body — **overhand** *adv* — **over·hand·ed** \,ō-vər-'han-dəd\ *adv*
2overhand \'ō-vər-,hand\ *n* **:** an overhand stroke (as in tennis)
3overhand \'ō-vər-,\ *vt* **:** to sew with short vertical stitches
overhand knot \,ō-vər-,han(d)-\ *n* **:** a small knot often used to prevent the end of a cord from fraying
1over·hang \'ō-vər-,haŋ, ,ō-vər-'\ *vt* **1 :** to project over **2 :** to impend over **:** THREATEN ~ *vi* **:** to project so as to be over something
2overhang \'ō-vər-,\ *n* **1 :** something that overhangs; *also* **:** the extent of the overhanging **2 :** the part of the bow or stern of a ship that projects over the water above the waterline **3 :** a projection of the roof or upper story of a building beyond the wall of the lower part
over·haul \,ō-vər-'hȯl\ *vt* **1 :** to haul or drag over **2 a :** to examine thoroughly **b :** REPAIR **3 :** OVERTAKE — used esp. of a ship — **overhaul** \'ō-vər-,\ *n*
1over·head \,ō-vər-'hed\ *adv* **:** above one's head **:** ALOFT
2overhead \'ō-vər-,\ *adj* **1 :** operating or lying above **2 :** of or relating to overhead expense
3overhead \'ō-vər-,\ *n* **1 :** business expenses not chargeable to a particular part of the work or product **2 :** CEILING; *esp* **:** the ceiling of a ship's compartment **3 :** a stroke in a racket game made above head height **:** SMASH
over·hear \,ō-vər-'hi(ə)r\ *vb* **:** to hear without the speaker's knowledge or intention
over·heat \-'hēt\ *vt* **1 :** to heat to excess **2 :** to agitate unduly ~ *vi* **:** to become overheated
over·in·dulge \,ō-və-rin-'dəlj\ *vb* **:** to indulge to excess — **over·in·dul·gence** \-'dəl-jən(t)s\ *n* — **over·in·dul·gent** \-jənt\ *adj*
over·is·sue \,ō-və-'rish-(,)ü, -'rish-ü\ *n* **:** an issue exceeding the limit of capital, credit, or authority — **overissue** *vt*
over·joy \,ō-vər-'jȯi\ *vt* **:** to fill with great joy
over·kill \,ō-vər-'kil\ *vt* **:** to obliterate (a target) with more nuclear force than required — **over·kill** \'ō-vər-,\ *n*
over·land \'ō-vər-,land, -lənd\ *adv* (*or adj*) **:** by, upon, or across land
over·lap \,ō-vər-'lap\ *vt* **1 :** to extend over and cover a part of **2 :** to have something in common with ~ *vi* **1 :** to lap over **2 :** to have something in common — **overlap** \'ō-vər-,\ *n*
1over·lay \,ō-vər-'lā\ *vt* **1 a :** to lay or spread over or across **:** SUPERIMPOSE **b :** to prepare an overlay for **2 :** OVERLIE 2
2overlay \'ō-vər-,\ *n* **:** a covering either permanent or temporary: as **a :** an ornamental veneer **b :** paper patches added to the packing on a printing press to make a stronger impression **c :** a decorative and contrasting design or article placed on top of a plain one **d :** a transparent sheet containing graphic matter to be superimposed on another sheet
over·leap \,ō-vər-'lēp\ *vt* **1 :** to leap over or across **2 :** to defeat (oneself) by going too far
over·lie \-'lī\ *vt* **1 :** to lie over or upon **2 :** to cause the death of by lying upon
over·load \-'lōd\ *vt* **:** to load to excess — **overload** \'ō-vər-,\ *n*
over·long \,ō-vər-'lȯŋ\ *adj* (*or adv*) **:** too long
over·look \-'lu̇k\ *vt* **1 :** to look over **:** INSPECT **2 a :** to look down upon from above **b :** to rise above or afford a view of **3 a :** to look past **:** MISS **b :** to pass over **:** IGNORE **c :** EXCUSE **4 :** to watch over **:** SUPERVISE **5 :** to look on with the evil eye **:** BEWITCH **syn** see NEGLECT
over·lord \'ō-vər-,lȯ(ə)rd\ *n* **1 :** a lord who is lord over other lords **:** a lord paramount **2 :** an absolute or supreme ruler — **over·lord·ship** \-,ship, ,ō-vər-'\ *n*
over·ly \'ō-vər-lē\ *adv* **:** EXCESSIVELY
1over·man \-mən, -,man\ *n* **:** a man in authority over others; *specif* **:** FOREMAN
2over·man \,ō-vər-'man\ *vt* **:** to have or get too many men for the needs of ⟨~ a ship⟩
over·mas·ter \-'mas-tər\ *vt* **:** OVERPOWER, SUBDUE
over·match \-'mach\ *vt* **1 :** to be more than a match for **:** DEFEAT **2 :** to match with a superior opponent
1over·much \-'məch\ *adj* (*or adv*) **:** too much
2overmuch \'ō-vər-,, ,ō-vər-'\ *n* **:** too great an amount **:** EXCESS
1over·night \,ō-vər-'nīt\ *adv* **1 :** on or during the evening or night ⟨stayed away ~⟩ **2 :** SUDDENLY ⟨became famous ~⟩
2overnight *adj* **:** of or lasting the night
1over·pass \,ō-vər-'pas\ *vt* **1 :** to pass across, over, or beyond **:** CROSS; *also* **:** SURPASS **2 :** TRANSGRESS **3 :** DISREGARD, IGNORE
2overpass \'ō-vər-,\ *n* **:** a crossing of two highways or of a highway and pedestrian path or railroad at different levels where clearance to traffic on the lower level is obtained by elevating the higher level; *also* **:** the upper level of such a crossing
over·per·suade \,ō-vər-pər-'swād\ *vt* **:** to persuade to act contrary to one's conviction or preference — **over·per·sua·sion** \-'swā-zhən\ *n*
over·play \,ō-vər-'plā\ *vt* **1 a :** to present (as a dramatic role) extravagantly **:** EXAGGERATE **b :** OVEREMPHASIZE **2 :** to rely too much upon the strength of **3 :** to strike a golf ball beyond (a putting green)
over·plus \'ō-vər-,pləs\ *n* [ME, part trans. of MF *surplus*] **:** SURPLUS
over·pow·er \,ō-vər-'pau̇(-ə)r\ *vt* **1 :** to overcome by superior force **:** DEFEAT **2 :** OVERWHELM — **over·pow·er·ing·ly** \-'pau̇r-iŋ-lē\ *adv*
over·praise \-'prāz\ *vt* **:** to praise excessively
over·price \-'prīs\ *vt* **:** to price too high
1over·print \-'print\ *vt* **:** to print over with something additional
2overprint \'ō-vər-,\ *n* **:** something added by overprinting; *specif* **:** a printed marking added to a postage or revenue stamp esp. to alter the original or to commemorate a special event
over·prize \,ō-vər-'prīz\ *vt* **:** to prize excessively
over·pro·duce \-prə-'d(y)üs\ *vt* **:** to produce beyond demand or allotment — **over·pro·duc·tion** \-prə-'dək-shən\ *n*

over·proof \\,ō-vər-'prüf\\ *adj* **:** containing more alcohol than proof spirit

over·pro·por·tion \\-p(r)ə-'pōr-shən, -'pȯr-\\ *vt* **:** to make disproportionately large — **overproportion** *n* — **over·pro·por·tion·ate** \\-sh(ə-)nət\\ *adj* — **over·pro·por·tion·ate·ly** *adv*

over·pro·tect \\,ō-vər-prə-'tekt\\ *vt* **:** to protect unduly — **over·pro·tec·tion** \\-'tek-shən\\ *n* — **over·pro·tec·tive** \\-'tek-tiv\\ *adj*

over·rate \\,ō-və(r)-'rāt\\ *vt* **:** to rate too highly

over·reach \\-'rēch\\ *vt* **1 :** to reach above or beyond **:** OVERTOP **2 :** to defeat (oneself) by seeking to do or gain too much **3 :** OUTWIT, TRICK ~ *vi* **1** *of a horse* **:** to strike the toe of the hind foot against the heel or quarter of the forefoot **2 a :** to go to excess **b :** EXAGGERATE **syn** see CHEAT — **over·reach·er** *n*

over·re·fine·ment \\-ri-'fīn-mənt\\ *n* **:** excessive refinement

1**over·ride** \\,ō-və(r)-'rīd\\ *vt* **1 :** to ride over or across **:** TRAMPLE **2 :** to ride (as a horse) too much or too hard **3 a :** to prevail over **:** DOMINATE **b :** to set aside **:** ANNUL **4 :** to extend or pass over; *esp* **:** OVERLAP

2**override** \\'ō-və(r)-,rīd\\ *n* **:** a commission paid to a sales manager on sales made by his salesmen

over·ripe \\,ō-və(r)-'rīp\\ *adj* **1 :** passed beyond maturity or ripeness toward decay **2 :** DECADENT

over·rule \\-'rül\\ *vt* **1 :** to rule over **:** GOVERN **2 :** to prevail over **:** OVERCOME **3 a :** to rule against **b :** to set aside **:** REVERSE

1**over·run** \\-'rən\\ *vt* **1 a :** to defeat decisively and occupy the positions of **b :** to swarm over **:** INFEST **2 a :** to run past **b :** EXCEED **c** (1) **:** to readjust (set type) by shifting letters or words from one line into another (2) **:** OVERSET **3 :** to flow over

2**overrun** \\'ō-və(r)-,rən\\ *n* **:** an act or instance of overrunning; *also* **:** the amount by which something overruns

over·sea \\,o-vər-'sē, 'ō-vər-,\\ *adj (or adv)* **:** OVERSEAS

over·seas \\-'sēz, -,sēz\\ *adv* **:** beyond or across the sea **:** ABROAD — **overseas** *adj*

over·see \\,ō-vər-'sē\\ *vt* **1 :** SURVEY, WATCH **2 a :** INSPECT, EXAMINE **b :** SUPERINTEND, SUPERVISE

over·seer \\'ō-və(r)-,si(ə)r, -,sē-ər, ,ō-və(r)-'\\ *n* **:** SUPERINTENDENT, SUPERVISOR

over·sell \\,ō-vər-'sel\\ *vt* **1 a :** to sell too much to **b :** to sell too much of **2 :** to make excessive claims for **:** OVERPRAISE

over·sen·si·tive \\-'sen(t)-sət-iv, -stiv\\ *adj* **:** unduly or extremely sensitive — **over·sen·si·tive·ness** *n*

over·set \\-'set\\ *vt* **1 :** to adorn with settings **2 :** to disturb mentally or physically **:** UPSET **3 :** to turn or tip over **:** OVERTURN **4 :** OVERTHROW **5 :** to set too much type matter for — **overset** \\'ō-vər-,\\ *n*

over·sexed \\,ō-vər-'sekst\\ *adj* **:** exhibiting an excessive sexual drive or interest

over·shad·ow \\-'shad-(,)ō, -ə(-w)\\ *vt* **1 :** to cast a shadow over **:** DARKEN **2 :** to exceed in importance **:** OUTWEIGH

over·shoe \\'ō-vər-,shü\\ *n* **:** an outer shoe; *esp* **:** GALOSH

over·shoot \\,ō-vər-'shüt\\ *vt* **1 :** to pass swiftly beyond **2 :** to shoot over or beyond so as to miss **3 :** to excel in shooting

1**over·shot** \\'ō-vər-,shät\\ *adj* **1 :** having the upper jaw extending beyond the lower **2 :** actuated by the weight of water passing over and flowing from above ⟨an ~ waterwheel⟩

2**overshot** *n* **:** a pattern or weave featuring filling floats which pass two or more warp yarns before reentering the fabric

over·sight \\-,sīt\\ *n* **1 :** MANAGEMENT, SUPERVISION **2 :** an inadvertent omission or error

over·sim·pli·fi·ca·tion \\,ō-vər-,sim-plə-fə-'kā-shən\\ *n* **1 :** the act or an instance of oversimplifying **2 :** something that oversimplifies

over·sim·pli·fy \\-'sim-plə-,fī\\ *vt* **:** to simplify to such an extent as to bring about distortion, misunderstanding, or error ~ *vi* **:** to engage in undue or extreme simplification

over·size \\,ō-vər-'sīz\\ *or* **over·sized** \\-'sīzd\\ *adj* **:** being of more than ordinary size

over·skirt \\'ō-vər-,skərt\\ *n* **:** a skirt worn over another skirt

over·slaugh \\,ō-vər-'slȯ\\ *vt* [D *overslaan* to pass over, omit] **:** to pass over for appointment or promotion in favor of another

over·sleep \\,ō-vər-'slēp\\ *vi* **:** to sleep beyond the time for waking

overslip *vt* **1** *obs* **:** OMIT **2** *obs* **:** ESCAPE

over·soul \\'ō-vər-,sōl\\ *n* **:** the absolute reality and ground of existences conceived as a spiritual being in which the ideal nature manifested in human beings is perfectly realized

over·spend \\,ō-vər-'spend\\ *vt* **1 :** to spend or use to excess **:** EXHAUST **2 :** to exceed in expenditure ~ *vi* **:** to spend beyond one's means

over·spread \\-'spred\\ *vt* **:** to spread over or above — **overspread** \\'ō-vər-,\\ *n*

over·state \\,ō-vər-'stāt\\ *vt* **:** to state in too strong terms **:** EXAGGERATE — **over·state·ment** \\-mənt\\ *n*

over·stay \\,ō-vər-'stā\\ *vt* **1 :** to stay beyond the time or the limits of ⟨~*ed* his leave⟩ **2 :** to carry a transaction in (a market) beyond the point at which the greatest profit is possible ⟨~*ed* his market⟩

over·step \\-'step\\ *vt* **:** EXCEED, TRANSGRESS

over·stock \\-'stäk\\ *vb* **:** to stock beyond requirements or facilities

over·strew \\-'strü\\ *vt* **1 :** to strew or scatter about **2 :** to cover here and there

over·stride \\-'strīd\\ *vt* **1 a :** to stride over, across, or beyond **b :** BESTRIDE **2 :** to stride faster than or beyond

over·strung \\,ō-vər-'strəŋ\\ *adj* **:** too highly strung **:** too sensitive

over·stuff \\-'stəf\\ *vt* **1 :** to stuff too full **2 :** to cover (as a chair or sofa) completely and deeply with upholstery

over·sub·scribe \\-səb-'skrīb\\ *vt* **:** to subscribe for more of than is offered for sale — **over·sub·scrip·tion** \\-'skrip-shən\\ *n*

over·sub·tle \\-'sət-ᵊl\\ *adj* **:** excessively or impracticably subtle

over·sup·ply \\-sə-'plī\\ *n* **:** an excessive supply — **oversupply** *vt*

overt \\ō-'vərt, 'ō-(,)\\ *adj* [ME, fr. MF *ouvert, overt*, fr. pp. of *ouvrir* to open, fr. (assumed) VL *operire*, alter. of L *aperire* — more at WEIR] **:** open to view **:** MANIFEST — **overt·ly** *adv*

over·take \\,ō-vər-'tāk\\ *vt* [ME *overtaken*, fr. 1*over* + *taken* to take] **1 a :** to catch up with **b :** to catch up with and pass by **2 :** to come upon suddenly **:** SEIZE

over·tax \\-'taks\\ *vt* **1 :** to tax too heavily **2 :** to put too great a burden or strain on

over–the–count·er \\,ō-vər-thə-'kaunt-ər\\ *adj* **1 :** sold otherwise than on an organized securities exchange **:** UNLISTED **2 :** sold lawfully without prescription

over·throw \\,ō-vər-'thrō\\ *vt* **1 :** OVERTURN, UPSET **2 :** to bring down **:** DEFEAT **3 :** to throw a baseball over or past (as a base) **syn** see CONQUER — **overthrow** \\'ō-vər-,\\ *n*

over·time \\'ō-vər-,tīm\\ *n, often attrib* **1 :** time in excess of a set limit; *esp* **:** working time in excess of a standard day or week **2 :** the wage paid for overtime — **overtime** *adv*

over·tone \\-,tōn\\ *n* **1 :** one of the higher tones that with the fundamental comprise a complex musical tone **:** HARMONIC 1a **2 :** the color of the light reflected (as by a paint) **3 :** a secondary effect, quality, or meaning **:** SUGGESTION

over·top \\,ō-vər-'täp\\ *vt* **1 :** to rise above the top of **2 :** to be superior to **3 :** SURPASS

over·trade \\-'trād\\ *vi* **:** to trade beyond one's capital

over·train \\-'trān\\ *vb* **:** to train more than is necessary or desirable

over·trick \\'ō-vər-,trik\\ *n* **:** a card trick won in excess of the number bid

over·trump \\,ō-vər-'trəmp\\ *vb* **:** to trump with a higher trump card than the highest previously played to the same trick

1**over·ture** \\'ō-və(r)-,chu̇(ə)r, -chər, -,t(y)u̇(ə)r\\ *n* [ME, lit., opening, fr. MF, fr. (assumed) VL *opertura*, alter. of L *apertura* — more at APERTURE] **1 a :** an initiative toward agreement or action **:** PROPOSAL **b :** something introductory **:** PRELUDE **2 :** the orchestral introduction to a musical dramatic work

2**overture** *vt* **1 :** to put forward as an overture **2 :** to make or present an overture to

over·turn \\,ō-vər-'tərn\\ *vt* **1 :** to cause to turn over **:** UPSET **2 :** OVERTHROW, DESTROY ~ *vi* **:** to turn over — **overturn** \\'ō-vər-,\\ *n*

over·use \\,ō-vər-'yüs\\ *n* **:** excessive use — **over·use** \\-'yüz\\ *vt*

over·watch \\-'wäch\\ *vt* **1** *archaic* **:** to weary or exhaust by keeping awake **2 :** to watch over

over·wear \\-'wa(ə)r, -'we(ə)r\\ *vt* **:** to wear out **:** EXHAUST

1**over·wea·ry** \\-'wi(ə)r-ē\\ *vt* **:** to tire out

2**overweary** *adj* **:** wearied to excess

over·ween·ing \\,ō-vər-'wē-niŋ\\ *adj* **1 :** ARROGANT, PRESUMPTUOUS **2 :** EXAGGERATED, IMMODERATE

over·weigh \\-'wā\\ *vt* **1 :** to exceed in weight **:** OVERBALANCE **2 :** to weigh down **:** OPPRESS

1**over·weight** \\'ō-vər-,wāt, *2 is usu* ,ō-vər-'\\ *n* **1 :** weight over and above what is required or allowed **2 :** excessive or burdensome weight — **overweight** \\,ō-vər-'\\ *adj*

2**overweight** \\,ō-vər-'wāt\\ *vt* **1 :** to give too much weight or consideration to **2 :** to weight excessively **3 :** to exceed in weight **:** OVERBALANCE

over·whelm \\-'hwelm, -'welm\\ *vt* [ME *overwhelmen*, fr. 1*over* + *whelmen* to turn over, cover up] **1 :** OVERTHROW, UPSET **2 a :** to cover over completely **:** SUBMERGE **b :** to overcome by superior force or numbers **:** CRUSH — **over·whelm·ing·ly** \\-'hwel-miŋ-lē, -'wel-\\ *adv*

over·wind \\-'wīnd\\ *vt* **:** to wind too much

over·win·ter \\-'wint-ər\\ *vi* **:** to survive the winter

over·word \\'ō-vər-,wərd\\ *n* **:** BURDEN, REFRAIN

over·work \\,ō-vər-'wərk\\ *vt* **1 :** to cause to work too hard, too long, or to exhaustion **2 :** to decorate all over **3 a :** to work too much on **:** OVERDO **b :** to make excessive use of ~ *vi* **:** to work too much or too long **:** OVERDO — **overwork** *n*

over·write \\,ō-və(r)-'rīt\\ *vt* **1 :** to write over the surface of **2 :** to write in inflated or pretentious style ~ *vi* **:** to write too much

over·wrought \\-'rȯt\\ *adj* [pp. of *overwork*] **1 :** extremely excited **:** AGITATED **2 :** elaborated to excess **:** OVERDONE

ovi- *or* **ovo-** — see OV-

ovi·ci·dal \\,ō-və-'sīd-ᵊl\\ *adj* **:** capable of killing eggs — **ovi·cide** \\'ō-və-,sīd\\ *n*

ovi·duct \\'ō-və-,dəkt\\ *n* [NL *oviductus*, fr. *ov-* + *ductus* duct] **:** a tube that serves exclusively or esp. for the passage of eggs from an ovary — **ovi·duc·tal** \\,ō-və-'dək-tᵊl\\ *adj*

ovine \\'ō-,vīn\\ *adj* [LL *ovinus*, fr. L *ovis* sheep — more at EWE] **:** of or relating to sheep — **ovine** *n*

ovip·a·rous \\ō-'vip-(ə-)rəs\\ *adj* [L *oviparus*, fr. *ov-* + *-parus* -parous] **:** producing eggs that develop and hatch outside the maternal body; *also* **:** involving the production of such eggs — **ovip·a·rous·ly** *adv* — **ovip·a·rous·ness** *n*

ovi·pos·it \\'ō-və-,päz-ət, ,ō-və-'\\ *vi* [prob. back-formation fr. *ovipositor*] **:** to lay eggs — used esp. of insects — **ovi·po·si·tion** \\,ō-və-pə-'zish-ən\\ *n*

ovi·pos·i·tor \\'ō-və-,päz-ət-ər, -,päz-tər, ,ō-və-'\\ *n* [NL, fr. L *ov-* + *positor* one that places, fr. *positus*, pp. of *ponere* to place — more at POSITION] **:** a specialized organ (as of an insect) for depositing eggs

ovoid \\'ō-,vȯid\\ *or* **ovoi·dal** \\ō-'vȯid-ᵊl\\ *adj* [F *ovoïde*, fr. L *ovum* egg — more at EGG] **:** shaped like an egg **:** OVATE — **ovoid** *n*

ovo·lo \\'ō-və-,lō\\ *n, pl* **ovo·li** \\-,lē\\ [It, dim. of *uovo*, *ovo* egg, fr. L *ovum*] **:** a rounded convex molding

ovo·tes·tis \\,ō-vō-'tes-təs\\ *n* [NL] **:** a hermaphrodite gonad

ovo·vi·vip·a·rous \\,ō-(,)vō-,vī-'vip-(ə-)rəs\\ *adj* [prob. fr. (assumed) NL *ovoviviparus*, fr. L *ov-* + *viviparus* viviparous] **:** producing eggs that develop within the maternal body and hatch within or immediately after extrusion from the parent — **ovo·vi·vip·a·rous·ly** *adv* — **ovo·vi·vip·a·rous·ness** *n*

ovu·lar \\'äv-yə-lər, 'ōv-\\ *adj* **:** relating to or being an ovule

ovu·late \\'äv-yə-,lāt, 'ōv-\\ *vi* **:** to produce eggs or discharge them from an ovary — **ovu·la·tion** \\,äv-yə-'lā-shən, ,ōv-\\ *n*

ovule \\'ō-(,)vyü(ə)l\\ *n* [NL *ovulum*, dim. of L *ovum*] **1 :** an outgrowth of the ovary of a seed plant that is a megasporangium and encloses an embryo sac within a nucellus **2 :** a small egg; *esp* **:** one in an early stage of growth

ovum \\'ō-vəm, 'ōv-ᵊm\\ *n, pl* **ova** \\'ō-və\\ [NL, fr. L, egg — more at EGG] **:** a female gamete **:** MACROGAMETE

owe \\'ō\\ *vb* [ME *owen* to possess, own, owe, fr. OE *āgan;* akin to OHG *eigun* (1st & 3d pl. pres. indic.) possess, Skt *īśe* he possesses] *vt* **1 a** *archaic* **:** POSSESS, OWN **b :** to have or bear (an emotion or attitude) to someone or something ⟨~*s* the boss a grudge⟩ **2 a** (1) **:** to be under obligation to pay or repay in return for something received **:** be indebted in the sum of ⟨~*s* me five dollars⟩ (2) **:** to be under obligation to render (as duty or service) **b :** to be indebted to ⟨~*s* the grocer for supplies⟩ **3 :** to be indebted for ⟨*owed* his wealth to his father⟩ ~ *vi* **:** to be in debt ⟨~*s* for his house⟩

owing to *prep* **:** because of ⟨delayed *owing to* a crash⟩

owl \\'au̇(ə)l\\ *n* [ME *owle*, fr. OE *ūle;* akin to OHG *uwila* owl] **:** any of an order (Strigiformes) of birds of prey with large head

and eyes, short hooked bill, strong talons, and more or less nocturnal habits

owl·et \'aů-lət\ *n* : a small or young owl

owl·ish \'aů-lish\ *adj* : resembling or suggesting an owl — **owl·ish·ly** *adv* — **owl·ish·ness** *n*

¹own \'ōn\ *adj* [ME *owen*, fr. OE *āgen*; akin to OHG *eigan* own, ON *eiginn*, OE *āgan* to possess — more at OWE] : belonging to oneself or itself — usu. used following a possessive case or pronoun

²own *vt* **1** : to have or hold as property : POSSESS **2** : ACKNOWLEDGE, ADMIT ⟨~ a debt⟩ ~ *vi* : ADMIT, CONFESS — used with *to* or *up* **syn** see ACKNOWLEDGE, HAVE — **own·er** \'ō-nər\ *n* — **own·er·ship** \-,ship\ *n*

³own *pron, sing or pl in constr* : one or ones belonging to oneself — used after a possessive and without a following noun as a pronoun equivalent in meaning to the adjective *own*

ox \'äks\ *n, pl* **ox·en** \'äk-sən\ *also* **ox** [ME, fr. OE *oxa*; akin to OHG *ohso* ox, Gk *hygros* wet — more at HUMOR] **1** : the domestic bovine mammal (*Bos taurus*); *esp* : an adult castrated male **2** : a bovine mammal

ox- *or* **oxo-** *comb form* [F, fr. *oxygène*] : oxygen ⟨*oxa*zine⟩

ox·a·late \'äk-sə-,lāt\ *n* : a salt or ester of oxalic acid

ox·al·ic acid \(,)äk-,sal-ik-\ *n* [F (*acide*) *oxalique*, fr. L *oxalis* wood sorrel] : a poisonous strong acid $(COOH)_2$ or $H_2C_2O_4$ that occurs in various plants as oxalates and is used esp. as a bleaching or cleaning agent and in making dyes

ox·al·is \äk-'sal-əs\ *n* [NL, genus name, fr. L, wood sorrel, fr. Gk, fr. *oxys* sharp — more at OXYGEN] : WOOD SORREL 1

ox·a·zine \'äk-sə-,zēn\ *n* [ISV *ox-* + *azine*] : any of several parent compounds C_4H_5NO containing a ring composed of four carbon atoms, one oxygen atom, and one nitrogen atom

ox·blood \'äks-,bləd\ *n* : a moderate reddish brown

ox·bow \'äks-,bō\ *n* **1** : a U-shaped frame forming a collar about an ox's neck and supporting the yoke **2** : something (as a bend in a river) resembling an oxbow — **oxbow** *adj*

ox·eye \'äk-,sī\ *n* : any of several composite plants having heads with both disk and ray flowers

ox·ford \'äks-fərd\ *n* [*Oxford*, England] : a low shoe laced or tied over the instep

Oxford down *n, often cap D* [*Oxford*shire, county of England] : any of a Down breed of large hornless sheep developed by crossing Cotswolds and Hampshire Downs

Oxford movement *n* [*Oxford*, England] : a High Church movement within the Church of England begun at Oxford in 1833

ox·heart \'äks-,härt\ *n* : any of various large sweet cherries

ox·i·dant \'äk-səd-ənt\ *n* : an oxidizing agent

ox·i·dase \'äk-sə-,dās, -,dāz\ *n* [ISV] : any of various enzymes that catalyze oxidations; *esp* : one able to react directly with molecular oxygen — **ox·i·da·sic** \,äk-sə-'dā-sik, -zik\ *adj*

ox·i·da·tion \,äk-sə-'dā-shən\ *n* [F, fr. *oxider*, *oxyder* to oxidize, fr. *oxide*] **1** : the act or process of oxidizing **2** : the state or result of being oxidized — **ox·i·da·tive** \'äk-sə-,dāt-iv\ *adj* — **ox·i·da·tive·ly** *adv*

oxidation–reduction *n* : a chemical reaction in which one or more electrons are transferred from one atom or molecule to another

ox·ide \'äk-,sīd\ *n* [F *oxide*, *oxyde*, fr. *ox-* (fr. *oxygène* oxygen) + *-ide* (fr. *acide* acid)] : a binary compound of oxygen with an element or radical — **ox·id·ic** \äk-'sid-ik\ *adj*

ox·i·diz·able \'äk-sə-,dī-zə-bəl\ *adj* : capable of being oxidized

ox·i·dize \-,dīz\ *vb* [*oxide* + *-ize*] *vt* **1** : to combine with oxygen **2** : to dehydrogenate esp. by the action of oxygen **3** : to change (a compound) by increasing the proportion of the electronegative part or change (an element or ion) from a lower to a higher positive valence : remove one or more electrons from (an atom, ion, or molecule) ~ *vi* : to become oxidized — **ox·i·diz·er** *n*

ox·ime \'äk-,sēm\ *n* [ISV *ox-* + *-ime* (fr. *imide*)] : any of various compounds obtained chiefly by the action of hydroxylamine on aldehydes and ketones and characterized by the grouping $>C=NOH$

ox·lip \'äk-,slip\ *n* [(assumed) ME *oxeslippe*, fr. OE *oxanslyppe*; lit., ox dung, fr. *oxa* ox + *slypa*, *slyppe* paste — more at SLIP] **1** : a hybrid primrose **2** : a Eurasian primula (*Primula elatior*) differing from the cowslip chiefly in the flat corolla limb

Ox·o·ni·an \äk-'sō-nē-ən\ *n* [ML *Oxonia* Oxford] **1** : a native or resident of Oxford, England **2** : a student or graduate of Oxford University — **Oxonian** *adj*

ox·tail \'äk-,stāl\ *n* : the tail of cattle; *esp* : the skinned tail used for soup

ox·ter \'äk-stər\ *n* [(assumed) ME, alter. of OE *ōxta*; akin to L *axilla* armpit — more at AXIS] **1** *chiefly Scot & Irish* : ARMPIT **2** *chiefly Scot & Irish* : ARM

ox·tongue \'äk-,stəŋ\ *n* : any of several plants (as a bugloss) having rough tongue-shaped leaves

oxy- *comb form* [F, fr. *oxygène* oxygen] **1** : oxygen : containing oxygen or additional oxygen ⟨*oxy*hemoglobin⟩ **2** : of oxygen and ⟨*oxy*hydrogen⟩ — **oxy** *adj*

oxy·acet·y·lene \,äk-sē-ə-'set-ᵊl-ən, -ᵊl-,ēn\ *adj* [ISV] : of, relating to, or utilizing a mixture of oxygen and acetylene ⟨~ torch⟩

oxy·cal·ci·um \,äk-si-'kal-sē-əm\ *adj* : of or relating to oxygen and calcium ⟨the ~ light or limelight⟩

ox·y·gen \'äk-si-jən\ *n, often attrib* [F *oxygène*, fr. Gk *oxys*, adj., acid, lit., sharp + F *-gène* -gen; akin to L *acer* sharp — more at EDGE] : an element that is found free as a colorless tasteless odorless gas in the atmosphere of which it forms about 21 percent or combined in water, in most rocks and minerals, and in numerous organic compounds, that is capable of combining with all elements except the inert gases, is active in physiological processes, and is involved esp. in combustion processes — see ELEMENT table —

ox·y·gen·ic \,äk-si-'jen-ik\ *adj* — **ox·y·gen·ic·i·ty** \-jə-'nis-ət-ē\ *n*

oxygen acid *n* : an acid (as sulfuric acid) containing oxygen

ox·y·gen·ate \'äk-si-jə-,nāt, äk-'sij-ə-\ *vt* : to impregnate, combine, or supply with oxygen — **ox·y·gen·ation** \,äk-si-jə-'nā-shən, (,)äk-,sij-ə-\ *n*

oxygen debt *n* : a cumulative oxygen deficit that develops during periods of intense bodily activity and must be made good when the body returns to rest

oxygen mask *n* : a device worn over the nose and mouth (as by airmen at high altitudes) through which oxygen is supplied from a storage tank

oxygen tent *n* : a canopy which can be placed over a bedridden person and within which a flow of oxygen can be maintained

oxy·he·mo·glo·bin \,äk-si-'hē-mə-,glō-bən, -'hem-ə-, -,hē-mə-', -,hem-ə-'\ *n* [ISV] : hemoglobin loosely combined with oxygen that it releases to the tissues

oxy·hy·dro·gen \-'hī-drə-jən\ *adj* : of, relating to, or utilizing a mixture of oxygen and hydrogen ⟨~ torch⟩

oxy·mo·ron \,äk-si-'mō(ə)r-,än, -'mò(ə)r-\ *n, pl* **oxy·mo·ra** \-'mōr-ə, -'mòr-\ [LGk *oxymōron*, fr. neut. of *oxymōros* pointedly foolish, fr. Gk *oxys* sharp, keen + *mōros* foolish — more at MORON] : a combination of contradictory or incongruous words (as *cruel kindness*)

oxy·phile \'äk-si-,fīl\ *or* **oxy·phil** \-,fil\ *or* **oxy·phil·ic** \,äk-si-'fil-ik\ *or* **ox·yph·i·lous** \äk-'sif-ə-ləs\ *adj* [Gk *oxys* acid + E *-phil*, *-philic*, *-philous*] : ACIDOPHILIC — **oxyphile** *n*

oxy·sul·fide \,äk-si-'səl-,fīd\ *n* [ISV] : a compound of oxygen and sulfur with an element or radical that may be regarded as a sulfide in which part of the sulfur is replaced by oxygen

oxy·tet·ra·cy·cline \-,te-trə-'sī-,klēn\ *n* : a yellow crystalline broad-spectrum antibiotic $C_{22}H_{24}N_2O_9$ produced by a soil actinomycete (*Streptomyces rimosus*)

oxy·to·cic \,äk-si-'tō-sik\ *adj* [ISV, fr. Gk *oxys* sharp, quick + *tokos* childbirth, fr. *tiktein* to bear — more at THANE] : hastening parturition; *also* : inducing contraction of uterine smooth muscle — **oxytocic** *n*

oxy·to·cin \-'tōs-ᵊn\ *n* [ISV, fr. *oxytocic*] : a postpituitary hormone $C_{43}H_{66}N_{12}O_{12}S_2$ that stimulates esp. the contraction of uterine muscle and the ejection of milk

oxy·tone \'äk-si-,tōn\ *adj* [F *oxyton*, fr. Gk *oxytonos*, fr. *oxys* sharp, acute in pitch + *tonos* tone] : having an acute accent on the last syllable — **oxytone** *n*

oxy·uri·a·sis \,äk-si-yù-'rī-ə-səs\ *n* [NL, fr. *Oxyuris*, genus of worms + *-iasis*] : infestation with or disease caused by pinworms (family Oxyuridae)

oyer and ter·mi·ner \,òi-(ə)-rən-'tər-mə-nər\ *n* [ME, part trans. of AF *oyer et terminer*, lit., to hear and determine] **1** : a commission authorizing a British judge to hear and determine a criminal case at the assizes **2** : a high criminal court in some U.S. states

oyez \ō-'yā, -'yes, -'yez\ *v imper* [ME, fr. AF, hear ye, imper. pl. of *oir* to hear, fr. L *audire* — more at AUDIBLE] — used by a court or public crier to gain attention before a proclamation — **oyez** *n, pl* **oyesses** \-'yāz, -'yes-əz, -'yez-əz\

oys·ter \'òi-stər\ *n, often attrib* [ME, *oistre*, fr. MF, fr. L *ostrea*, fr. Gk *ostreon*; akin to Gk *ostrakon* shell, *osteon* bone — more at OSSEOUS] **1 a** : any of various marine bivalve mollusks (family Ostreidae) having a rough irregular shell closed by a single adductor muscle and including important shellfish **b** : any of various mollusks resembling or related to the oysters **2** : a small mass of muscle contained in a concavity of the pelvic bone on each side of the back of a fowl **3** : an extremely taciturn person

oyster bed *n* : a place where oysters grow or are cultivated

oyster catcher *n* : any of a genus (*Haematopus*) of wading birds with stout legs and heavy wedge-shaped bill and often black and white plumage

oyster crab *n* : a crab (*Pinnotheres ostreum*) that lives as a commensal in the gill cavity of the oyster

oyster cracker *n* : a small salted cracker

oys·ter·man \-mən\ *n* : a gatherer, opener, breeder, or seller of oysters

oyster plant *n* : SALSIFY

ozo·ke·rite \,ō-zō-'ki(ə)r-,īt\ *or* **ozo·ce·rite** \-'si(ə)r-\ *n* [G *ozokerit*, fr. Gk *ozein* to smell + *kēros* wax — more at CERUMEN] : a waxy mineral mixture of hydrocarbons that is colorless or white when pure and often of unpleasant odor and is used esp. in making candles and in electrotyping

ozon- *or* **ozono-** *comb form* [ISV, fr. *ozone*] : ozone ⟨*ozon*ize⟩

ozone \'ō-,zōn\ *n* [G *ozon*, fr. Gk *ozōn*, prp. of *ozein* to smell — more at ODOR] **1** : an allotropic triatomic form of oxygen that is normally a faintly blue irritating gas with a characteristic pungent odor, is generated usu. in dilute form by a silent electric discharge in ordinary oxygen or air, and is used esp. in disinfection and deodorization and in oxidation and bleaching **2** : pure and refreshing air — **ozo·nic** \ō-'zō-nik, -'zän-ik\ *adj* — **ozo·nif·er·ous** \,ō-(,)zō-'nif-(ə-)rəs\ *adj* — **ozon·ous** \'ō-,zō-nəs, ō-'\ *adj*

ozon·ide \'ō-(,)zō-,nīd\ *n* : a compound of ozone

ozon·ize \-,nīz\ *vt* **1** : to convert (oxygen) into ozone **2** : to treat, impregnate, or combine with ozone ~ *vi* : to become converted into ozone — **ozon·iz·er** *n*

ozo·no·sphere \ō-'zō-nə-,sfi(ə)r\ *n* : an atmospheric layer at heights of approximately 20 to 30 miles characterized by high ozone content

p \'pē\ *n, often cap, often attrib* **1 a :** the 16th letter of the English alphabet **b :** a graphic representation of this letter **c :** a speech counterpart of orthographic *p* **2 :** a graphic device for reproducing the letter *p* **3 :** one designated *p* esp. as the 15th or when j is used for the 10th the 16th in order or class **4 :** something shaped like the letter P

pa \'pä, 'pȯ\ *n* [short for *papa*] **:** FATHER

PABA \'pab-ə, ˌpē-ˌā-'bē-ˌā\ *n* [*para-amino-benzoic acid*] **:** PARA-AMINOBENZOIC ACID

pab·u·lum \'pab-yə-ləm\ *n* [L, food, fodder; akin to L *pascere* to feed — more at FOOD] **1 :** FOOD; *esp* **:** a suspension or solution of nutrients in a state suitable for absorption **2 :** intellectual sustenance **3 :** an insipid piece of writing

pa·ca \'päk-ə, 'pak-\ *n* [Pg & Sp, fr. Tupi *páca*] **:** any of a genus (*Cuniculus,* esp. *C. paca*) of large So. and Central American rodents

¹pace \'pās\ *n* [ME *pas,* fr. OF, step, fr. L *passus,* fr. *passus,* pp. of *pandere* to spread — more at FATHOM] **1 a :** rate of movement esp. on foot; *esp* **:** an established rate of locomotion **b :** rate of progress; *specif* **:** parallel rate of growth or development **c :** an example to be emulated; *specif* **:** first place in a competition **d** (1) **:** rate of performance or delivery **:** TEMPO (2) **:** rhythmic animation **:** FLUENCY **2 :** a manner of walking **:** TREAD **3 a :** STEP 2a(1) **b :** any of various units of distance based on the length of a human step **4 a :** an exhibition of skills or capacities **b :** GAIT; *esp* **:** a fast 2-beat gait (as of the horse) in which the legs move in lateral pairs and support the animal alternately on the right and left legs

²pace *vi* **1 a :** to walk with slow or measured tread **b :** to move along **:** PROCEED **2 :** to go at a pace — used esp. of a horse ~ *vt* **1 a :** to measure by pacing **b :** to cover at a walk **2** *of a horse* **:** to cover (a course) by pacing **3 a :** to set or regulate the pace of **b** (1) **:** to go before **:** PRECEDE (2) **:** LEAD **c :** to keep pace with

³pa·ce \'pā-sē\ *prep* [L, abl. of *pac-, pax* peace, permission] **:** with due respect to

pace·mak·er \'pā-ˌsmā-kər\ *n* **1 :** one that sets the pace for another — called also *pacesetter* **2 :** one that takes the lead or sets an example — **pace·mak·ing** \-kiŋ\ *n*

pac·er \'pā-sər\ *n* **1 :** one that paces; *specif* **:** a horse whose gait is the pace **2 :** PACEMAKER

pa·chi·si \pə-'chē-zē, *esp Brit* -sē\ *n* [Hindi *pacīsī*] **:** an ancient board game resembling backgammon

pa·chu·co \pə-'chü-(ˌ)kō\ *n* [MexSp] **:** a young usu. underprivileged Mexican-American affecting special clothes and jargon, usu. belonging to a neighborhood gang, and often identified by a small tattoo

pachy·derm \'pak-i-ˌdərm\ *n* [F *pachyderme,* fr. Gk *pachydermos* thick-skinned, fr. *pachys* thick + *derma* skin; akin to ON *bingr* heap, Skt *bahu* dense, much — more at DERM-] **:** any of various nonruminant hoofed mammals that mostly have a thick skin and include the elephant, rhinoceros, and pig — **pachy·der·mal** \ˌpak-i-'dər-məl\ *adj* — **pachy·der·moid** \-ˌmȯid\ *adj*

pachy·der·ma·tous \ˌpak-i-'dər-mət-əs\ *adj* [deriv. of Gk *pachys* + *dermat-, derma* skin] **1 :** of or relating to the pachyderms **2 a :** THICK, THICKENED ⟨~ skin⟩ **b :** CALLOUS, INSENSITIVE — **pachy·der·ma·tous·ly** *adv*

pach·ys·an·dra \ˌpak-ə-'san-drə\ *n* [NL, genus name, fr. Gk *pachys* + NL *-andrus* -androus] **:** any of a genus (*Pachysandra*) of the box family of evergreen woody trailing plants often used as a ground cover

pac·i·fi·able \'pas-ə-ˌfī-ə-bəl\ *adj* **:** capable of being pacified

pa·cif·ic \pə-'sif-ik\ *adj* [MF *pacifique,* fr. L *pacificus,* fr. *pac-, pax* peace + *-i-* + *-ficus* -fic — more at PEACE] **1 a :** tending to lessen conflict **:** CONCILIATORY **b :** rejecting use of force **:** PEACEFUL **2 a :** CALM, TRANQUIL **b :** mild of temper **:** PEACEABLE **3** *cap* **:** of or relating to the Pacific ocean — **pa·cif·i·cal·ly** \-i-k(ə-)lē\ *adv*

pac·i·fi·ca·tion \ˌpas-(ə-)fə-'kā-shən\ *n* **1 :** the act or process of pacifying **:** the state of being pacified **2 :** a treaty of peace

pa·cif·i·ca·tor \pə-'sif-ə-ˌkāt-ər\ *n* **:** PACIFIER 1

pa·cif·i·ca·to·ry \pə-'sif-i-kə-ˌtōr-ē, -ˌtȯr-\ *adj* **:** CONCILIATORY

pa·cif·i·cism \pə-'sif-ə-ˌsiz-əm\ *n* **:** PACIFISM — **pa·cif·i·cist** \-ə-səst\ *n*

Pacific time *n* [*Pacific* ocean] **:** the time of the 8th time zone west of Greenwich that includes the Pacific coastal region of the U.S.

pac·i·fi·er \'pas-ə-ˌfī(-ə)r\ *n* **1 :** one that pacifies **2 :** a usu. nipple-shaped device for babies to suck or bite upon

pac·i·fism \'pas-ə-ˌfiz-əm\ *n* [F *pacifisme,* fr. *pacifique* pacific] **1 :** opposition to war or violence as a means of settling disputes; *specif* **:** refusal to bear arms on moral or religious grounds **2 :** an attitude or policy of nonresistance **:** PASSIVISM — **pac·i·fist** \-fəst\ *n* — **pacifist** *or* **pac·i·fis·tic** \ˌpas-ə-'fis-tik\ *adj*

pac·i·fy \'pas-ə-ˌfī\ *vt* [ME *pacifien,* fr. L *pacificare,* fr. *pac-, pax* peace] **1 a :** to allay anger or agitation in **b :** APPEASE, PROPITIATE **2 a :** to restore to a tranquil state **:** SETTLE **b :** to reduce to a submissive state **:** SUBDUE

syn APPEASE, PLACATE, MOLLIFY, PROPITIATE, CONCILIATE: PACIFY suggests a soothing or calming of anger or agitation or the forceful quelling of insurrection; APPEASE implies quieting insistent demands by making concessions; PLACATE suggests changing resentment or bitterness to goodwill; MOLLIFY implies soothing hurt feelings or rising anger; PROPITIATE implies averting anger or malevolence esp. of a superior being; CONCILIATE suggests ending an estrangement by persuasion, concession, or settling of differences

¹pack \'pak\ *n, often attrib* [ME, of LG or D origin; akin to MLG & MD *pak* pack, MFlem *pac*] **1 a :** a bundle arranged for convenience in carrying esp. on the back **b :** a group or pile of related objects: as (1) **:** a number of separate photographic films packed so as to be inserted together into a camera (2) **:** a set of two or three color films or plates for simultaneous exposure (3) **:** a stack of theatrical flats arranged in sequence **c** (1) **:** PACKET (2) **:** CONTAINER (3) **:** a compact unitized assembly to perform a specific function **2 a :** the contents of a bundle **b :** a large amount or number **:** HEAP **c :** a full set of playing cards **3 a :** an act or instance of packing **b :** a method of packing **4 a** (1) **:** a group trained to hunt or run together (2) **:** a group of often predatory animals of the same kind (3) **:** a set of persons with a common interest **:** CLIQUE **b :** an organized group of combat craft **5 :** a concentrated mass **6 :** wet absorbent material for therapeutic application to the body **7 a :** a cosmetic paste for the face **b :** an application or treatment of oils or creams for conditioning the scalp and hair **8 :** material used as packing

²pack *vt* **1 a :** to make into a compact bundle **b :** to fill completely **c :** to fill with packing **d :** to load with a pack **e :** to put in a protective container **2 a :** to crowd together **b :** to increase the density of **:** COMPRESS **3 a :** to cause or command to go without ceremony ⟨*~ed* off to school⟩ **b :** to bring to an end **:** FINISH **4 :** to gather into a tight formation **5 :** to cover or surround with a pack **6 a :** to transport on foot or on the back of an animal **b :** to wear or carry as regular equipment ⟨~ a gun⟩ **c :** to be supplied or equipped with **:** POSSESS ~ *vi* **1 :** to go away without ceremony **2 a :** to stow goods and equipment for transportation **b :** to be suitable for packing **3 a :** to assemble in a group **:** CONGREGATE **b :** to crowd together **4 :** to increase in density **5 a :** to carry goods or equipment **b :** to travel with one's baggage (as by horse) — **pack·abil·i·ty** \ˌpak-ə-'bil-ət-ē\ *n* — **pack·able** \'pak-ə-bəl\ *adj*

³pack *vt* [obs. *pack* (to make a secret agreement)] **1 :** to bring together or make up fraudulently to secure a favorable vote ⟨~ a jury⟩ **2** *archaic* **:** to arrange (the cards in a pack) so as to cheat

⁴pack *n* [perh. fr. obs. *pack* (secret compact)] **:** an unjustified surcharge added to a price by a dealer

⁵pack *adj* [perh. fr. obs. *pack* (to make a secret agreement)] *chiefly Scot* **:** INTIMATE

¹pack·age \'pak-ij\ *n* **1** *archaic* **:** the act or process of packing **2 a :** a small or moderate-sized pack **:** PARCEL **b :** a commodity or a unit of a product uniformly wrapped or sealed **c :** a preassembled unit **3 :** a covering wrapper or container **4 :** something that resembles a package: as **a :** PACKAGE DEAL **b :** a radio or television series offered for sale at a lump sum **c :** contract benefits gained through collective bargaining

²package *vt* **1 :** to make into a package **2 :** to enclose in a package or protective covering — **pack·ag·er** *n*

package deal *n* **1 :** an offer or agreement involving a number of related items or one making acceptance of one item dependent on the acceptance of another **2 :** the items offered in a package deal

package store *n* **:** a store that sells alcoholic beverages that may not lawfully be drunk on the premises

pack·er \'pak-ər\ *n* **1 :** one that packs; *specif* **:** a wholesale dealer **2 a :** ²PORTER 1 **b :** one who conveys goods on pack animals

pack·et \'pak-ət\ *n* [MF *pacquet,* of Gmc origin; akin to MD *pak* pack] **1 a :** a number of letters dispatched at one time **b :** a small group, cluster, or mass **2 :** a passenger boat carrying mail and cargo on a regular schedule **3 a :** a small bundle or parcel **b :** a small thin package

pack ice *n* **:** sea ice formed into a mass by the crushing together of pans, floes, and brash

pack·ing \'pak-iŋ\ *n* **1 a :** the act or process of packing goods; *specif* **:** the wholesale processing of food **b :** a method of packing **2 :** material used to pack

pack·ing·house \-ˌhau̇s\ *or* **packing plant** *n* **:** an establishment for slaughtering, processing, and packing livestock into meat, meat products, and by-products or for processing and packing other foodstuffs

pack·man \'pak-mən\ *n* **:** PEDDLER

pack rat *n* **:** WOOD RAT; *esp* **:** a large bushy-tailed rodent (*Neotoma cinerea*) of the Rocky Mountain area that hoards food and miscellaneous objects

pack·sack \'pak-ˌsak\ *n* **:** a canvas or leather case used to carry gear on the back when traveling on foot

pack·sad·dle \-ˌsad-ᵊl\ *n* **:** a saddle designed to support loads on the backs of pack animals

pack·thread \-ˌthred\ *n* **:** strong thread or small twine used for sewing or tying packs or parcels

pact \'pakt\ *n* [ME, fr. MF, fr. L *pactum,* fr. neut. of *pactus,* pp. of *pacisci* to agree, contract; akin to OE *fōn* to seize, L *pangere* to fix, fasten, Gk *pēgnynai*] **:** ⁴COMPACT; *specif* **:** an international treaty

¹pad \'pad\ *n* [origin unknown] **1 a :** a thin flat mat or cushion: as (1) **:** a piece of soft stuffed material used as or under a saddle (2) **:** padding used to shape an article of clothing (3) **:** a guard worn to shield body parts (4) **:** a piece of usu. folded absorbent material (as gauze) used as a surgical dressing or protective covering **b :** a piece of material saturated with ink for inking the surface of a rubber stamp **2 a :** the foot of an animal **b :** the cushioned thickening of the underside of the toes of an animal **3 :** a floating leaf of a water plant **4 :** TABLET **5 a :** a section of an airstrip used for warm-ups, takeoffs, or landings **b :** LAUNCHING PAD **6** *slang* **a :** living quarters **b :** BED

²pad *vt* **pad·ded; pad·ding 1 a :** to furnish with a pad or padding **b :** MUTE, MUFFLE **2 :** to expand with needless or fraudulent matter

³pad *vb* **pad·ded; pad·ding** [perh. fr. MD *paden* to follow a path, fr. *pad* path — more at PATH] *vt* **:** to traverse on foot ~ *vi* **1 :** to go on foot **:** WALK **2 :** to move along with a muffled step

⁴pad *n* [MD *pad*] **1** *dial Brit* **:** PATH **2 :** a horse that moves along at an easy pace **3** *archaic* **:** FOOTPAD

⁵pad *n* [imit.] **:** a soft muffled or slapping sound

pad·ding *n* **:** material with which something is padded

¹pad·dle \'pad-ᵊl\ *n* [ME *padell*] **1 :** an implement with a flat blade to propel and steer a small craft (as a canoe) **2 :** an implement used for stirring, mixing, or beating **3 :** one of the broad boards at the circumference of a paddle wheel or waterwheel

²paddle *vb* **pad·dling** \'pad-liŋ, -ᵊl-iŋ\ *vi* **:** to go on or through water by or as if by means of a paddle or paddle wheel ~ *vt* **1 a :** to propel by a paddle **b :** to transport in a paddled craft **2 :** to beat, stir, or punish by or as if by a paddle

³paddle *vi* **pad·dling** \'pad-liŋ, -ᵊl-iŋ\ [origin unknown] **1 :** to move the hands or feet about in shallow water **2** *archaic* **:** to use the hands or fingers in toying or caressing **3 :** TODDLE

pad·dle·ball \'pad-ᵊl-ˌbȯl\ *n* **:** a game for 2, 3, or 4 players played on a 1-, 3-, or 4-walled court with a wood or plastic paddle and a ball similar to a tennis ball; *also* **:** the ball used in this game

pad·dle·fish \'pad-ᵊl-ˌfish\ *n* **:** any of a family (Polyodontidae) of ganoid fishes; *esp* **:** one (*Polyodon spathula*) of the Mississippi valley about four feet long with a spatula-shaped snout

pad·dler \'pad-lər, -ᵊl-ər\ *n* **:** one that paddles

paddle wheel *n* **:** a wheel with paddles, floats, or boards around its circumference used to propel a vessel

pad·dock \'pad-ək, -ik\ *n* [alter. of ME *parrok,* fr. OE *pearroc;* akin to OHG *pfarrih* enclosure; both fr. a prehistoric Gmc word borrowed fr. (assumed) VL *parricus*] **:** a usu. enclosed area used esp. for pasturing or exercising animals; *esp* **:** an enclosure where

racehorses are saddled and paraded before a race

pad·dy \'pad-ē\ *n* [Malay *padi*] **1 :** RICE; *esp* **:** threshed unmilled rice **2 :** wet land in which rice is grown

pad·dy wagon \'pad-ē-\ *n* [prob. fr. E slang *Paddy* (Irishman, policeman)] **:** PATROL WAGON

padi·shah \'päd-(ə-),shä, -(ə-),shȯ\ *n* [Per *pādshāh*] **:** a chief ruler **:** SOVEREIGN; *esp* **:** the shah of Iran

pad·lock \'pad-,läk\ *n* [ME *padlok*, fr. *pad-* (of unknown origin) + *lok* lock] **:** a removable lock with a shackle that can be passed through a staple or link and then secured to fasten something — **padlock** *vt*

pa·dre \'päd-(,)rā, -rē\ *n* [Sp or It or Pg, lit., father, fr. L *pater* — more at FATHER] **1 :** a Christian clergyman; *esp* **:** PRIEST **2 :** a military chaplain

pa·dro·ne \pə-'drō-nē\ *n* [It, protector, owner, fr. L *patronus* patron] **1 :** an Italian innkeeper **2 :** one that secures employment for immigrants esp. of Italian extraction

pad·u·a·soy \'paj-(ə-)wə-,sȯi\ *n* [alter. of earlier *poudesoy*, fr. F *pou-de-soie*] **:** a rich corded silk fabric; *also* **:** a garment made of it

pae·an \'pē-ən\ *n* [L, hymn of thanksgiving esp. addressed to Apollo, fr. Gk *paian*, *paiōn*, fr. *Paian*, *Paiōn*, epithet of Apollo in the hymn] **:** a joyously exultant song or hymn of praise, tribute, thanksgiving, or triumph

paed- *or* **paedo-** *or* **ped-** *or* **pedo-** *comb form* [Gk *paid-*, *paido-*, fr. *paid-* *pais* child, boy — more at FEW] **:** child ⟨*pedi*atric⟩ **:** childhood ⟨*paedo*genesis⟩

pae·do·gen·e·sis \,pēd-ō-'jen-ə-səs\ *n* [NL] **:** reproduction by young or larval animals **:** NEOTENY — **pae·do·ge·net·ic** \-jə-'net-ik\ *or* **pae·do·gen·ic** \-'jen-ik\ *adj*

pae·do·mor·phic \,pēd-ə-'mȯr-fik\ *adj* **:** of, relating to, or involving paedomorphosis or paedomorphism

pae·do·mor·phism \-,fiz-əm\ *n* **:** retention in the adult of infantile or juvenile characters

pae·do·mor·pho·sis \-'mȯr-fə-səs\ *n* [NL] **:** phylogenetic change involving retention of juvenile characters by the adult with increased capacity for further change indicative of a potential for further evolution

pae·on \'pē-ən, -,än\ *n* [L, fr. Gk *paiōn*, fr. *paian*, *paiōn* paean] **:** a metrical foot of four syllables with one long and three short syllables (as in classical prosody) or with one stressed and three unstressed syllables (as in English prosody)

pa·gan \'pā-gən\ *n* [ME, fr. LL *paganus*, fr. L, country dweller, fr. *pagus* country district; akin to L *pangere* to fix — more at PACT] **1 :** HEATHEN 1 **2 :** an irreligious person — **pagan** *adj* — **pa·gan·ish** \-gə-nish\ *adj*

pa·gan·ism \'pā-gə-,niz-əm\ *n* **1 a :** pagan beliefs or practices **:** HEATHENISM **b :** a pagan religion **2 :** the quality or state of being a pagan

pa·gan·ize \-,nīz\ *vt* **:** to make pagan ~ *vi* **:** to become pagan — **pa·gan·iz·er** *n*

¹page \'pāj\ *n* [ME, fr. OF, fr. It *paggio*] **1 a** (1) **:** a youth being trained for the medieval rank of knight and in the personal service of a knight (2) **:** a youth attendant on a person of rank **b :** a boy serving as an honorary attendant at a formal function **2 :** one employed to deliver messages, assist patrons, serve as a guide, or attend to other duties

²page *vt* **1 :** to serve in the capacity of a page **2 :** to summon by repeatedly calling out the name of

³page *n* [MF, fr. L *pagina*; akin to L *pangere* to fix, fasten] **1 a :** one of the leaves of a book, magazine, or similar article **b :** a single side of one of these leaves **2 a :** a written record **b :** something suitable to a written record **3 :** a section of a printed or written work ⟨the most exciting ~s in the book⟩

⁴page *vt* **:** to number or mark the pages of

pag·eant \'paj-ənt\ *n* [ME *pagyn*, *padgeant*, lit., scene of a play, fr. ML *pagina*, fr. L, page] **1 a :** a mere show **:** PRETENSE **b :** an ostentatious display **2 :** SHOW, EXHIBITION; *esp* **:** an elaborate colorful exhibition or spectacle often with music that consists of a series of tableaux, of a loosely unified drama, or of a procession usu. with floats **3 :** PAGEANTRY 1

pag·eant·ry \'paj-ən-trē\ *n* **1 :** pageants and the presentation of pageants **2 :** colorful, rich, or splendid display **:** SPECTACLE **3 :** mere show

page boy *n* [¹*page*] **1 :** a boy serving as a page **2** *usu* **page·boy :** a woman's often shoulder-length bob with the ends of the hair turned under in a smooth roll

pag·i·nal \'paj-ən-ᵊl\ *adj* [LL *paginalis*, fr. L *pagina* page] **:** of, relating to, or consisting of pages

pag·i·nate \'paj-ə-,nāt\ *vt* [L *pagina* page] **:** ⁴PAGE

pag·i·na·tion \,paj-ə-'nā-shən\ *n* **1 :** the action of paging **:** the condition of being paged **2 a :** the numbers or other marks used to indicate the sequence of pages **b :** the number and arrangement of pages or an indication of these

pa·go·da \pə-'gōd-ə\ *n* [Pg *pagode* oriental idol, temple] **:** a Far Eastern tower usu. with roofs curving upward at the division of each of several stories and erected as a temple or memorial

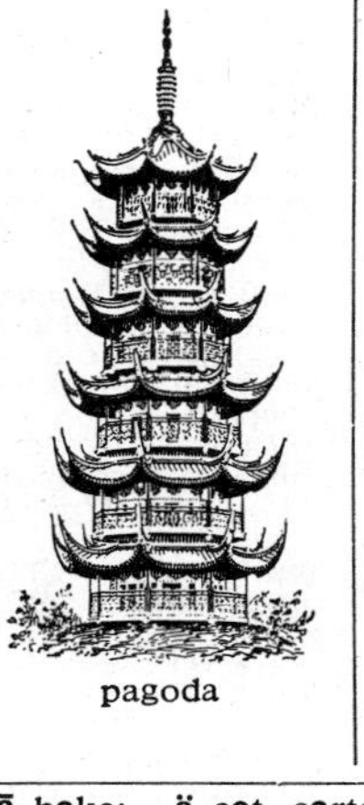

pagoda

pah·la·vi \'pal-ə-(,)vē\ *n*, *pl* **pahlavi** *or* **pahlavis** [Per *pahlawī*, fr. Riza Shah *Pahlawī* †1944 Shah of Iran] **1 :** a monetary unit of Iran equal to 100 rials **2 :** a coin representing one pahlavi

Pah·la·vi \'pal-ə-(,)vē\ *n* [Per *pahlawī*, fr. *Pahlav* Parthia, fr. OPer *Parthava-*] **1 :** the Iranian language of Sassanian Persia **2 :** a script used for writing Pahlavi

paid *past of* PAY

pai–hua \'bī-'hwä\ *n* [Chin (Pek) *pai²* *hua⁴*, lit., plain speech] **:** a form of written Chinese based on modern colloquial

pail \'pā(ə)l\ *n* [ME *payle*, *paille*] **1 :** a usu. cylindrical vessel with a handle **:** BUCKET **2 :** the quantity that a pail contains

pail·ful \-,fu̇l\ *n* **:** PAIL 2

pail·lette \pī-'(y)et, pā-'yet, 'pī-,, 'pā-,; pə-'let\ *n* [F, fr. *paille* straw — more at PALLET] **:** a small shiny object (as a spangle)

pail·lon \pī-'(y)ōⁿ\ *n* [F, fr. *paille* straw] **:** a thin sheet of metallic foil used esp. in enameling and gilding

¹pain \'pān\ *n* [ME, fr. OF *peine*, fr. L *poena*, fr. Gk *poinē* payment, penalty; akin to Gk *tinein* to pay, *tinesthai* to punish, *timē* price, value, honor] **1 :** PUNISHMENT **2 a :** unpleasant or distressing sensation due to bodily injury or disorder **b :** acute mental or emotional distress or suffering **:** GRIEF **3** *pl* **:** the throes of childbirth **4** *pl* **:** CARE, TROUBLE **syn** see EFFORT — **pain·less** \-ləs\ *adj* — **pain·less·ly** *adv* — **pain·less·ness** *n*

²pain *vt* **1 :** to make suffer or cause distress to **:** HURT **2** *archaic* **:** to put (oneself) to trouble or exertion ~ *vi* **1** *archaic* **:** SUFFER **2 :** to give or have a sensation of pain

pain·ful \'pān-fəl\ *adj* **1 a :** feeling or giving pain **b :** ANNOYING, IRKSOME, VEXATIOUS **2 :** requiring effort or exertion **3** *archaic* **:** CAREFUL, DILIGENT — **pain·ful·ly** \-f(ə-)lē\ *adv* — **pain·ful·ness** \-fəl-nəs\ *n*

pains·tak·ing \'pān-,stā-kiŋ\ *n* **:** the action of taking pains — **painstaking** *adj* — **pains·tak·ing·ly** \-kiŋ-lē\ *adv*

¹paint \'pānt\ *vb* [ME *painten*, fr. OF *peint*, pp. of *peindre*, fr. L *pingere* to tattoo, embroider, paint; akin to OE *fāh* variegated, Gk *poikilos* variegated, *pikros* sharp, bitter] *vt* **1 a** (1) **:** to apply color, pigment, or paint to (2) **:** to color with a cosmetic **b** (1) **:** to apply with a movement resembling that used in painting (2) **:** to treat with a liquid by brushing or swabbing ⟨~ the wound with iodine⟩ **2 a** (1) **:** to produce in lines and colors on a surface by applying pigments (2) **:** to depict by such lines and colors (3) **:** to depict as having specified or implied characteristics **b :** to decorate, adorn, or variegate by applying lines and colors **c :** to produce or evoke as if by painting ⟨~s glowing pictures of a promised utopia⟩ **3 :** to touch up or cover over by or as if by painting ~ *vi* **1 :** to practice the art of painting **2 :** to use cosmetics

²paint *n* **1 :** the action of painting **:** something produced by painting **2 :** MAKEUP; *esp* **:** a cosmetic to add color **3 a** (1) **:** a mixture of a pigment and a suitable liquid to form a thin closely adherent coating when spread on a surface in a thin coat (2) **:** the pigment used in this mixture esp. when in the form of a cake **b :** an applied coating of paint

paint·brush \-,brəsh\ *n* **1 :** a brush for applying paint **2 :** any of several plants with showy tufted flowers

painted bunting *n* **:** a brightly colored finch (*Passerina ciris*) of the southern U.S.

¹paint·er \'pānt-ər\ *n* **:** one that paints: as **a :** an artist who paints **b :** one who applies paint (as to a building) esp. as an occupation

²pain·ter \'pānt-ər\ *n* [ME *paynter*, prob. fr. MF *pendoir*, *pentoir* clothesline, fr. *pendre* to hang — more at PENDANT] **:** a line used for securing or towing a boat

³pain·ter *n* [alter. of *panther*] *chiefly South & Midland* **:** COUGAR

paint·er·ly \'pānt-ər-lē\ *adj* **:** of, relating to, or typical of a painter **:** ARTISTIC

painter's colic *n* **:** LEAD COLIC

paint·ing *n* **1 :** a product of painting; *esp* **:** a work produced through the art of painting **2 :** the art or occupation of painting

¹pair \'pa(ə)r, 'pe(ə)r\ *n*, *pl* **pairs** *also* **pair** [ME *paire*, fr. OF, fr. L *paria* equal things, fr. neut. pl. of *par* equal] **1 a** (1) **:** two corresponding things designed for use together ⟨~ of shoes⟩ (2) **:** two corresponding bodily parts or members **b :** something made up of two corresponding pieces ⟨~ of trousers⟩ **2 a :** two similar or associated things: as (1) **:** two mated animals (2) **:** a couple in love, engaged, or married (3) **:** two playing cards of the same value or denomination (4) **:** two horses harnessed side by side (5) **:** two members of a deliberative body that agree not to vote on a specific issue during a time agreed on **b :** a partnership esp. of two players in a contest against another partnership **c :** an agreement not to vote made by the two members of a pair (sense 2a(5)) **3** *chiefly dial* **:** a set or series of small objects (as beads)

²pair *vt* **1 a :** to make a pair of **b :** to arrange a voting pair between **2 :** to arrange in pairs ~ *vi* **1 :** to constitute a member of a pair **2 a :** to become associated with another **b :** to become grouped or separated into pairs ⟨~*ed* off for the next dance⟩

pair–oar \-,ō(ə)r, -,ȯ(ə)r\ *n* **:** a boat rowed by two men pulling one oar each and seated one abaft the other — **pair–oared** \-'ō(ə)rd, -'ȯ(ə)rd\ *adj*

pair production *n* **:** the simultaneous and complete transformation of a quantum of radiant energy into an electron and a positron when the quantum interacts with the intense electric field near a nucleus

pai·sa \pī-'sä\ *n*, *pl* **pai·se** \-'sā\ *or* **paisa** *or* **paisas** [Hindi *paisā*] — see MONEY table

pais·ley \'pāz-lē\ *adj*, *often cap* [*Paisley*, Scotland] **:** made typically of soft wool and woven or printed with colorful curved abstract figures — **paisley** *n*

Pai·ute \'pī-,(y)üt\ *n* **:** a member of a Shoshonean people of Utah, Arizona, Nevada, and California

pa·ja·ma \pə-'jäm-ə, -'jam-\ *n* [Hindi *pājāma*, fr. Per *pā* leg + *jāma* garment] **:** PAJAMAS

pa·ja·mas \pə-'jäm-əz, -'jam-\ *n pl* [pl. of *pajama*] **1 :** loose lightweight trousers formerly much worn in the Near East **2 :** a loose usu. two-piece lightweight suit designed for sleeping or lounging

¹pal \'pal\ *n* [Romany *phral*, *phal* brother, friend, fr. Skt *bhrātṛ* brother; akin to OE *brōthor* brother] **:** PARTNER; *esp* **:** a close friend

²pal *vi* **palled; pal·ling :** to be or become pals

pal·ace \'pal-əs\ *n* [ME *palais*, fr. OF, fr. L *palatium*, fr. *Palatium* the Palatine Hill in Rome where the emperors' residences were built] **1 a :** the official residence of a sovereign **b** *chiefly Brit* **:** the official residence of an archbishop or bishop **2 a :** a large stately house **b :** a large public building **c :** a gaudy place for public amusement or refreshment

pal·a·din \'pal-əd-ən\ *n* [F, fr. It *paladino*, fr. ML *palatinus* courtier, fr. L, palace official — more at PALATINE] **1 :** a champion of a medieval prince **2 :** an outstanding protagonist of a cause

Pa·lae·arc·tic *or* **Pa·le·arc·tic** \,pā-lē-'ärk-tik, -'ärt-ik, *esp Brit* ,pal-ē-\ *adj* [*pale-*] **:** of, relating to, or being a biogeographic region or subregion that includes Europe, Asia north of the Himalayas, northern Arabia, and Africa north of the Sahara

pa·laeo·an·throp·ic \,pā-lē-(,)ō-(,)an-'thräp-ik, *esp Brit* ,pal-ē-\ *adj* [*pale-* + Gk *anthrōpos* man] **:** of or relating to hominids more primitive than those included in the species (*Homo sapiens*) that includes recent man

pa·laes·tra \pə-ˈles-trə\ *n, pl* **pa·laes·trae** \-(ˌ)trē\ [L, fr. Gk *palaistra*, fr. *palaiein* to wrestle; akin to Gk *pallein* to brandish — more at POLEMIC] **1 :** a school in ancient Greece or Rome for wrestling and other sports **2 :** GYMNASIUM

pa·lan·quin \ˌpal-ən-ˈkēn, -ˈk(w)in; pə-ˈlaŋ-kwən, -ˈlan-\ *n* [Pg *palanquim*, fr. Jav *pĕlaṅki*] **:** a conveyance formerly used in eastern Asia esp. for one person that consists of an enclosed litter borne on the shoulders of men by means of poles

pal·at·abil·i·ty \ˌpal-ət-ə-ˈbil-ət-ē\ *n* **:** the quality or state of being palatable

pal·at·able \ˈpal-ət-ə-bəl\ *adj* **1 :** agreeable to the palate or taste **:** SAVORY **2 :** agreeable to the mind **:** ACCEPTABLE — **pal·at·able·ness** *n* — **pal·at·ably** \-blē\ *adv*

pal·a·tal \ˈpal-ət-ᵊl\ *adj* **1 :** of or relating to the palate **2 a :** formed with the front of the tongue behind the lowered tip near or touching the hard palate ⟨the \k̟\ in German \ik̟\ *ich* and the \y\ in English *yeast* are ~ sounds⟩ **b** (1) **:** formed with the blade of the tongue near the hard palate ⟨the ~ sounds represented by *sh* in *she* and *si* in *vision*⟩ (2) *of a vowel* **:** FRONT — **palatal** *n* — **pal·a·tal·ly** \-ᵊl-ē\ *adv*

pal·a·tal·iza·tion \ˌpal-ət-ᵊl-ə-ˈzā-shən\ *n* **1 :** the quality or state of being palatalized **2 :** an act or instance of palatalizing an utterance

pal·a·tal·ize \ˈpal-ət-ᵊl-ˌīz\ *vt* **1 :** to pronounce as or change into a palatal sound **2 :** to modify the utterance of (a nonpalatal sound) by simultaneously bringing the front of the tongue to or near the hard palate

pal·ate \ˈpal-ət\ *n* [ME, fr. L *palatum*] **1 :** the roof of the mouth separating the mouth from the nasal cavity **2 :** intellectual relish or taste **syn** see TASTE

pa·la·tial \pə-ˈlā-shəl\ *adj* [L *palatium* palace] **1 :** of, relating to, or being a palace **2 :** suitable to a palace **:** MAGNIFICENT — **pa·la·tial·ly** \-shə-lē\ *adv* — **pa·la·tial·ness** *n*

pa·lat·i·nate \pə-ˈlat-ᵊn-ət\ *n* **:** the territory of a palatine

1pal·a·tine \ˈpal-ə-ˌtīn\ *adj* [L *palatinus*, fr. *palatium*] **1 a :** of or relating to a palace esp. of a Roman or Holy Roman emperor **b :** PALATIAL **2 a :** possessing royal privileges **b :** of or relating to a palatine or a palatinate

2palatine \-ˌtīn, *3 is also* -ˌtēn\ *n* [L *palatinus*, fr. *palatinus*, adj.] **1 a :** a high officer of an imperial palace **b :** a feudal lord having sovereign power within his domains **2** *cap* **:** a native or inhabitant of the Palatinate **3** [F, fr. Elisabeth Charlotte of Bavaria †1722 Princess *Palatine*] **:** a fur cape or stole covering the neck and shoulders

3palatine \-ˌtīn\ *adj* **:** of, relating to, or lying near the palate

4palatine \-ˌtīn\ *n* **:** a palatine bone

1pa·la·ver \pə-ˈlav-ər, -ˈläv-\ *n* [Pg *palavra* word, speech, fr. LL *parabola* parable, speech] **1 a :** a long parley usu. between persons of different levels of culture or sophistication **b :** CONFERENCE, DISCUSSION **2 a :** idle talk **b :** misleading or beguiling speech

2palaver *vb* **pa·la·ver·ing** \-(ə-)riŋ\ *vi* **1 :** to talk profusely or idly **2 :** PARLEY ~ *vt* **:** to use palaver to **:** CAJOLE

1pale \ˈpā(ə)l\ *adj* [ME, fr. MF, fr. L *pallidus*, fr. *pallēre* to be pale — more at FALLOW] **1 :** deficient in color or intensity of color **:** PALLID **2 :** not bright or brilliant **:** DIM **3 :** FEEBLE, FAINT **4 :** deficient in chroma ⟨a ~ pink⟩ — **pale·ly** \ˈpā(ə)l-lē\ *adv* — **pale·ness** \-nəs\ *n*

2pale *vi* **:** to become pale ~ *vt* **:** to make pale

3pale *vt* [ME *palen*, fr. MF *paler*, fr. *pal*] **:** to enclose with pales **:** FENCE

4pale *n* [ME, fr. MF *pal* stake, fr. L *palus* — more at POLE] **1** *archaic* **:** PALISADE, PALING **2 a :** one of the stakes of a palisade **b :** PICKET **3 a :** ENCLOSURE **b :** a territory or district within certain bounds or under a particular jurisdiction **4 :** an area or the limits within which one is privileged or protected (as from censure) ⟨conduct that was beyond the ~⟩ **5 :** a perpendicular stripe in an escutcheon

pale- *or* **paleo-** *or* **palae-** *or* **palaeo-** *comb form* [Gk *palai-*, *palaio-* ancient, fr. *palaios*, fr. *palai* long ago; akin to Gk *tēle* far off, Skt *carama* last] **1 :** involving or dealing with ancient forms or conditions ⟨*paleo*botany⟩ **2 :** early **:** primitive **:** archaic ⟨*Paleo*lithic⟩

pa·lea \ˈpā-lē-ə\ *n, pl* **pa·le·ae** \-lē-ˌē\ [NL, fr. L, chaff — more at PALLET] **1 :** one of the chaffy scales on the receptacle of many composite plants **2 :** the upper bract that with the lemma encloses the flower in grasses — **pa·le·al** \ˈpā-lē-əl\ *adj*

pa·le·aceous \ˌpā-lē-ˈā-shəs\ *adj* [NL *palea* + E *-aceous*] **:** covered with or resembling chaffy scales

pa·le·eth·nol·o·gy \ˌpā-lē-(ˌ)eth-ˈnäl-ə-jē, *esp Brit* ˌpal-ē-\ *n* [ISV] **:** ethnology of early prehistoric man

pale·face \ˈpā(ə)l-ˌfās\ *n* **:** a white person **:** CAUCASIAN

pa·leo·bo·tan·i·cal \ˌpā-lē-ō-bə-ˈtan-i-kəl, *esp Brit* ˌpal-ē-\ *adj* **:** of or relating to paleobotany — **pa·leo·bo·tan·i·cal·ly** \-k(ə-)lē\ *adv*

pa·leo·bot·a·ny \-ˈbät-ᵊn-ē, -ˈbät-nē\ *n* [ISV] **:** a branch of botany dealing with fossil plants

Pa·leo·cene \ˈpā-lē-ə-ˌsēn, *esp Brit* ˈpal-ē-\ *adj* [ISV *pale-* + *-cene*] **:** of, relating to, or being the earliest epoch of the Tertiary or the corresponding system of rocks — **Paleocene** *n*

pa·le·og·ra·pher \ˌpā-lē-ˈäg-rə-fər, *esp Brit* ˌpal-ē-\ *n* **:** a specialist in paleography

pa·leo·graph·ic \-ə-ˈgraf-ik\ *adj* **:** of or relating to paleography — **pa·leo·graph·i·cal** \-i-kəl\ *adj* — **pa·leo·graph·i·cal·ly** \-k(ə-)lē\ *adv*

pa·le·og·ra·phy \-ˈäg-rə-fē\ *n* [NL *palaeographia*, fr. Gk *palai-* pale- + *-graphia* -graphy] **1 a :** an ancient manner of writing **b :** ancient writings **2 :** the study of ancient writings and inscriptions

pa·leo·lith \ˈpā-lē-ə-ˌlith, *esp Brit* ˈpal-ē-\ *n* **:** a Paleolithic stone implement

Pa·leo·lith·ic \ˌpā-lē-ə-ˈlith-ik, *esp Brit* ˌpal-ē-\ *adj* [ISV] **:** of or relating to the second period of the Stone Age characterized by rough or chipped stone implements

pa·le·on·to·log·i·cal \ˌpā-lē-ˌänt-ᵊl-ˈäj-i-kəl, *esp Brit* ˌpal-ē-\ *or* **pa·le·on·to·log·ic** \-ik\ *adj* **:** of or relating to paleontology

pa·le·on·tol·o·gist \-(ˌ)än-ˈtäl-ə-jəst, -ən-\ *n* **:** a specialist in paleontology

pa·le·on·tol·o·gy \-jē\ *n* [F *paléontologie*, fr. *palé-* pale- + Gk *onta* existing things (fr. neut. pl. of *ont-*, *ōn*, prp. of *einai* to be) + F *-logie* -logy — more at IS] **:** a science dealing with the life of past geological periods as known from fossil remains

Pa·leo·zo·ic \ˌpā-lē-ə-ˈzō-ik, *esp Brit* ˌpal-ē-\ *adj* **:** of, relating to, or being an era of geological history which extends from the beginning of the Cambrian to the close of the Permian and is marked by the culmination of nearly all classes of invertebrates except the insects and in the later epochs of which seed-bearing plants, amphibians, and reptiles first appeared; *also* **:** relating to the system of rocks formed in this era — **Paleozoic** *n*

pa·leo·zo·olog·i·cal \ˌpā-lē-(ˌ)ō-ˌzō-ə-ˈläj-i-kəl, *esp Brit* ˌpal-ē-\ *adj* **:** of or relating to paleozoology

pa·leo·zo·ol·o·gy \-zō-ˈäl-ə-jē, -zə-ˈwäl-\ *n* [F *paléozoologie*, fr. *palé-* pale- + *zoologie* zoology, fr. NL *zoologia*] **:** a branch of paleontology dealing with ancient and fossil animals

pal·et \pā-ˈlet, ˈpā-lət\ *n* [*pale* (palea) + *-et*] **:** PALEA

pal·ette \ˈpal-ət\ *n* [F, fr. MF, dim. of *pale* spade, shovel, fr. L *pala*] **1 :** a thin oval or rectangular board or tablet with a hole for the thumb at one end by which a painter holds it and on which he lays and mixes pigments **2 :** the set of colors put on the palette

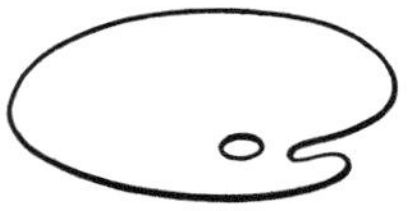
palette 1

palette knife *n* **:** a knife with a flexible steel blade and no cutting edge used to mix colors **:** SPATULA

pal·frey \ˈpȯl-frē\ *n* [ME, fr. OF *palefrei*, fr. ML *palafredus*, fr. LL *paraveredus* post-horse for secondary roads, fr. Gk *para-* beside, subsidiary + L *veredus* post-horse, fr. a Gaulish word akin to W *gorwydd* horse; akin to OIr *rīadaim* I ride — more at PARA-, RIDE] *archaic* **:** a saddle horse other than a war-horse; *esp* **:** a light easy-gaited horse suitable for a woman

Pa·li \ˈpäl-ē\ *n* [Skt *pāli* row, series of Buddhist sacred texts] **:** an Indic language used as the liturgical and scholarly language of Hinayana Buddhism

pa·limp·sest \ˈpal-əm(p)-ˌsest, pə-ˈlim(p)-\ *n* [L *palimpsestus*, fr. Gk *palimpsēstos* scraped again, fr. *palin* + *psēn* to rub, scrape — more at SAND] **:** writing material (as a parchment or tablet) used one or more times after earlier writing has been erased

pal·in·drome \ˈpal-ən-ˌdrōm\ *n* [Gk *palindromos* running back again, fr. *palin* back, again + *dramein* to run; akin to Gk *polos* axis, pole — more at POLE, DROMEDARY] **:** a word, verse, or sentence (as "Able was I ere I saw Elba") that reads the same backward or forward

pal·ing \ˈpā-liŋ\ *n* **1 :** a fence of pales or pickets **2 :** wood for pales **3 :** a pale for a fence

pal·in·gen·e·sis \ˌpal-ən-ˈjen-ə-səs\ *n* [NL, fr. Gk *palin* again + L *genesis*] **1 :** METEMPSYCHOSIS **2 :** reproduction during development of characters or structures that have been maintained essentially unchanged throughout the phylogeny of a strain — **pal·in·ge·net·ic** \-jə-ˈnet-ik\ *adj* — **pal·in·ge·net·i·cal·ly** \-i-k(ə-)lē\ *adv*

pal·in·ode \ˈpal-ə-ˌnōd\ *n* [Gk *palinōidia*, fr. *palin* back + *aeidein* to sing — more at ODE] **1 :** an ode or song recanting or retracting something in a former one **2 :** RETRACTION; *esp* **:** a formal retraction

1pal·i·sade \ˌpal-ə-ˈsād\ *n* [F *palissade*, deriv. of L *palus* stake — more at POLE] **1 a :** a fence of stakes esp. for defense **b :** a long strong stake pointed at the top and set close with others as a defense **2 :** a line of bold cliffs

2palisade *vt* **:** to surround or fortify with palisades

palisade parenchyma *n* **:** a layer of columnar cells rich in chloroplasts found beneath the upper epidermis of foliage leaves

pal·ish \ˈpā-lish\ *adj* **:** somewhat pale

1pall \ˈpȯl\ *n* [ME, cloak, mantle, fr. OE *pæll*, fr. L *pallium*] **1 :** PALLIUM 1b **2 a :** a square of linen usu. stiffened with cardboard **b** (1) **:** a heavy cloth draped over a coffin (2) **:** a coffin esp. when holding a body **3 :** something that covers or conceals; *esp* **:** an overspreading element that produces an effect of gloom

2pall *vt* **:** to cover with a pall **:** CLOAK

3pall *vb* [ME *pallen*, short for *appallen* to become pale — more at APPALL] *vi* **1 :** to lose strength or effectiveness **2 :** to lose in interest or attraction **3 :** to become tired of something ~ *vt* **1 :** to cause to become insipid **2 :** SATIATE, CLOY **syn** see SATIATE

Pal·la·di·an \pə-ˈläd-ē-ən\ *adj* **:** of or relating to a revived classic style in architecture based on the works of Andrea Palladio — **Pal·la·di·an·ism** \-ˌiz-əm\ *n*

1pal·la·di·um \pə-ˈlād-ē-əm\ *n* [L, fr. Gk *palladion*, fr. *Pallad-*, *Pallas*] **1** *cap* **:** a statue of Pallas Athena whose preservation was held to ensure the safety of Troy **2** *pl* **pal·la·dia** \-ē-ə\ **:** SAFEGUARD

2palladium *n* [NL, fr. *Pallad-*, *Pallas*, the asteroid] **:** a silver-white ductile malleable metallic element of the platinum group that is used esp. as a catalyst and in alloys — see ELEMENT table

Pal·las \ˈpal-əs\ *n* [L *Pallad-*, *Pallas*, fr. Gk] **1 :** ATHENA — called also *Pallas Athena* **2** [NL, fr. L, epithet of Athena] **:** one of the asteroids

pall·bear·er \ˈpȯl-ˌbar-ər, -ˌber-\ *n* [*1pall*] **:** a person who attends the coffin at a funeral

1pal·let \ˈpal-ət\ *n* [ME *pailet*, fr. (assumed) MF *paillet*, fr. *paille* straw, fr. L *palea* chaff, straw; akin to Skt *palāva* chaff] **1 :** a straw-filled tick or mattress **2 :** a small, hard, or temporary bed often on the floor

2pallet *n* [MF *palette*, lit., small shovel — more at PALETTE] **1 :** a wooden flat-bladed instrument: as **a :** an implement for forming, beating, or rounding clay **b :** PALETTE 1 **2 :** a lever or surface in a timepiece that receives an impulse from the escapement wheel and imparts motion to a balance or pendulum **3 :** a portable platform of wood or other material for handling, storage, or movement of materials and packages in warehouses, factories, or vehicles

pal·let·ize \ˈpal-ət-ˌīz\ *vt* **:** to place on, transport, or store by means of pallets

pal·lette \pa-ˈlet\ *n* [alter. of *palette*] **:** one of the plates at the armpits of a suit of armor

pal·li·al \ˈpal-ē-əl\ *adj* [NL *pallium*] **1 :** of or relating to the cerebral cortex **2 :** of, relating to, or produced by a mantle of a mollusk

pal·liasse \pal-ˈyas\ *n* [modif. of F *paillasse*, fr. *paille* straw] **:** a thin straw mattress used as a pallet

pal·li·ate \ˈpal-ē-ˌāt\ *vt* [LL *palliatus*, pp. of *palliare* to cloak, conceal, fr. *pallium* cloak] **1 :** to reduce the violence of **:** ABATE

2 : to cover by excuses and apologies **: EXCUSE — pal·li·a·tion** \ˌpal-ē-'ā-shən\ n **— pal·li·a·tor** \'pal-ē-ˌāt-ər\ n

pal·lia·tive \'pal-ē-ˌāt-iv, 'pal-yət-\ adj **:** serving to palliate **— palliative** n **— pal·lia·tive·ly** adv

pal·lid \'pal-əd\ adj [L pallidus — more at PALE] **:** deficient in color **: WAN — pal·lid·ly** adv **— pal·lid·ness** n

pal·li·um \'pal-ē-əm\ n, pl **pal·lia** \-ē-ə\ or **pal·li·ums** [L] **1 a :** a draped rectangular cloth worn by men of ancient Greece and Rome as a cloak **b :** a white woolen band with pendants in front and back worn over the chasuble by a pope or archbishop as a symbol of full episcopal authority **2** [NL, fr. L, cloak] **a :** the whole cerebral cortex **b :** the mantle of a mollusk, brachiopod, or bird

pall–mall \'pel-'mel, 'pal-'mal, US often 'pòl-'mòl\ n [MF pallemaille, fr. It pallamaglio, fr. palla ball (of Gmc origin; akin to OHG balla ball) + maglio mallet, fr. L malleus — more at BALL, MAUL] **:** a 17th century game in which a 4-inch wooden ball is driven with a mallet; also **:** the alley in which it is played

pal·lor \'pal-ər\ n [L, fr. pallēre to be pale — more at FALLOW] **:** deficiency of color esp. of the face **: PALENESS**

pal·ly \'pal-ē\ adj **:** sharing the relationship of pals **: INTIMATE**

¹palm \'päm, 'pälm\ n [in sense 1, fr. ME, fr. OE; akin to OHG palma palm tree; both fr. a prehistoric NGmc-WGmc word borrowed fr. L palma palm of the hand, palm tree; fr. the resemblance of the tree's leaves to an outstretched hand; in other senses, fr. ME paume, fr. MF, fr. L palma; akin to OE flōr floor] **1 a :** any of a family (Palmae, the palm family) of mostly tropical or subtropical monocotyledonous trees, shrubs, or vines with usu. a simple stem and terminal crown of large pinnate or fan-shaped leaves **b** (1) **:** a leaf of the palm as a symbol of victory or rejoicing (2) **:** a branch (as of laurel) similarly used **c :** a symbol of triumph; also **: VICTORY, TRIUMPH d :** an addition to a military decoration in the form of a palm frond esp. to indicate a second award of the basic decoration **2 :** the somewhat concave part of the human hand between the bases of the fingers and the wrist or the corresponding part of the forefoot of a lower mammal **3 a :** a flat expanded part esp. at the end of a base or stalk: as **a :** the blade of an oar or paddle **b** (1) **:** the flat inner face of an anchor fluke (2) **: ²FLUKE 1 4** [L palmus, fr. palma] **:** a unit of length based on the breadth or length of the hand **5 :** something (as a part of a glove) that covers the palm of the hand **— pal·ma·ceous** \pal-'mā-shəs, pä(l)-'mā-\ adj **— palm·like** \'pä(l)m-ˌlīk\ adj

²palm \'päm, 'pälm\ vt **1 :** to touch with the palm **2 a :** to conceal in or with the hand **b :** to pick up stealthily **3 :** to impose by fraud 〈trash ∼ed on the unwary〉

pal·mar \'pal-mər, 'pä(l)m-ər\ adj **:** of, relating to, situated in, or involving the palm of the hand

pal·ma·ry \'pal-mə-rē, 'pä(l)m-ə-\ adj [L palmarius deserving the palm, fr. palma] **: OUTSTANDING, BEST**

pal·mate \'pal-ˌmāt, 'pä(l)m-ˌāt\ also **pal·mat·ed** \-əd\ adj **:** resembling a hand with the fingers spread: **a :** having lobes radiating from a common point 〈∼ leaf〉 **b** (1) of an aquatic bird **:** having the anterior toes united by a web (2) **:** having the distal portion broad, flat, and lobed 〈a ∼ antler〉 **— pal·mate·ly** adv **— pal·ma·tion** \pal-'mā-shən, pä(l)-'mā-\ n

pal·mat·i·fid \pal-'mat-ə-fəd, pä(l)-'mat-, -ˌfid\ adj [ISV] **:** cleft in a palmate manner 〈a ∼ leaf〉

palm·er \'päm-ər, 'päl-mər\ n **:** a person wearing two crossed palm leaves as a sign of his pilgrimage to the Holy Land

palm–worm \-ˌwərm\ n **:** a caterpillar that suddenly appears in great numbers devouring herbage; esp **:** the larva of a No. American moth (Dichomeris ligulella) destructive to fruit trees

pal·met·to \pal-'met-(ˌ)ō also pä(l)-\ n, pl **palmettos** or **palmettoes** [modif. of Sp palmito, fr. palma palm, fr. L] **1 :** any of several usu. low-growing fan-leaved palms **2 :** strips of the leaf blade of a palmetto used in weaving

pal·mi·ped \'pal-mə-ˌped, 'pä(l)m-ə-\ adj [L palmiped-, palmipes, fr. palma palm of the foot + ped-, pes foot — more at FOOT] **: WEB≠FOOTED**

palm·ist \'päm-əst, 'päl-məst\ n [prob. back-formation fr. palm istry] **:** one who practices palmistry

palm·ist·ry \'päm-ə-strē, 'päl-mə-\ n [ME pawmestry, prob. fr. paume palm + maistrie mastery] **:** the art or practice of reading a person's character or future from the markings on his palms

pal·mi·tate \'pal-mə-ˌtāt, 'pä(l)m-ə-\ n **:** a salt or ester of palmitic acid

pal·mit·ic acid \ˌ(ˌ)pal-ˌmit-ik-, ˌ(ˌ)pä(l)-\ n [ISV, fr. palmitin] **:** a waxy crystalline fatty acid $C_{16}H_{32}O_2$ occurring free or in the form of glycerides and other esters in most fats and fatty oils and in several essential oils and waxes

pal·mi·tin \'pal-mət-ən, 'pä(l)m-ət-\ n [F palmitine, prob. fr. palmite pith of the palm tree, fr. Sp palmito, fr. palma palm, fr. L] **:** an ester of glycerol and palmitic acid; esp **:** a solid ester found with stearin and olein in animal fats

palm oil n **:** an edible fat obtained from the flesh of the fruit of several palms and used esp. in soap, candles, and lubricating greases

Palm Sunday n [fr. the palms strewn in Christ's way by the welcoming multitude] **:** the Sunday preceding Easter commemorating Christ's triumphal entry into Jerusalem when palm branches were strewn in his way

palmy \'päm-ē, 'päl-mē\ adj **1 :** abounding in or bearing palms **2 : FLOURISHING, PROSPEROUS**

pal·my·ra \pal-'mī-rə\ n [Pg palmeira, fr. palma palm, fr. L] **:** a tall African fan-leaved palm (Borassus flabellifer) cultivated for its hard resistant wood, fiber, and sugar-rich sap

pal·o·mi·no \ˌpal-ə-'mē-(ˌ)nō, -nə-(w)\ n [AmerSp, fr. Sp, like a dove, fr. L palumbinus, fr. palumbes ringdove; akin to Gk peleia dove, L pallēre to be pale — more at FALLOW] **:** a slender-legged short-coupled horse of largely Arabian ancestry and of a light tan or cream color with flaxen or white mane and tail

palp \'palp\ n [NL palpus] **: PALPUS — pal·pal** \'pal-pəl\ adj

pal·pa·bil·i·ty \ˌpal-pə-'bil-ət-ē\ n **:** the quality or state of being palpable

pal·pa·ble \'pal-pə-bəl\ adj [ME, fr. LL palpabilis, fr. L palpare to stroke, caress — more at FEEL] **1 :** capable of being touched or felt **: TANGIBLE 2 :** easily perceptible **: NOTICEABLE 3 :** easily perceptible by the mind **: MANIFEST syn** see PERCEPTIBLE **— pal·pa·bly** \-blē\ adv

¹pal·pate \'pal-ˌpāt\ vt [prob. back-formation fr. palpation, fr. L palpation- palpatio, fr. palpatus, pp. of palpare] **:** to examine by touch esp. medically **— pal·pa·tion** \pal-'pā-shən\ n

²palpate adj [NL palpatus, fr. palpus] **:** having a palpus

pal·pe·bral \'pal-pə-brəl; pal-'pē-brəl, -'peb-rəl\ adj [LL palpebralis, fr. L palpebra eyelid; akin to L palpare] **:** of, relating to, or located on or near the eyelids

pal·pi·tant \'pal-pət-ənt\ adj **: TREMBLING, THROBBING**

pal·pi·tate \'pal-pə-ˌtāt\ vi [L palpitatus, pp. of palpitare, freq. of palpare to stroke] **:** to beat rapidly and strongly **: THROB** 〈his heart ∼s〉 **— pal·pi·ta·tion** \ˌpal-pə-'tā-shən\ n

pal·pus \'pal-pəs\ n, pl **pal·pi** \-ˌpī, -ˌpē\ [NL, fr. L, caress, soft palm of the hand; akin to L palpare] **:** a segmented usu. tactile or gustatory process on an arthropod mouthpart

pals·grave \'pòlz-ˌgrāv\ n [D paltsgrave] **: COUNT PALATINE**

pal·sied \'pòl-zēd\ adj **:** affected with palsy

pal·sy \'pòl-zē\ n [ME parlesie, fr. MF paralisie, fr. L paralysis] **1 : PARALYSIS 2 :** a condition marked by uncontrollable tremor of the body or a part **— palsy** vt

pal·ter \'pòl-tər\ vi **pal·ter·ing** \-t(ə-)riŋ\ [origin unknown] **1 :** to act insincerely **: EQUIVOCATE 2 : HAGGLE, CHAFFER syn** see LIE **— pal·ter·er** \-tər-ər\ n

pal·tri·ness \'pòl-trē-nəs\ n **:** the quality or state of being paltry

pal·try \'pòl-trē\ adj [obs. paltry (trash)] **1 : INFERIOR, TRASHY 2 : MEAN, DESPICABLE 3 : TRIVIAL**

pa·lu·dal \pə-'lüd-ᵊl, 'pal-yəd-ᵊl\ adj [L palud-, palus marsh; akin to Skt palvala pond] **:** of or relating to marshes or fens **: MARSHY**

pal·u·dism \'pal-yə-ˌdiz-əm\ n [ISV, fr. L palud-, palus] **: MALARIA**

paly \'pā-lē\ adj **:** somewhat pale

pal·y·nol·o·gy \ˌpal-ə-'näl-ə-jē\ n [Gk palynein to sprinkle, fr. palē fine meal — more at POLLEN] **:** a branch of science dealing with pollen and spores

pam·pa \'pam-pə\ n, pl **pam·pas** \-pəz, -pəs\ [AmerSp, fr. Quechua & Aymara, plain] **:** an extensive generally grass-covered plain of So. America **: PRAIRIE**

pam·pe·an \'pam-pē-ən, pam-'\ adj **:** of or relating to the pampas of So. America or their Indian inhabitants

pam·per \'pam-pər\ vt **pam·per·ing** \-p(ə-)riŋ\ [ME pamperen, prob. of D origin; akin to Flem pamperen to pamper] **1** archaic **: GLUT 2 a :** to treat with extreme or excessive care and attention 〈∼ed their guests〉 **b : GRATIFY, HUMOR** 〈the job has enabled him to ∼ his wanderlust thoroughly —New Yorker〉 **syn** see INDULGE **— pam·per·er** \-pər-ər\ n

pam·pe·ro \pam-'pe(ə)r-(ˌ)ō, päm-\ n [AmerSp, fr. pampa] **:** a strong cold wind from the west or southwest that sweeps over the pampas

pam·phlet \'pam(p)-flət, 'pam-plət\ n [ME pamflet unbound booklet, fr. Pamphilus seu De Amore Pamphilus or On Love, popular Latin love poem of the 12th cent.] **:** an unbound printed publication with no cover or with a flush paper cover

¹pam·phle·teer \ˌpam(p)-flə-'ti(ə)r, ˌpam-plə-\ n **:** a writer of pamphlets attacking something or urging a cause

²pamphleteer vi **:** to write and publish pamphlets

¹pan \'pan\ n [ME panne, fr. OE; akin to OHG phanna pan; both fr. a prehistoric WGmc-NGmc word borrowed fr. L patina, fr. Gk patanē; akin to L patēre to be open — more at FATHOM] **1 a :** a container usu. broad, shallow, and open for domestic use **b :** any of various similar usu. metal receptacles: as (1) **:** either of the receptacles in a pair of scales (2) **:** a round shallow metal container used in separating gold or other metal from waste by washing **2 a :** a natural basin or depression **b :** an artificial basin **c :** a drifting fragment of the flat thin ice that forms in bays or along the shore **3 : HARDPAN 1 4** slang **: FACE**

²pan vb **panned; pan·ning** vi **1 :** to wash earth, gravel, or other material in a pan in search of gold or other metal **2 a :** to yield precious metal in the process of panning **b :** to turn out; esp **: SUCCEED** — usu. used with out ∼ vt **1 a :** to wash in a pan for the purpose of separating heavy particles **b :** to separate (as gold) by panning **2 :** to criticize severely

³pan \'pän\ n [Hindi pān, fr. Skt parṇa wing, leaf — more at FERN] **:** a betel leaf; also **:** a masticatory of betel nut, lime, and pan

⁴pan \'pan\ vb **panned; pan·ning** [panorama] vi **1 :** to rotate a motion-picture or television camera so as to keep an object in the picture or secure a panoramic effect **2** of a camera **:** to undergo such rotation ∼ vt **:** to cause to pan

⁵pan \'pan\ n **:** the process of panning a motion-picture or television camera

Pan \'pan\ n [L, fr. Gk] **:** the Greek god of forests, pastures, flocks, and shepherds represented as having the legs and sometimes the ears and horns of a goat

pan- comb form [Gk, fr. pan, neut. of pant-, pas all, every; akin to Skt śaśvat all, every, śvayati he swells] **1 :** all **:** completely 〈panchromatic〉 **2 a :** involving all of a (specified) group 〈Pan=American〉 **b :** advocating or involving the union of a (specified) group 〈Pan-Asian〉 **3 :** whole **:** general 〈panleucopenia〉

pan·a·cea \ˌpan-ə-'sē-ə\ n [L, fr. Gk panakeia, fr. pan- + akeisthai to heal, fr. akos remedy — more at AUTACOID] **:** a remedy for all ills or difficulties **: CURE-ALL — pan·a·ce·an** \-'sē-ən\ adj

pa·nache \pə-'nash, -'näsh\ n [MF pennache, fr. OIt pennacchio, fr. LL pinnaculum small wing — more at PINNACLE] **1 :** an ornamental tuft (as of feathers) esp. on a helmet **2 :** dash or flamboyance in style and action **: VERVE**

pa·na·da \pə-'näd-ə\ n [Sp, fr. pan bread, fr. L panis — more at FOOD] **:** a paste of flour or bread crumbs and water or stock used as a base for sauce or a binder for forcemeat or stuffing

pan·a·ma \'pan-ə-ˌmä, -ˌmò\ n, often cap [AmerSp panamá, fr. Panama, Central America] **:** a lightweight hat of natural-colored straw hand-plaited of narrow strips from the young leaves of the jipijapa

Pan–Amer·i·can \ˌpan-ə-'mer-ə-kən\ adj **:** of, relating to, or involving the independent republics of No. and So. America

Pan American Day n **:** April 14 observed as the anniversary of the founding of the Pan American Union in 1890

Pan–Amer·i·can·ism \-kə-ˌniz-əm\ n **:** a movement for greater cooperation among the Pan-American nations esp. in defense, commerce, and cultural relations

pan·a·tela \ˌpan-ə-'tel-ə\ n [Sp, fr. AmerSp, a long thin biscuit,

deriv. of L *panis* bread] **:** a long slender cigar with straight sides rounded off at the sealed end
[1]pan·cake \'pan-,kāk\ *n* **:** GRIDDLE CAKE
[2]pancake *vi* **:** to make a pancake landing ~ *vt* **:** to cause to pancake
pancake landing *n* **:** a landing in which the airplane is leveled off higher than for a normal landing causing it to stall and drop in an approximately horizontal position with little forward motion
pan·chax \'pan-,kaks\ *n* [NL] **:** any of numerous small brilliantly colored Old World killifishes (genus *Aplocheilus*) often kept in the tropical aquarium
Pan·chen Lama \,pän-chən-\ *n* [*Panchen* fr. Chin (Pek) *pan*1 *ch'an*2] **:** the lama next in rank to the Dalai Lama
pan·chro·mat·ic \,pan-krō-'mat-ik, ,paŋ-\ *adj* [ISV] **:** sensitive to light of all colors in the visible spectrum ⟨~ film⟩
pan·cra·ti·um \pan-'krā-shē-əm\ *n* [L, fr. Gk *pankration*, fr. *pan-* + *kratos* strength — more at HARD] **:** an ancient Greek athletic contest involving both boxing and wrestling
pan·cre·as \'paŋ-krē-əs, 'pan-\ *n* [NL, fr. Gk *pankreas*, fr. *pan-* + *kreas* flesh, meat — more at RAW] **:** a large compound racemose gland of vertebrates that secretes digestive enzymes and the hormone insulin — **pan·cre·at·ic** \,paŋ-krē-'at-ik, ,pan-\ *adj*
pancreat- *or* **pancreato-** *comb form* [NL, fr. Gk *pankreat-*, *pancreas*] **:** pancreas ⟨*pancreatic*⟩
pancreatic juice *n* **:** a clear alkaline secretion of pancreatic enzymes that is poured into the duodenum and acts on food already acted on by the gastric juice and saliva
pan·cre·atin \pan-'krē-ət-ən; 'paŋ-krē-, 'pan-\ *n* **:** a mixture of enzymes from the pancreatic juice or a preparation containing such a mixture
pan·da \'pan-də\ *n* [F, fr. native name in Nepal] **:** a large black-and-white mammal (*Ailuropoda melanoleuca*) of Tibet that suggests a bear but is related to the raccoons
pan·da·nus \pan-'dā-nəs, -'dan-əs\ *n* [NL, genus name, fr. Malay *pandan* screw pine] **:** SCREW PINE
Pan·da·rus \'pan-d(ə-)rəs\ *n* [L, fr. Gk *Pandaros*] **1 :** a leader of the Lycians in the Trojan War **2 :** the procurer of Cressida for Troilus
pan·dect \'pan-,dekt\ *n* [LL *Pandectae*, the Pandects, digest of Roman civil law (6th cent. A.D.), fr. L, pl. of *pandectes* encyclopedic work, fr. Gk *pandektēs* all-receiving, fr. *pan-* + *dechesthai* to receive; akin to Gk *dokein* to seem, seem good — more at DECENT] **1 :** a complete code of the laws of a country or system of law **2 :** a treatise covering an entire subject
[1]pan·dem·ic \pan-'dem-ik\ *adj* [LL *pandemus*, fr. Gk *pandēmos* of all the people, fr. *pan-* + *dēmos* people — more at DEMAGOGUE] **:** occurring over a wide geographic area and affecting an exceptionally high proportion of the population ⟨~ malaria⟩
[2]pandemic *n* **:** a pandemic outbreak of a disease
Pan·de·mo·ni·um \,pan-də-'mō-nē-əm\ *n* [NL, fr. Gk *pan-* + *daimōn* evil spirit — more at DEMON] **1 :** the capital of Hell in Milton's *Paradise Lost* **2 :** HELL **3** *not cap* **:** a wild uproar **:** TUMULT
[1]pan·der \'pan-dər\ *or* **pan·der·er** \-dər-ər\ *n* [*pander* fr. ME *Pandare* Pandarus, fr. L *Pandarus; panderer* fr. [2]*pander*] **1 a :** a go-between in love intrigues **b :** a man who solicits clients for a prostitute **2 :** someone who caters to or exploits the weaknesses of others
[2]pander *vi* **pan·der·ing** \-d(ə-)riŋ\ **:** to act as a pander; *esp* **:** to provide gratification for others' desires
pan·dit \'pan-dət, 'pən-\ *n* [Hindi *paṇḍit*, fr. Skt *paṇḍita*] **:** a wise or learned man in India — often used as an honorary title
pan·do·ra \pan-'dōr-ə, -'dȯr-\ *n* [It, fr. LL *pandura* 3-stringed lute] **:** BANDORE
Pandora *n* [L, fr. Gk *Pandōra*, lit., having all gifts] **:** a woman given a box by Zeus from which all human ills escaped when she opened it
pan·dow·dy \pan-'daủd-ē\ *n* [origin unknown] **:** a deep-dish apple dessert spiced, sweetened with sugar, molasses, or maple syrup, and covered with a rich crust
pan·du·rate \pan-'d(y)ủr-ət\ *adj* [LL *pandura*] **:** resembling a fiddle in outline
pan·du·ri·form \pan-'d(y)ủr-ə-,fȯrm\ *adj* [NL *panduriformis*, fr. LL *pandura* + L *-iformis* -iform] **:** PANDURATE
pane \'pān\ *n* [ME *pan*, *pane* strip of cloth, pane, fr. MF *pan*, fr. L *pannus* cloth, rag — more at VANE] **1 :** a piece, section, or side of something: as **a :** a framed sheet of glass in a window or door **b :** one of the sides of a nut or bolt head **2 :** one of the sections into which a sheet of postage stamps is cut for distribution
pan·e·gy·ric \,pan-ə-'jir-ik, -'jī-rik\ *n* [L *panegyricus*, fr. Gk *panēgyrikos*, fr. *panēgyrikos* of or for a festival assembly, fr. *panēgyris* festival assembly, fr. *pan-* + *agyris* assembly; akin to Gk *ageirein* to gather — more at GREGARIOUS] **:** a eulogistic oration or writing; *also* **:** formal or elaborate praise **syn** see ENCOMIUM — **pan·e·gy·ri·cal** \-'jir-i-kəl, -'jī-ri-\ *adj* — **pan·e·gy·ri·cal·ly** \-k(ə-)lē\ *adv*
pan·e·gy·rist \,pan-ə-'jir-əst, -'jī-rəst, 'pan-ə-,\ *n* **:** EULOGIST
[1]pan·el \'pan-ᵊl\ *n* [ME, piece of cloth, slip of parchment, jury schedule, fr. MF, piece of cloth, piece, prob. fr. (assumed) VL *pannellus*, dim. of L *pannus* cloth] **1 a** (1) **:** a schedule containing names of persons summoned as jurors (2) **:** the group of persons so summoned (3) **:** JURY 1 **b** (1) **:** a group of persons selected (as to advise) (2) **:** a group of persons who discuss before an audience a topic of usu. political or social interest; *also* **:** a discussion by such a panel (3) **:** a group of entertainers or guests engaged as players in a quiz or guessing game on a radio or television program **2 :** a separate or distinct part of a surface: as **a :** a fence section **:** HURDLE **b** (1) **:** a thin usu. rectangular board set in a frame (as in a door) (2) **:** a usu. sunken or raised section of a surface set off by a margin (3) **:** a flat usu. rectangular piece of construction material (as plywood) made to form part of a surface **c :** a vertical section of fabric (as a gore) **d :** any of several units of construction of an airplane wing surface **e :** a flat, smooth, or unmarked area on a container **3 :** a thin flat piece of wood on which a picture is painted; *also* **:** a painting on such a surface **4 a :** a section of a switchboard **b :** a flat insulating support for parts of an electrical device usu. with control handles on one face **c :** a usu. vertical mount for controls or dials of instruments of measurement
[2]panel *vt* **pan·eled** *or* **pan·elled**; **pan·el·ing** *or* **pan·el·ling** \'pan-ᵊl-iŋ, 'pan-liŋ\ **:** to furnish or decorate with panels
panel heating *n* **:** space heating by means of wall, floor, baseboard, or ceiling panels with embedded electric conductors or hot-air or hot-water pipes
pan·el·ing *n* **:** panels joined in a continuous surface; *esp* **:** decorative wood panels so combined
pan·el·ist \'pan-ᵊl-əst\ *n* **:** a member of a discussion or advisory panel or of a radio or television panel
panel truck *n* **:** a small light motortruck with a fully enclosed body used chiefly for delivery service
pan·e·tela *or* **pan·e·tel·la** *var of* PANATELA
pan·fish \'pan-,fish\ *n* **:** a small food fish (as a sunfish) usu. taken with hook and line and not available on the market
[1]pang \'paŋ\ *n* [origin unknown] **1 :** a brief piercing spasm of pain **2 :** a sudden sharp attack of mental anguish
[2]pang *vt* **:** to cause to have pangs **:** TORMENT
pan·gen·e·sis \(')pan-'jen-ə-səs\ *n* [NL] **:** a hypothetical mechanism of heredity in which the cells throw off particles that circulate freely throughout the system, multiply by subdivision, and collect in the reproductive products or in buds so that the egg or bud contains particles from all parts of the parent — **pan·ge·net·ic** \,pan-jə-'net-ik\ *adj* — **pan·ge·net·i·cal·ly** \-i-k(ə-)lē\ *adv*
pan·go·lin \pan-'gō-lən\ *n* [Malay *pĕngguling*] **:** any of several Asiatic and African edentate mammals (*Manis* or related genera of the order Pholidota) having the body covered with large imbricated horny scales
[1]pan·han·dle \'pan-,han-dᵊl\ *n* **:** a narrow projection of a larger territory (as a state)
[2]panhandle *vb* **pan·han·dling** \-,han-(d)liŋ, -dᵊl-iŋ\ [back-formation fr. *panhandler*, prob. fr. *panhandle*, n.; fr. the extended forearm] *vi* **:** BEG ~ *vt* **1 :** to accost on the street and beg from **2 :** to get by panhandling — **pan·han·dler** \-(d)lər, -dᵊl-ər\ *n*
Pan·hel·len·ic \,pan-hə-'len-ik\ *adj* **1 :** of or relating to all Greece or all the Greeks **2 :** of or relating to the Greek-letter sororities or fraternities in American colleges and universities or to an association representing them
[1]pan·ic \'pan-ik\ *adj* [F *panique*, fr. Gk *panikos*, lit., of Pan, fr. *Pan*] **1 :** of, relating to, or resembling the mental or emotional state believed induced by the god Pan ⟨~ fear⟩ **2 :** of, relating to, or arising from a panic **3 :** of or relating to the god Pan
[2]panic *n* **1 :** a sudden overpowering fright; *esp* **:** a sudden unreasoning terror often accompanied by mass flight **2 :** a sudden widespread fright concerning financial affairs and resulting in a depression in values caused by violent measures for protection of securities or other property **3** *slang* **:** something very funny **syn** see FEAR — **pan·icky** \'pan-i-kē\ *adj* — **pan·ic–strick·en** \-,strik-ən\ *adj*
[3]panic *vt* **pan·icked** \-ikt\ **pan·ick·ing 1 :** to affect with panic **2 :** to produce demonstrative appreciation on the part of ⟨~ an audience with a gag⟩
pan·ic grass \'pan-ik-\ *n* [ME *panik*, fr. MF or L; MF *panic* foxtail millet, fr. L *panicum*, fr. *panus* swelling, ear of millet] **:** any of various grasses (*Panicum* or related genera) including important forage and cereal grasses
pan·i·cle \'pan-i-kəl\ *n* [L *panicula*, fr. dim. of *panus* swelling] **:** a compound racemose inflorescence; *broadly* **:** a pyramidal loosely branched flower cluster — **pan·i·cled** \-kəld\ *adj* — **pa·nic·u·late** \pa-'nik-yə-lət\ *adj*
Pan·ja·bi \,pən-'jäb-ē, -'jab-\ *n* [Hindi *pañjābī*, fr. *pañjābī* of Punjab] **1 :** an Indic language of the Punjab **2 :** PUNJABI
pan·jan·drum \pan-'jan-drəm\ *n* [Grand *Panjandrum*, burlesque title of an imaginary personage in some nonsense lines by Samuel Foote] **:** a powerful personage or pretentious official
pan·leu·co·pe·nia \,pan-,lü-kə-'pē-nē-ə\ *n* [NL] **:** an acute usu. fatal viral epizootic disease of cats characterized by fever, diarrhea and dehydration, and extensive destruction of white blood cells
panne \'pan\ *n* [F, fr. OF *penne*, *panne* fur used for lining, fr. L *pinna* feather, wing — more at PEN] **1 :** a silk or rayon velvet with lustrous pile flattened in one direction **2 :** a heavy silk or rayon satin with high luster and waxy smoothness
pan·nier *or* **pan·ier** \'pan-yər, 'pan-ē-ər\ *n* [ME *panier*, fr. MF, fr. L *panarium*, fr. *panis* bread — more at FOOD] **1 :** a large basket; *esp* **:** one often carried on the back of an animal or the shoulders of a person **2 a :** one of a pair of hoops formerly used to expand women's skirts at the sides **b :** an overskirt draped at the sides
pan·ni·kin \'pan-i-kən\ *n* [[1]*pan* + *-nikin* (as in *cannikin*)] *Brit* **:** a small pan or cup
pa·no·cha \pə-'nō-chə\ *or* **pa·no·che** \-chē\ *var of* PENUCHE
pan·o·plied \'pan-ə-plēd\ *adj* **:** dressed in or having a panoply
pan·o·ply \'pan-ə-plē\ *n* [Gk *panoplia*, fr. *pan-* + *hopla* arms, armor, pl. of *hoplon* tool, weapon — more at HOPLITE] **1 a :** a full suit of armor **b :** ceremonial attire **2 :** something forming a protective covering **3 a :** a magnificent or impressive array **b :** a display of all appropriate appurtenances
pan·ora·ma \,pan-ə-'ram-ə, -'räm-\ *n* [*pan-* + Gk *horama* sight, fr. *horan* to see — more at WARY] **1 a :** CYCLORAMA 1 **b :** a picture exhibited a part at a time by being unrolled before the spectator **2 a :** an unobstructed or complete view of a region in every direction **b :** a comprehensive presentation of a subject **c :** RANGE **3 :** a mental picture of a series of images or events — **pan·oram·ic** \-'ram-ik\ *adj*
pan·pipe \'pan-,pīp\ *n* [*Pan*, its traditional inventor] **:** a primitive wind instrument consisting of a graduated series of short vertical flutes bound together with the mouthpieces in an even row — often used in pl.

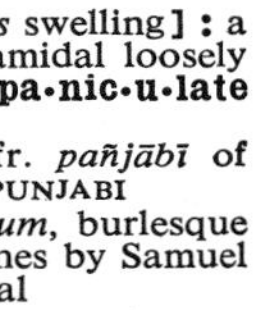

panpipe

pan·sy \'pan-zē\ *n* [MF *pensée*, fr. *pensée* thought, fr. fem. of *pensé*, pp. of *penser* to think, fr. L *pensare* to ponder — more at PENSIVE] **1 :** a garden plant (*Viola tricolor hortensis*) derived chiefly from the wild pansy of Europe by hybridizing the latter with other wild violets; *also* **:** its flower **2 a :** an effeminate youth **b :** a male homosexual
[1]pant \'pant\ *vb* [ME *panten*, fr. MF *pantaisier*, fr. (assumed) VL *phantasiare* to have hallucinations, fr. Gk *phantasioun*, fr. *phantasia* appearance, imagination — more at FANCY] *vi* **1 a :** to breathe quickly, spasmodically, or in a labored manner **b :** to run panting **c :** to move with or make a throbbing or puffing sound **2 :** to long eagerly **:** YEARN **3 :** THROB, PULSATE ~ *vt* **:** to utter with panting **:** GASP
[2]pant *n* **1 a :** a panting breath **b :** the visible movement of the chest accompanying such a breath **2 :** a throbbing or puffing sound

pant- or **panto-** comb form [MF, fr. L, fr. Gk, fr. pant-, pas — more at PAN-] : all ⟨pantology⟩

Pan·ta·gru·el \,pant-ə-'grü-əl; pan-'tag-rə-wəl, -,wel\ n [F] : the unrestrainedly humorous and huge son of Gargantua in Rabelais's Pantagruel — **Pan·ta·gru·el·ian** \,pant-ə-grü-'el-ē-ən, pan-,tag-rə-'wel-\ adj — **Pan·ta·gru·el·ism** \,pant-ə-'grü-əl-,iz-əm; pan-'tag-rə-wəl-,iz-əm, -,wel-\ n — **Pan·ta·gru·el·ist** \-əst\ n

pan·ta·lets or **pan·ta·lettes** \,pant-ᵊl-'ets\ n pl [pantaloons] : long drawers with a ruffle at the bottom of each leg usu. showing below the skirt and worn by women and children in the first half of the 19th century

pan·ta·loon \,pant-ᵊl-'ün\ n [MF & OIt; MF Pantalon, fr. OIt Pantaleone, Pantalone] **1 a** or **pan·ta·lo·ne** \-ᵊl-'ō-nē\ cap : a character in the commedia dell'arte that is usu. a lean old dotard who wears spectacles, slippers, and a tight-fitting combination of trousers and stockings **b** : a buffoon in pantomimes **2** pl **a** : BREECHES **b** : TROUSERS

pan·tech·ni·con \pan-'tek-ni-kən\ n [short for pantechnicon van, fr. pantechnicon (storage warehouse)] Brit : ³VAN 1

pan·the·ism \'pan(t)-thē-,iz-əm\ n [F panthéisme, fr. panthéiste pantheist, fr. E pantheist, fr. pan- + -theist] : a doctrine that equates God with the forces and laws of the universe — **pan·the·ist** \-thē-əst\ n — **pan·the·is·tic** \,pan(t)-thē-'is-tik\ or **pan·the·is·ti·cal** \-ti-kəl\ adj — **pan·the·is·ti·cal·ly** \-ti-k(ə-)lē\ adv

pan·the·on \'pan(t)-thē-,än, -ən\ n [ME Panteon, a temple at Rome, fr. L Pantheon, fr. Gk pantheion temple of all the gods, fr. neut. of pantheios of all gods, fr. pan- + theos god] **1** : a temple dedicated to all the gods **2** : a building serving as the burial place of or containing memorials to famous dead **3** : the gods of a people; esp : the gods officially recognized

pan·ther \'pan(t)-thər\ n, pl panthers also panther [ME pantere, fr. OF, fr. L panthera, fr. Gk panthēr] **1** : LEOPARD: as **a** : a leopard of a supposed exceptionally large fierce variety **b** : a leopard of the black color phase **2** : COUGAR **3** : JAGUAR

pant·ie or **panty** \'pant-ē\ n [pants] : a woman's or child's undergarment covering the lower trunk and made with closed crotch and very short legs — usu. used in pl.

pantie girdle n : a woman's girdle with a sewed-in or detachable crotch made with or without garters and boning

pan·tile \'pan-,tīl\ n [¹pan] **1** : a roofing tile whose cross section is a dissymmetric ogee curve **2** : a longitudinally curved roofing tile laid alternately with convex covering tiles

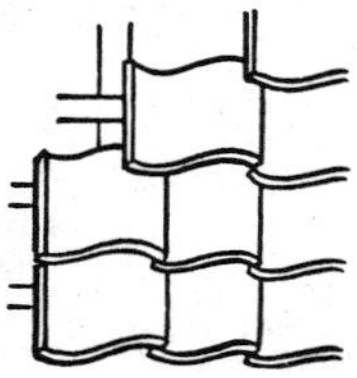

pan·to·fle \pan-'tōf-əl, -'täf-, -'tüf-; 'pant-ə-fəl\ n [ME pantufle, fr. MF pantoufle] : SLIPPER

pan·to·graph \'pant-ə-,graf\ n [F pantographe, fr. pant- + -graphe -graph] **1** : an instrument for copying on any predetermined scale consisting of four light rigid bars jointed in parallelogram form; also : a similar jointed device **2** : an electrical trolley carried by a collapsible and adjustable frame — **pan·to·graph·ic** \,pant-ə-'graf-ik\ adj

pantiles 1

pan·to·mime \'pant-ə-,mīm\ n [L pantomimus, fr. pant- + mimus mime] **1** : PANTOMIMIST **2 a** : an ancient Roman dramatic performance featuring a solo dancer and a narrative chorus **b** : any of various dramatic or dancing performances in which a story is told by expressive bodily or facial movements of the performers **3** : conveyance of a story by bodily or facial movements esp. in drama or dance **4** : the art or genre of conveying a story by bodily movements only — **pantomime** vb — **pan·to·mim·ic** \,pant-ə-'mim-ik\ adj

pan·to·mim·ist \'pant-ə-,mim-əst, -,mīm-\ n : an actor or dancer in or a composer of pantomimes

pan·to·the·nate \,pant-ə-'then-,āt, pan-'täth-ə-,nāt\ n : a salt or ester of pantothenic acid

pan·to·then·ic acid \,pant-ə-,then-ik-\ n [Gk pantothen from all sides, fr. pant-, pas all — more at PAN-] : a viscous oily acid $C_9H_{17}NO_5$ of the vitamin B complex found in all living tissues

pan·toum \pan-'tüm\ n [F, fr. Malay pantun] : a series of quatrains with interlaced rhyming (as abab, bcbc, cdcd) in which the second and fourth verses of each stanza are repeated as the first and third verses of the following stanza and the first and third verses of the opening stanza as the second and fourth verses of the final stanza

pan·trop·ic \(')pan-'träp-ik\ adj : occurring or distributed throughout the tropical regions of the earth

pan·try \'pan-trē\ n [ME panetrie, fr. MF paneterie, fr. OF, fr. panetier servant in charge of the pantry, irreg. fr. pan bread, fr. L panis — more at FOOD] **1** : a room or closet used for storing provisions or glassware and china or for serving **2** : a room for preparation of cold foods

pants \'pan(t)s\ n pl [short for pantaloons] **1** : TROUSERS **2** chiefly Brit : men's short underpants **3** : PANTIE

panty·waist \'pant-ē-,wāst\ n **1** : a child's garment consisting of short pants buttoned to a waist **2** : SISSY — **pantywaist** adj

Pan·urge \'pan-,ərj, pa-'nü(ə)rzh\ n [F] : a witty rascal and companion of Pantagruel in Rabelais's Pantagruel

¹pan·zer \'pan-zər, 'pän(t)-sər\ adj [G panzer-, fr. panzer coat of mail, armor, fr. OF pancière, fr. pance belly, paunch — more at PAUNCH] : of or relating to a panzer division or similar armored unit

²panzer n : TANK

panzer division n : a German armored division

¹pap \'pap\ n [ME pappe] **1** chiefly dial : NIPPLE, TEAT **2** : something shaped like a nipple

²pap n [ME] **1** : a soft food for infants or invalids **2** : political patronage **3** : something lacking solid value or substance

pa·pa \'päp-ə, chiefly Brit pə-'pä\ n [F (baby talk)] : FATHER

Papa — a communications code word for the letter p

pa·pa·cy \'pā-pə-sē\ n [ME papacie, fr. ML papatia, fr. LL papa pope — more at POPE] **1** : the office of pope **2** : a succession or line of popes **3** : the term of a pope's reign **4** cap : the system of government of the Roman Catholic Church of which the pope is the supreme head

pa·pa·in \pə-'pā-ən, -'pī-ən\ n [ISV, fr. papaya] : a proteinase

in the juice of unripe papaya used esp. as a tenderizer for meat and in medicine

pa·pal \'pā-pəl\ adj [ME, fr. MF, fr. ML papalis, fr. LL papa] : of or relating to a pope or to the Roman Catholic Church — **pa·pal·ly** \-pə-lē\ adv

papal cross n — see CROSS illustration

Pa·pa·ni·co·laou test \,päp-ə-'nē-kə-,laù-, ,pap-ə-'nik-ə-\ n [George N. Papanicolaou †1962 Am medical scientist] : a method for the early detection of cancer by special staining of exfoliated cells

pa·pav·er·ine \pə-'pav-ə-,rēn, -(ə-)rən\ n [ISV, fr. L papaver poppy] : a crystalline alkaloid $C_{20}H_{21}NO_4$ found in opium and used chiefly as an antispasmodic because of its ability to relax smooth muscle

pa·paw n [prob. modif. of Sp papaya] **1** \pə-'pò\ : PAPAYA **2** \'päp-,ò, 'pòp-\ : a No. American tree (Asimina triloba) of the custard-apple family with purple flowers and a yellow edible fruit; also : its fruit

pa·pa·ya \pə-'pī-ə\ n [Sp, of AmerInd origin; akin to Otomac papai] : a tropical American tree (Carica papaya of the family Caricaceae, the papaya family) with large oblong yellow edible fruit; also : its fruit

¹pa·per \'pā-pər\ n [ME papir, fr. MF papier, fr. L papyrus papyrus, paper, fr. Gk papyros papyrus] **1 a** : a felted sheet of usu. vegetable fibers laid down on a fine screen from a water suspension **b** : a sheet or piece of paper **2 a** : a piece of paper containing a written or printed statement : DOCUMENT **b** : a piece of paper containing writing or print **c** : a written composition **d** : a piece of written schoolwork **3** : a paper container or wrapper **4** : NEWSPAPER **5** : the negotiable notes or instruments of commerce **6** : WALLPAPER **7** : TICKETS; esp : free passes

²paper vt **pa·per·ing** \'pā-p(ə-)riŋ\ **1** archaic : to put down or describe in writing **2** : to fold or enclose in paper **3** : to cover or line with paper; esp : to apply wallpaper to **4** : to fill by giving out free passes ~ vi : to hang wallpaper — **pa·per·er** \-pər-ər\ n

³paper adj **1 a** : made of paper, paperboard, or papier-mâché ⟨~ carton⟩ **b** : resembling paper in texture, strength, or thickness : PAPERY **2** : of or relating to clerical work or written communication **3** : NOMINAL, THEORETICAL **4** : admitted by free passes ⟨~ audience⟩ **5** : issued as paper money

pa·per·back \'pā-pər-,bak\ n : a paper-covered book — **paperback** adj

paper birch n : an American birch (Betula papyrifera) with peeling white bark often worked into fancy articles

pa·per·board \'pā-pər-,bō(ə)rd, -,bò(ə)rd\ n : a composition board : CARDBOARD — **paperboard** adj

paper chase n : HARE AND HOUNDS

paper cutter n **1** : PAPER KNIFE **2** : a machine for simultaneous cutting of many sheets of paper

pa·per·hang·er \'pā-pər-,haŋ-ər\ n : one that applies wallpaper

pa·per·hang·ing \-,haŋ-iŋ\ n : the act of applying wallpaper

pa·per·i·ness \'pā-p(ə-)rē-nəs\ n : the condition of being papery

paper knife n **1** : a knife for slitting envelopes or uncut pages **2** : the knife of a paper cutter

paper money n **1** : money consisting of government notes and bank notes **2** : BANK MONEY

paper mulberry n : an Asiatic tree (Broussonetia papyrifera) of the mulberry family widely grown as a shade tree

paper profit n : a profit that can be realized by selling (as when market value exceeds book value)

pa·per·weight \'pā-pər-,wāt\ n : an object used to hold down loose papers by its weight

paper work n : routine clerical or record-keeping work often incidental to a more important task

pa·pery \'pā-p(ə-)rē\ adj : resembling paper in thinness or consistency

pa·pe·terie \'pap-ə-trē, ,pap-ə-'\ n [F] : packaged fancy writing papers

¹Pa·phi·an \'pā-fē-ən\ adj [L paphius, fr. Gk paphios, fr. Paphos, ancient city of Cyprus that was the center of worship of Aphrodite] **1** : of or relating to Paphos or its people **2** : of or relating to illicit love : WANTON

²Paphian n **1** : a native or inhabitant of Paphos **2** often not cap : PROSTITUTE

pa·pier col·lé \,päp-,yā-(,)kò-'lā, ,pap-\ n, pl **papiers collés** \-,yā-(,)kò-'lā(z)\ [F, glued paper] : COLLAGE

pa·pier-mâ·ché \,pā-pər-mə-'shā, ,pap-ər-mä-'shā, -(,)ma-\ n [F, lit., chewed paper] : a light strong molding material of wastepaper pulped with glue and other additives — **papier-mâché** adj

pa·pil·i·o·na·ceous \pə-,pil-ē-ə-'nā-shəs\ adj [L papilion-, papilio butterfly — more at PAVILION] **1** : resembling a butterfly esp. in irregular shape **2** : LEGUMINOUS 1

pa·pil·la \pə-'pil-ə\ n, pl **pa·pil·lae** \-'pil-(,)ē, -,ī\ [L; akin to L papula pimple, Lith papas nipple] **1** obs : the nipple of the breast **2** : a small projecting body part similar to a nipple in form: **a** : vascular process of connective tissue extending into and nourishing the root of a hair, feather, or developing tooth **b** : one of the vascular protuberances of the dermal layer of the skin extending into the epidermal layer and often containing tactile corpuscles **c** : one of the small protuberances on the upper surface of the tongue — **pa·pil·lar·y** \'pap-ə-,ler-ē, pə-'pil-ə-rē\ adj — **pa·pil·late** \'pap-ə-,lāt, pə-'pil-ət\ adj — **pa·pil·lose** \'pap-ə-,lōs, pə-'pil-,ōs\ adj

pap·il·lo·ma \,pap-ə-'lō-mə\ n, pl **papillomas** or **pap·il·lo·ma·ta** \-mət-ə\ **1** : a benign tumor (as a wart) due to overgrowth of epithelial tissue on papillae of vascular connective tissue (as of the skin) **2** : an epithelial tumor caused by a virus — **pap·il·lo·ma·tous** \,pap-ə-'läm-ət-əs, -'lō-mət-\ adj

pa·pil·lon \,päp-ē-'(y)ōⁿ, 'pap-\ n [F, lit., butterfly, fr. L papilion-, papilio] : any of a breed of small slender toy spaniels resembling long-haired Chihuahuas

pa·pil·lote \,päp-ē-'(y)ōt, ,pap-\ n [F, fr. papillon butterfly] **1** : CURLPAPER **2** : a greased paper wrapper in which food is cooked

pa·pist \'pā-pəst\ n, often cap [MF or NL; MF papiste, fr. pape pope; NL papista, fr. LL papa pope] : ROMAN CATHOLIC — usu. used disparagingly

pa·pist·ry \'pā-pə-strē\ *n* **:** ROMAN CATHOLICISM — usu. used disparagingly

pa·poose \pa-'püs, pə-\ *n* [Narraganset *papoòs*] **:** a young child of No. American Indian parents

pap·pose \'pap-,ōs\ *also* **pap·pous** \'pap-əs\ *adj* **:** having or being a pappus

pap·pus \'pap-əs\ *n, pl* **pap·pi** \'pap-,ī, -,ē\ [L, fr. Gk *pappos*] **:** an appendage or tuft of appendages crowning the ovary or fruit in various seed plants and functioning in dispersal of the fruit

pa·pri·ka \pə-'prē-kə, pa-\ *n* [Hung, fr. Serb, fr. *papar* pepper, fr. Gk *peperi*] **:** a condiment consisting of the dried finely ground pods of various cultivated sweet peppers; *also* **:** a sweet pepper used for making paprika

Pap·u·an \'pap-yə-wən\ *n* **1 :** a native or inhabitant of Papua **2 :** a member of any of the negroid native peoples of New Guinea and adjacent areas of Melanesia **3 :** any of a heterogeneous group of languages spoken in New Guinea, New Britain, and the Solomon islands — **Papuan** *adj*

pap·u·lar \'pap-yə-lər\ *adj* **:** consisting of or characterized by papules

pap·ule \'pap-(,)yü(ə)l\ *n* [L *papula*] **:** a small solid usu. conical elevation of the skin — **pap·u·lif·er·ous** \,pap-yə-'lif-(ə-)rəs\ *adj*

pa·py·rus \pə-'pī-rəs\ *n, pl* **pa·py·rus·es** *or* **pa·py·ri** \-'pī(ə)r-(,)ē, -,ī\ [ME, fr. L — more at PAPER] **1 :** a tall sedge (*Cyperus papyrus*) of the Nile valley **2 :** the pith of the papyrus plant esp. when cut in strips and pressed into a writing material **3 a :** a writing on papyrus **b :** a written scroll made of papyrus

par \'pär\ *n* [L, one that is equal, fr. *par* equal] **1 a :** the established value of the monetary unit of one country expressed in terms of the monetary unit of another country using the same metal as the standard of value **b** (1) **:** the face value of securities or certificates of value (2) **:** the price at which securities are issued — called also *par value* **2 :** common level **:** EQUALITY **3 a :** an amount taken as an average or norm **b :** an accepted standard; *specif* **:** a usual standard of physical condition or health **4 :** the score standard set for each hole of a golf course — **par** *adj*

1**pa·ra** *n* [Turk] **1** \pə-'rä\ **a :** a Turkish monetary unit equal in modern Turkey to $\frac{1}{4000}$ of a lira **b :** a coin representing one para **2** \'pär-(,)ä\ [Serbo-Croatian, fr. Turk] — see *dinar* at MONEY table

2**para** \'par-ə\ *adj* [1*para-*] **:** relating to or having an ortho-relation in the benzene ring

1**para-** *or* **par-** *prefix* [ME, fr. MF, fr. L, fr. Gk, fr. *para;* akin to Gk *pro* before — more at FOR] **1 :** beside **:** alongside of **:** beyond **:** aside from ⟨*para*thyroid⟩ ⟨*par*enteral⟩ **2 a :** closely related to ⟨*para*ldehyde⟩ **b :** involving substitution at or characterized by two opposite positions in the benzene ring that are separated by two carbon atoms ⟨*para*dichlorobenzene⟩ **3 a :** faulty **:** abnormal ⟨*par*esthesia⟩ **b :** associated in a subsidiary or accessory capacity ⟨*para*sympathetic⟩ **c :** closely resembling **:** almost ⟨*para*typhoid⟩

2**para-** *comb form* [*parachute*] **1 :** parachute ⟨*para*trooper⟩ **2 :** parachutist ⟨*para*spotter⟩

-p·a·ra \p-(ə-)rə\ *n comb form, pl* **-p·a·ras** \p-(ə-)rəz\ *or* **-p·a·rae** \p-ə-,rē, -,rī\ [L, fr. *parere* to give birth to — more at PARE] **:** woman delivered of (so many) children ⟨nulli*para*⟩

para-ami·no·ben·zo·ic acid \'par-ə-ə-,mē-(,)nō-(,)ben-,zō-ik-, 'par-ə-,am-ə-(,)nō-\ *n* [ISV] **:** a colorless para-substituted aminobenzoic acid of the vitamin B complex

para·bi·o·sis \,par-ə-(,)bī-'ō-səs, -bē-\ *n* [NL] **1 :** reversible suspension of obvious vital activities **2 :** anatomical and physiological union of two organisms — **para·bi·ot·ic** \-'ät-ik\ *adj* — **para·bi·ot·i·cal·ly** \-i-k(ə-)lē\ *adv*

par·a·ble \'par-ə-bəl\ *n* [ME, fr. MF, fr. LL *parabola*, fr. Gk *parabolē*, fr. *paraballein* to compare, fr. *para-* + *ballein* to throw — more at DEVIL] **:** COMPARISON; *specif* **:** a usu. short fictitious story that illustrates a moral attitude or a religious principle **syn** see ALLEGORY — **par·a·bol·ic** \,par-ə-'bäl-ik\ *adj*

pa·rab·o·la \pə-'rab-ə-lə\ *n* [NL, fr. Gk *parabolē*, lit., comparison] **1 :** a plane curve generated by a point moving so that its distance from a fixed point is equal to its distance from a fixed line **:** the intersection of a right circular cone with a plane parallel to an element of the cone **2 :** something bowl-shaped (as a microphone) — **par·a·bol·ic** \,par-ə-'bäl-ik\ *adj*

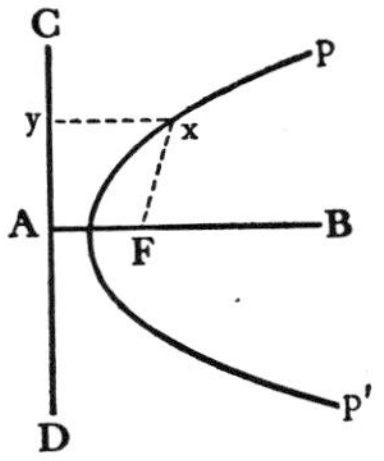

parabola: *F* focus; *AB* axis; *CD* directrix; *x* any point on parabola; *y* intersection of *CD* and perpendicular from *x; p p'* parabola

pa·rab·o·loid \pə-'rab-ə-,lȯid\ *n* **:** a surface all of whose intersections by planes are either parabolas and ellipses or parabolas and hyperbolas

1**para·chute** \'par-ə-,shüt\ *n* [F, fr. *para-* (as in *parasol*) + *chute* fall — more at CHUTE] **1 :** a folding umbrella-shaped device of light fabric used esp. for making a safe descent from an airplane **2 :** PATAGIUM **3 :** a device suggestive of a parachute in form, use, or operation — **para·chut·ic** \,par-ə-'shüt-ik\ *adj*

2**parachute** *vt* **:** to convey by means of a parachute ~ *vi* **:** to descend by means of a parachute

parachute spinnaker *n* **:** an exceptionally large spinnaker used esp. on racing yachts

para·chut·ist \'par-ə-,shüt-əst\ *n* **:** one that parachutes; *specif* **:** a soldier trained and equipped to parachute from an airplane

Par·a·clete \'par-ə-,klēt\ *n* [ME *Paraclit*, fr. MF *Paraclet*, fr. LL *Paracletus*, fr. Gk *Paraklētos*, lit., comforter, fr. *parakalein* to comfort, fr. *para-* + *kalein* to call — more at LOW] **:** HOLY SPIRIT

1**pa·rade** \pə-'rād\ *n* [F, fr. MF, fr. *parer* to prepare — more at PARE] **1 :** a pompous show **:** EXHIBITION **2 a :** the ceremonial formation of a body of troops before a superior officer **b :** a place where troops assemble regularly for parade **3 :** a public procession **4 a :** a place of promenade **b :** those who promenade

2**parade** *vt* **1 :** to cause to maneuver or march **:** MARSHAL **2 :** PROMENADE **3 :** to exhibit ostentatiously ~ *vi* **1 :** to march in a procession **2 :** PROMENADE **3 a :** to show off **b :** MASQUERADE **syn** see SHOW — **pa·rad·er** *n*

para·di·chlo·ro·ben·zene \,par-ə-,dī-,klōr-ə-'ben-,zēn, -,klȯr-, -,ben-'\ *n* [ISV] **:** a white crystalline compound $C_6H_4Cl_2$ made by chlorinating benzene and used chiefly as a fumigant

par·a·digm \'par-ə-,dīm, -,dim\ *n* [LL *paradigma*, fr. Gk *paradeigma*, fr. *paradeiknynai* to show side by side, fr. *para-* + *deiknynai* to show — more at DICTION] **1 :** EXAMPLE, PATTERN **2 :** an example of a conjugation or declension showing a word in all its inflectional forms — **par·a·dig·mat·ic** \,par-ə-dig-'mat-ik\ *adj*

par·a·di·sa·ic \,par-ə-,dī-'sā-ik, -'zā-\ *adj* [*paradise* + *-aic* (as in *Hebraic*)] **:** PARADISIACAL — **par·a·di·sa·i·cal** \-'sā-ə-kəl, -'zā-\ *adj* — **par·a·di·sa·i·cal·ly** \-k(ə-)lē\ *adv*

par·a·dis·al \,par-ə-'dī-səl, -'dī-zəl\ *adj* **:** PARADISIACAL

par·a·dise \'par-ə-,dīs, -,dīz\ *n* [ME *paradis*, fr. OF, fr. LL *paradisus*, fr. Gk *paradeisos*, lit., enclosed park, of Iranian origin; akin to Av *pairi-daēza-* enclosure; akin to Gk *peri* around and to Gk *teichos* wall — more at PERI-, DOUGH] **1 a :** the garden of Eden **b :** LIMBO **c :** HEAVEN **2 :** a place of bliss, felicity, or delight

par·a·di·si·a·cal \,par-ə-də-'sī-ə-kəl, -,dī-, -'zī-\ *or* **par·a·dis·i·ac** \-'diz-ē-,ak, -'dis-\ *adj* [LL *paradisiacus*, fr. *paradisus*] **:** of, relating to, or resembling paradise — **par·a·di·si·a·cal·ly** \-də-'sī-ə-k(ə-)lē, -,dī-, -'zī-\ *adv*

par·a·dox \'par-ə-,däks\ *n* [L *paradoxum*, fr. Gk *paradoxon*, fr. neut. of *paradoxos* contrary to expectation, fr. *para-* + *dokein* to think — more at DECENT] **1 :** a tenet contrary to received opinion **2 a :** a statement that is seemingly contradictory or opposed to common sense and yet is perhaps true **b :** a self-contradictory statement that at first seems true **c :** an argument that apparently derives self-contradictory conclusions by valid deduction from acceptable premises **3 :** something (as a person, condition, or act) with seemingly contradictory qualities or phases — **par·a·dox·i·cal** \,par-ə-'däk-si-kəl\ *adj* — **par·a·dox·i·cal·ly** \-k(ə-)lē\ *adv* — **par·a·dox·i·cal·ness** \-kəl-nəs\ *n*

par·aes·the·sia *var of* PARESTHESIA

1**par·af·fin** \'par-ə-fən\ *n* [G, fr. L *parum* too little + *affinis* bordering on; akin to L *paucus* few — more at FEW, AFFINITY] **1 a :** a waxy crystalline flammable substance obtained esp. from distillates of wood, coal, or petroleum or shale oil that is a complex mixture of hydrocarbons and is used chiefly in coating and sealing, in candles, in rubber compounding, and in pharmaceuticals and cosmetics **b :** any of various mixtures of similar hydrocarbons including mixtures that are semisolid or oily **2 :** a hydrocarbon of the methane series **3** *chiefly Brit* **:** KEROSINE — **par·af·fin·ic** \,par-ə-'fin-ik\ *adj*

2**paraffin** *vt* **:** to coat or saturate with paraffin

para·gen·e·sis \,par-ə-'jen-ə-səs\ *n* [NL] **:** the formation of minerals in contact so as to affect one another's development — **para·ge·net·ic** \-jə-'net-ik\ *adj*

1**par·a·gon** \'par-ə-,gän, -gən\ *n* [MF, fr. OIt *paragone*, lit., touchstone, fr. *paragonare* to test on a touchstone, fr. Gk *parakonan* to sharpen, fr. *para-* + *akonē* whetstone, fr. *akē* point; akin to Gk *akmē* point — more at EDGE] **1 :** a model of excellence or perfection **:** PATTERN **2 a :** a perfect diamond of 100 carats or more **b :** a perfectly spherical pearl of exceptional size

2**paragon** *vt* **1 :** to compare with **:** PARALLEL **2 :** to put in rivalry **:** MATCH **3** *obs* **:** SURPASS

pa·rag·o·nite \pə-'rag-ə-,nīt\ *n* [G *paragonit*, fr. Gk *paragōn*, prp. of *paragein* to divert, mislead, fr. *para-* + *agein* to lead — more at AGENT] **:** a mica $NaAl_3Si_3O_{10}(OH)_2$ corresponding to muscovite but with sodium instead of potassium — **pa·rag·o·nit·ic** \pə-,rag-ə-'nit-ik\ *adj*

1**para·graph** \'par-ə-,graf\ *n* [MF & ML; MF *paragraphe*, fr. ML *paragraphus* sign marking a paragraph, fr. Gk *paragraphos* line used to mark change of persons in a dialogue, fr. *paragraphein* to write alongside, fr. *para-* + *graphein* to write — more at CARVE] **1 a :** a subdivision of a written composition that consists of one or more sentences, deals with one point or gives the words of one speaker, and begins on a new usu. indented line **b :** a short composition or note that is complete in one paragraph **2 :** a character (as ¶) used to indicate the beginning of a paragraph and in printing as the sixth in series of the reference marks — **para·graph·ic** \,par-ə-'graf-ik\ *adj*

2**paragraph** *vt* **1 :** to write paragraphs about **2 :** to divide into paragraphs ~ *vi* **:** to write paragraphs; *specif* **:** to work as a paragrapher

para·graph·er \'par-ə-,graf-ər\ *n* **:** a writer of paragraphs esp. for the editorial page of a newspaper

par·a·keet *var of* PARRAKEET

par·al·de·hyde \pa-'ral-də-,hīd\ *n* **:** a colorless liquid polymeric modification $C_6H_{12}O_3$ of acetaldehyde used as a hypnotic

para·lim·ni·on \,par-ə-'lim-nē-,än, -nē-ən\ *n* [NL, fr. *para-* + Gk *limnion*, dim. of *limnē* marshy lake; akin to Gk *limēn* harbor — more at LIMB] **:** the littoral portion of a lake extending to the limit of rooted vegetation

par·al·lac·tic \,par-ə-'lak-tik\ *adj* [NL *parallacticus*, fr. Gk *parallaktikos*, fr. *parallaxis*] **:** of, relating to, or due to parallax

par·al·lax \'par-ə-,laks\ *n* [MF *parallaxe*, fr. Gk *parallaxis*, fr. *parallassein* to change, fr. *para-* + *allassein* to change, fr. *allos* other — more at ELSE] **:** the apparent displacement or the difference in apparent direction of an object as seen from two different points not on a straight line with the object; *specif* **:** the difference in direction of a celestial body as measured from two points on the earth

1**par·al·lel** \'par-ə-,lel, -ləl\ *adj* [L *parallelus*, fr. Gk *parallēlos*, fr. *para* beside + *allēlōn* of one another, fr. *allos* . . . *allos* one . . . another, fr. *allos* other — more at PARA-, ELSE] **1 a :** extending in the same direction, everywhere equidistant, and not meeting ⟨~ rows of trees⟩ **b :** everywhere equally distant ⟨concentric spheres are ~⟩ **2 a :** having parallel sides ⟨a ~ reamer⟩ **b :** being or relating to an electrical circuit having a number of conductors in parallel **3 a :** similar, analogous, or interdependent in tendency or development **b :** readily compared **:** COMPANION **c :** having corresponding syntactical elements **d :** keeping the same distance apart in musical pitch ⟨~ voice parts⟩ **syn** see SIMILAR

2**parallel** *n* **1 a :** a parallel line, curve, or surface **b** (1) **:** one of the imaginary circles on the surface of the earth paralleling the equator and marking the latitude (2) **:** the corresponding line on a globe or map **c :** a character ‖ used in printing as the fifth in series of the reference marks **2 a :** something equal or similar in all essential particulars **:** COUNTERPART **b :** SIMILARITY, ANALOGUE **3 :** a tracing of similarity **4 a :** the state of being physically parallel **:** PARALLELISM **b :** the arrangement of electrical devices in which all positive poles, electrodes, and terminals are joined to one conductor and all negative ones to another conductor so that each unit is in effect on a parallel branch

3**parallel** *vt* **1 :** to indicate analogy of **:** COMPARE **2 a :** to show

something equal to : MATCH **b** : to correspond to **3** : to place so as to be parallel in direction with something **4** : to extend, run, or move in a direction parallel to

4**parallel** *adv* : in a parallel manner

parallel bars *n pl* : a pair of bars on a support adjustable in height and spacing that are parallel to each other and are used for gymnastic exercises

par·al·lel·epi·ped \ˌpar-ə-ˌlel-ə-ˈpī-pəd, -ˈpip-əd; -ˌlel-ˈep-ə-ˌped\ *n* [Gk *parallēlepipedon*, fr. *parallēlos* + *epipedon* plane surface, fr. neut. of *epipedos* flat, fr. *epi-* + *pedon* ground; akin to L *ped-*, *pes* foot — more at FOOT] : a prism whose bases are parallelograms

parallel forces *n pl* : forces acting in parallel lines

par·al·lel·ism \ˈpar-ə-ˌlel-ˌiz-əm, -ləl-\ *n* **1** : the quality or state of being parallel **2** : RESEMBLANCE, CORRESPONDENCE **3** : recurrent syntactical similarities introduced for rhetorical effect **4** : a theory that mind and matter accompany one another but are not causally related **5** : the development of similar new characters by two or more related organisms in response to similarity of environment

par·al·lel·o·gram \ˌpar-ə-ˈlel-ə-ˌgram\ *n* [LL or Gk; LL *parallelogrammum*, fr. Gk *parallēlogrammon*, fr. neut. of *parallēlogrammos* bounded by parallel lines, fr. *parallēlos* + *grammē* line, fr. *graphein* to write — more at CARVE] : a quadrilateral with opposite sides parallel and equal

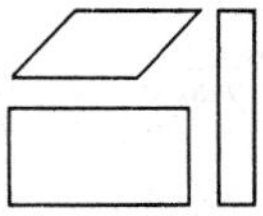

parallelograms

pa·ral·o·gism \pə-ˈral-ə-ˌjiz-əm\ *n* [MF *paralogisme*, fr. LL *paralogismus*, fr. Gk *paralogismos*, fr. *paralogos* unreasonable, fr. *para-* + *logos* speech, reason — more at LEGEND] : a fallacious argument contrary to logical rules

pa·ral·y·sis \pə-ˈral-ə-səs\ *n* [L, fr. Gk, fr. *paralyein* to loosen, disable, fr. *para-* + *lyein* to loosen — more at LOSE] **1** : complete or partial loss of function esp. when involving the motion or sensation in a part of the body **2** : loss of the ability to move **3** : a state of powerlessness or incapacity to act : IMPOTENCE — **par·a·lyt·ic** \ˌpar-ə-ˈlit-ik\ *adj or n*

paralysis agi·tans \-ˈaj-ə-ˌtanz\ *n* [NL, lit., shaking palsy] : a chronic progressive nervous disease of later life marked by tremor and weakness of resting muscles and a peculiar gait

par·a·ly·za·tion \ˌpar-ə-lə-ˈzā-shən\ *n* : paralyzed state; *also* : the act or process of paralyzing

par·a·lyze \ˈpar-ə-ˌlīz\ *vt* [F *paralyser*, back-formation fr. *paralysie* paralysis, fr. L *paralysis*] **1** : to affect with paralysis **2** : to make powerless or ineffective **3** : UNNERVE **4** : STUN, STUPEFY **5** : to bring to an end : PREVENT, DESTROY — **par·a·lyz·er** *n*

para·mag·net \ˈpar-ə-ˌmag-nət\ *n* [back-formation fr. *paramagnetic*] : a paramagnetic substance

para·mag·net·ic \ˌpar-ə-(ˌ)mag-ˈnet-ik\ *adj* [ISV] : being or relating to a magnetizable substance that like aluminum and platinum has small but positive susceptibility varying but little with magnetizing force — **para·mag·ne·tism** \-ˈmag-nə-ˌtiz-əm\ *n*

par·a·mat·ta \ˌpar-ə-ˈmat-ə\ *n* [*Parramatta*, Australia] : a fine lightweight dress fabric of silk and wool or cotton and wool

par·a·me·cium \ˌpar-ə-ˈmē-sh(ē-)əm, -sē-əm\ *n, pl* **par·a·me·cia** \-sh(ē-)ə, -sē-ə\ *also* **parameciums** [NL, genus name, fr. Gk *paramēkēs* oblong, fr. *para-* + *mēkos* length; akin to Gk *makros* long — more at MEAGER] : any of a genus (*Paramecium*) of ciliate protozoans having an elongate body rounded at the anterior end and an oblique funnel-shaped buccal groove bearing the mouth at the extremity

par·a·ment \ˈpar-ə-mənt\ *n* [ME, fr. ML *paramentum*, fr. *parare* to adorn, fr. L, to prepare — more at PARE] : an ornamental ecclesiastical hanging or vestment

pa·ram·e·ter \pə-ˈram-ət-ər\ *n* [NL, fr. *para-* + Gk *metron* measure — more at MEASURE] **1** : an arbitrary constant each of whose values characterizes a member of a system (as a family of curves); *specif* : a quantity that describes a statistical population **2 a** : one of a set of physical properties whose values determine the characteristics or behavior of a system **b** : something represented by a parameter — **para·met·ric** \ˌpar-ə-ˈme-trik\ *adj*

par·am·ne·sia \ˌpar-ˌam-ˈnē-zhə, -əm-\ *n* [NL, fr. *para-* + *-mnesia* (as in *amnesia*)] : a disorder of memory: as **a** : a condition in which the proper meaning of words cannot be remembered **b** : the illusion of remembering scenes and events when experienced for the first time

para·mor·phic \ˌpar-ə-ˈmȯr-fik\ *or* **para·mor·phous** \-fəs\ *adj* : affected by paramorphism

para·mor·phism \-ˌfiz-əm\ *n* : the changing of one mineral species to another by a change in physical characters without change in chemical composition

1**par·a·mount** \ˈpar-ə-ˌmau̇nt\ *adj* [AF *paramont*, fr. OF *par* by (fr. L *per*) + *amont* above, fr. *a* to (fr. L *ad*) + *mont* mountain — more at FOR, AT, MOUNT] : superior to all others : SUPREME **syn** see DOMINANT — **par·a·mount·cy** \-ˌmau̇n(t)-sē\ *n*

2**paramount** *n* : a supreme ruler

par·amour \ˈpar-ə-ˌmu̇(ə)r\ *n* [ME, fr. *par amour* by way of love, fr. OF] : an illicit lover; *esp* : MISTRESS

par·am·y·lum \(ˈ)pa(ə)r-ˈam-ə-ləm\ *n* [NL, fr. *para-* + L *amylum* starch — more at AMYL-] : a reserve carbohydrate of various protozoans and algae that resembles starch

pa·rang \ˈpär-ˌaŋ\ *n* [Malay] : a short sword, cleaver, or machete common in Malaya, British Borneo, and Indonesia

para·noia \ˌpar-ə-ˈnȯi-ə\ *n* [NL, fr. Gk, madness, fr. *paranous* demented, fr. *para-* + *nous* mind] **1** : a rare chronic psychosis characterized by systematized delusions of persecution or of grandeur usu. not associated with hallucinations **2** : a tendency on the part of individuals or of groups toward excessive or irrational suspiciousness and distrustfulness of others — **para·noi·ac** \-ˈnȯi-ˌak, -ˈnȯi-ik\ *adj or n*

para·noid \ˈpar-ə-ˌnȯid\ *adj* **1** : resembling paranoia **2** : characterized by suspiciousness, persecutory trends, or megalomania — **paranoid** *n*

paranoid schizophrenia *n* : a psychosis resembling paranoia but commonly displaying hallucinations and marked behavioral deterioration

para·nor·mal \ˌpar-ə-ˈnȯr-məl\ *adj* : not scientifically explainable : SUPERNATURAL — **para·nor·mal·i·ty** \-ˌnȯr-ˈmal-ət-ē\ *n* — **para·nor·mal·ly** \-ˈnȯr-mə-lē\ *adv*

para·nymph \ˈpar-ə-ˌnim(p)f\ *n* [LL *paranymphus*, fr. Gk *paranymphos*, fr. *para-* + *nymphē* bride — more at NUPTIAL] **1** : a friend going with a bridegroom to fetch home the bride in ancient Greece; *also* : the bridesmaid conducting the bride to the bridegroom **2 a** : BEST MAN **b** : BRIDESMAID

par·a·pet \ˈpar-ə-pət, -ˌpet\ *n* [It *parapetto*, fr. *parare* to shield (fr. L, to prepare) + *petto* chest, fr. L *pectus* — more at PARE, PECTORAL] **1** : a wall, rampart, or elevation of earth or stone to protect soldiers : BREASTWORK **2** : a low wall or railing to protect the edge of a platform, roof, or bridge — **par·a·pet·ed** \-ˌpet-əd\ *adj*

pa·raph \ˈpar-əf, pə-ˈraf\ *n* [MF, fr. L *paragraphus* paragraph] : a flourish at the end of a signature sometimes meant to safeguard against forgery

par·a·pher·na·lia \ˌpar-ə-fə(r)-ˈnāl-yə\ *n pl but sing or pl in constr* [ML, deriv. of Gk *parapherna* goods a bride brings over and above the dowry, fr. *para-* + *phernē* dowry, fr. *pherein* to bear — more at BEAR] **1** : the separate real or personal property of a married woman that she can dispose of by will and sometimes according to common law during her life **2** : personal belongings **3** : FURNISHINGS, APPARATUS

1**para·phrase** \ˈpar-ə-ˌfrāz\ *n* [MF, fr. L *paraphrasis*, fr. Gk, fr. *paraphrazein* to paraphrase, fr. *para-* + *phrazein* to point out] **1** : a restatement of a text, passage, or work giving the meaning in another form **2** : the use or process of paraphrasing in studying or teaching composition

2**paraphrase** *vt* : to make a paraphrase of ~ *vi* : to make a paraphrase — **para·phras·er** *n*

para·phras·tic \ˌpar-ə-ˈfras-tik\ *adj* [F *paraphrastique*, fr. Gk *paraphrastikos*, fr. *paraphrazein*] : PARAPHRASING : explaining or translating more clearly and amply — **para·phras·ti·cal·ly** \-ti-k(ə-)lē\ *adv*

pa·raph·y·sis \pə-ˈraf-ə-səs\ *n* [NL, fr. Gk, sucker, offshoot, fr. *paraphyein* to produce at the side, fr. *para-* + *phyein* to bring forth — more at PHYSICS] : one of the slender sterile filaments borne among the sporogenous or gametogenous organs in cryptogamic plants

para·ple·gia \ˌpar-ə-ˈplē-j(ē-)ə\ *n* [NL, fr. Gk *paraplēgiē* hemiplegia, fr. *para-* + *-plēgia* -plegia] : paralysis of the lower half of the body with involvement of both legs — **para·ple·gic** \-jik\ *adj or n*

para·psy·chol·o·gy \ˌpar-ə-(ˌ)sī-ˈkäl-ə-jē\ *n* [ISV] : a science concerned with the investigation of evidence for telepathy, clairvoyance, and psychokinesis

para·ros·an·i·line \ˌpar-ə-(ˌ)rō-ˈzan-ᵊl-ən\ *n* [ISV] : a white crystalline base $C_{19}H_{19}N_3O$ that is the parent compound of many dyes; *also* : its red chloride used esp. in coloring paper and as a biological stain

Pa·ra rubber \ˌpar-ə-, pə-ˌrä-\ *n* [*Pará*, Brazil] : native rubber from a So. American tree (genus *Hevea*, esp. *H. brasiliensis*) of the spurge family

par·a·sang \ˈpar-ə-ˌsaŋ\ *n* [L *parasanga*, fr. Gk *parasangēs*, of Iranian origin; akin to Per *farsung* parasang] : any of various Persian units of distance; *esp* : an ancient unit of about four miles

para·se·le·ne \ˌpar-ə-sə-ˈlē-nē\ *n, pl* **para·se·le·nae** \-(ˌ)nē, -ˌnī\ [NL, fr. *para-* + Gk *selēnē* moon — more at SELENIUM] : a luminous appearance seen in connection with lunar halos — **para·se·le·nic** \-ˈlēn-ik, -ˈlen-\ *adj*

pa·ra·shah \ˈpär-ə-ˌshä\ *n* [Heb *pārāshāh*, lit., explanation] : one of the portions into which the law is divided for synagogue reading on the Sabbath; *also* : a section (as for a holy day) of the weekly portion

par·a·site \ˈpar-ə-ˌsīt\ *n* [MF, fr. L *parasitus*, fr. Gk *parasitos*, fr. *para-* + *sitos* grain] **1** : one frequenting the tables of the rich and earning welcome by flattery : SYCOPHANT **2** : an organism living in or on another organism in parasitism **3** : something that resembles a biological parasite in dependence on something else for existence or support without making a useful or adequate return — **par·a·sit·ic** \ˌpar-ə-ˈsit-ik\ *also* **par·a·sit·i·cal** \-i-kəl\ *adj* — **par·a·sit·i·cal·ly** \-k(ə-)lē\ *adv*

par·a·sit·i·ci·dal \ˌpar-ə-ˌsit-ə-ˈsīd-ᵊl\ *adj* : destructive to parasites

par·a·sit·i·cide \-ˈsit-ə-ˌsīd\ *n* [L *parasitus* + E *-cide*] : a parasiticidal agent

par·a·sit·ism \ˈpar-ə-ˌsīt-ˌiz-əm\ *n* **1** : the behavior of a parasite **2** : an intimate association between organisms of two or more kinds; *esp* : one in which a parasite obtains benefits from a host which it usu. injures **3** : PARASITOSIS

par·a·sit·ize \ˈpar-ə-sə-ˌtīz, -ˌsīt-ˌīz\ *vt* : to infest or live on or with as a parasite

par·a·si·tol·o·gy \-sə-ˈtäl-ə-jē, -ˌsīt-ˈäl-\ *n* [L *parasitus* + ISV *-logy*] : a branch of biology dealing with parasites and parasitism esp. among animals

par·a·sit·osis \-ˌsīt-ˈō-səs\ *n* : infestation with or disease caused by parasites

para·sol \ˈpar-ə-ˌsȯl, -ˌsäl\ *n* [F, fr. OIt *parasole*, fr. *parare* to shield + *sole* sun, fr. L *sol* — more at PARAPET, SOLAR] **1** : a lightweight umbrella used as a sunshade esp. by women **2** : a monoplane with wings raised above a pilot's head to permit downward vision

para·sym·pa·thet·ic \ˌpar-ə-ˌsim-pə-ˈthet-ik\ *adj* [ISV] : of, relating to, being, or acting on the parasympathetic nervous system — **parasympathetic** *n*

parasympathetic nervous system *n* : the part of the autonomic nervous system that contains chiefly cholinergic fibers and tends to induce secretion, increase the tone and contractility of smooth muscle, and cause the dilatation of blood vessels and that consists of a cranial and a sacral part

para·sym·pa·tho·mi·met·ic \ˌpar-ə-ˈsim-pə-(ˌ)thō-(ˌ)mī-ˈmet-ik, -mə-\ *adj* [ISV] : simulating parasympathetic nervous action in physiological effect

para·syn·the·sis \ˌpar-ə-ˈsin(t)-thə-səs\ *n* [NL] : the formation of words by adding a derivative ending and prefixing a particle (as in *denationalize*) — **para·syn·thet·ic** \-(ˌ)sin-ˈthet-ik\ *adj*

para·tac·tic \ˌpar-ə-ˈtak-tik\ *adj* : of or relating to parataxis — **para·tac·ti·cal** \-ti-kəl\ *adj* — **para·tac·ti·cal·ly** \-k(ə-)lē\ *adv*

para·tax·is \ˌpar-ə-ˈtak-səs\ *n* [NL, fr. Gk, act of placing side by

side, fr. *paratassein* to place side by side, fr. *para-* + *tassein* to arrange — more at TACTICS] **:** the placing of clauses, phrases, or words one after another without coordinating or subordinating connectives

para·thi·on \\,par-ə-'thī-,än\\ *n* [*para-* + *thio*phosphate + *-on*] **:** an extremely toxic thiophosphate insecticide $C_{10}H_{14}NO_5PS$

para·thy·roid \\-'thī(ə)r-,ȯid\\ *adj* [ISV] **:** of, relating to, or produced by the parathyroid glands

parathyroid gland *n* [ISV] **:** any of usu. four small endocrine glands adjacent to or embedded in the thyroid gland that produce a hormone concerned with calcium metabolism

para·troop \\'par-ə-,trüp\\ *adj* **:** of or relating to paratroops ⟨~ boots⟩

para·troop·er \\-,trü-pər\\ *n* **:** a member of the paratroops

para·troops \\-,trüps\\ *n pl* **:** troops trained and equipped to parachute from an airplane

1**para·ty·phoid** \\,par-ə-'tī-,fȯid, -(,)tī-'\\ *adj* [ISV] **1 :** resembling typhoid fever **2 :** of or relating to paratyphoid or its causative organisms ⟨~ infection⟩

2**paratyphoid** *n* **:** a salmonellosis resembling typhoid fever and occurring as a food poisoning

para·vane \\'par-ə-,vān\\ *n* **:** a torpedo-shaped underwater protective device with serrate teeth in its forward end towed from the bow of a ship in mined areas to sever the moorings of mines

par·boil \\'pär-,bȯil\\ *vt* [ME *parboilen*, fr. *parboilen* to boil thoroughly, fr. MF *parboillir*, fr. LL *perbullire*, fr. L *per-* thoroughly (fr. *per* through) + *bullire* to boil, fr. *bulla* bubble — more at FOR] **:** to boil briefly as a preliminary or incomplete cooking procedure

1**par·buck·le** \\'pär-,bək-əl\\ *n* [origin unknown] **1 :** a purchase for hoisting or lowering a cylindrical object by making fast the middle of a long rope aloft and looping both ends around the object which rests in the loops and rolls in them as the ends are hauled up or paid out **2 :** a double sling made of a single rope for slinging a cask or gun

2**parbuckle** *vt* **par·buck·ling** \\-,bək-(ə-)liŋ\\ **:** to hoist or lower by means of a parbuckle

Par·cae \\'pär-,kī, -,sē\\ *n pl* [L] **:** the three Fates of Roman mythology

1**par·cel** \\'pär-səl\\ *n* [ME, fr. MF, fr. (assumed) VL *particella*, fr. L *particula* small part — more at PARTICLE] **1 :** FRAGMENT, PORTION **2 :** a tract or plot of land **3 :** a company, collection, or group of persons, animals, or things **:** LOT **4 a :** a wrapped bundle **:** PACKAGE **b :** a unit of salable merchandise **5 :** PARCELING 2

2**parcel** *adv, archaic* **:** PARTLY

3**parcel** *vt* **par·celed** *or* **par·celled; par·cel·ing** *or* **par·cel·ling** \\'pär-s(ə-)liŋ\\ **1 :** to divide into parts **:** DISTRIBUTE **2 :** to make up into a parcel **:** WRAP **3 :** to cover (as a rope) with strips of canvas

4**parcel** *adj* **:** PART-TIME, PARTIAL

par·cel·ing *or* **par·cel·ling** *n* **1 a :** the act of dividing and distributing in portions **b :** the act of wrapping into bundles **2 a :** the covering of a caulked seam with canvas and then tarring it **b :** long narrow tarred slips of canvas wound about a rope to exclude moisture

parcel post *n* **1 :** a mail service handling parcels **2 :** packages handled by parcel post

par·ce·nary \\'pärs-ᵊn-,er-ē\\ *n* [AF *parcenarie*, fr. OF *parçonerie*, fr. *parçon* portion, fr. L *partition-*, *partitio* partition] **:** COPARCENARY 1

par·ce·ner \\'pärs-nər, -ᵊn-ər\\ *n* [AF, fr. OF *parçonier*, fr. *parçon*] **:** COPARCENER

parch \\'pärch\\ *vb* [ME *parchen*] *vt* **1 :** to toast under dry heat **2 :** to shrivel with heat **3 :** to dry or shrivel with cold ~ *vi* **:** to become dry or scorched

Par·chee·si \\pär-'chē-zē *also* pər-, *esp Brit* pə-'chē-sē\\ *trademark* — used for a board game adapted from pachisi

parch·ment \\'pärch-mənt\\ *n* [ME *parchemin*, fr. OF, modif. of L *pergamena*, fr. Gk *pergamēnē*, fr. fem. of *Pergamēnos* of Pergamum, fr. *Pergamon* Pergamum] **1 :** the skin of a sheep or goat prepared for writing on **2 :** any of various superior papers made to resemble parchment **3 :** a parchment manuscript; *also* **:** an academic diploma

1**pard** \\'pärd\\ *n* [ME *parde*, fr. OF, fr. L *pardus*, fr. Gk *pardos*] *archaic* **:** LEOPARD

2**pard** *n* [short for *pardner*] *chiefly dial* **:** PARTNER, CHUM

par·die *or* **par·di** *or* **par·dy** \\(,)pər-'dē, pär-\\ *interj* [ME *pardee*, fr. OF *par Dé* by God] *archaic* — a mild oath

pard·ner \\'pärd-nər\\ *n, chiefly dial* **:** PARTNER, CHUM

1**par·don** \\'pärd-ᵊn\\ *n* **1 a :** the excusing of an offense without exacting a penalty **b :** divine forgiveness **2 :** INDULGENCE 1 **3 a :** a release from the legal penalties of an offense **b :** an official warrant of remission of penalty **4 :** excuse or forgiveness for a fault, offense, or discourtesy

2**pardon** *vt* **par·don·ing** \\'pärd-niŋ, -ᵊn-iŋ\\ [ME *pardonen*, fr. MF *pardoner*, fr. LL *perdonare* to grant freely, fr. L *per-* thoroughly + *donare* to give — more at PARBOIL, DONATION] **1 a :** to free from penalty **b :** to remit the penalty of **:** FORGIVE **2 :** TOLERATE **syn** see EXCUSE

par·don·able \\'pärd-nə-bəl, -ᵊn-ə-bəl\\ *adj* **:** admitting of being pardoned **:** EXCUSABLE — **par·don·able·ness** *n* — **par·don·ably** \\-blē\\ *adv*

par·don·er \\'pärd-nər, -ᵊn-ər\\ *n* **1 :** a medieval preacher delegated to raise money for religious works by soliciting offerings and granting indulgences **2 :** one that pardons

pare \\'pa(ə)r, 'pe(ə)r\\ *vt* [ME *paren*, fr. MF *parer*, fr. L *parare* to prepare, acquire; akin to OE *fearr* bull, ox, L *parere* to give birth to, produce] **1 :** to trim or shave off **2 :** to diminish gradually by or as if by paring

par·e·go·ric \\,par-ə-'gȯr-ik, -'gōr-, -'gär-\\ *n* [F *parégorique* mitigating pain, fr. LL *paregoricus*, fr. Gk *parēgorikos*, fr. *parēgorein* to talk over, soothe, fr. *para-* + *agora* assembly — more at GREGARIOUS] **:** camphorated tincture of opium used to relieve pain

pa·ren·chy·ma \\pə-'reŋ-kə-mə, -'ren-\\ *n* [NL, fr. Gk, visceral flesh, fr. *parenchein* to pour in beside, fr. *para-* + *en-* + *chein* to pour — more at FOUND] **1 :** a tissue of higher plants consisting of thin-walled living photosynthetic or storage cells capable of division even when mature that make up much of the substance of leaves and roots, the pulp of fruits, and parts of stems and supporting structures **2 :** the essential and distinctive tissue of an organ or an abnormal growth as distinguished from its supportive framework — **par·en·chym·a·tous** \\,par-ən-'kim-ət-əs\\ *also* **pa·ren·chy·mal** \\pə-'reŋ-kə-məl, -'ren-; ,par-ən-'kī-\\ *adj* — **par·en·chym·a·tous·ly** *adv*

par·ent \\'par-ənt, 'per-\\ *n* [ME, fr. MF, fr. L *parent-*, *parens*, fr. prp. of *parere* to give birth to] **1 :** one that begets or brings forth offspring **2 a :** an animal or plant regarded in relation to its offspring **b :** the material or source of something — **parent** *adj* — **pa·ren·tal** \\pə-'rent-ᵊl\\ *adj*

par·ent·age \\'par-ənt-ij, 'per-\\ *n* **1 a :** descent from parents or ancestors **:** LINEAGE **b :** DERIVATION, ORIGIN **2 :** the standing or position of a parent **:** PARENTHOOD

parental generation *n* **:** a generation of individuals of distinguishable genotypes crossed to produce hybrids

par·en·ter·al \\pə-'rent-ə-rəl\\ *adj* [ISV] **:** situated or occurring outside the intestine; *esp* **:** introduced otherwise than by way of the intestines — **par·en·ter·al·ly** \\-'rent-ə-rə-lē, -'ren-trə-lē\\ *adv*

pa·ren·the·sis \\pə-'ren(t)-thə-səs\\ *n, pl* **pa·ren·the·ses** \\-thə-,sēz\\ [LL, fr. Gk, lit., act of inserting, fr. *parentithenai* to insert, fr. *para-* + *en-* + *tithenai* to place — more at DO] **1 a :** an amplifying or explanatory word, phrase, or sentence inserted in a passage from which it is usu. set off by punctuation **b :** a remark or passage that departs from the theme of a discourse **:** DIGRESSION **2 :** INTERLUDE, INTERVAL **3 :** one or both of the curved marks ( ) used in writing and printing to enclose a parenthetic expression or to group a symbolic unit in a logical or mathematical expression — **par·en·thet·ic** \\,par-ən-'thet-ik\\ *or* **par·en·thet·i·cal** \\-i-kəl\\ *adj* — **par·en·thet·i·cal·ly** \\-k(ə-)lē\\ *adv*

pa·ren·the·size \\pə-'ren(t)-thə-,sīz\\ *vt* **:** to make a parenthesis of

par·ent·hood \\'par-ənt-,hu̇d, 'per-\\ *n* **:** the position, function, or standing of a parent

pa·re·sis \\pə-'rē-səs, 'par-ə-\\ *n, pl* **pa·re·ses** \\-'rē-,sēz, -ə-,sēz\\ [NL, fr. Gk, fr. *parienai* to let fall, fr. *para-* + *hienai* to let go, send — more at JET] **1 :** slight or partial paralysis **2 :** GENERAL PARESIS — **pa·ret·ic** \\pə-'ret-ik\\ *adj or n*

par·es·the·sia \\,par-əs-'thē-zhə\\ *n* [NL] **:** a sensation of pricking, tingling, or creeping on the skin without objective cause — **par·es·thet·ic** \\-'thet-ik\\ *adj*

pa·reu \\'pär-ē-,ü\\ *n* [Tahitian] **:** a wraparound skirt or loincloth of Polynesia

pa·re·ve \\,pär-ə-'vā, 'pär-və\\ *adj* [Yiddish *parev*] **:** made without milk, meat, or their derivatives

par ex·cel·lence \\,pär-,ek-sə-'läⁿs\\ *adv (or adj)* [F, lit., by excellence] **:** in the highest degree **:** PREEMINENTLY

par·fait \\pär-'fā\\ *n* [F, lit., something perfect, fr. *parfait* perfect, fr. L *perfectus*] **1 :** a flavored custard containing whipped cream and syrup frozen without stirring **2 :** a cold dessert made of layers of fruit, syrup, ice cream, and whipped cream

par·fleche \\'pär-,flesh, pär-'\\ *n* [CanF *parflèche*] **1 :** a rawhide soaked in lye to remove the hair and dried **2 :** an article made of parfleche

1**par·get** \\'pär-jət\\ *vt* **par·get·ed** *or* **par·get·ted; par·get·ing** *or* **par·get·ting** [ME *pargetten*, fr. MF *parjeter* to throw on top of, fr. *par-* thoroughly (fr. L *per-*) + *jeter* to throw — more at JET] **:** to coat with plaster; *esp* **:** to apply ornamental plaster to

2**parget** *n* **1 :** plaster, whitewash, or roughcast for coating a wall **2 :** plasterwork esp. in raised ornamental figures on walls

par·he·lic \\pär-'hē-lik\\ *or* **par·he·li·a·cal** \\,pär-hi-'lī-ə-kəl\\ *adj* **:** of or relating to a parhelion

parhelic circle *n* **:** a luminous circle or halo parallel to the horizon at the altitude of the sun — called also *parhelic ring*

par·he·lion \\pär-'hēl-yən\\ *n, pl* **par·he·lia** \\-yə\\ [L *parelion*, fr. Gk *parēlion*, fr. *para-* + *hēlios* sun — more at SOLAR] **:** any one of several bright spots often tinged with color that often appear on the parhelic circle

pa·ri·ah \\pə-'rī-ə\\ *n* [Tamil *paraiyan*, lit., drummer] **1 :** a member of a low caste of southern India and Burma **2 :** OUTCAST

par·i·an \\'par-ē-ən, 'per-\\ *adj* **1** *cap* **:** of or relating to the island of Paros noted for its marble used extensively for sculpture in ancient times **2 :** of or relating to a fine white porcelain or the clay used in making it

Parian ware *n* **:** a cream-colored soft china made from feldspar and kaolin and used unglazed esp. for making statuettes

par·i·es \\'par-ē-,ēz, 'per-; 'pär-ē-,ās\\ *n, pl* **pa·ri·etes** \\pə-'rī-ə-,tēz, pä-'rē-ə-,tās\\ [NL *pariet-*, *paries*, fr. L, wall; akin to L *sparus* spear — more at SPEAR] **:** the wall of a cavity or hollow organ — usu. used in pl.

pa·ri·etal \\pə-'rī-ət-ᵊl\\ *adj* **1 a :** of or relating to the walls of a part or cavity **b :** of, relating to, or forming the upper posterior wall of the head **2 :** attached to the main wall rather than the axis or a cross wall of an ovary — used of an ovule or a placenta **3 :** of or relating to college living or its regulation; *esp* **:** of or relating to regulations for dormitory visiting between sexes — **parietal** *n*

parietal bone *n* **:** either of a pair of membrane bones of the roof of the skull between the frontal bones and the occipital bones

pari–mu·tu·el \\,par-i-'myüch-(ə-)wəl, -'myü-chəl\\ *n, pl* **pari–mutuels** *also in sense 1* **paris–mu·tu·els** *both* ,par-i-'myüch-(ə-)wəlz, -'myü-chəlz\\ [F *pari mutuel*, lit., mutual stake] **1 :** a system of betting in which those who bet on the winners of the first three places share the total stakes minus a percentage for the management **2 :** a machine for registering the bets and computing the payoffs in pari-mutuel betting

pa·ri pas·su \\,par-ē-'pas-(,)ü, ,pär-ē-'päs-\\ *adv (or adj)* [L, with equal step] **:** at an equal rate or pace

Par·is \\'par-əs\\ *n* [L, fr. Gk] **:** a son of Priam whose abduction of Helen leads to the Trojan War

Par·is green \\,par-əs-\\ *n* [*Paris*, France] **1 :** an insecticide and pigment prepared as a very poisonous bright green powder (as from arsenic trioxide and copper acetate) **2 :** a variable color averaging a brilliant yellowish green

par·ish \\'par-ish\\ *n* [ME *parisshe*, fr. MF *parroche*, fr. LL *parochia*, fr. LGk *paroikia*, fr. *paroikos* Christian, fr. Gk, stranger, fr. *para-* + *oikos* house — more at VICINITY] **1 a (1) :** the ecclesiastical unit of area committed to one pastor **(2) :** the residents of such area **b** *Brit* **:** a subdivision of a county often coinciding with an original ecclesiastical parish and constituting the unit of local government **2 :** a local church community composed of the members or constituents of a Protestant church **3 :** a civil division of the state of Louisiana corresponding to a county in other states

pa·rish·io·ner \\pə-'rish-(ə-)nər\\ *n* [ME *parisshoner*, prob. modif.

of MF *parrochien*, fr. *parroche*] **:** a member or inhabitant of a parish

¹par·i·ty \ˈpar-ət-ē\ *n* [L *paritas*, fr. *par* equal] **1 :** the quality or state of being equal or equivalent **2 a :** equivalence of a commodity price expressed in one currency to its price expressed in another **b :** equality of purchasing power established by law between different kinds of money at a given ratio **3 :** an equivalence between farmers' current purchasing power and their purchasing power at a selected base period maintained by government support of agricultural commodity prices **4 :** the property of an integer with respect to being odd or even ⟨3 and 7 have the same ~⟩

²parity *n* **:** the state or fact of having borne offspring; *also* **:** the number of children previously borne

¹park \ˈpärk\ *n* [ME, fr. OF *parc* enclosure, fr. (assumed) VL *parricus*] **1 a :** an enclosed piece of ground stocked with beasts of the chase and held by royal prescription or grant **b :** a tract of land often including lawns, woodland, and pasture attached to a country house and used as a game preserve and for recreation **2 a :** a piece of ground in or near a city or town kept for ornament and recreation **b :** an area maintained in its natural state as a public property **3 a :** a level valley between mountain ranges **b :** an open space surrounded by woodland **4 a :** a space occupied by military animals, vehicles, or materials **b :** PARKING LOT **5 :** an enclosed arena or stadium used esp. for ball games

²park *vt* **1 :** to enclose in a park **2 a** (1) **:** to bring to a stop and keep standing at the edge of a public way (2) **:** to leave temporarily on a public way or in a parking lot or garage **b :** to land or leave an airplane **3 :** to set and leave temporarily **4 :** to assemble (as equipment or stores) in a military dump or park **~** *vi* **:** to park a vehicle — **parker** *n*

par·ka \ˈpär-kə\ *n* [Aleut, skin, outer garment, fr. Russ, pelt, fr. Yurak] **1 :** a hooded fur pullover garment for arctic wear **2 :** a fabric pullover or jacket for sports or military wear

parking lot *n* **:** an outdoor lot for the parking of motor vehicles

par·kin·son·ism \ˈpär-kən-sə-ˌniz-əm\ *n* **1 :** PARALYSIS AGITANS **2 :** a chronic nervous disorder marked by muscle rigidity but without tremor of resting muscles

Par·kin·son's disease \ˈpär-kən-sənz-\ *n* [James *Parkinson* †1824 E physician] **:** PARALYSIS AGITANS

park·way \ˈpär-ˌkwā\ *n* **:** a broad landscaped thoroughfare

par·lance \ˈpär-lən(t)s\ *n* [MF, fr. OF, fr. *parler*] **1 :** SPEECH; *esp* **:** formal debate or parley **2 :** manner or mode of speech **:** IDIOM

par·lan·do \pär-ˈlän-(ˌ)dō\ *or* **par·lan·te** \-(ˌ)tā\ *adj* [*parlando* fr. It, verbal of *parlare* to speak, fr. ML *parabolare*; *parlante* fr. It, prp. of *parlare*] **:** delivered or performed in an unsustained style suggestive of speech — used as a direction in music

¹par·lay \ˈpär-ˌlā, -lē\ *vt* [F *paroli*, n., parlay, fr. It dial., pl. of *parolo*, fr. *paro* equal, fr. L *par*] **1 :** to bet in a parlay **2 :** to exploit successfully **:** MAGNIFY

²parlay *n* **:** a series of two or more bets so set up in advance that the original stake plus its winnings are risked on the successive wagers; *broadly* **:** the fresh risking of an original stake together with its winnings

parle \ˈpär(ə)l\ *vi or n* [ME *parlen* to parley, fr. MF *parler*] *archaic* **:** PARLEY

¹par·ley \ˈpär-lē\ *vi* [MF *parler* to speak, fr. ML *parabolare*, fr. LL *parabola* speech, parable — more at PARABLE] **:** to speak with another **:** CONFER; *specif* **:** to discuss terms with an enemy

²parley *n* **1 a :** a conference for discussion of points in dispute **b :** a conference with an enemy **2 :** CONVERSATION, DISCUSSION

par·lia·ment \ˈpär-lə-mənt, *US also* ˈpärl-yə-\ *n* [ME, fr. OF *parlement*, fr. *parler*] **1 :** a formal conference for the discussion of public affairs; *specif* **:** a council of state in early medieval England **2 a :** an assemblage of the nobility, clergy, and commons called together by the British sovereign as the supreme legislative body in the United Kingdom **b :** a similar assemblage in another nation or state **3 a :** the supreme legislative body of a usu. major political unit that is a continuing institution comprising a series of individual parliaments **b :** the British House of Commons **4 :** one of several principal courts of justice existing in France before the revolution of 1789

par·lia·men·tar·i·an \ˌpär-lə-ˌmen-ˈter-ē-ən, -mən-, ˌpärl-yə-\ *n* **1** *often cap* **:** an adherent of the parliament in opposition to the king during the English Civil War **2 :** an expert in the rules and usages of a parliament or other deliberative assembly

par·lia·men·ta·ry \-ˈment-ə-rē, -ˈmen-trē\ *adj* **1 a :** of or relating to a parliament **b :** enacted, done, or ratified by a parliament **2 :** of or adhering to the parliament as opposed to the king during the English Civil War **3 :** of, based on, or having the characteristics of parliamentary government **4 :** of or relating to members of a parliament **5 :** of or according to parliamentary law

parliamentary government *n* **:** a system of government having the real executive power vested in a cabinet composed of members of the legislature who are individually and collectively responsible to the legislature

parliamentary law *n* **:** the rules and precedents governing the proceedings of deliberative assemblies and other organizations

par·lor *or chiefly Brit* **par·lour** \ˈpär-lər\ *n, often attrib* [ME *parlour*, fr. OF, fr. *parler*] **1 :** a room used primarily for conversation or the reception of guests: as **a :** a room in a private dwelling for the entertainment of guests **b :** a conference chamber or private reception room **c :** a room in an inn, hotel, or club for conversation or semiprivate uses **2 :** any of various business places ⟨funeral ~⟩ ⟨beauty ~⟩

parlor car *n* **:** an extra-fare railroad passenger car for day travel equipped with individual chairs

par·lor·maid \-ˌmād\ *n* **:** a maid in a private home who attends to the parlor, the table, and the door

¹par·lous \ˈpär-ləs\ *adj* [ME, alter. of *perilous*] **1 :** fraught with danger or risk **:** HAZARDOUS **2** *obs* **:** dangerously shrewd or cunning — **par·lous·ly** *adv*

²parlous *adv* **:** to a very great extent **:** EXCEEDINGLY

Par·me·san \ˈpär-mə-ˌzän, -ˌzan, -zən\ *n* [*parmesan* (of Parma)] **:** a very hard dry cheese with a sharp flavor

Par·nas·si·an \pär-ˈnas-ē-ən\ *adj* **1** [L *parnassius* of Parnassus, fr. Gk *parnasios*, fr. *Parnasos* Parnassus, mountain in Greece sacred to Apollo and the Muses] **:** of or relating to poetry **2** [F *parnassien*, fr. *Parnasse* Parnassus; fr. *Le Parnasse contemporain* (1866) an anthology of poetry] **:** of or relating to a school of French poets of the second half of the 19th century emphasizing metrical form rather than emotion — **Parnassian** *n*

pa·ro·chi·al \pə-ˈrō-kē-əl\ *adj* [ME *parochiall*, fr. MF *parochial*, fr. LL *parochialis*, fr. *parochia* parish — more at PARISH] **1 :** of or relating to a church parish **2 :** confined or restricted as if within the borders of a parish **:** PROVINCIAL — **pa·ro·chi·al·ly** \-kē-ə-lē\ *adv*

pa·ro·chi·al·ism \-kē-ə-ˌliz-əm\ *n* **:** the quality or state of being parochial; *esp* **:** NARROWNESS

parochial school *n* **:** a school maintained by a religious body

par·o·dist \ˈpar-əd-əst\ *n* **:** a writer of parodies

par·o·dy \ˈpar-əd-ē\ *n* [L *parodia*, fr. Gk *parōidia*, fr. *para-* + *aidein* to sing — more at ODE] **1 :** a literary or musical work in which the style of an author or work is closely imitated for comic effect or in ridicule **2 :** a feeble or ridiculous imitation **syn** see CARICATURE — **parody** *vt*

pa·rol \pə-ˈrōl\ *n* [MF *parole*] **:** WORD OF MOUTH ⟨prove by ~⟩ — **parol** *adj*

¹pa·role \pə-ˈrōl\ *n* [F, speech, parole, fr. LL *parabola* speech — more at PARABLE] **1 :** a promise made with or confirmed by a pledge of one's honor; *esp* **:** the promise of a prisoner of war to fulfill stated conditions in consideration of his release **2 :** a watchword given only to officers of the guard and of the day **3 :** a conditional release of a prisoner serving an indeterminate or unexpired sentence — **parole** *adj*

²parole *vt* **:** to release (a prisoner) on parole — **pa·ro·lee** \pə-ˌrō-ˈlē, ˌpar-ə-ˈlē\ *n*

par·ono·ma·sia \ˌpar-ə-nō-ˈmā-zh(ē-)ə, pə-ˌrän-ə-ˈmā-\ *n* [L, fr. Gk, fr. *paronomazein* to call with a slight change of name, fr. *para-* + *onoma* name — more at NAME] **:** a play on words **:** PUN — **par·ono·mas·tic** \-ˈmas-tik\ *adj*

par·onym \ˈpar-ə-ˌnim\ *n* [LL *paronymon*, fr. Gk *parōnymon*, neut. of *parōnymos*] **:** a paronymous word

par·on·y·mous \pə-ˈrän-ə-məs, pa-\ *adj* [Gk *parōnymos*, fr. *para-* + *-ōnymos* (as in *homōnymos* homonymous)] **1 :** CONJUGATE 4 **2 a :** formed from a word in another language **b :** having a form similar to that of a cognate foreign word

par·otid \pə-ˈrät-əd, -ˈrōt-\ *adj* [NL *parotid-*, *parotis* parotid gland, fr. L, tumor near the ear, fr. Gk *parōtid-*, *parōtis*, fr. *para-* + *ōt-*, *ous* ear — more at EAR] **:** of or relating to the parotid gland

parotid gland *n* **:** either of a pair of large serous salivary glands situated below and in front of the ear

par·oti·tis \ˌpar-ə-ˈtīt-əs, ˌpar-ō-\ *n* **:** inflammation of the parotid glands; *also* **:** MUMPS

-p·a·rous \p-(ə-)rəs\ *adj comb form* [L *-parus*, fr. *parere* to give birth to, produce] **:** giving birth to **:** producing ⟨bi*parous*⟩

Par·ou·sia \ˌpär-ü-ˈsē-ə, pə-ˈrü-zē-ə\ *n* [Gk, lit., presence, fr. *paront-*, *parōn*, prp. of *pareinai* to be present, fr. *para-* + *einai* to be — more at IS] **:** SECOND COMING

par·ox·ysm \ˈpar-ək-ˌsiz-əm\ *n* [F & ML; F *paroxysme*, fr. ML *paroxysmus*, fr. Gk *paroxysmos*, fr. *paroxynein* to stimulate, fr. *para-* + *oxynein* to provoke, fr. *oxys* sharp — more at OXYGEN] **1 :** a sudden attack (as of a disease) or sharp recurrence or increase of symptoms **:** CONVULSION **2 :** a sudden violent emotion or action — **par·ox·ys·mal** \ˌpar-ək-ˈsiz-məl\ *adj*

par·oxy·tone \(ˈ)pa(ə)r-ˈäk-si-ˌtōn\ *adj* [NL *paroxytonus*, fr. Gk *paroxytonos*, fr. *para-* + *oxytonos* oxytone] **:** having or characterized by an acute accent on the penult — **paroxytone** *n*

¹par·quet \ˈpär-ˈkā\ *vt* **par·queted** \-ˈkād\ **par·quet·ing** \-ˈkā-iŋ\ **1 :** to furnish with a floor of parquetry **2 :** to make of parquetry

²parquet *n* [F, fr. MF, small enclosure, fr. *parc* park] **1 a :** a patterned flooring; *esp* **:** one made of parquetry **b :** PARQUETRY **2 :** the lower floor of a theater; *specif* **:** the part from the front of the stage to the parquet circle

parquet circle *n* **:** the part of the lower floor of a theater beneath the galleries

par·que·try \ˈpär-kə-trē\ *n* **:** a patterned wood inlay used esp. for floors

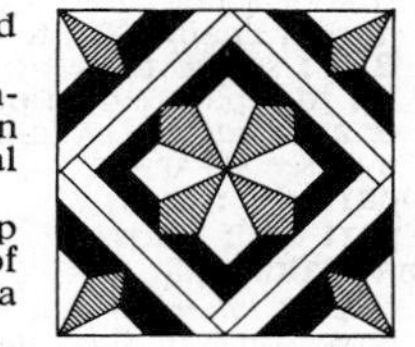
parquetry

parr \ˈpär\ *n, pl* **parr** *also* **parrs** [origin unknown] **:** a young salmon actively feeding in fresh water; *also* **:** the young of any of several other fishes

par·ra·keet \ˈpar-ə-ˌkēt\ *n* [Sp & MF; Sp *periquito*, fr. MF *perroquet* parrot] **:** any of numerous usu. small slender parrots with a long graduated tail

par·rel *or* **par·ral** \ˈpar-əl\ *n* [ME *perell*, fr. alter. of *parail* apparel, short for *apparail*, fr. MF *apareil*, fr. *apareillier* to prepare — more at APPAREL] **:** a rope loop or sliding collar by which a yard or spar is held to a mast in such a way that it may be hoisted or lowered

par·ri·ci·dal \ˌpar-ə-ˈsīd-ᵊl\ *adj* **:** of, relating to, or guilty of parricide

par·ri·cide \ˈpar-ə-ˌsīd\ *n* **1** [L *parricida* killer of a close relative, fr. *parri-* (akin to Gk *pēos* kinsman by marriage) + *-cida* -cide] **:** one that murders his father, mother, or a close relative **2** [L *parricidium* murder of a close relative, fr. *parri-* + *-cidium* -cide] **:** the act of a parricide

¹par·rot \ˈpar-ət\ *n* [prob. irreg. fr. MF *perroquet*] **1 :** any of numerous widely distributed tropical zygodactyl birds (order Psittaciformes) that have a distinctive stout curved hooked bill and are often crested and brightly variegated and excellent mimics **2 :** a person who sedulously echoes the words of another — **parrot** *adj*

²parrot *vt* **:** to repeat by rote

parrot disease *n* **:** PSITTACOSIS — called also *parrot fever*

parrot fish *n* **:** any of numerous marine percoid fish (as of the families Scaridae and Labridae) having the teeth in each jaw fused into a cutting plate like a beak

par·ry \ˈpar-ē\ *vb* [prob. fr. F *parez*, imper. of *parer* to parry, fr. OProv *parar*, fr. L *parare* to prepare — more of PARE] *vi* **1 :** to ward off a weapon or blow **2 :** to turn aside something **~** *vt* **1 :** to ward off (as a blow) **2 :** to evade esp. by an adroit answer — **parry** *n*

parse \ˈpärs, ˈpärz\ *vb* [L *pars orationis* part of speech] *vt* **1 :** to resolve (as a sentence) into component parts of speech and describe

them grammatically **2 :** to describe grammatically by stating the part of speech and explaining the inflection and syntactical relationships ~ *vi* **1 :** to give a grammatical description of a word or a group of words **2 :** to admit of being parsed

par·sec \'pär-,sek\ *n* [*par*allax + *sec*ond] **:** a unit of measure for interstellar space equal to a distance having a heliocentric parallax of one second or to 206,265 times the radius of the earth's orbit or to 3.26 light-years or to 19.2 trillion miles

Par·si *also* **Par·see** \'pär-,sē\ *n* [Per *pārsī*, fr. *Pārs* Persia] **1 :** a Zoroastrian descendant from Persian refugees settled principally at Bombay **2 :** the Iranian dialect of the Parsi religious literature — **Par·si·ism** \-,iz-əm\ *n*

Par·si·fal \'pär-zi-,fäl, -sə-,fòl\ *n* [G] **:** a knight of the Holy Grail and hero of Wagner's *Parsifal*

par·si·mo·ni·ous \,pär-sə-'mō-nē-əs\ *adj* **:** excessively frugal **:** NIGGARDLY **syn** see STINGY — **par·si·mo·ni·ous·ly** *adv*

par·si·mo·ny \'pär-sə-,mō-nē\ *n* [ME *parcimony*, fr. L *parsimonia*, fr. *parsus*, pp. of *parcere* to spare] **1 a :** carefulness with money or resources **:** THRIFT **b :** NIGGARDLINESS, STINGINESS **2 :** economy in the use of a means to an end

pars·ley \'pär-slē\ *n* [ME *persely*, fr. OE *petersilie*, fr. (assumed) VL *petrosilium*, alter. of L *petroselinum*, fr. Gk *petroselinon*, fr. *petros* stone + *selinon* celery] **:** a southern European annual or biennial herb (*Petroselinum crispum*) of the carrot family widely cultivated for its leaves which are used as a culinary herb or garnish

pars·nip \'pär-snəp\ *n* [ME *pasnepe*, modif. of MF *pasnaie*, fr. L *pastinaca*, fr. *pastinum* 2-pronged dibble] **:** a European biennial herb (*Pastinaca sativa*) of the carrot family with large pinnate leaves and yellow flowers; *also* **:** its long tapered root used in cultivated varieties as a vegetable

par·son \'pärs-ᵊn\ *n* [ME *persone*, fr. OF, fr. ML *persona*, lit., person, fr. L] **1 :** RECTOR **2 :** CLERGYMAN; *esp* **:** a Protestant pastor

par·son·age \'pär-snij, 'pärs-ᵊn-ij\ *n* **:** the house provided by a church for its pastor

¹**part** \'pärt\ *n* [ME, fr. OF & OE, both fr. L *part-*, *pars*; akin to L *parare* to prepare — more at PARE] **1 a** (1) **:** one of the portions into which something is or is regarded as divided and which together constitute the whole (2) **:** an essential portion or integral element **b :** one of several or many equal units of which something is composed **c** (1) **:** ALIQUOT (2) **:** PARTIAL FRACTION **d** *pl* **:** the external genital and excretory organs **e :** a division of a literary work **f** (1) **:** a vocal or instrumental line or melody in concerted music or in harmony (2) **:** a particular voice or instrument in concerted music; *also* **:** the score for it **g :** a constituent member of a machine or other apparatus; *also* **:** a spare part **2 :** something falling to one in a division or apportionment **:** SHARE **3 :** DUTY, FUNCTION **4 :** one of the opposing sides in a conflict or dispute **5 :** DISTRICT, REGION **6 :** a function or course of action performed **7 a :** an actor's lines in a play **b :** the role of a character in a play **8 :** a constituent of character or capacity **:** TALENT ⟨a man of many ~*s*⟩ **9 :** the line where the hair is parted

syn PART, PORTION, PIECE, MEMBER, DIVISION, SECTION, SEGMENT, FRAGMENT mean something less than the whole. PART is a general term interchangeable with any of the others; PORTION implies an assigned or allotted part; PIECE applies to a separate or detached part of a whole; MEMBER suggests one of the functional units composing a body; DIVISION and SECTION imply a part made by cutting, DIVISION usu. suggesting a larger or more diversified subordinate part than SECTION; SEGMENT applies to a part separated or marked out by natural lines of cleavage; FRAGMENT applies to a part produced accidentally as by breaking off or shattering

²**part** *vb* [ME *parten*, fr. OF *partir*, fr. L *partire* to divide, fr. *part-*, *pars*] *vi* **1 a :** to separate from or take leave of someone **b :** to take leave of one another **2 :** to become separated into parts **3 a :** to go away **:** DEPART **b :** DIE **4 :** to become separated, detached, or broken **5 :** to relinquish possession or control ~ *vt* **1 a :** to divide into parts **b :** to separate by combing on each side of a line **c :** to break or suffer the breaking of (as a rope or anchor chain) **2 :** to divide into shares and distribute **:** APPORTION **3 a :** SEPARATE, SUNDER **b :** to keep separate **c :** to hold apart **d :** to separate by a process of extraction, elimination, or secretion **4 a** *archaic* **:** LEAVE, QUIT **b** *dial Brit* **:** to give up **:** RELINQUISH **syn** see SEPARATE

³**part** *adv* **:** PARTLY

⁴**part** *adj* **:** PARTIAL

par·take \pär-'tāk, pər-\ *vb* [back-formation fr. *partaker*, alter. of *part taker*] *vi* **1 :** to take a part or share **:** PARTICIPATE **2 :** to have some of the qualities or attributes of something ~ *vt* **:** to take part in **syn** see SHARE — **par·tak·er** *n*

par·tan \'pärt-ᵊn\ *n* [ME (Sc), of Celt origin; akin to ScGael *partan* crab] **:** a European edible crab (*Cancer pagurus*)

part·ed \'pärt-əd\ *adj* **1 a :** divided into parts **b :** cleft so that the divisions reach nearly but not quite to the base ⟨3-*parted* corolla⟩ **2** *archaic* **:** DECEASED

par·terre \pär-'te(ə)r\ *n* [F, fr. MF, fr. *par terre* on the ground] **1 :** an ornamental garden with paths between the beds **2 :** the part of the floor of a theater behind the orchestra; *esp* **:** PARQUET CIRCLE

par·the·no·car·pic \,pär-thə-nō-'kär-pik\ *adj* **:** exhibiting parthenocarpy — **par·the·no·car·pi·cal·ly** \-pi-k(ə-)lē\ *adv*

par·the·no·car·py \'pär-thə-nō-,kär-pē\ *n* [ISV, fr. Gk *parthenos* virgin + *karpos* fruit — more at HARVEST] **:** the production of fruits without fertilization

par·the·no·gen·e·sis \,pär-thə-nō-'jen-ə-səs\ *n* [NL, fr. Gk *parthenos* + L *genesis*] **:** reproduction by development of an unfertilized gamete that occurs esp. among lower plants and invertebrate animals — **par·the·no·ge·net·ic** \,pär-thə-nō-jə-'net-ik\ *adj* — **par·the·no·ge·net·i·cal·ly** \-i-k(ə-)lē\ *adv*

Par·the·non \'pär-thə-,nän, -nən\ *n* [L, fr. Gk *Parthenōn*] **:** a celebrated Doric temple of Athena built on the acropolis at Athens in the 5th century B.C.

Par·thi·an \'pär-thē-ən\ *adj* **1 :** of, relating to, or characteristic of ancient Parthia or its people **2 :** of or relating to a shot fired while in real or feigned retreat — **Parthian** *n*

¹**par·tial** \'pär-shəl\ *adj* [ME *parcial*, fr. MF *partial*, fr. M *partialis*, fr. LL, of a part, fr. L *part-*, *pars* part] **1 :** inclined to favor one party more than the other **:** BIASED **2 :** markedly or foolishly fond — used with *to* ⟨~ to beans⟩ **3 :** of or relating to a part rather than the whole **:** not general or total — **par·tial·ly** \'pärsh-(ə-)lē\ *adv*

²**partial** *n* **:** OVERTONE 1 — called also *upper partial*

partial fraction *n* **:** one of the simpler fractions into the sum of which the quotient of two polynomials may be decomposed

par·tial·i·ty \,pär-shē-'al-ət-ē, pär-'shal-\ *n* **1 :** the quality or state of being partial **:** BIAS **2 :** a special taste or liking

partially ordered *adj* **:** having some elements connected by a relation that is transitive and not symmetric

part·ible \'pärt-ə-bəl\ *adj* **:** capable of being parted **:** DIVISIBLE

par·tic·i·pant \pər-'tis-(ə-)pənt, pär-\ *n* **:** one that participates — **participant** *adj*

par·tic·i·pate \pär-'tis-ə-,pāt, pər-\ *vb* [L *participatus*, pp. of *participare*, fr. *particip-*, *particeps* participant, fr. *part-*, *pars* part + *capere* to take — more at HEAVE] *vt* **:** PARTAKE ~ *vi* **1 :** to possess something of the nature of a person, thing, or quality **2 :** to take part **syn** see SHARE — **par·tic·i·pa·tive** \-,pāt-iv\ *adj* — **par·tic·i·pa·tor** \-,pāt-ər\ *n*

par·tic·i·pat·ing *adj* **1 :** involving participation by more than one person or agency ⟨~ mortgage⟩ **2 :** sharing in distributions

par·tic·i·pa·tion \pər-,tis-ə-'pā-shən, (,)pär-\ *n* **1 :** the act of participating **2 :** the state of being related to a larger whole

par·tic·i·pa·to·ry \pär-'tis-ə-pə-,tōr-ē, pər-, -,tòr-\ *adj* **:** characterized by or involving participation; *esp* **:** providing the opportunity for individual participation ⟨~ democracy⟩

par·ti·cip·i·al \,pärt-ə-'sip-ē-əl\ *adj* **:** of, relating to, or formed with or from a participle — **par·ti·cip·i·al·ly** \-ē-ə-lē\ *adv*

par·ti·ci·ple \'pärt-ə-,sip-əl\ *n* [ME, fr. MF, modif. of L *participium*, fr. *particip-*, *particeps*] **:** a word having the characteristics of both verb and adjective; *esp* **:** an English verbal form that has the function of an adjective and at the same time shows such verbal features as tense and voice and capacity to take an object

par·ti·cle \'pärt-i-kəl\ *n* [ME, fr. L *particula*, fr. dim. of *part-*, *pars*] **1** *archaic* **:** a clause or article of a composition or document **2 :** one of the minute subdivisions of matter **3 a :** a minute quantity or fragment **b :** the smallest possible portion or amount of something **4 a :** a unit of speech serving almost as a loose affix, expressing some general aspect of meaning or some connective or limiting relation, and including the articles, most prepositions and conjunctions, and some interjections and adverbs **b :** an element that resembles a word but that is used only in composition (as *un-* in *unfair* and *-ward* in *backward*) **5 :** a small eucharistic wafer distributed to a Roman Catholic layman at Communion

par·ti-col·ored \,pärt-ē-'kəl-ərd\ *adj* [obs. E *party* (parti-colored) + E *colored*] **:** showing different colors or tints

¹**par·tic·u·lar** \pə(r)-'tik-yə-lər\ *adj* [ME *particuler*, fr. MF, fr. LL *particularis*, fr. L *particula* small part] **1 :** of or relating to a single person or thing **2** *obs* **:** PARTIAL **3 :** of or relating to details **:** MINUTE **4 :** distinctive among others **:** SPECIAL **5 a :** being a particular in logic **b :** affirming or denying a predicate to a part of the subject — used of a proposition in logic ⟨"some men are wise" is a ~ affirmative⟩ **6 a :** attentive to details **:** EXACT **b :** nice in taste **:** FASTIDIOUS **c :** hard to please **:** EXACTING **syn** see CIRCUMSTANTIAL, NICE, SINGLE, SPECIAL

²**particular** *n* **1** *archaic* **:** a separate part of a whole **2 a :** an individual fact or detail **b :** a specific item or detail of information or news ⟨bill of ~*s*⟩ **3 a :** an individual or a specific subclass in logic falling under some general concept or term **b :** a particular proposition in logic **syn** see ITEM

par·tic·u·lar·ism \pə(r)-'tik-yə-lə-,riz-əm, pär-\ *n* **1 :** exclusive or special devotion to a particular interest **2 :** a theological doctrine that redemption through Christ is provided only for the elect **3 :** a political theory that each political group has a right to promote its own interests and esp. independence without regard to the interests of larger groups **4 :** a tendency to explain complex social phenomena in terms of a single causative factor — **par·tic·u·lar·ist** \-rəst\ *n*

par·tic·u·lar·i·ty \pə(r)-,tik-yə-'lar-ət-ē, (,)pär-\ *n* **1 a :** a minute detail **:** PARTICULAR **b :** an individual characteristic **:** PECULIARITY; *also* **:** SINGULARITY **2 a :** the quality or state of being particular as opposed to universal **b :** attentiveness to detail **:** EXACTNESS **c :** fastidiousness in behavior or expression

par·tic·u·lar·iza·tion \-yə-lə-rə-'zā-shən\ *n* **:** the act of particularizing **:** the condition of being particularized

par·tic·u·lar·ize \pə(r)-'tik-yə-lə-,rīz, pär-\ *vt* **:** to state in detail **:** SPECIFY ~ *vi* **:** to go into details

par·tic·u·lar·ly \pə(r)-'tik-yə-(lər-)lē, pə-'tik-yər-lē, pär-'tik-yə-lər-lē\ *adv* **1 :** in a particular manner **2 :** to an unusual degree

par·tic·u·late \pər-'tik-yə-lət, pär-, -,lāt\ *adj* [L *particula*] **:** of or relating to minute separate particles

particulate inheritance *n* **:** inheritance of characters specif. transmitted by genes in accord with Mendel's laws

par·ti pris \,pär-,tē-'prē\ *n*, *pl* **par·tis pris** \-,tē-'prē(z)\ [F, lit., side taken] **:** a preconceived opinion **:** PREJUDICE

¹**par·ti·san** *or* **par·ti·zan** \'pärt-ə-zən *also* -sən, *Brit usu* ,pär-tiz-'an\ *n* [MF *partisan*, fr. OIt *partigiano*, fr. *parte* part, party, fr. L *part-*, *pars* part] **1 :** one that takes the part of another **:** SUPPORTER **2 a :** a member of a body of detached light troops making forays and harassing an enemy **b :** a member of a guerrilla band operating within enemy lines **syn** see FOLLOWER — **partisan** *adj* — **par·ti·san·ship** \-,ship\ *n*

²**par·ti·san** *or* **par·ti·zan** \'pärt-ə-zən, -sən\ *n* [MF *partisane*, fr. OIt *partigiana*, fem. of *partigiano*] **:** a weapon of the 16th and 17th centuries with long shaft and broad blade

par·ti·ta \pär-'tēt-ə\ *n* [It, fr. *partire* to divide, fr. L — more at PART] **1 :** VARIATION 5 **2 :** SUITE 2b(1)

par·tite \'pär-,tīt\ *adj* [L *partitus*, fr. pp. of *partire*] **1 :** divided into a usu. specified number of parts **2 :** PARTED 1b

par·ti·tion \pər-'tish-ən, pär-\ *n* **1 a :** the action of parting **:** the state of being parted **:** DIVISION **b :** separation of a class or whole into constituent elements **2 :** something that divides; *esp* **:** an interior dividing wall **3 :** one of the parts or sections of a whole — **partition** *vt* **par·ti·tion·ing** \-'tish-(ə-)niŋ\ — **par·ti·tion·er** \-'tish-(ə-)nər\ *n* — **par·ti·tion·ist** \-(ə-)nəst\ *n*

par·ti·tive \'pärt-ət-iv\ *adj* **1 :** serving to part or divide into parts **2 a :** of, relating to, or denoting a part ⟨a ~ construction⟩ **b :** serving to indicate that of which a part is specified ⟨~ genitive⟩ — **partitive** *n* — **par·ti·tive·ly** *adv*

part·let \'pärt-lət\ *n* [ME (Sc) *patelet*, fr. MF *patelette*, fr. dim. of *patte* paw] **:** a 16th century chemisette with a band or collar

part·ly \'pärt-lē\ *adv* **:** in some measure or degree **:** PARTIALLY

part music *n* **:** vocal music for several voices in independent parts usu. without accompaniment

1part·ner \'pärt-nər, *as a term of address often* 'pärd-\ *n* [ME *partener*, alter. of *parcener*, fr. AF, coparcener — more at PARCENER] **1** *archaic* **:** PARTAKER, SHARER **2 a :** ASSOCIATE, COLLEAGUE **b :** either of a couple who dance together **c :** one of two or more persons who play together in a game against an opposing side **d :** HUSBAND, WIFE **3 :** a member of a partnership **4 :** one of the heavy timbers that strengthen a ship's deck to support a mast — usu. used in pl.

2partner *vt* **1 :** to join as partner **2 :** to provide with a partner ~ *vi* **:** to act as a partner

part·ner·ship \-,ship\ *n* **1 :** the state of being a partner **:** PARTICIPATION **2 :** a legal relation existing between two or more persons contractually associated as joint principals in a business

part of speech : a traditional class of words distinguished according to the kind of idea denoted and the function performed in a sentence **:** MAJOR FORM CLASS

par·tridge \'pär-trij, *dial or archaic* 'pa-trij\ *n, pl* **partridge** *or* **par·tridg·es** [ME *partrich*, modif. of OF *perdris*, modif. of L *perdic-, perdix*, fr. Gk *perdik-, perdix*] **1 :** any of various typically medium-sized stout-bodied Old World gallinaceous game birds (*Perdix*, *Alectoris*, and related genera) with variegated plumage **2 :** any of numerous gallinaceous birds (as the American ruffed grouse or bobwhite) more or less like the Old World partridges in size, habits, or value as game

par·tridge·ber·ry \-,ber-ē\ *n* **:** any of several plants with fruits eaten by partridges; *esp* **:** an American trailing evergreen plant (*Mitchella repens*) of the madder family with insipid scarlet berries

part–song \'pärt-,sȯŋ\ *n* **:** a song consisting of two or more voice parts

part–time \-'tīm\ *adj* **:** involving or working less than customary or standard hours

par·tu·ri·ent \pär-'t(y)u̇r-ē-ənt\ *adj* [L *parturient-, parturiens*, prp. of *parturire* to be in labor, fr. *parere* to produce — more at PARE] **1 a :** bringing forth or about to bring forth young **b :** of or relating to parturition **2 :** being at the point of producing something

par·tu·ri·tion \,pärt-ə-'rish-ən, ,pär-chə-\ *n* [LL *parturition-, parturitio*, fr. L *parturitus*, pp. of *parturire*] **:** the act or process of giving birth to offspring

par·ty \'pärt-ē\ *n* [ME *partie* part, party, fr. OF, fr. *partir* to divide — more at PART] **1 :** a person or group taking one side of a question, dispute, or contest **2 :** a group of persons organized for the purpose of directing the policies of a government **3 :** a person or group participating in an action or affair **:** PARTICIPANT ⟨a ~ to the transaction⟩ **4 :** a particular individual **:** PERSON ⟨a coquettish little ~⟩ **5 :** a detail of soldiers **6 :** a social gathering; *also* **:** the entertainment provided for it — **party** *adj*

party line *n* **1 :** the policy or practice of a political party ⟨elections fought on *party lines*⟩ **2 :** a single telephone circuit connecting two or more subscribers with the exchange — called also *party wire* **3 :** the principles or policies of an individual or organization; *esp* **:** the official policies of the Communist party — **par·ty–lin·er** \,pärt-ē-'lī-nər\ *n*

party wall *n* **:** a wall which divides two adjoining properties and in which each of the owners of the adjoining properties has rights of enjoyment

pa·rure \pə-'ru̇(ə)r\ *n* [F, lit., adornment, fr. OF *pareure*, fr. *parer* to prepare, adorn — more at PARE] **:** a matched set of jewelry or other ornaments

par·ve \'pär-və\ *var of* PAREVE

par·ve·nu \'pär-və-,n(y)ü\ *n* [F, fr. pp. of *parvenir* to arrive, fr. L *pervenire*, fr. *per* through + *venire* to come — more at FOR, COME] **:** one who has recently or suddenly attained to wealth or power and has not yet secured the social position appropriate to it **:** UPSTART — **parvenu** *or* **par·ve·nue** \-,n(y)ü\ *adj*

par·vis *also* **par·vise** \'pär-vəs\ *n* [ME *parvis*, fr. MF, modif. of LL *paradisus* enclosed park — more at PARADISE] **1 :** a court or enclosed space before a building (as a church) **2 :** a single portico or colonnade before a church

pas \'pä\ *n, pl* **pas** \'pä(z)\ [F, fr. L *passus* step — more at PACE] **1 :** the right of precedence **2 :** a dance step or combination of steps

Pasch \'pask\ *n* [ME *pasche* Passover, Easter, fr. OF, fr. LL *pascha*, fr. LGk, fr. Gk, Passover, fr. Heb *pesaḥ*] **1 :** PASSOVER **2 :** EASTER — **pas·chal** \'pas-kəl\ *adj*

paschal lamb *n* **1 :** a lamb slain and eaten at the Passover **2** *cap P & L* **a :** CHRIST **b :** AGNUS DEI

pas de deux \,päd-ə-'də(r), -'dü\ *n, pl* **pas de deux** \-'dər(z), -'də(z), -'dü(z)\ [F, lit., step for two] **:** a dance or figure for two performers

pas de trois \-'trwä, -trə-'wä\ *n, pl* **pas de trois** \-'trwä(z), -trə-'wä(z)\ [F, lit., step for three] **:** a dance or figure for three performers

pa·se \'päs-(,)ā\ *n* [Sp, lit., feint, fr. *pase* let him pass, fr. *pasar* to pass, fr. (assumed) VL *passare*] **:** a movement of a cape by a matador in drawing a bull and taking his charge

pa·seo \pə-'sā-(,)ō\ *n* [Sp] **1 a :** a leisurely stroll **:** PROMENADE **b :** a public walk or boulevard **2 :** a formal entrance march of bullfighters into an arena

1pash \'pash\ *vt* [ME *passhen*] *dial Eng* **:** SMASH

2pash *n* [origin unknown] *dial Eng* **:** HEAD

3pash *n* [by shortening & alter. fr. *passion*] *slang* **:** a schoolgirl infatuation

pa·sha \'päsh-ə, 'pash-; pə-'shä, -'shȯ\ *n* [Turk *paşa*] **:** a man of high rank (as a former governor in Turkey)

Pash·to \'pəsh-(,)tō\ *n* [Per *pashtu*, fr. Pashto] **:** the Iranian language of the Pathan people which is the chief vernacular of eastern Afghanistan and adjacent parts of West Pakistan

Pa·siph·aë \pə-'sif-ə-,ē\ *n* [L, fr. Gk *Pasiphaē*] **:** the wife of Minos and mother of the Minotaur by a white bull

pasque·flow·er \'pask-,flau̇(-ə)r\ *n* [MF *passefleur*, fr. *passer* to pass + *fleur* flower, fr. L *flor-, flos* — more at BLOW] **:** any of several low perennial herbs (genus *Anemone*) of the crowfoot family with palmately compound leaves and large usu. white or purple flowers in early spring

pas·qui·nade \,pas-kwə-'nād\ *n* [MF, fr. It *pasquinata*, fr. *Pasquino*, name given to a statue in Rome on which lampoons were posted] **1 :** a lampoon posted in a public place **2 :** satirical writing **:** SATIRE — **pasquinade** *vt*

1pass \'pas\ *vb* [ME *passen*, fr. OF *passer*, fr. (assumed) VL *passare*, fr. L *passus* step — more at PACE] *vi* **1 :** MOVE, PROCEED **2 a :** to go away **:** DEPART **b :** DIE — often used with *on* **3 a :** to go by or move past **b :** to glide by (as of time) **c :** to move past another vehicle going in the same direction **4 a :** to go or make one's way through **b :** to go uncensured or unchallenged ⟨let his remark ~⟩ **5 :** to go from **6** [AF *passer*, lit., to proceed, fr. OF] **a** *of a jury* (1) **:** to sit in inquest (2) **:** to sit in adjudication **b** (1) **:** to render a legal judgment (2) **:** to express a decided opinion **7 a :** to undergo transfer so as to become vested in another **b :** to go from the control or possession of one person or group to that of another ⟨throne ~*ed* to his son⟩ **8 a :** HAPPEN, OCCUR **b :** to take place as a mutual exchange or transaction ⟨words ~*ed*⟩ **9 a :** to secure the approval of a legislature or other body that has power to sanction or reject a proposal **b :** to go through an inspection, test, or course of study successfully **10 a :** to serve as a medium of exchange **b :** to be held or regarded **c :** to identify oneself or accept identification as a white person though having some Negro ancestry **11 a** *obs* **:** to make a pass in fencing **b :** to execute a pass (as in football) **12 a :** to decline to bid, double, or redouble in a card game **b :** to withdraw from the current poker pot ~ *vt* **1 :** to go beyond: as **a :** SURPASS **b :** to advance or develop beyond **c :** to go past (one moving in the same direction) **d :** to transcend the range or limitations of **2 a :** to omit a regularly scheduled declaration and payment of (a dividend) **b :** to leave out in an account or narration **3 a :** to go across, over, or through **:** CROSS **b :** to live through **:** UNDERGO **c :** to cause or permit to elapse **:** SPEND **4 a :** to secure the approval of **b :** to go through successfully ⟨~*ed* the exam⟩ **5 a :** to cause or permit to win approval or legal or official sanction **b :** to let go unnoticed **:** OVERLOOK **c :** to cause or allow to pass an examination or course of study **6 a :** PLEDGE **b :** to transfer the right or property in **7 a :** to put in circulation ⟨~*ing* bad checks⟩ **b :** to transfer from one person to another **c :** to cause or enable to go **:** TRANSPORT **d :** to take a turn with (as a rope) around something **e :** to transfer (as a ball) to another player on the same team **f :** THROW **8 a :** to pronounce judicially ⟨~*ed* sentence⟩ **b :** UTTER **9 a :** to cause or permit to go past or through a barrier **b :** to cause to march or go by in order ⟨~*ed* the troops in review⟩ **10 :** to emit or discharge from the bowels **11 :** to permit to reach first base by giving a base on balls — **pass·er** *n* — **pass muster :** to pass an inspection or examination — **pass the buck :** to shift a responsibility to someone else — **pass the hat :** to take up a collection of money

2pass *n* **1 :** an opening, road, channel, or other way by which a barrier may be passed or access gained to a particular place; *esp* **:** a low place in a mountain range **2 :** a position to be maintained usu. against odds

3pass *n* **1 :** the act or an instance of passing **:** PASSAGE **2 :** ACCOMPLISHMENT **3 :** a state of affairs **:** CONDITION **4 a :** a written permission to move about freely in a particular place or to leave or enter it **b :** a written leave of absence from a military post or station for a brief period **c :** a permit or ticket allowing one free transportation or free admission **5 :** a thrust or lunge in fencing **6 a :** a transference of objects by sleight of hand or other deceptive means **b :** a moving of the hands over or along something **7** *archaic* **:** an ingenious sally (as of wit) **8 :** the passing of an examination or course of study; *also* **:** the mark or certification of such passing **9 :** a single complete mechanical operation **10 :** a transfer of a ball or a puck from one player to another on the same team **11 :** BASE ON BALLS **12 a :** a refusal to bid, bet, or draw an additional card in a card game **b :** an election not to bid, double, or redouble in bridge **13 :** a throw of dice that wins the main bet **14 :** a single passage or movement of an airplane or other man-made object over a place or toward a target **15 a :** EFFORT, TRY **b :** a sexually inviting gesture or approach **16 :** PASE **syn** see JUNCTURE

pass·able \'pas-ə-bəl\ *adj* **1 a :** capable of being passed, crossed, or traveled on ⟨~ roads⟩ **b :** capable of being freely circulated **2 :** barely good enough **:** TOLERABLE

pass·ably \-blē\ *adv* **:** TOLERABLY, MODERATELY

pas·sa·ca·glia \,päs-ə-'käl-yə, ,pas-ə-'kal-yə\ *n* [modif. of Sp *pasacalle*] **1 a :** an old Italian or Spanish dance tune **b :** an instrumental musical composition consisting of variations usu. on a ground bass in moderately slow triple time **2 :** an old dance performed to a passacaglia

pas·sa·do \pə-'säd-(,)ō\ *n, pl* **passados** *or* **passadoes** [modif. of F *passade* (fr. It *passata*) or It *passata*, fr. *passare* to pass, fr. (assumed) VL] **:** a thrust in fencing with one foot advanced

1pas·sage \'pas-ij\ *n* **1 a :** the action or process of passing from one place or condition to another **b** *obs* **:** DEATH **2 a :** a road, path, channel, or course by which something passes **b :** a corridor or lobby giving access to the different rooms or parts of a building or apartment **3 a** (1) **:** a specific act of traveling or passing esp. by sea or air (2) **:** a privilege of conveyance as a passenger **:** ACCOMMODATIONS **b :** the passing of a legislative measure or law **:** ENACTMENT **4 :** a right, liberty, or permission to pass **5 a :** something that happens or is done **:** INCIDENT **b :** something that takes place between two persons mutually **6 a :** a usu. brief portion of a written work or speech that is relevant to a point under discussion or noteworthy for content or style **b :** a phrase or short section of a musical composition **c :** a detail of a painting or other work of art **7 :** the act or action of passing something or undergoing a passing

2passage *vi* **:** to go past or across **:** CROSS

pas·sage·way \-,wā\ *n* **:** a way that allows passage **:** PASSAGE 2

pas·sant \'pas-ᵊnt\ *adj* [MF, fr. prp. of *passer* to pass] **:** walking with the farther forepaw raised — used of a heraldic animal

pass away *vi* **1 :** to go out of existence **2 :** DIE

pass·book \'pas-,bu̇k\ *n* **:** BANKBOOK

pass degree *n* **:** a bachelor's degree without honors that is taken at a British university

pas·sé \pa-'sā\ *adj* [F, fr. pp. of *passer*] **1 :** past one's prime **2 a :** OUTMODED **b :** behind the times

passed ball *n* **:** a pitched ball not hit by the batter that passes the catcher when he should have stopped it and allows a base runner to advance a base

pas·sel \'pas-əl\ *n* [alter. of *parcel*] **:** a large number **:** GROUP

passe·men·terie \pa-'smen-trē, -'sment-ə-rē\ *n* [F, fr. *passement* ornamental braid, fr. *passer*] **:** a fancy edging or trimming made of braid, cord, gimp, beading, or metallic thread in various combinations

pas·sen·ger \'pas-ᵊn-jər\ *n, often attrib* [ME *passager*, fr. MF, fr. *passager*, adj., passing, fr. *passage* act of passing, fr. OF, fr. *passer*] **1 :** one who passes by **:** WAYFARER **2 :** a traveler in a public or private conveyance

passenger pigeon *n* **:** an extinct but formerly abundant No. American migratory pigeon (*Ectopistes migratorius*)

passe–par·tout \,pas-pər-'tü, -,pär-\ *n* [F, fr. *passe partout* pass everywhere] **1 :** something that passes or enables one to pass everywhere **:** MASTER KEY **2 a :** [5]MAT 1 **b :** a method of framing in which a picture, a mat, a glass, and a back (as of cardboard) are held together by strips of paper or cloth pasted over the edges **3 :** a strong paper gummed on one side and used esp. for mounting pictures

pas·ser·by \,pas-ər-'bī, 'pas-ər-,\ *n, pl* **pas·sers·by** \-ərz-\ **:** one who passes by

pas·ser·ine \'pas-ə-,rīn\ *adj* [L *passerinus* of sparrows, fr. *passer* sparrow] **1 :** of or relating to the largest order (Passeriformes) of birds including more than half of all living birds and consisting chiefly of altricial songbirds of perching habits **2 :** of or relating to a suborder (Passeres) of passerine birds comprising the true songbirds with specialized vocal apparatus — **passerine** *n*

pas seul \pä-'sər(-ə)l, -'səl\ *n* [F, lit., solo step] **:** a solo dance or dance figure

pas·si·ble \'pas-ə-bəl\ *adj* [ME, fr. MF, fr. LL *passibilis*, fr. L *passus*, pp. of *pati* to suffer — more at PATIENT] **:** capable of feeling or suffering

pas·sim \'pas-əm; 'pas-,im, 'päs-\ *adv* [L, fr. *passus* scattered, fr. pp. of *pandere* to spread — more at FATHOM] **:** here and there

[1]**pass·ing** *n* **:** the act of one that passes or causes to pass; *esp* **:** DEATH — **in passing :** by the way **:** PARENTHETICALLY

[2]**passing** *adj* **1 :** going by or past **2 :** having a brief duration **3** *obs* **:** SURPASSING **4 :** marked by haste, inattention, or inadequacy **:** SUPERFICIAL **5 a :** of, relating to, or used in or for the act or process of passing **b :** given on satisfactory completion of an examination or course of study

[3]**passing** *adv* **:** to a surpassing degree **:** EXCEEDINGLY ⟨~ fair⟩

passing note *n* **:** a note or tone foreign to the harmony and usu. unaccented that is interposed for melodic smoothness between essential notes or tones — called also *passing tone*

pas·sion \'pash-ən\ *n* [ME, fr. OF, fr. LL *passion-*, *passio* suffering, being acted upon, fr. L *passus*, pp. of *pati* to suffer — more at PATIENT] **1** *often cap* **a :** the sufferings of Christ between the night of the Last Supper and his death **b :** an oratorio based on a gospel narrative of the passion of Christ **2** *obs* **:** SUFFERING **3 :** the state or capacity of being acted on by external agents or forces **4 a** (1) **:** EMOTION (2) *pl* **:** the emotions as distinguished from reason **b :** violent, intense, or overmastering feeling **c :** an outbreak of anger **5 a :** ardent affection **:** LOVE **b :** a strong liking for or devotion to some activity, object, or concept **c :** sexual desire **d :** an object of desire or deep interest — **pas·sion·less** \-ləs\ *adj*

syn PASSION, FERVOR, ARDOR, ENTHUSIASM, ZEAL mean intense emotion compelling action. PASSION applies to an emotion that is deeply stirring or ungovernable; FERVOR implies a steadily glowing emotion; ARDOR suggests warm and excited feeling likely to be fitful or short-lived; ENTHUSIASM applies to lively or eager interest in or admiration for a proposal or cause or activity; ZEAL implies energetic and unflagging pursuit of an aim or devotion to a cause **syn** see in addition FEELING

pas·sion·al \'pash-ən-ᵊl, 'pash-nəl\ *adj* **:** of, relating to, or marked by passion

pas·sion·ate \'pash-(ə-)nət\ *adj* **1 a :** easily aroused to anger **b :** filled with anger **:** ANGRY **2 a :** capable of, affected by, or expressing intense feeling **b :** ENTHUSIASTIC **3 :** swayed by or affected with sexual desire **syn** see IMPASSIONED — **pas·sion·ate·ly** *adv* — **pas·sion·ate·ness** *n*

pas·sion·flow·er \'pash-ən-,flau̇(-ə)r\ *n* [fr. the fancied resemblance of parts of the flower to the instruments of Christ's crucifixion] **:** any of a genus (*Passiflora* of the family Passifloraceae, the passionflower family) of chiefly tropical woody tendril-climbing vines or erect herbs with usu. showy flowers and pulpy often edible berries

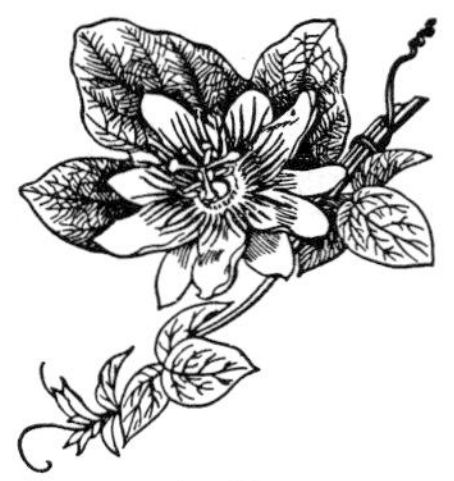

passionflower

Pas·sion·ist \'pash-(ə-)nəst\ *n, often attrib* [It *passionista*, fr. *passione* passion, fr. LL *passion-*, *passio*] **:** a priest of a Roman Catholic mendicant order founded in Italy in 1720 and devoted chiefly to missionary work and retreats

passion play *n, often cap 1st P* **:** a dramatic representation of the scenes connected with the passion of Christ

Passion Sunday *n* **:** the 5th Sunday in Lent

Pas·sion·tide \'pash-ən-,tīd\ *n* **:** the last two weeks of Lent

Passion Week *n* **1 :** HOLY WEEK **2 :** the second week before Easter

[1]**pas·sive** \'pas-iv\ *adj* [ME, fr. L *passivus*, fr. *passus*, pp.] **1 a** (1) **:** acted upon by an external agency (2) **:** receptive to outside impressions or influences **b** (1) *of a verb form or voice* **:** asserting that the person or thing represented by the grammatical subject is subjected to or affected by the action represented by the verb (2) *of a grammatical construction* **:** containing a passive verb form **c :** lacking in energy or will **:** LETHARGIC **d :** induced by an outside agency ⟨~ exercise⟩ **2 a :** not active or operating **:** INERT **b :** LATENT **c :** of, relating to, or characterized by a state of chemical inactivity; *esp* **:** resistant to corrosion **3 a :** receiving or enduring without resistance **:** SUBMISSIVE **b :** existing without being active or open ⟨~ support⟩ **syn** see INACTIVE — **pas·sive·ly** *adv* — **pas·sive·ness** *n* — **pas·siv·i·ty** \pa-'siv-ət-ē\ *n*

[2]**passive** *n* **1 :** a passive verb form **2 :** the passive voice of a language

passive resistance *n* **:** resistance esp. to a government or an occupying power characterized mainly by techniques and acts of noncooperation in place of violence or active measures of opposition

pas·siv·ism \'pas-iv-,iz-əm\ *n* **:** a passive attitude, behavior, or way of life

pass·key \'pas-,kē\ *n* **1 :** MASTER KEY **2 :** SKELETON KEY

pass off *vt* **1 :** to make public or offer for sale with intent to deceive **2 :** to give a false identity or character to

pass out *vi* **1 :** to lose consciousness **2 :** DIE

Pass·over \'pas-,ō-vər\ *n* **:** a Jewish holiday beginning on the 14th of Nisan and commemorating the Hebrews' liberation from slavery in Egypt

pass over *vt* **1 :** to ignore in passing **2 :** to pay no attention to the claims of **:** DISREGARD

pass·port \'pas-,pō(ə)rt, -,pȯ(ə)rt\ *n* [MF *passeport*, fr. *passer* to pass + *port* port, fr. L *portus* — more at FORD] **1 a :** a formal document that is issued by an authorized official of a country to one of its citizens and usu. necessary for exit from and reentry into the country, that allows him to travel in a foreign country in accordance with visa requirements, and that requests protection for him while abroad **b :** a license issued by a country permitting a foreign citizen to pass or take goods through its territory **:** SAFE-CONDUCT **c :** a document of identification required by the laws of a country to be carried by persons residing or traveling within that country **2 a :** a permission or authorization to go somewhere **b :** something that secures admission or acceptance

pass up *vt* **:** DECLINE, REJECT

pass·word \'pas-,wərd\ *n* **1 :** a word or phrase that must be spoken by a person before he is allowed to pass a guard **2:** WATCHWORD 1

[1]**past** \'past\ *adj* [ME, fr. pp. of *passen* to pass] **1 a :** AGO ⟨ten years ~⟩ **b :** just gone or elapsed ⟨for the ~ few months⟩ **2 :** having existed or taken place in a period before the present **:** BYGONE **3 :** of, relating to, or constituting a verb tense that in English is usu. formed by internal vowel change (as in *sang*) or by the addition of a suffix (as in *laughed*) and that is expressive of elapsed time **4 :** having served as a specified officer in an organization ⟨~ president⟩

[2]**past** \'past\ *prep* **1 a :** beyond the age for or of **b :** AFTER ⟨half ~ two⟩ **2 a :** at the farther side of **:** BEYOND **b :** in a course or direction going close to and then beyond **3** *obs* **:** more than **4 :** beyond the range, scope, or sphere of

[3]**past** \'past\ *n* **1 a :** time gone by **b :** something that happened or was done in the past **2 a :** the past tense of a language **b :** a verb form in the past tense **3 a :** a past life, history, or course of action **b :** a past life or career that is kept secret esp. because of criminal or immoral behavior

[4]**past** \'past\ *adv* **:** so as to reach and go beyond a point near at hand

pas·ta \'päs-tə\ *n* [It, fr. LL] **1 :** a paste in processed form (as spaghetti) or in the form of fresh dough (as ravioli) **2 :** a dish of cooked pasta

[1]**paste** \'pāst\ *n* [ME, fr. MF, fr. LL *pasta* dough, paste] **1 a :** a dough that contains a considerable proportion of fat and is used for pastry crust or fancy rolls **b :** a confection made by evaporating fruit with sugar or by flavoring a gelatin, starch, or gum arabic preparation **c :** a smooth food product made by evaporation or grinding **d :** a shaped dough (as spaghetti or ravioli) prepared from semolina, farina, or wheat flour **2 :** a soft plastic mixture or composition: as **a :** a preparation usu. of flour or starch and water used as an adhesive or a vehicle for mordant or color **b :** a moistened clay mixture used in making pottery or porcelain **3 :** a brilliant glass of high lead content used for the manufacture of artificial gems

[2]**paste** *vt* **1 :** to cause to adhere by paste **:** STICK **2 :** to cover with something pasted on

[3]**paste** *vt* [alter. of *baste*] **:** to strike hard at — **paste** *n*

[1]**paste·board** \'pās(t)-,bō(ə)rd, -,bȯ(ə)rd\ *n* **1 :** paperboard made by pasting together two or more sheets of paper; *broadly* **:** PAPERBOARD **2 a :** VISITING CARD **b :** PLAYING CARD **c :** TICKET

[2]**pasteboard** *adj* **1 :** made of pasteboard **2 :** SHAM, UNSUBSTANTIAL

paste·down \'pās(t)-,dau̇n\ *n* **:** the outer leaf of an endpaper that is pasted down to the inside of the front or back cover of a book

[1]**pas·tel** \pa-'stel\ *n* [F, fr. It *pastello*, fr. LL *pastellus* woad, fr. dim. of *pasta*] **1 :** a paste made of ground color and used for making crayons; *also* **:** a crayon made of such paste **2 a :** a drawing in pastel **b :** the process or art of drawing with pastels **3 :** a light literary sketch **4 :** any of various pale or light colors

[2]**pastel** *adj* **1 a :** of or relating to a pastel **b :** made with pastels **2 :** pale and light in color ⟨~ shades⟩ **3 :** lacking in body or vigor **:** DELICATE

pas·tel·ist *or* **pas·tel·list** \pa-'stel-əst\ *n* **:** a maker of pastel drawings

pas·tern \'pas-tərn\ *n* [MF *pasturon*, fr. *pasture* pasture, tether attached to a horse's foot] **:** a part of the foot of an equine extending from the fetlock to the coffin bone; *broadly* **:** a corresponding part of the leg of other animals

pas·teur·iza·tion \,pas-chə-rə-'zā-shən, ,pas-tə-\ *n* **:** partial sterilization of a substance (as a fluid) at a temperature that destroys objectionable organisms without major chemical alteration of the substance

pas·teur·ize \'pas-chə-,rīz, 'pas-tə-\ *vt* [Louis *Pasteur* †1895 F chemist] **:** to subject to pasteurization — **pas·teur·iz·er** *n*

Pas·teur treatment \pa-'stər-\ *n* **:** a method of aborting rabies by stimulating production of antibodies through successive inoculations with attenuated virus of gradually increasing strength

pas·tic·cio \pa-'stē-(,)chō, pä-, -chē-,ō\ *n, pl* **pas·tic·ci** \-(,)chē\ *or* **pas·tic·cios** [It, lit., pasty, fr. ML *pasticius*, fr. LL *pasta*] **:** PASTICHE

pas·tiche \pa-'stēsh, pä-\ *n* [F, fr. It *pasticcio*] **1 :** a literary, artistic, or musical work that imitates the style of previous work **2 a :** a musical composition or piece of writing made up of selections from different works **:** POTPOURRI **b :** HODGEPODGE

pas·tille \pa-'stē(ə)l\ *also* **pas·til** \'pas-tᵊl\ *n* [F *pastille*, fr. L *pastillus* small loaf, lozenge; akin to L *panis* bread — more at FOOD] **1 :** a small mass of aromatic paste for fumigating or scenting the air of a room **2 :** an aromatic or medicated lozenge **:** TROCHE

pas·time \'pas-,tīm\ *n* **:** something that amuses and serves to make time pass agreeably **:** DIVERSION

past·i·ness \'pā-stē-nəs\ *n* **:** the quality or state of being pasty

past master *n* **1 :** one who has held the office of worshipful master in a lodge of Freemasons or of master in some other society

2 [alter. of *passed master*] **:** one who is expert **:** ADEPT — **past mistress** *n*
pas·tor \'pas-tər\ *n* [ME *pastour*, fr. OF, fr. L *pastor*, fr. *pastus*, pp. of *pascere* to feed — more at FOOD] **1** *chiefly Southwest* **:** HERDSMAN **2 :** a spiritual overseer; *esp* **:** a clergyman serving a local church or parish — **pas·tor·ship** \-,ship\ *n*
¹**pas·to·ral** \'pas-t(ə-)rəl\ *adj* **1 a** (1) **:** of, relating to, or composed of shepherds or herdsmen (2) **:** devoted to or based on livestock raising **b :** RURAL **c :** portraying or expressive of the life of shepherds or country people esp. in an idealized and conventionalized manner ⟨~ poetry⟩ **d :** INNOCENT, IDYLLIC **2 a :** of or relating to spiritual care or guidance esp. of a congregation **b :** of or relating to the pastor of a church **syn** see RURAL — **pas·to·ral·ly** \-t(ə-)rə-lē\ *adv* — **pas·to·ral·ness** *n*
²**pastoral** \'pas-t(ə-)rəl, *2d is often* ,pas-tə-'räl, -'ral\ *n* **1 :** a letter of a pastor to his charge: as **a :** a letter addressed by a bishop to his diocese **b :** a letter of the house of bishops of the Protestant Episcopal Church to be read in each parish **2 a :** a literary work dealing with shepherds or rural life in a usu. artificial manner and typically drawing a contrast between the innocence and serenity of the simple life and the misery and corruption of city and esp. court life **b :** pastoral poetry or drama **c :** a rural picture or scene **d :** PASTORALE 1b **3 :** CROSIER
pas·to·rale \,pas-tə-'räl, -'ral *also* -'räl-ē\ *n* [It, fr. *pastorale* of herdsmen, fr. L *pastoralis*, fr. *pastor*] **1 a :** an opera of the 16th or 17th centuries having a pastoral plot **b :** an instrumental or vocal composition having a pastoral theme **2 :** PASTORAL 2a
Pastoral Epistle *n* **:** one of three New Testament letters including two addressed to Timothy and one to Titus and giving advice on matters of church government and discipline
pas·to·ral·ism \'pas-t(ə-)rə-,liz-əm\ *n* **1 :** the quality or style characteristic of pastoral writing **2 a :** livestock raising **b :** social organization based on livestock raising as the primary economic activity — **pas·to·ral·ist** \-ləst\ *n*
pas·tor·ate \'pas-t(ə-)rət\ *n* **1 a :** the office, state, jurisdiction, or tenure of office of a pastor **b :** a body of pastors **2 :** PARSONAGE
pas·to·ri·um \pa-'stōr-ē-əm, -'stȯr-\ *n* [irreg. fr. *pastor* + *-orium*] *chiefly South* **:** a Protestant parsonage
past participle *n* **:** a participle that typically expresses completed action, that is traditionally one of the principal parts of the verb, and that is traditionally used in English in the formation of perfect tenses in the active voice and of all tenses in the passive voice
past perfect *adj* **:** of, relating to, or constituting a verb tense that is traditionally formed in English with *had* and denotes an action or state as completed at or before a past time spoken of — **past perfect** *n*
pas·tra·mi \pə-'sträm-ē\ *n* [Yiddish, fr. Romanian *pastramă*] **:** a highly seasoned smoked beef prepared esp. from shoulder cuts
past·ry \'pā-strē\ *n, often attrib* [¹*paste*] **1 :** sweet baked goods made of dough or having a crust made of enriched dough **2 :** a piece of pastry
past tense *n* **:** a verb tense expressing action or state in or as if in the past: **a :** a verb tense expressive of elapsed time (as *wrote* in "on arriving I wrote a letter") **b :** a verb tense expressing action or state in progress or continuance or habitually done or customarily occurring at a past time (as *was writing* in "I was writing while he dictated" or *loved* in "their sons loved fishing")
pas·tur·age \'pas-chə-rij\ *n* **:** PASTURE
¹**pas·ture** \'pas-chər\ *n, often attrib* [ME, fr. MF, fr. LL *pastura*, fr. L *pastus*, pp. of *pascere* to feed — more at FOOD] **1 :** plants (as grass) grown for the feeding esp. of grazing animals **2 :** land or a plot of land used for grazing **3 :** the feeding of livestock **:** GRAZING
²**pasture** *vb* **pas·tur·ing** \'pas-chə-riŋ, 'pasch-riŋ\ *vi* **:** GRAZE, BROWSE ~ *vt* **1 :** to feed (as cattle) on pasture **2 :** to use as pasture — **pas·tur·er** \'pas-chər-ər\ *n*
¹**pas·ty** \'pas-tē\ *n* [ME *pastee*, fr. MF *pasté*, fr. *paste* dough, paste] **:** ²PIE 1, 2; *esp* **:** a meat pie
²**pasty** \'pā-stē\ *adj* **:** resembling paste; *esp* **:** pallid and unhealthy in appearance
PA system \pē-'ā-\ *n* **:** PUBLIC-ADDRESS SYSTEM
¹**pat** \'pat\ *n* [ME *patte*] **1 :** a light blow esp. with the hand or a flat instrument **2 :** a light tapping often rhythmical sound **3 :** a usu. square individual portion of butter or something resembling or suggesting it
²**pat** *vb* **pat·ted; pat·ting** *vt* **1 :** to strike lightly with a flat instrument **2 :** to flatten, smooth, or put into place or shape with light blows **3 :** to tap gently with the hand to soothe, caress, or show approval ~ *vi* **1 :** to strike or beat gently **2 :** to walk or run with a light beating sound
³**pat** *adv* **:** in a pat manner **:** APTLY, PROMPTLY
⁴**pat** *adj* **1 a :** exactly suited to the purpose or occasion **:** APT **b :** too exactly suitable **:** CONTRIVED **2 :** learned, mastered, or memorized exactly **3 :** FIRM, UNYIELDING ⟨stand ~⟩ **syn** see SEASONABLE
pa·ta·gi·um \pə-'tā-jē-əm, ,pat-ə-'jī-\ *n, pl* **pa·ta·gia** \-ə\ [NL, fr. L, gold edging on a tunic] **:** a wing membrane: as **a :** the fold of skin connecting the forelimbs and hind limbs of a flying squirrel or dragon lizard **b :** the fold of skin in front of the main segments of a bird's wing
¹**patch** \'pach\ *n* [ME *pacche*] **1 :** a piece of material used to mend or cover a hole or a weak spot **2 :** a tiny piece of black silk or court plaster worn on the face or neck esp. by women to hide a blemish or to heighten beauty **3 a :** a piece of adhesive plaster or other cover applied to a wound **b :** a shield worn over an injured eye **4 a :** a small piece **:** SCRAP **b :** a small area distinct from that about it ⟨cabbage ~⟩ **5 :** a piece of cloth sewed on a garment as an ornament or insignia; *esp* **:** SHOULDER PATCH
²**patch** *vt* **1 :** to mend, cover, or fill up a hole or weak spot in **2 :** to provide with a patch **3 a :** to make of patches or fragments **b :** to mend or put together esp. in hasty or shabby fashion — usu. used with *up* **syn** see MEND
³**patch** *n* [perh. by folk etymology fr. It dial. *paccio*] **:** FOOL, DOLT
pa·tchou·li *or* **pa·tchou·ly** \'pach-ə-lē, pə-'chü-lē\ *n* [Tamil *paccuḷi*] **1 :** an East Indian shrubby mint (*Pogostemon cablin*) that yields a fragrant essential oil **2 :** a heavy perfume made from patchouli
patch pocket *n* **:** a flat pocket applied to the outside of a garment
patch test *n* **:** a test for determining allergic sensitivity made by applying to the unbroken skin small pads soaked with the allergen in question
patch·work \'pach-,wərk\ *n* **1 :** something composed of miscellaneous or incongruous parts **:** HODGEPODGE **2 :** pieces of cloth of various colors and shapes sewed together usu. in a pattern to form a covering
patchy \'pach-ē\ *adj* **:** marked by, consisting of, or diversified with patches
¹**pate** \'pāt\ *n* [ME] **1 :** HEAD **2 :** the crown of the head **3 :** BRAIN — used chiefly disparagingly — **pat·ed** \'pāt-əd\ *adj*
²**pâ·té** \pä-'tā\ *n* [F, fr. OF *pasté*, fr. *paste*] **1 :** a meat or fish pie or patty **2 :** a spread of finely mashed seasoned and spiced meat
³**pâte** \'pät\ *n* [F, lit., paste, fr. OF *paste*] **:** the paste or plastic material for pottery or porcelain
pâ·té de foie gras \(,)pä-,tād-ə-,fwä-'grä, (,)pa-,tād-, ,pät-ēd-, ,pat-ēd-\ *n, pl* **pâ·tés de foie gras** \-,tā(z)d-ə-, -ē(z)d-ə-\ [F] **:** a paste of fat goose liver and truffles sometimes with added fat pork
pa·tel·la \pə-'tel-ə\ *n, pl* **pa·tel·lae** \-'tel-(,)ē, -,ī\ *or* **patellas** [L, fr. dim. of *patina* shallow dish] **:** a thick flat triangular movable bone that forms the anterior point of the knee and protects the front of the joint — called also *kneecap* — **pa·tel·lar** \-'tel-ər\ *adj*
pa·tel·late \pə-'tel-ət\ *adj* **1 :** having a patella **2 :** PATELLIFORM
pa·tel·li·form \pə-'tel-ə-,fȯrm\ *adj* **:** resembling a limpet or limpet shell; *esp* **:** disk-shaped with a narrow rim
pat·en \'pat-ᵊn, *esp by clergymen* -ən\ *n* [ME, fr. OF *patene*, fr. ML & L; ML *patina*, fr. L, shallow dish, fr. Gk *patanē*; akin to L *patēre* to be open — more at FATHOM] **1 :** a plate of precious metal for the eucharistic bread **2 :** PLATE **3 :** a thin metal disk or something resembling one
pa·ten·cy \'pat-ᵊn-sē, 'pāt-\ *n* **:** the quality or state of being patent
¹**pa·tent** *4–7 are* 'pat-ᵊnt, 'pāt-; *1–3 are* 'pat-, *Brit* 'pat- *or* 'pāt-\ *adj* [ME, fr. MF, fr. L *patent-, patens*, fr. prp. of *patēre*] **1 a :** open to public inspection — used chiefly in the phrase *letters patent* **b :** conferred or appointed by letters patent **c :** appropriated or protected by letters patent **:** PATENTED **2 :** of, relating to, or concerned with the granting of patents esp. for inventions **3 a :** marketed as a proprietary commodity ⟨a ~ can opener⟩ **b :** making exclusive or proprietary claims or pretensions **4 :** OPEN, UNOBSTRUCTED **5 :** PATULOUS, SPREADING **6** *archaic* **:** ACCESSIBLE, EXPOSED **7 :** OBVIOUS **syn** see EVIDENT — **pa·tent·ly** *adv*
²**pat·ent** \'pat-ᵊnt, *Brit also* 'pāt-\ *n* **1 :** an official document conferring a right or privilege **:** LETTERS PATENT **2 a :** a writing securing to an inventor for a term of years the exclusive right to make, use, or sell his invention **b :** the monopoly or right so granted **c :** a patented invention **3 :** PRIVILEGE, LICENSE **4 :** an instrument making a conveyance or grant of public lands; *also* **:** the land so conveyed
³**pat·ent** *vt* **1 :** to grant a privilege, right, or license to by patent **2 :** to obtain or secure by patent; *esp* **:** to secure by letters patent exclusive right to make, use, or sell **3 :** to obtain or grant a patent right to — **pat·ent·abil·i·ty** \,pat-ᵊnt-ə-'bil-ət-ē, *Brit also* ,pāt-\ *n* — **pat·ent·able** \'pat-ᵊnt-ə-bəl, *Brit also* 'pāt-\ *adj*
pat·en·tee \,pat-ᵊn-'tē, *Brit also* ,pāt-\ *n* **:** one to whom a grant is made or a privilege secured by patent
pat·ent flour \,pat-ᵊn(t)-, *Brit also* ,pāt-\ *n* **:** a high-grade wheat flour consisting solely of endosperm
pat·ent leather \,pat-ᵊn(t)-, *Brit usu* ,pāt-\ *n* **:** a leather with a hard smooth glossy surface
patent medicine *n* **:** PROPRIETARY 3
patent office *n* **:** a government office for examining claims to patents and granting patents
pat·en·tor \'pat-ᵊnt-ər, ,pat-ᵊn-'tȯ(ə)r, *Brit also* 'pāt-, ,pāt-\ *n* **:** one that grants a patent
patent right *n* **:** a right granted by letters patent; *esp* **:** the exclusive right to an invention
pa·ter *n* **1** *often cap* \'pä-,te(ə)r\ **:** PATERNOSTER **2** \'pāt-ər\ [L] *chiefly Brit* **:** FATHER
pa·ter·fa·mil·i·as \,pāt-ər-fə-'mil-ē-əs, ,pät-\ *n* [L, fr. *pater* father + *familias*, old gen. of *familia* family — more at FATHER] **1 :** the male head of a household **2 :** the father of a family
pa·ter·nal \pə-'tərn-ᵊl\ *adj* [L *paternus*, fr. *pater*] **1 :** of or relating to a father **2 :** received or inherited from one's father **3 :** related through one's father ⟨~ grandfather⟩ — **pa·ter·nal·ly** \-ᵊl-ē\ *adv*
pa·ter·nal·ism \-ᵊl-,iz-əm\ *n* **1 :** a system under which an authority treats those under its control in a fatherly way esp. in regulating their conduct and supplying their needs **2 :** a policy or practice based on or characteristic of the system of paternalism — **pa·ter·nal·ist** \-ᵊl-əst\ *n or adj* — **pa·ter·nal·is·tic** \-,tərn-ᵊl-'is-tik\ *adj*
pa·ter·ni·ty \pə-'tər-nət-ē\ *n* **1 :** the quality or state of being a father **2 :** origin or descent from a father
pa·ter·nos·ter \'pat-ər-,näs-tər; ,pät-ər-'näs-tər, -,te(ə)r\ *n* [ME, fr. ML, fr. L *pater noster* our father] **1** *often cap* **:** LORD'S PRAYER **2 :** a word formula repeated as a prayer or magical charm
path \'path, 'pȧth\ *n, pl* **paths** \'pat͟hz, 'paths, 'pȧt͟hz, 'pȧths\ [ME, fr. OE *pæth*; akin to OHG *pfad* path] **1 :** a trodden way **2 :** a track specially constructed for a particular use **3 a :** COURSE, ROUTE **b :** a way of life, conduct, or thought
path- *or* **patho-** *comb form* [NL, fr. Gk, fr. *pathos*, lit., suffering — more at PATHOS] **:** pathological state **:** DISEASE ⟨*path*ogen⟩
-path \,path\ *n comb form* **1** [G, back-formation fr. *-pathie* -pathy] **:** practitioner of a (specified) system of medicine that emphasizes one aspect of disease or its treatment ⟨naturo*path*⟩ **2** [ISV, fr. Gk *-pathēs*, adj., suffering, fr. *pathos*] **:** one suffering from (such) an ailment ⟨psycho*path*⟩
Pa·than \pə-'tän\ *n* [Hindi *Paṭhān*] **:** a member of the principal ethnic group of Afghanistan
pa·thet·ic \pə-'thet-ik\ *adj* [MF or LL; MF *pathetique*, fr. LL *patheticus*, fr. Gk *pathētikos* capable of feeling, pathetic, fr. *paschein* to experience, suffer — more at PATHOS] **1 :** evoking tenderness, pity, or sorrow **:** PITIABLE **2 :** marked by sorrow or melancholy **:** SAD **syn** see MOVING — **pa·thet·i·cal** \-i-kəl\ *adj* — **pa·thet·i·cal·ly** \-k(ə-)lē\ *adv*
pathetic fallacy *n* **:** the ascription of human traits or feelings to inanimate nature (as in *cruel sea*)

path·find·er \'path-,fīn-dər, 'päth-\ *n* **:** one that discovers a way; *esp* **:** one that explores untraversed regions to mark out a new route

path·less \-ləs\ *adj* **:** UNTRODDEN, TRACKLESS — **path·less·ness** *n*

patho·gen \'path-ə-jən\ *n* [ISV] **:** a specific cause of disease (as a bacterium or virus)

patho·gen·e·sis \,path-ə-'jen-ə-səs\ *n* [NL] **:** the origination and development of a disease

patho·ge·net·ic \-jə-'net-ik\ *adj* [ISV] **1 :** of or relating to pathogenesis **2 :** PATHOGENIC 2

patho·gen·ic \-'jen-ik\ *adj* [ISV] **1 :** PATHOGENETIC 1 **2 :** causing or capable of causing disease — **patho·gen·i·cal·ly** \-i-k(ə-)lē\ *adv* — **patho·ge·nic·i·ty** \-jə-'nis-ət-ē\ *n*

pa·tho·gno·mon·ic \,path-ə(g)-nō-'män-ik\ *adj* [Gk *pathognōmonikos*, fr. *path-* + *gnōmonikos* fit to judge, fr. *gnōmon* interpreter] **:** distinctively characteristic of a particular disease

patho·log·i·cal \,path-ə-'läj-i-kəl\ *or* **patho·log·ic** \-ik\ *adj* **1 :** of or relating to pathology **2 :** altered or caused by disease — **patho·log·i·cal·ly** \-i-k(ə-)lē\ *adv*

pa·thol·o·gist \pə-'thäl-ə-jəst, pa-\ *n* **:** a specialist in pathology; *specif* **:** one who interprets and diagnoses the changes caused by disease in tissues

pa·thol·o·gy \-jē\ *n* [NL *pathologia* & MF *pathologie*, fr. Gk *pathologia* study of the emotions, fr. *path-* + *-logia* -logy] **1 :** the study of the essential nature of diseases and esp. of the structural and functional changes produced by them **2 :** something abnormal: **a :** the anatomic and physiologic deviations from the normal that constitute disease or characterize a particular disease **b :** deviation from propriety or from an assumed normal state of something nonliving or nonmaterial

pa·thom·e·ter \pə-'thäm-ət-ər, pa-\ *n* **:** an instrument that measures changes in bodily electrical conductivity and is used as a lie detector

pa·thos \'pā-,thäs, -,thȯs\ *n* [Gk, suffering, experience, emotion, fr. *paschein* to experience, suffer; akin to Lith *kesti* to suffer] **1 :** an element in experience or in artistic representation evoking pity or compassion **2 :** an emotion of sympathetic pity

path·way \'path-,wā, 'päth-\ *n* **:** PATH, COURSE

-p·a·thy \p-ə-thē\ *n comb form* [L *-pathia*, fr. Gk *-patheia*, fr. *-pathēs* suffering — more at -PATH] **1 :** feeling **:** suffering ⟨em*pathy*⟩ ⟨tele*pathy*⟩ **2 :** disease of (such) a part or kind ⟨neuro*pathy*⟩ **3 :** system of medicine based on (such) a factor ⟨osteo*pathy*⟩

pa·tience \'pā-shən(t)s\ *n* **1 :** the capacity, habit, or fact of being patient **2** *chiefly Brit* **:** SOLITAIRE 2

1**pa·tient** \'pā-shənt\ *adj* [ME *pacient*, fr. MF, fr. L *patient-*, *patiens*, fr. prp. of *pati* to suffer; akin to L *paene* almost, *penuria* need, Gk *pēma* suffering] **1 :** bearing pains or trials calmly or without complaint **2 :** manifesting forbearance under provocation or strain **3 :** not hasty or impetuous **4 :** steadfast despite opposition, difficulty, or adversity **5 :** able or willing to bear — used with *of* **6 :** SUSCEPTIBLE, ADMITTING ⟨∼ of one interpretation⟩ — **pa·tient·ly** *adv*

2**patient** *n* **1 a :** an individual awaiting or under medical care and treatment **b :** the recipient of any of various personal services ⟨found the beauty shop filled with ∼*s*⟩ **2 :** one that is acted upon

pa·ti·na \'pat-ə-nə, pə-'tē-nə\ *n, pl* **pa·ti·nas** \-nəz\ *or* **pa·ti·nae** \'pat-ə-,nē, -,nī\ [NL, fr. L, shallow dish — more at PATEN] **1 a :** a usu. green film formed naturally on copper and bronze by long exposure or artificially (as by acids) and often valued aesthetically for its color **b :** a surface appearance of something grown beautiful esp. with age or use **c :** an appearance or aura that is derived from association, habit, or established character **2 :** PATEN 1

1**pa·tine** \pa-'tēn\ *n* [F, fr. NL *patina*] **:** PATINA 1

2**patine** *vt* **:** to coat with a patina

pa·tio \'pat-ē-,ō *also* 'pät-\ *n* [Sp] **1 :** COURTYARD; *esp* **:** an inner court open to the sky **2 :** a recreation area that adjoins a dwelling, is often paved, and is adapted esp. to outdoor dining

pa·tois \'pa-,twä, 'pä-\ *n, pl* **pa·tois** \-,twäz\ [F] **1 a :** a dialect other than the standard or literary dialect **b :** illiterate or provincial speech **2 :** the characteristic special language of an occupational or social group **:** JARGON

patr- *or* **patri-** *or* **patro-** *comb form* [*patr-*, *patri-* fr. L, fr. *patr-*, *pater*; *patr-*, *patro-* fr. Gk, fr. *patr-*, *patēr* — more at FATHER] **:** father ⟨*patr*istic⟩

pa·tri·arch \'pā-trē-,ärk\ *n* [ME *patriarche*, fr. OF, fr. LL *patriarcha*, fr. Gk *patriarchēs*, fr. *patria* lineage (fr. *patr-*, *patēr* father) + *-archēs* -arch — more at FATHER] **1 a :** one of the scriptural fathers of the human race or of the Hebrew people **b :** a man who is father or founder **c** (1) **:** the oldest member or representative of a group (2) **:** a venerable old man **2 a :** any of the bishops of the ancient or Eastern Orthodox sees of Constantinople, Alexandria, Antioch, and Jerusalem or the ancient and Western see of Rome with authority over other bishops **b :** the head of any of various Eastern churches **c :** a Roman Catholic bishop next in rank to the pope with purely titular or with metropolitan jurisdiction **3 :** the head of the Sanhedrin **4 :** a Mormon of the Melchizedek priesthood empowered to perform the ordinances of the church and pronounce blessings within a stake or other prescribed jurisdiction — **pa·tri·ar·chal** \,pā-trē-'är-kəl\ *adj*

patriarchal cross *n* — see CROSS illustration

pa·tri·arch·ate \'pā-trē-,är-kət, -,kāt\ *n* **1 a :** the office, jurisdiction, or time in office of a patriarch **b :** the residence or headquarters of a patriarch **2 :** PATRIARCHY

pa·tri·ar·chy \-,är-kē\ *n* **1 :** social organization marked by the supremacy of the father in the clan or family, the legal dependence of wives and children, and the reckoning of descent and inheritance in the male line **2 :** a society organized according to the principles of patriarchy

pa·tri·cian \pə-'trish-ən\ *n* [ME *patricion*, fr. MF *patricien*, fr. L *patricius*, fr. *patres* senators, fr. pl. of *pater* father — more at FATHER] **1 :** a member of one of the original citizen families of ancient Rome **2 a :** a person of high birth **:** ARISTOCRAT **b :** a person of breeding and cultivation — **patrician** *adj*

pa·tri·ci·ate \-'trish-ē-ət, -ē-,āt\ *n* **1 :** the position or dignity of a patrician **2 :** a patrician class

pat·ri·ci·dal \,pa-trə-'sīd-ᵊl\ *adj* **:** of or relating to patricide

pat·ri·cide \'pa-trə-,sīd\ *n* **1** [L *patricida*, fr. *patr-* + *-cida* -cide] **:** one who murders his own father **2** [LL *patricidium*, fr. L *patr-* + *-cidium* -cide] **:** the murder of one's own father

pat·ri·lin·eal \,pa-trə-'lin-ē-əl\ *adj* **:** relating to, based on, or tracing descent through the paternal line ⟨∼ society⟩

pat·ri·mo·ni·al \,pa-trə-'mō-nē-əl\ *adj* **:** of, relating to, or constituting a patrimony

pat·ri·mo·ny \'pa-trə-,mō-nē\ *n* [ME *patrimonie*, fr. MF, fr. L *patrimonium*, fr. *patr-*, *pater* father] **1 a :** an estate inherited from one's father or other ancestor **b :** anything derived from one's father or ancestors **:** HERITAGE **2 :** an estate or endowment belonging by ancient right to a church **syn** see HERITAGE

pa·tri·ot \'pā-trē-ət, -trē-,ät, *chiefly Brit* 'pa-\ *n, often attrib* [MF *patriote*, fr. LL *patriota*, fr. Gk *patriōtēs*, fr. *patrios* of one's father, fr. *patr-*, *patēr* father] **:** one who loves his country and zealously supports its authority and interests

pa·tri·ot·ic \,pā-trē-'ät-ik, *chiefly Brit* ,pa-\ *adj* **1 :** inspired by patriotism **2 :** befitting or characteristic of a patriot — **pa·tri·ot·i·cal·ly** \-i-k(ə-)lē\ *adv*

pa·tri·o·tism \'pā-trē-ə-,tiz-əm, *chiefly Brit* 'pa-\ *n* **:** love for or devotion to one's country

Patriots' Day *n* **:** April 19 observed as a legal holiday in Maine and Massachusetts in commemoration of the battles of Lexington and Concord in 1775

pa·tris·tic \pə-'tris-tik\ *adj* **:** of or relating to the church fathers or their writings — **pa·tris·ti·cal** \-ti-kəl\ *adj*

pa·tris·tics \-tiks\ *n pl but sing in constr* **:** the study of the writings and background of the church fathers

Pa·tro·clus \pə-'trō-kləs, -'trä-; 'pa-trə-\ *n* [L, fr. Gk *Patroklos*] **:** a Greek slain in the Trojan War by Hector and avenged by his friend Achilles

1**pa·trol** \pə-'trōl\ *n* **1 a :** the action of traversing a district or beat or of going the rounds along a chain of guards for the purpose of observation or of the maintenance of security **b :** the person performing such an action **c :** a detachment of two or more men employed for reconnaissance, security, or combat **2 a :** a subdivision of a boy scout troop made up of two or more boys **b :** a subdivision of a girl scout troop usu. composed of from six to eight girls

2**patrol** *vb* **pa·trolled; pa·trol·ling** [F *patrouiller*, fr. MF, to tramp around in the mud, fr. *patte* paw — more at PATTEN] *vi* **:** to carry out a patrol ∼ *vt* **:** to carry out a patrol of — **pa·trol·ler** *n*

pa·trol·man \pə-'trōl-mən\ *n* **:** one who patrols; *esp* **:** a policeman assigned to a beat

patrol wagon *n* **:** an enclosed police wagon or motor truck used to carry prisoners

pa·tron \'pā-trən\ *n* [ME, fr. MF, fr. ML & L; ML *patronus* patron saint, patron of a benefice, pattern, fr. L, defender, fr. *patr-*, *pater*] **1 a :** a person chosen, named, or honored as a special guardian, protector, or supporter **b :** a wealthy or influential supporter of an artist or writer **c :** a social or financial sponsor of an entertainment or other function **2 :** one who gives of his means or uses his influence to help an individual, an institution, or a cause **3 :** a regular client or customer **4 :** the holder of the right of presentation to an English ecclesiastical benefice **5 :** a master of antiquity who frees his slave but retains some rights over him **6 :** the proprietor of an establishment (as an inn) **7 :** the chief male officer in some fraternal lodges having both men and women members — **pa·tron·al** \'pā-trən-ᵊl\ *adj*

pa·tron·age \'pa-trə-nij, 'pā-\ *n* **1 :** ADVOWSON **2 :** the support or influence of a patron **3 :** kindness done with an air of superiority **4 :** the trade of customers **5 a :** the power to make appointments to government jobs on a basis other than merit alone **b :** the distribution of jobs on this basis **c :** the jobs so distributed

pa·tron·ess \'pā-trə-nəs\ *n* **:** a female patron

pa·tron·ize \'pā-trə-,nīz, 'pa-\ *vt* **1 :** to act as patron of **2 :** to adopt an air of condescension toward **3 :** to be a customer or client of

patron saint *n* **1 :** a saint to whose protection and intercession a person, a society, a church, or a place is dedicated **2 :** an original leader or prime exemplar

pat·ro·nym·ic \,pa-trə-'nim-ik\ *n* [LL *patronymicum*, fr. neut. of *patronymicus* of a patronymic, fr. Gk *patronymikos*, fr. *patronymia* patronymic, fr. *patr-* + *onyma* name — more at NAME] **:** a name derived from that of the father or a paternal ancestor usu. by the addition of an affix — **patronymic** *adj*

pa·troon \pə-'trün\ *n* [F *patron* & Sp *patrón*, fr. ML *patronus*, fr. L, patron] **1** *archaic* **:** the captain or officer commanding a ship **2** [D, fr. F *patron*] **:** the proprietor of a manorial estate esp. in New York originally granted under Dutch rule but in some cases existing until the mid-19th century

pat·sy \'pat-sē\ *n* [perh. fr. It *pazzo* fool] **:** one who is duped or victimized **:** SUCKER

pat·tée \pə-'tā, pa-\ *adj* [MF *pattee*, fr. *patte* paw] *of a heraldic cross* **:** FORMÉE

pat·ten \'pat-ᵊn\ *n* [ME *patin*, fr. MF, fr. *patte* paw, hoof, fr. (assumed) VL *patta*, of imit. origin] **:** a clog, sandal, or overshoe often with a wooden sole or metal device to elevate the foot and increase the wearer's height or aid in walking in mud

1**pat·ter** \'pat-ər\ *vb* [ME *patren*, fr. *paternoster*] *vt* **:** to say or speak in a rapid or mechanical manner ∼ *vi* **1 :** to recite paternosters or other prayers rapidly or mechanically **2 :** to talk glibly and volubly **3 :** to speak or sing rapid-fire words in a theatrical performance — **pat·ter·er** \-ər-ər\ *n*

2**patter** *n* **1 :** a specialized lingo **:** CANT; *esp* **:** the jargon of criminals (as thieves) **2 :** the spiel of a street hawker or of a circus barker **3 :** empty chattering talk **4 a** (1) **:** the rapid-fire talk of a comedian (2) **:** the talk with which any of various entertainers accompanies his routine **b :** the words of a comic song or of a rapidly spoken usu. humorous monologue introduced into such a song

3**patter** *vb* [freq. of 2*pat*] *vi* **1 :** to strike or pat rapidly and repeatedly **2 :** to run with quick light-sounding steps ∼ *vt* **:** to cause to patter

4**patter** *n* **:** a quick succession of slight sounds or pats

1**pat·tern** \'pat-ərn\ *n* [ME *patron*, fr. MF, fr. ML *patronus*] **1 :** a form or model proposed for imitation **:** EXEMPLAR **2 :** something designed or used as a model for making things ⟨a dressmaker's ∼⟩ **3 :** a model for making a mold into which molten metal is poured to form a casting **4 :** SPECIMEN, SAMPLE **5 a :** an artistic or mechanical design **b :** form or style in literary or musical composition **6 :** a natural or chance configuration **7 :** a length of fabric sufficient for an article **8 a :** the distribution of the shot from a shotgun or the bullets from an exploded shrapnel **b :** the

grouping made on a target by bullets **9 :** a reliable sample of traits, acts, or other observable features characterizing an individual **10 :** the flight path prescribed for an airplane that is coming in for a landing **11 :** a standard diagram transmitted for testing television circuits **syn** see MODEL — **pat·terned** \-ərnd\ *adj*

[2]**pattern** *vt* **1 :** to make or fashion according to a pattern **2** *dial chiefly Eng* **a :** MATCH **b :** IMITATE **3 :** to furnish, adorn, or mark with a design ~ *vi* **:** to form a pattern

pat·ty *also* **pat·tie** \'pat-ē\ *n* [F *pâté*] **1 :** a little pie **2 a :** a small flat cake of chopped food **b :** a small flat candy

patty shell *n* **:** a shell of puff paste made to hold a creamed meat, fish, or vegetable filling

pat·u·lous \'pach-ə-ləs\ *adj* [L *patulus*, fr. *patēre* to be open — more at FATHOM] **:** spreading widely from a center ⟨a tree with ~ branches⟩ — **pat·u·lous·ly** *adv* — **pat·u·lous·ness** *n*

pau·ci·ty \'pò-sət-ē\ *n* [ME *paucite*, fr. MF or L; MF *paucité*, fr. L *paucitat-*, *paucitas*, fr. *paucus* little — more at FEW] **1 :** smallness of number **:** FEWNESS **2 :** smallness of quantity **:** DEARTH

Paul \'pòl\ *n* [L *Paulus*, fr. Gk *Paulos*] **:** an early Christian missionary and author of several New Testament epistles — **Paul·ine** \'pò-,līn\ *adj*

Paul Bun·yan \-'bən-yən\ *n* **:** a lumberjack in American folklore noted for his ability to perform superhuman feats

Pau·li exclusion principle \'paù-lē-\ *n* [Wolfgang *Pauli* b1900 Swiss physicist] **:** EXCLUSION PRINCIPLE — called also *Pauli principle*

Paul·ist \'pò-ləst\ *n* **:** a member of the Roman Catholic Congregation of the Missionary Priests of St. Paul the Apostle founded in the U.S. in 1858

pau·low·nia \pò-'lō-nē-ə\ *n* [NL, genus name, fr. Anna *Pàulovna* †1865 Russ princess] **:** any of a genus (*Paulownia*) of Chinese trees of the figwort family; *esp* **:** one (*P. tomentosa*) widely cultivated for its panicles of fragrant violet flowers

paunch \'pònch, 'pänch\ *n* [ME, fr. MF *panche*, fr. L *pantic-*, *pantex*] **1 a :** the belly and its contents **b :** POTBELLY **2 :** RUMEN

paunch·i·ness \'pòn-chē-nəs, 'pän-\ *n* **:** the quality or state of being paunchy

paunchy \-chē\ *adj* **:** having a potbelly

pau·per \'pò-pər\ *n, often attrib* [L, poor] **1 :** a person destitute of means except such as are derived from charity; *specif* **:** one who receives aid from public poor funds **2 :** a very poor person — **pau·per·ism** \'pò-pə-,riz-əm\ *n* — **pau·per·ize** \-,rīz\ *vt*

[1]**pause** \'pòz\ *n* [ME, fr. L *pausa*, fr. Gk *pausis*, fr. *pauein* to stop; akin to Gk *paula* rest] **1 :** a temporary stop **2 a :** a break in a verse **b :** a brief suspension of the voice to indicate the limits and relations of sentences and their parts **3 :** temporary inaction esp. as caused by uncertainty **4 a :** the sign denoting a fermata **b :** a mark (as a period or comma) used in writing or printing to indicate or correspond to a pause of voice **5 :** a reason or cause for pausing ⟨give ~⟩

[2]**pause** *vi* **1 :** to stop temporarily **2 :** to linger for a time

pa·vane \pə-'vän, -'van\ *also* **pa·van** *same or* 'pav-ən\ *or* **pav·in** \'pav-ən\ *n* [MF *pavane*, fr. OSp *pavana*, fr. OIt] **1 :** a stately court dance by couples that was introduced from southern Europe into England in the 16th century **2 :** music for the pavane

pave \'pāv\ *vt* [ME *paven*, fr. MF *paver*, fr. L *pavire* to strike, stamp; akin to OHG *arfūrian* to castrate, L *putare* to prune, reckon, think, Gk *paiein* to strike] **1 :** to lay or cover with stone, concrete, or other material making a firm level surface for travel **2 :** to cover firmly and solidly as if with paving material **3 :** to serve as a covering or pavement of — **pav·er** *n* — **pave the way :** to prepare a smooth easy way **:** facilitate the development

paved \'pāvd\ *adj* **1 :** covered with a pavement **2** *or* **pa·vé** \pa-'vā\ *of jewels* **:** set as close together as possible to conceal a metal base

pave·ment \'pāv-mənt\ *n* [ME, fr. OF, fr. L *pavimentum*, fr. *pavire*] **1 :** a paved surface: as **a :** the artificially covered surface of a public thoroughfare **b** *chiefly Brit* **:** SIDEWALK **2 :** the material with which something is paved

pav·id \'pav-əd\ *adj* [L *pavidus*, fr. *pavere* to be frightened; akin to L *pavire*] **:** TIMID

[1]**pa·vil·ion** \pə-'vil-yən\ *n* [ME *pavilon*, fr. OF *paveillon*, fr. L *papilion-*, *papilio* butterfly; akin to OHG *fifaltra* butterfly, Lith *peteliške* flighty] **1 a :** a large often sumptuous tent **b :** something resembling a canopy or tent **2 a :** a part of a building projecting from the rest **b :** one of several detached or semidetached units into which a building is sometimes divided **3 a :** a light sometimes ornamental structure in a garden, park, or place of recreation that is used for entertainment or shelter **b :** a temporary structure erected at an exposition by an individual exhibitor **4 :** the lower faceted part of a brilliant between the girdle and the culet

[2]**pavilion** *vt* **:** to furnish or cover with or put in a pavilion

pav·ing \'pā-viŋ\ *n* **:** PAVEMENT

pav·ior *or* **pav·iour** \'pāv-yər\ *n* [ME *pavier*, fr. *paven* to pave] **:** one that paves

Pav·lov·ian \pav-'lò-vē-ən, -'lò-fē-\ *adj* **:** of or relating to Ivan Pavlov or to his work and theories

[1]**paw** \'pò\ *n* [ME, fr. MF *poue*] **1 :** the foot of a quadruped (as a lion or dog) having claws; *broadly* **:** the foot of an animal **2 :** a human hand esp. when large or clumsy

[2]**paw** *vt* **1 :** to feel of or touch clumsily, amorously, or rudely **2 :** to touch or strike at with a paw **3 :** to scrape or beat upon with a hoof **4 :** to flail at or grab for wildly ~ *vi* **1 :** to beat or scrape with a hoof **2 :** to touch or strike with a paw **3 :** to feel or touch clumsily, amorously, or rudely **4 :** to flail or grab wildly

paw·ky \'pò-kē\ *adj* [obs. E dial. *pawk* (trick)] *chiefly Brit* **:** artfully shrewd **:** CANNY

pawl \'pòl\ *n* [perh. modif. of D *pal* pawl] **:** a pivoted tongue or sliding bolt on one part of a machine that is adapted to fall into notches or interdental spaces on another part (as a ratchet wheel) so as to permit motion in only one direction

[1]**pawn** \'pòn, 'pän\ *n* [ME *paun*, modif. of MF *pan*] **1 a :** something delivered to or deposited with another as security for a loan **b :** HOSTAGE **2 :** the state of being pledged **3 :** something used as a pledge **:** GUARANTY **4 :** the act of pawning

[2]**pawn** *vt* **:** to deposit in pledge or as security **:** STAKE — **pawn·er** \'pò-nər, 'pän-ər\ *or* **paw·nor** *same or* pò-'nò(ə)r, pä-\ *n*

[3]**pawn** *n* [ME *pown*, fr. MF *poon*, fr. ML *pedon-*, *pedo* foot soldier, fr. LL, one with broad feet, fr. L *ped-*, *pes* foot — more at FOOT] **1 :** one of the chessmen of least value having the power to move only one square forward at a time or at option two on its first move and to capture an enemy only on either of the two squares diagonally forward **2 :** one that can be used to further the purposes of another

pawn·bro·ker \'pòn-,brō-kər, 'pän-\ *n* **:** one who loans money on the security of personal property pledged in his keeping — **pawn·bro·king** \-kiŋ\ *n*

Paw·nee \pò-'nē, pä-\ *n, pl* **Pawnee** *or* **Pawnees :** a member of an Indian people of the Platte and Republican river valleys in Nebraska and Kansas

pawn·shop \'pòn-,shäp, 'pän-\ *n* **:** a pawnbroker's shop

paw·paw *var of* PAPAW

pax \'paks, 'päks\ *n* [ME, fr. ML, fr. L, peace — more at PEACE] **1 :** a tablet or board decorated with a figure or symbol of Christ, the Virgin Mary, or a saint and used in medieval times to convey the kiss of peace **2 :** the kiss of peace in the Mass **3 :** PEACE

[1]**pay** \'pā\ *vb* **paid** \'pād\ *also in sense 7* **payed; pay·ing** [ME *payen*, fr. OF *paier*, fr. L *pacare* to pacify, fr. *pac-*, *pax* peace] *vt* **1 a :** to make due return to for services rendered or property delivered **b :** to engage for money **:** HIRE **2 a :** to give in return for goods or service ⟨~ wages⟩ **b :** to discharge indebtedness for **:** SETTLE ⟨~ a bill⟩ **c :** to make a disposal or transfer of (money) **3 :** to give or forfeit in expiation or retribution ⟨~ the penalty⟩ **4 a :** to make compensation for **b :** to requite according to what is deserved ⟨~ him back⟩ **5 :** to give, offer, or make freely or as fitting ⟨~ attention⟩ **6 a :** to return value or profit to ⟨it ~*s* you to stay open⟩ **b :** to bring in as a return ⟨an investment ~*ing* five percent⟩ **7 :** to slacken (as a rope) and allow to run out — used with *out* ~ *vi* **1 :** to discharge a debt or obligation **2 :** to be worth the expense or effort

syn PAY, COMPENSATE, REMUNERATE, SATISFY, REIMBURSE, INDEMNIFY, REPAY, RECOMPENSE, REQUITE mean to give money or its equivalent in return for something. PAY implies the discharge of an obligation incurred; COMPENSATE implies a making up for services rendered or help given; REMUNERATE more clearly suggests paying for services rendered and may extend to payment that is generous or not contracted for; SATISFY implies paying a person what is demanded or required by law; REIMBURSE implies a return of money that has been expended for another's benefit; INDEMNIFY implies making good a loss suffered through accident, disaster, warfare; REPAY stresses paying back an equivalent in kind or amount; RECOMPENSE suggests due return in amends, friendly repayment, or reward; REQUITE implies repaying not necessarily in kind but esp. according to the merits of the case

[2]**pay** *n* **1 a :** the act or fact of paying or being paid **b :** the status of being paid by an employer **:** EMPLOY **2 :** something paid; *esp* **:** WAGES, SALARY **3 :** a person reliable or prompt in paying debts or bills **syn** see WAGE

[3]**pay** *adj* **1 :** containing or leading to something precious or valuable **2 :** equipped with a coin slot for receiving a fee for use **3 :** requiring payment

[4]**pay** *vt* **payed** *also* **paid; pay·ing** [obs. F *peier*, fr. L *picare*, fr. *pic-*, *pix* pitch] **:** to coat with a waterproof composition

pay·able \'pā-ə-bəl\ *adj* **1 :** that may, can, or must be paid **2 :** PROFITABLE

pay·check \'pā-,chek\ *n* **1 :** a check in payment of wages or salary **2 :** WAGES, SALARY

pay dirt *n* **1 :** earth or ore that yields a profit to a miner **2 :** a useful or remunerative discovery or object

pay·ee \pā-'ē\ *n* **:** one to whom money is or is to be paid

pay·er \'pā-ər\ *also* **pay·or** \'pā-ər, pā-'ò(ə)r\ *n* **:** one that pays; *esp* **:** the person by whom a bill or note has been or should be paid

pay·load \'pā-,lōd\ *n* **1 :** the revenue-producing or useful load that a vehicle of transport can carry **2 :** the explosive charge carried in the warhead of a missile

pay·mas·ter \-,mas-tər\ *n* **:** an officer or agent of a government, a corporation, or an employer whose duty it is to pay salaries or wages

pay·ment \'pā-mənt\ *n* **1 :** the act of paying **2 :** something that is paid **:** PAY **3 :** REQUITAL

pay·nim \'pā-nəm\ *n* [ME *painim*, fr. OF *paienime* heathendom, fr. LL *paganismus*, fr. *paganus* pagan] *archaic* **:** PAGAN; *esp* **:** MUSLIM

pay off *vt* **1 a :** to give all due wages to; *esp* **:** to pay in full and discharge (an employee) **b :** to pay (a debt or a creditor) in full **2 :** to inflict retribution on **3 :** to allow (a thread or rope) to run off a spool or drum ~ *vi* **:** to yield returns

[1]**pay·off** \'pā-,òf\ *n* **1 :** the act or occasion of paying employees' wages or distributing gains **2 a :** PROFIT, REWARD **b :** RETRIBUTION **3 :** the climax of an incident or enterprise; *specif* **:** the denouement of a narrative **4 :** a decisive fact or factor resolving a situation or bringing about a definitive conclusion

[2]**payoff** *adj* **:** yielding results in the final test **:** DECISIVE

pay·ola \pā-'ō-lə\ *n* [prob. alter. of [1]*payoff*] **:** undercover or indirect payment (as to a disc jockey) for a commercial favor (as plugging a record)

pay·roll \'pā-,rōl\ *n* **1 :** a paymaster's or employer's list of those entitled to pay and of the amounts due to each **2 :** the sum necessary for distribution to those on a payroll; *also* **:** the money to be distributed

pay station *n* **:** a public telephone usu. equipped with a slot-machine device for payment of toll

pay up *vb* **:** to pay in full

PDQ \,pē-,dē-'kyü\ *adv, often not cap* [abbr. of *pretty damned quick*] **:** IMMEDIATELY

pe \'pā\ *n* [Heb *pē*] **:** the 17th letter of the Hebrew alphabet — symbol פ or ף

pea \'pē\ *n, pl* **peas** *also* **pease** \'pēz\ *often attrib* [back-formation fr. ME *pease* (taken as a pl.), fr. OE *pise*, fr. L *pisa*, pl. of *pisum*, fr. Gk *pison*] **1 a :** a variable annual leguminous vine (*Pisum sativum*) cultivated for its rounded smooth or wrinkled edible protein-rich seeds **b :** the seed of the pea **c** *pl* **:** the immature pods of the pea with their included seeds **2 a :** any of various leguminous plants related to or resembling the pea — usu. used with

a qualifying term **b :** the seed of such a plant **3 :** something resembling a pea usu. in size, shape, or formation

1peace \'pēs\ *n, often attrib* [ME *pees,* fr. OF *pais,* fr. L *pac-, pax;* akin to L *pacisci* to agree — more at PACT] **1 :** a state of tranquillity or quiet: as **a :** freedom from civil disturbance **b :** a state of security or order within a community provided for by law or custom ⟨a breach of the ~⟩ **2 :** freedom from disquieting or oppressive thoughts or emotions **3 :** harmony in personal relations **4 a :** a state or period of mutual concord between governments **b :** a pact or agreement to end hostilities between those who have been at war or in a state of enmity

2peace *vi* **:** to be, become, or keep silent or quiet — often used interjectionally

peace·able \'pē-sə-bəl\ *adj* **1 a :** disposed to peace **b :** quietly behaved **2 :** marked by freedom from strife or disorder — **peace·able·ness** *n* — **peace·ably** \-blē\ *adv*

peace corps *n* **:** a body of trained personnel sent out as volunteers to assist underdeveloped nations

peace·ful \'pēs-fəl\ *adj* **1 :** PEACEABLE 1 **2 :** untroubled by conflict, agitation, or commotion **:** QUIET, TRANQUIL **3 :** of or relating to a state or time of peace **4 :** devoid of violence or force **syn** see CALM — **peace·ful·ly** \-fə-lē\ *adv* — **peace·ful·ness** *n*

peace·mak·er \'pē-,smā-kər\ *n* **:** one who makes peace esp. by reconciling parties at variance — **peace·mak·ing** \-kiŋ\ *n or adj*

peace offering *n* **:** a gift or service to procure peace or reconciliation

peace officer *n* **:** a civil officer whose duty it is to preserve the public peace

peace pipe *n* **:** CALUMET

peace·time \'pē-,stīm\ *n, often attrib* **:** a time when a nation is not at war

1peach \'pēch\ *n* [ME *peche,* fr. MF (the fruit), fr. LL *persica,* fr. L *persicum,* fr. neut. of *persicus* Persian, fr. *Persia*] **1 a :** a low spreading freely branching Chinese tree (*Prunus persica*) of the rose family that is cosmopolitan in cultivation in temperate areas and has lanceolate leaves, sessile usu. pink flowers borne on the naked twigs in early spring, and a fruit which is a single-seeded drupe with a hard endocarp, a pulpy white or yellow mesocarp, and a thin downy epicarp **b :** the edible fruit of the peach **2 :** a variable color averaging a moderate yellowish pink **3 :** one likened to a peach in sweetness, beauty, or excellence

2peach *vb* [ME *pechen,* short for *apechen* to accuse, fr. (assumed) AF *apecher,* fr. LL *impedicare* to entangle — more at IMPEACH] *vt* **:** to inform against **:** BETRAY ~ *vi* **:** to turn informer **:** BLAB

peach·blow \-,blō\ *n* **:** a glaze of the color of peach blooms used on a Chinese porcelain

peachy \'pē-chē\ *adj* **1 :** resembling a peach **2 :** unusually fine **:** DANDY

1pea·cock \'pē-,käk\ *n* [ME *pecok,* fr. *pe-* (fr. OE *pēa* peafowl) + *cok* cock; akin to OHG *pfāwo* peacock; both fr. a prehistoric WGmc-NGmc word borrowed fr. L *pavon-, pavo* peacock] **1 :** a male peafowl distinguished by a crest of upright plumules and by greatly elongated loosely webbed upper tail coverts mostly tipped with ocellated spots and erected and spread at will in a fan shimmering with iridescent color; *broadly* **:** PEAFOWL **2 :** one making a proud display of himself — **pea·cock·ish** \-ish\ *adj* — **pea·cocky** \-ē\ *adj*

2peacock *vi* **:** to make a vainglorious display

peacock blue *n* **:** a variable color averaging a moderate greenish blue

pea·fowl \'pē-,faul\ *n* [*pea-* (as in *peacock*) + *fowl*] **:** a very large terrestrial pheasant (genus *Pavo*) of southeastern Asia and the East Indies that is often reared as an ornamental fowl

pea green *n* **:** a variable color averaging a moderate yellow-green

pea·hen \'pē-,hen, -'hen\ *n* [ME *pehenne,* fr. *pe-* + *henne* hen] **:** a female peafowl

pea jacket \'pē-\ *n* [by folk etymology fr. D *pijjekker,* fr. *pij,* a kind of cloth + *jekker* jacket] **:** a heavy woolen double-breasted jacket worn chiefly by sailors

1peak \'pēk\ *vi* [origin unknown] **1 :** to grow thin or sickly **2 :** to dwindle away

2peak *n* [perh. alter. of *pike*] **1 :** a pointed or projecting part of a garment; *esp* **:** the visor of a cap or hat **2 :** PROMONTORY **3 :** a sharp or pointed end **4 a** (1) **:** the top of a hill or mountain ending in a point (2) **:** a whole hill or mountain esp. when isolated **b :** something resembling a mountain peak **5 a :** the upper aftermost corner of a fore-and-aft sail **b :** the narrow part of a ship's bow or stern or the part of the hold in it **6 a :** the highest level or greatest degree **b :** a high point in a course of development esp. as represented on a graph **7 :** a point formed by the hair on the forehead **syn** see SUMMIT

3peak *vi* **:** to reach a maximum ~ *vt* **:** to cause to come to a peak, point, or maximum

4peak *adj* **:** being at or reaching the maximum

5peak *vt* [fr. *apeak* (held vertically)] **1 :** to set (as a gaff) nearer the perpendicular **2 :** to hold (oars) with blades well raised

1peaked \'pēkt *also* 'pē-kəd *or* 'pik-əd\ *adj* **:** having a peak **:** POINTED — **peaked·ness** \'pēk(t)-nəs; 'pē-kəd-nəs, 'pik-əd-\ *n*

2peak·ed \'pē-kəd *also* 'pik-əd\ *adj* **:** looking pale and wan **:** SICKLY

1peal \'pē(ə)l\ *n* [ME, appeal, summons to church, short for *appel* appeal, fr. *appelen* to appeal] **1 a :** the loud ringing of bells **b** (1) **:** a complete set of changes on a given number of bells; *esp* **:** the series on seven bells (2) **:** a shorter performance than a full peal **c :** a set of bells tuned to the tones of the major scale for change ringing **2 :** a loud sound or succession of sounds

2peal *vi* **:** to give out peals ~ *vt* **:** to utter or give forth loudly

pea·like \'pē-,līk\ *adj* **1 :** resembling a garden pea esp. in size, firmness, and shape **2** *of a flower* **:** being showy and papilionaceous

1pea·nut \'pē-(,)nət\ *n* **1 a :** a low-branching widely cultivated leguminous annual herb (*Arachis hypogaea*) with showy yellow flowers having a peduncle which elongates and bends into the soil where the ovary ripens into a pod containing one to three oily edible seeds **b :** the seed or seed-containing pod of the peanut **2 :** an insignificant or tiny person **3** *pl* **:** a trifling amount

2peanut *adj* **:** INSIGNIFICANT, PETTY ⟨~ politics⟩

peanut butter *n* **:** a paste made by grinding roasted skinned peanuts

pear \'pa(ə)r, 'pe(ə)r\ *n* [ME *pere,* fr. OE *peru,* fr. L *pirum*] **1 :** the fleshy pome fruit of a tree (genus *Pyrus,* esp. *P. communis*) of the rose family **2 :** a tree bearing pears

1pearl \'pər(-ə)l\ *n* [ME *perle,* fr. MF, fr. (assumed) VL *pernula,* dim. of L *perna* haunch, sea mussel; akin to OE *fiersn* heel, Gk *pternē*] **1 a :** a dense variously colored and usu. lustrous concretion formed of concentric layers of nacre as an abnormal growth within the shell of some mollusks and used as a gem **b :** MOTHER-OF-PEARL **2 :** one that is very choice or precious **3 :** something resembling a pearl intrinsically or physically **4 :** a nearly neutral slightly bluish medium gray

2pearl *vb* **pearl·ing** \'pər-liŋ\ *vt* **1 :** to set or adorn with pearls **2 :** to sprinkle or bead with pearly drops **3 :** to form into small round grains **4 :** to give a pearly color or luster to ~ *vi* **1 :** to form drops or beads like pearls **2 :** to fish or search for pearls — **pearl·er** \'pər-lər\ *n*

3pearl *adj* **1 a :** of, relating to, or resembling pearl **b :** made of or adorned with pearls **2 :** having grains of medium size

4pearl *n or vt* [alter. of *purl*] *Brit* **:** PICOT

pearl danio *n* **:** a small lustrous cyprinid fish (*Brachydanio albolineatus*) often kept in the tropical aquarium

pearl·es·cent \,pər-'les-ᵊnt\ *adj* **:** PEARLIZED

pearl gray *n* **1 :** a yellowish to light gray **2 :** a variable color averaging a pale blue

Pearl Harbor *n* [*Pearl Harbor,* Oahu, Hawaii, Am naval station attacked without warning by the Japanese] **:** a sneak attack usu. with devastating effect

pearl·ite \'pər(-ə)l-,īt\ *n* [F *perlite,* fr. *perle* pearl] **1 :** the lamellar mixture of ferrite and cementite in slowly cooled iron-carbon alloys occurring normally as a principal constituent of both steel and cast iron **2 :** PERLITE — **pearl·it·ic** \,pər-'lit-ik\ *adj*

pearl·ized \'pər(-ə)l-,īzd\ *adj* **:** resembling mother-of-pearl

pearl millet *n* **:** a tall cereal grass (*Pennisetum glaucum*) with large leaves and dense round spikes that is widely grown for its seeds and for forage

pearly \'pər-lē\ *adj* **1 :** resembling, containing, or adorned with pearls or mother-of-pearl **2 :** highly precious

pear-shaped \'pa(ə)r-,shāpt, 'pe(ə)r-\ *adj* **1 :** having an oval shape markedly tapering at one end **2** *of a vocal tone* **:** free from harshness, thinness, or nasality

peart \'pi(ə)rt\ *adj* [alter. of *pert*] *chiefly South & Midland* **:** in good spirits **:** LIVELY — **peart·ly** *adv*

peas·ant \'pez-ᵊnt\ *n, often attrib* [ME *paissaunt,* fr. MF *paisant,* fr. OF, fr. *païs* country, fr. LL *pagensis* inhabitant of a district, fr. L *pagus* district] **1 :** one of a chiefly European class of persons tilling the soil as small landowners or as laborers **2 :** a person of low social status esp. when comparatively uneducated or uncouth

peas·ant·ry \-ᵊn-trē\ *n* **1 :** PEASANTS **2 :** the position, rank, or behavior of a peasant

1pease \'pēz\ *n* [ME *pese*] *chiefly Brit* **:** PEA

2pease *pl of* PEA

pease·cod *or* **peas·cod** \'pēz-,käd\ *n* [ME *pesecod,* fr. *pese* + *cod* bag, husk — more at CODPIECE] **:** a pea pod

pea·shoot·er \'pē-'shüt-ər, -,shüt-\ *n* **:** a toy blowgun for shooting peas

pea soup *n* **1 :** a thick soup made of dried peas usu. pureed **2 :** a heavy fog

1peat \'pēt\ *n, often attrib* [ME *pete,* fr. ML *peta*] **1 :** TURF 2b **2 :** partially carbonized vegetable tissue formed by partial decomposition in water of various plants (as mosses of the genus *Sphagnum*) — **peaty** \'pēt-ē\ *adj*

2peat *n* [origin unknown] **:** a bold gay woman

pea·vey *or* **pea·vy** \'pē-vē\ *n* [prob. fr. the name *Peavey*] **:** a stout lever like a cant hook but with the end armed with a strong sharp spike used esp. in handling logs

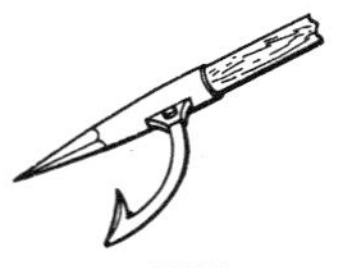

peavey

1peb·ble \'peb-əl\ *n* [ME *pobble,* fr. OE *papolstān,* fr. *papol-* (prob. imit.) + *stān* stone] **1 :** a small usu. rounded stone esp. when worn by the action of water **2 :** transparent and colorless quartz **:** ROCK CRYSTAL **3 :** an irregular, crinkled, or grainy surface — **peb·bly** \'peb-(ə-)lē\ *adj*

2pebble *vt* **peb·bling** \-(ə-)liŋ\ **1 :** to pelt with pebbles **2 :** to pave or cover with pebbles or something resembling pebbles **3 :** to grain (as leather) so as to produce a rough and irregularly indented surface

pe·can \pi-'kän, -'kan; 'pē-,kan\ *n* [of Algonquian origin; akin to Ojibwa *pagân,* a hard-shelled nut] **:** a large hickory (*Carya illinoensis*) of the south central U.S.; *also* **:** its edible oblong nut

pec·ca·ble \'pek-ə-bəl\ *adj* [MF, fr. L *peccare*] **:** liable or prone to sin

pec·ca·dil·lo \,pek-ə-'dil-(,)ō\ *n, pl* **peccadilloes** *or* **peccadillos** [Sp *pecadillo,* dim. of *pecado* sin, fr. L *peccatum,* fr. neut. of *peccatus,* pp. of *peccare*] **:** a slight offense

pec·can·cy \'pek-ən-sē\ *n* **1 :** the quality or state of being peccant **2 :** OFFENSE

pec·cant \'pek-ənt\ *adj* [L *peccant-, peccans,* prp. of *peccare* to stumble, sin] **1 :** guilty of a moral offense **:** SINNING **2 :** violating a principle or rule — **pec·cant·ly** *adv*

pec·ca·ry \'pek-ə-rē\ *n* [of Cariban origin; akin to Chayma *paquera* peccary] **:** either of two largely nocturnal gregarious American mammals resembling the related pigs: **a :** a grizzled animal (*Tayassu angulatus*) with an indistinct white collar **b :** a blackish animal (*Tayassu pecari*) with whitish cheeks

pec·ca·vi \pe-'kä-(,)wē, -(,)vē\ *n* [L, I have sinned, fr. *peccare*] **:** an acknowledgment of sin

1peck \'pek\ *n* [ME *pek,* fr. OF] **1** — see MEASURE table **2 :** a large quantity or number

2peck *vb* [ME *pecken,* alter. of *piken* to pierce — more at PICK] *vt* **1 a :** to strike or pierce esp. repeatedly with the bill or a pointed tool **b :** to make by pecking ⟨~ a hole⟩ **2 :** to pick up with the bill ~ *vi* **1 a :** to strike, pierce, or pick up something with or as if with the bill **b :** CARP, NAG **2 :** NIBBLE ⟨~ at food⟩

3peck *n* **1 :** an impression or hole made by pecking **2 :** a quick sharp stroke

peck·er \'pek-ər\ *n* **1 :** one that pecks **2** *chiefly Brit* **:** COURAGE ⟨keep your ~ up⟩

peck order *or* **pecking order** *n* **1 :** the basic pattern of social organization within a flock of poultry in which each bird pecks another lower in the scale without fear of retaliation and submits to pecking by one of higher rank **2 :** a hierarchy of social dominance or prestige

peck·sniff·ian \pek-'snif-ē-ən\ *adj* [Seth *Pecksniff,* character in *Martin Chuzzlewit* (1843–44) by Charles Dickens] **:** selfish and corrupt behind a display of seeming benevolence **:** SANCTIMONIOUS

pecky \'pek-ē\ *adj* [[3]*peck*] **:** marked by lens-shaped or finger-shaped pockets of decay caused by fungi ⟨~ cypress⟩
pec·tate \'pek-,tāt\ *n* **:** a salt or ester of a pectic acid
pec·ten \'pek-tən\ *n, pl* **pectens** [NL *pectin-, pecten,* fr. L, comb, scallop] **1** *pl usu* **pec·ti·nes** \-tə-,nēz\ **:** a body part felt to resemble a comb; *esp* **:** a folded vascular pigmented membrane projecting into the vitreous humor in the eye of a bird or reptile **2 :** [1]SCALLOP 1a
pec·tic \'pek-tik\ *adj* [F *pectique,* fr. Gk *pēktikos* coagulating, fr. *pēgnynai* to fix, coagulate — more at PACT] **:** of, relating to, or derived from pectin
pectic acid *n* **:** any of various water-insoluble substances formed by hydrolyzing the methyl ester groups of pectins
pec·tin \'pek-tən\ *n* [F *pectine,* fr. *pectique*] **:** any of various water-soluble substances in plant tissues that yield a gel which is the basis of fruit jellies; *also* **:** a commercial product rich in pectins — **pec·tin·ous** \-tə-nəs\ *adj*
pec·ti·nate \'pek-tə-,nāt\ *also* **pec·ti·nat·ed** \-,nāt-əd\ *adj* [L *pectinatus,* fr. *pectin-, pecten* comb; akin to Gk *kten-, kteis* comb, L *pectere* to comb — more at FEE] **:** having narrow parallel projections or divisions suggestive of the teeth of a comb — **pec·ti·na·tion** \,pek-tə-'nā-shən\ *n*
pec·tin·es·ter·ase \,pek-tə-'nes-tə-,rās, -,rāz\ *n* **:** an enzyme that catalyzes the hydrolysis of pectins into pectic acids and methanol
[1]pec·to·ral \'pek-t(ə-)rəl\ *n* **:** something worn on the breast
[2]pectoral *adj* [MF or L; MF, fr. L *pectoralis,* fr. *pector-, pectus* breast; akin to Toch A *päśśäm* the two breasts] **1 :** of, situated in or on, or worn on the chest **2 :** relating to or good for diseases of the respiratory tract **3 :** coming from the breast or heart as the seat of emotion **:** SUBJECTIVE
pectoral cross *n* **:** a cross worn on the breast esp. by a prelate
pectoral fin *n* **:** either of the fins of a fish that correspond to the forelimbs of a quadruped
pectoral girdle *n* **:** the bony or cartilaginous arch supporting the forelimbs of a vertebrate
pec·u·late \'pek-yə-,lāt\ *vt* [L *peculatus,* pp. of *peculari,* fr. *peculium*] **:** EMBEZZLE — **pec·u·la·tion** \,pek-yə-'lā-shən\ *n* — **pec·u·la·tor** \'pek-yə-,lāt-ər\ *n*
[1]pe·cu·liar \pi-'kyül-yər\ *adj* [ME *peculier,* fr. L *peculiaris* of private property, special, fr. *peculium* private property, fr. *pecu* cattle; akin to L *pecus* cattle — more at FEE] **1 :** belonging exclusively to one person or group **2 :** felt to be characteristic of one only **:** DISTINCTIVE **3 :** different from the usual or normal: **a :** SPECIAL, PARTICULAR **b :** CURIOUS **c :** ECCENTRIC, QUEER **syn** see CHARACTERISTIC, STRANGE — **pe·cu·liar·ly** *adv*
[2]peculiar *n* **:** something exempt from ordinary jurisdiction; *esp* **:** a church or parish exempt from the jurisdiction of the ordinary in whose territory it lies
pe·cu·liar·i·ty \pi-,kyül-'yar-ət-ē, -,kyü-lē-'ar-\ *n* **1 :** the quality or state of being peculiar **2 :** a distinguishing characteristic **3 :** ODDITY, QUIRK
pe·cu·niar·i·ly \pi-,kyün-'yer-ə-lē, -,kyü-nē-'er-\ *adv* **:** with respect to money
pe·cu·ni·ary \pi-'kyü-nē-,er-ē\ *adj* [L *pecuniarius,* fr. *pecunia* money — more at FEE] **1 :** consisting of or measured in money **2 :** of or relating to money **:** MONETARY **syn** see FINANCIAL
ped \'ped\ *n* [Gk *pedon* ground; akin to L *ped-, pes* foot — more at FOOT] **:** a natural soil aggregate
ped- — see PAED-
-ped \,ped *also* pəd\ *or* **-pede** \,pēd\ *n comb form* [L *ped-, pes*] **:** foot ⟨maxilli*ped*⟩ ⟨maxilli*pede*⟩
ped·a·gog·ic \,ped-ə-'gäj-ik *also* -'gōj-\ *adj* **:** of, relating to, or befitting a teacher — **ped·a·gog·i·cal** \-i-kəl\ *adj* — **ped·a·gog·i·cal·ly** \-k(ə-)lē\ *adv*
ped·a·gog·ics \-iks\ *n pl but sing in constr* **:** PEDAGOGY
ped·a·gogue *also* **ped·a·gog** \'ped-ə-,gäg\ *n* [ME *pedagoge,* fr. MF, fr. L *paedagogus,* fr. Gk *paidagōgos,* fr. *paid-* paed- + *agōgos* leader, fr. *agein* to lead — more at AGENT] **:** TEACHER, SCHOOLMASTER
ped·a·go·gy \'ped-ə-,gäj-ē, -,gōj-\ *n* **:** the art, science, or profession of teaching; *esp* **:** EDUCATION 2
[1]ped·al \'ped-ᵊl\ *n* [MF *pedale,* fr. It, fr. L *pedalis,* adj.] **1 :** a lever acted on by the foot in the playing of musical instruments **2 :** a foot lever or treadle by which a part is activated in a mechanism
[2]ped·al *adj* [L *pedalis,* fr. *ped-, pes*] **1** \'ped-ᵊl *also* 'pēd-\ **:** of or relating to the foot **2** \'ped-\ **:** of, relating to, or involving a pedal
[3]ped·al \'ped-ᵊl\ *vb* **ped·aled** *also* **ped·alled; ped·al·ing** *also* **ped·al·ling** \'ped-ᵊl-iŋ, 'ped-liŋ\ *vi* **1 :** to use or work a pedal **2 :** to ride a bicycle ~ *vt* **:** to work the pedals of
pe·dal·fer \pə-'dal-fər, -,fe(ə)r\ *n* [Gk *pedon* ground + E *al*umen + L *ferrum* iron] **:** a soil that lacks a hardened layer of accumulated carbonates — **ped·al·fer·ic** \,ped-(,)al'fer-ik\ *adj*
pedal point *n* **:** a single tone usu. the tonic or dominant that is normally sustained in the bass and sounds against changing harmonies in the other parts
pedal pushers *n pl* **:** women's and girls' calf-length trousers
ped·ant \'ped-ᵊnt\ *n* [MF, fr. It *pedante*] **1 :** a schoolmaster esp. in a petty school **2 a :** one who parades his learning **b :** one who is unimaginative or who unduly emphasizes minutiae in the presentation or use of knowledge **c :** a formalist or precisionist in teaching — **pe·dan·tic** \pə-'dant-ik\ *adj* — **pe·dan·ti·cal·ly** \-i-k(ə-)lē\ *adv*
ped·ant·ry \'ped-ᵊn-trē\ *n* **1 :** pedantic presentation or application of knowledge or learning **2 :** an instance of pedantry
ped·ate \'ped-,āt\ *adj* [L *pedatus,* fr. *ped-, pes* foot — more at FOOT] **1 a :** having a foot **b :** having tube feet **2 :** palmate with the lateral lobes cleft into two or more segments — **ped·ate·ly** *adv*
ped·dle \'ped-ᵊl\ *vb* **ped·dling** \'ped-liŋ, -ᵊl-iŋ\ [back-formation fr. *peddler,* fr. ME *pedlere*] *vi* **1 :** to travel about with wares for sale **2 :** to be busy with trifles **:** PIDDLE ~ *vt* **1 :** to sell or offer for sale from place to place **:** HAWK **2 :** to deal out or seek to disseminate — **ped·dler** \'ped-lər, *before "of" also* -ᵊl-ər\ *or* **ped·lar** \'ped-lər\ *n*
ped·dlery *or* **ped·lary** \'ped-lə-rē\ *n* **1 :** peddlers' merchandise **2 :** the trade of a peddler
ped·dling \'ped-lən, -ᵊl-ən, -liŋ, -ᵊl-iŋ\ *adj* [alter. of *piddling*] **:** PETTY

ped·er·ast \'ped-ə-,rast\ *n* [Gk *paiderastēs,* lit., lover of boys, fr. *paid-* paed- + *erastēs* lover, fr. *erasthai* to love — more at EROS] **:** one that practices pederasty — **ped·er·as·tic** \,ped-ə-'ras-tik\ *adj* — **ped·er·as·ti·cal·ly** \-ti-k(ə-)lē\ *adv*
ped·er·as·ty \'ped-ə-,ras-tē\ *n* **:** anal intercourse esp. with a boy
pedes *pl of* PES
[1]ped·es·tal \'ped-əst-ᵊl\ *n, often attrib* [MF *piedestal,* fr. OIt *piedestallo,* fr. *pie di stallo* foot of a stall] **1 a :** the support or foot of a late classic or neoclassic column **b :** the base of an upright structure **2 :** BASE, FOUNDATION **3 :** a position of esteem
[2]pedestal *vt* **ped·es·taled** *or* **ped·es·talled; ped·es·tal·ing** *or* **ped·es·tal·ling :** to place on or furnish with a pedestal
[1]pe·des·tri·an \pə-'des-trē-ən\ *adj* [L *pedestr-, pedester,* lit., going on foot, fr. *pedes* one going on foot, fr. *ped-, pes* foot — more at FOOT] **1 :** UNIMAGINATIVE, COMMONPLACE **2 a :** going or performed on foot **b :** of or relating to walking
[2]pedestrian *n* **:** a person going on foot **:** WALKER
pe·des·tri·an·ism \-,iz-əm\ *n* **1 a :** the practice of walking **b :** addiction to walking for exercise or recreation **2 :** the quality or state of being unimaginative or commonplace
pe·di·at·ric \,pēd-ē-'a-trik\ *adj* **:** of or relating to pediatrics
pe·di·a·tri·cian \,pēd-ē-ə-'trish-ən\ *also* **pe·di·a·trist** \,pēd-ē-'a-trəst, pē-'dī-ə-\ *n* **:** a specialist in pediatrics
pe·di·at·rics \,pēd-ē-'a-triks\ *n pl but sing or pl in constr* **:** a branch of medicine dealing with the child, its development, care, and diseases
pedi·cab \'ped-i-,kab\ *n* [L *ped-, pes* + E *cab*] **:** a small 3-wheeled hooded passenger vehicle that is pedaled
ped·i·cel \'ped-ə-,sel\ *n* [NL *pedicellus,* dim. of L *pediculus*] **1 :** a slender plant stalk; *esp* **:** one that supports a fruiting or spore-bearing organ **2 a :** a narrow basal part by which a larger part or organ of an animal is attached **b :** a small foot or footlike organ — **ped·i·cel·late** \,ped-ə-'sel-ət\ *adj*
ped·i·cle \'ped-i-kəl\ *n* [L *pediculus,* fr. dim. of *ped-, pes*] **:** PEDICEL — **ped·i·cled** \-kəld\ *adj*
pe·dic·u·lar \pi-'dik-yə-lər\ *adj* [L *pedicularis,* fr. *pediculus,* dim. of *pedis* louse] **:** of or relating to lice **:** LOUSY
pe·dic·u·late \-lət\ *adj* [deriv. of L *pediculus* footstalk] **:** of or relating to an order (Pediculati) of teleost fishes with jugular ventral fins, pectoral fins at the end of an armlike process, and part of the dorsal fin modified into a lure — **pediculate** *n*
pe·dic·u·lo·sis \pi-,dik-yə-'lō-səs\ *n* [NL, fr. L *pediculus* louse] **:** infestation with lice — called also *lousiness* — **pe·dic·u·lous** \-'dik-yə-ləs\ *adj*
ped·i·cure \'ped-i-,kyu̇(ə)r\ *n* [F *pédicure,* fr. L *ped-, pes* foot + *curare* to take care, fr. *cura* care — more at CURE] **1 :** CHIROPODIST **2 a :** care of the feet, toes, and nails **b :** a single treatment of these parts — **ped·i·cur·ist** \-,kyu̇r-əst\ *n*
ped·i·gree \'ped-ə-,grē\ *n* [ME *pedegru,* fr. MF *pie de grue* crane's foot; fr. the shape made by the lines of a genealogical chart] **1 :** a register recording a line of ancestors **2 a :** an ancestral line **:** LINEAGE **b :** the origin and the history of something **3 a :** distinguished ancestry **b :** recorded purity of breed of an individual or strain **syn** see ANCESTRY — **ped·i·greed** \-,grēd\ *adj*
ped·i·ment \'ped-ə-mənt\ *n* [obs. E *periment,* prob. alter. of E

pediments

pyramid] **:** a triangular space forming the gable of a 2-pitched roof in classic architecture; *also* **:** a similar form used as a decoration — **ped·i·men·tal** \,ped-ə-'ment-ᵊl\ *adj*
pedo- — see PAED-
ped·o·cal \'ped-ə-,kal\ *n* [Gk *pedon* earth + L *calc-, calx* lime — more at PED, CHALK] **:** a soil that includes a definite hardened layer of accumulated carbonates — **ped·o·cal·ic** \,ped-ə-'kal-ik\ *adj*
pedo·gen·e·sis \,ped-ə-'jen-ə-səs\ *n* [NL, fr. Gk *pedon* + L *genesis*] **:** the formation and development of soil — **pedo·gen·ic** \-'jen-ik\ *or* **pedo·ge·net·ic** \-jə-'net-ik\ *adj*
pe·do·log·ic *adj* **1** \,ped-ᵊl-'äj-ik\ **:** of or relating to soil science **2** \,pēd-\ **:** of or relating to child study — **pe·do·log·i·cal** \-i-kəl\ *adj*
[1]pe·dol·o·gist \pē-'däl-ə-jəst\ *n* **:** a specialist in child study
[2]pe·dol·o·gist \pi-'däl-ə-jəst, pe-\ *n* **:** a soil scientist
[1]pe·dol·o·gy \pē-'däl-ə-jē\ *n* **:** the scientific study of the life and development of children
[2]pe·dol·o·gy \pi-'däl-ə-jē, pe-\ *n* [Gk *pedon* + ISV *-logy*] **:** a science dealing with soils
pe·dom·e·ter \pi-'däm-ət-ər\ *n* [F *pédomètre,* fr. L *ped-, pes* foot + F *-mètre* -meter — more at FOOT] **:** an instrument usu. in watch form that records the distance a walker covers by responding to his body motion at each step
pe·dro \'pā-(,)drō, 'pē-\ *n* [Sp *Pedro* Peter] **:** the five of trumps in card games of the all fours family (as auction pitch or cinch)
pe·dun·cle \'pē-,dəŋ-kəl, pi-'\ *n* [NL *pedunculus,* dim. of L *ped-, pes*] **1 :** a stalk bearing a flower or flower cluster or a fructification **2 :** a narrow part by which some larger part or the whole body of an organism is attached **:** STALK, PEDICEL **3 :** a narrow stalk by which a tumor or polyp is attached — **pe·dun·cled** \-kəld\ *adj* — **pe·dun·cu·lar** \pi-'dəŋ-kyə-lər\ *adj*
pe·dun·cu·late \pi-'dəŋ-kyə-lət\ *or* **pe·dun·cu·lat·ed** \-,lāt-əd\ *adj* [NL *pedunculus*] **:** having, growing on, or being attached by a peduncle — **pe·dun·cu·la·tion** \pi-,dəŋ-kyə-'lā-shən, ,pē-\ *n*
pee \'pē\ *n* **:** the letter *p*
[1]peek \'pēk\ *vi* [ME *piken*] **1 a :** to look furtively **b :** to peer through a crack or hole or from a place of concealment **2 :** to take a brief look **:** GLANCE
[2]peek *n* **:** a brief or surreptitious look
[1]peel \'pē(ə)l\ *vb* [ME *pelen,* fr. MF *peler,* fr. L *pilare* to remove the hair from, fr. *pilus* hair — more at PILE] *vt* **1 :** to strip off an outer layer **2 :** to remove by stripping ~ *vi* **1 a :** to come off in sheets

or scales **b :** to lose an outer layer **2 :** to take off one's clothes
²peel *n* **:** the skin or rind of a fruit
³peel *n* [ME *pel* stockade, stake, fr. AF, stockade & MF, stake, fr. L *palus* stake — more at POLE] **:** a medieval small massive fortified tower along the Scottish-English border
⁴peel *n* [ME *pele*, fr. MF, fr. L *pala*] **:** a usu. long-handled spade-shaped instrument used chiefly by bakers
¹peel•er \'pē-lər\ *n* **1 :** one that peels **2 :** a log of wood (as Douglas fir) suitable for cutting into rotary veneer
²peeler *n* [Sir Robert *Peel* †1850 E statesman] *Brit* **:** POLICEMAN
peel•ing \'pē-liŋ\ *n* **:** a peeled-off piece or strip (as of skin or rind)
peel off *vi* **:** to veer away from an airplane formation esp. for diving or landing
¹peen \'pēn\ *vt* **:** to draw, bend, or flatten by or as if by hammering with a peen
²peen *or* **pein** \'pēn\ *n* [prob. of Scand origin; akin to Norw *penn* peen] **:** the hemispherical, wedge-shaped, or otherwise formed end of the head of a hammer opposite the face
¹peep \'pēp\ *vi* [ME *pepen*, of imit. origin] **1 :** to utter a feeble shrill sound as of a bird newly hatched **:** CHEEP **2 :** to utter the slightest sound
²peep *n* **1 :** a feeble shrill sound **:** CHEEP **2 :** a slight utterance esp. of complaint or protest
³peep *vb* [ME *pepen*, perh. alter. of *piken* to peek] *vi* **1 a :** to peer through a crevice **b :** to look cautiously or slyly **2 :** to begin to emerge from concealment **~** *vt* **:** to put forth or cause to protrude slightly
⁴peep *n* **1 :** the first glimpse or faint appearance ⟨at the ~ of dawn⟩ **2 :** a brief or furtive look
¹peep•er \'pē-pər\ *n* **1 :** one that peeps **2 :** any of various frogs (esp. of the family Hylidae) that peep
²peeper *n* **1 :** one that peeps; *specif* **:** VOYEUR **2 :** EYE
peep•hole \'pēp-,hōl\ *n* **:** a hole or crevice to peep through
Peeping Tom \-'täm\ *n* **1 :** a tailor of Coventry held to have peeped at Lady Godiva **2** *often not cap* **:** VOYEUR
peep show *n* **:** a small show or object exhibited that is viewed through an opening or a magnifying glass
peep sight *n* **:** a rear sight for a gun having an adjustable metal piece pierced with a small hole to peep through in aiming
¹peer \'pi(ə)r\ *n, often attrib* [ME, fr. OF *per*, fr. *per*, adj., equal, fr. L *par*] **1 :** one that is of equal standing with another **:** EQUAL **2** *archaic* **:** COMPANION, FELLOW **3 a :** a member of one of the five ranks (as duke, marquess, earl, viscount, or baron) of the British peerage **b :** NOBLE 1
²peer *vt, archaic* **:** RIVAL, MATCH
³peer *vi* [perh. by shortening & alter. fr. *appear*] **1 :** to look narrowly or curiously; *esp* **:** to look searchingly at something difficult to discern **2 :** to come slightly into view **syn** see GAZE
peer•age \'pi(ə)r-ij\ *n* **1 :** the body of peers **2 :** the rank or dignity of a peer **3 :** a book containing a list of peers
peer•ess \'pi(ə)r-əs\ *n* **1 :** the wife or widow of a peer **2 :** a woman who holds in her own right the rank of a peer
peer•less \'pi(ə)r-ləs\ *adj* **:** MATCHLESS, INCOMPARABLE — **peer•less•ly** *adv* — **peer•less•ness** *n*
¹peeve \'pēv\ *vt* [back-formation fr. *peevish*] **:** to make peevish or resentful **:** ANNOY **syn** see IRRITATE
²peeve *n* **1 :** a feeling or mood of resentment **2 :** a particular grievance **:** GRUDGE
pee•vish \'pē-vish\ *adj* [ME *pevish* spiteful] **1 :** querulous in temperament or mood **:** FRETFUL **2 :** perversely obstinate **:** CONTRARY **3 :** marked by ill temper — **pee•vish•ly** *adv* — **pee•vish•ness** *n*
pee•wee \'pē-(,)wē\ *n, often attrib* [imit.] **1 :** PEWEE **2 :** something or someone diminutive or tiny
pee•wit *var of* PEWIT
¹peg \'peg\ *n* [ME *pegge*] **1 a :** a small usu. cylindrical pointed or tapered piece (as of wood) used to pin down or fasten things or to fit into or close holes **:** PIN, PLUG **b** *Brit* **:** CLOTHESPIN **c :** a predetermined level at which something (as a price) is fixed **2 a :** a projecting piece used as a support or boundary marker **b :** something used as a support, pretext, or reason **3 a :** one of the pins of a stringed musical instrument that are turned to regulate the pitch of the strings **b :** a step or degree esp. in estimation **4 :** a pointed prong or claw for catching or tearing **5** *Brit* **:** DRINK **6 :** something resembling a peg **7 :** THROW
²peg *vb* **pegged; peg•ging** *vt* **1 a :** to put a peg into **b** *Brit* **:** to pin (laundry) on a clothesline **c :** to pin down **:** RESTRICT **d :** to fix or hold (as prices) at a predetermined level **e :** to place in a definite category **2 :** to mark by pegs **3 :** THROW **~** *vi* **1 :** to work steadily and diligently **2 :** to move along vigorously or hastily **:** HUSTLE
³peg \'peg\ *or* **pegged** \'pegd\ *adj* **:** wide at the top and narrow at the bottom ⟨~ pants⟩
Peg•a•sus \'peg-ə-səs\ *n* [L (gen. *Pegasi*, fr. Gk *Pēgasos*] **1 :** a winged horse that in Greek mythology caused Hippocrene to burst forth from Mount Helicon with a blow of his hoof **2 :** poetic inspiration **3 :** a northern constellation near the vernal equinoctial point
peg•ma•tite \'peg-mə-,tīt\ *n* [F, fr. Gk *pēgmat-*, *pēgma* something fastened together, fr. *pēgnynai* to fasten together — more at PACT] **1 :** a coarse variety of granite occurring in dikes or veins **2 :** a formation similar to pegmatite in other rocks ⟨syenite ~⟩ — **peg•ma•tit•ic** \,peg-mə-'tit-ik\ *adj*
peg top *n* **1 :** a pear-shaped top that is made to spin on a sharp metal peg by the unwinding of a string wound round its center **2** *pl* **:** peg-top trousers
peg-top \'peg-'täp\ *or* **peg-topped** \-'täpt\ *adj* **:** PEG
Peh•le•vi \'pel-ə-(,)vē\ *var of* PAHLAVI
pei•gnoir \pān-'wär, pen-', 'pān-,, 'pen-,\ *n* [F, lit., garment worn while combing the hair, fr. MF, fr. *peigner* to comb the hair, fr. L *pectinare*, fr. *pectin-*, *pecten* comb — more at PECTINATE] **:** a woman's loose negligee or dressing gown
pe•jo•ra•tive \pi-'jór-ət-iv, -'jär-; 'pej-(ə-)rət-, 'pej-ə-,rāt-, 'pēj-\ *adj* [LL *pejoratus*, pp. of *pejorare* to make or become worse, fr. L *pejor* worse; akin to L *pessimus* worst, Gk *pedon* ground — more at PARALLELEPIPED] **:** having a tendency to make or become worse **:** DEPRECIATORY, DISPARAGING — **pe•jo•ra•tive•ly** *adv*
Pe•kin \pi-'kin, 'pē-,\ *n* [*Peking, Pekin*, China] **:** any of a breed of large white ducks of Chinese origin used for meat production
Pe•king•ese *or* **Pe•kin•ese** \,pē-kən-'ēz, -kiŋ-, -'ēs\ *n, pl* **Peking-ese** *or* **Pekinese 1 a :** a native or resident of Peking **b :** the Chinese dialect of Peking **2 :** any of a Chinese breed of small short-legged dogs with a broad flat face and a profuse long soft coat
Pe•king man \,pē-,kiŋ-\ *n* **:** an extinct Pleistocene man that is known from skeletal and cultural remains in cave deposits at Choukoutien, China and that is more advanced in some details than Java man but nearer to him than to other fossil hominids or to recent man
pe•koe \'pek-(,)ō, *Brit also* 'pek-\ *n* [Chin (Amoy) *pek-ho*] **1 :** a tea made from the first three leaves on the spray **2 :** a tea of India or Ceylon made from leaves of approximately the same size obtained by screening fired tea
pel•age \'pel-ij\ *n* [F, fr. MF, fr. *poil* hair, fr. L *pilus* — more at PILE] **:** the hairy covering of a mammal
Pe•la•gian \pə-'lā-j(ē-)ən\ *n* **:** a follower of Pelagius who denied original sin and held that man has perfect freedom of the will — **Pelagian** *adj* — **Pe•la•gian•ism** \-j(ē-)ə-,niz-əm\ *n*
pe•lag•ic \pə-'laj-ik\ *adj* [L *pelagicus*, fr. Gk *pelagikos*, fr. *pelagos* sea — more at FLAKE] **:** of, relating to, or living or occurring in the open sea **:** OCEANIC
pel•ar•go•ni•um \,pel-(,)är-'gō-nē-əm, ,pel-ər-\ *n* [NL, genus name, irreg. fr. Gk *pelargos* stork] **:** any of a genus (*Pelargonium*) of southern African herbs of the geranium family that include the garden geraniums
Pe•las•gian \pə-'laz-j(ē-)ən, -'laz-gē-ən\ *n* [Gk *pelasgios*, adj., Pelasgian, fr. *Pelasgoi* Pelasgians] **:** one of an ancient people mentioned by classical writers as early inhabitants of Greece and the eastern islands of the Mediterranean — **Pelasgian** *adj* — **Pe•las•gic** \-jik, -gik\ *adj*
pel•er•ine \,pel-ə-'rēn, 'pel-ə-rən\ *n* [obs. F, neckerchief, fr. F *pèlerine*, fem. of *pèlerin* pilgrim, fr. LL *pelegrinus* — more at PILGRIM] **:** a woman's narrow cape of fabric or fur usu. with long ends hanging down in front
pelf \'pelf\ *n* [ME, fr. MF *pelfre* booty] **:** MONEY, RICHES
Pe•li•as \'pē-lē-əs, 'pel-ē-\ *n* [L, fr. Gk] **:** an uncle of Jason and king of Iolcus
pel•i•can \'pel-i-kən\ *n* [ME, fr. OE *pellican*, fr. LL *pelecanus*, fr. Gk *pelekan*] **:** any of a genus (*Pelecanus*) of large web-footed birds with a very large bill and distensible gular pouch in which fish are caught
pe•lisse \pə-'lēs, pe-\ *n* [F, fr. LL *pellicia*, fr. fem. of *pellicius* made of skin, fr. L *pellis* skin — more at FELL] **1 :** a long cloak or coat made of fur or lined or trimmed with fur **2 :** a woman's loose lightweight cloak with wide collar and fur trimming
pel•la•gra \pə-'lag-rə, -'läg-, -'läg-\ *n* [It, fr *pelle* skin (fr. L *pellis*) + *-agra* (as in *podagra*, fr. L)] **:** a disease marked by dermatitis, gastrointestinal disorders, and central nervous symptoms and associated with a diet deficient in niacin and protein — **pel•la•gric** \-rik\ *adj* — **pel•la•grin** \-rən\ *n* — **pel•la•groid** \-,ròid\ *adj* — **pel•la•grous** \-rəs\ *adj*
¹pel•let \'pel-ət\ *n* [ME *pelote*, fr. MF, fr. (assumed) VL *pilota*, dim. of L *pila* ball — more at PILE] **1 :** a usu. small round or spherical body (as of food, medicine, or debris) **2 a :** a usu stone ball used as a missile in medieval times **b :** CANNONBALL **c :** BULLET **d :** a piece of small shot **e :** an imitation bullet
²pellet *vt* **1 :** to form into pellets **2 :** to strike with pellets
pel•li•cle \'pel-i-kəl\ *n* [MF *pellicule*, fr. ML *pellicula*, fr. L, dim. of *pellis*] **:** a thin skin or film — **pel•lic•u•lar** \pə-'lik-yə-lər, pe-\ *adj* — **pel•lic•u•late** \-lət, -,lāt\ *adj*
pel•li•to•ry \'pel-ə-,tōr-ē, -,tòr-\ *n* **1** [ME *paritorie*, fr. MF *paritaire*, fr. LL *parietaria*, fr. fem. of *parietarius* of a wall, fr. L *pariet-*, *paries* wall — more at PARIES] **:** any of a genus (*Parietaria*) of herbs of the nettle family with alternate leaves and inconspicuous flowers **2** [ME *peletre*, fr. MF *piretre*, fr. L *pyrethrum*] **a :** a southern European composite plant (*Anacyclus pyrethrum*) resembling yarrow **b :** any of several similar plants (as the feverfew or yarrow)
pell-mell \'pel-'mel\ *adv* [MF *pelemele*] **1 :** in mingled confusion or disorder **2 :** in confused haste **:** HEADLONG — **pell-mell** *adj or n*
pel•lu•cid \pə-'lü-səd\ *adj* [L *pellucidus*, fr. *per* through + *lucidus* lucid — more at FOR] **1 :** admitting maximum passage of light without diffusion or distortion **2 :** reflecting light evenly from all surfaces **3 :** extremely easy to understand **syn** see CLEAR — **pel•lu•cid•i•ty** \,pel-yü-'sid-ət-ē\ *n* — **pel•lu•cid•ly** \pə-'lü-səd-lē\ *adv* — **pel•lu•cid•ness** *n*
Pe•lops \'pē-,läps, 'pel-,äps\ *n* [L, fr. Gk] **:** a son of Tantalus served by his father to the gods for food but restored to life by them
pe•lo•ria \pə-'lōr-ē-ə, -'lòr-\ *n* [NL, fr. Gk *pelōros* monstrous, fr. *pelōr* monster; akin to Gk *teras* marvel — more at TERATOLOGY] **:** an abnormal regularity of structure occurring in normally irregular flowers — **pe•lor•ic** \-'lòr-ik, -'lär-\ *adj*
pe•lo•rus \pə-'lōr-əs, -'lòr-\ *n* [origin unknown] **:** a navigational instrument resembling a mariner's compass without magnetic needles and having two sight vanes by which bearings are taken
pe•lo•ta \pə-'lōt-ə\ *n* [Sp, fr. OF *pelote* little ball — more at PELLET] **:** any of various Basque, Spanish, or Spanish-American games played in a court with a ball and a wickerwork racket; *specif* **:** JAI ALAI
¹pelt \'pelt\ *n* [ME] **1 :** a usu. undressed skin with its hair, wool, or fur **2 :** a skin stripped of hair or wool for tanning
²pelt *vt* **:** to strip off the skin of
³pelt *vb* [ME *pelten*] *vt* **1 :** to strike with a succession of blows or missiles **2 :** HURL, THROW **3 :** to beat or dash repeatedly against **~** *vi* **1 :** to deliver a succession of blows or missiles **2 :** to beat incessantly **3 :** to move rapidly and vigorously — **pelt•er** *n*
⁴pelt *n* **:** BLOW, WHACK
pel•tate \'pel-,tāt\ *adj* [prob. fr. (assumed) NL *peltatus*, fr. L *pelta* small shield, fr. Gk *peltē*] **:** shaped like a shield; *specif* **:** having the stem or support attached to the lower surface instead of at the base or margin ⟨a ~ leaf⟩ — **pel•tate•ly** *adv*
pelt•ing \'pel-tiŋ\ *adj* [prob. fr. E dial. *pelt* piece of trash] *archaic* **:** PALTRY, INSIGNIFICANT
pelt•ry \'pel-trē\ *n* [ME, fr. AF *pelterie*] **:** PELTS, FURS; *esp* **:** raw undressed skins
pel•vic \'pel-vik\ *adj* **:** of, relating to, or located in or near the pelvis — **pelvic** *n*
pelvic fin *n* **:** one of the paired fins of a fish homologous with the hind limbs of a quadruped — called also *ventral fin*
pelvic girdle *n* **:** a bony or cartilaginous arch that supports the hind limbs of a vertebrate
pel•vis \'pel-vəs\ *n, pl* **pel•vis•es** \-və-səz\ *or* **pel•ves** \'pel-,vēz\

[NL, fr. L, basin; akin to OE & ON *full* cup, Gk *pella* wooden bowl] **1 :** a basin-shaped structure in the skeleton of many vertebrates formed by the pelvic girdle and adjoining bones of the spine **2 :** the cavity of the pelvis **3 :** the funnel-shaped cavity of the kidney into which urine is discharged

Pem·broke \ˈpem-ˌbrōk, -ˌbru̇k\ *n* [*Pembroke*, Wales] **:** a Welsh corgi of a variety characterized by pointed erect ears, straight legs, and short tail

pem·mi·can *also* **pem·i·can** \ˈpem-i-kən\ *n* [Cree *pimikân*] **:** a concentrated food used by No. American Indians consisting of lean meat dried, pounded fine, and mixed with melted fat; *also* **:** a similar preparation (as of dried beef, flour, molasses, suet) used for emergency rations

pem·phi·gus \ˈpem(p)-fi-gəs, pem-ˈfī-\ *n* [NL, fr. Gk *pemphig-*, *pemphix* breath, pustule] **:** a disease characterized by large blisters on skin and mucous membranes and often by itching or burning

[1]**pen** \ˈpen\ *n* [ME, fr. OE *penn*] **1 a :** a small enclosure for animals **b :** animals in or in numbers to fill one such enclosure; *also* **:** a small group of animals functioning as a unit **2 :** a small place of confinement or storage **3 :** a dock or slip for reconditioning submarines

[2]**pen** *vt* **penned; pen·ning :** to shut in a pen

[3]**pen** *n, often attrib* [ME *penne*, fr. MF, feather, pen, fr. L *penna*, *pinna* feather; akin to Gk *pteron* wing — more at FEATHER] **1 :** an implement for writing or drawing with ink or a similar fluid: as **a :** QUILL **b :** a small thin convex metal device tapering to a split point and fitting into a holder **c :** a penholder containing a pen **d :** FOUNTAIN PEN **2 a :** a writing instrument that is a means of expression **b :** WRITER **3 :** the internal horny feather-shaped shell of a squid

[4]**pen** *vt* **penned; pen·ning :** WRITE, INDITE

[5]**pen** *n* [origin unknown] **:** a female swan

[6]**pen** *n, slang* **:** PENITENTIARY

pe·nal \ˈpēn-ᵊl\ *adj* [ME, fr. MF, fr. L *poenalis*, fr. *poena* punishment — more at PAIN] **1 :** of, relating to, or involving punishment, penalties, or punitive institutions **2 :** liable to punishment — **pe·nal·ly** \-ᵊl-ē\ *adv*

penal code *n* **:** a code of laws concerning crimes and offenses and their punishment

pe·nal·iza·tion \ˌpēn-ᵊl-ə-ˈzā-shən, ˌpen-\ *n* **1 :** the act of penalizing **2 :** the state of being penalized

pe·nal·ize \ˈpēn-ᵊl-ˌīz, ˈpen-\ *vt* **1 :** to inflict a penalty on **2 :** to put at a serious disadvantage

pen·al·ty \ˈpen-ᵊl-tē\ *n* [ML *poenalitas*, fr. L *poenalis*] **1 :** the suffering in person, rights, or property that is annexed by law or judicial decision to the commission of a crime or public offense **2 :** the suffering or the sum to be forfeited to which a person subjects himself by agreement in case of nonfulfillment of stipulations **3 :** disadvantage, loss, or hardship due to some action **4 :** points scored in bridge by the side that defeats the opposing contract — usu. used in pl. — **penalty** *adj*

[1]**pen·ance** \ˈpen-ən(t)s\ *n* [ME, fr. OF, fr. ML *poenitentia* penitence] **1 :** an act of self-abasement, mortification, or devotion performed to show sorrow or repentance for sin **2 :** a sacrament in the Roman Catholic and Eastern Churches consisting in repentance or contrition for sin, confession to a priest, satisfaction as imposed by the confessor, and absolution

[2]**penance** *vt* **:** to impose penance on

pe·na·tes \pə-ˈnāt-ēz, -ˈnät-\ *n pl* [L — more at PENETRATE] **:** the Roman gods of the household worshiped in close connection with Vesta and with the lares and household genius

pence \ˈpen(t)s\ *pl of* PENNY

pen·cel *or* **pen·cil** \ˈpen(t)-səl\ *n* [ME *pencel*, modif. of OF *penoncel*] **:** PENNONCEL

pen·chant \ˈpen-chənt, *esp Brit* ˈpä^{n}-ˌshä^{n}, pä^{n}-ˈ\ *n* [F, fr. prp. of *pencher* to incline, fr. (assumed) VL *pendicare*, fr. L *pendere* to weigh] **:** a strong leaning **:** LIKING **syn** see LEANING

[1]**pen·cil** \ˈpen(t)-səl\ *n, often attrib* [ME *pensel*, fr. MF *pincel*, fr. (assumed) VL *penicellus*, fr. L *penicillus*, lit., little tail, fr. dim. of *penis* tail, penis] **1 :** an artist's brush **2 :** an artist's individual skill or style **3 a :** an implement for writing, drawing, or marking consisting of or containing a slender cylinder or strip of a solid marking substance **b :** a small medicated or cosmetic roll or stick for local applications **4 a :** an aggregate of rays of light or other radiation esp. when diverging from or converging to a point **b :** a one-parameter family (as of the lines in a plane through a point) **5 :** something long and thin like a pencil

[2]**pencil** *vt* **pen·ciled** *or* **pen·cilled; pen·cil·ing** *or* **pen·cil·ling** \-s(ə-)liŋ\ **:** to paint, draw, or write with a pencil **:** SKETCH — **pen·cil·ler** \-s(ə-)lər\ *n*

pen·cil·ing *n* **:** the work of the pencil or brush or a product of this

pen·dant *also* **pen·dent** \ˈpen-dənt; *3 & 4 are also* ˈpen-ənt, *6 is also* pä^{n}-dä^{n}\ *n* [ME *pendaunt*, fr. MF *pendant*, fr. prp. of *pendre* to hang, fr. (assumed) VL *pendere*, fr. L *pendēre*; akin to L *pendere* to weigh, estimate, pay, *pondus* weight — more at SPAN] **1 :** something suspended: as **a :** an ornament allowed to hang free **b :** an electrical fixture suspended from the ceiling **2 :** a hanging ornament of roofs or ceilings much used in the later styles of Gothic architecture **3 :** a short rope hanging from a spar and having at its free end a block or spliced thimble **4** *chiefly Brit* **:** PENNANT 1a **5 :** the shank on a pocket watch stem to which the bow attaches **6 :** a companion piece or supplement

pen·den·cy \ˈpen-dən-sē\ *n* **:** the state of being pending

pen·dent *or* **pen·dant** \ˈpen-dənt\ *adj* [ME *pendaunt*] **1 :** supported from above **:** SUSPENDED **2 :** jutting or leaning over **:** OVERHANGING **3 :** remaining undetermined — **pen·dent·ly** *adv*

pen·den·tive \pen-ˈdent-iv\ *n* [F *pendentif*, fr. L *pendent-*, *pendens*, prp. of *pendēre*] **1 :** one of the triangular spherical sections of vaulting that spring from the corners of a rectangular ground plan and serve to allow the room enclosing it to be covered by a cupola of rounded or polygonal plan **2 :** the part of a groined vault that springs from a single pier or corbel

[1]**pend·ing** \ˈpen-diŋ\ *prep* [F *pendant*, fr. prp. of *pendre*] **1 :** DURING **2 :** while awaiting

[2]**pending** *adj* **1 :** not yet decided **2 :** IMPENDING, IMMINENT

pen·drag·on \pen-ˈdrag-ən\ *n* [ME, fr. W, fr. *pen* chief + *dragon* leader] **:** head of all the chiefs among the ancient Britons **:** KING

pen·du·lar \ˈpen-jə-lər, -dyə-lər, -dᵊl-ər\ *adj* **:** being or resembling the movement of a pendulum

pen·du·lous \-jə-ləs, -dyə-ləs, -dᵊl-əs\ *adj* [L *pendulus*, fr. *pendere* to weigh] **1** *archaic* **:** poised without visible support **2 a :** suspended so as to swing freely **b :** inclined or hanging downward **:** DROOPING **3 :** WAVERING, VACILLATING — **pen·du·lous·ly** *adv* — **pen·du·lous·ness** *n*

pen·du·lum \ˈpen-jə-ləm, -dyə-ləm, -dᵊl-əm\ *n, often attrib* [NL, fr. L, neut. of *pendulus*] **:** a body suspended from a fixed point so as to swing freely to and fro under the action of gravity and commonly used to regulate the movements of clockwork and other machinery

Pe·nel·o·pe \pə-ˈnel-ə-pē\ *n* [L, fr. Gk *Pēnelopē*] **:** the wife of Odysseus

pe·ne·plain *also* **pe·ne·plane** \ˈpēn-i-ˌplān, ˈpen-\ *n* [L *paene*, *pene* almost + E *plain* or *plane* — more at PATIENT] **:** a land surface of considerable area and slight relief shaped by erosion

pen·e·tra·bil·i·ty \ˌpen-ə-trə-ˈbil-ət-ē\ *n* **:** the quality or state of being penetrable

pen·e·tra·ble \ˈpen-ə-trə-bəl\ *adj* **:** capable of being penetrated — **pen·e·tra·ble·ness** *n* — **pen·e·tra·bly** \-blē\ *adv*

pen·e·tra·lia \ˌpen-ə-ˈtrā-lē-ə\ *n pl* [L, neut. pl. of *penetralis* inner, fr. *penetrare* to penetrate] **:** the innermost or most private parts

pen·e·tram·e·ter \ˌpen-ə-ˈtram-ət-ər\ *n* [*penetra*tion + *-meter*] **:** a device for measuring the penetrating power of X rays or other radiation

pen·e·trance \ˈpen-ə-trən(t)s\ *n* **:** the relative ability of a gene to produce its specific effect in any degree whatever in the organism of which it is a part

[1]**pen·e·trant** \-trənt\ *adj* **:** PENETRATING

[2]**penetrant** *n* **:** one that penetrates or is capable of penetrating

pen·e·trate \ˈpen-ə-ˌtrāt\ *vb* [L *penetratus*, pp. of *penetrare*; akin to L *penitus* inward, *Penates* household gods, Lith *peneti* to nourish] *vt* **1 a :** to pass into or through **b :** to enter by overcoming resistance **:** PIERCE **2 a :** to see into or through **b :** to discover the inner contents or meaning of **3 :** to affect profoundly with feeling **4 :** to diffuse through **:** PERMEATE ~ *vi* **1 a :** to pass, extend, pierce, or diffuse into or through something **b :** to pierce something with the eye or mind **2 :** to affect deeply the senses or feelings **syn** see ENTER

pen·e·trat·ing *adj* **1 :** having the power of entering, piercing, or pervading **2 :** ACUTE, DISCERNING — **pen·e·trat·ing·ly** \-ˌtrāt-iŋ-lē\ *adv*

pen·e·tra·tion \ˌpen-ə-ˈtrā-shən\ *n* **1 :** the act or process of penetrating: as **a :** the act of entering a country so that actual establishment of influence is accomplished **b :** an attack that penetrates the enemy's front or territory **2 a :** the depth to which something penetrates **b :** the power to penetrate; *specif* **:** the ability to discern deeply and acutely **syn** see DISCERNMENT

pen·e·tra·tive \ˈpen-ə-ˌtrāt-iv\ *adj* **1 :** tending to penetrate **:** PIERCING **2 :** ACUTE **3 :** IMPRESSIVE — **pen·e·tra·tive·ly** *adv* — **pen·e·tra·tive·ness** *n*

pen·e·trom·e·ter \ˌpen-ə-ˈträm-ət-ər\ *n* [L *penetrare* + ISV *-meter*] **1 :** an instrument for measuring the consistency of semisolids **2 :** PENETRAMETER

pen·gö \ˈpeŋ-ˌgə(r)\ *n, pl* **pengö** *or* **pengös** [Hung *pengő*, lit., jingling] **:** the basic monetary unit of Hungary from 1925 to 1946

pen·guin \ˈpen-gwən, ˈpeŋ-\ *n* [perh. fr. W *pen gwyn* white head] **:** any of various erect short-legged flightless aquatic birds (family Spheniscidae) of the southern hemisphere

pen·hold·er \ˈpen-ˌhōl-dər\ *n* **:** a holder or handle for a pen

pen·i·cil·late \ˌpen-ə-ˈsil-ət, -ˌāt\ *adj* [prob. fr. (assumed) NL *penicillatus*, fr. L *penicillus* brush — more at PENCIL] **:** furnished with a tuft of fine filaments — **pen·i·cil·late·ly** *adv* — **pen·i·cil·la·tion** \ˌpen-ə-sə-ˈlā-shən\ *n*

pen·i·cil·lin \ˌpen-ə-ˈsil-ən\ *n* **:** any of several relatively nontoxic antibiotic acids of the general constitution $C_9H_{11}N_2O_4SR$ or a salt or ester of one of these acids or a mixture produced by molds (genus *Penicillium* and esp. *P. notatum* or *P. chrysogenum*) or synthetically and used esp. against cocci

pen·i·cil·li·um \-ˈsil-ē-əm\ *n, pl* **pen·i·cil·lia** \-ē-ə\ [NL, genus name, fr. L *penicillus*] **:** any of a genus (*Pencillium*) of fungi (family Moniliaceae) comprising the blue molds found chiefly on moist nonliving organic matter

pe·nile \ˈpē-ˌnīl\ *adj* **:** of, relating to, or affecting the penis

pen·in·su·la \pə-ˈnin(t)-sə-lə; -ˈnin-chə-lə, -shə-; -ˈnin(t)s-lə, -ˈnin(t)s-yə-lə\ *n* [L *paeninsula*, fr. *paene* almost + *insula* island — more at PATIENT] **:** a portion of land nearly surrounded by water and connected with a larger body by an isthmus; *also* **:** a piece of land jutting out into the water whether with or without a well-defined isthmus — **pen·in·su·lar** \-lər\ *adj*

pe·nis \ˈpē-nəs\ *n, pl* **pe·nes** \ˈpē-(ˌ)nēz\ *or* **pe·nis·es** [L, penis, tail; akin to OHG *faselt* penis, Gk *peos*] **:** a male organ of copulation

pen·i·tence \ˈpen-ə-tən(t)s\ *n* [ME, fr. OF, fr. ML *poenitentia*, alter. of L *paenitentia* regret, fr. *paenitent-*, *paenitens*, prp.] **:** the quality or state of being penitent **:** sorrow for sins or faults

syn PENITENCE, REPENTANCE, CONTRITION, COMPUNCTION, REMORSE mean regret for sin or wrongdoing. PENITENCE implies humble realization of and regret for one's wrongdoing; REPENTANCE suggests additionally an awareness of one's general moral shortcomings and a resolve to change; CONTRITION suggests penitence shown by signs of grief or pain; COMPUNCTION implies a painful sting of conscience; REMORSE suggests prolonged and insistent self-reproach and mental anguish for consequences that cannot be escaped

[1]**pen·i·tent** \-tənt\ *adj* [ME, fr. MF, fr. L *paenitent-*, *paenitens*, fr. prp. of *paenitēre* to be sorry; akin to L *paene* almost — more at PATIENT] **:** feeling or expressing pain or sorrow for sins or offenses **:** REPENTANT — **pen·i·tent·ly** *adv*

[2]**penitent** *n* **1 :** a person who repents of sin **2 :** a person under church censure but admitted to penance esp. under the direction of a confessor

pen·i·ten·tial \ˌpen-ə-ˈten-chəl\ *adj* **:** of or relating to penitence or penance — **pen·i·ten·tial·ly** \-ˈtench-(ə-)lē\ *adv*

[1]**pen·i·ten·tia·ry** \ˌpen-ə-ˈtench-(ə-)rē, ˈpen-ˈtench-\ *n* [ME *penitenciary*, fr. ML *poenitentiarius*, fr. *poenitentia*] **1 a :** an officer in

some Roman Catholic dioceses vested with power from the bishop to absolve in cases reserved to him **b :** a tribunal of the Roman curia concerned with private spiritual matters **2 :** a public institution in which offenders against the law are confined for detention or punishment; *specif* **:** a state or federal prison in the U.S.

2**pen·i·ten·tia·ry** \ˌpen-ə-ˈtench-(ə-)rē, *1 also* -ˈtench-ē-ˌer-ē, *2 also* ˈpen-ˈtench-\ *adj* **1 :** PENITENTIAL **2 :** of, relating to, or incurring confinement in a penitentiary

pen·knife \ˈpen-ˌnīf\ *n* [fr. its original use for mending quill pens] **:** a small pocketknife usu. with only one blade

pen·man \ˈpen-mən\ *n* **1 a :** COPYIST, SCRIBE **b :** one who is expert in penmanship **2 :** AUTHOR

pen·man·ship \ˈpen-mən-ˌship\ *n* **1 :** the art or practice of writing with the pen **2 :** quality or style of handwriting

pen·na \ˈpen-ə\ *n, pl* **pen·nae** \ˈpen-ˌē, -ˌī\ [L, feather, wing — more at PEN] **:** a contour feather esp. as distinguished from a down feather or plume — **pen·na·ceous** \pe-ˈnā-shəs\ *adj*

pen name *n* **:** an author's pseudonym

pen·nant \ˈpen-ənt\ *n* [alter. of *pendant*] **1 a :** any of various nautical flags tapering usu. to a point or swallowtail and used for identification or signaling **b :** a flag or banner longer in the fly than in the hoist; *esp* **:** one that tapers to a point **2 :** a flag emblematic of championship

pen·nate \ˈpen-ˌāt\ *also* **pen·nat·ed** \-ˌāt-əd\ *adj* [L *pennatus*, fr. *penna*] **:** PINNATE

pen·ner \ˈpen-ər\ *n* **:** one that pens a document **:** WRITER

pen·ni \ˈpen-ē\ *n, pl* **pen·nia** \-ē-ə\ *or* **pen·nis** \-ēz\ [Finn] — see *markka* at MONEY table

pen·ni·less \ˈpen-i-ləs, ˈpen-ᵊl-əs\ *adj* **:** destitute of money **:** POOR

pen·non \ˈpen-ən\ *n* [ME, fr. MF *penon*, aug. of *penne* feather — more at PEN] **1 a :** a long usu. triangular or swallow-tailed streamer typically attached to the head of a lance as an ensign **b :** PENNANT 1a **2 :** a flag of any shape **:** BANNER **3 :** WING, PINION

pen·non·cel *or* **pen·on·cel** \ˈpen-ən-ˌsel\ *n* [ME *penoncell*, fr. MF *penoncel*, dim. of *penon*] **:** a small narrow flag or streamer borne esp. at the head of a lance in late medieval or Renaissance times

Penn·syl·va·nia Dutch \ˌpen(t)-səl-ˌvā-nyə-, -nē-ə-, *rapid* -sə-ˌvā-\ *n* **1 :** people living mostly in eastern Pennsylvania whose characteristic cultural traditions go back to the German migrations of the 18th century **2 :** a dialect of High German spoken in parts of Pennsylvania and Maryland — called also *Pennsylvania German* — **Pennsylvania Dutchman** *n*

Penn·syl·va·nian \-ˈvā-nyən, -nē-ən\ *adj* **1 :** of or relating to Pennsylvania or its people **2 :** of, relating to, or being the period of the Paleozoic era in No. America between the Mississippian and Permian or the corresponding system of rocks — **Pennsylvanian** *n*

pen·ny \ˈpen-ē\ *n, pl* **pen·nies** \-ēz\ *or* **pence** \ˈpen(t)s\ *often attrib* [ME, fr. OE *penning, penig*; akin to OHG *pfenning*, a coin] **1** — see *pound* at MONEY table **2 :** a coin of small denomination: as **a :** DENARIUS **b** *pl pennies* **:** a cent of the U.S. or Canada **3 :** a piece or sum of money

penny ante *n* **:** poker played for very low stakes

penny arcade *n* **:** an amusement center where each device for entertainment may be operated for a penny

penny dreadful *n* **:** a novel of violent adventure or crime orig. costing one penny

pen·ny–pinch \ˈpen-ē-ˌpinch\ *vt* [back-formation fr. *penny pincher*] **:** to give out money to in a niggardly or stingy manner — **penny pincher** *n*

pen·ny·roy·al \ˌpen-ē-ˈrȯi(-ə)l, ˈpen-i-ˌrīl\ *n* [prob. by folk etymology fr. MF *poullieul*, modif. of L *pulegium*] **1 :** a European perennial mint (*Mentha pulegium*) with small aromatic leaves **2 :** a similar American mint (*Hedeoma pulegioides*) that yields an oil used in folk medicine or to drive away mosquitoes

pen·ny·weight \ˈpen-ē-ˌwāt\ *n* — see MEASURE table

pen·ny–wise \ˈpen-ē-ˌwīz\ *adj* **:** wise or prudent only in small matters

pen·ny·wort \-ˌwərt, -ˌwȯ(ə)rt\ *n* **:** any of several round-leaved plants (as of the genera *Hydrocotyle* and *Centella*)

pen·ny·worth \ˈpen-ē-ˌwərth, *Brit often* ˈpen-ərth\ *n, pl* **pennyworth** *or* **pennyworths** **1 :** a penny's worth **2 :** BARGAIN **3 :** a small quantity **:** MODICUM

Pe·nob·scot \pə-ˈnäb-skət, -ˌskät\ *n, pl* **Penobscot** *or* **Penobscots** **1 :** an Indian people of the Penobscot river valley and Penobscot Bay region **2 :** a member of the Penobscot people

pe·no·che \pə-ˈnō-chē\ *var of* PENUCHE

pe·no·log·i·cal \ˌpēn-ᵊl-ˈäj-i-kəl\ *adj* **:** of or relating to penology

pe·nol·o·gist \pi-ˈnäl-ə-jəst\ *n* **:** a specialist in penology

pe·nol·o·gy \-jē\ *n* [Gk *poinē* penalty + E *-logy* — more at PAIN] **:** a branch of criminology dealing with prison management and the treatment of offenders

pen·sile \ˈpen-ˌsīl\ *adj* [L *pensilis*, fr. *pensus*, pp. of *pendere* to hang] **1 :** HANGING, PENDENT **2 :** having or building a hanging nest

1**pen·sion** *n, often attrib* [ME, fr. MF, fr. L *pension-, pensio*, fr. *pensus*, pp. of *pendere* to pay — more at PENDANT] **1** \ˈpen-chən\ **:** a fixed sum paid regularly to a person: **a** *archaic* **:** WAGE **b :** a gratuity granted (as by a government) as a favor or reward **c :** one paid under given conditions to a person following his retirement from service or to his surviving dependents **2** \päⁿs-yōⁿ\ **a :** payment for board and room **b :** a boardinghouse esp. in continental Europe — **pen·sion·less** \ˈpen-chən-ləs\ *adj*

2**pen·sion** \ˈpen-chən\ *vt* **pen·sion·ing** \ˈpench-(ə-)niŋ\ **:** to grant or pay a pension to — **pen·sion·able** \ˈpench-(ə-)nə-bəl\ *adj*

pen·sion·ary \ˈpen-chə-ˌner-ē\ *n* **:** PENSIONER; *esp* **:** HIRELING — **pensionary** *adj*

pen·sion·er \ˈpench-(ə-)nər\ *n* **1 :** a person who receives or lives on a pension **2** *obs* **a :** GENTLEMAN-AT-ARMS **b :** RETAINER **c :** MERCENARY, HIRELING

pen·sive \ˈpen(t)-siv\ *adj* [ME *pensif*, fr. MF, fr. *penser* to think, fr. L *pensare* to ponder, fr. *pensus*, pp. of *pendere* to weigh — more at PENDANT] **1 :** musingly or dreamily thoughtful **2 :** suggestive of sad thoughtfulness **:** MELANCHOLY — **pen·sive·ly** *adv* — **pen·sive·ness** *n*

pen·ster \ˈpenz-tər, ˈpen(t)-stər\ *n* [3*pen* + *-ster*] **:** WRITER; *esp* **:** a hack writer

pen·stock \ˈpen-ˌstäk\ *n* **1 :** a sluice or gate for regulating a flow (as of water) **2 :** a conduit or pipe for conducting water

pent \ˈpent\ *adj* [prob. fr. pp. of obs. E *pend* (to confine)] **:** shut up **:** CONFINED ⟨*pent*-up feelings⟩

penta- *or* **pent-** *comb form* [ME, fr. Gk, fr. *pente* — more at FIVE] **1 :** five ⟨*penta*hedron⟩ **2 :** containing five atoms, groups, or equivalents ⟨*pent*ane⟩

pen·ta·chlo·ro·phe·nol \ˌpent-ə-ˌklōr-ə-ˈfē-ˌnōl, -ˌklȯr-, -fi-ˈ\ *n* **:** a crystalline compound C_6Cl_5OH used as a wood preservative, fungicide, and disinfectant

pen·ta·cle \ˈpent-i-kəl\ *n* [OIt *pentacol*, fr. (assumed) ML *pentaculum*, prob. fr. Gk *pente*] **:** a 5-pointed or sometimes 6-pointed star used as a magical symbol

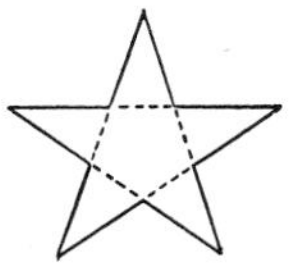

pentacle

pen·tad \ˈpen-ˌtad\ *n* [Gk *pentad-, pentas*, fr. *pente*] **:** a group of five

pen·ta·dac·tyl \ˌpent-ə-ˈdak-tᵊl\ *also* **pen·ta·dac·ty·late** \-tə-lət, -ˌlāt\ *adj* [L *pentadactylus*, fr. Gk *pentadaktylos*, fr. *penta-* + *daktylos* finger, toe] **:** having five digits to the hand or foot or five digitate parts — **pen·ta·dac·tyl·ism** \-tə-ˌliz-əm\ *n*

pen·ta·gon \ˈpent-i-ˌgän\ *n* [Gk *pentagōnon*, fr. neut. of *pentagōnos* pentagonal, fr. *penta-* + *gōnia* angle — more at -GON] **:** a polygon of five angles and five sides — **pen·tag·o·nal** \pen-ˈtag-ən-ᵊl\ *adj* — **pen·tag·o·nal·ly** \-ᵊl-ē\ *adv*

Pentagon *n* [the *Pentagon* building, headquarters of the Department of Defense] **:** the U.S. military establishment

pen·tag·o·noid \pen-ˈtag-ə-ˌnȯid\ *adj* **:** somewhat pentagonal

pen·ta·gram \ˈpent-ə-ˌgram\ *n* [Gk *pentagrammon*, fr. *penta-* + *-grammon* (akin to *gramma* letter) — more at GRAM] **:** PENTACLE

pen·ta·he·dron \ˌpent-ə-ˈhē-drən\ *n* [NL] **:** a solid bounded by five faces

pen·tam·er·ous \pen-ˈtam-ə-rəs\ *adj* [NL *pentamerus*, fr. *penta-* (fr. Gk) + *-merus* -merous] **:** divided into or consisting of five parts; *specif* **:** having each floral whorl consisting of five or a multiple of five members

pen·tam·e·ter \pen-ˈtam-ət-ər\ *n* [L, fr. Gk *pentametros* having five metrical feet, fr. *penta-* + *metron* measure — more at MEASURE] **:** a verse consisting of five feet

pen·tane \ˈpen-ˌtān\ *n* [ISV] **:** any of three isomeric hydrocarbons C_5H_{12} of the methane series occurring in petroleum

pent·an·gle \ˈpent-ˌaŋ-gəl\ *n* **:** PENTACLE

pen·ta·ploid \ˈpent-ə-ˌplȯid\ *adj* **:** fivefold in appearance or arrangement; *esp* **:** having or being a chromosome number that is five times the basic number — **pentaploid** *n* — **pen·ta·ploi·dy** \-ˌplȯid-ē\ *n*

pen·ta·quine *also* **pen·ta·quin** \ˈpent-ə-ˌkwēn, -kwən\ *n* [*penta-* + *quino*line] **:** an antimalarial $C_{18}H_{27}N_3O$ used esp. in the form of its pale yellow crystalline phosphate

pent·ar·chy \ˈpent-ˌär-kē\ *n* [Gk *pentarchia*, fr. *penta-* + *-archia* -archy] **:** a government by five persons

Pen·ta·teuch \ˈpent-ə-ˌt(y)ük\ *n* [LL *Pentateuchus*, fr. Gk *Pentateuchos*, fr. *penta-* + *teuchos* tool, vessel, book; akin to Gk *teuchein* to make — more at DOUGHTY] **:** the first five books of the Old Testament

pen·tath·lon \pen-ˈtath-lən, -ˌlän\ *n* [Gk, fr. *penta-* + *athlon* contest — more at ATHLETE] **:** an athletic contest involving participation by each contestant in five different events

pen·ta·ton·ic scale \ˌpent-ə-ˌtän-ik-\ *n* **:** a musical scale of five tones; *specif* **:** one in which the tones are arranged like a major scale with the fourth and seventh omitted

pen·ta·va·lent \ˌpent-ə-ˈvā-lənt\ *adj* **:** having a valence of five

Pen·te·cost \ˈpent-i-ˌkȯst, -ˌkäst\ *n* [ME, fr. OE *pentecosten*, fr. LL *pentecoste*, fr. Gk *pentēkostē*, lit., fiftieth day, fr. *pentēkostos* fiftieth, fr. *pentēkonta* fifty, fr. *penta-* + *-konta* (akin to L *viginti* twenty) — more at VIGESIMAL] **1 :** SHABUOTH **2 :** a Christian feast on the 7th Sunday after Easter commemorating the descent of the Holy Spirit on the apostles

Pen·te·cos·tal \ˌpent-i-ˈkäst-ᵊl, -ˈkȯst-\ *adj* **1 :** of, relating to, or suggesting Pentecost **2 :** of, relating to, or constituting any of various Christian religious bodies that employ revivalistic methods typically including the generating of great emotionalism and that are usu. fundamentalist in outlook — **Pentecostal** *n* — **Pen·te·cos·tal·ism** \-ˌiz-əm\ *n*

pent·house \ˈpent-ˌhau̇s\ *n* [ME *pentis*, fr. MF *appentis*, prob. fr. ML *appenticium* appendage, fr. L *appendic-, appendix* — more at APPENDIX] **1 a :** a shed or roof attached to and sloping from a wall or building **b :** a smaller structure joined to a building **:** ANNEX **2 :** a structure or dwelling built on the roof of a building

pent·land·ite \ˈpent-lən-ˌdīt\ *n* [F, fr. Joseph *Pentland* †1873 Irish scientist] **:** a bronzy yellow mineral $(Fe,Ni)_9S_8$ that is isometric nickel iron sulfide and the principal ore of nickel

pen·to·bar·bi·tal \ˌpent-ə-ˈbär-bə-ˌtȯl\ *n* **:** a granular barbiturate $C_{11}H_{18}N_2O_3$ used esp. in the form of its sodium or calcium salt as a sedative, hypnotic, and antispasmodic

pen·tom·ic \pen-ˈtäm-ik\ *adj* [blend of *penta-* and *atomic*] **1 :** made up of five battle groups ⟨∼ division⟩ **2 :** organized into pentomic divisions ⟨∼ army⟩

pen·to·san \ˈpent-ə-ˌsan\ *n* **:** any of various polysaccharides that yield only pentoses on hydrolysis and are widely distributed in plants

pen·tose \ˈpen-ˌtōs, -ˌtōz\ *n* [ISV] **:** any of various monosaccharides $C_5H_{10}O_5$ containing five carbon atoms in the molecule

pen·to·side \ˈpent-ə-ˌsīd\ *n* **:** a glycoside that yields a pentose on hydrolysis

Pen·to·thal \ˈpent-ə-ˌthȯl\ *trademark* — used for thiopental

pent·ox·ide \pent-ˈäk-ˌsīd\ *n* [ISV] **:** an oxide containing five atoms of oxygen in the molecule

pent·ste·mon *or* **pen·ste·mon** \pen(t)-ˈstē-mən, ˈpen(t)-stə-\ *n* [NL *pentstemon*, alter. of *Penstemon*, genus name, fr. Gk *penta-* + *stēmōn* thread — more at STAMEN] **:** any of a genus (*Penstemon*) of chiefly American herbs of the figwort family with showy blue, purple, red, yellow, or white flowers

pen·tyl \ˈpent-ᵊl\ *n* **:** any of eight isomeric alkyl radicals C_5H_{11} derived from pentanes

pentyl alcohol *n* **:** any of eight isomeric liquid alcohols $C_5H_{11}OH$ used chiefly as solvents and in making esters

pen·tyl·ene·tet·ra·zol \ˌpent-ᵊl-ˌēn-ˈte-trə-ˌzȯl, -ˌzōl\ *n* [*pent*amethy*lene-tetrazole*] **:** a compound $C_6H_{10}N_4$ used as a respiratory and circulatory stimulant and for producing a state of convulsion in treating mental disorders

pe·nu·che \pə-ˈnü-chē\ *n* [MexSp *panocha* raw sugar, fr. dim. of Sp *pan* bread, fr. L *panis* — more at FOOD] **:** fudge made usu. of brown

sugar, butter, cream or milk, and nuts

pe·nult \ˈpē-ˌnəlt, pi-ˈ\ *also* **pen·ul·ti·mate** \pi-ˈnəl-tə-mət\ *or* **pen·ul·ti·ma** \-mə\ *n* [L *paenultima* penult, fr. fem. of *paenultimus* almost last, fr. *paene* almost + *ultimus* last] **:** the next to the last member of a series; *esp* **:** the next to the last syllable of a word

penultimate *adj* **1 :** next to the last **2 :** of or relating to a penult — **pen·ul·ti·mate·ly** *adv*

pen·um·bra \pə-ˈnəm-brə\ *n, pl* **pe·num·brae** \-(ˌ)brē, -ˌbrī\ *or* **penumbras** [NL, fr. L *paene* almost + *umbra* shadow — more at PATIENT, UMBRAGE] **1 :** a space of partial illumination (as in an eclipse) between the perfect shadow on all sides and the full light **2 :** a shaded region surrounding the dark central portion of a sunspot **3 :** a surrounding or adjoining region in which something exists in a lesser degree **:** FRINGE — **pen·um·bral** \-brəl\ *adj*

pe·nu·ri·ous \pə-ˈn(y)u̇r-ē-əs\ *adj* **1 :** marked by or suffering from penury **2 :** given to or marked by extreme stinting frugality **syn** see STINGY — **pe·nu·ri·ous·ly** *adv* — **pe·nu·ri·ous·ness** *n*

pen·u·ry \ˈpen-yə-rē\ *n* [ME, fr. L *penuria* want — more at PATIENT] **1 :** extreme poverty **:** PRIVATION **2 :** absence of resources **:** SCANTINESS **syn** see POVERTY

pe·on \ˈpē-ˌän, -ən, *esp South* -ˌȯn; *also* pā-ˈōn *for 2, 3a; Brit also* ˈpyün *for 1*\ *n, pl* **peons** *or* **pe·o·nes** \pā-ˈō-nēz\ [Pg *peão* & F *pion*, fr. ML *pedon-, pedo* foot soldier — more at PAWN] **1 :** any of various Indian or Ceylonese workers **2 :** a member of the landless laboring class in Spanish America **3** *pl* **peons a :** a person held in compulsory servitude to a master for the working out of an indebtedness **b :** DRUDGE, MENIAL

pe·on·age \ˈpē-ə-nij\ *n* **1 :** the condition of a peon **2 a :** the use of laborers bound in servitude because of debt **b :** a system of convict labor by which convicts are leased to contractors

pe·o·ny \ˈpē-ə-nē, ˈpī-nē\ *n* [ME *piony*, fr. MF *pioine*, fr. L *paeonia*, fr. Gk *paiōnia*, fr. *Paiōn* Paeon, physician of the gods] **:** any of a genus (*Paeonia*) of plants of the crowfoot family with large usu. double flowers of red, pink, or white

[1]**peo·ple** \ˈpē-pəl\ *n, pl* **people** [ME *peple*, fr. OF *peuple*, fr. L *populus*] **1** *pl* **a :** persons who form part of the aggregate of human beings **b :** human beings as distinguished from the lower animals **2** *pl* **:** human beings making up a group or assembly or linked by a common interest **3** *pl* **:** the members of a family or kinship **4** *pl* **:** the mass of a community as distinguished from a special class ⟨disputes between the ~ and the nobles⟩ — often used by Communists to distinguish Communists or those under Communist control from other people ⟨Bulgarian *People's* Republic⟩ **5** *pl* **peoples :** a body of persons that are united by a common culture, tradition, or sense of kinship, that typically have common language, institutions, and beliefs, and that often constitute a politically organized group **6 :** lower animals usu. of a specified kind or situation **7 :** the body of enfranchised citizens of a state **:** ELECTORATE

[2]**people** *vt* **peo·pling** \-p(ə-)liŋ\ [MF *puepler*, fr. OF, fr. *peuple*] **1 :** to supply or fill with people **2 :** to dwell in **:** INHABIT

[1]**pep** \ˈpep\ *n* [short for *pepper*] **:** brisk energy or initiative and high spirits **:** LIVELINESS

[2]**pep** *vt* **pepped; pep·ping :** to inject pep into **:** STIMULATE ⟨~ him up⟩

pep·los \ˈpep-ləs, -ˌläs\ *also* **pep·lus** \-ləs\ *n* [L *peplus*, fr. Gk *peplos*] **:** a garment like a shawl worn by women of ancient Greece

pep·lum \-ləm\ *n* [L, fr. Gk *peplon* peplos] **:** a short section attached to the waistline of a blouse, jacket, or dress — **pep·lumed** \-ləmd\ *adj*

pe·po \ˈpē-(ˌ)pō\ *n* [L, a melon — more at PUMPKIN] **:** an indehiscent fleshy one-celled or falsely 3-celled many-seeded berry usu. with a hard rind (as a pumpkin, squash, melon, or cucumber) that is the characteristic fruit of the gourd family

[1]**pep·per** \ˈpep-ər\ *n, often attrib* [ME *peper*, fr. OE *pipor;* akin to OHG *pfeffar* pepper; both fr. a prehistoric WGmc-NGmc word borrowed fr. L *piper* pepper, fr. Gk *peperi*] **1 a :** a pungent product from the fruit of an East Indian plant (*Piper nigrum*) used as a condiment or as a carminative or stimulant and consisting of (1) the entire dried berry or (2) the dried seeds divested of membranes and pulp — called also (1) *black pepper*, (2) *white pepper* **b :** any of several somewhat similar products obtained from other plants of the same genus **c :** any of various pungent condiments obtained from plants of other genera — used with a qualifying term **2 :** any of a genus (*Piper* of the family Piperaceae, the pepper family) of tropical mostly jointed climbing shrubs with aromatic leaves **3 a :** CAPSICUM 1; *esp* **:** a New World capsicum (*Capsicum frutescens*) whose fruits are hot peppers or sweet peppers **b :** the usu. red or yellow fruit of a pepper

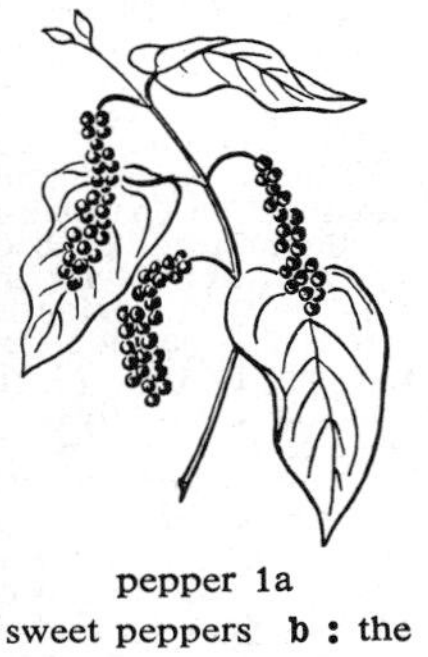
pepper 1a

[2]**pepper** *vt* **pep·per·ing** \-(ə-)riŋ\ **1 a :** to sprinkle or season with or as if with pepper **b :** to shower with shot or other missiles **2 :** to hit with rapid repeated blows **3 :** to sprinkle as pepper is sprinkled — **pep·per·er** \-ər-ər\ *n*

pepper-and-salt \ˌpep-ər(-ə)n-ˈsȯlt\ *adj* **:** having black and white or dark and light color intermingled in small flecks

pep·per·box \ˈpep-ər-ˌbäks\ *n* **1 :** a small box or bottle with a perforated top used for sprinkling ground pepper on food **2 :** something resembling a pepperbox

pep·per·corn \-ˌkȯ(ə)rn\ *n* **1 :** a dried berry of the black pepper **2 :** a trifling or nominal return by way of acknowledgment

pep·per·grass \-ˌgras\ *n* **:** any of a genus (*Lepidium*) of cresses; *esp* **:** GARDEN CRESS

pep·per·mint \-ˌmint, -mənt; ˈpep-mənt, -ᵊm-ənt\ *n* **1 a :** a pungent and aromatic mint (*Mentha piperita*) with dark green lanceolate leaves and whorls of small pink flowers in spikes **b :** any of several related mints (as *M. arvensis*) **2 :** candy flavored with peppermint

pepper pot *n* **1 :** PEPPERBOX **2 a :** a stew of vegetables, meat or fish, and various condiments common in the West Indies **b :** a thick soup of tripe, meat, dumplings, and vegetables highly seasoned esp. with crushed peppercorns

pep·per·tree \ˈpep-ər-ˌtrē\ *n* **:** a Peruvian evergreen tree (*Schinus molle*) of the sumac family grown as a shade tree in mild regions

pep·pery \ˈpep-(ə-)rē\ *adj* **1 :** of, relating to, or having the qualities of pepper **:** HOT, PUNGENT **2 :** having a hot temper **:** TOUCHY **3 :** FIERY, STINGING

pep·pi·ness \ˈpep-ē-nəs\ *n* **:** the quality or state of being peppy

pep·py \ˈpep-ē\ *adj* **:** full of pep

pep·sin \ˈpep-sən\ *n* [G, fr. Gk *pepsis* digestion, fr. *pessein*] **1 :** a proteinase of the stomach that digests most proteins to polypeptides **2 :** a preparation containing pepsin from the stomach esp. of the hog and used esp. as a digestive

pep·sin·o·gen \pep-ˈsin-ə-jən\ *n* [ISV *pepsin* + *-o-* + *-gen*] **:** a granular zymogen of the gastric glands readily converted into pepsin in a slightly acid medium

pep·tic \ˈpep-tik\ *adj* [L *pepticus*, fr. Gk *peptikos*, fr. *peptos* cooked, fr. *peptein, pessein* to cook, digest — more at COOK] **1 :** relating to or promoting digestion **:** DIGESTIVE **2 :** of, relating to, producing, or caused by pepsin ⟨~ digestion⟩ **3 :** connected with or resulting from the action of digestive juices ⟨a ~ ulcer⟩

pep·ti·dase \ˈpep-tə-ˌdās, -ˌdāz\ *n* **:** an enzyme that hydrolyzes simple peptides or their derivatives

pep·tide \ˈpep-ˌtīd\ *n* [ISV, fr. *peptone*] **:** any of various amides derived from two or more amino acids by combination of the amino group of one acid with the carboxyl group of another and usu. obtained by partial hydrolysis of proteins

pep·tize \-ˌtīz\ *vt* [prob. fr. Gk *peptein*] **:** to bring into colloidal solution; *also* **:** to convert into a sol — **pep·tiz·er** *n*

pep·tone \-ˌtōn\ *n* [G *pepton*, fr. Gk, neut. of *peptos*] **:** any of various water-soluble products of partial hydrolysis of proteins

pep·to·nize \ˈpep-tə-ˌnīz\ *vt* **1 :** to convert into peptone; *esp* **:** to digest or dissolve by a proteolytic enzyme **2 :** to combine with peptone

Pe·quot \ˈpē-ˌkwät\ *n* [prob. modif. of Narraganset *paquatanog* destroyers] **:** a member of an Algonquian people of southeastern Connecticut

per \(ˈ)pər\ *prep* [L, through, by means of, by — more at FOR] **1 :** by the means or agency of **:** THROUGH ⟨~ bearer⟩ **2 :** with respect to every member of a specified group **:** for each **3 :** as indicated by **:** according to ⟨~ list price⟩

per- *prefix* [L, through, throughout, thoroughly, to destruction, fr. *per*] **1 :** throughout **:** thoroughly ⟨*per*chlorinate⟩ **2 a :** containing the largest possible or a relatively large proportion of a (specified) chemical element ⟨*per*chloride⟩ **b :** containing an element in its highest or a high oxidation state ⟨*per*chloric acid⟩

per·ac·id \ˈpər-ˌas-əd\ *n* [ISV] **:** an acid containing a large proportion of oxygen as compared with the acid from which it is named

[1]**per·ad·ven·ture** \ˈpər-əd-ˌven-chər, ˈper-; ˌpər-əd-ˈ, ˌper-\ *adv* [ME *per aventure*, fr. OF, by chance] *archaic* **:** PERHAPS, POSSIBLY

[2]**peradventure** *n* **:** DOUBT, CHANCE

per·am·bu·late \pə-ˈram-byə-ˌlāt\ *vb* [L *perambulatus*, pp. of *perambulare*, fr. *per-* through + *ambulare* to walk — more at AMBLE] *vt* **1 :** to travel over or through esp. on foot **:** TRAVERSE **2 :** to make an official inspection of (a boundary) on foot ~ *vi* **:** STROLL, RAMBLE — **per·am·bu·la·tion** \-ˌram-byə-ˈlā-shən\ *n*

per·am·bu·la·tor \pə-ˈram-byə-ˌlāt-ər\ *n* **1 :** one that perambulates **2** *chiefly Brit* **:** a baby carriage — **per·am·bu·la·to·ry** \-lə-ˌtōr-ē, -ˌtȯr-\ *adj*

per an·num \(ˌ)pər-ˈan-əm\ *adv* [ML] **:** in or for each year **:** ANNUALLY

per·bo·rate \(ˈ)pər-ˈbō(ə)r-ˌāt, -ˈbȯ(ə)r-\ *n* [ISV] **:** a salt that is a compound of a borate with hydrogen peroxide

per·cale \(ˌ)pər-ˈkā(ə)l, ˈpər-ˌ; (ˌ)pər-ˈkal\ *n* [Per *pargālah*] **:** a fine closely woven cotton cloth variously finished for clothing, sheeting, and industrial uses

per·ca·line \ˌpər-kə-ˈlēn\ *n* [F, fr. *percale*] **:** a lightweight cotton fabric; *esp* **:** a glossy fabric used for bookbindings

per cap·i·ta \(ˌ)pər-ˈkap-ət-ə\ *adv (or adj)* [ML, by heads] **1 :** per unit of population **:** by or for each person **2 :** equally to each individual

per·ceiv·able \pər-ˈsē-və-bəl\ *adj* **:** PERCEPTIBLE, INTELLIGIBLE — **per·ceiv·ably** \-blē\ *adv*

per·ceive \pər-ˈsēv\ *vt* [ME *perceiven*, fr. OF *perceivre*, fr. L *percipere*, fr. *per-* thoroughly + *capere* to take — more at PER-, HEAVE] **1 :** to attain awareness or understanding of **2 :** to become aware of through the senses; *esp* **:** SEE, OBSERVE — **per·ceiv·er** *n*

[1]**per·cent** \pər-ˈsent\ *adv* [earlier *per cent*, fr. *per* + L *centum* hundred — more at HUNDRED] **:** in the hundred **:** of each hundred

[2]**percent** *n, pl* **percent** *or* **percents 1** *pl* **percent a :** one part in a hundred **:** HUNDREDTH **b :** PERCENTAGE **2** *percents pl, Brit* **:** securities bearing a specified rate of interest

[3]**percent** *adj* **1 :** reckoned on the basis of a whole divided into one hundred parts **2 :** paying interest at a specified percent

per·cent·age \pər-ˈsent-ij\ *n* **1 :** a part of a whole expressed in hundredths **2 a :** a share of winnings or profits **b :** ADVANTAGE, PROFIT **3 :** an indeterminate part **:** PROPORTION **4 a :** PROBABILITY **b :** favorable odds

per·cen·tile \pər-ˈsen-ˌtīl\ *n* [prob. fr. *percent* + *-ile* (as in *quartile*, n.)] **:** a value on a scale of one hundred that indicates the percent of a distribution that is equal to or below it ⟨a ~ score of 95 is a score equal to or better than 95 percent of the scores⟩

per cen·tum \pər-ˈsent-əm\ *n* [*per* + L *centum*] **:** PERCENT

per·cept \ˈpər-ˌsept\ *n* [back-formation fr. *perception*] **:** an impression of an object obtained by use of the senses

per·cep·ti·bil·i·ty \pər-ˌsep-tə-ˈbil-ət-ē\ *n* **:** capability of being perceived

per·cep·ti·ble \pər-ˈsep-tə-bəl\ *adj* **:** capable of being perceived — **per·cep·ti·bly** \-blē\ *adv*

syn PERCEPTIBLE, SENSIBLE, PALPABLE, TANGIBLE, APPRECIABLE, PONDERABLE mean apprehensible as real or existent. PERCEPTIBLE applies to what can be discerned by the senses to the smallest extent; SENSIBLE to what is clearly though not markedly seen, heard, smelled, sometimes in contrast to what is discerned only by the intellect; PALPABLE applies either to what has physical substance or to what is obvious and unmistakable; TANGIBLE suggests what is capable of being handled or grasped both physically and mentally; APPRECIABLE applies to what is distinctly discernible by the senses or definitely measurable; PONDERABLE

suggests having definitely measurable weight or importance esp. as distinguished from eluding such determination

per·cep·tion \pər-'sep-shən\ *n* [L *perception-, perceptio* act of perceiving, fr. *perceptus*, pp. of *percipere*] **1** *obs* **:** CONSCIOUSNESS **2 a :** a result of perceiving **:** OBSERVATION **b :** a mental image **:** CONCEPT **3 a :** awareness of the elements of environment through physical sensation ⟨color ~⟩ **b :** physical sensation interpreted in the light of experience **4 a :** direct or intuitive cognition **:** INSIGHT **b :** a capacity for comprehension **syn** see DISCERNMENT — **per·cep·tion·al** \-shnəl, -shən-ᵊl\ *adj*

per·cep·tive \pər-'sep-tiv\ *adj* **1 :** responsive to sensory stimulus **:** DISCERNING **2 a :** capable of or exhibiting keen perception **:** OBSERVANT **b :** characterized by sympathetic understanding or insight — **per·cep·tive·ly** *adv* — **per·cep·tive·ness** *n* — **per·cep·tiv·i·ty** \(,)pər-,sep-'tiv-ət-ē\ *n*

per·cep·tu·al \(,)pər-'sep-chə(-wə)l, -'sepsh-wəl\ *adj* [L *perceptus*] **:** of, relating to, or involving sensory stimulus as opposed to abstract concept — **per·cep·tu·al·ly** \-ē\ *adv*

1**perch** \'pərch\ *n* [ME *perche*, fr. OF, fr. L *pertica* pole] **1 :** the main shaft connecting the front and rear axles of a coach or other vehicle **2 :** a bar or peg on which something is hung **3 a :** a roost for a bird **b :** a resting place or vantage point **:** SEAT **c :** EMINENCE **4 a** *chiefly Brit* **:** ROD 2 **b :** any of various units of measure for stonework

2**perch** *vt* **:** to place on a perch, a height, or precarious spot ⟨~*ed* himself on the table⟩ **~** *vi* **:** to alight, settle, or rest often uneasily or precariously on a perch

3**perch** *n, pl* **perch** *or* **perch·es** [ME *perche*, fr. MF, fr. L *perca*, fr. Gk *perkē*; akin to OHG *faro* colored, L *porcus*, a spiny fish] **1 a :** a small European freshwater spiny-finned fish (*Perca fluviatilis*) **b :** a closely related American fish (*P. flavescens*) **2 :** any of numerous teleost fishes (as of the families Percidae, Centrarchidae, Serranidae)

per·chance \pər-'chan(t)s\ *adv* [ME *per chance*, fr. MF, by chance] **:** PERHAPS, POSSIBLY

Per·che·ron \'pər-chə-,rän, -shə-\ *n* [F] **:** any of a breed of powerful rugged draft horses from the Perche region of France

per·chlo·rate \(')pər-'klō(ə)r-,āt, -'klȯ(ə)r-, -ət\ *n* [ISV] **:** a salt or ester of perchloric acid

per·chlo·ric acid \(,)pər-,klōr-ik-, -,klȯr-\ *n* **:** a fuming corrosive strong acid $HClO_4$ that is the highest oxygen acid of chlorine and a powerful oxidizing agent when heated

per·cip·i·ence \pər-'sip-ē-ən(t)s\ *n* **:** PERCEPTION

per·cip·i·ent \-ənt\ *adj* [L *percipient-, percipiens*, prp. of *percipere* to perceive] **:** capable of or characterized by perception **:** DISCERNING — **percipient** *n*

Per·ci·vale \'pər-sə-vəl, -,vāl\ *n* **:** an Arthurian knight who wins a sight of the Holy Grail

per·coid \'pər-,kȯid\ *also* **per·coi·de·an** \,pər-'kȯid-ē-ən\ *adj* [deriv. of L *perca* perch] **:** of or relating to a very large suborder (Percoidea) of spiny-finned fishes including the true perches, sunfishes, sea basses, and sea breams — **percoid** *n*

per·co·late \'pər-kə-,lāt, *nonstand* -kyə-\ *vb* [L *percolatus*, pp. of *percolare*, fr. *per-* through + *colare* to sieve — more at PER-, COLANDER] *vt* **1 a :** to cause to pass through a permeable substance (as a powdered drug) esp. for extracting a soluble constituent **:** FILTER **b :** to prepare (coffee) in a percolator **2 :** to be diffused through **:** PENETRATE **~** *vi* **1 :** to ooze or trickle through a permeable substance **:** SEEP **2 a :** to become percolated **b :** to become lively or effervescent **3 :** to become diffused — **per·co·la·tion** \,pər-kə-'lā-shən\ *n*

per·co·la·tor \'pər-kə-,lāt-ər, *nonstand* -kyə-\ *n* **:** one that percolates; *specif* **:** a coffeepot in which boiling water rising through a tube is repeatedly deflected downward through a perforated basket containing ground coffee beans to extract their essence

per con·tra \(,)pər-'kän-trə, -'kōn-(,)trä\ *adv* [It, by the opposite side (of the ledger)] **1 a :** on the contrary **b :** by way of contrast **2 :** as an offset

per·cuss \pər-'kəs\ *vt* [L *percussus*] **:** to tap sharply; *esp* **:** to practice percussion on

per·cus·sion \pər-'kəsh-ən\ *n* [L *percussion-, percussio*, fr. *percussus*, pp. of *percutere* to beat, fr. *per-* thoroughly + *quatere* to shake — more at PER-, QUASH] **1 :** the act of percussing: as **a :** the striking of a percussion cap so as to set off the charge in a firearm **b :** the beating or striking of a musical instrument **c :** the act or technique of tapping the surface of a body part to learn the condition of the parts beneath by the resultant sound **2 :** the striking of sound on the ear **3 :** percussion instruments esp. as forming a section of a band or orchestra

percussion cap *n* **:** CAP 6

percussion instrument *n* **:** a musical instrument sounded by striking

per·cus·sion·ist \pər-'kəsh-(ə-)nəst\ *n* **:** one skilled in the playing of percussion instruments

percussion lock *n* **:** the lock of a gun fired by percussion

per·cus·sive \pər-'kəs-iv\ *adj* **:** of or relating to percussion; *esp* **:** operative or operated by striking — **per·cus·sive·ly** *adv* — **per·cus·sive·ness** *n*

per·cu·ta·ne·ous \,pər-kyu̇-'tā-nē-əs\ *adj* **:** effected or performed through the skin — **per·cu·ta·ne·ous·ly** *adv*

per·die \(,)pər-'dē\ *var of* PARDIE

per di·em \(,)pər-'dē-əm\ *adv* [ML] **:** by the day **:** for each day — **per diem** *adj or n*

per·di·tion \pər-'dish-ən\ *n* [ME *perdicion*, fr. LL *perdition-, perditio*, fr. L *perditus*, pp. of *perdere* to destroy, fr. *per-* to destruction + *dare* to give — more at PER-, DATE] **1 a** *archaic* **:** utter destruction **b** *obs* **:** LOSS **2 a :** eternal damnation **b :** HELL

1**per·du** *or* **per·due** \pər-'d(y)ü\ *adj* [MF *perdu*, masc., & *perdue*, fem., fr. pp. of *perdre* to lose, fr. L *perdere*] **:** remaining out of sight **:** CONCEALED

2**per·du** *or* **per·due** \'pər-(,)d(y)ü, (,)pər-'\ *n, obs* **:** a soldier assigned to extremely hazardous duty

per·du·ra·bil·i·ty \(,)pər-,d(y)u̇r-ə-'bil-ət-ē\ *n* **:** the quality or state of being perdurable **:** PERSISTENCE, PERMANENCE

per·du·ra·ble \(,)pər-'d(y)u̇r-ə-bəl, *archaic* 'pər-dyə-rə-, 'pər-jə-rə-\ *adj* [ME, fr. OF, fr. LL *perdurabilis*, fr. L *perdurare* to endure, fr. *per-* throughout + *durare* to last — more at DURING] **:** very durable — **per·du·ra·bly** \-blē\ *adv*

per·e·gri·nate \'per-ə-grə-,nāt\ *vi* **:** to travel esp. on foot **:** WALK **~** *vt* **:** to walk or travel over **:** TRAVERSE — **per·e·gri·na·tion** \,per-ə-grə-'nā-shən\ *n*

1**per·e·grine** \'per-ə-grən, -,grēn, -,grīn\ *adj* [ML *peregrinus*, fr. L, foreign — more at PILGRIM] **:** having a tendency to wander

2**peregrine** *n* **:** a swift nearly cosmopolitan falcon (*Falco peregrinus*) much used in falconry

pe·remp·to·ri·ly \pə-'rem(p)-t(ə-)rə-lē; -,rem(p)-'tōr-ə-, -'tȯr-\ *adv* **:** in a peremptory manner

pe·remp·to·ri·ness \pə-'rem(p)-t(ə-)rē-nəs\ *n* **:** the quality or state of being peremptory

pe·remp·to·ry \pə-'rem(p)-t(ə-)rē\ *adj* [LL & L; LL *peremptorius*, fr. L, destructive, fr. *peremptus*, pp. of *perimere* to take entirely, destroy, fr. *per-* to destruction + *emere* to take — more at REDEEM] **1 a :** putting an end to or precluding a right of action, debate, or delay **b :** ABSOLUTE, FINAL **2 :** expressive of urgency or command **:** IMPERATIVE ⟨~ tone⟩ **3 a :** marked by self-assurance **:** POSITIVE **b :** DECISIVE **4 :** HAUGHTY, DICTATORIAL **syn** see MASTERFUL

per·en·nate \'per-ə-,nāt\ *vi* [L *perennatus*, pp. of *perennare*, fr. *perennis*] **:** to live over from season to season — **per·en·na·tion** \,per-ə-'nā-shən\ *n*

pe·ren·ni·al \pə-'ren-ē-əl\ *adj* [L *perennis*, fr. *per-* throughout + *annus* year — more at PER-, ANNUAL] **1 :** present at all seasons of the year **2 :** persisting for several years usu. with new growth from a perennating part **3 a :** PERSISTENT, ENDURING **b :** continuing without interruption **:** CONSTANT **c :** regularly repeated **:** RECURRENT **syn** see CONTINUAL — **perennial** *n* — **pe·ren·ni·al·ly** \-ē-ə-lē\ *adv*

1**per·fect** \'pər-fikt\ *adj* [ME *parfit*, fr. OF, fr. L *perfectus*, fr. pp. of *perficere* to carry out, perfect, fr. *per-* thoroughly + *facere* to make, do — more at DO] **1 :** EXPERT, PROFICIENT **2 a :** being entirely without fault or defect **:** FLAWLESS **b :** satisfying all requirements **:** ACCURATE **c :** corresponding to an ideal standard **d :** faithfully reproducing the original; *specif* **:** LETTER-PERFECT **e :** legally valid **3 a :** PURE, TOTAL **b :** lacking in no essential detail **:** COMPLETE **c** *obs* **:** SANE **d :** ABSOLUTE, UNEQUIVOCAL **e :** of an extreme kind **:** UNMITIGATED **4** *obs* **:** MATURE **5 :** of, relating to, or constituting a verb form or verbal that expresses an action or state completed at the time of speaking or at a time spoken of **6** *obs* **a :** CERTAIN, SURE **b :** SATISFIED, CONTENT **7** *of an interval* **:** belonging to the consonances unison, fourth, fifth, and octave which retain their character when inverted and when raised or lowered by a half step become augmented or diminished **8 a :** sexually mature and fully differentiated **b :** MONOCLINOUS — **per·fect·ness** \-fik(t)-nəs\ *n*

syn WHOLE, ENTIRE, INTACT: PERFECT implies the soundness and the excellence of every part, element, or quality of a thing frequently as an unattainable or theoretical state; WHOLE suggests a completeness or perfection that can be sought, gained, or regained; ENTIRE implies perfection deriving from integrity, soundness, or completeness of a thing; INTACT implies retention of perfection of a thing in its natural or original state

2**per·fect** \pər-'fekt *also* 'pər-fikt\ *vt* **1 :** to make perfect **:** IMPROVE, REFINE **2 :** to bring to final form **:** COMPLETE — **per·fect·er** *n*

3**per·fect** \'pər-fikt\ *n* **:** the perfect tense of a language; *also* **:** a verb form in the perfect tense

perfect flower *n* **:** a monoclinous flower

per·fect·ibil·i·ty \pər-,fek-tə-'bil-ət-ē *also* ,pər-fik-\ *n* **:** a capacity for improvement esp. in moral qualities

per·fect·ible \pər-'fek-tə-bəl *also* 'pər-fik-\ *adj* **:** capable of improvement or perfection

per·fec·tion \pər-'fek-shən\ *n* **1 :** the quality or state of being perfect: as **a :** FLAWLESSNESS **b :** COMPLETENESS **c :** MATURITY **d :** SAINTLINESS **2 a :** an exemplification of supreme excellence **b :** an unsurpassable degree of accuracy or excellence **3 :** the act or process of perfecting

per·fec·tion·ism \-shə-,niz-əm\ *n* **1 a :** the doctrine that the perfection of moral character constitutes man's highest good **b :** the theological doctrine that a state of freedom from sin is attainable in the earthly life **2 :** a disposition to regard anything short of perfection as unacceptable — **per·fec·tion·ist** \-sh(ə-)nəst\ *n or adj*

per·fec·tive \pər-'fek-tiv *also* 'pər-fik-\ *adj* **1** *archaic* **a :** tending to make perfect **b :** becoming better **2 :** expressing action as complete or as implying the notion of completion, conclusion, or result ⟨~ verb⟩ — **perfective** *n* — **per·fec·tive·ly** *adv* — **per·fec·tive·ness** *n* — **per·fec·tiv·i·ty** \pər-,fek-'tiv-ət-ē *also* ,pər-fik-\ *n*

per·fect·ly \'pər-fik-(t)lē\ *adv* **1 :** in a perfect manner **2 :** to an adequate extent **:** QUITE

per·fec·to \pər-'fek-(,)tō\ *n* [Sp, perfect, fr. L *perfectus*] **:** a cigar that is thick in the middle and tapers almost to a point at each end

perfect participle *n* **:** PAST PARTICIPLE

perfect square *n* **:** an integer whose square root is an integer ⟨9 is a *perfect square* because it is the square of 3⟩

perfect year *n* **:** a common year of 355 days or a leap year of 385 days in the Jewish calendar

per·fer·vid \,pər-'fər-vəd, 'pər-\ *adj* [NL *perfervidus*, fr. L *per-* thoroughly + *fervidus* fervid] **:** extremely fervent **syn** see IMPASSIONED

per·fid·i·ous \(,)pər-'fid-ē-əs\ *adj* **:** of, relating to, or characterized by perfidy **syn** see FAITHLESS — **per·fid·i·ous·ly** *adv* — **per·fid·i·ous·ness** *n*

per·fi·dy \'pər-fəd-ē\ *n* [L *perfidia*, fr. *perfidus* faithless, fr. *per fidem decipere* to betray, lit., to deceive by trust] **:** the quality or state of being faithless or disloyal **:** TREACHERY

per·fo·li·ate \,pər-'fō-lē-ət, 'pər-\ *adj* [NL *perfoliata*, an herb having leaves pierced by the stem, fr. L *per* through + *foliata*, fem of *foliatus* foliate] **1 :** having the basal part naturally united around the stem **2 :** having the terminal joints expanded into flattened plates and encircling the stalk which connects them ⟨~ antenna of a beetle⟩ — **per·fo·li·a·tion** \,pər-,fō-lē-'ā-shən\ *n*

per·fo·rate \'pər-fə-,rāt\ *vb* [L *perforatus*, pp. of *perforare* to bore through, fr. *per-* through + *forare* to bore — more at BORE] *vt* **1 :** to make a hole through; *specif* **:** to make a line of holes in to facilitate separation **2 :** to pass through or into by or as if by making a hole **~** *vi* **:** to penetrate a surface — **per·fo·rate** \'pər-f(ə-)rət, -fə-,rāt\ *adj* — **per·fo·ra·tor** \-fə-,rāt-ər\ *n*

per·fo·ra·tion \,pər-fə-'rā-shən\ *n* **1 :** the act or process of perforating **2 a :** a hole or pattern made by or as if by piercing or boring **b :** one of the series of holes made between rows of postage stamps in a sheet

per·force \pər-ˈfō(ə)rs, -ˈfȯ(ə)rs\ *adv* [ME *par force*, fr. MF, by force] **1** *obs* **:** FORCIBLY **2 :** by force of circumstances

per·form \pə(r)-ˈfȯ(ə)rm\ *vb* [ME *performen*, fr. AF *performer*, alter. of OF *perfournir*, fr. *per-* thoroughly (fr. L) + *fournir* to complete — more at FURNISH] *vt* **1 :** to adhere to the terms of **:** FULFILL **2 :** to carry out **:** DO **3 a :** to do in a formal manner or according to prescribed ritual **b :** to give a rendition of **:** PRESENT ~ *vi* **1 :** to carry out an action or pattern of behavior **:** ACT, FUNCTION **2 :** to give a performance **:** PLAY — **per·form·able** \-ˈfȯr-mə-bəl\ *adj* — **per·form·er** *n*

syn EXECUTE, DISCHARGE, ACCOMPLISH, ACHIEVE, EFFECT, FULFILL: PERFORM implies action that follows established patterns or procedures or fulfills agreed-upon requirements and often connotes special skill; EXECUTE stresses the carrying out of what exists in plan or in intent; DISCHARGE implies execution and completion of appointed duties or tasks; ACCOMPLISH stresses the successful completion of a process rather than the means of carrying it out; ACHIEVE adds to ACCOMPLISH the implication of conquered difficulties; EFFECT adds to ACHIEVE an emphasis on the inherent force in the agent capable of surmounting obstacles; FULFILL implies a complete realization of ends or possibilities

per·for·mance \pə(r)-ˈfȯr-mən(t)s\ *n* **1 a :** the execution of an action **b :** something accomplished **:** DEED, FEAT **2 :** the fulfillment of a claim, promise, or request **:** IMPLEMENTATION **3 a :** the action of representing a character in a play **b :** a public presentation or exhibition **4 a :** the ability to perform **:** EFFICIENCY **b :** the manner in which a mechanism performs **5 :** the manner of reacting to stimuli **:** BEHAVIOR — **per·for·ma·to·ry** \-mə-ˌtōr-ē, -ˌtȯr-\ *adj*

per·form·ing *adj* **:** of, relating to, or constituting an art that involves public performance

[1]**per·fume** \ˈpər-ˌfyüm, (ˌ)pər-ˈ\ *n* [MF *perfum*, prob. fr. OProv, fr. *perfumar* to perfume, fr. *per-* thoroughly (fr. L) + *fumar* to smoke, fr. L *fumare* — more at FUME] **1 :** the scent of something sweet-smelling **2 :** a substance that emits a pleasant odor; *esp* **:** a fluid preparation of floral essences or synthetics and a fixative used for scenting **syn** see FRAGRANCE

[2]**per·fume** \(ˌ)pər-ˈfyüm, ˈpər-ˌ\ *vt* **:** to fill or imbue with an odor

per·fum·er \pə(r)-ˈfyü-mər\ *n* **:** one that makes or sells perfumes

per·fum·ery \pə(r)-ˈfyüm-(ə-)rē\ *n* **1 a :** the art or process of making perfume **b :** the products made by a perfumer **2 :** a perfume establishment

per·func·to·ri·ly \pər-ˈfəŋ(k)-t(ə-)rə-lē; (ˌ)pər-ˌfəŋ(k)-ˈtōr-ə-, -ˈtȯr-\ *adv* **:** in a perfunctory manner

per·func·to·ri·ness \pər-ˈfəŋ(k)-t(ə-)rē-nəs\ *n* **:** the quality or state of being perfunctory

per·func·to·ry \pər-ˈfəŋ(k)-t(ə-)rē\ *adj* [LL *perfunctorius*, fr. L *perfunctus*, pp. of *perfungi* to accomplish, get through with, fr. *per-* through + *fungi* to perform — more at PER-, FUNCTION] **1 :** characterized by routine or superficiality **:** MECHANICAL **2 :** lacking in interest or enthusiasm **:** APATHETIC

per·fuse \pər-ˈfyüz\ *vt* [L *perfusus*, pp. of *perfundere* to pour over, fr. *per-* through + *fundere* to pour — more at FOUND] **1 :** SUFFUSE **2 a :** to cause to flow or spread **:** DIFFUSE **b :** to force a fluid through (an organ or tissue) esp. by way of the blood vessels — **per·fu·sion** \-ˈfyü-zhən\ *n* — **per·fu·sive** \-ˈfyü-siv, -ziv\ *adj*

per·go·la \ˈpər-gə-lə, pər-ˈgō-\ *n* [It, fr. L *pergula* projecting roof] **1 :** ARBOR, TRELLIS **2 :** a structure usu. consisting of parallel colonnades supporting an open roof of girders and cross rafters

[1]**per·haps** \pər-ˈ(h)aps, ˈpraps\ *adv* [*per* + *hap*] **:** possibly but not certainly **:** MAYBE

[2]**perhaps** *n* **:** something open to doubt or conjecture

pe·ri \ˈpi(ə)r-ē\ *n* [Per *perī* fairy, genius, modif. of Av *pairikā* witch; akin to L *paelex* concubine] **1 :** a supernatural being in Persian folklore descended from fallen angels and excluded from paradise until penance is accomplished **2 :** a beautiful and graceful girl or woman

peri- *prefix* [L, fr. Gk, around, in excess, fr. *peri;* akin to Gk *peran* to pass through — more at FARE] **1 :** all around **:** about ⟨*peri*scope⟩ **2 :** near ⟨*peri*helion⟩ **3 :** enclosing **:** surrounding ⟨*peri*neurium⟩

peri·anth \ˈper-ē-ˌan(t)th\ *n, pl* **perianths** \-ˌan(t)s, -ˌan(t)ths\ [NL *perianthium*, fr. *peri-* + Gk *anthos* flower — more at ANTHOLOGY] **:** the external envelope of a flower esp. when not differentiated into calyx and corolla

peri·apt \ˈper-ē-ˌapt\ *n* [MF or Gk; MF *periapte*, fr. Gk *periapton*, fr. *periaptein* to fasten around (oneself), fr. *peri-* + *haptein* to fasten] **:** AMULET

peri·car·di·al \ˌper-ə-ˈkärd-ē-əl\ *also* **peri·car·di·ac** \-ē-ˌak\ *adj* **:** of, relating to, or affecting the pericardium; *also* **:** situated around the heart

peri·car·di·tis \-ˌkär-ˈdīt-əs\ *n* **:** inflammation of the pericardium

peri·car·di·um \ˌper-ə-ˈkärd-ē-əm\ *n, pl* **peri·car·dia** \-ē-ə\ [NL, fr. Gk *perikardion*, neut. of *perikardios* around the heart, fr. *peri-* + *kardia* heart — more at HEART] **:** the conical sac of serous membrane that encloses the heart and the roots of the great blood vessels of vertebrates

peri·carp \ˈper-ə-ˌkärp\ *n* [NL *pericarpium*, fr. Gk *perikarpion* pod, fr. *peri-* + *-karpion* -carp] **:** the ripened and variously modified walls of a plant ovary — see ENDOCARP illustration — **peri·car·pi·al** \ˌper-ə-ˈkär-pē-əl\ *or* **peri·car·pic** \-pik\ *adj*

peri·chon·dri·al \ˌper-ə-ˈkän-drē-əl\ *also* **peri·chon·dral** \-drəl\ *adj* **:** of or relating to the perichondrium

peri·chon·dri·um \-drē-əm\ *n, pl* **peri·chon·dria** \-drē-ə\ [NL, fr. *peri-* + Gk *chondros* grain, cartilage] **:** the membrane of fibrous connective tissue investing a cartilage except at joints

Per·i·cle·an \ˌper-ə-ˈklē-ən\ *adj* **:** of or relating to Pericles or his age

peri·cline \ˈper-ə-ˌklīn\ *n* [Gk *periklinēs* sloping on all sides, fr. *peri-* + *klinein* to lean — more at LEAN] **:** an albite occurring in white opaque crystals elongated

pe·ric·o·pe \pə-ˈrik-ə-pē\ *n* [LL, fr. Gk *perikopē* section, fr. *peri-* + *kopē* act of cutting; akin to Gk *koptein* to cut — more at CAPON] **:** a selection from a book; *specif* **:** LECTION 1

peri·cra·ni·al \ˌper-ə-ˈkrā-nē-əl\ *adj* **:** of or relating to the pericranium

peri·cra·ni·um \-nē-əm\ *n, pl* **peri·cra·nia** \-nē-ə\ [NL, fr. Gk *perikranion*, neut. of *perikranios* around the skull, fr. *peri-* + *kranion* skull] **:** the external periosteum of the skull

peri·cy·cle \ˈper-ə-ˌsī-kəl\ *n* [F *péricycle*, fr. Gk *perikyklos* spherical, fr. *peri-* + *kyklos* circle — more at WHEEL] **:** a thin layer of parenchymatous or sclerenchymatous cells surrounding the stele in most vascular plants — **peri·cy·clic** \ˌper-ə-ˈsī-klik, -ˈsik-lik\ *adj*

peri·cyn·thi·on \ˌper-ə-ˈsin(t)-thē-ən\ *n* [NL, fr. *peri-* + *Cynthia*] **:** PERILUNE

peri·derm \ˈper-ə-ˌdərm\ *n* [NL *peridermis*, fr. *peri-* + *-dermis*] **:** an outer layer of tissue; *esp* **:** a cortical protective layer of many roots and stems — **peri·der·mal** \ˌper-ə-ˈdər-məl\ *or* **peri·der·mic** \-mik\ *adj*

pe·rid·i·um \pə-ˈrid-ē-əm\ *n, pl* **pe·rid·ia** \-ē-ə\ [NL, fr. Gk *pēridion*, dim. of *pēra* leather bag] **:** the outer envelope of the sporophore of many fungi

per·i·dot \ˈper-ə-ˌdō(t), -ˌdät\ *n* [F *péridot*] **:** a deep yellowish green transparent olivine used as a gem — **per·i·do·tic** \ˌper-ə-ˈdōt-ik, -ˈdät-\ *adj*

pe·ri·do·tite \pə-ˈrid-ə-ˌtīt; ˈper-ə-ˌdōt-ˌīt, -ˌdät-\ *n* [F *péridotite*, fr. *péridot*] **:** any of a group of granitoid igneous rocks composed of olivine and usu. other ferromagnesian minerals — **pe·ri·do·tit·ic** \pə-ˌrid-ə-ˈtit-ik, ˌper-əd-ə-\ *adj*

peri·ge·an \ˌper-ə-ˈjē-ən\ *adj* **:** of or relating to perigee

peri·gee \ˈper-ə-(ˌ)jē\ *n* [MF & NL; MF, fr. NL *perigeum*, fr. Gk *perigeion*, fr. neut. of *perigeios* near the earth, fr. *peri-* + *gē* earth] **:** the point in the orbit of a satellite of the earth that is nearest to the earth

pe·rig·y·nous \pə-ˈrij-ə-nəs\ *adj* [NL *perigynus*, fr. *peri-* + *-gynus* -gynous] **:** borne on a ring or cup of the receptacle surrounding a pistil ⟨~ petals⟩; *also* **:** having perigynous stamens and petals ⟨~ flowers⟩ — **pe·rig·y·ny** \-nē\ *n*

peri·he·lial \ˌper-ə-ˈhēl-yəl\ *adj* **:** of or relating to perihelion

peri·he·lion \-ˈhēl-yən\ *n* [NL, fr. *peri-* + Gk *hēlios* sun — more at SOLAR] **:** the point in the path of a planet or other celestial body that is nearest to the sun

[1]**per·il** \ˈper-əl\ *n* [ME, fr. OF, fr. L *periculum* — more at FEAR] **1 :** exposure to the risk of being injured, destroyed, or lost **:** DANGER **2 :** something that imperils **:** RISK

[2]**peril** *vt* **per·iled** *also* **per·illed; per·il·ing** *also* **per·il·ling :** to expose to danger **:** HAZARD

per·il·ous \ˈper-ə-ləs\ *adj* **:** full of or involving peril **:** HAZARDOUS **syn** see DANGEROUS — **per·il·ous·ly** *adv* — **per·il·ous·ness** *n*

peri·lune \ˈper-ə-ˌlün\ *n* [*peri-* + L *luna* moon — more at LUNAR] **:** the point in the path of a body orbiting the moon that is nearest to the center of the moon

pe·rim·e·ter \pə-ˈrim-ət-ər\ *n* [F *périmètre*, fr. L *perimetros*, fr. Gk, fr. *peri-* + *metron* measure — more at MEASURE] **1 a :** the boundary of a closed plane figure **b :** the length of this boundary **2 :** a line or strip bounding or protecting an area **3 :** outer limits **syn** see CIRCUMFERENCE — **peri·met·ric** \ˌper-ə-ˈme-trik\ *or* **peri·met·ri·cal** \-tri-kəl\ *adj* — **peri·met·ri·cal·ly** \-k(ə-)lē\ *adv* — **pe·rim·e·try** \pə-ˈrim-ə-trē\ *n*

peri·morph \ˈper-ə-ˌmȯrf\ *n* [ISV] **:** a crystal of one species enclosing one of another species

peri·my·si·um \ˌper-ə-ˈmiz(h)-ē-əm\ *n, pl* **peri·my·sia** \-ē-ə\ [NL, irreg. fr. *peri-* + Gk *mys* mouse, muscle — more at MOUSE] **:** the connective-tissue sheath that surrounds a muscle and forms sheaths for the bundles of muscle fibers

per·i·ne·al \ˌper-ə-ˈnē-əl\ *adj* **:** of or relating to the perineum

per·i·ne·um \-ˈnē-əm\ *n, pl* **per·i·nea** \-ˈnē-ə\ [NL, fr. LL *perinaion*, fr. Gk, fr. *peri-* + *inein* to empty out; akin to L *ira* ire] **:** an area of tissue marking externally the approximate boundary of the outlet of the pelvis and giving passage to the urinogenital ducts and rectum; *also* **:** the area between the anus and the posterior part of the external genitalia esp. in the female

peri·neu·ri·um \ˌper-ə-ˈn(y)u̇r-ē-əm\ *n, pl* **peri·neu·ria** \-ē-ə\ [NL fr. *peri-* + Gk *neuron* nerve — more at NERVE] **:** the connective-tissue sheath that surrounds a bundle of nerve fibers

[1]**pe·ri·od** \ˈpir-ē-əd\ *n* [ME *pariode*, fr. MF *periode*, fr. ML, L, & Gk; ML *periodus* period of time, punctuation mark, fr. L & Gk; L, rhetorical period, fr. Gk *periodos* circuit, period of time, rhetorical period, fr. *peri-* + *hodos* way — more at CEDE] **1 a** (1) **:** an utterance from one full stop to another **:** SENTENCE (2) **:** a well-proportioned sentence of several clauses (3) **:** PERIODIC SENTENCE **b :** a musical structure or melodic section usu. of 8 or 16 measures and of 2 or more contrasting or complementary phrases and ending with a cadence **2 a :** the full pause with which the utterance of a sentence closes **b :** END, STOP **3** *obs* **:** GOAL, PURPOSE **4 a :** a point . used to mark the end (as of a declarative sentence or an abbreviation) **b :** a rhythmical unit in Greek verse composed of a series of two or more cola **5 :** the completion of a cycle, a series of events, or a single action **:** CONCLUSION **6 a :** a portion of time determined by some recurring phenomenon **b :** the interval of time required for a cyclic motion or phenomenon to complete a cycle and begin to repeat itself **c :** a single cyclic occurrence of menstruation **7 a :** a chronological division **:** STAGE **b :** a division of geologic time longer than an epoch and included in an era **c :** a stage of culture having a definable place in time and space **8 a :** one of the divisions of the academic day **b :** one of the divisions of the playing time of a game

syn PERIOD, EPOCH, ERA, AGE mean a division of time. PERIOD may designate an extent of time of any length; EPOCH applies to a period begun or set off by some significant or striking quality, change, or series of events; ERA suggests a period of history marked by a new or distinct order of things; AGE is used frequently of a fairly definite period dominated by a prominent figure or feature

[2]**period** *adj* **:** of, relating to, or representing a particular historical period

pe·ri·od·ic \ˌpir-ē-ˈäd-ik\ *adj* **1 a :** occurring at regular intervals **b :** RECURRENT **2 :** consisting of or containing a series of repeated stages **:** CYCLIC ⟨~ decimals⟩ **3 :** of or relating to a period **4 :** expressed in or characterized by periodic sentences **syn** see INTERMITTENT

per·iod·ic acid \ˌpər-(ˌ)ī-ˌäd-ik-\ *n* [ISV *per-* + *iodic*] **:** any of the strongly oxidizing acids (as H_5IO_6 or HIO_4) that are the highest oxygen acids of iodine

[1]**pe·ri·od·i·cal** \ˌpir-ē-ˈäd-i-kəl\ *adj* **1 :** PERIODIC 1 **2 a :** published with a fixed interval between the issues or numbers **b :** published

in, characteristic of, or connected with a periodical — **pe·ri·od·i·cal·ly** \-k(ə-)lē\ adv

²periodical n : a periodical publication

pe·ri·od·ic·i·ty \ˌpir-ē-ə-ˈdis-ət-ē\ n : the quality, state, or fact of being regularly recurrent

periodic law n : a law in chemistry: the elements when arranged in the order of their atomic numbers show a periodic variation in most of their properties

periodic sentence n : a sentence that has no subordinate or trailing elements following full grammatical statement of the essential idea (as in "yesterday while I was walking down the street, I saw him")

periodic table n : an arrangement of chemical elements based on the periodic law

peri·odon·tal \ˌper-ē-ō-ˈdänt-ᵊl\ adj 1 : investing or surrounding a tooth 2 : of or affecting periodontal tissues or regions

peri·odon·tics \-ˈdänt-iks\ n pl but sing or pl in constr [NL periodontium, fr. peri- + Gk odont-, odous, odōn tooth — more at TOOTH] : a branch of dentistry dealing with diseases of the supporting structures of the teeth — **peri·odon·tist** \-ˈdänt-əst\ n

peri·onych·i·um \ˌper-ē-ō-ˈnik-ē-əm\ n, pl **peri·onych·ia** \-ˈnik-ē-ə\ [NL, fr. peri- + Gk onych-, onyx nail — more at NAIL] : the tissue bordering the root and sides of a fingernail or toenail

periost- or **perioste-** or **periosteo-** comb form [NL periosteum] : periosteum ⟨periosteomyelitis⟩ ⟨periosteoma⟩ ⟨periostitis⟩

peri·os·te·al \ˌper-ē-ˈäs-tē-əl\ adj 1 : situated around or produced external to bone 2 : of, relating to, or involving the periosteum

peri·os·te·um \-tē-əm\ n, pl **peri·os·tea** \-tē-ə\ [NL, fr. LL periosteon, fr. Gk., neut. of periosteos around the bone, fr. peri- + osteon bone — more at OSSEOUS] : the membrane of connective tissue that closely invests all bones except at the articular surfaces

peri·os·ti·tis \-ˌäs-ˈtīt-əs\ n [NL] : inflammation of the periosteum

peri·otic \ˌper-ē-ˈōt-ik\ adj : situated around the ear; specif : being, relating to, or composed of the typically three bony elements that surround the internal ear and form or help to form its capsule

¹peri·pa·tet·ic \ˌper-ə-pə-ˈtet-ik\ n 1 cap : ARISTOTELIAN 2 : PEDESTRIAN, ITINERANT 3 pl : movements or journeyings hither and thither

²peripatetic adj [MF & L; MF peripatetique, fr. L peripateticus, fr. Gk peripatētikos, fr. peripatein to walk up and down, discourse while pacing (as did Aristotle), fr. peri- + patein to tread; akin to Skt patha path — more at FIND] : ITINERANT — **peri·pa·tet·i·cal·ly** \-i-k(ə-)lē\ adv — **Peri·pa·tet·i·cism** \-ˈtet-ə-ˌsiz-əm\ n

peri·pe·teia \ˌper-ə-pə-ˈtē-(y)ə, -ˈtī-ə\ n [Gk, fr. peripiptein to fall around, change suddenly, fr. peri- + piptein to fall — more at FEATHER] : a sudden or unexpected reversal of circumstances or situation esp. in a literary work

pe·rip·e·ty \pə-ˈrip-ət-ē\ n : PERIPETEIA

pe·riph·er·ad \pə-ˈrif-ə-ˌrad\ adv : toward the periphery

pe·riph·er·al \pə-ˈrif-(ə-)rəl\ adj 1 : of, relating to, or forming a periphery 2 : located away from a center or central portion : EXTERNAL 3 : of, relating to, or involving the surface of the body — **pe·riph·er·al·ly** \-ē\ adv

pe·riph·ery \pə-ˈrif-(ə-)rē\ n [MF peripherie, fr. LL peripheria, fr. Gk periphereia, fr. peripherein to carry around, fr. peri- + pherein to carry — more at BEAR] 1 : the perimeter of a circle or other closed curve; also : the perimeter of a polygon 2 : the external boundary or surface of a body 3 a : the outward bounds of something as distinguished from its internal regions or center : CONFINES b : an area lying beyond the strict limits of a thing 4 : the regions in which nerves terminate **syn** see CIRCUMFERENCE

pe·riph·ra·sis \pə-ˈrif-rə-səs\ n, pl **pe·riph·ra·ses** \-rə-ˌsēz\ [L, fr. Gk, fr. periphrazein to express periphrastically, fr. peri- + phrazein to point out] 1 : use of a longer phrasing in place of a

possible shorter and plainer form of expression : CIRCUMLOCUTION 2 : an instance of periphrasis

peri·phras·tic \ˌper-ə-ˈfras-tik\ adj 1 : of, relating to, or characterized by periphrasis 2 : formed by the use of function words or auxiliaries instead of by inflection ⟨more fair is a ∼ comparative⟩ — **peri·phras·ti·cal·ly** \-ti-k(ə-)lē\ adv

pe·rique \pə-ˈrēk\ n [LaF périque] : a strong-flavored Louisiana tobacco used in smoking mixtures

peri·sarc \ˈper-ə-ˌsärk\ n [ISV peri- + Gk sark-, sarx flesh — more at SARCASM] : the outer usu. chitinous integument of a hydroid — **peri·sar·cal** \ˌper-ə-ˈsär-kəl\ or **peri·sar·cous** \-kəs\ adj

peri·scope \ˈper-ə-ˌskōp\ n [ISV] : a tubular optical instrument containing lenses and mirrors by which an observer obtains an otherwise obstructed field of view

peri·scop·ic \ˌper-ə-ˈskäp-ik\ adj 1 : viewing all around or on all sides ⟨∼ lens⟩ 2 : of or relating to a periscope

periscope

per·ish \ˈper-ish\ vb [ME perisshen, fr. OF periss-, stem of perir, fr. L perire, fr. per- to destruction + ire to go — more at PER-, ISSUE] vi 1 : to become destroyed or ruined : DIE 2 chiefly dial : DETERIORATE, SPOIL ∼ vt 1 chiefly dial : to cause to die : DESTROY 2 : WEAKEN, BENUMB

per·ish·abil·i·ty \ˌper-i-shə-ˈbil-ət-ē\ n : the quality or condition of being perishable

per·ish·able \ˈper-i-shə-bəl\ adj : liable to perish — **perishable** n

pe·ris·so·dac·tyl \pə-ˌris-ə-ˈdak-tᵊl\ adj [deriv. of MGk perissodaktylos having more than the usual number of fingers or toes, fr. Gk perissos more than normal (fr. peri in excess) + daktylos toe, finger — more at PERI-] 1 : having the toes in odd numbers or unevenly disposed in relation to the axis of the foot 2 : of or relating to an order (Perissodactyla) of perissodactyl ungulate mammals — **perissodactyl** n — **pe·ris·so·dac·ty·lous** \-tə-ləs\ adj

peri·stal·sis \ˌper-ə-ˈstȯl-səs, -ˈstal-\ n, pl **peri·stal·ses** \-ˌsēz\ [NL, fr. Gk peristaltikos peristaltic, fr. peristellein to wrap around, fr. peri- + stellein to place — more at STALL] : successive waves of involuntary contraction passing along the walls of the intestine or other hollow muscular structure and forcing the contents onward — **peri·stal·tic** \-ˈstȯl-tik, -ˈstal-\ adj — **peri·stal·ti·cal·ly** \-ti-k(ə-)lē\ adv

peri·stome \ˈper-ə-ˌstōm\ n [NL peristoma, fr. peri- + Gk stoma mouth — more at STOMACH] 1 : the fringe of teeth surrounding the orifice of a moss capsule 2 : the region around the mouth in various invertebrates — **peri·sto·mi·al** \ˌper-ə-ˈstō-mē-əl\ adj

peri·style \ˈper-ə-ˌstīl\ n [F péristyle, fr. L peristylum, fr. Gk peristylon, fr. neut. of peristylos surrounded by a colonnade, fr. peri- + stylos pillar — more at STEER] 1 : a colonnade surrounding a building or court 2 : an open space enclosed by a colonnade

peri·the·cial \ˌper-ə-ˈthē-sh(ē-)əl, -sē-əl\ adj : of, relating to, or being a perithecium ⟨∼ wall⟩

peri·the·ci·um \-ˈthē-s(h)ē-əm\ n, pl **peri·the·cia** \-s(h)ē-ə\ [NL, fr. peri- + Gk thēkion, dim. of thēkē case — more at TICK] : a spherical, cylindrical, or flask-shaped hollow fruiting body in various ascomycetous fungi that contains the asci and usu. opens by a terminal pore

periton- or **peritone-** or **peritoneo-** comb form [LL peritoneum] : peritoneum ⟨peritonitis⟩

peri·to·ne·al \ˌper-ət-ᵊn-ˈē-əl\ adj : of, relating to, or affecting the peritoneum — **peri·to·ne·al·ly** \-ˈē-ə-lē\ adv

peri·to·ne·um \ˌper-ət-ᵊn-ˈē-əm\ n, pl **peri·to·ne·ums** \-ˈē-əmz\ or **peri·to·nea** \-ˈē-ə\ [LL, fr. Gk peritonaion, neut. of peritonaios stretched around, fr. peri- + teinein to stretch — more at THIN] 1 : the smooth transparent serous membrane that lines the cavity of the abdomen of a mammal and is reflected inward over the abdominal and pelvic viscera 2 : PLEUROPERITONEUM

PERIODIC TABLE

This is a common long form of the table. Roman numerals and letters heading the vertical columns indicate the groups (there are differences of opinion regarding the letter designations, those given here being probably the most generally used). The horizontal rows represent the periods, with two series removed from the two very long periods and represented below the main table. Atomic numbers are given above the symbols for the elements and atomic weights when known are given below. Compare ELEMENT table

IA																	VIIA	Zero
1 H 1.008	IIA																1 H 1.008	2 He 4.003
3 Li 6.940	4 Be 9.013											IIIA	IVA	VA	VIA			
												5 B 10.82	6 C 12.011	7 N 14.008	8 O 16.000	9 F 19.00	10 Ne 20.183	
11 Na 22.991	12 Mg 24.32	IIIB	IVB	VB	VIB	VIIB		VIII		IB	IIB	13 Al 26.98	14 Si 28.09	15 P 30.975	16 S 32.066	17 Cl 35.457	18 Ar 39.944	
19 K 39.100	20 Ca 40.08	21 Sc 44.96	22 Ti 47.90	23 V 50.95	24 Cr 52.01	25 Mn 54.94	26 Fe 55.85	27 Co 58.94	28 Ni 58.71	29 Cu 63.54	30 Zn 65.38	31 Ga 69.72	32 Ge 72.60	33 As 74.91	34 Se 78.96	35 Br 79.916	36 Kr 83.80	
37 Rb 85.48	38 Sr 87.63	39 Y 88.92	40 Zr 91.22	41 Nb 92.91	42 Mo 95.95	43 Tc	44 Ru 101.1	45 Rh 102.91	46 Pd 106.4	47 Ag 107.88	48 Cd 112.41	49 In 114.82	50 Sn 118.70	51 Sb 121.76	52 Te 127.61	53 I 126.91	54 Xe 131.31	
55 Cs 132.91	56 Ba 137.36	57 *La 138.92	72 Hf 178.50	73 Ta 180.95	74 W 183.86	75 Re 186.22	76 Os 190.2	77 Ir 192.2	78 Pt 195.09	79 Au 197.0	80 Hg 200.61	81 Tl 204.39	82 Pb 207.21	83 Bi 209.00	84 Po	85 At	86 Rn	
87 Fr	88 Ra	89 #Ac																

*LANTHANIDE SERIES	58 Ce 140.13	59 Pr 140.92	60 Nd 144.27	61 Pm	62 Sm 150.35	63 Eu 152.0	64 Gd 157.26	65 Tb 158.93	66 Dy 162.51	67 Ho 164.94	68 Er 167.27	69 Tm 168.94	70 Yb 173.04	71 Lu 174.99
#ACTINIDE SERIES	90 Th 232.05	91 Pa	92 U 238.07	93 Np	94 Pu	95 Am	96 Cm	97 Bk	98 Cf	99 Es	100 Fm	101 Md	102 No	103 Lw

peri·to·ni·tis \ˌper-ət-ᵊn-ˈīt-əs\ *n* [NL] **:** inflammation of the peritoneum

pe·rit·ri·chous \pə-ˈri-tri-kəs\ *adj* [*peri-* + Gk *trich-*, *thrix* hair — more at TRICH-] **:** having flagella uniformly distributed over the body — **pe·rit·ri·chous·ly** *adv*

peri·wig \ˈper-i-ˌwig\ *n* [modif. of MF *perruque*] **:** PERUKE — **peri·wigged** \-ˌwigd\ *adj*

1per·i·win·kle \ˈper-i-ˌwiŋ-kəl\ *n* [ME *perwinke*, fr. OE *perwince*, fr. L *pervinca*] **:** any of several trailing or woody evergreen herbs (genus *Vinca*) of the dogbane family; *esp* **:** a European creeper (*V. minor*) widely cultivated as a ground cover and for its blue or white flowers

2periwinkle *n* [(assumed) ME, alter. of OE *pīnewincle*, fr. L *pina*, a kind of mussel (fr. Gk) + OE *-wincle* (akin to Dan *vincle* snail shell); akin to OE *wincian* to wink] **:** any of various gastropod mollusks: as **a :** any of a genus (*Littorina*) of edible littoral marine snails; *also* **:** any of various similar or related marine snails (as various American members of *Thais*) **b :** any of several No. American freshwater snails

per·jure \ˈpər-jər\ *vt* **per·jur·ing** \ˈpərj-(ə-)riŋ\ [MF *perjurer*, fr. L *perjurare*, fr. *per-* to destruction, to the bad + *jurare* to swear — more at PER-, JURY] **1** *obs* **:** to cause to commit perjury **2 :** to make a perjurer of (oneself)

per·jur·er \ˈpər-jər-ər\ *n* **:** a person guilty of perjury

per·ju·ri·ous \(ˌ)pər-ˈju̇r-ē-əs\ *adj* **:** marked by perjury — **per·ju·ri·ous·ly** *adv*

per·ju·ry \ˈpərj-(ə-)rē\ *n* **:** the voluntary violation of an oath or vow either by swearing to what is untrue or by omission to do what has been promised under oath **:** false swearing

perk \ˈpərk\ *vb* [ME *perken*] *vi* **1 a :** to thrust up the head, stretch out the neck, or carry the body in a bold or insolent manner **b :** to stick up or out jauntily **2 :** to gain in vigor or cheerfulness esp. after a period of weakness or depression — usu. used with *up* ~ *vt* **1 :** to make smart or spruce in appearance **:** FRESHEN **2 :** to thrust up quickly or impudently

perk·i·ly \ˈpər-kə-lē\ *adv* **:** in a perky manner **:** SAUCILY

perk·i·ness \-kē-nəs\ *n* **:** the quality or state of being perky

perky \ˈpər-kē\ *adj* **1 :** briskly self-assured **:** COCKY **2 :** JAUNTY

per·lite \ˈpər(-ə)l-ˌīt\ *n* [F, fr. *perle* pearl] **:** volcanic glass that has a concentric shelly structure, appears as if composed of concretions, is usu. grayish and sometimes spherulitic, and when expanded by heat forms a lightweight aggregate used esp. in concrete and plaster — **per·lit·ic** \ˌpər-ˈlit-ik\ *adj*

per·ma·frost \ˈpər-mə-ˌfrȯst\ *n* [*perma*nent + *frost*] **:** a permanently frozen layer at variable depth below the earth's surface in frigid regions

per·ma·nence \ˈpərm-(ə-)nən(t)s\ *n* **:** the quality or state of being permanent **:** DURABILITY

per·ma·nen·cy \-(ə-)nən-sē\ *n* **1 :** PERMANENCE **2 :** something permanent

1per·ma·nent \ˈpərm-(ə-)nənt\ *adj* [ME, fr. MF, fr. L *permanent-*, *permanens*, prp. of *permanēre* to endure, fr. *per-* throughout + *manēre* to remain — more at PER-, MANSION] **:** continuing or enduring without fundamental or marked change **:** STABLE **syn** see LASTING — **per·ma·nent·ly** *adv* — **per·ma·nent·ness** *n*

2permanent *n* **:** a long-lasting hair wave produced by mechanical and chemical means

permanent magnet *n* **:** a magnet that retains its magnetism after removal of the magnetizing force

permanent tooth *n* **:** one of the second set of teeth of a mammal that follow the milk teeth, typically persist into old age, and in man are 32 in number

per·man·ga·nate \(ˌ)pər-ˈmaŋ-gə-ˌnāt\ *n* **:** a dark purple crystalline compound that is a salt of permanganic acid

per·man·gan·ic acid \ˌpər-(ˌ)man-ˌgan-ik-, -(ˌ)maŋ-\ *n* [ISV] **:** an unstable strong acid $HMnO_4$ known only in purple-colored strongly oxidizing aqueous solutions

per·me·abil·i·ty \ˌpər-mē-ə-ˈbil-ət-ē\ *n* **1 :** the quality or state of being permeable **2 :** the property of a magnetizable substance that determines the degree in which it modifies the magnetic flux in the region occupied by it in a magnetic field

per·me·able \ˈpər-mē-ə-bəl\ *adj* **:** capable of being permeated **:** PENETRABLE — **per·me·able·ness** *n* — **per·me·ably** \-blē\ *adv*

per·me·ance \ˈpər-mē-ən(t)s\ *n* **1 :** PERMEATION **2 :** the reciprocal of magnetic reluctance

per·me·ate \ˈpər-mē-ˌāt\ *vb* [L *permeatus*, pp. of *permeare*, fr. *per-* through + *meare* to go, pass; akin to MW *mynet* to go, OSlav *minǫti* to pass] *vi* **:** to diffuse through or penetrate something ~ *vt* **1 :** to spread or diffuse through **2 :** to pass through the pores or interstices of — **per·me·ation** \ˌpər-mē-ˈā-shən\ *n* — **per·me·ative** \ˈpər-mē-ˌāt-iv\ *adj*

per men·sem \(ˌ)pər-ˈmen(t)-səm\ *adv* [ML] **:** by the month

Perm·ian \ˈpər-mē-ən, ˈper-\ *adj* [*Perm*, region in eastern Russia] **:** of, relating to, or being the last period of the Paleozoic era or the corresponding system of rocks — **Permian** *n*

per mill \(ˌ)pər-ˈmil\ *adv* [*per* + L *mille* thousand — more at MILE] **:** per thousand — **per·mil·lage** \(ˌ)pər-ˈmil-ij\ *n*

per·mis·si·bil·i·ty \pər-ˌmis-ə-ˈbil-ət-ē\ *n* **:** the quality or state of being permissible

per·mis·si·ble \pər-ˈmis-ə-bəl\ *adj* [ME, fr. ML *permissibilis*, fr. L *permissus*, pp.] **:** that may be permitted **:** ALLOWABLE — **per·mis·si·ble·ness** *n* — **per·mis·si·bly** \-blē\ *adv*

per·mis·sion \pər-ˈmish-ən\ *n* [ME, fr. MF, fr. L *permission-*, *permissio*, fr. *permissus*, pp. of *permittere*] **1 :** the act of permitting **2 :** formal consent **:** AUTHORIZATION

per·mis·sive \pər-ˈmis-iv\ *adj* [F *permissif*, fr. L *permissus*, pp.] **1** *archaic* **:** granted on sufferance **:** TOLERATED **2 :** granting or tending to grant permission **:** TOLERANT **3 :** allowing discretion **:** OPTIONAL — **per·mis·sive·ly** *adv* — **per·mis·sive·ness** *n*

1per·mit \pər-ˈmit\ *vb* **per·mit·ted; per·mit·ting** [L *permittere* to let through, permit, fr. *per-* through + *mittere* to let go, send — more at PER-, SMITE] *vt* **1 :** to consent to expressly or formally ⟨~ access to records⟩ **2 :** to give leave **:** AUTHORIZE **3 :** to make possible ~ *vi* **:** to give an opportunity **:** ALLOW ⟨if time ~s⟩ **syn** see LET — **per·mit·ter** *n*

2per·mit \ˈpər-ˌmit, pər-ˈ\ *n* **1 :** a written warrant or license granted by one having authority **2 :** PERMISSION, ALLOWANCE

per·mit·tiv·i·ty \ˌpər-ˌmi-ˈtiv-ət-ē, -mə-\ *n* [1*permit* + *-ive* + *-ity*] **:** the ability of a dielectric to store electrical potential energy under the influence of an electric field measured by the ratio of the capacitance of a condenser with the material as dielectric to its capacitance with vacuum as dielectric

per·mu·ta·tion \ˌpər-myu̇-ˈtā-shən\ *n* [ME *permutacioun* exchange, transformation, fr. MF *permutation*, fr. L *permutation-*, *permutatio*, fr. *permutatus*, pp. of *permutare*] **1 :** a thorough change in character or condition **:** TRANSFORMATION **2 a :** the act or process of changing the lineal order of an ordered set of objects **b :** an ordered arrangement of a set of objects **syn** see CHANGE — **per·mu·ta·tion·al** \-shnəl, -shən-ᵊl\ *adj*

per·mute \pər-ˈmyüt\ *vt* [ME *permuten*, fr. MF or L; MF *permuter*, fr. L *permutare*, fr. *per-* + *mutare* to change — more at MISS] **:** to change the order or arrangement of; *esp* **:** to arrange in all possible ways

per·ni·cious \pər-ˈnish-əs\ *adj* [MF *pernicieus*, fr. L *perniciosus*, fr. *pernicies* destruction, fr. *per-* + *nec-*, *nex* violent death — more at NOXIOUS] **1 :** highly injurious or destructive **:** DEADLY **2** *archaic* **:** WICKED — **per·ni·cious·ly** *adv* — **per·ni·cious·ness** *n*

syn PERNICIOUS, BANEFUL, NOXIOUS, DELETERIOUS, DETRIMENTAL mean exceedingly harmful. PERNICIOUS and BANEFUL both imply causing irreparable or deadly injury, PERNICIOUS through evil or insidious corrupting or undermining, BANEFUL through poisoning or destroying; NOXIOUS applies to what is both offensive and injurious to the health of body or mind; DELETERIOUS applies to what has an unsuspected harmful effect when eaten or drunk or inhaled; DETRIMENTAL implies obvious harmfulness to something specified

pernicious anemia *n* **:** a severe hyperchromic anemia marked by a progressive decrease in number and increase in size of the red blood cells and by pallor, weakness, and gastrointestinal and nervous disturbances and associated with absence of gastric hydrochloric acid and intrinsic factor

per·nick·e·ty \pər-ˈnik-ət-ē\ *adj* [perh. alter. of *particular*] **1 :** having extremely exacting standards **:** FINICKY **2 :** requiring great precision **:** TICKLISH

Per·nod \per-ˈnō\ *trademark* — used for an aromatic French liqueur

pe·ro·ne·al \ˌper-ō-ˈnē-əl, pə-ˈrō-nē-\ *adj* [NL *peroneus*, fr. *perone* fibula, fr. Gk *peronē*, lit., pin; akin to L *per* through — more at FOR] **:** of, relating to, or located near the fibula

per·oral \(ˌ)pər-ˈōr-əl, pe(ə)r-, -ˈȯr-, -ˈär-\ *adj* [ISV, fr. L *per* through + *or-*, *os* mouth — more at ORAL] **:** occurring through or by way of the mouth — **per·oral·ly** \-ə-lē\ *adv*

per·orate \ˈper-ər-ˌāt *also* ˈpər-\ *vi* [L *peroratus*, pp. of *perorare* to declaim at length, wind up an oration, fr. *per-* through + *orare* to speak — more at PER-, ORATION] **1 :** to deliver a long or grandiloquent oration **:** DECLAIM **2 :** to make a peroration

per·ora·tion \ˌper-ər-ˈā-shən ˈper-ər- *also* ˌpər-ər-ˈ, ˈpər-ər-ˌ\ *n* **1 :** the concluding part of a discourse and esp. an oration **2 :** a highly rhetorical speech — **per·ora·tion·al** \-shnəl, -shən-ᵊl\ *adj*

per·ox·i·dase \pə-ˈräk-sə-ˌdās, -ˌdāz\ *n* **:** an enzyme that catalyzes the oxidation of various substances by peroxides

1per·ox·ide \pə-ˈräk-ˌsīd\ *n* [ISV] **:** an oxide containing a high proportion of oxygen; *esp* **:** a compound (as hydrogen peroxide H_2O_2) in which oxygen is held to be joined to oxygen

2peroxide *vt* **:** to treat with a peroxide; *esp* **:** to bleach (hair) with hydrogen peroxide

1per·pend \pər-ˈpend\ *vb* [L *perpendere*, fr. *per-* thoroughly + *pendere* to weigh — more at PER-, PENDANT] *vt* **:** to reflect on carefully **:** PONDER ~ *vi* **:** to be attentive **:** REFLECT

2per·pend \ˈpär-pən(d), ˈpər-\ *or* **per·pent** \-pən(t)\ *n* [ME *perpend*, *perpoynt*, fr. MF *perpain*] **:** a brick or large stone reaching through a wall so as to appear on both sides of it and acting as a binder

1per·pen·dic·u·lar \ˌpər-pən-ˈdik-yə-lər, ˌpərp-ᵊm-\ *adj* [ME *perpendiculer*, fr. MF, fr. L *perpendicularis*, fr. *perpendiculum* plumb line, fr. *per-* + *pendēre* to hang — more at PENDANT] **1 a :** exactly vertical or upright **b :** being at right angles to a given line or plane **2 :** extremely steep **:** PRECIPITOUS **3 :** of or relating to a medieval English Gothic style of architecture in which vertical lines predominate **4 :** relating to, uniting, or consisting of individuals of dissimilar type or on different levels **syn** see VERTICAL — **per·pen·dic·u·lar·i·ty** \ˌpər-pən-ˌdik-yə-ˈlar-ət-ē, ˌpərp-ᵊm-\ *n* — **per·pen·dic·u·lar·ly** \-ˈdik-yə-lər-lē\ *adv*

2perpendicular *n* **1 :** a line at right angles to the plane of the horizon or to another line or surface **2 :** an extremely steep face (as of a cliff)

per·pe·trate \ˈpər-pə-ˌtrāt\ *vt* [L *perpetratus*, pp. of *perpetrare*, fr. *per-* through + *patrare* to accomplish] **1 :** to be guilty of **:** COMMIT **2 :** to carry through **:** PERFORM — **per·pe·tra·tion** \ˌpər-pə-ˈtrā-shən\ *n* — **per·pe·tra·tor** \ˈpər-pə-ˌtrāt-ər\ *n*

per·pet·u·al \pər-ˈpech-(ə-)wəl, -ˈpech-əl\ *adj* [ME *perpetuel*, fr. MF, fr. L *perpetuus*, fr. *per-* through + *petere* to go to — more at FEATHER] **1 a :** continuing forever **:** EVERLASTING **b** (1) **:** valid for all time (2) **:** holding for life or for an unlimited time **2 :** occurring continually **:** indefinitely long-continued **:** CONSTANT **3 :** blooming continuously throughout the season **syn** see CONTINUAL — **per·pet·u·al·ly** \-ē\ *adv*

perpetual calendar *n* **1 :** a table for finding the day of the week for any one of a wide range of dates **2 :** a calendar having the years uniform in the correspondence of days and dates

per·pet·u·ate \pər-ˈpech-ə-ˌwāt\ *vt* [L *perpetuatus*, pp. of *perpetuare*, fr. *perpetuus*] **:** to make perpetual or cause to last indefinitely — **per·pet·u·a·tion** \-ˌpech-ə-ˈwā-shən\ *n* — **per·pet·u·a·tor** \-ˈpech-ə-ˌwāt-ər\ *n*

per·pe·tu·ity \ˌpər-pə-ˈt(y)ü-ət-ē\ *n* [ME *perpetuite*, fr. MF *perpetuité*, fr. L *perpetuitat-*, *perpetuitas*, fr. *perpetuus*] **1 :** endless time **:** ETERNITY **2 :** the quality or state of being perpetual ⟨bequeathed to them in ~⟩ **3 a :** the condition of an estate limited so that it will not take effect or vest within the period fixed by law **b :** an estate so limited **4 :** an annuity payable forever

per·plex \pər-ˈpleks\ *vt* [obs. *perplex*, adj., involved, perplexed, fr. L *perplexus*, fr. *per-* thoroughly + *plexus* involved, fr. pp. of *plectere* to braid, twine — more at PER-, PLY] **1 :** to disturb mentally; *esp* **:** CONFUSE, BEWILDER **2 :** to make intricate or involved **:** COMPLICATE **syn** see PUZZLE

per·plexed \-ˈplekst\ *adj* **1 :** filled with uncertainty **:** PUZZLED

2 : full of difficulty : COMPLICATED — **per·plexed·ly** \-'plek-səd-lē, -'pleks-tlē\ *adv*

per·plex·i·ty \pər-'plek-sət-ē\ *n* [ME *perplexite*, fr. OF *perplexité*, fr. LL *perplexitat-*, *perplexitas*, fr. L *perplexus*] **1** : the state of being perplexed : BEWILDERMENT **2** : something that perplexes **3** : ENTANGLEMENT

per·qui·site \'pər-kwə-zət\ *n* [ME, property acquired by other means than inheritance, fr. ML *perquisitum*, fr. neut. of *perquisitus*, pp. of *perquirere* to purchase, acquire, fr. L, to search for thoroughly, fr. *per-* thoroughly + *quaerere* to seek] **1** : a privilege, gain, or profit incidental to regular salary or wages; *esp* : one expected or promised **2** : GRATUITY, TIP **3** : something held or claimed as an exclusive right or possession

per·ron \'per-ən, pe-rōⁿ\ *n* [F, fr. OF, aug. of *perre*, *pierre* rock, stone, fr. L *petra*, fr. Gk] : an outdoor stairway leading up to a building entrance or a platform at its top

per·ry \'per-ē\ *n* [ME *peirrie*, fr. MF *peré*, fr. (assumed) VL *piratum*, fr. L *pirum* pear] : the expressed juice of pears often made alcoholic by fermentation

per·salt \'pər-,sölt\ *n* **1** : a salt containing a relatively large proportion of the acidic element or group **2** : a salt of a peracid

per se \(,)pər-'sā *also* pe(ə)r-'sā, (,)pər-'sē\ *adv* [L] : by, of, or in itself or oneself or themselves : as such : INTRINSICALLY

per second per second *adv* : per second every second — used of a rate of acceleration over an indefinite period

per·se·cute \'pər-si-,kyüt\ *vt* [MF *persecuter*, back-formation fr. *persecuteur* persecutor, fr. LL *persecutor*, fr. *persecutus*, pp. of *persequi* to persecute, fr. L, to pursue, fr. *per-* through + *sequi* to follow — more at SUE] **1** : to harass in a manner to injure, grieve, or afflict; *specif* : to cause to suffer because of belief **2** : to annoy with persistent or urgent approaches : PESTER **syn** see WRONG — **per·se·cu·tive** \-,kyüt-iv\ *adj* — **per·se·cu·tor** \-,kyüt-ər\ *n* — **per·se·cu·to·ry** \-kyü-,tōr-ē, -,tör-; -,kyüt-ə-rē\ *adj*

per·se·cu·tion \,pər-si-'kyü-shən\ *n* **1** : the act or practice of persecuting esp. those who differ in origin, religion, or social outlook **2** : the condition of being persecuted, harassed, or annoyed

Per·se·id \'pər-sē-əd\ *n* [L *Perseus*; fr. their appearing to radiate from a point in Perseus] : one of a group of meteors appearing annually about August 11

Per·seph·o·ne \pər-'sef-ə-nē\ *n* [L, fr. Gk *Persephonē*] : a daughter of Zeus and Demeter abducted by Pluto and made his wife and queen

Per·seus \'pər-,süs, -sē-əs\ *n* [L, fr. Gk] **1** : a son of Zeus and Danaë and slayer of Medusa **2** [L (gen. *Persei*), fr. Gk] : a northern constellation between Taurus and Cassiopeia

per·se·ver·ance \,pər-sə-'vir-ən(t)s\ *n* : the action, condition, or an instance of persevering : STEADFASTNESS

per·se·vere \-'vi(ə)r\ *vi* [ME *perseveren*, fr. MF *perseverer*, fr. L *perseverare*, fr. *per-* through + *severus* severe] : to persist in a state, enterprise, or undertaking in spite of counter influences, opposition, or discouragement

Per·sian \'pər-zhən, *esp Brit* -shən\ *n* **1** : one of the people of Persia: as **a** : one of the ancient Iranian Caucasians who under Cyrus and his successors became the dominant Asian race **b** : a member of one of the peoples forming the modern Iranian nationality **2 a** : any of several Iranian languages dominant in Persia at different periods **b** : the modern language of Iran and western Afghanistan used also in Pakistan and by Indian Muslims as a literary language **3** : a thin soft silk formerly used esp. for linings — **Persian** *adj*

Persian cat *n* : a stocky round-headed domestic cat with long and silky fur that is the long-haired cat of shows and fanciers

Persian lamb *n* **1** : the young of the karakul sheep that furnishes skins used in furriery **2** : a pelt obtained from karakul lambs older than those yielding broadtail and characterized by very silky tightly curled fur

per·si·flage \'pər-si-,fläzh, 'per-\ *n* [F, fr. *persifler* to banter, fr. *per-* thoroughly + *siffler* to whistle, hiss, boo, fr. L *sibilare*, of imit. origin] : frivolous or lightly derisive talk or manner of treating a subject

per·sim·mon \pər-'sim-ən\ *n* [of Algonquian origin; akin to Cree *pasiminan* dried fruit] **1** : any of a genus (*Diospyros*) of trees of the ebony family with hard fine wood, oblong leaves, and small bell-shaped white flowers; *esp* : an American tree (*D. virginiana*) or a Japanese tree (*D. kaki*) **2** : the usu. orange several-seeded berry of a persimmon that resembles a plum and is edible when fully ripe

per·sist \pər-'sist, -'zist\ *vi* [MF *persister*, fr. L *persistere*, fr. *per-* + *sistere* to take a stand, stand firm; akin to L *stare* to stand — more at STAND] **1** : to go on resolutely or stubbornly in spite of opposition, importunity, or warning **2** *obs* : to remain unchanged or fixed in a (specified) character, condition, or position **3** : to be insistent in the repetition or pressing of a question or an opinion **4** : to continue to exist **syn** see CONTINUE — **per·sist·er** *n*

per·sis·tence \pər-'sis-tən(t)s, -'zis-\ *n* **1** : the action or fact of persisting **2** : the quality or state of being persistent; *esp* : PERSEVERANCE

per·sis·ten·cy \-tən-sē\ *n* : PERSISTENCE 2

per·sis·tent \-tənt\ *adj* [L *persistent-*, *persistens*, prp. of *persistere*] **1 a** : continuing or inclined to persist in a course **b** : continuing to exist in spite of interference or treatment ⟨a ~ cough⟩ **2** : existing for a long or longer than usual time or continuously: as **a** : retained beyond the usual period ⟨a ~ leaf⟩ **b** : continuing without change in function or structure ⟨~ gills⟩ **c** : effective in the open for an appreciable time usu. through slow volatilizing ⟨mustard gas is ~⟩ — **per·sis·tent·ly** *adv*

per·snick·e·ty \pər-'snik-ət-ē\ *adj* : PERNICKETY

per·son \'pərs-ᵊn\ *n* [ME, fr. OF *persone*, fr. L *persona* actor's mask, character in a play, person, prob. fr. Etruscan *phersu* mask] **1 a** : a human being **b** : a human being as distinguished from an animal or thing **c** : an inferior human being **2** : CHARACTER, GUISE **3 a** : one of the three modes of being in the Godhead as understood by Trinitarians **b** : the unitary personality of Christ that unites the divine and human natures **4 a** *archaic* : bodily appearance **b** : the body of a human being **5 a** : the individual personality of a human being : SELF **b** : bodily presence ⟨appear in ~⟩ **6** : a human being, body of persons, corporation, partnership, or other legal entity recognized by law as the subject of rights and duties **7** : reference of a segment of discourse to the speaker, to one spoken to, or to one spoken of as indicated by means of certain pronouns or in many languages by verb inflection

per·so·na \pər-'sō-nə, -,nä\ *n* [L] **1 per·so·nae** \-(,)nē, -,nī\ *pl* : the characters of a fictional presentation (as a novel or play) ⟨comic *personae*⟩ **2** *pl* **personas** [NL, fr. L] : the social facade an individual assumes

per·son·able \'pərs-nə-bəl, -ᵊn-ə-bəl\ *adj* : pleasing in person : ATTRACTIVE — **per·son·able·ness** *n*

per·son·age \'pərs-nij, -ᵊn-ij\ *n* **1** : a person of rank, note, or distinction; *esp* : one distinguished for presence and personal power **2** : a dramatic, fictional, or historical character; *also* : IMPERSONATION **3** : a human individual : PERSON

per·so·na gra·ta \pər-,sō-nə-'grat-ə, -'grät-\ *n*, *pl* **per·so·nae gra·tae** \-nē-'grat-ē, -'grat-,ī, -'grät-\ *or* **persona grata** [NL] : an acceptable person; *specif* : a diplomatic official who is personally acceptable to the government of a foreign country to which he is accredited

¹**per·son·al** \'pərs-nəl, -ᵊn-əl\ *adj* [ME, fr. MF, fr. LL *personalis*, fr. L *persona*] **1** : of, relating to, or affecting a person : PRIVATE **2 a** : done in person without the intervention of another; *also* : proceeding from a single person **b** : carried on between individuals directly **3** : relating to the person or body **4** : relating to an individual or his character, conduct, motives, or private affairs often in an offensive manner **5** : rational and self-conscious **6** : of, relating to, or constituting personal property **7** : denoting grammatical person

²**personal** *n* : a short newspaper paragraph relating to a person or group or to personal matters

personal effects *n pl* : possessions having a close relationship to one's person

personal equation *n* : variation (as in observation) occasioned by the personal peculiarities of an individual; *also* : a correction or allowance made for such variation

per·son·al·ism \'pərs-nə-,liz-əm, -ᵊn-ə-\ *n* : a doctrine emphasizing the significance, uniqueness, and inviolability of personality — **per·son·al·ist** \-ləst\ *n or adj* — **per·son·al·is·tic** \,pərs-nə-'lis-tik, -ᵊn-ə-\ *adj*

per·son·al·i·ty \,pərs-ᵊn-'al-ət-ē, ,pər-'snal-\ *n* [ME *personalite*, fr. LL *personalitat-*, *personalitas*, fr. *personalis*] **1 a** : the quality or state of being a person **b** : personal existence **2 a** : the condition or fact of relating to a particular person; *specif* : the condition of referring directly to or being aimed disparagingly or hostilely at an individual **b** : an offensively personal remark **3 a** : the complex of characteristics that distinguishes an individual or a nation or group **b** (1) : the totality of an individual's behavioral and emotional tendencies (2) : the organization of the individual's distinguishing character traits, attitudes, or habits **4 a** : distinction or excellence of personal and social traits **b** : a person having such quality **c** : a person of importance, prominence, renown, or notoriety **syn** see DISPOSITION

per·son·al·ize \'pərs-nə-,līz, -ᵊn-ə-\ *vt* **1** : PERSONIFY **2** : to make personal or individual; *specif* : to mark as the property of a particular person

per·son·al·ly \'pərs-nə-lē, -ᵊn-ə-\ *adv* **1** : in a personal manner **2** : on or for one's own part **3** : in person

personal pronoun *n* : a pronoun (as *I*, *you*, *they*) expressing a distinction of person

personal property *n* : property other than real property consisting of things temporary or movable : CHATTELS

per·son·al·ty \'pərs-nəl-tē, -ᵊn-əl-\ *n* [AF *personalté*, fr. LL *personalitat-*, *personalitas* personality] : PERSONAL PROPERTY

per·so·na non gra·ta \pər-,sō-nə-,nän-'grat-ə, -'grät-\ *n*, *pl* **per·so·nae non gra·tae** \-nē-,nän-'grat-ē, -,nī-, -'grat-,ī, -'grät-\ *or* **persona non grata** [NL] : an unacceptable person; *specif* : a diplomatic official who is personally not acceptable to the government of a foreign country to which he is accredited

¹**per·so·nate** \'pərs-nət, -ᵊn-ət\ *adj* [L *personatus* masked, fr. *persona* mask] *of a bilabiate corolla* : having the throat nearly closed by a palate; *also* : having such a corolla ⟨a ~ flower⟩

²**per·son·ate** \'pərs-ᵊn-,āt\ *vt* **1 a** : IMPERSONATE, REPRESENT **b** : to assume without authority some character or capacity when done with fraudulent intent **2** : to invest with personality or personal characteristics — **per·son·ation** \,pərs-ᵊn-'ā-shən\ *n* — **per·son·ative** \'pərs-ᵊn-,āt-iv\ *adj* — **per·son·a·tor** \-,āt-ər\ *n*

per·son·i·fi·ca·tion \pər-,sän-ə-fə-'kā-shən\ *n* : an act of personifying or something that personifies: as **a** : attribution of personal qualities; *esp* : representation of a thing or abstraction as a person or by the human form **b** : a divinity or imaginary being thought of as representing a thing or abstraction **c** : EMBODIMENT, INCARNATION

per·son·i·fi·er \pər-'sän-ə-,fī(-ə)r\ *n* : one that personifies

per·son·i·fy \-,fī\ *vt* **1** : to conceive of or represent as a person or as having human qualities or powers **2** : to be the embodiment or personification of : INCARNATE

per·son·nel \,pərs-ᵊn-'el\ *n* [F, fr. G *personale*, *personal*, fr. ML *personale*, fr. LL, neut. of *personalis* personal] **1 a** : a body of persons usu. employed in some public service or in a factory, office, or organization **b personnel** *pl* : PERSONS **2** : a division of an organization concerned with personnel

¹**per·spec·tive** \pər-'spek-tiv\ *n* [ML *perspectivum*, fr. neut. of *perspectivus* of sight, optical, fr. L *perspectus*, pp. of *perspicere* to look through, see clearly, fr. *per-* through + *specere* to look — more at PER-, SPY] : an optical glass (as a telescope)

²**perspective** *adj* [ME, fr. ML *perspectivus*] **1** *obs* : aiding the vision ⟨~ glass⟩ **2** : of, relating to, or seen in perspective — **per·spec·tive·ly** *adv*

³**perspective** *n* [MF, prob. modif. of OIt *prospettiva*, fr. *prospetto* view, prospect, fr. L *prospectus* — more at PROSPECT] **1 a** : the technique or process of representing on a plane or curved surface the spatial relation of objects as they might appear to the eye; *specif* : LINEAR PERSPECTIVE **b** : the technique of adjusting the apparent sources of sounds (as on a radio program) into a natural-seeming and integrated whole **2 a** : the aspect in which a subject or its parts are mentally viewed **b** : capacity to view things in their true relations or relative importance **3 a** (1) : a visible scene; *esp* : one giving a distinctive impression of distance : VISTA (2) : a mental view or prospect **b** : a picture in linear perspective **4** : the appearance to the eye of objects in respect to their relative distance and positions

per·spi·ca·cious \,pər-spə-'kā-shəs\ *adj* [L *perspicac-*, *perspicax*, fr. *perspicere*] : of acute mental vision or discernment : KEEN **syn** see SHREWD — **per·spi·ca·cious·ly** *adv* — **per·spi·ca·cious·ness** *n*

per·spi·cac·i·ty \ˌpər-spə-ˈkas-ət-ē\ *n* **:** the quality or state of being perspicacious

per·spi·cu·ity \-ˈkyü-ət-ē\ *n* **1 :** the quality or state of being perspicuous **2 :** PERSPICACITY

per·spic·u·ous \pər-ˈspik-yə-wəs\ *adj* [L *perspicuus* transparent, perspicuous, fr. *perspicere*] **:** plain to the understanding **syn** see CLEAR — **per·spic·u·ous·ly** *adv* — **per·spic·u·ous·ness** *n*

per·spi·ra·tion \ˌpər-spə-ˈrā-shən, ˌpər-ˈsprā-\ *n* **1 :** the act or process of perspiring **2 :** a saline fluid secreted by the sweat glands **:** SWEAT

per·spi·ra·to·ry \pər-ˈspī-rə-ˌtōr-ē, ˈpər-sp(ə-)rə-, -ˌtȯr-\ *adj* **:** of, relating to, secreting, or inducing perspiration

per·spire \pər-ˈspī(ə)r\ *vi* [F *perspirer*, fr. MF, fr. L *per-* through + *spirare* to blow, breathe — more at PER-, SPIRIT] **:** to emit matter through the skin; *specif* **:** to secrete and emit perspiration

per·suad·able \pər-ˈswād-ə-bəl\ *adj* **:** capable of being persuaded

per·suade \pər-ˈswād\ *vt* [L *persuadēre*, fr. *per-* thoroughly + *suadēre* to advise, urge — more at SUASION] **1 :** to move by argument, entreaty, or expostulation to a belief, position, or course of action **2 :** to plead with **:** URGE **syn** see INDUCE — **per·suad·er** *n*

per·sua·si·ble \-ˈswā-zə-bəl, -ˈswā-sə-\ *n* [MF, fr. L *persuasibilis* persuasive, fr. *persuasus*] **:** PERSUADABLE

per·sua·sion \pər-ˈswā-zhən\ *n* [ME *persuasioun*, fr. MF or L; MF *persuasion*, fr. L *persuasion-*, *persuasio*, fr. *persuasus*, pp. of *persuadēre*] **1 a :** the act or process or an instance of persuading **b :** a persuading argument **:** INDUCEMENT **c :** PERSUASIVENESS **2 :** the condition of being persuaded **3 a :** OPINION, BELIEF; *esp* **:** a system of religious beliefs **b :** a group adhering to a particular system of beliefs **4 :** KIND, SORT **syn** see OPINION

per·sua·sive \-ˈswā-siv, -ziv\ *adj* **:** tending to persuade — **per·sua·sive·ly** *adv* — **per·sua·sive·ness** *n*

pert \ˈpərt\ *adj* [ME, open, bold, pert, modif. of OF *apert*, fr. L *apertus* open, fr. pp. of *aperire* to open] **1 a :** saucily free and forward **:** IMPUDENT **b :** being trim and chic **:** JAUNTY **c :** piquantly stimulating **2 :** LIVELY, VIVACIOUS — **pert·ly** *adv* — **pert·ness** *n*

per·tain \pər-ˈtān\ *vi* [ME *perteinen*, fr. MF *partenir*, fr. L *pertinēre* to reach to, belong, fr. *per-* through + *tenēre* to hold] **1 a (1) :** to belong as a part, member, accessory, or product **(2) :** to belong as an attribute, feature, or function **(3) :** to belong as a duty or right **b :** to be appropriate **2 :** to have reference **:** RELATE

per·ti·na·cious \ˌpərt-ᵊn-ˈā-shəs\ *adj* [L *pertinac-*, *pertinax*, fr. *per-* thoroughly + *tenac-*, *tenax* tenacious, fr. *tenēre*] **1 a :** adhering resolutely to an opinion, purpose, or design **b :** perversely persistent **2 :** stubbornly unyielding or tenacious **syn** see OBSTINATE — **per·ti·na·cious·ly** *adv* — **per·ti·na·cious·ness** *n*

per·ti·nac·i·ty \-ˈas-ət-ē\ *n* **:** the quality or state of being pertinacious

per·ti·nence \ˈpərt-ᵊn-ən(t)s, ˈpərt-nən(t)s\ *or* **per·ti·nen·cy** \ˈpərt-ᵊn-ən-sē, ˈpərt-nən-\ *n* **:** the quality or state of being pertinent **:** RELEVANCE

per·ti·nent \ˈpərt-ᵊn-ənt, ˈpərt-nənt\ *adj* [ME, fr. MF, fr. L *pertinent-*, *pertinens*, prp. of *pertinēre*] **:** relevant or applicable to the matter in hand **syn** see RELEVANT — **per·ti·nent·ly** *adv*

per·turb \pər-ˈtərb\ *vt* [ME *perturben*, fr. MF *perturber*, fr. L *perturbare* to throw into confusion, fr. *per-* + *turbare* to disturb — more at TURBID] **1 :** to disturb greatly in mind **:** DISQUIET **2 :** to throw into confusion **:** DERANGE **3 :** to cause (a celestial body) to deviate from a theoretically regular orbital motion **syn** see DISCOMPOSE — **per·turb·able** \-ˈtər-bə-bəl\ *adj*

per·tur·ba·tion \ˌpərt-ər-ˈbā-shən, ˌpər-ˌtər-\ *n* **1 :** the action of perturbing **:** the state of being perturbed **2 :** a disturbance of the regular elliptic or other motion of a celestial body produced by some force additional to that which causes its regular motion — **per·tur·ba·tion·al** \-shnəl, -shən-ᵊl\ *adj*

per·tus·sis \pər-ˈtəs-əs\ *n* [NL, fr. L *per-* thoroughly + *tussis* cough] **:** WHOOPING COUGH

pe·ruke \pə-ˈrük\ *n* [MF *perruque*, fr. OIt *parrucca*, *perrucca* hair, wig] **:** WIG; *specif* **:** one of a type popular from the 17th to the early 19th century

pe·rus·al \pə-ˈrü-zəl\ *n* **:** the action of perusing

pe·ruse \pə-ˈrüz\ *vt* [ME *perusen*, prob. fr. L *per-* thoroughly + ME *usen* to use] **1 :** to examine or consider with attention and in detail **:** STUDY **2 :** READ — **pe·rus·er** *n*

Pe·ru·vi·an bark \pə-ˌrü-vē-ən-\ *n* [NL *Peruvia* Peru, country of So. America, fr. Sp *Perú*] **:** CINCHONA 2

per·vade \pər-ˈvād\ *vt* [L *pervadere* to go through, pervade, fr. *per-* through + *vadere* to go — more at PER-, WADE] **:** to become diffused throughout every part of — **per·va·sion** \-ˈvā-zhən\ *n* — **per·va·sive** \-ˈvā-siv, -ziv\ *adj* — **per·va·sive·ly** *adv* — **per·va·sive·ness** *n*

per·verse \(ˌ)pər-ˈvərs, ˈpər-ˌ\ *adj* [ME, fr. L *perversus*, fr. pp. of *pervertere*] **1 a :** turned away from what is right or good **:** CORRUPT **b :** INCORRECT, IMPROPER **c :** contrary to the evidence or the direction of the judge on a point of law ⟨~ verdict⟩ **2 a :** obstinate in opposing what is right, reasonable, or accepted **:** WRONGHEADED **b :** arising from or indicative of stubbornness or obstinacy **3 :** marked by peevishness or petulance **:** CRANKY **syn** see CONTRARY — **per·verse·ly** *adv* — **per·verse·ness** *n*

per·ver·sion \pər-ˈvər-zhən, -shən\ *n* **1 :** the action of perverting **:** the condition of being perverted **2 :** a perverted form; *esp* **:** an aberrant sexual practice habitually preferred to normal coitus

per·ver·si·ty \pər-ˈvər-sət-ē\ *n* **:** the quality, state, or an instance of being perverse

per·ver·sive \-ˈvər-siv, -ziv\ *adj* **1 :** that perverts or tends to pervert **2 :** marked by perversion

[1]**per·vert** \pər-ˈvərt\ *vt* [ME *perverten*, fr. MF *pervertir*, fr. L *pervertere* to overturn, corrupt, pervert, fr. *per-* thoroughly + *vertere* to turn — more at PER-, WORTH] **1 a :** to cause to turn aside or away from what is good or true or morally right **:** CORRUPT **b :** to cause to turn aside or away from what is generally done or accepted **:** MISDIRECT **2 a :** to divert to a wrong end or purpose **:** MISUSE **b :** to twist the meaning or sense of **:** MISINTERPRET **syn** see DEBASE — **per·vert·er** *n*

[2]**per·vert** \ˈpər-ˌvərt\ *n* **:** one that has been perverted; *specif* **:** one given to some form of sexual perversion

per·vert·ed \pər-ˈvərt-əd\ *adj* **1 :** CORRUPT, VICIOUS **2 :** marked by perversion — **per·vert·ed·ly** *adv* — **per·vert·ed·ness** *n*

per·vi·ous \ˈpər-vē-əs\ *adj* [L *pervius*, fr. *per-* through + *via* way] **:** admitting passage **:** PERMEABLE — **per·vi·ous·ness** *n*

pes \ˈpās\ *n*, *pl* **pe·des** \ˈped-ˌās\ [NL *ped-*, *pes*, fr. L, foot — more at FOOT] **:** the distal segment of the hind limb of a vertebrate including the tarsus and foot

Pe·sach \ˈpā-ˌsäk\ *n* [Heb *pesaḥ*] **:** PASSOVER

pe·se·ta \pə-ˈsāt-ə\ *n* [Sp, fr. dim. of *peso*] — see MONEY table

pe·se·wa \pə-ˈsā-wə\ *n* [native name in Ghana] — see *cedi* at MONEY table

pes·ky \ˈpes-kē\ *adj* [prob. irreg. fr. *pest* + *-y*] **:** TROUBLESOME, VEXATIOUS

pe·so \ˈpā-(ˌ)sō, ˈpes-(ˌ)ō\ *n* [Sp, lit. weight, fr. L *pensum* — more at POISE] **1 :** an old silver coin of Spain or Spanish America equal to eight reals **2** — see MONEY table **3 :** the former basic monetary unit of Chile

pes·sa·ry \ˈpes-(ə-)rē\ *n* [ME *pessarie*, fr. LL *pessarium*, fr. *pessus*, *pessum* pessary, fr. Gk *pessos* oval stone for playing checkers, pessary] **1 :** a vaginal suppository **2 :** a device worn in the vagina to support the uterus, remedy a malposition, or prevent conception

pes·si·mism \ˈpes-ə-ˌmiz-əm *also* ˈpez-\ *n* [F *pessimisme*, fr. L *pessimus* worst — more at PEJORATIVE] **1 :** an inclination to emphasize adverse aspects, conditions, and possibilities or to expect the worst possible outcome **2 a :** the doctrine that reality is essentially evil **b :** the doctrine that evil overbalances happiness in life — **pes·si·mist** \-məst\ *n*

pes·si·mis·tic \ˌpes-ə-ˈmis-tik *also* ˌpez-\ *adj* **:** of, relating to, or characterized by pessimism **:** GLOOMY **syn** see CYNICAL — **pes·si·mis·ti·cal·ly** \-ti-k(ə-)lē\ *adv*

pest \ˈpest\ *n* [MF *peste*, fr. L *pestis*] **1 :** an epidemic disease associated with high mortality; *specif* **:** PLAGUE **2 :** something resembling a pest in destructiveness; *esp* **:** a plant or animal detrimental to man **3 :** one that pesters or annoys **:** NUISANCE

pes·ter \ˈpes-tər\ *vt* **pes·ter·ing** \-t(ə-)riŋ\ [modif. of MF *empestrer* to hobble, embarrass, fr. (assumed) VL *impastoriare*, fr. L *in-* + (assumed) VL *pastoria* hobble, fr. L *pastor* herdsman — more at PASTOR] **1** *obs* **:** OVERCROWD **2 :** to harass with petty irritations **:** ANNOY **syn** see WORRY

pest·hole \ˈpest-ˌhōl\ *n* **:** a place subject or liable to epidemic disease

pest·house \-ˌhau̇s\ *n* **:** a shelter or hospital for those infected with a pestilential or contagious disease

pes·ti·cide \ˈpes-tə-ˌsīd\ *n* **:** an agent used to destroy pests

pes·tif·er·ous \pe-ˈstif-(ə-)rəs\ *adj* [ME, fr. L *pestifer* pestilential, noxious, fr. *pestis* + *-fer* -ferous] **1 :** dangerous to society **:** PERNICIOUS **2 a :** carrying or propagating infection **:** PESTILENTIAL **b :** infected with a pestilential disease **3 :** ANNOYING, TROUBLESOME — **pes·tif·er·ous·ly** *adv* — **pes·tif·er·ous·ness** *n*

pes·ti·lence \ˈpes-tə-lən(t)s\ *n* **:** a contagious or infectious epidemic disease that is virulent and devastating; *specif* **:** BUBONIC PLAGUE

pes·ti·lent \-lənt\ *adj* [ME, fr. L *pestilent-*, *pestilens* pestilential, fr. *pestis*] **1 :** destructive of life **:** DEADLY **2 :** injuring or endangering society **:** PERNICIOUS **3 :** VEXING, IRRITATING **4 :** INFECTIOUS, CONTAGIOUS — **pes·ti·lent·ly** *adv*

pes·ti·len·tial \ˌpes-tə-ˈlen-chəl\ *adj* **1 a :** causing or tending to cause pestilence **:** DEADLY **b :** of or relating to pestilence **2 :** morally harmful **:** PERNICIOUS **3 :** IRRITATING, ANNOYING — **pes·ti·len·tial·ly** \-ˈlench-(ə-)lē\ *adv*

pes·tle \ˈpes-əl *also* ˈpest-ᵊl\ *n* [ME *pestel*, fr. MF, fr. L *pistillum;* akin to MLG *vīsel* pestle, L *pilum* pestle, javelin, *pinsere* to pound, crush] **1 :** a usu. club-shaped implement for pounding or grinding substances in a mortar **2 :** any of various devices for pounding, stamping, or pressing — **pestle** *vt* **pes·tling** \ˈpes-(ə-)liŋ; ˈpest-(ə-)liŋ\

[1]**pet** \ˈpet\ *n* [perh. back-formation fr. ME *pety* small — more at PETTY] **1 :** a domesticated animal kept for pleasure rather than utility **2 a :** a pampered and usu. spoiled child **b :** a person who is treated with unusual kindness or consideration **:** DARLING

[2]**pet** *adj* **1 :** kept or treated as a pet **2 :** expressing fondness or endearment **3 :** FAVORITE

[3]**pet** *vb* **pet·ted; pet·ting** *vt* **1 a :** to treat as a pet **b :** to stroke in a gentle or loving manner **2 :** to treat with unusual kindness and consideration **:** PAMPER ~ *vi* **:** to engage in amorous embracing, caressing, and kissing **syn** see CARESS — **pet·ter** *n*

[4]**pet** *n* [origin unknown] **:** a fit of peevishness, sulkiness, or anger

[5]**pet** *vi* **:** to take offense **:** SULK

pet·al \ˈpet-ᵊl\ *n* [NL *petalum*, fr. Gk *petalon;* akin to Gk *petannynai* to spread out — more at FATHOM] **:** one of the modified leaves of a corolla of a flower — **pet·aled** *or* **pet·alled** \-ᵊld\ *adj* — **pet·al·like** \-ᵊl-ˌ(l)īk\ *adj*

pet·al·oid \ˈpet-ᵊl-ˌȯid\ *adj* **1 :** resembling a flower petal **2 :** consisting of petaloid elements

pet·al·ous \ˈpet-ᵊl-əs\ *adj* **:** having petals

-pet·al·ous \ˈpet-ᵊl-əs\ *adj comb form* [NL *-petalus*, fr. *petalum*] **:** having (such or so many) petals ⟨poly*petalous*⟩

pe·tard \pə-ˈtär(d)\ *n* [MF, fr. *peter* to break wind, fr. *pet* expulsion of intestinal gas, fr. L *peditum*, fr. neut. of *peditus*, pp. of *pedere* to break wind; akin to Gk *bdein* to break wind] **1 :** a case containing an explosive to break down a door or gate or breach a wall **2 :** a firework that explodes with a loud report

pet·a·sos *or* **pet·a·sus** \ˈpet-ə-səs\ *n* [L & Gk; L *petasus*, fr. Gk *petasos;* akin to Gk *petannynai* to spread out] **:** a broad-brimmed low-crowned hat worn by ancient Greeks and Romans; *esp* **:** the winged hat of Hermes

pet cock \ˈpet-\ *n* **:** a small cock, faucet, or valve for letting out air, releasing compression, or draining

pe·te·chia \pə-ˈtē-kē-ə\ *n*, *pl* **pe·te·chi·ae** \-kē-ˌī, -kē-ˌē\ [NL, fr. It *petecchia*, deriv. of L *impetigo*] **:** a minute hemorrhagic or purpuric spot appearing esp. in some infectious diseases — **pe·te·chi·al** \-kē-əl\ *adj* — **pe·te·chi·ate** \-kē-ət\ *adj*

pe·ter \ˈpēt-ər\ *vi* [origin unknown] **1 :** to diminish gradually and come to an end **:** give out ⟨stream ~*s out*⟩ **2 :** to become exhausted — usu. used with *out*

Pe·ter \ˈpēt-ər\ *n* [LL *Petrus*, fr. Gk *Petros*, fr. *petra* rock] **:** a fisherman of Galilee and one of the twelve apostles

Pe·ter Pan \ˌpēt-ər-ˈpan\ *n* **1 :** a boy in Sir James Barrie's play *Peter Pan* who never grows up **2 :** a small close-fitting round

ə abut; ᵊ kitten; ər further; a back; ā bake; ä cot, cart; au̇ out; ch chin; e less; ē easy; g gift; i trip; ī life
j joke; ŋ sing; ō flow; ȯ flaw; ȯi coin; th thin; t͟h this; ü loot; u̇ foot; y yet; yü few; yu̇ furious; zh vision

collar used on women's and children's clothing

Pe·ter's pence \ˌpēt-ərz-\ *n pl but sing or pl in constr* [fr. the tradition that St. Peter founded the papal see] **1 :** an annual tribute of a penny formerly paid by each householder in England to the papal see **2 :** a voluntary annual contribution made by Roman Catholics to the pope

pet·i·o·lar \ˌpet-ē-ˈō-lər\ *adj* **:** of, relating to, or proceeding from a petiole

pet·i·o·late \ˈpet-ē-ə-ˌlāt, ˌpet-ē-ˈō-lət\ *also* **pet·i·o·lat·ed** \ˈpet-ē-ˌō-ˌlāt-əd\ *adj* **:** having a stalk or petiole

pet·i·ole \ˈpet-ē-ˌōl\ *n* [NL *petiolus*, fr. L, small foot, fruit stalk, alter. of *pediculus*, dim. of *ped-, pes* foot — more at FOOT] **1 :** a slender stem that supports the blade of a foliage leaf **2 :** PEDUNCLE; *specif* **:** a slender abdominal segment joining the rest of the abdomen to the thorax in an insect — **pet·i·oled** \-ˌōld\ *adj*

pet·i·o·lule \ˈpet-ē-ō-ˌlül, ˌpet-ē-ˈōl-(ˌ)yü(ə)l\ *n* [NL *petiolulus*, dim. of *petiolus*] **:** a stalk of a leaflet of a compound leaf

pet·it \ˈpet-ē, ˈpet-ət\ *adj* [ME, small, minor, fr. MF, small] **:** PETTY 1 — used chiefly in legal compounds

pe·tit bourgeois \pə-ˌtē-\ *adj* [F, lit., small bourgeois] **:** of, relating to, or characteristic of the petite bourgeoisie — **petit bourgeois** *n*

pe·tite \pə-ˈtēt\ *adj* [F, fem. of *petit*] **:** small and trim of figure **:** LITTLE — usu. used of a woman **syn** see SMALL — **pe·tite·ness** *n*

pe·tite bourgeoisie \pə-ˌtēt-\ *n* [F, lit., small bourgeoisie] **:** the lower middle class including esp. small shopkeepers and artisans

pe·tit four \ˌpet-ē-ˈfō(ə)r, -ˈfȯ(ə)r; pə-ˌtē-ˈfü(ə)r\ *n, pl* **petits fours** *or* **petit fours** \-ē-ˈfō(ə)rz, -ˈfȯ(ə)rz; -ˌtē-ˈfü(ə)r(z)\ [F, lit., small oven] **:** a small frosted and ornamented cake cut from pound or sponge cake

¹pe·ti·tion \pə-ˈtish-ən\ *n* [ME, fr. MF, fr. L *petition-, petitio*, fr. *petitus*, pp. of *petere* to seek, request — more at FEATHER] **1 :** an earnest request **:** ENTREATY **2 a :** a formal written request made to a superior **b :** a document embodying such a formal written request **3 :** something asked or requested — **pe·ti·tion·ary** \-ˈtish-ə-ˌner-ē\ *adj*

²petition *vb* **pe·ti·tion·ing** \-ˈtish-(ə-)niŋ\ *vt* **:** to make a request to or for **:** SOLICIT **~** *vi* **:** to make a request; *esp* **:** to make a formal written request — **pe·ti·tion·er** \-ˈtish-(ə-)nər\ *n*

pe·ti·tio prin·ci·pii \pə-ˈtēt-ē-ˌō-(ˌ)priŋ-ˈkip-ē-ˌē\ *n* [ML, lit., postulation of the beginning, begging the question] **:** a logical fallacy in which a premise is assumed to be true without warrant or in which what is to be proved is implicitly taken for granted

petit jury *n* **:** a jury of twelve persons impaneled to try and decide finally upon the facts at issue in causes for trial in a court

petit larceny *n* **:** larceny involving property of a value below a legally established minimum

pe·tit–maî·tre \pə-ˌtē-ˈmātrᵊ\ *n, pl* **petits–maîtres** *same*\ [F, lit., small master] **:** DANDY, FOP

pe·tit mal \pə-ˌtē-ˈmäl, -ˈmal\ *n* [F, lit., small illness] **:** epilepsy characterized by mild convulsive seizure with transient clouding of consciousness

pet·it point \ˈpet-ē-ˌpȯint\ *n* [F, lit., small point] **:** TENT STITCH

petr- *or* **petri-** *or* **petro-** *comb form* [NL, fr. Gk *petr-, petro-*, fr. *petros* stone & *petra* rock] **:** stone **:** rock ⟨*petro*logy⟩

Pe·trar·chan sonnet \pi-ˌträr-kən-, ˌpē-, (ˌ)pe-\ *n* [*Petrarch* (Francesco Petrarca) †1374 It poet] **:** ITALIAN SONNET

pe·trel \ˈpe-trəl *also* ˈpē-\ *n* [alter. of earlier *pitteral*] **1 :** any of numerous sea birds (families Procellariidae and Hydrobatidae); *esp* **:** one of the smaller long-winged birds that fly far from land **2 :** STORM PETREL

pe·tri dish \ˌpē-trē-\ *n* [Julius R. *Petri* †1921 G bacteriologist] **:** a small shallow dish of thin glass with a loose cover used esp. for cultures in bacteriology

pet·ri·fac·tion \ˌpe-trə-ˈfak-shən\ *n* **1 :** the process of petrifying **2 :** something petrified **3 :** the quality or state of being petrified

pet·ri·fac·tive \-ˈfak-tiv\ *adj* **:** having the quality of converting organic matter into stone **:** PETRIFYING

pet·ri·fi·ca·tion \ˌpe-trə-fə-ˈkā-shən\ *n* **:** PETRIFACTION

pet·ri·fy \ˈpe-trə-ˌfī\ *vb* [MF *petrifier*, fr. *petr-* + *-ifier* -ify] *vt* **1 :** to convert into stone or a stony substance **2 :** to make rigid or inert like stone: **a :** to make lifeless or inactive **:** DEADEN **b :** to confound with fear, amazement, or awe **:** PARALYZE **~** *vi* **:** to become stone or of stony hardness or rigidity

Pe·trine \ˈpē-ˌtrīn\ *adj* [LL *Petrus* Peter] **:** of, relating to, or characteristic of the apostle Peter or the doctrines associated with his name

pet·ro·chem·i·cal \ˌpe-trō-ˈkem-i-kəl\ *n, often attrib* [*petro*leum + *chemical*] **:** a chemical isolated or derived from petroleum or natural gas — **pet·ro·chem·is·try** \-ˈkem-ə-strē\ *n*

pet·ro·glyph \ˈpe-trə-ˌglif\ *n* [F *pétroglyphe*, fr. *pétr-* petr- + *-glyphe* (as in *hiéroglyphe* hieroglyph)] **:** a carving or inscription on a rock

pe·trog·ra·pher \pə-ˈträg-rə-fər\ *n* **:** a specialist in petrography

pet·ro·graph·ic \ˌpe-trə-ˈgraf-ik\ *adj* **:** of or relating to petrography — **pet·ro·graph·i·cal** \-i-kəl\ *adj*

pe·trog·ra·phy \pə-ˈträg-rə-fē\ *n* [NL *petrographia*, fr. *petr-* + L *-graphia* -graphy] **:** the description and systematic classification of rocks

pet·rol \ˈpe-trəl, -ˌträl\ *n* [F *essence de pétrole*, lit., essence of petroleum] *Brit* **:** GASOLINE

pet·ro·la·tum \ˌpe-trə-ˈlāt-əm, -ˈlät-\ *n* [NL, fr. ML *petroleum*] **:** a neutral unctuous odorless tasteless substance obtained from petroleum and used esp. in ointments and dressings

pe·tro·le·um \pə-ˈtrō-lē-əm, -ˈtrōl-yəm\ *n* [ML, fr. L *petr-* + *oleum* oil — more at OIL] **1 :** an oily flammable bituminous liquid that may vary from almost colorless to black, occurs in many places in the upper strata of the earth, is a complex mixture of hydrocarbons with small amounts of other substances, and is prepared for use as gasoline, naphtha, or other products by various refining processes **2 :** a substance similar in composition to petroleum

pet·ro·log·ic \ˌpe-trə-ˈläj-ik\ *adj* **:** of or relating to petrology — **pet·ro·log·i·cal** \-i-kəl\ *adj* — **pet·ro·log·i·cal·ly** \-k(ə-)lē\ *adv*

pe·trol·o·gist \pə-ˈträl-ə-jəst\ *n* **:** a specialist in petrology

pe·trol·o·gy \-jē\ *n* [ISV] **:** a science that deals with the origin, history, occurrence, structure, chemical composition, and classification of rocks

pet·ro·nel \ˌpe-trə-ˈnel\ *n* [perh. modif. of MF *poitrinal, petrinal*, fr. *poitrinal* of the chest, fr. *poitrine* chest] **:** a portable firearm resembling a carbine of large caliber

pe·tro·sal \pə-ˈtrō-səl\ *adj* [NL *petrosa* petrous portion of the temporal bone, fr. L, fem. of *petrosus*] **:** HARD, STONY; *specif* **:** of, relating to, or situated in the region of the petrous portion of the temporal bone or capsule of the internal ear

pe·trous \ˈpe-trəs\ *adj* [MF *petreux*, fr. L *petrosus*, fr. *petra* rock, fr. Gk] **:** resembling stone esp. in hardness **:** ROCKY; *specif* **:** of, relating to, or constituting the exceptionally hard and dense portion of the temporal bone of man that contains the internal auditory organs

¹pet·ti·coat \ˈpet-ē-ˌkōt\ *n* [ME *petycote* short tunic, petticoat, fr. *pety* small + *cote* coat] **1 :** a skirt worn by women, girls, or young children: as **a :** an outer skirt formerly worn by women and small children **b :** a fancy skirt made to show below a draped-up overskirt **c :** an underskirt usu. a little shorter than outer clothing and often made with a ruffled, pleated, or lace edge **d** *archaic* **:** the skirt of a woman's riding habit **2 a :** a garment characteristic or typical of women **b :** WOMAN **3 :** something (as a valance) resembling a petticoat

²petticoat *adj* **:** FEMALE ⟨~ government⟩

pet·ti·fog \ˈpet-ē-ˌfȯg, -ˌfäg\ *vi* **pet·ti·fogged; pet·ti·fog·ging** [back-formation fr. *pettifogger*, prob. fr. *petty* + obs. *fogger* (pettifogger)] **1 :** to engage in legal chicanery **2 :** to quibble over insignificant details **:** CAVIL — **pet·ti·fog·ger** *n* — **pet·ti·fog·gery** \-(ə-)rē\ *n*

pet·ti·ly \ˈpet-ᵊl-ē\ *adv* **:** in a petty manner

pet·ti·ness \ˈpet-ē-nəs\ *n* **1 :** the quality or state of being petty **2 :** something petty **:** TRIVIALITY

pet·tish \ˈpet-ish\ *adj* [prob. fr. ⁴*pet*] **:** FRETFUL, PEEVISH — **pet·tish·ly** *adv* — **pet·tish·ness** *n*

pet·ti·toes \ˈpet-ē-ˌtōz\ *n pl* [pl. of obs. *pettytoe* (offal)] **1 :** the feet of a pig used as food **2 :** TOES, FEET

pet·ty \ˈpet-ē\ *adj* [ME *pety* small, minor, alter. of *petit*] **1 :** having secondary rank or importance **:** MINOR, SUBORDINATE **2 :** having little or no importance or significance **3 :** marked by or reflective of narrow interests and sympathies **:** SMALL-MINDED

petty cash *n* **:** cash kept on hand for payment of minor items

petty larceny *n* **:** PETIT LARCENY

petty officer *n* **:** an enlisted man in the navy of a rank corresponding to a noncommissioned officer in the army; *esp* **:** one in one of the three lowest grades (as petty officer second class)

pet·u·lance \ˈpech-ə-lən(t)s\ *n* **:** the quality or state of being petulant **:** PEEVISHNESS

pet·u·lan·cy \-lən-sē\ *n, archaic* **:** PETULANCE

pet·u·lant \-lənt\ *adj* [L or MF; MF, fr. L *petulant-, petulans;* akin to L *petere* to go to, attack, seek — more at FEATHER] **1 :** insolent or rude in speech or behavior **2 :** characterized by temporary or capricious ill humor **:** PEEVISH — **pet·u·lant·ly** *adv*

pe·tu·nia \pə-ˈt(y)ün-yə\ *n* [NL, genus name, fr. obs. F *petun* tobacco, fr. Tupi *petyn*] **:** any of a genus (*Petunia*) of tropical American herbs of the nightshade family with funnel-shaped corollas

pew \ˈpyü\ *n* [ME *pewe*, fr. MF *puie* balustrade, fr. L *podia*, pl. of *podium* parapet, podium, fr. Gk *podion* base, dim. of *pod-, pous* foot — more at FOOT] **1 :** a compartment in the auditorium of a church providing seats for several persons **2 :** one of the benches with backs and sometimes doors fixed in rows in a church

pe·wee \ˈpē-(ˌ)wē\ *n* [imit.] **:** any of various small olivaceous flycatchers

pe·wit \ˈpē-ˌwit, ˈpyü-ət\ *n* [imit.] **:** any of several birds: as **a :** LAPWING **b :** a small black-headed European gull (*Larus ridibundus*) **c :** PEWEE

pew·ter \ˈpyüt-ər\ *n* [ME, fr. MF *peutre;* akin to It *peltro* pewter] **1 :** any of various alloys having tin as chief component; *esp* **:** a dull alloy with lead formerly used for domestic utensils **2 :** utensils of pewter — **pewter** *adj*

pew·ter·er \ˈpyüt-ər-ər\ *n* **:** one that makes pewter utensils or vessels

pey·o·te \pā-ˈōt-ē\ *or* **pey·otl** \-ˈōt-ᵊl\ *n* [MexSp *peyote*, fr. Nahuatl *peyotl*] **1 :** any of several American cacti (genus *Lophophora*); *esp* **:** MESCAL **2 :** a stimulant drug derived from mescal buttons

pfen·nig \ˈfen-ig, -ik, *G* ˈ(p)fen-ik\ *n, pl* **pfen·nigs** \ˈfen-igz, -iks\ *or* **pfen·ni·ge** \ˈ(p)fen-i-gə, -i-yə\ [G, fr. OHG *pfenning* — more at PENNY] — see *deutsche mark* at MONEY table

pH \pē-ˈāch\ *n* **:** the negative logarithm of the effective hydrogen-ion concentration or hydrogen-ion activity in gram equivalents per liter used in expressing both acidity and alkalinity on a scale whose values run from 0 to 14 with 7 representing neutrality, numbers less than 7 increasing acidity, and numbers greater than 7 increasing alkalinity

Phae·dra \ˈfē-drə\ *n* [L, fr. Gk *Phaidra*] **:** the wife of Theseus and stepmother of Hippolytus

Pha·ë·thon \ˈfā-ə-ˌthän, -thən\ *n* [L, fr. Gk *Phaethōn*] **:** a son of Helios permitted for a day to drive the chariot of the sun and struck down with a thunderbolt by Zeus to keep the world from being set on fire

pha·eton \ˈfā-ət-ᵊn\ *n* [*Phaëthon*] **1 :** any of various light four-wheeled horse-drawn vehicles **2 :** TOURING CAR

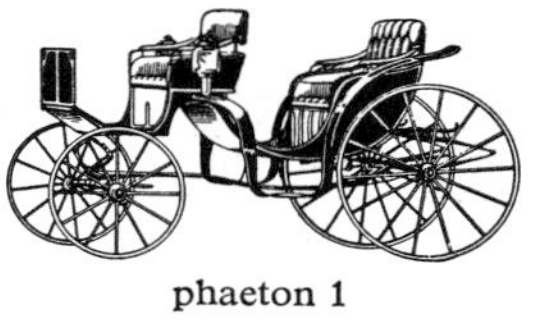

phaeton 1

phage \ˈfāj, ˈfäzh\ *n* [by shortening] **:** BACTERIOPHAGE

-phage \ˌfāj, ˌfäzh\ *n comb form* [Gk *-phagos*, fr. *-phagos* -phagous] **:** one that eats ⟨bacterio*phage*⟩

-pha·gia \ˈfā-j(ē-)ə\ *n comb form* [NL, fr. Gk] **:** -PHAGY ⟨dys*phagia*⟩

phago·cyte \ˈfag-ə-ˌsīt\ *n* [ISV, fr. Gk *phagein* + NL *-cyta* -cyte] **:** a cell (as a leukocyte) that characteristically engulfs foreign material and consumes debris and foreign bodies — **phago·cyt·ic** \ˌfag-ə-ˈsit-ik\ *adj*

phago·cyt·ize \ˈfag-ə-ˌsīt-ˌīz, -sə-ˌtīz\ *vt* **:** to consume by phagocytosis

phago·cy·to·sis \ˌfag-ə-(ˌ)sī-ˈtō-səs\ *n* **:** the engulfing and usu. destruction of particulate matter by phagocytes — **phago·cy·tot·ic** \-ˈtät-ik\ *adj*

-ph·a·gous \f-ə-gəs\ *adj comb form* [Gk *-phagos*, fr. *phagein* to eat — more at BAKSHEESH] **:** eating ⟨sapro*phagous*⟩

-ph·a·gy \f-ə-jē\ *n comb form* [Gk *-phagia*, fr. *phagein*] **:** eating of a (specified) type or substance ⟨geo*phagy*⟩
pha·lange \ˈfā-ˌlanj, fə-ˈ, fā-ˈ\ *n* [F, fr. Gk *phalang-*, *phalanx*] **:** PHALANX 2
pha·lan·geal \fə-ˈlan-j(ē-)əl, fā-; ˌfā-ˌlan-ˈjē-əl\ *adj* **:** of or relating to a phalanx or the phalanges
pha·lan·ger \fə-ˈlan-jər\ *n* [NL, fr. Gk *phalang-*, *phalanx*] **:** any of various marsupial mammals (family Phalangeridae) of the Australian region ranging in size from a mouse to a large cat
pha·lan·stery \ˈfal-ən-ˌster-ē, fə-ˈlan(t)-stə-rē\ *n* [F *phalanstère* dwelling of a Fourierist community, fr. L *phalang-*, *phalanx* + *-stère* (as in *monastère* monastery)] **1 a :** a Fourierist cooperative community **b :** a self-contained structure housing such a community **2 :** something resembling a Fourierist phalanstery
pha·lanx \ˈfā-ˌlaŋ(k)s, *Brit usu* ˈfal-ˌaŋ(k)s\ *n, pl* **pha·lanx·es** *or* **pha·lan·ges** \fə-ˈlan-(ˌ)jēz, fā-\ [L *phalang-*, *phalanx*, fr. Gk, battle line, digital bone, lit., log — more at BALK] **1 :** a body of heavily armed infantry formed in close deep ranks and files; *broadly* **:** a body of troops in close array **2** *pl* **phalanges :** one of the digital bones of the hand or foot of a vertebrate **3** *pl usu* **phalanxes a :** a massed arrangement of persons, animals, or things **b :** an organized body of persons
phal·a·rope \ˈfal-ə-ˌrōp\ *n* [F, fr. NL *phalaropod-*, *phalaropus*, fr. Gk *phalaris* coot + *pod-*, *pous* foot; akin to Gk *phalios* having a white spot — more at BALD, FOOT] **:** any of various small shorebirds (family Phalaropodidae) that resemble sandpipers but have lobate toes and are good swimmers
phal·lic \ˈfal-ik\ *adj* **1 :** of or relating to phallicism **2 :** of, relating to, or resembling a phallus
phal·li·cism \ˈfal-ə-ˌsiz-əm\ *n* **:** the worship of the generative principle as symbolized by the phallus
phal·lus \ˈfal-əs\ *n, pl* **phal·li** \ˈfal-ˌī, -ˌē\ *or* **phal·lus·es** [L, fr. Gk *phallos* penis, representation of the penis — more at BLOW] **1 :** a symbol or representation of the penis **2 :** PENIS
-phane \ˌfān\ *n comb form* [Gk *-phanēs* appearing, fr. *phainein* to show — more at FANCY] **:** substance having a (specified) form, quality, or appearance ⟨hydro*phane*⟩
pha·nero·gam \ˈfan-ə-rə-ˌgam, fə-ˈner-ə-\ *n* [F *phanérogame*, deriv. of Gk *phaneros* visible (fr. *phainein*) + *gamos* marriage — more at BIGAMY] **:** a seed plant or flowering plant **:** SPERMATOPHYTE — **pha·nero·gam·ic** \ˌfan-ə-rə-ˈgam-ik, fə-ˌner-ə-\ *adj* — **phan·er·og·a·mous** \ˌfan-ə-ˈräg-ə-məs\ *adj*
pha·nero·phyte \ˈfan-ə-rə-ˌfīt, fə-ˈner-ə-\ *n* [Gk *phaneros* + ISV *-phyte*] **:** a perennial plant that bears its overwintering buds well above the surface of the ground
phan·tasm \ˈfan-ˌtaz-əm\ *n* [ME *fantasme*, fr. OF, fr. L *phantasma*, fr. Gk, fr. *phantazein* to present to the mind — more at FANCY] **1 :** a product of phantasy: as **a :** delusive appearance **:** ILLUSION **b :** GHOST, SPECTER **c :** a figment of the imagination **:** FANTASY **2 :** a mental representation of a real object **3 :** a deceptive or illusory appearance of a thing — **phan·tas·mal** \fan-ˈtaz-məl\ *adj* — **phan·tas·mic** \-mik\ *adj*
phan·tas·ma \fan-ˈtaz-mə\ *n, pl* **phan·tas·ma·ta** \-mət-ə\ [L *phantasmat-*, *phantasma*] **:** PHANTASM 1
phan·tas·ma·go·ria \(ˌ)fan-ˌtaz-mə-ˈgōr-ē-ə, -ˈgȯr-\ *n* [F *phantasmagorie*, fr. *phantasme* phantasm (fr. OF *fantasme*) + *-agorie* (prob. fr. Gk *ageirein* to assemble, collect) — more at GREGARIOUS] **1 :** an optical effect by which figures on a screen appear to dwindle into the distance or to rush toward the observer with enormous increase of size **2 a :** a constantly shifting, complex succession of things seen or imagined **b :** a scene that constantly changes or fluctuates — **phan·tas·ma·go·ric** \-ˈgōr-ik, -ˈgȯr-, -ˈgär-\ *adj*
phantasy *var of* FANTASY
¹phan·tom \ˈfant-əm\ *n* [ME *fantosme*, *fantome*, fr. MF *fantosme*, modif. of L *phantasma*] **1 a :** something (as a specter) apparent to sense but with no substantial existence **:** APPARITION **b :** something elusive or visionary **:** WILL-O'-THE-WISP **c :** an object of continual dread or abhorrence **:** BUGBEAR **2 :** something existing in appearance only **:** SHADOW **3 :** a representation of something abstract, ideal, or incorporeal
²phantom *adj* **1 :** of the nature of, suggesting, or being a phantom **:** ILLUSORY **2 :** FICTITIOUS, DUMMY ⟨~ voters⟩
pha·raoh \ˈfe(ə)r-(ˌ)ō, ˈfā-(ˌ)rō, ˈfa(ə)r-(ˌ)ō\ *n, often cap* [LL *pharaon-*, *pharao*, fr. Gk *pharaō*, fr. Heb *par'ōh*, fr. Egypt *pr-'*;] **1 :** a ruler of ancient Egypt **2 :** TYRANT — **phar·a·on·ic** \ˌfer-ā-ˈän-ik, ˌfar-\ *adj, often cap*
pharaoh ant *n* **:** a little red ant (*Monomorium pharaonis*) that is a common household pest
phar·i·sa·ic \ˌfar-ə-ˈsā-ik\ *adj* [LL *pharisaicus*, fr. LGk *pharisaikos*, fr. Gk *pharisaios* Pharisee] **1** *cap* **:** of or relating to the Pharisees **2 :** PHARISAICAL
phar·i·sa·ical \-ˈsā-ə-kəl\ *adj* **:** marked by hypocritical censorious self-righteousness — **phar·i·sa·ical·ly** \-k(ə-)lē\ *adv* — **phar·i·sa·ical·ness** \-kəl-nəs\ *n*
phar·i·sa·ism \ˈfar-ə-(ˌ)sā-ˌiz-əm\ *n* [NL *pharisaismus*, fr. Gk *pharisaios*] **1** *cap* **:** the doctrines or practices of the Pharisees **2** *often cap* **:** pharisaical character, spirit, or attitude
phar·i·see \ˈfar-ə-(ˌ)sē\ *n* [ME *pharise*, fr. OE *farise*, fr. LL *pharisaeus*, fr. Gk *pharisaios*, fr. Aram *pĕrīshayyā*, pl. of *pĕrīshā*, lit., separated] **1** *cap* **:** a member of a Jewish sect of the intertestamental period noted for strict observance of rites and ceremonies of the written law and for insistence on the validity of the oral law **2 :** a pharisaical person
phar·ma·ceu·tic \ˌfär-mə-ˈsüt-ik\ *adj* **:** PHARMACEUTICAL
¹phar·ma·ceu·ti·cal \-i-kəl\ *adj* [LL *pharmaceuticus*, fr. Gk *pharmakeutikos*, fr. *pharmakeuein* to administer drugs — more at PHARMACY] **:** of or relating to pharmacy or pharmacists — **phar·ma·ceu·ti·cal·ly** \-k(ə-)lē\ *adv*
²pharmaceutical *n* **:** a pharmaceutical preparation
phar·ma·ceu·tics \-iks\ *n pl but sing in constr* **:** the science of preparing, using, or dispensing medicines **:** PHARMACY
phar·ma·cist \ˈfär-mə-səst\ *n* **:** one skilled or engaged in pharmacy
pharmaco- *comb form* [Gk *pharmako-*, fr. *pharmakon*] **:** medicine **:** drug ⟨*pharmaco*logy⟩
phar·ma·co·dy·nam·ic \ˌfär-mə-kō-ˌdī-ˈnam-ik\ *adj* [back-formation fr. *pharmacodynamics*] **:** of, relating to, or used in pharmacodynamics — **phar·ma·co·dy·nam·i·cal·ly** \-i-k(ə-)lē\ *adv*
phar·ma·co·dy·nam·ics \-iks\ *n pl but sing in constr* **:** a branch of pharmacology dealing with the reactions between drugs and living structures
phar·ma·cog·no·sy \ˌfär-mə-ˈkäg-nə-sē\ *n* [ISV, fr. Gk *pharmakon* + *-gnōsia* knowledge, fr. *gnōsis* — more at GNOSIS] **:** descriptive pharmacology dealing with crude drugs and simples
phar·ma·co·log·i·cal \ˌfär-mə-kə-ˈläj-i-kəl\ *or* **phar·ma·co·log·ic** \-ik\ *adj* **:** of, relating to, or determined by pharmacology — **phar·ma·co·log·i·cal·ly** \-i-k(ə-)lē\ *adv*
phar·ma·col·o·gist \ˌfär-mə-ˈkäl-ə-jəst\ *n* **:** a specialist in pharmacology
phar·ma·col·o·gy \-jē\ *n* **1 :** the science of drugs including materia medica, toxicology, and therapeutics **2 :** the properties and reactions of drugs esp. with relation to their therapeutic value
phar·ma·co·poe·ia \ˌfär-mə-kə-ˈpē-(y)ə\ *n* [NL, fr. LGk *pharmakopoiia* preparation of drugs, fr. Gk *pharmako-* + *poiein* to make — more at POET] **1 :** a book describing drugs, chemicals, and medicinal preparations; *esp* **:** one issued by official authority and recognized as a standard **2 :** a collection or stock of drugs — **phar·ma·co·poe·ial** \-(y)əl\ *adj*
phar·ma·cy \ˈfär-mə-sē\ *n* [LL *pharmacia* administration of drugs, fr. Gk *pharmakeia*, fr. *pharmakeuein* to administer drugs, fr. *pharmakon* magic charm, poison, drug; akin to Lith *burti* to practice magic] **1 :** the art or practice of preparing, preserving, compounding, and dispensing drugs **2 a :** a place where medicines are compounded or dispensed **b :** DRUGSTORE **3 :** PHARMACOPOEIA 2
phar·os \ˈfa(ə)r-ˌäs, ˈfe(ə)r-\ *n* [Gk, fr. *Pharos*, island in the bay of Alexandria, Egypt, famous for its lighthouse] **:** a lighthouse or beacon to guide seamen
pharyng- *or* **pharyngo-** *comb form* [Gk, fr. *pharyng-*, *pharynx*] **:** pharynx ⟨*pharyng*itis⟩ ⟨*pharyngo*logy⟩
pha·ryn·geal \fə-ˈrin-j(ē-)əl, ˌfar-ən-ˈjē-əl\ *adj* [NL *pharyngeus*, fr. *pharyng-*, *pharynx*] **:** relating to or located or produced in the region of the pharynx
phar·yn·gi·tis \ˌfar-ən-ˈjīt-əs\ *n* **:** inflammation of the pharynx
phar·yn·gol·o·gy \ˌfar-ən-ˈgäl-ə-jē\ *n* **:** a branch of medical science dealing with the pharynx and its diseases
phar·ynx \ˈfar-iŋ(k)s\ *n, pl* **pha·ryn·ges** \fə-ˈrin-(ˌ)jēz\ *also* **phar·ynx·es** [NL *pharyng-*, *pharynx*, fr. Gk, throat, pharynx; akin to ON *barki* throat, L *forare* to bore — more at BORE] **:** the part of the alimentary canal between the cavity of the mouth and the esophagus
¹phase \ˈfāz\ *n* [NL *phasis*, fr. Gk, appearance of a star, phase of the moon, fr. *phainein* to show (middle voice, to appear) — more at FANCY] **1 :** a particular appearance or state in a regularly recurring cycle of changes ⟨~s of the moon⟩ **2 a :** a stage or interval in a development or cycle **b :** an aspect or part under consideration **3 :** the point or stage in a period in uniform circular motion, harmonic motion, or the periodic changes of any magnitude varying according to a simple harmonic law to which the rotation, oscillation, or variation has advanced considered in its relation to a standard position or assumed instant of starting **4 :** a homogeneous, physically distinct, and mechanically separable portion of matter present in a nonhomogeneous physical-chemical system **5 :** an individual or subgroup distinguishably different in appearance or behavior from the norm of the group to which it belongs; *also* **:** the distinguishing peculiarity — **pha·sic** \ˈfā-zik\ *adj*
syn PHASE, ASPECT, SIDE, FACET, ANGLE mean one of the possible ways of viewing or being presented to view. PHASE implies a change in appearance often without clear reference to an observer; ASPECT may stress the point of view of an observer and its limitation of what is seen or considered; SIDE stresses one of several aspects from which something may be viewed; FACET implies one of a multiplicity of sides each of which manifests the central quality of the whole; ANGLE suggests an aspect seen from a very restricted or specific point of view
²phase *vt* **1 :** to adjust so as to be in phase **2 a :** to conduct or carry out by planned phases **b :** to schedule or contract for to be performed or supplied as required **3 :** to introduce in stages ⟨~ in new fighter models⟩
phase–con·trast \ˈfāz-ˌkän-ˌtrast\ *adj* **:** of or employing the phase microscope
phase microscope *n* **:** a microscope that translates differences in phase of the light transmitted through or reflected by the object into differences of intensity in the image
phase modulation *n* **:** modulation of the phase of a radio carrier wave by voice or other signal
phase·out \ˈfā-ˌzau̇t\ *n* **:** a gradual stopping of operations or production **:** a closing down by phases
-pha·sia \ˈfā-zh(ē-)ə\ *n comb form* [NL, fr. Gk, speech, fr. *phasis* utterance, fr. *phanai* to speak, say — more at BAN] **:** speech disorder of a (specified) type ⟨dys*phasia*⟩
phat \ˈfat\ *adj* [alter. of ¹*fat*] *of copy or type matter* **:** susceptible of easy and rapid setting
phat·ic \ˈfat-ik\ *adj* [Gk *phatos*, verbal of *phanai* to speak] **:** revealing or sharing feelings or establishing an atmosphere of sociability rather than communicating ideas ⟨~ communion⟩ — **phat·i·cal·ly** \-i-k(ə-)lē\ *adv*
pheas·ant \ˈfez-ᵊnt\ *n, pl* **pheasant** *or* **pheasants** [ME *fesaunt*, fr. AF, fr. OF *fesan*, fr. L *phasianus*, fr. Gk *phasianos*, fr. *phasianos* of the Phasis river, fr. *Phasis*, river in Colchis] **1 :** any of numerous large long-tailed brilliantly colored Old World gallinaceous birds (*Phasianus* and related genera of the family Phasianidae) many of which are reared as ornamental or game birds **2 :** any of various birds resembling a pheasant
phel·lem \ˈfel-ˌem\ *n* [Gk *phellos* cork + E *-em* (as in *phloem*)] **:** a layer of usu. suberized cells produced outwardly by a phellogen
phel·lo·derm \ˈfel-ə-ˌdərm\ *n* [Gk *phellos* + ISV *-derm*] **:** a layer of parenchyma produced inwardly by a phellogen — **phel·lo·der·mal** \ˌfel-ə-ˈdər-məl\ *adj*
phel·lo·gen \ˈfel-ə-jən\ *n* [Gk *phellos* + ISV *-gen*] **:** a secondary meristem that initiates phellem and phelloderm in the periderm of a stem — **phel·lo·ge·net·ic** \ˌfel-ə-jə-ˈnet-ik\ *adj* — **phel·lo·gen·ic** \-ˈjen-ik\ *adj*
phen- *or* **pheno-** *comb form* [obs. *phene* (benzene), fr. F *phène*, fr. Gk *phainein* to show; fr. its occurrence in illuminating gas — more at FANCY] **:** related to or derived from benzene ⟨*phen*ol⟩ **:** containing phenyl ⟨*pheno*barbital⟩

phe·na·caine *or* **phe·no·cain** \ˈfē-nə-ˌkān, ˈfen-ə-\ *n* [*phenacaine* prob. fr. *phene*tidine + acet- + *-caine; phenocain* prob. irreg. fr. *phen-* + *-caine*] **:** a crystalline base $C_{18}H_{22}N_2O_2$ or its hydrochloride used as a local anesthetic

phen·ac·e·tin \fi-ˈnas-ət-ən\ *n* [ISV] **:** ACETOPHENETIDIN

phen·a·kite \ˈfen-ə-ˌkīt\ *or* **phen·a·cite** \-ˌsīt\ *n* [G *phenakit,* fr. Gk *phenak-, phenax* deceiver; fr. its being easily mistaken for quartz] **:** a glassy mineral Be_2SiO_4 that consists of a beryllium silicate and occurs in rhombohedral crystals

phen·an·threne \fə-ˈnan-ˌthrēn\ *n* [ISV *phen-* + *anthracene*] **:** a crystalline aromatic hydrocarbon $C_{14}H_{10}$ of coal tar isomeric with anthracene

phen·azine \ˈfen-ə-ˌzēn\ *n* [ISV] **:** a yellowish crystalline base $C_{12}H_8N_2$ that is the parent compound of many azine dyes and a few antibiotics

phe·net·i·dine \fə-ˈnet-ə-ˌdēn\ *n* [*phenet*ole + *-idine*] **:** any of three liquid basic amino derivatives $C_6H_4(NH_2)OC_2H_5$ of phenetole used esp. in manufacturing dyestuffs

phen·e·tole \ˈfen-ə-ˌtōl\ *n* [ISV *phen-* + *et*hyl + *-ole*] **:** the aromatic liquid ethyl ether $C_8H_{10}O$ of phenol

phe·no·bar·bi·tal \ˌfē-nō-ˈbär-bə-ˌtȯl\ *n* **:** a crystalline barbiturate $C_{12}H_{12}N_2O_3$ used as a hypnotic and sedative

phe·no·copy \ˈfē-nə-ˌkäp-ē\ *n* [*pheno*type + *copy*] **:** a phenotypic variation due to modifying environmental influences that mimics the expression of a genotype other than its own

phe·no·cryst \-ˌkrist\ *n* [F *phénocryste,* fr. Gk *phainein* to show + *krystallos* crystal — more at FANCY] **:** one of the prominent embedded crystals of a porphyry

phe·nol \ˈfē-ˌnōl, fi-ˈ\ *n* [ISV *phen-* + *-ol*] **1 :** a caustic poisonous crystalline acidic compound C_6H_5OH present in coal tar and wood tar that in dilute solution is used as a disinfectant **2 :** any of various acidic compounds analogous to phenol and regarded as hydroxyl derivatives of aromatic hydrocarbons — **phe·no·lic** \fi-ˈnō-lik, -ˈnäl-ik\ *adj*

phe·no·late \ˈfē-nᵊl-ˌāt\ *n* **:** PHENOXIDE

phe·no·lic \fi-ˈnō-lik, -ˈnäl-ik\ *n* **:** a resin or plastic made by condensation of a phenol with an aldehyde and used esp. for molding and insulating and in coatings and adhesives

phe·no·log·i·cal \ˌfēn-ᵊl-ˈäj-i-kəl\ *adj* **:** of, relating to, or involving phenology — **phe·no·log·i·cal·ly** \-k(ə-)lē\ *adv*

phe·nol·o·gy \fi-ˈnäl-ə-jē\ *n* [*pheno*mena + *-logy*] **1 :** a branch of science dealing with the relations between climate and periodic biological phenomena **2 :** phenological phenomena (as of a kind of organism)

phe·nol·phtha·lein \ˌfē-ˌnōl-ˈthal-ē-ən, -ˈthal-ˌēn, -ˈthāl-\ *n* [ISV] **:** a white or yellowish white crystalline compound $C_{20}H_{14}O_4$ used in medicine as a laxative and in analysis as an indicator because its solution is brilliant red in alkalies and is decolorized by acids

phenol red *n* **:** a red crystalline compound $C_{19}H_{14}O_5S$ used esp. as an acid-base indicator

phe·nom·e·nal \fi-ˈnäm-ən-ᵊl\ *adj* **:** relating to or being a phenomenon: as **a :** known through the senses rather than through thought or intuition **b :** concerned with phenomena rather than with hypotheses **c :** EXTRAORDINARY, REMARKABLE **syn** see MATERIAL — **phe·nom·e·nal·ly** \-ə-nə-lē\ *adv*

phe·nom·e·nal·ism \-ən-ᵊl-ˌiz-əm\ *n* **1 :** a theory that limits knowledge to phenomena only **2 :** a theory that all knowledge is of phenomena and all existence is phenomenal — **phe·nom·e·nal·ist** \-ᵊl-əst\ *n* — **phe·nom·e·nal·is·tic** \-ˌnäm-ən-ᵊl-ˈis-tik\ *adj* — **phe·nom·e·nal·is·ti·cal·ly** \-ti-k(ə-)lē\ *adv*

phe·nom·e·no·log·i·cal \fi-ˌnäm-ən-ᵊl-ˈäj-i-kəl\ *adj* **:** of or relating to phenomenology or phenomena — **phe·nom·e·no·log·i·cal·ly** \-k(ə-)lē\ *adv*

phe·nom·e·nol·o·gist \fi-ˌnäm-ə-ˈnäl-ə-jəst\ *n* **:** an advocate of phenomenology

phe·nom·e·nol·o·gy \-jē\ *n* **1 :** the philosophical study of the progressive development of mind **2 :** the description of the formal structure of phenomena in abstraction from interpretation or evaluation esp. as a foundation for the sciences

phe·nom·e·non \fi-ˈnäm-ə-ˌnän, -nən\ *n, pl* **phe·nom·e·na** \-nə, -ˌnä\ *or* **phenomenons** [LL *phaenomenon,* fr. Gk *phainomenon,* fr. neut. of *phainomenos,* prp. of *phainesthai* to appear, middle voice of *phainein* to show — more at FANCY] **1** *pl phenomena* **:** an observable fact or event **2** *pl phenomena* **a :** an object or aspect known through the senses rather than by thought or intuition **b :** an object of experience in space and time as distinguished from a thing-in-itself **c :** a fact or event of scientific interest susceptible of scientific description and explanation **3 a :** a rare or significant fact or event **b** *pl phenomenons* **:** an exceptional, unusual, or abnormal person, thing, or occurrence **:** PRODIGY

phe·no·thi·azine \ˌfē-nō-ˈthī-ə-ˌzēn\ *n* [ISV] **:** a greenish yellow crystalline compound $C_{12}H_9NS$ used as an anthelmintic and insecticide esp. in veterinary practice

phe·no·type \ˈfē-nə-ˌtīp\ *n* [G *phänotypus,* fr. Gk *phainein* to show + *typos* type] **1 :** the detectable expression of the interaction of genotype and environment constituting the visible characters of an organism **2 :** a group of organisms sharing a particular phenotype — **phe·no·typ·ic** \ˌfē-nə-ˈtip-ik\ *or* **phe·no·typ·i·cal** \-i-kəl\ *adj* — **phe·no·typ·i·cal·ly** \-k(ə-)lē\ *adv*

phen·ox·ide \fi-ˈnäk-ˌsīd\ *n* **:** a salt of a phenol esp. in its capacity as a weak acid

phe·nyl \ˈfen-ᵊl, ˈfēn-\ *n* [ISV] **:** a univalent radical C_6H_5 derived from benzene by removal of one hydrogen atom — **phe·nyl·ic** \fi-ˈnil-ik\ *adj*

phe·nyl·al·a·nine \ˌfen-ᵊl-ˈal-ə-ˌnēn, ˌfēn-\ *n* [ISV] **:** an essential amino acid $C_9H_{11}NO_2$ obtained by the hydrolysis of proteins and converted in the normal body to tyrosine

phe·nyl·ene \ˈfen-ᵊl-ˌēn, ˈfēn-\ *n* [ISV] **:** any of three bivalent radicals — C_6H_4 — derived from benzene by removal of two hydrogen atoms

phi \ˈfī\ *n* [MGk, fr. Gk *phei*] **:** the 21st letter of the Greek alphabet — symbol Φ or ϕ

phi·al \ˈfī(-ə)l\ *n* [ME, fr. L *phiala,* fr. Gk *phialē*] **:** VIAL

phil- *or* **philo-** *comb form* [ME, fr. OF, fr. L, fr. Gk, fr. *philos* dear, friendly] **:** loving **:** having an affinity for ⟨*philo*progenitive⟩

[1]**-phil** \ˌfil\ *or* **-phile** \ˌfīl\ *n comb form* [F *-phile,* fr. Gk *-philos* -philous] **:** lover **:** one having an affinity for or a strong attraction to ⟨acido*phil*⟩ ⟨Slavo*phile*⟩

[2]**-phil** *or* **-phile** *adj comb form* [NL *-philus,* fr. L, fr. Gk *-philos*] **:** loving **:** having a fondness or affinity for ⟨hemo*phile*⟩ ⟨Franco*phil*⟩

Phil·a·del·phia lawyer \ˌfil-ə-ˌdel-fyə-, -fē-ə-\ *n* [*Philadelphia,* Pa.] **:** a shrewd lawyer versed in the intricacies of legal phraseology and adept at exploiting legal technicalities

phil·a·del·phus \ˌfil-ə-ˈdel-fəs\ *n* [NL, genus name, fr. Gk *philadelphos* brotherly, fr. *phil-* + *adelphos* brother — more at -ADELPHOUS] **:** any of a genus of ornamental shrubs of the saxifrage family widely distributed in temperate regions

phi·lan·der \fə-ˈlan-dər\ *vi* **phi·lan·der·ing** \-d(ə-)riŋ\ [fr. obs. *philander* (lover, philanderer), prob. fr. the name *Philander*] **:** to make love frivolously **:** FLIRT — **phi·lan·der·er** \-dər-ər\ *n*

phil·an·throp·ic \ˌfil-ən-ˈthräp-ik\ *adj* **1 :** of, relating to, or characterized by philanthropy **:** BENEVOLENT **2 :** ELEEMOSYNARY — **phil·an·throp·i·cal** \-i-kəl\ *adj* — **phil·an·throp·i·cal·ly** \-k(ə-)lē\ *adv*

phi·lan·thro·pist \fə-ˈlan(t)-thrə-pəst\ *n* **:** one who practices philanthropy

phi·lan·thro·py \-pē\ *n* [LL *philanthropia,* fr. Gk *philanthrōpia,* fr. *philanthrōpos* loving mankind, fr. *phil-* + *anthrōpos* man] **1 :** goodwill to fellow men; *esp* **:** active effort to promote human welfare **:** HUMANITARIANISM **2 :** a philanthropic act or gift or an organization distributing or supported by philanthropic funds

phil·a·tel·ic \ˌfil-ə-ˈtel-ik\ *adj* **:** of or relating to philately — **phil·a·tel·i·cal·ly** \-i-k(ə-)lē\ *adv*

phi·lat·e·list \fə-ˈlat-ᵊl-əst\ *n* **:** a specialist in philately

phi·lat·e·ly \fə-ˈlat-ᵊl-ē\ *n* [F *philatélie,* fr. *phil-* + Gk *ateleia* tax exemption, fr. *atelēs* free from tax, fr. *a-* + *telos* tax; akin to Gk *telein* to pay, *tlēnai* to bear; fr. the fact that a stamped letter frees the recipient from paying the mailing charges — more at TOLERATE] **:** the collection and study of postage and imprinted stamps

Phi·le·mon \fə-ˈlē-mən, fī-\ *n* [Gk *Philēmōn*] **:** a friend and probable convert of the apostle Paul

[1]**phil·har·mon·ic** \ˌfil-ər-ˈmän-ik, ˌfil-(ˌ)(h)är-\ *adj* [F *philharmonique,* lit., loving harmony, fr. It *filarmonico,* fr. *fil-* phil- + *armonia* harmony, fr. L *harmonia*] **:** of or relating to a musical organization and esp. a symphony orchestra

[2]**philharmonic** *n* **:** a musical organization

philharmonic pitch *n* **1 :** a tuning standard formerly common in England of about 450 vibrations per second for A above middle C — called also *high pitch* **2 :** INTERNATIONAL PITCH

phil·hel·lene \fil-ˈhel-ˌēn\ *or* **phil·hel·len·ic** \ˌfil-hə-ˈlen-ik\ *adj* [Gk *philellēn,* fr. *phil-* + *Hellēn* Hellene] **:** admiring Greece or the Greeks — **philhellene** *n* — **phil·hel·le·nism** \fil-ˈhel-ə-ˌniz-əm\ *n* — **phil·hel·le·nist** \-nəst\ *n*

-phil·ia \ˈfil-ē-ə\ *n comb form* [NL, fr. Gk *philia* friendship, fr. *philos* dear] **1 :** tendency toward ⟨hemo*philia*⟩ **2 :** abnormal appetite or liking for ⟨necro*philia*⟩

-phil·ic \ˈfil-ik\ *adj comb form* [Gk *-philos* -philous] **:** having an affinity for **:** loving ⟨photo*philic*⟩

phi·lip·pic \fə-ˈlip-ik\ *n* [MF *philippique,* fr. L & Gk; L *philippica, orationes philippicae,* speeches of Cicero against Mark Anthony, trans. of Gk *philippikoi logoi,* speeches of Demosthenes against Philip II of Macedon, lit., speeches relating to Philip] **:** a discourse or declamation full of acrimonious invective **:** TIRADE

Phil·ip·pine mahogany \ˌfil-ə-ˌpēn-\ *n* [*Philippine* islands] **:** any of several Philippine timber trees with wood resembling that of the true mahoganies; *also* **:** its wood

phi·lis·tia \fə-ˈlis-tē-ə\ *n pl, often cap* [*Philistia,* ancient country of southwest Palestine] **:** the class or world of cultural philistines

phi·lis·tine \ˈfil-ə-ˌstēn; fə-ˈlis-tən, -ˌtēn; ˈfil-ə-stən\ *n* **1** *cap* **:** a native or inhabitant of ancient Philistia **2** *often cap* **a :** a crass prosaic often priggish individual guided by material rather than intellectual or artistic values **:** BABBITT **b :** one uninformed in a special area of knowledge — **philistine** *adj* — **phi·lis·tin·ism** \-ˌiz-əm\ *n*

philo·den·dron \ˌfil-ə-ˈden-drən\ *n, pl* **philodendrons** *or* **philo·den·dra** \-drə\ [NL, fr. Gk, neut. of *philodendros* loving trees, fr. *phil-* + *dendron* tree — more at DENDR-] **:** any of various aroid plants (as of the genus *Philodendron*) cultivated for their showy foliage

phi·log·y·ny \fə-ˈläj-ə-nē\ *n* [Gk *philogynia,* fr. *phil-* + *gynē* woman — more at QUEEN] **:** fondness for women

philo·log·i·cal \ˌfil-ə-ˈläj-i-kəl *also* ˌfī-lə-\ *adj* **:** of, relating to, or dealing with philology — **philo·log·i·cal·ly** \-k(ə-)lē\ *adv*

phi·lol·o·gist \fə-ˈläl-ə-jəst *also* fī-\ *n* **:** a specialist in philology

phi·lol·o·gy \-jē\ *n* [F *philologie,* fr. L *philologia* love of learning and literature, fr. Gk, fr. *philologos* fond of learning and literature, fr. *phil-* + *logos* word, speech — more at LEGEND] **1 :** the study of literature and of relevant disciplines **2 a :** LINGUISTICS; *esp* **:** historical and comparative linguistics **b :** the study of human speech esp. as the vehicle of literature and as a field of study that sheds light on cultural history

Phil·o·mel \ˈfil-ə-ˌmel\ *n* [L *Philomela* Philomela, nightingale] **:** NIGHTINGALE

Phil·o·me·la \ˌfil-ə-ˈmē-lə\ *n* [L, fr. Gk *Philomēlē*] **:** an Athenian princess raped and deprived of her tongue by her brother-in-law Tereus and according to Ovid subsequently transformed into a nightingale

philo·pro·gen·i·tive \ˌfil-ə-prō-ˈjen-ət-iv\ *adj* [*phil-* + L *progenitus,* pp. of *progignere* to beget — more at PROGENITOR] **1 :** tending to produce offspring **:** PROLIFIC **2 :** of, relating to, or characterized by love of offspring — **philo·pro·gen·i·tive·ness** *n*

phi·lo·sophe \ˌfē-lə-ˈzȯf\ *n* [F, lit., philosopher] **:** one of the deistic or materialistic writers and thinkers of the 18th century French Enlightenment

phi·los·o·pher \fə-ˈläs-(ə-)fər\ *n* [ME, modif. of MF *philosophe,* fr. L *philosophus,* fr. Gk *philosophos,* fr. *phil-* + *sophia* wisdom, fr. *sophos* wise] **1 a :** SCHOLAR, THINKER **b :** a student of philosophy **2 a :** a person whose philosophical perspective enables him to meet trouble with equanimity **b :** the expounder of a theory in a particular area of experience **c :** PHILOSOPHIZER

philosophers' stone *n* **:** an imaginary stone, substance, or chemical preparation believed to have the power of transmuting baser metals into gold and sought for by alchemists

philo·soph·ic \ˌfil-ə-ˈsäf-ik *also* -ˈzäf-\ *adj* **1 a :** of or relating to philosophers or philosophy **b :** based on philosophy **2 :** characterized by the attitude of a philosopher; *specif* **:** calm in face of trouble **:** TEMPERATE — **philo·soph·i·cal** \-i-kəl\ *adj* — **philo·soph·i·cal·ly** \-k(ə-)lē\ *adv*

phi·los·o·phize \fə-ˈläs-ə-ˌfīz\ *vi* **1 :** to reason in the manner of a

philosopher **2 :** to expound an esp. superficial moralizing philosophy — **phi·los·o·phiz·er** *n*

phi·los·o·phy \fə-ˈläs-(ə-)fē\ *n* [ME *philosophie,* fr. OF, fr. L *philosophia,* fr. Gk, fr. *philosophos* philosopher] **1 a :** pursuit of wisdom **b :** a search for truth through logical reasoning rather than factual observation **c :** an analysis of the grounds of and concepts expressing fundamental beliefs **2 a** (1) *archaic* **:** PHYSICAL SCIENCE (2) **:** ETHICS **b** (1) **:** all learning exclusive of technical precepts and practical arts (2) **:** sciences and liberal arts exclusive of medicine, law, and theology ⟨doctor of ~⟩ (3) **:** the 4-year college course of a major seminary **c :** a discipline comprising logic, aesthetics, ethics, metaphysics, and epistemology **3 a :** a system of philosophical concepts **b :** a theory underlying or regarding a sphere of activity or thought **4 a :** the beliefs, concepts, and attitudes of an individual or group **b :** calmness of temper and judgment befitting a philosopher

-ph·i·lous \f-(ə-)ləs\ *adj comb form* [Gk *-philos,* fr. *philos* dear, friendly] **:** loving **:** having an affinity for ⟨acido*philous*⟩

phil·ter *or* **phil·tre** \ˈfil-tər\ *n* [MF *philtre,* fr. L *philtrum,* fr. Gk *philtron;* akin to Gk *philos* dear] **1 :** a potion, drug, or charm held to have the power to excite sexual passion **2 :** a potion credited with magical power

phiz \ˈfiz\ *n* [by shortening & alter. fr. *physiognomy*] **:** FACE

phleb- *or* **phlebo-** *comb form* [ME *fleb-,* fr. MF, fr. LL *phlebo-,* fr. Gk *phleb-, phlebo-,* fr. *phleb-, phleps;* akin to L *fluere* to flow — more at FLUID] **:** vein ⟨*phleb*itis⟩

phle·bi·tis \fli-ˈbīt-əs\ *n* [NL] **:** inflammation of a vein

phle·bot·o·mist \fli-ˈbät-ə-məst\ *n* **:** one that practices phlebotomy

phle·bot·o·mize \-ˌmīz\ *vt* **:** to draw blood from **:** BLEED ~ *vi* **:** to practice phlebotomy

phle·bot·o·my \-mē\ *n* [ME *fleobotomie,* fr. MF *flebotomie,* fr. LL *phlebotomia,* fr. Gk, fr. *phleb-* + *-tomia* -tomy] **:** the letting of blood in the treatment of disease **:** VENESECTION

Phleg·e·thon \ˈfleg-ə-ˌthän\ *n* [L, fr. Gk *Phlegethōn*] **:** a river of Hades in Greek mythology containing fire instead of water

phlegm \ˈflem\ *n* [ME *fleume,* fr. MF, fr. LL *phlegmat-, phlegma,* fr. Gk, flame, inflammation, phlegm, fr. *phlegein* to burn — more at BLACK] **1 :** one of the four humors of early physiology supposed to be cold and moist and to cause sluggishness **2 :** viscid mucus secreted in abnormal quantity in the respiratory passages **3 a :** dull or apathetic coldness or indifference **b :** intrepid coolness or calm fortitude **syn** see EQUANIMITY — **phlegmy** \ˈflem-ē\ *adj*

phleg·mat·ic \fleg-ˈmat-ik\ *adj* **1 :** resembling, consisting of, or producing the humor phlegm **2 :** having or showing a slow and stolid temperament **syn** see IMPASSIVE — **phleg·mat·i·cal** \-i-kəl\ *adj* — **phleg·mat·i·cal·ly** \-k(ə-)lē\ *adv*

phlo·em \ˈflō-ˌem\ *n* [G, fr. Gk *phloios, phloos* bark; akin to Gk *phallos* penis — more at BLOW] **:** a complex tissue in the vascular system of higher plants consisting mainly of sieve tubes and elongated parenchyma cells usu. with fibers and functioning in translocation and in support and storage

phloem necrosis *n* **:** a pathological state in a plant characterized by brown discoloration and disintegration of the phloem; *esp* **:** a fatal virus disease of the American elm

phloem ray *n* **:** a vascular ray or part of a vascular ray that is located in phloem — called also *bast ray;* compare XYLEM RAY

phlo·gis·tic \flō-ˈjis-tik\ *adj* **1** [NL *phlogiston*] **:** of or relating to phlogiston **2** [Gk *phlogistos*] **:** of or relating to inflammations and fevers

phlo·gis·ton \-tən\ *n* [NL, fr. Gk, neut. of *phlogistos* inflammable, fr. *phlogizein* to set on fire, fr. *phlog-, phlox* flame, fr. *phlegein*] **:** the hypothetical principle of fire regarded formerly as a material substance

phlog·o·pite \ˈfläg-ə-ˌpīt\ *n* [G *phlogopit,* fr. Gk *phlogōpos* fiery-looking, fr. *phlog-, phlox* + *ōps* face — more at EYE] **:** a usu. brown to red form of mica

phlox \ˈfläks\ *n, pl* **phlox** *or* **phlox·es** [NL, genus name, fr. L, a flower, fr. Gk, flame, wallflower] **:** any of a genus (*Phlox* of the family Polemoniaceae, the phlox family) of American annual or perennial herbs with red, purple, white, or variegated flowers

phlyc·ten·ule \flik-ˈten-(ˌ)yü(ə)l\ *n* [NL *phlyctenula,* dim. of *phlyctena* pustule, fr. Gk *phlyktaina* blister, fr. *phlyzein* to boil over — more at FLUID] **:** a small vesicle or pustule; *esp* **:** one on the conjunctiva or cornea of the eye

-phobe \ˌfōb\ *n comb form* [Gk *-phobos* fearing] **:** one fearing or averse to (something specified) ⟨Franco*phobe*⟩

pho·bia \ˈfō-bē-ə\ *n* [NL, fr. LL *-phobia,* fr. Gk, fr. *-phobos* fearing, fr. *phobos* fear, flight; akin to Gk *phebesthai* to flee, be frightened, Lith *bėgti* to flee] **:** an exaggerated usu. inexplicable and illogical fear of a particular object or class of objects

pho·bic \ˈfō-bik, ˈfäb-ik\ *adj* **1 :** of, relating to, or constituting phobia **2 :** tending to withdraw from something unpleasant

-pho·bic \ˈfō-bik, ˈfäb-ik\ *or* **-ph·o·bous** \f-ə-bəs\ *adj comb form* [*-phobic* fr. F *-phobique,* fr. LL *-phobicus,* fr. Gk *-phobikos,* fr. *-phobia; -phobous* fr. LL *-phobus,* fr. Gk *-phobos*] **1 :** having an aversion for ⟨calci*phobous*⟩ **2 :** lacking affinity for ⟨lyo*phobic*⟩

phoe·be \ˈfē-(ˌ)bē\ *n* [alter. of *pewee*] **:** any of several American flycatchers (genus *Sayornis*); *esp* **:** one (*S. phoebe*) of the eastern U.S. that has a slight crest and is plain grayish brown above and yellowish white below

Phoe·be \ˈfē-bē\ *n* [L, fr. Gk *Phoibē,* fr. *phoibē,* fem. of *phoibos*] **:** ARTEMIS

Phoe·bus \ˈfē-bəs\ *n* [L, fr. Gk *Phoibos,* fr. *phoibos* radiant] **:** APOLLO

Phoe·ni·cian \fi-ˈnish-ən, -ˈnē-shən\ *n* **1 :** a native or inhabitant of ancient Phoenicia **2 :** the Semitic language of ancient Phoenicia — **Phoenician** *adj*

phoe·nix \ˈfē-niks\ *n* [ME *fenix,* fr. OE, fr. L *phoenix,* fr. Gk *phoinix* purple, crimson, Phoenician, phoenix, date palm, fr. *phoinos* bloodred; akin to Gk *phonos* murder, *theinein* to strike — more at DEFEND] **:** a legendary bird represented by ancient Egyptians as living five or six centuries, being consumed in fire by its own act, and rising in youthful freshness from its own ashes

phon \ˈfän\ *n* [ISV, fr. Gk *phōnē* voice, sound] **:** the unit of loudness level on a scale beginning at zero for the faintest audible sound and corresponding to the decibel scale of sound intensity with the number of phons of a given sound being equal to the decibels of a pure 1000-cycle tone judged by the listener to be equally loud

phon- *or* **phono-** *comb form* [L, fr. Gk *phōn-, phōno-,* fr. *phōnē* — more at BAN] **:** sound **:** voice **:** speech ⟨*phon*ate⟩ ⟨*phono*graph⟩

pho·nate \ˈfō-ˌnāt\ *vi* **:** to produce speech sounds — **pho·na·tion** \fō-ˈnā-shən\ *n*

1phone \ˈfōn\ *n* [by shortening] **1 :** EARPHONE **2 :** TELEPHONE

2phone *vb* **:** TELEPHONE

3phone *n* [Gk *phōnē*] **:** a speech sound considered as a physical event without regard to its place in the structure of a language

-phone \ˌfōn\ *n comb form* [Gk *-phōnos* sounding, fr. *phōnē*] **:** sound ⟨homo*phone*⟩ — often in names of musical instruments and sound-transmitting devices ⟨radio*phone*⟩ ⟨xylo*phone*⟩

pho·ne·mat·ic \ˌfō-ni-ˈmat-ik\ *adj* **:** PHONEMIC

pho·neme \ˈfō-ˌnēm\ *n* [F *phonème,* fr. Gk *phōnēmat-, phōnēma* speech sound, utterance, fr. *phōnein* to sound] **:** a member of the set of the smallest units of speech that serve to distinguish one utterance from another in a language or dialect ⟨the *p* of English *pin* and the *f* of English *fin* are two different ~*s*⟩

pho·ne·mic \fə-ˈnē-mik, fō-\ *adj* **1 :** of, relating to, or having the characteristics of a phoneme **2 a :** constituting members of different phonemes ⟨in English \n\ and \ŋ\ are ~⟩ **b :** DISTINCTIVE 2 — **pho·ne·mi·cal·ly** \-mi-k(ə-)lē\ *adv*

pho·ne·mics \-miks\ *n pl but sing in constr* **1 :** a branch of linguistic analysis that consists of the study of phonemes **2 :** the structure of a language in terms of phonemes

pho·net·ic \fə-ˈnet-ik\ *adj* [NL *phoneticus,* fr. Gk *phōnētikos,* fr. *phōnein* to sound with the voice, fr. *phōnē* voice] **1 a :** of or relating to spoken language or speech sounds **b :** of or relating to the science of phonetics **2 :** representing the sounds and other phenomena of speech: **a :** constituting an alteration of ordinary spelling that better represents the spoken language, that employs only characters of the regular alphabet, and that is used in a context of conventional spelling **b :** representing speech sounds by means of symbols that have one value only **c :** employing for speech sounds more than the minimum number of symbols necessary to represent the significant differences in a speaker's speech — **pho·net·i·cal** \-i-kəl\ *adj* — **pho·net·i·cal·ly** \-k(ə-)lē\ *adv*

phonetic alphabet *n* **1 :** a set of symbols used for phonetic transcription **2 :** any of various systems of identifying letters of the alphabet by means of code words in voice communication

pho·ne·ti·cian \ˌfō-nə-ˈtish-ən *also* ˌfän-ə-\ *n* **:** a specialist in phonetics

pho·net·ics \fə-ˈnet-iks\ *n pl but sing in constr* **1 a :** the study and systematic classification of the sounds made in spoken utterance **b :** the practical application of this science to language study **2 :** the system of speech sounds of a language or group of languages

pho·nic \ˈfän-ik, *except 2b also* ˈfō-nik\ *adj* **1 :** of, relating to, or producing sound **:** ACOUSTIC **2 a :** of or relating to the sounds of speech **b :** of or relating to phonics — **pho·ni·cal·ly** \-(ə-)lē\ *adv*

pho·nics \ˈfän-iks, *1 is also* ˈfō-niks\ *n pl but sing in constr* **1 :** the science of sound **:** ACOUSTICS **2 :** a method of teaching beginners to read and pronounce words by learning the phonetic value of letters, letter groups, and esp. syllables

pho·ni·ly \ˈfōn-ᵊl-ē\ *adv* **:** in a phony manner **:** SPURIOUSLY

pho·ni·ness \ˈfō-nē-nəs\ *n* **:** the quality or state of being phony

pho·no·gram \ˈfō-nə-ˌgram\ *n* [ISV] **1 :** a character or symbol used to represent a word, syllable, or phoneme **2 :** a succession of orthographic letters that occurs with the same phonetic value in several words (as the *ight* of *bright, fight, flight*) — **pho·no·gram·mic** *or* **pho·no·gram·ic** \ˌfō-nə-ˈgram-ik\ *adj* — **pho·no·gram·mi·cal·ly** *or* **pho·no·gram·i·cal·ly** \-i-k(ə-)lē\ *adv*

pho·no·graph \ˈfō-nə-ˌgraf\ *n* **:** an instrument for reproducing sounds by means of the vibration of a stylus or needle following a spiral groove on a revolving disc or cylinder

pho·nog·ra·pher \fə-ˈnäg-rə-fər, fō-\ *n* **:** a specialist in phonography

pho·no·graph·ic \ˌfō-nə-ˈgraf-ik, *1 is also* ˌfän-ə-\ *adj* **1 :** of or relating to phonography **2 :** of or relating to a phonograph — **pho·no·graph·i·cal·ly** \-i-k(ə-)lē\ *adv*

pho·nog·ra·phy \fə-ˈnäg-rə-fē, fō-\ *n* **1 :** spelling based on pronunciation **2 :** a system of shorthand writing based on sound

pho·no·lite \ˈfōn-ᵊl-ˌīt\ *n* [F, fr. G *phonolith,* fr. *phon-* + *-lith;* fr. its ringing sound when struck] **:** a gray or green volcanic rock consisting essentially of orthoclase and nepheline — **pho·no·lit·ic** \ˌfōn-ᵊl-ˈit-ik\ *adj*

pho·no·log·i·cal \ˌfōn-ᵊl-ˈäj-i-kəl *also* ˌfän-ᵊl-\ *also* **pho·no·log·ic** \-ik\ *adj* **:** of or relating to phonology — **pho·no·log·i·cal·ly** \-i-k(ə-)lē\ *adv*

pho·nol·o·gist \fə-ˈnäl-ə-jəst, fō-\ *n* **:** a specialist in phonology

pho·nol·o·gy \-jē\ *n* **1 :** the science of speech sounds including esp. the history and theory of sound changes in a language or in two or more related languages **2 :** the phonetics and phonemics of a language at a particular time

pho·no·re·cep·tion \ˌfō-nō-ri-ˈsep-shən\ *n* **:** the perception of vibratory motion of relatively high frequency; *specif* **:** HEARING — **pho·no·re·cep·tor** \-ˈsep-tər\ *n*

1pho·ny *or* **pho·ney** \ˈfō-nē\ *adj* **pho·ni·er; pho·ni·est** [origin unknown] **:** marked by empty pretension **:** FALSE, SPURIOUS

2phony *or* **phoney** *n* **:** one that is fraudulent or spurious **:** FAKE

-pho·ny \f-ə-nē, ˌfō-nē\ *also* **-pho·nia** \ˈfō-nē-ə\ *n comb form* [ME *-phonie,* fr. OF, fr. L *-phonia,* fr. Gk *-phōnia,* fr. *-phōnos* sounding — more at -PHONE] **1 :** sound ⟨tele*phony*⟩ **2** *usu* *-phonia* **:** speech disorder of a (specified) type ⟨dys*phonia*⟩

-phore \ˌfō(ə)r, ˌfȯ(ə)r\ *n comb form* [NL *-phorus,* fr. Gk *-phoros,* fr. *-phoros* (adj. comb. form) carrying, fr. *pherein* to carry — more at BEAR] **:** carrier ⟨gameto*phore*⟩

-pho·re·sis \fə-ˈrē-səs\ *n comb form, pl* **-pho·re·ses** \-ˈrē-ˌsēz\ [NL, fr. Gk *phorēsis* act of carrying, fr. *phorein* to carry, wear, freq. of *pherein*] **:** transmission ⟨electro*phoresis*⟩

phos- *comb form* [Gk *phōs-,* fr. *phōs*] **:** light ⟨*phos*gene⟩

phos·gene \ˈfäz-ˌjēn\ *n* [fr. its originally having been obtained by the action of sunlight] **:** a colorless gas $COCl_2$ of unpleasant odor that is a severe respiratory irritant and used as a war gas

phosph- *or* **phospho-** *comb form* [*phosphorus*] **:** phosphorus ⟨*phosph*ide⟩ ⟨*phospho*protein⟩

phos·pha·tase \ˈfäs-fə-ˌtās, -ˌtāz\ *n* **:** any of numerous enzymes that accelerate the hydrolysis and synthesis of organic esters of phos-

ə abut; ᵊ kitten; ər further; a back; ā bake; ä cot, cart; aů out; ch chin; e less; ē easy; g gift; i trip; ī life
j joke; ŋ sing; ō flow; ȯ flaw; ȯi coin; th thin; t͟h this; ü loot; ů foot; y yet; yü few; yů furious; zh vision

phoric acid and the transfer of phosphate groups to other compounds

phos·phate \ˈfäs-ˌfāt\ *n* [F, fr. *acide phosphorique* phosphoric acid] **1 :** a salt or ester of a phosphoric acid **2 :** an effervescent drink of carbonated water with a small amount of phosphoric acid or an acid phosphate flavored with fruit syrup **3 :** a phosphatic material used for fertilizers

phosphate rock *n* **:** a rock that consists of calcium phosphate usu. together with calcium carbonate and other minerals, is used in making fertilizers, and is a source of phosphorus compounds

phos·phat·ic \fäs-ˈfat-ik, -ˈfāt-\ *adj* **:** of, relating to, or containing phosphoric acid or phosphates

phos·pha·tide \ˈfäs-fə-ˌtīd\ *n* **:** a complex phosphoric ester lipide found in all living cells in association with stored fats — **phos·pha·tid·ic** \ˌfäs-fə-ˈtid-ik\ *adj*

phos·pha·ti·za·tion \ˌfäs-ˌfāt-ə-ˈzā-shən, ˌfäs-fət-\ *n* **:** the process of phosphatizing

phos·pha·tize \ˈfäs-fə-ˌtīz\ *vt* **1 :** to change to a phosphate or phosphates **2 :** to treat with phosphoric acid or a phosphate

phos·pha·tu·ria \ˌfäs-fə-ˈt(y)u̇r-ē-ə\ *n* [NL, fr. ISV *phosphate* + NL *-uria*] **:** the excessive discharge of phosphates in the urine — **phos·pha·tu·ric** \-ˈt(y)u̇(ə)r-ik\ *adj*

phos·phene \ˈfäs-ˌfēn\ *n* [ISV *phos-* + Gk *phainein* to show — more at FANCY] **:** a luminous impression due to excitation of the retina

phos·phide \ˈfäs-ˌfīd\ *n* [ISV] **:** a binary compound of phosphorus usu. with a more electropositive element or radical

phos·phine \-ˌfēn\ *n* [ISV] **:** a colorless poisonous flammable gas PH_3 that is a weaker base than ammonia; *broadly* **:** any of various derivatives of phosphine analogous to amines but weaker as bases

phos·phite \-ˌfīt\ *n* **:** a salt or ester of phosphorous acid

phos·pho·cre·atine \ˌfäs-(ˌ)fō-ˈkrē-ə-ˌtēn\ *n* [ISV] **:** a compound $C_4H_{10}N_3O_5P$ of creatine and phosphoric acid found in vertebrate muscle and used as a source of physiologic energy

phos·pho·lip·ide \ˌfäs-fō-ˈlip-ˌīd\ *n* **:** PHOSPHATIDE

phos·pho·ni·um \fäs-ˈfō-nē-əm\ *n* [NL] **:** a univalent radical PH_4 analogous to ammonium and derived from phosphine

phos·pho·pro·tein \ˌfäs-fō-ˈprō-ˌtēn, -ˈprōt-ē-ən\ *n* **:** any of various proteins (as casein) containing combined phosphoric acid

phos·phor \ˈfäs-fər, -ˌfō(ə)r\ *n* [L *phosphorus*, fr. Gk *phōsphoros*, lit., light bringer, fr. *phōsphoros* light-bearing, fr. *phōs-* + *pherein* to carry, bring — more at BEAR] **1** *cap* **:** MORNING STAR; *specif* **:** Venus as morning star **2** *also* **phos·phore** *same or* -ˌfō(ə)r\ **:** a phosphorescent substance; *specif* **:** a substance that emits light when excited by radiation

phosphor bronze *n* **:** a bronze of great hardness, elasticity, and toughness that contains a small amount of phosphorus

phos·pho·resce \ˌfäs-fə-ˈres\ *vi* [prob. back-formation fr. *phosphorescent*] **:** to exhibit phosphorescence

phos·pho·res·cence \-ˈres-ᵊn(t)s\ *n* **1 :** luminescence that is caused by the absorption of radiations and continues for a noticeable time after these radiations have stopped **2 :** an enduring luminescence without sensible heat

phos·pho·res·cent \-ᵊnt\ *adj* **:** exhibiting phosphorescence — **phos·pho·res·cent·ly** *adv*

phos·pho·ret·ed *or* **phos·pho·ret·ted** \ˈfäs-fə-ˌret-əd\ *adj* [NL *phosphoretum* phosphide, fr. *phosphorus*] **:** impregnated or combined with phosphorus

phos·pho·ric \fäs-ˈfȯr-ik, -ˈfär-; ˈfäs-f(ə-)rik\ *adj* **:** of, relating to, or from phosphorus esp. with a valence higher than in phosphorous compounds

phosphoric acid *n* **:** an oxygen acid of phosphorus (as metaphosphoric acid, orthophosphoric acid, or pyrophosphoric acid)

phos·pho·rism \ˈfäs-fə-ˌriz-əm\ *n* **:** a poisoning by phosphorus esp. when chronic

phos·pho·rite \-ˌrīt\ *n* **1 :** a fibrous concretionary apatite **2 :** PHOSPHATE ROCK — **phos·pho·rit·ic** \ˌfäs-fə-ˈrit-ik\ *adj*

phos·pho·rol·y·sis \ˌfäs-fə-ˈräl-ə-səs\ *n* [NL] **:** a reversible reaction analogous to hydrolysis in which phosphoric acid functions in a manner similar to that of water with the formation of a phosphate — **phos·pho·ro·lyt·ic** \-rō-ˈlit-ik\ *adj*

phos·pho·rous \ˈfäs-f(ə-)rəs; fäs-ˈfōr-əs, -ˈfȯr-\ *adj* **:** of, relating to, or containing phosphorus esp. with a valence lower than in phosphoric compounds

phosphorous acid *n* **:** a deliquescent crystalline acid H_3PO_3 made esp. by hydrolysis of phosphorus trichloride and used esp. as a reducing agent and in making phosphites

phos·pho·rus \ˈfäs-f(ə-)rəs\ *n, often attrib* [NL, fr. Gk *phōsphoros* light-bearing — more at PHOSPHOR] **1 :** a phosphorescent substance or body; *esp* **:** one that shines or glows in the dark **2 :** a nonmetallic multivalent element of the nitrogen family that occurs widely esp. as phosphates — see ELEMENT table

phos·pho·ryl·ase \ˈfäs-f(ə-)rə-ˌlās, -ˌlāz\ *n* [*phosphoryl* (the radical PO)] **:** any enzyme that catalyzes phosphorolysis with the formation of organic phosphates

phos·pho·ryl·ate \-ˌlāt\ *vt* [*phosphoryl*] **:** to convert (an organic compound) into an organic phosphate — **phos·pho·ryl·ation** \ˌfäs-f(ə-)rə-ˈlā-shən\ *n* — **phos·pho·ryl·ative** \ˈfäs-f(ə-)rə-ˌlāt-iv\ *adj*

phot \ˈfōt, ˈfät\ *n* [ISV, fr. Gk *phōt-*, *phōs* light] **:** the cgs unit of illumination equal to one lumen per square centimeter

phot- *or* **photo-** *comb form* [Gk *phōt-*, *phōto-*, fr. *phōt-*, *phōs* — more at FANCY] **1 :** light ⟨*photon*⟩ ⟨*photography*⟩ **2 :** photograph **:** photographic ⟨*photoengraving*⟩ **3 :** photoelectric ⟨*photocell*⟩

pho·tic \ˈfōt-ik\ *adj* **1 :** of, relating to, or involving light esp. in relation to organisms **2 :** penetrated by light esp. of the sun

pho·to \ˈfōt-(ˌ)ō, -ə-w\ *n* **:** PHOTOGRAPH — **photo** *vb* — **photo** *adj*

pho·to·au·to·tro·phic \ˌfōt-ə-ˌwȯt-ə-ˈträf-ik, -ˈtrō-fik\ *adj* **:** autotrophic and obtaining energy from light

pho·to·bi·ot·ic \ˌfōt-ō-(ˌ)bī-ˈät-ik\ *adj* **:** requiring light in order to live or thrive

pho·to·cell \ˈfōt-ə-ˌsel\ *n* [ISV] **:** PHOTOELECTRIC CELL

pho·to·chem·i·cal \ˌfōt-ō-ˈkem-i-kəl\ *adj* **:** of or relating to photochemistry

pho·to·chem·is·try \-ˈkem-ə-strē\ *n* **:** a branch of chemistry that deals with the effect of radiant energy in producing chemical changes

pho·to·chrono·graph \-ˈkrän-ə-ˌgraf, -ˈkrō-nə-\ *n* [ISV *phot-* + *chron-* + *-graph*] **1 :** an apparatus for photographing a moving object at regular minute intervals; *also* **:** one of the photographs thus taken **2 :** an instrument for the photographic recording of star transits **3 :** an instrument for recording minute intervals of time photographically

pho·to·com·pose \-kəm-ˈpōz\ *vt* **:** to compose (reading matter) for reproduction by means of characters photographed on film — **pho·to·com·po·si·tion** \-ˌkäm-pə-ˈzish-ən\ *n*

pho·to·con·duc·tive \-kən-ˈdək-tiv\ *adj* **:** having or operating by photoconductivity

pho·to·con·duc·tiv·i·ty \-ˌkän-ˌdək-ˈtiv-ət-ē, -kən-\ *n* **:** electrical conductivity that is affected by exposure to light or other radiation

pho·to·copy \ˈfōt-ə-ˌkäp-ē\ *n* [ISV] **:** a photographic reproduction of graphic matter — **photocopy** *vb*

pho·to·cur·rent \ˈfōt-ō-ˌkər-ənt, -ˌkə-rənt\ *n* [*photo*electric *current*] **:** a stream of electrons produced by photoelectric or photovoltaic effects

pho·to·dis·in·te·gra·tion \ˌfōt-ō-(ˌ)dis-ˌint-ə-ˈgrā-shən\ *n* **:** disintegration of the nucleus of an atom produced by absorption of radiant energy

pho·to·dra·ma \ˈfōt-ə-ˌdräm-ə, -ˌdram-\ *n* **:** MOTION PICTURE

pho·to·du·pli·cate \ˌfōt-ō-ˈd(y)ü-plə-ˌkāt\ *vb* **:** PHOTOCOPY — **pho·to·du·pli·cate** \-pli-kət\ *n* — **pho·to·du·pli·ca·tion** \-ˌd(y)ü-plə-ˈkā-shən\ *n*

pho·to·dy·nam·ic \-(ˌ)dī-ˈnam-ik\ *adj* [ISV] **:** of, relating to, or having the property of intensifying or inducing a toxic reaction to light and esp. sunlight in living systems — **pho·to·dy·nam·i·cal·ly** \-i-k(ə-)lē\ *adv*

pho·to·elec·tric \ˌfōt-ə-wə-ˈlek-trik\ *adj* [ISV] **:** relating to or utilizing any of various electrical effects due to the interaction of light or other radiation with matter

photoelectric cell *n* **:** a cell whose electrical properties are modified by the action of light

pho·to·elec·tron \-ˈlek-ˌträn\ *n* [ISV] **:** an electron released in photoemission

pho·to·emis·sion \-ə-wi-ˈmish-ən\ *n* **:** the release of electrons from a metal by means of energy supplied by incidence of light or other radiation — **pho·to·emis·sive** \-ˈmis-iv\ *adj*

pho·to·en·grave \ˌfōt-ə-wən-ˈgrāv\ *vt* [back-formation fr. *photoengraving*] **:** to make a photoengraving of — **pho·to·en·grav·er** *n*

pho·to·en·grav·ing \-ˈgrā-viŋ\ *n* **1 :** a photomechanical process for making linecuts and halftone cuts by photographing an image on a metal plate and then etching **2 a :** a plate made by photoengraving **b :** a print made from such a plate

photo finish *n* **1 :** a race finish in which contestants are so close that a photograph of them as they cross the finish line has to be examined to determine the winner **2 :** a close contest

pho·to·flash \ˈfōt-ə-ˌflash\ *n* **:** an electrically operated flash lamp; *esp* **:** FLASHBULB

pho·to·flood \-ˌfləd\ *n* **:** an electric lamp using excess voltage to give intense sustained illumination for taking photographs

pho·to·flu·o·ro·gram \ˌfōt-ə-ˈflu̇r-ə-ˌgram\ *n* **:** a photograph made by photofluorography

pho·to·flu·o·ro·graph·ic \-ˌflu̇r-ə-ˈgraf-ik\ *adj* **:** of, used in, or relating to photofluorography

pho·to·flu·o·rog·ra·phy \-(ˌ)flu̇(-ə)r-ˈäg-rə-fē\ *n* **:** the photography of the image produced on a fluorescent screen by X rays

pho·to·gel·a·tin process \ˌfōt-ə-ˈjel-ət-ᵊn-\ *n* **:** COLLOTYPE 1

pho·to·gene \ˈfōt-ə-ˌjēn\ *n* [ISV] **:** an afterimage or retinal impression

pho·to·ge·nic \ˌfōt-ə-ˈjen-ik, -ˈjē-nik\ *adj* **1 :** produced or precipitated by light **2 :** producing or generating light **:** PHOSPHORESCENT **3 :** suitable for being photographed — **pho·to·ge·ni·cal·ly** \-i-k(ə-)lē, -ni\ *adv*

pho·to·gram \ˈfōt-ə-ˌgram\ *n* [ISV] **:** a shadowlike photograph made by placing objects between light-sensitive paper and a light source

pho·to·gram·met·ric \ˌfōt-ə-grə-ˈme-trik\ *adj* **:** of, made by, or relating to photogrammetry

pho·to·gram·me·try \-ˈgram-ə-trē\ *n* [ISV *photogram* photograph (fr. *phot-* + *-gram*) + *-metry*] **:** the science of making reliable measurements by the use of usu. aerial photographs in surveying and map making

[1]**pho·to·graph** \ˈfōt-ə-ˌgraf\ *n* **:** a picture or likeness obtained by photography

[2]**photograph** *vt* **:** to take a photograph of ~ *vi* **1 :** to take a photograph **2 :** to undergo being photographed — **pho·tog·ra·pher** \fə-ˈtäg-rə-fər, *rapid* -ˈtäg-ə-fər; *before "of" also* ˈfōt-ə-ˌgraf-ər\ *n*

pho·to·graph·ic \ˌfōt-ə-ˈgraf-ik\ *adj* **1 :** relating to, obtained by, or used in photography **2 :** representing nature and human beings with the exactness of a photograph **3 :** capable of retaining vivid impressions ⟨a ~ mind⟩ — **pho·to·graph·i·cal·ly** \-i-k(ə-)lē\ *adv*

pho·tog·ra·phy \fə-ˈtäg-rə-fē\ *n* **:** the art or process of producing images on a sensitized surface by the action of light or other radiant energy

pho·to·gra·vure \ˌfōt-ə-grə-ˈvyu̇(ə)r\ *n* [F, fr. *phot-* + *gravure*] **:** a process for making prints from an intaglio plate prepared by photographic methods; *also* **:** a print produced by photogravure — **photogravure** *vt*

pho·to·he·lio·graph \-ˈhē-lē-ə-ˌgraf\ *n* **:** a telescope adapted for photographing the sun

pho·to·ki·ne·sis \-kə-ˈnē-səs, -(ˌ)kī-\ *or* **pho·to·ci·ne·sis** *same or* -sə-, -(ˌ)sī-\ *n* [NL, fr. *phot-* + Gk *kinēsis* motion — more at KINESIOLOGY] **:** motion or activity induced by light — **pho·to·ki·net·ic** \-ˈnet-ik\ *adj*

pho·to·lith \ˈfōt-ᵊl-ˌith\ *n* **:** PHOTOLITHOGRAPHY — **photolith** *adj* — **photolith** *vb*

[1]**pho·to·litho·graph** \ˌfōt-ᵊl-ˈith-ə-ˌgraf\ *n* **:** a print made by photolithography — **pho·to·litho·graph·ic** \-ˌith-ə-ˈgraf-ik\ *adj*

[2]**photolithograph** *vt* **:** to make a photolithograph of — **pho·to·li·tho·gra·pher** \ˌfōt-ᵊl-ith-ˈäg-rə-fər, -ˈith-ə-ˌgraf-ər\ *n*

pho·to·li·thog·ra·phy \ˌfōt-ᵊl-ith-ˈäg-rə-fē\ *n* [ISV] **:** lithography in which photographically prepared plates are used

pho·tol·y·sis \fō-ˈtäl-ə-səs\ *n* [NL] **:** chemical decomposition by the action of radiant energy — **pho·to·lyt·ic** \ˌfōt-ᵊl-ˈit-ik\ *adj*

pho·to·map \ˈfōt-ə-ˌmap\ *n* **:** a photograph taken vertically from an airplane upon which a grid and data pertinent to maps have been added — **photomap** *vb*

pho·to·me·chan·i·cal \ˌfōt-ō-mi-ˈkan-i-kəl\ *adj* [ISV] **:** relating to or involving any process for producing printed matter from a photo-

graphically prepared surface — **pho·to·me·chan·i·cal·ly** \-i-k(ə-)lē\ *adv*

pho·tom·e·ter \fō-'täm-ət-ər\ *n* [NL *photometrum*, fr. *phot-* + *-metrum* -meter] **:** an instrument for measuring luminous intensity, luminous flux, illumination, or brightness

pho·to·met·ric \,fōt-ə-'me-trik\ *adj* **:** of or relating to photometry or the photometer — **pho·to·met·ri·cal·ly** \-tri-k(ə-)lē\ *adv*

pho·tom·e·try \fō-'täm-ə-trē\ *n* [NL *photometria*, fr. *phot-* + *-metria* -metry] **:** a branch of science that deals with measurement of the intensity of light; *also* **:** the practice of using a photometer

pho·to·mi·cro·graph \,fōt-ə-'mī-krə-,graf\ *n* [*phot-* + *micr-* + *-graph*] **:** a photograph of a magnified image of a small object — **photomicrograph** *vt* — **pho·to·mi·cro·graph·ic** \-,mī-krə-'graf-ik\ *adj* — **pho·to·mi·crog·ra·phy** \-(,)mī-'kräg-rə-fē\ *n*

pho·to·mon·tage \-(,)män-'täzh\ *n* [ISV] **:** montage using photographic images; *also* **:** a picture made by photomontage

pho·to·mu·ral \,fōt-ə-'myu̇r-əl\ *n* **:** an enlarged photograph usu. several yards long used on walls esp. as decoration

pho·ton \'fō-,tän\ *n* [*phot-* + *-on*] **1 :** a quantum of radiant energy **2 :** a unit of intensity of light at the retina equal to the illumination received per square millimeter of a pupillary area from a surface having a brightness of one candle per square meter

pho·to·neg·a·tive \,fōt-ə-'neg-ət-iv\ *adj* **:** exhibiting negative phototropism or phototaxis

pho·to–off·set \,fōt-ə-'wȯf-,set\ *n* **:** offset using a photographically prepared planographic printing plate

pho·to·pe·ri·od \,fōt-ə-'pir-ē-əd\ *n* **:** the relative lengths of alternating periods of lightness and darkness as they affect the growth and maturity of an organism — **pho·to·pe·ri·od·ic** \-,pir-ē-'äd-ik\ *or* **pho·to·pe·ri·od·i·cal** \-i-kəl\ *adj* — **pho·to·pe·ri·od·i·cal·ly** \-k(ə-)lē\ *adv* — **pho·to·pe·ri·od·ism** \-'pir-ē-ə-,diz-əm\ *n*

pho·to·phil·ic \-'fil-ik\ *adj* **:** thriving in full light **:** requiring abundant light ⟨~ plants⟩ — **pho·toph·i·ly** \fō-'täf-ə-lē\ *n*

pho·to·pho·bia \,fōt-ə-'fō-bē-ə\ *n* [NL] **:** intolerance to light

pho·to·pho·bic \,fōt-ə-'fō-bik, -'fäb-ik\ *adj* **1 a :** shunning or avoiding light **b :** growing best under reduced illumination **2 :** of or relating to photophobia

pho·to·pia \fō-'tō-pē-ə\ *n* [NL] **:** vision in bright light with light-adapted eyes believed to be mediated by the retina cones — **pho·to·pic** \fō-'tō-pik, -'täp-ik\ *adj*

pho·to·play \'fōt-ə-,plā\ *n* **:** MOTION PICTURE 2

pho·to·pos·i·tive \,fōt-ə-'päz-ət-iv, -'päz-tiv\ *adj* **:** exhibiting positive phototropism or phototaxis

pho·to·re·cep·tion \-ri-'sep-shən\ *n* **:** perception of waves in the range of visible light; *specif* **:** VISION — **pho·to·re·cep·tive** \-'sep-tiv\ *adj* — **pho·to·re·cep·tor** \-tər\ *n*

pho·to·re·con·nais·sance \-ri-'kän-ə-zən(t)s *also* -sən(t)s\ *n* **:** reconnaissance in which aerial photographs are taken

pho·to·sen·si·tive \-'sen(t)-sət-iv, -'sen(t)-stiv\ *adj* **:** sensitive or sensitized to the action of radiant energy — **pho·to·sen·si·tiv·i·ty** \-,sen(t)-sə-'tiv-ət-ē\ *n*

pho·to·sen·si·ti·za·tion \-,sen(t)-sət-ə-'zā-shən, -,sen(t)-stə-'zā-\ *n* **1 :** the process of photosensitizing **2 :** the condition of being photosensitized; *esp* **:** the development of an abnormal capacity to react to sunlight typically by edematous swelling and dermatitis

pho·to·sen·si·tize \-'sen(t)-sə-,tīz\ *vt* **:** to make photosensitive

pho·to·set \'fōt-ə-,set\ *vt* **:** PHOTOCOMPOSE

pho·to·sphere \-,sfi(ə)r\ *n* **1 :** a sphere of light **2 :** the luminous surface of the sun or a star — **pho·to·spher·ic** \,fōt-ə-'sfi(ə)r-ik, -'sfer-\ *adj*

pho·to·stat \'fōt-ə-,stat\ *vb* **:** to copy by a Photostat device — **pho·to·static** \,fōt-ə-'stat-ik\ *adj*

Photostat *trademark* **1** — used for a device for making a photographic copy of graphic matter directly upon the surface of prepared paper **2 :** a copy made by a Photostat device

pho·to·syn·the·sis \,fōt-ə-'sin(t)-thə-səs\ *n* [NL] **:** synthesis of chemical compounds with the aid of radiant energy and esp. light; *esp* **:** formation of carbohydrates in the chlorophyll-containing tissues of plants exposed to light — **pho·to·syn·the·size** \-,sīz\ *vi* — **pho·to·syn·thet·ic** \-(,)sin-'thet-ik\ *adj* — **pho·to·syn·thet·i·cal·ly** \-i-k(ə-)lē\ *adv*

pho·to·tac·tic \,fōt-ə-'tak-tik\ *adj* [ISV] **:** of, relating to, or exhibiting phototaxis

pho·to·tax·is \-'tak-səs\ *n* [NL] **:** a taxis in which light is the directive factor

pho·to·te·leg·ra·phy \-tə-'leg-rə-fē\ *n* [ISV] **:** FACSIMILE 2

pho·to·trop·ic \,fōt-ə-'träp-ik\ *adj* **:** of, relating to, or capable of phototropism

pho·tot·ro·pism \fō-'tä-trə-,piz-əm\ *n* [ISV] **:** a tropism in which light is the orienting stimulus

pho·to·tube \'fōt-ə-,t(y)üb\ *n* **:** an electron tube having a photoemissive cathode whose released electrons are drawn to the anode by reason of its positive potential

pho·to·type·set·ting \,fōt-ə-'tīp-,set-iŋ\ *n* **:** PHOTOCOMPOSITION; *esp* **:** photocomposition done on a keyboard composing machine

pho·to·ty·po·graph·ic \-,tī-pə-'graf-ik\ *adj* **:** producing matter used in phototypography — **pho·to·ty·po·graph·i·cal** \-i-kəl\ *adj*

pho·to·ty·pog·ra·phy \-(,)tī-'päg-rə-fē\ *n* [ISV] **:** a photomechanical process producing matter resembling that done by typographical printing

pho·to·vol·ta·ic \-,väl-'tā-ik, -,vōl-\ *adj* [ISV] **:** of, relating to, or utilizing the generation of an electromotive force when radiant energy falls on the boundary between dissimilar substances

pho·to·zin·co·graph \-'ziŋ-kə-,graf\ *n* **:** a print made by photozincography — **photozincograph** *vt*

pho·to·zin·cog·ra·phy \-(,)ziŋ-'käg-rə-fē\ *n* [ISV] **:** zincography using photographically prepared plates

phras·al \'frā-zəl\ *adj* **:** of, relating to, or consisting of a phrase — **phras·al·ly** \-zə-lē\ *adv*

[1]**phrase** \'frāz\ *n* [L *phrasis*, fr. Gk, fr. *phrazein* to point out, explain, tell] **1 :** a characteristic manner of style or expression **:** DICTION **2 a :** a brief expression; *esp* **:** CATCHWORD **b :** WORD **3 :** a short musical thought typically two to four measures long closing with a cadence **4 :** a group of two or more grammatically related words that form a sense unit expressing a thought either in a fragmentary manner or as a sentence element not containing a predication but having the force of a single part of speech

[2]**phrase** *vt* **1 a :** to express in words or in appropriate or telling terms **:** WORD **b :** to designate by a descriptive word or phrase **:** TERM **2 :** to divide into melodic phrases

phra·seo·gram \'frā-zē-ə-,gram\ *n* [*phraseo-* (as in *phraseology*) + *-gram*] **:** a symbol for a phrase in some shorthand systems — called also *phra·seo·graph* \-,graf\

phra·seo·log·i·cal \,frā-zē-ə-'läj-i-kəl\ *adj* **1 a :** expressed in formal often sententious phrases **b :** marked by frequently insincere use of such phrases **2 :** of or relating to phraseology — **phra·seo·log·i·cal·ly** \-k(ə-)lē\ *adv*

phrase·ol·o·gist \,frā-zē-'äl-ə-jəst, frā-'zäl-\ *n* **:** one who uses sententious or insincere phrases

phrase·ol·o·gy \-jē\ *n* [NL *phraseologia*, fr. Gk *phrase-*, *phrasis* + *-logia* -logy] **1 :** a manner of organization of words and phrases into longer elements **:** STYLE **2 :** choice of words **:** VOCABULARY

phras·ing \'frā-ziŋ\ *n* **1 :** style of expression **:** PHRASEOLOGY **2 :** the act, method, or result of grouping notes into musical phrases

phra·try \'frā-trē\ *n* [Gk *phratria*, fr. *phratēr* member of the same clan, member of a phratry — more at BROTHER] **1 :** a subdivision of a Greek phyle **2 :** a tribal subdivision; *specif* **:** an exogamous group typically comprising several totemic clans

phren- *or* **phreno-** *comb form* [Gk, fr. *phren-*, *phrēn* diaphragm, mind — more at FRENETIC] **1 :** mind ⟨*phren*ology⟩ **2 :** diaphragm ⟨*phren*ic⟩

phre·net·ic \fri-'net-ik\ *adj* [L *phreneticus*] **:** FRENETIC

-phre·nia \'frē-nē-ə *also* 'fren-ē-\ *n comb form* [NL, fr. Gk *phren-*, *phrēn*] **:** disordered condition of mental functions ⟨hebe*phrenia*⟩

phre·nic \'fren-ik *also* 'frē-nik\ *adj* [NL *phrenicus*, fr. *phren-*] **1 :** of or relating to the diaphragm **2 :** of or relating to the mind

phre·no·log·i·cal \,fren-ᵊl-'äj-i-kəl, ,frēn-\ *adj* **:** of or relating to phrenology — **phre·no·log·i·cal·ly** \-k(ə-)lē\ *adv*

phre·nol·o·gist \fri-'näl-ə-jəst\ *n* **:** one versed in phrenology

phre·nol·o·gy \-jē\ *n* **:** the study of the conformation of the skull as indicative of mental faculties and character

phrensy *var of* FRENZY

Phry·gian \'frij-(ē-)ən\ *n* **1 :** a native or inhabitant of ancient Phrygia **2 :** the language of the Phrygians usu. assumed to be Indo-European — **Phrygian** *adj*

phtha·lein \'thal-ē-ən, 'thal-,ēn, 'thāl-\ *n* [ISV, fr. *phthalic acid*] **:** any of various xanthene dyes that are intensely colored in alkaline solution

phtha·lic acid \,thal-ik-, ,thā-lik-\ *n* [ISV, short for obs. *naphthalic acid*, fr. *naphthalene*] **:** any of three isomeric acids $C_8H_6O_4$ obtained by oxidation of various benzene derivatives

phthalic anhydride *n* **:** a crystalline cyclic acid anhydride $C_8H_4O_3$ used esp. in making alkyd resins

phtha·lo·cy·a·nine \,thal-ō-'sī-ə-,nēn, ,thā-lō-\ *n* [ISV *phthal*ic acid + *-o-* + *cyanine*] **:** a bright greenish blue crystalline compound $C_{32}H_{18}N_8$; *also* **:** any of several metal derivatives that are brilliant fast blue to green dyes or pigments

phthi·ri·a·sis \thə-'rī-ə-səs, thī-\ *n* [L, fr. Gk *phtheiriasis*, fr. *phtheir* louse; akin to Gk *phtheirein* to destroy, Skt *kṣarati* it flows, perishes] **:** PEDICULOSIS; *esp* **:** infestation with crab lice

phthis·ic \'tiz-ik\ *n* [ME *tisike*, fr. MF *tisique*, fr. *tisique* tubercular, fr. L *phthisicus*, fr. Gk *phthisikos*, fr. *phthisis*] **:** PHTHISIS — **phthisic** *or* **phthis·i·cal** \-i-kəl\ *adj* — **phthis·icky** \-i-kē\ *adj*

phthi·sis \'thī-səs\ *n*, *pl* **phthi·ses** \'thī-,sēz\ [L, fr. Gk, fr. *phthinein* to waste away; akin to Skt *kṣiṇoti* he destroys] **:** a progressively wasting or consumptive condition; *esp* **:** pulmonary tuberculosis

phy·col·o·gy \fī-'käl-ə-jē\ *n* [Gk *phykos* seaweed + ISV *-logy* — more at FUCUS] **:** ALGOLOGY

phy·co·my·cete \,fī-kō-'mī-,sēt, -(,)mī-'sēt\ *n* [deriv. of Gk *phykos* + *mykēt-*, *mykēs* fungus — more at MYC-] **:** any of a large class (Phycomycetes) of highly variable lower fungi in many respects similar to algae — **phy·co·my·ce·tous** \-(,)mī-'sēt-əs\ *adj*

phyl- *or* **phylo-** *comb form* [L, fr. Gk, fr. *phylē*, *phylon*; akin to Gk *phyein* to bring forth — more at BE] **:** tribe **:** race **:** phylum ⟨*phylo*geny⟩

phy·lac·tery \fə-'lak-t(ə-)rē\ *n* [ME *philaterie*, fr. ML *philaterium*, alter. of LL *phylacterium*, fr. Gk *phylaktērion* amulet, phylactery, fr. *phylassein* to guard, fr. *phylak-*, *phylax* guard] **1 :** one of two small square leather boxes containing slips inscribed with scriptural passages and traditionally worn on the left arm and forehead by Jewish men during morning weekday prayers **2 :** AMULET

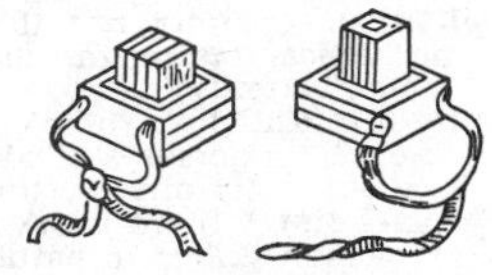

phylacteries

phy·lar \'fī-lər\ *adj* **:** of or relating to a phylum

phy·le \'fī-(,)lē\ *n*, *pl* **phy·lae** \-,lē\ [Gk *phylē* tribe, phyle] **:** the largest political subdivision among the ancient Athenians

phy·le·sis \fī-'lē-səs\ *n* [NL, fr. *phyl-* + *-esis* (as in *genesis*)] **:** the course of evolutionary or phylogenetic development — **phy·let·ic** \-'let-ik\ *adj* — **phy·let·i·cal·ly** \-i-k(ə-)lē\ *adv*

phyll- *or* **phyllo-** *comb form* [NL, fr. Gk, fr. *phyllon* — more at BLADE] **:** leaf ⟨*phyllo*me⟩

-phyll \,fil\ *n comb form* [NL *-phyllum*, fr. Gk *phyllon* leaf] **:** leaf ⟨sporo*phyll*⟩

phyl·line \'fil-,īn, -,ēn\ *adj* **:** LEAFLIKE

phyl·lo·clade \'fil-ə-,klād\ *n* [NL *phyllocladium*, fr. *phyll-* + Gk *klados* branch — more at GLADIATOR] **:** a flattened stem or branch that functions as a leaf — **phyl·lo·cla·di·oid** \,fil-ə-'klād-ē-,ȯid\ *adj* — **phyl·lo·cla·dous** \,fil-ə-'klād-əs\ *adj*

phyl·lode \'fil-,ōd\ *n* [NL *phyllodium*, fr. Gk *phyllōdēs* like a leaf, fr. *phyllon* leaf] **:** a flat expanded petiole that replaces the blade of a foliage leaf, fulfills the same functions, and is analogous to a cladophyll — **phyl·lo·di·al** \fə-'lōd-ē-əl\ *adj*

phyl·lo·di·um \fə-'lōd-ē-əm\ *n*, *pl* **phyl·lo·dia** \-ē-ə\ [NL] **:** PHYLLODE

phyl·loid \'fil-,ȯid\ *adj* **:** resembling a leaf — **phylloid** *n*

phyl·lome \'fil-,ōm\ *n* [ISV] **:** a plant part that is a leaf or is phylogenetically derived from a leaf — **phyl·lo·mic** \fil-'ōm-ik, -'äm-\ *adj*

phyl·loph·a·gous \fil-'äf-ə-gəs\ *adj* [prob. fr. (assumed) NL *phyllophagus*, fr. NL *phyll-* + *-phagus* -phagous] **:** feeding on leaves
phyl·lo·pod \'fil-ə-,päd\ *n* [deriv. of Gk *phyllon* leaf + *pod-*, *pous* foot — more at FOOT] **:** any of a group (Phyllopoda) of crustaceans (subclass Entomostraca) typically having leaflike swimming appendages that also serve as gills — **phyllopod** *adj* — **phyl·lop·o·dan** \fil-'äp-əd-ən\ *adj or n* — **phyl·lop·o·dous** \-əd-əs\ *adj*
phyl·lo·tac·tic \,fil-ə-'tak-tik\ *adj* **:** of or relating to phyllotaxy — **phyl·lo·tac·ti·cal** \-ti-kəl\ *adj*
phyl·lo·taxy \'fil-ə-,tak-sē\ *also* **phyl·lo·tax·is** \,fil-ə-'tak-səs\ *n* [NL *phyllotaxis*, fr. *phyll-* + *-taxis*] **1 :** the arrangement of leaves on a stem and in relation to one another **2 :** the study of phyllotaxy and of the laws that govern it
-phyl·lous \'fil-əs\ *adj comb form* [NL *-phyllus*, fr. Gk *-phyllos*, fr. *phyllon* leaf — more at BLADE] **:** having (such or so many) leaves, leaflets, or leaflike parts ⟨di*phyllous*⟩
phyl·lox·e·ra \,fil-,äk-'sir-ə, fə-'läk-sə-rə\ *n* [NL, genus name, fr. *phyll-* + Gk *xēros* dry — more at SERENE] **:** any of various plant lice (esp. genus *Phylloxera*) differing from aphids esp. in wing structure and in being continuously oviparous — **phyl·lox·e·ran** \-'sir-ən, -sə-rən\ *adj or n*
phy·lo·ge·net·ic \,fī-lō-jə-'net-ik\ *adj* [ISV, fr. NL *phylogenesis* phylogeny, fr. *phyl-* + *genesis*] **1 :** of or relating to phylogeny **2 :** based on natural evolutionary relationships **3 :** acquired in the course of phylogenetic development **:** RACIAL — **phy·lo·ge·net·i·cal·ly** \-i-k(ə-)lē\ *adv*
phy·log·e·ny \fī-'läj-ə-nē\ *n* [ISV] **1 :** the racial history of a kind of organism **2 :** the evolution of a genetically related group of organisms as distinguished from the development of the individual organism **3 :** the history or course of the development of something
phy·lon \'fī-,län\ *n, pl* **phy·la** \-lə\ [NL, fr. Gk] **:** a genetically related group (as a tribe or race)
phy·lum \'fī-ləm\ *n, pl* **phy·la** \-lə\ [NL, fr. Gk *phylon* tribe, race — more at PHYL-] **1 a :** a direct line of descent within a group **b :** a group that constitutes or has the unity of such a phylum; *esp* **:** one of the usu. primary divisions of the animal kingdom ⟨the ~ Arthropoda⟩ **2 :** a group of languages related more remotely than those of a family or stock
-phyre \,fī(ə)r\ *n comb form* [F, fr. *porphyre* porphyry, fr. ML *porphyrium*] **:** porphyritic rock ⟨grano*phyre*⟩
physi- *or* **physio-** *comb form* [L, fr. Gk, fr. *physis* — more at PHYSICS] **1 :** nature ⟨*physio*graphy⟩ **2 :** physical ⟨*physio*therapy⟩
phys·iat·rics \,fiz-ē-'a-triks\ *n pl but sing or pl in constr* [Gk *physis* + ISV *-iatrics*] **:** PHYSICAL THERAPY
[1]**physic** *var of* PHYSICS
[2]**phys·ic** \'fiz-ik\ *vt* **phys·icked** \-ikt\ **phys·ick·ing** \-i-kiŋ\ [ME *phisiken*, fr. *phisik* medicine — more at PHYSICS] **1 :** to treat with or administer medicine to; *esp* **:** PURGE **2 :** HEAL, CURE
phys·i·cal \'fiz-i-kəl\ *adj* [ME, fr. ML *physicalis*, fr. L *physica* physics] **1 :** of, relating to, or according with material things or natural laws as opposed to things mental, moral, spiritual, or imaginary **2 a :** of or relating to natural science **b** (1) **:** of or relating to physics (2) **:** characterized or produced by the forces and operations of physics **3 a :** of or relating to the body **b :** concerned or preoccupied with the body and its needs **:** CARNAL **syn** see BODILY, MATERIAL — **phys·i·cal·ly** \-k(ə-)lē\ *adv*
physical education *n* **:** instruction in the development and care of the body usu. involving training in hygiene and systematic exercises
physical geography *n* **:** geography that deals with the exterior physical features and changes of the earth
phys·i·cal·ism \'fiz-i-kə-,liz-əm\ *n* **:** a thesis that the descriptive terms of scientific language are reducible to terms which refer to spatiotemporal things or events or to their properties — **phys·i·cal·ist** \-ləst\ *n* — **phys·i·cal·is·tic** \,fiz-i-kə-'lis-tik\ *adj*
phys·i·cal·i·ty \,fiz-ə-'kal-ət-ē\ *n* **:** intensely physical orientation at the expense of the mental, spiritual, or social
physical science *n* **:** the natural sciences (as mineralogy, astronomy, meteorology, geology) that deal primarily with nonliving materials
physical therapy *n* **:** the treatment of disease by physical and mechanical means (as massage, regulated exercise, water, light, heat, electricity)
phy·si·cian \fə-'zish-ən\ *n* [ME *fisicien*, fr. OF, fr. *fisique* medicine] **1 :** a person skilled in the art of healing; *specif* **:** a doctor of medicine **2 :** one exerting a remedial or salutary influence
phys·i·cist \'fiz-(ə-)səst\ *n* **1 :** a specialist in physics **2** *archaic* **:** a person skilled in natural science
phys·i·co·chem·i·cal \,fiz-i-kō-'kem-i-kəl\ *adj* **1 :** being physical and chemical **2 :** relating to chemistry that deals with the physicochemical properties of substances — **phys·i·co·chem·i·cal·ly** \-k(ə-)lē\ *adv*
phys·ics \'fiz-iks\ *n pl but sing or pl in constr* [*physics* fr. L *physica*, pl., natural science, fr. Gk *physika*, fr. neut. pl. of *physikos* of nature, fr. *physis* growth, nature, fr. *phyein* to bring forth; *physic* fr. ME *phisik* natural science, art of medicine, fr. OF *fisique*, fr. L *physica*, sing., natural science, fr. Gk *physikē*, fr. fem. of *physikos* — more at BE] **1 physic** *n sing* **a** (1) **:** the art or practice of healing disease (2) **:** the practice or profession of medicine **b :** a medicinal agent or preparation; *esp* **:** a medicine that purges **2** *also* **physic** *archaic* **:** NATURAL SCIENCE **3 :** a science that deals with matter and energy and their interactions in the fields of mechanics, acoustics, optics, heat, electricity, magnetism, radiation, atomic structure, and nuclear phenomena **4 a :** the physical processes and phenomena of a particular system **b :** the physical properties and composition of something
Phys·io·crat \'fiz-ē-ə-,krat\ *n* [F *physiocrate*, fr. *physi-* + *-crate* -crat] **:** a member of a school of political economists founded in 18th century France and characterized chiefly by a belief that government policy should not interfere with the operation of natural economic laws and that land is the source of all wealth — **phys·io·crat·ic** \,fiz-ē-ə-'krat-ik\ *adj, often cap*
phys·i·og·nom·ic \,fiz-ē-ə(g)-'näm-ik\ *adj* **:** of, relating to, or characteristic of physiognomy or the physiognomy — **phys·i·og·nom·i·cal** \-i-kəl\ *adj* — **phys·i·og·nom·i·cal·ly** \-k(ə-)lē\ *adv*
phys·i·og·no·my \,fiz-ē-'ä(g)-nə-mē\ *n* [ME *phisonomie*, fr. MF, fr. LL *physiognomonia*, *physiognomia*, fr. Gk *physiognōmonia*, fr. *physiognōmōn* judging character by the features, fr. *physis* nature, physique, appearance + *gnōmōn* interpreter — more at GNOMON] **1 :** the art of discovering temperament and character from outward appearance **2 :** the facial features held to show qualities of mind or character by their configuration or expression **3 :** external aspect; *also* **:** inner character or quality revealed outwardly **syn** see FACE
phys·i·og·ra·pher \,fiz-ē-'äg-rə-fər\ *n* **:** a specialist in physiography
phys·io·graph·ic \,fiz-ē-ə-'graf-ik\ *adj* **:** of, relating to, or employing the methods of physiography — **phys·io·graph·i·cal** \-i-kəl\ *adj*
phys·i·og·ra·phy \,fiz-ē-'äg-rə-fē\ *n* [prob. fr. (assumed) NL *physiographia*, fr. NL *physi-* + L *-graphia* -graphy] **1 :** a description of nature or natural phenomena in general **2 :** PHYSICAL GEOGRAPHY
phys·i·o·log·i·cal \,fiz-ē-ə-'läj-i-kəl\ *or* **phys·i·o·log·ic** \-ik\ *adj* **1 :** of or relating to physiology **2 :** characteristic of or appropriate to an organism's healthy or normal functioning **3 :** differing in, involving, or affecting physiological factors — **phys·i·o·log·i·cal·ly** \-i-k(ə-)lē\ *adv*
physiological saline *n* **:** a solution of a salt or salts that is essentially isotonic with tissue fluids or blood
phys·i·ol·o·gist \,fiz-ē-'äl-ə-jəst\ *n* **:** a specialist in physiology
phys·i·ol·o·gy \-jē\ *n* [L *physiologia* natural science, fr. Gk, fr. *physi-* + *-logia* -logy] **1 :** a branch of biology dealing with the processes, activities, and phenomena incidental to and characteristic of life or of living matter **2 :** the organic processes and phenomena of an organism or any of its parts or of a particular bodily process
phys·io·ther·a·py \,fiz-ē-ō-'ther-ə-pē\ *n* [NL *physiotherapia*, fr. *physi-* + *therapia* therapy] **:** PHYSICAL THERAPY
phy·sique \fə-'zēk\ *n* [F, fr. *physique* physical, bodily, fr. L *physicus* of nature, fr. Gk *physikos*] **:** bodily makeup or type with reference to its structure, constitution, appearance, or strength — **phy·siqued** \-'zēkt\ *adj*
phy·so·stig·mine \,fī-sə-'stig-,mēn\ *n* [ISV, fr. NL *Physostigma*, genus of vines whose fruit is the Calabar bean] **:** a crystalline tasteless alkaloid $C_{15}H_{21}N_3O_2$ from the Calabar bean used in medicine esp. in the form of its salicylate
phyt- *or* **phyto-** *comb form* [NL, fr. Gk, fr. *phyton*, fr. *phyein* to bring forth — more at BE] **:** plant ⟨*phyto*phagous⟩
-phyte \,fīt\ *n comb form* [ISV, fr. Gk *phyton* plant] **1 :** plant having a (specified) characteristic or habitat ⟨xero*phyte*⟩ **2 :** pathological growth ⟨osteo*phyte*⟩
-phyt·ic \'fit-ik\ *adj comb form* [ISV, fr. Gk *phyton* plant] **:** like a plant ⟨holo*phytic*⟩
phy·to·fla·gel·late \,fīt-ō-'flaj-ə-lət, -,lāt; -flə-'jel-ət\ *n* **:** PLANTLIKE FLAGELLATE
phy·to·gen·ic \,fīt-ə-'jen-ik\ *adj* **:** of plant origin
phy·to·ge·og·ra·phy \,fīt-ō-jē-'äg-rə-fē\ *n* [ISV] **:** the biogeography of plants
phy·tog·ra·phy \fī-'täg-rə-fē\ *n* [NL *phytographia*, fr. *phyt-* + L *-graphia* -graphy] **:** descriptive botany sometimes including plant taxonomy
phy·to·hor·mone \,fīt-ə-'hȯr-,mōn\ *n* [ISV] **:** PLANT HORMONE
phy·to·lite \'fīt-ᵊl-,īt\ *or* **phy·to·lith** \-,ith\ *n* **:** a plant fossil
phy·to·log·ic \,fīt-ᵊl-'äj-ik\ *adj* **:** BOTANICAL — **phy·to·log·i·cal** \-i-kəl\ *adj* — **phy·to·log·i·cal·ly** \-k(ə-)lē\ *adv*
phy·tol·o·gy \fī-'täl-ə-jē\ *n* [NL *phytologia*, fr. *phyt-* + L *-logia* -logy] **:** BOTANY
phy·ton \'fī-,tän\ *n* [NL, fr. Gk, plant] **1 :** a structural unit of a plant consisting of a leaf and its associated portion of stem **2 :** the smallest part of a stem, root, or leaf that when severed may grow into a new plant — **phy·ton·ic** \fī-'tän-ik\ *adj*
phy·to·path·o·log·ic \,fīt-ō-,path-ə-'läj-ik\ *adj* [ISV *phytopathology* plant pathology, fr. *phyt-* + *pathology*] **:** of or relating to plant pathology — **phy·to·path·o·log·i·cal** \-i-kəl\ *adj*
phy·toph·a·gous \fī-'täf-ə-gəs\ *adj* **:** feeding on plants ⟨~ insect⟩ — **phy·toph·a·gy** \-ə-jē\ *n*
phy·to·plank·ton \,fīt-ō-'plaŋ(k)-tən, -,tän\ *n* [ISV] **:** planktonic plant life — **phy·to·plank·ton·ic** \-(,)plaŋ(k)-'tän-ik\ *adj*
phy·to·so·cio·log·i·cal \-,sō-s(h)ē-ə-'läj-i-kəl *also* -shə-'läj-\ *adj* **:** of or relating to phytosociology — **phy·to·so·cio·log·i·cal·ly** \-k(ə-)lē\ *adv*
phy·to·so·ci·ol·o·gist \-,sō-s(h)ē-'äl-ə-jəst\ *n* **:** a specialist in phytosociology
phy·to·so·ci·ol·o·gy \-jē\ *n* **:** a branch of ecology dealing with the interrelations among the flora of particular areas and esp. with plant communities
phy·tos·ter·ol \fī-'täs-tə-,rȯl, -,rōl\ *n* [ISV] **:** any of various sterols derived from plants
phy·to·tox·ic \,fīt-ə-'täk-sik\ *adj* **:** poisonous to plants — **phy·to·tox·ic·i·ty** \-,täk-'sis-ət-ē\ *n*
[1]**pi** \'pī\ *n* [MGk, fr. Gk *pei*, of Sem origin; akin to Heb *pē* pe] **1 :** the 16th letter of the Greek alphabet — symbol Π or π **2 a :** the symbol π denoting the ratio of the circumference of a circle to its diameter **b :** the ratio itself **:** a transcendental number having a value to eight decimal places of 3.14159265
[2]**pi** *n, pl* **pies** [origin unknown] **1 :** type or type matter that is spilled, mixed, or incorrectly distributed **2 :** a pi character or matrix
[3]**pi** *adj* **1 :** not intended to appear in final printing ⟨~ lines⟩ **2 :** capable of being inserted only by hand ⟨~ character⟩
[4]**pi** *vb* **pied; pi·ing** *vt* **:** to spill or throw (type or type matter) into disorder ~ *vi* **:** to become pied
pi·al \'pī-əl, 'pē-\ *adj* **:** of or relating to the pia mater
pia ma·ter \'pī-ə-,māt-ər, 'pē-ə-,mät-\ *n* [ME, fr. ML, fr. L, tender mother] **:** the thin vascular membrane investing the brain and spinal cord internal to the arachnoid and dura mater
pi·a·nis·si·mo \,pē-ə-'nis-ə-,mō\ *adv (or adj)* [It, fr. *piano* softly] **:** very softly — used as a direction in music
pi·a·nist \pē-'an-əst, 'pē-ə-nəst\ *n* **:** one who plays the piano; *esp* **:** a skilled or professional performer on the piano
[1]**pi·a·no** \pē-'än-(,)ō\ *adv (or adj)* [It, fr. LL *planus* smooth, fr. L, level — more at FLOOR] **:** SOFTLY, QUIETLY — used as a direction in music
[2]**pi·ano** \pē-'an-(,)ō, -ə(-w) *also* -'än-\ *n* [It, short for *pianoforte*, fr. *piano e forte* soft and strong; fr. the fact that its tones could be varied in loudness] **:** a stringed percussion instrument having steel wire strings that sound when struck by felt-covered hammers operated from a keyboard

piano accordion *n* **:** an accordion with a keyboard for the right hand resembling and corresponding to the middle register of a piano keyboard

pi·ano·forte \pē-ˈan-ə-ˌfō(ə)rt, -ˈän-, -ˌfȯ(ə)rt, -ˌfȯrt-ē; -ˌan-ə-ˈfȯrt-ē, -ˌän-\ *n* [It] **:** PIANO

pi·as·sa·va \ˌpē-ə-ˈsäv-ə\ *n* [Pg *piassaba*, fr. Tupi *piaçaba*] **1 :** any of several stiff coarse fibers obtained from palms and used esp. in cordage or brushes **2 :** a palm yielding piassava; *esp* **:** either of two Brazilian palms (*Attalia funifera* and *Leopoldinia piassaba*)

pi·as·ter *or* **pi·as·tre** \pē-ˈas-tər, -ˈäs-\ *n* [F *piastre*] **1 :** a Spanish dollar **:** PIECE OF EIGHT **2 a** — see *pound* at MONEY table **b :** a former monetary unit of Saudi Arabia equal to 1/22 riyal **c** — see MONEY table

pi·az·za \pē-ˈaz-ə, *1 is usu* -ˈat-sə, -ˈät-\ *n, pl* **pi·az·zas** \-ˈaz-əz\ *or* **pi·az·ze** \-ˈat-(ˌ)sā, -ˈät-\ [It, fr. L *platea* broad street — more at PLACE] **1** *pl piazze* **:** an open square in an Italian or other European town **2 a :** an arcaded and roofed gallery **b** *chiefly North & Midland* **:** VERANDA, PORCH

pi·broch \ˈpē-ˌbräk, -ˌbräk\ *n* [ScGael *piobaireachd* pipe-music] **:** a set of martial or mournful variations for the Scottish Highland bagpipe

1pi·ca \ˈpī-kə\ *n* [prob. fr. ML, collection of church rules] **1 :** 12-point type **2 :** a unit of 1/6 inch used in measuring typographical material

2pica *n* [NL, fr. L, magpie — more at PIE] **:** a craving for unnatural food

pic·a·dor \ˈpik-ə-ˌdȯ(ə)r, ˌpik-ə-ˈ\ *n, pl* **picadors** \-ˌdȯ(ə)rz\ *or* **pic·a·do·res** \ˌpik-ə-ˈdȯr-ēz, -ˈdȯr-\ [Sp, fr. *picar* to prick, fr. (assumed) VL *piccare* — more at PIKE] **:** a horseman in a bullfight who prods the bull with a lance to weaken its neck and shoulder muscles

pi·ca·ra \ˈpē-kä-ˌrä\ *n* [Sp, fem. of *pícaro*] **:** a female picaro

pi·ca·resque \ˌpik-ə-ˈresk, ˌpē-kə-\ *adj* [Sp *picaresco*, fr. *pícaro*] **:** of or relating to rogues or rascals; *also* **:** of or relating to a type of fiction of Spanish origin dealing with rogues and vagabonds

pi·ca·ro \ˈpē-kä-ˌrō\ *n* [Sp *pícaro*] **:** ROGUE, BOHEMIAN

1pic·a·roon *or* **pick·a·roon** \ˌpik-ə-ˈrün\ *n* [Sp *picarón*, aug. of *pícaro*] **1 :** PICARO **2 :** PIRATE

2picaroon *vi* **:** to act as a pirate

1pic·a·yune \ˌpik-ē-ˈ(y)ün, -ə-ˈyün\ *n* [F *picaillon* halfpenny, fr. Prov *picaioun*, fr. *picaio* money, fr. *pica* to prick, jingle, fr. (assumed) VL *piccare* to prick — more at PIKE] **1 a :** a Spanish half real piece formerly current in Louisiana and other southern states **b :** HALF DIME **2 :** something trivial

2picayune *adj* **:** of little value **:** PALTRY; *also* **:** PETTY, SMALL-MINDED

pic·a·yun·ish \-ish\ *adj* **:** PICAYUNE

pic·ca·lil·li \ˌpik-ə-ˈlil-ē\ *n* [prob. alter. of *pickle*] **:** a relish of chopped vegetables and pungent spices

1pic·co·lo \ˈpik-ə-ˌlō\ *n* [It, short for *piccolo flauto* small flute]

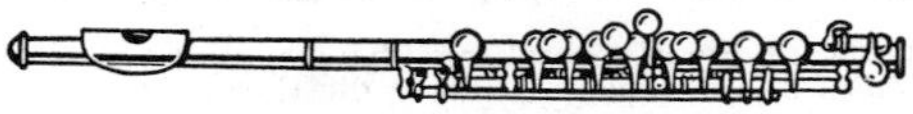

piccolo

: a small shrill flute pitched an octave higher than the ordinary flute — **pic·co·lo·ist** \-əst\ *n*

2piccolo *adj* [It, small] **:** smaller than ordinary size ⟨~ banjo⟩

pice \ˈpīs\ *n, pl* **pice** [Hindi *paisā*] **1 :** a former monetary unit of India and Pakistan equal to 1/64 of the rupee **2 :** PAISA

pi·ce·ous \ˈpī-sē-əs\ *adj* [L *piceus*, fr. *pic-*, *pix* pitch — more at PITCH] **:** of, relating to, or resembling pitch; *esp* **:** glossy brownish black in color

1pick \ˈpik\ *vb* [ME *piken*, partly fr. (assumed) OE *pīcian* (akin to MD *picken* to prick); partly fr. MF *piquer* to prick — more at PIKE] *vt* **1 :** to pierce, penetrate, or break up with a pointed instrument **2 a :** to remove bit by bit ⟨~ meat from bones⟩ **b :** to remove covering or adhering matter from ⟨~ the bones⟩ **3 a :** to gather by plucking ⟨~ apples⟩ **b :** CULL, SELECT **4 :** PILFER, ROB ⟨~ pockets⟩ **5 :** PROVOKE ⟨~ a quarrel⟩ **6 a :** to dig into or pull lightly at **b :** to pluck with a plectrum or with the fingers **c :** to loosen or pull apart with a sharp point **7 :** to unlock with a wire instead of the key ~ *vi* **1 :** to use or work with a pick **2 :** to gather or harvest something by plucking **3 :** PILFER **4 :** to eat sparingly or mincingly — **pick·er** *n* — **pick on 1 :** HARASS ⟨always *picked on* smaller boys⟩ **2 :** to single out or choose for a particular purpose or for special attention

2pick *n* **1 :** a blow or stroke with a pointed instrument **2 a :** the act or privilege of choosing or selecting **:** CHOICE **b :** the best or choicest one **3 :** the portion of a crop gathered at one time

3pick *vt* [ME *pykken*, alter. of *picchen* to pitch] **1** *chiefly dial* **:** to throw or thrust with effort **:** HURL **2 :** to throw (a shuttle) across the loom

4pick *n* **1** *dial Eng* **a :** the act of pitching or throwing **b :** something thrown **2 a :** a throw of the shuttle by which the speed of a loom is calculated **b :** one filling thread taken as a unit of fineness of fabric

5pick *n* [ME *pik*] **1 :** a heavy wooden-handled iron or steel tool pointed at one or both ends **2 a :** TOOTHPICK **b :** PICKLOCK **c :** PLECTRUM

pick·a·back \ˈpig-ē-ˌbak, ˈpik-ə-\ *var of* PIGGYBACK

pick·a·nin·ny *or* **pic·a·nin·ny** \ˈpik-ə-ˌnin-ē, ˌpik-ə-ˈ\ *n* [prob. modif. of Pg *pequenino* very little] **:** a Negro child

1pick·ax *or* **pick·axe** \ˈpik-ˌaks\ *n* [alter. of ME *pikois*, fr. OF *picois*, fr. *pic* pick, fr. L *picus* woodpecker — more at PIE] **:** 5PICK 1

2pickax *or* **pickaxe** *vt* **:** to break up or dig with a pickax ~ *vi* **:** to work with a pickax

1picked \ˈpikt\ *adj* **:** CHOICE, PRIME

2pick·ed \ˈpik-əd\ *adj* [ME, fr. 5*pick*] *chiefly dial* **:** POINTED, PEAKED

pick·eer \pik-ˈi(ə)r\ *vi* [prob. modif. of F *picorer* to steal sheep, maraud, fr. MF *pecore* sheep, fr. OIt *pecora*, fr. L, neut. pl. of *pecor-*, *pecus* cattle — more at FEE] *obs* **:** to skirmish in advance of an army; *also* **:** SCOUT, RECONNOITER

pick·er·el \ˈpik-(ə-)rəl\ *n, pl* **pickerel** *or* **pickerels** [ME *pikerel*, dim. of *pike*] **1 a** *dial chiefly Brit* **:** a young or small pike **b :** any of several comparatively small fishes (genus *Esox*) ⟨grass ~⟩ **2 :** WALLEYED PIKE

pick·er·el·weed \-ˌwēd\ *n* **:** any of various monocotyledonous aquatic plants: as **a :** any of a genus (*Pontederia*); *esp* **:** a blue-flowered American shallow-water herb (*P. cordata*) **b :** any of several still-water herbs (genus *Potamogeton*)

1pick·et \ˈpik-ət\ *n* [F *piquet*, fr. MF, fr. *piquer* to prick — more at PIKE] **1 :** a pointed or sharpened stake, post, or pale **2 a :** a detached body of soldiers serving to guard an army from surprise **b :** a detachment kept ready in camp for such duty **c :** SENTINEL **3 :** a person posted by a labor organization at a place of work affected by a strike; *also* **:** a person posted for a demonstration or protest

2picket *vt* **1 :** to enclose, fence, or fortify with pickets **2 a :** to guard with a picket **b :** to post as a picket **3 :** TETHER **4 a :** to post pickets at **b :** to walk or stand in front of as a picket ~ *vi* **:** to serve as a picket — **pick·et·er** *n*

pick·ings \ˈpik-iŋz, -ənz\ *n pl* **1 :** gleanable or eatable fragments **:** SCRAPS **2 :** yield or return for effort expended

1pick·le \ˈpik-əl\ *n* [ME *pekille*] **1 :** a solution or bath for preserving or cleaning: as **a :** a brine or vinegar solution in which foods are preserved **b :** any of various baths used in industrial cleaning or processing **2 :** a difficult situation **:** PLIGHT **3 :** an article of food that has been preserved in brine or in vinegar **syn** see PREDICAMENT

2pickle *vt* **pick·ling** \-(ə-)liŋ\ **:** to treat, preserve, or clean in or with a pickle

3pickle *n* [perh. fr. Sc *pickle* (to trifle, pilfer)] **1** *Scot* **:** GRAIN, KERNEL **2** *Scot* **:** a small quantity

pick·lock \ˈpik-ˌläk\ *n* **1 :** a tool for picking locks **2 :** BURGLAR

pick off *vt* **1 :** to shoot or bring down one by one **2 :** to catch off base with a quick throw **3 :** INTERCEPT ⟨*picked off* a pass⟩

pick out *vt* **1 a :** SELECT, CHOOSE **b :** DISTINGUISH **2 :** to play the notes of by ear or one by one

pick over *vt* **:** to examine in order to select the best or remove the unwanted

pick·pock·et \ˈpik-ˌpäk-ət\ *n* **:** one who steals from pockets

pick·thank \-ˌthaŋk\ *n* [fr. *pick a thank* to seek someone's favor] *archaic* **:** SYCOPHANT

pick up *vt* **1 a :** to take hold of and lift up **b :** to take into a vehicle **2 :** to acquire casually; *esp* **:** to strike up an acquaintance with casually **3 :** to bring within range of sight or hearing **4 :** to take into custody **5 a :** REVIVE **b :** INCREASE ~ *vi* **:** to recover speed, vigor, or activity **:** IMPROVE

pick·up \ˈpik-ˌəp\ *n* **1 a :** a revival of business activity **b :** ACCELERATION **2 a :** HITCHHIKER **b :** a temporary chance acquaintance **3 :** the conversion of mechanical movements into electrical impulses in the reproduction of sound; *also* **:** a device (as on a phonograph) for making such conversion **4 a :** the reception of sound or an image into a radio or television transmitting apparatus for conversion into electrical signals **b :** a device (as a microphone or a television camera) for converting sound or the image of a scene into electrical signals **c :** the place where a broadcast originates **d :** the electrical system for connecting to a broadcasting station a program produced outside the studio **5 :** a light truck having an open body with low sides and tailboard

Pick·wick·ian \pik-ˈwik-ē-ən\ *adj* [Samuel *Pickwick*, character in the novel *Pickwick Papers* (1836–37) by Charles Dickens] **1 :** marked by simplicity and generosity **2 :** intended or taken in a sense other than the obvious or literal one

picky \ˈpik-ē\ *adj* **:** FUSSY, FINICKY

1pic·nic \ˈpik-(ˌ)nik\ *n, often attrib* [G or F; G *picknick*, fr. F *pique-nique*] **1 :** an excursion or outing with food usu. provided by members of the group and eaten in the open **2 a :** a pleasant or amusing experience **b :** an easy task or feat **3 :** a shoulder of pork with much of the butt removed

2pic·nic \-(ˌ)nik\ *vi* **pic·nicked** \-(ˌ)nikt\ **pic·nick·ing** \-ˌnik-iŋ\ **:** to go on a picnic **:** eat in picnic fashion — **pic·nick·er** \-ˌnik-ər\ *n*

picnometer *var of* PYCNOMETER

pi·co- \ˈpē-(ˌ)kō, -kə\ *comb form* [ISV, perh. fr. It *piccolo* small] **:** one trillionth (10^{-12}) part of ⟨*picogram*⟩

pic·o·line \ˈpik-ə-ˌlēn, ˈpī-kə-\ *n* [L *pic-*, *pix* pitch + ISV *-ol* + *-ine* — more at PITCH] **:** any of the three liquid pyridine bases $CH_3C_5H_4N$ found in coal tar, ammonia liquor, and bone oil and used chiefly as solvents and in organic synthesis

1pi·cot \ˈpē-(ˌ)kō, pē-ˈ\ *n* [F, lit., small point, fr. MF, fr. *pic* prick, fr. *piquer* to prick — more at PIKE] **:** one of a series of small ornamental loops forming an edging on ribbon or lace

2picot *vt* **:** to finish with a picot

pic·o·tee \ˌpik-ə-ˈtē\ *n* [F *picoté* pointed, fr. *picoter* to mark with points, fr. *picot*] **:** a flower having one basic color with a margin of another color

picr- *or* **picro-** *comb form* [F, fr. Gk *pikr-*, *pikro-*, fr. *pikros* — more at PAINT] **1 :** bitter ⟨*picric* acid⟩ **2 :** picric acid ⟨*picrate*⟩

pic·rate \ˈpik-ˌrāt\ *n* **:** a salt or ester of picric acid

pic·ric acid \ˌpik-rik-\ *n* [ISV] **:** a bitter toxic explosive yellow crystalline strong acid $C_6H_3N_3O_7$ used esp. in high explosives, as a dye, or in medicine

pic·ro·tox·in \ˌpik-rə-ˈtäk-sən\ *n* [ISV] **:** a poisonous bitter crystalline stimulant and convulsive drug $C_{30}H_{34}O_{13}$ used intravenously as an antidote for barbiturate poisoning

Pict \ˈpikt\ *n* [ME *Pictes*, pl., Picts, fr. LL *Picti*] **:** one of a possibly non-Celtic people who once occupied Great Britain, were in many places displaced by the Britons, carried on continual border wars with the Romans, and about the 9th century became amalgamated with the Scots — **Pict·ish** \ˈpik-tish\ *adj or n*

pic·to·graph \ˈpik-tə-ˌgraf\ *n* [L *pictus* + E *-o-* + *-graph*] **1 :** an ancient or prehistoric drawing or painting on a rock wall **2 :** one of the symbols belonging to a pictorial graphic system **3 :** a diagram representing statistical data by pictorial forms varied in color, size, or number to indicate change — **pic·to·graph·ic** \ˌpik-tə-ˈgraf-ik\ *adj*

pic·tog·ra·phy \pik-ˈtäg-rə-fē\ *n* **:** use of pictographs **:** PICTURE WRITING 1

1pic·to·ri·al \pik-ˈtōr-ē-əl, -ˈtȯr-\ *adj* [LL *pictorius*, fr. L *pictor* painter] **1 :** of or relating to a painter, a painting, or the painting or drawing of pictures ⟨~ perspective⟩ **2 a :** consisting of pictures ⟨~ records⟩ **b :** illustrated by pictures ⟨~ weekly⟩ **c :** PICTO-

GRAPHIC **syn** see GRAPHIC — **pic·to·ri·al·ly** \-ə-lē\ *adv* — **pic·to·ri·al·ness** *n*

2pictorial *n* **:** a periodical having much pictorial matter

1pic·ture \'pik-chər\ *n* [ME, fr. L *pictura*, fr. *pictus*, pp. of *pingere* to paint — more at PAINT] **1 :** a representation made by painting, drawing, or photography **2 :** a description so vivid or graphic as to suggest a mental image or give an accurate idea of something **3 :** IMAGE, COPY ⟨the ~ of his father⟩ **4 a :** a transitory visible image or reproduction **b :** MOTION PICTURE **c** *pl, chiefly Brit* **:** MOVIES **5 :** TABLEAU 1, 2 ⟨stage ~⟩ **6 :** SITUATION

2picture *vt* **pic·tur·ing** \'pik-chə-riŋ, 'pik-shriŋ\ **1 :** to paint or draw a representation, image, or visual conception of **:** DEPICT; *also* **:** ILLUSTRATE **2 :** to describe graphically in words **3 :** to form a mental image of **:** IMAGINE

picture hat *n* **:** a woman's dressy hat with a broad brim

pic·tur·esque \,pik-chə-'resk\ *adj* [F & It; F *pittoresque*, fr. It *pittoresco*, fr. *pittore* painter, fr. L *pictor*, fr. *pictus*, pp.] **1 a :** resembling a picture **:** suggesting a painted scene **b :** CHARMING, QUAINT **2 :** evoking mental images **:** VIVID **syn** see GRAPHIC — **pic·tur·esque·ly** *adv* — **pic·tur·esque·ness** *n*

picture tube *n* **:** KINESCOPE 1

picture window *n* **:** an outsize window framing an exterior view

picture writing *n* **1 :** the recording of events or expression of messages by pictures representing actions or facts **2 :** the record or message so represented

pic·ul \'pik-əl\ *n* [Malay *pikul* to carry a heavy load] **:** any of various units of weight used in China and southeast Asia; *esp* **:** a Chinese unit equal to 133.33 pounds

pid·dle \'pid-ᵊl\ *vi* **pid·dling** \'pid-liŋ, -ᵊl-iŋ\ [origin unknown] **:** to act or work idly **:** DAWDLE

pid·dling \'pid-lən, -ᵊl-ən, -liŋ, -ᵊl-iŋ\ *adj* **:** TRIVIAL, PALTRY

pid·dock \'pid-ək, -ik\ *n* [origin unknown] **:** a bivalve mollusk (genus *Pholas* or family Pholadidae) that bores holes in wood, clay, and rocks

pid·gin \'pij-ən\ *n* [pidgin E, alter. of E *business*] **:** a simplified speech used for communication between people with different languages; *esp* **:** an English-based pidgin used in China ports

1pie \'pī\ *n* [ME, fr. OF, fr. L *pica*; akin to L *picus* woodpecker, OHG *speh*] **1 :** MAGPIE **2 :** a parti-colored animal

2pie *n* [ME] **1 :** a meat dish baked with biscuit or pastry crust **2 :** a dessert with a baked crust and various fillings (as of fruit) **3 :** a layer of cake split horizontally and filled with custard, cream, or jam

3pie *var of* PI

4pie *n* [Hindi *pāī*, fr. Skt *pādikā* quarter] **:** a former monetary unit of India and Pakistan equal to 1/192 of the rupee

1pie·bald \'pī-,bȯld\ *adj* **1 :** of different colors: **a :** spotted or blotched with black and white **b :** SKEWBALD **2 :** composed of incongruous parts **:** HETEROGENEOUS

2piebald *n* **:** a piebald animal (as a horse)

1piece \'pēs\ *n* [ME, fr. OF, fr. (assumed) VL *pettia*, of Gaulish origin; akin to Bret *peg* piece] **1 :** a part of a whole **:** FRAGMENT **2 :** an object or individual regarded as a unit of a kind or class **:** EXAMPLE **3 :** a length, weight, or size in which something is made or sold **4 a :** a literary composition **b :** PAINTING, SCULPTURE **c :** a theatrical production **:** PLAY **d :** a musical composition **5 :** FIREARM **6 :** COIN; *also* **:** TOKEN **7 :** a man used in playing a board game; *specif* **:** a chessman of superior rank **syn** see PART — **of a piece :** ALIKE, CONSISTENT

2piece *vt* **1 :** to repair, renew, or complete by adding pieces **:** PATCH **2 :** to join into a whole — **piec·er** *n*

pièce de ré·sis·tance \pē-,es-də-rə-,zē-'stän(t)s, -'stäⁿs\ *n, pl* **pièces de ré·sis·tance** *same*\ [F, lit., piece of resistance] **1 :** the chief dish of a meal **2 :** an outstanding item

piece-dye \'pēs-,dī\ *vt* **:** to dye after weaving or knitting

piece goods *n pl* **:** cloth fabrics sold from the bolt at retail in lengths specified by the customer — called also *yard goods*

1piece·meal \'pē-,smēl, -'smē(ə)l\ *adv* **1 :** one piece at a time **:** GRADUALLY **2 :** in pieces or fragments **:** APART

2piecemeal \-,smēl\ *adj* **:** done, made, or accomplished piece by piece or in a fragmentary way **:** GRADUAL

piece of eight : an old Spanish peso of eight reals

piece·work \'pē-,swərk\ *n* **:** work done by the piece and paid for at a standard rate per unit — **piece·work·er** \-,swər-kər\ *n*

pie chart *n* **:** a circular chart cut by radii into segments illustrating relative magnitudes or frequencies

pied \'pīd\ *adj* **:** of two or more colors in blotches **:** PARTI-COLORED; *also* **:** wearing or having a parti-colored coat

pied-à-terre \pē-,ād-ə-'te(ə)r\ *n, pl* **pieds-à-terre** *same*\ [F, lit., foot to the ground] **:** a temporary or second lodging

pied·mont \'pēd-,mänt\ *adj* [*Piedmont*, region of Italy] **:** lying or formed at the base of mountains — **piedmont** *n*

pie·plant \'pī-,plant\ *n* **:** garden rhubarb

pier \'pi(ə)r\ *n* [ME *per*, fr. OE, fr. ML *pera*] **1 :** an intermediate support for the adjacent ends of two bridge spans **2 :** a structure (as a breakwater) extending into navigable water for use as a landing place or promenade or to protect or form a harbor **3 :** a vertical structural support: as **a :** the wall between two openings **b :** PILLAR, PILASTER **c :** a vertical member that supports the end of an arch or lintel **d :** an auxiliary mass of masonry used to stiffen a wall **4 :** a structural mount usu. of stonework, concrete, or steel

pierce \'pi(ə)rs\ *vb* [ME *percen*, fr. OF *percer*] *vt* **1 a :** to run into or through as a pointed weapon does **:** STAB **b :** to enter or thrust into sharply or painfully **2 :** to make a hole through **:** PERFORATE **3 :** to force or make a way into or through **4 :** to penetrate with the eye or mind **:** DISCERN **5 :** to penetrate so as to move or touch the emotions of ~ *vi* **:** to force a way into or through something **syn** see ENTER — **pierc·ing·ly** \'pir-siŋ-lē\ *adv*

pier glass *n* **:** a large high mirror; *esp* **:** one designed to occupy the wall space between windows

Pi·eri·an \pī-'ir-ē-ən, -'er-\ *adj* **1 :** of or relating to the region of Pieria in ancient Macedonia or to the Muses as early worshiped there **2 :** of or relating to learning or poetry

Pierian spring *n* **:** a fountain in Pieria sacred to the Muses and held to be a source of poetic inspiration

Pier·rot \'pē-ə-,rō\ *n* [F, dim. of *Pierre* Peter] **:** a standard comic character of old French pantomime usu. with whitened face and loose white clothes

pier table *n* **:** a table to be placed under a pier glass

pies *pl of* PI *or of* PIE

pie·tà \,pē-ā-'tä, pyā-'tä\ *n, often cap* [It, lit., pity, fr. L *pietat-, pietas*] **:** a representation of the Virgin Mary mourning over the dead body of Christ

pi·etism \'pī-ə-,tiz-əm\ *n* **1** *cap* **:** a 17th century religious movement originating in Germany in reaction to formalism and intellectualism and stressing Bible study and personal religious experience **2 a :** emphasis on devotional experience and practices **b :** affectation of devotion — **pi·etist** \'pī-ət-əst\ *n, often cap* — **pi·etis·tic** \,pī-ə-'tis-tik\ *adj* — **pi·etis·ti·cal·ly** \-ti-k(ə-)lē\ *adv*

pi·ety \'pī-ət-ē\ *n* [F *pieté* piety, pity, fr. L *pietat-, pietas*, fr. *pius* dutiful — more at PIOUS] **1 :** the quality or state of being pious: as **a :** fidelity to natural obligations (as to parents) **b :** dutifulness in religion **:** DEVOUTNESS **2 :** an act inspired by piety **3 :** a conventional belief or standard **:** ORTHODOXY **syn** see FIDELITY

piezo- *comb form* [Gk *piezein* to press; akin to Skt *pīḍayati* he squeezes] **:** pressure ⟨*piezo*meter⟩

pi·ezo·elec·tric \pē-,ā-(,)zō-ə-'lek-trik, pē-,āt-(,)sō-\ *adj* [ISV] **:** of, relating to, or marked by piezoelectricity — **pi·ezo·elec·tri·cal·ly** \-tri-k(ə-)lē\ *adv*

pi·ezo·elec·tric·i·ty \-ə-,lek-'tris-ət-ē, -'tris-tē\ *n* [ISV] **:** electricity or electric polarity due to pressure esp. in a crystalline substance

pi·ezom·e·ter \,pē-ə-'zäm-ət-ər, pē-,āt-'säm-\ *n* **:** an instrument for measuring pressure or compressibility — **pi·ezo·met·ric** \pē-,ā-zə-'me-trik, pē-,āt-sə-\ *adj* — **pi·ezom·e·try** \,pē-ə-'zäm-ə-trē, pē-,āt-'säm-\ *n*

1pif·fle \'pif-əl\ *vi* **pif·fling** \-(ə-)liŋ\ [perh. blend of *piddle* and *trifle*] **:** to talk or act in a trivial, inept, or ineffective way **:** TRIFLE

2piffle *n* **:** trivial nonsense **:** INEPTITUDE

1pig \'pig\ *n, often attrib* [ME *pigge*] **1 :** a young swine not yet sexually mature; *broadly* **:** a wild or domestic swine **2 a :** PORK **b :** the dressed carcass of a young swine weighing less than 130 pounds **c :** PIGSKIN **3 a :** one resembling a pig **b :** an animal related to or resembling the pig — usu. used in combination **4 :** a crude casting of metal (as iron) **5** *slang* **:** an immoral woman

2pig *vb* **pigged; pig·ging** *vi* **1 :** FARROW **2 :** to live like a pig ⟨~ it⟩ ~ *vt* **:** FARROW

3pig *n* [ME *pygg*] **1** *chiefly Scot* **:** an earthenware vessel **2** *chiefly Scot* **:** CROCK

pig bed *n* **:** a bed of sand in which iron is cast into pigs

pig·boat \'pig-,bōt\ *n, slang* **:** SUBMARINE

pi·geon \'pij-ən\ *n* [ME, fr. MF *pijon*, fr. LL *pipion-, pipio* young bird, fr. L *pipire* to chirp] **1 :** any of a widely distributed family (Columbidae, order Columbiformes) of birds with a stout body, rather short legs, and smooth and compact plumage; *esp* **:** a member of one of the many domesticated varieties derived from the rock pigeon **2 :** a young woman **3 :** an easy mark **:** DUPE **4 :** CLAY PIGEON **5** [alter. of *pidgin*] **:** an object of special concern **:** BUSINESS

pigeon breast *n* **:** a rachitic deformity of the chest marked by sharp projection of the sternum — **pi·geon–breast·ed** \,pij-ən-'bres-təd\ *adj*

pigeon hawk *n* **:** any of several small hawks; *esp* **:** a small American falcon (*Falco columbarius*) related to the European merlin

pi·geon·heart·ed \,pij-ən-'härt-əd\ *adj* **:** TIMID, COWARDLY

1pi·geon·hole \'pij-ən-,hōl\ *n* **1 :** a hole or small recess for pigeons to nest **2 :** a small open compartment (as in a desk or cabinet) for keeping letters or documents

2pigeonhole *vt* **1 a :** to place in or as if in the pigeonhole of a desk **b :** to lay aside **:** SHELVE **2 :** to assign to a category **:** CLASSIFY

pi·geon–liv·ered \,pij-ən-'liv-ərd\ *adj* **:** GENTLE, MILD

pigeon pea *n* **:** a leguminous woody herb (*Cajanus cajan*) with trifoliate leaves, yellow flowers, and somewhat flat pods much cultivated esp. in the tropics; *also* **:** its small highly nutritious seed

pi·geon–toed \,pij-ən-'tōd\ *adj* **:** having the toes turned in

pi·geon·wing \'pij-ən-,wiŋ\ *n* **1 :** a fancy dance step executed by jumping and striking the legs together **2 :** a fancy figure in skating

pig·fish \'pig-,fish\ *n* **1 :** any of several saltwater grunts; *esp* **:** a food fish (*Orthopristis chrysopterus*) of the U.S. from Long Island southward **2 :** a grunt (*Lagodon rhomboides*)

pig·gery \'pig-(ə-)rē\ *n* **:** a place where swine are kept

pig·gin \'pig-ən\ *n* [origin unknown] *dial* **:** a small wooden pail with one stave extended upward as a handle

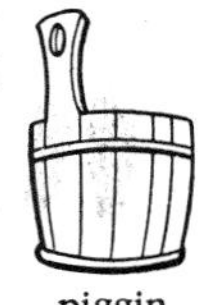

piggin

pig·gish \'pig-ish\ *adj* **:** resembling a pig **:** DIRTY, GREEDY, STUBBORN — **pig·gish·ly** *adv*

pig·gy·back \'pig-ē-,bak\ *adv (or adj)* [alter. of earlier *a pick pack*, of unknown origin] **1 :** up on the back and shoulders **2 :** on a railroad flatcar

piggy bank *n* **:** a child's coin bank often in the shape of a pig

pig·head·ed \'pig-'hed-əd\ *adj* **:** OBSTINATE, STUBBORN

pig iron *n* **:** crude iron that is the direct product of the blast furnace and is refined to produce steel, wrought iron, or ingot iron

pig latin *n, often cap L* **:** a jargon that is made by systematic mutilation of English (as *ipskay the ointjay* for *skip the joint*)

pig lead *n* **:** lead cast in pigs

1pig·ment \'pig-mənt\ *n* [L *pigmentum*, fr. *pingere* to paint — more at PAINT] **1 :** a substance that imparts black or white or a color to other materials; *esp* **:** a powdered substance mixed with a liquid in which it is relatively insoluble to impart color **2 a :** a coloring matter in animals and plants esp. in a cell or tissue **b :** any of various related colorless substances — **pig·men·tary** \-mən-,ter-ē\ *adj*

2pig·ment \-mənt, -,ment\ *vt* **:** to color with or as if with pigment

pig·men·ta·tion \,pig-mən-'tā-shən, -,men-\ *n* **:** coloration with or deposition of pigment; *esp* **:** an excessive deposition of bodily pigment

pigmy *var of* PYGMY

pig·nut \'pig-,nət\ *n* **1 :** any of several bitter-flavored hickory nuts **2 :** a hickory (as *Carya glabra*, *C. ovalis*, or *C. cordiformis*) bearing pignuts

pig·pen \-,pen\ *n* **1 :** PIGSTY **2 :** a dirty place

pig·skin \-,skin\ *n* **1 :** the skin of a swine or leather made of it **2 a :** a jockey's saddle **b :** FOOTBALL 2a

pig·stick \-,stik\ *vi* **:** to hunt the wild boar on horseback with a spear — **pig·stick·er** *n*

pig·sty \'pig-,stī\ *n* **:** a pen for pigs

pig·tail \-,tāl\ *n* **1 :** tobacco in small twisted strands or rolls **2 :** a tight braid of hair

pig–tailed \-,tāld\ *adj* **:** wearing a pigtail
pig·weed \-,wēd\ *n* **:** any of various strongly growing weedy plants esp. of the goosefoot or amaranth families
pi·ka \'pē-kə\ *n* [Tungusic *piika*] **:** any of various short-eared small lagomorph mammals (family Ochotonidae) of rocky uplands of Asia and western No. America that are related to the rabbits
1**pike** \'pīk\ *n* [ME, fr. OE *pīc* pickax] **1 :** PIKESTAFF 1 **2 :** a sharp point or spike; *also* **:** the tip of a spear — **piked** \'pīkt\ *adj*
2**pike** *vi* [ME *pyken* (refl.)] **1 :** to leave abruptly **2 :** to make one's way ⟨~ along⟩
3**pike** *n* [ME, perh. of Scand origin; akin to Norw dial. *pīk* pointed mountain] **1** *dial Eng* **:** a mountain or hill having a peaked summit — used esp. in place names **2** [Sp *pico*, fr. *picar* to prick — more at PICADOR] *archaic* **:** 2PEAK
4**pike** *n, pl* **pike** *or* **pikes** [ME, fr. 1*pike*] **1 a :** a large elongate long-snouted voracious teleost fish (*Esox lucius*) valued for food and sport and widely distributed in cooler parts of the northern hemisphere **b :** any of various related fishes (family Esocidae): as (1) **:** MUSKELLUNGE (2) **:** PICKEREL **2 :** any of various fishes resembling the pike in appearance or habits
5**pike** *n* [MF *pique*, fr. *piquer* to prick, fr. (assumed) VL *piccare*, fr. *piccus* woodpecker, fr. L *picus* — more at PIE] **:** a weapon formed of a long wooden shaft with a pointed steel head and used by the foot soldier until superseded by the bayonet
6**pike** *vt* **:** to pierce, kill, or wound with a pike
7**pike** *n* **:** TURNPIKE
pike·man \'pīk-mən\ *n* **:** a soldier armed with a pike
pike perch *n* **:** a walleye or other fish of the perch group that resembles the pike
pik·er \'pī-kər\ *n* [*Pike* county, Missouri, thought to be the original home of many shiftless farmers] **1 :** one who gambles or speculates with small amounts of money **2 :** one who does things in a small way; *also* **:** TIGHTWAD, CHEAPSKATE
pike·staff \'pīk-,staf\ *n* **1 :** a spiked staff for use on slippery ground **2 :** the staff of a foot soldier's pike
pil- *or* **pili-** *or* **pilo-** *comb form* [L *pilus* — more at PILE] **:** hair ⟨*pil*eous⟩ ⟨*pili*ferous⟩
pi·laf *or* **pi·laff** \pi-'läf, 'pē-,\ *or* **pi·lau** \pi-'lō, -'lȯ, 'pē-(,) ; *South often* 'pər-(,)lü, -(,)lō\ *n* [Per & Turk *pilāu*] **:** a dish made of rice with meat and seasoning
pi·las·ter \'pī-,las-tər *also* pə-'las-, pī-'\ *n* [MF *pilastre*, fr. It *pilastro*] **:** an upright architectural member that is rectangular in plan and is structurally a pier but architecturally treated as a column and that usu. projects a third of its width or less from the wall

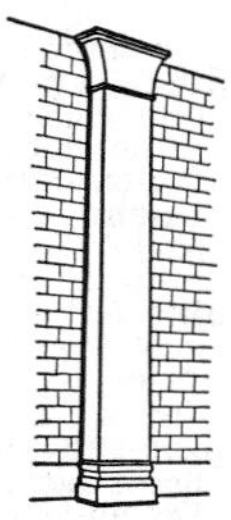
pilaster

pil·chard \'pil-chərd\ *n* [origin unknown] **1 :** a fish (*Sardinia pilchardus*) of the herring family resembling the herring and occurring in great schools along the coasts of Europe **2 :** any of several sardines related to the European pilchard
1**pile** \'pī(ə)l\ *n* [ME, dart, stake, fr. OE *pīl;* akin to OHG *pfīl* dart; both fr. a prehistoric WGmc word borrowed fr. L *pilum* javelin — more at PESTLE] **1 :** a long slender column usu. of timber, steel, or reinforced concrete driven into the ground to carry a vertical load **2 :** a wedge-shaped heraldic charge usu. placed vertically with the broad end up **3 a :** a target-shooting arrowhead without cutting edges **b** [L *pilum*] **:** an ancient Roman foot soldier's heavy javelin
2**pile** *vt* **:** to drive piles into
3**pile** *n* [ME, fr. MF, fr. L *pila* pillar] **1 a** (1) **:** a quantity of things heaped together (2) **:** a heap of wood for burning a corpse or a sacrifice **b :** any great number or quantity **:** LOT **2 :** a large building or group of buildings **3 :** a great amount of money **:** FORTUNE **4 a :** a vertical series of alternate disks of two dissimilar metals (as copper and zinc) with disks of cloth or paper moistened with an electrolyte between them for producing a current of electricity **b :** a battery made up of cells similarly constructed **5 :** REACTOR
4**pile** *vt* **1 :** to lay or place in a pile **:** STACK **2 :** to heap in abundance **:** LOAD ~ *vi* **1 :** to form a pile **:** ACCUMULATE **2 :** to move or press forward in or as if in a mass **:** CROWD ⟨*piled* into a car⟩
5**pile** *n* [ME, fr. L *pilus* hair; akin to L *pila* ball, *pilleus, pileus* felt cap, Gk *pilos*] **1 :** a coat or surface of usu. short close fine furry hairs **2 :** a velvety surface produced by an extra set of filling yarns that form raised loops which are cut and sheared
6**pile** *n* [ME, fr. L *pila* ball] **1 :** a single hemorrhoid **2** *pl* **:** HEMORRHOIDS; *also* **:** the condition of one affected with hemorrhoids
pi·le·ate \'pī-lē-,āt\ *or* **pi·le·at·ed** \-,āt-əd\ *adj* **1 :** having a pileus **2 :** having a crest covering the pileum ⟨a ~ woodpecker⟩
piled \'pī(ə)ld\ *adj* **:** having a pile
pile driver *n* **1 :** a machine for driving down piles with a pile hammer or a steam or air hammer **2 :** an operator of a pile driver
pile hammer *n* **:** the heavy weight of the pile driver whose impact forces a pile into the earth
pi·le·um \'pī-lē-əm\ *n, pl* **pi·lea** \-lē-ə\ [NL, fr. L *pileus, pileum* felt cap] **:** the top of the head of a bird from the bill to the nape
pi·le·us \'pī-lē-əs\ *n, pl* **pi·lei** \-lē-,ī\ [NL, fr. L] **1 :** the umbrella-shaped fruiting body of many fungi (as the mushrooms) **2** [L] **:** a pointed or close-fitting cap worn by ancient Romans
pile·wort \'pī(ə)l-,wərt, -,wȯ(ə)rt\ *n* **1 :** CELANDINE 2 **2 :** a coarse hairy perennial figwort (*Scrophularia marilandica*) of the eastern and central U.S.
pil·fer \'pil-fər\ *vb* **pil·fer·ing** \-f(ə-)riŋ\ [MF *pelfrer*, fr. *pelfre* booty] *vi* **:** PLUNDER, ROB; *esp* **:** to practice petty theft ~ *vt* **:** to steal in small quantities **:** FILCH **syn** see STEAL — **pil·fer·age** \-f(ə-)rij\ *n* — **pil·fer·er** \-fər-ər\ *n*
pil·gar·lic \pil-'gär-lik\ *n* [*pilled garlic*] **1 a :** a bald head **b :** a bald-headed man **2 :** a man looked upon with humorous contempt or mock pity
pil·grim \'pil-grəm\ *n* [ME, fr. OF *peligrin*, fr. LL *pelegrinus*, alter. of L *peregrinus* foreigner, fr. *peregrinus* foreign, fr. *pereger* being abroad, fr. *per* through + *agr-, ager* land — more at FOR, ACRE] **1 :** one who journeys in alien lands **:** WAYFARER **2 :** one who travels to a shrine or holy place as a devotee **3** *cap* **:** one of the English colonists founding the first permanent settlement in New England at Plymouth in 1620
1**pil·grim·age** \'pil-grə-mij\ *n* **1 :** a journey of a pilgrim; *esp* **:** one to a shrine or a sacred place **2 :** the course of life on earth
2**pilgrimage** *vi* **:** to go on a pilgrimage
pil·ing \'pī-liŋ\ *n* **:** a structure of piles; *also* **:** PILES
1**pill** \'pil\ *vb* [ME *pilen, pillen*, partly fr. OE *pilian* to peel, partly fr. MF *piller* to plunder] *vi, dial chiefly Eng* **:** come off in flakes or scales **:** PEEL ~ *vt* **1** *archaic* **:** to subject to depredation or extortion **2** *dial* **:** to peel or strip off **3** *obs* **:** to remove hair from
2**pill** *n* [L *pilula*, fr. dim. of *pila* ball — more at PILE] **1 :** medicine in a small rounded mass to be swallowed whole **2 :** something repugnant or unpleasant that must be accepted or endured **3 :** something resembling a pill in size or shape **4 :** a disagreeable or tiresome person **5 :** an oral contraceptive — usu. used with *the*
3**pill** *vt* **1 :** to dose with pills **2 :** BLACKBALL
1**pil·lage** \'pil-ij\ *n* [ME, fr. MF, fr. *piller* to plunder, fr. *peille* rag, fr. L *pilleum, pilleus* felt cap] **1 :** the act of looting or plundering esp. in war **2** *archaic* **:** something taken as booty **syn** see SPOIL
2**pillage** *vt* **:** LOOT, SACK ~ *vi* **:** to take booty **:** PLUNDER **syn** see RAVAGE — **pil·lag·er** *n*
1**pil·lar** \'pil-ər\ *n* [ME *piler*, fr. OF, fr. ML *pilare*, fr. L *pila*] **1 a :** a firm upright support for a superstructure **:** POST **b :** a column or shaft standing alone esp. for a monument **2 :** a chief supporter **:** PROP **3 :** a solid mass of coal, rock, or ore left standing to support a mine roof **4 :** a body part likened to a column — **from pillar to post :** from one place or one situation to another
2**pillar** *vt* **:** to support or strengthen with a pillar
pil·lar–box \-,bäks\ *n, Brit* **:** a pillar-shaped mailbox
pill·box \'pil-,bäks\ *n* **1 :** a box for pills; *esp* **:** a shallow round box of pasteboard **2 :** a small low concrete emplacement for machine guns and antitank weapons **3 :** a small round hat without a brim; *specif* **:** a woman's shallow hat with a flat crown and straight sides
pill bug *n* **:** WOOD LOUSE 1
1**pil·lion** \'pil-yən\ *n* [ScGael or IrGael; ScGael *pillean*, dim. of *peall* covering, couch; IrGael *pillīn*, dim. of *peall* covering, couch] **1 a :** a light saddle for women consisting chiefly of a cushion **b :** a pad or cushion put on behind a man's saddle chiefly for a woman to ride on **2 :** a motorcycle or bicycle riding saddle for a passenger
2**pillion** *adv* **:** on or as if on a pillion ⟨ride ~⟩
1**pil·lo·ry** \'pil-(ə-)rē\ *n* [ME, fr. OF *pilori*] **1 :** a device for publicly punishing offenders consisting of a wooden frame with holes in which the head and hands can be locked **2 :** a means for exposing to public scorn or ridicule
2**pillory** *vt* **1 :** to set in a pillory as punishment **2 :** to expose to public contempt, ridicule, or scorn

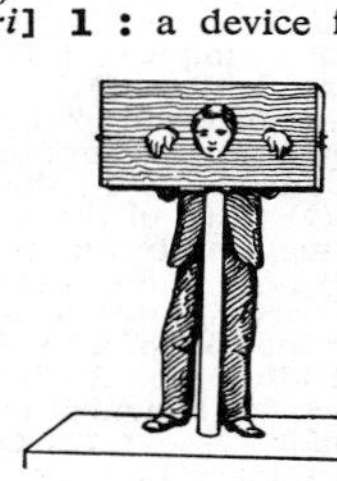
pillory 1

1**pil·low** \'pil-(,)ō, -ə(-w)\ *n* [ME *pilwe*, fr. OE *pyle;* akin to OHG *pfuliwi* pillow; both fr. a prehistoric WGmc word borrowed fr. L *pulvinus* pillow] **1 :** a support for the head of a sleeping person; *esp* **:** a cloth bag filled with feathers, down, or sponge rubber **:** CUSHION **2 :** a block or support used esp. to equalize or distribute pressure **3 :** a cushion or pad tightly stuffed and used as a support for the design and tools in making lace with a bobbin
2**pillow** *vt* **1 :** to rest or lay on or as if on a pillow **2 :** to serve as a pillow for ~ *vi* **:** to lay or rest one's head on or as if on a pillow
pillow block *n* **:** a block or standard to support a journal (as of a shaft) **:** BEARING
pil·low·case \'pil-ə-,kās, -ō-\ *n* **:** a removable covering for a pillow usu. of white linen or cotton
pillow lace *n* **:** lace made with a bobbin
pillow sham *n* **:** an ornamental covering for a bed pillow
pillow slip *n* **:** PILLOWCASE
pilo- — see PIL-
pi·lo·car·pine \,pī-lə-'kär-,pēn\ *n* [ISV, fr. NL *Pilocarpus jaborandi*, species of tropical shrubs] **:** an alkaloid $C_{11}H_{16}N_2O_2$ obtained from jaborandi that is a strong sialagogue and diaphoretic
pi·lose \'pī-,lōs\ *adj* [L *pilosus*, fr. *pilus* hair — more at PILE] **:** covered with usu. soft hair — **pi·los·i·ty** \pī-'läs-ət-ē\ *n*
1**pi·lot** \'pī-lət\ *n* [MF *pilote*, fr. It *pilota*, alter. of *pedota*, fr. (assumed) MGk *pēdōtēs*, fr. Gk *pēda* steering oars, pl. of *pēdon* oar; akin to Gk *pod-, pous* foot — more at FOOT] **1 a :** one employed to steer a ship **:** HELMSMAN **b :** a person who is qualified and usu. licensed to conduct a ship into and out of a port or in specified waters, often for fixed fees **2 :** GUIDE, LEADER **3 :** an inclined frame on the front of a railroad locomotive for throwing obstacles off the track — called also *cowcatcher* **4 :** one who flies or is qualified to fly an airplane **5 :** a piece that guides a tool or machine part — **pi·lot·less** \-ləs\ *adj*
2**pilot** *vt* **1 :** CONDUCT **2 a :** to set the course of **:** STEER ⟨~ a ship⟩ **b :** to act as pilot of **:** FLY ⟨~ a plane⟩ **syn** see GUIDE
3**pilot** *adj* **:** serving as a guiding or tracing device, an activating or auxiliary unit, or a trial or operation
pi·lot·age \'pī-lət-ij\ *n* **1 :** the act or business of piloting **2 :** the compensation paid to a pilot
pilot balloon *n* **:** a small unmanned balloon sent up to show the direction and speed of the wind
pilot biscuit *n* **:** HARDTACK
pilot bread *n* **:** HARDTACK
pilot burner *n* **:** a small burner kept lighted to rekindle the principal burner
pilot engine *n* **:** a locomotive going in advance of a train to make sure that the way is clear
pilot fish *n* **:** a pelagic carangid fish (*Naucrates ductor*) that often swims in company with a shark
pi·lot·house \'pī-lət-,haùs\ *n* **:** a forward deckhouse for a ship's helmsman containing the steering wheel, compass, and navigating equipment
pilot light *n* **1 :** an indicator light showing where a switch or circuit breaker is located or whether a motor is in operation or power is on — called also *pilot lamp* **2 :** a small permanent flame used to ignite gas at a burner
pil·sner *also* **pil·sen·er** \'pilz-(ə-)nər\ *n* [G, lit., of Pilsen, city in Czechoslovakia] **1 :** a light beer with a strong flavor of hops **2 :** a tall slender footed glass for beer

Pilt·down man \ˌpilt-ˌdau̇n-\ *n* [*Piltdown*, East Sussex, England] **:** a supposedly very early primitive modern man based on skull fragments uncovered in a gravel pit at Piltdown and used in combination with comparatively recent skeletal remains of various animals in the elaborate of an elaborate fraud
pil·u·lar *or* **pil·lu·lar** \ˈpil-yə-lər\ *adj* **:** of, relating to, or resembling a pill
pil·ule *or* **pil·lule** \ˈpil-(ˌ)yü(ə)l\ *n* [MF, fr. L *pilula* pill — more at PILE] **:** a little pill
pi·ma cotton \ˌpē-mə-, ˌpim-ə-\ *n* [*Pima* county, Arizona] **:** a cotton with fiber of exceptional strength and firmness developed in the southwestern U.S. by selection and breeding of Egyptian cottons
Pi·man \ˈpē-mən\ *adj* **:** of, relating to, or constituting a language family of the Uto-Aztecan phylum
pi·men·to \pə-ˈment-(ˌ)ō\ *n, pl* **pimentos** *or* **pimento** [Sp *pimienta* allspice, pepper, fr. LL *pigmenta*, pl. of *pigmentum* plant juice, fr. L, pigment] **1 :** PIMIENTO 1 **2 :** ALLSPICE
pimento cheese *n* **:** a Neufchâtel, process, cream, or occas. cheddar cheese to which ground pimientos have been added
pi–me·son \ˈpī-ˈmez-ˌän, -ˈmēz-, -ˈmes-, -ˈmēs-\ *n* **:** a short-lived meson having a mass approximately 270 times that of the electron and being responsible for a part of nuclear forces
pi·mien·to \pə-ˈment-(ˌ)ō, pəm-ˈyent-\ *n, pl* **pimientos** [Sp, fr. *pimienta*] **1 :** any of various bluntly conical thick-fleshed sweet peppers of European origin with a distinctive mild sweet flavor used esp. as a garnish, as a stuffing for olives, and as a source of paprika **2 :** a plant that bears pimientos
1pimp \ˈpimp\ *n* [origin unknown] **:** PROCURER, PANDER
2pimp *vi* **:** to act the pimp
pim·per·nel \ˈpim-pər-ˌnel, -pərn-ᵊl\ *n* [ME *pimpernele*, fr. MF *pimprenelle*, fr. LL *pimpinella*, a medicinal herb] **:** any of a genus (*Anagallis*) of herbs of the primrose family; *esp* **:** one (*A. arvensis*) whose scarlet, white, or purplish flowers close at the approach of rainy or cloudy weather — called also *scarlet pimpernel*
pimp·ing \ˈpim-pən, -piŋ\ *adj* [origin unknown] **1 :** PETTY, INSIGNIFICANT **2** *chiefly dial* **:** PUNY, SICKLY
pim·ple \ˈpim-pəl\ *n* [ME *pinple*] **1 :** a small inflamed elevation of the skin **:** PAPULE; *esp* **:** PUSTULE **2 :** a swelling or protuberance like a pimple — **pim·pled** \-pəld\ *adj* — **pim·ply** \-p(ə-)lē\ *adj*
1pin \ˈpin\ *n* [ME, fr. OE *pinn;* akin to OHG *pfinn* peg] **1 a :** a piece of wood or metal used esp. for fastening separate articles together or as a support by which one article may be suspended from another **b** *obs* **:** the center peg of a target; *also* **:** the center itself **c (1) :** one of the wooden pieces constituting the target in various games (as bowling) **(2) :** the peg at which a quoit is pitched **(3) :** the staff of the flag marking a hole on a golf course **d :** a peg for regulating the tension of the strings of a musical instrument **e :** the part of a key stem that enters a lock **f (1) :** THOLE 2 **(2) :** a belaying pin **2 a (1) :** a small pointed piece of wire with a head used for fastening clothes or attaching papers **(2) :** something of small value **:** TRIFLE **b :** an ornament or emblem fastened to clothing with a pin **c (1) :** BOBBY PIN **(2) :** HAIRPIN **(3) :** SAFETY PIN **3 :** LEG ⟨wobbly on his ~*s*⟩
2pin *vt* **pinned; pin·ning 1 a :** to fasten, join, or secure with a pin **b :** to press together and hold fast **2 a :** ATTACH, HANG ⟨*pinned* his hopes on a miracle⟩ **b :** to assign the blame or responsibility for ⟨~ the robbery on a night watchman⟩
3pin *adj* **1 :** of or relating to a pin **2** *of leather* **:** having a grain suggesting the heads of pins
pi·ña cloth \ˌpēn-yə-\ *n* [Sp *piña*] **:** a lustrous transparent cloth of Philippine origin that is woven of silky pineapple fibers
pin·afore \ˈpin-ə-ˌfō(ə)r, -ˌfȯ(ə)r\ *n* [*pin* + *afore*] **:** a low-necked sleeveless apron worn esp. by children
pi·nas·ter \pī-ˈnas-tər, ˈpī-ˌ\ *n* [L, wild pine, fr. *pinus* pine] **:** a pine (*Pinus pinaster*) of the Mediterranean region
pi·ña·ta *or* **pi·na·ta** \pēn-ˈyät-ə\ *n* [Sp *piñata*, lit., pot] **:** a decorated pottery jar filled with candies, fruits, and gifts and hung from the ceiling to be broken as part of Mexican Christmas festivities
pin·ball machine \ˈpin-ˌbȯl-\ *n* **:** an amusement device often used for gambling in which a ball propelled by a plunger scores points as it rolls down a slanting surface among pins and targets — called also *pinball game*
pin·bone \ˈpin-ˈbōn, -ˌbōn\ *n* **:** the hipbone esp. of a quadruped
pince–nez \paⁿ-ˈsnā, pan(t)-\ *n, pl* **pince–nez** \-ˈsnā(z)\ [F, fr. *pincer* to pinch + *nez* nose, fr. L *nasus* — more at NOSE] **:** eyeglasses clipped to the nose by a spring
pin·cer \ˈpin-chər (*usu US for 1*), ˈpin(t)-sər\ *n* [ME *pinceour*] **1** *pl but sing or pl in constr* **a :** an instrument having two short handles and two grasping jaws working on a pivot and used for gripping things **b :** a claw (as of a lobster) resembling a pair of pincers **:** CHELA **2 :** one part of a double envelopment in which two forces are driven one on each side of an enemy position so as to converge on it — **pin·cer·like** \-ˌlīk\ *adj*

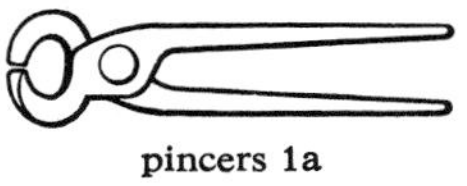
pincers 1a

1pinch \ˈpinch\ *vb* [ME *pinchen*, fr. (assumed) ONF *pinchier*] *vt* **1 a :** to squeeze between the finger and thumb or between the jaws of an instrument **b :** to prune the tip of (a plant or shoot) usu. to induce branching **c :** to squeeze or compress painfully **d :** to cause physical or mental pain to **e (1) :** to cause to appear thin or shrunken **(2) :** to cause to shrivel or wither **2 :** to subject to strict economy or want **:** STRAITEN **3 a :** STEAL **b :** ARREST **4 :** to sail too close to the wind ~ *vi* **1 :** COMPRESS, SQUEEZE **2 :** to be miserly or closefisted **3 :** to press painfully **4 :** NARROW, TAPER
2pinch *n* **1 a :** a critical juncture **:** EMERGENCY **b (1) :** PRESSURE, STRESS **(2) :** HARDSHIP, PRIVATION **c :** SHORTAGE **2 a :** an act of pinching **:** SQUEEZE **b :** as much as may be taken between the finger and thumb ⟨a ~ of salt⟩ **3 :** a marked thinning of a vein or bed **4 a :** THEFT **b :** a police raid **:** ARREST **syn** see JUNCTURE
pinch bar *n* **:** a lever with a pointed projection at one end that is used esp. to roll heavy wheels
pinch·beck \ˈpinch-ˌbek\ *n* [Christopher *Pinchbeck* †1732 E watchmaker] **1 :** an alloy of copper and zinc used esp. to imitate gold in cheap jewelry **2 :** something counterfeit or spurious — **pinchbeck** *adj*
pinch·cock \-ˌkäk\ *n* **:** a clamp used on a flexible tube to regulate the flow of a fluid through the tube
pinch·er \ˈpin-chər\ *n* **1 :** one that pinches **2** *pl* **:** PINCERS
pinch–hit \ˈpinch-ˈhit\ *vi* [back-formation fr. *pinch hitter*] **1 :** to bat in the place of another player esp. in an emergency when a hit is particularly needed **2 :** to act or serve in place of another — **pinch hit** *n*
pinch hitter *n* **:** one that pinch-hits
pin curl *n* **:** a curl made usu. by dampening a strand of hair with water or lotion, coiling it, and securing it by a hairpin or clip
pin·cush·ion \ˈpin-ˌku̇sh-ən\ *n* **:** a small cushion in which pins may be stuck ready for use
1Pin·dar·ic \pin-ˈdar-ik\ *adj* **1 :** of or relating to the poet Pindar **2 :** written in the manner or style characteristic of Pindar
2Pindaric *n* **1 :** a Pindaric ode **2** *pl* **:** loose irregular verses similar to those used in Pindaric odes
pin·dling \ˈpin-(d)lən, -dᵊl-ən, -(d)liŋ, -dᵊl-iŋ\ *adj* [perh. alter. of *spindling*] *dial* **:** PUNY, FRAIL
1pine \ˈpīn\ *vi* [ME *pinen*, fr. OE *pīnian*, fr. (assumed) OE *pīn* punishment, fr. L *poena* — more at PAIN] **1 :** to lose vigor, health, or flesh (as through grief) **:** LANGUISH **2 :** to yearn intensely **syn** see LONG
2pine *n, often attrib* [ME, fr. OE *pīn*, fr. L *pinus;* akin to Gk *pitys* pine, L *opimus* fat — more at FAT] **1 :** any of a genus (*Pinus* of the family Pinaceae, the pine family) of coniferous evergreen trees having slender elongated needles and including valuable timber trees as well as many ornamentals **2 :** the straight-grained white or yellow usu. durable and resinous wood of a pine varying from extreme softness in the white pine (*Pinus strobus*) to hardness in the longleaf pine (*P. palustris*) and related forms **3 :** any of various Australian coniferous trees (as of the genera *Callitris, Araucaria*, or *Cupressus*) **4 :** PINEAPPLE — **piny** *or* **pin·ey** \ˈpī-nē\ *adj*
pi·ne·al \ˈpin-ē-əl, ˈpī-nē-\ *adj* [F *pinéal*, fr. MF, fr. L *pinea* pinecone, fr. fem. of *pineus* of pine, fr. *pinus*] **:** of, relating to, or being the pineal body
pineal body *n* **:** a small usu. conical appendage of the brain of all craniate vertebrates that in a few reptiles has the essential structure of an eye and that is variously postulated to be a vestigial third eye, an endocrine organ, or the seat of the soul
pine·ap·ple \ˈpī-ˌnap-əl\ *n* **1 a :** a tropical monocotyledonous plant (*Ananas comosus* of the family Bromeliaceae, the pineapple family) with rigid spiny-margined recurved leaves and a short stalk with a dense oblong head of small abortive flowers **b :** the fruit of this plant consisting of the succulent fleshy inflorescence **2 a :** a dynamite bomb **b :** a hand grenade
pine·drops \ˈpīn-ˌdräps\ *n pl but sing or pl in constr* **1 :** a purplish brown leafless saprophytic plant (*Pterospora andromedea*) of the wintergreen family with racemose drooping white flowers **2 :** BEECHDROPS
pi·nene \ˈpī-ˌnēn\ *n* [ISV, fr. L *pinus*] **:** either of two liquid isomeric unsaturated bicyclic terpene hydrocarbons $C_{10}H_{16}$ found in turpentine oils
pine nut *n* **:** the edible seed of any of several chiefly western No. American pines
pin·ery \ˈpīn-(ə-)rē\ *n* **1 :** a hothouse or area where pineapples are grown **2 :** a grove or forest of pine
pine·sap \ˈpīn-ˌsap\ *n* **:** any of several parasitic or saprophytic herbs (genus *Monotropa*) of the wintergreen family resembling the Indian pipe but yellowish or reddish
pine siskin *n* **:** a No. American finch (*Spinus pinus*) with streaked plumage
pine tar *n* **:** tar obtained by destructive distillation of the wood of the pine tree and used esp. in roofing and soaps and in the treatment of skin diseases
pi·ne·tum \pī-ˈnēt-əm\ *n, pl* **pi·ne·ta** \-ˈnēt-ə\ [L, fr. *pinus*] **1 :** a plantation of pine trees; *esp* **:** a scientific collection of living coniferous trees **2 :** a treatise on pines
pine·wood \ˈpīn-ˌwu̇d\ *n* **1 :** a wood of pines — often used in pl. but sing. or pl. in constr. **2 :** the wood of the pine tree
pin·feath·er \ˈpin-ˌfeth-ər\ *n* **:** a feather not fully developed; *esp* **:** a feather just emerging through the skin — **pin·feath·ered** \-ərd\ *adj* — **pin·feath·ery** \-ˌfeth-(ə-)rē\ *adj*
pin·fish \ˈpin-ˌfish\ *n* **:** any of several fishes having sharp dorsal spines; *esp* **:** a small compressed dark green grunt (*Lagodon rhomboides*) of the Atlantic coast
pin·fold \-ˌfōld\ *n* [ME, fr. OE *pundfald*, fr. *pund-* enclosure + *fald* fold] **1 :** 4POUND 1 **2 :** a place of restraint
ping \ˈpiŋ\ *n* [imit.] **1 :** a sharp sound like that of a bullet striking **2 :** ignition knock — **ping** *vi*
Ping–Pong \ˈpiŋ-ˌpäŋ, -ˌpȯŋ\ *trademark* — used for table tennis
pin·head \ˈpin-ˌhed\ *n* **1 :** something very small or insignificant **2 :** a very dull or stupid person **:** FOOL
pin·head·ed \-ˈhed-əd\ *adj* **:** lacking intelligence or understanding **:** DULL, STUPID — **pin·head·ed·ness** *n*
pin·hole \-ˌhōl\ *n* **:** a small hole made by, for, or as if by a pin
1pin·ion \ˈpin-yən\ *n* [ME, fr. MF *pignon*] **1 :** the terminal section of a bird's wing including the carpus, metacarpus, and phalanges; *broadly* **:** WING **2 :** FEATHER, QUILL; *also* **:** FLIGHT FEATHERS — **pin·ioned** \-yənd\ *adj*
2pinion *vt* **1 :** to restrain (a bird) from flight esp. by cutting off the pinion of one wing **2 a :** to disable or restrain by binding the arms **b :** to bind fast **:** SHACKLE
3pi·nion \ˈpin-ˌyōn\ *n* [AmerSp *piñón*] **:** PIÑON
4pin·ion \ˈpin-yən\ *n* [F *pignon*, fr. MF *peignon*, fr. *peigne* comb, fr. L *pecten* — more at PECTINATE] **:** a gear with a small number of teeth designed to mesh with a larger wheel or rack **:** the smallest of a train or set of gear wheels
pi·nite \ˈpē-ˌnīt\ *n* [G *pinit*, fr. the *Pini* mine, Saxony, Germany] **:** a compact dull grayish, green, or brownish mineral essentially muscovite derived from the alteration of other minerals
1pink \ˈpiŋk\ *vt* [ME *pinken*] **1 a :** PIERCE, STAB **b :** to wound by irony, criticism, or ridicule **2 a :** to perforate in an ornamental pattern **b :** to cut a saw-toothed edge on
2pink *n* [ME, fr. MD *pinke*] **:** a ship with a narrow overhanging stern — called also *pin·kie* \ˈpiŋ-kē\
3pink *n* [origin unknown] **1 :** any of a genus (*Dianthus* of the family Caryophyllaceae, the pink family) of annual or perennial herbs often cultivated for their showy flowers **2 a :** the very embodiment **:** PARAGON ⟨~ of condition⟩ **b (1) :** one dressed in the height of fashion **:** SWELL **(2) :** ELITE
4pink *adj* **1 :** of the color pink **2 :** holding moderately radical and usu. socialistic political or economic views **3 :** ANGERED, EXCITED ⟨thrilled ~⟩ — **pink·ness** *n*

5pink *n* **1 :** any of a group of colors bluish red to red in hue, of medium to high lightness, and of low to moderate saturation **2 a** (1) **:** the scarlet color of a fox hunter's coat (2) **:** a fox hunter's coat of this color **b :** pink-colored clothing **c** *pl* **:** light-colored trousers formerly worn by army officers **3 :** a person who holds advanced or moderately radical political or economic views

pink elephants *n pl* **:** any of various hallucinations arising esp. from heavy drinking or use of narcotics

pink·eye \'piŋ-ˌkī\ *n* **:** an acute highly contagious conjunctivitis of man and various domestic animals

pin·kie *or* **pin·ky** \'piŋ-kē\ *n* [prob. fr. D *pinkje*, dim. of *pink* little finger] **:** a little finger

pinking shears *n pl* **:** shears with a saw-toothed inner edge on the blades for making a zigzag cut

pink·ish \'piŋ-kish\ *adj* **:** somewhat pink; *esp* **:** tending to be pink in politics — **pink·ish·ness** *n*

pink lady *n* **:** a cocktail consisting of gin, brandy, lemon juice, grenadine, and white of egg shaken with ice and strained

pink·ly \'piŋ-klē\ *adv* **:** in a pink manner **:** with a pink hue

pin knot *n* **:** a sound knot in lumber not over ½ inch in diameter

pinko \'piŋ-(ˌ)kō\ *n* **:** 5PINK 3

pink·root \'piŋ-ˌkrüt, -ˌkru̇t\ *n* **:** any of several plants (genus *Spigelia*) related to the nux vomica and used as anthelmintics; *esp* **:** an American woodland herb (*S. marilandica*) sometimes cultivated for its showy red and yellow flowers

pin money *n* **1 :** money given by a man to his wife for her own use **2 :** money set aside for the purchase of incidentals

pin·na \'pin-ə\ *n, pl* **pin·nae** \'pin-ˌē, -ˌī\ *or* **pinnas** [NL, fr. L, feather, wing — more at PEN] **1 :** a leaflet or primary division of a pinnate leaf or frond **2 a :** a feather, wing, or fin or some similar part **b :** the largely cartilaginous projecting portion of the external ear — **pin·nal** \'pin-ᵊl\ *adj*

pin·nace \'pin-əs\ *n* [MF *pinace*, prob. fr. OSp *pinaza*, fr. *pino* pine, fr. L *pinus*] **1 :** a light sailing ship used largely as a tender **2 :** any of various ship's boats

1pin·na·cle \'pin-i-kəl\ *n* [ME *pinacle*, fr. MF, fr. LL *pinnaculum* gable, fr. dim. of L *pinna* wing, battlement] **1 :** an upright architectural member generally ending in a small spire and used esp. in Gothic construction to give weight to a buttress or angle pier **2 :** a structure or formation suggesting a pinnacle; *specif* **:** a lofty peak **3 :** the highest point of development or achievement **:** ACME **syn** see SUMMIT

2pinnacle *vt* **pin·na·cling** \-k(ə-)liŋ\ **1 :** to surmount with a pinnacle **2 :** to raise or rear on a pinnacle

pin·nate \'pin-ˌāt\ *adj* [NL *pinnatus*, fr. L, feathered, fr. *pinna*] **:** resembling a feather esp. in having similar parts arranged on opposite sides of an axis like the barbs on the rachis of a feather ⟨~ leaf⟩ — **pin·nate·ly** *adv* — **pin·na·tion** \pin-'ā-shən\ *n*

pinnati- *comb form* [NL, fr. *pinnatus*] **:** pinnately ⟨*pinnati*sect⟩

pin·nati·fid \pə-'nat-ə-fəd, -ˌfid\ *adj* [NL *pinnatifidus*, fr. *pinnati-* + L *-fidus* -fid] **:** cleft in a pinnate manner ⟨a ~ leaf⟩ — **pin·nati·fid·ly** *adv*

pin·nati·sect \pə-'nat-ə-ˌsekt\ *adv* **:** cleft pinnately to or almost to the midrib

pin·ner \'pin-ər\ *n* **1 :** a woman's cap with long lappets worn in the 17th and 18th centuries **2 :** one that pins

pin·ni·ped \'pin-ə-ˌped\ *n* [deriv. of L *pinna* + *ped-*, *pes* foot — more at FOOT] **:** any of a suborder (Pinnipedia) of aquatic carnivorous mammals including the seals and the walruses — **pinniped** *adj*

pin·nu·la \'pin-yə-lə\ *n, pl* **pin·nu·lae** \-ˌlē, -ˌlī\ [NL, fr. L, dim. of *pinna*] **1 :** PINNULE **2 :** BARB 4 — **pin·nu·lar** \-lər\ *adj*

pin·nu·late \-ˌlāt\ *or* **pin·nu·lat·ed** \-ˌlāt-əd\ *adj* **:** having pinnules

pin·nule \'pin-(ˌ)yü(ə)l\ *n* [NL *pinnula*] **1 a :** one of the secondary branches of a plumose organ **b :** a small detached fish fin **2 :** one of the ultimate divisions of a twice pinnate leaf

pi·noch·le \'pē-ˌnək-əl\ *n* [prob. modif. of G dial. *binokel*, a game resembling bezique, fr. F dial. *binocle*] **:** a card game played with a 48-card pack containing two of each suit of A, K, Q, J, 10, 9; *also* **:** the meld of queen of spades and jack of diamonds scoring 40 points in this game

pi·no·le \pi-'nō-lē\ *n* [AmerSp, fr. Nahuatl *pinolli*] **1 :** a finely ground flour made from parched corn **2 :** any of various flours resembling pinole and ground from seeds of other plants

pi·ñon \'pin-ˌyän\ *n, pl* **piñons** *or* **pi·ño·nes** \pin-'yō-nēz\ [AmerSp *piñón*, fr. Sp, pine nut, fr. *piña* pine cone, fr. L *pinea* — more at PINEAL] **:** any of various low-growing nut pines (as *Pinus parryana*, *P. cembroides*, *P. edulis*, and *P. monophylla*) of western No. America; *also* **:** their edible seed

1pin·point \'pin-ˌpȯint\ *vt* **1 :** to locate or aim with great precision or accuracy **2 a :** to fix, determine, or identify with precision **b :** to cause to stand out conspicuously **:** HIGHLIGHT

2pinpoint *adj* **1 :** extremely fine or precise **2 :** located, fixed, or directed with extreme precision

1pin·prick \-ˌprik\ *n* **1 :** a small puncture made by or as if by a pin **2 :** a petty irritation or annoyance

2pinprick *vt* **:** to administer pinpricks to ~ *vi* **:** to administer pinpricks

pins and needles *n pl* **:** a pricking tingling sensation in a limb recovering from numbness — **on pins and needles :** in a nervous or jumpy state of anticipation

pin·set·ter \'pin-ˌset-ər\ *n* **:** an employee or a mechanical device that spots pins in a bowling alley

pin·spot·ter \-ˌspät-ər\ *n* **:** PINSETTER

pin·stripe \-ˌstrīp\ *n* **:** a fine stripe on a fabric; *also* **:** a suit with such stripes — **pin-striped** \-ˌstrīpt\ *adj*

pint \'pīnt\ *n* [ME *pinte*, fr. MF, fr. ML *pincta*, fr. (assumed) VL, fem. of *pinctus*, pp. of L *pingere* to paint — more at PAINT] **1** — see MEASURE table **2 :** a pint pot or vessel

pin·tail \'pin-ˌtāl\ *n, pl* **pintail** *or* **pintails :** a bird having elongated central tail feathers: as **a :** a river duck (*Dafila acuta*) **b :** any of several grouse

pin-tailed \-ˌtāld\ *adj* **1 :** having a tapered tail with the middle feathers longest **2 :** having the tail feathers spiny

pin·tle \'pint-ᵊl\ *n* [ME *pintel*, lit., penis, fr. OE; akin to MLG *pint* penis, OE *pinn* pin] **:** a usu. upright pivot pin on which another part turns

1pin·to \'pin-(ˌ)tō\ *n, pl* **pintos** *also* **pintoes** [AmerSp, fr. *pinto* spotted, fr. obs. Sp, fr. (assumed) VL *pinctus*] *chiefly West* **:** a spotted or calico horse or pony

2pinto *adj* **:** MOTTLED, PIED

Pintsch gas \'pinch-\ *n* [Richard *Pintsch* †1919 G inventor] **:** a gas obtained by cracking gas oil and formerly used in lighting railroad cars and buoys

pint-size \'pīnt-ˌsīz\ *or* **pint-sized** \-ˌsīzd\ *adj* **:** SMALL, DIMINUTIVE

1pin·up \'pin-ˌəp\ *n* **:** something fastened to a wall: as **a :** a photograph of a pinup girl **b :** a lamp or other accessory attached to a wall

2pinup *adj* **1 :** of or relating to pinup girls **2 :** designed for hanging on a wall

pinup girl *n* **1 :** a girl whose glamorous qualities make her a suitable subject of a photograph pinned up on an admirer's wall **2 :** a photograph of a pinup girl

pin·wale \'pin-ˌwāl\ *adj, of a fabric* **:** made with narrow wales

pin·weed \-ˌwēd\ *n* **1 :** any of a genus (*Lechea*) of herbs of the rockrose family with slender stems and leaves **2 :** ALFILARIA

pin·wheel \-ˌhwēl, -ˌwēl\ *n* **1 :** a toy consisting of lightweight vanes that revolve at the end of a stick **2 :** a fireworks device in the form of a revolving wheel of colored fire

pin·work \-ˌwərk\ *n* **:** fine stitches raised from the surface of a design in needlepoint lace to add lightness to the effect

pin·worm \-ˌwərm\ *n* **1 :** any of numerous small nematode worms (family Oxyuridae) that infest the intestines and esp. the cecum of various vertebrates; *esp* **:** a worm (*Enterobius vermicularis*) parasitic in man **2 :** any of several rather slender insect larvae that burrow in plant tissue

pin wrench *n* **:** a wrench having a projecting pin to enter a hole (as in a nut or cylinder) to make a hold

pinx·ter flower \'piŋ(k)-stər-\ *n* [D *pinkster* Whitsuntide] **:** a deciduous pink-flowered azalea (*Rhododendron nudiflorum*) native to rich moist woodlands of eastern No. America

pi·o·let \ˌpē-ə-'lā\ *n* [F] **:** a two-headed ice ax used in mountaineering

pi·on \'pī-ˌän\ *n* [by contr.] **:** PI-MESON

1pi·o·neer \ˌpī-ə-'ni(ə)r\ *n* [MF *pionier*, fr. OF *peonier* foot soldier fr. *peon* foot soldier, fr. ML *pedon-*, *pedo* — more at PAWN] **1 :** a member of a military unit usu. of construction engineers **2 a :** a person or group that originates or helps open up a new line of thought or activity or a new method or technical development **b :** one of the first to settle in a territory **3 :** a plant or animal capable of establishing itself in a bare or barren area and initiating an ecological cycle

2pioneer *adj* **1 :** EARLIEST, ORIGINAL **2 :** relating to or being a pioneer; *esp* **:** of, relating to, or characteristic of early settlers or their time

3pioneer *vi* **:** to act as a pioneer ~ *vt* **1 :** to open or prepare for others to follow; *esp* **:** SETTLE **2 :** to originate or take part in the development of

Pioneer Day *n* **:** July 24 observed as a legal holiday in Utah in commemoration of the arrival of Brigham Young at the present site of Salt Lake City in 1847

pi·os·i·ty \pī-'äs-ət-ē\ *n* **:** an exaggerated or superficial piousness

pi·ous \'pī-əs\ *adj* [L *pius*; akin to L *piare* to appease] **1 a :** marked by or showing reverence for deity and devotion to divine worship **:** DEVOUT **b :** marked by conspicuous religiosity **2 :** sacred or devotional as distinct from the profane or secular **:** RELIGIOUS ⟨a ~ opinion⟩ **3 :** showing loyal reverence for a person or thing **:** DUTIFUL **4 a :** marked by sham or hypocrisy **b :** marked by self-conscious virtue **:** VIRTUOUS **5 :** deserving commendation **:** WORTHY ⟨a ~ effort⟩ **syn** see DEVOUT — **pi·ous·ly** *adv* — **pi·ous·ness** *n*

1pip \'pip\ *n* [ME *pippe*, fr. MD; akin to OHG *pfiffiz* pip; both fr. a prehistoric WGmc word borrowed fr. (assumed) VL *pipita*, alter. of L *pituita* phlegm, pip; akin to L *opimus* fat — more at FAT] **1 a :** a disorder of a bird marked by formation of a scale or crust on the tongue **b :** the scale or crust of this disorder **2 :** any of various human ailments; *esp* **:** a slight nonspecific disorder

2pip *n* [origin unknown] **1 a :** one of the dots used on dice and dominoes to indicate numerical value **b :** SPOT 2c **2 a :** SPOT, SPECK **b :** an inverted V or a spot of light on a radarscope indicating the return of radar waves reflected from an object **3 :** an individual rootstock of the lily of the valley **4 :** a star worn to indicate rank by a second lieutenant, lieutenant, or captain in the British army

3pip *n* [short for *pippin*] **1 :** a small fruit seed; *esp* **:** one of a several-seeded fleshy fruit **2** *slang* **:** something extraordinary of its kind **:** PIPPIN

4pip *vb* **pipped; pip·ping** [imit.] *vi* **1 :** 1PEEP 1 **2 :** to break through the shell of the egg ⟨the chick *pipped*⟩ ~ *vt* **:** to break open (the shell of an egg) in hatching

5pip *n* [imit.] **:** a short high-pitched tone ⟨broadcast six ~*s* as a time signal⟩

pip·age *or* **pipe·age** \'pī-pij\ *n* **1 a :** transportation by means of pipes **b :** the charge for such transportation **2 :** PIPING, PIPES

pi·pal \'pē-(ˌ)pəl\ *n* [Hindi *pīpal*, fr. Skt *pippala*] **:** a large long-lived fig (*Ficus religiosa*) of India yielding a product like lac and lacking prop roots

1pipe \'pīp\ *n* [ME, fr. OE *pīpa*; akin to OHG *pfīfa* pipe; both fr. a prehistoric WGmc word borrowed fr. (assumed) VL *pipa* pipe, fr. L *pipare* to peep, of imit. origin] **1 a** (1) **:** a tubular wind instrument *specif* **:** a small fipple flute held in and played by the left hand (2) **:** one of the tubes of a pipe organ (3) **:** BAGPIPE — usu. used in pl. **b** (1) **:** VOICE, VOCAL CORD — usu. used in pl. (2) **:** PIPING 1 **2 :** a long tube or hollow body for conducting a liquid, gas, or finely divided solid or for structural purposes **3 a :** a tubular or cylindrical object, part, or passage **b :** a roughly cylindrical and vertical geological formation **c :** the eruptive channel opening into the crater of a volcano **4 a :** a large cask of varying capacity used esp. for wine and oil **b :** any of various units of liquid capacity based on the size of a pipe; *esp* **:** a unit equal to 2 hogsheads **5 :** a device for smoking usu. consisting of a tube having a bowl at one

end and a mouthpiece at the other 6 : something easy : SNAP ⟨considered the course a ~⟩

2**pipe** *vi* 1 a : to play on a pipe b : to convey orders by signals on a boatswain's pipe 2 a : to speak in a high or shrill voice b : to emit a shrill sound ~ *vt* 1 a : to play (a tune) on a pipe b : to utter in the shrill tone of a pipe 2 a : to cause to go or be with pipe music b (1) : to call or direct by the boatswain's pipe (2) : to receive aboard or attend the departure of by a boatswain's pipe 3 : to trim with piping 4 : to furnish or equip with pipes 5 : to convey by or as if by pipes; *specif* : to transmit by wire or coaxial cable 6 *slang* : NOTICE

pipe clay *n* : highly plastic grayish white clay used in making tobacco pipes, in calico printing, for marking and scouring, and for whitening leather

pipe–clay \'pīp-,klā\ *vt* : to whiten or clean with pipe clay

pipe cleaner *n* : something used to clean the inside of a pipe; *specif* : a piece of flexible wire in which tufted fabric is twisted and which is used to clean the stem of a tobacco pipe

pipe cutter *n* : a tool or machine for cutting pipe; *specif* : a hand tool comprising a grasping device and three sharp-edged wheels forced inward by screw pressure that cut into the pipe as the tool is rotated

pipe down *vi* [2*pipe*] : to become quiet : stop talking

pipe dream *n* [fr. the fantasies brought about by the smoking of opium] : an illusory or fantastic plan, hope, or story

pipe·fish \'pīp-,fish\ *n* : any of various long slender fishes that are related to the sea horses and have an elongate snout and an angular body covered with bony plates

pipe fitter *n* : one who installs and repairs piping

pipe fitting *n* 1 : a piece (as a coupling or elbow) used to connect pipe or as accessory to a pipe 2 : the work of a pipe fitter

pipe·ful \-,fu̇l\ *n* : a quantity of tobacco smoked in a pipe at one time

pipe·less \'pī-pləs\ *adj* : having no pipe

pipe·like \'pī-,plīk\ *adj* : resembling a pipe or piping

pipe·line \'pī-,plīn\ *n* 1 : a line of pipe with pumps, valves, and control devices for conveying liquids, gases, or finely divided solids 2 : a direct channel for information 3 : the processes through which supplies pass from source to user

pipe major *n* : the principal player in a band of bagpipes

pipe of peace : CALUMET

pip·er \'pī-pər\ *n* 1 : one that plays on a pipe 2 a : a maker, layer, or repairer of pipes b : a person or device that applies piping

pi·per·a·zine \pī-'per-ə-,zēn\ *n* [ISV, blend of *piperidine* and *az-*] : a crystalline heterocyclic base $C_4H_{10}N_2$ or $C_4H_{10}N_2.6H_2O$ used esp. as an anthelmintic

pi·per·i·dine \pī-'per-ə-,dēn\ *n* [ISV, blend of *piperine* and *-ide*] : a liquid heterocyclic base $C_5H_{10}NH$ having a peppery ammoniacal odor that is obtained usu. by hydrolysis of piperine

pip·er·ine \'pip-ə-,rēn\ *n* [ISV, fr. L *piper* pepper] : a white crystalline alkaloid $C_{17}H_{19}NO_3$ that is the chief active constituent of pepper

pi·per·o·nal \pī-'per-ə-,nal\ *n* [ISV *piperine* + *-one* + *-al*] : a crystalline aldehyde $C_8H_6O_3$ with an odor of heliotrope that is used in perfumery

pipe·stone \'pīp-,stōn\ *n* : a pink or mottled pink-and-white argillaceous stone carved by the Indians into tobacco pipes

pipe stop *n* : an organ stop composed of flue pipes

pi·pette *also* **pi·pet** \pī-'pet\ *n* [F *pipette*, dim. of *pipe* pipe, cask, fr. (assumed) VL *pipa, pippa* pipe] : a small piece of apparatus into which fluids are taken and which principally consists of a narrow glass tube into which the liquid is drawn by suction and retained by closing the upper end

pipe up *vi* : to begin to play or to sing or speak

pipe wrench *n* : a wrench for gripping and turning a pipe or other cylindrical surfaces usu. by use of two serrated jaws so designed as to grip the pipe when turning in one direction only

1**pip·ing** \'pī-piŋ\ *n* 1 a : the music of a pipe b : a sound, note, or call like that of a pipe 2 : a quantity or system of pipes 3 : trimming stitched in seams or along edges of clothing, slipcovers, curtains

2**piping** *adj* : marked by peaceful pipe music rather than martial drum and fife music : TRANQUIL

piping hot *adj* : so hot as to sizzle or hiss : very hot

pip·it \'pip-ət\ *n* [imit.] : any of various small singing birds (family Motacillidae and esp. genus *Anthus*) resembling the lark

pip·kin \'pip-kən\ *n* [perh. fr. *pipe*] : a small earthenware or metal pot usu. with a horizontal handle

pip·pin \'pip-ən\ *n* [ME *pepin*, fr. OF] 1 : any of numerous apples of superior dessert quality with usu. yellow or greenish yellow skins strongly flushed with red 2 : a highly admired or very admirable person or thing

pip–pip \'pip-'pip\ *interj* [origin unknown] *Brit* : GOOD-BYE

pip·sis·se·wa \pip-'sis-ə-,wȯ\ *n* [Cree *pipisisikweu*] : any of a genus (*Chimaphila*, esp. *C. corymbosa*) of evergreen herbs of the wintergreen family with astringent leaves used as a tonic and diuretic

pip–squeak \'pip-,skwēk\ *n* : a small or insignificant person

pi·quan·cy \'pē-kən-sē\ *n* : the quality or state of being piquant

pi·quant \'pē-kənt, -,känt\ *adj* [MF, fr. prp. of *piquer*] 1 : agreeably stimulating to the palate : PUNGENT 2 : engagingly provocative; *also* : having a lively arch charm ⟨~ face⟩ **syn** see PUNGENT — **pi·quant·ly** *adv* — **pi·quant·ness** *n*

1**pique** \'pēk\ *n* : offense taken by one slighted or disdained; *also* : a fit of resentment **syn** see OFFENSE

2**pique** *vt* [F *piquer*, lit., to prick — more at PIKE] 1 : to arouse anger or resentment in : IRRITATE; *specif* : to offend by slighting 2 : to excite or arouse by a provocation, challenge, or rebuff **syn** see PROVOKE

3**pi·qué** *or* **pi·que** \pi-'kā, 'pē-,\ *n* [F *piqué*, fr. pp. of *piquer* to prick, quilt] : a durable ribbed clothing fabric of cotton, rayon, or silk

pi·quet \pi-'kā\ *n* [F] : a two-handed card game played with 32 cards

pi·ra·cy \'pī-rə-sē\ *n* 1 : robbery on the high seas 2 : the unauthorized use of another's production, invention, or conception esp. in infringement of a copyright 3 a : an act of piracy b : an act resembling piracy

pi·ra·gua \pə-'räg-wə\ *n* [Sp] 1 : DUGOUT 1 2 : a 2-masted flat-bottomed boat

Pi·ran·del·li·an \,pir-ən-'del-ē-ən\ *adj* : of, relating to, or characteristic of Pirandello or his writings

pi·ra·nha \pə-'ran-yə, -'rän-\ *n* [Pg, fr. Tupi] : CARIBE

pi·ra·ru·cu \pi-,rär-ə-'kü\ *n* [Pg, fr. Tupi *pirá-rucú*] : a very large food fish (*Arapaima gigas*, order Isospondyli) of the rivers of northern So. America

1**pi·rate** \'pī-rət\ *n* [ME, fr. MF or L; MF, fr. L *pirata*, fr. Gk *peiratēs*, fr. *peiran* to attempt — more at FEAR] : one who commits or practices piracy — **pi·rat·i·cal** \pə-'rat-i-kəl, pī-\ *adj* — **pi·rat·i·cal·ly** \-k(ə-)lē\ *adv*

2**pirate** *vt* 1 : to commit piracy on 2 : to take or appropriate by piracy: as a : to reproduce without authorization esp. in infringement of copyright b : to lure away from another employer by offers of betterment ~ *vi* : to commit or practice piracy

pirn \'pərn, 'pi(ə)rn\ *n* [ME] 1 *chiefly Brit* : QUILL 1a(1) 2 *chiefly Scot* : a device resembling a reel

pi·rogue \'pē-,rōg\ *n* [F, fr. Sp *piragua*, of Cariban origin; akin to Galibi *piraua* pirogue] 1 : DUGOUT 1 2 : a boat like a canoe

piro·plasm \'pir-ə-,plaz-əm\ *or* **piro·plas·ma** \,pir-ə-'plaz-mə\ *n*, *pl* **piroplasms** *or* **piro·plas·ma·ta** \,pir-ə-'plaz-mət-ə\ [NL *Piroplasma*, genus of piroplasms] : any of a family (Babesiidae) of parasitic sporozoans — **piro·plas·mic** \,pir-ə-'plaz-mik\ *adj*

pir·ou·ette \,pir-ə-'wet\ *n* [F, lit., teetotum] : a rapid whirling about of the body; *specif* : a full turn on the toe or ball of one foot in ballet — **pirouette** *vi*

pis al·ler \,pē-(,)za-'lā\ *n*, *pl* **pis al·lers** \-'lā(z)\ [F, lit., to go worst] : a last resource or device : EXPEDIENT

pis·ca·ry \'pis-kə-rē\ *n* 1 [ME *piscarie*, fr. ML *piscaria*, fr. L, neut. pl. of *piscarius* of fish, fr. *piscis*] : FISHERY 4; *esp* : the right of fishing in waters belonging to another 2 [ML *piscaria*, fr. L, fem. of *piscarius*] : FISHERY 2

pis·ca·to·ri·al \,pis-kə-'tōr-ē-əl, -'tȯr-\ *adj* : PISCATORY — **pis·ca·to·ri·al·ly** \-ē-ə-lē\ *adv*

pis·ca·to·ry \'pis-kə-,tōr-ē, -,tȯr-\ *adj* [L *piscatorius*, fr. *piscatus*, pp. of *piscari* to fish, fr. *piscis*] : of, relating to, or dependent on fishermen or fishing

Pi·sces \'pī-(,)sēz, 'pis-,ēz, 'pis-,kās\ *n pl but sing in constr* [ME, fr. L (gen. *Piscium*), fr. pl. of *piscis* fish — more at FISH] 1 : a zodiacal constellation directly south of Andromeda 2 : the 12th sign of the zodiac

pi·sci·cul·ture \'pī-sə-,kəl-chər, 'pis-(k)ə-\ *n* [prob. F, fr. L *piscis* + F *culture*] : fish culture

pi·sci·na \piə-'s(h)ē-nə, -'sī-\ *n* [ML, fr. L, fishpond, fr. *piscis*] : a basin with a drain near the altar of a church for disposing of water from liturgical ablutions

pi·scine \'pī-,sēn, 'pis-,(k)īn\ *adj* [L *piscinus*, fr. *piscis*] : of, relating to, or characteristic of fish

pi·sciv·o·rous \pə-'siv-ə-rəs, pī-\ *adj* [L *piscis* + E *-vorous*] : feeding on fishes

pish *interj* — used to express disdain or contempt

1**pi·si·form** \'pī-sə-,fȯrm\ *adj* [L *pisum* pea + E *-iform* — more at PEA] : resembling a pea in size or shape

2**pisiform** *n* : a bone on the ulnar side of the carpus in most mammals

pis·mire \'pis-,mī(ə)r, 'piz-\ *n* [ME *pissemire*, fr. *pisse* urine + *mire* ant, of Scand. origin; akin to ON *maurr* ant; akin to L *formica* ant, Gk *myrmēx*] : ANT

pis·mo clam \,piz-(,)mō-\ *n*, *often cap P* [*Pismo* Beach, Calif.] : a thick-shelled clam (*Tivela stultorum*) of the southwest coast of No. America used extensively for food

pi·so·lite \'pī-sə-,līt\ *n* [NL *pisolithus*, fr. Gk *pisos* pea + *-lithos* -lith] : a limestone composed of pisiform concretions — **pi·so·lit·ic** \,pī-sə-'lit-ik\ *adj*

pis·soir \pi-'swär\ *n* [F, fr. MF, fr. *pisser* to urinate, fr. (assumed) VL *pissiare*, of imit. origin] : a public urinal usu. located on the street in some European countries

pis·ta·chio \pə-'stash-ē-,ō, -'stash-(,)ō, -'stäsh-\ *n* [It *pistacchio*, fr. L *pistacium* pistachio nut, fr. Gk *pistakion*, fr. *pistakē* pistachio tree, fr. Per *pistah*] : a small tree (*Pistacia vera*) of the sumac family whose drupaceous fruit contains a greenish edible seed; *also* : its seed

pis·til \'pist-ᵊl\ *n* [NL *pistillum*, fr. L, pestle — more at PESTLE] : the ovule-bearing organ of a seed plant consisting of the ovary with its appendages

pis·til·late \'pis-tə-,lāt\ *adj* : having pistils; *specif* : having pistils but no stamens

pis·tol \'pist-ᵊl\ *n* [MF *pistole*, fr. G, fr. MHG dial. *pischulle*, fr. Czech *píšťal*, lit., pipe; akin to Russ *pishchal* harquebus] 1 : a short firearm intended to be aimed and fired with one hand 2 : a handgun whose chamber is integral with the barrel — **pistol** *vt* **pis·toled** *or* **pis·tolled** \'pist-ᵊld\ **pis·tol·ing** *or* **pis·tol·ling** \'pis-tə-liŋ\

pis·tole \pis-'tōl\ *n* [ME] : an old gold 2-escudo piece of Spain or any of several old gold coins of Europe of approximately the same value

pis·tol·eer \,pis-tə-'li(ə)r\ *n* : one who uses a pistol or is armed with a pistol

pistol grip *n* 1 : a grip of a shotgun or rifle shaped like a pistol stock 2 : a handle (as of a saw) shaped like a pistol stock

pis·tol–whip \pist-ᵊl-,hwip, -,wip\ *vt* : to beat with a pistol

pis·ton \'pis-tən\ *n* [F, fr. It *pistone*, fr. *pistare* to pound, fr. ML *pistare*, fr. L *pistus*, pp. of *pinsere* to crush — more at PESTLE] 1 : a sliding piece moved by or moving against fluid pressure that usu. consists of a short cylinder fitting within a cylindrical vessel along which it moves back and forth 2 a : a valve sliding in a cylinder in a brass wind instrument and serving when depressed by a finger knob to lower its pitch b : a button on an organ console to bring in a previously selected registration

piston pin *n* : WRIST PIN

piston ring *n* : a springy split metal ring for sealing the gap between a piston and the cylinder wall

piston rod *n* : a rod by which a piston is moved or by which it communicates motion

1**pit** \'pit\ *n* [ME, fr. OE *pytt*; akin to OHG *pfuzzi* well] 1 a : a hole, shaft, or cavity in the ground b : an area often sunken or depressed below the adjacent floor area: as (1) : an enclosure in which animals are made to fight each other (2) : a space at

the front of a theater for the orchestra (3) : an area in a securities or commodities exchange in which members do trading **2 :** HELL — used with *the* **3 :** a hollow or indentation esp. in the surface of an organism: as **a :** a natural hollow in the surface of the body **b :** one of the indented scars left in the skin by a pustular disease **:** POCKMARK **c :** a minute depression in the secondary wall of a plant cell functioning in the intercellular movement of water and dissolved material

[2]**pit** *vb* **pit·ted; pit·ting** *vt* **1 a :** to place, cast, bury, or store in a pit **b :** to make pits in; *esp* **:** to scar or mark with pits **2 a :** to set (as gamecocks) into or as if into a pit to fight **b :** to set into opposition or rivalry **:** OPPOSE ~ *vi* **:** to become marked with pits; *esp* **:** to preserve for a time an indentation made by pressure

[3]**pit** *n* [D, fr. MD — more at PITH] **:** the stone of a drupaceous fruit

[4]**pit** *vt* **pit·ted; pit·ting :** to remove the pit from

pi·ta \'pēt-ə\ *n* [Sp & Pg] **1 :** any of several fiber-yielding plants: as **a :** CENTURY PLANT **b :** YUCCA **c :** a Central American wild pineapple (*Ananas magdalenae*) **2 a :** the fiber of a pita **b :** any of several other fibers

pit–a–pat \,pit-i-'pat\ *adv* (*or adj*) [imit.] **:** PITTER-PATTER — **pit–a–pat** *n* — **pit–a–pat** *vi*

[1]**pitch** \'pich\ *n* [ME *pich,* fr. OE *pic,* fr. L *pic-, pix;* akin to L *opimus* fat — more at FAT] **1 :** a black or dark viscous substance obtained as a residue in the distillation of tars or other organic materials **2 :** any of various bituminous substances **3 :** an often medicinal resin obtained from various conifers **4 :** any of various artificial mixtures resembling resinous or bituminous pitches

[2]**pitch** *vt* **:** to cover, smear, or treat with or as if with pitch

[3]**pitch** *vb* [ME *pichen*] *vt* **1 :** to erect and fix firmly in place ⟨~ a tent⟩ **2 :** THROW, FLING: as **a :** to deliver (a baseball) to a batter **b :** to toss (as coins) so as to fall at or near a mark ⟨~ pennies⟩ **3 :** to sell or advertise esp. in a high-pressure way **4 a** (1) **:** to cause to be at a particular level or of a particular quality (2) **:** to set in a particular musical key **b :** to cause to be set at a particular angle **5 :** to utter with glib insincerity **6 a :** to use as a starting pitcher **b :** to play as pitcher ~ *vi* **1 a :** to fall precipitately or headlong **b** *of a ship* **:** to have the bow alternately plunge precipitately down and rise abruptly up **c :** BUCK 1 **2 a :** ENCAMP **b :** to choose something usu. in a casual way **3 :** to incline downward **:** SLOPE **4 a :** to pitch something (as a baseball or softball) **b :** to play ball as a pitcher **syn** see THROW

[4]**pitch** *n* **1 :** the action or a manner of pitching **2 a :** degree of slope **:** RAKE **b** (1) **:** distance between one point on a gear tooth and the corresponding point on the next tooth (2) **:** distance from any point on the thread of a screw to the corresponding point on an adjacent thread measured parallel to the axis **c :** the distance advanced by a propeller in one revolution **d :** the number of teeth or of threads per inch **3** *archaic* **:** TOP, ZENITH **4 a :** the relative level, intensity, or extent of some quality or state **b** (1) **:** the property of a musical tone that is determined by the frequency of the sound waves producing it **:** highness or lowness of sound (2) **:** a standard frequency for tuning instruments **c** (1) **:** the difference in the relative vibration frequency of the human voice that contributes to the total meaning of speech (2) **:** a definite relative pitch that is a significant phenomenon in speech **5 :** a steep place **:** DECLIVITY **6 :** an all-fours game in which the first card led is a trump **7 a :** an often high-pressure sales talk **b :** ADVERTISEMENT **8 a :** the delivery of a baseball by a pitcher to a batter **b :** a baseball so thrown — **pitched** \'picht\ *adj*

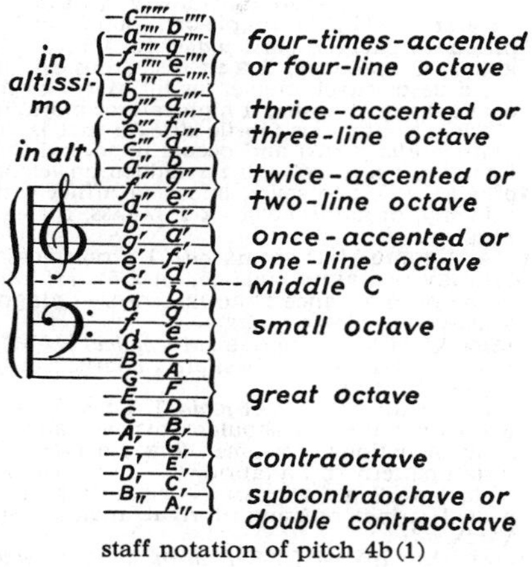
in altissimo
in alt
four-times-accented or four-line octave
thrice-accented or three-line octave
twice-accented or two-line octave
once-accented or one-line octave
middle C
small octave
great octave
contraoctave
subcontraoctave or double contraoctave
staff notation of pitch 4b(1)

pitch–and–toss \,pich-ən-'tȯs, -'täs\ *n* **:** a game in which the player who pitches coins nearest to a mark has first chance at tossing the pitched coins and winning those that fall heads up

pitch–black \'pich-'blak\ *adj* **:** extremely dark or black

pitch·blende \'pich-,blend\ *n* [part trans. of G *pechblende,* fr. *pech* pitch + *blende*] **:** a brown to black mineral that consists of massive uraninite, has a distinctive luster, contains radium, and is the chief ore-mineral source of uranium

pitch–dark \'pich-'därk\ *adj* **:** extremely dark **:** PITCH-BLACK

pitched battle \'pich(t)-\ *n* **:** an intensely fought battle in which the opposing forces are locked in close combat

[1]**pitch·er** \'pich-ər\ *n* [ME *picher,* fr. OF *pichier,* fr. ML *bicarius* goblet, fr. Gk *bikos* earthen jug] **1 :** a container for holding and pouring liquids that usu. has a lip or spout and a handle **2 :** ASCIDIUM; *esp* **:** a modified leaf of a pitcher plant in which the hollowed petiole and base of the blade form an elongated receptacle

[2]**pitcher** *n* **:** one that pitches; *specif* **:** the player that pitches in a game of baseball or softball

pitcher plant *n* **:** a plant (esp. family Sarraceniaceae, the pitcher-plant family) with leaves modified into pitchers in which insects are trapped and digested by the plant through liquids secreted by the leaves

pitch·fork \'pich-,fȯ(ə)rk\ *n* [ME *pikfork,* fr. *pik* pick + *fork*] **:** a usu. long-handled fork with two or three long somewhat curved prongs used esp. in pitching hay — **pitchfork** *vt*

pitch in *vi* **1 :** to begin to work **2 :** to contribute to a common endeavor

pitch·man \'pich-mən\ *n* **:** SALESMAN; *esp* **:** one who vends novelties or similar articles on the streets or from a concession

pitch·out \'pich-,au̇t\ *n* **1 :** a pitch in baseball deliberately out of reach of the batter to enable the catcher to check or put out a base runner **2 :** a lateral pass in football between two backs behind the scrimmage line

pitch pipe *n* **:** a small reed pipe or flue pipe producing one or more tones to establish the pitch in singing or in tuning an instrument

pitch·stone \'pich-,stōn\ *n* **:** a glassy rock with a resinous luster containing more water than obsidian

pitchy \'pich-ē\ *adj* **1 a :** full of pitch **:** TARRY **b :** of, relating to, or having the qualities of pitch **2 :** PITCH-BLACK

pit·e·ous \'pit-ē-əs\ *adj* **:** arousing or deserving pity or compassion **syn** see PITIFUL — **pit·e·ous·ly** *adv* — **pit·e·ous·ness** *n*

pit·fall \'pit-,fȯl\ *n* **1 :** TRAP, SNARE; *specif* **:** a pit flimsily covered or camouflaged and used to capture and hold animals or men **2 :** a hidden or not easily recognized danger or difficulty

[1]**pith** \'pith\ *n* [ME, fr. OE *pitha;* akin to MD & MLG *pit* pith, pit] **1 a :** a usu. continuous central strand of spongy tissue in the stems of most vascular plants that prob. functions chiefly in storage **b :** any of various loose spongy plant tissues that resemble true pith **c :** the soft or spongy interior of a part of the body **2 a :** the essential part **:** CORE **b :** substantial quality (as of meaning) **3 :** IMPORTANCE, SIGNIFICANCE

[2]**pith** *vt* **1 a :** to kill (as cattle) by piercing or severing the spinal cord **b :** to destroy the spinal cord or central nervous system of (as a frog) usu. by passing a wire or needle up and down the vertebral canal **2 :** to remove the pith from (a plant stem)

pit·head \'pit-,hed\ *n* **:** the top of a mining pit or coal shaft; *also* **:** the immediately adjacent ground and buildings

pith·ec·an·thro·poid \,pith-i-'kan(t)-thrə-,pȯid\ *adj* **:** of, relating to, or resembling the pithecanthropi — **pithecanthropoid** *n*

pith·ec·an·thro·pus \-'kan(t)-thrə-pəs, -(,)kan-'thrō-\ *n, pl* **pith·ec·an·thro·pi** \-,pī, -,pē\ [NL, fr. Gk *pithēkos* ape + *anthrōpos* human being; akin to OHG *bibēn* to tremble, L *foedus* ugly] **:** any of the primitive extinct men (genus *Pithecanthropus*) known from skeletal remains from Javanese Pliocene gravels

pith·i·ly \'pith-ə-lē\ *adv* **:** in a pithy manner

pith·i·ness \'pith-ē-nəs\ *n* **:** the quality or state of being pithy

pithy \'pith-ē\ *adj* **1 :** consisting of or abounding in pith **2 :** having substance and point **:** tersely cogent **syn** see CONCISE

piti·able \'pit-ē-ə-bəl\ *adj* **1 :** deserving or exciting pity **:** LAMENTABLE **2 :** pitifully insignificant **:** DESPICABLE **syn** see CONTEMPTIBLE, PITIFUL — **piti·able·ness** \-bəl-nəs\ *n* — **piti·ably** \-blē\ *adv*

piti·er \'pit-ē-ər\ *n* **:** one that pities

piti·ful \'pit-i-fəl\ *adj* **1 a :** deserving or arousing pity **b :** MEAN, MEAGER **2** *archaic* **:** full of pity **:** COMPASSIONATE — **piti·ful·ly** \-f(ə-)lē\ *adv* — **piti·ful·ness** \-fəl-nəs\ *n*

syn PITIFUL, PITEOUS, PITIABLE mean calling for pity. PITIFUL implies making a successful appeal to compassion or commiseration through being felt as pathetic; PITEOUS implies pleading for compassion or mercy whether successfully or not; PITIABLE suggests usu. arousing some contempt along with pity

piti·less \'pit-i-ləs, 'pit-ᵊl-əs\ *adj* **:** devoid of pity **.** MERCILESS — **piti·less·ly** *adv* — **piti·less·ness** *n*

pit·man \'pit-mən\ *n* **1** *pl* **pitmen :** one who works in or near a pit (as a worker in a coal mine) **2** *pl* **pitmans :** CONNECTING ROD

pi·ton \'pē-,tän\ *n* [F] **:** a spike, wedge, or peg driven into a rock or ice surface as a support often with an eye through which a rope may pass

Pi·tot–stat·ic tube \,pē-,tō-,stat-ik-\ *n* **:** a device that consists of a Pitot tube and a static tube and that measures pressures in such a way that the relative speed of a fluid can be determined

Pi·tot tube \,pē-,tō-\ *n* [F (*tube de*) *Pitot,* fr. Henri *Pitot* †1771 F physicist] **1 :** a device that consists of a tube having a short right-angled bend which is placed vertically in a moving body of fluid with the mouth of the bent part directed upstream and is used with a manometer to measure the velocity of fluid flow **2 :** PITOT-STATIC TUBE

pit saw *n* **:** a handsaw worked by two men one of whom stands on or above the log being sawed and the other below it usu. in a pit

pit·tance \'pit-ᵊn(t)s\ *n* [ME *pitance,* fr. OF, piety, pity, fr. ML *pietantia,* fr. *pietant-, pietans,* prp. of *pietari* to be charitable, fr. L *pietas*] **:** a small portion, amount, or allowance

pit·ted \'pit-əd\ *adj* **:** marked with pits

pit·ter–pat·ter \'pit-ər-,pat-ər, 'pit-ē-,\ *n* [imit.] **:** a rapid succession of light sounds or beats **:** PATTER — **pitter–patter** \,pit-ər-', ,pit-ē-'\ *adv* (*or adj*) — **pitter–patter** *like adv*\ *vi*

pit·ting *n* **1 :** the action or process of forming pits **2 :** an arrangement of pits **3 :** the bringing of gamecocks together to fight

pi·tu·itary \pə-'t(y)ü-ə-,ter-ē\ *adj* [L *pituita* phlegm; fr. the former belief that the pituitary body secreted phlegm — more at PIP] **1 :** of or relating to the pituitary body **2 :** of, relating to, or being a physique with a symptom complex characteristic of secretory disturbances of the pituitary body

pituitary body *n* **:** a small oval endocrine organ attached to the infundibulum of the brain that consists of an epithelial anterior lobe joined by an intermediate part to a posterior lobe of nervous origin and produces various internal secretions directly or indirectly impinging on most basic body functions

Pi·tu·itrin \pə-'t(y)ü-ə-trən\ *trademark* — used for an aqueous extract of the fresh pituitary body of cattle

pit viper *n* **:** any of various mostly New World specialized venomous snakes (family Crotalidae) with a sensory pit on each side of the head and hollow perforated fangs

[1]**pity** \'pit-ē\ *n* [ME *pite,* fr. OF *pité,* fr. L *pietat-, pietas* piety, pity, fr. *pius* pious] **1 a :** sympathetic sorrow for one suffering, distressed, or unhappy **:** COMPASSION **b :** capacity to feel pity **2 :** something to be regretted

syn COMPASSION, COMMISERATION, RUTH, CONDOLENCE, SYMPATHY: PITY implies tender or sometimes slightly contemptuous sorrow for one in misery or distress; COMPASSION implies pity coupled with an urgent desire to aid or to spare; COMMISERATION suggests pity expressed outwardly in exclamations, tears, words of comfort; RUTH implies pity coming from a change of heart or a relenting; CONDOLENCE applies chiefly to formal expression of grief to one

who has suffered loss; SYMPATHY implies a power to enter into another's emotional experiences of any sort

2**pity** *vt* **:** to feel pity for ~ *vi* **:** to feel pity

pity·ing *adj* **:** expressing or feeling pity — **pity·ing·ly** \-iŋ-lē\ *adv*

pit·y·ri·a·sis \ˌpit-i-ˈrī-ə-səs\ *n* [NL, fr. Gk, fr. *pityron* scurf] **:** a condition of man or domestic animals marked by dry scaling or scurfy patches of skin

piu \(ˌ)pyü, pē-ˈü\ *adv* [It *più*, fr. L *plus*] **:** MORE — used to qualify an adverb or adjective used as a direction in music

Pi·ute *var of* PAIUTE

1**piv·ot** \ˈpiv-ət\ *n* [F] **1 :** a shaft or pin on which something turns **2 :** a person, thing, or factor having a major or central role, function, or effect **3 :** the action of pivoting

2**pivot** *vi* **:** to turn on or as if on a pivot ~ *vt* **1 :** to provide with, mount on, or attach by a pivot **2 :** to cause to pivot

3**pivot** *adj* **1 :** turning on or as if on a pivot **2 :** PIVOTAL

piv·ot·al \ˈpiv-ət-ᵊl\ *adj* **1 :** of, relating to, or constituting a pivot **2 :** vitally important **:** CRUCIAL — **piv·ot·al·ly** \-ᵊl-ē\ *adv*

pivot tooth *n* **:** an artificial crown attached to the root of a tooth by a pivot — called also *pivot crown*

1**pix·ie** *or* **pixy** \ˈpik-sē\ *n* [origin unknown] **:** FAIRY; *specif* **:** a cheerful mischievous sprite — **pix·ie·ish** \-sē-ish\ *adj*

2**pixie** *or* **pixy** *adj* **:** playfully mischievous **:** given to or marked by pranks — **pixi·ness** \-sē-nəs\ *n*

pix·i·lat·ed \ˈpik-sə-ˌlāt-əd\ *adj* [irreg. fr. *pixie*] **1 :** somewhat unbalanced mentally; *also* **:** BEMUSED **2 :** WHIMSICAL — **pix·i·la·tion** \ˌpik-sə-ˈlā-shən\ *n*

piz·za \ˈpēt-sə\ *n* [It, fr. (assumed) VL *picea*, fr. L, fem. of *piceus* of pitch, fr. *pic-*, *pix* pitch — more at PITCH] **:** an open pie made typically of thinly rolled bread dough spread with a spiced mixture (as of tomatoes, cheese, ground meat) and baked

piz·zazz *or* **pi·zazz** \pə-ˈzaz\ *n* [origin unknown] **:** the quality of being exciting or attractive: as **a :** GLAMOUR **b :** VITALITY

piz·ze·ria \ˌpēt-sə-ˈrē-ə\ *n* [It, fr. *pizza*] **:** an establishment where pizzas are made or sold

piz·zi·ca·to \ˌpit-si-ˈkät-(ˌ)ō\ *adv* (*or adj*) [It] **:** by means of plucking instead of bowing — used as a direction in music

piz·zle \ˈpiz-əl\ *n* [prob. fr. Flem *pezel*; akin to LG *pesel* pizzle] **1 :** the penis of an animal (as a bull) **2 :** a whip made of a bull's pizzle

pj's \(ˈ)pē-ˈjāz\ *n pl* [*pa*jamas] **:** PAJAMAS

pla·ca·bil·i·ty \ˌplak-ə-ˈbil-ət-ē, ˌplā-kə-\ *n* **:** the quality or state of being placable

pla·ca·ble \ˈplak-ə-bəl, ˈplā-kə-\ *adj* **:** easily placated **:** TOLERANT, TRACTABLE — **pla·ca·bly** \-blē\ *adv*

1**plac·ard** \ˈplak-ˌärd, -ərd\ *n* [ME *placquart*, a formal document, fr. MF, fr. *plaquier* to plate — more at PLAQUE] **1 :** a notice posted in a public place **:** POSTER **2 :** a small card or metal plaque

2**placard** *vt* **1 a :** to cover with or as if with posters **b :** to post in a public place **2 :** to announce by or as if by posting

pla·cate \ˈplā-ˌkāt, ˈplak-ˌāt\ *vt* [L *placatus*, pp. of *placare* — more at PLEASE] **:** to soothe or mollify esp. by concessions **:** APPEASE **syn** see PACIFY — **pla·ca·tion** \plā-ˈkā-shən, pla-\ *n* — **pla·ca·tive** \ˈplā-ˌkāt-iv, -kət-; ˈplak-ˌāt-, -ət-\ *adj* — **pla·ca·to·ry** \ˈplā-kə-ˌtōr-ē, ˈplak-ə-, -ˌtȯr-\ *adj*

pla·cat·er \ˈplā-ˌkāt-ər, ˈplak-ˌāt-\ *n* **:** one that placates; *esp* **:** MEDIATOR

1**place** \ˈplās\ *n* [ME, fr. MF, open space, fr. L *platea* broad street, fr. Gk *plateia* (*hodos*), fr. fem. of *platys* broad, flat; akin to Skt *pṛthu* broad, L *planta* sole of the foot] **1 a :** a way for admission or transit **b :** physical environment **:** SPACE **c :** physical surroundings **:** ATMOSPHERE **2 a :** an indefinite region or expanse **:** AREA **b :** a building or locality used for a special purpose **c** *archaic* **:** the three-dimensional compass of a material object **3 a :** a particular region or center of population **b :** HOUSE, HOMESTEAD **4 :** a particular part of a surface or body **:** SPOT **5 a :** relative position in a scale or sequence **:** DEGREE **b :** a leading position at the conclusion of a competition **6 a :** a proper or designated niche **b :** an appropriate moment or point **7 a :** an available seat or accommodation **b :** an empty or vacated position **8 :** the position of a figure in relation to others of a row or series and esp. of one occurring after a decimal point **9 a :** remunerative employment **:** JOB; *esp* **:** public office **b :** prestige accorded to one of high rank **:** STATUS **10 :** a public square **:** PLAZA **syn** see POSITION — **place·less** \ˈplā-sləs\ *adj*

2**place** *vt* **1 :** to distribute in an orderly manner **:** ARRANGE **2 a :** to put in a particular place **:** SET **b :** to present for consideration ⟨a question *placed* before the group⟩ **c :** to put in a particular state **d :** to direct to a desired spot **e :** to cause (the voice) to produce free and well resonated singing or speaking tones **3 :** to appoint to a position **4 :** to find employment or a home for **5 a :** to assign to a position in a series or category **:** RANK **b :** ESTIMATE **c :** to identify by connecting with an associated context **6 a :** to give (an order) to a supplier **b :** to give an order for ⟨~ a bet⟩ ~ *vi* **:** to earn a top spot in a competition; *specif* **:** to come in second in a horse race — **place·able** \ˈplā-sə-bəl\ *adj*

pla·ce·bo *n* **1** \plä-ˈchā-(ˌ)bō\ [ME, fr. L, I shall please, fr. *placēre* to please — more at PLEASE] **:** the vespers for the dead in the Roman Catholic Church **2** \plə-ˈsē-\ [L, I shall please] **a :** an inert or innocuous medication given esp. to satisfy the patient **b :** something tending to soothe or gratify

place hitter *n* **:** a baseball player who is able to hit a pitched ball to a chosen part of the playing field

place–kick \ˈplā-ˌskik\ *n* **:** the kicking of a football placed or held in a stationary position on the ground — **place–kick** *vb*

place·less \ˈplā-sləs\ *adj* **:** lacking a fixed location — **place·less·ly** *adv*

place·man \ˈplā-smən\ *n* **:** a political appointee to a public office esp. in 18th century Britain

place·ment \ˈplā-smənt\ *n* **:** an act or instance of placing: as **a** (1) **:** the position of a ball for a place-kick (2) **:** PLACE-KICK **b :** the assignment of a person to a suitable place (as a job)

place–name \ˈplā-ˌsnām\ *n* **:** the name of a geographical locality

pla·cen·ta \plə-ˈsent-ə\ *n* [NL, fr. L, flat cake, fr. Gk *plakount-*, *plakous*, fr. *plak-*, *plax* flat surface — more at PLEASE] **1 a :** the vascular organ in mammals except monotremes and marsupials that unites the fetus to the maternal uterus and mediates its metabolic exchanges through a more or less intimate association of uterine mucosal with chorionic and usu. allantoic tissues **b :** an analogous organ in another animal **2 :** a sporangium-bearing surface; *esp* **:** the part of the carpel bearing ovules — **pla·cen·tal** \-ˈsent-ᵊl\ *adj or n*

pla·cen·ta·tion \ˌplas-ᵊn-ˈtā-shən, plə-ˌsen-\ *n* **1 :** the development or morphological type of a placenta **2 :** the arrangement of placentas and ovules in a plant ovary

plac·er \ˈplas-ər\ *n* [Sp, fr. Catal, submarine plain, fr. *plaza* place, fr. L *platea* broad street — more at PLACE] **:** an alluvial or glacial deposit containing particles of gold or other valuable mineral — **placer miner** *n* — **placer mining** *n*

place setting *n* **:** a table service for one person

plac·id \ˈplas-əd\ *adj* [L *placidus*, fr. *placēre*] **1 :** UNDISTURBED, PEACEFUL **2 :** COMPLACENT **syn** see CALM — **pla·cid·i·ty** \pla-ˈsid-ət-ē, plə-\ *n* — **plac·id·ly** \ˈplas-əd-lē\ *adv* — **plac·id·ness** *n*

plack·et \ˈplak-ət\ *n* [origin unknown] **1 a :** a slit in a garment **b** *archaic* **:** a pocket esp. in a woman's skirt **2** *archaic* **a :** PETTICOAT **b :** WOMAN

plac·oid \ˈplak-ˌȯid\ *adj* [Gk *plak-*, *plax*] **:** of, relating to, or being a scale of dermal origin with an enamel-tipped spine characteristic of the elasmobranchs

pla·fond \plȧ-ˈfōⁿ\ *n* [F, fr. MF, fr. *plat* flat + *fond* bottom, fr. L *fundus* — more at PLATE, BOTTOM] **:** a usu. elaborate ceiling formed by the underside of a floor

pla·gal \ˈplā-gəl\ *adj* [ML *plagalis*, deriv. of Gk *plagios* oblique, sideways, fr. *plagos* side; akin to L *plaga* net, region, Gk *pelagos* sea — more at FLAKE] **1 :** having the keynote on the 4th scale step ⟨~ church modes⟩ **2 :** progressing from the subdominant chord to the tonic ⟨~ cadence⟩

pla·gia·rism \ˈplā-jə-ˌriz-əm *also* -jē-ə-\ *n* **1 :** an act or instance of plagiarizing **2 :** something plagiarized — **pla·gia·rist** \-rəst\ *n* — **pla·gia·ris·tic** \ˌplā-jə-ˈris-tik *also* -jē-ə-\ *adj*

pla·gia·rize \ˈplā-jə-ˌrīz *also* -jē-ə-\ *vt* **:** to steal and pass off as one's own (the ideas or words of another) ~ *vi* **:** to present as one's own an idea or product derived from an existing source — **pla·gia·riz·er** *n*

pla·gia·ry \ˈplā-jē-ˌer-ē, -jə-rē\ *n* [L *plagiarius*, lit., plunderer, fr. *plagium* hunting net, fr. *plaga*] **1** *archaic* **:** PLAGIARIST **2 :** PLAGIARISM

pla·gio·clase \ˈplā-j(ē-)ə-ˌklās, ˈplaj-(ē-)ə-, -ˌklāz\ *n* [Gk *plagios* + *klasis* breaking, fr. *klan* to break — more at HALT] **:** a triclinic feldspar; *esp* **:** one having calcium or sodium in its composition

pla·gio·trop·ic \ˌplā-j(ē-)ə-ˈträp-ik, ˌplaj-(ē-)ə-\ *adj* [Gk *plagios* + ISV *-tropic*] **:** having the longer axis inclined away from the vertical — **pla·gio·trop·i·cal·ly** \-i-k(ə-)lē\ *adv* — **pla·gi·ot·ro·pism** \ˌplā-jē-ˈä-trə-ˌpiz-əm, ˌplaj-ē-\ *n*

1**plague** \ˈplāg\ *n* [ME *plage*, fr. MF, fr. LL *plaga*, fr. L, blow; akin to Gk *plēssein*] **1 a :** a disastrous evil or affliction **:** CALAMITY **b :** a destructively numerous influx ⟨~ of locusts⟩ **2 a :** an epidemic disease causing a high rate of mortality **:** PESTILENCE **b :** a virulent contagious febrile disease that is caused by a bacterium (*Pasteurella pestis*) and occurs in several forms **3 a :** a cause of irritation **:** NUISANCE **b :** a sudden unwelcome outbreak

2**plague** *vt* **1 :** to smite, infest, or afflict with or as if with disease, calamity, or natural evil **2 :** HARASS, TORMENT **syn** see WORRY — **plagu·er** *n*

plague·some \ˈplāg-səm\ *adj* **1 :** TROUBLESOME **2 :** PESTILENTIAL

plagu·ey *or* **plaguy** \ˈplā-gē, ˈpleg-ē\ *adj, chiefly dial* **:** causing irritation or annoyance **:** TROUBLESOME — **plagu·ey** *adv* — **plagu·i·ly** \ˈplā-gə-lē, ˈpleg-ə-\ *adv*

plaice \ˈplās\ *n, pl* **plaice** [ME *plaice*, fr. OF *plaïs*, fr. LL *platensis*] **:** any of various flatfishes; *esp* **:** a large European flounder (*Pleuronectes platessa*)

plaid \ˈplad\ *n* [ScGael *plaide*] **1 :** a rectangular length of tartan worn over the left shoulder by men and women as part of the Scottish national costume **2 a :** a twilled woolen fabric with a tartan pattern **b :** a fabric with a pattern of tartan or an imitation of tartan **3 a :** TARTAN 1 **b :** a pattern of unevenly spaced repeated stripes crossing at right angles — **plaid** *adj* — **plaid·ed** \-əd\ *adj*

1**plain** \ˈplān\ *vi* [ME *plainen*, fr. MF *plaindre*, fr. L *plangere*] *archaic* **:** COMPLAIN

2**plain** *n* [ME, fr. OF, fr. L *planum*, fr. neut. of *planus* flat, plain — more at FLOOR] **1 a :** an extensive area of level or rolling treeless country **b :** a broad unbroken expanse **2 :** something free from artifice, ornament, or extraneous matter

3**plain** *adj* **1** *archaic* **:** EVEN, LEVEL **2 :** lacking ornament **:** UNDECORATED **3 :** free of extraneous matter **:** PURE **4 :** free of impediments to view **:** UNOBSTRUCTED **5 a** (1) **:** evident to the mind or senses **:** OBVIOUS (2) **:** CLEAR **b :** marked by candor **:** BLUNT **6 a :** COMMON, ORDINARY **b :** characterized by lack of vanity or affectation **7 :** SIMPLE, UNCOMPLICATED **8 :** lacking beauty or ugliness **:** HOMELY **syn** see EVIDENT, FRANK — **plain·ly** *adv* — **plain·ness** \ˈplān-nəs\ *n*

4**plain** *adv* **:** in a plain manner

plain·chant \ˈplān-ˌchant\ *n* [F *plain-chant*, lit., plain song] **:** PLAINSONG

plain·clothes·man \ˈplān-ˈklō(th)z-mən, -ˌman\ *n* **:** DETECTIVE

plain–laid \ˈplān-ˈlād\ *adj, of a rope* **:** consisting of strands twisted opposite to the twist in the strands

Plain People *n* **:** members of any of various religious groups (as Mennonites) who wear plain clothes, adhere to old customs, and lead a simple life

Plains \ˈplānz\ *adj* **:** of or relating to No. American Indians of the Great Plains or to their culture

plain sail *n* **:** the ordinary working canvas of a sailing ship

plain sailing *n* **:** easy progress over an unobstructed course

plains·man \ˈplānz-mən\ *n* [Great *Plains* + *man*] **:** an inhabitant of the plains

plain·song \ˈplān-ˌsȯŋ\ *n* **1 :** GREGORIAN CHANT **2 :** liturgical chant of any of various Christian rites

plain·spo·ken \-ˈspō-kən\ *adj* **:** CANDID, FRANK — **plain·spo·ken·ness** \-kən-nəs\ *n*

plaint \ˈplānt\ *n* [ME, fr. MF, fr. L *planctus*, fr. *planctus*, pp. of *plangere* to strike, beat one's breast, lament; akin to OHG *fluokhōn* to curse, Gk *plēssein* to strike] **1 :** LAMENTATION, WAIL **2 :** PROTEST, COMPLAINT

plaint·ful \-fəl\ *adj* **:** MOURNFUL

plain·tiff \ˈplānt-əf\ *n* [ME *plaintif*, fr. MF, fr. *plaintif*, adj.] **1 :** one who commences a personal action or lawsuit to obtain a remedy for an injury to his rights **2 :** the complaining party in any litigation — compare DEFENDANT

plain·tive \'plānt-iv\ *adj* [ME *plaintif*, fr. MF, fr. *plaint*] **:** expressive of suffering or woe **:** MELANCHOLY — **plain·tive·ly** *adv* — **plain·tive·ness** *n*

plain weave *n* **:** a weave in which the threads interlace alternately

plais·ter \'plā-stər\ *var of* PLASTER.

1plait \'plāt, 'plat\ *n* [ME *pleit*, fr. MF, fr. (assumed) VL *plictus*, fr. *plictus*, pp. of L *plicare* to fold — more at PLY] **1 :** PLEAT **2 :** a braid of hair, straw, or other material; *specif* **:** PIGTAIL

2plait *vt* **1 :** PLEAT 1 **2 a :** to interweave the strands or locks of **:** BRAID **b :** to make by plaiting — **plait·er** *n*

plait·ing *n* **:** the interlacing of strands **:** BRAIDING

1plan \'plan\ *n* [F, plane, foundation, ground plan; partly fr. L *planum* level ground, fr. neut. of *planus* level; partly fr. F *planter* to plant, fix in place, fr. LL *plantare* — more at FLOOR, PLANT] **1 :** a drawing or diagram drawn on a plane: as **a :** a top or horizontal view of an object **b :** a large-scale map of a small area **2 a :** a method of carrying out a design **:** DEVICE **b :** a method of doing something **:** PROCEDURE **c :** a detailed program of action **d :** GOAL, AIM **3 :** an orderly arrangement of parts of an overall design or objective

syn PLAN, DESIGN, PLOT, SCHEME, PROJECT mean a method devised for making or doing something or achieving an end. PLAN always implies mental formulation and sometimes graphic representation; DESIGN often suggests a particular pattern and some degree of achieved order or harmony; PLOT implies a laying out in clearly distinguished sections with attention to their relations and proportions; SCHEME stresses calculation of the end in view and may apply to a plan motivated by craftiness and self-seeking; PROJECT often stresses imaginative scope and vision

2plan *vb* **planned; plan·ning** *vt* **1 :** to arrange the parts of **:** DESIGN **2 :** to devise or project the realization or achievement of **3 :** to have in mind **:** INTEND ~ *vi* **:** to make plans — **plan·ner** *n*

1plan- *or* **plano-** *comb form* [prob. fr. NL, fr. Gk, wandering, fr. *planos;* akin to Gk *planasthai* to wander — more at PLANET] **:** moving about **:** motile ⟨*plano*blast⟩

2plan- *or* **plano-** *comb form* [L *planus*] **1 :** flat ⟨*plano*sol⟩ **2 :** flatly ⟨*plano*spiral⟩ **3 :** flat and ⟨*plano*-concave⟩

pla·nar \'plā-nər, -,när\ *adj* **1 :** of, relating to, or lying in a plane **2 :** two-dimensional in quality

pla·nar·i·an \plə-'nar-ē-ən, -'ner-\ *n* [deriv. of L *planum* plane] **:** any of a family (Planariidae) or order (Tricladida) of small soft-bodied ciliated mostly aquatic turbellarian worms

pla·na·tion \plā-'nā-shən\ *n* **:** mechanical erosion producing flat surface

plan·chet \'plan-chət\ *n* [dim. of *planch* (flat plate)] **1 :** a metal disk to be stamped as a coin **2 :** a small metal or plastic disk sometimes with a raised edge

plan·chette \plan-'shet\ *n* [F, fr. dim. of *planche* plank, fr. L *planca*] **:** a small board supported on casters at two points and a vertical pencil at a third and believed to produce automatic writing when lightly touched by the fingers

1plane \'plān\ *vb* [ME *planen*, fr. MF *planer*, fr. LL *planare*, fr. L *planus* level — more at FLOOR] *vt* **1 a :** to make smooth or even **:** LEVEL **b :** to make plane by use of a plane **2 :** to remove by planing ~ *vi* **1 :** to work with a plane **2 :** to do the work of a plane — **plan·er** *n*

2plane *n* [ME, fr. MF, fr. L *platanus*, fr. Gk *platanos;* akin to Gk *platys* broad — more at PLACE] **:** any of a genus (*Platanus* of the family Platanaceae, the plane-tree family) of trees with large palmately lobed leaves and flowers in globose heads — called also *buttonwood, sycamore*

3plane *n* [ME, fr. MF, fr. LL *plana*, fr. *planare*] **:** a tool for smoothing or shaping a wood surface

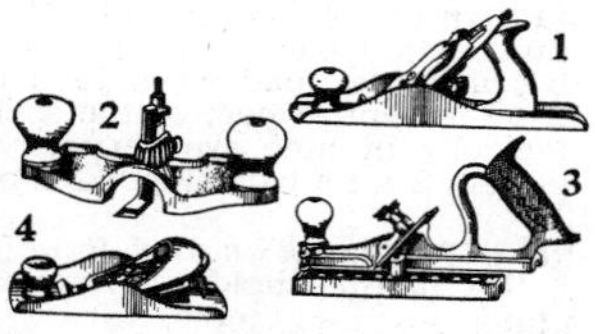

planes: *1* jack plane, *2* router plane, *3* tonguing and grooving plane, *4* block plane

4plane *n* [L *planum*, fr. neut. of *planus* level] **1 a :** a surface of such nature that a straight line joining two of its points lies wholly in the surface **b :** a flat or level surface **2 :** a level of existence, consciousness, or development **3 a :** one of the main supporting surfaces of an airplane **b** [by shortening] **:** AIRPLANE

5plane *adj* [L *planus*] **1 :** having no elevations or depressions **:** FLAT **2 a :** of, relating to, or dealing with geometric planes **b :** lying in a plane ⟨~ curve⟩ **syn** see LEVEL

6plane *vi* [F *planer*, fr. *plan* plane; fr. the plane formed by the wings of a soaring bird] **1 a :** to soar on wings **b :** to skim across the surface of the water **2 :** to travel by airplane

plane angle *n* **:** an angle formed by two lines

plane geometry *n* **:** a branch of elementary geometry that deals with plane figures

pla·ner tree \'plā-nər-\ *n* [J. J. *Planer* †1789 G botanist] **:** a small-leaved No. American tree (*Planera aquatica*) of the elm family with an oval ribbed fruit

plan·et \'plan-ət\ *n* [ME *planete*, fr. OF, fr. LL *planeta*, modif. of Gk *planēt-, planēs*, lit., wanderer, fr. *planasthai* to wander; akin to ON *flana* to rush around] **1 a :** any of the seven heavenly bodies sun, moon, Venus, Jupiter, Mars, Mercury, and Saturn that in ancient belief have motions of their own among the fixed stars **b :** one of the bodies except a comet, meteor, or satellite that revolves around the sun in the solar system; *specif* **:** EARTH **2 :** a heavenly body held to influence the fate of human beings **3 :** a person or thing of great importance **:** LUMINARY

PLANETS

SYMBOL	NAME	MEAN DISTANCE FROM THE SUN astronomical units	million miles	PERIOD IN DAYS OR YEARS	DIAMETER IN MILES
♃	Jupiter	5.20	483	12 years	86,800
♄	Saturn	9.54	886	29 years	71,500
♅	Uranus	19.18	1783	84 years	29,400
♆	Neptune	30.06	2794	165 years	28,000
⊕	Earth	1.00	93	365 ¼ days	7,913
♀	Venus	0.72	67	225 days	7,600
♂	Mars	1.52	142	687 days	4,200
♇	Pluto	39.52	3670	248 years	4,000?
☿	Mercury	0.39	36	88 days	2,900

plane table *n* **:** an instrument that consists essentially of a drawing board on a tripod with a ruler pointed at the object observed and is used for plotting the lines of a survey directly from the observation

plan·e·tar·i·um \,plan-ə-'ter-ē-əm\ *n, pl* **planetariums** *or* **plan·e·tar·ia** \-ē-ə\ **1 :** a model or representation of the solar system **2 a :** an optical device to project various celestial images and effects **b :** a building or room housing such a device

plan·e·tary \'plan-ə-,ter-ē\ *adj* **1 a :** of or relating to a planet **b** (1) **:** WANDERING (2) **:** having a motion like that of a planet **c :** IMMENSE **2 :** TERRESTRIAL, WORLDWIDE **3 :** having or consisting of an epicyclic train of gear wheels

plan·e·tes·i·mal \,plan-ə-'tes-ə-məl, -'tez-\ *n* [*planet* + *-esimal* (as in *infinitesimal*)] **:** one of numerous small solid heavenly bodies that may have existed at an early stage of the development of the solar system

planetesimal hypothesis *n* **:** a hypothesis in astronomy: the planets have evolved by aggregation from planetesimals

plan·e·toid \'plan-ə-,tȯid\ *n* **1 :** a body resembling a planet **2 :** ASTEROID — **plan·e·toi·dal** \,plan-ə-'tȯid-ᵊl\ *adj*

plan·et–strick·en \'plan-ət-,strik-ən\ *or* **plan·et–struck** \-,strək\ *adj* **1 :** affected by the influence of a planet **2 :** PANIC-STRICKEN

planet wheel *n* **:** a gear wheel that revolves around the wheel with which it meshes in an epicyclic train

plan·form \'plan-,fȯrm\ *n* **:** the contour of an airplane as viewed from above

plan·gen·cy \'plan-jən-sē\ *n* **:** the quality or state of being plangent

plan·gent \-jənt\ *adj* [L *plangent-, plangens*, prp. of *plangere* to strike, lament] **1 :** having a loud reverberating sound **2 :** having an expressive esp. plaintive quality — **plan·gent·ly** *adv*

pla·nim·e·ter \plā-'nim-ət-ər, plə-\ *n* [F *planimètre*, fr. L *planum* plane + F *-mètre* -meter] **:** an instrument for measuring the area of a plane figure by tracing its boundary line

pla·ni·met·ric \,plā-nə-'me-trik\ *adj* [F *planimétrie* measurement of plane surfaces, fr. ML *planimetria*, fr. L *planum* plane + *-metria* -metry] *of a map* **:** having no indications of contour

plan·ish \'plan-ish\ *vt* [MF *planiss-*, stem of *planir*, fr. *plan* level, fr. L *planus*] **:** to make smooth or plane; *specif* **:** to toughen and polish by hammering lightly — **plan·ish·er** *n*

pla·ni·sphere \'plā-nə-,sfi(ə)r\ *n* [ML *planisphaerium*, fr. L *planum* plane + *sphaera* sphere] **:** a representation of the circles of the sphere on a plane; *esp* **:** a polar projection of the celestial sphere and the stars on a plane with adjustable circles or other appendages for showing celestial phenomena for any given time

1plank \'plaŋk\ *n* [ME, fr. ONF *planke*, fr. L *planca*] **1 a :** a heavy thick board; *specif* **:** one 2 to 4 inches thick and at least 8 inches wide **b :** an object made of a plank or planking **c :** PLANKING **2 a :** an article in the platform of a political party **b :** a principal item of a policy or program

2plank *vt* **1 :** to cover or floor with planks **2 :** to set down **3 :** to cook and serve on a board usu. with an elaborate garnish

plank·ing *n* **1 :** the act or process of covering or fitting with planks **2 :** a quantity of planks

plank–sheer \'plaŋk-,shi(ə)r\ *n* [alter. of obs. *plancher* (planking)] **:** a heavy plank forming the outer edge of a ship's deck

plank·ter \'plaŋ(k)-tər\ *n* [Gk *planktēr* wanderer, fr. *plazesthai*] **:** a planktonic organism

plank·ton \'plaŋ(k)-tən, -,tän\ *n* [G, fr. Gk, neut. of *planktos* drifting, fr. *plazesthai* to wander, drift, pass. of *plazein* to drive astray; akin to L *plangere* to strike — more at PLAINT] **:** the passively floating or weakly swimming animal and plant life of a body of water — **plank·ton·ic** \plaŋ(k)-'tän-ik\ *adj*

plan·less \'plan-ləs\ *adj* **:** functioning or taking place without a plan or set goal — **plan·less·ly** *adv* — **plan·less·ness** *n*

plano- — see PLAN-

pla·no–con·cave \,plā-nō-(,)kän-'kāv, -'kän-,\ *adj* **:** flat on one side and concave on the other

pla·no–con·vex \-(,)kän-'veks, -'kän-,, -kən-'\ *adj* **:** flat on one side and convex on the other

pla·no·graph \'plā-nə-,graf, 'plan-ə-\ *vt* [back-formation fr. *planography*] **:** to print by planography — **planograph** *n*

pla·no·graph·ic \,plā-nə-'graf-ik, ,plan-ə-\ *adj* **:** involving planography

pla·nog·ra·phy \plā-'näg-rə-fē, plə-\ *n* **:** a process (as lithography) for printing from a plane surface; *also* **:** matter so printed

pla·no·sol \'plā-nə-,säl, -,sȯl\ *n* [²*plan-* + L *solum* ground, soil] **:** any of an intrazonal group of soils with strongly leached upper layer over a compacted clay or silt developed on smooth flat uplands

plan position indicator *n* **:** PPI

1plant \'plant\ *vb* [ME *planten*, fr. OE *plantian*, fr. LL *plantare* to plant, fix in place, fr. L, to plant, fr. *planta* plant] *vt* **1 a :** to put or set in the ground for growth ⟨~ seeds⟩ **b :** to set or sow with seeds or plants **c :** IMPLANT **2 a :** to establish or institute **b :** COLONIZE, SETTLE **c :** to place (animals) in a new locality to grow and multiply **d :** to stock with animals **3 a :** to place in or on the ground **b :** to place firmly or forcibly **4 a :** CONCEAL **b :** to covertly place for discovery, publication, or dissemination ~ *vi* **:** to plant something — **plant·able** \-ə-bəl\ *adj*

2plant *n* [ME *plante*, fr. OE, fr. L *planta*] **1 a :** a young tree, vine, shrub, or herb planted or suitable for planting **b :** any of a kingdom (Plantae) of living beings typically lacking locomotive movement or obvious nervous or sensory organs and possessing cellulose cell walls **2 a :** the land, buildings, machinery, apparatus, and fixtures employed in carrying on a trade or an industrial business **b :** a factory or workshop for the manufacture of a particular product **c :** the total facilities available for production or service **d :** the buildings and other physical equipment of an institution **3 :** an act of planting **4 :** something or someone planted — **plant·like** \-,līk\ *adj*

Plan·tag·e·net \plan-'taj-(ə)-nət\ *adj* [*Plantagenet*, nickname of the family adopted as surname] **:** of or relating to an English royal house furnishing sovereigns from 1154 to 1399 — **Plantagenet** *n*

1plan·tain \'plant-ᵊn\ *n* [ME, fr. OF, fr. L *plantagin-, plantago*, fr.

planta sole of the foot; fr. its broad leaves — more at PLACE] **:** any of a genus (*Plantago* of the family Plantaginaceae, the plantain family) of short-stemmed elliptic-leaved herbs with spikes of minute greenish flowers

2**plantain** *n* [Sp *plántano* plane tree, banana tree, fr. ML *plantanus*, alter. of L *platanus* — more at PLANE] **1 :** a banana plant (*Musa paradisiaca*) **2 :** the angular greenish starchy fruit of the plantain that is a staple food throughout the tropics when cooked

plantain lily *n* **:** a plant (genus *Hosta*) of the lily family with plaited basal leaves and racemose white or violet flowers

plan·tar \'plant-ər, 'plan-,tär\ *adj* [L *plantaris*, fr. *planta* sole — more at PLACE] **:** of or relating to the sole of the foot

plan·ta·tion \plan-'tā-shən, *South also* plant-'ā-\ *n* **1 :** a usu. large group of plants and esp. trees under cultivation **2 :** a settlement in a new country or region **:** COLONY **3 a :** a place that is planted or under cultivation **b :** a usu. large estate usu. worked by resident labor

plant·er \'plant-ər\ *n* **1 :** one that cultivates plants: as **a :** FARMER **b :** one who owns or operates a plantation **2 :** one who settles or founds a place and esp. a new colony **3 :** a container in which ornamental plants are grown

planter's punch *n* **:** a punch of rum, lime or lemon juice, sugar, water, and sometimes bitters

plant food *n* **1 :** FOOD 1b **2 :** FERTILIZER

plant hormone *n* **:** an organic substance other than a nutrient that in minute amounts modifies a plant physiological process; *esp* **:** one produced by a plant and active elsewhere than at the site of production

plan·ti·grade \'plant-ə-,grād\ *adj* [F, fr. L *planta* sole + F *-grade*] **:** walking on the sole with the heel touching the ground ⟨man is a ~ animal⟩ — **plantigrade** *n*

plant·like flagellate \,plant-,līk-\ *n* **:** any of various organisms constituting a subclass (Phytomastigina), having many characteristics in common with typical algae, and being considered as protozoans or as algae

plant louse *n* **:** an aphid or a related insect

plan·u·la \'plan-yə-lə\ *n, pl* **plan·u·lae** \-yə-,lē, -,lī\ [NL, fr. L *planus* level, flat — more at FLOOR] **:** the very young usu. flattened oval or oblong free-swimming ciliated larva of a coelenterate — **plan·u·lar** \-lər\ *adj* — **plan·u·loid** \-,lȯid\ *adj*

plaque \'plak\ *n* [F, fr. MF, metal sheet, fr. *plaquier* to plate, fr. MD *placken* to piece, patch; akin to MD *placke* piece, MHG *placke* patch] **1 a :** an ornamental brooch; *esp* **:** the badge of an honorary order **b :** a flat thin piece (as of metal) used for decoration **c :** a commemorative or identifying inscribed tablet **2 :** a localized abnormal patch on a body part or surface

plash \'plash\ *n* [prob. imit.] **:** SPLASH — **plash** *vb*

-pla·sia \'plā-zh(ē)ə\ *or* **-pla·sy** \,plā-sē, ,plas-ē, p-lə-sē\ *n comb form* [NL *-plasia*, fr. Gk *plasis* molding, fr. *plassein*] **:** development **:** formation ⟨hyper*plasia*⟩ ⟨homo*plasy*⟩

plasm \'plaz-əm\ *n* [LL *plasma* something molded] **:** PLASMA

plasm- *or* **plasmo-** *comb form* [F, fr. NL *plasma*] **:** plasma ⟨*plasmo*dium⟩ ⟨*plasmo*lysis⟩

-plasm \,plaz-əm\ *n comb form* [G *-plasma*, fr. NL *plasma*] **:** formative or formed material (as of a cell or tissue) ⟨endo*plasm*⟩

plas·ma \'plaz-mə\ *n* [G, fr. LL, something molded, fr. Gk, fr. *plassein* to mold — more at PLASTER] **1 :** a green faintly translucent quartz **2** [NL, fr. LL] **a :** the fluid part of blood, lymph, or milk as distinguished from suspended material **b :** the juice that can be expressed from muscle **3 :** PROTOPLASM **4 :** an ionized gas containing about equal numbers of positive ions and electrons — **plas·mat·ic** \plaz-'mat-ik\ *adj*

plas·ma·gel \'plaz-mə-,jel\ *n* **:** gelated protoplasm; *esp* **:** the outer firm zone of a pseudopodium

plas·ma·gene \-,jēn\ *n* [ISV] **:** a submicroscopic determiner held to be present in cytoplasm and to be comparable to genes — **plas·ma·gen·ic** \,plaz-mə-'jē-nik\ *adj*

plas·ma·lem·ma \,plaz-mə-'lem-ə\ *n* [NL, fr. *plasma* + Gk *lemma* husk — more at LEMMA] **:** the differentiated protoplasmic surface bounding a cell

plasma membrane *n* **:** a semipermeable limiting layer of cell protoplasm

plas·ma·sol \'plaz-mə-,säl, -,sȯl, -,sōl\ *n* **:** solated protoplasm; *esp* **:** the inner fluid zone of a pseudopodium or amoeboid cell

plas·min \'plaz-mən\ *n* **:** a proteolytic enzyme that dissolves the fibrin of blood clots

plas·mo·di·um \plaz-'mōd-ē-əm\ *n, pl* **plas·mo·dia** \-ē-ə\ [NL, fr. *plasm-* + *-odium* thing resembling, fr. Gk *-ōdēs* like] **1 a :** a motile multinucleate mass of protoplasm resulting from fusion of uninuclear amoeboid cells **b :** SYNCYTIUM 1 **2 :** an individual malaria parasite

plas·mol·y·sis \plaz-'mäl-ə-səs\ *n* [NL] **:** shrinking of the cytoplasm away from the wall of a living cell due to water loss by exosmosis — **plas·mo·lyt·ic** \,plaz-mə-'lit-ik\ *adj* — **plas·mo·lyt·i·cal·ly** \-i-k(ə-)lē\ *adv*

plas·mo·lyze \'plaz-mə-,līz\ *vt* **:** to subject to plasmolysis ~ *vi* **:** to undergo plasmolysis

-plast \,plast\ *n comb form* [MF *-plaste* thing molded, fr. LL *-plastus*, fr. Gk *-plastos*, fr. *plastos* molded, fr. *plassein*] **:** organized particle or granule **:** cell ⟨chromo*plast*⟩

1**plas·ter** \'plas-tər\ *n* [ME, fr. OE, fr. L *emplastrum*, fr. Gk *emplastron*, fr. *emplassein* to plaster on, fr. *en-* + *plassein* to mold, plaster; akin to L *planus* level, flat — more at FLOOR] **1 :** a pharmaceutical preparation stiffer than ointment usu. applied to the body spread on some surface (as of cloth); *broadly* **:** something applied to heal and soothe **2 :** a pasty composition (as of lime, water, and sand) that hardens on drying and is used for coating walls, ceilings, and partitions — **plas·ter·work** \-,wərk\ *n* — **plas·tery** \-t(ə-)rē\ *adj*

2**plaster** *vb* **plas·ter·ing** \-t(ə-)riŋ\ *vt* **1 :** to overlay or cover with plaster **:** COAT **2 :** to apply a plaster to **3 a :** to cover over or conceal as if with a coat of plaster **b :** to apply as a coating or incrustation **c :** to smooth down with a sticky or shiny substance **4 :** to fasten or apply tightly to another surface **5 :** to treat with plaster of paris **6 :** to affix to or place upon esp. conspicuously or in quantity ~ *vi* **:** to apply plaster — **plas·ter·er** \-tər-ər\ *n*

plas·ter·board \'plas-tər-,bō(ə)rd, -,bȯ(ə)rd\ *n* **:** a board used in large sheets as a backing or as a substitute for plaster in walls and consisting of several plies of fiberboard, paper, or felt usu. bonded to a hardened gypsum plaster core

plaster cast *n* **1 :** a sculptor's model in plaster of paris **2 :** a rigid dressing of gauze impregnated with plaster of paris

plas·tered \'plas-tərd\ *adj, slang* **:** DRUNK, INTOXICATED

plas·ter·ing *n* **1 :** the act or process of applying a plaster or a coating of plaster **2 :** a coating of plaster or similar substance **3 :** DRUBBING

plaster of par·is \-'par-əs\ *often cap 2d P* [*Paris*, France] **:** a white powdery slightly hydrated calcium sulfate $CaSO_4.\frac{1}{2}H_2O$ or $2CaSO_4.H_2O$ made by calcining gypsum and used chiefly for casts and molds in the form of a quick-setting paste with water

1**plas·tic** \'plas-tik\ *adj* [L *plasticus* of molding, fr. Gk *plastikos*, fr. *plassein* to mold, form] **1 :** FORMATIVE, CREATIVE ⟨~ forces in nature⟩ **2 a :** capable of being molded or modeled ⟨~ clay⟩ **b :** capable of adapting **:** PLIABLE ⟨ecologically ~ animals⟩ **3 :** characterized by or using modeling ⟨~ arts⟩ **4 :** SCULPTURAL **5 :** made or consisting of a plastic **6 :** capable of being deformed continuously and permanently in any direction without rupture

syn PLIABLE, PLIANT, DUCTILE, MALLEABLE, ADAPTABLE: PLASTIC applies to substances soft enough to be molded yet capable of hardening into the desired fixed form; PLIABLE suggests something easily bent, folded, twisted, or manipulated; PLIANT may stress flexibility and sometimes connote springiness and so lack some of the suggestion of submissiveness found in PLIABLE; DUCTILE applies to what can be drawn out at will and therefore suggests being easily led or influenced; MALLEABLE applies to what may be beaten into shape and may suggest lack of independent will or firm character; ADAPTABLE implies the capability of being easily modified to suit other conditions, needs, or uses

2**plastic** *n* **:** a plastic substance; *specif* **:** any of numerous organic synthetic or processed materials that are molded, cast, extruded, drawn, or laminated into objects, films, or filaments — often used in pl. with sing. constr.

-plas·tic \'plas-tik\ *adj comb form* [Gk *-plastikos*, fr. *plassein*] **1 :** developing **:** forming ⟨thrombo*plastic*⟩ **2 :** of or relating to (something designated by a term ending in *-plasm, -plast, -plasty*, or *-plasy*) ⟨homo*plastic*⟩ ⟨neo*plastic*⟩

plas·ti·cal·ly \'plas-ti-k(ə-)lē\ *adv* **1 :** in a plastic manner **2 :** with respect to plastic qualities

plas·tic·i·ty \pla-'stis-ət-ē\ *n* **1 :** the quality or state of being plastic; *esp* **:** capacity for being molded or altered **2 :** the ability to retain a shape attained by pressure deformation

plas·ti·cize \'plas-tə-,sīz\ *vt* **:** to make plastic

plas·ti·ciz·er \-,sī-zər\ *n* **:** one that plasticizes; *specif* **:** a chemical added to rubbers and resins to impart flexibility, workability, or stretchability

plastic surgeon *n* **:** a specialist in plastic surgery

plastic surgery *n* **:** a branch of surgery concerned with the repair or restoration of lost, injured, or deformed parts of the body chiefly by transfer of tissue

plas·tid \'plas-təd\ *n* [G, fr. Gk *plastos* molded] **:** any of various small bodies of specialized protoplasm lying in the cytoplasm of cells and serving in many cases as centers of special metabolic activities — **plas·tid·i·al** \pla-'stid-ē-əl\ *adj*

plas·to·gene \'plas-tə-,jēn\ *n* [*plast*ed + *-o-* + *-gene*] **:** a submicroscopic determiner held to be present in plant cell plastids and to influence phenomena of the plastids

plas·to·mer \'plas-tə-mər\ *n* [*plastic* + *-o-* + *-mer*] **:** a relatively tough usu. hard and rigid polymeric substance

plas·tral \'plas-trəl\ *adj* **:** of or relating to a plastron

plas·tron \'plas-trən\ *n* [MF, fr. OIt *piastrone*, aug. of *piastra* thin metal plate — more at PIASTER] **1 a :** a metal breastplate **b :** a quilted pad worn in fencing practice to protect the chest **2 :** the ventral part of the shell of a tortoise or turtle consisting typically of nine symmetrically placed bones overlaid by horny plates **3 a :** a trimming like a bib for a woman's dress **b :** DICKEY 1a

-plas·ty \,plas-tē\ *n comb form* [F *-plastie*, fr. LGk *-plastia* molding, fr. Gk *-plastēs* molder, fr. *plassein*] **:** plastic surgery ⟨osteo*plasty*⟩

-plasy — see -PLASIA

1**plat** \'plat\ *vt* **plat·ted; plat·ting** [ME *platen*, alter. of *plaiten*] **:** PLAIT

2**plat** *n* **:** PLAIT

3**plat** *n* [prob. alter. of *plot*] **1 :** a small piece of ground **:** PLOT **2 :** a plan, map, or chart of a piece of land (as a town) with actual or proposed features (as lots); *also* **:** the land represented

4**plat** *vt* **plat·ted; plat·ting :** to make a plat of

plat·an \'plat-ᵊn\ *n* [ME, fr. L *platanus*] **:** 2PLANE

1**plate** \'plāt\ *n* [ME, fr. OF, fr. *plate*, fem. of *plat* flat, fr. (assumed) VL *plattus*, prob. fr. Gk *platys* broad, flat — more at PLACE] **1 a :** a smooth flat thin piece of material **b** (1) **:** forged, rolled, or cast metal in sheets usu. thicker than ¼ inch (2) **:** a very thin layer of metal deposited on a surface of base metal by plating **c :** one of the broad metal pieces used in armor; *also* **:** armor of such plates **d** (1) **:** a lamina or plaque (as of bone or horn) that forms part of an animal body; *esp* **:** SCUTE (2) **:** the thin under portion of the forequarter of beef; *esp* **:** the fatty back part **e** (1) **:** HOME PLATE (2) **:** a rubber slab from which a softball or baseball pitcher delivers the ball **2** [ME; partly fr. OF *plate* plate, piece of silver; partly fr. OSp *plata* silver, fr. (assumed) VL *plattus* flat] **a** *obs* **:** a silver coin **b :** precious metal; *esp* **:** silver bullion **3** [ME, fr. MF *plat* dish, plate, fr. *plat* flat] **a :** domestic hollow ware of gold, silver, base metals, or plated **b :** a shallow usu. circular vessel from which food is eaten or served **c** (1) **:** PLATEFUL (2) **:** a main course served on a plate (3) **:** food and service supplied to one person **d** (1) **:** a prize given to the winner in a contest (2) **:** a sports competition; *esp* **:** a horse race in which the contestants compete for a prize rather than stakes **e :** a dish or pouch passed in taking collections **f :** a flat glass dish used chiefly for culturing microorganisms **4 a :** PRINTING SURFACE **b :** a sheet of material (as glass) coated with a light-sensitive photographic emulsion **c** (1) **:** the usu. flat or grid-formed anode of an electron tube at which electrons collect (2) **:** a metallic grid with its interstices filled with active material that forms one of the structural units of a storage cell or battery **5 :** a horizontal timber for carrying the trusses of a roof or the rafters directly **6 :** the part of a denture that fits to the mouth; *broadly* **:** DENTURE **7 :** a full-page illustration often on different paper from the text pages

2**plate** *vt* **1 :** to cover or equip with plate: as **a :** to arm with armor plate **b :** to cover with an adherent layer mechanically,

chemically, or electrically; *also* : to deposit (as a layer) on a surface **2** : to make a printing surface from or for **3** : to fix or secure with a plate

1pla·teau \pla-'tō, 'pla-,\ *n, pl* **plateaus** *or* **pla·teaux** \-'tōz, -,tōz\ [F, fr. MF, platter, fr. *plat* flat] **1 a** : a usu. extensive land area having a relatively level surface raised sharply above adjacent land on at least one side : TABLELAND **b** : a similar undersea feature **2 a** : a region of little or no change in a graphical representation **b** : a relatively stable level, period, or condition

2plateau *vi* : to reach a period or phase of stability : form a plateau : level off

plate·ful \'plāt-,fu̇l\ *n, pl* **platefuls** \'plāt-,fu̇lz\ *also* **plates·ful** \'plāts-,fu̇l\ : a quantity to fill a plate

plate glass *n* : fine rolled, ground, and polished sheet glass

plate·let \'plāt-lət\ *n* : a minute flattened body; *specif* : BLOOD PLATELET

plate·like \-,līk\ *adj* : resembling a plate esp. in smooth flat form

plat·en \'plat-ᵊn\ *n* [MF *plateine*, fr. *plate*] **1** : a flat plate of metal; *esp* : one that exerts or receives pressure **2** : the roller of a typewriter

plate proof *n* : a proof taken from a plated letterpress printing surface

plat·er \'plāt-ər\ *n* **1** : one that plates **2 a** : a horse that runs chiefly in plate races **b** : an inferior racehorse

plate rail *n* **1** *chiefly Brit* : a primitive type of flat rail of cast iron with an upright ledge on the outer edge to keep wheels on the rail **2** : a rail or narrow shelf along the upper part of a wall to hold plates or ornaments

plat·form \'plat-,fȯrm\ *n, often attrib* [MF *plate-forme* diagram, map, lit., flat form] **1 a** : PLAN, DESIGN **b** : a declaration of the principles on which a group of persons stand; *esp* : a declaration of principles and policies adopted by a political party or a candidate **2** : a horizontal flat surface usu. higher than the adjoining area; *esp* : a raised flooring for speakers, performers, or other persons **3 a** : a layer (as of leather) between the inner sole and outer sole of a shoe **b** : a shoe having such a sole

platform car *n* : FLATCAR

platform rocker *n* : a chair that rocks on a stable platform

platform scale *n* : a weighing machine with a flat platform on which objects are weighed — called also *platform balance*

platin- *or* **platino-** *comb form* [NL *platinum*] : platinum ⟨*platino*type⟩ ⟨*platin*iridium⟩

1pla·ti·na \plə-'tē-nə\ *n* [Sp] : PLATINUM; *esp* : crude native platinum

2platina *adj* : of the color platinum

plat·ing *n* **1** : the act or process of plating **2 a** : a coating of metal plates **b** : a thin coating of metal

pla·tin·ic \plə-'tin-ik\ *adj* : of, relating to, or containing platinum esp. when tetravalent — compare PLATINOUS

plat·i·nize \'plat-ᵊn-,īz\ *vt* : to cover, treat, or combine with platinum

plat·i·no·cy·a·nide \,plat-ᵊn-ō-'sī-ə-,nīd\ *n* : a fluorescent complex salt formed by the union of platinous cyanide with another cyanide

1plat·i·noid \'plat-ᵊn-,ȯid\ *adj* : resembling platinum

2platinoid *n* **1** : an alloy chiefly of copper, nickel, and zinc used for forming electrical resistance coils and standards **2** : a metal related to platinum

plat·i·no·type \'plat-ᵊn-ō-,tīp\ *n* : a permanent photographic print in platinum black obtained by the reduction of a platinum salt by a developer; *also* : the process of making such a print

plat·i·nous \'plat-nəs, -ᵊn-əs\ *adj* : of, relating to, or containing platinum esp. when bivalent — compare PLATINIC

plat·i·num \'plat-nəm, -ᵊn-əm\ *n, often attrib* [NL, fr. Sp *platina*, fr. dim. of *plata* silver — more at PLATE] **1** : a heavy precious grayish white noncorroding ductile malleable metallic element that fuses with difficulty and is used esp. in chemical ware and apparatus, as a catalyst, and in dental and jewelry alloys — see ELEMENT table **2** : a moderate gray

platinum black *n* : a soft dull black powder of metallic platinum obtained by reduction and precipitation from solutions of its salts and used as a catalyst

platinum blonde *n* **1** : a pale silvery blonde color that in human hair is usu. produced by bleach and a bluish rinse **2** : a person whose hair is of the color platinum blonde

plat·i·tude \'plat-ə-,t(y)üd\ *n* [F, fr. *plat* flat, dull] **1** : the quality or state of being dull or insipid : TRITENESS **2** : a flat, trite, or weak remark : COMMONPLACE — **plat·i·tu·di·nous** \,plat-ə-'t(y)üd-nəs, -ᵊn-əs\ *adj*

plat·i·tu·di·nal \,plat-ə-'t(y)üd-nəl, -ᵊn-əl\ *adj* : PLATITUDINOUS

plat·i·tu·di·nar·i·an \-,t(y)üd-ᵊn-'er-ē-ən\ *n* : one given to platitudes

plat·i·tu·di·nize \-'t(y)üd-ᵊn-,īz\ *vi* [*platitudinous*] : to utter platitudes

pla·ton·ic \plə-'tän-ik, plā-\ *adj* [L *platonicus*, fr. Gk *platōnikos* fr. *Platōn* Plato] **1** *cap* : of, relating to, or characteristic of Plato or Platonism **2 a** : relating to or based on platonic love; *also* : experiencing or professing platonic love **b** : NOMINAL, THEORETICAL — **pla·ton·i·cal·ly** \-i-k(ə-)lē\ *adv*

platonic love *n, often cap P* **1** : love conceived by Plato as ascending from passion for the individual to contemplation of the universal and ideal **2** : a close relationship between two persons in which sexual desire has been suppressed or sublimated

Pla·to·nism \'plāt-ᵊn-,iz-əm\ *n* **1 a** : the philosophy of Plato stressing esp. that actual things are copies of transcendent ideas and that these ideas are the objects of true knowledge apprehended by reminiscence **b** : NEOPLATONISM **2** : PLATONIC LOVE — **Pla·to·nist** \-ᵊn-əst\ *n* — **Pla·to·nis·tic** \,plāt-ᵊn-'is-tik\ *adj*

Pla·to·nize \'plāt-ᵊn-,īz\ *vi* : to adopt, imitate, or conform to Platonic opinions ~ *vt* : to explain in accordance with or adapt to Platonic doctrines; *esp* : IDEALIZE

pla·toon \plə-'tün, pla-\ *n* [F *peloton* small detachment, lit., ball, fr. *pelote* little ball — more at PELLET] **1** : a subdivision of a company-size military unit normally consisting of a headquarters and two or more squads or sections **2** : a group of persons sharing a common characteristic or activity; *specif* : a group of football players trained for either offense or defense and sent into or withdrawn from the game as a body

platoon sergeant *n* **1** : an army noncommissioned officer in charge of a platoon **2** : SERGEANT FIRST CLASS

Platt·deutsch \'plat-,dȯich, 'plät-\ *n* [G, fr. D *Platduitsch*, lit., Low German, fr. *plat* flat, low + *duitsch* German] : a colloquial language of northern Germany comprising several Low German dialects

plat·ter \'plat-ər\ *n* [ME *plater*, fr. AF, fr. MF *plat* plate] **1 a** : a large plate used esp. for serving meat **b** : PLATE 3c(2) **2** : a phonograph record

1platy \'plāt-ē\ *adj* **1** : resembling a plate **2** : consisting of plates or flaky layers — used chiefly of soil or mineral formations

2platy \'plat-ē\ *n, pl* **platy** *or* **plat·ys** *or* **plat·ies** [NL *Platypoecilus*, genus name] : any of various small stockily built Mexican topminnows highly favored for the tropical aquarium, noted for variability and brilliant color, and held to form a single species (*Platypoecilus maculatus*)

platy·hel·minth \,plat-i-'hel-,min(t)th\ *n* [deriv. of Gk *platys* broad, flat + *helminth-*, *helmis* helminth] : any of a phylum (Platyhelminthes) of soft-bodied usu. much flattened worms (as the planarians, flukes, and tapeworms) — **platy·hel·min·thic** \-(,)hel-'min(t)-thik, -'mint-ik\ *adj*

platy·pus \'plat-i-pəs, -,pu̇s\ *n* [NL, fr. Gk *platypous* flat-footed, fr. *platys* broad, flat + *pous* foot — more at PLACE, FOOT] : a small aquatic oviparous mammal (*Ornithorhynchus anatinus*) of southern and eastern Australia and Tasmania having a fleshy bill resembling that of a duck, dense fur, webbed feet, and a broad flattened tail

plat·yr·rhine \'plat-i-,rīn\ *adj* [Gk *platyrrhin-*, *platyrrhis* broad-nosed, fr. *platys* + *rhin-*, *rhis* nose] : having a short broad nose — **platyrrhine** *n* — **plat·yr·rhi·ny** \-,rī-nē\ *n*

plau·dit \'plȯd-ət\ *n* [L *plaudite* applaud, pl. imper. of *plaudere* to applaud] **1** : an act or round of applause **2** : enthusiastic approval

plau·si·bil·i·ty \,plȯ-zə-'bil-ət-ē\ *n* **1** : the quality or state of being plausible **2** : something plausible

plau·si·ble \'plȯ-zə-bəl\ *adj* [L *plausibilis* worthy of applause, fr. *plausus*, pp. of *plaudere*] **1** : superficially fair, reasonable, or valuable : SPECIOUS **2** : superficially pleasing or persuasive **3** : superficially worthy of belief : CREDIBLE — **plau·si·ble·ness** *n* — **plau·si·bly** \-blē\ *adv*

syn PLAUSIBLE, CREDIBLE, COLORABLE, SPECIOUS mean outwardly acceptable as true or genuine. PLAUSIBLE implies reasonableness at first sight or hearing usu. with some hint of a possibility of being deceived; CREDIBLE may suggest plausibility but more clearly stresses worthiness of belief; COLORABLE stresses credibility on merely outward grounds; SPECIOUS stresses plausibility usu. with a clear implication of dissimulation or fraud

plau·sive \'plȯ-ziv, -siv\ *adj* [L *plausus*, pp.] **1** : manifesting praise or approval : APPLAUDING **2** *obs* : PLEASING **3** *archaic* : SPECIOUS

Plau·tine \'plȯ-,tīn\ *adj* : of, relating to, or characteristic of Plautus or his writings

1play \'plā\ *n* [ME, fr. OE *plega*; akin to OE *plegan* to play, MD *pleyen*] **1 a** : an act of briskly handling or using a weapon or instrument **b** (1) *archaic* : GAME, SPORT (2) : the conduct, course, or action of a game (3) : a particular act or maneuver in a game **c** (1) *obs* : SEXUAL INTERCOURSE (2) : DALLIANCE **d** (1) : recreational activity; *esp* : the spontaneous activity of children (2) : JEST ⟨said it in ~⟩ (3) : the act or an instance of playing on words or speech sounds **e** : GAMBLING, GAMING **2 a** (1) : an act, way, or manner of proceeding (2) : DEAL, VENTURE **b** (1) : OPERATION, ACTIVITY (2) : brisk, fitful, or light movement (3) : free or unimpeded motion (as of a part of a machine); *also* : the length or measure of such motion (4) : scope or opportunity for action **3 a** : the stage representation of an action or story **b** : a dramatic composition : DRAMA **syn** see FUN — **in play** : in condition or position to be legitimately played

2play *vi* **1 a** : to engage in sport or recreation : FROLIC **b** (1) : to move aimlessly about : TRIFLE (2) : to deal or behave frivolously or mockingly : JEST (3) : to deal in a light, speculative, or sportive manner (4) : to make use of double meaning or of the similarity of sound of two words for stylistic or humorous effect **2 a** : to take advantage ⟨~*ing* upon fears⟩ **b** (1) : FLUTTER, FRISK (2) : to move or operate in a lively, irregular, or intermittent manner **c** : to move or function freely within prescribed limits **d** : to discharge, eject, or fire repeatedly or so as to make a stream ⟨hoses ~*ing* on a fire⟩ **3 a** (1) : to perform music ⟨~ on a violin⟩ (2) : to sound in performance ⟨the organ is ~*ing*⟩ **b** (1) : to act on a stage or other dramatic medium (2) : SHOW, RUN ⟨what's ~*ing* at the theater⟩ **c** : to lend itself to performance **4 a** : to engage or take part in a game **b** : GAMBLE **c** (1) : to behave or conduct oneself in a specified way ⟨~ safe⟩ (2) : to feign a specified state or quality ⟨~ dead⟩ (3) : to take part in or assent to some activity : COOPERATE ⟨~ along with his scheme⟩ ~ *vt* **1 a** (1) : to engage in or occupy oneself with ⟨~ baseball⟩ (2) : to engage in as if in a game (3) : to deal with, handle, or manage (4) : EXPLOIT, MANIPULATE **b** : to pretend to engage in ⟨children ~*ing* house⟩ **c** (1) : to perform or execute for amusement or to deceive or mock ⟨~ trick⟩ (2) : WREAK ⟨~ havoc⟩ **2 a** (1) : to put on a performance of (a play) (2) : to act in the character or part of (3) : to act or perform in ⟨~*ed* leading theaters⟩ **b** : to perform or act the part of ⟨~ the fool⟩ **3 a** : to contend against in a game **b** (1) : to wager in a game : STAKE (2) : to make wagers on ⟨~ the races⟩ (3) : to operate on the basis of ⟨~ a hunch⟩ **c** : to put into action in a game **4 a** : to perform (music) on an instrument ⟨~ a waltz⟩ **b** : to perform music upon ⟨~ the violin⟩ **5 a** : WIELD, PLY **b** : to discharge, fire, or set off with continuous effect **c** : to cause to move or operate lightly and irregularly or intermittently **d** : to keep (a hooked fish) in action — **play·able** \'plā-ə-bəl\ *adj* — **play ball** : COOPERATE

pla·ya \'plī-ə\ *n* [Sp, lit., beach] : the flat-floored bottom of an undrained desert basin that becomes at times a shallow lake

play·act \'plā-,akt\ *vb* [back-formation fr. *playacting*] *vi* **1 a** : to take part in theatrical performances esp. professionally **b** : to make believe **2** : to engage in theatrical or insincere behavior ~ *vt* : to act out — **play·act·ing** *n*

play back *vt* : to run through (a disc or tape) recently recorded

play·back \'plā-,bak\ *n* **1** : an act of reproducing a sound record-

ing often immediately after recording **2 :** a tape or disc sound reproducing device

play·bill \-,bil\ *n* **1 :** a bill advertising a play and usu. announcing the cast **2 :** a theater program

play·boy \-,bȯi\ *n* **:** a man who lives a life devoted chiefly to the pursuit of pleasure

play-by-play \,plā-bə-,plā, -,bī-\ *adj* **1 :** being a running commentary on a sports event **2 :** circumstantially related **:** DETAILED

play down *vt* **:** to refrain from emphasizing **:** DEPRECIATE

played out *adj* **1 :** worn out or used up **2 :** tired out **:** SPENT

play·er \'plā-ər\ *n* **:** one that plays: as **a :** a person who plays a game **b :** MUSICIAN **c :** ACTOR **d :** a mechanical device for automatically playing a musical instrument (as a piano)

player piano *n* **:** a piano containing a mechanical piano player

play·fel·low \'plā-,fel-(,)ō, -ə(-w)\ *n* **:** PLAYMATE

play·ful \'plā-fəl\ *adj* **1 :** full of play **:** SPORTIVE **2 :** HUMOROUS, JOCULAR — **play·ful·ly** \-fə-lē\ *adv* — **play·ful·ness** *n*

play·go·er \-,gō(-ə)r\ *n* **:** a person who frequently attends plays

play·ground \'plā-,graủnd\ *n* **:** a piece of ground used for and usu. having facilities for recreation esp. by children

play·house \-,haủs\ *n* **1 :** THEATER **2 :** a small house for children to play in

playing card *n* **:** one of a set of 24 to 78 cards marked to show its rank and suit and used in playing any of numerous games

playing field *n* **:** a field for various games; *esp* **:** the part of a field officially marked off for play

play·land \'plā-,land\ *n* **:** PLAYGROUND

play·let \-lət\ *n* **:** a short play

play·mate \'plā-,māt\ *n* **:** a companion in play

play off *vt* **1 :** to complete the playing of (an interrupted contest) **2 :** to break (a tie) by a play-off

play-off \'plā-,ȯf\ *n* **1 :** a final contest or series of contests to determine the winner between contestants or teams that have tied **2 :** a series of contests played after the end of the regular season to determine a championship

play out *vt* **1 a :** to perform to the end **b :** to use up **:** FINISH **2 :** UNREEL, UNFOLD ~ *vi* **:** to become spent or exhausted

play·pen \'plā-,pen\ *n* **:** a portable enclosure in which a baby or young child may play

play·room \-,rüm, -,rủm\ *n* **:** RUMPUS ROOM

play·suit \-,süt\ *n* **:** a sports and play outfit for women and children consisting usu. of a blouse and shorts

play·thing \-,thiŋ\ *n* **:** TOY

play·time \-,tīm\ *n* **:** a time for play or diversion

play up *vt* **:** to give emphasis or prominence to — **play up to** \plā-'əp-tə(-w), -(,)tü\ **:** to support or flatter by eager agreement

play·wright \'plā-,rīt\ *n* ['*play* + obs. *wright* (maker), fr. ME, fr. OE *wryhta* — more at WRIGHT] **:** a person who writes plays

pla·za \'plaz-ə, 'pläz-\ *n* [Sp, fr. L *platea* broad street — more at PLACE] **:** a public square in a city or town

plea \'plē\ *n* [ME *plaid, plai,* fr. OF *plait, plaid,* fr. ML *placitum,* fr. L decision, decree, fr. neut. of *placitus,* pp. of *placēre* to please, be decided — more at PLEASE] **1 :** a legal suit or action **2 :** an allegation made by a party in support of his cause: as **a :** an allegation of fact — compare DEMURRER **b** (1) **:** a defendant's answer to a plaintiff's declaration in common-law practice (2) **:** an accused person's answer to a charge or indictment in criminal practice **c :** a plea of guilty to an indictment **3 :** something alleged as an excuse **:** PRETEXT **4 :** an earnest entreaty **:** APPEAL **syn** see APOLOGY

pleach \'plēch, 'plāch\ *vt* [ME *plechen,* fr. ONF *plechier,* fr. L *plexus,* pp. of *plectere* to braid — more at PLY] **:** INTERLACE, PLAIT

plead \'plēd\ *vb* **plead·ed** \'plēd-əd\ *or* **pled** \'pled\ **plead·ing** [ME *plaiden* to institute a lawsuit, fr. OF *plaidier,* fr. *plaid* plea] *vi* **1 :** to argue a case or cause in a court of law **2 a :** to make an allegation in an action or other legal proceeding; *esp* **:** to answer the previous pleading of the other party by denying facts therein stated or by alleging new facts **b :** to conduct pleadings **3 :** to make a plea of a specified nature ⟨~ not guilty⟩ **4 a :** to argue for or against a claim **b :** to entreat or appeal earnestly **:** IMPLORE ~ *vt* **1 :** to maintain (as a case or cause) in a court of law or other tribunal **2 :** to allege in or by way of a legal plea **3 :** to offer as a plea usu. in defense, apology, or excuse — **plead·able** \'plēd-ə-bəl\ *adj* — **plead·er** *n*

plead·ing *n* **1 :** advocacy of a cause in a court of law **2 a :** one of the formal usu. written allegations and counter allegations made alternately by the parties in a legal action or proceeding **b :** the action or process performed by the parties in presenting such formal allegations until a single point at issue is produced **c :** the introduction of one of these allegations esp. the first one **d :** the body of rules according to which these allegations are framed **3 :** ADVOCACY, INTERCESSION

pleas·ance \'plez-ᵊn(t)s\ *n* **1 :** a feeling of pleasure **:** DELIGHT **2 :** a pleasant rest or recreation place usu. attached to a mansion

pleas·ant \'plez-ᵊnt\ *adj* [ME *plesaunt,* fr. MF *plaisant,* fr. prp. of *plaisir*] **1 :** giving pleasure **:** AGREEABLE **2 :** having or characterized by pleasing manners, behavior, or appearance — **pleas·ant·ly** *adv* — **pleas·ant·ness** *n*

syn PLEASANT, PLEASING, AGREEABLE, GRATEFUL, GRATIFYING, WELCOME mean highly acceptable to the mind or senses. PLEASANT usu. stresses this quality inherent in an object; PLEASING suggests the effect an object has upon one; AGREEABLE implies being in harmony with one's taste or likings; GRATEFUL implies the satisfaction or relief afforded by what is pleasing or agreeable; GRATIFYING suggests mental pleasure afforded by satisfaction of one's desires or hopes; WELCOME is stronger than PLEASING or GRATEFUL in stressing the pleasure given by satisfying a prior need or longing

pleas·ant·ry \-ᵊn-trē\ *n* **1 :** an agreeable playfulness in conversation **:** BANTER **2 :** a humorous act or speech **:** JEST

please \'plēz\ *vb* [ME *plesen,* fr. MF *plaisir,* fr. L *placēre;* akin to L *placare* to placate, OE *flōh* flat stone, Gk *plak-, plax* flat surface] *vi* **1 :** to afford or give pleasure or satisfaction **2 :** LIKE, WISH ⟨do as you ~⟩ **3** *archaic* **:** to have the kindness ~ *vt* **1 :** to give pleasure to **:** GRATIFY **2 :** to be the will or pleasure of ⟨may it ~ your Majesty⟩ **3 :** to be willing to — usu. used in the imperative to express a polite command or request ⟨~ come in⟩

pleas·ing \'plē-ziŋ\ *adj* **:** giving pleasure **:** AGREEABLE **syn** see PLEASANT — **pleas·ing·ly** \-ziŋ-lē\ *adv* — **pleas·ing·ness** *n*

plea·sur·abil·i·ty \,plezh-(ə-)rə-'bil-ət-ē, ,plāzh-\ *n* **:** the quality or state of being pleasurable

plea·sur·able \'plezh-(ə-)rə-bəl, 'plāzh-\ *adj* **:** GRATIFYING, PLEASANT — **plea·sur·able·ness** *n* — **plea·sur·ably** \-blē\ *adv*

1**plea·sure** \'plezh-ər, 'plāzh-\ *n* [ME *plesure,* alter. of *plesir,* fr. MF *plaisir,* fr. *plaisir* to please] **1 :** DESIRE, INCLINATION ⟨wait upon his ~ —Shak.⟩ **2 :** a state of gratification **:** ENJOYMENT **3 a :** sensual gratification **b :** frivolous amusement **4 :** a source of delight or joy

syn PLEASURE, DELIGHT, JOY, DELECTATION, ENJOYMENT, FRUITION mean the agreeable emotion accompanying the possession or expectation of what is good or greatly desired. PLEASURE stresses satisfaction or gratification rather than visible happiness; DELIGHT usu. reverses this emphasis; JOY may imply a more deep-rooted rapturous emotion than either; DELECTATION and ENJOYMENT imply reaction to pleasurable experience consciously sought or provided, DELECTATION suggesting amusement or diversion, ENJOYMENT gratification or happiness; FRUITION implies pleasure in possession or enjoyment in attainment

2**pleasure** *vb* **plea·sur·ing** \-(ə-)riŋ\ *vi* **1 :** to take pleasure **:** DELIGHT **2 :** to seek pleasure ~ *vt* **:** to afford pleasure to **:** GRATIFY

plea·sure·less \-ər-ləs\ *adj* **:** affording no pleasure

1**pleat** \'plēt\ *vt* [ME *pleten,* fr. *pleit, plete* plait] **1 :** FOLD; *esp* **:** to arrange in pleats **2 :** PLAIT 2 — **pleat·ed** *adj* — **pleat·er** *n*

2**pleat** *n* [ME *plete*] **:** a fold in cloth made by doubling material over on itself; *also* **:** something resembling such a fold

pleb \'pleb\ *n* **:** PLEBEIAN

plebe \'plēb\ *n* [obs. *plebe* (common people), fr. F *plèbe,* fr. L *plebs*] **:** a freshman at a military or naval academy

1**ple·be·ian** \pli-'bē-(y)ən\ *n* [L *plebeius* of the common people, fr. *plebs* common people; akin to Gk *plēthos* throng, *plēthein* to be full — more at FULL] **1 :** a member of the Roman plebs **2 :** one of the common people — **ple·be·ian·ism** \-,iz-əm\ *n*

2**plebeian** *adj* **1 :** of or relating to plebeians **2 :** crude or coarse in manner or style **:** COMMON — **ple·be·ian·ly** *adv*

pleb·i·scite \'pleb-ə-,sīt, -sət *also* -,sēt\ *n* [L *plebis scitum* law voted by the comitia, lit., decree of the common people] **:** a vote by which the people of an entire country or district express an opinion for or against a proposal esp. on a choice of government or ruler

plebs \'plebz, 'pleps\ *n, pl* **ple·bes** \'plē-bēz, 'plā-,bās\ [L] **1 :** the common people of ancient Rome **2 :** the general populace

plec·to·gnath \'plek-,täg-,nath, -tə(g)-\ *n* [deriv. of Gk *plektos* twisted (fr. *plekein* to braid) + *gnathos* jaw — more at PLY, GNATH-] **:** any of an order (Plectognathi) of bony fishes including the filefishes, puffers, and triggerfishes and usu. having the body covered with bony plates, spines, or ossicles — **plectognath** *adj*

plec·trum \'plek-trəm\ *n, pl* **plec·tra** \-trə\ *or* **plectrums** [L, fr. Gk *plēktron,* fr. *plēssein* to strike — more at PLAINT] **:** a small thin piece (as of ivory or metal) used to pluck a stringed instrument

1**pledge** \'plej\ *n* [ME, security, fr. MF *plege,* fr. LL *plebium,* fr. (assumed) LL *plebere* to pledge] **1 a :** a bailment of a chattel as security for a debt or other obligation without involving transfer of title **b :** the chattel so delivered **c :** the contract incidental to such a bailment **2 a :** the state of being held as a security or guaranty **b :** something given as security for the performance of an act **3 :** a token, sign, or earnest of something else **4 :** a gage of battle **5 :** TOAST 3 **6 a :** a binding promise or agreement to do or forbear **b** (1) **:** a promise to join a fraternity or secret society (2) **:** a person who has so promised

2**pledge** *vt* **1 :** to make a pledge of; *specif* **:** to deposit in pledge or pawn **2 :** to drink the health of **:** TOAST **3 :** to bind by a pledge **:** PLIGHT **4 :** to promise the performance of by a pledge **:** UNDERTAKE — **pledg·ee** \ple-'jē\ *n* — **pledg·er** \'plej-ər\ *n* — **pled·gor** \'plej-ər, ple-'jȯ(ə)r\ *n*

pled·get \'plej-ət\ *n* [origin unknown] **:** a compress or pad used esp. to apply medication to or absorb discharges from a wound or ulcer

-ple·gia \'plē-j(ē-)ə\ *n comb form* [NL, fr. Gk *-plēgia,* fr. *plēssein* to strike — more at PLAINT] **:** paralysis ⟨di*plegia*⟩

ple·iad \'plē-əd, *chiefly Brit* 'plī-əd\ *n* [F *Pléiade,* group of 7 16th cent. F poets, fr. MF, group of 7 tragic poets of ancient Alexandria, fr. Gk *Pleiad-, Pleias,* fr. sing. of *Pleiades*] **:** a group of usu. seven illustrious or brilliant persons or things

Pleiad *n* **:** any of the Pleiades

Ple·ia·des \'plē-ə-,dēz, *chiefly Brit* 'plī-\ *n pl* [L, fr. Gk] **1 :** the seven daughters of Atlas transformed according to Greek mythology into a group of stars **2 :** a conspicuous loose cluster of stars in the constellation Taurus consisting of six stars visible to the average eye

plein air \plā-'na(ə)r, ple(ⁿ)-, -'ne(ə)r\ *adj* [F, open air] **1 :** of or relating to painting in outdoor daylight **2 :** of or relating to a mid-19th century French art movement attempting to represent outdoor light and air — **plein·air·ism** \-,iz-əm\ *n* — **plein·air·ist** \-əst\ *n*

pleio- *or* **pleo-** *or* **plio-** *comb form* [Gk *pleiōn, pleōn* — more at PLUS] **:** more ⟨*pleio*tropic⟩ ⟨*pleo*morphism⟩ ⟨*Plio*cene⟩

pleio·taxy \'plī-ə-,tak-sē\ *n* [ISV] **:** development of more than the normal number of parts (as bracts in a flower or inflorescence)

pleio·trop·ic \,plī-ə-'träp-ik\ *adj* **:** producing more than one effect; *specif* **:** having multiple phenotypic expressions ⟨a ~ gene⟩ — **pleio·trop·i·cal·ly** \-i-k(ə-)lē\ *adv* — **plei·ot·ro·py** \plī-'ä-trə-pē\ *n*

Pleis·to·cene \'plī-stə-,sēn\ *adj* [Gk *pleistos* most + ISV *-cene;* akin to Gk *pleiōn* more] **:** of, relating to, or being the earlier epoch of the Quaternary or the corresponding system of rocks — **Pleistocene** *n*

ple·na·ry \'plē-nə-rē, 'plen-ə-\ *adj* [LL *plenarius,* fr. L *plenus* full — more at FULL] **1 :** COMPLETE, FULL **2 :** fully attended or constituted by all entitled to be present ⟨a ~ session⟩ **syn** see FULL

plenary indulgence *n* **:** a remission of the entire temporal punishment due to sin

plenary inspiration *n* **:** inspiration in all subjects dealt with

ple·nip·o·tent \pli-'nip-ət-ənt\ *adj* [LL *plenipotent-, plenipotens,* fr. L *plenus* + *potent-, potens* powerful — more at POTENT] **:** PLENIPOTENTIARY

pleni·po·ten·tia·ry \,plen-ə-pə-'tench-(ə-)rē, -'ten-chē-,er-ē\ *n* [ML *plenipotentiarius,* adj. & n., fr. (assumed) *plenipotentia* investment with full power, fr. LL *plenipotent-, plenipotens*] **:** a person and esp. a diplomatic agent invested with full power to transact any business — **plenipotentiary** *adj*

plen·ish \'plen-ish\ *vt* [ME (Sc) *plenyssen* to fill up, fr. MF *pleniss-*, stem of *plenir*, fr. *plen* full, fr. L *plenus*] *chiefly Brit* **:** EQUIP, FURNISH

plen·i·tude \'plen-ə-,t(y)üd\ *or* **plent·i·tude** \'plen(t)-ə-\ *n* [ME *plenitude*, fr. MF or L; MF, fr. L *plenitudo*, fr. *plenus* full] **1 :** the quality or state of being full **:** COMPLETENESS **2 :** a great sufficiency **:** ABUNDANCE

plen·i·tu·di·nous \,plen-ə-'t(y)üd-nəs, -ᵊn-əs\ *adj* [L *plenitudin-*, *plenitudo* plenitude] **1 :** characterized by plenitude **2 :** PORTLY, STOUT

plen·te·ous \'plent-ē-əs\ *adj* [ME *plentevous*, *plenteous*, fr. OF *plentiveus*, fr. *plentif* abundant, fr. *plenté* plenty] **1 :** FRUITFUL, PRODUCTIVE **2 :** constituting, characterized by, or existing in plenty — **plen·te·ous·ly** *adv* — **plen·te·ous·ness** *n*

plen·ti·ful \'plent-i-fəl\ *adj* **1 :** containing or yielding plenty **:** FRUITFUL **2 :** characterized by, constituting, or existing in plenty **:** NUMEROUS — **plen·ti·ful·ly** \-fə-lē\ *adv* — **plen·ti·ful·ness** *n*

syn PLENTIFUL, AMPLE, ABUNDANT, COPIOUS mean more than sufficient yet not in excess. PLENTIFUL implies a great or rich supply; AMPLE implies a generous sufficiency to satisfy a particular requirement; ABUNDANT suggests an even greater or richer supply than does PLENTIFUL; COPIOUS stresses largeness of supply rather than fullness or richness

¹**plen·ty** \'plent-ē\ *n* [ME *plente*, fr. OF *plenté*, fr. LL *plenitat-*, *plenitas*, fr. L, fullness, fr. *plenus* full — more at FULL] **1 a :** a full supply **:** ABUNDANCE **b :** a large number or amount **2 :** the quality or state of being copious **:** PLENTIFULNESS

²**plenty** *adj* **1 :** plentiful in amount, number, or supply **2 :** AMPLE

³**plenty** *adv* **:** ABUNDANTLY, PLENTIFULLY

ple·num \'plen-əm, 'plēn-əm\ *n, pl* **plenums** *or* **ple·na** \-ə\ [NL, fr. L, neut. of *plenus*] **1 a :** a space or all space every part of which is full of matter **b** (1) **:** a condition in which the pressure of the air in an enclosed space is greater than that of the outside atmosphere (2) **:** an enclosed space in which such a condition exists **2 :** a general assembly of all members esp. of a legislative body **3 :** the quality or state of being full

pleo·mor·phic \,plē-ə-'mȯr-fik\ *adj* **:** of, relating to, or characterized by pleomorphism

pleo·mor·phism \-,fiz-əm\ *n* [ISV] **1 :** the occurrence of more than one distinct form in the life cycle of a plant **2 :** POLYMORPHISM

ple·o·nasm \'plē-ə-,naz-əm\ *n* [LL *pleonasmus*, fr. Gk *pleonasmos*, fr. *pleonazein* to be excessive, fr. *pleiōn*, *pleōn* more — more at PLUS] **:** the use of more words than those necessary to denote mere sense (as in *the man he said*) **:** REDUNDANCY; *also* **:** an instance or example of such use of words — **ple·o·nas·tic** \,plē-ə-'nas-tik\ *adj* — **ple·o·nas·ti·cal·ly** \-ti-k(ə-)lē\ *adv*

ple·oph·a·gous \plē-'äf-ə-gəs\ *adj* **1 :** eating a variety of foods **2** *of a parasite* **:** not restricted to a single kind of host

pleo·pod \'plē-ə-,päd\ *n* [Gk *plein* to sail + E *-o-* + *-pod*; fr. its use in swimming — more at FLOW] **:** an abdominal limb of a crustacean

ple·ro·cer·coid \,plir-ō-'sər-,kȯid\ *n* [Gk *plērēs* full + *kerkos* tail] **:** the solid elongate infective larva of some tapeworms usu. occurring in the muscles of fishes

ple·sio·saur \'plē-sē-ə-,sȯ(ə)r, -zē-\ *n* [deriv. of Gk *plēsios* close (fr. *pelas* near) + *sauros* lizard — more at FELT] **:** any of a suborder (Plesiosauria) of Mesozoic marine reptiles

pleth·o·ra \'pleth-ə-rə\ *n* [ML, fr. Gk *plēthōra*, lit., fullness, fr. *plēthein* to be full — more at FULL] **1 :** a bodily condition characterized by an excess of blood and marked by turgescence and a florid complexion **2 :** SUPERFLUITY, EXCESS — **ple·tho·ric** \plə-'thȯr-ik, ple-, -'thär-; 'pleth-ə-rik\ *adj*

pleur- *or* **pleuro-** *comb form* [NL, fr. *pleura*] **1 a :** pleura ⟨*pleuro*pneumonia⟩ **b :** pleura and ⟨*pleuro*peritoneum⟩ **2** [Gk, fr. *pleura*] **:** side **:** lateral ⟨*pleur*odont⟩

pleu·ra \'plu̇r-ə\ *n, pl* **pleu·rae** \'plu̇(ə)r-,ē, -,ī\ *or* **pleuras** [Gk, rib, side] **:** the delicate serous membrane lining each half of the thorax of mammals and folded back over the surface of the lung of the same side — **pleu·ral** \'plu̇r-əl\ *adj*

pleu·ri·sy \'plu̇r-ə-sē\ *n* [ME *pluresie*, fr. MF *pleuresie*, fr. LL *pleurisis*, alter. of L *pleuritis*, fr. Gk, fr. *pleura* side] **:** inflammation of the pleura usu. with fever, painful and difficult respiration, cough, and exudation into the pleural cavity — **pleu·rit·ic** \plü-'rit-ik\ *adj*

pleur·odont \'plu̇r-ə-,dänt\ *adj* [Gk *pleura* side + ISV *-odont*] **1 :** consolidated with the inner surface of the alveolar ridge without sockets ⟨~ teeth⟩ **2 :** having pleurodont teeth — **pleurodont** *n*

pleu·ro·per·i·to·ne·um \,plu̇r-ō-,per-ət-ᵊn-'ē-əm\ *n* [NL] **:** the membrane lining the body cavity and covering the surface of the enclosed viscera of vertebrates that have no diaphragm

pleu·ro·pneu·mo·nia \-n(y)u̇-'mō-nyə\ *n* [NL] **1 :** combined inflammation of the pleura and lungs **2 :** an acute febrile and often fatal respiratory disorder of cattle and related animals caused by microorganisms (family Mycoplasmataceae) of uncertain affinities

pleus·ton \'plü-stən, -,stän\ *n* [(assumed) Gk *pleustos* (verbal of *plein* to sail, float) + ISV *-on* (as in *plankton*)] **:** macroscopic floating vegetation forming mats on or near the surface of a body of fresh water — **pleus·ton·ic** \plü-'stän-ik\ *adj*

plexi·form \'plek-sə-,fȯrm\ *adj* [NL *plexus* + E *-iform*] **:** of, relating to, or having the form or characteristics of a plexus

plex·us \'plek-səs\ *n* [NL, fr. L, braid, network, fr. *plexus*, pp. of *plectere* to braid — more at PLY] **1 :** a network of anastomosing or interlacing blood vessels or nerves **2 :** an interwoven combination of parts in a structure

pli·abil·i·ty \,plī-ə-'bil-ət-ē\ *n* **:** the quality or state of being pliable

pli·able \'plī-ə-bəl\ *adj* [ME, fr. MF, fr. *plier* to bend, fold — more at PLY] **1 :** FLEXIBLE, SUPPLE **2 :** yielding easily to others **:** COMPLIANT **3 :** ADAPTABLE **syn** see PLASTIC — **pli·able·ness** *n* — **pli·ably** \-blē\ *adv*

pli·an·cy \'plī-ən-sē\ *n* **:** the quality or state of being pliant

pli·ant \'plī-ənt\ *adj* **1 :** bending or folding easily **:** FLEXIBLE **2 :** easily influenced **:** YIELDING **3 :** SUITABLE, APT **4 :** ADAPTABLE **syn** see PLASTIC — **pli·ant·ly** *adv* — **pli·ant·ness** *n*

pli·ca \'plī-kə\ *n, pl* **pli·cae** \-,kē, -,sē\ [ML, fr. L *plicare* to fold — more at PLY] **:** a fold or folded part; *esp* **:** a groove or fold of skin — **pli·cal** \-kəl\ *adj*

pli·cate \'plī-,kāt\ *adj* [L *plicatus*, pp. of *plicare*] **1 :** folded lengthwise like a fan ⟨a ~ leaf⟩ **2 :** having the surface thrown up into or marked with parallel ridges ⟨~ wing cases⟩ — **pli·cate·ly** *adv* — **pli·cate·ness** *n*

pli·ca·tion \plī-'kā-shən\ *n* **1 :** the act or process of folding or state of being folded **2 :** FOLD

pli·ers \'plī(-ə)rz\ *n pl but sing or pl in constr* **:** a small pincers with long jaws for holding small objects or for bending and cutting wire ⟨a pair of ~⟩

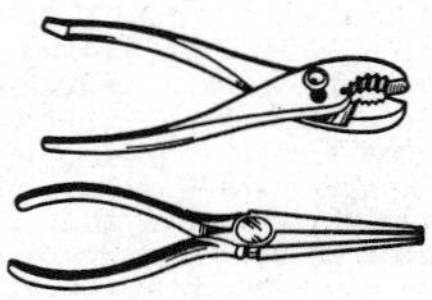

pliers

¹**plight** \'plīt\ *vt* [ME *plighten*, fr. OE *plihtan* to endanger, fr. *pliht* danger; akin to OHG *pflegan* to take care of] **:** to put or give in pledge **:** ENGAGE — **plight·er** *n*

²**plight** *n* **:** a solemnly given pledge **:** ENGAGEMENT

³**plight** *n* [ME *plit*, fr. AF, fr. (assumed) VL *plictus* fold — more at PLAIT] **:** CONDITION, STATE; *esp* **:** bad state or condition **syn** see PREDICAMENT

plim·soll \'plim(p)-səl, 'plim-,sȯl\ *n, Brit* **:** a light shoe with rubber sole and canvas top

Plimsoll mark *n* [Samuel *Plimsoll* †1898 E leader of shipping reform] **:** a load line or a set of load-line markings on an oceangoing cargo ship — called also *Plimsoll line*

¹**plink** \'pliŋk\ *vb* [imit.] *vi* **1 :** to make a tinkling sound **2 :** to shoot at random targets ~ *vt* **1 :** to cause to make a tinkling sound **2 :** to shoot at esp. in a casual manner

²**plink** *n* **:** a tinkling sound

plinth \'plin(t)th\ *n, pl* **plinths** \'plin(t)s, 'plin(t)ths\ [L *plinthus*, fr. Gk *plinthos*] **1 a :** the lowest member of a base **:** SUBBASE **b :** a block upon which the moldings of an architrave or trim are stopped at the bottom **2 :** a square block serving as a base **3 :** a course of stones forming a continuous foundation or base course

plio- — see PLEIO-

Plio·cene \'plī-ə-,sēn\ *adj* **:** of, relating to, or being the latest epoch of the Tertiary or the corresponding system of rocks

Plio·film \'plī-ə-,film\ *trademark* — used for a glossy membrane made of rubber hydrochloride and used chiefly for raincoats, packaging material, and as fruit wrapping

plis·kie \'plis-kē\ *n* [origin unknown] *chiefly Scot* **:** TRICK, PRACTICAL JOKE

plis·sé *or* **plis·se** \pli-'sā\ *n* [F *plissé*, fr. pp. of *plisser* to pleat, fr. MF, fr. *pli* fold, fr. *plier* to fold — more at PLY] **1 :** a textile finish of permanently puckered designs formed by treating with a caustic soda solution **2 :** a fabric usu. of cotton, rayon, or nylon with a plissé finish

plod \'pläd\ *vb* **plod·ded**; **plod·ding** [imit.] *vi* **1 :** to walk heavily or slowly **:** TRUDGE **2 :** to work laboriously and monotonously **:** DRUDGE ~ *vt* **:** to tread slowly or heavily along or over — **plod** *n* — **plod·der** *n* — **plod·ding·ly** \-iŋ-lē\ *adv*

-ploid \,plȯid\ *adj comb form* [ISV, fr. *diploid* & *haploid*] **:** having or being a chromosome number that bears (such) a relationship to or is (so many) times the basic chromosome number of a given group ⟨poly*ploid*⟩

ploi·dy \'plȯid-ē\ *n* [fr. such words as *diploidy*, *hexaploidy*] **:** degree of replication of chromosomes or genomes

plop \'pläp\ *vb* **plopped**; **plop·ping** [imit.] *vi* **1 :** to fall, drop, or move suddenly with a sound like that of something dropping into water **2 :** to allow the body to drop heavily ~ *vt* **:** to set, drop, or throw heavily — **plop** *n*

plo·sion \'plō-zhən\ *n* **:** EXPLOSION 2 — **plo·sive** \'plō-siv, -ziv\ *adj or n*

¹**plot** \'plät\ *n* [ME, fr. OE] **1 a :** a small area of planted ground **b :** a measured piece of land **:** LOT **2 :** GROUND PLAN, PLAT **3 :** the plan or main story of a literary work **4 :** a secret plan for accomplishing a usu. evil or unlawful end **:** INTRIGUE **5 :** a graphic representation (as a chart)

syn PLOT, INTRIGUE, MACHINATION, CONSPIRACY, CABAL mean a plan secretly devised to accomplish an evil or treacherous end. PLOT implies careful foresight in planning positive action; INTRIGUE suggests secret underhand maneuvering in an atmosphere of duplicity; MACHINATION implies a contriving of annoyances, injuries, or evils by indirect means; CONSPIRACY implies a secret agreement among many persons not necessarily for positive action; CABAL implies a political intrigue involving persons of some eminence **syn** see in addition PLAN

²**plot** *vb* **plot·ted**; **plot·ting** *vt* **1 a :** to make a plot, map, or plan of **b :** to mark or note on or as if on a map or chart **2 :** to lay out in plots **3 a :** to locate (a point) by means of coordinates **b :** to locate (a curve) by plotted points **c :** to represent (an equation) by means of a curve so constructed **4 :** to plan or contrive esp. secretly ~ *vi* **:** to form a plot **:** CONSPIRE, SCHEME **syn** see ¹PLAN — **plot·ter** *n*

Plo·ti·nism \plō-'tī-,niz-əm\ *n* **:** the Neoplatonic doctrines of the philosopher Plotinus — **Plo·ti·nist** \-nəst\ *n*

plot·tage \'plät-ij\ *n* **:** the area included in a plot of land

plotting board *n* **:** a device for showing graphically the position of a stationary target or the periodic positions of a moving target with reference to a battery in artillery firing

plo·ver \'pləv-ər, 'plō-vər\ *n, pl* **plover** *or* **plovers** [ME, fr. MF, fr. (assumed) VL *pluviarius*, fr. L *pluvia* rain — more at PLUVIAL] **1 :** any of numerous shore-inhabiting birds (family Charadriidae) that differ from the sandpipers in the short, hard-tipped bill and usu. a stouter, more compact build **2 :** any of various birds (as a turnstone or sandpiper) related to the plovers

¹**plow** *or* **plough** \'plau̇\ *n* [ME, plow, plowland, fr. OE *plōh* plowland; akin to OHG *pfluog* plow] **1 :** an implement used to cut, lift, and turn over soil esp. in preparing a seedbed **2 :** any of various devices operating like a plow

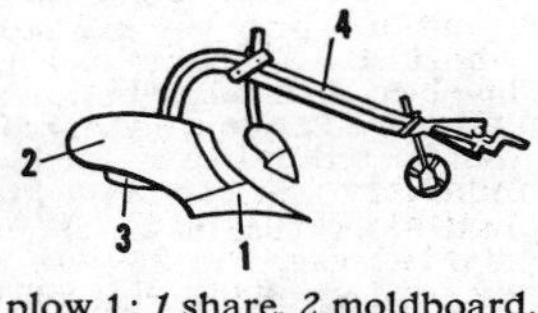

plow 1: *1* share, *2* moldboard, *3* landside, *4* beam

2plow *or* **plough** *vt* **1 a :** to turn, break up, or work with a plow **b :** to make (as a furrow) with a plow **2 :** to cut into, open, or make furrows or ridges in with a plow — often used with *up* **3 :** to cleave the surface of or move through (water) ~ *vi* **1 a :** to use a plow **b :** to bear or admit of plowing **2 a :** to move in a way resembling that of a plow cutting into or going through the soil **b :** to proceed steadily and laboriously **:** PLOD — **plow·boy** \-,bȯi\ *n* — **plow·er** \'plaů-(ə)r\ *n* — **plow·man** \'plaů-mən, -,man\ *n*
plow·able \'plaů-ə-bəl\ *adj* **:** capable of being plowed
plow back *vt* **:** to retain (profits) for reinvestment in a business
plow·head \'plaů-,hed\ *n* **:** the clevis of a plow
plow·share \'plaů-,she(ə)r, -,sha(ə)r\ *n* [ME *ploughshare*, fr. *plough* plow + *schare* plowshare — more at SHARE] **:** the part of a moldboard plow that cuts the furrow
plow sole *n* **:** a layer of earth at the bottom of the furrow compacted by repeated plowing at the same depth
plow·staff \-,staf\ *n* **:** a spade or paddle for cleaning the plowshare
plow under *vt* **:** to cause to disappear **:** BURY, OVERWHELM
ploy \'plȯi\ *n* [prob. fr. *employ*] **1 :** ESCAPADE, FROLIC **2 :** a tactic intended to embarrass or frustrate an opponent
1pluck \'plək\ *vb* [ME *plucken*, fr. OE *pluccian;* akin to MHG *pflücken* to pluck] *vt* **1 :** to pull or pick off or out **2 a :** to remove something (as hairs) from, by, or as if by plucking **b :** ROB, FLEECE **3 :** to move or separate forcibly **4 :** to pick, pull, or grasp at; *also* **:** to play (an instrument) in this manner ~ *vi* **:** to make a sharp pull or twitch **:** TUG — **pluck·er** *n*
2pluck *n* **1 :** an act or instance of plucking or pulling **2 :** the heart, liver, lungs and windpipe of a slaughtered animal esp. as an item of food **3 :** SPIRIT, COURAGE, RESOLUTION **syn** see FORTITUDE
pluck·i·ly \'plək-ə-lē\ *adv* **:** in a plucky manner
pluck·i·ness \'plək-ē-nəs\ *n* **:** the quality or state of being plucky
plucky \'plək-ē\ *adj* **:** COURAGEOUS, SPIRITED
1plug \'pləg\ *n* [D, fr. MD *plugge;* akin to MHG *pfloc* plug] **1 a :** a piece used to fill a hole **:** STOPPER **b :** an obtruding or obstructing mass of material resembling a stopper **2 :** a flat compressed cake of tobacco **3 :** SHOT **4 :** a small core or segment removed from a larger object **5 :** something inferior; *esp* **:** an inferior often aged or unsound horse; *also* **:** a quiet steady cold-blooded horse usu. of light or moderate weight **6 a :** FIREPLUG **b :** SPARK PLUG **7 :** an artificial angling lure used primarily for casting and made with one or more sets of gang hooks **8 :** any of various devices resembling or functioning like a plug: as **a :** a male fitting for making an electrical connection by insertion in a receptacle or body of electrical equipment to a circuit **b :** a device for connecting electric wires to a jack **9 :** a piece of favorable publicity usu. incorporated in general matter
2plug *vb* **plugged; plug·ging** *vt* **1 :** to stop, make tight, or secure by inserting a plug **2 :** to hit with a bullet **:** SHOOT **3 :** to advertise or publicize insistently ~ *vi* **1 :** to become plugged — usu. used with *up* **2 :** to work doggedly and persistently **3 :** to fire shots — **plug·ger** *n*
plugged \'pləgd\ *adj* **1 :** BLOCKED, OBSTRUCTED **2** *of a coin* **:** altered by the insertion of a plug of base metal
plug hat *n* **:** a man's stiff hat (as a bowler or top hat)
plug in *vi* **:** to establish an electric circuit by inserting a plug ~ *vt* **:** to attach or connect (as an electrical device) to a service outlet
plug–ug·ly \'pləg-,əg-lē\ *n* **:** THUG, TOUGH; *esp* **:** one hired to intimidate
plum \'pləm\ *n* [ME, fr. OE *plūme;* akin to OHG *pflūmo* plum tree; both fr. a prehistoric WGmc word borrowed fr. L *prunum* plum, fr. Gk *proumnon*] **1 a :** any of numerous trees and shrubs (genus *Prunus*) with globular to oval smooth-skinned fruits which are drupes with oblong seeds **b :** the edible fruit of a plum **2 :** any of various trees with edible fruits resembling plums; *also* **:** its fruit **3 a :** a raisin when used in puddings or other dishes **b :** SUGARPLUM **4 :** something excellent or superior; *esp* **:** something given as recompense for service **5 :** a variable color averaging a dark reddish purple
plum·age \'plü-mij\ *n* **:** the entire clothing of feathers of a bird
plu·mate \'plü-,māt\ *adj* **:** having a main shaft that bears small filaments ⟨~ antennae of an insect⟩
1plumb \'pləm\ *n* [ME, fr. (assumed) OF *plomb*, fr. OF *plon* lead, fr. L *plumbum*] **1 :** a lead weight attached to a line and used to indicate a vertical direction **2 :** a lead or other weight — **out of plumb** *or* **off plumb :** out of vertical or true
2plumb *adv* **1 :** straight down or up **:** VERTICALLY **2 :** DIRECTLY, EXACTLY; *also* **:** IMMEDIATELY **3** *chiefly dial* **:** COMPLETELY, ABSOLUTELY
3plumb *vb* [back-formation fr. *plumber*] *vt* **1 :** to weight with lead **2 a :** to measure the depth of with a plumb **b :** to examine minutely and critically **3 :** to adjust or test by a plumb line **4 :** to seal with lead **5 :** to supply with or install as plumbing ~ *vi* **:** to work as a plumber
4plumb *adj* **1 :** exactly vertical or true **2 :** DOWNRIGHT, COMPLETE **syn** see VERTICAL
plumb- *or* **plumbo-** *comb form* [L *plumb-*, fr. *plumbum*] **:** lead ⟨*plumbism*⟩
plum·bag·i·nous \,pləm-'baj-ə-nəs\ *adj* **:** resembling, consisting of, or containing graphite
plum·ba·go \,pləm-'bā-(,)gō\ *n* [L *plumbagin-, plumbago* galena, leadwort, fr. *plumbum*] **1 :** GRAPHITE **2** [NL, genus name, fr. L] **:** any of a genus (*Plumbago* of the family Plumbaginaceae, the plumbago family) of woody chiefly tropical plants with alternate leaves and spikes of showy flowers
plumb bob *n* **:** the metal bob of a plumb line
plum·be·ous \'pləm-bē-əs\ *adj* [L *plumbeus*, fr. *plumbum*] **:** consisting of or resembling lead **:** LEADEN
plumb·er \'pləm-ər\ *n* **1** *obs* **:** a dealer or worker in lead **2 :** one who installs, repairs, and maintains piping, fittings, and fixtures involved in the distribution and use of water in a building
plumber's snake *n* **:** a long flexible rod or cable usu. of spring steel that is used to free clogged pipes
plumb·ery \'pləm-ə-rē\ *n* **:** the business or work of a plumber
plum·bic \'pləm-bik\ *adj* **:** of, relating to, or containing lead and esp. tetravalent lead
plum·bif·er·ous \,pləm-'bif-(ə-)rəs\ *adj* **:** containing lead
plumb·ing \'pləm-iŋ\ *n* **1 :** the act of using a plumb **2 :** a plumber's occupation or trade **3 :** the pipes, fixtures, and other apparatus concerned in the distribution and use of water in a building
plum·bism \'pləm-,biz-əm\ *n* **:** lead poisoning esp. when chronic
plumb line *n* **1 :** a line or cord having at one end a weight (as a plumb bob) and serving to determine verticality **2 :** a line directed to the center of gravity of the earth **:** a vertical line **3 :** a sounding line
plum·bous \'pləm-bəs\ *adj* **:** of, relating to, or containing lead and esp. bivalent lead
plumb rule *n* **:** a narrow board with a plumb and bob used esp. by builders and carpenters
1plume \'plüm\ *n* [ME, fr. MF, fr. L *pluma* small soft feather — more at FLEECE] **1 :** a feather of a bird: as **a :** a large conspicuous or showy feather **b :** CONTOUR FEATHER **c :** PLUMAGE **d :** a cluster of distinctive feathers **2 a :** a feather, cluster of feathers, tuft of hair, or similar matter worn as an ornament **b :** a token of honor or prowess **:** PRIZE **3 a :** a plumose appendage of a plant **b :** a plumate animal structure; *esp* **:** a full bushy tail
2plume *vt* **1 a :** to provide or deck with feathers **b :** to array showily **2 :** to indulge (oneself) in pride **:** CONGRATULATE **3 a :** to dress the feathers of (itself) — used of a bird **b :** to preen and arrange (feathers)
plume·let \'plüm-lət\ *n* **:** a small tuft or plume
plum·like \'pləm-,līk\ *adj* **:** resembling a plum and esp. a plum fruit
1plum·met \'pləm-ət\ *n* [ME *plomet*, fr. MF *plombet* ball of lead, fr. *plomb* lead, fr. (assumed) OF — more at PLUMB] **:** PLUMB BOB; *also* **:** PLUMB LINE
2plummet *vi* **1 :** to fall perpendicularly **2 :** to drop sharply and abruptly
plu·mose \'plü-,mōs\ *adj* **1 :** having feathers or plumes **:** FEATHERED **2 :** PLUMATE, FEATHERY — **plu·mose·ly** *adv*
1plump \'pləmp\ *vb* [ME *plumpen*, of imit. origin] *vi* **1 :** to drop, sink, or come in contact suddenly or heavily **2 :** to favor someone or something strongly — used with *for* ~ *vt* **1 :** to drop, cast, or place suddenly or heavily **2 :** to give support and favorable publicity to
2plump *adv* **1 :** with a sudden or heavy drop **2 a :** straight down **b :** straight ahead **3 :** FLATLY, UNQUALIFIEDLY
3plump *n* **:** a sudden plunge, fall, or blow; *also* **:** the sound made by such an act
4plump *n* [ME *plumpe*] *chiefly dial* **:** GROUP, FLOCK
5plump *adj* [ME, dull, blunt] **1 :** having a full rounded usu. pleasing form **2 :** AMPLE
6plump *vt* **:** to make plump ~ *vi* **:** to become plump
1plump·er \'pləm-pər\ *n* **:** an object carried in the mouth to fill out the cheeks
2plumper *n* [¹*plump*] *chiefly Brit* **:** a vote for only one candidate when two or more are to be elected to the same office
plump·ish \'pləm-pish\ *adj* **:** somewhat plump **:** moderately stout
1plump·ly \'pləm-plē\ *adv* **:** in a plump way
2plumply *adv* **:** in a wholehearted manner and without hesitation or circumlocution **:** FORTHRIGHTLY
1plump·ness \'pləmp-nəs\ *n* **:** the quality or state of being plump
2plumpness *n* **:** FORTHRIGHTNESS
plum pudding *n* **:** a boiled or steamed pudding of flour or bread crumbs, raisins, currants, and other fruits, suet, eggs, and spices and other flavoring matters
plu·mu·late \'plü-myə-,lāt\ *adj* [L *plumula*, dim. of *pluma*] **:** finely plumose
plu·mule \'plü-(,)myü(ə)l\ *n* [NL *plumula*, fr. L] **1 :** the primary bud of a plant embryo usu. situated at the apex of the hypocotyl and consisting of leaves and an epicotyl **2 :** a down feather — **plu·mu·lose** \'plü-myə-,lōs\ *adj*

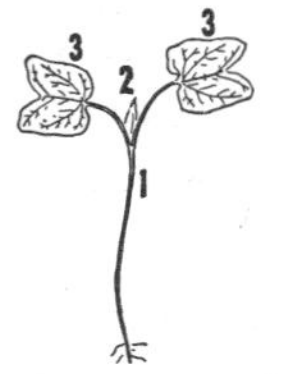

plumule of morning-glory seedling: *1* hypocotyl; *2* plumule; *3, 3* cotyledons

plumy \'plü-mē\ *adj* **1 :** DOWNY **2 :** having or resembling plumes
1plun·der \'plən-dər\ *vb* **plun·der·ing** \-d(ə-)riŋ\ [G *plündern*] *vt* **1 :** PILLAGE, SACK **2 :** to take by force or wrongfully **:** STEAL ~ *vi* **:** to commit robbery or looting — **plun·der·er** \-dər-ər\ *n*
2plunder *n* **1 :** an act of plundering **:** PILLAGING **2 :** something taken by force, theft, or fraud **:** LOOT **3** *chiefly dial* **:** personal or household effects **syn** see SPOIL
plun·der·able \'plən-d(ə-)rə-bəl\ *adj* **:** capable of being plundered **:** worth plundering **:** subject to plunder
plun·der·age \-d(ə-)rij\ *n* **1 :** an act or instance of plundering; *esp* **:** embezzlement of goods on shipboard **2 :** property obtained by plunderage
plun·der·ous \-d(ə-)rəs\ *adj* **:** given to or characterized by plundering
1plunge \'plənj\ *vb* [ME *plungen*, fr. MF *plonger*, fr. (assumed) VL *plumbicare*, fr. L *plumbum* lead — more at PLUMB] *vt* **1 a :** to cause to penetrate or enter quickly and forcibly into something **b :** to sink (a potted plant) in the ground or a prepared bed **2 :** to cause to enter a state or course of action usu. suddenly, unexpectedly, or violently ~ *vi* **1 :** to thrust or cast oneself into or as if into water **2 a :** to become pitched or thrown headlong or violently forward and downward **b :** to act with reckless haste **:** enter suddenly or unexpectedly **c :** to bet or gamble heavily and recklessly **3 :** to descend or dip suddenly
2plunge *n* **:** an act or instance of plunging (as a swim)
plung·er \'plən-jər\ *n* **:** one that plunges: as **a :** DIVER **b :** a reckless gambler or speculator **c :** the rod carrying the valves in the inner assembly of an automobile tire valve unit **d** (1) **:** a sliding reciprocating piece driven by or against fluid pressure; *esp* **:** PISTON (2) **:** a piece with a motion more or less like that of a ram or piston **e :** a rubber suction cup on a handle used to free plumbing traps and waste outlets of obstructions
plunging fire *n* **:** direct fire from a superior elevation resulting in the projectiles striking the target at a high angle
plunk \'pləŋk\ *vb* [imit.] *vt* **1 :** to pluck or hit so as to produce a quick, hollow, metallic, or harsh sound **2 :** to set down suddenly **:** PLUMP ~ *vi* **1 :** to make a plunking sound **2 :** to drop abruptly **:** DIVE **3 :** to come out in favor of someone or something — used with *for* — **plunk** *n* — **plunk·er** *n*
plu·per·fect \(')plü-'pər-fikt\ *adj* [modif. of LL *plusquamperfectus*, lit., more than perfect] **:** past perfect — **pluperfect** *n*
plu·ral \'plůr-əl\ *adj* [ME, fr. MF & L; MF *plurel*, fr. L *pluralis*, fr. *plur-, plus* more] **1 :** of, relating to, or constituting a class of

grammatical forms used to denote more than one or in some languages more than two **2 :** relating to or consisting of or containing more than one or more than one kind or class — **plural** *n* — **plu·ral·ly** \-ə-lē\ *adv*

plu·ral·ism \ˈplu̇r-ə-ˌliz-əm\ *n* **1 :** the quality or state of being plural **2 a :** the holding by one person of two or more offices or positions at the same time **b :** PLURALITY 2a **3 a :** a theory that there are more than one or more than two kinds of ultimate reality **b :** a theory that reality is composed of a plurality of entities **4 a :** a state of society in which members of diverse ethnic, racial, religious, or social groups maintain an autonomous participation in and development of their traditional culture or special interest within the confines of a common civilization **b :** a concept, doctrine, or policy advocating this state — **plu·ral·ist** \-ləst\ *n* — **plu·ral·is·tic** \ˌplu̇r-ə-ˈlis-tik\ *adj*

plu·ral·i·ty \plu̇-ˈral-ət-ē\ *n* **1 a :** the state of being plural **b :** the state of being numerous **c :** MULTITUDE **2 a :** the holding by one person of two or more benefices at one time **b :** any of the benefices so held **c :** PLURALISM 2a **3 a :** a number greater than another **b :** an excess of votes over those cast for an opposing candidate **c :** a number of votes cast for a candidate in a contest of more than two candidates that is greater than the number cast for any other candidate but not more than half the total votes cast

plu·ral·iza·tion \ˌplu̇r-ə-lə-ˈzā-shən\ *n* **:** the act or process of pluralizing

plu·ral·ize \ˈplu̇r-ə-ˌlīz\ *vt* **:** to make plural or express in the plural form

pluri- *comb form* [L, fr. *plur-, plus*] **:** having or being more than one **:** MULTI- ⟨*pluri*axial⟩

plu·ri·ax·i·al \ˌplu̇r-ē-ˈak-sē-əl, ˌplu̇(ə)r-ˌī-\ *adj* **:** having more than one axis; *specif* **:** having flowers developed on secondary shoots

1plus \ˈpləs\ *prep* [L, adv., more, fr. neut. of *plur-, plus*, adj., more; akin to Gk *pleiōn* more, L *plenus* full — more at FULL] **1 :** increased by **:** with the addition of ⟨four ~ five⟩ ⟨the debt ~ interest⟩ **2 :** having gained **:** WITH

2plus *n* **1 :** an added quantity **2 :** a positive factor or quality **:** ADVANTAGE **3 :** SURPLUS

3plus *adj* **1 a :** requiring addition **b :** algebraically positive **2 :** having, receiving, or being in addition to what is anticipated **3 a :** falling high in a specified range ⟨a grade of C ~⟩ **b :** greater than that specified **c :** possessing a specified quality to a high degree **4 :** electrically positive

plus fours *n pl* **:** loose sports knickers made four inches longer than ordinary knickers

1plush \ˈpləsh\ *n* [MF *peluche*] **:** a fabric with an even pile longer and less dense than velvet pile — **plushy** \-ē\ *adj*

2plush *adj* **1 :** relating to, resembling, or made of plush **2 :** notably luxurious

plush·ly \ˈpləsh-lē\ *adv* **:** LUXURIOUSLY

plus·sage \ˈpləs-ij\ *n* **:** amount over and above another

plus sign *n* **:** a sign + denoting addition or a positive quantity

Plu·to \ˈplüt-(ˌ)ō\ *n* [L *Pluton-, Pluto*, fr. Gk *Ploutōn*] **1 :** the god of the dead and the lower world in classical mythology **2** [NL] **:** the planet most remote from the sun — see PLANET table

plu·toc·ra·cy \plü-ˈtäk-rə-sē\ *n* [Gk *ploutokratia*, fr. *ploutos* wealth] **1 :** government by the wealthy **2 :** a controlling class of rich men — **plu·to·crat** \ˈplüt-ə-ˌkrat\ *n* — **plu·to·crat·ic** \ˌplüt-ə-ˈkrat-ik\ *adj* — **plu·to·crat·i·cal·ly** \-i-k(ə-)lē\ *adv*

plu·to·ni·an \plü-ˈtō-nē-ən\ *adj, often cap* **1 :** of, relating to, or characteristic of Pluto or the lower world **:** INFERNAL **2 :** of or relating to the planet Pluto

plu·ton·ic \plü-ˈtän-ik\ *adj* **1 :** formed by solidification of a molten magma deep within the earth and crystalline throughout ⟨~ rock⟩ **2** *often cap* **:** PLUTONIAN

plu·to·ni·um \plü-ˈtō-nē-əm\ *n* [NL, fr. *Pluton-, Pluto*, the planet Pluto] **:** a radioactive metallic element similar chemically to uranium that is formed as the isotope 239 by decay of neptunium and found in minute quantities in pitchblende, that undergoes slow disintegration with the emission of a helium nucleus to form uranium 235, and that is fissionable with slow neutrons to yield atomic energy — see ELEMENT table

Plu·tus \ˈplüt-əs\ *n* [L, fr. Gk *Ploutos*] **:** the god of wealth in Greek mythology

plu·vi·al \ˈplü-vē-əl\ *adj* [L *pluvialis*, fr. *pluvia* rain, fr. fem. of *pluvius* rainy, fr. *pluere* to rain — more at FLOW] **1 a :** of or relating to rain **b :** characterized by abundant rain **2** *of a geologic change* **:** resulting from the action of rain

plu·vi·an \-vē-ən\ *adj* **:** RAINY

plu·vi·om·e·ter \ˌplü-vē-ˈäm-ət-ər\ *n* [prob. fr. F *pluviomètre*, fr. L *pluvia* + F *-mètre* -meter] **:** RAIN GAUGE — **plu·vio·met·ric** \ˌplü-vē-ə-ˈme-trik\ *adj* — **plu·vi·om·e·try** \-vē-ˈäm-ə-trē\ *n*

plu·vi·ose \ˈplü-vē-ˌōs\ *adj* [L *pluviosus*] **:** marked by or regularly receiving heavy rainfall — **plu·vi·os·i·ty** \ˌplü-vē-ˈäs-ət-ē\ *n*

plu·vi·ous \-vē-əs\ *adj* [ME *pluvyous*, fr. L *pluviosus*, fr. *pluvia* rain] **:** of or relating to rain **:** RAINY

1ply \ˈplī\ *vt* **plied; ply·ing** [ME *plien* to fold, fr. MF *plier*, fr. L *plicare*; akin to OHG *flehtan* to braid, L *plectere*, Gk *plekein*] **:** to twist together ⟨~ two single yarns⟩

2ply *n* **1 a :** one of the strands in a yarn **b :** one of several layers of cloth usu. sewn or laminated together **c :** one of the veneer sheets forming plywood **d :** a layer of a paper or paperboard **2 :** INCLINATION, BIAS

3ply *vb* **plied; ply·ing** [ME *plien*, short for *applien* to apply] *vt* **1 a :** to use or wield diligently **b :** to practice or perform diligently **2 :** to keep furnishing or supplying to **3 :** to make a practice of rowing or sailing over or on ~ *vi* **1 :** to apply oneself steadily **2 :** to go or travel regularly

Plym·outh Rock \ˌplim-əth-\ *n* [fr. *Plymouth Rock*, on which the Pilgrims are supposed to have landed in 1620] **:** any of an American breed of medium-sized single-combed dual-purpose domestic fowls

ply·wood \ˈplī-ˌwu̇d\ *n* **:** a structural material consisting of sheets of wood glued or cemented together with the grains of adjacent layers arranged at right angles or at a wide angle

-pnea *or* **-pnoea** \(p)-(ˈ)nē-ə\ *n comb form* [NL, fr. Gk *-pnoia*, fr. *pnoia*, fr. *pnein* to breathe] **:** breath **:** breathing ⟨hyper*pnea*⟩ ⟨*apnoea*⟩

pneum- *or* **pneumo-** *comb form* [NL, fr. Gk *pneum-*, fr. *pneuma*] **1 :** air **:** gas ⟨*pneumo*thorax⟩ **2 :** lung ⟨*pneum*ectomy⟩ **:** pulmonary and ⟨*pneumo*gastric⟩ **3 :** respiration ⟨*pneumo*graph⟩ **4 :** pneumonia ⟨*pneumo*coccus⟩

pneu·ma \ˈn(y)ü-mə\ *n* [Gk] **:** SOUL, SPIRIT

pneumat- *or* **pneumato-** *comb form* [Gk, fr. *pneumat-, pneuma*] **1 :** air **:** vapor **:** gas ⟨*pneumat*ics⟩ **2 :** respiration ⟨*pneumato*meter⟩

pneu·mat·ic \n(y)u̇-ˈmat-ik\ *adj* [L *pneumaticus*, fr. Gk *pneumatikos*, fr. *pneumat-, pneuma* air, breath, spirit, fr. *pnein* to breathe — more at SNEEZE] **1 :** of, relating to, or using air, wind, or other gas: **a :** moved or worked by air pressure **b** (1) **:** adapted for holding or inflated with compressed air (2) **:** having air-filled cavities **2 :** SPIRITUAL — **pneu·mat·i·cal·ly** \-i-k(ə-)lē\ *adv*

pneu·ma·tic·i·ty \ˌn(y)ü-mə-ˈtis-ət-ē\ *n* **:** a condition marked by presence of air cavities

pneu·mat·ics \n(y)u̇-ˈmat-iks\ *n pl but sing in constr* **:** a branch of mechanics that deals with the mechanical properties of gases

pneu·ma·tol·o·gy \ˌn(y)ü-mə-ˈtäl-ə-jē\ *n* [NL *pneumatologia*, fr. Gk *pneumat-, pneuma* + NL *-logia* -logy] **:** the study of spiritual beings or phenomena

pneu·ma·tol·y·sis \-ˈtäl-ə-səs\ *n* [NL] **:** the process by which pneumatolytic minerals are formed

pneu·ma·to·lyt·ic \ˌn(y)ü-mət-ᵊl-ˈit-ik, n(y)u̇-ˌmat-ᵊl-ˈit-\ *adj* [ISV] **:** formed or forming by hot vapors or superheated liquids under pressure — used esp. of minerals and ores

pneu·ma·tom·e·ter \ˌn(y)ü-mə-ˈtäm-ət-ər\ *n* **1 :** an instrument for measuring the amount of force exerted by the lungs in respiration **2 :** SPIROMETER

pneu·mato·phore \n(y)u̇-ˈmat-ə-ˌfō(ə)r, -ˌfȯ(ə)r\ *n* [ISV] **1 :** a muscular gas-containing sac that serves as a float on a siphonophore colony **2 :** a root often functioning as a respiratory organ in a marsh plant — **pneu·mato·phor·ic** \n(y)u̇-ˌmat-ə-ˈfȯr-ik, -ˈfär-\ *adj*

pneu·mec·to·my \n(y)u̇-ˈmek-tə-mē\ *n* [ISV] **:** the surgical removal of lung tissue

pneu·mo·ba·cil·lus \ˌn(y)ü-mō-bə-ˈsil-əs\ *n* [NL] **:** a bacterium (*Klebsiella pneumoniae*) associated with pneumonia and other inflammations of the respiratory tract

pneu·mo·coc·cal \ˌn(y)ü-mə-ˈkäk-əl\ *also* **pneu·mo·coc·cic** \-ˈkäk-(s)ik\ *adj* **:** of, caused by, or derived from pneumococci

pneu·mo·coc·cus \-ˈkäk-əs\ *n* [NL] **:** a bacterium (*Diplococcus pneumoniae*) that causes lobar pneumonia

pneu·mo·co·ni·o·sis \-ˌkō-nē-ˈō-səs\ *n* [NL, fr. *pneum-* + Gk *konis* dust — more at INCINERATE] **:** a disease of the lungs caused by the habitual inhalation of irritant mineral or metallic particles

pneu·mo·gas·tric \-ˈgas-trik\ *adj* **1 :** of or relating to the lungs and the stomach **2 :** VAGAL

pneu·mo·graph \ˈn(y)ü-mə-ˌgraf\ *n* [ISV] **:** an instrument for recording the thoracic movements or volume change during respiration

pneu·mo·nec·to·my \ˌn(y)ü-mə-ˈnek-tə-mē\ *n* [Gk *pneumōn* + ISV *-ectomy*] **:** excision of lung or of one or more lobes of a lung

pneu·mo·nia \n(y)u̇-ˈmō-nyə\ *n* [NL, fr. Gk, fr. *pneumōn* lung, alter. of *pleumōn* — more at PULMONARY] **:** a disease of the lungs characterized by inflammation and consolidation followed by resolution and caused by infection or irritants

pneu·mon·ic \n(y)u̇-ˈmän-ik\ *adj* [NL *pneumonicus*, fr. Gk *pneumonikos*, fr. *pneumōn*] **1 :** of or relating to the lungs **:** PULMONIC **2 :** of, relating to, or affected with pneumonia

pneu·mo·no·ul·tra·mi·cro·scop·ic·sil·i·co·vol·ca·no·co·ni·o·sis \ˈn(y)ü-mə-(ˌ)nō-ˌəl-trə-ˌmī-krə-ˈskäp-ik-ˈsil-i-(ˌ)kō-(ˌ)väl-ˈkā-nō-ˌkō-nē-ˈō-səs\ *n* [NL, fr. Gk *pneumōn* + ISV *ultramicroscopic* + NL *silicon* + ISV *volcano* + Gk *konis* dust] **:** a pneumoconiosis caused by the inhalation of very fine silicate or quartz dust

pneu·mo·tho·rax \ˌn(y)ü-mə-ˈthō(ə)r-ˌaks, -ˈthȯ(ə)r-\ *n* [NL] **:** a state in which air or other gas is present in the pleural cavity and which occurs spontaneously as a result of disease or injury of lung tissue or puncture of the chest wall or is induced as a therapeutic measure to collapse the lung

pneu·mo·trop·ic \ˌn(y)ü-mə-ˈträp-ik\ *adj* **:** turning, directed toward, or having an affinity for lung tissues — used esp. of infective agents — **pneu·mot·ro·pism** \n(y)u̇-ˈmä-trə-ˌpiz-əm\ *n*

1poach \ˈpōch\ *vt* [ME *pochen*, fr. MF *pocher*, fr. OF *pochier*, lit., to put into a bag, fr. *poche* bag, pocket, of Gmc origin; akin to OE *pocca* bag — more at POKE] **:** to cook in simmering liquid ⟨~*ed* egg⟩

2poach *vb* [MF *pocher*, of Gmc origin; akin to ME *poken* to poke] *vt* **1 :** to trample or cut up (as sod) with or as if with hoofs **2 a :** to trespass on **b :** to take (game or fish) by illegal methods ~ *vi* **1 a :** to sink into mud or mire while walking **b :** to become soft or muddy and full of holes when trampled on **2 :** to trespass for the purpose of stealing game; *also* **:** to take game or fish illegally — **poach·er** *n*

po·chard \ˈpō-chərd\ *n* [origin unknown] **:** any of numerous rather heavy-bodied diving ducks (esp. genus *Aythya*) with large head and feet and legs placed far back under the body

1pock \ˈpäk\ *n* [ME *pokke*, fr. OE *pocc*; akin to MLG & MD *pocke* pock, L *bucca* cheek, mouth] **:** a pustule in an eruptive disease (as smallpox); *also* **:** a spot suggesting such a pustule

2pock *vt* **:** to mark with pocks **:** PIT

1pock·et \ˈpäk-ət\ *n* [ME *poket*, fr. ONF *pokete*, dim. of *poke* bag, of Gmc origin; akin to OE *pocca* bag] **1 a :** a small bag carried by a person **:** PURSE **b :** a small bag open at the top or side inserted in a garment **2 :** supply of money **:** MEANS **3 :** RECEPTACLE, CONTAINER: as **a :** a bag at the corner or side of a billiard table **b :** a superficial pouch in some animals **4 :** a small isolated area or group: **a** (1) **:** a cavity containing a deposit (as of gold or water) (2) **:** a small body of ore **b :** AIR HOLE **5 :** a place for a spar made by sewing a strip of canvas on a sail **6 a :** BLIND ALLEY **b :** the position of a contestant in a race hemmed in by others

2pocket *vt* **1 a :** to put or enclose in or as if in one's pocket **b :** to appropriate to one's own use **:** STEAL **c :** to veto (a bill) by retaining it unsigned until after a legislature has adjourned **2 :** to put up with **:** ACCEPT **3 :** to set aside **:** SUPPRESS **4 a :** to hem in **b :** to drive (a ball) into a pocket of a pool table **5 :** to cover or supply with pockets

3pocket *adj* **1 a :** small enough to be carried in the pocket **b :** SMALL, MINIATURE **2 :** MONETARY **3 :** carried in or paid from one's own pocket in or for small cash outlays

pocket battleship *n* **:** a small battleship built so as to come within treaty limitations of tonnage and armament
pocket billiards *n pl but usu sing in constr* **:** POOL 2b
pock·et·book \'päk-ət-,bu̇k\ *n* **1** *usu* **pocket book :** a small esp. paperback book that can be carried in the pocket **2 a** (1) **:** a pocket-size container for money and personal papers **:** WALLET (2) **:** PURSE **b :** HANDBAG 2 **3 a :** financial resources **:** INCOME **b :** economic interests
pocket borough *n* **:** an English constituency controlled before parliamentary reform by a single person or family
pocket edition *n* **1 :** POCKETBOOK 1 **2 :** a miniature form of something
pock·et·ful \'päk-ət-,fu̇l\ *n, pl* **pocketfuls** \-,fu̇lz\ *or* **pock·ets·ful** \-əts-,fu̇l\ **:** as much or as many as the pocket will contain
pock·et–hand·ker·chief \,päk-ət-'haŋ-kər-chəf, -(,)chif, -,chēf\ *n* **1 :** a handkerchief carried in the pocket **2 :** something tiny
pock·et·knife \'päk-ət-,nīf\ *n* **:** a knife with a folding blade to be carried in the pocket
pocket money *n* **:** money for small personal expenses
pocket mouse *n* **:** any of various nocturnal burrowing rodents (family Heteromyidae) resembling mice of arid parts of western No. America that have long hind legs and tail and fur-lined cheek pouches
pocket rat *n* **:** any of various rodents with cheek pouches
pocket veto *n* **:** an indirect veto of a legislative bill by an executive through retention of the bill unsigned until after adjournment of the legislature
pock·mark \'päk-,märk\ *n* **:** a mark, pit, or depressed scar caused by smallpox — **pockmark** *vt*
pocky \'päk-ē\ *adj* **1 :** covered with pocks; *specif* **:** SYPHILITIC **2 :** relating to or being a pock or the pox
po·co \,pō-(,)kō, ,pȯ-\ *adv* [It, little, fr. L *paucus* — more at FEW] **:** SOMEWHAT — used to qualify a direction in music
po·co a po·co \,pō-kō-(,)ä-'pō-(,)kō, ,pȯ-kō-(,)ä-'pȯ-(,)kō\ *adv* [It] **:** little by little **:** GRADUALLY — used as a direction in music
po·co·cu·ran·te \,pō-kō-k(y)u̇-'rant-ē\ *adj* [It *poco curante* caring little] **:** INDIFFERENT, NONCHALANT — **po·co·cu·ran·tism** \-'ran-,tiz-əm\ *n*
po·co·sin \pə-'kōs-ᵊn\ *n* [Delaware *pâkwesen*] **:** an upland swamp of the coastal plain of the southeastern U.S.
¹**pod** \'päd\ *n* [origin unknown] **1 :** a bit socket in a brace **2 :** a straight groove or channel in the barrel of an auger
²**pod** *n* [prob. alter. of *cod* bag — more at CODPIECE] **1 :** a dry dehiscent seed vessel or fruit that is either monocarpellary or composed of two or more carpels; *esp* **:** LEGUME **2 a :** an anatomical pouch **b :** a grasshopper egg case **3 :** a number of animals (as seals) clustered together **4 :** a streamlined compartment under the wings or fuselage of an airplane used as a container (as for fuel) **5 :** a detachable compartment (as for personnel, a power unit, or an instrument) on a spacecraft
³**pod** *vi* **pod·ded; pod·ding :** to produce pods
-pod \,päd\ *n comb form* [Gk *-podos*, fr. *pod-*, *pous* foot — more at FOOT] **:** foot **:** part resembling a foot ⟨pleo*pod*⟩
-p·o·da \p-əd-ə\ *n pl comb form* [NL, fr. Gk, neut. pl. of *-podos*] **:** creatures having (such or so many) feet — in taxonomic names in zoology ⟨Arthro*poda*⟩ ⟨Deca*poda*⟩
po·dag·ra \pə-'dag-rə\ *n* [ME, fr. L, fr. Gk, fr. *pod-*, *pous* + *agra* hunt, catch; akin to L *agere* to drive — more at AGENT] **:** GOUT — **po·dag·ral** \-rəl\ *adj*
po·de·sta \,pōd-ə-'stä\ *n* [It *podestà*, lit., power, fr. L *potestat-*, *potestas*, irreg. fr. *potis* able — more at POTENT] **:** a chief magistrate in a medieval Italian municipality
podgy \'päj-ē\ *adj* [*podge* (something pudgy)] **:** PUDGY
po·di·a·trist \pə-'dī-ə-trəst, pō-\ *n* [*podiatry* + *-ist*] **:** CHIROPODIST
po·di·a·try \pə-'dī-ə-trē, pō-\ *n* [Gk *pod-*, *pous* + E *-iatry*] **:** CHIROPODY
pod·ite \'päd-,īt\ *n* [*-podite*] **:** a limb segment of an arthropod — **po·dit·ic** \pä-'dit-ik\ *adj*
-p·o·dite \p-ə-,dīt\ *n comb form* [ISV, fr. Gk *pod-*, *pous*] **:** podite ⟨endo*podite*⟩
po·di·um \'pōd-ē-əm\ *n, pl* **podiums** *or* **po·dia** \-ē-ə\ [L — more at PEW] **1 :** a low wall serving as a foundation or terrace wall: as **a :** one around the arena of an ancient amphitheater serving as a base for the tiers of seats **b :** the masonry under the stylobate of a temple **2 a :** a dais esp. for an orchestral conductor **b :** LECTERN
-po·di·um \'pōd-ē-əm\ *n comb form, pl* **-po·dia** \-ē-ə\ [NL, fr. Gk *podion*, dim. of *pod-*, *pous* foot — more at FOOT] **:** foot **:** part resembling a foot ⟨pseudo*podium*⟩
podo·phyl·lin \,päd-ə-'fil-ən\ *n* [ISV, fr. NL *Podophyllum*, genus of herbs] **:** a bitter irritant purgative resin obtained from the rhizome of the mayapple and used esp. as a cathartic
Po·dunk \'pō-,dəŋk\ *n* [*Podunk*, village in Mass. or locality in Conn.] **:** a small, unimportant, and isolated town
pod·zol \'päd-,zȯl\ *n* [Russ] **:** any of a group of zonal soils that develop in a moist climate esp. under coniferous or mixed forest and have an organic mat and a thin organic-mineral layer above a gray leached layer resting on a dark illuvial horizon enriched with amorphous clay — **pod·zol·ic** \päd-'zäl-ik, -'zȯl-\ *adj*
pod·zol·iza·tion \,päd-,zȯ-lə-'zā-shən\ *n* **:** a process of soil formation esp. in humid regions involving principally leaching of the upper layers with accumulation of material in lower layers and development of characteristic horizons; *specif* **:** the development of a podzol — **pod·zol·ize** \'päd-,zō-,līz\ *vb*
po·em \'pō-əm, -,em\ *n* [MF *poeme*, fr. L *poema*, fr. Gk *poiēma*, fr. *poiein*] **1 :** a composition in verse **2 :** a piece of poetry communicating to the reader the sense of a complete experience **3 :** a creation, experience, or object likened to a poem
po·esy \'pō-ə-zē, -sē\ *n* [ME *poesie*, fr. MF, fr. L *poesis*, fr. Gk *poiēsis*, lit., creation, fr. *poiein*] **1 a :** a poem or body of poems **b :** POETRY **2 :** poetic inspiration
po·et \'pō-ət\ *n* [ME, fr. OF *poete*, fr. L *poeta*, fr. Gk *poiētēs* maker, poet, fr. *poiein* to make, create; akin to Skt *cinoti* he heaps up] **1 :** one who writes poetry **2 :** a creative artist of great imaginative and expressive gifts and special sensitivity to his medium
po·et·as·ter \'pō-ət-,as-tər\ *n* [NL, fr. L *poeta*] **:** an inferior poet
po·et·ess \'pō-ət-əs\ *n* **:** a female poet
po·et·ic \pō-'et-ik\ *adj* **1 a :** of, relating to, or characteristic of poets or poetry **b :** given to writing poetry **2 :** written in verse
po·et·i·cal \-i-kəl\ *adj* **1 :** POETIC **2 :** beyond or above the truth of history or nature **:** IDEALIZED — **po·et·i·cal·ly** \-k(ə-)lē\ *adv*
po·et·i·cal·ness \-nəs\ *n* **:** poetic quality
po·et·i·cism \pō-'et-ə-,siz-əm\ *n* **:** an archaic, trite, or strained form of poetic expression
po·et·i·cize \pō-'et-ə-,sīz\ *vt* **:** to give a poetic quality to
poetic justice *n* **:** an outcome in which vice is punished and virtue rewarded usu. in a manner peculiarly or ironically appropriate
po·et·ics \pō-'et-iks\ *n pl but sing or pl in constr* **1 a :** a treatise on poetry or aesthetics **b :** poetic theory or practice **2 :** poetic feelings or utterances
po·et·ize \'pō-ət-,īz\ *vi* **:** to compose poetry ~ *vt* **:** POETICIZE — **po·et·iz·er** *n*
poet laureate *n, pl* **poets laureate** *or* **poet laureates 1 :** a poet honored for achievement in his art **2 :** a poet appointed for life by an English sovereign as a member of the royal household and formerly expected to compose poems for court and national occasions **3 :** one regarded by a country or region as its most eminent or representative poet
po·et·ry \'pō-ə-trē, *esp South* -it-rē\ *n* **1 a :** metrical writing **:** VERSE **b :** the productions of a poet **:** POEMS **2 :** writing that formulates a concentrated imaginative awareness of experience in language chosen and arranged to create a specific emotional response through meaning, sound, and rhythm **3 a :** a quality that stirs the imagination **b :** a quality of spontaneity and grace
po·go·nia \pə-'gō-nē-ə\ *n* [NL, genus name, fr. Gk *pōgōn* beard] **:** any of a genus (*Pogonia*) of terrestrial orchids of the north temperate zone having terminal solitary flowers with a crested lip and including the snakemouth
pog·o·nip \'päg-ə-,nip\ *n* [Southern Paiute] **:** a dense winter fog containing frozen particles that is formed in deep mountain valleys of western U.S.
po·go stick \'pō-(,)gō-\ *n* [fr. *Pogo*, a trademark] **:** a pole with two footrests and a strong spring at the bottom propelled along the ground by jumping
¹**po·grom** \pō-'gräm, 'pō-grəm\ *n* [Yiddish, fr. Russ, lit., devastation] **:** an organized massacre of helpless people; *specif* **:** such a massacre of Jews
²**pogrom** *vt* **:** to massacre or destroy in a pogrom
po·grom·ist \-əst\ *n* **:** one who organizes or takes part in a pogrom
po·gy \'pō-gē\ *n* [of Algonquian origin; akin to Abnaki *p8kañgan* menhaden] **:** MENHADEN
poi \'pȯi\ *n, pl* **poi** *or* **pois** [Hawaiian & Samoan] **:** a Hawaiian food of taro root cooked, pounded, and kneaded to a paste and often allowed to ferment
-poi·e·sis \(,)pȯi-'ē-səs\ *n comb form, pl* **-poi·e·ses** \-'ē-,sēz\ [NL, fr. Gk *poiēsis* creation — more at POESY] **:** production **:** formation ⟨lympho*poiesis*⟩
-poi·et·ic \(,)pȯi-'et-ik\ *adj comb form* [Gk *poiētikos* creative, fr. *poiētēs* poet] **:** productive **:** formative ⟨lympho*poietic*⟩
poi·gnan·cy \'pȯi-nyən-sē\ *n* **1 :** the quality or state of being poignant **2 :** an instance of poignancy
poi·gnant \-nyənt\ *adj* [ME *poinaunt*, fr. MF *poignant*, prp. o *poindre* to prick, sting, fr. L *pungere* — more at PUNGENT] **1 :** PUNGENT **2 a** (1) **:** painfully affecting the feelings **:** PIERCING (2) **:** deeply affecting **:** TOUCHING **b :** CUTTING, INCISIVE ⟨~ satire⟩ **3 a :** pleasurably stimulating **b :** being to the point **:** APT **syn** see MOVING, PUNGENT — **poi·gnant·ly** *adv*
poi·kilo·therm \pȯi-'kil-ə-,thərm\ *n* [Gk *poikilos* variegated + ISV *-therm;* akin to L *pingere* to paint — more at PAINT] **:** a cold-blooded organism — **poi·kilo·ther·mic** \(,)pȯi-,kil-ə-'thər-mik\ *adj* — **poi·kilo·ther·mism** \-'thər-,miz-əm\ *n*
poi·lu \pwäl-'(y)ü, 'pwäl-,; pwȧ-lüē\ *n* [F, fr. *poilu* hairy, fr. MF, fr. *poil* hair, fr. L *pilus* — more at PILE] **:** a French soldier; *esp* **:** a front-line soldier in World War I
poin·ci·ana \,pȯin(t)-sē-'an-ə, ,p(w)än(t)-\ *n* [NL, genus name, fr. De *Poinci*, 17th cent. governor of part of the French West Indies] **:** any of a small genus (*Poinciana*) of ornamental tropical leguminous trees or shrubs with bright orange or red flowers; *also* **:** a showy closely related tree (*Delonix regia*) with immense racemes of scarlet and orange flowers, flat woody pods, and twice-pinnate leaves
poin·set·tia \pȯin-'set-ē-ə, -'set-ə\ *n* [NL, fr. Joel R. *Poinsett* †1851 Am diplomat] **:** any of various spurges (genus *Euphorbia*) with flower clusters subtended by showy involucral bracts; *esp* **:** a showy Mexican and So. American plant (*E. pulcherrima*) with tapering scarlet bracts suggestive of petals surrounding small yellow flowers
¹**point** \'pȯint\ *n* [ME, partly fr. OF, puncture, small spot, point in time or space, fr. L *punctum*, fr. neut. of *punctus*, pp. of *pungere* to prick; partly fr. OF *pointe* sharp end, fr. (assumed) VL *puncta*, fr. L, fem. of *punctus*, pp. — more at PUNGENT] **1 a** (1) **:** an individual detail **:** ITEM (2) **:** a distinguishing detail **b :** the most important essential in a discussion or matter ⟨~ of the joke⟩ **c :** COGENCY **2** *obs* **:** physical condition **3 :** an end or object to be achieved **:** PURPOSE **4 a** (1) **:** an undefined geometric element of which it is postulated that at least two exist and that two suffice to determine a line (2) **:** a geometric element determined by an ordered set of coordinates **b** (1) **:** a narrowly localized place having a precisely indicated position (2) **:** a particular place **:** LOCALITY **c** (1) **:** an exact moment (2) **:** a time interval immediately before something indicated **:** VERGE ⟨at the ~ of death⟩ **d** (1) **:** a particular step, stage, or degree in development (2) **:** a definite position in a scale ⟨boiling ~⟩ **5 a :** the terminal usu. sharp or narrowly rounded part of something **:** TIP **b :** a weapon or tool having such a part and used for stabbing or piercing **c** (1) **:** the contact or discharge extremity of an electric device (as a spark plug or contact break) (2) *chiefly Brit* **:** an electric outlet **6 a :** a projecting usu. tapering piece of land or a sharp prominence **b** (1) **:** the tip of a projecting body part (2) *pl* **:** terminal bodily projections esp. when differing from the rest of the body in color **c** (1) **:** a railroad switch (2) **:** the tip of the angle between two rails in a railroad frog **d :** the head of the bow of a stringed instrument **7 :** a short musical phrase; *esp* **:** a phrase in contrapuntal music **8 a :** a very small mark **b** (1) **:** PUNCTUATION MARK; *esp* **:** PERIOD (2) **:** DECIMAL POINT **c :** a note in medieval music **9 :** a lace for tying parts of a garment together used esp. in the 16th and 17th centuries **10 :** one of the nine divisions of a heraldic shield or escutcheon that determine the position of a charge **11 a :** one of the 32 equidistant spots of a compass card **b :** the difference of 11¼ degrees between

two such successive points **12** : a small detachment ahead of an advance guard or behind a rear guard **13 a** : NEEDLEPOINT 1 **b** : lace made with a bobbin **14** : one of 12 spaces marked off on each side of a backgammon board **15** : a unit of measurement: as **a** (1) : a unit of counting in the scoring of a game or contest (2) : a unit used in evaluating the strength of a bridge hand **b** : a unit of academic credit **c** : a unit used in quoting prices of stocks, shares, and various commodities **d** : a unit of about ½ inch used to measure the belly-to-back dimension of printing type **16** : the action of pointing: as **a** : the rigidly intent attitude of a hunting dog marking game for a gunner **b** : the action in dancing of extending one leg so that only the tips of the toes touch the floor **c** : a thrust or lunge in fencing **17** : a position of a player in various games (as lacrosse); *also* : the player of such a position — **to the point** : RELEVANT, PERTINENT

²point *vt* **1 a** : to furnish with a point **b** : to give added force, emphasis, or piquancy to ⟨~ up a remark⟩ **2** : to scratch out the old mortar from the joints of (as a brick wall) and fill in with new material **3 a** (1) : to mark the pauses or grammatical divisions in : PUNCTUATE (2) : to separate (a decimal fraction) from an integer by a decimal point — usu. used with *off* **b** : to mark (as Hebrew words) **4 a** (1) : to indicate the position or direction of esp. by extending a finger ⟨~ out a house⟩ (2) : to direct someone's attention to ⟨~ out a mistake⟩ **b** *of a hunting dog* : to indicate the presence and place of (game) by a point **5 a** : to cause to be turned in a particular direction ⟨~ a gun⟩ **b** : to extend (a leg) in executing a point in dancing ~ *vi* **1 a** : to indicate the fact or probability of something specified ⟨everything ~s to a bright future⟩ **b** : to indicate the position or direction of something esp. by extending a finger ⟨~ at the map⟩ **c** : to point game **2 a** : to lie extended, aimed, or turned in a particular direction **b** : to execute a point in dancing **3** *of a ship* : to sail close to the wind **4** : to train for a particular contest

point–blank \'point-'blaŋk\ *adj* **1 a** : marked by no appreciable drop below initial horizontal line of flight **b** : so close to a target that a missile fired will travel in a straight line to the mark **2** : DIRECT, BLUNT — **point-blank** *adv*

point count *n* : a method of evaluating the strength of a hand in bridge by counting points for each high card and often for long or short suits; *also* : the value of a hand so evaluated

point d'ap·pui \,pwaⁿ(n)-(,)dap-'wē\ *n, pl* **points d'appui** *same*\ [F, lit., point of support] : a foundation or base esp. for a military operation

point–de·vice \,point-di-'vīs\ *adj, archaic* [ME *at point devis* at a fixed point] : marked by punctilious attention to detail : METICULOUS — **point-device** *adv, archaic*

pointe \'pwaⁿ(n)t\ *n* [F, lit., point] : a position of balance in ballet on the extreme tip of the toe

¹point·ed \'point-əd\ *adj* **1 a** : having a point **b** : having a pointed crown characteristic of Gothic architecture **2 a** : to the point : PERTINENT **b** : aimed at a particular person or group : CONSPICUOUS, MARKED — **point·ed·ly** *adv* — **point·ed·ness** *n*

²pointed *adj* [by shortening] *dis* : APPOINTED

point·er \'point-ər\ *n* **1** : one that furnishes with points **2 a** : one that points out; *specif* : one used to direct attention **b** *pl, cap* : the two stars in the Great Bear a line through which points to the North Star **3** : a large strong slender smooth-haired gundog that hunts by scent and indicates the presence of game by pointing **4** : a useful suggestion or hint : TIP

poin·til·lism \'pwaⁿ(n)-tē-,(y)iz-əm\ *n* [F *pointillisme*, fr. *pointiller* to stipple, fr. *point* spot — more at POINT] : the practice or technique of applying dots of color to a surface so that from a distance they blend together — **poin·til·list** \'pwaⁿ(n)-tē-əst, ,pwaⁿ(n)-tē-'ēst\ *n*

poin·til·lis·tic \,pwaⁿ(n)-tē-'(y)is-tik\ *adj* : of, relating to, or characteristic of pointillism or pointillists

point lace *n* : NEEDLEPOINT 1

point·less \'point-ləs\ *adj* **1** : devoid of meaning : SENSELESS **2** : devoid of effectiveness : FLAT — **point·less·ly** *adv* — **point·less·ness** *n*

point of honor *n* : a matter seriously affecting one's honor

point of view : a position from which something is considered or evaluated : STANDPOINT

point system *n* : a system in which printing type and spacing materials are made in sizes that are exact multiples of the point

pointy \'point-ē\ *adj* **1** : coming to a rather sharp point : quite pointed **2** : having parts that stick out sharply here and there

¹poise \'poiz\ *vb* [ME *poisen* to weigh, ponder, fr. MF *pois-*, stem of *peser*, fr. L *pensare* — more at PENSIVE] *vt* **1 a** : BALANCE; *esp* : to hold or carry in equilibrium **b** : to hold supported or suspended without motion in a steady position **2** : to hold or carry (the head) in a particular way **3** : to put into readiness : BRACE ~ *vi* **1** : to become drawn up into readiness **2** : HOVER

²poise *n* **1** : BALANCE, EQUILIBRIUM **2 a** (1) : self-possessed composure, assurance, and dignity (2) : TRANQUILLITY, CALM, SERENITY **b** : a particular way of carrying oneself : BEARING, CARRIAGE **syn** see TACT

¹poi·son \'poiz-ᵊn\ *n* [ME, fr. OF, drink, poisonous drink, poison, fr. L *potion-, potio* drink — more at POTION] **1 a** : a substance that through its chemical action usu. kills, injures, or impairs an organism **b** (1) : something destructive or harmful (2) : an object of aversion or abhorrence **2** : a substance that inhibits the activity of another substance or the course of a reaction or process ⟨a catalyst ~⟩

²poison *vb* **poi·son·ing** \'poiz-niŋ, -ᵊn-iŋ\ *vt* **1 a** : to injure or kill with poison **b** : to treat, taint, or impregnate with poison **2** : to exert a baneful influence on : CORRUPT **3** : to inhibit the activity, course, or occurrence of ~ *vi* : to put poison into or on something

³poison *adj* **1** : POISONOUS ⟨a ~ plant⟩ : VENOMOUS ⟨a ~ tongue⟩ **2** : POISONED ⟨a ~ arrow⟩

poison bean *n* : a leguminous shrub (*Daubentonia drummondii*) of the southern U. S. with poisonous seeds

poi·son·er \'poiz-nər, -ᵊn-ər\ *n* : one that poisons

poison gas *n* : a poisonous gas or a liquid or a solid giving off poisonous vapors designed (as in chemical warfare) to kill, injure, or disable by inhalation or contact

poison hemlock *n* **1** : a large branching biennial poisonous herb (*Conium maculatum*) of the carrot family with finely divided leaves and white flowers **2** : WATER HEMLOCK

poison ivy *n* : any of several usu. climbing American plants (genus *Rhus*) of the sumac family with an acutely irritating oil that causes an itchy rash when the herbage is touched

poison oak *n* : any of several shrubby sumacs (genus *Rhus*) that are poison ivies; *esp* : POISON SUMAC

poi·son·ous \'poiz-nəs, -ᵊn-əs\ *adj* : having the properties or effects of poison — VENOMOUS — **poi·son·ous·ly** *adv*

poi·son–pen \,poiz-ᵊn-'pen\ *adj* : written with malice and spite and usu. anonymously ⟨~ letter⟩

poison sumac *n* : a smooth shrubby American swamp poison ivy (*Rhus vernix*) with greenish flowers and greenish white berries — called also *poison dogwood*

poison ivy: *1* leaves, *2* berries

Pois·son distribution \pwä-'sōⁿ-\ *n* [Siméon D. *Poisson* †1840 F mathematician] : a frequency distribution that is a good approximation to the binomial distribution as the number of trials increases and the probability of success in a single trial is small

¹poke \'pōk\ *n* [ME, fr. ONF — more at POCKET] *chiefly South & Midland* : BAG, SACK

²poke *vb* [ME *poken*; akin to MD *poken* to poke] *vt* **1 a** (1) : PROD, JAB (2) : to urge or stir by prodding or jabbing **b** (1) : PIERCE, STAB (2) : to produce by piercing, stabbing, or jabbing ⟨~ a hole⟩ **c** (1) : HIT, PUNCH (2) : to deliver (a blow) with the fist **2 a** : to cause to project **b** : to thrust forward obtrusively or suddenly ~ *vi* **1 a** : to make a prodding, jabbing, or thrusting movement esp. repeatedly **b** : to strike out at something **2 a** : to look about or through something without system : RUMMAGE **b** : MEDDLE **3** : to move or act slowly or aimlessly : DAWDLE **4** : to become stuck out or forward : PROTRUDE — **poke fun at** : RIDICULE, MOCK

³poke *n* **1 a** : a quick thrust : JAB **b** : a blow with the fist : PUNCH **2** : a projecting brim on the front of a woman's bonnet

⁴poke *n* [modif. of *puccoon* (in some Algonquian language of Virginia), a plant used in dyeing] : POKEWEED

poke·ber·ry \'pōk-,ber-ē\ *n* : the berry of the pokeweed; *also* : POKEWEED

poke bonnet *n* : a woman's bonnet with a projecting brim at the front

poke check *n* : an act or instance of attempting to knock the puck away from an opponent in ice hockey by jabbing or thrusting at it with the stick

¹pok·er \'pō-kər\ *n* : one that pokes; *esp* : a metal rod for stirring a fire

²po·ker \'pō-kər\ *n* [prob. modif. of F *poque*, a card game similar

poker hands in descending value: *1* royal flush, *2* straight flush, *3* four of a kind, *4* full house, *5* flush, *6* straight, *7* three of a kind, *8* two pairs, *9* one pair

to poker] : one of several card games in which a player bets that the value of his hand is greater than that of the hands held by others, each subsequent player must either equal or raise the bet or drop out, and at the end of the betting the player holding the highest hand wins

poker face *n* : an immobile inscrutable face characteristic of an expert poker player — **po·ker–faced** \,pō-kər-'fāst\ *adj*

poke·weed \'pō-,kwēd\ *n* : a coarse American perennial herb (*Phytolacca americana* of the family Phytolaccaceae, the pokeweed family) with racemose white flowers, dark purple juicy berries, a poisonous root, and young shoots sometimes used as potherbs

po·key \'pō-kē\ *n* [origin unknown] *slang* : JAIL

pok·i·ly \'pō-kə-lē\ *adv* : in a poky manner

pok·i·ness \-kē-nəs\ *n* : the quality or state of being poky

poky *also* **pok·ey** \'pō-kē\ *adj* [²*poke*] **1** : small and cramped **2** : SHABBY, DULL **3** : annoyingly slow

Po·lack \'pō-,läk\ *n* [Pol *Polak*] **1** *obs* : POLE 1 **2** : a person of Polish birth or descent — usu. used disparagingly

Po·land Chi·na \,pō-lən(d)-'chī-nə\ *n* [*Poland* country in Europe + *China* country in Asia] : any of an American breed of large white-marked black swine of the lard type

¹po·lar \'pō-lər\ *adj* [NL *polaris*, fr. L *polus* pole] **1 a** : of or relating to a geographical pole or the region around it **b** : coming from or having the characteristics of such a region **2** : of or relating to one or more poles (as of a magnet) **3** : serving as a guide **4** : diametrically opposite **5** : having a dipole or characterized by molecules having dipoles ⟨a ~ solvent⟩ **6** : resembling a pole or axis around which all else revolves : PIVOTAL

²polar *n* : a straight line related to a point; *specif* : the straight line joining the points of contact of the tangents from a point exterior to a conic section

polar body *n* : one of the minute bodies or cells that separate from an oocyte during maturation

polar circle *n* **:** one of the two parallels of latitude each at a distance from a pole of the earth equal to about 23 degrees 27 minutes

polar coordinate *n* **:** either of two numbers that locate a point in a plane by its distance from a fixed point on a line and the angle this line makes with a fixed line

polar front *n* **:** the boundary between the cold air of a polar region and the warmer air of lower latitudes

po·lar·im·e·ter \ˌpō-lə-ˈrim-ət-ər\ *n* [ISV, fr. *polarization*] **1 :** an instrument for determining the amount of polarization of light or the proportion of polarized light in a partially polarized ray **2 :** a polariscope for measuring the amount of rotation of the plane of polarization esp. by liquids — **po·lari·met·ric** \pō-ˌlar-ə-ˈme-trik\ *adj* — **po·lar·im·e·try** \ˌpō-lə-ˈrim-ə-trē\ *n*

Po·lar·is \pə-ˈlar-əs\ *n* [NL, fr. *polaris* polar] **:** NORTH STAR

po·lari·scope \pō-ˈlar-ə-ˌskōp\ *n* [ISV, fr. *polarization*] **1 :** an instrument for studying the properties of or examining substances in polarized light **2 :** POLARIMETER 2 — **po·lari·scop·ic** \-ˌlar-ə-ˈskäp-ik\ *adj*

po·lar·i·ty \pō-ˈlar-ət-ē, pə-\ *n* **1 :** the quality or condition inherent in a body that exhibits opposite properties or powers in opposite parts or directions or that exhibits contrasted properties or powers in contrasted parts or directions **2 :** attraction toward a particular object or in a specific direction **3 :** the particular state either positive or negative with reference to the two poles or to electrification **4 a :** diametrical opposition **b :** an instance of such opposition

po·lar·iz·able \ˈpō-lə-ˌrī-zə-bəl\ *adj* **:** capable of being polarized

po·lar·iza·tion \ˌpō-lə-rə-ˈzā-shən\ *n* **1 :** the action of polarizing or state of being polarized: as **a** (1) **:** the action or process of affecting light or other radiation so that the vibrations of the wave assume a definite form (2) **:** the state of radiation affected by this process **b :** the deposition of gas on one or both electrodes of an electrolytic cell increasing the resistance and setting up a counter electromotive force **c :** MAGNETIZATION **2 a :** division into two opposites **b :** concentration about opposing extremes of groups or interests formerly ranged on a continuum

po·lar·ize \ˈpō-lə-ˌrīz\ *vb* [F *polariser*, fr. NL *polaris* polar] *vt* **1 :** to cause (as light waves) to vibrate in a definite pattern **2 :** to give polarity to ~ *vi* **:** to become polarized — **po·lar·iz·er** *n*

Po·laro·graph \pō-ˈlar-ə-ˌgraf\ *trademark* — used for a registering instrument used in polarography

po·laro·graph·ic \pō-ˌlar-ə-ˈgraf-ik\ *adj* **:** of, relating to, or by means of polarography — **po·laro·graph·i·cal·ly** \-i-k(ə-)lē\ *adv*

po·lar·og·ra·phy \ˌpō-lə-ˈräg-rə-fē\ *n* [ISV, fr. *polarization*] **:** a method of qualitative or quantitative analysis based on current-voltage curves obtained during electrolysis of a solution with a steadily increasing electromotive force

Po·lar·oid \ˈpō-lə-ˌrȯid\ *trademark* — used for a light-polarizing material used esp. in eyeglasses and lamps to prevent glare and in various optical devices

pol·der \ˈpōl-dər, ˈpäl-\ *n* [D] **:** a tract of low land reclaimed from a body of water (as the sea)

¹pole \ˈpōl\ *n* [ME, fr. OE *pāl* stake, pole, fr. L *palus* stake; akin to L *pangere* to fix — more at PACT] **1 a :** a long slender usu. cylindrical substance (as wood) **b :** a shaft which extends from the front axle of a wagon between wheelhorses and by which the wagon is held back **:** TONGUE **2 a :** a varying unit of length; *esp* **:** one measuring 16½ feet **b :** a unit of area equal to a square rod or perch **3 :** a tree with a breast-high diameter of from 4 to 12 inches **4 :** the inside position on a racetrack

²pole *vt* **1 :** to act upon with a pole **2 :** to impel or push with a pole ~ *vi* **1 :** to propel a boat with a pole **2 :** to use ski poles to gain speed

³pole *n* [ME *pool*, fr. L *polus*, fr. Gk *polos* pivot, pole; akin to Gk *kyklos* wheel — more at WHEEL] **1 :** either extremity of an axis of a sphere and esp. of the earth's axis **2 a :** either of two related opposites **b :** a point of guidance or attraction **3 a :** one of the two terminals of an electric cell, battery, or dynamo **b :** one of two or more regions in a magnetized body at which the magnetic flux density is concentrated **4 :** either of two morphologically or physiologically differentiated areas at opposite ends of an axis in an organism or cell **5 a :** the vertex of the angle coordinate in a polar coordinate system **b :** the point of origin of two tangents to a conic that determine a polar

Pole \ˈpōl\ *n* [G, of Slavic origin; akin to Pol *Polak* Pole] **1 :** a native or inhabitant of Poland **2 :** a person of Polish descent

pole·ax \ˈpō-ˌlaks\ *n* [ME *polax, pollax*, fr. *pol, polle* poll + *ax*] **1 :** a battle-ax with short handle and cutting edge or point opposite the blade; *also* **:** one with a long handle used as an ornamental weapon **2 :** an ax used in slaughtering cattle

pole bean *n* **:** a cultivated bean having long internodes and twining stems and usu. trained to grow upright on supports

pole·cat \ˈpōl-ˌkat\ *n, pl* **polecats** *or* **polecat** [ME *polcat*, prob. fr. MF *poul, pol* cock + ME *cat*; prob. fr. its preying on poultry — more at PULLET] **1 :** a European carnivorous mammal (*Mustela putorius*) of which the ferret is considered a domesticated variety **2 :** SKUNK

pole horse *n* **1 :** a horse harnessed beside the pole of a wagon **2 :** the horse having a starting position next to the inside rail in a harness race

pole·less \ˈpōl-ləs\ *adj* **:** having no pole

po·lem·ic \pə-ˈlem-ik\ *n* [F *polémique*, fr. MF, fr. *polemique* controversial, fr. Gk *polemikos* warlike, hostile, fr. *polemos* war; akin to OE eal*felo* baleful, Gk *pallein* to brandish] **1 a :** an aggressive attack on or refutation of the opinions or principles of another **b :** the art or practice of disputation or controversy — usu. used in pl. but sing. or pl. in constr. **2 :** an aggressive controversialist **:** DISPUTANT **3** *pl but sing or pl in constr* **:** the branch of Christian theology devoted to the refutation of errors — **polemic** *or* **po·lem·i·cal** \-i-kəl\ *adj* — **po·lem·i·cal·ly** \-k(ə-)lē\ *adv* — **po·lem·i·cist** \-ˈlem-ə-səst\ *n*

po·lem·i·cize \-ˈlem-ə-ˌsīz\ *vi* **:** POLEMIZE

po·le·mist \pə-ˈlem-əst, ˈpäl-ə-məst\ *n* [irreg. fr. *polemic*] **:** one skilled in or given to polemics

pol·e·mize \ˈpäl-ə-ˌmīz\ *vi* **:** to engage in controversy **:** dispute aggressively

po·len·ta \pō-ˈlent-ə, -ˈlen-ˌtä\ *n* [It] **:** mush made of chestnut meal or principally of cornmeal or sometimes of semolina or farina

pol·er \ˈpō-lər\ *n* **:** one that poles: as **a :** POLE HORSE **b :** one that poles a boat

pole·star \ˈpōl-ˌstär\ *n* **1 :** NORTH STAR **2 a :** a directing principle **:** GUIDE **b :** a center of attraction

pole vault *n* **:** a vault with the aid of a pole; *specif* **:** a field event consisting of a vault for height over a crossbar — called also *pole jump* — **pole–vault** \ˈpōl-ˌvȯlt\ *vi* — **pole–vault·er** *n*

¹po·lice \pə-ˈlēs\ *n, pl* **police** [MF, fr. LL *politia*, fr. Gk *politeia*, fr. *politeuein* to be a citizen, engage in political activity, fr. *politēs* citizen, fr. *polis* city, state; akin to Skt *pur* city] **1 a :** the internal organization or regulation of a political unit through exercise of governmental powers esp. with respect to general comfort, health, morals, safety, or prosperity **b :** control and regulation of affairs affecting the general order and welfare of any unit or area **c :** the system of laws for effecting such control **2 a :** the department of government concerned primarily with maintenance of public order, safety, and health and enforcement of laws and possessing executive, judicial, and legislative powers **b :** the department of government charged with prevention, detection, and prosecution of public nuisances and crimes **3 a :** POLICE FORCE **b** *pl* **:** POLICEMEN **4 a :** a private organization resembling a police force **b** *pl* **:** the members of such an organization **5 a :** the action or process of cleaning and putting in order **b :** military personnel detailed to perform this function

²police *vt* **1** *archaic* **:** GOVERN **2 :** to control, regulate, or keep in order by use of police **3 :** to make clean and put in order **4 a :** to supervise the operation, execution, or administration of to prevent or detect and prosecute violations of rules and regulations **b :** to exercise such supervision over the policies and activities of **5 :** to perform the functions of a police force in or over

police action *n* **:** a localized military action undertaken without formal declaration of war by regular forces against persons held to be violators of international peace and order

police court *n* **:** a court of record with jurisdiction over various minor offenses and power to bind over for trial in a superior court or for a grand jury persons accused of more serious offenses

police dog *n* **1 :** a dog trained to assist police esp. in tracking criminals **2 :** GERMAN SHEPHERD

police force *n* **:** a body of trained officers and men entrusted by a government with maintenance of public peace and order, enforcement of laws, and prevention and detection of crime

po·lice·man \pə-ˈlē-smən\ *n* **:** a member of a police force

police power *n* **:** the inherent power of a government to exercise reasonable control over persons and property within its jurisdiction in the interest of the general security, health, safety, morals, and welfare except where legally prohibited

police reporter *n* **:** a reporter assigned to cover police news

police state *n* **:** a political unit characterized by repressive governmental control of political, economic, and social life usu. by an arbitrary exercise of power by police and esp. secret police in place of regular operation of administrative and judicial organs of the government according to established legal processes

police station *n* **:** the headquarters of the police for a particular locality

poli·clin·ic \ˌpäl-i-ˈklin-ik, ˌpō-lē-\ *n* [G *poliklinik*, fr. Gk *polis* city + G *klinik* clinic, fr. F *clinique*] **:** a dispensary or department of a hospital at which outpatients are treated

¹pol·i·cy \ˈpäl-ə-sē\ *n* [ME *policie*, government, policy, fr. MF, government, regulation, fr. LL *politia* — more at POLICE] **1 a :** prudence or wisdom in the management of affairs **:** SAGACITY **b :** management or procedure based primarily on material interest **2 :** a definite course or method of action selected from among alternatives and in light of given conditions to guide and determine present and future decisions

²policy *n* [alter. of earlier *police*, fr. MF, certificate, fr. OIt *polizza*, modif. of ML *apodixa* receipt, fr. MGk *apodeixis*, fr. Gk, proof, fr. *apodeiknynai* to demonstrate — more at APODICTIC] **1 :** a writing whereby a contract of insurance is made **2 a :** a daily lottery in which participants bet that certain numbers will be drawn from a lottery wheel **b :** NUMBER 6a

pol·i·cy·hold·er \-ˌhōl-dər\ *n* **:** one granted an insurance policy

po·lio \ˈpō-lē-ˌō\ *n* **:** POLIOMYELITIS

po·lio·my·elit·ic \ˌpō-lē-(ˌ)ō-ˌmī-ə-ˈlit-ik\ *adj* [ISV] **:** of, relating to, or affected with poliomyelitis

po·lio·my·eli·tis \-ˌmī-ə-ˈlīt-əs\ *n* [NL, fr. Gk *polios* gray + *myelos* marrow — more at FALLOW, MYEL-] **:** an acute infectious virus disease characterized by fever, motor paralysis, and atrophy of skeletal muscles often with permanent disability and deformity and marked by inflammation of nerve cells in the anterior horns of the spinal cord — called also *infantile paralysis*

po·lis \ˈpäl-əs\ *n, pl* **po·leis** \ˈpäl-ˌās\ [Gk — more at POLICE] **:** a Greek city-state

-p·o·lis \p-(ə-)ləs\ *n comb form* [LL, fr. Gk, fr. *polis*] **:** city ⟨megalo*polis*⟩

¹pol·ish \ˈpäl-ish\ *vb* [ME *polisshen*, fr. OF *poliss-*, stem of *polir*, fr. L *polire*] *vt* **1 :** to make smooth and glossy usu. by friction **:** BURNISH **2 :** to smooth, soften, or refine in manners or condition **3 :** to bring to a highly developed, finished, or refined state **:** PERFECT ~ *vi* **:** to become smooth or glossy by or as if by friction — **pol·ish·er** *n*

²polish *n* **1 a :** a smooth glossy surface **:** LUSTER **b :** REFINEMENT CULTURE **c :** a state of high development or refinement **2 :** the action or process of polishing **3 :** a preparation used in polishing

¹Pol·ish \ˈpō-lish\ *adj* [*Pole*] **:** of, relating to, or characteristic of Poland, the Poles, or Polish

²Polish *n* **:** the Slavic language of the Poles

polish off *vt* **:** to dispose of rapidly or completely

po·lit·bu·ro \ˈpäl-ət-ˌbyu̇(ə)r-(ˌ)ō, ˈpō-lət-, pə-ˈlit-\ *n* [Russ *politbyuro*, fr. *politicheskoye byuro* political bureau] **:** the principal policy-making and executive committee of a Communist party

po·lite \pə-ˈlīt\ *adj* [L *politus*, fr. pp. of *polire*] **1 a :** of, relating to or having the characteristics of advanced culture **b :** marked by refined cultured interests and pursuits esp. in arts and belles lettres **2 a :** showing or characterized by correct social usage **b :** marked by consideration, tact, deference, or courtesy **c :** gentle or moderate in tone **syn** see CIVIL — **po·lite·ly** *adv* — **po·lite·ness** *n*

po·li·tesse \ˌpäl-i-ˈtes, ˌpȯ-li-\ *n* [F, fr. MF, cleanness, fr. OIt *pulitezza*, fr. *pulito*, pp. of *pulire* to polish, clean, fr. L *polire*] **:** formal politeness **:** DECOROUSNESS

pol·i·tic \ˈpäl-ə-ˌtik\ *adj* [ME *politik*, fr. MF *politique*, fr. L *politicus*, fr. Gk *politikos*, fr. *politēs* citizen — more at POLICE] **1 :** POLITICAL

2 **:** characterized by shrewdness 3 **:** sagacious in promoting a policy 4 **:** shrewdly tactful **syn** see EXPEDIENT, SUAVE

po·lit·i·cal \pə-'lit-i-kəl\ *adj* [L *politicus*] 1 a **:** of or relating to government, a government, or the conduct of government b **:** of, relating to, or concerned with the making as distinguished from the administration of governmental policy 2 **:** of, relating to, or involving politics and esp. party politics 3 **:** organized in governmental terms ⟨~ units⟩ 4 **:** involving or charged or concerned with acts against a government or a political system — **po·lit·i·cal·ly** \-k(ə-)lē\ *adv*

political economist *n* **:** a specialist in political economy

political economy *n* 1 **:** a 19th century social science comprising the modern science of economics 2 **:** a modern social science dealing with the interrelationship of political and economic processes

political science *n* **:** a social science concerned chiefly with the description and analysis of political and esp. governmental institutions and processes — **political scientist** *n*

pol·i·ti·cian \,päl-ə-'tish-ən\ *n* 1 **:** one versed in the art or science of government; *esp* **:** one actively engaged in conducting the business of a government 2 a **:** one engaged in party politics as a profession b **:** one primarily interested in political offices from selfish or other narrow usu. short-run interests

po·lit·i·cize \pə-'lit-ə-,sīz\ *vi* **:** to discuss or discourse on politics ~ *vt* **:** to give a political tone or character to

pol·i·tick \'päl-ə-,tik\ *vi* [prob. back-formation fr. *politics*] **:** to engage in political discussion or activity — **pol·i·tick·er** *n*

po·lit·i·co \pə-'lit-i-,kō\ *n, pl* **politicos** *also* **politicoes** [It *politico* or Sp *político*, derivs. of L *politicus* political] **:** POLITICIAN 2

politico- *comb form* [L *politicus*] **:** political and ⟨*politico*-diplomatic⟩

pol·i·tics \'päl-ə-,tiks\ *n pl but sing or pl in constr* [Gk *politika*, fr. neut. pl. of *politikos* political] 1 a **:** the art or science of government b **:** the art or science concerned with guiding or influencing governmental policy c **:** the art or science concerned with winning and holding control over a government 2 **:** political actions, practices, or policies 3 a **:** political affairs or business; *specif* **:** competition between competing interest groups or individuals for power and leadership in a government or other group b **:** political life esp. as a principal activity or profession c **:** political activities characterized by artful and often dishonest practices 4 **:** the political opinions or sympathies of a person 5 **:** the total complex of relations between men in society

pol·i·ty \'päl-ət-ē\ *n* [LL *politia* — more at POLICE] 1 **:** political organization 2 **:** a specific form of political organization 3 **:** a politically organized unit 4 a **:** the form or constitution of a politically organized unit b **:** the form of government of a religious denomination

pol·ka \'pōl-kə\ *n* [Czech, fr. Pol *Polka* Polish woman, fem. of *Polak* Pole] 1 **:** a vivacious couple dance of Bohemian origin with three steps and a hop in duple time 2 **:** a lively Bohemian dance tune in 2/4 time — **polka** *vi*

pol·ka dot \'pō-kə-,dät\ *n* **:** a dot in a pattern of regularly distributed dots in textile design

[1]**poll** \'pōl\ *n* [ME *pol*, *polle*, fr. MLG] 1 **:** HEAD 2 a **:** the prominent hairy top or back of the head b **:** NAPE 3 **:** the broad or flat end of a hammer or similar tool 4 a (1) **:** the casting or recording of the votes of a body of persons (2) **:** a counting of votes cast b **:** the place where votes are cast or recorded — usu. used in pl. ⟨at the ~s⟩ c **:** the period of time during which votes may be cast at an election d **:** the total number of votes recorded ⟨a heavy ~⟩ 5 a **:** a questioning or canvassing of persons selected at random or by quota to obtain information or opinions to be analyzed b **:** a record of the information so obtained

[2]**poll** *vt* 1 a **:** to cut off or cut short the hair or wool of **:** CROP, SHEAR b **:** to cut off or cut short (as wool) 2 a **:** to cut off or back the top of (as a tree); *specif* **:** POLLARD b **:** to cut off or cut short the horns of (cattle) 3 a **:** to receive and record the votes of b **:** to request each member of to declare his vote individually 4 **:** to receive (as votes) in an election 5 **:** to question or canvass in a poll ~ *vi* **:** to cast one's vote at a poll — **poll·ee** \pō-'lē\ *n* — **poll·er** \'pō-lər\ *n*

[3]**poll** *n* [prob. fr. obs. E *poll*, adj., naturally hornless, short for E *polled*] **:** a polled animal

pol·lack *or* **pol·lock** \'päl-ək\ *n, pl* **pollack** *or* **pollacks** *or* **pollock** *or* **pollocks** [Sc *podlok*, of unknown origin] **:** a commercially important north Atlantic food fish (*Pollachius virens*) related to and resembling the cods but darker

[1]**pol·lard** \'päl-ərd\ *n* [[2]*poll*] 1 **:** a hornless animal of a usu. horned kind 2 **:** a tree cut back to the trunk to promote the growth of a dense head of foliage

[2]**pollard** *vt* **:** to make a pollard of (a tree)

polled \'pōld\ *adj* **:** having no horns

pol·len \'päl-ən\ *n* [NL *pollin-*, *pollen*, fr. L, fine flour; akin to L *pulvis* dust, Gk *palē* fine meal] 1 **:** a mass of microspores in a seed plant appearing usu. as a fine dust 2 **:** a dusty bloom on the body of an insect — **pol·lin·ic** \pä-'lin-ik\ *adj*

pol·len·ate \'päl-ə-,nāt\ *vt* **:** POLLINATE 1 — **pol·len·ation** \,päl-ə-'nā-shən\ *n*

pol·len·iz·er \'päl-ə-,nī-zər\ *n* [*pollenize* (to pollinize)] 1 **:** a plant that is a source of pollen 2 **:** POLLINATOR a

pol·lex \'päl-,eks\ *n, pl* **pol·li·ces** \'päl-ə-,sēz\ [NL *pollic-*, *pollex*, fr. L, thumb, big toe] **:** the first digit of the forelimb **:** THUMB — **pol·li·cal** \'päl-i-kəl\ *adj*

pollin- *or* **pollini-** *comb form* [NL *pollin-*, *pollen*] **:** pollen ⟨*pollinate*⟩

pol·li·nate \'päl-ə-,nāt\ *vt* 1 **:** to place pollen on the stigma of 2 **:** to mark or smudge with pollen — **pol·li·na·tion** \,päl-ə-'nā-shən\ *n*

pol·li·na·tor \'päl-ə-,nāt-ər\ *n* **:** one that pollinates: as a **:** an agent that pollinates flowers b **:** POLLENIZER 1

pol·li·nif·er·ous \,päl-ə-'nif-(ə-)rəs\ *adj* 1 **:** bearing or producing pollen 2 **:** adapted for the purpose of carrying pollen

pol·lin·i·um \pä-'lin-ē-əm\ *n, pl* **pol·lin·ia** \-ē-ə\ [NL, fr. *pollin-*] **:** a coherent mass of pollen grains

pol·li·nize \'päl-ə-,nīz\ *vt* [ISV] **:** POLLINATE 1

pol·li·niz·er \-,nī-zər\ *n* **:** POLLENIZER

pol·li·nose \'päl-ə-,nōs\ *adj, of an insect* **:** covered with pollen **:** PRUINOSE

pol·li·no·sis *or* **pol·len·osis** \,päl-ə-'nō-səs\ *n* [NL *pollinosis*, fr. *pollin-*] **:** an acute recurrent catarrhal disorder caused by allergic sensitivity to specific pollens

pol·li·wog *or* **pol·ly·wog** \'päl-ē-,wäg, -,wȯg\ *n* [alter. of ME *polwygle*, prob. fr. *pol* poll + *wiglen* to wiggle] **:** TADPOLE

poll·ster \'pōl-stər\ *n* **:** one that conducts a poll or compiles data obtained by a poll

poll tax *n* **:** a tax of a fixed amount per person levied on adults and often payable as a requirement for voting

pol·lu·tant \pə-'lüt-ᵊnt, 'päl-yə-tənt\ *n* **:** something that pollutes

pol·lute \pə-'lüt\ *vt* [ME *polluten*, fr. L *pollutus*, pp. of *polluere*, fr. *por-* (akin to L *per* through) + *-luere* (akin to L *lutum* mud, Gk *lyma* dirt, defilement) — more at FOR] 1 **:** to make ceremonially or morally impure **:** DEFILE 2 **:** to make physically impure or unclean **:** BEFOUL, DIRTY, TAINT **syn** see CONTAMINATE — **pol·lu·tion** \pə-'lü-shən\ *n*

pol·lut·er \-'lüt-ər\ *n* **:** one that pollutes

Pol·lux \'päl-əks\ *n* [L, modif. of Gk *Polydeukēs*] 1 **:** the immortal twin of Castor — compare DIOSCURI 2 **:** a first-magnitude star in the constellation Gemini

Pol·ly·an·na \,päl-ē-'an-ə\ *n* [*Pollyanna*, heroine of the novel *Pollyanna* (1913) by Eleanor Porter] **:** one characterized by irrepressible optimism and a tendency to find good in everything

po·lo \'pō-(,)lō\ *n* [Balti, ball] 1 **:** a game of oriental origin played by teams of players on horseback using mallets with long flexible handles to drive a wooden ball 2 **:** WATER POLO — **po·lo·ist** \'pō-lə-wəst\ *n*

polo coat *n* **:** a tailored overcoat for casual wear of tan camel's hair or other fabric

po·lo·naise \,päl-ə-'nāz, ,pō-lə-\ *n* [F, fr. fem. of *polonais* Polish, fr. *Pologne* Poland, fr. ML *Polonia*] 1 **:** an elaborate 18th century overdress with short-sleeved fitted waist and draped cutaway overskirt 2 a **:** a stately 19th century Polish processional dance b **:** music for this dance in moderate 3/4 time

po·lo·ni·um \pə-'lō-nē-əm\ *n* [NL, fr. ML *Polonia* Poland] **:** a radioactive metallic element similar chemically to tellurium and bismuth that occurs esp. in pitchblende and radium-lead residues and emits a helium nucleus to form an isotope of lead — see ELEMENT table

Po·lo·ni·us \pə-'lō-nē-əs\ *n* **:** a garrulous courtier and father of Ophelia and Laertes in Shakespeare's *Hamlet*

polo shirt *n* **:** a close-fitting pullover shirt of knitted cotton with short or long sleeves and turnover collar or round banded neck

pol·ter·geist \'pōl-tər-,gīst\ *n* [G, fr. *poltern* to knock + *geist* spirit, fr. OHG — more at GHOST] **:** a noisy usu. mischievous ghost held to be responsible for unexplained noises (as rappings)

[1]**pol·troon** \päl-'trün\ *n* [MF *poultron*, fr. OIt *poltrone*, fr. aug. of *poltro* colt, deriv. of L *pullus* young of an animal — more at FOAL] **:** a spiritless coward **:** CRAVEN

[2]**poltroon** *adj* **:** characterized by complete cowardice

pol·troon·ery \-'trün-(ə-)rē\ *n* **:** mean pusillanimity **:** COWARDICE

pol·troon·ish \-'trü-nish\ *adj* **:** resembling a poltroon **:** COWARDLY — **pol·troon·ish·ly** *adv*

poly \'päl-ē\ *n, pl* **pol·ys** \-ēz\ [by shortening] **:** a polymorphonuclear leukocyte

poly- *comb form* [ME, fr. L, fr. Gk, fr. *polys*; akin to OE *full* full] 1 a **:** many **:** several **:** much **:** MULTI- ⟨*poly*chotomous⟩ ⟨*poly*gyny⟩ b **:** excessive **:** abnormal **:** HYPER- ⟨*poly*phagia⟩ 2 a **:** containing an indefinite number more than one of a (specified) substance ⟨*poly*sulfide⟩ b **:** polymeric **:** polymer of a (specified) monomer ⟨*poly*ethylene⟩

poly·adel·phous \,päl-ē-ə-'del-fəs\ *adj* **:** united by the anthers into three or more groups ⟨~ stamens⟩

poly·am·ide \-'am-,īd\ *n* [ISV] **:** a compound characterized by more than one amide group; *esp* **:** a polymeric amide

poly·an·dric \-'an-drik\ *adj* **:** of or relating to polyandry

poly·an·drous \-drəs\ *adj* 1 [*poly-* + *-androus*] **:** having many usu. free hypogynous stamens 2 [*polyandry*] **:** relating to or practicing polyandry

poly·an·dry \'päl-ē-,an-drē\ *n* [Gk *polyandros*, adj., having many husbands, fr. *poly-* + *andr-*, *anēr* man, husband — more at ANDR-] 1 **:** the practice of having more than one husband at one time 2 **:** the state of being polyandrous

poly·an·tha \,päl-ē-'an(t)-thə\ *n* [NL, fr. Gk *polyanthos* blooming] **:** any of numerous dwarf hybrid bush roses characterized by the free production of large clusters of small flowers

poly·an·thus \-'an(t)-thəs\ *n, pl* **poly·an·thus·es** *or* **poly·an·thi** \-'an-,thī, -,thē\ [NL, fr. Gk *polyanthos* blooming, fr. *poly-* + *anthos* flower — more at ANTHOLOGY] 1 **:** any of various hybrid primroses 2 **:** a narcissus (*Narcissus tazetta*) having small umbeled white or yellow flowers with a spreading perianth

poly·ba·sic \,päl-i-'bā-sik\ *adj* **:** having more than one hydrogen atom replaceable by basic atoms or radicals — used of acids — **poly·ba·sic·i·ty** \-bā-'sis-ət-ē\ *n*

poly·ba·site \-'bā-,sīt\ *n* [G *polybasit*, fr. *poly-* + *basi-*] **:** an iron-black metallic-looking ore $(Ag,Cu)_{16}Sb_2S_{11}$ of silver consisting of silver, copper, sulfur, and antimony

poly·car·pel·lary \-'kär-pə-,ler-ē\ *adj* **:** consisting of several carpels

poly·car·pic \-'kär-pik\ *or* **poly·car·pous** \-pəs\ *adj* [prob. fr. NL *polycarpicus*, *polycarpus*, fr. *poly-* + *-carpicus* -carpic, *-carpus* -carpous] **:** having a gynoecium forming two or more distinct ovaries — **poly·car·py** \'päl-i-,kär-pē\ *n*

poly·chaete \'päl-i-,kēt\ *adj* [deriv. of Gk *polychaitēs* having much hair, fr. *poly-* + *chaitē* long hair — more at CHAETA] **:** of or relating to a class (Polychaeta) of annelid worms comprising most of the common marine worms usu. having paired segmental appendages — **polychaete** *n* — **poly·chae·tous** \,päl-i-'kēt-əs\ *adj*

poly·cha·si·um \,päl-i-'kā-z(h)ē-əm\ *n, pl* **poly·cha·sia** \-z(h)ē-ə\ [NL, fr. *poly-* + *-chasium* (as in *dichasium*)] **:** a cymose inflorescence in which each main axis produces more than two branches

poly·chot·o·mous \-'kät-ə-məs\ *adj* [*poly-* + *-chotomous* (as in *dichotomous*)] **:** dividing or marked by division into many parts, branches, or classes — **poly·chot·o·my** \-mē\ *n*

poly·chro·mat·ic \,päl-i-krō-'mat-ik\ *adj* [Gk *polychrōmatos*, fr. *poly-* + *chrōmat-*, *chrōma* color — more at CHROMATIC] **:** showing a variety or a change of colors **:** MULTICOLORED

poly·chro·mato·phil·ia \-krō-ˌmat-ə-'fil-ē-ə\ *n* [NL] **:** the quality of being stainable with more than one type of stain and esp. with both acid and basic dyes
poly·chrome \'päl-i-ˌkrōm\ *adj* [Gk *polychrōmos*, fr. *poly-* + *chrōma*] **:** relating to, made with, or decorated in several colors ⟨~ pottery⟩
poly·chro·my \-ˌkrō-mē\ *n* **:** the art or practice of decorating in several colors
poly·clin·ic \ˌpäl-i-'klin-ik\ *n* [ISV] **:** a clinic or hospital treating diseases of many sorts
poly·con·den·sa·tion \-ˌkän-ˌden-'sā-shən, -dən-\ *n* [ISV] **:** a chemical condensation leading to the formation of a compound of high molecular weight
poly·con·ic projection \ˌpäl-i-ˌkän-ik-\ *n* **:** a map projection of the earth's surface in which each narrow section is projected on the inside surface of a cone touching the sphere along this section and then the cone is unrolled
poly·cot \'päl-i-ˌkät\ *or* **poly·cot·yl** \-ˌkät-ᵊl\ *n* **:** POLYCOTYLEDON
poly·cot·y·le·don \-ˌkät-ᵊl-'ēd-ᵊn\ *n* [NL] **:** a plant having more than two cotyledons — **poly·cot·y·le·do·nous** \-'ēd-nəs, -ᵊn-əs\ *adj*
poly·cy·clic \-'sī-klik, -'sik-lik\ *adj* [ISV] **:** having more than one cyclic component
poly·cy·the·mia \ˌpäl-i-(ˌ)sī-'thē-mē-ə\ *n* [NL, fr. *poly-* + *cyt-* + *-hemia*] **:** any condition marked by an abnormal increase in the number of circulating red blood cells — **poly·cy·the·mic** \-mik\ *adj*
poly·dac·tyl \ˌpäl-i-'dak-tᵊl\ *adj* [Gk *polydaktylos*, fr. *poly-* + *daktylos* digit] **:** having several to many and esp. abnormally many digits — **poly·dac·ty·lous** \-tə-ləs\ *adj* — **poly·dac·ty·ly** \-lē\ *n*
poly·dip·sia \ˌpäl-i-'dip-sē-ə\ *n* [NL, fr. *poly-* + Gk *dipsa* thirst] **:** excessive or abnormal thirst — **poly·dip·sic** \-sik\ *adj*
poly·em·bry·on·ic \ˌpäl-ē-ˌem-brē-'än-ik\ *adj* [ISV] **:** producing two or more embryos from one ovule or egg — **poly·em·bry·o·ny** \-'em-brē-ə-nē, -(ˌ)em-'brī-\ *n*
poly·ene \'päl-ē-ˌēn\ *n* [ISV] **:** an organic compound containing many double bonds; *esp* **:** one having the double bonds in a long aliphatic hydrocarbon chain — **poly·enic** \-'ē-nik\ *adj*
poly·es·ter \'päl-ē-ˌes-tər\ *n* [ISV] **:** a complex ester formed by polymerization or condensation and used esp. in making fibers or plastics — **poly·es·ter·i·fi·ca·tion** \ˌpäl-ē-e-ˌster-ə-fə-'kā-shən\ *n*
poly·es·trous \ˌpäl-ē-'es-trəs\ *adj* **:** having more than one period of estrus in a year
poly·eth·yl·ene \-'eth-ə-ˌlēn\ *n* **:** a polymer of ethylene; *esp* **:** one of various partially crystalline lightweight thermoplastics $(-CH_2CH_2-)_x$ resistant to chemicals and moisture and with good insulating properties that are used esp. in packaging and insulation
po·lyg·a·la \pə-'lig-ə-lə\ *n* [NL, genus name, fr. L, milkwort, fr. Gk *polygalon*, fr. *poly-* + *gala* milk — more at GALAXY] **:** MILKWORT
poly·gam·ic \ˌpäl-i-'gam-ik\ *adj* **:** POLYGAMOUS — **poly·gam·i·cal** \-i-kəl\ *adj* — **poly·gam·i·cal·ly** \-k(ə-)lē\ *adv*
po·lyg·a·mist \pə-'lig-ə-məst\ *n* **:** one who practices polygamy
po·lyg·a·mize \-ˌmīz\ *vi* **:** to practice polygamy
po·lyg·a·mous \-məs\ *adj* [Gk *polygamos*, fr. *poly-* + *-gamos* -gamous] **1 a :** of or relating to polygamy **b :** having more than one spouse or mate at one time **2 :** bearing both hermaphrodite and unisexual flowers on the same plant — **po·lyg·a·mous·ly** *adv*
po·lyg·a·my \-mē\ *n* **:** the state or fact of being polygamous; *esp* **:** marriage in which a spouse of either sex may possess a plurality of mates at the same time
poly·gene \'päl-i-ˌjēn\ *n* [ISV] **:** any of a group of nonallelic genes that collectively control the inheritance of a quantitative character or modify the expression of a qualitative character — **poly·gen·ic** \ˌpäl-i-'jē-nik\ *adj*
poly·gen·e·sis \ˌpäl-i-'jen-ə-səs\ *n* [NL] **:** polyphyletic origin — **poly·gen·e·sist** \-səst\ *n* — **poly·ge·net·ic** \-jə-'net-ik\ *adj* — **poly·ge·net·i·cal·ly** \-i-k(ə-)lē\ *adv*
poly·glan·du·lar \-'glan-jə-lər\ *adj* [ISV] **:** of, relating to, or involving several glands ⟨~ therapy⟩
[1]**poly·glot** \'päl-i-ˌglät\ *n* [Gk *polyglōttos*, adj., polyglot, fr. *poly-* + *glōtta* language — more at GLOSS] **1 :** one who is polyglot **2** *cap* **:** a book containing versions of the same text in several languages; *esp* **:** the Scriptures in several languages **3 :** a mixture or confusion of languages or nomenclatures
[2]**polyglot** *adj* **1 a :** speaking or writing several languages **b :** composed of numerous linguistic groups **2 :** containing matter in several languages **3 :** composed of elements from different languages
poly·glot·ism *or* **poly·glot·tism** \-ˌglät-ˌiz-əm\ *n* **:** the use of many languages **:** the ability to speak many languages
poly·gon \'päl-i-ˌgän\ *n* [LL *polygonum*, fr. Gk *polygōnon*, fr. neut. of *polygōnos* polygonal, fr. *poly-* + *gōnia* angle — more at -GON] **1 :** a closed plane figure bounded by straight lines **2 :** a closed figure on a sphere bounded by arcs of great circles — **po·lyg·o·nal** \pə-'lig-ən-ᵊl\ *adj* — **po·lyg·o·nal·ly** \-ᵊl-ē\ *adv*

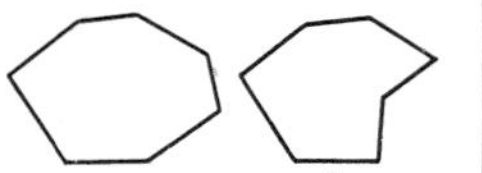

1 2
polygons: *1* convex, *2* concave

po·lyg·o·num \pə-'lig-ə-nəm\ *n* [NL, genus name, fr. Gk *polygonon* knotgrass, fr. *poly-* + *gony* knee — more at KNEE] **:** KNOTGRASS 1
poly·graph \'päl-i-ˌgraf\ *n* **:** an instrument for recording tracings of several different pulsations simultaneously; *broadly* **:** LIE DETECTOR — **poly·graph·ic** \ˌpäl-i-'graf-ik\ *adj*
poly·gy·noe·cial \ˌpäl-i-jin-'ē-s(h)ē-əl, -(ˌ)gī-'nē-, -shəl\ *adj* [*poly-* + NL *gynoecium*] **:** made up of several to many united gynoecia ⟨collective fruits are ~⟩
po·lyg·y·nous \pə-'lij-ə-nəs\ *adj* **1 :** relating to or practicing polygyny **2 :** having many pistils
po·lyg·y·ny \-nē\ *n* **:** the practice of having more than one wife or female mate at one time
poly·he·dral \ˌpäl-i-'hē-drəl\ *adj* **:** relating to or having the form of a polyhedron
poly·he·dron \-drən\ *n, pl* **polyhedrons** *or* **poly·he·dra** \-drə\ [NL] **:** a solid formed by plane faces
poly·he·dro·sis \-hē-'drō-səs\ *n* [NL, fr. *polyhedron*] **:** any of several virus diseases of insect larvae characterized by dissolution of tissues and accumulation of polyhedral granules in the resultant fluid
poly·his·tor \ˌpäl-i-'his-tər\ *n* [Gk *polyistōr* very learned, fr. *poly-* + *istōr* learned — more at HISTORY] **:** POLYMATH
poly·hy·droxy \-(ˌ)hī-'dräk-sē\ *adj* [*poly-* + *hydroxyl*] **:** containing more than one hydroxyl group in the molecule
Poly·hym·nia \ˌpäl-i-'him-nē-ə\ *n* [L, fr. Gk *Polyymnia*] **:** the Greek Muse of the sacred lyric
poly·iso·to·pic \ˌpäl-ē-ˌī-sə-'täp-ik, -'tō-pik *also* -ˌī-zə-\ *adj* **:** of, relating to, or consisting of more than one isotope
poly·mas·ti·gote \ˌpäl-i-'mas-tə-ˌgōt\ *adj* **:** having many flagella
poly·math \'päl-i-ˌmath\ *n* [Gk *polymathēs* very learned, fr. *poly-* + *manthanein* to learn — more at MATHEMATICAL] **:** one of encyclopedic learning — **polymath** *or* **poly·math·ic** \ˌpäl-i-'math-ik\ *adj* — **po·ly·ma·thy** \pə-'lim-ə-thē, 'päl-ə-ˌmath-ē\ *n*
poly·mer \'päl-ə-mər\ *n* [ISV, back-formation fr. *polymeric*] **:** a chemical compound or mixture of compounds formed by polymerization and consisting essentially of repeating structural units
poly·mer·ic \ˌpäl-ə-'mer-ik\ *adj* [ISV, fr. Gk *polymerēs* having many parts, fr. *poly-* + *meros* part — more at MERIT] **:** of, relating to, or consisting of a polymer; *broadly* **:** composed of or involving several similar parts or items — **poly·mer·i·cal·ly** \-i-k(ə-)lē\ *adv* — **po·ly·mer·ism** \pə-'lim-ə-ˌriz-əm, 'päl-ə-mə-\ *or* **po·ly·mery** \pə-'lim-ə-rē, 'päl-ə-ˌmer-ē\ *n*
po·ly·mer·iza·tion \pə-ˌlim-ə-rə-'zā-shən, ˌpäl-ə-mə-rə-\ *n* [ISV] **1 :** a chemical reaction in which two or more small molecules combine to form larger molecules; *broadly* **:** ASSOCIATION 5 **2 :** reduplication of parts in an organism
po·ly·mer·ize \pə-'lim-ə-ˌrīz, 'päl-ə-mə-\ *vt* **:** to subject to polymerization ~ *vi* **:** to undergo polymerization
po·lym·er·ous \pə-'lim-ə-rəs\ *adj* [*poly-* + *-merous*] **:** having many parts or members in a whorl
poly·morph \'päl-i-ˌmȯrf\ *n* [ISV] **1 :** a polymorphous organism; *also* **:** one of the several forms of such an organism **2 :** any of the crystalline forms of a polymorphous substance
poly·mor·phic \ˌpäl-i-'mȯr-fik\ *or* **poly·mor·phous** \-fəs\ *adj* [Gk *polymorphos*, fr. *poly-* + *-morphos* -morphous] **:** having, assuming, or occurring in various forms, characters, or styles — **poly·mor·phi·cal·ly** \-fi-k(ə-)lē\ *or* **poly·mor·phous·ly** *adv* — **poly·mor·phism** \-ˌfiz-əm\ *n*
poly·mor·pho·nu·cle·ar \-ˌmȯr-fə-'n(y)ü-klē-ər\ *adj*, *of a leukocyte* **:** having the nucleus complexly lobed — **polymorphonuclear** *n*
poly·myx·in \ˌpäl-i-'mik-sən\ *n* [ISV, fr. NL *polymyxa* (specific epithet of *Bacillus polymyxa*), fr. *poly-* + Gk *myxa* mucus — more at MUCUS] **:** any of several toxic antibiotics obtained from a soil bacterium (*Bacillus polymyxa*) and active against gram-negative bacteria
Poly·ne·sian \ˌpäl-ə-'nē-zhən, -shən\ *n* **1 :** a member of any of the native peoples of Polynesia **2 :** a group of Austronesian languages spoken in Polynesia — **Polynesian** *adj*
Poly·ni·ces \ˌpäl-ə-'nī-sēz\ *n* [L, fr. Gk *Polyneikēs*] **:** a son of Oedipus and intended beneficiary of the expedition of the Seven against Thebes
poly·no·mi·al \ˌpäl-i-'nō-mē-əl\ *n* [*poly-* + *-nomial* (as in *binomial*)] **1 :** a sum of two or more algebraic expressions **2 :** a sum of a finite number of terms each composed of a positive or zero power of a variable multiplied by a constant — **polynomial** *adj*
po·lyn·ya \ˌpäl-ən-'yä\ *n* [Russ *polyn'ya*] **:** an area of open water in sea ice
pol·yp \'päl-əp\ *n* [MF *polype* octopus, nasal tumor, fr. L *polypus*, fr. Gk *polypous*, fr. *poly-* + *pous* foot — more at FOOT] **1 :** a coelenterate having typically a hollow cylindrical body closed and attached at one end and opening at the other by a central mouth surrounded by tentacles armed with nematocysts **2 :** a projecting mass of swollen and hypertrophied or tumorous membrane — **pol·yp·oid** \'päl-ə-ˌpȯid\ *adj*
pol·yp·ary \'päl-ə-ˌper-ē\ *n* **:** the common investing structure or tissue in which the polyps of corals and other compound coelenterates are embedded
poly·pep·tide \ˌpäl-i-'pep-ˌtīd\ *n* [ISV] **:** a compound that yields amino acids on hydrolysis but has a lower molecular weight than a protein
poly·pet·al·ous \-'pet-ᵊl-əs\ *adj* [NL *polypetalus*, fr. *poly-* + *petalum* petal] **:** having or consisting of separate petals **:** CHORIPETALOUS
poly·pha·gia \-'fā-j(ē-)ə\ *n* [Gk *polyphagia*, fr. *polyphagos*] **:** excessive appetite or eating
po·lyph·a·gous \pə-'lif-ə-gəs\ *adj* [Gk *polyphagos* eating too much, fr. *poly-* + *-phagos* -phagous] **:** feeding on or utilizing many kinds of food
poly·phase \'päl-i-ˌfāz\ *adj* [ISV] **:** having or producing two or more phases ⟨a ~ machine⟩ ⟨a ~ current⟩
Poly·phe·mus \ˌpäl-ə-'fē-məs\ *n* [L, fr. Gk *Polyphēmos*] **:** a Cyclops blinded by Odysseus in order to escape from his cave
poly·phone \'päl-i-ˌfōn\ *n* **:** a symbol or sequence of symbols having more than one phonetic value (as *a* in English)
poly·phon·ic \ˌpäl-i-'fän-ik\ *or* **po·lyph·o·nous** \pə-'lif-ə-nəs\ *adj* **1 :** of, relating to, or marked by polyphony **2 :** being a polyphone — **poly·phon·i·cal·ly** \ˌpäl-i-'fän-i-k(ə-)lē\ *or* **po·lyph·o·nous·ly** *adv*
polyphonic prose *n* **:** a freely rhythmical prose employing characteristic devices of verse (as alliteration, assonance)
po·lyph·o·ny \pə-'lif-ə-nē\ *n* [Gk *polyphōnia* variety of tones, fr. *polyphōnos* having many tones or voices, fr. *poly-* + *phōnē* voice — more at BAN] **1 :** a style of musical composition in which two or more independent but organically related voice parts sound against one another **2 a :** multiplicity of polyphones **b :** representation so characterized
poly·phy·let·ic \ˌpäl-i-(ˌ)fī-'let-ik\ *adj* [ISV, fr. Gk *polyphylos* of many tribes, fr. *poly-* + *phylē* tribe — more at PHYL-] **:** of or relating to more than one stock; *specif* **:** derived from more than one ancestral line — **poly·phy·let·i·cal·ly** \-i-k(ə-)lē\ *adv* — **poly·phy·let·i·cism** \-'let-ə-ˌsiz-əm\ *n*
pol·yp·ide \'päl-ə-ˌpīd\ *n* **:** one of the individual zooids of a bryozoan colony
poly·ploid \'päl-i-ˌplȯid\ *adj* [ISV] **:** manifold in appearance or arrangement; *specif* **:** having or being a chromosome number that is a multiple greater than two of the monoploid number — **poly-**

ploid *n* — **poly·ploi·dic** \ˌpäl-i-ˈplȯid-ik\ *adj* — **poly·ploi·dy** \ˈpäl-i-ˌplȯid-ē\ *n*

poly·pnea \ˌpäl-i(p)-ˈnē-ə, pä-ˈlip-nē-ə\ *n* [NL] **:** rapid or panting respiration — **poly·pne·ic** \-(ˈ)nē-ik\ *adj*

poly·po·dy \ˈpäl-ə-ˌpōd-ē\ *n* [ME *polypodie*, fr. L *polypodium*, fr. Gk *polypodion*, fr. *poly-* + *pod-*, *pous* foot — more at FOOT] **:** a widely distributed fern (*Polypodium vulgare*) with creeping rootstocks and pinnatifid fronds with entire segments

pol·yp·ous \ˈpäl-ə-pəs\ *adj* **:** relating to, being, or resembling a polyp

pol·yp·tych \ˈpäl-əp-ˌtik\ *n* [Gk *polyptychos* having many folds, fr. *poly-* + *ptychē* fold, fr. *ptyssein* to fold] **:** an arrangement of four or more panels usu. hinged and folding together

poly·sac·cha·ride \ˌpäl-i-ˈsak-ə-ˌrīd\ *n* [ISV] **:** a carbohydrate that can be decomposed by hydrolysis into two or more molecules of monosaccharides; *esp* **:** one of the more complex carbohydrates

poly·sa·pro·bic \-sə-ˈprō-bik\ *adj* [ISV] **:** living in a medium that is rich in organic matter that can be decomposed and is nearly free from dissolved oxygen

poly·se·mous \ˌpäl-i-ˈsē-məs\ *adj* [LL *polysemus*, fr. Gk *polysēmos*, fr. *poly-* + *sēma* sign] **:** marked by multiplicity of meaning

poly·se·my \ˈpäl-i-ˌsē-mē\ *n* **:** multiplicity of meaning

poly·sep·al·ous \ˌpäl-i-ˈsep-ə-ləs\ *adj* **:** having separate sepals

poly·so·mic \-ˈsō-mik\ *adj* [ISV] **:** having one or a few chromosomes present in greater or smaller number than the rest — **polysomic** *n*

po·lys·ti·chous \pə-ˈlis-ti-kəs\ *adj* [Gk *polystichos*, fr. *poly-* + *stichos* row — more at DISTICH] **:** arranged in several rows

poly·sty·rene \ˌpäl-i-ˈstī(ə)r-ˌēn\ *n* **:** a polymer of styrene; *esp* **:** a rigid transparent thermoplastic of good physical and electrical insulating properties used esp. in containers and other molded products and sheet materials

poly·sul·fide \-ˈsəl-ˌfīd\ *n* [ISV] **:** a sulfide containing two or more atoms of sulfur in the molecule

poly·syl·lab·ic \ˌpäl-i-sə-ˈlab-ik\ *adj* [ML *polysyllabus*, fr. Gk *polysyllabos*, fr. *poly-* + *syllabē* syllable] **1 :** having more than three syllables **2 :** characterized by polysyllabic words — **poly·syl·lab·i·cal·ly** \-i-k(ə-)lē\ *adv*

poly·syl·la·ble \ˈpäl-i-ˌsil-ə-bəl, ˌpäl-i-ˈ\ *n* [modif. of ML *polysyllaba*, fr. fem. of *polysyllabus*] **:** a polysyllabic word

poly·syn·de·ton \ˌpäl-i-ˈsin-də-ˌtän\ *n* [NL, fr. LGk, neut. of *polysyndetos* using many conjunctions, fr. Gk *poly-* + *syndetos* bound together, conjunctive — more at ASYNDETON] **:** repetition of conjunctions in close succession

[1]**poly·tech·nic** \ˌpäl-i-ˈtek-nik\ *adj* [F *polytechnique*, fr. Gk *polytechnos* skilled in many arts, fr. *poly-* + *technē* art — more at TECHNICAL] **:** relating to or devoted to instruction in many technical arts or applied sciences

[2]**polytechnic** *n* **:** a polytechnic school

poly·the·ism \ˈpäl-i-(ˌ)thē-ˌiz-əm\ *n* [F *polythéisme*, fr. LGk *polytheos* polytheistic, fr. Gk, of many gods, fr. *poly-* + *theos* god] **:** belief in or worship of a plurality of gods — **poly·the·ist** \-ˌthē-əst\ *adj or n* — **poly·the·is·tic** \ˌpäl-i-thē-ˈis-tik\ *also* **poly·the·is·ti·cal** \-ˈis-ti-kəl\ *adj*

poly·thene \ˈpäl-ə-ˌthēn\ *n* [by contr.] **:** POLYETHYLENE

po·lyt·o·cous \pə-ˈlit-ə-kəs\ *adj* [Gk *polytokos*, fr. *poly-* + *tiktein* to beget — more at THANE] **:** producing many eggs or young at one time

poly·ton·al \ˌpäl-i-ˈtōn-ᵊl\ *adj* **:** of or relating to polytonality

poly·to·nal·i·ty \-tō-ˈnal-ət-ē\ *n* **:** the simultaneous use of two or more musical keys

poly·tro·phic \-ˈträf-ik, -ˈtrō-fik\ *adj* **:** deriving nourishment from more than one organic substance

poly·typ·ic \-ˈtip-ik\ *adj* **:** represented by several or many types or subdivisions

poly·un·sat·u·rat·ed \ˌpäl-ē-ˌən-ˈsach-ə-ˌrāt-əd\ *adj, of an oil or fatty acid* **:** rich in unsaturated bonds

poly·ure·thane \ˌpäl-ē-ˈ(y)u̇r-ə-ˌthān\ *or* **poly·ure·than** \-ˌthan\ *n* [ISV] **:** any of various polymers that contain —NHCOO— linkages and are used esp. in flexible and rigid foams, elastomers, and resins

poly·uria \ˌpäl-ē-ˈ(y)u̇r-ē-ə\ *n* [NL] **:** excessive secretion of urine

poly·va·lence \ˌpäl-i-ˈvā-lən(t)s\ *or* **poly·va·len·cy** \-lən-sē\ *n* **:** the state of being polyvalent

poly·va·lent \ˌpäl-i-ˈvā-lənt\ *adj* [ISV] **1 a :** having a valence greater usu. than two **b :** having variable valence **2 a :** effective against or sensitive toward more than one exciting agent **b :** MULTIVALENT 2

poly·vi·nyl \-ˈvīn-ᵊl\ *n, often attrib* [ISV] **:** a polymerized vinyl compound, resin, or plastic

poly·vi·nyl·i·dene \-(ˌ)vī-ˈnil-ə-ˌdēn\ *adj* **:** relating to or being a polymerized vinylidene compound

polyvinyl resin *n* **:** VINYL RESIN

poly·zo·an \ˌpäl-i-ˈzō-ən\ *adj or n* **1** [NL *Polyzoa*, phylum name, fr. *poly-* + *-zoa*] **:** BRYOZOAN **2** [NL *Polyzoa*, subclass name, fr. *poly-* + *-zoa*] **:** CESTODE

poly·zo·ar·i·um \-zə-ˈwar-ē-əm, -ˈwer-\ *n, pl* **poly·zo·ar·ia** \-ē-ə\ [NL, fr. *Polyzoa*] **:** a bryozoan colony or the supporting skeleton of such a colony

poly·zo·ic \-ˈzō-ik\ *adj* **1 :** composed of many zooids **2 :** producing many sporozoites

pom·ace \ˈpəm-əs, ˈpäm-\ *n* [prob. fr. ML *pomacium* cider, fr. LL *pomum* apple, fr. L, fruit] **1 :** the substance of apples or other fruit crushed by grinding or the residue remaining after pressing wine grapes **2 :** a substance crushed to a pulpy mass

po·ma·ceous \pō-ˈmā-shəs\ *adj* [NL *pomaceus*, fr. LL *pomum*] **1 :** of or relating to apples **2** [*pome*] **:** resembling a pome

po·made \pō-ˈmād, pə-, -ˈmäd\ *n* [MF *pommade* ointment formerly made from apples, fr. It *pomata*, fr. *pomo* apple, fr. LL *pomum*] **:** a perfumed ointment; *esp* **:** a fragrant unguent for the hair or scalp — **pomade** *vt*

po·man·der \ˈpō-ˌman-dər, pō-ˈ\ *n* [ME, modif. of MF *pome d'ambre*, lit., apple or ball of amber] **:** a mixture of aromatic substances enclosed in a perforated bag or box and formerly carried as a guard against infection

po·ma·tum \pō-ˈmāt-əm, pə-, -ˈmät-\ *n* [NL, fr. LL *pomum* apple] **:** OINTMENT; *esp* **:** a perfumed unguent for the hair or scalp

pome \ˈpōm\ *n* [ME, fr. MF *pome*, *pomme* apple, pome, ball, fr. LL *pomum* apple, fr. L, fruit] **:** a fleshy fruit consisting of a central core with usu. five seeds enclosed in a capsule and of an outer thickened fleshy layer

pome·gran·ate \ˈpäm-(ə-)ˌgran-ət, ˈpəm-ˌgran-\ *n* [ME *poumgarnet*, fr. MF *pomme grenate*, lit., seedy apple] **1 :** a thick-skinned several-celled reddish berry about the size of an orange having many seeds in a crimson pulp of agreeable acid flavor **2 :** a widely cultivated tropical Old World tree (*Punica granatum* of the family Punicaceae) bearing pomegranates

pom·e·lo \ˈpäm-ə-ˌlō\ *n* [alter. of earlier *pompelmous*, fr. D *pompelmoes*] **1 :** SHADDOCK **2 :** GRAPEFRUIT

Pom·er·a·nian \ˌpäm-ə-ˈrā-nē-ən, -nyən\ *n* **1 :** a native or inhabitant of Pomerania **2 :** any of a breed of very small compact long-haired dogs of the spitz type — **Pomeranian** *adj*

po·mif·er·ous \pō-ˈmif-(ə-)rəs\ *adj* [L *pomifer* fruitbearing, fr. *pomum* + *-fer* -ferous] **:** bearing pomes

pom·mée \pä-ˈmā\ *adj* [F, fr. MF *pomme* apple, ball] *of a heraldic cross* **:** having the end of each arm terminating in a ball or disk — see CROSS illustration

[1]**pom·mel** \ˈpəm-əl, ˈpäm-\ *n* [ME *pomel*, fr. MF, fr. (assumed) VL *pomellum* ball, knob, fr. dim. of LL *pomum* apple] **1 :** the knob on the hilt of a sword or saber **2 :** the protuberance at the front and top of a saddlebow

[2]**pom·mel** \ˈpəm-əl\ *vt* **pom·meled** *or* **pom·melled; pom·mel·ing** *or* **pom·mel·ling** \-(ə-)liŋ\ [[1]*pommel*] **:** PUMMEL

po·mo·log·i·cal \ˌpō-mə-ˈläj-i-kəl\ *adj* **:** of or relating to pomology — **po·mo·log·i·cal·ly** \-k(ə-)lē\ *adv*

po·mol·o·gist \pō-ˈmäl-ə-jəst, pə-\ *n* **:** a horticulturist who specializes in pomology

po·mol·o·gy \-jē\ *n* [NL *pomologia*, fr. L *pomum* fruit + *-logia* -logy] **:** the science and practice of fruit growing

Po·mo·na \pə-ˈmō-nə\ *n* [L] **:** the ancient Italian goddess of fruit trees

pomp \ˈpämp\ *n* [ME, fr. MF *pompe*, fr. L *pompa* procession, pomp, fr. Gk *pompē* act of sending, escort, procession, pomp] **1 :** brilliant display **:** SPLENDOR **2 :** PAGEANT **3 a :** ostentatious display **:** VAINGLORY **b :** an ostentatious gesture or act

pom·pa·dour \ˈpäm-pə-ˌdō(ə)r, -ˌdȯ(ə)r\ *n* [Marquise de *Pompadour* †1764 mistress of Louis XV of France] **1 a :** a woman's style of hairdressing in which the hair is brushed into a loose full roll around the face **b :** a man's style of hairdressing in which the hair is combed back to stand erect **2 :** hair dressed in a pompadour

pom·pa·no \ˈpäm-pə-ˌnō, ˈpəm-\ *n, pl* **pompano** *or* **pompanos** [Sp *pámpano* gilthead, lit., vine leaf, fr. L *pampinus*] **1 :** a marine percoid food fish (*Trachinotus carolinus*) of the southern Atlantic and Gulf coasts of No. America; *broadly* **:** any of several related fishes **2 :** a small bluish or greenish butterfish (*Palometa simillima*) of the Pacific coast

pom-pom \ˈpäm-ˌpäm\ *n* [imit.] **:** an automatic gun of 20 to 40 millimeters mounted on ships in pairs, fours, or eights

pom·pon \ˈpäm-ˌpän\ *n* [F, fr. MF *pompe* tuft of ribbons] **1 :** an ornamental ball or tuft used on clothing, caps, and fancy costumes **2 a :** any of various hardy garden chrysanthemums with flower heads resembling a pompon **b :** any of various dahlias with flower heads usu. not more than two inches in diameter

pom·pos·i·ty \päm-ˈpäs-ət-ē\ *n* **1 :** POMPOUSNESS **2 :** a pompous gesture, habit, or action

pomp·ous \ˈpäm-pəs\ *adj* **1 :** relating to or suggestive of pomp **:** MAGNIFICENT **2 :** SELF-IMPORTANT **3 :** excessively elevated or ornate ⟨~ rhetoric⟩ **syn** see SHOWY — **pomp·ous·ly** *adv* — **pomp·ous·ness** *n*

Pon·ceau \pän-ˈsō\ *n* [F, poppy red, fr. OF *pouncel* red poppy] **:** any of several azo dyes giving red colors

pon·cho \ˈpän-(ˌ)chō\ *n* [AmerSp, fr. Araucanian *pontho* woolen fabric] **1 :** a cloak resembling a blanket with a slit in the middle for the head **2 :** a waterproof garment resembling a poncho worn chiefly as a raincoat

pond \ˈpänd\ *n* [ME *ponde* artificially confined body of water, alter. of *pounde* enclosure — more at POUND] **:** a body of water usu. smaller than a lake

pon·der \ˈpän-dər\ *vb* **pon·der·ing** \-d(ə-)riŋ\ [ME *ponderen*, fr. MF *ponderer*, fr. L *ponderare* to weigh, ponder, fr. *ponder-*, *pondus* weight — more at PENDANT] *vt* **1 :** to weigh in the mind **2 :** to deliberate about **3 :** to muse over ~ *vi* **:** to think or consider esp. quietly, soberly, and deeply — **pon·der·er** \-dər-ər\ *n*

syn MEDITATE, MUSE, RUMINATE: PONDER implies a careful weighing of a problem or, often, prolonged inconclusive thinking about a matter; MEDITATE implies a definite focusing of one's thoughts on something so as to understand it deeply; MUSE suggests a more or less focused daydreaming as in remembrance; RUMINATE implies going over the same matter in one's thoughts again and again but suggests little of either purposive thinking or rapt absorption

pon·der·a·ble \ˈpän-d(ə-)rə-bəl\ *adj* [LL *ponderabilis*, fr. *ponderare*] **:** capable of being weighed or appraised **:** APPRECIABLE **syn** see PERCEPTIBLE

pon·der·ous \ˈpän-d(ə-)rəs\ *adj* [ME, fr. MF *pondereux*, fr. L *ponderosus*, fr. *ponder-*, *pondus* weight] **1 :** of very great weight **2 :** unwieldy or clumsy because of weight and size **3 :** oppressively or unpleasantly dull **:** PEDESTRIAN **syn** see HEAVY — **pon·der·ous·ly** *adv* — **pon·der·ous·ness** *n*

pond scum *n* **:** a spirogyra or a related alga; *also* **:** a mass of tangled filaments formed by these on stagnant waters

pond·weed \ˈpän-ˌdwēd\ *n* **:** any of a genus (*Potamogeton* of the family Zannichelliaceae, the pondweed family) of aquatic plants

pone \ˈpōn\ *n* [of Algonquian origin; akin to Delaware *äpân* baked] *South & Midland* **:** a cornmeal cake shaped into an oval in the palms and baked, fried, or boiled; *also* **:** corn bread in the form of pones

pon·gee \pän-ˈjē, ˈpän-ˌ\ *n* [Chin (Pek) *pen³ chi¹*, fr. *pen³* own + *chi¹* loom] **:** a thin soft ecru or tan fabric of Chinese origin woven from raw silk; *also* **:** an imitation of this fabric in cotton or rayon

pon·gid \ˈpän-jəd\ *n* [deriv. of Kongo *mpungu* ape] **:** an anthropoid ape

[1]**pon·iard** \ˈpän-yərd\ *n* [MF *poignard*, fr. *poing* fist, fr. L *pugnus* fist

— more at PUNGENT] **:** a dagger with a usu. slender triangular or square blade

2**poniard** *vt* **:** to pierce or kill with a poniard

pons \'pänz\ *n, pl* **pon·tes** \'pän-,tēz\ [NL *pons* (*Varolii*), lit., bridge of Varoli, fr. Costanzo *Varoli* †1575 It surgeon and anatomist] **:** a broad mass of chiefly transverse nerve fibers conspicuous on the ventral surface of the brain of man and lower mammals at the anterior end of the medulla oblongata — called also *pons Va·ro·lii* \,pänz-və-'rō-lē-,ī, -lē-,ē\

pons asi·no·rum \'pän-,zas-ə-'nōr-əm, -'nȯr-\ *n* [NL, lit., asses' bridge, name applied to the proposition that the base angles of an isosceles triangle are equal] **:** a critical test of ability imposed upon the inexperienced or ignorant

Pon·tic \'pänt-ik\ *adj* [L *ponticus*, fr. Gk *pontikos*, fr. *Pontos* Pontus & *Pontos* the Black sea (lit., the sea)] **:** of or relating to Pontus or the Black sea

pon·ti·fex \'pänt-ə-,feks\ *n, pl* **pon·tif·i·ces** \pän-'tif-ə-,sēz\ [L *pontific-, pontifex*] **:** a member of the council of priests forming the most important part of the Roman religious body

pon·tiff \'pänt-əf\ *n* [F *pontif*, fr. L *pontific-, pontifex*, lit., bridge maker, fr. *pont-, pons* bridge + *facere* to make — more at FIND, DO] **1 :** PONTIFEX **2 :** BISHOP; *specif* **:** POPE

1**pon·tif·i·cal** \pän-'tif-i-kəl\ *adj* [L *pontificalis*, fr. *pontific-, pontifex*] **1 a :** of or relating to a pontiff or pontifex **b :** celebrated by a prelate of episcopal rank with distinctive ceremonies ⟨~ mass⟩ **2 :** POMPOUS **3 :** pretentiously dogmatic — **pon·tif·i·cal·ly** \-k(ə-)lē\ *adv*

2**pontifical** *n* **1 :** episcopal attire; *specif* **:** the insignia of the episcopal order worn by a prelate when celebrating a pontifical mass — usu. used in pl. **2 :** a book containing the forms for sacraments and rites performed by a bishop

1**pon·tif·i·cate** \pän-'tif-i-kət, -ə-,kāt\ *n* [L *pontificatus*, fr. *pontific-, pontifex*] **:** the state, office, or term of office of a pontiff

2**pon·tif·i·cate** \-ə-,kāt\ *vi* [ML *pontificatus*, pp. of *pontificare*, fr. L. *pontific-, pontifex*] **1 a :** to officiate as a pontiff **b :** to celebrate pontifical mass **2 :** to deliver oracular utterances or dogmatic opinions — **pon·tif·i·ca·tor** \-,kāt-ər\ *n*

Pont l'É·vêque \pōⁿ-lā-'vek\ *n* [*Pont l'Évêque*, France] **:** a firm cheese with soft center and mild flavor made of whole milk and artificially colored yellow

pon·ton \'pänt-ᵊn, pän-'tün\ *n* [F] **:** PONTOON

pon·ton·ier \,pänt-ᵊn-'i(ə)r\ *n* [F *pontonnier*, fr. *ponton*] **:** an individual engaged in constructing a pontoon bridge

pon·toon \pän-'tün\ *n* [F *ponton*, floating bridge, punt, fr. L *ponton-, ponto*, fr. *pont-, pons* bridge] **1 :** a flat-bottomed boat (as a lighter); *esp* **:** a flat-bottomed boat or portable float used in building a floating temporary bridge **2 :** a float of an airplane

pontoon bridge *n* **:** a bridge whose deck is supported on pontoons

po·ny \'pō-nē\ *n* [prob. fr. obs. F *poulenet*, dim. of F *poulain* colt, fr. ML *pullanus*, fr. L *pullus* young of an animal, foal — more at FOAL] **1 a :** a small horse; *esp* **:** one of any of several breeds of very small stocky animals noted for their gentleness and endurance **b :** a bronco, mustang, or similar horse of the western U.S. **c :** RACEHORSE **2 :** something smaller than standard **3 :** a literal translation of a foreign language text; *esp* **:** one used surreptitiously by students in preparing or reciting lessons

pony express *n* **:** a rapid postal and express system operating by relays of ponies

po·ny·tail \'pō-nē-,tāl\ *n* **:** hair arranged to resemble a pony's tail

po·ny up \,pō-nē-'əp\ *vb* [origin unknown] *vt* **:** to pay (money) in settlement of an account ~ *vi* **:** PAY

pooch \'püch\ *n* [origin unknown] *slang* **:** DOG

pood \'püd, 'püt\ *n* [Russ *pud*, fr. ON *pund* pound — more at POUND] **:** a Russian unit of weight equal to about 36.11 pounds

poo·dle \'püd-ᵊl\ *n* [G *pudel*, short for *pudelhund*, fr. *pudeln* to splash (fr. *pudel* puddle, fr. LG) + *hund* dog (fr. OHG *hunt*)] **:** any of an old breed of active intelligent heavy-coated solid-colored dogs

pooh \'pü, 'pu̇\ *interj* — used to express contempt or disapproval

pooh–bah \'pü-,bä, -,bȯ\ *n, often cap P&B* [*Pooh-Bah*, character in Gilbert and Sullivan's opera *The Mikado* (1885) bearing the title Lord-High-Everything-Else] **1 :** one holding many public or private offices **2 :** one in high position

pooh–pooh \'pü-(,)pü, pü-'\ *also* **pooh** \'pü\ *vb* [*pooh* (interj. expressing contempt)] *vi* **:** to express contempt or impatience ~ *vt* **:** to express contempt for **:** SCORN

1**pool** \'pül\ *n* [ME, fr. OE *pōl*; akin to OHG *pfuol* pool] **1 :** a small and rather deep body of usu. fresh water **2 :** a small body of standing liquid **:** PUDDLE **3 :** a continuous area of porous sedimentary rock which yields petroleum or gas

2**pool** *n* [F *poule*, lit., hen, fr. OF, fem. of *poul* cock — more at PULLET] **1 a :** an aggregate stake to which each player of a game has contributed **b :** all the money bet by a number of persons on a particular event **2 a :** a game played on an English billiard table in which each of the players stakes a sum and the winner takes all **b :** any of various games of billiards played on a pool table having 6 pockets with usu. 15 object balls **3 :** an aggregation of the interests or property of different persons made to further a joint undertaking by subjecting them to the same control and a common liability: as **a :** a common fund or combination of interests for the common adventure in buying or selling; *esp* **:** one for speculating in or manipulating the market price of securities or commodities (as grain) **b :** a combination between competing business houses for the control of traffic by removing competition **4 :** a fencing contest in which each member of a team successively engages each member of another team **5 :** a readily available supply: as **a :** the whole quantity of a particular material present in the body and available for function or the satisfying of metabolic demands **b :** a body product (as blood) collected from many donors and stored for later use **syn** see MONOPOLY

3**pool** *vt* **:** to contribute to a common fund or effort

pool·room \-,rüm, -,ru̇m\ *n* **1 :** a room in which bookmaking is carried on **2 :** a room for the playing of pool

1**poop** \'püp\ *n* [MF *poupe*, fr. L *puppis*] **1** *obs* **:** STERN **2 :** an enclosed superstructure at the stern of a ship above the main deck

2**poop** *vt* **1 :** to break over the stern of **2 :** to ship (a sea or wave) over the stern

3**poop** *vb* [origin unknown] *vt, slang* **:** to put out of breath; *also* **:** to wear out **:** EXHAUST ~ *vi, slang* **:** to become exhausted ⟨~ out⟩

4**poop** *n* [origin unknown] *slang* **:** official or unofficial information

poop deck *n* **:** a partial deck above a ship's main afterdeck

poor \'pu̇(ə)r, 'pō(ə)r\ *adj* [ME *poure*, fr. OF *povre*, fr. L *pauper*; akin to L *paucus* little and to L *parere* to produce, *parare* to acquire — more at FEW, PARE] **1 a :** lacking material possessions **b :** of, relating to, or characterized by poverty **2 a :** less than adequate **:** MEAGER **b :** small in worth **3 :** exciting pity **4 a :** inferior in quality or value **b :** HUMBLE, UNPRETENTIOUS **c :** MEAN, PETTY **5 :** EMACIATED, LEAN **6 :** BARREN, UNPRODUCTIVE — used of land — **poor·ly** *adv* — **poor·ness** *n*

poor box *n* **:** a box (as in a church) for alms for the poor

Poor Clare \-'kla(ə)r, -'kle(ə)r\ *n* **:** a nun of an order founded early in the 13th century at Assisi by St. Clare under the direction of St. Francis

poor farm \'pu̇(ə)r-,färm, 'pō(ə)r-\ *n* **:** a farm maintained at public expense for the support and employment of needy persons

poor·house \-,hau̇s\ *n* **:** a place maintained at public expense to house needy or dependent persons

poor·ish \-ish\ *adj* **:** rather poor

poor law *n* **:** a law providing for or regulating the public relief or support of the poor

poor·ly \-lē\ *adj* **:** somewhat ill **:** INDISPOSED

poor–spir·it·ed \-'spir-ət-əd\ *adj* **:** lacking zest, confidence, or courage — **poor–spir·it·ed·ly** *adv* — **poor–spir·it·ed·ness** *n*

poor white *n* **:** a member of an inferior or underprivileged white social group — often taken to be offensive

1**pop** \'päp\ *vb* **popped; pop·ping** [ME *poppen*, of imit. origin] *vt* **1 :** to strike or knock sharply **:** HIT **2 :** to push, put, or thrust suddenly **3 :** to cause to explode or burst open **4 :** to fire at **:** SHOOT ~ *vi* **1 :** to go, come, or enter suddenly **2 :** to make or burst with a sharp sound **:** EXPLODE **3 :** to protrude from the sockets **4 :** to shoot with a firearm **5 :** to hit a pop fly — **pop the question :** to propose marriage

2**pop** *n* **1 :** a sharp explosive sound **2 :** a shot from a gun **3** [fr. the sound made by pulling a cork from a bottle] **:** a flavored carbonated beverage **4 :** POP FLY

3**pop** *adv* **:** like or with a pop **:** SUDDENLY

4**pop** *n* **1 :** pop music **2 :** POP ART **3 :** pop culture

5**pop** *adj* **1 :** POPULAR ⟨~ music⟩: as **a :** of or relating to pop music ⟨~ singer⟩ **b :** of, relating to, or constituting a mass culture esp. of the young widely disseminated through the mass media ⟨~ society⟩ **2 a :** of or relating to pop art ⟨~painter⟩ **b :** having, using, or imitating themes or techniques characteristic of pop art ⟨~ movie⟩

pop art *n* **:** art in which commonplace objects (as road signs, hamburgers, comic strips, or soup cans) are used as subject matter and are often physically incorporated in the work — **pop artist** *n*

pop·corn \'päp-,kȯ(ə)rn\ *n* **:** an Indian corn (*Zea mays everta*) whose kernels on exposure to dry heat burst open to form a white starchy mass; *also* **:** the popped kernels

pope \'pōp\ *n* [ME, fr. OE *pāpa*, fr. LL *papa*, fr. Gk *pappas, papas*, title of bishops, lit., papa] **1** *often cap* **:** the head of the Roman Catholic Church **2 :** one held to resemble a pope (as in authority)

pop·ery \'pō-p(ə-)rē\ *n* **:** ROMAN CATHOLICISM — usu. used disparagingly

pop·eyed \'päp-'īd\ *adj* **:** having eyes that bulge (as from excitement)

pop fly *n* **:** a short high fly ball in baseball

pop·gun \'päp-,gən\ *n* **:** a child's toy gun for shooting pellets with compressed air

Pop·i·an *also* **Pop·ean** \'pō-pē-ən\ *adj* **:** of, relating to, or characteristic of Alexander Pope or his poetry

pop·in·jay \'päp-ən-,jā\ *n* [ME *papejay*, fr. MF *papegai, papejai*, fr. Ar *babghā'*] **1** *obs* **:** PARROT **2 :** a strutting supercilious person

pop·ish \'pō-pish\ *adj* [*pope*] **:** Roman Catholic — often used disparagingly — **pop·ish·ly** *adv*

pop·lar \'päp-lər\ *n* [ME *poplere*, fr. MF *pouplier*, fr. *pouple* poplar, fr. L *populus*] **1 a :** any of a genus (*Populus*) of slender quick-growing trees of the willow family **b :** the wood of a poplar **2 a :** TULIP TREE **b :** the wood of a tulip tree

pop·lin \'päp-lən\ *n* [F *papeline*] **:** a strong fabric in plain weave with crosswise ribs

pop·li·te·al \pä-'plit-ē-əl, ,päp-lə-'tē-\ *adj* [NL *popliteus*, fr. L *poplit-, poples* ham of the knee] **:** of or relating to the back part of the leg behind the knee joint

pop off *vi* **1 a :** to leave suddenly **b :** to die unexpectedly **2 :** to talk thoughtlessly and often loudly or angrily

pop-off \'päp-,ȯf\ *n* **:** one who talks loosely or loudly

pop·over \'päp-,ō-vər\ *n* **:** a quick bread made from a thin batter of eggs, milk, and flour and baked into a hollow shell

pop·per \'päp-ər\ *n* **:** one that pops; *esp* **:** a utensil for popping corn

pop·pet \'päp-ət\ *n* [ME *popet* doll, puppet — more at PUPPET] **1** *chiefly Brit* **:** DEAR **2 a** *Midland* **:** DOLL **b** *obs* **:** MARIONETTE **3 a :** an upright support or guide of a machine that is fastened at the bottom only **b :** a valve that rises perpendicularly to or from its seat **4 :** any of the small pieces of wood on a boat's gunwale supporting or forming the rowlocks

pop·pied \'päp-ēd\ *adj* **1 :** growing or overgrown with poppies **2 a :** drugging or sleep-inducing like poppy juice **b :** DROWSY

1**pop·ple** \'päp-əl\ *n* [ME *popul*, fr. OE, fr. L *populus*] *chiefly dial* **:** POPLAR 1

2**popple** *n* [*popple*, vb., fr. ME *poplen*, prob. of imit. origin] **1 :** a heaving of water (as from boiling) **2 :** a choppy sea — **popple** *vi* **pop·pling** \-(ə-)liŋ\

pop·py \'päp-ē\ *n* [ME *popi*, fr. OE *popæg, popig*, modif. of L *papaver*] **1 a :** any of a genus (*Papaver* of the family Papaveraceae, the poppy family) of chiefly annual or perennial herbs with milky juice, showy regular flowers, and capsular fruits including one (*P. somniferum*) that is the source of opium and several that are cultivated as ornamentals **b :** an extract or decoction of poppy used medicinally **2 :** a strong reddish orange

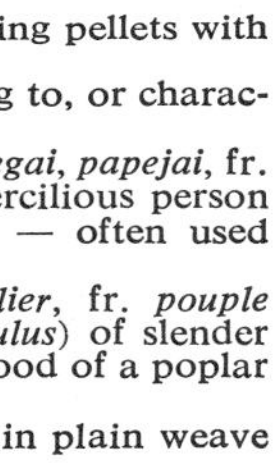
poppy

pop·py·cock \'päp-ē-,käk\ *n* [D dial. *pappekak*, lit. soft dung, fr. D *pap* pap + *kak* dung] **:** empty talk **:** NONSENSE

pop·py·head \-,hed\ *n* **:** a raised ornament often in the form of a finial generally used on the tops of the upright ends of seats in Gothic churches

pop·u·lace \'päp-yə-ləs\ *n* [MF, fr. It *popolaccio* rabble, pejorative of *popolo* the people, fr. L *populus*] **1 :** the common people **:** MASSES **2 :** POPULATION

pop·u·lar \'päp-yə-lər\ *adj* [L *popularis*, fr. *populus* the people, a

people] **1 :** of or relating to the general public **2 :** suitable to the majority: as **a :** easy to understand **:** PLAIN **b :** suited to the means of the majority **:** INEXPENSIVE **3 :** having general currency **4 :** commonly liked or approved **syn** see COMMON — **pop·u·lar·ly** *adv*

popular front *n, often cap P&F* **:** a working coalition esp. of leftist political parties against a common opponent; *specif* **:** one sponsored and dominated by Communists as a device for gaining power

pop·u·lar·i·ty \ˌpäp-yə-'lar-ət-ē\ *n* **:** the quality or state of being popular

pop·u·lar·iza·tion \ˌpäp-yə-lə-rə-'zā-shən\ *n* **1 :** the act of popularizing or the state of being popularized **2 :** something that is popularized

pop·u·lar·ize \'päp-yə-lə-ˌrīz\ *vi* **:** to cater to popular taste ~ *vt* **:** to make popular: as **a :** to cause to be liked or esteemed **b :** to present in generally understandable or interesting form — **pop·u·lar·iz·er** *n*

popular sovereignty *n* **:** a pre-Civil War doctrine asserting the right of the people living in a newly organized territory to decide by vote of their territorial legislature whether or not slavery would be permitted in the territory

pop·u·late \'päp-yə-ˌlāt\ *vt* [ML *populatus*, pp. of *populare* to people, fr. L *populus* people] **1 :** to have a place in **:** INHABIT **2 :** to furnish or provide with inhabitants **:** PEOPLE

pop·u·la·tion \ˌpäp-yə-'lā-shən\ *n* [LL *population-, populatio*, fr. L *populus*] **1 :** the whole number of people or inhabitants in a country or region **2 :** the act or process of populating **3 a :** a body of persons having a quality or characteristic in common **b** (1) **:** the organisms inhabiting a particular area or biotope (2) **:** a group of interbreeding biotypes that represents the level of organization at which speciation begins **4 :** a group of individual persons, objects, or items from which samples are taken for statistical measurement

population explosion *n* **:** a pyramiding of a living population; *esp* **:** the recent great increase in human numbers that is usu. related to both increased survival and increased reproduction

Pop·u·lism \'päp-yə-ˌliz-əm\ *n* **:** the political and economic doctrines advocated by the Populists

Pop·u·list \-ləst\ *n* [L *populus* the people] **:** a member of a U.S. political party formed in 1891 primarily to represent agrarian interests and to advocate the free coinage of silver and government control of monopolies — **populist** *also* **pop·u·lis·tic** \ˌpäp-yə-'lis-tik\ *adj, often cap*

pop·u·lous \'päp-yə-ləs\ *adj* [L *populosus*, fr. *populus* people] **1 :** densely populated **2 a :** NUMEROUS **b :** CROWDED — **pop·u·lous·ly** *adv* — **pop·u·lous·ness** *n*

por·bea·gle \'pȯ(ə)r-ˌbē-gəl\ *n* [Corn *porgh-bugel*] **:** a small voracious viviparous shark (*Lamna nasus*) of the north Atlantic and Pacific oceans with a pointed nose and crescent-shaped tail

por·ce·lain \'pōr-s(ə-)lən, 'pȯr-\ *n* [MF *porcelaine* cowrie shell, porcelain, fr. It *porcellana*, fr. *porcello* vulva, lit., little pig, fr. L *porcellus*, dim. of *porcus* pig, vulva; fr. the shape of the shell — more at FARROW] **:** a fine ceramic ware that is hard, translucent, white, sonorous, and nonporous and usu. consists essentially of kaolin, quartz, and feldspar — **por·ce·lain·like** \-ˌlīk\ *adj* — **por·ce·la·ne·ous** *or* **por·cel·la·ne·ous** \ˌpōr-sə-'lā-nē-əs, ˌpȯr-\ *adj*

porcelain enamel *n* **:** VITREOUS ENAMEL

por·ce·lain·ize \'pōr-s(ə-)lə-ˌnīz, 'pȯr-\ *vt* **:** to fire a vitreous coating on (as steel)

porch \'pō(ə)rch, 'pȯ(ə)rch\ *n* [ME *porche*, fr. OF, fr. L *porticus* portico, fr. *porta* gate — more at FORD] **1 :** a covered entrance to a building usu. with a separate roof **:** VERANDA **2** *obs* **:** PORTICO **3 :** a place for waiting before entering **:** PASSAGE

por·cine \'pȯr-ˌsīn\ *adj* [L *porcinus*, fr. *porcus* pig — more at FARROW] **:** of, relating to, or suggesting swine

por·cu·pine \'pȯr-kyə-ˌpīn\ *n, often attrib* [ME *porkepin*, fr. MF *porc espin*, fr. OIt *porcospino*, fr. L *porcus* pig + *spina* spine, prickle] **:** any of various relatively large rodents having stiff sharp erectile bristles mingled with the hair and constituting an Old World terrestrial family (Hystricidae) and a New World arboreal family (Erethizontidae)

[1]pore \'pō(ə)r, 'pȯ(ə)r\ *vi* [ME *pouren*] **1 :** to gaze intently **2 :** to read studiously or attentively **3 :** to reflect or meditate steadily

[2]pore *n* [ME, fr. MF, fr. L *porus*, fr. Gk *poros* passage, pore — more at FARE] **1 :** a minute opening esp. in an animal or plant; *esp* **:** one by which matter passes through a membrane **2 :** a small interstice (as in stone) admitting absorption or passage of liquid

pored \'pō(ə)rd, 'pȯ(ə)rd\ *adj* **:** having pores

pore fungus *n* **:** a fungus (family Boletaceae or Polyporaceae) having the spore-bearing surface within tubes or pores

por·gy \'pȯr-gē\ *n, pl* **porgies** *also* **porgy** [partly fr. earlier *pargo* (porgy); partly fr. earlier *scuppaug* (porgy)] **1 :** a blue-spotted crimson percoid food fish (*Pagrus pagrus*) of the coasts of Europe and America; *also* **:** any of various related fishes (family Sparidae) **2 :** any of various teleost fishes (as a menhaden) not closely related to the red porgy

po·rif·er·an \pə-'rif-(ə-)rən\ *n* [deriv. of L *porus* pore + *-fer* -ferous] **:** any of a phylum (Porifera) of primitive invertebrate animals comprising the sponges — **poriferan** *or* **po·rif·er·al** \-(ə-)rəl\ *adj*

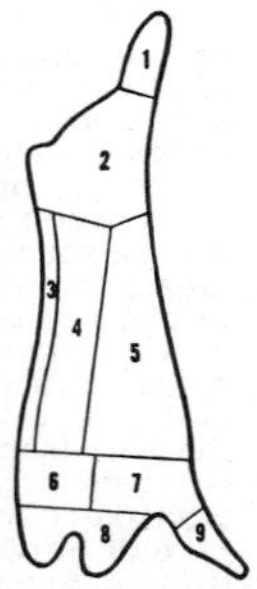

cuts of pork: *1* hind foot, *2* ham, *3* fatback, *4* loin, *5* side, *6* Boston butt, *7* picnic ham, *8* jowl, *9* forefoot

pork \'pō(ə)rk, 'pȯ(ə)rk\ *n* [ME, fr. OF, pig, fr. L *porcus*] **1 :** the fresh or salted flesh of swine when dressed for food **2 :** government money, jobs, or favors used by politicians as patronage

pork barrel *n* **:** a government project or appropriation yielding rich patronage benefits

pork·er \'pōr-kər, 'pȯr-\ *n* **:** HOG; *esp* **:** a young pig fattened for table use as fresh pork

pork·pie hat \ˌpōrk-ˌpī-, ˌpȯrk-\ *n* **:** a felt, straw, or cloth hat with a low crown, flat top, and turned-up or snap brim

por·nog·ra·pher \pȯr-'näg-rə-fər\ *n* **:** one who produces pornography

por·no·graph·ic \ˌpȯr-nə-'graf-ik\ *adj* **:** of or relating to pornography — **por·no·graph·i·cal·ly** \-i-k(ə-)lē\ *adv*

por·nog·ra·phy \pȯr-'näg-rə-fē\ *n* [Gk *pornographos*, adj., writing of harlots, fr. *pornē* harlot + *graphein* to write; akin to Gk *pernanai* to sell, *poros* journey — more at FARE, CARVE] **1 :** the depiction of erotic behavior (as in pictures or writing) intended to cause sexual excitement **2 :** pornographic material

po·ro·mer·ic \ˌpōr-ə-'mer-ik, ˌpȯr-\ *adj* [Gk *poros* pore + E *polymeric*] **:** full of very fine pores — used of tough synthetic leatherlike material (as for shoe uppers) — **poromeric** *n*

po·rose \'pō(ə)r-ˌōs, 'pȯ(ə)r-\ *adj* **:** divided into or forming a continuous series of pores

po·ros·i·ty \pə-'räs-ət-ē, pōr-'äs-, pȯ-'räs-\ *n* **1 :** the quality or state of being porous; *specif* **:** the ratio of the volume of interstices of a material to the volume of its mass **2 :** PORE

po·rous \'pōr-əs, 'pȯr-\ *adj* **1 :** possessing or full of pores **2 :** permeable to liquids — **po·rous·ly** *adv* — **po·rous·ness** *n*

por·phyr·a·tin \pȯr-'fir-ət-ᵊn\ *n* [*porphyr*in + hem*atin*] **:** a complex compound (as hematin) of porphyrins with metals

por·phyr·ia \pȯr-'fir-ē-ə\ *n* [NL, fr. ISV *porphyrin*] **:** a pathological state characterized by abnormalities of porphyrin metabolism and by excretion of excess porphyrins in the urine and by extreme sensitivity to light

por·phy·rin \'pȯr-fə-rən\ *n* [ISV, fr. Gk *porphyra* purple] **:** any of various metal-free derivatives of pyrrole obtained esp. from chlorophyll or hemoglobin

por·phy·rit·ic \ˌpȯr-fə-'rit-ik\ *adj* [ML *porphyriticus*, fr. Gk *porphyritikos*, fr. *porphyritēs* (*lithos*) porphyry] **1 :** of or relating to porphyry **2 :** having distinct crystals (as of feldspar) in a relatively fine-grained base

por·phy·roid \'pȯr-fə-ˌrȯid\ *n* [*porphyry*] **:** a more or less schistose metamorphic rock with porphyritic texture

por·phy·rop·sin \ˌpȯr-fə-'räp-sən\ *n* [Gk *porphyra* purple + E *-opsin* (as in *rhodopsin*)] **:** a purple pigment in the retinal rods of freshwater fishes that resembles rhodopsin

por·phy·ry \'pȯr-f(ə-)rē\ *n* [ME *porfurie*, fr. ML *porphyrium*, alter. of L *porphyrites*, fr. Gk *porphyritēs* (*lithos*), lit., stone like purple, fr. *porphyra* purple] **1 :** a rock consisting of feldspar crystals embedded in a compact dark red or purple groundmass **2 :** an igneous rock of porphyritic texture

por·poise \'pȯr-pəs\ *n* [ME *porpoys*, fr. MF *porpois*, fr. ML *porcopiscis*, fr. L *porcus* pig + *piscis* fish] **1 :** any of several small gregarious toothed whales (genus *Phocaena*); *esp* **:** a blunt-snouted usu. largely black whale (*P. phocaena*) of the north Atlantic and Pacific 5 to 8 feet long **2 :** any of several dolphins

por·rect \pə-'rekt\ *adj* [L *porrectus*, pp. of *porrigere* to stretch out, fr. *por-* forward + *regere* to direct] **:** extended forward

por·ridge \'pȯr-ij, 'pär-\ *n* [alter. of *pottage*] **:** a soft food made by boiling meal of grains or legumes in milk or water until thick

por·rin·ger \-ən-jər\ *n* [alter. of ME *poteger, potinger*, fr. AF *potageer*, fr. MF *potager* of pottage, fr. *potage* pottage] **:** a low one-handled metal bowl or cup for children

[1]port \'pō(ə)rt, 'pȯ(ə)rt\ *n* [ME, fr. OE & OF, fr. L *portus* — more at FORD] **1 :** a place where ships may ride secure from storms **:** HAVEN **2 a :** a harbor town or city where ships may take on or discharge cargo **b :** AIRPORT **3 :** PORT OF ENTRY

[2]port *n* [ME *porte*, fr. MF, gate, door, fr. L *porta* passage, gate; akin to L *portus* port] **1** *chiefly Scot* **:** GATE **2 a :** an opening for intake or exhaust of a fluid esp. in a valve seat or valve face **b :** the area of opening in a cylinder face of a passageway for the working fluid in an engine **c :** such a passageway **3 a :** an opening in a ship's side to admit light or air or to load cargo **b** *archaic* **:** the cover for a porthole **4 :** a hole in an armored vehicle or fortification through which guns may be fired

[3]port *n* [ME, fr. MF, fr. *porter* to carry] **1 :** the manner in which one bears himself **2** *archaic* **:** STATE 1a **3 :** the position in which a military weapon is carried when ported

[4]port *vt* [MF *porter* to carry, fr. L *portare*] **:** to carry (as a rifle) in a position sloping across the body from right to left

[5]port *n* [prob. fr. [1]*port* or [2]*port*] **:** the left side of a ship or airplane looking forward — called also *larboard;* compare STARBOARD — **port** *adj*

[6]port *vt* **:** to turn or put (a helm) to the left — used chiefly as a command

[7]port *n* [*Oporto*, Portugal] **:** a fortified sweet wine of rich taste and aroma

por·ta·bil·i·ty \ˌpōrt-ə-'bil-ət-ē, ˌpȯrt-\ *n* **:** the quality or state of being portable

por·ta·ble \'pōrt-ə-bəl, 'pȯrt-\ *adj* [ME, fr. MF, fr. LL *portabilis*, fr. L *portare* to carry — more at FARE] **1 :** capable of being carried **2** *obs* **:** BEARABLE — **portable** *n* — **por·ta·bly** \-blē\ *adv*

por·tage \'pōrt-ij, 'pȯrt-, *3 is also* pȯr-'täzh\ *n* [ME, fr. MF, fr. *porter* to carry] **1 :** the labor of carrying or transporting **2** *archaic* **:** the cost of carriage **:** PORTERAGE **3 a :** the carrying of boats or goods overland from one body of water to another **b :** the route followed in making such a transfer

[1]por·tal \'pōrt-ᵊl, 'pȯrt-\ *n* [ME, fr. MF, fr. ML *portale* city gate, porch, fr. neut. of *portalis* of a gate, fr. L *porta* gate — more at PORT] **1 :** DOOR, ENTRANCE; *esp* **:** a grand or imposing one **2 :** the whole architectural composition surrounding and including the doorways and porches of a church **3 :** the approach or entrance to a bridge or tunnel **4 :** a communicating part or area of an organism; *specif* **:** the point at which something enters the body

[2]portal *adj* [NL *porta* transverse fissure of the liver, fr. L, gate] **1 :** of or relating to the transverse fissure on the underside of the liver where most of the vessels enter **2 :** of, relating to, or being a large vein that collects blood from one part of the body and distributes it in another part through a capillary network

portal-to-portal *adj* **:** of or relating to the time spent by a workman in traveling from the entrance to his employer's property to his actual working place (as in a mine) and in returning after work

portal vein *n* **:** a vein carrying blood from the digestive organs and spleen to the liver

por·ta·men·to \ˌpōrt-ə-'men-(ˌ)tō, ˌpȯrt-\ *n, pl* **por·ta·men·ti** \-(ˌ)tē\ [It, lit., act of carrying, fr. *portare* to carry, fr. L] **:** a continuous glide effected by the voice, a trombone, or a bowed stringed musical instrument in passing from one tone to another

por·ta·tive \'pōrt-ət-iv, 'pȯrt-\ *adj* [ME *portatif*, fr. MF, fr. L *portatus*, pp. of *portare*] **:** PORTABLE

port·cul·lis \pōrt-'kəl-əs, pȯrt-\ *n* [ME *port colice*, fr. MF *porte*

coleïce, lit., sliding door] **:** a grating of iron hung over the gateway of a fortified place and lowered between grooves to prevent passage

Porte \'pō(ə)rt, 'pȯ(ə)rt\ *n* [F, short for *Sublime Porte*, lit., sublime gate; fr. the gate of the sultan's palace where justice was administered] **:** the government of the Ottoman empire

porte co·chere \,pōrt-kō-'she(ə)r, ,pȯrt-\ *n* [F *porte cochère*, lit., coach door] **1** *archaic* **:** a passageway through a building or screen wall designed to let vehicles pass from the street to an interior courtyard **2 :** a roofed structure extending from the entrance of a building over an adjacent driveway and sheltering those getting in or out of vehicles

porte–mon·naie \'pōrt-,mən-ē\ *n* [F, fr. *porter* to carry + *monnaie* coined money, fr. MF *moneie* — more at PORT, MONEY] **:** a small pocketbook or purse

por·tend \pȯr-'tend, pōr-\ *vt* [ME *portenden*, fr. L *portendere*, fr. *por-* forward (akin to *per* through) + *tendere* to stretch — more at FOR, THIN] **1 :** to give an omen or anticipatory sign of **:** BODE **2 :** INDICATE, SIGNIFY

por·tent \'pȯ(ə)r-,tent, 'pō(ə)r-\ *n* [L *portentum*, fr. neut. of *portentus*, pp. of *portendere*] **1 :** something that foreshadows a coming event **:** OMEN **2 :** prophetic indication or significance **3 :** MARVEL, PRODIGY

por·ten·tous \pȯr-'tent-əs, pōr-\ *adj* **1 :** of, relating to, or constituting a portent **2 :** eliciting amazement or wonder **:** PRODIGIOUS **3 :** self-consciously weighty **:** POMPOUS **syn** see OMINOUS — **por·ten·tous·ly** *adv* — **por·ten·tous·ness** *n*

1por·ter \'pōrt-ər, 'pȯrt-\ *n* [ME, fr. OF *portier*, fr. LL *portarius*, fr. L *porta* gate — more at PORT] *chiefly Brit* **:** a person stationed at a door or gate to admit or assist those entering

2porter *n* [ME *portour*, fr. MF *porteour*, fr. LL *portator*, fr. L *portatus*, pp. of *portare* to carry — more at FARE] **1 :** one who carries burdens; *specif* **:** one employed to carry baggage for patrons at a hotel or transportation terminal **2 :** a parlor-car or sleeping-car attendant who waits on passengers and makes up berths **3** [short for *porter's beer*] **:** a weak stout that is rich in saccharine matter and contains about four percent of alcohol

por·ter·age \-ə-rij\ *n* **:** the work of a porter; *also* **:** the charge for it

por·ter·house \'pōrt-ər-,hau̇s, 'pȯrt-\ *n* **1** *archaic* **:** a house where malt liquor (as porter) is sold **2 :** a large steak cut from the thick end of the short loin to contain a T-shaped bone and a large piece of tenderloin

port·fo·lio \pōrt-'fō-lē-,ō, pȯrt-\ *n* [It *portafoglio*, fr. *portare* to carry (fr. L) + *foglio* leaf, sheet, fr. L *folium* — more at BLADE] **1 :** a portable case for carrying papers or drawings **2** [fr. the use of such a case to carry documents of state] **:** the office and functions of a minister of state or member of a cabinet **3 :** the securities held by an investor or the commercial paper held by a bank or other financial house

port·hole \'pō(ə)rt-,hōl, 'pȯ(ə)rt-\ *n* [2*port*] **1 :** an opening (as a window) in the side of a ship or airplane **2 :** an embrasure or loophole through which to shoot **3 :** 2PORT 2

Por·tia \'pōr-shə, 'pȯr-\ *n* **:** the heroine in Shakespeare's *The Merchant of Venice*

por·ti·co \'pōrt-i-,kō, 'pȯrt-\ *n, pl* **porticoes** *or* **porticos** [It, fr. L *porticus* — more at PORCH] **:** a colonnade or covered ambulatory esp. in classical architecture and often at the entrance of a building

por·tiere \,pōrt-ē-'e(ə)r, ,pȯrt-; pōr-'ti(ə)r, pȯr-; 'pōrt-ē-ər, 'pȯrt-\ *n* [F *portière*, fr. OF, fem. of *portier* porter, doorkeeper] **:** a curtain hanging across a doorway

1por·tion \'pōr-shən, 'pȯr-\ *n* [ME, fr. OF, fr. L *portion-, portio;* akin to L *part-, pars* part] **1 :** an individual's part or share of something: as **a :** a share received by gift or inheritance **b :** DOWRY **c :** a helping of food **2 :** an individual's lot, fate, or fortune **3 a :** a part of a whole **b :** a limited amount or quantity **syn** see FATE, PART

2portion *vt* **por·tion·ing** \-sh(ə-)niŋ\ **1 :** to divide into portions **:** DISTRIBUTE **2 :** to allot a dowry to **:** DOWER

por·tion·less \-shən-ləs\ *adj* **:** having no portion; *esp* **:** having no dowry or inheritance

port·land cement \,pōrt-lən(d)-, ,pȯrt-\ *n* [Isle of *Portland*, England; fr. its resemblance to a limestone found there] **:** a hydraulic cement made by finely pulverizing the clinker produced by calcining to incipient fusion a mixture of argillaceous and calcareous materials

port·li·ness \'pōrt-lē-nəs, 'pȯrt-\ *n* **:** the quality or state of being portly

port·ly \-lē\ *adj* [3*port*] **1** *chiefly dial* **:** DIGNIFIED, STATELY **2 :** heavy or rotund of body **:** CORPULENT

1port·man·teau \pōrt-'man-(,)tō, pȯrt-\ *n, pl* **portmanteaus** *or* **port·man·teaux** \-(,)tōz\ [MF *portemanteau*, fr. *porter* to carry + *manteau* mantle, fr. L *mantellum* — more at PORT] **:** TRAVELING BAG; *esp* **:** a large gladstone bag

2portmanteau *adj* **:** combining more than one use or quality

portmanteau word *n* **:** 2BLEND b

port of call 1 : an intermediate port where ships customarily stop for supplies, repairs, or transshipment of cargo **2 :** a stop included on an itinerary

port of entry 1 : a place where foreign goods may be cleared through a customhouse **2 :** a place where an alien may be permitted to enter a country

por·trait \'pōr-trət, 'pȯr-, -,trāt\ *n* [MF, fr. pp. of *portraire*] **1 :** PICTURE; *esp* **:** a pictorial representation (as a painting) of a person usu. showing his face **2 :** BUST, STATUE **3 :** a graphic portrayal in words

por·trait·ist \-əst\ *n* **:** a maker of portraits

por·trai·ture \'pōr-trə-,chu̇(ə)r, 'pȯr-, -chər, -,t(y)u̇(ə)r\ *n* **1 :** the making of portraits **:** PORTRAYAL **2 :** PORTRAIT

por·tray \pōr-'trā, pȯr-, pər-\ *vt* [ME *portraien*, fr. MF *portraire*, fr. L *protrahere* to draw forth, reveal, expose, fr. *pro-* forth + *trahere* to draw] **1:** to make a picture of **:** DEPICT **2 a :** to describe in words **b :** to play the role of **:** ENACT — **por·tray·er** *n*

por·tray·al \-'trā(-ə)l\ *n* **1 :** the act or process of portraying **:** REPRESENTATION **2 :** PORTRAIT

por·tress \'pōr-trəs, 'pȯr-\ *n* **:** a female porter: as **a :** a doorkeeper in a convent or apartment house **b :** CHARWOMAN

Port Roy·al·ist \pōrt-'rȯi-ə-ləst, pȯrt-\ *n* [F *port-royaliste*, fr. *Port-Royal*, a convent near Versailles, France] **:** a member or adherent of a 17th century French Jansenist lay community distinguished as logicians and educators

Por·tu·guese \,pōr-chə-'gēz, ,pȯr-, -'gēs\ *n, pl* **Portuguese** [Pg *português*, adj. & n., fr. *Portugal*] **1 a :** a native or inhabitant of Portugal **b :** a person of Portuguese descent **2 :** the Romance language of Portugal and Brazil — **Portuguese** *adj*

Portuguese man–of–war *n* **:** any of several large siphonophores (genus *Physalia*) having a large bladderlike sac or cyst with a broad crest on the upper side by means of which they float at the surface

por·tu·laca \,pōr-chə-'lak-ə, ,pȯr-\ *n* [NL, genus name, fr. L, purslane, fr. *portula*, dim. of *porta* gate; fr. the lid of its capsule — more at PORT] **:** any of a genus (*Portulaca*) of mainly tropical succulent herbs of the purslane family; *esp* **:** a plant (*P. grandiflora*) cultivated for its showy flowers

po·sa·da \pə-'säd-ə\ *n* [Sp, fr. *posar* to lodge, fr. LL *pausare*] **:** an inn in Spanish-speaking countries

1pose \'pōz\ *vb* [ME *posen*, fr. MF *poser*, fr. (assumed) VL *pausare*, fr. LL, to stop, rest, pause, fr. L *pausa* pause] *vt* **1 a :** to put or set in place **b :** to place (as a model) in a studied attitude **2 :** to put or set forth **:** PROPOUND ~ *vi* **1 :** to assume a posture or attitude usu. for artistic purposes **2 :** to affect an attitude or character **:** POSTURE

2pose *n* **1 :** a sustained posture; *esp* **:** one assumed for artistic effect **2 :** a mental posture; *esp* **:** AFFECTATION

syn POSE, AIR, AIRS, AFFECTATION, MANNERISM mean an adopted way of speaking or behaving. POSE implies an attitude deliberately assumed in order to impress others; AIR may suggest natural acquirement through environment or way of life, but AIRS always implies artificiality and pretentiousness; AFFECTATION applies to a trick of speech or behavior that strikes the observer as insincere; MANNERISM applies to an acquired eccentricity that has become a habit

3pose *vt* [short for earlier *appose*, fr. ME *apposen*, alter. of *opposen* to oppose] **1** *obs* **:** QUESTION **2 :** PUZZLE, BAFFLE

Po·sei·don \pə-'sīd-ᵊn\ *n* [L, fr. Gk *Poseidōn*] **:** the god of the sea in Greek mythology

1pos·er \'pō-zər\ *n* **:** a puzzling or baffling question

2poser *n* **:** a person who poses

po·seur \pō-'zər\ *n* [F, lit., poser, fr. *poser*] **:** an affected or insincere person

posh \'päsh\ *adj* [origin unknown] **:** ELEGANT, FASHIONABLE

pos·it \'päz-ət\ *vt* **pos·it·ed** \'päz-ət-əd, 'päz-təd\ **pos·it·ing** \'päz-ət-iŋ, 'päz-tiŋ\ [L *positus*, pp.] **1 :** to dispose or set firmly **:** FIX **2 :** to assume or affirm the existence of **:** POSTULATE

1po·si·tion \pə-'zish-ən\ *n* [MF, fr. L *position-, positio*, fr. *positus*, pp. of *ponere* to lay down, put, place, fr. (assumed) OL *posinere*, fr. *po-* away (akin to Gk *apo-*) + L *sinere* to lay, leave — more at SITE] **1 :** an act of placing or arranging: as **a :** the laying down of a proposition or thesis **b :** an arranging in order **2 :** the stand taken on a question **3 :** a market commitment in securities or commodities; *also* **:** the inventory of a market trader **4 :** the point or area occupied by a physical object **5 a :** social or official rank or status **b :** EMPLOYMENT, JOB **c :** a situation that confers advantage or preference — **po·si·tion·al** \-'zish-nəl, -ən-ᵊl\ *adj*

syn POSITION, PLACE, SITUATION, OFFICE, POST, JOB mean employment for wages or salary. POSITION and PLACE may mean no more than this although POSITION commonly suggests higher social status; SITUATION adds an emphasis on a place needing to be filled or that is filled; OFFICE applies to a position of trust or authority; POST suggests a position involving responsibility or the discharge of onerous duties; JOB specifically stresses the work involved in a position

2position *vt* **po·si·tion·ing** \-'zish-(ə-)niŋ\ **:** to put in proper position; *also* **:** LOCATE

po·si·tion·er \-'zish-(ə-)nər\ *n* **:** one that positions

1pos·i·tive \'päz-ət-iv, 'päz-tiv\ *adj* [ME, fr. OF *positif*, fr. L *positivus*, fr. *positus*] **1 a :** formally laid down or imposed **:** PRESCRIBED ⟨~ laws⟩ **b :** expressed clearly or peremptorily **c** (1) **:** fully assured **:** CONFIDENT (2) **:** SELF-ASSURED, ARROGANT **2 a :** of, relating to, or constituting the degree of comparison that is expressed in English by the unmodified and uninflected form of an adjective or adverb and denotes no increase or diminution **b** (1) **:** independent of changing circumstances **:** UNCONDITIONED (2) **:** relating to or constituting a motion or device that is definite, unyielding, constant, or certain in its action ⟨~ system of levers⟩ **c :** INCONTESTABLE ⟨~ proof⟩ **:** UNQUALIFIED ⟨a ~ disgrace⟩ **3 a :** not fictitious **:** REAL **b :** active and effective in social or economic function rather than merely maintaining peace and order ⟨~ government⟩ **4 a :** having or expressing actual existence or quality as distinguished from deprivation or deficiency ⟨~ change in temperature⟩: as (1) **:** logically affirmative ⟨~ instance⟩ (2) **:** not speculative **:** EMPIRICAL **b :** having rendition of light and shade similar in tone to the tones of the original subject ⟨a ~ photographic image⟩ **c** (1) **:** that is or is generated in a direction arbitrarily or customarily taken as that of increase or progression ⟨~ rotation of the earth⟩ ⟨~ angles⟩ (2) **:** directed or moving toward a source of stimulation ⟨a ~ taxis⟩ **d :** real and numerically greater than zero ⟨+2 is a ~ integer⟩ **5 a** (1) **:** being, relating to, or charged with electricity of a kind of which the proton possesses an elementary unit and which predominates in a glass body after being rubbed with silk (2) **:** losing electrons **:** ELECTROPOSITIVE, BASIC **b** (1) **:** having higher electric potential and constituting the part from which the current flows to the external circuit ⟨the ~ terminal of a discharging storage battery⟩ (2) **:** being an electron-collecting electrode of an electron tube **6 a :** marked by or indicating agreement or affirmation ⟨a ~ response⟩ **b :** affirming the presence of that sought or suspected to be present ⟨~ test for blood⟩ **syn** see SURE — **pos·i·tive·ly** *adv* — **pos·i·tive·ness** *n*

2positive *n* **:** something positive: as **a** (1) **:** the positive degree of comparison in a language (2) **:** a positive form of an adjective or adverb **b :** something of which an affirmation can be made **:** REALITY **c :** a positive photograph or a print from a negative

positive electricity *n* **:** electricity of which the elementary unit is the proton

positive law *n* **:** law established or recognized by governmental authority — compare NATURAL LAW

pos·i·tiv·ism \-,iz-əm\ *n* **1 a :** a theory that theology and metaphysics are earlier imperfect modes of knowledge and that positive knowledge is based on natural phenomena and their properties and relations as verified by the empirical sciences **b :** LOGICAL POSITIVISM **2 :** the quality or state of being positive **:** DOGMATISM, CONFIDENCE, CERTAINTY

— **pos·i·tiv·ist** \-əst\ *adj or n* — **pos·i·tiv·is·tic** \ˌpäz-ət-iv-ˈis-tik, ˌpäz-tiv-\ *adj*

pos·i·tiv·i·ty \ˌpäz-ə-ˈtiv-ət-ē\ *n* **:** the quality or state of being positive **:** POSITIVENESS

pos·i·tron \ˈpäz-ə-ˌträn\ *n* [*positive* + *-tron* (as in *electron*)] **:** a positively charged particle having the same mass and magnitude of charge as the electron

pos·se \ˈpäs-ē\ *n* [ML *posse comitatus,* lit., power or authority of the county] **1 :** a body of persons summoned by a sheriff to assist in preserving the public peace usu. in an emergency **2 :** a group of people temporarily organized to make a search (as for a lost child)

pos·sess \pə-ˈzes *also* -ˈses\ *vt* [ME *possessen,* fr. MF *possesser* to have possession of, take possession of, fr. L *possessus,* pp. of *possidēre,* fr. *potis* able, in power + *sedēre* to sit — more at POTENT, SIT] **1 a** *obs* **:** to instate in as owner **b :** to make the owner or holder **c :** to have possession of **2 a :** to have and hold as property **:** OWN **b :** to have as an attribute, knowledge, or skill **3 a :** to take into one's possession **b :** to enter into and control firmly **:** DOMINATE ⟨~*ed* by a demon⟩ **syn** see HAVE

pos·sessed *adj* **1** *obs* **:** held as a possession **2 a** (1) **:** influenced or controlled by something (as an evil spirit or a passion) (2) **:** MAD, CRAZED **b :** urgently desirous to do or have something **3 :** SELF-POSSESSED, COOL, CALM — **pos·sessed·ly** *adv* — **pos·sessed·ness** *n*

pos·ses·sion \-ˈzesh-ən, *also* -ˈsesh-\ *n* **1 a :** the act of having or taking into control **b :** control or occupancy of property without regard to ownership **c :** OWNERSHIP **2 :** something owned, occupied, or controlled **:** PROPERTY **3 a :** domination by something **b :** a psychological state in which an individual's normal personality is replaced by another **c :** the fact or condition of being self-controlled — **pos·ses·sion·al** \-ˈzesh-nəl, -ən-ᵊl *also* -ˈsesh-\ *adj*

1**pos·ses·sive** \pə-ˈzes-iv *also* -ˈses-\ *adj* **1 :** of, relating to, or constituting a word, a word group, or a grammatical case that denotes ownership or a relation analogous to ownership **2 :** manifesting possession or the desire to possess or own — **pos·ses·sive·ly** *adv* — **pos·ses·sive·ness** *n*

2**possessive** *n* **1 a :** the possessive case **b :** a word in the possessive case **2 :** a possessive word or word group

possessive adjective *n* **:** a pronominal adjective expressing possession

possessive pronoun *n* **:** a pronoun that derives from a personal pronoun and denotes possession and analogous relationships

pos·ses·sor \pə-ˈzes-ər *also* -ˈses-\ *n* **:** one that possesses

pos·ses·so·ry \pə-ˈzes-(ə-)rē *also* -ˈses-\ *adj* **1 :** of, arising from, or having the nature of possession **2 :** having possession **3 :** characteristic of a possessor **:** POSSESSIVE

pos·set \ˈpäs-ət\ *n* [ME *poshet, possot*] **:** a hot drink of sweetened and spiced milk curdled with ale or wine

pos·si·bil·i·ty \ˌpäs-ə-ˈbil-ət-ē\ *n* **1 :** the condition or fact of being possible **2 :** something that is possible **3** *archaic* **:** one's utmost power, capacity, or ability

pos·si·ble \ˈpäs-ə-bəl\ *adj* [ME, fr. MF, fr. L *possibilis,* fr. *posse* to be able, fr. *potis, pote* able + *esse* to be — more at POTENT, IS] **1 a :** being within the limits of ability, capacity, or realization **b :** being what may be done or may occur according to nature, custom, or manners **2 :** being something that may or may not occur **3 :** able or fitted to become **:** POTENTIAL

syn POSSIBLE, PRACTICABLE, FEASIBLE mean capable of being realized. POSSIBLE implies that a thing may certainly exist or occur given the proper conditions; PRACTICABLE implies that something may be easily or readily effected by available means or under current conditions; FEASIBLE applies to what is likely to work or be useful in attaining the end desired **syn** see in addition PROBABLE

pos·si·bly \-blē\ *adv* **:** in a possible manner **:** PERHAPS

pos·sum \ˈpäs-əm\ *n* **:** OPOSSUM

1**post** \ˈpōst\ *n* [ME, fr. OE; akin to OHG *pfosto* post; both fr. a prehistoric WGmc word borrowed fr. L *postis;* akin to Gk *pro* before and to Gk *histasthai* to stand — more at FOR, STAND] **1 :** a piece of timber or metal fixed firmly in an upright position esp. as a stay or support **:** PILLAR, COLUMN **2 :** a pole or stake set up to mark or indicate something

2**post** *vt* **1 :** to affix to a usual place (as a wall) for public notices **:** PLACARD **2 a :** to publish, announce, or advertise by or as if by use of a placard **b :** to denounce by public notice **c :** to enter on a public listing **d :** to forbid (property) to trespassers under penalty of legal prosecution by notices placed along the boundaries **e :** SCORE

3**post** *n* [MF *poste* relay station, courier, fr. OIt *posta* relay station, fr. fem. of *posto,* pp. of *porre* to place, fr. L *ponere* — more at POSITION] **1** *obs* **:** COURIER **2** *archaic* **a :** one of a series of stations for keeping horses for relays **b :** the distance between any two such consecutive stations **:** STAGE **3** *chiefly Brit* **a :** a nation's organization for handling mail; *also* **:** the mail handled **b :** a single dispatch of mail **c :** POST OFFICE **d :** POSTBOX

4**post** *vi* **1 :** to travel with post-horses **2 :** to ride or travel with haste **:** HURRY ~ *vt* **1** *archaic* **:** to dispatch in haste **2 :** MAIL **3 a :** to transfer or carry from a book of original entry to a ledger **b :** to make transfer entries in **4 :** to make familiar with a subject

5**post** *adv* **:** with post-horses **:** EXPRESS

6**post** *n* [MF *poste,* fr. OIt *posto,* fr. pp. of *porre* to place] **1 a :** the place at which a soldier is stationed; *esp* **:** a sentry's beat or station **b :** a station or task to which anyone is assigned **c :** the place at which a body of troops is stationed **:** CAMP **d :** a local subdivision of a veterans' organization **e :** one of two bugle calls sounded at tattoo (as in the British Army) **2 :** an office or position to which a person is appointed **3 a :** TRADING POST, SETTLEMENT **b :** a trading station on the floor of a stock exchange **syn** see POSITION

7**post** *vt* **1 a :** to station in a given place **b :** to carry ceremoniously to a position ⟨~*ing* the colors⟩ **2 :** to put up (as bond)

post- *prefix* [ME, fr. L, fr. *post;* akin to Skt *paśca* behind, after, Gk *-apo* away from — more at OF] **1 a :** after **:** subsequent **:** later ⟨*post*date⟩ **b :** behind **:** posterior **:** following after ⟨*post*lude⟩ ⟨*post*consonantal⟩ **2 a :** subsequent to **:** later than ⟨*post*operative⟩ ⟨*post*war⟩ ⟨*post*-Pleistocene⟩ **b :** posterior to ⟨*post*orbital⟩

post·age \ˈpō-stij\ *n* **1 :** the fee for postal service **2 :** adhesive stamps or printed indicia representing postal fees

postage meter *n* **:** a machine that prints postal indicia on pieces of mail, records the amount of postage given in the indicia, and subtracts it from a total amount which has been paid at a post office and for which the machine has been set

postage stamp *n* **:** a government adhesive stamp or imprinted stamp for use on mail matter as evidence of prepayment of postage

post·al \ˈpōst-ᵊl\ *adj* **:** of or relating to the mails or the post office

postal card *n* **:** POSTCARD

postal union *n* **:** an association of governments setting up uniform regulations and practices for international mail

post·ax·i·al \(ˈ)pō-ˈstak-sē-əl\ *adj* **:** located behind an axis of the body; *esp* **:** of or relating to the posterior side of the axis of a vertebrate limb — **post·ax·i·al·ly** \-ə-lē\ *adv*

post·bel·lum \(ˈ)pōs(t)-ˈbel-əm\ *adj* [L *post bellum* after the war] **:** of, relating to, or characteristic of the period following a war and esp. following the American Civil War

post·box \ˈpōs(t)-ˌbäks\ *n* **:** MAILBOX; *esp* **:** a public mailbox

post·boy \-ˌbȯi\ *n* **:** POSTILION

post·breed·ing \ˌpōs(t)-ˌbrēd-iŋ\ *adj* **:** following a period of physiological fitness for reproduction ⟨~ regressive changes⟩

post·card \ˈpōs(t)-ˌkärd\ *n* **:** a card on which a message may be written for mailing without an envelope

post·car·di·nal \(ˈ)pōs(t)-ˈkärd-nəl, -ᵊn-əl\ *adj* **:** lying behind or caudal to the heart

post·ca·va \(ˈ)pōs(t)-ˈkäv-ə, -ˈkā-və\ *n* [NL] **:** the inferior vena cava of vertebrates higher than fishes — **post·ca·val** \-ˈkäv-əl, -ˈkā-vəl\ *adj*

post chaise *n* **:** a carriage usu. having a closed body on four wheels and seating two to four persons

post·clas·si·cal \(ˈ)pōs(t)-ˈklas-i-kəl\ *adj* **:** of or relating to a period following the classical

post–com·mu·nion \ˌpōs(t)-kə-ˈmyü-nyən\ *n, often cap P&C* [ML *postcommunion-, postcommunio,* fr. L *post-* + LL *communio* communion] **:** a prayer following the communion of the people at Mass

post·con·so·nan·tal \ˌpōs(t)-ˌkän(t)-sə-ˈnant-ᵊl\ *adj* **:** immediately following a consonant

post·date \(ˈ)pōs(t)-ˈdāt\ *vt* **:** to date with a date later than that of execution ⟨~ a check⟩

1**post·di·lu·vi·an** \ˌpōs(t)-də-ˈlü-vē-ən, -(ˌ)dī-\ *adj* **:** of or relating to the period after the flood described in the Bible ⟨~ man⟩

2**postdiluvian** *n* **:** one living after the flood described in the Bible

post·doc·tor·al \(ˈ)pōs(t)-ˈdäk-t(ə-)rəl\ *adj* **:** of, relating to, or engaged in advanced academic or professional work beyond a doctor's degree

1**post·er** \ˈpō-stər\ *n* [4*post*] **1** *archaic* **:** a swift traveler **2 :** POST-HORSE

2**poster** *n* [2*post*] **:** a bill or placard for posting in a public place

poster color *n* **:** a water-color paint with a gum or glue-size binder sold usu. in jars

poste res·tante \ˌpō-ˌstres-ˈtä(ⁿ)nt, -ˈtäⁿt, pō-ˈstres-ˌ\ *n* [F, lit., waiting mail] **:** GENERAL DELIVERY

pos·te·ri·ad \pä-ˈstir-ē-ˌad, pō-\ *adv* [*posterior* + *-ad*] **:** POSTERIORLY

1**pos·te·ri·or** \pä-ˈstir-ē-ər, pō-\ *adj* [L, compar. of *posterus* coming after, fr. *post* after — more at POST-] **1 a :** later in time **:** SUBSEQUENT **b :** logically consequent **2 :** situated behind: as **a :** CAUDAL **b :** DORSAL — used of human anatomy **3** *of a plant part* **:** ADAXIAL, SUPERIOR — **pos·te·ri·or·ly** *adv*

2**posterior** *n* **:** the hinder parts of the body; *specif* **:** BUTTOCKS

pos·te·ri·or·i·ty \(ˌ)pä-ˌstir-ē-ˈȯr-ət-e, (ˌ)pō-, -ˈär-\ *n* **:** the quality or state of being later or subsequent

pos·ter·i·ty \pä-ˈster-ət-ē\ *n* [ME *posterite,* fr. MF *posterité,* fr. L *posteritat-, posteritas,* fr. *posterus* coming after] **1 :** the offspring of one progenitor to the furthest generation **:** DESCENDANTS **2 :** all future generations

pos·tern \ˈpōs-tərn, ˈpäs-\ *n* [ME *posterne,* fr. OF, alter. of *posterle,* fr. LL *posterula,* dim. of *postera* back door, fr. L, fem. of *posterus*] **1 :** a back door or gate **2 :** a private or side entrance or way — **postern** *adj*

post exchange *n* **:** a store at a military installation that sells merchandise and services to military personnel and authorized civilians

post·ex·il·ic \ˌpō-(ˌ)steg-ˈzil-ik\ *adj* **:** of or relating to the period of Jewish history between the end of the exile in Babylon in 538 B.C. and A.D. 1

post·form \(ˈ)pōs(t)-ˈfȯ(ə)rm\ *vt* **:** to shape (as a sheet material after laminating) subsequently

post–free \ˈpōs(t)-ˈfrē\ *adj, chiefly Brit* **:** POSTPAID

post·gan·gli·on·ic \ˌpōs(t)-ˌgaŋ-glē-ˈän-ik\ *adj* **:** distal to a ganglion; *specif* **:** of, relating to, or being an axon arising from a cell body within an autonomic ganglion

post·gla·cial \(ˈ)pōs(t)-ˈglā-shəl\ *adj* [ISV] **:** occurring after a period of glaciation

1**post·grad·u·ate** \-ˈgraj-(ə-)wət, -ə-ˌwāt\ *adj* **:** GRADUATE 1b

2**postgraduate** *n* **:** a student continuing his education after graduation from high school or college

1**post·haste** \ˈpōst-ˈhāst\ *n* [3*post*] *archaic* **:** great haste

2**posthaste** *adv* **:** with all possible speed

3**posthaste** *adj, obs* **:** SPEEDY, IMMEDIATE ⟨requires your . . . ~ appearance —Shak.⟩

post hoc \ˈpōst-ˈhäk\ *n* [NL *post hoc, ergo propter hoc* after this, therefore because of this] **:** the fallacy of arguing from temporal sequence to a causal relation

post·hole \ˈpōst-ˌhōl\ *n* **:** a hole sunk in the ground to hold a fence post

post horn *n* **:** a simple straight or coiled brass or copper wind instrument with cupped mouthpiece used esp. by postilions of the 18th and 19th centuries

post–horse \ˈpōst-ˌhȯ(ə)rs\ *n* [3*post*] **:** a horse for use esp. by couriers or mail carriers

post·hu·mous \ˈpäs-chə-məs *also* ˈpäs-t(h)ə-, pä-ˈst(y)ü-, pōst-ˈhyü-\ *adj* [L *posthumus,* alter. of *postumus* late-born, posthumous, fr. superl. of *posterus* coming after — more at POSTERIOR] **1 :** born after the death of the father **2 :** published after the death of the author **3 :** following or occurring after one's death — **post·hu·mous·ly** *adv* — **post·hu·mous·ness** *n*

post·hyp·not·ic \ˌpōst-(h)ip-ˈnät-ik\ *adj* [ISV] **:** of, relating to, or characteristic of the period following a hypnotic trance

pos·tiche \pȯ-ˈstēsh\ *n* [F, fr. Sp *postizo*] **:** false hair: as **a :** SWITCH **b :** TOUPEE

pos·til·ion *or* **pos·til·lion** \pō-ˈstil-yən, pə-\ *n* [MF *postillon* mail carrier using post-horses, fr. It *postiglione*, fr. *posta* post] **:** one who rides as a guide on the near horse of one of the pairs attached to a coach or post chaise esp. without a coachman

Post·im·pres·sion·ism \ˌpō-stim-ˈpresh-ə-ˌniz-əm\ *n* [F *post-impressionisme*, fr. *post-* + *impressionisme* impressionism] **:** a theory or practice originating among French artists (as Cézanne, Matisse, Derain) in the last quarter of the 19th century that in revolt against impressionism stresses variously volume, picture structure, or expressionism — **Post·im·pres·sion·ist** \-ˈpresh-(ə-)nəst\ *adj or n* — **Post·im·pres·sion·is·tic** \-ˌpresh-ə-ˈnis-tik\ *adj*

post–ju·ve·nal \(ˈ)pōs(t)-ˈjü-vən-ᵊl\ *adj* **:** following or terminating the juvenal stage of a bird's life history ⟨a ~ molt⟩

post–Kant·ian \(ˈ)pōs(t)-ˈkant-ē-ən, -ˈkänt-\ *adj* **:** of or relating to the idealist philosophers (as Fichte, Schelling, and Hegel) following Kant and developing some of his ideas

post·lude \ˈpōst-ˌlüd\ *n* [*post-* + *-lude* (as in *prelude*)] **:** a closing piece of music; *esp* **:** an organ voluntary at the end of a church service

post·man \ˈpōs(t)-mən, -ˌman\ *n* **:** MAILMAN

1**post·mark** \-ˌmärk\ *n* **:** an official postal marking on a piece of mail; *specif* **:** a cancellation mark showing the post office and date of mailing

2**postmark** *vt* **:** to put a postmark on

post·mas·ter \-ˌmas-tər\ *n* **1 :** one who has charge of a post office **2 :** one who has charge of a station for accommodation of travelers or who supplies post-horses

postmaster general *n, pl* **postmasters general :** an official in charge of a national post office department

post me·ri·di·em \ˈpōs(t)-mə-ˈrid-ē-əm\ *adj* [L] **:** being after noon

post·mil·le·nar·i·an \ˌpōs(t)-ˌmil-ə-ˈner-ē-ən\ *n* **:** POSTMILLENNIALIST — **postmillenarian** *adj* — **post·mil·le·nar·i·an·ism** \-ē-ə-ˌniz-əm\ *n*

post·mil·len·ni·al \ˌpōs(t)-mə-ˈlen-ē-əl\ *adj* **1 :** coming after or relating to the period after the millennium **2 :** holding or relating to the view that the Parousia will follow the millennium — **post·mil·len·ni·al·ism** \-ē-ə-ˌliz-əm\ *n* — **post·mil·len·ni·al·ist** \-ē-ə-ləst\ *n* — **post·mil·len·ni·al·ly** \-ē-ə-lē\ *adv*

post·mis·tress \ˈpōs(t)-ˌmis-trəs\ *n* **:** a female postmaster

post·mor·tem \pōs(t)-ˈmȯrt-əm\ *adj* [L *post mortem* after death] **1 :** occurring after death **2 :** following the event ⟨~ analysis⟩ — **postmortem** *n*

postmortem examination *n* **:** an examination of a body after death for determining the cause of death or the character and extent of changes produced by disease

post·na·sal \(ˈ)pōs(t)-ˈnā-zəl\ *adj* **:** lying or occurring posterior to the nose — **postnasal** *n*

postnasal drip *n* **:** flow of mucous secretion from the posterior part of the nasal cavity onto the wall of the pharynx occurring usu. as a chronic accompaniment of an allergic state

post·na·tal \(ˈ)pōs(t)-ˈnāt-ᵊl\ *adj* [ISV] **:** subsequent to birth; *specif* **:** of or relating to an infant immediately after birth ⟨~ care⟩ — **post·na·tal·ly** \-ᵊl-ē\ *adv*

post·nup·tial \-ˈnəp-shəl, -chəl\ *adj* **:** made or occurring after marriage or mating — **post·nup·tial·ly** \-ē\ *adv*

post–obit \pō-ˈstō-bət, *esp Brit* -ˈstäb-it\ *adj* [L *post obit*um after death] **:** occurring or taking effect after death

post–obit bond *n* **:** a bond made by a reversioner to secure a loan and payable out of his reversion

post office *n* **1 :** a government department handling the transmission of mail **2 :** a local branch of a post office department handling the mail for a particular place

post·op·er·a·tive \(ˈ)pō-ˈstäp-(ə-)rət-iv, -ˈstäp-ə-ˌrāt-\ *adj* [ISV] **:** following a surgical operation ⟨~ nausea⟩ ⟨~ care⟩ — **post·op·er·a·tive·ly** *adv*

post·or·bit·al \(ˈ)pō-ˈstȯr-bət-ᵊl\ *adj* **:** situated behind the eye socket

post·paid \ˈpōs(t)-ˈpād\ *adv* **:** with the postage paid by the sender and not chargeable to the receiver

post·par·tum \pōs(t)-ˈpärt-əm\ *adj* [NL *post partum* after birth] **:** following parturition

post·pi·tu·itary \ˌpōs(t)-pə-ˈt(y)ü-ə-ˌter-ē\ *adj* **:** arising in or derived from the posterior lobe of the pituitary body

post·pon·able \pōs(t)-ˈpō-nə-bəl\ *adj* **:** capable of being postponed

post·pone \pōs(t)-ˈpōn\ *vt* [L *postponere* to place after, postpone, fr. *post-* + *ponere* to place] **1 :** to hold back to a later time **:** DEFER **2 a :** to place after ⟨~ an adjective⟩ **2 :** SUBORDINATE **syn** see DEFER — **post·pone·ment** \-mənt\ *n* — **post·pon·er** *n*

post·po·si·tion \ˌpōs(t)-pə-ˈzish-ən\ *n* [F, fr. *postposer* to place after, fr. L *postponere* (perf. indic. *postposui*)] **:** the placing of a grammatical element after a word to which it is primarily related in a sentence; *also* **:** such a word or particle esp. when functioning as a preposition — **post·po·si·tion·al** \-ˈzish-nəl, -ən-ᵊl\ *adj* — **post·po·si·tion·al·ly** \-ē\ *adv*

post·pos·i·tive \(ˈ)pōs(t)-ˈpäz-ət-iv, -ˈpäz-tiv\ *adj* **:** placed after or at the end of another word — **post·pos·i·tive·ly** *adv*

post·pran·di·al \pōs(t)-ˈpran-dē-əl\ *adj* [*post-* + L *prandium* late breakfast, midday meal] **:** following a meal ⟨~ blood sugar level⟩ ⟨~ nap⟩

post road *n* **:** a road used for the conveyance of mail

pos·trorse \ˈpōs-ˌtrȯ(ə)rs, ˈpäs-\ *adj* [*post-* + *-trorse* (as in *antrorse*)] **:** RETRORSE

post·script \ˈpō(s)-ˌskript\ *n* [NL *postscriptum*, fr. L, neut. of *postscriptus*, pp. of *postscribere* to write after, fr. *post-* + *scribere* to write — more at SCRIBE] **:** a note or series of notes appended to a completed letter, article, or book

post·syn·ap·tic \ˌpōs(t)-sə-ˈnap-tik\ *adj* **:** occurring after synapsis ⟨a ~ chromosome⟩

post·trau·mat·ic \ˌpōs(t)-trə-ˈmat-ik, -trȯ-, -trau̇-\ *adj* [ISV] **:** following or resulting from trauma

pos·tu·lan·cy \ˈpäs-chə-lən-sē\ *n* **1 :** the quality or state of being a postulant **2 :** the period during which a person remains a postulant

pos·tu·lant \ˈpäs-chə-lənt\ *n* [F, petitioner, candidate, postulant, fr. MF, fr. prp. of *postuler* to demand, solicit, fr. L *postulare*] **1 :** a person admitted to a religious house as a probationary candidate for membership **2 :** a person on probation before being admitted as a candidate for holy orders in the Episcopal Church

1**pos·tu·late** \ˈpäs-chə-ˌlāt\ *vt* [L *postulatus*, pp. of *postulare*, fr. (assumed) *postus*, pp. of L *poscere* to ask; akin to OHG *forsca* question, Skt *pṛcchati* he asks] **1 :** DEMAND, CLAIM **2 a :** to depend upon or start from the postulate of **b :** to assume as a postulate or axiom — **pos·tu·la·tion** \ˌpäs-chə-ˈlā-shən\ *n*

2**pos·tu·late** \ˈpäs-chə-lət, -ˌlāt\ *n* [ML *postulatum*, fr. neut. of *postulatus*, pp. of *postulare* to assume, fr. L, to demand] **1 :** a hypothesis advanced as an essential presupposition or premise of a train of reasoning **2 :** AXIOM 2a

pos·tu·la·tor \-ˌlāt-ər\ *n* **:** an official who presents a plea for beatification or canonization in the Roman Catholic Church

pos·tur·al \ˈpäs-chə-rəl\ *adj* **:** of, relating to, or involving posture

1**pos·ture** \ˈpäs-chər\ *n* [F, fr. It *postura*, fr. L *positura*, fr. *positus*, pp. of *ponere* to place — more at POSITION] **1 :** relative arrangement of the different parts esp. of the body: as **a :** the position or bearing of the body whether characteristic or assumed for a special purpose ⟨erect ~⟩ **b :** the pose of a model or artistic figure **2 :** relative place or position **:** SITUATION **3 :** state or condition at a given time esp. in relation to other persons or things **4 :** frame of mind **:** ATTITUDE

2**posture** *vt* **:** to make assume a given posture **:** POSE ~ *vi* **:** to assume a posture; *esp* **:** to strike a pose for effect — **pos·tur·er** \-chər-ər\ *n*

post·vo·cal·ic \ˌpōst-vō-ˈkal-ik, -və-\ *adj* [ISV] **:** immediately following a vowel

post·war \ˈpōs-ˈtwȯ(ə)r\ *adj* **:** of or relating to the period after a war

po·sy \ˈpō-zē\ *n* [alter. of *poesy*] **1 :** a brief sentiment, motto, or legend **2 :** BOUQUET, NOSEGAY

1**pot** \ˈpät\ *n* [ME, fr. OE *pott;* akin to MLG *pot* pot] **1 a :** a rounded metal or earthen container used chiefly for domestic purposes **b :** POTFUL **2 :** an enclosed framework of wire, wood, or wicker for catching fish or lobsters **3 a :** a large sum of money **b** (1) **:** the total of the bets at stake at one time (2) **:** one round in a poker game **c :** the total of a prize **d :** the common fund of a group **4 :** POTSHOT **5** *slang* **:** POTBELLY **6 :** RUIN, DETERIORATION ⟨business went to ~⟩ **7 :** a shot in which a billiard ball is pocketed **8 :** MARIJUANA

2**pot** *vt* **pot·ted; pot·ting 1 a :** to place in a pot **b :** to preserve in a sealed pot, jar, or can ⟨*potted* chicken⟩ **2 a :** to shoot for food **b :** to shoot by a potshot ~ *vi* **:** to take a potshot

po·ta·bil·i·ty \ˌpōt-ə-ˈbil-ət-ē\ *n* **:** the quality or state of being potable

po·ta·ble \ˈpōt-ə-bəl\ *adj* [LL *potabilis*, fr. L *potare* to drink; akin to L *bibere* to drink, Gk *pinein*] **:** suitable for drinking — **potable** *n* — **po·ta·ble·ness** *n*

po·tage \pȯ-ˈtäzh\ *n* [MF, fr. OF, pottage, fr. *pot*, of Gmc origin; akin to OE *pott*] **:** a thick soup

pot ale *n* **:** the residue of fermented wort left in a still after whiskey or alcohol has been distilled off and used for feeding swine

pot·ash \ˈpät-ˌash\ *n* [sing. of *pot ashes*] **1 a :** potassium carbonate esp. from wood ashes **b :** POTASSIUM HYDROXIDE **2 :** potassium or a potassium compound esp. as used in agriculture or industry

po·tas·sic \pə-ˈtas-ik\ *adj* **:** of, relating to, or containing potassium

po·tas·si·um \pə-ˈtas-ē-əm\ *n, often attrib* [NL, fr. *potassa* potash, fr. E *potash*] **:** a silver-white soft light low-melting univalent metallic element of the alkali metal group that occurs abundantly in nature esp. combined in minerals — see ELEMENT table

potassium bromide *n* **:** a crystalline salt KBr with a saline taste used as a sedative and in photography

potassium carbonate *n* **:** a white salt K_2CO_3 that forms a strongly alkaline solution and is used in making glass and soap

potassium chlorate *n* **:** a crystalline salt $KClO_3$ that is used as an oxidizing agent in matches, fireworks, and explosives

potassium chloride *n* **:** a crystalline salt KCl occurring as a mineral and in natural waters and used as a fertilizer

potassium cyanide *n* **:** a very poisonous crystalline salt KCN used in electroplating

potassium dichromate *n* **:** a soluble salt $K_2Cr_2O_7$ forming large orange-red crystals used in dyeing, in photography, and as an oxidizing agent

potassium hydroxide *n* **:** a white deliquescent solid KOH that dissolves in water with much heat to form a strongly alkaline and caustic liquid and is used chiefly in making soap and as a reagent

potassium nitrate *n* **:** a crystalline salt KNO_3 that occurs as a product of nitrification in arable soils, is a strong oxidizer, and is used in making gunpowder, in preserving meat, and in medicine

potassium permanganate *n* **:** a dark purple salt $KMnO_4$ used as an oxidizer and disinfectant

potassium sulfate *n* **:** a white crystalline compound K_2SO_4 used as a fertilizer

po·ta·tion \pō-ˈtā-shən\ *n* [ME *potacioun*, fr. MF *potation*, fr. L *potation-*, *potatio* act of drinking, fr. *potatus*, pp. of *potare*] **1 :** a usu. alcoholic drink or brew **2 a :** the act of drinking **b :** DRAFT 4a

po·ta·to \pə-ˈtāt-(ˌ)ō, pət-ˈāt-, -ə(-w)\ *n, pl* **potatoes** *often attrib* [Sp *batata*, fr. Taino] **1 :** SWEET POTATO **2 a :** an erect American herb (*Solanum tuberosum*) of the nightshade family widely cultivated as a vegetable crop **b :** its edible starchy tuber — called also *white potato*

potato beetle *n* **:** a black-and-yellow striped beetle (*Leptinotarsa decemlineata*) that feeds on the leaves of the potato — called also *potato bug*

potato chip *n* **:** a thin slice of white potato fried crisp

po·ta·to·ry \ˈpōt-ə-ˌtōr-ē, -ˌtȯr-\ *adj* [LL *potatorius*, fr. L *potatus*] **:** of, relating to, or given to drinking

pot–au–feu \ˌpät-ō-ˈfə(r), pȯ-tō-fœ\ *n, pl* **pot–au–feu** [F, lit., pot on the fire] **:** a thick French soup of meat and vegetables

pot·bel·lied \ˈpät-ˈbel-ēd\ *adj* **:** having a potbelly or a bulging part suggestive of a potbelly ⟨a ~ man⟩ ⟨a ~ stove⟩

pot·bel·ly \ˈpät-ˌbel-ē\ *n* **1 :** an enlarged, swollen, or protruding abdomen **2 :** a stove with a bulging body

pot·boil \-ˌbȯil\ *vi* **:** to produce potboilers

pot·boil·er \-ˌbȯi-lər\ *n* **:** a usu. inferior work of art or literature produced chiefly for monetary return

pot·boy \-ˌbȯi\ *n* **:** a boy who serves drinks in a tavern

pot cheese *n* **:** COTTAGE CHEESE

po·teen *also* **po·theen** \pə-'tēn, -'chēn, -'tyēn, -'thēn\ *n* [IrGael *poitín*] **:** illicitly distilled whiskey of Ireland

po·tence \'pōt-ᵊn(t)s\ *n* **:** POTENCY

po·ten·cy \'pōt-ᵊn-sē\ *n* **1 :** the quality or state of being potent **2 :** POTENTIALITY 1

1po·tent \'pōt-ᵊnt\ *adj* [obs. E *potent* crutch] *of a heraldic cross* **:** having flat bars across the ends of the arms — see CROSS illustration

2potent *adj* [ME (Sc), fr. L *potent-, potens,* fr. prp. of (assumed) L *potēre* to be powerful, fr. L *potis, pote* able; akin to Goth *brūth-faths* bridegroom, Gk *posis* husband, Skt *pati* master] **1 :** having or wielding force, authority, or influence **:** POWERFUL **2 :** producing an effect **:** PREGNANT **3 a :** chemically or medicinally effective ⟨a ~ vaccine⟩ **b :** rich in a characteristic constituent ⟨~ tea⟩ **4 :** able to copulate — usu. used of the male — **po·tent·ly** *adv*

po·ten·tate \'pōt-ᵊn-,tāt\ *n* **:** one who wields controlling power

1po·ten·tial \pə-'ten-chəl\ *adj* [ME, fr. LL *potentialis,* fr. *potentia* potentiality, fr. L, power, fr. *potent-, potens*] **1 :** existing in possibility **:** capable of development into actuality **2 :** expressing possibility; *specif* **:** of, relating to, or constituting a verb phrase expressing possibility, liberty, or power by the use of an auxiliary with the infinitive of the verb (as in "it may rain") **syn** see LATENT — **po·ten·tial·ly** \-'tench-(ə-)lē\ *adv*

2potential *n* **1 :** something that can develop or become actual **2 :** any of various functions from which the intensity or the velocity at any point in a field may be readily calculated; *specif* **:** the degree of electrification as referred to some standard

potential energy *n* **:** the energy that a piece of matter has because of its position or because of the arrangement of parts

po·ten·ti·al·i·ty \pə-,ten-chē-'al-ət-ē\ *n* **1 :** the ability to develop or come into existence **2 :** POTENTIAL 1

po·ten·ti·ate \pə-'ten-chē-,āt\ *vt* **:** to make potent; *specif* **:** to augment (as a drug) synergistically — **po·ten·ti·a·tion** \-,ten-chē-'ā-shən\ *n* — **po·ten·ti·a·tor** \-'ten-chē-,āt-ər\ *n*

po·ten·til·la \,pōt-ᵊn-'til-ə\ *n* [NL, genus name, fr. ML, garden valerian, fr. L *potent-, potens*] **:** any of a large genus (*Potentilla*) of herbs and shrubs of the rose family comprising cinquefoils and related plants and having opposite pinnate or palmate leaves

po·ten·ti·om·e·ter \pə-,ten-chē-'äm-ət-ər\ *n* [ISV *potential* + *-o-* + *-meter*] **1 :** an instrument for measuring electromotive forces **2 :** VOLTAGE DIVIDER — **po·ten·tio·met·ric** \-chē-ō-'me-trik\ *adj*

pot·ful \'pät-,fu̇l\ *n* **:** the quantity held by a pot

pot hat *n* **:** a hat with a stiff crown; *esp* **:** DERBY

poth·e·cary \'päth-ə-,ker-ē\ *n, chiefly dial* **:** APOTHECARY

1poth·er \'päth-ər\ *n* [origin unknown] **1 a :** a noisy disturbance **b :** FUSS **2 :** a choking cloud of dust or smoke **3 :** mental turmoil **syn** see STIR

2pother *vt* **poth·er·ing** \-(ə-)riŋ\ **:** to put into a pother ~ *vi* **:** to be in a pother

pot·herb \'pät-,(h)ərb\ *n* **:** an herb whose leaves or stems are cooked for use as greens; *also* **:** one (as mint) used to season food

pot·hole \-,hōl\ *n* **1 :** a circular hole formed in the rocky bed of a river by the grinding action of stones or gravel whirled round by the water **2 :** a pot-shaped hole in a road surface

pot·hook \-,hu̇k\ *n* **1 :** an S-shaped hook for hanging pots and kettles over an open fire **2 :** a written character resembling a pothook

pot·house \-,hau̇s\ *n* **:** TAVERN 1

pot·hunt·er \-,hənt-ər\ *n* **:** one who hunts game for food

po·tiche \pō-'tēsh\ *n, pl* **po·tiches** \-'tēsh(-əz)\ [F, fr. *pot* — more at POTAGE] **:** a vase having a separate cover, a body usu. rounded or polygonal with nearly vertical sides, a rounded shoulder, and a tapered neck

po·tion \'pō-shən\ *n* [ME *pocioun,* fr. MF *potion,* fr. L *potion-, potio* drink, potion, fr. *potus,* pp. of *potare* to drink — more at POTABLE] **:** a liquid mixture or dose

1pot·latch \'pät-,lach\ *n* [Chinook Jargon, fr. Nootka *patshatl* giving] **1 :** a ceremonial feast of the Indians of the northwest coast marked by the host's lavish distribution of gifts requiring reciprocation **2** *Northwest* **:** a social event or celebration

2potlatch *vt* **1 :** to hold or give a potlatch for (as a tribe or group) **2 :** to give (as a gift) esp. with the expectancy of reciprocation ~ *vi* **:** to hold or give a potlatch

pot liquor *n* **:** the liquid left in a pot after cooking meat or vegetables

pot·luck \'pät-'lək\ *n* **:** the regular meal available to a guest for whom no special preparations have been made

pot marigold *n* **:** a calendula (*Calendula officinalis*) grown esp. for ornament

pot·pie \'pät-'pī\ *n* **:** meat and vegetables covered with pastry and boiled or baked in a pot

pot·pour·ri \,pō-pu̇-'rē\ *n* [F *pot pourri,* lit., rotten pot] **1 :** a jar of flower petals and spices used for scent **2 :** a miscellaneous collection **:** MEDLEY

pot roast *n* **:** a piece of beef or other meat cooked by braising usu. on top of the stove

pot·sherd \'pät-,shərd\ *n* [ME *pot-sherd,* fr. *pot* + *sherd* shard] **:** a pottery fragment

pot·shot \-,shät\ *n* **1 a :** a pothunter's shot **b :** a shot taken in a casual manner or at an easy target **2 :** a critical remark made in a random or sporadic manner — **potshot** *vb*

pot still *n* **:** a still used esp. in the distillation of Irish grain whiskey and Scotch malt whiskey in which the heat of the fire is applied directly to the pot containing the mash

pot·stone \'pät-,stōn\ *n* **:** a more or less impure steatite used esp. in prehistoric times to make cooking vessels

pot·tage \'pät-ij\ *n* [ME *potage,* fr. OF] **:** a thick soup of vegetables or vegetables and meat

1pot·ter \'pät-ər\ *n* **:** one that makes pottery

2potter *vi* [prob. freq. of E dial. *pote* to poke] **:** PUTTER — **pot·ter·er** \'pät-ər-ər\ *n* — **pot·ter·ing·ly** \'pät-ə-riŋ-lē\ *adv*

potter's clay *n* **:** a plastic clay suitable for modeling or throwing pottery — called also *potter's earth*

potter's field *n* [fr. the mention in Mt 27:7 of the purchase of a potter's field for use as a graveyard] **:** a public burial place for paupers, unknown persons, and criminals

potter's wheel *n* **:** a usu. horizontal disk revolving on a vertical spindle and carrying the clay being shaped by a potter

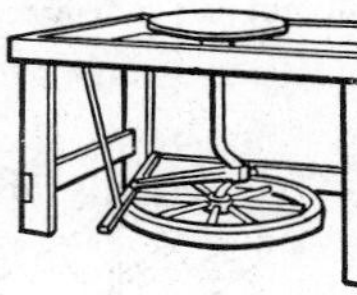

potter's wheel

pot·tery \'pät-ə-rē\ *n* **1 :** a shop or factory where earthen vessels are made **2 :** the art of the potter **:** CERAMICS **3 :** ware made usu. from clay that is shaped while moist and soft and hardened by heat; *specif* **:** coarser ware so made

pot·tle \'pät-ᵊl\ *n* [ME *potel,* fr. OF, fr. *pot*] **1** *archaic* **:** a measure equal to a half gallon **2 a :** a container holding one pottle **b :** a pottle of wine or liquor

Pott's disease \'päts-\ *n* [Percivall *Pott* †1788 E surgeon] **:** tuberculosis of the spine with destruction of bone resulting in curvature of the spine

1pot·ty \'pät-ē\ *adj* [prob. fr. 1*pot*] **1** *Brit* **:** TRIVIAL, INSIGNIFICANT **2** *slang chiefly Brit* **:** slightly crazy **3 :** SNOBBISH

2potty *n* **:** a small child's pot for voiding or defecation

pot·ty-chair \-,che(ə)r, -,cha(ə)r\ *n* **:** a child's chair having an open seat under which a receptacle is placed for toilet training

1pouch \'pau̇ch\ *n* [ME *pouche,* fr. MF, of Gmc origin; akin to OE *pocca* bag] **1 :** a small drawstring bag carried on the person **2 a :** a bag of small or moderate size for storing or transporting goods; *specif* **:** a locking bag for first class mail or diplomatic dispatches **b** *chiefly Scot* **:** POCKET **c :** PACKET **3 :** an anatomical structure resembling a pouch — **pouched** \'pau̇cht\ *adj*

2pouch *vt* **1 :** to put or form into or as if into a pouch **2 :** to transmit by pouch ~ *vi* **:** to form a pouch

pouchy \'pau̇-chē\ *adj* **:** having, tending to have, or resembling a pouch

pouf \'püf\ *n* [F, of imit. origin] **1 :** PUFF 3b(3) **2 :** a bouffant or fluffy part of a garment or accessory **3 :** OTTOMAN

pou·larde *also* **pou·lard** \pü-'lärd\ *n* [F *poularde*] **:** a pullet sterilized to produce fattening

poult \'pōlt\ *n* [ME *polet, pulte* young fowl — more at PULLET] **:** a young fowl; *esp* **:** a young turkey

poul·ter·er \'pōl-tər-ər\ *n* [alter. of ME *pulter,* fr. MF *pouletier*] **:** one that deals in poultry

poul·ter's measure \'pōl-tərz-\ *n* [obs. *poulter* poulterer, fr. ME *pulter;* fr. the former practice of occasionally giving one or two extra when counting eggs by dozens] **:** a meter in which lines of 12 and 14 syllables alternate

1poul·tice \'pōl-təs\ *n* [ML *pultes* pap, fr. L, pl. of *pult-, puls* porridge] **:** a soft usu. heated and sometimes medicated mass spread on cloth and applied to sores or other lesions

2poultice *vt* **:** to apply a poultice to

poul·try \'pōl-trē\ *n* [ME *pultrie,* fr. MF *pouleterie,* fr. OF, fr. *pouletier* poulterer, fr. *polet* — more at PULLET] **:** domesticated birds kept for eggs or meat

poul·try·man \-mən\ *n* **1 :** one that raises domestic fowls esp. on a commercial scale for the production of eggs and meat **2 :** a dealer in poultry or poultry products

1pounce \'pau̇n(t)s\ *n* [ME, talon] **:** the claw of a bird of prey

2pounce *vi* **1 :** to swoop upon and seize something with or as if with talons **2 :** to make an abrupt assault or approach

3pounce *n* **:** the act of pouncing

4pounce *vt* **:** to dust, rub, finish, or stencil with pounce

5pounce *n* [F *ponce* pumice, fr. LL *pomic-, pomex,* alter. of L *pumic-, pumex* — more at FOAM] **1 :** a fine powder formerly used to prevent ink from spreading **2 :** a fine powder for making stenciled patterns

poun·cet-box \'pau̇n(t)-sət-\ *n* [prob. fr. (assumed) MF *poncette* small pounce bag] *archaic* **:** a box for carrying pomander

1pound \'pau̇nd\ *n, pl* **pounds** *also* **pound** [ME, fr. OE *pund;* akin to ON *pund* pound; both fr. a prehistoric Gmc word borrowed fr. L *pondo* pound; akin to L *pondus* weight — more at PENDANT] **1 :** any of various units of mass and weight; *specif* **:** a unit now in general use among English-speaking peoples equal to 16 avoirdupois ounces or 7000 grains or 0.45359237 kilogram — called also *avoirdupois pound;* see MEASURE table **2 a :** the basic monetary unit of the United Kingdom — called also *pound sterling* **b :** any of numerous basic monetary units of other countries — see MONEY table

2pound *vb* [alter. of ME *pounen,* fr. OE *pūnian*] *vt* **1 :** to reduce to powder or pulp by beating **2 a :** to strike heavily or repeatedly **b :** to produce by means of repeated vigorous strokes **c :** to inculcate by insistent repetition **:** DRIVE **3 :** to move along heavily or persistently ~ *vi* **1 :** to strike heavy repeated blows **2 a :** to move with or make a heavy repetitive sound **b :** to work hard and continuously

3pound *n* **:** an act or sound of pounding

4pound *n* [ME, enclosure, fr. OE *pund-*] **1 a :** an enclosure for animals; *esp* **:** a public enclosure for stray or unlicensed animals **b :** a depot for holding personal property until redeemed by the owner **2 :** a place or condition of confinement **3 a :** an enclosure within which fish are kept or caught; *esp* **:** the inner compartment of a fish trap or pound net **b :** an establishment selling live lobsters

5pound *vt, archaic* **:** IMPOUND

1pound·age \'pau̇n-dij\ *n* **1 a :** a tax levied in pounds sterling **b :** COMMISSION **2 a :** a charge per pound of weight **b :** weight in pounds

2poundage *n* **1 :** the act of impounding **:** the state of being impounded **2 :** a fee for the release of an impounded animal

pound·al \'pau̇n-dᵊl\ *n* [*pound* + *-al* (as in *quintal*)] **:** a unit of force equal to the force that would give a free mass of one pound an acceleration of one foot per second per second

pound cake *n* **:** a rich butter cake made with a large proportion of eggs and shortening

1pound·er \'pau̇n-dər\ *n* **:** one that pounds

2pounder *n* **1 :** one having a usu. specified weight or value in pounds **2 :** a gun throwing a projectile of a specified weight

pound-fool·ish \'pau̇n(d)-'fü-lish\ *adj* [fr. the phrase *penny-wise and pound-foolish*] **:** imprudent in dealing with large sums or large matters

pound mile *n* **:** the transport of one pound of mail or express for one mile
pound net *n* **:** a fish trap consisting of a netting arranged into a

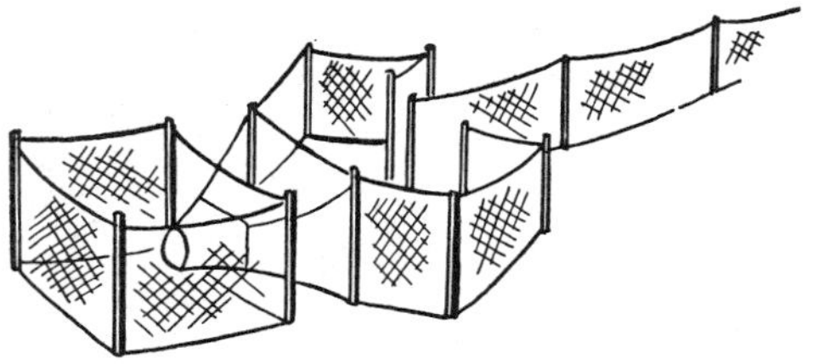

pound net

directing wing and an enclosure with a narrow entrance
¹pour \'pō(ə)r, 'pȯ(ə)r\ *vb* [ME *pouren*] *vt* **1 :** to cause to flow in a stream **2 :** to supply or produce freely or copiously ~ *vi* **1 :** to move with a continuous flow **2 :** to rain hard **3 :** to preside at a tea table — **pour·able** \'pōr-ə-bəl, 'pȯr-\ *adj* — **pour·er** \-ər\ *n* — **pour·ing·ly** \-iŋ-lē\ *adv*
²pour *n* **:** the action of pouring **:** STREAM; *esp* **:** a heavy fall of rain
pour·boire \pü(ə)rb-'wär\ *n* [F, fr. *pour boire* for drinking] **:** TIP, GRATUITY
pour·par·ler \ˌpü(ə)r-(ˌ)pär-'lā\ *n* [F] **:** a discussion preliminary to negotiations
pour·point \'pü(ə)r-ˌpȯint, -ˌpwant\ *n* [ME *purpoint*, fr. MF *pourpoint*] **:** a padded and quilted doublet
pour point \'pō(ə)r-ˌpȯint, 'pȯ(ə)r-\ *n* **:** the lowest temperature at which a substance flows under specified conditions
pousse–ca·fé \ˌpü-(ˌ)ska-'fā\ *n* [F, lit., coffee chaser] **1 :** an after-dinner drink consisting of several liqueurs of different colors and specific gravities poured so as to remain in separate layers **2 :** a small drink of brandy or a liqueur taken with black coffee after dinner
pous·sette \pü-'set\ *vi* [F] **:** to swing in a semicircle with hands joined with one's partner in a country-dance
¹pout \'pau̇t\ *n, pl* **pout** *or* **pouts** [prob. fr. (assumed) ME *poute*, a fish with a large head, fr. OE *-pūte;* akin to ME *pouten* to pout, Skt *budbuda* bubble] **:** any of several large-headed fishes (as a bullhead or eelpout)
²pout *vb* [ME *pouten*] *vi* **1 a :** to show displeasure by thrusting out the lips or wearing a sullen expression **b :** SULK **2 :** PROTRUDE ~ *vt* **:** to cause to protrude
³pout *n* **1 :** a protrusion of the lips expressive of displeasure **2** *pl* **:** a fit of pique
pout·er \'pau̇t-ər\ *n* **1 :** one that pouts **2 :** a domestic pigeon of a breed characterized by erect carriage and a distensible and dilatable crop
pouty \'pau̇t-ē\ *adj* **:** SULKY
pov·er·ty \'päv-ərt-ē\ *n* [ME *poverte*, fr. OF *poverté*, fr. L *paupertat-, paupertas*, fr. *pauper* poor — more at POOR] **1 a :** lack of money or material possessions **:** WANT **b :** renunciation as a member of a religious order of the right as an individual to own property **2 :** SCARCITY, DEARTH **3 a :** debility due to malnutrition **b :** lack of fertility
syn INDIGENCE, PENURY, WANT, DESTITUTION: POVERTY may cover a range from extreme want of necessities to a falling short of having comfortable means; INDIGENCE implies seriously straitened circumstances; PENURY suggests a cramping or oppressive lack of money; WANT and DESTITUTION imply extreme poverty that threatens life itself through starvation or exposure
pov·er·ty–strick·en \-ˌstrik-ən\ *adj* **:** afflicted with poverty **:** very poor **:** DESTITUTE
¹pow \'pō, 'pau̇\ *n* [by alter.] **:** POLL
²pow \'pau̇\ *n* [imit.] **:** a sound of a blow or explosion
¹pow·der \'pau̇d-ər\ *n, often attrib* [ME *poudre*, fr. OF, fr. L *pulver-, pulvis* dust — more at POLLEN] **1 :** a substance composed of fine particles **2 :** a medicinal, cosmetic, or other preparation in the form of fine particles **3 :** any of various solid explosives used chiefly in gunnery and blasting
²powder *vb* **pow·der·ing** \-(ə-)riŋ\ *vt* **1 :** to sprinkle or cover with or as if with powder **2 :** to reduce to powder ~ *vi* **1 :** to become powder **2 :** to apply cosmetic powder — **pow·der·er** \-ər-ər\ *n*
powder blue *n* **1 :** a pigment consisting of powdered smalt **2 :** a variable color averaging a pale blue
powder horn *n* **:** a flask for carrying gunpowder; *esp* **:** one made of the horn of an ox or cow
powder keg *n* **1 :** a small usu. metal cask for holding gunpowder or blasting powder **2 :** something liable to explode
powder metallurgy *n* **:** the production of metallic objects by compressing powdered metal or alloy with or without other materials and heating without thoroughly melting to solidify and strengthen
powder monkey *n* **:** one who transports powder from the magazine to the guns esp. on shipboard
powder puff *n* **:** a small fluffy device (as a pad) for applying cosmetic powder
powder room *n* **:** a rest room for women
pow·dery \'pau̇d-ə-rē\ *adj* **1 a :** resembling or consisting of powder **b :** easily reduced to powder **:** CRUMBLING **2 :** covered with or as if with powder
powdery mildew *n* **1 :** a perfect fungus (family Erysiphaceae) or an imperfect fungus (genus *Oidium*) producing abundant powdery conidia on the host **2 :** a plant disease caused by a powdery mildew
¹pow·er \'pau̇(-ə)r\ *n, often attrib* [ME, fr. OF *poeir*, fr. *poeir* to be able, fr. (assumed) L *potēre* to be powerful — more at POTENT] **1 a :** possession of control, authority, or influence over others **b :** one having such power; *specif* **:** a sovereign state **c** *archaic* **:** a force of armed men **d** *chiefly dial* **:** a large number or quantity **2 a** (1) **:** ability to act or produce an effect (2) **:** capacity for being acted upon or undergoing an effect **b :** legal or official authority, capacity, or right **3 a :** physical might **b :** mental or moral efficacy **c :** political control or influence **4 :** an angel of the fourth lowest rank **5 a :** the number of times as indicated by an exponent a number occurs as a factor in a product; *also* **:** the product itself **b :** CARDINAL NUMBER 2 **6 a :** a source or means of supplying energy; *esp* **:** ELECTRICITY **b :** MOTIVE POWER **c :** the time rate at which work is done or energy emitted or transferred **7 :** MAGNIFICATION 2b **8 :** SCOPE, COMPREHENSIVENESS
syn POWER, FORCE, ENERGY, STRENGTH, MIGHT mean the ability to exert effort. POWER may imply latent or exerted physical, mental, or spiritual ability to act or be acted upon; FORCE implies the actual and efficacious exercise of power; ENERGY applies to power expended or capable of being transformed into work; STRENGTH applies to the quality or property of a person or thing that enables him to exert force or withstand strain, pressure, or attack; MIGHT implies great or overwhelming power or strength
syn POWER, AUTHORITY, JURISDICTION, CONTROL, COMMAND, SWAY, DOMINION mean the right to govern or rule or determine. POWER implies possession of ability to wield coercive force, permissive authority, or substantial influence; AUTHORITY implies the granting of power for a specific purpose within specified limits; JURISDICTION applies to official power exercised within prescribed limits; CONTROL stresses the power to direct and restrain; COMMAND implies the power to make arbitrary decisions and compel obedience; SWAY suggests the extent or scope of exercised power or influence; DOMINION stresses sovereign power or supreme authority
²power *vt* **:** to supply with power esp. motive power
pow·er·boat \-'bōt\ *n* **:** MOTORBOAT
power dive *n* **:** a dive of an airplane accelerated by the power of the engine — **pow·er–dive** \-'dīv\ *vb*
pow·er·ful \'pau̇(-ə)r-fəl\ *adj* **1 :** having great power **2 :** leading to many or important deductions ⟨~ set of postulates⟩ — **pow·er·ful·ly** \-f(ə-)lē\ *adv*
pow·er·house \'pau̇(-ə)r-ˌhau̇s\ *n* **1 a :** an electric utility generating station **b :** a source of influence or inspiration **2 :** one having or wielding great power
pow·er·less \-ləs\ *adj* **1 :** devoid of strength or resources **2 :** lacking the authority or capacity to act **:** UNABLE — **pow·er·less·ly** *adv* — **pow·er·less·ness** *n*
power mower *n* **:** a motor-driven lawn mower
power of attorney : a legal instrument authorizing one to act as the attorney or agent of the grantor
power pack *n* **:** a unit for converting a power supply (as from a battery) to a voltage suitable for an electronic device
power plant *n* **1 :** POWERHOUSE 1a **2 :** an engine and related parts supplying the motive power of a self-propelled vehicle
power play *n* **:** an offensive maneuver (as in football or hockey) in which mass interference is provided at a particular point or in a particular zone
power politics *n pl but sing or pl in constr* **:** politics based primarily on the use of power as a coercive force rather than upon ethical precepts; *esp* **:** international politics characterized by attempts to advance national interests through coercion on the basis of military and economic strength
power series *n* **:** an infinite series whose terms are successive integral powers of a variable multiplied by constants
power shovel *n* **:** a power-operated excavating machine consisting of a boom or crane that supports a dipper handle with a dipper at the end of it
power steering *n* **:** automotive steering with engine power used to amplify the torque applied at the steering wheel by the driver
power take–off *n* **:** a supplementary mechanism on a truck or tractor enabling the engine power to be used to operate nonautomotive apparatus (as pumps or saws)
¹pow·wow \'pau̇-ˌwau̇\ *n* [of Algonquian origin; akin to Natick *pauwau* conjurer] **1 :** a No. American Indian medicine man **2 :** a No. American Indian ceremony (as for victory in war) **3 a :** a social get-together **b :** a meeting for discussion
²powwow *vi* **:** to hold a powwow
¹pox \'päks\ *n, pl* **pox** *or* **pox·es** [alter. of *pocks*, pl. of *pock*] **1 a :** a virus disease characterized by pustules or eruptions ⟨chicken *pox*⟩ **b** *archaic* **:** SMALLPOX **c :** SYPHILIS **2 :** an afflictive rash **:** PLAGUE ⟨a ~ on him⟩
²pox *vt, archaic* **:** to infect with a pox and esp. with syphilis
poz·zo·la·na \ˌpät-sə-'län-ə\ *or* **poz·zo·lan** \-'län\ *n* [It *pozzolana*] **:** a pulverulent siliceous or siliceous and aluminous substance that reacts chemically with slaked lime at ordinary temperature and in the presence of moisture to form a cement — **poz·zo·la·nic** \-'län-ik\ *adj*
PPI \ˌpē-(ˌ)pē-'ī\ *n* [*p*lan *p*osition *i*ndicator] **:** a radarscope on which spots of light representing reflections of radar waves indicate the range and bearing of objects
prac·tic \'prak-tik\ *adj* [ME *practik*, fr. MF *practique*, fr. LL *practicus*] **:** PRACTICAL
prac·ti·ca·bil·i·ty \ˌprak-ti-kə-'bil-ət-ē\ *n* **:** the quality or state of being practicable
prac·ti·ca·ble \'prak-ti-kə-bəl\ *adj* **1 :** possible to practice or perform **:** FEASIBLE **2 :** capable of being used **:** USABLE — **prac·ti·ca·ble·ness** *n* — **prac·ti·ca·bly** \-blē\ *adv*
syn PRACTICABLE, PRACTICAL both mean relating to practice or use but are not interchangeable. PRACTICABLE applies to what has been proposed and seems feasible but has not been actually tested in use; PRACTICAL applies to things and to persons and implies success in meeting the demands made by actual living or use **syn** see in addition POSSIBLE
prac·ti·cal \'prak-ti-kəl\ *adj* [LL *practicus*, fr. Gk *praktikos*, fr. *prassein* to pass over, fare, do; akin to Gk *peran* to pass through — more at FARE] **1 :** actively engaged in some course of action or occupation **2 a :** of, relating to, or manifested in practice or action ⟨for ~ purposes⟩ **b :** being such in practice or effect **:** VIRTUAL ⟨a ~ failure⟩ **3 :** capable of being put to use or account **:** USEFUL **4 a :** disposed to action as opposed to speculation or abstraction **b** (1) **:** qualified by practice or practical training (2) **:** designed to supplement theoretical training by experience **5 :** concerned with voluntary action and ethical decisions ⟨~ reason⟩ **syn** see PRACTICABLE — **prac·ti·cal·i·ty** \ˌprak-ti-'kal-ət-ē\ *n* — **prac·ti·cal·ly** \'prak-ti-k(ə-)lē\ *adv* — **prac·ti·cal·ness** \-kəl-nəs\ *n*
practical art *n* **:** an art (as woodworking) that serves ordinary or material needs — usu. used in pl.
practical joke *n* **:** a joke whose humor stems from the tricking or abuse of an individual placed somehow at a disadvantage — **practical joker** *n*
practical nurse *n* **:** a nurse that cares for the sick professionally without having the training or experience required of a registered nurse

practical theology *n* **:** the study of the institutional activities of religion (as preaching, church administration, and liturgics)

1**prac·tice** *or* **prac·tise** \ˈprak-təs\ *vb* [ME *practisen*, fr. MF *practiser*, fr. *practique* practice, fr. LL *practice*, fr. Gk *praktikē*, fr. fem. of *praktikos*] *vt* **1 a :** to perform or work at repeatedly so as to become proficient ⟨~ his act⟩ **b :** to train by repeated exercises ⟨~ pupils in penmanship⟩ **2 a :** to carry out **:** APPLY ⟨~ what he preaches⟩ **b :** to do or perform often, customarily, or habitually ⟨~ politeness⟩ **c :** to be professionally engaged in ⟨~ medicine⟩ **3** *obs* **:** PLOT **4** *obs* **:** FREQUENT **~** *vi* **1 :** to do repeated exercises for proficiency **2 :** to pursue a profession actively **3** *archaic* **a :** INTRIGUE **b :** to impose by artifice **4 :** to do something customarily — **prac·tic·er** *n*

syn PRACTICE, EXERCISE, DRILL mean to perform or make perform repeatedly. PRACTICE further implies the attainment of skill through much repetition; EXERCISE implies a strengthening or developing by keeping at work; DRILL stresses the forming of correct habit by mechanical repetition

2**practice** *also* **practise** *n, often attrib* **1 a :** actual performance or application **b :** a repeated or customary action **c :** the usual way of doing something ⟨local ~⟩ **d :** the form, manner, and order of conducting legal suits and prosecutions **2 a :** systematic exercise for proficiency ⟨~ makes perfect⟩ **b :** the condition of being proficient through systematic exercise ⟨get in ~⟩ **3 a :** the continuous exercise of a profession **b :** a professional business; *esp* **:** one constituting an incorporeal property **syn** see HABIT

prac·ticed *or* **prac·tised** \ˈprak-təst\ *adj* **1 :** EXPERIENCED, SKILLED **2 :** learned by practice

practice teacher *n* **:** one doing practice teaching

practice teaching *n* **:** teaching by a student preparing for a teaching career for the purpose of practicing educational skills and methods under the supervision of an experienced teacher

prac·ti·tion·er \prak-ˈtish-(ə-)nər\ *n* [alter. of earlier *practician*, fr. ME (Sc) *pratician*, fr. MF *praticien*, fr. *pratique*] **1 :** one who practices; *esp* **:** one who practices a profession **2** *Christian Science* **:** an authorized healer

prae·di·al \ˈprēd-ē-əl\ *adj* [ML *praedialis*, fr. L *praedium* landed property, fr. *praed-*, *praes* bondman — more at PREST] **:** of or relating to land or its products

prae·mu·ni·re \ˌprē-myu̇-ˈnī(ə)r-ē\ *n* [ME *praemunire facias*, fr. ML, that you cause to warn; fr. prominent words in the writ] **:** an offense against the English Crown punishable chiefly by forfeiture and originally committed by asserting papal legal supremacy in England

prae·no·men \prē-ˈnō-mən\ *n, pl* **praenomens** *or* **prae·no·mi·na** \-ˈnäm-ə-nə, -ˈnō-mə-\ [L, fr. *prae-* pre- + *nomen* name — more at NAME] **:** the first of the usual three names of an ancient Roman

prae·sid·i·um *var of* PRESIDIUM

prae·tor \ˈprēt-ər\ *n* [ME *pretor*, fr. L *praetor*] **:** an ancient Roman magistrate ranking below a consul and having chiefly judicial functions — **prae·to·ri·al** \prē-ˈtōr-ē-əl, -ˈtȯr-\ *adj* — **prae·tor·ship** \ˈprēt-ər-ˌship\ *n*

prae·to·ri·an \prē-ˈtōr-ē-ən, -ˈtȯr-\ *adj* **1 :** of or relating to a praetor **2** *often cap* **:** of, forming, or resembling the Roman imperial bodyguard — **praetorian** *n, often cap*

prag·mat·ic \prag-ˈmat-ik\ *adj* [L *pragmaticus* skilled in law or business, fr. Gk *pragmatikos*, fr. *pragmat-*, *pragma* deed, fr. *prassein* to do — more at PRACTICAL] **1** *archaic* **a** (1) **:** BUSY (2) **:** OFFICIOUS **b :** OPINIONATED **2 :** relating to matters of fact or practical affairs often to the exclusion of intellectual or artistic matters **3 :** relating to or in accordance with pragmatism — **pragmatic** *n* — **prag·mat·i·cal** \-i-kəl\ *adj* — **prag·mat·i·cal·ly** \-k(ə-)lē\ *adv*

prag·mat·i·cism \prag-ˈmat-ə-ˌsiz-əm\ *n* **:** the philosophic doctrine of C.S.Peirce — **prag·mat·i·cist** \-səst\ *n*

prag·mat·ics \prag-ˈmat-iks\ *n pl but sing or pl in constr* **:** a branch of semiotic that deals with the relation between signs or linguistic expressions and their users

pragmatic sanction *n* **:** a solemn decree of a sovereign on a matter of primary importance and with the force of fundamental law

prag·ma·tism \ˈprag-mə-ˌtiz-əm\ *n* **1 :** a practical approach to problems and affairs **2 :** an American movement in philosophy founded by C. S. Peirce and William James and marked by the doctrines that the meaning of conceptions is to be sought in their practical bearings, that the function of thought is to guide action, and that truth is preeminently to be tested by the practical consequences of belief — **prag·ma·tist** \-mət-əst\ *adj or n* — **prag·ma·tis·tic** \ˌprag-mə-ˈtis-tik\ *adj*

prai·rie \ˈpre(ə)r-ē\ *n, often attrib* [F, fr. (assumed) VL *prataria*, fr. L *pratum* meadow; akin to L *pravus* crooked, MIr *rāth* earthworks] **:** a tract of grassland**:** as **a :** a large area of level or rolling land in the Mississippi valley with generally deep fertile soil, a cover of tall coarse grasses, and few trees **b :** one of the dry treeless plateaus into which the prairies proper merge on the west

prairie breaker *n* **:** a plow with a long low moldboard designed to cut a wide shallow furrow and turn the slice completely over

prairie chicken *n* **:** a grouse (*Tympanuchus cupido pinnatus*) of the Mississippi valley; *also* **:** a closely related American grouse

prairie dog *n* **:** a colonial American burrowing rodent (genus *Cynomys*, esp. *C. ludovicianus* of the prairies) related to the marmots

prairie schooner *n* **:** a covered wagon used by pioneers in cross-country travel — called also *prairie wagon*

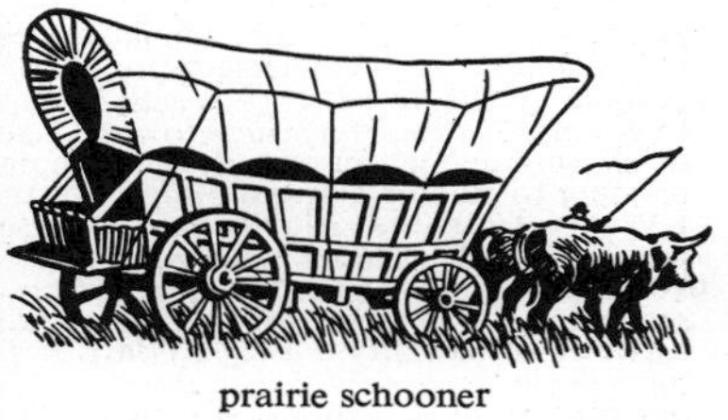

prairie schooner

prairie soil *n* **:** any of a zonal group of soils developed in a temperate relatively humid climate under tall grass

1**praise** \ˈprāz\ *vb* [ME *praisen*, fr. MF *preisier* to prize, praise, fr. LL *pretiare* to prize, fr. L *pretium* price — more at PRICE] *vt* **1 :** to express a favorable judgment of **:** COMMEND **2 :** to glorify esp. by ascription of perfections **~** *vi* **:** to express praise — **prais·er** *n*

2**praise** *n* **1 a :** an act of praising **:** COMMENDATION **b :** WORSHIP **2 a :** VALUE, MERIT **b :** one to be praised

praise·wor·thi·ly \ˈprāz-ˌwər-t͟hə-lē\ *adv* **:** in a praiseworthy manner

praise·wor·thi·ness \-t͟hē-nəs\ *n* **:** the quality or state of being praiseworthy

praise·wor·thy \-t͟hē\ *adj* **:** LAUDABLE

Pra·krit \ˈpräk-ˌrit, -rət\ *n* [Skt *prākṛta*, fr. *prākṛta* natural, vulgar] **1 :** any or all of the ancient Indic languages or dialects other than Sanskrit **2 :** any of the modern Indic languages

pra·line \ˈprä-ˌlēn, ˈprā-; ä *usual in La.*\ *n* [F, fr. Count Plessis-*Praslin* †1675 F soldier] **:** a confection of nut kernels**: a :** almonds roasted in boiling sugar until brown and crisp **b :** a patty of creamy brown sugar and pecan meats

prall·tril·ler \ˈpräl-ˌtril-ər\ *n* [G] **:** a musical mordent using the upper auxiliary note

1**pram** \ˈpräm\ *n* [D *praam;* akin to MLG *prām* pram] **:** a small lightweight nearly flat-bottomed boat with a broad transom and usu. squared-off bow

2**pram** \ˈpram\ *n, often attrib* [by shortening & alter. fr. *perambulator*] **1** *chiefly Brit* **:** PERAMBULATOR **2** *chiefly Brit* **:** HANDCART

1**prance** \ˈpran(t)s\ *vb* [ME *prauncen*] *vi* **1 :** to spring from the hind legs or move by so doing **2 :** to ride on a prancing horse **3 a :** SWAGGER **b :** CAPER **~** *vt* **:** to cause (a horse) to prance — **pranc·er** \ˈpran(t)-sər\ *n* — **pranc·ing·ly** \-siŋ-lē\ *adv*

2**prance** *n* **:** an act or instance of prancing; *specif* **:** a prancing movement

1**prank** \ˈpraŋk\ *n* [obs. *prank* to play tricks] **:** TRICK**: a** *obs* **:** a malicious act **b :** a ludicrous or mildly mischievous act

2**prank** *vb* [prob. fr. D *pronken* to strut; akin to MHG *gebrunkel* glitter of metal] *vt* **1 :** to dress or adorn gaily or showily **2 :** ADORN, SPANGLE **~** *vi* **:** to make ostentatious show

prank·ish \ˈpraŋ-kish\ *adj* **1 :** full of pranks **2 :** having the nature of a prank — **prank·ish·ly** *adv* — **prank·ish·ness** *n*

prank·ster \ˈpraŋ(k)-stər\ *n* **:** a player of pranks

prase \ˈprāz, ˈprās\ *n* [F, fr. L *prasius*, fr. Gk *prasios*, fr. *prasios*, adj., leek green, fr. *prason* leek; akin to L *porrum* leek] **:** a chalcedony that is translucent and leek green

pra·seo·dym·i·um \ˌprā-zē-ō-ˈdim-ē-əm\ *n* [NL, alter. of *praseodidymium*, irreg. fr. Gk *prasios*, adj. + NL *didymium*] **:** a yellowish white trivalent metallic element of the rare-earth group used chiefly in the form of its salts in coloring glass greenish yellow — see ELEMENT table

1**prate** \ˈprāt\ *vb* [ME *praten*, fr. MD; akin to MLG *pratten* to pout] *vi* **:** to talk long and idly **:** CHATTER **~** *vt* **:** to utter foolishly **:** BABBLE — **prat·er** \ˈprāt-ər\ *n* — **prat·ing·ly** \-iŋ-lē\ *adv*

2**prate** *n* **:** an act of prating

prat·fall \ˈprat-ˌfȯl\ *n* [*prat* (buttocks) + *fall*] **1 :** a fall on the buttocks **2 :** a humiliating mishap or blunder

pra·tin·cole \ˈprat-ᵊn-ˌkōl, ˈprāt-, -iŋ-\ *n* [deriv. of L *pratum* meadow + *incola* inhabitant, fr. *in-* + *colere* to cultivate — more at PRAIRIE, WHEEL] **:** any of a genus (*Glareola*) of limicoline birds

pra·tique \pra-ˈtēk\ *n* [F, lit., practice — more at PRACTICE] **:** clearance given an incoming ship by the health authority of a port

1**prat·tle** \ˈprat-ᵊl\ *vb* **prat·tling** \ˈprat-liŋ, -ᵊl-iŋ\ [LG *pratelen;* akin to MD *praten* to prate] *vi* **1 :** PRATE **2 :** to utter meaningless sounds suggestive of the chatter of children **~** *vt* **:** to say lightly and artlessly **:** BABBLE — **prat·tler** \ˈprat-lər, -ᵊl-ər\ *n* — **prat·tling·ly** \-liŋ-lē, -ᵊl-iŋ-\ *adv*

2**prattle** *n* **1 :** trifling or empty talk **2 :** a sound that is meaningless, repetitive, and suggestive of the chatter of children

prau \ˈprau̇, ˈprä-ˌü\ *n* [Malay *pĕrahu*] **:** any of several usu. undecked Indonesian boats propelled by sails, oars, or paddles

1**prawn** \ˈprȯn, ˈprän\ *n* [ME *prane*] **:** any of numerous widely distributed edible decapod crustaceans (as of the genera *Pandalus* and *Peneus*) resembling shrimps with large compressed abdomens; *also* **:** SHRIMP

2**prawn** *vi* **:** to fish for or with prawns — **prawn·er** *n*

prax·e·ol·o·gy \ˌprak-sē-ˈäl-ə-jē\ *n* [alter. of earlier *praxiology*, fr. *praxis* + *-o-* + *-logy*] **:** the study of human action and conduct

prax·is \ˈprak-səs\ *n, pl* **prax·es** \ˈprak-ˌsēz\ [ML, fr. Gk, doing, action, fr. *prassein* to pass through, practice — more at PRACTICAL] **1 :** exercise or practice of an art, science, or skill **2 :** customary practice or conduct

pray \ˈprā\ *vb* [ME *prayen*, fr. OF *preier*, fr. L *precari*, fr. *prec-*, *prex* request, prayer; akin to OHG *frāgēn* to ask, Skt *pṛcchati* he asks] *vt* **1 :** ENTREAT, IMPLORE — often used as a function word in introducing a question, request, or plea **2 :** to get or bring by praying **~** *vi* **1 :** to make entreaty or supplication **2 :** to address God with adoration, confession, supplication, or thanksgiving

1**prayer** \ˈpra(ə)r, ˈpre(ə)r\ *n, often attrib* [ME, fr. OF *preiere*, fr. ML *precaria*, fr. L, fem. of *precarius* obtained by entreaty, fr. *prec-*, *prex*] **1 a :** an approach to deity in word or thought **b :** an earnest request **2 :** the act or practice of praying to God **3** *often pl* **:** a religious service consisting chiefly of prayers **4 :** a form of words used in praying ⟨repeat a ~⟩ **5 :** something prayed for

2**pray·er** \ˈprā-ər, ˈpre(-ə)r\ *n* **:** one that prays **:** SUPPLIANT

prayer beads *n pl* **:** a string of beads by which prayers are counted; *specif* **:** ROSARY

prayer book *n* **:** a book containing prayers and often other forms and directions for worship

prayer·ful \ˈpra(ə)r-fəl, ˈpre(ə)r-\ *adj* **1 :** DEVOUT **2 :** EARNEST — **prayer·ful·ly** \-fə-lē\ *adv* — **prayer·ful·ness** *n*

prayer meeting *n* **:** a Protestant Christian service of evangelical worship usu. held regularly on a week night — called also *prayer service*

prayer wheel *n* **:** a cylinder of wood or metal revolving on an axis and containing written prayers that are considered efficacious by Tibetan Buddhists

pre- *prefix* [ME, fr. OF & L; OF, fr. L *prae-*, fr. *prae* in front of, before — more at FOR] **1 a** (1) **:** earlier than **:** prior to **:** before ⟨*Pre*cambrian⟩ ⟨*pre*historic⟩ ⟨*pre*-English⟩ (2) **:** preparatory or prerequisite to ⟨*pre*medical⟩ **b :** in advance **:** beforehand ⟨*pre*cancel⟩ ⟨*pre*pay⟩ **2 a :** in front of **:** anterior to ⟨*pre*axial⟩ ⟨*pre*molar⟩ **b :** front **:** anterior ⟨*pre*abdomen⟩

preach \ˈprēch\ *vb* [ME *prechen*, fr. OF *prechier*, fr. LL *praedicare*, fr. L, to proclaim publicly, fr. *prae-* pre- + *dicare* to proclaim

— more at DICTION] *vi* **1 :** to deliver a sermon **2 :** to urge acceptance or abandonment of an idea or course of action; *specif* **:** to exhort in an officious or tiresome manner ~ *vt* **1 :** to set forth in a sermon ⟨~ the gospel⟩ **2 :** to advocate earnestly **3 :** to utter (as a sermon) publicly **:** DELIVER **4 :** to bring, put, or affect by preaching — **preach·er** *n* — **preach·ing·ly** \'prē-chiŋ-lē\ *adv*

preach·ify \'prē-chə-ˌfī\ *vi* **:** to preach ineptly or tediously

preach·i·ly \-chə-lē\ *adv* **:** in a preachy manner

preach·i·ness \-chē-nəs\ *n* **:** the quality or state of being preachy

preach·ment \'prēch-mənt\ *n* **1 :** the act or practice of preaching **2 :** SERMON, EXHORTATION; *specif* **:** a tedious or unwelcome exhortation

preachy \'prē-chē\ *adj* **:** marked by obvious moral exhortation **:** DIDACTIC

pre·ad·o·les·cence \ˌprē-ˌad-ᵊl-'es-ᵊn(t)s\ *n* **:** the period of human development just preceding adolescence; *specif* **:** the period between the approximate ages of 9 and 12 — **pre·ad·o·les·cent** \-ᵊnt\ *adj or n*

pre·am·ble \'prē-ˌam-bəl, prē-'\ *n* [ME, fr. MF *preambule*, fr. ML *preambulum*, fr. LL, neut. of *praeambulus* walking in front of, fr. L *prae-* + *ambulare* to walk] **1 :** an introductory statement; *specif* **:** the introductory part of a constitution or statute that usu. states the reasons for and intent of the law **2 :** an introductory fact or circumstance; *esp* **:** one indicating what is to follow

pre·ar·range \ˌprē-ə-'rānj\ *vt* **:** to arrange beforehand — **pre·ar·range·ment** \-mənt\ *n*

pre·as·signed \ˌprē-ə-'sīnd\ *adj* **:** assigned beforehand

pre·atom·ic \-ə-'täm-ik\ *adj* **:** of or relating to a time before the use of the atom bomb and atomic energy

pre·ax·i·al \(')prē-'ak-sē-əl\ *adj* **:** situated in front of an axis of the body — **pre·ax·i·al·ly** \-ə-lē\ *adv*

preb·end \'preb-ənd\ *n* [ME *prebende*, fr. MF, fr. ML *praebenda*, fr. LL, subsistence allowance granted by the state, fr. L, fem. of *praebendus*, gerundive of *praebēre* to offer, fr. *prae-* + *habēre* to have — more at GIVE] **1 a :** an endowment held by a cathedral or collegiate church for the maintenance of a prebendary **b :** the stipend paid from this endowment **2 :** PREBENDARY — **pre·ben·dal** \pri-'ben-dᵊl, 'preb-ən-\ *adj*

preb·en·dary \'preb-ən-ˌder-ē\ *n* **1 :** a clergyman receiving a prebend for officiating and serving in the church **2 :** an honorary canon

Pre·cam·bri·an \(')prē-'kam-brē-ən\ *adj* **:** of, relating to, or being the earliest era of geological history equivalent to the Archeozoic and Proterozoic eras or the corresponding system of rocks — **Precambrian** *n*

pre·can·cel \(')prē-'kan(t)-səl\ *vt* **:** to cancel (a postage stamp) in advance of use — **pre·can·cel·la·tion** \ˌprē-ˌkan(t)-sə-'lā-shən\ *n*

pre·can·cer·ous \(')prē-'kan(t)s-(ə-)rəs\ *adj* [ISV] **:** likely to become cancerous ⟨a ~ lesion⟩

pre·car·i·ous \pri-'kar-ē-əs, -'ker-\ *adj* [L *precarius* obtained by entreaty, uncertain — more at PRAYER] **1** *archaic* **:** depending on the will or pleasure of another **2 :** dependent on uncertain premises **:** DUBIOUS **3 a :** dependent on chance circumstances, unknown conditions, or uncertain developments **b :** characterized by a lack of security or stability that threatens with danger **syn** see DANGEROUS — **pre·car·i·ous·ly** *adv* — **pre·car·i·ous·ness** *n*

pre·cau·tion \pri-'kȯ-shən\ *n* [F *précaution*, fr. LL *praecaution-*, *praecautio*, fr. L *praecautus*, pp. of *praecavēre* to guard against, fr. *prae-* + *cavēre* to be on one's guard — more at HEAR] **1 :** care taken in advance **:** FORESIGHT **2 :** a measure taken beforehand to prevent harm or secure good **:** SAFEGUARD — **pre·cau·tion·ary** \-shə-ˌner-ē\ *adj*

pre·ca·va \(')prē-'käv-ə, -'kā-və\ *n, pl* **pre·ca·vae** \-'käv-ˌī, -'kā-(ˌ)vē\ [NL] **:** SUPERIOR VENA CAVA — **pre·ca·val** \-'käv-əl, -'kā-vəl\ *adj*

pre·cede \pri-'sēd\ *vb* [ME *preceden*, fr. MF *preceder*, fr. L *praecedere*, fr. *prae-* pre- + *cedere* to go — more at CEDE] *vt* **1 :** to surpass in rank, dignity, or importance **2 :** to be, go, or come ahead or in front of **3 :** to be earlier than **4 :** to cause to be preceded **:** PREFACE ~ *vi* **:** to go or come before

pre·ce·dence \'pres-əd-ən(t)s, pri-'sēd-ᵊn(t)s\ *n* **1 a** *obs* **:** ANTECEDENT **b :** the fact of preceding in time **2 :** PRIORITY, PREFERENCE: **a :** the right to superior honor on a ceremonial or formal occasion **b :** the order of ceremonial or formal preference

pre·ce·den·cy \-ən-sē, -ᵊn-sē\ *n* **:** PRECEDENCE

1**pre·ce·dent** \pri-'sēd-ᵊnt, 'pres-əd-ənt\ *adj* [ME, fr. MF, fr. L *praecedent-*, *praecedens*, prp. of *praecedere*] **:** prior in time, order, arrangement, or significance

2**prec·e·dent** \'pres-əd-ənt\ *n* **1 :** an earlier occurrence of something similar **2 a :** something done or said that may serve as an example or rule to authorize or justify a subsequent act of the same or an analogous kind **b :** the convention established by such a precedent or by long practice

pre·ced·ing \pri-'sēd-iŋ\ *adj* **:** that precedes **:** going before
syn PRECEDING, ANTECEDENT, FOREGOING, PREVIOUS, PRIOR, FORMER, ANTERIOR mean being before. PRECEDING usu. implies being immediately before in time or in place; ANTECEDENT applies to order in time and may suggest a causal relation; FOREGOING applies to what has preceded esp. in a discourse; PREVIOUS and PRIOR imply existing or occurring earlier, but PRIOR often adds an implication of greater importance; FORMER implies always a definite comparison or contrast with something that is *latter*; ANTERIOR applies to position before or ahead of usu. in space, sometimes in time or order

pre·cen·sor \(')prē-'sen(t)-sər\ *vt* **:** to censor (a publication or film) before its release to the public

pre·cen·tor \pri-'sent-ər\ *n* [LL *praecentor*, fr. L *praecentus*, pp. of *praecinere* to sing before, fr. *prae-* + *canere* to sing — more at CHANT] **:** a leader of the singing of a choir or congregation — **pre·cen·to·ri·al** \ˌprē-ˌsen-'tōr-ē-əl, -'tȯr-\ *adj* — **pre·cen·tor·ship** \pri-'sent-ər-ˌship\ *n*

pre·cept \'prē-ˌsept\ *n* [ME, fr. L *praeceptum*, fr. neut. of *praeceptus*, pp. of *praecipere* to take beforehand, instruct, fr. *prae-* + *capere* to take — more at HEAVE] **1 :** a command or principle intended as a general rule of action **2 :** an order issued by legally constituted authority to a subordinate official **syn** see LAW

pre·cep·tive \pri-'sep-tiv\ *adj* **:** giving precepts — **pre·cep·tive·ly** *adv*

pre·cep·tor \pri-'sep-tər, 'prē-ˌ\ *n* **1 a :** TEACHER, TUTOR **b :** the headmaster or principal of a school **2 :** the head of a preceptory of Knights Templars — **pre·cep·to·ri·al** \pri-ˌsep-'tōr-ē-əl, ˌprē-, -'tȯr-\ *adj* — **pre·cep·tor·ship** \pri-'sep-tər-ˌship, 'prē-ˌ\ *n* — **pre·cep·tress** \-trəs\ *n*

pre·cep·to·ry \pri-'sep-t(ə-)rē, 'prē-ˌ\ *n* **1 :** a subordinate house or community of the Knights Templars; *broadly* **:** COMMANDERY 1 **2 :** COMMANDERY 2

pre·cess \prē-'ses\ *vi* [back-formation fr. *precession*] **:** to progress with a movement of precession

pre·ces·sion \prē-'sesh-ən\ *n* [NL *praecession-*, *praecessio*, fr. ML, act of preceding, fr. L *praecessus*, pp. of *praecedere* to precede] **:** a comparatively slow gyration of the rotation axis of a spinning body about another line intersecting it so as to describe a cone caused by the application of a torque tending to change the direction of the rotation axis — **pre·ces·sion·al** \-'sesh-nəl, -ən-ᵊl\ *adj*

precession of the equinoxes : a slow westward motion of the equinoctial points along the ecliptic caused by the action of sun and moon upon the protuberant matter about the earth's equator

pre–Chel·le·an \(')prē-'shel-ē-ən\ *adj* **:** of or relating to a lower Paleolithic culture preceding the Abbevillian and characterized by crudely flaked stone hand axes

pré·cieux \prā-syœ̄\ *or* **pré·cieuse** \-syœ̄z\ *adj* [F *précieux*, masc., & *précieuse*, fem., lit., precious, fr. OF *precios*] **:** extremely or excessively refined **:** AFFECTED

pre·cinct \'prē-ˌsiŋ(k)t\ *n* [ME, fr. ML *praecinctum*, fr. L, neut. of *praecinctus*, pp. of *praecingere* to gird about, fr. *prae-* pre- + *cingere* to gird — more at CINCTURE] **1 :** a part of a territory with definite bounds or functions often established for administrative purposes **:** DISTRICT: as **a :** a subdivision of a county, town, city, or ward for election purposes **b :** a division of a city for police control **2** *often pl* **:** the enclosure bounded by the walls or limits of a building or place **3** *pl* **:** the region immediately surrounding a place **:** ENVIRONS **4 :** BOUNDARY

pre·ci·os·i·ty \ˌpres(h)-ē-'äs-ət-ē\ *n* **:** fastidious refinement

1**pre·cious** \'presh-əs\ *adj* [ME, fr. OF *precios*, fr. L *pretiosus*, fr. *pretium* price — more at PRICE] **1 :** of great value or high price **2 :** highly esteemed or cherished **3 :** excessively refined **:** AFFECTED **4 :** GREAT, THOROUGHGOING ⟨~ scoundrel⟩ **syn** see COSTLY — **pre·cious·ly** *adv* — **pre·cious·ness** *n*

2**precious** *adv* **:** EXTREMELY, VERY

prec·i·pice \'pres-(ə-)pəs\ *n* [MF, fr. L *praecipitium*, fr. *praecipit-*, *praeceps* headlong, fr. *prae-* + *caput* head — more at HEAD] **1 :** a very steep or overhanging place **2 :** the brink of disaster

pre·cip·i·ta·ble \pri-'sip-ət-ə-bəl\ *adj* **:** capable of being precipitated

pre·cip·i·tance \pri-'sip-ət-ən(t)s\ *n* **:** PRECIPITANCY

pre·cip·i·tan·cy \-ən-sē\ *n* **:** precipitate action

1**pre·cip·i·tant** \-ənt\ *adj* **:** PRECIPITATE — **pre·cip·i·tant·ly** *adv* — **pre·cip·i·tant·ness** *n*

2**precipitant** *n* **:** a precipitating agent; *specif* **:** one that causes the formation of a precipitate

1**pre·cip·i·tate** \pri-'sip-ə-ˌtāt\ *vb* [L *praecipitatus*, pp. of *praecipitare*, fr. *praecipit-*, *praeceps*] *vt* **1 a :** to throw violently **:** HURL **b :** to throw down **2 a :** to urge or press on with haste or violence **b :** to bring on abruptly **3 a :** to cause to separate from solution or suspension **b :** to cause (vapor) to condense and fall or deposit ~ *vi* **1 a :** to fall headlong **b :** to fall or come suddenly into some condition **2 :** to move or act precipitately **3 a :** to separate from solution or suspension **b :** to condense from a vapor and fall as rain or snow — **pre·cip·i·ta·tive** \-ˌtāt-iv\ *adj* — **pre·cip·i·ta·tor** \-ˌtāt-ər\ *n*

2**pre·cip·i·tate** \pri-'sip-ət-ət, -ə-ˌtāt\ *n* [NL *praecipitatum*, fr. L, neut. of *praecipitatus*] **1 :** a substance separated from a solution or suspension by chemical or physical change usu. as an insoluble amorphous or crystalline solid **2 :** a product, result, or outcome of some process or action

3**pre·cip·i·tate** \pri-'sip-ət-ət\ *adj* **1 :** exhibiting violent or unwise speed **:** RASH **2 a :** falling, flowing, or rushing with steep descent **b :** PRECIPITOUS — **pre·cip·i·tate·ly** *adv* — **pre·cip·i·tate·ness** *n*
syn PRECIPITATE, HEADLONG, ABRUPT, IMPETUOUS, SUDDEN mean showing undue haste or unexpectedness. PRECIPITATE and HEADLONG imply rashness and lack of forethought, PRECIPITATE applying usu. to actions or decisions, HEADLONG to persons or qualities; ABRUPT stresses curtness and lack of warning or intimation; IMPETUOUS implies vehement impatience or impulsiveness; SUDDEN stresses unexpectedness and sharpness or violence of action

pre·cip·i·ta·tion \pri-ˌsip-ə-'tā-shən\ *n* **1 :** the quality or state of being precipitate **:** HASTE **2 :** an act, process, or instance of precipitating; *esp* **:** the process of forming a precipitate **3 :** something precipitated: as **a :** a deposit on the earth of hail, mist, rain, sleet, or snow; *also* **:** the quantity of water deposited **b :** PRECIPITATE 1

pre·cip·i·tin \pri-'sip-ət-ən\ *n* [ISV, fr. *precipitate*] **:** an antibody that forms an insoluble precipitate when it unites with its antigen

pre·cip·i·tin·o·gen \pri-ˌsip-ə-'tin-ə-jən\ *n* **:** an antigen that stimulates the production of a specific precipitin — **pre·cip·i·tin·o·gen·ic** \-ˌtin-ə-'jen-ik\ *adj*

pre·cip·i·tous \pri-'sip-ət-əs\ *adj* **1 :** PRECIPITATE **2 a :** having the character of a precipice **b :** containing precipices **c :** having a very steep ascent **syn** see STEEP — **pre·cip·i·tous·ly** *adv* — **pre·cip·i·tous·ness** *n*

pré·cis \prā-'sē, 'prā-(ˌ)sē\ *n, pl* **pré·cis** \-'sēz, -(ˌ)sēz\ [F, fr. *précis* precise] **:** a concise summary of essential points, statements, or facts **syn** see COMPENDIUM

pre·cise \pri-'sīs\ *adj* [MF *precis*, fr. L *praecisus*, pp. of *praecidere* to cut off, fr. *prae-* + *caedere* to cut — more at CONCISE] **1 :** exactly or sharply defined or stated **2 :** minutely exact **3 :** strictly conforming to rule or convention **4 :** distinguished from every other **:** VERY ⟨at just that ~ moment⟩ **syn** see CORRECT — **pre·cise·ly** *adv* — **pre·cise·ness** *n*

pre·ci·sian \pri-'sizh-ən\ *n* **:** a person who stresses or practices scrupulous adherence to a strict standard esp. of religious observance or morality; *specif* **:** PURITAN 1 — **pre·ci·sian·ism** \-ə-ˌniz-əm\ *n*

1**pre·ci·sion** \pri-'sizh-ən\ *n* **:** the quality or state of being precise **:** EXACTNESS; *specif* **:** the degree of refinement with which an operation is performed or a measurement stated — **pre·ci·sion·ist** \-'sizh-(ə-)nəst\ *n*

2**precision** *adj* **1 :** adapted for extremely accurate measurement or operation **2 :** held to low tolerance in manufacture **3 :** marked by precision of execution

pre·clin·i·cal \(')prē-'klin-i-kəl\ *adj* **:** of or relating to the period preceding clinical manifestations

pre·clude \pri-'klüd\ *vt* [L *praecludere*, fr. *prae-* + *claudere* to close — more at CLOSE] **1** *archaic* **:** CLOSE **2 :** to make impossible by necessary consequence **syn** see PREVENT — **pre·clu·sion** \-'klü-zhən\ *n* — **pre·clu·sive** \-'klü-siv, -ziv\ *adj* — **pre·clu·sive·ly** *adv*

pre·co·cial \pri-'kō-shəl\ *adj* [NL *praecoces* precocial birds, fr. L, pl. of *praecoc-*, *precox*] **:** capable of a high degree of independent activity from birth

pre·co·cious \pri-'kō-shəs\ *adj* [L *praecoc-*, *praecox* early ripening, precocious, fr. *prae-* + *coquere* to cook — more at COOK] **1 :** exceptionally early in development or occurrence **2 :** exhibiting mature qualities at an unusually early age — **pre·co·cious·ly** *adv* — **pre·co·cious·ness** *n* — **pre·coc·i·ty** \pri-'käs-ət-ē\ *n*

pre·cog·ni·tion \,prē-(,)käg-'nish-ən\ *n* [LL *praecognition-*, *praecognitio*, fr. L *praecognitus*, pp. of *praecognoscere* to know beforehand, fr. *prae-* + *cognoscere* to know — more at COGNITION] **:** clairvoyance relating to an event or state not yet experienced — **pre·cog·ni·tive** \(')prē-'käg-nət-iv\ *adj*

pre·con·ceive \,prē-kən-'sēv\ *vt* **:** to form an opinion of prior to actual knowledge or experience

pre·con·cep·tion \-'sep-shən\ *n* **1 :** a preconceived idea **2 :** PREJUDICE

pre·con·cert \,prē-kən-'sərt\ *vt* **:** to settle by prior agreement

1pre·con·di·tion \-'dish-ən\ *n* **:** something that must exist before something else can come about **:** PREREQUISITE

2precondition *vt* **:** to put in proper or desired condition or frame of mind in advance

pre·con·scious \(')prē-'kän-chəs\ *adj* **:** not present in consciousness but capable of being recalled without encountering any inner resistance or repression — **pre·con·scious·ly** *adv*

pre·cook \(')prē-'kůk\ *vt* **:** to cook partially or entirely before final cooking or reheating

pre·crit·i·cal \(')prē-'krit-i-kəl\ *adj* **:** prior to the development of critical capacity

pre·cur·sor \pri-'kər-sər, 'prē-,\ *n* [L *praecursor*, fr. *praecursus*, pp. of *praecurrere* to run before, fr. *prae-* pre- + *currere* to run — more at CURRENT] **1 a :** one that precedes and indicates the approach of another **b :** PREDECESSOR **2 :** a substance from which another substance is formed **syn** see FORERUNNER

pre·cur·so·ry \pri-'kərs-(ə-)rē\ *adj* **:** having the character of a precursor **:** PREMONITORY

pre·da·cious *or* **pre·da·ceous** \pri-'dā-shəs\ *adj* [L *praedari* to prey upon (fr. *praeda* prey) + E *-acious* (as in *rapacious*) — more at PREY] **:** living by preying on other animals **:** PREDATORY — **pre·da·cious·ness** *n* — **pre·dac·i·ty** \-'das-ət-ē\ *n*

pre·date \(')prē-'dāt\ *vt* **:** ANTEDATE

pre·da·tion \pri-'dā-shən\ *n* [L *praedation-*, *praedatio*, fr. *praedatus*, pp. of *praedari*] **1 :** the act of preying or plundering **:** DEPREDATION **2 :** a mode of life in which food is primarily obtained by killing and consuming animals

predation pressure *n* **:** the effects of predation on a natural community esp. with respect to the survival of species preyed upon

pred·a·tor \'pred-ət-ər, -ə-,tȯ(ə)r\ *n* **1 :** one that preys, destroys, or devours **2 :** an animal that lives by predation

pred·a·to·ri·al \,pred-ə-'tōr-ē-əl, -'tȯr-\ *adj* **:** PREDATORY

pred·a·to·ri·ly \-'tōr-ə-lē, -'tȯr-\ *adv* **:** in a predatory manner

pred·a·to·ry \'pred-ə-,tōr-ē, -,tȯr-\ *adj* **1 a :** of, relating to, or practicing plunder, pillage, or rapine **b :** disposed or showing a disposition to injure or exploit others for one's own gain **2 :** living by predation **:** PREDACIOUS; *also* **:** adapted to predation

pre·de·cease \,prēd-i-'sēs\ *vt* **:** to die before (another person) ~ *vi* **:** to die first — **predecease** *n*

pre·de·ces·sor \'pred-ə-,ses-ər, 'prēd-; ,pred-ə-', ,prēd-\ *n* [ME *predecessour*, fr. MF *predecesseur*, fr. LL *praedecessor*, fr. L *prae-* pre- + *decessor* retiring governor, fr. *decessus*, pp. of *decedere* to depart, retire from office — more at DECEASE] **1 :** one that precedes; *esp* **:** a person who has previously occupied a position or office to which another has succeeded **2** *archaic* **:** ANCESTOR

pre·des·ig·nate \(')prē-'dez-ig-,nāt\ *vt* **:** to designate beforehand — **pre·des·ig·na·tion** \,prē-,dez-ig-'nā-shən\ *n*

pre·des·ti·nar·i·an \(,)prē-,des-tə-'ner-ē-ən\ *adj* [*predestination* + *-arian*] **1 :** of or relating to predestination **2 :** holding the doctrine of predestination — **predestinarian** *n* — **pre·des·ti·nar·i·an·ism** \-ē-ə-,niz-əm\ *n*

1pre·des·ti·nate \prē-'des-tə-nət, -,nāt\ *adj* [ME, fr. L *praedestinatus*, pp. of *praedestinare*] **:** PREDESTINATED, PREDESTINED

2pre·des·ti·nate \-,nāt\ *vt* [ME *predestinaten*, fr. L *praedestinatus*, pp.] **1 :** to foreordain to an earthly or eternal lot or destiny by divine decree **2** *archaic* **:** PREDETERMINE

pre·des·ti·na·tion \(,)prē-,des-tə-'nā-shən\ *n* **:** the act of predestinating **:** the state of being predestinated

pre·des·ti·na·tor \(')prē-'des-tə-,nāt-ər\ *n* **1 :** one that predestinates **2** *archaic* **:** PREDESTINARIAN

pre·des·tine \(')prē-'des-tən\ *vt* [ME *predestinen*, fr. MF or L; MF *predestiner*, fr. L *praedestinare*, fr. *prae-* + *destinare* to determine — more at DESTINE] **:** to destine, decree, determine, appoint, or settle beforehand; *specif* **:** PREDESTINATE 1

pre·de·ter·mi·na·tion \,prē-di-,tər-mə-'nā-shən\ *n* **:** the act of predetermining **:** the state of being predetermined: as **a :** the ordaining of events beforehand **b :** a purpose formed beforehand **c :** a fixing or settling in advance

pre·de·ter·mine \-'tər-mən\ *vt* [LL *praedeterminare*, fr. L *prae-* + *determinare* to determine] **1 a :** FOREORDAIN, PREDESTINE **b :** to determine beforehand **2 :** to impose a direction or tendency on beforehand

pre·di·al \'prēd-ē-əl\ *var of* PRAEDIAL

1pred·i·ca·ble \'pred-i-kə-bəl\ *n* [ML *praedicabile*, fr. neut. of *praedicabilis*] **:** something that may be predicated; *esp* **:** one of the five most general kinds of attribution in traditional logic that include genus, species, difference, property, and accident

2predicable *adj* [ML *praedicabilis*, fr. LL *praedicare* to predicate] **:** capable of being asserted

pre·dic·a·ment \pri-'dik-ə-mənt, *1 is usu* 'pred-i-kə-\ *n* [ME, fr. LL *praedicamentum*, fr. *praedicare*] **1 :** the character, status, or classification assigned by a predication; *specif* **:** CATEGORY 1 **2** *archaic* **:** CONDITION, STATE **3 :** a difficult, perplexing, or trying situation **:** DILEMMA

syn DILEMMA, QUANDARY, PLIGHT, FIX, JAM, PICKLE: PREDICAMENT suggests a difficult situation usu. offering no satisfactory solution; DILEMMA implies a predicament presenting a choice between equally bad alternatives; QUANDARY stresses puzzlement and perplexity; PLIGHT suggests an unfortunate or trying situation; FIX and JAM are informal equivalents of PLIGHT but are more likely to suggest involvement through some fault or wrongdoing; PICKLE implies a distressing or embarrassing situation

1pred·i·cate \'pred-i-kət\ *n* [LL *praedicatum*, fr. neut. of *praedicatus*] **1 a :** something that is affirmed or denied of the subject in a proposition in logic ⟨in "paper is white", whiteness is the ~⟩ **b :** a term designating a property or relation **2 :** the part of a sentence or clause that expresses what is said of the subject and that usu. consists of a verb with or without objects, complements, or adverbial modifiers — **pred·i·ca·tive** \'pred-i-kət-iv, 'pred-ə-,kāt-\ *adj*

2pred·i·cate \'pred-ə-,kāt\ *vt* [LL *praedicatus*, pp. of *praedicare* to assert, predicate logically, preach, fr. L, to proclaim publicly, assert — more at PREACH] **1 a :** AFFIRM, DECLARE **b** *archaic* **:** PREACH **2 a :** to assert to be a quality, attribute, or property **b :** to make (a term) the predicate in a proposition **3 :** to cause to be based **:** FOUND **4 :** IMPLY

3pred·i·cate \'pred-i-kət\ *adj* **:** belonging to the predicate; *specif* **:** completing the meaning of a copula or linking verb

predicate nominative *n* **:** a noun or pronoun in the nominative or common case completing the meaning of a linking verb

pred·i·ca·tion \,pred-ə-'kā-shən\ *n* **1** *archaic* **a :** an act of proclaiming or preaching **b :** SERMON **2 :** an act or instance of predicating: as **a :** the expression of action, state, or quality by a grammatical predicate **b :** the logical affirmation of something about another; *esp* **:** assignment of something to a class

pred·i·ca·to·ry \'pred-i-kə-,tōr-ē, -,tȯr-\ *adj* [LL *praedicatorius*, fr. *praedicatus*, pp. of *praedicare* to preach] **:** of or relating to preaching

pre·dict \pri-'dikt\ *vt* [L *praedictus*, pp. of *praedicere*, fr. *prae-* pre- + *dicere* to say — more at DICTION] **:** to declare in advance **:** foretell on the basis of observation, experience, or scientific reason **syn** see FORETELL — **pre·dict·able** \-'dik-tə-bəl\ *adj* — **pre·dict·ably** \-blē\ *adv*

pre·dict·abil·i·ty \-,dik-tə-'bil-ət-ē\ *n* **:** the quality or state of being predictable

pre·dic·tion \pri-'dik-shən\ *n* **1 :** an act of predicting **2 :** something that is predicted **:** FORECAST — **pre·dic·tive** \-'dik-tiv\ *adj* — **pre·dic·tive·ly** *adv*

pre·dic·tor \-'dik-tər\ *n* **:** one that predicts

pre·di·gest \,prēd-ī-'jest, ,prēd-ə-\ *vt* **:** to subject to predigestion

pre·di·ges·tion \-'jes(h)-chən\ *n* **:** artificial partial digestion of food for use in illness or impaired digestion

pre·di·lec·tion \,pred-ᵊl-'ek-shən, ,prēd-\ *n* [F *prédilection*, fr. ML *praedilectus*, pp. of *praediligere* to love more, prefer, fr. L *prae-* + *diligere* to love — more at DILIGENT] **:** a prepossession in favor of something **:** PREFERENCE

syn PREPOSSESSION, PREJUDICE, BIAS: PREDILECTION implies a strong liking deriving from one's temperament or experience; PREPOSSESSION suggests a fixed conception likely to preclude objective judgment of anything seeming to be counter to it; PREJUDICE implies usu. but not always an unfavorable prepossession and connotes a feeling rooted in suspicion, fear, intolerance; BIAS implies an unreasoned and unfair distortion of judgment in favor of or against a person or thing

pre·dis·pose \,prē-dis-'pōz\ *vt* **:** to dispose in advance **:** make susceptible **syn** see INCLINE

pre·dis·po·si·tion \,prē-,dis-pə-'zish-ən\ *n* **:** a condition of being predisposed **:** INCLINATION

pre·dom·i·nance \pri-'däm(-ə)-nən(t)s\ *also* **pre·dom·i·nan·cy** \-nən-sē\ *n* **:** the quality or state of being predominant

pre·dom·i·nant \-nənt\ *adj* [MF, fr. ML *praedominant-*, *praedominans*, prp. of *praedominari* to predominate, fr. L *prae-* + *dominari* to rule, govern — more at DOMINATE] **:** having superior strength, influence, or authority **:** PREVAILING **syn** see DOMINANT — **pre·dom·i·nant·ly** *adv*

1pre·dom·i·nate \-nət\ *adj* [alter. of *predominant*] **:** PREDOMINANT — **pre·dom·i·nate·ly** *adv*

2pre·dom·i·nate \pri-'däm-ə-,nāt\ *vb* [ML *praedominatus*, pp. of *praedominari*] *vi* **1 :** to exert controlling power or influence **:** PREVAIL **2 :** to hold advantage in numbers or quantity **:** PREPONDERATE ~ *vt* **:** to exert control over **:** DOMINATE — **pre·dom·i·na·tion** \-,däm-ə-'nā-shən\ *n*

pree \'prē\ *vt* [short for *preve* to prove, test, fr. ME *preven*, fr. OF *preuv-*, stem of *prover* to prove] *Scot* **:** to taste tentatively **:** SAMPLE

pre·em·i·nence \prē-'em-ə-nən(t)s\ *n* **:** the quality or state of being preeminent **:** SUPERIORITY

pre·em·i·nent \-nənt\ *adj* [LL *praeeminent-*, *praeeminens*, fr. L, prp. of *praeeminēre* to be outstanding, fr. *prae-* + *eminēre* to stand out — more at EMINENT] **:** having paramount rank, dignity, or importance **:** OUTSTANDING, SUPREME — **pre·em·i·nent·ly** *adv*

pre·empt \prē-'em(p)t\ *vb* [back-formation fr. *preemption*] *vt* **1 :** to acquire (as land) by preemption **2 :** to seize upon to the exclusion of others **:** take for oneself ~ *vi* **:** to make a preemptive bid in bridge **syn** see APPROPRIATE

pre·emp·tion \-'em(p)-shən\ *n* [ML *praeemptus*, pp. of *praeemere* to buy before, fr. L *prae-* pre- + *emere* to buy — more at REDEEM] **1 a :** the right of purchasing before others; *esp* **:** one given by the government to the actual settler upon a tract of public land **b :** the purchase of something under this right **2 :** a prior seizure or appropriation **:** a taking possession before others

pre·emp·tive \-'em(p)-tiv\ *adj* **1 :** of or relating to preemption **:** having power to preempt **2 :** of a bid in bridge that is higher than necessary and designed to shut out bids by the opponents **3 :** giving a stockholder first option to purchase new stock in an amount proportionate to his existing holdings ⟨~ right⟩ — **pre·emp·tive·ly** *adv*

pre·emp·tor \-'em(p)-tər\ *n* **:** one that preempts

1preen \'prēn\ *n* [ME *prene*, fr. OE *prēon;* akin to MHG *pfrieme* awl] **1** *dial chiefly Brit* **:** PIN **2 :** BROOCH

ə abut; ᵊ kitten; ər further; a back; ā bake; ä cot, cart; aů out; ch chin; e less; ē easy; g gift; i trip; ī life
j joke; ŋ sing; ō flow; ȯ flaw; ȯi coin; th thin; th this; ü loot; ů foot; y yet; yü few; yů furious; zh vision

2**preen** *vt, chiefly Scot* : 2PIN

3**preen** *vb* [ME *preinen*] *vt* **1** : to trim or dress with the bill **2** : to dress or smooth (oneself) up : PRIMP **3** : to pride or congratulate (oneself) for achievement ~ *vi* **1** : to make oneself sleek **2** : GLOAT, SWELL — **preen·er** *n*

pre·ex·il·ian \ˌprē-(ˌ)eg-ˈzil-ē-ən, -ˈzil-yən\ *or* **pre·ex·il·ic** \-ˈzil-ik\ *adj* : previous to the exile of the Jews to Babylon in about 600 B.C.

pre·ex·ist \ˌprē-ig-ˈzist\ *vb* : to exist earlier or before

pre·ex·is·tence \-ˈzis-tən(t)s\ *n* : existence in a former state or previous to something else; *specif* : existence of the soul before its union with the body — **pre·ex·is·tent** \-tənt\ *adj*

pre·fab \(ˈ)prē-ˈfab, ˈprē-ˌ\ *n* : a prefabricated structure

pre·fab·ri·cate \(ˈ)prē-ˈfab-rə-ˌkāt\ *vt* **1** : to fabricate the parts of at a factory so that construction consists mainly of assembling and uniting standardized parts **2** : to produce synthetically or artificially — **pre·fab·ri·ca·tion** \ˌprē-ˌfab-rə-ˈkā-shən\ *n*

1**pref·ace** \ˈpref-əs\ *n* [ME, fr. MF, fr. ML *prephatia*, alter. of L *praefation-, praefatio* foreword, fr. *praefatus*, pp. of *praefari* to say beforehand, fr. *prae-* pre- + *fari* to say — more at BAN] **1** *often cap* : a eucharistic prayer of thanksgiving forming in the Roman rite an introduction to the canon **2** : the introductory remarks of a speaker or writer : FOREWORD, PROLOGUE **3** : PRELIMINARY

2**preface** *vi* : to make introductory remarks ~ *vt* **1** : to say or write as preface ⟨a note *prefaced* to the manuscript⟩ **2** : PRECEDE, HERALD **3** : to introduce by or begin with a preface **4** : to locate in front of **5** : to be a preliminary to — **pref·ac·er** *n*

pref·a·to·ri·al \ˌpref-ə-ˈtōr-ē-əl, -ˈtȯr-\ *adj* : PREFATORY — **pref·a·to·ri·al·ly** \-ē-ə-lē\ *adv*

pref·a·to·ri·ly \ˌpref-ə-ˈtōr-ə-lē, -ˈtȯr-\ *adv* : in a prefatory manner : as a preface

pref·a·to·ry \ˈpref-ə-ˌtōr-ē, -ˌtȯr-\ *adj* [L *praefatus*, pp.] **1** : of, relating to, or constituting a preface **2** : located in front

pre·fect \ˈprē-ˌfekt\ *n* [ME, fr. MF, fr. L *praefectus*, fr. pp. of *praeficere* to place at the head of, fr. *prae-* + *facere* to make — more at DO] **1** : any of various high officials or magistrates of differing functions and ranks **2** : a presiding or other chief officer or chief magistrate **3** : a student monitor in some usu. private schools

prefect apostolic *n* : a Roman Catholic priest with quasi-episcopal jurisdiction over a district of a missionary territory

pre·fec·tur·al \prē-ˈfek-chə-rəl, -ˈfek-shrəl\ *adj* : of or relating to a prefecture

pre·fec·ture \ˈprē-ˌfek-chər\ *n* **1** : the office or term of office of a prefect **2** : the official residence of a prefect **3** : the district governed by a prefect

pre·fer \pri-ˈfər\ *vt* **pre·ferred; pre·fer·ring** [ME *preferren*, fr. MF *preferer*, fr. L *praeferre* to put before, prefer, fr. *prae-* + *ferre* to carry — more at BEAR] **1** *archaic* : to promote or advance to a rank or position **2** : to choose or esteem above another **3** : to give (a creditor) priority **4** *archaic* : to put or set forward or before someone : RECOMMEND **5** : to bring or lay (as a complaint) against **6** : to bring forward or lay before one for consideration — **pre·fer·rer** *n*

pref·er·a·bil·i·ty \ˌpref-(ə-)rə-ˈbil-ət-ē\ *n* : the quality or state of being preferable

pref·er·a·ble \ˈpref-(ə-)rə-bəl, ˈpref-ər-bəl\ *adj* : worthy to be preferred — **pref·er·a·ble·ness** *n* — **pref·er·a·bly** \-blē\ *adv*

pref·er·ence \ˈpref-ərn(t)s, ˈpref-(ə-)rən(t)s\ *n* [F *préférence*, fr. ML *praeferentia*, fr. L *praeferent-, praeferens*, prp. of *praeferre*] **1 a** : the act of preferring : the state of being preferred **b** : the power or opportunity of choosing **2** : one that is preferred **3** : the act, fact, or principle of giving advantages to some over others **4** : priority in the right to demand and receive satisfaction of an obligation **syn** see CHOICE

pref·er·en·tial \ˌpref-ə-ˈren-chəl\ *adj* **1** : showing preference **2** : employing or creating a preference in trade relations **3** : designed to permit expression of preference among candidates **4** : giving preference esp. in hiring to union members ⟨~ shop⟩ — **pref·er·en·tial·ly** \-ˈrench-(ə-)lē\ *adv*

pre·fer·ment \pri-ˈfər-mənt\ *n* **1 a** : advancement or promotion in dignity, office, or station **b** : a position or office of honor or profit **2** : priority or seniority in right esp. to receive payment or to purchase property on equal terms with others **3** : the act of bringing forward (as charges)

preferred stock *n* : stock guaranteed priority by a corporation's charter over common stock in the payment of dividends and usu. in the distribution of assets

pre·fig·u·ra·tion \(ˌ)prē-ˌfig-(y)ə-ˈrā-shən\ *n* **1** : the act of prefiguring : the state of being prefigured **2** : something that prefigures

pre·fig·u·ra·tive \(ˈ)prē-ˈfig-(y)ə-rət-iv, -(y)ərt-iv\ *adj* : of, relating to, or showing by prefiguration — **pre·fig·u·ra·tive·ly** *adv* — **pre·fig·u·ra·tive·ness** *n*

pre·fig·ure \(ˈ)prē-ˈfig-yər, *esp Brit* -ˈfig-ər\ *vt* [ME *prefiguren*, fr. LL *praefigurare*, fr. L *prae-* pre- + *figurare* to shape, picture, fr. *figura* figure] **1** : to show, suggest, or announce by an antecedent type, image, or likeness **2** : to picture or imagine beforehand : FORESEE — **pre·fig·ure·ment** \-mənt\ *n*

1**pre·fix** *vt* [ME *prefixen*, fr. MF *prefixer*, fr. *pre-* + *fixer* to fix, fr. *fix* fixed, fr. L *fixus* — more at FIX] **1** \(ˈ)prē-ˈfiks\ *archaic* : to fix or appoint beforehand **2** \ˈprē-ˌ, prē-ˈ\ [2*prefix*] : to place in front : add as a prefix ⟨~ a syllable to a word⟩

2**pre·fix** \ˈprē-ˌfiks\ *n* [NL *praefixum*, fr. L, neut. of *praefixus*, pp. of *praefigere* to fasten before, fr. *prae-* + *figere* to fasten — more at DIKE] **1** : a sound or sequence of sounds or in writing a letter or sequence of letters occurring as a bound form attached to the beginning of a word, base, or phrase and serving to produce a derivative word or an inflectional form **2** : a title used before a person's name — **pre·fix·al** \ˈprē-ˌfik-səl, prē-ˈ\ *adj* — **pre·fix·al·ly** \-sə-lē\ *adv*

pre·flight \ˈprē-ˈflīt\ *adj* : preparing for or preliminary to airplane flight

pre·form \ˈprē-ˈfȯ(ə)rm\ *vt* [L *praeformare*, fr. *prae-* + *formare* to form, fr. *forma* form] : to form or shape beforehand — **preform** \ˈprē-ˌ\ *n*

pre·for·ma·tion \ˌprē-(ˌ)fȯr-ˈmā-shən\ *n* **1** : previous formation **2** : a now discredited theory holding that every germ cell contains the organism of its kind fully formed and that development consists merely in increase in size

pre·fron·tal \(ˈ)prē-ˈfrənt-ᵊl\ *adj* : anterior to or involving the anterior part of a frontal structure ⟨a ~ bone⟩

pre·gan·gli·on·ic \ˌprē-ˌgaŋ-glē-ˈän-ik\ *adj* : proximal to a ganglion; *specif* : of, relating to, or being a usu. medullated axon arising from a cell body in the central nervous system and terminating in an autonomic ganglion

preg·na·bil·i·ty \ˌpreg-nə-ˈbil-ət-ē\ *n* : the quality of being pregnable

preg·na·ble \ˈpreg-nə-bəl\ *adj* [modif. of ME *prenable*, fr. MF — more at IMPREGNABLE] : vulnerable to capture ⟨a ~ fort⟩

preg·nan·cy \ˈpreg-nən-sē\ *n* **1** : the condition of being pregnant : GESTATION **2** : the quality of being pregnant

1**preg·nant** \ˈpreg-nənt\ *adj* [ME *preignant*, fr. MF, fr. prp. of *preindre* to press, fr. L *premere* — more at PRESS] *archaic* : COGENT

2**pregnant** *adj* [ME, fr. L *praegnant-, praegnans*, alter. of *praegnas*, fr. *prae-* pre- + *-gnas* (akin to *gignere* to produce) — more at KIN] **1 a** : containing unborn young within the body : GRAVID **b** : capable of producing **2** : abounding in fancy, wit, or resourcefulness : INVENTIVE **3** : rich in significance or implication : MEANINGFUL **4** : containing the germ or shape of future events **5** : exhibiting fertility : TEEMING — **preg·nant·ly** *adv*

pre·heat \(ˈ)prē-ˈhēt\ *vt* : to heat beforehand; *specif* : to heat (an oven) to a designated temperature before placing food therein

pre·hen·sile \prē-ˈhen(t)-səl, -ˈhen-ˌsīl\ *adj* [F *préhensile*, fr. L *prehensus*, pp. of *prehendere* to grasp, fr. *prae-* + *-hendere* (akin to ON *geta* to get) — more at GET] : adapted for seizing or grasping esp. by wrapping around ⟨~ tail⟩ — **pre·hen·sil·i·ty** \ˌprē-ˌhen-ˈsil-ət-ē\ *n*

pre·hen·sion \prē-ˈhen-chən\ *n* **1** : the act of taking hold, seizing, or grasping **2 a** : UNDERSTANDING, COMPREHENSION **b** : apprehension by the senses

pre·his·tor·ic \ˌprē-is-ˈtȯr-ik, -(ˌ)his-, -ˈtär-\ *adj* **1** : of, relating to, or existing in times antedating written history **2** : of or relating to a language in a period of its development from which contemporary records of its actual sounds and forms have not been preserved — **pre·his·tor·i·cal** \-i-kəl\ *adj* — **pre·his·tor·i·cal·ly** \-k(ə-)lē\ *adv*

pre·his·to·ry \(ˈ)prē-ˈhis-t(ə-)rē\ *n* **1** : the study of prehistoric man **2** : a history of the antecedents of an event or situation

pre·hom·i·nid \-ˈhäm-ə-nəd\ *n* [deriv. of L *pre-* + *homin-, homo* man] : any of the extinct manlike primates that are often held to constitute a natural family (Prehominidae) — **prehominid** *adj*

pre·ig·ni·tion \ˌprē-ig-ˈnish-ən\ *n* : ignition in an internal-combustion engine while the inlet valve is open or before compression is completed

pre·judge \(ˈ)prē-ˈjəj\ *vt* [MF *prejuger*, fr. L *praejudicare*, fr. *prae-* + *judicare* to judge — more at JUDGE] : to judge before hearing or before full and sufficient examination — **pre·judg·er** *n* — **pre·judg·ment** \-ˈjəj-mənt\ *n*

1**prej·u·dice** \ˈprej-əd-əs\ *n* [ME, fr. OF, fr. L *praejudicium* previous judgment, damage, fr. *prae-* + *judicium* judgment — more at JUDICIAL] **1** : injury or damage resulting from some judgment or action of another in disregard of one's rights; *esp* : detriment to one's legal rights or claims **2 a** (1) : preconceived judgment or opinion (2) : an opinion or leaning adverse to anything without just grounds or before sufficient knowledge **b** : an instance of such judgment or opinion **c** : an irrational attitude of hostility directed against an individual, a group, a race, or their supposed characteristics **syn** see PREDILECTION

2**prejudice** *vt* **1** : to injure or damage by some judgment or action esp. at law **2** : to cause to have prejudice

prej·u·di·cial \ˌprej-ə-ˈdish-əl\ *adj* **1** : tending to injure or impair : DETRIMENTAL **2** : leading to premature judgment or unwarranted opinion — **prej·u·di·cial·ly** \-ˈdish-(ə-)lē\ *adv* — **prej·u·di·cial·ness** \-əl-nəs\ *n*

prej·u·di·cious \-ˈdish-əs\ *adj* : PREJUDICIAL — **prej·u·di·cious·ly** *adv*

prel·a·cy \ˈprel-ə-sē\ *n* **1** : the office or dignity of a prelate **2** : the whole body of prelates **3** : episcopal church government

prel·ate \ˈprel-ət *also* ˈprē-ˌlāt\ *n* [ME *prelat*, fr. OF, fr. ML *praelatus*, lit., one receiving preferment, fr. L, (pp. of *praeferre* to prefer) fr. *prae-* + *latus*, pp. of *ferre* to carry — more at TOLERATE, BEAR] : an ecclesiastic (as a bishop or abbot) of superior rank

prelate nul·li·us \-nü-ˈlē-əs\ *n* [*nullius* fr. NL *nullius dioeceseos* of no diocese] : a Roman Catholic prelate usu. a titular bishop with ordinary jurisdiction over a district independent of any diocese

prel·a·ture \ˈprel-ə-ˌchu̇(ə)r, -chər, -ˌt(y)u̇(ə)r\ *n* **1** : PRELACY 1,2 **2** : the jurisdiction of a prelate

pre·lect \pri-ˈlekt\ *vi* [L *praelectus*, pp. of *praelegere*, fr. *prae-* + *legere* to read — more at LEGEND] : to discourse publicly : LECTURE — **pre·lec·tion** \-ˈlek-shən\ *n*

pre·li·ba·tion \ˌprē-(ˌ)lī-ˈbā-shən\ *n* [L *praelibation-, praelibatio*, fr. *praelibatus*, pp. of *praelibare* to taste beforehand, fr. *prae-* + *libare* to pour as an offering, taste — more at LIBATION] : FORETASTE

pre·lim \ˈprē-ˌlim, pri-ˈ\ *n or adj* : PRELIMINARY

pre·lim·i·nar·i·ly \pri-ˌlim-ə-ˈner-ə-lē\ *adv* : in a preliminary manner : as a preliminary

1**pre·lim·i·nary** \pri-ˈlim-ə-ˌner-ē\ *n* [F *préliminaires*, pl., fr. ML *praeliminaris*, adj., preliminary, fr. L *prae-* pre- + *limin-, limen* threshold — more at LIMB] : something that precedes or is introductory or preparatory: as **a** : a preliminary scholastic examination **b** : a minor match preceding the main event

2**preliminary** *adj* : preceding the main discourse or business : INTRODUCTORY

1**pre·lude** \ˈprel-ˌyüd, ˈprā-ˌlüd\ *n* [MF, fr. ML *praeludium*, fr. *praeludere* to play beforehand, fr. *prae-* + *ludere* to play — more at LUDICROUS] : an introductory performance, action, or event preceding and preparing for the principal or a more important matter: as **a** : a musical section or movement introducing the theme or chief subject (as of a fugue or suite) or serving as an introduction to an opera or oratorio **b** : an opening voluntary **c** : a separate concert piece usu. for piano or orchestra and based entirely on a short motive

2**prelude** *vi* : to give or serve as a prelude; *esp* : to play a musical introduction ~ *vt* **1** : to serve as prelude to : FORESHADOW **2** : to play as a prelude — **pre·lud·er** *n*

pre·lu·sion \pri-ˈlü-zhən\ *n* [L *praelusion-, praelusio*, fr. *praelusus*, pp. of *praeludere*] : PRELUDE, INTRODUCTION

pre·lu·sive \-ˈlü-siv, -ziv\ *or* **pre·lu·so·ry** \-ˈlüs-(ə-)rē, -ˈlüz-\ *adj* : constituting or having the form of a prelude : INTRODUCTORY — **pre·lu·sive·ly** *or* **pre·lu·so·ri·ly** \-ˈlüs-(ə-)rə-lē, -ˈlüz-\ *adv*

pre·man \'prē-'man\ *n* **:** a hypothetical ancient primate constituting the immediate ancestor of man **:** PREHOMINID

pre·ma·ture \,prē-mə-'t(y)u̇(ə)r, -'chu̇(ə)r *also* ,prem-ə-\ *adj* [L *praematurus* too early, fr. *prae-* + *maturus* ripe, mature] **:** happening, arriving, existing, or performed before the proper or usual time; *specif* **:** born after a gestation period of less than 37 weeks ⟨~ babies⟩ — **premature** *n* — **pre·ma·ture·ly** *adv* — **pre·ma·ture·ness** *n* — **pre·ma·tu·ri·ty** \-'t(y)u̇r-ət-ē, -'chu̇r-\ *n*

pre·max·il·la \,prē-(,)mak-'sil-ə\ *n* [NL] **:** either of a pair of bones of the upper jaw of vertebrates between and in front of the maxillae — **pre·max·il·lary** \(')prē-'mak-sə-,ler-ē, *chiefly Brit* ,prē-(,)mak-'sil-ə-rē\ *adj or n*

pre·med \'prē-'med\ *adj* **:** PREMEDICAL — **premed** *n*

pre·me·di·an \(')prē-'mēd-ē-ən\ *or* **pre·me·di·al** \-ē-əl\ *adj* **:** lying in front of the middle (as of the body)

pre·med·i·cal \(')prē-'med-i-kəl\ *adj* **:** preceding and preparing for the professional study of medicine

pre·med·i·tate \pri-'med-ə-,tāt, 'prē-\ *vb* [L *praemeditatus*, pp. of *praemeditari*, fr. *prae-* + *meditari* to meditate] *vt* **:** to think about and revolve in the mind beforehand ~ *vi* **:** to think, consider, or deliberate beforehand — **pre·med·i·ta·tor** \-,tāt-ər\ *n*

pre·med·i·tat·ed *adj* **:** characterized by fully conscious willful intent and a measure of forethought and planning — **pre·med·i·tat·ed·ly** *adv*

pre·med·i·ta·tion \pri-,med-ə-'tā-shən, ,prē-\ *n* **:** an act or instance of premeditating; *specif* **:** consideration or planning of an act beforehand that shows intent to commit that act

pre·med·i·ta·tive \pri-'med-ə-,tāt-iv, 'prē-\ *adj* **:** given to or characterized by premeditation

pre·men·stru·al \(')prē-'men(t)-strə(-wə)l\ *adj* **:** of or relating to the period just preceding menstruation — **pre·men·stru·al·ly** \-ē\ *adv*

¹**pre·mier** \pri-'m(y)i(ə)r; 'prē-mē-ər, 'prem-ē-\ *adj* [ME *primier*, fr. MF *premier* first, chief, fr. L *primarius* of the first rank — more at PRIMARY] **1 :** first in position, rank, or importance **:** PRINCIPAL **2 :** first in time **:** EARLIEST

²**premier** *n* [F, fr. *premier*, adj.] **:** PRIME MINISTER

¹**pre·miere** \pri-'mye(ə)r, -'mi(ə)r; ,prim-ē-'e(ə)r\ *n* [F *première*, fr. fem. of *premier* first] **1 :** a first performance or exhibition **2 :** the leading lady of a group; *esp* **:** the chief actress of a theatrical cast

²**premiere** *or* **pre·mier** *like* ¹PREMIERE\ *vt* **:** to give a first public performance of ~ *vi* **1 :** to have a first public performance **2 :** to appear for the first time as a star

³**premiere** *adj* [alter. of ¹*premier*] **:** OUTSTANDING, CHIEF

pre·mier·ship \pri-'m(y)i(ə)r-,ship; 'prē-mē-ər-, 'prem-ē-\ *n* **:** the position or office of a premier

pre·mil·le·nar·i·an \,prē-,mil-ə-'ner-ē-ən\ *n* [*pre-* + *millenary*] **:** PREMILLENNIALIST — **premillenarian** *adj* — **pre·mil·le·nar·i·an·ism** \-ē-ə-,niz-əm\ *n*

pre·mil·len·ni·al \,prē-mə-'len-ē-əl\ *adj* [*pre-* + *millennium*] **1 :** coming before a millennium **2 :** holding or relating to the view that the Parousia ushers in the millennium — **pre·mil·len·ni·al·ism** \-ē-ə-,liz-əm\ *n* — **pre·mil·len·ni·al·ist** \-ə-ləst\ *n* — **pre·mil·len·ni·al·ly** \-ə-lē\ *adv*

¹**prem·ise** \'prem-əs\ *n* [In sense 1, fr. ME *premisse*, fr. MF, fr. ML *praemissa*, fr. L, fem. of *praemissus*, pp. of *praemittere* to place ahead, fr. *prae-* pre- + *mittere* to send; in other senses, fr. ME *premisses*, fr. ML *praemissa*, fr. L, neut. pl. of *praemissus* — more at SMITE] **1 :** a proposition antecedently supposed or proved as a basis of argument or inference; *specif* **:** either of the first two propositions of a syllogism from which the conclusion is drawn **2** *pl* **:** matters previously stated; *specif* **:** the preliminary and explanatory part of a deed or of a bill in equity **3** *pl* **a :** a tract of land with the buildings thereon **b :** a building or part of a building usu. with its grounds or other appurtenances

²**pre·mise** \'prem-əs *also* pri-'mīz\ *vt* **1 a :** to set forth beforehand as introductory or as postulated **b :** to offer as a premise in an argument **2 :** to presuppose or imply as preexistent **:** POSTULATE

¹**pre·mi·um** \'prē-mē-əm\ *n, pl* **premiums** *also* **pre·mia** \-mē-ə\ [L *praemium* booty, profit, reward, fr. *prae-* + *emere* to take, buy — more at REDEEM] **1 a :** a reward or recompense for a particular act **b :** a sum over and above a regular price paid chiefly as an inducement or incentive **c :** a sum in advance of or in addition to the nominal value of something **d :** something given free or at a reduced price with the purchase of a product or service **2 :** the consideration paid for a contract of insurance **3 :** a high value or a value in excess of that normally or usu. expected — **at a premium** **:** above par **:** unusually valuable esp. because of demand ⟨housing was *at a premium*⟩

²**premium** *adj* **:** of exceptional quality

pre·mix \(')prē-'miks\ *vt* **:** to mix before use

pre·mo·lar \(')prē-'mō-lər\ *adj* **:** situated in front of or preceding the molar teeth; *esp* **:** being or relating to those teeth of a mammal in front of the true molars and behind the canines when the latter are present — **premolar** *n*

pre·mon·ish \(')prē-'män-ish\ *vt* **:** FOREWARN ~ *vi* **:** to give warning in advance — **pre·mon·ish·ment** \-mənt\ *n*

pre·mo·ni·tion \,prē-mə-'nish-ən, ,prem-ə-\ *n* [MF, fr. LL *praemonition-*, *praemonitio*, fr. L *praemonitus*, pp. of *praemonēre* to warn in advance, fr. *prae-* + *monēre* to warn — more at MIND] **1 :** previous warning or notice **:** FOREWARNING **2 :** anticipation of an event without conscious reason **:** PRESENTIMENT

pre·mon·i·to·ri·ly \(,)prē-,män-ə-'tōr-ə-lē, -'tȯr-\ *adv* **:** in a premonitory manner

pre·mon·i·to·ry \prē-'män-ə-,tōr-ē, -,tȯr-\ *adj* **:** giving previous warning ⟨~ symptom⟩

Pre·mon·stra·ten·sian \,prē-,män(t)-strə-'ten-chən\ *n* [ML *praemonstratensis*, fr. *praemonstratensis* of Prémontré, fr. *Praemonstratus* Prémontré] **:** a member of an order of canons regular founded by St. Norbert at Prémontré near Laon, France, in 1119

pre·morse \pri-'mȯ(ə)rs\ *adj* [L *praemorsus*, fr. pp. of *praemordēre* to bite off in front, fr. *prae-* + *mordēre* to bite — more at SMART] **:** terminated abruptly but irregularly as if bitten off ⟨a ~ root⟩

pre·mune \(')prē-'myün\ *adj* [back-formation fr. *premunition*] **:** exhibiting premunition

pre·mu·ni·tion \,prē-myu̇-'nish-ən\ *n* [L *praemunition-*, *praemunitio* advance fortification, fr. *praemunitus*, pp. of *praemunire* to fortify in advance, fr. *prae-* + *munire* to fortify — more at MUNITION] **1** *archaic* **:** an advance provision of protection **2 a :** resistance to a disease due to the existence of its causative agent in a state of physiological equilibrium in the host **b :** immunity to a particular infection due to previous presence of the causative agent

pre·name \'prē-,nām\ *n* **:** FORENAME

pre·na·tal \(')prē-'nāt-ᵊl\ *adj* **:** occurring or existing before birth — **pre·na·tal·ly** \-ᵊl-ē\ *adv*

pre·no·men *var of* PRAENOMEN

¹**pre·nom·i·nate** \(')prē-'näm-ə-nət\ *adj* [LL *praenominatus*, pp. of *praenominare* to name before, fr. L *prae-* + *nominare* to name — more at NOMINATE] *obs* **:** previously mentioned

²**pre·nom·i·nate** \-,nāt\ *vt, obs* **:** to mention previously — **pre·nom·i·na·tion** \(,)prē-,näm-ə-'nā-shən\ *n, obs*

pre·no·tion \(')prē-'nō-shən\ *n* [L *praenotion-*, *praenotio* preconception, fr. *prae-* + *notio* idea, conception — more at NOTION] **1 :** PRESENTIMENT, PREMONITION **2 :** PRECONCEPTION

¹**pren·tice** \'prent-əs\ *n* [ME *prentis*, short for *apprentis*] **:** APPRENTICE 1, LEARNER — **prentice** *adj*

²**prentice** *vt* **:** APPRENTICE

pre·oc·cu·pan·cy \(')prē-'äk-yə-pən-sē\ *n* **1 :** an act or the right of taking possession before another **2 :** the condition of being completely busied or preoccupied

pre·oc·cu·pa·tion \(,)prē-,äk-yə-'pā-shən\ *n* [L *praeoccupation-*, *praeoccupatio* act of seizing beforehand, fr. *praeoccupatus*, pp. of *praeoccupare* to seize beforehand, fr. *prae-* + *occupare* to seize, occupy] **1 :** an act of preoccupying **:** the state of being preoccupied **2 a :** complete absorption of the mind or interests **b :** something that causes such absorption

pre·oc·cu·pied \prē-'äk-yə-,pīd\ *adj* **1 a :** lost in thought **:** ENGROSSED **b :** already occupied **2 :** previously applied to another group and unavailable for use in a new sense — used of a biological generic or specific name

pre·oc·cu·py *vt* [*pre-* + *occupy*] **1** \prē-'äk-yə-,pī\ **:** to engage or engross the interest or attention of beforehand or preferentially **2** \(')prē-\ **:** to take possession of or fill beforehand or before another

pre·op·er·a·tive \(')prē-'äp-(ə-)rət-iv, -'äp-ə-,rāt-\ *adj* **:** occurring during the period preceding a surgical operation — **pre·op·er·a·tive·ly** *adv*

pre·or·bit·al \-'ȯr-bət-ᵊl\ *adj* **:** occurring before going into orbit

pre·or·dain \,prē-(,)ȯr-'dān\ *vt* **:** to decree or ordain in advance **:** FOREORDAIN — **pre·or·dain·ment** \-mənt\ *n* — **pre·or·di·na·tion** \(,)prē-,ȯrd-ᵊn-'ā-shən\ *n*

pre·ovu·la·to·ry \(')prē-'äv-yə-lə-,tōr-ē, -,tȯr-, -'ōv-\ *adj* **:** occurring in or typical of the period immediately preceding ovulation

¹**prep** \'prep\ *n* **1** *Brit* **:** preparation of lessons **:** HOMEWORK **2 :** PREPARATORY SCHOOL

²**prep** *vb* **prepped**; **prep·ping** *vi* **:** to attend preparatory school or engage in preparatory study or training ~ *vt* **:** PREPARE

prep·a·ra·tion \,prep-ə-'rā-shən\ *n* [ME *preparacion*, fr. MF *preparation*, fr. L *praeparation-*, *praeparatio*, fr. *praeparatus*, pp. of *praeparare*] **1 :** the action or process of making something ready for use or service or of getting ready for some occasion, test, or duty **2 :** a state of being prepared **:** READINESS **3 :** a preparatory act or measure **4 :** something that is prepared; *specif* **:** a medicinal substance fitted for use

¹**pre·par·a·tive** \pri-'par-ət-iv\ *n* **:** something that prepares the way for or serves as a preliminary to something else **:** PREPARATION

²**preparative** *adj* **:** PREPARATORY — **pre·par·a·tive·ly** *adv*

pre·pa·ra·tor \pri-'par-ət-ər, 'prep-ə-,rāt-\ *n* **:** one that prepares; *specif* **:** one that prepares scientific specimens

pre·pa·ra·to·ri·ly \pri-,par-ə-'tōr-ə-lē, -'tȯr- *also* ,prep-(ə-)rə-\ *adv* **:** in a preparatory manner **:** by way of preparation

pre·pa·ra·to·ry \pri-'par-ə-,tōr-ē, -,tȯr- *also* 'prep-(ə-)rə-\ *adj* **:** preparing or serving to prepare for something **:** INTRODUCTORY, PRELIMINARY — **preparatory** *adv*

preparatory school *n* **1 :** a usu. private school preparing students primarily for college **2** *Brit* **:** a private elementary school preparing students primarily for public schools

pre·pare \pri-'pa(ə)r, -'pe(ə)r\ *vb* [ME *preparen*, fr. MF *preparer*, fr. L *praeparare*, fr. *prae-* pre- + *parare* to procure, prepare — more at PARE] *vt* **1 :** to make ready ⟨*prepared* her gradually for the shocking news⟩ **2 :** to procure as suitable or necessary **:** PROVIDE **3 a :** to put together **:** COMPOUND ⟨~ a vaccine⟩ ⟨~ a prescription⟩ **b :** to put into written form ~ *vi* **1 :** to get ready **2 :** to arrange things in readiness — **pre·par·er** *n*

pre·pared \-'pa(ə)rd, -'pe(ə)rd\ *adj* **1 :** made ready, fit, or suitable beforehand **:** READY, EQUIPPED **2 :** subjected to a special process or treatment ⟨~ chalk⟩ — **pre·pared·ly** \-lē; -'par-əd-lē, -'per-\ *adv*

pre·pared·ness \pri-'par-əd-nəs, -'per- *also* -'pa(ə)rd-nəs, -'pe(ə)rd-nəs\ *n* **:** the quality or state of being prepared; *specif* **:** a state of adequate preparation in case of war

pre·pay \(')prē-'pā\ *vt* **:** to pay or pay the charge on in advance — **pre·pay·ment** \-mənt\ *n*

pre·pense \pri-'pen(t)s\ *adj* [by shortening & alter. fr. earlier *purpensed*, fr. ME, pp. of *purpensen* to deliberate, premeditate, fr. MF *purpenser*, fr. OF, fr. *pur-* for + *penser* to think — more at PURCHASE, PENSIVE] **:** deliberated or planned beforehand **:** PREMEDITATED ⟨malice ~⟩ — **pre·pense·ly** *adv*

pre·pon·der·ance \pri-'pän-d(ə-)rən(t)s\ *n* **1 :** a superiority in weight or in power, importance, or strength **2 a :** a superiority or excess in number or quantity **b :** MAJORITY

pre·pon·der·an·cy \-d(ə-)rən-sē\ *n* **:** PREPONDERANCE

pre·pon·der·ant \pri-'pän-d(ə-)rənt\ *adj* **1 :** PREDOMINANT, PREPONDERATING **2 :** having greater prevalence **syn** see DOMINANT — **pre·pon·der·ant·ly** *adv*

pre·pon·der·ate \pri-'pän-də-,rāt\ *vb* [L *praeponderatus*, pp. of *praeponderare*, fr. *prae-* + *ponder-*, *pondus* weight — more at PENDANT] *vt* **1** *archaic* **:** OUTWEIGH **2** *archaic* **:** to weigh down ~ *vi* **1 a :** to exceed in weight **b :** to descend or incline downward **2 :** to exceed in influence, power, or importance **:** PREDOMINATE **3 :** to exceed in numbers — **pre·pon·der·a·tion** \pri-,pän-də-'rā-shən, ,prē-\ *n*

prep·o·si·tion \,prep-ə-'zish-ən\ *n* [ME *preposicioun*, fr. L

praeposition-, praepositio, fr. *praepositus*, pp. of *praeponere* to put in front, fr. *prae-* pre- + *ponere* to put — more at POSITION] **:** a linguistic form that combines with a noun, pronoun, or noun equivalent to form a phrase that typically has an adverbial, adjectival, or substantival relation to some other word — **prep·o·si·tion·al** \-'zish-nəl, -ən-ᵊl\ *adj* — **prep·o·si·tion·al·ly** \-ē\ *adv*

pre·pos·i·tive \pri-'päz-ət-iv, -'päz-tiv\ *adj* [LL *praepositivus*, fr. L *praepositus*] **:** put before **:** PREFIXED — **pre·pos·i·tive·ly** *adv*

pre·pos·sess \,prē-pə-'zes *also* -'ses\ *vt* **1** *obs* **:** to take previous possession of **2 :** to cause to be preoccupied with an idea, belief, or attitude **3 a :** to influence beforehand for or against someone or something **:** PREJUDICE **b :** to induce to a favorable opinion beforehand

pre·pos·sess·ing *adj* **1** *archaic* **:** creating prejudice **2 :** tending to create a favorable impression **:** ATTRACTIVE — **pre·pos·sess·ing·ly** \-iŋ-lē\ *adv* — **pre·pos·sess·ing·ness** *n*

pre·pos·ses·sion \,prē-pə-'zesh-ən *also* -'sesh-\ *n* **1** *archaic* **:** prior possession **2 :** an attitude, belief, or impression formed beforehand **:** PREJUDICE **3 :** an exclusive concern with one idea or object **:** PREOCCUPATION **syn** see PREDILECTION

pre·pos·ter·ous \pri-'päs-t(ə-)rəs\ *adj* [L *praeposterus*, lit., with the hindside in front, fr. *prae-* + *posterus* hinder, following — more at POSTERIOR] **:** contrary to nature, reason, or common sense **:** ABSURD — **pre·pos·ter·ous·ly** *adv* — **pre·pos·ter·ous·ness** *n*

pre·po·ten·cy \(')prē-'pōt-ᵊn-sē\ *n* **1 :** the quality or state of being prepotent **:** PREDOMINANCE **2 :** unusual ability of an individual or strain to transmit its characters to offspring

pre·po·tent \-ᵊnt\ *adj* [ME, fr. L *praepotent-, praepotens*, fr. *prae-* + *potens* powerful — more at POTENT] **1 a :** having exceptional power, authority, or influence **:** PREEMINENT **b :** exceeding others in power **2 :** exhibiting genetic prepotency — **pre·po·tent·ly** *adv*

pre·pu·ber·al \(')prē-'pyü-b(ə-)rəl\ *adj* **:** of or relating to prepuberty — **pre·pu·ber·al·ly** \-ē\ *adv*

pre·pu·ber·ty \(')prē-'pyü-bərt-ē\ *n* **:** the period immediately preceding puberty

pre·puce \'prē-,pyüs\ *n* [ME, fr. MF, fr. L *praeputium*, fr. *prae-* + *-putium* (akin to Belorussian *potka* penis)] **:** FORESKIN; *also* **:** a similar fold investing the clitoris — **pre·pu·tial** \prē-'pyü-shəl\ *adj*

Pre–Ra·pha·el·ite \(')prē-'raf-ē-ə-,līt, -'rā-fē-, -'räf-ē-\ *n* **1 a :** a member of a brotherhood of artists formed in England in 1848 to restore the artistic principles and practices regarded as characteristic of Italian art before Raphael **b :** an artist or writer influenced by this brotherhood **2 :** a modern artist dedicated to restoring early Renaissance ideals or methods **3 :** an Italian painter active before the time of Raphael's fame and influence — **Pre–Raphaelite** *adj* — **Pre–Ra·pha·el·it·ism** \-,līt-,iz-əm\ *n*

pre·re·cord \,prē-ri-'kȯ(ə)rd\ *vt* **:** to record (as a radio or television program) in advance of presentation or use **:** PRESCORE

pre·req·ui·site \(')prē-'rek-wə-zət\ *n* **:** something that is necessary to an end or to the carrying out of a function — **prerequisite** *adj*

pre·rog·a·tive \pri-'räg-ət-iv\ *n* [ME, fr. MF & L; MF, fr. L *praerogativa*, Roman century voting first in the comitia, privilege, fr. fem. of *praerogativus* voting first, fr. *praerogatus*, pp. of *praerogare* to ask for an opinion before another, fr. *prae-* + *rogare* to ask — more at RIGHT] **1 a :** an exclusive or special right, power, or privilege: as (1) **:** one belonging to an office or an official body (2) **:** one belonging to a person, group, or class of individuals (3) **:** one possessed by a nation as an attribute of sovereignty **b :** the discretionary power inhering in the British Crown **2 :** a distinctive excellence — **pre·rog·a·tived** \-ivd\ *adj*

pre·sa \'prā-sə, -,sä, -zə\ *n, pl* **pre·se** \-(,)sā, -(,)zā\ [It, lit., act of taking, fr. *prendere* to take, fr. L *prehendere* to grasp — more at PREHENSILE] **:** a mark or cue (as :S: or ※) indicating the point of entry of the successive voice parts of a canon

¹**pres·age** \'pres-ij, *archaic* pri-'sāj\ *n* [ME, fr. L *praesagium*, fr. *praesagire* to forebode, fr. *prae-* + *sagire* to perceive keenly — more at SEEK] **1 :** something that foreshadows or portends a future event **:** OMEN **2 :** FOREBODING, PRESENTIMENT **3** *archaic* **:** PROGNOSTICATION; *also* **:** FOREKNOWLEDGE **4 :** warning or indication of the future **:** AUGURY — **pre·sage·ful** \pri-'sāj-fəl\ *adj*

²**pre·sage** \'pres-ij, pri-'sāj\ *vt* **1 :** to give an omen or warning of **:** FORESHADOW, PORTEND **2 :** FORETELL, PREDICT **3 :** to have a presentiment of ~ *vi* **:** to make or utter a prediction — **pre·sag·er** *n, obs*

pre·sanc·ti·fied \(')prē-'saŋ(k)-ti-,fīd\ *adj* **:** consecrated at a previous service — used of eucharistic elements

presby- *or* **presbyo-** *comb form* [NL, fr. Gk *presby-* elder, fr. *presbys* old man] **:** old age ⟨*presbyopia*⟩ ⟨*presbyophrenia*⟩

pres·by·ope \'prez-bē-,ōp; 'pres-bē-, -pē-\ *n* [prob. fr. F, fr. Gk *presby-* + *ōps* eye — more at EYE] **:** a farsighted person

pres·by·opia \,prez-bē-'ō-pē-ə; ,pres-bē-, -pē-\ *n* [NL] **:** a condition of defective elasticity of the crystalline lens of the eye usu. in old age resulting in difficulty of accommodation and inability to attain a sharp focus for near vision — **pres·by·opic** \-'äp-ik, -'ō-pik\ *adj or n*

pres·by·ter \'prez-bət-ər; 'pres-bət-, -pət-\ *n* [LL, elder, priest — more at PRIEST] **1 :** a member of the governing body of an early Christian church **2 :** a Christian priest; *esp* **:** a member of the second order of clergy in the Anglican communion **3 :** ELDER 4b — **pres·byt·er·ate** \prez-'bit-ə-rət, pres-, -,rāt\ *n*

¹**pres·by·te·ri·al** \,prez-bə-'tir-ē-əl; ,pres-bə-, -pə-\ *adj* **:** of or relating to a presbyter or presbytery — **pres·by·te·ri·al·ly** \-ē-ə-lē\ *adv*

²**presbyterial** *n, often cap* **:** an organization of Presbyterian women associated with a presbytery

Pres·by·te·ri·an \-ē-ən\ *adj* **1** *often not cap* **:** characterized by a graded system of representative ecclesiastical bodies (as presbyteries) exercising legislative and judicial powers **2 :** of, relating to, or constituting a Protestant Christian church that is presbyterian in government and traditionally Calvinistic in doctrine — **Presbyterian** *n* — **Pres·by·te·ri·an·ism** \-ē-ə-,niz-əm\ *n*

pres·by·tery \'prez bə-,ter-ē, -trē; 'pres-bə-, -pə-\ *n* [ME & LL; ME *presbytory* part of church reserved for clergy, fr. LL *presbyterium* group of presbyters, part of church reserved for clergy, fr. Gk *presbyterion* group of presbyters, fr. *presbyteros* elder, priest — more at PRIEST] **1 :** the part of a church reserved for the officiating clergy **2 :** a ruling body in presbyterian churches consisting of the ministers and representative elders from congregations within a district **3 :** the jurisdiction of a presbytery **4 :** the house of a Roman Catholic parish priest

¹**pre·school** \'prē-'skül\ *adj* **:** of, relating to, or constituting the period in a child's life from infancy to the age of five or six that ordinarily precedes attendance at elementary school

²**pre·school** \'prē-,\ *n* **:** NURSERY SCHOOL, KINDERGARTEN

pre·science \'prēsh-(ē-)ən(t)s, 'presh-; 'prēs-ē-ən(t)s, 'pres-\ *n* [ME, fr. LL *praescientia*, fr. L *praescient-, praesciens*, prp. of *praescire* to know beforehand, fr. *prae-* + *scire* to know — more at SCIENCE] **:** foreknowledge of events; *specif* **:** omniscience with regard to the future — **pre·scient** \-(ē-)ənt\ *adj* — **pre·scient·ly** *adv*

pre·sci·en·tif·ic \,prē-,sī-ən-'tif-ik\ *adj* [*pre-* + *scientific*] **:** of, relating to, or having the characteristics of a period before the rise of modern science or a state prior to the application of scientific method

pre·scind \pri-'sind\ *vb* [L *praescindere* to cut off in front, fr. *prae-* + *scindere* to cut — more at SHED] *vt* **:** to detach for purposes of thought ~ *vi* **:** to abstract or detach oneself

pre·score \(')prē-'skō(ə)r, -'skȯ(ə)r\ *vt* **:** to record (sound) in advance for use when the corresponding scenes are photographed in making movies

pre·scribe \pri-'skrīb\ *vb* [L *praescribere* to write at the beginning, dictate, order, fr. *prae-* + *scribere* to write — more at SCRIBE] *vi* **1** [ME *prescriben*, fr. ML *praescribere*, fr. L, to write at the beginning] **:** to claim a title to something by right of prescription **2 :** to lay down a rule **:** DICTATE **3 :** to write or give medical prescriptions **4 :** to become by prescription invalid or unenforceable ~ *vt* **1 a :** to lay down as a guide, direction, or rule of action **:** ORDAIN **b :** to specify with authority **2 :** to designate or order the use of as a remedy — **pre·scrib·er** *n*

pre·script \'prē-,skript, pri-'\ *adj* [ME, fr. L *praescriptus*, pp.] **:** prescribed as a rule — **pre·script** \'prē-,\ *n*

pre·scrip·ti·ble \pri-'skrip-tə-bəl\ *adj* **:** depending on, derived from, or subject to prescription

pre·scrip·tion \pri-'skrip-shən\ *n* [partly fr. ME *prescripcion* establishment of a claim, fr. MF *prescription*, fr. LL *praescription-, praescriptio*, fr. L, act of writing at the beginning, order, limitation of subject matter, fr. *praescriptus*, pp. of *praescribere;* partly fr. L *praescription-, praescriptio* order] **1 a :** the establishment of a claim of title to something under common law usu. by use and enjoyment for a period fixed by statute **b :** the right or title acquired under common law by such possession **2 :** the process of making claim to something by long use and enjoyment **3 :** the action of laying down authoritative rules or directions **4 a :** a written direction for a therapeutic or corrective agent; *specif* **:** one for the preparation and use of a medicine **b :** a prescribed medicine **5 a :** ancient or long continued custom **b :** claim founded upon ancient custom or long continued use **6 :** PRESCRIPT

pre·scrip·tive \-'skrip-tiv\ *adj* **1 :** serving to prescribe **2 :** acquired by, founded on, or determined by prescription by long-standing custom — **pre·scrip·tive·ly** *adv*

pre·sell \(')prē-'sel\ *vt* **:** to precondition by advertising and devices of salesmanship for a subsequent purchase

pres·ence \'prez-ᵊn(t)s\ *n* **1 :** the fact or condition of being present **2 a :** the part of space within one's immediate vicinity **b :** the neighborhood of one of superior esp. royal rank **3** *archaic* **:** COMPANY 2a **4 :** one that is present: as **a :** the actual person or thing that is present **b :** something present of a visible or concrete nature **5 a :** the bearing, carriage, or air of a person; *esp* **:** stately or distinguished bearing **b :** a quality of poise and effectiveness that enables a performer to achieve a close relationship with his audience **6 :** something held to be present

presence chamber *n* **:** the room where a great personage receives those entitled to come into his presence

presence of mind : self-control so maintained in an emergency or in an embarrassing situation that one can say and do the right thing

¹**pres·ent** \'prez-ᵊnt\ *n* [ME, fr. OF, fr. *presenter*] **:** something presented **:** GIFT

²**pre·sent** \pri-'zent\ *vb* [ME *presenten*, fr. OF *presenter*, fr. L *praesentare*, fr. *praesent-, praesens*, adj.] *vt* **1 a :** to bring or introduce into the presence of someone **b :** to bring (as a play) before the public **2 :** to make a gift to **3 :** to give or bestow formally **4 a :** to lay (as a charge) before a court as an object of inquiry **b :** to bring a formal public charge, indictment, or presentment against **5 :** to nominate to a benefice **6 :** to offer to view **:** SHOW **7** *archaic* **:** PERFORM, PERSONATE **8 :** to aim, point, or direct (as a weapon) so as to face something or in a particular direction ~ *vi* **1 :** to present a weapon **2 :** to come forward or into view **syn** see GIVE — **pre·sent·er** *n*

³**pre·sent** \pri-'zent\ *n* **1 :** the position of a firearm ready to be fired or of a lance or similar weapon ready to be used in attack **2 :** the position of present arms

⁴**pres·ent** \'prez-ᵊnt\ *adj* [ME, fr. OF, fr. L *praesent-, praesens*, fr. prp. of *praeesse* to be before one, fr. *prae-* pre- + *esse* to be — more at IS] **1 :** now existing or in progress **2 a :** being in view or at hand **b :** existing in something mentioned or under consideration **3 :** constituting the one actually involved, at hand, or being considered **4 :** of, relating to, or constituting a verb tense that is expressive of present time or the time of speaking **5** *obs* **a :** ATTENTIVE **b :** SELF-POSSESSED, COLLECTED **6** *archaic* **:** immediately operative or effective **:** INSTANT — **pres·ent·ness** *n*

⁵**pres·ent** \'prez-ᵊnt\ *n* **1 a** *obs* **:** present occasion or affair **b** *pl* **:** the present words or statements; *specif* **:** the legal instrument or other writing in which these words are used **2 a :** the present tense of a language **b :** a verb form in the present tense **3 :** the present time

pre·sent·abil·i·ty \pri-,zent-ə-'bil-ət-ē\ *n* **:** the quality or state of being presentable

pre·sent·able \pri-'zent-ə-bəl\ *adj* **1 :** capable of being presented **2 :** being in condition to be seen or inspected esp. by the critical — **pre·sent·able·ness** *n* — **pre·sent·ably** \-blē\ *adv*

pre·sent arms \pri-,zent-\ *n* [²*present*] **:** a position in the manual of arms in which the rifle is held perpendicularly in front of the center of the body; *also* **:** the command to take this position

pre·sen·ta·tion \,prē-,zen-'tā-shən, ,prez-ᵊn-, ,prēz-ᵊn-\ *n* **1 a :** the act of presenting **b :** the act, power, or privilege esp. of a patron of applying to the bishop or ordinary for the institution of one nominated to a benefice **2 :** something presented: as **a :** a symbol or image that represents something **b :** something offered or given **:** GIFT **c :** something set forth for the attention of the mind **3 :** the position in which the fetus lies in the uterus in labor with respect to the mouth of the uterus **4 :** an object of perception, cognition, or memory; *specif* **:** the object of sensation abstracted from conscious awareness **5** *often cap* **:** a church

feast on November 21 celebrating the presentation of the Virgin Mary in the Temple **6 :** the method by which radio, navigation, or radar information is given to the operator (as the pilot of an airplane) — **pre·sen·ta·tion·al** \-shnəl, -shən-ᵊl\ *adj*

pre·sen·ta·tive \pri-ˈzent-ət-iv, ˈprez-ᵊn-ˌtāt-\ *adj* **1 :** known, knowing, or capable of being known directly rather than through cogitation **2 :** NONREPRESENTATIONAL

pres·ent-day \ˌprez-ᵊnt-ˌdā\ *adj* **:** now existing or occurring **:** CURRENT

pre·sen·tee \ˌprez-ᵊn-ˈtē, pri-ˌzen-\ *n* **:** one who is presented or to whom something is presented

pre·sen·tient \pri-ˈsen-ch(ē-)ənt, ˈprē-; pri-ˈzen-\ *adj* [L *praesentient-, praesentiens*, prp. of *praesentire*] **:** having a presentiment

pre·sen·ti·ment \pri-ˈzent-ə-mənt\ *n* [F *pressentiment*, fr. MF, fr. *pressentir* to have a presentiment, fr. L *praesentire* to feel beforehand, fr. *prae-* + *sentire* to feel — more at SENSE] **:** a feeling that something will or is about to happen **:** PREMONITION — **pre·sen·ti·men·tal** \-ˌzent-ə-ˈment-ᵊl\ *adj*

pres·ent·ly \ˈprez-ᵊnt-lē\ *adv* **1** *archaic* **:** at once **2 :** before long **:** SOON **3 :** at the present time **:** NOW

pre·sent·ment \pri-ˈzent-mənt\ *n* **1 :** the act of presenting to an authority a formal statement of a matter to be dealt with; *specif* **:** the notice taken or statement made by a grand jury of an offense from their own knowledge without a bill of indictment laid before them **2 :** the act of offering a document at the proper time and place requiring to be accepted or paid by another **3 a :** the act of presenting to view or consciousness **b :** something set forth, presented, or exhibited **c :** the aspect in which something is presented

present participle *n* **:** a participle that typically expresses present action in relation to the time expressed by the finite verb in its clause and that in English is formed with the suffix *-ing* and is used in the formation of the progressive tenses

present perfect *adj* **:** of, relating to, or constituting a verb tense that is formed in English with *have* and that expresses action or state completed at the time of speaking — **present perfect** *n*

present tense *n* **:** the tense of a verb that expresses action or state in the present time and is used of what occurs or is true at the time of speaking and of what is habitual or characteristic or is always or necessarily true, that is sometimes used to refer to action in the past (as in the historical present), and that is sometimes used for future events

pre·serv·able \pri-ˈzər-və-bəl\ *adj* **:** capable of being preserved

pres·er·va·tion \ˌprez-ər-ˈvā-shən\ *n* **:** the act of preserving **:** the state of being preserved

[1]**pre·ser·va·tive** \pri-ˈzər-vət-iv\ *adj* **:** having the power of preserving

[2]**preservative** *n* **:** something that preserves or has the power of preserving; *specif* **:** an additive used to protect against decay, discoloration, or spoilage

[1]**pre·serve** \pri-ˈzərv\ *vb* [ME *preserven*, fr. MF *preserver*, fr. ML *praeservare*, fr. LL, to observe beforehand, fr. L *prae-* + *servare* to keep, guard, observe — more at CONSERVE] *vt* **1 :** to keep safe from injury, harm, or destruction **:** PROTECT **2 a :** to keep alive, intact, or free from decay **b :** MAINTAIN **3 a :** to keep or save from decomposition **b :** to can, pickle, or similarly prepare for future use **4 :** to keep up and reserve for personal or special use ~ *vi* **1 :** to make preserves **2 :** to raise and protect game for purposes of sport **3 :** to stand preserving (as by canning) — **pre·serv·er** *n*

[2]**preserve** *n* **1 :** something that preserves or is designed to preserve **2 :** fruit canned or made into jams or jellies or cooked whole or in large pieces with sugar so as to keep its shape — often used in pl. **3 :** an area restricted for the protection and preservation of animals, trees, or other natural resources; *esp* **:** one used primarily for regulated hunting or fishing **4 :** something regarded as reserved for certain persons

pre·set \(ˈ)prē-ˈset\ *vt* **:** to set beforehand

pre·shrunk \ˈprē-ˈshrəŋk, *esp South* -ˈsrəŋk\ *adj* **:** of, relating to, or constituting a fabric subjected to a shrinking process during manufacture usu. to reduce later shrinking

pre·side \pri-ˈzīd\ *vi* [L *praesidēre* to guard, preside over, lit., to sit in front of, sit at the head of, fr. *prae-* + *sedēre* to sit — more at SIT] **1 a :** to occupy the place of authority **:** act as president, chairman, or moderator **b :** to occupy a position similar to that of a president or chairman **2 :** to exercise guidance, direction, or control **3 :** to occupy a position of featured instrumental performer

pres·i·den·cy \ˈprez-əd-ən-sē, ˈprez-dən- *also* ˈprez-ə-ˌden(t)-sē\ *n* **1 a :** the office of president **b** (1) **:** the office of president of the U.S. (2) **:** the American governmental institution comprising the office of president and various associated administrative and policy-making agencies **2 :** the term during which a president holds office **3 :** the action or function of one that presides **:** SUPERINTENDENCE **4 :** a Mormon executive council of the church or a stake consisting of a president and two counselors

pres·i·dent \ˈprez-əd-ənt, ˈprez-dənt *also* ˈprez-ə-ˌdent\ *n* [ME, fr. MF, fr. L *praesident-, praesidens*, fr. prp. of *praesidēre*] **1 :** an official chosen to preside over a meeting or assembly **2 :** an appointed governor of a subordinate political unit **3 :** the chief officer of a corporation, institution, or similar organization usu. entrusted with the direction and administration of its policies **4 :** the presiding officer of a governmental body **5 a :** an elected official serving as both chief of state and chief political executive in a republic having a presidential government **b :** an elected official having the position of chief of state but usu. only minimal political powers in a republic having a parliamentary government — **pres·i·den·tial** \(ˌ)prez-(ə-)ˈden-chəl\ *adj*

presidential government *n* **:** a system of government in which the president is constitutionally independent of the legislature

pres·i·dent·ship \ˈprez-əd-ənt-ˌship, ˈprez-dənt- *also* ˈprez-ə-ˌdent-\ *n* **:** PRESIDENCY

pre·sid·er \pri-ˈzīd-ər\ *n* **:** one that presides

pre·sid·i·al \pri-ˈsid-ē-əl, prī-, -ˈzid-\ *adj* [LL *praesidialis*, fr. L *praesidium* garrison, fr. *praesid-, praeses* guard, governor, fr. *praesidēre*] **1 :** of, having, or constituting a garrison **2 :** PRESIDENTIAL **3** [F *présidial*, fr. MF, alter. of *presidal*, fr. LL *praesidalis* of a provincial governor, fr. L *praesid-, praeses*] **:** of or relating to a province **:** PROVINCIAL

pre·sid·i·ary \-ē-ˌer-ē\ *adj* **:** PRESIDIAL 1

pre·si·dio \pri-ˈsēd-ē-ˌō, -ˈsid-, -ˈzēd-, -ˈzid-\ *n* [Sp, fr. L *praesidium*] **:** a garrisoned place; *esp* **:** a military post or fortified settlement in areas currently or orig. under Spanish control

pre·sid·i·um \pri-ˈsid-ē-əm, prī-, -ˈzid-\ *n, pl* **pre·sid·ia** \-ē-ə\ *or* **presidiums** [Russ *prezidium*, fr. L *praesidium* garrison] **:** a permanent executive committee selected in Communist countries to act for a larger body

pre·sig·ni·fy \(ˈ)prē-ˈsig-nə-ˌfī\ *vt* [L *praesignificare*, fr. *prae-* + *significare* to signify] **:** to intimate or signify beforehand **:** PRESAGE

pre–So·crat·ic \ˌprē-sə-ˈkrat-ik, -sō-\ *adj* **:** of or relating to Greek philosophers before Socrates — **pre–Socratic** *n*

[1]**press** \ˈpres\ *n* [ME *presse*, fr. OF, fr. *presser* to press] **1 a :** a crowd or crowded condition **:** THRONG **b :** a thronging or crowding forward or together **2 a :** an apparatus or machine by which a substance is cut or shaped, an impression of a body is taken, a material is compressed, pressure is applied to a body, liquid is expressed, or a cutting tool is fed into the work by pressure **b :** a building containing presses or a business using presses **3 :** CLOSET, CUPBOARD **4 :** an act of pressing or pushing **:** PRESSURE **5 :** the properly smoothed and creased condition of a freshly pressed garment **6 a :** PRINTING PRESS **b :** the act or the process of printing **c :** a printing or publishing establishment **7 a :** the gathering and publishing or broadcasting of news **:** JOURNALISM **b :** newspapers, periodicals, and often radio and television news broadcasting **c :** news reporters, publishers, and broadcasters **d :** comment or notice in newspapers and periodicals **8 :** any of various pressure devices (as one for keeping sporting gear from warping when not in use)

[2]**press** *vb* [ME *pressen*, fr. MF *presser*, fr. L *pressare*, fr. *pressus* pp. of *premere* to press; akin to L *prelum* press and perh. to Russ *peret'* to press] *vt* **1 :** to act upon through steady pushing or thrusting force exerted in contact **:** SQUEEZE **2 a :** ASSAIL, HARASS **b :** AFFLICT, OPPRESS **3 a :** to squeeze out the juice or contents of **b :** to squeeze with apparatus or instruments to a desired density, smoothness, or shape **4 a :** to exert influence on **:** CONSTRAIN **b :** to try hard to persuade **:** BESEECH, ENTREAT **5 :** to move by means of pressure **6 a :** to lay stress or emphasis on **b :** to insist on or request urgently **7 :** to follow through (a course of action) **8 :** to clasp in affection or courtesy **9 :** to make (a phonograph record) from a matrix ~ *vi* **1 :** to crowd closely **:** MASS **2 :** to force or push one's way **3 :** to seek urgently **:** CONTEND **4 :** to require haste or speed in action **5 :** to exert pressure **6 :** to take or hold a press — **press·er** *n*

[3]**press** *vb* [alter. of obs. *prest* (to enlist by giving pay in advance), fr. [2]*prest*] *vt* **1 :** to force into service esp. in the army or navy **:** IMPRESS **2 a :** to take by authority esp. for public use **:** COMMANDEER **b :** to take and force into any usu. emergency service ~ *vi* **:** to impress men as soldiers or sailors

[4]**press** *n* **1 :** impressment into service esp. in a navy **2** *obs* **:** a warrant for impressing recruits

press agent *n* [[1]*press*] **:** an agent employed to establish and maintain good public relations through publicity — **press–agent** \ˈpres-ˌā-jənt\ *vb* — **press–agent·ry** \-jən-trē\ *n*

press·board \ˈpres-ˌbō(ə)rd, -ˌbȯ(ə)rd\ *n* **1 :** a strong highly glazed board resembling vulcanized fiber **2 :** an ironing board; *esp* **:** a small one for sleeves

press box *n* **:** a space reserved for reporters (as at a game)

press conference *n* **:** an interview given by a public figure to newsmen by appointment

pressed \ˈprest\ *adj, of food* **:** shaped, molded, or having liquid or juices extracted under pressure ⟨~ duck⟩

press–gang \ˈpres-ˌgaŋ\ *n* [[4]*press*] **:** a detachment of men under command of an officer empowered to force men into military or naval service — **press–gang** *vt*

press·ing *adj* **1 :** urgently important **:** CRITICAL **2 :** EARNEST, WARM — **press·ing·ly** \-iŋ-lē\ *adv*

press·man \ˈpres-mən, -ˌman\ *n* **1 :** an operator of a press; *esp* **:** the operator of a printing press **2** *Brit* **:** NEWSPAPERMAN

press·mark \-ˌmärk\ *n, chiefly Brit* **:** a mark assigned to a book to indicate its location in a library

press money *n* **:** PREST MONEY

press of sail : the fullest amount of sail that a ship can crowd on — called also *press of canvas*

pres·sor \ˈpres-ˌȯ(ə)r, -ər\ *adj* [LL, one that presses, fr. L *pressus*, pp. of *premere* to press — more at PRESS] **:** raising or tending to raise blood pressure; *also* **:** involving vasoconstriction

press release *n* **:** HANDOUT 3

press·room \ˈpres-ˌrüm, -ˌru̇m\ *n* **1 :** a room in a printing plant containing the printing presses **2 :** a room (as at the White House) for the use of reporters

press·run \-ˌrən\ *n* **:** a continuous operation of a printing press producing a specified number of copies; *also* **:** the number of copies printed

[1]**pres·sure** \ˈpresh-ər\ *n* **1 a :** the burden of physical or mental distress **b :** the constraint of circumstance **2 :** the application of force to something by something else in direct contact with it **:** COMPRESSION **3** *archaic* **:** IMPRESSION, STAMP **4 a :** the action of a force against an opposing force **b :** the force or thrust exerted over a surface divided by its area **c :** ELECTROMOTIVE FORCE **5 :** the stress or urgency of matters demanding attention **:** EXIGENCY **6 :** a factor that tends to reduce a wild animal population esp. when arising from human activity **7 :** atmospheric pressure **8 :** a sensation aroused by moderate compression of a body part or surface

[2]**pressure** *vt* **pres·sur·ing** \-(ə-)riŋ\ **1 :** to apply pressure to **:** CONSTRAIN **2 :** PRESSURIZE **3 :** to cook in a pressure cooker

pressure cabin *n* **:** a pressurized cabin

pres·sure–cook \ˌpresh-ər-ˈku̇k\ *vb* [back-formation fr. *pressure cooker*] **:** to cook in a pressure cooker

pressure cooker *n* **:** an airtight utensil for quick cooking or preserving of foods by means of superheated steam under pressure

pressure gauge *n* **1 :** a gauge for indicating fluid pressure **2 :** a device to measure the pressure of an explosive

pressure group *n* **:** an interest group actively organized to in-

fluence public and esp. governmental policy but not to elect candidates to office

pressure suit *n* **:** an inflatable suit for high-altitude flying to protect a flier's body from low atmospheric pressure

pres·sur·iza·tion \,presh-(ə-)rə-'zā-shən\ *n* **:** the action or process of pressurizing **:** the state of being pressurized

pres·sur·ize \'presh-ə-,rīz\ *vt* **1 :** to maintain near-normal atmospheric pressure in during high-level flight by means of a supercharger **2 :** to apply pressure to **3 :** to design to withstand pressure — **pres·sur·iz·er** *n*

press·work \'pres-,wərk\ *n* **:** the operation, management, or product of a printing press; *esp* **:** the branch of printing concerned with the actual transfer of ink from form or plates to paper

¹prest \'prest\ *adj* [ME, fr. OF, fr. L *praestus* — more at PRESTO] *obs* **:** READY

²prest *n* [ME, fr. MF, fr. OF, fr. *prester* to lend, fr. L *praestare* to be surety for, pay, provide, fr. *praed-, praes* bondsman (fr. *prae-* pre- + *vad-, vas* security) + *stare* to stand — more at WED, STAND] **1** *obs* **:** a loan of money **2** *obs* **:** an advance on wages or on the cost of an undertaking

Pres·ter John \,pres-tər-'jän\ *n* [ME *Prestre Johan*, fr. MF *prestre Jehan*, fr. *prestre* priest + *Jehan* John — more at PRIEST] **:** a legendary medieval Christian priest and king

pre·ster·num \(')prē-'stər-nəm\ *n* [NL] **:** the anterior segment of the sternum of a mammal **:** MANUBRIUM

pres·ti·dig·i·ta·tion \,pres-tə-,dij-ə-'tā-shən\ *n* [F, fr. *prestidigitateur* prestidigitator, fr. *preste* nimble, quick (fr. It *presto*) + L *digitus* finger — more at DIGIT] **:** SLEIGHT OF HAND, LEGERDEMAIN — **pres·ti·dig·i·ta·tor** \-'dij-ə-,tāt-ər\ *n*

pres·tige \pre-'stēzh, -'stēj\ *n* [F, fr. MF, conjuror's trick, illusion, fr. LL *praestigium*, fr. L *praestigiae*, pl., conjuror's tricks, irreg. fr. *praestringere* to tie up, blindfold, fr. *prae-* + *stringere* to bind tight — more at STRAIN] **1 :** standing or estimation in the eyes of people **:** weight or credit in general opinion **2 :** commanding position in men's minds **:** ASCENDANCY **syn** see INFLUENCE

pres·ti·gious \pre-'stij-(ē-)əs, *2 is also* -'stēzh-, -'stēj-\ *adj* [L *praestigiosus*, fr. *praestigiae*] **1** *archaic* **:** of, relating to, or marked by illusion, conjuring, or trickery **2 :** having prestige **:** HONORED — **pres·ti·gious·ly** *adv* — **pres·ti·gious·ness** *n*

pres·tis·si·mo \pre-'stis-ə-,mō\ *adv (or adj)* [It, fr. superl. of *presto*] **:** at a very rapid tempo — used as a direction in music

prest money *n, obs* **:** money advanced to men enlisting in the British army or navy

¹pres·to \'pres-(,)tō\ *adv (or adj)* [It, quick, quickly, fr. L *praestus* ready, fr. *praesto*, adv. on hand; akin to L *prae* before — more at FOR] **1 :** at once **:** QUICKLY **2 :** at a rapid tempo — used as a direction in music

²presto *n* **:** a presto musical passage or movement

pre·stress \(')prē-'stres\ *vt* **:** to introduce internal stresses into to counteract the stresses that will result from applied load (as in incorporating cables under tension in concrete)

pre·sum·able \pri-'zü-mə-bəl\ *adj* **:** capable of being presumed **:** acceptable as an assumption **:** PROBABLE — **pre·sum·ably** \-blē\ *adv*

pre·sume \pri-'züm\ *vb* [ME *presumen*, fr. LL & MF; LL *praesumere* to dare, fr. L, to anticipate, assume, fr. *prae-* + *sumere* to take; MF *presumer* to assume, fr. L *praesumere* — more at CONSUME] *vt* **1 :** to take upon oneself without leave or warrant **:** DARE **2 :** to expect or assume esp. with confidence **3 :** to raise a presumption of or that ~ *vi* **1 :** to act or proceed presumptuously or on a presumption **2 :** to go beyond what is right or proper — **pre·sum·er** *n*

pre·sum·ing *adj* **:** PRESUMPTUOUS — **pre·sum·ing·ly** \-'zü-miŋ-lē\ *adv*

pre·sump·tion \pri-'zəm(p)-shən\ *n* [ME *presumpcioun*, fr. OF *presumption*, fr. LL *praesumption-, praesumptio* presumptuous attitude (fr. L) & L *praesumption-, praesumptio* assumption, fr. *praesumptus*, pp. of *praesumere*] **1 :** presumptuous attitude or conduct **:** AUDACITY **2 a :** an attitude or belief dictated by probability **:** ASSUMPTION **b :** the ground, reason, or evidence lending probability to a belief **3 :** a legal inference as to the existence or truth of a fact not certainly known drawn from the known or proved existence of some other fact

pre·sump·tive \-'zəm(p)-tiv\ *adj* **1 :** giving grounds for reasonable opinion or belief **2 :** based on probability or presumption — **pre·sump·tive·ly** *adv*

pre·sump·tu·ous \pri-'zəm(p)-chə-wəs; -'zəm(p)-shəs, -chəs\ *adj* [ME, fr. MF *presumptueux*, fr. LL *praesumptuosus*, irreg. fr. *praesumptio*] **:** overstepping due bounds **:** taking liberties **:** OVERWEENING — **pre·sump·tu·ous·ly** *adv* — **pre·sump·tu·ous·ness** *n*

pre·sup·pose \,prē-sə-'pōz\ *vt* [ME *presupposen*, fr. MF *presupposer*, fr. ML *praesupponere* (perf. indic. *praesupposui*), fr. L *prae-* + ML *supponere* to suppose — more at SUPPOSE] **1 :** to suppose beforehand **2 :** to require as an antecedent in logic or fact — **pre·sup·po·si·tion** \(,)prē-,səp-ə-'zish-ən\ *n*

pre·tend \pri-'tend\ *vb* [ME *pretenden*, fr. L *praetendere* to allege as an excuse, lit., to stretch in front of like a curtain, fr. *prae-* pre- + *tendere* to stretch — more at THIN] *vt* **1 :** to hold out the appearance of being, possessing, or performing **:** PROFESS **2 a :** to make believe **:** FEIGN **b :** to hold out, represent, or assert falsely **3 :** VENTURE, UNDERTAKE ~ *vi* **1 :** to feign an action, part, or role in play **2 :** to put in a claim **syn** see ASSUME

pre·tend·ed *adj* **:** professed or avowed but not genuine — **pre·tend·ed·ly** *adv*

pre·tend·er \-'ten-dər\ *n* **:** one that pretends: as **a :** CLAIMANT; *specif* **:** a claimant to a throne who is held to have no just title **b :** one who makes a false or hypocritical show

pre·tense *or* **pre·tence** \'prē-,ten(t)s, pri-'\ *n* [ME, fr. MF *pretensse*, fr. (assumed) ML *praetensa*, fr. LL, fem. of *praetensus*, pp. of L *praetendere*] **1 :** a claim made or implied; *esp* **:** one not supported by fact **2 a :** mere ostentation **:** PRETENTIOUSNESS **b :** a pretentious act or assertion **3 :** an attempt to attain a certain condition or quality **4 :** professed rather than real intention or purpose **:** PRETEXT **5 :** MAKE-BELIEVE, FICTION **6 :** false show **:** SIMULATION

pre·ten·sion \pri-'ten-chən\ *n* **1 :** an allegation of doubtful value **:** PRETEXT **2 :** a claim or an effort to establish a claim **3 :** a claim or right to attention or honor because of merit **4 :** ASPIRATION, INTENTION **5 :** PRETENTIOUSNESS, VANITY **syn** see AMBITION

pre·ten·sion·less \-chən-ləs\ *adj* **:** UNPRETENTIOUS

pre·ten·tious \-chəs\ *adj* [F *prétentieux*, fr. *prétention* pretension, fr. ML *praetention-, praetentio*, fr. L *praetentus*, pp. of *praetendere*] **1 :** making or possessing claims **:** OSTENTATIOUS **2 :** making demands on one's skill, ability, or means **:** AMBITIOUS **syn** see SHOWY — **pre·ten·tious·ly** *adv* — **pre·ten·tious·ness** *n*

pret·er·it *or* **pret·er·ite** \'pret-ə-rət\ *adj* [ME *preterit*, fr. MF, fr. L *praeteritus*, fr. pp. of *praeterire* to go by, pass, fr. *praeter* beyond, past, by (fr. compar. of *prae* before) + *ire* to go — more at FOR, ISSUE] **1** *archaic* **:** BYGONE, FORMER **2 :** of, relating to, or constituting a verb tense that indicates action in the past without reference to duration, continuance, or repetition — **preterit** *n*

pre·ter·mi·nal \(')prē-'tərm-nəl, -ən-ᵊl\ *adj* **:** occurring before death

pre·ter·mis·sion \,prēt-ər-'mish-ən\ *n* [L *praetermission-, praetermissio*, fr. *praetermissus*, pp. of *praetermittere*] **:** the act or an instance of pretermitting **:** OMISSION

pre·ter·mit \-'mit\ *vt* **pre·ter·mit·ted; pre·ter·mit·ting** [L *praetermittere*, fr. *praeter* by, past + *mittere* to let go, send — more at SMITE] **1 :** to let pass without mention or notice **:** OMIT **2 :** to leave undone **:** NEGLECT **3 :** to break off **:** SUSPEND

pre·ter·nat·u·ral \,prēt-ər-'nach-(ə-)rəl\ *adj* [ML *praeternaturalis*, fr. L *praeter naturam* beyond nature] **1 :** existing outside of nature **2 :** exceeding what is natural or regular in nature **:** ABNORMAL **3 :** inexplicable by ordinary means — **pre·ter·nat·u·ral·ly** \-rə-lē, -'nach-ər-lē\ *adv* — **pre·ter·nat·u·ral·ness** \-'nach-(ə-)rəl-nəs\ *n*

pre·test \'prē-,test, (')prē-'\ *n* **:** a preliminary test serving for exploration rather than evaluation — **pretest** *vt*

pre·text \'prē-,tekst\ *n* [L *praetextus*, fr. *praetextus*, pp. of *praetexere* to assign as a pretext, lit., to weave in front, fr. *prae-* + *texere* to weave — more at TECHNICAL] **:** a purpose or motive alleged or an appearance assumed in order to cloak the real intention or state of affairs **syn** see APOLOGY

pre·tor, pre·to·ri·an *var of* PRAETOR, PRAETORIAN

pre·treat \(')prē-'trēt\ *vt* **:** to treat beforehand — **pre·treat·ment** \-mənt\ *n*

pret·ti·fi·ca·tion \,prit-i-fə-'kā-shən, ,pu̇rt-, ,pru̇t-\ *n* **:** the act, process, or result of prettifying

pret·ti·fy \'prit-i-,fī, 'pu̇rt-, 'pru̇t-\ *vt* **:** to make pretty

pret·ti·ly \'prit-ᵊl-ē, 'pu̇rt-, 'pru̇t-\ *adv* **:** in a pretty manner

pret·ti·ness \'prit-ē-nəs, 'pu̇rt-, 'pru̇t-\ *n* **1 :** the quality or state of being pretty **2 :** something pretty

¹pret·ty \'prit-ē, 'pu̇rt-, 'pru̇t-\ *adj* [ME *praty, prety*, fr. OE *prættig* tricky, fr. *prætt* trick; akin to ON *prettr* trick] **1 a :** ARTFUL, CLEVER **b :** PAT, APT **2 a :** pleasing by delicacy or grace **b :** having conventionally accepted elements of beauty **c :** appearing or sounding pleasant or nice but lacking strength, force, manliness, purpose, or intensity **3 a :** FINE, GOOD — often used ironically **b** *chiefly Scot* **:** STOUT **4 :** moderately large **:** CONSIDERABLE **syn** see BEAUTIFUL — **pret·ty·ish** \-ish\ *adj*

²pret·ty \,pu̇rt-ē, pərt-ē (*unstressed* pərt-), ,prit-ē, ,pru̇t-ē; *before "near(ly)" often without* -ē\ *adv* **1 :** in some degree **:** MODERATELY **2** *chiefly dial* **:** PRETTILY

³pret·ty \'prit-ē, 'pu̇rt-ē, 'pru̇t-ē\ *vt* **:** to make pretty — usu. used with *up*

⁴pretty *like* ³\ *n* **1 :** a pretty person or thing **2** *pl* **:** dainty clothes; *esp* **:** LINGERIE

pre·tu·ber·cu·lous \,prē-t(y)ù-'bər-kyə-ləs\ *or* **pre·tu·ber·cu·lar** \-lər\ *adj* **1 :** preceding the development of lesions definitely identifiable as tuberculous **2 :** likely to develop tuberculosis

pre·typ·i·fy \(')prē-'tip-ə-,fī\ *vt* **:** to typify earlier **:** PREFIGURE

pret·zel \'pret-səl\ *n* [G *brezel*, deriv. of L *brachiatus* having branches like arms, fr. *brachium* arm — more at BRACE] **:** a brittle glazed and salted cracker typically having the form of a loose knot

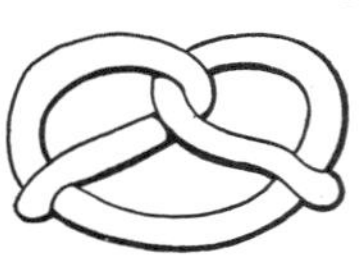

pretzel

pre·vail \pri-'vā(ə)l\ *vi* [ME *prevailen*, fr. L *praevalēre*, fr. *prae-* pre- + *valēre* to be strong — more at WIELD] **1 :** to gain ascendancy through strength or superiority **:** TRIUMPH **2 :** to be or become effective or effectual **3 :** to use persuasion successfully ⟨~*ed* on him to sing⟩ **4 :** to be frequent **:** PREDOMINATE **5 :** to be or continue in use or fashion **:** PERSIST **syn** see INDUCE

pre·vail·ing *adj* **1 :** having superior force or influence **2 a :** most frequent ⟨~ winds⟩ **b :** generally current **:** COMMON — **pre·vail·ing·ly** \-'vā-liŋ-lē\ *adv*

syn PREVAILING, PREVALENT, RIFE, CURRENT mean generally circulated, accepted, or used in a certain time or place. PREVAILING stresses predominance ⟨*prevailing* opinion⟩ PREVALENT implies only frequency ⟨*prevalent* custom⟩ RIFE implies a growing prevalence or rapid spread; CURRENT applies to what is subject to change and stresses prevalence at the present time

prev·a·lence \'prev-(ə-)lən(t)s\ *n* **:** the quality or state of being prevalent

prev·a·lent \-(ə-)lənt\ *adj* [L *praevalent-, praevalens* very powerful, fr. prp. of *praevalēre*] **1** *archaic* **:** POWERFUL **2 :** being in ascendancy **:** DOMINANT **3 :** generally or widely accepted, practiced, or favored **:** WIDESPREAD **syn** see PREVAILING — **prevalent** *n* — **prev·a·lent·ly** *adv*

pre·var·i·cate \pri-'var-ə-,kāt\ *vi* [L *praevaricatus*, pp. of *praevaricari* to walk crookedly, fr. *prae-* + *varicus* having the feet spread apart, fr. *varus* bent, knock-kneed; prob. akin to OE *wōh* crooked, L *vacillare* to sway, *vagus* wandering] **:** to deviate from the truth **:** EQUIVOCATE — **pre·var·i·ca·tion** \-,var-ə-'kā-shən\ *n* — **pre·var·i·ca·tor** \-'var-ə-,kāt-ər\ *n*

pré·ve·nance \,prāv-(ə-)'näⁿs\ *n* [F, fr. *prévenant*, prp. of *prévenir* to anticipate, fr. L *praevenire*] **:** attentiveness to or anticipation of others' needs

pre·ve·nience \pri-'vē-nyən(t)s\ *n* [*prevenient*] **1 :** PRÉVENANCE **2 :** prevenient character or action

pre·ve·nient \-nyənt\ *adj* [L *praevenient-, praeveniens*, prp. of *praevenire*] **:** ANTECEDENT, ANTICIPATORY — **pre·ve·nient·ly** *adv*

pre·vent \pri-'vent\ *vb* [ME *preventen* to anticipate, fr. L *praeventus*, pp. of *praevenire* to come before, anticipate, forestall, fr. *prae-* + *venire* to come — more at COME] *vt* **1** *archaic* **a :** to be in readiness for (as an occasion) **b :** to meet or satisfy in advance **c :** to act ahead of **d :** to arrive before **2 :** to deprive of power or hope of acting or succeeding **3 :** to keep from happening or

existing ⟨steps to ~ war⟩ **4 :** to hold or keep back **:** HINDER, STOP — often used with *from* ~ *vi* **:** to interpose an obstacle — **pre·vent·abil·i·ty** \-ˌvent-ə-ˈbil-ət-ē\ *n* — **pre·vent·able** *also* **pre·vent·ible** \-ˈvent-ə-bəl\ *adj* — **pre·vent·er** *n*

syn PREVENT, ANTICIPATE, FORESTALL mean to deal with beforehand. PREVENT implies taking advance measures against something possible or probable; ANTICIPATE implies a getting ahead of or being prior to (as in using, treating, accomplishing) often so as to prepare for something that will come later; FORESTALL implies a getting ahead so as to stop or interrupt something in its course

syn PREVENT, PRECLUDE, OBVIATE, AVERT, WARD OFF mean to stop something from coming or occurring. PREVENT implies the existence of or the placing of an insurmountable obstacle; PRECLUDE implies the shutting out of every possibility of a thing's happening or taking effect; OBVIATE suggests the use of forethought to avoid the necessity for unwelcome or disagreeable actions or measures; AVERT and WARD OFF imply taking immediate and effective measures to avoid, repel, or counteract threatening evil

pre·ven·ta·tive \-ˈvent-ət-iv\ *adj or n* **:** PREVENTIVE

pre·ven·tion \pri-ˈven-chən\ *n* **:** the act of preventing or hindering

1pre·ven·tive \-ˈvent-iv\ *n* **:** something that prevents; *esp* **:** something used to prevent disease

2preventive *adj* **1 :** devoted to or concerned with prevention **:** PRECAUTIONARY **2 :** undertaken to forestall anticipated hostile action ⟨~ war⟩ — **pre·ven·tive·ly** *adv* — **pre·ven·tive·ness** *n*

1pre·view \ˈprē-ˌvyü\ *vt* **1 :** to see beforehand; *specif* **:** to view or to show in advance of public presentation **2 :** to give a preliminary survey of

2preview *n* **1 :** an advance showing or viewing **2** *also* **pre·vue** \-ˌvyü\ **:** a showing of snatches from a motion picture advertised for appearance in the near future **3 :** a statement giving advance information **:** FORETASTE **4 :** a preliminary survey

pre·vi·ous \ˈprē-vē-əs\ *adj* [L *praevius* leading the way, fr. *prae-* pre- + *via* way — more at VIA] **1 :** going before in time or order **:** PRECEDING **2 :** acting too soon **:** PREMATURE **syn** see PRECEDING — **pre·vi·ous·ly** *adv* — **pre·vi·ous·ness** *n*

previous question *n* **:** a parliamentary motion that the pending question be put to an immediate vote without further debate or amendment and that if defeated has the effect of permitting resumption of debate

previous to *prep* **:** prior to **:** BEFORE

pre·vise \prē-ˈvīz\ *vt* [L *praevisus*, pp.] **1 :** FORESEE **2 :** FOREWARN

1pre·vi·sion \prē-ˈvizh-ən\ *n* [LL *praevision-*, *praevisio*, fr. L *praevisus*, pp. of *praevidēre* to foresee, fr. *prae-* + *vidēre* to see — more at WIT] **1 :** FORESIGHT, PRESCIENCE **2 :** PROGNOSTICATION, FORECAST — **pre·vi·sion·al** \-ˈvizh-nəl, -ən-ᵊl\ *adj* — **pre·vi·sion·ary** \-ˈvizh-ə-ˌner-ē\ *adj*

2prevision *vt* **pre·vi·sion·ing** \-ˈvizh-(ə-)niŋ\ **:** FORESEE

pre·vo·cal·ic \ˌprē-vō-ˈkal-ik, -və-\ *adj* [ISV] **:** immediately preceding a vowel

pre·vo·ca·tion·al \ˌprē-vō-ˈkā-shnəl, -shən-ᵊl\ *adj* **:** given or required before admission to a vocational school

pre·war \ˈprē-ˈwȯ(ə)r\ *adj* **:** occurring or existing before a war

prexy \ˈprek-sē\ *also* **prex** \ˈpreks\ *n* [*prexy* fr. *prex*, by shortening & alter. fr. *president*] *slang* **:** PRESIDENT — used chiefly of a college president

1prey \ˈprā\ *n* [ME *preie*, fr. OF, fr. L *praeda;* akin to L *prehendere* to grasp, seize — more at PREHENSILE] **1** *archaic* **:** SPOIL, BOOTY **2 a :** an animal taken by a predator as food **b :** one that is helpless or unable to resist attack **:** VICTIM **3 :** the act or habit of preying

2prey *vi* [ME *preyen*, fr. OF *preier*, fr. L *praedari*, fr. *praeda*] **1 :** to make raids for the sake of booty **2 a :** to seize and devour prey **b :** to commit violence or robbery or fraud **3 :** to have an injurious, destructive, or wasting effect — **prey·er** *n*

Pri·am \ˈprī-əm, -ˌam\ *n* [L *Priamus*, fr. Gk *Priamos*] **:** the father of Hector and Paris and king of Troy during the Trojan War

pri·a·pic \prī-ˈap-ik, -ˈā-pik\ *adj* [L *priapus* lecher] **:** PHALLIC

Pri·a·pus \prī-ˈā-pəs\ *n* [L, fr. Gk *Priapos*] **:** the god of male generative power in classical antiquity

1price \ˈprīs\ *n* [ME *pris*, fr. OF, fr. L *pretium* price, money; akin to Skt *prati-* against, in return — more at PROS-] **1** *archaic* **:** VALUE, WORTH **2 a :** the quantity of one thing that is exchanged or demanded in barter or sale for another **b :** the amount of money given or set as consideration for the sale of a specified thing **3 :** the terms for the sake of which something is done or undertaken: as **a :** an amount sufficient to bribe one **b :** a reward for the apprehension or death of a person **4 :** the cost at which something is obtained

2price *vt* **1 :** to set a price on **2 :** to ask the price of **3 :** to drive by raising prices excessively ⟨*priced* themselves out of the market⟩ — **pric·er** *n*

price–cut·ter \ˈprī-ˌskət-ər\ *n* **:** one that reduces prices esp. to a level designed to cripple competition

price index *n* **:** an index number expressing the level of a group of commodity prices relative to the level of the prices of the same commodities during an arbitrarily chosen base period and used to indicate changes in the level of prices from one period to another

price·less \ˈprī-sləs\ *adj* **1 a :** having a value beyond any price **:** INVALUABLE **b :** excessively high-priced **2 :** having worth in terms of other than market value **3 :** surprisingly amusing, odd, or absurd **syn** see COSTLY

price support *n* **:** artificial maintenance of prices (as of a particular raw material) at some predetermined level usu. through government action

price tag *n* **1 :** a tag on merchandise showing the price at which it is offered for sale **2 :** PRICE, COST

price war *n* **:** a period of commercial competition characterized by repeated cutting of prices below those of competitors

1prick \ˈprik\ *n* [ME *prikke*, fr. OE *prica;* akin to MD *pric* prick] **1 :** a mark or shallow hole made by a pointed instrument **2 a :** a pointed instrument or weapon **b :** a sharp projecting organ or part **3 :** an instance of pricking or the sensation of being pricked

2prick *vt* **1 :** to pierce slightly with a sharp point **2 :** to affect with anguish, grief, or remorse **3 :** to ride, guide, or urge on with spurs **4 :** to mark by means of a small mark **5 :** to trace or outline with punctures **6 :** to remove (a young seedling) from the seedbed to another suitable for further growth **7 :** to cause to be or stand erect ⟨a dog ~*ing* his ears⟩ ~ *vi* **1 a :** to prick something or cause a pricking sensation **b :** to feel discomfort as if from being pricked **2 a :** to urge a horse with the spur **b :** to ride fast **3 :** THRUST **4 :** to become directed upward **:** POINT — **prick up one's ears :** to listen intently

prick·er \ˈprik-ər\ *n* **1 :** one that pricks; *specif* **:** a military light horseman **2 :** BRIAR, PRICKLE, THORN

prick·et \ˈprik-ət\ *n* [ME *priket*, fr. *prikke*] **1 a :** a spike on which a candle is stuck **b :** a candlestick with such a point **2 :** a buck in his second year

1prick·le \ˈprik-əl\ *n* [ME *prikle*, fr. OE *pricle;* akin to OE *prica* prick] **1 :** a fine sharp process or projection; *esp* **:** a sharp pointed emergence arising from the epidermis or bark of a plant **2 :** a prickling sensation

2prickle *vb* **prick·ling** \-(ə-)liŋ\ *vt* **1 :** to prick slightly **2 :** to produce prickles in ~ *vi* **:** to cause or feel a prickling or stinging sensation **:** TINGLE

prick·li·ness \ˈprik-lē-nəs\ *n* **:** the quality or state of being prickly

prick·ly \ˈprik-lē, -ə-lē\ *adj* **1 :** full of or covered with prickles; *esp* **:** distinguished from related kinds by the presence of prickles **2 :** PRICKLING, STINGING **3 a :** VEXATIOUS **b :** easily irritated **:** SENSITIVE

prickly ash *n* **:** a prickly aromatic shrub or small tree (*Zanthoxylum americanum*) of the rue family with yellowish flowers

prickly heat *n* **:** a noncontagious cutaneous eruption of red pimples with intense itching and tingling caused by inflammation around the sweat ducts

prickly pear *n* **:** any of a large genus (*Opuntia*) of cacti with yellow flowers and flat or terete joints usu. studded with tubercles bearing spines or prickly hairs; *also* **:** its pulpy pear-shaped edible fruit

prickly poppy *n* **:** any of a genus (*Argemone*) of plants of the poppy family with prickly leaves and white or yellow flowers; *esp* **:** a yellow-flowered Mexican annual (*A. mexicana*)

1pride \ˈprīd\ *n* [ME, fr. OE *prȳde*, fr. *prūd* proud — more at PROUD] **1 :** the quality or state of being proud: as **a :** inordinate self-esteem **:** CONCEIT **b :** a reasonable or justifiable self-respect **c :** delight or elation arising from some act or possession **2 :** proud or disdainful behavior or treatment **:** DISDAIN **3 a :** ostentatious display **b :** highest pitch **:** PRIME **4 :** something that excites pride **:** PICK **5 :** a company of lions

2pride *vt* **:** to indulge in pride **:** PLUME ⟨~ oneself on one's skill⟩

pride·ful \ˈprīd-fəl\ *adj* **:** full of pride: as **a :** HAUGHTY **b :** ELATED — **pride·ful·ly** \-fə-lē\ *adv* — **pride·ful·ness** *n*

prie–dieu \prēd-ˈyə(r)\ *n, pl* **prie–dieux** \-ˈyə(r)(z)\ [F, lit., pray God] **1 :** a prayer desk with a kneeling bench and bookshelf **2 :** a low armless upholstered chair with a high straight back

pri·er \ˈprī(-ə)r\ *n* **:** one that pries

priest \ˈprēst\ *n* [ME *preist*, fr. OE *prēost*, modif. of LL *presbyter*, fr. Gk *presbyteros* elder, priest, compar. of *presbys* old man] **:** one authorized to perform the sacred rites of a religion esp. as a mediatory agent between man and God; *specif* **:** an Anglican, Eastern Orthodox, or Roman Catholic clergyman ranking below a bishop and above a deacon — **priest·ess** \ˈprē-stəs\ *n*

priest·hood \ˈprēst-ˌhu̇d, ˈprē-ˌstu̇d\ *n* **1 :** the office, dignity, or character of a priest **2 :** the whole body of priests

priest·li·ness \ˈprēst-lē-nəs\ *n* **:** the quality, manner, or characteristics of a priest

priest·ly \ˈprēst-lē\ *adj* **1 :** of or relating to a priest or the priesthood **:** SACERDOTAL **2 :** characteristic of or befitting a priest

priest–rid·den \ˈprē-ˌstrid-ᵊn\ *adj* **:** controlled or oppressed by a priest

1prig \ˈprig\ *n* [*prig* (to steal)] **:** THIEF

2prig *n* [prob. fr. 1*prig*] **1** *archaic* **:** FELLOW, PERSON **2** *archaic* **:** FOP **3 :** one who offends or irritates by observance of proprieties in a pointed manner or to an obnoxious degree — **prig·gery** \-ə-rē\ *n* — **prig·gish** \ˈprig-ish\ *adj* — **prig·gish·ly** *adv* — **prig·gish·ness** *n*

prig·gism \ˈprig-ˌiz-əm\ *n* **:** stilted adherence to convention **:** PRIGGISHNESS

prill \ˈpril\ *vt* [perh. fr. E dial. *prill* (a running stream)] **:** to convert (a solid) into spherical pellets

1prim \ˈprim\ *vt* **primmed; prim·ming** [origin unknown] **1 :** to make prim **2 :** to dress primly

2prim *adj* **prim·mer; prim·mest 1 a :** stiffly formal and precise **:** DECOROUS **b :** PRUDISH **2 :** NEAT, TRIM — **prim·ly** *adv* — **prim·ness** *n*

pri·ma ballerina \ˌprē-mə-\ *n* [It, leading ballerina] **:** the leading female dancer in a ballet company

pri·ma·cy \ˈprī-mə-sē\ *n* **1 :** the state of being first (as in rank) **2 :** the office, rank, or character of an ecclesiastical primate

pri·ma don·na \ˌprim-ə-ˈdän-ə, ˌprē-mə-\ *n, pl* **prima donnas** [It, lit., first lady] **1 :** a principal female singer in an opera or concert organization **2 :** an extremely sensitive, vain, or undisciplined performer

1pri·ma fa·cie \ˌprī-mə-ˈfā-shə, -s(h)ē *also* ˌprē-, -shē-ə, -shē-ˌē\ *adv* [L] **:** at first view **:** on the first appearance

2prima facie *adj* **1 :** true, valid, or sufficient at first impression **:** APPARENT **2 :** SELF-EVIDENT **3 :** legally sufficient to establish a fact or a case unless disproved

pri·mal \ˈprī-məl\ *adj* **1 :** ORIGINAL, PRIMITIVE **2 :** first in importance **:** FUNDAMENTAL

pri·mar·i·ly \prī-ˈmer-ə-lē *also* prə-\ *adv* **1 :** FUNDAMENTALLY **2 :** in the first place **:** ORIGINALLY

1pri·ma·ry \ˈprī-ˌmer-ē, ˈprīm-(ə-)rē\ *adj* [LL *primarius* basic, primary, fr. L, principal, fr. *primus*] **1 a :** first in order of time or development **:** PRIMITIVE **b :** of or relating to formations of the Paleozoic and earlier periods **2 a :** of first rank, importance, or value **:** PRINCIPAL **b :** BASIC, FUNDAMENTAL **c :** of, relating to, or constituting the principal quills of a bird's wing **d :** of or relating to agriculture, forestry, and the extractive industries or their products **e :** expressive of present or future time ⟨~ tense⟩ **f :** of, relating to, or constituting the strongest of the three or four degrees of stress recognized by most linguists ⟨the first syllable of *basketball* carries ~ stress⟩ **3 a :** DIRECT, FIRSTHAND **b :** not derivable from other colors ⟨~ color⟩ **c :** preparatory to something else in a continuing process ⟨~ school⟩ **d :** belonging

to the first group or order in successive divisions, combinations, or ramifications ⟨~ nerves⟩ **e :** of, relating to, or constituting the inducing current or its circuit in an induction coil or transformer **4 :** resulting from the substitution of one of two or more atoms or groups in a molecule; *esp* **:** being or characterized by a carbon atom united by a single valence to only one chain or ring member

[2]**primary** *n* **1 :** something that stands first in rank, importance, or value **:** FUNDAMENTAL — usu. used in pl. **2** [short for *primary planet*] **:** a planet as distinguished from its satellites **3 :** one of the usu. 9 or 10 strong quills on the distal joint of a bird's wing **4 a :** any of a set of colors from which all other colors may be derived **b :** a primary-color sensation **5 a :** CAUCUS **b :** an election in which qualified voters nominate or express a preference for a particular candidate or group of candidates for political office, choose party officials, or select delegates for a party convention

primary atypical pneumonia *n* **:** a usu. mild pneumonia believed to be caused by a virus

primary cell *n* **:** a cell that converts chemical energy into electrical energy by irreversible chemical reactions

primary coil *n* **:** the coil through which the inducing current passes in an induction coil or transformer

primary road *n* **:** a principal usu. state-maintained road in a recognized system of highways

pri·mate \'prī-,māt *or esp for 1* -mət\ *n* [ME *primat*, fr. OF, fr. ML *primat-*, *primas* archbishop, fr. L, leader, fr. *primus*] **1** *often cap* **:** a bishop who has precedence in a province, group of provinces, or a nation **2** *archaic* **:** one first in authority or rank **:** LEADER **3 :** any of an order (Primates) of mammals comprising man together with the apes, monkeys, and related forms (as lemurs and tarsiers) — **pri·mate·ship** \-,ship\ *n* — **pri·ma·tial** \prī-'mā-shəl\ *adj*

[1]**prime** \'prīm\ *n* [ME, fr. OE *prīm*, fr. L *prima hora* first hour] **1 a** *often cap* **:** the second of the canonical hours **b :** the 1st hour of the day **2 a :** the earliest stage **b :** SPRING **c :** YOUTH **3 :** the most active, thriving, or successful stage or period **4 :** the chief or best individual or part **:** PICK **5 :** a number that has no factor except itself and one **6 :** UNISON 2 **7 :** the first of the eight defensive positions in fencing **8 :** the symbol ′

[2]**prime** *adj* [ME, fr. MF, fem. of *prin* first, fr. L *primus;* akin to L *prior*] **1 :** first in time **:** ORIGINAL **2 a :** having no factor except itself and one ⟨3 is a ~ number⟩ **b :** having no common factor except one ⟨12 and 25 are relatively ~⟩ **3 a :** first in rank, authority, or significance **:** PRINCIPAL **b :** first in excellence, quality, or value ⟨~ beef⟩ **4 :** not deriving from something else **:** PRIMARY — **prime·ly** *adv* — **prime·ness** *n*

[3]**prime** *vb* [prob. fr. [1]*prime*] *vt* **1 :** FILL, LOAD **2 :** to prepare for firing by supplying with priming or a primer **3 :** to lay the first color, coating, or preparation on in painting **4 :** to put into working order by filling or charging with something **5 :** to instruct beforehand **:** COACH **6 :** STIMULATE ~ *vi* **:** to become prime

prime cost *n* **:** the combined total of raw material and direct labor costs incurred in production

prime meridian *n* **:** the meridian of 0° longitude which runs through the original site of the Royal Observatory at Greenwich, England, and from which other longitudes are reckoned east and west

prime minister *n* **1 :** the chief minister of a ruler or state **2 :** the official head of a cabinet or ministry; *esp* **:** the chief executive of a parliamentary government — **prime ministership** *n* — **prime ministry** *n*

prime mover *n* [trans. of ML *primus motor*] **1 :** the self-moved being that is the source of all motion **2 :** a powerful tractor or truck usu. with all-wheel drive **3 :** the original or most effective force in an undertaking or work

[1]**prim·er** \'prim-ər, *esp Brit* 'prī-mər\ *n* [ME, fr. ML *primarium*, fr. LL, neut. of *primarius* primary] **1 :** a small book for teaching children to read **2 :** a small introductory book on a subject

[2]**prim·er** \'prī-mər\ *n* **1 :** a device for priming; *esp* **:** a cap, tube, or wafer containing percussion powder or compound used to ignite an explosive charge **2 :** PRIMING

pri·me·ro \pri-'me(ə)r-(,)ō, -'mi(ə)r-\ *n* [modif. of Sp *primera*] **:** an old card game in which each player holds three or four cards

pri·me·val \prī-'mē-vəl\ *adj* [L *primaevus*, fr. *primus* first + *aevum* age — more at AYE] **:** of or relating to the earliest ages **:** PRIMITIVE — **pri·me·val·ly** \-və-lē\ *adv*

prim·ing *n* **1 :** the act of one that primes **2 :** the explosive used in priming a charge **3 :** the material used in priming a surface

pri·mip·a·ra \prī-'mip-ə-rə\ *n, pl* **primiparas** *or* **pri·mip·a·rae** \-,rē, -,rī\ [L, fr. *primus* first + *-para*] **1 :** an individual bearing a first offspring **2 :** an individual that has borne only one offspring — **pri·mi·par·i·ty** \,prī-mə-'par-ət-ē\ *n* — **pri·mip·a·rous** \prī-'mip-ə-rəs\ *adj*

[1]**prim·i·tive** \'prim-ət-iv\ *adj* [ME *primitif*, fr. L *primitivus*, fr. *primitus* originally, fr. *primus* first — more at PRIME] **1 a :** not derived **:** ORIGINAL, PRIMARY **b :** assumed as a basis; *esp* **:** AXIOMATIC **2 a :** of or relating to the earliest age or period **:** PRIMEVAL **b :** little evolved and closely approximating an early ancestral type **:** ARCHAIC **c :** belonging to or characteristic of an early stage of development **:** RUDIMENTARY **d :** of, relating to, or constituting the assumed parent speech of related languages ⟨~ Germanic⟩ **3 a :** ELEMENTAL, NATURAL **b :** of or relating to a relatively simple people or culture **c :** NAÏVE **d** (1) **:** SELF-TAUGHT, UNTUTORED (2) **:** produced by a self-taught artist — **prim·i·tive·ly** *adv* — **prim·i·tive·ness** *n*

[2]**primitive** *n* **1 a :** something primitive; *specif* **:** a primitive idea, term, or proposition **b :** a root word **2 a** (1) **:** an artist of an early period of a culture or artistic movement (2) **:** a later imitator or follower of such an artist **b** (1) **:** a self-taught artist (2) **:** an artist whose work is marked by directness and naïveté **c :** a work of art produced by a primitive artist **3 a :** a member of a primitive people **b :** an unsophisticated person

prim·i·tiv·ism \-iv-,iz-əm\ *n* **1 :** belief in the superiority of a simple way of life close to nature **2 :** the style of art of primitive peoples or primitive artists — **prim·i·tiv·ist** \-əst\ *n or adj* — **prim·i·tiv·is·tic** \,prim-ət-iv-'is-tik\ *adj*

[1]**pri·mo** \'prē-(,)mō, 'prī-\ *adv* (*or adj*) [L, fr. *primus*] **:** in the first place **:** FIRST

[2]**pri·mo** \'prē-(,)mō\ *n* [It, fr. *primo* first, fr. L *primus*] **:** the first or leading part (as in a duet or trio)

pri·mo·gen·i·tor \,prī-mō-'jen-ət-ər\ *n* [LL, fr. L *primus* + *genitor* begetter, fr. *genitus*, pp. of *gignere* to beget — more at KIN] **:** ANCESTOR, FOREFATHER

pri·mo·gen·i·ture \-'jen-ə-,chu̇(ə)r, -i-chər, -ə-,t(y)u̇(ə)r\ *n* [LL *primogenitura*, fr. L *primus* + *genitura* birth, fr. *genitus*, pp.] **1 :** the state of being the firstborn of the children of the same parents **2 :** an exclusive right of inheritance belonging to the eldest son

pri·mor·di·al \prī-'mȯrd-ē-əl\ *adj* [ME, fr. LL *primordialis*, fr. L *primordium* origin, fr. neut. of *primordius* original, fr. *primus* first + *ordiri* to begin — more at PRIME, ORDER] **1 a :** first created or developed **:** PRIMEVAL **b :** earliest formed in the growth of an individual or organ **:** PRIMITIVE **2 :** FUNDAMENTAL, PRIMARY — **pri·mor·di·al·ly** \-ə-lē\ *adv*

pri·mor·di·um \-ē-əm\ *n, pl* **pri·mor·dia** \-ē-ə\ [NL, fr. L] **:** the rudiment or commencement of a part or organ

primp \'primp\ *vb* [perh. alter. of [1]*prim*] *vt* **:** to dress, adorn, or arrange in a careful or finicky manner ~ *vi* **:** to dress or groom oneself carefully

prim·rose \'prim-,rōz\ *n* [ME *primerose*, fr. MF] **:** any of a genus (*Primula* of the family Primulaceae, the primrose family) of perennial herbs with large tufted basal leaves and showy variously colored flowers

primrose path *n* **1 :** a path of ease or pleasure and esp. sensual pleasure **2 :** a path of least resistance

primrose yellow *n* **1 :** a light to moderate greenish yellow **2 :** a light to moderate yellow

prim·u·la \'prim-yə-lə\ *n* [ML, fr. *primula veris*, lit., firstling of spring] **:** PRIMROSE

pri·mum mo·bi·le \,prē-,mu̇m-'mō-bi-,lā\ *n, pl* **primum mobiles** [ME, fr. ML, lit., first moving thing] **:** the outermost concentric sphere conceived in medieval astronomy as carrying the spheres of the fixed stars and the planets in its daily revolution

pri·mus \'prī-məs\ *n, often cap* [ML, one who is first, magnate, fr. L, first — more at PRIME] **:** the first in dignity of the bishops of the Episcopal Church in Scotland who has certain privileges but no metropolitan authority

pri·mus in·ter pa·res \'prē-mə-,sint-ər-'pär-,ās\ *n* [L] **:** first among equals

prince \'prin(t)s\ *n* [ME, fr. OF, fr. L *princip-*, *princeps*, lit., one who is taken as first, fr. *primus* first + *capere* to take — more at HEAVE] **1 a :** MONARCH, KING **b :** the ruler of a principality or state **2 :** a male member of a royal family; *esp* **:** a son of the king **3 :** a nobleman of varying rank and status **4 :** a person of high rank or of high standing in his class or profession — **prince·dom** \-dəm, 'prin(t)-stəm\ *n* — **prince·ship** \'prin(t)s-,ship\ *n*

Prince Al·bert \prin-'sal-bərt\ *n* [Prince *Albert* Edward (later Edward VII king of England) †1910] **:** a long double-breasted frock coat

prince charming *n* [*Prince Charming*, hero of the fairy-tale *Cinderella* by Charles Perrault] **:** a suitor who fulfills the dreams of his beloved; *also* **:** a man of often specious affability and charm toward women

prince consort *n, pl* **princes consort :** the husband of a reigning female sovereign

prince·kin \'prin(t)-skən\ *n* **:** a small prince

prince·let \'prin(t)-slət\ *n* **:** a petty prince

prince·li·ness \-slē-nəs\ *n* **1 :** princely conduct or character **2 :** LUXURY, MAGNIFICENCE

prince·ling \'prin(t)-sliŋ\ *n* **:** PRINCELET

prince·ly \'prin(t)-slē\ *adj* **1 :** of or relating to a prince **:** ROYAL **2 :** characteristic of a prince **:** NOBLE — **princely** *adv*

Prince of Wales \-'wā(ə)lz\ **:** the male heir apparent to the British throne — used only after the title has been specif. conferred by the sovereign

prince's-feath·er \'prin(t)-səz-,feth-ər\ *n* **:** a showy annual plant (*Amaranthus hybridus hypochondriacus*) of the amaranth family often cultivated for its dense usu. red spikes of bloom

[1]**prin·cess** \'prin(t)-səs, 'prin-,ses, (*usual Brit*) prin-'ses\ *n* **1** *archaic* **:** a woman having sovereign power **2 :** a female member of a royal family; *esp* **:** a daughter or granddaughter of a sovereign **3 :** the consort of a prince **4 :** a woman or something personified as female that is outstanding in some respect

[2]**princess** *like* [1]\ *or* **prin·cesse** \prin-'ses\ *adj* [F *princesse* princess, fr. *prince*] **:** close-fitting and usu. with gores from neck to flaring hemline ⟨~ gown⟩

princess royal *n, pl* **princesses royal :** the eldest daughter of a sovereign

[1]**prin·ci·pal** \'prin(t)-s(ə-)pəl, -sə-bəl\ *adj* [ME, fr. OF, fr. L *principalis*, fr. *princip-*, *princeps*] **1 :** most important, consequential, or influential **:** CHIEF **2 :** of, relating to, or constituting principal or a principal — **prin·ci·pal·ly** \-ē, 'prin(t)-splē\ *adv*

[2]**principal** *n* **1 :** a person who has controlling authority or is in a leading position: as **a :** a chief or head man or woman **b :** the chief executive officer of an educational institution (as a high school) **c :** one who employs another to act for him subject to his general control and instruction; *specif* **:** the person from whom an agent's authority derives **d :** the chief or an actual participant in a crime **e :** the person primarily or ultimately liable on a legal obligation **f :** a leading performer **:** STAR **2 :** a matter or thing of primary importance: as **a** (1) **:** a capital sum placed at interest, due as a debt, or used as a fund (2) **:** the corpus of an estate, portion, devise, or bequest **b :** the construction that gives shape and strength to a roof and is usu. one of several trusses — **prin·ci·pal·ship** \'prin(t)-s(ə-)pəl-,ship, -sə-bəl-\ *n*

prin·ci·pal·i·ty \,prin(t)s-(ə-)'pal-ət-ē\ *n* **1 :** the office or position of a prince or principal **2 :** the territory or jurisdiction of a prince or the country that gives title to a prince **3 :** an angel of the third lowest rank

principal parts *n pl* **:** a series of verb forms from which all the other forms of a verb can be derived including in English the infinitive, the past tense, and the past participle

prin·cip·i·um \prin-'sip-ē-əm, priŋ-'kip-\ *n, pl* **prin·cip·ia** \-ē-ə\ [L, beginning, basis] **:** a fundamental principle

prin·ci·ple \'prin(t)-s(ə-)pəl, -sə-bəl\ *n* [ME, modif. of MF *principe*, fr. L *principium* beginning, fr. *princip-*, *princeps* taken as first — more at PRINCE] **1 a :** a comprehensive and fundamental law, doctrine, or assumption **b** (1) **:** a rule or code of conduct (2) **:** habitual devotion to right principles **c :** the laws or facts of nature underlying the working of an artificial device **2 a :** a primary source **:** ORIGIN **b :** an underlying faculty or endowment **3 :** a distinguishable ingredient that exhibits or imparts a char-

acteristic quality **4** *cap, Christian Science* **:** a divine principle **:** GOD
prin·ci·pled \-s(ə-)pəld, -sə-bəld\ *adj* **:** exhibiting, based on, or characterized by principle — often used in combination ⟨high-*principled*⟩
prin·cox \'prin-,käks, 'priŋ-\ *n* [origin unknown] *archaic* **:** a pert youth **:** COXCOMB
prink \'priŋk\ *vb* [prob. alter. of 2*prank*] **:** PRIMP — **prink·er** *n*
1**print** \'print\ *n* [ME *preinte*, fr. OF, fr. *preint*, pp. of *preindre* to press, fr. L *premere* — more at PRESS] **1 a :** a mark made by pressure **:** IMPRESSION **b :** something impressed with a print or formed in a mold **2 :** a device or instrument for impressing or forming a print **3 a :** printed state or form **b :** the printing industry **4 :** printed matter **5 :** printed letters **:** TYPE **6 a :** a copy made by printing **b :** cloth with a pattern or figured design applied by printing; *also* **:** an article of such cloth **c :** a photographic copy; *esp* **:** one made from a negative — **in print :** procurable from the publisher — **out of print :** not procurable from the publisher
2**print** *vt* **1 a :** to impress something in or on **b :** to stamp (as a mark) in or on something **2 a :** to make a copy of by impressing paper against an inked printing surface **b** (1) **:** to impress (as wallpaper) with a design or pattern (2) **:** to impress (a pattern or design) on something **c :** to publish in print **3 :** to write in letters shaped like those of ordinary roman text type **4 :** to make (a positive picture) on sensitized photographic surface from a negative or a positive ~ *vi* **1 a :** to work as a printer **b :** to produce printed matter **2 :** to produce something in printed form
print·abil·i·ty \,print-ə-'bil-ət-ē\ *n* **:** the quality or state of being printable
print·able \'print-ə-bəl\ *adj* **1 :** capable of being printed or of being printed from **2 :** considered fit to publish
printed circuit *n* **:** a circuit for electronic apparatus made by depositing conductive material in continuous paths from terminal to terminal on an insulating surface
printed matter *n* **:** matter printed by any of various mechanical processes that is eligible for mailing at a special rate
print·er \'print-ər\ *n* **:** one that prints: as **a :** one engaged in printing **b :** a device used for printing; *specif* **:** a machine for printing from photographic negatives
printer's devil *n* **:** an apprentice in a printing office
printer's mark *n* **:** IMPRINT b
print·ery \'print-ə-rē\ *n* **:** PRINTING OFFICE
print·ing *n* **1 :** reproduction in printed form **2 :** the art, practice, or business of a printer **3 :** IMPRESSION 4c **4** *pl* **:** paper to be printed on
printing office *n* **:** an establishment where printing is done
printing plate *n* **:** PRINTING SURFACE
printing press *n* **:** a machine that produces printed copies (as by letterpress or lithography)
printing surface *n* **:** a prepared surface from which printing is done
print·less \'print-ləs\ *adj* **:** making, bearing, or taking no imprint
print·out \-,au̇t\ *n* **:** a printed record produced automatically (as by a computer)
1**pri·or** \'prī(-ə)r\ *n* [ME, fr. OE & MF, fr. ML, fr. LL, administrator, fr. L, former, superior, compar. of OL *pri* before; akin to L *priscus* ancient, *prae* before — more at FOR] **1 :** the superior ranking next to the abbot of a monastery **2 :** the superior of a house or group of houses of any of various religious communities — **pri·or·ate** \'prī-ə-rət\ *n* — **pri·or·ship** \'prī(-ə)r-,ship\ *n*
2**pri·or** \'prī(-ə)r\ *adj* **1 :** earlier in time or order **2 :** taking precedence (as in importance) **syn** see PRECEDING — **pri·or·ly** *adv*
pri·or·ess \'prī-ə-rəs\ *n* **:** a nun corresponding in rank to a prior
pri·or·i·ty \prī-'ȯr-ət-ē, -'är-\ *n* **1 a** (1) **:** the quality or state of being prior (2) **:** precedence in date or position of publication — used of taxa **b** (1) **:** superiority in rank, position, or privilege (2) **:** legal precedence in exercise of rights over the same subject matter **2 :** a preferential rating; *esp* **:** one that allocates rights to goods and services usu. in limited supply **3 :** something meriting prior attention
prior to *prep* **:** in advance of **:** BEFORE ⟨pay the balance due *prior to* receiving the goods⟩
pri·o·ry \'prī-(ə-)rē\ *n* **:** a religious house under a prior or prioress **syn** see CLOISTER
prise *chiefly Brit var of* PRIZE
pri·sere \'prī-,si(ə)r\ *n* [1*primary* + *sere*] **:** the succession of vegetational stages that occurs in passing from bare earth or water to a climax community
prism \'priz-əm\ *n* [LL *prismat-*, *prisma*, fr. Gk, lit., anything sawn, fr. *priein* to saw] **1 :** a polyhedron with two faces that are polygons in parallel planes and the other faces parallelograms — see VOLUME table **2 a :** a transparent body bounded in part by two plane faces that are not parallel used to deviate or disperse a beam of light **b :** a prism-shaped decorative glass luster **3 :** a crystal form whose faces are parallel to one axis; *specif* **:** one whose faces are parallel to the vertical axis

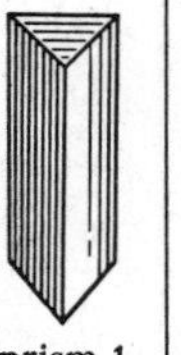
prism 1

pris·mat·ic \priz-'mat-ik\ *adj* **1 :** relating to, resembling, or constituting a prism **2 a :** formed by a prism **b :** resembling the colors formed by refraction of light through a prism ⟨~ effects⟩ **3 :** highly colored **:** BRILLIANT **4 :** having such symmetry that a general form with faces cutting all axes at unspecified intercepts is a prism ⟨~ crystals⟩ — **pris·mat·i·cal·ly** \-i-k(ə-)lē\ *adv*
pris·moid \'priz-,mȯid\ *n* **:** a polyhedron with two parallel similar and not congruent bases and faces that are trapezoids — **pris·moi·dal** \priz-'mȯid-ᵊl\ *adj*
1**pris·on** \'priz-ᵊn\ *n* [ME, fr. OF, fr. L *prehension-*, *prehensio* act of seizing, fr. *prehensus*, pp. of *prehendere* to seize — more at PREHENSILE] **1 :** a state of confinement or captivity **2 :** a place of confinement: as **a :** a building in which persons are confined for safe custody while on trial for an offense or for punishment after trial and conviction **b :** an institution for the imprisonment of persons convicted of serious crimes **:** PENITENTIARY
2**prison** *vt* **:** IMPRISON, CONFINE
prison camp *n* **1 :** a camp for the confinement of reasonably trustworthy prisoners usu. employed on government projects **2 :** a camp for prisoners of war
pris·on·er \'priz-nər, -ᵊn-ər\ *n* **:** a person deprived of his liberty and kept under involuntary restraint, confinement, or custody; *esp* **:** one on trial or in prison
prisoner of war : a person captured or interned by a belligerent power because of war with several exceptions provided by international law or agreements
prisoner's base *n* **:** a game in which players of one team seek to tag and imprison players of the other team who have ventured out of their home territory
prison fever *n* **:** typhus fever
pris·si·ly \'pris-ə-lē\ *adv* **:** in a prissy manner
pris·si·ness \'pris-ē-nəs\ *n* **:** the quality or state of being prissy
pris·sy \'pris-ē\ *adj* [prob. blend of *prim* and *sissy*] **:** being prim and precise **:** FINICKY
pris·tine \'pris-,tēn *also* pris-'\ *adj* [L *pristinus*; akin to L *prior*] **1 :** belonging to the earliest period or state **2 a :** UNCORRUPTED ⟨~ innocence⟩ **b :** being fresh and clean — **pris·tine·ly** *adv*
prith·ee \'prith-ē, 'prith-\ *interj* [alter. of (*I*) *pray thee*] *archaic* — used to express a wish or request
pri·va·cy \'prī-və-sē, *Brit also* 'priv-ə-\ *n* **1 :** the quality or state of being apart from company or observation **:** SECLUSION **2** *archaic* **:** a place of seclusion **3 :** SECRECY
pri·vat·do·cent *or* **pri·vat·do·zent** \pri-'vät-dō-,sent\ *n* [G *privatdozent*, fr. *privat* private + *dozent* teacher] **:** an unsalaried university lecturer or teacher in German-speaking countries remunerated directly by students' fees
1**pri·vate** \'prī-vət\ *adj* [ME *privat*, fr. L *privatus*, fr. pp. of *privare* to deprive, release, fr. *privus* private, set apart; akin to L *pro* for — more at FOR] **1 a :** intended for or affecting a particular person, group, or class ⟨~ park⟩ **b :** belonging to or concerning an individual person, company, or interest ⟨~ house⟩ **c** (1) **:** restricted to the individual or arising independently of others ⟨~ opinion⟩ (2) **:** carried on by the individual independently of the usual institutions ⟨~ study⟩; *also* **:** being educated by independent study or a tutor or in a private school ⟨~ students⟩ **d :** not general in effect ⟨~ statute⟩ **e :** of, relating to, or receiving hospital service in which the patient has more privileges than a semiprivate or ward patient **2 a** (1) **:** not holding public office or employment ⟨~ citizen⟩ (2) **:** not related to one's official position **:** PERSONAL **b :** being a private ⟨~ soldier⟩ **3 a :** withdrawn from company or observation **:** SEQUESTERED **b :** not known or intended to be known publicly **:** SECRET **c :** unsuitable for public mention, use, or display ⟨one's ~ parts⟩ — **pri·vate·ly** *adv* — **pri·vate·ness** *n*
2**private** *n* **1** *archaic* **:** one not in public office **2** *obs* **:** PRIVACY **3 a :** a person of low rank in various organizations (as a police or fire department) **b :** an enlisted man of the lowest rank in the marine corps or the next to lowest in the army; *broadly* **:** any enlisted man in the army or marine corps ranking below a noncommissioned officer — **in private :** PRIVATELY, SECRETLY
pri·va·teer \,prī-və-'ti(ə)r\ *n* **1 :** an armed private ship commissioned to cruise against the commerce or warships of an enemy **2 :** the commander or one of the crew of a privateer — **privateer** *vi* — **pri·va·teers·man** \-'ti(ə)rz-mən\ *n*
private first class *n* **:** an enlisted man ranking in the army above a private and below a corporal and in the marine corps above a private and below a lance corporal
private law *n* **:** a branch of law concerned with private persons, property, and relationships — compare PUBLIC LAW
private school *n* **:** a school that is established, conducted, and primarily supported by a nongovernmental agency
private treaty *n* **:** a sale of property on terms determined by conference of the seller and buyer — compare AUCTION
pri·va·tion \prī-'vā-shən\ *n* [ME *privacion*, fr. MF *privation*, fr. L *privation-*, *privatio*, fr. *privatus*, pp. of *privare*] **1 :** an act or instance of depriving **:** DEPRIVATION **2 :** the state of being deprived; *esp* **:** lack of what is needed for existence
1**priv·a·tive** \'priv-ət-iv\ *n* **:** a privative term, expression, or proposition; *also* **:** a privative prefix or suffix
2**privative** *adj* **:** constituting or predicating privation or absence of a quality ⟨*a-*, *un-*, *non-* are ~ prefixes⟩ ⟨*blind* is a ~ term⟩ — **priv·a·tive·ly** *adv*
priv·et \'priv-ət\ *n* [origin unknown] **:** an ornamental shrub (*Ligustrum vulgare*) of the olive family with half-evergreen leaves and small white flowers widely used for hedges; *broadly* **:** any of various similar shrubs of the same genus
1**priv·i·lege** \'priv-(ə-)lij\ *n* [ME, fr. OF, fr. L *privilegium* law for or against a private person, fr. *privus* private + *leg-*, *lex* law — more at LEGAL] **:** a right or immunity granted as a peculiar benefit, advantage, or favor; *esp* **:** one attached specif. to a position or an office
2**privilege** *vt* **:** to grant a privilege to
priv·i·leged \-(ə-)lijd\ *adj* **1 :** having or enjoying one or more privileges ⟨~ classes⟩ **2 :** not subject to the usual rules or penalties because of some special circumstance ⟨a ~ communication⟩ **3 :** having a plenary indulgence attached to a mass celebrated thereon ⟨a ~ altar⟩
priv·i·ly \'priv-ə-lē\ *adv* **:** in a privy manner **:** PRIVATELY, SECRETLY
priv·i·ty \'priv-ət-ē\ *n* [ME *privite*, fr. OF, fr. ML *privitat-*, *privitas*, fr. L *privus* private — more at PRIVATE] **1 :** private or joint knowledge of a private matter; *esp* **:** cognizance implying concurrence **2 a :** a relationship between persons who successively have a legal interest in the same right or property **b :** an interest in a transaction, contract, or legal action to which one is not a party arising out of a relationship to one of the parties
1**privy** \'priv-ē\ *adj* [ME *prive*, fr. OF *privé*, fr. L *privatus* private] **1 :** belonging or relating to a person in his individual rather than his official capacity **2 a :** WITHDRAWN, PRIVATE **b :** SECRET **3 :** admitted as one sharing in a secret ⟨~ to the conspiracy⟩
2**privy** *n* **1 :** a person having a legal interest of privity **2 a :** a small building having a bench with holes through which the user may evacuate and usu. lacking means of automatic discharge **b :** TOILET 3b
privy council *n* **1** *archaic* **:** a secret or private council **2** *cap P&C* **:** a body of officials and dignitaries chosen by the British monarch as an advisory council to the Crown usu. functioning through its committees **3 :** a usu. appointive advisory council to an executive — **privy councillor** *n*

privy purse *n, often cap both Ps* : an allowance for the private expenses of the British sovereign

prix fixe \'prē-'fēks, -'fiks\ *n* [F, fixed price] **1** : TABLE D'HÔTE **2** : the price charged for a table d'hôte meal

1**prize** \'prīz\ *n* [ME *pris* prize, price — more at PRICE] **1** : something offered or striven for in competition or in contests of chance; *also* : a premium given with merchandise as inducement to buy **2** : something exceptionally desirable **3** *archaic* : a contest for a reward : COMPETITON — **prize·win·ner** \-,win-ər\ *n* — **prize·win·ning** \-,win-iŋ\ *adj*

2**prize** *adj* **1 a** : awarded or worthy of a prize **b** : awarded as a prize **c** : entered for the sake of a prize **2** : OUTSTANDING

3**prize** *vt* [ME *prisen*, fr. MF *prisier*, fr. LL *pretiare*, fr. L *pretium* price, value — more at PRICE] **1** : to estimate the value of : RATE **2** : to value highly : ESTEEM **syn** see APPRECIATE

4**prize** *n* [ME *prise*, fr. OF, act of taking, fr. *prendre* to take, fr. L *prehendere* — more at PREHENSILE] **1** : something taken by force, stratagem, or threat; *esp* : property lawfully captured in time of war **2** : an act of capturing or taking; *esp* : the wartime capture of a ship and its cargo at sea **syn** see SPOIL

5**prize** *or chiefly Brit* **prise** \'prīz\ *vt* [*prize* (lever)] : to press, force, or move with a lever : PRY

prize·fight \'prīz-,fīt\ *n* [back-formation fr. *prizefighter*] : a contest between professional boxers for pay — **prize·fight·er** \-ər\ *n* — **prize·fight·ing** \-iŋ\ *n*

prize money *n* : a part of the proceeds of a captured ship formerly divided among the officers and men making the capture

priz·er \'prī-zər\ *n, archaic* : one that contends for a prize

prize ring *n* [*prizefight ring*] : a ring for a prizefight

1**pro** \'prō\ *n* [ME, fr. L, prep., for — more at FOR] : the affirmative side or one holding it

2**pro** *adv* [*pro-*] : on the affirmative side

3**pro** \(,)prō\ *prep* [L] : in favor of : FOR

4**pro** \'prō\ *n or adj* : PROFESSIONAL

1**pro-** *prefix* [ME, fr. OF, fr. L, fr. Gk, before, forward, forth, for, fr. *pro* — more at FOR] **1 a** : earlier than : prior to : before ⟨*pro*thalamion⟩ **b** : rudimentary : PROT- ⟨*pro*nucleus⟩ **2 a** : located in front of or at the front of : anterior to ⟨*pro*cephalic⟩ ⟨*pro*ventriculus⟩ **b** : front : anterior ⟨*pro*thorax⟩ **3** : projecting ⟨*pro*gnathous⟩

2**pro-** *prefix* [L, before, forward, forth, for, fr. *pro* in front of, before, for — more at FOR] **1** : taking the place of : substituting for ⟨*pro*cathedral⟩ **2** : favoring : supporting : championing ⟨*pro*-American⟩

proa \'prō-ə\ *var of* PRAU

prob·a·bi·lism \'präb-(ə-)bə-,liz-əm\ *n* [F *probabilisme*, fr. L *probabilis* probable] **1** : a theory that certainty is impossible esp. in the sciences and that probability suffices to govern belief and action **2** : a theory that in disputed moral questions any solidly probable course may be followed even though an opposed course is or appears more probable — **prob·a·bi·list** \-ləst\ *adj or n*

prob·a·bi·lis·tic \,präb-(ə-)bə-'lis-tik\ *adj* **1** : of or relating to probabilism **2** : of, relating to, or based on probability

prob·a·bil·i·ty \,präb-ə-'bil-ət-ē\ *n* **1** : the quality or state of being probable **2** : something probable **3** : a mathematical basis for prediction that for an exhaustive set of outcomes is the ratio of the outcomes that would produce a given event to the total number of possible outcomes **4** : a logical relation between statements such that evidence confirming one confirms the other to some degree

prob·a·ble \'präb-(ə-)bəl\ *adj* [ME, fr. MF, fr. L *probabilis*, fr. *probare* to test, approve, prove — more at PROVE] **1** : supported by evidence strong enough to establish presumption but not proof ⟨a ~ hypothesis⟩ **2** : establishing a probability ⟨~ evidence⟩ **3** : likely to be or become true or real ⟨~ events⟩ — **prob·a·bly** \'präb-(ə-)blē, 'präb-lē\ *adv*

syn PROBABLE, POSSIBLE, LIKELY mean such as may be or may become true or actual. PROBABLE applies to what is supported by evidence that is strong but not conclusive; POSSIBLE applies to what lies within the known limits of performance, attainment, nature, or mode of existence of a thing or person regardless of the chances for or against its actuality; LIKELY differs from PROBABLE in implying either more superficial or more general grounds for judgment or belief

probable cause *n* : a reasonable ground for supposing that a criminal charge is well-founded

pro·band \'prō-,band, prō-'\ *n* [L *probandus*, gerundive of *probare*] : 1SUBJECT 3c(2)

pro·bang \'prō-,baŋ\ *n* [origin unknown] : a slender flexible rod with a sponge on one end used esp. for removing obstructions from the esophagus

1**pro·bate** \'prō-,bāt, *esp Brit* -bit\ *n* [ME *probat*, fr. L *probatum*, neut. of *probatus*, pp. of *probare*] **1 a** : the action or process of proving before a competent judicial authority that a document offered for official recognition and registration as the last will and testament of a deceased person is genuine **b** : the judicial determination of the validity of a will **2** : the officially authenticated copy of a probated will

2**pro·bate** \-,bāt\ *vt* **1** : to establish (a will) by probate as genuine and valid **2** : to put (a convicted offender) on probation

probate court *n* : a court having jurisdiction chiefly over the probate of wills and the administration of estates of deceased persons

pro·ba·tion \prō-'bā-shən\ *n* **1** : critical examination and evaluation or subjection to such examination and evaluation **2 a** : subjection of an individual to a period of testing and trial to ascertain fitness (as for a job or school) **b** : the action of suspending the sentence of a convicted offender and giving him freedom during good behavior under the supervision of a probation officer **c** : the state or a period of being subject to probation — **pro·ba·tion·al** \-shnəl, -shən-ᵊl\ *adj* — **pro·ba·tion·al·ly** \-ē\ *adv* — **pro·ba·tion·ary** \-shə-,ner-ē\ *adj*

pro·ba·tion·er \-sh(ə-)nər\ *n* **1** : one (as a newly admitted student nurse) whose fitness is being tested during a trial period **2** : a convicted offender on probation

probation officer *n* : an officer appointed to investigate, report on, and supervise the conduct of convicted offenders on probation

pro·ba·tive \'prō-bət-iv\ *adj* **1** : serving to test or try **2** : serving to prove

pro·ba·to·ry \'prō-bə-,tōr-ē, -,tȯr-\ *adj* : PROBATIVE

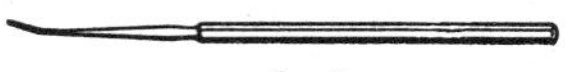

probe 1

1**probe** \'prōb\ *n* [ML *proba* examination, fr. L *probare*] **1** : a slender surgical instrument for examining a cavity **2 a** : a pointed metal tip for making electrical contact with a circuit element being checked **b** : a device used to penetrate or send back information from outer space **c** : a pipe on the receiving airplane thrust into the drogue of the delivering airplane in air refueling **3 a** : the action of probing **b** : a penetrating investigation **c** : a tentative exploratory advance or survey

2**probe** *vt* **1** : to examine with a probe **2** : to investigate thoroughly ~ *vi* : to make an exploratory investigation **syn** see ENTER — **prob·er** *n*

prob·it \'präb-ət\ *n* [*prob*ability un*it*] : a unit of measurement of statistical probability based on deviations from the mean of a normal frequency distribution

pro·bi·ty \'prō-bət-ē *also* 'präb-ət-\ *n* [MF *probité*, fr. L *probitat-*, *probitas*, fr. *probus* honest — more at PROVE] : adherence to the highest principles and ideals : UPRIGHTNESS **syn** see HONESTY

1**prob·lem** \'präb-ləm, 'präb-ᵊm, -,lem\ *n* [ME *probleme*, fr. MF, fr. L *problema*, fr. Gk *problēma*, lit., something thrown forward, fr. *proballein* to throw forward, fr. *pro-* forward + *ballein* to throw — more at PRO-, DEVIL] **1 a** : a question raised for inquiry, consideration, or solution **b** : a proposition in mathematics or physics stating something to be done **2 a** : an intricate unsettled question **b** : a source of perplexity or vexation **syn** see MYSTERY

2**problem** *adj* **1** : dealing with a problem of human conduct or social relationship **2** : difficult to deal with

prob·lem·at·ic \,präb-lə-'mat-ik\ *adj* **1 a** : difficult to solve or decide : PUZZLING **b** : not definite : DUBIOUS **c** : open to question or debate : QUESTIONABLE **2** : expressing or supporting a possibility **syn** see DOUBTFUL — **prob·lem·at·i·cal** \-i-kəl\ *adj* — **prob·lem·at·i·cal·ly** \-k(ə-)lē\ *adv*

pro·bos·ci·de·an \prə-,bäs-ə-'dē-ən\ *or* **pro·bos·cid·i·an** \prə-,bäs-'id-ē-ən, (,)prō-\ *n* [deriv. of L *proboscid-*, *proboscis*] : any of an order (Proboscidea) of large mammals comprising the elephants and extinct related forms — **proboscidean** *adj*

pro·bos·cis \prə-'bäs-əs\ *n, pl* **proboscises** *also* **pro·bos·ci·des** \-'bäs-ə-,dēz\ [L, fr. Gk *proboskis*, fr. *pro-* + *boskein* to feed; akin to Lith *gauja* herd] **1 a** : the trunk of an elephant; *also* : any long flexible snout **b** : the human nose esp. when prominent **2** : any of various elongated or extensible tubular processes of the oral region of an invertebrate

pro·caine \'prō-,kān\ *n* [ISV 2*pro-* + *cocaine*] : a basic ester $C_{13}H_{20}N_2O_2$ of para-aminobenzoic acid; *also* : its crystalline hydrochloride used as a local anesthetic

pro·cam·bi·al \(')prō-'kam-bē-əl\ *adj* : of, relating to, being, or derived from procambium

pro·cam·bi·um \-bē-əm\ *n* [NL] : the part of a plant meristem that forms cambium and primary vascular tissues

pro·ca·the·dral \,prō-kə-'thē-drəl\ *n* : a parish church used as a cathedral

pro·ce·dur·al \prə-'sēj-(ə-)rəl\ *adj* : of or relating to procedure esp. of courts or other bodies administering substantive law — **pro·ce·dur·al·ly** \-ē\ *adv*

pro·ce·dure \prə-'sē-jər\ *n* [F *procédure*, fr. MF, fr. *proceder*] **1 a** : a particular way of accomplishing something or of acting **b** : a step in a procedure **2** : a series of steps followed in a regular definite order **3 a** : a traditional or established way of doing things **b** : PROTOCOL 3

pro·ceed \prō-'sēd, prə-\ *vi* [ME *proceden*, fr. MF *proceder*, fr. L *procedere*, fr. *pro-* forward + *cedere* to go — more at PRO-, CEDE] **1** : to come forth from a source : ISSUE **2 a** : to continue after a pause or interruption **b** : to go on in an orderly regulated way **3 a** : to begin and carry on an action, process, or movement **b** : to be in the process of being accomplished **4** : to move along a course : ADVANCE **syn** see SPRING

pro·ceed·ing *n* **1** : PROCEDURE **2** *pl* : EVENTS, HAPPENINGS **3** *pl* : legal action ⟨divorce ~*s*⟩ **4** : AFFAIR, TRANSACTION **5** *pl* : an official record of things said or done

pro·ceeds \'prō-,sēdz\ *n pl* : the total amount or the profit arising from an investment, transaction, levy, or business : RETURN

pro·ce·phal·ic \,prō-sə-'fal-ik\ *adj* : relating to, forming, or situated on or near the front of the head

pro·cer·coid \(')prō-'sər-,kȯid\ *n* [*pro-* + Gk *kerkos* tail] : the solid first parasitic larva of some tapeworms that develops usu. in the body cavity of a copepod

1**pro·cess** \'präs-,es, 'prōs-, -əs\ *n, pl* **pro·cess·es** \-,es-əz, -ə-səz, -ə-,sēz\ [ME *proces*, fr. MF, fr. L *processus*, fr. *processus*, pp. of *procedere*] **1 a** : PROGRESS, ADVANCE **b** : something going on : PROCEEDING **2 a** : a natural phenomenon marked by gradual changes that lead toward a particular result ⟨~ of growth⟩ **b** : a series of actions or operations conducing to an end; *esp* : a continuous operation or treatment esp. in manufacture **3 a** : the whole course of proceedings in a legal action **b** : the summons, mandate, or writ used by a court to compel the appearance of the defendant in a legal action or compliance with its orders **4** : a prominent or projecting part of an organism or organic structure ⟨a bone ~⟩

2**process** *vt* **1 a** : to proceed against by law : PROSECUTE **b** (1) : to take out a summons against (2) : to serve a summons on **2** : to subject to a special process or treatment (as in the course of manufacture) — **pro·ces·sor** \-,es-ər, -ə-sər, -ə-,sō(ə)r\ *n*

3**process** *adj* **1** : treated or made by a special process esp. when involving synthesis or artificial modification **2** : made by or used in a mechanical or photomechanical duplicating process **3** : of or involving illusory effects usu. introduced during processing of the film ⟨~ motion-picture scene⟩

4**pro·cess** \prə-'ses\ *vi* [back-formation fr. 1*procession*] *chiefly Brit* : to move in a procession

process cheese *n* : a cheese made by blending several lots of cheese

1**pro·ces·sion** \prə-'sesh-ən\ *n* **1** : continuous forward movement : PROGRESSION **2 a** : a group of individuals moving along in an orderly often ceremonial way **b** : SUCCESSION, SEQUENCE

2**procession** \prə-'sesh-ən\ *vi* **pro·ces·sion·ing** \-'sesh-(ə-)niŋ\ *archaic* : to go in procession

1**pro·ces·sion·al** \prə-'sesh-nəl, -ən-ᵊl\ *n* **1** : a book containing material for a procession **2** : a musical composition (as a hymn) designed for a procession

2**processional** *adj* : of, relating to, or moving in a procession — **pro·ces·sion·al·ly** \-ē\ *adv*

process printing *n* : a method of printing from halftone plates in usu. three or more colors so that nearly any hue may be reproduced

pro·cès–ver·bal \prō-,sā-vər-'bäl, -(,)ver-\ *n, pl* **pro·cès–ver·baux**

\-ˈbō\ [F, lit., verbal trial] : an official written record

pro·claim \prō-ˈklām, prə-\ *vt* [ME *proclamen*, fr. MF or L; MF *proclamer*, fr. L *proclamare*, fr. *pro-* before + *clamare* to cry out — more at PRO-, CLAIM] **1 a :** to declare publicly through speech or writing **:** ANNOUNCE **b :** to give outward indication of **:** SHOW **2 :** to declare or declare to be solemnly, officially, or formally ⟨~ the country a republic⟩ **3 :** to praise or glorify openly or publicly **:** EXTOL **syn** see DECLARE — **pro·claim·er** *n*

proc·la·ma·tion \ˌpräk-lə-ˈmā-shən\ *n* [ME *proclamacion*, fr. MF *proclamation*, fr. L *proclamation-*, *proclamatio*, fr. *proclamatus*, pp. of *proclamare*] **1 :** the action of proclaiming **:** the state of being proclaimed **2 :** something proclaimed; *specif* **:** an official formal public announcement

pro·cli·max \(ˈ)prō-ˈklī-ˌmaks\ *n* **:** an ecological community that suggests a climax in stability and permanence but is not primarily the product of climate

pro·clit·ic \prō-ˈklit-ik\ *adj* [NL *procliticus*, fr. Gk *pro-* + LL *-cliticus* (as in *encliticus* enclitic)] **:** of, relating to, or constituting a word or particle without sentence stress that is accentually dependent upon a following stressed word and is pronounced with it as a phonetic unit — **proclitic** *n*

pro·cliv·i·ty \prō-ˈkliv-ət-ē\ *n* [L *proclivitas*, fr. *proclivis* sloping, prone, fr. *pro-* forward + *clivus* hill — more at PRO-, DECLIVITY] **:** an inclination or predisposition toward something; *esp* **:** a strong inherent inclination toward something objectionable **syn** see LEANING

Proc·ne \ˈpräk-nē\ *n* [L, fr. Gk *Proknē*] **:** a sister of Philomela transformed by the gods into a swallow

pro·con·sul \(ˈ)prō-ˈkän(t)-səl\ *n* [ME, fr. L, fr. *pro consule* for a consul] **1 :** a governor or military commander of an ancient Roman province **2 :** an administrator in a modern colony, dependency, or occupied area usu. with wide powers — **pro·con·su·lar** \-s(ə-)lər\ *adj* — **pro·con·su·late** \-s(ə-)lət\ *n* — **pro·con·sul·ship** \-səl-ˌship\ *n*

pro·cras·ti·nate \p(r)ə-ˈkras-tə-ˌnāt, prō-\ *vb* [L *procrastinatus*, pp. of *procrastinare*, fr. *pro-* forward + *crastinus* of tomorrow, fr. *cras* tomorrow] *vt* **:** to put off intentionally and habitually **:** POSTPONE ~ *vi* **:** to put off intentionally and reprehensibly the doing of something that should be done **syn** see DELAY — **pro·cras·ti·na·tion** \-ˌkras-tə-ˈnā-shən\ *n* — **pro·cras·ti·na·tor** \-ˈkras-tə-ˌnāt-ər\ *n*

pro·cre·ant \ˈprō-krē-ənt\ *adj* **:** PROCREATIVE

pro·cre·ate \-ˌāt\ *vb* [L *procreatus*, pp. of *procreare*, fr. *pro-* forth + *creare* to create — more at PRO-, CREATE] *vt* **:** to produce (offspring) by generation **:** PROPAGATE ~ *vi* **:** to produce offspring — **pro·cre·ation** \ˌprō-krē-ˈā-shən\ *n* — **pro·cre·ative** \ˈprō-krē-ˌāt-iv\ *adj* — **pro·cre·ator** \-ˌāt-ər\ *n*

pro·crus·te·an \p(r)ə-ˈkrəs-tē-ən, prō-\ *adj, often cap* **1 :** of, relating to, or typical of Procrustes **2 :** marked by arbitrary often ruthless disregard of individual differences or special circumstances

procrustean bed *n, often cap P* **:** a scheme or pattern into which someone or something is arbitrarily forced

Pro·crus·tes \-ˈkrəs-(ˌ)tēz\ *n* [L, fr. Gk *Prokroustēs*] **:** a legendary robber of ancient Greece noted for stretching or cutting off the legs of his victims to adapt them to the length of his bed

pro·cryp·tic \(ˈ)prō-ˈkrip-tik\ *adj* [*pro-* (as in *protect*) + *cryptic*] **:** of, relating to, or being a concealing pattern or shade of coloring esp. in insects

proc·to·dae·um \ˌpräk-tə-ˈdē-əm\ *n, pl* **proc·to·daea** \-ˈdē-ə\ *or* **proctodaeums** [NL, fr. Gk *prōktos* anus + *hodos* way — more at CEDE] **:** the posterior ectodermal part of the alimentary canal formed in the embryo by invagination of the outer body wall

proc·to·log·ic \ˌpräk-tə-ˈläj-ik\ *adj* **:** of or relating to proctology — **proc·to·log·i·cal** \-i-kəl\ *adj*

proc·tol·o·gist \präk-ˈtäl-ə-jəst\ *n* **:** a specialist in proctology

proc·tol·o·gy \-jē\ *n* [Gk *prōktos* anus + E *-logy*] **:** a branch of medicine dealing with the structure and diseases of the anus, rectum, and sigmoid colon

proc·tor \ˈpräk-tər\ *n* [ME *procutour* procurator, proctor, alter. of *procuratour*] **:** SUPERVISOR, MONITOR; *specif* **:** one appointed to supervise students (as at an examination) — **proctor** *vb* **proc·tor·ing** \-t(ə-)riŋ\ — **proc·to·ri·al** \präk-ˈtōr-ē-əl, -ˈtȯr-\ *adj* — **proc·tor·ship** \ˈpräk-tər-ˌship\ *n*

pro·cum·bent \prō-ˈkəm-bənt\ *adj* [L *procumbent-*, *procumbens*, prp. of *procumbere* to fall or lean forward, fr. *pro-* forward + *-cumbere* to lie down — more at HIP] **1 :** being or having stems that trail along the ground without rooting **2 :** lying face down

pro·cur·able \prə-ˈkyu̇r-ə-bəl, prō-\ *adj* **:** capable of being procured

pro·cur·ance \-ˈkyu̇r-ən(t)s\ *n* **:** the action of procuring **:** PROCUREMENT

proc·u·ra·tion \ˌpräk-yə-ˈrā-shən\ *n* [ME *procuratioun*, fr. MF *procuration*, fr. L *procuration-*, *procuratio*, fr. *procuratus*, pp. of *procurare*] **1 a :** the act of appointing another as one's agent or attorney **b :** the authority vested in one so appointed **2 :** PROCUREMENT

proc·u·ra·tor \ˈpräk-yə-ˌrāt-ər\ *n* **1 :** one that manages another's affairs **:** AGENT **2 :** an officer of the Roman empire entrusted with management of the financial affairs of a province and often having administrative powers as agent of the emperor **3 :** one that obtains or gets something (as supplies) esp. regularly or in an official capacity — **proc·u·ra·to·ri·al** \ˌpräk-yə-rə-ˈtōr-ē-əl, -ˈtȯr-\ *adj*

pro·cure \prə-ˈkyu̇(ə)r, prō-\ *vb* [ME *procuren*, fr. LL *procurare*, fr. L, to take care of, fr. *pro-* for + *cura* care] *vt* **1 a :** to get possession of **:** OBTAIN **b :** to get and make available for promiscuous sexual intercourse **2 :** to bring about **:** ACHIEVE ~ *vi* **:** to procure women **syn** see GET — **pro·cure·ment** \-mənt\ *n*

pro·cur·er \-ˈkyu̇r-ər\ *n* **:** one that procures; *esp* **:** PANDER — **pro·cur·ess** \-ˈkyu̇(ə)r-əs\ *n*

Pro·cy·on \ˈprō-sē-ˌän, ˈpräs-ē-, -ən\ *n* [L, fr. Gk *Prokyōn*, lit., fore-dog; fr. its rising before the Dog Star] **:** a first-magnitude star in Canis Minor

1**prod** \ˈpräd\ *vt* **prod·ded**; **prod·ding** [origin unknown] **1 a :** to thrust a pointed instrument into **:** PRICK **b :** to incite to action **:** STIR **2 :** to poke or stir as if with a prod — **prod·der** *n*

2**prod** *n* **1 :** a pointed instrument used to prod **2 :** an incitement to act

prod·i·gal \ˈpräd-i-gəl\ *adj* [L *prodigus*, fr. *prodigere* to drive away, squander, fr. *pro-*, *prod-* forth + *agere* to drive — more at PRO-, AGENT] **1 :** recklessly extravagant **2 :** characterized by wasteful expenditure **:** LAVISH **3 :** yielding abundantly **:** LUXURIANT **syn** see PROFUSE — **prodigal** *n* — **prod·i·gal·i·ty** \ˌpräd-ə-ˈgal-ət-ē\ *n* — **prod·i·gal·ly** \ˈpräd-i-gə-lē\ *adv*

pro·di·gious \prə-ˈdij-əs\ *adj* **1 a** *obs* **:** PORTENTOUS **b** *archaic* **:** UNUSUAL, EXTRAORDINARY **2 :** exciting amazement or wonder **3 :** extraordinary in bulk, quantity, or degree **:** ENORMOUS **syn** see MONSTROUS — **pro·di·gious·ly** *adv* — **pro·di·gious·ness** *n*

prod·i·gy \ˈpräd-ə-jē\ *n* [L *prodigium* omen, monster, fr. *pro-*, *prod-* + *-igium* (akin to *aio* I say) — more at ADAGE] **1 a** *archaic* **:** a portentous event **:** OMEN **b :** something extraordinary or inexplicable **2 a :** an extraordinary, marvelous, or unusual accomplishment, deed, or event **b :** a highly talented child

pro·dro·mal \prō-ˈdrō-məl\ *or* **pro·drom·ic** \-ˈdräm-ik\ *adj* **:** PRECURSORY; *esp* **:** marked by prodromes

pro·drome \ˈprō-ˌdrōm\ *n, pl* **pro·dro·ma·ta** \prō-ˈdrō-mət-ə\ *or* **pro·dromes** \ˈprō-ˌdrōmz\ [F, lit., precursor, fr. Gk *prodromos*, fr. *pro-* before + *dromos* running — more at PRO-, DROMEDARY] **:** a premonitory symptom of disease

1**pro·duce** \prə-ˈd(y)üs, prō-\ *vb* [ME (Sc) *producen*, fr. L *producere*, fr. *pro-* forward + *ducere* to lead — more at TOW] *vt* **1 :** to offer to view or notice **:** EXHIBIT **2 :** to give birth or rise to **:** YIELD **3 :** to extend in length, area, or volume ⟨~ a side of a triangle⟩ **4 :** to present to the public on the stage or screen or over radio or television **5 :** to give being, form, or shape to **:** MAKE; *esp* **:** MANUFACTURE **6 :** to accrue or cause to accrue ~ *vi* **:** to bear, make, or yield something

2**pro·duce** \ˈpräd-(ˌ)üs, ˈprōd- *also* -(ˌ)yüs\ *n* **1 a :** something produced **b :** the amount produced **:** YIELD **2 :** agricultural products and esp. fresh fruits and vegetables as distinguished from grain and other staple crops **3 :** the progeny usu. of a female animal

pro·duced \prə-ˈd(y)üst, prō-\ *adj* **:** disproportionately elongated ⟨a ~ leaf⟩

pro·duc·er \prə-ˈd(y)ü-sər, prō-\ *n* **1 :** one that produces; *esp* **:** one that grows agricultural products or manufactures crude materials into articles of use **2 :** a furnace or apparatus that produces combustible gas to be used for fuel by circulating air or a mixture of air and steam through a layer of incandescent fuel **3 :** a person who supervises or finances the production of a stage or screen production or radio or television program

producer gas *n* **:** gas made in a producer and consisting chiefly of carbon monoxide, hydrogen, and nitrogen

producer goods *n pl* **:** goods (as tools and raw materials) that are used to produce other goods and satisfy human wants only indirectly

pro·duc·ible \prə-ˈd(y)ü-sə-bəl, prō-\ *adj* **:** capable of being produced **:** PRESENTABLE

prod·uct \ˈpräd-(ˌ)əkt\ *n* [in sense 1, fr. ME, fr. ML *productum*, fr. L, something produced, fr. neut. of *productus*, pp. of *producere*; in other senses, fr. L *productum*] **1 :** the number or expression resulting from the multiplication together of two or more numbers or expressions **2 :** something produced **3 :** the amount, quantity, or total produced **4 :** CONJUNCTION 5

pro·duc·tion \prə-ˈdək-shən, prō-\ *n* **1 a :** something produced **:** PRODUCT **b** (1) **:** a literary or artistic work (2) **:** a work presented on the stage or screen or over the air **c :** an exaggerated action **2 a :** the act or process of producing **b :** the creation of utility; *esp* **:** the making of goods available for human wants **3 :** total output esp. of a commodity or an industry — **pro·duc·tion·al** \-shnəl, -shən-ᵊl\ *adj*

production control *n* **:** systematic planning, coordinating, and directing of all manufacturing activities and influences to insure having goods made on time, of adequate quality, and at reasonable cost

pro·duc·tive \-ˈdək-tiv\ *adj* **1 :** having the quality or power of producing esp. in abundance ⟨~ fishing waters⟩ **2 :** effective in bringing about **:** ORIGINATIVE **3 :** yielding or furnishing results, benefits, or profits **4 a :** effecting or contributing to effect production **b :** yielding or devoted to the satisfaction of wants or the creation of utilities **5 :** continuing to be used in the formation of new words or constructions ⟨*un-* is a ~ prefix⟩ **6 :** raising mucus or sputum (as from the bronchi) ⟨a ~ cough⟩ — **pro·duc·tive·ly** *adv* — **pro·duc·tive·ness** *n*

pro·duc·tiv·i·ty \(ˌ)prō-ˌdək-ˈtiv-ət-ē, ˌpräd-(ˌ)ək-, prə-ˌdək-\ *n* **:** the quality or state of being productive

pro·em \ˈprō-ˌem\ *n* [ME *proheme*, fr. MF, fr. L *prooemium*, fr. Gk *prooimion*, fr. *pro-* + *oimē* song] **1 :** preliminary comment **:** PREFACE **2 :** PRELUDE — **pro·emi·al** \prō-ˈē-mē-əl, -ˈem-ē-\ *adj*

pro·en·zyme \(ˈ)prō-ˈen-ˌzīm\ *n* [ISV] **:** ZYMOGEN

pro·es·trus \(ˈ)prō-ˈes-trəs\ *n* [NL] **:** a preparatory period immediately preceding estrus

prof \ˈpräf\ *n, slang* **:** PROFESSOR

pro·fa·na·tion \ˌpräf-ə-ˈnā-shən, ˌprō-fə-\ *n* **:** the act of profaning

syn PROFANATION, DESECRATION, SACRILEGE mean violation of that which is sacred. PROFANATION implies irreverence or contempt as shown by vulgar intrusion or vandalism; DESECRATION implies a loss of sacred character as through defilement or reduction to secular use; SACRILEGE may apply to technical violations not intrinsically outrageous such as improper reception of sacraments or theft of sacred objects, but it may also imply outrageous profanation

pro·fa·na·to·ry \prō-ˈfan-ə-ˌtōr-ē, prə-, -ˈfā-nə-, -ˌtȯr-\ *adj* **:** tending to profane **:** DESECRATING

1**pro·fane** \prō-ˈfān, prə-\ *vt* **1 :** to treat (something sacred) with abuse, irreverence, or contempt **:** DESECRATE, VIOLATE **2 :** to debase by a wrong, unworthy, or vulgar use — **pro·fan·er** *n*

2**profane** *adj* [ME *prophane*, fr. MF, fr. L *profanus*, fr. *pro-* before + *fanum* temple — more at PRO-, FEAST] **1 :** not concerned with religion or religious purposes **:** SECULAR **2 :** not holy because unconsecrated, impure, or defiled **:** UNSANCTIFIED **3 :** serving to debase or defile what is holy **:** IRREVERENT **4 a :** not among the initiated **b :** not possessing esoteric or expert knowledge — **pro·fane·ly** *adv* — **pro·fane·ness** \-ˈfān-nəs\ *n*

pro·fan·i·ty \prō-ˈfan-ət-ē, prə-\ *n* **1 a :** the quality or state of

being profane **b :** the use of profane language **2 :** profane language

pro·fess \prə-ˈfes, prō-\ *vb* [in sense 1, fr. ME *professen*, fr. *profes*, adj., having professed one's vows, fr. OF, fr. LL *professus*, fr. L, pp. of *profiteri* to profess, confess, fr. *pro-* before + *fateri* to acknowledge; in other senses, fr. L *professus*, pp. — more at CONFESS] *vt* **1 a :** to receive formally into a religious community following a novitiate by acceptance of the required vows **b :** to take (vows) as a member of a religious community or order **2 a :** to declare or admit openly or freely **:** AFFIRM **b :** to declare in words or appearances only **:** PRETEND **3 :** to confess one's faith in or allegiance to **:** PRACTICE **4 :** to practice or claim to be versed in (a calling or profession) ~ *vi* **1 :** to make a profession or avowal **2** *obs* **:** to profess friendship

pro·fessed \-ˈfest\ *adj* **1 :** openly and freely declared or acknowledged **:** AFFIRMED **2 :** professing to be qualified **:** EXPERT

pro·fessed·ly \prə-ˈfes-əd-lē, -ˈfest-lē\ *adv* **1 :** AVOWEDLY **2 :** ALLEGEDLY

pro·fes·sion \prə-ˈfesh-ən\ *n* **1 :** the act of taking the vows of a religious community **2 :** an act of openly declaring or publicly claiming a belief, faith, or opinion **:** PROTESTATION **3 :** an avowed religious faith **4 a :** a calling requiring specialized knowledge and often long and intensive academic preparation **b :** a principal calling, vocation, or employment **c :** the whole body of persons engaged in a calling

¹**pro·fes·sion·al** \prə-ˈfesh-nəl, -ən-ᵊl\ *adj* **1 a :** of, relating to, or characteristic of a profession **b :** engaged in one of the learned professions **c :** characterized by or conforming to the technical or ethical standards of a profession **2 a :** participating for gain or livelihood in an activity or field of endeavor often engaged in by amateurs **b :** engaged in by persons receiving financial return ⟨~ football⟩ **3 :** following a line of conduct as though it were a profession ⟨a ~ patriot⟩ — **pro·fes·sion·al·ly** \-ē\ *adv*

²**professional** *n* **:** one that engages in a pursuit or activity professionally

pro·fes·sion·al·ism \-ˌiz-əm\ *n* **1 :** the conduct, aims, or qualities that characterize or mark a profession or a professional person **2 :** the following of a profession (as athletics) for gain or livelihood

pro·fes·sion·al·ize \-ˌīz\ *vt* **:** to give a professional character to

pro·fes·sor \prə-ˈfes-ər\ *n* **1 :** one that professes, avows, or declares **2 a :** a faculty member of the highest academic rank at an institution of higher education **b :** a teacher at a university, college, or sometimes secondary school **c :** one that teaches or professes special knowledge of an art, sport, or occupation requiring skill — **pro·fes·so·ri·al** \ˌprō-fə-ˈsōr-ē-əl, ˌpräf-ə-, -ˈsȯr-\ *adj* — **pro·fes·so·ri·al·ly** \-ē-ə-lē\ *adv*

pro·fes·sor·ate \prə-ˈfes-ə-rət\ *n* **:** the office, term of office, or position of a professor

pro·fes·so·ri·at \ˌprō-fə-ˈsōr-ē-ət, ˌpräf-ə-, -ˈsȯr-, -ē-ˌat\ *or* **pro·fes·so·ri·ate** \-ət,-ˌāt\ *n* [modif. of F *professorat*, fr. *professeur* professor, fr. L *professor*, fr. *professus*] **1 :** the body of college and university teachers at an institution or in society **2 :** PROFESSORSHIP

pro·fes·sor·ship \prə-ˈfes-ər-ˌship\ *n* **:** the office, duties, or position of an academic professor

¹**prof·fer** \ˈpräf-ər\ *vb* **prof·fer·ing** \-(ə-)riŋ\ [ME *profren*, fr. AF *profrer*, fr. OF *poroffrir*, fr. *por-* forth (fr. L *pro-*) + *offrir* to offer — more at PRO-] *vt* **:** to present for acceptance **:** TENDER, OFFER ~ *vi*, *obs* **:** to move as if about to act

²**proffer** *n* **1 :** OFFER, SUGGESTION **2** *obs* **:** ATTEMPT

pro·fi·cien·cy \prə-ˈfish-ən-sē\ *n* **1 :** advancement in knowledge or skill **:** PROGRESS **2 :** the quality or state of being proficient

pro·fi·cient \prə-ˈfish-ənt\ *adj* [L *proficient-*, *proficiens*, prp. of *proficere* to go forward, accomplish, fr. *pro-* forward + *facere* to make — more at PRO-, DO] **:** well advanced in an art, occupation, or branch of knowledge **:** ADEPT — **proficient** *n* — **pro·fi·cient·ly** *adv*

syn PROFICIENT, ADEPT, SKILLED, SKILLFUL, EXPERT mean having great knowledge and experience in a trade or profession. PROFICIENT implies a thorough competence derived from training and practice; ADEPT implies special aptitude as well as proficiency; SKILLED stresses mastery of technique; SKILLFUL implies individual dexterity in execution or performance; EXPERT implies extraordinary proficiency and often connotes knowledge as well as technical skill

¹**pro·file** \ˈprō-ˌfīl, *Brit usu* -ˌfēl\ *n* [It *profilo*, fr. *profilare* to draw in outline, fr. *pro-* forward (fr. L) + *filare* to spin, fr. LL — more at FILE] **1 :** a representation of something in outline; *esp* **:** a human head or face represented or seen in a side view **2 :** an outline seen or represented in sharp relief **:** CONTOUR **3 :** a side or sectional elevation: as **a :** a drawing showing a vertical section of the ground **b :** a vertical section of a soil exposing its various zones or inclusions **4 :** a graph representing the extent to which an individual exhibits traits or abilities as determined by tests or ratings **5 :** a concise biographical sketch **syn** see OUTLINE

²**profile** *vt* **1 :** to represent in profile **:** draw or write a profile of **2 :** to shape the outline of by passing a cutter around

¹**prof·it** \ˈpräf-ət\ *n, often attrib* [ME, fr. MF, fr. L *profectus* advance, profit, fr. *profectus*, pp. of *proficere*] **1 :** a valuable return **:** GAIN **2 :** the excess of returns over expenditure in a transaction or series of transactions; *specif* **:** the excess of the selling price of goods over their cost **3 :** net income usu. for a given period of time **4 :** the ratio of profit for a given year to the amount of capital invested or to the value of sales **5 :** the compensation accruing to entrepreneurs for the assumption of risk in business enterprise as distinguished from wages or rent — **prof·it·less** \-ləs\ *adj*

²**profit** *vi* **1 :** to be of service or advantage **:** AVAIL **2 :** to derive benefit **:** GAIN ~ *vt* **:** to be of service to **:** BENEFIT

prof·it·abil·i·ty \ˌpräf-ət-ə-ˈbil-ət-ē, ˌpräf-tə-ˈbil-\ *n* **:** the quality or state of being profitable

prof·it·able \ˈpräf-ət-ə-bəl, ˈpräf-tə-bəl\ *adj* **:** affording profits **:** USEFUL **syn** see BENEFICIAL — **prof·it·able·ness** *n* — **prof·it·ably** \-blē\ *adv*

profit and loss *n* **:** a summary account used at the end of an accounting period to collect the balances of the nominal accounts that the net profit or loss may be shown

prof·i·teer \ˌpräf-ə-ˈti(ə)r\ *n* **:** one who makes what is considered an unreasonable profit esp. on the sale of essential goods during times of emergency — **profiteer** *vi*

profit sharing *n* **:** a system or process under which employees receive a part of the profits of an industrial or commercial enterprise

profit system *n* **:** FREE ENTERPRISE

prof·li·ga·cy \ˈpräf-li-gə-sē\ *n* **:** the quality or state of being profligate

prof·li·gate \ˈpräf-li-gət, -lə-ˌgāt\ *adj* [L *profligatus*, fr. pp. of *profligare* to strike down, fr. *pro-* forward, down + *-fligare* (akin to *fligere* to strike); akin to Gk *thlibein* to squeeze] **1 :** completely given up to dissipation and licentiousness **2 :** wildly extravagant **:** PRODIGAL — **profligate** *n* — **prof·li·gate·ly** *adv*

pro·flu·ent \ˈpräf-ˌlü-ənt, ˈprōf-, -lə-wənt\ *adj* [ME, fr. L *profluent-*, *profluens*, prp. of *profluere* to flow forth, fr. *pro-* forth + *fluere* to flow — more at PRO-, FLUENT] **:** flowing copiously or smoothly

pro for·ma \(ˈ)prō-ˈfȯr-mə\ *adj* [L] **1 :** for the sake of or as a matter of form **2 :** provided in advance to prescribe form or describe items ⟨*pro forma* invoice⟩

¹**pro·found** \prə-ˈfau̇nd, prō-\ *adj* [ME, fr. MF *profond* deep, fr. L *profundus*, fr. *pro-* before + *fundus* bottom — more at PRO-, BOTTOM] **1 a :** having intellectual depth and insight **b :** difficult to fathom or understand **2 a :** extending far below the surface **b :** coming from, reaching to, or situated at a depth **:** DEEP-SEATED ⟨~ sigh⟩ **3 a :** characterized by intensity of feeling or quality **b :** all encompassing **:** COMPLETE ⟨~ sleep⟩ **syn** see DEEP — **pro·found·ly** \-ˈfau̇n-(d)lē\ *adv* — **pro·found·ness** \-ˈfau̇n(d)-nəs\ *n*

²**profound** *n* **:** something that is very deep; *specif* **:** the deeps of the sea

pro·fun·di·ty \prə-ˈfən-dət-ē\ *n* [ME *profundite*, fr. MF *profundité*, fr. L *profunditat-*, *profunditas* depth, fr. *profundus*] **1 a :** intellectual depth **b :** something profound or abstruse **2 :** the quality or state of being very profound or deep

pro·fuse \prə-ˈfyüs, prō-\ *adj* [ME, fr. L *profusus*, pp. of *profundere* to pour forth, fr. *pro-* forth + *fundere* to pour — more at FOUND] **1 :** pouring forth liberally **:** EXTRAVAGANT ⟨~ in their thanks⟩ **2 :** exhibiting great abundance **:** BOUNTIFUL — **pro·fuse·ly** *adv* — **pro·fuse·ness** *n*

syn LAVISH, PRODIGAL, LUXURIANT, LUSH, EXUBERANT: PROFUSE implies pouring forth without restraint; LAVISH suggests an unstinted or unmeasured profusion; PRODIGAL implies reckless lavishness threatening to lead to early exhaustion of resources; LUXURIANT suggests a rich and splendid abundance; LUSH suggests rich, soft luxuriance; EXUBERANT implies marked vitality or vigor in what produces abundantly

pro·fu·sion \-ˈfyü-zhən\ *n* **1 :** lavish expenditure **:** EXTRAVAGANCE **2 :** the quality or state of being profuse **:** PRODIGALITY **3 :** lavish display **:** ABUNDANCE

¹**prog** \ˈpräg\ *vi* **progged; prog·ging** [origin unknown] *chiefly dial* **:** to search about; *esp* **:** FORAGE

²**prog** *n, chiefly dial* **:** FOOD, VICTUALS

pro·ga·mete \ˌprō-gə-ˈmēt, (ˈ)prō-ˈgam-ˌēt\ *n* [ISV] **:** an oocyte or a spermatocyte

pro·gen·i·tor \prō-ˈjen-ət-ər, prə-\ *n* [ME, fr. MF *progeniteur*, fr. L *progenitor*, fr. *progenitus*, pp. of *progignere* to beget, fr. *pro-* forth + *gignere* to beget — more at KIN] **1 a :** an ancestor in the direct line **:** FOREFATHER **b :** a biologically ancestral form **2 :** ORIGINATOR, PRECURSOR

prog·e·ny \ˈpräj-(ə-)nē\ *n* [ME *progenie*, fr. OF, fr. L *progenies*, fr. *progignere*] **1 a :** DESCENDANTS, CHILDREN **b :** offspring of animals or plants **2 :** OUTCOME, PRODUCT

pro·ges·ta·tion·al \ˌprō-ˌjes-ˈtā-shnəl, -shən-ᵊl\ *adj* **:** preceding pregnancy or gestation; *esp* **:** of, relating to, or constituting the modifications of the female mammalian system associated with ovulation

pro·ges·ter·one \prō-ˈjes-tə-ˌrōn\ *n* [*progestin* + *sterol* + *-one*] **:** a steroid progestational hormone $C_{21}H_{30}O_2$

pro·ges·tin \-ˈjes-tən\ *n* [*pro-* + *gestation* + *-in*] **:** a progestational hormone; *esp* **:** PROGESTERONE

pro·glot·tid \(ˈ)prō-ˈglät-əd\ *n* **:** a segment of a tapeworm containing both male and female reproductive organs — **pro·glot·ti·de·an** \ˌprō-ˌglät-ə-ˈdē-ən, ˌprō-ˌglä-ˈtid-ē-\ *adj*

pro·glot·tis \(ˈ)prō-ˈglät-əs\ *n, pl* **pro·glot·ti·des** \-ˈglät-ə-ˌdēz\ [NL *proglottid-*, *proglottis*, fr. Gk *proglōttis* tip of the tongue, fr. *pro-* before + *glōtta* tongue — more at PRO-, GLOSS] **:** PROGLOTTID

prog·na·thic \präg-ˈnath-ik, -ˈnā-thik\ *adj* **:** PROGNATHOUS

prog·na·thism \ˈpräg-nə-ˌthiz-əm, präg-ˈnā-\ *n* **:** prognathous condition

prog·na·thous \-thəs\ *adj* **:** having the jaws projecting beyond the upper part of the face

prog·no·sis \präg-ˈnō-səs\ *n* [LL, fr. Gk *prognōsis*, lit., foreknowledge, fr. *progignōskein* to know before, fr. *pro-* before + *gignōskein* to know — more at PRO-, KNOW] **1 :** the prospect of recovery as anticipated from the usual course of disease or peculiarities of the case **2 :** FORECAST, PROGNOSTICATION

prog·nos·tic \präg-ˈnäs-tik\ *n* [ME *pronostique*, fr. MF, fr. L *prognosticum*, fr. Gk *prognōstikon*, fr. neut. of *prognōstikos* foretelling, fr. *progignōskein*] **1 :** something that foretells **:** PORTENT **2 :** PROGNOSTICATION, PROPHECY — **prognostic** *adj*

prog·nos·ti·cate \präg-ˈnäs-tə-ˌkāt\ *vt* **1 :** to foretell from signs or symptoms **:** PREDICT, PROGNOSTICATE **2 :** FORESHOW, PRESAGE **syn** see FORETELL — **prog·nos·ti·ca·tive** \-ˌkāt-iv\ *adj* — **prog·nos·ti·ca·tor** \-ˌkāt-ər\ *n*

prog·nos·ti·ca·tion \(ˌ)präg-ˌnäs-tə-ˈkā-shən\ *n* **1 :** an indication in advance **:** FORETOKEN **2 a :** an act, the fact, or the power of prognosticating **:** FORECAST **b :** FOREBODING

¹**pro·gram** *or* **pro·gramme** \ˈprō-ˌgram, -grəm\ *n* [F *programme* agenda, public notice, fr. Gk *programma*, fr. *prographein* to write before, fr. *pro-* before + *graphein* to write] **1** [LL *programma*, fr. Gk] **:** a public notice **2 a :** a brief outline of the order to be pursued or the subjects embraced (as in a public entertainment) **b :** the performance of a program; *esp* **:** a performance broadcast on radio or television **3 a :** a plan of procedure **b :** a proposed project or scheme **c:** a comprehensive schedule **4 :** PROSPECTUS, SYLLABUS **5 :** a printed bill, card, or booklet giving a program **6 a :** a plan for the programming of a mechanism (as a computer) **b :** a sequence of coded instructions for insertion into a mechanism (as a computer) **7 :** matter for programmed instruction

²**program** *also* **programme** *vt* **pro·grammed** *or* **pro·gramed; pro·gram·ming** *or* **pro·gram·ing** **1 a :** to arrange or furnish a program of or for **:** BILL **b :** to enter in a program **2 :** to work out a sequence of operations to be performed by (a mechanism) **3 :** to insert a program for (a particular action) into a mechanism — **pro·gram·mer** *n*

program director *n* **:** one that is in charge of planning and scheduling program material for a radio or television station or network

pro·gram·mat·ic \ˌprō-grə-ˈmat-ik\ *adj* **1 :** relating to program music **2 :** of, resembling, or having a program — **pro·gram·mat·i·cal·ly** \-i-k(ə-)lē\ *adv*

programmed instruction *n* **:** instruction through information given in small steps with each requiring a correct response by the learner before going on to the next step

program music *n* **:** music intended to suggest a sequence of images or incidents

1**prog·ress** \ˈpräg-rəs, -ˌres, *chiefly Brit* ˈprō-ˌgres\ *n* [ME, fr. L *progressus* advance, fr. *progressus*, pp. of *progredi* to go forth, fr. *pro-* forward + *gradi* to go — more at PRO-, GRADE] **1 a :** a royal journey or tour marked by pomp and pageant **b :** an official journey or circuit **c :** a journeying forward **:** TOUR **2 :** a forward or onward movement **:** ADVANCE **3 :** gradual betterment; *esp* **:** the progressive development of mankind

2**pro·gress** \prə-ˈgres\ *vi* **1 :** to move forward **:** PROCEED **2 :** to develop to a higher, better, or more advanced stage

pro·gres·sion \prə-ˈgresh-ən\ *n* **1 :** a sequence of numbers in which each term is related to its predecessor by a uniform law **2 a :** an act of progressing **:** ADVANCE **b :** a continuous and connected series **:** SEQUENCE **c :** PROGRESS **3 a :** succession of musical tones or chords **b :** the movement of musical parts in harmony **c :** SEQUENCE 2c — **pro·gres·sion·al** \-ˈgresh-nəl, -ən-ᵊl\ *adj*

pro·gres·sion·ist \-ˈgresh-(ə-)nəst\ *n* **:** one who believes in progress; *esp* **:** one who believes in the continuous progress of the human race or of society

pro·gres·sist \ˈpräg-rəs-əst, -ˌres-; prə-ˈgres-\ *n* **1 :** PROGRESSIONIST **2 :** PROGRESSIVE 1

1**pro·gres·sive** \prə-ˈgres-iv\ *adj* **1 a :** of, relating to, or characterized by progress **b :** of, relating to, or constituting an educational theory marked by emphasis on the individual child, informality of classroom procedure, and encouragement of self-expression **2 :** of, relating to, or characterized by progression **3 :** moving forward or onward **:** ADVANCING **4 :** increasing in extent or severity ⟨a ~ disease⟩ **5** *often cap* **:** of or relating to political Progressives **6 :** of, relating to, or constituting a verb form that expresses action or state in progress at the time of speaking or a time spoken of — **pro·gres·sive·ly** *adv* — **pro·gres·sive·ness** *n*

2**progressive** *n* **1 a :** one that is progressive **b :** one believing in moderate political change and esp. social improvement by governmental action **2** *cap* **:** a member of a U.S. political party: as **a :** a member of a predominantly agrarian minor party split off from the Republicans about 1912; *specif* **:** BULL MOOSE **b :** a follower of Robert M. La Follette in the presidential campaign of 1924 **c :** a follower of Henry A. Wallace in the presidential campaign of 1948

Progressive Conservative *adj* **:** of or relating to a major political party in Canada traditionally advocating economic nationalism and close ties with the United Kingdom — **Progressive Conservative** *n*

progressive jazz *n* **:** jazz of the 1950s characterized by harmonic, contrapuntal, and rhythmic experimentation

pro·gres·siv·ism \prə-ˈgres-i-ˌviz-əm\ *n* **1 :** the principles or beliefs of progressives **2** *cap* **:** the political and economic doctrines advocated by the Progressives **3 :** the theories of progressive education — **pro·gres·siv·ist** \-vəst\ *n or adj*

pro·hib·it \prō-ˈhib-ət, prə-\ *vt* [ME *prohibiten*, fr. L *prohibitus*, pp. of *prohibēre* to hold away, fr. *pro-* forward + *habēre* to hold] **1 :** to forbid by authority **:** ENJOIN **2 a :** to prevent from doing something **b :** to make impossible **:** DEBAR **syn** see FORBID

pro·hi·bi·tion \ˌprō-ə-ˈbish-ən *also* ˌprō-hə-\ *n* **1 :** the act of prohibiting by authority **2 :** an order to restrain or stop **3 :** the forbidding by law of the sale and sometimes the manufacture and transportation of alcoholic liquors as beverages

pro·hi·bi·tion·ist \-ˈbish-(ə-)nəst\ *n* **:** one who favors the prohibition of the sale or manufacture of alcoholic liquors as beverages; *specif, cap* **:** a member of a minor U.S. political party advocating the prohibition by law of the manufacture, importation, transportation, and sale of alcoholic beverages

pro·hib·i·tive \prō-ˈhib-ət-iv, prə-\ *adj* **1 :** tending to prohibit or restrain **2 :** serving to preclude the use of something — **pro·hib·i·tive·ly** *adv*

pro·hib·i·to·ry \-ˈhib-ə-ˌtōr-ē, -ˌtȯr-\ *adj* **:** PROHIBITIVE

1**proj·ect** \ˈpräj-ˌekt, -ikt\ *n* [ME *proiecte*, modif. of MF *pourjet*, fr. *pourjeter* to throw out, spy, plan, fr. *pour-* (fr. L *porro* forward) + *jeter* to throw; akin to Gk *pro* forward — more at FOR, JET] **1 :** a specific plan or design **:** SCHEME **2** *obs* **:** IDEA **3 :** a planned undertaking: as **a :** a definitely formulated piece of research **b :** a large usu. government-supported undertaking **4 :** a task or problem engaged in usu. by a group of students to supplement and apply classroom studies **syn** see PLAN

2**pro·ject** \prə-ˈjekt\ *vt* [partly modif. of MF *pourjeter;* partly fr. L *projectus*, pp. of *proicere* to throw forward, fr. *pro-* + *jacere* to throw — more at JET] **1 :** to devise in the mind **:** DESIGN **2 :** to throw or cast forward **3 :** to present for consideration characteristics of **4 :** to cause to protrude **5 :** to cause (light or shadow) to fall into space, or (an image) upon a surface **6 :** to reproduce (as a point, line, or area) on a surface by motion in a prescribed direction **7 :** to communicate vividly esp. to an audience **8 :** to externalize and regard as objective or outside oneself ~ *vi* **:** to jut out **:** PROTRUDE

pro·ject·able \prə-ˈjek-tə-bəl\ *adj* **:** capable of being projected

1**pro·jec·tile** \prə-ˈjek-tᵊl *also* -ˌtīl, *chiefly Brit* ˈpräj-ik-ˌtīl\ *n* **1 :** a body projected by external force and continuing in motion by its own inertia; *specif* **:** a missile for a firearm, cannon, or other weapon **2 :** a self-propelling weapon (as a rocket)

2**projectile** *adj* **1 :** projecting or impelling forward **2 :** capable of being thrust forward

pro·jec·tion \prə-ˈjek-shən\ *n* **1 a :** a systematic presentation of intersecting coordinate lines on a flat surface upon which features from the curved surface of the earth or the celestial sphere may be mapped **b :** the process or technique of reproducing a spatial object upon a plane or curved surface by projecting its points; *also* **:** the graphic reproduction so formed **2 :** a transforming change **3 :** the act of throwing or shooting forward **:** EJECTION **4 :** the forming of a plan **:** SCHEMING **5 a** (1) **:** a jutting out (2) **:** a part that juts out **b :** a view of a building or architectural element **6 a :** the act of perceiving a mental object as spatially and sensibly objective; *also* **:** something so perceived **b :** the act of externalizing or objectifying what is primarily subjective **7 :** the display of motion pictures by projecting an image from them upon a screen **8 :** an estimate of future possibilities based on a current trend — **pro·jec·tion·al** \-shnəl, -shən-ᵊl\ *adj*

syn PROJECTION, PROTRUSION, PROTUBERANCE, BULGE mean an extension beyond the normal line or surface. PROJECTION implies a jutting out esp. at a sharp angle; PROTRUSION suggests a thrusting out so as to seem a deformity; PROTUBERANCE implies a growing or swelling out in rounded form; BULGE suggests an expansion caused by internal pressure

pro·jec·tion·ist \-sh(ə-)nəst\ *n* **:** one that makes projections: as **a :** a map maker **b :** one that operates a motion-picture projector or television equipment

pro·jec·tive \prə-ˈjek-tiv\ *adj* **1 :** relating to, produced by, or involving geometric projection **2 :** jutting out **:** PROJECTING **3 :** of or relating to a test or device designed to analyze the psychodynamic constitution of an individual

projective geometry *n* **:** a branch of geometry that deals with the properties of configurations that are unaltered by projection

pro·jec·tor \prə-ˈjek-tər\ *n* **1 :** one that plans a project; *specif* **:** PROMOTER **2 :** one that projects: as **a :** a device for projecting a beam of light **b :** an optical instrument for projecting an image upon a surface **c :** a machine for projecting motion pictures on a screen **3 :** an imagined line from an object to a surface along which projection takes place

pro·jet \prō-ˈzhā\ *n, pl* **projets** \-ˈzhā(z)\ [F, fr. MF *pourjet*] **1 :** PLAN; *esp* **:** a draft of a proposed measure or treaty **2 :** a projected or proposed design

pro·lac·tin \prō-ˈlak-tən\ *n* [2*pro-* + *lact-* + *-in*] **:** a pituitary lactogenic hormone

pro·la·min *or* **pro·la·mine** \ˈprō-lə-mən, -ˌmēn\ *n* [ISV *pro*line + *am*monia + *-in, -ine*] **:** any of various simple proteins found esp. in seeds and insoluble in absolute alcohol or water

pro·lan \ˈprō-ˌlan\ *n* [G, fr. L *proles* progeny] **:** either of two gonadotrophic hormones found esp. in urine in pregnancy

1**pro·lapse** \prō-ˈlaps, ˈprō-ˌ\ *n* [NL *prolapsus*, fr. LL, fall, fr. L *prolapsus*, pp. of *prolabi* to fall or slide forward, fr. *pro-* forward + *labi* to slide — more at PRO-, SLEEP] **:** the falling down or slipping of a body part from its usual position or relations

2**pro·lapse** \prō-ˈlaps\ *vi* **:** to undergo prolapse

pro·late \ˈprō-ˌlāt\ *adj* [L *prolatus* (pp. of *proferre* to bring forward, extend) fr. *pro-* forward + *latus*, pp. of *ferre* to carry] **:** EXTENDED; *esp* **:** elongated in the direction of a line joining the poles

pro·leg \ˈprō-ˌleg, -ˌlāg\ *n* **:** a fleshy leg on an abdominal segment of some insect larvae

pro·le·gom·e·non \ˌprō-li-ˈgäm-ə-ˌnän, -nən\ *n, pl* **pro·le·gom·e·na** \-nə\ [Gk, neut. pres. pass. part. of *prolegein* to say beforehand, fr. *pro-* before + *legein* to say] **:** prefatory remarks; *specif* **:** a formal essay or critical discussion serving to introduce and interpret an extended work — **pro·le·gom·e·nous** \-nəs\ *adj*

pro·lep·sis \prō-ˈlep-səs\ *n, pl* **pro·lep·ses** \-ˈlep-ˌsēz\ [Gk *prolēpsis*, fr. *prolambanein* to take beforehand, fr. *pro-* before + *lambanein* to take — more at LATCH] **:** ANTICIPATION: as **a :** the representation or assumption of a future act or development as if presently existing or accomplished **b :** the application of an adjective to a noun in anticipation of the result of the action of the verb (as in "while yon slow oxen turn the *furrowed* plain") — **pro·lep·tic** \-ˈlep-tik\ *adj*

1**pro·le·tar·i·an** \ˌprō-lə-ˈter-ē-ən\ *n* [L *proletarius*, fr. *proles* progeny, fr. *pro-* forth + *-olescere* (fr. *alescere* to grow) — more at OLD] **:** a member of the proletariat

2**proletarian** *adj* **:** of, relating to, or representative of the proletariat

pro·le·tar·i·an·iza·tion \-ˌter-ē-ə-nə-ˈzā-shən\ *n* **:** reduction to a proletarian status or level

pro·le·tar·i·an·ize \-ˈter-ē-ə-ˌnīz\ *vt* **:** to cause to undergo proletarianization

pro·le·tar·i·at \ˌprō-lə-ˈter-ē-ət, -ˈtar-\ *n* [F *prolétariat*, fr. L *proletarius*] **1 :** the lowest social or economic class of a community **2 :** industrial workers who lack their own means of production and hence sell their labor to live

1**pro·lif·er·ate** \prə-ˈlif-ə-ˌrāt\ *vi* [back-formation fr. *proliferation*, fr. F *prolifération*, fr. *proliférer* to proliferate, fr. *prolifère* proliferous, fr. L *proles* + *-fer* -ferous] **:** to grow by rapid production of new parts, cells, buds, or offspring — **pro·lif·er·a·tion** \-ˌlif-ə-ˈrā-shən\ *n* — **pro·lif·er·a·tive** \-ˈlif-ə-ˌrāt-iv\ *adj*

2**pro·lif·er·ate** \-ˈlif-ə-rət, -ˌrāt\ *adj* [back-formation fr. *proliferation*] **:** developing a leafy shoot from a normally terminal organ ⟨~ flowers⟩

pro·lif·er·ous \prə-ˈlif-(ə-)rəs\ *adj* **1 :** reproducing freely by vegetative means (as offsets, bulbils, gemmae) **2 :** PROLIFERATING; *specif* **:** producing a cluster of branchlets from a larger branch ⟨a ~ coral⟩ — **pro·lif·er·ous·ly** *adv*

pro·lif·ic \prə-ˈlif-ik\ *adj* [F *prolifique*, fr. L *proles* progeny] **1 :** producing young or fruit esp. freely **:** FRUITFUL **2** *archaic* **:** causing abundant growth, generation, or reproduction **3 :** marked by abundant inventiveness or productivity ⟨a ~ writer⟩ **syn** see FERTILE — **pro·lif·i·ca·cy** \-ˈlif-i-kə-sē\ *n* — **pro·lif·i·cal·ly** \-i-k(ə-)lē\ *adv* — **pro·lif·ic·ness** \-ik-nəs\ *n*

pro·line \ˈprō-ˌlēn\ *n* [G *prolin*] **:** an amino acid $C_5H_9NO_2$ of many proteins that may be freed by hydrolysis

pro·lix \prō-ˈliks, ˈprō-(ˌ)\ *adj* [ME, fr. MF & L; MF *prolixe*, fr. L *prolixus* extended, fr. *pro-* forward + *liquēre* to be fluid — more at LIQUID] **1 :** unduly prolonged or drawn out **2 :** given to verbosity and diffuseness in speaking or writing **:** LONG-WINDED **syn** see WORDY — **pro·lix·ly** *adv*

pro·lix·i·ty \prō-ˈlik-sət-ē\ *n* **:** the quality or state of being prolix

pro·loc·u·tor \prō-ˈläk-yət-ər\ *n* [L, fr. *pro-* for + *locutor* speaker, fr. *locutus*, pp. of *loqui* to speak] **1 :** one who speaks for another **:** SPOKESMAN **2 :** presiding officer **:** CHAIRMAN

pro·lo·gize \ˈprō-ˌlȯg-ˌīz, -ˌläg-; -lə-ˌjīz\ *or* **pro·logu·ize** \-ˌlȯg-ˌīz, -ˌläg-\ *vi* **:** to write or speak a prologue

pro·logue \ˈprō-ˌlȯg, -ˌläg\ *n* [ME *prolog*, fr. OF *prologue*, fr. L *prologus* preface to a play, fr. Gk *prologos* part of a Greek play preceding the entry of the chorus, fr. *pro-* before + *legein* to speak — more at PRO-, LEGEND] **1 :** the preface or introduction (as to

a discourse or play) **2 :** the actor speaking a prologue **3 :** an introductory or preceding act, event, or development

pro·long \prə-ˈlȯŋ\ *vt* [ME *prolongen*, fr. MF *prolonguer*, fr. LL *prolongare*, fr. L *pro-* forward + *longus* long] **1 :** to lengthen in time **:** CONTINUE **2 :** to lengthen in extent, scope, or range ⟨~ the boundary northward⟩ **syn** see EXTEND — **pro·long·er** \-ˈlȯŋ-ər\ *n*

pro·lon·gate \prə-ˈlȯŋ-ˌgāt, prō-\ *vt* **:** PROLONG — **pro·lon·ga·tion** \(ˌ)prō-ˌlȯŋ-ˈgā-shən, prə-\ *n*

pro·lo·ther·a·py \ˌprō-lō-ˈther-ə-pē\ *n* [L *proles* progeny + E *-o-* + *therapy* — more at PROLETARIAN] **:** the rehabilitation of an incompetent structure (as a ligament or tendon) by the induced proliferation of new cells

pro·lu·sion \prō-ˈlü-zhən\ *n* [L *prolusion-*, *prolusio*, fr. *prolusus*, pp. of *proludere* to play beforehand, fr. *pro-* before + *ludere* to play — more at LUDICROUS] **1 :** a preliminary trial **:** EXERCISE, PRELUDE **2 :** an introductory and often tentative discourse — **pro·lu·so·ry** \-ˈlüs-(ə-)rē, -ˈlüz-\ *adj*

prom \ˈpräm\ *n* [short for *promenade*] **:** a formal dance given by a high school or college class

1prom·e·nade \ˌpräm-ə-ˈnād, -ˈnäd\ *n* [F, fr. *promener* to take for a walk, fr. L *prominare* to drive forward, fr. *pro-* forward + *minare* to drive — more at AMENABLE] **1 :** a leisurely walk or ride esp. in a public place for pleasure or display **2 :** a place for strolling **3 a :** a ceremonious opening of a formal ball consisting of a grand march of all the guests **b :** a figure in a square dance

2promenade *vi* **1 :** to take or go on a promenade **2 :** to perform a promenade in a dance ~ *vt* **:** to walk about in or on — **prom·e·nad·er** *n*

promenade deck *n* **:** an upper deck or an area on a deck of a passenger ship where passengers promenade

Pro·me·the·an \prə-ˈmē-thē-ən\ *adj* **:** of, relating to, or resembling Prometheus, his experiences, or his art

Pro·me·theus \-ˌth(y)üs, -thē-əs\ *n* [L, fr. Gk *Promētheus*] **:** a Titan in Greek legend who steals fire from heaven as a gift for man

pro·me·thi·um \-thē-əm\ *n* [NL, fr. *Prometheus*] **:** a metallic element of the rare-earth group obtained as a fission product of uranium or from neutron-irradiated neodymium — see ELEMENT table

prom·i·nence \ˈpräm-(ə-)nən(t)s\ *n* **1 :** the quality, state, or fact of being prominent or conspicuous **:** SALIENCE **2 :** something prominent **:** PROJECTION **3 :** a mass of gas resembling a cloud that arises from the chromosphere of the sun

prom·i·nent \-(ə-)nənt\ *adj* [L *prominent-*, *prominens*, fr. prp. of *prominēre* to jut forward, fr. *pro-* forward + *-minēre* (akin to *mont-*, *mons* mountain) — more at MOUNT] **1 :** standing out or projecting beyond a surface or line **:** PROTUBERANT **2 :** readily noticeable **:** CONSPICUOUS **3 :** NOTABLE, EMINENT **syn** see NOTICEABLE — **prom·i·nent·ly** *adv*

pro·mis·cu·ity \ˌpräm-(ˌ)is-ˈkyü-ət-ē, (ˌ)prō-ˌmis-, prə-ˌmis-\ *n* **1 :** indiscriminate mingling **:** PROMISCUOUSNESS **2 :** promiscuous sexual union

pro·mis·cu·ous \prə-ˈmis-kyə-wəs\ *adj* [L *promiscuus*, fr. *pro-* forth + *miscēre* to mix — more at PRO-, MIX] **1 :** consisting of a heterogeneous mixture **2 :** not restricted to one class, sort, or person; *specif* **:** not restricted to one sexual partner **3 :** CASUAL, IRREGULAR — **pro·mis·cu·ous·ly** *adv* — **pro·mis·cu·ous·ness** *n*

1prom·ise \ˈpräm-əs\ *n* [ME *promis*, fr. L *promissum*, fr. neut. of *promissus*, pp. of *promittere* to send forth, promise, fr. *pro-* forth + *mittere* to send — more at PRO-, SMITE] **1 a :** a declaration that one will do or refrain from doing something specified **b :** a declaration that gives the person to whom it is made a right to expect or to claim the performance or forbearance of a specified act **2 :** ground for expectation usu. of success, improvement, or excellence **3 :** something that is promised

2promise *vt* **1 :** to engage to do, bring about, or provide ⟨~ aid⟩ **2** *archaic* **:** WARRANT, ASSURE **3** *chiefly dial* **:** BETROTH **4 :** to suggest beforehand **:** FORETOKEN ⟨dark clouds ~ rain⟩ ~ *vi* **1 :** to make a promise **2 :** to give ground for expectation **:** be imminent — **prom·is·er** *n*

promised land *n* **:** a place or condition believed to promise final satisfaction or realization of hopes

prom·is·ee \ˌpräm-ə-ˈsē\ *n* **:** a person to whom a promise is made

prom·is·ing \ˈpräm-ə-siŋ\ *adj* **:** full of promise **:** AUSPICIOUS — **prom·is·ing·ly** \-siŋ-lē\ *adv*

prom·i·sor \ˌpräm-ə-ˈsȯ(ə)r\ *n* **:** one who engages or undertakes

prom·is·so·ry \ˈpräm-ə-ˌsōr-ē, -ˌsȯr-\ *adj* [ML *promissorius*, fr. L *promissus*, pp.] **:** containing or conveying a promise or assurance ⟨~ oath⟩

promissory note *n* **:** a written promise to pay on demand or at a fixed future time a sum of money to a specified person

prom·on·to·ry \ˈpräm-ən-ˌtōr-ē, -ˌtȯr-\ *n* [L *promunturium*, *promonturium*; prob. akin to *prominēre* to jut forth — more at PROMINENT] **1 :** a high point of land or rock projecting into a body of water **:** HEADLAND **2 :** a bodily prominence

pro·mot·able \prə-ˈmōt-ə-bəl\ *adj* **:** likely or deserving to be advanced in rank or position

pro·mote \prə-ˈmōt\ *vt* [L *promotus*, pp. of *promovēre*, lit., to move forward, fr. *pro-* forward + *movēre* to move] **1 a :** to advance in station, rank, or honor **:** RAISE **b :** to advance (a student) from one grade to the next higher grade **2 a :** to contribute to the growth or prosperity of **:** FURTHER **b :** to help bring (as an enterprise) into being **:** LAUNCH **3** *slang* **:** to get possession of by doubtful means or by ingenuity **syn** see ADVANCE

pro·mot·er \-ˈmōt-ər\ *n* **1 :** one that promotes; *esp* **:** one who assumes the financial responsibilities of a sporting event including contracting with the principals, renting the site, and collecting gate receipts **2** *obs* **:** PROSECUTOR **3 :** a substance that in very small amounts is able to increase the activity of a catalyst

pro·mo·tion \prə-ˈmō-shən\ *n* **1 :** the act or fact of being raised in position or rank **:** PREFERMENT **2 :** the act of furthering the growth or development of something — **pro·mo·tion·al** \-shnəl, -shən-ᵊl\ *adj*

pro·mo·tive \-ˈmōt-iv\ *adj* **1 :** tending to further or encourage **2 :** PROMOTIONAL — **pro·mo·tive·ness** *n*

1prompt \ˈpräm(p)t\ *vt* [ME *prompten*, fr. ML *promptare*, fr. L *promptus* prompt] **1 :** to move to action **:** INCITE **2 :** to assist (one acting or reciting) by suggesting the next words of something forgotten or imperfectly learned **:** CUE **3 :** to serve as the inciting cause of **:** URGE — **prompt·er** *n*

2prompt *adj* [ME, fr. MF or L; MF, fr. L *promptus* ready, prompt, fr. pp. of *promere* to bring forth, fr. *pro-* forth + *emere* to take — more at REDEEM] **1 :** being ready and quick to act as occasion demands **:** PUNCTUAL **2 :** performed readily or immediately ⟨~ assistance⟩ **3 :** of or relating to prompting actors ⟨~ side⟩ **syn** see QUICK — **prompt·ly** \ˈpräm(p)-tlē, ˈpräm-plē\ *adv* — **prompt·ness** \ˈprämt-nəs, ˈprämp-nəs\ *n*

3prompt *n*, *pl* **prompts** \ˈpräm(t)s, ˈprämps\ **1 :** REMINDER **2 :** a limit of time given for payment of an account for goods purchased; *also* **:** the contract by which this time is fixed

prompt·book \ˈprämt-ˌbu̇k, ˈprämp-ˌbu̇k\ *n* **:** a copy of a play with directions for performance used by a theater prompter

promp·ti·tude \ˈpräm(p)-tə-ˌt(y)üd\ *n* [ME, fr. MF or LL; MF, fr. LL *promptitudo*, fr. L *promptus*] **:** the quality or habit of being prompt **:** PROMPTNESS

pro·mul·gate \ˈpräm-əl-ˌgāt; prō-ˈməl-, prə-ˈ, ˈprō-(ˌ)\ *vt* [L *promulgatus*, pp. of *promulgare*] **1 :** to make known by open declaration **:** PROCLAIM **2 a :** to make known or public the terms of (a proposed law) **b :** to issue or give out (a law) by way of putting into execution **syn** see DECLARE — **pro·mul·ga·tion** \ˌpräm-əl-ˈgā-shən; ˌprō-(ˌ)məl-, (ˌ)prō-ˌ, prə-ˌ\ *n* — **pro·mul·ga·tor** \ˈpräm-əl-ˌgāt-ər; prō-ˈməl-, prə-ˈ, ˈprō-(ˌ)\ *n*

pro·mulge \prō-ˈməlj\ *vt* [ME *promulgen*, fr. L *promulgare*] *archaic* **:** PROMULGATE

pro·nate \ˈprō-ˌnāt\ *vt* [LL *pronatus*, pp. of *pronare* to bend forward, fr. L *pronus*] **:** to rotate (as the hand or forearm) so as to bring the palm facing downward or backward; *broadly* **:** to rotate (a joint or part) forward and toward the midline — **pro·na·tion** \prō-ˈnā-shən\ *n*

pro·na·tor \ˈprō-ˌnāt-ər\ *n* **:** a muscle that produces pronation

prone \ˈprōn\ *adj* [ME, fr. L *pronus* bent forward, tending; akin to L *pro* forward — more at FOR] **1 :** having a tendency or inclination **:** DISPOSED ⟨man is ~ to error⟩ **2 :** DOWNWARD: as **a :** having the front or ventral downward **b :** lying flat or prostrate — **prone·ly** *adv* — **prone·ness** \ˈprōn-nəs\ *n*

syn PRONE, SUPINE, PROSTRATE, RECUMBENT mean lying down. PRONE implies a position with the front of the body turned toward the supporting surface; SUPINE implies lying on one's back and suggests inertness or abjectness; PROSTRATE implies lying full-length as in submission, defeat, or physical collapse; RECUMBENT implies the posture of one sleeping or resting **syn** see in addition LIABLE

pro·neph·ric \(ˈ)prō-ˈnef-rik\ *adj* **:** of or relating to a pronephros

pro·neph·ros \(ˈ)prō-ˈnef-rəs, -ˌräs\ *n* [NL, fr. Gk *pro-* + *nephros* kidney — more at NEPHRITIS] **:** one of the anterior of the three pairs of embryonic renal organs of higher vertebrates

1prong \ˈprȯŋ, ˈpräŋ\ *n* [ME *pronge*] **1 :** FORK **2 :** a tine of a fork **3 :** a slender pointed or projecting part: as **a :** a fang of a tooth **b :** a point of an antler — **pronged** \ˈprȯŋd, ˈpräŋd\ *adj*

2prong *vt* **:** to stab, pierce, or break up with a prong

prong·horn \ˈprȯŋ-ˌhȯ(ə)rn, ˈpräŋ-\ *n*, *pl* **pronghorn** *also* **pronghorns :** a ruminant mammal (*Antilocapra americana*) of treeless parts of western No. America resembling an antelope

pro·nom·i·nal \prō-ˈnäm-ən-ᵊl, -ˈnäm-nəl\ *adj* [LL *pronominalis*, fr. L *pronomin-*, *pronomen*] **1 :** of, relating to, or constituting a pronoun **2 :** resembling a pronoun in identifying or specifying without describing ⟨the ~ adjective *this* in *this* dog⟩ — **pro·nom·i·nal·ly** \-ē\ *adv*

pro·noun \ˈprō-ˌnau̇n\ *n* [ME *pronom*, fr. L *pronomin-*, *pronomen*, fr. *pro-* for + *nomin-*, *nomen* name — more at PRO-, NAME] **:** a word belonging to one of the major form classes in any of a great many languages that is used as a substitute for a noun or noun equivalent, takes noun constructions, and refers to persons or things named, asked for, or understood in the context

pro·nounce \prə-ˈnau̇n(t)s\ *vb* [ME *pronouncen*, fr. MF *prononcier*, fr. L *pronuntiare*, fr. *pro-* forth + *nuntiare* to report, fr. *nuntius* messenger — more at PRO-] *vt* **1 :** to utter officially or ceremoniously **2 :** to declare authoritatively or as an opinion **3 :** to employ the organs of speech to produce ⟨~ these words⟩ **4 :** RECITE ~ *vi* **1 :** to pass judgment **2 :** to produce the components of spoken language ⟨~ faultlessly⟩ — **pro·nounce·able** \-ˈnau̇n(t)-sə-bəl\ *adj* — **pro·nounc·er** *n*

pro·nounced \-ˈnau̇n(t)st\ *adj* **:** strongly marked **:** DECIDED — **pro·nounced·ly** \-ˈnau̇n(t)-səd-lē, -ˈnau̇n(t)s-tlē\ *adv*

pro·nounce·ment \prə-ˈnau̇n(t)-smənt\ *n* **1 :** a usu. formal declaration of opinion **2 :** an authoritative announcement

pro·nounc·ing *adj* **:** relating to or indicating pronunciation ⟨~ dictionary⟩

pron·to \ˈprän-(ˌ)tō\ *adv* [Sp, fr. L *promptus* prompt] **:** QUICKLY

pro·nu·cle·ar \(ˈ)prō-ˈn(y)ü-klē-ər\ *adj* **:** of, relating to, or resembling a pronucleus

pro·nu·cle·us \(ˈ)prō-ˈn(y)ü-klē-əs\ *n* [NL] **:** a gamete nucleus after completion of maturation and entry of a sperm into the egg

pro·nun·ci·a·men·to \prō-ˌnən(t)-sē-ə-ˈment-(ˌ)ō\ *n*, *pl* **pronunciamentos** *or* **pronunciamentoes** [Sp *pronunciamiento*, fr. *pronunciar* to pronounce, fr. L *pronuntiare*] **:** PROCLAMATION

pro·nun·ci·a·tion \prə-ˌnən(t)-sē-ˈā-shən\ *n* [ME *pronunciacion*, fr. MF *prononciation*, fr. L *pronuntiation-*, *pronuntiatio*, fr. *pronuntiatus*, pp. of *pronuntiare*] **:** the act or manner of pronouncing something **:** articulate utterance — **pro·nun·ci·a·tion·al** \-shnəl, -shən-ᵊl\ *adj*

1proof \ˈprüf\ *n* [ME, alter. of *preove*, fr. OF *preuve*, fr. LL *proba*, fr. L *probare* to prove — more at PROVE] **1 a :** the cogency of evidence that compels acceptance by the mind of a truth or a fact **b :** the process or an instance of establishing the validity of a statement esp. by derivation from other statements in accordance with accepted or stipulated principles of reasoning **2** *obs* **:** EXPERIENCE **3 :** an act, effort, or operation designed to establish or discover a fact or truth **:** TEST **4** *archaic* **:** the quality or state of having been tested or tried; *esp* **:** unyielding hardness **5 :** evidence operating to determine the finding or judgment of a tribunal **6 a :** an impression (as from type) taken for correction or examination **b :** a proof impression of an engraving, etching, or lithograph **c :** a test photographic print made from a negative **7 :** a test applied to articles or substances to determine whether they are of standard or satisfactory quality **8 a :** the minimum alcoholic strength of proof spirit **b :** strength with reference to the standard for proof spirit; *specif* **:** alcoholic strength indicated by a number that is twice the percent by volume of alcohol present ⟨whiskey of 90 ~ is 45% alcohol⟩ ⟨alcohol of 200 ~ is 100% alcohol⟩

2proof *adj* **1 :** firm or successful in resisting or repelling — often used in combination **2 :** used in proving or testing or a standard of

comparison **3 :** of standard strength or quality or alcoholic content

³proof *vt* **1 a :** to make or take a proof or test of **b :** PROOFREAD **2 :** to bring (dough) to the proper lightness **3 :** to give a resistant quality to — **proof·er** *n*

proof·read \'prü-,frēd\ *vt* [back-formation fr. *proofreader*] **:** to read and mark corrections in (a proof) — **proof·read·er** *n*

proof·room \'prü-,früm, -,frům\ *n* **:** a room in which proofreading is done

proof spirit *n* **:** alcoholic liquor or mixture of alcohol and water that contains one half of its volume of alcohol of a specific gravity 0.7939 at 60°F

¹prop \'präp\ *n* [ME *proppe*, fr. MD, stopper; akin to MLG *proppe* stopper] **:** something that props or sustains **:** SUPPORT

²prop *vt* **propped; prop·ping 1 a :** to support by placing something under or against **b :** to support by placing against something **2 :** SUSTAIN, STRENGTHEN

³prop *n* **:** PROPERTY 3

⁴prop *n* **:** PROPELLER

prop- *comb form* [ISV, fr. *propionic (acid)*] **:** related to propionic acid ⟨propane⟩ ⟨propyl⟩

¹pro·pae·deu·tic \,prō-pi-'d(y)üt-ik\ *n* [Gk *propaideuein* to teach beforehand, fr. *pro-* before + *paideuein* to teach, fr. *paid-, pais* child — more at PRO-, FEW] **:** preparatory study or instruction **:** INTRODUCTION

²propaedeutic *adj* **:** needed as preparation for learning or study

prop·a·ga·ble \'präp-ə-gə-bəl\ *adj* **:** capable of being propagated

pro·pa·gan·da \,präp-ə-'gan-də, ,prō-pə-\ *n* [NL, fr. *Congregatio de propaganda fide* Congregation for propagating the faith, organization established by Pope Gregory XV] **1** *cap* **:** a congregation of the Roman curia having jurisdiction over missionary territories and related institutions **2 :** the spreading of ideas, information, or rumor for the purpose of helping or injuring an institution, a cause, or a person **3 :** ideas, facts, or allegations spread deliberately to further one's cause or to damage an opposing cause; *also* **:** a public action having such an effect

pro·pa·gan·dism \-'gan-,diz-əm\ *n* **:** the action, practice, or art of propagating doctrines or of spreading or employing propaganda — **pro·pa·gan·dist** \-dəst\ *n or adj* — **pro·pa·gan·dis·tic** \-,gan-'dis-tik\ *adj* — **pro·pa·gan·dis·ti·cal·ly** \-ti-k(ə-)lē\ *adv*

pro·pa·gan·dize \-'gan-,dīz\ *vt* **:** to subject to propaganda **~** *vi* **:** to carry on propaganda

prop·a·gate \'präp-ə-,gāt\ *vb* [L *propagatus*, pp. of *propagare* to set slips, propagate, fr. *propages* slip, offspring, fr. *pro-* before + *pangere* to fasten — more at PRO-, PACT] *vt* **1 :** to cause to continue or increase by sexual or asexual reproduction **2 :** to pass along to offspring **3 a :** to cause to spread out and affect a greater number or greater area **:** EXTEND **b :** PUBLICIZE **c :** TRANSMIT **~** *vi* **1 :** to multiply sexually or asexually **2 :** INCREASE, EXTEND — **prop·a·ga·tive** \-,gāt-iv\ *adj* — **prop·a·ga·tor** \-,gāt-ər\ *n*

prop·a·ga·tion \,präp-ə-'gā-shən\ *n* **:** the act or action of propagating: as **a :** increase (as of a kind of organism) in numbers **b :** the spreading of something (as a belief) abroad or into new regions **:** DISSEMINATION **c :** enlargement or extension (as of a crack) in a solid body — **prop·a·ga·tion·al** \-shnəl, -shən-ᵊl\ *adj*

pro·pane \'prō-,pān\ *n* [ISV] **:** a heavy flammable gaseous paraffin hydrocarbon $CH_3CH_2CH_3$ found in crude petroleum and natural gas and used esp. as fuel and in chemical synthesis

pro·par·oxy·tone \,prō-pə-'räk-si-,tōn, ,prō-,pa(ə)r-'äk-\ *adj* [Gk *proparoxytonos*] **:** having or characterized by an acute accent on the antepenult — **proparoxytone** *n*

pro·pel \prə-'pel\ *vt* **pro·pelled; pro·pel·ling** [ME *propellen*, fr. L *propellere*, fr. *pro-* before + *pellere* to drive — more at FELT] **1 :** to drive forward or onward **2 :** to urge on **:** MOTIVATE **syn** see PUSH

¹pro·pel·lant *or* **pro·pel·lent** \-'pel-ənt\ *adj* **:** capable of propelling

²propellant *also* **propellent** *n* **:** something that propels: as **a :** an explosive for propelling projectiles **b :** fuel plus oxidizer used by a rocket engine **c :** a gas in a pressure bottle for expelling the contents when the pressure is released

pro·pel·ler *also* **pro·pel·lor** \prə-'pel-ər\ *n* **:** one that propels; *specif* **:** SCREW PROPELLER

pro·pend \prō-'pend\ *vi* [L *propendēre*, fr. *pro-* before + *pendēre* to hang — more at PENDANT] *obs* **:** INCLINE

pro·pense \prō-'pen(t)s\ *adj* [L *propensus*, pp. of *propendēre*] *archaic* **:** INCLINED, DISPOSED

pro·pen·si·ty \prə-'pen(t)-sət-ē\ *n* **:** a natural inclination **syn** see LEANING

¹prop·er \'präp-ər\ *adj* [ME *propre* proper, own, fr. OF, fr. L *proprius* own] **1 :** marked by suitability, rightness, or appropriateness **:** FIT **2 a :** appointed for the liturgy of a particular day **b :** belonging to one **:** OWN **c :** referring to one individual only ⟨~ noun⟩ **d :** represented heraldically in natural color **3 :** belonging characteristically to a species or individual **:** PECULIAR **4 :** very good **:** EXCELLENT **5** *chiefly Brit* **:** UTTER, ABSOLUTE ⟨a ~ villain⟩ **6** *chiefly dial* **:** BECOMING, HANDSOME **7 :** strictly limited to a specified thing, place, or idea ⟨the city ~⟩ **8 a :** strictly accurate **:** CORRECT **b** *archaic* **:** VIRTUOUS, RESPECTABLE **c :** strictly decorous **:** GENTEEL **syn** see FIT

²proper *n* **1 a :** the special liturgical office for a particular day **b :** the parts of the mass that vary according to the day or feast **2 :** the part of a missal or breviary containing the offices proper to certain feasts or saints

³proper *adv, chiefly dial* **:** THOROUGHLY, COMPLETELY

proper adjective *n* **:** an adjective that is formed from a proper noun and is usu. capitalized in English

pro·per·din \prō-'pərd-ᵊn\ *n* [prob. fr. ¹*pro-* + L *perdere* to destroy + E *-in* — more at PERDITION] **:** a serum protein that participates in destruction of bacteria, neutralization of viruses, and lysis of red blood cells

proper fraction *n* **:** a fraction in which the numerator is less or of lower degree than the denominator

prop·er·ly \'präp-ər-lē\ *adv* **:** in a proper manner: as **a :** SUITABLY **b :** STRICTLY, CORRECTLY **c** *chiefly Brit* **:** UTTERLY

proper noun *n* **:** a noun that designates a particular being or thing, does not take a limiting modifier, and is usu. capitalized in English — called also *proper name*

proper subset *n* **:** a subset containing fewer elements than does the class to which it is subordinate

prop·er·tied \'präp-ərt-ēd\ *adj* **:** possessing property

prop·er·ty \'präp-ərt-ē\ *n* [ME *proprete*, fr. MF *propreté*, fr. L *proprietat-, proprietas*, fr. *proprius* own] **1 a :** a quality or trait belonging and esp. peculiar to an individual or thing **b :** an effect that an object has on another object or on the senses **c :** VIRTUE 3 **d :** an attribute common to all members of a class **2 a :** something owned or possessed; *specif* **:** a piece of real estate **b :** the exclusive right to possess, enjoy, and dispose of a thing **:** OWNERSHIP **c :** something to which a person has a legal title **3 :** an article or object used in a play or motion picture except painted scenery and actors' costumes **syn** see QUALITY

property damage insurance *n* **:** protection against the legal liability of the insured for damage caused by his automobile to the property of others

prop·er·ty·less \'präp-ərt-ē-ləs\ *adj* **:** lacking property

property man *n* **:** one who is in charge of theater or motion-picture stage properties

pro·phage \'prō-,fāj, -,fäzh\ *n* **:** an intracellular form of a bacterial virus in which it is harmless to the host which it protects against active viruses

pro·phase \'prō-,fāz\ *n* [ISV] **:** the initial phase of mitosis in which chromosomes are condensed from the resting form and split into paired chromatids — **pro·pha·sic** \(')prō-'fā-zik\ *adj*

proph·e·cy \'präf-ə-sē\ *n* [ME *prophecie*, fr. OF, fr. LL *prophetia*, fr. Gk *prophēteia*, fr. *prophētēs* prophet] **1 :** the vocation of a prophet; *specif* **:** the inspired declaration of divine will and purpose **2 :** an inspired utterance of a prophet **3 :** a declaration of something to come **:** PREDICTION

proph·e·si·er \-,sī(-ə)r\ *n* **:** one that prophesies

proph·e·sy \'präf-ə-,sī\ *vb* [ME *prophesien*, fr. MF *prophesier*, fr. OF, fr. *prophecie*] *vt* **1 :** to utter by divine inspiration **2 :** PREDICT **3 :** FORESHOW, PREFIGURE **~** *vi* **1 :** to speak as if divinely inspired **2 :** to give instruction in religious matters **:** PREACH **3 :** to make a prediction **syn** see FORETELL

proph·et \'präf-ət\ *n* [ME *prophete*, fr. OF, fr. L *propheta*, fr. Gk *prophētēs*, fr. *pro-* before + *phanai* to speak — more at PRO-, BAN] **1 :** one who utters divinely inspired revelations; *specif, often cap* **:** the writer of one of the prophetic books of the Old Testament **2 :** one gifted with more than ordinary spiritual and moral insight; *esp* **:** an inspired poet **3 :** one who foretells future events **:** PREDICTOR **4 :** an effective or leading spokesman for a cause, doctrine, or group **5** *Christian Science* **a :** a spiritual seer **b :** disappearance of material sense before the conscious facts of spiritual Truth — **proph·et·ess** \-ət-əs\ *n*

pro·phet·ic \prə-'fet-ik\ *adj* **1 :** of, relating to, or characteristic of a prophet or prophecy **2 :** foretelling events **:** PREDICTIVE — **pro·phet·i·cal** \-i-kəl\ *adj* — **pro·phet·i·cal·ly** \-k(ə-)lē\ *adv*

Proph·ets \'präf-əts\ *n pl* **:** the second part of the Jewish scriptures — compare HAGIOGRAPHA, LAW

¹pro·phy·lac·tic \,prō-fə-'lak-tik *also* ,präf-ə-\ *adj* [Gk *prophylaktikos*, fr. *prophylassein* to keep guard before, fr. *pro-* before + *phylassein* to guard, fr. *phylak-, phylax* guard] **1 :** guarding from or preventing disease **2 :** tending to prevent or ward off **:** PREVENTIVE — **pro·phy·lac·ti·cal·ly** \-ti-k(ə-)lē\ *adv*

²prophylactic *n* **:** something that is prophylactic: as **a :** a device for preventing venereal infection **b :** CONTRACEPTIVE

pro·phy·lax·is \-'lak-səs\ *n, pl* **pro·phy·lax·es** \-'lak-,sēz\ [NL, fr. Gk *prophylaktikos*] **:** measures designed to preserve health and prevent the spread of disease

¹pro·pine \prə-'pēn, -'pīn\ *vt* [ME *propinen*, fr. MF *propiner*, fr. L *propinare* to present, drink to someone's health, fr. Gk *propinein* lit., to drink first, fr. *pro-* ¹pro- + *pinein* to drink — more at POTABLE] *chiefly Scot* **:** PRESENT, PLEDGE 2

²propine *n, Scot* **:** a gift in return for a favor

pro·pin·qui·ty \prō-'piŋ-kwət-ē\ *n* [ME *propinquite*, fr. L *propinquitat-, propinquitas* kinship, proximity, fr. *propinquus* near, akin, fr. *prope* near — more at APPROACH] **1 :** nearness of blood **:** KINSHIP **2 :** nearness in place or time **:** PROXIMITY

pro·pi·o·nate \'prō-pē-ə-,nāt\ *n* [ISV] **:** a salt or ester of propionic acid

pro·pi·on·ic acid \,prō-pē-,än-ik-\ *n* [ISV ¹*pro-* + Gk *piōn* fat; akin to L *opimus* fat — more at FAT] **:** a liquid sharp-odored fatty acid $C_3H_6O_2$ found in milk and distillates of wood, coal, and petroleum

pro·pi·tia·ble \prō-'pish-(ē-)ə-bəl\ *adj* **:** capable of being propitiated

pro·pi·ti·ate \prō-'pish-ē-,āt\ *vt* [L *propitiatus*, pp. of *propitiare*, fr. *propitius* propitious] **:** to appease and make favorable **:** CONCILIATE **syn** see PACIFY — **pro·pi·ti·a·tor** \-,āt-ər\ *n*

pro·pi·ti·a·tion \(,)prō-,pis(h)-ē-'ā-shən\ *n* **1 :** the act of propitiating **2 :** something that propitiates; *specif* **:** an atoning sacrifice

pro·pi·tia·to·ry \prō-'pish-(ē-)ə-,tōr-ē, -,tòr-\ *adj* **1 :** of or relating to propitiation **2 :** intended to propitiate **:** EXPIATORY

pro·pi·tious \prə-'pish-əs\ *adj* [ME *propicious*, fr. L *propitius*, fr. *pro-* before + *petere* to seek — more at PRO-, FEATHER] **1 :** favorably disposed **:** BENEVOLENT **2 :** being of good omen **:** AUSPICIOUS ⟨~ sign⟩ **3 :** tending to favor **:** ADVANTAGEOUS **syn** see FAVORABLE — **pro·pi·tious·ly** *adv* — **pro·pi·tious·ness** *n*

prop·jet engine \,präp-,jet-\ *n* **:** TURBO-PROPELLER ENGINE

prop·man \'präp-,man\ *n* **:** PROPERTY MAN

prop·o·lis \'präp-ə-ləs\ *n* [L, fr. Gk, fr. *pro-* for + *polis* city — more at PRO-, POLICE] **:** a brownish resinous material of waxy consistency collected by bees from the buds of trees and used as a cement

pro·pone \prə-'pōn\ *vt* [ME (Sc) *proponen*, fr. L *proponere* — more at PROPOUND] **1** *Scot* **:** PROPOSE, PROPOUND **2** *Scot* **:** to put forward (a defense)

pro·po·nent \prə-'pō-nənt\ *n* [L *proponent-, proponens*, prp. of *proponere*] **:** one who argues in favor of something **:** ADVOCATE

¹pro·por·tion \p(r)ə-'pōr-shən, -'pòr-\ *n* [ME *proporcion*, fr. MF *proportion*, fr. L *proportion-, proportio*, fr. *pro* for + *portion-, portio* portion — more at FOR] **1 :** the relation of one part to another or to the whole with respect to magnitude, quantity, or degree **:** RATIO **2 :** BALANCE, SYMMETRY **3 :** a relation of equality of two ratios in which the first of the four terms divided by the second equals the third divided by the fourth (as in $4/2=10/5$)

4 a : proper or equal share b : QUOTA, PERCENTAGE 5 : SIZE, DEGREE
[2]proportion *vt* **pro·por·tion·ing** \-sh(ə-)niŋ\ 1 : to adjust (a part or thing) in size relative to other parts or things 2 : to make the parts of harmonious or symmetrical 3 : APPORTION, ALLOT
pro·por·tion·able \-sh(ə-)nə-bəl\ *adj, archaic* : PROPORTIONAL, PROPORTIONATE — **pro·por·tion·ably** \-blē\ *adv, archaic*
[1]pro·por·tion·al \p(r)ə-'pōr-shnəl, -'pȯr-, -shən-ᵊl\ *adj* 1 a : being in proportion : PROPORTIONATE b : having the same or a constant ratio 2 : regulated or determined in size or degree with reference to proportions — **pro·por·tion·al·i·ty** \-,pōr-shə-'nal-ət-ē, -,pȯr-\ *n* — **pro·por·tion·al·ly** \-'pōr-shnə-lē, -'pȯr-, -shən-ᵊl-ē\ *adv*
syn PROPORTIONAL, PROPORTIONATE, COMMENSURATE, COMMENSURABLE mean duly proportioned to something else. PROPORTIONAL and PROPORTIONATE are often interchangeable but PROPORTIONAL may apply to several closely related things that change without altering their relations; PROPORTIONATE to one thing that bears a reciprocal relationship to another; COMMENSURATE stresses an equality between things different from but in some way dependent on each other; COMMENSURABLE more strongly implies a common scale by which two quite different things can be shown to be significantly equal or proportionate
[2]proportional *n* : a number or quantity in a proportion
proportional parts *n pl* : fractional parts of the difference between successive entries in a table for use in linear interpolation
proportional representation *n* : an electoral system designed to represent in a legislative body each political group or party in proportion to its actual voting strength in the electorate
[1]pro·por·tion·ate \p(r)ə-'pōr-sh(ə-)nət, -'pȯr-\ *adj* : being in proportion **syn** see PROPORTIONAL — **pro·por·tion·ate·ly** *adv*
[2]pro·por·tion·ate \-shə-,nāt\ *vt* : to make proportionate : PROPORTION
pro·pos·al \prə-'pō-zəl\ *n* 1 : an act of putting forward or stating something for consideration 2 a : something proposed : SUGGESTION b : OFFER; *specif* : an offer of marriage
pro·pose \prə-'pōz\ *vb* [ME *proposen*, fr. MF *proposer*, fr. L *proponere* (perf. indic. *proposui*)] *vi* 1 : to form or declare a plan or intention 2 *obs* : CONVERSE, DISCOURSE 3 : to make an offer of marriage ~ *vt* 1 a : to bring forward : PROPOUND b : INTEND 2 : to offer for consideration or adoption 3 : to declare as a purpose or goal 4 : to offer as a toast — **pro·pos·er** *n*
[1]prop·o·si·tion \,präp-ə-'zish-ən\ *n* 1 a : something proposed or offered for consideration or acceptance : PROPOSAL b : the point to be discussed or maintained in argument usu. stated in sentence form near the outset c : a theorem or problem to be demonstrated or performed 2 a : an expression in language or signs of something that can be believed, doubted, or denied or is either true or false b : the objective meaning of a proposition 3 : a project or situation requiring some action with reference to it : AFFAIR — **prop·o·si·tion·al** \-'zish-nəl, -ən-ᵊl\ *adj*
[2]proposition *vt* **prop·o·si·tion·ing** \-'zish-(ə-)niŋ\ : to make a proposal to; *specif* : to suggest sexual intercourse to
propositional function *n* 1 : SENTENTIAL FUNCTION 2 : something that is designated or expressed by a sentential function
pro·pos·i·tus \prə-'päz-ət-əs\ *n* [NL, fr. L, pp. of *proponere*] : the person immediately concerned : SUBJECT
pro·pound \prə-'pau̇nd\ *vt* [alter. of earlier *propone*, fr. ME (Sc) *proponen*, fr. L *proponere* to display, propound, fr. *pro-* before + *ponere* to put, place — more at PRO-, POSITION] : to offer for consideration : PROPOSE — **pro·pound·er** *n*
pro·prae·tor *or* **pro·pre·tor** \(')prō-'prēt-ər\ *n* [L *propraetor*, fr. *pro-* (as in *proconsul*) + *praetor*] : a praetor of ancient Rome sent out to govern a province
[1]pro·pri·etary \p(r)ə-'prī-ə-,ter-ē\ *n* 1 a : PROPRIETOR, OWNER b : an owner or grantee of a proprietary colony 2 : a body of proprietors 3 : a drug that is protected by secrecy, patent, or copyright against free competition as to name, product, composition, or process of manufacture
[2]proprietary *adj* [LL *proprietarius*, fr. L *proprietas* property — more at PROPERTY] 1 : of, relating to, or characteristic of a proprietor 2 : made and marketed by one having the exclusive right to manufacture and sell 3 : privately owned and managed
proprietary colony *n* : a colony granted to a proprietor with full prerogatives of government
pro·pri·etor \p(r)ə-'prī-ət-ər\ *n* [alter. of [1]*proprietary*] 1 : PROPRIETARY 1b 2 a : one who has the legal right or exclusive title to something : OWNER b : one having an interest less than absolute and exclusive right — **pro·pri·etor·ship** \-,ship\ *n* — **pro·pri·etress** \-'prī-ə-trəs\ *n*
pro·pri·ety \p(r)ə-'prī-ət-ē\ *n* [ME *propriete*, fr. MF *proprieté* property, quality of a person or thing — more at PROPERTY] 1 *obs* : true nature 2 *obs* : a special characteristic : PECULIARITY 3 : the quality or state of being proper 4 a : the standard of what is socially acceptable in conduct or speech : DECORUM b : fear of offending against conventional rules of behavior esp. as between the sexes c *pl* : the customs and manners of polite society **syn** see DECORUM
pro·prio·cep·tive \,prō-prē-ō-'sep-tiv\ *adj* [L *proprius* own + E *-ceptive* (as in *receptive*)] : of, relating to, or being stimuli arising within the organism
pro·prio·cep·tor \-tər\ *n* : a sensory receptor excited by proprioceptive stimuli
prop root *n* : a root that serves as a prop or support to the plant
pro·pto·sis \(')prō-'tō-səs, präp-'tō-\ *n* [NL, fr. LL, falling forward, fr. Gk *proptōsis*, fr. *propiptein* to fall forward, fr. *pro-* + *piptein* to fall — more at FEATHER] : forward projection or displacement esp. of the eyeball
pro·pul·sion \prə-'pəl-shən\ *n* [L *propulsus*, pp. of *propellere* to propel] 1 : the action or process of propelling 2 : something that propels
pro·pul·sive \-'pəl-siv\ *adj* [L *propulsus*] : tending or having power to propel
pro·pyl \'prō-pəl\ *n* : either of two isomeric alkyl radicals C_3H_7 derived from propane or an isomer — **pro·pyl·ic** \prō-'pil-ik\ *adj*
prop·y·lae·um \,präp-ə-'lē-əm\ *n, pl* **prop·y·laea** \-'lē-ə\ [L, fr. Gk *propylaion*, fr. *pro-* before + *pylē* gate — more at PRO-] : a vestibule or entrance of architectural importance before a building or enclosure — often used in pl.
pro·pyl·ene \'prō-pə-,lēn\ *n* : a flammable gaseous hydrocarbon $CH_3CH{=}CH_2$ obtained by cracking petroleum hydrocarbons and used chiefly in organic synthesis
propylene glycol *n* : a sweet hygroscopic viscous liquid preservative $C_3H_8O_2$ made esp. from propylene and used as an antifreeze and solvent and in brake fluids
pro ra·ta \(')prō-'rāt-ə, -'rät-\ *adv* [L] : proportionately according to some exactly calculable factor — **pro rata** *adj*
pro·rate \(')prō-'rāt\ *vb* [*pro rata*] *vt* : to divide, distribute, or assess proportionately ~ *vi* : to make a pro rata distribution
pro·ra·tion \prō-'rā-shən\ *n* : the act or an instance of prorating; *specif* : the limitation of production of crude oil or gas to some fractional part of the total productive capacity of each producer
pro·ro·gate \'prōr-ō-,gāt, 'prȯr-\ *vt* : PROROGUE
pro·ro·ga·tion \,prōr-ō-'gā-shən, ,prȯr-ō-, p(r)ə-,rō-\ *n* : the act of proroguing : the state of being prorogued
pro·rogue \p(r)ə-'rōg\ *vb* [ME *prorogen*, fr. MF *proroguer*, fr. L *prorogare*, fr. *pro-* before + *rogare* to ask — more at PRO-, RIGHT] *vt* 1 : DEFER, POSTPONE 2 : to terminate a session of (as a British parliament) by royal prerogative ~ *vi* : to suspend or end a legislative session **syn** see ADJOURN
pros- *prefix* [LL, fr. Gk, fr. *proti*, *pros* face to face with, towards, in addition to, near; akin to Skt *prati-* near, towards, against, in return, Gk *pro* before — more at FOR] 1 : near : toward ⟨*pros*enchyma⟩ 2 : in front ⟨*pros*encephalon⟩
pro·sa·ic \prō-'zā-ik\ *adj* [LL *prosaicus*, fr. L *prosa* prose] 1 a : characteristic of prose as distinguished from poetry : FACTUAL b : DULL, UNIMAGINATIVE 2 : belonging to the everyday world : COMMONPLACE — **pro·sa·i·cal·ly** \-'zā-ə-k(ə-)lē\ *adv*
pro·sa·ism \'prō-(,)zā-,iz-əm\ *n* 1 : a prosaic manner, style, or quality 2 : a prosaic expression
pro·sa·ist \-(,)zā-əst\ *n* [L *prosa* prose] 1 : a prose writer 2 : a prosaic person
pro·sa·teur \,prō-zə-'tər\ *n* [F, fr. It *prosatore*, fr. ML *prosator*, fr. L *prosa*] : a writer of prose
pro·sce·ni·um \prō-'sē-nē-əm\ *n* [L, fr. Gk *proskēnion* front of the building forming the background for a dramatic performance, stage, fr. *pro-* + *skēnē* building forming the background for a dramatic performance — more at SCENE] 1 a : the stage of an ancient theater b : the part of a modern stage in front of the curtain c : the wall that separates the stage from the auditorium and provides the arch that frames it 2 : FOREGROUND
proscenium arch *n* : the arch that encloses the opening in the proscenium wall through which the spectator sees the stage
pro·scribe \prō-'skrīb\ *vt* [L *proscribere* to publish, proscribe, fr. *pro-* before + *scribere* to write — more at SCRIBE] 1 a : to publish the name of (a person) as condemned to death with his property forfeited to the state b : OUTLAW 2 : to condemn or forbid as harmful : PROHIBIT — **pro·scrib·er** *n*
pro·scrip·tion \prō-'skrip-shən\ *n* [ME *proscripcion*, fr. L *proscription-*, *proscriptio*, fr. *proscriptus*, pp. of *proscribere*] 1 : the act of proscribing : the state of being proscribed 2 : an imposed restraint or restriction : PROHIBITION — **pro·scrip·tive** \-'skrip-tiv\ *adj* — **pro·scrip·tive·ly** *adv*
[1]prose \'prōz\ *n* [ME, fr. MF, fr. L *prosa*, fr. fem. of *prorsus*, *prosus*, straightforward, being in prose, contr. of *proversus*, pp. of *provertere* to turn forward, fr *pro-* forward + *vertere* to turn — more at PRO-, WORTH] 1 a : the ordinary language of men in speaking or writing b : a literary medium distinguished from poetry esp. by its greater irregularity and variety of rhythm and its closer correspondence to the patterns of everyday speech 2 : a prosaic style, quality, character, or condition : ORDINARINESS, MATTER-OF-FACTNESS
[2]prose *vi* 1 : to write prose 2 : to write or speak in a dull prosy manner
[3]prose *adj* 1 : of, relating to, or written in prose 2 : MATTER-OF-FACT, PROSAIC
pro·sec·tor \prō-'sek-tər\ *n* [prob. fr. F *prosecteur*, fr. LL *prosector* anatomist, fr. L *prosectus*, pp. of *prosecare* to cut away, fr. *pro-* forth + *secare* to cut — more at PRO-, SAW] : one that makes dissections for anatomic demonstrations — **pro·sec·to·ri·al** \,prō-,sek-'tōr-ē-əl, -'tȯr-\ *adj*
pros·e·cut·able \'präs-i-,kyüt-ə-bəl\ *adj* : subject to prosecution ⟨a ~ offense⟩
pros·e·cute \'präs-i-,kyüt\ *vb* [ME *prosecuten*, fr. L *prosecutus*, pp. of *prosequi* to pursue — more at PURSUE] *vt* 1 : to follow to the end ⟨~ the investigation⟩ 2 : to engage in 3 a : to pursue for redress or punishment of a crime or violation of law in due legal form before a legal tribunal b : to institute legal proceedings with reference to ⟨~ a claim⟩ ~ *vi* : to institute and carry on a legal suit or prosecution
prosecuting attorney *n* : an attorney who conducts proceedings in a court on behalf of the government : DISTRICT ATTORNEY
pros·e·cu·tion \,präs-i-'kyü-shən\ *n* 1 : the act or process of prosecuting; *specif* : the institution and continuance of a criminal suit involving the process of pursuing formal charges against an offender to final judgment 2 : the party by whom criminal proceedings are instituted or conducted 3 *obs* : PURSUIT
pros·e·cu·tor \'präs-i-,kyüt-ər\ *n* 1 : a person who institutes an official prosecution before a court 2 : PROSECUTING ATTORNEY
[1]pros·e·lyte \'präs-ə-,līt\ *n* [ME *proselite*, fr. LL *proselytus* proselyte, alien resident, fr. Gk *prosēlytos*, fr. *pros* near + *-ēlytos* (akin to *elthein* to go); akin to Gk *elaunein* to drive — more at PROS-, ELASTIC] : a new convert : NEOPHYTE; *specif* : a convert to Judaism **syn** see CONVERT
[2]proselyte *vt* : to convert from one religion, belief, or party to another ~ *vi* 1 : to make proselytes 2 : to recruit members esp. by the offer of special inducements
pros·e·ly·tism \'präs-ə-,līt-,iz-əm, 'präs-(ə-)lə-,tiz-\ *n* 1 : the act of becoming or condition of being a proselyte : CONVERSION 2 : the act or process of proselyting
pros·e·ly·tize \'präs-(ə-)lə-,tīz\ *vb* : PROSELYTE
pro·sem·i·nar \(')prō-'sem-ə-,när\ *n* : a directed course of study conducted in the manner of a graduate seminar but often open to advanced undergraduate students
pros·en·ce·phal·ic \,präs-,en(t)-sə-'fal-ik\ *adj* : of, relating to, or derived from the forebrain
pros·en·ceph·a·lon \,präs-,en-'sef-ə-,län, -lən\ *n* [NL] : FOREBRAIN
pros·en·chy·ma \prä-'seŋ-kə-mə, -'sen-\ *n, pl* **pros·en·chym·a·ta** \,präs-ᵊn-'kim-ət-ə\ *or* **prosenchymas** [NL] : a tissue of higher plants composed of elongated cells with little protoplasm and

specialized for conduction and support — **pros·en·chym·a·tous** \ˌpräs-ᵊn-ˈkim-ət-əs\ *adj*

prose poem *n* **:** a work in prose that has some of the qualities of a poem (as rhythm, patterned structure, or imaginative heightening) — **prose poet** *n*

pros·er \ˈprō-zər\ *n* **1 :** a writer of prose **2 :** one who talks or writes tediously

Pro·ser·pi·na \prə-ˈsər-pə-nə\ *or* **Pros·er·pine** \ˈpräs-ər-ˌpīn\ *n* [L *Proserpina*] **:** PERSEPHONE

pros·i·ly \ˈprō-zə-lē\ *adv* **:** in a prosy manner

pros·i·ness \-zē-nəs\ *n* **:** the quality or state of being prosy

pro·sit \ˈprō-zət, -sət\ *or* **prost** \ˈprōst\ *interj* [G, fr. L *prosit* may it be beneficial, fr. *prodesse* to be useful — more at PROUD] — used to wish good health esp. before drinking

pro·so \ˈprō-(ˌ)sō\ *n* [Russ] **:** MILLET 1a

pro·sod·ic \prə-ˈsäd-ik *also* -ˈzäd-\ *adj* **:** of or relating to prosody — **pro·sod·i·cal** \-i-kəl\ *adj* — **pro·sod·i·cal·ly** \-i-k(ə-)lē\ *adv*

pros·o·dist \ˈpräs-əd-əst\ *n* **:** a specialist in prosody

pros·o·dy \ˈpräs-əd-ē\ *n* [ME, fr. L *prosodia* accent of a syllable, fr. Gk *prosōidia* song sung to instrumental music, accent, fr. *pros* in addition to + *ōidē* song — more at PROS-, ODE] **1 :** the study of versification; *esp* **:** the systematic study of metrical structure **:** METRICS **2 :** a particular system, theory, or style of versification

pro·so·ma \prə-ˈsō-mə\ *n* [NL, fr. Gk *pro-* + *sōma* body; akin to L *tumēre* to swell — more at THUMB] **:** the anterior region of the body of an invertebrate when not readily analyzable into its primitive segmentation; *esp* **:** CEPHALOTHORAX — **pro·so·mal** \-məl\ *adj*

pro·so·po·poe·ia \prə-ˌsō-pə-ˈpē-(y)ə, ˌpräs-ə-pə-\ *n* [L, fr. Gk *prosōpopoiia*, fr. *prosōpon* mask, person (fr. *pros-* + *ōps* face) + *poiein* to make — more at EYE, POET] **1 :** a figure of speech in which an imaginary or absent person is represented as speaking or acting **2 :** PERSONIFICATION

1pros·pect \ˈpräs-ˌpekt\ *n* [ME, fr. L *prospectus* view, prospect, fr. *prospectus*, pp. of *prospicere* to look forward, exercise foresight, fr. *pro-* forward + *specere* to look — more at PRO-, SKY] **1 :** OUTLOOK, EXPOSURE 2b **2 a** (1) **:** an extensive view (2) **:** a mental consideration **:** SURVEY **b :** a place that commands an extensive view **:** LOOKOUT **c :** something extended to the view **:** SCENE **d** *archaic* **:** a sketch or picture of a scene **3** *obs* **:** ASPECT **4 a :** act of looking forward **:** ANTICIPATION **b :** a mental picture of something to come **:** VISION **c :** something that is awaited or expected **:** POSSIBILITY **d** *pl* (1) **:** financial expectations (2) **:** CHANCES **5 a :** a place showing signs of containing a mineral deposit **b :** a partly developed mine **c :** the mineral yield of a tested sample of ore or gravel **6 a :** a potential buyer or customer **b :** a likely candidate

syn PROSPECT, OUTLOOK, ANTICIPATION, FORETASTE mean an advance realization of something to come. PROSPECT implies expectation of a particular event, condition, or development of definite interest or concern; OUTLOOK suggests a forecasting of the future; ANTICIPATION implies a prospect or outlook that involves advance suffering or enjoyment of what is foreseen; FORETASTE implies an actual though brief or partial experience of something that will or may come later in full force

2pros·pect \ˈpräs-ˌpekt, *chiefly Brit* prəs-ˈ\ *vi* **:** to explore an area esp. for mineral deposits ~ *vt* **:** to inspect (a region) for mineral deposits; *broadly* **:** EXPLORE — **pros·pec·tor** \-ˌpek-tər, -ˈpek-\ *n*

pro·spec·tive \prə-ˈspek-tiv *also* ˈprä-, ˌprō-ˈ, prä-ˈ\ *adj* **1 :** relating to or effective in the future **2 :** EXPECTANT, EXPECTED — **pro·spec·tive·ly** *adv*

pro·spec·tus \prə-ˈspek-təs, prä-\ *n* [L, prospect] **:** a preliminary printed statement that describes an enterprise (as a business) and is distributed to prospective buyers, investors, or participants

pros·per \ˈpräs-pər\ *vb* **pros·per·ing** \-p(ə-)riŋ\ [ME *prosperen*, fr. MF *prosperer*, fr. L *prosperare* to cause to succeed, fr. *prosperus* favorable] *vi* **1 :** SUCCEED; *esp* **:** to achieve economic success **2 :** FLOURISH, THRIVE ~ *vt* **:** to cause to succeed or thrive

pros·per·i·ty \prä-ˈsper-ət-ē\ *n* **:** the condition of being successful or thriving; *esp* **:** economic well-being

Pros·pero \ˈpräs-pə-ˌrō\ *n* **:** the rightful duke of Milan in Shakespeare's *The Tempest*

pros·per·ous \ˈpräs-p(ə-)rəs\ *adj* [ME, fr. MF *prospereux*, fr. *prosperer* to prosper + *-eux* -ous] **1 :** AUSPICIOUS, FAVORABLE **2 a :** marked by success or economic well-being **b :** FLOURISHING — **pros·per·ous·ly** *adv* — **pros·per·ous·ness** *n*

pros·tate \ˈpräs-ˌtāt\ *also* **pros·tat·ic** \prä-ˈstat-ik\ *adj* [NL *prostata* prostate gland, fr. Gk *prostatēs*, fr. *proïstanai* to put in front, fr. *pro-* before + *histanai* to cause to stand — more at PRO-, STAND] **:** of or relating to or being the prostate gland

pros·ta·tec·to·my \ˌpräs-tə-ˈtek-tə-mē\ *n* **:** surgical removal of the prostate gland

prostate gland *n* **:** a firm partly muscular partly glandular body about the base of the mammalian male urethra

pros·ta·tism \ˈpräs-tə-ˌtiz-əm\ *n* **:** disease of the prostate; *esp* **:** a disorder resulting from obstruction of the bladder neck by an enlarged prostate

pros·the·sis \präs-ˈthē-səs, ˈpräs-thə-\ *n, pl* **pros·the·ses** \-ˌsēz\ [NL, fr. Gk, addition, fr. *prostithenai* to add to, fr. *pros-* in addition to + *tithenai* to put — more at PROS-, DO] **:** an artificial device to replace a missing part of the body

pros·thet·ic \präs-ˈthet-ik\ *adj* **1 :** of or relating to a prosthesis or prosthetics **2 :** of, relating to, or constituting a nonprotein group of a conjugated protein — **pros·thet·i·cal·ly** \-i-k(ə-)lē\ *adv*

pros·thet·ics \-iks\ *n pl but sing or pl in constr* **:** the surgical and dental specialties concerned with the artificial replacement of missing parts

prosth·odon·tics \ˌpräs-thə-ˈdänt-iks\ *n pl but sing or pl in constr* [NL *prosthodontia*, fr. *prosthesis* + *-odontia*] **:** prosthetic dentistry — **prosth·odon·tist** \-ˈdänt-əst\ *n*

1pros·ti·tute \ˈpräs-tə-ˌt(y)üt\ *vt* [L *prostitutus*, pp. of *prostituere*, fr. *pro-* before + *statuere* to station — more at PRO-, STATUTE] **1 :** to offer indiscriminately for sexual intercourse esp. for money **2 :** to devote to corrupt or unworthy purposes **:** DEBASE — **pros·ti·tu·tor** \-ˌt(y)üt-ər\ *n*

2prostitute *adj* **:** devoted to corrupt purposes **:** PROSTITUTED

3prostitute *n* **1 :** a woman who engages in promiscuous sexual intercourse esp. for money **:** WHORE **2 :** a person who deliberately debases himself for consideration (as money)

pros·ti·tu·tion \ˌpräs-tə-ˈt(y)ü-shən\ *n* **1 :** the act or practice of indulging in promiscuous sexual relations esp. for money **2 :** the state of being prostituted **:** DEBASEMENT

pro·sto·mi·al \prō-ˈstō-mē-əl\ *adj* **:** of or relating to the prostomium

pro·sto·mi·um \prō-ˈstō-mē-əm\ *n, pl* **pro·sto·mia** \-mē-ə\ [NL, fr. Gk *pro-* + *stoma* mouth — more at STOMACH] **:** the portion of the head of various worms and mollusks situated in front of the mouth and usu. held to be nonmetameric

1pros·trate \ˈpräs-ˌtrāt\ *adj* [ME *prostrat*, fr. L *prostratus*, pp. of *prosternere*, fr. *pro-* before + *sternere* to spread out, throw down — more at STREW] **1 a :** stretched out with face on the ground in adoration or submission **b :** extended in a horizontal position **:** FLAT **2 :** lacking in vitality or will **:** OVERCOME **3 :** trailing on the ground **:** PROCUMBENT ⟨~ shrub⟩ **syn** see PRONE

2prostrate *vt* **1 :** to throw or put into a prostrate position **2 :** to reduce to submission, helplessness, or exhaustion **:** OVERCOME

pros·tra·tion \prä-ˈstrā-shən\ *n* **1 a :** the act of assuming a prostrate position **b :** the state of being in a prostrate position **:** ABASEMENT **2 a :** complete physical or mental exhaustion **:** COLLAPSE **b :** HELPLESSNESS, POWERLESSNESS

prosy \ˈprō-zē\ *adj* **1 :** PROSAIC **2 :** TEDIOUS

prot- *or* **proto-** *comb form* [ME *protho-*, fr. MF, fr. LL *proto-*, fr. Gk *prōt-*, *prōto-*, fr. *prōtos*; akin to Gk *pro* before — more at FOR] **1 :** first in time ⟨*proto*lithic⟩ ⟨*proto*nymph⟩ **2 a :** first or lowest of a series and as such usu. having the smallest relative amount of a (specified) element or radical ⟨*prot*oxide⟩ **b :** parent substance of a (specified) substance ⟨*prot*actinium⟩ **3 :** first formed **:** primary ⟨*proto*xylem⟩ **4** *cap* **:** relating to or constituting the recorded or assumed language that is ancestral to a language or to a group of related languages or dialects ⟨*Proto*-Indo-European⟩

prot·ac·tin·i·um \ˌprōt-ˌak-ˈtin-ē-əm\ *n* [NL] **:** a shiny metallic radioelement of relatively short life — see ELEMENT table

pro·tag·o·nist \prō-ˈtag-ə-nəst\ *n* [Gk *prōtagōnistēs*, fr. *prōt-* prot- + *agōnistēs* competitor at games, actor, fr. *agōnizesthai* to compete, fr. *agōn* contest, competition at games — more at AGONY] **1 :** one who takes the leading part in a drama, novel, or story **2 :** the leader of a cause **:** CHAMPION **3 :** a muscle that by its contraction actually causes a particular movement

prot·amine \ˈprōt-ə-ˌmēn\ *n* [ISV] **:** any of various simple strongly basic proteins that are not coagulable by heat but are soluble in water and dilute ammonia

prot·a·sis \ˈprät-ə-səs\ *n, pl* **prot·a·ses** \-ə-ˌsēz\ [LL, fr. Gk, premise of a syllogism, conditional clause, fr. *proteinein* to stretch out before, put forward, fr. *pro-* + *teinein* to stretch — more at THIN] **1 :** the introductory part of a play or narrative poem **2 :** CONDITION 2b — **pro·tat·ic** \prä-ˈtat-ik\ *adj*

prote- *or* **proteo-** *comb form* [ISV, fr. F *protéine*] **:** protein ⟨*prote*olysis⟩ ⟨*proteo*se⟩

pro·tea \ˈprōt-ē-ə\ *n* [NL, genus name, fr. L *Proteus*, sea god able to assume various shapes] **:** any of a genus (*Protea* of the family Proteaceae, the protea family) of evergreen shrubs often grown for their showy bracts and dense flower heads

pro·te·an \ˈprōt-ē-ən, prō-ˈtē-\ *adj* **1 :** of or resembling Proteus **:** VARIABLE **2 :** readily assuming different shapes or roles

pro·te·ase \ˈprōt-ē-ˌās, -ˌāz\ *n* [ISV] **:** PROTEINASE, PEPTIDASE

pro·tect \prə-ˈtekt\ *vt* [L *protectus*, pp. of *protegere*, fr. *pro-* in front + *tegere* to cover — more at PRO-, THATCH] **1 a :** to cover or shield from injury or destruction **:** GUARD **b :** to save from contingent financial loss **2 :** to shield or foster by a protective tariff **syn** see DEFEND

pro·tec·tion \prə-ˈtek-shən\ *n* **1 :** the act of protecting **:** the state of being protected **2 a :** one that protects **b :** the oversight or support of one that is smaller and weaker **3 :** the freeing of the producers of a country from foreign competition in their home market by high duties or other restrictions on foreign competitive goods **4 a :** immunity from prosecution purchased by criminals through bribery **b :** money extorted by racketeers posing as a protective association **5 :** COVERAGE 2a — **pro·tec·tive** \-ˈtektiv\ *adj* — **pro·tec·tive·ly** *adv*

pro·tec·tion·ism \-shə-ˌniz-əm\ *n* **:** the doctrine or policy of protectionists

pro·tec·tion·ist \-sh(ə-)nəst\ *n* **:** an advocate of government economic protection for domestic producers through restrictions on foreign competitors — **protectionist** *adj*

protective tariff *n* **:** a tariff intended primarily to protect domestic producers rather than to yield revenue

pro·tec·tor \prə-ˈtek-tər\ *n* **1 a :** one that protects **:** GUARDIAN **b :** a device used to prevent injury **:** GUARD **2 :** one having the care of a kingdom during the king's minority **:** REGENT — **pro·tec·tor·ship** \-ˌship\ *n* — **pro·tec·tress** \-ˈtek-trəs\ *n*

pro·tec·tor·al \-ˈtek-t(ə-)rəl\ *adj* **:** of or relating to a protector or protectorate

pro·tec·tor·ate \-ˈtek-t(ə-)rət\ *n* **1 a :** government by a protector **b :** the government of England (1653–59) under the Cromwells **c :** the rank, office, or period of rule of a protector **2 a :** the relationship of superior authority assumed by one power or state over a dependent one **b :** the dependent political unit in such a relationship

pro·tec·to·ry \-t(ə-)rē\ *n* **:** an institution for the protection and care usu. of homeless or delinquent children

pro·té·gé \ˈprōt-ə-ˌzhā, ˌprōt-ə-ˈ\ *n* [F, fr. pp. of *protéger* to protect, fr. L *protegere*] **:** a man under the care and protection of an influential person usu. for the furthering of his career

pro·té·gée \ˈprōt-ə-ˌzhā, ˌprōt-ə-ˈ\ *n* [F, fem. of *protégé*] **:** a female protégé

pro·teid \ˈprō-ˌtēd, ˈprōt-ē-əd\ *n* [ISV, fr. *protein*] **:** PROTEIN 1

pro·te·ide \ˈprōt-ē-ˌīd\ *n* [ISV, fr. *protein*] **:** PROTEIN 1

pro·tein \ˈprō-ˌtēn, ˈprōt-ē-ən\ *n, often attrib* [F *protéine*, fr. LGk *prōteios* primary, fr. Gk *prōtos* first — more at PROT-] **1 :** any of numerous naturally occurring extremely complex combinations of amino acids that contain the elements carbon, hydrogen, nitrogen, oxygen, usu. sulfur, occas. phosphorus, iron, or other elements, are essential constituents of all living cells, and are synthesized from raw materials by plants but assimilated as separate amino acids by animals **2 :** the total nitrogenous material in plant or animal substances

pro·tein·aceous \ˌprō-ˌtē-ˈnā-shəs, ˌprōt-ē-ə-ˈnā-\ *adj* **:** of, relating to, resembling, or being protein
pro·tein·ase \ˈprō-ˌtē-ˌnās, ˈprōt-ē-ə-, -ˌnāz\ *n* [ISV] **:** an enzyme that hydrolyzes proteins esp. to peptides
pro·tein·ate \-ˌnāt\ *n* **:** a compound of a protein ⟨silver ~⟩
pro·tein·uria \ˌprō-ˌtē-ˈn(y)u̇r-ē-ə, ˌprōt-ē-ə-\ *n* [NL, fr. ISV *protein* + NL *-uria*] **:** the presence of protein in the urine — **pro·tein·uric** \-ˈn(y)u̇r-ik\ *adj*
pro tem \prō-ˈtem\ *adv* [short for *pro tempore*] **:** for the time being
pro tem·po·re \prō-ˈtem-pə-rē\ *adv* [L] **:** for the time being **:** TEMPORARILY
pro·tend \prō-ˈtend\ *vb* [ME *protenden*, fr. L *protendere*, fr. *pro-* + *tendere* to stretch — more at THIN] **:** to stretch forth **:** EXTEND
pro·ten·sive \-ˈten(t)-siv\ *adj* [L *protensus*, pp. of *protendere*] **1 :** having continuance in time **2 :** having lengthwise extent or extensiveness — **pro·ten·sive·ly** *adv*
pro·teo·clas·tic \ˌprōt-ē-ō-ˈklas-tik\ *adj* [*prote-* + Gk *klan* to break — more at HALT] **:** PROTEOLYTIC
pro·te·ol·y·sis \ˌprōt-ē-ˈäl-ə-səs\ *n* [NL] **:** the hydrolysis of proteins or peptides with formation of simpler and soluble products — **pro·teo·lyt·ic** \ˌprōt-ē-ə-ˈlit-ik\ *adj*
pro·te·ose \ˈprōt-ē-ˌōs, -ˌōz\ *n* [ISV] **:** any of various water-soluble protein derivatives formed by partial hydrolysis of proteins
pro·ter·an·thous \ˌprät-ə-ˈran(t)-thəs, ˌprōt-\ *adj* [Gk *proteros* + *anthos* flower — more at ANTHOLOGY] **:** having flowers appearing before the leaves — **pro·ter·an·thy** \ˈprät-ə-ˌran(t)-thē, ˈprōt-\ *n*
Pro·tero·zo·ic \ˌprät-ə-rə-ˈzō-ik, ˌprōt-\ *adj* [Gk *proteros* former, earlier (fr. *pro* before) + ISV *-zoic* — more at FOR] **:** of, relating to, or being an era of geological history that includes the interval between the Archeozoic and the Paleozoic, perhaps exceeds in length all of subsequent geological time, and is marked by rocks that contain a few fossils indicating the existence of annelid worms and algae; *also* **:** relating to the system of rocks formed in this era — **Proterozoic** *n*
[1]**pro·test** \ˈprō-ˌtest\ *n* **1 :** a solemn declaration of opinion and usu. of dissent: as **a :** a sworn declaration that payment of a note or bill has been refused and that all responsible signers or debtors are liable for resulting loss or damage **b :** a formal declaration of dissent by a member to an act or resolution of a legislature; *esp* **:** one made by a member of the House of Lords **c :** a declaration made esp. before or while paying that a tax is illegal and that payment is not voluntary **d :** a solemn declaration of disapproval **2 :** the act of protesting **3 a :** a complaint, objection, or display of unwillingness usu. to an idea or a course of action **b :** a gesture of extreme disapproval **4 :** an objection made to an official or a governing body of a sport
[2]**pro·test** \prə-ˈtest, ˈprō-ˌ, prō-ˈ\ *vb* [ME *protesten*, fr. MF *protester*, fr. L *protestari*, fr. *pro-* forth + *testari* to call to witness — more at PRO-, TESTAMENT] *vt* **1 :** to make solemn declaration or affirmation of **:** AVOW **2 :** to make or procure to be made a notarial protest of **3 :** to make a protest against **4 :** to object to ~ *vi* **1 :** to make a protestation **2 :** to make or enter a protest **syn** see ASSERT, OBJECT
prot·es·tant \ˈprät-əs-tənt, *2 is also* prə-ˈtes-\ *n* [MF, fr. L *protestant-, protestans*, prp. of *protestari*] **1** *cap* **a :** one of a group of German princes and cities presenting a defense of freedom of conscience against an edict of the Diet of Spires in 1529 intended to suppress the Lutheran movement **b :** a member or adherent of one of the Christian churches deriving from the Reformation and affirming justification by faith, the priesthood of all believers, and the primacy of the Bible **c :** a Christian not of a Catholic or Eastern church **2 :** one who makes or enters a protest — **protestant** *adj, often cap* — **Prot·es·tant·ism** \ˈprät-əs-tənt-ˌiz-əm\ *n*
pro·tes·ta·tion \ˌprät-əs-ˈtā-shən, ˌprō-ˌtes-, ˌprōt-əs-, ˌprät-ˌes-\ *n* **:** the act of protesting **:** a solemn declaration or avowal
Pro·teus \ˈprō-ˌt(y)üs, ˈprōt-ē-əs\ *n* [L, fr. Gk *Prōteus*] **:** a sea god in Greek mythology capable of assuming different forms
pro·tha·la·mi·on \ˌprō-thə-ˈlā-mē-ən, -ˌän\ *or* **pro·tha·la·mi·um** \-mē-əm\ *n, pl* **pro·tha·la·mia** \-mē-ə\ [NL, fr. Gk *pro-* + *-thalamion* (as in *epithalamion*)] **:** a song in celebration of a marriage
pro·thal·li·al \(ˈ)prō-ˈthal-ē-əl\ *adj* **:** of or relating to a prothallium
pro·thal·li·um \-ē-əm\ *n, pl* **pro·thal·lia** \-ē-ə\ [NL, fr. *pro-* + *thallus*] **1 :** the gametophyte of a fern or other pteridophyte that is typically a small flat green thallus attached to the soil by rhizoids **2 :** a greatly reduced structure of a seed plant corresponding to the pteridophyte prothallium
proth·e·sis \ˈpräth-ə-səs\ *n, pl* **proth·e·ses** \-ə-ˌsēz\ [LL, alter. of *prosthesis*, fr. Gk, lit., addition — more at PROSTHESIS] **:** the addition of a sound to the beginning of a word — **pro·thet·ic** \prä-ˈthet-ik\ *adj*
prothe·tely \ˈpräth-ə-ˌtel-ē\ *n* [prob. fr. Gk *protithenai* to put before (fr. *pro-* + *tithenai* to put) + *telein* to complete, perfect, fr. *telos* end — more at DO, WHEEL] **:** relatively precocious differentiation of a structure usu. associated with a later stage of development
pro·tho·no·tar·i·al \(ˌ)prō-ˌthän-ə-ˈter-ē-əl, ˌprō-thə-nō-ˈter-\ *adj* **:** of or relating to a prothonotary
pro·tho·no·ta·ry \prō-ˈthän-ə-ˌter-ē, ˌprō-thə-ˈnōt-ə-rē\ *or* **pro·to·no·ta·ry** \prō-ˈtän-ə-ˌter-ē, ˌprōt-ə-ˈnōt-ə-rē\ *n* [ME *prothonotarie*, fr. LL *protonotarius*, fr. *prot-* + L *notarius* notary] **:** a chief clerk of any of various courts of law
prothonotary apostolic *n, pl* **prothonotaries apostolic :** a priest of the chief college of the papal curia who keeps records of consistories and canonizations and signs papal bulls; *also* **:** an honorary member of this college
pro·tho·rac·ic \ˌprō-thə-ˈras-ik\ *adj* **:** of or relating to the prothorax
pro·tho·rax \(ˈ)prō-ˈthō(ə)r-ˌaks, -ˈthȯ(ə)r-\ *n* [NL *prothorac-, prothorax*, fr. [1]*pro-* + *thorax*] **:** the anterior segment of the thorax of an insect
pro·throm·bin \(ˈ)prō-ˈthräm-bən\ *n* [ISV] **:** a plasma protein produced in the liver in the presence of vitamin K and converted into thrombin in the clotting of blood
pro·tist \ˈprōt-əst, ˈprō-ˌtist\ *n* [deriv. of Gk *prōtistos* very first, primal, fr. superl. of *prōtos* first — more at PROT-] **:** any of a kingdom or other group (Protista) of unicellular or acellular organisms comprising bacteria, protozoans, various algae and fungi, and sometimes viruses — **pro·tis·tan** \prō-ˈtis-tən\ *adj or n*
pro·ti·um \ˈprōt-ē-əm, ˈprō-shē-\ *n* [NL, fr. Gk *prōtos* first] **:** the ordinary light hydrogen isotope of atomic mass 1
proto- — see PROT-
pro·to·ac·tin·i·um \ˌprōt-(ˌ)ō-ˌak-ˈtin-ē-əm\ *var of* PROTACTINIUM
pro·to·col \ˈprōt-ə-ˌkȯl, -ˌkōl, -ˌkäl, -kəl\ *n* [MF *prothocole*, fr. ML *protocollum*, fr. LGk *prōtokollon* first sheet of a papyrus roll bearing data of manufacture, fr. Gk *prōt-* prot- + *kollan* to glue together, fr. *kolla* glue; akin to MD *helen* to glue] **1 :** an original draft, minute, or record of a document or transaction **2 a :** a preliminary memorandum of diplomatic negotiation **b :** the records or minutes of a diplomatic conference or congress **3 :** a code of diplomatic or military etiquette and precedence
pro·to·his·tor·ic \ˌprōt-(ˌ)ō-his-ˈtȯr-ik, -ˈtär-\ *adj* **:** of or relating to protohistory
pro·to·his·to·ry \-ˈhis-t(ə-)rē\ *n* [ISV] **:** the study of man in the times that just antedate recorded history
pro·to·hu·man \-ˈhyü-mən, -ˈyü-\ *adj* **:** of, relating to, or resembling an early primitive human or a manlike primate
pro·to·lan·guage \ˈprōt-ō-ˌlaŋ-gwij\ *n* **:** an assumed or fragmentary ancestral language
pro·to·lith·ic \ˌprōt-ə-ˈlith-ik\ *adj* **:** of or relating to the earliest period of the Stone Age **:** EOLITHIC
pro·to·mar·tyr \ˈprōt-ō-ˌmärt-ər\ *n* [ME *prothomartir*, fr. MF, fr. LL *protomartyr*, fr. LGk *prōtomartyr-, prōtomartys*, fr. Gk *prōt-* + *martyr-, martys* martyr] **:** the first martyr in a cause or region
pro·ton \ˈprō-ˌtän\ *n* [Gk *prōton*, neut. of *prōtos* first — more at PROT-] **:** an elementary particle that is identical with the nucleus of the hydrogen atom, that along with neutrons is a constituent of all other atomic nuclei, that carries a positive charge numerically equal to the charge of an electron, and that has a mass of 1.672×10^{-24} gram — **pro·ton·ic** \prō-ˈtän-ik\ *adj*
pro·to·ne·ma \ˌprōt-ə-ˈnē-mə\ *n, pl* **pro·to·ne·ma·ta** \-ˈnē-mət-ə, -ˈnem-ət-\ [NL *protonemat-, protonema*, fr. *prot-* + Gk *nēma* thread — more at NEMAT-] **:** the primary usu. filamentous thalloid stage of the gametophyte in mosses and in some liverworts corresponding somewhat to the prothallium in ferns — **pro·to·ne·mal** \-ˈnē-məl\ *adj* — **pro·to·ne·ma·tal** \-ˈnē-mət-ᵊl, -ˈnem-ət-\ *adj*
pro·ton–syn·chro·tron \ˈprō-ˌtän-ˈsiŋ-k(r)ə-ˌträn, -ˈsin-\ *n* **:** a synchrotron in which protons are accelerated by means of frequency modulation of the radio-frequency accelerating voltage so that they have energies of billions of electron volts
pro·to·nymph \ˈprōt-ə-ˌnim(p)f\ *n* **:** any of various acarids in their first developmental stage — **pro·to·nym·phal** \ˌprōt-ə-ˈnim(p)-fəl\ *adj*
pro·to·path·ic \ˌprōt-ə-ˈpath-ik\ *adj* [ISV, fr. MGk *prōtopathēs* affected first, fr. Gk *prōt-* prot- + *pathos* experience, suffering — more at PATHOS] **:** of, relating to, or being cutaneous sensory reception responsive only to rather gross stimuli
pro·to·phlo·em \-ˈflō-ˌem\ *n* **:** the first-formed phloem developing from procambium and consisting of narrow thin-walled cells capable of a limited amount of stretching and usu. associated with a region of rapid growth
pro·to·plasm \ˈprōt-ə-ˌplaz-əm\ *n* [G *protoplasma*, fr. *prot-* + NL *plasma*] **1 :** the colloidal complex of protein, other organic and inorganic substances, and water that constitutes the living nucleus, cytoplasm, plastids, and mitochondria of the cell and is regarded as the only form of matter in which the vital phenomena are manifested **2 :** CYTOPLASM — **pro·to·plas·mic** \ˌprōt-ə-ˈplaz-mik\ *adj*
pro·to·plast \ˈprōt-ə-ˌplast\ *n* [MF *protoplaste*, fr. LL *protoplastus* first man, fr. Gk *prōtoplastos* first formed, fr. *prōt-* prot- + *plastos* formed, fr. *plassein* to mold — more at PLASTER] **1 :** one that is formed first **:** PROTOTYPE **2 a :** the nucleus, cytoplasm, and plasma membrane of a cell constituting a living unit distinct from inert walls and inclusions **b :** ENERGID — **pro·to·plas·tic** \ˌprōt-ə-ˈplas-tik\ *adj*
pro·to·por·phy·rin \ˌprōt-ō-ˈpȯr-f(ə-)rən\ *n* [ISV] **:** a purple porphyrin acid $C_{34}H_{34}N_4O_4$ obtained from hemin or heme by removal of bound iron
pro·to·stele \ˈprōt-ə-ˌstēl, ˌprōt-ə-ˈstē-lē\ *n* **:** a stele forming a solid rod with the phloem surrounding the xylem — **pro·to·ste·lic** \ˌprōt-ə-ˈstē-lik\ *adj*
pro·to·tro·phic \ˌprōt-ə-ˈträf-ik, -ˈtrō-fik\ *adj* [ISV] **:** deriving nutriment from inorganic sources
pro·to·typ·al \ˌprōt-ə-ˈtī-pəl\ *adj* **:** of, relating to, or constituting a prototype **:** ARCHETYPAL
pro·to·type \ˈprōt-ə-ˌtīp\ *n* [F, fr. Gk *prōtotypon*, fr. neut. of *prōtotypos* archetypal, fr. *prōt-* + *typos* type] **1 :** an original model on which something is patterned **:** ARCHETYPE **2 :** an individual that exhibits the essential features of a later type **3 :** a standard or typical example — **pro·to·typ·ic** \ˌprōt-ə-ˈtip-ik\ *adj*
pro·to·xy·lem \ˌprōt-ə-ˈzī-ləm, -ˌlem\ *n* **:** the first-formed xylem developing from procambium and consisting of narrow cells with annular, spiral, or scalariform wall thickenings
pro·to·zo·al \ˌprōt-ə-ˈzō-əl\ *adj* **:** PROTOZOAN
pro·to·zo·an \ˌprōt-ə-ˈzō-ən\ *n* [NL *Protozoa*, phylum name, fr. *prot-* + *-zoa*] **:** any of a phylum or subkingdom (Protozoa) of minute protoplasmic acellular or unicellular animals with varied morphology and physiology and often complex life cycles that are represented in most habitats including the parasitic — **protozoan** *adj* — **pro·to·zo·ic** \-ˈzō-ik\ *adj*
pro·to·zo·ol·o·gy \-zō-ˈäl-ə-jē, -zə-ˈwäl-\ *n* [NL *Protozoa* + ISV *-logy*] **:** a branch of zoology dealing with protozoans
pro·to·zo·on \-ˈzō-ˌän\ *n, pl* **pro·to·zoa** \-ˈzō-ə\ [NL, fr. sing. of *Protozoa*] **:** PROTOZOAN
pro·tract \prō-ˈtrakt, p(r)ə-\ *vt* [L *protractus*, pp. of *protrahere*, lit., to draw forward, fr. *pro-* forward + *trahere* to draw — more at PRO-, DRAW] **1** *archaic* **:** DELAY, DEFER **2 :** to prolong in time or space **3 :** to lay down the lines and angles of with scale and protractor **:** PLOT **syn** see EXTEND — **pro·trac·tive** \-ˈtrak-tiv\ *adj*
protracted meeting *n* **:** a series of revival meetings extending over a period of time
pro·trac·tile \-ˈtrak-tᵊl, -ˌtīl\ *adj* [L *protractus*] **:** capable of being thrust out **:** PROTRUSILE
pro·trac·tion \-ˈtrak-shən\ *n* [LL *protraction-, protractio* act of drawing out, fr. *protractus*] **1 :** the act of protracting **:** the state of being protracted **:** PROLONGATION **2 :** the drawing to scale of an area of land
pro·trac·tor \-ˈtrak-tər\ *n* **1 a :** one that protracts, prolongs, or delays **b :** a muscle that extends a part **2 :** an instrument for laying down and measuring

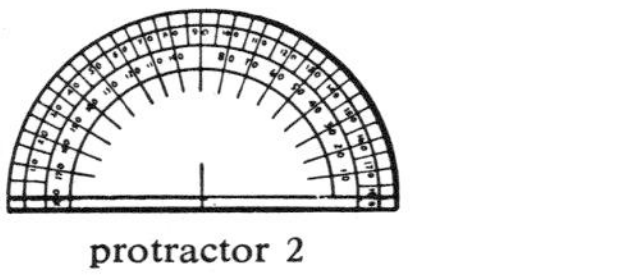

protractor 2

angles that is used in drawing and plotting

1pro·trep·tic \prō-'trep-tik\ *n* [LL *protrepticus* hortatory, encouraging, fr. Gk *protreptikos*, fr. *protrepein* to turn forward, urge on, fr. *pro-* + *trepein* to turn — more at TROPE] **:** EXHORTATION

2protreptic *adj* [LL *protrepticus*] **:** HORTATORY, PERSUASIVE

pro·trude \prō-'trüd\ *vb* [L *protrudere*, fr. *pro-* + *trudere* to thrust — more at THREAT] *vt* **1** *archaic* **:** to thrust forward **2 :** to cause to project or stick out ~ *vi* **:** to jut out from the surroundings — **pro·tru·si·ble** \-'trü-sə-bəl, -zə-\ *adj*

pro·tru·sile \prō-'trü-səl, -ˌsīl, -zəl, -ˌzīl\ *adj* **:** capable of being protruded — **pro·tru·sil·i·ty** \(ˌ)prō-ˌtrü-'sil-ət-ē\ *n*

pro·tru·sion \prō-'trü-zhən\ *n* [L *protrusus*, pp. of *protrudere*] **1 :** the act of protruding **:** the state of being protruded **2 :** something that protrudes **syn** see PROJECTION

pro·tru·sive \-'trü-siv, -ziv\ *adj* **1** *archaic* **:** thrusting forward **2 :** PROTUBERANT **3 :** OBTRUSIVE, PUSHING — **pro·tru·sive·ly** *adv* — **pro·tru·sive·ness** *n*

pro·tu·ber·ance \prō-'t(y)ü-b(ə-)rən(t)s\ *n* **1 :** the quality or state of being protuberant **2 :** something that is protuberant **:** BULGE **syn** see PROJECTION

pro·tu·ber·ant \-b(ə-)rənt\ *adj* [LL *protuberant-*, *protuberans*, prp. of *protuberare* to bulge out, fr. L *pro-* forward + *tuber* hump, swelling] **1 :** bulging beyond the surrounding or adjacent surface **:** PROMINENT **2 :** forcing itself into consciousness **:** OBTRUSIVE — **pro·tu·ber·ant·ly** *adv*

proud \'prau̇d\ *adj* [ME, fr. OE *prūd*, prob. fr. OF *prod*, *prud*, *prou* capable, good, valiant, fr. LL *prode* advantage, advantageous, back-formation fr. L *prodesse* to be advantageous, fr. *pro-*, *prod-* for, in favor + *esse* to be — more at PRO-, IS] **1 :** feeling or showing pride: as **a :** having or displaying excessive self-esteem **b :** much pleased **:** EXULTANT **c :** having proper self-respect **2 :** MAGNIFICENT, GLORIOUS **3 :** VIGOROUS, SPIRITED — **proud·ly** *adv*

syn PROUD, ARROGANT, HAUGHTY, LORDLY, INSOLENT, OVERBEARING, SUPERCILIOUS, DISDAINFUL mean showing scorn for inferiors. PROUD may suggest an assumed superiority or loftiness but just as often implies strong self-respect or sense of accomplishment; ARROGANT implies a claiming for oneself more consideration or importance than is warranted; HAUGHTY suggests a consciousness of superior birth or position; LORDLY implies pomposity or an arrogant display of power; INSOLENT implies contemptuous haughtiness; OVERBEARING suggests a tyrannical manner or an intolerable insolence; SUPERCILIOUS implies a cool, patronizing haughtiness; DISDAINFUL suggests a more active and openly scornful superciliousness

syn PROUD, VAIN, VAINGLORIOUS mean aware of one's excellence or superiority. PROUD may imply justified as well as excessive self-esteem; VAIN suggests an excessive desire to win the notice or praise of others often in trivialities; VAINGLORIOUS implies a boastful or arrogant display of power, skill, or achievement

proud flesh *n* **:** an excessive growth of granulation tissue (as in an ulcer)

proud·ful \'prau̇d-fəl\ *adj*, *chiefly dial* **:** marked by or full of pride

proud·heart·ed \-'härt-əd\ *adj* **:** proud in spirit **:** HAUGHTY

Proust·ian \'prü-stē-ən\ *adj* **:** of, relating to, or characteristic of Proust or his writings

prov·able \'prü-və-bəl\ *adj* **:** capable of being proved — **prov·able·ness** *n* — **prov·ably** \-blē\ *adv*

pro·vas·cu·lar \(')prō-'vas-kyə-lər\ *adj* **:** of, relating to, or being procambium

prove \'prüv\ *vb* **proved**; **proved** *or* **prov·en** \'prü-vən, *Brit also* 'prō-\ **prov·ing** \'prü-viŋ\ [ME *proven*, fr. OF *prover*, fr. L *probare* to test, approve, prove, fr. *probus* good, honest, fr. *pro-* for, in favor + *-bus* (akin to OE *bēon* to be)] *vt* **1** *archaic* **:** EXPERIENCE **2 :** to try or ascertain by an experiment or a standard; *esp* **:** to subject to a technical testing process **3 a :** to establish the truth or validity of by evidence or demonstration **b :** to check the correctness of (as an arithmetic operation) **4 a :** to ascertain the genuineness of **:** VERIFY; *specif* **:** to obtain probate of (a will) **b :** PROOF 1 ~ *vi* **:** to turn out esp. after trial or test

prov·e·nance \'präv-(ə-)nən(t)s, -ə-ˌnän(t)s\ *n* [F, fr. *provenir* to come forth, originate, fr. L *provenire*, fr. *pro-* forth + *venire* to come — more at PRO-, COME] **:** ORIGIN, SOURCE

Pro·ven·çal \ˌpräv-ən-'säl, ˌprōv-, -ˌäⁿ-; prə-'ven(t)-səl\ *n* [MF, fr. *provençal* of Provence, fr. *Provence*] **1 :** a native or inhabitant of Provence **2 :** a Romance language spoken in southeastern France — **Provençal** *adj*

prov·en·der \'präv-ən-dər\ *n* [ME, fr. MF *provende*, *provendre*, fr. ML *provenda*, alter. of *praebenda* prebend] **1 :** dry food for domestic animals **:** FEED **2 :** FOOD, VICTUALS

pro·ve·nience \prə-'vē-nyən(t)s, -nē-ən(t)s\ *n* [alter. of *provenance*] **:** ORIGIN, SOURCE

prov·en·ly \'prü-vən-lē\ *adv* **:** in a proven manner

pro·ven·tric·u·lus \ˌprō-(ˌ)ven-'trik-yə-ləs\ *n*, *pl* **pro·ven·tric·u·li** \-ˌlī, -ˌlē\ [NL] **:** the glandular or true stomach of a bird situated between the crop and gizzard

prove out *vi* **:** to turn out to be adequate or satisfactory

prov·er \'prü-vər\ *n* **:** one that proves; *specif* **:** PROOFER

1prov·erb \'präv-ˌərb\ *n* [ME *proverbe*, fr. MF, fr. L *proverbium*, fr. *pro-* + *verbum* word — more at WORD] **1 :** a brief popular epigram or maxim **:** ADAGE **2 :** BYWORD 4

2proverb *vt* **1** *obs* **:** to provide with a proverb **2 :** to turn into a proverb or byword

pro·ver·bi·al \prə-'vər-bē-əl\ *adj* **1 :** of, relating to, or resembling a proverb **2 :** commonly spoken of — **pro·ver·bi·al·ly** \-ə-lē\ *adv*

pro·vide \prə-'vīd\ *vb* [ME *providen*, fr. L *providēre*, lit., to see ahead, fr. *pro-* forward + *vidēre* to see — more at PRO-, WIT] *vi* **1 :** to take precautionary measures **2 :** to make a proviso or stipulation **3 :** to supply what is needed for sustenance or support ~ *vt* **1** *archaic* **:** to procure in advance **:** PREPARE **2 a :** to fit out **:** EQUIP **b :** to supply for use **:** AFFORD, YIELD **3 :** STIPULATE — **pro·vid·er** *n*

pro·vid·ed *conj* [pp. of *provide*] **:** on condition that **:** with the understanding **:** IF

prov·i·dence \'präv-əd-ən(t)s, -ə-ˌden(t)s\ *n* [ME, fr. MF, fr. L *providentia*, fr. *provident-*, *providens*] **1 a** *often cap* **:** divine guidance or care **b** *cap* **:** God conceived as the power sustaining and guiding human destiny **2 :** the quality or state of being provident

prov·i·dent \-əd-ənt, -ə-ˌdent\ *adj* [L *provident-*, *providens*, fr. prp. of *providēre*] **1 :** making provision for the future **:** PRUDENT **2 :** FRUGAL, SAVING — **prov·i·dent·ly** *adv*

prov·i·den·tial \ˌpräv-ə-'den-chəl\ *adj* **1** *archaic* **:** FORESIGHTED **2 :** of, relating to, or determined by Providence **3 :** occurring by or as if by an intervention of Providence **:** OPPORTUNE ⟨~ escape⟩ **syn** see LUCKY — **prov·i·den·tial·ly** \-'dench-(ə-)lē\ *adv*

pro·vid·ing *conj* [prp. of *provide*] **:** on condition that **:** in case **:** PROVIDED

prov·ince \'präv-ən(t)s\ *n* [F, fr. L *provincia*] **1 a :** a country or region brought under the control of the ancient Roman government **b :** an administrative district or division of a country **c** *pl* **:** all of a country except the metropolis **2 a :** a division of a country forming the jurisdiction of an archbishop or metropolitan **b :** a territorial unit of a religious order **3 :** a biogeographic division of less rank than a region **4 a :** proper or appropriate business or scope **:** SPHERE **b :** a department of knowledge or activity **syn** see FUNCTION

1pro·vin·cial \prə-'vin-chəl\ *n* **1 :** the superior of a province of a Roman Catholic religious order **2 :** one living in or coming from a province **3 a :** a person of local or restricted interests or outlook **b :** a person lacking metropolitan polish or refinement

2provincial *adj* **1 :** of or relating to a province **2 :** confined to a province or region **:** NARROW **3 :** of or relating to a decorative style (as in furniture) marked by simplicity, informality, and relative plainness — **pro·vin·cial·ly** \-'vinch-(ə-)lē\ *adv*

pro·vin·cial·ism \-chə-ˌliz-əm\ *n* **1 :** a dialectal or local word, phrase, or idiom **2 :** the quality or state of being provincial

pro·vin·cial·ist \-ləst\ *n* **:** a native or inhabitant of a province

pro·vin·ci·al·i·ty \prə-ˌvin-chē-'al-ət-ē\ *n* **:** PROVINCIALISM

pro·vin·cial·ize \-'vin-chə-ˌlīz\ *vt* **:** to make provincial

proving ground *n* **:** a place for scientific experimentation or testing

1pro·vi·sion \prə-'vizh-ən\ *n* [ME, fr. MF, fr. LL & L; LL *provision-*, *provisio* act of providing, fr. L, foresight, fr. *provisus*, pp. of *providēre* to see ahead] **1 a :** the act or process of providing **b :** the quality or state of being prepared beforehand **c :** a measure taken beforehand **:** PREPARATION **2 :** a stock of needed materials or supplies; *esp* **:** a stock of food **:** VICTUALS — usu. used in pl. **3 :** PROVISO, STIPULATION

2provision *vt* **pro·vi·sion·ing** \-'vizh-(ə-)niŋ\ **:** to supply with provisions

1pro·vi·sion·al \prə-'vizh-nəl, -ən-ᵊl\ *adj* **:** provided for a temporary need but subject to change **:** CONDITIONAL — **pro·vi·sion·al·ly** \-ē\ *adv*

2provisional *n* **:** a postage stamp for use until a regular issue appears

pro·vi·sion·ary \-'vizh-ə-ˌner-ē\ *adj* **:** PROVISIONAL

pro·vi·sion·er \-'vizh-(ə-)nər\ *n* **:** VICTUALLER

pro·vi·so \prə-'vī-(ˌ)zō\ *n*, *pl* **provisos** *or* **provisoes** [ME, fr. ML *proviso quod* provided that] **:** an article or clause that introduces a condition **:** STIPULATION

pro·vi·so·ry \-'vīz-(ə-)rē\ *adj* **1 :** containing or subject to a proviso **:** CONDITIONAL **2 :** PROVISIONAL

pro·vi·ta·min \(')prō-'vīt-ə-mən\ *n* **:** a precursor of a vitamin convertible into the vitamin in an organism

prov·o·ca·tion \ˌpräv-ə-'kā-shən\ *n* [ME *provocacioun*, fr. MF *provocation*, fr. L *provocation-*, *provocatio*, fr. *provocatus*, pp. of *provocare*] **:** the act of provoking **:** INCITEMENT; *also* **:** something that provokes, arouses, or stimulates

pro·voc·a·tive \prə-'väk-ət-iv\ *adj* **:** serving or tending to provoke, excite, or stimulate — **provocative** *n* — **pro·voc·a·tive·ly** *adv* — **pro·voc·a·tive·ness** *n*

pro·voke \prə-'vōk\ *vt* [ME *provoken*, fr. MF *provoquer*, fr. L *provocare*, fr. *pro-* forth + *vocare* to call — more at PRO-, VOICE] **1 a** *archaic* **:** AROUSE, STIR **b :** to incite to anger **:** INCENSE **2 a :** to call forth **:** EVOKE **b :** to stir up purposely **:** INDUCE **c :** to provide the needed stimulus for **:** OCCASION

syn PROVOKE, EXCITE, STIMULATE, PIQUE, QUICKEN mean to arouse as if by pricking. PROVOKE directs attention to the response called forth and most often applies to an angry or vexed reaction; EXCITE implies a stirring up or moving profoundly; STIMULATE suggests a rousing out of lethargy, quiescence, or indifference; PIQUE suggests stimulating by mild irritation or challenge; QUICKEN implies beneficially stimulating and making active or lively **syn** see in addition IRRITATE

pro·vok·ing \-'vō-kiŋ\ *adj* **:** causing mild anger **:** ANNOYING — **pro·vok·ing·ly** \-kiŋ-lē\ *adv*

pro·vost \'prō-ˌvōst, 'präv-əst, 'prō-vəst, *esp attrib* ˌprō-(ˌ)vō\ *n* [ME, fr. OE *profost* & OF *provost*, fr. ML *propositus*, alter. of *praepositus*, fr. L, one in charge, director, fr. pp. of *praeponere* to place at the head — more at PREPOSITION] **1 :** the chief dignitary of a collegiate or cathedral chapter **2 :** the chief magistrate of a Scottish burgh **3 :** the keeper of a prison **4 :** a high-ranking university administrative officer

provost court *n* **:** a military court usu. for the trial of minor offenses within an occupied hostile territory

provost guard *n* **:** a police detail of soldiers under the authority of the provost marshal

provost marshal *n* **:** an officer who supervises the military police of a command esp. outside an installation

1prow \'prau̇\ *adj* [ME, fr. MF *prou* — more at PROUD] *archaic* **:** VALIANT, GALLANT

2prow \'prau̇, *archaic* 'prō\ *n* [MF *proue*, prob. fr. OIt dial. *prua*, fr. L *prora*, fr. Gk *prōira*] **1 :** the bow of a ship **:** STEM **2 :** a pointed projecting front part (as of an airplane)

prow·ess \'prau̇-əs *also* 'prō-\ *n* [ME *prouesse*, fr. OF *proesse*, fr. *prou* valiant — more at PROUD] **1 :** distinguished bravery; *esp* **:** military valor and skill **2 :** extraordinary ability **syn** see HEROISM

prowl \'prau̇(ə)l\ *vb* [ME *prollen*] *vi* **:** to move about or wander stealthily ~ *vt* **:** to roam over in a predatory manner — **prowl** *n* — **prowl·er** *n*

prowl car *n* **:** SQUAD CAR

prox·i·mal \'präk-sə-məl\ *adj* [L *proximus*] **1 :** NEAREST, PROXIMATE **2 :** next to or nearest the point of attachment or origin, a central point, or the point of view; *esp* **:** located toward the center of the body — **prox·i·mal·ly** \-mə-lē\ *adv*

prox·i·mate \-mət\ *adj* [L *proximatus*, pp. of *proximare* to ap-

proach, fr. *proximus* nearest, next, superl. of *prope* near] **1 a :** very near **:** CLOSE **b :** soon forthcoming **:** IMMINENT **2 :** next preceding or following — **prox·i·mate·ly** *adv* — **prox·i·mate·ness** *n*

prox·im·i·ty \präk-'sim-ət-ē\ *n* [MF *proximité*, fr. L *proximitat-, proximitas*, fr. *proximus*] **:** the quality or state of being proximate

proximity fuze *n* **:** an electronic device that detonates a projectile within effective range of the target by means of the radio waves sent out from a tiny radio set in the nose of the projectile and reflected back to the set from the target

prox·i·mo \'präk-sə-,mō\ *adj* [L *proximo mense* in the next month] **:** of or occurring in the next month after the present

proxy \'präk-sē\ *n* [ME *procucie*, contr. of *procuracie*, fr. AF, fr. ML *procuratia*, alter. of L *procuratio* procuration] **1 :** the agency, function, or office of a deputy who acts as a substitute for another **2 a :** authority or power to act for another **b :** a document giving such authority; *specif* **:** a power of attorney authorizing a specified person to vote corporate stock **3 :** PROCURATOR — **proxy** *adj*

proxy marriage *n* **:** a marriage celebrated in the absence of one of the contracting parties who authorizes a proxy to represent him at the ceremony

prude \'prüd\ *n* [F, good woman, prudish woman, short for *prudefemme* good woman, fr. OF *prode femme*] **:** a person who is excessively or priggishly attentive to propriety or decorum; *esp* **:** a woman who shows or affects extreme modesty

pru·dence \'prüd-ᵊn(t)s\ *n* **1 :** the ability to govern and discipline oneself by the use of reason **2 :** sagacity or shrewdness in the management of affairs **:** DISCRETION **3 :** providence in the use of resources **4 :** caution or circumspection as to danger or risk

pru·dent \-ᵊnt\ *adj* [ME, fr. MF, fr. L *prudent-, prudens*, contr. of *provident-, providens* — more at PROVIDENT] **1 :** FORESIGHTED, WISE **2 :** shrewd in the management of practical affairs **3 :** CIRCUMSPECT, DISCREET **4 :** PROVIDENT, FRUGAL **syn** see WISE— **pru·dent·ly** *adv*

pru·den·tial \prü-'den-chəl\ *adj* **1 :** of, relating to, or proceeding from prudence **2 :** exercising prudence esp. in business matters — **pru·den·tial·ly** \-chə-lē\ *adv*

prud·ery \'prüd-(ə-)rē\ *n* **:** the quality or state of being a prude

prud·ish \'prüd-ish\ *adj* **:** marked by prudery **:** PRIGGISH — **prud·ish·ly** *adv* — **prud·ish·ness** *n*

pru·inose \'prü-ə-,nōs\ *adj* [L *pruinosus* covered with hoarfrost, fr. *pruina* hoarfrost] **:** covered with whitish dust or bloom

1**prune** \'prün\ *n* [ME, fr. MF, plum, fr. L *prunum* — more at PLUM] **:** a plum dried or capable of drying without fermentation

2**prune** *vb* [ME *prouynen*, fr. MF *proignier*, prob. alter. of *provigner* to layer, fr. *provain* layer, fr. L *propagin-, propago*, fr. *pro-* forward + *pangere* to fix] *vt* **1 :** to cut off or cut back parts of for better shape or more fruitful growth **2 a :** to reduce by eliminating superfluous matter **b :** to remove as superfluous **c :** to effect a reduction in ~ *vi* **:** to cut away what is unwanted — **prun·er** *n*

pru·nel·la \prü-'nel-ə\ *also* **pru·nelle** \-'nel\ *n* [F *prunelle*, lit., sloe, fr. dim. of *prune* plum] **1 :** a twilled woolen dress fabric **2 :** a heavy woolen fabric used for the uppers of shoes

pruning hook *n* **:** a pole bearing a curved blade for pruning plants

pru·ri·ence \'prür-ē-ən(t)s\ *n* **:** the quality or state of being prurient

pru·ri·en·cy \-ən-sē\ *n* **:** PRURIENCE

pru·ri·ent \'prür-ē-ənt\ *adj* [L *prurient-, pruriens*, prp. of *prurire* to itch, crave, be wanton; akin to L *pruna* glowing coal, Skt *ploṣati* he singes] **1 :** craving restlessly **2 :** lascivious in thought or desire **3 :** exciting to lasciviousness — **pru·ri·ent·ly** *adv*

pru·rig·i·nous \prü-'rij-ə-nəs\ *adj* [L *pruriginosus* having the itch, fr. *prurigin-, prurigo*] **:** resembling, caused by, affected with, or being prurigo

pru·ri·go \prü-'rī-(,)gō, -'rē-\ *n* [NL, fr. L, itch, fr. *prurire*] **:** a chronic inflammatory skin disease marked by itching papules

pru·rit·ic \-'rit-ik\ *adj* **:** of, relating to, or marked by itching

pru·ri·tus \-'rīt-əs, -'rēt-\ *n* [L, fr. *pruritus*, pp. of *prurire*] **:** ITCHING

Prus·sian blue \,prəsh-ən-\ *n* [*Prussian* (of Prussia)] **1 :** any of numerous blue iron pigments formerly regarded as ferric ferrocyanide **2 :** a dark blue crystalline hydrated ferric ferrocyanide $Fe_4[Fe(CN)_6]_3.xH_2O$ used as a test for ferric iron

Prus·sian·ism \'prəsh-ə-,niz-əm\ *n* **:** the practices or policies (as the advocacy of militarism) held to be typically Prussian

prus·sian·ize \-,nīz\ *vt, often cap* **:** to make Prussian in character or principle (as in authoritarian control or rigid discipline)

prus·si·ate \'prəs-ē-,āt\ *n* [F, fr. (*acide*) *prussique*] **1 :** a salt of hydrocyanic acid **:** CYANIDE **2 a :** FERROCYANIDE **b :** FERRICYANIDE

prus·sic acid \,prəs-ik-\ *n* [F (*acide*) *prussique*, fr. (*bleu de*) *Prusse* Prussian blue] **:** HYDROCYANIC ACID

1**pry** \'prī\ *vi* **pried; pry·ing** [ME *prien*] **:** to look closely or inquisitively **:** PEER; *esp* **:** to make a presumptuous inquiry

2**pry** *vt* **pried; pry·ing** [alter. of 5*prize*] **1 :** to raise, move, or pull apart with a pry or lever **:** PRIZE **2 :** to extract, detach, or open with difficulty

3**pry** *n* **1 :** a tool for prying **2 :** LEVERAGE

pry·er *var of* PRIER

pry·ing *adj* **:** impertinently or officiously inquisitive or interrogatory **syn** see CURIOUS — **pry·ing·ly** \-iŋ-lē\ *adv*

psalm \'säm, 'sälm\ *n, often cap* [ME, fr. OE *psealm*, fr. LL *psalmus*, fr. Gk *psalmos*, lit., twanging of a harp, fr. *psallein* to pluck, play a stringed instrument] **:** a sacred song or poem used in the praise or worship of the Deity; *esp* **:** one of the biblical hymns collected in the Book of Psalms — **psalm** *vt*

psalm·book \-,bu̇k\ *n* **1 :** PSALTER **2 :** a book of sacred poems or songs for use in public worship

psalm·ist \'säm-əst, 'säl-məst\ *n* **:** a writer or composer of psalms

psalm·o·dy \'säm-əd-ē, 'säl-məd-\ *n* [ME *psalmodie*, fr. LL *psalmodia*, fr. LGk *psalmōidia*, lit., singing to the harp, fr. *psalmos* + *aidein* to sing — more at ODE] **1 :** the act, practice, or art of singing psalms in worship **2 :** a collection of psalms

Psal·ter \'sȯl-tər\ *n* [ME, fr. OE *psalter* & OF *psaltier*, fr. LL *psalterium*, fr. LGk *psaltērion*, fr. Gk, psaltery] **:** the Book of Psalms; *also* **:** a collection of the Psalms or some of them for liturgical or devotional use

psal·te·ri·um \sȯl-'tir-ē-əm\ *n, pl* **psal·te·ria** \-ē-ə\ [NL, fr. LL, psalter; fr. the resemblance of the folds to the pages of a book] **:** OMASUM

psal·tery *also* **psal·try** \'sȯl-t(ə-)rē\ *n* [ME *psalterie*, fr. MF, fr. L *psalterium*, fr. Gk *psaltērion*, fr. *psallein* to play on a stringed instrument] **:** an ancient musical instrument resembling the zither

pseud- *or* **pseudo-** *comb form* [ME, fr. LL, fr. Gk, fr. *pseudēs*] **:** false **:** spurious ⟨*pseud*axis⟩ ⟨*pseudo*classic⟩ ⟨*pseudo*podium⟩

pseud·epig·ra·pha \,süd-i-'pig-rə-fə\ *n pl* [NL, fr. Gk, neut. pl. of *pseudepigraphos* falsely ascribed, fr. *pseud-* + *epigraphein* to inscribe, ascribe — more at EPIGRAM] **1 :** APOCRYPHA 1 **2** *cap* **:** Jewish nonrabbinic religious writings of the period 200 B.C. to 200 A.D. not included in the Old Testament or Apocrypha — **pseud·epig·ra·phal** \-fəl\ *adj* — **pseud·epi·graph·ic** \,süd-,ep-ə-'graf-ik\ *adj*

pseud·epig·ra·phy \,süd-i-'pig-rə-fē\ *n* [Gk *pseudepigraphos*] **:** the ascription of false names of authors to works

pseu·do \'süd-(,)ō\ *adj* [ME, fr. *pseudo-*] **:** SHAM, SPURIOUS

pseu·do·al·lele \,süd-ō-ə-'lē(ə)l\ *n* **:** any of two or more closely linked genes acting as if a single member of an allelic pair — **pseu·do·al·le·lic** \-'lē-lik, -'lel-ik\ *adj* — **pseu·do·al·lel·ism** \-'lē(ə)l-,iz-əm, -'lel-,iz-\ *n*

pseu·do·al·um \-'al-əm\ *n* **:** any of various double sulphates of aluminum and a bivalent metal (as zinc) not isomorphous with common alum

pseu·do·carp \'süd-ə-,kärp\ *n* **:** ACCESSORY FRUIT — **pseu·do·car·pous** \,süd-ə-'kär-pəs\ *adj*

pseu·do·clas·sic \,süd-ō-'klas-ik\ *adj* **:** pretending to be or erroneously regarded as classic — **pseudoclassic** *n* — **pseu·do·clas·si·cism** \-'klas-ə-,siz-əm\ *n*

pseu·do·morph \'süd-ə-,mȯrf\ *n* [prob. fr. F *pseudomorphe*, fr. *pseud-* + *-morphe* -morph] **1 :** a mineral having the characteristic outward form of another species **2 :** a deceptive or irregular form — **pseu·do·mor·phic** \,süd-ə-'mȯr-fik\ *adj* — **pseu·do·mor·phism** \-,fiz-əm\ *n* — **pseu·do·mor·phous** \-fəs\ *adj*

pseu·do·my·ce·li·al \,süd-ō-(,)mī-'sē-lē-əl\ *adj* **:** of, relating to, or forming pseudomycelium

pseu·do·my·ce·li·um \-lē-əm\ *n* [NL] **:** a cellular association occurring among higher bacteria and yeasts in which cells form chains resembling small mycelia

pseud·onym \'süd-ᵊn-,im\ *n* [F *pseudonyme*, fr. Gk *pseudōnymos* bearing a false name] **:** a fictitious name; *esp* **:** PEN NAME

pseud·on·y·mous \sü-'dän-ə-məs\ *adj* [Gk *pseudōnymos*, fr. *pseud-* + *onoma, onyma* name] **:** bearing or using a fictitious name — **pseud·on·y·mous·ly** *adv* — **pseud·on·y·mous·ness** *n*

pseu·do·pa·ren·chy·ma \,süd-(,)ō-pə-'reŋ-kə-mə, -'ren-\ *n* [NL] **:** compactly interwoven short-celled filaments in a thallophyte suggesting parenchyma of higher plants — **pseu·do·par·en·chym·a·tous** \,süd-ō-,par-ən-'kim-ət-əs\ *adj*

pseu·do·pod \'süd-ə-,päd\ *n* [NL *pseudopodium*] **1 :** PSEUDOPODIUM **2 :** a supposed or apparent psychic projection — **pseu·dop·o·dal** \sü-'däp-əd-ᵊl\ *or* **pseu·do·po·di·al** \,süd-ə-'pōd-ē-əl\ *adj*

pseu·do·po·di·um \,süd-ə-'pōd-ē-əm\ *n, pl* **pseu·do·po·dia** \-ē-ə\ [NL] **:** a temporary protrusion or retractile process of the protoplasm of a cell

pseu·do·preg·nan·cy \,süd-(,)ō-'preg-nən-sē\ *n* **:** an anestrous state resembling pregnancy that occurs in various mammals usu. after an infertile copulation — **pseu·do·preg·nant** \-nənt\ *adj*

pseu·do·salt \'süd-ō-,sȯlt\ *n* **:** a compound analogous in formula to a salt but not ionized as such

pseu·do·sci·ence \,süd-ō-'sī-ən(t)s\ *n* **:** a system of theories, assumptions, and methods erroneously regarded as scientific — **pseu·do·sci·en·tif·ic** \-,sī-ən-'tif-ik\ *adj*

pseu·do·tu·ber·cu·lo·sis \-t(y)ü-,bər-kyə-'lō-səs\ *n* [NL] **:** any of several diseases characterized by the formation of granulomas resembling tubercular nodules but not caused by the tubercle bacillus

pshaw \'shȯ\ *interj* — used to express irritation, disapproval, contempt, or disbelief

psi \'sī\ *n* [LGk, fr. Gk *psei*] **:** the 23d letter of the Greek alphabet — symbol Ψ or ψ

psi·lo·cin \'sī-lə-sən\ *n* [NL *Psilocybe*, genus of fungi + E *-in*] **:** a hallucinogenic organic compound obtained from a fungus (*Psilocybe mexicana*)

psi·lo·cy·bin \,sī-lə-'sī-bən\ *n* [NL *Psilocybe* + *-in*] **:** a hallucinogenic organic compound obtained from a fungus (*Psilocybe mexicana*)

psit·ta·ceous \sə-'tā-shəs, si-\ *adj* [L *psittacus* parrot] **1 :** PSITTACINE **2 :** resembling a parrot ⟨~ chatter⟩

psit·ta·cine \'sit-ə-,sīn\ *adj* [L *psittacinus*, fr. *psittacus* parrot, fr. Gk *psittakos*] **:** of or relating to the parrots — **psittacine** *n*

psit·ta·co·sis \,sit-ə-'kō-səs\ *n* [NL, fr. L *psittacus*] **:** an infectious disease of birds caused by a rickettsia (*Miyagawanella psittaci*), marked by diarrhea and wasting, and transmissible to man in whom it usu. occurs as an atypical pneumonia accompanied by high fever — **psit·ta·co·tic** \-'kät-ik, -'kōt-\ *adj*

pso·cid \'sō-səd\ *n* [deriv. of NL *Psocus*, genus of lice] **:** any of an order (Corrodentia) of minute usu. winged primitive insects

pso·ri·a·sis \sə-'rī-ə-səs\ *n* [NL, fr. Gk *psōriasis*, fr. *psōrian* to have the itch, fr. *psōra* itch; akin to Gk *psēn* to rub] **:** a chronic skin disease characterized by circumscribed red patches covered with white scales — **pso·ri·at·ic** \,sȯr-ē-'at-ik, ,sȯr-\ *adj or n*

psych- *or* **psycho-** *comb form* [Gk, fr. *psychē* breath, principle of life, life, soul; akin to Gk *psychein* to breathe, blow, cool, Skt *babhasti* he blows] **1 :** soul **:** spirit ⟨*psycho*gnosis⟩ **2 a :** mind **:** mental processes and activities ⟨*psycho*dynamic⟩ ⟨*psycho*logy⟩ **b :** psychological methods ⟨*psycho*analysis⟩ ⟨*psycho*therapy⟩ **c :** brain ⟨*psycho*surgery⟩ **d :** mental and ⟨*psycho*somatic⟩

psych·as·the·nia \,sī-kəs-'thē-nē-ə\ *n* [NL] **:** an incapacity to resolve doubts or uncertainties or to resist phobias, obsessions, or compulsions that one knows are irrational — **psych·as·then·ic** \-'then-ik\ *adj or n*

Psy·che \'sī-kē\ *n* [L] **1 :** a beautiful princess of classical mythology loved by Cupid **2** *not cap* [Gk *psychē*] **:** SOUL; *also* **:** MIND

psy·che·de·lia \,sī-kə-'dēl-yə\ *n* [NL, fr. E *psychedelic* + NL *-ia*] **:** the world of people or items associated with psychedelic drugs

psy·che·del·ic *also* **psy·cho·del·ic** \,sī-kə-'del-ik\ *adj* [Gk *psychē* soul + *dēloun* to show] **1 a :** of, relating to, or causing an exposure of normally repressed psychic elements ⟨~ drugs⟩ **b :** relating to the taking of psychedelic drugs ⟨~ experience⟩ **2 a :** imitating the effects of psychedelic drugs ⟨~ art⟩ **b :** FLUORESCENT ⟨~ colors⟩ **3 :** selling items that appeal to those interested in psychedelic drugs or effects ⟨a ~ shop⟩ — **psychedelic** *n* — **psy·che·del·i·cal·ly** \-i-k(ə-)lē\ *adv*

Psyche knot *n* [fr. the frequent representation of Psyche in works

of art with this style] **:** a woman's hair style in which the hair is brushed back and twisted into a conical coil usu. just above the nape

psy·chi·at·ric \ˌsī-kē-ˈa-trik\ *adj* **:** of or relating to psychiatry — **psy·chi·at·ri·cal·ly** \-tri-k(ə-)lē\ *adv*

psy·chi·a·trist \sə-ˈkī-ə-trəst, sī-\ *n* **:** a physician specializing in psychiatry

psy·chi·a·try \-trē\ *n* [prob. fr. (assumed) NL *psychiatria,* fr. *psych-* + *-iatria* -iatry] **:** a branch of medicine that deals with mental, emotional, or behavioral disorders

[1]**psy·chic** \ˈsī-kik\ *adj* [Gk *psychikos* of the soul, fr. *psychē* soul] **1 :** of or relating to the psyche **:** PSYCHOGENIC **2 :** lying outside the sphere of physical science or knowledge **:** immaterial, moral, or spiritual in origin or force **3 :** sensitive to nonphysical or supernatural forces and influences — **psy·chi·cal** \-ki-kəl\ *adj* — **psy·chi·cal·ly** \-ki-k(ə-)lē\ *adv*

[2]**psychic** *n* **1 a :** a person apparently sensitive to nonphysical forces **b :** MEDIUM 2d **2 :** psychic phenomena

psy·cho \ˈsī-(ˌ)kō\ *n* **1** *slang* **:** PSYCHOANALYSIS **2** [short for *psychoneurotic*] *slang* **:** a victim of severe mental or emotional disorder **:** MADMAN — **psycho** *adj, slang*

psy·cho·anal·y·sis \ˌsī-kə-wə-ˈnal-ə-səs\ *n* [ISV] **:** a method of analysis esp. for therapeutic purposes based on the theory that abnormal mental reactions are due to repression of desires consciously rejected but subconsciously persistent — **psy·cho·an·a·lyt·ic** \ˌsī-kō-ˌan-ᵊl-ˈit-ik\ *or* **psy·cho·an·a·lyt·i·cal** \-i-kəl\ *adj* — **psy·cho·an·a·lyt·i·cal·ly** \-k(ə-)lē\ *adv*

psy·cho·an·a·lyst \ˌsī-kō-ˈan-ᵊl-əst\ *n* **:** one who practices psychoanalysis

psy·cho·an·a·lyze \-ˌīz\ *vt* **:** to treat by means of psychoanalysis

psy·cho·bio·log·i·cal \ˌsī-kō-ˌbī-ə-ˈläj-i-kəl\ *or* **psy·cho·bio·log·ic** \-ik\ *adj* **:** of or relating to psychobiology

psy·cho·bi·ol·o·gy \-(ˌ)bī-ˈäl-ə-jē\ *n* [ISV] **:** the study of mental life and behavior in relation to other biological processes

psy·cho·dra·ma \ˌsī-kə-ˈdräm-ə, -ˈdram-\ *n* **:** an extemporized dramatization designed to afford catharsis and social relearning for one or more of the participants from whose life history the plot is abstracted — **psy·cho·dra·mat·ic** \-kō-drə-ˈmat-ik\ *adj*

psy·cho·dy·nam·ic \ˌsī-kō-(ˌ)dī-ˈnam-ik\ *adj* **:** of or relating to mental or emotional forces or processes developing esp. in early childhood and their effects on behavior and mental states — **psy·cho·dy·nam·i·cal·ly** \-i-k(ə-)lē\ *adv* — **psy·cho·dy·nam·ics** \-iks\ *n pl but sing or pl in constr*

psy·cho·gen·e·sis \ˌsī-kə-ˈjen-ə-səs\ *n* [NL] **1 :** the origin and development of the mind or of a mental function or trait **2 :** development from psychic as distinguished from somatic origins — **psy·cho·ge·net·ic** \-jə-ˈnet-ik\ *adj*

psy·cho·gen·ic \-ˈjen-ik\ *adj* **:** originating in the mind or in mental or emotional conflict — **psy·cho·gen·i·cal·ly** \-i-k(ə-)lē\ *adv*

psy·chog·no·sis \ˌsī-kəg-ˈnō-səs, -ˌkäg-\ *also* **psy·chog·no·sy** \sī-ˈkäg-nə-sē\ *n* [NL *psychognosis,* fr. *psych-* + *-gnosis*] **:** the study of the psyche in relation to character

psy·cho·graph \ˈsī-kə-ˌgraf\ *n* **:** PROFILE 4

psy·cho·ki·ne·sis \ˌsī-kō-kə-ˈnē-səs, -(ˌ)kī-\ *n* [NL, fr. *psych-* + Gk *kinēsis* motion — more at KINESIOLOGY] **:** movement of physical objects by the mind without use of physical means — compare PRECOGNITION, TELEKINESIS — **psy·cho·ki·net·ic** \-ˈnet-ik\ *adj*

psy·cho·log·i·cal \ˌsī-kə-ˈläj-i-kəl\ *also* **psy·cho·log·ic** \-ik\ *adj* **1 a :** of or relating to psychology **b :** MENTAL **2 :** directed toward the will or toward the mind specif. in its conative function ⟨~ warfare⟩ — **psy·cho·log·i·cal·ly** \-i-k(ə-)lē\ *adv*

psychological hedonism *n* **:** the theory that conduct is fundamentally motivated by the pursuit of pleasure or the avoidance of pain

psychological moment *n* **:** the occasion when the mental atmosphere is most certain to be favorable to the full effect of an action or event

psy·chol·o·gism \sī-ˈkäl-ə-ˌjiz-əm\ *n* **:** a theory that applies psychological conceptions to the interpretation of historical events or logical thought

psy·chol·o·gist \-jəst\ *n* **:** a specialist in psychology

psy·chol·o·gize \-ˌjīz\ *vt* **:** to explain or interpret in psychological terms ~ *vi* **:** to speculate in psychological terms or upon psychological motivations

psy·chol·o·gy \-jē\ *n, often attrib* [NL *psychologia,* fr. *psych-* + *-logia* -logy] **1 :** the science of mind and behavior **2 a :** the mental or behavioral characteristics of an individual or group **b :** the study of mind and behavior in relation to a particular field of knowledge or activity **3 :** a treatise on psychology

psy·cho·met·ric \ˌsī-kə-ˈme-trik\ *adj* **:** of or relating to psychometrics or psychometry — **psy·cho·met·ri·cal·ly** \-tri-k(ə-)lē\ *adv*

psy·cho·met·rics \-triks\ *n pl but sing in constr* **:** the psychological theory or technique of mental measurement

psy·chom·e·try \sī-ˈkäm-ə-trē\ *n* **1 :** divination of facts concerning an object or its owner through contact with or proximity to the object **2 :** PSYCHOMETRICS

psy·cho·mo·tor \ˌsī-kə-ˈmōt-ər\ *adj* [ISV] **:** of or relating to muscular action believed to ensue from prior esp. conscious mental activity

psy·cho·neu·ro·sis \ˌsī-kō-n(y)u̇-ˈrō-səs\ *n* [NL] **1 :** a neurosis based on emotional conflict in which an impulse that has been blocked seeks expression in a disguised response or symptom **2 :** NEUROSIS — **psy·cho·neu·rot·ic** \-ˈrät-ik\ *adj or n*

psy·cho·path \ˈsī-kə-ˌpath\ *n* [ISV] **1 :** a mentally ill or unstable person **2 :** PSYCHOPATHIC PERSONALITY 2

psy·cho·path·ic \ˌsī-kə-ˈpath-ik\ *adj* **:** of or relating to psychopathy — **psychopathic** *n* — **psy·cho·path·i·cal·ly** \-i-k(ə-)lē\ *adv*

psychopathic personality *n* **1 :** a disorder of behavior toward other individuals or toward society in which reality is usu. clearly perceived except for an individual's social and moral obligations and which often seeks immediate personal gratification in criminal acts, drug addiction, or sexual perversion **2 :** an individual having a psychopathic personality

psy·cho·patho·log·i·cal \ˌsī-kō-ˌpath-ə-ˈläj-i-kəl\ *or* **psy·cho·patho·log·ic** \-ik\ *adj* **:** of, relating to, or exhibiting psychopathology

psy·cho·pa·thol·o·gist \-pə-ˈthäl-ə-jəst\ *n* **:** a specialist in psychopathology

psy·cho·pa·thol·o·gy \-jē\ *n* [ISV *psych-* + *pathology*] **:** the study of psychologic and behavioral dysfunction occurring in mental disorder or in social disorganization; *also* **:** such dysfunction

psy·chop·a·thy \sī-ˈkäp-ə-thē\ *n* [ISV] **:** mental disorder; *esp* **:** extreme mental disorder marked usu. by egocentric and antisocial activity

psy·cho·phys·i·cal \ˌsī-kō-ˈfiz-i-kəl\ *adj* **:** of or relating to psychophysics; *also* **:** sharing mental and physical qualities — **psy·cho·phys·i·cal·ly** \-k(ə-)lē\ *adv*

psychophysical parallelism *n* **:** a theory that parallel physical and psychical events do not interact

psy·cho·phys·i·cist \-ˈfiz-(ə-)səst\ *n* **:** a specialist in psychophysics

psy·cho·phys·ics \-ˈfiz-iks\ *n pl but sing in constr* [ISV] **:** a branch of psychology that studies the effect of physical processes upon the mental processes of an organism

psy·cho·sis \sī-ˈkō-səs\ *n* [NL] **:** fundamental lasting mental derangement characterized by defective or lost contact with reality **syn** see INSANITY — **psy·chot·ic** \-ˈkät-ik\ *adj or n* — **psy·chot·i·cal·ly** \-i-k(ə-)lē\ *adv*

[1]**psy·cho·so·mat·ic** \ˌsī-kə-sə-ˈmat-ik\ *adj* [ISV] **1 :** of, relating to, or resulting from the interaction and interdependence of psychic and somatic phenomena **2 :** of or relating to psychosomatics or psychosomatic disorders — **psy·cho·so·mat·i·cal·ly** \-i-k(ə-)lē\ *adv*

[2]**psychosomatic** *n* **:** one who evidences bodily symptoms or bodily and mental symptoms as a result of mental conflict

psy·cho·so·mat·ics \-iks\ *n pl but sing in constr* **:** a branch of medical science dealing with psychosomatic interrelationships and esp. with the relation of psychic conflict to somatic symptomatology

psy·cho·sur·gery \ˌsī-kō-ˈsərj-(ə-)rē\ *n* **:** cerebral surgery employed in treating psychic symptoms

psy·cho·ther·a·peu·tic \ˌsī-kō-ˌther-ə-ˈpyüt-ik\ *adj* [ISV] **:** of or relating to psychotherapy — **psy·cho·ther·a·peu·ti·cal·ly** \-i-k(ə-)lē\ *adv*

psy·cho·ther·a·peu·tics \-iks\ *n pl but sing or pl in constr* **:** PSYCHOTHERAPY

psy·cho·ther·a·pist \-ˈther-ə-pəst\ *n* **:** a practitioner of psychotherapy

psy·cho·ther·a·py \-pē\ *n* [ISV] **:** treatment of mental or emotional disorder or of related bodily ills by psychological means

psychro- *comb form* [Gk, fr. *psychros,* fr. *psychein* to cool — more at PSYCH-] **:** cold ⟨*psychro*meter⟩

psy·chrom·e·ter \sī-ˈkräm-ət-ər\ *n* [ISV] **:** a hygrometer consisting essentially of two similar thermometers with the bulb of one being kept wet so that the cooling that results from evaporation makes it register a lower temperature than the dry one and with the difference between the readings constituting a measure of the dryness of the atmosphere

psy·chro·phil·ic \ˌsī-krō-ˈfil-ik\ *adj* **:** thriving at a relatively low temperature ⟨~ bacteria⟩

psyl·la \ˈsil-ə\ *n* [NL, genus name, fr. Gk, flea; akin to L *pulex* flea, Skt *pluṣi*] **:** any of various plant lice (family Psyllidae) including economically important plant pests

psyl·lid \ˈsil-əd\ *n* [deriv. of NL *Psylla*] **:** PSYLLA — **psyllid** *adj*

ptar·mi·gan \ˈtär-mi-gən\ *n, pl* **ptarmigan** *or* **ptarmigans** [modif. of ScGael *tàrmachan*] **:** any of various grouses (genus *Lagopus*) of northern regions with completely feathered feet

P T boat \(ˈ)pē-ˈtē-\ *n* [*p*atrol *t*orpedo] **:** MOTOR TORPEDO BOAT

pterid- *or* **pterido-** *comb form* [Gk *pterid-, pteris;* akin to Gk *pteron* wing, feather] **:** fern ⟨*pterid*oid⟩ ⟨*pterido*logy⟩

pter·i·doid \ˈter-ə-ˌdȯid\ *adj* **:** related to or resembling a fern

pte·ri·do·log·i·cal \tə-ˌrid-ᵊl-ˈäj-i-kəl, ˌter-əd-ᵊl-\ *adj* **:** of or relating to pteridology

pter·i·dol·o·gist \ˌter-ə-ˈdäl-ə-jəst\ *n* **:** a specialist in pteridology

pter·i·dol·o·gy \ˌter-ə-ˈdäl-ə-jē\ *n* **:** the study of ferns

pte·ri·do·phyte \tə-ˈrid-ə-ˌfīt, ˈter-əd-ō-\ *n* [deriv. of Gk *pterid-, pteris* fern + *phyton* plant — more at PHYT-] **:** any of a division (Pteridophyta) of vascular plants comprising the ferns and related forms — **pte·ri·do·phyt·ic** \tə-ˌrid-ə-ˈfit-ik, ˌter-əd-ō-\ *or* **pter·i·doph·y·tous** \ˌter-ə-ˈdäf-ət-əs\ *adj*

pte·ri·do·sperm \tə-ˈrid-ə-ˌspərm, ˈter-əd-ō-\ *n* [ISV] **:** SEED FERN

ptero·dac·tyl \ˌter-ə-ˈdak-tᵊl\ *n* [NL *Pterodactylus,* genus of reptiles, fr. Gk *pteron* wing + *daktylos* finger — more at FEATHER] **:** any of an order (Pterosauria) of extinct flying reptiles existing from the Lower Jurassic nearly to the close of the Mesozoic and having a wing membrane but no feathers extending from the side of the body along the arm to the end of the greatly enlarged fourth digit — **ptero·dac·ty·loid** \-tə-ˌlȯid\ *adj* — **ptero·dac·ty·lous** \-ləs\ *adj*

pte·ro·ic acid \tə-ˌrō-ik-\ *n* [*pter*in (a component of butterfly-wing pigments) + *-oic*] **:** a crystalline amino acid $C_{14}H_{12}N_6O_3$ formed with glutamic acid by hydrolysis of folic acid or other pteroylglutamic acids

ptero·pod \ˈter-ə-ˌpäd\ *n* [NL *Pteropoda,* group name, fr. Gk *pteron* wing + NL *-poda*] **:** any of a group (Pteropoda) of small gastropod mollusks having the anterior lobes of the foot expanded into broad thin winglike organs with which they swim — **pteropod** *adj* — **pte·rop·o·dan** \tə-ˈräp-əd-ən\ *adj or n*

ptero·saur \ˈter-ə-ˌsȯ(ə)r\ *n* [deriv. of Gk *pteron* wing + *sauros* lizard] **:** PTERODACTYL

pter·o·yl·glu·tam·ic acid \ˈter-ə-ˌwil-ˌglü-ˌtam-ik-\ *n* [ISV *pteroyl* (the radical $(C_{13}H_{11}N_6O)CO$) + *glutamic*] **:** an acid that is a conjugate of pteroic acid and glutamic acid; *esp* **:** FOLIC ACID

pter·y·goid \ˈter-ə-ˌgȯid\ *adj* [NL *pterygoides,* fr. Gk *pterygoeidēs,* lit., shaped like a wing, fr. *pteryg-, pteryx* wing; akin to Gk *pteron* wing — more at FEATHER] **:** of, relating to, or lying in the region of the inferior part of the sphenoid bone of the vertebrate skull — **pterygoid** *n*

pterygoid bone *n* **:** a horizontally placed bone or group of bones of the upper jaw or roof of the mouth in most lower vertebrates

pterygoid process *n* **:** a process extending downward from each side of the sphenoid bone in man and other mammals

ə abut; ᵊ kitten; ər further; a back; ā bake; ä cot, cart; au̇ out; ch chin; e less; ē easy; g gift; i trip; ī life
j joke; ŋ sing; ō flow; ȯ flaw; ȯi coin; th thin; th this; ü loot; u̇ foot; y yet; yü few; yu̇ furious; zh vision

pter·y·la \ˈter-ə-lə\ *n, pl* **pter·y·lae** \-ˌlē, -ˌlī\ [NL, fr. Gk *pteron* + *hylē* wood, forest] **:** one of the definite areas of the skin of a bird on which feathers grow

pti·san \tiz-ˈan, ˈtiz-ᵊn\ *n* [ME *tisane*, fr. MF, fr. L *ptisana* — more at TISANE] **:** a decoction of barley with other ingredients; *broadly* **:** TEA, TISANE

Ptol·e·ma·ic \ˌtäl-ə-ˈmā-ik\ *adj* [Gk *Ptolemaikos*, fr. *Ptolemaios* Ptolemy] **1 :** of or relating to Ptolemy the geographer and astronomer who flourished at Alexandria about A.D. 130 **2 :** of or relating to the Greco-Egyptian Ptolemies ruling Egypt from 323 B.C. to 30 B.C.

Ptolemaic system *n* [after Ptolemy *fl* 2d cent. A.D. who maintained it] **:** the system of planetary motions according to which the earth is at the center with the sun, moon, and planets revolving around it

Ptol·e·ma·ist \ˈtäl-ə-ˌmā-əst\ *n* **:** an adherent of the Ptolemaic system

pto·maine \ˈtō-ˌmān, tō-ˈ\ *n* [It *ptomaina*, fr. Gk *ptōma* fall, fallen body, corpse, fr. *piptein* to fall — more at FEATHER] **:** any of various organic bases formed by the action of putrefactive bacteria on nitrogenous matter

ptomaine poisoning *n* **:** food poisoning caused by bacteria or bacterial products

pto·sis \ˈtō-səs\ *n* [NL, fr. Gk *ptōsis* act of falling, fr. *piptein*] **:** a sagging or prolapse of an organ or part; *esp* **:** drooping of the upper eyelid

pty·a·lin \ˈtī-ə-lən\ *n* [Gk *ptyalon* saliva, fr. *ptyein* to spit — more at SPEW] **:** an amylase found in the saliva of many animals

pty·a·lism \-ˌliz-əm\ *n* [NL *ptyalismus*, fr. Gk *ptyalismos*, fr. *ptyalizein* to salivate, fr. *ptyalon*] **:** an excessive flow of saliva

pub \ˈpəb\ *n* **1** *chiefly Brit* **:** PUBLIC HOUSE **2 :** an establishment where alcoholic beverages are sold and consumed

pub crawler *n* **:** one that goes from bar to bar

pu·ber·tal \ˈpyü-bərt-ᵊl\ *adj* **:** of or relating to puberty

pu·ber·ty \ˈpyü-bərt-ē\ *n* [ME *puberte*, fr. L *pubertas*, fr. *puber* pubescent] **1 :** the condition of being or the period of becoming first capable of reproducing sexually **2 :** the age at which puberty occurs often construed legally as 14 in boys and 12 in girls

pu·ber·u·lent \pyü-ˈber-(y)ə-lənt\ *adj* [L *puber* pubescent + E *-ulent* (as in *pulverulent*)] **:** covered with fine pubescence

pu·bes \ˈpyü-(ˌ)bēz\ *n, pl* **pubes** [NL, fr. L, manhood, body hair, pubic region; akin to L *puber* pubescent] **1 :** the hair that appears upon the lower part of the hypogastric region at puberty **2 :** the pubic region

pu·bes·cence \pyü-ˈbes-ᵊn(t)s\ *n* **1 :** the quality or state of being pubescent **2 :** a pubescent covering or surface

pu·bes·cent \-ᵊnt\ *adj* [L *pubescent-, pubescens*, prp. of *pubescere* to reach puberty, become covered as with hair, fr. *pubes*] **1 :** arriving at or having reached puberty **2 :** covered with fine soft short hairs

pu·bic \ˈpyü-bik\ *adj* **:** of, relating to, or lying in the region of the pubes or the pubis

pu·bis \ˈpyü-bəs\ *n, pl* **pu·bes** \-(ˌ)bēz\ [NL *os pubis*, lit., bone of the pubic region] **:** the ventral and anterior of the three principal bones composing either half of the pelvis

1**pub·lic** \ˈpəb-lik\ *adj* [ME *publique*, fr. MF, fr. L *publicus*, prob. alter. of *poplicus*, fr. *populus* the people] **1 a :** of, relating to, or affecting all the people or the whole area of a nation or state ⟨~ law⟩ **b :** GOVERNMENTAL **c :** in the service of the community or nation **2 a :** of or relating to mankind in general **:** UNIVERSAL **b :** GENERAL, POPULAR **3 :** of or relating to business or community interests as opposed to private affairs **:** SOCIAL **4 :** devoted to the general or national welfare **:** HUMANITARIAN **5 :** accessible to or shared by all members of the community **6 a :** exposed to general view **:** OPEN **b :** WELL-KNOWN, PROMINENT **c :** PERCEPTIBLE, MATERIAL — **pub·lic·ness** *n*

2**public** *n* **1 :** a place accessible or visible to the public — usu. used in the phrase *in public* **2 :** the people as a whole **:** POPULACE **3 :** a group of people having common interests or characteristics

public-address system *n* **:** an apparatus including a microphone and loudspeakers used for broadcasting to a large audience in an auditorium or out of doors

pub·li·can \ˈpəb-li-kən\ *n* [ME, fr. MF, fr. L *publicanus* tax farmer, fr. *publicum* public revenue, fr. neut. of *publicus*] **1 a :** a Jewish tax collector for the ancient Romans **b :** a collector of taxes or tribute **2** *chiefly Brit* **:** the licensee of a public house

pub·li·ca·tion \ˌpəb-lə-ˈkā-shən\ *n* [ME *publicacioun*, fr. MF *publication*, fr. LL *publication-, publicatio*, fr. L *publicatus*, pp. of *publicare*] **1 :** the act or process of publishing **2 :** a published work

public defender *n* **:** a lawyer usu. holding public office whose duty is to defend accused persons unable to pay for legal assistance

public domain *n* **1 :** land owned directly by the government **2 :** the realm embracing property rights that belong to the community at large, are unprotected by copyright or patent, and are subject to appropriation by anyone

public house *n* **1 :** INN, HOSTELRY **2** *chiefly Brit* **:** a licensed saloon or bar

pub·li·cist \ˈpəb-lə-səst\ *n* **1 a :** an expert in international law **b :** an expert or commentator on public affairs **2 :** one that publicizes; *specif* **:** PRESS AGENT

pub·lic·i·ty \(ˌ)pə-ˈblis-ət-ē, -ˈblis-tē\ *n* **1 :** the quality or state of being public **2 a :** an act or device designed to attract public interest; *specif* **:** information with news value issued as a means of gaining public attention or support **b :** the dissemination of information or promotional material **c :** paid advertising **d :** public attention or acclaim

pub·li·cize \ˈpəb-lə-ˌsīz\ *vt* **:** to give publicity to **:** ADVERTISE

public law *n* **1 :** a legislative enactment affecting the public at large **2 :** a branch of law concerned with regulating the relations of individuals with the government and the organization and conduct of the government itself

pub·lic·ly \ˈpəb-li-klē\ *adv* **1 :** in a public manner **:** OPENLY **2 a :** by the people generally **b :** by a government

public relations *n pl but usu sing in constr* **:** the art or science of developing reciprocal understanding and goodwill between a person, firm, or institution and the public; *also* **:** the degree of understanding and goodwill achieved

public sale *n* **:** AUCTION 1

public school *n* **1 :** an endowed secondary boarding school in Great Britain offering a classical curriculum and preparation for the universities or public service **2 :** a free tax-supported school controlled by a local governmental authority

public servant *n* **:** a government official or employee

public service *n* **1 :** the business of supplying some commodity (as electricity or gas) or service (as transportation) to any or all members of a community **2 :** a service rendered in the public interest **3 :** governmental employment; *esp* **:** CIVIL SERVICE

public-service corporation *n* **:** a quasi-public corporation

public speaking *n* **1 :** the act or process of making speeches in public **2 :** the art or science of effective oral communication with an audience ⟨took a course in *public speaking*⟩

pub·lic-spir·it·ed \ˌpəb-lik-ˈspir-ət-əd\ *adj* **:** motivated by devotion to the general or national welfare — **pub·lic-spir·it·ed·ness** *n*

public utility *n* **:** a business organization (as a public-service corporation) performing some public service and subject to special governmental regulation

public works *n pl* **:** works (as schools, highways, docks) constructed for public use or enjoyment esp. when financed and owned by the government

pub·lish \ˈpəb-lish\ *vb* [ME *publishen*, modif. of MF *publier*, fr. L *publicare*, fr. *publicus*] *vt* **1 a :** to make generally known **b :** to make public announcement of **2** *obs* **:** ADVERTISE **3 a :** to place before the public **:** DISSEMINATE **b :** to produce or release for publication; *specif* **:** PRINT **c :** to issue the work of (an author) ~ *vi* **1 :** to put out an edition **2 :** to have one's work accepted for publication ⟨a ~*ing* scholar⟩ **syn** see DECLARE — **pub·lish·able** \-ə-bəl\ *adj*

pub·lish·er \-ər\ *n* **:** one that publishes; *esp* **:** one that issues and offers for sale books or other printed matter

puc·coon \pə-ˈkün\ *n* [fr. *puccoon* (in some Algonquian language of Virginia)] **1 :** any of several American plants yielding a red or yellow pigment; *esp* **:** BLOODROOT **2 :** a pigment from a puccoon

puce \ˈpyüs\ *n* [F, lit., flea, fr. L *pulic-, pulex* — more at PSYLLA] **:** a dark red

1**puck** \ˈpək\ *n* [ME *puke*, fr. OE *pūca;* akin to ON *pūki* devil] **1** *archaic* **:** an evil spirit **:** DEMON **2 :** a mischievous sprite **:** HOBGOBLIN; *specif, cap* **:** ROBIN GOODFELLOW

2**puck** *n* [E dial. *puck* to poke, hit, alter. of E 2*poke*] **:** a vulcanized rubber disk used in ice hockey

pucka *var of* PUKKA

1**puck·er** \ˈpək-ər\ *vb* **puck·er·ing** \-(ə-)riŋ\ [prob. irreg. fr. 1*poke*] *vi* **:** to become wrinkled or constricted ~ *vt* **:** to contract into folds or wrinkles

2**pucker** *n* **:** a fold or wrinkle in a normally even surface

puck·ery \ˈpək-(ə-)rē\ *adj* **:** that puckers or causes puckering

puck·ish \ˈpək-ish\ *adj* **:** IMPISH, WHIMSICAL — **puck·ish·ly** *adv* — **puck·ish·ness** *n*

pud·ding \ˈpu̇d-iŋ\ *n* [ME] **1 :** BLOOD SAUSAGE **2 a** (1) **:** a boiled or baked soft food usu. with a cereal base (2) **:** a dessert of a soft, spongy, or thick creamy consistency **b :** a dish often containing suet or having a suet crust and orig. boiled in a bag

pudding stone *n* **:** CONGLOMERATE

1**pud·dle** \ˈpəd-ᵊl\ *n* [ME *podel;* akin to LG *pudel* puddle, OE *pudd* ditch] **1 :** a very small pool of usu. dirty or muddy water **2 :** an earthy mixture (as of clay, sand, and gravel) worked while wet into a compact mass that becomes impervious to water when dry

2**puddle** *vb* **pud·dling** \ˈpəd-liŋ, -ᵊl-iŋ\ *vi* **:** to dabble or wade around in a puddle ~ *vt* **1 :** to make muddy or turbid **:** MUDDLE **2 a :** to work (a wet mixture of earth or concrete) into a dense impervious mass **b :** to subject (iron) to the process of puddling **3 a :** to strew with puddles **b :** to compact (soil) esp. by working when too wet **c :** to dip the roots of (a plant) in a thin mud before transplanting — **pud·dler** \-lər, -ᵊl-ər\ *n*

pud·dling \ˈpəd-liŋ, -ᵊl-iŋ\ *n* **:** the process of converting pig iron into wrought iron or rarely steel by subjecting it to heat and frequent stirring in a furnace in the presence of oxidizing substances

pu·den·cy \ˈpyüd-ᵊn-sē\ *n* [L *pudentia*, fr. *pudent-, pudens*, prp. of *pudēre* to be ashamed, make ashamed] **:** MODESTY, PRUDISHNESS

pu·den·dal \pyu̇-ˈden-dᵊl\ *adj* **:** of or relating to the external genital organs

pu·den·dum \-dəm\ *n, pl* **pu·den·da** \-də\ [NL, sing. of L *pudenda*, fr. neut. pl. of *pudendus*, gerundive of *pudēre* to be ashamed] **:** the external genital organs of a human being and esp. of a woman — usu. used in pl.

pudg·i·ness \ˈpəj-ē-nəs\ *n* **:** the quality or state of being pudgy

pudgy \ˈpəj-ē\ *adj* [origin unknown] **:** being short and plump **:** CHUBBY

pueb·lo \pü-ˈeb-(ˌ)lō, ˈpweb-, pyü-ˈeb-\ *n* [Sp, village, lit., people, fr. L *populus*] **1 a :** the communal dwelling of an Indian village of Arizona, New Mexico, and adjacent areas consisting of contiguous flat-roofed stone or adobe houses in groups sometimes several stories high **b :** an Indian village of the southwestern U.S. **2** *cap* **:** a member of any of several Indian peoples of Arizona and New Mexico

pu·er·ile \ˈpyu̇(-ə)r-əl, -ˌīl\ *adj* [F or L; F *puéril*, fr. L *puerilis*, fr. *puer* boy, child; akin to Gk *pais* boy, child — more at FEW] **1 :** JUVENILE **2 :** CHILDISH, SILLY ⟨~ remarks⟩ — **pu·er·ile·ly** \-ə(l)-lē, -ˌīl-lē\ *adv* — **pu·er·il·i·ty** \ˌpyu̇(-ə)r-ˈil-ət-ē\ *n*

pu·er·il·ism \ˈpyu̇(-ə)r-ə-ˌliz-əm, ˈpyu̇(-ə)r-ˌī-\ *n* **:** childish behavior esp. as a symptom of mental disorder

pu·er·per·al \pyü-ˈər-p(ə-)rəl\ *adj* [L *puerpera* woman in childbirth, fr. *puer* child + *parere* to give birth to — more at PARE] **:** of or relating to parturition ⟨~ infection⟩

pu·er·pe·ri·um \ˌpyü-ər-ˈpir-ē-əm\ *n, pl* **pu·er·pe·ria** \-ē-ə\ [L, fr. *puerpera*] **:** the condition of a woman immediately following childbirth

1**puff** \ˈpəf\ *vb* [ME *puffen*, fr. OE *pyffan*, of imit. origin] *vi* **1 a** (1) **:** to blow in short gusts (2) **:** to exhale forcibly **b :** to breathe hard **:** PANT **c :** to emit small whiffs or clouds (as of smoke) **2 :** to speak or act in a scornful, conceited, or exaggerated manner **3 a :** to become distended **:** SWELL — usu. used with *up* **b :** to open or appear in or as if in a puff ~ *vt* **1 :** to emit, propel, blow, or expel by or as if by puffs **:** WAFT **2 a :** to distend with or as if with air or gas **:** INFLATE **b :** to make proud or conceited **:** ELATE **c :** to praise extravagantly; *specif* **:** ADVERTISE

2**puff** *n* **1 a :** an act or instance of puffing **:** WHIFF **b :** a slight explosive sound accompanying a puff **c :** a perceptible cloud or aura emitted in a puff **2 :** a light pastry that rises high in baking **3 a :** a slight swelling **:** PROTUBERANCE **b :** a fluffy mass: as

(1) : POUF 2 (2) : a small fluffy pad for applying cosmetic powder (3) : a soft loose roll of hair (4) : a quilted bed covering **4 :** a commendatory notice or review — **puff·i·ness** \'pəf-ē-nəs\ n — **puffy** \'pəf-ē\ adj

puff adder n : HOGNOSE SNAKE

puff·ball \'pəf-,bȯl\ n : any of various globose fungi (esp. family Lycoperdaceae) that discharge ripe spores in a smokelike cloud when pressed or struck and are often edible

puff·er \'pəf-ər\ n **1 :** one that puffs **2 :** GLOBEFISH; broadly : any of various similar fishes (order Plectognathi)

puff·ery \'pəf-(ə-)rē\ n : flattering publicity or extravagant commendation

puf·fin \'pəf-ən\ n [ME pophyn] : any of several sea birds (genera Fratercula and Lunda) having a short neck and a deep grooved parti-colored laterally compressed bill

puffin

puff paste n : dough used in making light flaky pastries

¹pug \'pəg\ n [obs. pug (hobgoblin, monkey)] **1 :** a small sturdy compact dog of a breed of Asiatic origin with a close coat, tightly curled tail, and broad wrinkled face **2 a :** PUG NOSE **b :** a close knot or coil of hair : BUN

²pug vt **pugged; pug·ging** [perh. alter. of ²poke] **1 :** to plug or pack with a substance (as clay or mortar) esp. for deadening sound **2 :** to mix and stir (clay) when wet for making bricks or pottery

³pug n : pugged clay for making pottery

⁴pug n [by shortening & alter. fr. pugilist] : BOXER

⁵pug n [Hindi pag foot] : FOOTPRINT; esp : a print of a wild mammal

pug·ga·ree or **pug·a·ree** or **pug·gree** \'pəg-(ə-)rē\ n [Hindi pagrī turban] : a light scarf wrapped around a sun helmet

pu·gi·lism \'pyü-jə-,liz-əm\ n [L pugil boxer; akin to L pugnus fist — more at PUNGENT] : ²BOXING — **pu·gi·lis·tic** \,pyü-jə-'lis-tik\ adj

pu·gi·list \'pyü-jə-ləst\ n : FIGHTER; esp : a professional boxer

pug·mark \'pəg-,märk\ n : ⁵PUG

pug·na·cious \,pəg-'nā-shəs\ adj [L pugnac-, pugnax, fr. pugnare to fight — more at PUNGENT] : having a belligerent nature : TRUCULENT, COMBATIVE **syn** see BELLIGERENT — **pug·na·cious·ly** adv — **pug·na·cious·ness** n — **pug·nac·i·ty** \-'nas-ət-ē\ n

pug nose n [¹pug] : a nose having a slightly concave bridge and flattened nostrils — **pug-nosed** \'pəg-'nōzd\ adj

puis·ne \'pyü-nē\ adj [MF puisné younger — more at PUNY] chiefly Brit : inferior in rank — **puisne** n

puis·sance \'pwis-ᵊn(t)s, 'pyü-ə-sən(t)s, pyü-'is-ᵊn(t)s\ n [ME, fr. MF, fr. OF, fr. puissant powerful, fr. poeir to be able, be powerful — more at POWER] : STRENGTH, POWER — **puis·sant** \-ᵊnt, -sənt\ adj — **puis·sant·ly** adv

puke \'pyük\ vb [perh. imit.] : VOMIT — **puke** n

puk·ka \'pək-ə\ adj [Hindi pakkā cooked, ripe, solid, fr. Skt pakva; akin to Gk pessein to cook — more at COOK] : GENUINE, AUTHENTIC; also : FIRST-CLASS, COMPLETE

pul \'pül\ n, pl **puls** \'pülz\ or **pu·li** \'pü-lē\ [Per pūl] — see afghani at MONEY table

pul·chri·tude \'pəl-krə-,t(y)üd\ n [ME, fr. L pulchritudin-, pulchritudo, fr. pulchr-, pulcher beautiful] : physical comeliness : BEAUTY

pul·chri·tu·di·nous \,pəl-krə-'t(y)üd-nəs, -ᵊn-əs\ adj : having or marked by pulchritude

pule \'pyü(ə)l\ vi [prob. imit.] : WHINE, WHIMPER — **pul·er** \'pyü-lər\ n, archaic

pu·li \'pül-ē, 'pyü-lē\ n, pl **pu·lik** \'pül-ēk, 'pyü-lēk\ [Hung] : an intelligent vigorous medium-sized farm dog of a Hungarian breed with long usu. corded coat

pu·li·cide \'pyü-lə-,sīd\ n [blend of L pulic-, pulex flea and E -cide] : an agent used for destroying fleas

¹pull \'pül\ vb [ME pullen, fr. OE pullian] vt **1 a :** to draw out from the skin **b :** to pluck from a plant or by the roots ⟨~ flowers⟩ ⟨~ turnips⟩ **c :** EXTRACT ⟨~ a tooth⟩ **2 a :** to exert force upon so as to cause or tend to cause motion toward the force **b :** to stretch (cooling candy) repeatedly **c :** to strain abnormally ⟨~ a tendon⟩ **d :** to hold back (a racehorse) from winning **e :** to work (an oar) by drawing back strongly **3 :** to hit (a ball) toward the left from a right-handed swing **4 :** to draw apart : REND, TEAR **5 :** to print a proof from by impression **6 :** REMOVE ⟨~ a crankshaft⟩ ⟨~ed the pitcher in the third inning⟩ **7 :** to bring (a weapon) into the open ⟨~ a knife⟩ **8 a :** to carry out with daring ⟨~ a robbery⟩ **b :** to be guilty of : COMMIT, PERPETRATE **9 :** to draw the support or attention of : ATTRACT ⟨~ votes⟩ ~ vi **1 a :** to use force in drawing, dragging, or tugging **b :** MOVE ⟨the car ~ed out of the driveway⟩ **c** (1) : to take a drink (2) : to draw hard in smoking ⟨~ed at his pipe⟩ **d :** to strain against the bit **2 :** to draw a gun **3 :** to admit of being pulled **4 :** to feel or express strong sympathy : ROOT ⟨~ing for his team to win⟩ — **pull·er** n

syn PULL, DRAW, DRAG, HAUL, TUG mean to cause to move toward or after one. PULL is the general term but may emphasize the force exerted rather than resulting motion; DRAW implies a smoother, steadier motion and generally a lighter force than PULL; DRAG suggests great effort overcoming resistance or friction; HAUL implies sustained pulling or dragging of heavy or bulky objects; TUG applies to strenuous often spasmodic efforts to move not necessarily with success

— **pull oneself together :** to regain one's self-possession — **pull one's leg :** to deceive someone playfully : HOAX — **pull one's teeth :** to make one harmless — **pull one's weight :** to do one's full share of the work — **pull stakes** or **pull up stakes :** to move out : LEAVE — **pull strings** or **pull wires :** to exert secret influence or control — **pull the string :** to throw a slow pitch

²pull n, often attrib **1 a :** the act or an instance of pulling **b :** a draft of liquid ⟨a long ~ uphill⟩ **c :** an inhalation of smoke **d :** force required to overcome resistance to pulling **2 a :** ADVANTAGE **b :** special influence **3 :** PROOF **6a 4 :** a device for pulling something or for operating by pulling ⟨bell ~⟩ **5 :** a force that attracts, compels, or influences : ATTRACTION

pull away vi : to draw oneself back or away : WITHDRAW, ESCAPE

pull·back \'pül-,bak\ n **1 :** a pulling back; esp : an orderly withdrawal of troops from a position **2 :** a skirt style marked by fullness drawn to the back

pull down vt **1 a :** DEMOLISH, DESTROY **b :** to hunt down : OVERCOME **2 a :** to bring to a lower level : REDUCE **b :** to depress in health, strength, or spirits : ENFEEBLE **3 :** to draw as wages or salary

pul·let \'pul-ət\ n [ME polet young fowl, fr. MF poulet, fr. OF, dim. of poul cock, fr. LL pullus, fr. L, young of an animal, chicken, sprout — more at FOAL] : a young hen; specif : a hen of the common fowl less than a year old

pul·ley \'pul-ē\ n [ME pouley, fr. MF poulie, prob. deriv. of Gk polos axis, pole] **1 a :** a sheave or small wheel with a grooved rim and with or without the block in which it runs used singly with a rope or chain to change the direction and point of application of a pulling force and in various combinations to increase the applied force esp. for lifting weights

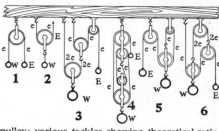

pulley: various tackles showing theoretical ratios of weights lifted, W, to effort, E, and tensions in various cords, e: 1 W=E; 2 W=2E; 3,4,6, W=4E; 5 W=3E

2 : a pulley or pulleys with ropes to form a tackle that constitutes one of the simple machines **3 :** a wheel used to transmit power by means of a band, belt, cord, rope, or chain

pull in vt **1 :** CHECK, RESTRAIN **2 :** ARREST ~ vi : to arrive at a destination or come to a stop

Pull·man \'pul-mən\ n [George M. Pullman †1897 Am inventor] : a railroad passenger car with specially comfortable furnishings for day or esp. for night travel

pull off vt : to carry out despite difficulties : accomplish successfully against odds

pul·lo·rum disease \pə-'lȯr-əm-, -'lȯr-\ n [NL pullorum (specific epithet of Salmonella pullorum), fr. L, gen. pl. of pullus)] : a destructive typically diarrheal salmonellosis of the chicken and less often other birds caused by a bacterium (Salmonella pullorum) which is transmitted either in the egg or from chick to chick

pull out vi **1 :** LEAVE, DEPART **2 :** WITHDRAW **3 :** to emerge or escape from difficulty

pull·out \'pul-,aut\ n **1 :** something that can be pulled out **2 :** the action in which an airplane goes from a dive to horizontal flight **3 :** PULLBACK

pull over vi : to steer one's vehicle to the side of the road

¹pull·over \,pul-,ō-vər\ adj : put on by being pulled over the head

²pullover \'pul-,ō-vər\ n : a pullover garment

pull round vt : to restore to good health ~ vi : to regain one's health

pull through vt : to help through a dangerous or difficult period or situation ~ vi : to survive a dangerous or difficult period or situation

pull together vi : to work in harmony : COOPERATE

pul·lu·late \'pul-yə-,lāt\ vi [L pullulatus, pp. of pullulare, fr. pullulus, dim. of pullus] **1 a :** GERMINATE, SPROUT **b :** to breed or produce freely **2 :** SWARM, TEEM — **pul·lu·la·tion** \,pəl-yə-'lā-shən\ n

pull up vt **1 :** CHECK, REBUKE **2 :** to bring to a stop : HALT ~ vi **1 a :** to check oneself **b :** to come to a halt : STOP **2 :** to draw even with others in a race

pul·mo·nary \'pul-mə-,ner-ē, 'pəl-\ adj [L pulmonarius, fr. pulmon-, pulmo lung; akin to Gk pleumōn lung] **1 :** relating to, functioning like, or associated with the lungs **2 :** PULMONATE **3 :** carried on by the lungs

pulmonary artery n : an artery that conveys venous blood from the heart to the lungs

pulmonary vein n : a valveless vein that returns oxygenated blood from the lungs to the heart

¹pul·mo·nate \'pul-mə-,nāt, 'pəl-\ adj [L pulmon-, pulmo lung] **1 :** having lungs or organs resembling lungs **2 :** of or relating to a large order (Pulmonata) of gastropod mollusks having a lung or respiratory sac and comprising most land snails and slugs and many freshwater snails

²pulmonate n : a pulmonate gastropod

pul·mon·ic \pul-'män-ik, ,pəl-\ adj [L pulmon-, pulmo] : PULMONARY

pul·mo·tor \'pul-,mōt-ər, 'pəl-\ n [fr. Pulmotor, a trademark] : a respiratory apparatus for pumping oxygen or air into and out of the lungs (as of an asphyxiated person)

¹pulp \'pəlp\ n [MF poulpe, fr. L pulpa flesh, pulp] **1 :** a moist usu. coherent mass of soft animal or plant tissue: as **a** (1) : the soft, succulent, usu. mesocarpic part of fruit (2) : stem pith when soft and spongy **b :** a soft mass of vegetable matter (as of apples) from which most of the water has been extracted by pressure **c :** a material prepared by chemical or mechanical means chiefly from wood but also from rags and other materials and used in making paper and cellulose products **2 :** pulverized ore mixed with water **3 a :** pulpy condition or character **b :** something in such a condition or having such a character **4 :** a magazine or book using rough-surfaced paper made of wood pulp and often dealing with sensational material — **pulp·i·ness** \'pəl-pē-nəs\ n — **pulpy** \'pəl-pē\ adj

²pulp vt **1 :** to reduce to pulp : cause to appear pulpy **2 :** to deprive of the pulp **3 :** to produce or reproduce (written matter) in pulp form ~ vi : to become pulp or pulpy — **pulp·er** n

pul·pit \'pul-,pit also 'pəl-, -pət\ n [ME, fr. LL pulpitum, fr. L,

staging, platform] **1 :** an elevated platform or high reading desk used in preaching or conducting a worship service **2 a :** the preaching profession **b :** a preaching position

pulp·wood \'pəlp-,wu̇d\ *n* **:** a wood (as of aspen, hemlock, pine, spruce) used in making pulp for paper

pul·que \'pül-,kā; 'pül-kē, 'pu̇l-\ *n* [MexSp] **:** a fermented drink made in Mexico from the juice of various magueys

pul·sant \'pəl-sənt\ *adj* **:** PULSATING

pul·sar \'pəl-,sär\ *n* [*pulse* + *-ar* (as in *quasar*)] **:** a celestial source of pulsating radio waves characterized by a short interval (as 1.33 or 0.25 seconds) between pulses and uniformity of the repetition rate of the pulses

pul·sate \'pəl-,sāt *also* ,pəl-'\ *vi* [L *pulsatus*, pp. of *pulsare*, fr. *pulsus*, pp. of *pellere*] **1 :** to exhibit a pulse **:** BEAT **2 :** to throb or move rhythmically **:** VIBRATE

pul·sa·tile \'pəl-sət-ᵊl, -sə-,tīl\ *adj* **:** PULSATING, THROBBING

pul·sa·tion \,pəl-'sā-shən\ *n* **:** rhythmical throbbing or vibrating (as of an artery); *also* **:** a single beat or throb

pul·sa·tor \'pəl-,sāt-ər, ,pəl-'\ *n* **:** something that beats or throbs in working (as a pulsometer pump)

pul·sa·to·ry \'pəl-sə-,tōr-ē, -,tȯr-\ *adj* **:** capable of or characterized by pulsation **:** THROBBING

1pulse \'pəls\ *n* [ME *puls*, fr. OF *pouls* porridge, fr. L *pult-*, *puls*; akin to L *pollen* fine flour — more at POLLEN] **:** the edible seeds of various leguminous crops (as peas, beans, lentils); *also* **:** a plant yielding pulse

2pulse *n* [ME *puls*, fr MF *pouls*, fr. L *pulsus*, lit., beating, fr. *pulsus*, pp. of *pellere* to drive, push, beat — more at FELT] **1 :** a regular throbbing caused in the arteries by the contractions of the heart; *also* **:** a single excursion of such throbbing **2 a :** underlying sentiment or opinion or an indication of it **b :** VITALITY **3 a :** rhythmical beating, vibrating, or sounding **b :** BEAT, THROB **4 a :** a transient variation of a quantity (as electrical current or voltage) whose value is normally constant **b :** an electromagnetic wave or modulation thereof of brief duration

3pulse *vi* **:** to exhibit a pulse or pulsation **:** THROB ~ *vt* **1 :** to drive by or as if by a pulsation **2 :** to cause to pulsate **3 a :** to produce or modulate (as electromagnetic waves) in the form of pulses ⟨*pulsed* waves⟩ **b :** to cause (an apparatus) to produce pulses

pulse–jet engine \,pəls-,jet-\ *n* **:** a jet engine having in its forward end intermittent air-inlet valves designed to produce a pulsating thrust by the intermittent flow of hot gases

pulse modulation *n* **:** modulation of a radio wave or signal by pulses

pul·sim·e·ter \,pəl-'sim-ət-ər\ *n* **:** an instrument for measuring the pulse and esp. its force and rate

pul·sion \'pəl-shən\ *n* [LL *pulsion-*, *pulsio*, fr. L *pulsus*, pp.] **:** PROPULSION

pul·sive \'pəl-siv\ *adj* **:** PROPULSIVE

pul·som·e·ter \,pəl-'säm-ət-ər\ *n* [ISV] **:** a pump with valves for raising water by steam and atmospheric pressure without intervention of a piston — called also *vacuum pump*

pul·ver·a·ble \'pəlv-(ə-)rə-bəl\ *adj* **:** capable of being pulverized

pul·ver·iz·able \'pəl-və-,rī-zə-bəl\ *adj* **:** capable of being pulverized

pul·ver·i·za·tion \,pəlv-(ə-)rə-'zā-shən\ *n* **:** the act or process of pulverizing

pul·ver·ize \'pəl-və-,rīz\ *vb* [MF *pulveriser*, fr. LL *pulverizare*, fr. L *pulver-*, *pulvis* dust, powder — more at POLLEN] *vt* **1 :** to reduce (as by crushing, beating, or grinding) to very small particles **:** ATOMIZE **2 :** ANNIHILATE, DEMOLISH ~ *vi* **:** to become pulverized — **pul·ver·iz·er** *n*

pul·ver·u·lent \,pəl-'ver-(y)ə-lənt\ *adj* [L *pulverulentus* dusty, fr. *pulver-*, *pulvis*] **1 :** consisting of or reducible to fine powder **2 :** being or looking dusty **:** CRUMBLY

pul·vil·lus \,pəl-'vil-əs\ *n*, *pl* **pul·vil·li** \-'vil-,ī, -(,)ē\ [NL, fr. L, dim. of *pulvinus* cushion] **:** a pad often covered with short hairs on an insect's foot

pul·vi·nate \,pəl-'vī-nət, -'vē-; 'pəl-və-,nāt\ *or* **pul·vi·nat·ed** \'pəl-və-,nāt-əd, -(,)vī-\ *adj* [L *pulvinatus*, fr. *pulvinus* cushion] **1 :** cushion-shaped **2 :** having a pulvinus — **pul·vi·nate·ly** *adv*

pul·vi·nus \,pəl-'vī-nəs, -'vē-\ *n*, *pl* **pul·vi·ni** \-'vī-,nī, -'vē-(,)nē\ [NL, fr. L, cushion] **:** a mass of large thin-walled cells surrounding a vascular strand at the base of a petiole or petiolule and functioning in turgor movements

pu·ma \'p(y)ü-mə\ *n*, *pl* **pumas** *also* **puma** [Sp, fr. Quechua] **:** COUGAR; *also* **:** the fur or pelt of a cougar

pum·ice \'pəm-əs\ *n* [ME *pomis*, fr. MF, fr. L *pumic-*, *pumex* — more at FOAM] **:** a volcanic glass full of cavities and very light in weight used esp. in powder form for smoothing and polishing — **pumice** *vt* — **pu·mi·ceous** \pyü-'mish-əs, ,pə-\ *adj*

pum·ic·ite \'pəm-ə-,sīt\ *n* **1 :** PUMICE **2 :** a volcanic dust

pum·mel \'pəm-əl\ *vb* **pum·meled** *or* **pum·melled**; **pum·mel·ing** *or* **pum·mel·ling** \-(ə-)liŋ\ [alter. of *pommel*] **:** POUND, BEAT

1pump \'pəmp\ *n* [ME *pumpe*, *pompe*, fr. MLG *pumpe* or MD *pompe*, prob. fr. Sp *bomba*, of imit. origin] **1 :** a device that raises, transfers, or compresses fluids or that attenuates gases esp. by suction or pressure or both **2 :** HEART

2pump *vt* **1 :** to raise (as water) with a pump **2 :** to pour forth, deliver, or draw with or as if with a pump **3 a :** to question persistently **b :** to elicit by such means **4 :** to draw fluid from with a pump **5 a :** to manipulate as or as if a pump handle **b :** to operate by manipulating a lever **6 :** to fill with air by means of a pump or bellows ~ *vi* **1 :** to work a pump **:** raise or move a fluid with a pump **2 :** to move up and down like a pump handle **3 :** to spurt out intermittently — **pump·er** *n*

3pump *n* [origin unknown] **:** a low shoe not fastened on and gripping the foot chiefly at the toe and heel

pum·per·nick·el \'pəm-pər-,nik-əl\ *n* [G] **:** a dark coarse sourdough bread made of unbolted rye flour

pump·kin \'pəŋ-kən, 'pəm(p)-kən\ *n*, *often attrib* [alter. of earlier *pumpion*, modif. of F *popon*, *pompon* melon, pumpkin, fr. L *pepon-*, *pepo*, fr. Gk *pepōn*, fr. *pepōn* ripened, fr. *pessein* to cook, ripen — more at COOK] **1 a :** the usu. round deep yellow fruit of a vine (*Cucurbita pepo*) of the gourd family widely cultivated as food **b :** a winter crookneck squash (*C. moschata*) **c** *Brit* **:** any of various large-fruited winter squashes (*C. maxima*) **2 :** a usu. hairy prickly vine that produces pumpkins

pump·kin·seed \-,sēd\ *n* **:** a small brilliantly colored No. American freshwater sunfish (*Lepomis gibbosus*) or the related bluegill

pump priming *n* **:** investment expenditures by government designed to induce a self-sustaining expansion of economic activity

1pun \'pən\ *n* [perh. fr. It *puntiglio* fine point, quibble — more at PUNCTILIO] **:** the humorous use of a word in such a way as to suggest different meanings or applications or of words having the same or nearly the same sound but different meanings

2pun *vi* **punned**; **pun·ning :** to make puns

pu·na \'pü-nə\ *n* [AmerSp, fr. Quechua] **1 :** a treeless windswept tableland or basin in the higher Andes **2 :** a cold mountain wind in Peru

1punch \'pənch\ *vb* [ME *punchen*, fr. MF *poinçonner* to prick, stamp, fr. *poinçon* puncheon] *vt* **1 a :** PROD, POKE **b :** to drive or herd (cattle) **2 a :** to strike with a forward thrust of the fist **b :** to drive or push forcibly by or as if by a punch **3 :** to emboss, cut, perforate, or make with a punch **4 :** to strike or press sharply ~ *vi* **:** to perform the action of punching something **syn** see STRIKE — **punch·er** *n*

2punch *n* **1 :** the action of punching **2 :** a quick blow with or as if with the fist **3 :** energy that commands attention

3punch *n* [prob. short for *puncheon*] **1 a :** a tool usu. in the form of a short rod of steel that is variously shaped at one end for different operations (as perforating or cutting) **b :** a short tapering steel rod for driving the heads of nails below the surface **c :** a steel die faced with a letter in relief that is forced into a softer metal to form an intaglio matrix from which foundry type is cast **d :** a device for cutting holes or notches in paper or cardboard **2 :** a hole or notch resulting from a perforating operation

4punch *n* [perh. fr. Hindi *pāc* five, fr. Skt *pañca*; akin to Gk *pente* five; fr. the number of ingredients] **:** a beverage usu. composed of wine or alcoholic liquor, citrus juice, spices, tea, and water; *also* **:** a beverage composed of nonalcoholic liquids (as fruit juices)

Punch–and–Judy show \,pən-chən-'jüd-ē-\ *n* **:** a puppet show in which a little hook-nosed humpback Punch quarrels ludicrously with his wife Judy

punch·board \'pənch-,bō(ə)rd, -,bȯ(ə)rd\ *n* **:** a small board that has many holes each filled with a rolled-up printed slip to be punched out on payment of a nominal sum in an effort to obtain a slip that entitles the player to a designated prize

punch bowl *n* **:** a large bowl from which a beverage (as punch) is served

punch–drunk \'pənch-,drəŋk\ *adj* [2*punch*] **1 :** suffering cerebral injury and bleeding from blows received in prizefighting **2 :** GROGGY, DAZED

punched card *or* **punch card** *n* **:** a card with holes punched in particular positions each with its own signification for use in data processing; *also* **:** a similar card with holes and notches cut along the edge

1pun·cheon \'pən-chən\ *n* [ME *ponson*, fr. MF *poinçon* pointed tool, king post (perh. fr. its being marked by the builder with a pointed tool), fr. (assumed) VL *punction-*, *punctio* pointed tool, fr. *punctiare* to prick, fr. L *punctus*, pp. of *pungere* to prick — more at PUNGENT] **1 :** a pointed tool for piercing or for working on stone **2 a :** a short upright framing timber **b :** a split log or heavy slab with the face smoothed **3 :** a figured stamp die or punch used esp. by goldsmiths, cutlers, and engravers

2puncheon *n* [ME *poncion*, fr. MF *ponchon*, *poinçon*, of unknown origin] **1 :** a large cask of varying capacity **2 :** any of various units of liquid capacity (as a unit equal to 70 gallons)

punch in *vi* **:** to record the time of one's presence (as for work) by punching a time clock

pun·chi·nel·lo \,pən-chə-'nel-(,)ō\ *n* [modif. of It dial. *polecenella*] **1 :** a fat short humpbacked clown or buffoon in Italian puppet shows **2 :** a squat grotesque person

punching bag *n* **:** a usu. suspended stuffed or inflated bag to be punched for exercise or for training in boxing

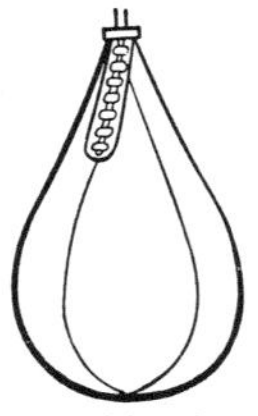
punching bag

punch line *n* **:** a sentence, statement, or phrase (as in a humorous story) that makes the point

punch out *vi* **:** to record the time of one's stopping work or departure by punching a time clock

punch press *n* **:** a press for working on material (as metal) by the use of cutting, shaping, or combination dies

punchy \'pən-chē\ *adj* **:** PUNCH-DRUNK

punc·tate \'pəŋ(k)-,tāt\ *adj* [NL *punctatus*, fr. L *punctum* point — more at POINT] **1 :** ending in or resembling a point **2 :** marked with minute spots or depressions ⟨a ~ leaf⟩ — **punc·ta·tion** \,pəŋ(k)-'tā-shən\ *n*

punc·til·io \,pəŋ(k)-'til-ē-,ō\ *n* [It & Sp; It *puntiglio* point of honor, scruple, fr. Sp *puntillo*, fr. dim. of *punto* point, fr. L *punctum*] **1 :** a nice detail of conduct in a ceremony or in observance of a code **2 :** careful observance of forms (as in social conduct)

punc·til·i·ous \-ē-əs\ *adj* **:** marked by precise exact accordance with the details of codes or conventions **syn** see CAREFUL — **punc·til·i·ous·ly** *adv* — **punc·til·i·ous·ness** *n*

punc·tu·al \'pəŋ(k)-chə(-wə)l, 'pəŋ(k)sh-wəl\ *adj* [ML *punctualis*, fr. L *punctus* pricking, point, fr. *punctus*, pp. of *pungere* to prick — more at PUNGENT] **1 :** relating to or having the nature of a point **2 :** to the point **:** POINTED **3 :** PUNCTILIOUS **4 :** acting or habitually acting at an appointed time or at a regularly scheduled time **:** PROMPT — **punc·tu·al·i·ty** \,pəŋ(k)-chə-'wal-ət-ē, ,pəŋ(k)sh-'wal-\ *n* — **punc·tu·al·ly** \'pəŋ(k)-chə(-wə)-lē, 'pəŋ(k)sh-wə-\ *adv* — **punc·tu·al·ness** \-chə(-wə)l-nəs, 'pəŋ(k)sh-wəl-\ *n*

punc·tu·ate \'pəŋ(k)-chə-,wāt\ *vb* [ML *punctuatus*, pp. of *punctuare* to point, provide with punctuation marks, fr. L *punctus* point] *vt* **1 :** to mark or divide (written matter) with punctuation marks **2 :** to break into or interrupt at intervals **:** EMPHASIZE ~ *vi* **:** to use punctuation marks — **punc·tu·a·tor** \-,wāt-ər\ *n*

punc·tu·a·tion \,pəŋ(k)-chə-'wā-shən\ *n* **:** the act, practice, or system of inserting standardized marks or signs in written matter to clarify the meaning and separate structural units

punctuation mark *n* **:** any of various standardized marks or signs used in punctuation

punc·tu·late \'pəŋ(k)-chə-,lāt\ *adj* [NL *punctulatus*, fr. L *punctulum*, dim. of *punctum* point] **:** marked with small spots; *specif* **:** minutely punctate — **punc·tu·la·tion** \,pəŋ(k)-chə-'lā-shən\ *n*

1punc·ture \'pəŋ(k)-chər\ *n* [L *punctura*, fr. *punctus*, pp. of *pungere*] **1 :** an act of puncturing **2 :** a hole, slight wound, or other perforation made by puncturing **3 :** a minute depression

2puncture *vb* **punc·tur·ing** \'pəŋ(k)-chə-riŋ, 'pəŋ(k)-shriŋ\ *vt* **1 :** to pierce with a pointed instrument or object **2 :** to suffer a

puncture of 3 : to make useless or absurd as if by a puncture : DESTROY ~ *vi* : to become punctured

punc·tured *adj* : having the surface covered with minute indentations or dots : PUNCTATE

pun·dit \'pən-dət\ *n* [Hindi *paṇḍit*, fr. Skt *paṇḍita*, fr *paṇḍita* learned] 1 : PANDIT 2 : a learned man : TEACHER 3 : an authority or one who gives opinions in an authoritative manner : CRITIC

pung \'pəŋ\ *n* [short for earlier *tow-pong*, of Algonquian origin; akin to Micmac *tobâgun* drag made with skin] *NewEng* : a sleigh with a box-shaped body

pun·gen·cy \'pən-jən-sē\ *n* : the quality or state of being pungent : SHARPNESS

pun·gent \-jənt\ *adj* [L *pungent-, pungens*, prp. of *pungere* to prick, sting; akin to L *pugnus* fist, *pugnare* to fight, Gk *pygmē* fist] 1 : having a stiff and sharp point ⟨~ leaves⟩ 2 : sharply painful : POIGNANT 3 a : CAUSTIC, STINGING b : POINTED, TELLING 4 : causing a sharp or irritating sensation; *esp* : ACRID — **pun·gent·ly** *adv*

syn PUNGENT, PIQUANT, POIGNANT, RACY mean sharp and stimulating to the senses. PUNGENT implies a stinging or biting quality esp. of odors; PIQUANT suggests a power to whet the appetite or interest through tartness or mild pungency; POIGNANT suggests a power to enter deeply as if by piercing or stabbing; RACY implies having a strongly characteristic natural quality fresh and unimpaired

[1]**Pu·nic** \'pyü-nik\ *adj* [L *punicus*, fr. *Poenus* inhabitant of Carthage, modif. of Gk *Phoinix* Phoenician] 1 : of or relating to Carthage or the Carthaginians 2 : FAITHLESS, TREACHEROUS

[2]**Punic** *n* : the Phoenician dialect of ancient Carthage

pu·ni·ly \'pyün-ᵊl-ē\ *adv* : in a puny manner

pu·ni·ness \'pyü-nē-nəs\ *n* : the quality or state of being puny

pun·ish \'pən-ish\ *vb* [ME *punisshen*, fr. MF *puniss-*, stem of *punir*, fr. L *punire*, fr. *poena* penalty — more at PAIN] *vt* 1 a : to impose a penalty on for a fault, offense, or violation b : to inflict a penalty for the commission of (an offense) in retribution or retaliation 2 a : to deal with roughly or harshly b : to inflict injury upon : HURT ~ *vi* : to inflict punishment — **pun·ish·abil·i·ty** \,pən-ish-ə-'bil-ət-ē\ *n* — **pun·ish·able** \'pən-ish-ə-bəl\ *adj* — **pun·ish·er** *n*

syn CHASTISE, CASTIGATE, CHASTEN, DISCIPLINE, CORRECT: PUNISH implies subjecting to a penalty for wrongdoing; CHASTISE implies corporal punishment; CASTIGATE implies a lashing with words; CHASTEN suggests any affliction or trial that leaves one humbled or subdued; DISCIPLINE implies a punishing or chastening in order to bring under control; CORRECT implies punishing aimed at reforming an offender

pun·ish·ment \'pən-ish-mənt\ *n* 1 : the act of punishing 2 a : retributive suffering, pain, or loss b : a penalty inflicted on an offender through judicial procedure 3 : severe, rough, or disastrous treatment

pu·ni·tion \pyü-'nish-ən\ *n* [ME *punicion*, fr. MF *punition*, fr. L *punition-, punitio*, fr. *punitus*] : PUNISHMENT

pu·ni·tive \'pyü-nət-iv\ *adj* [F *punitif*, fr. ML *punitivus*, fr. L *punitus*, pp. of *punire*] : inflicting, involving, or aiming at punishment — **pu·ni·tive·ly** *adv* — **pu·ni·tive·ness** *n*

punitive damages *n pl* : damages awarded in excess of normal compensation to the plaintiff to punish a defendant for a gross wrong

Pun·jabi \,pən-'jäb-ē, -'jab-\ *n* [Hindi *pañjābī*, fr. *pañjābī* of Punjab, fr. Per, fr. *Pañjāb* Punjab] 1 : a native or inhabitant of the Punjab region of northwestern India 2 : PANJABI — **Punjabi** *adj*

[1]**punk** \'pəŋk\ *n* [origin unknown] 1 *archaic* : PROSTITUTE 2 [prob. partly fr. [3]*punk*] : NONSENSE, BUNKUM 3 a : a young inexperienced person; *esp* : a young man : BOY b : a young gangster, hoodlum, or ruffian

[2]**punk** *adj* : very poor : INFERIOR; *also* : being in poor health

[3]**punk** *n* [perh. alter. of *spunk*] 1 : wood so decayed as to be dry, crumbly, and useful for tinder 2 : a dry spongy substance prepared from fungi (genus *Fomes*) and used to ignite fuses esp. of fireworks

pun·kah \'pəŋ-kə\ *n* [Hindi *pākhā*] : a large fan or a canvas-covered frame suspended from the ceiling and used esp. in India for fanning a room

pun·kie *also* **pun·ky** \'pəŋ-kē\ *n* [D dial. *punki*, fr. Delaware *punk*, lit., fine ashes, powder] : BITING MIDGE

pun·kin *var of* PUMPKIN

punky \'pəŋ-kē\ *adj* 1 : of, relating to, or like punk 2 : burning slowly : SMOLDERING

pun·ster \'pən(t)-stər\ *n* : one who is given to punning

[1]**punt** \'pənt\ *n* [(assumed) ME, fr. OE, fr. L *ponton-, ponto* — more at PONTOON] : a long narrow flat-bottomed boat with square ends usu. propelled with a pole

[2]**punt** *vt* : to propel by pushing with a pole against the bottom

[3]**punt** *vi* [F *ponter*, fr. *ponte* point in some games, play against the banker, fr. Sp *punto* point, fr. L *punctum* — more at POINT] 1 : to play at a gambling game against the banker 2 *Brit* : GAMBLE, BET

[4]**punt** *vb* [origin unknown] *vt* : to kick (a football) before the ball dropped from the hands hits the ground ~ *vi* : to punt a ball

[5]**punt** *n* : the act or an instance of punting a ball

punt·er \'pənt-ər\ *n* : one that punts

punt formation *n* : an offensive football formation in which a back making a punt stands approximately 10 yards behind the line and the other backs are in blocking position close to the line of scrimmage

pun·ty \'pənt-ē\ *n* [F *pontil*] : a metal rod used for fashioning hot glass

pu·ny \'pyü-nē\ *adj* [MF *puisné* younger, lit. born afterward, fr. *puis* afterward + *né* born] : slight or inferior in power, size, or importance : WEAK

[1]**pup** \'pəp\ *n* [short for *puppy*] : a young dog; *also* : one of the young of various animals (as seals)

[2]**pup** *vi* **pupped; pup·ping** : to give birth to pups

pu·pa \'pyü-pə\ *n, pl* **pu·pae** \-(,)pē, -,pī\ *or* **pupas** [NL, fr. L *pupa* girl, doll] : a metamorphic insect in an intermediate usu. quiescent form assumed between the larval and the imaginal stages and characterized by internal dedifferentiation of larva structures and their replacement by structures typical of the imago — **pu·pal** \'pyü-pəl\ *adj*

pu·pate \'pyü-,pāt\ *vi* : to become a pupa : pass through a pupal stage — **pu·pa·tion** \pyü-'pā-shən\ *n*

[1]**pu·pil** \'pyü-pəl\ *n* [ME *pupille* minor ward, fr. MF, fr. L *pupillus* male ward (fr. dim. of *pupus* boy) & *pupilla* female ward, fr. dim. of *pupa* girl, doll, puppet] 1 : a child or young person in school or in the charge of a tutor or instructor : STUDENT 2 : one who has been taught or influenced by a person of fame or distinction : DISCIPLE **syn** see SCHOLAR

[2]**pupil** *n* [MF *pupille*, fr. L *pupilla*, fr. dim. of *pupa* doll; fr. the tiny image of oneself seen reflected in another's eye] : the contractile usu. round aperture in the iris of the eye — **pu·pil·ar** \-pə-lər\ *adj* — **pu·pil·lary** \-,ler-ē\ *adj*

pu·pil·age *or* **pu·pil·lage** \'pyü-pə-lij\ *n* : the state or period of being a pupil

pupil load *n* : the total number of pupils assigned to a single teacher in a school for classroom or other instruction

pu·pip·a·rous \pyü-'pip-ə-rəs\ *adj* [NL *pupa* + E *-i-* + *-parous*] : producing mature larvae that are ready to pupate at birth; *also* : of or relating to a division (Pupipara) of two-winged flies with such larvae

pup·pet \'pəp-ət\ *n* [ME *popet*, fr. MF *poupette*, dim. of (assumed) *poupe* doll, fr. L *pupa*] 1 : a small-scale figure of a human or other living being often with jointed limbs and moved by hand or by strings or wires 2 : DOLL 1 3 : one whose acts are controlled by an outside force or influence

pup·pe·teer \,pəp-ə-'ti(ə)r\ *n* : one who manipulates puppets or marionettes

pup·pet·ry \'pəp-ə-trē\ *n* : the production or creation of puppets or puppet shows

pup·py \'pəp-ē\ *n* [ME *popi*, fr. MF *poupée* doll, toy, fr. (assumed) *poupe* doll] : a young domestic dog; *specif* : one less than a year old

pup·py·ish \-ish\ *adj* : of, relating to, or characteristic of a puppy

puppy love *n* : CALF LOVE

pup tent *n* : a wedge-shaped shelter tent

Pu·ra·na \pu̇-'rän-ə\ *n, often cap* [Skt *purāṇa*, fr. *purāṇa* ancient, fr. *purā* formerly; akin to OE *fore*] : one of a class of Hindu sacred writings chiefly from A.D. 300 to A.D. 750 comprising popular myths and legends and other traditional lore — **Pu·ra·nic** \-ik\ *adj*

pur·blind \'pər-,blīnd\ *adj* [ME *pur blind*, fr. *pur* purely, wholly, fr. *pur* pure] 1 a *obs* : wholly blind b : partly blind 2 : lacking in vision, insight, or understanding : OBTUSE — **pur·blind·ly** \-,blīn-(d)lē\ *adv* — **pur·blind·ness** \-,blīn(d)-nəs\ *n*

pur·chas·able \'pər-chə-sə-bəl\ *adj* : capable of being purchased

[1]**pur·chase** \'pər-chəs\ *vt* [ME *purchacen*, fr. OF *purchacier* to seek to obtain, fr. *por-, pur-* for, forward (modif. of L *pro-*) + *chacier* to pursue, chase — more at PRO-] 1 a *archaic* : GAIN, ACQUIRE b : to acquire (real estate) by means other than descent or inheritance c : to obtain by paying money or its equivalent : BUY d : to obtain by labor, danger, or sacrifice : EARN 2 : to apply a device for obtaining a mechanical advantage to (as something to be moved); *also* : to move by a purchase 3 : to constitute the means for buying

[2]**purchase** *n* 1 : an act or instance of purchasing 2 a : something gotten by any means : GAIN b : something obtained for a price in money 3 a (1) : a mechanical hold or advantage applied to the raising or moving of heavy bodies (2) : an apparatus or device by which advantage is gained b (1) : an advantage used in applying one's power in any effort (2) : position or means of exerting power

pur·chas·er \'pər-chə-sər\ *n* : one that purchases

pur·dah \'pərd-ə\ *n* [Hindi *parda*, lit., screen, veil] : seclusion of women from public observation among Muslims and some Hindus esp. in India

pure \'pyu̇(ə)r\ *adj* [ME *pur*, fr. OF, fr. L *purus*; akin to Skt *punāti* he cleanses, MIr *ūr* fresh, green] 1 a (1) : unmixed with any other matter ⟨~ gold⟩ (2) : free from dust, dirt, or taint ⟨~ food⟩ (3) : SPOTLESS, STAINLESS b : free from harshness or roughness ⟨~ tone⟩ c *of a vowel* : characterized by no appreciable alteration of articulation during utterance 2 a : SHEER, UNALLOYED ⟨~ folly⟩ b (1) : ABSTRACT, THEORETICAL (2) : a priori ⟨~ mechanics⟩ c : not directed toward exposition of reality or solution of practical problems ⟨~ literature⟩; *esp* : being nonobjective and to be appraised on formal and technical qualities only ⟨~ form⟩ 3 a (1) : free from what vitiates, weakens, or pollutes (2) : containing nothing that does not properly belong b : free from moral fault or guilt c : marked by chastity : CONTINENT d (1) : of pure blood and unmixed ancestry (2) : homozygous in and breeding true for one or more characters e : ritually clean **syn** see CHASTE — **pure·ness** *n*

pure·blood \-,bləd\ *or* **pure–blood·ed** \-'bləd-əd\ *adj* : of unmixed ancestry : PUREBRED — **pureblood** *n*

pure·bred \-'bred\ *adj* : bred from members of a recognized breed, strain, or kind without admixture of other blood over many generations — **purebred** \-,bred\ *n*

[1]**pu·ree** \pyu̇-'rā, -'rē\ *n* [F, fr. MF, fr. fem. of *puré*, pp. of *purer* to purify, strain, fr. L *purare* to purify, fr. *purus*] 1 : a paste or thick liquid suspension usu. produced by rubbing cooked food through a sieve 2 : a thick soup having pureed vegetables as a base

[2]**puree** *vt* **pu·reed; pu·ree·ing** : to boil soft and then rub through a sieve

pure imaginary *n* : the product of a real number other than zero and the imaginary unit

pure·ly \'pyu̇(ə)r-lē\ *adv* 1 : without admixture of anything injurious or foreign 2 : MERELY, SOLELY 3 : CHASTELY, INNOCENTLY 4 : COMPLETELY

pur·fle \'pər-fəl\ *vt* **pur·fling** \-f(ə-)liŋ\ [ME *purfilen*, fr. MF *porfiler*] 1 : to ornament the border of 2 : to ornament with metallic threads, jewels, or fur, or with tracery or inlay — **purfle** *n*

pur·ga·tion \,pər-'gā-shən\ *n* : the act or result of purging

[1]**pur·ga·tive** \'pər-gət-iv\ *adj* [ME *purgatif*, fr. MF, fr. LL *purgativus*, fr. L *purgatus*, pp.] : purging or tending to purge : CATHARTIC

[2]**purgative** *n* : a purging medicine : CATHARTIC

pur·ga·to·ri·al \,pər-gə-'tōr-ē-əl, -'tȯr-\ *adj* 1 : cleansing of sin : EXPIATORY 2 : of or relating to purgatory

pur·ga·to·ry \'pər-gə-,tōr-ē, -,tȯr-\ *n* [ME, fr. AF or ML; AF *purgatorie*, fr. ML *purgatorium*, fr. LL, neut. of *purgatorius* purging, fr. L *purgatus*, pp. of *purgare*] **1 :** an intermediate state after death for expiatory purification; *specif* **:** a place or state of punishment wherein according to Roman Catholic doctrine the souls of those who die in God's grace may expiate venial sins or satisfy divine justice for the temporal punishment still due to remitted mortal sin **2 :** a place or state of temporary punishment

¹purge \'pərj\ *vb* [ME *purgen*, fr. OF *purgier*, fr. L *purigare*, *purgare* to purify, purge, fr. *purus* pure + *-igare* (akin to *agere* to drive, do) — more at ACT] *vt* **1 :** to clear of guilt or of moral or ceremonial defilement **2 :** to remove by cleansing **3 a :** to cause evacuation from (as the bowels) **b :** to free (as a boiler) of sediment or relieve (as a steam pipe) of trapped air by bleeding **c** (1) **:** to rid (as a state) by a purge (2) **:** to get rid of (undesirable persons) **:** ELIMINATE ~ *vi* **1 :** to become purged **2 :** to have or produce frequent evacuations **3 :** to cause purgation — **purg·er** *n*

²purge *n* **1 a :** an act or instance of purging **b :** a ridding of elements or members regarded as treacherous or disloyal **2 :** something that purges; *esp* **:** PURGATIVE

pu·ri·fi·ca·tion \,pyu̇r-ə-fə-'kā-shən\ *n* **:** an act or instance of purifying or of being purified

pu·ri·fi·ca·tor \'pyu̇r-ə-fə-,kāt-ər\ *n* **1 :** PURIFIER **2 :** a linen cloth used to wipe the chalice after celebration of the Eucharist

pu·ri·fi·ca·to·ry \pyu̇r-'if-i-kə-,tōr-ē, 'pyu̇r-(ə-)fə-kə-, -,tȯr-\ *adj* **:** serving, tending, or intended to purify

pu·ri·fi·er \'pyu̇r-ə-,fī(-ə)r\ *n* **:** one that purifies

pu·ri·fy \-,fī\ *vt* **:** to make pure: as **a :** to clear from material defilement or imperfection **b :** to free from guilt or moral or ceremonial blemish **c :** to free from anything alien, extraneous, improper, corrupting, or otherwise damaging ~ *vi* **:** to grow or become pure or clean

Pu·rim \'pu̇r-əm, pu̇-'rim\ *n* [Heb *pūrīm*, lit., the lots; fr. the casting of lots by Haman, Esth 9:24–26] **:** a Jewish holiday celebrated on the 14th of Adar in commemoration of the rescue of the Jews from Haman's plotting

pu·rine \'pyu̇(ə)r-,ēn\ *n* [G *purin*, fr. L *purus* pure + NL *uricus* uric, fr. E *uric*] **:** a crystalline base $C_5H_4N_4$ that is the parent of compounds of the uric-acid group; *also* **:** a derivative of this

pur·ism \'pyu̇(ə)r-,iz-əm\ *n* **1 :** rigid adherence to or insistence on purity or nicety esp. in use of words **2 :** an example of purism; *esp* **:** a word, phrase, or sense used chiefly by purists **3 :** a 20th century theory and practice in art that reduces all natural appearances to geometric simplicity — **pur·ist** \-əst\ *n* — **pu·ris·tic** \pyu̇r-'is-tik\ *adj*

pu·ri·tan \'pyu̇r-ət-ᵊn\ *n* [prob. fr. LL *puritas* purity] **1** *cap* **:** a member of a 16th and 17th century Protestant group in England and New England opposing as unscriptural the traditional and formal usages of the Church of England **2 :** one who practices or preaches a more rigorous or professedly purer moral code than that which prevails — **puritan** *adj, often cap* — **pu·ri·tan·i·cal** \,pyu̇r-ə-'tan-i-kəl\ *adj* — **pu·ri·tan·i·cal·ly** \-k(ə-)lē\ *adv* — **pu·ri·tan·ism** \'pyu̇r-ət-ᵊn-,iz-əm\ *n, often cap*

pu·ri·ty \'pyu̇r-ət-ē\ *n* [ME *purete*, fr. OF *pureté*, fr. LL *puritat-, puritas*, fr. L *purus* pure] **1 :** the quality or state of being pure **2 :** SATURATION 4a

¹purl \'pər(-ə)l\ *n* [obs. *pirl* (to twist)] **1 :** gold or silver thread or wire for embroidering or edging **2 :** the intertwist of thread knotting a stitch usu. along an edge

²purl *vt* **1 a :** to embroider with gold or silver thread **b :** to edge or border with gold or silver embroidery **2 :** to knit in purl stitch ~ *vi* **:** to do knitting in purl stitch

³purl *n* [perh. of Scand origin; akin to Norw *purla* to ripple] **1 :** a purling or swirling stream or rill **2 :** a gentle murmur or movement (as of purling water)

⁴purl *vi* **1 :** EDDY, SWIRL **2 :** to make a soft murmuring sound like that of a purling stream

pur·lieu \'pərl-(,)yü\ *n* [ME *purlewe* land severed from an English royal forest by perambulation, fr. AF *puralé* perambulation, fr. OF *puraler* to go through, fr. *pur-* for, through + *aler* to go — more at PURCHASE, ALLEY] **1 a :** a place of resort **:** HAUNT **b** *pl* **:** CONFINES, BOUNDS **2 a :** an outlying or adjacent district **b** *pl* **:** ENVIRONS, NEIGHBORHOOD

pur·lin \'pər-lən\ *n* [origin unknown] **:** a horizontal member in a roof supporting the common rafters

pur·loin \(,)pər-'lȯin, 'pər-,\ *vb* [ME *purloinen* to put away, render ineffectual, fr. AF *purloigner*, fr. OF *porloigner* to put off, delay, fr. *por-* forward + *loing* at a distance, fr. L *longe*, fr. *longus* long — more at PURCHASE] *vt* **:** to appropriate wrongfully **:** FILCH ~ *vi* **:** to practice theft **syn** see STEAL — **pur·loin·er** *n*

purl stitch *n* [¹*purl*] **:** a knitting stitch usu. made by inserting the right needle into the front of a loop on the left needle from the right, catching the yarn with the right needle, and bringing it through to form a new loop

¹pur·ple \'pər-pəl\ *adj* [ME *purpel*, alter. of *purper*, fr. OE *purpuran*, gen. of *purpure* purple color, fr. L *purpura*, fr. Gk *porphyra*] **1 :** IMPERIAL, REGAL **2 :** of the color purple **3 a :** highly rhetorical **:** ORNATE **b :** marked by profanity

²purple *n* **1 a** (1) **:** TYRIAN PURPLE (2) **:** any of various colors that fall about midway between red and blue in hue **b** (1) **:** cloth dyed purple (2) **:** a garment of such color; *esp* **:** a purple robe worn as an emblem of rank or authority **c** (1) **:** a mollusk (as of the genus *Purpura*) yielding a purple dye and esp. the Tyrian purple of ancient times (2) **:** a pigment or dye that colors purple **2 a :** imperial or regal rank or power **b :** exalted station

³purple *vb* **pur·pling** \'pər-p(ə-)liŋ\ **:** to turn purple

Purple Heart *n* **:** a U.S. military decoration awarded to any member of the armed forces wounded by enemy action

purple passage *n* [trans. of L *pannus purpureus* purple patch; fr. the traditional splendor of purple cloth as contrasted with more shabby materials] **1 :** a passage conspicuous for brilliance or effectiveness in a work that is characteristically dull, commonplace, or uninspired **2 :** a piece of obtrusively ornate writing — called also *purple patch*

pur·plish \'pər-p(ə-)lish\ *adj* **:** somewhat purple

¹pur·port \'pər-,pō(ə)rt, -,pȯ(ə)rt\ *n* [ME, fr. AF, content, tenor, fr. *purporter* to contain, fr. OF *porporter* to convey, fr. *por-* forward + *porter* to carry — more at PURCHASE, PORT] **:** meaning conveyed, professed, or implied **:** IMPORT; *also* **:** SUBSTANCE, GIST

²pur·port \(,)pər-'pō(ə)rt, -'pȯ(ə)rt\ *vt* **1 :** to convey or profess outwardly; *specif* **:** to have the often specious appearance of being, intending, or claiming (something implied or inferred) **:** PROFESS **2 :** INTEND, PURPOSE

pur·port·ed *adj* **:** REPUTED, RUMORED — **pur·port·ed·ly** *adv*

¹pur·pose \'pər-pəs\ *n* [ME *purpos*, fr. OF, fr. *purposer* to purpose, fr. L *proponere* (perf. indic. *proposui*) to propose — more at PROPOSE] **1 a :** something set up as an object or end to be attained **:** INTENTION **b :** RESOLUTION, DETERMINATION **2 :** an object or result aimed at **3 :** a subject under discussion or an action in course of execution **syn** see INTENTION — **pur·pose·ful** \-fəl\ *adj* — **pur·pose·ful·ly** \-fə-lē\ *adv* — **pur·pose·ful·ness** \-fəl-nəs\ *n* — **pur·pose·less** \-ləs\ *adj* — **on purpose :** by intent **:** INTENTIONALLY

²purpose *vt* **:** to propose as an aim to oneself

pur·pose·ly \'pər-pə-slē\ *adv* **:** with a deliberate or express purpose **:** INTENTIONALLY

pur·pos·ive \'pər-pə-siv\ *adj* **1 :** serving or effecting a useful function though not as a result of design **2 :** having or tending to fulfill a conscious purpose or design **:** PURPOSEFUL — **pur·pos·ive·ly** *adv* — **pur·pos·ive·ness** *n*

pur·pu·ra \'pər-pyə-rə\ *n* [NL, fr. L, purple color] **:** any of several hemorrhagic states characterized by extravasation of blood into the skin and mucous membranes resulting in patches of purplish discoloration — **pur·pu·ric** \,pər-'pyu̇(ə)r-ik\ *adj*

purr \'pər\ *n* [imit.] **:** a low vibratory murmur typical of a cat apparently contented or pleased — **purr** *vb*

¹purse \'pərs\ *n* [ME *purs*, fr. OE, modif. of ML *bursa*, fr. LL, oxhide, fr. Gk *byrsa*] **1 a** (1) **:** a small bag for money (2) **:** a receptacle (as a wallet) to carry money and often other small objects in **b :** a receptacle (as a pouch) shaped like a purse **2 a :** RESOURCES, FUNDS **b :** a sum of money offered as a prize or present

²purse *vt* **1 :** to put into a purse **2 :** PUCKER, KNIT

purse crab *n* **:** a land crab (*Birgus latro*) widely distributed about islands of the tropical Indian and Pacific oceans where it burrows in the soil and feeds on coconuts and related to the hermit crabs but distinguished by its large size and broad symmetrical abdomen the oily flesh of which is esteemed a delicacy

purse–proud \'pər-,sprau̇d\ *adj* **:** proud because of one's wealth

purs·er \'pər-sər\ *n* **:** an official on a ship responsible for papers and accounts and on a passenger ship also for the comfort and welfare of passengers

purse race *n* **:** a race for a fixed purse

purse seine *n* **:** a large seine designed to be set by two boats around

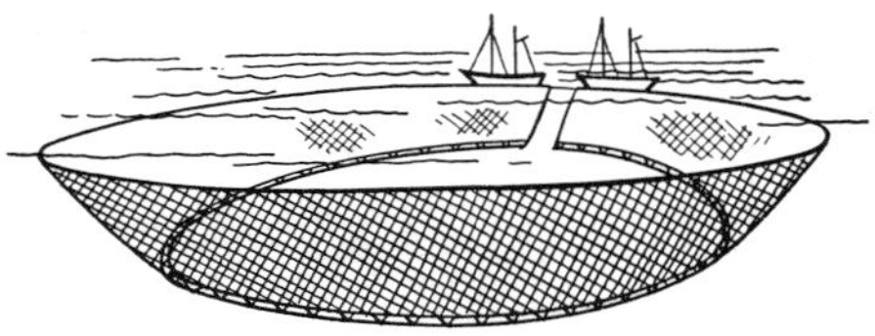

purse seine

a school of fish and so arranged that after the ends have been brought together the bottom can be closed — **purse seiner** *n*

pur·si·ness \'pəs-ē-nəs, 'pər-sē-\ *n* **:** the quality or state of being pursy

purs·lane \'pər-slən, -,slān\ *n* [ME, fr. MF *porcelaine*, fr. LL *porcillagin-*, *porcillago*, alter. of L *porcillaca*, alter. of *portulaca*] **:** any of a family (Portulacaceae, the purslane family) of usu. succulent herbs having perfect regular flowers with two sepals and 4 to 5 hypogynous petals; *esp* **:** an annual herb (*Portulaca oleracea*) with fleshy leaves used as a potherb or for salads and common as a weed in gardens

pur·su·ance \pər-'sü-ən(t)s\ *n* **:** the act of pursuing; *esp* **:** a carrying out or into effect **:** PROSECUTION

pur·su·ant \-ənt\ *adj* **:** being in pursuit **:** PURSUING

pur·su·ant·ly *adv* **:** CONSEQUENTLY

pursuant to *prep* **:** in carrying out **:** in conformance to **:** according to

pur·sue \pər-'sü\ *vb* [ME *pursuen*, fr. AF *pursuer*, fr. OF *poursuir*, fr. L *prosequi*, fr. *pro-* forward + *sequi* to follow — more at PRO-, SUE] *vt* **1 :** to follow in order to overtake, capture, kill, or defeat **2 :** to find or employ measures to obtain or accomplish **:** SEEK ⟨~ a goal⟩ **3 :** to proceed along **:** FOLLOW ⟨~s a northern course⟩ **4 :** to engage in **:** PRACTICE ⟨~ a hobby⟩ **5 :** to continue to afflict **:** HAUNT **6 :** COURT, ¹CHASE 1c ~ *vi* **:** to go in pursuit **syn** see CHASE — **pur·su·er** *n*

pur·suit \pər-'süt\ *n* [ME, fr. OF *poursuite*, fr. *poursuir*] **1 :** the act of pursuing **2 :** an activity that one engages in as a vocation, profession, or avocation **:** OCCUPATION **syn** see WORK

pursuit plane *n* **:** a fighter plane for pursuit of and attack on enemy airplanes

pur·sui·vant \'pər-s(w)i-vənt\ *n* [ME *pursevant* attendant of a herald, fr. MF *poursuivant*, lit., follower, fr. prp. of *poursuir*, *poursuivre* to pursue] **1 :** an officer of arms ranking below a herald but having similar duties **2 :** FOLLOWER, ATTENDANT

¹pur·sy \'pəs-ē, 'pər-sē\ *or* **pus·sy** \'pəs-ē\ *adj* [ME *pursy*, fr. AF *pursif*, alter. of MF *polsif*, fr. *poulser*, *polser* to beat, push, pant — more at PUSH] **1 a :** short-winded esp. because of corpulence **b :** FAT **2 :** characterized by or arising from arrogance of wealth, self-indulgence, or luxury

²pursy \'pər-sē\ *adj* [*purse*] **1 :** PUCKERED **2 :** PURSE-PROUD

pur·te·nance \'pərt-nən(t)s, -ᵊn-ən(t)s\ *n* [ME, lit., appendage, modif. of MF *partenance*, fr. *partenir* to pertain — more at PERTAIN] **:** ENTRAILS, PLUCK

pu·ru·lence \'p(y)u̇r-(y)ə-lən(t)s\ *n* **:** the quality or state of being purulent; *also* **:** PUS

pu·ru·lent \-lənt\ *adj* [L *purulentus*, fr. *pur-*, *pus* pus] **1 :** containing, consisting of, or being pus ⟨a ~ discharge⟩ **2 :** accompanied by suppuration

pur·vey \(,)pər-'vā, 'pər-,\ *vt* [ME *purveien*, fr. MF *porveeir*, fr. L *providēre* to provide] **:** to supply (as provisions) usu. as a matter of business

pur·vey·ance \-ən(t)s\ *n* **:** the act or process of purveying or procuring

pur·vey·or \-ər\ *n* **:** VICTUALLER, CATERER

pur·view \'pər-(,)vyü\ *n* [ME *purveu*, fr. AF *purveu est* it is provided (opening phrase of a statute)] **1 a :** the body or enacting part of a statute **b :** the limit, purpose, or scope of a statute **2 :** the range or limit of authority, competence, responsibility, concern, or intention **3 :** range of vision, understanding, or cognizance

pus \'pəs\ *n* [L *pur-, pus* — more at FOUL] **:** thick opaque usu. yellowish white fluid matter formed by suppuration and composed of exudate containing leukocytes, tissue debris, and microorganisms

Pu·sey·ism \'pyü-zē-,iz-əm, -sē-\ *n* [E. B. *Pusey* †1882 Eng. theologian] **:** TRACTARIANISM — **Pu·sey·ite** \-,īt\ *n*

[1]**push** \'pu̇sh\ *vb* [ME *pusshen*, fr. OF *poulser* to beat, push, fr. L *pulsare*, fr. *pulsus*, pp. of *pellere* to drive, strike — more at FELT] *vt* **1 a :** to press against with force in order to drive or impel **b :** to move or endeavor to move away or ahead by steady pressure without striking **2 :** to thrust forward, downward, or outward **3 a :** to press or urge forward to completion with insistence **b :** to prosecute with vigor or effectiveness **4 :** to bear hard upon so as to involve in difficulty **~** *vi* **1 :** to press against something with steady force in or as if in order to impel **2 :** to press forward against opposition or with energy **3 :** to exert oneself continuously, vigorously, or obtrusively to gain an end (as success or social advancement) — **push·er** *n* — **pushy** \'pu̇sh-ē\ *adj*

syn PUSH, SHOVE, THRUST, PROPEL mean to cause to move ahead or aside by force. PUSH implies application of force by a body already in contact with the body to be moved; SHOVE implies a fast or rough pushing of something usu. along a surface; THRUST suggests less steadiness and greater violence than PUSH; PROPEL suggests rapidly driving forward or onward by force applied in any manner

[2]**push** *n* **1 :** a vigorous effort to attain an end **:** DRIVE: **a :** a military assault or offensive **b :** an advance overcoming obstacles **c :** a campaign to promote a product **2 :** a time for action **:** EMERGENCY **3 a :** an act of pushing **:** SHOVE **b** (1) **:** a physical force steadily applied in a direction away from the body exerting it (2) **:** INFLUENCE, URGE **c :** vigorous enterprise or energy **4 a :** an exertion of influence to promote another's interests **b :** stimulation to activity **:** IMPETUS

push·ball \-,bȯl\ *n* **:** a game in which each of two sides endeavors to push an inflated leather-covered ball six feet in diameter across its opponents' goal; *also* **:** the ball used

push button *n* **:** a small button or knob that when pushed operates something esp. by closing an electric circuit

push–but·ton \,pu̇sh-,bət-ᵊn\ *adj, of warfare* **:** using complex and more or less self-operating mechanisms against an enemy that are put in operation by a simple act comparable to pushing a button

push·cart \'pu̇sh-,kärt\ *n* **:** a cart or barrow pushed by hand

push·i·ly \'pu̇sh-ə-lē\ *adv* **:** in a pushy manner

push·i·ness \'pu̇sh-ē-nəs\ *n* **:** the quality or state of being pushy

push·ing *adj* **1 :** marked by ambition, energy, enterprise, and initiative **2 :** marked by tactless forwardness or officious intrusiveness **syn** see AGGRESSIVE

push off *vi* **:** to set out

push·over \'pu̇sh-,ō-vər\ *n* **1 :** an opponent easy to defeat or a victim capable of no effective resistance **2 :** someone unwilling or unable to resist the power of a particular attraction or appeal **:** SUCKER **3 :** something accomplished without difficulty **:** SNAP

push·pin \-,pin\ *n* **:** a steel point having a projecting head for sticking into a wall or board

push–pull \'pu̇sh-'pu̇l\ *adj* **:** constituting or relating to an arrangement of two electron tubes such that an alternating input causes them to send current through a load alternately ⟨a ~ circuit⟩ — **push–pull** *n*

Push·tu \'pəsh-(,)tü\ *var of* PASHTO

push–up \'pu̇sh-,əp\ *n* **:** an exercise for strengthening arm and shoulder muscles by bending and extending the elbows with the body in a prone position supported by the hands and toes

pu·sil·la·nim·i·ty \,pyü-s(ə-)lə-'nim-ət-ē *also* ,pyü-zə-lə-\ *n* **:** the quality or state of being pusillanimous **:** COWARDLINESS

pu·sil·lan·i·mous \,pyü-sə-'lan-ə-məs *also* ,pyü-zə-\ *adj* [LL *pusillanimis*, fr. L *pusillus* very small (dim. of *pusus* small child) + *animus* soul; akin to L *puer* child — more at PUERILE, ANIMATE] **:** lacking courage and resolution **:** marked by contemptible timidity **syn** see COWARDLY — **pu·sil·lan·i·mous·ly** *adv*

[1]**puss** \'pu̇s\ *n* [origin unknown] **1 :** CAT **2 :** GIRL

[2]**puss** *n* [IrGael *pus* mouth, fr. MIr *bus*] *slang* **:** FACE

puss·ley \'pəs-lē\ *n* [by alter.] **:** PURSLANE

[1]**pussy** \'pu̇s-ē\ *n* **1 :** PUSS **2 :** a catkin of the pussy willow

[2]**pus·sy** \'pəs-ē\ *adj* **:** full of or resembling pus

[3]**pus·sy** \'pəs-ē\ *var of* PURSY

[1]**pussy·foot** \'pu̇s-ē-,fu̇t\ *vi* **1 :** to tread or move warily or stealthily **2 :** to refrain from committing oneself

[2]**pussyfoot** *n* **:** any of several plants having leaf clusters or flower heads that suggest a cat's foot

pussy willow \,pu̇s-ē-\ *n* **:** a willow (as the American *Salix discolor*) having large cylindrical silky aments

pus·tu·lant \'pəs-chə-lənt, 'pəs-t(y)ə-\ *adj* **:** producing pustules — **pustulant** *n*

pus·tu·lar \-lər\ *adj* **1 :** of, relating to, or resembling pustules **2 :** covered with pustular prominences **:** PUSTULATE

pus·tu·late \-lət, -,lāt\ *or* **pus·tu·lat·ed** \-,lāt-əd\ *adj* **:** covered with pustules

pus·tu·la·tion \,pəs-chə-'lā-shən, ,pəs-t(y)ə-\ *n* **1 :** the act of producing or state of having pustules **2 :** PUSTULE

pus·tule \'pəs-(,)chü(ə)l, -(,)t(y)ü(ə)l\ *n* [ME, fr. L *pustula* — more at FOG] **1 :** a small circumscribed elevation of the skin containing pus and having an inflamed base **2 :** a small often distinctively colored elevation or spot resembling a blister or pimple

[1]**put** \'pu̇t\ *vb* **put; put·ting** [ME *putten*; akin to OE *putung* instigation, MD *poten* to plant] *vt* **1 a :** to place in a specified position or relationship **:** LAY **b :** to move in a specified direction **c** (1) **:** to send (as a weapon or missile) into or through something **:** THRUST (2) **:** to throw with an overhand pushing motion ⟨~ the shot⟩ **d :** to bring into a specified state or condition ⟨~ it to use⟩ ⟨~ the matter right⟩ **2 a :** to cause to endure something **:** SUBJECT ⟨~ him to death⟩ **b :** IMPOSE, INFLICT ⟨~ a special tax on luxuries⟩ **3 a :** to set before one for judgment or decision ⟨~ the question⟩ **b :** to call for a formal vote on ⟨~ the motion⟩ **4 a** (1) **:** to turn into language or literary form ⟨~ his feelings in words⟩ (2) **:** to translate into another language ⟨~ the poem into English⟩ (3) **:** ADAPT ⟨lyrics ~ to music⟩ **b :** EXPRESS, STATE ⟨*putting* it mildly⟩ **5 a :** to devote (oneself) to an activity or end **b :** APPLY ⟨~ his mind to the problem⟩ **c :** ASSIGN ⟨~ them to work⟩ **d :** to cause to perform an action **:** URGE ⟨~ the horse over the fence⟩ **e :** IMPEL, INCITE ⟨~ them into a frenzy⟩ **6 a :** REPOSE, REST ⟨~*s* his faith in reason⟩ **b :** INVEST ⟨~ his money in the company⟩ **7 a :** to give as an estimate ⟨~ the time as about eleven⟩ **b :** ATTACH, ATTRIBUTE ⟨~*s* a high value on his friendship⟩ **c :** IMPUTE ⟨~ the blame on his partner⟩ **8 :** BET, WAGER ⟨~ two dollars on the favorite⟩ **~** *vi* **1 :** to start in motion **:** GO; *esp* **:** to leave in a hurry **2** *of a ship* **:** to take a specified course ⟨~ down the river⟩ **syn** see SET — **put forth 1 a :** ASSERT **:** IMPOSE **b :** to make public **:** ISSUE **2 :** to bring into action **:** EXERT **3 :** to produce or send out by growth ⟨*put forth* leaves⟩ **4 :** to start out — **put forward :** PROPOSE ⟨*put forward* a theory⟩ — **put in mind :** REMIND — **put paid to** *Brit* **:** to finish off **:** wipe out — **put the arm on 1 :** to ask for money **2 :** to hold up **:** HIJACK — **put to bed :** to make the final preparations for printing (as a newspaper) — **put together 1 :** to create as a unified whole **:** CONSTRUCT ⟨*put* a book *together*⟩ **2 :** ADD, COMBINE — **put to it :** to give difficulty to **:** press hard ⟨had been *put to it* to keep up⟩

[2]**put** *n* **1 :** a throw made with an overhand pushing motion; *specif* **:** the act or an instance of putting the shot **2 :** an option to sell a specified amount of stock or commodity at a fixed price at or within a certain time

[3]**put** *adj* **:** being in place **:** FIXED, SET ⟨stay ~ until I come for you⟩

put about *vi, of a ship* **:** to change direction **:** go on another tack **~** *vt* **:** to cause to change course or direction

put across *vt* **1 :** to achieve or carry through by deceit or trickery **2 :** to convey effectively or forcefully

pu·ta·tive \'pyüt-ət-iv\ *adj* [ME, fr. LL *putativus*, fr. L *putatus*, pp. of *putare* to think] **1 :** commonly accepted or supposed **2 :** assumed to exist or to have existed — **pu·ta·tive·ly** *adv*

put away *vt* **1 a :** DISCARD, RENOUNCE **b :** DIVORCE **2 :** to eat or drink up **:** CONSUME **3 a :** to confine esp. in a mental institution **b :** BURY **c :** KILL ⟨*put away* a sick dog⟩

put by *vt* **1** *archaic* **:** to turn aside **:** REJECT **2 :** to lay aside **:** SAVE

put down *vt* **1 :** to bring to an end **:** STOP ⟨*put down* a riot⟩ **2 a :** DEPOSE, DEGRADE **b :** DISPARAGE, BELITTLE ⟨mentioned his poetry only to *put* it *down*⟩ **c :** DISAPPROVE, CRITICIZE ⟨was *put down* for the way she dressed⟩ **d :** HUMILIATE, SQUELCH ⟨*put* him *down* with a sharp retort⟩ **3 :** PUNCTURE, CHECK ⟨*put down* the gossip⟩ **4 a :** to put in writing ⟨*put* it *down* truthfully⟩ **b :** to enter in a list ⟨*put* me *down* for a donation⟩ **5 a :** to place in a category ⟨I *put* him *down* as a hypochondriac — O.S.J. Gogarty⟩ **b :** ATTRIBUTE ⟨*put* it *down* to inexperience⟩ **6 :** CONSUME ⟨*putting down* helping after helping — Carson McCullers⟩ **7 :** to pack or preserve for future use

put–down \'pu̇t-,dau̇n\ *n* **:** an act or instance of putting down; *esp* **:** a deflating remark

put in *vt* **1 :** to make a formal offer or declaration of ⟨*put in* a plea of guilty⟩ **2 :** to come in with **:** INTERPOSE ⟨*put in* a word for his brother⟩ **3 :** to spend (time) at some occupation or job ⟨*put in* six hours at the office⟩ **4 :** PLANT ⟨*put in* a crop⟩ **~** *vi* **1 :** to call at or enter a place; *esp* **:** to enter a harbor or port **2 :** to make an application, request, or offer

put·log \'pu̇t-,lȯg, 'pət-, -,läg\ *n* [prob. alter. of earlier *putlock*, perh. fr. [3]*put* + *lock*] **:** one of the short timbers that support the flooring of a scaffold

put off *vt* **1 :** DISCONCERT, REPEL **2 a :** to hold back to a later time **b :** to induce to wait ⟨*put* the bill collector *off* for another month⟩ **3 :** to take off **:** rid oneself of **4 :** to sell or pass fraudulently

put on *vt* **1 a :** to dress oneself in **:** DON **b :** to make part of one's appearance or behavior **c :** FEIGN **2 :** to cause to act or operate **:** APPLY ⟨*put on* more speed⟩ **3 a :** ADD ⟨*put on* weight⟩ **b :** EXAGGERATE, OVERSTATE ⟨he's *putting* it *on* when he makes such claims⟩ **4 :** PERFORM, PRODUCE ⟨*put on* a play⟩ **5 a :** to mislead deliberately esp. for amusement ⟨the interviewer must be put down — or possibly, *put on* — Melvin Maddocks⟩ **b :** KID ⟨you're *putting* me *on*⟩

[1]**put–on** \,pu̇t-,ȯn, -,än\ *adj* **:** ASSUMED, PRETENDED

[2]**put–on** \'pu̇t-,ȯn, -,än\ *n* **:** an instance of putting someone on; *also* **:** PARODY, SPOOF ⟨a kind of *put-on* of every pretentious film ever made — C.A. Ridley⟩

put out *vt* **1 :** EXERT, USE ⟨*put out* considerable effort⟩ **2 :** EXTINGUISH ⟨*put* the fire *out*⟩ **3 :** PUBLISH, ISSUE **4 :** to produce for sale **5 a :** DISCONCERT, EMBARRASS **b :** ANNOY, IRRITATE **c :** INCONVENIENCE ⟨don't *put* yourself *out* for us⟩ **6 :** to cause to be out (as in baseball or cricket) **:** RETIRE **~** *vi* **1 :** to set out from shore **2 :** to make an effort

put·out \'pu̇t-,au̇t\ *n* **:** the retiring of a base runner or batter by a defensive player in baseball

put over *vt* **1 :** DELAY, POSTPONE **2 :** to put across ⟨*put over* a deliberate deception⟩

pu·tre·fac·tion \,pyü-trə-'fak-shən\ *n* [ME *putrefaccion*, fr. LL *putrefaction-, putrefactio*, fr. L *putrefactus*, pp. of *putrefacere*] **1 :** the decomposition of organic matter; *esp* **:** the typically anaerobic splitting of proteins by bacteria and fungi with the formation of foul-smelling incompletely oxidized products **2 :** the state of being putrefied **:** CORRUPTION — **pu·tre·fac·tive** \-'fak-tiv\ *adj*

pu·tre·fy \'pyü-trə-,fī\ *vb* [ME *putrefien*, fr. MF & L; MF *putrefier*, fr. L *putrefacere*, fr. *putrēre* to be rotten + *facere* to make — more at DO] *vt* **:** to make putrid **~** *vi* **:** to become putrid **syn** see DECAY

pu·tres·cence \pyü-'tres-ᵊn(t)s\ *n* **:** the state of being putrescent

pu·tres·cent \-ᵊnt\ *adj* [L *putrescent-, putrescens*, prp. of *putrescere* to grow rotten, fr. *putrēre*] **1 :** undergoing putrefaction **:** becoming putrid **2 :** of or relating to putrefaction

pu·tres·ci·ble \-'tres-ə-bəl\ *adj* **:** liable to become putrid

pu·tres·cine \-'tres-,ēn\ *n* [ISV, fr. L *putrescere*] **:** a crystalline slightly poisonous ptomaine $C_4H_{12}N_2$ found esp. in putrid flesh

pu·trid \'pyü-trəd\ *adj* [L *putridus*, fr. *putrēre* to be rotten, fr. *puter, putris* rotten; akin to L *putēre* to stink] **1 a :** being in a state of putrefaction **:** ROTTEN **b :** of, relating to, or characteristic of putrefaction **:** FOUL **2 a :** morally corrupt **b :** totally disagreeable or objectionable **syn** see MALODOROUS — **pu·trid·i·ty** \pyü-'trid-ət-ē\ *n* — **pu·trid·ly** \'pyü-trəd-lē\ *adv* — **pu·trid·ness** *n*

putsch \'pu̇ch\ *n* [G] **:** a secretly plotted and suddenly executed attempt to overthrow a government

putsch·ist \'pu̇ch-əst\ *n* **:** one who advocates or organizes a putsch

putt \'pət\ *n* [alter. of ²*put*] **:** a golf stroke made on a putting green to cause the ball to roll into or near the hole — **putt** *vb*

put·tee \ˌpə-'tē, pu̇-; 'pət-ē\ *n* [Hindi *paṭṭī* strip of cloth, fr. Skt *paṭṭikā*] **1 :** a cloth strip wrapped around the leg from ankle to knee **2 :** a leather legging secured by a strap or catch or by laces

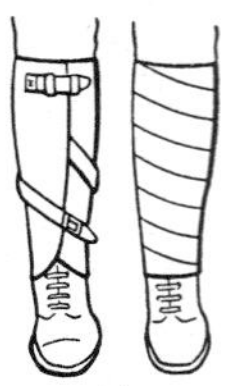

puttees

¹put·ter \'pu̇t-ər\ *n* **:** one that puts

²putt·er \'pət-ər\ *n* **1 :** a golf club used in putting **2 :** one that putts

³put·ter \'pət-ər\ *vi* [alter. of *potter*] **1 :** to move or act aimlessly or idly **:** DAWDLE **2 :** to work at random **:** TINKER — **put·ter·er** \-ər-ər\ *n*

put through *vt* **1 :** to carry to a successful conclusion ⟨*put through* a number of reforms⟩ **2 a :** to make a telephone connection for **b :** to obtain a connection for (a telephone call)

put·ti·er \'pət-ē-ər\ *n* **:** one that putties **:** GLAZIER

putt·ing green \'pət-iŋ-\ *n* **:** a grassy area at the end of a golf fairway containing the hole into which the ball must be played

put to *vi, of a ship* **:** to put in to shore (as for shelter)

¹put·ty \'pət-ē\ *n* [F *potée,* lit., potful, fr. OF, fr. *pot* — more at POTAGE] **1 :** a pasty substance consisting of hydrated lime and water **2 :** a polishing material containing chiefly an oxide of tin **3 a :** a cement usu. made of whiting and boiled linseed oil beaten or kneaded to the consistency of dough and used in fastening glass in sashes and stopping crevices in woodwork **b :** any of various substances resembling such cement in appearance, consistency, or use: as (1) **:** an acid-resistant mixture of ferric oxide and boiled linseed oil (2) **:** a mixture of red and white lead and boiled linseed oil used as a lute in pipe fitting **4 :** *of textiles* **:** a light brownish gray to light grayish brown

²putty *vt* **:** to use putty on or apply putty to

put·ty·root \'pət-ē-ˌrüt, -ˌru̇t\ *n* **:** a No. American orchid (*Aplectrum hyemale*) having a slender naked rootstock and producing brown flowers

put up *vt* **1 a :** to place in a container or receptacle ⟨*put* his lunch *up* in a bag⟩ **b :** to put away (a sword) in a scabbard **:** SHEATHE **c :** to prepare so as to preserve for later use **:** CAN **d :** COMPOUND, PREPARE **e :** to put away out of use **2 :** to start (game) from cover **3 :** to nominate for election **4 :** to offer up (as a prayer) **5 :** to set (hair) in pin curls **6 :** to offer for public sale ⟨*puts* his possessions *up* for auction⟩ **7 :** to give food and shelter to **:** ACCOMMODATE **8 :** to arrange (as a plot or scheme) with others **:** PRECONCERT ⟨*put up* a job to steal the jewels⟩ **9 :** BUILD, ERECT **10 a :** to make a display of **:** EXHIBIT, SHOW ⟨*put up* a bluff⟩ **b :** to carry on ⟨*put up* a struggle against odds⟩ **11 a :** CONTRIBUTE, PAY **b :** to offer as a prize or stake **12 :** to increase the amount of **:** RAISE ~ *vi* **:** LODGE **syn** see RESIDE — **put up to :** INCITE, INSTIGATE — **put up with :** to endure or tolerate without complaint or attempt at reprisal

put–up \ˌpu̇t-ˌəp\ *adj* **:** underhandedly arranged **:** PRECONCERTED

put–upon \'pu̇t-ə-ˌpȯn, -ˌpän\ *adj* **:** taken advantage of

¹puz·zle \'pəz-əl\ *vb* **puz·zling** \-(ə-)liŋ\ [origin unknown] *vt* **1** *obs* **:** BAFFLE, CONFOUND **2 :** PERPLEX, NONPLUS **3** *archaic* **:** COMPLICATE, ENTANGLE **4 :** to solve with difficulty or ingenuity ~ *vi* **1 :** to be uncertain as to action or choice **2 :** to attempt a solution of a puzzle by guesswork or experiment — **puz·zler** \-(ə-)lər\ *n*

syn PUZZLE, PERPLEX, BEWILDER, DISTRACT, NONPLUS, CONFOUND, DUMBFOUND mean to disturb and baffle. PUZZLE implies presenting a problem difficult to solve; PERPLEX suggests worry and uncertainty in making a decision; BEWILDER implies a confusion of mind preventing clear thinking; DISTRACT suggests agitation caused by conflicting preoccupations or interests; NONPLUS implies a bafflement causing complete blankness of mind; CONFOUND implies temporary mental paralysis caused by astonishment or thorough abashment; DUMBFOUND suggests a stronger but momentary confounding

²puzzle *n* **1 :** the state of being puzzled **:** PERPLEXITY **2 a :** something that puzzles **b :** a question, problem, or contrivance designed for testing ingenuity **syn** see MYSTERY

puz·zle·head·ed \ˌpəz-əl-'hed-əd\ *adj* **:** having or based on confused attitudes or ideas — **puz·zle·head·ed·ness** *n*

puz·zle·ment \'pəz-əl-mənt\ *n* **1 :** the state of being puzzled **:** PERPLEXITY **2 :** PUZZLE

py- *or* **pyo-** *comb form* [Gk, fr. *pyon* pus — more at FOUL] **:** pus ⟨*pyemia*⟩ ⟨*pyorrhea*⟩

pya \pē-'(y)ä\ *n* [Burmese] — see *kyat* at MONEY table

pyc·nid·i·al \pik-'nid-ē-əl\ *adj* **:** of or relating to pycnidia

pyc·nid·i·um \-ē-əm\ *n, pl* **pyc·nid·ia** \-ē-ə\ [NL, fr. Gk *pyknos* close; akin to Gk *pyka* thickly, Alb *puth* kiss] **:** a flask-shaped spore fruit bearing conidiophores and conidia on the interior and occurring in various imperfect fungi and ascomycetes

pyc·no·gon·id \ˌpik-nə-'gän-əd\ *n* [deriv. of Gk *pyknos* + *gony* knee — more at KNEE] **:** SEA SPIDER

pyc·nom·e·ter \pik-'näm-ət-ər\ *n* [Gk *pyknos* + ISV *-meter*] **:** a standard vessel often provided with a thermometer for measuring and comparing the densities of liquids or solids

pye–dog \'pī-ˌdȯg\ *n* [prob. by shortening and alter. fr. *pariah dog*] **:** a half-wild dog common about Asian villages

py·eli·tis \ˌpī-ə-'līt-əs\ *n* [NL, fr. Gk *pyelos* trough; akin to Gk *plein* to sail — more at FLOW] **:** inflammation of the pelvis of a kidney

py·elo·ne·phri·tis \ˌpī-ə-lō-ni-'frīt-əs\ *n* [NL, fr. Gk *pyelos* + NL *nephritis*] **:** inflammation of both the pelvis and the substance of the kidney

py·emia \pī-'ē-mē-ə\ *n* [NL] **:** purulent septicemia — **py·emic** \-mik\ *adj*

py·gid·i·al \pī-'jid-ē-əl\ *adj* **:** of, relating to, or constituting a pygidium

py·gid·i·um \-ē-əm\ *n, pl* **py·gid·ia** \-ē-ə\ [NL, fr. Gk *pygidion,* dim. of *pygē* rump; akin to L *pustula* pustule] **:** a caudal structure or the terminal body region of various invertebrates

pyg·mae·an *or* **pyg·me·an** \pig-'mē-ən, 'pig-mē-\ *adj* [L *pygmaeus*] **:** PYGMY

Pyg·ma·lion \pig-'māl-yən, -'mā-lē-ən\ *n* [Gk *Pygmaliōn*] **:** a sculptor and king of Cyprus — compare GALATEA

pyg·moid \'pig-ˌmȯid\ *adj* **:** resembling or partaking of the characteristics of the Pygmies

pyg·my \'pig-mē\ *n* [ME *pigmei,* fr. L *pygmaeus* of a pygmy, dwarfish, fr. Gk *pygmaios,* fr. *pygmē* fist, measure of length — more at PUNGENT] **1** *often cap* **:** one of a race of dwarfs described by ancient Greek authors **2** *cap* **:** one of a small people of equatorial Africa ranging under five feet in height **3 :** a short insignificant person **:** DWARF — **pygmy** *adj*

pyg·my·ish \-ish\ *adj* **:** DWARFISH, STUNTED

pyg·my·ism \-ˌiz-əm\ *n* **:** the condition of a pygmy **:** a stunted or dwarfish state

py·ja·mas \pə-'jä-məz\ *chiefly Brit var of* PAJAMAS

pyk·nic \'pik-nik\ *adj* [ISV, fr. Gk *pyknos* close — more at PYCNIDIUM] **:** characterized by shortness of stature, broadness of girth, and powerful muscularity **:** ENDOMORPHIC — **pyknic** *n*

py·lon \'pī-ˌlän, -lən\ *n* [Gk *pylōn,* fr. *pylē* gate] **1 a :** a usu. massive gateway **b :** an ancient Egyptian gateway building in a truncated pyramidal form **c :** a monumental mass flanking an entranceway or an approach to a bridge **2 :** a tower for supporting either end of a wire over a long span **3 :** a projection (as a post or tower) marking a prescribed course of flight for an airplane

py·lo·ric \pī-'lȯr-ik, pə-, -'lȯr-\ *adj* **:** of, relating to, or lying in the region of the pylorus or the part of the stomach from which the intestine leads

py·lo·rus \-əs\ *n, pl* **py·lo·ri** \pī-'lō(ə)r-ˌī; pə-'lō(ə)r-ˌī, -(ˌ)ē; -'lȯ(ə)r-\ [LL, fr. Gk *pylōros,* lit., gatekeeper, fr. *pylē*] **:** the opening in a vertebrate from the stomach into the intestine

pyo·der·ma \ˌpī-ə-'dər-mə\ *n* [NL] **:** a bacterial skin inflammation marked by pussy lesions — **pyo·der·mic** \-mik\ *adj*

pyo·gen·ic \ˌpī-ə-'jen-ik\ *adj* [ISV] **:** producing pus **:** marked by pus production

py·or·rhea \ˌpī-ə-'rē-ə\ *n* [NL] **:** a discharge of pus; *specif* **:** purulent inflammation of the sockets of the teeth leading usu. to loosening of the teeth — **py·or·rhe·al** \-'rē-əl\ *adj*

pyr- *or* **pyro-** *comb form* [ME, fr. MF, fr. LL, fr. Gk, fr. *pyr* — more at FIRE] **1 :** fire **:** heat ⟨*pyro*meter⟩ ⟨*pyr*heliometer⟩ **2 :** produced by or as if by the action of heat ⟨*pyro*electricity⟩; *esp* **:** derived from a corresponding ortho acid by loss usu. of one molecule of water from two molecules of acid ⟨*pyro*phosphoric acid⟩ **3 :** fever ⟨*pyro*toxin⟩

pyr·acan·tha \ˌpir-ə-'kan(t)-thə, ˌpī-rə-\ *n* [NL, genus name, fr. Gk *pyrakantha,* a tree, fr. *pyr-* + *akantha* thorn — more at ACANTH-] **:** any of a small genus (*Pyracantha*) of Eurasian thorny evergreen or half-evergreen shrubs of the rose family with alternate leaves, corymbs of white flowers, and small reddish pomes

py·ral·i·did \pə-'ral-əd-əd, pī-\ *n* [deriv. of L *pyralis,* fly fabled as living in fire, fr. Gk, fr. *pyr*] **:** any of a very large heterogeneous family (Pyralididae) of mostly small slender long-legged moths — **pyralidid** *adj*

¹pyr·a·mid \'pir-ə-ˌmid\ *n* [L *pyramid-, pyramis,* fr. Gk, of unknown origin] **1 a :** an ancient massive structure found esp. in Egypt having typically a square ground plan, outside walls in the form of four triangles that meet in a point at the top, and inner sepulchral chambers **b :** a structure or object of similar form **2 :** a polyhedron having for its base a polygon and for faces triangles with a common vertex — see VOLUME table **3 :** a crystalline form each face of which intersects the vertical axis and either two lateral axes or in the tetragonal system one lateral axis **4 :** an immaterial structure built on a broad supporting base and narrowing gradually to an apex ⟨socioeconomic ~⟩ — **py·ra·mi·dal** \pə-'ram-əd-ᵊl, ˌpir-ə-'mid-ᵊl\ *adj* — **py·ra·mi·dal·ly** \-ᵊl-ē\ *adv* — **pyr·a·mid·i·cal** \ˌpir-ə-'mid-i-kəl\ *adj*

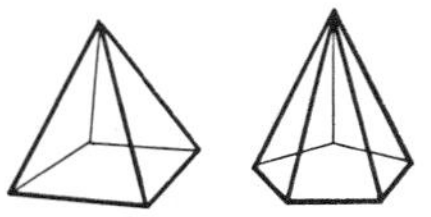

pyramids 2

²pyramid *vi* **1 :** to enlarge one's holdings on an exchange on a continued rise by using paper profits as margin to buy additional amounts **2 :** to increase rapidly and progressively step by step on a broad base ~ *vt* **1 :** to arrange or build up as if on the base of a pyramid **2 :** to use or to deal in

Py·ram·i·don \pə-'ram-ə-ˌdän\ *trademark* — used for aminopyrine

Pyr·a·mus \'pir-ə-məs\ *n* [L, fr. Gk *Pyramos*] **:** a legendary Babylonian and lover of Thisbe

py·ran \'pī(ə)r-ˌan\ *n* [ISV] **:** either of two parent cyclic compounds C_5H_6O that contain five carbon atoms and one oxygen atom in the ring — **py·ra·noid** \'pir-ə-ˌnȯid, 'pī-rə-\ *adj*

pyr·ar·gy·rite \pī-'rär-jə-ˌrīt, pə-\ *n* [G *pyrargyrit,* fr. Gk *pyr-* + *argyros* silver — more at ARGENT] **:** a mineral Ag_3SbS_3 consisting of silver antimony sulfide that occurs in rhombohedral crystals or massive and has a dark red or black color with a metallic adamantine luster

pyre \'pī(ə)r\ *n* [L *pyra,* fr. Gk, fr. *pyr* fire — more at FIRE] **:** a combustible heap for burning a dead body as a funeral rite; *broadly* **:** a pile to be burned

py·rene \'pī(ə)r-ˌēn, pī-'rēn\ *n* [NL *pyrena,* fr. Gk *pyrēn* stone of a fruit; akin to Gk *pyros* wheat — more at FURZE] **:** the stone of a drupelet; *broadly* **:** a small hard nutlet

py·re·noid \pī-'rē-ˌnȯid, 'pī-rə-\ *n* [ISV, fr. NL *pyrena*] **:** one of the protein bodies in the chromatophores of various low organisms that act as centers for starch deposition

py·re·thrin \pī-'rē-thrən, -'reth-rən\ *n* [ISV, fr. L *pyrethrum*] **:** either of two oily liquid esters $C_{21}H_{28}O_3$ and $C_{22}H_{28}O_5$ that have high insecticidal properties and that occur esp. in pyrethrum flowers

py·re·thrum \-'rē-thrəm, -'reth-rəm\ *n* [L, pellitory, fr. Gk *pyrethron,* fr. *pyr* fire] **1 :** any of several chrysanthemums with finely divided often aromatic leaves including ornamentals as well as important sources of insecticides **2 :** an insecticide consisting of the dried heads of any of several Old World chrysanthemums

py·ret·ic \pī-'ret-ik\ *adj* [NL *pyreticus,* fr. Gk *pyretikos,* fr. *pyretos* fever, fr. *pyr*] **:** of or relating to fever **:** FEBRILE

Py·rex \'pī(ə)r-ˌeks\ *trademark* — used for glass and glassware resistant to heat, chemicals, or electricity

py·rex·ia \pī-'rek-sē-ə\ *n* [NL, fr. Gk *pyressein* to be feverish, fr. *pyretos*] **:** abnormal elevation of body temperature **:** FEVER — **py·rex·i·al** \-sē-əl\ *adj* — **py·rex·ic** \-sik\ *adj*

pyr·he·li·om·e·ter \'pī(ə)r-ˌhē-lē-'äm-ət-ər, 'pi(ə)r-\ *n* [ISV] **:** an instrument for measuring the sun's radiant energy as received at the earth

py·ric \'pī(ə)r-ik, 'pi(ə)r-\ *adj* [F *pyrique,* fr. Gk *pyr*] **:** resulting from, induced by, or associated with burning

pyr·i·dine \'pir-ə-ˌdēn\ *n* [*pyr-* + *-id* + *-ine*] **:** a toxic water-soluble flammable liquid base C_5H_5N of pungent odor obtained by dis-

tillation of bone oil or as a by-product of coking that is the parent of many naturally occurring organic compounds and is used as a solvent and a denaturant for alcohol and in the manufacture of pharmaceuticals and waterproofing agents

pyr·i·dox·al \‚pir-ə-'däk-‚sal\ n [ISV, fr. pyridoxine] : a crystalline aldehyde $C_8H_9NO_3$ of the vitamin B_6 group that occurs as a phosphate active as a coenzyme

pyr·i·dox·amine \‚pir-ə-'däk-sə-‚mēn\ n [ISV pyridoxine + amine] : a crystalline amine $C_8H_{12}N_2O_2$ of the vitamin B_6 group that occurs as a phosphate active as a coenzyme

pyr·i·dox·ine also **pyr·i·dox·in** \-‚sēn, -‚däk-‚sēn, -sən\ n [pyridine + ox- + -ine] : a crystalline phenolic alcohol $C_8H_{11}NO_3$ of the vitamin B_6 group found esp. in cereals and convertible in the organism into pyridoxal and pyridoxamine

pyr·i·form \'pir-ə-‚form\ adj [NL pyriformis, fr. ML pyrum pear (alter. of L pirum) + -iformis -iform — more at PEAR] : having he form of a pear

py·rim·i·dine \pī-'rim-ə-‚dēn, pə-\ n [ISV, alter. of pyridine] **1** : a feeble organic base $C_4H_4N_2$ of penetrating odor **2** : a derivative of pyrimidine; esp : a base (as cytosine) that is an important component of nucleotides

py·rite \'pī(ə)r-‚īt\ n [L pyrites] : a common mineral that consists of iron disulfide FeS_2, has a pale brass-yellow color and metallic luster, and is burned in making sulfur dioxide and sulfuric acid

py·rites \pə-'rīt-ēz, pī-; 'pī-‚rīts\ n, pl **py·rites** [L, flint, fr. Gk pyritēs of or in fire, fr. pyr fire] : any of various metallic-looking sulfides of which pyrite is the commonest — **py·rit·ic** \-'rit-ik\ adj

py·ro·cat·e·chol \‚pī-rō-'kat-ə-‚chól, -‚shól, -‚chōl, -‚shōl\ n [ISV pyr- + catechol ($C_{15}H_{14}O_6$)] : a crystalline phenol $C_6H_4(OH)_2$ obtained by pyrolysis of various natural substances (as resins and lignins) but usu. made synthetically and used esp. as a photographic developer and in organic synthesis

py·ro·cel·lu·lose \-'sel-yə-‚lōs, -‚lōz\ n : cellulose nitrate that is of lower degree of nitration than guncotton and is used in smokeless powders

py·ro·chem·i·cal \-'kem-i-kəl\ adj : relating to or involving chemical activity at high temperatures — **py·ro·chem·i·cal·ly** \-k(ə-)lē\ adv

py·ro·clas·tic \-'klas-tik\ adj : formed by fragmentation as a result of volcanic or igneous action

py·ro·con·den·sa·tion \-‚kän-‚den-'sā-shən, -dən-\ n : chemical condensation brought about by heat

py·ro·cot·ton \'pī-rō-‚kät-ən\ n : cellulose nitrate containing about 12.6 percent nitrogen and used in smokeless powders

py·ro·elec·tric \‚pī-rō-ə-'lek-trik\ adj [ISV, back-formation fr. pyroelectricity] : of, relating to, or exhibiting pyroelectricity

py·ro·elec·tric·i·ty \-‚lek-'tris-ət-ē, -'tris-tē\ n [ISV] : electrification produced on various crystals by change of temperature

py·ro·gal·late \‚pī-rō-'gal-‚āt, -'gó-‚lāt\ n : a salt or ether of pyrogallol

py·ro·gal·lic acid \‚pī-rō-‚gal-ik-, -‚gó-lik-\ n [ISV] : PYROGALLOL

py·ro·gal·lol \‚pī-rō-'gal-‚ól, -‚ōl\ n : a poisonous bitter crystalline phenol $C_6H_3(OH)_3$ with weak acid properties obtained usu. by pyrolysis of gallic acid and used esp. as a photographic developer

py·ro·gen \'pī-rə-jən\ n [ISV] : a fever-producing substance

py·ro·gen·ic \‚pī-rō-'jen-ik\ also **py·rog·e·nous** \pī-'räj-ə-nəs\ adj [ISV] **1** : producing or produced by heat or fever **2** : of igneous origin — **py·ro·ge·nic·i·ty** \‚pī-rō-jə-'nis-ət-ē\ n

py·ro·lig·ne·ous \‚pī-rō-'lig-nē-əs\ adj [F pyroligneux, fr. pyr- + ligneux woody, fr. L lignosus, fr. lignum wood — more at LIGNEOUS] : obtained by destructive distillation of wood

pyroligneous acid n : an acid reddish brown aqueous liquid containing chiefly acetic acid, methanol, wood oils, and tars

py·ro·lu·site \‚pī-rō-'lü-‚sīt\ n [G pyrolusit, fr. Gk pyr- + lousis washing, fr. louein to wash — more at LYE] : a mineral MnO_2 consisting of manganese dioxide that is of an iron-black or dark steel-gray color and metallic luster, is usu. soft, and is the most important ore of manganese

py·rol·y·sis \pī-'räl-ə-səs\ n [NL] : chemical change brought about by the action of heat — **py·ro·lyt·ic** \‚pī-rə-'lit-ik\ adj — **py·ro·lyt·i·cal·ly** \-i-k(ə-)lē\ adv

py·rol·y·zate \pī-'räl-ə-‚zāt\ n : a product of pyrolysis

py·ro·lyze \'pī-rə-‚līz\ vt : to subject to pyrolysis

py·ro·man·cy \'pī-rə-‚man(t)-sē\ n [ME pyromancie, fr. MF, fr. LL pyromantia, fr. Gk pyromanteia, fr. pyr fire + manteia divination — more at -MANCY] : divination by means of fire or flames

py·ro·ma·nia \‚pī-rō-'mā-nē-ə, -nyə\ n [NL] : an irresistible impulse to start fires — **py·ro·ma·ni·ac** \-nē-‚ak\ n — **py·ro·ma·ni·a·cal** \-‚(‚)rō-mə-'nī-ə-kəl\ adj

py·ro·met·al·lur·gy \-'met-əl-‚ər-jē\ n [ISV] : chemical metallurgy depending on heat action (as roasting and smelting)

py·rom·e·ter \pī-'räm-ət-ər\ n [ISV] : an instrument for measuring temperatures esp. when beyond the range of mercurial thermometers usu. by the increase of electric resistance in a metal, by the generation of electric current by a thermocouple, or by the increase in intensity of light radiated by an incandescent body — **py·ro·met·ric** \‚pī-rə-'me-trik\ adj — **py·ro·met·ri·cal·ly** \-tri-k(ə-)lē\ adv — **py·rom·e·try** \pī-'räm-ə-trē\ n

py·ro·mor·phite \‚pī-rō-'mór-‚fīt\ n [G pyromorphit, fr. Gk pyr- + morphē form] : a mineral $Pb_5(PO_4)_3Cl$ consisting of a lead chloride and phosphate and occurring in green, yellow, brown, gray, or white crystals or masses

py·rone \'pī(ə)r-‚ōn\ n [ISV] : either of two isomeric carbonyl compounds $C_5H_4O_2$ derived from pyran; also : a derivative of either

py·ro·nine \'pī-rə-‚nēn\ n [ISV pyr- + -on -one + -ine] : any of several basic xanthene dyes used chiefly as biological stains — **py·ro·ni·no·phil·ic** \‚pī-rə-‚nē-nə-'fil-ik\ adj

py·rope \'pī(ə)r-‚ōp\ n [ME pirope, a red gem, fr. MF, fr. L pyropus, a red bronze, fr. Gk pyrōpos, lit., fiery-eyed, fr. pyr- + ōp-, ōps eye — more at EYE] : a magnesium-aluminum garnet that is deep red in color and is frequently used as a gem

py·ro·phor·ic \‚pī-rō-'fòr-ik, -'fär-\ adj [NL pyrophorus, fr. Gk pyrophoros fire-bearing, fr. pyr- + -phoros -phorous] **1** : igniting spontaneously **2** : emitting sparks when scratched or struck esp. with steel

py·ro·phos·phate \‚pī-rō-'fäs-‚fāt\ n : a salt or ester of pyro-

phosphoric acid — **py·ro·phos·phat·ic** \-(‚)fäs-'fat-ik\ adj

py·ro·phos·pho·ric acid \-(‚)fäs-‚fór-ik-, -‚fär-; -‚fäs-f(ə-)rik-\ n [ISV] : a crystalline acid $H_4P_2O_7$ formed when orthophosphoric acid is heated or prepared in the form of salts by heating acid salts of orthophosphoric acid

py·ro·phyl·lite \‚pī-rō-'fil-‚īt, pī-'räf-ə-‚līt\ n [G pyrophyllit, fr. Gk pyr- + phyllon leaf — more at BLADE] : a white or greenish mineral $AlSi_2O_5(OH)$ that is a hydrous aluminum silicate, resembles talc, and occurs in a foliated form or in compact masses

py·ro·sis \pī-'rō-səs\ n [NL, fr. Gk pyrōsis burning, fr. pyroun to burn, fr. pyr fire — more at FIRE] : HEARTBURN

py·ro·sul·fate \‚pī-rō-'səl-‚fāt\ n : a salt of pyrosulfuric acid

py·ro·sul·fu·ric acid \-‚səl-‚fyúr-ik-\ n [ISV] : an unstable crystalline acid $H_2S_2O_7$ usu. handled commercially as a thick oily fuming liquid and converted to sulfuric acid when mixed with water

¹py·ro·tech·nic \‚pī-rə-'tek-nik\ adj [F pyrotechnique, fr. Gk pyr fire + technē art] : of or relating to pyrotechnics — **py·ro·tech·ni·cal** \-ni-kəl\ adj — **py·ro·tech·ni·cal·ly** \-k(ə-)lē\ adv

²pyrotechnic n **1** pl but sing or pl in constr : the art of making or the manufacture and use of fireworks **2** pl **a** : materials (as fireworks) for flares or signals **b** : a display of fireworks **3** : a spectacular display (as of oratory) — usu. used in pl. — **py·ro·tech·nist** \-'tek-nəst\ n

py·rox·ene \'pī-‚räk-‚sēn, pə-\ n [F pyroxène, fr. Gk pyr- + xenos stranger] : any of a group of igneous-rock-forming silicate minerals that contain calcium, sodium, magnesium, iron, or aluminum, usu. occur in short prismatic crystals or massive, are often laminated, and vary in color from white to dark green or black — **py·rox·e·nic** \‚pī-‚räk-'sēn-ik, pə-, -'sen-\ adj

py·rox·e·nite \pī-'räk-sə-‚nīt, pə-\ n : an igneous rock that is free from olivine and is composed essentially of pyroxene

py·rox·y·lin \-sə-lən\ n [ISV pyr- + Gk xylon wood] **1** : a flammable mixture of cellulose nitrates usu. with less than 12.5 percent nitrogen that is less explosive than guncotton, soluble in a mixture of ether and alcohol or other organic solvents, and used esp. in making plastics, lacquers, and other coatings **2** : a pyroxylin product

Pyr·rha \'pir-ə\ n [L, fr. Gk] : the wife of Deucalion

pyr·rhic \'pir-ik\ n [L pyrrhichius, fr. Gk (pous) pyrrhichios, fr. pyrrhichē, a kind of dance] : a metrical foot consisting of two short or unaccented syllables — **pyrrhic** adj

Pyr·rhic victory \‚pir-ik-\ n [Pyrrhus †272 B.C. king of Epirus who sustained heavy losses in defeating the Romans] : a victory won at excessive cost

Pyr·rho·nism \'pir-ə-‚niz-əm\ n [F pyrrhonisme, fr. Pyrrhon Pyrrho, 4th cent. B.C. Gk philosopher, fr. Gk Pyrrhōn] **1** : the doctrines of the founder of a school of skeptics in Greece **2** : total or radical skepticism — **Pyr·rho·nist** \-nəst\ n

pyr·rho·tite \'pir-ə-‚tīt\ n [modif. of G pyrrhotin, fr. Gk pyrrhotēs redness; fr. pyrrhos red, fr. pyr fire — more at FIRE] : a bronze-colored mineral FeS of metallic luster that consists of ferrous sulfide and is attracted by the magnet

pyr·rhu·lox·ia \‚pir-(y)ə-'läk-sē-ə\ n [NL, genus name, fr. Pyr-rhula, genus of finches + Loxia, genus constituted by the crossbills] : a large showy finch (Pyrrhuloxia sinuata) of the southwestern U.S. and Mexico having the back gray and the breast and crest rose-colored in the male and yellowish in the female

pyr·role \'pi(‚)r-‚ōl\ n [Gk pyrrhos red, fr. pyr fire — more at FIRE] : a colorless weakly basic liquid C_4H_5N that smells like chloroform and is the parent of many compounds

pyr·uvate \pī-'rü-‚vāt, pī(ə)r-'yü-\ n : a salt or ester of pyruvic acid

pyr·uvic acid \‚(‚)pī-‚rü-vik-, ‚pī(ə)r-‚yü-\ n [ISV pyr- + L uva grape — more at UVULA] : a liquid keto acid CH_3COCO_2H that smells like acetic acid and is an important intermediate in metabolism and fermentation

Py·thag·o·re·an \pə-‚thag-ə-'rē-ən (‚)pī-\ n : one of a group professing to be followers of the Greek philosopher Pythagoras and stressing mathematics, astronomy, music, metempsychosis, and the mystical significance of numbers — **Pythagorean** adj — **Py·thag·o·re·an·ism** \-'rē-ə-‚niz-əm\ n

Pyth·ia \'pith-ē-ə\ n [L, fr. Gk, fem. of pythios] : a priestess and prophetess of Apollo at Delphi

Pyth·i·ad \'pith-ē-‚ad\ n [Gk Pythia, the Pythian games, fr. neut. pl. of pythios] : the four-year period between celebrations of the Pythian games in ancient Greece

Pyth·i·an \'pith-ē-ən\ adj [L pythius of Delphi, fr. Gk pythios, fr. Pythō Pytho, former name of Delphi, Greece] **1** : of or relating to the ancient Greek god Apollo esp. as patron deity of Delphi **2** : of or relating to games celebrated at Delphi every four years

Pyth·i·as \'pith-ē-əs\ n [Gk] : a friend of Damon condemned to death by Dionysius of Syracuse

py·thon \'pī-‚thän, -thən\ n [L, monstrous serpent killed by Apollo, fr. Gk Pythōn] : a large constricting snake (as a boa); esp : any of a genus (Python) including the largest recent snakes — **py·tho·nine** \'pī-thə-‚nīn\ adj

py·tho·ness \'pī-thə-nəs, 'pith-ə-\ n [ME Phitonesse, fr. MF pithonisse, fr. LL pythonissa, fr. Gk Pythōn, spirit of divination, fr. Pythō, seat of the Delphic oracle] **1** : a woman believed to have a spirit of divination **2** : a priestess of Apollo held to have prophetic powers — **py·thon·ic** \pī-'thän-ik\ adj

py·uria \pī-'(y)ùr-ē-ə\ n [NL] : pus in the urine; also : a condition in which this occurs

pyx \'piks\ n [ME, fr. ML pyxis, fr. L, box, fr. Gk — more at BOX] **1** : a container for the reserved Host; esp : a usu. watch-shaped case used to carry the Eucharist to the sick **2** : a box used in a mint for deposit of sample coins reserved for testing weight and fineness

pyx·id·i·um \pik-'sid-ē-əm\ n, pl **pyx·id·ia** \-ē-ə\ [NL, fr. Gk pyxidion, dim. of pyxis] **1** : a capsular fruit that dehisces so that the upper part falls off like a cap **2** : CAPSULE 2b

pyx·ie \'pik-sē\ n [by shortening & alter. fr. NL Pyxidanthera, genus name] : a creeping evergreen shrub (Pyxidanthera barbulata) of the sandy pine barrens of the Atlantic coast of the U.S. that is related to the true heaths and has usu. white star-shaped flowers

pyx·is \'pik-səs\ n, pl **pyx·i·des** \-sə-‚dēz\ [NL, fr. L, box] : PYXIDIUM 1

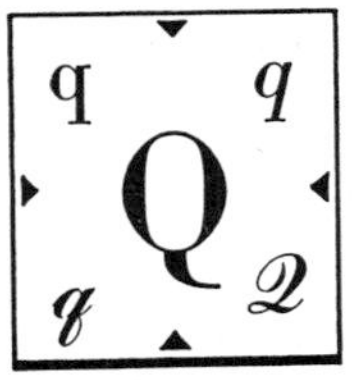

q \'kyü\ *n, often cap, often attrib* **1 a :** the 17th letter of the English alphabet **b :** a graphic representation of this letter **c :** a speech counterpart of orthographic *q* **2 :** a graphic device for reproducing the letter *q* **3 :** one designated *q* esp. as the 16th or when j is used for the 10th the 17th in order or class **4 :** something shaped like the letter Q

Q fever \'kyü-\ *n* [query] **:** a mild disease characterized by high fever, chills, and muscular pains, caused by a rickettsia (*Coxiella burnetii*), and transmitted by raw milk, by contact, or by ticks

qin·tar \kin-'tär\ *n* [Alb] — see *lek* at MONEY table

qoph \'kōf\ *n* [Heb *qōph*] **:** the 19th letter of the Hebrew alphabet — symbol ק

qua \'kwā, 'kwä\ *prep* [L, fr. abl. sing. fem. of *qui* who — more at WHO] **:** in the capacity or character of **:** AS

¹**quack** \'kwak\ *vi* [imit.] **:** to make the characteristic cry of a duck

²**quack** *n* **:** a noise made by quacking

³**quack** *n* [short for *quacksalver*] **1 :** a pretender to medical skill **2 :** CHARLATAN — **quack·ish** \-ish\ *adj*

⁴**quack** *vi* **:** to play the quack

⁵**quack** *adj* **:** of, relating to, or characteristic of a quack; *esp* **:** pretending to cure diseases

quack·ery \'kwak-(ə-)rē\ *n* **:** the practices or pretensions of a quack

quack·sal·ver \'kwak-,sal-vər\ *n* [obs. D (now *kwakzalver*)] **:** CHARLATAN, QUACK

¹**quad** \'kwäd\ *n* **:** QUADRANGLE

²**quad** *n* [short for *quadrat*] **:** a type-metal space that is 1 en or more in width

³**quad** *vt* **quad·ded; quad·ding :** to fill out (as a typeset line) with quads

⁴**quad** *n* **:** QUADRUPLET

quad·ran·gle \'kwäd-,raŋ-gəl\ *n* [ME, fr. MF, fr. LL *quadrangulum*, fr. L, neut. of *quadriangulus* quadrangular, fr. *quadri-* + *angulus* angle] **1 :** QUADRILATERAL **2 a :** a four-sided enclosure esp. when surrounded by buildings **b :** the buildings enclosing a quadrangle **3 :** a tract of country represented by one atlas sheet (as published by the U. S. Geological Survey) — **qua·dran·gu·lar** \kwä-'draŋ-gyə-lər\ *adj*

quad·rant \'kwäd-rənt\ *n* [ME, fr. L *quadrant-*, *quadrans* fourth part; akin to L *quattuor* four — more at FOUR] **1 a :** an instrument for measuring altitudes consisting commonly of a graduated arc of 90° with an index or vernier and usu. having a plumb line or spirit level for fixing the vertical or horizontal direction **b :** a device or mechanical part shaped like or suggestive of the quadrant of a circle **2 a :** an arc of 90° that is one quarter of a circle **b :** the area bounded by a quadrant and two radii **3 a :** any of the four parts into which a plane is divided by rectangular coordinate axes lying in that plane **b :** any of the four quarters into which something is divided by two real or imaginary lines that intersect each other at right angles — **qua·dran·tal** \kwä-'drant-ᵊl\ *adj*

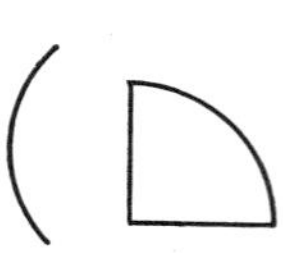

quadrants 2

quad·rat \'kwäd-rət, -,rat\ *n* [alter. of ²*quadrate*] **1 :** ²QUAD **2 :** a usu. rectangular plot used for ecological or population studies

¹**quad·rate** \'kwäd-,rāt, -rət\ *adj* [ME, fr. L *quadratus*, pp. of *quadrare* to make square, fit; akin to L *quattuor*] **1 :** being square or approximately square **2** *of a heraldic cross* **:** expanded into a square at the junction of the arms — see CROSS illustration **3 :** of, relating to, or constituting a bony or cartilaginous element of each side of the skull to which the lower jaw is articulated in most vertebrates below mammals

²**quadrate** *n* **1 :** an approximately square or cubical area, space, or body **2 :** a quadrate bone

³**quad·rate** \'kwäd-,rāt\ *vi* **:** AGREE, CORRESPOND

qua·drat·ic \kwä-'drat-ik\ *adj* **:** involving terms of second degree at most ⟨~ function⟩ — **quadratic** *n*

qua·drat·ics \-iks\ *n pl but sing or pl in constr* **:** a branch of algebra dealing with quadratic equations

quad·ra·ture \'kwäd-rə-,chù(ə)r, -chər, -,t(y)ù(ə)r\ *n* **1 :** the process of finding a square equal in area to a given area ⟨~ of the circle is impossible with ruler and compass⟩ **2 a :** a configuration in which two celestial bodies have a separation of 90 degrees **b :** either of two points on an orbit in a middle position between the syzygies

qua·dren·ni·al \kwä-'dren-ē-əl\ *adj* **1 :** consisting of or lasting for four years **2 :** occurring or being done every four years — **quadrennial** *n* — **qua·dren·ni·al·ly** \-ē-ə-lē\ *adv*

qua·dren·ni·um \-ē-əm\ *n, pl* **quadrenniums** *or* **qua·dren·nia** \-ē-ə\ [L *quadriennium*, fr. *quadri-* + *annus* year — more at ANNUAL] **:** a period of four years

quadri- *or* **quadr-** *or* **quadru-** *comb form* [ME, fr. L; akin to L *quattuor* four] **1 a :** four ⟨*quadri*lingual⟩ ⟨*quadru*mana⟩ **b :** square ⟨*quadr*ic⟩ **2 :** fourth ⟨*quadri*centennial⟩

quad·ric \'kwäd-rik\ *adj* [ISV] **:** QUADRATIC ⟨~ surface⟩ — used where there are more than two variables — **quadric** *n*

quad·ri·ceps \'kwäd-rə-,seps\ *n* [NL *quadricipit-*, *quadriceps*, fr. *quadri-* + *-cipit-*, *-ceps* (as in *bicipit-*, *biceps* biceps)] **:** the great extensor muscle of the front of the thigh divided above into four parts — **quad·ri·cip·i·tal** \,kwäd-rə-'sip-ət-ᵊl\ *adj*

quad·ri·fid \'kwäd-rə-fəd, -,fid\ *adj* [L *quadrifidus*, fr. *quadri-* + *-fidus* -fid] **:** divided or deeply cleft into four parts ⟨a ~ petal⟩

qua·dri·ga \kwä-'drē-gə\ *n, pl* **qua·dri·gae** \-,gī\ [L, sing. of *quadrigae* team of four, contr. of *quadrijugae*, fem. pl. of *quadrijugus* yoked four abreast, fr. *quadri-* + *jungere* to yoke, join — more at JOIN] **:** a chariot drawn by four horses abreast

¹**quad·ri·lat·er·al** \,kwäd-rə-'lat-ə-rəl, -'la-trəl\ *adj* [prob. fr. (assumed) NL *quadrilateralis*, fr. L *quadrilaterus*, fr. *quadri-* + *later-*, *latus* side] **:** having four sides

²**quadrilateral** *n* **:** a polygon of four sides

¹**qua·drille** \kwä-'dril, k(w)ə-\ *n* [F, lit., knights engaged in a carrousel] **:** a 4-handed card game popular esp. in the 18th century

²**quadrille** *n* [F, group of knights engaged in a carrousel, fr. Sp *cuadrilla* troop] **:** a square dance for four couples made up of five or six figures chiefly in 6/8 and 2/4 time; *also* **:** music for this dance

³**quadrille** *adj* **:** marked with squares or rectangles ⟨~ paper⟩

qua·dril·lion \kwä-'dril-yən\ *n* [F, fr. MF, fr. *quadri-* + *-illion* (as in *million*)] — see NUMBER table — **quadrillion** *adj* — **qua·dril·lionth** \-yən(t)th\ *adj* — **quadrillionth** *n, pl* **qua·dril·lionths** \-yən(t)s, -yən(t)ths\

quad·ri·par·tite \,kwäd-rə-'pär-,tīt\ *adj* [ME, fr. L *quadripartitus*, fr. *quadri-* + *partitus*, pp. of *partire* to divide, fr. *part-*, *pars* part] **1 :** consisting of or divided into four parts **2 :** shared or participated in by four parties or persons

quad·ri·va·lent \-'vā-lənt\ *adj* [ISV] **:** TETRAVALENT — **quadrivalent** *n*

qua·driv·i·al \kwä-'driv-ē-əl\ *adj* **1 :** of or relating to the quadrivium **2 :** having four ways or roads meeting in a point

qua·driv·i·um \-ē-əm\ *n* [LL, fr. L, crossroads, fr. *quadri-* + *via* way — more at VIA] **:** a group of studies consisting of arithmetic, music, geometry, and astronomy and forming the course for the three years of study between the B.A. and M.A. degrees in a medieval university — compare TRIVIUM

qua·droon \kwä-'drün\ *n* [modif. of Sp *cuarterón*, fr. *cuarto* fourth, fr. L *quartus*] **:** a person of quarter Negro ancestry

qua·dru·ma·na \kwä-'drü-mə-nə\ *n pl* [NL, fr. *quadri-* + L *manus* hand — more at MANUAL] **:** primates excluding man considered as a group distinguished by hand-shaped feet — **qua·dru·ma·nal** \-mən-ᵊl\ *adj* — **quad·ru·mane** \'kwäd-rù-,mān\ *adj or n* — **qua·dru·ma·nous** \kwä-'drü-mə-nəs\ *adj*

qua·drum·vir \kwä-'drəm-vər\ *n* [back-formation fr. *quadrumvirate*] **:** a member of a quadrumvirate

qua·drum·vi·rate \-və-rət\ *n* [*quadri-* + *-umvirate* (as in *triumvirate*)] **:** a group or association of four men

quad·ru·ped \'kwäd-rə-,ped\ *n* [L *quadruped-*, *quadrupes*, fr. *quadruped-*, *quadrupes*, adj., having four feet, fr. *quadri-* + *ped-*, *pes* foot — more at FOOT] **:** an animal having four feet — **quadruped** *adj* — **qua·dru·pe·dal** \kwä-'drü-pəd-ᵊl, ,kwäd-rə-'ped-\ *adj*

¹**qua·dru·ple** \kwä-'drüp-əl, -'drəp-; 'kwäd-rəp-\ *vb* **qua·dru·pling** \-(ə-)liŋ\ *vt* **:** to make four times as great or as many ~ *vi* **:** to become four times as great or as numerous

²**quadruple** *adj* [MF or L; MF, fr. L *quadruplus*, fr. *quadri-* + *-plus* multiplied by — more at DOUBLE] **1 :** having four units or members **2 :** being four times as great or as many **3 :** marked by four beats per measure ⟨~ meter⟩ — **quadruple** *n*

qua·dru·plet \kwä-'drəp-lət, -'drüp-; 'kwäd-rəp-\ *n* **1 :** one of four offspring born at one birth **2 :** a combination of four of a kind

¹**qua·dru·pli·cate** \kwä-'drü-pli-kət\ *adj* [L *quadruplicatus*, pp. of *quadruplicare* to quadruple, fr. *quadruplic-*, *quadruplex* fourfold, fr. *quadri-* + *-plic-*, *-plex* fold — more at SIMPLE] **1 :** repeated four times **2 :** FOURTH ⟨file the ~ copy⟩ — **quadruplicate** *n*

²**qua·dru·pli·cate** \-plə-,kāt\ *vt* **1 :** QUADRUPLE **2 :** to provide in quadruplicate

quae·re \'kwi(ə)r-ē, 'kwe(ə)r-\ *n* [L, imper. of *quaerere* to seek] *archaic* **:** QUERY, QUESTION

quaes·tor \'kwes-tər, 'kwē-stər\ *n* [ME *questor*, fr. L *quaestor*, fr. *quaestus*, pp. of *quaerere*] **:** one of numerous ancient Roman officials concerned chiefly with financial administration

¹**quaff** \'kwäf, 'kwaf\ *vb* [origin unknown] **:** to drink deeply or repeatedly — **quaff·er** *n*

²**quaff** *n* **:** a deep drink

quag \'kwag, 'kwäg\ *n* [origin unknown] **:** MARSH, BOG

quag·ga \'kwag-ə, 'kwäg-\ *n* [obs. Afrik (now *kwagga*)] **:** an extinct wild ass (*Equus quagga*) of southern Africa related to the zebras

quag·gy \'kwag-ē, 'kwäg-\ *adj* **1 :** MARSHY **2 :** FLABBY, YIELDING

quag·mire \'kwag-,mī(ə)r, 'kwäg-\ *n* **1 :** soft miry land that shakes or yields under the foot **2 :** a complex or precarious position

qua·hog *also* **qua·haug** \'kwò-,hòg, 'k(w)ō-, -,häg\ *n* [Narraganset *poquaûhock*] **:** a thick-shelled American clam (*Mercenaria mercenaria*)

quai \'kā\ *n* [F] **:** QUAY

quaich *or* **quaigh** \'kwāḵ\ *n* [ScGael *cuach*] *chiefly Scot* **:** a small shallow drinking vessel with ears for use as handles

Quai d' Or·say \,kād-(,)òr-'sā, ,kēd-, -'zā\ *n* [F, lit., quay of Orsay, a French general] **:** the French government; *specif* **:** the French foreign office

¹**quail** \'kwā(ə)l\ *n, pl* **quail** *or* **quails** [ME *quaille*, fr. MF, fr. ML *quaccula*, of imit. origin] **1 :** any of various Old World gallinaceous birds (genus *Coturnix*); *esp* **:** a migratory game bird (*C. coturnix* syn. *C. communis*) **2 :** any of various small American game birds (order Galliformes); *esp* **:** BOBWHITE

²**quail** *vb* [ME *quailen* to curdle, fr. MF *quailler*, fr. L *coagulare* — more at COAGULATE] *vi* **1** *chiefly dial* **:** WITHER, DECLINE **2 :** to lose courage **:** COWER ~ *vt, archaic* **:** to make fearful **syn** see RECOIL

quaint \'kwānt\ *adj* [ME *cointe*, fr. OF, fr. L *cognitus*, pp. of *cognoscere* to know — more at COGNITION] **1** *obs* **:** EXPERT, SKILLED **2 :** marked by cleverness, ingenuity, or refinement **3 a :** unusual or different in character or appearance **:** ODD **b :** pleasingly old-fashioned or unfamiliar **:** PICTURESQUE **syn** see STRANGE — **quaint·ly** *adv* — **quaint·ness** *n*

¹**quake** \'kwāk\ *vi* [ME *quaken*, fr. OE *cwacian*] **1 :** to shake or vibrate usu. from shock or instability **2 :** to tremble or shudder usu. from cold or fear

²**quake** *n* **:** a shaking or trembling **:** EARTHQUAKE

quak·er \'kwā-kər\ *n* **1 :** one that quakes **2** *cap* **:** FRIEND 5 — **Quak·er·ish** \'kwā-k(ə-)rish\ *adj* — **Quak·er·ism** \-kə-,riz-əm\ *n* — **Quak·er·ly** \-kər-lē\ *adj*

Quaker gun *n* [fr. the Quakers' opposition to war] **:** a dummy piece of artillery usu. made of wood

quak·er–la·dies \,kwā-kər-'lād-ēz\ *n pl* **:** BLUETS

Quaker meeting *n* **1 :** a meeting of Friends for worship marked often by long periods of silence **2 :** a social gathering marked by many periods of silence

qua·le \'kwäl-ē\ *n, pl* **qua·lia** \-ē-ə\ [L, neut. of *qualis* of what kind — more at QUALITY] **:** a property considered as an object of experience esp. in abstraction from a physical entity

qual·i·fi·ca·tion \,kwäl-ə-fə-'kā-shən\ *n* **1 :** something that qualifies **:** MODIFICATION **2 a** *obs* **:** NATURE **b** *archaic* (1) **:** CHARACTERISTIC (2) **:** ACCOMPLISHMENT **3 a :** an endowment or acquirement that fits a person (as for an office) **b :** a condition that must be complied with (as for the attainment of a privilege)

qual·i·fied \'kwäl-ə-,fīd\ *adj* **1 a :** fitted for a given purpose **:** COMPETENT **b :** having complied with the specific requirements or precedent conditions for an office or employment **:** ELIGIBLE **2 :** limited or modified in some way ⟨~ approval⟩ **syn** see ABLE — **qual·i·fied·ly** \-,fī(-ə)d-lē\ *adv*

qual·i·fi·er \-ˌfī(-ə)r\ *n* **:** one that qualifies: as **a :** one that satisfies requirements or meets a specified standard **b :** a word or word group that limits or modifies the meaning of another word or word group

qual·i·fy \'kwäl-ə-ˌfī\ *vb* [MF *qualifier*, fr. ML *qualificare*, fr. L *qualis*] *vt* **1 a :** to reduce from a general to a particular or restricted form **:** MODIFY **b :** to make less harsh or strict **:** MODERATE **c :** to alter the strength or flavor of **d :** to limit or modify the meaning of (as a noun) **2 :** to characterize by naming an attribute **:** DESCRIBE **3 a :** to fit by training, skill, or ability for a special purpose **b** (1) **:** to declare competent or adequate **:** CERTIFY (2) **:** to invest with legal capacity **:** LICENSE ~ *vi* **1 :** to be fit (as for an office) **2 :** to obtain legal or competent power or capacity **3 a :** to exhibit a required degree of ability in a preliminary contest **b :** to fire a score that makes one eligible for the award of a marksmanship badge

qual·i·ta·tive \'kwäl-ə-ˌtāt-iv\ *adj* **:** of, relating to, or involving quality or kind — **qual·i·ta·tive·ly** *adv*

qualitative analysis *n* **:** chemical analysis designed to identify the components of a substance or mixture

qual·i·ty \'kwäl-ət-ē\ *n* [ME *qualite*, fr. OF *qualité*, fr. L *qualitat-*, *qualitas*, fr. *qualis* of what kind; akin to L *qui* who — more at WHO] **1 a :** peculiar and essential character **:** NATURE **b :** an inherent feature **:** PROPERTY **c :** CAPACITY, ROLE **2 a :** degree of excellence **:** GRADE **b :** superiority in kind **3 a :** social status **:** RANK **b :** ARISTOCRACY **4 a :** a distinguishing attribute **:** CHARACTERISTIC **b :** the character in a logical proposition of being affirmative or negative **c** *archaic* **:** ACCOMPLISHMENT **5 a :** vividness of hue **b :** TIMBRE **c :** the identifying character of a vowel sound determined chiefly by the resonance of the vocal chambers in uttering it **d :** the attribute of an elementary sensation that makes it fundamentally unlike any other sensation

syn PROPERTY, CHARACTER, ATTRIBUTE: QUALITY is a general term applicable to any trait or characteristic whether individual or generic; PROPERTY implies a characteristic that belongs to a thing's essential nature and may be used to describe a type or species; CHARACTER applies to a peculiar and distinctive quality of a thing or a class; ATTRIBUTE implies a quality ascribed to a thing or a being

qualm \'kwäm *also* 'kwälm, 'kwȯm\ *n* [origin unknown] **1 :** a sudden attack of illness, faintness, or nausea **2 a :** a sudden misgiving or fear **b :** an emotional pang **:** TWINGE **3 :** COMPUNCTION, SCRUPLE — **qualmy** \-ē\ *adj*

syn QUALM, SCRUPLE, COMPUNCTION, DEMUR mean a misgiving about what one is doing or going to do. QUALM implies an uneasy fear that one is not following his conscience or better judgment; SCRUPLE implies doubt of the rightness of an act on grounds of principle; COMPUNCTION implies a spontaneous feeling of responsibility or compassion for a potential victim; DEMUR implies hesitation caused by objection to an outside suggestion or influence

qualm·ish \-ish\ *adj* **1 a :** feeling qualms **:** NAUSEATED **b :** overly scrupulous **:** SQUEAMISH **2 :** of, relating to, or producing qualms — **qualm·ish·ly** *adv* — **qualm·ish·ness** *n*

qua·mash \'kwäm-ish\ *var of* CAMAS

quan·da·ry \'kwän-d(ə-)rē\ *n* [origin unknown] **:** a state of perplexity or doubt **:** DILEMMA **syn** see PREDICAMENT

quan·tal \'kwänt-ᵊl\ *adj* [L *quanti* how many, pl. of *quantus*] **1 :** of or relating to a quantum **2 :** relating to a sensitivity response marked by the presence or absence of a definite reaction

quan·ti·fi·able \'kwänt-ə-ˌfī-ə-bəl\ *adj* **:** capable of being quantified

quan·ti·fi·ca·tion \ˌkwänt-ə-fə-'kā-shən\ *n* **:** the operation of quantifying — **quan·ti·fi·ca·tion·al** \-shnəl, -shən-ᵊl\ *adj* — **quan·ti·fi·ca·tion·al·ly** \-ē\ *adv*

quan·ti·fi·er \'kwänt-ə-ˌfī(-ə)r\ *n* **:** a prefixed operator that binds the variables in a logical formula by specifying their quantity

quan·ti·fy \-ˌfī\ *vt* [ML *quantificare*, fr. L *quantus* how much] **1 a** (1) **:** to limit by a quantifier (2) **:** to bind by prefixing a quantifier **b :** to make explicit the logical quantity of **2 :** to determine, express, or measure the quantity of

quan·ti·tate \'kwän(t)-ə-ˌtāt\ *vt* [back-formation fr. *quantitative*] **1 :** to measure or estimate the quantity of **2 :** to express in quantitative terms — **quan·ti·ta·tion** \ˌkwän(t)-ə-'tā-shən\ *n*

quan·ti·ta·tive \'kwän(t)-ə-ˌtāt-iv\ *adj* [ML *quantitativus*, fr. L *quantitat-*, *quantitas* quantity + *-ivus* -ive] **1 :** of, relating to, or expressible in terms of quantity ⟨~ relation⟩ **2 :** of, relating to, or involving the measurement of quantity or amount **3 :** based upon quantity; *specif, of classical verse* **:** based upon temporal quantity or duration of sounds — **quan·ti·ta·tive·ly** *adv* — **quan·ti·ta·tive·ness** *n*

quantitative analysis *n* **:** chemical analysis designed to determine the amounts or proportions of the components of a substance or mixture

quantitative inheritance *n* **:** particulate inheritance of a character (as height or skin color in man) mediated by groups of multiple factors each allelic pair of which adds or subtracts a specific increment

quan·ti·ty \'kwän(t)-ət-ē\ *n, often attrib* [ME *quantite*, fr. OF *quantité*, fr. L *quantitat-*, *quantitas*, fr. *quantus* how much, how large; akin to L *quam* how, as, *quando* when, *qui* who — more at WHO] **1 a :** an indefinite amount or number **b :** a determinate or estimated amount **c :** total amount or number **d :** a considerable amount or number — often used in pl. **2 a :** the aspect in which a thing is measurable in terms of greater, less, or equal or of increasing or decreasing magnitude **b :** the subject of a mathematical operation **3 a :** duration and intensity of speech sounds as distinct from their individual quality or phonemic character; *specif* **:** the relative length or brevity of a prosodic syllable in some languages (as Greek and Latin) **b :** the relative duration or time length of a speech sound or sound sequence **4 :** the character of a logical proposition as universal, particular, or singular **syn** see SUM

quan·ti·za·tion \ˌkwänt-ə-'zā-shən\ *n* **:** the act or process of quantizing

quan·tize \'kwän-ˌtīz\ *vt* [*quantum*] **1 :** to subdivide (as energy) into small finite increments **2 :** to calculate or express in terms of quantum mechanics

quan·tum \'kwänt-əm\ *n, pl* **quan·ta** \-ə\ [L, neut. of *quantus* how much] **1 a :** QUANTITY, AMOUNT **b :** PORTION, PART **c :** gross quantity **:** BULK **2 a :** one of the very small increments or parcels into which many forms of energy are subdivided **b :** one of the small subdivisions (as velocity) of a physical magnitude

quantum mechanics *n pl but sing or pl in constr* **:** a general mathematical theory dealing with the interactions of matter and radiation in terms of observable quantities only

quantum theory *n* **:** a branch of physical theory based on the concept of the subdivision of radiant energy into finite quanta and applied to numerous processes involving transference or transformation of energy in an atomic or molecular scale

quar·an·tin·able \'kwȯr-ən-ˌtē-nə-bəl, ˌkwȯr-ən-', 'kwär-, ˌkwär-\ *adj* **:** subject to or constituting grounds for quarantine ⟨a ~ disease⟩

¹**quar·an·tine** \'kwȯr-ən-ˌtēn, ˌkwȯr-ən-', 'kwär-, ˌkwär-\ *n* [It *quarantina*, fr. MF *quarantaine*, fr. OF, fr. *quarante* forty, fr. L *quadraginta*, fr. *quadra-* (akin to *quattuor* four) + *-ginta* (akin to *viginti* twenty) — more at FOUR, VIGESIMAL] **1 :** a period of 40 days **2 a :** a term during which a ship arriving in port and suspected of carrying contagious disease is forbidden all intercourse with the shore **b :** a regulation enforcing such a quarantine **c :** a place where a ship is detained during quarantine **3 a :** a restraint upon the activities or communication of persons or the transport of goods designed to prevent the spread of disease or pests **b :** a place in which persons under quarantine are kept **4 :** a state of enforced isolation

²**quarantine** *vt* **1 :** to detain in or exclude by quarantine **2 :** to isolate from normal relations or intercourse ⟨~ an aggressor⟩ ~ *vi* **:** to establish or declare a quarantine

quare \'kwa(ə)r, 'kwe(ə)r, 'kwär\ *dial var of* ¹QUEER

¹**quar·rel** \'kwȯr(-ə)l, 'kwär(-ə)l\ *n* [ME, fr. MF & OF; MF, square of glass, fr. OF, square-headed arrow, building stone, fr. (assumed) VL *quadrellum*, dim. of L *quadrum* square; akin to L *quattuor* four — more at FOUR] **1 :** a square-headed bolt or arrow esp. for a crossbow **2 :** a small quadrangular building member (as a diamond-shaped pane of glass)

²**quarrel** *n* [ME *querele*, fr. MF, complaint, fr. L *querela*, fr. *queri* to complain — more at WHEEZE] **1 :** a ground of dispute or complaint **2 :** a conflict between antagonists **:** ALTERCATION

syn WRANGLE, ALTERCATION, SQUABBLE, SPAT, TIFF: QUARREL implies a verbal clash followed by strained or severed relations; WRANGLE suggests a noisy, insistent dispute; ALTERCATION suggests determined verbal quarreling often with blows; SQUABBLE implies childish and unseemly wrangling; SPAT implies a lively but brief dispute over a trifle; TIFF suggests a trivial dispute without serious consequence

³**quarrel** *vi* **quar·reled** *or* **quar·relled**; **quar·rel·ing** *or* **quar·rel·ling 1 a :** to find fault **:** CAVIL **b :** DISAGREE **2 :** to contend or dispute actively **:** SQUABBLE — **quar·rel·er** *or* **quar·rel·ler** *n*

quar·rel·some \'kwȯr(-ə)l-səm, 'kwär(-ə)l-\ *adj* **:** apt or disposed to quarrel **:** CONTENTIOUS **syn** see BELLIGERENT — **quar·rel·some·ly** *adv* — **quar·rel·some·ness** *n*

quar·ri·er \'kwȯr-ē-ər, 'kwär-\ *n* **:** a worker in a stone quarry

¹**quar·ry** \'kwȯr-ē, 'kwär-\ *n* [ME *querre* entrails of game given to the hounds, fr. MF *cuiriee*] **1** *obs* **:** a heap of the game killed in a hunt **2 :** the object of a chase **:** GAME; *esp* **:** game hunted with hawks **3 :** PREY

²**quarry** *n* [ME *quarey*, alter. of *quarrere*, fr. MF *quarriere*, fr. (assumed) OF *quarre* squared stone, fr. L *quadrum* square] **:** an open excavation usu. for obtaining building stone, slate, or limestone

³**quarry** *vt* **1 :** to dig or take from or as if from a quarry **2 :** to make a quarry in

⁴**quarry** *n* [alter. of ¹*quarrel*] **:** a diamond-shaped pane of glass, stone, or tile

quar·ry·ing *n* **:** the business, occupation, or act of extracting stone, marble, or slate from quarries

quart \'kwȯ(ə)rt\ *n, often attrib* [ME, one fourth of a gallon, fr. MF *quarte*, fr. OF, fr. fem. of *quart*, adj., fourth, fr. L *quartus*; akin to L *quattuor* four — more at FOUR] **1** — see MEASURE table **2 :** a vessel or measure having a capacity of one quart

¹**quar·tan** \'kwȯrt-ᵊn\ *adj* [ME *quarteyne*, fr. OF (*fievre*) *quartaine* quartan fever, fr. L (*febris*) *quartana*, fr. *quartanus* of the fourth, fr. *quartus*] **:** occurring every fourth day reckoning inclusively

²**quartan** *n* **:** an intermittent fever that recurs at approximately 72-hour intervals; *esp* **:** a quartan malaria

quarte \'kärt\ *n* [F, fr. fem. of *quart* fourth] **:** the fourth of the eight defensive positions in fencing

¹**quar·ter** \'kwȯ(r)t-ər\ *n* [ME, fr. OF *quartier*, fr. L *quartarius*, fr. *quartus* fourth] **1 :** one of four equal parts into which something is divisible **:** a fourth part **2 :** any of various units of capacity or weight equal to or derived from one fourth of some larger unit **3 :** any of various units of length or area equal to one fourth of some larger unit **4 :** the fourth part of a measure of time: as **a :** one of a set of four 3-month divisions of a year **b :** a school term of about 12 weeks **c :** QUARTER HOUR **5 a :** a coin worth a quarter of a dollar **b :** the sum of 25 cents **6 :** one limb of a quadruped with the adjacent parts; *esp* **:** one fourth part of the carcass of a slaughtered animal including a leg **7 a :** the region or direction lying under any of the four divisions of the horizon **b :** one of the four parts into which the horizon is divided or the cardinal point corresponding to it **c :** a compass point or direction other than the cardinal points **d** (1) **:** a person or group not definitely specified (2) **:** a point, direction, or place not identified **8 a :** a division or district of a town or city **b :** the inhabitants of such a quarter **9 a :** an assigned station or post **b** *pl* **:** an assembly of a ship's company for ceremony, drill, or emergency **c** *pl* **:** living accommodations **:** LODGINGS **10 :** MERCY, CONSIDERATION; *esp* **:** the clemency of not killing a defeated enemy **11 :** a fourth part of the moon's period **12 :** the side of a horse's hoof between the toe and the heel **13 a :** any of the four parts into which a heraldic field is divided **b :** a bearing or charge occupying the first fourth part of a heraldic field **14 :** the state of two machine parts that are exactly at right angles to one another or are spaced about a circle so as to subtend a right angle at the center of the circle **15 a :** the stern area of a ship's side **b :** the part of the yardarm outside of the slings **16 :** one side of the upper of a shoe or boot from heel to vamp **17 :** one of the four equal periods into which the playing time of some games is divided — **at close quarters :** at close range or in immediate contact

²**quarter** *vt* **1 a :** to divide into four equal or nearly equal parts

b : to separate into either more or fewer than four parts ⟨~ an orange⟩ c *archaic* : to divide (a human body) into four parts 2 : to provide with lodging or shelter 3 : to crisscross (an area) in many directions 4 a : to arrange or bear (as different coats of arms) quarterly on one escutcheon b : to add (a coat of arms) to others on one escutcheon 5 : to adjust or locate (as cranks) at right angles in a machine ~ *vi* 1 : LODGE, DWELL 2 : to crisscross a district 3 : to change from one quarter to another ⟨the moon ~*s*⟩ 4 : to strike on a ship's quarter ⟨the wind ~*s*⟩

³**quarter** *adj* : consisting of or equal to a quarter

quar·ter·age \'kwȯ(r)t-ə-rij\ *n* : a quarterly payment, tax, wage, or allowance

¹**quar·ter·back** \'kwȯ(r)t-ər-ˌbak, 'kwȯrt-ə-ˌbak\ *n* : a backfield player in football who calls the signals and directs the offensive play of his team

²**quarterback** *vt* 1 : to call the signals and direct the offensive play of (a football team) 2 : to give executive direction to : BOSS ~ *vi* : to play quarterback

quarter crack *n* : a sand crack usu. in a horse's forefoot

quarter day *n* : the day beginning a quarter of the year and often when a quarterly payment falls due

quar·ter·deck \'kwȯ(r)t-ər-ˌdek\ *n* 1 : the stern area of a ship's upper deck 2 : a part of a deck on a naval vessel set aside by the captain for ceremonial and official use

¹**quar·ter·fi·nal** \'kwȯ(r)t-ər-'fīn-ᵊl\ *adj* 1 : being next to the semifinal in an elimination tournament 2 : of or participating in a quarterfinal

²**quarterfinal** *n* 1 : a quarterfinal match 2 *pl* : a quarterfinal round — **quar·ter·fi·nal·ist** \-ᵊl-əst\ *n*

quarter horse *n* [fr. its high speed for distances up to a quarter of a mile] : an alert cobby muscular horse developed for great endurance under the saddle

quarter hour *n* 1 : 15 minutes 2 : any of the quarter points of an hour

¹**quar·ter·ing** \'kwȯ(r)t-ə-riŋ\ *n* 1 : a division into quarters or some other number of parts 2 a : the providing of living quarters b : LODGING 3 : a ranging to and fro : CRISSCROSSING 4 a : the division of an escutcheon containing different coats of arms into four or more compartments b : a quarter of an escutcheon or the coat of arms on it

²**quartering** *adj* 1 : coming from a point well abaft the beam of a ship but not directly astern ⟨~ waves⟩ 2 : lying at right angles ⟨~ cranks of a locomotive⟩

¹**quar·ter·ly** \'kwȯ(r)t-ər-lē, 'kwȯrt-ᵊl-ē\ *adv* : at 3-month intervals

²**quarterly** *adj* 1 : computed for or payable at 3-month intervals ⟨~ premium⟩ 2 : recurring, issued, or spaced at 3-month intervals ⟨~ meeting⟩ 3 : divided into heraldic quarters or compartments

³**quarterly** *n* : a periodical published four times a year

Quarterly Meeting *n* : an organizational unit of the Society of Friends usu. composed of several Monthly Meetings

quar·ter·mas·ter \'kwȯ(r)t-ər-ˌmas-tər, 'kwȯrt-ə-ˌmas-\ *n* 1 : a petty officer who attends to a ship's helm, binnacle, and signals 2 : an army officer who provides clothing and subsistence for a body of troops

quar·tern \'kwȯ(r)t-ərn\ *n* [ME *quarteron*, fr. OF, quarter of a pound, quarter of a hundred, fr. *quartier* quarter] 1 : a fourth part : QUARTER 2 *Brit* : a loaf of bread weighing about four pounds

quarter note *n* : a musical note equal in time value to a fourth of a whole note — called also *crotchet*

quar·ter–phase \ˌkwȯ(r)t-ər-'fāz\ *adj* : DIPHASE

quar·ter·saw \'kwȯ(r)t-ər-ˌsȯ\ *vt* : to saw (a log) into quarters and then into planks in which the annual rings are nearly at right angles to the wide face

quarter section *n* : a tract of land that is half a mile square and contains 160 acres in the U.S. government system of land surveying

quarter sessions *n pl* 1 : an English local court with limited original and appellate criminal and sometimes civil jurisdiction and often administrative functions held quarterly usu. by two justices of the peace in a county or by a recorder in a borough 2 : a local court with criminal jurisdiction and sometimes administrative functions in some states of the U.S.

quar·ter·staff \'kwȯ(r)t-ər-ˌstaf\ *n* : a long stout staff formerly used as a weapon and wielded with one hand in the middle and the other between the middle and the end

quarter tone *n* 1 : a musical interval of one half a semitone 2 : a tone at an interval of one quarter

quar·tet *also* **quar·tette** \kwȯr-'tet\ *n* [It *quartetto*, fr. *quarto* fourth, fr. L *quartus* — more at QUART] 1 : a musical composition for four instruments or voices 2 : a group or set of four; *esp* : the musicians that perform a quartet

quar·tic \'kwȯrt-ik\ *adj* [L *quartus* fourth] : of the fourth degree ⟨~ equation⟩ — **quartic** *n*

quar·tile \'kwȯ(ə)r-ˌtīl, 'kwȯrt-ᵊl\ *n* [ISV, fr. L *quartus*] : the value that marks the boundary between two consecutive intervals in a frequency distribution of four intervals each containing one quarter of the total population

quar·to \'kwȯrt-(ˌ)ō\ *n* [L, abl. of *quartus* fourth] 1 : the size of a piece of paper cut four from a sheet; *also* : paper or a page of this size 2 : a book printed on quarto pages

quartz \'kwȯ(ə)rts\ *n* [G *quarz*] : a mineral SiO_2 consisting of a silicon dioxide that occurs in colorless and transparent or colored hexagonal crystals and also in crystalline masses — **quartz·ose** \'kwȯrt-ˌsōs\ *adj*

quartz battery *n* : STAMP MILL — called also *quartz mill*

quartz glass *n* : vitreous silica prepared from pure quartz and noted for its transparency to ultraviolet radiation

quartz·if·er·ous \kwȯrt-'sif-(ə-)rəs\ *adj* : bearing quartz

quartz·ite \'kwȯrt-ˌsīt\ *n* [ISV] : a compact granular rock composed of quartz and derived from sandstone by metamorphism — **quartz·it·ic** \kwȯrt-'sit-ik\ *adj*

qua·sar \'kwā-ˌzär, -ˌsär\ *n* [*quasi*-stell*ar* radio source] : any of various very distant celestial objects that resemble stars but emit unusually bright blue and ultraviolet light and radio waves

¹**quash** \'kwäsh, 'kwȯsh\ *vt* [ME *quassen*, fr. MF *casser*, *quasser* to annul, fr. LL *cassare*, fr. L *cassus* void, without effect; akin to L *carēre* to be without — more at CASTE] : to put an end to, set aside, or make void esp. by judicial action ⟨~ an indictment⟩

²**quash** *vt* [ME *quashen* to smash, fr. MF *quasser*, *casser*, fr. L *quassare* to shake violently, shatter, fr. *quassus*, pp. of *quatere* to shake; akin to OE *hūdenian* to shake] : to suppress or extinguish completely : QUELL ⟨~ a rebellion⟩

¹**qua·si** \'kwā-ˌzī, -ˌsī; 'kwäz-ē, 'kwäs-; 'kwā-zē\ *adv* [L, as if, as it were, approximately, fr. *quam* as + *si* if — more at QUANTITY, SO] : in some sense or degree : SEEMINGLY ⟨*quasi*-historical⟩ ⟨*quasi*-officially⟩

²**quasi** *adj* 1 : having some resemblance usu. by possession of certain attributes (as function) ⟨a ~ corporation⟩ 2 : having a legal status only by operation or construction of law and without reference to intent ⟨~ contract⟩

qua·si–ju·di·cial \-jü-'dish-əl\ *adj* 1 : having a partly judicial character by possession of the right to hold hearings on and conduct investigations into disputed claims and alleged infractions of rules and regulations and to make decisions in the general manner of courts ⟨~ bodies⟩ 2 : essentially judicial in character but not within the judicial power or function esp. as constitutionally defined ⟨~ review⟩ — **qua·si–ju·di·cial·ly** \-'dish-(ə-)lē\ *adv*

qua·si–leg·is·la·tive \-'lej-ə-ˌslāt-iv\ *adj* 1 : having a partly legislative character by possession of the right to make rules and regulations having the force of law ⟨a ~ agency⟩ 2 : essentially legislative in character but not within the legislative power or function esp. as constitutionally defined ⟨~ powers⟩

Qua·si·mo·do \ˌkwäs-i-'mōd-(ˌ)ō, ˌkwäz-\ *n* [ML *quasi modo geniti infantes* as newborn babes (words of the introit for Low Sunday)] : LOW SUNDAY

qua·si–pub·lic \-'pəb-lik; *see* ¹QUASI\ *adj* : essentially public (as in services rendered) although under private ownership or control ⟨~ corporations⟩

quas·qui·cen·ten·ni·al \ˌkwäs-kwi-sen-'ten-ē-əl\ *n* [fr. L *quadrans* quarter, after L *semis* half: E *sesquicentennial*] : a 125th anniversary

quas·sia \'kwäsh-ə\ *n* [NL, genus name, fr. *Quassi* 18th cent. Surinam Negro slave who discovered the medicinal value of quassia] : a drug from the heartwood of various tropical trees of the ailanthus family used esp. as a bitter tonic and remedy for roundworms in children and as an insecticide

¹**qua·ter·na·ry** \'kwät-ə(r)-ˌner-ē, kwə-'tər-nə-rē\ *adj* [L *quaternarius*, fr. *quaterni* four each] 1 : of, relating to, or consisting of four units or members 2 *cap* : of, relating to, or being the geological period from the end of the Tertiary to the present time or the corresponding system of rocks 3 : consisting of, containing, or being an atom united by four bonds to carbon atoms

²**quaternary** *n* 1 : a member of a group fourth in order or rank 2 *cap* : the Quaternary period or system of rocks

quaternary ammonium compound *n* : any of numerous strong bases and their salts derived from ammonium by replacement of the hydrogen atoms with organic radicals and important esp. as surface-active agents, disinfectants, and drugs

qua·ter·ni·on \kwə-'tər-nē-ən\ *n* [ME *quaternyoun*, fr. LL *quaternion-*, *quaternio*, fr. L *quaterni* four each, fr. *quater* four times; akin to L *quattuor* four — more at FOUR] 1 : a set of four parts, things, or persons : TETRAD 2 a : a generalized complex number composed of a real number and a vector and depending on one real and three imaginary units b *pl* : the calculus of the quaternion

qua·train \'kwä-ˌtrān, kwä-'\ *n* [F, fr. MF, fr. *quatre* four, fr. L *quattuor*] : a unit or group of four lines of verse

qua·tre·foil \'kat-ər-ˌfȯil, 'ka-trə-\ *n* [ME *quaterfoil* set of four leaves, fr. MF *quatre* + ME *-foil* (as in *trefoil*)] 1 : a conventionalized representation of a flower with four petals or of a leaf with four leaflets 2 : a 4-lobed foliation in architecture

quat·tro·cen·to \ˌkwä-trō-'chen-(ˌ)tō\ *n*, *often cap* [It, lit., four hundred, fr. *quattro* four (fr. L *quattuor*) + *cento* hundred] : the 15th century esp. with reference to Italian literature and art

quat·tu·or·de·cil·lion \ˌkwät-ə-ˌwȯr-di-'sil-yən\ *n*, *often attrib* [L *quattuordecim* fourteen (fr. *quattuor* four + *decem* ten) + E *-illion* (as in *million*) — more at TEN] — see NUMBER table

¹**qua·ver** \'kwā-vər\ *vb* **qua·ver·ing** \'kwāv-(ə-)riŋ\ [ME *quaveren*, freq. of *quaven* to tremble] *vi* 1 : TREMBLE, SHAKE ⟨~*ing* inwardly⟩ 2 : TRILL 3 : to utter sound in tremulous tones ~ *vt* : to utter quaveringly — **qua·ver·ing·ly** \'kwāv-(ə-)riŋ-lē\ *adv* — **qua·very** \-(ə-)rē\ *adj*

²**quaver** *n* 1 : EIGHTH NOTE 2 : TRILL 1 3 : a tremulous sound

quay \'kē, 'k(w)ā\ *n* [alter. of earlier *key*, fr. ME, fr. MF *cai*, of Celt origin; akin to Corn *kē* hedge, fence; akin to OE *hecg* hedge] : a stretch of paved bank or a solid artificial landing place beside navigable water for convenience in loading and unloading ships

quay·age \-ij\ *n* 1 : a charge for use of a quay 2 : room on or for quays 3 : a system of quays

quay·side \-ˌsīd\ *n*, *often attrib* : land bordering on a quay

quean \'kwēn\ *n* [ME *quene*, fr. OE *cwene*; akin to OE *cwēn* woman, queen] 1 : a disreputable woman; *specif* : PROSTITUTE 2 *chiefly Scot* : WOMAN; *esp* : one that is young or unmarried

quea·si·ly \'kwē-zə-lē\ *adv* : in a queasy manner

quea·si·ness \-zē-nəs\ *n* : the quality or state of being queasy

quea·sy *also* **quea·zy** \'kwē-zē\ *adj* [ME *coysy*, *qwesye*] 1 : full of doubt : HAZARDOUS 2 a : causing nausea ⟨~ motion⟩ b : NAUSEATED 3 a : causing uneasiness b (1) : DELICATE, SQUEAMISH (2) : ill at ease

Que·bec \kwi-'bek\ — a communications code word for the letter *q*

que·bra·cho \kā-'bräch-(ˌ)ō\ *n* [AmerSp, alter. of *quiebracha*, fr. Sp *quiebra* it breaks + *hacha* ax] 1 : any of several tropical American trees with hard wood; *esp* : a chiefly Argentine tree (*Schinopsis lorentzii*) of the sumac family with dense wood rich in tannins — called also *red quebracho* 2 a : the wood of a quebracho b : a tannin-rich extract of the Argentine quebracho used in tanning leather

Que·chua \'kech-(ə-)wə, kə-'chü-ə\ *n*, *pl* **Quechua** *or* **Quechuas** [Sp, fr. Quechua *kkechuwa* plunderer, robber] 1 a (1) : a people of central Peru (2) : a group of peoples constituting the dominant element of the Inca Empire b : a member of any of these peoples 2 a : the language of the Quechua people widely spoken by other Indian peoples of Peru, Bolivia, Ecuador, Chile, and Argentina b : a language family comprising the Quechua language — **Que·chu·an** \-(ə-)wən, -'chü-ən\ *adj or n*

¹**queen** \'kwēn\ *n* [ME *quene*, fr. OE *cwēn* woman, wife, queen; akin to Goth *qens* wife, Gk *gynē* woman, wife] 1 a : the wife or widow of a king b : the wife or widow of a tribal chief 2 a : a female monarch b : a female chieftain 3 a : a woman eminent in rank, power, or attractions b : a goddess or a thing personified as female and having supremacy in a specified realm c : an attractive girl or woman; *esp* : a beauty contest winner 4 : the most privileged piece in a set of chessmen having the power to move

as either a rook or a bishop **5 :** a playing card picturing a queen **6 :** the fertile fully developed female of social bees, ants, and termites whose function is to lay eggs **7 :** a mature female cat **8** *slang* **:** HOMOSEXUAL — **queen·dom** \-dəm\ *n* — **queen·like** \-ˌlīk\ *adj* — **queen·li·ness** \-lē-nəs\ *n* — **queen·ly** \-lē\ *adj or adv*

[2]**queen** *vi* **1 a :** to act like a queen **b :** to put on airs — usu. used with formulary *it* **2 :** to become a queen in chess **~** *vt* **:** to promote (a pawn) to a queen in chess

Queen Anne \kwē-'nan\ *adj* [*Queen Anne* of England †1714] **1 :** of, relating to, or having the characteristics of a style of furniture prevalent in England under Dutch influence esp. during the first half of the 18th century that is marked by extensive use of upholstery, marquetry, and Oriental fabrics **2 :** of, relating to, or having the characteristics of a style of English building of the early 18th century characterized by modified classic ornament and the use of red brickwork in which even relief ornament is carved

Queen Anne's lace *n* **:** WILD CARROT

queen consort, *n, pl* **queens consort :** the wife of a reigning king

queen mother *n* **:** a queen dowager who is mother of the reigning sovereign

queen olive *n* **:** any of various olives with large oblong fruits grown esp. in the region of Seville, Spain

queen post *n* **:** one of two vertical tie posts in a truss (as of a roof)

queen regent *n, pl* **queens regent :** a queen ruling in behalf of another or in her own right

queen regnant *n, pl* **queens regnant :** a queen reigning in her own right

Queen's Birthday *n* **:** a legal holiday in parts of the British Commonwealth celebrating the birthday of the queen

Queen's Counsel *n* — used instead of *King's Counsel* when the British monarch is a queen

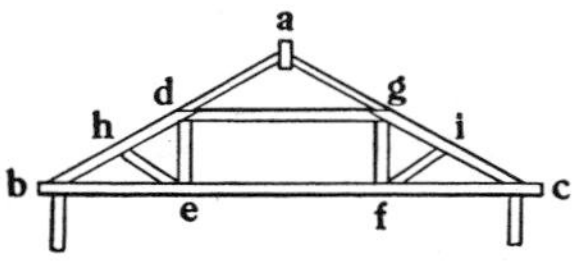

de, gf, queen posts; *bc,* beam; *dg,* straining piece; *bd, cg,* principal rafters; *ba, ca,* rafters; *eh, fi,* struts

queen truss *n* **:** a truss framed with queen posts

[1]**queer** \'kwi(ə)r\ *adj* [origin unknown] **1 a :** differing in some odd way from what is usual or normal **b** (1) **:** ECCENTRIC, UNCONVENTIONAL (2) **:** mildly insane **:** TOUCHED **c :** OBSESSED, HIPPED **d** *slang* **:** sexually deviate **:** HOMOSEXUAL **2 a** *slang* **:** WORTHLESS, COUNTERFEIT ⟨~ money⟩ **b :** QUESTIONABLE, SUSPICIOUS **3 :** not quite well **:** QUEASY **syn** see STRANGE — **queer·ish** \-ish\ *adj* — **queer·ly** *adv* — **queer·ness** *n*

[2]**queer** *adv* **:** QUEERLY

[3]**queer** *vt* **1 :** to spoil the effect or success of **:** DISRUPT ⟨~ one's plans⟩ **2 :** to put or get into an embarrassing or disadvantageous situation

[4]**queer** *n* **1** *slang* **:** one that is queer; *esp* **:** HOMOSEXUAL **2** *slang* **:** counterfeit money

[1]**quell** \'kwel\ *vt* [ME *quellen* to kill, quell, fr. OE *cwellan* to kill; akin to OHG *quellen* to torture, kill, *quāla* torment, Gk *belonē* needle] **1 :** to put down **:** SUPPRESS ⟨~ a riot⟩ **2 :** QUIET, PACIFY ⟨~ fears⟩ — **quell·er** *n*

[2]**quell** *n* [ME, fr. *quellen*] *archaic* **:** KILLING, SLAUGHTER; *also* **:** the power of quelling

quench \'kwench\ *vb* [ME *quenchen,* fr. OE *-cwencan;* akin to OE *-cwincan* to vanish, OFris *quinka*] *vt* **1 a :** to put out **:** EXTINGUISH **b :** to put out the fire or light of ⟨~ a lamp⟩ **2 :** SUBDUE, OVERCOME ⟨~ hatred⟩ **3 :** DESTROY ⟨~ rebellion⟩ **4 :** to relieve or satisfy with liquid ⟨~*ed* his thirst⟩ **5 :** to cool (as heated steel) suddenly by immersion esp. in water or oil **6 :** SUPPRESS, INHIBIT **~** *vi* **1 :** to become extinguished **:** COOL **2 :** to become calm **:** SUBSIDE — **quench·able** \-ə-bəl\ *adj* — **quench·er** *n* — **quench·less** \-ləs\ *adj*

quer·ce·tin \'kwər-sət-ən\ *n* [ISV, fr. L *quercetum* oak forest, fr. *quercus* oak — more at FIR] **:** a yellow crystalline pigment $C_{15}H_{10}O_7$ occurring usu. in the form of glycosides in various plants

quer·ci·tron \'kwər-sə-trən, -ˌträn; (ˌ)kwər-'si-trən\ *n* [blend of NL *Quercus* (genus name) and ISV *citron*] **1 :** an oak (*Quercus velutina*) **2 :** the bark of this oak rich in tannin and yellow coloring matter and used in tanning and dyeing

que·rist \'kwi(ə)r-əst, 'kwe(ə)r-\ *n* [L *quaerere* to ask] **:** INQUIRER

quern \'kwərn\ *n* [ME, fr. OE *cweorn;* akin to OHG *quirn* mill, OSlav *žrŭny*] **:** a primitive hand mill for grinding grain

quer·u·lous \'kwer-(y)ə-ləs *also* 'kwir-\ *adj* [L *querulus,* fr. *queri* to complain] **1 :** habitually complaining **2 :** FRETFUL, WHINING ⟨~ voice⟩ — **quer·u·lous·ly** *adv* — **quer·u·lous·ness** *n*

[1]**que·ry** \'kwi(ə)r-ē, 'kwe(ə)r-\ *n* [alter. of earlier *quere,* fr. L *quaere,* imper. of *quaerere* to ask] **1 :** QUESTION, INQUIRY **2 :** a question in the mind **:** DOUBT **3 :** QUESTION MARK

[2]**query** *vt* **1 :** to put as a question **2 :** to ask questions about esp. in order to resolve a doubt **3 :** to ask questions of esp. with a desire for authoritative information **4 :** to mark with a query **syn** see ASK

[1]**quest** \'kwest\ *n* [ME, search, pursuit, investigation, inquest, fr. MF *queste* search, pursuit, fr. (assumed) VL *quaesta,* fr. L, fem. of *quaestus*] **1 a :** a jury of inquest **b :** INVESTIGATION **2 :** an act or instance of seeking: **a :** PURSUIT, SEARCH **b :** a chivalrous enterprise in medieval romance usu. involving an adventurous journey **3** *obs* **:** ones who search or make inquiry

[2]**quest** *vi* **1** *of a dog* **a :** to search a trail **b :** BAY **2 :** to go on a quest **~** *vt* **1 :** to search for **2 :** to ask for **:** DEMAND — **quest·er** *n*

[1]**ques·tion** \'kwes(h)-chən\ *n* [ME, fr. MF, fr. L *quaestion-, quaestio,* fr. *quaesitus, quaestus,* pp. of *quaerere* to seek, ask] **1 a** (1) **:** an interrogative expression often used to test knowledge (2) **:** an interrogative sentence or clause **b :** a subject or aspect in dispute or open for discussion **:** ISSUE; *broadly* **:** PROBLEM, MATTER **c** (1) **:** a subject or point of debate or a proposition to be voted on in a meeting (2) **:** the bringing of such to a vote **d :** the specific point at issue **2 a :** an act or instance of asking **:** INQUIRY **b :** INTERROGATION; *also* **:** a judicial or official investigation **c :** torture as part of an examination **d** (1) **:** OBJECTION, DISPUTE (2) **:** room for doubt or objection (3) **:** CHANCE, POSSIBILITY ⟨no ~ of escape⟩

[2]**question** *vt* **1 :** to ask a question of or about **2 :** CROSS-EXAMINE **3 a :** DOUBT, DISPUTE **b :** to subject to analysis **:** EXAMINE **~** *vi* to ask questions **:** INQUIRE **syn** see ASK — **ques·tion·er** *n*

ques·tion·able \'kwes(h)-chə-nə-bəl, *rapid* 'kwesh-nə-\ *adj* **1** *obs* **:** inviting inquiry **2** *obs* **:** liable or amenable to judicial inquiry or action **3 :** affording reason for being doubted, questioned, or challenged **:** not certain or exact **:** PROBLEMATIC ⟨milk of ~ purity⟩ ⟨~ decision⟩ **4 :** attended by well-grounded suspicions of being immoral, crude, false, or unsound **:** DUBIOUS ⟨~ motives⟩ **syn** see DOUBTFUL — **ques·tion·able·ness** *n* — **ques·tion·ably** \-blē\ *adv*

ques·tion·ary \'kwes(h)-chə-ˌner-ē\ *n* **:** a collection of questions; *esp* **:** QUESTIONNAIRE

ques·tion·less \'kwes(h)-chən-ləs\ *adj* **1 :** INDUBITABLE, UNQUESTIONABLE **2 :** UNQUESTIONING

question mark *n* **:** a mark ? used in writing and printing at the conclusion of a sentence to indicate a direct question

ques·tion·naire \ˌkwes(h)-chə-'na(ə)r, -'ne(ə)r\ *n* [F, fr. *questionner* to question, fr. MF, fr. *question,* n.] **1 :** a set of questions for obtaining statistically useful or personal information from individuals **2 :** a sheet of paper containing a questionnaire **3 :** a survey made by the use of a questionnaire

question time *n* **:** a period in a session of a British parliamentary body during which members may put to a minister questions on matters concerning his department

ques·tor \'kwes-tər\ *var of* QUAESTOR

quet·zal \ket-'säl, -'sal\ *n, pl* **quetzals** *or* **quet·za·les** \-'säl-(ˌ)ās, -'sal-\ [AmerSp, fr. Nahuatl *quetzaltototl,* fr. *quetzalli* brilliant tail feather + *tototl* bird] **1 :** a Central American trogon (*Pharomachrus mocino*) having brilliant plumage and in the male long upper tail coverts **2** — see MONEY table

Quet·zal·coatl \ket-'säl-ˌkwät-ᵊl, -'sal-, -kə-ˌwät-\ *n* [Nahuatl] **:** the chief deity of the Aztecs

[1]**queue** \'kyü\ *n* [F, lit., tail, fr. L *cauda, coda*] **1 :** a braid of hair usu. worn hanging at the back of the head **2 :** a line esp. of persons or vehicles

[2]**queue** *vb* **queued; queu·ing** *or* **queue·ing** *vt* **:** to arrange or form in a queue **~** *vi* **:** to line up or wait in a queue — **queu·er** *n*

[1]**quib·ble** \'kwib-əl\ *n* [prob. dim. of obs. *quib* (quibble)] **1 :** an evasion of or shift from the point **:** EQUIVOCATION **2 :** a minor objection or criticism

[2]**quibble** *vb* **quib·bling** \-(ə-)liŋ\ *vi* **1 :** EQUIVOCATE **2 a :** CAVIL, CARP **b :** BICKER **~** *vt* **:** to subject to quibbles — **quib·bler** \-(ə-)lər\ *n*

[1]**quick** \'kwik\ *adj* [ME *quik,* fr. OE *cwic;* akin to ON *kvikr* living, L *vivus* living, *vivere* to live, Gk *bios, zōē* life] **1** *archaic* **:** not dead **:** LIVING, ALIVE **2 :** RAPID, SPEEDY: as **a** (1) **:** fast in understanding, thinking, or learning **:** mentally agile ⟨a ~ mind⟩ ⟨~ thinking⟩ (2) **:** reacting to stimuli with speed and keen sensitivity (3) **:** aroused immediately and intensely ⟨~ temper⟩ **b** (1) **:** fast in development or occurrence ⟨a ~ succession of events⟩ (2) **:** done or taking place with rapidity ⟨gave them a ~ look⟩ **c :** marked by speed, readiness, or promptness of physical movement ⟨walked with ~ steps⟩ **3 :** easily aroused to impatience or anger **4** *archaic* **a :** not stagnant **:** RUNNING, FLOWING **b :** SHIFTING, MOVING ⟨~ mud⟩ **5** *archaic* **:** FIERY, GLOWING **6** *obs* **a :** PUNGENT **b :** CAUSTIC **7** *archaic* **:** PREGNANT **8 :** turning or bending at a sharp angle ⟨a ~ turn in the road⟩ — **quick·ly** *adv* — **quick·ness** *n*

syn QUICK, PROMPT, READY, APT mean able to respond without delay or hesitation. QUICK implies native ability rather than acquired power; PROMPT usu. implies training and discipline that fits one for instant response; READY suggests facility or fluency in response; APT implies quickness in responding because of unusual intelligence or particular talent **syn** see in addition FAST

[2]**quick** *adv* **:** QUICKLY

[3]**quick** *n* **1** *obs* **:** a living thing **2** [prob. of Scand origin; akin to ON *kvika* sensitive flesh, fr. *kvikr* living] **a :** a painfully sensitive spot or area of flesh (as that underlying a fingernail or toenail) **b :** the inmost sensibilities ⟨hurt to the ~ by the remark⟩ **c :** the very center of something **:** HEART ⟨the ~ of the matter⟩ **3** *archaic* **:** LIFE 11 **4 :** QUICKIE

[4]**quick** *vb, archaic* **:** QUICKEN

quick assets *n pl* **:** cash, accounts receivable, and other current assets excluding inventories

quick bread *n* **:** a bread made with a leavening agent that permits immediate baking of the dough or batter mixture

quick·en \'kwik-ən\ *vb* **quick·en·ing** \-(ə-)niŋ\ *vt* **1 a :** to make alive **:** REVIVE **b :** to cause to be enlivened **:** STIMULATE **2** *archaic* **a :** KINDLE **b :** to cause to burn more intensely **3 :** to make more rapid **:** HASTEN, ACCELERATE ⟨~*ed* her steps⟩ **4 a :** to make (a curve) sharper **b :** to make (a slope) steeper **~** *vi* **1 :** to quicken something **2 :** to come to life; *esp* **:** to enter into a phase of active growth and development ⟨seeds ~*ing* in the soil⟩ **3 :** to reach the stage of gestation at which fetal motion is felt **4 :** to shine more brightly ⟨watched the dawn ~*ing* in the east⟩ **5 :** to become more rapid ⟨her pulse ~*ed* at the sight⟩ — **quick·en·er** \-(ə-)nər\ *n*

syn QUICKEN, ANIMATE, ENLIVEN, VIVIFY mean to make alive or lively. QUICKEN stresses a sudden renewal of life or activity esp. in something inert; ANIMATE emphasizes the imparting of motion or activity to what is mechanical or artificial; ENLIVEN suggests a stimulus that arouses from dullness or torpidity; VIVIFY implies a freshening or energizing through renewal of vitality **syn** see in addition PROVOKE

quick-freeze \'kwik-'frēz\ *vt* **:** to freeze (food) for preservation so rapidly that ice crystals formed are too small to rupture the cells and the natural juices and flavor are preserved

quick·ie \'kwik-ē\ *n* **:** something done or made in less than the usual time; *esp* **:** an alcoholic drink hurriedly tossed off

quick·lime \'kwik-ˌlīm\ *n* **:** the first solid product that is obtained by calcining limestone and that develops great heat and becomes crumbly when treated with water

quick-lunch \-'lənch\ *n* **:** a luncheonette specializing in short-order food

quick·sand \'kwik-ˌsand\ *n* **:** sand readily yielding to pressure; *esp* **:** a deep mass of loose sand mixed with water into which heavy objects sink

quick·set \-ˌset\ *n, chiefly Brit* **:** plant cuttings set in the ground to grow esp. in a hedgerow; *also* **:** a hedge or thicket esp. of hawthorn grown from quickset

quick·sil·ver \-ˌsil-vər\ *n* **:** MERCURY 2a — **quicksilver** *adj*

quick·step \-ˌstep\ *n* **:** a spirited march tune esp. accompanying a march in quick time

quick–tem·pered \-'tem-pərd\ *adj* **:** easily angered **:** IRASCIBLE

quick time *n* **:** a rate of marching in which 120 steps each 30 inches in length are taken in one minute

quick–wit·ted \'kwik-'wit-əd\ *adj* **:** quick in perception and understanding **:** mentally alert **syn** see INTELLIGENT — **quick–wit·ted·ly** *adv* — **quick–wit·ted·ness** *n*

1quid \'kwid\ *n, pl* **quid** *also* **quids** [origin unknown] *slang Brit* **:** a pound sterling **:** SOVEREIGN

2quid *n* [E dial., cud, fr. ME *quide*, fr. OE *cwidu* — more at CUD] **:** a cut or wad of something chewable

quid·di·ty \'kwid-ət-ē\ *n* [ML *quidditas* essence, lit., whatness, fr. L *quid* what, neut. of *quis* who — more at WHO] **1 a :** a trifling point **:** QUIBBLE **b :** CROTCHET, ECCENTRICITY **2 :** whatever makes something to be of the type that it is **:** ESSENCE

quid·nunc \'kwid-ˌnəŋk\ *n* [L *quid nunc* what now?] **:** an inquisitive usu. small-minded individual **:** BUSYBODY

quid pro quo \ˌkwid-ˌprō-'kwō\ *n* [NL, something for something] **:** something given or received for something else

qui·es·cence \kwī-'es-ᵊn(t)s, kwē-\ *n* **:** the quality or state of being quiescent

qui·es·cent \-ᵊnt\ *adj* [L *quiescent-, quiescens*, prp. of *quiescere* to become quiet, rest, fr. *quies*] **1 :** being at rest **:** INACTIVE **2 :** causing no trouble or symptoms **syn** see LATENT — **qui·es·cent·ly** *adv*

1qui·et \'kwī-ət\ *n* [ME, fr. L *quiet-, quies* rest, quiet — more at WHILE] **:** the quality or state of being quiet **:** TRANQUILLITY — **on the quiet :** in a secretive manner

2quiet *adj* [ME, fr. MF, fr. L *quietus*, fr. pp. of *quiescere*] **1 a :** marked by little or no motion or activity **:** CALM **b :** GENTLE, EASYGOING ⟨~ temperament⟩ **c :** UNDISTURBED ⟨~ reading⟩ **d :** enjoyed in peace and relaxation ⟨a ~ cup of tea⟩ **2 a :** free from noise or uproar **:** STILL **b :** UNOBTRUSIVE, CONSERVATIVE ⟨~ clothes⟩ **3 :** RETIRED, SECLUDED ⟨~ nook⟩ — **qui·et·ly** *adv* — **qui·et·ness** *n*

3quiet *adv* **:** QUIETLY ⟨*quiet*-running engine⟩

4quiet *vt* **1 :** to cause to be quiet **:** CALM **2 :** to make secure by freeing from dispute or question ⟨~ title⟩ ~ *vi* **:** to become quiet — usu. used with *down* — **qui·et·er** *n*

qui·et·en \'kwī-ət-ᵊn\ *vb* **qui·et·en·ing** \-ət-niŋ, -ᵊn-iŋ\ *chiefly Brit* **:** QUIET

qui·et·ism \'kwī-ət-ˌiz-əm\ *n* **1 :** a system of religious mysticism teaching that perfection and spiritual peace are attained by annihilation of the self and passive absorption in contemplation of God and divine things **2 :** a state of calmness or passivity — **qui·et·ist** \-ət-əst\ *adj or n*

qui·etude \'kwī-ə-ˌt(y)üd\ *n* [MF, fr. LL *quietudo*, fr. L *quietus*] **:** QUIETNESS, REPOSE

qui·etus \kwī-'ēt-əs\ *n* [ME *quietus est*, fr. ML, he is quit, formula of discharge from obligation] **1 :** final settlement (as of a debt) **2 :** removal from activity; *esp* **:** DEATH **3 :** something that quiets or represses **4 :** a state of inactivity

quiff \'kwif\ *n* [origin unknown] *Brit* **:** a prominent forelock

1quill \'kwil\ *n* [ME *quil* hollow reed, bobbin; akin to MHG *kil* large feather] **1 a** (1) **:** a bobbin, spool, or spindle on which filling yarn is wound (2) **:** a hollow shaft often surrounding another shaft and used in various mechanical devices **b :** a roll of dried bark **2 a** (1) **:** the hollow horny barrel of a feather (2) **:** FEATHER; *esp* **:** one of the large stiff feathers of the wing or tail **b :** one of the hollow sharp spines of a porcupine or hedgehog **3 :** one of various articles made from or resembling the quill of a feather; *esp* **:** a pen for writing **4 :** a float for a fishing line

2quill *vt* **1 :** to pierce with quills **2 a :** to wind (thread or yarn) on a quill **b :** to make a series of small rounded ridges in (cloth)

quill·back \'kwil-ˌbak\ *n, pl* **quillback** *or* **quillbacks :** any of several suckers; *esp* **:** a small fish (*Carpiodes velifer*) of central and eastern No. America

1quilt \'kwilt\ *n* [ME *quilte* mattress, quilt, fr. OF *cuilte*, fr. L *culcita* mattress] **1 :** a bed coverlet of two layers of cloth filled with wool, cotton, or down and held in place by stitched designs **2 :** something that is quilted or resembles a quilt

2quilt *vt* **1 a :** to fill, pad, or line like a quilt **b** (1) **:** to stitch, sew, or cover with lines or patterns like those used in quilts (2) **:** to stitch (designs) through layers of cloth **c :** to fasten between two pieces of material **2 :** to stitch or sew in layers with padding in between ~ *vi* **1 :** to make quilts **2 :** to do quilted work — **quilt·er** *n*

quilt·ing *n* **1 :** the process of quilting **2 :** material that is quilted or used for making quilts

quin- *or* **quino-** *comb form* [Sp *quina* — more at QUININE] **1 :** cinchona **:** cinchona bark ⟨*quin*oline⟩ **2 :** quinone ⟨*quin*oid⟩

quin·a·crine \'kwin-ə-ˌkrēn\ *n* [*quin-* + *acridine*] **:** an antimalarial drug derived from acridine and used esp. as the dihydrochloride $C_{23}H_{30}ClN_3O.2HCl.2H_2O$

quince \'kwin(t)s\ *n* [ME *quynce* quinces, pl. of *coyn, quyn* quince, fr. MF *coin*, fr. L *cydonium*, fr. Gk *kydōnion*] **1 :** the fruit of a central Asiatic tree (*Cydonia oblonga*) of the rose family that resembles a hard-fleshed yellow apple and is used for marmalade, jelly, and preserves **2 :** the tree bearing quinces

quin·cun·cial \kwin-'kən-chəl\ *or* **quin·cunx·ial** \-'kəŋ(k)-sē-əl\ *adj* **1 :** of, relating to, or arranged in a quincunx **2 :** having the members of a pentamerous bud or flower so imbricated that two are exterior, two are interior, and one has one edge exterior and one interior — **quin·cun·cial·ly** \-'kən-chə-lē\ *adv*

quin·cunx \'kwin-ˌkəŋ(k)s\ *n* [L *quincunc-, quincunx*, lit., five twelfths, fr. *quinque* five + *uncia* twelfth part — more at FIVE, OUNCE] **1 :** an arrangement of five things with one at each corner and one in the middle of a square or rectangle **2 :** a quincuncial arrangement of plant parts

quin·de·cil·lion \ˌkwin-di-'sil-yən\ *n, often attrib* [L *quindec*im fifteen (fr. *quinque* five + *decem* ten) + E *-illion* (as in *million*) — more at TEN] — see NUMBER table

quin·i·dine \'kwin-ə-ˌdēn\ *n* [ISV, fr. *quinine*] **:** an alkaloid $C_{20}H_{24}N_2O_2$ stereoisomeric with and resembling quinine that is found in some cinchonas

qui·nine \'kwī-ˌnīn, *Brit* kwin-'ēn\ *n* [Sp *quina* cinchona, short for *quinaquina*, fr. Quechua] **1 :** a bitter crystalline alkaloid $C_{20}H_{24}N_2O_2$ from cinchona bark used in medicine **2 :** a salt of quinine used as a febrifuge, antimalarial, antiperiodic, and bitter tonic

quinine water *n* **:** a carbonated beverage flavored with a small amount of quinine, lemon, and lime

qui·noa \ki-'nō-ə\ *n* [Sp, fr. Quechua *quinua*] **:** a pigweed (*Chenopodium quinoa*) of the high Andes whose seeds are locally a staple food

quin·oid \'kwin-ˌȯid\ *n* **:** a quinonoid compound

qui·noi·dine \kwə-'nȯid-ᵊn\ *n* [ISV] **:** a bitter brownish resinous mixture of alkaloids obtained as a by-product in the extraction of cinchona bark for crystalline alkaloids and formerly used as a quinine substitute

quin·o·line \'kwin-ᵊl-ˌēn\ *n* [ISV] **1 :** a pungent oily nitrogenous base C_9H_7N obtained usu. by distillation of coal tar or by synthesis from aniline that is the parent compound of many alkaloids, drugs, and dyes **2 :** a derivative of quinoline

qui·none \kwin-'ōn, 'kwin-ˌōn\ *n* [ISV, fr. *quinine*] **1 :** either of two isomeric cyclic crystalline compounds $C_6H_4O_2$; *esp* **:** the pungent yellow para isomer usu. made by oxidation of aniline and used esp. as an oxidizing agent **2 :** a usu. yellow, orange, or red compound containing quinone structures

qui·no·noid \kwin-'ō-ˌnȯid, 'kwin-ə-\ *or* **quin·oid** \'kwin-ˌȯid\ *adj* **:** resembling quinone esp. in having a benzene nucleus containing two double bonds within the nucleus

Quin·qua·ge·si·ma \ˌkwiŋ-kwə-'jes-ə-mə, -'jā-zə-\ *n* [ML, fr. L, fem. of *quinquagesimus* fiftieth, fr. *quinquaginta* fifty, fr. *quinque* + *-ginta* (akin to *viginti* twenty) — more at VIGESIMAL] **:** the Sunday before Lent

quinque- *or* **quinqu-** *comb form* [L, fr. *quinque* — more at FIVE] **:** five ⟨*quinque*foliolate⟩

quin·que·fo·li·o·late \ˌkwiŋ-kwi-'fō-lē-ə-ˌlāt\ *adj* **:** having five leaflets

quin·quen·ni·al \kwin-'kwen-ē-əl, kwiŋ-\ *adj* **1 :** consisting of or lasting for five years **2 :** occurring or being done every five years — **quinquennial** *n* — **quin·quen·ni·al·ly** \-ē-ə-lē\ *adv*

quin·quen·ni·um \-ē-əm\ *n, pl* **quinquenniums** *or* **quin·quen·nia** \-ē-ə\ [L, fr. *quinque-* + *annus* year — more at ANNUAL] **:** a period of five years

quin·que·va·lent *also* **quin·qui·va·lent** \ˌkwiŋ-kwi-'vā-lənt\ *adj* **:** PENTAVALENT

quin·sy \'kwin-zē\ *n* [ME *quinesie*, fr. MF *quinancie*, fr. LL *cynanche*, fr. Gk *kynanchē*, fr. *kyn-, kyōn* dog + *anchein* to strangle — more at HOUND, ANGER] **:** a severe inflammation of the throat or adjacent parts with swelling and fever

1quint \'kint, 'kwint\ *n* [F *quinte*, fr. fem. of *quint* fifth, fr. L *quintus* — more at QUINTUPLE] **:** a sequence of five playing cards of the same suit

2quint \'kwint\ *n* **:** QUINTUPLET

quin·tain \'kwint-ᵊn\ *n* [ME *quintaine*, fr. MF, fr. L *quintana* street in a Roman camp separating the fifth maniple from the sixth where military exercises were performed, fr. fem. of *quintanus* fifth in rank, fr. *quintus* fifth] **:** an object to be tilted at; *esp* **:** a post with a crosspiece supporting a target

quin·tal \'kwint-ᵊl\ *n* [ME, fr. MF, fr. ML *quintale*, fr. Ar *qinṭār*, fr. LGk *kentēnarion*, fr. LL *centenarium*, fr. L, neut. of *centenarius* consisting of a hundred — more at CENTENARY] **1 :** HUNDREDWEIGHT **2** — see METRIC SYSTEM table

quinte \'kant\ *n* [F, fr. fem. of *quint*] **:** the fifth of the eight defensive positions in fencing

quin·tes·sence \kwin-'tes-ᵊn(t)s\ *n* [ME, fr. MF *quinte essence*, fr. ML *quinta essentia*, lit., fifth essence] **1 :** the fifth and highest essence in ancient and medieval philosophy that permeates all nature and is the substance composing the heavenly bodies **2 :** the essence of a thing in its purest and most concentrated form **3 :** the most typical example or representative — **quint·es·sen·tial** \ˌkwint-ə-'sen-chəl\ *adj*

quin·tet *also* **quin·tette** \kwin-'tet\ *n* [*quintet* fr. It *quintetto*, fr. *quinto* fifth, fr. L *quintus*; *quintette* fr. F, fr. It *quintetto*] **1 :** a musical composition or movement for five instruments or voices **2 :** a group or set of five: as **a :** the musicians that perform a quintet **b :** a male basketball team

quin·tile \'kwin-ˌtīl, 'kwint-ᵊl\ *n* [L *quintus* fifth] *archaic* **:** the aspect of planets when separated a fifth part of a circle or 72 degrees

quin·til·lion \kwin-'til-yən\ *n* [L *quint*us + E *-illion* (as in *million*)] — see NUMBER table — **quintillion** *adj* — **quin·til·lionth** \-yən(t)th\ *adj* — **quintillionth** *n, pl* **quin·til·lionths** \-yən(t)s, -yən(t)ths\

1quin·tu·ple \kwin-'t(y)üp-əl, -'təp-; 'kwint-əp-\ *adj* [MF, fr. LL *quintuplex*, fr. L *quintus* fifth + *-plex* -fold; akin to L *quinque* five — more at FIVE, SIMPLE] **1 :** having five units or members **2 :** being five times as great or as many **3 :** marked by five beats per measure ⟨~ meter⟩ — **quintuple** *n*

2quintuple *vb* **quin·tu·pling** \-(ə-)liŋ\ *vt* **:** to make five times as great or as many ~ *vi* **:** to become five times as much or as numerous

quin·tu·plet \kwin-'təp-lət, -'t(y)üp-; 'kwint-əp-\ *n* **1 :** a combination of five of a kind **2 a :** one of five children or offspring born at one birth **b** *pl* **:** a group of five such offspring

1quin·tu·pli·cate \kwin-'t(y)ü-pli-kət\ *adj* [L *quintuplicatus*, pp. of *quintuplicare* to quintuple, fr. *quintuplic-, quintuplex* quintuple] **1 :** repeated five times **2 :** FIFTH ⟨the ~ copy⟩ — **quintuplicate** *n*

2quin·tu·pli·cate \-plə-ˌkāt\ *vt* **1 :** QUINTUPLE **2 :** to provide in quintuplicate

1quip \'kwip\ *n* [earlier *quippy*, perh. fr. L *quippe* indeed, to be sure (often ironical), fr. *quid* what — more at QUIDDITY] **1 a :** a clever usu. taunting remark **:** GIBE **b :** a witty or funny observation or response usu. made on the spur of the moment **2 :** QUIBBLE, EQUIVOCATION **3 :** something strange, droll, curious, or eccentric **:** ODDITY **syn** see JEST — **quip·ster** \-stər\ *n*

2quip *vb* **quipped; quip·ping** *vi* **:** to make quips **:** SCOFF, GIBE ~ *vt* **:** to jest or gibe at

qui·pu \'kē-(ˌ)pü\ *n* [Sp *quipo*, fr. Quechua *quipu*] **:** a device made of a main cord with smaller varicolored cords attached and knotted and used by the ancient Peruvians for calculating and record keeping

1quire \'kwī(ə)r\ *n* [ME *quair* four sheets of paper folded once, collection of sheets, fr. MF *quaer*, fr. (assumed) VL *quadernum*, alter. of L *quaterni* four each, set of four — more at QUATERNION] **:** a collection of 24 or sometimes 25 sheets of paper of the same size and quality **:** $\frac{1}{20}$ ream

2quire *var of* CHOIR

1quirk \'kwərk\ *n* [origin unknown] **1 a :** an abrupt twist or

curve   **b** : a peculiar trait : IDIOSYNCRASY   **c** : ACCIDENT, VAGARY   **2** : a groove separating a bead or other molding from adjoining members — **quirk·i·ly** \ˈkwər-kə-lē\ adv — **quirk·i·ness** \-kē-nəs\ n — **quirky** \-kē\ adj

²**quirk** vt : to give a quirk to ~ vi : to make or exhibit a quirk

¹**quirt** \ˈkwərt\ n [MexSp cuarta] : a riding whip with a short handle and a rawhide lash

²**quirt** vt : to strike or drive with a quirt

quis·ling \ˈkwiz-liŋ\ n [Vidkun Quisling †1945 Norw politician] : a traitor who collaborates with the invaders of his country esp. by serving in a puppet government — **quis·ling·ism** \-liŋ-ˌiz-əm\ n

¹**quit** \ˈkwit\ adj [ME quite, quit, fr. OF quite] : released from obligation, cnarge, or penalty : ABSOLVED; esp : FREE ⟨~ of unnecessary fears⟩

²**quit** vb **quit** also **quit·ted; quit·ting** [ME quiten, quitten, fr. MF quiter, quitter, fr. OF, fr. quite free of, released, lit., at rest, fr. L quietus quiet, at rest] vt **1** : to set free : RELIEVE, RELEASE ⟨~ oneself of fear⟩ **2** : to make full payment of : pay up ⟨~ a debt⟩ **3** : CONDUCT, ACQUIT ⟨the youths ~ themselves like men⟩ **4 a** : to depart from or out of   **b** : to leave the company of   **c** : to relinquish, abandon, or give over (as a way of thought, acting, or living) : FORSAKE   **d** : to give up (an action, activity, or employment) : LEAVE ⟨~ a job⟩ ~ vi **1** : to cease normal, expected, or necessary action   **2** : to give up employment   **3** : to give up : admit defeat **syn** see GO, STOP

³**quit** n : the act of quitting

quitch \ˈkwich\ n [(assumed) ME quicche, fr. OE cwice; akin to OHG quecca couch grass, OE cwic living — more at QUICK] : a couch grass (Agropyron repens)

quit·claim \ˈkwit-ˌklām\ vt : to release or relinquish a legal claim to; esp : to release a claim to or convey by a quitclaim deed — **quitclaim** n

quitclaim deed n : a legal instrument used to release one person's right, title, or interest to another without providing a guarantee or warranty of title

quite \ˈkwīt\ adv [ME, fr. quite, adj., quit] **1** : COMPLETELY, WHOLLY ⟨not ~ all⟩ **2** : to an extreme : POSITIVELY ⟨~ sure⟩ **3** : to a considerable extent : RATHER ⟨~ near⟩

quit·rent \ˈkwit-ˌrent\ n : a fixed rent payable to a feudal superior in commutation of services; specif : a fixed rent due from a socage tenant

quits \ˈkwits\ adj [ME, var. prob. fr. ML quittus, alter. of L quietus at rest] : on even terms by repayment or requital

quit·tance \ˈkwit-ᵊn(t)s\ n **1 a** : discharge from a debt or an obligation   **b** : a document evidencing quittance   **2** : RECOMPENSE, REQUITAL

quit·ter \ˈkwit-ər\ n : one that gives up too easily; esp : DEFEATIST

quit·tor \ˈkwit-ər\ n [ME quiture pus, prob. fr. OF, act of boiling, fr. L coctura, fr. coctus, pp. of coquere to cook — more at COOK] : a purulent inflammation of the feet esp. of horses and asses affecting chiefly the cartilage

¹**quiv·er** \ˈkwiv-ər\ n [ME, fr. OF quivre, of Gmc origin; akin to OE cocer quiver, OHG kohhari] **1** : a case for carrying arrows   **2** : the arrows in a quiver

²**quiver** vi **quiv·er·ing** \-(ə-)riŋ\ : to come to rest — used of an arrow

³**quiver** vb **quiv·er·ing** \-(ə-)riŋ\ [ME quiveren, prob. fr. quiver agile, quick, fr. (assumed) OE cwifer] : to shake or move with a slight trembling motion

⁴**quiver** n : the act or action of quivering : TREMOR

qui vive \kē-ˈvēv\ n [F qui-vive, fr. qui vive? long live who ?, challenge of a French sentry] **1** : CHALLENGE   **2** : ALERT, LOOKOUT — used in the phrase on the qui vive

qui·xote \ˈkwik-sət, kē-ˈ(h)ōt-ē\ n, often cap [Don Quixote] : a quixotic person — **quix·o·tism** \ˈkwik-sə-ˌtiz-əm\ n — **quix·o·try** \-sə-trē\ n

quix·ot·ic \kwik-ˈsät-ik\ adj [Don Quixote, hero of the novel Don Quixote de la Mancha (1605, 1615) by Cervantes] : idealistic to an impractical degree; esp : marked by rash lofty romantic ideas or extravagantly chivalrous action **syn** see IMAGINARY — **quix·ot·i·cal** \-i-kəl\ adj — **quix·ot·i·cal·ly** \-k(ə-)lē\ adv

¹**quiz** \ˈkwiz\ n, pl **quiz·zes** [origin unknown] **1** : an eccentric person   **2** : a practical joke   **3** : the act or action of quizzing; specif : a short oral or written test

²**quiz** vt **quizzed; quiz·zing 1** : to make fun of : MOCK   **2** : to look at inquisitively   **3** : to question closely : EXAMINE — **quiz·zer** n

quiz·zi·cal \ˈkwiz-i-kəl\ adj **1** : slightly eccentric : ODD   **2** : BANTERING, TEASING   **3** : QUESTIONING, INQUISITIVE — **quiz·zi·cal·i·ty** \ˌkwiz-ə-ˈkal-ət-ē\ n — **quiz·zi·cal·ly** \ˈkwiz-i-k(ə-)lē\ adv

quod \ˈkwäd\ n [origin unknown] slang Brit : PRISON

quirt

quod·li·bet \ˈkwäd-lə-ˌbet\ n [ME, subtle theological question proposed as an exercise for argument, fr. ML quodlibetum, fr. L quodlibet, neut. of quilibet any whatever, fr. qui who, what + libet it pleases, fr. libēre to please — more at WHO, LOVE] : a whimsical combination of familiar melodies or texts

quo·hog var of QUAHOG

¹**quoin** \ˈk(w)oin\ n [alter. of ¹coin] **1 a** : a solid exterior angle (as of a building)   **b** : one of the blocks forming it   **2** : the keystone or a voussoir of an arch   **3** : a wooden or expandable metal block used by printers to lock up a form within a chase

²**quoin** vt **1** : to equip (a type form) with quoins   **2** : to provide with quoins ⟨~ed walls⟩

¹**quoit** \ˈkwät, ˈk(w)oit\ n [ME coite] **1** : a flattened ring of iron or circle of rope used in a throwing game   **2** pl but sing in constr : a game played with quoits

²**quoit** vt : to throw like a quoit

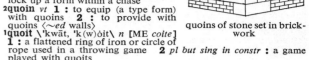

quoins of stone set in brick-work

quon·dam \ˈkwän-dəm, -ˌdam\ adj [L, at one time, formerly, fr. quom, cum when; akin to L qui who — more at WHO, SOMETIME ⟨a ~ friend⟩ : FORMER,

Quon·set \ˌkwän(t)-sət, ˌkwän-zət\ trademark — used for a prefabricated shelter set on a foundation of bolted steel trusses and built of a semicircular arching roof of corrugated metal insulated with wood fiber

quo·rum \ˈkwōr-əm, ˈkwȯr-\ n [ME, quorum of justices of the peace, fr. L, of whom, gen. pl. of qui who; fr. the wording of the commission formerly issued to justices of the peace] **1** : the number usu. a majority of officers or members of a body that when duly assembled is legally competent to transact business   **2** : a select group   **3** : a Mormon body comprising those in the same grade of priesthood

quo·ta \ˈkwōt-ə\ n [ML, fr. L quota pars how great a part] **1** : a proportional part or share; esp : the share or proportion assigned to each in a division or to each member of a body   **2** : the number or amount constituting a proportional share

quot·able \ˈkwōt-ə-bəl\ adj : fit for or worth quoting

quo·ta·tion \kwō-ˈtā-shən also kō-\ n **1** : something that is quoted; esp : a passage referred to, repeated, or adduced   **2 a** : the act or process of quoting   **b** : the naming or publishing of current bids and offers or prices of securities or commodities; also : the bids, offers, or prices so named or published

quotation mark n : one of a pair of punctuation marks " " or " " or ' ' or ' ' used chiefly to indicate the beginning and the end of a quotation in which the exact phraseology of another or of a text is directly cited

¹**quote** \ˈkwōt also ˈkōt\ vb [ME quotare to mark the number of, number references, fr. L quotus of what number or quantity, fr. quot how many, (as) many as; akin to L qui who — more at WHO] vt **1 a** : to speak or write (a passage) from another usu. with credit acknowledgment   **b** : to repeat a passage from esp. in substantiation or illustration   **2** : to cite in illustration ⟨~ cases⟩ **3 a** : to name (the current price) of a commodity, stock, or bond   **b** : to give exact information on   **4** : to set off by quotation marks ~ vi : to inform a hearer or reader that matter following is quoted

²**quote** n **1** : QUOTATION   **2** : QUOTATION MARK

quoth \ˈkwōth\ vb past [ME, past of quethen to say, fr. OE cwethan; akin to OHG quedan to say] archaic : SAID — used chiefly in the first and third persons with a postpositive subject

quotha \ˈkwō-thə\ interj [alter. of quoth he] archaic — used esp. to express surprise or contempt

quo·tid·i·an \kwō-ˈtid-ē-ən\ adj [ME cotidian, fr. MF, fr. L quotidi-anus, cotidianus, fr. quotidie every day, fr. quot (as) many as + dies day — more at DEITY] **1** : occurring every day ⟨~ fever⟩ **2** : COMMONPLACE, ORDINARY **syn** see DAILY

quo·tient \ˈkwō-shənt\ n [ME quocient, modif. of L quotiens how many times, fr. quot how many] **1** : the number resulting from the division of one number by another   **2** : the numerical ratio usu. multiplied by 100 between a test score and a measurement on which that score might be expected largely to depend ⟨intelligence ~⟩ ⟨accomplishment ~⟩ **3** : QUOTA, SHARE

quo war·ran·to \ˌkwō-wə-ˈränt-(ˌ)ō, -ˈrant-; (ˈ)kwō-ˈwȯr-ənt-ˌō, -ˈwär-\ n [ML, by what warrant; fr. the wording of the writ] **1 a** : an English writ formerly requiring a person to show by what authority he exercises a public office, franchise, or liberty   **b** : a legal proceeding for a like purpose begun by an information   **2** : the legal action begun by a quo warranto

Qur·'an or **Qur·an** \kə-ˈran, -ˈrän; kù-(ə)r-ˈan, -ˈän\ var of KORAN

qursh \ˈkù-(ə)rsh\ or **qu·rush** \ˈkùr-əsh\ n [Ar qirsh] — see riyal at MONEY table

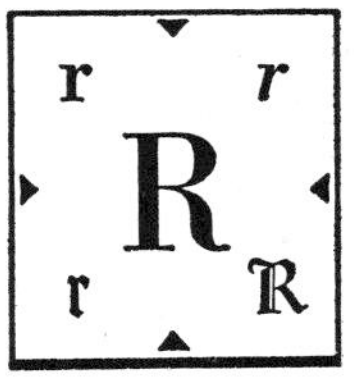

r \'är\ *n, often cap, often attrib* **1 a :** the 18th letter of the English alphabet **b :** a graphic representation of this letter **c :** a speech counterpart of orthographic *r* **2 :** a graphic device for reproducing the letter *r* **3 :** one designated *r* esp. as the 17th or when j is used for the 10th the 18th in order or class **4 :** something shaped like the letter R
Ra \'rä\ *n* [Egypt *rʿ*] **:** the great god of the sun and the chief deity of historical Egypt
ra·ba·to \rə-'bät-(,)ō\ *n* [modif. of MF *rabat,* lit., act of turning down] **:** a wide lace-edged collar of the early 17th century often stiffened to stand high at the back
1**rab·bet** \'rab-ət\ *n* [ME *rabet,* fr. MF *rabat* act of beating down, fr. OF *rabattre* to beat down, reduce — more at REBATE] **:** a channel, groove, or recess cut out of the edge or face of any body; *esp* **:** one intended to receive another member (as a panel)
2**rabbet** *vt* **1 :** to cut a rabbet in **2 :** to unite the edges of in a rabbet joint ~ *vi* **:** to become joined by a rabbet
rabbet joint *n* **:** a joint formed by fitting together rabbeted boards or timbers
rab·bi \'rab-,ī\ *n* [LL, fr. Gk *rhabbi,* fr. Heb *rabbī* my master, fr. *rabh* master + *-ī* my] **1 :** MASTER, TEACHER — used by Jews as a term of address **2 a :** a Jew qualified to expound and apply the halakah and other Jewish law **b** *often cap* **:** one of the scholars who developed the Talmudic basis of orthodox Judaism during the first centuries of the Christian era **3 :** a Jew trained and ordained for professional religious leadership; *specif* **:** the official leader of a Jewish congregation
rab·bin \'rab-ən\ *n* [F] **:** RABBI
rab·bin·ate \'rab-ə-nət, -,nāt\ *n* **1 :** the office or tenure of a rabbi **2 :** a group of rabbis
rab·bin·ic \rə-'bin-ik, ra-\ *adj* **1 :** of or relating to rabbis or their writings **2 :** of or preparing for the rabbinate **3 :** comprising or belonging to any of several sets of Hebrew characters simpler than the square Hebrew letters — **rab·bin·i·cal** \-i-kəl\ *adj* — **rab·bin·i·cal·ly** \-k(ə-)lē\ *adv*
Rabbinic Hebrew *n* **:** the Hebrew used esp. by medieval rabbis
rab·bin·ism \'rab-ə-,niz-əm\ *n* **:** rabbinic teachings and traditions
1**rab·bit** \'rab-ət\ *n, pl* **rabbit** *or* **rabbits** *often attrib* [ME *rabet*] **1 a :** a small long-eared mammal (*Oryctolagus cuniculus*) of the hare family that differs from ordinary hares in producing naked young and in its burrowing habits **b :** HARE **2 :** the pelt of a rabbit **3 :** WELSH RABBIT — **rab·bity** \-ē\ *adj*
2**rabbit** *vi* **:** to hunt rabbits — **rab·bit·er** *n*
rab·bit-eye \-,ī\ *n* **:** a blueberry (*Vaccinium ashei*) of the southeastern U.S.
rabbit fever *n* **:** TULAREMIA
rabbit punch *n* **:** a short chopping blow delivered to the back of the neck or the base of the skull
rab·bit·ry \'rab-ə-trē\ *n* **:** a place where domestic rabbits are kept; *also* **:** a rabbit-raising enterprise
1**rab·ble** \'rab-əl\ *n* [ME *rabel*] **1 :** a pack or swarm of animals or insects **2 :** a disorganized or confused collection of things **3 a :** a disorganized or disorderly crowd of people **:** MOB **b :** the lowest class of people
2**rabble** *vt* **rab·bling** \-(ə-)liŋ\ **:** to insult or assault by a mob
3**rabble** *n* [F *râble* fire shovel, fr. ML *rotabulum,* alter. of L *rutabulum,* fr. *rutus,* pp. of *ruere* to dig up — more at RUG] **:** an iron bar with the end bent for use like a rake in puddling iron; *also* **:** a similar device used in a melting, refining, or roasting furnace
4**rabble** *vt* **rab·bling** \-(ə-)liŋ\ **:** to stir or skim with a rabble — **rab·bler** \'rab-(ə-)lər\ *n*
rab·ble·ment \'rab-əl-mənt\ *n* **1 :** RABBLE **2 :** DISTURBANCE
rab·ble–rous·er \'rab-əl-,rau̇-zər\ *n* **:** one that stirs up (as to hatred or violence) the masses of the people **:** DEMAGOGUE
Ra·be·lai·sian \,rab-ə-'lā-zhən, -zē-ən\ *adj* **1 :** of, relating to, or characteristic of Rabelais or his works **2 :** marked by or manifesting gross robust humor, extravagance of caricature, or bold naturalism
Ra·bi \'rəb-ē\ *n* [Ar *rabīʿ*] **:** either of two months of the Muhammadan year: **a :** the 3d month **b :** the 4th month
ra·bic \'rā-bik\ *adj* **:** of or relating to rabies
ra·bid \'rab-əd *also* 'rā-bəd\ *adj* [L *rabidus* mad, fr. *rabere*] **1 a :** extremely violent **:** FURIOUS **b :** going to extreme lengths in expressing or pursuing a feeling, interest, or opinion **2 :** affected with rabies — **ra·bid·i·ty** \rə-'bid-ət-ē, ra-, rā-\ *n* — **ra·bid·ly** \'rab-əd-lē *also* 'rā-bəd-\ *adv* — **ra·bid·ness** *n*
ra·bies \'rā-bēz\ *n, pl* **rabies** [NL, fr. L, madness, fr. *rabere* to rave — more at RAGE] **:** an acute virus disease of the nervous system of warm-blooded animals usu. transmitted through the bite of a rabid animal
rac·coon \ra-'kün *also* rə-\ *n, pl* **raccoon** *or* **raccoons** [*ärähkun* (in some Algonquian language of Virginia)] **1 a :** a small flesh-eating mammal (*Procyon lotor*) of No. America that is chiefly gray, has a bushy ringed tail, and lives chiefly in trees **b :** the pelt of this animal **2 :** any of several animals resembling or related to the raccoon
1**race** \'rās\ *n* [ME *ras,* fr. ON *rās;* akin to OE *rǣs* rush, L *rorarii* skirmishers, Gk *erōē* rush] **1** *chiefly Scot* **:** the act of running **2 a :** a strong or rapid current of water through a narrow channel **b :** a heavy or choppy sea **c :** a watercourse used industrially **d :** the current flowing in such a course **3 a :** a set course or duration of time **b :** the course of life **4 a :** a running in competition **b** *pl* **:** a meeting for contests in the running esp. of horses **c :** a contest involving progress toward a goal **5 :** a track or channel in which something rolls or slides; *specif* **:** a groove (as for the balls) in a bearing **6 :** SLIPSTREAM
2**race** *vi* **1 :** to run in a race **2 :** to go or move at top speed or out of control **3 :** to revolve too fast under a diminished load ~ *vt* **1 :** to engage in a race with **2 a :** to enter in a race **b :** to race against **c :** to drive at high speed **d :** to transport or propel at maximum speed **3 :** to speed (as an engine) without a working load or with the transmission disengaged
3**race** *n* [MF, generation, fr. OIt *razza*] **1 :** a breeding stock of animals **2 a :** a family, tribe, people, or nation belonging to the same stock **b :** a class or kind of individuals with common characteristics, interests, or habits **3 :** any of various infraspecific taxonomic groups: as **a :** SUBSPECIES **b :** a permanent or fixed variety **c :** BREED **d :** a division of mankind possessing traits that are transmissible by descent and sufficient to characterize it as a distinct human type **4** *obs* **:** inherited temperament or disposition **5 :** distinctive flavor, taste, or strength
race·course \'rā-,skō(ə)rs, -,skȯ(ə)rs\ *n* **1 :** a course for racing; *esp* **:** a turf course for steeplechase or cross-country racing **2 :** RACEWAY 1
race·horse \'rās-,hȯ(ə)rs\ *n* **:** a horse bred or kept for racing
ra·ce·mate \rā-'sē-,māt, rə-; 'ras-ə-\ *n* **1 :** a salt or ester of racemic acid **2 :** a racemic compound or mixture
ra·ceme \rā-'sēm, rə-\ *n* [L *racemus* bunch of grapes] **:** a simple inflorescence in which the elongated axis bears flowers on short stems in succession toward the apex
ra·ce·mic \-'sē-mik\ *adj* **1 :** relating to or derived from racemic acid **2 :** of, relating to, or constituting a compound or mixture that is composed of equal amounts of dextrorotatory and levorotatory forms of the same compound and is optically inactive
racemic acid *n* **:** optically inactive tartaric acid that consists of equal parts of *dextro-* and *levo-*tartaric acids and is often found with *dextro-*tartaric acid in the juice of grapes
ra·ce·mi·form \-'sē-mə-,fȯrm\ *adj* [ISV] **:** having the form of a raceme
ra·ce·mi·za·tion \rā-,sē-mə-'zā-shən, rə-; ,ras-ə-mə-\ *n* **:** the action or process of changing from an optically active compound into a racemic compound or mixture — **ra·ce·mize** \rā-'sē-,mīz, rə-; 'ras-ə-\ *vb*
ra·ce·mose \'ras-ə-,mōs; rā-'sē-, rə-\ *adj* [L *racemosus* full of clusters, fr. *racemus*] **:** having or growing in the form of a raceme
racemose gland *n* **:** a compound gland of freely branching ducts that end in acini
rac·er \'rā-sər\ *n* **1 :** one that races **2 :** any of various active American snakes (genera *Coluber* and *Mastigophis*)
race riot *n* **:** a riot caused by racial dissensions or hatreds
race runner *n* **:** a No. American lizard (*Cnemidophorus sexlineatus*) that moves swiftly
race·track \'rā-,strak\ *n* **:** a usu. oval course on which races are run
race·way \'rā-,swā\ *n* **1 :** a canal for a current of water **2 :** a channel for loosely holding electrical wires in buildings **3 :** 1RACE 5 **4 :** a track for harness racing
rach·et \'rach-ət\ *var of* RATCHET
rachi- *or* **rachio-** *comb form* [Gk *rhachi-,* fr. *rhachis;* akin to Gk *rhachos* thorn, Lith *ražas* stubble] **:** spine ⟨*rachio*dont⟩
ra·chi·odont \'rā-kē-ō-,dänt, 'rak-ē-\ *adj* **:** having gular teeth that are modified vertebral spines ⟨~ snake⟩
ra·chis \'rā-kəs, 'rak-əs\ *n, pl* **ra·chis·es** *also* **ra·chi·des** \'rak-ə-,dēz, 'rā-kə-\ [NL *rachid-, rachis,* modif. of Gk *rhachis*] **1 :** SPINAL COLUMN **2 :** an axial structure: as **a** (1) **:** the elongated axis of an inflorescence (2) **:** an extension of the petiole of a compound leaf that bears the leaflets **b :** the distal part of the shaft of a feather that bears the web
ra·chit·ic \rə-'kit-ik\ *adj* **1 :** RICKETY 1 **2 :** suggesting the condition of one affected with rickets
ra·chi·tis \rə-'kīt-əs\ *n* [NL, fr. Gk *rhachitis* disease of the spine, fr. *rhachis*] **:** RICKETS
ra·cial \'rā-shəl\ *adj* **1 :** of, relating to, or based on a race **2 :** existing or occurring between races — **ra·cial·ly** \-shə-lē\ *adv*
ra·cial·ism \'rā-shə-,liz-əm\ *n* **1 :** racial prejudice or discrimination **2 :** RACISM 1 — **ra·cial·ist** \-ləst\ *n* — **ra·cial·is·tic** \,rā-shə-'lis-tik\ *adj*
rac·i·ly \'rā-sə-lē\ *adv* **:** in a racy manner
rac·i·ness \-sē-nəs\ *n* **:** the quality or state of being racy
rac·ing *n* **1 :** the sport or profession of engaging in or holding races **2 :** horse races that are a sport or business
racing form *n* **:** an information sheet giving pertinent data about horse races
rac·ism \'rā-,siz-əm\ *n* **1 :** a belief that race is the primary determinant of human traits and capacities and that racial differences produce an inherent superiority of a particular race **2 :** RACIALISM 1 — **rac·ist** \-səst\ *n*
1**rack** \'rak\ *n* [ME *rak,* prob. of Scand origin; akin to Sw dial. *rak* wreck; akin to OE *wrecan* to drive — more at WREAK] **:** a wind-driven mass of high often broken clouds
2**rack** *vi* **:** to fly or scud in high wind
3**rack** *n* [ME, prob. fr. MD *rec* framework; akin to OE *reccan* to stretch, Gk *oregein* — more at RIGHT] **1 :** a framework for holding fodder for livestock **2 :** an instrument of torture on which a body is stretched **3 a** (1) **:** a cause of anguish or pain (2) **:** acute suffering **b :** STRAINING, WRENCHING **4 :** a framework, stand, or grating on or in which articles are placed **5 :** a frame placed in a stream to stop fish and floating or suspended matter **6 a :** a bar with teeth on one face for gearing with a pinion or worm gear **b :** a notched bar used as a ratchet to engage with a pawl, click, or detent **7 :** a triangular frame used to set up the balls in a pool game; *also* **:** the balls as set up — **on the rack :** under great mental or emotional stress

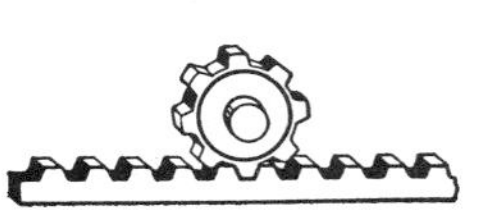

rack 6 with pinion

4**rack** *vt* **1 :** to torture on the rack **2 :** to cause to suffer torture, pain, or anguish **3 a :** to stretch or strain violently ⟨~*ed* his brains⟩ **b :** to raise (rents) oppressively **c :** to harass or oppress with high rents or extortions **4 :** to work or treat (material) on a rack **5 :** to seize (as parallel ropes of a tackle) together **6 :** to place (as pool balls) in a rack ~ *vi* **:** to become forced out of shape or out of plumb **syn** see AFFLICT — **rack·er** *n*
5**rack** *vt* [ME *rakken,* fr. OProv *arraca*] **:** to draw off (as wine) from the lees
6**rack** *vi* [prob. alter. of 1*rock*] *of a horse* **:** to go at a rack
7**rack** *n* **:** either of two gaits of a horse: **a :** PACE 4b **b :** a fast showy usu. artificial 4-beat gait
8**rack** *n* [perh. fr. 3*rack*] **1 :** the neck and spine of a forequarter of veal, pork, or esp. mutton **2 :** the rib section of a forequarter
9**rack** *n* [alter. of *wrack*] **:** DESTRUCTION ⟨~ and ruin⟩
1**rack·et** *also* **rac·quet** \'rak-ət\ *n* [MF *raquette,* fr. Ar *rāḥah* palm of the hand] **1 a :** a light bat that consists of a netting (as of nylon) stretched in an oval open frame and that is used for striking the ball in tennis and similar games **b :** a small round paddle with a short handle used in table tennis **2 :** *usu* **racquets** *pl but sing in constr* **:** a game for two or four played with ball and racket on a four-walled court

2racket *n* [prob. imit.] 1 : confused clattering noise : CLAMOR 2 a : social whirl or excitement b : the strain of exciting or trying experiences 3 a : a fraudulent scheme, enterprise, or activity b : a usu. illegitimate enterprise made workable by bribery or intimidation c : an easy and lucrative means of livelihood d *slang* : OCCUPATION, BUSINESS

3racket *vi* 1 : to engage in active social life 2 : to move with or make a racket

1rack·e·teer \ˌrak-ə-'ti(ə)r\ *n* : one who extorts money or advantages by threats of violence, by blackmail, or by unlawful interference with business or employment

2racketeer *vi* : to carry on a racket ~ *vt* : to practice extortion on

rack·ety \'rak-ət-ē\ *adj* 1 : NOISY 2 : FLASHY, ROWDY 3 : RICKETY

rack·le \'rak-əl\ *adj* [ME *rakel*] *chiefly Scot* : IMPETUOUS, HEADSTRONG

rack railway *n* : a railway having between its rails a rack that meshes with a gear wheel or pinion of the locomotive for traction on steep grades

rack rent *n* [4*rack*] : an excessive or unreasonably high rent; *esp* : one equal or nearly equal to the full annual value of the property

rack–rent \'rak-'rent\ *vt* : to subject to rack rent

rack–rent·er \-'rent-ər\ *n* : one that pays or exacts rack rent

rack up *vt* : SCORE ⟨*racked* 30 points *up* in the first half⟩

ra·con \'rā-ˌkän\ *n* [*ra*dar bea*con*] : RADAR BEACON

ra·con·teur \ˌrak-ˌän-'tər, -ən-\ *n* [F, fr. MF, fr. *raconter* to tell, fr. OF, fr. *re-* + *aconter, acompter* to tell, count — more at ACCOUNT] : one who excels in telling anecdotes

ra·coon *var of* RACCOON

1racy \'rā-sē\ *adj* [3*race*] 1 : having the distinctive quality of something in its original or most characteristic form 2 a : full of zest or vigor b : PIQUANT, PUNGENT c : RISQUÉ, SUGGESTIVE **syn** see PUNGENT

2racy *adj* : having a build fitted for racing : long-bodied and lean

ra·dar \'rā-ˌdär\ *n* [*ra*dio *d*etecting *a*nd *r*anging] : a radio device or system for locating an object by means of ultrahigh-frequency radio waves reflected from the object and received, observed, and analyzed by the receiving part of the device in such a way that characteristics (as distance and direction) of the object may be determined — ra·dar·man \-mən, -ˌman\ *n*

radar beacon *n* : a radar transmitter that upon receiving a radar signal emits a signal which reinforces the normal reflected signal or which introduces a code into the reflected signal esp. for identification purposes

ra·dar·scope \'rā-ˌdär-ˌskōp\ *n* [*radar* + oscillo*scope*] : the oscilloscope or screen serving as the visual indicator in a radar receiver

1rad·dle \'rad-əl\ *n* [prob. alter. of *ruddle*] : RED OCHER

2raddle *vt* rad·dling \'rad-liŋ, -əl-iŋ\ : to mark or paint with raddle

3raddle *vt* [E dial. *raddle* (supple stick interwoven with others as in making a fence)] : to twist together : INTERWEAVE

rad·dled \'rad-əld\ *adj* [origin unknown] 1 : CONFUSED, BEFUDDLED 2 : broken down : WORN

1ra·di·al \'rād-ē-əl\ *adj* [ML *radialis*, fr. L *radius* ray] 1 : arranged or having parts arranged like rays 2 a : relating to, placed like, or moving along a radius b : characterized by divergence from a center 3 : of, relating to, or adjacent to a bodily radius 4 : developing uniformly around a central axis — ra·di·al·ly \-ē-ə-lē\ *adv*

2radial *n* 1 a : a radial part b : RAY 2 : a body part lying near or following the course of the radius

ra·di·a·le \ˌrād-ē-'al-(ˌ)ē, -'āl-, -'äl-\ *n, pl* ra·di·a·lia \-ē-ə\ [NL, fr. ML, neut. of *radialis*] : a bone or cartilage of the carpus that articulates with the radius; *specif* : the navicular in man

radial engine *n* : a usu. internal-combustion engine with cylinders arranged radially like the spokes of a wheel

ra·di·an \'rād-ē-ən\ *n* : a unit of plane angular measurement equal to the angle at the center of a circle subtended by an arc equal in length to the radius

ra·di·ance \'rād-ē-ən(t)s\ *also* ra·di·an·cy \-ən-sē\ *n* 1 : the quality or state of being radiant : SPLENDOR 2 : a deep pink

1ra·di·ant \'rād-ē-ənt\ *adj* 1 a : radiating rays or reflecting beams of light b : vividly bright and shining : GLOWING 2 : marked by or expressive of love, confidence, or happiness 3 a : emitted or transmitted by radiation b : emitting or relating to radiant heat 4 : of, relating to, or exhibiting biological radiation **syn** see BRIGHT — ra·di·ant·ly *adv*

2radiant *n* : something that radiates: as a : a point in the heavens at which the visible parallel paths of meteors appear to meet when traced backward b : a point or object from which light emanates c : the part of a gas or electric heater that becomes incandescent

radiant energy *n* : energy traveling as a wave motion; *specif* : the energy of electromagnetic waves

radiant flux *n* : the rate of emission or transmission of radiant energy

radiant heating *n* : PANEL HEATING

1ra·di·ate \'rād-ē-ˌāt\ *vb* [L *radiatus*, pp. of *radiare*, fr. *radius* ray] *vi* 1 : to send out rays : shine brightly 2 : to issue in rays 3 : to proceed in a direct line from or toward a center ~ *vt* 1 : to send out in rays 2 : IRRADIATE, ILLUMINATE 3 : to spread abroad or around as if from a center

2ra·di·ate \-ē-ət, -ē-ˌāt\ *adj* : having rays or radial parts: as a : having ray flowers b : characterized by radial symmetry — ra·di·ate·ly *adv*

ra·di·a·tion \ˌrād-ē-'ā-shən\ *n* 1 a : the action or process of radiating b (1) : the process of emitting radiant energy in the form of waves or particles (2) : the combined processes of emission, transmission, and absorption of radiant energy 2 a : something that is radiated b : energy radiated in the form of waves or particles 3 : radial arrangement 4 : RADIATOR — ra·di·a·tion·al \-shnəl, -shən-əl\ *adj* — ra·di·a·tive \'rād-ē-ˌāt-iv\ *adj*

ra·di·a·tor \'rād-ē-ˌāt-ər\ *n* : one that radiates: as a : any of various devices (as a nest of pipes or tubes) for heating external objects or cooling internal substances b : a transmitting antenna

1rad·i·cal \'rad-i-kəl\ *adj* [ME, fr. LL *radicalis*, fr. L *radic-, radix* root — more at ROOT] 1 : of, relating to, or proceeding from a root 2 : of or relating to the origin : FUNDAMENTAL 3 a : marked by a considerable departure from the usual or traditional : EXTREME b : tending or disposed to make extreme changes in existing views, habits, conditions, or institutions c : of, relating to, or constituting a political group associated with views, practices, and policies of extreme change — rad·i·cal·ness *n*

2radical *n* 1 a : a root part b : basic principle : FOUNDATION 2 a : ROOT 6 b : a sound or letter belonging to a radical 3 : one who is radical 4 a : a single replaceable atom or the reactive atomic form of an element b : a group of atoms that is replaceable by a single atom, that is capable of remaining unchanged during a series of reactions, or that may show a definite transitory existence in the course of a reaction 5a : RADICAL EXPRESSION b : RADICAL SIGN

radical expression *n* : a mathematical expression involving radical signs

rad·i·cal·ism \'rad-i-kə-ˌliz-əm\ *n* 1 : the quality or state of being radical 2 : the doctrines or principles of radicals

rad·i·cal·ly \-k(ə-)lē\ *adv* 1 : in origin or essence 2 : in a radical or extreme manner

radical sign *n* : the sign √ placed before an expression to denote that the square root is to be extracted or that some other root is to be extracted when a corresponding index is placed over the sign

rad·i·cand \ˌrad-ə-'kand\ *n* [L *radicandum*, neut. of *radicandus*, gerundive of *radicari*] : the quantity under a radical sign

rad·i·cate \'rad-ə-ˌkāt\ *vt* [ME *radicaten*, fr. L *radicatus*, pp. of *radicari* to take root, fr. *radic-, radix* root] : to cause to take root

radices *pl of* RADIX

rad·i·cle \'rad-i-kəl\ *n* [L *radicula*, dim. of *radic-, radix*] 1 : the lower part of the axis of a plant embryo or seedling: a : the root portion b : HYPOCOTYL c : the hypocotyl and the root together 2 : the rootlike beginning of an anatomical vessel or part 3 : RADICAL — ra·dic·u·lar \ra-'dik-yə-lər\ *adj*

radii *pl of* RADIUS

1ra·dio \'rād-ē-ˌō\ *n* [short for *radiotelegraphy*] 1 a : the wireless transmission and reception of electric impulses or signals by means of electric waves b : the use of these waves for the wireless transmission of electric impulses into which sound is converted 2 : a radio message 3 : a radio receiving set 4 a : a radio transmitting station b : a radio broadcasting organization c : the radio broadcasting industry d : communication by radio

2radio *adj* 1 : of, relating to, or operated by radiant energy 2 : of or relating to electric currents or phenomena of frequencies between about 15,000 and $(10)^{11}$ per second 3 a : of, relating to, or used in radio or a radio set b : specializing in radio or associated with the radio industry c (1) : transmitted by radio (2) : making or participating in radio broadcasts d : controlled or directed by radio

3radio *vt* 1 : to send or communicate by radio 2 : to send a radio message to ~ *vi* : to send or communicate something by radio

radio- *comb form* [F, fr. L *radius* ray] 1 a : radial : radially ⟨*radio*symmetrical⟩ b : radial and ⟨*radio*bicipital⟩ 2 a : radiant energy : radiation ⟨*radio*active⟩ ⟨*radio*dermatitis⟩ b : radioactive ⟨*radio*element⟩ c : radium : X rays ⟨*radio*therapy⟩ d : radioactive isotopes esp. as produced artificially ⟨*radio*carbon⟩ e : radio ⟨*radio*telegraphy⟩

ra·dio·ac·tive \ˌrād-ē-ō-'ak-tiv\ *adj* [ISV] : of, caused by, or exhibiting radioactivity — ra·dio·ac·tive·ly *adv*

ra·dio·ac·tiv·i·ty \-ˌak-'tiv-ət-ē\ *n* [ISV] : the property possessed by some elements (as uranium) of spontaneously emitting alpha or beta rays and sometimes also gamma rays by the disintegration of the nuclei of atoms

radio astronomy *n* : a branch of astronomy dealing with electromagnetic radiations of radio frequency received from outside the earth's atmosphere

ra·dio·au·to·graph \ˌrād-ē-ō-'ȯt-ə-ˌgraf\ *n* : AUTORADIOGRAPH — ra·dio·au·to·graph·ic \-ˌȯt-ə-'graf-ik\ *adj* — ra·dio·au·tog·ra·phy \-(ˌ)ȯ-'täg-rə-fē\ *n*

radio beacon *n* : a radio transmitting station that transmits special radio signals for use (as on a landing field) in determining the direction or position of those receiving them

ra·dio·bio·log·i·cal \ˌrād-ē-ō-ˌbī-ə-'läj-i-kəl\ *or* ra·dio·bio·log·ic \-'läj-ik\ *adj* : relating to, produced by, or employing radiobiology

ra·dio·bi·ol·o·gy \-(ˌ)bī-'äl-ə-jē\ *n* : a branch of biology dealing with the interaction of biological systems and radiant energy or radioactive materials

ra·dio·broad·cast \-'brȯd-ˌkast\ *vt* : BROADCAST 3 — ra·dio·broad·cast·er *n*

radio car *n* : an automobile equipped with radio communication

ra·dio·car·bon \ˌrād-ē-ō-'kär-bən\ *n* [ISV] : radioactive carbon; *esp* : CARBON 14

ra·dio·cast \'rād-ē-ō-ˌkast\ *vt* [*radio-* + broad*cast*] : BROADCAST 3 — ra·dio·cast·er *n*

ra·dio·chem·i·cal \ˌrād-ē-ō-'kem-i-kəl\ *adj* : of, relating to, or using the methods of radiochemistry

ra·dio·chem·is·try \-'kem-ə-strē\ *n* : a branch of chemistry dealing with radioactive phenomena

radio compass *n* : a direction finder used in navigation

ra·dio·el·e·ment \ˌrād-ē-ō-'el-ə-mənt\ *n* [ISV] : a radioactive element

radio frequency *n* : an electromagnetic wave frequency intermediate between audio frequencies and infrared frequencies used esp. in radio and television transmission

RADIO FREQUENCIES

CLASS	ABBREVIATION	RANGE
very low frequency	vlf	10 to 30 kilocycles
low frequency	lf	30 to 300 kilocycles
medium frequency	mf	300 to 3000 kilocycles
high frequency	hf	3 to 30 megacycles
very high frequency	vhf	30 to 300 megacycles
ultrahigh frequency	uhf	300 to 3000 megacycles
superhigh frequency	shf	3000 to 30,000 megacycles
extremely high frequency	ehf	30,000 to 300,000 megacycles

ra·dio·gen·ic \ˌrād-ē-ō-ˈjen-ik\ *adj* : produced by radioactivity

ra·dio·gram \ˈrād-ē-ō-ˌgram\ *n* **1** : RADIOGRAPH **2** : a message transmitted by radiotelegraphy

[1]**ra·dio·graph** \-ˌgraf\ *n* : a picture produced on a sensitive surface by a form of radiation other than light; *specif* : an X ray or gamma ray photograph — **ra·dio·graph·ic** \ˌrād-ē-ō-ˈgraf-ik\ *adj* — **ra·dio·graph·i·cal·ly** \-i-k(ə-)lē\ *adv*

[2]**radiograph** *vt* : to make a radiograph of

[3]**radiograph** *vt* [*radio-* + tele*graph*] : to send a radiogram to

ra·di·og·ra·phy \ˌrād-ē-ˈäg-rə-fē\ *n* [ISV] : the art, act, or process of making radiographs

ra·dio·iso·tope \ˌrād-ē-ō-ˈī-sə-ˌtōp, -ˈī-zə-\ *n* [ISV] : a radioactive isotope

ra·di·o·lar·i·an \ˌrād-ē-ō-ˈlar-ē-ən, -ˈler-\ *n* [deriv. of LL *radiolus* small sunbeam, fr. dim. of L *radius* ray — more at RAY] : any of a large order (Radiolaria) of marine protozoans having a siliceous skeleton of spicules and radiating threadlike pseudopodia

ra·dio·lo·ca·tion \ˌrād-ē-(ˌ)ō-lō-ˈkā-shən\ *n* : the detection or the determination of the position and course of distant objects by radar

ra·dio·log·i·cal \ˌrād-ē-ə-ˈläj-i-kəl\ *adj* **1** : of or relating to radiology **2** : of or relating to nuclear radiation — **ra·dio·log·i·cal·ly** \-k(ə-)lē\ *adv*

ra·di·ol·o·gist \ˌrād-ē-ˈäl-ə-jəst\ *n* : a specialist in the use of radiant energy

ra·di·ol·o·gy \-jē\ *n* : the science of radioactive substances and high-energy radiations; *specif* : the use of radiant energy in medicine

ra·dio·lu·cen·cy \ˌrād-ē-ō-ˈlüs-ᵊn-sē\ *n* : the quality or state of being permeable to radiation — **ra·dio·lu·cent** \-ᵊnt\ *adj*

ra·dio·man \ˈrād-ē-(ˌ)ō-ˌman\ *n* : a radio operator or technician

ra·dio·me·te·or·o·graph \ˌrād-ē-(ˌ)ō-ˌmēt-ē-ˈȯr-ə-ˌgraf, -ˈär-\ *n* : RADIOSONDE

ra·di·om·e·ter \ˌrād-ē-ˈäm-ət-ər\ *n* : an instrument for measuring the intensity of radiant energy by the torsional twist of suspended vanes that are blackened on one side and exposed to a source of radiant energy; *also* : an instrument for measuring electromagnetic or acoustic radiation — **ra·dio·met·ric** \ˌrād-ē-ō-ˈme-trik\ *adj* — **ra·di·om·e·try** \ˌrād-ē-ˈäm-ə-trē\ *n*

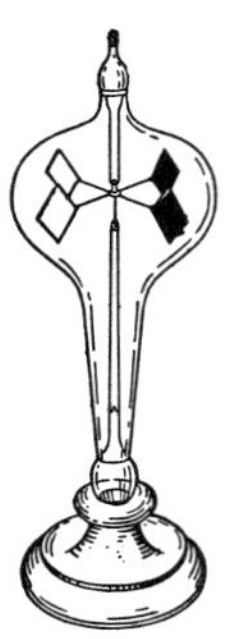

radiometer

ra·dio·mi·met·ic \ˌrād-ē-ō-mə-ˈmet-ik, -(ˌ)mī-\ *adj* [ISV] : producing effects similar to those of radiation

ra·di·on·ics \ˌrād-ē-ˈän-iks\ *n pl but sing in constr* [*radio-* + electr*onics*] : ELECTRONICS

ra·dio·phone \ˈrād-ē-ə-ˌfōn\ *n* **1** : an apparatus for the production of sound by radiant energy **2** : RADIOTELEPHONE

ra·dio·pho·to \ˌrād-ē-ō-ˈfōt-(ˌ)ō\ *n* **1** *also* **ra·dio·pho·to·graph** \-ˈfōt-ə-ˌgraf\ : a picture transmitted by radio **2** : the process of transmitting a picture by radio

radio range *n* : a radio facility aiding in the navigation of airplanes

ra·dio·scop·ic \ˌrād-ē-ə-ˈskäp-ik\ *adj* : of or relating to radioscopy

ra·di·os·co·py \-ˈäs-kə-pē\ *n* [ISV] : direct observation of objects opaque to light by means of some other form of radiant energy

ra·dio·sen·si·tive \ˌrād-ē-ō-ˈsen(t)-sət-iv, -ˈsen(t)-stiv\ *adj* : sensitive to the effects of radiant energy ⟨~ cancer cells⟩

ra·dio·sonde \ˈrād-ē-ō-ˌsänd\ *n* [ISV] : a miniature radio transmitter that is carried (as by an unmanned balloon) aloft with instruments for broadcasting (as by means of precise tone signals) the humidity, temperature, and pressure

radio spectrum *n* : the region of the electromagnetic spectrum usu. including frequencies below 30,000 megacycles in which radio or radar transmission and detection techniques may be used

ra·dio·stron·tium \ˌrād-ē-ō-ˈsträn-ch(ē-)əm, -ˈstränt-ē-əm\ *n* [NL] : radioactive strontium; *esp* : STRONTIUM 90

ra·dio·sym·met·ri·cal \ˌrād-ē-(ˌ)ō-sə-ˈme-tri-kəl\ *adj* : radially symmetrical; *specif* : ACTINOMORPHIC

ra·dio·tel·e·graph \-ˈtel-ə-ˌgraf\ *n* [ISV] : WIRELESS TELEGRAPHY — **ra·dio·tel·e·graph·ic** \-ˌtel-ə-ˈgraf-ik\ *adj* — **ra·dio·te·leg·ra·phy** \-tə-ˈleg-rə-fē\ *n*

ra·dio·tel·e·phone \-ˈtel-ə-ˌfōn\ *n* [ISV] : an apparatus for carrying on wireless telephony by radio waves — **ra·dio·te·le·pho·ny** \-tə-ˈlef-ə-nē, -ˈtel-ə-ˌfō-nē\ *n*

radio telescope *n* : a radio receiver-antenna combination used for observation in radio astronomy

ra·dio·ther·a·py \ˌrād-ē-ō-ˈther-ə-pē\ *n* [ISV] : the treatment of disease by means of X rays or radioactive substances

radio–ulna *n* : a bone of some lower vertebrates (as the toad) equivalent to the combined radius and ulna of higher forms

radio wave *n* : an electromagnetic wave with radio frequency

rad·ish \ˈrad-ish, ˈred-\ *n* [ME, alter. of OE *rædic*, fr. L *radic-, radix* root, radish — more at ROOT] : the pungent fleshy root of a plant (*Raphanus sativus*) of the mustard family usu. eaten raw; *also* : the plant that produces radishes

ra·di·um \ˈrād-ē-əm\ *n, often attrib* [NL, fr. L *radius* ray] : an intensely radioactive shining white metallic element that resembles barium chemically, occurs in combination in minute quantities in minerals (as pitchblende or carnotite), emits alpha particles and gamma rays to form radon, and is used chiefly in luminous materials and in the treatment of cancer — see ELEMENT table

radium therapy *n* : RADIOTHERAPY

[1]**ra·di·us** \ˈrād-ē-əs\ *n, pl* **ra·dii** \-ē-ˌī\ *also* **ra·di·us·es** [L, ray, radius] **1 a** : the anterior and thicker and shorter bone of the human forearm or of the corresponding part of the forelimb of vertebrates above fishes **b** : the third and usu. largest vein of an insect's wing **2** : a line segment extending from the center of a circle or sphere to the curve or surface **3 a** : the distance of a radius **b** : the circular area defined by a stated radius **c** : a bounded or circumscribed area **4** : a radial part **5** : the distance from a center line or point to an axis of rotation **6** : an imaginary radial plane dividing the body of a radially symmetrical animal into similar parts

[2]**radius** *vt* : to cut (as a fillet) on an arc of a circle

radius vector *n* **1** : a line segment or its length from a fixed point to a variable point; *also* : the linear polar coordinate of the variable point **2** : a straight line joining the center of an attracting body (as the sun) with that of a body (as a planet) in orbit around it

ra·dix \ˈrād-iks\ *n, pl* **ra·di·ces** \ˈrad-ə-ˌsēz, ˈrād-\ *or* **ra·dix·es** \ˈrād-ik-səz\ [L, root] **1** : BASE 5d **2** : the primary source **3** : the root of a plant **4** : RADICLE; *esp* : a root of a cranial or spinal nerve

ra·dome \ˈrā-ˌdōm\ *n* [*ra*dar *dome*] : a plastic housing sheltering the antenna assembly of a radar set esp. on an airplane

ra·don \ˈrā-ˌdän\ *n* [ISV, fr. *radium*] : a heavy radioactive gaseous element of the group of inert gases formed by distintegration of radium — see ELEMENT table

rad·u·la \ˈraj-ə-lə\ *n, pl* **rad·u·lae** \-ˌlē, -ˌlī\ *also* **radulas** [NL, fr. L, scraper, fr. *radere* to scrape — more at RAT] : a horny band or ribbon in mollusks other than bivalves that bears minute teeth on its dorsal surface and tears up food and draws it into the mouth — **rad·u·lar** \-lər\ *adj*

raff \ˈraf\ *n* [ME *raf* rubbish] : RIFFRAFF

raf·fia \ˈraf-ē-ə\ *n* [Malagasy *rafia*] : the fiber of the raffia palm used for tying plants and making baskets and hats

raffia palm *n* : a pinnate-leaved palm (*Raphia ruffia*) of Madagascar valued for the fiber from its leafstalks

raf·fi·nose \ˈraf-ə-ˌnōs, -ˌnōz\ *n* [F, fr. *raffiner* to refine, fr. *re-* + *affiner* to make fine, fr. *a-* ad- (fr. L *ad-*) + *fin* fine] : a crystalline slightly sweet sugar $C_{18}H_{32}O_{16}$ obtained commercially from cottonseed meal but found in many plant products

raff·ish \ˈraf-ish\ *adj* **1** : marked by or suggestive of flashy vulgarity or crudeness **2** : marked by a careless unconventionality : RAKISH — **raff·ish·ly** *adv* — **raff·ish·ness** *n*

[1]**raf·fle** \ˈraf-əl\ *n* [ME *rafle*, a dice game, fr. MF] : a lottery in which the prize is won by one of numerous persons buying chances

[2]**raffle** *vb* **raf·fling** \ˈraf-(ə-)liŋ\ *vi* : to engage in a raffle ~ *vt* : to dispose of by means of a raffle ⟨~ off a turkey⟩

[3]**raffle** *n* [prob. fr. F *rafle* act of snatching, sweeping, fr. MF *rafle, raffe*, fr. MHG *raffen* to snatch; akin to OE *hreppan* to touch, *hearpe* harp — more at HARP] : RUBBISH; *specif* : a jumble or tangle of nautical material

raf·fle·sia \rə-ˈflē-zh(ē-)ə, ra-\ *n* [NL, fr. Sir Thomas *Raffles* †1826 E colonial administrator] : any of a genus (*Rafflesia* of the family Rafflesiaceae) of Malaysian dicotyledonous plants that are parasitic in other plants and have fleshy usu. foul-smelling apetalous flowers emerging from the host, imbricated scales in place of leaves, and no stems

[1]**raft** \ˈraft\ *n* [ME *rafte* rafter, raft, fr. ON *raptr* rafter] **1 a** : a collection of logs or timber fastened together for conveyance by water **b** : a flat structure for support or transportation on water **2** : a floating cohesive mass

[2]**raft** *vt* **1** : to transport in the form of or by means of a raft **2** : to make into a raft ~ *vi* : to travel by raft

[3]**raft** *n* [alter. (influenced by [1]*raft*) of *raff* (jumble)] : a large collection

[1]**raf·ter** \ˈraf-tər\ *n* [ME, fr. OE *ræfter* akin to ON *raptr* rafter] : any of the parallel beams that support a roof

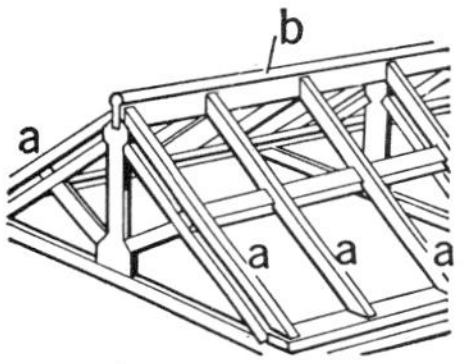

a rafters, *b* ridgepole

[2]**raft·er** \ˈraf-tər\ *n* [[2]*raft*] : one who maneuvers logs into position and binds them into rafts

rafts·man \ˈraf(t)-smən\ *n* : a man engaged in rafting

[1]**rag** \ˈrag\ *n* [ME *ragge*, fr. (assumed) OE *ragg*, fr. ON *rögg* tuft, shagginess — more at RUG] **1 a** : a waste piece of cloth **b** *pl* : clothes usu. in poor or ragged condition **2** : something resembling a rag **3** : NEWSPAPER **4** : the stringy axis and white fibrous membrane of a citrus fruit

[2]**rag** *n* [origin unknown] **1** : any of various hard rocks **2** : a large roofing slate rough on one side

[3]**rag** *vt* **ragged** \ˈragd\; **rag·ging** [origin unknown] **1** : to rail at : SCOLD **2** : TORMENT, TEASE

[4]**rag** *n, chiefly Brit* : an outburst of boisterous fun; *also* : PRANK

[5]**rag** *n* [short for *ragtime*] : a composition in ragtime

ra·ga \ˈräg-ə\ *n* [Skt *rāga*, lit., color, tone] : one of the ancient traditional melodic patterns or modes in Indian music

rag·a·muf·fin \ˈrag-ə-ˌməf-ən\ *n* [*Ragamoffyn*, a demon in *Piers Plowman* (1393), attributed to William Langland] : a ragged often disreputable person; *esp* : a poorly clothed often dirty child

rag·bag \ˈrag-ˌbag\ *n* **1** : a bag for scraps **2** : a miscellaneous collection

rag doll *n* **1** : a stuffed usu. painted cloth doll **2** : a rolled strip of moist cloth for testing the germination of seed

[1]**rage** \ˈrāj\ *n* [ME, fr. MF, fr. LL *rabia*, fr. L *rabies* rage, madness, fr. *rabere* to be mad; akin to Skt *rabhas* violence] **1 a** : violent and uncontrolled anger : FURY **b** : a fit of violent wrath **c** *archaic* : INSANITY **2** : violent action (as of wind or sea) **3** : an intense feeling : PASSION **4** : VOGUE ⟨was all the ~⟩ **syn** see ANGER, FASHION

[2]**rage** *vi* **1** : to be in a rage **2** : to be in tumult **3** : to prevail uncontrollably

rag·ged \ˈrag-əd\ *adj* **1** : roughly unkempt **2** : having an irregular edge or outline **3 a** : torn or worn to tatters **b** : worn out from stress and strain ⟨run ~⟩ **4** : wearing tattered clothes **5 a** : STRAGGLY **b** : executed in an irregular or uneven manner **c** *of a sound* : HARSH, DISSONANT — **rag·ged·ly** *adv* — **rag·ged·ness** *n*

ragged robin *n* : a perennial herb (*Lychnis floscuculi*) cultivated for its pink flowers with narrow-lobed petals

rag·gedy \ˈrag-əd-ē\ *adj* : somewhat ragged

rag·gee *or* **ragi** \ˈrag-ē\ *n* [Hindi *rāgī*] : an East Indian cereal grass (*Eleusine coracana*) yielding a staple food crop in the Orient

rag·gle \ˈrag-əl\ *n* [*raggle* (to cut a raggle in)] : a groove cut in masonry

rag·gle–tag·gle \ˈrag-əl-ˌtag-əl\ *adj* [irreg. fr. *ragtag* (motley crowd)] : MOTLEY

rag·ing *adj* **1** : causing great pain or distress **2** : VIOLENT, WILD **3** : EXTRAORDINARY, TREMENDOUS

rag·lan \ˈrag-lən\ *n* [F.J.H. Somerset, Baron *Raglan* †1855 Brit field marshal] : a loose overcoat having sleeves that extend to the neckline with slanted seams from the underarm to the neck

rag·man \ˈrag-ˌman\ *n* : a man who collects or deals in rags and refuse

Rag·na·rok \ˈrag-nə-ˌräk, -ˌrə(r)k\ *n* [ON *ragna rök*, lit., doom of the gods] : the final destruction of the world in the conflict between the Aesir and the powers of Hel led by Loki — called also *Twilight of the Gods*

ra·gout \ra-'gü\ *n* [F *ragoût*, fr. *ragoûter* to revive the taste, fr. *re-* + *a-* ad- (fr. L *ad-*) + *goût* taste, fr. L *gustus;* akin to L *gustare* to taste — more at CHOOSE] **:** well-seasoned meat and vegetables cooked in a thick sauce

rag·pick·er \'rag-,pik-ər\ *n* **:** one who collects rags and refuse for a livelihood

rag·tag and bobtail \,rag-,tag-\ *n* **:** RABBLE

rag·time \'rag-,tīm\ *n* [prob. fr. *ragged* + *time*] **1 :** rhythm characterized by strong syncopation in the melody with a regularly accented accompaniment **2 :** music having ragtime rhythm

rag·weed \'rag-,wēd\ *n* **1 :** any of various chiefly No. American weedy composite herbs (genus *Ambrosia*) that produce highly allergenic pollen **2 :** FRANSERIA

rag·wort \'rag-,wərt, -,wȯ(ə)rt\ *n* **:** any of several composite herbs (genus *Senecio*); *esp* **:** TANSY RAGWORT

rah \'rä, 'rȯ\ *interj* **:** HURRAH — used esp. to cheer on a team ⟨*rah, rah,* team⟩

rah-rah \'rä-(,)rä, 'rȯ-(,)rȯ\ *adj* [redupl. of *rah* (*hurrah*)] **:** marked by the enthusiastic expression of college spirit

[1]**raid** \'rād\ *n* [Sc dial., fr. OE *rād* ride, raid — more at ROAD] **1 a :** a hostile or predatory incursion **b :** a surprise attack by a small force **2 a :** a brief foray outside one's usual sphere **b :** a sudden invasion by officers of the law **c :** a daring operation against a competitor **3 :** the act of mulcting public money **4 :** an attempt by professional operators to depress stock prices by concerted selling

[2]**raid** *vt* **:** to make a raid on **~** *vi* **:** to conduct or take part in a raid

raid·er \'rād-ər\ *n* **:** one that raids: as **a :** a fast lightly armed ship operating against merchant shipping **b :** a soldier specially trained for close-range fighting

[1]**rail** \'rā(ə)l\ *n* [ME *raile*, fr. MF *reille* ruler, bar, fr. L *regula* ruler, fr. *regere* to keep straight, direct, rule — more at RIGHT] **1 a :** a bar extending from one post or support to another and serving as a guard or barrier **b :** a structural member or support **2 a :** RAILING **b :** a light structure serving as a guard at the outer edge of a ship's deck **c :** a fence bounding a racetrack **3 a :** a bar of rolled steel forming a track for wheeled vehicles **b :** TRACK **c :** RAILROAD

[2]**rail** *vt* **:** to provide with a railing **:** FENCE

[3]**rail** *n, pl* **rail** *or* **rails** [ME *raile*, fr. MF *raale*] **:** any of numerous precocial wading birds (family Rallidae) that are structurally related to the cranes but of small or medium size and have short rounded wings, a short tail, and usu. very long toes which enable them to run on the soft mud of swamps

[4]**rail** *vi* [ME *railen*, fr. MF *railler* to mock, fr. OProv *ralhar* to babble, joke, fr. (assumed) VL *ragulare* to bray, fr. LL *ragere* to neigh] **:** to revile or scold in harsh, insolent, or abusive language **syn** see SCOLD — **rail·er** *n*

rail fence *n* **:** a fence of posts and split rails

rail·head \'rā(ə)l-,hed\ *n* **1 :** a point on a railroad in a theater of operations at which military supplies are unloaded for distribution **2 :** the end of a railroad line

rail·ing \'rā-liŋ\ *n* **1 :** a barrier consisting of a rail and supports **2 :** RAILS

rail·lery \'rā-lə-rē\ *n* [F *raillerie*, fr. MF, fr. *railler* to mock] **1 :** good-natured ridicule **:** BANTER **2 :** JEST

[1]**rail·road** \'rā(ə)l-,rōd\ *n* **:** a permanent road having a line of rails fixed to ties and laid on a roadbed and providing a track for rolling stock drawn by locomotives or propelled by self-contained motors; *also* **:** such a road and its assets constituting a single property

[2]**railroad** *vt* **1 :** to transport by railroad **2 a :** to push through hastily or without due consideration **b :** to convict with undue haste and by means of false charges or insufficient evidence **~** *vi* **:** to work for a railroad company — **rail·road·er** *n*

railroad flat *n* **:** an apartment having a series of narrow rooms arranged in line

rail·road·ing *n* **:** construction or operation of a railroad

railroad worm *n* **:** APPLE MAGGOT

rail-split·ter \'rā(ə)l-,split-ər\ *n* **:** one that makes logs into fence rails

rail·way \'rā(ə)l-,wā\ *n* **1 :** RAILROAD; *esp* **:** a railroad operating with light equipment or within a small area **2 :** a line of track providing a runway for wheels ⟨a cash or parcel **~** in a department store⟩

rai·ment \'rā-mənt\ *n* [ME *rayment*, short for *arrayment*, fr. *arrayen* to array] **:** CLOTHING, GARMENTS

[1]**rain** \'rān\ *n, often attrib* [ME *reyn*, fr. OE *regn, rēn;* akin to OHG *regan* rain] **1 a :** water falling in drops condensed from vapor in the atmosphere **b :** the descent of such water **2 a :** a fall of rain **:** RAINSTORM **b** *pl* **:** the rainy season **3 :** rainy weather **4 :** a heavy fall of particles or bodies

[2]**rain** *vi* **1 :** to fall as water in drops from the clouds **2 :** to send down rain **3 :** to fall like rain **~** *vt* **1 :** to pour down **2 :** to bestow abundantly

rain·bird \'rān-,bərd\ *n* **:** any of numerous birds (esp. of the family Cuculidae) whose cries are popularly believed to augur rain

rain·bow \'rān-,bō\ *n* **1 :** an arc or circle that exhibits in concentric bands the colors of the spectrum and that is formed opposite the sun by the refraction and reflection of the sun's rays in raindrops, spray, or mist **2 a :** a multicolored array **b :** a wide assortment or range **3 :** ILLUSION

rainbow fish *n* **:** any of numerous brilliantly colored fishes (as a wrasse, parrot fish, or guppy)

rainbow perch *n* **:** a small brilliantly striped, red, orange, and blue surf fish (*Hypsurus caryi*) of the Pacific coast of No. America

rainbow runner *n* **:** a large brilliantly marked blue and yellow food and sport fish (*Elagatis bipinnulatus*) common in warm seas

rain check *n* **1 :** a ticket stub good for a later performance when the scheduled one is rained out **2 :** an assurance of a deferred extension of an offer

rain·coat \'rān-,kōt\ *n* **:** a coat of waterproof or water-resistant material

rain·drop \-,dräp\ *n* **:** a drop of rain

rain·fall \-,fȯl\ *n* **1 :** RAIN 2a **2 :** the amount of precipitation usu. measured by the depth in inches

rain forest *n* **:** a tropical woodland with an annual rainfall of at least 100 inches and marked by lofty broad-leaved evergreen trees forming a continuous canopy — called also *tropical rain forest*

rain gauge *n* **:** an instrument for measuring the quantity of precipitation

rain·mak·ing \'rān-,mā-kiŋ\ *n* **:** the act or process of attempting to produce rain by artificial means

rain out *vt* **:** to interrupt or prevent by rain

rain·proof \'rān-'prüf\ *adj* **:** impervious to rain

rain·spout \-,spau̇t\ *n* **:** a pipe, duct, or orifice draining a roof gutter

rain·squall \-,skwȯl\ *n* **:** a squall accompanied by rain

rain·storm \-,stȯ(ə)rm\ *n* **:** a storm of or with rain

rain·wash \-,wȯsh, -,wäsh\ *n* **:** the washing away of material by rain; *also* **:** the material so washed away

rain·wa·ter \-,wȯt-ər, -,wät-\ *n* **:** water fallen as rain that has not collected soluble matter from the soil and is therefore soft

rain·wear \-,wa(ə)r, -,we(ə)r\ *n* **:** waterproof or water-resistant clothing

rainy \'rā-nē\ *adj* **:** marked by, abounding with, or bringing rain

rainy day *n* **:** a period of want or need

[1]**raise** \'rāz\ *vb* [ME *raisen*, fr. ON *reisa* — more at REAR] *vt* **1 :** to cause or help to rise to a standing position **2 a :** AWAKEN, AROUSE **b :** to stir up **:** INCITE ⟨~ a rebellion⟩ **c :** to flush (game) from cover **d :** to recall from or as if from death **e :** to establish radio communication with **3 a :** to set upright by lifting or building **b :** to lift higher **c :** to place higher in rank or dignity **:** ELEVATE **d :** HEIGHTEN, INVIGORATE ⟨~ the spirits⟩ **e :** to end or suspend the operation or validity of ⟨~ a siege⟩ **4 :** to get together for a purpose **:** COLLECT ⟨~ funds⟩ **5 a :** to breed and bring (an animal) to maturity **b :** GROW, CULTIVATE ⟨~ cotton⟩ **c :** to bring up (a child) **:** REAR **6 a :** to give rise to **:** PROVOKE **b :** to give voice to ⟨~ a cheer⟩ **7 :** to bring up for consideration or debate ⟨~ an issue⟩ **8 a :** to increase the strength, intensity, or pitch of **b :** to increase the degree of **c :** to cause to rise in level or amount ⟨~ the rent⟩ **d** (1) **:** to increase the amount of (a poker bet) (2) **:** to bet more than (a previous bettor) **e** (1) **:** to make a higher bridge bid in (a partner's suit) (2) **:** to increase the bid of (one's partner) **9 :** to make light and porous ⟨~ dough⟩ **10 :** to cause to ascend **11 :** to multiply (a quantity) by itself a specified number of times **12 :** to bring in sight on the horizon by approaching ⟨~ land⟩ **13 a :** to bring up the nap of (cloth) **b :** to cause (as a blister) to form on the skin **14 :** to increase the nominal value of fraudulently ⟨~ a check⟩ **15 :** to articulate (a sound) with the tongue in a higher position **~** *vi* **1** *dial* **:** RISE **2 :** to increase a bet or bid **syn** see LIFT — **rais·er** *n*

[2]**raise** *n* **1 :** an act of raising or lifting **2 :** an upward grade **:** RISE **3 :** an increase in amount; *esp* **:** an increase of a bet or bid

raised *adj* **1 a :** done in relief **b :** NAPPED **2 :** leavened with yeast rather than with baking powder or soda

rai·sin \'rāz-ən\ *n* [ME, fr. MF, grape, fr. L *racemus* cluster of grapes or berries] **:** a grape usu. of a special type dried in the sun or by artificial heat

rai·son d'être \,rā-,zōn-'detr\ *n* [F] **:** reason or justification for existence

raj \'räj\ *n* [Hindi *rāj*, fr. Skt *rājya;* akin to Skt *rājan* king] **:** REIGN

ra·ja *or* **ra·jah** \'räj-ə\ *n* [Hindi *rājā*, fr. Skt *rājan* king — more at ROYAL] **1 :** an Indian or Malay prince or chief **2 :** the bearer of a title of nobility among the Hindus

Ra·jab \rə-'jab\ *n* [Ar] **:** the 7th month of the Muhammadan year

Raj·put *or* **Raj·poot** \'räj-,pu̇t\ *n* [Hindi *rājpūt*, fr. Skt *rājaputra* king's son, fr. *rājan* king + *putra* son — more at FEW] **:** a member of an Indo-Aryan caste of northern India

[1]**rake** \'rāk\ *n* [ME, fr. OE *racu;* akin to OHG *rehho* rake] **1 a :** an implement equipped with projecting prongs to gather material (as grass) or for loosening or smoothing the surface of the ground **b :** a machine for gathering hay **2 :** an implement like a rake

[2]**rake** *vt* **1 :** to gather, loosen, or smooth with or as if with a rake **2 :** to gain rapidly or in abundance ⟨~ in a fortune⟩ **3 a :** to touch in passing over lightly **b :** SCRATCH **4 :** to censure severely **5 :** to search through **:** RANSACK **6 :** to sweep the length of esp. with gunfire **:** ENFILADE **7 :** to glance over rapidly — **rak·er** *n*

[3]**rake** *vi* [origin unknown] **:** to incline from the perpendicular

[4]**rake** *n* **1 :** inclination from the perpendicular; *esp* **:** the overhang of a ship's bow or stern **2 :** inclination from the horizontal **:** SLOPE **3 :** the angle between the top cutting surface of a tool and a plane perpendicular to the surface of the work **4 :** the angle between a wing-tip edge that is sensibly straight in planform and the plane of symmetry of an airplane

[5]**rake** *n* [short for *rakehell*] **:** a dissolute person **:** LIBERTINE

rake·hell \'rāk-,hel\ *n* **:** RAKE — **rakehell** *or* **rake·helly** \-,hel-ē\ *adj*

rake-off \'rā-,kȯf\ *n* [[2]*rake* + *off;* fr. the use of a rake by a croupier to collect the operator's profits in a gambling casino] **:** a percentage or cut taken (as by an operator)

rake up *vt* **:** to dig out **:** UNCOVER ⟨*rake up* a scandal⟩

[1]**rak·ish** \'rā-kish\ *adj* **:** of, relating to, or characteristic of a rake **:** DISSOLUTE — **rak·ish·ly** *adv* — **rak·ish·ness** *n*

[2]**rakish** *adj* [prob. fr. [3]*rake;* fr. the raking masts of pirate ships] **1 :** having a smart stylish appearance suggestive of speed ⟨a ~ ship⟩ **2 :** negligent of convention or formality **:** JAUNTY ⟨~ clothes⟩ — **rak·ish·ly** *adv* — **rak·ish·ness** *n*

rale \'ral, 'räl\ *n* [F *râle*] **:** an abnormal sound heard accompanying the normal respiratory sounds

ral·len·tan·do \,räl-ən-'tän-(,)dō\ *adv* (*or adj*) [It, lit., slowing down, verbal of *rallentare* to slow down again, fr. *re-* + *allentare* to slow down] **:** with a gradual decrease in tempo — used as a direction in music

ral·li·form \'ral-ə-,fȯrm\ *adj* [ML *rall*us rail (fr. MF *raale*) + E *-iform*] **:** resembling or related to the rails

[1]**ral·ly** \'ral-ē\ *vb* [F *rallier*, fr. OF *ralier*, fr. *re-* + *alier* to unite — more at ALLY] *vt* **1 a :** to muster for a common purpose **b :** to recall to order **2 a :** to arouse for action **b :** to rouse from depression or weakness **~** *vi* **1 :** to come together again to renew an effort **2 :** to join in a common cause **3 :** RECOVER, REBOUND **4 :** to engage in a rally

[2]**rally** *n* **1 a :** a mustering of scattered forces to renew an effort **b :** a summoning up of strength or courage after weakness or dejection **c :** a recovery of price after a decline **2 :** a mass meeting intended to arouse group enthusiasm **3 :** a series of strokes inter-

changed between players (as in tennis) before a point is won **4 :** a competitive automobile run esp. over public roads

[3]**rally** *vt* [F *railler* to mock, rally — more at RAIL] **:** to attack with raillery **:** BANTER **syn** see RIDICULE

[1]**ram** \'ram\ *n* [ME, fr. OE *ramm;* akin to OHG *ram*] **1 :** a male sheep **2 a :** BATTERING RAM **b :** a warship with a heavy beak at the prow for piercing an enemy ship **3 :** any of various guided pieces for exerting pressure or for driving or forcing something by impact: as **a :** the plunger of a hydrostatic press or force pump **b :** the weight that strikes the blow in a pile driver

[2]**ram** *vb* **rammed; ram·ming** [ME *rammen*] *vi* **1 :** to strike with violence **:** CRASH **2 :** to move with extreme rapidity ~ *vt* **1 :** to force in by driving **2 a :** to make compact (as by pounding) **b :** CRAM, CROWD **3 :** to force passage or acceptance of ⟨~ home an idea⟩ **4 :** to strike against violently — **ram·mer** *n*

Ram·a·dan \'ram-ə-,dän, -,dan\ *n* [Ar *Ramaḍān*] **:** the 9th month of the Muhammadan year observed as sacred with fasting practiced daily from dawn to sunset

Ra·ma·ism \'räm-ə-,iz-əm\ *n* [*Rama*, 7th avatar of Vishnu, fr. Skt *Rāma*] **:** the worship of the Hindu epic hero Rama as an incarnation of the god Vishnu

ra·mate \'rā-,māt\ *adj* [L *ramus* branch] **:** having branches

[1]**ram·ble** \'ram-bəl\ *vb* **ram·bling** \-b(ə-)liŋ\ [perh. fr. ME *romblen*, freq. of *romen* to roam] *vi* **1 a :** to move aimlessly from place to place **b :** to explore idly **2 :** to talk or write in a desultory fashion **3 :** to grow or extend irregularly ~ *vt* **:** to wander over **:** ROAM

[2]**ramble** *n* **:** a leisurely excursion for pleasure; *esp* **:** an aimless walk

ram·bler \'ram-blər\ *n* **1 :** one that rambles **2 :** any of various climbing roses with rather small often double flowers in large clusters

ram·bling \'ram-bliŋ\ *adj* **:** DISCURSIVE — **ram·bling·ly** \-bliŋ-lē\ *adv*

ram·bouil·let \,ram-bə-'lā, -(,)bü-'yā\ *n, often cap* [*Rambouillet*, France] **:** a large sturdy sheep developed in France for mutton and wool

ram·bunc·tious \ram-'bəŋ(k)-shəs\ *adj* [prob. irreg. fr. *robust*] **:** marked by uncontrollable exuberance **:** UNRULY — **ram·bunc·tious·ly** *adv* — **ram·bunc·tious·ness** *n*

ram·bu·tan \ram-'büt-ᵊn\ *n* [Malay] **:** a bright red spiny Malayan fruit closely related to the litchi nut; *also* **:** a tree (*Nephelium lappaceum*) of the soapberry family that bears this fruit

ram·e·kin *or* **ram·e·quin** \'ram-i-kən\ *n* [F *ramequin*, fr. LG *ramken*, dim. of *ram* cream] **1 :** a preparation of cheese with bread crumbs, puff paste, or eggs baked in a mold or shell **2 :** an individual baking dish

ra·men·tum \rə-'ment-əm\ *n, pl* **ra·men·ta** \-ə\ [NL, fr. L, a shaving, fr. *radere* to scratch, scrape — more at RAT] **:** a thin brownish scale on a leaf or young shoot of a fern

ra·met \'rā-,met\ *n* [L *ramus* branch] **:** an independent member of a clone

ra·mie \'ram-ē, 'rā-mē\ *n* [Malay *rami*] **:** an Asian perennial plant (*Boehmeria nivea*) of the nettle family; *also* **:** the strong lustrous bast fiber of this plant

ram·i·fi·ca·tion \,ram-ə-fə-'kā-shən\ *n* **1 a :** the act or process of branching **b :** arrangement of branches (as on a plant) **2 a :** BRANCH, OFFSHOOT **b :** a branched structure **3 :** OUTGROWTH, CONSEQUENCE ⟨the ~*s* of a problem⟩

ra·mi·form \'ram-ə-,fȯrm, 'rā-mə-\ *adj* [L *ramus* + E *-iform*] **:** resembling or constituting branches **:** BRANCHED

ram·i·fy \'ram-ə-,fī\ *vb* [MF *ramifier*, fr. ML *ramificare*, fr. L *ramus* branch; akin to L *radix* root] *vt* **1 :** to cause to branch **2 :** to separate into divisions ~ *vi* **1 :** to split up into branches or constituent parts **2 :** to send forth branches or extensions

Ra·mism \'rā-,miz-əm\ *n* **:** the doctrines of the French reformer Ramus (†1572) based on opposition to scholasticism and advocacy of Calvinism and on a new logic blended with rhetoric — **Ra·mist** \-məst\ *n or adj*

ram·jet engine \,ram-,jet-\ *n* **:** a jet engine having in its forward end a continuous inlet of air so that there is a compressing effect produced on the air taken in while the engine is in motion

ra·mose \'rā-,mōs\ *adj* [L *ramosus*, fr. *ramus* branch] **:** consisting of or having branches — **ra·mose·ly** *adv*

ra·mous \'rā-məs\ *adj* [L *ramosus*] **1 :** RAMOSE **2 :** resembling branches

[1]**ramp** \'ramp\ *vi* [ME *rampen*, fr. OF *ramper* to crawl, rear, of Gmc origin; akin to OHG *rimpfan* to wrinkle — more at RUMPLE] **1 a :** to be rampant **b** (1) **:** to stand or advance menacingly with forelegs or with arms raised (2) **:** to move or act furiously **:** STORM **2 :** to creep up — used esp. of plants

[2]**ramp** *n* **:** the act or an instance of ramping

[3]**ramp** *n* [F *rampe*, fr. *ramper*] **1 :** a short bend, slope, or curve usu. in the vertical plane where a handrail or coping changes its direction **2 :** a sloping way: as **a :** a sloping floor, walk, or roadway leading from one level to another **b :** a stairway for entering or leaving the main door of an airplane

[1]**ram·page** \'ram-,pāj, (')ram-'\ *vi* [Sc] **:** to rush wildly about

[2]**ram·page** \'ram-,pāj\ *n* **:** a course of violent, riotous, or reckless action or behavior — **ram·pa·geous** \ram-'pā-jəs\ *adj* — **ram·pa·geous·ly** *adv* — **ram·pa·geous·ness** *n*

ram·pan·cy \'ram-pən-sē\ *n* **:** the quality or state of being rampant

ram·pant \'ram-pənt, -,pant\ *adj* [ME, fr. MF, prp. of *ramper*] **1 a :** rearing upon the hind legs with forelegs extended **b** *of a heraldic beast* **:** standing on one hind foot with one foreleg raised above the other and the head in profile **2 a :** marked by a menacing wildness, extravagance, or absence of restraint **b :** WIDESPREAD **3 :** having one impost or abutment higher than the other ⟨a ~ arch⟩ — **ram·pant·ly** *adv*

ram·part \'ram-,pärt, -pərt\ *n* [MF] **1 :** a broad embankment raised as a fortification and usu. surmounted by a parapet **2 :** a protective barrier **:** BULWARK **3 :** a wall-like ridge of rock fragments, earth, or other debris

ram·pike \-,pīk\ *n* [origin unknown] **:** an erect broken or dead tree

ram·pi·on \'ram-pē-ən\ *n* [prob. modif. of MF *raiponce*, fr. OIt *raponzo*] **:** a European bellflower (*Campanula rapunculus*) with a tuberous root used with the leaves in salad

[1]**ram·rod** \'ram-,räd\ *n* **1 :** a rod for ramming home the charge in a muzzle-loading firearm **2 :** a cleaning rod for small arms

[2]**ramrod** *adj* **:** marked by rigidity, severity, or stiffness

ram·shack·le \'ram-,shak-əl\ *adj* [alter. of earlier *ransackled*, fr. pp. of obs. *ransackle*, freq. of *ransack*] **1 :** appearing ready to collapse **:** RICKETY **2 :** carelessly or loosely constructed

ram's horn *n* **:** SHOFAR

rams·horn \'ramz-,hȯ(ə)rn\ *n* **:** a snail (genus *Planorbis*) often used as an aquarium scavenger

ram·til \'ram-,til\ *n* [Hindi *rāmtil*, fr. Skt *Rāma* Rama, Hindu epic hero + *tila* sesame] **:** a tropical composite herb (*Guizotia abyssinica*) cultivated in India for its oil seeds

ram·u·lose \'ram-yə-,lōs\ *or* **ram·u·lous** \-ləs\ *adj* [L *ramulosus*, fr. *ramulus* small branch, dim. of *ramus*] **:** having many small branches

ra·mus \'rā-məs\ *n, pl* **ra·mi** \-,mī\ [NL, fr. L, branch — more at RAMIFY] **:** a projecting part or elongated process **:** BRANCH

ran *past of* RUN

[1]**ranch** \'ranch\ *n* [MexSp *rancho* small ranch, fr. Sp, camp, hut & Sp dial., small farm, fr. OSp *ranchear(se)* to take up quarters, fr. MF *(se) ranger* to take up a position, fr. *ranger* to set in a row — more at RANGE] **1 :** a large farm for raising horses, cattle, or sheep **2 :** a farm or area devoted to a particular specialty

[2]**ranch** *vi* **:** to live or work on a ranch ~ *vt* **1 :** to work as a rancher on **2 :** to raise on a ranch

ranch·er \'ran-chər\ *n* **:** one who owns, operates, or works on a ranch

ran·che·ro \ran-'che(ə)r-(,)ō, rän-\ *n, pl* **rancheros** [MexSp, fr. *rancho*] **:** RANCHER

ranch house *n* **:** a one-story house typically with a low-pitched roof and an open plan

ranch·man \'ranch-mən\ *n* **:** RANCHER

ran·cho \'ran-(,)chō, 'rän-\ *n, pl* **ranchos** [MexSp, small ranch] **:** RANCH 1

ranch wagon *n* **:** STATION WAGON

ran·cid \'ran(t)-səd\ *adj* [L *rancidus*, fr. *rancēre* to be rancid] **1 :** having a rank smell or taste **2 :** OFFENSIVE — **ran·cid·i·ty** \ran-'sid-ət-ē\ *n* — **ran·cid·ness** \'ran(t)-səd-nəs\ *n*

ran·cor \'raŋ-kər, -,kȯ(ə)r\ *n* [ME *rancour*, fr. MF *ranceur*, fr. LL *rancor* rancidity, rancor, fr. L *rancēre*] **:** bitter deep-seated ill will **syn** see ENMITY

ran·cor·ous \'raŋ-k(ə-)rəs\ *adj* **:** marked by rancor — **ran·cor·ous·ly** *adv*

rand \'rand, 'ränd\ *n, pl* **rand** [the *Rand*, So. Africa] — see MONEY table

[1]**ran·dom** \'ran-dəm\ *n* [ME, impetuosity, fr. MF *randon*, fr. OF, fr. *randir* to run, of Gmc origin; akin to OHG *rinnan* to run — more at RUN] **:** a haphazard course — **at random :** without definite aim, direction, rule, or method

[2]**random** *adj* **1 :** lacking a definite plan, purpose, or pattern **2 :** being a member of, consisting of, or relating to a set of elements that have a definite probability of occurring with a specific frequency ⟨~ variable⟩; *specif* **:** being or relating to a member of a set whose members have an equal probability of occurring ⟨table of ~ numbers⟩ — **ran·dom·ly** *adv* — **ran·dom·ness** *n*

syn RANDOM, HAPHAZARD, CASUAL, DESULTORY mean determined by accident rather than design. RANDOM stresses lack of definite aim, fixed goal, or regular procedure; HAPHAZARD applies to what is done without regard for regularity or fitness or ultimate consequence; CASUAL suggests working or acting without deliberation, intention, or purpose; DESULTORY implies a jumping or skipping from one thing to another ungoverned by method or system

[3]**random** *adv* **:** in a random manner

ran·dom·iza·tion \,ran-də-mə-'zā-shən\ *n* **:** arrangement (as of samples) so as to simulate a chance distribution, reduce interference by irrelevant variables, and yield unbiased statistical data

ran·dom·ize \'ran-də-,mīz\ *vt* **:** to use randomization on

[1]**randy** \'ran-dē\ *adj* [prob. fr. obs. *rand* (to rant)] **1** *chiefly Scot* **:** having a coarse manner **2 :** LECHEROUS, SEXY

[2]**randy** *n, chiefly Scot* **:** a scolding or dissolute woman

rang *past of* RING

[1]**range** \'rānj\ *n, often attrib* [ME, row of persons, fr. OF *renge*, fr. *rengier* to range] **1 a** (1) **:** a series of things in a line **:** ROW (2) **:** a series of mountains (3) **:** one of the north-south rows of a township in a U.S. public-land survey that are numbered east and west from the principal meridian of the survey **b :** an aggregate of individuals in one order **c :** a direction line **2 :** a cooking stove that has a flat top with plates or racks to hold utensils over flames or coils and an oven **3 a :** a place that may be ranged over **b :** an open region over which livestock may roam and feed **c :** the region throughout which a kind of organism or ecological community naturally lives or occurs **4 :** the act of ranging about **5 a** (1) **:** the horizontal distance to which a projectile can be propelled (2) **:** the maximum distance a vehicle can travel without refueling **b :** a place where shooting is practiced **6 a :** the space or extent included, covered, or used **:** SCOPE **b :** the extent of pitch covered by a melody or lying within the capacity of a voice or instrument **7 a :** a sequence, series, or scale between limits **b :** the limits of a series **c :** the difference between the least and greatest values of the attribute or variable of a frequency distribution **8 a :** the set of values a function may take on **b :** the class of admissible values of a variable

[2]**range** *vb* [ME *rangen*, fr. MF *ranger* to set in a row, place, fr. OF *rengier*, fr. *renc, reng* line, place, row — more at RANK] *vt* **1 a :** to set in a row or in the proper order **b :** to place among others in a position or situation **c :** to assign to a category **:** CLASSIFY **2 a :** to rove over or through **b :** to sail or pass along **3 :** to arrange (an anchor cable) on deck **4 :** to graze (livestock) on a range **5 :** to determine or give the elevation necessary for (a gun) to propel a projectile to a given distance ~ *vi* **1 a :** to roam at large or freely **b :** to move over an area so as to explore it **2 :** to take a position **3 a :** to correspond in direction or line **:** ALIGN **b :** to extend in a particular direction **4 :** to have range **5 :** to change or differ within limits **6** *of an organism* **:** to live or occur in or be native to a region **syn** see LINE

range finder *n* **1 :** an instrument used in gunnery to determine the distance of a target **2 :** TACHYMETER **3 :** a camera attachment for measuring the distance between the camera and an object

range paralysis *n* **:** an avian leukosis involving flaccid paralysis esp. of the legs and wings of maturing chickens

rang·er \'rān-jər\ *n* **1 a :** the keeper of a British royal park or forest **b :** an officer charged with patrolling and protecting a forest **2 :** one that ranges **3 a :** one of a body of organized armed men

who range over a region **b :** a soldier specially trained in close-range fighting and raiding tactics

rang·i·ness \'rān-jē-nəs\ *n* **:** the quality or state of being rangy

rangy \'rān-jē\ *adj* **1 :** able to range for considerable distances **2 a :** long-limbed and long-bodied ⟨~ cattle⟩ **b :** being tall and slender **3 :** having room for ranging **4 :** having great scope

ra·ni *or* **ra·nee** \rä-'nē\ *n* [Hindi *rānī*, fr. Skt *rājñī*, fem. of *rājan* king — more at ROYAL] **:** a Hindu queen **:** a rajah's wife

ra·nid \'ran-əd, 'rā-nəd\ *n* [deriv. of L *rana* frog] **:** any of a large family (Ranidae) of frogs distinguished by slightly dilated transverse sacral processes and comprising the typical frogs

ra·nine \'rā-,nīn\ *adj* [L *rana* frog] **1 :** of or relating to frogs **2 :** of or relating to the region beneath the tip of the tongue

[1]**rank** \'raŋk\ *adj* [ME, fr. OE *ranc* overbearing, strong; akin to OE *riht* right — more at RIGHT] **1 :** luxuriantly or excessively vigorous in growth **2 :** offensively gross or coarse **:** FOUL **3** *obs* **:** grown too large **4 a :** DOWNRIGHT **b :** COMPLETE, UTTER **5** *archaic* **:** LUSTFUL, RUTTISH **6 :** RANCID **7 :** PUTRID, FESTERING **8 :** high in amount **:** EXCESSIVE **syn** see FLAGRANT, MALODOROUS — **rank·ly** *adv* — **rank·ness** *n*

[2]**rank** *n* [MF *renc, reng*, of Gmc origin; akin to OHG *hring* ring — more at RING] **1 a :** ROW, SERIES **b :** a row of people **c** (1) **:** a line of soldiers ranged side by side in close order (2) *pl* **:** ARMED FORCES (3) *pl* **:** the body of enlisted men **d :** a row of squares extending horizontally across a chessboard **e** *Brit* **:** STAND 6 **2 :** an orderly arrangement **:** FORMATION **3 :** a social class **4 a :** relative standing or position **b :** a degree or position of dignity, eminence, or excellence **:** DISTINCTION **c :** high social position **d :** a grade of official standing

[3]**rank** *vt* **1 :** to arrange in lines or in a regular formation **2 :** to determine the relative position of **:** RATE **3 :** to take precedence of ~ *vi* **1 :** to form or move in ranks **2 :** to take or have a position in relation to others

rank and file *n* **1 :** the enlisted men of an armed force **2 :** the individuals who constitute the body of an organization, society, or nation as distinguished from the leaders

rank·er \'raŋ-kər\ *n* **:** one who serves or has served in the ranks; *esp* **:** a commissioned officer promoted from the ranks

Ran·kine \'raŋ-kən\ *adj* [William J. M. *Rankine* †1872 Sc engineer & physicist] **:** being, according to, or relating to an absolute-temperature scale on which the unit of measurement equals a Fahrenheit degree and on which the freezing point of water is 491.69° and the boiling point 671.69°

rank·ing *adj* **:** having a high position: as **a :** FOREMOST ⟨~ poet⟩ **b :** being next to the chairman in seniority ⟨~ committee member⟩

ran·kle \'raŋ-kəl\ *vb* **ran·kling** \-k(ə-)liŋ\ [ME *ranclen* to fester, fr. MF *rancler*, fr. OF *draoncler, raoncler*, fr. *draoncle, raoncle* festering sore, fr. (assumed) VL *dracunculus*, fr. L, dim. of *draco* serpent — more at DRAGON] *vi* **1 :** to cause anger, irritation, or deep bitterness **2 :** to chafe with anger ~ *vt* **:** to cause irritation or bitterness in

ran·sack \'ran-,sak, (')ran-'\ *vt* [ME *ransaken*, fr. ON *rannsaka*, fr. *rann* house + *-saka* (akin to OE *sēcan* to seek)] **1 a :** to search thoroughly **b :** to examine closely and carefully **2 :** to search through to commit robbery **:** PLUNDER — **ran·sack·er** *n*

[1]**ran·som** \'ran(t)-səm\ *n* [ME *ransoun*, fr. OF *rançon*, fr. L *redemption-, redemptio* — more at REDEMPTION] **1 :** a consideration paid or demanded for the redemption of a captured person **2 :** the act of ransoming

[2]**ransom** *vt* **1 :** to deliver esp. from sin or its penalty **2 :** to free from captivity or punishment by paying a price **syn** see RESCUE — **ran·som·er** *n*

[1]**rant** \'rant\ *vb* [obs. D *ranten, randen*] *vi* **1 :** to talk in a noisy, excited, or declamatory manner **2 :** to scold vehemently ~ *vt* **:** to utter in a bombastic declamatory fashion — **rant·er** *n* — **rant·ing·ly** \-iŋ-lē\ *adv*

[2]**rant** *n* **1 a :** a bombastic extravagant speech **b :** bombastic extravagant language **2** *dial Brit* **:** a rousing good time **syn** see BOMBAST

ran·u·la \'ran-yə-lə\ *n* [NL, fr. L, swelling on the tongue of cattle, fr. dim. of *rana* frog] **:** a cyst formed under the tongue by obstruction of a gland duct

ra·nun·cu·lus \rə-'nəŋ-kyə-ləs\ *n, pl* **ra·nun·cu·lus·es** *or* **ra·nun·cu·li** \-,lī, -,lē\ [NL, genus name, fr. L, tadpole, crowfoot, dim. of *rana* frog] **:** any of a large widely distributed genus (*Ranunculus*) of dicotyledonous herbs (as a buttercup)

[1]**rap** \'rap\ *n* [ME *rappe*] **1 :** a sharp blow or knock **2 :** a sharp rebuke or criticism **3** *slang* **a :** the responsibility for or adverse consequences of an action **b :** a criminal charge **c :** a prison sentence

[2]**rap** *vb* **rapped; rap·ping** *vt* **1 :** to strike with a sharp blow **2 :** to utter suddenly and forcibly **3 :** to cause to be or come by raps ⟨~ the meeting to order⟩ **4 :** to criticize sharply **5** *slang* **:** to arrest, hold, or sentence on a criminal charge ~ *vi* **1 :** to strike a quick sharp blow **2 :** to make a short sharp sound

[3]**rap** *vt* **rapped** *also* **rapt; rap·ping** [back-formation fr. *rapt*] **1 :** to snatch away or upward **2 :** to transport out of oneself **:** ENRAPTURE

[4]**rap** *n* [perh. fr. [1]*rap*] **:** something of little value

ra·pa·cious \rə-'pā-shəs\ *adj* [L *rapac-, rapax*, fr. *rapere* to seize] **1 :** excessively grasping or covetous **2 :** living on prey **3 :** RAVENOUS, VORACIOUS — **ra·pa·cious·ly** *adv* — **ra·pa·cious·ness** *n*

ra·pac·i·ty \rə-'pas-ət-ē\ *n* **:** the quality of being rapacious

[1]**rape** \'rāp\ *n* [ME, fr. L *rapa, rapum* turnip, rape; akin to OHG *rāba* turnip, rape] **:** a European herb (*Brassica napus*) of the mustard family grown as a forage crop for sheep and hogs and for its seeds which yield rape oil and are a bird food

[2]**rape** *vt* [ME *rapen*, fr. L *rapere*] **1** *archaic* **:** to seize and take away by force **2 :** to commit rape on — **rap·er** *n* — **rap·ist** \'rā-pəst\ *n*

[3]**rape** *n* **1 :** an act or instance of robbing or despoiling or carrying away a person by force **2 a :** the unlawful carnal knowledge of a woman by a man without her consent and chiefly by force or deception —compare STATUTORY RAPE **b :** unlawful carnal knowledge other than of a woman by a man **3 :** an outrageous violation

[4]**rape** *n* [F *râpe* grape stalk] **:** grape pomace

rape oil *n* **:** a nondrying or semidrying oil obtained from rapeseed and turnip seed and used chiefly as a lubricant, illuminant, and food — called also *rapeseed oil*

rape·seed \'rāp-,sēd\ *n* **:** the seed of rape

Ra·pha·el \'raf-ē-əl, 'rā-fē-\ *n* [LL, fr. Gk *Rhaphaēl*, fr. Heb *Rěphā'ēl*] **:** one of the archangels

ra·phe \'rā-(,)fē\ *n* [NL, fr. Gk *rhaphē* seam, fr. *rhaptein* to sew — more at RHAPSODY] **1 :** the seamlike union of the two lateral halves of a part or organ (as the tongue) having externally a ridge or furrow **2 a :** the part of the stalk of an anatropous ovary that is united in growth to the outside covering and forms a ridge along the body of the ovule **b :** the median line of a diatom's valve

ra·phia \'rā-fē-ə, 'raf-ē-\ *n* [NL, genus of palms, fr. Malagasy *rafia* raffia] **:** RAFFIA

ra·phide \'rā-fəd, 'raf-əd\ *n, pl* **ra·phides** \'rā-fədz, -fə-,dēz; 'raf-ədz, -ə-,dēz\ [NL *raphides*, pl., modif. of Gk *rhaphides*, pl. of *rhaphid-, rhaphis* needle, fr. *rhaptein*] **:** one of the needle-shaped crystals, usu. of calcium oxalate that develop as metabolic by-products in plant cells — **ra·phi·dif·er·ous** \,rā-fə-'dif-(ə-)rəs, ,raf-ə-\ *adj*

[1]**rap·id** \'rap-əd\ *adj* [L *rapidus* seizing, sweeping, rapid, fr. *rapere* to seize, sweep away; akin to OE *refsan* to blame] **:** marked by a fast rate of motion, activity, succession, or occurrence **:** SWIFT **syn** see FAST — **rap·id·ly** *adv* — **rap·id·ness** *n*

[2]**rapid** *n* **:** a part of a river where the current is fast and the surface is usu. broken by obstructions — usu. used in pl. but sing. or pl. in constr.

rap·id–fire \,rap-əd-'fī(ə)r\ *adj* **1 :** firing or adapted for firing shots in rapid succession **2 :** marked by rapidity, liveliness, or sharpness

ra·pid·i·ty \rə-'pid-ət-ē, ra-\ *n* **:** the quality or state of being rapid

rapid transit *n* **:** fast passenger transportation (as by subway) in urban areas

ra·pi·er \'rā-pē-ər\ *n* [MF *(espee) rapiere*] **:** a straight 2-edged sword with a narrow pointed blade

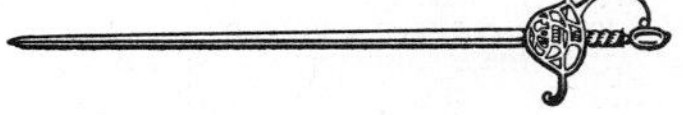

rapier

rap·ine \'rap-ən\ *n* [ME *rapyne*, fr. L *rapina*, fr. *rapere* to seize, rob] **:** PILLAGE, PLUNDER

rap·pa·ree \,rap-ə-'rē\ *n* [IrGael *rāpaire*] **1 :** an Irish irregular soldier or freebooter **2 :** PLUNDERER, VAGABOND

rap·pee \ra-'pā\ *n* [F *(tabac) râpé*, lit., grated tobacco] **:** a pungent snuff made from dark rank tobacco leaves

rap·pel \ra-'pel, rə-\ *n* [F, lit., recall, fr. OF *rapel*, fr. *rapeler* to recall, fr. *re-* + *apeler* to appeal, call — more at APPEAL] **:** descent of a cliff by means of a double rope passed under one thigh, across the body, and over the opposite shoulder — **rappel** *vi* **rap·pelled; rap·pel·ling**

rap·pen \'räp-ən\ *n, pl* **rappen** [G, lit., raven; akin to OHG *hraban* raven — more at RAVEN] **:** the centime of Switzerland

rap·per \'rap-ər\ *n* **:** one that raps; *specif* **:** a door knocker

rap·pi·ni \ra-'pē-nē\ *n pl* [It *rapini*, pl. of *rapino*, dim. of *rapo* turnip, fr. L *rapum* — more at RAPE] **:** immature turnip plants for use as greens

rap·port \ra-'pō(ə)r, -'pȯ(ə)r\ *n* [F, fr. *rapporter* to bring back, refer, fr. OF *raporter* to bring back, fr. *re-* + *aporter* to bring, fr. L *apportare*, fr. *ad-* + *portare* to carry — more at FARE] **:** RELATION; *esp* **:** relation marked by harmony, conformity, accord, or affinity

rap·proche·ment \,rap-,rōsh-'mäⁿ\ *n* [F, fr. *rapprocher* to bring together, fr. MF, fr. *re-* + *approcher* to approach, fr. OF *aprochier*] **:** establishment or state of cordial relations

rap·scal·lion \rap-'skal-yən\ *n* [alter. of earlier *rascallion*, fr. [1]*rascal*] **:** RASCAL, NE'ER-DO-WELL

rapt \'rapt\ *adj* [ME, fr. L *raptus*, pp. of *rapere* to seize — more at RAPID] **1 :** lifted up and carried away **2 :** transported with emotion **:** ENRAPTURED **3 :** wholly absorbed **:** ENGROSSED — **rapt·ly** \'rap-(t)lē\ *adv* — **rapt·ness** \'rap(t)-nəs\ *n*

rap·ta·to·ri·al \,rap-tə-'tōr-ē-əl, -'tȯr-\ *adj* [alter. of *raptorial*] **:** PREDACIOUS

rap·tor \'rap-tər, -,tȯ(ə)r\ *n* [deriv. of L *raptor* plunderer, fr. *raptus*] **:** a bird of prey

rap·to·ri·al \rap-'tōr-ē-əl, -'tȯr-\ *adj* **1 :** PREDACIOUS **2 :** adapted to seize prey **3 :** of, relating to, or being a bird of prey

[1]**rap·ture** \'rap-chər\ *n* [L *raptus*] **1 :** a state or experience of being carried away by overwhelming emotion **2 :** an expression or manifestation of ecstasy or passion — **rap·tur·ous** \'rap-chə-rəs, 'rap-shrəs\ *adj* — **rap·tur·ous·ly** *adv* — **rap·tur·ous·ness** *n*

[2]**rapture** *vt* **:** ENRAPTURE

ra·ra avis \,rar-ə-'ā-vəs, ,rer-; ,rär-ə-'ä-wəs\ *n, pl* **ra·ra avis·es** \-'ā-və-səz\ *or* **ra·rae aves** \,rär-,ī-'ä-,wās\ [L, rare bird] **:** a rare person or thing **:** RARITY

[1]**rare** \'ra(ə)r, 're(ə)r\ *adj* [alter. of earlier *rere*, fr. ME, fr. OE *hrēre* boiled lightly; akin to OE *hrēran* to stir, OHG *hruoren*] **:** cooked a short time **:** UNDERDONE

[2]**rare** *adj* [ME, fr. L *rarus*] **1 :** marked by wide separation of component particles **:** THIN ⟨~ air⟩ **2 a :** marked by unusual quality, merit, or appeal **:** DISTINCTIVE **b :** superlative or extreme of its kind **3 :** seldom occurring or found **:** UNCOMMON **syn** see INFREQUENT, CHOICE — **rare·ness** *n*

rare·bit \'ra(ə)r-bət, 're(ə)r-\ *n* [(*Welsh*) *rarebit*] **:** WELSH RABBIT

rare earth *n* **1 :** any of a group of similar oxides of metals or a mixture of such oxides occurring together in widely distributed but relatively scarce minerals **2 :** any of the series of chiefly trivalent metallic elements whose oxides are the rare earths and which include the elements with atomic numbers 58 through 71, usu. lanthanum, and sometimes yttrium and scandium — called also *rare-earth element, rare-earth metal;* compare ELEMENT table

rar·ee–show \'rar-ē-,shō, 'rer-\ *n* [alter. of *rare show*] **1 :** PEEP SHOW **2 :** SHOW, SPECTACLE; *specif* **:** a cheap street show

rar·efac·tion \,rar-ə-'fak-shən, ,rer-\ *n* [F or ML; F *raréfaction*, fr. ML *rarefaction-, rarefactio*, fr. L *rarefactus*, pp. of *rarefacere* to rarefy] **1 :** the act or process of rarefying **2 :** the quality or state of being rarefied — **rar·efac·tion·al** \-shnəl, -shən-ᵊl\ *adj* — **rar·e·fac·tive** \-'fak-tiv\ *adj*

rar·efied \'rar-ə-,fīd, 'rer-\ *adj* **1 :** of, relating to, or interesting to a select group **:** ESOTERIC **2 :** very high

rar·efy *also* **rar·i·fy** \-ə-,fī\ *vb* [ME *rarefien, rarifien*, fr. MF *rarefier*, modif. of L *rarefacere*, fr. *rarus* rare + *facere* to make — more at DO] *vt* **1 :** to make rare, thin, porous, or less dense **2 :** to

make more spiritual, refined, tenuous, or abstruse ~ *vi* **:** to become less dense

rare·ly *adv* **1 :** not often **:** SELDOM **2 :** with rare skill **:** EXCELLENTLY **3 :** EXTREMELY

¹rare·ripe \'ra(ə)r-,rīp, 're(ə)r-\ *adj* [E dial. *rare* (early) + E *ripe*] **:** ripe before others or earlier than usual

²rareripe *n* **1 :** an early ripening fruit or vegetable **2** *dial* **:** GREEN ONION

rar·ing \'ra(ə)r-iŋ, 're(ə)r-\ *adj* [fr. prp. of E dial. *rare* to rear, alter. of E *rear*] **:** full of enthusiasm or eagerness

rar·i·ty \'rar-ət-ē, 'rer-\ *n* **1 :** the quality, state, or fact of being rare **2 :** someone or something rare

ras·bo·ra \raz-'bōr-ə, -'bȯr-\ *n* [NL, genus name, fr. native name in the East Indies] **:** any of a genus (*Rasbora*) of tiny brilliantly colored cyprinid freshwater fishes often kept in the tropical aquarium

¹ras·cal \'ras-kəl\ *n* [ME *rascaile* rabble, one of the rabble] **1 :** a mean, unprincipled, or dishonest person **2 :** a mischievous person

²rascal *adj* **:** of, forming, or befitting the rabble **:** LOW

ras·cal·i·ty \ra-'skal-ət-ē\ *n* **1 :** RABBLE **2 a :** the character or actions of a rascal **:** KNAVERY **b :** a rascally act

ras·cal·ly \'ras-kə-lē\ *adj* **:** of or characteristic of a rascal — **rascally** *adv*

rase \'rāz\ *vt* [ME *rasen*, fr. MF *raser*, fr. (assumed) VL *rasare*, fr. L *rasus*, pp. of *radere* to scrape, shave] **1 :** ERASE **2 :** RAZE 1

¹rash \'rash\ *adj* [ME (northern dial.) *rasch* quick; akin to OHG *rasc* fast] **1 :** marked by or proceeding from undue haste or lack of deliberation or caution **:** PRECIPITATE **2** *obs* **:** quickly effective **syn** see ADVENTUROUS — **rash·ly** *adv* — **rash·ness** *n*

²rash *adv, archaic* **:** RASHLY

³rash *n* [obs. F *rache* scurf, fr. (assumed) VL *rasica*, fr. *rasicare* to scratch, fr. L *rasus*, pp. of *radere*] **1 :** an eruption on the body **2 :** a large number of instances in a short period

rash·er \'rash-ər\ *n* [perh. fr. obs. *rash* to cut, fr. ME *rashen*] **:** a thin slice of bacon or ham broiled or fried; *also* **:** a portion consisting of several such slices

ra·so·ri·al \rə-'zōr-ē-əl, -'sōr-, -'zȯr-, -'sȯr-\ *adj* [deriv. of LL *rasor* scraper, fr. L *rasus*] **1 :** habitually scratching the ground in search of food ⟨~ birds⟩ **2 :** GALLINACEOUS

¹rasp \'rasp\ *vb* [ME *raspen*, fr. (assumed) MF *rasper*, of Gmc origin; akin to OHG *raspōn* to scrape together] *vt* **1 :** to rub with something rough; *specif* **:** to abrade with a rasp **2 :** to grate upon **:** IRRITATE **3 :** to utter in an irritated tone ~ *vi* **1 :** SCRAPE **2 :** to produce a grating sound — **rasp·er** *n* — **rasp·ing·ly** \'ras-piŋ-lē\ *adv*

²rasp *n* **1 :** a coarse file with cutting points instead of lines **2 :** something used for rasping **3 a :** an act of rasping **b :** a rasping sound, sensation, or effect

rasp·ber·ry \'raz-,ber-ē, -b(ə-)rē\ *n* [E dial. *rasp* (raspberry) + E *berry*] **1 a :** any of various usu. black or red edible berries that are aggregate fruits consisting of numerous small drupes on a fleshy receptacle and that are usu. rounder and smaller than the closely related blackberries **b :** a plant (genus *Rubus*) that bears raspberries **2 :** a sound of contempt made by protruding the tongue between the lips and expelling air forcibly to produce a vibration

raspy \'ras-pē\ *adj* **1 :** GRATING, HARSH **2 :** IRRITABLE

ras·ter \'ras-tər\ *n* [G, fr. L *raster*, *rastrum* rake, fr. *radere* to scrape] **:** the area on which the image is reproduced in a kinescope

ra·sure \'rā-shər, -zhər\ *n* [MF, fr. L *rasura*, fr. *rasus*, pp. of *radere*] **:** ERASURE, OBLITERATION

¹rat \'rat\ *n* [ME, fr. OE *ræt;* akin to OHG *ratta* rat, L *rodere* to gnaw, *radere* to scrape, shave] **1 a :** any of numerous rodents (*Rattus* and related genera) differing from the related mice by considerably larger size and by features of the teeth and other structures **b :** any of various similar rodents **2 :** a contemptible person: as **a :** BETRAYER **b :** SCAB 3b **c :** INFORMER **3 :** a pad over which a woman's hair is arranged

²rat *vi* **rat·ted; rat·ting 1 :** to desert or inform on one's associates **2 :** to catch or hunt rats **3 :** to work as a scab **4 :** to reverse one's position **:** RECANT

rat·able *or* **rate·able** \'rāt-ə-bəl\ *adj* **:** capable of being rated, estimated, or apportioned — **rat·ably** \-blē\ *adv*

rat·a·fia \,rat-ə-'fē-ə\ *n* [F] **1 :** a liqueur flavored with fruit kernels and bitter almonds **2 :** a sweet biscuit made of almond paste

rat·a·plan \'rat-ə-,plan\ *n* [F, of imit. origin] **:** the iterative sound of beating

rat-a-tat \'rat-ə-,tat\ *or* **rat-a-tat-tat** \,rat-ə-,ta(t)-'tat\ *n* [imit.] **:** a sharp repeated knocking, tapping, or cracking sound

rat-bite fever *n* **:** either of two febrile bacterial diseases of man usu. transmitted by the bite of a rat

ratch \'rach\ *n* [G *ratsche*, fr. *ratschen* to rattle, fr. MHG *ratzen;* akin to MHG *razzeln* to rattle] **1 :** RATCHET 2 **2 :** a notched bar with which a pawl or detent works to prevent reversal of motion

rat cheese *n* **:** CHEDDAR

ratch·et \'rach-ət\ *n* [alter. of earlier *rochet*, fr. F, alter. of MF *rocquet* lance head, of Gmc origin; akin to OHG *rocko* distaff — more at ROCK] **1 :** a mechanism that consists of a bar or wheel having inclined teeth into which a pawl drops so that motion can be imparted to the wheel or bar, governed, or prevented and that is used in a hand tool (as a brace or screwdriver) to allow effective motion in one direction only **2 :** a pawl or detent for holding or propelling a ratchet wheel

ratchet wheel *n* **:** a toothed wheel held in position or turned by an engaging pawl

¹rate \'rāt\ *vb* [ME *raten*] *vt* **1 :** to rebuke angrily or violently **2** *obs* **:** to drive away by scolding ~ *vi* **:** to voice angry reprimands

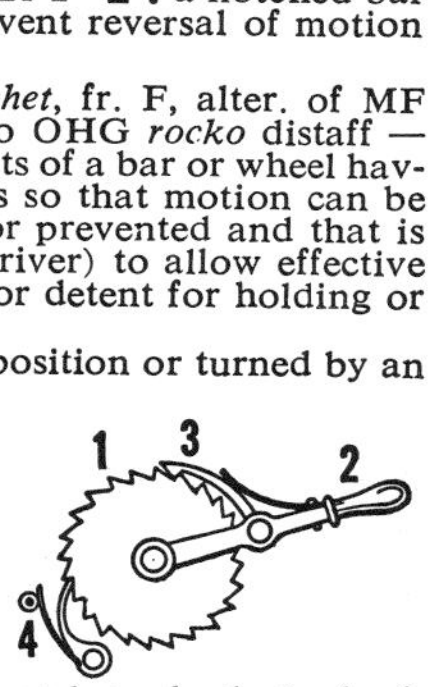

ratchet wheel: *1* wheel, *2* reciprocating lever, *3* pawl for communicating motion, *4* pawl for preventing backward motion

²rate *n* [ME, fr. MF, fr. ML *rata*, fr. L (*pro*) *rata* (*parte*) according to a fixed proportion] **1 a :** reckoned value **:** VALUATION **b** *obs* **:** ESTIMATION **2** *obs* **:** a fixed quantity **3 a :** a fixed ratio between two things **b :** a charge, payment, or price fixed according to a ratio, scale, or standard: as (1) **:** a charge per unit of a public-service commodity (2) **:** a charge per unit of freight or passenger service (3) **:** a unit charge or ratio used by a government for assessing property taxes (4) *Brit* **:** a local tax **4 a :** a quantity, amount, or degree of something measured per unit of something else **b :** an amount of payment or charge based on another amount; *specif* **:** the amount of premium per unit of insurance **5 :** relative condition or quality **:** CLASS — **at any rate :** in any case **:** at least

³rate *vt* **1** *obs* **:** ALLOT **2 :** CONSIDER, REGARD **3 a :** APPRAISE, ESTIMATE **b :** to determine or assign the relative rank or class of **:** GRADE **c :** to estimate the normal capacity or power of **4 :** to fix the amount of premium to be charged per unit of insurance on **5 :** to have a right to **:** DESERVE ⟨~ special privileges⟩ ~ *vi* **:** to be of consequence **syn** see ESTIMATE

rated load *n* **:** the load a machine is designed to carry

ra·tel \'rāt-ᵊl, 'rät-\ *n* [Afrik, lit., rattle, fr. MD — more at RATTLE] **:** an African or Asiatic nocturnal carnivorous mammal (genus *Mellivora*) resembling the badger

rate·pay·er \'rāt-,pā-ər\ *n, Brit* **:** TAXPAYER

rat·er \'rāt-ər\ *n* **1 :** one that rates; *specif* **:** a person who estimates or determines a rating **2 :** one having a specified rating or class ⟨first-*rater*⟩

rat·fish \'rat-,fish\ *n* **:** CHIMAERA

rathe \'rāth, 'rath\ *adj* [ME, quick, fr. OE *hræth*, alter. of *hræd;* akin to OHG *hrad* quick] *archaic* **:** EARLY — **rathe·ness** *n*

rath·er \'rath-ər, 'rəth-, 'räth-; *interjectionally* (')ra-'thər, 'rə-', ,rə-', (')rä-'\ *adv* [ME, OE *hrathor*, compar. of *hrathe* quickly; akin to OHG *rado* quickly, OE *hræd* quick] **1 :** with better reason or more propriety **2 :** more readily or willingly **:** PREFERABLY — often used interjectionally to express affirmation **3 :** more properly or truly **4 :** to the contrary **:** INSTEAD **5 :** in some degree **:** SOMEWHAT

raths·kel·ler \'rät-,skel-ər, 'rat(h)-\ *n* [obs. G (now *ratskeller*), city-hall basement restaurant, fr. *rat* council + *keller* cellar] **:** a restaurant patterned after the cellar of a German city hall where beer is sold

rat·icide \'rat-ə-,sīd\ *n* **:** a substance for killing rats

rat·i·fi·ca·tion \,rat-ə-fə-'kā-shən\ *n* **:** the act or process of ratifying

rat·i·fy \'rat-ə-,fī\ *vt* [ME *ratifien*, fr. MF *ratifier*, fr. ML *ratificare*, fr. L *ratus* determined, fr. pp. of *reri* to calculate — more at REASON] **:** to approve and sanction formally **:** CONFIRM

ra·ti·né \,rat-ᵊn-'ā\ *or* **ra·tine** \,rat-ᵊn-'ā, ra-'tēn\ *n* [F *ratiné*] **1 :** a nubby ply yarn of various fibers made by twisting under tension a thick and a thin yarn **2 :** a rough bulky fabric usu. woven loosely in plain weave from ratiné yarns

rat·ing *n* **1 :** a classification according to grade; *specif* **:** a military or naval specialist classification **2** *chiefly Brit* **:** a naval enlisted man **3 a :** relative estimate or evaluation **:** STANDING **b :** an estimate of an individual's or business's credit and responsibility **4 :** a stated operating limit of a machine expressible in power units or in characteristics

ra·tio \'rā-(,)shō, -shē-,ō\ *n* [L, computation, reason — more at REASON] **1 a :** the indicated quotient of two mathematical expressions **b :** the relationship in quantity, amount, or size between two or more things **:** PROPORTION **2 :** the expression of the relative values of gold and silver as determined by a country's currency laws

ra·ti·o·ci·nate \,rat-ē-'ōs-ᵊn-,āt, ,rash-ē-, -'äs-\ *vi* [L *ratiocinatus*, pp. of *ratiocinari* to reckon, fr. *ratio*] **:** REASON — **ra·ti·o·ci·na·tor** \-,āt-ər\ *n*

ra·ti·o·ci·na·tion \-,ōs-ᵊn-'ā-shən, -,äs-\ *n* **1 :** the process of exact thinking **:** REASONING **2 :** a reasoned train of thought — **ra·ti·o·ci·na·tive** \-'ōs-ᵊn-,āt-iv, -'äs-\ *adj*

¹ra·tion \'rash-ən, 'rā-shən\ *n* [F, fr. L *ration-*, *ratio* computation, reason] **1 a :** a food allowance for one day **b** *pl* **:** FOOD, PROVISIONS **2 :** a share esp. as determined by supply

²ration *vt* **ra·tion·ing** \'rash-(ə-)niŋ, 'rāsh-\ **1 :** to supply with or put on rations **2 a :** to distribute as rations **b :** to distribute equitably **c :** to use sparingly

¹ra·tio·nal \'rash-nəl, -ən-ᵊl\ *adj* [ME *racional*, fr. L *rationalis*, fr. *ration-*, *ratio*] **1 a :** having reason or understanding **b :** relating to, based on, or agreeable to reason **2 :** relating to or resulting from the application of the arithmetic operations to integers or to polynomials ⟨division is a ~ operation⟩ — **ra·tio·nal·ly** \-ē\ *adv* — **ra·tio·nal·ness** *n*

²rational *n* **:** something rational; *specif* **:** a rational number or fraction

ra·tio·nale \,rash-ə-'nal *also* -'nä-lē\ *n* [L, neut. of *rationalis*] **1 :** an explanation of controlling principles of opinion, belief, practice, or phenomena **2 :** an underlying reason **:** BASIS

ra·tio·nal·ism \'rash-nə-,liz-əm, -ən-ᵊl-,iz-\ *n* **1 :** reliance on reason as the basis for establishment of religious truth **2 a :** a theory that reason is in itself a source of knowledge superior to and independent of sense perceptions **b :** a view that reason and experience rather than the nonrational are the fundamental criteria in the solution of problems **3 :** FUNCTIONALISM — **ra·tio·nal·ist** \-nə-ləst, -ən-ᵊl-əst\ *n* — **rationalist** *or* **ra·tio·nal·is·tic** \,rash-nə-'lis-tik, -ən-ᵊl-'is-\ *adj* — **ra·tio·nal·is·ti·cal·ly** \-ti-k(ə-)lē\ *adv*

ra·tio·nal·i·ty \,rash-ə-'nal-ət-ē\ *n* **1 :** the quality or state of being rational **2 :** acceptability to reason **:** REASONABLENESS **3 :** a rational opinion, belief, or practice — usu. used in pl.

ra·tio·nal·iza·tion \,rash-nə-lə-'zā-shən, -ən-ᵊl-ə-'zā-\ *n* **:** an act, process, or result of rationalizing

ra·tio·nal·ize \'rash-nə-,līz, -ən-ᵊl-,īz\ *vt* **1 :** to free (a mathematical equation) from irrational expressions **2 a :** to make conformable with rational principles **b :** to substitute a natural for a supernatural explanation of **3 :** to attribute (one's actions) to rational and creditable motives without analysis of true esp. unconscious motives ~ *vi* **:** to provide plausible but untrue reasons for conduct

rational number *n* **:** an integer or the quotient of two integers

¹rat·ite \'ra-,tīt\ *adj* [deriv. of L *ratitus* marked with the figure of a raft, fr. *ratis* raft] **:** having a flat breastbone

²ratite *n* **:** a bird with a flat breastbone

rat·like \'rat-,līk\ *adj* **:** of, relating to, or resembling a rat

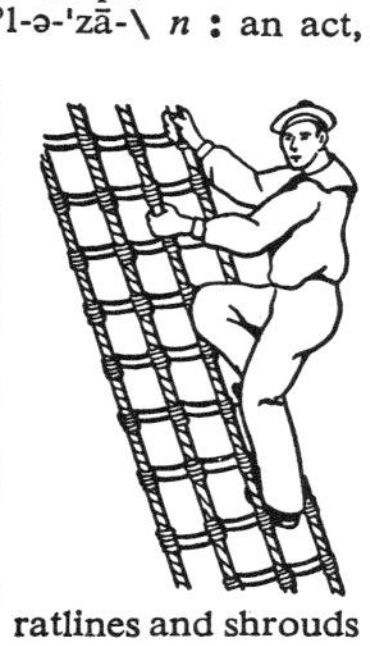

ratlines and shrouds

rat·line \'rat-lən\ *n* [origin unknown] **:** one of the small transverse ropes attached to the shrouds of a ship so as to form the steps of a rope ladder

rat mite *n* **:** a widely distributed mite (*Bdellonyssus bacoti*) that may cause dermatitis in man and is a vector of typhus

1**ra·toon** \ra-'tün\ *n* [Sp *retoño,* fr. *retoñar* to sprout, fr. *re-* (fr. L) + *otoñar* to grow in autumn, fr. *otoño* autumn, fr. L *autumnus*] **1 :** a shoot of a perennial plant (as cotton) **2 :** a crop (as of bananas) produced on ratoons

2**ratoon** *vi* **:** to sprout or spring up from the root ~ *vt* **:** to grow or produce (a crop) from or on ratoons

ra·to unit \'rāt-(,)ō-\ *n* [*r*ocket-*a*ssisted *t*ake*o*ff] **:** JATO UNIT

rat race *n* **:** violent, senseless, and usu. competitive activity or rush

rats·bane \'rats-,bān\ *n* **1 :** arsenic trioxide **2 :** any of various plants held to be poisonous to rats

rat snake *n* **:** any of numerous rat-eating colubrid snakes

rat·tail \'rat-,tāl\ *n* **1 :** a horse's tail with little or no hair **2 :** any of several plants with elongated terete spikes

rattail cactus *n* **:** a commonly cultivated tropical American cactus (*Aporocactus flagelliformis*) with creeping stems and showy crimson flowers

rat·tan \ra-'tan, rə-\ *n* [Malay *rotan*] **1 a :** a climbing palm (esp. of the genera *Calamus* and *Daemonorops*) with very long tough stems **b :** a part of one of these stems used esp. for walking sticks and wickerwork **2 :** a rattan cane or switch

rat·teen \ra-'tēn\ *n* [F *ratine*] *archaic* **:** a coarse woolen fabric

rat·ter \'rat-ər\ *n* **:** one that catches rats; *specif* **:** a rat-catching dog or cat

1**rat·tle** \'rat-ᵊl\ *vb* **rat·tling** \'rat-liŋ, -ᵊl-iŋ\ [ME *ratelen;* akin to MD *ratel* rattle, OE *hratian* to rush — more at CARDINAL] *vi* **1 :** to make a rapid succession of short sharp noises **2 :** to chatter incessantly and aimlessly **3 a :** to move with a clatter or rattle **b :** to have room to move about aimlessly ~ *vt* **1 :** to say, perform, or affect in a brisk lively fashion **2 :** to cause to make a rattling sound **3 :** ROUSE; *specif* **:** to beat (a cover) for game **4 :** to disturb the composure of **syn** see EMBARRASS

2**rattle** *n* **1 a :** a rapid succession of sharp clattering sounds **b :** NOISE, RACKET **2 a :** a device that produces a rattle; *specif* **:** a case containing pellets used as a baby's toy **b :** the sound-producing organ on a rattlesnake's tail **3 :** a throat noise caused by air passing through mucus and heard esp. at the approach of death

3**rattle** *vt* [irreg. fr. *ratline*] **:** to furnish with ratlines

rat·tle·brain \'rat-ᵊl-,brān\ *n* **:** a flighty or thoughtless person — **rat·tle·brained** \,rat-ᵊl-'brānd\ *adj*

rat·tler \'rat-lər, -ᵊl-ər\ *n* **1 :** one that rattles **2 :** a freight train **3 :** RATTLESNAKE

rat·tle·snake \'rat-ᵊl-,snāk\ *n* **:** any of various thick-bodied American venomous snakes (family Crotalidae, genera *Sistrurus* and *Crotalus*) with horny interlocking joints at the end of the tail that make a sharp rattling sound when shaken

rattlesnake plantain *n* **:** an orchid (genus *Goodyera*) with checked or mottled leaves

rattlesnake root *n* **1 :** a composite plant (genus *Prenanthes,* esp. *P. altissima*) formerly held to be a remedy for snake bites **2 :** SENEGA ROOT

rattlesnake weed *n* **1 :** a hawkweed (*Hieracium venosum*) with purple-veined leaves **2 :** a weedy herb (*Daucus pusillus*) of the western U.S. related to the carrot **3 :** BUTTON SNAKEROOT

rat·tle·trap \'rat-ᵊl-,trap\ *n* **:** something rattly or rickety; *esp* **:** an old car — **rattletrap** *adj*

rat·tling *adj* **1 :** LIVELY, BRISK **2 :** extraordinarily good **:** SPLENDID — **rat·tling·ly** \'rat-liŋ-lē, -ᵊl-iŋ-\ *adv*

rat·tly \'rat-lē, -ᵊl-ē\ *adj* **:** likely to rattle **:** making a rattle

rat·ton \'rat-ᵊn\ *n* [ME *ratoun,* fr. MF *raton,* dim. of *rat,* prob. of Gmc origin; akin to OE *ræt* rat] *chiefly dial* **:** RAT

rat·trap \'rat-,trap\ *n* **1 :** a trap for rats **2 :** a dirty dilapidated structure **3 :** a hopeless situation

rat·ty \'rat-ē\ *adj* **1 a :** infested with rats **b :** of, relating to, or suggestive of a rat **c :** SHABBY, UNKEMPT **2 a :** DESPICABLE, TREACHEROUS **b :** IRRITABLE

rat unit *n* **:** a bioassay unit consisting of the amount of a material that under standardized conditions is just sufficient to produce a response in experimental rats

rau·cous \'rȯ-kəs\ *adj* [L *raucus* hoarse; akin to OE *rēon* to lament — more at RUMOR] **1 :** disagreeably harsh or strident **:** HOARSE **2 :** boisterously disorderly — **rau·cous·ly** *adv* — **rau·cous·ness** *n*

raun·chy \'rȯn-chē, 'rän-\ *adj* [origin unknown] **1 :** falling below standard; *esp* **:** SLOVENLY **2 :** SMUTTY

rau·wol·fia \raù-'wùl-fē-ə, rȯ-\ *n* [NL, genus name, fr. Leonhard *Rauwolf* †1596 G botanist] **1 :** any of a large pantropic genus (*Rauwolfia*) of the dogbane family of somewhat poisonous trees and shrubs yielding emetic and purgative substances **2 :** a medicinal extract from the root of an Indian rauwolfia (*Rauwolfia serpentina*) used in the treatment of hypertension and mental disorders

1**rav·age** \'rav-ij\ *n* [F, fr. MF, fr. *ravir* to ravish — more at RAVISH] **1 :** an act or practice of ravaging **2 :** damage resulting from ravaging

2**ravage** *vt* **:** to lay waste **:** PLUNDER ~ *vi* **:** to commit destructive actions — **rav·ag·er** *n*

syn RAVAGE, DEVASTATE, WASTE, SACK, PILLAGE, DESPOIL mean to lay waste by plundering or destroying. RAVAGE implies violent often cumulative depredation and destruction; DEVASTATE implies causing ruin and desolation over a wide area; WASTE may imply producing the same result by a slow process rather than sudden and violent action; SACK implies carrying off all valuable possessions from a helpless city; PILLAGE implies ruthless plundering at will but without the completeness suggested by SACK; DESPOIL applies to looting or robbing of a particular place or person without suggesting accompanying destruction

1**rave** \'rāv\ *vb* [ME *raven*] *vi* **1 a :** to talk irrationally in or as if in delirium **b :** to declaim wildly **c :** to talk with extreme enthusiasm **2 :** to move or advance violently **:** STORM ~ *vt* **:** to utter in madness or frenzy — **rav·er** *n*

2**rave** *n, often attrib* **1 :** an act or instance or raving **2 :** an extravagantly favorable criticism

1**rav·el** \'rav-əl\ *vb* **rav·eled** *or* **rav·elled; rav·el·ing** *or* **rav·el·ling** \'rav-(ə-)liŋ\ [D *rafelen,* fr. *rafel* loose thread; akin to OE *ræfter* rafter] *vt* **1 a :** to separate or undo the texture of **:** UNRAVEL **b :** to undo the intricacies of **:** DISENTANGLE **2 :** ENTANGLE, CONFUSE ~ *vi* **1** *obs* **:** to become entangled or confused **2 :** to become unwoven, untwisted, or unwound **:** FRAY — **rav·el·er** *or* **rav·el·ler** \-(ə-)lər\ *n*

2**ravel** *n* **:** an act or result of raveling: as **a :** something tangled **b :** something raveled out; *specif* **:** a loose thread

rav·el·ment \'rav-əl-mənt\ *n* **:** RAVEL, TANGLE

1**ra·ven** \'rā-vən\ *n* [ME, fr. OE *hræfn;* akin to OHG *hraban* raven, L *corvus,* Gk *korax,* L *crepare* to rattle, crack] **:** a glossy black corvine bird (*Corvus corax*) of northern Europe, Asia, and America — compare CROW

2**raven** *adj* **:** of the color or glossy sheen of the raven

3**rav·en** \'rav-ən\ *vb* **rav·en·ing** \-(ə-)niŋ\ [MF *raviner* to rush, take by force, fr. *ravine* rapine] *vt* **:** to devour greedily ~ *vi* **1 :** to feed greedily **2 :** to prowl for food **:** PREY **3 :** PLUNDER — **rav·en·er** \-ə-nər\ *n*

rav·en·ing *adj* **:** greedily devouring **:** RAPACIOUS

rav·en·ous \'rav-ə-nəs\ *adj* **1 :** RAPACIOUS, VORACIOUS **2 :** very eager for food, satisfaction, or gratification — **rav·en·ous·ly** *adv* — **rav·en·ous·ness** *n*

rav·in \'rav-ən\ *n* [ME, fr. MF *ravine*] **1 :** RAPINE, RAPACITY **2 a :** an act or habit of preying **b :** something seized as prey

ra·vine \rə-'vēn\ *n* [F, fr. MF, rapine, rush, fr. L *rapina* rapine] **:** a small narrow steep-sided valley larger than a gully, smaller than a canyon, and usu. worn by running water

rav·ined \'rav-ənd\ *adj, obs* **:** RAVENOUS

rav·i·o·li \,rav-ē-'ō-lē\ *n* [It, fr. It dial., pl. of *raviolo,* lit., little turnip, dim. of *rava* turnip, fr. L *rapa* — more at RAPE] **:** little cases of dough containing a savory filling

rav·ish \'rav-ish\ *vt* [ME *ravisshen,* fr. MF *raviss-,* stem of *ravir,* fr. (assumed) VL *rapire,* alter. of L *rapere* to seize, rob — more at RAPID] **1 a :** to seize and take away by violence **b :** to transport with emotion **c :** RAPE, VIOLATE **2 :** PLUNDER, ROB — **rav·ish·er** *n*

rav·ish·ing \'rav-i-shiŋ\ *adj* **:** unusually attractive, pleasing, or striking — **rav·ish·ing·ly** \-shiŋ-lē\ *adv*

rav·ish·ment \'rav-ish-mənt\ *n* **1 :** an act, means, or effect of ravishing **2 :** the state of being ravished; *specif* **:** a transport of delight

1**raw** \'rȯ\ *adj* **raw·er** \'rȯ(-ə)r\ **raw·est** \'rȯ-əst\ [ME, fr. OE *hrēaw;* akin to OHG *hrō* raw, L *crudus* raw, *cruor* blood, Gk *kreas* flesh] **1 :** not cooked **2 a** (1) **:** being in or nearly in the natural state ⟨~ fibers⟩ (2) **:** not diluted or blended ⟨~ spirits⟩ **b :** unprepared or imperfectly prepared for use **3 a** (1) **:** having the underlying tissues exposed (2) **:** very irritated **b :** lacking covering **:** NAKED **4 a :** lacking experience or understanding **:** GREEN **b** (1) **:** marked by absence of refinements (2) **:** VULGAR, COARSE ⟨a ~ story⟩ **5 :** disagreeably damp or cold **syn** see RUDE — **raw·ly** *adv* — **raw·ness** *n*

2**raw** *n* **:** a raw place or state; *specif* **:** NUDITY

raw·boned \'rȯ-'bōnd\ *adj* **:** having little flesh **:** GAUNT **syn** see LEAN

raw deal *n* **:** an instance of unfair treatment

1**raw·hide** \'rȯ-,hīd\ *n* **1 :** untanned cattle skin **2 :** a whip of untanned hide

2**rawhide** *vt* **:** to whip or drive with or as if with a rawhide

ra·win·sonde \'rā-wən-,sänd\ *n* [*ra*dar + *win*d + radio*sonde*] **:** a radiosonde tracked by a radio direction-finding device to determine the velocity of winds aloft

raw material *n* **:** material available or suitable for manufacture, use, or finishing

rax \'raks\ *vb* [ME (northern dial.) *raxen,* fr. OE *raxan;* akin to OE *reccan* to stretch — more at RACK] *chiefly Scot* **:** STRETCH

1**ray** \'rā\ *n* [ME *raye,* fr. MF *raie,* fr. L *raia*] **:** any of numerous elasmobranch fishes (order Hypotremata) having the body flattened dorsoventrally, the eyes on the upper surface, and a much-reduced caudal region

2**ray** *n* [ME, fr. MF *rai,* fr. L *radius* rod, ray] **1 a :** one of the lines of light that appear to radiate from a bright object **b :** a beam of light or other radiant energy of small cross section **c** (1) **:** a stream of material particles traveling in the same line (as in radioactive phenomena) (2) **:** a single particle of such a stream **2 a :** light cast by rays **:** RADIANCE **b :** a moral or intellectual light **3 :** a thin line suggesting a ray: as **a :** any of a group of lines diverging from a common center **b :** HALF LINE **4 a :** one of the bony rods that extend and support the membrane in the fin of a fish **b :** one of the radiating divisions of the body of a radiate animal **c :** a longitudinal vein of an insect's wing **5 a :** a branch or flower stalk of an umbel **b** (1) **:** MEDULLARY RAY (2) **:** VASCULAR RAY **6 :** PARTICLE, TRACE

3**ray** *vi* **1 a :** to shine in or as if in rays **b :** to issue as rays **2 :** to extend like the radii of a circle **:** RADIATE ~ *vt* **1 :** to emit in rays **2 :** to furnish or mark with rays

rayed \'rād\ *adj* **:** having ray flowers

ray flower *n* **:** one of the marginal flowers of the head in a composite plant (as the aster) that also has disk flowers; *also* **:** the entire head in a plant (as chicory) that lacks disk flowers — called also *ray floret*

ray·less \'rā-ləs\ *adj* **1 :** having, admitting, or emitting no rays; *esp* **:** DARK **2 :** lacking ray flowers — **ray·less·ness** *n*

rayless goldenrod *n* **:** any of several composite plants (*Haplopappus* or related genera) some of which produce trembles in cattle

ray·on \'rā-,än\ *n* [irreg. fr. 2*ray*] **1 :** any of a group of smooth textile fibers made in filament and staple form from regenerated cellulose or other cellulosic material by extrusion through minute holes **2 :** a rayon yarn, thread, or fabric

raze \'rāz\ *vt* [alter. of *rase*] **1 :** to destroy to the ground **:** DEMOLISH **2 a :** to scrape, cut, or shave off **b** *archaic* **:** ERASE — **raz·er** *n*

1**ra·zee** \rā-'zē\ *n* [F (*vaisseau*) *rasé,* lit., cut-off ship] **:** a wooden ship with the upper deck cut away

2**razee** *vt* **ra·zeed; ra·zee·ing :** to convert to a razee

ra·zor \'rā-zər\ *n* [ME *rasour,* fr. OF *raseor,* fr. *raser* to raze, shave — more at RASE] **:** a keen-edged instrument for shaving or cutting hair

ra·zor·back \'rā-zər-,bak\ *n* **:** a thin-bodied long-legged half-wild mongrel hog chiefly of the southeastern U.S.

ra·zor–backed \,rā-zər-'bakt\ *or* **ra·zor·back** \'rā-zər-,bak\ *adj* **:** having a sharp narrow back ⟨a ~ horse⟩

ra·zor·bill \'rā-zər-,bil\ *n* **:** a No. Atlantic auk (*Alca torda*) with

the plumage black above and white below and a compressed sharp-edged bill — called also *razor-billed auk* \ˌrā-zər-ˌbild-\
razor clam *n* **:** any of numerous marine bivalve mollusks (family Solenidae) having a long narrow curved thin shell
1**razz** \ˈraz\ *n* [short for *razzberry* (sound of contempt), alter. of *raspberry*] **:** RASPBERRY 2
2**razz** *vt* **:** RIDICULE, TEASE
raz·zle–daz·zle \ˌraz-əl-ˈdaz-əl\ *n* [irreg. redupl. of *dazzle*] **1 :** a state of confusion or hilarity **2 :** a confusing or colorful often gaudy action or display
razz·ma·tazz \ˌraz-mə-ˈtaz\ *n* [prob. alter. of *razzle-dazzle*] **1 :** RAZZLE-DAZZLE 2 **2 :** DOUBLE-TALK 2 **3 :** VIM, ZING
r color *n* **:** an acoustic effect of a simultaneously articulated \r\ imparted to a vowel by retroflexion or contraction of the tongue — **r–col·ored** \ˈär-ˌkəl-ərd\ *adj*
1**re** \ˈrā\ *n* [ML, fr. the syllable sung to this note in a medieval hymn to St. John the Baptist] **:** the second tone of the diatonic scale in solmization
2**re** \(ˈ)rā, (ˈ)rē\ *prep* [L, abl. of *res* thing — more at REAL] **:** with regard to **:** in re
re- \(ˈ)rē *before* ˈ*-stressed syll,* (ˌ)rē *before* ˌ*-stressed syll,* ˌrē *before unstressed syll*\ *prefix* [ME, fr. OF, fr. L *re-*, *red-* back, again, against] **1 :** again **:** anew ⟨*re*tell⟩ **2 :** back **:** backward ⟨*re*call⟩
're \(ə)r\ *vb* **:** ARE ⟨what'*re* you doing⟩
re·ab·sorb \ˌrē-əb-ˈsȯ(ə)rb, -ˈzȯ(ə)rb\ *vt* **:** to absorb again; *specif* **:** RESORB 2 — **re·ab·sorp·tion** \-ˈsȯrp-shən, -ˈzȯrp-\ *n*
1**reach** \ˈrēch\ *vb* [ME *rechen*, fr. OE *rǣcan;* akin to OHG *reichen* to reach, Lith *raižytis* to stretch oneself repeatedly] *vt* **1 a :** to stretch out **:** EXTEND **b :** THRUST **2 a** *obs* **:** to get by seizing **b :** to touch or grasp by extending a part of the body (as a hand) or an object ⟨~*ed* a cup from the shelf⟩ **c** (1) **:** to extend to ⟨the shadow ~*ed* the wall⟩ (2) **:** to arrive at ⟨his letter ~*ed* me⟩ (3) **:** to go as far as **:** ATTAIN ⟨try to ~ happiness⟩ **d** (1) **:** ENCOMPASS (2) **:** to make an impression on (3) **:** to communicate with **3 :** to hand over **:** PASS ~ *vi* **1 a :** to make a stretch with or as if with one's hand **b :** to strain after something **2 a :** PROJECT, EXTEND **b :** to arrive at or come to something ⟨as far as the eye could ~⟩ **3 :** to sail on a reach — **reach·able** \ˈrē-chə-bəl\ *adj* — **reach·er** *n*
syn GAIN, COMPASS, ACHIEVE, ATTAIN: REACH may be used in reference to anything arrived at by any degree of effort; GAIN implies some degree of struggle to reach; COMPASS implies efforts to get around difficulties or transcend limitations; ACHIEVE may imply skill, courage, or endurance as well as effort; ATTAIN suggests a reaching to the extreme, the difficult, or the unusual
2**reach** *n* **1 a** (1) **:** the action or an act of reaching (2) **:** an individual part of a progression or journey **b :** the distance or extent of reaching or of ability to reach **c :** COMPREHENSION, RANGE **2 :** a continuous unbroken stretch or expanse; *esp* **:** a straight portion of a stream or river **3 :** a bearing shaft or coupling pole; *esp* **:** the rod joining the hind axle to the forward bolster of a wagon **4 :** the tack sailed by a ship with the wind coming just forward of the beam or with the wind directly abeam or abaft the beam
reach–me–down \ˈrēch-mē-ˌdau̇n\ *adj or n, chiefly Brit* **:** HAND-ME-DOWN
re·act \rē-ˈakt\ *vb* [NL *reactus*, pp. of *reagere*, fr. L *re-* + *agere* to act — more at AGENT] *vi* **1 :** to exert a reciprocal or counteracting force or influence — often used with *on* or *upon* **2 :** to respond to a stimulus **3 :** to act in opposition to a force or influence — usu. used with *against* **4 :** to move or tend in a reverse direction **5 :** to undergo chemical reaction ~ *vt* **:** to cause to react
re·ac·tance \rē-ˈak-tən(t)s\ *n* **:** the part of the impedance of an alternating-current circuit due to capacitance or inductance or both and expressed in ohms
re·ac·tant \-tənt\ *n* **1 :** a chemically reacting substance **2 :** an initial factor in a chemical reaction
re·ac·tion \rē-ˈak-shən\ *n* **1 a :** the act or process or an instance of reacting **b :** tendency toward a former esp. outmoded political or social order or policy **2 :** bodily response to or activity aroused by a stimulus: **a :** an action induced by vital resistance to another action; *esp* **:** the result characteristically evoked in tissues by a foreign substance and used to determine specific sensitivities or presence of infection **b :** depression or exhaustion due to excessive exertion or stimulation **c :** heightened activity and overaction succeeding depression or shock **d :** a mental or emotional disorder forming an individual's response to his life situation **3 :** the force that a body subjected to the action of a force from another body exerts in the opposite direction **4 a** (1) **:** chemical transformation or change (2) **:** the state resulting from such a reaction **b :** a process involving change in atomic nuclei — **re·ac·tion·al** \-shnəl, -shən-ᵊl\ *adj* — **re·ac·tion·al·ly** \-ē\ *adv*
1**re·ac·tion·ary** \rē-ˈak-shə-ˌner-ē\ *adj* **:** relating to, marked by, or favoring esp. political reaction
2**reactionary** *n* **:** a reactionary person
reaction engine *n* **:** an engine (as a jet engine) that develops thrust by expelling a jet of fluid or a stream of particles
re·ac·ti·vate \(ˈ)rē-ˈak-tə-ˌvāt\ *vt* **:** to activate again ~ *vi* **:** to become active again — **re·ac·ti·va·tion** \(ˌ)rē-ˌak-tə-ˈvā-shən\ *n*
re·ac·tive \rē-ˈak-tiv\ *adj* **1 :** of, relating to, or marked by reaction or reactance **2 :** tending to or resulting from reaction — **re·ac·tive·ly** *adv* — **re·ac·tive·ness** *n* — **re·ac·tiv·i·ty** \(ˌ)rē-ˌak-ˈtiv-ət-ē\ *n*
re·ac·tor \rē-ˈak-tər\ *n* **1 :** one that reacts; *specif* **:** a subject reacting positively to a foreign substance **2 :** a device (as a coil, winding, or conductor of small resistance) used to introduce reactance into an alternating-current circuit **3 a :** a vat for an industrial chemical reaction **b :** an apparatus in which a chain reaction of fissionable material is initiated and controlled
1**read** \ˈrēd\ *vb* **read** \ˈred\ **read·ing** \ˈrēd-iŋ\ [ME *reden* to advise, interpret, read, fr. OE *rǣdan;* akin to OHG *rātan* to advise, Gk *arariskein* to fit — more at ARM] *vt* **1 a** (1) **:** to receive or take in the sense of (as letters or symbols) by scanning (2) **:** to study the movements of (as lips) with mental formulation of the communication expressed (3) **:** to utter aloud the printed or written words of ⟨~ them a story⟩ (4) **:** to understand the meaning of (written or printed matter) **b :** to learn from what one has seen or found in writing or printing **c :** to deliver aloud by or as if by reading; *specif* **:** to utter interpretively **d** (1) **:** to become acquainted with or look over the contents of (as a book) **:** PERUSE (2) **:** to make a study of ⟨~ law⟩ **e** (1) **:** COPYREAD (2) **:** PROOFREAD **f :** to receive and understand (a voice message) by radio **2 a :** to interpret the meaning or significance of ⟨~ palms⟩ **b :** FORETELL, PREDICT **3 :** to discover by interpreting outward expression or signs **4 a :** to attribute a meaning or interpretation to (something read) **b :** to attribute (a meaning) to something read or considered **5 :** to use as a substitute for or in preference to another word or phrase in a particular passage, text, or version ⟨~ *hurry* for *harry*⟩ **6 :** INDICATE ⟨thermometer ~*s* zero⟩ **7 :** to interpret (a musical work) in performance ~ *vi* **1 a :** to perform the act of reading words **b** (1) **:** to learn something by reading (2) **:** to pursue a course of study **2 a :** to yield a particular meaning or impression when read **b :** to have qualities that affect comprehension or enjoyment **3 :** to consist of specific words, phrases, or other similar elements ⟨a passage ~*s* differently in older versions⟩ — **read·abil·i·ty** \ˌrēd-ə-ˈbil-ət-ē\ *n* — **read·able** \ˈrēd-ə-bəl\ *adj* — **read·able·ness** *n* — **read·ably** \-blē\ *adv* — **read between the lines :** to understand more than is directly stated — **read the riot act 1 :** to order a mob to disperse **2 a :** to order or warn to cease something **b :** to protest vehemently **c :** to reprimand severely
2**read** \ˈrēd\ *n, chiefly Brit* **:** a period of reading
3**read** \ˈred\ *adj* **:** instructed by or informed through reading
read·er \ˈrēd-ər\ *n* **1 a :** one that reads **b :** one appointed to read to others: as (1) **:** LECTOR (2) **:** one chosen to read aloud selected material in a Christian Science church or society **c** (1) **:** PROOFREADER (2) **:** one that evaluates manuscripts (3) **:** one that reads periodical literature to discover items of special interest or value **d :** an employee that reads and records the indications of meters **e :** a teacher's assistant who reads and marks student papers **2** *Brit* **:** one who reads lectures or expounds subjects to students **3 a :** a device for projecting a readable image of a transparency **b :** a unit that scans material recorded (as on punched cards) for storage or computation **4 a :** a book for instruction and practice esp. in reading **b :** ANTHOLOGY
read·er·ship \-ˌship\ *n* **1 a :** the quality or state of being a reader **b :** the office or position of a reader **2 :** the mass or a particular group of readers
read·i·ly \ˈred-ᵊl-ē\ *adv* **:** in a ready manner: as **a :** WILLINGLY **b :** SPEEDILY **c :** EASILY
read·i·ness \ˈred-ē-nəs\ *n* **:** the quality or state of being ready
read·ing \ˈrēd-iŋ\ *n* **1 a :** material read or for reading **b :** extent of material read **2 a :** a particular version **b :** data indicated by an instrument **3 :** a particular interpretation or performance
reading desk *n* **:** a desk to support a book in a convenient position for a standing reader
read out *vt* **:** to expel from an organization
read·out \ˈrē-ˌdau̇t\ *n* **:** a device that displays in digits data computed or registered
1**ready** \ˈred-ē\ *adj* [ME *redy;* akin to OHG *reiti* ready, Goth *garaiths* arrayed, Gk *arariskein* to fit — more at ARM] **1 :** prepared mentally or physically for some experience or action **2 a** (1) **:** willingly disposed **:** INCLINED (2) **:** likely to do something indicated **b :** spontaneously prompt **3 :** notably dexterous, adroit, or skilled **4 :** immediately available **syn** see QUICK
2**ready** *vt* **:** to make ready
3**ready** *n* **:** the state of being ready; *esp* **:** preparation of a gun for immediate aiming and firing
ready box *n* **:** a box placed near a gun (as on a ship) to hold ammunition kept ready for immediate use
ready–made \ˌred-ē-ˈmād\ *adj* **1 :** made beforehand esp. for general sale ⟨~ suit⟩ **2 :** lacking individuality **:** COMMONPLACE — **ready–made** *n*
ready room *n* **:** a room in which pilots are briefed and await orders
ready–to–wear \ˌred-ēt-ə-ˈwa(ə)r, -ˈwe(ə)r\ *adj* **:** READY-MADE
ready–wit·ted \ˌred-ē-ˈwit-əd\ *adj* **:** QUICK-WITTED
re·agent \rē-ˈā-jənt\ *n* [NL *reagent-*, *reagens*, prp. of *reagere* to react — more at REACT] **:** a substance that takes part in one or more chemical reactions or biological processes and is used to detect other substances and for other purposes
re·agin \rē-ˈā-jən\ *n* [ISV, fr. *reagent*] **1 :** a substance in the blood of persons with syphilis responsible for positive serological reactions for syphilis **2 :** an antibody in the blood of individuals with some forms of allergy possessing the power of passively sensitizing the skin of normal individuals — **re·agin·ic** \ˌrē-ə-ˈjin-ik\ *adj* — **re·agin·i·cal·ly** \-i-k(ə-)lē\ *adv*
1**re·al** \ˈrē(-ə)l, ˈri(-ə)l\ *adj* [ME, real, relating to things (in law), fr. MF, fr. ML & LL; ML *realis* relating to things (in law), fr. LL, real, fr. L *res* thing, fact; akin to Skt *rai* property] **1 :** of or relating to fixed, permanent, or immovable things (as lands or tenements) **2 a :** not artificial, fraudulent, illusory, or apparent **:** GENUINE **b :** occurring in fact **c** (1) **:** necessarily existent (2) **:** FUNDAMENTAL, ESSENTIAL **d :** having no imaginary part ⟨~ number⟩ **e :** measured by purchasing power ⟨~ income⟩ **3 :** exact as regards repetition of musical intervals in transposition — **re·al·ness** *n*
syn REAL, ACTUAL, TRUE mean corresponding to known facts. REAL implies agreement between what a thing seems to be and what it is; ACTUAL stresses occurrence or manifest existence; TRUE implies conformity to what is real or actual esp. as a model or standard
2**real** *n* **:** a real thing; *esp* **:** a mathematical real quantity
3**real** *adv* **:** VERY
4**re·al** \rā-ˈäl\ *n, pl* **re·als** *or* **re·ales** \-ˈäl-(ˌ)ās\ [Sp] **:** the chief former monetary unit of Spain
real estate *n* **:** property in houses and land
re·al·gar \rē-ˈal-ˌgär, -gər\ *n* [ME, fr. ML, fr. Catal, fr. Ar *rahj al-ghār* powder of the mine] **:** an orange-red mineral consisting of arsenic sulfide and having a resinous luster
re·alia \rē-ˈal-ē-ə, -ˈā-lē-\ *n pl* [LL, neut. pl. of *realis* real] **:** objects or activities used to relate classroom teaching to the real life esp. of peoples studied
re·al·ism \ˈrē-ə-ˌliz-əm, ˈrē-ˌliz-\ *n* **1 :** preoccupation with fact or reality and rejection of the impractical and visionary **2 a :** a doctrine that universals exist outside the mind; *specif* **:** the conception that an abstract term names an independent and unitary reality **b :** the conception that objects of sense perception or cogni-

See *re-* and 2d element	**reactuate**	**readjust**	**readmission**	**readopt**	**reaffirmation**
reaccommodate	**readapt**	**readjustable**	**readmit**	**readoption**	**realign**
reacquire	**readdress**	**readjustment**	**readmittance**	**reaffirm**	**realignment**

tion exist independently of the mind **3 :** fidelity in art and literature to nature or to real life and to accurate representation without idealization — **re·al·ist** \-ləst\ *adj or n* — **re·al·is·tic** \ˌrē-(ə-)ˈlis-tik\ *adj* — **re·al·is·ti·cal·ly** \-ti-k(ə-)lē\ *adv*

re·al·i·ty \rē-ˈal-ət-ē\ *n* **1 :** the quality or state of being real **2 a** (1) **:** a real event, entity, or state of affairs (2) **:** the totality of real things and events **b :** something that is neither derivative nor dependent but exists necessarily

re·al·iz·able \ˈrē-ə-ˌlī-zə-bəl, ˈrē-ˌlī-\ *adj* **:** capable of being realized

re·al·iza·tion \ˌrē-(ə-)lə-ˈzā-shən\ *n* **1 :** the action of realizing **:** the state of being realized **2 :** something realized

re·al·ize \ˈrē-ə-ˌlīz, ˈrē-ˌlīz\ *vt* [F *réaliser*, fr. MF *realiser*, fr. *real* real] **1 :** to make real or apparently real **:** ACCOMPLISH **2 a :** to convert into actual money ⟨*realized* assets⟩ **b :** to bring or get by sale, investment, or effort **:** GAIN **3 :** to understand clearly **syn** see THINK — **re·al·iz·er** *n*

re·al·ly \ˈrē-(ə-)lē, ˈri(-ə)-lē\ *adv* **1 a :** in reality **:** ACTUALLY **b :** UNQUESTIONABLY, TRULY **2 :** INDEED

realm \ˈrelm\ *n* [ME *realme*, fr. OF, modif. of L *regimen* rule — more at REGIMEN] **1 :** KINGDOM **2 :** SPHERE, DOMAIN **3 :** a primary marine or terrestrial biogeographic division of the earth's surface

re·al·po·li·tik \rā-ˈäl-ˌpō-li-ˌtēk\ *n* [G, fr. *real* practical + *politik* politics] **:** politics based on practical and material rather than theoretical or ethical factors

real presence *n, often cap R&P* **:** the doctrine that Christ is actually present in the Eucharist

Re·al·tor \ˈrē(-ə)l-tər, -ˌtȯ(ə)r *also* rē-ˈal-\ *n* [*Realtor*, a service mark] **:** a real estate agent who is a member of the National Association of Real Estate Boards

re·al·ty \ˈrē(-ə)l-tē\ *n* [*real* + *-ty* (as in *property*)] **:** REAL ESTATE

¹ream \ˈrēm\ *n* [ME *reme*, fr. MF *raime*, fr. Ar *rizmah*, lit., bundle] **1 :** a quantity of paper being 20 quires or variously 480, 500, or 516 sheets **2 :** a great amount — usu. used in pl.

²ream *vt* [perh. fr. (assumed) ME dial. *remen* to open up, fr. OE dial. *rēman;* akin to OE *rȳman* to open up, *rūm* roomy — more at ROOM] **1 a :** to widen the opening of (a hole) **:** COUNTERSINK **b** (1) **:** to enlarge or dress out (a hole) with a reamer (2) **:** to enlarge the bore of (as a gun) in this way **c :** to remove by reaming **2 a :** to press out with a reamer **b :** to press out the juice of with a reamer

ream·er \ˈrē-mər\ *n* **:** one that reams: as **a :** a rotating finishing tool with cutting edges used to enlarge or shape a hole **b :** a fruit squeezer

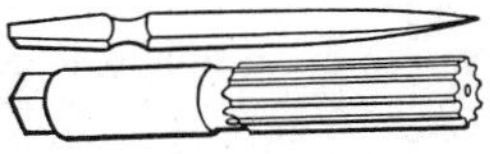

reamers

reap \ˈrēp\ *vb* [ME *repen*, fr. OE *reopan;* akin to OE *rāw* row — more at ROW] *vt* **1 a** (1) **:** to cut with a sickle, scythe, or reaping machine (2) **:** to clear of a crop by so cutting **b :** to gather by so cutting **:** HARVEST **2 :** OBTAIN, WIN ~ *vi* **:** to reap something

reap·er \ˈrē-pər\ *n* **:** one that reaps; *esp* **:** any of various machines for reaping grain

reaping hook *n* **:** a hand implement with a hook-shaped blade used in reaping — called also *reap hook*

re·ap·prais·al \ˌrē-ə-ˈprā-zəl\ *n* **:** a fresh appraisal

¹rear \ˈri(ə)r\ *vb* [ME *reren*, fr. OE *rǣran;* akin to ON *reisa* to raise, OE *rīsan* to rise] *vt* **1 :** to erect by building **:** CONSTRUCT **2 :** to raise upright **3 a** (1) **:** to breed and raise (an animal) for use or market (2) **:** to bring up (a person) **b :** to cause (as plants) to grow **4 :** to cause (a horse) to rise up on the hind legs ~ *vi* **1 :** to rise high **2** *of a horse* **:** to rise up on the hind legs **syn** see LIFT

²rear *n* [prob. fr. *rear* (in such terms as *rear guard*)] **1 :** the back part of something: as **a :** the unit (as of an army) or area farthest from the enemy **b :** the part of something located opposite its front **c :** BUTTOCKS **2 :** the space or position at the back

³rear *adj* **:** being at the back — **rear** *adv*

rear admiral *n* **:** a commissioned officer in the navy ranking below a vice admiral and above a captain

rear echelon *n* **:** an element of a military headquarters or unit located at a considerable distance from the front and concerned esp. with administrative and supply duties

rear guard *n* [ME *reregarde*, fr. MF, fr. OF, fr. *rere* backward, behind (fr. L *retro*) + *garde* guard — more at RETRO-] **:** a military detachment detailed to bring up and protect the rear of a main body or force

rear·guard action \ˌri(ə)r-ˌgärd-\ *n* **1 :** a defensive or delaying fight engaged in by forces covering the rear **2 :** a preventive or delaying effort in defense of the existing order

rear·horse \ˈri(ə)r-ˌhȯ(ə)rs\ *n* [fr. the way it rears up when disturbed] **:** MANTIS

re·arm \(ˈ)rē-ˈärm\ *vb* **:** to arm again with new or better weapons — **re·ar·ma·ment** \-ˈär-mə-mənt\ *n*

rear·most \ˈri(ə)r-ˌmōst\ *adj* **:** farthest in the rear **:** LAST

rear·mouse *var of* REREMOUSE

¹rear·ward \ˈri(ə)r-ˌwȯrd\ *n* [ME *rerewarde*, fr. AF; akin to OF *reregarde* rear guard] **:** REAR; *esp* **:** the rear division (as of an army)

²rear·ward \-wərd\ *adj* **1 :** located at, near, or toward the rear **2 :** directed toward the rear **:** BACKWARD — **rear·ward·ly** *adv*

³rear·ward \-wərd\ *also* **rear·wards** \-wərdz\ *adv* **:** at, near, or toward the rear **:** BACKWARD

¹rea·son \ˈrēz-ᵊn\ *n* [ME *resoun*, fr. OF *raison*, fr. L *ration-*, *ratio* reason, computation; akin to Goth *garathjan* to count, L *reri* to calculate, think, Gk *arariskein* to fit — more at ARM] **1 a :** a statement offered in explanation or justification **b :** a rational ground or motive **c :** a sufficient ground of explanation or of logical defense **d :** the thing that makes some fact intelligible **:** CAUSE **2 a** (1) **:** the power of comprehending, inferring, or thinking esp. in orderly rational ways **:** INTELLIGENCE (2) **:** proper exercise of the mind (3) **:** SANITY **b :** the sum of the intellectual powers **3** *archaic* **a :** treatment that affords satisfaction **b :** a formal accounting **syn** see CAUSE — **in reason :** JUSTIFIABLY, RIGHTLY — **within reason :** within reasonable limits **:** REASONABLE

²reason *vb* **rea·son·ing** \ˈrēz-niŋ, -ᵊn-iŋ\ *vi* **1 :** to use the faculty of reason **:** THINK **2 a** *obs* **:** to take part in conversation, discussion, or argument **b :** to talk with another so as to influence his actions or opinions ~ *vt* **1** *archaic* **:** to justify or support with reasons **2 :** to persuade or influence by use of reason **3 :** to discover, formulate, or conclude by use of reason **syn** see THINK — **rea·son·er** \-nər, -ᵊn-ər\ *n*

rea·son·abil·i·ty \ˌrēz-nə-ˈbil-ət-ē, -ᵊn-ə-ˈbil-\ *n* **:** the quality or state of being reasonable

rea·son·able \ˈrēz-nə-bəl, -ᵊn-ə-bəl\ *adj* **1 a :** agreeable to reason **b :** not extreme or excessive **c :** MODERATE, FAIR **d :** INEXPENSIVE **2 a :** having the faculty of reason **:** RATIONAL **b :** possessing sound judgment — **rea·son·able·ness** *n* — **rea·son·ably** \-blē\ *adv*

rea·son·ing *n* **1 :** the use of reason; *esp* **:** the drawing of inferences or conclusions through the use of reason **2 :** an instance of the use of reason **:** ARGUMENT

rea·son·less \ˈrēz-ᵊn-ləs\ *adj* **1 :** not having the faculty of reason **2 :** not reasoned **:** SENSELESS **3 :** not based on or supported by reasons — **rea·son·less·ly** *adv*

re·as·sur·ance \ˌrē-ə-ˈshu̇r-ən(t)s\ *n* **1 :** the action of reassuring **:** the state of being reassured **2 :** REINSURANCE

re·as·sure \ˌrē-ə-ˈshu̇(ə)r\ *vt* **1 :** to assure anew **2 :** to restore to confidence **3 :** REINSURE

re·ata \rē-ˈat-ə, -ˈät-\ *n* [AmerSp] **:** LARIAT

Re·au·mur \ˌrā-ō-ˈmyu̇(ə)r\ *adj* [René Antoine Ferchault de *Réaumur* †1757 F physicist] **:** relating or conforming to a thermometric scale on which the boiling point of water is at 80° above the zero of the scale and the freezing point is at zero

¹reave \ˈrēv\ *vb* **reaved** *or* **reft** \ˈreft\ **reav·ing** [ME *reven*, fr. OE *rēafian;* akin to OHG *roubōn* to rob, L *rumpere* to break, *ruere* to rush, dig up — more at RUG] *vi, archaic* **:** PLUNDER, ROB ~ *vt* **1** *archaic* **:** ROB, DESPOIL **2** *archaic* **a :** to deprive of **b :** SEIZE **3** *archaic* **:** to carry or tear away — **reav·er** *n*

²reave *vb* **reaved** *or* **reft** \ˈreft\ **reav·ing** [ME *reven*] *archaic* **:** BURST

reb \ˈreb\ *n* [short for *rebel*] **:** JOHNNY REB

re·bar·ba·tive \ri-ˈbär-bət-iv\ *adj* [F *rébarbatif*, fr. MF, fr. *rebarber* to be repellent, fr. *re-* + *barbe* beard, fr. L *barba* — more at BEARD] **:** CRABBED, REPELLENT

¹re·bate \ˈrē-ˌbāt, ri-ˈ\ *vb* [ME *rebaten*, fr. MF *rabattre* to beat down again, fr. OF, fr. *re-* + *abattre* to beat down, fr. *a-* (fr. L *ad-*) + *battre* to beat, fr. L *battuere* — more at BATTLE] *vt* **1 :** to reduce the force or activity of **:** DIMINISH **2 :** to reduce the sharpness of **:** BLUNT **3 a :** to make a rebate of **b :** to give a rebate to ~ *vi* **:** to give rebates — **re·bat·er** *n*

²re·bate \ˈrē-ˌbāt\ *n* **:** a return of a portion of a payment **:** ABATEMENT

³re·bate \ˈrē-ˌbāt, ˈrab-ət\ *var of* RABBET

re·ba·to \ri-ˈbät-(ˌ)ō\ *var of* RABATO

re·bec *or* **re·beck** \ˈrē-ˌbek\ *n* [MF *rebec*, alter. of OF *rebebe*, fr. OProv *rebeb*, fr. Ar *rebāb*] **:** an old bowed usu. 3-stringed musical instrument with a pear-shaped body and slender neck

Re·bek·ah \ri-ˈbek-ə\ *n* [Heb *Ribhqāh*] **:** the wife of Isaac

¹reb·el \ˈreb-əl\ *adj* [ME, fr. OF *rebelle*, fr. L *rebellis*, fr. *re-* + *bellum* war, fr. OL *duellum* — more at DUEL] **1 a :** opposing or taking arms against the government or ruler **b :** of or relating to rebels **2 :** DISOBEDIENT, REBELLIOUS

²rebel *n* **:** one who rebels or participates in a rebellion

³re·bel \ri-ˈbel\ *vi* **re·belled; re·bel·ling 1 a :** to oppose or disobey one in authority or control **b :** to renounce and resist by force the authority of one's government **2 a :** to act in or show disobedience **b :** to feel or exhibit anger or revulsion

re·bel·lion \ri-ˈbel-yən\ *n* **1 :** opposition to one in authority or dominance **2 a :** open defiance of or resistance to an established government **b :** an instance of such defiance or resistance

syn REVOLUTION, UPRISING, REVOLT, INSURRECTION, MUTINY: REBELLION implies open, organized, and often armed resistance to authority; REVOLUTION applies to a successful rebellion resulting in a change usu. in government; UPRISING implies no more than an effort at rebellion; REVOLT and INSURRECTION imply an armed uprising that quickly fails or succeeds; MUTINY applies to group insubordination or insurrection esp. against maritime authority

re·bel·lious \-yəs\ *adj* **1 a :** given to or engaged in rebellion **b :** of, relating to, or characteristic of a rebel or rebellion **c :** resistant to authority or tradition **2 :** resisting treatment or management **:** REFRACTORY **syn** see INSUBORDINATE — **re·bel·lious·ly** *adv* — **re·bel·lious·ness** *n*

re·bind \(ˈ)rē-ˈbīnd\ *vt* **:** to bind anew or again

re·birth \(ˈ)rē-ˈbərth, ˈrē-ˌ\ *n* **1 a :** a new or second birth **:** METEMPSYCHOSIS **b :** spiritual regeneration **2 :** RENAISSANCE, REVIVAL

reb·o·ant \ˈreb-ə-wənt\ *adj* [L *reboant-*, *reboans*, prp. of *reboare* to resound, fr. *re-* + *boare* to cry aloud, roar, fr. Gk *boan*, of imit. origin] **:** REVERBERATING

re·born \(ˈ)rē-ˈbȯ(ə)rn\ *adj* **:** born again **:** REGENERATED

¹re·bound \ˈrē-ˈbau̇nd, ri-\ *vb* [ME *rebounden*, fr. MF *rebondir*, fr. OF, fr. *re-* + *bondir* to bound — more at BOUND] *vi* **1 a :** to spring back on or as if on collision or impact with another body **b :** to recover from setback or frustration **2 :** REECHO ~ *vt* **:** to cause to rebound

²re·bound \ˈrē-ˌbau̇nd, ri-ˈ\ *n* **1 a :** the action of rebounding **:** RECOIL **b :** an upward leap or movement **:** RECOVERY **2 a :** a basketball or hockey puck that rebounds **b :** the act of taking

See *re-* and 2d element	**reappear**	**rearouse**	**reassertion**	**reassume**	**reauthorize**
reallocate	**reappearance**	**rearrange**	**reassess**	**reassumption**	**reawake**
reallocation	**reapplication**	**rearrangement**	**reassessment**	**reattach**	**reawaken**
reanalysis	**reapply**	**rearrest**	**reassign**	**reattachment**	**rebaptism**
reanalyze	**reappoint**	**reascend**	**reassignment**	**reattack**	**rebaptize**
reanimate	**reappointment**	**reassail**	**reassociate**	**reattain**	**rebid**
reanimation	**reapportion**	**reassemble**	**reassociation**	**reattainment**	**rebiddable**
reannex	**reapportionment**	**reassembly**	**reassort**	**reattempt**	**reboil**
reannexation	**reappraise**	**reassert**	**reassortment**		

a basketball rebound **3 :** an immediate spontaneous reaction to setback, frustration, or crisis

re·bo·zo \ri-ˈbō-(ˌ)sō\ *n* [Sp, shawl, fr. *rebozar* to muffle, fr. *re-* (fr. L) + *bozo* mouth, fr. (assumed) VL *bucceum*, fr. L *bucca* cheek] **:** a long scarf worn chiefly by Mexican women

re·broad·cast \(ˈ)rē-ˈbrȯd-ˌkast\ *vt* **1 :** to broadcast again (a radio or television program being simultaneously received from another source) **2 :** to repeat (a broadcast) at a later time — **rebroadcast** *n*

re·buff \ri-ˈbəf\ *vt* [MF *rebuffer*, fr. OIt *ribuffare* to reprimand] **:** REPULSE, SNUB — **rebuff** *n*

re·build \(ˈ)rē-ˈbild\ *vt* **1 a :** to make extensive repairs to **:** RECONSTRUCT **b :** to restore to a previous state **2 :** to make extensive changes in **:** REMODEL ~ *vi* **:** to build again ⟨planned to ~ after the fire⟩ **syn** see MEND

¹re·buke \ri-ˈbyük\ *vt* [ME *rebuken*, fr. ONF *rebuker*] **1 a :** to criticize sharply **:** REPRIMAND **b :** to serve as a rebuke to **2 :** to turn back or keep down **:** CHECK **syn** see REPROVE — **re·buk·er** *n*

²rebuke *n* **:** REPRIMAND, REPROOF

re·bus \ˈrē-bəs\ *n* [L, by things, abl. pl. of *res* thing — more at REAL] **:** a representation of words or syllables by pictures of objects whose names resemble the intended words or syllables in sound; *also* **:** a riddle made up of such pictures or symbols

re·but \ri-ˈbət\ *vb* **re·but·ted; re·but·ting** [ME *rebuten*, fr. OF *reboter*, fr. *re-* + *boter* to butt — more at BUTT] *vt* **1 :** to drive or beat back **:** REPEL **2 a :** to contradict or oppose by formal legal argument, plea, or countervailing proof **b :** to expose the falsity of **:** REFUTE ~ *vi* **:** to make or furnish an answer or counter proof **syn** see DISPROVE — **re·but·ta·ble** \-ˈbət-ə-bəl\ *adj*

re·but·tal \ri-ˈbət-ᵊl\ *n* **:** the act of rebutting esp. in a legal suit

¹re·but·ter \-ˈbət-ər\ *n* [AF *rebuter*, fr. OF *reboter* to rebut] **:** the answer of a defendant in matter of fact to a plaintiff's surrejoinder

²rebutter *n* **:** something that rebuts

re·cal·ci·trance \ri-ˈkal-sə-trən(t)s\ *or* **re·cal·ci·tran·cy** \-trən-sē\ *n* **:** the state of being recalcitrant

re·cal·ci·trant \-trənt\ *adj* [LL *recalcitrant-*, *recalcitrans*, prp. of *recalcitrare* to be stubbornly disobedient, fr. L, to kick back, fr. *re-* + *calcitrare* to kick, fr. *calc-*, *calx* heel — more at CALK] **1 :** obstinately defiant of authority or restraint **2 :** not responsive to handling or treatment **syn** see UNRULY — **recalcitrant** *n*

re·cal·cu·late \(ˈ)rē-ˈkal-kyə-ˌlāt\ *vt* **:** to calculate again esp. to discover the source of an error — **re·cal·cu·la·tion** \(ˌ)rē-ˌkal-kyə-ˈlā-shən\ *n*

re·ca·les·cence \ˌrē-kə-ˈles-ᵊn(t)s\ *n* [L *recalescere* to grow warm again, fr. *re-* + *calescere* to grow warm, incho. of *calēre* to be warm — more at LEE] **:** an increase in temperature that occurs while cooling metal through a range of temperatures in which change in structure occurs

¹re·call \ri-ˈkȯl\ *vt* **1 a :** to call back **b :** to bring back to mind **2 :** ANNUL **3 :** RESTORE, REVIVE **syn** see REMEMBER — **re·call·able** \-ˈkȯ-lə-bəl\ *adj*

²re·call \ri-ˈkȯl, ˈrē-ˌ\ *n* **1 :** a summons to return **2 :** the right or procedure by which an official may be removed by vote of the people on petition **3 :** remembrance of what has been learned or experienced **4 :** the act of revoking

re·cant \ri-ˈkant\ *vb* [L *recantare*, fr. *re-* + *cantare* to sing — more at CHANT] *vt* **1 :** to withdraw or repudiate (a statement or belief) formally and publicly **:** RENOUNCE **2 :** REVOKE ~ *vi* **:** to make an open confession of error **syn** see ABJURE — **re·can·ta·tion** \ˌrē-ˌkan-ˈtā-shən\ *n*

¹re·cap \(ˈ)rē-ˈkap\ *vt* **:** to cement, mold, and vulcanize a strip of camelback upon the buffed and roughened surface of the tread of (a worn pneumatic tire) — **re·cap·pa·ble** \-ˈkap-ə-bəl\ *adj*

²re·cap \ˈrē-ˌkap\ *n* **:** a recapped tire

³re·cap \ri-ˈkap\ *vt* **re·capped; re·cap·ping** [by shortening] **:** RECAPITULATE

⁴re·cap \ri-ˈkap\ *n* **:** RECAPITULATION

re·cap·i·tal·iza·tion \(ˌ)rē-ˌkap-ət-ᵊl-ə-ˈzā-shən, -ˌkap-tᵊl-\ *n* **:** a revision of the capital structure of a corporation

re·cap·i·tal·ize \(ˈ)rē-ˈkap-ət-ᵊl-ˌīz, -ˈkap-tᵊl-\ *vt* **:** to change the capital structure of

re·ca·pit·u·late \ˌrē-kə-ˈpich-ə-ˌlāt\ *vb* [LL *recapitulatus*, pp. of *recapitulare* to restate by heads, sum up, fr. L *re-* + *capitulum* division of a book] **:** to repeat briefly **:** SUMMARIZE

re·ca·pit·u·la·tion \-ˌpich-ə-ˈlā-shən\ *n* **1 :** a concise summary **2 :** the supposed repetition in an individual of the phylogenetic history of its group **3 :** the third section of a sonata form

re·cap·ture \(ˈ)rē-ˈkap-chər\ *n* **1 :** the act of retaking **:** the fact of being retaken **:** RECOVERY **2 :** the retaking of a prize or goods under international law **3 :** a governmental seizure under law of earnings or profits beyond a fixed amount — **recapture** *vt*

re·cast \(ˈ)rē-ˈkast\ *vt* **:** to cast again ⟨~ a gun⟩ ⟨~ a play⟩ — **recast** \(ˈ)rē-ˈ, ˈrē-ˌ\ *n*

¹re·cede \ri-ˈsēd\ *vi* [L *recedere* to go back, fr. *re-* + *cedere* to go — more at CEDE] **1 a :** to move back or away **:** WITHDRAW **b :** to slant backward **2 :** to grow less **:** CONTRACT

syn RECEDE, RETREAT, RETROGRADE, RETRACT, BACK mean to move backward. RECEDE implies a withdrawing from a forward or high fixed point in time or space; RETREAT implies withdrawal from a point or position reached; RETROGRADE implies movement contrary to a normally progressive direction; RETRACT implies drawing back from an extended position; BACK is used, with *up, down, out, off*, interchangeably with any of the others

²re·cede \(ˈ)rē-ˈsēd\ *vt* [*re-* + *cede*] **:** to cede back

¹re·ceipt \ri-ˈsēt\ *n* [ME *receite*, fr. ONF, fr. ML *recepta*, prob. fr. L, neut. pl. of *receptus*, pp. of *recipere*] **1 :** RECIPE **2 a** *obs* **:** RECEPTACLE **b** *archaic* **:** a revenue office **3 :** the act or process of receiving **4 :** something received — usu. used in pl. **5 :** a writing acknowledging the receiving of goods or money

²receipt *vt* **1 :** to give a receipt for or acknowledge the receipt of **2 :** to mark as paid

re·ceiv·able \ri-ˈsē-və-bəl\ *adj* **1 :** capable of being received **2 :** subject to call for payment ⟨accounts ~⟩

re·ceiv·ables \-bəlz\ *n pl* **:** amounts of money receivable

re·ceive \ri-ˈsēv\ *vb* [ME *receiven*, fr. ONF *receivre*, fr. L *recipere*, fr. *re-* + *capere* to take — more at HEAVE] *vt* **1 :** to take or come into possession of **:** GET **2 a** (1) **:** to take in **:** HOLD (2) **:** CONTAIN **b :** to take in through the mind or senses **3 a :** to permit to enter **:** ADMIT **b :** WELCOME, GREET **4 :** to accept as true **:** BELIEVE **5 a :** TAKE, BEAR ⟨some clay ~*s* clear impressions⟩ **b :** UNDERGO, EXPERIENCE ⟨*received* his early schooling at home⟩ ~ *vi* **1 :** to be a recipient **2 :** to be at home to visitors ⟨~*s* on Tuesdays⟩ **3 :** to convert incoming radio waves into perceptible signals

syn ACCEPT, ADMIT, TAKE: RECEIVE ordinarily implies passiveness in the one receiving; ACCEPT implies some element of consent or approval but a minimum of definite activity; ADMIT may often suggest a relaxation of refusal or denial or an overcoming of reluctance to receive or accept; TAKE applies to a receiving by letting into one's hands, mind, or possession and implies a positive act

re·ceiv·er \ri-ˈsē-vər\ *n* **:** one that receives: as **a :** TREASURER **b** (1) **:** a person appointed to hold in trust and administer property under litigation (2) **:** a person appointed to wind up the affairs of a business involving a public interest or to manage a corporation during reorganization **c :** one that receives stolen goods **:** FENCE **d :** a vessel to receive and contain gases **e** (1) **:** RECEIVING SET (2) **:** the portion of a telegraphic or telephonic apparatus that converts the electric currents or waves into visible or audible signals

re·ceiv·er·ship \-vər-ˌship\ *n* **1 :** the office or function of a receiver **2 :** the state of being in the hands of a receiver

receiving set *n* **:** an apparatus for receiving radio or television signals

re·cen·cy \ˈrēs-ᵊn-sē\ *n* **:** the quality or state of being recent

re·cen·sion \ri-ˈsen-chən\ *n* [L *recension-*, *recensio* enumeration, fr. *recensēre* to review, fr. *re-* + *censēre* to assess, tax] **1 :** a critical revision of a text **2 :** a text established by critical revision

re·cent \ˈrēs-ᵊnt\ *adj* [MF or L; MF, fr. L *recent-*, *recens;* akin to Gk *kainos* new] **1 a :** of or relating to a time not long past **b :** having lately come into existence **:** NEW, FRESH **2** *cap* **:** of, relating to, or being the present or post-Pleistocene geologic epoch — **re·cent·ly** *adv* — **re·cent·ness** *n*

re·cep·ta·cle \ri-ˈsep-ti-kəl\ *n* [L *receptaculum*, fr. *receptare* to receive, fr. *receptus*, pp. of *recipere* to receive] **1 :** one that receives and contains something **:** CONTAINER **2** [NL *receptaculum*, fr. L] **a :** an intercellular cavity containing secretion products **b :** the end of the flower stalk upon which the floral organs are borne **c :** a modified branch bearing sporangia in a cryptogamous plant **3 :** a mounted female electrical fitting that contains the live parts of the circuit

re·cep·tac·u·lum \ˌrē-ˌsep-ˈtak-yə-ləm, ri-\ *n, pl* **re·cep·tac·u·la** \-lə\ [NL, fr. L] **:** RECEPTACLE 2

re·cep·tion \ri-ˈsep-shən\ *n* [ME *recepcion*, fr. MF or L; MF *reception*, fr. L *reception-*, *receptio*, fr. *receptus*, pp. of *recipere*] **:** the act or action of receiving: as **a :** RECEIPT **b :** ADMISSION **c** (1) **:** WELCOME, RESPONSE (2) **:** a social gathering **d :** the receiving of a radio or television broadcast

re·cep·tion·ist \-sh(ə-)nəst\ *n* **:** one employed to greet callers

re·cep·tive \ri-ˈsep-tiv\ *adj* **1 :** able or inclined to receive ideas **2 a** *of a sensory end organ* **:** fit to receive and transmit stimuli **b :** SENSORY — **re·cep·tive·ly** *adv* — **re·cep·tive·ness** *n* — **re·cep·tiv·i·ty** \ˌrē-ˌsep-ˈtiv-ət-ē, ri-\ *n*

re·cep·tor \ri-ˈsep-tər\ *n* **:** RECEIVER: as **a :** a cell or group of cells that receives stimuli **:** SENSE ORGAN **b :** a chemical group having a specific affinity for a particular antibody or a virus

¹re·cess \ˈrē-ˌses, ri-ˈ\ *n* [L *recessus*, fr. *recessus*, pp. of *recedere* to recede] **1 :** RECESSION **2 :** a hidden, secret, or secluded place **3 a :** INDENTATION, CLEFT **b :** ALCOVE **4 :** a suspension of business or procedure

²recess *vt* **1 :** to put into a recess ⟨~*ed* lighting⟩ **2 :** to make a recess in **3 :** to interrupt for a recess ~ *vi* **:** to take a recess

¹re·ces·sion \ri-ˈsesh-ən\ *n* **1 :** the act or action of receding **:** WITHDRAWAL **2 :** a return procession **3 :** a period of reduced economic activity — **re·ces·sion·ary** \-ə-ˌner-ē\ *adj*

²re·ces·sion \(ˈ)rē-ˈsesh-ən\ *n* [*re-* + *cession*] **:** the act of ceding back

¹re·ces·sion·al \ri-ˈsesh-nəl, -ən-ᵊl\ *adj* **:** of or relating to a withdrawal

²recessional *n* **1 :** a hymn or musical piece at the conclusion of a service or program **2 :** ¹RECESSION 2

¹re·ces·sive \ri-ˈses-iv\ *adj* **1 a :** tending to go back **:** RECEDING **b :** RETIRING, WITHDRAWN **2** *of an allele* **:** subordinate to a contrasting allele in manifestation — **re·ces·sive·ly** *adv* — **re·ces·sive·ness** *n*

²recessive *n* **:** a recessive character or factor or an organism possessing one or more such characters

ré·chauf·fé \ˌrā-(ˌ)shō-ˈfā\ *n* [F] **1 :** a warmed-over dish of food **2 :** REHASH

re·cheat \ri-ˈchēt\ *n* [ME *rechate*, fr. *rechaten* to blow the recheat, fr. MF *rachater* to assemble, rally, fr. *re-* + *achater* to acquire, fr. (assumed) VL *accaptare*, fr. L *ac-* + *captare* to seek to obtain, intens. of *capere* to take, receive — more at HEAVE] **:** a hunting call sounded on a horn to assemble the hounds

re·cher·ché \rə-ˌsher-ˈshā, -ˈshe(ə)r-ˌ\ *adj* [F] **1 a :** EXQUISITE, CHOICE **b :** EXOTIC, RARE **2 :** excessively refined **:** PRECIOUS **3 :** OVERBLOWN, PRETENTIOUS

re·cid·i·vism \ri-ˈsid-ə-ˌviz-əm\ *n* **:** a tendency to relapse into a previous condition or mode of behavior

re·cid·i·vist \-vəst\ *n* [F *récidiviste*, fr. *récidiver* to relapse, fr. ML *recidivare*, fr. L *recidivus* recurring, fr. *recidere* to fall back, fr. *re-* + *cadere* to fall — more at CHANCE] **:** one who relapses; *specif* **:** an habitual criminal — **recidivist** *adj*

rec·i·pe \ˈres-ə-(ˌ)pē\ *n* [L, take, imper. of *recipere* to take, receive — more at RECEIVE] **1 :** PRESCRIPTION 4 **2 :** a set of instructions for making something (as a food dish) from various ingredients **3 :** method of procedure

re·cip·i·ent \ri-ˈsip-ē-ənt\ *n* [L *recipient-*, *recipiens*, prp. of *recipere*] **:** one that receives **:** RECEIVER — **recipient** *adj*

¹re·cip·ro·cal \ri-ˈsip-rə-kəl\ *adj* [L *reciprocus* returning the same way, alternating, irreg. fr. *re-* + *pro-*] **1 a :** inversely related **:** OPPOSITE **b :** of, constituting, or resulting from paired crosses in which the kind that supplies the male parent of the first cross supplies the female parent of the second cross and vice versa **2 :** shared, felt, or shown by both sides **3 :** serving to reciprocate **4 a :** mutually corresponding **b :** marked by or based upon reciprocity — **re·cip·ro·cal·ly** \-k(ə-)lē\ *adv*

See *re-* and 2d element	rebury	rechannel	recharge	recheck	rechristen
reburial	**recarbonize**				

syn RECIPROCAL, MUTUAL, COMMON mean shared or experienced by each. RECIPROCAL implies an equal return or counteraction by each of two sides toward or against or in relation to the other; MUTUAL applies to feelings or effects shared by two jointly; COMMON does not suggest reciprocity but merely a sharing with others

²reciprocal *n* **1 :** something in a reciprocal relationship to another **2 :** one of a pair of numbers (as ⅔, ³⁄₂) whose product is one

reciprocal pronoun *n* **:** a pronoun (as *each other*) used to denote mutual action or cross relationship between the members comprised in a plural subject

re·cip·ro·cate \ri-ˈsip-rə-ˌkāt\ *vt* **1 :** to give and take mutually **2 :** REPAY ~ *vi* **1 :** to make a return for something **2 :** to move forward and backward alternately — **re·cip·ro·ca·tor** \-ˌkāt-ər\ *n*

reciprocating engine *n* **:** an engine in which the to-and-fro motion of a piston is transformed into circular motion of the crankshaft

re·cip·ro·ca·tion \ri-ˌsip-rə-ˈkā-shən\ *n* **1 a :** a mutual exchange **b :** a return in kind or of like value **2 :** an alternating motion — **re·cip·ro·ca·tive** \ri-ˈsip-rə-ˌkāt-iv, -kət-\ *adj*

rec·i·proc·i·ty \ˌres-ə-ˈpräs-ət-ē, -ˈpräs-tē\ *n* **1 :** the quality or state of being reciprocal **2 :** a mutual exchange of privileges; *specif* **:** a recognition by one of two countries or institutions of the validity of licenses or privileges granted by the other

re·ci·sion \ri-ˈsizh-ən\ *n* [MF, alter. of *rescision*, fr. LL *rescission-, rescissio* rescission] **:** CANCELLATION

re·cit·al \ri-ˈsīt-ᵊl\ *n* **1 a :** the act, process, or an instance of reciting **b :** ENUMERATION **c :** DISCOURSE, NARRATION **2 :** a public reading or recitation of a piece of writing **3 a :** a public performance given by a musician or dancer or by a dance troupe **b :** an exhibition concert given by music or dance pupils — **re·cit·al·ist** \-ᵊl-əst\ *n*

rec·i·ta·tion \ˌres-ə-ˈtā-shən\ *n* **1 :** ENUMERATION **2 :** the act or an instance of reading or repeating aloud esp. publicly **3 a :** a student's oral reply to questions **b :** a class period

rec·i·ta·tive \ˌres-(ə-)tə-ˈtēv\ *n* [It *recitativo*, fr. *recitare* to recite, fr. L] **:** a rhythmically free declamatory vocal style for delivering a narrative text; *also* **:** a passage to be delivered in this style — **recitative** *adj*

rec·i·ta·ti·vo \ˌres-(ə-)tə-ˈtē-(ˌ)vō\ *n, pl* **rec·i·ta·ti·vi** \-(ˌ)vē\ *or* **recitativos** [It] **:** RECITATIVE

re·cite \ri-ˈsīt\ *vb* [ME *reciten* to state formally, fr. MF or L; MF *reciter* to recite, fr. L *recitare*, fr. *re-* + *citare* to summon — more at CITE] *vt* **1 :** to repeat from memory or read aloud publicly **2 a :** to give a detailed narration of **b :** ENUMERATE **3 :** to repeat or answer questions about (a lesson) ~ *vi* **1 :** to repeat or read aloud something memorized or prepared **2 :** to reply to a teacher's question on a lesson — **re·cit·er** *n*

reck \ˈrek\ *vb* [ME *recken*, fr. OE *reccan;* akin to OHG *ruohhen* to take heed] *vi* **1 :** WORRY, CARE **2 :** MATTER ~ *vt* **1 :** to care for **:** REGARD **2 :** to matter to **:** CONCERN

reck·less \ˈrek-ləs\ *adj* **1 a :** marked by lack of caution **:** RASH **b :** IRRESPONSIBLE, WILD **2 :** CARELESS, NEGLIGENT **syn** see ADVENTUROUS — **reck·less·ly** *adv* — **reck·less·ness** *n*

reck·on \ˈrek-ən\ *vb* **reck·on·ing** \-(ə-)niŋ\ [ME *rekenen*, fr. OE *-recenian* (as in *gerecenian* to narrate); akin to OE *reccan*] *vt* **1 a :** COUNT **b :** ESTIMATE, COMPUTE **c :** to determine by reference to a fixed basis **2 :** to regard **:** CONSIDER **3** *chiefly dial* **:** THINK ~ *vi* **1 :** to settle accounts **2 :** to make a calculation **3 a :** JUDGE **b** *chiefly dial* **:** SUPPOSE **4 :** DEPEND **syn** see CALCULATE, RELY

reck·on·ing *n* **1 :** the act or an instance of reckoning: as **a :** ACCOUNT, BILL **b :** COMPUTATION **c :** calculation of a ship's position **2 :** a settling of accounts ⟨day of ~⟩ **3 :** APPRAISAL

re·claim \ri-ˈklām\ *vt* [ME *reclamen*, fr. OF *reclamer* to call back, fr. L *reclamare* to cry out against, fr. *re-* + *clamare* to cry out — more at CLAIM] **1 a :** to recall from wrong or improper conduct **:** REFORM **b :** TAME **2 :** to rescue from an undesirable or uncultivated state **3 :** to obtain from a waste product or by-product **:** RECOVER **syn** see RESCUE — **re·claim·able** \-ˈklā-mə-bəl\ *adj*

re–claim \(ˈ)rē-ˈklām\ *vt* **:** to demand or obtain the return of

rec·la·ma·tion \ˌrek-lə-ˈmā-shən\ *n* [MF, fr. L *reclamation-, reclamatio*, fr. *reclamatus*, pp. of *reclamare*] **:** the act or process of reclaiming: as **a :** REFORMATION **b :** restoration to use **:** RECOVERY

ré·clame \rā-ˈkläm\ *n* [F, advertising, fr. *réclamer* to appeal, fr. OF *reclamer*] **1 :** public acclaim **:** VOGUE **2 :** SHOWMANSHIP

rec·li·nate \ˈrek-lə-ˌnāt\ *adj* **:** bent downward so that the apex is below the base

re·cline \ri-ˈklīn\ *vb* [ME *reclinen*, fr. MF or L; MF *recliner*, fr. L *reclinare*, fr. *re-* + *clinare* to bend] *vt* **:** to cause or permit to incline backwards ~ *vi* **1 :** to lean or incline backwards **2 :** REPOSE, LIE

¹re·cluse \ˈrek-ˌlüs, ri-ˈklüs, ˈrek-ˌlüz\ *adj* [ME, fr. OF *reclus*, lit., shut up, fr. LL *reclusus*, pp. of *recludere* to shut up, fr. L *re-* + *claudere* to close — more at CLOSE] **:** marked by withdrawal from society **:** SOLITARY — **re·clu·sive** \ri-ˈklü-siv, -ziv\ *adj*

²recluse *n* **:** a person who leads a secluded or solitary life **:** HERMIT

re·clu·sion \ri-ˈklü-zhən\ *n* **:** the state of being recluse

rec·og·ni·tion \ˌrek-ig-ˈnish-ən, -əg-\ *n* **1 :** the action of recognizing **:** the state of being recognized: as **a :** ACKNOWLEDGMENT **b :** knowledge or feeling that an object present has been met before **2 :** special notice or attention

rec·og·niz·abil·i·ty \-ˌnī-zə-ˈbil-ət-ē\ *n* **:** the quality or state of being recognizable

rec·og·niz·able \ˈrek-ig-ˌnī-zə-bəl, -əg-\ *adj* **:** capable of being recognized — **rec·og·niz·ably** \-blē\ *adv*

re·cog·ni·zance \ri-ˈkäg-nə-zən(t)s, -ˈkän-ə-\ *n* [alter. of ME *reconissaunce*, fr. MF *reconoissance* recognition, fr. *reconoistre* to recognize] **1 a :** an obligation of record entered into before a court or magistrate requiring the performance of an act (as appearance in court) usu. on penalty of a money forfeiture **b :** the sum liable to forfeiture upon such an obligation **2** *archaic* **:** TOKEN, PLEDGE

rec·og·nize \ˈrek-ig-ˌnīz, -əg-\ *vt* [modif. of MF *reconoiss-*, stem of *reconoistre*, fr. L *recognoscere*, fr. *re-* + *cognoscere* to know — more at COGNITION] **1 a :** to perceive to be something previously known ⟨*recognized* the word⟩ **b :** to perceive clearly **:** REALIZE **2 a :** to acknowledge with a show of appreciation ⟨*recognizing* services⟩ **b :** to acknowledge acquaintance with ⟨~ an old crony⟩ **c :** to admit the fact of **3 :** to acknowledge formally: as **a :** to admit as being lord or sovereign **b :** to admit as being of a particular status **c :** to admit as being one entitled to be heard **d :** to acknowledge the de facto existence or the independence of

¹re·coil \ri-ˈkȯi(ə)l\ *vi* [ME *reculen*, fr. OF *reculer*, fr. *re-* + *cul* backside — more at CULET] **1 a :** to fall back under pressure **b :** to shrink back **2 :** to spring back to or as if to a starting point **3** *obs* **:** DEGENERATE

syn RECOIL, SHRINK, FLINCH, WINCE, BLENCH, QUAIL mean to draw back through fear or distaste. RECOIL implies a start or movement away through shock, fear, or disgust; SHRINK suggests an instinctive recoil through sensitiveness, scrupulousness, or cowardice; FLINCH implies a failure to endure pain or face something dangerous or frightening with resolution; WINCE suggests an involuntary movement of recoil; BLENCH implies fainthearted flinching; QUAIL suggests shrinking and cowering in fright or consternation

²re·coil \ri-ˈkȯi(ə)l, ˈrē-ˌkȯil\ *n* **:** the action of recoiling **:** REACTION; *esp* **:** the kickback of a gun upon firing

re·coil·less \-ˈkȯi(ə)l-ləs, -ˌkȯil-ləs\ *adj* **:** having a minimum of recoil ⟨a ~ gun⟩

re·coin \(ˈ)rē-ˈkȯin\ *vt* **:** to coin again or anew — **re·coin·age** \-ˈkȯi-nij\ *n*

re–col·lect \ˌrē-kə-ˈlekt\ *vt* [partly fr. L *recollectus*, pp. of *recolligere*, fr. *re-* + *colligere* to collect; partly fr. *re-* + *collect*] **:** to collect again; *esp* **:** RALLY, RECOVER

rec·ol·lect \ˌrek-ə-ˈlekt\ *vb* [ML *recollectus*, pp. of *recolligere*, fr. L, to gather again] *vt* **1 :** to recall to mind **:** REMEMBER **2 :** to remind (oneself) of something temporarily forgotten ~ *vi* **:** to call something to mind **syn** see REMEMBER

re·col·lect·ed \ˌrē-kə-ˈlek-təd\ *adj* **:** COMPOSED, CALM

rec·ol·lec·tion \ˌrek-ə-ˈlek-shən\ *n* **1 a :** tranquillity of mind **b :** religious contemplation **2 a :** the action or power of recalling to mind **b :** something recalled to the mind **syn** see MEMORY

re·com·bi·nant \(ˈ)rē-ˈkäm-bə-nənt\ *n* **:** an individual exhibiting genetic recombination

re·com·bi·na·tion \ˌrē-ˌkäm-bə-ˈnā-shən\ *n* **1 :** the formation of new combinations of genes in fertilization **2 :** the formation of new combinations of linked genes (as by crossing-over) resulting in new heritable characters or new combinations of such characters — **re·com·bi·na·tion·al** \-shnəl, -shən-ᵊl\ *adj*

rec·om·mend \ˌrek-ə-ˈmend\ *vt* [ME *recommenden* to praise, fr. ML *recommendare*, fr. L *re-* + *commendare* to commend] **1 a :** to present as worthy of acceptance or trial **b :** to urge the fitness of **2 :** ENTRUST **3 :** to attract favor to **4 :** ADVISE — **rec·om·mend·able** \-ˈmen-də-bəl\ *adj* — **rec·om·men·da·to·ry** \-də-ˌtōr-ē, -ˌtȯr-\ *adj* — **rec·om·mend·er** *n*

rec·om·men·da·tion \ˌrek-ə-mən-ˈdā-shən, -ˌmen-\ *n* **1 :** the action of recommending **2 :** something that recommends or expresses commendation

re·com·mit \ˌrē-kə-ˈmit\ *vt* **1 :** to refer (as a bill) again to a committee **2 :** to consign again — **re·com·mit·ment** \-mənt\ *n* — **re·com·mit·tal** \-ˈmit-ᵊl\ *n*

¹rec·om·pense \ˈrek-əm-ˌpen(t)s\ *vt* [ME *recompensen*, fr. MF *recompenser*, fr. LL *recompensare*, fr. L *re-* + *compensare* to compensate] **1 a :** to give compensation to **:** REPAY **b :** to pay for **2 :** to return in kind **:** REQUITE **syn** see PAY

²recompense *n* **:** an equivalent or a return for something done, suffered, or given **:** COMPENSATION

re·com·pose \ˌrē-kəm-ˈpōz\ *vt* **1 :** to compose again **:** REARRANGE **2 :** to restore to composure — **re·com·po·si·tion** \(ˌ)rē-ˌkäm-pə-ˈzish-ən\ *n*

rec·on·cil·abil·i·ty \ˌrek-ən-ˌsī-lə-ˈbil-ət-ē\ *n* **:** the quality or state of being reconcilable

rec·on·cil·able \ˌrek-ən-ˈsī-lə-bəl, ˈrek-ən-ˌ\ *adj* **:** capable of being reconciled — **rec·on·cil·able·ness** *n*

rec·on·cile \ˈrek-ən-ˌsīl\ *vt* [ME *reconcilen*, fr. MF or L; MF *reconcilier*, fr. L *reconciliare*, fr. *re-* + *conciliare* to conciliate] **1 a :** to restore to friendship, harmony, or communion ⟨*reconciled* the factions⟩ **b :** ADJUST, SETTLE ⟨~ differences⟩ **2 :** to make congruous ⟨~ an ideal with reality⟩ **3 :** to cause to submit to or accept **syn** see ADAPT — **rec·on·cile·ment** \-mənt\ *n* — **rec·on·cil·i·a·tion** \ˌrek-ən-ˌsil-ē-ˈā-shən\ *n* — **rec·on·cil·ia·to·ry** \-ˈsil-yə-ˌtōr-ē, -ˈsil-ē-ə-, -ˌtȯr-\ *adj*

re·con·dite \ˈrek-ən-ˌdīt, ri-ˈkän-\ *adj* [L *reconditus*, pp. of *recondere* to conceal, fr. *re-* + *condere* to store up, fr. *com-* + *-dere* to put — more at DO] **1** *archaic* **:** hidden from sight **:** CONCEALED ⟨produced some ~ flasks of wine —T.L.Peacock⟩ **2 :** incomprehensible to one of ordinary understanding or knowledge **:** DEEP ⟨a ~ subject⟩ **3 :** of, relating to, or dealing with something little known or obscure ⟨~ fact about the origin of the holiday —Floyd Dell⟩ — **re·con·dite·ly** *adv* — **re·con·dite·ness** *n*

re·con·di·tion \ˌrē-kən-ˈdish-ən\ *vt* **1 :** to restore to good condition (as by repairing or replacing parts) **2 :** REFORM

re·con·firm \ˌrē-kən-ˈfərm\ *vt* **:** to confirm again; *also* **:** to establish more strongly — **re·con·fir·ma·tion** \(ˌ)rē-ˌkän-fər-ˈmā-shən\ *n*

re·con·nais·sance \ri-ˈkän-ə-zən(t)s *also* -sən(t)s\ *n* [F, lit., recognition, fr. MF *reconoissance*] **:** a preliminary survey to gain information; *esp* **:** an exploratory military survey of enemy territory

re·con·noi·ter \ˌrē-kə-ˈnȯit-ər *also* ˌrek-ə-\ *vb* **re·con·noi·ter·ing** \-ˈnȯit-ə-riŋ, -ˈnȯi-triŋ\ [obs. F *reconnoître*, lit., to recognize, fr. MF *reconoistre* — more at RECOGNIZE] *vt* **:** to make a reconnaissance of ~ *vi* **:** to engage in reconnaissance

re·con·sid·er \ˌrē-kən-ˈsid-ər\ *vt* **:** to consider again with a view to changing or reversing; *specif* **:** to take up again in a meeting ~ *vi* **:** to engage in reconsideration — **re·con·sid·er·a·tion** \-ˌsid-ə-ˈrā-shən\ *n*

See *re-* and 2d element	**recodify**	**recommencement**	**recompress**	**reconcentration**	**reconnect**
reclassification	**recolonization**	**recommission**	**recompression**	**reconception**	**reconquer**
reclassify	**recolonize**	**recompile**	**recomputation**	**recondensation**	**reconquest**
reclean	**recolor**	**recomplete**	**recompute**	**recondense**	**reconsecrate**
recoal	**recombine**	**recompletion**	**reconceive**	**reconduct**	**reconsecration**
recodification	**recommence**	**recompound**	**reconcentrate**	**reconfine**	**reconsign**

ə abut; ᵊ kitten; ər further; a back; ā bake; ä cot, cart; au̇ out; ch chin; e less; ē easy; g gift; i trip; ī life
j joke; ŋ sing; ō flow; ȯ flaw; ȯi coin; th thin; t͟h this; ü loot; u̇ foot; y yet; yü few; yu̇ furious; zh vision

re·con·struc·tion \ˌrē-kən-ˈstrək-shən\ *n* **1 a :** the action of reconstructing **:** the state of being reconstructed **b** *often cap* **:** the reorganization and reestablishment of the seceded states in the Union after the American Civil War **2 :** something reconstructed

re·con·struc·tion·ism \-shə-ˌniz-əm\ *n, often cap* **1 :** advocacy of post-Civil War reconstruction **2 :** a movement in 20th century American Judaism that advocates a creative adjustment to contemporary conditions through the cultivation of traditions and folkways shared by all Jews — **re·con·struc·tion·ist** \-sh(ə-)nəst\ *n, often cap*

re·con·ver·sion \ˌrē-kən-ˈvər-zhən, -shən\ *n* **:** conversion back to a previous state

re·con·vert \ˌrē-kən-ˈvərt\ *vb* **:** to convert back

re·con·vey \ˌrē-kən-ˈvā\ *vt* **:** to convey back to a previous position or owner — **re·con·vey·ance** \-ˈvā-ən(t)s\ *n*

[1]**re·cord** \ri-ˈkȯ(ə)rd\ *vb* [ME *recorden,* lit., to recall, fr. OF *recorder,* fr. L *recordari,* fr. *re-* + *cord-, cor* heart — more at HEART] *vt* **1 a** (1) **:** to set down in writing (2) **:** to deposit an authentic official copy of **b** (1) **:** to register permanently (2) **:** INDICATE, READ **2 :** to give evidence of **3 :** to cause (as sound) to be registered (as on a phonograph disc) in reproducible form **~** *vi* **:** to engage in recording

[2]**rec·ord** \ˈrek-ərd *also* -ˌȯ(ə)rd\ *n* **1 :** the state or fact of being recorded **2 :** something that records: as **a :** something that recalls or relates past events **b :** an official writing that records the acts of a public body or officer **c :** an authentic official copy of a document deposited with a legally designated officer **d :** the official copy of the papers used in a law case **3 a :** the known or recorded facts regarding something or someone **b :** an attested top performance **4 :** something on which sound or visual images have been recorded; *specif* **:** a disc with a spiral groove carrying recorded sound for phonograph reproduction

[3]**record** *like* [2]\ *adj* **:** surpassing others of its kind

re·cor·da·tion \ˌrek-ˌȯr-ˈdā-shən; ˌrē-ˌkȯr-, ri-\ *n* **:** the action or process of recording

record changer *n* **:** a phonograph attachment that automatically positions and plays successively each of a stack of records

re·cord·er \ri-ˈkȯrd-ər\ *n* **1 :** a person or device that records **2 a :** the chief judicial magistrate of some British cities and boroughs **b :** a municipal judge with criminal jurisdiction of first instance and sometimes limited civil jurisdiction **3 :** a fipple flute with eight finger holes

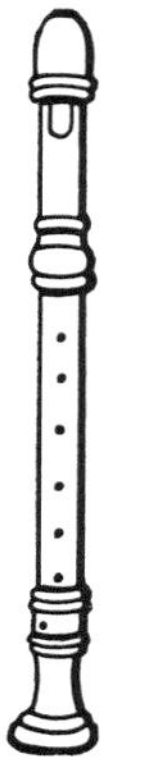

recorder 3

re·cord·ing \ri-ˈkȯrd-iŋ\ *n* **:** RECORD 4

re·cord·ist \ri-ˈkȯrd-əst\ *n* **:** one who records sound esp. on film

record player *n* **:** an electronic instrument for playing phonograph records through a usu. incorporated loudspeaker

[1]**re·count** \ri-ˈkau̇nt\ *vt* [ME *recounten,* fr. MF *reconter,* fr. *re-* + *conter* to count, relate — more at COUNT] **1 :** to relate in detail **:** NARRATE **2 :** ENUMERATE

[2]**re·count** \(ˈ)rē-ˈkau̇nt\ *vt* [*re-* + *count*] **:** to count again

[3]**re·count** \(ˈ)rē-ˈkau̇nt, ˈrē-ˌ\ *n* **:** a second or fresh count

re·coup \ri-ˈküp\ *vb* [F *recouper* to cut back, fr. OF, fr. *re-* + *couper* to cut — more at COPE] *vt* **1 :** to withhold rightfully part of (a sum legally claimed) instead of filing a counterclaim **2 a :** to get an equivalent for (as losses) **b :** REIMBURSE **3 :** REGAIN **~** *vi* **:** to make up for something lost — **re·coup·able** \-ˈkü-pə-bəl\ *adj* — **re·coup·ment** \-ˈküp-mənt\ *n*

re·course \ˈrē-ˌkō(ə)rs, -ˌkȯ(ə)rs, ri-ˈ\ *n* [ME *recours,* fr. MF, fr. LL *recursus,* fr. L, act of running back, fr. *recursus,* pp. of *recurrere* to run back — more at RECUR] **1 a :** a turning to someone or something for help or protection **b :** a source of help or strength **:** RESORT **2 :** the right to demand payment from the maker or endorser of a negotiable instrument

re·cov·er \ri-ˈkəv-ər\ *vb* **re·cov·er·ing** \-(ə-)riŋ\ [ME *recoveren,* fr. MF *recoverer,* fr. L *recuperare;* akin to L *recipere* to receive — more at RECEIVE] *vt* **1 :** to get back **:** REGAIN **2 a :** to bring back to normal position or condition **b** *archaic* **:** RESCUE **3 a :** to make up for **b :** to gain by legal process **4** *archaic* **:** REACH **5 :** RECLAIM **~** *vi* **1 :** to regain a normal position or condition (as of health) ⟨*~ing* from a cold⟩ **2 :** to obtain a final legal judgment in one's favor — **re·cov·er·able** \-ˈkəv-(ə-)rə-bəl\ *adj*

re–cov·er \(ˈ)rē-ˈkəv-ər\ *vt* **:** to cover again or anew

re·cov·ery \ri-ˈkəv-(ə-)rē\ *n* **:** the act, process, or an instance of recovering

recovery room *n* **:** a hospital room equipped for meeting postoperative emergencies

[1]**rec·re·ant** \ˈrek-rē-ənt\ *adj* [ME, fr. MF, fr. prp. of *recroire* to renounce one's cause in a trial by battle, fr. *re-* + *croire* to believe, fr. L *credere* — more at CREED] **1 :** crying for mercy **:** COWARDLY **2 :** unfaithful to duty or allegiance

[2]**recreant** *n* **1 :** COWARD **2 :** DESERTER, APOSTATE

rec·re·ate \ˈrek-rē-ˌāt\ *vt* [L *recreatus,* pp.] **:** to give new life or freshness to — **rec·re·ative** \-ˌāt-iv\ *adj*

re–cre·ate \ˌrē-krē-ˈāt\ *vt* **:** to create anew esp. in the imagination — **re–cre·ation** \-ˈā-shən\ *n* — **re–cre·ative** \-ˈāt-iv\ *adj*

rec·re·ation \ˌrek-rē-ˈā-shən\ *n* [ME *recreacion,* fr. MF *recreation,* fr. L *recreation-, recreatio* restoration to health, fr. *recreatus,* pp. of *recreare* to create anew, restore, refresh, fr. *re-* + *creare* to create] **:** refreshment of strength and spirits after toil **:** DIVERSION; *also* **:** a means of refreshment or diversion — **rec·re·ation·al** \-shnəl, -shən-ᵊl\ *adj*

re·crim·i·nate \ri-ˈkrim-ə-ˌnāt\ *vi* [ML *recriminatus,* pp. of *recriminare,* fr. L *re-* + *criminari* to accuse — more at CRIMINATE] **1 :** to make a retaliatory charge against an accuser **2 :** to retort bitterly — **re·crim·i·na·tion** \ri-ˌkrim-ə-ˈnā-shən, ˌrē-\ *n* — **re·crim·i·na·to·ry** \ri-ˈkrim-(ə-)nə-ˌtōr-ē, -ˌtȯr-\ *adj*

re·cru·desce \ˌrē-krü-ˈdes\ *vi* [L *recrudescere* to become raw again, fr. *re-* + *crudescere* to become raw, fr. *crudus* raw — more at RAW] **:** to break out or become active again **syn** see RETURN

re·cru·des·cence \-ˈdes-ᵊn(t)s\ *n* **:** a new outbreak after a period of abatement or inactivity — **re·cru·des·cent** \-ᵊnt\ *adj*

[1]**re·cruit** \ri-ˈkrüt\ *n* [F *recrute, recrue* fresh growth, new levy of soldiers, fr. MF, fr. *recroistre* to grow up again, fr. L *recrescere,* fr. *re-* + *crescere* to grow — more at CRESCENT] **1 :** a fresh or additional supply **2 :** a newcomer to a field or activity; *specif* **:** a newly enlisted or drafted member of the armed forces **3 :** an enlisted man of the lowest rank in the army

[2]**recruit** *vt* **1 a :** to fill up the number of (as an army) with new members **:** REINFORCE **b :** ENLIST, RAISE **c :** to secure the services of **:** ENGAGE **2 :** REPLENISH **3 :** to restore or increase the health, vigor, or intensity of **~** *vi* **:** to enlist new members — **re·cruit·ment** \-mənt\ *n*

re·crys·tal·lize \(ˈ)rē-ˈkris-tə-ˌlīz\ *vb* **:** to crystallize again or repeatedly

rect- *or* **recto-** *comb form* [NL *rectum*] **:** rectum ⟨*rectal*⟩

rec·tal \ˈrek-tᵊl\ *adj* **:** relating to, affecting, or near the rectum — **rec·tal·ly** \-ē\ *adv*

rec·tan·gle \ˈrek-ˌtaŋ-gəl\ *n* [ML *rectangulus* having a right angle, fr. L *rectus* right + *angulus* angle — more at RIGHT, ANGLE] **:** a parallelogram all of whose angles are right angles

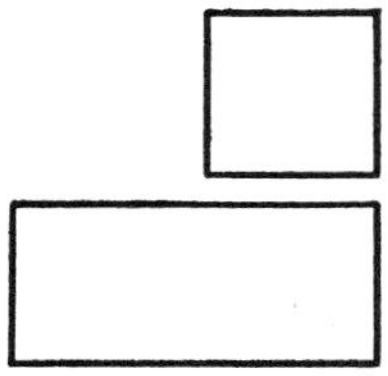

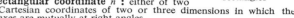

rectangles

rec·tan·gu·lar \rek-ˈtaŋ-gyə-lər\ *adj* **1 :** having a flat surface shaped like a rectangle **2 a :** crossing, lying, or meeting at a right angle **b :** having lines or surfaces that meet at right angles — **rec·tan·gu·lar·i·ty** \(ˌ)rek-ˌtaŋ-gyə-ˈlar-ət-ē\ *n* — **rec·tan·gu·lar·ly** \rek-ˈtaŋ-gyə-lər-lē\ *adv*

rectangular coordinate *n* **:** either of two Cartesian coordinates of two or three dimensions in which the axes are mutually at right angles

rec·ti·fi·able \ˈrek-tə-ˌfī-ə-bəl\ *adj* **:** capable of being rectified

rec·ti·fi·ca·tion \ˌrek-tə-fə-ˈkā-shən\ *n* **:** the act or process of rectifying

rec·ti·fi·er \ˈrek-tə-ˌfī(-ə)r\ *n* **:** one that rectifies; *specif* **:** a device for converting alternating current into direct current

rec·ti·fy \ˈrek-tə-ˌfī\ *vt* [ME *rectifien,* fr. MF *rectifier,* fr. ML *rectificare,* fr. L *rectus* right] **1 :** to set right **:** REMEDY **2 :** to purify (as alcohol) esp. by repeated or fractional distillation **3 :** to correct by removing errors **:** ADJUST ⟨~ the calendar⟩ **4 :** to make (an alternating current) unidirectional **syn** see CORRECT

rec·ti·lin·ear \ˌrek-tə-ˈlin-ē-ər\ *adj* [LL *rectilineus,* fr. L *rectus* + *linea* line] **1 :** moving in or forming a straight line **2 :** characterized by straight lines **3 :** PERPENDICULAR 3 **4 :** corrected for distortion so that straight lines are imaged accurately ⟨~ lens⟩ — **rec·ti·lin·ear·ly** *adv*

rec·ti·tude \ˈrek-tə-ˌt(y)üd\ *n* [ME, fr. MF, fr. LL *rectitudo,* fr. L *rectus* straight, right] **1 :** STRAIGHTNESS **2 :** moral integrity **:** RIGHTEOUSNESS **3 :** correctness of judgment or procedure

rec·to \ˈrek-(ˌ)tō\ *n* [NL *recto* (*folio*) the page being straight] **1 :** the side of a leaf (as of a manuscript) that is to be read first **2 :** a right-hand page — compare VERSO

rec·tor \ˈrek-tər\ *n* [L, fr. *rectus,* pp. of *regere* to direct — more at RIGHT] **1 :** one that directs **:** LEADER **2 a :** a clergyman (as of the Protestant Episcopal Church) in charge of a parish; *specif* **:** an incumbent of an Anglican benefice in full possession of its rights **b :** a Roman Catholic priest directing a church with no pastor or one whose pastor has other duties **3 :** the head of a university or school — **rec·tor·ate** \-t(ə-)rət\ *n* — **rec·to·ri·al** \rek-ˈtōr-ē-əl, -ˈtȯr-\ *adj*

rec·to·ry \ˈrek-t(ə-)rē\ *n* **1 :** a benefice held by a rector **2 :** a rector's residence

rec·trix \ˈrek-triks\ *n, pl* **rec·tri·ces** \ˈrek-trə-ˌsēz, rek-ˈtrī-(ˌ)sēz\ [NL, fr. L, fem. of *rector* one that directs] **:** any of the quill feathers of a bird's tail important in controlling flight direction — usu. used in pl.

rec·tum \ˈrek-təm\ *n, pl* **rectums** *or* **rec·ta** \-tə\ [NL, fr. *rectum intestinum,* lit., straight intestine] **:** the terminal part of the intestine from the sigmoid flexure to the anus

rec·tus \ˈrek-təs\ *n, pl* **rec·ti** \-ˌtī, -ˌtē\ [NL, fr. *rectus musculus* straight muscle] **:** any of several straight muscles (as of the abdomen)

re·cum·ben·cy \ri-ˈkəm-bən-sē\ *n* **:** recumbent position **:** REPOSE

re·cum·bent \-bənt\ *adj* [L *recumbent-, recumbens,* prp. of *recumbere* to lie down, fr. *re-* + *-cumbere* to lie down (akin to L *cubare* to lie, recline)] **1 a :** suggestive of repose **:** RESTING **b :** lying down **c :** representing a person lying down ⟨a ~ statue⟩ **2** *of an anatomical structure* **:** tending to rest upon the surface from which it extends **syn** see PRONE — **re·cum·bent·ly** *adv*

re·cu·per·ate \ri-ˈk(y)ü-pə-ˌrāt\ *vb* [L *recuperatus,* pp. of *recuperare* — more at RECOVER] *vt* **:** to get back **:** REGAIN **~** *vi* **:** to recover health or strength — **re·cu·per·a·tion** \-ˌk(y)ü-pə-ˈrā-shən\ *n* — **re·cu·per·a·tive** \-ˈk(y)ü-pə-ˌrāt-iv, -p(ə-)rət-\ *adj*

re·cur \ri-ˈkər\ *vi* **re·curred; re·cur·ring** [ME *recurren* to return, fr. L *recurrere,* lit., to run back, fr. *re-* + *currere* to run — more at CURRENT] **1 :** to have recourse **:** RESORT **2 :** to go back in thought or discourse **3 a :** to come up again for consideration **b :** to come again to mind **4 :** to occur again after an interval **syn** see RETURN — **re·cur·rence** \-ˈkər-ən(t)s, -ˈkə-rən(t)s\ *n*

re·cur·rent \-ˈkər-ənt, -ˈkə-rənt\ *adj* [L *recurrent-, recurrens,* prp. of *recurrere*] **1 :** running or turning back in a direction opposite to a former course ⟨~ laryngeal nerve⟩ **2 :** returning from time to time ⟨~ problem⟩ **syn** see INTERMITTENT — **re·cur·rent·ly** *adv*

recurring decimal *n* **:** REPEATING DECIMAL

re·cur·vate \ri-ˈkər-ˌvāt, ˈrē-, -vət\ *adj* **:** RECURVED

re·curve \(ˈ)rē-ˈkərv\ *vb* [L *recurvare,* fr. *re-* + *curvare* to curve, fr. *curvus* curved — more at CROWN] **:** to curve backward or inward

re·cu·san·cy \ˈrek-yə-zən-sē, ri-ˈkyüz-ᵊn-\ *n* [*recusant,* n., fr. L *recusant-, recusans,* prp. of *recusare* to refuse, fr. *re-* + *causari* to give a reason, fr. *causa* cause, reason] **:** refusal to accept or obey established authority; *specif* **:** the refusal of Roman Catholics to attend services of the Church of England constituting a statutory offense from about 1570 till 1791 — **re·cu·sant** \ˈrek-yə-zənt, ri-ˈkyüz-ᵊnt\ *n or adj*

See *re-* and 2d element
reconsignment
reconstitute
reconstitution
reconstruct
reconstructible
reconstructive
reconsult
reconsultation
recontact
recontaminate
recontamination
recontract
reconvene
recook
recopy
recouple
recross
recrystallization
recurved
recut

1red \'red\ *adj* **red·der; red·dest** [ME, fr. OE *rēad;* akin to OHG *rōt* red, L *ruber* & *rufus,* Gk *erythros*] **1 a :** of the color red **b :** having red as a distinguishing color **2 a** (1) **:** FLUSHED (2) **:** RUDDY, FLORID (3) **:** of a coppery hue **b :** BLOODSHOT **c :** in the color range between a moderate orange and russet or bay **d :** tinged with red **:** REDDISH **3 :** heated to redness **:** GLOWING **4 a :** inciting or endorsing radical social or political change esp. by force **b :** COMMUNIST **c :** of or relating to the U.S.S.R. or its allies — **red·ly** *adv* — **red·ness** *n*

2red *n* **1 :** a color whose hue resembles that of blood or of the ruby or is that of the long-wave extreme of the visible spectrum **2 :** one that is of a red or reddish color; *esp* **:** an animal with a reddish coat **3 a :** a pigment or dye that colors red **b :** a shade or tint of red **4 a :** one who advocates or is thought to advocate or endorse the violent overthrow of an existing social or political order **b** *cap* **:** COMMUNIST **5** [fr. the bookkeeping practice of entering debit items in red ink] **:** the condition of showing a loss ⟨in the ~⟩

re·dact \ri-'dakt\ *vt* [back-formation fr. *redaction*] **1 :** to put in writing **:** FRAME **2 :** EDIT — **re·dac·tor** \-'dak-tər, -,tȯ(ə)r\ *n*

re·dac·tion \ri-'dak-shən\ *n* [F *rédaction,* fr. LL *redaction-, redactio* act of reducing, compressing, fr. L *redactus,* pp. of *redigere* to bring back, reduce, fr. *re-, red-* re- + *agere* to lead — more at AGENT] **1 :** an act or instance of redacting **2 :** EDITION — **re·dac·tion·al** \-shnəl, -shən-ᵊl\ *adj*

red alert *n* **:** the final stage of alert in which enemy attack appears imminent

red alga *n* **:** an alga (division Rhodophyta) having predominantly red pigmentation

re·dan \ri-'dan\ *n* [F, alter. of *redent,* fr. *re-* + *dent* tooth, fr. L *dent-, dens* — more at TOOTH] **:** a fortification having two parapets forming a salient angle

red ant *n* **:** any of various reddish ants (as the pharaoh ant)

red·ar·gue \ri-'där-(,)gyü, re-, -gyə-w\ *vt* [ME *redarguen,* fr. L *redarguere,* fr. *red-* + *arguere* assert, make clear — more at ARGENT] *archaic* **:** CONFUTE, DISPROVE

red·bel·ly dace \,red-,bel-ē-'dās\ *or* **red–bel·lied dace** \-ē(d)-'dās\ *n* **:** either of two small brightly-marked No. American cyprinid fishes (*Chrosomus eos* and *C. erythrogaster*)

red birch *n* **1 :** the heartwood lumber of the yellow birch (*Betula lutea*) and of the sweet birch (*Betula lenta*) **2 :** a valuable New Zealand timber tree (*Nothofagus fusca*); *also* **:** its hard wood

red·bird \'red-,bərd\ *n* **:** any of several birds (as a cardinal, several tanagers, or the bullfinch) with predominantly red plumage

red blood cell *n* **:** one of the cells responsible for the red color of vertebrate blood — called also *red blood corpuscle*

red–blood·ed \'red-'bləd-əd\ *adj* **:** VIGOROUS, LUSTY

red·bone \'red-,bōn\ *n* **:** a moderate-sized speedy dark red or red and tan American hound

red·breast \'red-,brest\ *n* **1 :** a bird (as a robin) with a reddish breast **2** *or* **red–breast·ed bream** \,red-,bres-təd-\ **:** a reddish-bellied sunfish (*Lepomis auritus*) of the eastern U.S.

red·bud \'red-,bəd\ *n* **:** an American tree (genus *Cercis*) with usu. pale rosy pink flowers

red·cap \'red-,kap\ *n* **:** a baggage porter (as at a railroad station)

red–car·pet \'red-'kär-pət\ *adj* [fr. the traditional laying down of a red carpet for important guests to walk on] **:** marked by ceremonial courtesy ⟨~ treatment⟩

red clover *n* **:** a Eurasian clover (*Trifolium pratense*) with globose heads of reddish purple flowers widely cultivated as a hay, forage, and cover crop

red·coat \'red-,kōt\ *n* **:** a British soldier esp. during the Revolutionary War

red coral *n* **:** a gorgonian (*Corallium nobile*) of the Mediterranean and adjacent parts of the Atlantic having a hard stony skeleton of a delicate red or pink color used for ornaments and jewelry

Red Cross *n* **:** a red Greek cross on a white ground used as the emblem of the International Red Cross

1redd \'red\ *vb* **redd·ed** *or* **redd; redd·ing** [ME *redden* to clear, prob. alter. of *ridden* — more at RID] *vt, chiefly dial* **:** to set in order ~ *vi, chiefly dial* **:** to make things tidy

2redd *n* [origin unknown] **:** the spawning ground or nest of various fishes

red deer *n* **1 :** the common deer of temperate Europe and Asia (*Cervus elaphus*) which is related to but smaller than the elk **2 :** the whitetail in its summer coat

red·den \'red-ᵊn\ *vb* **red·den·ing** \'red-niŋ, -ᵊn-iŋ\ *vt* **:** to make red or reddish ~ *vi* **:** to become red; *esp* **:** BLUSH

red·dish \'red-ish\ *adj* **:** tinged with red — **red·dish·ness** *n*

red·dle \'red-ᵊl\, **red·dle·man** \-mən\ *var of* RUDDLE, RUDDLEMAN

1rede \'rēd\ *vt* [ME *reden* — more at READ] **1** *dial* **:** to give counsel to **:** ADVISE **2** *dial* **:** INTERPRET, EXPLAIN

2rede *n* **1** *chiefly dial* **:** COUNSEL, ADVICE **2** *archaic* **:** ACCOUNT, STORY

red·ear \'red-,i(ə)r\ *n* **:** a common sunfish (*Lepomis microlophus*) of the southern and eastern U.S. resembling the bluegill but having the back part of the gill cover bright orange-red

re·dec·o·rate \(')rē-'dek-ə-,rāt\ *vt* **:** to freshen or change in appearance **:** REFURBISH ~ *vi* **:** to freshen or change a decorative scheme — **re·dec·o·ra·tion** \(,)rē-,dek-ə-'rā-shən\ *n*

re·ded·i·ca·tion \(,)rē-,ded-i-'kā-shən\ *n* **:** a second or additional dedication

re·deem \ri-'dēm\ *vt* [ME *redemen,* modif. of MF *redimer,* fr. L *redimere,* fr. *re-, red-* re- + *emere* to take, buy; akin to Lith *imti* to take] **1 a :** to buy back **:** REPURCHASE **b :** to get or win back **2 a :** to liberate by payment **:** RANSOM **b :** to free by force **:** LIBERATE **c :** to release from blame or debt **:** CLEAR **d :** to free from the bondage of sin **3 :** to change for the better **:** REFORM **4 a :** REPAIR, RESTORE **b** *archaic* **:** RECLAIM **5 a :** to free from a lien by payment of an amount secured thereby **b** (1) **:** to remove the obligation of by payment (2) **:** to convert (as certificates) into cash **c :** to make good **:** FULFILL **6 a :** to atone for **:** EXPIATE **b** (1) **:** to offset the bad effect of (2) **:** to make worthwhile **:** RETRIEVE **syn** see RESCUE — **re·deem·able** \-'dē-mə-bəl\ *adj* — **re·deem·er** *n*

re·de·liv·er \,rēd-ᵊl-'iv-ər\ *vt* **:** to deliver back or again

re·demp·tion \ri-'dem(p)-shən\ *n* [ME *redempcioun,* fr. MF *redemption,* fr. L *redemption-, redemptio,* fr. *redemptus,* pp. of *redimere* to redeem] **:** the act, process, or an instance of redeeming — **re·demp·tion·al** \-'dem(p)-shnəl, -shən-ᵊl\ *adj* — **re·demp·tive** \-'dem(p)-tiv\ *adj*

re·demp·tion·er \-'dem(p)-sh(ə-)nər\ *n* **:** an immigrant to America in the 18th and 19th centuries obtaining passage by becoming an indentured servant

Re·demp·tor·ist \ri-'dem(p)-t(ə-)rəst\ *n* [F *rédemptoriste,* fr. LL *redemptor* redeemer, fr. L, contractor, fr. *redemptus*] **:** a member of the Roman Catholic Congregation of the Most Holy Redeemer

re·demp·to·ry \ri-'dem(p)-t(ə-)rē\ *adj* **:** serving to redeem

re·de·ploy \,rēd-i-'plȯi\ *vt* **:** to transfer from one area to another ~ *vi* **:** to relocate men or equipment — **re·de·ploy·ment** \-mənt\ *n*

re·de·sign \,rēd-i-'zīn\ *vt* **:** to revise in appearance, function, or content — **redesign** *n*

re·de·ter·mi·na·tion \,rēd-i-,tər-mə-'nā-shən\ *n* **:** an act or instance of determining again

re·de·ter·mine \-'tər-mən\ *vt* **:** to determine again **:** CONFIRM

re·de·vel·op·ment \,rēd-i-'vel-əp-mənt\ *n* **:** the act or process of redeveloping; *esp* **:** renovation of a blighted area

red–eye \'red-,ī\ *n* **:** cheap whiskey

red feed *n* **:** small red marine planktonic copepods that are a leading food of some commercial fishes

red·fin \'red-,fin\ *n* **:** a fish (as any of several American shiners or suckers) with more or less red fins

red fire *n* **:** a pyrotechnic composition usu. containing a strontium or lithium salt that burns with a red light

red·fish \'red-,fish\ *n* **:** any of various reddish fishes

red fox *n* **:** a fox (*Vulpes vulpes*) with bright orange-red to dusky reddish brown fur

red gum *n* **1 :** any of several Australian trees of the genus *Eucalyptus* (esp. *E. camaldulensis, E. amygdalina,* and *E. calophylla*) **2 :** eucalyptus gum

red–hand·ed \'red-'han-dəd\ *adv* (*or adj*) **:** in the act of committing a crime or misdeed

red·head \'red-,hed\ *n* **1 :** a person having red hair **2 :** an American duck (*Aythya americana*) related to the canvasback but having in the male a brighter rufous head and shorter bill

red heat *n* **:** the state of being red-hot; *also* **:** the temperature at which a substance is red-hot

red herring *n* **1 :** a herring cured by salting and slow smoking to a dark brown color **2** [fr. the practice of drawing a red herring across a trail to confuse hunting dogs] **:** a diversion intended to distract attention from the real issue

red–hot \'red-'hät\ *adj* **1 :** glowing with heat **2 :** exhibiting or marked by intense emotion, enthusiasm, or violence ⟨*red-hot* line drive⟩ **3 :** FRESH, NEW

re·dia \'rēd-ē-ə\ *n, pl* **re·di·ae** \-ē-,ē\ *also* **re·di·as** [NL, fr. Francesco *Redi* †1698? It naturalist] **:** a larva produced within the sporocyst of many trematodes that produces another generation of rediae or develops into a cercaria — **re·di·al** \-ē-əl\ *adj*

Red Indian *n* **:** AMERICAN INDIAN — called also *Red Man*

red·in·gote \'red-iŋ-,gōt\ *n* [F, modif. of E *riding coat*] **:** a fitted outer garment: as **a :** a woman's lightweight coat open at the front **b :** a dress with a front gore of contrasting material

red·in·te·grate \ri-'dint-ə-,grāt, re-\ *vt* [ME *redintegraten,* fr. L *redintegratus,* pp. of *redintegrare,* fr. *re-, red-* re- + *integrare* to make complete — more at INTEGRATE] *archaic* **:** to restore to a former or sound state — **red·in·te·gra·tion** \ri-,dint-ə-'grā-shən, ,rē-, (,)re-\ *n* — **red·in·te·gra·tive** \ri-'dint-ə-,grāt-iv, re-\ *adj*

re·di·rect \,rēd-ə-'rekt, ,rē-(,)dī-\ *vt* **:** to change the direction of — **re·di·rec·tion** \-'rek-shən\ *n*

1re·dis·count \(')rē-'dis-,kau̇nt, ,rē-dis-'\ *vt* **:** to discount again (as commercial paper) — **re·dis·count·able** \-ə-bəl\ *adj*

2rediscount \(')rē-'dis-,\ *n* **:** the act or process of rediscounting or negotiable paper rediscounted

re·dis·trib·ute \,rēd-ə-'strib-yət\ *vt* **:** to alter the distribution of **:** REALLOCATE — **re·dis·tri·bu·tion** \(,)rē-,dis-trə-'byü-shən\ *n* — **re·dis·trib·u·tive** \,rēd-ə-'strib-yət-iv\ *adj*

re·dis·trict \(')rē-'dis-(,)trikt\ *vt* **:** to divide anew into districts; *specif* **:** to revise the legislative districts of

red·i·vi·vus \,red-ə-'vī-vəs, -'vē-\ *adj* [LL, fr. L, renovated] **:** brought back to life **:** REBORN

red jasmine *n* **1 :** a widely cultivated frangipani (*Plumeria rubra*) with large terminal cymes of pink, red, or purple fragrant flowers **2 :** CYPRESS VINE

red lead *n* **:** an orange-red to brick-red lead oxide Pb_3O_4 used in storage-battery plates, in glass and ceramics, and as a paint pigment — called also *minium*

red leaf *n* **:** any of several plant diseases characterized by reddening of the foliage

red·leg \'red-,leg, -,lāg\ *n* **:** any of several birds (as a redshank) with red legs

red–let·ter \'red-'let-ər\ *adj* **:** of special significance **:** MEMORABLE

red light *n* **1 :** a warning signal; *esp* **:** a red traffic signal **2 :** a cautionary sign **:** DETERRENT

red–light district *n* **:** a district in which brothels are frequent

red mass *n, often cap R & M* **:** a votive mass of the Holy Ghost celebrated in red vestments esp. at the opening of courts and congresses

red mulberry *n* **:** a No. American forest tree (*Morus rubra*) with soft weak but durable wood; *also* **:** its edible purple fruit

red–neck \'red-,nek\ *n* **:** a member of the Southern rural laboring class

re·do \(')rē-'dü\ *vt* **1 :** to do over or again **2 :** REDECORATE

red oak *n* **:** any of numerous American oaks (as *Quercus borealis* and *Quercus falcata*); *also* **:** the wood of red oak

See *re-* and 2d element	**redelivery**	**redevelop**	**redigestion**	**rediscovery**	**redissolve**
rededicate	**redemand**	**redeveloper**	**redip**	**redispose**	**redistill**
redefine	**redemandable**	**redifferentiation**	**rediscover**	**redisposition**	**redistillation**
redefinition	**redeposit**	**redigest**			

red ocher *n* **:** a red earthy hematite used as a pigment

red·o·lence \'red-ᵊl-ən(t)s\ *n* **1 :** the quality or state of being redolent **2 :** SCENT, AROMA **syn** see FRAGRANCE

red·o·lent \-ənt\ *adj* [ME, fr. MF, fr. L *redolent-, redolens,* prp. of *redolēre* to emit a scent, fr. *re-* + *olēre* to smell — more at ODOR] **1 :** exuding fragrance **:** AROMATIC **2 a :** full of a specified fragrance **:** SCENTED **b :** EVOCATIVE, REMINISCENT — **red·o·lent·ly** *adv*

re·dou·ble \(')rē-'dəb-əl\ *vt* **1 :** to make twice as great in size or amount **:** INTENSIFY **2 a** *obs* **:** to echo back **b** *archaic* **:** REPEAT ~ *vi* **1 :** to become redoubled **2** *archaic* **:** RESOUND **3 :** to double again **4 :** to double an opponent's double in bridge — **redouble** *n*

re·doubt \ri-'daùt\ *n* [F *redoute,* fr. It *ridotto,* fr. ML *reductus* secret place, fr. L, withdrawn, fr. pp. of *reducere* to lead back — more at REDUCE] **1 a :** a small usu. temporary enclosed defensive work **b :** a defended position or protective barrier **2 :** a secure retreat **:** STRONGHOLD

re·doubt·able \ri-'daùt-ə-bəl\ *adj* [ME *redoutable,* fr. MF, fr. *redouter* to dread, fr. *re-* + *douter* to doubt] **1 :** causing fear or alarm **:** FORMIDABLE **2 :** inspiring or worthy of awe or reverence **:** DOUGHTY — **re·doubt·ably** \-blē\ *adv*

re·dound \ri-'daùnd\ *vi* [ME *redounden,* fr. MF *redonder,* fr. L *redundare,* fr. *re-, red-* re- + *unda* wave — more at WATER] **1** *archaic* **:** to become swollen **:** OVERFLOW **2 :** to have an effect **:** CONDUCE **3 :** to become transferred or added **:** ACCRUE **4 :** REBOUND, REFLECT **syn** see CONDUCE

red·out \'red-,aùt\ *n* **:** a condition in which centripetal acceleration drives blood to the head and causes reddening of the visual field and headache

re·dox \'rē-,däks\ *n* **:** OXIDATION-REDUCTION

red–pen·cil \'red-'pen(t)-səl\ *vt* **1 :** CENSOR **2 :** CORRECT, REVISE

red pepper *n* **:** CAYENNE PEPPER

red·poll \'red-,pōl\ *n* **:** any of several small finches (genus *Carduelis* or *Acanthis*) which resemble siskins and in which the males usu. have a red or rosy crown

red poll *n, often cap R&P* [alter. of *red polled*] **:** any of a British breed of large hornless dual-purpose cattle that are red with a little white on switch and belly

¹re·dress \ri-'dres\ *vt* [ME *redressen,* fr. MF *redresser,* fr. OF *redrecier,* fr. *re-* + *drecier* to make straight — more at DRESS] **1 a** (1) **:** to set right **:** REMEDY (2) **:** to make up for **:** COMPENSATE **b :** to remove the cause of (a grievance or complaint) **c :** to exact reparation for **:** AVENGE **2** *archaic* **a :** to requite (a person) for a wrong or loss **b :** HEAL **syn** see CORRECT — **re·dress·er** *n*

²re·dress \ri-'dres, 'rē-,\ *n* **1 a :** relief from distress **b :** means or possibility of seeking a remedy **2 :** compensation for wrong or loss **:** REPARATION **3 a :** an act or instance of redressing **b :** CORRECTION, RETRIBUTION

red ribbon *n* **:** a red ribbon usu. with appropriate words or markings awarded the second-place winner in a competition

red·root \'red-,rüt, -,rùt\ *n* **1 :** a perennial herb (*Lachnanthes tinctoria*) of the bloodwort family of the eastern U.S. whose red root is the source of a dye **2 :** BLOODROOT

red rust *n* **:** the uredinial stage of a rust; *also* **:** the diseased condition produced by such fungi

red salmon *n* **:** SOCKEYE

red·shank \'red-,shaŋk\ *n* **:** a common Old World limicoline bird (*Tringa totanus*) with pale red legs and feet

red sind·hi \-'sin-dē\ *n* ['*red* + *sindhi* (one belonging to Sind, Pakistan)] **:** any of an Indian breed of rather small red humped dairy cattle extensively used for crossbreeding with European stock in tropical areas

red siskin *n* **:** a finch (*Carduelis cucullata*) of northern So. America that is scarlet with black head, wings, and tail and often kept as a cage bird

red·skin \'red-,skin\ *n* **:** a No. American Indian

red snapper *n* **:** any of various reddish fishes (as of the genera *Lutjanus* and *Sebastodes*) including several esteemed food fishes

red snow *n* **:** snow colored by various airborne dusts or by a growth of algae (as of the genus *Chlamydomonas*) that contain red pigment and live in the upper layer of snow; *also* **:** an alga causing red snow

red spider *n* **:** any small web-spinning mite (family Tetranychidae) that attacks forage and crop plants

red squill *n* **:** a European squill (*Urginea maritima*) having a reddish brown bulb used chiefly in rat poison

red·start \'red-,stärt\ *n* [*red* + obs. *start* (handle, tail)] **:** a small European singing bird (*Phoenicurus phoenicurus*) related to the redbreast

red tape *n* [fr. the red tape formerly used to bind legal documents in England] **:** bureaucratic procedure esp. as marked by delay or inaction

red tide *n* **:** seawater discolored by the presence of large numbers of dinoflagellates (esp. of the genera *Peridinium* and *Gymnodinium*)

red·top \'red-,täp\ *n* **:** any of various grasses (genus *Agrostis*) with usu. reddish panicles; *esp* **:** an important forage and lawn grass (*A. alba*) of eastern No. America

re·duce \ri-'d(y)üs\ *vb* [ME *reducen* to lead back, fr. L *reducere,* fr. *re-* + *ducere* to lead — more at TOW] *vt* **1 a :** to draw together or cause to converge **:** CONSOLIDATE **b :** to diminish in size, amount, extent, or number **c :** to narrow down **:** RESTRICT **d :** to make shorter **:** ABRIDGE **2** *archaic* **:** to restore to righteousness **:** SAVE **3 :** to bring to a specified state or condition **4 a :** to force to capitulate **b :** FORCE, COMPEL **5 a :** to bring to a systematic form or character **b :** to endow with (a definite shape) **6 :** to correct (as a fracture) by bringing displaced or broken parts back into their normal positions **7 a :** to lower in grade or rank **:** DEMOTE **b :** to lower in condition or status **:** DOWNGRADE **8 a :** to diminish in strength or density **b :** to diminish in value **9 a** (1) **:** to change the denominations or form of without changing the value (2) **:** to construct a geometrical figure similar to but smaller than (a given figure) **b :** to transpose from one form into another **c :** to change (an expression) to an equivalent but more fundamental expression **10 :** to break down (as by crushing or grinding) **:** PULVERIZE **11 a :** to bring to the metallic state by removal of nonmetallic elements **b :** DEOXIDIZE **c :** to combine with or subject to the action of hydrogen **d** (1) **:** to change (an element or ion) from a higher to a lower oxidation state (2) **:** to add one or more electrons to (an atom or ion or molecule) **12 :** to change (a stressed vowel) to an unstressed vowel ~ *vi* **1 a :** to become diminished or lessened; *esp* **:** to lose weight by dieting **b :** to become concentrated or consolidated **c :** to undergo meiosis **2 :** to become converted or equated **syn** see CONQUER, DECREASE — **re·duc·er** *n* — **re·duc·ibil·i·ty** \-,d(y)ü-sə-'bil-ət-ē\ *n* — **re·duc·ible** \-'d(y)ü-sə-bəl\ *adj* — **re·duc·ibly** \-blē\ *adv*

re·duc·tant \ri-'dək-tənt\ *n* **:** a reducing agent

re·duc·tase \-,tās, -,tāz\ *n* **:** an enzyme that catalyzes reduction

re·duc·tio ad ab·sur·dum \ri-'dək-tē-,ō-,ad-əb-'sərd-əm, -s(h)ē-,ō-, -'zərd-\ *n* [LL] **:** disproof of a proposition by showing an absurdity to which it leads when carried to its logical conclusion

re·duc·tion \ri-'dək-shən\ *n* [ME *reduccion* restoration, fr. MF *reduction,* fr. LL & L; LL *reduction-, reductio* reduction (in a syllogism), fr. L, restoration, fr. *reductus,* past part. of *reducere*] **1 :** the act or process of reducing **:** the state of being reduced **2 :** something made by reducing **3 :** MEIOSIS; *specif* **:** production of the gametic chromosome number in the first meiotic division — **re·duc·tion·al** \-shnəl, -shən-ᵊl\ *adj* — **re·duc·tive** \-'dək-tiv\ *adj*

re·duc·tion·ism \-'dək-shə-,niz-əm\ *n* **:** a procedure or theory that reduces complex data or phenomena to simple terms — **re·duc·tion·ist** \-sh(ə-)nəst\ *n* — **re·duc·tion·is·tic** \-,dək-shə-'nis-tik\ *adj*

re·dun·dan·cy \ri-'dən-dən-sē\ *n* **1 :** the quality or state of being redundant **:** SUPERFLUITY **2 :** PROFUSION, ABUNDANCE **3 a :** superfluous repetition **:** PROLIXITY **b :** an act or instance of needless repetition **4 :** the part of a message that can be eliminated without loss of essential information

re·dun·dant \ri-'dən-dənt\ *adj* [L *redundant-, redundans,* prp. of *redundare* to overflow — more at REDOUND] **1 a :** exceeding what is necessary or normal **:** SUPERFLUOUS **b :** characterized by or containing an excess; *specif* **:** using more words than necessary **2 :** PROFUSE, LAVISH **syn** see WORDY — **re·dun·dant·ly** *adv*

re·du·pli·cate \ri-'d(y)ü-pli-,kāt, 'rē-\ *vt* [LL *reduplicatus,* pp. of *reduplicare,* fr. L *re-* + *duplicare* to double — more at DUPLICATE] **1 :** to make or perform again **:** COPY **2 :** to form (a word) by reduplication — **re·du·pli·cate** \-kət\ *adj*

re·du·pli·ca·tion \ri-,d(y)ü-pli-'kā-shən, ,rē-\ *n* **1 :** an act or instance of doubling or reiterating **2 a :** repetition of a radical element or a part of it occurring usu. at the beginning of a word and often accompanied by change of the radical vowel **b** (1) **:** a word or form produced by reduplication (2) **:** the repeated element in such a word or form **3 :** ANADIPLOSIS — **re·du·pli·ca·tive** \ri-'d(y)ü-pli-,kāt-iv, 'rē-\ *adj* — **re·du·pli·ca·tive·ly** *adv*

re·du·vi·id \ri-'d(y)ü-vē-əd\ *adj* [deriv. of L *reduvia* hangnail] **:** of or relating to a large and widely distributed family of blood-sucking hemipterous insects comprising the assassin bugs

red water *n* **:** a disease of cattle marked by hematuria

red·wing \'red-,wiŋ\ *n* **:** a European thrush (*Turdus musicus*) having the under wing coverts red

red·wing blackbird *or* **red–winged blackbird** \,red-,wiŋ(d)-\ *n* **:** a No. American blackbird (*Agelaius phoeniceus*) of which the adult male is black with a patch of bright scarlet bordered behind with white or buff on the wing coverts

red·wood \'red-,wùd\ *n* **1 :** a wood yielding a red dye **2 :** a tree that yields a red dyewood or produces red or reddish wood **3 a :** a commercially important coniferous timber tree (*Sequoia sempervirens*) of California that often reaches a height of 300 feet **b :** the brownish red light wood of the California redwood

red worm *n* **:** BLOODWORM; *esp* **:** a small reddish aquatic oligochaete worm (genus *Tubifex*)

re·echo \(')rē-'ek-(,)ō\ *vi* **:** to repeat or return an echo again or repeatedly **:** REVERBERATE ~ *vt* **:** to send (an echo) back

reechy \'rē-chē\ *adj* [ME *rechy,* fr. *rek, rech* reek] *archaic* **:** FILTHY, RANCID

reed \'rēd\ *n* [ME *rede,* fr. OE *hrēod;* akin to OHG *hriot* reed, Lith *krutėti* to stir] **1 a :** any of various tall grasses with slender often prominently jointed stems that grow esp. in wet areas **b :** a stem of such a grass **c :** one too weak to rely on **2 :** a growth or mass of reeds; *specif* **:** reeds for thatching **3 :** ARROW **4 :** a musical instrument made of the hollow joint of a plant **5 :** an ancient Hebrew unit of length equal to 6 cubits **6 a :** a thin elastic tongue of cane, wood, or metal fastened at one end to the mouthpiece of a musical instrument (as a clarinet or organ pipe) or to a reed block or other fixture over an air opening (as in an accordion) and set in vibration by the breath or other air current **b :** a reed instrument ⟨the ~s of an orchestra⟩ **7 :** a device on a loom resembling a comb and used to space warp yarns evenly **8 :** REEDING 1

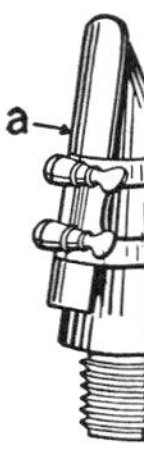

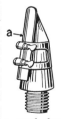

a, reed 6a: in mouthpiece of a clarinet

reed·bird \'rēd-,bərd\ *n, chiefly South* **:** BOBOLINK

reed·buck \'rēd-,bək\ *n, pl* **reedbuck** *also* **reedbucks :** any of a genus (*Redunca*) of fawn-colored African antelopes with hornless females

re·ed·i·fy \(')rē-'ed-ə-,fī\ *vt* [ME *reedifien,* fr. MF *reedifier,* fr. LL *reaedificare,* fr. L *re-* + *aedificare* to build] **:** REBUILD

reed·i·ness \'rēd-ē-nəs\ *n* **:** the quality or state of being reedy

reed·ing \'rēd-iŋ\ *n* **1 :** a small convex molding **2 :** decoration by series of parallel reeds

reed organ *n* **:** a keyboard wind instrument in which the wind acts on a set of metal reeds

reed pipe *n* **:** a pipe-organ pipe producing its tone by vibration of a beating reed in a current of air

reed stop *n* **:** a set of reed pipes in an organ controlled by a single stop knob

re·ed·u·cate \(')rē-'ej-ə-,kāt\ *vt* **:** to train again; *esp* **:** to rehabilitate through education — **re·ed·u·ca·tion** \(,)rē-,ej-ə-'kā-shən\ *n* — **re·ed·u·ca·tive** \(')rē-'ej-ə-,kāt-iv\ *adj*

reedy \'rēd-ē\ *adj* **1 :** abounding in or covered with reeds **2 :** made of or resembling reeds; *esp* **:** SLENDER, FRAIL **3 :** having the tone quality of a reed instrument

¹reef \'rēf\ *n* [ME *riff,* fr. ON *rif*] **1 :** a part of a sail taken in or let out in regulating size **2 :** reduction in sail area by reefing

²reef *vt* **1 :** to reduce the area of (a sail) by rolling or folding a portion **2 :** to lower or bring inboard (a spar) wholly or partially ~ *vi* **:** to reduce a sail by taking in a reef

³reef *n* [D *rif,* prob. of Scand origin; akin to ON *rif* reef of a sail] **1 a :** a chain of rocks or ridge of sand at or near the surface of water **b :** a hazardous obstruction **2 :** VEIN, LODE

See *re-* and 2d element **redomesticate** | **redraft** | **redraw** | **redrawer** | **reedification**

1reef·er \'rē-fər\ *n* **1 :** one that reefs **2 :** a close-fitting usu. double-breasted jacket of thick cloth
2reefer *n* [*2reef*] **:** a marijuana cigarette
3ree·fer \'rē-fər\ *n* [by shortening & alter.] **1 :** REFRIGERATOR **2 :** a refrigerator car, truck, trailer, or ship
reef knot *n* **:** a square knot used in reefing a sail
1reek \'rēk\ *n* [ME *rek*, fr. OE *rēc;* akin to OHG *rouh* smoke] **1** *chiefly dial* **:** SMOKE **2 :** VAPOR, FOG **3 :** a strong or disagreeable fume or odor
2reek *vi* **1 :** to emit smoke or vapor **2 a :** to give off or become permeated with a strong or offensive odor **b :** to give a strong impression of some constituent quality or feature **3 :** EMANATE ~ *vt* **1 :** to subject to the action of smoke or vapor **2 :** to give off as or as if a reek **:** EXUDE — **reek·er** *n* — **reeky** \'rē-kē\ *adj*
1reel \'rē(ə)l\ *n* [ME, fr. OE *hrēol;* akin to ON *hræll* weaver's reed, Gk *krekein* to weave] **1 :** a revolvable device on which something flexible is wound: as **a :** a small windlass at the butt of a fishing rod for the line **b** *chiefly Brit* **:** a spool or bobbin for sewing thread **c :** a flanged spool for photographic film **2 :** a quantity of something wound on a reel **3 :** a frame for drying clothes usu. having radial arms on a vertical pole
2reel *vt* **1 :** to wind upon or as if upon a reel **2 :** to draw by reeling a line ~ *vi* **:** to wind on a reel — **reel·able** \'rē-lə-bəl\ *adj* — **reel·er** *n*
3reel *vb* [ME *relen*, prob. fr. *reel*, n.] *vi* **1 a :** to turn or move round and round **:** WHIRL **b :** to be giddy **2 :** to behave in a violent disorderly manner **3 :** to waver or fall back from a blow **:** RECOIL **4 :** to walk or move unsteadily **:** SWAY ~ *vt* **:** to cause to reel
4reel *n* **:** a reeling motion
5reel *n* [prob. fr. *4reel*] **:** a lively Scottish-Highland dance or its music
re·elect \,rē-ə-'lekt\ *vt* **:** to elect for another term in office — **re·elec·tion** \-'lek-shən\ *n*
re·em·ploy \,rē-əm-'plȯi\ *vt* **:** to hire back — **re·em·ploy·ment** \-mənt\ *n*
re·en·act \,rē-ə-'nakt\ *vt* **1 :** to enact again **2 :** to perform again — **re·en·act·ment** \-'nak(t)-mənt\ *n*
re·en·force \,rē-ən-'fō(ə)rs, -'fȯ(ə)rs\ *var of* REINFORCE
re·en·trance \(')rē-'en-trən(t)s\ *n* **:** REENTRY
1re·en·trant \-trənt\ *adj* **:** directed inward
2reentrant *n* **:** one that reenters or is reentrant
re·en·try \(')rē-'en-trē\ *n* **1 :** a retaking possession; *esp* **:** entry by a lessor on leased premises on the tenant's failure to perform the conditions of the lease **2 :** a second or new entry **3 :** a playing card that will enable a player to retake the lead **4 :** the action of reentering the earth's atmosphere after travel in space
reest \'rēst\ *vi* [prob. short for Sc *arreest* to arrest, fr. ME (Sc) *arreisten*, fr. MF *arester* — more at ARREST] *chiefly Scot* **:** BALK
1reeve \'rēv\ *n* [ME *reve*, fr. OE *gerēfa*, fr. *ge-* (associative prefix) + *-rēfa* (akin to OE *-rōf* number, OHG *ruova*) — more at CO-] **1 :** a local administrative agent of an Anglo-Saxon king **2 :** a medieval English manor officer responsible chiefly for overseeing the discharge of feudal obligations **3 a :** the council president in some Canadian municipalities **b :** a local official charged with enforcement of specific regulations ⟨deer ~⟩
2reeve *vb* **rove** \'rōv\ *or* **reeved; reev·ing** [origin unknown] *vt* **1 :** to pass (as a rope) through a hole or opening **2 :** to fasten by passing through a hole or around something **3 :** to pass a rope through ~ *vi, of a rope* **:** to pass through a block or similar device
3reeve *n* [prob. alter. of *ruff*] **:** the female of the ruff
re·ex·am·i·na·tion \,rē-ig-,zam-ə-'nā-shən\ *n* **:** a second or new examination
re·ex·am·ine \-'zam-ən\ *vt* **:** to subject to reexamination
re·fash·ion \(')rē-'fash-ən\ *vt* **:** to make over **:** ALTER
re·fect \ri-'fekt\ *vt* [L *refectus*, pp.] *archaic* **:** to refresh with food or drink
re·fec·tion \ri-'fek-shən\ *n* [ME *refeccioun*, fr. MF *refection*, fr. L *refection-, refectio*, fr. *refectus*, pp. of *reficere* to restore, fr. *re-* + *facere* to make — more at DO] **1 :** refreshment of mind, spirit, or body; *esp* **:** NOURISHMENT **2 a :** the taking of refreshment **b :** food and drink together **:** REPAST
re·fec·to·ry \ri-'fek-t(ə-)rē\ *n* [LL *refectorium*, fr. L *refectus*] **:** a dining hall esp. in a monastery
refectory table *n* **:** a long narrow table with heavy legs
re·fel \ri-'fel\ *vt* **re·felled; re·fel·ling** [L *refellere* to prove false, refute, fr. *re-* + *fallere* to deceive] *obs* **:** REJECT, REPULSE
re·fer \ri-'fər\ *vb* **re·ferred; re·fer·ring** [ME *referren*, fr. L *referre* to bring back, report, refer, fr. *re-* + *ferre* to carry — more at BEAR] *vt* **1 a** (1) **:** to think of, regard, or classify within a general category or group (2) **:** to explain in terms of a general cause **b :** to allot to a particular place, stage, or period **c :** to regard as coming from or located in a specific area **2 a :** to send or direct for treatment, aid, information, or decision **b :** to direct for testimony or guaranty as to character or ability ~ *vi* **1 a :** to have relation or connection **:** RELATE **b :** to direct attention **:** make reference **2 :** to have recourse — **re·fer·able** \'ref-(ə-)rə-bəl, ri-'fər-ə-bəl\ *adj* — **re·fer·rer** \ri-'fər-ər\ *n*

syn REFER, ALLUDE mean to call or direct attention to something. REFER usu. implies intentional introduction and distinct mention as by direct naming; ALLUDE suggests indirect mention (as by a hint, roundabout expression, or figure of speech) **syn** see in addition ASCRIBE

ref·er·ee \,ref-ə-'rē\ *n* **1 :** a person to whom a legal matter is referred for investigation and report or for settlement **2 :** a sports official usu. having final authority in administering a game — **referee** *vb* **ref·er·eed; ref·er·ee·ing**
1ref·er·ence \'ref-ərn(t)s, 'ref-(ə-)rən(t)s\ *n* **1 :** the act of referring or consulting **2 :** a bearing on a matter **:** RELATION **3 :** something that refers: as **a :** ALLUSION, MENTION **b :** a sign or indication referring a reader to another passage or book **c :** consultation of sources of information **4 :** one referred to: as **a :** a person to whom inquiries as to character or ability can be made **b :** a statement of the qualifications of a person seeking employment or appointment given by someone familiar with them **c :** a book or passage to which a reader is referred **d :** DENOTATION, MEANING
2reference *vt* **:** to supply with references
ref·er·en·dum \,ref-ə-'ren-dəm\ *n, pl* **ref·er·en·da** \-də\ *or* **referendums** [NL, fr. L, neut. of *referendus*, gerundive of *referre* to refer] **1 a :** the principle or practice of submitting to popular vote a measure passed upon or proposed by a legislative body or by popular initiative **b :** a vote on a measure so submitted **2 :** a diplomatic agent's note asking his government for instructions
re·fer·ent \ri-'fər-ənt, 'ref-(ə-)rənt\ *n* [L *referent-, referens*, prp. of *referre*] **:** something that refers or is referred to — **referent** *adj*
ref·er·en·tial \,ref-ə-'ren-chəl\ *adj* **:** containing or constituting a reference — **ref·er·en·tial·ly** \-'rench-(ə-)lē\ *adv*
re·fer·ral \ri-'fər-əl\ *n* **1 :** the act or an instance of referring **2 :** one that is referred
1re·fill \(')rē-'fil\ *vt* **:** to fill again **:** REPLENISH ~ *vi* **:** to become filled again — **re·fill·able** \-'fil-ə-bəl\ *adj*
2re·fill \'rē-,fil\ *n* **1 :** a product or a container and a product used to refill the exhausted supply of a device **2 :** something provided again; *esp* **:** a second filling of a medical prescription
re·fi·nance \,rē-fə-'nan(t)s, (')rē-'fī-,, ,rē-(,)fī-'\ *vt* **:** to renew or reorganize the financing of
re·fine \ri-'fīn\ *vt* **1 :** to reduce to a pure state ⟨~ sugar⟩ **2 :** to free from moral imperfection **:** ELEVATE **3 :** to improve or perfect by pruning or polishing **4 :** to free from what is coarse, vulgar, or uncouth ~ *vi* **1 :** to become pure or perfected **2 :** to make improvement by introducing subtleties or distinctions — **re·fin·er** *n*
re·fined \ri-'fīnd\ *adj* **1 :** free from impurities **2 :** FASTIDIOUS, CULTIVATED **3 :** PRECISE, EXACT
re·fine·ment \ri-'fīn-mənt\ *n* **1 :** the action or process of refining **2 :** the quality or state of being refined **:** CULTIVATION **3 a :** a refined feature or method **b :** SUBTLETY **c :** a contrivance or device intended to improve or perfect
re·fin·ery \ri-'fīn-(ə-)rē\ *n* **:** a building and equipment for refining or purifying metals, oil, or sugar
re·fin·ish \(')rē-'fin-ish\ *vt* **:** to give (as furniture) a new surface — **re·fin·ish·er** *n*
re·fit \(')rē-'fit\ *vt* **:** to fit out or supply again ~ *vi* **:** to obtain repairs or fresh supplies or equipment — **refit** \'rē-, , (')rē-'\ *n*
re·flect \ri-'flekt\ *vb* [ME *reflecten*, fr. L *reflectere* to bend back, fr. *re-* + *flectere* to bend] *vt* **1** *archaic* **:** to turn into or away from a course **:** DEFLECT **2 a :** to turn, throw, or bend off or backward at an angle ⟨mirror ~s light⟩ **b :** to cast back **3 :** to bend or fold back **4 :** to give back or exhibit as an image, likeness, or outline **:** MIRROR **5 :** to bring or cast as a result **6 :** to make manifest or apparent **:** SHOW **7 :** REALIZE, CONSIDER ~ *vi* **1** *obs* **:** to become turned or thrown back **2 :** to throw back light or sound **3 :** to think quietly and calmly **4 a :** to tend to bring reproach **b :** to have a bearing or influence **syn** see THINK
re·flec·tance \ri-'flek-tən(t)s\ *n* **:** the fraction of the total luminous flux incident upon a surface that is reflected and that varies according to the wavelength distribution of the incident light
reflecting telescope *n* **:** REFLECTOR 2
re·flec·tion *or chiefly Brit* **re·flex·ion** \ri-'flek-shən\ *n* [ME, alter. of *reflexion*, fr. MF, fr. LL *reflexion-, reflexio* act of bending back, fr. L *reflexus*, pp. of *reflectere*] **1 :** an instance of reflecting; *esp* **:** the return of light or sound waves from a surface **2 :** the production of an image by or as if by a mirror **3 a :** the action of bending or folding back **b :** a reflected part **:** FOLD **4 :** something produced by reflecting; *esp* **:** an image given back by a reflecting surface **5 :** REPROACH, CENSURE **6 :** a thought, idea, or opinion formed or a remark made as a result of meditation **7 :** consideration of some subject matter, idea, or purpose **8** *obs* **:** turning back **:** RETURN **syn** see ANIMADVERSION — **re·flec·tion·al** \-shnəl, -shən-ᵊl\ *adj*
re·flec·tive \ri-'flek-tiv\ *adj* **1 :** capable of reflecting light, images, sound waves **2 :** marked by reflection **3 :** of, relating to, or caused by reflection **4 :** REFLEXIVE — **re·flec·tive·ly** *adv* — **re·flec·tive·ness** *n* — **re·flec·tiv·i·ty** \,rē-,flek-'tiv-ət-ē, ri-\ *n*
re·flec·tom·e·ter \,rē-,flek-'täm-ət-ər, ri-\ *n* **:** a device for measuring the reflectance of light
re·flec·tor \ri-'flek-tər\ *n* **1 :** a polished surface for reflecting light or other radiation **2 :** a telescope in which the principal focusing element is a mirror
re·flec·tor·ize \-tə-,rīz\ *vt* **1 :** to make reflecting **2 :** to provide with reflectors
1re·flex \'rē-,fleks\ *n* [L *reflexus*, pp. of *reflectere* to reflect] **1 a :** reflected heat, light, or color **b :** a mirrored image **c :** a copy exact in essential or peculiar features **2 a :** an act performed involuntarily in consequence of a nervous impulse transmitted inward from a receptor to a nerve center and outward to an effector (as a muscle or gland) **b :** the process comprising reception, transmission, and reaction culminating in a reflex act **c** *pl* **:** the power of acting or responding with adequate speed **d :** an habitual and predictable way of thinking or behaving
2reflex *adj* [L *reflexus*] **1 :** bent, turned, or directed back **:** REFLECTED **2 :** INTROSPECTIVE **3 :** produced in reaction, resistance, or return **4** *of an angle* **:** being between 180° and 360° **5 :** of, relating to, or produced by reflex action without intervention or consciousness — **re·flex·ly** *adv*
reflex arc *n* **:** the complete nervous path involved in a reflex
reflex camera *n* **:** a camera in which the image formed by the lens is reflected onto a screen for focusing and composition
1re·flex·ive \ri-'flek-siv\ *adj* [ML *reflexivus*, fr. L *reflexus*] **1 :** directed or turned back upon itself **2 :** of, relating to, or constituting an action (as in "he perjured himself") directed back upon the agent or the grammatical subject — **re·flex·ive·ly** *adv* — **re·flex·ive·ness** *n* — **re·flex·iv·i·ty** \,rē-,flek-'siv-ət-ē, ri-\ *n*

See *re-* and 2d element	**reemergence**	**reenlistment**	**reevaluation**	**reexporter**	**refilm**
reeligibility	**reemergent**	**reenter**	**reevaporation**	**reface**	**refilter**
reeligible	**reemission**	**reequip**	**reevoke**	**refall**	**refind**
reembodiment	**reemphasis**	**reestablish**	**reexchange**	**refasten**	**refinish**
reembody	**reemphasize**	**reestablishment**	**reexport**	**refight**	**refinisher**
reemerge	**reenlist**	**reevaluate**	**reexportation**	**refigure**	**refix**

2**reflexive** *n* : a reflexive pronoun or verb

reflexive pronoun *n* : a pronoun referring to the subject of the sentence, clause, or verbal phrase in which it stands; *specif* : a personal pronoun compounded with *-self*

re·flex·ol·o·gy \ˌrē-ˌflek-ˈsäl-ə-jē, ri-\ *n* [ISV] : the study and interpretation of behavior in terms of simple and complex reflexes

re·flo·res·cence \ˌrē-flə-ˈres-ᵊn(t)s, -flȯ-\ *n* [L *reflorescere* to blossom again, fr. *re-* + *florescere* to bloom — more at FLORESCENCE] : a renewed blossoming

re·flow \(ˈ)rē-ˈflō\ *vi* **1** : to flow back : EBB **2** : to flow in again — **reflow** \ˈrē-ˌ\ *n*

ref·lu·ence \ˈref-ˌlü-ən(t)s, -lə-wən(t)s\ *n* [L *refluere* to flow back, fr. *re-* + *fluere* to flow — more at FLUID] : REFLUX — **ref·lu·ent** \-ˌlü-ənt, -lə-wənt\ *adj*

re·flux \ˈrē-ˌfləks\ *n* [ME, fr. ML *refluxus*, fr. L *re-* + *fluxus* flow — more at FLUX] : a flowing back : EBB

re·foc·il·late \(ˈ)rē-ˈfäs-ə-ˌlāt\ *vt* [LL *refocillatus*, pp. of *refocillare*, *refocilare* to warm into life again, fr. L *re-* + *focilare* to revive by warmth, fr. *foculum* chafing dish, brazier, fr. *fovēre* to warm] : REFRESH, REVIVE

re·for·est \(ˈ)rē-ˈfȯr-əst, -ˈfär-\ *vt* : to renew forest cover on by seeding or planting — **re·for·es·ta·tion** \(ˌ)rē-ˌfȯr-ə-ˈstā-shən, -ˌfär-\ *n*

re·forge \(ˈ)rē-ˈfō(ə)rj, -ˈfȯ(ə)rj\ *vt* [ME *reforgen*, fr. MF *reforgier*, fr. *re-* + *forgier* to forge] : to forge again : make over

1**re·form** \ri-ˈfȯ(ə)rm\ *vb* [ME *reformen*, fr. MF *reformer*, fr. L *reformare*, fr. *re-* + *formare* to form] *vt* **1 a** : to amend or improve by change of form or removal of faults or abuses **b** : to put or change into an improved form or condition **2** : to put an end to (an evil) by enforcing or introducing a better method or course of action **3** : to induce or cause to abandon evil ways ⟨~ a drunkard⟩ **4 a** : to subject (oil or gas) to cracking **b** : to produce (as gasoline or gas) by cracking ~ *vi* : to become changed for the better **syn** see CORRECT — **re·form·able** \-ˈfȯr-mə-bəl\ *adj*

2**reform** *n* **1** : amendment of what is defective, vicious, corrupt, or depraved **2** : a removal or correction of an abuse, a wrong, or errors

ref·or·ma·tion \ˌref-ər-ˈmā-shən\ *n* **1** : the act of reforming : the state of being reformed **2** *cap* : a 16th century religious movement marked ultimately by rejection or modification of much of Roman Catholic doctrine and practice and establishment of the Protestant churches — **ref·or·ma·tion·al** \-shnəl, -shən-ᵊl\ *adj*

re·for·ma·tive \ri-ˈfȯr-mət-iv\ *adj* : tending or disposed to reform

1**re·for·ma·to·ry** \ri-ˈfȯr-mə-ˌtōr-ē, -ˌtȯr-\ *adj* : REFORMATIVE ⟨~ measures⟩

2**reformatory** *n* : a penal institution to which young or first offenders or women are committed for training and reformation

re·formed *adj* **1** : restored to purity or excellence : CORRECTED **2** *cap* **a** : PROTESTANT **b** : of or relating to the chiefly Calvinist Protestant churches formed in various continental European countries

reformed spelling *n* : any of several methods of spelling English words that use letters with more phonetic consistency than conventional spelling and usu. discard some silent letters (as in *thoro* for *thorough*)

re·form·er \ri-ˈfȯr-mər\ *n* **1** : one that works for or urges reform **2** *cap* : a leader of the Protestant Reformation

re·form·ism \ri-ˈfȯr-ˌmiz-əm\ *n* : a doctrine, policy, or movement of reform — **re·form·ist** \-məst\ *n*

Reform Judaism *n* : a 19th and 20th century development of Judaism marked by rationalization of belief, simplification of many observances, and affirmation of the religious rather than national character of Judaism

reform school *n* : a reformatory for boys or girls

re·for·mu·late \(ˈ)rē-ˈfȯr-myə-ˌlāt\ *vt* : to formulate again esp. in a different way — **re·for·mu·la·tion** \(ˌ)rē-ˌfȯr-myə-ˈlā-shən\ *n*

re·fract \ri-ˈfrakt\ *vt* [L *refractus*, pp. of *refringere* to break open, break up, refract, fr. *re-* + *frangere* to break — more at BREAK] **1** : to subject to refraction **2** : to determine the refracting power of

re·frac·tile \-ˈfrak-tᵊl, -ˌtīl\ *adj* : REFRACTIVE

refracting telescope *n* : REFRACTOR

re·frac·tion \ri-ˈfrak-shən\ *n* **1** : deflection from a straight path undergone by a light ray or energy wave in passing obliquely from one medium (as air) into another (as glass) in which its velocity is different **2** : the change in the apparent position of a celestial body due to bending of the light rays emanating from it as they pass through the atmosphere; *also* : the correction to be applied to the apparent position of a body because of this bending

re·frac·tive \ri-ˈfrak-tiv\ *adj* **1** : having power to refract **2** : relating or due to refraction — **re·frac·tive·ly** *adv* — **re·frac·tive·ness** *n* — **re·frac·tiv·i·ty** \ˌrē-ˌfrak-ˈtiv-ət-ē, ri-\ *n*

refractive index *n* : INDEX OF REFRACTION

re·frac·tom·e·ter \ˌrē-ˌfrak-ˈtäm-ət-ər, ri-\ *n* [ISV] : an instrument for measuring indices of refraction — **re·frac·to·met·ric** \ri-ˌfrak-tə-ˈme-trik\ *adj* — **re·frac·tom·e·try** \ˌrē-ˌfrak-ˈtäm-ə-trē, ri-\ *n*

re·frac·tor \ri-ˈfrak-tər\ *n* : a telescope whose principal focusing element is usu. an achromatic lens

re·frac·to·ri·ly \ri-ˈfrak-t(ə-)rə-lē\ *adv* : in a refractory manner

re·frac·to·ri·ness \ri-ˈfrak-t(ə-)rē-nəs\ *n* : the quality or state of being refractory

1**re·frac·to·ry** \ri-ˈfrak-t(ə-)rē\ *adj* [alter. of *refractary*, fr. L *refractarius*, irreg. fr. *refragari* to oppose, fr. *re-* + *-fragari* (as in *suffragari* to support with one's vote) — more at SUFFRAGE] **1** : resisting control or authority : STUBBORN **2 a** : resistant to treatment or cure **b** : unresponsive to stimulus **c** : IMMUNE, INSUSCEPTIBLE **3** : difficult to fuse, corrode, or draw out; *esp* : capable of enduring high temperature **syn** see UNRULY

2**refractory** *n* : a refractory person or thing; *esp* : a heat-resisting nonmetallic ceramic material

1**re·frain** \ri-ˈfrān\ *vb* [ME *refreynen*, fr. MF *refraindre* to restrain, fr. L *refringere* to break up, destroy, check — more at REFRACT] *vt*, *archaic* : CURB, RESTRAIN ~ *vi* : to keep oneself from doing, feeling, or indulging in something : ABSTAIN — **re·frain·ment** \-mənt\ *n*

syn REFRAIN, ABSTAIN, FORBEAR mean to keep oneself from doing or indulging in something. REFRAIN commonly suggests the checking of a passing impulse; ABSTAIN implies deliberate renunciation or self-denial; FORBEAR suggests self-restraint motivated by compassion, charity, or stoicism

2**refrain** *n* [ME *refreyn*, fr. MF *refrain*, fr. *refraindre* to resound, fr. L *refringere* to break up, refract] : a regularly recurring phrase or verse esp. at the end of each stanza or division of a poem or song : CHORUS; *also* : the musical setting of a refrain

re·fran·gi·bil·i·ty \ri-ˌfran-jə-ˈbil-ət-ē, ˌrē-\ *n* : the quality or state of being refrangible

re·fran·gi·ble \ri-ˈfran-jə-bəl\ *adj* [irreg. fr. L *refringere* to refract] : capable of being refracted — **re·fran·gi·ble·ness** *n*

re·fresh \ri-ˈfresh\ *vb* [ME *refresshen*, fr. MF *refreschir*, fr. OF, fr. *re-* + *freis* fresh — more at FRESH] *vt* **1** : to restore strength and animation to : REVIVE **2** : to freshen up : RENOVATE **3 a** : to restore or maintain by renewing supply : REPLENISH **b** : AROUSE, STIMULATE **4** : to restore water to ~ *vi* **1** : to become refreshed **2** : to take refreshment **3** : to lay in fresh provisions **syn** see RENEW

re·fresh·en \ri-ˈfresh-ən\ *vt* [*re-* + *freshen*] : REFRESH

re·fresh·er \ri-ˈfresh-ər\ *n* **1** : something that refreshes **2** : REMINDER **3** : review or instruction designed esp. to keep one abreast of professional developments

re·fresh·ment \ri-ˈfresh-mənt\ *n* **1** : the act of refreshing : the state of being refreshed **2 a** : something that refreshes **b** *pl* : a light meal : LUNCH

1**re·frig·er·ant** \ri-ˈfrij-(ə-)rənt\ *adj* **1** : COOLING **2** : allaying heat or fever

2**refrigerant** *n* : a refrigerant agent or agency: as **a** : a medication for reducing body heat **b** : a substance used in refrigeration

re·frig·er·ate \ri-ˈfrij-ə-ˌrāt\ *vt* [L *refrigeratus*, pp. of *refrigerare*, fr. *re-* + *frigerare* to cool, fr. *frigor-*, *frigus* cold — more at FRIGID] : to make or keep cold or cool; *specif* : to freeze or chill (food) for preservation — **re·frig·er·a·tion** \ri-ˌfrij-ə-ˈrā-shən\ *n*

re·frig·er·a·tor \ri-ˈfrij-ə-ˌrāt-ər\ *n* : something that refrigerates or keeps cool: **a** : a cabinet or room for keeping food or other items cool **b** : an apparatus for rapidly cooling heated liquids or vapors in a distilling process

re·frin·gent \ri-ˈfrin-jənt\ *adj* [L *refringent-*, *refringens*, prp. of *refringere* to refract] : REFRACTIVE, REFRACTING

reft *past of* REAVE

re·fu·el \(ˈ)rē-ˈfyü(-ə)l, -ˈfyü(-ə)l\ *vt* : to provide with additional fuel ~ *vi* : to take on additional fuel

1**ref·uge** \ˈref-(ˌ)yüj\ *n* [ME, fr. MF, fr. L *refugium*, fr. *refugere* to escape, fr. *re-* + *fugere* to flee — more at FUGITIVE] **1** : shelter or protection from danger or distress **2** : a place that provides shelter or protection **3** : a means of resort for help in difficulty : RESOURCE

2**refuge** *vt* : to give refuge to ~ *vi* : to seek or take refuge

ref·u·gee \ˌref-yu̇-ˈjē\ *n* [F *réfugié*, pp. of (*se*) *réfugier* to take refuge, fr. L *refugium*] : one that flees for safety; *esp* : one who flees to a foreign country or power to escape danger or persecution

re·ful·gence \ri-ˈfu̇l-jən(t)s, -ˈfəl-\ *n* [L *refulgentia*, fr. *refulgent-*, *refulgens*, prp. of *refulgēre* to shine brightly, fr. *re-* + *fulgēre* to shine — more at FULGENT] : a radiant or resplendent quality or state : BRILLIANCE — **re·ful·gent** \-jənt\ *adj*

1**re·fund** \ri-ˈfənd, ˈrē-ˌfənd\ *vt* [ME *refunden*, fr. MF & L; MF *refonder*, fr. L *refundere*, lit., to pour back, fr. *re-* + *fundere* to pour — more at FOUND] **1** : to give or put back **2** : to return (money) in restitution, repayment, or balancing of accounts — **re·fund·able** \-ə-bəl\ *adj*

2**re·fund** \ˈrē-ˌfənd\ *n* **1** : the act of refunding **2** : a sum refunded

3**re·fund** \(ˈ)rē-ˈfənd\ *vt* [*re-* + *fund*] : to fund (a debt) again or anew

re·fur·bish \(ˈ)rē-ˈfər-bish\ *vt* : to brighten or freshen up : RENOVATE — **re·fur·bish·ment** \-mənt\ *n*

re·fus·al \ri-ˈfyü-zəl\ *n* **1** : the act of refusing or denying **2** : the opportunity or right of refusing or taking before others

1**re·fuse** \ri-ˈfyüz\ *vb* [ME *refusen*, fr. MF *refuser*, fr. (assumed) VL *refusare*, fr. L *refusus*, pp. of *refundere* to pour back] *vt* **1** : to decline to accept : REJECT **2 a** : to show or express unwillingness to do or comply with **b** : DENY ⟨was *refused* entrance⟩ **3** *obs* : to give up : RENOUNCE **4** *of a horse* : to decline to jump or leap over ~ *vi* : to withhold acceptance, compliance, or permission **syn** see DECLINE — **re·fus·er** *n*

2**ref·use** \ˈref-ˌyüs, -ˌyüz\ *n* [ME, fr. MF *refus* rejection, fr. OF, fr. *refuser*] **1** : the worthless or useless part of something : LEAVINGS **2** : TRASH, GARBAGE

3**ref·use** \ˈref-ˌyüs, -ˌyüz\ *adj* : thrown aside or left as worthless : USELESS

re·fut·able \ri-ˈfyüt-ə-bəl, ˈref-yət-\ *adj* [LL *refutabilis*, fr. L *refutare*] : capable of being refuted — **re·fut·ably** \-blē\ *adv*

ref·u·ta·tion \ˌref-yu̇-ˈtā-shən\ *n* : the act or process of refuting : DISPROOF

re·fute \ri-ˈfyüt\ *vt* [L *refutare*, fr. *re-* + *-futare* to beat — more at BEAT] **1** : to overthrow by argument, evidence, or proof **2** : to prove to be false or erroneous **syn** see DISPROVE — **re·fut·er** *n*

re·gain \(ˈ)rē-ˈgān\ *vt* : to gain or reach anew : RECOVER

re·gal \ˈrē-gəl\ *adj* [ME, fr. MF or L; MF, fr. L *regalis* — more at ROYAL] **1** : of, relating to, or suitable for a king **2** : of notable excellence or magnificence : SPLENDID — **re·gal·i·ty** \ri-ˈgal-ət-ē\ *n* — **re·gal·ly** \ˈrē-gə-lē\ *adv*

1**re·gale** \ri-ˈgā(ə)l\ *vb* [F *régaler*, fr. MF, fr. *regale*, n.] *vt* **1** : to entertain sumptuously or agreeably **2** : to give pleasure or amusement to ~ *vi* : to feast oneself : FEED — **re·gale·ment** \-mənt\ *n*

2**regale** *n* [F *régal*, fr. MF *regale*, fr. *re-* + *galer* to have a good time — more at GALLANT] **1** : a choice or sumptuous feast **2** : a choice piece esp. of food

re·ga·lia \ri-ˈgāl-yə\ *n pl* [ML, fr. L, neut. pl. of *regalis*] **1** : royal rights or prerogatives **2** : the emblems, symbols, or paraphernalia indicative of royalty or of office or membership **3** : special costume : FINERY

1**re·gard** \ri-ˈgärd\ *n* [ME, fr. MF, fr. OF, fr. *regarder*] **1** *archaic* : ASPECT **2 a** : CONSIDERATION, HEED **b** : LOOK, GAZE **3 a** : the worth or estimation in which something is held **b** (1) : a feeling of respect and affection : ESTEEM (2) : friendly greetings implying

See *re-* and 2d element	reflorescent	reflower	refold	reframe	refront
refloat	reflourish	refly	refortify	refreeze	refurnish
reflorescence	reflow	refocus	refound		

such feeling ⟨give him my ~*s*⟩ **c :** a protective interest **:** CARE **4 :** a ground of action or opinion **:** MOTIVE **5 :** an aspect to be taken into consideration **:** RESPECT **6** *obs* **:** INTENTION

2**regard** *vb* [ME *regarden*, fr. MF *regarder* to look back at, regard, fr. OF, fr. *re-* + *garder* to guard, look at] *vt* **1 :** to pay attention to **2 a :** to show respect or consideration for **b :** to hold in high esteem **3 :** to look at **4 :** to take into consideration or account **5 :** to relate to **6 :** to think of as ~ *vi* **1 :** to look attentively **:** GAZE **2 :** to pay attention **:** HEED

syn REGARD, RESPECT, ESTEEM, ADMIRE mean to recognize the worth of a person or thing. REGARD is a formal term and may stress the fact of caring or feeling; RESPECT usu. adds the implication that the feeling is justly due; ESTEEM implies somewhat greater warmth of feeling accompanying high evaluation; ADMIRE connotes enthusiastic often uncritical appreciation

re·gar·dant \ri-'gärd-ᵊnt\ *adj* [ME, fr. MF, prp. of *regarder*] **:** looking backward over the shoulder — used of a heraldic animal

re·gard·ful \ri-'gärd-fəl\ *adj* **1 :** HEEDFUL, OBSERVANT **2 :** full or expressive of regard or respect **:** RESPECTFUL — **re·gard·ful·ly** \-fə-lē\ *adv* — **re·gard·ful·ness** *n*

re·gard·ing *prep* **:** with respect to **:** CONCERNING

1**re·gard·less** \ri-'gärd-ləs\ *adj* **:** HEEDLESS, CARELESS — **re·gard·less·ly** *adv* — **re·gard·less·ness** *n*

2**regardless** *adv* **:** without prudent regard to impediments

regardless of *prep* **:** in spite of ⟨*regardless of* our mistakes⟩

re·gat·ta \ri-'gät-ə, -'gat-\ *n* [It] **:** a rowing, speedboat, or sailing race or a series of such races

re·ge·la·tion \,rē-jə-'lā-shən\ *n* **:** the freezing again of water derived from ice melting under pressure when the pressure is relieved

1**re·gen·cy** \'rē-jən-sē\ *n* **1 a :** the office, jurisdiction, or government of a regent or of a body of regents **b** *archaic* **:** governmental authority **:** RULE **2 :** a body of regents **3 :** the period of rule of a regent or body of regents

2**regency** *adj* [fr. the regency of George, Prince of Wales (afterwards George IV) during the period 1811–20] **:** of, relating to, or resembling furniture or dress of the regency of George, Prince of Wales

re·gen·er·a·cy \ri-'jen-(ə-)rə-sē\ *n* **:** the state of being regenerated

1**re·gen·er·ate** \ri-'jen-(ə-)rət\ *adj* [ME *regenerat*, fr. L *regeneratus*, pp. of *regenerare* to regenerate, fr. *re-* + *generare* to beget — more at GENERATE] **1 :** formed or created again **2 :** spiritually reborn or converted **3 :** restored to a better, higher, or more worthy state — **regenerate** *n* — **re·gen·er·ate·ly** *adv* — **re·gen·er·ate·ness** *n*

2**re·gen·er·ate** \ri-'jen-ə-,rāt\ *vi* **1 :** to become formed again **2 :** to become regenerate **:** REFORM **3 :** to undergo regeneration ~ *vt* **1 a :** to subject to spiritual regeneration **b :** to change radically for the better **2 a :** to generate or produce anew; *esp* **:** to replace (a body part) by a new growth of tissue **b :** to produce again chemically sometimes in a physically changed form **3 :** to reestablish on a new and usu. better basis **4 :** to restore to original strength or properties **5 :** to increase the amplification of (an electron current) by causing part of the power in the output circuit to act upon the input circuit

regenerated cellulose *n* **:** cellulose obtained in a changed form by chemical treatment (as of a cellulose solution or derivative)

re·gen·er·a·tion \ri-,jen-ə-'rā-shən, ,rē-\ *n* **1 :** an act or the process of regenerating **:** the state of being regenerated **2 :** spiritual renewal or revival **3 :** renewal or restoration of a body or bodily part after injury or as a normal process **4 :** utilization by special devices of heat or other products that would ordinarily be lost

re·gen·er·a·tive \ri-'jen-ə-,rāt-iv, -'jen-(ə-)rət-\ *adj* **1 :** of, relating to, or marked by regeneration **2 :** tending to regenerate — **re·gen·er·a·tive·ly** *adv*

re·gen·er·a·tor \ri-'jen-ə-,rāt-ər\ *n* **1 :** one that regenerates **2 :** a device used esp. with hot-air engines or gas furnaces in which incoming air or gas is heated by contact with masses (as of brick) previously heated by outgoing hot air or gas

re·gent \'rē-jənt\ *n* [ME, fr. MF or ML; MF, fr. ML *regent-*, *regens*, fr. L, prp. of *regere* to rule — more at RIGHT] **1 a** *archaic* **:** a ruling authority or principle **b :** one who rules or reigns **:** GOVERNOR **2 :** one who governs a kingdom in the minority, absence, or disability of the sovereign **3 :** a member of a governing board (as of a state university) — **regent** *adj*

reg·i·ci·dal \,rej-ə-'sīd-ᵊl\ *adj* **:** relating to, constituting, or disposed to regicide

reg·i·cide \'rej-ə-,sīd\ *n* **1** [prob. fr. (assumed) NL *regicida*, fr. L *reg-*, *rex* king + *-cida* -cide — more at ROYAL] **:** one who kills a king or assists in his death **2** [prob. fr. (assumed) NL *regicidium*, fr. L *reg-*, *rex* + *-cidium* -cide] **:** the killing of a king

re·gime *also* **ré·gime** \rā-'zhēm, ri-\ *n* [F *régime*, fr. L *regimin-*, *regimen*] **1 a :** REGIMEN 1 **b :** a regular pattern of occurrence or action **2 a :** mode of rule or management **b :** a form of government or administration; *specif* **:** a governmental or social system

reg·i·men \'rej-ə-mən, -,men\ *n* [ME, fr. L *regimin-*, *regimen* rule, fr. *regere*] **1 :** a systematic course of therapy **2 :** GOVERNMENT, RULE **3 :** the characteristic behavior or orderly procedure of a natural phenomenon or process

1**reg·i·ment** \'rej-(ə-)mənt\ *n* [ME, fr. MF, fr. LL *regimentum*, fr. L *regere*] **1 :** governmental rule **2 :** a military unit consisting of a variable number of battalions or other units — **reg·i·men·tal** \,rej-ə-'ment-ᵊl\ *adj* — **reg·i·men·tal·ly** \-ᵊl-ē\ *adv*

2**reg·i·ment** \'rej-ə-,ment\ *vt* **1 :** to form into or assign to a regiment **2 a :** to organize rigidly esp. for the sake of regulation or control **b :** to subject to order or uniformity — **reg·i·men·ta·tion** \,rej-ə-mən-'tā-shən, -,men-\ *n*

reg·i·men·tals \,rej-ə-'ment-ᵊlz\ *n pl* **1 :** a regimental uniform **2 :** military dress

re·gion \'rē-jən\ *n* [ME, fr. MF, fr. L *region-*, *regio*, fr. *regere* to rule] **1 :** an administrative area, division, or district **2 a :** a major indefinite division of inanimate creation **b :** a sphere of activity or interest **:** FIELD **3 a :** an indefinite area **b :** a broad homogeneous geographical area **c** (1) **:** a major world area that supports a characteristic fauna (2) **:** an area characterized by prevalence of one or more vegetational climax types **4 :** one of the major subdivisions into which the body or one of its parts is divisible **5 :** one of the zones into which the atmosphere is divided according to height or the sea according to depth

re·gion·al \'rēj-nəl, -ən-ᵊl\ *adj* **1 :** of, relating to, or characteristic of a region ⟨a ~ turn of speech⟩ **2 :** affecting a particular region **:** LOCALIZED — **re·gion·al·ly** \-ē\ *adv*

re·gion·al·ism \'rēj-nəl-,iz-əm, -ən-ᵊl-\ *n* **1 a :** consciousness of and loyalty to a distinct region with a homogeneous population **b :** development of a political or social system based on one or more such areas **2 :** emphasis on regional locale and characteristics in art or literature **3 :** a peculiarity characteristic of a geographic area — **re·gion·al·ist** \-əst\ *n or adj* — **re·gion·al·is·tic** \,rēj-nəl-'is-tik, -ən-ᵊl-\ *adj*

ré·gis·seur \,rā-zhi-'sər\ *n* [F *régisseur*] **:** a director responsible for staging a theatrical work (as a ballet)

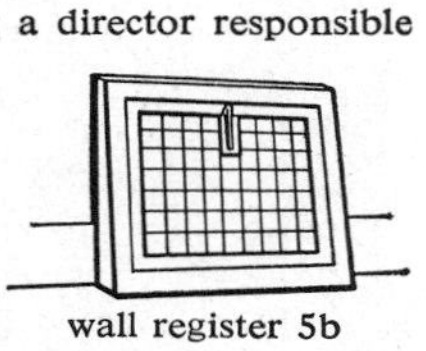

wall register 5b

1**reg·is·ter** \'rej-ə-stər\ *n* [ME *registre*, fr. MF, fr. ML *registrum*, alter. of LL *regesta*, pl., register, fr. L, neut. pl. of *regestus*, pp. of *regerere* to bring back, fr. *re-* + *gerere* to bear — more at CAST] **1 :** a written record containing regular entries of items or details **2 a :** a book or system of public records **b :** a roster of qualified or available individuals **3 :** an entry in a register **4 a :** a set of organ pipes of like quality **:** STOP **b** (1) **:** the range of a human voice or a musical instrument (2) **:** a portion of such a range similarly produced or of the same quality **5a :** a device regulating admission of air to fuel **b :** a grille often with shutters for admitting heated air or for ventilation **6 :** REGISTRATION, REGISTRY **7 a :** an automatic device registering a number or a quantity **b :** a number or quantity so registered **8 :** a condition of correct alignment or proper relative position

2**register** *vb* **reg·is·ter·ing** \-st(ə-)riŋ\ *vt* **1 a :** to make or secure official entry of in a register **b :** to enroll formally esp. as a voter or student **c :** to record automatically **:** INDICATE **2 :** to make or adjust so as to correspond exactly **3 :** to secure special protection for (a piece of mail) by prepayment of a fee **4 :** to convey by expression and bodily movements alone ~ *vi* **1 a :** to enroll one's name in a register **b :** to enroll one's name officially as a prerequisite for voting **c :** to enroll formally as a student **2 a :** to correspond exactly **b :** to be in correct alignment or register **3 :** to make or convey an impression

3**register** *n* [prob. alter. of ME *registrer*] **:** REGISTRAR

reg·is·tered *adj* **1 a :** having the owner's name entered in a register ⟨~ security⟩ **b :** recorded as the owner of a security **2 :** recorded on the basis of pedigree or breed characteristics in the studbook of a breed association **3 :** qualified formally or officially

registered mail *n* **:** mail recorded in the post office of mailing and at each successive point of transmission and guaranteed special care in delivery

registered nurse *n* **:** a graduate trained nurse who has been licensed by a state authority after passing examinations for registration

reg·is·tra·ble \'rej-ə-st(ə-)rə-bəl\ *adj* **:** capable of being registered

reg·is·trant \-strənt\ *n* **:** one that registers or is registered

reg·is·trar \'rej-ə-,strär\ *n* [alter. of ME *registrer*, fr. MF *registreur*, fr. *registrer* to register, fr. ML *registrare*, fr. *registrum*] **:** an official recorder or keeper of records

reg·is·tra·tion \,rej-ə-'strā-shən\ *n* **1 :** an act or the fact of registering **2 :** an entry in a register **3 :** the number of individuals registered **:** ENROLLMENT **4 a :** the art or act of selecting and adjusting pipe organ stops **b :** the combination of stops selected for performing a particular organ work **5 :** a document certifying an act of registering

reg·is·try \'rej-ə-strē\ *n* **1 :** ENROLLMENT, REGISTRATION **2 :** the nationality of a ship as evidenced by its being entered in a register **:** FLAG **3 :** a place of registration **4 :** an official record book or an entry in one

re·gius professor \,rē-j(ē-)əs-\ *n* [NL, royal professor] **:** a holder of a professorship founded by royal bounty at a British university

reg·let \'reg-lət\ *n* [F *réglet*, fr. MF *reglet* straightedge, fr. *regle*, fr. L *regula* — more at RULE] **1 :** a flat narrow architectural molding **2 a :** a low strip of wood used like leads between lines of type **b :** reglets or material for them

reg·nal \'reg-nᵊl\ *adj* [ML *regnalis*, fr. L *regnum* reign — more at REIGN] **:** of or relating to a king or his reign; *specif* **:** calculated from a monarch's accession to the throne ⟨~ year⟩

reg·nant \'reg-nənt\ *adj* [L *regnant-*, *regnans*, prp. of *regnare* to reign, fr. *regnum*] **1 :** exercising rule **:** REIGNING **2 a :** having the chief power **:** DOMINANT **b :** of common or widespread occurrence **:** PREVALENT

reg·num \'reg-nəm\ *n, pl* **reg·na** \-nə\ [L] **:** KINGDOM

rego·lith \'reg-ə-,lith\ *n* [Gk *rhēgos* blanket + E *-lith;* akin to Skt *rāga* color] **:** MANTLEROCK

re·gorge \(')rē-'gȯ(ə)rj\ *vt* [F *regorger*, fr. MF, fr. *re-* + *gorger* to gorge] **:** DISGORGE

rego·sol \'reg-ə-,säl, -,sȯl\ *n* [*rego-* (as in *regolith*) + L *solum* soil — more at SOLE] **:** an azonal soil consisting chiefly of imperfectly consolidated material and having no clear-cut and specific morphology

re·grant \(')rē-'grant\ *vt* **:** to grant back or again — **regrant** \(')rē-', 'rē-,\ *n*

re·greet \(')rē-'grēt\ *vt, archaic* **:** to greet in return

regrets *n pl, obs* **:** GREETINGS

1**re·gress** \'rē-,gres\ *n* [ME, fr. L *regressus*, fr. *regressus*, pp. of *regredi* to go back, fr. *re-* + *gradi* to go — more at GRADE] **1 a :** an act or the privilege of going or coming back **:** WITHDRAWAL **b :** RE-ENTRY 1 **2 :** RETROGRESSION, RETROGRADATION **3 :** the act of reasoning backward

2**re·gress** \ri-'gres\ *vi* **1 :** to make or undergo regress **:** RETROGRADE **2 :** to tend to approach or revert to a mean ~ *vt* **:** to induce a state of psychological regression in — **re·gres·sor** \-'gres-ər\ *n*

re·gres·sion \ri-'gresh-ən\ *n* **1 :** an act or the fact of regressing **:** RETROGRESSION **2 :** a trend or shift toward a lower or less perfect state: as **a :** progressive decline of a manifestation of disease **b :** gradual loss of differentiation and function by a body part or

See *re-* and 2d element regather	regild regive	reglaze	reglow	reglue	regrade

of memories and acquired skills esp. as a physiological change accompanying aging **c** : reversion to an earlier mental or behavioral level **d** : the amount by which the conditional expectation of one of two correlated variables is closer to the mean of its set than are given values of the second to the mean of its set **3** : retrograde motion esp. of an astronomical orbital characteristic

re·gres·sive \ri-'gres-iv\ adj **1** : tending to regress or produce regression **2** : being, characterized by, or developing in the course of an evolutionary process involving increasing simplification of bodily structure **3** : decreasing in rate as the base increases ⟨~ tax⟩ — **re·gres·sive·ly** adv — **re·gres·sive·ness** n

¹re·gret \ri-'gret\ vb **re·gret·ted; re·gret·ting** [ME regretten, fr. MF regreter, fr. OF, fr. re- + -greter (of Scand origin; akin to ON grāta to weep) — more at GREET] vt **1 a** : to mourn the loss or death of **b** : to miss poignantly **2** : to be keenly sorry for ~ vi : to experience regret — **re·gret·ta·ble** \-'gret-ə-bəl\ adj — **re·gret·ta·bly** \-blē\ adv — **re·gret·ter** n

²regret n **1** : sorrow aroused by circumstances beyond one's power to remedy **2 a** : an expression of sorrow, disappointment, or other distressing emotion **b** pl : a note politely declining an invitation **syn** see SORROW — **re·gret·ful** \-'gret-fəl\ adj — **re·gret·ful·ly** \-fə-lē\ adv — **re·gret·ful·ness** n

re·gret·less \ri-'gret-ləs\ adj : feeling no regret

re·group \(')rē-'grüp\ vb : to form into a new grouping — **re·group·ment** \-mənt\ n

re·grow \(')rē-'grō\ vt : to grow (as a missing part) anew ~ vi : to continue growth after interruption or injury

¹reg·u·lar \'reg-yə-lər\ adj [ME reguler, fr. MF, fr. LL regularis regular, fr. L, of a bar, fr. regula rule — more at RULE] **1** : belonging to a religious order **2 a** : formed, built, arranged, or ordered according to some established rule, law, principle, or type **b** (1) : both equilateral and equiangular ⟨a ~ polygon⟩ (2) : having faces that are congruent regular polygons and all the polyhedral angles congruent ⟨a ~ polyhedron⟩ **c** of a flower : having the members of each whorl symmetrical with respect to form **d** : having or constituting an isometric system ⟨~ crystals⟩ **3 a** : ORDERLY, METHODICAL **b** : recurring or functioning at fixed or uniform intervals **4 a** : constituted, conducted, or done in conformity with established or prescribed usages, rules, or discipline **b** : NORMAL, CORRECT: as (1) : undeviating in conformance to a set standard (2) : COMPLETE, UNMITIGATED ⟨a ~ scoundrel⟩ **c** (1) : conforming to the normal or usual manner of inflection (2) : WEAK **7 5 a** : of, relating to, or constituting the regular army of a state **b** : constituting or made up of individuals properly recognized as legitimate combatants in war — **reg·u·lar·i·ty** \,reg-yə-'lar-ət-ē\ n — **reg·u·lar·ly** \'reg-yə-lər-lē\ adv

syn NORMAL, TYPICAL, NATURAL: REGULAR stresses conformity to a rule, standard, or pattern; NORMAL implies lack of deviation from what has been discovered or established as the most usual or expected; TYPICAL implies showing all important traits of a type, class, or group and may suggest lack of strong individuality; NATURAL applies to what conforms to a thing's essential nature, function, or mode of being

²regular n **1** : one who is regular: as **a** : one of the regular clergy **b** : a soldier in a regular army **c** : a player on an athletic team who usu. starts every game **2** : a clothing size designed to fit the person of average height

regular army n : a permanently organized body constituting the army of a state and being often identical with the standing army maintained by a federal government

reg·u·lar·ize \'reg-yə-lə-,rīz\ vt : to make regular by conformance to law, rules, or custom — **reg·u·lar·iz·er** n

regular solid n : any of the five regular polyhedrons

regular year n : a common year of 354 days or a leap year of 384 days in the Jewish calendar

reg·u·late \'reg-yə-,lāt\ vt [LL regulatus, pp. of regulare, fr. L regula] **1 a** : to govern or direct according to rule **b** : to bring under the control of law or constituted authority **2** : to reduce to order, method, or uniformity **3** : to fix or adjust the time, amount, degree, or rate of — **reg·u·la·tive** \-,lāt-iv\ adj — **reg·u·la·tor** \-,lāt-ər\ n — **reg·u·la·to·ry** \-lə-,tōr-ē, -,tor-\ adj

reg·u·la·tion \,reg-yə-'lā-shən\ n **1** : the act of regulating : state of being regulated **2 a** : an authoritative rule dealing with details of procedure **b** : a rule or order having the force of law issued by an executive authority of a government **3 a** : redistribution of material (as in an embryo) to restore a damaged or lost part independent of new tissue growth **b** : the mechanism by which an early embryo maintains normal development **syn** see LAW

reg·u·lus \'reg-yə-ləs\ n [NL, fr. L, petty king, fr. reg-, rex king — more at ROYAL] **1** cap : a first-magnitude star in the constellation Leo **2** [ML, metallic antimony, fr. L] : the more or less impure mass of metal formed beneath the slag in smelting and reducing ores

re·gur·gi·tate \(')rē-'gər-jə-,tāt\ vb [ML regurgitatus, pp. of regurgitare, fr. L re- + LL gurgitare to engulf, fr. L gurgit-, gurges whirlpool — more at VORACIOUS] vi : to become thrown or poured back ~ vt : to throw or pour back or out

re·gur·gi·ta·tion \(,)rē-,gər-jə-'tā-shən\ n : a regurgitating: as **a** : the casting up of incompletely digested food (as by some birds in feeding their young) **b** : the backward flow of blood through a defective heart valve

re·ha·bil·i·tant \,rē-(h)ə-'bil-ə-tənt\ n : a disabled person undergoing rehabilitation

re·ha·bil·i·tate \,rē-(h)ə-'bil-ə-,tāt\ vt [ML rehabilitatus, pp. of rehabilitare, fr. L re- + LL habilitare to habilitate] **1 a** : to restore to a former capacity : REINSTATE **b** : to restore to good repute by vindicating **2 a** : to restore to a state of efficiency, good management, or solvency **b** : to restore to a condition of health or useful and constructive activity — **re·ha·bil·i·ta·tion** \-,bil-ə-'tā-shən\ n — **re·ha·bil·i·ta·tive** \-'bil-ə-,tāt-iv\ adj

re·hash \(')rē-'hash\ vt : to present or use again in another form without substantial change or improvement — **rehash** \'rē-,\ n

re·hear·ing \(')rē-'hi(ə)r-iŋ\ n : a second or new hearing by the same tribunal

re·hears·al \ri-'hər-səl\ n **1** : something recounted or told again : RECITAL **2 a** : a private performance or practice session preparatory to a public appearance **b** : a practice exercise : TRIAL

re·hearse \ri-'hərs\ vb [ME rehersen, fr. MF rehercier, lit., to harrow again, fr. re- + hercier to harrow, fr. herce harrow — more at HEARSE] vt **1 a** : to say again : REPEAT **b** : to recite aloud in a formal manner **2** archaic : to present an account of : RELATE **3** : to recount in order : ENUMERATE **4 a** : to give a rehearsal of **b** : to train or make proficient by rehearsal **5** : to perform or practice as if in a rehearsal ~ vi : to engage in a rehearsal — **re·hears·er** n

re·house \(')rē-'haùz\ vt : to establish in a new or different housing unit of a better quality

re·hy·drate \(')rē-'hī-,drāt\ vt : to restore fluid lost in dehydration to — **re·hy·dra·tion** \(,)rē-,hī-'drā-shən\ n

reichs·mark \'rīk-,smärk\ n, pl **reichsmarks** also **reichsmark** [G, fr. reich empire + mark] : the German mark from 1925 to 1948

re·ifi·ca·tion \,rā-ə-fə-'kā-shən, ,rē-\ n : the process or result of reifying

re·ify \'rā-ə-,fī, 'rē-\ vt [L res thing — more at REAL] : to regard (something abstract) as a material thing

¹reign \'rān\ n [ME regne, fr. OF, fr. L regnum, fr. reg-, rex king — more at ROYAL] **1 a** : royal authority : SOVEREIGNTY **b** : the dominion, sway, or influence of one resembling a monarch **2** : the period of reign of a sovereign

²reign vi **1 a** : to possess or exercise sovereign power : RULE **b** : to hold office as chief of state although exercising minimal powers of making and executing governmental policy **2** : to exercise authority or hold sway in the manner of a monarch **3** : to be predominant or prevalent

reign of terror [Reign of Terror, a period of the French Revolution that was conspicuous for mass executions of political suspects] : a state or a period of time marked by conditions of violence that produce terror among the people involved

re·im·burs·able \,rē-əm-'bər-sə-bəl\ adj : REPAYABLE

re·im·burse \,rē-əm-'bərs\ vt [re- + obs. E imburse (to pocket money, pay)] **1** : to pay back to someone : REPAY **2** : to make restoration or payment of an equivalent to **syn** see PAY — **re·im·burse·ment** \-'bər-smənt\ n

re·im·pres·sion \,rē-əm-'presh-ən\ n : REPRINT 1

¹rein \'rān\ n [ME reine, fr. MF rene, fr. (assumed) VL retina, fr. L retinēre to restrain — more at RETAIN] **1** : a line fastened to a bit on each side by which a rider or driver controls an animal — usu. used in pl. **2 a** : a restraining influence : CHECK **b** : controlling or guiding power **3** : complete freedom : SCOPE — usu. used in the phrase give rein to

²rein vt **1** : to check or stop by or as if by a pull at the reins **2** : to control or direct with or as if with reins ~ vi **1** archaic : to submit to the use of reins **2** : to stop or slow up one's horse or oneself by or as if by pulling the reins

re·in·car·na·tion \(,)rē-,in-,kär-'nā-shən\ n **1 a** : the action of reincarnating : the state of being reincarnated **b** : rebirth in new bodies or forms of life; esp : a rebirth of a soul in a new human body **2** : a fresh embodiment — **re·in·car·na·tion·ist** \-sh(ə-)nəst\ n

rein·deer \'rān-,di(ə)r\ n, pl **reindeer** also **reindeers** [ME reindere, fr. ON hreinn reindeer + ME deer] : any of several deer (genus Rangifer) inhabiting northern Europe, Asia, and America and having antlers in both sexes

reindeer moss n : a gray, erect, tufted, and much-branched lichen (Cladonia rangiferina) that forms extensive patches in arctic and north-temperate regions, constitutes a large part of the food of reindeer, and is sometimes eaten by man

re·in·fec·tion \,rē-ən-'fek-shən\ n : infection following recovery from or superimposed on infection of the same type

re·in·force \,rē-ən-'fō(ə)rs, -'fo(ə)rs\ vb [re- + inforce, alter. of enforce] vt **1** : to strengthen by additional assistance, material, or support **2 a** : to strengthen with additional forces **b** : to strengthen or increase by fresh additions ~ vi : to seek or get reinforcements — **re·in·forc·er** n

reinforced concrete n : concrete in which metal (as steel) is embedded so that the two materials act together in resisting forces

re·in·force·ment \,rē-ən-'fōr-smənt, -'for-\ n **1** : the action of reinforcing or the state of being reinforced **2** : something that reinforces

rein·less \'rān-ləs\ adj : having no reins : UNCHECKED

reins \'rānz\ n pl [ME, fr. MF & L; MF, fr. L renes] **1 a** : KIDNEYS **b** : the region of the kidneys : LOINS **2** : the seat of the feelings or passions

reins·man \'rānz-mən\ n : a harness driver : JOCKEY

re·in·state \,rē-ən-'stāt\ vt **1** : to place again **2** : to restore to a previous effective state — **re·in·state·ment** \-mənt\ n

re·in·sur·ance \,rē-ən-'shùr-ən(t)s, esp South (')rē-'in-,\ n : insurance by a reinsurer

re·in·sure \,rē-ən-'shù(ə)r\ vt **1** : to insure again by transferring to another insurance company all or a part of a liability assumed **2** : to insure again by assuming all or a part of the liability of an insurance company already covering a risk ~ vi : to provide increased insurance — **re·in·sur·er** n

re·in·te·grate \(')rē-'int-ə-,grāt\ vt [ML reintegratus, pp. of reintegrare to renew, reinstate, fr. L re- + integrare to integrate] : to integrate again into an entity or restore to unity after disintegration — **re·in·te·gra·tion** \(,)rē-,int-ə-'grā-shən\ n — **re·in·te·gra·tive** \(')rē-'int-ə-,grāt-iv\ adj

re·in·ter·pret \,rē-ən-'tər-prət, rapid -pət\ vt : to interpret again; specif : to give a new or different interpretation to — **re·in·ter·pre·ta·tion** \-,tər-prə-'tā-shən, rapid -pə-\ n

re·in·vest \,rē-ən-'vest\ vt **1** : to invest again or anew **2 a** : to invest (as income from investments) in additional securities **b** : to invest in a business rather than distribute as dividends or profits — **re·in·vest·ment** \-'ves(t)-mənt\ n

re·in·vig·o·rate \,rē-ən-'vig-ə-,rāt\ vt : to give renewed or fresh vigor to — **re·in·vig·o·ra·tion** \-,vig-ə-'rā-shən\ n

re·is·sue \(')rē-'ish-(,)ü, -ù\ vt : to come forth again ~ vt : to issue again; esp : to cause to become available again — **reissue** n

re·it·er·ate \(')rē-'it-ə-,rāt\ vt [L reiteratus, pp. of reiterare to repeat, fr. re- + iterare to iterate] : to say or do over again or repeatedly sometimes with wearying effect **syn** see REPEAT — **re·it·er·a·tion**

See re- and 2d element

regrind	rehammer	rehearing	reimpose	reincorporate	reintroduce
regrow	rehandle	reheat	reimposition	reinsert	reintroduction
regrowth	rehear	rehouse	reincarnate	reinsertion	reinvasion

\(,)rē-,it-ə-'rā-shən\ *n* — **re·it·er·a·tive** \rē-'it-ə-,rāt-iv, -rət-iv; -'i-trət-iv\ *adj* — **re·it·er·a·tive·ly** *adv* — **re·it·er·a·tive·ness** *n*

reive \'rēv\ *vb* [ME (Sc) *reijen*, fr. OE *rēafian* to rob — more at REAVE] *Scot* : RAID — **reiv·er** *n*, *Scot*

¹re·ject \ri-'jekt\ *vt* [ME *rejecten*, fr. L *rejectus*, pp. of *reicere*, fr. *re-* + *jacere* to throw — more at JET] **1 :** to refuse to acknowledge, acquiesce in, or submit to **2** *obs* **:** to cast off **3 :** to refuse to have, use, or take for some purpose **4 a :** to refuse to hear, receive, or admit **:** REBUFF **b :** to refuse as lover or spouse **5 :** to refuse to grant, consider, or accede to **6 :** to throw back **:** REPULSE **7 :** to spew out **syn** see DECLINE — **re·ject·ee** \ri-,jek-'tē, ,rē-\ *n* — **re·ject·er** *or* **re·jec·tor** \ri-'jek-tər\ *n* — **re·jec·tive** \-tiv\ *adj*

²re·ject \'rē-,jekt\ *n* **:** a rejected person or thing

re·jec·tion \ri-'jek-shən\ *n* **1 :** the action of rejecting **:** the state of being rejected **2 :** something rejected

re·joice \ri-'jȯis\ *vb* [ME *rejoicen*, fr. MF *rejoiss-*, stem of *rejoir*, fr. *re-* + *joir* to rejoice, fr. L *gaudēre* — more at JOY] *vt* **:** to give joy to **:** GLADDEN ~ *vi* **:** to feel joy or great delight — **re·joic·er** \-'jȯi-sər\ *n* — **re·joic·ing·ly** \-siŋ-lē\ *adv* — **rejoice in :** HAVE, POSSESS

re·joic·ing *n* **1 :** the action of one that rejoices **2 :** an instance, occasion, or expression of joy **:** FESTIVITY

re·join \ri-'jȯin, *vt 1 is* (')rē-\ *vb* [ME *rejoinen* to answer to a legal charge, fr. MF *rejoin-*, stem of *rejoindre*, fr. *re-* + *joindre* to join — more at JOIN] *vi* **:** to answer the replication of the plaintiff ~ *vt* **1 :** to join again **2 :** to state in reply esp. to a reply **syn** see ANSWER

re·join·der \ri-'jȯin-dər\ *n* [ME *rejoiner*, fr. MF *rejoindre* to rejoin] **1 :** the defendant's answer to the plaintiff's replication **2 :** REPLY; *specif* **:** an answer to a reply

re·ju·ve·nate \ri-'jü-və-,nāt\ *vb* [*re-* + L *juvenis* young — more at YOUNG] *vt* **1 a :** to make young or youthful again **:** REINVIGORATE **b :** to restore to an original or new state **2 a :** to stimulate (as by uplift) to renewed erosive activity — used of streams **b :** to develop youthful features of topography in ~ *vi* **:** to cause or undergo rejuvenation **syn** see RENEW — **re·ju·ve·na·tion** \ri-,jü-və-'nā-shən, ,rē-\ *n* — **re·ju·ve·na·tor** \ri-'jü-və-,nāt-ər\ *n* — **re·ju·ve·nes·cence** \ri-,jü-və-'nes-ᵊn(t)s, ,rē-\ *n* — **re·ju·ve·nes·cent** \-ᵊnt\ *adj*

re·kin·dle \(')rē-'kin-dᵊl\ *vb* **:** to kindle again

re·knit \(')rē-'nit\ *vt* **:** to knit up or together again

¹re·lapse \ri-'laps, 'rē-,\ *n* [L *relapsus*, pp. of *relabi* to slide back, fr. *re-* + *labi* to slide — more at SLEEP] **1 :** the act or fact of backsliding, worsening, or subsiding **2 :** a recurrence of symptoms of a disease after a prolonged abatement

²re·lapse \ri-'laps\ *vi* **1 :** to slip or fall back into a former worse state **2 :** SINK, SUBSIDE **3 :** BACKSLIDE — **re·laps·er** *n*

relapsing fever *n* **:** a variable acute epidemic disease marked by recurring high fever lasting five to seven days and caused by a spirochete transmitted by the bites of lice and ticks

re·lat·able \ri-'lāt-ə-bəl\ *adj* **:** capable of being related

re·late \ri-'lāt\ *vb* [L *relatus* (pp. of *referre* to carry back), fr. *re-* + *latus*, pp. of *ferre* to carry — more at TOLERATE, BEAR] *vt* **1 :** to give an account of **:** TELL **2 :** to show or establish logical or causal connection between ~ *vi* **1 :** to apply or take effect retroactively **2 :** to have reference **3 :** to have meaningful social relationships **syn** see JOIN — **re·lat·er** *n*

re·lat·ed *adj* **1 :** connected by relation **2 :** allied by kindred; *esp* **:** connected by consanguinity **3 :** having close harmonic connection — **re·lat·ed·ly** *adv* — **re·lat·ed·ness** *n*

re·la·tion \ri-'lā-shən\ *n* **1 :** the act of telling or recounting **:** ACCOUNT **2 :** an aspect or quality (as resemblance) that can be predicated only of two or more things or parts taken together **:** CONNECTION **3 :** the referring by a legal fiction of an act to a prior date as the time of its taking effect **4 a** (1) **:** a person connected by consanguinity or affinity **:** RELATIVE (2) **:** a person legally entitled to a share of the property of an intestate **b :** relationship by consanguinity or affinity **:** KINSHIP **5 :** REFERENCE, RESPECT ⟨in ~ to⟩ **6 a :** the state of being mutually or reciprocally interested (as in social or commercial matters) **b** *pl* (1) **:** DEALINGS, AFFAIRS (2) **:** INTERCOURSE (3) **:** SEXUAL INTERCOURSE

re·la·tion·al \-shnəl, -shən-ᵊl\ *adj* **1 :** of or relating to kinship **2 :** characterized or constituted by relations **3 :** having the function chiefly of indicating a relation of syntax

re·la·tion·ship \-shən-,ship\ *n* **1 :** the state or character of being related or interrelated **2 :** KINSHIP; *also* **:** a specific instance or type of this

¹rel·a·tive \'rel-ət-iv\ *n* **1 :** a word referring grammatically to an antecedent **2 :** a thing having a relation to or connection with or necessary dependence upon another thing **3 a :** a person connected with another by blood or affinity **b :** an animal or plant related to another by common descent **4 :** a relative term

²relative *adj* **1 :** introducing a subordinate clause qualifying an expressed or implied antecedent ⟨~ pronoun⟩; *also* **:** introduced by such a connective ⟨~ clause⟩ **2 :** RELEVANT, PERTINENT **3 :** not absolute or independent **:** COMPARATIVE **4 :** having the same key signature — used of major and minor keys and scales **5 :** expressed as the ratio of the specified quantity to the total magnitude or to the mean of all the quantities involved — **rel·a·tive·ly** *adv* — **rel·a·tive·ness** *n*

relative humidity *n* **:** the ratio of the amount of water vapor actually present in the air to the greatest amount possible at the same temperature

rel·a·tiv·ism \'rel-ət-iv-,iz-əm\ *n* **1 a :** a theory that knowledge is relative to the limited nature of the mind and the conditions of knowing **b :** a view that ethical truths depend upon the individuals and groups holding them **2 :** RELATIVITY — **rel·a·tiv·ist** \-əst\ *n* — **rel·a·tiv·is·tic** \,rel-ət-iv-'is-tik\ *adj* — **rel·a·tiv·is·ti·cal·ly** \-ti-k(ə-)lē\ *adv*

rel·a·tiv·i·ty \,rel-ə-'tiv-ət-ē\ *n* **1 :** the quality or state of being relative **2 :** the state of being dependent for existence on or determined in nature, value, or quality by relation to something else **3 a :** a theory formulated by Albert Einstein and leading to the assertion of the equivalence of mass and energy and of the increase of the mass of a body with increased velocity and based on the two postulates that if two systems are in relative motion with uniform linear velocity it is impossible for observers in either system by observation and measurement of phenomena in the other to learn more about the motion than the fact that it is relative motion and that measurements of the velocity of light in either system regardless of the position of the source of light always give the same numerical value — called also *special theory of relativity* **b :** an extension of the theory to include a discussion of gravitation and related phenomena — called also *general theory of relativity* **4 :** RELATIVISM 1b

rel·a·tiv·ize \'rel-ət-iv-,īz\ *vt* **:** to treat or describe as relative

re·la·tor \ri-'lāt-ər\ *n* **:** one who relates **:** NARRATOR

re·lax \ri-'laks\ *vb* [ME *relaxen* to make less compact, fr. L *relaxare*, fr. *re-* + *laxare* to loosen, fr. *laxus* loose — more at SLACK] *vt* **1 :** to make less tense or rigid **:** SLACKEN **2 :** to make less severe or stringent **3 :** to make soft or enervated **4 :** to relieve from nervous tension ~ *vi* **1 :** to become lax, weak, or loose **:** REST **2 :** to abate in intensity **3** *of a muscle or muscle fiber* **:** to become inactive and lengthen **4 :** to cast off social restraint, nervous tension, or attitude of anxiety or suspicion **5 :** to seek rest or recreation **6 :** to relieve constipation — **re·lax·er** *n*

¹re·lax·ant \-'lak-sənt\ *adj* **:** of, relating to, or producing relaxation

²relaxant *n* **:** a drug that relaxes; *specif* **:** one that relieves muscular tension

re·lax·ation \,rē-,lak-'sā-shən, ri-\ *n* **1 :** the act or fact of relaxing or of being relaxed **2 :** a relaxing or recreative state, activity, or pastime **:** DIVERSION **3 :** the lengthening that characterizes inactive muscle fibers or muscles

re·laxed \ri-'lakst\ *adj* **1 :** lacking in precision or strictness **2 :** set at rest or at ease **3 :** easy of manner **:** INFORMAL — **re·laxed·ly** \-'lak-səd-lē, -'laks-tlē\ *adv* — **re·laxed·ness** \-'lak-səd-nəs, -'laks(t)-nəs\ *n*

re·lax·in \ri-'lak-sən\ *n* **:** a sex hormone of the corpus luteum that facilitates birth by causing relaxation of the pelvic ligaments

¹re·lay \'rē-,lā\ *n* **1 a :** a supply (as of horses) arranged beforehand for successive relief **b :** a number of men who relieve others in some work **2 a :** a race between teams in which each team member covers a specified portion of the course **b :** one of the divisions of a relay **3 :** an electromagnetic device for remote or automatic control actuated by variation in conditions of an electric circuit and operating in turn other devices (as switches) in the same or a different circuit **4 :** SERVOMOTOR **5 :** the act of passing along by stages; *also* **:** one of such stages

²re·lay \'rē-,lā, ri-'lā\ *vt* [ME *relayen*, fr. MF *relaier*, fr. OF, fr. *re-* + *laier* to leave — more at DELAY] **1 a :** to place or dispose in relays **b :** to provide with relays **2 :** to pass along by relays **3 :** to control or operate by a relay

³re·lay \(')rē-'lā\ *vt* **:** to lay again

re·leas·abil·i·ty \ri-,lē-sə-'bil-ət-ē\ *n* **:** the quality or state of being releasable

re·leas·able \ri-'lē-sə-bəl\ *adj* **:** capable of being released — **re·leas·ably** \-blē\ *adv*

¹re·lease \ri-'lēs\ *vt* [ME *relesen*, fr. OF *relessier*, fr. L *relaxare* to relax] **1 :** to set free from restraint, confinement, or servitude **2 :** to relieve from something that confines, burdens, or oppresses **3 :** to give up in favor of another **:** RELINQUISH ⟨~ a claim to property⟩ **4 :** to give permission for publication, performance, exhibition, or sale of on but not before a specified date **syn** see FREE

²release *n* **1 :** relief or deliverance from sorrow, suffering, or trouble **2 a :** discharge from obligation or responsibility **b** (1) **:** relinquishment of a right or claim (2) **:** an act by which a legal right is discharged; *specif* **:** a conveyance of a right in lands or tenements to another having an estate in possession **3 a :** the act or an instance of liberating or freeing **b :** the act or manner of concluding a musical tone or phrase or ending a sound **4 :** an instrument effecting a legal release **5 a :** the permitting of a working fluid (as steam) to escape from the cylinder at the end of the working stroke **b :** the point in a cycle at which this act occurs **6 :** the state of being freed **7 :** a device adapted to hold or release a mechanism as required **8 a :** the act of permitting performance or publication **b :** the matter released; *esp* **:** a statement prepared for the press

re–lease \(')rē-'lēs\ *vt* **:** to lease again

released time *n* **:** a scheduled time when children are dismissed from public school to receive religious instruction

re·leas·er \ri-'lē-sər\ *n* **:** one that releases; *specif* **:** a stimulus that serves as the initiator of complex reflex behavior

rel·e·gate \'rel-ə-,gāt\ *vt* [L *relegatus*, pp. of *relegare*, fr. *re-* + *legare* to send with a commission — more at LEGATE] **1 a :** to send into exile **:** BANISH **b :** to consign to insignificance or oblivion **2 :** to consign by classifying or appraising **3 :** to submit or refer for decision, judgment, or execution **syn** see COMMIT — **rel·e·ga·tion** \,rel-ə-'gā-shən\ *n*

re·lent \ri-'lent\ *vb* [ME *relenten*] *vi* **1 :** to become less severe, harsh, or strict **2 :** to let up **:** SLACKEN ~ *vt*, *obs* **:** SOFTEN, MOLLIFY **syn** see YIELD

re·lent·less \-ləs\ *adj* **:** mercilessly hard or harsh — **re·lent·less·ly** *adv* — **re·lent·less·ness** *n*

rel·e·vance \'rel-ə-vən(t)s\ *also* **rel·e·van·cy** \-vən-sē\ *n* **:** relation to the matter at hand **:** PERTINENCE

rel·e·vant \'rel-ə-vənt, *substand* 'rev-ə-lənt\ *adj* [ML *relevant-*, *relevans*, fr. L, prp. of *relevare* to raise up — more at RELIEVE] **1 a :** bearing upon the matter at hand **:** PERTINENT **b :** affording evidence tending to prove or disprove the matters at issue or under discussion ⟨~ testimony⟩ **2 :** PROPORTIONAL, RELATIVE — **rel·e·vant·ly** *adv*

syn RELEVANT, GERMANE, MATERIAL, PERTINENT, APPOSITE, APPLICABLE, APROPOS mean related to or bearing upon the matter in hand. RELEVANT implies a traceable, significant, logical connection; GERMANE may additionally imply a fitness for or appropriateness to the situation or occasion; MATERIAL implies so close a relationship that it cannot be dispensed with without serious alteration of the case; PERTINENT stresses a clear and decisive relevance; APPOSITE suggests a felicitous relevance; APPLICABLE suggests the fitness of bringing a general rule or principle to bear upon a particular in hand; APROPOS suggests being both relevant and opportune

See *re-* and 2d element **rejudge** **relearn** **relet** **reletter**

re·li·abil·i·ty \ri-ˌlī-ə-'bil-ət-ē\ *n* **:** the quality or state of being reliable

re·li·able \ri-'lī-ə-bəl\ *adj* **:** suitable or fit to be relied on — **re·li·able·ness** *n* — **re·li·ably** \-blē\ *adv*

re·li·ance \ri-'lī-ən(t)s\ *n* **1 :** the act of relying **2 :** the condition or attitude of one who relies **:** DEPENDENCE **3 :** something or someone relied on

re·li·ant \-ənt\ *adj* **:** having reliance on something or someone **:** TRUSTING — **re·li·ant·ly** *adv*

rel·ic \'rel-ik\ *n* [ME *relik*, fr. OF *relique*, fr. ML *reliquia*, fr. LL *reliquiae*, pl., remains of a martyr, fr. L, remains, fr. *relinquere* to leave behind — more at RELINQUISH] **1 a :** an object esteemed and venerated because of association with a saint or martyr **b :** SOUVENIR, MEMENTO **2** *pl* **:** REMAINS, CORPSE **3 :** something left behind after decay, disintegration, or disappearance **4 :** a trace of some past or outmoded practice, custom, or belief **:** VESTIGE

rel·ict \'rel-ikt\ *n* [in sense 1, fr. LL *relicta*, fr. L, fem. of *relictus*, pp. of *relinquere;* in senses 2 & 3, fr. *relict* (residual), adj., fr. L *relictus*] **1 :** WIDOW **2 :** a persistent remnant of an otherwise extinct flora or fauna or kind of organism **3 a :** a relief feature or rock remaining after other parts have disappeared **b :** something left unchanged in a process of change

re·lic·tion \ri-'lik-shən\ *n* [L *reliction-*, *relictio* act of leaving behind, fr. *relictus*] **1 :** the gradual recession of water leaving permanently uncovered land **2 :** land uncovered by reliction

re·lief \ri-'lēf\ *n* [ME, fr. MF, fr. OF, fr. *relever*] **1 :** a payment made by a feudal tenant to his lord upon succeeding to an inherited estate **2 a :** removal or lightening of something oppressive, painful, or distressing **b :** aid in the form of money or necessities for the indigent, aged, or handicapped **c :** military assistance in or rescue from a position of extreme difficulty or encirclement **d :** means of breaking or avoiding monotony or boredom **:** DIVERSION **3 :** release from a post or from the performance of duty **4 :** one that relieves another from duty by taking his place **5 :** legal remedy or redress **6** [F] **a :** a mode of sculpture in which forms and figures are distinguished from a surrounding plane surface **b :** sculpture or a sculptural form executed in this mode **c :** projecting detail, ornament, or figures **7 a :** the suggestion in pictorial art of spatial dimensions and relations **b :** sharpness of outline due to contrast **8 :** the elevations or inequalities of a land surface

relief map *n* **:** a map representing topographic relief

relief pitcher *n* **:** a baseball pitcher who takes over for another during a game; *esp* **:** one who is regularly held in readiness for relief

re·li·er \ri-'lī(-ə)r\ *n* **:** one that relies

re·liev·able \ri-'lē-və-bəl\ *adj* **:** capable of being relieved

re·lieve \ri-'lēv\ *vb* [ME *releven*, fr. MF *relever* to raise, relieve, fr. L *relevare*, fr. *re-* + *levare* to raise — more at LEVER] *vt* **1 :** to free from a burden, evil, or distress **:** SUCCOR **2 :** to bring about the removal or alleviation of **:** MITIGATE **3 a :** to release from a post, station, or duty **b :** to take the place of **4 :** to set free from an obligation, condition, or restriction **5 :** to ease of a burden, wrong, or oppression by judicial or legislative interposition **6 :** to remove or lessen the monotony **7 a :** to set off by contrast **b :** to raise in relief ~ *vi* **1 :** to bring or give relief **2 :** to stand out in relief — **re·liev·er** *n*

syn RELIEVE, ALLEVIATE, LIGHTEN, ASSUAGE, MITIGATE, ALLAY mean to make something less grievous. RELIEVE implies a lifting of enough of a burden to make it tolerable; ALLEVIATE implies temporary or partial lessening of pain or distress; LIGHTEN implies reducing a burdensome or depressing weight; ASSUAGE implies softening or sweetening what is harsh or disagreeable; MITIGATE suggests a moderating or countering the effect of something violent or painful; ALLAY implies an effective calming or soothing of fears or alarms

re·lie·vo \ri-'lē-(ˌ)vō, rēl-'yā-\ *n, pl* **relievos** [It *rilievo*, fr. *rilevare* to raise, fr. L *relevare*] **:** RELIEF 6

re·li·gion \ri-'lij-ən\ *n* [ME *religioun*, fr. L *religion-*, *religio* reverence, religion, prob. fr. *religare* to tie back — more at RELY] **1 a** (1) **:** the service and worship of God or the supernatural (2) **:** commitment or devotion to religious faith or observance **b :** the state of a religious **2 :** a personal set or institutionalized system of religious attitudes, beliefs, and practices **3** *archaic* **:** scrupulous conformity **:** CONSCIENTIOUSNESS **4 :** a cause, principle, or system of beliefs held to with ardor and faith

re·li·gion·ist \-'lij-(ə-)nəst\ *n* **:** a person adhering to a religion

re·li·gi·ose \ri-'lij-ē-ˌōs\ *adj* **:** excessively, obtrusively, or sentimentally religious — **re·li·gi·os·i·ty** \-ˌlij-ē-'äs-ət-ē\ *n*

¹re·li·gious \ri-'lij-əs\ *adj* [ME, fr. OF *religieus*, fr. L *religiosus*, fr. *religio*] **1 :** relating or devoted to the divine or that which is held to be of ultimate importance **2 :** of or relating to religious beliefs or observances **3 a :** scrupulously and conscientiously faithful **b :** FERVENT, ZEALOUS **syn** see DEVOUT — **re·li·gious·ly** *adv* — **re·li·gious·ness** *n*

²religious *n, pl* **religious** [ME, fr. OF *religieus*, fr. *religieus*, adj.] **:** one (as a monk) bound by vows, sequestered from secular concerns, and devoted to a life of piety

syn RELIGIOUS, MONK, FRIAR, NUN mean a member of a religious order bound by vows of poverty, chastity, and obedience. RELIGIOUS is the general term applicable to a man or woman; MONK applies to a male religious living in a cloister and devoted to contemplation, prayer, and some chosen work; FRIAR applies to a male religious of an order of originally mendicant preachers of the gospel; NUN applies to any female religious but suggests esp. one of the severer orders

re·line \(')rē-'līn\ *vt* **:** to put new lines on or a new lining in

re·lin·quish \ri-'liŋ-kwish, -'lin-\ *vt* [ME *relinquisshen*, fr. MF *relinquiss-*, stem of *relinquir*, fr. L *relinquere* to leave behind, fr. *re-* + *linquere* to leave — more at LOAN] **1 :** to withdraw or retreat from **:** ABANDON **2 a :** to desist from **b :** to assent to withdrawal, dropping, or cessation of **:** RENOUNCE **3 a :** to let go of **:** RELEASE **b :** to give over possession or control of **:** YIELD — **re·lin·quish·ment** \-mənt\ *n*

syn RELINQUISH, YIELD, RESIGN, SURRENDER, ABANDON, WAIVE mean to give up completely. RELINQUISH usu. does not imply strong feeling but may suggest some regret, reluctance, or weakness; YIELD implies concession or compliance or submission to force; RESIGN emphasizes voluntary relinquishment or sacrifice without struggle; SURRENDER implies a giving up after a struggle to retain or resist; ABANDON stresses finality and completeness in giving up; WAIVE implies conceding or forgoing with little or no compulsion

rel·i·quary \'rel-ə-ˌkwer-ē\ *n* [F *reliquaire*, fr. ML *reliquiarium*, fr. *reliquia* relic — more at RELIC] **:** a container for religious relics

re·lique \ri-'lēk, 'rel-ik\ *archaic var of* RELIC

re·liq·ui·ae \ri-'lik-wē-ˌī, -wē-ˌē\ *n pl* [L — more at RELIC] **:** remains of the dead **:** RELICS

¹rel·ish \'rel-ish\ *n* [alter. of ME *reles* taste, fr. OF, something left behind, release, fr. *relessier* to release] **1 :** characteristic flavor; *esp* **:** pleasing or zestful flavor **2 :** a quantity just sufficient to flavor or characterize **:** TRACE **3 a :** enjoyment of or delight in something that satisfies one's tastes, inclinations, or desires **b :** APPETITE, INCLINATION **4 a :** something adding a zestful flavor **:** CONDIMENT **b :** APPETIZER, HORS D'OEUVRE **syn** see TASTE

²relish *vt* **1 :** to add relish to **2 :** to be pleased or gratified by **:** ENJOY **3 :** to eat or drink with pleasure **4 :** to appreciate with taste and discernment ~ *vi* **:** to have a characteristic or pleasing taste — **rel·ish·able** \-ə-bəl\ *adj*

re·live \(')rē-'liv\ *vt* **:** to live over again ~ *vi* **:** to live again

re·lu·cent \ri-'lüs-ᵊnt\ *adj* [L *relucent-*, *relucens*, pp. of *relucēre* to shine back, fr. *re-* + *lucēre* to shine — more at LIGHT] **:** reflecting light **:** SHINING

re·luct \ri-'ləkt\ *vi* [L *reluctari*] **:** to feel or show repugnance or opposition **:** REVOLT

re·luc·tance \ri-'lək-tən(t)s\ *n* **1 :** the quality or state of being reluctant **2 :** the opposition offered by a magnetic substance to magnetic flux; *specif* **:** the ratio of the magnetic potential difference to the corresponding flux

re·luc·tan·cy \-tən-sē\ *n* **:** RELUCTANCE

re·luc·tant \ri-'lək-tənt\ *adj* [L *reluctant-*, *reluctans*, prp. of *reluctari* to struggle against, fr. *re-* + *luctari* to struggle — more at LOCK] **1 :** struggling against **:** OPPOSING **2 :** holding back **:** AVERSE, UNWILLING ⟨~ to condemn him⟩ **syn** see DISINCLINED — **re·luc·tant·ly** *adv*

re·luc·tate \-ˌtāt\ *vi* **:** to show reluctance — **re·luc·ta·tion** \ri-ˌlək-'tā-shən, ˌrē-\ *n*

re·luc·tiv·i·ty \ri-ˌlək-'tiv-ət-ē, ˌrē-\ *n* [*reluct*ance + *-ivity* (as in *conductivity*)] **:** the reciprocal of magnetic permeability

re·lume \(')rē-'lüm\ *vt* [irreg. fr. LL *reluminare*] **:** to light or light up again **:** REKINDLE

re·lu·mine \-'lü-mən\ *vt* [LL *reluminare*, fr. L *re-* + *luminare* to light up — more at ILLUMINATE] **:** RELUME

re·ly \ri-'lī\ *vi* [ME *relien* to rally, fr. MF *relier* to connect, rally, fr. L *religare* to tie back, fr. *re-* + *ligare* to tie — more at LIGATURE] **1 :** to have confidence **:** TRUST **2 :** to be dependent **:** COUNT

syn RELY, TRUST, DEPEND, COUNT, RECKON mean to place full confidence. RELY (*on* or *upon*) implies a judgment based on experience or association; TRUST (*in* or *to*) implies assurance based on faith that another will not fail one; DEPEND (*on* or *upon*) suggests a resting confidently for support or assistance; COUNT (*on*) and RECKON (*on*) imply a taking into one's calculations as certain or assured

¹re·main \ri-'mān\ *vi* [ME *remainen*, fr. MF *remaindre*, fr. L *remanēre*, fr. *re-* + *manēre* to remain — more at MANSION] **1 a :** to be a part not destroyed, taken, or used up **b :** to be something yet to be shown, done, or treated **2 :** to stay in the same place or with the same person or group; *specif* **:** to stay behind **3 :** to continue unchanged **:** STAND **syn** see STAY

²remain *n* **1** *obs* **:** STAY **2 :** a remaining part or trace — usu. used in pl. **3** *pl* **:** writings left unpublished at a writer's death **4** *pl* **:** a dead body

¹re·main·der \ri-'mān-dər\ *n* [ME, fr. AF, fr. MF *remaindre*] **1 :** an estate in expectancy that becomes an estate in possession upon the determination of a particular prior estate created at the same time by the same instrument — compare REVERSION **2 a :** a remaining group, part, or trace **b** (1) **:** the number left after a subtraction (2) **:** the final undivided part after division that is less or of lower degree than the divisor **3 :** a book sold at a reduced price by the publisher after sales have slowed

²remainder *adj* **:** LEFTOVER, REMAINING

³remainder *vt* **re·main·der·ing** \-d(ə-)riŋ\ **:** to dispose of as remainders

re·make \(')rē-'māk\ *vt* **:** to make anew or in a different form — **remake** \'rē-ˌ\ *n*

re·man \(')rē-'man\ *vt* **1 :** to man again or anew **2 :** to imbue with courage again

re·mand \ri-'mand\ *vt* [ME *remaunden*, fr. MF *remander*, fr. LL *remandare* to send back word, fr. L *re-* + *mandare* to order — more at MANDATE] **:** to order back: as **a :** to send back (a case) to another court or agency for further action **b :** to return to custody pending trial or for further detention — **remand** *n*

re·ma·nence \'rem-ə-nən(t)s, ri-'mā-\ *n* **:** the magnetic induction remaining in a magnetized substance when the magnetizing force has become zero

re·ma·nent \-nənt\ *adj* [ME, fr. L *remanent-*, *remanens*, prp. of *remanēre* to remain] **:** REMAINING, RESIDUAL

¹re·mark \ri-'märk\ *vb* [F *remarquer*, fr. MF, fr. *re-* + *marquer* to mark — more at MARQUE] *vt* **1** *obs* **:** to mark distinctively **2 :** to take notice of **:** OBSERVE **3 :** to express as an observation or comment **:** SAY ~ *vi* **:** to make an observation or comment — used with *on* or *upon*

²remark *n* **1 :** the act of remarking **:** NOTICE **2 :** mention of that which deserves attention or notice **3 :** an expression of opinion or judgment

re·mark·able \ri-'mär-kə-bəl\ *adj* **1 :** worthy of being or likely to be noticed **2 :** UNCOMMON, EXTRAORDINARY **syn** see NOTICEABLE — **re·mark·able·ness** *n* — **re·mark·ably** \-blē\ *adv*

re·marque \ri-'märk\ *n* [F *remarque* remark, note, fr. MF, fr. *remarquer*] **1 :** a drawn, etched, or incised scribble or sketch done on the margin of a plate or stone and removed before the regular printing **2 :** a proof taken before remarques have been removed

re·mar·riage \(')rē-'mar-ij\ *n* **1 :** an act or instance of remarrying **2 :** the state of being remarried

re·match \(')rē-'mach, 'rē-ˌ\ *n* **:** a second match between the same contestants or teams

re·me·di·a·ble \ri-'mēd-ē-ə-bəl\ *adj* **:** capable of being remedied — **re·me·di·a·ble·ness** *n* — **re·me·di·a·bly** \-blē\ *adv*

See *re-* and 2d element **relight** | **reload** **reloader** | **relocate** | **relocation** | **remanufacture** | **remarry**

re·me·di·al \ri-'mēd-ē-əl\ *adj* **1 :** affording a remedy **2 :** concerned with the correction of faulty study habits ⟨~ reading⟩ — **re·me·di·al·ly** \-ə-lē\ *adv*
re·me·di·ate \-ē-ət\ *adj, obs* **:** REMEDIAL
rem·e·di·less \'rem-əd-ē-ləs\ *adj* **1 :** not admitting remedy **:** IRREMEDIABLE, IRREPARABLE **2 :** having no legal remedy — **rem·e·di·less·ly** *adv*
[1]**rem·e·dy** \'rem-əd-ē\ *n* [ME *remedie,* fr. AF, fr. L *remedium,* fr. *re-* + *mederi* to heal — more at MEDICAL] **1 :** a medicine or application that relieves or cures a disease **2 :** something that corrects or counteracts an evil **:** CORRECTIVE **3 :** the legal means to recover a right or to prevent or obtain redress for a wrong
[2]**remedy** *vt* **:** to provide or serve as a remedy for **:** RELIEVE **syn** see CORRECT, CURE
re·mem·ber \ri-'mem-bər\ *vb* **re·mem·ber·ing** \-b(ə-)riŋ\ [ME *remembren,* fr. MF *remembrer,* fr. LL *rememorari,* fr. L *re-* + LL *memorari* to be mindful of, fr. L *memor* mindful — more at MEMORY] *vt* **1 :** to bring to mind or think of again **2** *archaic* **a :** BETHINK **b :** REMIND **3 a :** to keep in mind for attention or consideration **b :** REWARD **4 :** to retain in the memory **5 :** to convey greetings from **6 :** RECORD, COMMEMORATE ~ *vi* **1 :** to exercise or have the power of memory **2 :** to have a recollection or remembrance — **re·mem·ber·able** \-b(ə-)rə-bəl\ *adj* — **re·mem·ber·er** \-bər-ər\ *n*
syn RECOLLECT, RECALL, REMIND, REMINISCE: REMEMBER implies a keeping in memory that may be effortless or unwilled; RECOLLECT implies a bringing back to mind what is lost or scattered; RECALL suggests an effort to bring back to mind and often to re-create in speech; REMIND suggests a jogging of one's memory by an association or similarity; REMINISCE implies a casual often nostalgic recalling of experiences long past and gone
re·mem·brance \ri-'mem-brən(t)s, -bə-rən(t)s\ *n* **1 :** the state of bearing in mind **2 a :** the ability to remember **:** MEMORY **b :** the period over which one's memory extends **3 :** an act of recalling to mind **4 :** a memory of a person, thing, or event **5 a :** something that serves to keep in or bring to mind **:** REMINDER **b :** COMMEMORATION, MEMORIAL **c :** a greeting or gift recalling or expressing friendship or affection **syn** see MEMORY
Remembrance Day *n, Brit* **:** VETERANS DAY
re·mem·branc·er \-brən-sər\ *n* **:** one that reminds; *esp* **:** one of several English officials originally appointed to remind a governmental authority
re·mex \'rā-,meks, 'rē-\ *n, pl* **re·mi·ges** \'rā-mə-,gās, 'rem-ə-,jēz\ [NL *remig-, remex,* fr. L, oarsman, fr. *remus* oar + *agere* to drive — more at ROW, AGENT] **:** a primary or secondary quill feather of the wing of a bird — **re·mi·gial** \ri-'mij-(ē-)əl\ *adj*
re·mil·i·ta·rize \(')rē-'mil-ə-tə-,rīz\ *vt* **:** to equip again with military forces and installations
re·mind \ri-'mīnd\ *vt* **:** to put in mind of something or someone **syn** see REMEMBER — **re·mind·er** *n*
re·mind·ful \-'mīn(d)-fəl\ *adj* **1 :** MINDFUL **2 :** tending to remind
rem·i·nisce \,rem-ə-'nis\ *vi* [back-formation fr. *reminiscence*] **:** to indulge in reminiscence **syn** see REMEMBER
rem·i·nis·cence \-'nis-ᵊn(t)s\ *n* **1 :** apprehension of a Platonic idea as if it had been known in a previous existence **2 a :** recall to mind of a long-forgotten experience or fact **b :** the process or practice of thinking or telling about past experiences **3 a :** a remembered experience **b :** an account of a memorable experience — often used in pl. **4 :** something so like another as to be regarded as an unconscious repetition, imitation, or survival **syn** see MEMORY
rem·i·nis·cent \-ᵊnt\ *adj* [L *reminiscent-, reminiscens,* prp. of *reminisci* to remember, fr. *re-* + *-minisci* (akin to L *ment-, mens* mind) — more at MIND] **1 :** of the character of or relating to reminiscence **2 :** marked by or given to reminiscence **3 :** serving to remind **:** SUGGESTIVE — **rem·i·nis·cent·ly** *adv*
rem·i·nis·cen·tial \,rem-ə-(,)nis-'en-chəl\ *adj* **:** REMINISCENT
re·mise \ri-'mīz\ *vt* [ME *remisen,* fr. MF *remis,* pp. of *remettre* to put back, fr. L *remittere* to send back] **:** to give, grant, or release a claim to **:** DEED
re·miss \ri-'mis\ *adj* [ME, fr. L *remissus,* fr. pp. of *remittere* to send back, relax] **1 :** negligent in the performance of work or duty **:** CARELESS **2 :** showing neglect or inattention **:** LAX **syn** see NEGLIGENT — **re·miss·ly** *adv* — **re·miss·ness** *n*
re·mis·si·ble \ri-'mis-ə-bəl\ *adj* **:** that may be forgiven ⟨~ sins⟩ — **re·mis·si·bly** \-blē\ *adv*
re·mis·sion \ri-'mish-ən\ *n* **:** the act or process of remitting
re·mit \ri-'mit\ *vb* **re·mit·ted; re·mit·ting** [ME *remitten,* fr. L *remittere* to send back, fr. *re-* + *mittere* to send — more at SMITE] *vt* **1 a :** to release from the guilt or penalty of ⟨~ sins⟩ **b :** to refrain from exacting **c :** to cancel or refrain from inflicting **d :** to give relief from (suffering) **2 a :** to lay aside (a mood or disposition) partly or wholly **b :** to desist from **c :** to let slacken **:** RELAX **3 :** to submit or refer for consideration, judgment, decision, or action; *specif* **:** REMAND **4 :** to restore or consign to a former status or condition **5 :** POSTPONE, DEFER **6 :** to send (money) to a person or place esp. in payment of a demand, account, or draft ~ *vi* **1 a :** to abate in force or intensity **:** MODERATE **b** *of a disease or abnormality* **:** to abate symptoms for a period **2 :** to send money (as in payment) — **re·mit** \ri-'mit, 'rē-,\ *n* — **re·mit·ment** \ri-'mit-mənt\ *n* — **re·mit·ta·ble** \-'mit-ə-bəl\ *adj* — **re·mit·ter** *n*
re·mit·tal \ri-'mit-ᵊl\ *n* **:** REMISSION
re·mit·tance \ri-'mit-ᵊn(t)s\ *n* **1 a :** a sum of money remitted **b :** an instrument by which money is remitted **2 :** transmittal of money
remittance man *n* **:** a person living abroad on remittances from home
re·mit·tent \ri-'mit-ᵊnt\ *adj* [L *remittent-, remittens,* prp. of *remittere*] *of a disease* **:** marked by alternating periods of abatement and increase of symptoms — **re·mit·tent·ly** *adv*
[1]**rem·nant** \'rem-nənt\ *n* [ME, contr. of *remenant,* fr. MF, fr. prp. of *remenoir* to remain, fr. L *remanēre* — more at REMAIN] **1 a :** a usu. small part, member, or trace remaining **b :** REMAINDER **c :** a small surviving group — often used in pl. **2 :** an unsold or unused end of piece goods
[2]**remnant** *adj* **:** LEFT, REMAINING
re·mod·el \(')rē-'mäd-ᵊl\ *vt* **:** to alter the structure of **:** RECONSTRUCT **syn** see MEND
re·mon·e·tize \(')rē-'män-ə-,tīz, -'mən-\ *vt* **:** to restore to use as legal tender ⟨~ silver⟩
re·mon·strance \ri-'män(t)-strən(t)s\ *n* **1** *archaic* **:** REPRESENTATION, DEMONSTRATION; *specif* **:** a document formally stating points of opposition or grievance **2 :** an act or instance of remonstrating **:** EXPOSTULATION
re·mon·strant \-strənt\ *adj* **:** vigorously objecting or opposing — **remonstrant** *n* — **re·mon·strant·ly** *adv*
re·mon·strate \ri-'män-,strāt\ *vb* [ML *remonstratus,* pp. of *remonstrare* to demonstrate, fr. L *re-* + *monstrare* to show — more at MUSTER] *vt* **:** to say or plead in protest, reproof, or opposition ~ *vi* **:** to present and urge reasons in opposition **:** EXPOSTULATE **syn** see OBJECT — **re·mon·stra·tion** \ri-,män-'strā-shən, ,rem-ən-\ *n* — **re·mon·stra·tive** \ri-'män(t)-strət-iv\ *adj* — **re·mon·stra·tive·ly** *adv* — **re·mon·stra·tor** \ri-'män-,strāt-ər\ *n*
rem·o·ra \'rem-ə-rə\ *n* [L, lit., delay, fr. *remorari* to delay, fr. *re-* + *morari* to delay — more at MORATORY] **1 :** any of several specialized fishes (of *Echeneis* and related genera) having the anterior dorsal fin converted into a suctorial disk on the head by means of which they cling to other fishes and to ships **2 :** HINDRANCE, DRAG — **rem·o·rid** \-rəd\ *adj*
re·morse \ri-'mȯ(ə)rs\ *n* [ME, fr. MF *remors,* fr. ML *remorsus,* fr. LL, act of biting again, fr. L *remorsus,* pp. of *remordēre* to bite again, fr. *re-* + *mordēre* to bite — more at SMART] **1 :** a gnawing distress arising from a sense of guilt for past wrongs **:** SELF-REPROACH **2** *obs* **:** COMPASSION **syn** see PENITENCE
re·morse·ful \-'mȯrs-fəl\ *adj* **:** springing from or marked by remorse — **re·morse·ful·ly** \-fə-lē\ *adv* — **re·morse·ful·ness** *n*
re·morse·less \-'mȯr-sləs\ *adj* **:** being without remorse **:** MERCILESS — **re·morse·less·ly** *adv* — **re·morse·less·ness** *n*
re·mote \ri-'mōt\ *adj* [L *remotus,* fr. pp. of *removēre* to remove] **1 :** separated by great intervals **2 a :** far removed in space, time, or relation ⟨the ~ past⟩ **b :** DIVERGENT ⟨comments ~ from the truth⟩ **3 :** located out of the way **:** SECLUDED **4 a :** acting on or controlling indirectly or from a distance **b :** not arising from a primary or proximate action **5 :** small in degree **:** SLIGHT **6 :** distant in manner **:** ALOOF **syn** see DISTANT — **re·mote·ly** *adv* — **re·mote·ness** *n*
re·mo·tion \ri-'mō-shən\ *n* **1 :** the act of removing **:** REMOVAL **2** *obs* **:** DEPARTURE
[1]**re·mount** \(')rē-'maůnt\ *vb* [ME *remounten,* partly fr. *re-* + *mounten* to mount, partly fr. MF *remonter,* fr. *re-* + *monter* to mount] *vt* **1 :** to mount again **2 :** to furnish remounts to ~ *vi* **1 :** to become remounted **2 :** REVERT
[2]**re·mount** \'rē-,maůnt, (')rē-'\ *n* **:** a fresh horse to replace one no longer available
re·mov·abil·i·ty \ri-,mü-və-'bil-ət-ē\ *n* **:** the quality or state of being removable
re·mov·able \ri-'mü-və-bəl\ *adj* **:** capable of being removed — **re·mov·able·ness** *n* — **re·mov·ably** \-blē\ *adv*
re·mov·al \ri-'mü-vəl\ *n* **:** the act of removing **:** the fact of being removed
[1]**re·move** \ri-'müv\ *vb* [ME *removen,* fr. OF *removoir,* fr. L *removēre,* fr. *re-* + *movēre* to move] *vt* **1 a :** to change the location, position, station, or residence of **b :** to transfer (a legal proceeding) from one court to another **2 :** to move by lifting, pushing aside, or taking away or off **3 :** to dismiss from office **4 :** ELIMINATE ~ *vi* **1 :** to change location, station, or residence **2 :** to go away **3 :** to be capable of being removed — **re·mov·er** *n*
[2]**remove** *n* **1 :** REMOVAL; *specif* **:** MOVE 2c **2 a :** a distance or interval separating one person or thing from another **b :** a degree or stage of separation
re·moved *adj* **1 a :** distant in degree of relationship **b :** of a younger or older generation ⟨a second cousin's child is a second cousin once ~⟩ **2 :** separate or remote in space, time, or character **syn** see DISTANT
re·mu·da \ri-'müd-ə\ *n* [AmerSp, relay of horses, fr. Sp, exchange] **:** the herd of horses from which are chosen those to be used for the day
re·mu·ner·ate \ri-'myü-nə-,rāt\ *vt* [L *remuneratus,* pp. of *remunerare* to recompense, fr. *re-* + *munerare* to give, fr. *muner-, munus* gift] **1 :** to pay an equivalent for **2 :** to pay an equivalent to for a service, loss, or expense **:** RECOMPENSE **syn** see PAY — **re·mu·ner·a·tor** \-,rāt-ər\ *n* — **re·mu·ner·a·to·ry** \ri-'myün-(ə-)rə-,tōr-ē, -,tȯr-\ *adj*
re·mu·ner·a·tion \ri-,myü-nə-'rā-shən\ *n* **1 :** an act or fact of remunerating **2 :** something that remunerates **:** RECOMPENSE
re·mu·ner·a·tive \ri-'myü-nə-,rāt-iv, -'myün-(ə-)rət-\ *adj* **1 :** serving to remunerate **2 :** affording remuneration **:** PROFITABLE — **re·mu·ner·a·tive·ly** *adv* — **re·mu·ner·a·tive·ness** *n*
Re·mus \'rē-məs\ *n* [L] **:** the twin brother of Romulus
re·nais·sance \,ren-ə-'sän(t)s, -'zän(t)s, -'sä^{n}s, -'zä^{n}s, *chiefly Brit* ri-'nās-ᵊn(t)s\ *n, often attrib* [F, fr. MF, rebirth, fr. *renaistre* to be born again, fr. L *renasci,* fr. *re-* + *nasci* to be born — more at NATION] **1** *cap* **a :** the transitional movement in Europe between medieval and modern times beginning in the 14th century in Italy, lasting into the 17th century, and marked by a humanistic revival of classical influence expressed in a flowering of the arts and literature and by the beginnings of modern science **b :** the period of the Renaissance **c :** the neoclassic style of architecture prevailing during the Renaissance **2** *cap* **:** a movement or period of vigorous artistic and intellectual activity **3 :** REBIRTH, REVIVAL
re·nal \'rēn-ᵊl\ *adj* [F or LL; F *rénal,* fr. LL *renalis,* fr. L *renes* kidneys] **:** relating to, involving, or located in the region of the kidneys **:** NEPHRITIC
re·na·scence \ri-'nas-ᵊn(t)s, -'nās-\ *n, often cap* **:** RENAISSANCE
re·na·scent \-ᵊnt\ *adj* [L *renascent-, renascens,* prp. of *renasci*] **:** rising again into being or vigor
ren·con·tre \rä^{n}-kō^{n}trᵊ, ren-'känt-ər\ *or* **ren·coun·ter** \ren-

See *re-* and 2d element remelt	remigrant remigrate	remigration remilitarization	remix remold	remonetization rename	renature

\'kaünt-ər\ *n* [*rencounter* fr. MF *rencontre*, fr. *rencontrer; rencontre* fr. F] **1 :** a hostile meeting or a contest between forces or individuals **:** COMBAT **2 :** a casual meeting

rencounter *vt* [MF *rencontrer* to meet by chance or in hostility, fr. *re-* + *encontrer* to encounter] **:** to meet casually

rend \'rend\ *vb* **rent** \'rent\ *also* **rend·ed; rend·ing** [ME *renden*, fr. OE *rendan;* akin to OFris *renda* to tear, Skt *randhra* hole] *vt* **1 :** to remove from place by violence **:** WREST **2 :** to split or tear apart or in pieces by violence **3 :** to tear (the hair or clothing) as a sign of anger, grief, or despair **4 a :** to lacerate with painful feelings **b :** to pierce with sound **c :** to divide (as a nation) into parties ~ *vi* **1 :** to perform an act of tearing or splitting **2 :** to become torn or split **syn** see TEAR

1**ren·der** \'ren-dər\ *vb* **ren·der·ing** \-d(ə-)riŋ\ [ME *rendren*, fr. MF *rendre* to give back, yield, fr. (assumed) VL *rendere*, alter. of L *reddere*, partly fr. *re-* + *dare* to give & partly fr. *re-* + *-dere* to put — more at DATE, DO] *vt* **1 a :** to melt down **:** TRY **b :** to treat so as to convert into industrial fats and oils or fertilizer **2 a :** to transmit to another **:** DELIVER **b :** to give up **:** YIELD **c :** to furnish for consideration, approval, or information: as (1) **:** to hand down (a legal judgment) (2) **:** to agree upon and report (a verdict) **3 a :** to give in return or retribution **b** (1) **:** to give back **:** RESTORE (2) **:** REFLECT, ECHO **c :** to give in acknowledgment of dependence or obligation **:** PAY **d :** to do (a service) for another **4 a** (1) **:** to cause to be or become **:** MAKE (2) **:** IMPART **b** (1) **:** to reproduce or represent by artistic or verbal means **:** DEPICT (2) **:** to give a performance of (3) **:** to produce a copy or version of (4) **:** to execute the motions of ⟨~ a salute⟩ **c :** TRANSLATE **5 :** to direct the execution of **:** ADMINISTER ⟨~ justice⟩ **6 :** to apply a coat of plaster or cement directly to ~ *vi* **:** to give recompense — **ren·der·able** \-d(ə-)rə-bəl\ *adj* — **ren·der·er** \-dər-ər\ *n*

2**render** *n* **:** a return esp. in kind or services due from a feudal tenant to his lord

1**ren·dez·vous** \'rän-di-ˌvü, -dā-\ *n, pl* **ren·dez·vous** \-ˌvüz\ [MF, fr. *rendez vous* present yourselves] **1 a :** a place appointed for assembling or meeting **b :** a place of popular resort **:** HAUNT **2 :** an appointed meeting

2**rendezvous** *vb* **ren·dez·voused** \-ˌvüd\ **ren·dez·vous·ing** \-ˌvü-iŋ\ **ren·dez·vouses** \-ˌvüz\ *vi* **:** to come together at a rendezvous ~ *vt* **:** to bring together at a rendezvous

ren·di·tion \ren-'dish-ən\ *n* [obs. F, fr. MF, alter. of *reddition*, fr. LL *reddition-*, *redditio*, fr. L *redditus*, pp. of *reddere*] **:** the act or result of rendering: as **a :** SURRENDER **b :** TRANSLATION **c :** PERFORMANCE, INTERPRETATION

ren·dzi·na \ren-'jē-nə\ *n* [Pol, rich limy soil] **:** a dark grayish brown intrazonal soil developed in grassy regions of high to moderate humidity from soft calcareous marl or chalk

1**ren·e·gade** \'ren-i-ˌgād\ *n* [Sp *renegado*, fr. ML *renegatus*, fr. pp. of *renegare* to deny, fr. L *re-* + *negare* to deny — more at NEGATE] **:** a deserter from one faith, cause, or allegiance to another

2**renegade** *vi* **:** to become a renegade

3**renegade** *adj* **:** TRAITOROUS, APOSTATE

ren·e·ga·do \ˌren-i-'gäd-(ˌ)ō, -'gād-\ *n* [Sp] **:** RENEGADE

re·nege \ri-'nig, -'neg, -'nēg, -'nāg\ *vb* [ML *renegare*] *vt* **:** DENY, RENOUNCE ~ *vi* **1** *obs* **:** to make a denial **2 :** to fail to follow suit when able in a card game in violation of the rules of the game **3 :** to go back on a promise or commitment — **re·neg·er** *n*

re·ne·go·tia·ble \ˌrē-ni-'gō-sh(ē-)ə-bəl\ *adj* **:** subject to renegotiation

re·ne·go·ti·ate \ˌrē-ni-'gō-shē-ˌāt\ *vt* **:** to negotiate again; *esp* **:** to readjust by negotiation to eliminate or recover excessive profits — **re·ne·go·ti·a·tion** \ˌrē-ni-ˌgō-s(h)ē-'ā-shən\ *n*

re·new \ri-'n(y)ü\ *vt* **1 :** to make new again; *also* **:** to gain again as new **2 :** to make new spiritually **:** REGENERATE **3 :** to restore to existence **:** REVIVE **4 :** to do again **:** REPEAT **5 :** to begin again **:** RESUME **6 :** REPLACE **7 :** to grant or obtain an extension of or on ~ *vi* **1 :** to become new or as new **2 :** to begin again **:** RESUME **3 :** to make a renewal — **re·new·abil·i·ty** \ri-ˌn(y)ü-ə-'bil-ət-ē\ *n* — **re·new·able** \ri-'n(y)ü-ə-bəl\ *adj* — **re·new·ably** \-blē\ *adv* — **re·new·er** *n*

syn RENEW, RESTORE, REFRESH, RENOVATE, REJUVENATE mean to make like new. RENEW implies esp. a replacing damaged or decayed parts; RESTORE implies a return to an original state after depletion or loss; REFRESH suggests a supplying of what restores lost animation or zest; RENOVATE implies a renewing or restoring of a material thing; REJUVENATE suggests the restoring of youthful vigor, powers, and appearance

re·new·al \ri-'n(y)ü-əl\ *n* **1 :** the act or process of renewing **:** REPETITION **2 :** the quality or state of being renewed **3 :** something renewed **4 :** something used for renewing; *specif* **:** an expenditure that betters existing fixed assets

reni- *or* **reno-** *comb form* [L *renes* kidneys] **:** kidney ⟨*reni*form⟩

re·ni·form \'ren-ə-ˌfȯrm, 'rē-nə-\ *adj* [NL *reniformis*, fr. *reni-* + *-formis* -form] **:** suggesting a kidney in outline

re·nig \ri-'nig\ *vi* **re·nigged; re·nig·ging :** RENEGE

re·nin \'rē-nən, 'ren-ən\ *n* [ISV, fr. L *renes*] **:** a proteolytic enzyme found in kidney

re·ni·ten·cy \'ren-ə-tən-sē, ri-'nīt-ᵊn-\ *n* **:** RESISTANCE, OPPOSITION

re·ni·tent \'ren-ə-tənt, ri-'nīt-ᵊnt\ *adj* [F or L; F *rénitent*, fr. L *renitent-*, *renitens*, prp. of *reniti* to struggle against, fr. *re-* + *niti* to strive — more at NISUS] **1 :** resisting pressure **2 :** resisting constraint or compulsion **:** RECALCITRANT

ren·net \'ren-ət\ *n* [ME, fr. (assumed) ME *rennen* to cause to coagulate, fr. OE *gerennan*, fr. *ge-* together + (assumed) OE *rennan* to cause to run; akin to OHG *rennen* to cause to run, OE *rinnan* to run — more at CO-, RUN] **1 a :** the contents of the stomach of an unweaned animal (as a calf) **b :** the lining membrane of a stomach (as the fourth of a ruminant) used for curdling milk; *also* **:** a preparation of the stomach of animals used for this purpose **2 a :** RENNIN **b :** a substitute for rennin

ren·nin \'ren-ən\ *n* **:** an enzyme that coagulates milk, is obtained from the mucous membrane of the stomach of calves, and is used in making cheese and junkets

re·nom·i·nate \(')rē-'näm-ə-ˌnāt\ *vt* **:** to nominate again esp. for a succeeding term — **re·nom·i·na·tion** \(ˌ)rē-ˌnäm-ə-'nā-shən\ *n*

1**re·nounce** \ri-'naün(t)s\ *vb* [ME *renouncen*, fr. MF *renoncer*, fr. L *renuntiare*, fr. *re-* + *nuntiare* to report, fr. *nuntius* messenger] *vt* **1 :** to give up, refuse, or resign usu. by formal declaration ⟨~ his errors⟩ **2 :** to refuse further to follow, obey, or recognize **:** REPUDIATE **3 :** to fail to follow with a card from (the suit led) ~ *vi* **:** to make a renounce or renunciation **syn** see ABDICATE, ABJURE — **re·nounce·ment** \-'naün(t)-smənt\ *n* — **re·nounc·er** *n*

2**re·nounce** \ri-'naün(t)s, 'rē-ˌ\ *n* **:** failure to follow suit in a card game

ren·o·vate \'ren-ə-ˌvāt\ *vt* [L *renovatus*, pp. of *renovare*, fr. *re-* + *novare* to make new, fr. *novus* new — more at NEW] **1 :** to restore to life, vigor, or activity **:** REVIVE **2 :** to restore to a former state **syn** see RENEW — **ren·o·va·tion** \ˌren-ə-'vā-shən\ *n* — **ren·o·va·tor** \'ren-ə-ˌvāt-ər\ *n*

1**re·nown** \ri-'naün\ *n* [ME, fr. MF *renon*, fr. OF, fr. *renomer* to celebrate, fr. *re-* + *nomer* to name, fr. L *nominare*, fr. *nomin-*, *nomen* name — more at NAME] **1 :** a state of being widely acclaimed and highly honored **:** FAME **2** *obs* **:** REPORT, RUMOR

2**renown** *vt* **:** to give renown to

re·nowned *adj* **:** having renown **:** CELEBRATED **syn** see FAMOUS

rens·se·laer·ite \ˌren(t)-sə-'li(ə)r-ˌīt, ren(t)-'sli(ə)r-; 'ren(t)-s(ə-)lə-ˌrīt\ *n* [Stephen Van *Rensselaer* †1839 Am army officer] **:** a soft compact talc often worked in a lathe into articles (as inkstands)

1**rent** \'rent\ *n* [ME *rente*, fr. OF, income from a property, fr. (assumed) VL *rendita*, fr. fem. of *renditus*, pp. of *rendere* to yield — more at RENDER] **1 :** property (as a house) rented or for rent **2 a :** a usu. fixed periodical return made by a tenant or occupant of property to the owner for the possession and use thereof; *esp* **:** an agreed sum paid at fixed intervals by a tenant to his landlord for the use of land or its appendages **b :** the amount paid by a hirer of personal property to the owner for the use thereof **3 a :** the portion of the income of an economy (as of a nation) attributable to land as a factor of production in addition to capital and labor **b :** ECONOMIC RENT

2**rent** *vt* **1 :** to take and hold under an agreement to pay rent **2 :** to grant the possession and enjoyment of for rent **:** LET ~ *vi* **1 :** to be for rent **2 a :** to obtain the possession and use of a place or article for rent **b :** to allow the possession and use of property for rent **syn** see HIRE — **rent·able** \-ə-bəl\ *adj*

3**rent** *past of* REND

4**rent** *n* [E dial. *rent* (to rend)] **1 :** an opening made by or as if by rending **2 :** a split in a party or organized group **:** SCHISM **3 :** an act or instance of rending

1**rent·al** \'rent-ᵊl\ *n* **1 :** an amount paid or collected as rent **2 :** a property rented **3 :** an act of renting **4 :** a business that rents something

2**rental** *adj* **1 :** of, relating to, or available for rent **2 :** dealing in rental property

rental library *n* **:** a commercially operated library (as in a store) that lends books at a fixed charge per book per day

rente \räⁿt\ *n* [F] **1 :** annual income under French law resembling an annuity **2 a :** interest payable by the French and other European governments on the consolidated debt **b :** a government security yielding rente

rent·er \'rent-ər\ *n* **:** one that rents; *specif* **:** the lessee or tenant of property

ren·tier \räⁿ-tyā\ *n* [F, fr. OF, fr. *rente*] **1 :** one who owns rentes **2 :** a person who receives a fixed income from investments

re·num·ber \(')rē-'nəm-bər\ *vt* **:** to number again or differently

re·nun·ci·a·tion \ri-ˌnən(t)-sē-'ā-shən\ *n* [ME, fr. L *renuntiation-*, *renuntiatio*, fr. *renuntiatus*, pp. of *renuntiare*] **:** the act or practice of renouncing **:** REPUDIATION; *specif* **:** ascetic self-denial — **re·nun·ci·a·tive** \ri-'nən(t)-sē-ˌāt-iv\ *adj* — **re·nun·ci·a·to·ry** \-sē-ə-ˌtōr-ē, -ˌtȯr-\ *adj*

re·open \(')rē-'ō-pən, -'ōp-ᵊm\ *vt* **1 :** to open again **2 a :** to take up again **:** RESUME **b :** to resume discussion or consideration of **3 :** to begin again ~ *vi* **:** to open again

1**re·or·der** \(')rē-'ȯrd-ər\ *vt* **1 :** REORGANIZE **2 :** to give a reorder for ~ *vi* **:** to place a reorder

2**reorder** *n* **:** an order like a previous order from the same supplier

re·or·ga·ni·za·tion \(ˌ)rē-ˌȯrg-(ə-)nə-'zā-shən\ *n* **:** the act of reorganizing **:** the state of being reorganized; *specif* **:** the financial reconstruction of a business concern

rep \'rep\ *n* [F *reps*, modif. of E *ribs*, pl. of *rib*] **:** a plain-weave fabric with prominent rounded crosswise ribs

re·pack·age \'rē-'pak-ij\ *vt* **:** to package again or anew; *specif* **:** to put into a more efficient or attractive form

1**re·pair** \ri-'pa(ə)r, -'pe(ə)r\ *vi* [ME *repairen*, fr. MF *repairier* to go back to one's country, fr. LL *repatriare*, fr. L *re-* + *patria* native country — more at EXPATRIATE] **1 a :** to betake oneself **:** GO **b :** RALLY **2** *obs* **:** RETURN

2**repair** *n* **1 :** the act of repairing **:** RESORT **2 :** a place of resort

3**repair** *vb* [ME *repairen*, fr. MF *reparer*, fr. L *reparare*, fr. *re-* + *parare* to prepare — more at PARE] *vt* **1 a :** to restore by replacing a part or putting together what is torn or broken **:** FIX **b :** to restore to a sound or healthy state **:** RENEW **2 :** to make good **:** REMEDY **3 :** to make up for **:** compensate for ~ *vi* **:** to make repairs **syn** see MEND — **re·pair·able** \-'par-ə-bəl, -'per-\ *adj* — **re·pair·er** \-ər\ *n* — **re·pair·man** \-'pa(ə)r-mən, -'pe(ə)r-, -ˌman\ *n*

4**repair** *n* **1 a :** the act or process of repairing **b :** an instance or result of repairing **c :** the replacement of destroyed cells or tissues by new formations **2 a :** relative condition with respect to soundness or need of repairing **b :** the state of being in good or sound condition

re·pand \ri-'pand\ *adj* [L *repandus* bent backward, fr. *re-* + *pandus* bent; akin to ON *fattr* bent backward] **:** having a slightly undulating margin ⟨a ~ leaf⟩

rep·a·ra·ble \'rep-(ə-)rə-bəl\ *adj* **:** capable of being repaired

rep·a·ra·tion \ˌrep-ə-'rā-shən\ *n* [ME, fr. MF, fr. LL *reparation-*, *reparatio*, fr. L *reparatus*, pp. of *reparare*] **1 a :** a repairing or keeping in repair **b** *pl* **:** REPAIRS **2 a :** the act of making amends, offering expiation, or giving satisfaction for a wrong or injury **b :** something done or given as amends or satisfaction **3 :** the payment of damages **:** INDEMNIFICATION; *specif* **:** compensation in money or materials payable by a defeated nation for damages to or expenditures sustained by another nation as a result of hostilities with the defeated nation — usu. used in pl.

See *re-* and 2d element **reoccupy** | **reoccurrence** **reordination** | **reorganize** **reorganizer** | **reorient** **reorientate** | **reorientation** **repack** | **repackage** **repaint**

re·par·a·tive \ri-'par-ət-iv\ *adj* **1 :** of, relating to, or effecting repair **2 :** serving to make amends
rep·ar·tee \ˌrep-ər-'tē, -ˌär-, -'tā\ *n* [F *repartie,* fr. *repartir* to retort, fr. MF, fr. *re-* + *partir* to divide — more at PART] **1 a :** a quick and witty reply **b :** a succession of clever retorts **2 :** adroitness and cleverness in reply **syn** see WIT
re·par·ti·tion *n* [prob. fr. Sp *repartición,* fr. *repartir* to distribute, fr. *re-* + *partir* to divide, fr. L *partire* — more at PART] **1** \ˌrep-ˌär-'tish-ən, ˌrē-ˌpär-\ **:** DISTRIBUTION **2** \ˌrē-ˌpär-\ **:** a second or additional partition
re·pass \(')rē-'pas\ *vb* [ME *repassen,* fr. MF *repasser,* fr. OF, fr. *re-* + *passer* to pass] *vi* **:** to pass again esp. in the opposite direction **:** RETURN ~ *vt* **1 :** to pass through, over, or by again **2 :** to cause to pass again **3 :** to adopt again — **re·pas·sage** \-'pas-ij\ *n*
[1]**re·past** \ri-'past, 'rē-ˌ\ *n* [ME, fr. MF, fr. OF, fr. *repaistre* to feed, fr. *re-* + *paistre* to feed, fr. L *pascere* — more at FOOD] **1 :** something taken as food **:** MEAL **2 :** the act or time of taking food
[2]**re·past** \ri-'past\ *vt, obs* **:** to supply food to **:** FEED ~ *vi* **:** to take food **:** FEAST
re·pa·tri·ate \(')rē-'pā-trē-ˌāt, -'pa-\ *vt* [LL *repatriatus,* pp. of *repatriare* to go back to one's country — more at REPAIR] **:** to restore or return to the country of origin, allegiance, or citizenship — **re·pa·tri·ate** \-trē-ət, -trē-ˌāt\ *n* — **re·pa·tri·a·tion** \(ˌ)rē-ˌpā-trē-'ā-shən, -ˌpa-\ *n*
re·pay \(')rē-'pā\ *vt* **1 a :** to pay back **:** REFUND **b :** to give or inflict in return or requital **2 :** to make a return payment to **:** COMPENSATE, REQUITE **3 :** to make requital for **:** RECOMPENSE ~ *vi* **:** to make return payment or requital **syn** see PAY — **re·pay·able** \-ə-bəl\ *adj* — **re·pay·ment** \-mənt\ *n*
re·peal \ri-'pē(ə)l\ *vt* [ME *repelen,* fr. MF *repeler,* fr. OF, fr. *re-* + *apeler* to appeal, call] **1 :** to rescind or annul by authoritative act; *esp* **:** to revoke or abrogate by legislative enactment **2 :** ABANDON, RENOUNCE **3** *obs* **:** to summon to return **:** RECALL — **repeal** *n* — **re·peal·able** \-'pē-lə-bəl\ *adj* — **re·peal·er** *n*
[1]**re·peat** \ri-'pēt\ *vb* [ME *repeten,* fr. MF *repeter,* fr. L *repetere,* fr. *re-* + *petere* to go to or toward — more at FEATHER] *vt* **1 a :** to say or state again **:** REITERATE **b :** to say over from memory **:** RECITE **c :** to say after another **2 a :** to make, do, or perform again **b :** to make appear again **c :** to go through or experience again **3 :** to express or present (oneself) again in the same words, terms, or form ~ *vi* **:** to say, do, or accomplish something again — **re·peat·able** \-ə-bəl\ *adj*
syn REPEAT, ITERATE, REITERATE mean to say or do again. REPEAT is the general term and may imply once or many times by the same agent or different agents; ITERATE and REITERATE stress exact repetition of something said; REITERATE may be stronger in implying manifold repetition
[2]**re·peat** \ri-'pēt, 'rē-ˌ\ *n* **1 :** the act of repeating **2 a :** something repeated **b** (1) **:** a musical passage to be repeated in performance (2) **:** a sign consisting typically of two vertical dots placed before and after a passage to be repeated **c :** a rebroadcast of a radio or television program
re·peat·ed \ri-'pēt-əd\ *adj* **1 :** renewed or recurring again and again **:** CONSTANT **2 :** said, done, or presented again — **re·peat·ed·ly** *adv*
re·peat·er \ri-'pēt-ər\ *n* **:** one that repeats: as **a :** one who relates or recites **b :** a watch or clock with a striking mechanism that upon pressure of a spring will indicate the time **c :** a firearm having a magazine that holds a number of cartridges loaded into the firing chamber automatically by the action of the piece **d :** an habitual violator of the laws **e :** a student enrolled in a class or course for a second or subsequent time
repeating decimal *n* **:** a decimal in which after a certain point a particular digit or sequence of digits repeats itself indefinitely
repeating firearm *n* **:** a firearm having a magazine or a revolving cylinder holding several rounds and an action that makes possible rapid firing of successive shots
re·pel \ri-'pel\ *vb* **re·pelled; re·pel·ling** [ME *repellen,* fr. L *repellere,* fr. *re-* + *pellere* to drive — more at FELT] *vt* **1 a :** to drive back **:** REPULSE **b :** to fight against **:** RESIST **2 :** to turn away **:** REJECT ⟨*repelled* the insinuation⟩ **3 a :** to drive away **:** DISCOURAGE **b :** to be incapable of adhering to, mixing with, taking up, or holding **c :** to force away or apart or tend to do so by mutual action at a distance **4 :** to cause aversion in **:** DISGUST ~ *vi* **:** to cause aversion — **re·pel·ler** *n*
re·pel·len·cy \ri-'pel-ən-sē\ *n* **:** the quality or capacity of repelling
[1]**re·pel·lent** \-ənt\ *adj* [L *repellent-, repellens,* prp. of *repellere*] **1 :** serving or tending to drive away or ward off **2 :** arousing aversion or disgust **:** REPULSIVE **syn** see REPUGNANT — **re·pel·lent·ly** *adv*
[2]**repellent** *n* **:** something that repels; *esp* **:** a substance employed to prevent insect attacks
[1]**re·pent** \ri-'pent\ *vb* [ME *repenten,* fr. OF *repentir,* fr. *re-* + *pentir* to be sorry, fr. L *paenitēre* — more at PENITENCE] *vi* **1 :** to turn from sin and dedicate oneself to the amendment of one's life **2 a :** to feel regret or contrition **b :** to change one's mind ~ *vt* **1 :** to cause to feel regret or contrition **2 :** to feel sorrow, regret, or contrition for — **re·pent·er** *n*
[2]**re·pent** \'rē-pənt\ *adj* [L *repent-, repens,* prp. of *repere* to creep — more at REPTILE] **:** CREEPING, PROSTRATE
re·pen·tance \ri-'pent-ᵊn(t)s\ *n* **:** the act or process of repenting **syn** see PENITENCE
re·pen·tant \-ᵊnt\ *adj* **1 :** experiencing repentance **:** PENITENT **2 :** expressing or showing repentance ⟨~ tears⟩ — **re·pen·tant·ly** *adv*
re·peo·ple \(')rē-'pē-pəl\ *vt* [MF *repeupler,* fr. OF *repuepler,* fr. *re-* + *puepler* to people] **1 :** to people anew **2 :** RESTOCK
re·per·cus·sion \ˌrē-pər-'kəsh-ən, ˌrep-ər-\ *n* [L *repercussion-, repercussio,* fr. *repercussus,* pp. of *repercutere* to drive back, fr. *re-* + *percutere* to beat — more at PERCUSSION] **1 :** REFLECTION, REVERBERATION **2 a :** a reciprocal action or effect **b :** a widespread, indirect, or unforeseen effect of an act, action, or event — **re·per·cus·sive** \-'kəs-iv\ *adj*
rep·er·toire \'rep-ə(r)-ˌtwär\ *n* [F *répertoire,* fr. LL *repertorium*] **1 a :** a list or supply of dramas, operas, pieces, or parts that a company or person is prepared to perform **b :** a supply of skills, devices, or expedients possessed by a person **2 a :** the complete list or supply of dramas, operas, or musical works available for performance **b :** the complete list or supply of skills, devices, or ingredients used in a particular field, occupation, or practice
rep·er·to·ry \'rep-ə(r)-ˌtōr-ē, -ˌtȯr-\ *n* [LL *repertorium* list, fr. L *repertus,* pp. of *reperire* to find, fr. *re-* + *parere* to produce — more at PARE] **1 :** a place where something may be found **:** REPOSITORY **2 a :** REPERTOIRE **b :** the practice of presenting several plays in succession or alternately in the same season
rep·e·tend \'rep-ə-ˌtend\ *n* [L *repetendus* to be repeated, gerundive of *repetere* to repeat] **:** a repeated sound, word, or phrase; *specif* **:** REFRAIN
rep·e·ti·tion \ˌrep-ə-'tish-ən\ *n* [L *repetition-, repetitio,* fr. *repetitus,* pp. of *repetere* to repeat] **1 a :** the act or an instance of repeating **b :** MENTION, RECITAL **2 :** the fact of being repeated
rep·e·ti·tious \-'tish-əs\ *adj* **:** marked by repetition; *esp* **:** tediously repeating — **rep·e·ti·tious·ly** *adv* — **rep·e·ti·tious·ness** *n*
re·pet·i·tive \ri-'pet-ət-iv\ *adj* **:** REPETITIOUS — **re·pet·i·tive·ly** *adv* — **re·pet·i·tive·ness** *n*
re·pine \ri-'pīn\ *vi* **1 :** to feel or express dejection or discontent **:** COMPLAIN **2 :** to wish discontentedly — **re·pin·er** *n*
re·place \ri-'plās\ *vt* **1 :** to restore to a former place or position **2 :** to take the place of **:** SUPPLANT **3 :** to fill the place of — **re·place·able** \-'plā-sə-bəl\ *adj* — **re·plac·er** *n*
syn DISPLACE, SUPPLANT SUPERSEDE: REPLACE implies a filling of a place once occupied by something lost, destroyed, or no longer usable or adequate; DISPLACE implies an ousting or dislodging preceding a replacing; SUPPLANT applies to taking the place of one forced out by craft or fraud; applied to things it implies the new and usu. more efficient displacing the old; SUPERSEDE implies replacing a person or thing that has become superannuated, obsolete, or otherwise inferior
re·place·ment \ri-'plā-smənt\ *n* **1 :** the act of replacing **:** the state of being replaced **:** SUBSTITUTION **2 :** something that replaces; *esp* **:** an individual assigned to a military unit to replace a loss or complete a quota
re·plant \(')rē-'plant\ *vt* **1 :** to plant again or anew **2 :** to provide with new plants
re·plead·er \(')rē-'plēd-ər\ *n* [*replead* (to plead again) + *-er* (as in *misnomer*)] **1 :** a second legal pleading **2 :** the right of pleading again granted usu. when the issue raised is immaterial or insufficient
re·plen·ish \ri-'plen-ish\ *vb* [ME *replenisshen,* fr. MF *repleniss-,* stem of *replenir* to fill, fr. OF, fr. *re-* + *plein* full, fr. L *plenus* — more at FULL] *vt* **1 a :** to fill with persons or animals **:** STOCK **b** *archaic* **:** to supply fully **:** PERFECT **c :** to fill with a source of inspiration or power **:** NOURISH **2 a :** to fill or build up again **b :** to make good **:** REPLACE ~ *vi* **:** to become full **:** fill up again — **re·plen·ish·er** *n* — **re·plen·ish·ment** \-ish-mənt\ *n*
re·plete \ri-'plēt\ *adj* [ME, fr. MF & L; MF *replet,* fr. L *repletus,* pp. of *replēre* to fill up, fr. *re-* + *plēre* to fill — more at FULL] **1 :** fully or abundantly provided **2 a :** FILLED **b :** abundantly fed **:** GORGED **c :** FAT, STOUT **3 :** COMPLETE **syn** see FULL — **re·plete·ness** *n*
re·ple·tion \ri-'plē-shən\ *n* **1 :** the act of eating to excess **:** the state of being fed to excess **:** SURFEIT **2 :** the condition of being filled up or overcrowded **3 :** fulfillment of a need or desire **:** SATISFACTION
re·plevi·able \ri-'plev-ē-ə-bəl\ *or* **re·plev·i·sa·ble** \-'plev-ə-sə-bəl\ *adj* **:** capable of being replevied
[1]**re·plev·in** \ri-'plev-ən\ *n* [ME, fr. AF *replevine,* fr. *replevir* to give security, fr. OF, fr. *re-* + *plevir* to pledge, fr. (assumed) LL *plebere*] **1 :** the recovery by a person of goods or chattels claimed to be wrongfully taken or detained upon the person's giving security to try the matter in court and return the goods if defeated in the action **2 :** the writ or the common-law action whereby goods and chattels are replevied
[2]**replevin** *vt* **:** REPLEVY
[1]**re·plevy** \ri-'plev-ē\ *n* [ME, fr. AF *replevir,* v.] **:** REPLEVIN
[2]**replevy** *vt* **re·plev·ied; re·plevy·ing :** to take or get back by a writ for replevin
rep·li·ca \'rep-li-kə\ *n* [It, repetition, fr. *replicare* to repeat, fr. LL, fr. L, to fold back — more at REPLY] **1 :** a close reproduction or facsimile esp. by the maker of the original **2 :** COPY, DUPLICATE **syn** see REPRODUCTION
[1]**rep·li·cate** \'rep-lə-ˌkāt\ *vt* [LL *replicatus,* pp. of *replicare*] **1 :** DUPLICATE, REPEAT **2** [L *replicatus*] **:** to fold or bend back ⟨*replicated* leaf⟩
[2]**rep·li·cate** \-li-kət\ *n* **:** one of several identical experiments, procedures, or samples
[3]**replicate** \-li-kət\ *adj* **1 :** folded over or backward **:** folded back upon itself **2 :** MANIFOLD, REPEATED
rep·li·ca·tion \ˌrep-lə-'kā-shən\ *n* **1 a :** ANSWER, REPLY **b** (1) **:** an answer to a reply **:** REJOINDER (2) **:** a plaintiff's reply to a defendant's plea, answer, or counterclaim **2 :** ECHO, REVERBERATION **3 a :** COPY, REPRODUCTION **b :** the act or process of reproducing **4 :** repetition of an experiment or procedure at the same time and place; *esp* **:** systematic or random repetition of agricultural test rows or plats to reduce error
re·pli·er \ri-'plī(-ə)r\ *n* **:** one that replies
[1]**re·ply** \ri-'plī\ *vb* **re·plied; re·ply·ing** [ME *replien,* fr. MF *replier* to fold again, fr. L *replicare* to fold back, fr. *re-* + *plicare* to fold — more at PLY] *vi* **1 a :** to respond in words or writing **b :** ECHO, RESOUND **c :** to make a legal replication **2 :** to do something in response; *specif* **:** to return an attack ~ *vt* **:** to give as an answer **syn** see ANSWER
[2]**reply** *n* **1 :** something said, written, or done in answer or response **2 :** REPLICATION 1b(2)
[1]**re·port** \ri-'pō(ə)rt, -'pȯ(ə)rt\ *n* [ME, fr. MF, fr. OF, fr. *reporter* to report, fr. L *reportare,* fr. *re-* + *portare* to carry — more at FARE] **1 a :** common talk or an account spread by common talk **:** RUMOR **b :** FAME, REPUTATION **2 a :** a usu. detailed account or statement **b :** an account or statement of a judicial opinion or decision **c :** a usu. formal record of the proceedings of a meeting or session **3 :** an explosive noise

See *re-* and 2d element | **rephotograph** | **rephrase** | **replay**

2report *vt* **1 a :** to give an account of **:** RELATE **b :** to describe as being in a specified state **2 a :** to serve as carrier of (a message) **b :** to relate the words or sense of (something said) **c :** to make a written record or summary of **d** (1) **:** to watch for and write about the newsworthy aspects or developments of **:** COVER (2) **:** to prepare or present an account of for broadcast **3 a** (1) **:** to give a formal or official account or statement of (2) **:** to return or present (a matter referred for consideration) with conclusions or recommendations **b :** to announce or relate as the result of investigation **c :** to announce the presence, arrival, or sighting of **d :** to make known to the authorities **e :** to make a charge of misconduct against ~ *vi* **1 a :** to give an account **:** TELL **b :** to present oneself **2 :** to make, issue, or submit a report **3 :** to act in the capacity of a reporter — **re·port·able** \-ˈpōrt-ə-bəl, -ˈpȯrt-\ *adj*

re·port·age \ri-ˈpōrt-ij, -ˈpȯrt-, *esp for 2* ˌrep-ər-ˈtäzh, ˌrep-ˌȯr-\ *n* **1 :** the act or process of reporting news **2 :** writing intended to give an account of observed or documented events

report card *n* **:** a report on a student that is periodically submitted by a school to the student's parents or guardian

re·port·ed·ly \ri-ˈpōrt-əd-lē, -ˈpȯrt-\ *adv* **:** according to report

re·port·er \ri-ˈpōrt-ər, -ˈpȯrt-\ *n* **:** one that reports: as **a :** one that makes authorized statements of law decisions or legislative proceedings **b :** one that makes a shorthand record of a speech or proceeding **c** (1) **:** one employed by a newspaper or magazine to gather and write news (2) **:** one that broadcasts news — **re·por·to·ri·al** \ˌrep-ə(r)-ˈtōr-ē-əl, ˌrēp-, -ˈtȯr-; -ˌōr-ˈtōr-, -ˌȯr-ˈtȯr-\ *adj* — **re·por·to·ri·al·ly** \-ē-ə-lē\ *adv*

report out *vt* **:** to return after consideration and often with revisions to a legislative body for action ⟨the committee after much debate *reported* the bill *out*⟩

report stage *n* **:** the stage in the British legislative process preceding the third reading and concerned esp. with amendments and details

re·pos·al \ri-ˈpō-zəl\ *n, obs* **:** the act of reposing

1re·pose \ri-ˈpōz\ *vt* [ME *reposen* to replace, fr. L *reponere* (perf. indic. *reposui*)] **1** *archaic* **:** to put away or set down **:** DEPOSIT **2 :** to place unquestioningly (as trust) **:** SET **3 :** to place for control, management, or use

2repose *vb* [ME *reposen*, fr. MF *reposer*, fr. OF, fr. LL *repausare*, fr. L *re-* + LL *pausare* to stop — more at PAUSE] *vt* **:** to lay at rest ~ *vi* **1 a :** to lie at rest **b :** to lie dead ⟨*reposing* in state⟩ **c :** to remain still or concealed **2 :** to take rest **3** *archaic* **:** RELY **4 :** to rest for support **:** LIE

3repose *n* **1 :** a state of resting after exertion or strain; *esp* **:** rest in sleep **2 a :** a place of rest **b :** CALM, PEACE **c :** a harmony in the disposition of parts and colors restful to the eye **3 :** cessation or absence of activity, movement, or animation **4 :** composure of manner **:** POISE

re·pose·ful \ri-ˈpōz-fəl\ *adj* **:** full of repose **:** QUIET **syn** see COMFORTABLE — **re·pose·ful·ly** \-fə-lē\ *adv* — **re·pose·ful·ness** *n*

re·pos·it *vt* **re·pos·it·ing** \-ˈpäz-ət-iŋ, -ˈpäz-tiŋ\ [L *repositus*, pp. of *reponere* to replace, fr. *re-* + *ponere* to place — more at POSITION] **1** \ri-ˈpäz-ət\ **:** DEPOSIT, STORE **2** \(ˈ)rē\ **:** to put back in place **:** REPLACE

1re·po·si·tion \ˌrē-pə-ˈzish-ən, ˌrep-ə-\ *n* **:** the act of repositing **:** the state of being reposited

2re·po·si·tion \ˌrē-pə-ˈzish-ən\ *vt* **:** to change the position of

1re·pos·i·to·ry \ri-ˈpäz-ə-ˌtōr-ē, -ˌtȯr-\ *n* **1 :** a place, room, or container where something is deposited or stored **:** DEPOSITORY **2 :** a side altar in a Roman Catholic church where the consecrated Host is reserved from Holy Thursday until Good Friday **3 :** one that contains or stores something nonmaterial **4 :** a place or region richly supplied with a natural resource **5 :** a person to whom something is confided or entrusted

2repository *adj, of a drug* **:** designed to act over a prolonged period

re·pos·sess \ˌrē-pə-ˈzes *also* -ˈses\ *vt* **1 a :** to regain possession of **b :** to resume possession of in default of the payment of installments due **2 :** to restore to possession — **re·pos·ses·sion** \-ˈzesh-ən *also* -ˈsesh-\ *n*

re·pous·sé \rə-ˌpü-ˈsā\ *adj* [F] **1 :** shaped or ornamented with patterns in relief made by hammering or pressing on the reverse side — used of metal **2 :** formed in relief

repp *var of* REP

rep·re·hend \ˌrep-ri-ˈhend\ *vt* [ME *reprehenden*, fr. L *reprehendere*, lit., to hold back, fr. *re-* + *prehendere* to grasp — more at PREHENSILE] **:** to voice disapproval of **:** CENSURE **syn** see CRITICIZE

rep·re·hen·si·ble \ˌrep-ri-ˈhen(t)-sə-bəl\ *adj* **:** worthy of or deserving reprehension **:** CULPABLE — **rep·re·hen·si·ble·ness** *n* — **rep·re·hen·si·bly** \-blē\ *adv*

rep·re·hen·sion \-ˈhen-chən\ *n* [ME *reprehensioun*, fr. MF or L; MF *reprehension*, fr. L *reprehension-*, *reprehensio*, fr. *reprehensus*, pp. of *reprehendere*] **:** the act of reprehending **:** REPROOF — **rep·re·hen·sive** \-ˈhen(t)-siv\ *adj*

rep·re·sent \ˌrep-ri-ˈzent\ *vb* [ME *representen*, fr. MF *representer*, fr. L *repraesentare*, fr. *re-* + *praesentare* to present] *vt* **1 :** to bring clearly before the mind **:** PRESENT **2 :** to serve as a sign or symbol of **3 :** to portray or exhibit in art **:** DEPICT **4 :** to serve as the counterpart or image of **:** TYPIFY **5 a :** to produce on the stage **b :** to act the part or role of **6 a** (1) **:** to take the place of in some respect (2) **:** to act in the place of or for usu. by legal right **b :** to serve esp. in a legislative body by delegated authority usu. resulting from election **7 :** to describe as having a specified character or quality **8 a :** to state to affect action or judgment **:** ADVOCATE **b :** to point out in protest or remonstrance **9 :** to serve as a specimen, example, or instance of **10 a :** to form an image or representation of in the mind **b** (1) **:** to apprehend (an object) by means of an idea (2) **:** to recall in memory **11 :** to correspond to in kind ~ *vi* **:** to make representations against something **:** PROTEST — **rep·re·sent·able** \-ə-bəl\ *adj* — **rep·re·sent·er** *n*

rep·re·sen·ta·tion \ˌrep-ri-ˌzen-ˈtā-shən, -zən-\ *n* **1 :** one that represents: as **a :** an artistic likeness or image **b** (1) **:** a statement or account esp. of an opinion and made to influence opinion or action (2) **:** an incidental or collateral statement of fact on the faith of which a contract is entered into **c :** a dramatic production or performance **d** (1) **:** a usu. formal statement made against something or to effect a change (2) **:** a usu. formal protest **2 :** the act or action of representing or state of being represented: as **a** (1) **:** the action or fact of one person standing for another so as to have rights and obligations of the person represented (2) **:** the substitution of an individual or class in place of a person (as a child for a deceased parent) **b :** the action of representing or the fact of being represented esp. in a legislative body **3 :** the body of persons representing a constituency — **rep·re·sen·ta·tion·al** \-shnəl, -shən-ᵊl\ *adj*

rep·re·sen·ta·tion·al·ism \-shnəl-ˌiz-əm, -shən-ᵊl-\ *n* **1 :** the doctrine that the immediate object of knowledge is an idea in the mind distinct from the external object which is the occasion of perception **2 :** the theory or practice of realistic representation in art — **rep·re·sen·ta·tion·al·ist** \-əst\ *n*

1rep·re·sen·ta·tive \ˌrep-ri-ˈzent-ət-iv\ *adj* **1 :** serving to represent **2 :** standing or acting for another esp. through delegated authority **3 :** of, based upon, or constituting a government in which the many are represented by persons chosen from among them usu. by election **4 :** of or relating to representation or representationalism — **rep·re·sen·ta·tive·ly** *adv* — **rep·re·sen·ta·tive·ness** *n*

2representative *n* **1 :** a typical example of a group, class, or quality **:** SPECIMEN **2 :** one that represents another or others: as **a** (1) **:** one that represents a constituency as a member of a legislative body (2) **:** a member of the house of representatives of the U.S. Congress or a state legislature **b :** one that represents another as agent, deputy, substitute, or delegate usu. being invested with the authority of the principal **c :** one that represents a business organization **d :** one that represents another as successor or heir

re·press \ri-ˈpres\ *vb* [ME *repressen*, fr. L *repressus*, pp. of *reprimere* to check, fr. *re-* + *premere* to press — more at PRESS] *vt* **1 :** to check by or as if by pressure **:** CURB **2 :** to hold in by self-control **3 :** to put down by force **:** SUBDUE **4 :** to prevent the natural or normal expression, activity, or development of **5 :** to exclude from consciousness ~ *vi* **:** to take repressive action — **re·pres·sive** \-ˈpres-iv\ *adj* — **re·pres·sive·ly** *adv* — **re·pres·sive·ness** *n* — **re·pres·sor** \-ˈpres-ər\ *n*

re·pressed *adj* **1 :** subjected to or marked by repression **2 :** characterized by restraint

re·pres·sion \ri-ˈpresh-ən\ *n* **1 a :** the act of repressing **:** the state of being repressed **b :** an instance of repressing **2 a :** a process by which unacceptable desires or impulses are excluded from consciousness and left to operate in the unconscious **b :** an item so excluded

re·priev·al \ri-ˈprē-vəl\ *n, archaic* **:** REPRIEVE

1re·prieve \ri-ˈprēv\ *vt* [perh. fr. MF *repris*, pp. of *reprendre* to take back] **1 :** to delay the punishment of (as a condemned prisoner) **:** RESPITE **2 :** to give relief or deliverance to for a time

2reprieve *n* **1 a :** the act of reprieving **:** the state of being reprieved **b :** a formal temporary suspension of the execution of a sentence esp. of death **2 :** an order or warrant for a reprieve **3 :** a temporary respite

1rep·ri·mand \ˈrep-rə-ˌmand\ *n* [F *réprimande*, fr. L *reprimenda*, fem. of *reprimendus*, gerundive of *reprimere* to check] **:** a severe or formal reproof

2reprimand *vt* **:** to censure formally **syn** see REPROVE

1re·print \(ˈ)rē-ˈprint\ *vt* **:** to print again — **re·print·er** *n*

2re·print \ˈrē-ˌprint\ *n* **1 :** a subsequent printing of a book already published having the identical text of the previous printing **2 :** OFFPRINT

re·pri·sal \ri-ˈprī-zəl\ *n* [ME *reprisail*, fr. MF *reprisaille*, fr. OIt *ripresaglia*, fr. *ripreso*, pp. of *riprendere* to take back, fr. *ri-* re- (fr. L *re-*) + *prendere* to take, fr. L *prehendere* — more at PREHENSILE] **1 a :** the act or practice in international law of resorting to force short of war to procure redress of grievances **b :** an instance of such action **2** *obs* **:** PRIZE **3 :** the regaining of something (as by recapture) **4 :** COMPENSATION — usu. used in pl. **5 :** a retaliatory act

1re·prise \ri-ˈprēz, *1 is also* -ˈprīz\ *n* [ME, fr. MF, lit., action of taking back, fr. OF, fr. *reprendre* to take back, fr. *re-* + *prendre* to take, fr. L *prehendere*] **1 :** a deduction or charge made yearly out of a manor or estate — usu. used in pl. **2 :** a recurrence, renewal, or resumption of an action **3 a** (1) **:** the repetition of the exposition preceding the development (2) **:** RECAPITULATION **b :** a repeated instance **:** REPETITION

2re·prise \ri-ˈprīz, *3 is* -ˈprēz\ *vt* [MF *reprise* action of taking back] **1** *archaic* **:** to take back; *esp* **:** to recover by force **2** *archaic* **:** COMPENSATE **3 :** to repeat the performance of ⟨~ a song⟩

re·pris·ti·nate \(ˈ)rē-ˈpris-tə-ˌnāt\ *vt* [*re-* + *pristine* + *-ate*] **:** to restore to an original state or condition — **re·pris·ti·na·tion** \(ˌ)rē-ˌpris-tə-ˈnā-shən\ *n*

re·pro \ˈrē-(ˌ)prō\ *n* [short for *reproduction*] **:** a clear sharp proof made esp. from a letterpress printing surface to serve as photographic copy for a printing plate

1re·proach \ri-ˈprōch\ *n* [ME *reproche*, fr. MF, fr. OF, fr., *reprochier* to reproach, fr. (assumed) VL *repropiare*, fr. L *re-* + *prope* near — more at APPROACH] **1 a :** a cause or occasion of blame, discredit, or disgrace **b :** DISCREDIT, DISGRACE **2 :** the act or action of reproaching **:** REBUKE **3** *obs* **:** one subjected to censure or scorn — **re·proach·ful** \-fəl\ *adj* — **re·proach·ful·ly** \-fə-lē\ *adv* — **re·proach·ful·ness** *n*

2reproach *vt* **1 :** to cast up to someone as deserving reproach **2 :** to utter a reproach to **:** REBUKE **3 :** to bring into discredit **4 :** to cast reproach on **syn** see REPROVE — **re·proach·able** \-ˈprō-chə-bəl\ *adj* — **re·proach·er** *n* — **re·proach·ing·ly** \-ˈprō-chiŋ-lē\ *adv*

rep·ro·bance \ˈrep-rə-bən(t)s\ *n, archaic* **:** REPROBATION

1rep·ro·bate \ˈrep-rə-ˌbāt\ *vt* [ME *reprobaten*, fr. LL *reprobatus*, pp. of *reprobare* — more at REPROVE] **1 :** to condemn as unworthy or evil **2 :** to foreordain to damnation **3 :** to refuse to accept **:** REJECT **syn** see CRITICIZE — **rep·ro·ba·tion** \ˌrep-rə-ˈbā-shən\ *n* — **rep·ro·ba·tive** \ˈrep-rə-ˌbāt-iv\ *adj* — **rep·ro·ba·to·ry** \-bə-ˌtōr-ē, -ˌtȯr-\ *adj*

2reprobate *adj* **1** *archaic* **:** rejected as not enduring proof or trial **:** CONDEMNED **2 a :** foreordained to damnation **b :** morally abandoned **:** DEPRAVED **3 :** expressing or involving reprobation **4 :** of, relating to, or characteristic of a reprobate **:** CORRUPT

3reprobate *n* **:** a reprobate person

re·pro·duce \ˌrē-prə-ˈd(y)üs\ *vt* **:** to produce again: as **a :** to

produce again by generation **b :** to cause to exist again or anew **c :** to cause to be or seem to be repeated **:** REPEAT **d :** to present again **e :** to make a representation of **f :** to revive mentally **g :** to translate (a recording) into sound ~ *vi* **1 :** to undergo reproduction **2 :** to produce offspring — **re·pro·duc·er** *n* — **re·pro·duc·ibil·i·ty** \-,d(y)ü-sə-'bil-ət-ē\ *n* — **re·pro·duc·ible** \-'d(y)ü-sə-bəl\ *adj*

re·pro·duc·tion \,rē-prə-'dək-shən\ *n* **1 :** the act or process of reproducing; *specif* **:** the process by which plants and animals give rise to offspring and which fundamentally consists of the segregation of a portion of the parental body by a sexual or an asexual process and its subsequent growth and differentiation into a new individual **2 :** something reproduced **:** COPY **3 :** young seedling trees in a forest

syn DUPLICATE, COPY, FACSIMILE, REPLICA: REPRODUCTION implies an exact or close imitation of an existing thing; DUPLICATE implies a double or counterpart exactly corresponding to another thing; COPY applies to one of a number of things reproduced mechanically as from the same type format, die, or mold; FACSIMILE suggests a close reproduction in the same materials that may differ in scale; REPLICA applies strictly to an exact reproduction of a work of art made by the same artist and not clearly distinguishable from the original

1re·pro·duc·tive \,rē-prə-'dək-tiv\ *adj* **:** relating to, capable of, or concerned with reproduction — **re·pro·duc·tive·ly** *adv* — **re·pro·duc·tive·ness** *n* — **re·pro·duc·tiv·i·ty** \,rē-prə-,dək-'tiv-ət-ē\ *n*

2reproductive *n* **:** an actual or potential parent; *specif* **:** a sexually functional social insect

re·prog·ra·phy \ri-'präg-rə-fē\ *n* [*repro*duction + *-graphy*] **:** facsimile reproduction (as by photocopying) of graphic matter

re·proof \ri-'prüf\ *n* [ME *reprof*, fr. MF *reprove*, fr. OF, fr. *reprover*] **:** censure for a fault **:** REBUKE

re·prove \ri-'prüv\ *vt* [ME *reproven*, fr. MF *reprover*, fr. LL *reprobare* to disapprove, condemn, fr. L *re-* + *probare* to test, approve — more at PROVE] **1 :** to administer a rebuke to **2 :** to express disapproval of **:** CENSURE, CONDEMN **3** *obs* **:** DISPROVE, REFUTE **4** *obs* **:** CONVINCE, CONVICT — **re·prov·er** *n* — **re·prov·ing·ly** \-'prü-viŋ-lē\ *adv*

syn REPROVE, REBUKE, REPRIMAND, ADMONISH, REPROACH, CHIDE mean to criticize adversely. REPROVE implies an often kindly intent to correct a fault; REBUKE suggests a sharp or stern reproof; REPRIMAND implies a severe, formal, often public or official rebuke; ADMONISH suggests earnest or friendly warning and counsel; REPROACH and CHIDE suggest displeasure or disappointment expressed in mild reproof or scolding

rep·tant \'rep-tənt\ *adj* [L *reptant-*, *reptans*, prp. of *reptare* to creep, fr. *reptus*] **:** CREEPING, REPENT

1rep·tile \'rep-tᵊl, -,tīl\ *n* [ME *reptil*, fr. MF or LL; MF *reptile* (fem.), fr. LL *reptile* (neut.), fr. neut. of *reptilis* reptant, fr. L *reptus*, pp. of *repere* to creep; akin to OHG *reba* tendril] **1 :** an animal that crawls or moves (as a snake) on its belly or (as a lizard) on small short legs **2 a :** any of a class (Reptilia) of air-breathing vertebrates including the alligators and crocodiles, lizards, snakes, turtles, and extinct related forms with a completely ossified skeleton including a single occipital condyle, a distinct quadrate bone usu. immovably articulated with the skull, ribs attached to the sternum, and a body usu. covered with scales or bony plates **b :** AMPHIBIAN **3 :** a groveling or despicable person

2reptile *adj* **:** characteristic of a reptile **:** REPTILIAN

1rep·til·ian \rep-'til-ē-ən, -'til-yən\ *adj* **1 :** resembling or having the characteristics of the reptiles **2 :** of or relating to the reptiles

2reptilian *n* **:** REPTILE 2a

re·pub·lic \ri-'pəb-lik\ *n* [F *république*, fr. MF *republique*, fr. L *respublica*, fr. *res* thing, wealth + *publica*, fem. of *publicus* public — more at REAL, PUBLIC] **1 a** (1) **:** a government having a chief of state who is not a monarch and who in modern times is usu. a president (2) **:** a nation or other political unit having such a form of government **b** (1) **:** a government in which supreme power resides in a body of citizens entitled to vote and is exercised by elected officers and representatives responsible to them and governing according to law (2) **:** a nation or other political unit having such a form of government **c :** a usu. specified republican government of a political unit ⟨the French Fourth *Republic*⟩ **2 :** a body of persons freely engaged in a specified activity **3 :** a constituent political and territorial unit of the U.S.S.R. or Yugoslavia

1re·pub·li·can \ri-'pəb-li-kən\ *adj* **1 a :** of, relating to, or having the characteristics of a republic **b :** favoring, supporting, or advocating a republic **c :** belonging or appropriate to one living in or supporting a republic ⟨~ simplicity⟩ **2** *cap* **a :** of, relating to, or constituting the Democratic-Republican party **b :** of, relating to, or constituting one of the two major political parties in the U.S. evolving in the mid-19th century and usu. associated with business, financial, and some agricultural interests and with favoring a restricted governmental role in social and economic life

2republican *n* **1 :** one that favors or supports a republican form of government **2** *cap* **a :** a member of a political party advocating republicanism **b :** a member of the Democratic-Republican party or of the Republican party of the U.S.

re·pub·li·can·ism \-kə-,niz-əm\ *n* **1 :** adherence to or sympathy for a republican form of government **2 :** the principles or theory of republican government **3** *cap* **a :** the principles, policy, or practices of the Republican party of the U.S. **b :** the Republican party or its members

re·pub·li·can·ize \-kə-,nīz\ *vt* **:** to make republican in character, form, or principle

re·pub·li·ca·tion \(,)rē-,pəb-lə-'kā-shən\ *n* **1 :** the act or action of republishing **:** the state of being republished **2 :** something republished

re·pub·lish \(')rē-'pəb-lish\ *vt* **1 :** to publish again or anew **2 :** to execute (a will) anew — **re·pub·lish·er** *n*

re·pu·di·ate \ri-'pyüd-ē-,āt\ *vt* [L *repudiatus*, pp. of *repudiare*, fr. *repudium* divorce] **1 :** to divorce or separate formally from (a woman) **2 :** to refuse to have anything to do with **:** DISOWN **3 a :** to refuse to accept; *esp* **:** to reject as unauthorized or as having no binding force **b :** to reject as untrue or unjust ⟨~ a charge⟩ **4 :** to refuse to acknowledge or pay **syn** see DECLINE — **re·pu·di·a·tor** \-,āt-ər\ *n*

re·pu·di·a·tion \ri-,pyüd-ē-'ā-shən\ *n* **:** the action of repudiating **:** the state of being repudiated; *esp* **:** the refusal of public authorities to acknowledge or pay a debt — **re·pu·di·a·tion·ist** \-sh(ə-)nəst\ *n*

re·pugn \ri-'pyün\ *vb* [ME *repugnen*, fr. MF & L; MF *repugner*, fr. L *repugnare*] *vi*, *archaic* **:** to offer opposition, objection, or resistance ~ *vt* **:** to contend against **:** OPPOSE

re·pug·nance \ri-'pəg-nən(t)s\ *also* **re·pug·nan·cy** \-nən-sē\ *n* **1 a :** the quality or fact of being opposed and esp. reciprocally opposed **b :** an instance of such opposition **2 :** strong dislike, distaste, or antagonism

re·pug·nant \-nənt\ *adj* [ME, opposed, contradictory, incompatible, fr. MF, fr. L *repugnant-*, *repugnans*, prp. of *repugnare* to fight against, fr. *re-* + *pugnare* to fight — more at PUNGENT] **1 :** marked by repugnance **2** *archaic* **:** HOSTILE **3 :** exciting distaste or aversion — **re·pug·nant·ly** *adv*

syn REPELLENT, ABHORRENT, DISTASTEFUL, OBNOXIOUS, INVIDIOUS: REPUGNANT implies being alien to one's ideas, principles, or tastes and arousing resistance or loathing; REPELLENT suggests a generally forbidding or unlovely quality that causes one to back away; ABHORRENT implies a repugnance causing active antagonism; DISTASTEFUL implies a contrariness to one's tastes or inclinations that causes shrinking or reluctance to accept or agree; OBNOXIOUS suggests an objectionableness too great to tolerate; INVIDIOUS applies to what cannot be used or performed without creating ill will, odium, or envy

1re·pulse \ri-'pəls\ *vt* [L *repulsus*, pp. of *repellere* to repel] **1 :** to drive or beat back **:** REPEL **2 :** to repel by discourtesy, coldness, or denial **:** REBUFF **3 :** to cause repulsion in **:** DISGUST

2repulse *n* **1 :** REBUFF, REJECTION **2 :** the action of repelling an attacker **:** the fact of being repelled

re·pul·sion \ri-'pəl-shən\ *n* **1 :** the action of repulsing **:** the state of being repulsed **2 :** the action of repelling **:** the force with which bodies, particles, or like forces repel one another **3 :** a feeling of aversion **:** REPUGNANCE

re·pul·sive \ri-'pəl-siv\ *adj* **1 :** tending to repel or reject **:** FORBIDDING **2 :** serving to repulse **3 :** arousing aversion or disgust — **re·pul·sive·ly** *adv* — **re·pul·sive·ness** *n*

rep·u·ta·bil·i·ty \,rep-yət-ə-'bil-ət-ē\ *n* **:** the quality or state of being reputable

rep·u·ta·ble \'rep-yət-ə-bəl\ *adj* **1 :** enjoying good repute **:** ESTIMABLE **2 :** employed widely or sanctioned by good writers — **rep·u·ta·bly** \-blē\ *adv*

rep·u·ta·tion \,rep-yə-'tā-shən\ *n* **1 :** the fact of being highly esteemed **2 :** the character commonly imputed to one as distinct from real character **3 :** the honor or credit belonging to one **4 :** a particular character in popular estimation **syn** see FAME

1re·pute \ri-'pyüt\ *vt* [ME *reputen*, fr. MF *reputer*, fr. L *reputare* to reckon up, think over, fr. *re-* + *putare* to reckon — more at PAVE] **:** to hold in thought **:** ACCOUNT

2repute *n* **1 :** the character or status commonly ascribed to one **2 :** the state of being favorably known, spoken of, or esteemed

re·put·ed *adj* **1 :** having a good repute **:** REPUTABLE **2 :** according to reputation or popular belief **:** SUPPOSED — **re·put·ed·ly** *adv*

1re·quest \ri-'kwest\ *n* [ME *requeste*, fr. MF, fr. (assumed) VL *requaesta*, fr. fem. of *requaestus*, pp. of *requaerere* to require] **1 :** the act or an instance of asking for something **2 :** a thing asked for **3 :** the condition or fact of being requested **4 :** the state of being sought after **:** DEMAND

2request *vt* **1 :** to make a request to or of **2 :** to ask as a favor or privilege **3** *obs* **:** to ask to come or go to something or someplace **4 :** to ask for **syn** see ASK — **re·quest·er** *n*

re·qui·em \'rek-wē-əm *also* 'räk-, 'rēk-\ *n* [ME, fr. L (first word of the introit of the requiem mass), accus. of *requies* rest, fr. *re-* + *quies* quiet, rest — more at WHILE] **1 :** a mass for the repose of one or more departed souls commonly sung at funerals and on All Souls' Day **2 :** a dirge or other solemn chant for the repose of the dead **3** *cap* **a :** a musical setting of the mass for the dead **b :** a musical composition in honor of the dead

re·qui·es·cat \,rek-wē-'es-,kät, -,kat; ,rā-kwē-'es-,kät\ *n* [L, may he (or she) rest, fr. *requiescere* to rest, fr. *re-* + *quiescere* to be quiet, fr. *quies*] **:** a prayer for the repose of a dead person

re·quin \rə-'kan\ *n* [F] **:** a voracious shark (family Carcharhinidae)

re·quire \ri-'kwī(ə)r\ *vb* [ME *requeren*, fr. MF *requerre*, fr. (assumed) VL *requaerere* to seek for, need, require, alter. of L *requirere*, fr. *re-* + *quaerere* to seek, ask] *vt* **1 a :** to claim by right and authority **:** DEMAND **b** *archaic* **:** REQUEST **2 a :** to call for as suitable or appropriate **b :** to demand as necessary or essential **:** NEED, WANT **3 :** to impose a compulsion or command on **:** COMPEL **4 :** to feel or be constrained — used with a following infinitive ~ *vi*, *archaic* **:** ASK **syn** see DEMAND, LACK

re·quire·ment \-mənt\ *n* **:** something required: **a :** something wanted or needed **:** NECESSITY **b :** an essential requisite **:** CONDITION

req·ui·site \'rek-wə-zət\ *adj* [ME, fr. L *requisitus*, pp. of *requirere*] **:** ESSENTIAL, NECESSARY — **requisite** *n* — **req·ui·site·ness** *n*

req·ui·si·tion \,rek-wə-'zish-ən\ *n* [MF or ML; MF, fr. ML *requisition-*, *requisitio*, fr. L, act of searching, fr. *requisitus*] **1 a** *archaic* **:** the act of requiring **b** *archaic* **:** REQUEST, DEMAND **2 a :** the act of formally requiring or calling upon someone to perform an action **b :** a formal demand made by one nation upon another for the surrender or extradition of a fugitive from justice **3 a :** the act of requiring something to be furnished **b :** a demand or application made usu. with authority: as (1) **:** a demand made by military authorities upon civilians for supplies or other needs (2) **:** a written request for something authorized but not made available automatically **4 :** the state of being in demand or use — **requisition** *vt*

re·quit·al \ri-'kwīt-ᵊl\ *n* **1 :** the act or action of requiting **:** the state of being requited **2 :** something given in requital

re·quite \ri-'kwīt\ *vt* [*re-* + obs. *quite* (to quit, pay), fr. ME *quiten* — more at QUIT] **1 a :** to make return for **:** REPAY **b :** to make retaliation for **:** AVENGE **2 :** to make return to for a benefit or service or for an injury — **re·quit·er** *n*

re·ra·di·a·tion \(,)rē-,rād-ē-'ā-shən\ *n* **:** radiation emitted by a

See *re-* and 2d element | **repurchase** | **reradiate** | **reread** | **rerecord**

ə abut; ᵊ kitten; ər further; a back; ā bake; ä cot, cart; aù out; ch chin; e less; ē easy; g gift; i trip; ī life
j joke; ŋ sing; ō flow; ȯ flaw; ȯi coin; th thin; th this; ü loot; ù foot; y yet; yü few; yù furious; zh vision

body or system as a result of its absorbing radiation incident on it
re·re·dos \'rer-ə-,däs *also* 'rir-ə-,däs, 'ri(ə)r-,däs\ *n* [ME, fr. AF *areredos*, fr. MF *arrere* behind + *dos* back, fr. L *dorsum* — more at ARREAR] **1** : a usu. ornamental wood or stone screen or partition wall behind an altar **2** : the back of a fireplace or open hearth
rere·mouse \'ri(ə)r-,maùs\ *n* [ME *reremous*, fr. OE *hrēremūs*, prob. fr. *hrēran* to stir + *mūs* mouse] *chiefly dial* : BAT
[1]**re·run** \(')rē-'rən\ *vt* : to run again or anew
[2]**re·run** \'rē-,rən, (')rē-'\ *n* : the act or action or an instance of rerunning; *esp* : presentation of a motion picture or television film after its first run
res \'rās, 'rēz\ *n, pl* **res** [L — more at REAL] : a particular thing : MATTER — used esp. in legal phrases
res ad·ju·di·ca·ta \,rā-sə-,jüd-i-'kät-ə\ *n* [LL] : RES JUDICATA
re·sail \(')rē-'sā(ə)l\ *vi* : to sail back or again
re·sal·able \(')rē-'sā-lə-bəl\ *adj* : fit for resale
re·sale \'rē-,sāl, (')rē-'sā(ə)l\ *n* **1** : the act of selling again usu. to a new party **2** : a second sale
re·scale \(')rē-'skā(ə)l\ *vt* : to plan, establish, or formulate on a new and usu. smaller scale
re·scind \ri-'sind\ *vt* [L *rescindere* to annul, fr. *re-* + *scindere* to cut — more at SHED] **1** : to take away : REMOVE **2 a** : ANNUL, CANCEL **b** : to abrogate (a contract) by restoration of preexisting conditions **3** : to make void (as an act) by action of the enacting or a superior authority : REPEAL — **re·scind·er** *n*
re·scis·sion \ri-'sizh-ən\ *n* [LL *rescission-*, *rescissio*, fr. L *rescissus*, pp. of *rescindere*] : an act of rescinding
re·scis·so·ry \-'siz-ə-rē, -'sis-\ *adj* : relating or tending to or having the effect of rescission
re·script \'rē-,skript\ *n* [L *rescriptum*, fr. neut. of *rescriptus*, pp. of *rescribere* to write in reply, fr. *re-* + *scribere* to write — more at SCRIBE] **1** : a written answer of a Roman emperor or of a pope to a legal inquiry or petition **2** : an official or authoritative order, decree, edict, or announcement **3** : an act or instance of rewriting
res·cue \'res-(,)kyü\ *vt* [ME *rescuen*, fr. MF *rescourre*, fr. OF, fr. *re-* + *escourre* to shake out, fr. L *excutere*, fr. *ex-* + *quatere* to shake — more at QUASH] **1 a** : to free from confinement, danger, or evil : SAVE, DELIVER **b** : to take (as a prisoner) forcibly from legal custody **2 a** : to recover (as a prize) by force **b** : to deliver (as a place besieged) by force of arms — **rescue** *n* — **res·cu·er** *n*
syn DELIVER, REDEEM, RANSOM, RECLAIM, SAVE: RESCUE implies freeing from imminent danger by prompt or vigorous action; DELIVER implies release usu. of a person from confinement, temptation, slavery, suffering; REDEEM implies releasing from bondage or penalties by giving what is demanded or necessary; RANSOM specifically applies to buying out of captivity; RECLAIM suggests a bringing back to a former state or condition someone or something abandoned or debased; SAVE may replace any of the foregoing terms; it may further imply a preserving or maintaining for usefulness or continued existence
rescue mission *n* : a city religious mission seeking to convert and rehabilitate human derelicts
re·search \ri-'sərch, 'rē-,\ *n* [MF *recerche*, fr. *recerchier* to investigate thoroughly, fr. OF, fr. *re-* + *cerchier* to search — more at SEARCH] **1** : careful or diligent search **2** : studious inquiry or examination; *esp* : investigation or experimentation aimed at the discovery and interpretation of facts, revision of accepted theories or laws in the light of new facts, or practical application of such new or revised theories or laws — **research** *vb* — **re·search·er** *n*
re·search·ist \-'sər-chəst, -,sər-\ *n* : one engaged in research
re·seau \rā-'zō, rə-\ *n, pl* **re·seaux** \-'zōz\ [F *réseau*, fr. OF *resel*, dim. of *rais* net, fr. L *retis*, *rete* — more at RETINA] **1** : a system of lines forming small squares of standard size photographed by a separate exposure on the same plate with star images to facilitate measurements **2** : a net ground or foundation in lace **3** : a screen with minute elements of three colors in a regular geometric pattern used for taking color photographs
re·sect \ri-'sekt\ *vt* [L *resectus*, pp. of *resecare* to cut off, fr. *re-* + *secare* to cut — more at SAW] : to perform resection on — **re·sect·abil·i·ty** \ri-,sek-tə-'bil-ət-ē\ *n* — **re·sect·able** \ri-'sek-tə-bəl\ *adj*
re·sec·tion \ri-'sek-shən\ *n* : the surgical removal of part of an organ or structure
re·se·da *n* [NL, genus name, fr. L, a plant used to reduce tumors] **1** \ri-'sēd-ə\ : any of a genus (*Reseda*) of Old World herbs of the mignonette family having racemose flowers with cleft petals and numerous stamens **2** \'rā-zə-,dä\ : a variable color averaging a grayish green
re·seed \(')rē-'sēd\ *vt* **1** : to sow seed on again or anew **2** : to maintain (itself) by self-sown seed ~ *vi* : to maintain itself by self-sown seed
re·sem·blance \ri-'zem-blən(t)s\ *n* **1** : the quality or state of resembling : SIMILARITY; *also* : a point of likeness **2** : REPRESENTATION, IMAGE **3** *archaic* : characteristic appearance : SEMBLANCE **4** *obs* : PROBABILITY **syn** see LIKENESS
re·sem·blant \-blənt\ *adj* : marked by or showing resemblance
re·sem·ble \ri-'zem-bəl\ *vt* **re·sem·bling** \-b(ə-)liŋ\ [ME *resemblen*, fr. MF *resembler*, fr. OF, fr. *re-* + *sembler* to be like, seem, fr. L *similare* to copy, fr. *similis* like — more at SAME] **1** : to be like or similar to **2** *archaic* : to represent as like : COMPARE
re·send \(')rē-'send\ *vt* : to send again or back
re·sent \ri-'zent\ *vt* [F *ressentir* to be emotionally sensible of, fr. OF, fr. *re-* + *sentir* to feel, fr. L *sentire* — more at SENSE] : to feel, express, or exhibit indignant displeasure at
re·sent·ful \-fəl\ *adj* **1** : full of resentment : inclined to resent **2** : caused or marked by resentment — **re·sent·ful·ly** \-fə-lē\ *adv* — **re·sent·ful·ness** *n*
re·sent·ment \ri-'zent-mənt\ *n* : a feeling of indignant displeasure at something regarded as a wrong, insult, or injury : UMBRAGE **syn** see OFFENSE
re·ser·pine \ri-'sər-pən, -'zər-, -,pēn; 'res-ər-,pēn, 'rez-\ *n* [G *reserpin*, prob. irreg. fr. NL *Rauwolfia serpentina*, a species of rauwolfia] : a drug extracted esp. from the root of rauwolfias and used in the treatment of hypertension, mental diseases, and tension states
res·er·va·tion \,rez-ər-'vā-shən\ *n* **1** : an act of reserving something: as **a** (1) : the act or fact of a grantor's reserving some newly created thing out of the thing granted (2) : the right or interest so reserved **b** : the setting of limiting conditions or withholding from complete exposition **c** : an engaging in advance of an accommodation or service; *also* : a promise, guarantee, or record of such engagement **2** : something reserved: as **a** : a limiting condition **b** (1) : a tract of public land set aside (as for the use of Indians) (2) : an area in which hunting is not permitted; *esp* : one set aside as a secure breeding place
[1]**re·serve** \ri-'zərv\ *vt* [ME *reserven*, fr. MF *reserver*, fr. L *reservare*, lit., to keep back, fr. *re-* + *servare* to keep — more at CONSERVE] **1 a** : to keep in store for future or special use **b** (1) : to retain power of absolution of to oneself — used of a religious superior (2) : to set aside (part of the consecrated elements) at the Eucharist for future use **c** : to retain or hold over to a future time or place : DEFER **d** : to make legal reservation of **2** : to set or have set aside or apart **syn** see KEEP
[2]**reserve** *n, often attrib* **1** : something stored for future use : STOCK **2** : something reserved or set aside for a particular purpose, use, or reason: as **a** (1) : a military force withheld from action for later decisive use — usu. used in pl. (2) : forces not in the field but available (3) : the military forces of a country not part of the regular services; *also* : RESERVIST **b** : a tract set apart : RESERVATION **3** : an act of reserving : EXCEPTION **4 a** : restraint, closeness, or caution in one's words and bearing **b** : forbearance from making a full explanation, complete disclosure, or free expression of one's mind **5** : SECRET **6 a** : money or its equivalent kept in hand or set apart usu. to meet liabilities **b** : the liquid resources of a nation for meeting international payments **7** : the capacity of blood or bacteriological media to react with acid or alkali within predetermined usu. physiological limits of hydrogen-ion concentration **8** : SUBSTITUTE
reserve bank *n* : a central bank holding reserves of other banks
re·served \ri-'zərvd\ *adj* **1** : restrained in words and actions **2** : kept or set apart or aside for future or special use **syn** see SILENT — **re·serv·ed·ly** \-'zər-vəd-lē\ *adv* — **re·served·ness** \-'zər-vəd-nəs, -'zərv(d)-nəs\ *n*
reserved power *n* : a political power reserved by a constitution to the exclusive jurisdiction of a specified political authority
re·serv·ist \ri-'zər-vəst\ *n* : a member of a military reserve
res·er·voir \'rez-ə(r)v-,wär, -ə(r)v-,(w)ȯr, -ər-,vȯi\ *n* [F *réservoir*, fr. MF, fr. *reserver*] **1** : a place where something is kept in store: as **a** : an artificial lake where water is collected and kept in quantity for use **b** : a part of an apparatus in which a liquid is held **2** : an extra supply : RESERVE **3** : an organism in which a parasite that is pathogenic for some other species lives and multiplies without damaging its host; *also* : a noneconomic organism within which a pathogen of economic or medical importance flourishes
res ges·tae \'rās-'ges-,tī\ *n pl* [L] : things done; *esp* : the facts that form the environment of a litigated issue and are admissible in evidence
resh \'rāsh\ *n* [Heb *rēsh*] : the 20th letter of the Hebrew alphabet — symbol ר
re·shape \(')rē-'shāp\ *vt* : to give a new form or orientation to
re·ship \(')rē-'ship\ *vt* : to ship again; *specif* : to put on board a second time ~ *vi* : to embark on a ship again or anew — **re·ship·ment** \-mənt\ *n* — **re·ship·per** *n*
re·shuf·fle \(')rē-'shəf-əl\ *vt* **1** : to shuffle again **2** : to reorganize usu. by redistribution of existing elements — **reshuffle** *n*
re·side \ri-'zīd\ *vi* [ME *residen*, fr. MF or L; MF *resider*, fr. L *residēre* to sit back, remain, abide, fr. *re-* + *sedēre* to sit — more at SIT] **1 a** : to be in residence as the incumbent of a benefice or office **b** : to dwell permanently or continuously **2 a** : to be present as an element or quality **b** : to be vested as a right — **re·sid·er** *n*
res·i·dence \'rez-əd-ən(t)s, 'rez-dən(t)s, 'rez-ə-,den(t)s\ *n* **1 a** : the act or fact of dwelling in a place for some time **b** : the act or fact of living or regularly staying at or in some place for the discharge of a duty or the enjoyment of a benefit **2 a** (1) : the place where one actually lives as distinguished from his domicile or a place of temporary sojourn (2) : DOMICILE 2a **b** : the place where a corporation is actually or officially established **c** : the status of a legal resident **3 a** : DWELLING **b** : housing or a unit of housing provided for students **4 a** : the period or duration of abode in a place **b** : a period of active study, research, or teaching at a college or university
res·i·den·cy \'rez-əd-ən-sē, 'rez-dən-, 'rez-ə-,den(t)-\ *n* **1** : a usu. official place of residence **2** : a territorial unit in which a political resident exercises authority **3** : a period of advanced training in a medical specialty
[1]**res·i·dent** \'rez-əd-ənt, 'rez-dənt, 'rez-ə-,dent\ *adj* [ME, fr. L *resident-*, *residens*, prp. of *residēre*] **1 a** : RESIDING **b** : being in residence **2** : PRESENT, INHERENT **3** : not migratory
[2]**resident** *n* **1** : one who resides in a place **2** : a diplomatic agent residing at a foreign court or seat of government; *esp* : one exercising authority in a protected state as representative of the protecting power **3** : a physician serving a residency
resident commissioner *n* **1** : a nonvoting representative of a dependency in the U.S. House of Representatives **2** : a resident administrator in a British colony or possession
res·i·den·tial \,rez(-ə)-'den-chəl\ *adj* **1 a** : used as a residence or by residents **b** : providing living accommodations for students ⟨a ~ college⟩ **2** : restricted to or occupied by residences **3** : of or relating to residence or residences — **res·i·den·tial·ly** \-'dench-(ə-)lē\ *adv*
[1]**re·sid·u·al** \ri-'zij-(ə-)wəl, -'zij-əl\ *adj* [L *residuum* residue] **1** : of, relating to, or constituting a residue **2** : leaving a residue remaining effective for some time — **re·sid·u·al·ly** \-ē\ *adv*
[2]**residual** *n* **1** : REMAINDER, RESIDUUM: as **a** : the difference between results obtained by observation and by computation from a formula or between the mean of several observations and any one of them **b** : a residual product or substance **c** : an internal aftereffect of experience or activity that influences later behavior; *esp* : a disability remaining from a disease or operation **2** : a payment (as to an actor or writer) for each rerun after an initial showing (as of a TV tape)
residual power *n* : power held to remain at the disposal of a govern-

See *re-* and 2d element
reroll
reroller
resaw
resay
rescale
rescore
rescreen
reseal
reseat
resecrete
resegregation
resell
resensitize
reset
resettle
resettlement
resew
reshow

mental authority after an enumeration or delegation of specified powers to other authorities

re·sid·u·ary \ri-'zij-ə-,wer-ē, -'zij-ə-rē\ *adj* **:** of, relating to, consisting or disposing of, or constituting a residue ⟨~ clause⟩

res·i·due \'rez-ə-,d(y)ü\ *n* [ME, fr. MF *residu*, fr. L *residuum*, fr. neut. of *residuus* left over, fr. *residēre* to remain] **:** something that remains after a part is taken, separated, or designated **:** REMNANT, REMAINDER: as **a :** the part of a testator's estate remaining after the satisfaction of all debts, charges, allowances, and previous devises and bequests **b :** the remainder after subtracting a multiple of a modulus from an integer or a power of the integer **:** the second of two terms in a congruence ⟨2 and 7 are ~*s* of 12 modulo 5⟩ ⟨9 is a quadratic ~ of 7 modulo 5 since $7^2-8\times5=9$⟩

re·sid·u·um \ri-'zij-ə-wəm\ *n, pl* **re·sid·ua** \-wə\ [L] **:** something residual: as **a :** RESIDUE a **b :** a residual product (as from the distillation of crude petroleum)

re·sign \ri-'zīn\ *vb* [ME *resignen*, fr. MF *resigner*, fr. L *resignare*, lit., to unseal, cancel, fr. *re-* + *signare* to sign, seal — more at SIGN] *vt* **1 :** to give up deliberately; *specif* **:** to renounce by a formal act **2 :** RELEGATE, CONSIGN; *esp* **:** to give (oneself) over without resistance ~ *vi* **1 :** to give up one's office or position **:** QUIT **2 :** to accept something as inevitable **:** SUBMIT **syn** see ABDICATE, RELINQUISH — **re·sign·ed·ly** \-'zī-nəd-lē\ *adv* — **re·signed·ness** \-'zī-nəd-nəs, -'zīn(d)-nəs\ *n* — **re·sign·er** \-'zī-nər\ *n*

res·ig·na·tion \,rez-ig-'nā-shən\ *n* **1 a :** an act or instance of resigning something **:** SURRENDER **b :** a formal notification of relinquishment **2 :** the quality or state of being resigned **:** SUBMISSION

re·sile \ri-'zī(ə)l\ *vi* [LL & L; LL *resilire* to withdraw, fr. L, to recoil] **:** RECOIL, RETRACT; *esp* **:** to return to a prior position

re·sil·ience \ri-'zil-yən(t)s\ *n* **1 :** the capability of a strained body to recover its size and shape after deformation caused esp. by compressive stress **2 :** an ability to recover from or adjust easily to misfortune or change

re·sil·ien·cy \-yən-sē\ *n* **:** RESILIENCE

re·sil·ient \-yənt\ *adj* [L *resilient-*, *resiliens*, prp. of *resilire* to jump back, recoil, fr. *re-* + *salire* to leap — more at SALLY] **:** marked by resilience; *specif* **:** capable of withstanding shock without permanent deformation or rupture **syn** see ELASTIC — **re·sil·ient·ly** *adv*

1res·in \'rez-ᵊn\ *n* [ME, fr. MF *resine*, fr. L *resina*, fr. Gk *rhētinē* pine resin] **1 a :** any of various solid or semisolid amorphous fusible flammable natural organic substances that are usu. transparent or translucent and yellowish to brown, are formed esp. in plant secretions, are soluble in ether and other organic solvents but not in water, are electrical nonconductors, and are used chiefly in varnishes, printing inks, plastics, and sizes, and in medicine **b :** ROSIN **2 a :** any of a large class of synthetic products that have some of the physical properties of natural resins but are different chemically and are used chiefly as plastics **b :** any of various products made from a natural resin or a natural polymer — **res·in·ous** \'rez-ᵊn-əs, 'rez-nəs\ *adj*

2resin *vt* **res·in·ing** \'rez-ᵊn-iŋ, 'rez-niŋ\ **:** to treat with resin

res·in·ate \'rez-ᵊn-,āt\ *vt* **:** to impregnate or flavor with resin

resin canal *n* **:** a tubular intercellular space in gymnosperms and some angiosperms that is lined with epithelial cells which secrete resin — called also *resin duct*

re·sin·i·fy \re-'zin-ə-,fī\ *vt* **:** to convert into or treat with resin ~ *vi* **1 :** to change into resin **2 :** to form a gummy material

1res·in·oid \'rez-ᵊn-,ȯid\ *adj* **:** somewhat resinous

2resinoid *n* **1 :** a resinoid substance; *esp* **:** a thermosetting synthetic resin **2 :** GUM RESIN

1re·sist \ri-'zist\ *vb* [ME *resisten*, fr. MF or L; MF *resister*, fr. L *resistere*, fr. *re-* + *sistere* to take a stand; akin to L *stare* to stand — more at STAND] *vt* **1 :** to withstand the force or effect of **2 :** to exert oneself to counteract or defeat ~ *vi* **:** to exert force in opposition **syn** see OPPOSE — **re·sist·er** *n*

2resist *n* **:** something that resists or prevents a particular action

re·sis·tance \ri-'zis-tən(t)s\ *n* **1 a :** an act or instance of resisting **:** OPPOSITION **b :** a means of resisting **2 :** the ability to resist **3 :** an opposing or retarding force **4 a :** the opposition offered by a body or substance to the passage through it of a steady electric current **b :** a source of resistance **5** *often cap* **:** an underground organization of a conquered country engaging in sabotage and secret operations against occupation forces and collaborators

1re·sis·tant \-tənt\ *adj* **:** giving or capable of resistance

2resistant *n* **:** one who resists **:** RESISTER

re·sist·ibil·i·ty \ri-,zis-tə-'bil-ət-ē\ *n* **1 :** the quality or state of being resistible **2 :** the ability to resist

re·sist·ible \ri-'zis-tə-bəl\ *adj* **:** capable of being resisted

re·sis·tive \ri-'zis-tiv\ *adj* **:** marked by resistance — **re·sis·tive·ness** *n*

re·sis·tiv·i·ty \ri-,zis-'tiv-ət-ē, ,rē-\ *n* **1 :** capacity for resisting **:** RESISTANCE **2 :** the longitudinal electrical resistance of a uniform rod of unit length and unit cross-sectional area **:** the reciprocal of conductivity

re·sist·less \ri-'zis(t)-ləs\ *adj* **1 :** IRRESISTIBLE **2 :** offering no resistance — **re·sist·less·ly** *adv* — **re·sist·less·ness** *n*

re·sis·tor \ri-'zis-tər\ *n* **:** a device that has electrical resistance and is used in an electric circuit for protection, operation, or current control

res ju·di·ca·ta \,rās-,yüd-i-'kät-ə, ,rā-,shüd-; ,rās-,jüd-\ *n* [L] **:** a matter finally decided on its merits by a court having competent jurisdiction and not subject to litigation again between the same parties

reso·jet engine \,rez-ō-,jet-\ *n* [*resonance* + *jet* + *engine*] **:** a jet engine that consists of a continuously open air inlet, a diffuser, a combustion chamber, and an exhaust nozzle, has fuel admitted continuously, and has resonance established within the engine so that there is a pulsating thrust produced by the intermittent flow of hot gases

re·sol·u·ble \ri-'zäl-yə-bəl\ *adj* [LL *resolubilis*, fr. L *resolvere* to resolve] **:** SOLUBLE

1res·o·lute \'rez-ə-,lüt, -lət\ *adj* [L *resolutus*, pp. of *resolvere*] **1 :** marked by firm determination **:** RESOLVED **2 :** BOLD, STEADY **syn** see FAITHFUL — **res·o·lute·ly** \-,lüt-lē, -lət-; ,rez-ə-'lüt-\ *adv* — **res·o·lute·ness** \-,lüt-nəs, -lət-, -'lüt-\ *n*

2resolute *n* **:** one who is resolute

res·o·lu·tion \,rez-ə-'lü-shən\ *n* **1 :** the act or process of reducing to simpler form: as **a :** the act of analyzing a complex notion into simpler ones **b :** the act of answering **:** SOLVING **c :** the act of determining **2 :** the passing of a voice part from a dissonant to a consonant tone or the progression of a chord from dissonance to consonance **3 a :** the division of a prosodic element into its component parts **b :** the substitution in Greek or Latin prosody of two short syllables for a long syllable **4 :** the process or capability of making distinguishable the individual parts of an object, closely adjacent optical images, or sources of light **5 :** the subsidence of inflammation esp. in a lung **6 a :** something that is resolved **b :** firmness of resolve **7 :** a formal expression of opinion, will, or intent voted by an official body or assembled group **8 :** the point in a play or other work of literature at which the chief dramatic complication is worked out **syn** see COURAGE

re·solv·able \ri-'zäl-və-bəl, -'zȯl-\ *adj* **:** capable of being resolved

1re·solve \ri-'zälv, -'zȯlv\ *vb* [L *resolvere* to unloose, dissolve, fr. *re-* + *solvere* to loosen, release — more at SOLVE] *vt* **1** *obs* **:** DISSOLVE, MELT **2 a :** to break up **:** SEPARATE; *also* **:** to change by disintegration **b :** to reduce by analysis **c :** to distinguish between or make independently visible adjacent parts of **d :** to separate (a racemic compound or mixture) into the two components **3 :** to cause resolution of (as inflammation) **4 a :** to clear up **:** DISPEL ⟨~ doubts⟩ **b :** to find an answer to **c :** to find a mathematical solution of **5 :** to reach a decision about **6 a :** to declare or decide by a formal resolution and vote **b :** to change by resolution or formal vote **7 :** to make (as voice parts) progress from dissonance to consonance **8 :** to work out the resolution of (as a play) ~ *vi* **1 :** to become separated into component parts; *also* **:** to become reduced by dissolving or analysis **2 :** to form a resolution **:** DETERMINE **3 :** CONSULT, DELIBERATE **4 :** to progress from dissonance to consonance **syn** see ANALYZE, DECIDE — **re·solv·er** *n*

2resolve *n* **1 :** something resolved **:** DETERMINATION, RESOLUTION **2 :** fixity of purpose

1re·sol·vent \ri-'zäl-vənt, -'zȯl-\ *adj* [L *resolvent-*, *resolvens*, prp. of *resolvere*] **:** having power to resolve ⟨a ~ drug⟩

2resolvent *n* **1 :** an agent capable of dispersing or absorbing inflammatory or effused products **2 :** SOLVENT **3 :** a means of solving something

resolving power *n* **1 :** the ability of an optical system to form distinguishable images of objects separated by small angular distances **2 :** the ability of a photographic film or plate to reproduce the fine detail of an optical image

res·o·nance \'rez-ᵊn-ən(t)s, 'rez-nən(t)s\ *n* **1 a :** the quality or state of being resonant **b (1) :** a vibration of large amplitude in a mechanical or electrical system caused by a relatively small periodic stimulus of the same or nearly the same period as the natural vibration period of the system **(2) :** the state of adjustment that produces resonance in a mechanical or electrical system **2 a :** the intensification and enriching of a musical tone by supplementary vibration **b :** a quality imparted to voiced sounds by the resonance-chamber action of mouth and pharynx configurations and in some cases also of the nostrils **3 :** the sound elicited on percussion of the chest **4 :** a phenomenon that is shown by a molecule, ion, or radical to which two or more structures differing only in the distribution of electrons can be assigned and that gives rise to stabilization of the structure

res·o·nant \'rez-ᵊn-ənt, 'rez-nənt\ *adj* **1 :** continuing to sound **:** ECHOING **2 a :** inducing resonance **b :** relating to or exhibiting resonance **3 a :** intensified and enriched by resonance **b :** marked by grandiloquence — **resonant** *n* — **res·o·nant·ly** *adv*

res·o·nate \'rez-ᵊn-,āt\ *vb* [L *resonatus*, pp. of *resonare* to resound — more at RESOUND] *vi* **1 :** to produce or exhibit resonance **2 :** REECHO, RESOUND ~ *vt* **:** to subject to resonating

res·o·na·tor \-,āt-ər\ *n* **:** something that resounds or resonates: as **a :** a hollow metallic container for producing microwaves or a piezoelectric crystal put into oscillation by the oscillations of an outside source **b :** a device for increasing the resonance of a musical instrument

re·sorb \(')rē-'sȯ(ə)rb, -'zȯ(ə)rb\ *vb* [L *resorbēre*, fr. *re-* + *sorbēre* to suck up — more at ABSORB] *vt* **1 :** to swallow or suck in again **2 :** to lyse and assimilate something previously differentiated ~ *vi* **:** to undergo resorption

res·or·cin \rə-'zȯrs-ᵊn\ *n* [L *res*ina resin + ISV *orcin*] **:** RESORCINOL

res·or·cin·ol \-,ȯl, -,ōl\ *n* **:** a crystalline phenol $C_6H_4(OH)_2$ obtained from various resins or artificially and used in making dyes, pharmaceuticals, and resins

re·sorp·tion \(')rē-'sȯrp-shən, -'zȯrp-\ *n* [L *resorptus*, pp. of *resorbēre*] **:** the act or process of resorbing — **re·sorp·tive** \-tiv\ *adj*

1re·sort \ri-'zȯ(ə)rt\ *n* [ME, fr. MF, resource, recourse, fr. *resortir* rebound, resort, fr. OF, fr. *re-* + *sortir* to escape, sally] **1 a :** one who is looked to for help **:** REFUGE, RESOURCE **b :** RECOURSE **2 a :** frequent, habitual, or general visiting **b :** persons who frequent a place **:** THRONG **c (1) :** a frequently visited place **:** HAUNT **(2) :** a place providing recreation and entertainment esp. to vacationers **syn** see RESOURCE

2resort *vi* **1 :** to go esp. frequently or habitually **:** REPAIR **2 :** to have recourse

re·sort·er \ri-'zȯrt-ər\ *n* **:** a frequenter of resorts

re·sound \ri-'zaund *also* -'saund\ *vb* [ME *resounen*, fr. MF *resoner*, fr. L *resonare*, fr. *re-* + *sonare* to sound; akin to L *sonus* sound — more at SOUND] *vi* **1 :** to become filled with sound **:** REVERBERATE **2 a :** to sound loudly **b :** to produce a sonorous or echoing sound **3 :** to become renowned ~ *vt* **1 :** to extol loudly or widely **:** CELEBRATE **2 :** ECHO, REVERBERATE **3 :** to sound or utter in full resonant tones

re·sound·ing *adj* **1 :** RESONATING, RESONANT **2 a :** impressively sonorous ⟨~ name⟩ **b :** EMPHATIC, UNEQUIVOCAL ⟨a ~ success⟩ — **re·sound·ing·ly** \-'zaun-diŋ-lē *also* -'saun-\ *adv*

re·source \'rē-,sō(ə)rs, -,sȯ(ə)rs, -,zō(ə)rs, -,zȯ(ə)rs, ri-'\ *n* [F *ressource*, fr. OF *ressourse* relief, resource, fr. *resourdre* to relieve, lit., to rise again, fr. L *resurgere* — more at RESURRECTION] **1 a :** a

See *re-* and 2d element | resilver | resitting | resmooth

ə abut; ᵊ kitten; ər further; a back; ā bake; ä cot, cart; au̇ out; ch chin; e less; ē easy; g gift; i trip; ī life
j joke; ŋ sing; ō flow; ȯ flaw; ȯi coin; th thin; t͟h this; ü loot; u̇ foot; y yet; yü few; yu̇ furious; zh vision

new or a reserve source of supply or support **b** *pl* (1) **:** available means (2) **:** computable wealth (3) **:** immediate and possible sources of revenue **2 :** something to which one has recourse in difficulty **:** EXPEDIENT **3 :** a possibility of relief or recovery **4 :** a means of spending one's leisure time **5 :** an ability to meet and handle a situation — **re·source·ful** \-fəl\ *adj* — **re·source·ful·ly** \-fə-lē\ *adv* — **re·source·ful·ness** *n*

syn RESOURCE, RESORT, EXPEDIENT, SHIFT, MAKESHIFT, STOPGAP mean something one turns to in the absence of the usual means or source of supply. RESOURCE and RESORT apply to anything one falls back upon; EXPEDIENT may apply to any device or contrivance used when the usual one is not at hand or not possible; SHIFT implies a tentative or temporary imperfect expedient; MAKESHIFT implies an inferior expedient adopted because of urgent need or countenanced through indifference; STOPGAP applies to something used temporarily as an emergency measure

1**re·spect** \ri-'spekt\ *n* [ME, fr. L *respectus*, lit., act of looking back, fr. *respectus*, pp. of *respicere* to look back, regard, fr. *re-* + *specere* to look — more at SPY] **1 :** a relation to or concern with something usu. specified **:** REFERENCE **2 :** an act of giving particular attention **:** CONSIDERATION **3 a :** high or special regard **:** ESTEEM **b :** the quality or state of being esteemed **:** HONOR **c** *pl* **:** expressions of respect or deference **4 :** PARTICULAR, DETAIL — **re·spect·ful** \-'spek(t)-fəl\ *adj* — **re·spect·ful·ly** \-fə-lē\ *adv* — **re·spect·ful·ness** *n*

2**respect** *vt* **1 a :** to consider worthy of high regard **:** ESTEEM **b :** to refrain from interfering with ⟨~ one's privacy⟩ **2 :** to have reference to **:** CONCERN **syn** see REGARD — **re·spect·er** *n*

re·spect·abil·i·ty \ri-,spek-tə-'bil-ət-ē\ *n* **1 :** the quality or state of being respectable **2 a :** respectable persons **b :** a respectable convention

re·spect·able \ri-'spek-tə-bəl\ *adj* **1 :** worthy of respect **:** ESTIMABLE **2 :** decent or correct in character or behavior **:** PROPER **3 a :** fair in size or quantity ⟨~ amount⟩ **b :** moderately good **:** TOLERABLE **4 :** fit to be seen **:** PRESENTABLE ⟨~ clothes⟩ — **re·spect·able·ness** *n* — **re·spect·ably** \-blē\ *adv*

re·spect·ing *prep* **1 :** in view of **2 :** with regard to

re·spec·tive \ri-'spek-tiv\ *adj* **1 :** PARTIAL, DISCRIMINATIVE **2 :** PARTICULAR, SEVERAL ⟨their ~ homes⟩ **syn** see SPECIAL — **re·spec·tive·ness** *n*

re·spec·tive·ly *adv* **1 :** in a respective manner **2 :** each in the order given

re·spell \(')rē-'spel\ *vt* **:** to spell again or in another way; *esp* **:** to spell out according to a phonetic system

res·pi·ra·ble \'res-p(ə-)rə-bəl, ri-'spī-rə-\ *adj* **1 :** fit for breathing **2 :** capable of breathing

res·pi·ra·tion \,res-pə-'rā-shən\ *n* **1 a :** the placing of air or dissolved gases in intimate contact with the circulating medium of a multicellular organism (as by breathing) **b :** a single complete act of breathing **2 :** the physical and chemical processes by which an organism supplies its cells and tissues with the oxygen needed for metabolism and relieves them of the carbon dioxide formed in energy-producing reactions **3 :** any of various energy-yielding oxidative reactions in living matter — **res·pi·ra·tion·al** \-shnəl, -shən-ᵊl\ *adj* — **re·spi·ra·to·ry** \'res-p(ə-)rə-,tōr-ē, ri-'spī-rə-, 'res-pə-,tōr-, -,tȯr-\ *adj*

res·pi·ra·tor \'res-pə-,rāt-ər\ *n* **1 :** a device worn over the mouth or nose for protecting the respiratory tract **2 :** a device for maintaining artificial respiration

respiratory pigment *n* **:** any of various permanently or intermittently colored conjugated proteins that function in the transfer of oxygen in cellular respiration

respiratory quotient *n* **:** a ratio indicating the relation of the volume of carbon dioxide given off in respiration to that of the oxygen consumed

respiratory system *n* **:** a system of organs subserving the function of respiration and in air-breathing vertebrates consisting typically of the lungs and their nervous and circulatory supply and the channels by which these are continuous with the outer air

re·spire \ri-'spī(ə)r\ *vb* [ME *respiren*, fr. L *respirare*, fr. *re-* + *spirare* to blow, breathe — more at SPIRIT] *vi* **1 :** BREATHE; *specif* **:** to inhale and exhale air successively **2** *of a cell or tissue* **:** to take up oxygen and produce carbon dioxide through oxidation **~** *vt* **:** BREATHE

1**re·spite** \'res-pət *also* ri-'spīt, 'res-,pīt\ *n* [ME *respit*, fr. OF, fr. ML *respectus*, fr. L, act of looking back — more at RESPECT] **1 :** a temporary delay **:** POSTPONEMENT; *specif* **:** REPRIEVE 1b **2 :** an interval of rest or relief

2**respite** *vt* **1 :** to grant a respite to **2 :** to put off **:** DELAY

re·splen·dence \ri-'splen-dən(t)s\ *n* **:** the quality or state of being resplendent **:** SPLENDOR — **re·splen·den·cy** \-dən-sē\ *n*

re·splen·dent \-dənt\ *adj* [L *resplendent-*, *resplendens*, prp. of *resplendēre* to shine back, fr. *re-* + *splendēre* to shine — more at SPLENDID] **:** shining brilliantly **:** LUSTROUS **syn** see SPLENDID — **re·splen·dent·ly** *adv*

1**re·spond** \ri-'spänd\ *vb* [MF *respondre*, fr. L *respondēre* to promise in return, answer, fr. *re-* + *spondēre* to promise — more at SPOUSE] *vi* **1 :** to say something in return **:** make an answer **2 a :** to react in response **b :** to show favorable reaction ⟨~ to surgery⟩ **3 :** to be answerable ⟨~ in damages⟩ **~** *vt* **:** REPLY **syn** see ANSWER

2**respond** *n* **:** an engaged pillar supporting an arch or closing a colonnade or arcade

1**re·spon·dent** \ri-'spän-dənt\ *n* [L *respondent-*, *respondens*, prp. of *respondēre*] **:** one who responds: as **a :** one who maintains a thesis in reply **b** (1) **:** one who answers in various legal proceedings (as in equity cases) (2) **:** the prevailing party in the lower court — compare APPELLANT

2**respondent** *adj* **1** *obs* **:** serving to correspond **2 :** RESPONSIVE; *esp* **:** being a respondent at law

re·spond·er \ri-'spän-dər\ *n* **:** one that responds; *specif* **:** the part of a transponder that transmits a radio signal

re·sponse \ri-'spän(t)s\ *n* [ME & L; ME *respounse*, fr. MF *respons*, fr. L *responsum* reply, fr. neut. of *responsus*, pp. of *respondēre*] **1 :** an act of responding **2 :** something constituting a reply or a reaction: as **a :** the activity or inhibition of previous activity of an organism or any of its parts resulting from stimulation **b :** the output of a transducer or detecting device resulting from a given input

re·spon·si·bil·i·ty \ri-,spän(t)-sə-'bil-ət-ē\ *n* **1 :** the quality or state of being responsible: as **a :** moral, legal, or mental accountability **b :** RELIABILITY, TRUSTWORTHINESS **2 :** something for which one is responsible **:** BURDEN

re·spon·si·ble \-'spän(t)-sə-bəl\ *adj* **1 a :** liable to be called upon to answer as the primary cause, motive, or agent **b :** liable to legal review or in case of fault to penalties **2 a :** able to answer for one's conduct and obligations **:** TRUSTWORTHY **b :** being a free moral agent **3 :** involving responsibility or accountability **4 :** politically answerable; *esp* **:** required to submit to the electorate if defeated by the legislature — **re·spon·si·ble·ness** *n* — **re·spon·si·bly** \-blē\ *adv*

syn RESPONSIBLE, ANSWERABLE, ACCOUNTABLE, AMENABLE, LIABLE mean subject to an authority that may punish default. RESPONSIBLE implies holding a formal organizational role, duty, or trust; ANSWERABLE suggests a relation between one having a moral or legal obligation and a court or other authority charged with oversight of its observance; ACCOUNTABLE suggests imminence of retribution for unfulfilled trust or violated obligation; AMENABLE and LIABLE stress the fact of subjection to review, censure, or control by a designated authority under certain conditions

re·spon·sions \ri-'spän-chənz\ *n pl* **:** the first examination for the B.A. degree at Oxford University

re·spon·sive \ri-'spän(t)-siv\ *adj* **1 :** giving response **:** ANSWERING ⟨~ glance⟩ **2 :** quick to respond or react sympathetically **:** SENSITIVE **3 :** using responses ⟨~ worship⟩ — **re·spon·sive·ly** *adv* — **re·spon·sive·ness** *n*

re·spon·so·ry \-'spän(t)s-(ə-)rē\ *n* **:** a set of versicles and responses sung or said after or during a lection

res pu·bli·ca \(')rā-'spü-bli-,kä\ *n* [L — more at REPUBLIC] **:** COMMONWEAL, COMMONWEALTH, STATE, REPUBLIC

1**rest** \'rest\ *n* [ME, fr. OE; akin to OHG *rasta* rest, *ruowa* calm,

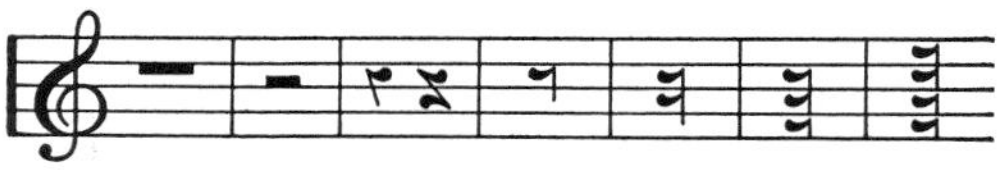

rests 5a(2)

Gk *erōē* respite] **1 :** REPOSE, SLEEP; *specif* **:** a bodily state characterized by minimal functional and metabolic activities **2 a :** freedom from activity **b :** a state of motionlessness or inactivity **c :** the repose of death **3 :** a place for resting or lodging **4 :** peace of mind or spirit **5 a** (1) **:** a rhythmic silence in music (2) **:** a character representing such a silence **b :** a brief pause in reading **6 :** something used for support **7 :** renewed vigor

2**rest** *vi* **1 a :** to get rest by lying down; *esp* **:** SLEEP **b :** to lie dead **2 :** to cease from action or motion **3 :** to be free from anxiety or disturbance **4 :** to sit or lie fixed or supported **5 a :** to remain confident **:** TRUST **b :** to remain based or founded **6 :** to remain for action or accomplishment ⟨the answer ~s with him⟩ **7** *of farmland* **:** to remain idle or uncropped **8 :** to bring to an end voluntarily the introduction of evidence in a law case **~** *vt* **1 :** to give rest to **2 :** to set at rest **3 :** to place on or against a support **:** LEAN **4 a :** to cause to be firmly fixed **:** GROUND **b :** to stop voluntarily from presenting evidence pertinent to (a case at law) — **rest·er** *n*

3**rest** *n* [ME *reste*, lit., stoppage, short for *areste*, fr. MF, fr. OF, fr. *arester* to arrest] **:** a projection or attachment on the side of the breastplate of medieval armor for supporting the butt of a lance

4**rest** *n* [ME, fr. MF *reste*, fr. *rester* to remain, fr. L *restare*, lit., to stand back, fr. *re-* + *stare* to stand — more at STAND] **:** something that remains over **:** REMAINDER

re·start \(')rē-'stärt\ *vt* **1 :** to start anew **2 :** RESUME **~** *vi* **:** to resume operation

re·state \(')rē-'stāt\ *vt* **:** to state again or in another way — **re·state·ment** \-mənt\ *n*

res·tau·rant \'res-t(ə-)rənt, -tə-,ränt, -,tränt, -tərnt\ *n* [F, fr. prp. of *restaurer* to restore, fr. L *restaurare*] **:** a public eating place

res·tau·ra·teur \,res-tə-rə-'tər\ *also* **res·tau·ran·teur** \-,rän-\ *n* [F *restaurateur*, fr. LL *restaurator* restorer, fr. L *restauratus*, pp. of *restaurare*] **:** the operator or proprietor of a restaurant

rest·ful \'rest-fəl\ *adj* **1 :** marked by, giving, or suggesting rest **2 :** being at rest **:** QUIET **syn** see COMFORTABLE — **rest·ful·ly** \-fə-lē\ *adv* — **rest·ful·ness** *n*

rest home *n* **:** SANATORIUM

rest house *n* **:** a building used for shelter by travelers

rest·ing *adj* **1 :** DORMANT, QUIESCENT ⟨a ~ spore⟩ **2 :** not undergoing or marked by division **:** VEGETATIVE ⟨a ~ nucleus⟩

res·ti·tute \'res-tə-,t(y)üt\ *vb* [L *restitutus*, pp.] *vt* **1 :** to restore to a former state or position **2 :** REFUND **~** *vi* **:** to undergo restitution

res·ti·tu·tion \,res-tə-'t(y)ü-shən\ *n* [ME, fr. OF, fr. L *restitution-*, *restitutio*, fr. *restitutus*, pp. of *restituere* to restore, fr. *re-* + *statuere* to set up — more at STATUTE] **1 :** an act of restoring or a condition of being restored: as **a :** a restoration of something to its rightful owner **b :** a making good of or giving an equivalent for some injury **2 :** a legal action serving to cause restoration of a previous state

res·tive \'res-tiv\ *adj* [ME, fr. MF, fr. *rester* to stop behind, remain] **1 :** stubbornly resisting control **:** BALKY **2 :** fidgeting about **:** UNEASY — **syn** see CONTRARY — **res·tive·ly** *adv* — **res·tive·ness** *n*

rest·less \'rest-ləs\ *adj* **1 :** lacking or giving no rest **:** UNEASY **2 :** continuously moving **:** UNQUIET **3 :** DESULTORY, DISCONTENTED — **rest·less·ly** *adv* — **rest·less·ness** *n*

rest mass *n* **:** the mass of a body exclusive of additional mass acquired by the body when in motion according to the theory of relativity

re·stor·able \ri-'stōr-ə-bəl, -'stȯr-\ *adj* **:** fit for restoring or reclaiming

res·to·ra·tion \,res-tə-'rā-shən\ *n* **1 :** an act of restoring or the condition of being restored: as **a :** a bringing back to a former position or condition **:** REINSTATEMENT **b :** RESTITUTION **c :** a restoring to an unimpaired or improved condition **d :** the replacing of missing teeth or crowns **2 :** something that is restored; *specif* **:** a representation or reconstruction of the original form (as of a fossil or a building) **3** *cap* **a :** the reestablishment of the monarchy in England in 1660 under Charles II **b :** the period in English

See *re-* and 2d element | **resow** | **respring** | **restaff** | **restage** | **restimulate** | **restock**

history usu. held to coincide with the reign of Charles II but sometimes to extend through the reign of James II

1**re·stor·ative** \ri-ˈstōr-ət-iv, -ˈstȯr-\ *adj* **:** of or relating to restoration; *esp* **:** having power to restore — **re·stor·ative·ly** *adv* — **re·stor·ative·ness** *n*

2**restorative** *n* **:** something that serves to restore to consciousness or health

re·store \ri-ˈstō(ə)r, -ˈstȯ(ə)r\ *vt* [ME *restoren*, fr. OF *restorer*, fr. L *restaurare* to renew, rebuild, alter. of *instaurare* to renew — more at STORE] **1 :** to give back **:** RETURN **2 :** to put or bring back into existence or use **3 :** to bring back to or put back into a former or original state **:** RENEW; *esp* **:** RECONSTRUCT **4 :** to put again in possession of something ⟨~ the king to the throne⟩ **syn** see RENEW — **re·stor·er** *n*

re·strain \ri-ˈstrān\ *vt* [ME *restraynen*, fr. MF *restraindre*, fr. L *restringere* to restrain, restrict, fr. *re-* + *stringere* to bind tight — more at STRAIN] **1 a** (1) **:** to prevent from doing something (2) **:** CURB, REPRESS ⟨~ anger⟩ **b :** to limit, restrict, or keep under control **2 :** to moderate or limit the force, effect, development, or full exercise of ⟨~ trade⟩ **3 :** to deprive of liberty; *esp* **:** to place under arrest or restraint — **re·strain·able** \-ˈstrā-nə-bəl\ *adj* — **re·strain·ed·ly** \-nəd-lē\ *adv* — **re·strain·er** \-ˈstrā-nər\ *n*

syn CHECK, CURB, BRIDLE: RESTRAIN suggests holding back by force or persuasion from acting or from going to extremes; CHECK implies restraining or impeding a progress, activity, or impetus; CURB suggests a quick and drastic checking; BRIDLE implies keeping under control by subduing or holding in

re·straint \ri-ˈstrānt\ *n* [ME, fr. MF *restrainte*, fr. *restraindre*] **1 a :** an act of restraining **:** the state of being restrained **b :** a means, force, or agency that restrains **:** INHIBITION **2 :** a control over the expression of one's emotions or thoughts **:** RESERVE

re·strict \ri-ˈstrikt\ *vt* [L *restrictus*, pp. of *restringere*] **1 :** to confine within bounds **:** RESTRAIN **2 :** to place under restrictions as to use **syn** see LIMIT — **re·strict·ed** *adj* — **re·strict·ed·ly** *adv*

re·stric·tion \ri-ˈstrik-shən\ *n* **1 :** something that restricts; *specif* **:** a limitation on the use or enjoyment of property or a facility **2 :** an act of restricting or the condition of being restricted

re·stric·tion·ism \-shə-ˌniz-əm\ *n* **:** a policy or philosophy advocating restriction (as of trade) — **re·stric·tion·ist** \-sh(ə-)nəst\ *adj or n*

re·stric·tive \ri-ˈstrik-tiv\ *adj* **1 :** serving or tending to restrict **2 :** limiting the reference of a modified word or phrase ⟨~ clause⟩ **3 :** prohibiting further negotiation — **restrictive** *n* — **re·stric·tive·ly** *adv* — **re·stric·tive·ness** *n*

rest room *n* **:** a room or suite of rooms providing personal facilities (as toilets)

1**re·sult** \ri-ˈzəlt\ *vi* [ME *resulten*, fr. ML *resultare*, fr. L, to rebound, fr. *re-* + *saltare* to leap — more at SALTATION] **1 :** to proceed or arise as a consequence, effect, or conclusion **:** TERMINATE, END **2 :** REVERT 2

2**result** *n* **1 :** something that results as a consequence, issue, or conclusion; *also* **:** beneficial or tangible effect **:** FRUIT **2 :** something obtained by calculation or investigation **syn** see EFFECT — **re·sult·ful** \-fəl\ *adj* — **re·sult·less** \-ləs\ *adj*

1**re·sul·tant** \ri-ˈzəlt-ᵊnt\ *adj* **:** derived from or resulting from something else — **re·sul·tant·ly** *adv*

2**resultant** *n* **:** something that results **:** OUTCOME; *specif* **:** the single vector that is the sum of a given set of vectors

1**re·sume** \ri-ˈzüm\ *vb* [ME *resumen*, fr. MF or L; MF *resumer*, fr. L *resumere*, fr. *re-* + *sumere* to take up, take — more at CONSUME] *vt* **1 :** to assume or take again **:** REOCCUPY **2 :** to return to or begin again after interruption **3 :** to take back to oneself **4 :** to pick up again **5 :** REITERATE, SUMMARIZE ~ *vi* **:** RECOMMENCE

2**ré·su·mé** *or* **re·su·me** \ˈrez-ə-ˌmā, ˌrez-ə-ˈ\ *n* [F *résumé*, fr. pp. of *résumer* to resume, summarize] **:** a summing up **:** SUMMARY; *specif* **:** a short account of one's career and qualifications prepared typically by an applicant for a position

re·sump·tion \ri-ˈzəm(p)-shən\ *n* [ME, fr. MF or LL; MF *resomption*, fr. LL *resumption-*, *resumptio*, fr. L *resumptus*, pp. of *resumere*] **1 :** an act or instance of resuming **:** RECOMMENCEMENT **2 :** a return to payment in specie

re·su·pi·nate \ri-ˈsü-pə-nət, -ˌnāt\ *adj* [L *resupinatus*, pp. of *resupinare* to bend back to a supine position, fr. *re-* + *supinus* supine] **:** inverted in position; *also* **:** appearing by a twist of the axis to be upside down

re·su·pi·na·tion \ri-ˌsü-pə-ˈnā-shən\ *n* **:** a twisting to an inverted or apparently inverted position

res·u·pine \ˌres-ə-ˈpīn\ *adj* [L *resupinus*, back-formation fr. *resupinare*] **:** SUPINE 1

re·sur·gence \ri-ˈsər-jən(t)s\ *n* **:** a rising again into life or prominence **:** RENASCENCE

re·sur·gent \-jənt\ *adj* [L *resurgent-*, *resurgens*, prp. of *resurgere*] **:** undergoing or tending to produce resurgence

res·ur·rect \ˌrez-ə-ˈrekt\ *vt* [back-formation fr. *resurrection*] **1 :** to raise from the dead **2 :** to bring to view, attention, or use again

res·ur·rec·tion \ˌrez-ə-ˈrek-shən\ *n* [ME, fr. LL *resurrection-*, *resurrectio* act of rising from the dead, fr. *resurrectus*, pp. of *resurgere* to rise from the dead, fr. L, to rise again, fr. *re-* + *surgere* to rise — more at SURGE] **1 a** *cap* **:** the rising of Christ from the dead **b** *often cap* **:** the rising again to life of all the human dead before the final judgment **c :** the state of one risen from the dead **2 :** RESURGENCE, REVIVAL **3** *Christian Science* **:** a spiritualization of thought **:** material belief that yields to spiritual understanding — **res·ur·rec·tion·al** \-shnəl, -shən-ᵊl\ *adj*

res·ur·rec·tion·ist \-sh(ə-)nəst\ *n* **1 :** BODY SNATCHER **2 :** one who resurrects

re·sus·ci·tate \ri-ˈsəs-ə-ˌtāt\ *vb* [L *resuscitatus*, pp. of *resuscitare*, lit., to stir up again, fr. *re-* + *suscitare* to stir up, fr. *sub-*, *sus-* up + *citare* to put in motion, stir — more at SUB-, CITE] *vt* **:** to revive from apparent death or from unconsciousness; *also* **:** REVITALIZE ~ *vi* **:** to come to **:** REVIVE — **re·sus·ci·ta·tion** \ri-ˌsəs-ə-ˈtā-shən, ˌrē-\ *n* — **re·sus·ci·ta·tive** \ri-ˈsəs-ə-ˌtāt-iv\ *adj*

re·sus·ci·ta·tor \ri-ˈsəs-ə-ˌtāt-ər\ *n* **:** one that resuscitates; *specif* **:** an apparatus used to relieve asphyxiation

ret \ˈret\ *vb* **ret·ted; ret·ting** [ME *reten*, fr. MD] *vt* **:** to soak (as flax) to loosen the fiber from the woody tissue ~ *vi* **:** to become retted

re·ta·ble \ˈrē-ˌtā-bəl\ *n* [F, fr. Sp *retablo*, deriv. of L *retro-* + *tabula* board, tablet] **:** a raised shelf above an altar for the altar cross, the altar lights, and flowers

1**re·tail** \ˈrē-ˌtāl, *esp for 2 also* ri-ˈtā(-ə)l\ *vb* [ME *retailen*, fr. MF *retaillier* to cut back, divide into pieces, fr. OF, fr. *re-* + *taillier* to cut — more at TAILOR] *vt* **1 a :** to sell in small quantities **b :** to sell directly to the ultimate consumer **2 :** TELL, RETELL ~ *vi* **:** to sell at retail — **re·tail·er** *n*

2**re·tail** \ˈrē-ˌtāl\ *n* **:** the sale of commodities or goods in small quantities to ultimate consumers — **at retail 1 :** at a retailer's price **2 :** 4RETAIL

3**retail** \ˈrē-ˌ\ *adj* **:** of, relating to, or engaged in the sale of commodities at retail ⟨~ trade⟩

4**retail** \ˈrē-ˌ\ *adv* **1 :** in small quantities **2 :** from a retailer

re·tain \ri-ˈtān\ *vt* [ME *reteinen*, *retainen*, fr. MF *retenir*, fr. L *retinēre* to hold back, keep, restrain, fr. *re-* + *tenēre* to hold — more at THIN] **1 a :** to keep in possession or use **b :** to keep in pay or in one's service; *specif* **:** to employ by paying a retainer **2 :** to hold secure or intact ⟨lead ~*s* heat⟩ **syn** see KEEP

retained object *n* **:** an object in a passive construction ⟨*me* in *a book was given me* and *book* in *I was given a book* are *retained objects*⟩

1**re·tain·er** \ri-ˈtā-nər\ *n* [ME *reteiner* act of withholding, fr. *reteinen* + AF *-er* (as in *weyver* waiver)] **1 :** the act of a client by which he engages the services of a lawyer, counselor, or adviser **2 :** a fee paid to a lawyer or professional adviser for advice or services or for a claim upon his services in case of need

2**retainer** *n* [*retain*] **1 :** one that retains **2 a :** a person attached or owing service to a household; *esp* **:** SERVANT **b :** EMPLOYEE **3 :** any of various devices used for holding something

1**re·take** \(ˈ)rē-ˈtāk\ *vt* **1 :** to take or receive again **2 :** RECAPTURE **3 :** to photograph again

2**re·take** \ˈrē-ˌtāk\ *n* **:** a second photographing or photograph

re·tal·i·ate \ri-ˈtal-ē-ˌāt\ *vb* [LL *retaliatus*, pp. of *retaliare*, fr. *re-* + *talio* legal retaliation] *vt* **:** to repay (as an injury) in kind ~ *vi* **:** to return like for like; *esp* **:** to get revenge — **re·tal·i·a·tion** \ri-ˌtal-ē-ˈā-shən, ˌrē-\ *n* — **re·tal·i·a·tive** \ri-ˈtal-ē-ˌāt-iv\ *adj* — **re·tal·ia·to·ry** \-ˈtal-yə-ˌtōr-ē, -ˈtal-ē-ə-, -ˌtȯr-\ *adj*

1**re·tard** \ri-ˈtärd\ *vb* [L *retardare*, fr. *re-* + *tardus* slow] *vt* **1 :** to make slow or slower **:** IMPEDE **2 :** to delay academic progress by failure to promote ~ *vi* **:** to undergo retardation **syn** see DELAY — **re·tard·er** *n*

2**retard** *n* **:** a holding back or slowing down **:** RETARDATION

re·tar·dant \ri-ˈtärd-ᵊnt\ *adj* **:** serving or tending to retard — **retardant** *n*

re·tar·date \-ˈtär-ˌdāt, -ˈtärd-ət\ *n* **:** one who is mentally retarded

re·tar·da·tion \ˌrē-ˌtär-ˈdā-shən, ri-\ *n* **1 :** an act or instance of retarding **2 :** the extent to which anything is retarded **3 a :** an abnormal slowness of thought or action **b :** slowness in development or progress

re·tard·ed \ri-ˈtärd-əd\ *adj* **:** slow or limited in intellectual or emotional development or academic progress

retch \ˈrech, *Brit* ˈrēch\ *vb* [(assumed) ME *rechen* to spit, retch, fr. OE *hrǣcan* to spit, hawk; akin to L *crepare* to rattle — more at RAVEN] *vi* **:** to make an effort to vomit ~ *vt* **:** VOMIT — **retch** *n*

re·te \ˈrēt-ē, ˈrāt-\ *n, pl* **re·tia** \ˈrēt-ē-ə, ˈrāt-\ [NL, fr. L, net — more at RETINA] **1 :** a network esp. of blood vessels or nerves **:** PLEXUS **2 :** an anatomical part resembling or including a network

re·tell \(ˈ)rē-ˈtel\ *vt* **1 :** to count again **2 :** to tell again or in another form

re·tem \rə-ˈtem\ *n* [Ar *ratam*] **:** a desert shrub (*Retama raetam*) of western Asia that is the juniper of the Old Testament and has tiny white flowers

re·tene \ˈrē-ˌtēn, ˈret-ˌēn\ *n* [Gk *rhētinē* resin] **:** a crystalline hydrocarbon $C_{18}H_{18}$ isolated esp. from pine tar and fossil resins but usu. prepared artificially

re·ten·tion \ri-ˈten-chən\ *n* [ME *retencioun*, fr. L *retention-*, *retentio*, fr. *retentus*, pp. of *retinēre* to retain — more at RETAIN] **1 a :** the act of retaining **:** the state of being retained **b :** abnormal retaining of a fluid or secretion in a body cavity **2 a :** power of retaining **:** RETENTIVENESS **b :** an ability to retain things in mind **:** MEMORY **3 :** something retained

re·ten·tive \-ˈtent-iv\ *adj* **:** having the power, property, or capacity of retaining; *specif* **:** retaining knowledge easily — **re·ten·tive·ly** *adv* — **re·ten·tive·ness** *n*

re·ten·tiv·i·ty \ˌrē-ˌten-ˈtiv-ət-ē, ri-\ *n* **:** the power of retaining; *specif* **:** the capacity for retaining magnetism after the action of the magnetizing force has ceased

re·ten·tor \ri-ˈtent-ər\ *n* **:** a muscle that retains a part in place esp. when retracted

re·test \ˈrē-ˌtest, (ˈ)rē-ˈ\ *n* **:** a repeated test

re·ti·a·ri·us \ˌrāt-ē-ˈär-ē-əs, -ē-ˌu̇s\ *n, pl* **re·ti·a·rii** \-ē-ˌē\ [L, fr. *rete* net] **:** a Roman gladiator armed with a net and a trident

ret·i·cence \ˈret-ə-sən(t)s\ *n* **1 :** RESERVE, RESTRAINT **2 :** an instance of being reticent

ret·i·cen·cy \-sən-sē\ *n* **:** RETICENCE

ret·i·cent \-sənt\ *adj* [L *reticent-*, *reticens*, prp. of *reticēre* to keep silent, fr. *re-* + *tacēre* to be silent — more at TACIT] **1 :** inclined to be silent or secretive **:** UNCOMMUNICATIVE **2 :** restrained in expression, presentation, or appearance **syn** see SILENT — **ret·i·cent·ly** *adv*

ret·i·cle \ˈret-i-kəl\ *n* [L *reticulum* network] **:** a system of lines, dots, cross hairs, or wires in the focus of the eyepiece of an optical instrument

re·tic·u·lar \ri-ˈtik-yə-lər\ *adj* **1 :** RETICULATE; *specif* **:** of, relating to, or being a reticulum **2 :** INTRICATE

1**re·tic·u·late** \-lət, -ˌlāt\ *adj* [L *reticulatus*, fr. *reticulum*] **1 :** re-

See *re-* and 2d element	**restring**	**restyle**	**resupply**	**resurrender**	**resynthesize**
restraighten	**restructure**	**resubmission**	**resurface**	**resurvey**	**retaste**
restrengthen	**restudy**	**resubmit**	**resurge**	**resynthesis**	**rethink**
restrike	**restuff**	**resummon**			

sembling a net; *specif* **:** having veins, fibers, or lines crossing ⟨a ~ leaf⟩ **2 :** of, relating to, or constituting evolutionary change dependent on complex new combinations of genes from varied strains of a diversified interbreeding population — **re·tic·u·late·ly** *adv* — **re·tic·u·lose** \-ˌlōs\ *adj*

2**re·tic·u·late** \-ˌlāt\ *vb* [back-formation fr. *reticulated,* adj. (reticulate)] *vt* **1 :** to divide, mark, or construct so as to form a network **2 :** to distribute by a network ~ *vi* **:** to become reticulated

re·tic·u·la·tion \ri-ˌtik-yə-ˈlā-shən\ *n* **:** reticulated formation **:** NETWORK; *also* **:** something reticulated

ret·i·cule \ˈret-i-ˌkyü(ə)l\ *n* [F *réticule,* fr. L *reticulum* network, network bag, fr. dim. of *rete* net] **1 :** RETICLE **2 :** a woman's drawstring bag used esp. as a carryall

re·tic·u·lo·cyte \ri-ˈtik-yə-lō-ˌsīt\ *n* [NL *reticulum* + ISV *-cyte*] **:** a young red blood cell with a fine basophilic reticulum appearing esp. in conditions in which many red cells are lost — **re·tic·u·lo·cyt·ic** \-ˌtik-yə-lō-ˈsit-ik\ *adj*

re·tic·u·lo·en·do·the·li·al \ri-ˈtik-yə-lō-ˌen-də-ˈthē-lē-əl\ *adj* [NL *reticulum* + *endothelium*] **:** of, relating to, or being the reticuloendothelial system

reticuloendothelial system *n* **:** a diffuse system of cells arising from mesenchyme and comprising all the phagocytic cells of the body except the circulating leukocytes

re·tic·u·lum \ri-ˈtik-yə-ləm\ *n, pl* **re·tic·u·la** \-lə\ [NL, fr. L, network] **1 :** the second stomach of a ruminant in which folds of the mucous membrane form hexagonal cells **2 :** NETWORK; *esp* **:** interstitial tissue composed of reticulum cells

reticulum cell *n* **:** one of the branched anastomosing reticuloendothelial cells that form an intricate interstitial network ramifying through other tissues and organs

re·ti·form \ˈrēt-ə-ˌfȯrm, ˈret-\ *adj* [NL *retiformis,* fr. L *rete* + *-iformis* -iform] **:** composed of crossing lines and interstices **:** RETICULAR

retin- *or* **retino-** *comb form* [*retina*] **:** retina ⟨*retin*itis⟩ ⟨*retino*scopy⟩

ret·i·na \ˈret-ᵊn-ə, ˈret-nə\ *n, pl* **retinas** *or* **ret·i·nae** \-ᵊn-ˌē, -ˌī\ [ME *rethina,* fr. ML *retina,* prob. fr. L *rete* net; akin to Gk *erēmos* lonely, solitary, Lith *rètis* sieve] **:** the sensory membrane of the eye that receives the image formed by the lens, is the immediate instrument of vision, and is connected with the brain by the optic nerve — **ret·i·nal** \ˈret-ᵊn-əl, ˈret-nəl\ *adj*

ret·i·nac·u·lar \ˌret-ᵊn-ˈak-yə-lər\ *adj* **:** relating to or resembling a retinaculum

ret·i·nac·u·lum \-ləm\ *n, pl* **ret·i·nac·u·la** \-lə\ [NL, fr. L, halter, cable, fr. *retinēre* to hold back — more at RETAIN] **:** a connecting or retaining band or body

ret·i·nene \ˈret-ᵊn-ˌēn\ *n* [*retina*] **:** either a yellowish or an orange aldehyde derived from vitamin A that in combination with proteins forms the visual pigments of the retinal rods and cones

ret·i·nis·po·ra \ˌret-ᵊn-ˈis-pə-rə\ *or* **ret·i·nos·po·ra** \-ˈäs-\ *n* [NL, fr. Gk *rhētinē* resin + NL *spora* spore] **1 :** any of various Japanese ornamental dwarf shrubs (genus *Chamaecyparis*) that resemble cypresses **2 :** any of several shrubs (genus *Thuja*) that retain the needlelike juvenile foliage permanently

ret·i·ni·tis \ˌret-ᵊn-ˈīt-əs\ *n* [NL] **:** inflammation of the retina

ret·i·nos·co·py \ˌret-ᵊn-ˈäs-kə-pē\ *n* **:** observation of the retina of the eye esp. to determine the state of refraction

ret·i·nue \ˈret-ᵊn-ˌ(y)ü\ *n* [ME *retenue,* fr. MF, fr. fem. of *retenu,* pp. of *retenir* to retain] **:** the body of retainers who follow a distinguished person **:** SUITE

re·tin·u·la \re-ˈtin-yə-lə\ *n, pl* **re·tin·u·lae** \-ˌlē, -ˌlī\ [NL, dim. of ML *retina*] **:** the neural receptor of a single facet of an arthropodan compound eye — **re·tin·u·lar** \-lər\ *adj*

re·tire \ri-ˈtī(ə)r\ *vb* [MF *retirer,* fr. *re-* + *tirer* to draw — more at TIRADE] *vi* **1 :** to withdraw from action or danger **:** RETREAT **2 :** to withdraw esp. for privacy **3 :** to fall back **:** RECEDE **4 :** to withdraw from one's position or occupation **5 :** to go to bed ~ *vt* **1 a :** WITHDRAW **b :** to march (a military force) away from the enemy **2 a :** to withdraw from circulation or from the market **:** RECALL **b :** to withdraw from usual use or service **3 :** to cause to retire from one's position or occupation **4 :** to put out (a batter or side) in baseball **syn** see GO

re·tired \ri-ˈtī(ə)rd\ *adj* **1 :** QUIET ⟨~ village⟩ **2 :** withdrawn from one's position or occupation **3 :** received by or due to one in retirement — **re·tired·ly** \-ˈtī-rəd-lē, -ˈtī(ə)rd-\ *adv* — **re·tired·ness** \-ˈtī(ə)rd-nəs\ *n*

re·tir·ee \ri-ˌtī-ˈrē\ *n* **:** a person who has retired from his vocation or profession

re·tire·ment \ri-ˈtī(ə)r-mənt\ *n* **1 :** an act of retiring **:** the state of being retired; *esp* **:** withdrawal from one's position or occupation **2 :** a place of seclusion or privacy

re·tir·ing \ri-ˈtī(ə)r-iŋ\ *adj* **:** RESERVED, SHY — **re·tir·ing·ly** \-iŋ-lē\ *adv* — **re·tir·ing·ness** *n*

re·tool \(ˈ)rē-ˈtül\ *vt* **1 :** to reequip with tools **2 :** REORGANIZE

1**re·tort** \ri-ˈtȯ(ə)rt\ *vb* [L *retortus,* pp. of *retorquēre,* lit., to twist back, hurl back, fr. *re-* + *torquēre* to twist — more at TORTURE] *vt* **1 :** to pay back **:** RETURN ⟨~ an insult⟩ **2 a :** to make a reply to **b :** to say in reply **3 :** to answer by a counter argument ~ *vi* **1 :** to answer back usu. sharply **2 :** to return an argument or charge **3 :** RETALIATE **syn** see ANSWER

2**retort** *n* **:** a quick, witty, or cutting reply; *esp* **:** one that turns the first speaker's words against him

3**re·tort** \ri-ˈtȯ(ə)rt, ˈrē-ˌ\ *n* [MF *retorte,* fr. ML *retorta,* fr. L, fem. of *retortus,* pp.; fr. its shape] **:** a vessel in which substances are distilled or decomposed by heat

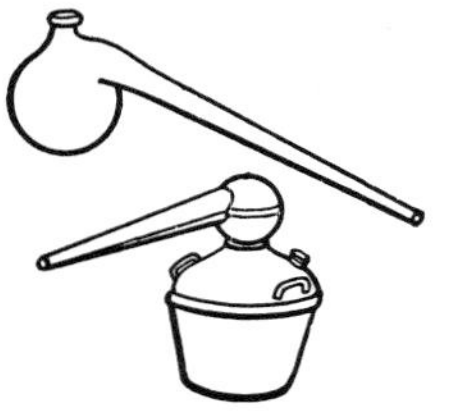

retorts

re·tor·tion \ri-ˈtȯr-shən\ *n* **:** an act of retorting

re·touch \(ˈ)rē-ˈtəch\ *vb* [F *retoucher,* fr. MF, fr. *re-* + *toucher* to touch] *vt* **1 :** to touch up **2 :** to alter (as a photographic negative) to produce a more desirable appearance ~ *vi* **:** to make or give retouches — **re·touch** \ˈrē-ˌtəch, (ˈ)rē-ˈ\ *n* — **re·touch·er** \(ˈ)rē-ˈtəch-ər\ *n*

re·trace \(ˈ)rē-ˈtrās\ *vt* [F *retracer,* fr. MF *retracier,* fr. *re-* + *tracier* to trace] **:** to trace again or back

re·tract \ri-ˈtrakt\ *vb* [ME *retracten,* fr. L *retractus,* pp. of *retrahere*] *vt* **1 a :** to draw back or in ⟨cats ~ their claws⟩ **b :** to move (the tongue) further back **2 a :** to take back (as a promise) **:** RECANT **b :** DISAVOW ~ *vi* **1 :** to draw back **2 :** to recant or disavow something **syn** see ABJURE, RECEDE — **re·tract·able** \-ˈtrak-tə-bəl\ *adj*

re·trac·tile \ri-ˈtrak-tᵊl, -ˌtīl\ *adj* **:** capable of being drawn back or in — **re·trac·til·i·ty** \ˌrē-ˌtrak-ˈtil-ət-ē, ri-\ *n*

re·trac·tion \ri-ˈtrak-shən\ *n* **1 :** RECANTATION; *specif* **:** a statement made by one retracting **2 :** an act of retracting **:** the state of being retracted **3 :** the ability to retract

re·trac·tor \ri-ˈtrak-tər\ *n* **:** one that retracts: as **a :** a surgical instrument for holding open the edges of a wound **b :** a muscle that draws in an organ or part

re·tral \ˈrē-trəl, ˈre-\ *adj* [L *retro* — more at RETRO-] **1 :** situated at or toward the back **:** POSTERIOR **2 :** BACKWARD, RETROGRADE — **re·tral·ly** \-trə-lē\ *adv*

re–tread \(ˈ)rē-ˈtred\ *vt* **:** to tread again

1**re·tread** \(ˈ)rē-ˈtred\ *vt* **:** to cement, mold, and vulcanize a new tread of camelback upon the bare cord fabric of (a worn tire)

2**re·tread** \ˈrē-ˌtred\ *n* **1 :** a new tread on a tire **2 :** a retreaded tire **3 :** one pressed into service again; *also* **:** REMAKE

1**re·treat** \ri-ˈtrēt\ *n* [ME *retret,* fr. MF *retrait,* fr. pp. of *retraire* to withdraw, fr. L *retrahere,* lit., to draw back, fr. *re-* + *trahere* to draw — more at DRAW] **1 a :** an act or process of withdrawing esp. from what is difficult, dangerous, or disagreeable **b** (1) **:** the usu. forced withdrawal of troops from an enemy or from an advanced position (2) **:** a signal for retreating **c** (1) **:** a signal given by bugle at the beginning of a military flag-lowering ceremony (2) **:** a military flag-lowering ceremony **2 :** a place of privacy or safety **:** REFUGE **3 :** a period of group withdrawal for prayer, meditation, study, and instruction under a director

2**retreat** *vi* **1 :** to make a retreat **:** WITHDRAW **2 :** to slope backward ~ *vt* **:** to draw or lead back **:** REMOVE; *specif* **:** to move (a piece) back in chess **syn** see RECEDE

re·trench \ri-ˈtrench\ *vb* [obs. F *retrencher* (now *retrancher*), fr. MF *retrenchier,* fr. *re-* + *trenchier* to cut] *vt* **1 a :** to cut down **:** REDUCE **b :** to cut out **:** EXCISE **2 :** to pare away **:** REMOVE ~ *vi* **:** to make retrenchments; *specif* **:** ECONOMIZE **syn** see SHORTEN

re·trench·ment \-mənt\ *n* **:** REDUCTION, CURTAILMENT; *specif* **:** a cutting of expenses

re·tri·al \(ˈ)rē-ˈtrī(-ə)l\ *n* **:** a second trial, experiment, or test

ret·ri·bu·tion \ˌre-trə-ˈbyü-shən\ *n* [ME *retribucioun,* fr. MF *retribution,* fr. LL *retribution-, retributio,* fr. L *retributus,* pp. of *retribuere* to pay back, fr. *re-* + *tribuere* to pay — more at TRIBUTE] **1 :** RECOMPENSE, REWARD **2 :** the dispensing or receiving of reward or punishment esp. in the hereafter **3 :** something given or exacted in recompense; *esp* **:** PUNISHMENT

re·trib·u·tive \ri-ˈtrib-yət-iv\ *adj* **:** of, relating to, or marked by retribution — **re·trib·u·tive·ly** *adv*

re·trib·u·to·ry \-yə-ˌtōr-ē, -ˌtȯr-\ *adj* **:** RETRIBUTIVE

re·triev·able \ri-ˈtrē-və-bəl\ *adj* **:** capable of being retrieved

re·triev·al \-ˈtrē-vəl\ *n* **1 :** an act or process of retrieving **2 :** possibility of being retrieved or of recovering

1**re·trieve** \ri-ˈtrēv\ *vb* [ME *retreven,* modif. of MF *retrouver* to find again, fr. *re-* + *trouver* to find, prob. fr. (assumed) VL *tropare* to compose — more at TROUBADOUR] *vt* **1 :** to discover and bring in (killed or wounded game) **2 :** to call to mind again **3 :** REGAIN, REPOSSESS **4 a :** RESCUE, SALVAGE **b :** to return (as a ball that is difficult to reach) successfully **5 :** RESTORE, REVIVE **6 :** to remedy the evil consequences of **:** CORRECT ~ *vi* **:** to bring in game; *also* **:** to bring back an object thrown by a person

2**retrieve** *n* **1 :** RETRIEVAL **2 :** the successful return of a ball that is difficult to reach or control (as in tennis)

re·triev·er \ri-ˈtrē-vər\ *n* **:** one that retrieves; *specif* **:** a vigorous active medium-sized dog with heavy water-resistant coat developed by crossbreeding and used esp. for retrieving game

retro- *prefix* [ME, fr. L, fr. *retro,* fr. *re-* + *-tro* (as in *intro* within) — more at INTRO-] **1 :** backward **:** back ⟨*retro*-rocket⟩ **2 :** situated behind ⟨*retro*choir⟩

re·tro·ac·tion \ˌre-trō-ˈak-shən *also* ˌrē-\ *n* **1** [*retroactive* + *-ion*] **:** retroactive or retrospective operation **2** [*retro-* + *action*] **:** a reciprocal action **:** REACTION

re·tro·ac·tive \-ˈak-tiv\ *adj* [F *retroactif,* fr. L *retroactus,* pp. of *retroagere* to drive back, reverse, fr. *retro-* + *agere* to drive — more at AGENT] **:** extending in scope or effect to a prior time; *esp* **:** made effective as of a date prior to enactment, promulgation, or imposition ⟨~ tax⟩ — **re·tro·ac·tive·ly** *adv* — **re·tro·ac·tiv·i·ty** \-ˌak-ˈtiv-ət-ē\ *n*

re·tro·cede \ˌre-trō-ˈsēd *also* ˌrē-\ *vi* [L *retrocedere,* fr. *retro-* + *cedere* to go, cede — more at CEDE] **:** to go back **:** RECEDE ~ *vt* [F *rétrocéder,* fr. ML *retrocedere,* fr. L *retro-* + *cedere* to cede] **:** to cede back (as a territory) — **re·tro·ces·sion** \-ˈsesh-ən\ *n*

ret·ro·fire \ˈre-trō-ˌfī(ə)r\ *vb* **:** to ignite a retro-rocket — **retrofire** *n*

ret·ro·flex \ˈre-trə-ˌfleks\ *or* **ret·ro·flexed** \-ˌflekst\ *adj* [ISV, fr. NL *retroflexus,* fr. L *retro-* + *flexus,* pp. of *flectere* to bend] **1 :** turned or bent abruptly backward **2 :** articulated with or involving the participation of the tongue tip turned up or curled back just under the hard palate ⟨~ vowel⟩

ret·ro·flex·ion *or* **ret·ro·flec·tion** \ˌre-trə-ˈflek-shən\ *n* **1 :** the act or process of bending back **2 :** the state of being bent back; *specif* **:** the bending back of an organ (as a uterus) upon itself **3 :** retroflex articulation

ret·ro·gra·da·tion \ˌre-trō-grā-ˈdā-shən, -grə-\ *n* **:** the act or process of retrograding

1**ret·ro·grade** \ˈre-trə-ˌgrād\ *adj* [ME, fr. L *retrogradus,* fr. *retro-* + *gradi* to go] **1 a** *of a celestial body* **:** having a direction contrary to that of the general motion of similar bodies **b :** moving or directed backward ⟨a ~ step⟩ **c :** contrary to the normal order **:** INVERSE; *specif* **:** written from right to left ⟨~ alphabet⟩ **2 :** tending toward or resulting in a worse state **3** *archaic* **:** OPPOSED, CONTRADICTORY **4 :** characterized by retrogression

2**retrograde** *adv* **:** BACKWARD, REVERSELY

3**retrograde** *vb* [L *retrogradi,* fr. *retro-* + *gradi* to go — more at GRADE] *vt, archaic* **:** to turn back **:** REVERSE ~ *vi* **1 a :** to go back **:** RETREAT ⟨a glacier ~*s*⟩ **b :** RECAPITULATE **2 :** to decline to a worse condition **syn** see RECEDE

See *re-* and 2d element | **retrack** | **retrain** | **retransmission** | **retransmit** | **retraverse**

re·tro·gress \ˌre-trə-ˈgres\ *vi* [L *retrogressus*, pp. of *retrogradi*] **:** to move backward **:** REVERT

re·tro·gres·sion \-ˈgresh-ən\ *n* **1 :** REGRESSION 3 **2 :** a reversal in development or condition; *esp* **:** a passing from a higher to a lower or from a more to a less specialized state or type in the course of development

re·tro·gres·sive \-ˈgres-iv\ *adj* **:** characterized by or tending to retrogression: as **a :** going or directed backward **b :** declining from a better to a worse state **c :** passing from a higher to a lower organization — **re·tro·gres·sive·ly** *adv*

ret·ro·len·tal \ˌre-trō-ˈlent-ᵊl *also* ˌrē-\ *adj* [*retro-* + L *lent-*, *lens* lens] **:** situated or occurring behind a lens (as of the eye)

re·tro·lin·gual \-ˈliŋ-gwəl\ *adj* **:** situated behind or near the base of the tongue ⟨~ salivary glands⟩

re·tro·per·i·to·ne·al \-ˌper-ət-ᵊn-ˈē-əl\ *adj* **:** situated behind the peritoneum — **re·tro·per·i·to·ne·al·ly** \-ə-lē\ *adv*

ret·ro–rock·et \ˈre-trō-ˌräk-ət\ *n* **:** an auxiliary rocket on an airplane, missile, or space vehicle that produces thrust in a direction opposite to or at an oblique angle to the motion of the object for deceleration

re·trorse \ˈrē-ˌtrȯ(ə)rs\ *adj* [L *retrorsus*, contr. of *retroversus* — more at RETROVERSION] **:** bent backward or downward — **re·trorse·ly** *adv*

re·tro·ser·rate \ˌre-trō-ˈse(ə)r-ˌāt, -ˈser-ət *also* ˌrē-\ *adj* **:** having retrorse teeth or barbs ⟨a ~ leaf⟩

1**re·tro·spect** \ˈre-trə-ˌspekt *also* ˈrē-\ *n* [*retro-* + *-spect* (as in *prospect*)] **1** *archaic* **:** reference to or regard of a precedent or authority **2 :** a review of or meditation upon past events

2**retrospect** *adj* **:** retrospective

3**retrospect** *vb* [L *retrospectus*, pp. of *retrospicere* to look back at, fr. *retro-* + *specere* to look — more at SPY] *vi* **1 :** to practice retrospection **2 :** to refer back **:** REFLECT ~ *vt* **:** to go back over in thought

re·tro·spec·tion \ˌre-trə-ˈspek-shən *also* ˌrē-\ *n* **1** *archaic* **:** reference to a past event **2 :** an act or instance or the process of surveying the past

1**re·tro·spec·tive** \-ˈspek-tiv\ *adj* **1 :** of, relating to, characteristic of, or given to retrospection **2 :** affecting things past **:** RETROACTIVE — **re·tro·spec·tive·ly** *adv*

2**retrospective** *n* **:** a generally comprehensive exhibition showing the work of an artist over a span of years

re·trous·sé \rə-ˌtrü-ˈsā, ˌre-trü-\ *adj* [F, fr. pp. of *retrousser* to tuck up, fr. MF, fr. *re-* + *trousser* to truss, tuck up] **:** turned up ⟨~ nose⟩

re·tro·ver·sion \ˌre-trō-ˈvər-zhən *also* ˌrē-, -shən\ *n* [L *retroversus* turned backward, fr. *retro-* + *versus*, pp. of *vertere* to turn — more at WORTH] **1 :** the act or process of turning back or regressing **2 :** the bending backward of the uterus and cervix

re–try \(ˈ)rē-ˈtrī\ *vt* **:** to try again

1**re·turn** \ri-ˈtərn\ *vb* [ME *retournen*, fr. MF *retourner*, fr. *re-* + *tourner* to turn — more at TURN] *vi* **1 a :** to go back or come back again ⟨~ home⟩ **b :** to go back in thought or practice **:** REVERT **2 :** to pass back to an earlier possessor **3 :** REPLY, RETORT ~ *vt* **1 a :** to give (as an official account) to a superior **b :** to elect (a candidate) as attested by official report or returns **c :** to bring back (as a writ or verdict) to an office or tribunal **2 a :** to bring, send, or put back to a former or proper place ⟨~ the gun to its holster⟩ **b :** to restore to a former or to a normal state **3 a :** to send back upon **:** VISIT **b** *obs* **:** to retort (as an accusation) upon **4 :** to bring in (as profit) **:** YIELD **5 a :** to give or perform in return **:** REPAY ⟨~ a compliment⟩ **b :** to give back to the owner **c :** REFLECT ⟨~ an echo⟩ **6 :** to cause (as a wall) to continue in a different direction (as at a right angle) **7 :** to lead (a specified suit or specified card of a suit) in response to a partner's earlier lead **8 a :** to play back (as a ball) to an opponent **b :** to throw back (as a fielded baseball) — **re·turn·er** *n*

syn RETURN, REVERT, RECUR, RECRUDESCE mean to go or come back. RETURN may imply a going back to a starting place or to a condition or place where it belongs; REVERT implies going back to a former state, an original owner, or a previous decision; RECUR implies a return of something that has happened or been experienced before; RECRUDESCE applies to a return to activity of something that has been suppressed, controlled, or lying dormant

2**return** *n* **1 a :** the act of coming back to or from a place or condition **b :** a regular or frequent returning **:** RECURRENCE **2 a** (1) **:** the delivery of a legal order (as a writ) to the proper officer or court (2) **:** the endorsed certificate of an official stating his action in the execution of such an order (3) **:** the sending back of a commission with the certificate of the commissioners **b :** an account or formal report **c** (1) **:** a report of the results of balloting — usu. used in pl. ⟨election ~*s*⟩ (2) **:** an official declaration of the election of a candidate (3) *chiefly Brit* **:** ELECTION **d** (1) **:** a formal statement on a required legal form showing taxable income, allowable deductions and exemptions, and the computation of the tax due (2) **:** a list of taxable property **3 a :** the continuation usu. at a right angle of the face or of a member of a building or of a molding or group of moldings **b :** a turn, bend, or winding back **c :** a means for conveying something (as water) back to its starting point **4 a :** a quantity of goods, consignment, or cargo coming back in exchange for goods sent out as a mercantile venture **b :** the value of or profit from such venture **c** (1) **:** the profit from labor, investment, or business **:** YIELD (2) *pl* **:** RESULTS **d :** the rate of profit in a process of production per unit of cost **5 a :** the act of returning something to a former place, condition, or ownership **:** RESTITUTION **b :** something returned; *esp, pl* **:** unsold publications returned to the publisher for cash or credit **6 a :** something given in repayment or reciprocation **b :** ANSWER, RETORT **c :** a lead in a suit previously led by one's partner in a card game **d :** an answering or retaliatory play: as (1) **:** the act of returning a ball to an opponent (2) **:** the run of a football after a kick by the other team

3**return** *adj* **1 a :** having or formed by a change of direction ⟨~ facade⟩ **b :** doubled on itself ⟨~ flue⟩ **2 :** played, delivered, or given in return **3 :** used or taken on returning **4 :** returning or permitting return ⟨~ valve⟩ **5 :** RECURRING

re·turn·able \ri-ˈtər-nə-bəl\ *adj* **1 :** legally required to be returned, delivered, or argued at a specified time or place ⟨a writ ~ on the date indicated⟩ **2 a :** capable of returning or of being returned **b :** permitted to be returned ⟨merchandise not ~⟩

re·turn·ee \ri-ˌtər-ˈnē\ *n* **:** one who returns; *esp* **:** one returning to the U.S. after military service abroad

re·tuse \ri-ˈt(y)üs\ *adj* [L *retusus* blunted, fr. pp. of *retundere* to pound back, blunt, fr. *re-* + *tundere* to beat, pound — more at STINT] **:** having the apex rounded or obtuse with a slight notch ⟨a ~ leaf⟩

Reu·ben \ˈrü-bən\ *n* [Heb *Rĕʼūbhēn*] **:** a son of Jacob and ancestor of one of the tribes of Israel

re·uni·fi·ca·tion \ˌrē-ˌyü-nə-fə-ˈkā-shən\ *n* **:** the act or process of reunifying

re·uni·fy \(ˈ)rē-ˈyü-nə-ˌfī\ *vt* **:** to restore unity to

re·union \(ˈ)rē-ˈyü-nyən\ *n* **1 :** an act of reuniting **:** the state of being reunited **2 :** a reuniting of persons after separation

re·union·ist \-nyə-nəst\ *n* **:** an advocate of reunion (as of sects) — **re·union·is·tic** \(ˌ)rē-ˌyü-nyə-ˈnis-tik\ *adj*

re·unite \ˌrē-yü-ˈnīt\ *vb* [ML *reunitus*, pp. of *reunire*, fr. L *re-* + LL *unire* to unite — more at UNITE] *vt* **:** to bring together again ~ *vi* **:** to come together again **:** REJOIN

re–up \(ˈ)rē-ˈəp\ *vi, slang* **:** REENLIST

re·us·able \(ˈ)rē-ˈyü-zə-bəl\ *adj* **:** capable of being used again or repeatedly

re·use \(ˈ)rē-ˈyüz\ *vt* **:** to use again — **re·use** \-ˈyüs\ *n*

1**rev** \ˈrev\ *n* [short for *revolution*] **:** a revolution of a motor

2**rev** *vb* **revved; rev·ving** *vt* **:** to step up the number of revolutions per minute of ⟨~ up the engine⟩ ~ *vi* **:** to operate at an increased speed of revolution — usu. used with *up*

re·val·u·ate \(ˈ)rē-ˈval-yə-ˌwāt\ *vt* [back-formation fr. *revaluation*] **:** REVALUE — **re·val·u·a·tion** \(ˌ)rē-ˌval-yə-ˈwā-shən\ *n*

re·val·ue \(ˈ)rē-ˈval-(ˌ)yü, -yə-w\ *vt* **1 :** to value (as currency) anew **2 :** to make a new valuation of **:** REAPPRAISE

re·vamp \(ˈ)rē-ˈvamp\ *vt* **1 :** RENOVATE, RECONSTRUCT **2 :** to work over **:** REVISE

re·vanche \rə-ˈväⁿsh\ *n* [F, fr. MF, alter. of *revenche* — more at REVENGE] **:** REVENGE; *esp* **:** a usu. political policy designed to recover lost territory or status — **re·vanch·ist** \-ˈväⁿ-shəst\ *adj or n*

1**re·veal** \ri-ˈvē(ə)l\ *vt* [ME *revelen*, fr. MF *reveler*, fr. L *revelare* to uncover, reveal, fr. *re-* + *velare* to cover, veil, fr. *velum* veil] **1 :** to make known through divine inspiration **2 :** to make publicly known **:** DIVULGE ⟨~ a secret⟩ **3 :** to show plainly **:** DISPLAY — **re·veal·able** \-ˈvē-lə-bəl\ *adj* — **re·veal·er** *n*

syn REVEAL, DISCOVER, DISCLOSE, DIVULGE, TELL, BETRAY mean to make known what has been or should be concealed. REVEAL may imply an unveiling of what is not clear to human vision or it may suggest public or dramatic disclosure; DISCOVER implies an uncovering of matters kept secret and not previously known; DISCLOSE may also imply a discovering but more often an imparting of information previously kept secret; DIVULGE implies a disclosure involving some impropriety or breach of confidence; TELL implies an imparting of necessary or useful information but often suggests indiscretion; BETRAY implies a divulging that represents a breach of faith or an involuntary or unconscious disclosure

2**reveal** *n* [alter. of earlier *revale*, fr. ME *revalen* to lower, fr. MF *revaler*, fr. *re-* + *val* valley — more at VALE] **:** the side of an opening (as for a window) between a frame and the outer surface of a wall; *also* **:** JAMB

re·veal·ment \ri-ˈvē(ə)l-mənt\ *n* **:** an act of revealing **:** REVELATION

re·ve·hent \ˈrev-ə-hənt, ri-ˈvē-ənt\ *adj* [L *revehent-*, *revehens*, prp. of *revehere* to carry back, fr. *re-* + *vehere* to carry — more at WAY] **:** carrying back ⟨~ veins⟩

rev·eil·le \ˈrev-ə-lē\ *n* [modif. of F *réveillez*, imper. pl. of *réveiller* to awaken, fr. *re-* + *eveiller* to awaken, fr. (assumed) VL *exvigilare*, fr. L *ex-* + *vigilare* to keep watch, stay awake — more at VIGILANT] **1 :** a bugle call at about sunrise signaling the first military formation of the day; *also* **:** the formation so signaled **2 :** a signal to get up mornings

1**rev·el** \ˈrev-əl\ *vi* **rev·eled** *or* **rev·elled; rev·el·ing** *or* **rev·el·ling** \ˈrev-(ə-)liŋ\ [ME *revelen*, fr. MF *reveler*, lit., to rebel, fr. L *rebellare*] **1 :** to take part in a revel **:** ROISTER **2 :** to take intense satisfaction ⟨~*ing* in success⟩ — **rev·el·er** *or* **rev·el·ler** \-(ə-)lər\ *n*

2**revel** *n* **:** a usu. wild party or celebration — **rev·el·ous** \ˈrev-ə-ləs\ *adj*

rev·e·la·tion \ˌrev-ə-ˈlā-shən\ *n* [ME, fr. MF, fr. LL *revelation-*, *revelatio*, fr. L *revelatus*, pp. of *revelare* to reveal] **1 :** an act of revealing or communicating divine truth **2 a :** an act of revealing to view **b :** something that is revealed; *esp* **:** an enlightening or astonishing disclosure

rev·e·la·tor \ˈrev-ə-ˌlāt-ər\ *n* **:** REVEALER; *esp* **:** one that reveals the will of God

re·ve·la·to·ry \ri-ˈvel-ə-ˌtōr-ē, ˈrev-(ə-)lə-, -ˌtȯr-\ *adj* **:** of, relating to, or characteristic of revelation

rev·el·ry \ˈrev-əl-rē\ *n* **:** an act or instance of reveling

rev·e·nant \ˈrev-ə-ˌnäⁿ, -nənt\ *n* [F, fr. prp. of *revenir* to return] **:** one that returns after death or a long absence — **revenant** *adj*

1**re·venge** \ri-ˈvenj\ *vt* [ME *revengen*, fr. MF *revengier*, fr. OF, fr. *re-* + *vengier* to avenge — more at VENGEANCE] **1 :** to inflict injury in return for ⟨~ an insult⟩ **2 :** to avenge for a wrong done ⟨~ oneself⟩ **syn** see AVENGE — **re·veng·er** *n*

2**revenge** *n* [MF *revenge*, *revenche*, fr. *revengier*, *revenchier* to revenge] **1 :** an act or instance of revenging **2 :** a desire for revenge **3 :** an opportunity for getting satisfaction or retrieving oneself

re·venge·ful \-fəl\ *adj* **:** full of or prone to revenge **:** VINDICTIVE — **re·venge·ful·ly** \-fə-lē\ *adv* — **re·venge·ful·ness** *n*

rev·e·nue \ˈrev-ə-ˌn(y)ü\ *n, often attrib* [ME, fr. MF, fr. *revenir* to return, fr. L *revenire*, fr. *re-* + *venire* to come — more at COME] **1 :** the income that comes back from an investment **2 :** the yield of taxes and other sources of income that a political unit (as a nation or state) collects and receives into the treasury for public use **3 :** the total income produced by a given source

rev·e·nu·er \ˈrev-ə-ˌn(y)ü-ər\ *n* **:** a revenue officer or boat

revenue stamp *n* **:** a stamp for use as evidence of payment of a tax (as on a cigarette pack)

re·ver·ber·ant \ri-ˈvər-b(ə-)rənt\ *adj* **1 :** tending to reverberate **2 :** marked by reverberation **:** RESONANT — **re·ver·ber·ant·ly** *adv*

1**re·ver·ber·ate** \-bə-ˌrāt\ *vb* [L *reverberatus*, pp. of *reverberare*, fr. *re-* + *verberare* to lash, fr. *verber* rod — more at VERVAIN] *vt* **1 :** to force back: as **a :** REPEL **b :** ECHO ⟨~ sound⟩ **c :** REFLECT ⟨~ light or heat⟩ **2 :** to subject to the action of a reverberatory

ə abut; ᵊ kitten; ər further; a back; ā bake; ä cot, cart; aù out; ch chin; e less; ē easy; g gift; i trip; ī life
j joke; ŋ sing; ō flow; ȯ flaw; ȯi coin; th thin; th̲ this; ü loot; ù foot; y yet; yü few; yù furious; zh vision

furnace ~ *vt* **1 a :** to become driven back **b :** to become reflected **2 :** to continue in or as if in a series of echoes **:** RESOUND

2**re·ver·ber·ate** \-b(ə-)rət\ *adj* **:** REVERBERATED, REVERBERANT ⟨~ sound⟩

re·ver·ber·a·tion \ri-ˌvər-bə-ˈrā-shən\ *n* **1 a :** an act of reverberating **b :** the state of being reverberated **2 :** something that is reverberated

re·ver·ber·a·tive \ri-ˈvər-bə-ˌrāt-iv, -b(ə-)rət-\ *adj* **1 :** constituting reverberation **2 :** tending to reverberate **:** REFLECTIVE

1**re·ver·ber·a·to·ry** \ri-ˈvər-b(ə-)rə-ˌtōr-ē, -bə-ˌtōr-, -ˌtȯr-\ *adj* **:** acting by reverberation; *esp* **:** forced back or diverted onto material under treatment

2**reverberatory** *n* **:** a furnace or kiln in which heat is radiated from the roof onto the material treated

1**re·vere** \ri-ˈvi(ə)r\ *vt* [L *revereri*, fr. *re-* + *vereri* to fear, respect — more at WARY] **:** to show devotion and honor to

syn REVERE, REVERENCE, VENERATE, WORSHIP, ADORE mean to regard with profound respect and honor. REVERE further implies deference and tenderness of feeling; REVERENCE suggests a self-denying acknowledging of what has an intrinsic and inviolate claim to respect; VENERATE implies a regarding as holy or sacrosanct esp. because of age; WORSHIP implies homage by word or ceremony esp. to a divine being; ADORE adds to WORSHIP a more personal emotion or may apply to any great and unquestioning love

2**revere** *n* [by alter.] **:** REVERS

1**rev·er·ence** \ˈrev-(ə-)rən(t)s, ˈrev-ərn(t)s\ *n* **1 :** honor or respect felt or shown **:** DEFERENCE; *esp* **:** profound adoring awed respect **2 :** a gesture of respect (as a bow) **3 :** the state of being revered or honored **4 :** one held in reverence — used as a title for a clergyman **syn** see HONOR

2**reverence** *vt* **:** to regard or treat with reverence **syn** see REVERE

1**rev·er·end** \ˈrev-(ə-)rənd, ˈrev-ərnd\ *adj* [ME, fr. MF, fr. L *reverendus*, gerundive of *revereri*] **1 :** worthy of reverence **:** REVERED **2 a :** of or relating to the clergy **b :** being a member of the clergy — used as a title usu. preceded by *the* and followed by a title or a full name ⟨the *Reverend* Mr. Doe⟩ ⟨the *Reverend* John Doe⟩ ⟨the *Reverend* Mother Superior⟩

2**reverend** *n* **:** a member of the clergy ⟨the ~ spoke⟩

rev·er·ent \ˈrev-(ə-)rənt, ˈrev-ərnt\ *adj* [ME, fr. L *reverent-*, *reverens*, prp. of *revereri*] **:** expressing or characterized by reverence **:** WORSHIPFUL — **rev·er·ent·ly** *adv*

rev·er·en·tial \ˌrev-ə-ˈren-chəl\ *adj* **1 :** proceeding from or expressing reverence ⟨~ awe⟩ **2 :** inspiring reverence — **rev·er·en·tial·ly** \-ˈrench-(ə-)lē\ *adv*

rev·er·ie *or* **rev·ery** \ˈrev-(ə-)rē\ *n* [F *rêverie*, fr. MF, delirium, fr. *resver, rever* to wander, be delirious] **1 :** DAYDREAM **2 :** the condition of being lost in thought

re·vers \ri-ˈvi(ə)r, -ˈve(ə)r\ *n, pl* **re·vers** \-ˈvi(ə)rz, -ˈve(ə)rz\ [F, lit., reverse, fr. MF, fr. *revers*, adj.] **:** a lapel esp. on a woman's garment

re·ver·sal \ri-ˈvər-səl\ *n* **1 :** an act or the process of reversing: as **a :** a change or overthrowing of a legal proceeding or judgment **b :** a causing to move or face in an opposite direction or to appear in an inverted position **2 :** a conversion of a photographic positive into a negative or vice versa

1**re·verse** \ri-ˈvərs\ *adj* [ME *revers*, fr. MF, fr. L *reversus*, pp. of *revertere* to turn back — more at REVERT] **1 a :** opposite or contrary to a previous or normal condition ⟨~ order⟩ **b :** having the back presented to the observer or opponent **2 :** acting or operating in a manner contrary to the usual **3 :** effecting reverse movement ⟨~ gear⟩ **4 :** so made that the part normally black is white and vice versa ⟨~ photoengraving⟩ — **re·verse·ly** *adv*

2**reverse** *vt* **1 a :** to turn completely about in position or direction **b :** to turn upside down **:** INVERT **2 :** ANNUL: as **a :** to overthrow, set aside, or make void (a legal decision) by a contrary decision **b :** to cause to take an opposite point of view **c :** to change to the contrary ⟨~ a policy⟩ **3 :** to cause to go in the opposite direction; *esp* **:** to cause (as an engine) to perform its action in the opposite direction ~ *vi* **1 :** to turn or move in the opposite direction **2 :** to put a mechanism (as an engine) in reverse — **re·vers·er** *n*

syn REVERSE, TRANSPOSE, INVERT mean to change to the opposite position. REVERSE is the most general term and may imply change in order, side, direction, meaning; TRANSPOSE implies a change in order or relative position of units often through exchange of position; INVERT applies chiefly to turning upside down or inside out or less often end for end

3**reverse** *n* **1 :** something directly contrary to something else **:** OPPOSITE **2 :** an act or instance of reversing; *specif* **:** a change for the worse **3 :** the back part of something; *esp* **:** VERSO 2 **4 a** (1) **:** a gear that reverses something; *also* **:** the whole mechanism brought into play when such a gear is used (2) **:** movement in reverse **b :** an offensive play in football in which a back moving in one direction gives the ball to a player moving in the opposite direction

re·vers·ibil·i·ty \ri-ˌvər-sə-ˈbil-ət-ē\ *n* **:** the quality or state of being reversible

1**re·vers·ible** \ri-ˈvər-sə-bəl\ *adj* **:** capable of being reversed or of reversing: as **a :** capable of going through a series of actions (as changes) either backward or forward ⟨~ chemical reaction⟩ **b** (1) **:** having two finished usable sides ⟨~ fabric⟩ (2) **:** wearable with either side out ⟨~ coat⟩ — **re·vers·ibly** \-blē\ *adv*

2**reversible** *n* **:** a reversible cloth or garment

re·ver·sion \ri-ˈvər-zhən, -shən\ *n* [ME, fr. MF, fr. L *reversion-*, *reversio* act of returning, fr. *reversus*, pp.] **1 a :** the part of a simple estate remaining in its owner after he has granted therefrom a lesser particular estate **b :** a future interest in property left in a grantor or his successor **2 :** the right of succession or future possession or enjoyment **3 :** an act or the process of returning (as to a former condition); *esp* **:** a return toward some ancestral type or condition **4 :** an act or instance of turning the opposite way **:** the state of being so turned **5 :** a product of reversion; *specif* **:** an organism with an atavistic character

re·ver·sion·al \-ˈvərzh-nəl, -ˈvərsh-, -ən-ᵊl\ *adj* **:** REVERSIONARY

re·ver·sion·ary \-ˈvər-zhə-ˌner-ē, -shə-\ *adj* **:** of, relating to, constituting, or involving esp. a legal reversion

re·ver·sion·er \-ˈvərzh-nər, -ˈvərsh-, -ə-nər\ *n* **:** one that has or is entitled to a reversion

re·vert \ri-ˈvərt\ *vi* [ME *reverten*, fr. MF *revertir*, fr. L *revertere*, v.t. to turn back & *reverti* v.i. to return, come back, fr. *re-* + *vertere*, *verti* to turn — more at WORTH] **1 :** to come or go back ⟨many ~*ed* to savagery⟩ **2 :** to return to the proprietor or his heirs at the end of a reversion **3 :** to return to an ancestral type **syn** see RETURN — **re·vert·er** *n* — **re·vert·ible** \-ˈvərt-ə-bəl\ *adj*

re·vert·ed \ri-ˈvərt-əd\ *adj* **:** turned or curled back or the wrong way ⟨~ leaf⟩; *also* **:** affected with reversion ⟨~ bacteria culture⟩ ⟨~ black currants⟩

re·vest \(ˈ)rē-ˈvest\ *vt* **:** REINSTATE, REINVEST ⟨lands ~*ed* in a former owner⟩

re·vet \ri-ˈvet\ *vt* **re·vet·ted; re·vet·ting** [F *revêtir*, lit., to clothe again, dress up, fr. L *revestire*, fr. *re-* + *vestire* to clothe — more at VEST] **:** to face (as an embankment) with a revetment

re·vet·ment \-mənt\ *n* **1 :** a facing (as of stone or concrete) to sustain an embankment **2 :** EMBANKMENT; *esp* **:** a barricade to provide shelter (as against bomb splinters or strafing)

re·vict·ual \(ˈ)rē-ˈvit-ᵊl\ *vb* **:** to victual again

1**re·view** \ri-ˈvyü\ *n* [MF *revue*, fr. *revoir* to look over, fr. *re-* + *voir* to see — more at VIEW] **1 :** REVISION 1 **2 a :** a formal military inspection **b :** a military ceremony honoring a person or an event **3 :** a general survey **4 :** an act of inspecting or examining **5 :** judicial reexamination (as of the proceedings of a lower tribunal by a higher) **6 a :** a critical evaluation (as of a book or play) **b :** a magazine devoted chiefly to reviews and essays **7 a :** a retrospective view or survey **b** (1) **:** renewed study of material previously studied (2) **:** an exercise facilitating such study **8 :** REVUE

2**re·view** \ri-ˈvyü, *1 is also* ˈrē-\ *vb* [in senses 1 & 2, fr. *re-* + *view*; in other senses, fr. 1*review*] *vt* **1** *archaic* **:** to view or see again **2 :** to examine again; *esp* **:** to reexamine judicially **3 :** to take a retrospective view of **4 a :** to go over or examine critically or deliberately **b :** to write a critical examination of ⟨~ a novel⟩ **5 :** to hold a review of ⟨~ troops⟩ ~ *vi* **1 :** to study material again **:** to make a review ⟨~ for a test⟩ **2 :** to write reviews

re·view·er \ri-ˈvyü-ər\ *n* **:** one that reviews; *esp* **:** a writer of critical reviews

re·vile \ri-ˈvī(ə)l\ *vb* [ME *revilen*, fr. MF *reviler* to despise, fr. *re-* + *vil* vile] *vt* **:** to subject to verbal abuse **:** VITUPERATE ~ *vi* **:** to use abusive language **:** RAIL **syn** see SCOLD — **re·vile·ment** \-mənt\ *n* — **re·vil·er** *n*

re·vis·able \ri-ˈvī-zə-bəl\ *adj* **:** capable of being revised

re·vis·al \-zəl\ *n* **:** an act of revising **:** REVISION

1**re·vise** \ri-ˈvīz\ *vt* [F *reviser*, fr. L *revisere* to look at again, fr. *revisus*, pp. of *revidēre* to see again, fr. *re-* + *vidēre* to see — more at WIT] **1 :** to look over again in order to correct or improve ⟨~ a manuscript⟩ **2 a :** to make a new, amended, improved, or up-to-date version of ⟨~ a dictionary⟩ **b :** to provide with a new taxonomic arrangement ⟨*revising* the alpine ferns⟩ **syn** see CORRECT — **re·vis·er** *or* **re·vi·sor** \-ˈvī-zər\ *n*

2**re·vise** \ˈrē-ˌvīz, ri-ˈ\ *n* **1 :** an act of revising **:** REVISION **2 :** a printing proof taken from matter that incorporates changes marked in a previous proof

Revised Standard Version *n* **:** a revision of the American Standard Version of the Bible published in 1946 and 1952

Revised Version *n* **:** a British revision of the Authorized Version of the Bible published in 1881 and 1885

re·vi·sion \ri-ˈvizh-ən\ *n* **1 :** an act of revising (as a manuscript) **2 :** a revised version — **re·vi·sion·ary** \-ə-ˌner-ē\ *adj*

re·vi·sion·ism \ri-ˈvizh-ə-ˌniz-əm\ *n* **1 :** advocacy of revision (as of a doctrine or treaty) **2 :** a movement in revolutionary Marxian socialism favoring an evolutionary spirit — **re·vi·sion·ist** \-ˈvizh-(ə-)nəst\ *adj or n*

1**re·vis·it** \(ˈ)rē-ˈviz-ət\ *vt* **:** to visit again **:** return to

2**revisit** *n* **:** a second or subsequent visit

re·vi·so·ry \ri-ˈvīz-(ə-)rē\ *adj* **:** having the power or purpose to revise ⟨~ body⟩ ⟨a ~ function⟩

re·vi·tal·iza·tion \(ˌ)rē-ˌvīt-ᵊl-ə-ˈzā-shən\ *n* **1 :** an act or instance of revitalizing **2 :** something revitalized

re·vi·tal·ize \(ˈ)rē-ˈvīt-ᵊl-ˌīz\ *vt* **:** to give new life or vigor to

re·viv·al \ri-ˈvī-vəl\ *n* **1 :** an act or instance of reviving **:** the state of being revived: as **a :** renewed attention to or interest in something **b :** a new presentation or publication **c** (1) **:** a period of renewed religious interest (2) **:** an often highly emotional evangelistic meeting or series of meetings **d :** REVITALIZATION 1 **2 :** restoration of force, validity, or effect (as to a contract)

re·viv·al·ism \-ˈvī-və-ˌliz-əm\ *n* **:** the spirit or methods characteristic of religious revivals

re·viv·al·ist \-ˈvīv-(ə-)ləst\ *n* **1 :** one who promotes religious revivals; *specif* **:** EVANGELIST **2 :** a reviver or restorer of something disused — **re·viv·al·is·tic** \-ˌvī-və-ˈlis-tik\ *adj*

re·vive \ri-ˈvīv\ *vb* [ME *reviven*, fr. MF *revivre*, fr. L *revivere* to live again, fr. *re-* + *vivere* to live — more at QUICK] *vi* **:** to return to consciousness or life **:** to become active or flourishing again ~ *vt* **1 :** to restore to consciousness or life **:** REANIMATE **2 :** to restore from a depressed, inactive, or unused state **3 :** to renew mentally **:** RECALL — **re·viv·er** *n*

re·viv·i·fi·ca·tion \(ˌ)rē-ˌviv-ə-fə-ˈkā-shən\ *n* **:** an act or instance of revivifying

re·viv·i·fy \rē-ˈviv-ə-ˌfī\ *vt* [F *révivifier*, fr. LL *revivificare*, fr. L *re-* + LL *vivificare* to vivify] **:** to give new life to **:** REVIVE

re·vi·vis·cence \ri-ˌvī-ˈvis-ᵊn(t)s, ˌrev-ə-\ *n* [L *reviviscere* to come to life again, fr. *re-* + *viviscere* to come to life, fr. *vivus* alive, living — more at QUICK] **:** an act of reviving **:** the state of being revived — **re·vi·vis·cent** \-ᵊnt\ *adj*

re·vo·ca·ble \ˈrev-ə-kə-bəl *also* ri-ˈvō-\ *adj* [ME, fr. MF, fr. L *revocabilis*, fr. *revocare*] **:** capable of being revoked

re·vo·ca·tion \ˌrev-ə-ˈkā-shən; ri-ˌvō-, ˌrē-\ *n* [ME, fr. MF, fr. L *revocation-*, *revocatio*, fr. *revocatus*, pp. of *revocare*] **:** an act or instance of revoking

re·vok·able \ri-ˈvō-kə-bəl\ *adj* **:** REVOCABLE

1**re·voke** \ri-ˈvōk\ *vb* [ME *revoken*, fr. MF *revoquer*, fr. L *revocare*, fr. *re-* + *vocare* to call — more at VOICE] *vt* **1 :** to bring or call back **2 :** to annul by recalling or taking back **:** RESCIND ⟨~ a will⟩ ~ *vi* **:** to fail to follow suit when able in a card game in violation of the rules — **re·vok·er** *n*

2**revoke** *n* **:** an act or instance of revoking in a card game

1**re·volt** \ri-ˈvōlt *also* -ˈvȯlt\ *vb* [MF *revolter*, fr. OIt *rivoltare* to overthrow, fr. (assumed) VL *revolvitare*, freq. of L *revolvere* to revolve, roll back] *vi* **1 :** to renounce allegiance or subjection (as

to a government) : REBEL **2 a :** to experience disgust or shock ⟨his nature ~*s* against such treatment⟩ **b :** to turn away with disgust ~ *vt* **:** to cause to turn away or shrink with disgust or abhorrence **:** NAUSEATE — **re·volt·er** *n*

[2]**revolt** *n* **1 :** an act or instance of revolting **2 :** a renunciation of allegiance to a government or other legitimate authority; *esp* **:** INSURRECTION **syn** see REBELLION

rev·o·lute \'rev-ə-,lüt\ *adj* [L *revolutus*, pp.] **:** rolled backward or downward ⟨~ margins⟩

rev·o·lu·tion \,rev-ə-'lü-shən\ *n* [ME *revolucioun*, fr. MF *revolution*, fr. LL *revolution-*, *revolutio*, fr. L *revolutus*, pp. of *revolvere*] **1 a** (1) **:** the action by a celestial body of going round in an orbit or elliptic course; *also* **:** apparent movement of such a body round the earth (2) **:** the time taken by a celestial body to make a complete round in its orbit (3) **:** the rotation of a celestial body on its axis **b :** completion of a course (as of years); *also* **:** the period made by the regular succession of a measure of time or by a succession of similar events **c** (1) **:** a progressive motion of a body round a center or axis so that any line of the body remains parallel to and returns to an initial position (2) **:** motion of any figure about a center or axis (3) **:** ROTATION 1b **2 a :** a sudden, radical, or complete change **b :** a fundamental change in political organization; *esp* **:** the overthrow or renunciation of one government or ruler and the substitution of another by the governed **syn** see REBELLION

[1]**rev·o·lu·tion·ary** \-shə-,ner-ē\ *adj* **1 a :** of, relating to, or constituting a revolution ⟨~ war⟩ **b** (1) **:** tending to or promoting revolution (2) **:** RADICAL, EXTREMIST **2** *cap* **:** of or relating to the American Revolution or the period of its occurrence

[2]**revolutionary** *n* **:** REVOLUTIONIST

Revolutionary calendar *n* **:** the calendar of the first French republic adopted in 1793, dated from September 22, 1792, and divided into 12 months of 30 days with five extra days in a regular year

rev·o·lu·tion·ist \,rev-ə-'lü-sh(ə-)nəst\ *n* **1 :** one engaged in a revolution **2 :** an adherent or advocate of revolutionary doctrines — **revolutionist** *adj*

rev·o·lu·tion·ize \-shə-,nīz\ *vt* **1 :** to overthrow the established government of **2 :** to imbue with revolutionary doctrines **3 :** to change fundamentally or completely ~ *vi* **:** to undergo revolution — **rev·o·lu·tion·iz·er** *n*

re·volv·able \ri-'väl-və-bəl, -'vȯl-\ *adj* **:** capable of being revolved

re·volve \ri-'välv, -'vȯlv\ *vb* [ME *revolven*, fr. L *revolvere* to roll back, cause to return, fr. *re-* + *volvere* to roll — more at VOLUBLE] *vt* **1 :** to turn over at length in the mind **:** PONDER ⟨~ a scheme⟩ **2 a :** to cause to go round in an orbit **b :** to cause to turn round on or as if on an axis **:** ROTATE ~ *vi* **1 :** RECUR **2 a :** to meditate on something **b :** to remain under consideration ⟨ideas *revolved* in his mind⟩ **3 a :** to move in a curved path round a center or axis **b :** to turn or roll round on an axis **4 :** to move in response to or dependence on a specified agent ⟨whole household ~*s* about the baby⟩ **syn** see CONSIDER

re·volv·er \-'väl-vər, -'vȯl-\ *n* **1 :** a handgun with a cylinder of several chambers brought successively into line with the barrel and discharged with the same hammer **2 :** one that revolves

re·volv·ing *adj* **:** tending to revolve or recur; *esp* **:** recurrently available ⟨~ credit⟩

revolving fund *n* **:** a fund set up for specified purposes to yield repayments restoring the fund for use again

re·vue \ri-'vyü\ *n* [F, fr. MF, review — more at REVIEW] **:** a theatrical production consisting typically of brief often satirical sketches and songs

re·vul·sion \ri-'vəl-shən\ *n* [L *revulsion-*, *revulsio* act of tearing away, fr. *revulsus*, pp. of *revellere* to pluck away, fr. *re-* + *vellere* to pluck — more at VULNERABLE] **1 :** a strong pulling or drawing away **:** WITHDRAWAL **2 a :** a sudden or strong reaction or change **b :** a sense of utter repugnance **:** REPULSION — **re·vul·sive** \-'vəl-siv\ *adj*

re·wake \(')rē-'wāk\ *or* **re·wak·en** \-'wā-kən\ *vb* **:** to waken again or anew

[1]**re·ward** \ri-'wȯ(ə)rd\ *vt* [ME *rewarden*, fr. ONF *rewarder* to regard, reward, fr. *re-* + *warder* to watch, guard, of Gmc origin; akin to OHG *wartēn* to watch — more at WARD] **1 :** to give a reward to or for **2 :** RECOMPENSE — **re·ward·able** \-'wȯrd-ə-bəl\ *adj* — **re·ward·er** *n*

[2]**reward** *n* **:** something that is given in return for good or evil done or received and esp. that is offered or given for some service or attainment

[1]**re·wind** \(')rē-'wīnd\ *vt* **:** to wind again; *esp* **:** to reverse the winding of (as film)

[2]**re·wind** \'rē-,wīnd, (')rē-'\ *n* **1 :** something that rewinds or is rewound **2 :** an act of rewinding

re·wire \(')rē-'wī(ə)r\ *vt* **:** to wire (as a house) anew

re·word \(')rē-'wərd\ *vt* **1 :** to repeat in the same words **2 :** to alter the wording of; *also* **:** to restate in other words

re·work \(')rē-'wərk\ *vt* **:** to work again or anew: as **a :** REVISE **b :** to reprocess (as used material) for further use

[1]**re·write** \(')rē-'rīt\ *vt* **1 :** to write in reply **2 :** to make a revision of (as a story): as **a :** to put (contributed material) into form for publication **b :** to alter (previously published material) for use in another publication ~ *vi* **:** to revise something previously written — **re·writ·er** *n*

[2]**re·write** \'rē-,rīt\ *n* **:** a piece of writing constructed by rewriting

rex \'reks\ *n, pl* **rex·es** *or* **rex** [F *castorrex*, *castorex*, a variety of rabbit, fr. L *castor* beaver + *rex* king — more at CASTOR, ROYAL] **:** an animal showing a genetic recessive variation in which the guard hairs are shorter than the undercoat or entirely lacking

rey·nard \'rān-ərd, 'ren-, -,är(d); rā-'när(d), re-\ *n, often cap* [ME *Renard*, name of the fox who is hero of the F beast epic *Roman de Renart*, fr. MF *Renart*, *Renard*] **:** FOX

re·zone \(')rē-'zōn\ *vt* **:** to alter the zoning of

rhab·do·coele \'rab-də-,sēl\ *n* [deriv. of Gk *rhabdos* rod + *koilos* hollow — more at CAVE] **:** a turbellarian worm (order Rhabdocoela) with an unbranched intestine

rhab·do·man·cy \-,man(t)-sē\ *n* [LGk *rhabdomanteia*, fr. Gk *rhabdos* rod + *-manteia* -mancy — more at VERVAIN] **:** divination by rods or wands

rhad·a·man·thine \,rad-ə-'man(t)-thən, -'man-,thīn\ *adj, often cap* [*Rhadamanthus*, mythical judge in the lower world] **:** rigorously strict or just

Rhae·to–Ro·man·ic \,rēt-ō-rō-'man-ik\ *n* [L *Rhaetus* of Rhaetia, ancient Roman province + *Romanic*] **:** a Romance language of eastern Switzerland, northeastern Italy, and adjacent parts of Austria

rham·na·ceous \ram-'nā-shəs\ *adj* [deriv. of Gk *rhamnos*] **:** of, relating to, or being the buckthorn family (Rhamnaceae)

rham·nose \'ram-,nōs, -,nōz\ *n* [ISV fr. NL *Rhamnus*, genus of the buckthorn; fr. its being produced from a plant of this genus] **:** a crystalline sugar $C_6H_{12}O_5$ that occurs combined in many plants and is obtained in the common dextrorotatory L form

rham·nus \-nəs\ *n* [NL, genus name, fr. Gk *rhamnos* buckthorn; akin to Gk *rhabdos* rod] **:** any of a genus (*Rhamnus*) of trees and shrubs of the buckthorn family with pinnately veined leaves, small perfect or polygamous flowers with the ovary free from the disk, and a fruit that is a drupe

rhaphe *var of* RAPHE

rhap·sod·ic \rap-'säd-ik\ *adj* **1 :** resembling or characteristic of a rhapsody **2 :** extravagantly emotional **:** RAPTUROUS — **rhap·sod·i·cal** \-i-kəl\ *adj* — **rhap·sod·i·cal·ly** \-k(ə-)lē\ *adv*

rhap·so·dist \'rap-səd-əst\ *n* **1 :** a professional reciter of epic poems **2 :** one who writes or speaks rhapsodically

rhap·so·dize \-sə-,dīz\ *vi* **:** to speak or write rhapsodically ⟨~ about a new book⟩

rhap·so·dy \'rap-səd-ē\ *n* [L *rhapsodia*, fr. Gk *rhapsōidia* recitation of selections from epic poetry, rhapsody, fr. *rhaptein* to sew, stitch together + *aidein* to sing; akin to OHG *worf* scythe handle, Gk *rhepein* to bend, incline — more at ODE] **1 :** a portion of an epic poem adapted for recitation **2** *archaic* **:** a miscellaneous collection **3 a** (1) **:** a highly emotional utterance or literary work (2) **:** extravagant rapturous discourse **b :** RAPTURE, ECSTASY **4 :** a musical composition of irregular form having an improvisatory character **syn** see BOMBAST

rhat·a·ny \'rat-ᵊn-ē\ *n* [Sp *ratania* & Pg *ratânhia*, fr. Quechua *ratánya*] **1 :** the dried root of either of two American shrubs (*Krameria triandra* and *K. argentea*) used as an astringent **2 :** a plant yielding rhatany

rhea \'rē-ə\ *n* [NL, genus of birds, prob. fr. L *Rhea*, mother of Zeus, fr. Gk] **:** any of several large tall flightless So. American birds (order Rheiformes) that resemble but are smaller than the African ostrich, have three toes, a fully feathered head and neck, an undeveloped tail, and pale gray to brownish feathers that droop over the rump and back

rhe·bok \'rē-,bäk\ *n* [Afrik *reebok*, fr. MD, male roe deer, fr. *ree* roe + *boc* buck] **:** a large gray southern African antelope (*Pelea capreolus*)

Rheims Version \'rēmz-\ *n* [*Rheims* (*Reims*), France, where it was made] **:** the New Testament portion of the Douay Version of the Bible

rhe·ni·um \'rē-nē-əm\ *n* [NL, fr. L *Rhenus* Rhine river] **:** a rare heavy metallic element that resembles manganese, is obtained either as a powder or as a silver-white hard metal, and is used in catalysts and thermocouples — see ELEMENT table

rheo- *comb form* [Gk *rhein* to flow — more at STREAM] **:** flow **:** CURRENT ⟨*rheo*stat⟩

rheo·log·i·cal \,rē-ə-'läj-i-kəl\ *adj* **:** of or relating to rheology

rhe·ol·o·gy \rē-'äl-ə-jē\ *n* [ISV] **:** a science dealing with the deformation and flow of matter

rhe·om·e·ter \rē-'äm-ət-ər\ *n* [ISV] **:** an instrument for measuring the flow of viscous substances

rheo·phile \'rē-ə-,fīl\ *also* **rheo·phil** \-,fil\ *adj* [ISV] **:** preferring or living in flowing water ⟨~ fauna⟩

rheo·stat \'rē-ə-,stat\ *n* **:** a resistor for regulating a current by means of variable resistances — **rheo·stat·ic** \,rē-ə-'stat-ik\ *adj*

rhe·sus monkey \,rē-səs-\ *n* [NL *Rhesus*, genus of monkeys, fr. L, a mythical king of Thrace, fr. Gk *Rhēsos*] **:** a pale brown Indian monkey (*Macaca mulata*) often kept in zoos and used in medical research

rhe·tor \'rē-,tȯ(ə)r, 're-; 'rēt-ər, 'ret-\ *n* [ME *rethor*, fr. L *rhetor*, fr. Gk *rhētōr*] **:** RHETORICIAN 1

rhet·o·ric \'ret-ə-rik\ *n* [ME *rethorik*, fr. MF *rethorique*, fr. L *rhetorica*, fr. Gk *rhētorikē*, lit., art of oratory, fr. fem. of *rhētorikos* of an orator, fr. *rhētōr* orator, rhetorician, fr. *eirein* to say, speak — more at WORD] **1 :** the art of speaking or writing effectively; *specif* **:** the study of principles and rules of composition formulated by ancient critics **2 a :** skill in the effective use of speech **b :** insincere or grandiloquent language **3 :** verbal communication **:** DISCOURSE

rhe·tor·i·cal \ri-'tȯr-i-kəl, -'tär-\ *also* **rhe·tor·ic** \ri-'tȯr-ik, -'tär-\ *adj* **1 a :** of, relating to, or concerned with rhetoric **b :** employed for rhetorical effect **2 a :** given to rhetoric **:** GRANDILOQUENT **b :** VERBAL — **rhe·tor·i·cal·ly** \-i-k(ə-)lē\ *adv* — **rhe·tor·i·cal·ness** \-kəl-nəs\ *n*

rhetorical question *n* **:** a question asked merely for effect with no answer expected

rhet·o·ri·cian \,ret-ə-'rish-ən\ *n* **1 a :** a master or teacher of rhetoric **b :** ORATOR **2 :** an eloquent or grandiloquent writer or speaker

rheum \'rüm\ *n* [ME *reume*, fr. MF, fr. L *rheuma*, fr. Gk, lit., flow, flux, fr. *rhein* to flow — more at STREAM] **1 :** a watery discharge from the mucous membranes esp. of the eyes or nose **2** *archaic* **:** TEARS — **rheumy** \'rü-mē\ *adj*

[1]**rheu·mat·ic** \rù-'mat-ik\ *adj* [ME *rewmatik* subject to rheum, fr. L *rheumaticus*, fr. Gk *rheumatikos*, fr. *rheumat-*, *rheuma*] **:** of, relating to, characteristic of, or affected with rheumatism — **rheu·mat·i·cal·ly** \-i-k(ə-)lē\ *adv*

[2]**rheumatic** *n* **:** one affected with rheumatism

rheumatic disease *n* **:** any of several diseases (as rheumatic fever or fibrositis) characterized by inflammation and pain in muscles or joints

rheumatic fever *n* **:** an acute disease occurring chiefly in children and young adults and characterized by fever, inflammation and

See *re-* and 2d element	rewarm	rewater	rewed	reweigher	reweld
revote	rewash	reweave	reweigh		

ə abut; ᵊ kitten; ər further; a back; ā bake; ä cot, cart; au̇ out; ch chin; e less; ē easy; g gift; i trip; ī life
j joke; ŋ sing; ō flow; ȯ flaw; ȯi coin; th thin; th this; ü loot; u̇ foot; y yet; yü few; yu̇ furious; zh vision

pain in and around the joints, and inflammatory involvement of the pericardium and heart valves

rheu·ma·tism \'rü-mə-,tiz-əm, 'rüm-ə-\ *n* [L *rheumatismus* flux, rheum, fr. Gk *rheumatismos,* fr. *rheumatizesthai* to suffer from a flux, fr. *rheumat-, rheuma* flux] **1 :** any of various conditions characterized by inflammation or pain in muscles, joints, or fibrous tissue ⟨muscular ~⟩ **2 :** RHEUMATOID ARTHRITIS

rheu·ma·tiz \-,tiz\ *n, chiefly dial* **:** RHEUMATISM

rheu·ma·toid \-,tȯid\ *adj* [ISV, fr. *rheumatism*] **:** characteristic of or affected with rheumatoid arthritis

rheumatoid arthritis *n* **:** a constitutional disease of unknown cause and progressive course characterized by inflammation and swelling of joint structures

Rh factor \ä-'räch-\ *n* [*rh*esus monkey (in which it was first detected)] **:** any of one or more substances present in the red blood cells of most persons and of higher animals, inherited according to Mendelian principles, and capable of inducing intense antigenic reactions

rhin- *or* **rhino-** *comb form* [NL, fr. Gk, fr. *rhin-, rhis*] **:** nose ⟨*rhin*itis⟩ **:** nose and ⟨*rhino*laryngology⟩

rhi·nal \'rīn-ᵊl\ *adj* **:** of or relating to the nose **:** NASAL

-rhine — see -RRHINE

rhin·en·ce·phal·ic \,rī-,nen(t)-sə-'fal-ik\ *adj* **:** of or relating to the rhinencephalon

rhin·en·ceph·a·lon \,rī-(,)nen-'sef-ə-,län, -lən\ *n* [NL] **:** the chiefly olfactory part of the forebrain

rhine·stone \'rīn-,stōn\ *n* [*Rhine* river, western Europe] **:** a colorless imitation stone of high luster made of glass, paste, or gem quartz

Rhine wine \'rīn-\ *n* **1 :** a typically light-bodied dry white wine produced in the Rhine valley **2 :** a wine similar to Rhine wine produced elsewhere

rhi·ni·tis \rī-'nīt-əs\ *n* [NL] **:** inflammation of the mucous membrane of the nose

[1]**rhi·no** \'rī-(,)nō\ *n* [origin unknown] **:** MONEY, CASH

[2]**rhino** *n, pl* **rhino** *or* **rhinos :** RHINOCEROS

rhi·noc·er·os \rī-'näs-(ə-)rəs\ *n, pl* **rhi·noc·er·os·es** *or* **rhinoceros** *or* **rhi·noc·eri** \-'näs-ə-,rī\ [ME *rinoceros,* fr. L *rhinocerot-, rhinoceros,* fr. Gk *rhinokerōt-, rhinokerōs,* fr. *rhin-* + *keras* horn — more at HORN] **:** any of various large powerful herbivorous thick-skinned perissodactyl mammals (family Rhinocerotidae) that have one or two heavy upright horns on the snout — **rhi·noc·er·ot·ic** \(,)rī-,näs-ə-'rät-ik\ *adj*

rhinoceros beetle *n* **:** any of various large chiefly tropical beetles (of *Dynastes* and closely related genera) having projecting horns on thorax and head

rhi·no·lar·yn·gol·o·gy \,rī-(,)nō-,lar-ən-'gäl-ə-jē\ *n* **:** a branch of medical science dealing with the nose and larynx

rhi·no·phar·yn·gi·tis \-,far-ən-'jīt-əs\ *n* [NL] **:** inflammation of the mucous membrane of the nose and pharynx

rhi·nos·co·py \rī-'näs-kə-pē\ *n* [ISV] **:** examination of the nasal passages

rhi·no·spo·rid·i·um \,rī-nō-spə-'rid-ē-əm\ *n* [NL, genus name, fr. *rhin-* + *sporidium* small spore] **:** any of a genus (*Rhinosporidium*) of microparasites of uncertain relationship associated with some nasal polyps in man and in horses

rhiz- *or* **rhizo-** *comb form* [NL, fr. Gk, fr. *rhiza* — more at ROOT] **:** root ⟨*rhiz*anthous⟩ ⟨*rhizo*carpous⟩

-rhi·za *or* **-r·rhi·za** \'rī-zə\ *n comb form, pl* **-rhi·zae** *or* **-r·rhi·zae** \-(,)zē\ *also* **-rhi·zas** *or* **-r·rhi·zas** \-zəz\ [NL, fr. Gk *rhiza*] **:** root **:** part resembling or connected with a root ⟨coleo*rhiza*⟩ ⟨myco*rrhiza*⟩

rhiz·an·thous \rī-'zan(t)-thəs\ *adj* [ISV *rhiz-* + Gk *anthos* flower — more at ANTHOLOGY] **:** producing flowers apparently directly from the root

rhi·zo·bi·um \rī-'zō-bē-əm\ *n, pl* **rhi·zo·bia** \-bē-ə\ [NL, genus name, fr. *rhiz-* + Gk *bios* life — more at QUICK] **:** any of a genus (*Rhizobium*) of small heterotrophic soil bacteria capable of forming symbiotic nodules on the roots of leguminous plants and of there becoming bacteroids that fix atmospheric nitrogen

rhi·zo·car·pous \,rī-zə-'kär-pəs\ *or* **rhi·zo·car·pic** \-pik\ *adj* [ISV] **:** having perennial underground parts but annual stems and foliage ⟨~ herbs⟩

rhi·zo·ceph·a·lan \,rī-zō-'sef-ə-lən\ *or* **rhi·zo·ceph·a·lid** \-ləd\ *n* [deriv. of Gk *rhiza* root + *kephalē* head — more at ROOT, CEPHALIC] **:** a crustacean of an order (Rhizocephala) comprising degenerate forms living as parasites on crabs and hermit crabs

rhi·zoc·to·nia \,rī-,zäk-'tō-nē-ə\ *n* [NL, genus name, fr. *rhiz-* + Gk *-ktonos* killing, fr. *kteinein* to kill; akin to Skt *kṣaṇoti* he wounds] **:** a fungus belonging to a form genus (*Rhizoctonia*) and including major plant pathogens

rhizoctonia disease *n* **:** a plant disease caused by a rhizoctonia; *esp* **:** one of potatoes characterized esp. by black scurfy spots on the tubers

rhi·zo·gen·ic \,rī-zə-'jen-ik\ *or* **rhi·zo·ge·net·ic** \-zō-jə-'net-ik\ *adj* **:** producing roots ⟨~ tissue⟩

rhi·zoid \'rī-,zȯid\ *n* **:** a rootlike structure — **rhi·zoi·dal** \rī-'zȯid-ᵊl\ *adj*

rhi·zo·ma·tous \rī-'zōm-ət-əs, -'zäm-\ *adj* [ISV, fr. NL *rhizomat-, rhizoma*] **:** having or resembling a rhizome

rhi·zome \'rī-,zōm\ *n* [NL *rhizomat-, rhizoma,* fr. Gk *rhizōmat-, rhizōma* mass of roots, fr. *rhizoun* to cause to take root, fr. *rhiza* root — more at ROOT] **:** a somewhat elongate usu. horizontal subterraneous plant stem that is often thickened by deposits of reserve food material, produces shoots above and roots below, and is distinguished from a true root in possessing buds, nodes, and usu. scalelike leaves — **rhi·zo·mic** \rī-'zō-mik, -'zäm-ik\ *adj*

rhi·zo·mor·phous \,rī-zə-'mȯr-fəs\ *adj* [ISV] **:** shaped like a root

rhi·zo·plane \'rī-zə-,plān\ *n* **:** the external surface of roots together with closely adhering soil particles and debris

rhi·zo·pod \'rī-zə-,päd\ *n* [deriv. of Gk *rhiza* + *pod-, pous* foot — more at FOOT] **:** any of a subclass (Rhizopoda) of usu. creeping protozoans having lobate or rootlike pseudopods and including the typical amoebas, foraminifers, and related forms — **rhi·zop·o·dal** \rī-'zäp-əd-ᵊl\ *adj* — **rhi·zop·o·dous** \-əd-əs\ *adj*

rhi·zo·pus \'rī-zə-pəs, -,pùs\ *n* [NL, genus name, fr. *rhiz-* + Gk *pous* foot] **:** any of a genus (*Rhizopus*) of mold fungi including economic pests causing decay

rhi·zo·sphere \'rī-zə-,sfi(ə)r\ *n* [ISV] **:** soil that surrounds and is influenced by the roots of a plant

rhi·zot·o·my \rī-'zät-ə-mē\ *n* [ISV] **:** the operation of cutting the anterior or posterior spinal nerve roots for therapeutic purposes

Rh–neg·a·tive \,är-,äch-'neg-ət-iv\ *adj* **:** lacking Rh factor in the blood

rho \'rō\ *n* [Gk *rhō,* of Sem origin; akin to Heb *rēsh* resh] **:** the 17th letter of the Greek alphabet — symbol P or ρ

rhod- *or* **rhodo-** *comb form* [NL, fr. L, fr. Gk, fr. *rhodon* rose] **:** rose **:** red ⟨*rhod*ium⟩ ⟨*rhodo*lite⟩

rho·da·mine \'rōd-ə-,mēn\ *n, often cap* [ISV] **1 :** any of a group of yellowish red to blue fluorescent dyes **2 :** a brilliant bluish red dye made by fusing an amino derivative of phenol with phthalic anhydride and used in coloring paper and as a biological stain — called also *rhodamine B*

Rhode Is·land bent \rō-,dī-lən(d)-\ *n* [*Rhode Island,* state of U.S.] **:** a lawn grass (*Agrostis tenuis*) of eastern No. America — called also *colonial bent*

Rhode Island Red *n* **:** any of an American breed of general-purpose domestic fowls having a long heavy body, smooth yellow or reddish legs, and rich brownish red plumage

Rhode Island White *n* **:** any of an American breed of domestic fowls resembling Rhode Island Reds but having pure white plumage

Rhodes grass \'rōdz-\ *n* [Cecil J. *Rhodes* †1902 E statesman and financier] **:** an African perennial grass (*Chloris gayana*) widely cultivated as a forage grass esp. in dry regions

Rho·de·sian man \rō-,dē-zh(ē-)ən-\ *n* [Northern *Rhodesia,* Africa] **:** an extinct African man (*Homo rhodesiensis* or *Africanthropus rhodesiensis*) having long bones of modern type, a skull with prominent brow ridges and large face but human palate and dentition, and a simple but relatively large brain

Rhodesian Ridge·back \-'rij-,bak\ *n* **:** any of an African breed of powerful long-bodied hunting dogs having a dense harsh short tan coat with a characteristic crest of reversed hair along the spine

Rhodes scholar \'rōd(z)-\ *n* **:** a holder of one of numerous scholarships founded under the will of Cecil J. Rhodes that are tenable at Oxford University for two or three years and are open to candidates from the British Commonwealth and the U.S.

rho·di·um \'rōd-ē-əm\ *n* [NL, fr. Gk *rhodon* rose] **:** a white hard ductile metallic element that is chiefly trivalent and resistant to attack by acids, occurs in platinum ores, and is used in alloys with platinum — see ELEMENT table

rho·do·chro·site \,rōd-ə-'krō-,sīt, ,räd-\ *n* [G *rhodocrosit,* fr. Gk *rhodochrōs* rose-colored, fr. *rhod-* + *chrōs* color; akin to Gk *chrōma* color — more at CHROMATIC] **:** a rose red mineral $MnCO_3$ consisting essentially of manganese carbonate

rho·do·den·dron \,rōd-ə-'den-drən\ *n* [NL, genus name, fr. L, rosebay, fr. Gk, fr. *rhod-* + *dendron* tree — more at DENDR-] **:** any of a genus (*Rhododendron*) of the heath family of widely cultivated shrubs and trees with alternate leaves and showy flowers; *esp* **:** one with leathery evergreen leaves as distinguished from a deciduous azalea

rho·do·lite \'rōd-ᵊl-,īt\ *n* **:** a pink or purple garnet used as a gem

rhodomontade *var of* RODOMONTADE

rho·don·ite \'rōd-ᵊn-,īt\ *n* [G *rhodonit,* fr. Gk *rhodon* rose] **:** a pale red triclinic mineral $MnSiO_3$ that consists essentially of manganese silicate and is used as an ornamental stone

rho·do·plast \'rōd-ə-,plast\ *n* [ISV] **:** one of the reddish chromatophores occurring in the red algae

rho·dop·sin \rō-'däp-sən\ *n* [ISV *rhod-* + Gk *opsis* sight, vision + ISV *-in* — more at OPTIC] **:** a red photosensitive pigment in the retinal rods of marine fishes and most higher vertebrates that is important in vision in dim light — called also *visual purple*

rho·do·ra \rō-'dōr-ə, -'dȯr-\ *n* [NL, genus name, fr. L, a plant] **:** any of a genus (*Rhodora*) of the heath family of shrubs that are found in Canada and New England and have delicate pink flowers produced before or with the leaves in the spring

rhomb \'räm(b)\ *n, pl* **rhombs** \'rämz\ [MF *rhombe,* fr. L *rhombus*] **:** RHOMBUS

rhomb- *or* **rhombo-** *comb form* [MF, fr. L, fr. Gk, fr. *rhombos*] **:** rhomb ⟨*rhomb*encephalon⟩ ⟨*rhombo*hedron⟩

rhomb·en·ceph·a·lon \,räm-(,)ben-'sef-ə-,län, -lən\ *n* [NL] **:** the parts of the vertebrate brain that develop from the embryonic hindbrain; *also* **:** HINDBRAIN 1a

rhom·bic \'räm-bik\ *adj* **1 :** having the form of a rhombus **2 :** ORTHORHOMBIC

rhom·bo·he·dral \,räm-bō-'hē-drəl\ *adj* **:** relating to or having the form of a rhombohedron

rhom·bo·he·dron \-drən\ *n, pl* **rhombohedrons** *or* **rhom·bo·he·dra** \-drə\ [NL] **:** a parallelepiped whose faces are rhombuses

rhom·boid \'räm-,bȯid\ *n* [MF *rhomboïde,* fr. L *rhomboides,* fr. Gk *rhomboeidēs* resembling a rhombus, fr. *rhombos*] **:** a parallelogram in which the angles are oblique and adjacent sides are unequal — **rhomboid** *adj* — **rhom·boi·dal** \räm-'bȯid-ᵊl\ *adj*

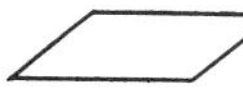

rhomboid

rhom·boi·de·us \räm-'bȯid-ē-əs\ *n, pl* **rhomboi·dei** \-ē-,ī\ [NL, fr. L *rhomboides* rhomboid] **:** either of two muscles that lie beneath the trapezius muscle and connect the spinous processes of various vertebrae with the medial border of the scapula

rhom·bus \'räm-bəs\ *n, pl* **rhom·bus·es** *or* **rhom·bi** \-,bī, -,bē\ [L, fr. Gk *rhombos*] **:** an equilateral parallelogram usu. having oblique angles

rhon·chus \'räŋ-kəs\ *n, pl* **rhon·chi** \'rän-,kī, 'räŋ-, -,kē\ [LGk, fr. *rhenchein* to snore, wheeze; akin to OIr *srennim* I snore] **:** a whistling or snoring sound heard on auscultation of the chest when the air channels are partly obstructed

Rh–pos·i·tive \,är-,äch-'päz-ət-iv, -'päz-tiv\ *adj* **:** containing Rh factor in the red blood cells

rhu·barb \'rü-,bärb\ *n* [ME *rubarbe,* fr. MF *reubarbe,* fr. ML *reubarbarum,* alter. of *rha barbarum,* lit., barbarian rhubarb] **1 :** any of several plants (genus *Rheum*) of the buckwheat family having large leaves with thick succulent petioles often used as food **2 :** the dried rhizome and roots of any of several rhubarbs grown in China and Tibet and used as a purgative and stomachic bitter **3 :** a heated dispute or controversy

rhumb \'rəm(b)\ *n, pl* **rhumbs** \'rəmz\ [Sp *rumbo* rhumb, rhumb line] **:** any of the points of the mariner's compass

rhumba *var of* RUMBA

rhumb line *n* [Sp *rumbo*] **:** a line on the surface of the earth that makes equal oblique angles with all meridians and is the path of a

ship sailing always oblique to the meridian in the direction of one and the same point of the compass

rhus dermatitis \ˌrəs-, ˌrüs-\ *n* [NL *Rhus*, genus name, fr. L, sumac, fr. Gk *rhous*] **:** dermatitis caused by contact with poison ivy or related plants (genus *Rhus*)

[1]rhyme \ˈrīm\ *n* [alter. of ME *rime*, fr. OF] **1 a :** correspondence in terminal sounds of two or more words, lines of verse, or other units of composition or utterance **b :** one of two or more words thus corresponding in sound **c :** correspondence of other than terminal word sounds: as (1) **:** ALLITERATION (2) **:** INTERNAL RHYME **2 a** (1) **:** rhyming verse (2) **:** POETRY **b :** a composition in verse that rhymes **3 :** RHYTHM, MEASURE

[2]rhyme *vi* **1 :** to make rhymes; *also* **:** to compose rhyming verse **2 a** *of a word or verse* **:** to end in syllables that rhyme **b :** to be a rhyme ⟨*cover* ~*s* with *lover*⟩ **3 :** to be in accord **:** HARMONIZE ~ *vt* **1 :** to relate or praise in rhyming verse **2 a :** to put into rhyme **b :** to compose (verse) in rhyme **c :** to cause to rhyme **:** use as rhyme

rhym·er \ˈrī-mər\ *n* **:** one that makes rhymes; *specif* **:** RHYMESTER

rhyme royal \-ˈrȯi(-ə)l\ *n* **:** a stanza of seven lines in iambic pentameter with a rhyme scheme of *ababbcc*

rhyme scheme *n* **:** the arrangement of rhymes in a stanza or a poem

rhyme·ster \ˈrīm(p)-stər\ *n* **:** an inferior poet **:** a maker of poor verse

[1]rhyn·cho·ce·pha·lian \ˌriŋ-(ˌ)kō-sə-ˈfāl-yən\ *adj* [deriv. of Gk *rhynchos* beak, snout + *kephalē* head] **:** of or relating to an order (Rhynchocephalia) of reptiles resembling lizards

[2]rhynchocephalian *n* **:** a rhynchocephalian reptile **:** TUATARA

rhyn·choph·o·ran \rin-ˈkäf-ə-rən, riŋ-\ *or* **rhyn·cho·phore** \ˈriŋ-kə-ˌfō(ə)r, -ˌfȯ(ə)r\ *n* [deriv. of Gk *rhynchos* + *pherein* to bear] **:** any of a group (Rhynchophora) of beetles with the head usu. prolonged as a snout **:** SNOUT BEETLE, WEEVIL

rhyn·choph·o·rous \rin-ˈkäf-ə-rəs, riŋ-\ *adj* [Gk *rhynchos* beak + *pherein* to bear — more at BEAR] **:** having a beak

rhy·o·lite \ˈrī-ə-ˌlīt\ *n* [G *rhyolith*, fr. Gk *rhyax* stream, stream of lava (fr. *rhein*) + G *-lith* -lite] **:** a very acid volcanic rock that is the lava form of granite — **rhy·o·lit·ic** \ˌrī-ə-ˈlit-ik\ *adj*

rhythm \ˈrith-əm\ *n* [MF & L; MF *rhythme*, fr. L *rhythmus*, fr. Gk *rhythmos*, fr. *rhein* to flow — more at STREAM] **1 a :** an ordered recurrent alternation of strong and weak elements in the flow of sound and silence in speech **b :** a particular example or form of rhythm ⟨iambic ~⟩ **2 a :** the aspect of music comprising all the elements (as accent, meter) that relate to forward movement **b :** a characteristic rhythmic pattern ⟨rumba ~⟩; *also* **:** [1]METER 2 **c :** the group of instruments in a band supplying the rhythm **3 a :** movement or fluctuation marked by the regular recurrence or natural flow of related elements **b :** the repetition in a literary work of phrase, incident, character type, or symbol **4 :** a regularly recurrent quantitative change in a variable biological process **5 :** the effect created by the elements in a play, movie, or novel that relate to the temporal development of the action — **rhyth·mic** \ˈrith-mik\ *or* **rhyth·mi·cal** \-mi-kəl\ *adj* — **rhyth·mi·cal·ly** \-mi-k(ə-)lē\ *adv*

rhythm band *n* **:** a band usu. composed of school children who play simple percussion instruments (as rhythm sticks, sleigh bells, or tambourines) to learn fundamentals of coordination and music

rhyth·mic·i·ty \rith-ˈmis-ət-ē\ *n* **:** the state of being rhythmic or of responding rhythmically

rhyth·mics \ˈrith-miks\ *n pl but sing or pl in constr* **:** the science or theory of rhythms

rhyth·mist \ˈrith-(ə-)məst\ *n* **:** one who studies or has a feeling for rhythm

rhyth·mi·za·tion \ˌrith-(ə-)mə-ˈzā-shən\ *n* **:** the organization of a series of events or processes into a rhythmic whole

rhyth·mize \ˈrith-(ə-)ˌmīz\ *vt* **:** to order or compose rhythmically

rhythm method *n* **:** a method of birth control involving continence during the period in which ovulation is most likely to occur

rhythm stick *n* **:** one of a pair of plain or notched wood sticks that are struck or rubbed together to produce various percussive sounds and are used esp. by young children in rhythm bands

rhyt·i·dome \ˈrit-ə-ˌdōm\ *n* [prob. fr. (assumed) NL *rhytidoma*, fr. Gk *rhytidōma* wrinkle, fr. *rhytidoun* to wrinkle, fr. *rhytid-*, *rhytis* wrinkle] **:** the bark external to the last formed periderm

[1]ri·al \rē-ˈȯl, -ˈäl\ *n* [Per, fr. Ar *riyāl* riyal] **1** — see MONEY table **2** — see *pound* at MONEY table

[2]rial *var of* RIYAL

ri·al·to \rē-ˈal-(ˌ)tō\ *n* [*Rialto*, island and district in Venice] **1 :** EXCHANGE, MARKETPLACE **2 :** a theater district

ri·ant \ˈrī-ənt, ˈrē-; rē-ˈäⁿ\ *adj* [MF, prp. of *rire* to laugh, fr. L *ridēre* — more at RIDICULOUS] **:** MIRTHFUL, GAY — **ri·ant·ly** \ˈrī-ənt-lē, ˈrē-\ *adv*

ri·a·ta \rē-ˈat-ə, -ˈät-\ *n* [modif. of AmerSp *reata*] **:** LARIAT

[1]rib \ˈrib\ *n* [ME, fr. OE; akin to OHG *rippi* rib, Gk *erephein* to roof over] **1 a :** one of the paired curved bony or partly cartilaginous rods that stiffen the walls of the body of most vertebrates and protect the viscera **b :** a cut of meat including a rib **c** [fr. the account of Eve's creation from Adam's rib, Gen 2:21–22] **:** WIFE **2 :** something resembling a rib in shape or function: as **a** (1) **:** a traverse member of the frame of a ship that runs from keel to deck (2) **:** a light fore-and-aft member in an airplane's wing **b :** one of the stiff strips supporting an umbrella's fabric **c :** one of the arches in Romanesque and Gothic vaulting meeting and crossing one another and dividing the whole vaulted space into triangles **3 :** an elongated ridge: as **a** (1) **:** a vein of an insect's wing (2) **:** one of the primary veins of a leaf **b :** one of the ridges in a knitted or woven fabric

[2]rib *vt* **ribbed; rib·bing 1 :** to furnish or enclose with ribs **2 :** to form vertical ridges in in knitting — **rib·ber** *n*

[3]rib *vt* **ribbed; rib·bing** [prob. fr. [1]*rib;* fr. the tickling of the ribs to cause laughter] **:** to poke fun at **:** KID — **rib·ber** *n*

[4]rib *n* **1 :** JOKE **2 :** PARODY

[1]rib·ald \ˈrib-əld *also* ˈrib-ˌȯld, ˈrī-ˌbȯld\ *n* [ME, fr. OF *ribaut*, *ribauld* wanton, rascal, fr. *riber* to be wanton, of Gmc origin; akin to OHG *rīban* to be wanton, lit., to twist; akin to Gk *rhiptein* to throw] **:** a ribald person

[2]ribald *adj* **1 :** CRUDE, OFFENSIVE ⟨~ language⟩ **2 :** characterized by or using broad indecent humor **syn** see COARSE

rib·ald·ry \ˈrib-əl-drē\ *n* **1 :** ribald quality or element **2 :** ribald language or humor

rib·and \ˈrib-ənd\ *n* [ME, alter. of *riban*] **:** a ribbon used esp. as a decoration

rib·band \ˈrib-ˌ(b)and, ˈrib-ən(d)\ *n* [[1]*rib* + *band*] **:** a long narrow strip or bar used in shipbuilding; *esp* **:** one bent and bolted longitudinally to the frames to hold them in position during construction

rib·bing \ˈrib-iŋ\ *n* **:** an arrangement of ribs (as in timberwork or leaves)

[1]rib·bon \ˈrib-ən\ *n* [ME *riban*, fr. MF *riban*, *ruban*] **1 a :** a flat or tubular narrow closely woven fabric (as of silk or rayon) used for trimmings or knitting **b :** a narrow fabric used for tying packages **c :** a piece of usu. multicolored ribbon worn as a military decoration or in place of a medal **d :** a strip of colored satin given for winning a place in a competition **2 :** a long narrow strip resembling a ribbon: as **a :** a board framed into the studs to support the ceiling or floor joists **b :** a strip of inked fabric (as in a typewriter) **3** *pl* **:** REINS **4 :** TATTER, SHRED — usu. used in pl. **5 :** RIBBAND — **rib·bon·like** \-ˌlīk\ *adj*

[2]ribbon *vt* **1 a :** to adorn with ribbons **b :** to divide into ribbons **2 :** to rip to shreds

ribbon candy *n* **:** a thin brittle usu. colored sugar candy folded back and forth upon itself

ribbon development *n* **:** a system of buildings built side by side along a road

rib·bon·fish \ˈrib-ən-ˌfish, ˈrib-ᵊm-\ *n* **:** any of various elongate greatly compressed marine fishes (as a dealfish or oarfish)

rib·by \ˈrib-ē\ *adj* **:** showing or marked by ribs

rib cage *n* **:** the bony enclosing wall of the chest consisting chiefly of the ribs and their connectives

ri·bes \ˈrī-(ˌ)bēz\ *n, pl* **ribes** [NL, genus name, fr. ML, currant, fr. Ar *rībās* rhubarb] **:** any of a genus (*Ribes*) of shrubs of the saxifrage family including the currants and usu. the gooseberries

rib·grass \ˈrib-ˌgras\ *n* **:** [1]PLANTAIN; *specif* **:** an Old World plantain (*Plantago lanceolata*) with long narrow ribbed leaves

rib·let \ˈrib-lət\ *n* **:** one of the rib ends in the strip of breast of lamb or veal

ri·bo·fla·vin \ˌrī-bə-ˈflā-vən\ *n* [ISV *ribose* + L *flavus* yellow — more at BLUE] **:** a yellow crystalline compound $C_{17}H_{20}N_4O_6$ that is a growth-promoting member of the vitamin B complex occurring both free (as in milk) and combined (as in liver) — called also *lactoflavin, vitamin B_2, vitamin G*

ri·bo·nu·cle·ic acid \ˌrī-bō-n(y)ü-ˌklē-ik-, -ˌklā-\ *n* [*ribose* + *nucleic*] **:** any of various nucleic acids that yield ribose as one product of hydrolysis, occur esp. in cytoplasm, and are associated with control of cellular chemical activities

ri·bose \ˈrī-ˌbōs, -ˌbōz\ *n* [ISV, fr. *ribonic acid* ($HOCH_2(CHOH)_3$-$COOH$)] **:** a pentose $C_5H_{10}O_5$ found esp. in the D-form (as adenosine) and obtained from nucleic acids

ri·bo·some \ˈrī-bə-ˌsōm\ *n* [*ribo*nucleic + *-some*] **:** a protoplasmic granule containing ribonucleic acid and held to be a center of protein synthesis

rib roast *n* **:** a cut of meat containing the large piece that lies along the outer side of the rib

rib·wort \ˈrib-ˌwərt, -ˌwȯ(ə)rt\ *n* **:** RIBGRASS

rice \ˈrīs\ *n, pl* **rice** [ME *rys*, fr. OF *ris*, fr. OIt *riso*, fr. Gk *oryza*, *oryzon*] **:** an annual cereal grass (*Oryza sativa*) widely cultivated in warm climates for its seed that is used for food and for its by-products

rice·bird \ˈrīs-ˌbərd\ *n* **:** any of several small birds common in rice fields; *esp* **:** BOBOLINK

rice Christian *n* **:** a convert to Christianity for material benefits

rice paper *n* [fr. its resemblance to paper made from rice straw] **:** a thin papery material made by cutting the rice-paper tree pith into a sheet and pressing it flat

rice–paper tree *n* **:** a small Asiatic tree or shrub (*Tetrapanax papyriferum*) of the ginseng family

rice polishings *n pl* **:** the inner bran layer of rice rubbed off in milling

ric·er \ˈrī-sər\ *n* **:** a kitchen utensil in which soft foods are pressed through a perforated container to produce strings about the diameter of a rice grain

ri·cer·car \ˌrē-ˌcher-ˈkär\ *n* [It, fr. *ricercare* to seek again, fr. *ri-* re- (fr. L *re-*) + *cercare* to seek, fr. LL *circare* to go about; fr. the disguising of the subjects by various alterations] **:** any of various contrapuntal instrumental forms esp. of the 16th and 17th centuries

rich \ˈrich\ *adj* [ME *riche*, fr. OE *rīce;* akin to OHG *rīhhi* rich, OE *rīce* kingdom, OHG *rīhhi;* all fr. prehistoric Gmc words borrowed fr. Celt words akin to OIr *rī* (gen. *rīg*) king — more at ROYAL] **1 :** possessing or controlling great wealth **:** WEALTHY **2 a :** having high value or quality **b :** well supplied **3 :** magnificently impressive **:** SUMPTUOUS **4 a :** vivid and deep in color ⟨~ red⟩ **b :** full and mellow in tone and quality ⟨~ voice⟩ **c :** PUNGENT ⟨~ odors⟩ **5 :** highly productive ⟨~ mine⟩ **6 a :** having abundant plant nutrients ⟨~ soil⟩ **b :** highly seasoned, fatty, oily, or sweet ⟨~ foods⟩ **c :** high in the combustible component ⟨~ fuel mixture⟩ **7 a :** AMUSING; *also* **:** LAUGHABLE **b :** MEANINGFUL, SIGNIFICANT ⟨~ allusions⟩ **c :** LUSH ⟨~ meadows⟩ **8 :** pure or nearly pure ⟨~ lime⟩ — **rich·ness** *n*

syn RICH, WEALTHY, AFFLUENT, OPULENT mean having goods, property, and money in abundance. RICH implies having more than enough to gratify normal needs or desires; WEALTHY stresses the possession of property and intrinsically valuable things; AFFLUENT suggests prosperity and an increasing wealth; OPULENT suggests lavish expenditure and display of great wealth

Rich·ard Roe \ˌrich-ər-ˈdrō\ *n* **:** a party to legal proceedings whose true name is unknown — compare JOHN DOE

rich·en \ˈrich-ən\ *vt* **rich·en·ing** \-(ə-)niŋ\ **:** to make rich or richer

rich·es \ˈrich-əz\ *n pl* [ME, sing. or pl., fr. *richesse*, lit., richness, fr. OF, fr. *riche* rich, of Gmc origin; akin to OE *rīce* rich] **:** things that make one rich **:** WEALTH

rich·ly \ˈrich-lē\ *adv* **1 :** in a rich manner **2 :** in full measure **:** AMPLY ⟨praise ~ deserved⟩

ri·cin \ˈrīs-ᵊn, ˈris-\ *n* [L *ricinus* castor-oil plant] **:** a poisonous protein in the castor bean

ri·cin·ole·ic acid \ˌrīs-ᵊn-ō-ˌlē-ik-, ˌris-, -ˌlā-\ *n* [L *ricinus* + E *oleic*] **:** an oily unsaturated hydroxy fatty acid $C_{18}H_{34}O_3$ found in castor oil in the form of a glyceride

ric·i·nus \ˈris-ᵊn-əs\ *n* [NL, genus name, fr. L, castor-oil plant] **:** any of a genus (*Ricinus*) of plants (as the castor-oil plant) of the spurge family with large palmate leaves

[1]**rick** \ˈrik\ *n* [ME *reek*, fr. OE *hrēac;* akin to ON *hraukr* rick] **1 :** a stack (as of hay) in the open air **2 :** a pile of material (as cordwood) split from short logs

[2]**rick** *vt* **:** to pile (as hay) in ricks

[3]**rick** *vt* [perh. fr. ME *wrikken* to move unsteadily] *chiefly Brit* **:** WRENCH, SPRAIN

rick·ets \ˈrik-əts\ *n pl but sing in constr* [origin unknown] **:** a childhood disease characterized esp. by faulty ossification of bone from defective deposition and utilization of calcium and phosphorus due to inadequate sunlight or vitamin D

ric·ket·tsia \rik-ˈet-sē-ə\ *n, pl* **ric·ket·tsi·as** *or* **ric·ket·tsi·ae** \-sē-ˌē, -ˌī\ [NL, genus of microorganisms, fr. Howard T. *Ricketts* †1910 Am pathologist] **:** any of a family (Rickettsiaceae) of pleomorphic rod-shaped nonfilterable microorganisms that cause various diseases (as typhus) — **ric·ket·tsi·al** \-sē-əl\ *adj*

rick·ety \ˈrik-ət-ē\ *adj* **1 :** affected with rickets **2 a :** feeble in the joints ⟨a ~ old man⟩ **b :** SHAKY, UNSOUND ⟨~ stairs⟩

rick·ey \ˈrik-ē\ *n* [prob. fr. the name *Rickey*] **:** a drink containing liquor, lime juice, sugar, and soda water; *also* **:** a similar drink without liquor

rick·rack *or* **ric·rac** \ˈrik-ˌrak\ *n* [redupl. of [4]*rack*] **:** a flat braid woven to form zigzags and used esp. as trimming on clothing

rick·sha *or* **rick·shaw** \ˈrik-ˌshȯ\ *n* **:** JINRIKISHA

[1]**ric·o·chet** \ˈrik-ə-ˌshā, ˌrik-ə-ˈ, *Brit also* -ˌshet, -ˈshet\ *n* [F] **:** a glancing rebound (as of a projectile off a flat surface); *also* **:** an object that ricochets

[2]**ricochet** *vi* **ric·o·cheted** *or* **ric·o·chet·ted; ric·o·chet·ing** *or* **ric·o·chet·ting :** to skip with or as if with glancing rebounds

ric·tal \ˈrik-tᵊl\ *adj* **:** of or relating to the rictus

ric·tus \ˈrik-təs\ *n* [NL, fr. L, open mouth, fr. *rictus*, pp. of *ringi* to open the mouth; akin to OSlav *ręgnǫti*] **1 :** the gape of a bird's mouth **2 a :** the mouth orifice **b :** a gaping grin or grimace

rid \ˈrid\ *vt* **rid** *also* **rid·ded; rid·ding** [ME *ridden* to clear, fr. ON *rythja;* akin to L *ruere* to dig up — more at RUG] **1** *archaic* **:** SAVE, RESCUE **2 :** to make free **:** RELIEVE, DISENCUMBER ⟨~ himself of his troubles⟩ ⟨be ~ of worries⟩ ⟨get ~ of that junk⟩

rid·able *or* **ride·able** \ˈrīd-ə-bəl\ *adj* **:** fit for riding

rid·dance \ˈrid-ᵊn(t)s\ *n* **1 :** an act of ridding **2 :** DELIVERANCE, RELIEF — often used in the phrase *good riddance*

[1]**rid·dle** \ˈrid-ᵊl\ *n* [ME *redels*, *ridel*, fr. OE *rǣdelse* opinion, conjecture, riddle; akin to OE *rǣdan* to interpret — more at READ] **1 :** a mystifying, misleading, or puzzling question posed as a problem to be solved or guessed **:** CONUNDRUM, ENIGMA **2 :** something or someone difficult to understand **syn** see MYSTERY

[2]**riddle** *vb* **rid·dling** \ˈrid-liŋ, -ᵊl-iŋ\ *vt* **1 :** to find the solution of **:** EXPLAIN, INTERPRET **2 :** to set a riddle for **:** MYSTIFY, PUZZLE **~** *vi* **:** to speak in or propound riddles — **rid·dler** \-lər, -ᵊl-ər\ *n*

[3]**riddle** *n* [ME *riddil*, fr. OE *hriddel;* akin to L *cribrum* sieve, *cernere* to sift — more at CERTAIN] **:** a coarse sieve

[4]**riddle** *vt* **rid·dling** \ˈrid-liŋ, -ᵊl-iŋ\ **1 :** to separate (as grain from the chaff) with a riddle **:** pass through a riddle **:** SCREEN **2 a :** to fill (something or someone) as full of holes as a sieve **:** puncture often and thoroughly ⟨*riddled* the ship with a broadside⟩ **b :** to corrupt throughout **:** PERMEATE ⟨slums *riddled* with disease⟩

[1]**ride** \ˈrīd\ *vb* **rode** \ˈrōd\ *or chiefly dial* **rid** \ˈrid\ **rid·den** \ˈrid-ᵊn\ *or chiefly dial* **rid** *or* **rode; rid·ing** \ˈrīd-iŋ\ [ME *riden*, fr. OE *rīdan;* akin to OHG *rītan* to ride] *vi* **1 a :** to sit and travel on the back of an animal that one directs **b :** to travel in or on a conveyance **2 :** to become sustained ⟨*rode* on a wave of popularity⟩ **3 a :** to lie moored or anchored ⟨ship ~*s* at anchor⟩ **b :** SAIL **c :** to move like a floating object ⟨moon *rode* in the sky⟩ **4 :** to become supported on a point or surface **5 :** to travel over a surface ⟨car ~*s* well⟩ **6 :** to continue without interference ⟨let it ~⟩ **7 :** to be contingent **:** DEPEND ⟨plans ~ on his nomination⟩ **8 :** to climb up on the body ⟨shorts that ~ up⟩ **9 :** to become bet ⟨his money is *riding* on the favorite⟩ **~** *vt* **1 a :** to mount and travel on while controlling ⟨~ a bike⟩ **b :** to move with ⟨~ the waves⟩ **2 a :** to traverse by conveyance ⟨*rode* 500 miles⟩ **b :** to ride a horse in ⟨~ a race⟩ **3 :** SURVIVE, OUTLAST — usu. used with *out* ⟨*rode* out the gale⟩ **4 :** to traverse on horseback to inspect or maintain ⟨~ fence⟩ **5 :** to mount in copulation **6 a :** OBSESS, OPPRESS ⟨*ridden* by anxiety⟩ **b :** to harass persistently **:** NAG **c :** TEASE, RIB **7 :** CARRY, CONVEY **8 :** to project over **:** OVERLAP **9 :** to give with (a punch) to soften the impact **10 :** to keep in partial engagement by resting a foot continuously on the pedal ⟨~ the clutch⟩

syn DRIVE: RIDE stresses a being borne along on the back of an animal or in a conveyance and implies control only when the rider is mounted astride ⟨*ride* a bicycle⟩ ⟨*ride* in a train⟩ DRIVE primarily refers to the action of controlling the movements of an animal or a powered vehicle whether or not the agent is borne along ⟨*drive* a team⟩ ⟨*drive* a bus⟩

— **ride circuit :** to hold court in the various towns of a judicial circuit — **ride for a fall :** to court disaster — **ride herd on :** to keep a check on — **ride roughshod over :** to treat with disdain or abuse

[2]**ride** *n* **1 :** an act of riding; *esp* **:** a trip on horseback or by vehicle **2 :** a way (as a road or path) suitable for riding **3 :** any of various mechanical devices (as at an amusement park) for riding on **4 a :** a trip on which gangsters take a victim to murder him **b :** HOODWINKING, SWINDLING ⟨take the taxpayers for a ~⟩ **5 :** a means of transportation **6 :** the qualities of travel comfort in a vehicle

rid·er \ˈrīd-ər\ *n* **1 :** one that rides **2 a :** an addition to a document often attached on a separate piece of paper **b :** a clause appended to a legislative bill to secure a usu. distinct object **3 :** something used to overlie another or to move along on another piece — **rid·er·less** \-ləs\ *adj*

[1]**ridge** \ˈrij\ *n* [ME *rigge*, fr. OE *hrycg;* akin to OHG *hrukki* ridge, back, L *cruc-*, *crux* cross, *curvus* curved — more at CROWN] **1 :** an elevated body part (as along the backbone) **2 a :** a range of hills or mountains **b :** an elongate elevation on an ocean bottom **3 :** an elongate crest or a linear series of crests **4 :** a raised strip (as of plowed ground) **5 :** the line of intersection at the top between the opposite slopes or sides of a roof

[2]**ridge** *vt* **:** to form into a ridge **~** *vi* **:** to extend in ridges

ridge·ling *or* **ridg·ling** \ˈrij-liŋ\ *n* [perh. fr. [1]*ridge*, fr. the supposition that the undescended testis remains near the animal's back] **1 :** a male animal having one or both testes retained in the intestinal canal **2 :** an imperfectly castrated male animal

ridge·pole \ˈrij-ˌpōl\ *n* **1 :** the highest horizontal timber in a roof and the receiver of the upper ends of the rafters **2 :** the horizontal pole at the top of a tent

ridgy \ˈrij-ē\ *adj* **:** having or rising in ridges

[1]**rid·i·cule** \ˈrid-ə-ˌkyü(ə)l\ *n* [F or L; F, fr. L *ridiculum* jest] **:** the act of exposing to laughter **:** DERISION, MOCKERY

[2]**ridicule** *vt* **:** to make fun of **:** DERIDE — **rid·i·cul·er** *n*

syn RIDICULE, DERIDE, MOCK, TAUNT, TWIT, RALLY mean to make an object of laughter. RIDICULE implies an often malicious belittling; DERIDE suggests contemptuous and often bitter ridicule; MOCK implies scorn often ironically expressed; TAUNT suggests jeeringly provoking insult or challenge; TWIT is now usu. milder and more good-humored than TAUNT; RALLY implies a light teasing or mocking without malice

ri·dic·u·lous \rə-ˈdik-yə-ləs\ *adj* [L *ridiculosus* (fr. *ridiculum* jest, fr. neut. of *ridiculus*) or *ridiculus*, lit., laughable, fr. *ridēre* to laugh; akin to Skt *vrīḍate* he is ashamed] **:** arousing or deserving ridicule **:** ABSURD, PREPOSTEROUS **syn** see LAUGHABLE — **ri·dic·u·lous·ly** *adv* — **ri·dic·u·lous·ness** *n*

[1]**ri·ding** \ˈrīd-iŋ\ *n* [ME, alter. of (assumed) OE *thriding*, fr. ON *thrithjungr* third part, fr. *thrithi* third; akin to OE *thridda* third — more at THIRD] **1 :** one of the three administrative jurisdictions into which Yorkshire, England, is divided **2 :** an administrative jurisdiction or electoral district in a British dominion (as Canada)

[2]**rid·ing** \ˈrīd-iŋ\ *n* **:** the act or state of one that rides

[3]**rid·ing** *adj* **1 :** used for or when riding ⟨~ horse⟩ **2 :** operated by a rider ⟨~ plow⟩

rid·ley \ˈrid-lē\ *n* [prob. fr. the name *Ridley*] **:** a marine turtle (*Caretta kempii* or *Lepidochelys kempii*) found off the Atlantic coast of the U.S.

ri·dot·to \ri-ˈdät-(ˌ)ō\ *n* [It, retreat, place of entertainment, redoubt] **:** a public entertainment consisting of music and dancing often in masquerade popular in 18th century England

ri·el \rē-ˈel\ *n* [origin unknown] — see MONEY table

Rie·mann·ian geometry \rē-ˌmän-ē-ən-\ *n* [G. F. B. *Riemann* †1866 G mathematician] **:** a non-euclidean geometry in which straight lines are geodesics and meet every other straight line ⟨great circles are straight lines in the *Riemannian geometry* of the sphere⟩

Ries·ling \ˈrēz-liŋ, ˈrē-sliŋ\ *n* [G] **:** a dry white table wine resembling Rhine wine

rife \ˈrīf\ *adj* [ME *ryfe*, fr. OE *rȳfe;* akin to ON *rīfr* abundant] **1 :** WIDESPREAD, PREVALENT **2 :** ABUNDANT, PLENTIFUL **3 :** ABOUNDING — usu. used with *with* ⟨~ with rumors⟩ **syn** see PREVAILING — **rife** *adv*

[1]**riff** \ˈrif\ *vb* [short for *riffle*] **:** RIFFLE, SKIM ⟨~ pages⟩

[2]**riff** *n* [prob. by shortening & alter. fr. *refrain*] **:** an ostinato phrase in jazz typically supporting a solo improvisation

[3]**riff** *vi* **:** to perform a jazz riff

Riff \ˈrif\ *n, pl* **Riffs** *or* **Riffi** \ˈrif-ē\ *or* **Riff** [Er *Rif*] **:** a Berber of the Rif in northern Morocco — called also *Riff·ian* \ˈrif-ē-ən\

[1]**rif·fle** \ˈrif-əl\ *n* [perh. alter. of *ruffle*] **1 a :** a shallow extending across a stream bed and causing broken water **b :** a stretch of water flowing over a riffle **2 :** a small wave or succession of small waves **:** RIPPLE **3** [[2]*riffle*] **a :** the act or process of shuffling (as cards) **b :** the sound made while doing this

[2]**riffle** *vb* **rif·fling** \ˈrif-(ə-)liŋ\ *vi* **1 :** to form, flow over, or move in riffles **2 :** to flip cursorily **:** THUMB ⟨~ through files⟩ **~** *vt* **1 :** to ruffle slightly **:** RIPPLE **2 a :** to leaf through hastily; *specif* **:** to leaf (as a stack of paper) by sliding a thumb along the edge of the leaves **b :** to shuffle (playing cards) by separating the deck into two parts and riffling with the thumbs so the cards intermix **3 :** to manipulate (small objects) idly between the fingers

[3]**riffle** *n* [prob. fr. [1]*riffle*] **1 a :** any of various contrivances (as blocks or rails) laid on the bottom of a sluice or launder to make a series of grooves or interstices to catch and retain a mineral (as gold) **b :** a groove or interstice so formed **2 :** a cleat or bar fastened to an inclined surface in a gold-washing apparatus to catch and hold mineral grains

[4]**riffle** *vt* **rif·fling** \ˈrif-(ə-)liŋ\ **:** to run through a riffle or over a series of riffles ⟨~ ground ore⟩

rif·fler \ˈrif-lər\ *n* [F *rifloir*, fr. *rifler* to file, rifle] **:** a small filing or scraping tool

riff·raff \ˈrif-ˌraf\ *n* [ME *riffe raffe*, fr. *rif and raf* every single one, fr. MF *rif et raf* completely, fr. *rifler* to plunder + *raffe* act of sweeping] **1 a :** disreputable persons **b :** RABBLE **c :** one of the riffraff **2 :** REFUSE, RUBBISH — **riffraff** *adj*

[1]**ri·fle** \ˈrī-fəl\ *vb* **ri·fling** \-f(ə-)liŋ\ [ME *riflen*, fr. MF *rifler* to scratch, file, plunder, of Gmc origin; akin to obs. D *rijffelen* to scrape] *vt* **1 :** to ransack esp. with the intent to steal **2 :** to steal and carry away **~** *vi* **:** to engage in rifling — **ri·fler** \-f(ə-)lər\ *n*

[2]**rifle** *vt* **ri·fling** \-f(ə-)liŋ\ [F *rifler* to scratch, file] **:** to cut spiral grooves into the bore of ⟨*rifled* arms⟩ ⟨*rifled* pipe⟩

[3]**rifle** *n* **1 a :** a shoulder weapon with a rifled bore **b :** a rifled artillery piece **2** *pl* **:** a body of soldiers armed with rifles — **ri·fle·man** \-fəl-mən\ *n*

[4]**rifle** *vt* **ri·fling** \-f(ə-)liŋ\ [[3]*rifle*] **:** to hit or throw (a ball) with great force

ri·fle·bird \ˈrī-fəl-ˌbərd\ *n* **:** any of several birds of paradise

ri·fle·ry \ˈrī-fəl-rē\ *n* **:** the practice of shooting at targets with a rifle

ri·fle·scope \ˈrī-fəl-ˌskōp\ *n* **:** a telescopic sight for a rifle

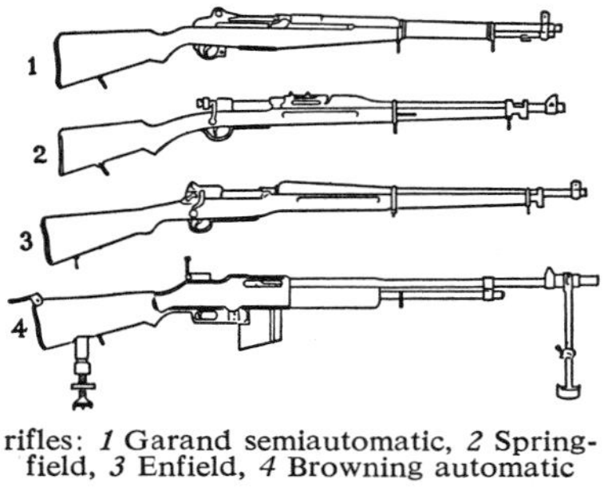

rifles: *1* Garand semiautomatic, *2* Springfield, *3* Enfield, *4* Browning automatic

ri·fling \ˈrī-f(ə-)liŋ\ *n* **1 :** the act or process of making spiral grooves **2 :** a system of spiral grooves in the surface

of the bore of a gun causing a projectile when fired to rotate about its longer axis

[1]**rift** \ˈrift\ *n* [ME, of Scand origin; akin to Dan & Norw *rift* fissure, ON *rīfa* to rive — more at RIVE] **1 a :** FISSURE, CREVASSE **b :** a normal geological fault **2 :** a clear space or interval **3 :** ESTRANGEMENT, BREACH

[2]**rift** *vt* **1 :** CLEAVE, DIVIDE **2 :** PENETRATE ~ *vi* **:** to burst open **:** SPLIT ⟨clouds ~*ed*⟩

[3]**rift** *n* [prob. alter. of E dial. *riff* (reef)] **:** a shallow or rocky place in a stream

[1]**rig** \ˈrig\ *vt* **rigged; rig·ging** [ME *riggen*] **1 :** to fit out (as a ship) with rigging **2 :** CLOTHE, DRESS — usu. used with *out* **3 :** to furnish with special gear **:** EQUIP **4 a :** ADJUST, ARRANGE **b :** CONSTRUCT ⟨~ up a temporary shelter⟩

[2]**rig** *n* **1 :** the distinctive shape, number, and arrangement of sails and masts of a ship **2 :** EQUIPAGE; *esp* **:** a carriage with its horse **3 :** DRESS, CLOTHING **4 :** tackle, equipment, or machinery fitted for a specified purpose ⟨oil-drilling ~⟩

[3]**rig** *vt* **rigged; rig·ging** [*rig* (swindle)] **1 :** to manipulate or control usu. by deceptive or dishonest means ⟨~ an election⟩ **2 :** to fix in advance for a desired result ⟨~ a quiz⟩ ⟨~ prices⟩

rig·a·doon \ˌrig-ə-ˈdün\ *or* **ri·gau·don** \rē-gō-dōⁿ\ *n* [F *rigaudon*] **:** a lively dance of the 17th and 18th centuries; *also* **:** the music for this

rig·a·ma·role *var of* RIGMAROLE

rig·a·to·ni \ˌrig-ə-ˈtō-nē\ *n* [It, pl., fr. *rigato* furrowed, fluted, fr. pp. of *rigare* to furrow, flute fr. *riga* line, of Gmc origin; akin to OHG *rīga* line — more at ROW] **:** macaroni made in short curved fluted pieces

Ri·gel \ˈrī-jəl, -gəl\ *n* [Ar *Rijl*, lit., foot] **:** a first-magnitude star in the left foot of the constellation Orion

rig·ger \ˈrig-ər\ *n* **1 :** one that rigs **2 :** a long slender and pointed sable brush used in painting pictures **3 :** a ship of a specified rig ⟨square-*rigger*⟩

rig·ging \ˈrig-iŋ, -ən\ *n* **1 a :** the lines (as ropes and chains) used aboard a ship esp. in working sail and supporting masts and spars **b :** a similar network (as in theater scenery) used for support and manipulation **2 :** CLOTHING

[1]**right** \ˈrīt\ *adj* [ME, fr. OE *riht;* akin to OHG *reht* right, L *rectus* straight, right, *regere* to lead straight, direct, rule, *rogare* to ask, Gk *oregein* to stretch out] **1 :** RIGHTEOUS, UPRIGHT **2 :** being in accordance with what is just, good, or proper ⟨~ conduct⟩ **3 a :** agreeable to a standard **b :** conforming to facts or truth **:** CORRECT ⟨~ answer⟩ **4 :** SUITABLE, APPROPRIATE ⟨~ man for the job⟩ ⟨~ tool⟩ **5 :** STRAIGHT ⟨~ line⟩ **6 :** GENUINE, REAL **7 a :** of, relating to, or being the stronger hand in most persons **b :** located nearer to the right hand than to the left ⟨~ pocket⟩; *esp* **:** located on the right hand when facing in the same direction as an observer ⟨~ wing of an army⟩ **8 :** having its axis perpendicular to the base ⟨~ cone⟩ **9 :** of, relating to, or constituting the principal or more prominent side of an object ⟨~ side out⟩ **10 :** acting or judging in accordance with truth or fact ⟨time proved him ~⟩ **11 a :** being in good physical or mental health or order ⟨~ mind⟩ **b :** being in a correct or proper state ⟨put things ~⟩ **12 :** most favorable or desired **:** PREFERABLE **13** *often cap* **:** of, adhering to, or constituted by the Right esp. in politics **syn** see CORRECT — **right·ness** *n*

[2]**right** *n* [ME, fr. OE *riht*, fr. *riht*, adj.] **1 :** adherence to duty, obedience to lawful authority, or other qualities that together constitute the ideal of moral propriety or merit moral approval **2 :** something to which one has a just claim: as **a :** the power or privilege to which one is justly entitled **b (1) :** the interest that one has in a piece of property — often used in pl. ⟨mineral ~*s*⟩ **(2)** *pl* **:** the property interest possessed under law or custom and agreement in an intangible thing esp. of a literary and artistic nature ⟨film ~*s* of the novel⟩ **3 :** something that one may properly claim as due **4 :** the cause of truth or justice **5 a :** the right hand **b :** the location or direction of the right side ⟨woods on his ~⟩ **c :** the part on the right side **6 a :** the true account or correct interpretation **b :** the quality or state of being factually correct **7** *often cap* **a :** the part of a legislative chamber located to the right of the presiding officer **b :** the members of a continental European legislative body occupying the right as a result of holding more conservative political views than other members **8 a (1)** *cap* **:** individuals sometimes professing opposition to change in the established order and favoring traditional attitudes and practices and sometimes advocating the forced establishment of an authoritarian political order **(2) :** a group or party in another organization that favors conservative, traditional, or sometimes authoritarian attitudes and policies **b** *often cap* **:** a conservative position **9 a :** a privilege given stockholders to subscribe pro rata to a new issue of securities generally below market price **b :** the negotiable certificate evidencing such privilege — usu. used in pl. — **right·ward** \-wərd\ *adj* — **by rights :** with reason or justice **:** PROPERLY — **to rights :** into proper order

[3]**right** *adv* **1 :** according to right ⟨live ~⟩ **2 :** EXACTLY, PRECISELY ⟨~ at his fingertips⟩ **3 :** in a suitable, proper, or desired manner ⟨hold your pen ~⟩ **4 :** in a direct line or course ⟨go ~ home⟩ **5 :** according to fact or truth **:** TRULY ⟨guess ~⟩ ⟨heard ~⟩ **6 a :** all the way ⟨windows ~ to the floor⟩ **b :** COMPLETELY **7 :** IMMEDIATELY ⟨~ after lunch⟩ **8 :** EXTREMELY, VERY ⟨~ pleasant day⟩ **9 :** on or to the right ⟨looked ~ and left⟩

[4]**right** *vt* **1 a :** to relieve from wrong **b :** JUSTIFY, VINDICATE **2 a :** to adjust or restore to the proper state or condition **b :** to bring or restore to an upright position ~ *vi* **:** to become upright — **right·er** *n*

right angle *n* **:** the angle bounded by two radii intercepting a quarter of a circle or by two lines perpendicular to each other — **right–an·gled** \ˈrīt-ˈaŋ-gəld\ *or* **right–an·gle** \-gəl\ *adj*

right ascension *n* **:** the arc of the celestial equator between the vernal equinox and the point where the hour circle through the given body intersects the equator reckoned eastward commonly in terms of the corresponding interval of sidereal time in hours, minutes, and seconds

righ·teous \ˈrī-chəs\ *adj* [alter. of earlier *rightuous*, alter. of ME *rightwise, rightwos*, fr. OE *rihtwīs*, fr. *riht*, n., right + *wīs* wise] **1 :** acting rightly **:** UPRIGHT **2 a :** according to what is right ⟨~ actions⟩ **b :** arising from an outraged sense of justice or morality ⟨~ indignation⟩ **syn** see MORAL — **righ·teous·ly** *adv* — **righ·teous·ness** *n*

right field *n* **1 :** the part of the baseball outfield to the right facing from the plate **2 :** the position of the player defending right field — **right fielder** *n*

right·ful \ˈrīt-fəl\ *adj* **1 :** JUST, EQUITABLE **2 :** having a just or legally established claim **:** LEGITIMATE ⟨~ owner⟩ **3 :** FITTING, PROPER **4 :** held by right or just claim **:** LEGAL ⟨~ authority⟩ — **right·ful·ly** \-fə-lē\ *adv* — **right·ful·ness** *n*

right hand *n* **1 a :** the hand on a person's right side **b :** a reliable or indispensable person **2 a :** the right side **b :** a place of honor

right–hand \ˈrīt-ˌhand\ *adj* **1 :** situated on the right **2 :** RIGHT-HANDED **3 :** chiefly relied on ⟨~ man⟩

right–hand·ed \-ˈhan-dəd\ *adj* **1 :** using the right hand habitually or more easily than the left **2 :** relating to, designed for, or done with the right hand **3 :** having the same direction or course as the movement of the hands of a watch viewed from in front **:** CLOCKWISE — used of a twist, rotary motion, or spiral curve as viewed from a given direction with respect to the axis of rotation **4 :** RIGHT-HAND — **right–handed** *adv* — **right–hand·ed·ly** *adv* — **right–hand·ed·ness** *n* — **right–hand·er** \-ˈhan-dər\ *n*

right·ism \ˈrīt-ˌiz-əm\ *n, often cap* **1 :** the principles and views of the Right **2 :** advocacy of or adherence to the doctrines of the Right — **right·ist** \ˈrīt-əst\ *n or adj, often cap*

right·ly \ˈrīt-lē\ *adv* **1 :** FAIRLY, JUSTLY **2 :** PROPERLY, FITLY **3 :** CORRECTLY, EXACTLY

right of asylum : the right of receiving protection at a place recognized by custom or treaty

right of search : the right to stop a merchant vessel on the high seas and make a reasonable search to determine its liability to capture by violation of international or revenue law

right–of–way \ˌrīt-ə(v)-ˈwā\ *n* **1 :** a legal right of passage over another person's ground **2 a :** the area over which a right-of-way exists **b :** the strip of land over which is built a public road **c :** the land occupied by a railroad esp. for its main line **d :** the land used by a public utility (as for transmission line) **3 a :** a precedence in passing accorded to one vehicle over another by custom, decision, or statute **b :** the right of traffic to take precedence

Right Reverend — used as a title for high ecclesiastical officials (as Episcopal bishops and some monsignors)

right triangle *n* **:** a triangle having a right angle

right whale *n* **:** a large whalebone whale (family Balaenidae) having no dorsal fin, very long baleen, a large head, an unwrinkled throat, and small eyes near the angles of the mouth

right wing *n* **1 :** the rightist division of a group **2 :** RIGHT 8 — **right–wing·er** \-ˈwiŋ-ər\ *n*

rig·id \ˈrij-əd\ *adj* [MF or L; MF *rigide*, fr. L *rigidus*, fr. *rigēre* to be stiff] **1 :** lacking flexibility **:** STIFF, HARD **2 a :** inflexibly set **:** UNYIELDING **b :** strictly observed **:** SCRUPULOUS **3 :** RIGOROUS, SEVERE ⟨~ treatment⟩ **4 :** precise and accurate in procedure **5 a :** having the gas containers enclosed within compartments of a fixed fabric-covered framework ⟨~ airship⟩ **b :** having the outer shape maintained by a fixed framework — **ri·gid·i·ty** \rə-ˈjid-ət-ē\ *n* — **rig·id·ly** \ˈrij-əd-lē\ *adv* — **rig·id·ness** *n*

syn RIGID, RIGOROUS, STRICT, STRINGENT mean extremely severe or stern. RIGID implies uncompromising inflexibility; RIGOROUS implies the imposition of hardship and difficulty; STRICT emphasizes undeviating conformity to rules, standards, or requirements; STRINGENT suggests restrictions or limitations that curb or coerce **syn** see in addition STIFF

ri·gid·i·fi·ca·tion \rə-ˌjid-ə-fə-ˈkā-shən\ *n* **:** the action of rigidifying **:** the state of being rigidified

ri·gid·i·fy \rə-ˈjid-ə-ˌfī\ *vt* **:** to make rigid ~ *vi* **:** to become rigid

rig·ma·role \ˈrig-ə-mə-ˌrōl, ˈrig-mə-\ *n* [alter. of obs. *ragman roll* (long list, catalog)] **1 :** confused or meaningless talk **2 :** a complex and ritualistic procedure

rig·or \ˈrig-ər, *2 & 5 are also* ˈrī-ˌgȯ(ə)r\ *or chiefly Brit* **rig·our** \ˈrig-ər\ *n* [ME *rigour*, fr. MF *rigueur*, fr. L *rigor*, lit., stiffness, fr. *rigēre* to be stiff] **1 a (1) :** harsh inflexibility in opinion, temper, or judgment **:** SEVERITY **(2) :** the quality of being unyielding or inflexible **:** STRICTNESS **(3) :** AUSTERITY **b :** an act or instance of strictness, severity, or cruelty **2 :** a tremor caused by a chill **3 :** a condition that makes life difficult, challenging, or uncomfortable; *esp* **:** extremity of cold **4 :** strict precision **:** EXACTNESS ⟨logical ~⟩ **5 a** *obs* **:** RIGIDITY, STIFFNESS **b :** rigidness or torpor of organs or tissue that prevents response to stimuli **syn** see DIFFICULTY

rig·or·ism \ˈrig-ə-ˌriz-əm\ *n* **:** rigidity in principle or practice — **rig·or·ist** \-ə-rəst\ *n or adj* — **rig·or·is·tic** \ˌrig-ə-ˈris-tik\ *adj*

rig·or mor·tis \ˌrig-ər-ˈmȯrt-əs *also chiefly Brit* ˌrī-ˌgȯ(ə)r-\ *n* [NL, stiffness of death] **:** temporary rigidity of muscles occurring after death

rig·or·ous \ˈrig-(ə-)rəs\ *adj* **1 :** manifesting, exercising, or favoring rigor **:** very strict **2 :** marked by extremes of temperature or climate **:** HARSH, SEVERE **3 :** scrupulously accurate **:** PRECISE **syn** see RIGID — **rig·or·ous·ly** *adv* — **rig·or·ous·ness** *n*

rile \ˈrī(ə)l\ *vt* [by alter.] **1 :** ROIL 1 **2 :** to make angry **syn** see IRRITATE

ril·ey \ˈrī-lē\ *adj* **1 :** TURBID **2 :** ANGRY

[1]**rill** \ˈril\ *n* [D *ril* or LG *rille;* akin to OE *rīth* rivulet] **:** a very small brook

[2]**rill** *vi* **:** to flow like a rill

[3]**rill** \ˈril\ *or* **rille** \ˈril, ˈril-ə\ *n* [G *rille*, lit., channel made by a small stream, fr. LG, rill] **:** any of several long narrow valleys on the moon's surface

rill·et \ˈril-ət\ *n* **:** a little rill

rill·stone \ˈril-ˌstōn\ *n* **:** VENTIFACT

[1]**rim** \ˈrim\ *n* [ME, fr. OE *rima;* akin to ON *rimi* strip of land, Gk *ērema* gently, Lith *remti* to support] **1 a :** the outer often curved or circular edge or border of something **b :** BRINK **2 a :** the outer part of a wheel joined to the hub usu. by spokes **b :** a removable outer metal band on an automobile wheel to which the tire is attached **3 :** FRAME 3a **syn** see BORDER — **rim·less** \-ləs\ *adj*

[2]**rim** *vb* **rimmed; rim·ming** *vt* **1 :** to furnish with a rim **:** serve as a rim for **:** BORDER **2 :** to run around the rim of ⟨putts that ~ the cup⟩ ~ *vi* **:** to form or show a rim

[1]**rime** \ˈrīm\ *n* [ME *rim*, fr. OE *hrīm;* akin to ON *hrīm* frost, Latvian *kreims* cream] **1 :** FROST 1c **2 :** an accumulation of granular ice tufts on the windward sides of exposed objects that is formed

from supercooled fog or cloud and built out directly against the wind **3 :** CRUST, INCRUSTATION

[2]**rime** *vt* **:** to cover with or as if with rime

[3]**rime, rimer, rimester** *var of* RHYME, RHYMER, RHYMESTER

rim·land \'rim-ˌland\ *n* **:** a region on the periphery of the heartland

ri·mose \'rī-ˌmōs\ *or* **ri·mous** \-məs\ *adj* [L *rimosus*, fr. *rima* slit, crack — more at ROW] **:** having numerous clefts, cracks, or fissures ⟨~ tree bark⟩

rim·rock \'rim-ˌräk\ *n* **1 :** overlying rock of a plateau outcrop forming a vertical face **2 :** the edge or face of a rimrock outcrop

rimy \'rī-mē\ *adj* **:** covered with rime **:** FROSTY

rind \'rīnd, *esp dial* 'rind\ *n* [ME, fr. OE; akin to OHG *rinda* bark, OE *rendan* to rend] **:** the bark of a tree; *also* **:** a usu. hard or tough outer layer **:** PEEL, CRUST — **rind·ed** \-əd\ *adj*

rin·der·pest \'rin-dər-ˌpest\ *n* [G, fr. *rinder*, pl., cattle + *pest* pestilence] **:** an acute infectious febrile disease esp. of cattle caused by a filterable virus and marked by diphtheritic inflammation of mucous membranes

[1]**ring** \'riŋ\ *n* [ME, fr. OE *hring*; akin to OHG *hring* ring, L *curvus* curved — more at CROWN] **1 :** a circular band for holding, connecting, hanging, or pulling ⟨curtain ~⟩ ⟨key ~⟩ ⟨towel ~⟩ or for packing or sealing **2 :** a circlet usu. of precious metal worn on the finger **3 a :** a circular line, figure, or object **b :** an encircling arrangement **c :** a circular or spiral course **4 a** (1) **:** an often circular space esp. for exhibitions or competitions; *esp* **:** such a space at a circus (2) **:** a structure containing such a ring **b** (1) **:** a square enclosure in which boxers or wrestlers contest (2) **:** PRIZEFIGHTING **5 :** one of three concentric bands usu. believed to be composed of meteoric fragments revolving around the planet Saturn **6 :** ANNUAL RING **7 :** an exclusive combination of persons for a selfish and often corrupt purpose (as to control the market) **8 :** the field of a political contest **:** RACE **9 :** food in the shape of a circle **10 :** an arrangement of atoms represented in formulas or models as a ring — called also *cycle* **11 :** a set of elements subject to two operations which is a commutative group under the first operation and in which the second operation is associative and distributive relative to the first — **ring·like** \'riŋ-ˌlīk\ *adj*

[2]**ring** *vt* **1 :** to place or form a ring around **:** ENCIRCLE **2 :** to provide with a ring **3 :** GIRDLE 3 **4 :** to throw a ring over (the mark) in a game where curved objects (as horseshoes) are tossed at a mark **~** *vi* **1 a :** to move in a ring **b :** to rise in the air spirally **2 :** to form or take the shape of a ring

[3]**ring** *vb* **rang** \'raŋ\ **rung** \'rəŋ\ **ring·ing** \'riŋ-iŋ\ [ME *ringen*, fr. OE *hringan*; akin to MD *ringen* to ring, Lith *krankti* to croak] *vi* **1 :** to sound resonantly ⟨the doorbell *rang*⟩ or sonorously ⟨cheers *rang* out⟩ **2 a :** to be filled with a reverberating sound **:** RESOUND **b :** to have the sensation of being filled with a humming sound ⟨his ears *rang*⟩ **3 :** to cause something to ring **4 a :** to be filled with talk or report **b :** to have great renown **5 :** to have a sound or character expressive of some quality ⟨a story that ~*s* true⟩ **~** *vt* **1 :** to cause to sound esp. by striking **2 :** to make (a sound) by or as if by ringing a bell **3 :** to announce by or as if by ringing ⟨~ an alarm⟩ **4 :** to repeat often, loudly, or earnestly **5 :** to summon esp. by bell — **ring a bell :** to arouse a response — **ring the changes** *or* **ring changes :** to run through the range of possible variations

[4]**ring** *n* **1 :** a set of bells **2 :** a clear resonant sound made by or resembling that made by vibrating metal **3 :** resonant tone **:** SONORITY **4 :** a loud sound continued, repeated, or reverberated **5 :** a sound or character expressive of some particular quality **6 a :** the act or an instance of ringing **b :** a telephone call

ring·bark \'riŋ-ˌbärk\ *vt* **:** GIRDLE 3

ring·bolt \-ˌbōlt\ *n* **:** an eyebolt with a ring through its eye

ring·bone \-ˌbōn\ *n* **:** an exostosis on the pastern bones of the horse usu. producing lameness — **ring·boned** \-ˌbōnd\ *adj*

ring·dove \-ˌdəv\ *n* **1 :** a common European pigeon (*Columba palumbus*) with a whitish patch on each side of the neck and wings edged with white **2 :** a small dove (*Streptopelia risoria*) of southeastern Europe and Asia

rin·gent \'rin-jənt\ *adj* [L *ringent-, ringens*, prp. of *ringi* to open the mouth — more at RICTUS] **:** GAPING; *esp* **:** having lips separated like an open mouth ⟨a ~ corolla⟩ ⟨a clamshell with ~ valves⟩

[1]**ring·er** \'riŋ-ər\ *n* **1 :** one that sounds esp. by ringing **2 a :** one that enters a competition under false representations **b :** one that strongly resembles another

[2]**ringer** *n* **:** one that encircles or puts a ring around (as a quoit or horseshoe that lodges so as to surround the peg)

ring finger *n* **:** the third finger of the left hand

ring·lead·er \'riŋ-ˌlēd-ər\ *n* **:** a leader of a group of individuals engaged esp. in a violation of law or an improper enterprise

ring·let \'riŋ-lət\ *n* **1** *archaic* **:** a small ring or circle **2 :** CURL; *esp* **:** a long curl of hair

ring·mas·ter \'riŋ-ˌmas-tər\ *n* **:** one in charge of performances in a ring (as of a circus)

ring·neck \-ˌnek\ *n* **:** a ring-necked bird or animal (as a ring-necked pheasant)

ring–necked \'riŋ-'nek(t), ˌriŋ-ˌ\ *or* **ring–neck** \ˌriŋ-ˌnek\ *adj* **:** having a ring of color about the neck

ring–necked pheasant *n* **:** any of various pheasants with white neck rings widely introduced in temperate regions as game birds that are varieties of or hybrids between varieties of the common Old World pheasant (*Phasianus colchicus*)

Ring of the Ni·be·lung \-'nē-bə-ˌlu̇ŋ\ **:** a ring made by the dwarf Alberich whose story is the theme of a tetralogy of music dramas by Richard Wagner

[1]**ring·side** \'riŋ-ˌsīd\ *n* **1 :** the area just outside a ring esp. in which a contest occurs **2 :** a place from which one may have a close view

[2]**ringside** *adv* (*or adj*) **:** at the ringside

ring spot *n* **:** a lesion of plant tissue consisting of yellowish, purplish, or necrotic, often concentric rings; *also* **:** a plant disease of which ring spots are the characteristic lesion

ring·straked \'riŋ-ˌstrākt\ *adj, archaic* **:** marked with circular stripes

ring·tail \-ˌtāl\ *n* **1 :** CACOMISTLE **2 :** RACCOON **3 :** CAPUCHIN 3

ring–tailed \-'tā(ə)ld\ *adj* **1 :** having a tail marked with rings of differing colors **2 :** having a tail carried in the form of a circle ⟨a ~ dog⟩

ring·taw \'riŋ-ˌtȯ\ *n* **:** a game of marbles in which marbles are placed in a circle on the ground and shot at from a distance with the object of knocking them out of the circle

ring·toss \-ˌtȯs, -ˌtäs\ *n* **:** a game the object of which is to toss a ring so that it will fall over an upright stick

ring·worm \'riŋ-ˌwərm\ *n* **:** any of several contagious diseases of the skin, hair, or nails of man and domestic animals caused by fungi and characterized on the skin by ring-shaped discolored patches covered with vesicles and scales

rink \'riŋk\ *n* [ME (Sc) *rinc* area in which a contest takes place, fr. MF *renc* place, row — more at RANK] **1 a :** a smooth extent of ice marked off for curling or ice hockey **b :** a usu. artificial sheet of ice for ice-skating; *also* **:** a building containing such a rink **c :** an enclosure for roller-skating **2 :** a division of a bowling green large enough for a match **3 :** a team in bowls or curling

[1]**rinse** \'rin(t)s, *esp dial* 'rench\ *vt* [ME *rincen*, fr. MF *rincer*, fr. (assumed) VL *recentiare*, fr. L *recent-, recens* fresh, recent] **1 :** to cleanse by introduction of water or other liquid **2 a :** to cleanse (as from soap used in washing) by clear water **b :** to treat (hair) with a rinse **3 :** to remove (dirt or impurities) by washing lightly or in water only — **rins·er** *n*

[2]**rinse** *n* **1 :** the act or process of rinsing **2 a :** liquid used for rinsing **b :** a solution that temporarily tints hair

rins·ing *n* **1 :** water that has been used for rinsing — usu. used in pl. **2 :** DREGS, RESIDUE — usu. used in pl.

[1]**ri·ot** \'rī-ət\ *n* [ME, fr. OF, dispute] **1** *archaic* **a :** profligate behavior **:** DEBAUCHERY **b :** unrestrained revelry **c :** noise, uproar, or disturbance made by revelers **2 a :** public violence, tumult, or disorder **b :** a violent public disorder; *specif* **:** a tumultuous disturbance of the public peace by three or more persons assembled together and acting with a common intent **3 :** a random or disorderly profusion **4 :** something or someone wildly amusing

[2]**riot** *vi* **1 :** to indulge in revelry or wantonness **2 :** to create or engage in a riot **~** *vt* **:** to waste or spend recklessly — **ri·ot·er** *n*

riot act *n* [the *Riot Act*, English law of 1715 providing for the dispersal of riots upon command of legal authority] **:** a vigorous reprimand or warning — used in the phrase *read the riot act*

riot gun *n* **:** a small arm used to disperse rioters rather than to inflict serious injury or death; *esp* **:** a short-barreled shotgun

ri·ot·ous \'rī-ət-əs\ *adj* **1 :** ABUNDANT, EXUBERANT **2 a :** of the nature of a riot **:** TURBULENT **b :** participating in riot — **ri·ot·ous·ly** *adv* — **ri·ot·ous·ness** *n*

[1]**rip** \'rip\ *vb* **ripped; rip·ping** [prob. fr. Flem *rippen* to strip off roughly] *vt* **1 a :** to tear or split apart or open **b :** to saw or split (wood) with the grain **2 :** to slash or slit with or as if with a sharp blade **~** *vi* **1 :** to become ripped **:** REND **2 :** to rush headlong **syn** see TEAR — **rip·per** *n*

[2]**rip** *n* **:** a rent made by ripping **:** TEAR

[3]**rip** *n* [perh. fr. [2]*rip*] **1 :** a body of water made rough by the meeting of opposing tides or currents **2 :** a current of water roughened by passing over an irregular bottom

[4]**rip** *n* [perh. by shortening & alter. fr. *reprobate*] **1 :** a worn-out worthless horse **2 :** a dissolute person **:** LIBERTINE

ri·par·i·an \rə-'per-ē-ən, rī-\ *adj* [L *riparius* — more at RIVER] **:** relating to or living or located on the bank of a natural watercourse (as a stream or river) or sometimes of a lake or a tidewater

riparian right *n* **:** a right (as access to or use of the shore, bed, and water) of one owning riparian land

rip cord *n* **1 :** a cord by which the gasbag of a balloon may be ripped open for a limited distance to release the gas quickly and so cause immediate descent **2 :** a cord or wire pulled in making a descent to release the pilot parachute which lifts the main parachute out of its container

rip current *n* **:** a strong surface current flowing outward from a shore

ripe \'rīp\ *adj* [ME, fr. OE *rīpe*; akin to OE *rīpan* to reap — more at REAP] **1 :** fully grown and developed **:** MATURE **2 :** having mature knowledge, understanding, or judgment **3 a :** of advanced years **:** LATE **b :** fully arrived **:** SUITABLE ⟨the time seemed ~⟩ **4 :** fully prepared **:** READY **5 :** brought by aging to full flavor or the best state **:** MELLOW ⟨~ cheese⟩ **6 :** ruddy, plump, or full like ripened fruit — **ripe·ly** *adv* — **ripe·ness** *n*

rip·en \'rī-pən, 'rīp-ᵊm\ *vb* **ri·pen·ing** \'rīp-(ə-)niŋ\ *vi* **:** to grow or become ripe **~** *vt* **1 :** to make ripe **2 a :** to bring to completeness or perfection **b :** to age or cure (cheese) to develop characteristic flavor, odor, body, texture, and color **c :** to improve flavor and tenderness of (beef or game) through a period of refrigeration — **rip·en·er** \'rīp-(ə-)nər\ *n*

ri·pie·no \ri-'pyā-(ˌ)nō, -'pyen-(ˌ)ō\ *n* [It, lit., filled up] **:** TUTTI

ri·poste \ri-'pōst\ *n* [F, modif. of It *risposta*, lit., answer, fr. *rispondere* to respond, fr. L *respondēre*] **1 :** a fencer's quick return thrust following a parry **2 :** a retaliatory verbal sally **:** RETORT **3 :** a retaliatory maneuver or measure — **riposte** *vi*

rip·ping \'rip-iŋ\ *adj* [prob. fr. pp. of [1]*rip*] **:** EXCELLENT, SWELL

[1]**rip·ple** \'rip-əl\ *vb* **rip·pling** \-(ə-)liŋ\ [perh. freq. of [1]*rip*] *vi* **1 a :** to become lightly ruffled or covered with small waves **b :** to flow in small waves **c :** to fall in soft undulating folds **2 :** to flow with a light rise and fall of sound or inflection **3 :** to move with an undulating motion or so as to cause ripples **~** *vt* **1 :** to stir up small waves on **2 :** to impart a wavy motion or appearance to **3 :** to utter or play with a slight rise and fall of sound — **rip·pler** \-(ə-)lər\ *n*

[2]**ripple** *n* **1 a :** a shallow stretch of rough water in a stream **b** (1) **:** the ruffling of the surface of water (2) **:** a small wave **2 :** a sound like that of rippling water

ripple mark *n* **1 :** one of a series of small ridges produced esp. on sand by the action of wind, a current of water, or waves **2 :** a striation across the grain of wood esp. on the tangential surface — **rip·ple–marked** \'rip-əl-ˌmärkt\ *adj*

[1]**rip·rap** \'rip-ˌrap\ *n* [obs. *riprap* (sound of rapping)] **1 :** a foundation or sustaining wall of stones thrown together without order (as in deep water or on an embankment slope to prevent erosion) **2 :** stone used for riprap

[2]**riprap** *vt* **1 :** to form a riprap in or upon **2 :** to strengthen or support with a riprap

rip–roar·ing \'rip-'rōr-iŋ, -'rȯr-\ *adj* **:** noisily excited or exciting **:** HILARIOUS

rip·saw \'rip-ˌsȯ\ *n* **:** a coarse-toothed saw for cutting wood in the direction of the grain

rip·snort·er \'rip-'snȯrt-ər\ *n* **:** something extraordinary **:** HUMDINGER — **rip·snort·ing** \-iŋ\ *adj*

rip·tide \'rip-ˌtīd\ *n* **:** RIP CURRENT

Rip·u·ar·i·an \ˌrip-yə-'wer-ē-ən\ *adj* [ML *Ripuarius*] **:** of, relating

to, or constituting a group of Franks settling in the 4th century on the Rhine near Cologne

Rip van Win·kle \ˌrip-(ˌ)van-ˈwiŋ-kəl, -vən-\ *n* **:** a ne'er-do-well in a story in Washington Irving's *Sketch Book* who sleeps for 20 years

[1]**rise** \ˈrīz\ *vi* **rose** \ˈrōz\ **ris·en** \ˈriz-ᵊn\ **ris·ing** \ˈrī-ziŋ\ [ME *risen,* fr. OE *rīsan;* akin to OHG *rīsan* to rise, L *oriri* to rise, *rivus* stream, Gk *ornynai* to rouse] **1 a :** to assume an upright position esp. from lying, kneeling, or sitting **b :** to get up from sleep or from one's bed **2 :** to return from death **3 :** to take up arms **4 :** to respond warmly — usu. used with *to* **5 :** to end a session **:** ADJOURN **6 :** to appear above the horizon ⟨sun ~s at six⟩ **7 a :** to move upward **:** ASCEND **b :** to increase in height, size, or volume **8 :** to extend above other objects **9 a :** to become heartened or elated ⟨his spirits *rose*⟩ **b :** to increase in fervor or intensity **10 a :** to attain a higher level or rank **b :** to increase in quantity or number **11 a :** to take place **:** HAPPEN **b :** to come into being **:** ORIGINATE **12 :** to follow as a consequence **:** RESULT **13 :** to exert oneself to meet a challenge ⟨~ to the occasion⟩ **syn** see SPRING

[2]**rise** \ˈrīz *also* ˈrīs\ *n* **1 :** an act of rising or a state of being risen: as **a :** a movement upward **:** ASCENT **b :** emergence (as of the sun) above the horizon **c :** the upward movement of a fish to seize food or bait **2 :** BEGINNING, ORIGIN **3 :** the distance or elevation of one point above another **4 a :** an increase in amount, number, or volume **b :** an increase in price, value, rate, or sum **5 a :** an upward slope **b :** a spot higher than surrounding ground **6 :** an angry reaction

ris·er \ˈrī-zər\ *n* **1 :** one that rises (as from sleep) **2 :** the upright member between two stair treads

ris·i·bil·i·ty \ˌriz-ə-ˈbil-ət-ē\ *n* **1 :** the ability or inclination to laugh — often used in pl. **2 :** LAUGHTER, MERRIMENT

ris·i·ble \ˈriz-ə-bəl\ *adj* [LL *risibilis,* fr. L *risus,* pp. of *ridēre* to laugh — more at RIDICULOUS] **1 a :** capable of laughing **b :** disposed to laugh **2 :** arousing or provoking laughter **:** FUNNY **3 :** associated with, relating to, or used in laughter ⟨~ muscles⟩

ris·ing \ˈrī-ziŋ\ *adj* **1** *of an animal's age* **:** slightly less than a specified number of years **2 :** approaching a stated age

[1]**risk** \ˈrisk\ *n* [F *risque,* fr. It *risco*] **1 :** possibility of loss or injury **:** PERIL **2 :** a dangerous element or factor **3 a** (1) **:** the chance of loss or the perils to the subject matter of an insurance contract (2) **:** the degree of probability of such loss **b :** a person or thing that is a specified hazard to an insurer ⟨a poor ~ for insurance⟩ **c :** an insurance hazard from a specified cause or source ⟨war ~⟩

[2]**risk** *vt* **risked** \ˈriskt, *nonstand* ˈrist\ **risk·ing 1 :** to expose to hazard or danger **2 :** to incur the risk or danger of — **risk·er** *n*

risk capital *n* **:** VENTURE CAPITAL

risk·i·ness \ˈris-kē-nəs\ *n* **:** the quality or state of being risky

risky \ˈris-kē\ *adj* **:** attended with risk or danger **:** HAZARDOUS **syn** see DANGEROUS

ri·sor·gi·men·to \ri-ˌzȯr-ji-ˈmen-(ˌ)tō, -ˌsȯr-\ *n, pl* **risorgimentos** [It] **:** REVIVAL; *specif* **:** the 19th century movement for Italian political unity

ri·sot·to \ri-ˈsȯt-(ˌ)ō, -ˈzȯt-\ *n, pl* **risottos** [It] **:** rice cooked in meat stock and seasoned (as with cheese)

ris·qué \ri-ˈskā\ *adj* [F, fr. pp. of *risquer* to risk, fr. *risque*] **:** verging on impropriety or indecency **:** OFF-COLOR

[1]**ri·tar·dan·do** \ri-ˌtär-ˈdän-(ˌ)dō, ˌrē-\ *adv (or adj)* [It, fr. L *retardandum,* gerund of *retardare* to retard] **:** with a gradual slackening in tempo — used as a direction in music

[2]**ritardando** *n, pl* **ritardandos :** a ritardando passage

rite \ˈrīt\ *n* [ME, fr. L *ritus;* akin to OE *rīm* number, Gk *arithmos* number — more at ARITHMETIC] **1 a :** a prescribed form or manner governing the words or actions for a ceremony **b :** the liturgy of a church or group of churches **2 :** a ceremonial act or action **3 :** a division of the Christian church using a distinctive liturgy

ri·tor·nel·lo \ˌrit-ər-ˈnel-(ˌ)ō, ˌri-ˌtȯr-\ *n, pl* **ri·tor·nel·li** \-ˈnel-(ˌ)ē\ *or* **ritornellos** [It] **1 a :** a short recurrent instrumental passage in a vocal composition **b :** an instrumental interlude in early opera **2 :** a tutti passage in a concerto or rondo refrain

[1]**rit·u·al** \ˈrich-(ə-)wəl, ˈrich-əl\ *adj* **1 :** of or relating to rites **2 :** forming a ritual — **rit·u·al·ly** \-ē\ *adv*

[2]**ritual** *n* **1 :** the established form for a ceremony; *specif* **:** the order of words prescribed for a religious ceremony **2 a :** ritual observance; *specif* **:** a system of rites **b :** a ceremonial act or action **c :** any formal and customarily repeated act or series of acts

rit·u·al·ism \-ˌiz-əm\ *n* **1 :** the use of ritual **2 :** excessive devotion to ritual — **rit·u·al·ist** \-əst\ *n* — **rit·u·al·is·tic** \ˌrich-(ə-)wəl-ˈis-tik, ˌrich-əl-\ *adj* — **rit·u·al·is·ti·cal·ly** \-ti-k(ə-)lē\ *adv*

rit·u·al·iza·tion \ˌrich-(ə-)wəl-ə-ˈzā-shən, ˌrich-əl-\ *n* **:** the act of ritualizing **:** the condition of being ritualized

rit·u·al·ize \ˈrich-(ə-)wə-ˌlīz, ˈrich-ə-\ *vi* **:** to practice ritualism ~ *vt* **1 :** to make a ritual of **2 :** to impose a ritual on

ritzy \ˈrit-sē\ *adj* [*Ritz* hotels, noted for their opulence] **1 :** ostentatiously smart **:** FASHIONABLE **2 :** SNOBBISH

[1]**ri·val** \ˈrī-vəl\ *n* [MF or L; MF, fr. L *rivalis* one using the same stream as another, rival in love, fr. *rivalis* of a stream, fr. *rivus* stream — more at RISE] **1 a :** one of two or more striving to reach or obtain that which only one can possess **b :** one who tries to excel **2** *obs* **:** ASSOCIATE, COMPANION **3 :** one that equals another in desired qualities **:** PEER

[2]**rival** *adj* **:** having the same pretensions or claims **:** COMPETING

[3]**rival** *vb* **ri·valed** *or* **ri·valled; ri·val·ing** *or* **ri·val·ling** \ˈrīv-(ə-)liŋ\ *vi* **:** to act as a rival **:** COMPETE ~ *vt* **1 :** to be in competition with **2 :** to strive to equal or excel **:** EMULATE **3 :** to possess qualities or aptitudes that equal (those of another)

ri·val·ry \ˈrī-vəl-rē\ *n* **:** the act of rivaling **:** the state of being a rival **:** COMPETITION

rive \ˈrīv\ *vb* **rived** \ˈrīvd\ **riv·en** \ˈriv-ən\ *also* **rived; riv·ing** \ˈrī-viŋ\ [ME *riven,* fr. ON *rīfa;* akin to L *ripa* shore, Gk *ereipein* to tear down, OE *rāw* row] *vt* **1 a :** to tear apart **:** REND **b :** SPLIT, CLEAVE **2 a :** to divide into pieces **:** SHATTER **b :** FRACTURE ~ *vi* **:** to become split **:** CRACK **syn** see TEAR

riv·er \ˈriv-ər\ *n* [ME *rivere,* fr. OF, fr. (assumed) VL *riparia,* fr. L, fem. of *riparius* riparian, fr. *ripa*] **1 a :** a natural stream of water of considerable volume **b :** WATERCOURSE **2 a :** something resembling a river **b** *pl* **:** large or overwhelming quantities

riv·er·bed \-ˌbed\ *n* **:** the channel occupied or formerly occupied by a river

riv·er·boat \-ˌbōt\ *n* **:** a boat for use on a river

river horse *n* **:** HIPPOPOTAMUS

riv·er·ine \ˈriv-ə-ˌrīn, -ˌrēn\ *adj* **1 :** relating to, formed by, or resembling a river **2 :** living or situated on the banks of a river

riv·er·side \ˈriv-ər-ˌsīd\ *n* **:** the side or bank of a river

riv·er·ward \-wərd\ *or* **riv·er·wards** \-wərdz\ *adv (or adj)* [[1]*river* + *-ward, -wards*] **:** toward a river

riv·er·weed \-ˌwēd\ *n* **:** any of a genus (*Podostemon* of the family Podostemaceae) of frondose aquatic dicotyledonous herbs somewhat resembling seaweeds

[1]**riv·et** \ˈriv-ət\ *n* [ME *rivette,* fr. MF *river* to be attached] **:** a headed pin or bolt of metal used for uniting two or more pieces by passing the shank through a hole in each piece and then beating or pressing down the plain end so as to make a second head

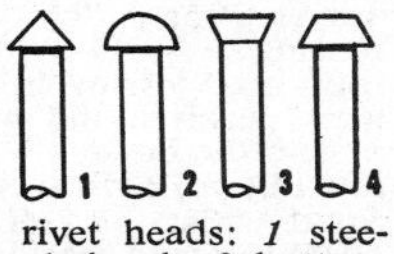

rivet heads: *1* steeple-head, *2* button-head, *3* countersunk, *4* conehead

[2]**rivet** *vt* **1 :** to fasten with or as if with rivets **2 :** to upset the end or point of (as a metallic pin, rod, or bolt) by beating or pressing so as to form a head **3 :** to fasten firmly **4 :** to attract and hold (as the attention) completely — **riv·et·er** *n*

riv·i·era \ˌriv-ē-ˈer-ə\ *n, often cap* [fr. the *Riviera,* region in southeastern France and northwestern Italy] **:** a coastal region frequented as a resort area and usu. marked by a mild climate

riv·i·ère \ˌriv-ē-ˈe(ə)r\ *n* [F, lit., river, fr. OF *rivere*] **:** a necklace of precious stones (as diamonds)

riv·u·let \ˈriv-(y)ə-lət, ˈriv-lət\ *n* [It *rivoletto,* dim. of *rivolo,* fr. L *rivulus,* dim. of *rivus* stream — more at RISE] **:** a small stream **:** BROOK

riv·u·lose \ˈriv-yə-ˌlōs\ *adj* [L *rivulus*] **:** marked with irregular, narrow, sinuous, or crooked lines ⟨a ~ thallus⟩

ri·yal \rē-ˈ(y)ȯl, -ˈ(y)äl\ *n* [Ar *riyāl,* fr. Sp *real* real] **1** — see *dinar* at MONEY table **2** — see MONEY table

[1]**roach** \ˈrōch\ *n, pl* **roach** *also* **roach·es** [ME *roche,* fr. MF] **1 :** a silver-white European freshwater cyprinid fish (*Rutilus rutilus*) with a greenish back; *also* **:** any of various related fishes (as some shiners) **2 :** any of several American freshwater sunfishes (family Centrarchidae)

[2]**roach** *vt* [origin unknown] **1 :** to cause to arch; *specif* **:** to brush (the hair) in a roach — often used with *up* **2 :** to cut (as a horse's mane) so the part left stands upright

[3]**roach** *n* **1 :** a curved cut in the edge of a sail to prevent chafing or secure a better fit **2 :** a roll of hair brushed straight back from the forehead or side of the head

[4]**roach** *n* **:** COCKROACH

roach back *n* **:** an arched back

road \ˈrōd\ *n* [ME *rode,* fr. OE *rād* ride, journey; akin to OE *rīdan* to ride] **1 :** a place less enclosed than a harbor where ships may ride at anchor — often used in pl.; called also *roadstead* **2 a :** an open way for vehicles, persons, and animals; *esp* **:** one lying outside of an urban district **:** HIGHWAY **b :** ROADBED 2b **3 :** ROUTE, PATH **4 :** RAILWAY — **road·side** \-ˌsīd\ *adj or n*

road·abil·i·ty \ˌrōd-ə-ˈbil-ət-ē\ *n* **:** the qualities (as steadiness and balance) desirable in an automobile on the road

road·able \ˈrōd-ə-bəl\ *adj* **:** capable of being driven along roads like an automobile

road agent *n* **:** a highwayman esp. on stage routes in unsettled districts

road·bed \ˈrōd-ˌbed\ *n* **1 a :** the bed on which the ties, rails, and ballast of a railroad rest **b :** the ballast or the upper surface of the ballast on which the ties rest **2 a :** the earth foundation of a road prepared for surfacing **b :** the part of the surface of a road traveled by vehicles

road·block \-ˌbläk\ *n* **1 a :** a barricade often with traps or mines for holding up an enemy at a point on a road covered by fire **b :** a road barricade set up esp. by law enforcement officers **2 :** an obstruction in a road

road hog *n* **:** a driver of an automotive vehicle who obstructs others esp. by occupying part of another's traffic lane

road·house \-ˌhau̇s\ *n* **:** an inn usu. outside city limits providing liquor and usu. meals, dancing, and often gambling

road metal *n* **:** broken stone or cinders used in making and repairing roads or ballasting railroads

road roller *n* **:** one that rolls roadways; *specif* **:** a machine equipped with heavy wide smooth rollers for compacting roads and pavements

road·run·ner \ˈrō-ˌdrən-ər\ *n* **:** a largely terrestrial bird (*Geococcyx californianus*) of the cuckoo family that is a speedy runner and ranges from California to Mexico and eastward to Texas — called also *chaparral cock; also* **:** a closely related Mexican bird (*G. velox*)

road·stead \ˈrōd-ˌsted\ *n* **:** ROAD 1

road·ster \ˈrōd-stər\ *n* **1 a :** a horse for riding or driving on roads **b :** a utility saddle horse of the hackney type **2 a :** a light carriage **:** BUGGY **b :** an automobile with an open body and one cross seat with a luggage compartment or rumble seat in the rear

road test *n* **:** a test of a vehicle under practical operating conditions on the road

road·way \ˈrō-ˌdwā\ *n* **1 a :** the strip of land over which a road passes **b :** ROAD; *specif* **:** ROADBED 2b **2 :** a railroad right-of-way with tracks, structures, and appurtenances **3 :** the part of a bridge used by vehicles

road·work \ˈrō-ˌdwərk\ *n* **:** conditioning for an athletic contest (as a boxing match) consisting mainly of long runs

roam \ˈrōm\ *vb* [ME *romen*] *vi* **1 :** to go from place to place without purpose or direction **:** WANDER **2 :** to travel purposefully unhindered through a wide area ~ *vt* **:** to range or wander over — **roam** *n* — **roam·er** *n*

[1]**roan** \ˈrōn *also* ˈrō-ən\ *adj* [MF, fr. OSp *roano*] **:** having the base color (as black, red, gray, or brown) muted and lightened by admixture of white hairs ⟨~ horse⟩ ⟨~ calf⟩

[2]**roan** *n* **1 :** an animal (as a horse) with a roan coat — usu. used of a red roan when unqualified **2 :** the color of a roan horse — used

esp. when the base color is red **3 :** a sheepskin tanned with sumac and colored and finished to imitate morocco

1**roar** \'rō(ə)r, 'rȯ(ə)r\ *vb* [ME *roren*, fr. OE *rārian;* akin to OHG *rērēn* to bleat, Skt *rāyati* he barks] *vi* **1 a :** to utter or emit a full loud prolonged sound **b :** to sing or shout with full force **2 a :** to make or emit a loud confused sound **b :** to laugh loudly **3 :** to be boisterous or disorderly **4 :** to make a loud noise in breathing (as horses afflicted with roaring) ~ *vt* **1 :** to utter or proclaim with a roar **2 :** to cause to roar

2**roar** *n* **1 :** the deep cry of a wild beast **2 :** a loud deep cry (as of pain or anger) **3 :** a loud continuous confused sound **4 :** a boisterous outcry

roar·er \'rōr-ər, 'rȯr-\ *n* **1 :** one that roars **2 :** a horse subject to roaring

1**roar·ing** \'rōr-iŋ, 'rȯr-\ *n* **:** noisy respiration in a horse caused by nerve paralysis and muscular atrophy and constituting an unsoundness in the horse

2**roaring** *adj* **:** THRIVING, BOOMING

1**roast** \'rōst\ *vb* [ME *rosten*, fr. OF *rostir*, of Gmc origin; akin to OHG *rōsten* to roast] *vt* **1 a :** to cook by exposing to dry heat (as in an oven or before a fire) or by surrounding with hot embers, sand, or stones ⟨~ a potato in ashes⟩ **b :** to dry and parch by exposure to heat ⟨~ coffee⟩ ⟨~ chestnuts⟩ **2 :** to heat (inorganic material) with access of air and without fusing to effect change (as expulsion of volatile matter, oxidation, or removal of sulfur from sulfide ores) **3 :** to heat to excess **4 :** to criticize severely ~ *vi* **1 :** to cook food by heat **2 :** to undergo being roasted

2**roast** *n* **1 :** a piece of meat suitable for roasting **2 :** a gathering at which food is roasted before an open fire or in hot ashes or sand **3 :** an act or process of roasting; *specif* **:** severe banter or criticism

3**roast** *adj* **:** ROASTED ⟨~ beef⟩

roast·er \'rō-stər\ *n* **1 :** one that roasts **2 :** a device for roasting **3 :** something adapted to roasting: as **a :** a suckling pig **b :** a young domestic fowl

rob \'räb\ *vb* **robbed; rob·bing** [ME *robben*, fr. OF *rober*, of Gmc origin; akin to OHG *roubōn* to rob — more at REAVE] *vt* **1 a** (1) **:** to take something away from by force **:** steal from (2) **:** to take personal property from by violence or threat **b** (1) **:** to remove valuables without right from (a place) (2) **:** to take the contents of (a receptacle) **c :** to take away as loot **:** STEAL **2 a :** to deprive of something due, expected, or desired **b :** to withhold unjustly or injuriously ~ *vi* **:** to commit robbery — **rob·ber** *n*

ro·ba·lo \'rō-bə-,lō, rō-'bäl-(,)ō\ *n, pl* **robalos** *or* **robalo** [Sp] **:** a snook (*Centropomus undecimalis*)

ro·band \'rō-,band\ *n* [prob. fr. MD *rabant*] **:** a piece of spun yarn or marline used to fasten the head of a sail to a spar

robber fly *n* **:** any of numerous predaceous flies (family Asilidae) that sometimes closely resemble the bumblebees

rob·bery \'räb-(ə-)rē\ *n* **:** the act or practice of robbing; *specif* **:** larceny from the person or presence of another by violence or threat

1**robe** \'rōb\ *n* [ME, fr. OF, robe, booty, of Gmc origin; akin to OHG *roubōn* to rob] **1 a :** a long flowing outer garment; *esp* **:** one used for ceremonial occasions or as a symbol of office or profession **b :** a loose garment for informal wear esp. at home (as a bathrobe) **2 :** COVERING, MANTLE **3 :** a covering of pelts or fabric for the lower body used while driving or at outdoor events

2**robe** *vt* **:** to clothe or invest with or cover as if with a robe ~ *vi* **1 :** to put on a robe **2 :** DRESS

robe de cham·bre \,rōb-də-'shäⁿbrᵊ\ *n, pl* **robes de chambre** \,rōb(z)-\ [F] **:** DRESSING GOWN

rob·in \'räb-ən\ *n* [short for *robin redbreast*] **1 a :** a small European thrush (*Erithacus rubecola*) resembling a warbler and having a brownish olive back and yellowish red throat and breast **b :** any of various Old World songbirds that are related to or resemble the European robin **2 :** a large No. American thrush (*Turdus migratorius*) with olivaceous gray upper parts, blackish head and tail, black and whitish streaked throat, and chiefly dull reddish breast and underparts

Rob·in Good·fel·low \,räb-ən-'gu̇d-,fel-(,)ō, -ə(-w)\ *n* **:** a mischievous sprite in English folklore

Robin Hood \-'hu̇d\ *n* **:** a legendary English outlaw noted for his courage, courtesy, and skill in archery and for his habit of robbing the rich to aid the poor

robin red·breast \-'red-,brest\ *n* [ME, fr. *Robin*, nickname for *Robert*] **:** ROBIN

Rob·in·son Cru·soe \,räb-ə(n)-sən-'krü-(,)sō\ *n* **:** a shipwrecked sailor in Defoe's *Robinson Crusoe* who lives for many years on an uninhabited island

ro·ble \'rō-(,)blā\ *n* [AmerSp, fr. Sp, oak, fr. L *robur*] **:** any of several oaks of California and Mexico

ro·bot \'rō-,bät, -bət\ *n* [Czech, fr. *robota* work; akin to OHG *arabeit* trouble, L *orbus* orphaned] **1 a :** a machine that looks like a human being and performs various complex acts (as walking or talking) of a human being; *also* **:** a similar but fictional machine whose lack of capacity for human emotions is often emphasized **b :** an efficient, insensitive, often brutalized person **2 :** an automatic apparatus or device that performs functions ordinarily ascribed to human beings or operates with what appears to be almost human intelligence **3 :** a mechanism guided by automatic controls — **ro·bot·ism** \-,iz-əm\ *n*

robot bomb *n* **1 :** GUIDED MISSILE **2 :** a powered missile not subject to control after launching

ro·bot·iza·tion \,rō-,bät-ə-'zā-shən, -bət-\ *n* **1 :** the process of turning a human being into a robot **2 :** AUTOMATION

ro·bot·ize \'rō-,bät-,īz, -bət-\ *vt* **:** to make automatic

ro·bust \rō-'bəst, 'rō-(,)bəst\ *adj* [L *robustus* oaken, strong, fr. *robor-*, *robur* oak, strength] **1 a :** having or exhibiting strength or vigorous health **:** VIGOROUS **b :** firm in purpose or outlook **2 :** ROUGH, RUDE **3 :** requiring strength or vigor **4 :** FULL-BODIED ⟨~ coffee⟩ **syn** see HEALTHY — **ro·bust·ly** *adv* — **ro·bust·ness** \-'bəs(t)-nəs, -(,)bəs(t)-\ *n*

ro·bus·tious \rō-'bəs-chəs\ *adj* **1 :** ROBUST **2 :** rudely vigorous **:** BOISTEROUS — **ro·bus·tious·ly** *adv* — **ro·bus·tious·ness** *n*

roc \'räk\ *n* [Ar *rukhkh*] **:** a legendary bird of great size and strength believed to inhabit the Indian ocean area

roc·am·bole \'räk-əm-,bōl\ *n* [F, fr. G *rockenbolle*, fr. *rocken*, *roggen* rye + *bolle* bulb] **:** a European leek (*Allium scorodoprasum*) used for flavoring

Ro·chelle powders \rō-,shel-\ *n pl* [La *Rochelle*, France] **:** SEIDLITZ POWDERS

Rochelle salt *n* **:** a crystalline salt $KNaC_4H_4O_6.4H_2O$ that is a mild purgative

roche mou·ton·née \'rȯsh-,müt-ᵊn-'ā, 'rōsh-\ *n, pl* **roches mou·ton·nées** *same or* -'āz\ [F, lit., fleecy rock] **:** an elongate rounded ice-sculptured hillock of bedrock

roch·et \'räch-ət\ *n* [ME, MF, fr. OF, fr. (assumed) OF *roc* coat, of Gmc origin; akin to OHG *roc* coat] **:** a white linen vestment resembling a surplice with close-fitting sleeves worn by bishops and privileged prelates in some ceremonies

1**rock** \'räk\ *vb* [ME *rokken*, fr. OE *roccian;* akin to OHG *rucken* to cause to move] *vt* **1 a :** to move back and forth in or as if in a cradle **b :** to wash (placer gravel) in a cradle **2 a :** to cause to sway back and forth **b** (1) **:** DAZE, STUN (2) **:** DISTURB, UPSET ~ *vi* **1 :** to become moved backward and forward under impact **2 :** to move oneself or itself rhythmically back and forth **syn** see SHAKE

2**rock** *n* **1 :** a rocking movement **2 :** ROCK 'N' ROLL

3**rock** *n* [ME *roc*, fr. MD *rocke;* akin to OHG *rocko* distaff, *roc* coat] **:** DISTAFF

4**rock** *n, often attrib* [ME *rokke*, fr. ONF *roque*, fr. (assumed) VL *rocca*] **1 :** a large mass of stone forming a cliff, promontory, or peak **2 :** a concreted mass of stony material; *also* **:** broken pieces of such masses **3 :** consolidated or unconsolidated solid mineral matter; *also* **:** a particular mass of it **4 a :** something like a rock in firmness: (1) **:** FOUNDATION, SUPPORT (2) **:** REFUGE **b :** something that threatens or causes disaster — often used in pl. **5 :** a stick candy with color running through **6** *slang* **:** DIAMOND — **on the rocks 1 :** in or into a state of destruction or wreckage **2 :** on ice cubes ⟨bourbon *on the rocks*⟩

rock and roll *var of* ROCK 'N' ROLL

rock and rye *n* **:** rye whiskey flavored with orange, lemon, and occas. pineapple and cherry

rock·a·way \'räk-ə-,wā\ *n* [*Rockaway*, New Jersey] **:** a light low four-wheeled carriage with a fixed top and open sides

rock bass *n* **1 :** a sunfish (*Ambloplites rupestris*) found esp. in the upper Mississippi valley and Great Lakes region **2 a :** a striped bass (*Roccus saxatilis*) **b :** any of several sea basses (genus *Paralabrax*) of the California and adjoining Mexican coast

rock bottom *n* **:** the absolute bottom or foundation

rock·bound \'räk-'bau̇nd\ *adj* **:** fringed, surrounded, or covered with rocks **:** ROCKY

rock brake *n* **:** any of several ferns that grow chiefly on or among rocks

rock candy *n* **:** boiled sugar crystallized in large masses on string

Rock Cornish *n* **:** a crossbred domestic fowl produced by interbreeding Cornish and white Plymouth Rock fowls and used esp. for small roasters

rock crystal *n* **:** transparent quartz

rock·er \'räk-ər\ *n* **1 a :** either of two curving pieces of wood or metal on which an object (as a cradle) rocks **b :** any of various objects that rock upon rockers (as an infant's toy having a seat placed between side pieces) **c :** any of various objects in the form of a rocker or with parts resembling a rocker **2 :** any of various devices that work with a rocking motion

rocker arm *n* **:** a center-pivoted lever to push an automotive engine valve down

1**rock·et** \'räk-ət, rä-'ket\ *n* [MF *roquette*, fr. OIt *rochetta*, dim. of *ruca* garden rocket, fr. L *eruca*] **1 :** a yellowish flowered European herb (*Eruca sativa*) of the mustard family sometimes grown for salad **2 :** DAME'S VIOLET; *also* **:** any of several plants resembling dame's violet

2**rock·et** \'räk-ət\ *n, often attrib* [It *rocchetta*, lit., small distaff, fr. dim. of *rocca* distaff, of Gmc origin; akin to OHG *rocko* distaff] **1 :** a firework consisting of a case partly filled with a combustible composition fastened to a guiding stick and projected through the air by the reaction resulting from the rearward discharge of the gases liberated by combustion; *also* **:** such a device used as an incendiary weapon or as a propelling unit (as for a lifesaving line or a whaling harpoon) **2 :** a jet engine that operates on the same principle as the firework rocket, consists essentially of a combustion chamber and an exhaust nozzle, carries either liquid or solid propellants which provide the fuel and oxygen needed for combustion and thus make the engine independent of the oxygen of the air, and is used esp. for the propulsion of a missile (as a bomb or shell) or a vehicle (as an airplane) **3 :** a rocket-propelled bomb, missile, or projectile

3**rock·et** \'räk-ət\ *vt* **:** to convey by means of a rocket ~ *vi* **1 :** to rise up swiftly, spectacularly, and with force **2 :** to travel rapidly in or as if in a rocket

rocket bomb *n* **1 :** an aerial bomb designed for release at low altitude and equipped with a rocket apparatus for giving it added momentum **2 :** a rocket-propelled bomb launched from the ground

rock·e·teer \,räk-ə-'ti(ə)r\ *n* **1 :** one who fires, pilots, or rides in a rocket **2 :** a scientist who specializes in rocketry

rocket plane *n* **:** an airplane propelled by rockets or armed with rocket launchers

rocket propulsion *n* **:** propulsion by means of a rocket engine

rock·et·ry \'räk-ə-trē\ *n* **:** the study of, experimentation with, or use of rockets

rocket ship *n* **:** a rocket-propelled craft capable of navigation beyond the earth's atmosphere

rock·fish \'räk-,fish\ *n* **:** any of various valuable market fishes that live among rocks or on rocky bottoms: as **a :** any of several fishes (family Scorpaenidae) **b :** a striped bass (*Roccus saxatilis*) **c :** any of several groupers **d :** GREENLING 1a

rock garden *n* **:** a garden laid out among rocks or decorated with rocks and adapted for the growth of particular kinds of plants (as alpines)

rock hind *n* **:** any of various spotted groupers commonly found about rocky coasts or reefs

rocking chair *n* **:** a chair mounted on rockers

rocking horse *n* **:** a toy horse mounted on rockers — called also *hobbyhorse*

rock·ling \'räk-liŋ\ *n* **:** any of several small rather elongate marine cods (family Gadidae)

rock lobster *n* **1 :** SPINY LOBSTER **2 :** the flesh of the Cape crawfish esp. when canned or frozen for use as food

rock maple *n* **:** a sugar maple (*Acer saccharum*)

rock 'n' roll \,räk-ən-'rōl\ *n* **1 :** music characterized by a strong

beat and much repetition often with both blues and folk song elements **2 :** improvisatory popular dancing associated with rock 'n' roll music
rock oil *n* **:** PETROLEUM
roc·koon \rä-'kün\ *n* [[2]rocket + balloon] **:** a small rocket carried to a high altitude by a balloon and then fired
rock pigeon *n* **:** a bluish gray wild pigeon (*Columba livia*) of Europe and Asia
rock rabbit *n* **1 :** HYRAX **2 :** PIKA
rock–ribbed \'räk-'ribd\ *adj* **1 :** ROCKY **2 :** firm and inflexible in doctrine or integrity
rock·rose \'räk-,rōz\ *n* **:** a shrub or woody herb (family Cistaceae, the rockrose family)
rock salt *n* **:** common salt occurring in solid form as a mineral; *also* **:** salt artificially prepared in large crystals or masses
rock·shaft \'räk-,shaft\ *n* **:** a shaft that oscillates on its journals instead of revolving
rock·skip·per \-,skip-ər\ *n* **:** any of several blennies
rock tripe *n* **:** an edible lichen (of *Umbilicaria* or the related genus *Gyrophora*) that is common on rocks in arctic and subarctic regions
rock wallaby *n* **:** any of various medium-sized kangaroos (genus *Petrogale*)
rock·weed \'räk-,wēd\ *n* **:** a coarse brown seaweed (family Fucaceae) growing attached to rocks
rock wool *n* **:** mineral wool made by blowing a jet of steam through molten rock (as limestone or siliceous rock) or through slag and used chiefly for heat and sound insulation
[1]**rocky** \'räk-ē\ *adj* **1 :** abounding in or consisting of rocks **2 :** difficult to impress or affect **:** INSENSITIVE ⟨his ~ heart⟩ **3 :** firmly held **:** STEADFAST
[2]**rocky** *adj* **1 :** UNSTABLE, WOBBLY **2 :** physically upset (as from drinking excessively) **3 :** marked by obstacles **:** DIFFICULT
Rocky Mountain sheep *n* [*Rocky mountains*, No. America] **:** BIGHORN
Rocky Mountain spotted fever *n* **:** an acute rickettsial disease characterized by chills, fever, prostration, pains in muscles and joints, and a red to purple eruption and transmitted by the bite of a wood tick (*Dermacentor andersoni*)
[1]**ro·co·co** \rə-'kō-(,)kō, ,rō-kə-'kō\ *adj* [F, irreg. fr. *rocaille* rock-work, fr. *roc* rock, alter. of MF *roche*, fr. (assumed) VL *rocca*] **1 a :** of or relating to an artistic style esp. of the 18th century characterized by fanciful curved spatial forms and ornament of pierced shellwork **b :** of or relating to an 18th century musical style marked by light gay ornamentation and departure from thorough bass and polyphony **2 :** excessively ornate or intricate
[2]**rococo** *n* **:** rococo work or style
rod \'räd\ *n* [ME, fr. OE *rodd;* akin to ON *rudda* club] **1 a** (1) **:** a straight slender stick growing on or cut from a tree or bush (2) **:** OSIER (3) **:** a stick or bundle of twigs used to punish; *also* **:** PUNISHMENT (4) **:** a shepherd's cudgel (5) **:** a pole with a line and usu. a reel attached for fishing **b** (1) **:** a slender bar (as of wood or metal) (2) **:** a bar or staff for measuring (3) **:** SCEPTER; *also* **:** a wand or staff carried as a badge of office (as of marshal) **2 a :** a unit of length — see MEASURE table **b :** a square rod **3 :** any of the long rod-shaped sensory bodies in the retina responsive to faint light **4 :** a bacterium shaped like a rod **5** *slang* **:** PISTOL — **rod·less** \-ləs\ *adj* — **rod·like** \-,līk\ *adj*
rode *past of* RIDE
[1]**ro·dent** \'rōd-ᵊnt\ *adj* **1 :** GNAWING, BITING **2 :** of or relating to rodents
[2]**rodent** *n* [deriv. of L *rodent-, rodens*, prp. of *rodere* to gnaw — more at RAT] **:** any of an order (Rodentia) of relatively small gnawing mammals having a single pair of upper incisors with a chisel-shaped edge; *also* **:** a lagomorph (as a rabbit) or other small mammal (as a shrew)
ro·den·ti·cide \rō-'dent-ə-,sīd\ *n* **:** an agent that kills, repels, or controls rodents
ro·deo \'rōd-ē-,ō, rə-'dā-(,)ō\ *n* [Sp, fr. *rodear* to surround, fr. *rueda* wheel, fr. L *rota* — more at ROLL] **1 :** ROUNDUP **2 a :** a public performance featuring bronco riding, calf roping, steer wrestling, and Brahma bull riding **b :** a contest likened to a rodeo
rod·man \'räd-mən, -,man\ *n* **:** a surveyor's assistant who holds the leveling rod
ro·do·mon·tade \,räd-ə-mən-'tād, ,rōd-, -,män-; -mən-'täd\ *n* [MF, fr. *Rodomonte*, character in *Orlando Innamorato* by Matteo M. Boiardo] **1 :** a bragging speech **2 :** vain boasting or bluster **:** RANT — **rodomontade** *adj*
[1]**roe** \'rō\ *n, pl* **roe** *or* **roes** [ME *ro*, fr. OE *rā;* akin to OHG *rēh* roe, OIr *rīabach* dappled] **:** DOE
[2]**roe** *n* [ME *roof;* akin to OHG *rogo* roe, Lith *kurkulai* frog's eggs] **1 a :** the eggs of a fish esp. when still enclosed in the ovarian membrane **b :** the eggs or ovaries of an invertebrate (as the coral of a lobster) **2 :** a dark mottled or flecked figure appearing esp. in quartersawed lumber
roe·buck \'rō-,bək\ *n, pl* **roebuck** *or* **roebucks :** ROE DEER; *esp* **:** the male roe deer
roe deer *n* **:** a small European and Asiatic deer (*Capreolus capreolus*) that has erect cylindrical antlers forked at the summit, is reddish brown in summer and grayish in winter, has a white rump patch, and is noted for its nimbleness and grace
[1]**roent·gen** \'rent-gən, 'rənt-, -jən; 'ren-chən, 'rən-\ *adj* [ISV, fr. Wilhelm *Röntgen* †1923 G physicist] **:** of or relating to X rays ⟨~ examinations⟩
[2]**roentgen** *n* **:** the international unit of X-radiation or gamma radiation equal to the amount of radiation that produces in one cubic centimeter of dry air under standard conditions of temperature and pressure ionization of either sign equal to one electrostatic unit of charge
roent·gen·ize \-,īz\ *vt* **1 :** to make (air or other gas) conducting by the passage of X rays **2 :** to subject to the action of X rays
roent·gen·o·gram \-ə-,gram\ *n* [ISV] **:** a photograph made with X rays
roent·gen·o·graph \-,graf\ *n* **:** ROENTGENOGRAM
roent·gen·o·graph·ic \,rent-gən-ə-'graf-ik, ,rənt-, -jən-; ,ren-chən-, ,rən-\ *adj* **:** of or relating to roentgenography — **roent·gen·o·graph·i·cal·ly** \-i-k(ə-)lē\ *adv*
roent·gen·og·ra·phy \-'äg-rə-fē\ *n* [ISV] **:** photography by means of X rays
roent·gen·o·log·ic \-ə-'läj-ik\ *adj* **:** of or relating to roentgenology — **roent·gen·o·log·i·cal** \-i-kəl\ *adj* — **roent·gen·o·log·i·cal·ly** \-i-k(ə-)lē\ *adv*
roent·gen·ol·o·gist \-'äl-ə-jəst\ *n* **:** a specialist in roentgenology
roent·gen·ol·o·gy \-jē\ *n* [ISV] **:** a branch of radiology that deals with the use of X rays for diagnosis or treatment of disease
roent·gen·o·scope \'rent-gən-ə-,skōp, 'rənt-, -jən-; 'ren-chən-, 'rən-\ *n* **:** FLUOROSCOPE — **roent·gen·o·scop·ic** \,rent-gən-ə-'skäp-ik, ,rənt-, -jən-; ,ren-chən-, ,rən-\ *adj* — **roent·gen·os·co·py** \-'äs-kə-pē\ *n*
roent·gen·o·ther·a·py \,rent-gən-ə-'ther-ə-pē, ,rənt-, -jən-; ,ren-chən-, ,rən-\ *n* [ISV] **:** radiotherapy by means of X rays
roentgen ray *n, often cap 1st R* **:** X RAY
ro·ga·tion \rō-'gā-shən\ *n* [ME *rogacion*, fr. LL *rogation-, rogatio*, fr. L, questioning, fr. *rogatus*, pp. of *rogare* to ask — more at RIGHT] **1 :** LITANY, SUPPLICATION **2** *pl* **:** the ceremonies of the Rogation Days
Rogation Day *n* **:** one of the days of prayer esp. for the harvest observed on the three days before Ascension Day and by Roman Catholics also on April 25
rog·er \'räj-ər\ *interj* [fr. *Roger*] — used esp. in radio and signaling to indicate that a message has been received and understood
Rog·er \'räj-ər\ [fr. the name *Roger*] — a communications code word for the letter *r*
[1]**rogue** \'rōg\ *n* [origin unknown] **1 :** VAGRANT, TRAMP **2 :** a dishonest or worthless person **:** SCOUNDREL **3 :** a mischievous person **:** SCAMP **4 :** a horse inclined to shirk or misbehave **5 :** an individual exhibiting a chance and usu. inferior biological variation — **rogu·ish** \'rō-gish\ *adj* — **rogu·ish·ly** *adv* — **rogu·ish·ness** *n*
[2]**rogue** *vi* **rogued; rogu·ing** *or* **rogue·ing :** to weed out inferior, diseased, or nontypical individuals from a crop plant or a field
[3]**rogue** *adj, of an animal* **:** being vicious and destructive ⟨~ otter⟩
rogue elephant *n* **:** a vicious elephant that separates from the herd and roams alone
rogu·ery \'rō-g(ə-)rē\ *n* **1 :** an act characteristic of a rogue **2 :** mischievous play
rogues' gallery *n* **:** a collection of portraits of persons arrested as criminals
roil \'rȯi(ə)l, *vt 2 is also* 'rī(ə)l\ *vb* [origin unknown] *vt* **1 a :** to make turbid by stirring up the sediment or dregs of **b :** to stir up **:** DISTURB, DISORDER **2 :** RILE 2 **~** *vi* **:** to move turbulently **syn** see IRRITATE
roily \'rȯi-lē\ *adj* **1 :** full of sediment or dregs **:** MUDDY **2 :** TURBULENT **syn** see TURBID
rois·ter \'rȯi-stər\ *vi* **rois·ter·ing** \-st(ə-)riŋ\ [earlier *roister* (roisterer)] **:** to engage in noisy revelry **:** CAROUSE — **rois·ter·er** \-stər-ər\ *n*
Ro·land \'rō-lənd\ *n* [F] **:** a stalwart defender of the Christians against the Saracens in French romance killed at Roncesvalles in 778
role *also* **rôle** \'rōl\ *n* [F *rôle*, lit., roll, fr. OF *rolle*] **1 a :** a character assigned or assumed **b :** a part played by an actor or singer **2 :** FUNCTION
[1]**roll** \'rōl\ *n* [ME *rolle*, fr. OF, fr. L *rotula*, dim. of *rota* wheel; akin to OHG *rad* wheel, Skt *ratha* wagon] **1 a** (1) **:** a written document that may be rolled up **:** SCROLL; *specif* **:** a document containing an official or formal record ⟨~*s* of parliament⟩ (2) **:** a manuscript book **b :** a list of names or related items **:** CATALOG **c :** an official list: as (1) **:** MUSTER ROLL (2) **:** a list of members of a school or class or of members of a legislative body **2 :** something that is rolled up into a cylinder or ball: as **a :** a quantity (as of fabric or paper) rolled up to form a single package **b :** a hairdo in which some or all of the hair is rolled or curled up or under ⟨pageboy ~⟩ **c :** any of various food preparations rolled up for cooking or serving; *specif* **:** a small piece of baked yeast dough **d :** a cylindrical twist of tobacco **e :** a flexible case (as of leather) in which articles may be rolled and fastened by straps or clasps **f** (1) **:** paper money folded or rolled into a wad (2) *slang* **:** BANKROLL **3 :** something that performs a rolling action or movement **:** ROLLER; as **a :** a wheel for making decorative lines on book covers; *also* **:** a design impressed by such a tool **b :** a typewriter platen
[2]**roll** *vt* **1 a :** to impel forward by causing to turn over and over on a surface **b :** to cause to revolve by turning over and over on or as if on an axis **c :** to cause to move in a circular manner **d :** to form into a mass by turning over and over **e :** to impel forward with an easy continuous motion **2 a :** to put a wrapping around **:** ENFOLD, ENVELOP **b :** to wrap round on itself **:** shape into a ball or roll **3 a :** to press, spread, or level with a roller **:** make smooth, even, or compact **b :** to spread out **:** EXTEND ⟨~ out the red carpet⟩ **4 a :** to move on rollers or wheels **b :** to cause to begin operating or moving ⟨~ the cameras⟩ **5 a :** to sound with a full reverberating tone ⟨~*ed* out the words⟩ **b :** to make a continuous beating sound upon **:** sound a roll upon ⟨~*ed* their drums⟩ **c :** to utter with a trill ⟨~*ed* his *r's*⟩ **d :** to play (a chord) in arpeggio style **6 :** to rob (a drunk, sleeping, or unconscious person) usu. by going through the pockets **~** *vi* **1 a :** to move along a surface by rotation without sliding **b** (1) **:** to turn over and over ⟨the children ~*ed* in the grass⟩ (2) **:** to luxuriate in an abundant supply **:** WALLOW ⟨fairly ~*ing* in money⟩ **2 a :** to move onward or around as if by completing a revolution ⟨the months ~ on⟩ **:** ELAPSE, PASS **b :** to shift the gaze continually ⟨eyes ~*ing* in terror⟩ **c :** to revolve on an axis **3 :** to move about **:** ROAM, WANDER **4 a :** to flow with a rising and falling motion ⟨the clouds ~ past⟩ **b :** to flow in a continuous stream **:** POUR ⟨money was ~*ing* in⟩ **c :** to have an undulating contour ⟨~*ing* prairie⟩ **d :** to lie extended **:** STRETCH **5 a :** to travel in a vehicle **b :** to become carried on a stream **c :** to move on wheels **6 a :** to make a deep reverberating sound ⟨the thunder ~*s*⟩ **b :** TRILL **7 a :** to swing from side to side ⟨the ship heaved and ~*ed*⟩ **b :** to walk with a swinging gait **:** SWAY **c :** to move so as to cushion the impact of a blow — used with *with* ⟨~*ed* with the punch⟩ **8 a :** to take the form of a cylinder or ball **b :** to respond to rolling in a specified way or to be in a specified condition after being rolled **9 a :** to get under way **:** begin to move or operate **b :** to move forward **:** develop and maintain impetus **10 a :** BOWL **b :** to execute a roll in tumbling — **roll**

one's hoop *slang* : to attend to one's own business — **roll the bones** : to shoot craps

³roll *n* **1 a** : a sound produced by rapid strokes on a drum **b** : a sonorous and often rhythmical flow of speech **c** : a heavy reverberatory sound ⟨the ~ of cannon⟩ **d** : a chord in arpeggio style **e** : a trill of some birds (as a canary) **2** : a rolling movement or an action or process involving such movement ⟨a ~ of the dice⟩: as **a** : a swaying movement of the body **b** : a side to side movement (as of a ship or train) **c** : a flight maneuver in which a complete revolution about the longitudinal axis of an airplane is made with the horizontal direction of flight being approximately maintained **d** (1) : any of several acrobatic and modern dance exercises in which the body is rotated on the floor ⟨chest ~⟩ (2) : a pivot of ballroom dance partners away from or toward each other or toward a new partner **e** : SOMERSAULT **f** : the movement of a curling stone after impact with another stone

roll back *vt* **1** : to reduce (a commodity price) to or toward a previous level on a national scale by government control devices **2** : to cause to retreat or withdraw : push back

roll·back \ˈrōl-ˌbak\ *n* : the act or an instance of rolling back

roll call *n* : the act or an instance of calling off a list of names (as for checking attendance); *also* : a time for a roll call

¹roll·er \ˈrō-lər\ *n* **1 a** : a revolving cylinder over or on which something is moved or which is used to press, shape, or smooth something **b** : a rod on which something (as a shade) is rolled up **2 a** : a long heavy wave on a coast **b** : a tumbler pigeon

²rol·ler \ˈrō-lər\ *n* [G, fr. *rollen* to roll, reverberate, fr. MF *roller*, fr. (assumed) VL *rotulare*, fr. L *rotula*] **1** : any of numerous mostly brightly colored nonpasserine Old World birds (family Coraciidae) related to the motmots and todies **2** : a canary having a song in which the notes are soft and run together

roller bearing *n* : a bearing in which the journal rotates in peripheral contact with a number of rollers usu. contained in a cage

roll·er coast·er \ˈrō-lər-ˌkō-stər, ˈrō-lē-ˌkō-\ *n* : an elevated railway (as in an amusement park) constructed with curves and inclines on which cars roll

roller skate *n* : a skate with wheels instead of a runner for skating on a surface other than ice — **roll·er–skate** \ˌrō-lər-ˈskāt\ *vi* — **roller skater** *n*

roller towel *n* : an endless towel hung from a roller

roll film *n* : a strip of film for still camera use wound on a spool

rol·lick \ˈräl-ik\ *vi* [origin unknown] : to move or behave in a carefree joyous manner : FROLIC — **rollick** *n* — **rol·lick·ing** *adj*

rolling hitch *n* : a hitch for fastening a line to a spar or to the standing part of another line that will not slip when the pull is parallel to the spar or line

rolling mill *n* : an establishment where metal is rolled into plates and bars

rolling pin *n* : a long cylinder for rolling out dough

rolling stock *n* : the wheeled vehicles owned and used by a railroad or motor carrier

roll·man \ˈrōl-mən, -ˌman\ *n* : one who operates a rolling machine

roll out *vi* : to get out of bed

roll·top desk \ˌrōl-ˌtäp-\ *n* : a writing desk with a sliding cover of parallel slats fastened to a flexible backing

roll up *vt* : to increase by successive accumulations : ACCUMULATE ⟨*rolled up* a large majority⟩ ~ *vi* **1** : to become larger by successive accumulations **2** : to arrive in a vehicle

¹ro·ly–po·ly \ˌrō-lē-ˈpō-lē\ *n* [redupl. of *roly*, fr. ²*roll*] **1** : a sweet dough spread with a filling, rolled, and baked or steamed **2** : a roly-poly person or thing

²roly–poly *adj* : being short and pudgy : ROTUND

Ro·ma·ic \rō-ˈmā-ik\ *n* [NGk *Rhōmaiikos*, fr. Gk *Rhōmaïkos* Roman, fr. *Rhōmē* Rome] : the modern Greek vernacular — **Romaic** *adj*

ro·maine \rō-ˈmān\ *n* [F, fr. fem. of *romain* Roman, fr. L *Romanus*] : COS LETTUCE

ro·man \rō-ˈmäⁿ\ *n* [MF, fr. OF *romans* romance] : a metrical romance

¹Ro·man \ˈrō-mən\ *n* [partly fr. ME, fr. OE, fr. L *Romanus*, adj. & n., fr. *Roma* Rome; partly fr. ME *Romain*, fr. OF, fr. L *Romanus*] **1** : a native or resident of Rome **2** : ROMAN CATHOLIC — often taken to be offensive **3** *not cap* : roman letters or type

²Roman *adj* **1** : of or relating to Rome or the people of Rome; *specif* : characteristic of the ancient Romans ⟨~ fortitude⟩ **2** : LATIN **3** *not cap* : UPRIGHT — used of numbers and letters whose capital forms are modeled on ancient Roman inscriptions **4** : of or relating to the see of Rome or the Roman Catholic Church **5** : having a semicircular intrados ⟨~ arch⟩ **6** : having a prominent slightly aquiline bridge ⟨~ nose⟩

ro·man à clef \rō-ˌmä(ⁿ)n-(ˌ)ä-ˈklā\ *n, pl* **ro·mans à clef** *same or* -ˌmäⁿz-(ˌ)ä-\ [F, lit., novel with a key] : a novel in which real persons or actual events figure under disguise

Roman architecture *n* : the classical architectural style of the Roman empire marked by the use of the orders, pediment, arch, dome, and vault

Roman calendar *n* : a calendar of ancient Rome preceding the Julian calendar and having 12 months with the days of the month reckoned backward from fixed points — compare CALENDS

Roman candle *n* : a straight cylindrical firework that discharges at intervals balls or stars of fire

Roman Catholic *adj* : of or relating to the body of Christians in communion with the pope having a hierarchy of priests and bishops under the pope, a liturgy centered in the Mass, and a body of dogma formulated by the church as the infallible interpreter of revealed truth; *esp* : of or relating to the Western rite of this church marked by a Latin liturgy — **Roman Catholic** *n* — **Roman Catholicism** *n*

¹ro·mance \rō-ˈman(t)s, rə-; ˈrō-ˌ\ *n* [ME *romauns*, fr. OF *romans* French, something written in French, fr. L *romanice* in the Roman manner, fr. *romanicus* Roman, fr. *Romanus*] **1 a** (1) : a medieval tale in verse or prose based on legend, chivalric love and adventure, or the supernatural (2) : a prose narrative treating imaginary characters involved in events remote in time or place and usu. heroic, adventurous, or mysterious (3) : a love story **b** : a class of such literature **2** : something that lacks basis in fact **3** : an emotional attraction or aura belonging to an esp. heroic era, adventure, or calling **4** : a passionate love affair **5** *cap* : the Romance languages

²romance *vi* **1** : to exaggerate or invent detail or incident **2** : to entertain romantic thoughts or ideas ~ *vt* : to carry on a love affair with

³romance *n* : a short instrumental piece in ballad style

Ro·mance \rō-ˈman(t)s, rə-; ˈrō-ˌ\ *adj* : of, relating to, or constituting the languages developed from Latin

ro·manc·er \-ər\ *n* **1** : a writer of romance **2** : one that romances

Roman collar *n* : CLERICAL COLLAR

Ro·man·esque \ˌrō-mə-ˈnesk\ *adj* : of or relating to a style of architecture developed in Italy and western Europe between the Roman and the Gothic styles and characterized in its development after 1000 by the use of the round arch and vault, substitution of piers for columns, decorative use of arcades, and profuse ornament — **Romanesque** *n*

ro·man–fleuve \rō-ˌmäⁿ-ˈflœv, -ˈflə(r)v\ *n, pl* **ro·mans–fleuves** \-ˌmäⁿ-ˈflœv, -ˈflə(r)v(z)\ [F, lit., river novel] : a distinctively French novel in the form of a long usu. easygoing chronicle of a family, community, or other social group

Ro·ma·nian \ru̇-ˈmā-nē-ən, rō-, -nyən\ *n* **1** : a native or inhabitant of Romania **2** : the Romance language of the Romanians — **Romanian** *adj*

Ro·man·ic \rō-ˈman-ik\ *adj* : ROMANCE — **Romanic** *n*

Ro·man·ism \ˈrō-mə-ˌniz-əm\ *n* : ROMAN CATHOLICISM — often taken to be offensive

Ro·man·ist \-nəst\ *n* **1** : ROMAN CATHOLIC — often taken to be offensive **2** : a specialist in the language, culture, or law of ancient Rome — **Romanist** *or* **Ro·man·is·tic** \ˌrō-mə-ˈnis-tik\ *adj*

ro·man·ize \ˈrō-mə-ˌnīz\ *vt* **1** *often cap* : to make Roman : LATINIZE **2** : to write or print (as a language) in roman characters

roman numeral *n, often cap R* : a numeral in a system of notation based on the ancient Roman system — see NUMBER table

Ro·ma·no \rə-ˈmän-(ˌ)ō, rō-\ *n* [It, Roman, fr. L *Romanus*] : a sharp hard cheese with blackish green rind

Ro·mansh *or* **Ro·mansch** \rō-ˈmänch, -ˈmanch\ *n* [Romansh *romonsch*] : the Rhaeto-Romanic dialects spoken in the Grisons, Switzerland and adjacent parts of Italy

¹ro·man·tic \rō-ˈmant-ik, rə-\ *adj* [F *romantique*, fr. obs. *romant* romance, fr. OF *romans*] **1** : consisting of or resembling a romance **2** : having no basis in fact : IMAGINARY **3** : impractical in conception or plan : VISIONARY **4 a** : marked by the imaginative or emotional appeal of the heroic, adventurous, remote, mysterious, or idealized **b** *often cap* : of, relating to, or having the characteristics of romanticism **5 a** : having an inclination for romance **b** : ARDENT, FERVENT; *esp* : marked by or constituting passionate love **6** : of, relating to, or constituting the part of the hero in a comedy — **ro·man·ti·cal·ly** \-i-k(ə-)lē\ *adv*

²romantic *n* **1** : a romantic person, trait, or component **2** *cap* : ROMANTICIST

ro·man·ti·cism \rō-ˈmant-ə-ˌsiz-əm, rə-\ *n* **1** : the quality or state of being romantic **2** *often cap* **a** (1) : a literary, artistic, and philosophical movement originating in the 18th century, characterized chiefly by a reaction against neoclassicism and an emphasis on the imagination and emotions, and marked esp. in English literature by sensibility and the use of autobiographical material, an exaltation of the primitive and the common man, an appreciation of external nature, an interest in the remote, a predilection for melancholy, and the use in poetry of older verse forms (2) : an aspect of romanticism **b** : adherence to or practice of romantic doctrine or assumptions — **ro·man·ti·cist** \-səst\ *n, often cap*

ro·man·ti·ci·za·tion \-ˌmant-ə-sə-ˈzā-shən\ *n* : the act or process of romanticizing

ro·man·ti·cize \-ˈmant-ə-ˌsīz\ *vt* : to make romantic ~ *vi* **1** : to hold romantic ideas **2** : to present details, incidents, or people in a romantic way

Ro·ma·ny \ˈräm-ə-nē, ˈrō-mə-\ *n* [Romany *romani*, adj., gypsy, fr. *rom* gypsy man, fr. Skt *ḍomba* man of a low caste of musicians] **1** : GYPSY 1 **2** : the Indic language of the Gypsies — **Romany** *adj*

ro·maunt \rō-ˈmȯnt, -ˈmänt\ *n* [ME, fr. MF *romant*] *archaic* : ROMANCE 1a(1)

rom·el·dale \ˈräm-əl-ˌdāl\ *n, often cap* [blend of *Romney*, *Rambouillet*, and *Corriedale*] : any of an American breed of utility sheep yielding a heavy fleece of fine wool and producing a quickly maturing high-grade market lamb

¹Ro·meo \ˈrō-mē-ˌō, *in Shak also* ˈrōm-(ˌ)yō\ *n* **1** : a son of Montague in love with Juliet in Shakespeare's *Romeo and Juliet* **2** : a male lover

²Romeo — a communications code word for the letter *r*

Rom·ish \ˈrō-mish\ *adj* : Roman Catholic — usu. used disparagingly — **Rom·ish·ly** *adv* — **Rom·ish·ness** *n*

Rom·ney \ˈräm-nē\ *n* [*Romney* Marsh, pasture tract in England] : any of a British breed of hardy long-wooled mutton-type sheep esp. adapted to damp or marshy regions — called also *Romney marsh, often cap M*

¹romp \ˈrämp, ˈrȯmp\ *n* [partly alter. of ²*ramp*; partly alter. of *ramp* (bold woman)] **1** : one that romps; *esp* : a romping girl or woman **2** : boisterous play : FROLIC **3** : an easy winning pace

²romp *vi* [alter. of ¹*ramp*] **1** : to play in a boisterous manner : FROLIC **2 a** : to proceed in a gay or animated manner **b** : to run so as to win easily

romp·er \ˈräm-pər, ˈrȯm-\ *n* **1** : one that romps **2** : a child's one-piece garment with the lower part shaped like bloomers — usu. used in pl.

Rom·u·lus \ˈräm-yə-ləs\ *n* [L] : the legendary founder and first king of Rome

ron·deau \ˈrän-(ˌ)dō, rän-ˈdō\ *n, pl* **ron·deaux** \-(ˌ)dōz, -ˈdōz\ [MF *rondel*, *rondeau*] **1 a** : a fixed form of verse running on two rhymes and consisting usu. of 15 lines of eight or ten syllables divided into three stanzas in which the opening words of the first line of the first stanza serve as the refrain of the second and third stanzas — called also *rondel* **b** : a poem in this form **2** : a monophonic trouvère song with a 2-part refrain

rondeau re·dou·blé \-rə-ˌdü-ˈblā\ *n, pl* **rondeaux re·dou·blés** *same or* -(ˌ)dōz-rə-ˌdü-ˈblā, -ˈdōz- *or* -(ˌ)dō-rə-ˌdü-ˈblāz, -ˈdō-\ [F, lit., double rondeau] **1** : a fixed form of verse running on two alternating rhymes that usu. consists of five quatrains in which the lines of the 1st quatrain are used consecutively to end each of the remaining four quatrains which are in turn sometimes followed by an envoi of four lines that terminates with the opening words of the poem **2** : a poem in the rondeau redoublé form

ron·del \'rän-d⁰l, rän-'del\ *or* **ron·delle** \rän-'del\ *n* [ME, fr. OF, lit., small circle — more at ROUNDEL] **1** *usu* rondelle : a circular object **2 a** *usu rondel* : a fixed form of verse running on two rhymes and consisting usu. of 14 lines of eight or ten syllables divided into three stanzas in which the 1st two lines of the 1st stanza serve as the refrain of the 2nd and 3d stanzas **b** : a poem in this form **c** : RONDEAU 1

ron·de·let \,rän-d⁰l-'et\ *n* : a modified rondeau running on two rhymes and consisting usu. of seven lines in which the 1st line of four syllables is repeated as the 3d line and as the final line or refrain and the remaining lines are made up of eight syllables each

ron·do \'rän-(,)dō, rän-'dō\ *n* [It *rondò*, fr. MF *rondeau*] **1** : an instrumental composition typically with a refrain recurring four times in the tonic and with three couplets in contrasting keys **2** : the musical form of a rondo

ron·dure \'rän-jər, -(,)dyu̇(ə)r\ *n* [F *rondeur* roundness, fr. MF, fr. *rond* round, fr. OF *roont* — more at ROUND] **1** : ROUND 1a **2** : gracefully rounded curvature

röntgen *var of* ROENTGEN

ron·yon \'rən-yən\ *n* [perh. modif. of F *rogne* scab] *obs* : a mangy or scabby creature

rood \'rüd\ *n* [ME, fr. OE *rōd* rod, rood; akin to OHG *ruota* rod, OSlav *ratište* shaft of a lance] **1** : a cross or crucifix symbolizing the cross on which Jesus Christ died; *specif* : a large crucifix on a beam or screen at the entrance of the chancel of a medieval church **2 a** : any of various units of land area; *esp* : a British unit equal to ¼ acre **b** : any of various units of length; *esp* : a British unit equal to seven or eight yards or sometimes a rod

¹roof \'rüf, 'ru̇f\ *n*, *pl* **roofs** \'rüfs, 'ru̇fs *also* 'rüvz, 'ru̇vz\ [ME, fr. OE *hrōf*; akin to ON *hrōf* roof of a boathouse, OSlav *stropŭ* roof] **1 a** : the cover of a building **b** : DWELLING, HOME **c** : ROOFING ⟨slag or gravel ∼⟩ ⟨coal tar, pitch, and felt ∼⟩ **2 a** (1) : the highest point : SUMMIT (2) : CEILING 5 **b** : something resembling a roof in form or function **3 a** : the vaulted upper boundary of the mouth **b** : a covering structure of any of various parts of the body — **roofed** \'rüft, 'ru̇ft\ *adj* — **roof·less** \'rü-fləs, 'ru̇f-ləs\ *adj* — **roof·like** \'rü-,flīk, 'ru̇f-,līk\ *adj*

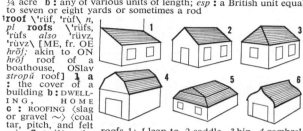

roofs 1: *1* lean-to, 2 saddle, *3* hip, *4* gambrel, *5* mansard, *6* ogee

²roof *vt* **1 a** : to cover with or as if with a roof **b** : to provide (a roof) with a protective exterior **2** : to constitute a roof over — **roof·er** *n*

roof garden *n* : a restaurant at the top of a building usu. with facilities for music and dancing

roof·ing *n* : material for a roof

roof·top \'rüf-,täp, 'ru̇f-\ *n* : ROOF; *esp* : the outer surface of a usu. flat roof ⟨sunning themselves on the ∼⟩

roof·tree \-,trē\ *n* : RIDGEPOLE

¹rook \'ru̇k\ *n* [ME, fr. OE *hrōc*; akin to OE *hræfn* raven — more at RAVEN] : a common Old World gregarious bird (*Corvus frugilegus*) about the size and color of the related American crow

²rook *vt* : to defraud by cheating or swindling

³rook *n* [ME *rok*, fr. MF *roc*, fr. Ar *rukhkh*, fr. Per] : a chess piece that moves parallel to the sides of the board across any number of unoccupied squares — called also *castle*

rook·ery \'ru̇k-ə-rē\ *n* **1 a** : the nests or breeding place of a colony of rooks; *also* : a colony of rooks **b** : a breeding ground or haunt of gregarious birds or mammals; *also* : a colony of such birds or mammals **2** : a crowded dilapidated tenement or group of dwellings : WARREN **3** : a place teeming with like individuals

rook·ie \'ru̇k-ē\ *n* [perh. alter. of *recruit*] : RECRUIT; *also* : NOVICE

rooky \'ru̇k-ē\ *adj* : full of or containing rooks

¹room \'rüm, 'ru̇m\ *n* [ME, fr. OE *rūm*; akin to OHG *rūm* room, L *rur-, rus* open land] **1 a** : unoccupied area : SPACE **b** : sufficient unoccupied space ⟨∼ to swing a cat⟩ **2** : a delimited space : COMPASS **3 a** *obs* : a place or station assigned or in a hierarchy : POST **b** : a place or station formerly occupied by another **4 a** : a partitioned part of the inside of a building; *esp* : such a part used as a lodging **b** : the people in a room ∼ *n* sing **5** : OPPORTUNITY, CAPACITY

²room *vi* : to occupy a room ∼ *vt* : to accommodate with lodgings

room·er \'rü-mər, 'ru̇m-ər\ *n* : LODGER

room·ette \rü-'met, ru̇m-'et\ *n* : a small private single room on a railroad sleeping car

room·ful \'rüm-,fu̇l, 'ru̇m-\ *n*, *pl* **roomfuls** \-,fu̇lz\ *or* **rooms·ful** \'rümz-,fu̇l, 'ru̇mz-\ : as much or as many as a room will hold; *also* : the persons or objects in a room

room·i·ness \'rü-mē-nəs, 'ru̇m-ē-\ *n* : the quality or state of being roomy

rooming house *n* : LODGING HOUSE

room·mate \'rüm-,māt, 'ru̇m-\ *n* : one of two or more persons occupying the same room

roomy \'rü-mē, 'ru̇m-ē\ *adj* **1** : having ample room : SPACIOUS **2** *of a female mammal* : having a large or well-proportioned body suited for breeding

roor·back \'ru̇(ə)r-,bak\ *n* [fr. an attack on James K. Polk in 1844 purporting to quote from an invented book by a Baron von *Roorback*] : a defamatory falsehood published for political effect

roose \'rüz\ *vt* [ME *rusen*, fr. ON *hrōsa*] *chiefly dial* : PRAISE

¹roost \'rüst\ *n* [ME, fr. OE *hrōst*; akin to MD *roest* roost, OSlav *krada* pile of wood] **1 a** : a support on which birds rest **b** : a place where birds customarily roost **2** : a group of birds (as fowl) roosting together

²roost *vi* **1** : to settle down for rest or sleep : PERCH **2** : to settle oneself as if on a roost ∼ *vt* : to supply a roost for or put to roost

roost·er \'rüs-tər *also* 'ru̇s-\ *n* **1 a** : an adult male domestic fowl : COCK **b** : an adult male of various other birds **2** : a cocky or vain person

roost·ers \-tərz\ *n pl but sing in constr* : a common No. American blue violet (*Viola palmata*)

¹root \'rüt, 'ru̇t\ *n, often attrib* [ME, fr. OE *rōt*, fr. ON; akin to OE *wyrt* root, L *radix*, Gk *rhiza*] **1 a** : the usu. underground part of a seed plant body that originates usu. from the hypocotyl, functions as an organ of absorption, aeration, and food storage or as a means of anchorage and support, and differs from a stem esp. in lacking nodes, buds, and leaves **b** : any subterranean plant part (as a true root or a bulb, tuber, rootstock, or other modified stem) esp. when fleshy and edible **2 a** : the part of a tooth within the socket **b** : the enlarged basal part of a hair within the skin **c** : the proximal end of a nerve **d** : the part of an organ or physical structure by which it is attached to the body ⟨∼ of the tongue⟩ **3 a** : an original cause or quality : SOURCE **b** : one or more progenitors of a group of descendants **c** : an underlying support : BASIS **d** : the essential core : HEART **e** : close relationship with an environment : TIE — usu. used in pl. **4 a** : a quantity taken an indicated number of times as an equal factor ⟨2 is a fourth ∼ of 16⟩ **b** : a solution of a polynomial equation in one unknown **5 a** : the lower part : BASE **b** : the part by which an object is attached to something else **6** : the simple element inferred as the basis from which a word is derived by phonetic change or by extension (as composition or the addition of an affix or inflectional ending) **7 a** : the tone from whose overtones a chord is composed **b** : the lowest tone of a chord in normal position **syn** see ORIGIN — **root·like** \-,līk\ *adj*

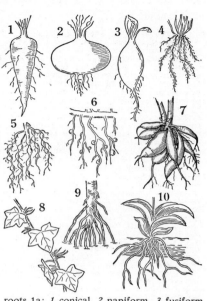

roots 1a: *1* conical, *2* napiform, *3* fusiform, *4* fibrous, *5* moniliform, *6* nodulose, *7* tuberous, *8* adventitious root, *9* prop root, *10* aerial root

²root *vt* **1 a** : to furnish with or enable to develop roots **b** : to fix or implant by or as if by roots **2** : to remove altogether often by force ⟨∼ out dissenters⟩ ∼ *vi* **1** : to grow roots or take root **2** : to have an origin

³root *vb* [ME *wroten*, fr. OE *wrōtan*; akin to OHG *ruozzan* to root] *vi* **1** : to turn up or dig in the earth with the snout : GRUB **2** : to poke or dig about ∼ *vt* : to turn over, dig up, or discover and bring to light — usu. used with *out*

⁴root \'rüt *also* 'ru̇t\ *vi* [perh. alter. of ²rout] **1** : to noisily applaud or encourage a contestant or team : CHEER **2** : to wish the success of or lend support to someone or something — **root·er** *n*

root·age \'rüt-ij, 'ru̇t-\ *n* **1** : a developed system of roots **2** : ROOT 3a

root beer *n* : a sweetened effervescent or carbonated beverage flavored with extracts of roots and herbs

root borer *n* : an insect or insect larva that bores into the roots of plants

root cap *n* : a protective cap of parenchyma cells that covers the terminal meristem in most root tips

root cellar *n* : a pit used for the storage of root crops or other vegetables

root climber *n* : a plant that climbs by adventitious roots

root crop *n* : a crop (as turnips or sweet potatoes) grown for its enlarged roots

root graft *n* **1** : a plant graft in which the stock is a root or piece of a root **2** : a natural anastomosis between roots of compatible plants

root hair *n* : a filamentous outgrowth near the tip of a rootlet that functions in absorption of water and minerals

root·hold \'rüt-,hōld, 'ru̇t-\ *n* **1** : the anchorage of a plant to soil through the growing and spreading of roots **2** : a place where plants may obtain a roothold

root·less \'rüt-ləs, 'ru̇t-\ *adj* : having no roots ⟨∼ nomads⟩

root·let \-lət\ *n* : a small root

root rot *n* : a plant disease characterized by a decay of the roots

root·stalk \'rüt-,stȯk, 'ru̇t-\ *n* : RHIZOME

root·stock \-,stäk\ *n* **1** : a rhizomatous underground part of a plant **2** : a stock for grafting consisting of a root or a piece of root; *broadly* : STOCK

rooty \'rüt-ē, 'ru̇t-\ *adj* : full of or consisting of roots ⟨∼ soil⟩

¹rope \'rōp\ *n* [ME, fr. OE *rāp*; akin to OHG *reif* hoop] **1 a** : a large stout cord of strands of fibers or wire twisted or braided together **b** : a long slender strip of material used as rope ⟨rawhide ∼⟩ **c** : a hangman's noose **2** : a row or string consisting of things united by or as if by braiding, twining, or threading

²rope *vt* **1 a** : to bind, fasten, or tie with a rope or cord **b** : to partition, separate, or divide by a rope ⟨∼ off the street⟩ **c** : LASSO **2** : to draw as if with a rope : LURE ∼ *vi* : to take the form of or twist in the manner of rope — **rop·er** *n*

rope·danc·er \'rōp-ˌdan(t)-sər\ *n* **:** one that dances, walks, or performs acrobatic feats on a rope high in the air — **rope·danc·ing** \-siŋ\ *n*

rop·ery \'rō-p(ə-)rē\ *n, archaic* **:** roguish tricks or banter

rope·walk \'rōp-ˌwȯk\ *n* **:** a long covered walk, building, or room where ropes are manufactured

rope·walk·er \-ˌwȯ-kər\ *n* **:** an acrobat that walks on a rope high in the air

rope·way \-ˌwā\ *n* **1 :** a fixed cable or a pair of fixed cables between supporting towers serving as a track for suspended passenger or freight carriers **2 :** an endless aerial cable moved by a stationary engine and used to transport logs, ore, and other freight

rope yarn *n* **1 :** the yarn or thread composing the strands of a rope **2 :** a yarn of fibers loosely twisted up right-handedly

rop·i·ness \'rō-pē-nəs\ *n* **:** the quality or state of being ropy

ropy \'rō-pē\ *adj* **1 a :** capable of being drawn into a thread **:** VISCOUS **b :** having a gelatinous or slimy quality from bacterial or fungal contamination ⟨~ milk⟩ ⟨~ flour⟩ **2 a :** resembling rope **:** STRINGY **b :** MUSCULAR, SINEWY

roque \'rōk\ *n* [alter. of *croquet*] **:** croquet played on a hard-surfaced court with a raised border

ro·que·laure \ˌrō-kə-'lō(ə)r, ˌräk-ə-, -'lȯ(ə)r\ *n* [F, fr. the Duc de *Roquelaure* †1738 F marshal] **:** a knee-length cloak worn esp. in the 18th and 19th centuries

ror·qual \'rȯ(ə)r-kwəl, -ˌkwȯl\ *n* [F, fr. Norw *rørhval*, fr. ON *reytharhvalr*, fr. *reythr* rorqual + *hvalr* whale] **:** a large whalebone whale (genus *Balaenoptera*) having the skin of the throat marked with deep longitudinal furrows

Ror·schach \'rȯ(ə)r-ˌshäk, 'rō(ə)r-\ *n* [Hermann *Rorschach* †1922 Swiss psychiatrist] **:** a personality and intelligence test in which a subject interprets inkblot designs in terms that reveal intellectual and emotional factors

ro·sa·ceous \rō-'zā-shəs\ *adj* [deriv. of L *rosa*] **1 :** of or relating to the rose family **2 :** of, relating to, or resembling a rose esp. in having a 5-petaled regular corolla

ros·an·i·line \rō-'zan-ᵊl-ən\ *n* [L *rosa* rose + ISV *aniline*] **1 :** a white crystalline base $C_{20}H_{21}N_3O$ that is the parent of many dyes **2 :** FUCHSINE

ro·sar·i·an \rō-'zar-ē-ən, -'zer-\ *n* **:** a cultivator of roses

ro·sa·ry \'rōz-(ə-)rē\ *n* [ML *rosarium*, fr. L, rose garden, fr. neut. of *rosarius* of roses, fr. *rosa* rose] **1 :** a string of beads used in counting prayers esp. of the Roman Catholic rosary **2** *often cap* **:** a Roman Catholic devotion consisting of meditation on usu. five sacred mysteries during recitation of five decades of Ave Marias of which each begins with a paternoster and ends with a Gloria

ros·coe \'räs-(ˌ)kō\ *n* [prob. fr. the name *Roscoe*] *slang* **:** PISTOL

[1]**rose** *past of* RISE

[2]**rose** \'rōz\ *n* [ME, fr. OE, fr. L *rosa*] **1 a :** any of a genus (*Rosa* of the family Rosaceae, the rose family) of usu. prickly shrubs with pinnate leaves and showy flowers having five petals in the wild state but being often double or semidouble under cultivation **b :** the flower of a rose **2 :** something resembling a rose in form: as **a** (1) **:** COMPASS CARD (2) **:** a circular card with radiating lines used in other instruments **b :** a rosette esp. on a shoe **c** (1) **:** a form in which diamonds and other gems are cut that usu. has a flat circular base and facets in two ranges rising to a point (2) **:** a gem with a rose cut **3 :** a variable color averaging a moderate purplish red — **rose·like** \-ˌlīk\ *adj* — **under the rose :** in secret or private

[3]**rose** *adj* **1 a :** of or relating to a rose **b :** containing or used for roses **c :** flavored, scented, or colored with or like roses **2 :** of the color rose

[4]**ro·sé** \rō-'zā\ *n* [F] **:** a light pink table wine made from red grapes by removing the skins after fermentation has begun

ro·se·ate \'rō-zē-ət, -zē-ˌāt\ *adj* [L *roseus* rosy, fr. *rosa*] **1 :** resembling a rose esp. in color **2 :** overly optimistic **:** viewed favorably — **ro·se·ate·ly** *adv*

rose·bay \'rōz-ˌbā\ *n* **1 :** OLEANDER **2 :** RHODODENDRON; *esp* **:** one (*Rhododendron maxima*) of eastern No. America with rosy bell-shaped flowers — called also *big laurel* **3 :** a fireweed (*Epilobium angustifolium*) of the evening-primrose family with racemes of usu. pink flowers

rose chafer *n* **:** a common No. American beetle (*Macrodactylus subspinosus*) whose larva feeds on plant roots and adult on leaves and flowers (as of rose or grapevines) — called also *rose bug*

rose–col·ored \'rōz-ˌkəl-ərd\ *adj* **1 :** having a rose color **2 :** seeing or seen in a promising light **:** OPTIMISTIC

rose comb *n* **:** a flat broad comb of a domestic fowl having the upper surface studded with small tubercles and terminating posteriorly in a fleshly spike

rose daphne *n* **:** a low evergreen shrub (*Daphne cneorum*) with trailing pubescent branches and fragrant rose-pink flowers

rose fever *n* **:** hay fever occurring in the spring or early summer — called also *rose cold*

rose·fish \'rōz-ˌfish\ *n* **:** a marine food fish (*Sebastes marinus*) of northern coasts of Europe and America that when mature is usu. bright rose red

rose geranium *n* **:** any of several pelargoniums grown for their fragrant 3- to 5-lobed leaves and small pink flowers

rose mallow *n* **1 :** any of several plants (genus *Hibiscus*) with large rose-colored flowers; *esp* **:** a showy plant (*H. moscheutos*) of the salt marshes of the eastern U. S. **2 :** HOLLYHOCK

rose·mary \'rōz-ˌmer-ē\ *n* [ME *rosmarine*, fr. L *rosmarinus*, fr. *ror-*, *ros* dew + *marinus* of the sea; akin to ON *rās* race — more at RACE, MARINE] **1 :** a fragrant shrubby mint (*Rosmarinus officinalis*) of southern Europe and Asia Minor used in cookery and in perfumery **2 :** COSTMARY

rose of Jer·i·cho \-'jer-i-ˌkō\ [ME, fr. *Jericho*, ancient city in Palestine] **:** an Asiatic plant (*Anastatica hierochuntica*) that rolls up when dry and expands when moistened — called also *resurrection plant*

rose of Shar·on \-'shar-ən, -'sher-\ [Plain of *Sharon*, Palestine] **1 :** a Eurasian St.-John's-wort (*Hypericum calycinum*) often cultivated for its large yellow flowers **2 :** a commonly cultivated Asiatic small shrubby tree (*Hibiscus syriacus*) having showy bell-shaped rose, purple, or white flowers

ro·se·o·la \rō-'zē-ə-lə, ˌrō-zē-'ō-\ *n* [NL, fr. L *roseus* rosy, fr. *rosa* rose] **:** a rose-colored eruption in spots; *specif* **:** GERMAN MEASLES — **ro·se·o·lar** \-lər\ *adj*

rose pink *n* **:** a variable color averaging a moderate pink

ros·ery \'rōz-(ə-)rē\ *n* **:** a place where roses are grown

rose slug *n* **:** either of two slimy green larval sawflies (*Claudius isomerus* and *Endelomyia aethiops*) that feed on the parenchyma of and skeletonize the leaves of roses

ros·et \'räz-ət\ *n* [alter. of ME *rosin*] *chiefly Scot* **:** RESIN

Ro·set·ta stone \rō-ˌzet-ə-\ *n* [*Rosetta*, Egypt] **:** a black basalt stone found in 1799 that bears an inscription in hieroglyphics, demotic characters, and Greek and is celebrated for having given the first clue to the decipherment of Egyptian hieroglyphics

ro·sette \rō-'zet\ *n* [F, lit., small rose, fr. OF, fr. *rose*, fr. L *rosa*] **1 :** an ornament resembling a rose usu. gathered or pleated and worn as a badge of office, as evidence of having won a decoration (as the medal of honor), or as trimming **2 :** a disk of foliage or a floral design usu. in relief used as a decorative motif **3 :** a structure or color marking on an animal suggestive of a rosette; *esp* **:** one of the groups of spots on a leopard **4 :** a cluster of leaves in crowded circles or spirals arising basally from a crown (as in the dandelion) or apically from an axis with greatly shortened internodes (as in many tropical palms)

rose water *n* **:** a watery solution of the odoriferous constituents of the rose used as a perfume

rose·wa·ter \'rōz-ˌwȯt-ər, -ˌwät-\ *adj* **1 :** having the odor of rose water **2 :** affectedly nice or delicate

rose window *n* **:** a circular window filled with tracery

rose window

rose·wood \'rōz-ˌwu̇d\ *n* **1 :** any of various tropical trees yielding valuable cabinet woods of a dark red or purplish color streaked and variegated with black **2 :** the wood of a rosewood

Rosh Ha·sha·nah \ˌrōsh-(h)ə-'shō-nə\ *n* [LHeb *rōsh hashshānāh*, lit., beginning of the year] **:** the Jewish New Year observed on the 1st and by Orthodox and Conservative Jews also on the 2d of Tishri

Ro·si·cru·cian \ˌrō-zə-'krü-shən, ˌräz-ə-\ *n* [Christian *Rosenkreutz* (NL *Rosae Crucis*) reputed 15th cent. founder of the movement] **1 :** an adherent of a 17th and 18th century movement devoted to esoteric wisdom **2 :** a member of one of several organizations held to be descended from the Rosicrucians — **Rosicrucian** *adj* — **Ro·si·cru·cian·ism** \-shə-ˌniz-əm\ *n*

ros·i·ly \'rō-zə-lē\ *adv* **1 :** with a rosy color or tinge **2 :** CHEERFULLY, PLEASANTLY

[1]**ros·in** \'räz-ᵊn, 'rȯz-, *dial* 'rȯ-zəm\ *n* [ME, modif. of MF *resine* resin] **:** a translucent amber-colored to almost black brittle friable resin that is obtained by chemical means from the oleoresin or dead wood of pine trees or from tall oil and used in making varnish, paper size, soap, and soldering flux and on violin bows

[2]**rosin** *vt* **ros·in·ing** \'räz-niŋ, 'rȯz-, -ᵊn-iŋ\ **:** to rub with rosin (as the bow of a violin)

ros·i·ness \'rō-zē-nəs\ *n* **:** the quality or state of being rosy

ros·in·ous \'räz-ᵊn-əs, 'räz-nəs, 'rȯz-\ *adj* **:** containing or resembling rosin

ros·in·weed \'räz-ᵊn-ˌwēd, 'rȯz-\ *n* **:** any of various American plants having resinous foliage or a resinous odor; *esp* **:** a coarse yellow-flowered composite herb (*Silphium laciniatum*)

ross \'rȯs\ *n* [origin unknown] **:** the rough often scaly exterior of bark

ros·tel·lar \rä-'stel-ər\ *adj* **:** of, relating to, or having the form of a rostellum

ros·tel·late \'räs-tə-ˌlāt, rä-'stel-ət\ *adj* **:** having a rostellum

ros·tel·lum \rä-'stel-əm\ *n* [NL, fr. L, dim. of *rostrum* beak] **:** a small process resembling a beak **:** a diminutive rostrum: as **a :** the apex of the gynoecium of an orchid flower **b :** the sucking beak of an insect (as a louse or aphid) **c :** an anterior prolongation of the head of a tapeworm bearing hooks

ros·ter \'räs-tər\ *n* [D *rooster*, lit., gridiron; fr. the parallel lines] **1 :** a roll or list of personnel; *esp* **:** one that gives the order in which a duty is to be performed **2 :** an itemized list

ros·tral \'räs-trəl\ *adj* **:** of or relating to a rostrum — **ros·tral·ly** \-trə-lē\ *adv*

ros·trate \'räs-ˌtrāt, -trət\ *adj* **:** having a rostrum

ros·trum \'räs-trəm\ *n, pl* **rostrums** *or* **ros·tra** \-trə\ [L, beak, ship's beak, fr. *rodere* to gnaw — more at RAT] **1** [L *Rostra*, pl., a platform for speakers in the Roman Forum decorated with the beaks of captured ships, fr. pl. of *rostrum*] **a :** an ancient Roman platform for public orators **b :** a stage for public speaking **c :** a raised platform on a stage **2 :** the curved end of a ship's prow; *esp* **:** the beak of a war galley **3 :** a bodily part or process (as a snout or median projection) suggesting a bird's bill

ro·su·late \'räz(h)-ə-ˌlāt, 'rōz(h)-\ *adj* [LL *rosula*, dim. of L *rosa* rose] **:** arranged in the form of a rosette or in rosettes

rosy \'rō-zē\ *adj* **1 a :** of the color rose **b :** having a rosy complexion **:** BLOOMING **c :** BLUSHING **2 :** characterized by or tending to promote optimism

[1]**rot** \'rät\ *vb* **rot·ted; rot·ting** [ME *roten*, fr. OE *rotian*; akin to OHG *rōzzēn* to rot, L *rudus* rubble — more at RUDE] *vi* **1 a :** to undergo decomposition from the action of bacteria or fungi **b :** to become unsound or weak (as from use or chemical action) **2 a :** to go to ruin **:** DETERIORATE **b :** to become morally corrupt **:** DEGENERATE ~ *vt* **:** to cause to decompose or deteriorate with rot
syn see DECAY

[2]**rot** *n* **1 a :** the process of rotting **:** the state of being rotten **:** DECAY **b :** something rotten or rotting **2 a :** *archaic* **:** a wasting putrescent disease **b :** any of several parasitic diseases esp. of sheep marked by necrosis and wasting **c :** plant disease marked by breakdown of tissues and caused esp. by fungi or bacteria **3 :** NONSENSE — often used interjectionally

ro·ta \'rōt-ə\ *n* [L, wheel — more at ROLL] **1** *chiefly Brit* **:** ROSTER **2** *cap* [ML, fr. L] **:** a tribunal of the papal curia exercising jurisdiction esp. in matrimonial cases appealed from diocesan courts

ro·ta·me·ter \'rōt-ə-ˌmēt-ər, rō-'tam-ət-\ *n* [L *rota* + E *-meter*] **:** a gauge that consists of a graduated glass tube containing a free float for measuring the flow of a fluid

Ro·tar·i·an \rō-'ter-ē-ən\ *n* [*Rotary* (club)] **:** a member of one of the major service clubs

[1]**ro·ta·ry** \'rōt-ə-rē\ *adj* [ML *rotarius*, fr. L *rota* wheel] **1 a :** turn-

ing on an axis like a wheel **b :** taking place about an axis ⟨~ motion⟩ **2 :** having an important part that turns on an axis ⟨~ cutter⟩ **3 :** characterized by rotation **4 :** of, relating to, or being a press in which paper is printed by rotation in contact with a curved printing surface attached to a cylinder

[2]**rotary** *n* **1 :** a rotary machine **2 :** a road junction formed around a central circle about which traffic moves in one direction only — called also *circle, traffic circle*

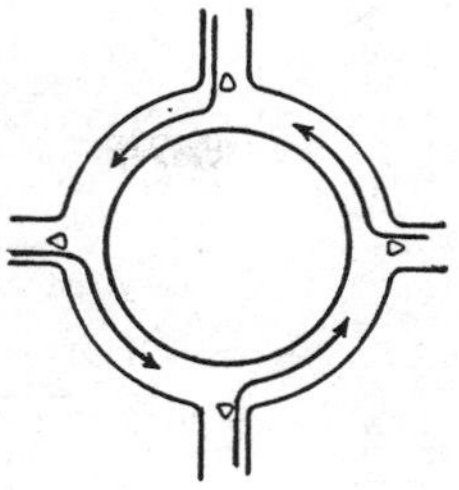

rotary 2

rotary cultivator *n* **:** an implement having blades or claws that revolve rapidly and till or stir the soil

rotary engine *n* **1 :** any of various engines (as a turbine) in which power is applied to vanes or similar parts constrained to move in a circular path **2 :** a radial engine in which the cylinders revolve about a stationary crankshaft

rotary plow *n* **1 :** a plow having a rotating propeller-shaped element for throwing snow aside **2 :** ROTARY CULTIVATOR

rotary-wing aircraft *n* **:** an aircraft supported in flight partially or wholly by rotating airfoils

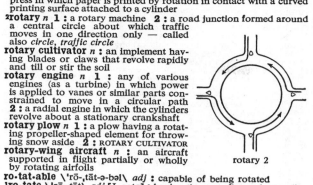

ro·tat·able \ˈrō-ˌtāt-ə-bəl\ *adj* **:** capable of being rotated

[1]**ro·tate** \ˈrō-ˌtāt\ *adj* [L *rota*] **:** having the parts flat and spreading or radiating like the spokes of a wheel ⟨~ blue flowers⟩

[2]**rotate** *vb* [L *rotatus*, pp. of *rotare*, fr. *rota* wheel — more at ROLL] *vi* **1 :** to turn about an axis or a center **:** REVOLVE; *specif* **:** to move in such a way that all particles follow circles with a common angular velocity about a common axis **2 :** to perform an act, function, or operation in turn ~ *vt* **1 :** to cause to turn about an axis or a center **:** REVOLVE **2 :** to cause to grow in rotation **3 :** to cause to pass or act in a series **:** ALTERNATE **4 :** to exchange (individuals or units) with other personnel

ro·ta·tion \rō-ˈtā-shən\ *n* **1 a :** the act of rotating on or as if on an axis **b :** one complete turn **:** the angular displacement required to return a rotating body or figure to its original orientation **2 :** return or succession in a series (as of different crops in succession on one field) **3 :** the turning of a body part about its long axis as if on a pivot — **ro·ta·tion·al** \-shnəl, -shən-ᵊl\ *adj*

ro·ta·tive \ˈrō-ˌtāt-iv\ *adj* **1 :** turning like a wheel **:** ROTARY **2 :** relating to, occurring in, or characterized by rotation — **ro·ta·tive·ly** *adv*

ro·ta·tor \ˈrō-ˌtāt-ər\ *n* **:** one that rotates or causes rotation; *specif* **:** a muscle that partially rotates a part on its axis

ro·ta·to·ry \ˈrōt-ə-ˌtōr-ē, -ˌtȯr-\ *adj* **1 :** of, relating to, or producing rotation **2 :** occurring in rotation

[1]**rote** \ˈrōt\ *n* [ME, fr. OF, of Gmc origin; akin to OHG *hruozza* crowd] **:** [3]CROWD 1

[2]**rote** *n* [ME] **1 :** the use of memory usu. with little intelligence ⟨learn by ~⟩ **2 :** routine or repetition carried out without understanding or mechanically

[3]**rote** *n* [perh. of Scand origin; akin to ON *rauta* to roar — more at ROUT] **:** the noise of surf on the shore

ro·te·none \ˈrōt-ᵊn-ˌōn\ *n* [ISV, fr. Jap *roten* derris plant] **:** a crystalline insecticide $C_{23}H_{22}O_6$ that is of low toxicity for warm-blooded animals and is used esp. in home gardens

ro·ti·fer \ˈrōt-ə-fər\ *n* [deriv. of L *rota* + *-fer*] **:** any of a class (Rotifera) of minute usu. microscopic but many-celled aquatic invertebrate animals having the anterior end modified into a retractile disk bearing circles of strong cilia that often give the appearance of rapidly revolving wheels — **ro·tif·er·al** \rō-ˈtif-(ə-)rəl\ *adj* — **ro·tif·er·an** \-(ə-)rən\ *n or adj*

ro·ti·form \ˈrōt-ə-ˌfȯrm\ *adj* [NL *rotiformis*, fr. L *rota* wheel + *-iformis* -iform] **:** ROTATE

ro·tis·ser·ie \rō-ˈtis-(ə-)rē\ *n* [F *rôtisserie*, fr. MF *rostisserie*, fr. *rostir* to roast — more at ROAST] **1 :** a restaurant specializing in broiled and barbecued meats **2 :** an appliance fitted with a spit on which food is rotated before or over a source of heat

rotl \ˈrät-ᵊl\ *n* [Ar *raṭl*] **:** any of various units of weight of Mediterranean and Near Eastern countries ranging from slightly less than one pound to more than six pounds

ro·to \ˈrōt-(ˌ)ō\ *n* **:** ROTOGRAVURE

ro·to·gra·vure \ˌrōt-ə-grə-ˈvyu̇(ə)r\ *n* [L *rota* + E *-o-* + *gravure*] **1 a :** a photogravure process in which the impression is produced by a rotary press **b :** a print made by rotogravure **2 :** a section of a newspaper devoted to rotogravure pictures

ro·to·me·ter \ˈrōt-ə-ˌmēt-ər, rō-ˈtäm-ət-\ *n* **:** ROTAMETER

ro·tor \ˈrōt-ər\ *n* [contr. of *rotator*] **1 :** a part that revolves in a stationary part; *esp* **:** the rotating member of an electrical machine **2 :** a revolving vertical cylinder of a rotor ship **3 :** a complete system of more or less horizontal blades that supplies all or a major part of the force supporting an aircraft in flight

ro·tor·craft \-ˌkraft\ *n* **:** ROTARY-WING AIRCRAFT

rotor plane *n* **:** ROTARY-WING AIRCRAFT

rotor ship *n* **:** a ship propelled by the pressure and suction of the wind acting on one or more revolving vertical cylinders

ro·to·till \ˈrōt-ə-ˌtil\ *vt* [back-formation fr. *Rototiller*] **:** to stir with a rotary cultivator

Ro·to·till·er \-ˌtil-ər\ *trademark* — used for a rotary cultivator

rot·ten \ˈrät-ᵊn\ *adj* [ME *roten*, fr. ON *rotinn*; akin to OE *rotian* to rot] **1 :** having rotted **:** PUTRID **2 :** morally corrupt **3 :** extremely unpleasant or inferior **4 :** marked by weakness or unsoundness — **rot·ten·ly** *adv* — **rot·ten·ness** \-ᵊn-(n)əs\ *n*

rotten borough *n* **:** an election district that has many fewer inhabitants than other election districts with the same voting power

rot·ten·stone \ˈrät-ᵊn-ˌstōn\ *n* **:** a decomposed siliceous limestone used for polishing

rot·ter \ˈrät-ər\ *n* **:** a thoroughly objectionable person

rott·wei·ler \ˈrät-ˌwī-lər, ˈrȯt-ˌvī-\ *n, often cap* [G, fr. *Rottweil*, Germany] **:** any of a German breed of tall vigorous black short-haired cattle dogs

ro·tund \rō-ˈtənd, ˈrō-ˌ\ *adj* [L *rotundus* — more at ROUND] **1 :** marked by roundness **:** ROUNDED **2 :** FULL, SONOROUS **3 :** PLUMP, CHUBBY — **ro·tun·di·ty** \rō-ˈtən-dət-ē\ *n* — **ro·tund·ly** \-ˈtən-dlē, ˈrō-ˌ\ *adv* — **ro·tund·ness** \rō-ˈtən(d)-nəs, ˈrō-ˌ\ *n*

ro·tun·da \rō-ˈtən-də\ *or* **ro·ton·da** \-ˈtän-\ *n* [It *rotonda*, fr. L *rotunda*, fem. of *rotundus*] **1 :** a round building; *esp* **:** one covered by a dome **2 a :** a large round room **b :** a large central area (as in a hotel)

ro·tu·ri·er \rō-ˈt(y)u̇r-ē-ˌā\ *n* [MF] **:** a person not of noble birth

rou·ble *var of* RUBLE

roué \rü-ˈā\ *n* [F, lit., broken on the wheel, fr. pp. of *rouer* to break on the wheel, fr. ML *rotare*, fr. L, to rotate; fr. the feeling that such a person deserves this punishment] **:** DEBAUCHEE, RAKE

rou·en \rü-ˈä^{n}, -ˈän\ *n* [*Rouen*, France] *often cap* **:** any of a breed of domestic ducks resembling wild mallards in coloring

[1]**rouge** \ˈrüzh, *esp South* ˈrüj\ *n* [F, fr. MF, fr. *rouge* red, fr. L *rubeus* reddish — more at RUBY] **1 :** any of various cosmetics to color the cheeks or lips red **2 :** a red powder consisting essentially of ferric oxide used in polishing glass, metal, or gems and as a pigment **3 :** the red compartments in roulette

[2]**rouge** *vt* **:** to apply rouge to ~ *vi* **:** to use rouge

rouge et noir \ˌrü-(ˌ)zhā-ˈnwär\ *n* [F, lit., red and black] **:** a game in which two rows of cards are dealt and players may bet on which row will have a count nearer 31 or on the color of the cards

[1]**rough** \ˈrəf\ *adj* [ME, fr. OE *rūh*; akin to L *ruga* wrinkle, Gk *oryssein* to dig, ON *rögg* tuft — more at RUG] **1 a :** marked by inequalities, ridges, or projections on the surface **:** COARSE **b :** covered with or made up of coarse and often shaggy hair **c** (1) **:** having a broken, uneven, or bumpy surface (2) **:** difficult to travel over or penetrate **:** WILD **2 a :** TURBULENT, TEMPESTUOUS **b** (1) **:** characterized by harshness, violence, or force (2) **:** DIFFICULT, TRYING **3 :** coarse or rugged in character or appearance: as **a :** harsh to the ear **b :** crude in style or expression **c :** INDELICATE **d :** marked by a lack of refinement or grace **:** UNCOUTH **4 a :** CRUDE, UNFINISHED **b :** executed hastily, tentatively, or imperfectly ⟨a ~ draft⟩ ⟨~ estimate⟩ **5 :** pronounced with aspiration ⟨a ~ vowel⟩ — **rough·ly** *adv* — **rough·ness** *n*

syn ROUGH, HARSH, UNEVEN, RUGGED, SCABROUS mean not smooth or even. ROUGH implies points, bristles, ridges, or projections on the surface; HARSH implies a surface or texture distinctly unpleasant to the touch; UNEVEN implies a lack of uniformity in height, breadth, or quality; RUGGED implies irregularity or roughness of land surface and connotes difficulty of travel; SCABROUS implies scaliness or prickliness of surface and may connote diseased or decayed appearance **syn** see in addition RUDE

[2]**rough** *n* **1 :** uneven ground covered with high grass, brush, and stones; *specif* **:** such ground bordering a golf fairway **2 :** the disagreeable side or aspect **3 a :** something in a crude, unfinished, or preliminary state **b :** broad outline **:** general terms **c :** a hasty preliminary drawing or layout **4 :** ROWDY, TOUGH

[3]**rough** *vt* **1 :** ROUGHEN **2 a :** MANHANDLE, BEAT — usu. used with *up* **b :** to subject to unnecessary and intentional violence in a sport **3 :** to calk or otherwise roughen (a horse's shoes) to prevent slipping **4 a :** to shape, make, or dress in a rough or preliminary way **b :** to indicate the chief lines of ⟨~ out the structure of a building⟩ — **rough·er** *n* — **rough it :** to live under primitive conditions

rough·age \ˈrəf-ij\ *n* **:** coarse bulky food (as bran) that is relatively high in fiber and low in digestible nutrients and that by its bulk stimulates peristalsis

rough-and-ready \ˌrəf-ən-ˈred-ē\ *adj* **:** crude in nature, method, or manner but effective in action or use

rough-and-tum·ble \-ˈtəm-bəl\ *n* **:** a rough disorderly unrestrained struggle — **rough-and-tumble** *adj*

rough bluegrass *n* **:** a European forage grass (*Poa trivialis*) naturalized in eastern No. America

rough breathing *n* **1 :** a mark ʽ used in Greek over some initial vowels or over ρ to show that they are aspirated (as in ὡς pronounced \ˈhōs\ or ῥήτωρ pronounced \ˈhrā-ˌtōr\) **2 :** the sound indicated by a mark ʽ over a Greek vowel or ρ

[1]**rough·cast** \ˈrəf-ˌkast\ *n* **1 :** a rough model **2 :** a plastic of lime mixed with shells or pebbles used for covering buildings **3 :** a rough surface finish (as of a plaster wall)

[2]**roughcast** *vt* **1 :** to plaster (as a wall) with roughcast **2 :** to shape or form roughly

rough·dry \-ˈdrī\ *vt* **:** to dry (laundry) without smoothing or ironing — **roughdry** *adj*

rough·en \ˈrəf-ən\ *vb* **rough·en·ing** \-(ə-)niŋ\ *vt* **:** to make rough ~ *vi* **:** to become rough

rough fish *n* **:** a fish that is neither a sport fish nor an important food for sport fishes

rough-foot·ed \ˈrəf-ˈfu̇t-əd\ *adj* **:** having feathered feet ⟨the *rough-footed* eagles⟩

rough·hew \ˈrəf-ˈhyü\ *vt* **1 :** to hew (as timber) coarsely without smoothing or finishing **2 :** to form crudely **:** ROUGHCAST — **rough-hewn** \-ˈhyün\ *adj*

rough·house \ˈrəf-ˌhau̇s\ *n* **:** violence or rough boisterous play esp. among occupants of a room — **rough·house** \-ˌhau̇s, -ˌhau̇z\ *vb* — **rough·house** \-ˌhau̇s\ *adj*

rough·ish \ˈrəf-ish\ *adj* **:** somewhat rough

rough-legged hawk \ˌrəf-ˌleg(-ə)d-, -ˌlāg(-ə)d-\ *or* **rough·leg** \ˈrəf-ˌleg, -ˌlāg\ *n* **:** any of several large heavily built hawks (genus *Buteo*) that have the tarsus feathered to the base of the toes, feed chiefly on rodents (as mice), and are beneficial to the farmer

rough·neck \ˈrəf-ˌnek\ *n* **:** a rough or uncouth person; *esp* **:** ROWDY, TOUGH

rough·rid·er \ˈrəf-ˈrīd-ər\ *n* **1 :** one who breaks horses to the saddle or is accustomed to riding little-trained horses **2 a :** irregular cavalryman **b** *cap* **:** a member of the 1st U.S. Volunteer Cavalry regiment in the Spanish-American War commanded by Theodore Roosevelt

rough·shod \-ˈshäd\ *adj* **:** shod with calked shoes

[1]**rou·lade** \rü-ˈläd\ *n* [F, lit., act of rolling] **:** a florid vocal embellishment sung to one syllable

[2]**roulade** *n* [F] **:** a slice of meat rolled with or without a stuffing

rou·leau \rü-ˈlō\ *n, pl* **rou·leaux** \-ˈlōz\ [F] **1 :** a little roll; *esp* **:** a roll of coins put up in paper **2 :** a bundle of fascines used in groups in siege operations

rou·lette \rü-ˈlet\ *n* [F, lit., small wheel, fr. OF *roelete*, dim. of *roele* small wheel, fr. LL *rotella*, dim. of L *rota* wheel — more at

ROLL] **1 :** a gambling game in which players bet on which compartment of a revolving wheel a small ball will come to rest in **2 a :** any of various toothed wheels or disks (as for producing rows of dots on engraved plates or for making short consecutive incisions in paper to facilitate subsequent division) **b :** tiny slits in a sheet of stamps made by a roulette — **roulette** *vt*

Rou·ma·nian \rü-ˈmā-nē-ən, -nyən\ *var of* ROMANIAN

1**round** \ˈraůnd\ *vt* [ME *rounen*, fr. OE *rūnian;* akin to OE *rūn* mystery — more at RUNE] **1 :** WHISPER **2 :** to speak to in a whisper

2**round** *adj* [ME, fr. OF *roont*, fr. L *rotundus;* akin to L *rota* wheel — more at ROLL] **1 a :** having every part of the surface or circumference equidistant from the center **b :** CYLINDRICAL **2 :** PLUMP, SHAPELY **3 a :** COMPLETE, FULL ⟨a ~ dozen⟩ ⟨a ~ ton⟩ **b :** approximately correct; *esp* **:** exact only to a specific decimal **c :** AMPLE, LARGE **4 :** BLUNT, OUTSPOKEN **5 :** moving in or forming a circle **6 a :** brought to completion or perfection **:** FINISHED **b :** presented with lifelike fullness or vividness **7 a :** having full or unimpeded resonance or tone **:** SONOROUS **b :** pronounced with rounded lips **:** LABIALIZED **8 :** of or relating to handwriting predominantly curved rather than angular — **round·ly** \ˈraůn-(d)lē\ *adv* — **round·ness** \ˈraůn(d)-nəs\ *n*

3**round** *adv* **:** AROUND

4**round** \(ˈ)raůnd\ *prep* **1 :** AROUND **2 :** all during **:** THROUGHOUT ⟨~ the year⟩

5**round** \ˈraůnd\ *n* **1 a :** something (as a circle, globe, ring) round **b :** a knot of people **:** a circle of things **2 :** ROUND DANCE 1 **3 :** a polyphonic vocal composition in which three or four voices follow each other around in a canon at the unison or octave **4 a :** a rung of a ladder or a chair **b :** a rounded molding **5 a :** a circling or circuitous path or course **b :** motion in a circle or a curving path **6 a :** a route or circuit habitually covered (as by a watchman or policeman) **b :** a series of professional calls on hospital patients made by a doctor or nurse **c :** a series of similar or customary calls or stops **7 :** a drink of liquor served at one time to each person in a group **8 :** a sequence of recurring routine or repetitive actions or events **9 :** a period of time that recurs in a fixed pattern **10 a :** one shot fired by a weapon or by each man in a military unit **b :** a unit of ammunition consisting of the parts necessary to fire one shot **11 :** a unit of play in a contest or game which occupies a stated period, covers a prescribed distance, includes a specified number of plays, or gives each player one turn **12 :** an outburst of applause **13 :** a cut of beef esp. between the rump and the lower leg **14 :** a rounded or curved part — **in the round 1 :** in full sculptured form unattached to a background **:** FREESTANDING — compare RELIEF **2 :** with an inclusive or comprehensive view or representation **3 :** with a center stage surrounded by an audience on all sides ⟨theater *in the round*⟩

6**round** \ˈraůnd\ *vt* **1 a :** to make round **b** (1) **:** to make (the lips) round and protruded (as in the pronunciation of \ü\) (2) **:** to pronounce (a sound) with rounding of the lips **:** LABIALIZE **2 a :** to go around **b :** to pass part way around **3 :** ENCIRCLE, ENCOMPASS **4 a :** to bring to completion **:** FINISH **b :** to bring to perfection of style **:** POLISH **5 :** to express as a round number ⟨11.3572 *~ed* to three decimals becomes 11.357⟩ **~** *vi* **1 a :** to become round, plump, or shapely **b :** to become complete **2 :** to follow a winding course **:** BEND — **round on :** to turn against **:** ASSAIL

1**round·about** \ˈraůn-də-ˌbaůt\ *n* **1 :** a circuitous route **:** DETOUR **2** *Brit* **:** MERRY-GO-ROUND **3 :** a short close-fitting jacket worn by men and boys esp. in the 19th century

2**roundabout** \ˌraůn-də-ˈ\ *adj* **:** CIRCUITOUS, INDIRECT — **round·about·ness** *n*

round angle *n* **:** the 360 degree angle described by a half line turning positively in a plane about its extremity as a center until it returns to its original position

round clam *n* **:** QUAHOG

round dance *n* **1 :** a folk dance in which participants form a ring and move in a prescribed direction **2 :** a ballroom dance in which couples progress around the room

round·ed *adj* **1 a :** made round **:** SPHERICAL; *also* **:** POLISHED, FINISHED **b :** FULL, COMPLETE **2 :** produced with rounded lips **:** LABIALIZED

roun·del \ˈraůn-dᵊl\ *n* [ME, fr. OF *rondel*, fr. *roont* round — more at ROUND] **1 :** a round figure or object; *esp* **:** a circular panel, window, or niche **2 a :** RONDEL 2a **b :** an English modified rondeau

roun·de·lay \ˈraůn-də-ˌlā\ *n* [modif. of MF *rondelet*, dim. of *rondel*] **1 :** a simple song with refrain **2 :** a poem with a refrain recurring frequently or at fixed intervals as in a rondel

round·er \ˈraůn-dər\ *n* **1 :** a dissolute person **:** WASTREL **2** *pl but sing in constr* **:** an English game played with ball and bat somewhat resembling baseball **3 a :** one that rounds by hand or by machine **b :** a tool for making an edge or a surface round **4 :** a boxing match lasting a specified number of rounds

round·head \ˈraůnd-ˌhed\ *n* **1** *cap* **:** a Puritan or member of the parliamentary party in England at the time of Charles I and Oliver Cromwell **2 :** a brachycephalic person

round·head·ed \-ˈhed-əd\ *adj* **:** having a round head; *specif* **:** BRACHYCEPHALIC — **round·head·ed·ness** *n*

round·house \ˈraůnd-ˌhaůs\ *n* **1** *archaic* **:** LOCKUP **2 :** a circular building for housing and repairing locomotives **3 :** a cabin or apartment on the stern of a quarterdeck **4 :** a hook in boxing delivered with a wide swing

round·ish \ˈraůn-dish\ *adj* **:** somewhat round

round·let \ˈraůn(d)-lət\ *n* [ME *roundelet*, fr. MF *rondelet* — more at ROUNDELAY] **:** a small circle or round object **:** DISK

round robin *n* **1 a :** a written petition, memorial, or protest to which the signatures are affixed in a circle so as not to indicate who signed first **b :** a statement signed by several persons **c :** a letter sent in turn to the members of a group each of whom signs and forwards it sometimes after adding comment **2 :** ROUND TABLE **3 :** a tournament in which every contestant meets every other contestant in turn **4 :** SERIES, ROUND

round scale *n* **:** any of various armored scales (genus *Aspidiotus*) that have a nearly circular covering

round–shoul·dered \ˈraůn(d)-ˈshōl-dərd\ *adj* **:** having the shoulders stooping or rounded

rounds·man \ˈraůn(d)z-mən\ *n* **1 :** one that makes rounds **2 :** a supervisory police officer of the grade of sergeant or just below

round steak *n* **:** a steak cut from the whole round

round table *n* **1 a** *cap R & T* **:** a large circular table for King Arthur and his knights **b :** the knights of King Arthur **2 :** a conference for discussion or deliberation by several participants; *also* **:** the participants in such a conference or the discussion carried on

round trip *n* **:** a trip to a place and back usu. over the same route

round up *vt* **1 :** to collect (cattle) by means of a roundup **2 :** to gather in or bring together

round·up \ˈraůn-ˌdəp\ *n* **1 a** (1) **:** the act or process of collecting cattle by riding around them and driving them in (2) **:** the men and horses so engaged **b :** a gathering in of scattered persons or things **2 :** SUMMARY, RÉSUMÉ

round·worm \ˈraůn-ˌdwərm\ *n* **:** a nematode worm or sometimes a related round-bodied unsegmented worm (as an acanthocephalan worm) as distinguished from a flatworm

roup \ˈrüp, ˈraůp\ *n* [origin unknown] **:** a virus disease of poultry marked by cheesy lesions of the mouth, throat, and eyes

1**rouse** \ˈraůz\ *vb* [ME *rousen*] *vi* **1 :** to become aroused **:** AWAKEN **2 :** to become stirred **~** *vt* **1** *archaic* **:** to cause to break from cover **2 a :** to stir up **:** EXCITE **b :** to arouse from sleep or repose **:** AWAKEN — **rous·er** *n*

2**rouse** *n* **:** an act or instance of rousing; *esp* **:** an excited stir

3**rouse** *n* [alter. (resulting fr. incorrect division of *to drink carouse*) of *carouse*] **1** *obs* **:** DRINK, TOAST **2** *archaic* **:** CAROUSAL

rous·ing \ˈraů-ziŋ\ *adj* **1 a :** EXCITING, STIRRING **b :** BRISK, LIVELY **2 :** EXCEPTIONAL, SUPERLATIVE

roust \ˈraůst\ *vt* [alter. of 1*rouse*] **:** to rout esp. from bed **:** ROUSE

roust·about \ˈraů-stə-ˌbaůt\ *n* **1 :** DECKHAND, LONGSHOREMAN **2 :** an unskilled or semiskilled laborer esp. in an oil field or refinery **3 :** a circus worker who erects and dismantles tents, cares for the grounds, and handles animals and equipment

roust·er \ˈraů-stər\ *n* **:** ROUSTABOUT

1**rout** \ˈraůt\ *n* [ME *route*, fr. MF, troop, defeat, fr. (assumed) VL *rupta*, fr. L, fem. of *ruptus*, pp. of *rumpere* to break — more at REAVE] **1 :** MOB, THRONG; *specif* **:** RABBLE **2 a :** DISTURBANCE **b** *archaic* **:** FUSS **3 :** a fashionable gathering **:** RECEPTION **syn** see CROWD

2**rout** *vi* [ME *rowten*, fr. ON *rauta;* akin to OE *rēotan* to weep, L *rudere* to roar] *dial chiefly Brit* **:** to low loudly **:** BELLOW — used of cattle

3**rout** *vb* [alter. of 3*root*] *vi* **1 :** to poke around with the snout **:** ROOT **2 :** to search haphazardly **:** RUMMAGE **~** *vt* **1 a** *archaic* **:** to dig up with the snout **b :** to gouge out or make a furrow in (as wood or metal); *specif* **:** to cut away (as blank parts) from a printing surface (as an engraving or electrotype) with a router **2 a :** to expel by force **:** EJECT — usu. used with *out* **b :** to cause to emerge esp. from bed **:** ROUSE **3 :** to come up with **:** DISCOVER, UNCOVER

4**rout** *n* [MF *route* troop, defeat] **1 :** a state of wild confusion or disorderly retreat **2 a :** a disastrous defeat **:** DEBACLE **b :** a precipitate flight **c :** an act or instance of routing

5**rout** *vt* **1 a :** to disorganize completely **:** DEMORALIZE; *esp* **:** to put to precipitate flight **b :** to defeat decisively **:** OVERWHELM **2 :** to drive out **:** DISPEL **syn** see CONQUER

1**route** \ˈrüt, ˈraůt\ *n* [ME, fr. OF, fr. (assumed) VL *rupta* (*via*), lit., broken way, fr. L *rupta*, fem. of *ruptus*, pp.] **1 a :** a traveled way **:** HIGHWAY **b :** a means of access **:** CHANNEL **2 :** a line of travel **:** COURSE **3 a :** an established or selected course of travel **b :** an assigned territory to be systematically covered

2**route** *vt* **1 a :** to send by a selected route **:** DIRECT **b :** to divert in a specified direction **2 :** to prearrange and direct the order and execution of (a series of operations)

route·man \-mən, -ˌman\ *n* **:** one who is responsible for making sales or deliveries on an assigned route

route march *n* **:** a practice march in which troops maintain prescribed interval and distance but are not required to keep step or maintain silence

1**rout·er** \ˈraůt-ər\ *n* **:** one that routs: as **a :** a routing plane **b :** a machine with a revolving vertical spindle and cutter for milling out the surface of wood or metal

2**rout·er** \ˈrüt-ər, ˈraůt-\ *n* **:** one that routes

3**rout·er** \ˈrüt-ər, ˈraůt-\ *n* **:** a horse trained for distance races

routh \ˈrüth, ˈraůth\ *n* [origin unknown] *chiefly Scot* **:** PLENTY, ABUNDANCE

1**rou·tine** \rü-ˈtēn\ *n* [F, fr. MF, fr. *route* traveled way] **1 a :** a regular course of procedure **b :** habitual or mechanical performance of an established procedure **2 :** a reiterated speech or formula **3 :** a sequence of coded instructions for an electronic computer **4 :** a fixed piece of entertainment often repeated **:** ACT; *specif* **:** a theatrical number

2**rou·tine** \ˌrü-ˈtēn, ˌrü-ˌ\ *adj* **1 :** COMMONPLACE, UNINSPIRED **2 :** of, relating to, or in accordance with established procedure — **rou·tine·ly** *adv*

rou·tin·ize \rü-ˈtē-ˌnīz\ *vt* **:** to discipline in or reduce to a routine

roux \ˈrü\ *n, pl* **roux** \ˈrüz\ [F, fr. *beurre roux* browned butter] **:** a cooked mixture of flour and fat

1**rove** \ˈrōv\ *vb* [ME *roven* to shoot at rovers] *vi* **:** to move aimlessly **:** ROAM **~** *vt* **:** to wander through or over

2**rove** *n* **:** an act or instance of wandering

3**rove** *past of* REEVE

4**rove** *vt* [origin unknown] **:** to join (textile fibers) with a slight twist and draw out into roving

5**rove** *n* **:** ROVING

rove beetle *n* [perh. fr. 1*rove*] **:** any of numerous often predatory active beetles (family Staphylinidae) having a long body and very short wing covers beneath which the wings are folded transversely

1**ro·ver** \ˈrō-vər\ *n* [ME, fr. MD, fr. *roven* to rob; akin to OE *rēafian* to reave — more at REAVE] **:** PIRATE

2**rov·er** \ˈrō-vər\ *n* [ME, fr. *roven* to shoot at random, wander] **1 :** a random or long-distance mark in archery — usu. used in pl. **2 :** WANDERER, ROAMER

rov·ing \ˈrō-viŋ\ *n* **:** a slightly twisted roll or strand of textile fibers

1**row** \ˈrō\ *vb* [ME *rowen*, fr. OE *rōwan;* akin to MHG *rüejen* to row, L *remus* oar] *vi* **1 :** to propel a boat by means of oars **2 :** to move by or as if by the propulsion of oars **~** *vt* **1 a :** to propel with or as if with oars **b :** to be equipped with (a specified number of oars) **c** (1) **:** to participate in (a rowing match) (2) **:** to compete against in rowing (3) **:** to pull (an oar) in a crew **2 :** to transport in a boat propelled by oars — **row·er** \ˈrō(-ə)r\ *n*

2**row** *n* **:** an act or instance of rowing

³**row** *n* [ME *rawe;* akin to OE *rǣw* row, OHG *rīga* line, L *rima* slit] **1 :** a number of objects in an orderly series or sequence **2 a :** WAY, STREET **b :** a street or area dominated by a specific kind of enterprise or occupancy **3 :** a continuous strip usu. running horizontally or parallel to a base line

⁴**row** *vt* **:** to form into rows

⁵**row** \'raù\ *n* [origin unknown] **:** a noisy disturbance or quarrel **:** BRAWL

⁶**row** \'raù\ *vi* **:** to engage in a row

row·an \'raù-ən, 'rō-\ *n* [of Scand origin; akin to ON *reynir* rowan; akin to OE *rēad* red — more at RED] **1 a :** a Eurasian tree (*Sorbus aucuparia*) of the rose family with flat corymbs of white flowers followed by small red pomes **b :** an American mountain ash (*Sorbus americana*) **2** *or* **row·an·ber·ry** \-,ber-ē\ **:** the fruit of a rowan

row·boat \'rō-,bōt\ *n* **:** a boat designed to be rowed

row·di·ly \'raùd-ᵊl-ē\ *adv* **:** in a rowdy manner

row·di·ness \'raùd-ē-nəs\ *n* **:** the quality or state of being rowdy

¹**row·dy** \'raùd-ē\ *adj* [perh. irreg. fr. ⁵*row*] **:** coarse or boisterous in behavior **:** ROUGH — **row·dy·ish** \-ē-ish\ *adj* — **row·dy·ism** \-,iz-əm\ *n*

²**rowdy** *n* **:** a rowdy person **:** TOUGH

¹**row·el** \'raù(-ə)l\ *n* [ME *rowelle,* fr. MF *rouelle* small wheel, fr. OF *roele* — more at ROULETTE] **:** a revolving disk at the end of a spur with sharp marginal points

²**rowel** *vt* **row·eled** *or* **row·elled; row·el·ing** *or* **row·el·ling** **:** to goad with or as if with a rowel **:** SPUR

row·en \'raù-ən\ *n* [ME *rowein,* fr. (assumed) ONF *rewain;* akin to OF *regaïn* aftermath, fr. *re-* + *gaaignier* to till— more at GAIN] **1 :** a stubble field left unplowed for late grazing **2 :** AFTERMATH 1 — often used in pl.

row house \'rō-\ *n* **:** one of a series of houses connected by common sidewalls and forming a continuous group

row·lock \'räl-ək, 'rəl-; ¹rō-,läk\ *n* [prob. by alter.] *chiefly Brit* **:** OARLOCK

¹**roy·al** \'ròi(-ə)l\ *adj* [ME *roial,* fr. MF, fr. L *regalis,* fr. *reg-, rex* king; akin to OIr *rī* (gen. *rīg*) king, Skt *rājan,* L *regere* to rule — more at RIGHT] **1 a :** of kingly ancestry **b :** of, relating to, or subject to the crown **c :** being in the Crown's service ⟨~ prosecutor⟩ ⟨*Royal* Air Force⟩ **2 a :** suitable for royalty **:** MAGNIFICENT **b :** requiring no exertion **:** EASY **3 a :** of superior size, magnitude, or quality **b :** established or chartered by the Crown **4 :** of, relating to, or being a part (as a mast, sail, or yard) next above the topgallant — **roy·al·ly** \'ròi-ə-lē\ *adv*

²**royal** *n* **1 :** a stag of eight years or more having antlers with at least twelve points **2 :** a small sail on the royal mast immediately above the topgallant sail **3 :** a size of paper usu. 20 x 25 or 19 x 24 inches

royal antler *n* — see ANTLER illustration

royal blue *n* **:** a variable color averaging a vivid purplish blue

roy·al·ism \'ròi-ə-,liz-əm\ *n* **:** MONARCHISM

roy·al·ist \-ə-ləst\ *n* **1** *often cap* **:** an adherent of a king or of monarchical government: as **a :** CAVALIER 2 — compare ROUNDHEAD **b :** TORY 4 **2 :** a reactionary business tycoon — **royalist** *adj*

royal jelly *n* **:** a highly nutritious secretion of the pharyngeal glands of the honeybee that is fed to the very young larvae in a colony and to all queen larvae

royal palm *n* **:** any of several palms (genus *Roystonea*); *esp* **:** a tall graceful pinnate-leaved palm (*R. regia*) of southern Florida and Cuba that is widely planted for ornament

royal poinciana *n* **:** a showy tropical tree (*Delonix regia* syn. *Poinciana regia*) widely planted for its immense racemes of scarlet and orange flowers — called also *flamboyant, peacock flower*

royal purple *n* **:** a dark reddish purple

roy·al·ty \'ròi(-ə)l-tē\ *n* [ME *roialte,* fr. MF *roialté,* fr. OF, fr. *roial*] **1 a :** royal status or power **:** SOVEREIGNTY **b :** a right or perquisite of a sovereign (as a percentage paid to the crown of gold or silver taken from mines) **2 :** regal character or bearing **:** NOBILITY **3 a :** persons of royal lineage **b :** a person of royal rank **c :** a privileged class **4 :** a right of jurisdiction granted to an individual or corporation by a sovereign **5 a :** a share of the product or profit reserved by the grantor esp. of an oil or mining lease **b :** a payment made to an author or composer for each copy of his work sold or to an inventor for each article sold under a patent

royster *var of* ROISTER

-r·rha·gia \'rā-j(ē-)ə\ *n comb form* [NL, fr. Gk, fr. *rhēgnynai* to break, burst; akin to OSlav *rězati* to cut] **:** abnormal or excessive discharge or flow ⟨metro*rrhagia*⟩

-r·rhea *also* **-r·rhoea** \'rē-ə\ *n comb form* [ME *-ria,* fr. LL *-rrhoea,* fr. Gk *-rrhoia,* fr. *rhoia,* fr. *rhein* to flow — more at STREAM] **:** flow **:** discharge ⟨logo*rrhea*⟩ ⟨leuko*rrhea*⟩

-r·rhine *or* **-rhine** \,rīn\ *adj comb form* [ISV, fr. Gk *-rrhin-, -rrhis,* fr. *rhin-, rhis* nose] **:** having (such) a nose ⟨platy*rrhine*⟩

-rrhiza — see -RHIZA

¹**rub** \'rəb\ *vb* **rubbed; rub·bing** [ME *rubben;* akin to Icel *rubba* to scrape] *vi* **1 a :** to move along the surface of a body with pressure **:** GRATE **b** (1) **:** to fret or chafe with friction (2) **:** to cause discontent, irritation, or anger **2 :** to admit of being rubbed (as for erasure or obliteration) ~ *vt* **1 a :** to subject to the action of something moving esp. back and forth with pressure and friction **b** (1) **:** to cause (a body) to move with pressure and friction along a surface (2) **:** to treat in any of various ways by rubbing **c :** to bring into reciprocal back-and-forth or rotary contact **2 :** ANNOY, IRRITATE

²**rub** *n* **1 a :** an unevenness of surface (as of the ground in lawn bowling) **b :** OBSTRUCTION, DIFFICULTY **c :** something grating to the feelings (as a gibe, sarcasm, or harsh criticism) **d :** something that mars or upsets serenity **2 :** the application of friction with pressure **:** RUBBING

rub–a–dub \'rəb-ə-,dəb\ *n* [imit.] **:** the sound of drumbeats

Ru·bai·yat stanza \'rü-bē-,ät-\ *n* [*Rubáiyát,* collection of quatrains by Omar Khayyam] **:** an iambic pentameter quatrain with a rhyme scheme *aaba* — called also *Omar stanza* \'ō-,mär-, -mər-\

Ru·barth's disease \'rü-,bärts-\ *n* [C. Sven *Rubarth* b1905 Sw veterinarian] **:** a highly fatal febrile virus hepatitis of dogs

ru·basse \rü-'bas\ *n* [F *rubace,* irreg. fr. *rubis* ruby — more at RUBY] **:** a quartz stained a ruby red

ru·ba·to \rü-'bät-(,)ō\ *n* [It, lit., robbed] **:** fluctuation of speed within a musical phrase typically against a rhythmically steady accompaniment

¹**rub·ber** \'rəb-ər\ *n, often attrib* **1 a :** one that rubs **b :** an instrument or object (as a rubber eraser) used in rubbing, polishing, scraping, or cleaning **c :** something that prevents rubbing or chafing **2** [fr. its use in erasers] **a :** an elastic substance obtained by coagulating the milky juice of any of various tropical plants (as of the genera *Hevea* and *Ficus*) and prepared as sheets and then dried — called also *caoutchouc, india rubber* **b :** any of various synthetic rubberlike substances **c :** natural or synthetic rubber modified by chemical treatment to increase its useful properties (as toughness and resistance to wear) and used in tires, electrical insulation, and waterproof materials **3 :** something made of or resembling rubber: as **a :** a rubber overshoe **b :** the pitcher's plate in baseball or softball — **rub·bery** \'rəb-(ə-)rē\ *adj*

²**rubber** *n* [origin unknown] **1 :** a contest consisting of an odd number of games won by the side that takes a majority (as two out of three) **2 :** an odd game played to determine the winner of a tie

rubber–base paint *n* **:** a paint having a rubber derivative or a synthetic resin as its binder or vehicle

rubber cement *n* **:** an adhesive consisting typically of a dispersion of vulcanized rubber in an organic solvent

rub·ber·ize \'rəb-ə-,rīz\ *vt* **:** to coat or impregnate with rubber or a rubber solution

rub·ber·like \'rəb-ər-,līk\ *adj* **:** resembling rubber esp. in physical properties (as elasticity and toughness)

rub·ber·neck \-,nek\ *n* **1 :** an inquisitive person **2 :** TOURIST; *esp* **:** one on a guided tour — **rubberneck** *vi*

rubber plant *n* **:** a plant that yields rubber; *esp* **:** a tall tropical Asian tree (*Ficus elastica*) that is frequently dwarfed in pots as an ornamental

rubber stamp *n* **1 a :** a person who echoes or imitates others **b :** a body or person that approves or endorses a program or policy with little or no dissent or discussion **2 a :** a stereotyped copy or expression **b :** a routine endorsement or approval

rub·ber–stamp \,rəb-ər-'stamp\ *vt* **:** to approve, endorse, or dispose of as a matter of routine usu. without exercise of judgment or at the command of another

rub·bing \'rəb-iŋ\ *n* **:** an image of a raised, indented, or textured surface obtained by placing paper over it and rubbing the paper

rub·bish \'rəb-ish\ *n* [ME *robys*] **:** useless waste or rejected matter **:** TRASH — **rub·bishy** \'rəb-i-shē\ *adj*

rub·ble \'rəb-əl\ *n* [ME *robyl*] **1 :** rough stone as it comes from the quarry **2 :** waterworn or rough broken stones or bricks used in coarse masonry or in filling courses of walls; *also* **:** RUBBLEWORK **3 :** a mass made up of rough irregular pieces — **rub·bly** \'rəb-(ə-)lē\ *adj*

rub·ble·work \'rəb-əl-,wərk\ *n* **:** masonry of unsquared or rudely squared stones that are irregular in size and shape

rub·down \'rəb-,daùn\ *n* **:** a brisk rubbing of the body (as after a bath)

rube \'rüb\ *n* [*Rube,* nickname for *Reuben*] **:** an awkward unsophisticated person **:** RUSTIC

¹**ru·be·fa·cient** \,rü-bə-'fā-shənt\ *adj* [L *rubefacient-, rubefaciens,* prp. of *rubefacere* to make red, fr. *rubeus* reddish + *facere* to make — more at RUBY, DO] **:** causing redness (as of the skin)

²**rubefacient** *n* **:** a substance for external application that produces redness of the skin — **ru·be·fac·tion** \-'fak-shən\ *n*

ru·bel·la \rü-'bel-ə\ *n* [NL, fr. L, fem. of *rubellus* reddish, fr. *ruber* red — more at RED] **:** GERMAN MEASLES

ru·bel·lite \rü-'bel-,īt, 'rü-bə-,līt\ *n* [L *rubellus*] **:** a red tourmaline used as a gem

ru·be·o·la \rü-'bē-ə-lə, ,rü-bē-'ō-\ *n* [NL, fr. neut. pl. of (assumed) NL *rubeolus* reddish, fr. L *rubeus* — more at RUBY] **:** MEASLES — **ru·be·o·lar** \-lər\ *adj*

Ru·bi·con \'rü-bi-,kän\ *n* [L *Rubicon-, Rubico,* river of northern Italy forming part of the boundary between Cisalpine Gaul and Italy whose crossing by Julius Caesar in 49 B.C. was regarded by the Senate as an act of war] **:** a bounding or limiting line; *esp* **:** one that when crossed commits a person irrevocably

ru·bi·cund \'rü-bi-(,)kənd\ *adj* [L *rubicundus,* fr. *rubēre* to be red; akin to L *rubeus*] **:** RED, RUDDY — **ru·bi·cun·di·ty** \,rü-bi-'kən-dət-ē\ *n*

ru·bid·i·um \rü-'bid-ē-əm\ *n* [NL, fr. L *rubidus* red, fr. *rubēre*] **:** a soft silvery metallic element that decomposes water with violence and inflames spontaneously in air — see ELEMENT table

ru·big·i·nous \rü-'bij-ə-nəs\ *adj* [L *robiginosus, rubiginosus* rusty, fr. *robigin-, robigo* rust; akin to L *rubēre*] **:** of a rusty red color

ru·bi·ous \'rü-bē-əs\ *adj* **:** RED, RUBY

ru·ble \'rü-bəl\ *n* [Russ *rubl'*] — see MONEY table

ru·bric \'rü-brik, -,brik\ *n* [ME *rubrike* red ocher, heading in red letters of part of a book, fr. MF *rubrique,* fr. L *rubrica,* fr. *rubr-, ruber* red] **1 :** a heading of a part of a book or manuscript done or underlined in a color (as red) different from the rest **2 a :** NAME, TITLE; *specif* **:** the title of a statute **b :** an authoritative rule; *esp* **:** a rule for conduct of a liturgical service **c :** an explanatory or introductory commentary **:** GLOSS; *specif* **:** an editorial interpolation **3 :** an established rule or custom — **rubric** *or* **ru·bri·cal** \-bri-kəl\ *adj* — **ru·bri·cal·ly** \-k(ə-)lē\ *adv*

ru·bri·cate \'rü-bri-,kāt\ *vt* **1 :** to write or print as a rubric **2 :** to provide with a rubric — **ru·bri·ca·tion** \,rü-bri-'kā-shən\ *n* — **ru·bri·ca·tor** \'rü-bri-,kāt-ər\ *n*

ru·bus \'rü-bəs\ *n, pl* **rubus** [NL, genus name, fr. L, blackberry] **:** a plant (as a blackberry or raspberry) of a genus (*Rubus*) of the rose family having 3- to 7-foliolate or simple lobed leaves, white or pink flowers, and a mass of carpels ripening into an aggregate fruit composed of many drupelets

¹**ru·by** \'rü-bē\ *n* [ME, fr. MF *rubis, rubi,* irreg. fr. L *rubeus* reddish; akin to L *ruber* red — more at RED] **1 a :** a precious stone that is a red corundum **b :** something made of ruby; *esp* **:** a watch bearing or other part of ruby or a substitute material **2 a :** the dark red color of the ruby **b :** something resembling a

ruby in color **3 :** a Brazilian hummingbird (genus *Clytolaema*) whose male has a ruby throat or breast
²ruby *adj* **:** of the color ruby
ruby glass *n* **:** glass of a deep red color containing selenium, an oxide of copper, or gold chloride
ruby spinel *n* **:** a spinel used as a gem
ru·by–throat·ed hummingbird \ˌrü-bē-ˌthrōt-əd-\ *n* **:** a hummingbird (*Archilochus colubris*) of eastern No. America having a bright bronzy green back, whitish underparts, and in the adult male a red throat with metallic reflections
ruche \ˈrüsh\ *or* **ruch·ing** \ˈrü-shiŋ\ *n* [F *ruche*] **:** a pleated, fluted, or gathered strip of fabric used for trimming
¹ruck \ˈrək\ *n* [ME *ruke* pile of combustible material, of Scand origin; akin to ON *hraukr* rick — more at RICK] **1 a :** an indistinguishable gathering **:** JUMBLE **b :** the usual run of persons or things **:** GENERALITY **2 :** the persons or things following the vanguard
²ruck *vb* [*ruck*, n. (wrinkle)] **:** PUCKER, WRINKLE
ruck·sack \ˈrək-ˌsak, ˈrůk-\ *n* [G] **:** KNAPSACK
ruck·us \ˈrək-əs, ˈrük-, ˈrůk-\ *n* [prob. blend of *ruction* and *rumpus*] **:** ROW, DISTURBANCE
ruc·tion \ˈrək-shən\ *n* [perh. by shortening & alter. fr. *insurrection*] **1 :** a noisy fight **2 :** DISTURBANCE, UPROAR
rud·beck·ia \ˌrəd-ˈbek-ē-ə, rüd-\ *n* [NL, genus name, fr. Olof *Rudbeck* †1702 Sw scientist] **:** any of a genus (*Rudbeckia*) of No. American perennial composite herbs having showy flower heads with mostly yellow ray flowers and a conical chaffy receptacle
rudd \ˈrəd, ˈrůd\ *n* [prob. fr. *rud* redness, red ocher, fr. ME *rude*, fr. OE *rudu* — more at RUDDY] **:** a freshwater European cyprinid fish (*Scardinius erythrophthalmus*) resembling the roach
rud·der \ˈrəd-ər\ *n* [ME *rother*, fr. OE *rōther* paddle; akin to OE *rōwan* to row] **1 a :** a flat piece or structure of wood or metal attached upright to a ship's stern so that it can be turned causing the ship's head to turn in the same direction **b :** a movable auxiliary airfoil usu. attached at the rear end that serves to control direction of flight of an airplane in the horizontal plane **2 :** GUIDE, GOVERNOR

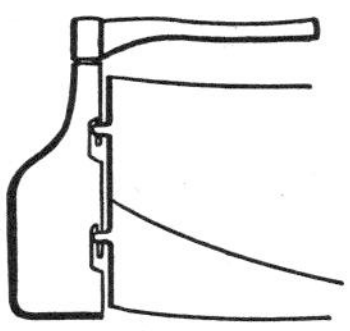
rudder 1a

rud·der·post \-ˌpōst\ *n* **1 :** RUDDERSTOCK **2 :** an additional sternpost in a single-screw ship to which the rudder is attached
rud·der·stock \-ˌstäk\ *n* **:** the shaft of a rudder
rud·di·ly \ˈrəd-ᵊl-ē\ *adv* **:** with a ruddy hue or tinge
rud·di·ness \ˈrəd-ē-nəs\ *n* **:** the quality or state of being ruddy
¹rud·dle \ˈrəd-ᵊl\ *n* [dim. of *rud* red ocher] **:** RED OCHER
²ruddle *vt* **rud·dling** \ˈrəd-liŋ, -ᵊl-iŋ\ **:** to color with or as if with red ocher **:** REDDEN
rud·dle·man \ˈrəd-ᵊl-mən\ *n* **:** a dealer in red ocher
rud·dock \ˈrəd-ək, ˈrůd-\ *n* [ME *ruddok*, fr. OE *rudduc;* akin to OE *rudu*] **:** ROBIN 1a
rud·dy \ˈrəd-ē\ *adj* [ME *rudi*, fr. OE *rudig*, fr. *rudu* redness; akin to OE *rēad* red — more at RED] **1 :** having a healthy reddish color **2 :** RED, REDDISH
rude \ˈrüd\ *adj* [ME, fr. MF, fr. L *rudis;* akin to L *rudus* rubble, *ruere* to fall — more at RUG] **1 a :** being in a rough or unfinished state **:** CRUDE **b :** NATURAL, RAW **c :** PRIMITIVE, UNDEVELOPED **d :** SIMPLE, ELEMENTAL **2 :** lacking refinement or delicacy: **a :** IGNORANT, UNLEARNED **b :** INELEGANT, UNCOUTH **c :** offensive in manner or action **:** DISCOURTEOUS **d :** UNCIVILIZED, SAVAGE **e :** COARSE, VULGAR **3 :** marked by lack of training or skill **:** INEXPERIENCED **4 :** ROBUST, STURDY **5 :** FORCEFUL, ABRUPT — **rude·ly** *adv* — **rude·ness** *n*
syn RUDE, ROUGH, CRUDE, RAW, CALLOW, GREEN mean lacking in social refinement. RUDE implies ignorance of or indifference to good form; it may suggest intentional discourtesy; ROUGH is likely to stress lack of polish, but it need not imply positively unpleasant qualities; CRUDE may apply to thought or behavior limited to the gross, the obvious, or the primitive and ignorant of civilized amenities; RAW suggests being untested, inexperienced, or unfinished; CALLOW suggests the immaturity of adolescence or early manhood; GREEN implies nothing worse than simple unfamiliarity with a new environment or pursuit
¹ru·der·al \ˈrüd-ə-rəl\ *adj* [NL *ruderalis*, fr. L *ruder-*, *rudus* rubble] *of a plant* **:** growing in rubbish or in a waste or in a place (as a roadside) where the vegetation has been disturbed by man
²ruderal *n* **:** a weedy and commonly introduced plant growing where the vegetational cover has been interrupted
rudes·by \ˈrüdz-bē\ *n* [*rude* + *-sby* (as in the name *Crosby*)] *archaic* **:** a rude person
ru·di·ment \ˈrüd-ə-mənt\ *n* [L *rudimentum* beginning, fr. *rudis* raw, rude] **1 :** a basic principle or element or a fundamental skill — usu. used in pl. **2 a :** something unformed or undeveloped **:** BEGINNING — usu. used in pl. **b :** a body part or organ so deficient in size or structure as to entirely prevent its performing its normal function — **ru·di·men·tal** \ˌrüd-ə-ˈment-ᵊl\ *adj* — **ru·di·men·tar·i·ly** \-(ˌ)men-ˈter-ə-lē, -mən-\ *adv* — **ru·di·men·ta·ri·ness** \-ˈment-ə-rē-nəs, -ˈmen-trē-\ *n* — **ru·di·men·ta·ry** \-ˈment-ə-rē, -ˈmen-trē\ *adj*
¹rue \ˈrü\ *vb* [ME *ruen*, fr. OE *hrēowan;* akin to OHG *hriuwan* to regret] *vt* **:** to feel penitence, remorse, or regret for ~ *vi* **:** to feel sorrow, regret, or remorse
²rue *n* **:** REGRET, SORROW
³rue *n* [ME, fr. MF, fr. L *ruta*, fr. Gk *rhytē*] **:** a strong-scented perennial woody herb (*Ruta graveolens* of the family Rutaceae, the rue family) that has bitter leaves used in medicine and is related to the citrus
rue anemone *n* **:** a delicate vernal herb (*Anemonella thalictroides*) of the crowfoot family with white flowers resembling those of the wood anemone
rue·ful \ˈrü-fəl\ *adj* **1 :** exciting pity or sympathy **:** PITIABLE **2 :** MOURNFUL, REGRETFUL — **rue·ful·ly** \-fə-lē\ *adv* — **rue·ful·ness** *n*
ru·fes·cent \rü-ˈfes-ᵊnt\ *adj* [L *rufescent-*, *rufescens*, pp. of *rufescere* to become reddish, fr. *rufus* red — more at RED] **:** REDDISH
¹ruff \ˈrəf\ *n* [ME *ruf*] **1** *also* **ruffe** \ˈrəf\ **:** a small freshwater European perch (*Acerina cernua*) **2 :** a pumpkinseed (*Lepomis gibbosus*)
²ruff *n* [prob. back-formation fr. *ruffle*] **1 :** a wheel-shaped stiff collar worn by men and women of the late 16th and early 17th centuries **2 :** a fringe or frill of long hairs or feathers growing around or on the neck **3 :** a common Eurasian sandpiper (*Philomachus pugnax*) whose male during the breeding season has a large ruff of erectile feathers on the neck — **ruffed** \ˈrəft\ *adj*

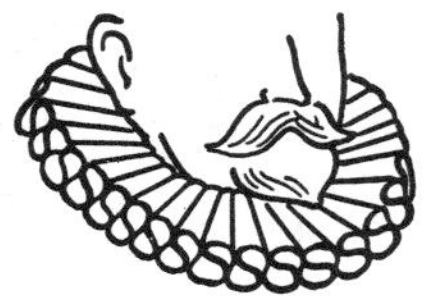
ruff 1

³ruff *n* [MF *roffle*] **:** the act of trumping
⁴ruff *vb* **:** TRUMP
ruffed grouse *n* **:** a No. American grouse (*Bonasa umbellus*) valued as a game bird in the eastern U.S. and Canada
ruf·fi·an \ˈrəf-ē-ən\ *n* [MF *rufian*] **:** a brutal cruel fellow — **ruffian** *adj* — **ruf·fi·an·ism** \-ē-ə-ˌniz-əm\ *n* — **ruf·fi·an·ly** *adj*
¹ruf·fle \ˈrəf-əl\ *vb* **ruf·fling** \-(ə-)liŋ\ [ME *ruffelen;* akin to LG *ruffelen* to crumple] *vt* **1 a :** ROUGHEN, ABRADE **b :** TROUBLE, VEX **2 :** to erect (as feathers) in or like a ruff **3 a :** to flip through (as pages) **b :** SHUFFLE **4 :** to make into a ruffle ~ *vi* **:** to become ruffled
²ruffle *n* **1 :** a state or cause of irritation **2 :** COMMOTION, BRAWL **3 :** an unevenness or disturbance of surface **:** RIPPLE **4 a :** a strip of fabric gathered or pleated on one edge **b :** ²RUFF 2 — **ruf·fly** \ˈrəf-(ə-)lē\ *adj*
³ruffle *n* [*ruff* (a drumbeat)] **:** a low vibrating drumbeat less loud than a roll
ru·fous \ˈrü-fəs\ *adj* [L *rufus* red — more at RED] **:** REDDISH
rug \ˈrəg\ *n* [(assumed) ME, rag, tuft, of Scand origin; akin to ON *rögg* tuft; akin to L *ruere* to rush, fall, dig up, Skt *ravate* he breaks up] **1 :** a piece of thick heavy fabric usu. with a nap or pile used as a floor covering **2 :** a floor mat of an animal pelt ⟨bearskin ~⟩ **3 :** a lap robe
ru·ga \ˈrü-gə\ *n, pl* **ru·gae** \-ˌgī, -ˌgē, -ˌjē\ [NL, fr. L, wrinkle — more at ROUGH] **:** a visceral fold or wrinkle — used chiefly in pl. — **ru·gal** \ˈrü-gəl\ *adj* — **ru·gate** \ˈrü-ˌgāt\ *adj*
rug·by \ˈrəg-bē\ *n, often cap* [*Rugby* School, Rugby, Warwickshire, England] **:** a football game in which play is continuous, kicking, dribbling, lateral passing, tackling, and the scrum are featured, and interference and substitution are not permitted
rug·ged \ˈrəg-əd\ *adj* [ME, fr. (assumed) ME *rug*] **1** *obs* **:** SHAGGY, HAIRY **2 :** having a rough uneven surface **:** JAGGED ⟨~ mountains⟩ **3 :** TURBULENT, STORMY **4 a :** seamed with wrinkles and furrows **:** WEATHERED **b :** showing signs of strength **:** STURDY **5 a :** AUSTERE, STERN **b :** COARSE, RUDE **6 a :** strongly built or constituted **:** ROBUST **b :** presenting a severe test of ability, stamina, or resolution **syn** see ROUGH — **rug·ged·ly** *adv* — **rug·ged·ness** *n*
rug·ged·iza·tion \ˌrəg-əd-ə-ˈzā-shən\ *n* **:** the act of ruggedizing **:** the state of being ruggedized
rug·ged·ize \ˈrəg-ə-ˌdīz\ *vt* **:** to strengthen (as a machine) for better resistance to wear, stress, and abuse ⟨a *ruggedized* camera⟩
rug·ger \ˈrəg-ər\ *n* [by alter.] *Brit* **:** RUGBY
ru·go·sa rose \rü-ˌgō-sə-, -zə-\ *n* [NL *rugosa*, specific epithet of *Rosa rugosa* rugose rose] **:** any of various garden roses descended from a Japanese rose (*Rosa rugosa*)
ru·gose \ˈrü-ˌgōs\ *adj* [L *rugosus*, fr. *ruga*] **1 :** full of wrinkles ⟨~ cheeks⟩ **2 :** having the veinlets sunken and the spaces between elevated ⟨~ leaves of the sage⟩ — **ru·gose·ly** *adv* — **ru·gos·i·ty** \rü-ˈgäs-ət-ē\ *n*
ru·gu·lose \ˈrü-gyə-ˌlōs\ *adj* [prob. fr. (assumed) NL *rugulosus*, fr. NL *rugula*, dim. of L *ruga*] **:** having small rugae **:** finely wrinkled
Ruhm·korff coil \ˌrüm-ˌkȯrf-\ *n* [Heinrich *Ruhmkorff* †1877 G physicist] **:** INDUCTION COIL
¹ru·in \ˈrü-ən, ˈrü-, -ˌin\ *n* [ME *ruine*, fr. MF, fr. L *ruina;* akin to L *ruere* to fall — more at RUG] **1 a** *archaic* **:** a falling down **:** COLLAPSE **b :** physical, moral, economic, or social collapse **2 a** *archaic* **:** the state of being ruined **b :** the remains of something destroyed — usu. used in pl. **3 :** a cause of destruction **4 a :** the action of destroying, laying waste, or wrecking **b :** DAMAGE, INJURY **5 :** a ruined building, person, or object
²ruin *vt* **1 :** to reduce to ruins **:** DEVASTATE **2 a :** to damage irreparably **b :** BANKRUPT, IMPOVERISH **3 :** to subject to frustration or failure ~ *vi* **:** to become ruined — **ru·in·er** \ˈrü-ə-nər, ˈrü-\ *n*
ru·in·ate \ˈrü-ə-ˌnāt, ˈrü-\ *adj* **:** RUINED — **ruinate** *vt*
ru·in·a·tion \ˌrü-ə-ˈnā-shən, ˌrü-\ *n* **:** RUIN, DESTRUCTION
ru·in·ous \ˈrü-ə-nəs, ˈrü-\ *adj* **1 :** RUINED, DILAPIDATED **2 :** causing or tending to cause ruin **:** DESTRUCTIVE — **ru·in·ous·ly** *adv* — **ru·in·ous·ness** *n*
¹rule \ˈrül\ *n* [ME *reule*, fr. OF, fr. L *regula* straightedge, rule, fr. *regere* to lead straight — more at RIGHT] **1 a :** a prescribed guide for conduct or action **b :** the laws or regulations prescribed by the founder of a religious order for observance by its members **c :** an accepted procedure, custom, or habit **d** (1) **:** a usu. written order or direction made by a court regulating court practice or the action of parties (2) **:** a legal precept or doctrine **e :** a regulation or bylaw governing procedure or controlling conduct **2 a** (1) **:** a usu. valid generalization (2) **:** a generally prevailing quality, state, or mode **b :** a standard of judgment **:** CRITERION **c :** a regulating principle **3 a :** the exercise of authority or control **:** DOMINION **b :** a period during which a specified ruler or government exercises control **4 a :** a strip of material marked off in units used for measuring or ruling off lengths **b :** a metal strip with a type-high face that prints a linear design; *also* **:** the design so printed **syn** see LAW
²rule *vt* **1 a :** CONTROL, DIRECT **b :** GUIDE, MANAGE **2 a :** to exercise authority or power over **:** GOVERN **b :** to be preeminent in **:** DOMINATE **3 :** to declare authoritatively; *specif* **:** to command or determine judicially **4 a** (1) **:** to mark with lines drawn along or as if along the straight edge of a ruler (2) **:** to mark (a line) on a paper with a ruler **b :** to arrange in a line ~ *vi* **1 a :** to exercise supreme authority **b :** PREDOMINATE, PREVAIL **2 :** to exist in a specified state or condition **3 :** to lay down a legal rule **syn** see DECIDE, GOVERN
ruled surface *n* **:** a surface generated by a moving straight line
rule·less \ˈrül-ləs\ *adj* **:** not restrained or regulated by law
rule of thumb **1 :** a rough measurement or calculation **2 :** a judgment based on practical experience rather than on scientific knowledge
rule out *vt* **1 :** EXCLUDE, ELIMINATE **2 :** to make impossible **:** PREVENT
rul·er \ˈrü-lər\ *n* **1 :** one that rules; *specif* **:** SOVEREIGN **2 :** a

worker or a machine that rules paper **3 :** a smooth-edged strip (as of wood or metal) used for guiding a pen or pencil in drawing lines or for measuring — **rul·er·ship** \-ˌship\ *n*

1rul·ing \'rü-liŋ\ *n* **:** an official or authoritative decision, decree, statement, or interpretation

2ruling *adj* **1 a :** exerting power or authority **b :** CHIEF, PREDOMINATING **2 :** generally prevailing **:** CURRENT

1rum \'rəm\ *adj* [earlier *rome*, perh. fr. Romany *rom* gypsy man] **1** *chiefly Brit* **:** QUEER, ODD **2** *chiefly Brit* **:** DIFFICULT, DANGEROUS

2rum *n* [prob. short for obs. *rumbullion* (rum)] **1 :** an alcoholic liquor distilled from a fermented cane product (as molasses) **2 :** alcoholic liquor

Ru·ma·nian \rü-'mā-nē-ən, -nyən\ *var of* ROMANIAN

rum·ba \'rəm-bə, 'rüm-, 'rüm-\ *n* [AmerSp] **1 :** a Cuban Negro dance marked by violent movements **2 :** an American ballroom dance imitative of the Cuban rumba

1rum·ble \'rəm-bəl\ *vb* **rum·bling** \-b(ə-)liŋ\ [ME *rumblen;* akin to MHG *rummeln* to rumble] *vi* **1 :** to make a low heavy rolling sound **2 :** to travel as or with a low reverberating sound **3 :** to speak in a low rolling tone ~ *vt* **1 :** to utter or emit in a low rolling voice **2 :** to polish or otherwise treat (metal parts) in a tumbling barrel — **rum·bler** \-b(ə-)lər\ *n*

2rumble *n* **1 :** a low heavy continuous reverberating often muffled sound **2 :** a seat for servants behind the body of a carriage **3 :** TUMBLING BARREL **4 a :** widespread expression of dissatisfaction or unrest **b** *slang* **:** a street fight esp. among teen-age gangs

rumble seat *n* **:** a folding seat in the back of an automobile (as a coupe or roadster) not covered by the top

rum·bly \'rəm-b(ə-)lē\ *adj* **:** tending to rumble or rattle

ru·men \'rü-mən\ *n, pl* **ru·mi·na** \-mə-nə\ *or* **rumens** [NL, fr. L, gullet] **:** the large first compartment of the stomach of a ruminant in which cellulose is broken down by the action of symbionts — **ru·mi·nal** \-mən-ᵊl\ *adj*

1ru·mi·nant \'rü-mə-nənt\ *n* **:** a ruminant mammal

2ruminant *adj* **1 a** (1) **:** chewing the cud (2) **:** characterized by chewing again what has been swallowed **b :** of or relating to a suborder (Ruminantia) of even-toed hoofed mammals (as sheep, giraffes, deer, and camels) that chew the cud and have a complex 3- or 4-chambered stomach **2 :** given to or engaged in contemplation **:** MEDITATIVE — **ru·mi·nant·ly** *adv*

ru·mi·nate \'rü-mə-ˌnāt\ *vb* [L *ruminatus*, pp. of *ruminari* to chew the cud, muse upon, fr. *rumin-, rumen* gullet; akin to Skt *romantha* ruminant] *vt* **1 :** to muse upon **:** CONTEMPLATE **2 :** to chew repeatedly for an extended period ~ *vi* **1 :** to chew again what has been chewed slightly and swallowed **:** chew a cud **2 :** to engage in contemplation **:** REFLECT **syn** see PONDER — **ru·mi·na·tion** \ˌrü-mə-'nā-shən\ *n* — **ru·mi·na·tive** \'rü-mə-ˌnāt-iv\ *adj* — **ru·mi·na·tive·ly** *adv* — **ru·mi·na·tor** \-ˌnāt-ər\ *n*

1rum·mage \'rəm-ij\ *n* [obs. E *rummage* act of packing cargo, modif. of MF *arrimage*] **1 :** a thorough search esp. among a confusion of objects or into every section **2 a :** a confused miscellaneous collection **b :** items for sale at a rummage sale

2rummage *vt* **1 :** to make a thorough search through **:** RANSACK **2 :** to discover by searching **3 :** to examine minutely and completely ~ *vi* **1 :** to make a thorough search or investigation **2 :** to engage in a haphazard search — **rum·mag·er** *n*

rummage sale *n* **:** a sale of donated articles usu. by a church or charitable organization

rum·mer \'rəm-ər\ *n* [G or D; G *römer*, fr. D *roemer*] **:** a large tall glass drinking cup

1rum·my \'rəm-ē\ *adj* **:** QUEER, ODD

2rummy *n* **:** DRUNKARD

3rummy *n* [perh. fr. *1rummy*] **:** a card game in which each player tries to assemble groups of three or more cards of the same rank or suit and to be the first to meld all his cards

1ru·mor \'rü-mər\ *n* [ME *rumour*, fr. MF, fr. L *rumor;* akin to OE *rēon* to lament, Gk *ōryesthai* to howl] **1 :** talk or opinion widely disseminated with no discernible source **:** HEARSAY **2 :** a statement or report current without known authority for its truth **3 :** a soft low indistinct sound **:** MURMUR

2rumor *vt* **ru·mor·ing** \'rüm-(ə-)riŋ\ **:** to tell or spread by rumor

ru·mor·mon·ger \'rü-mər-ˌməŋ-gər, -ˌmäŋ-\ *n* **:** one who spreads rumors

rump \'rəmp\ *n* [ME, of Scand origin; akin to Icel *rumpr* rump; akin to MHG *rumph* torso] **1 a :** the upper rounded part of the hindquarters of a quadruped mammal **b :** BUTTOCKS **c :** the sacral or dorsal part of the posterior end of a bird **2 :** a cut of beef between the loin and round **3 :** a small fragment remaining after the separation of the larger part of a group or an area; *esp* **:** a group (as a parliament) carrying on in the name of the original body after the departure or expulsion of a large number of its members

1rum·ple \'rəm-pəl\ *n* **:** FOLD, WRINKLE

2rumple *vb* **rum·pling** \-p(ə-)liŋ\ [D *rompelen;* akin to OHG *rimpfan* to wrinkle, L *curvus* curved] *vt* **1 :** WRINKLE, CRUMPLE **2 :** to make unkempt **:** TOUSLE ~ *vi* **:** to become rumpled

rum·ply \'rəm-p(ə-)lē\ *adj* **:** RUMPLED

rum·pus \'rəm-pəs\ *n* [origin unknown] **:** DISTURBANCE, FRACAS

rumpus room *n* **:** a room usu. in the basement of a home set apart for games, parties, and recreation

rum·run·ner \'rəm-ˌrən-ər\ *n* **:** a person or ship engaged in bringing prohibited alcoholic liquor ashore or across a border — **rum-running** \-ˌrən-iŋ\ *adj*

1run \'rən\ *vb* **ran** \'ran\ **run; run·ning** [ME *ronnen*, alter. of *rinnen*, v.i. (fr. OE *iernan, rinnan* & ON *rinna*) & of *rennen*, v.t., fr. ON *renna;* akin to OHG *rinnan*, v.i., to run, OE *rīsan* to rise] *vi* **1 a :** to go faster than a walk; *specif* **:** to go steadily by springing steps so that both feet leave the ground for an instant in each step **b** *of a horse* **:** to move at a fast gallop **c :** FLEE, RETREAT, ESCAPE ⟨dropped his gun and *ran*⟩ **2 a :** to go without restraint **:** move freely about at will ⟨let his chickens ~ loose⟩ **b :** to keep company **:** CONSORT — used with *with* chiefly of male animals ⟨a ram *running* with ewes⟩ **c :** to sail before the wind in distinction from reaching or sailing close-hauled **d :** ROAM, ROVE ⟨*running* about with no overcoat⟩ **3 a :** to go rapidly or hurriedly **:** HASTEN ⟨~ and fetch the doctor⟩ **b :** to go in urgency or distress **:** RESORT ⟨~*s* to his mother at every little difficulty⟩ **c :** to make a quick, easy, or casual trip or visit ⟨*ran* over to borrow some sugar⟩ **4 a :** to contend in a race **b :** to enter into an election contest **5 a :** to move on or as if on wheels **:** GLIDE ⟨file drawers *running* on ball bearings⟩ **b :** to roll forward rapidly or freely **c :** to pass or slide freely ⟨rope ~*s* through the pulley⟩ **d :** to ravel lengthwise ⟨stockings guaranteed not to ~⟩ **6 :** to sing or play a musical passage quickly ⟨~ up the scale⟩ **7 a :** to go back and forth **:** PLY **b** *of fish* **:** to migrate or move in schools; *esp* **:** to ascend a river to spawn **8 a :** TURN, ROTATE ⟨a swiftly *running* grindstone⟩ **b :** FUNCTION, OPERATE ⟨engine ~*s* on gasoline⟩ **9 a :** to continue in force or operation ⟨the contract has two more years to ~⟩ **b :** to accompany as a valid obligation or right **c :** to continue to accrue or become payable ⟨interest on the loan ~*s* from last July 1st⟩ **10 :** to pass from one state to another ⟨~ into debt⟩ **11 a :** to flow rapidly or under pressure **b :** MELT, FUSE **c :** SPREAD, DISSOLVE ⟨colors guaranteed not to ~⟩ **d :** to discharge pus or serum ⟨a *running* sore⟩ **12 a :** to develop rapidly in some specific direction; *esp* **:** to throw out an elongated shoot of growth **b :** to tend to produce or develop a specified quality or feature ⟨they ~ to big noses in that family⟩ **13 a :** to lie in or take a certain direction ⟨the boundary line ~*s* east⟩ **b :** to lie or extend in relation to something **c :** to go back **:** REACH **d :** to be in a certain form or expression ⟨letter ~*s* as follows⟩ or order of succession ⟨house numbers ~ in odd numbers from 3 to 57⟩ **14 a :** to occur persistently **:** RECUR ⟨musical talent seems to ~ in his family⟩ **b :** to continue to be of a specified size or character or quality ⟨profits were *running* high⟩ **c :** to exist or occur in a continuous range of variation **d :** to play on a stage a number of successive days or nights ⟨the piece *ran* for six months⟩ **15 a :** to spread or pass quickly from point to point ⟨chills *ran* up his spine⟩ **b :** to be current **:** CIRCULATE ⟨speculation *ran* rife on who the candidate would be⟩ ~ *vt* **1 a :** to cause (an animal) to go at speed **:** ride or drive fast **b :** to bring to a specified condition by or as if by running ⟨*ran* himself to death⟩ **c :** to go in pursuit of **:** HUNT, CHASE **d :** to follow the trail of backward **:** TRACE ⟨*ran* the rumor to its source⟩ **e :** to enter, register, or enroll as a contestant in a race **f :** to put forward as a candidate for office **2 a :** to drive (livestock) esp. to a grazing place **b :** to provide pasturage for (livestock) **c :** to keep or maintain (livestock) on or as if on pasturage **3 a :** to pass over or traverse with speed **b :** to accomplish or perform by running ⟨*running* errands for a bank⟩ **c :** to flee from **d :** to slip through or past ⟨~ a blockade⟩ **4 a :** to cause to penetrate or enter **:** THRUST ⟨*ran* a splinter into his toe⟩ **b :** STITCH **c :** to cause to pass **:** LEAD ⟨~ a wire in from the antenna⟩ **d :** to cause to collide ⟨*ran* his head into a post⟩ **e :** SMUGGLE **5 :** to cause to pass lightly or quickly over, along, or into something ⟨*ran* his eye down the list⟩ **6 a :** to cause or allow (as a vehicle, a vessel) to go in a specified manner or direction ⟨*ran* his car off the road⟩ **b :** OPERATE ⟨~ a taxi⟩ **c :** to carry on **:** MANAGE, CONDUCT ⟨~ a factory⟩ **7 a :** to be full of or drenched with ⟨streets *ran* blood⟩ **b :** CONTAIN, ASSAY **8 :** to cause to move or flow in a specified way or into a specified position ⟨~ cards into a file⟩ **9 a :** to melt and cast in a mold ⟨~ bullets⟩ **b :** TREAT, PROCESS, REFINE ⟨~ oil in a still⟩ **10 :** to make oneself liable to **:** INCUR ⟨*ran* the risk of discovery⟩ **11 :** to mark out ⟨~ a contour line on a map⟩ **:** DRAW ⟨~ a line through the word to be deleted⟩ **12 :** to permit (as charges, accounts, bills) to accumulate before settling ⟨~ an account at the grocery⟩ **13 a :** to run off ⟨a book to be ~ on lightweight paper⟩ ⟨a job to be ~ 4-up⟩ **b :** to carry in a printed medium **:** PRINT **14 a :** to make (a series of counts) without a miss ⟨~ 19 in an inning in billiards⟩ **b :** to lead winning cards of (a suit) successively **15 :** to make (a golf ball) roll forward after alighting — **run across :** to meet with or discover by chance — **run after 1 :** PURSUE, CHASE; *esp* **:** to seek the company of **2 :** to take up with **:** FOLLOW ⟨*run after* new theories⟩ — **run against 1 :** to meet suddenly or unexpectedly **2 :** to work or take effect unfavorably to **:** DISFAVOR, OPPOSE — **run a temperature :** to have a fever — **run false :** to save distance by running directly for the game instead of following the scent or track — **run foul of :** to collide with ⟨*ran foul of* a hidden reef⟩ **:** run into conflict with or hostility to ⟨*run foul of* the law⟩ — **run into 1 a :** to change or transform into **:** BECOME **b :** to merge with **c :** to mount up to ⟨a boat like that one *runs into* money⟩ **2 a :** to collide with **b :** ENCOUNTER, MEET ⟨*ran into* an old classmate the other day⟩ — **run riot 1 :** to act wildly or without restraint **2 :** to occur in profusion — **run short :** to become insufficient — **run short of :** to use up — **run to seed 1 :** to exhaust vitality in producing seed **2 :** to cease growing — **run upon :** to run across **:** meet with

2run *n* **1 a :** an act or the action of running **:** continued rapid movement **b :** a quickened gallop **c** (1) **:** the act of migrating or ascending a river to spawn (2) **:** an assemblage of fish so migrating **d :** a running race ⟨a mile ~⟩ **e** (1) **:** a score made in cricket each time the batsmen safely change ends (2) **:** a score made in baseball by a runner reaching home plate safely **f :** strength or ability to run ⟨two laps took most of the ~ out of him⟩ **2 a** *chiefly Midland* **:** CREEK 2 **b :** something that flows in the course of a certain operation or during a certain time ⟨the first ~ of sap in sugar maples⟩ **3 a :** the stern of the underwater body of a ship from where it begins to curve or slope upward and inward **b :** the direction in which a vein of ore lies **c :** a direction of secondary or minor cleavage **:** GRAIN ⟨~ of a mass of granite⟩ **d** (1) **:** the horizontal distance covered by a flight of steps (2) **:** the horizontal distance from the wall plate to the center line of a building **e :** general tendency or direction **4 :** a continuous series esp. of things of identical or similar sort: as **a :** a rapid scale passage **b :** a number of rapid, small dance steps executed in even tempo **c :** the act of making successively a number of successful shots or strokes; *also* **:** the score thus made ⟨a ~ of 20 in billiards⟩ **d :** an unbroken course of performances or showings **e :** a set of consecutive measurements, readings, or observations **f :** persistent and heavy demands from depositors, creditors, or customers ⟨a ~ on a bank⟩ **g :** SEQUENCE 2b **5 :** the quantity of work turned out in a continuous operation **6 :** the usual or normal kind, character, type, or group ⟨average ~ of college graduates⟩ **7 a :** the distance covered in a period of continuous traveling or sailing **b :** a course or route mapped out and traveled with regularity **:** TRIP **c :** a news reporter's regular territory **:** BEAT **d :** the distance a golf ball travels after touching the ground **e :** freedom of movement in or access to a place or area ⟨has the ~ of his friend's house⟩ **8 :** the period during which a machine or plant is in continuous operation **9 a :** a way, track, or path frequented by animals **b :** an enclosure for livestock where they may feed or exercise **c** *Austral* **:** a large area of land

used for grazing ⟨sheep ~⟩ : RANCH, STATION ⟨run-holder⟩ **d** : an inclined passageway **10 a** : an inclined course (as for skiing or bobsledding) **b** : a support (as a track, pipe, or trough) on which something runs **11 a** : a ravel in a knitted fabric (as in hosiery) caused by the breaking of stitches **b** : a paint defect caused by excessive flow — **in the long run** : in the course of sufficiently prolonged time, trial, or experience — **on the run 1** : in haste : without pausing **2** : in retreat : running away

³run *adj* **1 a** : MELTED ⟨~ butter⟩ **b** : made from molten material : cast in a mold ⟨~ metal⟩ ⟨~ joint⟩ **2** *of fish* : having made a migration or spawning run **3** : exhausted or winded from running

run·about \ˈrən-ə-ˌbau̇t\ *n* **1** : one who wanders about : STRAY **2** : a light open wagon, roadster, or motorboat

run·a·gate \ˈrən-ə-ˌgāt\ *n* [alter. of *renegate*, fr. ML *renegatus* — more at RENEGADE] **1** : FUGITIVE, RUNAWAY **2** : VAGABOND

run along *vi* : to go away : be on one's way : DEPART

run·around \ˈrən-ə-ˌrau̇nd\ *n* **1** : matter typeset in shortened measure to run around something (as a cut) **2** : deceptive or delaying action esp. in response to a request

run away *vi* **1** : FLEE, DESERT **2** : to leave home; *esp* : ELOPE **3** : to run out of control : STAMPEDE, BOLT — **run away with 1** : to take away in haste r secretly; *esp* : STEAL **2** : to outshine the others in (a theatrical performance) **3** : to carry or drive beyond prudent or reasonable limits ⟨his imagination *ran away with* him⟩

¹run·away \ˈrən-ə-ˌwā\ *n* **1** : FUGITIVE **2** : the act of running away out of control; *also* : a horse that is running out of control

²runaway *adj* **1** : running away : FUGITIVE **2** : accomplished by elopement or during flight **3** : won by or having a long lead **4** : subject to uncontrolled changes ⟨~ inflation⟩

run·ci·ble spoon \ˌrən(t)-sə-bəl-\ *n* [coined with an obscure meaning by Edward Lear] : a sharp-edged fork with three broad curved prongs

run·ci·nate \ˈrən(t)-sə-ˌnāt\ *adj* [L *runcinatus*, pp. of *runcinare* to plane off, fr. *runcina* plane] : pinnately cut with the lobes pointing downward

run·dle \ˈrən-dᵊl\ *n* [ME *roundel* circle — more at ROUNDEL] **1** : a step of a ladder : RUNG **2** : the drum of a windlass or capstan

rund·let *or* **run·let** \ˈrən-(d)lət\ *n* [ME *roundelet* — more at ROUNDLET] **1** : a small barrel : KEG **2** : an old unit of liquid capacity equal to 18 U.S. gallons

run down *vt* **1 a** : to collide with and knock down **b** : to run against and sink **2 a** : to chase until exhausted or captured **b** : to find by search : trace the source of **c** : to tag out (a base runner) between bases **3** : DISPARAGE ~ *vi* **1** : to cease to operate because of the exhaustion of motive power ⟨that clock *ran down* hours ago⟩ **2** : to decline in physical condition

run–down \ˈrən-ˈdau̇n\ *adj* **1** : being in poor repair : DILAPIDATED **2** : worn out : EXHAUSTED **3** : completely unwound

run·down \-ˌdau̇n\ *n* : an item-by-item report : SUMMARY

rune \ˈrün\ *n* [ON & OE *rūn* mystery, runic character, writing; akin to OHG *rūna* secret discussion] **1** : one of the characters of an alphabet prob. derived from Latin and Greek and used by the Germanic peoples from about the 3d to the 13th centuries **2** : MYSTERY, MAGIC **3** [Finn *runo*, of Gmc origin; akin to ON *rūn*] **a** : a Finnish or Old Norse poem **b** : POEM, SONG — **ru·nic** \ˈrü-nik\ *adj*

¹rung *past of* RING

²rung \ˈrəŋ\ *n* [ME, fr. OE *hrung*; akin to OE *hring* ring — more at RING] **1** *archaic Scot* : a heavy staff or cudgel **2** : a spoke of a wheel **3 a** : one of the rounds of a chair **b** : one of the crosspieces of a ladder **4** : a stage in an ascent : DEGREE

run in *vt* **1 a** : to make (typeset matter) continuous without a paragraph or other break **b** : to insert as additional matter **2** : to arrest for a minor offense ~ *vi* : to pay a casual visit

run–in \ˈrən-ˌin\ *n* **1** : something inserted as a substantial addition in copy or typeset matter **2** : ALTERCATION, QUARREL

run·less \ˈrən-ləs\ *adj* : scoring no runs

run·let \ˈrən-lət\ *n* : RUNNEL

run·nel \ˈrən-ᵊl\ *n* [alter. of ME *rinel*, fr. OE *rynel*; akin to OE *rinnan* to run — more at RUN] : RIVULET, STREAMLET

run·ner \ˈrən-ər\ *n* **1 a** : one that runs : RACER **b** : BASE RUNNER **c** : a football player in possession of a live ball **2 a** : MESSENGER **b** one that smuggles or distributes illicit or contraband goods (as drugs, liquor, or guns) **3 a** : any of various large active carangid fishes **b** : BLACKSNAKE **4 a** : either of the longitudinal pieces on which a sled or sleigh slides **b** : the part of a skate that slides on the ice : BLADE **c** : the support of a drawer or a sliding door **5 a** : a growth produced by a plant in running; *esp* : STOLON 1 **b** : a plant that forms or spreads by means of runners **c** : a twining vine (as a scarlet runner) **6 a** : a long narrow carpet for a hall or staircase **b** : a narrow decorative cloth cover for a table or dresser top

runner bean *n, chiefly Brit* : SCARLET RUNNER

run·ner–up \ˈrən-ə-ˌrəp, ˌrən-ə-ˈ\ *n* : the competitor in a contest that finishes next to the winner

¹run·ning *adj* **1** : FLUID, RUNNY **2** : INCESSANT, CONTINUOUS ⟨a ~ battle⟩ **3** : measured in a straight line ⟨cost of lumber per ~ foot⟩ **4** : FLOWING, CURSIVE **5** : initiated or performed while running or with a running start **6** : fitted or trained for running rather than walking, trotting, or jumping ⟨~ horse⟩

²running *adv* : in succession : CONSECUTIVELY

running board *n* : a footboard esp. at the side of an automobile

running gear *n* **1** : the parts of an automobile chassis not used in developing, transmitting, and controlling power **2** : the working and carrying parts of a machine (as a locomotive)

running hand *n* : handwriting in which the letters are usu. slanted and the words formed without lifting the pen

running head *n* : a headline repeated on consecutive pages (as of a book) — called also *running headline*

running knot *n* : a knot that slips along the rope or line round which it is tied; *esp* : an overhand slipknot

running light *n* : one of the lights carried by a ship under way at night or on the wing and fuselage of an airplane

running mate *n* **1** : a horse entered in a race to set the pace for a horse of the same owner or stable **2** : a candidate running for a subordinate place on a ticket; *esp* : the candidate for vice-president **3** : a person frequently seen in close association with another

running stitch *n* : a small even stitch run in and out in cloth

running title *n* : the title or short title of a volume printed at the top of left-hand text pages or sometimes of all text pages

run·ny \ˈrən-ē\ *adj* : having a tendency to run ⟨watery eyes and ~ nose⟩

run off *vt* **1 a** : to recite or compose rapidly or glibly **b** : to produce by a printing press **c** : to cause to be run or played to a finish **d** : to decide (as a race) by a runoff **e** : to carry out (a test) **2** : to draw off : drain off **3 a** : to drive off (as trespassers) **b** : to steal (as cattle) by driving away ~ *vi* : to run away — **run off with** : to carry off : STEAL

run·off \ˈrən-ˌȯf\ *n* **1** : the portion of the precipitation on the land that ultimately reaches streams; *esp* : the water from rain or melted snow that flows over the surface **2** : a final race, contest, or election to decide an earlier one that has not resulted in a decision in favor of any one competitor

run–of–the–mill \ˌrən-ə(v)-t͟hə-ˈmil\ *adj* : not outstanding in quality or rarity : AVERAGE

run–of–the–mine \-ˈmīn\ *adj* **1** : UNGRADED ⟨~ coal⟩ **2** : RUN-OF-THE-MILL

run on *vi* **1** : to keep going : CONTINUE **2** : to talk or narrate at length ~ *vt* **1** : to carry on (matter in type) without a break or a new paragraph : run in **2** : to place or add (as an entry in a dictionary) at the end of a paragraphed item

¹run–on \ˈrən-ˈȯn, -ˈän\ *adj* : continuing without rhetorical pause from one line of verse into another

²run–on \-ˌȯn, -ˌän\ *n* : something (as a dictionary entry) that is run on

run–on sentence *n* : a sentence formed with a comma fault

run out *vi* **1 a** : to come to an end : EXPIRE **b** : to become exhausted or used up : FAIL **2** : to jut out ~ *vt* **1** : to finish out (as a course, series, a contest) : COMPLETE **2 a** : to fill out (a line) with quads, leaders, or ornaments **b** : to set (as the first line of a paragraph) with a hanging indention **3** : to exhaust (oneself) in running **4** : to cause to leave by force or coercion : EXPEL — **run out of** : to use up the available supply of

run over *vi* **1** : OVERFLOW **2** : to exceed a limit ~ *vt* **1** : to go over, examine, repeat, or rehearse quickly **2** : to run down ⟨*ran over* a dog in the road⟩

run–over \ˈrən-ˈō-vər\ *adj* : extending beyond the allotted space

run·over \-ˌō-vər\ *n* : matter for publication that exceeds the space allotted

runt \ˈrənt\ *n* [origin unknown] **1** *chiefly Scot* : a hardened stalk or stem of a plant **2** : an animal unusually small of its kind; *esp* : the smallest of a litter of pigs **3** : a person of small stature or stunted growth — **runt·i·ness** \ˈrənt-ē-nəs\ *n* — **runty** \ˈrənt-ē\ *adj*

run through *vt* **1** : PIERCE **2** : to spend or consume wastefully and rapidly **3** : to read or rehearse without pausing

run–through \ˈrən-ˌthrü\ *n* : a cursory reading, summary, or rehearsal

run up *vi* : to grow rapidly : shoot up ~ *vt* **1** : to increase by bidding : bid up **2** : to stitch quickly **3** : to erect hastily **4** : to run (an airplane engine) at high speed for testing, checking, or warming

run·way \ˈrən-ˌwā\ *n* **1** : the channel of a stream **2 a** : a beaten path made by animals **b** : a passageway for animals **3** : an artificially surfaced strip of ground on a landing field for the landing and takeoff of airplanes **4** : a narrow platform from a stage into an auditorium

ru·pee \rü-ˈpē, ˈrü-(ˌ)pē\ *n* [Hindi *rūpaiyā*, fr. Skt *rūpya* coined silver] — see MONEY table

ru·pi·ah \rü-ˈpē-ə\ *n, pl* **rupiah** *or* **rupiahs** [Hindi *rūpaiyā*] — see MONEY table

ru·pic·o·lous \rü-ˈpik-ə-ləs\ *or* **ru·pic·o·line** \-ˌlīn\ *adj* [L *rupes* rock + *-cola* inhabitant; akin to L *rumpere* — more at WHEEL] : living among, inhabiting, or growing on rocks

¹rup·ture \ˈrəp-chər\ *n* [ME *ruptur*, fr. MF or L; MF *rupture*, fr. L *ruptura* fracture, fr. *ruptus*, pp. of *rumpere* to break — more at REAVE] **1** : breach of peace or concord; *specif* : open hostility or war between nations **2 a** : the tearing apart of a tissue ⟨~ of the heart muscle⟩ ⟨~ of an intervertebral disk⟩ **b** : HERNIA **3** : a breaking apart or the state of being broken apart **syn** see FRACTURE

²rupture *vb* **rup·tur·ing** \-chə-riŋ, -shriŋ\ *vt* **1 a** : to part by violence : BREAK **b** : to create or induce a breach of **2** : to produce a rupture in ~ *vi* : to have a rupture

rup·tured *adj* **1** : torn apart : BROKEN **2** : having a rupture ⟨a ~ appendix⟩

ru·ral \ˈru̇(ə)r-əl\ *adj* [ME, fr. MF, fr. L *ruralis*, fr. *rur-*, *rus* open land — more at ROOM] : of or relating to the country, country people or life, or agriculture — **ru·ral·ism** \-ə-ˌliz-əm\ *n* — **ru·ral·ist** \-ləst\ *n* — **ru·ral·i·ty** \ru̇(ə)r-ˈal-ət-ē\ *n* — **ru·ral·iza·tion** \ˌru̇r-ə-lə-ˈzā-shən\ *n* — **ru·ral·ize** \ˈru̇r-ə-ˌlīz\ *vb* — **ru·ral·ly** \-ə-lē\ *adv*

syn RURAL, RUSTIC, PASTORAL, BUCOLIC mean characteristic of the country. RURAL suggests open country and farming; RUSTIC suggests more clearly a contrast with city life and connotes rudeness and lack of polish; PASTORAL implies an idealized simplicity and peacefulness and apartness from the world; BUCOLIC is stronger than RUSTIC in suggesting loutishness

rural dean *n* : DEAN 1b

rural free delivery *n* : free delivery of mail to a rural area — called also *rural delivery*

rural route *n* : a mail-delivery route in a rural free delivery area

rur·ban \ˈrər-bən, ˈru̇(ə)r-\ *adj* [blend of *rural* and *urban*] : of, relating to, or constituting an area which is chiefly residential but where some farming is carried on

ruse \ˈrüs, ˈrüz\ *n* [F, fr. MF, fr. *ruser* to dodge, deceive] : STRATAGEM, SUBTERFUGE **syn** see TRICK

¹rush \ˈrəsh\ *n* [ME, fr. OE *risc*; akin to MHG *rusch* rush, L *restis* rope] : any of various monocotyledonous often tufted marsh plants (as of the genera *Juncus* and *Scirpus* of the family Juncaceae, the rush family) with cylindrical often hollow stems which are used in bottoming chairs and plaiting mats — **rushy** \-ē\ *adj*

²rush *vb* [ME *russhen*, fr. MF *ruser* to put to flight, repel, deceive, fr. L *recusare* to refuse — more at RECUSANCY] *vi* **1** : to move forward, progress, or act with haste or eagerness or without preparation **2** : to act as carrier of a football in a running play ~ *vt* **1** : to push or impel on or forward with speed, impetuosity, or violence **2** : to perform in a short time or at high speed **3** : to urge to an unnatural speed **4** : to run towards or against in attack : CHARGE **5** : to carry (a ball) forward in a running play **6** : to lavish attention on : COURT — **rush·er** *n*

³rush *n* **1 a** : a violent forward motion **b** : ONSET, ATTACK **c** : a surging of emotion **2 a** : a burst of activity, productivity, or speed

b **:** a sudden insistent demand **3 :** a thronging of people usu. to a new place in search of wealth ⟨gold ∼⟩ **4 :** the act of carrying a football during a game **:** running play **5 :** a round of attention usu. involving extensive social activity **6 :** a print of a motion-picture scene processed directly after the shooting for review by the director or producer

⁴rush *adj* **:** requiring or marked by special speed or urgency ⟨∼ orders⟩ ⟨∼ season⟩

rush candle *n* **:** RUSHLIGHT

rush·ee \ˌrəsh-'ē\ *n* **:** a college or university student who is being rushed by a fraternity or sorority

rush·light \'rəsh-ˌlīt\ *n* **:** a candle made of the pith of various rushes and dipped in grease

rusk \'rəsk\ *n* [modif. of Sp & Pg *rosca* coil, twisted roll] **1 :** hard crisp bread orig. used as ship's stores **2 :** a sweet or plain bread baked, sliced, and baked again until dry and crisp

Russ \'rəs, 'rüs, 'rüs\ *n, pl* **Russ** *or* **Russ·es** [Russ *Rus'*] **:** RUSSIAN — **Russ** *adj*

Rus·sell's viper \ˌrəs-əlz-\ *n* [Patrick *Russell* †1805 Brit physician] **:** a strikingly marked highly venomous snake (*Vipera russellii*) of southeastern Asia

¹rus·set \'rəs-ət\ *n* [ME, fr. OF *rousset*, fr. *rousset*, adj., russet, fr. *rous* russet, fr. L *russus* red; akin to L *ruber* red — more at RED] **1 :** coarse homespun usu. reddish brown cloth **2 :** a variable color averaging a strong brown **3 :** any of various winter apples having russet rough skins

²russet *adj* **:** of the color russet

rus·set·ing *also* **rus·set·ting** \'rəs-ət-iŋ\ *n* **:** a brownish roughened area on the skin of fruit (as apples, pears, and citrus fruit) caused by injury

Rus·sia leather \ˌrəsh-ə-\ *n* [*Russia*, country in Europe] **:** leather made by tanning various skins with willow, birch, or oak and then rubbing the flesh side with birch oil — called also *Russia calf*

Rus·sian \'rəsh-ən\ *n* **1 a :** one of the people of Russia; *esp* **:** a member of the dominant Slavic-speaking Great Russian ethnic group of Russia **:** one that is of Russian descent **2 a :** a Slavic language of the Russian people that is the official language of the U.S.S.R. **b :** the three Slavic languages of the Russian people including Belorussian and Ukrainian — **Russian** *adj*

Russian blue *n, often cap* **:** a slender long-bodied large-eared domestic cat with short silky bluish gray fur

Russian dressing *n* **:** mayonnaise with added chili sauce, chopped pickles, or pimientos

rus·sian·ize \'rəsh-ə-ˌnīz\ *vt, often cap* **:** to make Russian

Russian olive *n* **:** a chiefly silvery Eurasian large shrub or small tree (*Elaeagnus angustifolia*) cultivated in arid windy regions esp. as a shelterbelt plant

Russian thistle *n* **:** a prickly European herb (*Salsola kali tenuifolia*) that is a serious pest in No. America — called also *Russian tumbleweed*

Russian wolfhound *n* **:** BORZOI

rus·si·fi·ca·tion \ˌrəs-ə-fə-'kā-shən\ *n, often cap* **:** the act or process of being russianized

rus·si·fy \'rəs-ə-ˌfī\ *vt, often cap* **:** RUSSIANIZE

Rus·so- *comb form* [*Russia* & *Russian*] **1** \ˌrəs-ə, 'rəs-, -ō\ **:** Russia **:** Russians ⟨*Russo*phobia⟩ **2** \ˌrəs(h)-(ˌ)ō, ˌrəs(h)-\ **:** Russian and ⟨*Russo*-Japanese⟩

¹rust \'rəst\ *n* [ME, fr. OE *rūst;* akin to OE *rēad* red — more at RED] **1 a :** the reddish brittle coating formed on iron esp. when chemically attacked by moist air and composed essentially of hydrated ferric oxide **b :** the similar coating produced on any of various other metals by corrosion **c :** something resembling rust **:** ACCRETION **2 :** corrosive or injurious influence or effect **3 :** any of numerous destructive diseases of plants produced by fungi (order Uredinales) and characterized by reddish brown pustular lesions; *also* **:** a fungus causing this **4 :** a strong brown

²rust *vi* **1 :** to form rust **:** become oxidized ⟨iron ∼s⟩ **2 :** to degenerate esp. from inaction, lack of use, or passage of time ⟨most men would . . . have allowed their faculties to ∼ —T.B.Macaulay⟩ **3 :** to become reddish brown as if with rust ⟨the leaves slowly ∼*ed*⟩ **4 :** to be affected with a rust fungus ∼ *vt* **1 :** to cause (a metal) to form rust ⟨keep up your bright swords, for the dew will ∼ them —Shak.⟩ **2 :** to impair or corrode by or as if by time, inactivity, or deleterious use **3 :** to cause to become reddish brown **:** turn the color of rust

¹rus·tic \'rəs-tik\ *adj* [ME *rustik*, fr. MF *rustique*, fr. L *rusticus*, fr. *rus* open land — more at ROOM] **1 :** of, relating to, or suitable for the country **:** RURAL **2 a :** made of the rough limbs of trees ⟨∼ furniture⟩ **b :** RUSTICATED ⟨a ∼ joint in masonry⟩ **3 a :** characteristic of or resembling country people **b :** AWKWARD, BOORISH **4 :** PLAIN, STURDY **syn** see RURAL — **rus·ti·cal** \-ti-kəl\ *adj* — **rus·ti·cal·ly** \-ti-k(ə-)lē\ *adv* — **rus·tic·i·ty** \ˌrəs-'tis-ət-ē\ *n*

²rustic *n* **1 :** an inhabitant of a rural area **2 a :** an awkward coarse person **b :** an unsophisticated rural person

rus·ti·cate \'rəs-ti-ˌkāt\ *vi* **:** to go into or reside in the country

: follow a rustic life ∼ *vt* **1 :** to suspend from school or college ⟨had been first *rusticated* from Oxford and then expelled —Anthony Trollope⟩ **2 :** to bevel or rebate (as the edges of stone blocks) to make the joints conspicuous ⟨a *rusticated* stone wall⟩ **3 a :** to compel to reside in the country **b :** to cause to become rustic **:** implant rustic mannerisms in — **rus·ti·ca·tion** \ˌrəs-ti-'kā-shən\ *n* — **rus·ti·ca·tor** \'rəs-ti-ˌkāt-ər\ *n*

rust·i·ly \'rəs-tə-lē\ *adv* **:** in a rusty manner

rust·i·ness \-tē-nəs\ *n* **:** the quality or state of being rusty

¹rus·tle \'rəs-əl\ *vb* **rus·tling** \'rəs-(ə-)liŋ\ [ME *rustelen*] *vi* **1 :** to make or cause a rustle **2 a :** to act or move with energy or speed **b :** to forage food **3 :** to steal cattle ∼ *vt* **1 :** to cause to rustle **2 :** to procure by rustling; *esp* **:** FORAGE **3 :** to take (as cattle) feloniously **:** STEAL — **rus·tler** \-(ə-)lər\ *n*

²rustle *n* **:** a quick succession or confusion of small sounds

rust mite *n* **:** any of various small gall mites that burrow in the surface of leaves or fruits usu. producing brown or reddish patches

rust·proof \'rəst-'prüf\ *adj* **:** incapable of rusting

¹rusty \'rəs-tē\ *adj* **1 :** affected by or as if by rust; *esp* **:** stiff with or as if with rust **2 :** inept and slow through lack of practice or old age **3 a :** of the color rust **b :** dulled in color or appearance by age and use ⟨a ∼ old suit of clothes⟩ **4 :** OUTMODED **5 :** GRATING, HOARSE

²rus·ty \'rəs-tē\ *adj* [alter. of *restive*] *chiefly dial* **:** ill-tempered **:** SURLY

¹rut \'rət\ *n* [ME *rutte*, fr. MF *rut* roar, fr. LL *rugitus*, fr. L *rugitus*, pp. of *rugire* to roar; akin to OE *rēoc* wild, MIr *rucht* roar] **1 :** an annually recurrent state of sexual excitement in the male deer; *broadly* **:** sexual excitement in a mammal esp. when periodic **:** ESTRUS, HEAT **2 :** the period during which rut normally occurs — often used with *the*

²rut *vi* **rut·ted; rut·ting :** to be in or enter into a state of rut

³rut *n* [perh. modif. of MF *route* way, route] **1 a :** a track worn by a wheel or by habitual passage **b :** a groove in which something runs **c :** CHANNEL, FURROW **2 :** a usual or fixed practice **:** a regular course; *esp* **:** a monotonous routine ⟨fall easily into a conversational ∼⟩

⁴rut *vt* **rut·ted; rut·ting :** to make a rut in **:** FURROW

ru·ta·ba·ga \ˌrüt-ə-'bā-gə, ˌrüt-\ *n* [Sw dial. *rotabagge*, fr. *rot* root + *bagge* bag] **:** a turnip (*Brassica napobrassica*) commonly with a very large yellowish root

ruth \'rüth\ *n* [ME *ruthe*, fr. *ruen* to rue] **1 :** compassion for the misery of another **2 :** sorrow for one's own faults **:** REMORSE **syn** see PITY

ru·the·nic \rü-'then-ik, -'thē-nik\ *adj* **:** of, relating to, or derived from ruthenium esp. with a relatively high valence

ru·the·ni·ous \rü-'thē-nē-əs\ *adj* **:** of, relating to, or derived from ruthenium esp. with a relatively low valence

ru·the·ni·um \-nē-əm\ *n* [NL, fr. ML *Ruthenia* Russia] **:** a hard brittle grayish polyvalent rare metallic element occurring in platinum ores and used in hardening platinum alloys — see ELEMENT table

Ruth·er·ford atom \ˌrəth-ə(r)-fərd-\ *n* [Baron Ernest *Rutherford* †1937 E physicist] **:** the atom held to consist of a small dense positively charged nucleus surrounded by planetary electrons

ruth·ful \'rüth-fəl\ *adj* **1 :** full of ruth **:** PITIFUL **2 :** full of sorrow **:** WOEFUL **3 :** causing sorrow — **ruth·ful·ly** \-fə-lē\ *adv* — **ruth·ful·ness** *n*

ruth·less \'rüth-ləs *also* 'rüth-\ *adj* **:** having no ruth **:** MERCILESS, CRUEL ⟨act of savage, ∼ ferocity —J.A.Froude⟩ — **ruth·less·ly** *adv* — **ruth·less·ness** *n*

ru·ti·lant \'rüt-°l-ənt\ *adj* [ME *rutilaunt*, fr. L *rutilant-, rutilans*, pp. of *rutilare* to be reddish, fr. *rutilus* red; akin to L *ruber* red — more at RED] **:** having a reddish glow

ru·tile \'rü-ˌtēl\ *n* [G *rutil*, fr. L *rutilus* reddish; akin to L *ruber* red — more at RED] **:** a mineral TiO_2 that consists of titanium dioxide usu. with a little iron, is of a reddish brown color but when deep red or black is sometimes cut into a gem, and has a brilliant metallic or adamantine luster

rut·tish \'rət-ish\ *adj* **:** inclined to rut **:** LUSTFUL — **rut·tish·ly** *adv* — **rut·tish·ness** *n*

rut·ty \'rət-ē\ *adj* **:** full of ruts

-ry \rē\ *n suffix* [ME *-rie*, fr. OF, short for *-erie* *-ery*] **:** -ERY ⟨wizard*ry*⟩ ⟨citizen*ry*⟩ ⟨ancient*ry*⟩

¹rye \'rī\ *n* [ME, fr. OE *ryge*; akin to OHG *rocko* rye, Lith *rugys*] **1 :** a hardy annual grass (*Secale cereale*) that is widely cultivated as a cereal grass and cover crop **2 :** the seeds of rye

²rye *n* [Romany *rai*, fr. Skt *rājan* king — more at ROYAL] **:** a gypsy gentleman

rye bread *n* **:** bread made wholly or in part of rye flour; *esp* **:** a light bread often with caraway seeds

rye·grass \'rī-ˌgras\ *n* **:** any of several grasses (genus *Lolium*); *esp* **:** perennial ryegrass (*L. perenne*)

rye whiskey *n* **:** a whiskey distilled from rye or from rye and malt

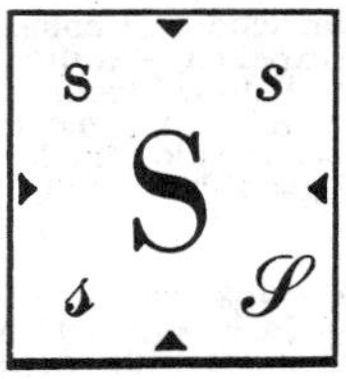

s \ˈes\ *n, often cap, often attrib* **1 a :** the 19th letter of the English alphabet **b :** a graphic representation of this letter **c :** a speech counterpart of orthographic *s* **2 :** a graphic device for reproducing the letter *s* **3 :** one designated *s* esp. as the 18th or when j is used for the 10th the 19th in order or class **4 a :** a grade rating a student's work as satisfactory **b :** one graded or rated with an S **5 :** something shaped like the letter S

¹-s \s *after a voiceless consonant sound,* z *after a voiced consonant sound or a vowel sound*\ *n pl suffix* [ME *-es, -s,* fr. OE *-as,* nom. & acc. pl. ending of some masc. nouns; akin to OS *-os*] **1** — used to form the plural of most nouns that do not end in *s, z, sh, ch,* or postconsonantal *y* ⟨head*s*⟩ ⟨book*s*⟩ ⟨boy*s*⟩ ⟨belief*s*⟩, to form the plural of proper nouns that end in postconsonantal *y* ⟨Mary*s*⟩, and with or without a preceding apostrophe to form the plural of abbreviations, numbers, letters, and symbols used as nouns ⟨MC*s*⟩ ⟨4*s*⟩ ⟨#*s*⟩ ⟨B'*s*⟩ — compare ¹-ES 1 **2** [ME *-es, -s,* pl. ending of nouns, fr. *-es,* gen. sing. ending of nouns (functioning adverbally), fr. OE *-es*] — used to form adverbs denoting usual or repeated action or state ⟨always at home Sunday*s*⟩ ⟨morning*s* he stops by the newsstand⟩

²-s *vb suffix* [ME (Northern & North Midland dial.) *-es,* fr. OE (Northumbrian dial.) *-es, -as,* prob. fr. OE *-es, -as,* 2d sing. pres. indic. ending — more at -EST] — used to form the third person singular present of most verbs that do not end in *s, z, sh, ch,* or postconsonantal *y* ⟨fall*s*⟩ ⟨take*s*⟩ ⟨play*s*⟩ — compare ²-ES

-'s \s *after voiceless consonant sounds other than* s, sh, ch; z *after vowel sounds and voiced consonant sounds other than* z, zh, j; əz *after* s, sh, ch, z, zh, j\ *n suffix or pron suffix* [ME *-es, -s,* gen. sing. ending, fr. OE *-es;* akin to OHG *-es,* gen. sing. ending, Gk *-oio, -ou,* Skt *-asya*] — used to form the possessive of singular nouns ⟨boy'*s*⟩, of plural nouns not ending in *s* ⟨children'*s*⟩, of some pronouns ⟨anyone'*s*⟩, and of word groups functioning as nouns ⟨the man in the corner'*s* hat⟩ or pronouns ⟨someone else'*s*⟩

¹'s *like* -'s\ *vb* [contr. of *is, has, does*] **1 :** IS ⟨she'*s* here⟩ **2 :** HAS ⟨he'*s* seen them⟩ **3 :** DOES ⟨what'*s* he want?⟩

²'s \s\ *pron* [by contr.] **:** US — used with *let* ⟨let'*s*⟩

Saa·nen \ˈsän-ən, ˈzän-\ *n* [*Saanen,* locality in southwest Switzerland] **:** any of a Swiss breed of usu. white and hornless short-haired dairy goats

sab·a·dil·la \ˌsab-ə-ˈdil-ə, -ˈdē-(y)ə\ *n* [Sp *cebadilla*] **:** a Mexican plant (*Schoenocaulon officinalis*) of the lily family; *also* **:** its seeds used as a source of veratrine and in insecticides

sab·bat \ˈsab-ət, sə-ˈbä\ *n, often cap* [F, lit., sabbath, fr. L *sabbatum*] **:** a midnight assembly of diabolists (as witches and sorcerers) held esp. in medieval and Renaissance times to renew allegiance to the devil through mystic and licentious rites

Sab·ba·tar·i·an \ˌsab-ə-ˈter-ē-ən\ *n* [L *sabbatarius,* fr. *sabbatum* sabbath] **1 :** one who keeps tne seventh day of the week as holy in conformity with the letter of the fourth commandment **2 :** one who favors strict observance of the Sabbath — **Sabbatarian** *adj* — **Sab·ba·tar·i·an·ism** \-ē-ə-ˌniz-əm\ *n*

Sab·bath \ˈsab-əth\ *n* [ME *sabat,* fr. OF & OE, fr. L *sabbatum,* fr. Gk *sabbaton,* fr. Heb *shabbāth,* lit., rest] **1** *often cap* **a :** the seventh day of the week observed from Friday evening to Saturday evening as a day of rest and worship by Jews and some Christians **b :** Sunday observed among Christians as a day of rest and worship **2 :** a time of rest

sab·bat·i·cal \sə-ˈbat-i-kəl\ *or* **sab·bat·ic** \-ik\ *adj* [LL *sabbaticus,* fr. Gk *sabbatikos,* fr. *sabbaton*] **1 :** of or relating to the sabbath **2 :** being a recurring period of rest or renewal

sabbatical year *n* **1** *often cap S* **:** a year of rest for the land observed every seventh year in ancient Judea **2 :** a leave granted usu. every seventh year (as to a college professor) for rest, travel, or research — called also *sabbatical leave*

Sa·bel·li·an \sə-ˈbel-ē-ən\ *n* [L *Sabellus* Sabine] **1 :** a member of one of a group of early Italian peoples including Sabines and Samnites **2 :** one or all of several little known languages or dialects of ancient Italy presumably closely related to Oscan and Umbrian — **Sabellian** *adj*

¹sa·ber *or* **sa·bre** \ˈsā-bər\ *n* [F *sabre,* modif. of G dial. *sabel,* fr. MHG, of Slav origin; akin to Russ *sablya* saber] **1 :** a cavalry sword with a curved blade, thick back, and guard **2 :** a light fencing or dueling sword

²saber *or* **sabre** *vt* **sa·bered** *or* **sa·bred; sa·ber·ing** *or* **sa·bring** \-b(ə-)riŋ\ **:** to strike, cut, or kill with a saber

saber rattling *n* **:** ostentatious display of military power

sa·ber–toothed \ˌsā-bər-ˈtütht\ *adj* **:** having long sharp canine teeth

saber–toothed tiger \-ˌtüth(t)-\ *n* **:** any of numerous extinct cats (esp. genus *Smilodon*) widely distributed from the Oligocene through the Pleistocene and characterized by extreme development of the upper canines into curved swordlike piercing or slashing weapons — called also *sa·ber-tooth* \ˈsā-bər-ˌtüth\

sa·bin \ˈsā-bən\ *n* [Wallace C. W. *Sabine* †1919 Am physicist] **:** a unit of acoustic absorption equivalent to the absorption by one square foot of a perfect absorber

Sa·bine \ˈsā-ˌbīn, *esp Brit* ˈsab-ˌīn\ *n* [ME *Sabin,* fr. L *Sabinus*] **1 :** a member of an ancient people of the Apennines northeast of Latium **2 :** the Italic language of the Sabine people — **Sabine** *adj*

¹sa·ble \ˈsā-bəl\ *n, pl* **sables** [ME, sable or its fur, the heraldic color black, black, fr. MF, sable or its fur, the heraldic color black, fr. MLG *sabel* sable or its fur, fr. MHG *zobel,* of Slav origin; akin to Russ *sobol'* sable or its fur] **1 a :** the color black **b :** black clothing worn in mourning — usu. used in pl. **2 a** *or pl* **sable** (1) **:** a carnivorous mammal (*Martes zibellina*) of northern Europe and parts of northern Asia related to the martens and valued for its fur (2) **:** any of various related animals **b :** the fur or pelt of a sable **3 a :** the usu. dark brown color of the fur of the sable **b :** a grayish yellowish brown

²sable *adj* **1 :** of the color black **2 :** DARK

sa·ble·fish \ˈsā-bəl-ˌfish\ *n* **:** a large spiny-finned gray to blackish fish (*Anoplopoma fimbria*) of the Pacific coast that is a leading market fish with a liver rich in vitamins — called also *black cod*

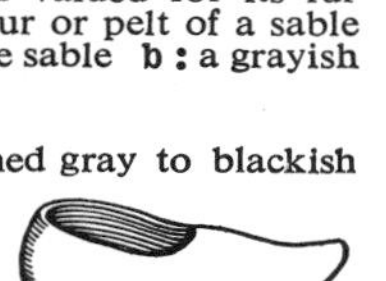

sabot 1a

sa·bot \sa-ˈbō, ˈsab-(ˌ)ō, *for 1b also* ˈsab-ət\ *n* [F] **1 a :** a wooden shoe worn in various European countries **b** (1) **:** a band across the instep in a shoe esp. of the sandal type (2) **:** a shoe having a sabot strap **2 :** a thrust-transmitting carrier that positions a projectile in a tube

¹sab·o·tage \ˈsab-ə-ˌtäzh\ *n* [F, fr. *saboter* to clatter with sabots, botch, sabotage, fr. *sabot*] **1 :** destruction of an employer's property (as tools or materials) or the hindering of manufacturing by discontented workmen **2 :** destructive or obstructive action carried on by a civilian or enemy agent designed to hinder a nation's war effort **3 :** an act or process tending to hamper or hurt

²sabotage *vt* **:** to practice sabotage on **:** WRECK, DESTROY

sab·o·teur \ˌsab-ə-ˈtər, -ˈt(y)u̇(ə)r\ *n* [F, fr. *saboter*] **:** one that commits sabotage

sa·bra \ˈsäb-rə\ *n* [NHeb *sābrāh*] **:** a native-born Israeli

sab·u·lous \ˈsab-yə-ləs\ *adj* [L *sabulosus,* fr. *sabulum* sand — more at SAND] **:** SANDY, GRITTY

sac \ˈsak\ *n* [F, lit., bag, fr. L *saccus* — more at SACK] **:** a pouch within an animal or plant often containing a fluid ⟨a synovial ~⟩ — **sac·like** \ˈsak-ˌlīk\ *adj*

sa·ca·huis·te \ˌsak-ə-ˈwis-tə, ˌsäk-, -tē\ *n* [AmerSp *zacahuiscle,* of AmerInd origin; akin to Nahuatl *zacatl* coarse grass] **:** a bear grass (*Nolina texana*) with long linear leaves used in some areas for forage

sac·a·ton \ˈsak-ə-ˌtōn\ *n* [AmerSp *zacatón,* fr. *zacate* coarse grass, fr. Nahuatl *zacatl*] **:** a coarse perennial grass (*Sporobolus wrightii*) of the southwestern U.S. useful for hay in alkaline regions

sac·cate \ˈsak-ˌāt\ *adj* [NL *saccatus,* fr. L *saccus*] **:** having the form of a sac or pouch

sacchar- *or* **sacchari-** *or* **saccharo-** *comb form* [L *saccharum,* fr. Gk *sakcharon,* fr. Pali *sakkharā,* fr. Skt *śarkarā* gravel, sugar] **:** sugar ⟨*sacchar*ic⟩ ⟨*sacchari*fy⟩ ⟨*saccharo*meter⟩

sac·cha·rase \ˈsak-ə-ˌrās, -ˌrāz\ *n* [ISV] **:** INVERTASE

sac·cha·rate \ˈsak-ə-ˌrāt, -rət\ *n* **1 :** a salt or ester of saccharic acid **2 :** a compound of a sugar usu. with a bivalent metal; *esp* **:** SUCRATE

sac·char·ic \sə-ˈkar-ik, sa-\ *adj* **:** of, relating to, or obtained from saccharine substances

saccharic acid *n* **:** a dicarboxylic acid $C_6H_{10}O_8$ obtained by oxidation of glucose by nitric acid

sac·cha·ride \ˈsak-ə-ˌrīd\ *n* **:** a simple sugar, combination of sugars, or polymerized sugar **:** CARBOHYDRATE

sac·char·i·fi·ca·tion \sə-ˌkar-ə-fə-ˈkā-shən, sa-\ *n* **:** an act or process of saccharifying

sac·char·i·fy \-ˈkar-ə-ˌfī\ *vt* **:** to break (as a complex carbohydrate) into simple sugars

sac·cha·rim·e·ter \ˌsak-ə-ˈrim-ət-ər\ *n* [ISV] **:** a device for measuring the amount of sugar in a solution; *esp* **:** a polarimeter so used

sac·cha·rin \ˈsak-(ə-)rən\ *n* [ISV] **:** a crystalline compound $C_7H_5NO_3S$ that is several hundred times sweeter than cane sugar and is used as a calorie-free sweetener

sac·cha·rine \ˈsak-(ə-)rən, -ə-ˌrēn, -ə-ˌrīn\ *adj* [L *saccharum*] **1 a :** of, relating to, or resembling that of sugar ⟨~ taste⟩ ⟨~ fermentation⟩ **b :** yielding or containing sugar ⟨~ vegetables⟩ **2 :** overly sweet ⟨~ flavor⟩ **3 :** ingratiatingly agreeable or friendly — **sac·cha·rin·i·ty** \ˌsak-ə-ˈrin-ət-ē\ *n*

sac·cha·roi·dal \ˌsak-ə-ˈrȯid-ᵊl\ *adj* **:** having a granular texture like that of loaf sugar

sac·cha·rom·e·ter \-ˈräm-ət-ər\ *n* **:** SACCHARIMETER; *esp* **:** a hydrometer with a special scale

sac·cha·ro·my·cete \ˌsak-ə-rō-ˈmī-ˌsēt, -(ˌ)mī-ˈsēt\ *n* [ISV] **:** a yeast fungus — **sac·cha·ro·my·ce·tic** \-(ˌ)mī-ˈsēt-ik, -ˈset-\ *adj*

sac·cha·rose \ˈsak-ə-ˌrōs, -ˌrōz\ *n* **:** SUCROSE; *broadly* **:** DISACCHARIDE

sac·cu·lar \ˈsak-yə-lər\ *adj* **:** resembling a sac

sac·cu·lat·ed \-ˌlāt-əd\ *adj* **:** having or formed of a series of saccular expansions — **sac·cu·la·tion** \ˌsak-yə-ˈlā-shən\ *n*

sac·cule \ˈsak-(ˌ)yü(ə)l\ *n* [NL *sacculus,* fr. L, dim. of *saccus* bag — more at SACK] **:** a little sac; *specif* **:** the smaller chamber of the membranous labyrinth of the ear

sac·er·do·tal \ˌsas-ər-ˈdōt-ᵊl, ˌsak-\ *adj* [ME, fr. MF, fr. L *sacerdotalis,* fr. *sacerdot-, sacerdos* priest, fr. *sacer* sacred + *-dot-, -dos* (akin to *facere* to make) — more at SACRED, DO] **1 :** of or relating to priests or a priesthood **:** PRIESTLY **2 :** of, relating to, or suggesting sacerdotalism — **sac·er·do·tal·ly** \-ᵊl-ē\ *adv*

sac·er·do·tal·ism \-ᵊl-ˌiz-əm\ *n* **:** religious belief emphasizing the powers of priests as essential mediators between God and man — **sac·er·do·tal·ist** \-ᵊl-əst\ *n*

sa·chem \ˈsā-chəm\ *n* [Narraganset & Pequot *sachima*] **1 :** a No. American Indian chief; *specif* **:** the chief of a confederation of Algonquian tribes of the north Atlantic coast **2 :** a Tammany leader — **sa·chem·ic** \sā-ˈchem-ik, ˈsā-chə-mik\ *adj*

sa·chet \sa-ˈshā\ *n* [F, fr. OF, dim. of *sac* bag — more at SAC] **:** a small bag containing a perfumed powder used to scent clothes

¹sack \ˈsak\ *n* [ME *sak* bag, sackcloth, fr. OE *sacc;* akin to OHG *sac* bag; both fr. a prehistoric Gmc word borrowed fr. L *saccus* bag & LL *saccus* sackcloth, both fr. Gk *sakkos* bag, sackcloth, of Sem origin; akin to Heb *śaq* bag, sackcloth] **1 a :** a large bag of coarse strong material **b :** a small container of paper or similar material **2 :** the amount contained in a sack; *esp* **:** a fixed amount of a certain commodity sometimes used as a unit of measure **3 a :** a woman's loose-fitting dress **b :** a short usu. loose-fitting coat for women and children **c :** SACQUE 2 **4 :** DISMISSAL — usu. used with *get* or *give* **5 :** BUNK, BED **6 :** a base in baseball

²sack *vt* **1 :** to put or place in a sack **2 :** to dismiss esp. summarily

³sack *n* [modif. of MF *sec* dry, fr. L *siccus;* akin to OHG *sīhan* to filter, Gk *hikmas* moisture] **:** a usu. dry white wine imported to England from the south of Europe during the 16th and 17th centuries

⁴sack *n* [MF *sac,* fr. OIt *sacco,* lit., bag, fr. L *saccus*] **:** the plundering of a captured town

⁵sack *vt* **1 :** to plunder (as a town) after capture **2 :** to strip of valuables **:** LOOT **syn** see RAVAGE — **sack·er** *n*

sack·but \ˈsak-(ˌ)bət\ *n* [MF *saqueboute,* lit., hooked lance, fr. OF, fr. *saquer* to pull + *bouter* to push — more at BUTT] **1 :** the medieval trombone **2 :** TRIGON

sack·cloth \ˈsak-ˌ(k)lȯth\ *n* **1 :** a coarse cloth of goat or camel's hair or of flax, hemp, or cotton **2 :** a garment of sackcloth worn as a sign of mourning or penitence

sack coat *n* **:** a man's single-breasted or double-breasted jacket with a straight unfitted back

sack·ful \'sak-ˌfu̇l\ *n, pl* **sackfuls** \-ˌfu̇lz\ *or* **sacks·ful** \'saks-ˌfu̇l\ **:** the quantity that fills a sack

sack·ing \'sak-iŋ\ *n* **:** material for sacks; *esp* **:** a coarse fabric (as burlap or gunny)

sack race *n* **:** a race run by persons each with his legs in a sack

sacque \'sak\ *n* [alter. of ¹*sack*] **1 :** SACK 3a, 3b **2 :** a jacket for a baby

¹**sacr-** *or* **sacro-** *comb form* [ME *sacr-*, fr. MF & L; MF, fr. L *sacr-*, *sacer* — more at SACRED] **:** sacred ⟨*sacral*⟩

²**sacr-** *or* **sacro-** *comb form* [NL, fr. *sacrum*, fr. L, neut. of *sacr-*, *sacer* sacred] **1 :** sacrum ⟨*sacral*⟩ **2 :** sacral and ⟨*sacroiliac*⟩

sa·crad \'sak-ˌrad, 'sā-ˌkrad\ *adv* **:** toward the sacrum

¹**sa·cral** \'sak-rəl, 'sā-krəl\ *adj* **:** of, relating to, or lying near the sacrum

²**sa·cral** \'sā-krəl\ *adj* **:** HOLY, SACRED

sac·ra·ment \'sak-rə-mənt\ *n* [ME *sacrement, sacrament*, fr. OF & LL; OF, fr. LL *sacramentum*, fr. L, oath of allegiance, obligation, fr. *sacrare* to consecrate] **1 :** a formal religious act that is sacred as a sign or symbol of a spiritual reality; *esp* **:** one instituted or recognized by Jesus Christ **2 a** *cap* **:** BLESSED SACRAMENT **b :** the elements or action of a sacrament

¹**sac·ra·men·tal** \ˌsak-rə-'ment-ᵊl\ *adj* **1 :** of, relating to, or having the character of a sacrament **2 :** suggesting a sacrament (as in sacredness) — **sac·ra·men·tal·ly** \-ᵊl-ē\ *adv*

²**sacramental** *n* **:** an action or object (as the rosary) of ecclesiastical origin serving as an indirect means of grace by producing devotion

sac·ra·men·tal·ism \-ᵊl-ˌiz-əm\ *n* **:** belief in or use of sacramental rites, acts, or objects; *specif* **:** belief that the sacraments are inherently efficacious and necessary for salvation — **sac·ra·men·tal·ist** \-ᵊl-əst\ *n*

Sac·ra·men·tar·i·an \ˌsak-rə-ˌmen-'ter-ē-ən, -mən-\ *n* **1 :** one who interprets sacraments as merely visible symbols **2 :** SACRAMENTALIST — **Sacramentarian** *adj* — **Sac·ra·men·tar·i·an·ism** \-ē-ə-ˌniz-əm\ *n*

sa·cred \'sā-krəd\ *adj* [ME, fr. pp. of *sacren* to consecrate, fr. OF *sacrer*, fr. L *sacrare*, fr. *sacr-*, *sacer* holy, cursed; akin to L *sancire* to make sacred, Hitt *saklais* rite] **1 a :** set apart for the service or worship of deity **b :** devoted exclusively to one service or use (as of a person or purpose) **2 a :** worthy of religious veneration **:** HOLY **b :** entitled to reverence **3 :** of or relating to religion **:** RELIGIOUS **4** *obs* **:** ACCURSED — **sa·cred·ly** *adv* — **sa·cred·ness** *n*

sacred cow *n* **:** a person or thing immune from criticism

sacred mushroom *n* **:** MESCAL BUTTON

¹**sac·ri·fice** \'sak-rə-ˌfīs, -fəs *also* -ˌfīz\ *n* [ME, fr. OF, fr. L *sacrificium*, fr. *sacr-*, *sacer*] **1 :** an act of offering something precious to deity; *specif* **:** the offering of an immolated victim **2 :** something offered in sacrifice **3 a :** destruction or surrender of something for the sake of something else **b :** something given up or lost ⟨the ~*s* made by parents⟩ **4 :** LOSS, DEPRIVATION

²**sac·ri·fice** \-ˌfīs, -ˌfīz *also* -fəs\ *vt* **1 :** to offer as a sacrifice **:** IMMOLATE **2 :** to suffer loss of, give up, renounce, injure, or destroy for an ideal, belief, or end **3 :** to sell at a loss ~ *vi* **1 :** to offer up or perform rites of a sacrifice **2 :** to make a sacrifice hit in baseball — **sac·ri·fic·er** *n*

sacrifice fly *n* **:** an outfield fly in baseball caught by a fielder after which a runner scores

sacrifice hit *n* **:** a bunt in baseball that allows a runner to advance one base while the batter is put out

sac·ri·fi·cial \ˌsak-rə-'fish-əl\ *adj* **:** of, relating to, of the nature of, or involving sacrifice — **sac·ri·fi·cial·ly** \-ə-lē\ *adv*

sac·ri·lege \'sak-rə-lij\ *n* [ME, fr. OF, fr. L *sacrilegium*, fr. *sacrilegus* one who steals sacred things, fr. *sacr-*, *sacer* + *legere* to gather, steal — more at LEGEND] **1 :** theft or violation of something consecrated to God **2 :** gross irreverence toward a hallowed person, place, or thing **syn** see PROFANATION — **sac·ri·le·gious** \ˌsak-rə-'lij-əs, -'lē-jəs\ *adj* — **sac·ri·le·gious·ly** *adv* — **sac·ri·le·gious·ness** *n*

sac·ris·tan \'sak-rə-stən\ *n* **:** an officer of a church in charge of the sacristy and ceremonial equipment; *also* **:** SEXTON

sac·ris·ty \-rə-stē\ *n* [ML *sacristia*, fr. *sacrista* sacristan, fr. L *sacr-*, *sacer*] **:** a room in a church where sacred utensils and vestments are kept **:** VESTRY

¹**sa·cro·il·i·ac** \ˌsak-rō-'il-ē-ˌak, ˌsā-krō-\ *adj* [ISV] **:** of, relating to, or being the region of juncture of the sacrum and ilium

²**sacroiliac** *n* **:** the sacroiliac region; *also* **:** its firm fibrous cartilage

sac·ro·sanct \'sak-rō-ˌsaŋ(k)t\ *adj* [L *sacrosanctus*, prob. fr. *sacro sanctus* hallowed by a sacred rite] **:** SACRED, INVIOLABLE — **sac·ro·sanc·ti·ty** \ˌsak-rō-'saŋ(k)-tət-ē\ *n*

sa·crum \'sak-rəm, 'sā-krəm\ *n, pl* **sa·cra** \'sak-rə, 'sā-krə\ [NL, fr. LL *os sacrum* last bone of the spine, lit., holy bone] **:** the part of the vertebral column that is directly connected with or forms a part of the pelvis and in man consists of five united vertebrae

sad \'sad\ *adj* **sad·der; sad·dest** [ME, fr. OE *sæd* sated; akin to OHG *sat* sated, L *satis* enough] **1 a :** affected with or expressive of grief or unhappiness **:** DOWNCAST **b** (1) **:** causing or associated with grief or unhappiness **:** DEPRESSING ⟨~ news⟩ (2) **:** DISMAYING, DEPLORABLE **c :** INFERIOR **2 :** of a dull somber color **:** DRAB — **sad·ly** *adv*

sad·den \'sad-ᵊn\ *vb* **sad·den·ing** \'sad-niŋ, -ᵊn-iŋ\ *vt* **:** to make sad ~ *vi* **:** to become sad

¹**sad·dle** \'sad-ᵊl\ *n, often attrib* [ME *sadel*, fr. OE *sadol*; akin to OHG *satul* saddle] **1 a** (1) **:** a girthed usu. padded and leather-covered seat for a rider on horseback (2) **:** a comparable part of a driving harness used to keep the breeching in place **b :** a similar seat on a bicycle or similar vehicle **2 :** an often shaped mounted support for an object **3 a :** a ridge connecting two higher elevations **b :** COL 2 **4 a :** both sides of the unsplit back of a carcass including both loins **b :** a colored marking on the back of an animal **c :** the rear part of a male fowl's back extending to the tail **5 :** the central part of the backbone of the binding of a book **6 :** a piece of leather across the instep of a shoe

²**saddle** *vb* **sad·dling** \'sad-liŋ, -ᵊl-iŋ\ *vt* **1 :** to put a saddle upon **2 a :** to place under a burden or encumbrance **b :** to place (an onerous responsibility) on a person or group ~ *vi* **:** to mount a saddled horse

sad·dle·bag \'sad-ᵊl-ˌbag\ *n* **:** a large pouch carried hanging from one side of a saddle or over the rear wheel of a bicycle or motorcycle and usu. one of a pair

sad·dle–bill \'sad-ᵊl-ˌbil\ *n* **:** a large black-and-white West African stork (*Ephippiorhynchus senegalensis*) having the bill red with a black median band

sad·dle·bow \'sad-ᵊl-ˌbō\ *n* **:** the arch in or the pieces forming the front of a saddle

sad·dle·cloth \-ˌklȯth\ *n* **:** a cloth placed under or over a saddle

saddle horse *n* **:** a horse suited for or trained for riding

saddle leather *n* **:** leather made of the hide of cattle that is vegetable tanned and used for saddlery; *also* **:** smooth polished leather simulating this

sad·dler \'sad-lər\ *n* **:** one that makes, repairs, or sells saddles and other furnishings for horses

saddle roof *n* **:** a roof having two gables and one ridge

sad·dlery \'sad-lə-rē, 'sad-ᵊl-rē\ *n* **:** the trade, articles of trade, or shop of a saddler

saddle shoe *n* **:** an oxford-style shoe having a saddle of contrasting color or leather

saddle soap *n* **:** a mild soap made with added unsaponified oil and used for cleansing and conditioning leather

saddle sore *n* **1 :** a gall or open sore developing on the back of a horse at points of pressure from an ill-fitting or ill-adjusted saddle **2 :** an irritation or sore on parts of the rider chafed by the saddle

sad·dle·tree \'sad-ᵊl-ˌtrē\ *n* **:** the frame of a saddle

Sad·du·ce·an \ˌsaj-ə-'sē-ən, ˌsad-yə-\ *adj* **:** of or relating to the Sadducees

Sad·du·cee \'saj-ə-ˌsē, 'sad-yə-\ *n* [ME *saducee*, fr. OE *sadduce*, fr. LL *sadducaeus*, fr. Gk *saddoukaios*, fr. LHeb *ṣaddūqi*] **:** a member of a Jewish party of the intertestamental period consisting largely of the priestly aristocracy and rejecting doctrines not in the Law (as resurrection, retribution in a future life, and the existence of angels) — **Sad·du·cee·ism** \-ˌiz-əm\ *n*

sa·dhe \'(t)säd-ə, -ē\ *n* [Heb *ṣādhē*] **:** the 18th letter of the Hebrew alphabet — symbol צ or ץ

sa·dhu *or* **sad·dhu** \'säd-(ˌ)ü\ *n* [Skt *sādhu*] **:** a Hindu mendicant ascetic

sad·iron \'sad-ˌī(-ə)rn\ *n* [*sad* (compact, heavy) + *iron*] **:** a flatiron pointed at both ends and having a removable handle

sa·dism \'sā-ˌdiz-əm, 'sad-ˌiz-\ *n* [ISV, fr. Marquis de *Sade* †1814 F author] **1 :** the infliction of pain (as upon a love object) as a means of obtaining sexual release — compare MASOCHISM **2 a :** delight in cruelty **b :** excessive cruelty — **sa·dist** \'sād-əst, 'sad-\ *adj or n* — **sa·dis·tic** \sə-'dis-tik *also* sā-, sa-\ *adj* — **sa·dis·ti·cal·ly** \-ti-k(ə-)lē\ *adv*

sad·ness \'sad-nəs\ *n* **:** quality, state, or fact of being sad

syn DEPRESSION, MELANCHOLY, MELANCHOLIA, DEJECTION, GLOOM: SADNESS is a general term that carries no suggestion of the cause, extent, or exact nature of low spirits; DEPRESSION suggests a condition in which one feels let down, disheartened, or enervated; MELANCHOLY suggests a mood of sad and serious but not wholly unpleasant pensiveness; MELANCHOLIA applies to a settled deep depression verging on insanity; DEJECTION implies a usu. passing mood of being downcast or dispirited from a natural or logical cause; GLOOM applies to the atmosphere or the effect on others created by one afflicted with any of these moods or conditions

sa·do·mas·och·ism \ˌsād-(ˌ)ō-'mas-ə-ˌkiz-əm, ˌsad-, -'maz-\ *n* [ISV *sadism* + *-o-* + *masochism*] **:** the derivation of pleasure from the infliction of physical or mental pain either on others or on oneself — **sa·do·mas·och·ist** \-kəst\ *n* — **sa·do·mas·och·is·tic** \-ˌmas-ə-'kis-tik, -ˌmaz-\ *adj*

sad sack *n* **:** an inept person; *esp* **:** an inept serviceman

Sa·far \sə-'fär\ *n* [Ar *ṣafar*] **:** the second month of the Muhammadan year

sa·fa·ri \sə-'fär-ē, -'far-\ *n* [Ar *safarīy* of a trip] **:** a hunting or other expedition esp. in East Africa or its caravan and equipment — **safari** *vi*

¹**safe** \'sāf\ *adj* [ME *sauf*, fr. OF, fr. L *salvus* safe, healthy; akin to L *salus* health, safety, *salubris* healthful, *solidus* solid, Gk *holos* whole, safe] **1 :** freed from harm or risk **:** UNHURT **2 a :** secure from threat of danger, harm, or loss **b :** successful in reaching base in baseball **3 :** affording safety from danger **4** *obs, of mental or moral faculties* **:** HEALTHY, SOUND **5 :** not threatening danger **:** HARMLESS **6 a :** CAUTIOUS **b :** TRUSTWORTHY — **safe·ly** *adv* — **safe·ness** *n*

syn SAFE, SECURE mean free from danger. SAFE may or may not imply danger successfully avoided or risk run without harm but always suggests present or immediate freedom from threatening harm; SECURE implies freedom from anxiety or apprehension of danger or risk

²**safe** *n* **:** a place or receptacle to keep articles (as valuables) safe

safe–con·duct \'sāf-'kän-(ˌ)dəkt\ *n* [ME *sauf conduit*, fr. OF, safe conduct] **1 :** protection given a person passing through a military zone or occupied area **2 :** a document authorizing safe-conduct

safe·crack·er \'sāf-ˌkrak-ər\ *n* **:** one that breaks open safes to steal

safe–de·pos·it \ˌsāf-di-'päz-ət, ˌsāf-ti-\ *adj* **:** of, providing, or constituting a box or vault for the safe storage of valuables

¹**safe·guard** \'sāf-ˌgärd\ *n* [ME *saufgarde*, fr. MF *saufegarde*, fr. OF, fr. *sauve* safe + *garde* guard] **1 a :** CONVOY, ESCORT **b :** PASS, SAFE-CONDUCT **2 a :** a precautionary measure or stipulation **b :** a technical contrivance to prevent accident

²**safeguard** *vt* **1 :** to provide a safeguard for **2 :** to make safe **:** PROTECT **syn** see DEFEND

safe·keep·ing \'sāf-'kē-piŋ\ *n* **1 :** the act or process of preserving in safety **2 :** the state of being preserved in safety

safe·light \'sā-ˌflīt\ *n* **:** a darkroom lamp with a filter to screen out rays that are harmful to sensitive film or paper

¹**safe·ty** \'sāf-tē\ *n, often attrib* [ME *saufte*, fr. MF *sauveté*, fr. OF, fr. *sauve*, fem. of *sauf* safe] **1 :** the condition of being safe from undergoing or causing hurt, injury, or loss **2 a :** a device on a military apparatus (as a mine or missile) that prevents it from being fired accidentally **b :** a device on a piece of equipment to reduce hazard **3 a :** a football play in which the ball is downed by the offensive team behind its own goal line counting two points for the defensive team — compare TOUCHBACK **b :** a member of a defensive backfield in football in the deepest position

ə abut; ᵊ kitten; ər further; a back; ā bake; ä cot, cart; au̇ out; ch chin; e less; ē easy; g gift; i trip; ī life
j joke; ŋ sing; ō flow; ȯ flaw; ȯi coin; th thin; t͟h this; ü loot; u̇ foot; y yet; yü few; yu̇ furious; zh vision

2**safety** *vt* **:** to protect against failure, breakage, or accident ⟨~ a rifle⟩

safety belt *n* **:** a belt fastening a person to an object to prevent falling or injury

safety glass *n* **:** laminated glass

safety island *n* **:** an area within a roadway from which vehicular traffic is excluded

safety lamp *n* **:** a miner's lamp constructed to avoid explosion in an atmosphere containing flammable gas usu. by enclosing the flame in fine wire gauze

safety match *n* **:** a match capable of being struck and ignited only on a specially prepared friction surface

safety pin *n* **:** a pin in the form of a clasp with a guard covering the point to prevent pricking

safety razor *n* **:** a razor provided with a guard for the blade to prevent deep cuts in the skin

safety valve *n* **1 :** an automatic escape or relief valve (as for a steam boiler or hydraulic system) **2 :** an outlet for an excess (as of energy or emotion)

safety zone *n* **:** a safety island for pedestrians or for street car or bus passengers

saf·flow·er \'saf-ˌlau̇(-ə)r\ *n* [MF *saffleur,* fr. OIt *saffiore,* fr. Ar *aṣfar* a yellow plant] **:** a widely grown Old World composite herb (*Carthamus tinctorius*) with large orange or red flower heads and seeds rich in oil; *also* **:** a red dyestuff prepared from the flower heads

saf·fron \'saf-rən\ *n* [ME, fr. OF *safran,* fr. ML *safranum,* fr. Ar *za'farān*] **1 :** a purple-flowered crocus (*Crocus sativus*) **2 :** the deep orange aromatic pungent dried stigmas of saffron used to color and flavor foods and formerly as a dyestuff and in medicine **3 :** a moderate orange to orange yellow

saf·ra·nine *or* **saf·ra·nin** \'saf-rə-ˌnen, -nən\ *n* [ISV, fr. F or G *safran* saffron] **1 :** any of various usu. red synthetic dyes that are amino derivatives of bases **2 :** any of various mixtures of safranine salts used in dyeing and as a microscopic stain

saf·role \'saf-ˌrōl\ *n* [ISV, fr. F or G *safran*] **:** a poisonous oily cyclic ether $C_{10}H_{10}O_2$ that is the principal component of sassafras oil and is used chiefly for perfuming and flavoring

1**sag** \'sag\ *vb* **sagged; sag·ging** [ME *saggen,* prob. of Scand origin; akin to Sw *sacka* to sag] *vi* **1 :** to droop, sink, or settle from or as if from pressure or loss of tautness **2 a :** to lose firmness, resiliency, or vigor ⟨spirits *sagging* from overwork⟩ **b :** to fall from a thriving state **3 :** DRIFT **~** *vt* **:** to cause to sag

2**sag** *n* **1 :** a tendency to drift (as of a ship to leeward) **2 :** a drop or depression below the surrounding area **3 :** a temporary economic decline

sa·ga \'säg-ə *also* 'sag-\ *n* [ON — more at SAW] **1 :** a prose narrative recorded in Iceland in the 12th and 13th centuries of historic or legendary figures and events of Norway and Iceland **2 :** a modern heroic narrative resembling the Icelandic saga

sa·ga·cious \sə-'gā-shəs, sig-'ā-\ *adj* [L *sagac-, sagax* sagacious; akin to L *sagire* to perceive keenly — more at SEEK] **1** *obs* **:** keen in sense perception **2 a :** of keen and farsighted penetration and judgment **:** DISCERNING ⟨~ judge of character⟩ **b :** caused by or indicating acute discernment ⟨~ purchase of stock⟩ **syn** see SHREWD — **sa·ga·cious·ly** *adv* — **sa·ga·cious·ness** *n*

sa·gac·i·ty \sə-'gas-ət-ē, sig-'as-\ *n* **:** the quality of being sagacious

sag·a·more \'sag-ə-ˌmō(ə)r, -ˌmȯ(ə)r\ *n* [Abnaki *sāgimau,* lit., he prevails over] **1 :** a subordinate chief of the Algonquian Indians of the north Atlantic coast **2 :** SACHEM 1

saga novel *n* **:** ROMAN-FLEUVE

1**sage** \'sāj\ *adj* [ME, fr. OF, fr. (assumed) VL *sapius,* fr. L *sapere* to taste, have good taste, be wise; akin to OE *sefa* mind, Oscan *sipus* knowing] **1 a :** wise through reflection and experience **b** *archaic* **:** GRAVE, SOLEMN **2 :** proceeding from or characterized by wisdom, prudence, and good judgment ⟨~ counsel⟩ **syn** see WISE — **sage·ly** *adv* — **sage·ness** *n*

2**sage** *n* **1 :** one (as a profound philosopher) distinguished for wisdom **2 :** a mature or venerable man sound in judgment

3**sage** *n* [ME, fr. MF *sauge,* fr. L *salvia,* fr. *salvus* healthy; fr. its use as a medicinal herb — more at SAFE] **1 :** a mint (*Salvia officinalis*) with grayish green aromatic leaves used esp. in flavoring meats; *broadly* **:** a plant of this genus several of which (as the scarlet-flowered *S. splendens*) are grown as ornamentals **2 :** SAGEBRUSH

sage·brush \'sāj-ˌbrəsh\ *n* **:** any of several No. American hoary composite undershrubs (genus *Artemisia*); *esp* **:** a common plant (*A. tridentata*) having a bitter juice and an odor resembling sage and often covering vast tracts of alkaline plains in the western U.S.

sag·ger *or* **sag·gar** \'sag-ər\ *n* [prob. alter. of *safeguard*] **:** a box made of fireclay in which delicate ceramic pieces are fired either for biscuit or for glaze; *also* **:** the clay of which saggers are made

sa·git·tal \'saj-ət-ᵊl, sə-'jit-\ *adj* [L *sagitta* arrow] **1 :** of or relating to the suture between the parietal bones of the skull **2 :** of, relating to, or situated in the median plane of the body or any plane parallel thereto — **sa·git·tal·ly** \-ᵊl-ē\ *adv*

Sag·it·tar·i·us \ˌsaj-ə-'ter-ē-əs, ˌsag-, -'tar-\ *n* [L (gen. *Sagittarii*), lit., archer, fr. *sagitta*] **1 :** a southern constellation pictured as a centaur shooting an arrow **2 :** the 9th sign of the zodiac

sag·it·tate \'saj-ə-ˌtāt\ *adj* [L *sagitta*] **:** shaped like an arrowhead; *specif* **:** elongated, triangular, and having the two basal lobes prolonged downward ⟨~ leaf⟩

sa·go \'sā-(ˌ)gō\ *n* [Malay *sagu* sago palm] **:** a dry granulated or powdered starch prepared from the pith of a sago palm and used in foods and as textile stiffening

sago palm *n* **:** a plant that yields sago; *esp* **:** any of various lofty pinnate-leaved Indian and Malaysian palms (genus *Metroxylon*)

sa·gua·ro \sə-'(g)wär-(ˌ)ō\ *n* [MexSp] **:** an arborescent cactus (*Carnegiea gigantea*) of desert regions of the southwestern U.S. and Mexico that has a tall columnar simple or sparsely branched trunk of up to 60 feet and bears white flowers and edible fruit

sa·hib \'sä-ˌ(h)ib\ *n* [Hindi *ṣāḥib,* fr. Ar] **:** SIR, MASTER — used esp. among Hindus and Muslims in colonial India when addressing or speaking of a European of some social or official status

said \'sed\ *adj* [pp. of *say*] **:** AFOREMENTIONED

1**sail** \'sā(ə)l, *as last element in compounds often* səl\ *n* [ME, fr. OE *segl;* akin to OHG *segal* sail, L *secare* to cut — more at SAW] **1 a** (1) **:** an extent of fabric (as canvas) by means of which wind is used to propel a ship through water (2) **:** the sails of a ship **b** *pl usu* **sail :** a ship equipped with sails **2 :** an extent of fabric

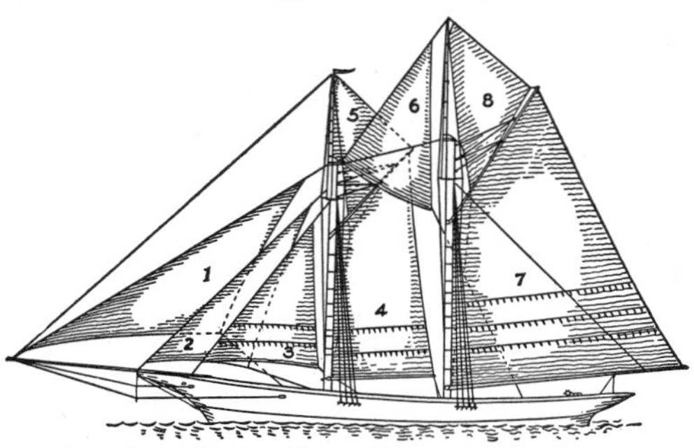

schooner's sails: *1* flying jib, *2* jib, *3* forestaysail, *4* foresail, *5* fore gaff-topsail, *6* main-topmast staysail, *7* mainsail, *8* main gaff-topsail

used in propelling a wind-driven vehicle (as an iceboat) **3 :** something that resembles a sail **4 :** a passage by a sailing ship **:** CRUISE

2**sail** *vi* **1 a :** to travel on water in a ship propelled by wind or by any means **b :** YACHT **2 a :** to travel on water by the action of wind upon sails or by other means **b :** to move without visible effort or in a stately manner (as through water) **3 :** to begin a water voyage ⟨~ with the tide⟩ **4 :** to attack something with gusto **~** *vt* **1 a :** to travel upon (water) by means of motive power (as sail) **b :** to glide through **2 :** to direct or manage the motion of (as a ship)

sail·boat \'sā(ə)l-ˌbōt\ *n* **:** a boat usu. propelled by sail

sail·cloth \-ˌklȯth\ *n* **1 :** a heavy canvas for sails, tents, or upholstery **2 :** a piece of sailcloth

sail·er \'sā-lər\ *n* **:** a ship or boat esp. having specified sailing qualities

sail·fish \'sā(ə)l-ˌfish\ *n* **:** any of a genus (*Istiophorus*) of large pelagic fishes related to the swordfish but having teeth, scales, and a very large dorsal fin

sail·ing \'sā-liŋ\ *n* **1 a :** the technical skill of managing a ship **:** NAVIGATION **b :** the method of determining the course to be followed to reach a given point **2 a :** the sport of navigating or riding in a sailboat **b :** a departure from a port

sail·or \'sā-lər\ *n* [alter. of *sailer*] **1 a :** one that sails; *esp* **:** MARINER **b** (1) **:** a member of a ship's crew (2) **:** SEAMAN 2 **2 :** a traveler by water **3 :** a stiff straw hat with low flat crown and straight circular brim

sail·or's–choice \ˌsā-lərz-'chȯis\ *n* **:** any of several small grunts of the western Atlantic: as **a :** PINFISH **b :** a pigfish (*Orthopristis chrysopterus*)

sail·plane \'sā(ə)l-ˌplān\ *n* **:** a glider of such design that it is able to rise in an upward air current

sain \'sān\ *vt* [ME *sainen,* fr. OE *segnian,* fr. LL *signare* — more at SIGN] **1** *dial Brit* **:** to make the sign of the cross on (oneself) **2** *dial Brit* **:** BLESS

sain·foin \'sān-ˌfȯin, 'san-\ *n* [F, fr. MF, fr. *sain* healthy (fr. L *sanus*) + *foin* hay, fr. L *fenum*] **:** a Eurasian pink-flowered perennial leguminous forage herb (*Onobrychis viciaefolia*); *also* **:** any of several New World legumes

1**saint** \'sānt, *before a name* (ˌ)sānt *or* sənt\ *n* [ME, fr. MF, fr. LL *sanctus,* fr. L, sacred, fr. pp. of *sancire* to make sacred — more at SACRED] **1 :** one officially recognized as preeminent for holiness esp. through canonization **2 a :** one of the spirits of the departed in heaven **b :** ANGEL **3 a :** one of God's chosen people **b :** one belonging to the entire company of baptized Christians **c** *cap* **:** a member of any of various religious bodies; *specif* **:** LATTER-DAY SAINT **4 :** a holy or godly person **5 :** an illustrious predecessor

2**saint** \'sānt\ *vt* **:** to recognize or designate as a saint; *specif* **:** CANONIZE

Saint Ag·nes's Eve \-ˌag-nə-sə-'zēv\ *n* [*St. Agnes* †A.D. 304? Roman virgin-martyr] **:** the night of January 20 when a woman is traditionally held to have a revelation of her future husband

Saint An·drew's cross \-ˌan-ˌdrüz-\ *n* [St. *Andrew* †*ab* A.D. 60, one of the twelve apostles] — see CROSS illustration

Saint An·tho·ny's cross \-ˌan(t)-thə-nēz-, *chiefly Brit* -ˌan-tə-\ *n* [St. *Anthony* †*ab* A.D. 350 Egyptian abbot] **:** TAU CROSS

Saint Anthony's fire *n* **:** any of several inflammations or gangrenous conditions (as erysipelas or ergotism) of the skin

Saint Ber·nard \ˌsānt-bə(r)-'närd\ *n* [the hospice of Grand *St. Bernard,* where such dogs were first bred] **:** any of a Swiss alpine breed of tall powerful dogs used esp. formerly in aiding lost travelers

saint·dom \'sānt-dəm\ *n* **:** the quality or state of being a saint

saint·ed \'sānt-əd\ *adj* **1 :** befitting or relating to a saint **2 :** SAINTLY, PIOUS **3 :** entered into heaven **:** DEAD

Saint El·mo's fire \-ˌel-(ˌ)mōz-\ *n* [St. *Elmo* (*Erasmus*) †303 It bishop & patron saint of sailors] **:** a flaming phenomenon sometimes seen in stormy weather at prominent points on an airplane or ship and on land that is of the nature of a brush discharge of electricity — called also *St. Elmo's light*

saint·hood \'sānt-ˌhu̇d\ *n* **1 :** the quality or state of being a saint **2 :** SAINTS

Saint–John's–wort \-'jänz-ˌwərt, -ˌwȯ(ə)rt\ *n* [St. *John* the Baptist] **:** any of a genus (*Hypericum* of the family Guttiferae, the Saint-John's-wort family) of herbs and shrubs with showy pentamerous yellow flowers

saint·less \'sānt-ləs\ *adj* **:** having no patron saint

saint·li·ness \'sānt-lē-nəs\ *n* **:** the quality or state of being saintly **:** SANCTITY

Saint Lou·is encephalitis \sānt-ˌlü-əs-, sənt-\ *n* [*St. Louis,* Mo.] **:** a No. American viral encephalitis

saint·ly \'sānt-lē\ *adj* **:** relating to, resembling, or befitting a saint **:** HOLY

Saint Mar·tin's summer \-ˌmärt-ᵊn(z)-'səm-ər\ *n* [*Saint Martin's* Day, November 11] **:** Indian summer when occurring in November

Saint Pat·rick's Day \-'pa-triks-\ *n* [*St. Patrick* †*ab*461 Brit

prelate who converted Ireland to Christianity] **:** March 17 celebrated in honor of St. Patrick and observed as a legal holiday in Ireland in commemoration of his death

saint·ship \'sānt-,ship\ *n* **:** SAINTHOOD 1

Saint Val·en·tine's Day \-'val-ən-,tīnz-\ *n* [*St. Valentine* †*ab*270 It priest] **:** Feb. 14 observed in honor of St. Valentine and as a time for sending valentines

Saint Vi·tus's dance \-,vīt-əs(-əz)-\ *n* [*St. Vitus,* 3d cent. Christian child martyr] **:** CHOREA

saith \(')seth, 'sā-əth\ *archaic pres 3d sing of* SAY

saithe \'sāth, 'sā<u>th</u>\ *n, pl* **saithe** [of Scand origin; akin to ON *seithr* coalfish] **:** POLLACK

Sai·va \'s(h)ī-və\ *n* [Skt *Śaiva,* fr. *Śiva* Siva] **:** a worshiper of Siva — **Sai·vism** \-,viz-əm\ *n*

[1]**sake** \'sāk\ *n* [ME, dispute, guilt, purpose, fr. OE *sacu* guilt, action at law; akin to OHG *sahha* action at law, cause, OE *sēcan* to seek — more at SEEK] **1 :** END, PURPOSE ⟨for the ~ of argument⟩ **2 a :** GOOD, ADVANTAGE **b :** personal or social welfare, safety, or benefit ⟨died for the ~ of his country⟩

[2]**sa·ke** *or* **sa·ki** \'säk-ē\ *n* [Jap *sake*] **:** a Japanese alcoholic beverage of fermented rice usu. served hot

sa·ker \'sā-kər\ *n* [ME *sagre,* fr. MF *sacre,* fr. Ar *ṣaqr*] **:** an Old World falcon (*Falco cherrug*) used in falconry

Sakti \'s(h)äk-tē\, **Saktism** *var of* SHAKTI, SHAKTISM

sal \'sal\ *n* [L — more at SALT] **:** SALT

sa·laam \sə-'läm\ *n* [Ar *salām,* lit., peace] **1 :** a salutation or ceremonial greeting in the East **2 :** an obeisance performed by bowing very low and placing the right palm on the forehead — **salaam** *vb*

sal·abil·i·ty \,sā-lə-'bil-ət-ē\ *n* **:** the quality or state of being salable

sal·able *or* **sale·able** \'sā-lə-bəl\ *adj* **:** capable of being or fit to be sold **:** MARKETABLE

sa·la·cious \sə-'lā-shəs\ *adj* [L *salac-, salax* fond of leaping, lustful, fr. *salire* to leap — more at SALLY] **1 :** arousing sexual desire or imagination **:** LASCIVIOUS **2 :** LECHEROUS, LUSTFUL — **sa·la·cious·ly** *adv* — **sa·la·cious·ness** *n*

sal·ad \'sal-əd\ *n* [ME *salade,* fr. MF, fr. OProv *salada,* fr. *salar* to salt, fr. *sal* salt, fr. L — more at SALT] **1 a :** green vegetables (as lettuce, endive, romaine) often with tomato, cucumber, or radish served with dressing **b :** a cold dish of meat, fish, or shellfish served with fruits or vegetables and a dressing usu. on lettuce and sometimes with hard-boiled eggs or gelatin **2 :** a green vegetable or herb grown for salad; *esp* **:** LETTUCE

salad days *n pl* **:** time of youthful inexperience or indiscretion ⟨my *salad days* when I was green in judgment —Shak.⟩

salad dressing *n* **:** a savory sauce (as mayonnaise) for a salad

sal·a·man·der \'sal-ə-,man-dər *also* ,sal-ə-'\ *n* [ME *salamandre,* fr. MF, fr. L *salamandra,* fr. Gk] **1 :** a mythical animal having the power to endure fire without harm **2 :** an elemental being in the theory of Paracelsus inhabiting fire **3 :** any of numerous amphibians (order Caudata) superficially resembling lizards but scaleless and covered with a soft moist skin and breathing by gills in the larval stage **4 :** an article (as a culinary utensil for browning pastry or a portable stove or incinerator) used in connection with fire — **sal·a·man·drine** \,sal-ə-'man-drən\ *adj*

sa·la·mi \sə-'läm-ē\ *n* [It, pl. of *salame* salami, fr. *salare* to salt, fr. *sale* salt, fr. L *sal* — more at SALT] **:** highly seasoned sausage of pork and beef either dried and of good keeping qualities or fresh and requiring refrigeration

sal am·mo·ni·ac \,sal-ə-'mō-nē-,ak\ *n* [ME *sal armoniak,* fr. L *sal ammoniacus,* lit., salt of Ammon] **:** AMMONIUM CHLORIDE

sal·a·ried \'sal-(ə-)rēd\ *adj* **:** receiving or yielding a salary

sal·a·ry \'sal-(ə-)rē\ *n* [ME *salarie,* fr. L *salarium* salt money, pension, salary, fr. neut. of *salarius* of salt, fr. *sal* salt — more at SALT] **:** fixed compensation paid regularly for services **:** STIPEND **syn** see WAGE

sale \'sā(ə)l\ *n* [ME, fr. OE *sala,* fr. ON — more at SELL] **1 :** the act of selling; *specif* **:** the transfer of ownership of and title to property from one person to another for a price **2 :** availability for purchase — usu. used in the phrases *for sale* and *on sale* **3 a :** opportunity of selling or being sold **:** DEMAND **b :** distribution by selling **4 :** public disposal to the highest bidder **:** AUCTION **5 :** a selling of goods at bargain prices **6** *pl* **a :** operations and activities involved in promoting and selling goods or services **b :** gross receipts

sa·lep \'sal-əp, sə-'lep\ *n* [F or Sp, fr. Ar dial. *saḥlab,* alter. of Ar (*khuṣy ath-*) *tha'lab,* lit., testicles of the fox] **:** the starchy or mucilaginous dried tubers of various Old World orchids (esp. genus *Orchis*) used for food or in medicine

sal·era·tus \,sal-ə-'rāt-əs\ *n* [NL *sal aeratus* aerated salt] **:** a leavening agent consisting of potassium or sodium bicarbonate **:** BAKING SODA

sales \'sā(ə)lz\ *adj* **:** of, relating to, or used in selling

sales check *n* **:** a strip or piece of paper used by retail stores as a memorandum, record, or receipt of a purchase or sale

sales·clerk \-,klərk\ *n* **:** a salesman or saleswoman in a store

Sa·le·sian \sə-'lē-zhən, sā-\ *n* **:** a member of the Society of St. Francis de Sales founded as a Roman Catholic religious congregation in the 19th century by St. John Bosco in Turin and devoted chiefly to education

sales·man \'sā(ə)lz-mən\ *n* **:** one that sells either in a given territory or in a store — **sales·man·ship** \-,ship\ *n* — **sales·wom·an** \-,wu̇m-ən\ *n*

sales promotion *n* **:** activities and devices designed to create goodwill and sell a product; *esp* **:** selling activities that supplement advertising and personal selling, coordinate them, and make them effective

sales register *n* **:** CASH REGISTER

sales resistance *n* **1 :** the power, capacity, or disposition to resist buying goods or services offered for sale **2 :** disinclination to accept or approve new ideas or proposals

sales·room \'sā(ə)lz-,rüm, -,ru̇m\ *n* **:** a place where goods are displayed for sale; *esp* **:** an auction room

sales talk *n* **:** argument often accompanied by demonstration used to persuade others to buy a product or service or to accept an idea or proposal

sales tax *n* **:** a tax levied on the sale of goods and services that is usu. calculated as a percentage of the purchase price and collected by the seller

sali- *comb form* [L, fr. *sal* — more at SALT] **:** salt ⟨*sali*ferous⟩

Sa·lic \'sā-lik, 'sal-ik\ *adj* [MF or ML; MF *salique,* fr. ML *Salicus,* fr. LL *Salii* Salic Franks] **:** of, relating to, or being a Frankish people settling early in the 4th century on the IJssel river

sal·i·cin \'sal-ə-sən\ *n* [F *salicine,* fr. L *salic-, salix* willow — more at SALLOW] **:** a bitter white crystalline glucoside $C_{13}H_{18}O_7$ found in the bark and leaves of several willows and poplars and used in medicine like salicylic acid

Salic law *n* **1 :** the legal code of the Salic Franks **2 :** a rule held to derive from the Salic code excluding females from the line of succession to a throne

sa·li·cy·late \sə-'lis-ə-,lāt, -lət; ,sal-ə-'sil-ət\ *n* **:** a salt or ester of salicylic acid; *also* **:** SALICYLIC ACID

sal·i·cyl·ic acid \,sal-ə-,sil-ik-\ *n* [ISV, fr. *salicyl* (the radical HOC_6H_4CO)] **:** a crystalline phenolic acid $C_7H_6O_3$ used esp. in the form of salts as an analgesic and antipyretic and in the treatment of rheumatism

sa·lience \'sā-lyən(t)s, -lē-ən(t)s\ *or* **sa·lien·cy** \-lyən-sē, -lē-ən-\ *n* **1 :** the quality or state of being salient **2 :** a striking point or feature **:** HIGHLIGHT

[1]**sa·lient** \'sā-lyənt, -lē-ənt\ *adj* [L *salient-, saliens,* prp. of *salire* to leap — more at SALLY] **1 :** moving by leaps or springs **:** JUMPING; *specif* **:** SALIENTIAN ⟨a ~ amphibian⟩ **2 :** jetting upward ⟨~ fountain⟩ **3 a :** projecting beyond a line, surface, or level **:** PROTUBERANT **b :** standing out conspicuously **:** PROMINENT, STRIKING ⟨~ traits⟩ **syn** see NOTICEABLE — **sa·lient·ly** *adv*

[2]**salient** *n* **:** something that projects outward or upward from its surroundings; *specif* **:** an outwardly projecting part of a fortification, trench system, or line of defense

sa·li·en·tian \,sā-lē-'en-chən\ *n* [deriv. of L *salient-, saliens*] **:** any of an order (Salientia) of amphibians comprising the frogs, toads, and tree toads all of which lack a tail in the adult stage and have long strong hind limbs suited to leaping and swimming — **salientian** *adj*

sal·i·fy \'sal-ə-,fī\ *vt* [F *salifier,* fr. L *sal* salt] **1 :** to combine or impregnate with a salt **2 :** to form a salt with or convert into a salt ⟨~ a base by treatment with an acid⟩

sa·lim·e·ter \sə-'lim-ət-ər, sa-\ *n* **:** a hydrometer for indicating the percentage of a salt in a solution

sa·li·na \sə-'lī-nə, -'lē-\ *n* [Sp, fr. L *salinae* saltworks, fr. fem. pl. of *salinus*] **1 :** a salt-encrusted playa or flat **2 :** a salt marsh, pond, or lake

[1]**sa·line** \'sā-,lēn, -,līn\ *adj* [ME, fr. L *salinus,* fr. *sal* salt — more at SALT] **1 :** consisting of or containing salt ⟨a ~ solution⟩ **2 :** of, relating to, or resembling salt **:** SALTY ⟨a ~ taste⟩ ⟨~ compounds⟩ **3 :** consisting of or relating to the salts of the alkali metals or of magnesium ⟨a ~ cathartic⟩ — **sa·lin·i·ty** \sā-'lin-ət-ē, sə-\ *n*

[2]**sa·line** *1 usu* sə-'lēn, *2 & 3 usu* 'sā-,lēn *or* 'sā-,līn\ *n* **1 a :** a natural deposit of common salt or other soluble salt **b :** SALINA 2 **2 :** a metallic salt; *esp* **:** a salt of potassium, sodium, or magnesium with a cathartic action **3 :** a saline solution; *esp* **:** one isotonic with body fluids

sa·lin·om·e·ter \,sal-ə-'näm-ət-ər, ,sā-,lē-, ,sā-,lī-\ *n* [ISV *saline* + *-o-* + *-meter*] **:** an instrument (as a hydrometer) for measuring the amount of salt in a solution

Sa·lique \'sā-lik, 'sal-ik; sa-'lēk, sā-\ *var of* SALIC

Salis·bury steak \,sȯlz-,ber-ē-, ,salz-, -b(ə-)rē-\ *n* [J. H. *Salisbury,* 19th cent. E physician] **:** ground beef mixed with egg, milk, bread crumbs, and seasonings and formed into patties

Sa·lish \'sā-lish\ *n* **1 :** a language stock of the Mosan phylum **2 :** the peoples speaking Salish dialects — **Sa·lish·an** \-ən\ *adj*

sa·li·va \sə-'lī-və\ *n* [L — more at SALLOW] **:** a slightly alkaline secretion of water, mucin, protein, salts, and often a starch-splitting enzyme secreted into the mouth by salivary glands

sal·i·vary \'sal-ə-,ver-ē\ *adj* **:** of or relating to saliva or the glands that secrete it; *esp* **:** producing or carrying saliva

sal·i·vate \-,vāt\ *vt* **:** to produce an abnormal flow of saliva in (as by the use of mercury) **~** *vi* **:** to have a flow of saliva esp. in excess **:** DROOL — **sal·i·va·tion** \,sal-ə-'vā-shən\ *n*

Salk vaccine \(,)sȯ(l)k-\ *n* [Jonas *Salk b*1914 Am physician] **:** a vaccine consisting of poliomyelitis virus inactivated with formaldehyde

sal·let \'sal-ət\ *n* [ME, fr. MF *sallade*] **:** a light 15th century helmet with a projection over the neck

[1]**sal·low** \'sal-(,)ō, -ə(-w)\ *n* [ME, fr. OE *sealh;* akin to OHG *salha* sallow, L *salix* willow] **:** any of various Old World broad-leaved willows (as *Salix caprea*) including important sources of charcoal and tanbark

[2]**sallow** *adj* [ME *salowe,* fr. OE *salu;* akin to OHG *salo* murky, L *saliva* spittle] **:** of a grayish greenish yellow color ⟨~ complexion⟩ — **sal·low·ish** \'sal-ə-wish\ *adj* — **sal·low·ness** \'sal-ō-nəs, 'sal-ə-\ *n*

[1]**sal·ly** \'sal-ē\ *n* [MF *saillie,* fr. OF, fr. *saillir* to rush forward, fr. L *salire* to leap; akin to Gk *hallesthai* to leap] **1 :** an action of rushing or bursting forth; *specif* **:** a sortie of besieged troops upon the attackers **2 a :** a brief outbreak **:** OUTBURST **b :** a witty or imaginative saying **:** QUIP **3 :** an excursion usu. off the beaten track **:** JAUNT

[2]**sally** *vi* **1 :** to leap out or burst forth suddenly **2 :** to set out **:** DEPART — usu. used with *forth*

Sal·ly Lunn \,sal-ē-'lən\ *n* [*Sally Lunn,* 18th cent. E baker] **:** a slightly sweetened tea cake

sally port *n* **:** a gate or passage in a fortified place for use of troops making a sortie

sal·ma·gun·di \,sal-mə-'gən-dē\ *n* [F *salmigondis*] **1 :** a salad plate of chopped meats, anchovies, eggs, vegetables arranged in rows for contrast and dressed with a salad dressing **2 :** a heterogeneous mixture **:** POTPOURRI

sal·mi \'sal-mē\ *n* [F *salmis,* short for *salmigondis*] **:** a ragout of half roasted game stewed in a rich sauce

salm·on \'sam-ən\ *n, pl* **salmon** *also* **salmons** *often attrib* [ME *samon,* fr. MF, fr. L *salmon-, salmo*] **1 a :** a large soft-finned anadromous game fish (*Salmo salar*) of the northern Atlantic noted as a table fish **b :** any of various other anadromous fishes

(family Salmonidae); *esp* **:** a fish (genus *Oncorhynchus*) that breeds in rivers tributary to the northern Pacific **c :** a fish (as a barramunda) resembling a salmon **2 :** the variable color of salmon's flesh averaging a strong yellowish pink

salm·on·ber·ry \-ˌber-ē\ *n* **:** a showy red-flowered raspberry (*Rubus spectabilis*) of the Pacific coast; *also* **:** its edible salmon-colored fruit

sal·mo·nel·la \ˌsal-mə-ˈnel-ə\ *n, pl* **salmonellas** *or* **salmonella** *also* **sal·mo·nel·lae** \-ˈnel-(ˌ)ē, -ˌī\ [NL, genus name, fr. Daniel E. Salmon †1914 Am veterinarian] **:** any of a genus (*Salmonella*) of aerobic rod-shaped usu. motile bacteria that are pathogenic for man and other warm-blooded animals and cause food poisoning, gastrointestinal inflammation, or diseases of the genital tract — **sal·mo·nel·lo·sis** \-ˌnel-ˈō-səs\ *n*

salm·on·oid \ˈsam-ə-ˌnȯid\ *adj* **:** resembling or related to the typical salmons — **salmonoid** *n*

salmon pink *n* **:** a strong yellowish pink

Sa·lo·me \sə-ˈlō-mē\ *n* [LL, fr. Gk *Salōmē*] **:** a niece of Herod Antipas given the head of John the Baptist as a reward for her dancing

sa·lon \sa-ˈlōⁿ, -ˈlän; ˈsal-ˌōⁿ; *1–3 also, 4 usu* sə-ˈlän, ˈsal-ˌän\ *n* [F] **1 :** an elegant apartment or living room (as in a fashionable French home) **2 :** a fashionable assemblage of notables (as literary figures, artists, or statesmen) held by custom at the home of a prominent person **3 a :** a hall for exhibition of art **b** *cap* **:** an annual exhibition of such works **4 :** a stylish business establishment or shop

sa·loon \sə-ˈlün\ *n* [F *salon*, fr. It *salone*, aug. of *sala* hall, of Gmc origin; akin to OHG *sal* hall; akin to Lith *sala* village] **1 :** SALON 1 **2 :** SALON 2 **3 a :** an elaborately decorated public apartment or hall (as a large cabin for social use of a ship's passengers) **b :** SALON 4 **c :** a room or establishment in which alcoholic beverages are sold and consumed **:** BARROOM, TAPROOM **4** *Brit* **a :** PARLOR CAR **b :** SEDAN 2a

sa·loop \sə-ˈlüp\ *n* [modif. of F or Sp *salep*] **1 :** SALEP **2 :** a hot drink made from an infusion of salep or sassafras

salp \ˈsalp\ *n* [NL *Salpa*] **:** SALPA

sal·pa \ˈsal-pə\ *n* [NL, genus name, fr. L, a kind of stockfish, fr. Gk *salpē*] **:** a transparent barrel-shaped or fusiform free-swimming oceanic tunicate (family Salpidae and esp. genus *Salpa*) that is abundant in warm seas

sal·pi·glos·sis \ˌsal-pə-ˈgläs-əs\ *n* [NL, genus name, irreg. fr. Gk *salpinx* trumpet + *glōssa* tongue — more at GLOSS] **:** any of a small genus (*Salpiglossis*) of Chilean herbs of the nightshade family with large funnel-shaped varicolored flowers often strikingly marked

salping- *or* **salpingo-** *comb form* [NL, fr. *salping-*, *salpinx*] **:** salpinx ⟨*salping*itis⟩

sal·pin·gian \sal-ˈpin-j(ē-)ən\ *adj* **:** of or relating to a salpinx

sal·pin·gi·tis \ˌsal-pən-ˈjīt-əs\ *n* **:** inflammation of a fallopian or eustachian tube

sal·pinx \ˈsal-(ˌ)piŋ(k)s\ *n, pl* **sal·pin·ges** \sal-ˈpin-(ˌ)jēz\ [NL *salping-*, *salpinx*, fr. Gk, trumpet] **1 :** EUSTACHIAN TUBE **2 :** FALLOPIAN TUBE

sal·si·fy \ˈsal-sə-fē, -ˌfī\ *n* [F *salsifis*, modif. of It *sassefrica*, fr. LL *saxifrica*, any of various herbs, fr. L *saxum* rock + *fricare* to rub — more at SAXIFRAGE, FRICTION] **:** a European biennial composite herb (*Tragopogon porrifolius*) with a long fusiform edible root — called also *oyster plant*, *vegetable oyster*

sal soda \ˈsal-ˈsōd-ə\ *n* **:** a transparent crystalline hydrated sodium carbonate $Na_2CO_3.10H_2O$

1**salt** \ˈsȯlt\ *n* [ME, fr. OE *sealt;* akin to OHG *salz* salt, L *sal*, Gk *hals* salt, sea] **1 a :** a crystalline compound NaCl that is the chloride of sodium, abundant in nature, and used esp. for seasoning or preserving food or in industry — called also *common salt* **b :** a substance (as sal soda) resembling common salt in some property **c** *pl* (1) **:** a mineral or saline mixture (as Epsom salts) used as an aperient or cathartic (2) **:** SMELLING SALTS **d :** any of numerous compounds formed by replacement of part or all of the acid hydrogen of an acid by a metal or radical acting like a metal **2 a :** an element that gives savor, piquancy, or zest **:** FLAVOR **b :** sharpness of wit **:** PUNGENCY **c :** EARTHINESS **d :** RESERVE, SKEPTICISM — often used in the phrase *with a grain of salt* **e :** a scattered elite — usu. used in the phrase *salt of the earth* **3 :** SAILOR

2**salt** *vt* **1 a :** to sprinkle, rub, impregnate, or season with salt **b :** to preserve (food) with salt or in brine **2 :** to give flavor or piquancy to **3 :** to enrich (as a mine) artificially by secretly placing valuable mineral in some of the working places **4 :** to supply (as an animal) with salt **5 :** to sprinkle as if with salt ⟨~*ing* clouds with silver iodide⟩

3**salt** *adj* **1 a :** SALINE, SALTY **b :** being or inducing one of the four basic taste sensations **2 :** cured or seasoned with salt **:** SALTED **3 :** overflowed with salt water **4 :** SHARP, PUNGENT — **salt·ness** *n*

4**salt** *adj* [by shortening & alter. fr. *assaut*, fr. ME *a sawt*, fr. MF *a saut*, lit., on the jump] *obs* **:** LUSTFUL, LASCIVIOUS

sal·ta·rel·lo \ˌsal-tə-ˈrel-(ˌ)ō, ˌsäl-\ *n* [It] **:** an Italian dance with a lively hop step beginning each measure

sal·ta·tion \sal-ˈtā-shən, sȯl-\ *n* [L *saltation-*, *saltatio*, fr. *saltatus*, pp. of *saltare* to leap, dance, fr. *saltus*, pp. of *salire* to leap — more at SALLY] **1 a :** the action of leaping or jumping **b :** DANCING **2 a :** an abrupt change **b :** the reputed direct transformation of one form into another in the course of evolution; *broadly* **:** discontinuous variation

sal·ta·to·ri·al \ˌsal-tə-ˈtōr-ē-əl, ˌsȯl-, -ˈtȯr-\ *adj* **:** relating to, marked by, or adapted for leaping

sal·ta·to·ry \ˈsal-tə-ˌtōr-ē, ˈsȯl-, -ˌtȯr-\ *adj* **1 :** of or relating to dancing ⟨the ~ art⟩ **2 :** proceeding by leaps rather than by gradual transitions **:** DISCONTINUOUS — compare SALTATION 2b

salt away *vt* **:** to lay away safely **:** SAVE

salt·box \ˈsȯlt-ˌbäks\ *n* **:** a frame dwelling with two stories in front and one behind and a roof with a long rear slope

salt·bush \-ˌbu̇sh\ *n* **:** any of various shrubby plants of the goosefoot family that thrive in dry alkaline soil; *esp* **:** one of the oraches that are important browse plants in dry regions

salt·cel·lar \-ˌsel-ər\ *n* [ME *salt saler*, fr. *salt* + *saler* salt cellar, fr. MF, fr. L *salarius* of salt — more at SALARY] **:** a small vessel for holding salt at table

salt·ed \ˈsȯl-təd\ *adj, of an animal* **:** immune against a contagious disease because of prior infection and recovery

salt·er \ˈsȯl-tər\ *n* **1 :** one that manufactures or deals in salt **2 :** one that salts something (as meat, fish, or hides)

sal·tern \ˈsȯl-tərn\ *n* [OE *sealtern*, fr. *sealt* salt + *ærn* house; akin to ON *rann* house] **:** a place where salt is made (as by boiling)

salt grass *n* **:** a grass native to an alkaline habitat (as a salt meadow)

sal·ti·grade \ˈsal-tə-ˌgrād, ˈsȯl-\ *adj* [L *saltus* leap (fr. *saltus*, pp. of *salire* to leap) + *-i-* + *gradi* to step — more at SALLY, GRADE] **:** having feet or legs adapted to leaping

sal·tine \sȯl-ˈtēn\ *n* **:** a thin crisp cracker sprinkled with salt

salt·i·ness \ˈsȯl-tē-nəs\ *n* **:** the quality or state of being salty

sal·tire \ˈsȯl-ˌtī(ə)r, ˈsal-\ *n* [ME *sautire*, fr. MF *saultoir* X-shaped animal barricade that can be jumped over by people, saltire, fr. *saulter* to jump, fr. L *saltare* — more at SALTATION] **:** a heraldic ordinary consisting of a cross formed by a bend dexter and a bend sinister crossing in the center

salt·ish \ˈsȯl-tish\ *adj* **:** somewhat salty

salt lick *n* **:** LICK 3

salt marsh *n* **:** flat land subject to overflow by salt water

salt out *vt* **:** to precipitate, coagulate, or separate (a dissolved substance or lyophilic sol) from a solution by the addition of salt ~ *vi* **:** to become salted out

salt·pe·ter \ˈsȯlt-ˈpēt-ər\ *n* [alter. of earlier *salpeter*, fr. ME, fr. MF *salpetre*, fr. ML *sal petrae*, lit., salt of the rock] **1 :** POTASSIUM NITRATE **2 :** SODIUM NITRATE

salt·shak·er \-ˌshā-kər\ *n* **:** a container with a perforated top for sprinkling salt

salt·wa·ter \ˌsȯlt-ˌwȯt-ər, -ˌwät-\ *adj* **:** relating to, living in, or consisting of salt water

salt·works \ˈsȯlt-ˌwərks\ *n pl but sing or pl in constr* **:** a plant where salt is made on a commercial scale

salt·wort \-ˌwərt, -ˌwȯ(ə)rt\ *n* **1 :** any of a genus (*Salsola*) of plants of the goosefoot family used in making soda ash **2 :** GLASSWORT 1

salty \ˈsȯl-tē\ *adj* **1 :** of, seasoned with, or containing salt **:** SALINE **2 :** smacking of the sea or nautical life **3 a :** PIQUANT **b :** EARTHY

sa·lu·bri·ous \sə-ˈlü-brē-əs\ *adj* [L *salubris* — more at SAFE] **:** favorable to or promoting health or well-being **:** BENEFICIAL, HEALTHFUL — **sa·lu·bri·ous·ly** *adv* — **sa·lu·bri·ous·ness** *n* — **sa·lu·bri·ty** \-brət-ē\ *n*

sa·lu·ki \sə-ˈlü-kē\ *n* [Ar *salūqīy* of Saluq, fr. *Salūq* Saluq, ancient city in Arabia] **:** any of an old northern African and Asiatic breed of tall slender swift-footed keen-eyed hunting dogs having long narrow skulls, long silky ears, and a smooth silky coat ranging from white or cream to black or black and tan

sal·u·tar·i·ly \ˌsal-yə-ˈter-ə-lē\ *adv* **:** in a salutary manner

sal·u·tar·i·ness \ˈsal-yə-ˌter-ē-nəs\ *n* **:** the quality or state of being salutary

sal·u·tary \ˈsal-yə-ˌter-ē\ *adj* [MF *salutaire*, fr. L *salutaris*, fr. *salut-*, *salus* health] **1 :** promoting health **:** CURATIVE **2 :** producing a beneficial effect **:** REMEDIAL

sal·u·ta·tion \ˌsal-yə-ˈtā-shən\ *n* **1 a :** an expression of greeting, goodwill, or courtesy by word, gesture, or ceremony **b** *pl* **:** REGARDS **2 :** the word or phrase of greeting (as *Gentlemen* or *Dear Sir*) that conventionally comes immediately before the body of a letter — **sal·u·ta·tion·al** \-shnəl, -shən-ᵊl\ *adj*

sa·lu·ta·to·ri·an \sə-ˌlüt-ə-ˈtōr-ē-ən, -ˈtȯr-\ *n* **:** the graduating student usu. second highest in rank who pronounces the salutatory oration

1**sa·lu·ta·to·ry** \sə-ˈlüt-ə-ˌtōr-ē, -ˌtȯr-\ *adj* **:** expressing salutations or welcome

2**salutatory** *n* **:** a salutatory oration delivered at the commencement exercises of an educational institution

1**sa·lute** \sə-ˈlüt\ *vb* [ME *saluten*, fr. L *salutare*, fr. *salut-*, *salus* health, safety, greeting — more at SAFE] *vt* **1 a :** to address with expressions of kind wishes, courtesy, or honor or with a sign of respect, courtesy, or goodwill **:** GREET **b :** to become apparent to **2 a :** to honor by a conventional military or naval ceremony **b :** to show respect and recognition to (a military superior) by assuming a prescribed position **c :** to express commendation of **:** PRAISE ~ *vi* **:** to make a salute — **sa·lut·er** *n*

2**salute** *n* **1 :** GREETING, SALUTATION **2 a :** a sign, token, or ceremony (as a kiss or a bow) expressing goodwill, compliment, or respect **b :** the position of the hand or weapon or the entire attitude of a person saluting a superior **3 :** FIRECRACKER

sal·u·tif·er·ous \ˌsal-yə-ˈtif-(ə-)rəs\ *adj* [L *salutifer*, fr. *salut-*, *salus* + *-i-* + *-fer* -ferous] **:** SALUTARY

salv·able \ˈsal-və-bəl\ *adj* [LL *salvare* to save — more at SAVE] **:** capable of being saved or salvaged

1**sal·vage** \ˈsal-vij\ *n* [F, fr. MF, fr. *salver* to save — more at SAVE] **1 a :** compensation paid for saving a ship or its cargo from the perils of the sea or for the lives and property rescued in a wreck **b :** the act of saving or rescuing a ship or its cargo **c :** the act of saving or rescuing property in danger (as from fire) **2 :** property saved from destruction in a calamity (as a wreck or fire)

2**salvage** *vt* **:** to rescue or save (as from wreckage or ruin) — **salvage·able** \-ə-bəl\ *adj* — **sal·vag·er** *n*

Sal·var·san \ˈsal-vər-ˌsan\ *trademark* — used for arsphenamine

sal·va·tion \sal-ˈvā-shən\ *n* [ME, fr. OF, fr. LL *salvation-*, *salvatio*, fr. *salvatus*, pp. of *salvare* to save — more at SAVE] **1 :** the saving of man from the power and effects of sin **2 :** liberation from clinging to the phenomenal world of appearance and final union with ultimate reality **3** *Christian Science* **:** the realization of the supremacy of infinite Mind over all bringing with it the destruction of the illusion of sin, sickness, and death **4 a :** preservation from destruction or failure **b :** deliverance from danger or difficulty **5 :** the agent or means or the course of spiritual experiences determining the soul's redemption **6 :** something that saves from danger or difficulty **:** a source, cause, or means of preservation

sal·va·tion·al \-shnəl, -shən-ᵊl\ *adj* **:** of, relating to, or conducive to salvation

Salvation Army *n* **:** a religious and charitable organization on military lines founded in 1865 by William Booth for evangelizing and social betterment (as of the poor)

sal·va·tion·ism \sal-ˈvā-shə-ˌniz-əm\ *n* **:** religious teaching emphasizing the saving of the soul

Sal·va·tion·ist \-sh(ə-)nəst\ *n* **1 :** a soldier or officer of the Salvation Army **2** *often not cap* **:** EVANGELIST — **salvationist** *adj, often cap*

1**salve** \ˈsav, ˈsȧv\ *n* [ME, fr. OE *sealf;* akin to OHG *salba* salve, Gk *olpē* oil flask] **1 :** a healing ointment **2 :** a remedial or soothing

influence or agency **3 :** something laid on like a salve
[2]**salve** *vt* **:** QUIET, ASSUAGE
[3]**salve** \'salv\ *vt* [back-formation fr. *salvage*] **:** SALVAGE — **sal·vor** \'sal-vər, -,vȯ(ə)r\ *n*
sal·ver \'sal-vər\ *n* [modif. of F *salve*, fr. Sp *salva* sampling of food to detect poison, tray, fr. *salvar* to save, sample food to detect poison, fr. LL *salvare* to save — more at SAVE] **:** a tray esp. for serving food or beverages
sal·ver·form \'sal-vər-,fȯrm\ *or* **sal·ver–shaped** \-,shāpt\ *adj* **:** tubular with a spreading limb — used of a gamopetalous corolla
sal·via \'sal-vē-ə\ *n* [NL, genus name, fr. L, sage — more at SAGE] **:** any of a large and widely distributed genus (*Salvia*) of herbs or shrubs of the mint family having a 2-lipped open calyx and two anthers; *esp* **:** the scarlet-flowered sage
[1]**sal·vo** \'sal-(,)vō\ *n, pl* **salvos** *or* **salvoes** [It *salva*, fr. F *salve*, fr. L, hail!, imper. of *salvēre* to be healthy, fr. *salvus* healthy — more at SAFE] **1 a :** a simultaneous discharge of two or more guns in action or as a salute **b :** the release all at one time of a rack of bombs or rockets (as from an airplane) **c :** a series of shots by an artillery battery with each gun firing one round in turn after a prescribed interval **d :** the bombs or projectiles released in a salvo **2 :** SALUTE, TRIBUTE **3 :** a sudden burst (as of cheers)
[2]**salvo** *n* [ML *salvo jure* with the right reserved] **1 :** a mental reservation **:** PROVISO **2 :** a means of safeguarding one's honor or allaying one's conscience **:** SALVE
sal vo·la·ti·le \,sal-və-'lat-ᵊl-ē\ *n* [NL, lit., volatile salt] **:** an aromatic solution of ammonium carbonate in alcohol or ammonia water or both
sa·ma·ra \'sam-ə-rə; sə-'mar-ə, -'mär-\ *n* [NL, fr. L, seed of the elm] **:** a dry indehiscent usu. one-seeded winged fruit (as of an ash or elm tree) — called also *key*

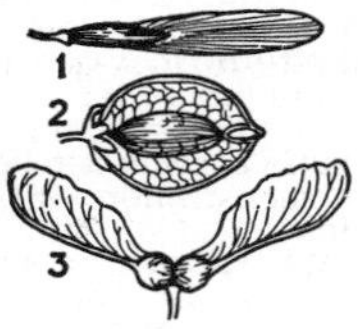

samaras: *1* ash, *2* elm, *3* maple

Sa·mar·i·tan \sə-'mar-ət-ᵊn, -'mer-\ *n* [ME, fr. LL *samaritanus*, n. & adj., fr. Gk *samaritēs* inhabitant of Samaria, fr. *Samaria*, district of ancient Palestine] **1 :** a native or inhabitant of Samaria **2** *often not cap* [fr. the parable of the good Samaritan, Lk 10:30–37] **:** one ready and generous in helping those in distress — **samaritan** *adj, often cap*
sa·mar·i·um \sə-'mer-ē-əm, -'mar-\ *n* [NL, fr. F *samarskite*] **:** a pale gray lustrous metallic element — see ELEMENT table
sa·mar·skite \sə-'mär-,skīt, 'sam-ər-\ *n* [F, fr. Col. von *Samarski*, 19th cent. Russ mine official] **:** a velvet-black orthorhombic mineral consisting of an oxide of rare earths, uranium, iron, lead, thorium, columbium, tantalum, titanium, and tin
sam·ba \'sam-bə, 'säm-\ *n* [Pg] **:** a Brazilian dance of African origin characterized by a dip and spring upward with a bending of the knee at each beat of the music — **samba** *vi*
sam·bar *or* **sam·bur** \'säm-bər, 'sam-\ *n* [Hindi *sābar*, fr. Skt *śambara*] **:** a large Asiatic deer (*Cervus unicolor*) having long coarse hair on the throat and the antlers strong and three-pointed
Sam Browne belt \,sam-,braůn-\ *n* [Sir *Samuel* James *Browne* †1901 Brit army officer] **:** a leather belt for a dress uniform supported by a light strap passing over the right shoulder
[1]**same** \'sām\ *adj* [ME, fr. ON *samr;* akin to OHG *sama* same, L *simulis* like, *simul* together, at the same time, *sem-* one, Gk *homos* same, *hama* together, *hen-*, *heis* one] **1 a :** resembling in every relevant respect **b :** conforming in every respect — used with *as* **2 a :** being one without addition, change or discontinuance **:** IDENTICAL **b :** being the one under discussion or already referred to **3 :** corresponding so closely as to be indistinguishable **:** COMPARABLE ⟨the ~ day last year⟩
syn SAME, SELFSAME, VERY, IDENTICAL, EQUIVALENT, EQUAL mean not different or not differing from one another. SAME may imply and SELFSAME always implies that the things under consideration are one thing and not two or more things, or SAME may imply numerical difference without difference in kind, appearance, or other essential aspect; VERY implies no difference in number and may additionally stress agreement with a desire or intent; IDENTICAL may imply selfsameness or suggest absolute agreement in all details; EQUIVALENT implies amounting to the same thing in worth or significance; EQUAL implies being identical in value, magnitude, or some specified quality
[2]**same** *pron* **1 :** something identical with or similar to another **2 :** something previously defined or described
[3]**same** *adv* **:** in the same manner
same here *adv* **:** similarly with me
sa·mekh \'säm-,ek\ *n* [Heb *sāmekh*] **:** the 15th letter of the Hebrew alphabet — symbol ס
same·ness \'sām-nəs\ *n* **1 :** the quality or state of being the same **:** IDENTITY **2 :** MONOTONY, UNIFORMITY
sam·iel \səm-'yel\ *n* [Turk *samyeli*] **:** SIMOOM
sam·i·sen \'sam-ə-,sen\ *n* [Jap] **:** a 3-stringed Japanese musical instrument resembling a banjo
sa·mite \'sam-,īt, 'sā-,mīt\ *n* [ME *samit*, fr. MF, fr. ML *examitum*, *samitum*, fr. MGk *hexamiton*, fr. Gk, neut. of *hexamitos* of six threads, fr. *hexa-* + *mitos* thread of the warp] **:** a rich medieval silk fabric interwoven with gold or silver
sam·let \'sam-lət\ *n* [irreg. fr. *salmon* + *-let*] **:** PARR
Sa·mo·an \sə-'mō-ən\ *n* **1 :** a native or inhabitant of Samoa **2 :** the Polynesian language of the Samoans — **Samoan** *adj*
sam·o·var \'sam-ə-,vär, ,sam-ə-'\ *n* [Russ, fr. *samo-* self + *varit'* to boil] **1 :** an urn with a spigot at its base used esp. in Russia to boil water for tea **2 :** an urn similar to a Russian samovar with a device for heating the contents
Sam·o·yed *also* **Sam·o·yede** \'sam-ə-,yed, 'sam-,ȯi-,ed\ *n* [Russ *samoed*] **1 :** a member of a people of the Nenets district of the Arkhangelsk region of the U.S.S.R. **2 :** any of a group of Uralic languages spoken by the Samoyed people **3 :** any of a Siberian breed of medium-sized deep-chested white or cream-colored arctic dogs — **Samoyed** *adj* — **Sam·o·yed·ic** \,sam-ə-'yed-ik, -,ȯi-'ed-\ *adj*
samp \'samp\ *n* [Narraganset *nasaump* corn mush] **:** coarse hominy or a boiled cereal made from it
sam·pan \'sam-,pan\ *n* [Chin (Pek) *san*[1] *pan*[3], fr. *san*[1] three + *pan*[3] board, plank] **:** a flat-bottomed Chinese skiff usu. propelled by two short oars
sam·phire \'sam-,fī(ə)r\ *n* [alter. of earlier *sampiere*, fr. MF (*herbe de*) *Saint Pierre*, lit., St. Peter's herb] **1 :** a fleshy European seacoast plant (*Crithmum maritimum*) of the carrot family sometimes pickled **2 :** a common glasswort (*Salicornia europaea*) that is sometimes pickled
[1]**sam·ple** \'sam-pəl\ *n* [ME, fr. MF *essample*, fr. L *exemplum* — more at EXAMPLE] **1 :** a representative part or a single item from a larger whole or group presented for inspection or shown as evidence of quality **:** SPECIMEN **2 :** a part of a statistical population whose properties are studied to gain information about the whole **syn** see INSTANCE
[2]**sample** *vt* **sam·pling** \-p(ə-)liŋ\ **1 :** to take a sample of; *esp* **:** to judge the quality of by a sample **:** TEST **2 :** to present a sample of
[1]**sam·pler** \'sam-plər\ *n* **:** a decorative piece of needlework typically having letters or verses embroidered on it in various stitches as an example of skill
[2]**sam·pler** \-plər, *before "of" also* -pə-lər\ *n* **1 :** one that collects or examines samples **2 :** something containing representative specimens or selections
sample room *n* **:** a room in which samples are displayed; *esp* **:** a hotel room in which salesmen display merchandise for the inspection of buyers for retail stores
sam·pling *n* **1** \-pliŋ\ **:** a small part selected as a sample for inspection or analysis **2** \-p(ə-)liŋ\ **:** the act, process, or technique of selecting a suitable sample
sam·sa·ra \səm-'sär-ə\ *n* [Skt *saṁsāra*, lit., passing through] **:** the indefinitely repeated cycles of birth, misery, and death caused by karma
sam·shu \'sam-(,)shü, -'shü\ *n* [perh. fr. Chin (Pek) *shao*[1] *chiu*[3], lit., spirits that will burn] **:** an alcoholic liquor distilled in China usu. from rice or large millet
Sam·son \'sam(p)-sən\ *n* [LL, fr. Gk *Sampsōn*, fr. Heb *Shimshōn*] **:** an Israelite judge of great physical strength
Sam·so·ni·an \sam(p)-'sō-nē-ən\ *adj* [*Samson*, judge of Israel] **:** of heroic strength or proportions **:** MIGHTY
Sam·u·el \'sam-yə(-wə)l\ *n* [LL, fr. Gk *Samouel*, fr. Heb *Shĕmū'ēl*] **:** an early Hebrew judge and prophet
sam·u·rai \'sam-(y)ə-,rī\ *n, pl* **samurai** [Jap] **1 :** a military retainer of a Japanese daimyo practicing the chivalric code of Bushido **2 :** the warrior aristocracy of Japan
san·a·tar·i·um \,san-ə-'ter-ē-əm\ *n, pl* **sanatariums** *or* **san·a·tar·ia** \-ē-ə\ [by alter.] **:** SANATORIUM
san·a·tive \'san-ət-iv\ *adj* [ME *sanatif*, fr. MF, fr. LL *sanativus*, fr. L *sanatus*, pp. of *sanare* to cure, fr. *sanus* healthy] **:** CURATIVE, RESTORATIVE
san·a·to·ri·um \,san-ə-'tōr-ē-əm, -'tȯr-\ *n, pl* **sanatoriums** *or* **san·a·to·ria** \-ē-ə\ [NL, fr. LL, neut. of *sanatorius* curative, fr. *sanatus*] **1 :** an establishment that provides physical therapy and other treatment **2 a :** an institution for rest and recuperation (as of convalescents) **b :** an establishment for the treatment of the chronically ill
san·be·ni·to \,san-bə-'nēt-(,)ō, ,sam-\ *n* [Sp *sambenito*, fr. *San Benito* St. Benedict of Nursia †*ab* 543] **1 :** a sackcloth coat worn by penitents on being reconciled to the church **2 :** a Spanish Inquisition garment resembling a scapular, yellow with red crosses for the penitent, and black with painted devils and flames for the impenitent condemned to an auto-da-fé
San·cho Pan·za \,san-chō-'pan-zə\ *n* **:** the squire of Don Quixote in Cervantes' *Don Quixote*
sanc·ti·fi·ca·tion \,saŋ(k)-ti-fə-'kā-shən\ *n* **1 :** an act of sanctifying **2 :** the state of being sanctified
sanc·ti·fi·er \'saŋ(k)-ti-,fī(-ə)r\ *n* **:** one that sanctifies; *specif, cap* **:** HOLY SPIRIT
sanc·ti·fy \-,fī\ *vt* [ME *sanctifien*, fr. MF *sanctifier*, fr. LL *sanctificare*, fr. L *sanctus* sacred — more at SAINT] **1 :** to set apart to a sacred purpose or to religious use **:** CONSECRATE **2 :** to free from sin **:** PURIFY **3 :** to give moral or social sanction to **4 :** to make efficient as the means of holiness
sanc·ti·mo·nious \,saŋ(k)-tə-'mō-nē-əs, -nyəs\ *adj* **1 :** affecting piousness **:** hypocritically devout **2** *obs* **:** possessing sanctity **:** HOLY **syn** see DEVOUT — **sanc·ti·mo·nious·ly** *adv* — **sanc·ti·mo·nious·ness** *n*
sanc·ti·mo·ny \'saŋ(k)-tə-,mō-nē\ *n* [MF *sanctimonie*, fr. L *sanctimonia*, fr. *sanctus*] **1** *obs* **:** HOLINESS **2 :** assumed or hypocritical holiness
[1]**sanc·tion** \'saŋ(k)-shən\ *n* [MF or L; MF, fr. L *sanction-*, *sanctio*, fr. *sanctus*, pp. of *sancire* to make holy — more at SACRED] **1 :** a formal decree; *esp* **:** an ecclesiastical decree **2 a** *obs* **:** a solemn agreement **:** OATH **b :** something that makes an oath binding **3 :** the detriment, loss of reward, or other coercive intervention annexed to a violation of a law as a means of enforcing the law **4 a :** a consideration, principle, or influence (as of conscience) that impels to moral action or determines moral judgment **b :** a mechanism of social control for enforcing a society's standards **c :** explicit or official permission or ratification **:** APPROBATION **5 :** an economic or military coercive measure adopted usu. by several nations in concert for forcing a nation violating international law to desist or yield to adjudication
[2]**sanction** *vt* **sanc·tion·ing** \-sh(ə-)niŋ\ **1 :** RATIFY, VALIDATE **2 :** to give effective approval or consent to **syn** see APPROVE
sanc·ti·ty \'saŋ(k)-tət-ē\ *n* [ME *saunctite*, fr. MF *sainctété*, fr. L *sanctitat-*, *sanctitas*, fr. *sanctus* sacred] **1 :** holiness of life and character **:** GODLINESS **2 a :** INVIOLABILITY, SACREDNESS **b** *pl* **:** sacred objects, obligations, or rights
sanc·tu·ary \'saŋ(k)-chə-,wer-ē\ *n* [ME *sanctuarie*, fr. MF *sainctuarie*, fr. LL *sanctuarium*, fr. L *sanctus*] **1 :** a consecrated place: as **a :** the ancient Hebrew temple at Jerusalem or its holy of holies **b :** the most sacred part of a religious building (as the part of a Christian church in which the altar is placed) **2 a :** a place of refuge and protection **b :** the immunity from law attached to a sanctuary
sanc·tum \'saŋ(k)-təm\ *n, pl* **sanctums** *also* **sanc·ta** \-tə\ [LL, fr. L, neut. of *sanctus* sacred] **1 :** a sacred place **2 :** a study, office, or place where one is free from intrusion ⟨an editor's ~⟩

sanc·tum sanc·to·rum \ˌsaŋ(k)-təm-ˌsaŋ(k)-'tōr-əm, -'tȯr-\ *n* [LL] : HOLY OF HOLIES
Sanc·tus \'saŋ(k)-təs; 'säŋ(k)-təs, -ˌtüs\ *n* [ME, fr. LL *Sanctus, sanctus, sanctus* Holy, holy, holy, opening of a hymn sung by the angels in Isa 6:3] : an ancient Christian hymn closing the preface of most Christian liturgies and commencing with the words *Sanctus, sanctus, sanctus* or *Holy, holy, holy*
Sanctus bell *n* : a bell rung by the server at the Sanctus of the mass
¹**sand** \'sand\ *n* [ME, fr. OE; akin to OHG *sant* sand, L *sabulum*, Gk *psammos* & *ammos* sand, *psēn* to rub] **1 a** : a loose granular material resulting from the disintegration of rocks that is used in mortar, glass, abrasives, and foundry molds **b** : soil containing 85 percent or more of sand and a maximum of 10 percent of clay **2 a** : a tract of sand : BEACH **b** : a sandbank or sandbar **3** : the sand in an hourglass; *also* : the moments of a lifetime **4** : an oil-producing formation of sandstone or unconsolidated sand **5** : firm resolution : COURAGE, BOLDNESS **6** : a variable color averaging a yellowish gray **syn** see FORTITUDE
²**sand** *vt* **1** : to sprinkle or powder with sand **2** : to cover or fill with sand **3** : to smooth by grinding or rubbing with an abrasive (as sandpaper)
san·dal \'san-dᵊl\ *n* [ME *sandalie*, fr. L *sandalium*, fr. Gk *sandalion*, dim. of *sandalon* sandal] **1** : a shoe consisting of a sole strapped to the foot **2** : a low-cut shoe that fastens by an ankle strap **3** : a strap to hold on a slipper or low shoe **4** : a rubber overshoe cut very low
san·dal·wood \-ˌwu̇d\ *n* [*sandal* (sandalwood) (fr. ME, fr. MF, fr. ML *sandalum*, fr. LGk *santalon*, deriv. of Skt *candana*, of Dravidian origin; akin to Tamil *cāntu* sandalwood tree) + *wood*] **1** : the compact close-grained fragrant yellowish heartwood of an Indo-Malayan parasitic tree (*Santalum album* of the family Santalaceae, the sandalwood family) much used in ornamental carving and cabinetwork; *also* : the tree that yields this wood **2** : any of various other trees or their fragrant wood some of which yield dyewoods
san·da·rac \'san-də-ˌrak\ *n* [L *sandaraca* red coloring, fr. Gk *sandarakē* realgar, red pigment from realgar] **1** : REALGAR **2** : a brittle faintly aromatic translucent resin obtained esp. from the African sandarac tree and used chiefly in making varnish and as incense
sandarac tree *n* : a large northern African tree (*Callitris articulata*) of the pine family with a hard durable fragrant wood much used in building; *also* : any of several related Australian trees
¹**sand·bag** \'san(d)-ˌbag\ *n* : a bag filled with sand and used as in fortifications, as ballast, or as a weapon
²**sandbag** *vt* **1** : to bank, stop up, or weight with sandbags **2 a** : to hit or stun with a sandbag **b** : to coerce by crude means — **sand·bag·ger** *n*
sand·bank \-ˌbaŋk\ *n* : a large deposit of sand in a mound, hillside, bar, or shoal
sand·bar \-ˌbär\ *n* : a ridge of sand built up by currents in a river or in coastal waters
¹**sand·blast** \-ˌblast\ *n* : a stream of sand projected by air or steam for engraving, cutting, or cleaning glass or stone, for cleaning and sharpening files, or for removing scale from metals
²**sandblast** *vt* : to engrave, cut, or clean with a high-velocity stream of sand — **sand·blast·er** *n*
sand–blind \'san(d)-ˌblīnd\ *adj* [ME, prob. fr. (assumed) ME *samblind*, fr. OE *sam-* half + *blind*; akin to OHG *sāmi-* half — more at SEMI-] : having poor eyesight : PURBLIND
sand bluestem *n* : a tall rhizomatous American grass (*Andropogon hallii*) used for forage and as a soil binder
sand·box \'san(d)-ˌbäks\ *n* : a box or other receptacle containing loose sand: as **a** : a shaker for sprinkling sand upon wet ink **b** : a box that contains sand for children to play in
sand·boy \-ˌbȯi\ *n* : any of various hopping insects (as a sand flea) found on sandy beaches
sand·bur \'san(d)-ˌbər\ *n* : any of several weeds of waste places with burry fruit: as **a** : a No. American nightshade (*Solanum rostratum*) with prickly foliage and racemose yellow flowers **b** : an annual bristly herb (*Franseria acanthicarpa*) of western No. America related to the cocklebur
sand–cast \-ˌkast\ *vt* : to make (a casting) by pouring metal in a sand mold (as in ordinary founding)
sand casting *n* : a casting made in a mold of sand
sand column *n* : DUST DEVIL
sand crack *n* : a fissure in the wall of a horse's hoof often causing lameness
sand dollar *n* : any of numerous flat circular sea urchins (order Exocycloida) that live on sandy bottoms
sand·er \'san-dər\ *n* : one that sands: as **a** : a device on a locomotive for sanding the rails **b** : SANDING MACHINE **c** : one that sands surfaces (as of wood, metal, plastic) to smooth, clean, or roughen them in preparation for finishing
sand·er·ling \'san-dər-liŋ\ *n* [perh. irreg. fr. *sand* + *-ling*] : a small sandpiper (*Crocethia alba*) with largely gray-and-white plumage
sand flea *n* **1** : a flea (as a chigoe) found in sandy places **2** : BEACH FLEA
sand fly *n* : any of various small biting two-winged flies (families Psychodidae, Simuliidae, and Ceratopogonidae)
sand·glass \'san(d)-ˌglas\ *n* : an instrument like an hourglass for measuring time by the running of sand
sand grouse *n* : any of numerous birds (family Pteroclidae) of arid parts of southern Europe, Asia, and Africa closely related to the pigeons but having precocial downy young
san·dhi \'san-dē, 'sän-, 'sən-\ *n* [Skt *saṁdhi*, lit., placing together] : modification of the sound of a morpheme (as a word or affix) conditioned by the context in which it is uttered ⟨pronunciation of *-ed* as \d\ in *glazed* and as \t\ in *paced*, and occurrence of *a* in *a cow* and of *an* in *an old cow*, are examples of ∼⟩
sand·hog \'sand-ˌhȯg, -ˌhäg\ *n* : a laborer who works in a caisson in driving underwater tunnels
sand·i·ness \'san-dē-nəs\ *n* : the quality or state of being sandy
sanding machine *n* : a machine for smoothing, polishing, or scouring with an abrasive disk or belt
sand jack *n* : a device for lowering a heavy weight (as a bridge section) into place by allowing sand on which it is supported to run out
sand launce *n* : any of several small elongate marine teleost fishes (genus *Ammodytes*) that associate in large schools and remain buried in sandy beaches at ebb tide — called also *sand eel*
sand lily *n* : a western No. American spring herb (*Leucocrinum montanum*) of the lily family with narrow linear leaves and fragrant salver-shaped flowers
sand·ling \'san-(d)liŋ\ *n* : a small flounder
sand·lot \'san-ˌ(d)lät\ *n* : a vacant lot esp. when used for the unorganized sports of boys from city streets — **sandlot** *adj* — **sand·lot·ter** \-ər\ *n*
sand·man \'san(d)-ˌman\ *n* : the genie of folklore who makes children sleepy supposedly by sprinkling sand in their eyes
sand myrtle *n* : a variable low-branching evergreen upland shrub (*Leiophyllum buxifolium*) of the heath family found in the southeastern U.S.
sand painting *n* : a Navaho and Pueblo Indian ceremonial design made of various materials (as colored sands) upon a flat surface of sand or buckskin
¹**sand·pa·per** \'san(d)-ˌpā-pər\ *n* : paper covered on one side with sand or other abrasive material glued fast and used for smoothing and polishing
²**sandpaper** *vt* : to rub with sandpaper
sand·pile \-ˌpīl\ *n* : a pile of sand; *esp* : sand for children to play in
sand·pip·er \-ˌpī-pər\ *n* : any of numerous small shore birds distinguished from the related plovers chiefly by the longer and soft-tipped bill
sand rat *n* : any of various rodents (as of Africa) native to sandy or desert areas
sand smelt *n* : SILVERSIDES 1
sand·soap \'san(d)-ˌsōp\ *n* : a gritty soap for all-purpose cleaning
sand·stone \'san(d)-ˌstōn\ *n* : a sedimentary rock consisting of usu. quartz sand united by some cement (as silica, iron oxide, or calcium carbonate)
sand·storm \-ˌstȯ(ə)rm\ *n* : a desert windstorm driving clouds of sand before it
sand table *n* **1 a** : a table holding sand for children to mold **b** : a table bearing a relief model of a terrain built to scale for study or demonstration **2** : an inclined table for concentrating ores by shaking
sand trap *n* : an artificial hazard on a golf course consisting of a depression containing sand
sand verbena *n* : any of several western American herbs (genus *Abronia*) of the four-o'clock family having flowers like the verbena; *esp* : either of two plants (*A. latifolia* and *A. umbellata*) of the Pacific coast
¹**sand·wich** \'san-(ˌ)(d)wich\ *n* [John Montagu, 4th Earl of *Sandwich* †1792 E diplomat] **1** : two or more slices of bread with a layer (as of meat, cheese, or savory mixture) spread between them **2** : something resembling a sandwich
²**sandwich** *vt* : to make into a sandwich; *also* : to insert between two things of different quality or character
sandwich board *n* : two usu. hinged boards designed for hanging from the shoulders with one board before and one behind and used esp. for advertising
sandwich man *n* : one who advertises or pickets a place of business by wearing a sandwich board
sand·worm \'san-ˌ(d)wərm\ *n* : any of various sand-dwelling polychaete worms: as **a** : any of several large burrowing worms (esp. genus *Nereis*) often used as bait **b** : LUGWORM
sand·wort \'san-ˌ(d)wərt, -ˌ(d)wȯ(ə)rt\ *n* : any of a genus (*Arenaria*) of low tufted herbs of the pink family growing usu. in dry sandy regions
sandy \'san-dē\ *adj* **1** : consisting of, containing, or sprinkled with sand **2** : of the color sand ⟨∼ hair⟩
sandy loam *n* : a loam low in clay and high in sand
sane \'sān\ *adj* [L *sanus* healthy, sane] **1** : free from hurt or disease : HEALTHY **2** : mentally sound; *esp* : able to anticipate and judge of the effect of one's actions **3** : proceeding from a sound mind : RATIONAL **syn** see WISE — **sane·ly** *adv* — **sane·ness** \'sān-nəs\ *n*
sang *past of* SING
san·ga·ree \ˌsaŋ-gə-'rē\ *n* [Sp *sangría*] : a cooling drink of wine or sometimes of ale, beer, or liquor sweetened, iced, and garnished with nutmeg
sang·froid \'säⁿ-'f(r)wä, ˌsäⁿ-frə-'wä\ *n* [F *sang-froid*, lit., cold blood] : self-possession or imperturbability esp. under strain **syn** see EQUANIMITY
San·greal \'san-'grā(ə)l\ *n* [ME *Sangrayll*, fr. MF *Saint Graal* Holy Grail] : GRAIL
san·gui·nar·ia \ˌsaŋ-gwə-'ner-ē-ə, -'nar-\ *n* [NL, fr. L, an herb that stanches blood, fr. fem. of *sanguinarius* sanguinary] **1** : BLOODROOT **2** : the rhizome and roots of a bloodroot used as an expectorant and emetic
san·gui·nar·i·ly \-'ner-ə-lē\ *adv* : in a sanguinary manner
san·gui·nary \'saŋ-gwə-ˌner-ē\ *adj* [L *sanguinarius*, fr. *sanguin-*, *sanguis* blood] **1** : BLOODTHIRSTY, MURDEROUS **2** : attended by bloodshed : BLOODY **3** : consisting of blood ⟨a ∼ stream⟩
¹**san·guine** \'saŋ-gwən\ *adj* [ME *sanguin*, fr. MF, fr. L *sanguineus*, fr. *sanguin-*, *sanguis*] **1** : BLOODRED **2 a** : consisting of or relating to blood **b** : SANGUINARY 1 **c** *of the complexion* : RUDDY **3 a** : having blood as the predominating bodily humor **b** : having the bodily conformation and temperament held characteristic of such predominance and marked by sturdiness, high color, and cheerfulness **4** : CONFIDENT, OPTIMISTIC — **san·guine·ly** *adv* — **san·guine·ness** \-gwən-nəs\ *n*
²**sanguine** *n* : a moderate to strong red
san·guin·e·ous \san-'gwin-ē-əs, saŋ-\ *adj* **1** : BLOODRED **2** : of, relating to, or involving bloodshed : BLOODTHIRSTY **3** : of, relating to, or containing blood
san·guin·i·ty \-'gwin-ət-ē\ *n* : the quality or state of being sanguine
san·guin·o·lent \-'gwin-ᵊl-ənt\ *adj* [L *sanguinolentus*, fr. *sanguin-*, *sanguis*] : of, containing, or tinged with blood ⟨∼ sputum⟩
san·gui·no·pu·ru·lent \ˌsaŋ-gwə-nō-'p(y)u̇r-(y)ə-lənt\ *adj* [L *sanguin-*, *sanguis* blood + E *-o-* + *purulent*] : containing blood and pus ⟨∼ discharge⟩
San·he·drin \san-'hēd-rən; sän-'hed-, san-\ *n* [LHeb *sanhedhrīn gĕdhōlāh* great council] : the supreme council and tribunal of the Jews in New Testament times having religious, civil, and criminal jurisdiction
san·i·cle \'san-i-kəl\ *n* [ME, fr. MF, fr. MF *sanicula*] : any of several plants reputed to have healing powers; *esp* : a plant (genus *Sanicula*) of the carrot family with a root used in folk medicine as an anodyne or astringent
sa·nies \'sān-(ē-ˌ)ēz, 'san-\ *n, pl* **sanies** [L] : a thin blood-tinged

seropurulent discharge from ulcers or infected wounds — **sa·ni·ous** \-ē-əs\ *adj*

san·i·tar·i·an \ˌsan-ə-ˈter-ē-ən\ *n* **:** a specialist in sanitary science and public health ⟨milk ~⟩

san·i·tar·i·ly \-ˈter-ə-lē\ *adv* **:** in a sanitary manner **:** with regard to sanitation

san·i·tar·i·um \ˌsan-ə-ˈter-ē-əm\ *n* [NL, fr. L *sanitat-*, *sanitas* health] **:** SANATORIUM

san·i·tary \ˈsan-ə-ˌter-ē\ *adj* [F *sanitaire*, fr. L *sanitas*] **1 :** of or relating to health **:** HYGIENIC ⟨~ measures⟩ **2 :** of, relating to, or used in the disposal esp. of domestic waterborne waste ⟨~ sewage⟩ **3 :** characterized by or readily kept in cleanliness ⟨~ packages⟩

sanitary napkin *n* **:** a disposable absorbent pad (as of cellulose) in a gauze covering used to absorb the uterine flow during menstruation or postpartum

san·i·tate \ˈsan-ə-ˌtāt\ *vt* [back-formation fr. *sanitation*] **:** to provide with sanitary appliances or facilities

san·i·ta·tion \ˌsan-ə-ˈtā-shən\ *n* **1 :** the act or process of making sanitary **2 :** the promotion of hygiene and prevention of disease by maintenance of sanitary conditions

san·i·tize \ˈsan-ə-ˌtīz\ *vt* [L *sanitas*] **:** to make sanitary (as by cleaning or sterilizing)

san·i·ty \ˈsan-ət-ē\ *n* [ME *sanite*, fr. L *sanitat-*, *sanitas* health, sanity, fr. *sanus* healthy, sane] **:** the quality or state of being sane; *esp* **:** soundness or health of mind

San Ja·cin·to Day \ˌsan-jə-ˈsint-ə-\ *n* **:** April 21 observed as a legal holiday in Texas in commemoration of the battle of San Jacinto in 1836

San Jo·se scale \ˌsan-ə-ˌzā-\ *n* [*San Jose*, Calif.] **:** a prob. Asiatic scale insect (*Aspidiotus perniciosus*) naturalized in the U.S. and a most damaging pest to fruit trees

sank *past of* SINK

San·khya \ˈsäŋ-kyə\ *n* [Skt *sāṁkhya*, lit., based on calculation] **:** an orthodox Hindu philosophy teaching salvation through knowledge of the distinction between matter and souls

san·nup \ˈsan-əp\ *n* [Abnaki *senanbe*] **:** a married male American Indian — compare SQUAW

sann·ya·si \(ˌ)sən-ˈyäs-ē\ *or* **sann·ya·sin** \-ˈyäs-ᵊn\ *n* [Hindi *sannyāsī*] **:** a Hindu mendicant ascetic

sans \(ˌ)sanz\ *prep* [ME *saun*, *sans*, fr. MF *san*, *sans*, modif. of L *sine* without — more at SUNDER] **:** WITHOUT

sans-cu·lotte \ˌsanz-skyu̇-ˈlät\ *n* [F *sans-culotte*, lit., without breeches] **1 :** an extreme radical republican in France at the time of the Revolution **2 :** a person of the lower class: as **a :** one lacking culture and refinement **b :** a radical or violent extremist in politics — **sans-cu·lott·ic** \-ˈlät-ik\ *adj* — **sans-cu·lott·ish** \-ish\ *adj* — **sans-cu·lott·ism** \-ˌiz-əm, ˈsan-skyü-ˌlät-\ *n*

san·sei \(ˈ)sän-ˈsā, ˈsän-ˌ\ *n, pl* **sansei** *also* **sanseis** *often cap* [Jap *san* third + *sei* generation] **:** a son or daughter of nisei parents who is born and educated in America and esp. in the U.S.

san·se·vie·ria \ˌsan(t)-sə-ˈvir-ē-ə\ *n* [NL, genus name, fr. Raimondo di Sangro, prince of *San Severo* †1774 It scholar] **:** any of a genus (*Sansevieria*) of tropical herbs of the lily family with showy mottled sword-shaped leaves usu. yielding a strong fiber

San·skrit \ˈsan-ˌskrit, ˈsan(t)-skrət\ *n* [Skt *saṁskṛta*, lit., perfected, fr. *sam* together + *karoti* he makes] **1 :** an ancient Indic language that is the classical language of India and of Hinduism as described by the Indian grammarians **2 :** classical Sanskrit together with the older Vedic and various later modifications of classical Sanskrit — **Sanskrit** *adj* — **San·skrit·ist** \-əst\ *n*

San·skrit·ic \san-ˈskrit-ik\ *n* **1 :** INDIC **2 :** a group of Indic languages developed directly from Sanskrit — **Sanskritic** *adj*

sans ser·if *or* **san·ser·if** \san-ˈser-əf\ *n* [prob. fr. *sans* + modif. of D *schreef* stroke — more at SERIF] **:** a letter or typeface with no serifs

San·ta Claus \ˈsant-ē-ˌklȯz, ˈsant-ə-\ *n* [modif. of D *Sinterklaus*, alter. of *Sint Nikolaas* Saint Nicholas *fl* 4th cent., bishop of Myra, Asia Minor and patron saint of children] **:** the religious and holiday spirit of Christmas personified

San·ta Ger·tru·dis \ˌsant-ə-(ˌ)gər-ˈtrüd-əs\ *n* [*Santa Gertrudis*, section of the King Ranch, Kingsville, Texas] **:** any of a breed of cherry-red beef cattle developed from a Brahman-Shorthorn cross and valued for their hardiness in hot climes and thrifty growth on grass

san·ton·i·ca \san-ˈtän-i-kə\ *n* [NL, fr. L (*herba*) *santonica* an herb, prob. wormwood, fem. of *santonicus* of the Santoni, fr. *Santoni*, a people of Aquitania] **1 :** a European wormwood (*Artemisia pauciflora*) **2 :** the unexpanded dried flower heads of santonica or a related plant used as an anthelmintic

san·to·nin \ˈsant-ᵊn-ən, san-ˈtän-ən\ *n* [ISV, fr. NL *santonica*] **:** a poisonous slightly bitter crystalline compound $C_{15}H_{18}O_3$ found esp. in santonica and used as an anthelmintic

San·tos \ˈsant-əs\ *n* [*Santos*, Brazil] **:** a Brazilian coffee of moderate body and somewhat acid flavor produced chiefly in São Paulo

¹sap \ˈsap\ *n* [ME, fr. OE *sæp*; akin to OHG *saf* sap] **1 a :** the fluid part of a plant; *specif* **:** a watery solution that circulates through a plant's vascular system **b** (1) **:** a body fluid (as blood) essential to life, health, or vigor (2) **:** bodily health and vigor **:** VITALITY **2 :** a foolish gullible person **3 :** BLACKJACK, BLUDGEON

²sap *vt* **sapped; sap·ping 1 :** to drain or deprive of sap **2 :** to knock out with a sap

³sap *n* [MF & OIt; MF *sappe* hoe, fr. OIt *zappa*] **:** the extension of a trench from within the trench itself to a point beneath an enemy's fortifications

⁴sap *vb* **sapped; sap·ping** *vi* **:** to proceed by or execute a sap ~ *vt* **1 :** to subvert by digging or eroding the substratum or foundation **:** UNDERMINE **2 :** to weaken or exhaust the energy or vitality of **3 :** to operate against or pierce by a sap **syn** see WEAKEN

sap green *n* **:** a strong yellow green

sap·head \ˈsap-ˌhed\ *n* **:** a weak-minded stupid person **:** SAP — **sap·head·ed** \-ˈhed-əd\ *adj*

sa·phe·nous \sə-ˈfē-nəs\ *adj* [*saphena* (saphenous vein), fr. ME, fr. ML, fr. Ar *ṣāfin*] **:** of or relating to the two chief superficial veins of the leg

sap·id \ˈsap-əd\ *adj* [L *sapidus* tasty, fr. *sapere* to taste — more at SAGE] **1 a :** affecting the organs of taste **:** possessing flavor **b :** having a strong agreeable flavor **2 :** agreeable to the mind

sa·pid·i·ty \sə-ˈpid-ət-ē, sa-\ *n* **:** the quality or state of being sapid **:** SAVOR **syn** see TASTE

sa·pi·ence \ˈsā-pē-ən(t)s, ˈsap-ē-\ *n* **:** WISDOM, SAGENESS

sa·pi·ens \ˈsap-ē-ənz, ˈsā-pē-, -ˌenz\ *adj* [NL (specific epithet of *Homo sapiens*), fr. L, pp. of *sapere*] **:** of, relating to, or being recent man (*Homo sapiens*) as distinguished from various fossil men

sa·pi·ent \ˈsā-pē-ənt, ˈsap-ē-\ *adj* [ME, fr. MF, fr. L *sapient-*, *sapiens*, fr. prp. of *sapere* to taste, be wise] **:** SAGE, DISCERNING **syn** see WISE — **sa·pi·ent·ly** *adv*

sap·less \ˈsap-ləs\ *adj* **1 :** destitute of sap **:** DRY **2 :** lacking vitality or vigor **:** FEEBLE — **sap·less·ness** *n*

sap·ling \ˈsap-liŋ, -lən\ *n* **1 :** a young tree; *specif* **:** one not over four inches in diameter at breast height **2 :** YOUTH 2a

sap·o·dil·la \ˌsap-ə-ˈdil-ə, -ˈdē-(y)ə\ *n* [Sp *zapotillo*, dim. of *zapote* sapodilla — more at SAPOTA] **:** a tropical evergreen tree (*Achras zapota* of the family Sapotaceae, the sapodilla family) with hard reddish wood, a latex that yields chicle, and a rough-skinned brownish edible fruit; *also* **:** its fruit

sa·po·na·ceous \ˌsap-ə-ˈnā-shəs, sə-ˌpō-\ *adj* [NL *saponaceus*, fr. L *sapon-*, *sapo* soap, of Gmc origin; akin to OE *sāpe* soap] **1 :** resembling or having the qualities of soap **:** SOAPY ⟨a ~ root⟩ **2 :** ELUSIVE, SLIPPERY — **sa·po·na·ceous·ness** *n*

sa·po·nat·ed \ˈsap-ə-ˌnāt-əd, sə-ˈpō-\ *adj* **:** treated or combined with a soap ⟨~ cresol solution⟩

sa·pon·i·fi·able \sə-ˈpän-ə-ˌfī-ə-bəl\ *adj* **:** capable of being saponified ⟨~ oils⟩

sa·pon·i·fi·ca·tion \sə-ˌpän-ə-fə-ˈkā-shən\ *n* **1 :** the hydrolysis of a fat by alkali with the formation of a soap and glycerol **2 :** the hydrolysis esp. by alkali of an ester into the corresponding alcohol and acid; *broadly* **:** HYDROLYSIS

sa·pon·i·fi·er \sə-ˈpän-ə-ˌfī(-ə)r\ *n* **:** a reagent or apparatus used in saponification

sa·pon·i·fy \-ˌfī\ *vb* [F *saponifier*, fr. L *sapon-*, *sapo*] *vt* **:** to convert (as fat) into soap; *broadly* **:** to subject to saponification ~ *vi* **:** to undergo saponification

sa·po·nin \ˈsap-ə-nən, sə-ˈpō-\ *n* [F *saponine*, fr. L *sapon-*, *sapo*] **:** any of various glucosides found in plants (as soapwort or soapbark), and marked by the property of producing a soapy lather; *esp* **:** a hygroscopic amorphous saponin mixture used esp. as a foaming and emulsifying agent and detergent

sap·o·nite \ˈsap-ə-ˌnīt, sə-ˈpō-\ *n* [Sw *saponit*, fr. L *sapon-*, *sapo* soap] **:** a hydrous magnesium aluminum silicate occurring in soft soapy amorphous masses and filling veins and cavities (as in serpentine or diabase)

sa·por \ˈsā-pər, -ˌpȯ(ə)r\ *n* [ME, fr. L — more at SAVOR] **:** a property (as bitterness) affecting the sense of taste **:** SAVOR, FLAVOR — **sa·po·rif·ic** \ˌsā-pə-ˈrif-ik, ˌsap-ə-\ *adj* — **sa·po·rous** \ˈsā-pə-rəs, ˈsap-ə-\ *adj*

sa·po·ta \sə-ˈpōt-ə\ *n* [modif. of Sp *zapote*, fr. Nahuatl *tzapotl*] **:** SAPODILLA

sap·pan·wood \sə-ˈpan-ˌwu̇d; ˈsap-ˌan-, -ən-\ *n* [Malay *sapang* heartwood of sappanwood + E *wood*] **:** a red soluble brazilwood obtained from an East Indian leguminous tree (*Caesalpinia sappan*); *also* **:** this tree

sap·per \ˈsap-ər\ *n* **1 :** a military engineer who does field fortification work (as sapping) **2 :** an engineer who lays, detects, and disarms mines

¹sap·phic \ˈsaf-ik\ *adj* **1** *cap* **:** of or relating to the Greek lyric poet Sappho **2 :** of, relating to, or consisting of a 4-line strophe made up of chiefly trochaic and dactylic feet **3 :** LESBIAN 2

²sapphic *n* **1 :** a sapphic strophe **2 :** a verse having the metrical pattern of one of the first three lines of a sapphic strophe

Sap·phi·ra \sə-ˈfī-rə\ *n* [Gk *Sappheirē*] **:** the wife of Ananias

sap·phire \ˈsaf-ˌī(ə)r\ *n* [ME *safir*, fr. OF, fr. L *sapphirus*, fr. Gk *sappheiros*, fr. Heb *sappīr*, fr. Skt *śanipriya*, lit., dear to the planet Saturn, fr. *Śani* Saturn + *priya* dear] **1 a :** a precious stone of transparent rich blue corundum **b :** a pure variety of corundum in transparent or translucent crystals used as a gem; *also* **:** such a gem **2 :** a variable color averaging a deep purplish blue — **sapphire** *adj*

¹sap·phi·rine \ˈsaf-ə-ˌrīn, ˈsaf-ˌī(ə)r-ˌēn, sa-ˈfī-rən\ *adj* **1 :** made of sapphire **2 :** resembling sapphire esp. in color

²sap·phi·rine \ˈsaf-ˌī(ə)r-ˌēn\ *n* **:** a mineral $(MgFe)_{15}(Al,Fe)_{34}Si_7O_{80}$ consisting of a green or pale blue magnesium aluminum iron silicate and oxide and occurring usu. in granular form

sap·phism \ˈsaf-ˌiz-əm\ *n* [*Sappho fl ab* 600 B.C. Greek poetess of Lesbos; fr. the belief that Sappho was homosexual] **:** LESBIANISM

sap·pi·ness \ˈsap-ē-nəs\ *n* **1 :** the state of being full of or smelling of sap **2 :** the quality or state of being sappy **:** FOOLISHNESS

sap·py \ˈsap-ē\ *adj* **1 :** abounding with sap **2 :** resembling or consisting largely of sapwood **3 a :** foolishly or immaturely sentimental **:** MAWKISH **b :** lacking in good sense **:** SILLY

sapr- *or* **sapro-** *comb form* [Gk, fr. *sapros*] **1 :** rotten **:** putrid ⟨sapremia⟩ **2 :** dead or decaying organic matter ⟨saprophyte⟩

sa·pre·mia \sa-ˈprē-mē-ə\ *n* [NL] **:** a toxic state in which toxic products of putrefactive bacteria are present in the blood — **sa·pre·mic** \-mik\ *adj*

sap·robe \ˈsap-ˌrōb\ *or* **sap·ro·bi·ont** \ˌsap-rō-ˈbī-ˌänt\ *n* [*saprobe* ISV *sapr-* + Gk *bios* life; *saprobiont* irreg. fr. *sapr-* + Gk *biount-*, *biōn*, prp. of *bioun* to live, fr. *bios* — more at QUICK] **:** a saprobic organism

sa·pro·bic \sa-ˈprō-bik\ *adj* **:** SAPROPHYTIC; *also* **:** living in or being an environment rich in organic matter and relatively free from oxygen — **sa·pro·bi·cal·ly** \-bi-k(ə-)lē\ *adv*

sap·ro·gen·ic \ˌsap-rə-ˈjen-ik\ *adj* **:** of, causing, or resulting from putrefaction — **sap·ro·ge·nic·i·ty** \-rō-jə-ˈnis-ət-ē\ *n*

sap·ro·lite \ˈsap-rə-ˌlīt\ *n* **:** disintegrated rock that lies in its original place

sap·ro·pe·lic \ˌsap-rə-ˈpel-ik, -ˈpē-lik\ *adj* [ISV *sapr-* + Gk *pēlos* clay, mud] **:** living in mud or ooze rich in decaying organic matter

sa·proph·a·gous \sa-ˈpräf-ə-gəs\ *adj* [NL *saprophagus*, fr. *sapr-* + *-phagus* -phagous] **:** feeding on decaying matter

sap·ro·phyte \ˈsap-rə-ˌfīt\ *n* [ISV] **1 :** a plant living on dead or decaying organic matter **2 :** an organism engaging in saprophytic nutrition

sap·ro·phyt·ic \ˌsap-rə-ˈfit-ik\ *adj* **:** obtaining food by absorbing

dissolved organic material; *esp* **:** obtaining nourishment osmotically from the products of organic breakdown and decay — **sap·ro·phyt·i·cal·ly** \-i-k(ə-)lē\ *adj*

sap·ro·zo·ic \ˌsap-rə-ˈzō-ik\ *adj* **:** SAPROPHYTIC — used of animals (as protozoans) — **sap·ro·zo·on** \-ˈzō-ˌän\ *n*

sap·sa·go \sap-ˈsā-(ˌ)gō, ˈsap-sə-ˌgō\ *n* [modif. of G *schabziger*] **:** a hard green skim-milk cheese containing dried leaf of an aromatic legume (*Trigonella coerulea*)

sap·suck·er \ˈsap-ˌsək-ər\ *n* **:** any of various small American woodpeckers (esp. genus *Sphyrapicus*) reputed to feed on sap

sap·wood \-ˌwu̇d\ *n* **:** the younger softer living or physiologically active outer portion of wood that lies between the cambium and the heartwood and is more permeable, less durable, and usu. lighter in color than the heartwood

sar·a·band *or* **sar·a·bande** \ˈsar-ə-ˌband\ *n* [F *sarabande*, fr. Sp *zarabanda*] **1 :** a stately court dance of the 17th and 18th centuries **2 :** the music for the saraband in slow triple time with accent on the second beat

Sar·a·cen \ˈsar-ə-sən\ *n* [ME, fr. LL *Saracenus*, fr. LGk *Sarakēnos*] **:** a member of a nomadic people of the deserts between Syria and Arabia; *broadly* **:** ARAB — **Saracen** *adj* — **Sar·a·cen·ic** \ˌsar-ə-ˈsen-ik\ *adj*

Sa·rah \ˈser-ə, ˈsar-ə, ˈsā-rə\ *n* [Heb *Śārāh*] **:** the wife of Abraham and mother of Isaac

sa·ran \sə-ˈran\ *n* [fr. *Saran*, a trademark] **:** a tough flexible thermoplastic that can be formed into waterproof and chemically resistant products (as filaments, tubing, and coating)

sa·ra·pe \sə-ˈräp-ē\ *n* [MexSp] **:** a woolen blanket worn by Spanish-American men as a cloak or poncho

Sar·a·to·ga trunk \ˌsar-ə-ˌtō-gə-\ *n* [*Saratoga* Springs, N.Y.] **:** a large traveling trunk usu. with a rounded top

sarc- *or* **sarco-** *comb form* [Gk *sark-*, *sarko-*, fr. *sark-*, *sarx*] **:** flesh ⟨*sarcous*⟩

sar·casm \ˈsär-ˌkaz-əm\ *n* [F *sarcasme*, fr. LL *sarcasmos*, fr. Gk *sarkasmos*, fr. *sarkazein* to tear flesh, bite the lips in rage, sneer, fr. *sark-*, *sarx* flesh; akin to Av *thwarəs* to cut] **1 :** a cutting, hostile, or contemptuous remark **:** GIBE **2 :** the use of caustic or ironic language **syn** see WIT — **sar·cas·tic** \sär-ˈkas-tik\ *adj* — **sar·cas·ti·cal·ly** \-ti-k(ə-)lē\ *adv*

sarce·net *or* **sarse·net** \ˈsär-snət\ *n* [ME *sarcenet*, fr. AF *sarzinett*] **:** a soft thin silk in plain or twill weaves used for dresses, veilings, or trimmings — **sarcenet** *adj*

sar·co·carp \ˈsär-kə-ˌkärp\ *n* [F *sarcocarpe*, fr. *sarc-* + *-carpe* -carp] **1 :** a usu. thickened and fleshy mesocarp **2 :** a fleshy fruit

sar·coid \ˈsär-ˌkȯid\ *adj* [Gk *sarkoeidēs*, fr. *sark-*, *sarx* flesh] **:** of or resembling flesh **:** FLESHY

sar·co·ma \sär-ˈkō-mə\ *n* [NL, fr. Gk *sarkōmat-*, *sarkōma* fleshy growth, fr. *sarkoun* to grow flesh, fr. *sark-*, *sarx*] **:** a malignant neoplasm arising in tissue of mesodermal origin (as connective tissue, bone, cartilage, or striated muscle) — **sar·co·ma·to·sis** \(ˌ)sär-ˌkō-mə-ˈtō-səs\ *n* — **sar·co·ma·tous** \sär-ˈkäm-ət-əs, -ˈkōm-\ *adj*

sar·coph·a·gous \sär-ˈkäf-ə-gəs\ *or* **sar·co·phag·ic** \ˌsär-kə-ˈfaj-ik\ *adj* [L *sarcophagus* flesh-eating, fr. Gk *sarkophagos*] **:** CARNIVOROUS — **sar·coph·a·gy** \sär-ˈkäf-ə-jē\ *n*

sar·coph·a·gus \sär-ˈkäf-ə-gəs\ *n, pl* **sar·coph·a·gi** \-ˌgī, -ˌjī, -ˌgē\ *also* **sar·coph·a·gus·es** [L *sarcophagus* (*lapis*) limestone used for coffins, fr. Gk (*lithos*) *sarkophagos*, lit., flesh-eating stone, fr. *sark-* sarc- + *phagein* to eat — more at BAKSHEESH] **1** *obs* **:** a limestone used among the Greeks for coffins and held to disintegrate the flesh of bodies deposited in it **2 :** a stone coffin

sar·cop·tic mange \ˌsär-ˌkäp-tik-\ *n* [NL *Sarcoptes*, genus of mites, fr. *sarc-* + Gk *koptein* to cut — more at CAPON] **:** mange caused by mites (genus *Sarcoptes*) burrowing in the skin esp. of the head and face

sar·cous \ˈsär-kəs\ *adj* **:** of, relating to, or consisting of muscle tissue **:** FLESHY

sard \ˈsärd\ *n* [F *sarde*, fr. L *sarda*] **:** a deep orange-red variety of chalcedony classed by some as a variety of carnelian

sardar *var of* SIRDAR

1sar·dine \ˈsär-ˌdīn\ *n* [ME, fr. LL (*lapis*) *sardinus*, fr. Gk *sardinos* (*lithos*), lit., stone of Sardis, ancient city in Asia Minor] **:** SARD

2sar·dine \sär-ˈdēn\ *n, pl* **sardines** *also* **sardine** [ME *sardeine*, fr. MF *sardine*, fr. L *sardina*] **1 :** any of several small or immature clupeid fishes; *esp* **:** the young of the European pilchard (*Sardinia pilchardus*) when of a size suitable for preserving for food **2 :** any of various small fishes (as an anchovy) resembling the true sardines or similarly preserved for food

Sar·din·ian \sär-ˈdin-ē-ən, -ˈdin-yən\ *n* **1 :** a native or inhabitant of Sardinia **2 :** the Romance language of central and southern Sardinia — **Sardinian** *adj*

sar·di·us \ˈsärd-ē-əs\ *n* [LL, fr. (*lapis*) *sardius*, fr. Gk *sardios* (*lithos*), lit., stone of Sardis] **:** SARD

sar·don·ic \sär-ˈdän-ik\ *adj* [F *sardonique*, fr. Gk *sardonios*] **:** BITTER, MOCKING — **sar·don·i·cal·ly** \-i-k(ə-)lē\ *adv*

sard·onyx \sär-ˈdän-iks *also* ˈsärd-ᵊn-\ *n* [ME *sardonix*, fr. L *sardonyx*, fr. Gk] **:** an onyx having parallel layers of sard

sar·gas·so \sär-ˈgas-(ˌ)ō\ *n* [Pg *sargaço*] **1 :** GULFWEED, SARGASSUM **2 :** a mass of floating vegetation and esp. sargassums

sar·gas·sum \-ˈgas-əm\ *n* [NL, fr. ISV *sargasso*] **:** any of a genus (*Sargassum*) of brown algae having a branching thallus with lateral outgrowths differentiated as leafy segments, air bladders, or spore-bearing structures **:** GULFWEED

sarge \ˈsärj\ *n* [by shortening & alter.] **:** SERGEANT

sa·ri *or* **sa·ree** \ˈsär-ē\ *n* [Hindi *sārī*, fr. Skt *śāṭī*] **:** a garment of Hindu women that consists of yards of lightweight cloth draped so that one end forms a skirt and the other a head or shoulder covering

sark \ˈsärk\ *n* [ME (Sc) *serk*, fr. OE *serc;* akin to ON *serkr* shirt] *dial chiefly Brit* **:** SHIRT

sar·men·tose \sär-ˈmen-ˌtōs, ˈsär-mən-\ *adj* [L *sarmentosus*, fr. *sarmentum* twig, fr. *sarpere* to prune] **:** producing slender prostrate branches or runners

sa·rong \sə-ˈrȯŋ, -ˈräŋ\ *n* [Malay *kain sarong* cloth sheath] **1 :** a loose skirt made of a long strip of cloth wrapped around the body and worn by men and women of the Malay archipelago and the Pacific islands **2 :** cloth for sarongs

Sar·pe·don \sär-ˈpēd-ᵊn\ *n* [L, fr. Gk *Sarpēdōn*] **:** a son of Zeus and Europa and king of Lycia killed in the Trojan War

sar·ra·ce·nia \ˌsar-ə-ˈsē-nē-ə, -ˈsen-ē-\ *n* [NL, genus name, fr. Michel *Sarrazin* †1734 F physician & naturalist] **:** any of a genus (*Sarracenia* of the family Sarraceniaceae, the pitcher-plant family) comprising insectivorous bog herbs of eastern No. America with pitcher-shaped or tubular leaves having an arched or hooded flap at the apex

sar·sa·pa·ril·la \ˌsas-(ə-)pə-ˈril-ə, ˌsär-s(ə-)pə-, -ˈrel-\ *n* [Sp *zarzaparilla*] **1 a :** any of various tropical American greenbriers **b :** the dried roots of a sarsaparilla plant used esp. as a flavoring **2 :** a sweetened carbonated beverage similar to root beer with the predominant flavor from birch oil and sassafras

sar·to·ri·al \sär-ˈtōr-ē-əl, sə(r)-, -ˈtȯr-\ *adj* [L *sartor*] **:** of or relating to a tailor or tailored clothes — **sar·to·ri·al·ly** \-ē-ə-lē\ *adv*

sar·to·ri·us \sär-ˈtōr-ē-əs, -ˈtȯr-\ *n* [NL, fr. L *sartor* tailor, fr. *sartus*, pp. of *sarcire* to mend — more at EXORCISE] **:** a muscle that crosses the front of the thigh obliquely, assists in rotating the leg to the position assumed in sitting like a tailor, and in man is the longest muscle

Sar·um \ˈsar-əm, ˈser-\ *adj* [*Sarum*, old borough near Salisbury, England] **:** of or relating to the Roman rite as modified in Salisbury and used in England, Wales, and Ireland before the Reformation

1sash \ˈsash\ *n* [Ar *shāsh* muslin] **:** any of various bands worn about the waist or over one shoulder as a dress accessory or the emblem of an order

2sash *n, pl* **sash** *also* **sash·es** [prob. modif. of F *châssis* chassis (taken as pl.)] **:** the framework in which panes of glass are set in a window or door; *also* **:** a movable part of a window

1sa·shay \sa-ˈshā, sī-\ *vi* [alter. of *chassé*] **1 :** CHASSÉ **2 a :** WALK, GLIDE, GO **b :** to strut or move about in an ostentatious or conspicuous manner **c :** to proceed or move in a diagonal or sideways manner

2sashay *n* [by alter.] **1 :** CHASSÉ **2 :** TRIP, EXCURSION

sas·ka·toon \ˌsas-kə-ˈtün\ *n* [*Saskatoon*, Saskatchewan, Canada] **:** JUNEBERRY; *esp* **:** a shrubby western Juneberry (*Amelanchier alnifolia*) with sweet usu. purple fruit

1sass \ˈsas\ *n* [back-formation fr. *sassy*] **:** BACK TALK

2sass *vt* **:** to talk impudently or disrespectfully to

sas·sa·fras \ˈsas-(ə-)ˌfras\ *n* [Sp *sasafrás*] **1 :** a tall eastern No. American tree (*Sassafras albidum*) of the laurel family with mucilaginous twigs and leaves **2 :** the dried root bark of the sassafras used esp. as a diaphoretic or flavoring agent

1Sas·sa·ni·an *or* **Sa·sa·ni·an** \sə-ˈsā-nē-ən, sa-ˈsā-\ *adj* **:** of, relating to, or having the characteristics of the Sassanid dynasty of ancient Persia or its art or architecture

2Sassanian *or* **Sasanian** *n* **:** SASSANID

Sas·sa·nid \sə-ˈsän-əd, -ˈsan-; ˈsas-ᵊn-\ *n* [NL *Sassanidae* Sassanids, fr. *Sassan*, founder of the dynasty] **:** a member of a dynasty of Persian kings of the 3d to 7th centuries — **Sassanid** *adj*

sas·se·nach \ˈsas-ᵊn-ˌak, -ək, -ˌäk\ *n, often cap* [Ir *sasanach*, of Gmc origin; akin to OE *Seaxan* Saxons] **:** a typical Englishman **:** something considered typical of England — often used disparagingly

sass·wood \ˈsas-ˌwu̇d\ *n* [earlier *sassywood*, fr. *sassy* sasswood + *wood*] **:** a western African leguminous tree (*Erythrophloeum guineënse*) with a poisonous bark and a hard strong insect-resistant wood

sassy \ˈsas-ē\ *adj* [by alter.] **:** SAUCY

sas·sy bark \ˈsas-ē-\ *n* [*sassy* sasswood, prob. of African origin; akin to Ewe *se3se3wu3* African oak] **:** sasswood bark formerly used locally as an ordeal poison

sat *past of* SIT

Sa·tan \ˈsāt-ᵊn\ *n* [ME, fr. OE, fr. LL, fr. Gk, fr. Heb *śāṭān*] **:** DEVIL 1 — **sa·tan·ic** \sə-ˈtan-ik, sā-\ *adj* — **sa·tan·i·cal·ly** \-i-k(ə-)lē\ *adv*

sa·tang \sə-ˈtäŋ\ *n* [Thai *satāṅ*] — see *baht* at MONEY table

sa·tan·ism \ˈsāt-ᵊn-ˌiz-əm\ *n, often cap* **1 :** innate wickedness **:** DIABOLISM **2 :** obsession with or affinity for evil; *specif* **:** a reputed Parisian cult of Satan in the 1890s marked by the travesty of Christian rites — **sa·tan·ist** \-ᵊn-əst\ *n, often cap*

satch·el \ˈsach-əl\ *n* [ME *sachel*, fr. MF, fr. L *sacellus*, dim. of *saccus* bag — more at SACK] **:** a small bag often with a shoulder strap

1sate \ˈsāt, ˈsat\ *archaic past of* SIT

2sate \ˈsāt\ *vt* [prob. by shortening & alter. fr. *satiate*] **1 :** to cloy with overabundance **:** GLUT **2 :** to appease (as a thirst or violent emotion) by indulging to the full **syn** see SATIATE

sa·teen \sa-ˈtēn, sə-\ *n* [alter. of *satin*] **:** a smooth durable lustrous fabric usu. made of cotton in satin weave

sat·el·lite \ˈsat-ᵊl-ˌīt\ *n* [MF, fr. L *satellit-*, *satelles* attendant] **1 :** a hired agent or obsequious follower **:** MINION, SYCOPHANT **2 a :** a celestial body orbiting another of larger size **b :** a man-made object or vehicle intended to orbit the earth, the moon, or another celestial body **3 :** someone or something attendant, subordinate, or dependent **syn** see FOLLOWER — **satellite** *adj*

sa·tem \ˈsät-əm\ *adj* [Av *satəm* hundred; fr. the fact that its initial sound (derived fr. an alveolar fricative) is the representative of an IE palatal stop — more at HUNDRED] **:** of, relating to, or constituting that part of the Indo-European language family in which the palatal stops became in prehistoric times palatal or alveolar fricatives — compare CENTUM

sa·ti \(ˌ)sə-ˈtē, ˈsə-ˌtē\ *var of* SUTTEE

sa·tia·ble \ˈsā-shə-bəl\ *adj* **:** capable of being appeased or satisfied

1sa·tiate \ˈsā-sh(ē-)ət\ *adj* **:** SATIATED

2sa·ti·ate \ˈsā-shē-ˌāt\ *vt* [L *satiatus*, pp. of *satiare*, fr. *satis* enough — more at SAD] **1 :** to satisfy fully **2 :** GLUT, SATE — **sa·ti·a·tion** \ˌsā-s(h)ē-ˈā-shən\ *n*

syn SATIATE, SATE, SURFEIT, CLOY, PALL, GLUT, GORGE mean to fill to repletion. SATIATE and SATE may sometimes imply only complete satisfaction but more often suggest repletion that has destroyed interest or desire; SURFEIT implies a nauseating repletion; CLOY stresses the resulting disgust or boredom of such surfeiting; PALL emphasizes the loss of power to stimulate interest or appetite; GLUT implies excess in feeding or supplying; GORGE suggests glutting to the point of bursting or choking

sa·ti·ety \sə-ˈtī-ət-ē *also* ˈsā-sh(ē-)ət-\ *n* [MF *satieté*, fr. L *satietat-*, *satietas*, fr. *satis*] **1 :** FULLNESS, SURFEIT **2 :** the revulsion or disgust of overindulgence or excess

sat·in \ˈsat-ᵊn\ *n* [ME, fr. MF] **:** a fabric in satin weave with lustrous face and dull back woven of fiber (as of silk) — **satin** *adj*

sat·in·et \ˌsat-ᵊn-ˈet\ *n* **1 :** a thin silk satin or imitation satin **2 :** a variation of satin weave used in making satinet

satin stitch *n* : an embroidery stitch nearly alike on both sides and worked so closely as to resemble satin

satin weave *n* : a weave in which warp threads interlace with filling threads to produce a smooth-faced fabric

sat·in·wood \'sat-ᵊn-,wu̇d\ *n* **1** : an East Indian tree (*Chloroxylon swietenia*) of the mahogany family; *also* : its lustrous yellowish brown wood **2** : a tree (as several yellowwoods) with wood resembling true satinwood; *also* : its wood

sat·iny \'sat-nē, 'sat-ᵊn-ē\ *adj* : having the soft lustrous smoothness of satin

sat·ire \'sa-,tī(ə)r\ *n* [MF, fr. L *satura*, *satira*, fr. (*lanx*) *satura* full plate, medley, fr. fem. of *satur* sated; akin to L *satis* enough — more at SAD] **1** : a literary work holding up human vices and follies to ridicule or scorn **2** : trenchant wit, irony, or sarcasm used to expose and discredit vice or folly **syn** see WIT — **sa·tir·ic** \sə-'tir-ik\ *or* **sa·tir·i·cal** \-i-kəl\ *adj* — **sa·tir·i·cal·ly** \-i-k(ə-)lē\ *adv*

sat·i·rist \'sat-ə-rəst\ *n* : one that satirizes; *esp* : a satirical writer

sat·i·rize \-,rīz\ *vi* : to utter or write satires ~ *vt* : to censure or ridicule by means of satire

sat·is·fac·tion \,sat-əs-'fak-shən\ *n* [ME, fr. MF, fr. LL *satisfaction-*, *satisfactio*, fr. L, reparation, amends, fr. *satisfactus*, pp. of *satisfacere* to satisfy] **1 a** : the payment through penance of the temporal punishment incurred by a sin **b** : reparation for sin that meets the demands of divine justice **2 a** : fulfillment of a need or want **b** : the quality or state of being satisfied : CONTENTMENT **c** : a cause or means of enjoyment : GRATIFICATION **3 a** : compensation for a loss or injury : ATONEMENT, RESTITUTION **b** : the discharge of a legal obligation or claim **c** : VINDICATION **4** : convinced assurance or certainty

sat·is·fac·to·ri·ly \-'fak-t(ə-)rə-lē\ *adv* : in a satisfactory manner

sat·is·fac·to·ri·ness \-t(ə-)rē-nəs\ *n* : the quality or state of being satisfactory

sat·is·fac·to·ry \,sat-əs-'fak-t(ə-)rē\ *adj* : giving satisfaction : ADEQUATE

sat·is·fi·able \'sat-əs-,fī-ə-bəl\ *adj* : capable of being satisfied

sat·is·fy \'sat-əs-,fī\ *vb* [ME *satisfien*, fr. MF *satisfier*, modif. of L *satisfacere*, fr. *satis* enough + *facere* to do, make — more at SAD, DO] *vt* **1 a** : to carry out the terms of (as a contract) : DISCHARGE **b** : to meet a financial obligation to **2** : to make reparation to (an injured party) : INDEMNIFY **3 a** : to make happy : PLEASE **b** : to gratify to the full : APPEASE **4 a** : CONVINCE **b** : to put an end to (doubt or uncertainty) : DISPEL **5 a** : FULFILL, MEET **b** : to make true by fulfilling a condition ⟨values that ~ an equation⟩ ⟨~ a hypothesis⟩ ~ *vi* : to be adequate : SUFFICE; *also* : PLEASE

syn SATISFY, CONTENT mean to appease one's desires or longings. SATISFY implies full appeasement esp. of a need or requirement; CONTENT implies gratification to the point where one is not disturbed or disquieted even though every wish is not fully realized **syn** see in addition PAY

sa·to·ri \sə-'tōr-ē, -'tȯr-\ *n* [Jap] : a state of intuitive illumination sought in Zen Buddhism

sa·trap \'sā-,trap, 'sa-\ *n* [ME, fr. L *satrapes*, fr. Gk *satrapēs*, fr. OPer *xshathrapāvan*, lit., protector of the dominion] **1** : the governor of a province in ancient Persia **2 a** : RULER **b** : a subordinate official : HENCHMAN

sa·tra·py \'sā-trə-pē, 'sa-, -,trap-ē\ *n* : the territory or jurisdiction of a satrap

sat·u·ra·ble \'sach-(ə-)rə-bəl\ *adj* : capable of being saturated

sat·u·rant \'sach-(ə-)rənt\ *n* : something that saturates

1**sat·u·rate** \'sach-ə-,rāt\ *vt* [L *saturatus*, pp. of *saturare*, fr. *satur* sated — more at SATIRE] **1** : to cloy with overabundance : SURFEIT **2** : to treat, furnish, or charge with something to the point where no more can be absorbed, dissolved, or retained ⟨water *saturated* with salt⟩ **3 a** : to infuse thoroughly or cause to be pervaded : STEEP **b** : to fill completely : IMBUE **c** : to load to capacity **4** : to cause to combine till there is no further tendency to combine : NEUTRALIZE **syn** see SOAK — **sat·u·ra·tor** \-,rāt-ər\ *n*

2**sat·u·rate** \'sach-(ə-)rət\ *adj* : SATURATED

sat·u·rat·ed \'sach-ə-,rāt-əd\ *adj* **1** : steeped in moisture : SOAKED **2 a** : being the most concentrated solution that can remain in the presence of an excess of the dissolved substance **b** : being a compound that does not tend to unite directly with another compound — used esp. of organic compounds containing no double or triple bonds

sat·u·ra·tion \,sach-ə-'rā-shən\ *n* **1** : the act of saturating : the state of being saturated **2** : SATIETY, SURFEIT **3** : magnetization to the point beyond which a further increase in the intensity of the magnetizing force will produce no futher magnetization **4 a** : chromatic purity : freedom from dilution with white : INTENSITY **b** (1) : degree of difference from the gray having the same lightness — used of an object color (2) : degree of difference from the achromatic light-source color of the same brightness — used of a light-source color **5** : the supplying of a market with all the goods it will absorb **6** : an overwhelming concentration of military forces or firepower

Sat·ur·day \'sat-ərd-ē\ *n* [ME *saterday*, fr. OE *sæterndæg*; akin to OFris *sāterdei*; both fr. a prehistoric WGmc compound whose first component was borrowed fr. L *Saturnus* Saturn and whose second component is represented by OE *dæg* day] : the seventh day of the week — **Sat·ur·days** \-ēz\ *adv*

Sat·urn \'sat-ərn\ *n* [L *Saturnus*] **1** : an ancient Roman god of agriculture held to have reigned during a golden age **2** : the planet 6th in order from the sun — see PLANET table

sat·ur·na·lia \,sat-ər-'nāl-yə, -'nā-lē-ə\ *n pl but sing or pl in constr* [L, fr. neut. pl. of *saturnalis* of Saturn, fr. *Saturnus*] **1** *cap* : the festival of Saturn in ancient Rome beginning on Dec. 17 **2** *sing, pl* **saturnalias** *also* **saturnalia a** : an unrestrained often licentious celebration : ORGY **b** : EXCESS, EXTRAVAGANCE — **sat·ur·na·lian** \-'nāl-yən, -'nā-lē-ən\ *adj* — **sat·ur·na·lian·ly** *adv*

Sa·tur·ni·an \sa-'tər-nē-ən, sə-\ *adj* **1** : of, relating to, or influenced by the planet Saturn **2** *archaic* : of or relating to the god Saturn or the golden age of his reign

sa·tur·ni·id \-nē-əd\ *n* [deriv. of NL *Saturnia*, genus of moths, fr. L, daughter of the god Saturn] : any of a large family (Saturniidae) of stout strong-winged moth with hairy bodies — **saturniid** *adj*

sat·ur·nine \'sat-ər-,nīn\ *adj* **1** : born under or influenced astrologically by the planet Saturn **2 a** : of a gloomy or surly disposition **b** : having a sardonic aspect ⟨~ smile⟩ **3** : of, relating to, or produced by the absorption of lead into the system ⟨~ poisoning⟩ **syn** see SULLEN — **sat·ur·nine·ly** *adv*

sat·urn·ism \'sat-ər-,niz-əm\ *n* [*saturn* (lead)] : LEAD POISONING

sa·tya·gra·ha \(,)sə-'tyä-grə-hə, 'sə-tyə-grə-\ *n* [Skt *satyāgraha*, lit., insistence on truth] : pressure for social and political reform through friendly passive resistance practiced by M. K. Gandhi and his followers in India

sa·tyr \'sāt-ər, 'sat-\ *n* [ME, fr. L *satyrus*, fr. Gk *satyros*] **1** *often cap* : a sylvan deity of Greek mythology often represented with certain characteristics of a horse or goat and fond of Dionysian revelry **2** : a lecherous man : one having satyriasis **3** : any of many usu. brown and gray butterflies (family Satyridae) often with ocelli on the wings — **sa·tyr·ic** \sā-'tir-ik, sə-, sa-\ *adj*

sa·ty·ri·a·sis \,sāt-ə-'rī-ə-səs, ,sat-\ *n* [LL, fr. Gk, fr. *satyros*] : excessive or abnormal sexual craving in the male

satyr play *n* : a comic play of ancient Greece burlesquing a mythological subject and having a chorus representing satyrs

1**sauce** \'sȯs, *usu* 'sas *for 3 & 5*\ *n* [ME, fr. MF, fr. L *salsa*, fem. of *salsus* salted, fr. pp. of *sallere* to salt, fr. *sal* salt — more at SALT] **1** : a condiment or relish for food; *esp* : a fluid dressing or topping **2** : something that adds zest or piquancy **3** : vegetables eaten with meat or as a relish **4** : stewed or canned fruit eaten with other food or as a dessert **5** : pert or impudent language or actions

2**sauce** \'sȯs, *usu* 'sas *for 3*\ *vt* **1** : to dress with relish or seasoning **2 a** *archaic* : to modify the harsh or unpleasant characteristics of **b** : to give zest or piquancy to **3** : to be rude or impudent to

sauce·box \'sas-,bäks *also* 'sȯs-\ *n* : a saucy impudent person

sauce·pan \'sȯ-,span, *esp Brit* -spən\ *n* : a cooking utensil with a handle for stewing or boiling

sau·cer \'sȯ-sər\ *n* [ME, plate containing sauce, fr. MF *saussier*, fr. *sausse*, *sauce*] **1** : a small shallow dish in which a cup is set at table **2** : something like a saucer esp. in shape

sauc·i·ly \'sas-ə-lē *also* 'sȯs-\ *adv* : in a saucy manner

sauc·i·ness \-ē-nəs\ *n* : the quality or state of being saucy

saucy \'sas-ē *also* 'sȯs-ē\ *adj* **1** : BOLD, IMPUDENT **2** : IRREPRESSIBLE, PERT **3** : SMART, TRIM ⟨a ~ ship⟩

sau·er·bra·ten \'sau̇(-ə)r-,brät-ᵊn, 'zau̇(-ə)r-\ *n* [G, fr. *sauer* sour + *braten* roast meat] : oven-roasted or pot-roasted beef marinated before cooking in vinegar with peppercorns, garlic, onions, and bay leaves

sau·er·kraut \'sau̇(-ə)r-,krau̇t\ *n* [G, fr. *sauer* sour + *kraut* cabbage] : cabbage cut fine and fermented in a brine made of its own juice with salt

sau·ger \'sȯ-gər\ *n* [origin unknown] : a pike perch (*Stizostedion canadense*) similar to the walleye but smaller; *also* : WALLEYE

saugh *or* **sauch** \'sau̇k̲, 'sȯk̲\ *n* [ME (Sc) *sauch*, fr. OE *salh*, alter. of *sealh*] *chiefly Scot* : SALLOW

Saul \'sȯl\ *n* [LL *Saulus*, fr. Gk *Saulos*, fr. Heb *Shā'ūl*] **1** : the first king of Israel **2** : the apostle Paul — called also *Saul of Tarsus*

sau·na \'sau̇-nə\ *n* [Finn] : a Finnish steam bath; *also* : the bathhouse with steam provided by water thrown on hot stones

saun·ter \'sȯnt-ər, 'sänt-\ *vi* [prob. fr. ME *santren* to muse] : to walk about in an idle or leisurely manner : STROLL — **saunter** *n* — **saun·ter·er** \-ər-ər\ *n*

sau·rel \sȯ-'rel\ *n* [F, fr. LL *saurus* horse mackerel, fr. Gk *sauros*] : any of a genus (*Trachurus*) of carangid fishes (esp. *T. trachurus* and *T. symmetricus*) of Europe and America

sau·ri·an \'sȯr-ē-ən\ *n* [deriv. of Gk *sauros* horse mackerel, lizard; akin to Gk *psauein* to touch, graze] : any of a group (Sauria) of reptiles including the lizards and in older classifications the crocodiles and various extinct forms (as the dinosaurs and ichthyosaurs) suggesting lizards — **saurian** *adj*

sau·ro·pod \'sȯr-ə-,päd\ *n* [NL *Sauropoda*, suborder of dinosaurs, fr. Gk *sauros* lizard + NL *-poda*] : any of a suborder (Sauropoda) of dinosaurs comprising herbivorous forms with long neck and tail, small head, and more or less plantigrade 5-toed limbs — **sauropod** *adj* — **sau·rop·o·dous** \sȯ-'räp-əd-əs\ *adj*

sau·ry \'sȯr-ē\ *n* [NL *saurus* lizard, fr. Gk *sauros*] : a slender long-beaked fish (*Scombresox saurus*) related to the needlefishes and found in temperate parts of the Atlantic

sau·sage \'sȯ-sij\ *n* [ME *sausige*, fr. ONF *saussiche*, fr. LL *salsicia*, fr. L *salsus* salted — more at SAUCE] **1** : a highly seasoned minced meat (as pork) usu. stuffed in casings of prepared animal intestine and used either fresh or cured **2** : a captive observation or barrage balloon

1**sau·té** \sȯ-'tā, sō-\ *n* [F, pp. of *sauter* to jump, fr. L *saltare* — more at SALTATION] : a sautéed dish — **sauté** *adj*

2**sauté** *vt* **sau·téed** *or* **sau·téd**; **sau·té·ing** : to fry in shallow fat

sau·terne \sō-'tərn, sȯ-, -'te(ə)rn\ *n*, *often cap* [F *sauternes*, fr. *Sauternes*, commune in France] : a usu. semisweet golden-colored table wine

1**sav·age** \'sav-ij\ *adj* [ME *sauvage*, fr. MF, fr. ML *salvaticus*, alter. of L *silvaticus* of the woods, wild, fr. *silva* wood, forest] **1 a** : not domesticated or under human control : UNTAMED ⟨~ beasts⟩ **b** : CRUEL, FEROCIOUS ⟨a ~ attack⟩ **2** : UNCULTIVATED, WILD ⟨~ scenery⟩ **3** : BOORISH, RUDE ⟨~ bad manners⟩ **4 a** : UNCIVILIZED ⟨~ peoples⟩ **b** : PRIMITIVE ⟨~ art⟩ **syn** see BARBARIAN, FIERCE — **sav·age·ly** *adv* — **sav·age·ness** *n*

2**savage** *n* **1** : a person belonging to a primitive society **2** : a brutal person **3** : a rude or unmannerly person

3**savage** *vt* **1** : to attack or treat violently or brutally **2** : to attack furiously (as by biting or trampling)

sav·age·ry \'sav-ij-(ə-)rē\ *n* **1 a** : the quality of being savage **b** : an act of cruelty or violence **2** : a rude or uncivilized state

sav·ag·ism \'sav-ij-,iz-əm\ *n* : SAVAGERY

sa·van·na *or* **sa·van·nah** \sə-'van-ə\ *n* [Sp *zavana*, fr. Taino *zabana*] **1** : a treeless plain esp. in Florida **2** : a tropical or subtropical grassland containing scattered trees and drought-resistant undergrowth

sa·vant \sa-'vänt, sə-, -'vä͞ⁿ; sə-'vant, 'sav-ənt\ *n* [F, fr. prp. of *savoir* to know, fr. L *sapere* to be wise — more at SAGE] : a man of learning; *esp* : a person with detailed knowledge in some specialized field (as of science or literature) : SCHOLAR

1**save** \'sāv\ *vb* [ME *saven*, fr. OF *salver*, fr. LL *salvare*, fr. L *salvus* safe — more at SAFE] *vt* **1 a** : to deliver from sin **b** : to rescue or deliver from danger or harm **c** : to preserve or guard from injury,

destruction, or loss **2 :** to put by as a store or reserve **:** ACCUMULATE **3 a :** to make unnecessary **:** AVOID ⟨it ~*s* an hour's waiting⟩ **b** (1) **:** to keep from being lost to an opponent (2) **:** to prevent an opponent from scoring or winning **4 :** MAINTAIN, PRESERVE ⟨~ appearances⟩ ~ *vi* **1 :** to rescue or deliver someone **2 a :** to put by money ⟨would rather ~ than spend⟩ **b :** to avoid unnecessary waste or expense **:** ECONOMIZE **3 :** to make a save **syn** see RESCUE — **sav·able** *or* **save·able** \'sā-və-bəl\ *adj* — **sav·er** *n*

²**save** *n* **:** a play that prevents an opponent from scoring or winning

³**save** \(,)sāv\ *prep* [ME *sauf,* fr. OF, fr. *sauf,* adj., safe — more at SAFE] **1 :** with the exception of **:** BARRING ⟨nothing in common ~ their fears⟩ **2 :** other than **:** BUT, EXCEPT ⟨no hope ~ one⟩

⁴**save** \(,)sāv\ *conj* **1 :** were it not **:** ONLY — used with *that* **2 :** BUT, EXCEPT — used before a word often taken to be the subject of a clause ⟨no one knows about it ~ she⟩ **3 :** UNLESS ⟨~ they could be plucked asunder, all my quest were but in vain —Alfred Tennyson⟩

save–all \'sā-,vȯl\ *n* **:** something that prevents waste, loss, or damage: as **a :** a device to hold a candle end in a candlestick and permit it to burn to the very end **b** (1) **:** a small sail sometimes set under the foot of another sail or between two sails (2) **:** a net hung between ship and pier to catch articles lost over the side **c :** a receptacle for catching waste products for further utilization

sav·e·loy \'sav-ə-,lȯi\ *n* [modif. of F *cervelas*] *Brit* **:** a ready-cooked dry sausage

sav·in *or* **sav·ine** \'sav-ən\ *n* [ME, fr. OE *safene,* fr. L *sabina*] **:** a Eurasian juniper (*Juniperus sabina*) with dark foliage and small yellowish green berries; *also* **:** either of two No. American junipers (*J. virginiana* and *J. horizontalis*)

¹**sav·ing** \,sā-viŋ, 'sā-\ *prep* **1 :** EXCEPT, SAVE **2 :** without disrespect to

²**saving** *conj* **:** EXCEPT, SAVE

savings and loan association *n* **:** a cooperative association that solicits savings in the form of share capital and invests its funds in mortgages

savings bank *n* **:** a bank organized to receive savings accounts only

savings bond *n* **:** a nontransferable registered U.S. bond issued in denominations of $25 to $1000

sav·ior *or* **sav·iour** \'sāv-yər *also* -,yō(ə)r\ *n* [ME *saveour,* fr. MF, fr. LL *salvator,* fr. *salvatus,* pp. of *salvare* to save] **1 :** one that saves from danger or destruction **2** *cap* **:** JESUS

sa·voir faire \,sav-,wär-'fa(ə)r, -'fe(ə)r\ *n* [F *savoir-faire,* lit., knowing how to do] **:** social adroitness **syn** see TACT

¹**sa·vor** \'sā-vər\ *n* [ME, fr. OF, fr. L *sapor;* akin to L *sapere* to taste — more at SAGE] **1 :** the taste or smell of something **2 :** a particular flavor or smell **3 :** a distinctive quality **:** SMACK **syn** see TASTE — **sa·vor·ous** \'sāv-(ə-)rəs\ *adj*

²**savor** *vb* **sa·vor·ing** \'sāv-(ə-)riŋ\ *vi* **:** to have a specified smell or quality **:** SMACK ~ *vt* **1 :** to give flavor to **:** SEASON **2 a :** to have experience of **:** TASTE **b :** to taste or smell with pleasure **:** RELISH **c :** to delight in **:** ENJOY — **sa·vor·er** \'sā-vər-ər\ *n*

sa·vor·i·ly \'sāv-(ə-)rə-lē\ *adv* **:** in a savory manner

sa·vor·i·ness \-(ə-)rē-nəs\ *n* **:** the quality or state of being savory

¹**sa·vory** \'sāv-(ə-)rē\ *adj* **1 a :** AGREEABLE, PLEASANT **b :** morally attractive **:** WHOLESOME **2 :** agreeable to the taste **:** APPETIZING; *also* **:** FRAGRANT

²**savory** *n, Brit* **:** a cooked or uncooked dish of stimulating flavor served usu. at the end of dinner but sometimes as an appetizer before the meal

³**sa·vo·ry** \'sāv-(ə-)rē\ *n* [ME *saverey*] **:** an aromatic mint (genus *Satureia*); *esp* **:** a European herb (*S. hortensis*) used in cookery — called also *summer savory*

Sa·voy·ard \sə-'vȯi-,ärd, ,sav-,ȯi-'ärd, ,sav-,wä-'yär(d)\ *n* [*Savoy* theater, London, built for the presentation of Gilbert and Sullivan operas] **:** a devotee, performer, or producer of the comic operas of W. S. Gilbert and A. S. Sullivan

sa·voy cabbage \sə-,vȯi-, ,sav-,ȯi-\ *n* [trans. of F *chou de Savoie* cabbage of Savoy] **:** a cabbage with compact heads of wrinkled and curled leaves

¹**sav·vy** \'sav-ē\ *vb* [modif. of Sp *sabe* he knows, fr. *saber* to know, fr. L *sapere* to be wise — more at SAGE] *slang* **:** COMPREHEND, UNDERSTAND

²**savvy** *n, slang* **:** practical grasp **:** SHREWDNESS ⟨political ~⟩ — **savvy** *adj, slang*

¹**saw** *past of* SEE

²**saw** \'sȯ\ *n* [ME *sawe,* fr. OE *sagu;* akin to OHG *sega* saw, L *secare* to cut, *secula* sickle] **1 :** a hand or power tool used to cut hard material (as wood, metal, or bone) and made of a toothed blade or disk **2 :** a machine mounting a saw (as a band saw or circular saw)

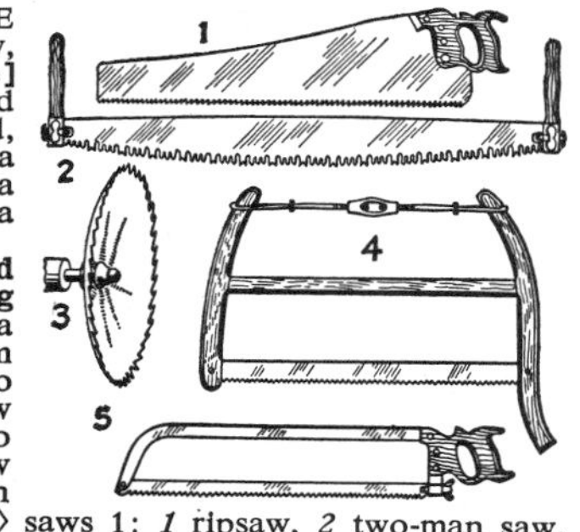

saws 1: *1* ripsaw, *2* two-man saw, *3* concave circular saw, *4* bucksaw, *5* butcher's saw

³**saw** *vb* **sawed** \'sȯd\ **sawed** *or* **sawn** \'sȯn\ **saw·ing** \'sȯ(-)iŋ\ *vt* **1 :** to cut with a saw **2 :** to produce or form by cutting with a saw **3 :** to slash as though with a saw ~ *vi* **1 a :** to use a saw **b :** to cut with or as if with a saw **2 :** to admit of being cut with a saw ⟨the timber ~*s* smoothly⟩ **3 :** to make motions as though using a saw ⟨~*ed* at the reins⟩ — **saw·er** \'sȯ(-ə)r\ *n*

⁴**saw** *n* [ME *sawe,* fr. OE *sagu* discourse; akin to OHG & ON *saga* tale, OE *secgan* to say — more at SAY] **:** MAXIM, PROVERB

saw·buck \'sȯ-,bək\ *n* **1 :** SAWHORSE **2** [prob. fr. the resemblance of the Roman numeral X to the ends of a sawhorse] *slang* **:** a 10-dollar bill

saw·dust \'sȯd-(,)əst\ *n* **:** dust or fine particles (as of wood or stone) made by a saw in cutting

saw–edged \'sȯ-'ejd\ *adj* **:** having a toothed or badly nicked edge

sawed–off \'sȯ-'dȯf\ *adj* **1 :** having an end sawed off ⟨a ~ shotgun⟩ **2 :** of less than average height

saw·fish \'sȯ-,fish\ *n* **:** any of several large elongate viviparous rays (family Pristidae) having a long flattened snout with a row of stout serrate structures along each edge and living principally in tropical America and Africa

saw·fly \-,flī\ *n* **:** any of numerous hymenopterous insects (superfamily Tenthredinoidea) having the female usu. with a pair of serrated blades in her ovipositor and larvae like caterpillars that feed on plants

saw grass *n* **:** a sedge (as of the genus *Cladium*) having the edges of the leaves set with minute sharp teeth

saw·horse \'sȯ-,hȯ(ə)rs\ *n* **:** a rack on which wood is laid for sawing by hand; *esp* **:** one with X-shaped ends

saw·log \-,lȯg, -,läg\ *n* **:** a log of suitable size for sawing into lumber

saw·mill \-,mil\ *n* **:** a mill or machine for sawing logs

saw·ney \'sȯ-nē\ *n* [prob. alter. of *zany*] *chiefly Brit* **:** FOOL, SIMPLETON — **sawney** *adj*

saw palmetto *n* **:** any of several shrubby palms with spiny-toothed leafstalks esp. of the southern U.S. and West Indies

saw set *n* **:** an instrument used to set sawteeth

saw·tim·ber \'sȯ-,tim-bər\ *n* **:** timber suitable for sawing into lumber

saw·tooth \'sȯ-,tüth\ *adj* **:** SAW-TOOTHED

saw–toothed \-'tütht\ *adj* **:** having teeth like those of a saw; *also* **:** SERRATE

saw–whet \'sȯ-,(h)wet\ *n* [imit.] **:** a very small harsh-voiced No. American owl (*Cryptoglaux acadica*) largely dark brown above and white beneath

saw·yer \'sȯ-yər, 'sȯi-ər\ *n* **1 :** one that saws **2 :** any of several large longicorn beetles whose larvae bore large holes in timber or dead wood **3 :** a tree fast in the bed of a stream with its branches projecting to the surface

sax \'saks\ *n* **:** SAXOPHONE

sax·a·tile \'sak-sə-,tīl, -sət-ᵊl\ *adj* [L *saxatilis,* fr. *saxum* rock] **:** SAXICOLOUS

sax·horn \'saks-,hȯ(ə)rn\ *n* [A. J. *Sax* †1894 + E *horn*] **:** one of a complete family of valved conical-bore brass-wind musical instruments of full even tone and large compass

sax·ic·o·lous \sak-'sik-ə-ləs\ *or* **sax·ic·o·line** \-'sik-ə-,līn\ *adj* [L *saxum* rock + *-cola* inhabitant; akin to L *colere* to inhabit — more at WHEEL] **:** inhabiting or growing among rocks

sax·i·frage \'sak-sə-frij, -,frāj\ *n* [ME, fr. MF, fr. LL *saxifraga,* fr. L, fem. of *saxifragus* breaking rocks, fr. *saxum* rock + *frangere* to break; akin to OE *sæx* knife, *sagu* saw — more at SAW, BREAK] **:** any of a genus (*Saxifraga* of the family Saxifragaceae, the saxifrage family) of mostly perennial herbs with showy pentamerous flowers and often with basal tufted leaves

Sax·on \'sak-sən\ *n* [ME, fr. LL *Saxones* Saxons, of Gmc origin; akin to OE *Seaxan* Saxons] **1 a** (1) **:** a member of a Germanic people entering and conquering England with the Angles and Jutes in the 5th century A.D. and merging with them to form the Anglo-Saxon people (2) **:** an Englishman or lowlander as distinguished from a Welshman, Irishman, or Highlander **b :** a native or inhabitant of Saxony **2 a :** the Germanic language or dialect of any of the Saxon peoples **b :** the Germanic element in the English language esp. as distinguished from the French and Latin — **Saxon** *adj*

sax·o·ny \'sak-s(ə-)nē\ *n, often cap* [*Saxony,* former state in Germany] **1 a :** a fine soft woolen fabric **b :** a fine closely twisted knitting yarn **2 :** a Wilton jacquard carpet

sax·o·phone \'sak-sə-,fōn\ *n* [F, fr. Antoine J. (known as Adolphe) *Sax* †1894 Belgian maker of musical instruments + F *-phone*] **:** a wind instrument with reed mouthpiece, curved conical metal tube, and finger keys — **sax·o·phon·ic** \,sak-sə-'fōn-ik, -'fän-\ *adj* — **sax·o·phon·ist** \'sak-sə-,fō-nəst\ *n*

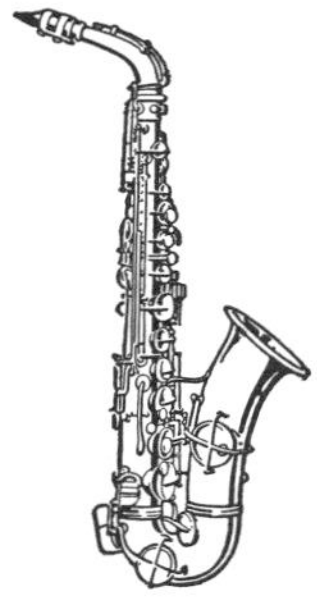
alto saxophone

sax·tu·ba \'sak-'st(y)ü-bə\ *n* [Antoine *Sax* + E *tuba*] **:** a bass saxhorn

¹**say** \'sā, *South also* 'se\ *vb* **said** \'sed, *esp when subject follows* səd\ **say·ing; says** \'sez\ [ME *sayen,* fr. OE *secgan;* akin to OHG *sagēn* to say, Gk en*nepein* to speak, tell] *vt* **1 a :** to express in words **:** STATE **b :** to state as opinion or belief **:** DECLARE **2 a :** UTTER, PRONOUNCE **b :** RECITE, REPEAT ⟨*said* his prayers⟩ **3 a :** INDICATE, SHOW ⟨the clock ~*s* five minutes after twelve⟩ **b :** to give expression to **:** COMMUNICATE ⟨a glance that *said* all that was necessary⟩ ~ *vi* **:** to express oneself **:** SPEAK — **say·er** *n*

²**say** *n, pl* **says** \'sāz, *South also* 'sez\ **1** *archaic* **:** something that is said **:** STATEMENT **2 :** an expression of opinion ⟨had his ~⟩ **3 :** a voice that decides or helps decide: **a :** COMMAND **b :** VOTE

³**say** *adv* [fr. imper. of ¹*say*] **1 :** ABOUT, APPROXIMATELY ⟨the property is worth, ~, four million dollars⟩ **2 :** for example **:** AS ⟨if we compress any gas, ~ oxygen⟩

say·able \'sā-ə-bəl\ *adj* **1 :** capable of being said **2 :** capable of being spoken effectively or easily

say·ing \'sā-iŋ, 'se-\ *n* **:** something said; *esp* **:** ADAGE

say–so \'sā-(,)sō, *South also* 'se-\ *n* **1 a :** one's bare word or assurance **b :** an authoritative pronouncement **:** DICTUM **2 :** a right of final decision **:** AUTHORITY

say·yid \'sī-(y)əd, 'sā-(y)əd\ *n* [Ar] **1 :** an Islamic chief or leader **2 :** LORD, SIR — used as a courtesy title for a Muslim of rank or lineage

Saz·e·rac \'saz-ə-,rak\ *n* [origin unknown] **:** a cocktail of bourbon, absinthe flavoring, bitters, and sugar with lemon peel

¹**scab** \'skab\ *n* [ME, of Scand origin; akin to OSw *skabbr* scab; akin to OE *sceabb* scab, L *scabies* mange, *scabere* to scratch — more at SHAVE] **1 :** scabies of domestic animals **2 :** a crust of hardened blood and serum over a wound **3 a :** a contemptible person **b** (1) **:** one who refuses to join a labor union (2) **:** a union member who refuses to strike or returns to work before a strike has ended (3) **:** a worker who accepts employment or replaces a union worker during a strike (4) **:** one who works for less than union wages or on nonunion terms **4 :** any of various bacterial or fungous diseases of plants characterized by crustaceous spots; *also* **:** one of the spots

²**scab** *vi* **scabbed; scab·bing 1 :** to become covered with a scab **2 :** to act as a scab

¹**scab·bard** \'skab-ərd\ *n* [ME *scaubert,* fr. AF *escaubers*] **:** a sheath for a sword, dagger, or bayonet

²**scabbard** *vt* **:** to put in a scabbard

scab·ble \'skab-əl\ *vt* **scab·bling** \-(ə-)liŋ\ [ME *scaplen,* fr. MF *escapler* to dress timber] **:** to dress (as stone) roughly

scab·by \'skab-ē\ *adj* **1 a :** covered with or full of scabs ⟨~ skin⟩ **b :** diseased with scab ⟨a ~ animal⟩ ⟨~ potatoes⟩ **2 :** MEAN, CONTEMPTIBLE ⟨a ~ trick⟩

sca·bies \'skā-bēz\ *n, pl* **scabies** [L] **:** itch or mange esp. with exudative crusts — **sca·bi·et·ic** \ˌskā-bē-'et-ik\ *adj*

sca·bi·o·sa \ˌskā-bē-'ō-sə, ˌskab-ē-, -zə\ *n* [NL, genus name, fr. ML, scabious, n.] **:** any of a genus (*Scabiosa*) of herbs of the teasel family with terminal flower heads subtended by a leafy involucre

[1]**sca·bi·ous** \'skā-bē-əs, 'skab-ē-\ *n* [ME *scabiose*, fr. ML *scabiosa*, fr. L, fem. of *scabiosus*, adj.] **1 :** SCABIOSA **2 :** any of several fleabanes (genus *Erigeron*)

[2]**scabious** *adj* [L *scabiosus*, fr. *scabies*] **1 :** SCABBY **2 :** of, relating to, or like scabies ⟨~ eruptions⟩

sca·brous \'skab-rəs *also* 'skāb-\ *adj* [L *scabr-*, *scaber* rough, scurfy; akin to L *scabies* mange — more at SCAB] **1 :** DIFFICULT, KNOTTY ⟨a ~ problem⟩ **2 :** rough to the touch **:** SCALY, SCURFY ⟨a ~ leaf⟩ **3 :** dealing with suggestive, indecent, or scandalous themes **:** SALACIOUS; *also* **:** SQUALID **syn** see ROUGH — **sca·brous·ly** *adv* — **sca·brous·ness** *n*

[1]**scad** \'skad\ *n, pl* **scad** *also* **scads** [origin unknown] **:** any of several carangid fishes

[2]**scad** *n* [prob. alter. of E dial. *scald* a multitude, fr. [2]*scald*] **1 :** a large number or quantity **2** *pl* **:** a great abundance ⟨~*s* of money⟩

scaf·fold \'skaf-əld *also* -ˌōld\ *n* [ME, fr. ONF *escafaut*, modif. of (assumed) VL *cutafalicum*, irreg. fr. Gk *kata-* cata- + L *fala* tower] **1 a :** a temporary or movable platform for workmen (as bricklayers, painters, or miners) to stand or sit on when working at a height above floor or ground **b :** a platform on which a criminal is executed (as by hanging or beheading) **c :** any platform at a height above ground or floor level **2 :** a supporting framework

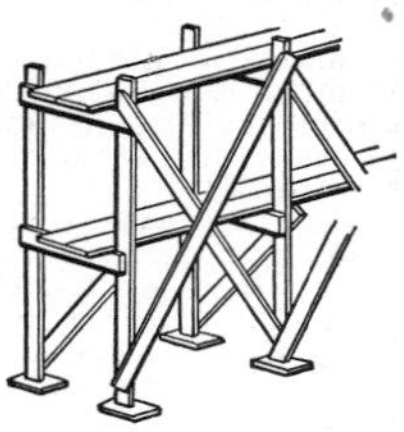
scaffold 1a

scaf·fold·ing \-iŋ\ *n* **:** a system of scaffolds; *also* **:** materials for scaffolds

sca·glio·la \skal-'yō-lə, -'yȯ-\ *n* [It, lit., little chip] **:** an imitation of ornamental marble consisting of finely ground gypsum mixed with glue

scal·able \'skā-lə-bəl\ *adj* **:** capable of being scaled

sca·lade \skə-'lād, -'läd\ *or* **sca·la·do** \-'lād-(ˌ)ō, -'läd-\ *n* [obs. It *scalada*, fr. *scalare* to scale, fr. *scala* ladder, staircase, fr. LL — more at SCALE] *archaic* **:** ESCALADE

scal·age \'skā-lij\ *n* **1 :** an allowance or percentage by which something (as listed weights, bulks, or prices of goods) is scaled down to compensate for loss (as by shrinkage) **2 :** the act of scaling in weight, quantity, or dimensions **3 :** the amount that logs or timber scale

[1]**sca·lar** \'skā-lər\ *adj* [L *scalaris*, fr. *scalae* stairs, ladder — more at SCALE] **1 :** arranged like a ladder **:** GRADUATED ⟨~ chain of authority⟩ ⟨~ cells⟩ **2 a :** that can be represented by a point on a scale ⟨~ quantity⟩ **b :** of or relating to a scalar or scalar product ⟨~ multiplication⟩

[2]**scalar** *n* **1 :** a real number rather than a vector **2 :** a quantity (as mass or time) that has a magnitude describable by a real number and no direction

sca·la·re \skə-'la(ə)r-ē, -'le(ə)r-, -'lär-\ *n* [NL specific epithet], fr. L, neut. of *scalaris*; fr. the barred pattern on its body] **:** a black and silver laterally compressed So. American cichlid fish (*Pterophyllum scalare*) popular in aquariums

sca·lar·i·form \skə-'lar-ə-ˌfȯrm\ *n* [NL *scalariformis*, fr. L *scalaris* + *-iformis* -iform] **:** resembling a ladder esp. in having transverse bars or markings like the rounds of a ladder ⟨~ cells in plants⟩

scalar product *n* **:** a real number that is the product of the lengths of two vectors and the cosine of the angle between them — called also *dot product*, *inner product*

scal·ation \skā-'lā-shən\ *n* [[3]*scale*] **:** LEPIDOSIS

scal·a·wag \'skal-i-ˌwag\ *n* [origin unknown] **1 :** an animal of little value esp. because of poor feeding, smallness, or age **2 :** SCAMP, REPROBATE **3 :** a white Southerner acting as a Republican in the time of reconstruction after the Civil War

[1]**scald** \'skȯld\ *vb* [ME *scalden*, fr. ONF *escalder*, fr. LL *excaldare* to wash in warm water, fr. L *ex-* + *calida*, *calda* warm water, fr. fem. of *calidus* warm — more at CALDRON] *vt* **1 :** to burn with hot liquid or steam **2 a :** to subject to the action of boiling water or steam **b :** to bring to a temperature just below the boiling point **3 :** SCORCH ~ *vi* **1 :** to scald something **2 :** to become scalded

[2]**scald** *n* **1 :** an injury to the body caused by scalding **2 :** an act or process of scalding **3 a :** a plant disease marked esp. by discoloration suggesting injury by heat **b :** a burning and browning of plant tissues resulting from high temperatures or high temperature and intense light

[3]**scald** *adj* [*scall* + *-ed*] **1** *archaic* **:** SCABBY, SCURFY **2** *archaic* **:** SHABBY, CONTEMPTIBLE ⟨~ rogues⟩

[4]**scald** *var of* SKALD

[5]**scald** \'skȯld\ *adj* **:** SCALDED

scald·ing *adj* **1 :** causing the sensation of scalding or burning **2 :** BOILING **3 :** SCORCHING, ARDENT ⟨the ~ sun⟩ **4 :** BITING, SCATHING ⟨a series of ~ editorials⟩

[1]**scale** \'skā(ə)l\ *n* [ME, bowl, scale of a balance fr. ON *skāl*; akin to ON *skel* shell — more at SHELL] **1 a :** either pan or tray of a balance **b :** a beam that is supported freely in the center and has two pans of equal weight suspended from its ends — usu. used in pl. **2 :** an instrument or machine for weighing

[2]**scale** *vt* **:** to weigh in scales ~ *vi* **:** to have a specified weight on scales

[3]**scale** *n* [ME, fr. MF *escale*, of Gmc origin; akin to OE *scealu* shell, husk — more at SHELL] **1 a :** a small, flattened, rigid, and definitely circumscribed plate forming part of the external body covering esp. of a fish **b :** a small thin plate suggesting a fish scale ⟨~*s* of mica⟩ ⟨the ~*s* on a moth's wing⟩ **c :** the scaly covering of a scaled animal **2 :** a small thin dry lamina shed (as in many skin diseases) from the skin **3 :** a thin coating, layer, or incrustation: **a :** a black scaly coating of oxide (as magnetic oxide) forming on the surface of iron when heated for processing **b :** a similar coating forming on other metals **4 a :** a modified leaf protecting a seed plant bud before expansion **b :** a thin, membranous, chaffy, or woody bract **5 a :** one of the small overlapping usu. metal pieces forming the outer surface of scale armor **b :** SCALE ARMOR **6 a :** SCALE INSECT **b :** infestation with or disease caused by scale insects — **scaled** \'skā(ə)ld\ *adj* — **scale·less** \'skā(ə)l-ləs\ *adj*

[4]**scale** *vt* **1 :** to remove the scale or scales from (as by scraping) ⟨~ a fish⟩ **2 :** to take off in thin layers or scales **3 :** to form scale on **4 :** to throw (as a thin flat stone) so that the edge cuts the air or so that it skips on water **:** SKIM ~ *vi* **1 :** to separate and come off in scales **:** FLAKE **2 :** to shed scales ⟨*scaling* skin⟩ **3 :** to become encrusted with scale

[5]**scale** *n* [ME, fr. LL *scala* ladder, staircase, fr. L *scalae*, pl., stairs, rungs, ladder; akin to L *scandere* to climb — more at SCAN] **1 a** *obs* **:** LADDER **b** *obs* **:** a flight of stairs **c** *archaic* **:** a means of ascent **2 :** a graduated series of musical tones ascending or descending in order of pitch according to a specified scheme of their intervals **3 :** something graduated esp. when used as a measure or rule: as **a :** a series of spaces marked by lines and used to measure distances or to register something (as the height of the mercury in a thermometer) **b :** a divided line on a map or chart indicating the length used to represent a larger unit of measure (as an inch to a mile) **c :** an instrument consisting of a strip (as of wood, plastic, or metal) with one or more sets of spaces graduated and numbered on its surface for measuring or laying off distances or dimensions **4 :** a graduated series or scheme of rank or order **5 :** a proportion between two sets of dimensions (as between those of a drawing and its original) **6 :** a graded series of tests or of performances used in rating individual intelligence or achievement — **scale** *adj*

[6]**scale** *vt* **1 a :** to attack with or take by means of scaling ladders ⟨~ a castle wall⟩ **b :** to climb up or reach by means of a ladder **c :** to reach the highest point of **:** SURMOUNT **2 a :** to arrange in a graduated series ⟨~ a test⟩ **b (1) :** to measure by or as if by a scale **(2) :** to measure or estimate the sound content of (as logs) **c :** to pattern, make, regulate, set, or estimate according to some rate or standard ~ *vi* **1 :** to climb by or as if by a ladder ⟨firemen given the command to ~⟩ **2 :** to rise in a graduated series ⟨windows *scaling* beside a stairway⟩ **3 :** MEASURE **syn** see ASCEND

[7]**scale** *n* **1** *obs* **:** ESCALADE **2 :** an estimate of the amount of sound lumber in logs or standing timber

scale armor *n* **:** armor made of small metallic scales on leather or cloth

scale–down \'skā(ə)l-ˌdau̇n\ *n* **:** a reduction according to a fixed ratio ⟨a ~ of debts⟩

scale insect *n* **:** any of numerous small but very prolific homopterous insects (esp. family Coccidae) including various economic pests and having winged males, degenerated scale-covered females attached to the host plant, and young that suck the juices of plants — compare COCHINEAL, LAC

scale leaf *n* **:** a modified usu. small and scaly leaf (as a bud scale or bract or the leaf of cypress)

scale·like \'skā(ə)l-ˌlīk\ *adj* **:** resembling a scale ⟨~ design⟩; *specif* **:** reduced to a minute appressed element resembling a scale ⟨~ leaves⟩

scale moss *n* **:** a foliose hepatic or liverwort

sca·lene \'skā-ˌlēn, skā-'\ *adj* [LL *scalenus*, fr. Gk *skalēnos*, lit., uneven; akin to Gk *skolios* crooked — more at CYLINDER] *of a triangle* **:** having the sides unequal

scale·pan \'skā(ə)l-ˌpan\ *n* **:** a pan of a scale for weighing

scal·er \'skā-lər\ *n* **1 :** one that scales **2 :** an electronic device that operates a recorder after a specified number of impulses appearing too rapidly for individual recording

scale·tail \'skā(ə)l-ˌtāl\ *n* **:** a rodent (genus *Anomalurus*) with horny scales under the base of the tail

scale–up \'skā-ˌləp\ *n* **:** an increase according to a fixed ratio ⟨a ~ of wages⟩

scal·i·ness \'skā-lē-nəs\ *n* **:** the quality or state of being scaly

scall \'skȯl\ *n* [ME, fr. ON *skalli* bald head] **:** a scurf or scabby disorder (as of the scalp)

scal·lion \'skal-yən\ *n* [ME *scaloun*, fr. AF *scalun*, fr. (assumed) VL *escalonia*, fr. L *ascalonia* (*caepa*) onion of Ascalon, fr. fem. of *ascalonius* of Ascalon, fr. *Ascalon-*, *Ascalo* Ascalon, seaport in southern Palestine] **1 :** SHALLOT **2 :** LEEK **3 :** an onion forming a thick basal portion without a bulb; *also* **:** GREEN ONION

[1]**scal·lop** \'skäl-əp, 'skal-\ *n* [ME *scalop*, fr. MF *escalope* shell, of Gmc origin; akin to MD *schelpe* shell] **1 a :** any of many marine bivalve mollusks (family Pectinidae) with the shell radially ribbed and the edge undulated that swim by opening and closing the valves **b :** the adductor muscle of a scallop as an article of food **2 :** a scallop-shell valve or a similarly shaped dish used for baking **3 :** one of a continuous series of circle segments or angular projections forming a border **4 :** CYMLING **5** [F *escalope*, perh. fr. E [1]*scallop*; fr. its being served curled like a scallop-shell valve] **:** a thin slice of boneless meat

[2]**scallop** *vt* **1** [*escallop* fr. earlier *escallop* scallop shell, alter. (influenced by MF *escalope* shell) of [1]*scallop*] **:** to bake in a sauce usu. covered with seasoned bread or cracker crumbs ⟨~ potatoes⟩ **2 a :** to shape, cut, or finish in scallops **b :** to form scallops in ~ *vi* **:** to gather or dredge scallops — **scal·lop·er** *n*

scal·lo·pi·ni \ˌskäl-ə-'pē-nē\ *n* [modif. of It *scaloppine*] **:** thin slices of meat (as veal) sautéed or coated with flour and fried

scal·ly·wag \'skal-i-ˌwag\ *var of* SCALAWAG

sca·lo·gram \'skā-lə-ˌgram\ *n* [[5]*scale* + *-o-* + *-gram*] **:** an arrangement of items (as of a psychological or sociological test) in ascending order of difficulty ⟨analysis by ~⟩

[1]**scalp** \'skalp\ *n* [ME, of Scand origin; akin to ON *skālpr* sheath; akin to MD *schelpe* shell] **1 a :** the part of the integument of the human head usu. covered with hair **b :** the corresponding part of a lower animal (as a wolf or fox) **2 a :** a part of the human scalp with attached hair cut or torn from an enemy as a token of victory by Indian warriors of No. America **b :** a trophy of victory **3** *chiefly Scot* **:** a projecting mass of bare ground or rock

[2]**scalp** *vt* **1 a :** to deprive of the scalp **b :** to remove an upper or better part from **2 :** to screen or sift in order to remove foreign materials or to separate out coarser grades **3 a :** to buy and sell so as to make small quick profits ⟨~ stocks⟩ ⟨~ grain⟩ **b :** to obtain and resell at greatly increased prices ~ *vi* **1 :** to take scalps **2 a :** to profit by slight market fluctuations **b :** to scalp tickets — **scalp·er** *n*

scal·pel \'skal-pəl *also* skal-'pel\ *n* [L *scalpellus, scalpellum,* dim. of *scalper, scalprum* chisel, knife, fr. *scalpere* to carve — more at SHELF] **:** a small straight thin-bladed knife used esp. in surgery

scalp lock *n* **:** a long tuft of hair on the crown of the otherwise shaved head of a warrior of some American Indian tribes

scaly \'skā-lē\ *adj* **1 a :** covered with, composed of, or rich in scale or scales **b :** FLAKY **2 :** of or relating to scaly animals **3 :** DESPICABLE, POOR **4 :** infested with scale insects ⟨~ fruit⟩

scaly anteater *n* **:** PANGOLIN; *esp* **:** a southern African pangolin

scaly–finned \ˌskā-lē-'find\ *adj* **:** having scales on the fins

scam·mo·ny \'skam-ə-nē\ *n* [ME *scamonie,* fr. L *scammonia,* fr. Gk *skammōnia*] **:** a twining convolvulus (*Convolvulus scammonia*) of Asia Minor with a large thick root; *also* **:** this root or a cathartic resin obtained from it

¹scamp \'skamp\ *n* [obs. *scamp* (to roam about idly)] **1 :** RASCAL, ROGUE **2 :** an impish or playful young person

²scamp *vt* [perh. of Scand origin; akin to ON *skammr* short — more at SCANT] **:** to perform in a hasty, neglectful, or imperfect manner

¹scam·per \'skam-pər\ *vi* **scam·per·ing** \-p(ə-)riŋ\ [prob. fr. obs. D *schampen* to flee, fr. MF *escamper,* fr. It *scampare,* fr. (assumed) VL *excampare* to decamp, fr. L *ex-* + *campus* field — more at CAMP] **:** to run nimbly and playfully about

²scamper *n* **:** a playful scurry

scam·pi \'skam-pē, 'skäm-\ *n, pl* **scampi** [It, pl. of *scampo,* a European lobster] **:** SHRIMP; *esp* **:** large shrimp prepared with a garlic-flavored sauce

scan \'skan\ *vb* **scanned; scan·ning** [ME *scannen,* fr. LL *scandere,* fr. L, to climb; akin to Gk *skandalon* trap, stumbling block, offense, Skt *skandati* he leaps] *vt* **1 :** to read or mark so as to show metrical structure **2 a** (1) **:** to examine intensively (2) **:** to check (as a magnetic tape or a punched card) for recorded data by means of an electronic or other device **b :** to make a wide sweeping search of **c :** to look through or over hastily **3 a :** to bring under a moving electron beam for conversion of light and dark picture or image values into corresponding electrical values to be transmitted by facsimile or television **b :** to direct a succession of radar beams over in searching for a target ~ *vi* **1 :** to scan verse **2 :** to conform to a metrical pattern **syn** see SCRUTINIZE — **scan** *n*

¹scan·dal \'skan-dᵊl\ *n* [LL *scandalum* stumbling block, offense, fr. Gk *skandalon*] **1 a :** discredit brought upon religion by unseemly conduct in a religious person **b :** conduct that causes or encourages a lapse of faith or of religious obedience in another **2 :** loss of or damage to reputation caused by actual or apparent violation of morality or propriety **:** DISGRACE **3 a :** a circumstance or action that offends propriety or established moral conceptions or disgraces those associated with it **b :** a person whose conduct offends propriety or morality **4 :** malicious or defamatory gossip **5 :** indignation, chagrin, or bewilderment brought about by a flagrant violation of morality, propriety, or religious opinion **syn** see OFFENSE

²scandal *vt* **1** *obs* **:** DISGRACE **2** *chiefly dial* **:** DEFAME, SLANDER

scan·dal·iza·tion \ˌskan-də-lə-'zā-shən\ *n* **:** the act of scandalizing or the state of being scandalized

scan·dal·ize \'skan-də-ˌlīz\ *vt* **1 :** to speak falsely or maliciously of **:** MALIGN **2** *archaic* **:** to bring into reproach **:** DISHONOR, DISGRACE **3 :** to offend the moral sense of **:** SHOCK — **scan·dal·iz·er** *n*

scan·dal·mon·ger \'skan-dᵊl-ˌməŋ-gər, -ˌmäŋ-\ *n* **:** a person who circulates scandal

scan·dal·ous \'skan-d(ə-)ləs\ *adj* **1 :** DEFAMATORY, LIBELOUS **2 :** offensive to propriety or morality **:** SHOCKING — **scan·dal·ous·ly** *adv* — **scan·dal·ous·ness** *n*

scandal sheet *n* **:** a newspaper or periodical dealing to a large extent in scandal and gossip

scan·dent \'skan-dənt\ *adj* [L *scandent-, scandens,* prp. of *scandere* to climb] **:** CLIMBING ⟨~ stems⟩

Scan·di·an \'skan-dē-ən\ *adj* [L *Scandia*] **1 :** SCANDINAVIAN **2 :** of or relating to the languages of Scandinavia — **Scandian** *n*

Scan·di·na·vian \ˌskan-də-'nā-vē-ən, -vyən\ *n* **1 a :** a native or inhabitant of Scandinavia **b :** a person of Scandinavian descent **2 :** the No. Germanic languages — **Scandinavian** *adj*

scan·di·um \'skan-dē-əm\ *n* [NL, fr. L *Scandia,* ancient name of southern Scandinavian peninsula] **:** a white trivalent metallic element found in association with the rare-earth metals — see ELEMENT table

scan·ner \'skan-ər\ *n* **:** one that scans: as **a :** a device that automatically checks a process or condition and may initiate a desired corrective action **b :** a device for sensing recorded data ⟨a punched-card ~⟩

scan·sion \'skan-chən\ *n* [LL *scansion-, scansio,* fr. L, act of climbing, fr. (assumed) L *scansus,* pp. of L *scandere*] **:** the analysis of verse to show its meter

scan·so·ri·al \skan-'sōr-ē-əl, -'sȯr-\ *adj* [L *scansorius,* fr. (assumed) L *scansus*] **:** relating to, capable of, or adapted for climbing

¹scant \'skant\ *adj* [ME, fr. ON *skamt,* neut. of *skammr* short; akin to Gk *koptein* to cut — more at CAPON] **1** *dial* **a :** excessively frugal **:** PARSIMONIOUS **b :** not prodigal **:** CHARY **2 a :** barely or scarcely sufficient; *specif* **:** not quite coming up to a stated measure **b :** lacking in amplitude or quantity **:** MEAGER **3 :** having a small or insufficient supply **syn** see MEAGER — **scant·ly** *adv*

²scant *adv, dial* **:** SCARCELY, HARDLY

³scant *vt* **1 :** to provide with a meager or inadequate portion or allowance **:** STINT **2 :** to make small, narrow, or meager **:** SKIMP **3 :** to provide an incomplete supply of **:** WITHHOLD **4 :** to give scant attention to **:** SLIGHT

scant·ies \'skant-ēz\ *n pl* [blend of ¹*scant* and *panties*] **:** abbreviated panties for women

scant·i·ly \'skant-ᵊl-ē\ *adv* **:** in a scanty manner

scant·i·ness \'skant-ē-nəs\ *n* **:** the quality or state of being scanty

scant·ling \'skant-liŋ, -lən\ *n* [alter. of ME *scantilon,* lit., mason's or carpenter's gauge, fr. ONF *escantillon*] **1 a :** the breadth and thickness of timber and stone used in building **b :** the dimensions of a frame or strake used in shipbuilding **2 :** a small quantity, amount, or proportion **:** MODICUM **3 :** a small piece of lumber (as an upright piece in house framing)

scant·ness \-nəs\ *n* **:** the quality or state of being scant

scanty \'skant-ē\ *adj* [E dial. *scant* scanty supply, fr. ME, fr. ON *skant,* fr. neut. of *skammr* short] **1 :** barely sufficient **2 :** somewhat less than is needed **:** INSUFFICIENT **syn** see MEAGER

¹scape \'skāp\ *vb* [ME *scapen,* short for *escapen*] **:** ESCAPE

²scape *n* [L *scapus* shaft, stalk — more at SHAFT] **1 :** a peduncle arising at or beneath the surface of the ground in an acaulescent plant (as the tulip); *broadly* **:** a flower stalk **2 a :** the shaft of a column **b :** the small concave curve at the top or bottom of the shaft of a column where it joins the capital or the base **3 :** the shaft of an animal part (as an antenna or feather) — **sca·pi·form** \'skā-pə-ˌfȯrm\ *adj*

-scape \ˌskāp\ *n comb form* [*landscape*] **:** view or picture of a (specified) type of scene ⟨moon*scape*⟩

scape·goat \'skāp-ˌgōt\ *n* [¹*scape;* intended as trans. of Heb *'azāzēl* (prob. name of a demon), as if *'ēz 'ōzēl* goat that departs, Lev 16:8 (AV)] **1 :** a goat upon whose head are symbolically placed the sins of the people after which he is sent into the wilderness in the biblical ceremony for Yom Kippur **2 :** a person or thing bearing the blame for others

scape·grace \-ˌgrās\ *n* [¹*scape*] **:** an incorrigible rascal

¹scaph·oid \'skaf-ˌȯid\ *adj* [NL *scaphoides,* fr. Gk *skaphoeidēs,* fr. *skaphos* boat] **:** shaped like a boat **:** NAVICULAR

²scaphoid *n* **:** the navicular of the carpus or tarsus

scap·o·lite \'skap-ə-ˌlīt\ *n* [F, fr. L *scapus* shaft + F *-o-* + *-lite;* fr. the prismatic shape of its crystals] **:** any of a group of minerals consisting essentially of silicates of aluminum, calcium, and sodium; *specif* **:** a species containing 46 to 54 percent of silica — called also *wernerite*

sca·pose \'skā-ˌpōs\ *adj* **:** bearing, resembling, or consisting of a scape

scap·u·la \'skap-yə-lə\ *n, pl* **scap·u·lae** \-yə-ˌlē, -ˌlī\ *or* **scapulas** [NL, fr. L, shoulder blade, shoulder] **:** either of a pair of large triangular bones lying one in each dorsal lateral part of the thorax, forming the principal bone of the corresponding half of the shoulder girdle, and articulating with the corresponding clavicle or coracoid — called also *shoulder blade*

¹scap·u·lar \-lər\ *n* [ME *scapulare,* fr. LL, fr. L *scapula* shoulder] **1 a :** a long wide band of cloth with an opening for the head worn front and back over the shoulders as part of a monastic habit **b :** a pair of small cloth squares joined by shoulder tapes and worn under the clothing on the breast and back as a sacramental and often also as a badge of a third order or confraternity **2 a :** SCAPULA **b :** a scapular feather

²scapular *adj* [NL *scapularis,* fr. *scapula*] **:** of or relating to the shoulder, the scapula, or scapulars

scapular medal *n* **:** a medal worn in place of a sacramental scapular

¹scar \'skär\ *n* [ME *skere,* fr. ON *sker* skerry; akin to ON *skera* to cut — more at SHEAR] **1 :** an isolated or protruding rock **2 :** a steep rocky eminence **:** a bare place on the side of a mountain

²scar *n* [ME *escare, scar,* fr. MF *escare* scab, fr. LL *eschara,* fr. Gk, hearth, scab] **1 :** a mark left (as in the skin) by the healing of injured tissue **2 a :** a mark left on a stem or branch by a fallen leaf or harvested fruit **b :** CICATRIX 2 **3 :** a lasting moral or emotional injury

³scar *vb* **scarred; scar·ring** *vt* **1 :** to mark with a scar **2 :** to do lasting injury to ~ *vi* **1 :** to form a scar **2 :** to become scarred

scar·ab \'skar-əb\ *n* [MF *scarabee,* fr. L *scarabaeus*] **1 :** SCARABAEUS 1; *broadly* **:** a scarabaeid beetle **2 :** SCARABAEUS 2

scar·a·bae·id \ˌskar-ə-'bē-əd\ *n* [deriv. of L *scarabaeus*] **:** any of a family (Scarabaeidae) of stout-bodied beetles with lamellate antennae including the dung beetles — **scarabaeid** *adj* — **scar·a·bae·oid** \-'bē-ˌȯid\ *adj*

scar·a·bae·us \ˌskar-ə-'bē-əs\ *n* [L] **1** *pl* **scar·a·bae·us·es** *or* **scar·a·baei** \-'bē-ˌī\ **:** a large black or nearly black dung beetle (*Scarabaeus sacer*) **2 :** a stone or faience beetle used in ancient Egypt as a talisman, ornament, and a symbol of the resurrection

scar·a·mouch *or* **scar·a·mouche** \'skar-ə-ˌmüsh, -ˌmüch, -ˌmau̇ch\ *n* [F *Scaramouche,* fr. It *Scaramuccia*] **1** *cap* **:** a stock character in the Italian commedia dell'arte drawn to burlesque the Spanish don and characterized by boastfulness and poltroonery **2 a :** a cowardly buffoon **b :** RASCAL, SCAMP

¹scarce \'ske(ə)rs, 'ska(ə)rs\ *adj* [ME *scars,* fr. ONF *escars,* fr. (assumed) VL *excarpsus,* lit., plucked out, pp. of L *excerpere* to pluck out — more at EXCERPT] **1 :** deficient in quantity or number compared with the demand **:** not plentiful or abundant **2 :** not provided in sufficient abundance to be free **syn** see INFREQUENT — **scarce·ly** *adv* — **scarce·ness** *n*

²scarce *adv* **:** SCARCELY, HARDLY

scarce·ment \-mənt\ *n* [obs. *scarce* (to diminish)] **:** an offset in the thickness of a wall or bank of earth

scar·ci·ty \'sker-sət-ē, 'sker-stē, 'skar-\ *n* **:** the quality or condition of being scarce; *esp* **:** want of provisions for the support of life

¹scare \'ske(ə)r, 'ska(ə)r\ *vb* [ME *skerren,* fr. ON *skirra,* fr. *skjarr* shy, timid] *vt* **:** to frighten suddenly **:** ALARM ~ *vi* **:** to become scared

²scare *n* **1 :** a sudden fright **2 :** a widespread state of alarm **:** PANIC — **scare** *adj*

scare·crow \-ˌkrō\ *n* **1 a :** an object typically suggesting a human figure set up to frighten crows or other birds away from crops **b :** something frightening but innocuous **2 :** a skinny or ragged person

scare·head \-ˌhed\ *n* **:** a big, sensational, or alarming newspaper headline

scare·mon·ger \-ˌməŋ-gər, -ˌmäŋ-\ *n* **:** ALARMIST

scar·er \'sker-ər, 'skar-\ *n* **:** one that scares

scare up *vt* **:** to bring to light or get together with considerable labor or difficulty

¹scarf \'skärf\ *n, pl* **scarves** \'skärvz\ *or* **scarfs** \'skärfs\ [ONF *escarpe* sash, sling] **1 :** a broad band of cloth worn about the shoulders, around the neck, or over the head **2 a :** a military or official sash usu. indicative of rank **b :** TIPPET 3 **3 :** RUNNER 6b

²scarf *vt* **1 :** to wrap, cover, or adorn with or as if with a scarf **2 :** to wrap or throw on (a scarf or mantle) loosely

³scarf *n* [ME *skarf,* prob. of Scand origin; akin to ON *skarfr* scarf; akin to Gk *skorpios* scorpion] **1 :** either of the chamfered or cutaway ends that fit together to form a scarf joint **2 :** a joint made by chamfering, halving, or notching two pieces to correspond and lapping and bolting them

⁴scarf *or* **scarph** \'skärf\ *vt* **1 :** to unite by a scarf joint **2 :** to form a scarf on

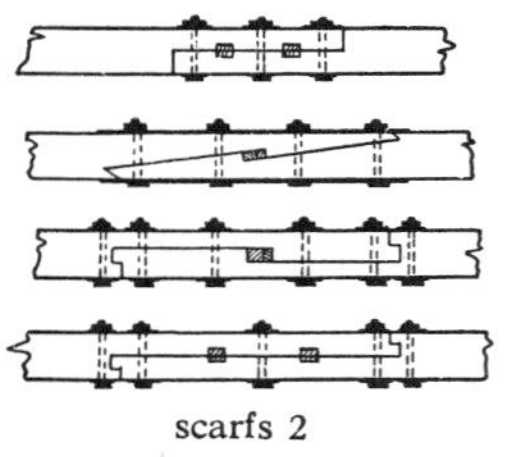
scarfs 2

scarf·pin \'skärf-,pin\ *n* : TIEPIN

scarf·skin \'skärf-,skin\ *n* [1*scarf*] : EPIDERMIS; *esp* : that forming the cuticle of a nail

scar·i·fi·ca·tion \,skar-ə-fə-'kā-shən, ,sker-\ *n* **1** : the act or process of scarifying **2** : a mark or marks made by scarifying

scar·i·fi·er \'skar-ə-,fī(-ə)r, 'sker-\ *n* : one that scarifies

scar·i·fy \-,fī\ *vt* [MF *scarifier*, fr. LL *scarificare*, alter. of L *scarifare*, fr. Gk *skariphasthai* to scratch an outline, sketch — more at SCRIBE] **1** : to make scratches or small cuts in (as the skin) ⟨~ an area for vaccination⟩ **2** : to lacerate the feelings of : FLAY **3** : to break up and loosen the surface of (as a field or road) **4** : to cut or soften the wall of (a hard seed) to hasten germination

scar·i·ous \'sker-ē-əs, 'skar-\ *adj* [NL *scariosus*] : dry and membranous in texture ⟨a ~ bract⟩

scar·la·ti·na \,skär-lə-'tē-nə\ *n* [NL, fr. ML *scarlata* scarlet] : SCARLET FEVER — **scar·la·ti·nal** \-'tēn-ᵊl\ *adj*

scar·less \'skär-ləs\ *adj* : having or leaving no scar

1**scar·let** \'skär-lət\ *n* [ME *scarlat, scarlet*, fr. OF or ML; OF *escarlate*, fr. ML *scarlata*, fr. Per *saqalāt*, a kind of rich cloth] **1** : scarlet cloth or clothes **2** : any of various bright reds

2**scarlet** *adj* **1** : of the color scarlet **2** [fr. the use of the word in Isa 1:18 & Rev 17:1–6 (AV)] : WHORISH; *also* : FLAGRANT

scarlet fever *n* : an acute contagious febrile disease caused by a hemolytic streptococcus and characterized by inflammation of the nose, throat, and mouth, generalized toxemia, and a red rash

scarlet letter *n* [fr. the novel *The Scarlet Letter* (1850) by Nathaniel Hawthorne] : a scarlet A worn as a punitive mark of adultery

scarlet runner *n* : a tropical American high-climbing bean (*Phaseolus coccineus*) with large bright red flowers and red-and-black seeds grown widely as an ornamental and in Great Britain as a preferred food bean

scarlet sage *n* : any of several red-flowered salvias

1**scarp** \'skärp\ *n* [It *scarpa*] **1** : the inner side of a ditch below the parapet of a fortification **2 a** : a line of cliffs produced by faulting or erosion **b** : a low steep slope along a beach caused by wave erosion

2**scarp** *vt* : to cut down vertically or to a steep slope

scar·per \'skär-pər\ *vi* [perh. fr. It *scappare*, fr. (assumed) VL *excappare* — more at ESCAPE] *Brit* : to run away

1**scar·ry** \'skär-ē\ *adj* [1*scar*] : characterized by bare and rugged projections of rock

2**scarry** *adj* [2*scar*] : bearing marks of wounds : SCARRED

1**scart** \'skärt\ *vb* [ME *skarten*, alter. of *scratten*] *chiefly Scot* : SCRATCH, SCRAPE

2**scart** *n, chiefly Scot* : SCRATCH, MARK; *esp* : one made in writing

scar tissue *n* : the connective tissue forming a scar and composed chiefly of fibroblasts in recent scars and largely of dense collagenous fibers in old scars

scary *also* **scar·ey** \'ske(ə)r-ē, 'ska(ə)r-\ *adj* **scarier**; **scariest** **1** : causing fright : ALARMING **2** : easily scared : TIMID **3** : SCARED, FRIGHTENED ⟨~ feeling⟩

1**scat** \'skat\ *vi* **scat·ted**; **scat·ting** [*scat*, interj. used to drive away a cat] **1** : to go away quickly — often used interjectionally to drive away an animal (as a cat) **2** : to move fast : SCOOT

2**scat** *n* [perh. imit.] : jazz singing with nonsense syllables

3**scat** *vi* **scat·ted**; **scat·ting** : to improvise nonsense syllables to an instrumental accompaniment : sing scat

scat- *or* **scato-** *comb form* [Gk *skato-*, fr. *skat-*, *skōr*; akin to OE *scearn* dung, L *muscerda* mouse dropping] : ordure ⟨*scato*logy⟩

scat·back \'skat-,bak\ *n* [1*scat* + *back*] : a backfield player in football who is an esp. fast and elusive runner

1**scathe** \'skāth, *dial also* 'skāth, 'skath\ *n* [ME *skathe*, fr. ON *skathi*; akin to OE *sceatha* injury, Gk *askēthēs* unharmed] : HARM, INJURY — **scathe·less** \-ləs\ *adj*

2**scathe** *vt* **1** : to do harm to : INJURE; *specif* : SCORCH, SEAR **2** : to assail with withering denunciation

scath·ing \'skā-thiŋ\ *adj* : bitterly severe ⟨~ rebuke⟩ — **scath·ing·ly** \-thiŋ-lē\ *adv*

scat·o·log·i·cal \,skat-ᵊl-'äj-i-kəl\ *adj* : of or relating to excrement or scatology

sca·tol·o·gy \skə-'täl-ə-jē, ska-\ *n* **1** : the study of excrement **2** : interest in or treatment of obscene matters esp. in literature

sca·toph·a·gous \ska-'täf-ə-gəs\ *adj* [Gk *skatophagos*, fr. *skat-*, *skōr* + *-phagos* -phagous] : habitually feeding on dung ⟨a ~ beetle⟩ : COPROPHAGOUS

scatt \'skat\ *n* [ON *skattr*; akin to OE *sceat* property, money, a small coin] *archaic* : TAX, TRIBUTE

1**scat·ter** \'skat-ər\ *vb* [ME *scateren*] *vt* **1** *archaic* : to fling away heedlessly : SQUANDER **2 a** : to cause to separate widely **b** : to cause to vanish **3** : to distribute irregularly **4** : to sow broadcast : STREW **5 a** : to reflect irregularly and diffusely **b** : to diffuse or disperse (a beam of radiation) **6** : to divide into ineffectual small portions ~ *vi* **1** : to separate and go in various directions : DISPERSE **2** : to occur or fall irregularly or at random — **scat·ter·er** \-ər-ər\ *n* — **scat·ter·ing·ly** \'skat-ə-riŋ-lē\ *adv*

syn SCATTER, DISPERSE, DISSIPATE, DISPEL mean to cause to separate or break up. SCATTER implies a force that drives parts or units irregularly in many directions; DISPERSE implies a wider separation and a complete breaking up of a mass or group; DISSIPATE stresses complete disintegration or dissolution and final disappearance; DISPEL stresses a driving away or getting rid of as if by scattering

2**scatter** *n* **1** : the act of scattering **2** : a small supply or number irregularly distributed or strewn about **3** : the state or extent of being scattered; *specif* : DISPERSION

scat·ter·brain \-,brān\ *n* : a giddy heedless person : FLIBBERTIGIBBET — **scat·ter·brained** \-,brānd\ *adj*

scat·ter·good \-,gu̇d\ *n* : a wasteful person : SPENDTHRIFT

1**scat·ter·ing** *n* **1** : an act or process in which something scatters or is scattered **2** : something scattered; *esp* : a small number or quantity interspersed here and there ⟨a ~ of visitors⟩

2**scattering** *adj* **1** : going in various directions **2** : found or placed far apart and in no order **3** : divided among many or several ⟨~ votes⟩ — **scat·ter·ing·ly** \-ə-riŋ-lē\ *adv*

scatter pin *n* : a small pin used as jewelry and worn usu. in groups of two or more on a woman's dress

scatter rug *n* : a rug of such a size that several can be used (as to fill vacant places) in a room

scaup \'skȯp\ *n, pl* **scaup** *or* **scaups** [perh. alter. of *scalp* (bed of shellfish); fr. its fondness for shellfish] : any of several diving ducks (genus *Aythya*)

scav·enge \'skav-ənj\ *vb* [back-formation fr. *scavenger*] *vt* **1 a** (1) : to remove (as dirt or refuse) from an area (2) : to clean away dirt or refuse from : CLEANSE ⟨~ a street⟩ **b** : to feed on (carrion or refuse) **2 a** : to remove (burned gases) from the cylinder of an internal combustion engine after a working stroke **b** : to clean and purify (molten metal) by taking up foreign elements in chemical union **3** : to salvage from discarded or refuse material; *also* : to salvage usable material from ~ *vi* : to work or act as a scavenger

scav·en·ger \-ən-jər\ *n* [alter. of earlier *scavager*, fr. ME *skawager* collector of a toll on goods sold by nonresident merchants, fr. *skawage* toll on goods sold by nonresident merchants, fr. ONF *escauwage* inspection] **1** *chiefly Brit* : a person employed to remove dirt and refuse from streets **2** : one that scavenges: as **a** : a garbage collector **b** : JUNKMAN **c** : a chemically active substance acting to make innocuous or remove an undesirable substance **3** : an organism that feeds habitually on refuse or carrion

sce·nar·io \sə-'nar-ē-,ō, -'ner-, -'när-\ *n* [It, fr. L *scaenarium*, fr. *scaena* stage] **1 a** : an outline or synopsis of a play; *esp* : a plot outline used by actors of the commedia dell'arte **b** : the book of an opera **2 a** : SCREENPLAY **b** : SHOOTING SCRIPT

sce·nar·ist \-'nar-əst, -'ner-, -'när-\ *n* : a writer of scenarios

1**scend** \'send\ *vi* [alter. of *send*] : to rise or heave upward under the influence of a natural force (as on a wave)

2**scend** *n* **1** : the upward movement of a pitching ship **2** : the lift of a wave : SEND

scene \'sēn\ *n* [MF, stage, fr. L *scena*, *scaena*, fr. Gk *skēnē* temporary shelter, tent, building forming the background for a dramatic performance, stage; akin to Gk *skia* shadow — more at SHINE] **1** : one of the subdivisions of a play: as **a** : a division of an act presenting continuous action in one place **b** : a single situation or unit of dialogue in a play **c** : a motion picture or television episode or sequence **2 a** : a stage setting **b** : a real or imaginary prospect suggesting a stage setting ⟨a sylvan ~⟩ ⟨the passing ~⟩ **3** : the place of an occurrence or action : LOCALE ⟨~ of the crime⟩ **4** : an exhibition of anger or indecorous behavior ⟨make a ~⟩

scen·ery \'sēn-(ə-)rē\ *n* **1** : the painted scenes or hangings and accessories used on a theater stage **2** : a picturesque view or landscape

scene·shift·er \'sēn-,shif-tər\ *n* : a worker who moves the scenes in a theater

scene–steal·er \-,stē-lər\ *n* : an actor who skillfully or ostentatiously diverts attention to himself when he is not intended to be the center of attention

sce·nic \'sēn-ik *also* 'sen-\ *adj* **1** : of or relating to the stage, a stage setting, or stage representation **2** : of or relating to natural scenery **3** : representing graphically an action, event, or episode ⟨a ~ bas-relief⟩

sce·ni·cal \-i-kəl\ *adj* : SCENIC — **sce·ni·cal·ly** \-k(ə-)lē\ *adv*

scenic railway *n* : a miniature railway (as in an amusement park) with artificial scenery along the way

sce·no·graph·ic \,sē-nə-'graf-ik\ *adj* : of or relating to scenography — **sce·no·graph·i·cal·ly** \-i-k(ə-)lē\ *adv*

sce·nog·ra·phy \sē-'näg-rə-fē\ *n* [Gk *skēnographia* painting of scenery, fr. *skēnē* + *-graphia* -graphy] : the art of perspective representation applied to the painting of stage scenery (as by the Greeks)

1**scent** \'sent\ *vb* [ME *senten*, fr. MF *sentir* to feel, smell, fr. L *sentire* to perceive, feel — more at SENSE] *vt* **1 a** : to perceive by the olfactory organs : SMELL **b** : to get or have an inkling of ⟨~ trouble⟩ **2** : to imbue or fill with odor ~ *vi* **1** : to yield an odor of some specified kind ⟨this ~*s* of sulfur⟩; *also* : to bear indication or suggestions ⟨the very air ~*s* of treachery⟩ **2** : to use the nose in seeking or tracking prey

2**scent** *n* **1** : effluvia from a substance that affect the sense of smell: as **a** : an odor left by an animal on a surface passed over; *also* : a course of pursuit or discovery ⟨throw one off the ~⟩ **b** : a characteristic or particular odor; *esp* : one that is agreeable **2 a** : power of smelling : sense of smell ⟨a keen ~⟩ **b** : power of detection ⟨a ~ for heresy⟩ : NOSE **3** : INKLING, INTIMATION ⟨a ~ of trouble⟩ **4** : PERFUME 2 **5** : bits of paper dropped in the game of hare and hounds **6** : a mixture prepared for use as a lure for an animal or fish **syn** see FRAGRANCE, SMELL

scent·ed *adj* : having scent: as **a** : having the sense of smell **b** : PERFUMED **c** : having or exhaling an odor

scent·less \'sent-ləs\ *adj* **1** : lacking the sense of smell **2** : emitting no odor **3 a** : holding no scent **b** : yielding no scent — **scent·less·ness** *n*

1**scep·ter** \'sep-tər\ *n* [ME *sceptre*, fr. OF *ceptre*, fr. L *sceptrum*, fr. Gk *skēptron* staff, scepter — more at SHAFT] **1** : a staff or baton borne by a sovereign as an emblem of authority **2** : royal or imperial authority : SOVEREIGNTY

2**scepter** *vt* **scep·ter·ing** \-t(ə-)riŋ\ : to endow with the scepter in token of royal authority

scep·tered \-tərd\ *adj* **1** : invested with a scepter or sovereign authority **2** : of or relating to a sovereign or to royalty

sceptic *var of* SKEPTIC

sched·u·lar \'skej-ə-lər — *see next*\ *adj* : of or relating to a schedule

1**sched·ule** \'skej-(,)ü(ə)l, 'skej-əl, *Canad also* 'shej-, *Brit usu* 'shed-(,)yü(ə)l\ *n* [ME *cedule*, fr. MF, slip of paper, note, fr. LL *schedula* slip of paper, dim. of L *scheda*, *scida* sheet of papyrus, fr. (assumed) Gk *schidē*; akin to Gk *schizein* to split — more at SHED] **1 a** *obs* : a written document **b** : a statement of supplementary details appended to a legal or legislative document **2** : a written or printed list, catalog, or inventory; *also* : TIMETABLE **3** : PROGRAM, PROPOSAL **4** : AGENDA

2**schedule** *vt* **1 a** : to place in a schedule **b** : to make a schedule of **2** : to appoint, assign, or designate for a fixed future time

schee·lite \'shā(ə)l-,īt\ *n* [G *scheelit*, fr. Karl W. *Scheele* †1786 Sw chemist] : a mineral $CaWO_4$ consisting of calcium tungstate that is a source of tungsten and its compounds

Sche·her·a·zade \shə-ˌher-ə-ˈzäd(-ə)\ *n* [G *Scheherezade*, fr. Per *Shīrazād*] **:** the wife of the sultan of India and narrator of the tales in the *Arabian Nights' Entertainments*

sche·ma \ˈskē-mə\ *n, pl* **sche·ma·ta** \-mət-ə\ [Gk *schēmat-, schēma*] **:** a diagrammatic presentation **:** OUTLINE, PLAN; *specif* **:** FIGURE 6

sche·mat·ic \ski-ˈmat-ik\ *adj* [NL *schematicus*, fr. Gk *schēmat-, schēma*] **:** of or relating to a scheme or schema **:** DIAGRAMMATIC — **schematic** *n* — **sche·mat·i·cal·ly** \-i-k(ə-)lē\ *adv*

sche·ma·tism \ˈskē-mə-ˌtiz-əm\ *n* **:** the disposition of constituents in a pattern or according to a scheme **:** DESIGN; *also* **:** a particular systematic disposition of parts — **sche·ma·tist** \-mət-əst\ *n*

sche·ma·ti·za·tion \ˌskē-mət-ə-ˈzā-shən\ *n* **:** an act or product of schematizing

sche·ma·tize \ˈskē-mə-ˌtīz\ *vt* [Gk *schēmatizein*, fr. *schēmat-, schēma*] **1 :** to form or to form into a scheme or systematic arrangement **2 :** to express or depict schematically

[1]**scheme** \ˈskēm\ *n* [L *schemat-, schema* arrangement, figure, fr. Gk *schēmat-, schēma*, fr. *echein* to have, hold, be in (such) a condition; akin to OE *sige* victory, Skt *sahate* he prevails] **1 a** *archaic* (1) **:** a mathematical or astronomical diagram (2) **:** a representation of the astrological aspects of the planets at a particular time **b :** a graphic sketch or outline **2 :** a concise statement or table **:** EPITOME **3 :** a plan or program of action; *esp* **:** a crafty or secret one **4 :** a systematic or organized framework **:** DESIGN
syn see PLAN

[2]**scheme** *vt* **:** to form a scheme for ∼ *vi* **:** to form plans; *also* **:** PLOT, INTRIGUE — **schem·er** *n*

schem·ing *adj* **:** given to forming schemes; *esp* **:** shrewdly devious and intriguing

[1]**scher·zan·do** \skert-ˈsän-(ˌ)dō\ *adv (or adj)* [It, fr. verbal of *scherzare* to joke, of Gmc origin; akin to MHG *scherzen* to leap for joy, joke; akin to Gk *skairein* to gambol — more at CARDINAL] **:** in sportive manner **:** PLAYFULLY — used as a direction in music indicating style and tempo ⟨allegretto ∼⟩

[2]**scherzando** *n* **:** a passage or movement in scherzando style

scher·zo \ˈske(ə)rt-(ˌ)sō\ *n, pl* **scherzos** *or* **scher·zi** \-(ˌ)sē\ [It, lit., joke, fr. *scherzare*] **:** a sprightly humorous instrumental musical composition or movement commonly in quick triple time

Schick test \ˈshik-\ *n* [Béla *Schick* †1967 Am pediatrician] **:** a test by cutaneous injection of a diluted diphtheria toxin that causes an area of reddening and induration in a subject susceptible to diphtheria

schil·ler \ˈshil-ər\ *n* [G] **:** a bronzy iridescent luster (as of a mineral)

schil·ling \ˈshil-iŋ\ *n* [G, fr. OHG *skilling*, a gold coin — more at SHILLING] — see MONEY table

schip·per·ke \ˈskip-ər-kē, -ər-kə, -ərk\ *n* [Flem, dim. of *schipper* skipper; fr. its use as a watchdog on boats — more at SKIPPER] **:** any of a Belgian breed of small stocky black dogs with foxy head and erect triangular ears

schism \ˈsiz-əm (*by theologians usu so*), ˈskiz-\ *n* [ME *scisme*, fr. MF *cisme*, fr. LL *schismat-, schisma*, fr. Gk, cleft, division, fr. *schizein* to split] **1 :** DIVISION, SEPARATION; *also* **:** DISCORD, DISHARMONY **2 a :** formal division in or separation from a church or religious body **b :** the offense of promoting schism

[1]**schis·mat·ic** \s(k)iz-ˈmat-ik\ *n* **:** one who creates or takes part in schism

[2]**schismatic** *adj* **:** of, relating to, or guilty of schism — **schis·mat·i·cal** \-i-kəl\ *adj* — **schis·mat·i·cal·ly** \-k(ə-)lē\ *adv*

schis·ma·tist \ˈs(k)iz-mət-əst\ *n* [prob. fr. *schismatize*] **:** SCHISMATIC

schis·ma·tize \-mə-ˌtīz\ *vi* **:** to take part in schism; *esp* **:** to make a breach of union (as in the church) ∼ *vt* **:** to induce into schism

schist \ˈshist\ *n* [F *schiste*, fr. L *schistos* (*lapis*), lit., fissile stone, fr. Gk *schistos* that may be split, fr. *schizein*] **:** a metamorphic crystalline rock having a closely foliated structure and admitting of division along approximately parallel planes

schis·tose \ˈshis-ˌtōs\ *or* **schis·tous** \-təs\ *adj* **:** of or relating to schist

schis·to·some \ˈshis-tə-ˌsōm, ˈskis-\ *n* [NL *Schistosoma*, genus name, fr. Gk *schistos* + *sōma* body — more at SOMAT-] **:** any of a genus (*Schistosoma*) of elongated trematode worms with the sexes separate that parasitize the blood vessels of birds and mammals and in man cause destructive schistosomiases; *broadly* **:** a worm of the family (Schistosomatidae) that includes this genus — **schistosome** *adj*

schis·to·so·mi·a·sis \ˌshis-tə-sō-ˈmī-ə-səs, ˌskis-\ *n* [NL, fr. *Schistosoma*] **:** infestation with or disease caused by schistosomes; *specif* **:** a severe endemic disease of man in much of Asia, Africa, and So. America marked esp. by blood loss and tissue damage

schiz- *or* **schizo-** *comb form* [NL, fr. Gk *schizo-*, fr. *schizein* to split] **1 :** split **:** cleft ⟨*schizo*carp⟩ **2 :** characterized by or involving cleavage ⟨*schizo*genesis⟩ **3 :** schizophrenia ⟨*schizo*thymia⟩

schizo \ˈskit-(ˌ)sō\ *n* **:** a schizophrenic individual

schizo·carp \ˈskiz-ə-ˌkärp, ˈskit-sə-\ *n* [ISV] **:** a dry compound fruit that splits at maturity into several indehiscent one-seeded carpels — **schizo·car·pic** \ˌskiz-ə-ˈkär-pik, ˌskit-sə-\ *adj* — **schizo·car·pous** \-pəs\ *adj*

schizo·gen·e·sis \ˌskiz-ō-ˈjen-ə-səs, ˌskit-sō-\ *n* [NL] **:** reproduction by fission

schi·zog·o·ny \skiz-ˈäg-ə-nē, skit-ˈsäg-\ *n* [NL *schizogonia*, fr. *schiz-* + L *-gonia* -gony] **:** asexual reproduction by multiple segmentation characteristic of sporozoans (as the malaria parasite)

schiz·oid \ˈskit-ˌsȯid\ *adj* [ISV] **:** characterized by, resulting from, or suggestive of a split personality — **schizoid** *n*

schizo·my·cete \ˌskiz-ə-ˈmī-ˌsēt, ˌskit-sə-, -(ˌ)mī-ˈ\ *n* [deriv. of Gk *schizo-* schiz- + *mykēt-, mykēs* fungus — more at MYC-] **:** BACTERIUM — **schizo·my·ce·tous** \-(ˌ)mī-ˈsēt-əs\ *adj*

schiz·ont \ˈskiz-ˌänt, ˈskit-ˌsänt\ *n* [ISV] **:** a multinucleate sporozoan that reproduces by schizogony

schizo·phrene \ˈskit-sə-ˌfrēn\ *n* [ISV, prob. back-formation fr. NL *schizophrenia*] **:** SCHIZOPHRENIC

schizo·phre·nia \ˌskit-sə-ˈfrē-nē-ə *also* -ˈfren-ē-\ *n* [NL] **:** a psychotic disorder characterized by loss of contact with environment and by disintegration of personality — **schizo·phre·nic** \-ˈfren-ik *also* -ˈfrē-nik\ *adj or n*

schizo·phyte \ˈskiz-ə-ˌfīt, ˈskit-sə-\ *n* [deriv. of Gk *schizo-* + *phyton* plant — more at PLANT] **:** any of a division (Schizophyta) of plants comprising the blue-green algae and bacteria and characterized by unicellular or loosely colonial and often filamentous organization, by lack of an obvious nucleus, and by chiefly asexual reproduction — **schizo·phyt·ic** \ˌskiz-ə-ˈfit-ik, ˌskit-sə-\ *adj*

schizo·pod \ˈskiz-ə-ˌpäd, ˈskit-sə-\ *n* [deriv. of Gk *schizo-* + *pod-, pous* foot — more at FOOT] **:** any of various crustaceans (orders Mysidacea and Euphausiacea) with a soft carapace — **schizopod** *adj* — **schi·zop·o·dous** \skiz-ˈäp-əd-əs, skit-ˈsäp-\ *adj*

schizo·thy·mia \ˌskit-sə-ˈthī-mē-ə\ *n* [NL] **:** a schizoid tendency or temperament remaining within the bounds of normality — **schizo·thy·mic** \-ˈthī-mik\ *adj*

schle·miel \shlə-ˈmē(ə)l\ *n* [Yiddish *shlumiel*] **:** an unlucky bungler **:** CHUMP

schlie·ren \ˈshlir-ən, ˈshlē-rən\ *n pl* [G] **1 :** small masses or streaks in an igneous rock that differ in composition from the main body **2 :** regions of varying refraction in a transparent medium often caused by pressure or temperature differences and detectable esp. by photographing the passage of a beam of light — **schlie·ric** \ˈshli(ə)r-ik, ˈshlē-rik\ *adj*

schmaltz *or* **schmalz** \ˈshmȯlts, ˈshmälts\ *n* [Yiddish *shmalts*, lit., rendered fat, fr. MHG *smalz*; akin to OHG *smelzan* to melt — more at SMELT] **:** sentimental or florid music or art — **schmaltzy** \-ē\ *adj*

Schmidt system \ˈs(h)mit-\ *n* [B. *Schmidt* †1935 G optical scientist] **:** an optical system (as for a telescope or camera) that utilizes an objective composed of a concave spherical mirror having in front of it a transparent plate to offset spherical aberration

schmo *or* **schmoe** \ˈshmō\ *n, pl* **schmoes** [prob. modif. of Yiddish *shmok* penis, fool, fr. G *schmuck* adornment] *slang* **:** JERK 4

schnapps \ˈshnaps\ *n, pl* **schnapps** [G *schnaps*, lit., dram of liquor, fr. LG, fr. *snappen* to snap] **:** any of various distilled liquors; *esp* **:** strong Holland gin

schnau·zer \ˈshnaủ-sər, ˈs(h)naủ-zər\ *n* [G, fr. *schnauze* snout — more at SNOUT] **:** any of an old German breed of terriers with a long head, small ears, heavy eyebrows, moustache, beard, and wiry coat

schnit·zel \ˈs(h)nit-səl\ *n* [G, lit., shaving, chip, fr. MHG, dim. of *sniz* slice; akin to OHG *snīdan* to cut, OE *snithan*, Czech *snět* bough] **:** a veal cutlet variously seasoned and garnished

schnook \ˈshnủk\ *n* [origin unknown] *slang* **:** a stupid or unimportant person **:** DOLT

schnor·kel \ˈs(h)nȯr-kəl\ *var of* SNORKEL

schnor·rer \ˈshnȯr-ər, ˈshnōr-\ *n* [Yiddish *shnorer*] **:** BEGGAR; *esp* **:** one who wheedles others into supplying his wants

schnoz·zle \ˈs(h)näz-əl\ *n* [prob. modif. of Yiddish *shnoitsl*, dim. of *shnoits* snout, fr. G *schnauze* snout, muzzle — more at SNOUT] *slang* **:** NOSE

scho·la can·to·rum \ˌskō-lə-ˌkan-ˈtōr-əm, -ˈtȯr-\ *n, pl* **scho·lae cantorum** \-ˌlē-, -ˌlā-, -ˌlī-\ [ML, school of singers] **1 :** a singing school; *specif* **:** the choir or choir school of a monastery or of a cathedral **2 :** the part of an ecclesiastical edifice reserved to the choir

schol·ar \ˈskäl-ər\ *n* [ME *scoler*, fr. OE *scolere* & OF *escoler*, fr. ML *scholaris*, fr. LL, of a school, fr. L *schola* school] **1 :** one who attends a school or studies under a teacher **:** PUPIL **2 a :** one who has done advanced study in a special field **b :** a learned person **3 :** a holder of a scholarship
syn SCHOLAR, PUPIL, STUDENT, DISCIPLE mean one who studies under a teacher. SCHOLAR stresses enrollment and instruction in a school; PUPIL stresses having a teacher's personal care and oversight; STUDENT commonly applies specifically to one attending a higher institution of learning; DISCIPLE suggests devoted adherence to the teachings and precepts of a master without directly implying either attendance at school or academic discipline

schol·ar·ism \-ə-ˌriz-əm\ *n* **:** scholastic often pedantic learning

schol·ar·ly \-ər-lē\ *adj* **:** characteristic of or suitable to learned persons **:** LEARNED, ACADEMIC

schol·ar·ship \-ər-ˌship\ *n* **1 :** a grant-in-aid to a student (as by a college or foundation) **2 :** the character, qualities, or attainments of a scholar **:** LEARNING **3 :** the fund of knowledge and learning

[1]**scho·las·tic** \skə-ˈlas-tik\ *adj* [ML & L; ML *scholasticus* of the schoolmen, fr. L, of a school, fr. Gk *scholastikos*, fr. *scholazein* to keep a school, fr. *scholē* school] **1 a** *often cap* **:** of or relating to Scholasticism ⟨∼ theology⟩ ⟨∼ philosophy⟩ **b :** excessively subtle **:** PEDANTIC **2 :** of or relating to schools or scholars — **scho·las·ti·cal·ly** \-ti-k(ə-)lē\ *adv*

[2]**scholastic** *n* **1 a** *cap* **:** a Scholastic philosopher **b :** PEDANT, FORMALIST **2** [NL *scholasticus*, fr. L *scholasticus*, adj.] **:** a student in a scholasticate **3 :** one who adopts scholastic or traditional methods in art

scho·las·ti·cate \skə-ˈlas-tə-ˌkāt, -ti-kət\ *n* [NL *scholasticatus*, fr. *scholasticus* student in a scholasticate] **:** a school of general study for those preparing for membership in a Roman Catholic religious order

scho·las·ti·cism \skə-ˈlas-tə-ˌsiz-əm\ *n* **1** *cap* **a :** a philosophical movement dominant in western Christian civilization from the 9th until the 17th century and combining a fixed religious dogma with the mystical and intuitional tradition of patristic philosophy esp. of St. Augustine and later with Aristotelianism **b :** NEO-SCHOLASTICISM **2 :** close adherence to the traditional teachings or methods of a school or sect

scho·li·ast \ˈskō-lē-ˌast, -lē-əst\ *n* [MGk *scholiastēs*, fr. *scholiazein* to write scholia on, fr. Gk *scholion*] **:** a maker of scholia **:** COMMENTATOR, ANNOTATOR — **scho·li·as·tic** \ˌskō-lē-ˈas-tik\ *adj*

scho·li·um \ˈskō-lē-əm\ *n, pl* **scho·lia** \-lē-ə\ *or* **scho·li·ums** [NL, fr. Gk *scholion* comment, scholium, fr. dim. of *scholē* lecture] **1 :** a marginal annotation or comment (as on the text of a classic by an early grammarian) **2 :** a remark or observation subjoined but not essential to a demonstration or a train of reasoning

[1]**school** \ˈskül\ *n* [ME *scole*, fr. OE *scōl*, fr. L *schola*, fr. Gk *scholē* leisure, discussion, lecture, school; akin to Gk *echein* to hold — more at SCHEME] **1 a** (1) **:** a group of scholars and teachers pursuing knowledge (as in a particular field) and constituting a college of a medieval university (2) *pl* **:** the academic or learned world **:** UNIVERSITIES **b :** the students attending a school; *also* **:** its teachers and students **c** (1) **:** persons who hold a common doctrine or follow the same teacher (as in philosophy, theology, or medicine) (2) **:** a group of artists under a common influence **2 a :** an institution for the teaching of children **b :** an institution

for specialized higher education usu. within a university **c :** a school building **3 a :** the process of teaching or learning **b :** attendance at a school **c :** a session of a school **4 :** the regulations governing military drill of individuals or units; *also* **:** the exercises carried out ⟨the ~ of the soldier⟩

²**school** *vt* **1 :** to educate in an institution of learning **2 a :** to teach or drill in a specific knowledge or skill ⟨well ~*ed* in languages⟩ **b :** to discipline or habituate to something ⟨~ oneself in patience⟩ **syn** see TEACH

³**school** *n* [ME *scole,* fr. MD *schole;* akin to OE *scolu* multitude, *scylian* to separate — more at SKILL] **:** a large number of fish or aquatic animals of one kind swimming together

⁴**school** *vi* **:** to swim or feed in a school ⟨bluefish are ~*ing*⟩

school age *n* **:** the period of life during which a child is considered mentally and physically fit to attend school and is commonly required to do so by law

school·bag \'skül-,bag\ *n* **:** a usu. cloth bag in which a pupil may carry school books and school supplies needed at school or for homework

school board *n* **:** a board in charge of local public schools

school·boy \'skül-,bȯi\ *n* **:** a boy attending school

school bus *n* **:** a vehicle that is either publicly owned or privately owned and operated for compensation and that is used for transporting children to or from school or on activities connected with school

school·child \-,chīld\ *n* **:** a child attending school

school edition *n* **:** an edition of a book issued esp. for use in schools and usu. simplified, condensed, or emended esp. with glossarial or explanatory matter

school·fel·low \'skül-,fel-(,)ō, -ə(-w)\ *n* **:** SCHOOLMATE

school·girl \-,gər(-ə)l\ *n* **:** a girl attending school

school·house \-,hau̇s\ *n* **:** a building used as a school and esp. as an elementary school ⟨little red ~⟩

school·ing *n* **1 a :** instruction in school **b :** discipline derived from experience **2** *archaic* **:** chastisement for correction **:** REPROOF **3 :** the cost of instruction and maintenance at school **4 :** the training of a horse to service; *esp* **:** the teaching and exercising of horse and rider in the formal techniques of equitation

school·man \'skül-mən, -,man\ *n* **1 a :** one skilled in academic disputation **b** *cap* **:** SCHOLASTIC 1a **2 :** a schoolteacher or school administrator

school·marm \-,mä(r)m\ *or* **school·ma'am** \-,mäm, -,mam\ *n* [*school* + *marm,* alter. of ma'am] **1 :** a woman schoolteacher esp. in an old-type rural or small-town school **2 :** a person who exhibits characteristics (as pedantry and priggishness) attributed to schoolteachers

school·mas·ter \-,mas-tər\ *n* **1 :** a male schoolteacher **2 :** one that disciplines or directs **3 :** a reddish brown edible snapper (*Lutjanus apodus*) of the tropical Atlantic and the Gulf of Mexico

school·mate \-,māt\ *n* **:** a school companion

school·mis·tress \-,mis-trəs\ *n* **:** a woman schoolteacher

school·room \-,rüm, -,ru̇m\ *n* **:** CLASSROOM

school·teach·er \-,tē-chər\ *n* **:** a person who teaches in a school

school·time \-,tīm\ *n* **1 :** the time for beginning a session of school or during which school is held **2 :** the period of life spent in school or in study

school·work \-,wərk\ *n* **:** lessons done in classes at school or assigned to be done at home

schoo·ner \'skü-nər\ *n* [origin unknown] **1 :** a fore-and-aft rigged ship having two masts with a smaller sail on the foremast and with the mainmast stepped nearly amidships; *broadly* **:** any of various larger fore-and-aft rigged ships with three to seven masts **2 :** a large tall drinking glass (as for beer or ale) **3 :** PRAIRIE SCHOONER

schooner rig *n* **:** FORE-AND-AFT RIG — **schoo·ner–rigged** \,skü-nə(r)-'rigd\ *adj*

schorl \'shȯr(ə)l, 'shər(-ə)l\ *n* [G *schörl*] **:** TOURMALINE; *esp* **:** tourmaline of the black variety — **schorl·aceous** \shȯr-'lā-shəs, ,shər-\ *adj*

schot·tische \'shät-ish, shä-'tēsh\ *n* [G, fr. *schottisch* Scottish, fr. *Schotte* Scotchman; akin to OE *Scottas* Scotchmen] **1 :** a round dance in duple measure similar to the polka but slower **2 :** music for the schottische

¹**schuss** \'shu̇s, 'shüs\ *n* [G, lit., shot, fr. OHG *scuz* — more at SHOT] **1 :** a straight high-speed run on skis **2 :** a straightaway downhill skiing course

²**schuss** *vt* **:** to make a schuss over ⟨~ a slope⟩ **~** *vi* **:** to ski directly down a slope

schuyt \'skīt\ *n* [D *schuit*] **:** a bluff-bowed Dutch ship used chiefly on canals and for coasting

schwa \'shwä *also* 'shfä\ *n* [G, fr. Heb *shĕwā*] **1 :** an unstressed mid-central vowel that is the usual sound of the first and last vowels of the English word *America* **2 :** the symbol ə commonly used for a schwa and sometimes also for a similarly articulated stressed vowel (as in *cut*)

schwar·me·rei \,shfer-mə-'rī\ *n* [G *schwärmerei,* fr. *schwärmen* to be enthusiastic, lit., to swarm] **:** excessive or unwholesome sentiment

sci·ae·nid \sī-'ē-nəd\ *n* [deriv. of Gk *skiaina,* a fish] **:** any of a family (Sciaenidae) of carnivorous mostly marine percoid fishes comprising the croakers and including numerous food fishes — **sciaenid** *adj* — **sci·ae·noid** \-,nȯid\ *adj or n*

sci·at·ic \sī-'at-ik\ *adj* [MF *sciatique,* fr. LL *sciaticus,* alter. of L *ischiadicus* of sciatica, fr. Gk *ischiadikos,* fr. *ischiad-, ischias* sciatica, fr. *ischion* ischium] **1 :** of, relating to, or situated near the hip **2 :** of, relating to, or caused by sciatica

sci·at·i·ca \sī-'at-i-kə\ *n* [ME, fr. ML, fr. LL, fem. of *sciaticus*] **:** pain along the course of a sciatic nerve esp. in the back of the thigh; *broadly* **:** pain in the lower back, buttocks, hips, or adjacent parts

sci·ence \'sī-ən(t)s\ *n* [ME, fr. MF, fr. L *scientia,* fr. *scient-, sciens* having knowledge, fr. prp. of *scire* to know; akin to L *scindere* to cut — more at SHED] **1 a :** possession of knowledge as distinguished from ignorance or misunderstanding **b :** knowledge attained through study or practice **2 a :** a department of systematized knowledge as an object of study ⟨the ~ of theology⟩ **b :** something (as a sport or technique) that may be studied or learned like systematized knowledge **c :** one of the natural sciences **3 :** knowledge covering general truths or the operation of general laws esp. as obtained and tested through scientific method; *specif* **:** NATURAL SCIENCE **4 :** a system or method based or purporting to be based upon scientific principles **5** *cap* **:** CHRISTIAN SCIENCE

science fiction *n* **:** fiction dealing principally with the impact of actual or imagined science upon society or individuals; *broadly* **:** literary fantasy including a scientific factor as an essential orienting component

sci·ent \'sī-ənt\ *adj* [ME, fr. L *scient-, sciens,* prp.] **:** KNOWING, SKILLFUL

sci·en·tial \sī-'en-chəl\ *adj* **1 :** relating to or producing knowledge or science **2 :** having efficient knowledge **:** CAPABLE

sci·en·tif·ic \,sī-ən-'tif-ik\ *adj* [ML *scientificus* producing knowledge, fr. L *scient-, sciens* + *-i-* + *-ficus* -fic] **:** of, relating to, or exhibiting the methods or principles of science — **sci·en·tif·i·cal·ly** \-i-k(ə-)lē\ *adv*

scientific method *n* **:** principles and procedures for the systematic pursuit of knowledge involving the recognition and formulation of a problem, the collection of data through observation and experiment, and the formulation and testing of hypotheses

sci·en·tism \'sī-ən-,tiz-əm\ *n* **1 :** methods and attitudes typical of or attributed to the natural scientist **2 :** the proposition that only scientific and esp. materialistic methods can be used effectively in the pursuit of knowledge (as in philosophy or the social sciences)

sci·en·tist \'sī-ənt-əst\ *n* [L *scientia*] **1 :** one learned in science and esp. natural science **:** a scientific investigator **2** *cap* **:** CHRISTIAN SCIENTIST

sci·en·tis·tic \,sī-ən-'tis-tik\ *adj* **1 :** devoted to scientific method **2 :** relating to or characterized by scientism

sci·li·cet \'skē-li-,ket, 'sī-lə-,set\ *adv* [ME, fr. L, surely, to wit, fr. *scire* to know + *licet* it is permitted, fr. *licēre* to be permitted — more at LICENSE] **:** to wit **:** NAMELY, VIDELICET

scil·la \'s(k)il-ə\ *n* [NL, genus name, fr. L, squill — more at SQUILL] **:** any of a genus (*Scilla*) of Old World bulbous herbs of the lily family with narrow basal leaves and pink, blue, or white racemose flowers

scim·i·tar \'sim-ət-ər, -ə-,tär\ *n* [It *scimitarra*] **:** a saber made of a curved blade with the edge on the convex side and used chiefly by Arabs and Turks

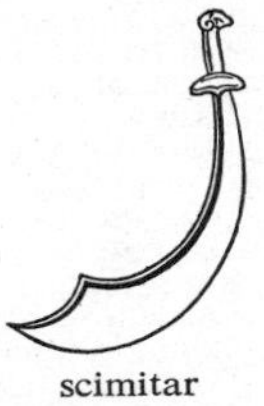

scimitar

scin·coid \'s(k)iŋ-,kȯid\ *adj* [L *scincus* skink — more at SKINK] **:** resembling or relating to the skinks — **scincoid** *n*

scin·til·la \sin-'til-ə\ *n* [L] **:** SPARK, TRACE

scin·til·lant \'sint-ᵊl-ənt\ *adj* **:** SCINTILLATING, SPARKLING — **scin·til·lant·ly** *adv*

scin·til·late \'sint-ᵊl-,āt\ *vb* [L *scintillatus,* pp. of *scintillare* to sparkle, fr. *scintilla* spark] *vi* **1 :** to emit sparks **:** SPARK **2 :** to emit quick flashes as if throwing off sparks; *also* **:** SPARKLE, TWINKLE **~** *vt* **:** to throw off as a spark or as sparkling flashes ⟨~ witticisms⟩ — **scin·til·la·tor** \-,āt-ər\ *n*

scin·til·la·tion \,sint-ᵊl-'ā-shən\ *n* **1 :** an act or instance of scintillating; *esp* **:** rapid changes in the brightness of a celestial body **2 a** (1) **:** a spark or flash emitted in scintillating (2) **:** a flash of light produced in a phosphor by an ionizing event **b :** a scintillating or brilliant outburst (as of wit) **c :** a flash of the eye **3 :** SCINTILLA

scintillation counter *n* **:** a device for detecting and registering individual scintillations (as in radioactive emission)

scin·til·lom·e·ter \,sint-ᵊl-'äm-ət-ər\ *n* [L *scintilla* + ISV *-o-* + *-meter*] **:** SCINTILLATION COUNTER

sci·o·lism \'sī-ə-,liz-əm\ *n* [LL *sciolus* smatterer, fr. dim. of L *scius* knowing, fr. *scire* to know — more at SCIENCE] **:** a superficial show of learning — **sci·o·list** \-ləst\ *n* — **sci·o·lis·tic** \,sī-ə-'lis-tik\ *adj*

scio·man·cy \'sī-ə-,man(t)-sē, 'skē-ə-\ *n* [LL *sciomantia,* fr. L Gk *skiomanteia,* fr. Gk *skia* shadow, shade + *-manteia* -mancy — more at SHINE] **:** divination by consulting the shades of the dead — **scio·man·tic** \,sī-ə-'mant-ik, ,skē-ə-\ *adj*

sci·on \'sī-ən\ *n* [ME, fr. MF *cion,* of Gmc origin; akin to OHG *chīnan* to sprout, split open, OE *cīnan* to gape] **1 :** a detached living portion of a plant joined to a stock in grafting and usu. supplying solely aerial parts to a graft **2 :** DESCENDANT, CHILD ⟨a ~ of royalty⟩

sci·re fa·cias \,sī-rē-'fā-sh(ē-)əs, ,skē-,rā-'fäk-ē-,äs\ *n* [ME, fr. ML, you should cause to know] **1 :** a judicial writ founded upon some matter of record and requiring the party proceeded against to show cause why the record should not be enforced, annulled, or vacated **2 :** a legal proceeding instituted by a scire facias

sci·roc·co \shi-\ *var of* SIROCCO

scir·rhoid \'s(k)i(ə)r-,ȯid\ *adj* **:** resembling a scirrhus

scir·rhous \'s(k)ir-əs\ *adj* **1 :** of, relating to, or being a scirrhus **2 :** hard or indurated with or as if with fibrous tissue

scir·rhus \'s(k)ir-əs\ *n, pl* **scir·rhi** \'s(k)i(ə)r-,ī, 'ski(ə)r-,ē\ [NL, fr. Gk *skiros, skirrhos,* fr. *skiros* hard] **:** a hard slow-growing malignant tumor having a preponderance of fibrous tissue

scis·sile \'sis-əl, -,īl\ *adj* [F, fr. L *scissilis,* fr. *scissus,* pp. of *scindere* to split — more at SHED] **:** capable of being cut smoothly or split easily

scis·sion \'sizh-ən\ *n* [F, fr. LL *scission-, scissio,* fr. L *scissus,* pp.] **1 :** a division or split in a group or union **:** SCHISM **2 :** an act of cutting, dividing, or splitting **:** the state of being cut, divided, or split

¹**scis·sor** \'siz-ər\ *n* [ME *sisoure,* fr. MF *cisoire,* fr. LL *cisorium* cutting instrument, irreg. fr. L *caesus,* pp. of *caedere* to cut — more at CONCISE] **:** SCISSORS

²**scissor** *vt* **scis·sor·ing** \-(ə-)riŋ\ **:** to cut, cut up, or cut off with scissors or shears

scis·sors \'siz-ərz\ *n pl but sing or pl in constr* **1 :** a cutting instrument having two blades whose cutting

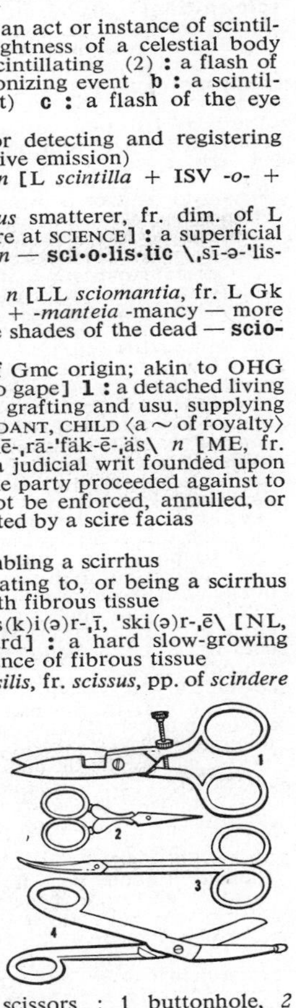

scissors : 1 buttonhole, *2* embroidery, *3* manicure, *4* bandage

edges slide past each other **2 :** any of several gymnastic or wrestling feats in which the leg movements suggest the opening and closing of scissors

scissors kick *n* **:** a swimming kick used in trudgen strokes and sidestrokes in which the legs move like scissors

scis·sor·tail \'siz-ər-ˌtāl\ *n* **:** a flycatcher (*Muscivora forficata*) of the southern U.S. and Mexico with a deeply forked tail

sci·uroid \'sī-(y)ə-ˌrȯid, sī-'(y)u̇(ə)r-ˌȯid\ *adj* [L *sciurus* squirrel — more at SQUIRREL] **1 :** resembling or related to the squirrels **2 :** resembling the tail of a squirrel ⟨barley has a ~ spike⟩

1sclaff \'sklaf\ *n* [prob. imit.] **1** *Scot* **:** a slight blow **:** SLAP **2 :** a golf stroke in which the club head strikes the ground behind the ball before touching the ball

2sclaff *vi* **1** *Scot* **:** to scuff or shuffle along **2 :** to make a sclaff in golf ~ *vt* **1** *Scot* **:** to strike with something flat **:** SLAP **2 a :** to cause (a golf club) to make a sclaff **b :** to strike (the ground) in making a sclaff — **sclaff·er** *n*

scler- *or* **sclero-** *comb form* [NL, fr. Gk *sklēr-*, *sklēro-*, fr. *sklēros* hard — more at SKELETON] **1 a :** hard ⟨*scler*ite⟩ ⟨*sclero*derma⟩ **b :** hardness ⟨*sclero*meter⟩ **2 :** sclera ⟨*scler*itis⟩

scle·ra \'sklir-ə\ *n* [NL, fr. Gk *sklēros* hard] **:** the dense fibrous opaque white outer coat enclosing the eyeball except the part covered by the cornea

scle·ren·chy·ma \sklə-'reŋ-kə-mə, -'ren-\ *n* [NL] **:** a protective or supporting tissue in higher plants composed of cells with walls thickened and lignified and often mineralized — **scle·ren·chym·a·tous** \ˌsklir-ən-'kim-ət-əs, ˌskler-\ *adj*

scle·rite \'skli(ə)r-ˌīt, 'skle(ə)r-\ *n* [ISV] **:** a hard chitinous or calcareous plate, piece, or spicule (as of the arthropod integument)

scle·ro·der·ma \ˌsklir-ō-'dər-mə, ˌskler-\ *n* [NL] **:** a disease of the skin characterized by thickening and hardening of the subcutaneous tissues

scle·ro·der·ma·tous \-'dər-mət-əs\ *adj* **:** having a hard external covering (as of bony plates or horny scales)

scle·roid \'skli(ə)r-ˌȯid, 'skle(ə)r-\ *adj* [ISV] **:** HARD, INDURATED ⟨~ tissue cells⟩

scle·rom·e·ter \sklir-'äm-ət-ər, skler-\ *n* [ISV] **:** an instrument for determining the relative hardnesses of materials

scle·ro·pro·tein \ˌsklir-ō-'prō-ˌtēn, ˌskler-, -'prōt-ē-ən\ *n* [ISV] **:** any of various fibrous proteins esp. from connective and skeletal tissues

scle·rose \sklə-'rōs, -'rōz\ *vb* [back-formation fr. *sclerosis*] *vt* **:** to cause sclerosis in **:** INDURATE ~ *vi* **:** to undergo sclerosis **:** become sclerotic

scle·ro·sis \sklə-'rō-səs\ *n* [ME *sclirosis*, fr. ML, fr. Gk *sklērōsis* hardening, fr. *sklēroun* to harden, fr. *sklēros*] **1 :** pathological hardening of tissue esp. from overgrowth of fibrous tissue or increase in interstitial tissue; *also* **:** a disease characterized by sclerosis **2 :** hardening of plant cell walls usu. by lignification

1scle·rot·ic \-'rät-ik\ *adj* **1 :** being or relating to the sclera **2 :** of, relating to, or affected with sclerosis

2sclerotic *n* [ML *sclerotica*, fr. Gk *sklēroun* to harden] **:** SCLERA

scle·ro·tium \sklə-'rō-sh(ē-)əm\ *n, pl* **scle·ro·tia** \-sh(ē-)ə\ [NL, fr. Gk *sklēroun* to harden] **:** a compact mass of hardened mycelium stored with reserve food material that in some higher fungi functions as a resistant form

scle·rous \'sklir-əs, 'skler-\ *adj* [Gk *sklēros*] **:** HARD, INDURATED

1scoff \'skäf, 'skȯf\ *n* [ME *scof*, prob. of Scand origin; akin to obs. Dan *skof* jest; akin to OFris *skof* mockery] **1 :** an expression of scorn, derision, or contempt **:** GIBE **2 :** an object of scorn, mockery, or derision

2scoff *vi* **:** to show contempt by derisive acts or language **:** MOCK ~ *vt* **:** to treat or address with derision **:** mock at — **scoff·er** *n*

syn SCOFF, JEER, GIBE, FLEER, SNEER, FLOUT mean to show one's contempt in derision or mockery. SCOFF stresses insolence, disrespect, or incredulity as motivating the derision; JEER suggests a coarser more undiscriminating derision; GIBE implies taunting either good-naturedly or in sarcastic derision; FLEER suggests grinning or grimacing derisively; SNEER stresses insulting by contemptuous facial expression, phrasing, or tone of voice; FLOUT stresses contempt shown by refusal to heed

scoff·law \-ˌlȯ\ *n* **:** a contemptuous law violator

1scold \'skōld\ *n* [ME *scald*, *scold*, prob. of Scand origin; akin to ON *skāld* poet, skald, Icel *skālda* to make scurrilous verse] **1 :** one addicted to abusive ribald speech **2 :** one who scolds habitually or persistently **3 :** SCOLDING ⟨a writing that is a ~⟩

2scold *vi* **1** *obs* **:** to quarrel noisily **:** BRAWL **2 :** to find fault noisily ~ *vt* **1 :** to censure severely or angrily **2 :** REBUKE — **scold·er** *n*

syn SCOLD, UPBRAID, BERATE, RAIL, REVILE, VITUPERATE mean to reproach angrily and abusively. SCOLD implies rebuking in irritation or ill temper justly or unjustly; UPBRAID implies censuring on definite and usu. justifiable grounds; BERATE suggests prolonged and often abusive scolding; RAIL (*at* or *against*) stresses an unrestrained berating; REVILE implies a scurrilous, abusive attack prompted by anger or hatred; VITUPERATE suggests a violent reviling

scold·ing *n* **1 :** the action of one who scolds **2 :** a harsh or severe reproof

sco·le·cite \'skäl-ə-ˌsīt, 'skō-lə-\ *n* [G *skolezit*, fr. Gk *skōlēk-*, *skōlēx* worm; fr. the motion of some forms when heated] **:** a zeolite mineral $CaAl_2Si_3O_{10}.3H_2O$ that is a hydrous calcium aluminum silicate and occurs in radiating groups of crystals, in fibrous masses, and in nodules

sco·lex \'skō-ˌleks\ *n, pl* **sco·li·ces** \-lə-ˌsēz\ [NL *scolic-*, *scolex*, fr. Gk *skōlēk-*, *skōlēx* worm; akin to Gk *skelos* leg — more at CYLINDER] **:** the head of a tapeworm either in the larva or adult stage

sco·li·o·sis \ˌskō-lē-'ō-səs, ˌskäl-ē-\ *n* [NL, fr. Gk *skoliōsis* crookedness of a bodily part, fr. *skolios* crooked — more at CYLINDER] **:** a lateral curvature of the spine — **sco·li·ot·ic** \-'ät-ik\ *adj*

scol·lop \'skäl-əp\ *var of* SCALLOP

scol·o·pen·dra \ˌskäl-ə-'pen-drə\ *n* [NL, genus of centipedes, fr. L, a kind of millipede, fr. Gk *skolopendra*] **:** CENTIPEDE — **scol·o·pen·drid** \-drəd\ *adj or n* — **scol·o·pen·dri·form** \-drə-ˌfȯrm\ *adj* — **scol·o·pen·drine** \-ˌdrīn, -drən\ *adj*

scom·broid \'skäm-ˌbrȯid\ *n* [deriv. of Gk *skombros* mackerel] **:** any of a suborder (Scombroidea) of marine spiny-finned fishes (as mackerels, tunas, albacores, bonitos, and swordfishes) of great economic importance as food fishes — **scombroid** *adj*

1sconce \'skän(t)s\ *n* [ME, fr. MF *esconse* screened lantern, fr. OF, fr. fem. of *escons*, pp. of *escondre* to hide, fr. L *abscondere* — more at ABSCOND] **:** a bracket candlestick or group of candlesticks

2sconce *n* [D *schans*, fr. G *schanze*] **1 :** a detached defensive work **2** *obs* **:** a protecting cover or screen **:** SHELTER

3sconce *vt* [origin unknown] **:** FINE

scone \'skōn, 'skän\ *n* [perh. fr. D *schoonbrood* fine white bread, fr. *schoon* pure, clean + *brood* bread] **:** a quick bread of oatmeal or barley flour rolled round, cut into quarters, and baked on a griddle

1scoop \'sküp\ *n* [ME *scope*, fr. MD *schope*; akin to OHG *skepfen* to shape — more at SHAPE] **1 a :** a large ladle **b :** a deep shovel or similar implement for digging, dipping, or shoveling **c :** a hemispherical utensil for dipping soft food **d :** a small spoon-shaped utensil or instrument for cutting or gouging **2 :** the action of scooping **3 :** a hollow place **:** CAVITY **4 a :** information esp. of immediate interest **b :** BEAT 6b — **scoop·ful** \-ˌfu̇l\ *n*

2scoop *vt* **1 :** to take out or up with or as if with a scoop **:** DIP **2 :** to empty by lading **3 :** to make hollow **:** dig out **4 :** BEAT 5a(2) — **scoop·er** *n*

scoot \'sküt\ *vi* [prob. of Scand origin; akin to ON *skjōta* to shoot — more at SHOOT] **:** to go suddenly and swiftly **:** DART — **scoot** *n*

scoot·er \'sküt-ər\ *n* **1 :** a child's foot-operated vehicle consisting of a narrow board mounted between two wheels tandem with an upright steering handle attached to the front wheel **2 :** MOTOR SCOOTER

scop \'skäp, 'skōp, 'shōp\ *n* [OE; akin to OHG *schof* poet] **:** an Old English bard or poet

1scope \'skōp\ *n* [It *scopo* purpose, goal, fr. Gk *skopos*, fr. *skeptesthai* to watch, look at — more at SPY] **1 :** space or opportunity for unhampered motion, activity, or thought **2 :** INTENTION, OBJECT **3 :** extent of treatment, activity, or influence **4 :** range of operation

2scope *n* [*-scope*] **1 :** any of various instruments for viewing: as **a :** MICROSCOPE **b :** TELESCOPE **c :** OSCILLOSCOPE **d :** RADARSCOPE **2 :** HOROSCOPE

-scope \ˌskōp\ *n comb form* [NL *-scopium*, fr. Gk *-skopion*, fr. *skeptesthai*] **:** means (as an instrument) for viewing or observing ⟨micro*scope*⟩

sco·pol·amine \skō-'päl-ə-ˌmēn\ *n* [G *scopolamin*, fr. NL *Scopolia*, genus of plants + G *amin* amine] **:** a poisonous alkaloid $C_{17}H_{21}NO_4$ found in the roots of various plants (esp. genus *Scopolia*) of the nightshade family and used as a truth serum or esp. with morphine as a sedative in surgery and obstetrics

scop·u·la \'skäp-yə-lə\ *n* [NL, fr. LL, dim. of L *scopa* broom — more at SCULLION] **:** a bushy tuft of hairs — **scop·u·late** \-ˌlāt\ *adj*

-s·co·py \s-kə-pē\ *n comb form* [Gk *-skopia*, fr. *skeptesthai*] **:** viewing **:** observation ⟨radio*scopy*⟩

scor·bu·tic \skȯr-'byüt-ik\ *adj* [NL *scorbuticus*, fr. *scorbutus* scurvy, prob. of Gmc origin; akin to OE *scurf*] **:** of, relating to, or resembling scurvy; *also* **:** diseased with scurvy — **scor·bu·ti·cal·ly** \-i-k(ə-)lē\ *adv*

1scorch \'skȯ(ə)rch\ *vb* [ME *scorcnen*, *scorchen*, prob. of Scand origin; akin to ON *skorpna* to shrivel up — more at SHRIMP] *vt* **1 :** to burn a surface so as to change its color and texture **2 a :** to parch with or as if with intense heat **b :** to afflict painfully with or as if with censure or sarcasm **3 :** to devastate completely esp. before abandoning to the enemy — used in the phrase *scorched earth* esp. of property of possible use to an enemy ~ *vi* **1 :** to become scorched **2 :** to travel at great usu. excessive speed

2scorch *n* **1 :** a result of scorching **2 :** a browning of plant tissues usu. from disease or heat

3scorch *vt* [alter. of *2score*] *dial chiefly Eng* **:** CUT, SLASH

scorched *adj* **:** parched or discolored by scorching

scorch·er \'skȯr-chər\ *n* **:** one that scorches; *esp* **:** a very hot day

scorch·ing \-chiŋ\ *adj* **1 :** BURNING ⟨~ heat⟩ **2 :** SCATHING, STINGING ⟨a ~ denunciation⟩ — **scorch·ing·ly** *adv*

1score \'skō(ə)r, 'skȯ(ə)r\ *n, pl* **scores** *or* **score** [ME *scor*, fr. ON *skor* notch, tally, twenty; akin to OE *scieran* to cut — more at SHEAR] **1 a :** TWENTY **b :** a group of 20 things — often used in combination with a cardinal number ⟨five*score*⟩ **c** *pl* **:** a group of an indefinite large number **2 a :** a line made with or as if with a sharp instrument **:** INCISION **b** (1) **:** a mark used as a starting point or goal by traffic (2) **:** one used for keeping account **3 a :** an account or reckoning kept by making marks on a tally **b :** ACCOUNT **c :** amount due **:** INDEBTEDNESS **4 :** an obligation or injury kept in mind for requital **:** GRUDGE **5 a :** REASON, GROUND **b :** SUBJECT, TOPIC **6 a :** the copy of a musical composition in written or printed notation **b :** a musical composition; *specif* **:** the music for a movie or theatrical production **c :** a complete description of a dance composition in choreographic notation **7 a :** a number that expresses accomplishment (as in a game or test) or excellence (as in quality) either absolutely in points gained or by comparison to a standard **b :** the making of a score **:** HIT **8 :** the stark inescapable facts of a situation

2score *vt* **1 a :** to keep a record or account of by or as if by notches on a tally **:** RECORD **b :** to enter in a record **c :** to mark with significant lines or notches (as in keeping account) **2 :** to mark with lines, grooves, scratches, or notches **3 :** BERATE, SCOLD **4 a** (1) **:** to gain for addition to the score ⟨~ a run⟩ (2) **:** to enable (a base runner) to make a score **b :** to have as a value in a game or contest **:** COUNT ⟨touchdown ~*s* six points⟩ **c :** ACHIEVE, WIN **5 :** to determine the merit of **:** GRADE **6 a :** to write or arrange (music) for a specific performance medium **b :** to make an orchestration of **c :** to compose a score for (a movie) ~ *vi* **1 :** to keep score in a game or contest **2 :** to make a count as a score in or as if in a game **:** TALLY **3 a :** to gain or have the advantage **b :** to be successful **c :** 3RATE — **scor·er** *n*

score·board \-ˌbō(ə)rd, -ˌbȯ(ə)rd\ *n* **:** a large board for displaying the score of a game or match and sometimes other information

score·card \-ˌkärd\ *n* **:** a card for recording the score of a game

score·keep·er \-ˌkē-pər\ *n* **:** an official who records the score during the progress of a game or contest

score·less \-ləs\ *adj* **:** having no score; *specif* **:** involving no points ⟨a ~ tie⟩

sco·ria \'skōr-ē-ə, 'skȯr-\ *n, pl* **sco·ri·ae** \-ē-ˌē, -ē-ˌī\ [ME, fr. L, fr. Gk *skōria*, fr. *skōr* excrement — more at SCAT-] **1 :** the refuse from melting of metals or reduction of ores **:** SLAG **2 :** rough vesicular cindery lava — **sco·ri·a·ceous** \ˌskōr-ē-'ā-shəs, ˌskȯr-\ *adj*

sco·ri·fi·ca·tion \ˌskōr-ə-fə-ˈkā-shən, ˌskȯr-\ *n* **:** the act, process, or result of scorifying

sco·ri·fy \ˈskōr-ə-ˌfī, ˈskȯr-\ *vt* **:** to reduce to scoria

1scorn \ˈskȯ(ə)rn\ *n* [ME, fr. OF *escarn*, of Gmc origin; akin to OHG *scern* jest; akin to Gk *skairein* to gambol — more at CARDINAL] **1 :** an emotion involving both anger and disgust **:** vigorous contempt **:** DISDAIN **2 :** an expression of extreme contempt **:** TAUNT **3 :** an object of extreme disdain, contempt, or derision

2scorn *vt* **1 :** to reject with vigorous or angry contempt **:** CONTEMN ⟨~*ed* all warnings of disaster⟩ **2 :** to refuse because of scorn **:** DISDAIN ⟨~*ed* to reply to the charge⟩ **~** *vi* **:** to show disdain or derision **:** SCOFF **syn** see DESPISE — **scorn·er** *n*

scorn·ful \ˈskȯrn-fəl\ *adj* **:** full of scorn **:** CONTEMPTUOUS — **scorn·ful·ly** \-fə-lē\ *adv* — **scorn·ful·ness** *n*

scor·pae·nid \skȯr-ˈpē-nəd\ *n* [deriv. of Gk *skorpaina*, a kind of fish] **:** any of a family (Scorpaenidae) of marine spiny-finned fishes comprising the scorpion fishes — **scorpaenid** *adj* — **scor·pae·noid** \-ˌnȯid\ *adj or n*

Scor·pio \ˈskȯr-pē-ˌō\ *n* [L *Scorpius* (gen. *Scorpii*) & *Scorpio* (gen. *Scorpionis*), fr. Gk *Skorpios*, lit., scorpion] **1 :** a southern constellation partly in the Milky Way and next to Libra **2 :** the 8th sign of the zodiac

scor·pi·oid \-pē-ˌȯid\ *adj* [Gk *skorpioeidēs*, fr. *skorpios*] **1 a :** resembling a scorpion **b :** of or relating to the order (Scorpionida) of arachnids comprising the scorpions **2 :** curved at the end like a scorpion's tail **:** CIRCINATE ⟨a ~ inflorescence⟩

scor·pi·on \ˈskȯr-pē-ən\ *n* [ME, fr. OF, fr. L *scorpion-*, *scorpio*, fr. Gk *skorpios*; akin to OE *scieran* to cut — more at SHEAR] **1 :** any of an order (Scorpionida) of arachnids having an elongated body and a narrow segmented tail bearing a venomous sting at the tip **2 :** a scourge prob. studded with metal **3 :** something that incites to action like the sting of an insect

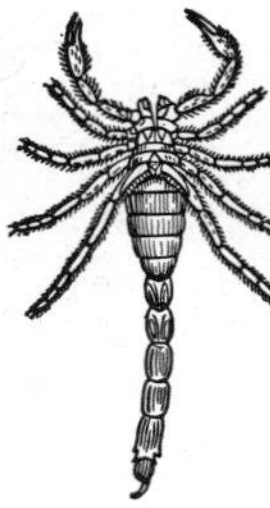

scorpion

scorpion fish *n* **1 :** a scorpaenid fish; *esp* **:** one with a venomous spine on the dorsal fin **2 :** the common toadfish (*Opsanus tau*)

scot \ˈskät\ *n* [ME, fr. ON *skot* shot, contribution — more at SHOT] **:** money assessed or paid

Scot \ˈskät\ *n* [ME *Scottes* Scotchmen, fr. OE *Scottas* Irishmen, Scotchmen, fr. LL *Scotus* Irishman] **1 :** one of a Gaelic people of northern Ireland settling in Scotland about A.D.500 **2 a :** a native or inhabitant of Scotland **b :** a person of Scotch descent

scot and lot *n* **1 :** a parish assessment formerly laid on subjects in Great Britain according to their ability to pay **2 :** obligations of all kinds taken as a whole

1scotch \ˈskäch\ *vt* [ME *scocchen* to gash] **1 :** to injure so as to make temporarily harmless **2 a :** to stamp out **:** CRUSH **b :** to end decisively by demonstrating the falsity of

2scotch *n* **:** a slight cut **:** SCORE

3scotch *n* [origin unknown] **:** a chock to prevent rolling or slipping

4scotch *vt* **1 :** to block with a chock to prevent rolling or slipping **2 :** HINDER, THWART

1Scotch \ˈskäch\ *adj* [contr. of *Scottish*] **1 :** of, relating to, or characteristic of Scotland, the Scotch, or Scots **2 :** FRUGAL

2Scotch *n* **1 :** SCOTS **2** *pl in constr* **:** the people of Scotland

3Scotch *trademark* — used for any of numerous adhesive tapes that can be made to adhere under slight pressure without heating or moistening

Scotch broth *n* **:** a soup made from beef or mutton and vegetables and thickened with barley

Scotch–Irish *adj* **1 :** of, relating to, or characteristic of the population of northern Ireland that is descended from Scotch settlers **2 :** of, relating to, or characteristic of the people of Scotch descent emigrating from northern Ireland to the U.S. before 1846 or their descendants

Scotch·man \ˈskäch-mən\ *n* **:** a man of Scotch descent **:** a male Scot — **Scotch·wom·an** \-ˌwu̇m-ən\ *n*

Scotch terrier *n* **:** SCOTTISH TERRIER

Scotch verdict *n* **1 :** a verdict of not proven that is allowed by Scottish criminal law in some cases instead of a verdict of not guilty **2 :** an inconclusive decision or pronouncement

Scotch whisky *n* **:** whiskey distilled in Scotland esp. from malted barley

Scotch woodcock *n* **:** toast spread with anchovy paste and scrambled egg

sco·ter \ˈskōt-ər\ *n, pl* **scoters** *or* **scoter** [origin unknown] **:** any of several sea ducks (genera *Oidemia* and *Melanitta*) of northern coasts of Europe and No. America and some larger inland waters

scot–free \ˈskät-ˈfrē\ *adj* [*scot* + *free*] **:** completely free from obligation, harm, or penalty

sco·tia \ˈskō-sh(ē-)ə, ˈskōt-ē-ə\ *n* [L, fr. Gk *skotia*, fr. fem. of *skotios* dark, shadowy, fr. *skotos* darkness — more at SHADE] **:** a concave molding used esp. in classical architecture in the bases of columns

Scot·ic \ˈskät-ik\ *adj* **:** of or relating to the ancient Scots

Sco·tism \ˈskōt-ˌiz-əm\ *n* **:** the doctrines of Duns Scotus (as voluntarism, logical realism, and the plurality of substantial forms) — **Sco·tist** \ˈskōt-əst\ *n*

Scot·land Yard \ˌskät-lən(d)-ˈyärd\ *n* [*Scotland Yard*, street in London formerly the headquarters of the Metropolitan Police] **:** the detective department of the Metropolitan Police force of London

sco·to·ma \skə-ˈtō-mə\ *n, pl* **scotomas** *or* **sco·to·ma·ta** \-mət-ə\ [NL *scotomat-*, *scotoma*, fr. ML, dimness of vision, fr. Gk *skotōmat-*, *skotōma*, fr. *skotoun* to darken, fr. *skotos*] **:** a blind or dark spot in the visual field — **sco·tom·a·tous** \-ˈtäm-ət-əs, -ˈtōm-\ *adj*

sco·to·pia \skə-ˈtō-pē-ə\ *n* [NL, fr. Gk *skotos* darkness + NL *-opia*] **:** vision in dim light with dark-adapted eyes believed to be mediated by the rods of the retina — **sco·to·pic** \-ˈtō-pik, -ˈtäp-ik\ *adj*

1Scots \ˈskäts\ *adj* [ME *scottis*, alter. of *scottish*] **:** SCOTCH 1

2Scots *n* **:** the English language of Scotland

Scots·man \ˈskät-smən\ *n* **:** SCOTCHMAN

Scot·ti·cism \ˈskät-ə-ˌsiz-əm\ *n* [LL *scotticus* of the ancient Scots, fr. *Scotus* Scot] **:** a characteristic feature of Scottish English esp. as contrasted with standard English

scot·tie \ˈskät-ē\ *n* **1** *cap* **:** SCOTCHMAN **2 :** SCOTTISH TERRIER

1Scot·tish \ˈskät-ish\ *adj* **:** SCOTCH 1

2Scottish *n* **:** SCOTS

Scottish Gaelic *n* **:** the Gaelic language of Scotland

Scottish rite *n* **1 :** a ceremonial observed by one of the Masonic systems **2 :** a system or organization that observes the Scottish rite and confers 33 degrees

Scottish terrier *n* **:** any of an old Scottish breed of terrier that has short legs, a large head with small prick ears and a powerful muzzle, a broad deep chest, and a very hard coat of wiry hair

scoun·drel \ˈskau̇n-drəl\ *n* [origin unknown] **:** a mean worthless fellow **:** VILLAIN — **scoundrel** *adj* — **scoun·drel·ly** \-drə-lē\ *adj*

1scour \ˈskau̇(ə)r\ *vb* [ME *scuren*, prob. of Scand origin; akin to Sw *skura* to rush] *vi* **:** to move about quickly esp. in search **~** *vt* **1 :** to move through or range over usu. rapidly **2 :** to examine minutely and rapidly — **scour·er** *n*

2scour *vb* [ME *scouren*] *vt* **1 a :** to rub hard for the purpose of cleansing **b :** to remove by rubbing hard and washing **2** *archaic* **:** to make (a region) free (as from undesired occupants) **3 :** to clean by purging **:** PURGE **4 :** to clear (as a pipe or ditch) by removing dirt and debris **5 :** to free from foreign matter or impurities by or as if by washing ⟨~ wool⟩ **6 :** to clear, dig, or remove by a powerful current of water **~** *vi* **1 :** to perform a process of scouring **2 :** to suffer from diarrhea or dysentery **:** PURGE **3 :** to become clean and bright by rubbing — **scour·er** *n*

3scour *n* **1 :** a place scoured by running water **2 :** scouring action **3 :** DIARRHEA, DYSENTERY — usu. used in pl. but sing. or pl. in constr.

1scourge \ˈskərj *also* ˈskō(ə)rj, ˈskȯ(ə)rj\ *n* [ME, fr. AF *escorge*, fr. (assumed) OF *escorgier* to whip, fr. OF *es-* ex- + L *corrigia* whip] **1 :** WHIP; *esp* **:** one used to inflict pain or punishment **2 a :** an instrument of punishment or criticism **b :** a cause of widespread or great affliction

2scourge *vt* **1 :** to whip severely **:** FLOG **2 a :** to punish severely **b :** to subject to affliction **:** DEVASTATE **c :** to force as if by blows of a whip **d :** to subject to severe criticism or satire — **scourg·er** *n*

scour·ing *n* **1 :** material removed by scouring or cleaning **:** REFUSE **2 :** the lowest rank of society **:** SCUM — usu. used in pl.

scouring rush *n* **:** HORSETAIL; *esp* **:** one (*Equisetum hyemale*) with strongly siliceous stems formerly used for scouring

scouse \ˈskau̇s\ *n* **:** LOBSCOUSE

1scout \ˈskau̇t\ *vb* [ME *scouten*, fr. MF *escouter* to listen, fr. L *auscultare* — more at AUSCULTATION] *vi* **1 :** to explore an area to obtain information (as about an enemy) **2 a :** to make a search **b :** to act as an athletic scout **~** *vt* **1 :** to observe in order to obtain information or evaluate **2 :** to explore in order to obtain information **:** RECONNOITER **3 :** to find by making a search

2scout *n* **1 a :** the act of scouting **b :** a scouting expedition **:** RECONNAISSANCE **2 a :** one sent to obtain information; *esp* **:** a soldier, ship, or plane sent out in war to reconnoiter **b :** WATCHMAN, LOOKOUT **c :** a person who searches for talented newcomers (as to acting or a sport) **3 a :** BOY SCOUT **b :** GIRL SCOUT **4 :** FELLOW, GUY

3scout *vb* [of Scand origin; akin to ON *skūti* taunt; akin to OE *scēotan* to shoot — more at SHOOT] *vt* **1 :** to make fun of **:** MOCK **2 :** to reject scornfully as absurd ⟨~ a theory⟩ **~** *vi* **:** SCOFF ⟨~ at popular remedies⟩ **syn** see DESPISE

scout car *n* **:** a fast armored military reconnaissance vehicle with four-wheel drive and open top

scout·craft \-ˌkraft\ *n* **:** the craft, skill, or practice of a scout

scout·er \ˈskau̇t-ər\ *n* **1 :** one that scouts **2 :** a member of the Boy Scouts of America over 18 years of age

scouth \ˈsküth\ *n* [origin unknown] *Scot* **:** PLENTY

scout·ing \ˈskau̇t-iŋ\ *n* **1 :** the action of one that scouts **2 :** the activities of the various boy scout and girl scout movements

scout·mas·ter \ˈskau̇t-ˌmas-tər\ *n* **:** the leader of a band of scouts; *specif* **:** the adult leader of a troop of boy scouts

scow \ˈskau̇\ *n* [D *schouw*; akin to OHG *scalta* punt pole] **:** a large flat-bottomed boat with broad square ends used chiefly for transporting sand, gravel, or refuse

1scowl \ˈskau̇(ə)l\ *vb* [ME *skoulen*, prob. of Scand origin; akin to Dan *skule* to scowl] *vi* **1 :** to draw down the forehead and make a face in expression of displeasure **2 :** to exhibit a threatening aspect **~** *vt* **:** to express with a scowl **syn** see FROWN — **scowl·er** *n*

2scowl *n* **:** a facial expression of displeasure **:** FROWN

scow·man \ˈskau̇-mən, -ˌman\ *n* **:** one who works on a scow

1scrab·ble \ˈskrab-əl\ *vb* **scrab·bling** \-(ə-)liŋ\ [D *schrabbelen* to scratch] *vi* **1 :** SCRAWL, SCRIBBLE **2 :** to scratch or claw about clumsily or frantically **3 a :** SCRAMBLE, CLAMBER **b :** to struggle by or as if by scraping or scratching **~** *vt* **1 :** SCRAMBLE **2 :** SCRIBBLE — **scrab·bler** \-(ə-)lər\ *n*

2scrabble *n* **1 :** SCRIBBLE **2 :** a repeated scratching or clawing **3 :** SCRAMBLE

scrab·bly \ˈskrab-(ə-)lē\ *adj* **1 :** SCRATCHY, RASPY **2 :** SPARSE, SCRUBBY

1scrag \ˈskrag\ *n* [perh. alter. of *2crag*] **1 :** a rawboned or scrawny person or animal **2 :** the lean end of a neck of mutton or veal; *broadly* **:** NECK

2scrag *vt* **scragged; scrag·ging 1 a :** to execute by hanging or garroting **b :** to wring the neck of **2 :** CHOKE

scrag·gly \ˈskrag-(ə-)lē\ *adj* **:** IRREGULAR; *also* **:** RAGGED, UNKEMPT

scrag·gy \ˈskrag-ē\ *adj* **1 :** ROUGH, JAGGED **2 :** being lean and long **:** SCRAWNY

scram \ˈskram\ *vi* **scrammed; scram·ming** [short for *1scramble*] **:** to go away at once ⟨~, you're not wanted⟩

scram·ble \ˈskram-bəl\ *vb* **scram·bling** \-b(ə-)liŋ\ [perh. alter. of *1scrabble*] *vi* **1 a :** to move or climb hastily on all fours **b :** to move with urgency or panic **2 a :** to struggle eagerly or unceremoniously for possession of something ⟨~ for front seats⟩ **b :** to get or gather something with difficulty or in irregular ways **3 a :** SPRAWL, STRAGGLE **b** *of a plant* **:** to climb over a support **4 :** to take off quickly in response to an alert **~** *vt* **1 :** to collect by scrambling **2 a :** to toss or mix together **:** JUMBLE **b :** to prepare (eggs) by stirring during frying **3 :** to cause or order (a fighter-interceptor group) to scramble — **scramble** *n* — **scram·bler** \-b(ə-)lər\ *n*

scran·nel \'skran-ᵊl\ *adj* [origin unknown] **:** HARSH, UNMELODIOUS

¹scrap \'skrap\ *n* [ME, fr. ON *skrap* scraps; akin to ON *skrapa* to scrape] **1** *pl* **:** fragments of discarded or leftover food **2 a :** a small detached piece **:** BIT ⟨~ of paper⟩ **b :** a fragment of something written or printed **c :** the least piece ⟨not a ~ of evidence⟩ **3** *pl* **:** CRACKLINGS **4 a :** fragments of stock removed in manufacturing **b :** manufactured articles or parts rejected or discarded and useful only as material for reprocessing

²scrap *vt* **scrapped; scrap·ping 1 :** to make into scrap ⟨~ a battleship⟩ **2 :** to abandon or get rid of as no longer of enough worth or effectiveness to retain ⟨~ outworn methods⟩ **syn** see DISCARD

³scrap *n* [origin unknown] **:** FIGHT

⁴scrap *vi* **scrapped; scrap·ping :** QUARREL, FIGHT

scrap·book \'skrap-,bu̇k\ *n* **:** a blank book in which miscellaneous items (as newspaper clippings or pictures) may be pasted or inserted

¹scrape \'skrāp\ *vb* [ME *scrapen,* fr. ON *skrapa;* akin to OE *scrapian* to scrape, L *scrobis* ditch, Gk *keirein* to cut — more at SHEAR] *vt* **1 a :** to remove (excrescent matter) from a surface by usu. repeated strokes of an edged instrument **b :** to make (a surface) smooth or clean with strokes of an edged instrument or an abrasive **2 a :** to grate harshly over or against **b :** to damage or injure the surface of by contact with a rough surface **c :** to draw roughly or noisily over a surface **3 :** to collect by or as if by scraping **:** SCRAMBLE **~** *vi* **1 :** to move in sliding contact with a rough surface **2 :** to accumulate money by small economies **3 :** to draw back the foot along the ground in making a bow **4 :** to make one's way with difficulty or succeed by a narrow margin — **scrap·er** *n* — **scrape a leg :** to make a low bow

²scrape *n* **1 a :** the act or process of scraping **b :** a sound made by scraping **2 :** a bow made by drawing back the foot **3 a :** a disagreeable predicament **b :** QUARREL, FIGHT

scrap heap *n* **1 :** a pile of discarded metal **2 :** the place to which useless things are relegated **:** DISCARD

scrap·per \'skrap-ər\ *n* **:** QUARRELER, FIGHTER

scrap·pi·ness \'skrap-ē-nəs\ *n* **:** the quality or state of being scrappy; *esp* **:** DISCONNECTEDNESS

scrap·ple \'skrap-əl\ *n* [dim. of ¹*scrap*] **:** a seasoned mush of meat scraps and cornmeal set in a mold and served sliced and fried

¹scrap·py \'skrap-ē\ *adj* **:** consisting of scraps **:** FRAGMENTARY

²scrappy *adj* **1 :** QUARRELSOME **2 :** aggressive and determined in spirit

¹scratch \'skrach\ *vb* [blend of E dial. *scrat* (to scratch) and obs. E *cratch* (to scratch)] *vt* **1 :** to scrape or dig with the claws or nails **2 :** to rub and tear or mark the surface of with something sharp or jagged **3 :** to scrape or rub lightly (as to relieve itching) **4 :** to scrape together **5 :** to write or draw on a surface **6 a :** to cancel or erase by or as if by drawing a line through **b :** to withdraw (an entry) from competition **7 :** SCRIBBLE, SCRAWL **8 :** to scrape along a rough surface ⟨~ a match⟩ **~** *vi* **1 :** to use the claws or nails in digging, tearing, or wounding **2 :** to scrape or rub oneself lightly (as to relieve itching) **3 :** to gather money or get a living by hard work and saving **4 :** to make a thin grating sound ⟨this pen ~*es*⟩ — **scratch·er** *n*

²scratch *n* **1 :** a mark or injury produced by scratching; *also* **:** a slight wound **2 :** SCRAWL, SCRIBBLE **3 :** the sound made by scratching **4 a :** the starting line in a race **b :** NOTHING **5 a :** a test of courage **b :** satisfactory condition or performance ⟨up to ~⟩ **6 :** a contestant whose name is withdrawn **7 a :** a shot in billiards or pool that involves a penalty **b :** a shot that scores by chance **:** FLUKE

³scratch *adj* **1 :** made as or used for a tentative effort ⟨~ paper⟩ **2 :** made or done by chance and not as intended ⟨~ shot⟩ **3 :** arranged or put together with little selection **:** HAPHAZARD ⟨~ team⟩ **4 :** without handicap or allowance ⟨~ golfer⟩

scratch hit *n* **:** a batted ball not solidly hit or cleanly fielded yet credited to the batter as a base hit

scratch·i·ness \'skrach-ē-nəs\ *n* **:** the quality or state of being scratchy

scratch line *n* **1 :** a starting line for a race **2 :** a line that marks the extreme limit of the takeoff for a broad jump **3 :** a line from which the javelin is thrown and which must not be overstepped by the thrower

scratch paper *n* **:** paper that may be used for jottings, memoranda, or other casual writing

scratch sheet *n* **:** a racing publication listing horses scratched from races and giving the handicapper's grading of the horses in order of winning chances

scratch test *n* **:** a test for allergic susceptibility made by rubbing an extract of an allergy-producing substance into small breaks or scratches in the skin

scratchy \'skrach-ē\ *adj* **1 :** likely to scratch **:** PRICKLY ⟨~ undergrowth⟩ **2 :** making a scratching noise **3 :** marked or made with scratches ⟨~ drawing⟩ ⟨~ handwriting⟩ **4 :** uneven in quality **:** RAGGED **5 :** causing tingling or itching **:** IRRITATING ⟨~ wool⟩

scrawl \'skrȯl\ *vb* [origin unknown] *vt* **:** to write or draw awkwardly, hastily, or carelessly **:** SCRIBBLE **~** *vi* **:** to write awkwardly or carelessly — **scrawl** *n* — **scrawl·er** *n* — **scrawly** \'skrȯ-lē\ *adj*

scrawl·i·ness \'skrȯ-lē-nəs\ *n* **:** the quality of being scrawly

scraw·ni·ness \'skrȯn-ē-nəs, 'skrän-\ *n* **:** the quality or state of being scrawny

scraw·ny \-ē\ *adj* [origin unknown] **:** ill-nourished **:** SKINNY ⟨~ cattle⟩ **syn** see LEAN

screak \'skrēk\ *vi* [of Scand origin; akin to ON *skrækja* to screak; akin to ME *scremen* to scream] **:** to make a harsh shrill noise **:** SCREECH — **screak** *n* — **screaky** \-ē\ *adj*

¹scream \'skrēm\ *vb* [ME *scremen;* akin to OHG *scrīan* to scream] *vi* **1 a** (1) **:** to voice a sudden sharp loud cry (2) **:** to produce harsh high tones **b :** to make or move with a noise resembling a scream **2 :** to speak or write with intense hysterical expressions **3 :** to produce a vivid startling effect **~** *vt* **:** to utter with or as if with a scream

²scream *n* **1 :** a loud sharp penetrating cry or noise **2 :** one that provokes mirth

scream·er \'skrē-mər\ *n* **1 :** one that screams **2 :** any of several So. American birds (family Anhimidae) **3 :** a sensationally startling headline

scream·ing·ly \-miŋ-lē\ *adv* **:** to an extreme degree

scree \'skrē\ *n* [of Scand origin; akin to ON *skritha* landslide, fr. *skrītha* to creep; akin to OHG *scrītan* to go, Lith *skrytis* felly, n.] **1 :** PEBBLE, STONE **2 :** a heap of stones or rocky debris **:** TALUS

¹screech \'skrēch\ *vb* [alter. of earlier *scritch,* fr. ME *scrichen;* akin to ON *skrækja* to screak] *vi* **1 :** to utter a high shrill piercing cry **:** make an outcry usu. in terror or pain **2 :** to make a sound resembling a screech **~** *vt* **:** to utter with or as if with a screech — **screech·er** *n*

²screech *n* **1 :** a high shrill piercing cry usu. expressing pain or terror **2 :** a sound resembling a screech

screed \'skrēd\ *n* [ME *screde* fragment, fr. OE *scrēade* — more at SHRED] **1** *Scot* **:** RENT, TEAR **2 a :** a lengthy discourse **b :** an informal piece of writing **3 :** a strip (as of plaster of the thickness planned for the coat) laid on as a guide

¹screen \'skrēn\ *n* [ME *screne,* fr. MF *escren,* fr. MD *scherm;* akin to OHG *skirm* screen, L *corium* skin — more at CUIRASS] **1 a :** a device used as a protection from heat or drafts or as an ornament **b :** a nonbearing partition often ornamental carried up to a height necessary for separation and protection **2 a :** something that shelters, protects, or conceals; *specif* **:** a body of troops, ships, or planes thrown to protect a command, an area, or larger force **b :** a shield for secret usu. evil practices **3 a :** a perforated plate or cylinder or a meshed wire or cloth fabric usu. mounted and used to separate coarser from finer parts **b :** a system for examining and separating into different groups **c :** a piece of apparatus designed to prevent agencies in one part from affecting other parts ⟨optical ~⟩ ⟨electric ~⟩ ⟨magnetic ~⟩ **d :** a frame holding a usu. metallic netting used esp. in a window or door to exclude insects **4 a** (1) **:** a flat surface upon which a picture or series of pictures is projected (2) **:** the motion-picture industry **b :** something that receives or retains a mental image or impression **c :** the surface upon which the image appears in a television or radar receiver **5 :** a glass plate ruled with crossing opaque lines through which an image is photographed in making a halftone

²screen *vt* **1 :** to guard from injury or danger **2 a :** to give shelter or protection to with or as if with a screen **b :** to separate with or as if with a screen **3 a :** to pass (as coal, gravel, ashes) through a screen to separate the fine part from the coarse; *also* **:** to remove by a screen **b** (1) **:** to examine usu. methodically in order to make a separation into different groups (2) **:** to select or eliminate by a screening process **4 :** to provide with a screen to keep out insects **5 a :** to project (as a motion-picture film) on a screen **b :** to present in a motion picture **~** *vi* **:** to appear on a motion-picture screen **syn** see HIDE — **screen·able** \'skrē-nə-bəl\ *adj* — **screen·er** *n*

screen·ing \'skrē-niŋ\ *n* **1** *pl but sing or pl in constr* **:** material (as waste or fine coal) separated out by passage through or retention on a screen **2 :** a metal or plastic mesh

screen·land \'skrēn-,land\ *n* **:** FILMDOM

screen memory *n* **:** an imagined or real recollection of early childhood that masks another memory of deep emotional significance

screen pass *n* **:** a forward pass in football in which the receiver is protected by a screen of blockers

screen·play \'skrēn-,plā\ *n* **:** the written form of a story prepared for motion-picture production including description of characters, details of scenes and settings, dialogue, and stage directions

screen test *n* **:** a short film sequence testing the ability of a prospective motion-picture actor — **screen–test** \'skrēn-,test\ *vt*

screen·writ·er \'skrēn-,rīt-ər\ *n* **:** a writer of screenplays

¹screw \'skrü\ *n* [ME, fr. MF *escroe* female screw, nut, fr. ML *scrofa,* fr. L, sow] **1 a :** a mechanical device consisting in its simplest form of a continuous helical rib with the cylindrical or conical shank from which it projects **b :** a usu. pointed and headed cylindrical fastener that is helically or spirally threaded and designed for insertion into material by rotating (as with a screwdriver) **2 a :** a screwlike form **:** SPIRAL **b :** a turn of a screw; *also* **:** a twist like the turn of a screw **c :** a screwlike device (as a corkscrew) **3 :** a worn-out horse **4** *chiefly Brit* **:** a small packet (as of tobacco) **5 :** a sharp bargainer **:** SKINFLINT **6 :** a prison guard **:** TURNKEY **7 :** SCREW PROPELLER **8 :** THUMBSCREW 2 — **screw·like** \-,līk\ *adj*

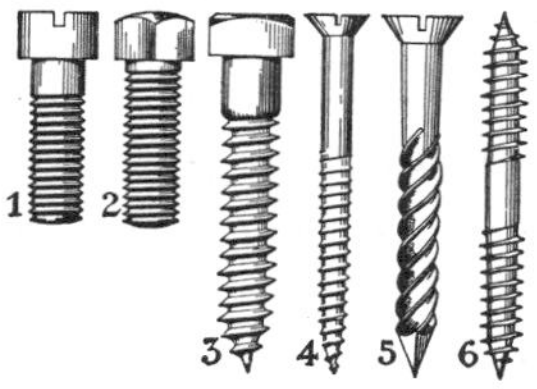

screws 1b: *1* cap, *2* setscrew, *3* lag, *4* flathead, *5* drivescrew, *6* dowel

²screw *vt* **1 a** (1) **:** to attach, fasten, or close by means of a screw (2) **:** to unite or separate by means of a screw or a twisting motion ⟨~ the two pieces together⟩ (3) **:** to press tightly in a device (as a vise) operated by a screw (4) **:** to operate, tighten, or adjust by means of a screw (5) **:** to torture by means of a thumbscrew **b :** to cause to rotate spirally about an axis **2 a** (1) **:** to twist into strained configurations **:** CONTORT (2) **:** SQUINT (3) **:** CRUMPLE **b :** to furnish with a spiral groove or ridge **:** THREAD **3 :** to increase the intensity, quantity, or capability of **4 a :** to practice extortion upon **:** OPPRESS **b :** to extract by pressure or threat **~** *vi* **1 :** to rotate like or as a screw **2 :** to turn or move with a twisting or writhing motion — **screw·er** *n*

¹screw·ball \'skrü-,bȯl\ *n* **1 :** a baseball pitch having reverse spin and a break in opposite direction to a curve **2 :** a whimsical, eccentric, or crazy person **:** ZANY

²screwball *adj* **:** crazily eccentric or whimsical **:** ZANY

screw bean *n* **:** the twisted sweet pod of a leguminous shrub or small tree (*Prosopis pubescens*) of the southwestern U.S.; *also* **:** this plant

screw·driv·er \'skrü-,drī-vər\ *n* **1 :** a tool for turning screws **2 :** vodka and orange juice served with ice

screw eye *n* **:** a wood screw with a head in the form of a loop

screw·fly \'skrü-,flī\ *n* **:** the adult of a screwworm

screw jack *n* **:** JACKSCREW

screw pine *n* **:** any of a genus (*Pandanus* of the family Pandanaceae, the screw-pine family) of tropical monocotyledonous plants with slender palmlike stems, often huge prop roots, and terminal crowns of swordlike leaves

screw propeller *n* **:** a device that consists of a central hub with radiating blades placed and twisted so that each forms part of a helical surface and that is used to propel a vehicle (as a ship or airplane)

screw thread *n* **1 :** the projecting helical rib of a screw **2 :** one complete turn of a screw thread

screw·worm \'skrü-,wərm\ *n* **:** the grub of a two-winged fly (*Cochliomyia hominivorax*) of the warmer parts of America that develops in sores or wounds or in the nostrils of mammals including

man with serious or sometimes fatal results; *broadly* **:** any of several fly larvae that parasitize the flesh of mammals

screwy \'skrü-ē\ *adj* **1 :** crazily absurd, eccentric, or unusual **2 :** CRAZY, INSANE

scrib·al \'skrī-bəl\ *adj* **:** of, relating to, or due to a scribe ⟨~ error⟩

scrib·ble \'skrib-əl\ *vb* **scrib·bling** \-(ə-)liŋ\ [ME *scriblen*, fr. ML *scribillare*, fr. L *scribere* to write] *vt* **1 :** to write hastily or carelessly without regard to legibility or thought **2 :** to cover with careless or worthless writings ~ *vi* **:** to write or draw hastily and carelessly — **scribble** *n*

scrib·bler \'skrib-lər, *before "of" also* -ə-lər\ *n* **1 :** one that scribbles **2 :** a minor or worthless author

1scribe \'skrīb\ *n* [ME, fr. L *scriba* official writer, fr. *scribere* to write; akin to Gk *skariphasthai* to scratch an outline, *keirein* to cut — more at SHEAR] **1 :** one of a learned class in ancient Palestine studying the Scriptures and serving as copyists, editors, teachers, and jurists **2 a :** an official or public secretary or clerk **b :** a copier of manuscripts **3 :** AUTHOR; *specif* **:** JOURNALIST

2scribe *vi* **:** to work as a scribe **:** WRITE

3scribe *vt* [prob. short for *describe*] **:** to mark a line on by cutting or scratching with a pointed instrument; *also* **:** to make by cutting or scratching

4scribe *n* **:** SCRIBER

scrib·er \'skrī-bər\ *n* **:** a sharp-pointed tool for marking off material (as wood or metal) to be cut — called also *scratch awl*

scrieve \'skrēv\ *vi* [of Scand origin; akin to ON *skrefa* to stride] *Scot* **:** to move along swiftly and smoothly

scrim \'skrim\ *n* [origin unknown] **:** a durable plain-woven usu. cotton fabric for use in clothing, curtains, building, and industry

1scrim·mage \'skrim-ij\ *n* [alter. of *1skirmish*] **1 a :** a minor battle **:** SKIRMISH **b :** a confused fight **:** SCUFFLE **2 a :** SCRUMMAGE **b :** the interplay between two football teams that begins with the snap of the ball and continues until the ball is dead **c :** practice play between a team's squads (as in football) **d :** the first line of scrimmage formed after kickoff in football

2scrimmage *vi* **:** to take part in a scrimmage — **scrim·mag·er** *n*

scrimp \'skrimp\ *vb* [perh. of Scand origin; akin to Sw *skrympa* to shrink, ON *skorpna* to shrivel up — more at SHRIMP] *vt* **1 :** to be niggardly in providing for **2 :** to make too small, short, or scanty **:** SKIMP ~ *vi* **:** to be frugal or niggardly — **scrimpy** \'skrim-pē\ *adj*

scrim·shaw \'skrim-(,)shȯ\ *n* [origin unknown] **1 :** any of various carved or engraved articles made esp. by American whalers usu. from whalebone or whale ivory **2 :** scrimshawed work **3 :** the art, practice, or technique of producing scrimshaw — **scrimshaw** *vb*

1scrip \'skrip\ *n* [ME *scrippe*, fr. ML *scrippum* pilgrim's knapsack] *archaic* **:** a small bag or wallet

2scrip *n* [short for *script*] **1 :** a short writing (as a certificate, schedule, or list) **2 :** a small piece **3 a :** any of various documents used as evidence that the holder or bearer is entitled to receive something (as a fractional share of stock or an allotment of land) **b :** paper currency or a token issued for temporary use in an emergency

script \'skript\ *n* [L *scriptum* thing written, fr. neut. of *scriptus*, pp. of *scribere* to write — more at SCRIBE] **1 a :** something written **:** TEXT **b :** an original or principal instrument or document **c** (1) **:** MANUSCRIPT 1 (2) **:** the written text of a stage play, screenplay, or broadcast; *specif* **:** the one used in production or performance **2 a :** printed lettering resembling handwritten lettering **b :** written characters **:** HANDWRITING **c :** ALPHABET

scrip·to·ri·um \skrip-'tōr-ē-əm, -'tȯr-\ *n, pl* **scrip·to·ria** \-ē-ə\ [ML, fr. L *scriptus*] **:** a copying room in a medieval monastery set apart for the scribes

scrip·tur·al \'skrip-chə-rəl, 'skrip-shrəl\ *adj* **:** of, relating to, contained in, or according to a sacred writing; *specif* **:** BIBLICAL — **scrip·tur·al·ly** \-ē\ *adv*

scrip·ture \'skrip-chər\ *n* [ME, fr. LL *scriptura*, fr. L, act or product of writing, fr. *scriptus*] **1 a** (1) *cap* **:** the books of the Old and New Testaments or of either of them **:** BIBLE — often used in pl. (2) *often cap* **:** a passage from the Bible **b :** the sacred writings of a religion **c :** a body of writings considered as authoritative **2 :** something written

script·writ·er \'skrip-,trīt-ər\ *n* **:** one that writes screenplays or radio or television programs

scriv·en·er \'skriv-(ə-)nər\ *n* [ME *scriveiner*, alter. of *scrivein*, fr. MF *escrivein*, fr. (assumed) VL *scriban-*, *scriba*, alter. of L *scriba* scribe] **1 :** a professional or public copyist or writer **:** SCRIBE **2 :** NOTARY

scro·bic·u·late \skrō-'bik-yə-lət\ *adj* [L *scrobiculus*, dim. of *scrobis* ditch — more at SCRAPE] **:** having shallow grooves or pits

scrod \'skräd\ *n* [perh. fr. obs. D *schrood* shred; akin to OE *scrēade* shred — more at SHRED] **:** a young fish (as a cod or haddock); *esp* **:** one split and boned for cooking

scrof·u·la \'skrȯf-yə-lə, 'skräf-\ *n* [ML, fr. LL *scrofulae*, pl., swellings of the lymph glands of the neck, fr. pl. of *scrofula*, dim. of L *scrofa* breeding sow] **:** tuberculosis of lymph glands esp. in the neck

scrof·u·lous \-ləs\ *adj* **1 :** of, relating to, or affected with scrofula **2 a :** resembling scrofula **b :** morally contaminated

scroll \'skrōl\ *n* [ME *scrowle*, alter. of *scrowe*, fr. MF *escroue* scrap, scroll, of Gmc origin; akin to OE *scrēade* shred] **1 a :** a roll (as of papyrus, leather, or parchment) for writing a document **b** *archaic* **:** a written message **c :** ROSTER, LIST **d :** a riband with rolled ends often inscribed with a motto **2 a :** something resembling a scroll in shape; *esp* **:** a spiral or convoluted form in ornamental design derived from the curves of a loosely or partly rolled parchment scroll **b :** the curved head of a bowed stringed musical instrument

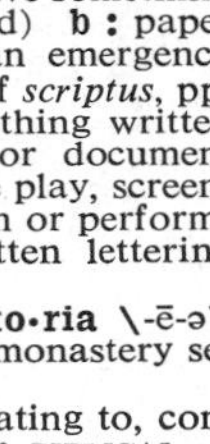

scroll 1a

scroll saw *n* **1 :** a thin handsaw for cutting curves or irregular designs **2 :** FRETSAW **3 :** JIGSAW

scroll·work \'skrōl-,wərk\ *n* **:** ornamentation characterized by scrolls; *esp* **:** fancy designs in wood often made with a scroll saw

scrooge \'skrüj\ *n, often cap* [Ebenezer *Scrooge*, character in *A Christmas Carol*, story by Charles Dickens] **:** a miserly person

scro·tal \'skrōt-ᵊl\ *adj* **:** of, relating to, or having a scrotum

scro·tum \'skrōt-əm\ *n, pl* **scro·ta** \-ə\ *or* **scrotums** [L; akin to L *scrupus* sharp stone — more at SHRED] **:** the external pouch that in most mammals contains the testes

scrouge \'skrau̇j, 'skrüj\ *vb* [alter. of E dial. *scruze* (to squeeze)] *chiefly dial* **:** CROWD, PRESS

scrounge \'skrau̇nj\ *vb* [alter. of E dial. *scrunge* (to wander about idly)] *vt* **1 :** to collect by or as if by foraging **2 :** CADGE, WHEEDLE ~ *vi* **1 :** FORAGE, HUNT **2 :** WHEEDLE — **scroung·er** *n*

scroung·ing *n* **:** the acquisition of goods or services other than by direct purchase

1scrub \'skrəb\ *n, often attrib* [ME, alter. of *schrobbe* shrub — more at SHRUB] **1 a :** a stunted tree or shrub **b :** vegetation consisting chiefly of such scrubs **c :** a tract covered with such vegetation **2 :** a domestic animal of mixed or unknown parentage and usu. inferior conformation **:** MONGREL **3 :** a person of insignificant size or standing **4 :** a player not belonging to the first string

2scrub *vb* **scrubbed; scrub·bing** [of LG or Scand origin; akin to MLG & MD *schrubben* to scrub, Sw *skrubba*] *vt* **1 a** (1) **:** to clean with hard rubbing **:** SCOUR (2) **:** to remove by scrubbing **b :** to subject to friction **:** RUB **2 :** WASH 6c(2) **3 :** CANCEL, ELIMINATE ~ *vi* **:** to use hard rubbing in cleaning

3scrub *n* **1 :** an act or instance of scrubbing **2 :** one that scrubs

scrub·bed \'skrəb-əd\ *adj* [*1scrub*] *archaic* **:** SCRUBBY

scrub·ber \'skrəb-ər\ *n* **:** one that scrubs; *specif* **:** an apparatus for removing impurities esp. from gases

scrub brush *n* **:** a brush with hard bristles for heavy cleaning — called also *scrubbing brush*

scrub·by \'skrəb-ē\ *adj* **1 :** inferior in size or quality **:** STUNTED ⟨~ cattle⟩ **2 :** covered with or consisting of scrub **3 :** lacking distinction **:** PALTRY

scrub typhus *n* **:** TSUTSUGAMUSHI DISEASE

scrub·wom·an \'skrəb-,wu̇m-ən\ *n* **:** a woman who hires herself out for cleaning **:** CHARWOMAN

scruff \'skrəf\ *n* [alter. of earlier *scuff*, of unknown origin] **:** the back of the neck **:** NAPE

scruffy \'skrəf-ē\ *adj* [E dial. *scruff* (something worthless)] **:** SHABBY, CONTEMPTIBLE

scrum \'skrəm\ *or* **scrum·mage** \'skrəm-ij\ *n* [*scrum* short for *scrummage*, alter. of *scrimmage*] **:** a Rugby play in which the forwards of each side crouch side by side typically in 3-2-3 formation and with locked arms with the two front lines meeting shoulder to shoulder — **scrummage** *vi*

scrump·tious \'skrəm(p)-shəs\ *adj* [prob. alter. of *sumptuous*] **:** DELIGHTFUL, EXCELLENT — **scrump·tious·ly** *adv*

1scrunch \'skrənch, 'skru̇nch\ *vb* [alter. of *1crunch*] *vt* **1 :** CRUNCH, CRUSH **2 a :** CONTRACT, HUNCH **b :** CRUMPLE, RUMPLE ~ *vi* **1 :** to make or move with a crunching sound **2 :** CROUCH, SQUEEZE

2scrunch *n* **:** a crunching sound

1scru·ple \'skrü-pəl\ *n* [ME *scriple*, fr. L *scrupulus* a unit of weight, fr. *scrupulus* small sharp stone] **1** — see MEASURE table **2 :** a minute part or quantity **:** IOTA

2scruple *n* [MF *scrupule*, fr. L *scrupulus* small sharp stone, cause of mental discomfort, scruple, dim. of *scrupus* sharp stone — more at SHRED] **1 :** an ethical consideration or principle that inhibits action **2 :** SCRUPULOUSNESS **syn** see QUALM

3scruple *vi* **scru·pling** \-p(ə-)liŋ\ **1 :** to have scruples **2 :** to be reluctant on grounds of conscience **:** HESITATE

scru·pu·los·i·ty \,skrü-pyə-'läs-ət-ē\ *n* **1 :** the quality or state of being scrupulous **2 :** SCRUPLE

scru·pu·lous \'skrü-pyə-ləs\ *adj* [L *scrupulus*] **:** full of or having scruples **:** inclined to scruple **:** STRICT, EXACT, PUNCTILIOUS **syn** see CAREFUL, UPRIGHT — **scru·pu·lous·ly** *adv* — **scru·pu·lous·ness** *n*

scru·ta·ble \'skrüt-ə-bəl\ *adj* [LL *scrutabilis* searchable, fr. L *scrutari* to search, investigate, examine — more at SCRUTINY] **:** capable of being deciphered **:** COMPREHENSIBLE

scru·ta·tor \'skrü-,tāt-ər, skrü-'\ *n* [L, fr. *scrutatus*, pp. of *scrutari* to search] **:** OBSERVER, EXAMINER

scru·ti·neer \,skrüt-ᵊn-'i(ə)r\ *n* **1 :** EXAMINER **2** *Brit* **:** a canvasser of votes

scru·ti·nize \'skrüt-ᵊn-,īz\ *vt* **:** to examine closely **:** INSPECT ~ *vi* **:** to make a scrutiny — **scru·ti·niz·er** *n*

syn SCRUTINIZE, SCAN, INSPECT, EXAMINE mean to look at critically or searchingly. SCRUTINIZE stresses close attention to minute detail; SCAN implies a surveying from point to point often suggesting a cursory overall observation; INSPECT implies scrutinizing for errors or defects; EXAMINE suggests a scrutiny in order to determine the nature, condition, or quality of a thing

scru·ti·ny \'skrüt-ᵊn-ē, 'skrüt-nē\ *n* [L *scrutinium*, fr. *scrutari* to search, examine, fr. *scruta* trash] **1 :** a searching study, inquiry, or inspection **:** EXAMINATION **2 :** a searching look **3 :** close watch **:** SURVEILLANCE

scu·ba \'sk(y)ü-bə\ *n* [*s*elf-*c*ontained *u*nderwater *b*reathing *a*pparatus] **:** an apparatus used for breathing while swimming under water

1scud \'skəd\ *vi* **scud·ded; scud·ding** [prob. of Scand origin; akin to Norw *skudda* to push; akin to L *quatere* to shake — more at QUASH] **1 :** to move or run swiftly esp. as if driven forward **2 :** to run before a gale

2scud *n* **1 :** the act of scudding **:** RUSH **2 a :** loose vapory clouds driven swiftly by the wind **b** (1) **:** a slight sudden shower (2) **:** a gust of wind (3) **:** mist, rain, snow, or spray driven by the wind

scu·do \'sküd-(,)ō\ *n, pl* **scu·di** \-(,)ē\ [It, lit., shield] **1 :** a gold coin first issued in the 15th century or a silver coin first issued in the 16th century and used in Italy to the 19th century approximately equivalent to a dollar **2 :** a unit of value equivalent to a scudo

1scuff \'skəf\ *vb* [prob. of Scand origin; akin to Sw *skuffa* to push] *vi* **1 a :** to walk without lifting the feet **:** SHUFFLE **b :** to poke or shuffle a foot in exploration or embarrassment **2 :** to become scratched, chipped, or roughened by wear ~ *vt* **1 :** CUFF **2 a :** to scrape (the feet) along a surface while walking or back and forth while standing **b :** to poke at with the toe **3 :** to scratch, gouge, or wear away the surface of

2scuff *n* **1 a :** a noise of or as if of scuffing **b :** the act or an instance of scuffing **c :** a mark or injury caused by scuffing **2 :** a flat-soled house slipper without quarter or counter

scuf·fle \'skəf-əl\ *vi* **scuf·fling** \-(ə-)liŋ\ [prob. of Scand origin; akin to Sw *skuffa* to push] **1 :** to struggle at close quarters with disorder and confusion **2 a :** to move with a quick shuffling gait **:** SCURRY **b :** SHUFFLE — **scuffle** *n*

scuffle hoe *n* **:** a garden hoe with both edges sharpened

1scull \'skəl\ *n* [ME *sculle*] **1 a :** an oar used at the stern of a boat to propel it forward with a thwartwise motion **b :** one of a pair of oars usu. less than 10 feet in length and operated by one person **2 :** a boat usu. for racing propelled by one or two persons using sculls

2scull *vt* **:** to propel (a boat) by sculls or by a large oar worked thwartwise **~** *vi* **:** to scull a boat — **scull·er** *n*

scul·lery \'skəl-(ə-)rē\ *n* [ME, department of household in charge of dishes, fr. MF *escuelerie*, fr. *escuelle* bowl, fr. L *scutella* drinking bowl — more at SCUTTLE] **:** a room for cleaning and storing dishes and culinary utensils, washing vegetables, and similar coarse work

scul·lion \'skəl-yən\ *n* [ME *sculion*, fr. MF *escouillon* dishcloth, alter. of *escouvillon*, fr. *escouve* broom, fr. L *scopa*, lit., twig; akin to L *scapus* stalk — more at SHAFT] **:** a kitchen helper whose chief task is washing

scul·pin \'skəl-pən\ *n, pl* **sculpins** *also* **sculpin** [origin unknown] **:** any of numerous spiny large-headed broad-mouthed usu. scaleless scorpaenoid fishes (esp. family Cottidae); *esp* **:** a scorpion fish (*Scorpaena guttata*) of the southern California coast esteemed for food and sport

sculpt \'skəlpt\ *vb* [F *sculpter*, alter. of obs. *sculper*, fr. L *sculpere*] **:** CARVE, SCULPTURE

sculp·tor \'skəlp-tər\ *n* [L, fr. *sculptus*, pp. of *sculpere*] **:** one that sculptures **:** an artist who produces works of sculpture — **sculp·tress** \-trəs\ *n*

sculp·tur·al \'skəlp-chə-rəl, 'skəlp-shrəl\ *adj* **1 :** of or relating to sculpture **2 :** resembling sculpture **:** SCULPTURESQUE — **sculp·tur·al·ly** \-ē\ *adv*

1sculp·ture \'skəlp-chər\ *n* [ME, fr. L *sculptura*, fr. *sculptus*, pp. of *sculpere* to carve, alter. of *scalpere* — more at SHELF] **1 a :** the act, process, or art of carving, cutting, or otherwise processing plastic or hard materials into works of art **b** (1) **:** work produced by sculpture (2) **:** a three-dimensional work of art (as a statue) **2 :** impressed or raised markings or a pattern of such on a plant or animal part

2sculpture *vb* **sculp·tur·ing** \'skəlp-chə-riŋ, 'skəlp-shriŋ\ *vt* **1 a :** to form an image or representation of from solid material (as wood or stone) **b :** to carve or otherwise form into a three-dimensional work of art **2 :** to change (the form of the earth's surface) by erosion **~** *vi* **:** to work as a sculptor

sculp·tur·esque \,skəlp-chə-'resk\ *adj* **:** done in the manner of or resembling sculpture — **sculp·tur·esque·ly** *adv*

1scum \'skəm\ *n* [ME, fr. MD *schum*; akin to OHG *scūm* foam] **1 a :** extraneous matter or impurities risen to or formed on the surface of a liquid often with a foul filmy covering **b :** the scoria of metals in a molten state **:** DROSS **2 a :** REFUSE **b :** the lowest class **:** RABBLE — **scum·my** \'skəm-ē\ *adj*

2scum *vi* **scummed; scum·ming :** to become covered with or as if with scum

1scum·ble \'skəm-bəl\ *vt* **scum·bling** \-b(ə-)liŋ\ [freq. of *2scum*] **1 a :** to make (color or a painting) less brilliant by covering with a thin coat of opaque or semiopaque color **b :** to apply (a color) in this manner **2 :** to soften the lines or colors of (a drawing) by rubbing lightly

2scumble *n* **1 :** the act or effect of scumbling **2 :** a material used for scumbling

1scun·ner \'skən-ər\ *vi* [ME (Sc dial.) *skunniren*] *chiefly Scot* **:** to be in a state of disgusted irritation

2scunner *n* **:** an unreasonable or extreme dislike or prejudice

scup \'skəp\ *n, pl* **scup** *also* **scups** [Narraganset *mishcùp*] **:** either of two porgies (genus *Stenostomus*) of the Atlantic coast of the U.S.: **a :** a fish (*S. chrysops*) occurring from So. Carolina to Maine and esteemed as a panfish **b :** a related fish (*S. aculeatus*) of more southerly distribution

scup·per \'skəp-ər\ *n* [ME *skopper*] **:** an opening cut through the waterway and bulwarks of a ship so that water falling on deck may flow overboard

scup·per·nong \-,nȯŋ, -,näŋ\ *n* [*Scuppernong*, river and lake in No. Carolina] **1 :** MUSCADINE; *esp* **:** a cultivated muscadine with yellowish green plum-flavored fruits **2 :** a white aromatic table wine made from scuppernongs

scurf \'skərf\ *n* [ME, of Scand origin; akin to Icel *skurfa* scurf; akin to OHG *scorf* scurf, L *carpere* to pluck — more at HARVEST] **1 :** thin dry scales detached from the epidermis esp. in an abnormal skin condition **2 a :** something like flakes or scales adhering to a surface **b :** the foul remains of something adherent **3 a :** a scaly deposit or covering on some plant parts; *also* **:** a localized or general darkening and roughening of a plant surface usu. more pronounced than russeting **b :** a plant disease characterized by scurf — **scurfy** \'skər-fē\ *adj*

scur·rile *or* **scur·ril** \'skər-əl, 'skə-rəl\ *adj* [MF *scurrile*, fr. L *scurrilis*, fr. *scurra* buffoon] **:** SCURRILOUS

scur·ril·i·ty \skə-'ril-ət-ē\ *n* **1 :** the quality or state of being scurrilous **2 a :** scurrilous or abusive language **b :** an offensively rude or abusive remark **syn** see ABUSE

scur·ri·lous \'skər-ə-ləs, 'skə-rə-\ *adj* **1 a :** using or given to the language of low buffoonery **b :** being vulgar and evil **:** LOW **2 :** containing low obscenities or coarse abuse — **scur·ri·lous·ly** *adv* — **scur·ri·lous·ness** *n*

scur·ry \'skər-ē, 'skə-rē\ *vi* [short for *hurry-scurry*, redupl. of *hurry*] **1 :** to move in or as if in a brisk rapidly alternating step **:** SCAMPER **2 :** to circulate in an agitated, confused, or fluttering manner — **scurry** *n*

scur·vi·ly \'skər-və-lē\ *adv* **:** in a scurvy manner

scur·vi·ness \-vē-nəs\ *n* **:** the quality or state of being scurvy

1scur·vy \'skər-vē\ *adj* [*scurf*] **1 :** SCURFY **2 :** MEAN, DESPICABLE ⟨~ tricks⟩ **syn** see CONTEMPTIBLE

2scurvy *n* **:** a disease marked by spongy gums, loosening of the teeth, and a bleeding into the skin and mucous membranes and caused by a lack of ascorbic acid

scurvy grass *n* **:** a cress (as *Cochlearia officinalis*) believed useful in preventing or treating scurvy

1scut \'skət\ *n* [origin unknown] **:** a short erect tail (as of a hare or rabbit)

2scut *n* [prob. alter. of obs. E *scout*, fr. ME] **:** a contemptible fellow

scu·tage \'sk(y)üt-ij\ *n* [ME, fr. ML *scutagium*, fr. L *scutum* shield — more at ESQUIRE] **:** a tax levied upon a tenant of a knight's fee in commutation for military service

scu·tate \'sk(y)ü-,tāt\ *or* **scu·tat·ed** \-,tāt-əd\ *adj* [NL *scutatus*, fr. L, armed with a shield, fr. *scutum*] **1 :** PELTATE **2 :** covered by bony or horny plates or large scales

1scutch \'skəch\ *vt* [(assumed) F *escoucher* to beat, fr. (assumed) VL *excuticare* to beat out, fr. L *executere*, fr. *ex-* + *quatere* to shake, strike — more at QUASH] **:** to separate the woody fiber from (flax or hemp) by beating

2scutch *n* **1 :** SCUTCHER **2 :** a bricklayer's hammer for cutting, trimming, and dressing bricks

scutch·eon \'skəch-ən\ *n* [ME *scochon*, fr. MF *escuchon*] **:** ESCUTCHEON

scutch·er \'skəch-ər\ *n* **:** an implement or machine for scutching flax, cotton, or cloth

scute \'sk(y)üt\ *n* [NL *scutum*, fr. L, shield — more at ESQUIRE] **:** an external bony or horny plate or large scale

scu·tel·late \sk(y)ü-'tel-ət, 'sk(y)üt-ᵊl-,āt\ *adj* **1 :** of or resembling a scutellum **2** *or* **scu·tel·lat·ed** \'sk(y)üt-ᵊl-,āt-əd\ **:** having or covered with scutella

scu·tel·la·tion \,sk(y)üt-ᵊl-'ā-shən\ *n* **:** LEPIDOSIS

scu·tel·lum \sk(y)ü-'tel-əm\ *n, pl* **scu·tel·la** \-ə\ [NL, dim. of L *scutum* shield] **1 :** any of several small shield-shaped plant structures **2 :** a hard plate or scale (as on the thorax of an insect or the tarsus of a bird)

scu·ti·form \'sk(y)üt-ə-,fȯrm\ *adj* [NL *scutiformis*, fr. L *scutum* + *-iformis* -iform] **:** PELTATE

scut·ter \'skət-ər\ *vi* [alter. of *4scuttle*] **:** SCURRY, SCUTTLE

1scut·tle \'skət-ᵊl\ *n* [ME *scutel*, fr. L *scutella* drinking bowl, tray, dim. of *scutra* platter] **1 :** a shallow open basket for carrying something (as grain or garden produce) **2 :** a metal pail for carrying coal

2scuttle *n* [ME *skottell*] **1 :** a small opening in a wall or roof furnished with a lid: as **a :** a small opening or hatchway in the deck of a ship large enough to admit a man and with a lid for covering it **b :** a small hole in the side or bottom of a ship furnished with a lid or glazed **2 :** a lid that closes a scuttle

3scuttle *vt* **scut·tling** \'skət-liŋ, -ᵊl-iŋ\ **:** to cut a hole through the bottom, deck, or sides of (a ship); *specif* **:** to sink or attempt to sink by making holes through the bottom of

4scuttle *vi* **scut·tling** \'skət-liŋ, -ᵊl-iŋ\ [prob. blend of *scud* and *shuttle*] **:** SCURRY

5scuttle *n* **1 :** a quick shuffling pace **:** SCURRY **2 :** a short swift run

scut·tle·butt \'skət-ᵊl-,bət\ *n* **1 a :** a cask on shipboard to contain fresh water for a day's use **b :** a drinking fountain on a ship or at a naval or marine installation **2 :** RUMOR, GOSSIP

scu·tum \'sk(y)üt-əm\ *n, pl* **scu·ta** \-ə\ [NL, fr. L, shield — more at ESQUIRE] **:** a bony, horny, or chitinous plate **:** SCUTE

Scyl·la \'sil-ə\ *n* [L, fr. Gk *Skylla*] **:** a rock on the Italian coast personified by the ancients as a female monster — **between Scylla and Cha·ryb·dis** \-kə-'rib-dəs\ **:** between two equally hazardous alternatives

scy·phis·to·ma \sī-'fis-tə-mə\ *n, pl* **scy·phis·to·mae** \-(,)mē\ *also* **scyphistomas** [NL, fr. L *scyphus* cup + Gk *stoma* mouth] **:** a sexually produced scyphozoan larva that ultimately repeatedly constricts transversely to form free-swimming medusae

scy·pho·zo·an \,sī-fə-'zō-ən\ *n* [NL *Scyphozoa*, class name, fr. L *scyphus* + NL *-zoa*] **:** any of a class (Scyphozoa) of coelenterates comprising jellyfishes lacking a true polyp and usu. a velum — **scyphozoan** *adj*

scy·phus \'sī-fəs\ *n, pl* **scy·phi** \-,fī\ [L, fr. Gk *skyphos*] **1 :** a deep drinking vessel with two horizontal handles used esp. in ancient Greece **2 :** a cup-shaped plant part

1scythe \'sīth\ *n* [ME *sithe*, fr. OE *sīthe*; akin to OE *sagu* saw — more at SAW] **:** an implement used for mowing (as grass) and composed of a long curving blade fastened at an angle to a long handle

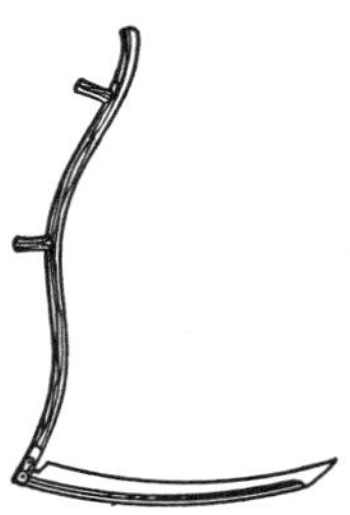
scythe

2scythe *vt* **:** to cut with or as if with a scythe **:** MOW

Scyth·i·an \'sith-ē-ən, 'sith-\ *n* [L *Scytha*, fr. Gk *Skythēs*] **1 :** one of an ancient nomadic people inhabiting Scythia **2 :** the Iranian language of the Scythians — **Scythian** *adj*

sea \'sē\ *n* [ME *see*, fr. OE *sǣ*; akin to OS & OHG *sē* sea] **1 a :** a great body of salty water that covers much of the earth; *broadly* **:** the waters of the earth as distinguished from the land and air **b :** a body of salt water of second rank more or less landlocked ⟨the Mediterranean ~⟩ **c :** OCEAN **d :** an inland body of water esp. if large or if salt or brackish ⟨the Caspian ~⟩ **e :** a small freshwater lake ⟨the *Sea* of Galilee⟩ **2 a :** surface motion on a large body of water or its direction; *also* **:** rough water **:** a heavy swell or wave **b :** the disturbance of the ocean or other body of water due to the wind **3 :** something vast or overwhelming likened to the sea **4 :** the seafaring life **5 :** 3MARE — **sea** *adj* — **at sea 1 :** on the sea; *specif* **:** on a sea voyage **2 :** LOST, BEWILDERED — **to sea :** to or upon the open waters of the sea

sea anchor *n* **:** a drag typically of canvas thrown overboard to retard the drifting of a ship or seaplane and to keep its head to the wind

sea anemone *n* **:** any of numerous usu. solitary polyps (order Actiniaria) that in form, bright and varied colors, and cluster of tentacles superficially resemble a flower

sea·bag \'sē-,bag\ *n* **:** a cylindrical canvas bag used esp. by a sailor for clothes and other gear

sea bass *n* **1 :** any of numerous marine fishes (family Serranidae) including usu. the smaller more active members of the family as distinguished from the groupers; *esp* **:** a food and sport fish (*Centropristes striatus*) of the Atlantic coast of the U.S. **2 :** any of numerous croakers or drums including noted sport and food fishes

sea·beach \-,bēch\ *n* **:** a beach lying along the sea

sea·bed \-,bed\ *n* **:** the floor of a sea or ocean

Sea·bee \'sē-(,)bē\ *n* [alter. of *cee* + *bee*; fr. the initials of *construction battalion*] **:** a member of one of the volunteer construction

battalions for building naval aviation facilities and defending them

sea·bird \'sē-ˌbərd\ n : a bird (as a gull or albatross) frequenting the open ocean

sea biscuit n : hard biscuit or loaf bread prepared for use on ship-board : HARDTACK

sea·board \'sē-ˌbō(ə)rd, -ˌbȯ(ə)rd\ n : SEACOAST; also : the country bordering a seacoast — **seaboard** adj

sea·boot \-ˌbüt\ n : a very high waterproof boot used esp. by sailors and fishermen

sea·borne \-ˌbō(ə)rn, -ˌbȯ(ə)rn\ adj 1 : borne over or upon the sea ⟨a ~ invasion⟩ 2 : engaged in or carried on by oversea shipping ⟨~ trade⟩

sea bread n : HARDTACK

sea bream n : any of numerous marine percoid fishes (as of the families Sparidae or Bramidae)

sea breeze n : a cooling breeze blowing generally in the daytime inland from the sea

sea cabin n : an emergency cabin near a ship's bridge for the use of captain and officers

sea captain n : the master of a merchant vessel

sea card n : the card of a mariner's compass

sea change n 1 : a change made by the sea 2 : TRANSFORMATION

sea chest n : a sailor's storage chest for personal property

sea·coast \'sē-ˌkōst\ n : the shore or border of the land adjacent to the sea

sea cow n 1 : MANATEE, DUGONG 2 : WALRUS 3 : HIPPOPOTAMUS

sea·craft \'sē-ˌkraft\ n 1 : seagoing ships 2 : skill in navigation

sea crawfish n : SPINY LOBSTER — called also sea crayfish

sea cucumber n : HOLOTHURIAN; esp : one whose contracted body suggests a cucumber in form

sea devil n 1 : DEVILFISH 1 2 : STONEFISH

sea dog n 1 : any of several seals 2 : DOGFISH 3 : a veteran sailor

sea·dog \'sē-ˌdȯg\ n : FOGBOW

sea·drome \-ˌdrōm\ n : a floating airdrome serving as an inter-mediate or emergency landing place

sea duck n : a diving duck (as a scoter, merganser, or eider) that frequents the sea

sea duty n : duty in the U.S. Navy performed outside the continental U.S. or specified dependencies thereof

sea eagle n 1 : any of various fish-eating eagles 2 : OSPREY

sea-ear \'sē-ˌi(ə)r\ n : ABALONE

sea fan n : a gorgonian with a fan-shaped skeleton; esp : one (Gorgonia flabellum) of Florida and the West Indies

sea·far·er \'sē-ˌfar-ər, -ˌfer-\ n : MARINER

sea·far·ing \-ˌfar-iŋ, -ˌfer-\ n : a mariner's calling — **seafaring** adj

sea feather n : a gorgonian with a plumose skeleton; esp : SEA PEN

sea fight n : an engagement between ships at sea

sea fire n : marine bioluminescence

sea·folk \'sē-ˌfōk\ n : seafaring people : MARINERS

sea·food \'sē-ˌfüd\ n : edible marine fish and shellfish

sea·fowl \-ˌfaul\ n : SEABIRD

sea·front \-ˌfrənt\ n : the waterfront of a seaside place

sea gate n : a gate, beach, or channel that gives access to the sea

sea·girt \'sē-ˌgərt\ adj : surrounded by the sea

sea·go·er \-ˌgō-(ə)r\ n : one that travels by sea : SEAFARER

sea·go·ing \-ˌgō-iŋ, -ˌgȯ-(ə)iŋ\ adj : OCEANGOING

sea green n 1 : a moderate green or bluish green 2 : a moderate yellow green

sea gull n : a gull frequenting the sea; broadly : GULL

sea hare n : any of various large naked mollusks (genus Tethys) with arched backs and anterior tentacles that project like ears

sea holly n : a European coastal herb (Eryngium maritimum) of the carrot family with spiny leaves and pale blue flowers

sea horse n 1 : WALRUS 2 : a fabulous creature half horse and half fish 3 : any of numerous small fishes (family Syng-nathidae) related to the pipefishes but stockier with the head and forepart of the body sharply flexed like the head and neck of a horse 4 : a large whitecap on a wave

sea is·land cotton \ˌsē-ˌī-lən(d)-\ n, often cap S&I [Sea islands, chain of islands in the Atlantic] : a cotton (Gossypium barbadense) with esp. long silky fiber

sea kale n : a European fleshy plant (Crambe maritima) of the mustard family used as a potherb

sea king n : a Norse pirate chief

¹seal \'sē(ə)l\ n, pl **seals** also **seal** [ME sele, fr. OE seolh; akin to OHG selah seal] 1 : any of numerous marine aquatic carnivorous mammals (families Pho-cidae and Otariidae) chiefly of cold regions with limbs modified into webbed flippers adapted primarily to swimming; esp : one (family Otariidae) valued for its soft dense underfur — called also fur seal 2 a : the pelt of a fur seal b : leather made from the skin of a seal 3 : a dark grayish yellowish brown

²seal vi : to hunt seals

³seal n [ME seel, fr. OF, fr. L sigillum seal, fr. dim. of signum sign, seal] 1 a : something that confirms, ratifies, or makes secure : GUARANTEE, ASSURANCE b (1) : a device with a cut or raised em-blem, symbol, or word used to certify a signature or authenticate a document (2) : a medallion or ring face bearing such a device in-cised so that it can be impressed on wax or moist clay; also : a piece of wax or a wafer bearing such an impression c : an impres-sion, device, or mark given the effect of a common-law seal by statute law or by American local custom recognized by judicial decision d : an adhesive stamp given in fund-raising campaigns 2 a : something that secures (as a wax seal on a document) b : a closure that must be broken to be opened and that thus reveals tampering c (1) : a tight and perfect closure (as against the passage of gas or water) (2) : a device to prevent the passage or return of gas or air into a pipe or container 3 chiefly Brit : a seal that is a symbol or mark of office — **under seal** : with an authenti-cating seal affixed

⁴seal vt 1 a : to confirm or make secure by or as if by a seal b : to solemnize for eternity (as a marriage or an adoption of a child) by a Mormon rite 2 a : to set or affix an authenticating seal to; also : AUTHENTICATE, RATIFY b : to mark with a stamp usu. as an evi-

dence of standard exactness, legal size, weight, or capacity, or merchantable quality 3 a : to fasten with or as if with a seal to prevent tampering b : to secure with a closure against access or leakage c : to make fast with cement or plaster 4 : to determine irrevocably or indisputably ⟨this answer ~ed our fate⟩

sea lace n : a seaweed (Chorda filum) with blackish fronds resem-bling cords — usu. used in pl.

sea ladder n 1 : a rope ladder or set of steps to be lowered over a ship's side for use in coming aboard (as at sea) 2 : SEA STEPS

sea lamprey n : a large anadromous lamprey (Petromyzon marinus) that is sometimes used as food and is a pest destructive of native fish fauna in the Great Lakes

sea-lane \'sē-ˌlān\ n : an established sea route

seal·ant \'sē-lənt\ n : a sealing agent ⟨radiator ~⟩

sea lavender n : any of a genus (Limonium) of mostly coastal plants of the plumbago family

sea lawyer n : an argumentative captious sailor

sea legs n pl 1 : ability to walk steadily on a ship at sea 2 : freedom from seasickness

¹seal·er \'sē-lər\ n 1 : an official who attests or certifies con-formity to a standard of correctness ⟨~ of weights and measures⟩ 2 : a coat (as of size) applied to prevent subsequent coats of paint or varnish from sinking in

²sealer n : a mariner or a ship engaged in hunting seals

seal·ery \'sē-lə-rē\ n : a seal fishery

sea lettuce n : any of a genus (Ulva, of the family Ulvaceae) of seaweeds with green fronds sometimes eaten as salad

sea level n : the level of the surface of the sea esp. at its mean posi-tion midway between mean high and low water

sea lily n : CRINOID; esp : a stalked crinoid

sealing wax n : a resinous composition that is plastic when warm and is used for sealing (as letters, dry cells, or cans)

sea lion n : any of several large Pacific eared seals (genus Zalophus and Otaria) related to the fur seals but lacking their valuable coat

seal off vt : to close tightly ⟨sealed the airport off with a cordon of police⟩

seal ring n : a finger ring engraved with a seal : SIGNET RING

seal·skin \'sē(ə)l-ˌskin\ n 1 : the fur or pelt of a fur seal 2 : a garment (as a jacket, coat, or cape) of sealskin — **sealskin** adj

Sea·ly·ham terrier \ˌsē-lē-ˌham-, esp Brit -lē-əm-\ n [Sealyham, Pembrokeshire, Wales] : a short-legged long-headed strong-jawed heavy-boned chiefly white terrier of a breed developed in Wales

¹seam \'sēm\ n [ME seem, fr. OE sēam; akin to OE sīwian to sew — more at SEW] 1 a : the joining of two pieces (as of cloth or leath-er) by sewing usu. near the edge b : the stitching used in such a joining 2 : the space between adjacent planks or strakes of a ship 3 a : a line, groove, or ridge formed by the abutment of edges b : a thin layer or stratum (as of rock) between distinctive layers; also : a bed of coal or other valuable mineral of any thickness c : a line left by a cut or wound; also : WRINKLE — **seam·like** \-ˌlīk\ adj

²seam vt 1 a : to join by sewing b : to join as if by sewing (as by welding, riveting, or heat-sealing) 2 : to mark with lines suggesting seams : FURROW ~ vi : to become fissured or ridgy — **seam·er** n

sea-maid \'sē-ˌmād\ or **sea-maid·en** \-ˌmād-ᵊn\ n : MERMAID; also : a goddess or nymph of the sea

sea·man \'sē-mən\ n 1 : SAILOR 1, MARINER 2 : an enlisted man in the navy ranking above a seaman apprentice and below a petty officer third class

seaman apprentice n : an enlisted man in the navy ranking above a seaman recruit and below a seaman

sea·man·like \'sē-mən-ˌlīk\ adj : characteristic of or befitting a competent seaman

sea·man·ly \-lē\ adj : SEAMANLIKE

seaman recruit n : an enlisted man of the lowest rank in the navy

sea·man·ship \'sē-mən-ˌship\ n : the art or skill of handling, working, and navigating a ship

sea·mark \-ˌmärk\ n 1 : a line on a coast marking the tidal limit 2 : an elevated object serving as a beacon to mariners

sea mew n : SEA GULL; esp : a European gull (Larus canus)

sea mile n : NAUTICAL MILE

seam·i·ness \'sē-mē-nəs\ n : seamy condition

seam·less \'sēm-ləs\ adj : having no seam — **seam·less·ly** adv — **seam·less·ness** n

sea·most \-ˌmōst\ adj : situated nearest the sea

sea·mount \-ˌmaunt\ n : a submarine mountain rising above the deep sea floor

sea mouse n : a large broad marine polychaete worm (Aphrodite or a related genus) covered with hairlike setae

seam·ster \'sēm(p)-stər also 'sem(p)-\ n [ME semester, semster, fr. OE sēamestre seamstress, tailor, fr. sēam seam] : a person employed at sewing; esp : TAILOR

seam·stress \'sēm(p)-strəs also 'sem(p)-\ n : a woman whose occupation is sewing

seamy \'sē-mē\ adj 1 archaic : having the rough side of the seam showing 2 a : UNPLEASANT b : DEGRADED, SORDID

sé·ance \'sā-ˌän(t)s, -ˌäⁿs, sā-¹\ n [F, fr. seoir to sit, fr. L sedēre — more at SIT] 1 : SESSION, SITTING 2 : a spiritualist meeting to receive spirit communications

sea nettle n : a stinging jellyfish

sea onion n 1 : a squill (Urginea maritima) 2 : a delicate blue-flowered European scilla (Scilla verna)

sea otter n : a rare large marine otter (Enhydra lutris) of the north-ern Pacific coasts whose pelt furnishes an extremely valuable fur

sea-otter's-cabbage n : a gigantic kelp (Nereocystis lütkeana) of the northern Pacific

sea pen n : any of numerous anthozoans (as of the genus Pennatula) whose colonies have a feathery form

sea·piece \'sē-ˌpēs\ n : a representation of the sea (as in a painting) : SEASCAPE

sea·plane \'sē-ˌplān\ n : an airplane designed to take off from and alight on the water

sea·port \-ˌpō(ə)rt, -ˌpȯ(ə)rt\ n : a port, harbor, or town accessible to seagoing ships

sea power n 1 : a nation having formidable naval strength 2 : na-val strength

sea horse

sea purse *n* : the horny egg case of skates and of some sharks

sea puss \-ˌpu̇s\ *n* [by folk etymology fr. a word of Algonquian origin; akin to Delaware *sepus* small brook] : a swirling or alongshore undertow

sea·quake \ˈsē-ˌkwāk\ *n* [*sea* + *-quake* (as in *earthquake*)] : a submarine earthquake

[1]**sear** *var of* SERE

[2]**sear** \ˈsi(ə)r\ *vb* [ME *seren*, fr. OE *sēarian*, fr. *sēar* sere] *vi* **1** *obs* : to wither away : become sere **2** : to cause withering or drying ⟨harsh winds that ~ and burn⟩ ~ *vt* **1** : to make withered and dry : PARCH, SHRIVEL **2** : to burn, scorch, or injure with or as if with sudden application of intense heat

[3]**sear** *n* : a mark or scar left by searing

[4]**sear** *n* [prob. fr. MF *serre* grasp, fr. *serrer* to press, grasp, fr. LL *serare* to bolt, latch, fr. L *sera* bar for fastening a door] : the catch that holds the hammer of a gunlock at cock or half cock

sea raven *n* : a large sculpin (*Hemitripterus americanus*) of the northern Atlantic coast of America

[1]**search** \ˈsərch\ *vb* [ME *cerchen*, fr. MF *cerchier* to go about, survey, search, fr. LL *circare* to go about, fr. L *circum* round about] *vt* **1** : to look into or over carefully or thoroughly in an effort to find or discover something: as **a** : to examine in seeking something ⟨~*ed* the north field⟩ **b** : to look through or explore by inspecting possible places of concealment or investigating suspicious circumstances **c** : to read thoroughly : CHECK; *esp* : to examine a public record or register for information about ⟨~*ing* titles⟩ **d** : to examine for articles concealed on the person **e** : to look at as if to discover or penetrate intention or nature **2** : to uncover, find, or come to know by inquiry or scrutiny ~ *vi* **1** : to look or inquire carefully — usu. used with *for* ⟨~*ed* for the papers⟩ **2** : to make painstaking investigation or examination — **search·able** \ˈsər-chə-bəl\ *adj* — **search·er** *n* — **search·ing·ly** \-chiŋ-lē\ *adv*

[2]**search** *n* **1 a** : an act of searching **b** : an act of boarding and inspecting a ship on the high seas in exercise of right of search **2** : a person or party that searches **3** : power or range of searching and esp. of penetrating; *also* : a penetrating effect

search·less \-ləs\ *adj* : INSCRUTABLE, IMPENETRABLE

search·light \ˈsərch-ˌlīt\ *n* **1** : an apparatus for projecting a beam of light; *also* : a beam of light projected by it **2** : FLASHLIGHT 3

search warrant *n* : a warrant authorizing a search (as of a house) for stolen goods or unlawful possessions (as gambling implements)

sea robin *n* : any of several gurnards; *esp* : an American gurnard (genus *Prionotus*) with red or brown on the body and fins

sea room *n* : room for maneuver at sea

sea rover *n* : one that roves the sea; *specif* : PIRATE

sea–run \ˌsē-ˌrən\ *adj* : ANADROMOUS ⟨a ~ salmon⟩

sea·scape \ˈsē-ˌskāp\ *n* **1** : a view of the sea **2** : a picture representing a scene at sea

sea scorpion *n* : SCULPIN

sea scout *n* : a boy enrolled in the boy-scout program that provides training for older boys in seamanship and water activities

sea serpent *n* : a large marine animal resembling a serpent often reported to have been seen but never proved to exist

sea·shell \ˈsē-ˌshel\ *n* : the shell of a marine animal and esp. a mollusk

sea·shine \-ˌshīn\ *n* : the shine of the sea; *esp* : light reflected off the sea

sea·shore \-ˌshō(ə)r, -ˌshȯ(ə)r\ *n* **1** : land adjacent to the sea : SEACOAST **2** : all the ground between the ordinary high-water and low-water marks : FORESHORE

sea·sick \-ˌsik\ *adj* : affected with or suggestive of seasickness

sea·sick·ness \-nəs\ *n* : motion sickness experienced on the water

sea·side \ˈsē-ˌsīd\ *n* : the district or land bordering the sea : country adjacent to the sea : SEASHORE

sea·sid·er \-ˌsīd-ər\ *n* : a resident or frequenter of the seaside

Sea Sled *trademark* — used for a gliding shallow-draft high-powered motorboat

sea slug *n* **1** : HOLOTHURIAN **2** : a naked marine gastropod; *specif* : NUDIBRANCH

sea snake *n* **1** : any of numerous venomous aquatic viviparous snakes (family Hydrophidae) of warm seas **2** : SEA SERPENT

[1]**sea·son** \ˈsēz-ᵊn\ *n* [ME, fr. OF *saison*, fr. L *sation-*, *satio* action of sowing, fr. *satus*, pp. of *serere* to sow — more at SOW] **1** : a suitable or natural time or occasion **2 a** : a period of the year associated with some phase or activity of agriculture (as growth or harvesting) **b** : the period normally characterized by a particular kind of weather ⟨a long rainy ~⟩ **c** : a period of the year marked by special activity in some field (as social, cultural, or business) ⟨theatrical ~⟩ ⟨social ~⟩ **d** : the time of a major holiday **3** [ME *sesoun*, fr. *sesounen*] *obs* : something that gives relish : SEASONING

[2]**season** *vb* **sea·son·ing** \ˈsēz-niŋ, -ᵊn-iŋ\ [ME *sesounen*, fr. MF *assaisoner* to ripen, season, fr. OF, fr. *a-* (fr. L *ad-*) + *saison* season] *vt* **1 a** : to make palatable by adding salt or condiment **b** *archaic* : to qualify by admixture : TEMPER **2 a** : to treat (as lumber) so as to prepare for use **b** : to make fit by experience ~ *vi* : to become seasoned — **sea·son·er** \ˈsēz-nər, -ᵊn-ər\ *n*

sea·son·able \ˈsēz-nə-bəl, -ᵊn-ə-bəl\ *adj* **1** : occurring in good or proper time : OPPORTUNE ⟨a ~ time for discussion⟩ **2** : suitable to the season or circumstances : TIMELY ⟨a ~ frost⟩ — **sea·son·able·ness** *n* — **sea·son·ably** \-blē\ *adv*

syn TIMELY, OPPORTUNE, PAT: SEASONABLE implies being appropriate to the season, occasion, or situation; TIMELY applies to what occurs or appears at the time or moment when it is most useful or valuable; OPPORTUNE implies coming at a time when circumstances happen to be favorable; PAT may apply to what is notably apt, ready, or well-timed, often so as to raise suspicion of being contrived to mislead or conceal

sea·son·al \ˈsēz-nəl, -ᵊn-əl\ *adj* : of or relating to the season or seasons ⟨~ storms⟩ ⟨~ industries⟩ — **sea·son·al·ly** \-ē\ *adv*

sea·son·er \ˈsēz-nər, -ᵊn-ər\ *n* : one that seasons: as **a** : a user of seasonings ⟨a heavy ~⟩ **b** : SEASONING

sea·son·ing \ˈsēz-niŋ, -ᵊn-iŋ\ *n* : something that serves to season; *esp* : an ingredient (as a condiment, spice, or herb) added to food primarily for the savor that it imparts

season ticket *n* : a ticket (as to all of a club's games or for specified daily transportation) valid during a specified time

sea spider *n* : any of various small long-legged marine arthropods (class Pycnogonida)

sea squirt *n* : a simple ascidian

sea steps *n pl* : projecting metal plates or bars attached to the side of a ship by which it may be boarded

sea stores *n pl* : supplies (as of foodstuffs) laid in before starting on a sea voyage

sea·strand \ˈsē-ˌstrand\ *n* : SEASHORE

[1]**seat** \ˈsēt\ *n* [ME *sete*, fr. ON *sæti*; akin to OE *sittan* to sit] **1 a** : a special chair of one in eminence; *also* : the status represented by it **b** : a chair, stool, or bench intended to be sat in or on **c** : the particular part of something on which one rests in sitting ⟨~ of a chair⟩ ⟨trouser ~⟩; *also* : the part of the body that bears the weight in sitting : BUTTOCKS **2 a** : a seating accommodation ⟨a ~ for the game⟩ **b** : a right of sitting **c** : membership on an exchange **3 a** : a place occupied by something **b** : a place from which authority is exercised **c** : a bodily part in which some function or condition is centered **4** : posture in or way of sitting on horseback **5 a** : a part at or forming the base of something **b** : a part or surface on which another part or surface rests

[2]**seat** *vt* **1 a** : to install in a seat of dignity or office **b** (1) : to cause to sit or assist in finding a seat (2) : to provide seats for ⟨a theater ~*ing* 1000 persons⟩ **c** : to put in a sitting position ⟨~*ed* himself at table⟩ **2** : to repair the seat of or provide a new seat for **3** : to fit to or with a seat ⟨~ a valve⟩ ~ *vi* **1** *archaic* : to take one's seat or place **2** : to fit correctly on a seat — **seat·er** *n*

sea tangle *n* : any of various kelp (esp. genus *Laminaria*)

seat belt *n* : straps designed to hold a person steady in a seat (as during the takeoff of an airplane)

seat·ing *n* **1** : the act of providing with seats **2 a** : material for covering or upholstering seats **b** : a seat in which something rests ⟨a valve ~⟩

seat·mate \ˈsēt-ˌmāt\ *n* : one with whom one shares a seat (as in a vehicle equipped with double or paired seats)

sea train *n* **1** : a seagoing ship equipped for carrying a train of railroad cars **2** : several army or navy transports forming a convoy at sea

sea trout *n* **1** : any of various trouts or chars that as adults inhabit the sea but ascend rivers to spawn **2** : any of various marine fishes (as a weakfish or greenling) felt to resemble trouts

sea urchin *n* : any of a class (Echinoidea) of echinoderms usu. of somewhat flattened globular form with a thin brittle shell covered with movable spines

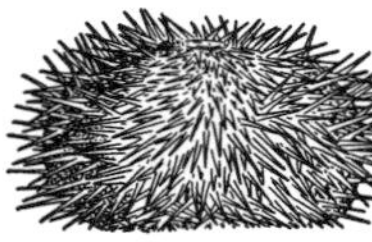
sea urchin

sea·wall \ˈsē-ˌwȯl\ *n* : a wall or embankment to protect the shore from erosion or to act as a breakwater

[1]**sea·ward** \-wərd\ *also* **sea·wards** \-wərdz\ *adv (or adj)* : toward the sea

[2]**seaward** *n* : the direction or side away from land and toward the open sea

sea·ware \ˈsē-ˌwa(ə)r, -ˌwe(ə)r\ *n* : sea wrack for use as manure

sea·wa·ter \-ˌwȯt-ər, -ˌwät-\ *n* : water in or from the sea

sea·way \-ˌwā\ *n* **1** : a moderate or rough sea ⟨caught in a ~⟩ **2** : a ship's headway **3** : the sea as a route for travel; *also* : an ocean traffic lane **4** : a deep inland waterway that admits ocean shipping

sea·weed \-ˌwēd\ *n* **1** : a mass or growth of marine plants **2** : a plant growing in the sea; *esp* : a marine alga

sea·worn \ˈsē-ˌwō(ə)rn, -ˌwȯ(ə)rn\ *adj* **1** : impaired or eaten away by the sea ⟨~ shores⟩ **2** : worn out by sea voyaging

sea·wor·thi·ness \-ˌwər-thē-nəs\ *n* : the quality or state of being seaworthy

sea·wor·thy \-ˌwər-thē\ *adj* : fit or safe for a sea voyage ⟨a ~ ship⟩

sea wrack *n* : SEAWEED; *esp* : that cast ashore in masses

se·ba·ceous \si-ˈbā-shəs\ *adj* [L *sebaceus* made of tallow, fr. *sebum* tallow — more at SOAP] : of, relating to, or being fatty material : FATTY ⟨a ~ exudate⟩; *also* : secreting sebum ⟨~ glands⟩

se·bac·ic acid \si-ˌbas-ik-, -ˌbā-sik-\ *n* [ISV, fr. L *sebaceus*] : a crystalline dicarboxylic acid $C_{10}H_{18}O_4$ used esp. in the manufacture of synthetic resins

se·bor·rhea \ˌseb-ə-ˈrē-ə, ˌsēb-\ *n* [NL, fr. L *sebum* + NL *-rrhea*] : abnormally increased secretion and discharge of sebum — **se·bor·rhe·ic** \-ˈrē-ik\ *adj*

se·bum \ˈsēb-əm, -ᵊm\ *n* [L, tallow, grease] : fatty lubricant matter secreted by sebaceous glands of the skin

sec \ˈsek\ *adj* [F, lit., dry — more at SACK] *of champagne* : containing three to five percent sugar by volume : DRY

se·cant \ˈsē-ˌkant, -kənt\ *n* [NL *secant-*, *secans*, fr. L, prp. of *secare* to cut — more at SAW] **1** : a straight line cutting a curve at two or more points **2 a** : a right line drawn from the center of a circle through one end of a circular arc to a tangent drawn from the other end of the arc **b** : the trigonometric function that for an acute angle in a right triangle is the ratio of the hypotenuse to the side adjacent to the angle

sec·a·teur \ˈsek-ə-ˌtər\ *n* [F *sécateur*, fr. L *secare* to cut] *chiefly Brit* : pruning shears — usu. used in pl.

sec·co \ˈsek-(ˌ)ō\ *n* [It, fr. *secco* dry, fr. L *siccus* — more at SACK] : the art of painting on dry plaster

se·cede \si-ˈsēd\ *vi* [L *secedere*, fr. *sed-*, *se-* apart (*fr. sed*, *se* without) + *cedere* to go — more at IDIOT, CEDE] : to withdraw from an organization or communion (as a church or political party) — **se·ced·er** *n*

se·cern \si-ˈsərn\ *vb* [L *secernere* to separate — more at SECRET] *vt* : SEPARATE; *esp* : to discriminate in thought : DISTINGUISH ~ *vi* : SEPARATE — **se·cern·ment** \-mənt\ *n*

se·ces·sion \si-ˈsesh-ən\ *n* [L *secession-*, *secessio*, fr. *secessus*, pp. of *secedere*] **1** : withdrawal into privacy or solitude : RETIREMENT **2** : formal withdrawal from an organization (as a religious communion or political party or federation)

se·ces·sion·ism \-ˈsesh-ə-ˌniz-əm\ *n* : the doctrine or policy of secession

se·ces·sion·ist \-ˈsesh-(ə-)nəst\ *n* : one who joins in a secession or maintains that secession is a right

se·clude \si-ˈklüd\ *vt* [ME *secluden* to keep away, fr. L *secludere* to separate, seclude, fr. *se-* apart + *claudere* to close — more at SECEDE, CLOSE] **1 a** : to confine in a retired or inaccessible place **b** : to remove or separate from intercourse or outside influence : ISOLATE **2** *obs* : to exclude or expel from a privilege, rank, or dignity : DEBAR **3** : to shut off : SCREEN

se·clud·ed *adj* **1** : screened or hidden from view : SEQUESTERED ⟨a ~ valley⟩ **2** : living in seclusion : SOLITARY ⟨~ monks⟩ — **se·clud·ed·ly** *adv* — **se·clud·ed·ness** *n*

se·clu·sion \-'klü-zhən\ *n* [ML *seclusion-, seclusio,* fr. L *seclusus,* pp. of *secludere*] **1 :** the act of secluding **:** the condition of being secluded **2 :** a secluded or isolated place **syn** see SOLITUDE — **se·clu·sive** \-'klü-siv, -ziv\ *adj* — **se·clu·sive·ly** *adv* — **se·clu·sive·ness** *n*

1**sec·ond** \'sek-ənd, -ənt, *esp. before a consonant* -ən, -ᵊŋ\ *adj* [ME, fr. OF, fr. L *secundus* second, following, favorable, fr. *sequi* to follow — more at SUE] **1 a** (1) — see NUMBER table (2) **:** being a type of grammatical declension or conjugation conventionally placed second in a sequential arrangement **b :** next to the first in place or time ⟨~ in line⟩ **c** (1) **:** next to the first in value, excellence or degree ⟨the ~ man in the department⟩ (2) **:** INFERIOR, SUBORDINATE **d :** ranking next below the top of a grade or degree in authority or precedence — used in titles ⟨~ mate⟩ **e :** ALTERNATE, OTHER ⟨elects a mayor every ~ year⟩ **f :** resembling or suggesting a prototype **:** ANOTHER ⟨a ~ Cato⟩ **g :** ingrained by discipline training, or effort **:** ACQUIRED ⟨~ nature⟩ **2 :** of or relating to a part in concerted or ensemble music typically lower in pitch than the first or to the player or singer performing this part ⟨~ violin⟩ ⟨~ bass⟩ — **second** *or* **sec·ond·ly** *adv*

2**second** *n* **1 a** — see NUMBER table **b :** one that is next after the first in rank, position, or other serial order ⟨the ~ in line⟩ **2 :** one who assists or supports another; *esp* **:** the supporter of a duelist or pugilist **3 a :** the musical interval embracing two diatonic degrees **b :** a tone at this interval; *specif* **:** the second note or tone of a scale **:** SUPERTONIC **c :** the harmonic combination of two tones a second apart **4 :** an inferior article of merchandise **5 a :** a second-in-command **b :** one having authority or precedence next below the first in a grade or degree **6 :** the act or declaration by which a parliamentary motion is seconded **7 :** a place next below the first (as in an examination, competition, or contest) **8 :** the second gear or speed in an automotive vehicle **9** *pl* **:** a second helping of food

3**second** *n* [ME *secunde,* fr. ML *secunda,* fr. L, fem. of *secundus* second; fr. its being the second sexagesimal division of a unit, as a minute is the first] **1 :** the 60th part of a minute of time or of a minute of angular measure **2 :** an instant of time **:** MOMENT

4**second** *vt* **1 a :** to give support or encouragement to **:** ASSIST **b** *obs* **:** to serve as follower or retainer of **:** ATTEND, ACCOMPANY **c :** to support in combat as reinforcement or second **2 a :** to support or assist in contention or debate **b :** to endorse (a motion or a nomination) so that it may be debated or voted on — **sec·ond·er** *n*

sec·ond·ar·i·ly \,sek-ən-'der-ə-lē\ *adv* **:** in a secondary manner or degree

sec·ond·ari·ness \'sek-ən-der-ē-nəs\ *n* **:** the quality or state of being secondary

1**sec·ond·ary** \'sek-ən-,der-ē\ *adj* **1 a :** of second rank, importance, or value **b :** of, relating to, or constituting the second strongest of the three or four degrees of stress recognized by most linguists ⟨the fourth syllable of *basketball team* carries ~ stress⟩ **c** *of a tense* **:** expressive of past time **2 a :** immediately derived from something original, primary, or basic **b :** of or relating to the induced current or its circuit in an induction coil or transformer ⟨a ~ coil⟩ ⟨~ voltage⟩ **c :** characterized by or resulting from the substitution of two atoms or groups in a molecule ⟨a ~ salt⟩; *esp* **:** being or characterized by a carbon atom united by two valences to chain or ring members **3 a :** of or relating to the second order or stage in a series **b :** of, relating to, or being the second segment of the wing of a bird or the quills of this segment **c :** intermediate between elementary and collegiate ⟨~ school⟩

2**secondary** *n* **1 :** one occupying a subordinate or auxiliary position rather than that of a principal **2 :** a defensive football backfield **3 :** a secondary electrical circuit or coil **4 :** any of the quill feathers of the forearm of a bird

secondary cell *n* **:** STORAGE CELL

secondary color *n* **:** a color formed by mixing primary colors in equal or equivalent quantities

secondary emission *n* **:** the emission of electrons from a surface that is bombarded by electrons or other charged particles from a primary source

secondary radiation *n* **:** rays (as X rays or beta rays) emitted by molecules or atoms as the result of the incidence of a primary radiation

secondary road *n* **1 :** a road not of primary importance **2 :** a feeder road

secondary sex characteristic *n* **:** a morphological or psychological peculiarity differentiated at puberty or in seasonal breeders at the breeding season in members of one sex and not directly concerned with reproduction

second base *n* **1 :** the base that must be touched second by a base runner in baseball **2 :** the player position for defending the area of the baseball infield on the first-base side of second base

sec·ond–best \,sek-ən-'best, -ᵊŋ-\ *adj* **:** next to the best ⟨give unto my wife my ~ bed —Shak.⟩

1**second best** *n* **:** one that is below or after the best

2**second best** *adv* **:** in second place

second blessing *n* **:** sanctification as a second gift of the Holy Spirit subsequent to justification

second childhood *n* **:** DOTAGE

second class *n* **1 :** the second and usu. next to highest group in a classification **2 :** CABIN CLASS **3 :** a class of U.S. or Canadian mail comprising newspapers and periodicals sent to regular subscribers

sec·ond–class \,sek-ᵊŋ-'klas, -ən-\ *adj* **1 :** of or relating to a second class **2 :** INFERIOR, MEDIOCRE; *also* **:** socially or economically deprived

Second Coming *n* **:** the coming of Christ as judge on the last day

second–degree burn *n* **:** a burn marked by pain, blistering, and superficial destruction of dermis with edema and hyperemia of the tissues beneath the burn

se·conde \sə-'känd, -'gänd\ *n* [F, fr. fem. of *second*] **:** the second of the eight defensive positions in fencing

Second Empire \,sek-ən-'dem-,pī(ə)r\ *adj* **:** of, relating to, or characteristic of a style (as of furniture) developed in France under Napoleon III and marked by heavy ornate modification of Empire styles

second fiddle *n* **:** one who fills a subordinate or secondary role or function — usu. used in the phrase *to play second fiddle*

second growth *n* **:** forest trees that come up naturally after removal of the first growth by cutting or by fire

sec·ond–guess \,sek-ᵊŋ-'ges, -ən-\ *vt* **1 :** to think out alternative strategies or explanations for after the event **2 a :** OUTGUESS **b :** PREDICT — **sec·ond–guess·er** *n*

1**second hand** \,sek-ən-'hand\ *n* **:** an intermediate person or means **:** INTERMEDIARY — usu. used in the phrase *at second hand*

2**second hand** \'sek-ən-,\ *n* **:** the hand marking seconds on a timepiece

1**sec·ond·hand** \,sek-ən-'\ *adj* **1 :** received from or through an intermediary **:** BORROWED **2 a :** acquired after being used by another **:** not new ⟨~ books⟩ **b :** dealing in secondhand merchandise ⟨a ~ bookstore⟩

2**secondhand** \,sek-ən-'\ *adv* **:** at second hand **:** INDIRECTLY

second lieutenant *n* **:** a commissioned officer in the army, air force, or marine corps of the lowest commissioned rank

second mortgage *n* **:** a mortgage the lien of which is subordinate to that of a first mortgage

se·con·do \si-'kōn-(,)dō, -'kän-\ *n, pl* **se·con·di** \-(,)dē\ [It, fr. *secondo,* adj., second, fr. L *secundus*] **:** the second part in a concerted piece; *esp* **:** the lower part (as in a piano duet)

second person *n* **1 a :** a set of linguistic forms (as verb forms, pronouns, and inflectional affixes) referring to the person or thing addressed in the utterance in which they occur **b :** a linguistic form belonging to such a set **2 :** reference of a linguistic form to the person or thing addressed in the utterance in which it occurs

sec·ond–rate \,sek-ən-'(d)rāt\ *adj* **:** of second or inferior quality or value **:** MEDIOCRE — **sec·ond–rate·ness** *n* — **sec·ond–rat·er** \-'(d)rāt-ər\ *n*

Second Reader *n* **:** a member of a Christian Science church or society chosen for a term of office to assist the First Reader in conducting services by reading aloud selections from the Bible

second reading *n* **1 :** the stage in the British legislative process following the first reading and usu. providing for debate on the principal features of a bill before its submission to a committee for consideration of details **2 :** the stage in the U.S. legislative process that occurs when a bill has been reported back from committee and that provides an opportunity for full debate and amendment before a vote is taken on the question of a third reading

second sight *n* **:** the capacity to see remote or future objects or events **:** CLAIRVOYANCE, PRECOGNITION

second–story man *n* **:** a burglar who enters a house by an upstairs window

se·cre·cy \'sē-krə-sē\ *n* [alter. of earlier *secretie,* fr. ME *secretee,* fr. *secre* secret, fr. MF *secré,* fr. L *secretus*] **1 :** the habit or practice of keeping secrets or maintaining privacy or concealment **:** SECRETIVENESS **2 :** the condition of being hidden or concealed

1**se·cret** \'sē-krət\ *adj* [ME, fr. MF, fr. L *secretus,* fr. pp. of *secernere* to separate, distinguish, fr. *se-* apart + *cernere* to sift — more at SECEDE, CERTAIN] **1 a :** kept from knowledge or view **:** HIDDEN **b :** marked by the habit of discretion **:** CLOSEMOUTHED **c :** working with hidden aims or methods **:** UNDERCOVER ⟨a ~ agent⟩ **d :** UNACKNOWLEDGED, UNAVOWED ⟨a ~ bride⟩ **2 :** remote from human frequentation or notice **:** SECLUDED **3 :** revealed only to the initiated **:** ESOTERIC **4 :** constructed so as to elude observation or detection ⟨a ~ panel⟩ — **se·cret·ly** *adv*

syn SECRET, COVERT, STEALTHY, FURTIVE, CLANDESTINE, SURREPTITIOUS, UNDERHAND mean done without attracting observation. SECRET implies concealment on any grounds for any motive; COVERT stresses the fact of not being open or declared; STEALTHY suggests taking pains to avoid being seen or heard esp. in some misdoing; FURTIVE implies a sly or timid stealthiness; CLANDESTINE implies secrecy usu. for an evil or illicit purpose; SURREPTITIOUS applies to action or behavior done secretly often with skilful avoidance of detection and in violation of usage, law, or authority; UNDERHAND stresses dishonest deception

2**secret** *n* **1 a :** something kept hidden or unexplained **:** MYSTERY **b :** something kept from the knowledge of others or shared only confidentially with a few **c :** a method, formula, or process used in an art or a manufacturing operation and divulged only to those of one's own company or craft **d** *pl* **:** the practices or knowledge making up the shared discipline or culture of an esoteric society **2 :** a prayer said inaudibly by the celebrant just before the preface of the mass **3 :** something taken to be a specific or key to a desired end ⟨the ~ of longevity⟩

se·cre·ta·gogue \si-'krēt-ə-,gäg\ *n* [*secret*ion + *-agogue*] **:** a substance stimulating secretion

sec·re·tar·i·al \,sek-rə-'ter-ē-əl\ *adj* **:** of or relating to a secretary or a secretary's work

sec·re·tar·i·at \-'ter-ē-ət\ *n* [F *secrétariat,* fr. ML *secretariatus,* fr. *secretarius*] **1 :** the office of secretary **2 :** a secretarial corps; *specif* **:** the clerical staff of an organization **3 :** the administrative department of a governmental organization ⟨the United Nations ~⟩

sec·re·tary \'sek-rə-,ter-ē\ *n* [ME *secretarie,* fr. ML *secretarius,* fr. L *secretum* secret, fr. neut. of *secretus,* pp.] **1** *obs* **:** one entrusted with the secrets or confidences of a superior **:** CONFIDANT **2 :** one employed to handle correspondence and manage routine and detail work for a superior **3 a :** an officer of a business concern who may keep records of directors' and stockholders' meetings and of stock ownership and transfer and help supervise the company's legal interests **b :** an officer of an organization or society responsible for its records and correspondence **4 :** an officer of state who superintends a government administrative department **5 a :** WRITING DESK, ESCRITOIRE **b :** a writing desk with a top section for books — **sec·re·tary·ship** \-,ship\ *n*

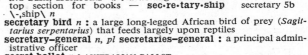

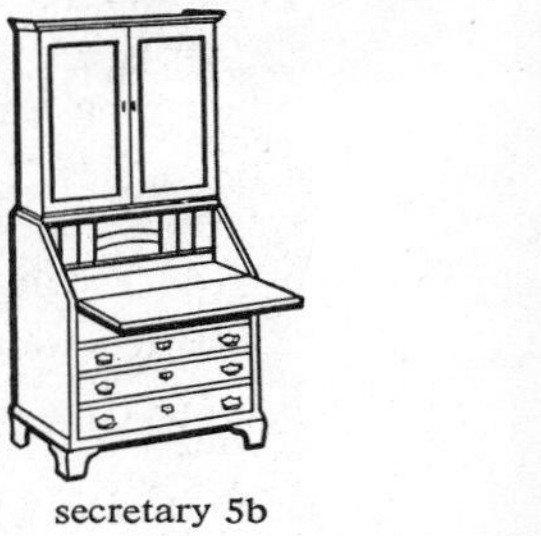
secretary 5b

secretary bird *n* **:** a large long-legged African bird of prey (*Sagittarius serpentarius*) that feeds largely upon reptiles

secretary–general *n, pl* **secretaries–general :** a principal administrative officer

secret ballot *n* **:** AUSTRALIAN BALLOT

1**se·crete** \si-ˈkrēt\ *vt* [back-formation fr. *secretion*] **:** to form and give off (a secretion)
2**se·crete** \si-ˈkrēt, ˈsē-krət\ *vt* [alter. of obs. *secret*] **1 :** to deposit or conceal in a hiding place **2 :** to appropriate secretly **:** ABSTRACT **syn** see HIDE
se·cre·tin \si-ˈkrēt-ᵊn\ *n* [*secret*ion + *-in*] **:** an intestinal hormone capable of stimulating the pancreas and liver to secrete
se·cre·tion \si-ˈkrē-shən\ *n* [F *sécrétion*, fr. L *secretion-, secretio* separation, fr. *secretus*, pp. of *secernere* to separate — more at SECRET] **1 a :** the process of segregating, elaborating, and releasing some material either functionally specialized (as saliva) or isolated for excretion (as urine) **b :** a product of such secretion formed by an animal or plant; *esp* **:** one performing a specific useful function in the organism **2** [2*secrete*] **:** the act of hiding something **:** CONCEALMENT — **se·cre·tion·ary** \-shə-ˌner-ē\ *adj*
se·cre·tive \ˈsē-krət-iv, si-ˈkrēt-\ *adj* [back-formation fr. *secretiveness*, trans. of F *secrétivité*] **:** disposed to secrecy, concealment, or privacy **syn** see SILENT — **se·cre·tive·ly** *adv* — **se·cre·tive·ness** *n*
se·cre·to·ry \si-ˈkrēt-ə-rē\ *adj* **:** of, relating to, or promoting secretion; *also* **:** produced by secretion
secret police *n* **:** a police organization operating for the most part in secrecy and esp. for the political purposes of its government often with terroristic methods
secret service *n* **1 :** a governmental service of a secret nature **2** *cap both Ss* **:** a division of the U.S. Treasury Department charged chiefly with the suppression of counterfeiting and the protection of the president
secret society *n* **:** any of various oath-bound societies often devoted to brotherhood, moral discipline, and mutual assistance
sect \ˈsekt\ *n* [ME *secte*, fr. MF & LL & L; MF, group, sect, fr. LL *secta* organized ecclesiastical body, fr. L, way of life, class of persons, fr. *sequi* to follow] **1 a :** a dissenting or schismatic religious body; *esp* **:** one regarded as extreme or heretical **b :** a religious denomination **2 a** *obs* **:** a class, order, or kind of persons **b** *archaic* **:** SEX ⟨so is all her ~ —Shak.⟩ **3 a :** a group adhering to a distinctive doctrine or to a leader **b :** PARTY **c :** FACTION
1**-sect** \ˌsekt\ *adj comb form* [L *sectus*, pp. of *secare* to cut — more at SAW] **:** cut **:** divided ⟨pinnati*sect*⟩
2**-sect** \ˌsekt, ˈsekt\ *vb comb form* [L *sectus*] **:** cut **:** divide ⟨bi*sect*⟩
1**sec·tar·i·an** \sek-ˈter-ē-ən\ *adj* **1 :** of, relating to, or characteristic of a sect or sectarian **2 :** limited in character or scope **:** PAROCHIAL — **sec·tar·i·an·ism** \-ē-ə-ˌniz-əm\ *n*
2**sectarian** *n* **1 :** an adherent of a sect **2 :** a narrow or bigoted person
sec·tar·i·an·ize \-ē-ə-ˌnīz\ *vi* **:** to act as sectarians **~** *vt* **:** to make sectarian
sec·ta·ry \ˈsek-tə-rē\ *n* **:** a member of a sect
sec·tile \ˈsek-tᵊl, -ˌtīl\ *adj* [L *sectilis*, fr. *sectus*] **1 :** capable of being severed by a knife with a smooth cut **2 :** cut into small divisions ⟨a ~ leaf⟩ — **sec·til·i·ty** \sek-ˈtil-ət-ē\ *n*
1**sec·tion** \ˈsek-shən\ *n* [L *section-, sectio*, fr. *sectus*] **1 a :** the action or an instance of cutting or separating by cutting **b :** a part set off by or as if by cutting **2 :** a distinct part or portion of a writing: as **a :** a subdivision of a chapter **b :** a division of a law **c :** a distinct component part of a newspaper **3 a :** the profile of something as it would appear if cut through by an intersecting plane **b :** the plane figure resulting from the cutting of a solid by a plane **4 :** a natural subdivision of a taxonomic group **5 :** a character § commonly used in printing as a mark for the beginning of a section and as the fourth in series of the reference marks **6 :** a piece of land one square mile in area forming one of the 36 subdivisions of a township **7 :** a distinct part of a territorial or political area, community, or group of people **8 a :** PORTION, SLICE **b :** one segment of a fruit **:** CARPEL **9 :** a basic military unit usu. having a special function **10 :** a very thin slice (as of tissue) suitable for microscopic examination **11 a :** a division of a railroad sleeping car with an upper and a lower berth **b :** a part of a permanent railroad way under the care of a particular set of men **c :** one of two or more vehicles which run on the same schedule **12 :** one of several component parts that may be assembled or reassembled **13 :** a division of an orchestra composed of one class of instruments **14 :** SIGNATURE 3b **syn** see PART
2**section** *vb* **sec·tion·ing** \-sh(ə-)niŋ\ *vt* **1 :** to cut or separate into sections **2 :** to represent in sections **~** *vi* **:** to become cut or separated into parts
1**sec·tion·al** \ˈsek-shnəl, -shən-ᵊl\ *adj* **1 a :** of or relating to a section **b :** local or regional rather than general in character ⟨~ interests⟩ **2 :** consisting of or divided into sections ⟨~ furniture⟩ — **sec·tion·al·ly** \-ē\ *adv*
2**sectional** *n* **:** a piece of furniture made up of modular units capable of use separately or in various combinations
sec·tion·al·ism \-shnə-ˌliz-əm, -shən-ᵊl-ˌiz-\ *n* **:** an exaggerated devotion to the interests of a region
Section Eight *n* [*Section VIII*, Army Regulation 615-360, in effect from December 1922 to July 1944] **1 :** a discharge from the U.S. Army for military inaptitude or undesirable habits or traits of character **2 :** a soldier discharged for military inaptitude or undesirable habits or traits of character
section gang *n* **:** a gang or crew of track workers employed to maintain a railroad section
section hand *n* **:** a laborer belonging to a section gang
1**sec·tor** \ˈsek-tər, -ˌtȯ(ə)r\ *n* [LL, fr. L, cutter, fr. *sectus*, pp. of *secare* to cut — more at SAW] **1 a :** a geometrical figure bounded by two radii and the included arc of a circle **b** (1) **:** a subdivision of a defensive military position (2) **:** a portion of a military front **2 :** a mathematical instrument consisting of two rulers connected at one end by a joint and marked with several scales **3 :** a distinctive part (as of an economy) ⟨the industrial ~⟩
2**sec·tor** \-tər\ *vt* **sec·tor·ing** \-t(ə-)riŋ\ **:** to divide into or furnish with sectors
sec·to·ri·al \sek-ˈtōr-ē-əl, -ˈtȯr-\ *adj* **1 :** of, relating to, or having the shape of a sector of a circle **2** *of a chimera* **:** having a sector of variant growth interposed in an otherwise normal body of tissue
1**sec·u·lar** \ˈsek-yə-lər\ *adj* [ME, fr. OF *seculer*, fr. LL *saecularis*, fr. L, coming once in an age, fr. *saeculum* breed, generation; akin to L *serere* to sow — more at SOW] **1 a :** of or relating to the worldly or temporal ⟨~ concerns⟩ **b :** not overtly or specif. religious ⟨~ music⟩ **c :** not ecclesiastical or clerical ⟨~ courts⟩ ⟨~ landowners⟩ **2 :** not bound by monastic vows or rules; *specif* **:** of, relating to, or forming clergy not belonging to a religious order or congregation ⟨a ~ priest⟩ **3 a :** occurring once in an age or a century **b :** existing or continuing through ages or centuries **c :** of or relating to a long term of indefinite duration — **sec·u·lar·ly** *adv*
2**secular** *n* **1 :** a secular ecclesiastic (as a parish priest) **2 :** LAYMAN
sec·u·lar·ism \ˈsek-yə-lə-ˌriz-əm\ *n* **:** indifference to or rejection or exclusion of religion and religious considerations — **sec·u·lar·ist** \-rəst\ *n* — **secularist** *or* **sec·u·lar·is·tic** \ˌsek-yə-lə-ˈris-tik\ *adj*
sec·u·lar·i·ty \ˌsek-yə-ˈlar-ət-ē\ *n* **1 :** something secular **2 :** the quality or state of being secular
sec·u·lar·iza·tion \ˌsek-yə-lə-rə-ˈzā-shən\ *n* **1 :** the act or process of secularizing **2 :** the condition of being secularized
sec·u·lar·ize \ˈsek-yə-lə-ˌrīz\ *vt* **1 :** to make secular **2 :** to transfer from ecclesiastical to civil or lay use, possession, or control **3 :** to convert to or imbue with secularism — **sec·u·lar·iz·er** *n*
se·cund \si-ˈkənd, ˈsē-ˌ\ *adj* [L *secundus* following — more at SECOND] **:** having some part or element arranged on one side only **:** UNILATERAL ⟨~ racemes⟩
se·cun·dines \ˈsek-ən-ˌdīnz, si-ˈkən-dənz\ *n pl* [pl. of obs. E *secundine* afterbirth, fr. ME, fr. LL *secundinae*, pl., fr. L *secundus*] **:** AFTERBIRTH
se·cur·ance \si-ˈkyu̇r-ən(t)s\ *n* **:** the act of making secure **:** ASSURANCE
1**se·cure** \si-ˈkyu̇(ə)r\ *adj* [L *securus* safe, secure, fr. *se* without + *cura* care — more at IDIOT, CURE] **1 a** *archaic* **:** unwisely free from fear or distrust **:** OVERCONFIDENT **b :** easy in mind **:** CONFIDENT **c :** assured in opinion or expectation **:** having no doubt **2 a :** free from danger **b :** free from risk of loss **c :** affording safety **:** INVIOLABLE ⟨~ hideaway⟩ **d :** TRUSTWORTHY, DEPENDABLE ⟨~ foundation⟩ **3 :** ASSURED, CERTAIN ⟨~ victory⟩ **syn** see SAFE — **se·cure·ly** *adv* — **se·cure·ness** *n*
2**secure** *vt* **1 a :** to relieve from exposure to danger **:** make safe **:** GUARD, SHIELD ⟨~ a supply line from enemy raids⟩ **b :** to put beyond hazard of losing or of not receiving **:** GUARANTEE ⟨~ the blessings of liberty —*U.S. Constitution*⟩ **c :** to give pledge of payment to (a creditor) or of (an obligation) ⟨*secured* by mortgage⟩ ⟨~ a note by a pledge of collateral security⟩ **2 a :** to take (a person) into custody **:** hold fast **:** PINION **b :** to make fast **:** SEAL ⟨~ a door⟩ **3 a :** to get secure possession of **:** PROCURE ⟨~ employment⟩ **b :** to bring about **:** EFFECT **4 :** to release (naval personnel) from work or duty **:** EXCUSE **~** *vi* **1** *of naval personnel* **:** to stop work **:** go off duty **2** *of a ship* **:** to tie up **:** BERTH **syn** see ENSURE, GET — **se·cur·er** *n*
se·cure·ment \si-ˈkyu̇(ə)r-mənt\ *n* **:** the act or process of making secure: as **a :** ASSURANCE, CERTAINTY **b :** PROCUREMENT
se·cu·ri·ty \si-ˈkyu̇r-ət-ē\ *n* **1 :** the quality or state of being secure: as **a :** freedom from danger **:** SAFETY **b :** freedom from fear or anxiety **2 a :** something given, deposited, or pledged to make certain the fulfillment of an obligation **b :** SURETY **3 :** an evidence of debt or of property (as a stock certificate or bond) **4 a :** something that secures **:** PROTECTION **b :** measures taken esp. to guard against espionage or sabotage
Security Council *n* **:** a permanent council of the United Nations having primary responsibility for the maintenance of peace and security
se·dan \si-ˈdan\ *n* [origin unknown] **1 :** a portable often covered chair designed to carry one person that is borne on poles by two men **2 a :** an enclosed automobile seating four to seven persons including the driver and having a single compartment and a permanent top **b :** a motorboat having one passenger compartment

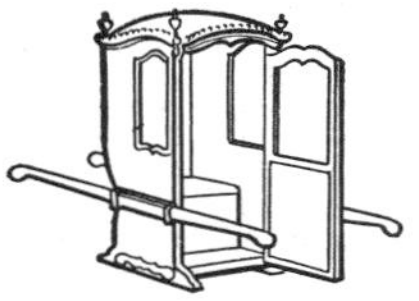

sedan 1

1**se·date** \si-ˈdāt\ *adj* [L *sedatus*, fr. pp. of *sedare* to calm; akin to *sedēre* to sit — more at SIT] **:** keeping a quiet steady attitude or pace **:** UNRUFFLED **syn** see SERIOUS — **se·date·ly** *adv* — **se·date·ness** *n*
2**sedate** *vt* [back-formation fr. *sedative*] **:** to dose with sedatives
se·da·tion \si-ˈdā-shən\ *n* **1 :** the inducing of a relaxed easy state esp. by the use of sedatives **2 :** a state resulting from or like that resulting from sedation
1**sed·a·tive** \ˈsed-ət-iv\ *adj* **:** tending to calm, moderate, or tranquilize nervousness or excitement
2**sedative** *n* **:** a sedative agent or drug
sed·en·tary \ˈsed-ᵊn-ˌter-ē\ *adj* [MF *sedentaire*, fr. L *sedentarius*, fr. *sedent-, sedens*, prp. of *sedēre* to sit] **1 :** not migratory **:** SETTLED ⟨~ birds⟩ **2 :** doing or requiring much sitting **3 :** permanently attached ⟨~ barnacles⟩
se·der \ˈsād-ər\ *n, pl* **se·da·rim** \si-ˈdär-əm\ *or* **seders** *often cap* [Heb *sēdher* order] **:** a Jewish home or community service and ceremonial dinner held on the first evening of the Passover and repeated on the second by Orthodox Jews except in Israel in commemoration of the exodus from Egypt
se·de·runt \sə-ˈdir-ənt, -ˈdā-rənt\ *n* [L, there sat (fr. *sedēre* to sit), word used to introduce list of those attending a session — more at SIT] **:** a prolonged sitting (as for discussion)
sedge \ˈsej, *dial* ˈsaj\ *n* [ME *segge*, fr. OE *secg*; akin to MHG *segge* sedge, OE *sagu* saw — more at SAW] **:** any of a family (Cyperaceae, the sedge family) of usu. tufted marsh plants differing from the related grasses in having achenes and solid stems; *esp* **:** any of a cosmopolitan genus (*Carex*) — **sedgy** \ˈsej-ē, *dial* ˈsā-jē\ *adj*
se·dil·ia \sə-ˈdē-lē-ə\ *n pl* [L, pl. of *sedile* seat, fr. *sedēre*] **:** seats on the south side of the chancel for the celebrant, deacon, and subdeacon
sed·i·ment \ˈsed-ə-mənt\ *n* [MF, fr. L *sedimentum* settling, fr. *sedēre* to sit, sink down] **1 :** the matter that settles to the bottom of a liquid **:** DREGS **2 :** material deposited by water, wind, or glaciers — **sed·i·ment** \-ˌment\ *vb*
sed·i·men·ta·ry \ˌsed-ə-ˈment-ə-rē, -ˈmen-trē\ *adj* **1 :** of, relating to, or containing sediment ⟨~ deposits⟩ **2 :** formed by or from deposits of sediment: as **a :** formed of fragments of other rock transported from its source and deposited in water ⟨sandstone and shale are ~ rocks⟩ **b :** formed by precipitation from solution ⟨rock salt and gypsum are ~ rocks⟩ **c :** formed from secretions of organisms ⟨limestone is ~ rock⟩
sed·i·men·ta·tion \ˌsed-ə-mən-ˈtā-shən, -ˌmen-\ *n* **:** the action or process of depositing sediment **:** SETTLING
se·di·tion \si-ˈdish-ən\ *n* [ME, fr. MF, fr. L *sedition-, seditio*, lit., separation, fr. *se-* apart + *ition-, itio* act of going, fr. *itus*, pp. of *ire* to go — more at SECEDE, ISSUE] **:** incitement of resistance to or insurrection against lawful authority

syn SEDITION, TREASON mean a serious breach of allegiance. SEDITION implies conduct leading to or inciting commotion or resistance to authority but without overt acts of violence or betrayal; TREASON implies an overt act aiming at overthrow of government or betrayal to the enemy

se·di·tion·ary \si-ˈdish-ə-ˌner-ē\ *n* **:** an inciter or promoter of sedition

se·di·tious \si-ˈdish-əs\ *adj* **1 :** disposed to arouse or take part in or guilty of sedition **2 :** of, relating to, or inciting to sedition — **se·di·tious·ly** *adv* — **se·di·tious·ness** *n*

se·duce \si-ˈd(y)üs\ *vt* [L *seducere* to lead away, fr. *se-* apart + *ducere* to lead — more at TOW] **1 :** to persuade to disobedience or disloyalty **2 :** to lead astray **3 :** to entice into unchastity **4 :** ATTRACT **syn** see LURE — **se·duc·er** *n*

se·duce·ment \-ˈd(y)ü-smənt\ *n* **1 :** SEDUCTION **2 :** something that serves to seduce

se·duc·tion \si-ˈdək-shən\ *n* [MF, fr. LL *seduction-, seductio,* fr. L, act of leading aside, fr. *seductus,* pp. of *seducere*] **1 :** the act of seducing to wrong; *specif* **:** the enticement of a female to unlawful sexual intercourse without use of force **2 :** something that seduces **:** TEMPTATION **3 :** something that attracts or charms **:** ALLUREMENT

se·duc·tive \-ˈdək-tiv\ *adj* **:** ALLURING, TEMPTING — **se·duc·tive·ly** *adv* — **se·duc·tive·ness** *n*

se·duc·tress \-ˈdək-trəs\ *n* [obs. *seductor* male seducer, fr. LL, fr. *seductus,* pp. of *seducere* to seduce, fr. L, to lead away] **:** a female seducer

se·du·li·ty \si-ˈd(y)ü-lət-ē\ *n* **:** sedulous activity **:** DILIGENCE

sed·u·lous \ˈsej-ə-ləs\ *adj* [L *sedulus,* fr. *sedulo* sincerely, diligently, fr. *se* without + *dolus* guile — more at IDIOT, TALE] **:** diligent in application or pursuit **:** ASSIDUOUS **syn** see BUSY — **sed·u·lous·ly** *adv* — **sed·u·lous·ness** *n*

se·dum \ˈsēd-əm\ *n* [NL, genus name, fr. L, houseleek] **:** any of a genus (*Sedum*) of fleshy widely distributed herbs of the orpine family **:** STONECROP

1see \ˈsē\ *vb* **saw** \ˈsȯ\ **seen** \ˈsēn\ **see·ing** \ˈsē-iŋ\ [ME *seen,* fr. OE *sēon;* akin to OHG *sehan* to see, OE *secgan* to say — more at SAY] *vt* **1 :** to perceive by the eye **2 a :** to have experience of **:** UNDERGO ⟨~ army service⟩ **b :** to come to know **:** DISCOVER **3 a :** to form a mental picture of **:** VISUALIZE **b :** to perceive the meaning or importance of **:** UNDERSTAND **c :** to be aware of **:** RECOGNIZE **d :** to imagine as a possibility **:** SUPPOSE ⟨couldn't ~ him as a crook⟩ **4 a :** EXAMINE, WATCH ⟨want to ~ how he handles the problem⟩ **b** (1) **:** READ (2) **:** to read of **c :** to attend as a spectator ⟨~ a play⟩ **5 a :** to take care of **:** provide for ⟨~ him through⟩ **b :** to make sure ⟨~ that order is kept⟩ **6 a :** to regard as **:** JUDGE **b :** to prefer to have ⟨I'll ~ him hanged first⟩ ⟨I'll ~ you dead before I accept your terms⟩ **c :** to find acceptable or attractive ⟨still can't ~ the design⟩ **7 a :** to call on **:** VISIT **b** (1) **:** to keep company with esp. in courtship or dating ⟨had been ~*ing* each other for a year⟩ (2) **:** to grant an interview to **:** RECEIVE ⟨the president will ~ you⟩ **8 :** ACCOMPANY, ESCORT ⟨~ the girls home⟩ **9 :** to meet (a bet) in poker or to equal the bet of (a player) **:** CALL ~ *vi* **1 a :** to give or pay attention **b :** to look about **2 a :** to have the power of sight **b :** to apprehend objects by sight **3 :** to grasp something mentally **:** UNDERSTAND **4 :** to make investigation or inquiry

syn SEE, LOOK, WATCH mean to perceive something by use of the eyes. SEE stresses the reception of visual impressions; LOOK stresses the directing of the eyes in order to see; WATCH implies a persistent observing or following with the eyes

2see *n* [ME *se,* fr. OF, fr. L *sedes* seat; akin to L *sedēre* to sit — more at SIT] **1 a** *archaic* **:** CATHEDRA **b :** a cathedral town **2 :** the charge or territory of a bishop **3 :** a person or official body vested with episcopal authority ⟨acts of the apostolic ~⟩

see·able \ˈsē-ə-bəl\ *adj* **:** capable of being seen

1seed \ˈsēd\ *n, pl* **seed** *or* **seeds** [ME, fr. OE *sǣd;* akin to OHG *sāt* seed, OE *sāwan* to sow — more at SOW] **1 a** (1) **:** the grains or ripened ovules of plants used for sowing (2) **:** the fertilized ripened ovule of a flowering plant containing an embryo and capable normally of germination to produce a new plant; *broadly* **:** a propagative plant structure (as a spore or small dry fruit) **b :** a propagative animal structure: (1) **:** MILT, SEMEN (2) **:** a small egg (as of an insect) (3) **:** a developmental form of a lower animal suitable for transplanting; *specif* **:** SPAT **c :** the condition or stage of bearing seed ⟨in ~⟩ **2 :** PROGENY **3 :** a source of development or growth **:** GERM ⟨sowed the ~*s* of discord⟩ **4 :** something that resembles a seed in shape or size (as a small bubble in glass) — **seed** *adj* — **seed·bed** \-ˌbed\ *n* — **seed·ed** \-əd\ *adj* — **seed·less** \-ləs\ *adj*

2seed *vi* **1 :** to sow seed **:** PLANT **2 :** to bear or shed seed ~ *vt* **1 a :** to plant seeds in **:** SOW ⟨~ land to grass⟩ **b :** to furnish with something that causes or stimulates growth or development **c :** INOCULATE **d :** NUCLEATE **2;** *esp* **:** to treat (a cloud) with solid particles to convert water droplets into ice crystals in an attempt to produce precipitation **2 :** PLANT 1a **3 :** to extract the seeds from (as raisins) **4 :** to schedule (tournament players or teams) so that superior ones will not meet in early rounds

seed·cake \ˈsēd-ˌkāk\ *n* **1 :** a cake or cookie containing aromatic seeds (as sesame or caraway) **2 :** OIL CAKE

seed·case \-ˌkās\ *n* **:** 2POD 1

seed coat *n* **:** an outer protective covering of a seed

seed·eat·er \ˈsēd-ˌēt-ər\ *n* **:** a bird (as a finch) whose diet consists basically of seeds — called also *hard-bill*

seed·er \ˈsēd-ər\ *n* **1 :** an implement for planting or sowing seeds **2 :** a device for seeding fruit **3 :** one that seeds clouds

seed fern *n* **:** any of an order (Cycadofilicales) of ancient plants with fronds like ferns and naked seeds

seed·ful \ˈsēd-fəl\ *adj* **:** full of seed **:** GENERATIVE

seed·i·ly \ˈsēd-ᵊl-ē\ *adv* **:** in a seedy manner

seed·i·ness \ˈsēd-ē-nəs\ *n* **:** the quality or state of being seedy

seed leaf *n* **:** COTYLEDON 2

seed·like \ˈsēd-ˌlīk\ *adj* **:** resembling a seed

seed·ling \-liŋ\ *n* **1 :** a plant grown from seed **2 :** a young plant: as **a :** a tree smaller than a sapling **b :** a nursery plant not yet transplanted — **seedling** *adj*

seed oyster *n* **:** a young oyster esp. of a size for transplantation

seed pearl *n* **1 :** a very small and often irregular pearl **2 :** minute pearls imbedded in some binding material

seed plant *n* **:** a plant that bears seeds; *specif* **:** SPERMATOPHYTE

seed·pod \ˈsēd-ˌpäd\ *n* **:** 2POD 1

seeds·man \ˈsēdz-mən\ *n* **1 :** SOWER **2 :** a dealer in seeds

seed stock *n* **:** a supply (as of seed) for planting; *broadly* **:** a source of new individuals ⟨leaving a ~ of trout in the streams⟩

seed·time \ˈsēd-ˌtīm\ *n* **:** the season of sowing

seed vessel *n* **:** PERICARP

seedy \ˈsēd-ē\ *adj* **1 a :** containing or full of seeds ⟨a ~ fruit⟩ **b :** containing many small similar inclusions ⟨glass ~ with air bubbles⟩ **2 :** inferior in condition or quality: as **a :** SHABBY, RUN-DOWN ⟨~ clothes⟩ ⟨a ~ settlement⟩ **b :** somewhat disreputable **:** SQUALID ⟨a ~ district⟩ ⟨~ entertainment⟩ **c :** slightly unwell **:** DEBILITATED ⟨felt ~ and went home early⟩

see·ing \ˈsē-iŋ\ *conj* **:** inasmuch as

Seeing Eye *trademark* — used for a guide dog trained to lead the blind

seek \ˈsēk\ *vb* **sought** \ˈsȯt\ **seek·ing** [ME *seken,* fr. OE *sēcan;* akin to OHG *suohhen* to seek, L *sagire* to perceive keenly, Gk *hēgeisthai* to lead] *vt* **1 :** to resort to **:** go to **2 a :** to go in search of **:** look for **b :** to try to discover **3 :** to ask for **:** REQUEST ⟨~*s* advice⟩ **4 :** to try to acquire or gain **:** aim at **5 :** to make an attempt **:** TRY — used with an infinitive ~ *vi* **:** to make a search or inquiry — **seek·er** *n*

seel \ˈsē(ə)l\ *vt* [alter. of ME *silen,* fr. MF *siller,* fr. ML *ciliare,* fr. L *cilium* eyelid — more at CILIA] **1 :** to close the eyes of (as a hawk) by drawing threads through the eyelids **2** *archaic* **:** to close up (one's eyes) **:** BLIND

see·ly \ˈsē-lē\ *adj* [ME *sely* — more at SILLY] *archaic* **:** pitiable esp. because of weak physical or mental condition **:** FRAIL

seem \ˈsēm\ *vi* [ME *semen,* of Scand origin; akin to ON *sōma* to beseem, *samr* same — more at SAME] **1 a** (1) **:** to give the impression of being **:** APPEAR (2) **:** to pretend to be **:** FEIGN **b :** to appear to the observation or understanding **c :** to appear to one's own mind or opinion ⟨~ to feel no pain⟩ **2 :** to give evidence of existing or being present ⟨there ~*ed* to be nothing amiss⟩

1seem·ing *n* **:** external appearance as distinguished from true character **:** LOOK

2seeming *adj* **:** apparent on superficial view **:** OSTENSIBLE **syn** see APPARENT — **seem·ing·ly** \ˈsē-miŋ-lē\ *adv*

seem·li·ness \ˈsēm-lē-nəs\ *n* **:** the quality or state of being seemly

seem·ly \-lē\ *adj* [ME *semely,* fr. ON *sœmiligr,* fr. *sœmr* becoming; akin to ON *sōma* to beseem] **1 a :** good-looking **:** HANDSOME **b :** agreeably fashioned **:** ATTRACTIVE **2 :** conventionally proper **:** DECOROUS **3 :** suited to the occasion, purpose, or person **:** FIT — **seemly** *adv*

1seep \ˈsēp\ *vi* [alter. of earlier *sipe,* fr. ME *sipen,* fr. OE *sipian;* akin to MLG *sipen* to seep] **:** to flow or pass slowly through fine pores or small openings **:** OOZE ⟨water had ~*ed* in through a crack in the ceiling⟩

2seep *n* **1 a :** a spot where a fluid (as water, oil, or gas) contained in the ground oozes slowly to the surface and often forms a pool **b :** a small spring **2 :** SEEPAGE — **seepy** \ˈsē-pē\ *adj*

seep·age \ˈsē-pij\ *n* **1 :** the process of seeping **:** OOZING **2 :** a quantity of fluid that has seeped through porous material

1seer \ˈsi(ə)r, *esp for 1 also* ˈsē-ər\ *n* **1 :** one that sees **2 a :** one that predicts events or developments **:** PROPHET **b :** a person credited with extraordinary moral and spiritual insight **3 :** one that practices divination; *specif* **:** CRYSTAL GAZER

2seer \ˈsi(ə)r\ *n, pl* **seers** *or* **seer** [Hindi *ser*] **1 :** any of various Indian units of weight; *esp* **:** a unit equal to 2.057 pounds **2 :** an Afghan unit of weight equal to 15.6 pounds

seer·ess \ˈsi(ə)r-əs\ *n* **:** a female seer **:** PROPHETESS

seer·suck·er \ˈsi(ə)r-ˌsək-ər\ *n* [Hindi *śīrśaker,* fr. Per *shīr-o-shakar,* lit., milk and sugar] **:** a light fabric of linen, cotton, or rayon usu. striped and slightly puckered

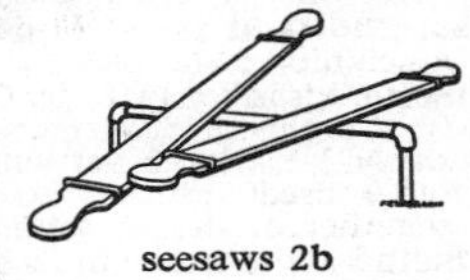

seesaws 2b

1see·saw \ˈsē-(ˌ)sȯ\ *n* [prob. fr. redupl. of 3*saw*] **1 :** an alternating up-and-down or backward-and-forward motion or movement; *also* **:** a contest or struggle in which now one side now the other has the lead **2 a :** a game in which two children or groups of children ride on opposite ends of a plank balanced in the middle so that one end goes up as the other goes down **b :** the plank or apparatus so used — **seesaw** *adj*

2seesaw *vi* **1 a :** to move backward and forward or up and down **b :** to play at seesaw **2 :** ALTERNATE ~ *vt* **:** to cause to move in seesaw fashion

1seethe \ˈsēth\ *vb* [ME *sethen,* fr. OE *sēothan;* akin to OHG *siodan* to seethe, Lith *siausti* to rage] *vt* **1 :** BOIL, STEW **2 :** to soak or saturate in a liquid ~ *vi* **1** *archaic* **:** BOIL **2 a :** to be in a state of rapid agitated movement **b :** to churn or foam as if boiling **3 :** to suffer violent internal excitement

2seethe *n* **:** a state of seething **:** EBULLITION

seeth·ing *adj* **1 :** intensely hot **:** BOILING ⟨a ~ inferno⟩ **2 :** constantly moving or active **:** AGITATED

1seg·ment \ˈseg-mənt\ *n, often attrib* [L *segmentum,* fr. *secare* to cut — more at SAW] **1 a :** a piece or separate fragment of something **:** PORTION **b** (1) **:** a portion cut off from a geometrical figure by a line or plane; *esp* **:** the part of a circular area bounded by a chord and an arc of that circle or so much of the area as is cut off by the chord (2) **:** the part of a sphere cut off by a plane or included between two parallel planes (3) **:** the finite part of a line between two points in the line **2 :** one of the constituent parts into which a body, entity, or quantity naturally divides **:** DIVISION **syn** see PART — **seg·men·tary** \ˈseg-mən-ˌter-ē\ *adj*

2seg·ment \ˈseg-ˌment\ *vt* **:** to separate into segments **:** give off as segments ~ *vi* **:** to be made up of or give off linear segments

seg·men·tal \seg-ˈment-ᵊl\ *adj* **1 :** of, relating to, or having the form of the segment or sector of a circle ⟨~ fanlight⟩ ⟨~ pediment⟩ **2 :** METAMERIC **3 :** of relating to, or resulting from segmentation **:** SUBSIDIARY ⟨~ data⟩ — **seg·men·tal·ly** \-ᵊl-ē\ *adv*

seg·men·ta·tion \ˌseg-mən-ˈtā-shən, -ˌmen-\ *n* **:** the process of dividing into segments; *esp* **:** the formation of many cells from a single cell (as in a developing egg)

segmentation cavity *n* **:** BLASTOCOEL

se·gno \ˈsān-(ˌ)yō\ *n* [It, sign, fr. L *signum*] **:** a notational sign; *specif* **:** the sign that marks the beginning or end of a musical repeat

se·go \'sē-(,)gō\ *n* [Paiute] **:** the edible bulb of the sego lily

sego lily *n* **:** a western No. American perennial herb (*Calochortus nuttallii*) of the lily family with bell-shaped flowers white within and largely green without

1**seg·re·gate** \'seg-ri-,gāt\ *vb* [L *segregatus*, pp. of *segregare*, fr. *se-* apart + *greg-*, *grex* herd — more at SECEDE, GREGARIOUS] *vt* **1 :** to separate or set apart from others or from the general mass **:** ISOLATE **2 :** to cause or force the separation of (as from the rest of society) ~ *vi* **1 :** SEPARATE, WITHDRAW **2 :** to practice or enforce a policy of segregation **3 :** to separate during meiosis — used esp. of allelic genes — **seg·re·ga·tive** \'seg-ri-,gāt-iv\ *adj*

2**seg·re·gate** \'seg-ri-gət, -,gāt\ *n* **:** a segregated individual or class of individuals

seg·re·gat·ed *adj* **1 a :** set apart or separated from others of the same kind or group ⟨a ~ account in a bank⟩ **b :** divided in facilities or administered separately for members of different groups or races ⟨~ education⟩ **c :** restricted to members of one group or one race by a policy of segregation ⟨~ schools⟩ **2 :** practicing or maintaining segregation esp. of races ⟨~ states⟩

seg·re·ga·tion \,seg-ri-'gā-shən\ *n* **1 :** the act or process of segregating **:** the state of being segregated **2 a :** the separation or isolation of a race, class, or ethnic group by enforced or voluntary residence in a restricted area, by barriers to social intercourse, by separate educational facilities, or by other discriminatory means **b :** the separation for special treatment or observation of individuals or items from a larger group ⟨~ of gifted children into accelerated classes⟩ ⟨~ of incorrigibles at a prison⟩

seg·re·ga·tion·ist \,seg-ri-'gā-sh(ə-)nəst\ *n* **:** a person who believes in or practices segregation esp. of races

se·gue \'sāg-(,)wā, 'seg-\ *v imper* [It, there follows, fr. *seguire* to follow, fr. L *sequi* — more at SUE] **:** proceed to what follows without pause — used as a direction in music

se·gui·di·lla \,seg-ə-'dē-(y)ə, -'dēl-yə\ *n* [Sp] **1 :** a Spanish stanza of four or seven short verses partly assonant **2 a :** a Spanish dance with many regional variations **b :** the music for such a dance

sei·cen·to \sā-'chen-(,)tō\ *n* [It, lit., six-hundred, fr. *sei* six (fr. L *sex*) + *cento* hundred — more at SIX, CINQUECENTO] **:** the 17th century; *specif* **:** the 17th century period in Italian literature and art

seiche \'sāsh\ *n* [F] **:** an oscillation of the surface of a lake or landlocked sea that varies in period from a few minutes to several hours

sei·del \'sīd-ᵊl, 'zīd-\ *n* [G, fr. L *situla* bucket] **:** a large glass for beer

Seid·litz powders \'sed-ləts-\ *n pl* [*Sedlitz*, Bohemia, Czechoslovakia; fr. the similarity of their effect to the water of the village] **:** effervescing salts consisting of one powder of sodium bicarbonate and Rochelle salt and another of tartaric acid that are mixed in water and drunk as a mild cathartic

sei·gneur \sān-'yər\ *n, often cap* [MF, fr. ML *senior*, fr. L, adj., elder — more at SENIOR] **:** LORD, SEIGNIOR; *esp* **:** a feudal lord

sei·gneur·ial \-'yu̇r-ē-əl, -'yər-\ *adj* **:** of, relating to, or befitting a seigneur

sei·gneury \'sān-yə-rē\ *n* **1 a :** the territory under the government of a feudal lord **b :** a landed estate held in Canada by feudal tenure until 1854 **2 :** the manor house of a Canadian seigneur

sei·gnior \sān-'yō(ə)r, 'sān-,\ *n* [ME *seignour*, fr. MF *seigneur*] **:** a man of rank or authority; *esp* **:** the feudal lord of a manor

sei·gnior·age *or* **sei·gnor·age** \'sān-yə-rij\ *n* [ME *seigneurage*, fr. MF, right of the lord (esp. to coin money), fr. *seigneur*] **:** a government revenue from the manufacture of coins calculated as the difference between the monetary and the bullion value of the silver contained in silver coins

sei·gniory *or* **sei·gnory** \'sān-yə-rē\ *n* **1 :** LORDSHIP, DOMINION; *specif* **:** the power or authority of a feudal lord **2 :** the territory over which a lord holds jurisdiction **:** DOMAIN

sei·gno·ri·al \sān-'yōr-ē-əl, -'yȯr-\ *adj* **:** of, relating to, or befitting a seignior **:** MANORIAL

1**seine** \'sān\ *n* [ME, fr. OE *segne*; akin to OHG *segīna* seine; both fr. a prehistoric WGmc word borrowed fr. L *sagena* seine, fr. Gk *sagēnē*] **:** a large net with sinkers on one edge and floats on the other used vertically to enclose fish when its ends are brought together or drawn ashore

2**seine** *vi* **:** to fish with or catch fish with a seine ~ *vt* **:** to fish for or in with a seine — **sein·er** *n*

sei·sin *or* **sei·zin** \'sēz-ᵊn\ *n* [ME *seisine*, fr. OF *saisine*, fr. *saisir* to seize — more at SEIZE] **1 :** the possession of land or chattels **2 :** the possession of a freehold estate in land by one having title thereto

seism \'sī-zəm\ *n* [Gk *seismos*] **:** EARTHQUAKE

seis·mic \'sīz-mik, 'sīs-\ *adj* [Gk *seismos* shock, earthquake, fr. *seiein* to shake; akin to Skt *tveṣati* he is violently moved] **:** of, subject to, or caused by an earthquake or an artificial earth vibration — **seis·mi·cal·ly** \-mi-k(ə-)lē\ *adv*

seis·mic·i·ty \sīz-'mis-ət-ē, sīs-\ *n* **:** the quality or state of being seismic

seis·mism \'sīz-,miz-əm\ *n* **:** earthquake phenomena

seismo- *comb form* [Gk, fr. *seismos*] **:** earthquake **:** vibration ⟨*seismo*meter⟩

seis·mo·gram \'sīz-mə-,gram, 'sīs-\ *n* [ISV] **:** the record of an earth tremor by a seismograph

seis·mo·graph \-,graf\ *n* [ISV] **:** an apparatus to measure and record vibrations within the earth and of the ground — **seis·mog·ra·pher** \sīz-'mäg-rə-fər, sīs-\ *n* — **seis·mo·graph·ic** \,sīz-mə-'graf-ik, ,sīs-\ *adj* — **seis·mog·ra·phy** \sīz-'mäg-rə-fē, sīs-\ *n*

seis·mo·log·i·cal \,sīz-mə-'läj-i-kəl, ,sīs-\ *adj* **:** of or relating to seismology — **seis·mo·log·i·cal·ly** \-k(ə-)lē\ *adv*

seis·mol·o·gist \sīz-'mäl-ə-jəst, sīs-\ *n* **:** a geophysicist who specializes in seismology **:** SEISMOGRAPHER

seis·mol·o·gy \-jē\ *n* [ISV] **:** a science that deals with earthquakes and with artificially produced vibrations of the earth

seis·mom·e·ter \-'mäm-ət-ər\ *n* **:** a seismograph measuring the actual movements of the ground — **seis·mo·met·ric** \,sīz-mə-'me-trik, ,sīs-\ *adj* — **seis·mo·met·ri·cal** \-tri-kəl\ *adj*

seis·mom·e·try \sīz-'mäm-ə-trē, sīs-\ *n* [ISV] **:** the scientific study of earthquakes

seis·mo·scope \'sīz-mə-,skōp, 'sīs-\ *n* [ISV] **:** an instrument for recording only the time or fact of occurrence of earthquakes — **seis·mo·scop·ic** \,sīz-mə-'skäp-ik, ,sīs-\ *adj*

seize \'sēz\ *vb* [ME *saisen*, fr. OF *saisir* to put in possession of, fr. ML *sacire*, of Gmc origin; akin to OHG *sezzen* to set — more at SET] *vt* **1 a** *usu* **seise** \'sēz\ **:** to vest ownership of a freehold estate in **b** *often* **seise :** to put in possession of something ⟨the biographer will be *seized* of all pertinent papers⟩ **2 a :** to take possession of **:** CONFISCATE **b :** to take possession of by legal process **3 a :** to possess or take by force **:** CAPTURE **b :** to take prisoner **:** ARREST **4 a :** to take hold of **:** CLUTCH **b :** to possess oneself of **:** GRASP **c :** to understand fully and distinctly **:** APPREHEND **5 a :** to attack or overwhelm physically **:** AFFLICT **b :** to possess (one's mind) completely or overwhelmingly **6 :** to bind or fasten together with a lashing of small stuff (as yarn, marline, or fine wire) ~ *vi* **1 :** to take or lay hold suddenly or forcibly **2 :** to cohere to a relatively moving part through excessive pressure, temperature, or friction **syn** see TAKE — **seiz·er** *n*

seiz·ing *n* **1 :** the operation of fastening together or lashing with tarred small stuff **2 a :** the cord or lashing used in seizing **b :** the fastening so made

sei·zor \'sē-,zȯ(ə)r\ *n* **:** one that seizes or takes possession esp. of a freehold estate

sei·zure \'sē-zhər\ *n* **1 a :** the act or process of seizing **:** the state of being seized **b :** the taking possession of person or property by legal process **2 :** a sudden attack (as of disease) **:** FIT

se·jant \'sē-jənt\ *adj* [modif. of MF *seant*, prp. of *seoir* to sit, fr. L *sedēre* — more at SIT] *heraldry* **:** SITTING ⟨a lion ~⟩

sel \'sel\ *chiefly Scot var of* SELF

se·la·chi·an \sə-'lā-kē-ən\ *n* [deriv. of Gk *selachos* cartilaginous phosphorescent fish; akin to Gk *selas* brightness — more at SELENIUM] **:** any of a variable group (Selachii) of elasmobranch fishes comprising all the elasmobranchs, all except the chimaeras, the existing sharks and rays, or in its most restricted use the existing sharks as distinguished from the rays — **selachian** *adj*

se·lag·i·nel·la \sə-,laj-ə-'nel-ə\ *n* [NL, genus name, fr. L *selagin-*, *selago*, a plant resembling the savin] **:** any of a genus (*Selaginella*) of mossy lower tracheophytes constituting a family (Selaginellaceae)

se·lah \'sē-lə, -,lä\ *interj* [Heb *selāh*] — a biblical term found in the Psalms and in Habakkuk and believed to have been an exclamation or musical direction

sel·couth \'sel-,küth\ *adj* [ME, fr. OE *seldcūth*, fr. *seldan* seldom + *cūth* known — more at UNCOUTH] *archaic* **:** UNUSUAL, STRANGE

1**sel·dom** \'sel-dəm\ *adv* [ME, fr. OE *seldan*; akin to OHG *seltan* seldom, L *sed*, *se* without — more at IDIOT] **:** in few instances **:** RARELY, INFREQUENTLY

2**seldom** *adj* **:** RARE, INFREQUENT

sel·dom·ness *n* **:** INFREQUENCY, RARENESS

1**se·lect** \sə-'lekt\ *adj* [L *selectus*, pp. of *seligere* to select, fr. *se-* apart (fr. *sed*, *se*) without) + *legere* to gather, select — more at LEGEND] **1 :** chosen from a number or group by fitness or preference **2 a :** of special value or excellence **:** SUPERIOR, CHOICE **b :** exclusively or fastidiously chosen often with regard to social, economic, or cultural characteristics **3 :** judicious or restrictive in choice **:** DISCRIMINATING — **se·lect·ness** \sə-'lek(t)-nəs\ *n*

2**select** *n* **:** one that is select — often used in pl.

3**select** *vt* **:** to take by preference from a number or group **:** pick out **:** CHOOSE ~ *vi* **:** to make a choice

se·lect·ed *adj* **:** SELECT; *specif* **:** of a higher grade or quality than the ordinary

se·lect·ee \sə-,lek-'tē\ *n* **:** one inducted into military service under selective service

se·lec·tion \sə-'lek-shən\ *n* **1 :** the act or process of selecting **:** the state of being selected **2 :** one that is selected **:** CHOICE; *also* **:** a collection of selected things **3 :** a natural or artificial process that prevents or tends to prevent some individuals or groups of organisms from surviving and propagating and allows others to do so **syn** see CHOICE

se·lec·tive \sə-'lek-tiv\ *adj* **1 :** of, relating to, or characterized by selection **:** selecting or tending to select **2 :** of, relating to, or constituting the ability of a radio circuit or apparatus to respond to a specific frequency without interference — **se·lec·tive·ly** *adv* — **se·lec·tive·ness** *n* — **se·lec·tiv·i·ty** \si-,lek-'tiv-ət-ē, ,sē-\ *n*

selective service *n* **:** the service of a person in the armed forces consequent to induction under a governmental act or decree

se·lect·man \si-'lek(t)-,man, -,lek(t)-'man, -'lek(t)-mən; 'sē-,lek(t)-,man\ *n* **:** one of a board of officials elected in towns of all New England states except Rhode Island to serve as the chief administrative authority of the town

se·lec·tor \-'lek-tər\ *n* **:** one that selects

1**selen-** *or* **seleno-** *comb form* [L *selen-*, fr. Gk *selēn-*, fr. *selēnē*] **:** moon ⟨*selen*ium⟩ ⟨*seleno*graphy⟩

2**selen-** *or* **seleni-** *or* **seleno-** *comb form* [Sw, fr. NL *selenium*] **:** selenium ⟨*seleni*ferous⟩ ⟨*selen*ious⟩

sel·e·nate \'sel-ə-,nāt\ *n* [Sw *selenat*, fr. *selen* selenic] **:** a salt ester of selenic acid

Se·le·ne \sə-'lē-nē\ *n* [Gk *Selēnē*] **:** the goddess of the moon in Greek mythology

se·le·nic \sə-'lēn-ik, -'len-\ *adj* [Sw *selen*, fr. NL *selenium*] **:** of, relating to, or containing selenium esp. with a relatively high valence

selenic acid *n* **:** a strong acid H_2SeO_4 whose aqueous solution attacks gold and platinum

sel·e·nif·er·ous \,sel-ə-'nif-(ə-)rəs\ *adj* [ISV] **:** containing or yielding selenium ⟨~ vegetation⟩

se·le·ni·ous \sə-'lē-nē-əs\ *adj* [ISV] **:** of, relating to, or containing selenium esp. with a relatively low valence

sel·e·nite \'sel-ə-,nīt\ *n* [L *selenites*, fr. Gk *selēnitēs* (*lithos*), lit., stone of the moon, fr. *selēnē*; fr. the belief that it waxed and waned with the moon] **:** a variety of gypsum occurring in transparent crystals or crystalline masses

se·le·ni·um \sə-'lē-nē-əm\ *n* [NL, fr. Gk *selēnē* moon; akin to Gk *selas* brightness, L *sol* sun — more at SOLAR] **:** a nonmetallic element that resembles sulfur and tellurium chemically, is obtained chiefly as a by-product in copper refining, and occurs in allotropic forms of which a gray stable form varies in electrical conductivity with the intensity of its illumination and is used in electronic devices — see ELEMENT table

selenium cell *n* **:** an insulated strip of selenium mounted with electrodes and used as a photoconductive element

se·le·no·cen·tric \sə-'lē-nə-'sen-trik\ *adj* [ISV] **:** of or relating to the center of the moon **:** referred to the moon as a center

sel·e·nog·ra·pher \,sel-ə-'näg-rə-fər\ *n* **:** a specialist in selenography

se·le·no·graph·ic \sə-ˌlē-nə-ˈgraf-ik\ *adj* **:** of or relating to selenography
sel·e·nog·ra·phy \ˌsel-ə-ˈnäg-rə-fē\ *n* **1 :** the science of the physical features of the moon **2 :** the physical geography of the moon
sel·e·nol·o·gist \-ˈnäl-ə-jəst\ *n* **:** a specialist in selenology
sel·e·nol·o·gy \-jē\ *n* **:** a branch of astronomy that deals with the moon
sel·e·no·sis \ˌsel-ə-ˈnō-səs\ *n* [NL] **:** poisoning of livestock by selenium due to ingestion of plants grown in seleniferous soils
1**self** \ˈself, *South also* ˈsef\ *pron* [ME (intensive pron.), fr. OE; akin to OHG *selb*, intensive pron., L *sui* (reflexive pron.) of oneself — more at SUICIDE] **:** MYSELF, HIMSELF, HERSELF ⟨check payable to ~⟩ ⟨accommodations for ~ and wife⟩
2**self** *adj* **1** *obs* **:** belonging to oneself **:** OWN **2** *obs* **:** IDENTICAL, SAME **3 a :** having a single character or quality throughout; *specif* **:** having one color only ⟨a ~ flower⟩ **b :** of the same kind (as in color, material, or pattern) as something with which it is used ⟨a ~ belt⟩ ⟨~ trimming⟩
3**self** *n, pl* **selves** \ˈselvz, *South also* ˈsevz\ **1 a :** the entire person of an individual **b :** the realization or embodiment of an abstraction **2 a :** an individual's typical or temporary character or behavior ⟨his true ~ was revealed⟩ ⟨his better ~⟩ **b :** a person in his normal or best condition ⟨looked like his old ~⟩ **3 :** the union of elements (as body, emotions, thoughts, sensations) that constitute the individuality and identity of a person **4 :** personal interest or advantage
4**self** *vt* **1 :** INBREED **2 :** to pollinate with pollen from the same flower or plant ~ *vi* **:** to undergo self-pollination
self- *comb form* [ME, fr. OE, fr. *self*] **1 a :** oneself or itself ⟨*self*-supporting⟩ **b :** of oneself or itself ⟨*self*-abasement⟩ **c :** by oneself or itself ⟨*self*-propelled⟩ ⟨*self*-acting⟩ **2 a :** to, with, for, or toward oneself or itself ⟨*self*-consistent⟩ ⟨*self*-addressed⟩ ⟨*self*-love⟩ ⟨*self*-satisfaction⟩ **b :** of or in oneself or itself inherently ⟨*self*-evident⟩ **c :** from or by means of oneself or itself ⟨*self*-fertile⟩
self-aban·doned \ˌsel-fə-ˈban-dənd\ *adj* **:** abandoned by oneself; *esp* **:** given up to one's impulses
self-aban·don·ment \-dən-mənt\ *n* **1 :** a surrender of one's selfish interests or desires **2 :** a lack of self-restraint
self-abase·ment \ˌsel-fə-ˈbā-smənt\ *n* **:** humiliation of oneself based on feelings of inferiority, guilt, or shame
self-ab·ne·gat·ing \ˈsel-ˈfab-ni-ˌgāt-iŋ\ *adj* **:** SELF-DENYING
self-ab·ne·ga·tion \ˌsel-ˌfab-ni-ˈgā-shən\ *n* **:** SELF-DENIAL
self-ab·sorbed \ˌsel-fəb-ˈsȯ(ə)rbd, -ˈzȯ(ə)rbd\ *adj* **:** absorbed in one's own thoughts, activities, or interests
self-ab·sorp·tion \-ˈsȯrp-shən, -ˈzȯrp-\ *n* **:** preoccupation with oneself
self-abuse \ˌsel-fə-ˈbyüs\ *n* **1** *obs* **:** SELF-DECEPTION **2 :** reproach of oneself **3 :** MASTURBATION
self-ac·cu·sa·tion \ˌsel-ˌfak-yə-ˈzā-shən\ *n* **:** the act or an instance of accusing oneself
self-ac·cu·sa·to·ry \ˌsel-fə-ˈkyü-zə-ˌtōr-ē, -ˌtȯr-\ *adj* **:** SELF-ACCUSING
self-ac·cus·ing \-ˈkyü-ziŋ\ *adj* **:** acting or serving to accuse oneself
self-ac·quired \ˌsel-fə-ˈkwī(ə)rd\ *adj* **:** acquired by oneself or for one's own use and benefit
self-act·ing \ˈsel-ˈfak-tiŋ\ *adj* **:** acting or capable of acting of or by itself **:** AUTOMATIC
self-ac·tion \-ˈfak-shən\ *n* **:** action not dependent on an external agency or force **:** independent action
self-ac·tive \-ˈfak-tiv\ *adj* **:** acting of itself without dependence on an external agency or force
self-ac·tiv·i·ty \ˌsel-ˌfak-ˈtiv-ət-ē\ *n* **:** SELF-ACTION
self-ad·dressed \ˌsel-fə-ˈdrest, ˈsel-ˈfad-ˌrest\ *adj* **:** addressed for return to the sender ⟨~ envelope⟩
self-ad·just·ing \ˌsel-fə-ˈjəs-tiŋ\ *adj* **:** adjusting by itself ⟨a ~ wrench⟩
self-ad·just·ment \-ˈjəs(t)-mənt\ *n* **:** adjustment to oneself or one's environment
self-ad·min·is·tered \ˌsel-fəd-ˈmin-ə-stərd\ *adj* **:** administered, managed, or dispensed by oneself
self-ad·mi·ra·tion \ˌsel-ˌfad-mə-ˈrā-shən\ *n* **:** SELF-CONCEIT
self-ad·vance·ment \ˌsel fəd-ˈvan(t)-smənt\ *n* **:** the act of advancing oneself
self-af·fect·ed \ˌsel-fə-ˈfek-təd\ *adj* **:** SELF-LOVING, CONCEITED
self-ag·gran·dize·ment \ˌsel-fə-ˈgran-dəz-mənt, -ˌdīz-; ˌsel-ˌfag-rən-ˈdīz-\ *n* **:** the act or process of making oneself greater (as in power or influence)
self-ag·gran·diz·ing \ˌsel-fə-ˈgran-ˌdī-ziŋ, ˈsel-ˈfag-rən-\ *adj* **:** acting or seeking to make oneself greater
self-anal·y·sis \ˌsel fə-ˈnal-ə-səs\ *n* **:** a systematic attempt by an individual to understand his own personality without the aid of another person
self-an·a·lyt·i·cal \ˌsel-ˌfan-ᵊl-ˈit-i-kəl\ *adj* **:** using self-analysis
self-an·ni·hi·la·tion \ˌsel-fə-ˌnī-ə-ˈlā-shən\ *n* **:** annihilation of the self (as in mystical contemplation of God)
self-ap·plaud·ing \ˌsel-fə-ˈplȯd-iŋ\ *adj* **:** applauding oneself
self-ap·plause \-ˈplȯz\ *n* **:** an expression or feeling of approval of oneself
self-ap·point·ed \ˌsel-fə-ˈpȯint-əd\ *adj* **:** appointed by oneself usu. without warrant or qualifications
self-ap·pro·ba·tion \ˌsel-ˌfap-rə-ˈbā-shən\ *n* **:** satisfaction with one's actions and achievements
self-as·sert·ing \ˌsel-fə-ˈsərt-iŋ\ *adj* **1 :** asserting oneself or one's own rights or claims **2 :** putting oneself forward in a confident or arrogant manner — **self-as·sert·ing·ly** \-iŋ-lē\ *adv*
self-as·ser·tion \ˌsel-fə-ˈsər-shən\ *n* **1 :** the act of asserting oneself or one's own rights or claims **2 :** the act of asserting one's superiority over others
self-as·sert·ive \-ˈsərt-iv\ *adj* **:** given to or characterized by self-assertion **syn** see AGGRESSIVE — **self-as·sert·ive·ly** *adv* — **self-as·sert·ive·ness** *n*
self-as·sump·tion \ˌsel-fə-ˈsəm(p)-shən\ *n* **:** SELF-CONCEIT
self-as·sur·ance \ˌsel-fə-ˈshu̇r-ən(t)s\ *n* **:** SELF-CONFIDENCE
self-as·sured \-ˈshu̇(ə)rd\ *adj* **:** SELF-CONFIDENT — **self-as·sured·ness** \-ˈshu̇r-əd-nəs, -ˈshu̇(ə)rd-\ *n*
self-aware·ness \ˌsel-fə-ˈwa(ə)r-nəs, -ˈwe(ə)r-\ *n* **:** an awareness of one's own personality or individuality
self-be·tray·al \ˌself-bi-ˈtrā(-ə)l\ *n* **:** SELF-REVELATION
self-bind·er \ˈself-ˈbīn-dər\ *n* **:** a harvesting machine that cuts grain and binds it into bundles
self-blind·ed \-ˈblīn-dəd\ *adj* **:** blinded or misled by oneself — **self-blind·ed·ness** *n*
self-born \-ˈbȯ(ə)rn\ *adj* **1 :** arising within the self ⟨~ sorrows⟩ **2 :** springing from a prior self ⟨phoenix rising ~ from the fire⟩
self-bur·ied \-ˈber-ēd\ *adj* **:** buried by natural forces rather than by an intentional act of man ⟨ancient ~ implements⟩
self-care \-ˈke(ə)r, -ˈka(ə)r\ *n* **:** care for oneself
self-cas·ti·ga·tion \ˌself-ˌkas-tə-ˈgā-shən\ *n* **:** SELF-PUNISHMENT
self-cen·tered \ˈself-ˈsent-ərd\ *adj* **1 :** independent of outside force or influence **:** SELF-SUFFICIENT **2 :** concerned solely with one's own desires, needs, or interests **:** SELFISH — **self-cen·tered·ly** *adv* — **self-cen·tered·ness** *n*
self-charg·ing \-ˈchär-jiŋ\ *adj* **:** that charges itself
self-clos·ing \-ˈklō-ziŋ\ *adj* **:** closing or shutting automatically after being opened
self-cock·ing \-ˈkäk-iŋ\ *adj* **:** cocked by the operation of some part of the action ⟨~ on closing the bolt⟩
self-col·lect·ed \ˌself-kə-ˈlek-təd\ *adj* **:** SELF-POSSESSED
self-col·ored \-ˈkəl-ərd\ *adj* **:** of a single color ⟨a ~ flower⟩
self-com·mand \ˌself-kə-ˈmand\ *n* **:** control of one's own behavior and emotions **:** SELF-CONTROL
self-com·pat·i·ble \-kəm-ˈpat-ə-bəl\ *adj* **:** capable of effective self-pollination that results in the production of seeds and fruits
self-com·pla·cen·cy \ˌself-kəm-ˈplās-ᵊn-sē\ *n* **:** SELF-SATISFACTION
self-com·pla·cent \-ᵊnt\ *adj* **:** SELF-SATISFIED — **self-com·pla·cent·ly** *adv*
self-com·posed \-kəm-ˈpōzd\ *adj* **:** having control over one's emotions **:** CALM — **self-com·posed·ly** \ˈpō-zəd-lē, -ˈpōz-dlē\ *adv* — **self-com·posed·ness** \-ˈpō-zəd-nəs, -ˈpōz(d)-nəs\ *n*
self-con·ceit \ˌself-kən-ˈsēt\ *n* **:** an exaggerated opinion of one's own qualities or abilities **:** VANITY — **self-con·ceit·ed** \-əd\ *adj*
self-con·cern \-ˈsərn\ *n* **:** a selfish or morbid concern for oneself — **self-con·cerned** \-ˈsərnd\ *adj*
self-con·dem·na·tion \-ˌkän-ˌdem-ˈnā-shən, -dəm-\ *n* **:** condemnation of one's own character or actions
self-con·demned \-kən-ˈdemd\ *adj* **:** condemned by oneself
self-con·fessed \-kən-ˈfest\ *adj* **:** openly acknowledged **:** AVOWED
self-con·fes·sion \-ˈfesh-ən\ *n* **:** AVOWAL
self-con·fi·dence \ˈself-ˈkän-fəd-ən(t)s, -fə-ˌden(t)s\ *n* **:** confidence in oneself and in one's powers and abilities — **self-con·fi·dent** \-fəd-ənt, -fə-ˌdent\ *adj* — **self-con·fi·dent·ly** *adv*
self-con·grat·u·la·tion \ˌself-kən-ˌgrach-ə-ˈlā-shən\ *n* **:** congratulation of oneself; *esp* **:** a complacent acknowledgment of one's own superiority or good fortune
self-con·grat·u·la·to·ry \-ˈgrach-(ə-)lə-ˌtōr-ē, -ˌtȯr-\ *adj* **:** indulging in self-congratulation
self-con·scious \ˈself-ˈkän-chəs\ *adj* **1 :** conscious of one's own acts or states as belonging to or originating in oneself **:** aware of oneself as an individual **2 :** uncomfortably conscious of oneself as an object of the observation of others **:** ill at ease — **self-con·scious·ly** *adv* — **self-con·scious·ness** *n*
self-con·se·cra·tion \ˌself-ˌkän(t)-sə-ˈkrā-shən\ *n* **:** the act or an instance of consecrating oneself
self-con·se·quence \ˈself-ˈkän(t)-sə-ˌkwen(t)s, -si-kwən(t)s\ *n* **:** SELF-IMPORTANCE
self-con·sis·ten·cy \ˌself-kən-ˈsis-tən-sē\ *n* **:** the quality or state of being self-consistent
self-con·sis·tent \ˌself-kən-ˈsis-tənt\ *adj* **:** having each part logically consistent with the rest
self-con·sti·tut·ed \ˈself-ˈkän(t)-stə-ˌt(y)üt-əd\ *adj* **:** constituted by oneself
self-con·tained \ˌself-kən-ˈtānd\ *adj* **1 :** sufficient in itself **2 a :** showing self-command **b :** formal and reserved in manner **3 :** complete in itself ⟨a ~ machine⟩ — **self-con·tained·ly** \-ˈtā-nəd-lē, -ˈtān-dlē\ *adv* — **self-con·tained·ness** \-ˈtā-nəd-nəs, -ˈtān(d)-nəs\ *n* — **self-con·tain·ment** \-ˈtān-mənt\ *n*
self-con·tam·i·na·tion \-ˌtam-ə-ˈnā-shən\ *n* **1 :** contamination by oneself **2 :** contamination from within
self-con·tem·pla·tion \ˌself-ˌkänt-əm-ˈplā-shən, -ˌkän-ˌtem-\ *n* **:** the act or an instance of contemplating oneself
self-con·tempt \ˌself-kən-ˈtem(p)t\ *n* **:** contempt for oneself
self-con·tent \-kən-ˈtent\ *n* **:** SELF-SATISFACTION
self-con·tent·ed \-əd\ *adj* **:** SELF-SATISFIED — **self-con·tent·ed·ly** *adv* — **self-con·tent·ed·ness** *n*
self-con·tent·ment \-ˈtent-mənt\ *n* **:** SELF-SATISFACTION
self-con·tra·dic·tion \ˌself-ˌkän-trə-ˈdik-shən\ *n* **1 :** contradiction of oneself **2 :** a self-contradictory statement or proposition
self-con·tra·dic·to·ry \-ˈdik-t(ə-)rē\ *adj* **:** consisting of two contradictory members or parts
self-con·trol \ˌself-kən-ˈtrōl\ *n* **:** restraint exercised over one's own impulses, emotions, or desires — **self-con·trolled** \-ˈtrōld\ *adj*
self-cor·rect·ing \ˌself-kə-ˈrek-tiŋ\ *adj* **:** acting automatically to correct or compensate for errors or weaknesses
self-cre·at·ed \ˌself-krē-ˈāt-əd, ˈself-ˈkrē-ˌāt-\ *adj* **:** created or appointed by oneself
self-crit·i·cal \ˈself-ˈkrit-i-kəl\ *adj* **:** critical of oneself
self-crit·i·cism \-ˈkrit-ə-ˌsiz-əm\ *n* **:** the act or capacity of criticizing one's own faults or shortcomings
self-cul·ti·va·tion \ˌself-ˌkəl-tə-ˈvā-shən\ *n* **:** the act of cultivating oneself
self-cul·ture \ˈself-ˈkəl-chər\ *n* **:** the development of one's mind or capacities through one's own efforts
self-de·ceit \ˌself-di-ˈsēt\ *n* **:** SELF-DECEPTION
self-de·ceived \-ˈsēvd\ *adj* **:** deceived or misled esp. respecting oneself by one's own mistake
self-de·ceiv·er \-ˈsē-vər\ *n* **:** one who practices self-deception
self-de·ceiv·ing \-viŋ\ *adj* **1 :** given to self-deception ⟨a ~ hypocrite⟩ **2 :** serving to deceive oneself ⟨~ excuses⟩
self-de·cep·tion \-ˈsep-shən\ *n* **:** the act of deceiving oneself **:** the

state of being deceived by oneself — **self–de·cep·tive** \-'sep-tiv\ *adj*
self–ded·i·ca·tion \ˌself-ˌded-i-'kā-shən\ *n* **:** dedication of oneself to a cause or ideal
self–de·feat·ing \ˌself-di-'fēt-iŋ\ *adj* **:** acting to defeat its own purpose
self–de·fense \-di-'fen(t)s\ *n* **1 :** the act of defending oneself or something that belongs or relates to oneself **2 :** a plea of justification for the use of force and esp. homicide
self–de·fen·sive \-'fen(t)-siv\ *adj* **:** given to or involving self-defense ⟨a ~ person⟩ ⟨a ~ attitude⟩
self–de·lud·ed \-di-'lüd-əd\ *adj* **:** SELF-DECEIVED
self–de·lu·sion \-di-'lü-zhən\ *n* **:** SELF-DECEPTION
self–de·ni·al \-di-'nī(-ə)l\ *n* **:** a restraint or limitation of one's own desires or interests — **self–de·ny·ing** \-'nī-iŋ\ *adj* — **self–de·ny·ing·ly** \-iŋ-lē\ *adv*
self–de·pen·dence \-'pen-dən(t)s\ *n* **:** dependence on one's own resources or exertions **:** SELF-RELIANCE — **self–de·pen·dent** \-dənt\ *adj*
self–dep·re·cat·ing \'self-'dep-ri-ˌkāt-iŋ\ *adj* **:** given to self-depreciation
self–de·pre·ci·a·tion \ˌself-di-ˌprē-shē-'ā-shən\ *n* **:** disparagement or undervaluation of oneself
self–de·spair \-di-'spa(ə)r, -'spe(ə)r\ *n* **:** despair of oneself **:** HOPELESSNESS
self–de·stroy·er \-di-'strȯi(-ə)r\ *n* **:** one who destroys himself
self–de·stroy·ing \-'strȯi-iŋ\ *adj* **:** SELF-DESTRUCTIVE
self–de·struc·tion \-di-'strək-shən\ *n* **:** destruction of oneself; *esp* **:** SUICIDE — **self–de·struc·tive** \-'strək-tiv\ *adj*
self–de·ter·mi·na·tion \-di-ˌtər-mə-'nā-shən\ *n* **1 :** free choice of one's own acts or states without external compulsion **2 :** determination by the people of a territorial unit of their own future political status — **self–de·ter·min·ing** \-di-'tərm-(ə-)niŋ\ *adj*
self–de·ter·mined \-di-'tər-mənd\ *adj* **:** determined by oneself
self–de·ter·min·ism \-di-'tər-mə-ˌniz-əm\ *n* **:** a doctrine that the actions of a self are determined by itself
self–de·vel·op·ment \-di-'vel-əp-mənt\ *n* **:** development of the capabilities or possibilities of oneself
self–de·vot·ed \-di-'vōt-əd\ *adj* **:** characterized by self-devotion — **self–de·vot·ed·ly** *adv* — **self–de·vot·ed·ness** *n*
self–de·vot·ing \-'vōt-iŋ\ *adj* **:** SELF-DEVOTED
self–de·vo·tion \-'vō-shən\ *n* **:** devotion of oneself esp. in service or sacrifice
self–de·vour·ing \ˌself-di-'vau̇(ə)r-iŋ\ *adj* **:** devouring itself
self–di·ges·tion \ˌself-(ˌ)dī-'jes(h)-chən, -də-\ *n* **:** decomposition of plant or animal tissue by internal process **:** AUTOLYSIS
self–di·rect·ed \ˌself-də-'rek-təd, -(ˌ)dī-\ *adj* **:** directed by oneself; *specif* **:** not guided or impelled by an outside force or agency ⟨a ~ personality⟩
self–di·rect·ing \-tiŋ\ *adj* **:** directing oneself
self–di·rec·tion \-'rek-shən\ *n* **:** guidance by oneself
self–dis·charg·ing \ˌself-dis(h)-'chär-jiŋ, 'self-'dis(h)-ˌ\ *adj* **:** discharging by itself
self–dis·ci·pline \'self-'dis-ə-plən, -(ˌ)plin\ *n* **:** correction or regulation of oneself for the sake of improvement
self–dis·ci·plined \-plənd, -(ˌ)plind\ *adj* **:** capable of or subject to self-discipline
self–dis·cov·ery \ˌself-dis-'kəv-(ə-)rē\ *n* **:** the act or process of achieving self-knowledge
self–dis·trib·ut·ing \-dis-'trib-yət-iŋ\ *adj* **:** distributing itself automatically
self–dis·trust \-dis-'trəst\ *n* **:** a lack of confidence in oneself **:** DIFFIDENCE — **self–dis·trust·ful** \-fəl\ *adj*
self–di·vi·sion \-də-'vizh-ən\ *n* **:** division of itself by its own action or process of growth
self·dom \'self-dəm, 'self-təm\ *n* **:** the essence of one's self **:** INDIVIDUALITY
self–doubt \'self-'dau̇t\ *n* **:** a lack of faith in oneself — **self–doubting** \-iŋ\ *adj*
self–dra·ma·ti·za·tion \ˌself-ˌdram-ət-ə-'zā-shən, -ˌdräm-\ *n* **:** the act or an instance of dramatizing oneself
self–dra·ma·tiz·ing \'self-'dram-ə-ˌtī-ziŋ, -'dräm-\ *adj* **:** seeing and presenting oneself as an actor in a drama
self–driv·en \-'driv-ən\ *adj* **:** driven by itself **:** AUTOMOTIVE
self–ed·u·cat·ed \'sel-'fej-ə-ˌkāt-əd\ *adj* **:** educated by one's own efforts without formal instruction — **self–ed·u·ca·tion** \ˌsel-ˌfej-ə-'kā-shən\ *n*
self–ef·face·ment \ˌsel-fə-'fā-smənt\ *n* **:** the placing or keeping of oneself in the background
self–ef·fac·ing \-'fā-siŋ\ *adj* **:** RETIRING — **self–ef·fac·ing·ly** \-siŋ-lē\ *adv*
self–elect·ed \ˌsel-fə-'lek-təd\ *adj* **:** SELF-APPOINTED
self–em·ployed \ˌsel-fim-'plȯid\ *adj* **:** earning income directly from one's own business, trade, or profession rather than as a specified salary or wages from an employer
self–em·ploy·ment \-'plȯi-mənt\ *n* **:** the state of being self-employed
self–en·er·giz·ing \'sel-'fen-ər-ˌjī-ziŋ\ *adj* **:** containing means for augmentation of power within itself ⟨~ brake⟩
self–en·forc·ing \ˌsel-fin-'fōr-siŋ, -'fȯr-\ *adj* **:** containing in itself the authority or means that provide for its enforcement ⟨a ~ treaty⟩
self–en·rich·ment \-fin-'rich-mənt\ *n* **:** the act or process of increasing one's intellectual or spiritual resources
self–es·teem \ˌsel-fə-'stēm\ *n* **1 :** SELF-RESPECT **2 :** SELF-CONCEIT
self–ev·i·dence \'sel-'fev-əd-ənts, -ə-ˌden(t)s\ *n* **:** the quality or state of being self-evident
self–ev·i·dent \-əd-ənt, -ə-ˌdent\ *adj* **:** evident without proof or reasoning — **self–ev·i·dent·ly** *adv*
self–ex·al·ta·tion \ˌsel-ˌfeg-ˌzȯl-'tā-shən, -ˌfek-ˌsȯl-\ *n* **:** exaltation of oneself
self–ex·alt·ing \ˌsel-fig-'zȯl-tiŋ\ *adj* **:** VAINGLORIOUS — **self–ex·alt·ing·ly** \-tiŋ-lē\ *adv*
self–ex·am·i·na·tion \ˌsel-fig-ˌzam-ə-'nā-shən\ *n* **:** INTROSPECTION
self–ex·cit·ed \ˌsel-fik-'sīt-əd\ *adj* **:** excited by a current produced by the dynamo itself ⟨~ generator⟩
self–ex·e·cut·ing \'sel-'fek-sə-ˌkyüt-iŋ\ *adj* **:** taking effect immediately without implementing legislation ⟨~ treaty⟩
self–ex·iled \'sel-'feg-ˌzīld, -'fek-ˌsīld\ *adj* **:** exiled by one's own wish or decision
self–ex·is·tence \ˌsel-fig-'zis-tən(t)s\ *n* **:** the quality or state of being self-existent
self–ex·is·tent \ˌsel-fig-'zis-tənt\ *adj* **:** existing of or by itself
self–ex·plain·ing \ˌsel-fik-'splā-niŋ\ *adj* **:** SELF-EXPLANATORY
self–ex·plan·a·to·ry \ˌsel-fik-'splan-ə-ˌtōr-ē, -ˌtȯr-\ *adj* **:** explaining itself **:** capable of being understood without explanation
self–ex·pres·sion \ˌsel-fik-'spresh-ən\ *n* **:** the expression of one's own personality **:** assertion of one's individual traits — **self–ex·pres·sive** \-'spres-iv\ *adj*
self–feed \'self-'fēd\ *vt* **:** to provide rations to (animals) in bulk so as to permit selecting food in kind and quantity as wanted — compare HAND-FEED
self–feed·er \-ər\ *n* **:** one that feeds itself automatically; *specif* **:** a device for feeding livestock that is equipped with a feed hopper that automatically supplies a trough below
self–feel·ing \'self-'fē-liŋ\ *n* **:** self-centered emotion
self–fer·tile \-'fərt-ᵊl\ *adj* **:** fertile by means of its own pollen or sperm — **self–fer·til·i·ty** \ˌself-(ˌ)fər-'til-ət-ē\ *n*
self–fer·til·iza·tion \ˌself-ˌfərt-ᵊl-ə-'zā-shən\ *n* **:** fertilization effected by pollen or sperm from the same individual — **self–fer·til·ized** \'self-'fərt-ᵊl-ˌīzd\ *adj*
self–flat·ter·ing \'self-'flat-ə-riŋ\ *adj* **:** given to self-flattery
self–flat·tery \-ə-rē\ *n* **:** the glossing over of one's own weaknesses or mistakes and the exaggeration of one's own qualities and achievements
self–for·get·ful \ˌself-fər-'get-fəl\ *adj* **:** having or showing no thought of self or selfish interests — **self–for·get·ful·ly** \-fə-lē\ *adv* — **self–for·get·ful·ness** *n*
self–for·get·ting \-'get-iŋ\ *adj* **:** SELF-FORGETFUL — **self–for·getting·ly** \-iŋ-lē\ *adv*
self–formed \'self-'fȯ(ə)rmd\ *adj* **:** formed or developed by one's own efforts
self–fruit·ful \-'früt-fəl\ *adj* **:** capable of setting a crop of self-pollinated fruit — **self–fruit·ful·ness** *n*
self–ful·fill·ing \ˌself-fu̇l-'fil-iŋ\ *adj* **:** marked by or achieving self-fulfillment
self–ful·fill·ment \-'fil-mənt\ *n* **:** fulfillment of oneself
self–giv·en \'self-'giv-ən\ *adj* **1 :** derived from itself ⟨a ~ entity⟩ **2 :** given by oneself ⟨~ authority⟩
self–giv·ing \'self-'giv-iŋ\ *adj* **:** SELF-SACRIFICING, UNSELFISH
self–glo·ri·fi·ca·tion \ˌself-ˌglōr-ə-fə-'kā-shən, -ˌglȯr-\ *n* **:** a feeling or expression of one's superiority to others
self–glor·i·fy·ing \'self-'glōr-ə-ˌfī-iŋ, -'glȯr-\ *adj* **:** BOASTFUL
self–glo·ry \-'glōr-ē, -'glȯr-ē\ *n* **:** personal vanity **:** PRIDE
self–gov·erned \-'gəv-ərnd\ *adj* **1 :** not influenced or controlled by others **2 :** exercising self-control
self–gov·ern·ing \-'gəv-ər-niŋ\ *adj* **:** having control or rule over oneself **:** not subject to outside authority; *specif* **:** having self-government **:** AUTONOMOUS
self–gov·ern·ment \-'gəv-ər(n)-mənt, -'gəv-ᵊm-ənt\ *n* **1 :** SELF-COMMAND, SELF-CONTROL **2 :** government under the control and direction of the inhabitants of a political unit rather than by an outside authority
self–grat·i·fi·ca·tion \ˌself-ˌgrat-ə-fə-'kā-shən\ *n* **:** the act of pleasing oneself or of satisfying one's desires
self–grat·u·la·tion \-ˌgrach-ə-'lā-shən\ *n* **:** SELF-CONGRATULATION
self–grat·u·la·to·ry \'self-'grach-(ə-)lə-ˌtōr-ē, -ˌtȯr-\ *adj* **:** SELF-CONGRATULATORY
self–hard·en·ing \-'härd-niŋ, -ᵊn-iŋ\ *adj* **:** hardening by itself or without quenching after heating ⟨~ steel⟩
self–hate \-'hāt\ *n* **:** hatred redirected toward one's self rather than toward others
self–hat·ing \-'hāt-iŋ\ *adj* **:** given to self-hate
self–ha·tred \-'hā-trəd\ *n* **:** SELF-HATE
self–heal \'self-ˌhēl\ *n* **:** any of several plants held to possess healing properties; *esp* **:** a blue-flowered Eurasian mint (*Prunella vulgaris*) naturalized throughout No. America
self–help \'self-'help\ *n* **:** the act or an instance of providing for or helping oneself without dependence on others
self·hood \-ˌhu̇d\ *n* **1 a :** INDIVIDUALITY **b :** PERSONALITY **2 :** SELFISHNESS
self–hum·bling \-'həm-b(ə-)liŋ, -'əm-, -bliŋ\ *adj* **:** acting or serving to humble oneself
self–hu·mil·i·a·tion \ˌself-hyü-ˌmil-ē-'ā-shən, ˌself-yü-\ *n* **:** the act or an instance of humbling oneself
self–hyp·no·sis \ˌself-hip-'nō-səs\ *n* **:** hypnosis of oneself
self–iden·ti·cal \ˌsel-ˌfī-'dent-i-kəl, -fə-\ *adj* **:** having self-identity
self–iden·ti·fi·ca·tion \-ˌdent-ə-fə-'kā-shən\ *n* **:** identification with someone or something outside oneself
self–iden·ti·ty \-'den(t)-ət-ē\ *n* **:** sameness of a thing with itself
self–ig·nite \ˌsel-fig-'nīt\ *vi* **:** to become ignited without flame or spark (as under high compression)
self–ig·ni·tion \-'nish-ən\ *n* **:** ignition without flame or spark
self–im·age \'sel-'fim-ij\ *n* **:** one's conception of oneself or of one's role
self–im·mo·la·tion \ˌsel-ˌfim-ə-'lā-shən\ *n* **:** a deliberate and willing sacrifice of oneself
self–im·por·tance \ˌself-ᵊm-'pȯrt-ᵊn(t)s, -ən(t)s\ *n* **1 :** an exaggerated estimate of one's own importance **:** SELF-CONCEIT **2 :** arrogant or pompous bearing or behavior — **self–im·por·tant** \-ᵊnt, -ənt\ *adj* — **self–im·por·tant·ly** *adv*
self–im·posed \ˌself-ᵊm-'pōzd\ *adj* **:** imposed on one by oneself **:** voluntarily assumed
self–im·prove·ment \ˌself-ᵊm-'prüv-mənt\ *n* **:** improvement of oneself by one's own action
self–in·clu·sive \ˌsel-fin-'klü-siv, -ziv\ *adj* **:** enclosing itself **:** complete in itself
self–in·crim·i·nat·ing \ˌsel-fin-'krim-ə-ˌnāt-iŋ\ *adj* **:** serving or tending to incriminate oneself
self–in·crim·i·na·tion \-ˌkrim-ə-'nā-shən\ *n* **:** incrimination of oneself; *specif* **:** the giving of evidence or answering of questions the tendency of which would be to subject one to criminal prosecution
self–in·duced \ˌsel-fin-'d(y)üst\ *adj* **:** induced by oneself; *specif* **:** produced by self-induction ⟨a ~ voltage⟩
self–in·duc·tance \-'dək-tən(t)s\ *n* **:** inductance that induces an

electromotive force in the same circuit as the one in which the current varies

self–in·duc·tion \-ˈdək-shən\ *n* **:** induction of an electromotive force in a circuit by a varying current in the same circuit

self–in·dul·gence \-ˈdəl-jən(t)s\ *n* **:** indulgence of one's own appetites, desires, or whims — **self–in·dul·gent** \-jənt\ *adj* — **self–in·dul·gent·ly** *adv*

self–in·flict·ed \ˌsel-fin-ˈflik-təd\ *adj* **:** inflicted by oneself or by one's own hand ⟨a ~ wound⟩

self–ini·ti·at·ed \ˌsel-fin-ˈish-ē-ˌāt-əd\ *adj* **:** initiated by oneself

self–in·struct·ed \-ˈstrək-təd\ *adj* **:** SELF-TAUGHT

self–in·sur·ance \ˌsel-fin-ˈshu̇r-ən(t)s, ˈsel-ˈfin-ˌ\ *n* **:** insurance of oneself or of one's own interests by the setting aside of money at regular intervals to provide a fund to cover possible losses (as in the event of fire)

self–in·sured \ˌsel-fin-ˈshu̇(ə)rd\ *adj* **:** insured by oneself

self–in·sur·er \ˌsel-fin-ˈshu̇r-ər\ *n* **:** one who practices self-insurance

self–in·ter·est \ˈsel-ˈfin-trəst; -ˈfint-ə-rəst, -ə-ˌrest, -ərst; -ˈfin-ˌtrest\ *n* **1 :** one's own interest or advantage **2 :** a concern for one's own advantage and well-being — **self–in·ter·est·ed** \-əd\ *adj* — **self–in·ter·est·ed·ness** *n*

self–in·volved \ˌsel-fin-ˈvälvd, -ˈvȯlvd\ *adj* **:** SELF-ABSORBED

self·ish \ˈsel-fish\ *adj* **1 :** concerned excessively or exclusively with oneself **:** seeking or concentrating on one's own advantage, pleasure, or well-being without regard for others **2 :** arising from concern with one's own welfare or advantage in disregard of others ⟨a ~ act⟩ — **self·ish·ly** *adv* — **self·ish·ness** *n*

self–jus·ti·fi·ca·tion \ˌself-ˌjəs-tə-fə-ˈkā-shən\ *n* **:** the act or an instance of making excuses for oneself

self–jus·ti·fy·ing \ˈself-ˈjəs-tə-ˌfī-iŋ\ *adj* **1 :** seeking to excuse oneself **2 :** automatically justifying itself ⟨a ~ typewriter⟩

self–know·ing \ˈself-ˈnō-iŋ\ *adj* **:** having self-knowledge

self–knowl·edge \ˈself-ˈnäl-ij\ *n* **:** knowledge or understanding of one's own capabilities, character, feelings, or motivations

self·less \ˈsel-fləs\ *adj* **:** having no concern for self **:** UNSELFISH — **self·less·ly** *adv* — **self·less·ness** *n*

self–lim·i·ta·tion \ˌsel-ˌflim-ə-ˈtā-shən\ *n* **:** the quality or state of being self-limiting

self–lim·it·ed \ˈsel-ˈflim-ət-əd\ *adj* **:** limited by one's or its own nature; *specif* **:** running a definite and limited course ⟨a ~ disease⟩

self–lim·it·ing \-ət-iŋ\ *adj* **:** limiting oneself or itself

self–liq·ui·dat·ing \ˈsel-ˈflik-wə-ˌdāt-iŋ\ *adj* **1 :** of or relating to a commercial transaction in which goods are converted into cash in a short time **2 :** generating funds from its own operations to repay the investment made to create it ⟨a ~ housing project⟩

self–load·er \ˈsel-ˈflōd-ər\ *n* **:** a semiautomatic firearm

self–load·ing \ˈsel-ˈflōd-iŋ\ *adj, of a firearm* **:** SEMIAUTOMATIC

self–lock·ing \ˈsel-ˈfläk-iŋ\ *adj* **:** locking by its own action

self–love \ˈsel-ˈfləv\ *n* **:** love of self: **a :** AMOUR PROPRE, VANITY **b :** regard for one's own happiness or advantage — **self–lov·ing** \-ˈfləv-iŋ\ *adj*

self–lu·bri·cat·ing \ˈsel-ˈflü-brə-ˌkāt-iŋ\ *adj* **:** lubricating itself

self–lu·mi·nous \ˈsel-ˈflü-mə-nəs\ *adj* **:** having in itself the property of emitting light

self–made \ˈself-ˈmād\ *adj* **1 :** made by oneself or itself **2 :** raised from poverty or obscurity by one's own efforts ⟨~ man⟩

self–mail·er \-ˈmā-lər\ *n* **:** a folder or broadside that can be sent by mail without enclosure in an envelope by use of a gummed sticker or a precanceled stamp to hold the leaves together

self–mail·ing \-liŋ\ *adj* **:** capable of being mailed without being enclosed in an envelope

self–mas·tery \ˈself-ˈmas-t(ə-)rē\ *n* **:** SELF-COMMAND, SELF-CONTROL

self–moved \-ˈmüvd\ *adj* **:** moved by inherent power

self–mov·er \-ˈmü-vər\ *n* **:** one that moves itself

self–mov·ing \-viŋ\ *adj* **:** capable of moving by itself

self–mur·der \-ˈmərd-ər\ *n* **:** SELF-DESTRUCTION, SUICIDE

self–naught·ing \ˈself-ˈnȯt-iŋ, -ˈnät-\ *n* **:** SELF-EFFACEMENT

self·ness \ˈself-nəs\ *n* **1 :** EGOISM, SELFISHNESS **2 :** PERSONALITY, SELFHOOD

self–ob·ser·va·tion \ˌsel-ˌfäb-sər-ˈvā-shən, -zər-\ *n* **1 :** observation of one's own appearance **2 :** INTROSPECTION

self–op·er·at·ing \ˈsel-ˈfäp-(ə-)ˌrāt-iŋ\ *or* **self–op·er·a·tive** \-ˈfäp-(ə-)rət-iv, -ˈfäp-ə-ˌrāt-\ *adj* **:** SELF-ACTING

self–opin·ion \ˌsel-fə-ˈpin-yən\ *n* **:** high or exaggerated opinion of oneself **:** SELF-CONCEIT

self–opin·ion·at·ed \-yə-ˌnāt-əd\ *adj* **1 :** CONCEITED **2 :** stubbornly holding to one's own opinion **:** OPINIONATED — **self–opin·ion·at·ed·ness** *n*

self–opin·ioned \-ˈpin-yənd\ *adj* **:** SELF-OPINIONATED

self–or·ga·ni·za·tion \ˌsel-ˌfȯrg-(ə-)nə-ˈzā-shən\ *n* **:** organization of oneself; *specif* **:** the act or process of forming or joining a labor union

self–orig·i·nat·ed \ˌsel-fə-ˈrij-ə-ˌnāt-əd\ *adj* **:** originated by oneself

self–orig·i·nat·ing \-ˌnāt-iŋ\ *adj* **:** originating by or from oneself

self–par·tial·i·ty \ˌself-ˌpär-shē-ˈal-ət-ē, -ˌpär-ˈshal-\ *n* **1 :** an excessive estimate of oneself as compared with others **2 :** a prejudice in favor of one's own claims or interests

self–per·pet·u·at·ing \ˌself-pər-ˈpech-ə-ˌwāt-iŋ\ *adj* **:** capable of continuing or renewing oneself indefinitely ⟨~ board of trustees⟩

self–per·pet·u·a·tion \-ˌpech-ə-ˈwā-shən\ *n* **:** perpetuation of oneself

self–pity \ˈself-ˈpit-ē\ *n* **:** pity for oneself; *esp* **:** a self-indulgent lingering on one's own sorrows or misfortunes — **self–pity·ing** \-ē-iŋ\ *adj* — **self–pity·ing·ly** \-iŋ-lē\ *adv*

self–pleased \-ˈplēzd\ *adj* **:** SELF-SATISFIED

self–pleas·ing \-ˈplē-ziŋ\ *adj* **:** pleasing to oneself

self–poise \-ˈpȯiz\ *n* **:** the quality or state of being self-poised

self–poised \-ˈpȯizd\ *adj* **1 :** balanced without support **2 :** having poise through self-command

self–pol·li·nate \ˈself-ˈpäl-ə-ˌnāt\ *vi* **:** to undergo self-pollination ~ *vt* **:** SELF 2

self–pol·li·na·tion \ˌself-ˌpäl-ə-ˈnā-shən\ *n* **:** the transfer of pollen from the anther of a flower to the stigma of the same flower or sometimes to that of another flower of the same plant or of another plant of the same clone

self–por·trait \ˈself-ˈpōr-trət, -ˈpȯr-, -ˌtrāt\ *n* **:** a portrait of oneself done by oneself

self–pos·sessed \ˌself-pə-ˈzest, *also* -ˈsest\ *adj* **:** having or showing self-possession **:** composed in mind or manner **:** CALM — **self–pos·sessed·ly** \-ˈzes-əd-lē, -ˈses-; -ˈzest-lē, -ˈsest-\ *adv*

self–pos·ses·sion \ˌself-pə-ˈzesh-ən, *also* -ˈsesh-\ *n* **:** control of one's emotions or reactions **:** PRESENCE OF MIND, COMPOSURE **syn** see CONFIDENCE

self–praise \ˈself-ˈprāz\ *n* **:** praise of oneself

self–pres·er·va·tion \ˌself-ˌprez-ər-ˈvā-shən\ *n* **1 :** preservation of oneself from destruction or harm **2 :** a natural or instinctive tendency to act so as to preserve one's own existence

self–pre·serv·ing \ˌself-pri-ˈzər-viŋ\ *adj* **:** acting or tending to preserve oneself

self–pride \ˈself-ˈprīd\ *n* **:** pride in oneself or that which relates to oneself

self–pro·claimed \ˌself-prō-ˈklāmd, -prə-\ *adj* **:** based on one's own say-so ⟨a ~ genius⟩

self–pro·duced \ˌself-prə-ˈd(y)üst, -prō-\ *adj* **:** produced by oneself

self–pro·pelled \ˌself-prə-ˈpeld\ *adj* **1 :** containing within itself the means for its own propulsion **2 :** mounted on or fired from a moving vehicle ⟨a ~ gun⟩

self–pro·pel·ling \-ˈpel-iŋ\ *adj* **:** SELF-PROPELLED

self–pro·pul·sion \-prə-ˈpəl-shən\ *n* **:** propulsion by one's or its own power

self–pro·tec·tion \-prə-ˈtek-shən\ *n* **:** protection of oneself **:** SELF-DEFENSE

self–pro·tec·tive \-ˈtek-tiv\ *adj* **:** serving or tending to protect oneself

self–pun·ish·ment \ˈself-ˈpən-ish-mənt\ *n* **:** punishment of oneself

self–pu·ri·fi·ca·tion \ˌself-ˌpyu̇r-ə-fə-ˈkā-shən\ *n* **:** purification of oneself ⟨moral ~⟩

self–ques·tion \ˈself-ˈkwes(h)-chən\ *n* **:** a question put to a person by himself

self–ques·tion·ing \ˈself-ˈkwes(h)-chə-niŋ\ *n* **:** examination of one's own actions and motives

self–raised \ˈsel-ˈfrāzd\ *adj* **:** raised by one's own power or effort

self–rat·ing \ˈsel-ˈfrāt-iŋ\ *n* **:** determination of one's own rating with reference to a standard educational scale or other rating device

self–re·act·ing \ˌsel-frē-ˈak-tiŋ\ *adj* **:** automatically compensating or adjusting to changed conditions

self–re·al·iza·tion \ˌsel-ˌfrē-(ə-)lə-ˈzā-shən\ *n* **:** fulfillment by oneself of the possibilities of one's character or personality

self–re·al·iza·tion·ism \-shə-ˌniz-əm\ *n* **:** the ethical theory that the highest good for man consists in realizing or fulfilling himself usu. on the assumption that he has certain inborn abilities constituting his real or ideal self

self–re·al·iza·tion·ist \-sh(ə-)nəst\ *n* **:** an advocate of self-realizationism

self–re·cord·ing \ˌsel-fri-ˈkȯrd-iŋ\ *adj* **:** making an automatic record **:** AUTOGRAPHIC ⟨~ instruments⟩

self–rec·ti·fy·ing \ˈsel-ˈfrek-tə-ˌfī-iŋ\ *adj* **:** capable of accomplishing rectification by itself

self–re·flec·tion \ˌsel-fri-ˈflek-shən\ *n* **:** INTROSPECTION

self–re·flec·tive \-ˈflek-tiv\ *adj* **:** INTROSPECTIVE

self–re·flex·ive \-ˈflek-siv\ *adj* **:** reflecting itself — **self–re·flex·ive·ness** *n*

self–ref·or·ma·tion \ˌsel-ˌfref-ər-ˈmā-shən\ *n* **:** the act or an instance of reforming oneself

self–re·gard \ˌsel-fri-ˈgärd\ *n* **1 :** regard for or consideration of oneself or one's own interests **2 :** SELF-RESPECT — **self–re·gard·ing** \-iŋ\ *adj*

self–reg·is·ter·ing \ˈsel-ˈfrej-ə-st(ə-)riŋ\ *adj* **:** registering automatically ⟨a ~ barometer⟩

self–reg·u·lat·ing \ˈsel-ˈfreg-yə-ˌlāt-iŋ\ *adj* **:** regulating oneself; *specif* **:** AUTOMATIC ⟨a ~ mechanism⟩ — **self–reg·u·la·tion** \ˌsel-ˌfreg-yə-ˈlā-shən\ *n*

self–re·li·ance \ˌsel-fri-ˈlī-ən(t)s\ *n* **:** reliance upon one's own efforts and abilities — **self–re·li·ant** \-ənt\ *adj*

self–re·nounc·ing \ˌsel-fri-ˈnau̇n(t)-siŋ\ *adj* **:** marked by self-renunciation

self–re·nun·ci·a·tion \ˌsel-fri-ˌnən(t)-sē-ˈā-shən\ *n* **:** renunciation of one's own desires or ambitions

self–re·pres·sion \ˌsel-fri-ˈpresh-ən\ *n* **:** the keeping to oneself of one's thoughts, wishes, or feelings

self–re·proach \ˌsel-fri-ˈprōch\ *n* **:** the act of blaming or accusing oneself — **self–re·proach·ful** \-fəl\ *adj*

self–re·proach·ing \-ˈprō-chiŋ\ *adj* **:** reproaching oneself — **self–re·proach·ing·ly** \-chiŋ-lē\ *adv* — **self–re·proach·ing·ness** *n*

self–re·proof \ˌsel-fri-ˈprüf\ *n* **:** the act of reproving oneself

self–re·prov·ing \-ˈprü-viŋ\ *adj* **:** feeling or expressing self-reproof — **self–re·prov·ing·ly** \-viŋ-lē\ *adv*

self–re·spect \ˌsel-fri-ˈspekt\ *n* **1 :** a proper respect for oneself as a human being **2 :** regard for one's own standing or position — **self–re·spect·ing** \-ˈspek-tiŋ\ *adj*

self–re·strain·ing \-ˈstrā-niŋ\ *adj* **:** marked by self-restraint

self–re·straint \ˌsel-fri-ˈstrānt\ *n* **:** restraint imposed on oneself **:** SELF-CONTROL

self–re·veal·ing \ˌsel-fri-ˈvē-liŋ\ *adj* **:** marked by self-revelation

self–rev·e·la·tion \ˌsel-ˌfrev-ə-ˈlā-shən\ *n* **:** revelation of one's own thoughts, feelings, and attitudes esp. without deliberate intent

self–re·ward·ing \ˌsel-fri-ˈwȯrd-iŋ\ *adj* **:** containing or producing its own reward ⟨a ~ virtue⟩

self–righ·teous \ˈsel-ˈfrī-chəs\ *adj* **:** convinced of one's own righteousness esp. in contrast with the actions and beliefs of others — **self–righ·teous·ly** *adv* — **self–righ·teous·ness** *n*

self–right·ing \ˈsel-ˈfrīt-iŋ\ *adj* **:** capable of righting itself when capsized ⟨a ~ boat⟩

self–ris·ing \ˈsel-ˈfrī-ziŋ\ *adj* **:** rising or able to rise by itself ⟨~ flour⟩

self–rule \ˈsel-ˈfrül\ *n* **:** SELF-GOVERNMENT

self–rul·ing \-ˈfrü-liŋ\ *adj* **:** SELF-GOVERNING

self–sac·ri·fice \ˈself-ˈsak-rə-ˌfīs, -fəs *also* -ˌfīz\ *n* **:** sacrifice of

oneself or one's interest for others or for a cause or ideal — **self–sac·ri·fic·ing** \-ˌfīs-iŋ, -ˌfīz- *also* -fəs-\ *adj* — **self–sac·ri·fic·ing·ly** \-iŋ-lē\ *adv*
self–sac·ri·fic·er \-ˌfīs-ər, -ˌfīz- *also* -fəs-\ *n* **:** one that practices self-sacrifice
self·same \'self-ˌsām\ *adj* **:** precisely the same **:** IDENTICAL **syn** see SAME — **self·same·ness** \-ˌsām-nəs, -'sām-\ *n*
self–sat·is·fac·tion \ˌself-ˌsat-əs-'fak-shən\ *n* **:** a usu. smug satisfaction with oneself or one's position or achievements **:** SELF-COMPLACENCY
self–sat·is·fied \'self-'sat-əs-ˌfīd\ *adj* **:** feeling or showing self-satisfaction
self–sat·is·fy·ing \-ˌfī-iŋ\ *adj* **:** giving satisfaction to oneself
self–scru·ti·ny \'self-'skrüt-ᵊn-ē, -'skrüt-nē\ *n* **:** INTROSPECTION
self–seal·ing \'self-'sē-liŋ\ *adj* **:** capable of sealing itself (as after puncture) ⟨a ~ tire⟩
self–search·ing \-'sər-chiŋ\ *adj* **:** SELF-QUESTIONING
self–seek·er \-'sē-kər\ *n* **:** one that seeks only or mainly his own advantage or pleasure — **self–seek·ing** \-kiŋ\ *n or adj*
self–se·lec·tion \ˌself-sə-'lek-shən\ *n* **:** selection of goods by retail customers from display racks or counters in a store having clerks available to help
self–ser·vice \'self-'sər-vəs\ *n* **:** the serving of oneself (as in a cafeteria or supermarket) with things to be paid for at a cashier's desk usu. upon leaving — **self–service** *adj*
self–serv·ing \-'sər-viŋ\ *adj* **:** serving one's own interests often in disregard of the truth or the reasonable interests of others
self–slaugh·ter \'self-'slȯt-ər\ *n* **:** SUICIDE
self–slaught·ered \-ərd\ *adj* **:** killed by oneself
self–slay·er \'self-ˌslā-ər\ *n* **:** one who kills himself
self–sow \'self-'sō\ *vi* **:** to sow itself by dropping seeds or by natural action (as of wind or water)
self–start·er \-'stärt-ər\ *n* **:** a more or less automatic attachment for starting an internal-combustion engine other than a crank or auxiliary engine
self–start·ing \-'stärt-iŋ\ *adj* **:** capable of starting by oneself
self–ster·ile \-'ster-əl\ *adj* **:** sterile to its own pollen or sperm
self–ste·ril·i·ty \ˌself-stə-'ril-ət-ē\ *n* **:** the quality or state of being self-sterile
self–study \'self-'stəd-ē\ *n* **:** study of oneself; *also* **:** a record of observations from such study
self–styled \-'stī(ə)ld\ *adj* **:** called by oneself ⟨~ experts⟩
self–sub·sis·tence \ˌself-səb-'sis-tən(t)s\ *n* **:** the quality or state of being self-subsistent
self–sub·sis·tent \-'sis-tənt\ *adj* **:** subsisting independently of anything external to itself
self–sub·sist·ing \-'sis-tiŋ\ *adj* **:** SELF-SUBSISTENT
self–suf·fi·cien·cy \ˌself-sə-'fish-ən-sē\ *n* **:** the quality or state of being self-sufficient
self–suf·fi·cient \-ənt\ *adj* **1 :** able to maintain oneself without outside aid **:** capable of providing for one's own needs **2 :** having an extreme confidence in one's own ability or worth **:** HAUGHTY, OVERBEARING
self–suf·fic·ing \-'fī-siŋ *also* -ziŋ\ *adj* **:** SELF-SUFFICIENT — **self–suf·fic·ing·ly** \-siŋ-lē\ *adv* — **self–suf·fic·ing·ness** *n*
self–sug·ges·tion \ˌself-sə(g)-'jes(h)-chən\ *n* **:** AUTOSUGGESTION
self–sup·port \ˌself-sə-'pō(ə)rt, -'pȯ(ə)rt\ *n* **:** independent support of oneself or itself — **self–sup·port·ed** \-əd\ *adj* — **self–sup·port·ing** \-iŋ\ *adj*
self–sur·ren·der \-sə-'ren-dər\ *n* **:** surrender of the self **:** a yielding up (as to some influence or to another person) of oneself or one's will
self–sus·tained \-sə-'stānd\ *adj* **:** sustained by oneself
self–sus·tain·ing \-sə-'stā-niŋ\ *adj* **1 :** maintaining or able to maintain oneself by independent effort **2 :** maintaining or able to maintain itself once commenced ⟨a ~ nuclear reaction⟩
self–taught \'self-'tȯt\ *adj* **1 :** having knowledge or skills acquired by one's own efforts without formal instruction **2 :** learned by oneself ⟨~ knowledge⟩
self–tight·en·ing \'self-'tīt-niŋ, -ᵊn-iŋ\ *adj* **:** tightening by itself
self–tor·ment \'self-'tȯr-ˌment\ *n* **:** the act of tormenting oneself — **self–tor·ment·ing** \ˌself-tȯr-'ment-iŋ, 'self-'tȯr-ˌ\ *adj* — **self–tor·men·tor** \ˌself-tȯr-'ment-ər, 'self-'tȯr-ˌ\ *n*
self–treat·ment \'self-'trēt-mənt\ *n* **:** medication of oneself or treatment of one's own disease without medical supervision or prescription
self–trust \'self-'trəst\ *n* **:** SELF-CONFIDENCE
self–un·der·stand·ing \ˌsel-ˌfən-dər-'stan-diŋ\ *n* **:** SELF-KNOWLEDGE
self–un·fruit·ful \ˌsel-ˌfən-'früt-fəl\ *adj* **:** setting few or no fruits in the absence of cross-pollination — **self–un·fruit·ful·ness** *n*
self–un·load·ing \ˌsel-ˌfən-'lōd-iŋ\ *adj* **:** unloading itself ⟨~ freighter⟩
self–will \'self-'wil\ *n* **:** stubborn or willful adherence to one's own desires or ideas **:** OBSTINACY
self–willed \-'wild\ *adj* **:** governed by one's own will **:** not yielding to the wishes of others **:** OBSTINATE — **self–willed·ly** \-'wil-(d)lē\ *adv* — **self–willed·ness** \-'wil(d)-nəs\ *n*
self–wind·ing \'self-'wīn-diŋ\ *adj* **:** not needing to be wound by hand ⟨a ~ watch⟩
self–wor·ship \'self-'wər-shəp\ *n* **:** worship of oneself — **self–wor·ship·er** *n*
Sel·juk \'sel-ˌjük, sel-'\ *or* **Sel·ju·ki·an** \sel-'jü-kē-ən\ *adj* [Turk *Selçuk*, eponymous ancestor of the dynasties] **1 :** of or relating to any of several Turkish dynasties ruling over a great part of western Asia in the 11th, 12th, and 13th centuries **2 :** of, relating to, or characteristic of a Turkish people ruled over by a Seljuk dynasty — **Seljuk** *or* **Seljukian** *n*
¹**sell** \'sel\ *vb* **sold** \'sōld\ **sell·ing** [ME *sellen*, fr. OE *sellan;* akin to OHG *sellen* to sell, ON *sala* sale, Gk *helein* to take] *vt* **1 :** to deliver or give up in violation of duty, trust, or loyalty **:** BETRAY **2 a** (1) **:** to give up (property) to another for money or other valuable consideration (2) **:** to offer for sale **b :** to give up in return for something else esp. foolishly or dishonorably ⟨*sold* his birthright for a mess of pottage⟩ **c :** to exact a price for **3 a :** to deliver into slavery for money **b :** to give into the power of another **c :** to deliver the personal services of for money **4 :** to dispose of or manage for profit instead of in accordance with conscience, justice, or duty ⟨*sold* his vote⟩ **5 a :** to develop a belief in the truth, value, or desirability of **b :** to persuade or influence to a course of action or to the acceptance of something ⟨~ children on reading⟩ **6 :** to impose upon **:** CHEAT ⟨realized that he had been *sold*⟩ **7 a :** to cause or promote the sale of **b :** to make or attempt to make sales to **c :** to influence or induce to make a purchase ~ *vi* **1 :** to dispose of something by sale **2 :** to achieve a sale **3 :** to have a specified price — **sell·able** \-ə-bəl\ *adj* — **sell short 1 :** to make a short sale ⟨made a fortune by *selling short*⟩ **2 :** to fail to value properly **:** UNDERESTIMATE ⟨made the mistake of *selling* his rival *short*⟩
²**sell** *n* **1 :** a deliberate deception **:** HOAX **2 :** the act or an instance of selling **:** SALESMANSHIP
³**sell** *or* **selle** \'sel\ *n* [ME *selle*, fr. MF, fr. L *sella* — more at SETTLE] *archaic* **:** SADDLE
⁴**sell** \'sel\ *chiefly Scot var of* SELF
sell·er \'sel-ər\ *n* **1 :** one that offers for sale **2 :** a product offered for sale and selling well or to a specified extent
sell·ing–plat·er \'sel-iŋ-ˌplāt-ər\ *n* **:** a horse that runs in selling races
selling race *n* **:** a claiming race in which the winning horse is put up for auction
sell off *vt* **:** to dispose of by selling esp. completely ~ *vi* **:** to suffer a drop in prices
sell–off \'sel-ˌȯf\ *n* **:** a decline in prices of stocks or bonds
sell out *vt* **1 :** to dispose of entirely by sale **2 :** to sell the goods of (a debtor) in order to satisfy creditors **3 a :** to sell (as stocks or commodities) in open market to satisfy an uncovered margin or other unpaid obligation **b :** to sell the stocks or commodities of in such manner ~ *vi* **1 :** to dispose of one's goods by sale **2 :** to betray one's cause or associates
sell·out \'sel-ˌau̇t\ *n* **1 :** the act or an instance of selling out **2 :** a show, exhibition, or contest for which all seats are sold
sel·syn \'sel-ˌsin\ *n* [*self-syn*chronizing] **:** a system comprising a generator and a motor so connected by wire that angular rotation or position in the generator is reproduced simultaneously in the motor — called also *synchro*
selt·zer \'selt-sər\ *n* [modif. of G *Selterser* (*wasser*) water of Selters, fr. Nieder *Selters*, Germany] **:** an artificially prepared mineral water containing carbon dioxide
sel·vage *or* **sel·vedge** \'sel-vij\ *n* [ME *selvage*, prob. fr. MFlem *selvegge*, *selvage*, fr. *selv* self + *egge* edge; akin to OE *self* and to OE *ecg* edge — more at EDGE] **1 a :** the edge on either side of a woven or flat-knitted fabric so finished as to prevent raveling; *specif* **:** a narrow border often of different or heavier threads than the fabric and sometimes in a different weave **b :** an edge (as of fabric or paper) meant to be cut off and discarded **2 :** BORDER, EDGE **3 :** the edge plate of a lock through which the bolt is projected — **sel·vaged** *or* **sel·vedged** \-vijd\ *adj*
selves *pl of* SELF
se·man·tic \si-'mant-ik\ *adj* [Gk *sēmantikos* significant, fr. *sēmainein* to signify, mean, fr. *sēma* sign, token; akin to Skt *dhyāti* he thinks] **1 :** of or relating to meaning in language **2 :** of or relating to semantics — **se·man·ti·cal** \-i-kəl\ *adj* — **se·man·ti·cal·ly** \-k(ə-)lē\ *adv*
se·man·ti·cist \-'mant-ə-səst\ *n* **:** a specialist in semantics
se·man·tics \si-'mant-iks\ *n pl but sing or pl in constr* **1 :** the study of meanings: **a :** the historical and psychological study and the classification of changes in the signification of words or forms viewed as factors in linguistic development **b** (1) **:** SEMIOTIC (2) **:** a branch of semiotic dealing with the relations between signs and what they refer to and including theories of denotation, extension, naming, and truth **2 :** GENERAL SEMANTICS **3 a :** the meaning or relationship of meanings of a sign or set of signs; *esp* **:** connotative meaning **b :** the exploitation of connotation and ambiguity (as in propaganda)
¹**sema·phore** \'sem-ə-ˌfō(ə)r, -ˌfȯ(ə)r\ *n* [Gk *sēma* sign, signal + ISV *-phore*] **1 :** an apparatus for visual signaling (as by the position of one or more movable arms) **2 :** a system of visual signaling by two flags held one in each hand
²**semaphore** *vb* **:** to signal by or as if by semaphore
se·ma·si·o·log·i·cal \si-ˌmā-sē-ə-'läj-i-kəl, -zē-\ *adj* **:** SEMANTIC — **se·ma·si·o·log·i·cal·ly** \-k(ə-)lē\ *adv*
se·ma·si·ol·o·gist \-'äl-ə-jəst\ *n* **:** SEMANTICIST
se·ma·si·ol·o·gy \-jē\ *n* [ISV, fr. Gk *sēmasia* meaning, fr. *sēmainein* to mean] **:** SEMANTICS 1a, 1b

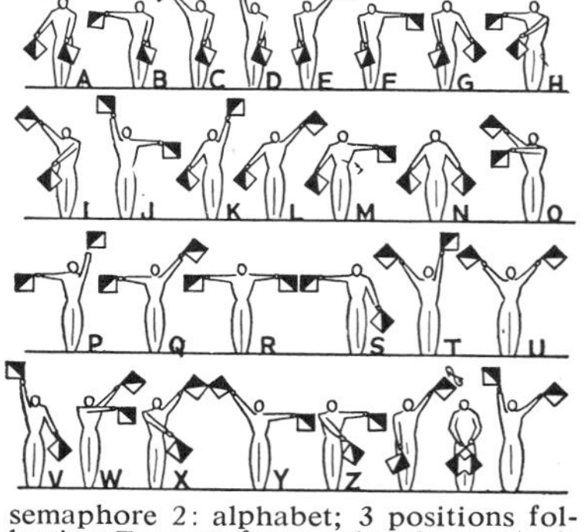

semaphore 2: alphabet; 3 positions following *Z:* error, front *or* break, numerals follow; numerals *1, 2, 3, 4, 5, 6, 7, 8, 9, 0* same as *A* through *J*

se·mat·ic \si-'mat-ik\ *adj* [Gk *sēmat-*, *sēma* sign] **:** warning of danger — used of conspicuous colors of a poisonous or noxious animal
¹**sem·bla·ble** \'sem-blə-bəl\ *adj* [ME, fr. MF, fr. OF, fr. *sembler* to be like, seem] **1 :** SIMILAR **2 :** SUITABLE **3 :** APPARENT, SEEMING — **sem·bla·bly** \-blə-blē\ *adv*
²**semblable** *n* **1** *archaic* **:** something similar **:** LIKE **2 :** one that is like oneself **:** one's fellow
sem·blance \'sem-blən(t)s\ *n* [ME, fr. MF, fr. OF *sembler* to be like, seem — more at RESEMBLE] **1 :** the outward appearance **:** FORM **2 :** COUNTENANCE, ASPECT **3 a :** phantasmal form **:** APPARITION **b :** IMAGE, LIKENESS **4 :** actual or apparent resemblance **5 :** specious appearance **6 :** slightest appearance
se·mé \sə-'mā, 'sem-(ˌ)ā\ *adj* [MF, pp. of *semer* to sow, fr. L *seminare*, fr. *semen*] **:** having an ornamental pattern consisting of usu. regularly disposed separate objects or groups of small figures (as flowers or stars) **:** SOWN, DOTTED — **semé** *n*
se·men \'sē-mən\ *n, pl* **sem·i·na** \'sem-ə-nə\ *or* **semens** [NL, fr. L, seed; akin to OHG *sāmo* seed, L *serere* to sow — more at SOW] **:** a viscid whitish fluid of the male reproductive tract con-

sisting of spermatozoa suspended in secretions of accessory glands
se·mes·ter \sə-'mes-tər\ *n* [G, fr. L *semestris* half-yearly, fr. *sex* six + *mensis* month — more at SIX, MOON] **1 :** a period of six months **2 :** either of the two usu. 18-week periods of instruction into which an academic year is usu. divided — **se·mes·tral** \-trəl\ *or* **se·mes·tri·al** \-trē-əl\ *adj*
semi- \,sem-i, 'sem-, -,ī\ *prefix* [ME, fr. L; akin to OHG *sāmi-* half, Gk *hēmi-*] **1 a :** precisely half of: (1) **:** forming a bisection of ⟨*semi*ellipse⟩ ⟨*semi*oval⟩ (2) **:** being a usu. vertically bisected form of (a specified architectural feature) ⟨*semi*arch⟩ ⟨*semi*dome⟩ **b :** half in quantity or value **:** half of or occurring halfway through a specified period of time ⟨*semi*annual⟩ ⟨*semi*centenary⟩ — compare BI- **2 :** to some extent **:** partly **:** incompletely ⟨*semi*civilized⟩ ⟨*semi*-independent⟩ ⟨*semi*dry⟩ — compare DEMI-, HEMI- **3 a :** partial **:** incomplete ⟨*semi*consciousness⟩ ⟨*semi*darkness⟩ **b :** having some of the characteristics of ⟨*semi*porcelain⟩ **c :** quasi ⟨*semi*governmental⟩ ⟨*semi*monastic⟩
semi·ab·stract \,sem-ē-(,)ab-'strakt, ,sem-,ī-, -'ab-,\ *adj* **:** having the character of a semiabstraction
semi·ab·strac·tion \-(,)ab-'strak-shən\ *n* **:** a composition or creation (as in painting or sculpture) in which the subject matter is easily recognizable though the form is stylized according to an abstract system or device
semi·an·nu·al \,sem-ē-'an-yə(-wə)l, ,sem-,ī-\ *adj* **:** occurring every six months or twice a year — **semi·an·nu·al·ly** \-ē\ *adv*
semi·aquat·ic \-ə-'kwät-ik, -'kwat-\ *adj* **:** growing indifferently in or adjacent to water; *also* **:** frequenting but not living wholly in water
semi·ar·bo·re·al \-(,)är-'bōr-ē-əl, -'bȯr-\ *adj* **:** often inhabiting and frequenting trees
semi·ar·id \-'ar-əd\ *adj* **:** characterized by light rainfall; *specif* **:** having from about 10 to 20 inches of annual precipitation
semi·au·to·mat·ic \-,ȯt-ə-'mat-ik\ *adj* **:** not fully automatic: as **a :** operated partly automatically and partly by hand **b** *of a firearm* **:** employing gas pressure or force of recoil and mechanical spring action to eject the empty cartridge case after the first shot and load the next cartridge from the magazine but requiring release and another pressure of the trigger for each successive shot — **semiautomatic** *n* — **semi·au·to·mat·i·cal·ly** \-i-k(ə-)lē\ *adv*
semi·au·ton·o·mous \-(,)ȯ-'tän-ə-məs\ *adj* **:** chiefly self-governing within a larger political or organizational entity
semi·base·ment \'sem-i-,bā-smənt, 'sem-,ī-\ *n* **:** a basement that is below ground level for only part of its depth
semi·breve \'sem-i-,brēv, 'sem-,ī-, -,brev\ *n* **:** WHOLE NOTE
semi·cen·te·na·ry \,sem-i-(,)sen-'ten-ə-rē, ,sem-,ī-, -'sent-ᵊn-,er-ē\ *adj or n* **:** SEMICENTENNIAL
semi·cen·ten·ni·al \-(,)sen-'ten-ē-əl\ *n* **:** a 50th anniversary or its celebration — **semicentennial** *adj*
semi·cir·cle \'sem-i-,sər-kəl\ *n* [L *semicirculus*, fr. *semi-* + *circulus* circle] **1 :** a half of a circle **2 :** an object or arrangement of objects in the form of a half circle — **semi·cir·cu·lar** \,sem-i-'sər-kyə-lər\ *adj*
semicircular canal *n* **:** any one of the loop-shaped tubular parts of the labyrinth of the ear that together constitute a sensory organ associated with the maintenance of bodily equilibrium
semi·civ·i·lized \,sem-i-'siv-ə-,līzd, ,sem-,ī-\ *adj* **:** partly civilized
semi·clas·sic \-'klas-ik\ *n* **:** a semiclassical work (as of music)
semi·clas·si·cal \-i-kəl\ *adj* **1 :** having some of the characteristics of the classical: as **a :** of, relating to, or being a musical composition that acts as a bridge between classical and popular music **b :** of, relating to, or being a classical composition that has developed popular appeal **2 :** inferior to the classical in importance or quality ⟨a ~ theory in physics⟩
semi·co·lon \'sem-i-,kō-lən\ *n* **:** a punctuation mark ; used chiefly in a coordinating function between major sentence elements
semi·co·lo·nial \,sem-i-kə-'lō-nyəl, -nē-əl\ *adj* **1 :** nominally independent but actually under foreign domination **2 :** dependent on foreign nations for supplying manufactured goods and for purchasing raw materials — **semi·co·lo·nial·ism** \-nyə-,liz-əm, -nē-ə-,liz-\ *n*
semi·com·mer·cial \-kə-'mər-shəl\ *adj* **:** of, relating to, or adapted to limited marketing of an experimental product
semi·con·duct·ing \-kən-'dək-tiŋ\ *adj* **:** of, relating to, or having the characteristics of a semiconductor
semi·con·duc·tor \,sem-i-kən-'dək-tər, ,sem-,ī-\ *n* **:** one of a class of solids (as germanium or silicon) whose electrical conductivity is between that of a conductor and that of an insulator in being nearly metallic at high temperatures and nearly absent at low temperatures
semi·con·scious \-'kän-chəs\ *adj* **:** half conscious — **semi·con·scious·ly** *adv* — **semi·con·scious·ness** *n*
semi·crus·ta·ceous \-,krəs-'tā-shəs\ *adj* **:** tending to form a somewhat crisp or brittle layer
semi·crys·tal·line \-'kris-tə-lən\ *adj* **:** partly crystalline
semi·dark·ness \-'därk-nəs\ *n* **:** partial darkness
semi·des·ert \-'dez-ərt\ *n* **:** an area having some of the characteristics of a desert and often lying between a desert and grassland or woodland
semi·de·tached \-di-'tacht\ *adj* **:** forming one of a pair of residences joined into one building by a common side wall
semi·di·am·e·ter \,sem-i-(,)dī-'am-ət-ər\ *n* **:** RADIUS; *specif* **:** the apparent radius of a generally spherical heavenly body
semi·di·ur·nal \,sem-i-(,)dī-'ərn-ᵊl\ *adj* **1 :** relating to or accomplished in half a day **2 :** occurring twice a day **3 :** occurring approximately every half day ⟨the ~ tides⟩
semi·di·vine \,sem-i-də-'vīn, ,sem-,ī-\ *adj* **:** more than mortal but not fully divine
semi·doc·u·men·ta·ry \,sem-i-,däk-yə-'ment-ə-rē, ,sem-,ī-, -'men-trē\ *n* **:** a motion picture that sets a fictional story in a factual background or tells a story true to the type of an actual story or true in outline but not literally true — **semidocumentary** *adj*
semi·dome \'sem-i-,dōm, 'sem-,ī-\ *n* **:** a roof or ceiling covering a semicircular or nearly semicircular room or recess — **semi·domed** \-,dōmd\ *adj*
semi·do·mes·ti·cat·ed \,sem-i-də-'mes-ti-,kāt-əd, ,sem-,ī-\ *adj* **:** of, relating to, or living in semidomestication
semi·do·mes·ti·ca·tion \-,mes-ti-'kā-shən\ *n* **:** a captive state (as in a zoo) of a wild animal in which its living conditions and often its breeding are controlled by man
semi·dou·ble \-'dəb-əl\ *adj* **:** having more than the normal number of petals or ray florets though retaining some pollen-bearing stamens or some perfect disk florets ⟨~ flowers⟩
semi·dry \,sem-i-'drī\ *adj* **:** moderately dry
semi·dry·ing \,sem-i-'drī-iŋ\ *adj* **:** that dries imperfectly or slowly — used of some oils (as cottonseed oil)
semi·ear·ly \,sem-ē-'ər-lē, ,sem-,ī-\ *adj, of a plant* **:** intermediate in bloom or maturity between an early and a later variety
semi·el·lipse \-ə-'lips\ *n* **:** the part of an ellipse from one end of usu. the transverse diameter to the other — **semi·el·lip·tic** \-ə-'lip-tik\ *or* **semi·el·lip·ti·cal** \-ti-kəl\ *adj*
semi·erect \,sem-ē-ə-'rekt, ,sem-,ī-ə-\ *adj* **:** imperfectly erect ⟨~ primates⟩
semi·ev·er·green \-'ev-ər-,grēn\ *adj* **:** HALF-EVERGREEN
[1]**semi·fi·nal** \,sem-i-'fīn-ᵊl\ *adj* **1 :** being next to the last in an elimination tournament ⟨~ pairings⟩ **2 :** of or participating in a semifinal
[2]**semi·fi·nal** \'sem-i-,\ *n* **1 :** a semifinal match **2 :** a semifinal round — **semi·fi·nal·ist** \,sem-i-'fīn-ᵊl-əst\ *n*
semi·fin·ished \,sem-i-'fin-isht, ,sem-,ī-\ *adj, of steel* **:** rolled from raw ingots into shapes (as bars, billets, or plates) ready for further processes
semi·fit·ted \-'fit-əd\ *adj* **:** partly fitted
semi·flex·i·ble \-'flek-sə-bəl\ *adj* **1 :** somewhat flexible **2** *of a book cover* **:** consisting of a heavy flexible board under the covering material
semi·flu·id \-'flü-əd\ *adj* **:** having the qualities of both a fluid and a solid **:** VISCOUS ⟨fluid and ~ greases⟩ — **semifluid** *n*
semi·for·mal \-'fȯr-məl\ *adj* **:** being or suitable for an occasion of moderate formality ⟨a ~ dinner⟩ ⟨~ gowns⟩
semi·fos·sil \-'fäs-əl\ *adj* **:** incompletely fossilized
semi·glob·u·lar \-'gläb-yə-lər\ *adj* **:** having the form of half a sphere
semi·gloss \'sem-i-,gläs, 'sem-,ī-, -,glȯs\ *adj* **:** having a low luster
semi·gov·ern·men·tal \,sem-i-,gəv-ər(n)-'ment-ᵊl, ,sem-,ī-, -,gəv-ᵊm-'ent-\ *adj* **:** having some governmental functions and powers
semi·hard \-'härd\ *adj* **:** moderately hard; *specif* **:** that can be cut with little difficulty
semi·hol·i·day \,sem-i-'häl-ə-,dā, ,sem-,ī-\ *n* **:** a weekday during a religious festival (as the Passover) on which ceremonial observances continue but activities prohibited on full festival days are permitted though discouraged
semi–in·de·pen·dent \,sem-ē-,in-də-'pen-dənt, ,sem-,ī-\ *adj* **:** partially independent; *specif* **:** SEMIAUTONOMOUS
semi–in·di·rect \-,in-də-'rekt, -(,)dī-\ *adj, of lighting* **:** using a translucent reflector that transmits some primary light while reflecting most of it
semi·late \-'lāt\ *adj, of a plant* **:** intermediate in season between middle-of-the-season and late forms
semi·leg·en·dary \-'lej-ən-,der-ē\ *adj* **:** elaborated in legend but having a dubious historical existence
semi·liq·uid \-'lik-wəd\ *adj* **:** having the qualities of both a liquid and a solid **:** SEMIFLUID ⟨~ peat⟩ — **semiliquid** *n*
semi·lit·er·ate \-'lit-ə-rət, -'li-trət\ *adj* **1 :** able to read and write on an elementary level **2 :** able to read but unable to write
semi·log·a·rith·mic \-,lȯg-ə-'rith-mik, -,läg-\ *also* **semi·log** \'sem-i-,lȯg, 'sem-,ī-, -,läg\ *adj* **:** having one scale logarithmic and the other arithmetic — used of graph paper or of a graph on such paper
semi·lu·nar \,sem-i-'lü-nər, ,sem-,ī-\ *adj* [NL *semilunaris*, fr. L *semi-* + *lunaris* lunar] **:** shaped like a crescent
semilunar valve *n* **:** any of the crescentic cusps that occur as a set of three between the heart and the aorta and another of three between the heart and the pulmonary artery, are forced apart by pressure in the ventricles during systole and pushed together by pressure in the arteries during diastole, and prevent regurgitation of blood into the ventricles; *also* **:** either set of three cusps
semi·lus·trous \-'ləs-trəs\ *adj* **:** slightly lustrous
semi·man·u·fac·tures \-,man-(y)ə-'fak-chərz\ *n pl* **:** products (as steel, rubber, newsprint) made from raw materials and used to manufacture finished goods
semi·mat *or* **semi·matt** *or* **semi·matte** \,sem-i-'mat, ,sem-,ī-\ *adj* [*semi-* + [4]*mat*] **:** having a slight luster
semi·met·al \-'met-ᵊl\ *n* **:** an element (as arsenic) possessing metallic properties in an inferior degree and not malleable — **semi·me·tal·lic** \-mə-'tal-ik\ *adj*
semi·moist \-'mȯist\ *adj* **:** slightly moist
semi·mo·nas·tic \-mə-'nas-tik\ *adj* **:** having some features characteristic of a monastic order
[1]**semi·month·ly** \,sem-i-'mən(t)th-lē, ,sem-,ī-\ *adj* **:** occurring twice a month
[2]**semimonthly** *n* **:** a semimonthly publication
[3]**semimonthly** *adv* **:** twice a month
semi·mys·ti·cal \,sem-i-'mis-ti-kəl, ,sem-,ī-\ *adj* **:** having some of the qualities of mysticism
sem·i·nal \'sem-ən-ᵊl\ *adj* [ME, fr. MF, fr. L *seminalis*, fr. *semin-*, *semen* seed — more at SEMEN] **1 :** of, relating to, or consisting of seed or semen **2 :** having the character of an originative power, principle, or source **:** containing or contributing the seeds of later development **:** GERMINATIVE, ORIGINAL — **sem·i·nal·ly** \-ᵊl-ē\ *adv*
sem·i·nar \'sem-ə-,när\ *n* [G, fr. L *seminarium* seminary] **1 :** a group of advanced students studying under a professor with each doing original research and all exchanging results through reports and discussions **2 a :** a course of study pursued by a seminar **b :** a scheduled meeting of a seminar or a room for such meetings **3 :** a meeting for giving and discussing information **:** CONFERENCE ⟨a three-day sales ~⟩
sem·i·nar·i·an \,sem-ə-'ner-ē-ən\ *n* **:** a student in a seminary esp. of the Roman Catholic Church
sem·i·nary \'sem-ə-,ner-ē\ *n* [ME, seedbed, nursery, seminary, fr. L *seminarium*, fr. *semin-*, *semen* seed] **1 :** an environment in which something originates and from which it is propagated ⟨a ~ of vice and crime⟩ **2 a :** an institution of secondary or higher education; *specif* **:** an academy for girls **b :** an institution for the training of candidates for the priesthood, ministry, or rabbinate

sem·i·nif·er·ous \,sem-ə-'nif-(ə-)rəs\ *adj* [L *semin-*, *semen* seed + E *-iferous*] : producing or bearing seed or semen

sem·i·niv·o·rous \-'niv-ə-rəs\ *adj* [prob. fr. (assumed) NL *seminivorus*, fr. L *semin-*, *semen* + *-vorus* *-vorous*] : feeding on seeds

Sem·i·nole \'sem-ə-,nōl\ *n*, *pl* **Seminole** *or* **Seminoles** [Creek *simaló-ni*, *simanó-li*, lit., wild, fr. AmerSp *cimarrón*] 1 : a Muskogean people of Florida 2 : a member of the Seminole people

semi·no·mad \,sem-i-'nō-,mad, ,sem-,ī-\ *n* : a member of a people living usu. in portable or temporary dwellings and practicing seasonal migration but having a base camp at which some crops are cultivated — **semi·no·mad·ic** \-nō-'mad-ik\ *adj*

semi·of·fi·cial \,sem-ē-ə-'fish-əl, ,sem-,ī-\ *adj* : having some official authority or standing ⟨a ∼ statement⟩ — **semi·of·fi·cial·ly** \-'fish-(ə-)lē\ *adv*

semi·opaque \-ō-'pāk\ *adj* : nearly opaque

semi·o·sis \,sem-ē-'ō-səs, ,sem-,ī-\ *n* [NL, fr. Gk *sēmeiōsis* observation of signs, fr. *sēmeioun*] : a process in which something functions as a sign to an organism

semi·ot·ic \,sem-ē-'ät-ik, ,sem-ē-, -'ōt-\ *n*, *pl* **semi·o·tics** \-iks\ *but sing or pl in constr* [Gk *sēmeiōtikos* observant of signs, fr. *sēmeiousthai* to interpret signs, fr. *sēmeion* sign; akin to Gk *sēma* sign — more at SEMANTIC] : a general philosophical theory of signs and symbols that deals esp. with their function in both artificially constructed and natural languages and comprises syntactics, semantics, and pragmatics — **semiotic** *also* **semi·o·ti·cal** \-i-kəl\ *adj* — **semi·o·ti·cian** \,sem-ē-ə-'tish-ən\ *n*

semi·pal·mate \,sem-i-'pal-,māt, ,sem-,ī-, -'pä(l)m-,āt\ *or* **semi·pal·mat·ed** \-əd\ *adj* : having the anterior toes joined only part way down with a web — **semi·pal·ma·tion** \,pal-'mā-shən, -(,)pä(l)-\ *n*

semi·par·a·site \-'par-ə-,sīt\ *n* : HEMIPARASITE — **semi·par·a·sit·ic** \-,par-ə-'sit-ik\ *adj*

semi·per·ma·nent \-'pərm-(ə-)nənt\ *adj* 1 : permanent in some respects 2 : lasting for an indefinite time

semi·per·me·able \-'pər-mē-ə-bəl\ *adj* : partially but not freely or wholly permeable; *specif* : permeable to some usu. small molecules but not to other usu. larger particles

semi·po·lit·i·cal \-pə-'lit-i-kəl\ *adj* : of, relating to, or involving some political features or activity

semi·por·ce·lain \-'pōr-s(ə-)lən, -'pór-\ *n* : a well-fired china not sufficiently translucent or nonporous to qualify as porcelain

semi·post·al \,sem-i-'pōst-ᵊl, ,sem-,ī-\ *n* : a postage stamp sold (as for various humanitarian purposes) at a premium over its postal value

semi·pre·cious \-'presh-əs\ *adj, of a gem stone* : of less commercial value than precious

semi·pri·vate \-'prī-vət\ *adj* : of, receiving, or associated with hospital service giving a patient more privileges than a ward patient but fewer than a private patient

semi·pro \'sem-i-,prō, 'sem-,ī-\ *adj* : SEMIPROFESSIONAL

semi·pro·fes·sion·al \,sem-i-prə-'fesh-nəl, -ən-ᵊl, ,sem-,ī-\ *adj* 1 : engaging in an activity for pay or gain but not as a full-time occupation 2 : engaged in by semiprofessional players ⟨∼ baseball⟩ — **semiprofessional** *n* — **semi·pro·fes·sion·al·ly** \-ē\ *adv*

semi·pub·lic \-'pəb-lik\ *adj* 1 : having some features of a public institution; *specif* : maintained as a public service by a private nonprofit organization 2 : open to some persons outside the regular constituency

semi·qua·ver \'sem-i-,kwā-vər, 'sem-,ī-\ *n* : SIXTEENTH NOTE

semi·re·li·gious \,sem-i-ri-'lij-əs, ,sem-,ī-\ *adj* : somewhat religious in character

semi·rig·id \,sem-i-'rij-əd, ,sem-,ī-\ *adj* 1 : rigid to some degree or in some parts 2 *of an airship* : having a flexible cylindrical gas container with an attached stiffening keel that carries the load

semi·sa·cred \-'sā-krəd\ *adj* : SEMIRELIGIOUS

semi·sed·en·tary \-'sed-ᵊn-,ter-ē\ *adj* : sedentary during part of the year and nomadic otherwise ⟨∼ tribes⟩

semi·shrub \'sem-i-,shrəb, 'sem-,ī-, *esp South* -,srəb\ *n* : SUBSHRUB, UNDERSHRUB — **semi·shrub·by** \-ē\ *adj*

semi·skilled \,sem-i-'skild, ,sem-,ī-\ *adj* : having or requiring less training than that skilled labor and more than unskilled labor

semi·soft \-'sȯft\ *adj* : moderately soft; *specif* : firm but easily cut ⟨∼ cheese⟩

semi·sol·id \,sem-i-'säl-əd, ,sem-,ī-\ *adj* : having the qualities of both a solid and a liquid : highly viscous — **semisolid** *n*

semi·sweet \-'swēt\ *adj* : slightly sweetened ⟨∼ chocolate⟩

semi·syn·thet·ic \-sin-'thet-ik\ *adj* : relating to or produced by synthesis from natural starting materials (as cellulose)

Sem·ite \'sem-,īt\ *n* [F *sémite*, fr. *Sem* Shem, fr. LL, fr. Gk *Sēm*, fr. Heb. *Shēm*] 1 : a member of any of the peoples descended from Shem 2 : a member of any of a group of peoples of southwestern Asia chiefly represented now by the Jews and Arabs but in ancient times also by the Babylonians, Assyrians, Aramaeans, Canaanites, and Phoenicians

semi·ter·res·tri·al \,sem-i-tə-'res-t(r)ē-əl, -'res(h)-chəl, ,sem-,ī-\ *adj* 1 : growing on boggy ground 2 : frequenting but not living wholly on land

¹Se·mit·ic \sə-'mit-ik\ *adj* 1 : of, relating to, or characteristic of the Semites; *specif* : JEWISH 2 : of, relating to, or constituting a branch of the Afro-Asiatic language family that includes Hebrew, Aramaic, Arabic, and Ethiopic

²Semitic *n* : any or all of the Semitic languages

Se·mit·ics \-iks\ *n pl but sing in constr* : the study of the language, literature, and history of Semitic peoples; *specif* : Semitic philology

Sem·i·tism \'sem-ə-,tiz-əm\ *n* 1 a : Semitic character or qualities b : a Semitic idiom or expression 2 : policy favorable to Jews : predisposition in favor of Jews

Sem·i·tist \-ət-əst\ *also* **Se·mit·i·cist** \sə-'mit-ə-səst\ *n* 1 : a scholar of the Semitic languages, cultures, or histories 2 *often not cap* : favoring or disposed to favor the Jews

semi·to·n·al \,sem-i-'tōn-ᵊl, ,sem-,ī-\ *adj* : CHROMATIC 3a, SEMITONIC — **semi·ton·al·ly** \-ᵊl-ē\ *adv*

semi·tone \'sem-i-,tōn, 'sem-,ī-\ *n* : the tone at a half step; *also* : HALF STEP — **semi·ton·ic** \,sem-i-'tän-ik, ,sem-,ī-\ *adj* — **semi·ton·i·cal·ly** \-i-k(ə-)lē\ *adv*

semi·trail·er \'sem-i-,trā-lər, 'sem-,ī-\ *n* 1 : a freight trailer that when attached is supported at its forward end by the fifth wheel device of the truck tractor 2 : a trucking rig made up of a tractor and a semitrailer

semi·trans·lu·cent \,sem-i-,tran(t)s-'lüs-ᵊnt, -,tranz-\ *adj* : partly translucent

semi·trans·par·ent \-,tran(t)s-'par-ənt, -'per-\ *adj* : imperfectly transparent

semi·trop·ic \-'träp-ik\ *adj* : SUBTROPICAL — **semi·trop·i·cal** \-i-kəl\ *adj*

semi·trop·ics \-iks\ *n pl* : SUBTROPICS

semi·vow·el \'sem-i-,vau̇(-ə)l\ *n* 1 : any speech sound not a stop, aspirate, or vowel and not at any stage of the language having a stop as a component 2 : one of the glides \y\, \w\, \r\ 3 : a letter representing a semivowel

¹semi·week·ly \,sem-i-'wē-klē, ,sem-,ī-\ *adj* : occurring twice a week — **semiweekly** *adv*

²semiweekly *n* : a semiweekly publication

semi·woody \-'wu̇d-ē\ *adj* : somewhat woody

semi·works \'sem-i-,wərks, 'sem-,ī-\ *n pl* : a manufacturing plant operating on a limited commercial scale to provide final tests of a new product or process

semi·year·ly \,sem-i-'yi(ə)r-lē, ,sem-,ī-\ *adj* : occurring twice a year

sem·o·li·na \,sem-ə-'lē-nə\ *n* [It *semolino*, dim. of *semola* bran, fr. L *simila* finest wheat flour] : the purified middlings of durum or other hard wheat used for macaroni, spaghetti, or vermicelli

sem·per·vi·vum \,sem-pər-'vī-vəm\ *n* [NL, fr. L, neuter of *sempervivus* ever-living, fr. *semper* ever + *vivus* living — more at QUICK] : any of a large genus (*Sempervivum*) of Old World fleshy herbs of the orpine family often grown as ornamentals

sem·pi·ter·nal \,sem-pi-'tərn-ᵊl\ *adj* [ME, fr. LL *sempiternalis*, fr. L *sempiternus*, fr. *semper* ever, always, fr. *sem-* one, same (akin to ON *samr* same) + *per* through — more at SAME, FOR] : of neverending duration : EVERLASTING, ETERNAL — **sem·pi·ter·nal·ly** \-ᵊl-ē\ *adv* — **sem·pi·ter·ni·ty** \-'tər-nət-ē\ *n*

sem·ple \'sem-pəl\ *adj* [alter. of *simple*] *Scot* : of humble birth : SIMPLE

sem·pli·ce \'sem-pli-,chā\ *adj (or adv)* [It, fr. L *simplic-, simplex* — more at SIMPLE] : SIMPLE, UNAFFECTED — used as a direction in music

sem·pre \'sem-(,)prā\ *adv* [It, fr. L *semper*] : ALWAYS — used to qualify an adverb or adjective used as a direction in music

semp·stress *var* SEAMSTRESS

¹sen \'sen\ *n*, *pl* **sen** [Jap] — see *yen* at MONEY table

²sen *n*, *pl* **sen** [native name in Indonesia] — see *rupiah* at MONEY table

³sen *n*, *pl* **sen** [native name in Cambodia] — see *riel* at MONEY table

se·nar·i·us \sə-'nar-ē-əs, -'ner-\ *n*, *pl* **se·nar·ii** \-ē-,ī, -ē-,ē\ [L, fr. *senarius* consisting of six each, fr. *seni* six each, fr. *sex* six — more at SIX] : a verse consisting of six feet esp. in Latin prosody

se·na·ry \'sen-ə-rē, 'sēn-\ *adj* [L *senarius*, fr. *seni* six each, fr. *sex* six — more at SIX] : of, based upon, or characterized by six : compounded of six things or six parts ⟨∼ scale⟩ ⟨∼ division⟩

sen·ate \'sen-ət\ *n* [ME *senat*, fr. OF, fr. L *senatus*, lit., council of elders, fr. *sen-, senex* old, old man — more at SENIOR] 1 : an assembly or council usu. possessing high deliberative and legislative functions: as **a** : the supreme council of the ancient Roman republic and empire **b** : the second chamber in the bicameral legislature of a major political unit (as a nation, state, or province) 2 : the hall or chamber in which a senate meets 3 : a governing body of some universities charged with maintaining academic standards and regulations and usu. composed of the principal or representative members of the faculty

sen·a·tor \'sen-ət-ər\ *n* [ME *senatour*, fr. OF *senateur*, fr. L *senator*, fr. *senatus*] : a member of a senate

sen·a·to·ri·al \,sen-ə-'tōr-ē-əl, -'tȯr-\ *adj* : of, relating to, or befitting a senator or a senate ⟨∼ office⟩ ⟨∼ rank⟩

senatorial courtesy *n* : a custom of the U.S. Senate of refusing to confirm a presidential appointment of an official in or from a state when the appointment is opposed by the senators or senior senator of the president's party from that state

senatorial district *n* : a territorial division from which a senator is elected — compare CONGRESSIONAL DISTRICT

sen·a·to·ri·an \,sen-ə-'tōr-ē-ən, -'tȯr-\ *adj* : SENATORIAL; *specif* : of or relating to the ancient Roman senate

sen·a·tor·ship \'sen-ət-ər-,ship\ *n* : the office or position of senator

se·na·tus con·sul·tum \sə-,nät-ə-skən-'səl-təm, -,nä-,tü-skən-, -'su̇l-\ *n, pl* **senatus con·sul·ta** \-tə\ [L, decree of the senate] : a decree of the ancient Roman senate

¹send \'send\ *vb* **sent** \'sent\; **send·ing** [ME *senden*, fr. OE *sendan;* akin to OHG *sendan* to send, OE *sith* road, journey, OIr *sēt*] *vt* 1 : to cause to go: as **a** : to propel or throw in a particular direction **b** : DELIVER ⟨*sent* a blow to his chin⟩ **c** : DRIVE ⟨*sent* the ball between the goalposts⟩ 2 : to cause to happen ⟨whatever fate may ∼⟩ 3 : to dispatch by a means of communication 4 **a** : to direct, order, or request to go **b** : to permit or enable to attend a term or session **c** : to direct by advice or reference **d** : to cause or order to depart : DISMISS 5 **a** : to force to go : DRIVE **b** : to cause to assume a specified state ⟨*sent* him mad⟩ 6 : to cause to issue: as **a** : to pour out : DISCHARGE ⟨clouds ∼*ing* forth rain⟩ **b** : UTTER ⟨∼ forth a cry⟩ **c** : EMIT ⟨*sent* out waves of perfume⟩ 7 : to cause to be carried to a destination; *esp* : to consign to death or a place of punishment 8 : to convey or cause to be conveyed or transmitted by an agent 9 : to strike or thrust so as to impel violently ⟨*sent* him sprawling⟩ ∼ *vi* 1 : to dispatch someone to convey a message or do an errand ⟨∼ out for coffee⟩ 2 : SCEND 3 : TRANSMIT — **send·er** — **send for** : to request by message to come : SUMMON — **send packing** : to send off roughly or in disgrace : DISMISS

²send *n* 1 : the lift of a wave 2 : an impetus or accelerating impulse

sen·dal \'sen-dᵊl\ *n* [ME, fr. OF *cendal*, fr. ML *sendallum, cendalum*] : a thin medieval silk of oriental origin used for fine clothing and church vestments

send away *vt* 1 : DISPATCH ⟨*sent* his application *away* in the evening mail⟩ 2 : to banish from a place ⟨*sent* him *away* for misconduct⟩

send down *vt, Brit* : to suspend or expel (a student) from a university

send in *vt* 1 : to cause to be delivered ⟨*send in* a letter of complaint⟩ 2 : to give (one's name or card) to a servant when making a call 3 : to send (a player) into an athletic contest ⟨coach *sent* several substitutes *in*⟩

send-off \'sen-,dȯf\ *n* : a demonstration of goodwill and enthusiasm for the beginning of a new venture (as a trip or a new business)

send out *vt* 1 : ISSUE ⟨had *sent* the wedding invitations *out*⟩ 2 : to

dispatch (as an order or shipment) from a store or similar establishment

send round *vt* **1 :** CIRCULATE ⟨a notice is being *sent round* to all employees⟩ **2 :** to dispatch (as a message or a messenger) for some object or purpose

send up *vt* **:** to sentence to imprisonment **:** send to jail

Sen·e·ca \ˈsen-i-kə\ *n, pl* **Seneca** *or* **Senecas** [D *Sennecaas*, pl., the Seneca, Oneida, Onondaga, and Cayuga people collectively, fr. Mahican *A'sinnika* Oneida] **1 :** a member of an Iroquoian people of western New York **2 :** the language of the Seneca people

Sen·e·can \-kən\ *adj* **:** of, relating to, or characteristic of Seneca, his philosophy, or his writings

Seneca oil *n* [fr. its discovery in the territory of the Senecas] **:** a crude petroleum formerly in medicinal use

se·nec·ti·tude \si-ˈnek-tə-ˌt(y)üd\ *n* [ML *senectitudo*, alter. of L *senectus* old age, fr. *sen-, senic-, senex* old, old man — more at SENIOR] **:** the final stage of the normal life span

sen·e·ga \ˈsen-i-gə\ *or* **sen·e·ca** \-kə\ *n* **:** the dried root of senega root or a related plant containing an irritating saponin

senega root *n* [alter. of *Seneca root;* fr. its use by the Seneca as a remedy for snakebite] **:** a No. American milkwort (*Polygala senega*) with leafy stems and small white flowers

se·nesce \si-ˈnes\ *vi* [L *senescere*, fr. *sen-, senex*] **:** to grow old — **se·nes·cence** \-ˈnes-ᵊn(t)s\ *n* — **se·nes·cent** \-ᵊnt\ *adj*

sen·e·schal \ˈsen-ə-shəl\ *n* [ME, fr. MF, of Gmc origin; akin to Goth *sineigs* old, and to OHG *scalc* servant — more at SENIOR] **:** an agent or bailiff in charge of a lord's estate in feudal times

se·nhor \si-ˈnyō(ə)r, -ˈnyȯ(ə)r\ *n, pl* **senhors** *or* **se·nho·res** \-ˈnyōr-ēs(h), -ˈnyȯr-, -ēz(h)\ [Pg, fr. ML *senior* superior, lord, fr. L, adj., elder] **:** a Portuguese or Brazilian gentleman — used as a title equivalent to *Mister*

se·nho·ra \-ˈnyōr-ə, -ˈnyȯr-\ *n* [Pg, fem. of *senhor*] **:** a married Portuguese or Brazilian woman — used as a title equivalent to *Mrs.*

se·nho·ri·ta \ˌsē-nyə-ˈrēt-ə\ *n* [Pg, fr. dim. of *senhora*] **:** an unmarried Portuguese or Brazilian woman — used as a title equivalent to *Miss*

se·nile \ˈsēn-ˌīl *also* ˈsen-\ *adj* [L *senilis*, fr. *sen-, senex* old, old man] **1 :** of, relating to, exhibiting, or characteristic of old age ⟨~ weakness⟩; *esp* **:** exhibiting a loss of mental faculties associated with old age **2 :** approaching the end of a geological cycle of erosion — **se·nile·ly** \-ˌīl-lē\ *adv*

se·nil·i·ty \si-ˈnil-ət-ē, se-\ *n* **:** the quality or state of being senile; *specif* **:** the physical and mental infirmity of old age

¹se·nior \ˈsē-nyər\ *n* [ME, fr. L, fr. *senior*, adj.] **1 :** a person older than another **2 a :** a person with higher standing or rank **b :** a senior fellow of a college at an English university **c :** a student in the year preceding graduation from a school of secondary or higher level

²senior *adj* [ME, fr. L, older, elder, compar. of *sen-, senex* old; akin to Goth *sineigs* old, Gk *henos*] **1 a :** of prior birth, establishment, or enrollment — often used to distinguish a father with the same given name as his son **b :** having reached the age of retirement ⟨~ citizens⟩ **2 :** SUPERIOR ⟨the ~ officers⟩ **3 :** of or relating to seniors ⟨the ~ class⟩ **4 :** having a claim on corporate assets and income prior to other securities

senior chief petty officer *n* **:** a petty officer in the navy ranking above a chief petty officer and below a master chief petty officer

senior high school *n* **:** a school usu. including the last three years of high school

se·nior·i·ty \sēn-ˈyȯr-ət-ē, -ˈyär-\ *n, often attrib* **1 :** the quality or state of being senior **:** PRIORITY **2 :** a privileged status attained by length of continuous service (as in a company)

senior master sergeant *n* **:** a noncommissioned officer in the air force ranking above a master sergeant and below a chief master sergeant

sen·na \ˈsen-ə\ *n* [NL, fr. Ar *sanā*] **1 :** any of a genus (*Cassia*) of leguminous herbs, shrubs, and trees native to warm regions; *esp* **:** one used medicinally **2 :** the dried leaflets of various sennas (esp. *Cassia acutifolia, C. angustifolia*) used as a purgative

sen·net \ˈsen-ət\ *n* [prob. alter. of obs. *signet* (signal)] **:** a signal call on a trumpet or cornet for entrance or exit on the stage

sen·night *also* **se'n·night** \ˈsen-ˌīt\ *n* [ME, fr. OE *seofon nihta* seven nights] *archaic* **:** the space of seven nights and days **:** WEEK

sen·nit \ˈsen-ət\ *n* [perh. fr. F *coussinet*, dim. of *coussin* cushion; fr. its use to protect cables from fraying] **1 :** a braided cord or fabric (as of plaited rope yarns) **2 :** a straw or grass braid for hats

se·nor *or* **se·ñor** \sān-ˈyō(ə)r\ *n, pl* **senors** *or* **se·ño·res** \-ˈyō(ə)r-(ˌ)ās, -ˈyȯ(ə)r-\ [Sp *señor*, fr. ML *senior* superior, lord, fr. L, adj., elder] **:** a Spanish or Spanish-speaking man — used as a title equivalent to *Mister*

se·no·ra *or* **se·ño·ra** \sān-ˈyōr-ə, -ˈyȯr-\ *n* [Sp *señora*, fem. of *señor*] **:** a married Spanish or Spanish-speaking woman — used as a title equivalent to *Mrs.*

se·no·ri·ta *or* **se·ño·ri·ta** \ˌsān-yə-ˈrēt-ə\ *n* [Sp *señorita*, fr. dim. of *señora*] **:** an unmarried Spanish or Spanish-speaking girl or woman — used as a title equivalent to *Miss*

sen·sate \ˈsen-ˌsāt\ *adj* [ML, fr. LL, endowed with sense, fr. L *sensus* sense] **:** apprehended through the senses or preoccupied with things that can be experienced through a sense modality — **sen·sate·ly** *adv*

sen·sa·tion \sen-ˈsā-shən, sən-\ *n* [ML *sensation-, sensatio*, fr. LL *sensatus* endowed with sense] **1 a :** a mental process (as seeing, hearing, or smelling) due to immediate bodily stimulation often as distinguished from awareness of the process — compare PERCEPTION **b :** awareness (as of heat or pain) due to stimulation of a sense organ **c :** a state of consciousness usu. due to physical objects or internal bodily changes ⟨binding ~ in his chest⟩ **d :** an indefinite bodily feeling ⟨a ~ of buoyancy⟩ **2 :** something (as a physical object, sense-datum, pain, or afterimage) that causes or is the object of sensation **3 a :** a state of excited interest or feeling **b :** a cause of such excitement

sen·sa·tion·al \-shnəl, -shən-ᵊl\ *adj* **1 :** of or relating to sensation or the senses **2 :** arousing or tending to arouse (as by lurid details) a quick, intense, and usu. superficial interest, curiosity, or emotional reaction **3 :** exceedingly or unexpectedly excellent or great — **sen·sa·tion·al·ly** \-ē\ *adv*

sen·sa·tion·al·ism \-ˌiz-əm\ *n* **1 :** the use or effect of sensational subject matter or treatment **2 :** empiricism that limits experience as a source of knowledge to sensation or sense perceptions — **sen·sa·tion·al·ist** \-əst\ *n* — **sen·sa·tion·al·is·tic** \-ˌsā-shnəl-ˈis-tik, -shən-ᵊl-\ *adj*

¹sense \ˈsen(t)s\ *n* [MF or L; MF *sens* sensation, feeling, mechanism of perception, meaning, fr. L *sensus*, fr. *sensus*, pp. of *sentire* to perceive, feel; akin to OHG *sin* mind, sense, OE *sith* journey — more at SEND] **1 :** a meaning conveyed or intended **:** IMPORT, SIGNIFICATION; *specif* **:** one of a set of meanings a word or phrase may bear esp. as segregated in a dictionary entry **2 a :** the faculty of perceiving by means of sense organs **b :** a specialized animal function or mechanism (as sight, hearing, smell, taste, or touch) basically involving a stimulus and a sense organ **c :** the sensory mechanisms constituting a unit distinct from other functions (as movement or thought) **3 :** CONSCIOUSNESS, SANITY — usu. used in pl. **4 a :** a particular sensation or kind or quality of sensation ⟨~ of balance⟩ **b :** a definite but often vague awareness or impression ⟨~ of insecurity⟩ ⟨~ of danger⟩ **c :** a motivating awareness ⟨~ of shame⟩ **d :** a discerning awareness and appreciation ⟨~ of humor⟩ ⟨~ of value⟩ **5 :** CONSENSUS ⟨the ~ of the meeting⟩ **6 a :** SENTIENCE, INTELLIGENCE **b :** sound mental capacity and understanding; *also* **:** agreement with or satisfaction of such power ⟨this decision makes ~⟩ **7 :** one of two opposite directions describable by the motion of a point, line, or surface

syn SENSE, COMMON SENSE, GUMPTION, JUDGMENT, WISDOM mean ability to reach intelligent conclusions. SENSE implies a reliable ability to judge and decide with soundness, prudence, and intelligence; COMMON SENSE suggests an average degree of such ability without sophistication or special knowledge; GUMPTION suggests a readiness to use or apply common sense; JUDGMENT implies sense tempered and refined by experience, training, and maturity; WISDOM implies sense and judgment far above average **syn** see in addition MEANING

²sense *vt* **1 a :** to perceive by the senses **b :** to be or become conscious of ⟨~ danger⟩ **2 :** GRASP, COMPREHEND **3 :** to detect (as a symbol or radiation) automatically

sense–datum *n, pl* **sense–data :** an immediate unanalyzable private object of sensation directly due to the stimulation of a sense organ

sense·ful \ˈsen(t)s-fəl\ *adj* **:** full of sense or reason **:** JUDICIOUS

sense·less \ˈsen(t)-sləs\ *adj* **:** destitute of, deficient in, or contrary to sense: as **a :** UNCONSCIOUS ⟨knocked ~⟩ **b :** FOOLISH, STUPID **c :** PURPOSELESS, MEANINGLESS ⟨a ~ act⟩ — **sense·less·ly** *adv* — **sense·less·ness** *n*

sense organ *n* **:** a bodily structure affected by a stimulus (as heat or sound waves) in such a manner as to initiate a wave of excitation in associated sensory nerve fibers that conveys specific impulses to the central nervous system where they are interpreted as corresponding sensations **:** RECEPTOR

sen·si·bil·i·ty \ˌsen(t)-sə-ˈbil-ət-ē\ *n* **1 :** SENSITIVENESS ⟨tactile ~⟩ **2 :** peculiar susceptibility to a pleasurable or painful impression (as a slight or unkindness) — often used in pl. **3 :** awareness of and responsiveness toward something (as emotion in another) **4 :** refined sensitiveness in emotion and taste with especial responsiveness to the pathetic

¹sen·si·ble \ˈsen(t)-sə-bəl\ *adj* [ME, fr. MF, fr. L *sensibilis*, fr. *sensus*, pp.] **1 a :** capable of being perceived by the senses or by reason or understanding **b :** of a significant size, amount, or degree ⟨a ~ error⟩ **c** (1) **:** readily perceptible by the senses (2) *archaic* **:** tending to produce an acute emotional response either positive or negative (3) **:** MATERIAL ⟨~ marks of his approval⟩ **2 a :** capable of receiving sense impressions ⟨~ to pain⟩ **b :** having nice perception or acute feeling **:** easily affected **3 a :** COGNIZANT, AWARE; *also* **:** CONVINCED **b :** emotionally aware **4 :** having or containing good sense or reason **:** REASONABLE **syn** see AWARE, MATERIAL, PERCEPTIBLE, WISE — **sen·si·ble·ness** *n* — **sen·si·bly** \-blē\ *adv*

²sensible *n* **:** something that can be sensed

sen·si·tive \ˈsen(t)-sət-iv, ˈsen(t)-stiv\ *adj* [ME, fr. MF *sensitif*, fr. ML *sensitivus*, irreg. fr. L *sensus*] **1 :** SENSORY 2 **2 a :** receptive to sense impressions **b :** subject to excitation by external agents (as light, gravity, or contact) **:** exhibiting irritability (sense c) **3 :** highly responsive or susceptible: as **a :** easily hurt **b :** excessively or abnormally susceptible **:** HYPERSENSITIVE ⟨~ to egg protein⟩ **c :** readily fluctuating in price or demand ⟨~ commodities⟩ **d :** capable of indicating minute differences **:** DELICATE ⟨~ scales⟩ **e :** readily affected or changed by various agents (as light or mechanical shock) **f :** high in radio sensitivity **4 :** concerned with highly classified government information or involving discretionary authority over important policy matters **syn** see LIABLE — **sen·si·tive·ly** *adv* — **sen·si·tive·ness** *n*

sensitive plant *n* **:** any of several mimosas (esp. *Mimosa pudica*) with leaves sensitive to tactile stimulation; *broadly* **:** a plant responding to touch with movement (as folding of leaves or drooping)

sen·si·tiv·i·ty \ˌsen(t)-sə-ˈtiv-ət-ē\ *n* **:** the quality or state of being sensitive: as **a :** the capacity of an organism or sense organ to respond to stimulation **b :** HYPERSENSITIVITY **c :** the degree to which a radio receiving set responds to incoming waves

sen·si·ti·za·tion \ˌsen(t)-sət-ə-ˈzā-shən, ˌsen(t)-stə-ˈzā-\ *n* **1 :** the quality or state of being sensitized (as to an antigen) **2 :** the act or process of sensitizing

sen·si·tize \ˈsen(t)-sə-ˌtīz\ *vb* [*sensitive* + *-ize*] *vt* **:** to make sensitive or hypersensitive ~ *vi* **:** to become sensitive — **sen·si·tiz·er** *n*

sen·si·tom·e·ter \ˌsen(t)-sə-ˈtäm-ət-ər\ *n* [ISV *sensitive* + *-o-* + *-meter*] **:** an instrument for measuring sensitivity of photographic material — **sen·si·to·met·ric** \ˌsen(t)-sət-ə-ˈme-trik\ *adj* — **sen·si·tom·e·try** \-sə-ˈtäm-ə-trē\ *n*

sen·sor \ˈsen-ˌsȯ(ə)r, ˈsen(t)-sər\ *n* [L *sensus*, pp. of *sentire* to perceive — more at SENSE] **:** a device that responds to a physical stimulus (as heat, light, or a particular motion) and transmits a resulting impulse (as for operating a control)

sen·so·ri·al \sen-ˈsōr-ē-əl, -ˈsȯr-\ *adj* **:** SENSORY — **sen·so·ri·al·ly** \-ə-lē\ *adv*

sen·so·ri·mo·tor \ˌsen(t)s-(ə-)rē-ˈmōt-ər\ *adj* **:** of, relating to, or functioning in both sensory and motor aspects of bodily activity

sen·so·ri·um \sen-ˈsōr-ē-əm, -ˈsȯr-\ *n, pl* **sensoriums** *or* **sen·so·ria** \-ē-ə\ [LL, sense organ, fr. L *sensus* sense] **:** the parts of the brain concerned with the reception and interpretation of sensory stimuli; *broadly* **:** the entire sensory apparatus

sen·so·ry \ˈsen(t)s-(ə-)rē\ *adj* **1 :** of or relating to sensation or to

the senses **2 :** conveying nerve impulses from the sense organs to the nerve centers **:** AFFERENT

sen·su·al \'sench-(ə-)wəl\ *adj* [ME, fr. LL *sensualis*, fr. L *sensus* sense + *-alis* -al] **1 :** SENSORY **2 :** relating to or consisting in the gratification of the senses or the indulgence of appetite **:** FLESHLY **3 a :** devoted to or preoccupied with the senses or appetites **b :** VOLUPTUOUS **c :** deficient in moral, spiritual, or intellectual interests **:** WORLDLY; *esp* **:** IRRELIGIOUS **syn** see CARNAL, SENSUOUS — **sen·su·al·i·ty** \,sen-chə-'wal-ət-ē\ *n* — **sen·su·al·ly** \'sench-(ə-)wə-lē\ *adv*

sen·su·al·ism \'sench-(ə-)wə-,liz-əm\ *n* **:** SENSUALITY — **sen·su·al·ist** \-ləst\ *n* — **sen·su·al·is·tic** \,sench-(ə-)wə-'lis-tik\ *adj*

sen·su·al·iza·tion \,sench-(ə-)wə-lə-'zā-shən\ *n* **:** the act of sensualizing **:** the state of being sensualized

sen·su·al·ize \'sench-(ə-)wə-,līz\ *vt* **:** to make sensual

sen·su·ous \'sench-(ə-)wəs\ *adj* [L *sensus* sense + E *-ous*] **1 :** of or relating to the senses or sensible objects **:** addressing the senses ⟨~ pleasure⟩ **2 :** characterized by sense impressions or imagery addressing the senses **3 :** highly susceptible to influence through the senses — **sen·su·ous·ly** *adv* — **sen·su·ous·ness** *n*

syn SENSUOUS, SENSUAL, LUXURIOUS, VOLUPTUOUS, EPICUREAN mean relating to or providing pleasure through gratification of the senses. SENSUOUS implies delight in beauty of color, sound, texture, or artistic form; SENSUAL stresses indulgence of appetite esp. for sexual pleasure; LUXURIOUS suggests the providing of or indulgence of sensuous pleasure inducing bodily ease and languor; VOLUPTUOUS implies more strongly an abandonment to sensuous or sensual pleasure for its own sake; EPICUREAN suggests the satisfaction of refined or fastidious taste in physical pleasures

sent *past of* SEND

1sen·tence \'sent-ᵊn(t)s, -ᵊnz\ *n, often attrib* [ME, fr. OF, fr. L *sententia*, lit. feeling, opinion, fr. (assumed) *sentent-*, *sentens*, irreg. prp. of *sentire* to feel — more at SENSE] **1** *obs* **:** OPINION; *esp* **:** a conclusion given on request or reached after deliberation **2 a :** JUDGMENT 2a; *specif* **:** one formally pronounced by a court or judge in a criminal proceeding and specifying the punishment to be inflicted upon the convict **b :** the punishment so imposed **3 :** AXIOM, MAXIM **4 :** a grammatically self-contained speech unit consisting of a word or a syntactically related group of words that expresses an assertion, a question, a command, a wish, or an exclamation, that in writing usu. begins with a capital letter and concludes with appropriate end punctuation, and that in speaking is phonetically distinguished by various patterns of stress, pitch, and pauses **5 :** PERIOD 1b **6 :** a meaningful logical formula **:** PROPOSITION 2a — **sen·ten·tial** \sen-'ten-chəl\ *adj* — **sen·ten·tial·ly** \-chə-lē\ *adv*

2sentence *vt* **1 :** to pronounce sentence on **2 :** to condemn to a specified punishment **3 :** to cause to suffer something

sentence fragment *n* **:** a word, phrase, or clause that usu. has in speech the intonation of a sentence but lacks the grammatically self-contained structure usu. found in the sentences of formal and esp. written composition

sentence stress *n* **:** the manner in which stresses are distributed on the syllables of words assembled into sentences — called also *sentence accent*

sentential function *n* **:** an expression that contains one or more variables and becomes a declarative sentence when constants are substituted for the variables

sen·ten·tious \sen-'ten-chəs\ *adj* [ME, fr. L *sententiosus*, fr. *sententia* sentence, maxim] **1 :** terse, aphoristic, or moralistic in expression **:** PITHY, EPIGRAMMATIC **2 a :** given to or abounding in aphoristic expression **b :** given to or abounding in excessive moralizing — **sen·ten·tious·ly** *adv* — **sen·ten·tious·ness** *n*

sen·tience \'sen-ch(ē-)ən(t)s\ *n* **1 :** a sentient quality or state **2 :** a state of elementary or undifferentiated consciousness

sen·tient \-ch(ē-)ənt\ *adj* [L *sentient-*, *sentiens*, prp. of *sentire* to perceive, feel] **1 :** responsive to or conscious of sense impressions **2 :** AWARE **3 :** finely sensitive in perception or feeling — **sen·tient·ly** *adv*

sen·ti·ment \'sent-ə-mənt\ *n* [F or ML; F, fr. ML *sentimentum*, fr. L *sentire*] **1 a :** an attitude, thought, or judgment prompted by feeling **:** PREDILECTION **b :** a specific view or notion **:** OPINION **2 a :** EMOTION **b :** refined feeling **:** delicate sensibility esp. as expressed in a work of art **c :** emotional idealism **d :** a romantic or nostalgic feeling verging on sentimentality **3 a :** an idea colored by emotion **b :** the emotional significance of a passage or expression as distinguished from its verbal context **syn** see FEELING, OPINION

sen·ti·men·tal \,sent-ə-'ment-ᵊl\ *adj* **1 a :** marked or governed by feeling, sensibility, or emotional idealism **b :** resulting from feeling rather than reason or thought **2 :** having an excess or affectation of sentiment or sensibility — **sen·ti·men·tal·ly** \-ᵊl-ē\ *adv*

sen·ti·men·tal·ism \,sent-ə-'ment-ᵊl-,iz-əm\ *n* **1 :** the disposition to favor or indulge in sentiment **2 :** an excessively sentimental conception or statement — **sen·ti·men·tal·ist** \-ᵊl-əst\ *n*

sen·ti·men·tal·i·ty \,sent-ə-,men-'tal-ət-ē, -mən-\ *n* **1 :** the quality or state of being sentimental esp. to excess or in affectation **2 :** a sentimental idea or its expression

sen·ti·men·tal·iza·tion \-,ment-ᵊl-ə-'zā-shən\ *n* **:** the act or process of sentimentalizing **:** the state of being sentimentalized

sen·ti·men·tal·ize \-'ment-ᵊl-,īz\ *vi* **:** to indulge in sentiment ~ *vt* **:** to look upon or imbue with sentiment

1sen·ti·nel \'sent-nəl, -ᵊn-əl\ *n* [MF *sentinelle*, fr. OIt *sentinella*, fr. *sentina* vigilance, fr. *sentire* to perceive, fr. L] **:** one that watches or guards **:** SENTRY

2sentinel *vt* **sen·ti·neled** *or* **sen·ti·nelled**; **sen·ti·nel·ing** *or* **sen·ti·nel·ling 1 :** to watch over as a sentinel **2 :** to furnish with a sentinel **3 :** to post as sentinel

sen·try \'sen-trē\ *n* [perh. fr. obs. *sentry* (sanctuary, watch tower)] **:** GUARD, WATCH; *esp* **:** a soldier standing guard at a passing point

sentry box *n* **:** a shelter for a sentry on his post

se·pal \'sēp-əl, 'sep-\ *n* [NL *sepalum*, fr. *sepa-* (fr. Gk *skepē* covering) + *-lum* (as in *petalum* petal); akin to Lith *kepurė* head covering] **:** one of the modified leaves comprising a calyx — **se·paled** *or* **se·palled** \-əld\ *adj*

se·pal·oid \-ə-,lȯid\ *adj* **:** resembling or functioning as a sepal

-sep·al·ous \'sep-ə-ləs\ *adj comb form* [*sepal*] **:** having (such or so many) sepals ⟨gamo*sepalous*⟩

sep·a·ra·bil·i·ty \,sep-(ə-)rə-'bil-ət-ē\ *n* **:** the quality or state of being separable

sep·a·ra·ble \'sep-(ə-)rə-bəl\ *adj* **1 :** capable of being separated or dissociated **2** *obs* **:** causing separation — **sep·a·ra·ble·ness** *n* — **sep·a·ra·bly** \-blē\ *adv*

1sep·a·rate \'sep-(ə-),rāt\ *vb* [ME *separaten*, fr. L *separatus*, pp. of *separare*, fr. *se-* apart + *parare* to prepare, procure — more at SECEDE, PARE] *vt* **1 a :** to set or keep apart **:** DISCONNECT, SEVER **b :** to make a distinction between **:** DISCRIMINATE, DISTINGUISH ⟨~ religion from magic⟩ **c :** SORT ⟨~ mail⟩ **d :** to disperse in space or time **:** SCATTER ⟨widely *separated* homesteads⟩ **2** *archaic* **:** to set aside for a special purpose **:** CHOOSE, DEDICATE **3 :** to part by a legal separation: **a :** to sever conjugal ties with **b :** to sever contractual relations with **:** DISCHARGE ⟨*separated* from the army⟩ **4 :** to block off **:** SEGREGATE **5 :** to isolate from a mixture **:** EXTRACT ⟨~ cream from milk⟩ ~ *vi* **1 :** to become divided or detached **2 a :** to sever an association **:** WITHDRAW **b :** to cease to live together as man and wife **3 :** to go in different directions **4 :** to become isolated from a mixture

syn SEPARATE, PART, DIVIDE, SEVER, SUNDER, DIVORCE mean to break into parts or to keep apart. SEPARATE may imply any of several causes such as dispersion, removal of one from others, or presence of an intervening thing; PART implies the separating of things or persons in close union or association; DIVIDE implies separating into pieces or sections by cutting or breaking; SEVER implies violence esp. in the removal of a part or member; SUNDER suggests violent rending or wrenching apart; DIVORCE implies separating two things that commonly interact and belong together

2sep·a·rate \'sep-(ə-)rət\ *adj* **1 a** *archaic* **:** SOLITARY, SECLUDED **b :** DISEMBODIED, IMMATERIAL **c :** set or kept apart **:** DETACHED **2 a :** not shared with another **:** INDIVIDUAL ⟨~ rooms⟩ **b** *often cap* **:** estranged from a parent body ⟨*Separate* churches⟩ **3 a :** existing by itself **:** AUTONOMOUS **b :** dissimilar in nature or identity **syn** see DISTINCT, SINGLE — **sep·a·rate·ly** \-(ə-)rət-lē, 'sep-ərt-lē\ *adv* — **sep·a·rate·ness** \-(ə-)rət-nəs\ *n*

3sep·a·rate \'sep-(ə-)rət\ *n* **1 :** OFFPRINT **2 :** an article of dress designed to be worn interchangeably with others to form various costume combinations — usu. used in pl.

sep·a·ra·tion \,sep-ə-'rā-shən\ *n* **1 :** the act or process of separating **:** the state of being separated **2 a :** a point, line, or means of division **b :** an intervening space **:** GAP **3 a :** cessation of cohabitation between husband and wife by mutual agreement or judicial decree **b :** termination of a contractual relationship (as employment or military service)

sep·a·rat·ism \'sep-(ə-)rət-,iz-əm\ *n* **:** a belief in, movement for, or state of separation (as schism, secession, or segregation)

sep·a·rat·ist \'sep-(ə-)rət-əst, 'sep-ə-,rāt-\ *n, often cap* **:** one that favors separatism: as **a** *cap* **:** one of a group of 16th and 17th century English Protestants preferring to separate from rather than to reform the Church of England **b :** an advocate of independence or autonomy for a part of a nation or other political unit — **separatist** *adj, often cap* — **sep·a·ra·tis·tic** \,sep-(ə-)rə-'tis-tik\ *adj*

sep·a·ra·tive \'sep-ə-,rāt-iv, 'sep-(ə-)rət-\ *adj* **:** tending toward, causing, or expressing separation

sep·a·ra·tor \'sep-(ə-),rāt-ər\ *n, often attrib* **:** one that separates; *specif* **:** a device for separating liquids of different specific gravities (as cream from milk) or liquids from solids

Se·phar·di \sə-'färd-ē\ *n, pl* **Se·phar·dim** \-'färd-əm\ [LHeb *sĕphāradhī*, fr. *Sĕphāradh* Spain, fr. Heb, region where Jews were once exiled (Obad 1: 20)] **:** a member of the occidental branch of European Jews settling in Spain and Portugal or one of their descendants — **Se·phar·dic** \-'färd-ik\ *adj*

1se·pia \'sē-pē-ə\ *n* [NL, genus comprising cuttlefish, fr. L, cuttlefish, fr. Gk *sēpia*; akin to Gk *sēpein* to make putrid, *sapros* rotten] **1 a :** the inky secretion of a cuttlefish **b :** a brown melanin-containing pigment from the ink of cuttlefishes **2 :** a print or photograph of a brown color resembling sepia **3 :** a brownish gray to dark olive brown

2sepia *adj* **1 :** of the color sepia **2 :** made of or done in sepia ⟨~ print⟩

se·pi·o·lite \'sē-pē-ə-,līt\ *n* [G *sepiolith*, fr. Gk *sēpion* cuttlebone (fr. *sēpia*) + G *-lith* -lite] **:** MEERSCHAUM 1

se·poy \'sē-,pȯi\ *n* [Pg *sipai*, fr. Hindi *sipāhī*, fr. Per, cavalryman] **:** a native of India employed as a soldier by a European power (as Great Britain)

sep·pu·ku \se-'pü-(,)kü, 'sep-ə-,kü\ *n* [Jap] **:** HARA-KIRI

sep·sis \'sep-səs\ *n, pl* **sep·ses** \'sep-,sēz\ [NL, fr. Gk *sēpsis* decay, fr. *sēpein* to make putrid] **:** a toxic condition resulting from the spread of bacteria or their products from a focus of infection; *esp* **:** SEPTICEMIA

sept \'sept\ *n* [prob. alter. of *sect*] **:** a branch of a family; *esp* **:** CLAN

sep·tal \'sep-tᵊl\ *adj* **:** of or relating to a septum

sep·tar·i·um \sep-'ter-ē-əm, -'tar-\ *n, pl* **sep·tar·ia** \-ē-ə\ [NL, fr. L *saeptum* partition — more at SEPTUM] **:** a concretionary nodule usu. of limestone or clay ironstone intersected within by cracks filled with minerals (as calcite or barite)

sep·tate \'sep-,tāt\ *adj* **:** divided by or having a septum

Sep·tem·ber \sep-'tem-bər, səp-\ *n* [ME *Septembre*, fr. OF, fr. L *September* (seventh month), fr. *septem* seven — more at SEVEN] **:** the 9th month of the Gregorian calendar

sep·te·nar·i·us \,sep-tə-'nar-ē-əs, -'ner-\ *n, pl* **sep·te·nar·ii** \-ē-,ī, -ē-,ē\ [L, fr. *septenarius* of seven, fr. *septeni* seven each, fr. *septem* seven] **:** a verse consisting of seven feet esp. in Latin prosody

sep·ten·de·cil·lion \,sep-,ten-di-'sil-yən\ *n, often attrib* [L *septendecim* seventeen (fr. *septem* seven + *decem* ten) + E *-illion* (as in *million*) — more at TEN] — see NUMBER table

sep·ten·ni·al \sep-'ten-ē-əl\ *adj* [LL *septennium* period of seven years, fr. L *septem* + *-ennium* (as in *biennium*)] **1 :** consisting of or lasting for seven years **2 :** occurring or being done every seven years — **sep·ten·ni·al·ly** \-ə-lē\ *adv*

sep·ten·tri·on \sep-'ten-trē-,än, -trē-ən\ *n* [ME, fr. MF, fr. L *septentrio*, sing. of *septentriones* the seven stars of Ursa Major or Ursa Minor, lit. the seven plow oxen, fr. *septem* seven + *trio* plow ox] *obs* **:** the northern regions **:** NORTH

sep·ten·tri·o·nal \-trē-ən-ᵊl\ *adj* **:** NORTHERN

sep·tet *also* **sep·tette** \sep-'tet\ *n* [G *septet*, fr. L *septem*] **1 :** a musical composition for seven instruments or voices **2 :** a group or set of seven; *esp* **:** the musicians that perform a septet

sep·tic \'sep-tik\ *adj* [L *septicus*, fr. Gk *sēptikos*, fr. *sēpein* to make putrid — more at SEPIA] **1 :** PUTREFACTIVE **2 :** of or characteristic of septicemia

sep·ti·ce·mia \,sep-tə-'sē-mē-ə\ *n* [NL, fr. L *septicus* + NL *-emia*] **:** invasion of the bloodstream by virulent microorganisms from a focus of infection accompanied esp. by chills, fever, and prostration — called also *blood poisoning* — **sep·ti·ce·mic** \-'sē-mik\ *adj*

sep·ti·ci·dal \ˌsep-tə-ˈsīd-ᵊl\ *adj* [NL *septum* + L *-cidere* to cut, fr. *caedere* — more at CONCISE] **:** dehiscent longitudinally at or along a septum ⟨a ~ fruit⟩ — **sep·ti·ci·dal·ly** \-ᵊl-ē\ *adv*

septic sore throat *n* **:** an inflammatory sore throat caused by hemolytic streptococci and marked by fever, prostration, and toxemia

septic tank *n* **:** a tank in which the solid matter of continuously flowing sewage is disintegrated by bacteria

sep·tif·ra·gal \sep-ˈtif-ri-gəl\ *adj* [NL *septum* + L *frangere* to break — more at BREAK] **:** dehiscing by breaking away from the dissepiments ⟨a ~ pod⟩ — **sep·tif·ra·gal·ly** \-gə-lē\ *adv*

sep·til·lion \sep-ˈtil-yən\ *n, often attrib* [F, fr. L *septem* + F *-illion* (as in *million*) — more at SEVEN] — see NUMBER table

sep·time \ˈsep-ˌtēm, sep-ˈ\ *n* [L *septima*, fem. of *septimus* seventh, fr. *septem*] **:** the seventh of the eight defensive positions in fencing

sep·tu·a·ge·nar·i·an \ˌsep-ˌt(y)ü-ə-jə-ˈner-ē-ən, ˌsep-tə-wə-jə-\ *n* [LL *septuagenarius* 70 years old, fr. L, of or containing 70, fr. *septuageni* 70 each, fr. *septuaginta*] **:** a person who is in his seventies — **septuagenarian** *adj*

Sep·tu·a·ge·si·ma \ˌsep-tə-wə-ˈjes-ə-mə, -ˈjā-zə-\ *n* [ME, fr. LL, fr. L, fem. of *septuagesimus* seventieth, fr. *septuaginta* 70] **:** the third Sunday before Lent

Sep·tu·a·gint \sep-ˈt(y)ü-ə-jənt, ˈsep-tə-wə-ˌjint\ *n* [LL *Septuaginta*, fr. L, seventy, irreg. fr. *septem* seven + *-ginta* (akin to L *viginti* twenty); fr. the approximate number of its translators — more at SEVEN, VIGESIMAL] **:** a pre-Christian Greek version of the Old Testament used by Greek-speaking Christians

sep·tum \ˈsep-təm\ *n, pl* **sep·ta** \-tə\ [NL, fr. L *saeptum* enclosure, fence, wall, fr. *saepire* to fence in, fr. *saepes* fence, hedge; akin to Gk *haimasia* stone wall] **:** a dividing wall or membrane — compare DISSEPIMENT

¹**sep·ul·cher** *or* **sep·ul·chre** \ˈsep-əl-kər\ *n* [ME *sepulcre*, fr. OF, fr. L *sepulcrum*, *sepulchrum*, fr. *sepelire* to bury; akin to Gk *hepein* to care for, Skt *sapati* he serves] **1 :** a place of burial **:** TOMB **2 :** a receptacle for religious relics esp. in an altar

²**sepulcher** *or* **sepulchre** *vt* **sep·ul·cher·ing** *or* **sep·ul·chring** \-k(ə-)riŋ\ **:** to place or receive in a sepulcher **:** BURY, ENTOMB

se·pul·chral \sə-ˈpəl-krəl\ *adj* **1 :** MORTUARY **2 :** suited to or suggestive of a sepulcher **:** FUNEREAL — **se·pul·chral·ly** \-krə-lē\ *adv*

sep·ul·ture \ˈsep-əl-ˌchu̇(ə)r\ *n* [ME, fr. OF, fr. L *sepultura*, fr. *sepultus*, pp. of *sepelire*] **1 :** BURIAL **2 :** SEPULCHER

se·qua·cious \si-ˈkwā-shəs\ *adj* [L *sequac-*, *sequax* inclined to follow, fr. *sequi*] **1** *archaic* **:** SUBSERVIENT, TRACTABLE **2 :** intellectually servile — **se·qua·cious·ly** *adv* — **se·quac·i·ty** \-ˈkwas-ət-ē\ *n*

se·quel \ˈsē-kwəl\ *n* [ME, fr. MF *sequelle*, fr. L *sequela*, fr. *sequi* to follow — more at SUE] **1 :** CONSEQUENCE, RESULT **2 a :** subsequent development **b :** the next installment (as of a speech or narrative) *esp* **:** a literary work continuing the course of a narrative begun in a preceding one

se·que·la \si-ˈkwel-ə, -ˈkwē-lə\ *n, pl* **se·que·lae** \-ˈkwel-(ˌ)ē, -ˌī; -ˈkwē-(ˌ)lē\ [NL, fr. L, sequel] **1 :** an aftereffect of disease or injury **2 :** a secondary result **:** CONSEQUENCE

¹**se·quence** \ˈsē-kwən(t)s, -ˌkwen(t)s\ *n* [ME, fr. ML *sequentia*, fr. LL, sequel, lit., act of following, fr. L *sequent-*, *sequens*, prp. of *sequi*] **1 :** a hymn in irregular meter between the gradual and Gospel in some masses **2 :** a continuous or connected series: as **a :** an extended series of poems united by a single theme ⟨sonnet ~⟩ **b :** three or more playing cards usu. of the same suit in consecutive order of rank **c :** a succession of repetitions of a melodic phrase or harmonic pattern each in a new position **d :** a set of elements ordered as are the natural numbers **e (1) :** a succession of related shots or scenes developing a single subject or phase of a film story (2) **:** EPISODE **3 a :** order of succession **b :** an arrangement of the tenses of successive verbs in a sentence designed to express a coherent relationship esp. between main and subordinate parts **4 a :** CONSEQUENCE, RESULT **b :** a subsequent development **5 :** continuity of progression

²**sequence** *vt* **:** to arrange in a sequence

se·quenc·er \-kwən-sər, -ˌkwen(t)-sər\ *n* **:** a device that determines a sequence

se·quen·cy \ˈsē-kwən-sē\ *n* [LL *sequentia*] **:** SEQUENCE

se·quent \ˈsē-kwənt\ *adj* [L *sequent-*, *sequens*, prp.] **1 :** SUCCEEDING, CONSECUTIVE **2 :** CONSEQUENT, RESULTANT — **sequent** *n*

se·quen·tial \si-ˈkwen-chəl\ *adj* **1 :** that is sequent **2 :** based on a method of determining at each of a series of samples whether to accept or reject a hypothesis or to continue the sampling ⟨~ analysis⟩ — **se·quen·tial·ly** \-chə-lē\ *adv*

¹**se·ques·ter** \si-ˈkwes-tər\ *vt* **se·ques·ter·ing** \-t(ə-)riŋ\ [ME *sequestren*, fr. MF *sequestrer*, fr. LL *sequestrare* to surrender for safekeeping, set apart, fr. L *sequester* agent, depositary, bailee; akin to L *sequi* to follow] **1 a :** to set apart **:** SEGREGATE **b :** SECLUDE, WITHDRAW **2 a :** to seize esp. by a writ of sequestration **b :** to place (property) in custody esp. in sequestration

²**sequester** *n, obs* **:** SEPARATION, ISOLATION

se·que·strate \si-ˈkwes-ˌtrāt; ˈsē-kwəs-, ˈsek-\ *vt* [LL *sequestratus*, pp. of *sequestrare*] **:** SEQUESTER

se·ques·tra·tion \ˌsē-kwəs-ˈtrā-shən, ˌsek-; si-ˌkwes-\ *n* **1 :** the act of sequestering **:** the state of being sequestered **2 a :** a legal writ authorizing a sheriff or commissioner to take into custody the property of a defendant who is in contempt until he complies with the orders of a court **b :** a deposit whereby a neutral depositary agrees to hold property in litigation and to restore it to the party to whom it is adjudged to belong **3 :** the formation of a sequestrum

se·ques·trum \si-ˈkwes-trəm\ *n, pl* **sequestrums** *also* **se·ques·tra** \-trə\ [NL, fr. L, legal sequestration; akin to L *sequester* bailee] **:** a fragment of dead bone detached from adjoining sound bone

se·quin \ˈsē-kwən\ *n* [F, fr. It *zecchino*, fr. *zecca* mint, fr. Ar *sikkah* die, coin] **1 :** an old gold coin of Italy and Turkey **2 :** SPANGLE

se·quined *or* **se·quinned** \-kwənd\ *adj* **:** ornamented with or as if with sequins

se·quoia \si-ˈkwȯi-ə\ *n* [NL, genus name, fr. *Sequoya* (George Guess) †1843 Am Indian scholar] **:** either of two huge coniferous California trees of the pine family that reach a height of over 300 feet: **a :** BIG TREE **b :** REDWOOD 3a

sera *pl of* SERUM

se·rac \sə-ˈrak, sā-\ *n* [F *sérac*, lit., a kind of white cheese, fr. ML *seracium* whey, fr. L *serum* whey — more at SERUM] **:** a pinnacle, sharp ridge, or block of ice among the crevasses of a glacier

se·ra·glio \sə-ˈral-(ˌ)yō, -ˈräl-\ *n* [It *serraglio* enclosure, seraglio, partly fr. ML *serraculum* bar of a door, bolt, fr. LL *serare* to bolt; partly fr. Turk *saray* palace — more at SEAR] **1 :** HAREM 1a **2 :** a palace of a sultan

se·rai \sə-ˈrī\ *n* [Turk & Per; Turk *saray* mansion, palace, fr. Per *sarāī* mansion, inn] **1 :** CARAVANSARY **2 :** SERAGLIO 2

se·rail \sā-ˈrä-yə, -ˈrī, -ˈrī(ə)l\ *n* [MF, fr. OIt *serraglio*] **:** SERAGLIO

ser·al \ˈsir-əl\ *adj* **:** of, relating to, or constituting an ecological sere

serape *var of* SARAPE

ser·aph \ˈser-əf\ *also* **ser·a·phim** \-ə-ˌfim\ *n, pl* **seraphim** *or* **seraphs** [LL *seraphim*, pl., seraphs, fr. Heb *śĕrāphīm*] **1 :** one of the 6-winged angels of the highest rank believed in ancient Judaism to guard God's throne with sacred ardor **2 :** one resembling or befitting an angel — **seraph** *adj* — **se·raph·ic** \sə-ˈraf-ik\ *adj* — **se·raph·i·cal·ly** \-i-k(ə-)lē\ *adv*

Se·ra·pis \sə-ˈrā-pəs\ *n* [L, fr. Gk *Sarapis*] **:** an Egyptian god combining attributes of Osiris and Apis and having a widespread cult throughout Greece and Rome

Serb \ˈsərb\ *n* [Serb *Srb*] **1 :** one of the south Slavic nationality and dominant ethnic group of Serbia and of adjacent states of Yugoslavia **2 :** SERBIAN 2 — **Serb** *adj*

Ser·bi·an \ˈsər-bē-ən\ *n* **1 :** SERB 1 **2 a :** the Serbo-Croatian language as spoken in Serbia **b :** a literary form of Serbo-Croatian using the Cyrillic alphabet — **Serbian** *adj*

Ser·bo-Cro·atian \ˌsər-(ˌ)bō-krō-ˈā-shən\ *n* **1 :** the Slavic language of the Serbs and Croats consisting of Serbian written in the Cyrillic alphabet and Croatian written in the Roman alphabet **2 :** one whose native language is Serbo-Croatian — **Serbo-Croatian** *adj*

¹**sere** \ˈsi(ə)r\ *adj* [ME, fr. OE *sēar* dry; akin to OHG *sōrēn* to wither, Gk *hauos* dry] **1 :** WITHERED **2** *archaic* **:** THREADBARE

²**sere** *n* [L *series* series] **:** a series of ecological communities succeeding one another in the biotic development of an area or formation

¹**ser·e·nade** \ˌser-ə-ˈnād\ *n* [F *sérénade*, fr. It *serenata*, fr. *sereno* clear, calm (of weather), fr. L *serenus*] **1 a :** a complimentary vocal or instrumental performance; *esp* **:** one given outdoors at night for a woman **b :** a work so performed **2 :** a work for chamber orchestra resembling a suite

²**serenade** *vt* **:** to perform a serenade in honor of **~** *vi* **:** to play a serenade — **ser·e·nad·er** *n*

ser·e·na·ta \ˌser-ə-ˈnät-ə\ *n* [It, serenade] **:** an 18th century secular cantata

ser·en·dip·i·tous \ˌser-ən-ˈdip-ət-əs\ *adj* **:** obtained or characterized by serendipity ⟨~ discoveries⟩

ser·en·dip·i·ty \-ˈdip-ət-ē\ *n* [fr. its possession by the heroes of the Per fairy tale *The Three Princes of Serendip*] **:** the gift of finding valuable or agreeable things not sought for

¹**se·rene** \sə-ˈrēn\ *adj* [L *serenus*; akin to OHG *serawēn* to become dry, Gk *xēros* dry] **1 a :** clear and free of storms or unpleasant change ⟨~ skies⟩ **b :** shining bright and steady **2 :** marked by utter calm **:** TRANQUIL **3 :** AUGUST — used as part of a title ⟨His *Serene* Highness⟩ **syn** see CALM — **se·rene·ly** *adv* — **se·rene·ness** \-ˈrēn-nəs\ *n*

²**serene** *n* **1 :** a serene condition or expanse (as of sky, sea, or light) **2 :** SERENITY, TRANQUILLITY

se·ren·i·ty \sə-ˈren-ət-ē\ *n* **:** the quality or state of being serene

serf \ˈsərf\ *n* [F, fr. L *servus* slave, servant, serf — more at SERVE] **:** a member of a servile feudal class bound to the soil and more or less subject to the will of his lord — **serf·age** \ˈsər-fij\ *n* — **serf·dom** \ˈsərf-dəm\ *n* — **serf·hood** \ˈsərf-ˌhu̇d\ *n* — **serf·ish** \ˈsər-fish\ *adj* — **serf·ism** \-ˌfiz-əm\ *n*

serge \ˈsərj\ *n* [ME *sarge*, fr. MF, fr. (assumed) VL *sarica*, fr. L *serica*, fem. of *sericus* silken — more at SERICEOUS] **:** a durable twilled fabric having a smooth clear face and a pronounced diagonal rib on the front and the back

ser·gean·cy \ˈsär-jən-sē\ *n* **:** the function, office, or rank of a sergeant

ser·geant \ˈsär-jənt\ *n* [ME, servant, attendant, sergeant, fr. OF *sergent*, *serjant*, fr. L *servient-*, *serviens*, prp. of *servire* to serve] **1 :** SERGEANT AT ARMS **2** *obs* **:** an officer who enforces the judgments of a court or the commands of one in authority **3 :** an officer in a police force ranking in the U. S. just below captain or sometimes lieutenant and in England just below inspector **4 :** a noncommissioned officer in the army or marine corps ranking above a corporal and below a staff sergeant; *broadly* **:** any of the noncommissioned officers ranking above a corporal in the army and marine corps and above an airman first class in the air force

sergeant at arms : an officer of an organization (as a legislative body or court of law) who preserves order and executes commands

sergeant first class *n* **:** a noncommissioned officer in the army ranking above a staff sergeant and below a master sergeant

sergeant fish *n* **1 :** COBIA **2 :** a snook (*Centropomus undecimalis*)

sergeant major *n, pl* **sergeants major** *or* **sergeant majors 1 :** a noncommissioned officer in the army, air force, or marine corps serving as chief administrative assistant in a headquarters **2 :** a noncommissioned officer of the highest enlisted rank in the army or marine corps

ser·geanty \ˈsär-jənt-ē\ *n* [ME *sergeantie*, fr. MF *sergentie*, fr. *sergent* sergeant] **:** any of numerous feudal services by which an estate is held of the king or other lord distinct from military tenure and from socage tenure

¹**se·ri·al** \ˈsir-ē-əl\ *adj* **1 :** of, consisting of, or arranged in a series, rank, or row ⟨~ order⟩ **2 :** belonging to a series maturing periodically rather than on a single date ⟨~ bonds⟩ **3 :** TWELVE-TONE ⟨~ technique⟩ — **se·ri·al·ly** \-ə-lē\ *adv*

²**serial** *n* **1 :** a work appearing (as in a magazine or on television) in parts at intervals **2 :** one part of a serial work **:** INSTALLMENT — **se·ri·al·ist** \-ə-ləst\ *n*

se·ri·al·iza·tion \ˌsir-ē-ə-lə-ˈzā-shən\ *n* **:** the act or process of serializing

se·ri·al·ize \ˈsir-ē-ə-ˌlīz\ *vt* **:** to arrange or publish in serial form

se·ri·ate \ˈsir-ē-ˌāt, -ē-ət\ *adj* [(assumed) NL *seriatus*, fr. L *series*] **:** arranged in a series or succession — **se·ri·ate** \-ē-ˌāt\ *vb* — **se·ri·ate·ly** *adv*

¹**se·ri·a·tim** \ˌsir-ē-ˈāt-əm, -ˈat-\ *adv* [ML, fr. L *series*] **:** in a series **:** SERIALLY

²seriatim *adj* **:** following seriatim

se·ri·ceous \sə-ˈrish-əs\ *adj* [LL *sericeus,* fr. L *sericum* silk garment, silk, fr. neut. of *sericus* silken, fr. Gk *sērikos,* fr. *Sēres,* an eastern Asiatic people producing silk in ancient times] **1 :** of, relating to, or consisting of silk **:** SILKY **2 :** finely pubescent ⟨~ leaf⟩

ser·i·cin \ˈser-ə-sən\ *n* [ISV, fr. L *sericum* silk] **:** a gelatinous protein that cements the two fibroin filaments in a silk fiber

seri·cul·tu·ral \ˌser-ə-ˈkəlch-(ə-)rəl\ *adj* **:** of or relating to sericulture

seri·cul·ture \ˈser-ə-ˌkəl-chər\ *n* [L *sericum* silk + E *culture*] **:** the production of raw silk by raising silkworms — **seri·cul·tur·ist** \ˌser-ə-ˈkəlch-(ə-)rəst\ *n*

se·ries \ˈsi(ə)r-(ˌ)ēz\ *n, pl* **series** *often attrib* [L, fr. *serere* to join, link together; akin to Gk *eirein* to string together, *hormos* chain, necklace] **1 a :** a number of things or events of the same class coming one after another **b :** a group with an order of arrangement exhibiting progression **2 :** the indicated sum of a usu. infinite sequence of numbers **3 :** a succession of volumes or issues published with related subjects or authors, similar format and price, or continuous numbering **4 :** a division of rock formations smaller than a system comprising rocks deposited during an epoch **5 :** an arrangement of the parts of or elements in an electric circuit whereby the whole current passes through each part or element without branching **6 :** a set of vowels connected by ablaut (as *i, a, u* in *ring, rang, rung*) **7 :** a group of successive coordinate sentence elements joined together ⟨an, a, b, and c ~⟩ **8 :** three consecutive games in bowling — **in series :** in a serial arrangement

series winding *n* **:** a winding in which the armature coil and the field-magnet coil are in series with the external circuit — **se·ries-wound** \ˌsir-ēz-ˈwau̇nd\ *adj*

ser·if \ˈser-əf\ *n* [prob. fr. D *schreef* stroke, line, fr. MD, fr. *schriven* to write, fr. L *scribere* — more at SCRIBE] **:** any of the short lines stemming from and at an angle to the upper and lower ends of the strokes of a letter

seri·graph \ˈser-ə-ˌgraf\ *n* [L *sericum* silk + Gk *graphein* to write, draw — more at CARVE] **:** an original color print made by pressing pigments through a silk screen with a stencil design — **se·rig·ra·pher** \sə-ˈrig-rə-fər\ *n* — **se·rig·ra·phy** \-fē\ *n*

se·rin \sə-ˈra^{n}\ *n* [F] **:** a small European finch (*Serinus canarius*) related to the canary

ser·ine \ˈse(ə)r-ˌēn\ *n* [ISV *sericin* + *-ine*] **:** a crystalline amino acid $C_3H_7NO_3$ obtained by hydrolysis of many proteins or cephalins

se·rio·com·ic \ˌsir-ē-ō-ˈkäm-ik\ *adj* [*serious* + *-o-* + *comic*] **:** having a mixture of the serious and the comic — **se·rio·com·i·cal·ly** \-i-k(ə-)lē\ *adv*

se·ri·ous \ˈsir-ē-əs\ *adj* [ME *seryows,* fr. MF or LL; MF *serieux,* fr. LL *seriosus,* alter. of L *serius*] **1 :** thoughtful or subdued in appearance or manner **:** SOBER **2 a :** requiring much thought or work ⟨~ study⟩ **b :** of or relating to a matter of importance ⟨a ~ play⟩ **3 a :** not joking or trifling **:** EARNEST **b** *archaic* **:** PIOUS **c :** deeply interested **:** DEVOTED ⟨~ fishermen⟩ **4 a :** not easily answered or solved ⟨~ objections⟩ **b :** having important or dangerous possible consequences ⟨a ~ injury⟩

syn GRAVE, SOLEMN, SEDATE, STAID, SOBER, EARNEST: SERIOUS implies a concern for what really matters; GRAVE implies both seriousness and dignity in expression or attitude; SOLEMN suggests an impressive gravity utterly free from levity; SEDATE implies a composed and decorous seriousness; STAID suggests a settled, accustomed sedateness and prim self-restraint; SOBER stresses seriousness of purpose and absence of levity or frivolity; EARNEST suggests sincerity or often zealousness of purpose

se·ri·ous·ly *adv* **:** in a serious manner or vein **:** to a serious extent **:** EARNESTLY, SEVERELY

se·ri·ous–mind·ed \ˌsir-ē-ə-ˈsmīn-dəd\ *adj* **:** having a serious disposition or trend of thought — **se·ri·ous–mind·ed·ly** *adv* — **se·ri·ous–mind·ed·ness** *n*

se·ri·ous·ness *n* **:** the quality or state of being serious

ser·jeant, ser·jeanty *var of* SERGEANT, SERGEANTY

ser·jeant–at–law \ˌsär-jənt-ət-ˈlȯ\ *n, pl* **ser·jeants–at–law** \-jən(t)-sət-\ **:** a barrister of the highest rank

ser·mon \ˈsər-mən\ *n* [ME, fr. OF, fr. ML *sermon-, sermo,* fr. L, speech, conversation, fr. *serere* to link together — more at SERIES] **1 :** a religious discourse delivered in public usu. by a clergyman as a part of a worship service **2 a :** a lecture on conduct or duty **b :** an annoying harangue — **ser·mon·ic** \ˌsər-ˈmän-ik\ *adj*

ser·mon·ize \ˈsər-mə-ˌnīz\ *vi* **1 :** to compose or deliver a sermon **2 :** to discourse didactically or dogmatically ~ *vt* **:** to preach at length — **ser·mon·iz·er** *n*

Sermon on the Mount : a discourse delivered by Jesus and recorded in Matthew 5–7 and Luke 6: 20–49

sero- *comb form* [L *serum*] **:** serum ⟨*serology*⟩

se·ro·log·ic \ˌsir-ə-ˈläj-ik, ˌser-\ *adj* **:** of, relating to, or employing the methods of serology — **se·ro·log·i·cal** \-i-kəl\ *adj* — **se·ro·log·i·cal·ly** \-k(ə-)lē\ *adv*

se·rol·o·gist \sə-ˈräl-ə-jəst\ *n* **:** a specialist in serology

se·rol·o·gy \-jē\ *n* [ISV] **:** a science dealing with serums and esp. their reactions and properties

se·ro·pu·ru·lent \ˌsir-ō-ˈp(y)u̇r-(y)ə-lənt, ˌser-\ *adj* **:** consisting of a mixture of serum and pus ⟨a ~ exudate⟩

se·ro·sa \sə-ˈrō-sə, -zə\ *n* [NL, fr. fem. of *serosus* serous, fr. L *serum*] **:** a usu. enclosing serous membrane — **se·ro·sal** \-ˈrō-səl, -zəl\ *adj*

se·rot·i·nal \sə-ˈrät-nəl, -ᵊn-əl\ *adj* **:** of or relating to the latter and usu. drier part of summer

se·rot·i·nous \sə-ˈrät-nəs, -ᵊn-əs\ *adj* [L *serotinus* coming late, fr. *sero* late — more at SOIREE] **:** late esp. in developing or flowering

se·ro·to·nin \ˌsir-ə-ˈtō-nən, ˌser-, -ˈtän-ən\ *n* [*sero-* + *tonic* + *-in*] **:** a powerful vasoconstrictor compound $C_{10}H_{12}N_2O$ derived from indole and found esp. in the blood serum and gastric mucosa of mammals

se·rous \ˈsir-əs, ˈser-\ *adj* [MF *sereux,* fr. *serum,* fr. L] **:** of, relating to, or resembling serum; *esp* **:** of thin watery constitution ⟨a ~ exudate⟩

serous membrane *n* **:** a thin membrane (as the peritoneum) with cells that secrete a serous fluid; *esp* **:** SEROSA

se·row \sə-ˈrō\ *n* [Lepcha *să-ro* long-haired Tibetan goat] **:** any of several goat antelopes (genus *Capricornis*) of eastern Asia usu. rather dark and heavily built including some with distinct manes

ser·pent \ˈsər-pənt\ *n, often attrib* [ME, fr. MF, fr. L *serpent-, serpens,* fr. prp. of *serpere* to creep; akin to Gk *herpein* to creep, Skt *sarpati* he creeps] **1 a** *archaic* **:** a noxious creature that creeps, hisses, or stings **b :** SNAKE; *esp* **:** a large snake **2 :** DEVIL 1 **3 :** a subtle treacherous malicious person **4 :** an obsolete bass wind instrument made of wood

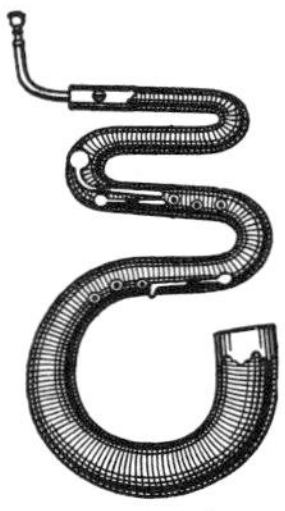

serpent 4

¹ser·pen·tine \ˈsər-pən-ˌtēn, -ˌtīn\ *adj* [ME, fr. MF *serpentin,* fr. LL *serpentinus,* fr. L *serpent-, serpens*] **1 :** of or resembling a serpent (as in form or movement) **2 :** subtly wily or tempting **:** DIABOLIC **3 :** winding or turning one way and another **:** SINUOUS

²serpentine *n* **:** something that winds sinuously

³serpentine *n* [ME, fr. ML *serpentina, serpentinum,* fr. LL, fem. & neut. of *serpentinus* resembling a serpent] **:** a mineral or rock consisting essentially of a hydrous magnesium silicate $H_4Mg_3Si_2O$ usu. having a dull green color and often a mottled appearance

ser·pen·tine·ly \-lē\ *adv* **:** in a serpentine manner

ser·pig·i·nous \(ˌ)sər-ˈpij-ə-nəs\ *adj* [ML *serpigin-, serpigo* creeping skin disease, fr. L *serpere* to creep] **:** CREEPING, SPREADING; *esp* **:** healing over in one portion while continuing to advance in another ⟨~ ulcer⟩ — **ser·pig·i·nous·ly** *adv*

ser·ra·nid \sə-ˈrā-nəd, -ˈran-əd\ *n* [deriv. of L *serra* saw] **:** any of a large family (Serranidae) of carnivorous marine percoid fishes having an oblong compressed body covered with ctenoid scales and including many important food and sport fishes (as the sea basses) esp. of warm seas — **serranid** *adj* — **ser·ra·noid** \-ˈrā-ˌnȯid, -ˈran-ˌȯid\ *adj or n*

¹ser·rate \sə-ˈrāt, ˈse(ə)r-ˌāt\ *vt* [LL *serratus,* pp. of *serrare* to saw, fr. L *serra*] **:** to mark with serrations **:** NOTCH

²ser·rate \ˈse(ə)r-ˌāt, ˈser-ət\ *adj* [L *serratus,* fr. *serra* saw] **1 :** notched or toothed on the edge **2 :** having marginal teeth pointing forward or toward the apex ⟨~ leaf⟩

ser·ra·tion \sə-ˈrā-shən, se-\ *n* **1 :** the condition of being serrate **2 :** a formation resembling the toothed edge of a saw **3 :** one of the teeth in a serrate margin

ser·ried \ˈser-ēd\ *adj* **1 :** crowded or pressed together **:** COMPACT **2** [by alter.] **:** SERRATE — **ser·ried·ly** *adv* — **ser·ried·ness** *n*

ser·ru·late \ˈser-(y)ə-lət, -ˌlāt\ *also* **ser·ru·lat·ed** \-ˌlāt-əd\ *adj* [NL *serrulatus,* fr. L *serrula,* dim. of *serra*] **:** finely serrate

ser·ru·la·tion \ˌser-(y)ə-ˈlā-shən\ *n* **1 :** the state of being serrulate **2 :** a serrulate formation

ser·ry \ˈser-ē\ *vb* [MF *serré,* pp. of *serrer* to press, crowd — more at SEAR] *vi, archaic* **:** to press together esp. in ranks ~ *vt* **:** to crowd together

ser·tu·lar·i·an \ˌsər-chə-ˈler-ē-ən, ˌsȯrt-ᵊl-ˈer-\ *n* [NL *Sertularia,* genus name, fr. L *sertula,* dim. of *serta* melilot, fr. fem. of *sertus,* pp. of *serere* to link together, entwine — more at SERIES] **:** any of a genus (*Sertularia*) of delicate branching hydroids — **sertularian** *adj*

se·rum \ˈsir-əm, ˈser-\ *n, pl* **serums** *or* **se·ra** \-ə\ *often attrib* [L, whey, serum; akin to Gk *oros* whey, serum, *hormē* onset, assault, Skt *sarati* it flows] **1 :** the watery portion of an animal fluid remaining after coagulation: **a :** BLOOD SERUM; *esp* **:** immune blood serum that contains specific immune bodies (as antitoxins or agglutinins) ⟨antitoxin ~⟩ **b :** WHEY **c :** a normal or pathological serous fluid (as in a blister) **2 :** the watery part of a plant fluid

serum albumin *n* **:** a crystallizable albumin or mixture of albumins that normally constitutes more than half of the protein in blood serum and serves to maintain the osmotic pressure of the blood

serum globulin *n* **:** a globulin or mixture of globulins occurring in blood serum and containing most of the antibodies of the blood

ser·val \ˈsər-vəl, (ˌ)sər-ˈval\ *n* [F, fr. Pg *lobo cerval* lynx, fr. ML *lupus cervalis,* lit., cervine wolf] **:** a long-legged African wildcat (*Felis capensis*) having large untufted ears and a tawny black-spotted coat — **ser·va·line** \ˈsər-və-ˌlīn\ *adj*

ser·vant \ˈsər-vənt\ *n* [ME, fr. OF, fr. prp. of *servir*] **:** one that serves others; *specif* **:** one that performs duties about the person or home of a master or personal employer

¹serve \ˈsərv\ *vb* [ME *serven,* fr. OF *servir,* fr. L *servire* to be a slave, serve, fr. *servus* slave, servant, perh. of Etruscan origin] *vi* **1 a :** to be a servant **b :** to do military or naval service **2 :** to assist a celebrant as server at mass **3 a :** to be of use **b :** to be favorable, opportune, or convenient **c :** to stand by **:** ASSIST **d :** to hold an office **:** discharge a duty or function ⟨~ on a jury⟩ **4 a :** to prove adequate or satisfactory **b :** to hold good **5 :** to help persons to food: as **a :** to wait at table **b :** to set out portions of food or drink **6 :** to wait on customers **7 :** to put the ball in play (as in tennis) ~ *vt* **1 a :** to be a servant to **:** ATTEND **b :** to give the service and respect due to (a superior) **c :** to comply with the commands or demands of **:** GRATIFY **d :** to give military or naval service to **e :** to perform the duties of (an office or post) **2 :** to act as server at (mass) **3** *archaic* **:** to pay a lover's or suitor's court to (a lady) **4 a :** to work through or perform a term of service ⟨*served* his time as a mate⟩ **b :** to put in (a term of imprisonment) **5 a :** to wait on at table **b :** to bring (food) to a diner **6 a :** to furnish or supply with something needed or desired **b :** to wait on (a customer) in a store **c :** to furnish professional service to **7 a :** to answer the needs of **:** AVAIL **b :** to be enough for **:** SUFFICE **c :** to contribute or conduce to **:** PROMOTE **8 :** to treat or act toward in a specified way **:** REQUITE ⟨he *served* me ill⟩ **9 a :** to bring to notice, deliver, or execute as required by law **b :** to make legal service upon (a person named in a writ) **10** *of an animal* **:** to copulate with **11 :** to wind yarn or wire tightly around (a rope or stay) for protection **12 :** to provide services that benefit or help **13 :** to put (the ball) in play (as in tennis)

²serve *n* **:** the act of putting the ball in play in any of various net or court games (as tennis)

serv·er \ˈsər-vər\ *n* **1 :** one that serves food or drink **2 :** the player who puts a ball in play **3 :** the celebrant's assistant at low mass **4 :** something used in serving food or drink

¹ser·vice \ˈsər-vəs\ *n* [ME, fr. OF, fr. L *servitium* condition of a slave, body of slaves, fr. *servus* slave] **1 :** the occupation or function of serving ⟨in active ~⟩; *specif* **:** employment as a servant ⟨entered his ~⟩ **2 a :** the work or action performed by one that serves ⟨gives good and quick ~⟩ **b :** HELP, USE, BENEFIT ⟨be of ~ to them⟩ **c :** contribution to the welfare of others **d :** disposal for use ⟨at your ~⟩ **3 a :** a form followed in worship or in a religious

ceremony ⟨the burial ~⟩ **b :** a meeting for worship ⟨held an evening ~⟩ **4 :** the act of serving: as **a :** a helpful act **:** good turn ⟨did him a ~⟩ **b :** useful labor that does not produce a tangible commodity — usu. used in pl. ⟨charge for professional ~*s*⟩ **c :** SERVE **5 :** a set of articles for a particular use ⟨a silver ~ for 12⟩ **6 :** an administrative division (as of a government or business) ⟨the consular ~⟩ **:** one of a nation's military forces ⟨called into the ~⟩ **7 :** a facility supplying some public demand ⟨bus ~⟩; *specif* **:** one providing maintenance and repair ⟨television ~⟩ **8 :** the materials used for serving (as a rope)

[2]**service** *adj* **1 a :** of or relating to the armed services **b :** of, relating to, or constituting a branch of an army that exists to provide service and supplies **2 :** used in serving or supplying **3 :** intended for everyday use **:** DURABLE **4 a :** providing services or producer goods **b :** offering repair, maintenance, or incidental services

[3]**service** *vt* **:** to perform services for: as **a :** to repair or provide maintenance for **b :** to meet interest and sinking fund payments on debt (as government debt) **c :** to perform any of the business functions auxiliary to production or distribution

[4]**ser·vice** \'sär-vəs, 'sər-\ *n* [ME *serves,* pl. of *serve* serviceberry, service tree, fr. OE *syrfe,* fr. (assumed) VL *sorbea,* fr. L *sorbus* service tree] **:** an Old World tree (*Sorbus domestica*) resembling the related mountain ashes but having larger flowers and larger edible fruit; *also* **:** a related Old World tree (*S. torminalis*) with bitter fruits

ser·vice·abil·i·ty \,sər-və-sə-'bil-ət-ē\ *n* **:** SERVICEABLENESS

ser·vice·able \'sər-və-sə-bəl\ *adj* **1 :** HELPFUL, USEFUL **2 :** wearing well in use — **ser·vice·able·ness** *n* — **ser·vice·ably** \-blē\ *adv*

ser·vice·ber·ry \'sär-vəs-,ber-ē, 'sər-\ *n* **1 :** the fruit of a service tree **2 :** JUNEBERRY

service book *n* **:** a book setting forth forms of worship used in religious services

service box *n* **:** the area in which a player stands while serving in various wall and net games

service ceiling *n* **:** the altitude at which under standard air conditions a particular airplane can no longer rise at a rate greater than a small designated rate (as 100 feet per minute)

service charge *n* **:** a fee charged for a particular service often in addition to a standard or basic fee

service club *n* **1 :** a club of business or professional men or women organized for their common benefit and active in community service **2 :** a recreation center for enlisted men provided by one of the armed services

ser·vice·man \'sər-və-,sman, -smən\ *n* **1 :** a male member of the armed forces **2 :** a man employed to repair or maintain equipment

service mark *n* **:** a mark or device used to identify a service (as transportation or insurance) offered to customers

service medal *n* **:** a medal awarded to an individual who does military service in a specified war or campaign — compare DECORATION

service station *n* **1 :** FILLING STATION **2 :** a depot or place at which some service is offered

service stripe *n* **:** a stripe worn on an enlisted man's left sleeve to indicate three years of service in the army or air force or four years in the navy

ser·vice tree \'sär-vəs-, 'sər-\ *n* [[4]*service*] **1 a :** [4]SERVICE **b :** MOUNTAIN ASH **2 :** JUNEBERRY

ser·vi·ette \,sər-vē-'et\ *n* [F, fr. MF, fr. *servir* to serve] *chiefly Brit* **:** a table napkin

ser·vile \'sər-vəl, -,vīl\ *adj* [ME, fr. L *servilis,* fr. *servus* slave — more at SERVE] **1 :** of or befitting a slave or an enslaved or menial class **2 :** lacking spirit or independence **syn** see SUBSERVIENT — **ser·vile·ly** \-və(l)-lē, -,vīl-lē\ *adv* — **ser·vile·ness** \-vəl-nəs, -,vīl-\ *n* — **ser·vil·i·ty** \(,)sər-'vil-ət-ē\ *n*

serv·ing \'sər-viŋ\ *n* **:** a helping of food or drink

Ser·vite \'sər-,vīt\ *n* [ML *Servitae,* pl. Servites, fr. L *servus*] **:** a member of the mendicant Order of Servants of Mary founded at Florence in 1233 — **Servite** *adj*

ser·vi·tor \'sər-vət-ər, -və-,tȯ(ə)r\ *n* [ME *servitour,* fr. MF, fr. LL *servitor,* fr. L *servitus,* pp. of *servire* to serve] **:** a male servant

ser·vi·tude \'sər-və-,t(y)üd\ *n* [ME, fr. MF, fr. L *servitudo* slavery, fr. *servus* slave] **1 :** the state of subjection to another that constitutes or resembles slavery or serfdom **2 :** a right by which something (as a piece of land) owned by one person is subject to a specified use or enjoyment by another

syn SERVITUDE, SLAVERY, BONDAGE mean the state of being subject to a master. SERVITUDE is chiefly rhetorical and imprecise in use; it implies in general lack of liberty to do as one pleases, specifically lack of freedom to determine one's course of action and conditions of living; SLAVERY implies subjection to a master who owns one's person and may treat one as property; BONDAGE implies a state of being bound in law or by physical restraint to a state of complete subjection to the will of another

ser·vo \'sər-(,)vō\ *n, often attrib* **1 :** SERVOMOTOR **2 :** SERVOMECHANISM

ser·vo·mech·a·nism \'sər-(,)vō-,mek-ə-,niz-əm\ *n* [*servo-* (as in *servomotor*) + *mechanism*] **:** an automatic device for controlling large amounts of power by means of very small amounts of power and automatically correcting performance of a mechanism

ser·vo·mo·tor \'sər-vō-,mōt-ər\ *n* [F *servo-moteur,* fr. L *servus* slave, servant + F *-o-* + *moteur* motor, fr. L *motor* one that moves — more at MOTOR] **:** a power-driven mechanism that supplements a primary control operated by a comparatively feeble force (as in a servomechanism)

ses·a·me \'ses-ə-mē\ *n* [alter. of earlier *sesam, sesama,* fr. L *sesamum, sesama,* fr. Gk *sēsamon, sēsamē,* of Sem origin; akin to Assyr *šamaššamu* sesame, Ar *simsim*] **1 :** an East Indian annual erect herb (*Sesamum indicum* of the family Pedaliaceae); *also* **:** its small flattish seeds used as a source of oil and a flavoring agent **2 :** OPEN SESAME

ses·a·moid \-,mȯid\ *adj* [Gk *sēsamoeidēs,* lit., resembling sesame seed, fr. *sēsamon*] **:** of, relating to, or being a nodular mass of bone or cartilage in a tendon esp. at a joint or bony prominence — **sesamoid** *n*

sesqui- *comb form* [L, one and a half, half again, lit., and a half, fr. *semis* half (fr. *semi-*) + *-que* (enclitic) and; akin to Gk *te* and, Skt *ca,* Goth *-h, -uh*] **1 :** one and a half times ⟨*sesqui*centennial⟩ **2 a :** containing three atoms or equivalents of a specified element or radical esp. combined with two of another ⟨*sesqui*oxide⟩ **b :** intermediate **:** combination ⟨*sesqui*carbonate⟩

ses·qui·car·bon·ate \,ses-kwi-'kär-bə-,nāt, -nət\ *n* **:** a salt that is neither a simple normal carbonate nor a simple bicarbonate but often a combination of the two

ses·qui·cen·ten·ni·al \,ses-kwi-(,)sen-'ten-ē-əl\ *n* **:** a 150th anniversary or its celebration — **sesquicentennial** *adj*

ses·qui·pe·da·lian \,ses-kwə-pə-'dāl-yən\ *adj* [L *sesquipedalis,* lit., a foot and a half long, fr. *sesqui-* + *ped-, pes* foot — more at FOOT] **1 :** having many syllables **:** LONG **2 :** given to or characterized by the use of long words

ses·sile \'ses-əl, -,īl\ *adj* [L *sessilis* of or fit for sitting, low, dwarf (of plants), fr. *sessus,* pp.] **1 :** attached directly by the base and not raised upon a stalk or peduncle ⟨a ~ leaf⟩ **2 :** permanently attached **:** not free to move about **:** SEDENTARY ⟨~ polyps⟩ — **ses·sil·i·ty** \se-'sil-ət-ē\ *n*

ses·sion \'sesh-ən\ *n* [ME, fr. MF, fr. L *session-, sessio,* lit., act of sitting, fr. *sessus,* pp. of *sedēre* to sit — more at SIT] **1 :** a meeting or series of meetings of a body (as a court or legislature) for the transaction of business ⟨morning ~⟩ **2** *pl* **a** (1) **:** a sitting of English justices of peace in execution of the powers conferred by their commissions (2) **:** an English court holding such sessions **b :** any of various courts answering more or less to the English sessions **3 :** the period between the first meeting of a legislative or judicial body and the prorogation or final adjournment **4 :** the ruling body of a Presbyterian congregation consisting of the elders in active service **5 :** the period during the year or day in which a school conducts classes **6 :** a meeting or period devoted to a particular activity ⟨recording ~⟩ — **ses·sion·al** \'sesh-nəl, -ən-ᵊl\ *adj*

ses·terce \'ses-,tərs\ *n* [L *sestertius,* fr. *sestertius* two and a half times as great (fr. its being equal originally to two and a half asses), fr. *semis* half (fr. *semi-*) + *tertius* third — more at THIRD] **:** an ancient Roman coin equal to ¼ denarius

ses·ter·tium \se-'stər-sh(ē-)əm\ *n, pl* **ses·ter·tia** \-sh(ē-)ə\ [L, fr. gen. pl. of *sestertius* (in the phrase *milia sestertium* thousands of sesterces)] **:** a unit of value in ancient Rome equal to one thousand sesterces

ses·tet \se-'stet\ *n* [It *sestetto,* fr. *sesto* sixth, fr. L *sextus* — more at SEXT] **:** a stanza or a poem of six lines; *specif* **:** the last six lines of an Italian sonnet

ses·ti·na \se-'stē-nə\ *n* [It, fr. *sesto* sixth] **:** a lyrical fixed form consisting of six six-line usu. unrhymed stanzas in which the end words of the first stanza recur as end words of the following five stanzas in a successively rotating order and as the middle and end words of the three verses of the concluding tercet

[1]**set** \'set\ *vb* **set; set·ting** [ME *setten,* fr. OE *settan;* akin to OHG *sezzen* to set, OE *sittan* to sit] *vt* **1 a :** to cause to sit **b :** to place in or on a seat ⟨~ a king on a throne⟩ **2 a :** to put (a fowl) on eggs to hatch them **b :** to put (eggs) for hatching under a fowl or into an incubator **3 :** to place (oneself) in a position to start running in a race **4 a :** to place with care or deliberate purpose ⟨~ a ladder against the wall⟩ **b :** TRANSPLANT 1 ⟨~ seedlings⟩ **c** (1) **:** to make (as a trap) ready to catch prey (2) **:** to fix (a hook) firmly into the jaw of a fish **d :** to put aside for fermenting **5 :** to direct with fixed attention ⟨had ~ his heart on going with us⟩ **6 :** to put in writing ⟨~ down all the items in one column⟩ **7 :** to cause to assume a specified condition, relation, or occupation ⟨slaves were ~ free⟩ **8 :** to appoint or assign to an office or duty **:** POST, STATION **9 :** to cause to assume a specified posture or position ⟨~ the door ajar⟩ **10 a :** to fix as a distinguishing imprint, sign, or appearance ⟨the years have ~ their mark on him⟩ **b :** AFFIX **c :** APPLY ⟨~ a match to kindling⟩ **11 a :** to fix or decide upon as a time, limit, or regulation **:** PRESCRIBE ⟨~ a wedding day⟩ **b :** to establish by authority **:** DECREE **12 a :** to establish as the highest level or best performance ⟨~ a record for the half mile⟩ **b :** to furnish as a pattern or model ⟨~ an example of generosity⟩ **c :** to allot as a task **13 a :** to put into a desired position, adjustment, or condition ⟨~ a thermostat at 70⟩ **b :** to restore to normal position or connection when dislocated or fractured ⟨~ a broken bone⟩ **c :** to spread to the wind ⟨~ the sails⟩ **14 a :** to put in order for immediate use ⟨~ a place for a guest⟩ **b :** to provide (as words, verses) with melody and instrumental accompaniment **c :** to make scenically ready for a performance ⟨~ the stage⟩ **d :** to compose (type) for printing **:** put into type **15 a :** to put a fine edge on by grinding or honing ⟨~ a razor⟩ **b :** to bend slightly the tooth points of (a saw) alternately in opposite directions **c :** to adjust (a measuring instrument) to a desired position **d :** to sink (a nailhead) below the surface **16 :** to fix in a desired position (as by heating or stretching) **17 a :** to adorn with something affixed or infixed **:** STUD, DOT ⟨clear sky ~ with stars⟩ **b :** to fix (as a precious stone) in a border of metal **:** place in a setting **18 a :** to hold something in regard or esteem at the rate of ⟨~*s* a great deal by daily exercise⟩ **b :** to place in a relative rank or category ⟨~ duty before pleasure⟩ **c :** to fix at a certain amount ⟨~ bail at $500⟩ **d :** VALUE, RATE ⟨his promises were ~ at naught⟩ **e :** to place as an estimate of worth ⟨~ a high value on life⟩ **19 :** to place in relation for comparison or balance ⟨theory ~ against practice⟩ **20 a :** to direct to action **b :** to incite to attack or antagonism ⟨war ~*s* brother against brother⟩ **21 a :** to place by transporting ⟨~ ashore on the island⟩ **b :** to put in motion **c :** to put and fix in a direction ⟨~ our faces toward home once more⟩ **d** *of a dog* **:** to point out the position of (game) by holding a fixed attitude **22 :** to adjust (as a clock) in conformity with some standard **23 :** to defeat (an opponent or his contract) in bridge **24 a :** to fix firmly **:** make immobile **:** give rigid form or condition to ⟨~ his jaw in determination⟩ **b :** to make unyielding or obstinate **25 :** to cause to become firm or solid ⟨~ milk for cheese⟩ **26 :** to cause (as fruit) to develop ~ *vi* **1** *chiefly dial* **:** SIT **2 :** to be becoming **:** be suitable **:** FIT ⟨his behavior does not ~ well with his years⟩ **3 :** to cover and warm eggs to hatch them **4 :** to become lodged or fixed ⟨the pudding ~ heavily on his stomach⟩ **5** *of a plant part* **:** to undergo development usu. as a result of pollination **6 a :** to pass below the horizon **:** go down ⟨the sun ~*s*⟩ **b :** to sink out of sight **:** pass away **7 :** to apply oneself to some activity ⟨~ to work⟩ **8 :** to have a specified direction in motion **:** FLOW, TEND **9** *of a dog* **:** to indicate the position of game by crouching or pointing **10 :** to dance face to face with another in a square dance ⟨~ to your partner and turn⟩ **11 a :** to become solid or thickened by chemical or physical alteration ⟨the

cement ~s rapidly⟩ **b** *of a dye or color* **:** to become permanent **c** *of a bone* **:** to become whole by knitting **d** *of metal* **:** to acquire a permanent twist or bend from strain — **set about :** to begin to do — **set aside 1 :** DISCARD **2 :** RESERVE, SAVE **3 :** DISMISS **4 :** ANNUL, OVERRULE — **set at :** ATTACK, ASSAIL — **set forth 1 :** PUBLISH **2 :** to give an account or statement of **3 :** to start out on a journey **:** set out — **set forward 1 :** FURTHER **2 :** to set out on a journey **:** START — **set upon :** to attack with violence **:** ASSAULT

²**set** *adj* [ME *sett*, fr. pp. of *setten* to set] **1 :** INTENT, DETERMINED ⟨~ upon going⟩ **2 :** PITCHED ⟨~ battle⟩ **3 :** PRESCRIBED, SPECIFIED ⟨~ hours of study⟩ **4 :** INTENTIONAL, PREMEDITATED ⟨did it of ~ purpose⟩ **5 :** reluctant to change **:** OBSTINATE ⟨an old man very ~ in his ways⟩ **6 a :** IMMOVABLE, RIGID ⟨~ frown⟩ **b :** BUILT-IN **7 :** SETTLED, PERSISTENT ⟨~ defiance⟩ **8 a :** securely balanced for delivering a blow **b :** poised to start running or to dive in at the instant the signal is given ⟨ready, ~, go⟩

³**set** *n* **1 a :** the act or action of setting **b :** the condition of being set **2 :** inclination to an action **3 :** a number of things of the same kind that belong or are used together **4 :** direction of flow **5 :** form or carriage of the body or of its parts **6 :** the manner of fitting or of being placed or suspended **7 :** amount of deflection from a straight line **8 :** permanent change of form (as of metal) due to repeated or excessive stress **9 a :** a young plant or rooted cutting ready for transplanting **b :** a small bulb, corm, or tuber or a piece of tuber used for propagation ⟨an onion ~⟩ **10 :** the width of the body of a piece of type **11 :** an artificial setting for a scene of a play or motion picture **12 :** a group of tennis games in which one side wins six to opponent's four or less or in case of a deuced score wins two consecutive games **13 :** a collection of books or periodicals forming a unit **14 :** a clutch of eggs **15 :** the basic formation in a country-dance or square dance **16 :** a group of persons associated by common interests **17 :** a collection of mathematical elements (as numbers or points) that are actually listed or are identified by a common characteristic or by a rule of formation **18 :** an apparatus of electronic components assembled so as to function as a unit ⟨radio ~⟩

se·ta \ˈsēt-ə\ *n, pl* **se·tae** \ˈsē-ˌtē\ [NL, fr. L *saeta, seta* bristle — more at SINEW] **:** a slender usu. rigid or bristly and springy organ or part of an animal or plant — **se·tal** \ˈsēt-ᵊl\ *adj*

se·ta·ceous \si-ˈtā-shəs\ *adj* [L *saeta, seta*] **1 :** set with or consisting of bristles **2 :** resembling a bristle in form or texture — **se·ta·ceous·ly** *adv*

set·back \ˈset-ˌbak\ *n* **1 :** a checking of progress **2 :** DEFEAT, REVERSE **3 :** a game of pitch in which players bid for the lead **4 :** a withdrawal of the face of a building to a line some distance to the rear of the building line or of the wall below

set chisel *n* **:** a chisel or punch with a broad flat end

set down *vt* **1 :** to cause to sit down **:** SEAT **2 :** to place at rest on a surface or on the ground **3 :** to suspend (a jockey) from racing **4 :** to cause or allow to get off a vehicle **:** DELIVER **5 :** to land (an airplane) on the ground or water **6 a :** ORDAIN, ESTABLISH **b :** to put in writing **7 a :** REGARD, CONSIDER ⟨*set* him *down* as a liar⟩ **b :** ATTRIBUTE **8 :** to defeat (an opponent) in a game or contest

Seth \ˈseth\ *n* [Heb *Shēth*] **:** a son of Adam

set in *vt* **1 :** INSERT; *esp* **:** to stitch (a small part) within a large article **2 :** to direct (a ship) towards shore ~ *vi* **1 :** to enter upon a particular state **2 :** to blow or flow toward shore ⟨the wind was beginning to *set in*⟩

¹**set–in** \ˌset-ˌin\ *adj* **1 :** placed, located, or built as a part of some other construction ⟨~ bookcase⟩ ⟨~ wash basin⟩ **2 :** cut separately and stitched in ⟨~ sleeves⟩

²**set–in** \ˈset-ˌin\ *n* **1 :** an instance or time of something setting in ⟨early ~ of frosty nights⟩ **2 :** INSERT

set·line \ˈset-ˌlīn\ *n* **:** a long heavy fishing line to which several hooks are attached in series

set off *vt* **1 a :** to put in relief **:** show up by contrast **b :** ADORN, EMBELLISH **c :** to set apart **:** make distinct or outstanding **2 a :** OFFSET, COMPENSATE **b :** to make a setoff of **3 a :** to set in motion **:** cause to begin **b :** to cause to explode **4 :** to measure off on a surface **:** lay off ~ *vi* **1 :** to start out on a course or a journey ⟨*set off* for home⟩ **2 :** OFFSET

set·off \ˈset-ˌȯf\ *n* **1 :** something that is set off against another thing: **a :** DECORATION, ORNAMENT **b :** COMPENSATION, COUNTERBALANCE **2 :** the discharge of a debt by setting against it a distinct claim in favor of the debtor; *also* **:** the claim itself **3 :** OFFSET 7a

set on *vt* **1 :** ATTACK **2 a** *obs* **:** PROMOTE **b :** to urge (as a dog) to attack or pursue **c :** to incite to action **:** INSTIGATE **d :** to set to work ~ *vi* **:** to go on **:** ADVANCE

se·tose \ˈsē-ˌtōs\ *adj* [L *saetosus*, fr. *saeta*] **:** BRISTLY, SETACEOUS

set out *vt* **1 a :** ISSUE, PROMULGATE **b :** to recite, describe, or state at large **2 a :** to arrange and present graphically or systematically **b :** to mark out (as a design) **:** lay out the plan of **3 :** to begin with a definite purpose **:** INTEND, UNDERTAKE ~ *vi* **:** to start out on a course, a journey, or a career

set·out \ˈset-ˌau̇t\ *n* **1 a** (1) **:** ARRAY, DISPLAY (2) **:** ARRANGEMENT, LAYOUT **b :** BUFFET, SPREAD **c :** TURNOUT 5 **2 :** PARTY, ENTERTAINMENT **3 :** BEGINNING, OUTSET

set·over \ˈset-ˌō-vər\ *n* **:** distance or amount set over

set piece *n* **1 :** a realistic piece of stage scenery standing by itself **2 :** a composition (as in literature) executed in a fixed or ideal form often with studied artistry and brilliant effect

set point *n* **:** a point that decides a tennis set if won by the side having an advantage in the score

set·screw \ˈset-ˌskrü\ *n* **1 :** a screw screwed through one part tightly upon or into another part to prevent relative movement **2 :** a screw for regulating a valve opening or a spring tension

set·tee \se-ˈtē\ *n* [alter. of *settle*] **1 :** a long seat with a back **2 :** a medium-sized sofa with arms and a back

set·ter \ˈset-ər\ *n* **1 :** one that sets ⟨brick*setter*⟩ **2 :** a large bird dog of a type formerly trained to crouch on finding game but now to point

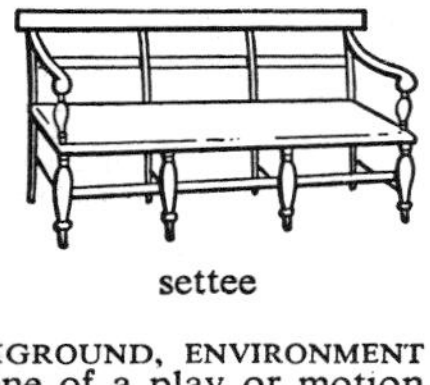

settee

set theory *n* **:** a branch of mathematics or of symbolic logic that deals with the nature and relations of sets

set·ting \ˈset-iŋ\ *n* **1 :** the manner, position, or direction in which something is set **2 :** the frame or bed in which a gem is set; *also* **:** style of mounting **3 a :** BACKGROUND, ENVIRONMENT **b :** the time and place within which a scene of a play or motion picture is enacted **4 :** the music composed for a poem or other text **5 :** the articles of tableware required for setting a place at table **6 :** a batch of eggs for incubation

¹**set·tle** \ˈset-ᵊl\ *n* [ME, place for sitting, seat, chair, fr. OE *setl*; akin to OHG *sezzal* seat, L *sella* seat, chair, saddle, OE *sittan* to sit] **:** a wooden bench with arms, a high solid back, and an enclosed foundation which can be a chest

²**set·tle** \ˈset-ᵊl\ *vb* **set·tling** \ˈset-liŋ, -ᵊl-iŋ\ [ME *settlen* to seat, bring to rest, come to rest, fr. OE *setlan*, fr. *setl* seat] *vt* **1 :** to place so as to stay **2 a :** to establish in residence **b :** to furnish with inhabitants **3 a :** to cause to pack down **b :** to clarify by causing dregs or impurities to sink **4 :** to make quiet or orderly **5 a :** to fix or resolve conclusively ⟨~ the question⟩ **b :** to establish or secure permanently **6 :** to arrange in a desired position **7 :** to make or arrange for final disposition of **8** *of an animal* **:** IMPREGNATE ~ *vi* **1 :** to come to rest **2 a :** to sink gradually or to the bottom **b :** to become clear by the deposit of sediment or scum **c :** to become compact by sinking **3 a :** to become fixed, resolved, or established **b :** to establish a residence or colony **4 a :** to become quiet or orderly **b :** to take up an ordered or stable life ⟨marry and ~ down⟩ **5 :** to adjust differences or accounts **6** *of an animal* **:** CONCEIVE **syn** see DECIDE

set·tle·ment \ˈset-ᵊl-mənt\ *n* **1 :** the act or process of settling **2 :** the sum, estate, or income secured to one by a settlement **3 a :** a place or region newly settled **b :** a small village **4 :** an institution providing various community services to people in a crowded part of a city **5 :** an agreement composing differences

set·tler \ˈset-lər, -ᵊl-ər\ *n* **:** one that settles (as a new region)

set·tling \ˈset-liŋ, -ᵊl-iŋ\ *n* **:** SEDIMENT, DREGS — usu. used in pl.

set·tlor \ˈset-lər, -ᵊl-ər\ *n* **:** one that makes a settlement or creates a trust of property

set to *vi* **1 :** to begin actively and earnestly **2 :** to begin fighting

set–to \ˈset-(ˌ)tü\ *n* **:** a usu. brief and vigorous contest

set up *vt* **1 a :** to raise to and place in a high position **b :** to place in view **:** POST **c :** to put forward for acceptance **2 a :** to make (a loud noise) with the voice **b :** to cause (a condition) to come into effect ⟨the wind *sets up* a humming in the wires⟩ **3 a :** to make taut (a stay, hawser) **b :** to raise the pitch of (a string) by tightening **c :** to tighten firmly **4 :** to place in power or in office **5 a :** to raise from depression **:** ELATE, GRATIFY **b :** to make proud or vain **6 a :** to put forward or extol as a model **b :** to claim (oneself) to be ⟨*sets* himself *up* as an authority⟩ **7 a :** to place upright **:** ERECT **b :** to assemble the parts of and erect in position ⟨*set up* a printing press⟩ **c :** to put (a machine) in readiness or adjustment for a tooling operation **8 :** to erect (a perpendicular or a figure) on a base in a drawing **9 a :** FOUND, INAUGURATE **b :** to put in operation as a way of living ⟨*set up* housekeeping⟩ or a means of livelihood ⟨*set up* shop in a new neighborhood⟩ **10 a :** to provide with means of making a living **b :** to bring or restore to normal health and strength **c :** to cause (one) to take on a soldierly or athletic appearance esp. through drill ⟨*set up* recruits⟩ **11 :** to make carefully worked out plans for ⟨*set up* a bank robbery⟩ **12 a :** to pay for (drinks) **b :** to treat (someone) to something ~ *vi* **1 :** to come into active operation or use **2 :** to begin business **3 :** to make pretensions ⟨*setting up* for a wit⟩

set·up \ˈset-ˌəp\ *n* **1 a :** carriage of the body; *esp* **:** erect and soldierly bearing **b :** CONSTITUTION, MAKEUP **2 a :** the assembly and arrangement of the tools and apparatus required for the performance of an operation **b :** the preparation and adjustment of machines for an assigned task **3 a :** a table setting **b :** glass, ice, and mixer served to patrons who supply their own liquor **4 :** a camera position from which a scene is filmed; *also* **:** the footage taken from one camera position **5 a :** a position of the balls in billiards or pool from which it is easy to score **b :** a task or contest purposely made easy **c :** something easy to get or accomplish **d :** a boxer who engages in a match which he has no chance to win **6 a :** the manner in which the elements or components of a machine, apparatus, or mechanical, electrical, or hydraulic system are arranged, designed, or assembled **b :** the patterns within which political, social, or administrative forces operate **:** customary or established practice **7 :** PROJECT, PLAN

sev·en \ˈsev-ən\ *n* [ME, fr. *seven*, adj., fr. OE *seofon;* akin to OHG *sibun* seven, L *septem*, Gk *hepta*] **1** — see NUMBER table **2 :** the seventh in a set or series ⟨the ~ of hearts⟩ **3 :** something having seven units or members **4 :** a score in a dice game made by throwing any combination of numbers that totals seven — **seven** *adj or pron*

Seven against Thebes \-ˈthēbz\ **:** an expedition undertaken by seven heroes of Greek legend to help Polynices recover a share in the kingship of Thebes

seven seas *n pl* **:** all the waters or oceans of the world

sev·en·teen \ˌsev-ən-ˈtēn\ *n* [*seventeen*, adj., fr. ME *seventene*, fr. OE *seofontēne*; akin to OE *tien* ten] — see NUMBER table — **seventeen** *adj or pron* — **sev·en·teenth** \-ˈtēn(t)th\ *adj* — **seventeenth** *n, pl* **sev·en·teenths** \-ˈtēn(t)s, -ˈtēn(t)ths\

seventeen–year locust *n* **:** a cicada (*Cicada septendecim*) of the U. S. that has in the North a life of seventeen years and in the South of thirteen years mostly spent underground in the nymphal condition from which it emerges as an adult and survives only a few weeks

sev·enth \ˈsev-ən(t)th\ *n, pl* **sev·enths** \ˈsev-ən(t)s, -ən(t)ths\ **1** — see NUMBER table **2 a :** a musical interval embracing seven diatonic degrees **b :** LEADING TONE **c :** the harmonic combination of two tones a seventh apart — **seventh** *adj or adv*

seventh chord *n* **:** a chord comprising a fundamental tone with its third, fifth, and seventh

sev·enth–day \ˌsev-ən(t)th-ˌdā\ *adj* **:** advocating or practicing observance of Saturday as the Sabbath

seventh heaven *n* **1 :** the highest of the abodes of bliss of the Muslim and cabalist systems **2 :** a state of extreme joy

sev·en·ti·eth \ˈsev-ən-tē-əth, -ən-dē-\ *n* — see NUMBER table — **seventieth** *adj*

sev·en·ty \ˈsev-ən-tē, -dē\ *n* [*seventy*, adj., fr. ME, fr. OE *seofontig*, short for *hundseofontig*, fr. *hundseofontig*, n., group of 70, fr. *hund* hundred + *seofon* seven + *-tig* group of ten — more at HUNDRED, EIGHTY] **1** — see NUMBER table **2** *pl* **:** the numbers 70 to 79; *specif* **:** the years 70 to 79 in a lifetime or century **3** *cap* **:** a Mormon elder ordained for missionary work under the apostles — **seventy** *adj or pron*

sev·en·ty–eight \ˌsev-ən-tē-ˈāt, -ən-dē-\ *n* **1** — see NUMBER table **2 :** a phonograph record designed to be played at 78 revolutions per minute — usu. written 78 — **seventy–eight** *adj or pron*

sev·en·ty-five \-'fīv\ *n* **1** — see NUMBER table **2** : a 75 millimeter gun; *esp* : the fieldpiece of this caliber used in the armies of France and of the U.S. in World War I — often written *75*
sev·en-up \,sev-ə-'nəp\ *n* : an American variety of all fours in which a total of seven points is game
sev·er \'sev-ər\ *vb* **sev·er·ing** \-(ə-)riŋ\ [ME *severen*, fr. MF *severer*, fr. L *separare* — more at SEPARATE] *vt* : to put or keep apart : DIVIDE; *specif* : to part by violence (as by cutting) ~ *vi* : to become separated — **syn** see SEPARATE
sev·er·abil·i·ty \,sev-(ə-)rə-'bil-ət-ē\ *n* : the quality or state of being severable
sev·er·able \'sev-(ə-)rə-bəl\ *adj* : capable of being severed; *esp* : capable of being divided into legally independent rights or obligations ⟨a ~ contract⟩
[1]**sev·er·al** \'sev-(ə-)rəl\ *adj* [ME, fr. AF, fr. ML *separalis*, fr. L *separ* separate, back-formation fr. *separare* to separate] **1 a** : separate or distinct from others : DIFFERENT ⟨federal union of the ~ states⟩ **b** (1) : individually owned or controlled : EXCLUSIVE ⟨a ~ fishery⟩ — compare COMMON (2) : of or relating separately to each individual involved : SEVERABLE ⟨a ~ judgment⟩ **c** : PARTICULAR, RESPECTIVE ⟨specialists in their ~ fields⟩ **2 a** : more than one ⟨~ pleas⟩ **b** : more than two but fewer than many ⟨moved ~ inches⟩ **c** *chiefly dial* : being a great many **syn** see DISTINCT — **sev·er·al·ly** \-ē\ *adv*
[2]**several** *pron, pl in constr* : an indefinite number more than two and fewer than many ⟨~ of the guests⟩
sev·er·al·fold \,sev-(ə-)rəl-'fōld\ *adj* **1** : having several parts or aspects **2** : being several times as large, as great, or as many as some understood size, degree, or amount ⟨a ~ increase⟩ — **severalfold** *adv*
sev·er·al·ty \'sev-(ə-)rəl-tē\ *n* [ME *severalte*, fr. AF *severalté*, fr. *several*] **1** : the quality or state of being several : DISTINCTNESS, SEPARATENESS **2 a** : a sole, separate, and exclusive possession, dominion, or ownership : one's own right without a joint interest in any other person ⟨tenants in ~⟩ **b** : the quality or state of being individual or particular **3 a** : land owned in severalty **b** : the quality or state of being held in severalty
sev·er·ance \'sev-(ə-)rən(t)s\ *n* : the act or process of severing : the state of being severed
se·vere \sə-'vi(ə)r\ *adj* [MF or L; MF, fr. L *severus*] **1 a** : strict in judgment, discipline, or government **b** : of a strict or stern bearing or manner : AUSTERE **2** : rigorous in restraint, punishment, or requirement : STRINGENT, RESTRICTIVE **3** : strongly critical or condemnatory : CENSORIOUS ⟨~ critic⟩ **4 a** : maintaining a scrupulously exacting standard of behavior or self-discipline **b** : establishing exacting standards of accuracy and integrity in intellectual processes ⟨~ logician⟩ **5** : sober or restrained in decoration or manner : PLAIN **6 a** : inflicting physical discomfort or hardship : HARSH ⟨~ winter⟩ **b** : inflicting pain or distress : GRIEVOUS ⟨~ wound⟩ **7** : requiring great effort : ARDUOUS ⟨~ test⟩ **8** : of a great degree : MARKED, SERIOUS ⟨~ economic depression⟩ — **se·vere·ly** *adv* — **se·vere·ness** *n*
syn SEVERE, STERN, AUSTERE, ASCETIC mean showing or requiring discipline or restraint. SEVERE implies standards enforced without indulgence or laxity and may suggest harshness; STERN stresses inflexibility and inexorability of temper or character; AUSTERE stresses absence of warmth, color, or feeling and may apply to rigorous restraint, simplicity, or self-denial; ASCETIC implies abstention from pleasure and comfort or self-indulgence as spiritual discipline and may even suggest the courting of what is hard or painful or disagreeable
se·ver·i·ty \sə-'ver-ət-ē\ *n* : the quality or state of being severe
Sè·vres \'sevrᵊ\ *n* [*Sèvres*, France] : a fine often elaborately decorated French porcelain
sew \'sō\ *vb* **sewed; sewn** \'sōn\ *or* **sewed; sew·ing** [ME *sewen*, fr. OE *sīwian*; akin to OHG *siuwen* to sew, L *suere*] *vt* **1** : to unite or fasten by stitches made with a flexible thread or filament ⟨~*s* on the button⟩ **2** : to close or enclose by sewing ⟨~ the money in a bag⟩ ~ *vi* : to practice or engage in sewing
sew·age \'sü-ij\ *n* [[3]*sewer*] : refuse liquids or waste matter carried off by sewers
[1]**sew·er** \'sü-ər, 'sů(-ə)r\ *n* [ME, fr. AF *asseour*, lit., seater, fr. OF *asseoir* to seat — more at ASSIZE] : a medieval household officer often of high rank in charge of serving the dishes at table and sometimes of seating and tasting
[2]**sew·er** \'sō(-ə)r\ *n* : one that sews
[3]**sew·er** \'sü-ər, 'sů(-ə)r\ *n* [ME, fr. MF *esseweur*, *seweur*, fr. *essewer* to drain, fr. (assumed) VL *exaquare*, fr. L *ex-* + *aqua* water — more at ISLAND] : an artificial usu. subterranean conduit to carry off water and waste matter
sew·er·age \'sü-ə-rij, 'sů(-ə)r-ij\ *n* **1** : SEWAGE **2** : the removal and disposal of sewage and surface water by sewers **3** : a system of sewers
sew·ing \'sō-iŋ\ *n* **1** : the act, method, or occupation of one that sews **2** : material that has been or is to be sewed
sew up *vt* **1** : to restrict completly : CONFINE **2** : to get exclusive use or control of **3** : to make certain of : ASSURE
[1]**sex** \'seks\ *n* [ME, fr. L *sexus*] **1** : either of two divisions of organisms distinguished respectively as male or female **2** : the sum of the structural, functional, and behavioral peculiarities of living beings that subserve reproduction by two interacting parents and distinguish males and females **3 a** : sexually motivated phenomena or behavior **b** : SEXUAL INTERCOURSE
[2]**sex** *vt* **1** : to identify the sex of ⟨~ chicks⟩ **2 a** : to increase the sexual appeal of **b** : to arouse the sexual desires of
sex- *or* **sexi-** *comb form* [L *sex* — more at SIX] : six ⟨*sexi*valent⟩ ⟨*sex*partite⟩
Sex·a·ges·i·ma \,sek-sə-'jes-ə-mə, -'jā-zə-\ *n* [LL, fr. L, fem. of *sexagesimus* sixtieth] : the second Sunday before Lent
[1]**sex·a·ges·i·mal** \-'jes-ə-məl\ *adj* [L *sexagesimus* sixtieth, irreg. fr. *sex* six + *-ginta* (akin to *viginti* twenty) — more at VIGESIMAL] : of, relating to, or based on the number 60 ⟨~ measurement of angles⟩ ⟨~ system of numeration⟩
[2]**sexagesimal** *n* : a sexagesimal fraction
sex appeal *n* : personal appeal or physical attractiveness for members of the opposite sex
sex chromosome *n* : a chromosome inherited differently in the two sexes that is or is held to be concerned directly with the inheritance of sex and is the seat of factors governing the inheritance of various sex-linked and sex-limited characters
sex·de·cil·lion \,seks-di-'sil-yən\ *n, often attrib* [L *sedecim*, *sexdecim* sixteen (fr. *sex* six + *decem* ten) + E *-illion* (as in *million*) — more at TEN] — see NUMBER table
sexed \'sekst\ *adj* **1** : having sex or sexual instincts **2** : having sex appeal
sex hormone *n* : a hormone (as from the gonads or adrenal cortex) having an effect on the growth or function of the reproductive organs or on the development of secondary sex characteristics
sex hygiene *n* : a division of hygiene that deals with sex and sexual conduct as bearing on the health of the individual and the community
sex·i·ness \'sek-sē-nəs\ *n* : the quality or state of being sexy
sex·less \'sek-sləs\ *adj* : lacking sex : NEUTER — **sex·less·ly** *adv* — **sex·less·ness** *n*
sex-link·age \'sek-,sliŋ-kij\ *n* : the quality or state of being sex-linked
sex-linked \'sek-,sliŋ(k)t\ *adj* **1** : located in a sex chromosome and heterozygous in one sex but homozygous in the other ⟨a ~ gene⟩ **2** : mediated by a sex-linked gene ⟨a ~ character⟩
sex·ol·o·gy \sek-'säl-ə-jē\ *n* : the study of sex or of the interaction of the sexes esp. among human beings
sext \'sekst\ *n, often cap* [ME *sexte*, fr. LL *sexta*, fr. L, sixth hour of the day, fr. fem. of *sextus* sixth, fr. *sex* six] : the fourth of the canonical hours
Sex·tans \'sek-,stanz\ *n* [NL (gen. *Sextantis*), lit., sextant] : a constellation on the equator south of Leo
sex·tant \'sek-stənt\ *n* [NL *sextant-*, *sextans* sixth part of a circle, fr. L, sixth part, fr. *sextus* sixth] : an instrument for measuring altitudes of celestial bodies from a moving ship or airplane
sex·tet *also* **sex·tette** \sek-'stet\ *n* [alter. of *sestet*] **1** : a musical composition for six instruments or voices **2** : a group or set of six: as **a** : the musicians that perform a sextet **b** : a hockey team
sex·tile \'sek-,stīl, -stəl\ *n* [L *sextilis* sixth, fr. *sextus*] : the aspect of two heavenly bodies when 60 degrees distant from each other
sex·til·lion \sek-'stil-yən\ *n, often attrib* [F, irreg. fr. *sex-* (fr. L *sex*) + *-illion* (as in *million*)] — see NUMBER table
sex·to \'sek-(,)stō\ *n* [L *sexto*, abl. of *sextus* sixth] : SIXMO
sex·to·dec·i·mo \,sek-stə-'des-ə-,mō\ *n* [L, abl. of *sextus decimus* sixteenth, fr. *sextus* sixth + *decimus* tenth — more at DIME] : SIXTEENMO
sex·ton \'sek-stən\ *n* [ME *secresteyn*, *sexteyn*, fr. MF *secrestain*, fr. ML *sacristanus* — more at SACRISTAN] : a church officer or employee who takes care of the church property and sometimes rings the bell for services and digs graves
[1]**sex·tu·ple** \sek-'st(y)üp-əl, -'stəp-; 'sek-stəp-\ *adj* [prob. fr. ML *sextuplus*, fr. L *sextus* sixth + *-plus* multiplied by — more at DOUBLE] **1** : having six units or members **2** : being six times as great or as many **3** : marked by six beats per measure ⟨~ meter⟩ — **sextuple** *n*
[2]**sextuple** *vb* **sex·tu·pling** \-(ə-)liŋ\ *vt* : to make six times as much or as many ~ *vi* : to become six times as much or as numerous
sex·tu·plet \sek-'stəp-lət, -'st(y)üp-; 'sek-st(y)əp-\ *n* **1** : a combination of six of a kind **2** : one of six offspring born at one birth **3** : a group of six equal musical notes performed in the time ordinarily given to four of the same value
[1]**sex·tu·pli·cate** \sek-'st(y)ü-pli-kət\ *adj* [blend of *sextuple* and *-plicate* (as in *duplicate*)] **1** : repeated six times **2** : SIXTH ⟨file the ~ copy⟩ — **sextuplicate** *n*
[2]**sex·tu·pli·cate** \-plə-,kāt\ *vt* **1** : SEXTUPLE **2** : to provide in sextuplicate
sex·u·al \'seksh-(ə-)wəl, 'sek-shəl\ *adj* [LL *sexualis*, fr. L *sexus* sex] **1** : of, relating to, or associated with sex or the sexes ⟨~ differentiation⟩ ⟨~ conflict⟩ **2** : having or involving sex ⟨~ reproduction⟩ ⟨~ spores⟩ — **sex·u·al·ly** \'seksh-(ə-)wə-lē, 'seksh-(ə-)lē\ *adv*
sexual generation *n* : the generation of an organism with alternation of generations that reproduces sexually
sexual intercourse *n* : sexual connection esp. between humans
sex·u·al·i·ty \,sek-shə-'wal-ət-ē\ *n* : the quality or state of being sexual: **a** : the condition of having sex **b** : sexual activity or interest esp. when excessive
sexual relations *n pl* : COITUS
sexy \'sek-sē\ *adj* : sexually suggestive or stimulating : EROTIC
sfer·ics \'sfi(ə)r-iks, 'sfer-\ *n pl* [by shortening & alteration] **1** : ATMOSPHERICS **2** *sing in constr* : an electronic detector of storms
[1]**sfor·zan·do** \sfȯrt-'sän-(,)dō\ *adj* [It, verbal of *sforzare* to force] : ACCENTED — used as a direction in music
[2]**sforzando** *n* : an accented tone or chord
sgraf·fi·to \zgra-'fē-(,)tō, skra-\ *n, pl* **sgraf·fi·ti** \-(,)tē\ [It, fr. pp. of *sgraffire* to scratch, produce sgraffito] **1** : decoration produced by scratching through a surface layer (as of plaster or glazing) to reveal a different colored ground **2** : pottery or ware decorated with sgraffito
sh \sh *often prolonged*\ *interj* — used often in prolonged or reduplicated form to enjoin silence
Sha'·ban \shə-'bän\ *n* [Ar *sha'bān*] : the 8th month of the Muhammadan year
Shab·bat \shə-'bät, 'shäb-əs\ *n, pl* **Shab·ba·tim** \shə-'bät-əm, -'bō-səm\ [Heb *shabbāth*] : the Jewish Sabbath
shab·bi·ly \'shab-ə-lē\ *adv* : in a shabby manner
shab·bi·ness \'shab-ē-nəs\ *n* : the quality or state of being shabby
shab·by \'shab-ē\ *adj* [obs. E *shab* (a low fellow)] **1 a** : threadbare and faded from wear **b** : ill kept : DILAPIDATED **2** : clothed with worn or seedy garments **3 a** : MEAN, DESPICABLE **b** : UNGENEROUS, UNFAIR **c** : inferior in quality : SLOVENLY
Sha·bu·oth \shə-'vü-,ōt(h), -,ōs, -əs\ *n* [Heb *shābhū'oth*] : a Jewish holiday observed on the 6th and 7th of Sivan in commemoration of the revelation of the Law at Mt. Sinai and of a wheat festival held in biblical times
[1]**shack** \'shak\ *n* [prob. back-formation fr. E dial. *shackly* (rickety)] **1** : HUT, SHANTY **2** : a room or similar enclosed structure for a particular person or use
[2]**shack** *vi* : LIVE, STAY — often used with *up*
[1]**shack·le** \'shak-əl\ *n* [ME *schakel*, fr. OE *sceacul*; akin to ON *skökull* pole of a cart] **1 a** : something (as a manacle or fetter) that

confines the legs or arms **b :** a hobble for a horse **2 :** something that checks or prevents free action as if by fetters — usu. used in pl. **3 :** any of various devices for making something fast (as a clevis) **4 :** a length of cable or anchor chain usu. 15 feet

2shackle *vt* **shack·ling** \-(ə-)liŋ\ **1 a :** to bind with shackles **:** FETTER **b :** to make fast with a shackle **2 :** to deprive of freedom esp. of action by means of restrictions or handicaps **:** IMPEDE **syn** see HAMPER — **shack·ler** \-(ə-)lər\ *n*

shack·le·bone \ˈshak-əl-ˌbōn\ *n, Scot* **:** WRIST

shad \ˈshad\ *n, pl* **shad** [(assumed) ME, fr. OE *sceadd;* akin to L *scatēre* to bubble] **:** any of several clupeid fishes (genus *Alosa*) that differ from the typical herrings in having a relatively deep body and in being anadromous and that are extremely important food fishes of Europe and No. America

shad·ber·ry \-ˌber-ē\ *n* **1 :** the fruit of the Juneberry **2 :** JUNEBERRY

shad·blow \ˈshad-ˌblō\ *n* **:** JUNEBERRY

shad·bush \-ˌbu̇sh\ *n* **:** JUNEBERRY

shad·dock \ˈshad-ək\ *n* [Captain *Shaddock,* 17th cent. E ship commander] **:** a very large thick-rinded usu. pear-shaped citrus fruit differing from the closely related grapefruit esp. in its loose rind and often coarse dry pulp; *also* **:** the tree (*Citrus grandis*) that bears it

1shade \ˈshād\ *n* [ME, fr. OE *sceadu;* akin to OHG *scato* shadow, Gk *skotos* darkness] **1 a :** comparative darkness or obscurity owing to interception of the rays of light **b :** relative obscurity or retirement **2 a :** shelter (as by foliage) from the heat and glare of sunlight **b :** a place sheltered from the sun **c :** a secluded retreat **3 :** an evanescent or unreal appearance **4** *pl* **a :** the shadows that gather as darkness comes on **b :** NETHERWORLD, HADES **5 :** a disembodied spirit **:** GHOST **6 :** something that intercepts or shelters from light, sun, or heat: as **a :** a device partially covering a lamp so as to reduce glare **b :** a flexible screen for regulating the light or the view through a window **7 a :** the reproduction of the effect of shade in painting or drawing **b :** a subdued or somber feature **8 a :** a color produced by a pigment or dye mixture having some black in it **b :** a color slightly different from the one under consideration **9 a :** a minute difference or variation **:** NUANCE **b :** a minute degree or quantity **10 :** a facial expression of sadness or displeasure **syn** see COLOR — **shade·less** \-ləs\ *adj*

2shade *vt* **1 a :** to shelter or screen by intercepting radiated light or heat **b :** to cover with a shade **2 :** to hide partly by or as if by a shadow **3 :** to darken with or as if with a shadow **4 :** to cast into the shade **:** OBSCURE **5 a :** to represent the effect of shade or shadow on **b :** to add shading to **c :** to color so that the shades pass gradually from one to another **6 :** to change by gradual transition or qualification **7 :** to reduce slightly (as a price) ~ *vi* **1 :** to pass by slight changes or imperceptible degrees into something else **2 :** to undergo or exhibit minute difference or variation — **shad·er** *n*

shad·i·ly \ˈshād-ᵊl-ē\ *adv* **:** in a shady manner

shad·i·ness \ˈshād-ē-nəs\ *n* **:** the quality or state of being shady

shad·ing \ˈshād-iŋ\ *n* **:** the filling up within outlines that represents the effect of more or less darkness in a picture or drawing

1shad·ow \ˈshad-(ˌ)ō, -ə(-w)\ *n* [ME *shadwe,* fr. OE *sceaduw-, sceadu* shade, shadow] **1 :** shade within defined bounds **2 :** a reflected image **3 :** shelter from danger or observation **4 a :** an imperfect and faint representation **b :** an imitation of something **:** COPY **5 :** the image made by an obscured space on a surface that cuts across it usu. representing in silhouette the form of the interposed body **6 :** PHANTOM **7** *pl* **:** DARKNESS **8 :** a shaded or darker portion of a picture **9 :** an attenuated form or a vestigial remnant **10 a :** an inseparable companion or follower **b :** one that shadows as a spy or detective **11 :** a small degree or portion **:** TRACE **12 :** influence casting a spell, gloom, or unhappiness **13 a :** an area within or held to be within the shadow cast by an object **:** VICINITY **b :** pervasive and dominant influence — **shad·ow·less** \ˈshad-ō-ləs, -ə-ləs\ *adj* — **shad·ow·like** \-ˌlīk\ *adj*

2shadow *vt* **1** *archaic* **:** SHELTER, PROTECT **2 :** to cast a shadow upon **3** *obs* **:** to shelter from the sun **4** *obs* **:** CONCEAL **5 :** to represent or indicate obscurely or faintly — often used with *forth* or *out* **6 :** to follow esp. secretly **:** TRAIL **7** *archaic* **:** SHADE 5 ~ *vi* **1 :** to shade off **2 :** to become overcast with or as if with shadows — **shad·ow·er** \-ə-wər\ *n*

3shadow *adj* **1 :** having form without substance ⟨~ government⟩ **2 a :** having an indistinct pattern ⟨~ plaid⟩ **b :** having darker sections of design ⟨~ lace⟩

shadow box *n* **:** a shallow enclosing case usu. with a glass front in which something is set for protection and display

shad·ow·box \ˈshad-ō-ˌbäks, -ə-ˌbäks\ *vi* **:** to box with an imaginary opponent esp. as a form of training — **shad·ow·box·ing** \-ˌbäk-siŋ\ *n*

shadow cabinet *n* **:** a group of leaders of a parliamentary opposition who constitute the probable membership of the cabinet when their party is returned to power

shadow dance *n* **:** a dance shown by throwing the shadows of invisible dancers on a screen

shad·ow·graph \ˈshad-ō-ˌgraf, -ə-ˌgraf\ *n* **1 :** SHADOW PLAY **2 :** a photographic image resembling a shadow

shadow play *n* **:** a drama exhibited by throwing shadows of puppets or actors on a screen

shad·owy \ˈshad-ə-wē\ *adj* **1 a :** of the nature of or resembling a shadow **:** UNSUBSTANTIAL **b :** INDISTINCT, VAGUE **2 :** being in or obscured by shadow **3 :** SHADY 1

shady \ˈshād-ē\ *adj* **1 :** producing or affording shade **2 :** sheltered from the sun's rays **3 a :** of questionable merit **b :** DISREPUTABLE

1shaft \ˈshaft\ *n* [ME, fr. OE *sceaft;* akin to OHG *scaft* shaft, L *scapus* shaft, stalk, Gk *skēptron* staff, L *capo* capon — more at CAPON] **1 a** (1) **:** the long handle of a spear or similar weapon (2) **:** SPEAR, LANCE **b** *or pl* **shaves** \ˈshāvz\ **:** POLE; *specif* **:** either of two long pieces of wood between which a horse is hitched to a vehicle **c** (1) **:** an arrow esp. for a longbow (2) **:** the body or stem of an arrow extending from the nock to the head **2 :** a sharply delineated beam shining through an opening **3 :** something suggestive of the shaft of a spear or arrow esp. in long slender cylindrical form: as **a :** the trunk of a tree **b :** the cylindrical pillar between the capital and the base **c :** the handle or helve of any of various tools or instruments **d :** a commonly cylindrical bar used to support rotating pieces or to transmit power or motion by rotation **e :** the stem or midrib of a feather **f :** the upright member of a cross esp. below the arms **g :** a small architectural column **h :** a column, obelisk, or other spire-shaped or columnar monument **i :** a vertical or inclined opening of uniform and limited cross section made for finding or mining ore, raising water, or ventilating underground workings (as in a cave) **j :** a vertical opening or passage through the floors of a building **4 a :** a projectile thrown like a spear or shot like an arrow **b :** a scornful, satirical, or pithily critical remark

2shaft *vt* **:** to fit with a shaft

shaft·ing \ˈshaf-tiŋ\ *n* **:** shafts or material for shafts

1shag \ˈshag\ *n* [(assumed) ME *shagge,* fr. OE *sceacga;* akin to ON *skegg* beard, OSlav *skokŭ* leap] **1 a :** a shaggy tangled mass or covering **b :** long coarse or matted fiber or nap **2 :** a strong coarse tobacco cut into fine shreds **3 :** CORMORANT

2shag *adj* **:** SHAGGY

3shag *vb* **shagged; shag·ging** *vi* **:** to fall or hang in shaggy masses ~ *vt* **:** to make rough or shaggy

4shag *vt* **shagged; shag·ging** [origin unknown] **1 :** to chase after (as a ball) **2 :** to chase away

5shag *vi* [perh. alter. of *shack* (to lumber along)] **1 :** to move or lope along **2 :** to dance the shag

6shag *n* **:** a dance step consisting of a lively hopping on each foot in turn

shag·bark \ˈshag-ˌbärk\ *n* **:** a hickory (*Carya ovata*) with a gray shaggy outer bark that peels off in long strips and sweet edible nuts; *also* **:** its wood

shag·gi·ly \ˈshag-ə-lē\ *adv* **:** in a shaggy manner

shag·gi·ness \ˈshag-ē-nəs\ *n* **:** the quality or state of being shaggy

shag·gy \ˈshag-ē\ *adj* **1 a :** covered with or consisting of long, coarse, or matted hair **b :** covered with or consisting of thick, tangled, or unkempt vegetation **c :** having a rough nap, texture, or surface **d :** having hairlike processes **2 a :** UNKEMPT **b :** RUDE, UNPOLISHED **c :** CONFUSED

shag·gy–dog story \ˌshag-ē-ˈdȯg-\ *n* **1 a :** a long-drawn-out circumstantial story concerning an inconsequential happening that impresses the teller as humorous but the hearer as tiresome and pointless **b :** a similar humorous story whose humor lies in the pointlessness or irrelevance of the punch line **2 :** a humorous anecdote involving a talking animal (as a horse or dog)

shag·gy·mane \ˈshag-ē-ˌmān\ *n* **:** a common edible mushroom (*Coprinus comatus*) having an elongated shaggy white pileus and black spores — called also *shaggy cap*

sha·green \sha-ˈgrēn, shə-\ *n* [by folk etymology fr. F *chagrin,* fr. Turk *sağrı*] **1 :** an untanned leather covered with small round granulations and usu. dyed green **2 :** the rough skin of various sharks and rays when covered with small close-set tubercles — **shagreen** *adj*

shah \ˈshä, ˈshȯ\ *n, often cap* [Per *shāh* king — more at CHECK] **:** the sovereign of Iran — **shah·dom** \ˈshäd-əm, ˈshȯd-əm\ *n*

Sha·hap·ti·an \shə-ˈhap-tē-ən\ *n, pl* **Shahaptian** *or* **Shahaptians** **1 :** a member of an Indian people of a large territory along the Columbia river and its tributaries **2 :** the language of the Shahaptian people including Nez Percé and Yakima

shai·tan \shā-ˈtän, shī-\ *n* [Ar *shayṭān*] **:** an evil spirit; *specif* **:** one of the rebellious jinn that lead men astray

shak·able *or* **shake·able** \ˈshā-kə-bəl\ *adj* **:** capable of being shaken

1shake \ˈshāk\ *vb* **shook** \ˈshu̇k\ **shak·en** \ˈshā-kən\ **shak·ing** [ME *shaken,* fr. OE *sceacan;* akin to ON *skaka* to shake, Skt *khajati* he agitates] *vi* **1 :** to move irregularly to and fro **:** QUIVER **2 :** to vibrate esp. as the result of a blow or shock **3 :** to tremble as a result of physical or emotional disturbance **4 :** to experience a state of instability **:** TOTTER **5 :** to clasp hands **6 :** TRILL ~ *vt* **1 :** to brandish, wave, or flourish often in a threatening manner **2 :** to cause to move in a quick jerky manner **3 :** to cause to quake, quiver, or tremble **4 :** to free oneself from ⟨~ a habit⟩ ⟨~ off a cold⟩ **5 :** to cause to waver **:** WEAKEN ⟨~ one's faith⟩ **6 :** to bring to a specified condition by repeated quick jerky movements **7 :** to dislodge or eject by quick jerky movements of the support or container **8 :** to clasp (hands) in greeting or farewell or as a sign of goodwill or agreement **9 :** to stir the feelings of **:** UPSET ⟨*shook* her up⟩ **10 :** TRILL

syn SHAKE, AGITATE, ROCK, CONVULSE mean to move up and down or to and fro with some violence. SHAKE often carries a further implication of a particular purpose; AGITATE suggests a violent and somewhat prolonged tossing or stirring; ROCK suggests a swinging or swaying motion resulting from violent impact or upheaval; CONVULSE suggests a violent pulling or wrenching as of a body in a paroxysm

— **shake a leg** **1 :** DANCE **2 :** to hurry up

2shake *n* **1 :** an act of shaking: as **a :** an act of shaking hands **b :** an act of shaking oneself **2 a :** a blow or shock that upsets the equilibrium or disturbs the balance of something **b :** EARTHQUAKE **3** *pl* **a :** a condition of trembling (as from chill) **b :** MALARIA 2a **4 :** something produced by shaking: as **a :** a fissure separating annual rings of growth in timber **b :** a fissure in strata **c :** MILK SHAKE **5 :** a wavering, quivering, or alternating motion caused by a blow or shock **6 :** TRILL **7 :** a very brief period of time **8** *pl* **:** one of importance or ability ⟨no great ~s⟩ **9 :** a shingle split from a piece of log usu. three or four feet long **10 :** 3DEAL 2 ⟨a fair ~⟩

shake down *vi* **1 a :** to take up temporary quarters **b :** to occupy an improvised or makeshift bed **2 a :** to become accustomed esp. to new surroundings or duties **b :** to settle down ~ *vt* **1 :** to obtain money from in a dishonest or illegal manner **2 :** to make a thorough search of **3 :** to bring about a reduction of **4 :** to test on a shakedown cruise

1shake·down \ˈshāk-ˌdau̇n\ *n* **1 :** an improvised bed (as made up on the floor) **2 :** a boisterous dance **3 :** an act or instance of shaking someone down; *esp* **:** EXTORTION **4 :** a thorough search **5 :** a process or period of adjustment

2shakedown *adj* **:** designed to test a new ship or airplane under operating conditions and to familiarize the crew with it ⟨~ cruise⟩

shake–out \ˈshā-ˌkau̇t\ *n* **:** a moderate stock market or business recession usu. corrective of an inflationary condition

shak·er \ˈshā-kər\ *n* **1 :** one that shakes; *esp* **:** any of various utensils or machines used in shaking ⟨pepper ~⟩ ⟨cocktail ~⟩ **2** *cap* **:** a member of a millenarian sect originating in England in 1747 and practicing celibacy and an ascetic communal life — **Shaker** *adj* — **Shak·er·ism** \-kə-ˌriz-əm\ *n*

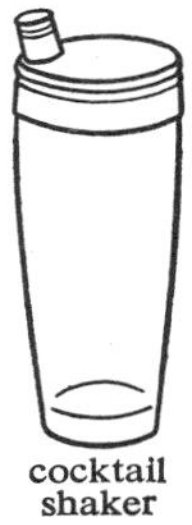
cocktail shaker

1Shake·spear·ean *or* **Shake·spear·ian** *also* **Shak-**

sper·ean *or* **Shak·sper·ian** \shāk-'spir-ē-ən\ *adj* **:** of, relating to, or having the characteristics of Shakespeare or his writings
[2]**Shakespearean** *or* **Shakespearian** *also* **Shakespearean** *or* **Shaksperian** *n* **:** an authority on or devotee of Shakespeare
Shake·spear·eana *or* **Shake·spear·iana** \ˌshāk-ˌspir-ē-'an-ə, -'än-ə, -'ā-nə\ *n pl* **:** collected items by, about, or relating to Shakespeare
Shakespearean sonnet *n* **:** ENGLISH SONNET
shake up *vt* **1** *obs* **:** CHIDE, SCOLD **2 :** to jar by or as if by a physical shock ⟨collision *shook up* both drivers⟩ **3 :** to effect an extensive and often drastic reorganization of
shake–up \'shā-ˌkəp\ *n* **:** an act or instance of shaking up; *specif* **:** an extensive and often drastic reorganization
shak·i·ly \'shā-kə-lē\ *adv* **:** in a shaky manner
shak·i·ness \-kē-nəs\ *n* **:** the quality or state of being shaky
shaking palsy *n* **:** PARALYSIS AGITANS
sha·ko \'shak-(ˌ)ō, 'shāk-, 'shäk-\ *n, pl* **shakos** *or* **shakoes** [F, fr. Hung *csákó*] **:** a stiff military cap with a high crown and plume
Shak·ta \'s(h)äk-tə\ *n or adj* [Skt *śākta*, fr. *Śakti*] **:** SHAKTIST
Shak·ti \-tē\ *n* [Skt *Śakti*] **:** the dynamic energy of a Hindu god personified as his female consort
Shak·tism \-ˌtiz-əm\ *n* **:** a Hindu sect worshiping Shakti under various names (as Kali, Durga) in a mother cult of devotion and a tantric cult with magical orgiastic rites — **Shak·tist** \-təst\ *n or adj*
shaky \'shā-kē\ *adj* **1 :** characterized by shakes ⟨~ timber⟩ **2 a :** lacking stability **b :** lacking in firmness **c :** lacking in authority or reliability **:** QUESTIONABLE **3 a :** somewhat unsound in health **b :** characterized by shaking **:** TREMBLING **4 :** easily shaken **:** RICKETY
shale \'shā(ə)l\ *n* [ME, shell, scale, fr. OE *scealu* — more at SHELL] **:** a fissile rock that is formed by the consolidation of clay, mud, or silt, has a finely stratified or laminated structure, and is composed of minerals essentially unaltered since deposition
shall \shəl, (')shal\ *vb, past* **should** \shəd, (')shu̇d\ *pres sing & pl* **shall** [ME *shal* (1st & 3d sing. pres. indic.), fr. OE *sceal;* akin to OHG *scal* (1st & 3d sing. pres. indic.) ought to, must, Lith *skola* debt] *verbal auxiliary* **1** *archaic* **a :** will have to **:** MUST **b :** will be able to **:** CAN **2 a** — used to express a command or exhortation ⟨you ~ go⟩ **b** — used in laws, regulations, or directives to express what is mandatory ⟨it ~ be unlawful to carry firearms⟩ **3 a** — used to express what is inevitable or likely to happen in the future ⟨we ~ have to be ready⟩ ⟨we ~ see⟩ **b** — used to express simple futurity ⟨when ~ we expect you⟩ **4** — used to express determination ⟨they ~ not pass⟩ **~** *vi* **:** will go ⟨he to England ~ along with you —Shak.⟩
shal·loon \shə-'lün, sha-\ *n* [*Châlons*-sur-Marne, France] **:** a lightweight twilled fabric of wool or worsted used chiefly for linings of coats and uniforms
shal·lop \'shal-əp\ *n* [MF *chaloupe*] **1 :** a usu. two-masted ship with lugsails **2 :** a small open boat propelled by oars or sails and used chiefly in shallow waters
shal·lot \shə-'lät\ *n* [modif. of F *échalote*, deriv. of (assumed) VL *escalonia* — more at SCALLION] **1 :** a bulbous perennial herb (*Allium ascalonicum*) that resembles an onion and produces small clustered bulbs used in seasoning **2 :** GREEN ONION
[1]**shal·low** \'shal-(ˌ)ō, -ə(-w)\ *adj* [ME *schalowe*] **1 :** having little depth **2 :** lacking intellectual depth **syn** see SUPERFICIAL — **shal·low·ly** \-ō-lē, -ə-lē\ *adv* — **shal·low·ness** *n*
[2]**shallow** *vt* **:** to make shallow **~** *vi* **:** to become shallow
[3]**shallow** *n* **:** a shallow place or area in a body of water — usu. used in pl. but sing. or pl. in constr.
sha·lom \shä-'lōm\ *interj* [Heb *shālōm* peace] — used as a Jewish greeting and farewell
sha·lom alei·chem \ˌshȯ-lə-mə-'lā-k͟əm\ *interj* [Heb *shālōm ʽalēkhem* peace unto you] — used as a traditional Jewish greeting
shalt \shəlt, (')shalt\ *archaic pres 2d sing of* SHALL
[1]**sham** \'sham\ *n* [perh. fr. E dial. *sham* shame, alter. of E *shame*] **1 :** a trick that deludes **:** HOAX **2 :** cheap falseness **:** HYPOCRISY **3 :** a decorative piece of cloth made to simulate an article of personal or household linen and used in place of or over it **4 :** an imitation or counterfeit purporting to be genuine **5 :** a person who shams **syn** see IMPOSTURE
[2]**sham** *vb* **shammed; sham·ming** *vt* **1** *archaic* **:** TRICK, DECEIVE **2 :** to go through the external motions necessary to counterfeit **~** *vi* **:** to act intentionally so as to give a false impression **:** FEIGN **syn** see ASSUME
[3]**sham** *adj* **:** FALSE: as **a :** FEIGNED, PRETENDED ⟨~ battle⟩ **b :** that shams or is made or used as a sham ⟨~ jewelry⟩
sha·man \'shäm-ən, 'shā-mən\ *n* [Russ or Tungus; Russ, fr. Tungus *šaman*] **:** a priest who uses magic to cure the sick, to divine the hidden, and to control events
sha·man·ism \-ˌiz-əm\ *n* **:** a religion of the Ural-Altaic peoples of northern Asia and Europe characterized by belief in an unseen world of gods, demons, and ancestral spirits responsive only to the shamans; *also* **:** any similar religion — **sha·man·ist** \-əst\ *n* — **sha·man·is·tic** \ˌshäm-ən-'is-tik, ˌshā-mən-\ *adj*
sham·ble \'sham-bəl\ *vi* **sham·bling** \-b(ə-)liŋ\ [*shamble* (bowed, malformed)] **:** to walk awkwardly with dragging feet **:** SHUFFLE — **shamble** *n*
sham·bles \'sham-bəlz\ *n pl but sing or pl in constr* [*shamble* (meat market) & obs. E *shamble* (table for exhibition of meat for sale)] **1** *archaic* **:** a meat market **2 :** SLAUGHTERHOUSE **3 a :** a place of mass slaughter or bloodshed **b :** a scene or a state of great destruction **:** RUIN, WRECKAGE **c :** a state of great disorder or confusion
sham·bling *adj* **:** characterized by slow awkward movement
[1]**shame** \'shām\ *n* [ME, fr. OE *scamu;* akin to OHG *scama* shame] **1 a :** a painful emotion caused by consciousness of guilt, shortcoming, or impropriety **b :** the susceptibility to such emotion **2 :** DISHONOR, DISGRACE **3 a :** something that brings strong regret, censure, or reproach **b :** a cause of feeling shame **syn** see DISGRACE
[2]**shame** *vt* **1 :** to bring shame to **:** DISGRACE **2 :** to put to shame by outdoing **3 :** to cause to feel shame **4 :** to force by causing to feel guilty ⟨*shamed* into confessing⟩
shame·faced \'shām-'fāst\ *adj* [alter. of *shamefast*] **1 :** showing modesty **:** BASHFUL **2 :** showing shame **:** ASHAMED — **shame·faced·ly** \-'fā-səd-lē, -'fāst-lē\ *adv* — **shame·faced·ness** \-'fā-səd-nəs, -'fās(t)-nəs\ *n*
shame·fast \'shām-ˌfast\ *adj* [ME, fr. OE *scamfæst*, fr. *scamu* + *fæst* fixed, fast] *archaic* **:** SHAMEFACED
shame·ful \'shām-fəl\ *adj* **1 a :** bringing shame **:** DISGRACEFUL **b :** arousing the feeling of shame **:** INDECENT **2** *archaic* **:** full of the feeling of shame **:** ASHAMED — **shame·ful·ly** \-fə-lē\ *adv* — **shame·ful·ness** *n*
shame·less \'shām-ləs\ *adj* **1 :** having no shame **:** BRAZEN **2 :** showing lack of shame **:** DISGRACEFUL — **shame·less·ly** *adv* — **shame·less·ness** *n*
sham·mer \'sham-ər\ *n* **:** one that shams
sham·mes \'shäm-əs\ *n, pl* **sham·mo·sim** *or* **sham·ma·shim** \shä-'mȯ-səm\ [Yiddish *shames*, fr. MHeb *shāmmāsh*] **1 :** the sexton of a synagogue **2 :** the candle or taper used to light the other candles in a Hanukkah menorah
sham·my \'sham-ē\ *var of* CHAMOIS
[1]**sham·poo** \sham-'pü\ *vt* [Hindi *cāpo*, imper. of *cāpnā* to press, shampoo] **1** *archaic* **:** MASSAGE **2 a :** to wash (as the hair) with soap and water or with a special preparation **b :** to wash the hair of — **sham·poo·er** *n*
[2]**shampoo** *n* **1 :** an act or instance of shampooing **2 :** a preparation used in shampooing
sham·rock \'sham-ˌräk\ *n* [IrGael *seamrōg*] **:** a trifoliolate leguminous plant used as a floral emblem by the Irish: as **a :** a yellow-flowered clover (*Trifolium dubium*) often regarded as the true shamrock **b :** a wood sorrel (*Oxalis acetosella*) **c :** WHITE DUTCH CLOVER **d :** a yellow-flowered medic (*Medicago lupulina*) with black pods

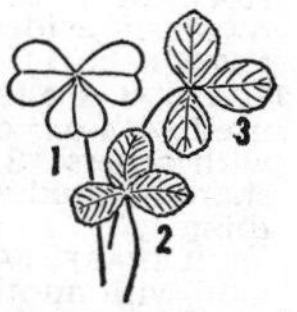

shamrocks: *1* wood sorrel, *2* white Dutch clover, *3* black medic

sha·mus \'shäm-əs, 'shā-məs\ *n* [prob. fr. Yiddish *shames* sexton of a synagogue; prob. fr. a jocular comparison of the duties of a sexton and those of a store detective] **1** *slang* **:** POLICEMAN **2** *slang* **:** a private detective
Shan \'shän, 'shan\ *n, pl* **Shan** *or* **Shans 1 a :** a group of Mongoloid peoples of southeastern Asia **b :** a member of any of these peoples **2 :** the Thai language of the Shan
shan·dry·dan \'shan-drē-ˌdan\ *n* [origin unknown] **1 :** a chaise with a hood **2 :** a rickety vehicle
shan·dy·gaff \'shan-dē-ˌgaf\ *or* **shandy** *n* [origin unknown] **:** a drink consisting of beer and ginger beer or ginger ale
shang·hai \shaŋ-'hī\ *vt* **shang·haied; shang·hai·ing** [*Shanghai*, China; fr. the formerly widespread use of this method to secure sailors for voyages to the Orient] **1 :** to drug, intoxicate, or make insensible and put aboard a ship esp. as a sailor **2 :** to bring by deceit or coercion — **shang·hai·er** \-'hī(-ə)r\ *n*
Shan·gri-la \ˌshaŋ-gri-'lä\ *n* [*Shangri-La*, imaginary land depicted in the novel *Lost Horizon* by James Hilton] **1 :** a remote beautiful imaginary place where life approaches perfection **:** UTOPIA **2 :** a remote usu. idyllic hideaway
shank \'shaŋk\ *n* [ME *shanke*, fr. OE *scanca;* akin to ON *skakkr* crooked, Gk *skazein* to limp] **1 a :** the part of the leg between the knee and the ankle in man or the corresponding part in various other vertebrates **b :** LEG **c :** a cut of beef, veal, mutton, or lamb from the upper or the lower part of the leg **:** SHIN **2 :** a straight narrow usu. essential part of an object: as **a :** the straight part of a nail or pin **b :** a straight part of a plant **:** STEM, STALK **c :** the part of an anchor between the ring and the crown **d :** the part of a fishhook between the eye and the bend **e :** the part of a key between the handle and the bit **f :** the stem of a tobacco pipe or the part between the stem and the bowl **g :** TANG 1 **h** (1) **:** the narrow part of the sole of a shoe beneath the instep (2) **:** SHANKPIECE **3 :** a part of an object by which it can be attached: as **a** (1) **:** a projection on the back of a solid button (2) **:** a short bar of thread that holds a sewn button away from the cloth **b :** the projecting part of a knob handle that contains the spindle socket **c :** the end (as of a drill) that is gripped in a chuck **4 :** BODY 7 **5 a :** the latter part of a period of time **b :** the early or main part of a period of time
shank·piece \-ˌpēs\ *n* **:** a support for the arch of the foot inserted in the shank of a shoe
shan't \(')shant, (')shȧnt\ **:** shall not
shantey *or* **shanty** *var of* CHANTEY
shan·tung \(')shan-'təŋ\ *n* [*Shantung*, China] **:** a fabric in plain weave having a slightly irregular surface
shan·ty \'shant-ē\ *n* [CanF *chantier*, fr. F, gantry, fr. L *cantherius* trellis] **:** a small crudely built dwelling or shelter usu. of wood
shan·ty·man \-mən, -ˌman\ *n* **:** one (as a logger) who lives in a shanty
shan·ty·town \-ˌtau̇n\ *n* **:** a town or section of a town consisting mostly of shanties
shap·able *or* **shape·able** \'shā-pə-bəl\ *adj* **1 :** capable of being shaped **2 :** SHAPELY
[1]**shape** \'shāp\ *vb* [ME *shapen*, alter. of OE *sceppan;* akin to OHG *skepfen* to shape] *vt* **1 :** FORM, CREATE; *esp* **:** to give a particular form or shape to **2** *obs* **:** ORDAIN, DECREE **3 :** to cut out and fashion (as a garment) by a pattern **4 a :** DEVISE, PLAN **b :** to embody in definite form ⟨*shaping* a folktale into an epic⟩ **5 a :** to make fit for **:** ADAPT **b :** to determine or direct the course of (as life) **~** *vi* **1 :** HAPPEN, BEFALL **2 :** to take on or approach a mature form — often used with *up* **syn** see MAKE — **shap·er** *n*
[2]**shape** *n* **1 a :** the visible makeup characteristic of a particular item or kind of item **b** (1) **:** spatial form (2) **:** a standard or universally recognized spatial form **2 :** the appearance of the body as distinguished from that of the face **:** FIGURE **3 a :** PHANTOM, APPARITION **b :** assumed appearance **:** GUISE **4 :** form of embodiment **5 :** a mode of existence or form of being having identifying features **6 :** something having a particular form **7 :** the condition in which someone or something exists at a particular time ⟨in excellent ~ for his age⟩ **syn** see FORM — **shaped** \ˌshāpt\ *adj*
shape·less \'shā-pləs\ *adj* **1 :** having no definite shape **2 a :** deprived of usual or normal shape **:** MISSHAPEN **b :** not shapely — **shape·less·ly** *adv* — **shape·less·ness** *n*
shape·li·ness \'shā-plē-nəs\ *n* **:** the quality or state of being shapely
shape·ly \'shā-plē\ *adj* **:** having a regular or pleasing shape

shap·en \'shā-pən\ *adj* **:** fashioned in or provided with a definite shape — usu. used in combination ⟨an ill-*shapen* body⟩
shape note *n* **:** one of a system of seven notes showing the musical scale degree by the shape of the note head
shape–up \'shā-,pəp\ *n* **:** a system of hiring longshoremen by the day or shift by having applicants gather usu. in a semicircle for selection by a union-appointed hiring boss
shard \'shärd\ *also* **sherd** \'shərd\ *n* [ME, fr. OE *sceard;* akin to OE *scieran* to cut — more at SHEAR] **1 a :** a piece or fragment of a brittle substance; *broadly* **:** a small piece **b :** SHELL, SCALE; *esp* **:** ELYTRON **2** *usu sherd* **:** fragments of pottery vessels found on sites and in refuse deposits where pottery-making peoples have lived
1share \'she(ə)r, 'sha(ə)r\ *n* [ME, fr. OE *scearu* cutting, tonsure; akin to OE *scieran* to cut — more at SHEAR] **1 a :** a portion belonging to, due to, or contributed by an individual **b :** one's full or fair portion **2 a :** the part allotted or belonging to one of a number owning together property or interest **b :** any of the equal portions into which property or invested capital is divided; *specif* **:** any of the equal interests or rights into which the entire capital stock of a corporation is divided and ownership of which is regularly evidenced by one or more certificates **c** *pl, chiefly Brit* **:** STOCK 6b(1)
2share *vt* **1 :** to divide and distribute in shares **:** APPORTION — usu. used with *out* or *with* **2 :** to partake of, use, experience, or enjoy with others **3 :** to grant or give a share in ~ *vi* **1 :** to have a share — used with *in* **2 :** to apportion and take shares of something
syn SHARE, PARTICIPATE, PARTAKE mean to have, get, use in common with another or others. SHARE implies that one as the original holder grants to another the partial use, enjoyment, or possession of a thing though it may merely imply a mutual use or possession; PARTICIPATE implies a having or taking part in an undertaking, activity, or discussion; PARTAKE implies accepting or acquiring a share esp. of food or drink
3share *n* [ME *schare,* fr. OE *scear;* akin to OHG *scaro* plowshare, OE *scieran* to cut] **:** PLOWSHARE
share·crop \-,kräp\ *vb* [back-formation fr. *sharecropper*] *vi* **:** to farm as a sharecropper ~ *vt* **:** to farm (land) or produce (a crop) as a sharecropper
share·crop·per \-,kräp-ər\ *n* **:** a tenant farmer esp. in the southern U.S. who is provided with credit for seed, tools, living quarters, and food, works the land, and receives an agreed share of the value of the crop minus charges
share·hold·er \-,hōl-dər\ *n* **:** one that holds or owns a share in a joint fund or property; *esp* **:** STOCKHOLDER
shar·er \'sher-ər, 'shar-\ *n* **:** one that shares
sha·rif \shə-'rēf\ *n* [Ar *sharīf,* lit., illustrious] **:** a descendant of the prophet Muhammad through his daughter Fatima; *broadly* **:** one of noble ancestry or religious preeminence in Islam — **sha·rif·ian** \-'rē-fē-ən\ *adj*
1shark \'shärk\ *n* [origin unknown] **:** any of numerous mostly marine elasmobranch fishes of medium to large size that have a fusiform body, lateral gill clefts, and a tough usu. dull gray skin roughened by minute tubercles, are typically active, voracious, and rapacious predators, and are of economic importance esp. for their large livers which are a source of oil and for their hides from which leather is made
2shark *n* [prob. modif. of G *schurke* scoundrel] **1 :** a rapacious crafty person who preys upon others through usury, extortion, or trickery **2 :** one who excels greatly esp. in a particular field
3shark *vt, archaic* **:** to get by playing the shark ~ *vi* **1 :** to play the shark **2 :** to live by shifts and stratagems
shark·skin \-,skin\ *n* **1 :** the hide of a shark or leather made from it **2 a :** a smooth durable woolen or worsted suiting in twill or basket weave with small woven designs **b :** a smooth crisp fabric with a dull finish made usu. of rayon in basket weave
1sharp \'shärp\ *adj* [ME, fr. OE *scearp;* akin to OE *scieran* to cut — more at SHEAR] **1 :** adapted to cutting or piercing: as **a :** having a thin keen edge or fine point **b :** briskly or sharply cold **:** NIPPING **c :** composed of hard angular particles **:** GRITTY **2 a :** keen in intellect **:** QUICK-WITTED **b :** keen in perception **:** ACUTE **c :** keen in attention **:** VIGILANT **d :** keen in attention to one's own interest sometimes to the point of being unethical ⟨a ~ trader⟩ **3 :** keen in spirit or action: as **a :** EAGER, BRISK **b :** capable of acting or reacting strongly; *esp* **:** CAUSTIC **4:** SEVERE, HARSH: as **a :** inclined to or marked by irritability or anger **b :** causing intense mental or physical distress **c :** cutting in language or import **5 :** affecting the senses or sense organs intensely: as **a** (1) **:** having a strong odor or flavor ⟨~ cheese⟩ (2) **:** ACRID **b :** having a strong piercing sound **c :** having the effect of or involving a sudden brilliant display of light **6 a :** terminating in a point or edge ⟨~ features⟩ **b :** involving an abrupt change in direction ⟨a ~ turn⟩ **c :** clear in outline or detail **:** DISTINCT **d :** set forth with clarity and distinctness ⟨~ contrast⟩ **7 a** *of a tone* **:** raised a half step in pitch **b :** higher than the proper pitch **c :** MAJOR, AUGMENTED — used of an interval in music **d :** having a sharp in the signature ⟨key of F ~⟩ **8 :** STYLISH, DRESSY — **sharp·ly** *adv* — **sharp·ness** *n*
syn KEEN, ACUTE: SHARP applies to things with an edge or point making cutting or piercing easy; applied to persons it implies quick perception or analysis, clever resourcefulness, or questionable trickiness; KEEN applies esp. to a very sharp edge or may suggest a poignant, a zestful, or a bracing quality; ACUTE stresses a power to penetrate and may apply to the senses or to mental faculties such as logical discrimination
2sharp *vt* **:** to raise (as a musical tone) in pitch; *esp* **:** to raise in pitch by a half step ~ *vi* **:** to sing or play above the proper pitch
3sharp *adv* **1 :** in a sharp manner **:** SHARPLY **2 :** PRECISELY, EXACTLY ⟨4 o'clock ~⟩
4sharp *n* **:** one that is sharp: as **a :** a sharp edge or point **b** (1) **:** a musical note or tone one half step higher than a note or tone named (2) **:** a character ♯ on a line or space of the musical staff indicating a pitch a half step higher than the degree would indicate without it **c :** a long sewing needle with sharp point **d :** a real or self-styled expert; *also* **:** SHARPER
sharp·en \'shär-pən\ *vb* **sharp·en·ing** \'shärp-(ə-)niŋ\ *vt* **:** to make sharp or sharper ~ *vi* **:** to grow or become sharp or sharper — **sharp·en·er** \'shärp-(ə-)nər\ *n*
sharp·er \'shär-pər\ *n* **:** CHEAT, SWINDLER; *esp* **:** a cheating gamester

sharp–eyed \'shär-'pīd\ *adj* **:** having keen sight; *also* **:** keen in observing or penetrating
sharp–fanged \'shärp-'faŋd\ *adj* **:** having sharp teeth; *also* **:** SARCASTIC
sharp–freeze \-'frēz\ *vt* **:** QUICK-FREEZE
sharp·ie *or* **sharpy** \'shär-pē\ *n* [1sharp] **1 :** a long narrow shallow-draft boat with flat or slightly V-shaped bottom and one or two masts that bear a triangular sail **2 a :** SHARPER **b :** an exceptionally keen or alert person

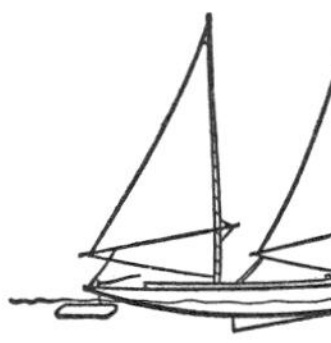
sharpie

sharp–nosed \'shärp-'nōzd\ *adj* **1 :** having a pointed nose or snout **2 :** keen of scent
sharp practice *n* **:** dealing in which advantage is taken or sought unscrupulously
sharp–set \'shärp-'set\ *adj* **1 :** set at a sharp angle or so as to present a sharp edge **2 :** eager in appetite or desire — **sharp–set·ness** *n*
sharp·shoot·er \-,shüt-ər\ *n* **:** one skilled in shooting **:** a good marksman — **sharp·shoot·ing** \-iŋ\ *n*
sharp–sight·ed \-'sīt-əd\ *adj* **1 :** having acute sight **2 :** mentally keen or alert
sharp–tongued \-'təŋd\ *adj* **:** having a sharp tongue **:** bitter of speech
sharp–wit·ted \-'wit-əd\ *adj* **:** having or showing an acute mind
shash·lik *also* **shash·lick** *or* **shas·lik** \shäsh-'lik\ *n* [Russ *shashlyk,* of Turkic origin; akin to Kazan Tatar *šyšlyk* kabob] **:** KABOB
1shat·ter \'shat-ər\ *vb* [ME *schateren*] *vt* **1 :** DISPERSE, SCATTER **2 a :** to break at once into pieces **b :** to damage badly **:** RUIN ~ *vi* **1 :** CLATTER, RATTLE **2 a :** to break apart **:** DISINTEGRATE **b :** to drop off parts
2shatter *n* **1 :** FRAGMENT, SHRED ⟨in ~*s*⟩ **2 :** an act of shattering **:** the state of being shattered **3 :** a result of shattering **:** SHOWER
shat·ter·proof \,shat-ər-'prüf\ *adj* **:** proof against shattering ⟨~ glass⟩
1shave \'shāv\ *vb* **shaved; shaved** *or* **shav·en** \'shā-vən\ **shav·ing** [ME *shaven,* fr. OE *scafan;* akin to L *scabere* to shave, *capo* capon] *vt* **1 a :** to remove a thin layer from **b :** to cut off in thin layers or shreds **:** SLICE **c :** to cut off closely **2 :** to sever the hair from close to the skin with a razor **3 a :** to discount (a note) at an exorbitant rate **b :** DEDUCT, REDUCE **4 :** to come close to or touch lightly in passing ~ *vi* **1 :** to cut off hair or beard close to the skin **2 :** to proceed with difficulty **:** SCRAPE
2shave *n* **1 :** SHAVER 3 **2 :** a thin slice **:** SHAVING **3 :** an act or process of shaving **4 :** an act of passing very near to so as almost to graze
shave·ling \'shāv-liŋ\ *n* **1 :** a tonsured clergyman **:** PRIEST — usu. used disparagingly **2 :** STRIPLING
shav·er \'shā-vər\ *n* **1 :** a person who shaves **2** *archaic* **:** SWINDLER **3 :** a tool or machine for shaving; *specif* **:** an electric-powered razor **4 :** BOY, YOUNGSTER
shaves *pl of* SHAFT
shave·tail \'shāv-,tāl\ *n* [fr. the practice of shaving the tails of newly broken mules to distinguish them from untrained ones] **1 :** a pack mule esp. when newly broken in **2 :** SECOND LIEUTENANT — usu. used disparagingly
Sha·vi·an \'shā-vē-ən\ *n* [*Shavius,* latinized form of George Bernard *Shaw*] **:** an admirer or devotee of G. B. Shaw, his writings, or his social and political theories — **Shavian** *adj*
sha·vie \'shā-vē\ *n* [perh. fr. *shave* (swindle)] *Scot* **:** PRACTICAL JOKE, PRANK
shav·ing \'shā-viŋ\ *n* **1 :** the act of one that shaves **2 :** something shaved off ⟨wood ~*s*⟩
1shaw \'shò\ *n* [ME, fr. OE *sceaga;* akin to ON *skegg* beard — more at SHAG] *dial* **:** COPPICE, THICKET
2shaw *n* [prob. alter. of *show*] *chiefly Brit* **:** the tops and stalks of a cultivated crop (as potatoes or turnips)
1shawl \'shòl\ *n* [Per *shāl*] **:** a square or oblong fabric garment or wrapper used esp. as a covering for the head or shoulders
2shawl *vt* **:** to wrap in or as if in a shawl
shawm \'shòm\ *n* [ME *schalme,* fr. MF *chalemie,* modif. of LL *calamellus,* dim. of *calamus* reed, fr. Gk *kalamos* —more at HAULM] **:** an early double-reed woodwind instrument
Shaw·nee \shò-'nē, shä-\ *n, pl* **Shawnee** *or* **Shawnees** [back-formation fr. obs E *Shawnese,* fr. Shawnee *Shaawanwaaki*] **1 :** an Algonquian people ranging through most of the states east of the Mississippi and south of the Great Lakes **2 :** a member of the Shawnee people
Shaw·wal \shə-'wäl\ *n* [Ar *shawwāl*] **:** the 10th month of the Muhammadan year
shay \'shā\ *n* [back-formation fr. *chaise,* taken as pl.] *chiefly dial* **:** CHAISE 1
1she \(')shē\ *pron* [ME, prob. alter. of *hye,* alter. of OE *hēo* she — more at HE] **:** that female one ⟨~ is my wife⟩ **:** that one regarded as feminine (as by personification) ⟨~ was a fine ship⟩ — compare HE, HER, HERS, IT, THEY
2she \'shē\ *n* **:** a female person or animal ⟨*she*-cat⟩ ⟨*she*-cousin⟩
shea butter \'shē-, 'shā-\ *n* **:** a pale solid fat from the seeds of the shea tree used in food, soap, and candles
sheaf \'shēf\ *n, pl* **sheaves** \'shēvz\ [ME *sheef,* fr. OE *scēaf;* akin to OHG *scoub* sheaf, Russ *chub* forelock] **1 :** a quantity of the stalks and ears of a cereal grass or sometimes other plant material bound together **2 :** something resembling a sheaf of grain — **sheaf·like** \'shē-,flīk\ *adj*
1shear \'shi(ə)r\ *vb* **sheared; sheared** *or* **shorn** \'shō(ə)rn, 'shò(ə)rn\ **shear·ing** [ME *sheren,* fr. OE *scieran;* akin to ON *skera* to cut, L *curtus* shortened, Gk *keirein* to cut, shear] *vt* **1 a :** to cut off the hair from ⟨with crown *shorn*⟩ **b :** to cut or clip (as hair or wool) from someone or something; *also* **:** to cut something from ⟨*shorn* sheep⟩ **c** *chiefly Scot* **:** to reap with a sickle **d :** to cut with shears or a similar instrument **2 :** to cut with something sharp **3 :** to deprive of something as if by cutting ~ *vi* **1 :** to cut through something with or as if with a sharp instrument **2** *chiefly Scot* **:** to reap crops with a sickle **3 :** to become divided under the action of a shear ⟨bolt may ~ off⟩ — **shear·er** *n*
2shear *n, often attrib* **1 a** (1) **:** a cutting implement similar or identical to a pair of scissors but typically larger — usu. used in pl.

(2) **:** one blade of a pair of shears **b :** any of various cutting tools or machines operating by the action of opposed cutting edges of metal — usu. used in pl. **c** (1) **:** something resembling a shear or a pair of shears (2) **:** a hoisting apparatus consisting of two or sometimes more spars fastened together at their upper ends and having tackle for masting or dismasting ships or lifting guns or other heavy loads — usu. used in pl. but sing. or pl. in constr. **2** *chiefly Brit* **:** SHEARING — used to indicate the age of sheep **3 a :** internal force tangential to the section on which it acts **:** shearing force **b :** an action or stress resulting from applied forces that causes two contiguous parts of a body to slide relatively to each other in a direction parallel to their plane of contact

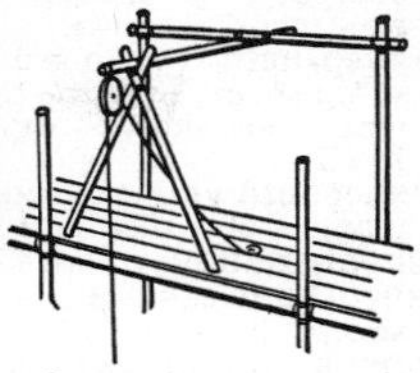

a form of shears 1c(2)

sheared *adj* **:** formed or finished by shearing; *esp* **:** cut to uniform length ⟨~ beaver coat⟩

shear·wa·ter \'shi(ə)r-,wȯt-ər, -,wät-\ *n* **:** any of numerous oceanic birds (esp. genus *Puffinus*) related to the petrels and albatrosses that in flight usu. skim close to the waves

sheat·fish \'shēt-,fish\ *n* [alter. of *sheathfish*, fr. *sheath* + *fish*] **:** a large catfish (*Silurus glanis*) of central and eastern Europe

sheath \'shēth\ *n, pl* **sheaths** \'shēthz, 'shēths\ [ME *shethe*, fr. OE *scēath;* akin to OHG *sceida* sheath, L *scindere* to cut — more at SHED] **1 :** a case for a blade (as of a knife) **2 :** an investing cover or case of a plant or animal body or body part: as **a :** the tubular fold of skin into which the penis of many mammals is retracted **b** (1) **:** the lower part of a leaf (as of a grass) when surrounding the stem (2) **:** an ensheathing spathe (3) **:** OCREA **3 :** any of various covering or supporting structures that are applied like or resemble the sheath of a blade: as **a :** SHEATHING 2 **b :** a woman's close-fitting dress having narrow straight unbroken lines and usu. worn without a belt

sheath·bill \'shēth-,bil\ *n* **:** any of several white shore birds (family Chionididae) of colder parts of the southern hemisphere that have a horny sheath over the base of the upper mandible and suggest the pigeons in general appearance

sheathe \'shēth\ *also* **sheath** \'shēth\ *vt* **1 :** to put into or furnish with a sheath **2 a :** to plunge or bury in flesh **b :** to withdraw (a claw) into a sheath **3 :** to case or cover with something (as thin boards or sheets of metal) that protects — **sheath·er** \'shē-thər, -thər\ *n*

sheath·ing \'shē-thiŋ, -thiŋ\ *n* **1 :** the action of one that sheathes something **2 :** material used to sheathe something; *esp* **:** the first covering of boards or of waterproof material on the outside wall of a frame house or on a timber roof

sheath knife *n* **:** a knife having a fixed blade and designed to be carried in a sheath

shea tree \'shē-, 'shā-\ *n* [Bambara *si*] **:** a tropical African tree (*Butyrospermum parkii*) of the sapodilla family with fatty nuts yielding shea butter

1sheave \'shiv, 'shēv\ *n* [ME *sheve;* akin to OE *scēath* sheath] **1 :** the grooved wheel or pulley of a pulley block **2 :** any grooved wheel or pulley

2sheave \'shēv\ *vt* [*sheaf*] **:** to gather and bind into a sheaf

3sheave \'shēv\ *vi* [perh. fr. ME *scheven* to shove, fr. OE *scēofan*, alter. of *scūfan* — more at SHOVE] **:** to reverse the action of the oars in rowing a boat

she·bang \shi-'baŋ\ *n* [perh. alter. of *shebeen*] **:** CONTRIVANCE, AFFAIR, CONCERN ⟨the whole ~⟩

She·bat \shə-'bät, -'vät\ *n* [Heb *shĕbhāṭ*] **:** the 5th month of the civil year or the 11th month of the ecclesiastical year in the Jewish calendar

she·been \shə-'bēn\ *n* [IrGael *sībīn* bad ale] *chiefly Irish* **:** an unlicensed or illegally operated drinking establishment

1shed \'shed\ *vb* **shed; shed·ding** [ME *sheden* to divide, separate, fr. OE *scēadan;* akin to OHG *skeidan* to separate, L *scindere* to cut, split, Gk *schizein* to split] *vt* **1** *chiefly dial* **:** to set apart **:** SEGREGATE **2 :** to cause to be dispersed without penetrating ⟨duck's plumage ~s water⟩ **3 a :** to cause (blood) to flow by cutting or wounding **b :** to pour forth in drops ⟨~ tears⟩ **c :** to give off in a stream **d :** to give off or out **4 a :** to cast off (as a body covering) **:** MOLT **b :** to let fall (as leaves) **c :** to eject (as seed or spores) from a natural receptacle ~ *vi* **1 :** to pour out **:** SPILL **2 :** to become dispersed **:** SCATTER **3 :** to cast off some natural covering **syn** see DISCARD — **shed blood :** to cause death by violence

2shed *n* **1** *obs* **:** DISTINCTION, DIFFERENCE **2 :** something that is discarded in shedding **3 :** a divide of land

3shed *n* [alter. of earlier *shadde*, prob. fr. ME *shade*] **1 :** a slight structure built for shelter or storage; *esp* **:** a single-storied building with one or more sides unenclosed **2** *archaic* **:** HUT

4shed *vt* **shed·ded; shed·ding :** to put or house in a shed

she'd \(,)shēd\ **:** she had **:** she would

shed·der \'shed-ər\ *n* **:** one that sheds something: as **a** (1) **:** a crab or lobster about to molt (2) **:** a newly molted crab **b :** a female salmon after spawning

shed dormer *n* **:** a dormer with a roof sloping in the same direction as the roof from which the dormer projects

1sheen \'shēn\ *adj* [ME *shene*, fr. OE *sciene;* akin to OE *scēawian* to look — more at SHOW] **:** BEAUTIFUL, RESPLENDENT

2sheen *vi* **:** to be bright **:** show a sheen

3sheen *n* **1 a :** BRIGHTNESS **b :** a subdued glitter approaching but short of optical reflection **c :** a lustrous surface imparted to textiles through finishing processes or use of shiny yarns **2 a :** bright or showy clothing **b :** a textile exhibiting notable sheen — **sheeny** \'shē-nē\ *adj*

sheep \'shēp\ *n, pl* **sheep** *often attrib* [ME, fr. OE *scēap;* akin to OHG *scāf* sheep] **1 :** any of numerous ruminant mammals (genus *Ovis*) related to the goats but stockier and lacking a beard in the male; *specif* **:** one (*O. aries*) long domesticated for its flesh, wool, and other products **2 a :** a timid defenseless creature **b :** a silly bashful fellow **3 :** leather prepared from the skins of sheep **:** SHEEPSKIN

sheep·ber·ry \'shēp-,ber-ē\ *n* **:** an often shrubby No. American viburnum (*Viburnum lentago*) with white flowers in flat cymes; *also* **:** its black edible berry

sheep·cote \-,kōt, -,kät\ *n, chiefly Brit* **:** SHEEPFOLD

sheep-dip \-,dip\ *n* **:** a liquid preparation of toxic chemicals into which sheep are plunged esp. to destroy parasitic arthropods

sheep dog *n* **:** a dog used to tend, drive, or guard sheep

sheep fescue *n* **:** a hardy fine-foliaged European perennial grass (*Festuca ovina*) widely used as a lawn grass

sheep·fold \'shēp-,fōld\ *n* **:** a pen or shelter for sheep

sheep·herd·er \'shēp-,hərd-ər\ *n* **:** a worker in charge of sheep esp. on open range — **sheep·herd·ing** \-iŋ\ *n*

sheep·ish \'shē-pish\ *adj* **1 :** resembling a sheep in meekness, stupidity, or timidity ⟨the ~ wisdom of the conventional —G.B. Shaw⟩ **2 :** embarrassed by consciousness of a fault ⟨a ~ look⟩ — **sheep·ish·ly** *adv* — **sheep·ish·ness** *n*

sheep ked *n* **:** a wingless bloodsucking dipterous fly (*Melophagus ovinus*) that feeds chiefly on sheep and is a vector of sheep trypanosomiasis — called also *sheep tick*

sheep's eye *n* **:** a shy longing and usu. amorous glance — usu. used in pl.

sheep·shank \'shēp-,shaŋk\ *n* **1 :** a knot for shortening a line **2** *Scot* **:** something of no worth or importance

sheeps·head \'shēps-,hed\ *n* **1** *archaic* **:** a silly or stupid person **2 a :** a sparid food fish (*Archosargus probatocephalus*) of the Atlantic and Gulf coasts of the U.S. with broad incisor teeth **b :** a large croaker (*Aplodinotus grunniens*) of the Great Lakes and Mississippi valley **c :** a common largely red or rose California wrasse (*Pimelometopon pulcher*)

sheep·shear·er \'shēp-,shir-ər\ *n* **:** one that shears sheep

sheep·shear·ing \'shēp-,shi(ə)r-iŋ\ *n* **1 :** the act of shearing sheep **2 :** the time or season for shearing sheep; *also* **:** a festival held at this time

sheep·skin \-,skin\ *n* **1 a :** the skin of a sheep; *also* **:** leather prepared from it **b :** PARCHMENT **c :** a garment made of or lined with sheepskin **2 :** DIPLOMA

sheep sorrel *n* **:** a small acid dock (*Rumex acetosella*)

sheep·walk \'shēp-,wȯk\ *n, chiefly Brit* **:** a pasture or range for sheep

1sheer \'shi(ə)r\ *adj* [ME *schere* freed from guilt, prob. alter. of *skere*, fr. ON *skǣrr* pure; akin to OE *scīnan* to shine] **1** *obs* **:** BRIGHT, SHINING **2 :** of very thin or transparent texture **:** DIAPHANOUS **3 a :** UNQUALIFIED, UTTER ⟨~ folly⟩ **b :** PURE, UNMIXED **c :** viewed or acting in dissociation from all else ⟨won through by ~ determination⟩ **4 :** PRECIPITOUS, PERPENDICULAR **syn** see STEEP — **sheer·ly** *adv* — **sheer·ness** *n*

2sheer *adv* **1 :** ALTOGETHER, COMPLETELY **2 :** PERPENDICULARLY

3sheer *vb* [perh. alter. of *1shear*] *vi* **:** to deviate from a course **:** SWERVE ~ *vt* **:** to cause to sheer

4sheer *n* **1 :** a turn, deviation, or change in a course **2 :** the position of a ship riding to a single anchor and heading toward it

5sheer *n* [perh. alter. of *2shear*] **:** the fore-and-aft curvature from bow to stern of a ship's deck as shown in side elevation

sheer·legs \'shi(ə)r-,legz, -,lāgz\ *n pl but sing or pl in constr* **:** SHEAR 1c(2)

1sheet \'shēt\ *n* [ME *shete*, fr. OE *scȳte;* akin to OE *scēotan* to shoot — more at SHOOT] **1 a :** a broad piece of cloth; *esp* **:** an oblong of usu. linen or cotton cloth used as an article of bedding next to the person **b :** SAIL 1 **2 a :** a usu. rectangular piece of paper; *specif* **:** one of full manufactured size **b :** a printed signature for a book esp. before it has been folded, cut, or bound — usu. used in pl. **c :** a newspaper, periodical, or occasional publication **d :** the unseparated postage stamps printed by one impression of a plate on a single piece of paper; *also* **:** a pane of stamps **3 :** a broad stretch or surface of something ⟨~ of ice⟩ **4 :** a suspended or moving expanse (as of fire or rain) **5 a :** a portion of something that is thin in comparison to its length and breadth **b :** a flat baking utensil of tinned metal usu. with a lip on the front edge for handling — **sheet·like** \-,līk\ *adj*

2sheet *vt* **1 :** to cover with a sheet **:** SHROUD **2 :** to furnish with sheets **3 :** to form into sheets ~ *vi* **:** to fall, spread, or flow in a sheet

3sheet *adj* **1 :** rolled or spread out in a sheet **2 :** of, relating to, or concerned with the making of sheet metal

4sheet *n* [ME *shete*, fr. OE *scēata* lower corner of a sail; akin to OE *scȳte* sheet] **1 :** a rope or chain that regulates the angle at which a sail is set in relation to the wind **2** *pl* **:** the spaces at either end of an open boat not occupied by thwarts **:** foresheets and stern sheets together

sheet anchor *n* **1 :** a large strong anchor carried in the waist of a ship **2 :** something that constitutes a main support or dependence in danger

sheet bend *n* **:** a bend or hitch used for temporarily fastening a rope to the bight of another rope or to an eye

sheet glass *n* **:** glass made in large sheets directly from the furnace or by making a cylinder and then flattening it

sheet home *vt* **1 :** to extend (a sail) and set as flat as possible by hauling upon the sheets **2 :** to fix the responsibility for **:** bring home to one

sheet·ing \'shēt-iŋ\ *n* **:** material in the form of sheets or suitable for forming into sheets

sheet lightning *n* **:** lightning in diffused or sheet form due to reflection and diffusion by the clouds and sky

sheet metal *n* **:** metal in the form of a sheet

sheet music *n* **:** music printed on large unbound sheets of paper

Sheet·rock \'shēt-,räk\ *trademark* — used for plasterboard

sheikh *or* **sheik** \'shēk, *also* 'shāk & 'shīk *for 1*\ *n* [Ar *shaykh*] **1 :** an Arab chief **2** *usu sheik* **:** a man supposed to be endowed with an irresistible fascination in the eyes of romantic young women

sheikh·dom *or* **sheik·dom** \-dəm\ *n* **:** a region under the rule of a sheikh

shek·el \'shek-əl\ *n* [Heb *sheqel*] **1 a :** any of various ancient units of weight; *esp* **:** a Hebrew unit equal to about 252 grains troy **b :** a unit of value based on a shekel weight of gold or silver **2 :** a coin weighing one shekel

shel·drake \'shel-,drāk\ *n* [ME, fr. *sheld-* (akin to MD *schillede*

parti-colored) + *drake*] **1 :** any of various Old World ducks (genus *Tadorna*); *esp* **:** a common mostly black-and-white European duck (*T. tadorna*) slightly larger than the mallard **2 :** MERGANSER

shelf \'shelf\ *n, pl* **shelves** \'shelvz\ [ME, prob. fr. OE *scylfe;* akin to L *scalpere, sculpere* to carve, OE *sciell* shell] **1 a :** a thin flat usu. long and narrow piece of wood or other material fastened horizontally (as on a wall) at a distance from the floor to hold objects **b :** one of several similar pieces in a closet, bookcase, or similar structure **c :** the contents of a shelf **2 :** something resembling a shelf in form or position: as **a :** a sandbank or ledge of rocks usu. partially submerged **b :** a stratum with a shelflike surface **c :** a flat projecting layer of rock — **shelf·like** \'shel-,flīk\ *adj* — **on the shelf :** in a state of inactivity or uselessness

shelf ice *n* **:** an extensive ice sheet originating on land but continuing out to sea beyond the depths at which it rests on the sea bottom

¹shell \'shel\ *n* [ME, fr. OE *sciell;* akin to OE *scealu* shell, ON *skel,* L *silex* pebble, flint, Gk *skallein* to hoe] **1 a :** a hard rigid usu. largely calcareous covering of an animal **b :** the hard or tough outer covering of an egg esp. of a bird **2 :** the covering or outside part of a fruit or seed esp. when hard or fibrous **3 :** shell material (as of mollusks or turtles) or their substance **4 :** something that resembles a shell: as **a :** a framework or exterior structure; *esp* **:** a building with an unfinished interior **b :** an external case or outside covering **c :** an edible case for holding a filling **d :** a reinforced concrete arched or domed roof that is used primarily over large unpartitioned areas **e :** a small beer glass **5 :** a thin hard layer of rock **6 :** a shell-bearing mollusk **7 :** an impersonal attitude or manner that conceals the presence or absence of feeling **8 :** a narrow light racing boat propelled by one or more oarsmen **9 :** any of the spaces occupied by the orbits of a group of electrons of approximately equal energy surrounding the nucleus of an atom **10 a :** a hollow projectile for cannon containing an explosive bursting charge **b :** a metal or paper case which holds the charge of powder and shot or bullet used with breech-loading small arms — **shell** *adj* — **shelled** \'sheld\ *adj* — **shell·work** \'shel-,wərk\ *n* — **shelly** \'shel-ē\ *adj*

²shell *vt* **1 a :** to take out of a natural enclosing cover (as a shell, husk, pod, capsule) **:** strip, break off, or remove the shell of **b :** to separate the kernels of (as an ear of Indian corn, wheat, or oats) from the cob, ear, or husk **2 :** to throw shells at, upon, or into **:** BOMBARD ~ *vi* **1 :** to fall or scale off in thin pieces **2 :** to cast the shell or exterior covering **:** fall out of the pod or husk **3 :** to gather shells (as from a beach) **:** collect shells

she'll \(,)shē(ə)l, shil\ **:** she will **:** she shall

¹shel·lac \shə-'lak\ *n* **1 :** purified lac usu. prepared in thin orange or yellow flakes by heating and filtering and often bleached white **2 :** a preparation of lac dissolved usu. in alcohol and used chiefly as a wood filler and finish **3 :** a composition containing shellac used for making phonograph records

²shellac *vt* **shel·lacked; shel·lack·ing 1 :** to coat or otherwise treat with shellac or a shellac varnish **2 :** to defeat decisively or ignominiously

shel·lack·ing *n* **:** a decisive defeat **:** DRUBBING

shell·back \'shel-,bak\ *n* **:** an old or veteran sailor **:** old salt

shell bean *n* **1 :** a bean grown primarily for its edible seeds **2 :** the edible seed of a bean

Shel·ley·an \'shel-ē-ən\ *adj* **:** of, relating to, or characteristic of Shelley or his writings

Shel·ley·esque \,shel-ē-'esk\ *adj* **:** of, relating to, or characteristic of Shelley or his writings

shell·fire \'shel-,fī(ə)r\ *n* **:** firing or shooting of shells

shell·fish \-,fish\ *n* **:** an aquatic invertebrate animal with a shell; *esp* **:** an edible mollusk or crustacean

shell game *n* **:** a gambling and swindling game resembling thimblerig but played with three walnut shells

shell jacket *n* **1 :** a short tight military jacket worn buttoned up the front **2 :** MESS JACKET

shell out *vb* **:** PAY

shell pink *n* **:** a variable color averaging a light yellowish pink

shell·proof \'shel-'prüf\ *adj* **:** capable of resisting shells or bombs

shell shock *n* **:** any of numerous psychoneurotic conditions appearing in soldiers exposed to modern warfare — **shell–shock** \'shel-,shäk\ *vt*

¹shel·ter \'shel-tər\ *n* [origin unknown] **1 :** something that covers or affords protection **:** means or place of protection ⟨fallout ~⟩ **2 :** the state of being covered and protected — **shel·ter·less** \-ləs\ *adj*

²shelter *vb* **shel·ter·ing** \-t(ə-)riŋ\ *vt* **1 :** to constitute or provide a shelter for **:** PROTECT **2 :** to place under shelter or protection ~ *vi* **:** to take shelter — **shel·ter·er** \-tər-ər\ *n*

shel·ter·belt \'shel-tər-,belt\ *n* **:** a barrier of trees and shrubs that protects (as soil and crops) from wind and storm and lessens erosion

shelter half *n* **:** one of the interchangeable halves of a two-man shelter tent

shelter tent *n* **:** a small tent usu. consisting of two interchangeable pieces of waterproof cotton duck fixed for buttoning or tying

shel·ty *or* **shel·tie** \'shel-tē\ *n* [prob. of Scand origin; akin to ON *Hjalti* Shetlander] **1 :** SHETLAND PONY **2 :** SHETLAND SHEEPDOG

shelve \'shelv\ *vb* [*shelf*] *vt* **1 :** to furnish with shelves **2 :** to place on a shelf **3 a :** to put on the shelf **:** DISMISS **b :** to put off or aside ~ *vi* **:** to slope in a formation like a shelf **:** INCLINE — **shelv·er** *n*

¹shelv·ing \'shel-viŋ\ *n* **1 :** the state or degree of sloping **2 :** a sloping surface or place

²shelving *n* **1 :** material for shelves **2 :** SHELVES

shelvy \'shel-vē\ *adj* **:** sloping or inclining in the manner of a geologic shelf

Shem \'shem\ *n* [Heb *Shēm*] **:** the eldest son of Noah

She·ma \shə-'mä\ *n* [Heb *shĕma'* hear, first word of Deut 6:4] **:** the central creed of Judaism comprising Deut 6:4–9 and 11:13–21 and Num 15:37–41

Shem·ite \'shem-,īt\ *n* [*Shem*] **:** SEMITE — **She·mit·ic** \shə-'mit-ik\ *or* **Shem·it·ish** \'shem-,īt-ish\ *adj*

she·nan·i·gan \shə-'nan-i-gən\ *n* [origin unknown] **1 :** a devious trick used esp. for an underhand purpose **2 a :** tricky or questionable practices or conduct **b :** high-spirited or mischievous activity

shend \'shend\ *vt* **shent** \'shent\ **shend·ing** [ME *shenden,* fr. OE *scendan;* akin to OE *scamu* shame — more at SHAME] **1** *archaic* **:** to put to shame or confusion **2** *archaic* **:** REPROVE, REVILE **3** *chiefly dial* **a :** INJURE, MAR **b :** RUIN, DESTROY

She·ol \shē-'ōl, 'shē-,\ *n* [Heb *Shĕ'ōl*] **1 :** an underworld where according to ancient Hebrew belief the dead have a shadowy existence **2 :** HELL

¹shep·herd \'shep-ərd\ *n* [ME *sheepherde,* fr. OE *scēaphyrde,* fr. *scēap* sheep + *hierde* herdsman; akin to OE *heord* herd] **1 :** a man who tends and guards sheep esp. in a flock that is grazing **2 :** PASTOR 2

²shepherd *vt* **1 :** to tend as a shepherd **2 :** to guide or guard in the manner of a shepherd

shepherd dog *n* **:** SHEEP DOG

shep·herd·ess \'shep-ərd-əs\ *n* **1 :** a woman or girl who tends sheep **2 :** a rural lass

shepherd's check *n* **:** a pattern of small even black-and-white checks; *also* **:** a fabric woven in this pattern — called also *shepherd's plaid*

shepherd's pie *n* **:** a meat pie with a mashed potato crust

shepherd's purse *n* **:** a white-flowered weedy annual herb (*Capsella bursa-pastoris*) of the mustard family with triangular notched pods

Sher·a·ton \'sher-ət-ᵊn\ *adj* [Thomas *Sheraton* †1806 E furniture maker] **:** of or relating to a style of furniture marked by straight lines and graceful proportions

sher·bet \'shər-bət\ *also* **sher·bert** \-bərt\ *n* [Turk & Per; Turk *şerbet,* fr. Per *sharbat,* fr. Ar *sharbah* drink] **1 :** a cooling drink of sweetened and diluted fruit juice **2 :** a water ice with milk, egg white, or gelatin added

sherd *var of* SHARD

she·rif \shə-'rēf\ *var of* SHARIF

sher·iff \'sher-əf\ *n* [ME *shirreve,* fr. OE *scīrgerēfa,* fr. *scīr* shire + *gerēfa* reeve — more at REEVE] **:** an important official of a shire or county charged primarily with judicial duties (as executing the processes and orders of courts and judges) — **sher·iff·dom** \-əf-dəm, -əf-təm\ *n*

sher·lock \'shər-,läk, 'she(ə)r-\ *n, often cap* [*Sherlock* Holmes, detective in stories by Sir Arthur Conan Doyle] **:** DETECTIVE

Sher·pa \'she(ə)r-pə, 'shər-\ *n* **1 :** a Tibetan people living on the high southern slopes of the Himalayas and skilled in mountain climbing **2 :** a member of the Sherpa people

sher·ris \'sher-is\ *archaic var of* SHERRY

sher·ry \'sher-ē\ *n* [alter. of earlier *sherris* (taken as pl.), fr. *Xeres* (now *Jerez*), Spain] **:** a fortified wine of Spanish origin with a distinctive nutty flavor; *also* **:** a similar wine produced elsewhere

she's \(,)shēz\ **:** she is **:** she has

Shet·land \'shet-lənd\ *n* **1 a :** SHETLAND PONY **b :** SHETLAND SHEEPDOG **2** *often not cap* **a :** a lightweight loosely twisted yarn of Shetland wool used for knitting and weaving **b :** a fabric made from Shetland wool

Shet·land pony \,shet-lən(d)-\ *n* **:** any of a breed of small stocky shaggy hardy ponies that originated in the Shetland islands

Shetland sheepdog *n* **:** any of a breed of small dogs resembling miniature collies with a short dense undercoat and a profuse outer coat of long hair developed in the Shetland islands

Shetland wool *n* **:** the fine undercoat of sheep raised in the Shetland islands; *also* **:** yarn spun from this

sheugh \'shük\ *n* [ME *sough,* fr. *swoughen* to sough — more at SOUGH] *chiefly Scot* **:** DITCH, TRENCH

shew \'shō\ *archaic var of* SHOW

shew·bread \'shō-,bred\ *n* [trans. of G *schaubrot*] **:** consecrated unleavened bread ritually placed by the Jewish priests on a table in the sanctuary of the Tabernacle on the Sabbath

Shia \'shē-(,)ä\ *n, pl* **Shia** *or* **Shi·as** [Ar *shī'ah* sect] **1** *pl* **:** the Muslims of the branch of Islam comprising sects believing in Ali and the Imams as the only rightful successors of Muhammad and in the concealment and messianic return of the last recognized Imam **2 :** SHIISM — **Shia** *adj*

shib·bo·leth \'shib-ə-ləth, -,leth\ *n* [Heb *shibbōleth* stream; fr. the use of this word as a test to distinguish Gileadites from Ephraimites, who pronounced it *sibbōleth*] **1 a :** CATCHWORD, SLOGAN **b :** a use of language regarded as distinctive of a particular group **2 :** a custom or usage regarded as a criterion for distinguishing members of one group

shiel \'shē(ə)l\ *n* [ME (northern dial.) *schele*] *chiefly Scot* **:** SHIELING

¹shield \'shē(ə)ld\ *n* [ME *sheld,* fr. OE *scield;* akin to OE *sciell* shell] **1 :** a broad piece of defensive armor carried on the arm **2 :** one that protects or defends **:** DEFENSE **3 :** an adjunct of dress worn inside a part of the clothing liable to be soiled by perspiration **4 :** a fixture designed to protect persons from injury from moving parts of machinery or parts carrying electricity **5 :** ESCUTCHEON **6 :** an armored screen protecting an otherwise exposed gun **7 :** an iron or steel framework moved forward in excavating to support the ground ahead of the lining **8 :** a protective structure (as a carapace) of some animals **9 :** something shaped like or resembling a shield: as **a :** APOTHECIUM **b :** a policeman's badge **c :** a decorative or identifying emblem

²shield *vt* **1 a :** to protect with a shield **b :** to cut off from observation **:** HIDE **2** *obs* **:** FORBID **syn** see DEFEND — **shield·er** *n*

shiel·ing \'shē-lən, -liŋ\ *n* **1** *dial Brit* **:** a mountain hut used as a shelter by shepherds **2** *dial Brit* **:** a summer pasture in the mountains

shier *comparative of* SHY

shiest *superlative of* SHY

¹shift \'shift\ *vb* [ME *shiften,* fr. OE *sciftan* to divide, arrange; akin to OE *scēadan* to divide — more at SHED] *vt* **1 :** to exchange for or replace by another **:** CHANGE **2 a :** to change the place, position, or direction of **:** MOVE **b :** to make a change in (place) **3 :** to change phonetically ~ *vi* **1 a :** to change place or position **b :** to change direction **c :** to change the gear rotating the transmission shaft of an automobile **2 a :** to manage by or for oneself **b :** to resort to expedients **3 a :** to go through a change **b :** to change one's clothes **c :** to become changed phonetically — **shift·able** \'shif-tə-bəl\ *adj* — **shift·er** *n*

²shift *n* **1 a :** a means or device for effecting an end **b (1) :** a deceitful or underhand scheme **:** DODGE **(2) :** an expedient tried in difficult circumstances **:** EXTREMITY **2 a** *chiefly dial* **:** a change of clothes **b (1)** *chiefly dial* **:** SHIRT **(2) :** a woman's slip or chemise **3 :** a change in direction **4 a :** a group of people who work or occupy themselves in turn with other groups **b (1) :** a change of one group of people (as workers) for another in regular alternation **(2) :** a scheduled period of work or duty **5 :** a change in place or position: as **a :** a change in the position of the hand on a fingerboard (as of a violin) **b (1) :** FAULT **(2) :** the relative displacement

of rock masses on opposite sides of a fault or fault zone **c :** a change in frequency resulting in a change in position of a spectral line or band **6 :** a removal from one person or thing to another **:** TRANSFER **7 :** CONSONANT SHIFT **syn** see RESOURCE
shift·i·ly \'shif-tə-lē\ *adv* **:** in a shifty manner
shift·i·ness \-tē-nəs\ *n* **:** the quality or state of being shifty
shifting pedal *n* **:** SOFT PEDAL 1
shift·less \'shif(t)-ləs\ *adj* [*shift* (resourcefulness)] **1 :** lacking in resourcefulness **:** INEFFICIENT **2 :** lacking in ambition or incentive **:** LAZY — **shift·less·ly** *adv* — **shift·less·ness** *n*
shifty \'shif-tē\ *adj* **1 :** full of or ready with expedients **:** RESOURCEFUL **2 a :** given to deception, evasion, or fraud **:** TRICKY **b :** capable of evasive movement **:** ELUSIVE **3 :** indicative of a tricky nature ⟨~ eyes⟩
Shi·ism \'shē-ˌiz-əm\ *n* **:** Shia Islam
Shi·ite \'shē-ˌīt\ *n* **:** a Shia Muslim
1**shi·kar** \shik-'är\ *n* [Hindi *shikār*, fr. Per] *India* **:** HUNTING
2**shikar** *vb* **shi·karred; shi·kar·ring** *India* **:** HUNT
shi·ka·ri \shik-'är-ē\ *n* [Hindi *shikārī*, fr. Per, fr. *shikār*] *India* **:** a big game hunter; *esp* **:** a professional hunter or guide
shill \'shil\ *n* [prob. short for *shillaber*, of unknown origin] **:** one who acts as a decoy (as for a pitchman or gambler) — **shill** *vi*
shil·le·lagh *also* **shil·la·lah** \shə-'lā-lē\ *n* [*Shillelagh*, Ireland] **:** CUDGEL
shil·ling \'shil-iŋ\ *n* [ME, fr. OE *scilling;* akin to OHG *skilling*, a gold coin; both fr. a prehistoric Gmc compound represented by OE *scield* shield and by OE *-ling*] **1 a :** a British monetary unit equal to 12 pence or 1/20 pound — see *pound* at MONEY table **b :** a coin representing this unit **2 :** a unit of value equal to 1/20 pound and a corresponding coin in any of several countries in or formerly in the British Commonwealth **3 :** any of several early American coins **4** — see MONEY table
Shil·luk \shil-'ük, 'shil-ˌ\ *n, pl* **Shilluk** *or* **Shilluks 1 a :** a Nilotic Negro people of the Sudan dwelling mainly on the west bank of the White Nile **b :** a member of such people **2 :** a Nilotic language of the Shilluk people
1**shilly–shally** \'shil-ē-ˌshal-ē\ *adv* [irreg. redupl. of *shall I*] **:** in an irresolute, undecided, or hesitating manner
2**shilly–shally** *adj* **:** IRRESOLUTE, VACILLATING
3**shilly–shally** *n* **:** INDECISION, IRRESOLUTION
4**shilly–shally** *vi* **1 :** to show hesitation or lack of decisiveness or resolution **:** VACILLATE **2 :** to waste time **:** DAWDLE
shil·pit \'shil-pət\ *adj* [origin unknown] **1** *Scot* **:** pinched and starved in appearance **:** PUNY **2** *Scot* **:** WEAK, INSIPID — used of drink
1**shim** \'shim\ *n* [origin unknown] **:** a thin often tapered slip of wood, metal, or stone used to fill in (as in leveling a stone in a building)
2**shim** *vt* **shimmed; shim·ming :** to fill out or level up by the use of a shim
1**shim·mer** \'shim-ər\ *vb* **shim·mer·ing** \-(ə-)riŋ\ [ME *schimeren*, fr. OE *scimerian;* akin to OE *scīnan* to shine — more at SHINE] *vi* **1 :** to shine with a tremulous or fitful light **:** GLIMMER **2 :** to reflect a wavering sometimes distorted visual image **~** *vt* **:** to cause to shimmer **syn** see FLASH
2**shimmer** *n* **1 :** a fitful tremulous light **:** subdued sparkle or sheen **:** GLIMMER **2 :** a wavering sometimes distorted visual image usu. produced by a reflection from heat waves — **shim·mery** \'shim-(ə-)rē\ *adj*
1**shim·my** \'shim-ē\ *n* **1** [by alter] **:** CHEMISE **2** [short for *shimmy-shake*] **:** a jazz dance characterized by a shaking of the body from the shoulders down **3 :** an abnormal vibration esp. in the front wheels of a motor vehicle
2**shimmy** *vi* **1 :** to shake, quiver, or tremble in or as if in dancing a shimmy **2 :** to vibrate abnormally — used esp. of automobiles
1**shin** \'shin\ *n* [ME *shine*, fr. OE *scinu;* akin to OHG *scina* shin, OE *scēadan* to divide — more at SHED] **:** the front part of the vertebrate leg below the knee
2**shin** *vb* **shinned; shin·ning** *vi* **1 :** to climb by moving oneself along alternately with the arms or hands and legs **2 :** to move forward rapidly on foot **~** *vt* **1 :** to kick or strike on the shins **2 :** to climb by shinning
3**shin** \'shēn, 'shin\ *n* [Heb *shīn*] **:** the 22d letter of the Hebrew alphabet — symbol ש
Shin \'shin, 'shēn\ *n* [Jap, lit., belief, faith] **:** a major Japanese Buddhist sect that emphasizes salvation by faith alone, has a married clergy, and holds to the exclusive worship of Amida Buddha
shin·bone \'shin-'bōn, -ˌbōn\ *n* **:** TIBIA 1a
shin·dig \'shin-ˌdig\ *n* [prob. alter. of *shindy*] **1 a :** a social gathering with dancing **b :** a usu. large or lavish party **2 :** SHINDY 2
shin·dy \'shin-dē\ *n, pl* **shindys** *or* **shindies** [prob. alter. of *shinny*] **1 :** SHINDIG 1 **2 :** FRACAS, UPROAR
1**shine** \'shīn\ *vb* **shone** \'shōn, *esp Brit* 'shän\ *or* **shined; shin·ing** [ME *shinen*, fr. OE *scīnan;* akin to OHG *skīnan* to shine, Gk *skia* shadow] *vi* **1 :** to emit rays of light **2 :** to be bright by reflection of light **3 :** to be eminent, conspicuous, or distinguished **4 :** to have a bright glowing appearance **5 :** to be conspicuously evident or clear **~** *vt* **1 a :** to cause to emit light **b :** to throw or flash the light of **2 :** to make bright by polishing
2**shine** *n* **1 :** brightness caused by the emission of light **2 :** brightness caused by the reflection of light **:** LUSTER **3 :** BRILLIANCE, SPLENDOR **4 :** fair weather **:** SUNSHINE **5 :** TRICK, CAPER — usu. used in pl. **6 :** LIKING, FANCY ⟨took a ~ to him⟩ **7 a :** a polish or gloss given to shoes **b :** a single polishing of a pair of shoes
shin·er \'shī-nər\ *n* **1 :** one that shines **2 :** a silvery fish; *esp* **:** any of numerous small freshwater American cyprinid fishes (esp. genus *Notropis*) **3 :** a black eye
1**shin·gle** \'shiŋ-gəl\ *n* [ME *schingel*] **1 :** a small thin piece of building material often with one end thicker than the other for laying in overlapping rows as a covering for the roof or sides of a building **2 :** a small signboard **3 :** a woman's haircut with the hair trimmed short from the back of the head to the nape
2**shingle** *vt* **shin·gling** \-g(ə-)liŋ\ **1 :** to cover with or as if with shingles **2 :** to bob and shape (the hair) in a shingle **3 :** to lay or dispose so as to overlap
3**shingle** *n* [prob. of Scand origin; akin to Norw *singel* coarse gravel] **1 :** coarse rounded detritus or alluvial material esp. on the seashore that differs from ordinary gravel only in the larger size of the stones **2 :** a place strewn with shingle
4**shingle** *vt* **shin·gling** \-g(ə-)liŋ\ [F dial. *chingler*, lit., to whip, fr. MF dial., fr. *chingle* strap, fr. L *cingula*, fr. *cingere* to gird — more at CINCTURE] **:** to subject (as iron) to the process of expelling cinder and impurities by hammering and squeezing
shin·gler \-g(ə-)lər\ *n* **:** one that shingles
shin·gles \'shiŋ-gəlz\ *n pl but sing in constr* [ME *schingles*, by folk etymology fr. ML *cingulus*, fr. L *cingulum* girdle — more at CINGULUM] **:** HERPES ZOSTER
shin·gly \-g(ə-)lē\ *adj* **:** composed of or abounding in shingle ⟨a ~ beach⟩
Shin·gon \'shin-ˌgän, 'shēn-\ *n* [Jap, lit., true word] **:** an esoteric Japanese Buddhist sect using mystical symbols
shin·i·ness \'shī-nē-nəs\ *n* **:** the quality or state of being shiny
shin·ing *adj* **1 :** emitting or reflecting light **2 :** bright and often splendid in appearance **:** RESPLENDENT **3 :** possessing a distinguished quality **:** ILLUSTRIOUS **4 :** full of sunshine
shin·leaf \'shin-ˌlēf\ *n, pl* **shinleafs :** either of two wintergreens (genus *Pyrola*) with lustrous evergreen basal leaves and racemose white or pinkish flowers
shin·nery \'shin-ə-rē\ *n* [modif. of LaF *chênière*, fr. F *chêne* oak] **:** a dense growth of small trees or an area of such growth; *esp* **:** one of scrub oak in the West and Southwest
1**shin·ny** *also* **shin·ney** \'shin-ē\ *n* [perh. fr. 1*shin*] **:** the game of hockey as informally played with a curved stick and a ball or block of wood by schoolboys; *also* **:** the stick used
2**shinny** *vi* [alter. of 2*shin*] **:** SHIN 1
shin·plas·ter \'shin-ˌplas-tər\ *n* **1 :** a piece of privately-issued paper currency; *esp* **:** one poorly secured and depreciated in value **2 :** a piece of fractional currency
Shin·to \'shin-(ˌ)tō\ *n* [Jap *shintō*] **:** the indigenous religious cult of Japan consisting chiefly in the reverence of the spirits of natural forces, emperors, and heroes — **Shinto** *adj* — **Shin·to·ism** \-(ˌ)tō-ˌiz-əm\ *n* — **Shin·to·ist** \-ˌtō-əst\ *n or adj* — **Shin·to·is·tic** \ˌshin-(ˌ)tō-'is-tik\ *adj*
shiny \'shī-nē\ *adj* **1 a :** SUNSHINY **b :** filled with light **2 :** bright in appearance **:** GLITTERING, POLISHED **3 :** rubbed or worn smooth **4 :** scrubbed clean; *esp* **:** lacking face powder
1**ship** \'ship\ *n, often attrib* [ME, fr. OE *scip;* akin to OHG *skif* ship, OE *scēadan* to divide — more at SHED] **1 a :** a large seagoing boat **b :** a sailing boat having a bowsprit and usu. three masts each composed of a lower mast, a topmast, and a topgallant mast **2 :** BOAT; *esp* **:** one propelled by power or sail **3 :** a ship's crew **4 :** FORTUNE ⟨when his ~ comes in⟩ **5 :** AIRSHIP, AIRPLANE — **ship·build·ing** \-ˌbil-diŋ\ *n*
2**ship** *vb* **shipped; ship·ping** *vt* **1 a :** to place or receive on board a ship for transportation by water **b :** to cause to be transported **2** *obs* **:** to provide with a ship **3 :** to put in place for use ⟨~ the tiller⟩ **4 :** to take into a ship or boat ⟨~ the gangplank⟩ **5 :** to engage for service on a ship **6 :** to take (as water) over the side **~** *vi* **1 :** to embark on a ship **2 :** to go or travel by ship **3 :** to engage to serve on shipboard
-ship \ˌship\ *n suffix* [ME, fr. OE *-scipe;* akin to OHG *-scaft* -ship, OE *sceppan* to shape — more at SHAPE] **1 :** state **:** condition **:** quality ⟨friend*ship*⟩ **2 :** office **:** dignity **:** profession ⟨clerk*ship*⟩ ⟨lord*ship*⟩ ⟨author*ship*⟩ **3 :** art **:** skill ⟨horseman*ship*⟩ **4 :** something showing, exhibiting, or embodying a quality or state ⟨town*ship*⟩ **5 :** one entitled to a (specified) rank, title, or appellation ⟨his Lord*ship*⟩
ship biscuit *n* **:** HARDTACK — called also *ship bread*
ship·board \'ship-ˌbō(ə)rd, -ˌbȯ(ə)rd\ *n* **1 :** the side of a ship **2 :** SHIP ⟨met on ~⟩
ship canal *n* **:** a canal large enough for seagoing ships
ship chandler *n* **:** a dealer in supplies and equipment for ships
ship fever *n* **:** typhus fever
ship·fit·ter \-ˌfit-ər\ *n* **1 :** one that fits together the structural members of ships and puts them into position for riveting or welding **2 :** a naval enlisted man who works in sheet metal and performs the work of a plumber aboard ship
ship·lap \'ship-ˌlap\ *n* **:** wooden sheathing in which the boards are rabbeted so that the edges of each board lap over the edges of adjacent boards to make a flush joint
ship·man \'ship-mən\ *n* **1 :** SEAMAN, SAILOR **2 :** SHIPMASTER
ship·mas·ter \-ˌmas-tər\ *n* **:** the master or commander of a ship other than a warship
ship·mate \-ˌmāt\ *n* **:** a fellow sailor
ship·ment \'ship-mənt\ *n* **1 :** the act or process of shipping **2 :** the goods shipped
ship money *n* **:** an impost levied at various times in England to provide ships for the national defense
ship of the line : a ship of war large enough to have a place in the line of battle
ship·pa·ble \'ship-ə-bəl\ *adj* **:** suitable for shipping
ship·per \'ship-ər\ *n* **:** one that sends goods by any form of conveyance
ship·ping \'ship-iŋ\ *n* **1 a :** passage on a ship **b :** SHIPS **c :** the body of ships in one place or belonging to one port or country **2 :** the act or business of one that ships
shipping articles *n pl* **:** the articles of agreement between the captain of a ship and the seamen in respect to wages, length of time for which they are shipped, and related matters
shipping clerk *n* **:** one who is employed in a shipping room to assemble, pack, and send out or receive goods
ship railway *n* **:** an inclined railway running into the water with a car on which a vessel may be drawn out on land for repairs or storage
ship–rigged \'ship-'rigd\ *adj* **:** SQUARE-RIGGED
ship·shape \'ship-'shāp\ *adj* [short for earlier *shipshapen*, fr. *ship* + *shapen*, archaic pp. of *shape*] **:** TRIM, TIDY
ship·side \-ˌsīd\ *n* **:** the area adjacent to shipping that is used for storage and loading of freight and passengers **:** DOCK
ship's papers *n pl* **:** the papers with which a ship is legally required to be provided for due inspection to show the character of the ship and cargo

ship's service *n* **:** a ship or navy post exchange — called also *navy exchange*
ship·way \'ship-ˌwā\ *n* **1 :** the ways on which a ship is built **2 :** a ship canal
ship·worm \-ˌwərm\ *n* **:** any of various elongated marine clams (esp. family Teredinidae) that resemble worms, burrow in submerged wood, and damage wharf piles and wooden ships
¹**ship·wreck** \-ˌrek\ *n* [alter. of earlier *shipwrack*, fr. ME *schipwrak*, fr. OE *scipwræc*, fr. *scip* ship + *wræc* something driven by the sea — more at WRACK] **1 :** a wrecked ship or its parts **:** WRECKAGE **2 :** the destruction or loss of a ship **3 :** an irretrievable loss or failure **:** RUIN
²**shipwreck** *vt* **1 a :** to cause to experience shipwreck **b :** RUIN **2 :** to destroy (a ship) by grounding or foundering
ship·wright \-ˌrīt\ *n* **:** a carpenter skilled in ship construction and repair
ship·yard \-ˌyärd\ *n* **:** a yard, place, or enclosure where ships are built or repaired
shire \'shī(ə)r, *in place-name compounds* ˌshi(ə)r, shər\ *n* [ME, fr. OE *scīr* office, shire; akin to OHG *scīra* care] **1 :** an administrative subdivision; *esp* **:** a county in England **2 :** any of a British breed of large heavy draft horses with heavily feathered legs
shire town *n* **1 :** a town that is the seat of the government of a county **:** COUNTY SEAT **2 :** a town where a court of superior jurisdiction (as a circuit court or a court with a jury) sits ⟨there are three *shire towns* in our county⟩
shirk \'shərk\ *vb* [origin unknown] *vi* **1 :** to go stealthily **:** SNEAK **2 :** to evade the performance of an obligation ~ *vt* **:** AVOID, EVADE — **shirk·er** *n*
Shir·ley poppy \ˌshər-lē-\ *n* [*Shirley* vicarage, Croydon, Eng.] **:** a variable annual garden poppy with bright solitary single or double flowers
shirr \'shər\ *vt* [origin unknown] **1 :** to draw (as cloth) together in a shirring **2 :** to bake (eggs removed from the shell) until set
shirr·ing \'shər-iŋ\ *n* **:** a decorative gathering of material made by drawing up the material along two or more parallel lines of stitching
shirt \'shərt\ *n* [ME *shirte*, fr. OE *scyrte;* akin to ON *skyrta* shirt, OE *scort* short] **:** a garment for the upper part of the body: as **a :** a loose cloth garment usu. having a collar, sleeves, a front opening, and a tail long enough to be tucked inside trousers or a skirt **b :** UNDERSHIRT
shirt·front \-ˌfrənt\ *n* **:** the front of a man's shirt
shirt·ing \'shərt-iŋ\ *n* **:** fabric suitable for shirts
shirt·mak·er \'shərt-ˌmā-kər\ *n* **1 :** one that makes shirts **2 :** a woman's tailored garment (as a dress or blouse) with details copied from a man's shirt
shirt·tail \-ˌtāl\ *n* **:** the part of a shirt that reaches below the waist esp. in the back
shirt·waist \'shərt-ˌwāst\ *n* **:** a woman's tailored blouse with details copied from men's shirts
shish ke·bab \'shish-kə-ˌbäb\ *n* [Arm *shish kabab*] **:** kabob cooked on skewers
shit·tah \'shit-ə\ *n, pl* **shittahs** *or* **shit·tim** \'shit-əm\ [Heb *shiṭṭāh*] **:** a tree of uncertain identity but prob. an acacia (as *Acacia seyal*) from the wood of which the ark and fittings of the Hebrew tabernacle were made
shit·tim·wood \'shit-əm-ˌwu̇d\ *also* **shittim** *n* [Heb *shiṭṭīm* (pl. of *shiṭṭāh*) + E *wood*] **1 :** the wood of the shittah tree **2 :** any of several buckthorns; *also* **:** their hard heavy dense wood used for turning and for inlay
shiv \'shiv\ *n* [prob. fr. Romany *chiv* blade] *slang* **:** KNIFE
Shi·va \'shē-və\ *var of* SIVA
shiv·a·ree \ˌshiv-ə-'rē, 'shiv-ə-ˌ\ *n* [F *charivari*] **:** a noisy mock serenade to a newly married couple — **shivaree** *vt*
¹**shiv·er** \'shiv-ər\ *n* [ME; akin to OE *scēadan* to divide — more at SHED] **:** one of the small pieces into which a brittle thing is broken by sudden violence
²**shiver** *vb* **shiv·er·ing** \-(ə-)riŋ\ **:** to break into many small pieces **:** SHATTER
³**shiver** *vb* **shiv·er·ing** \-(ə-)riŋ\ [ME *shiveren*, alter. of *chiveren*] *vi* **:** to undergo trembling **:** QUIVER; *specif* **:** to tremble in the wind as it strikes first one and then the other side (of a sail) ~ *vt* **:** to cause (a sail) to shiver by steering close to the wind
⁴**shiver** *n* **:** an instance of shivering **:** TREMBLE
¹**shiv·ery** \'shiv-(ə-)rē\ *adj* **:** inclined to break into flakes **:** BRITTLE
²**shivery** *adj* **1 :** characterized by shivers **:** TREMULOUS **2 :** causing shivers
¹**shoal** \'shōl\ *adj* [alter. of ME *shold*, fr. OE *sceald* — more at SKELETON] **:** SHALLOW
²**shoal** *n* **1 :** SHALLOW **2 :** a sandbank or sandbar that makes the water shoal; *specif* **:** an elevation which is not rocky and on which there is a depth of water of six fathoms or less
³**shoal** *vi* **:** to become shallow ~ *vt* **1 :** to come to a shallow or less deep part of **2 :** to cause to become shallow or less deep
⁴**shoal** *n* [(assumed) ME *shole*, fr. OE *scolu* multitude — more at SCHOOL] **:** a large group (as of fish) **:** CROWD
⁵**shoal** *vi* **:** THRONG, SCHOOL
shoat \'shōt\ *n* [ME *shote;* akin to Flem *schote* shoat] **:** a young hog usu. less than one year old
¹**shock** \'shäk\ *n* [ME; akin to MHG *schoc* heap, OE *hēah* high — more at HIGH] **:** a pile of sheaves of grain or stalks of Indian corn set up in a field with the butt ends down
²**shock** *vt* **:** to collect into shocks
³**shock** *n, often attrib* [MF *choc*, fr. *choquer* to strike against, fr. OF *choquier*, prob. of Gmc origin; akin to MD *schocken* to jolt] **1 :** the impact or encounter of individuals or groups in combat **2 a :** a violent shake or jar **:** CONCUSSION **b :** an effect of such violence **3 a** (1) **:** a disturbance in the equilibrium or permanence of something (2) **:** a sudden or violent disturbance in the mental or emotional faculties **b :** something that causes such disturbance **4 :** a state of profound depression of the vital processes associated with reduced blood volume and pressure and caused usu. by severe esp. crushing injuries, hemorrhage, or burns **5 :** sudden stimulation of the nerves and convulsive contraction of the muscles caused by the discharge of electricity through the animal body **6 a :** APOPLEXY **b :** CORONARY THROMBOSIS
⁴**shock** *vt* **1 a :** to strike with surprise, terror, horror, or disgust **b :** to cause to undergo a physical or nervous shock **c :** to subject to the action of an electrical discharge **2 :** to drive into or out of by or as if by a shock ~ *vi* **:** to meet with a shock **:** COLLIDE
⁵**shock** *n* [perh. fr. ¹*shock*] **:** a thick bushy mass (as of hair)
⁶**shock** *adj* **:** BUSHY, SHAGGY
shock absorber *n* **:** any of several devices for absorbing the energy of sudden impulses or shocks in machinery or structures (as springs of automobiles)
shock·er \'shäk-ər\ *n* **:** one that shocks **:** something horrifying or offensive; *specif* **:** a sensational work of fiction or drama
shock·ing *adj* **:** extremely startling and offensive — **shock·ing·ly** \-iŋ-lē\ *adv*
shock therapy *n* **:** the treatment of mental disorder by the artificial induction of coma or convulsions through use of drugs or electricity
shock troops *n pl* **:** troops esp. suited and chosen for offensive work because of their high morale, training, and discipline
shock wave *n* **1 :** BLAST 5c **2 :** a compressional wave formed whenever the speed of a body relative to a medium exceeds that at which the medium can transmit sound
shod \'shäd\ *adj* [ME, fr. pp. of *shoen* to shoe, fr. OE *scōgan*, fr. *scōh* shoe — more at SHOE] **1 a :** wearing shoes **b :** equipped with tires **2 :** furnished or equipped with a shoe
shod·di·ly \'shäd-ᵊl-ē\ *adv* **:** in a shoddy manner
shod·di·ness \'shäd-ē-nəs\ *n* **:** the quality or state of being shoddy
¹**shod·dy** \'shäd-ē\ *n* [origin unknown] **1 a :** wool of better quality and longer staple than mungo reclaimed from materials that are not felted **b :** a fabric often of inferior quality manufactured wholly or partly from reclaimed wool **2 a :** inferior, imitation, or pretentious articles or matter **b :** pretentious vulgarity
²**shoddy** *adj* **1 :** made wholly or partly of shoddy **2 a :** cheaply imitative **:** vulgarly pretentious **b :** hastily or poorly done **:** INFERIOR **c :** SHABBY
¹**shoe** \'shü\ *n* [ME *shoo*, fr. OE *scōh;* akin to OHG *scuoh* shoe, OE *hȳd* hide] **1 a :** an outer covering for the human foot usu. made of leather with a thick or stiff sole and an attached heel **b :** a metal plate or rim for the hoof of an animal **2 :** something resembling a shoe: as **a :** a metal band on the runner of a sled **b :** the casing of a pneumatic tire; *broadly* **:** TIRE **3** *pl* **:** STATUS, POSITION; *also* **:** PLIGHT **4 :** a device that retards, stops, or controls the motion of an object **5 :** any of various devices that are inserted in or run along a track or groove to guide a movement, provide a contact or friction grip, or protect against wear, damage, or slipping

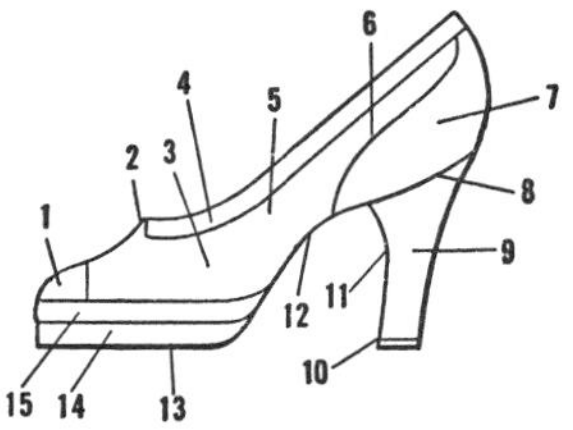

shoe 1a: *1* tip, *2* throat, *3* vamp, *4* collar, *5* arch, *6* foxing, *7* quarter, *8* heel seat, *9* heel, *10* top lift, *11* breasting, *12* shank, *13* sole, *14* platform, *15* mudguard

²**shoe** *vt* **shod** \'shäd\ *also* **shoed** \'shüd\ **shoe·ing** **1 :** to furnish with a shoe **2 :** to cover for protection, strength, or ornament
shoe·bill \'shü-ˌbil\ *n* **:** a large broad-billed wading bird (*Balaeniceps rex*) of the valley of the White Nile that is related to the storks and herons
shoe·black \-ˌblak\ *n* **:** BOOTBLACK
¹**shoe·horn** \-ˌhȯ(ə)rn\ *n* **:** a curved piece (as of horn, wood, or metal) to aid in slipping on a shoe
²**shoehorn** *vt* **:** to force into a small, narrow, or insufficient space
shoe·lace \-ˌlās\ *n* **:** a lace or string for fastening a shoe
shoe·mak·er \-ˌmā-kər\ *n* **:** a shopkeeper whose business is selling or repairing shoes
shoe·pac *or* **shoe·pack** \'shü-ˌpak\ *n* [by folk etymology fr. Del *shipak*] **:** a waterproof laced boot worn esp. over heavy socks in cold weather
sho·er \'shü-ər\ *n* **:** HORSESHOER
shoe·string \'shü-ˌstriŋ\ *n* **1 :** SHOELACE **2** [fr. shoestrings' being a typical item sold by itinerant vendors] **:** a small sum of money **:** capital inadequate or barely adequate to the needs of a transaction ⟨start a business on a ~⟩
shoe tree *n* **:** a foot-shaped device for inserting in a shoe to preserve its shape
sho·far \'shō-ˌfär, -fər\ *n, pl* **sho·froth** \shō-'frōt(h)\ [Heb *shōphār*] **:** a ram's-horn trumpet blown by the ancient Hebrews in battle and high religious observances and used in synagogues before and during Rosh Hashanah and at the conclusion of Yom Kippur
¹**shog** \'shäg\ *vi* **shogged; shog·ging** [ME *shoggen*] *chiefly dial* **:** to move along
²**shog** *n, chiefly dial* **:** SHAKE, JOLT
sho·gun \'shō-gən, -ˌgün\ *n* [Jap *shōgun* general] **:** one of a line of military governors ruling Japan until the revolution of 1867–68 — **sho·gun·ate** \'shō-gə-nət, -ˌgü-; -gə-ˌnāt\ *n*
sho·ji \'shō-jē\ *n, pl* **shoji** *also* **shojis** [Jap *shōji*] **:** a paper screen serving as a wall, partition, or sliding door
sho·lom \shä-'lōm\ *var of* SHALOM
shone *past of* SHINE
shoo \'shü\ *vt* [ME *schowe*, interj. used to drive away an animal] **:** to scare, drive, or send away by or as if by crying *shoo*
shoo·fly \'shü-ˌflī\ *n* [*shoo*, interj. (fr. ME *schowe*) + *fly*] **1 :** a child's rocker having the seat built on or usu. between supports representing an animal figure **2 :** any of several plants held to repel flies
shoo–in \'shü-ˌin\ *n* **:** one that is a certain and easy winner (as among candidates for an office or contestants in a race)
¹**shook** *past or chiefly dial past part of* SHAKE
²**shook** \'shu̇k\ *n* [origin unknown] **1 a :** a set of staves and headings for one hogshead, cask, or barrel **b :** a bundle of parts (as of boxes) ready to be put together **2 :** ¹SHOCK
shoon \'shün\ *chiefly dial pl of* SHOE
¹**shoot** \'shüt\ *vb* **shot** \'shät\ **shoot·ing** [ME *sheten, shuten*, fr. OE *scēotan;* akin to ON *skjōta* to shoot, Lith *skudrus* quick] *vt* **1 a** (1) **:** to let fly or cause to be driven forward with force (as an arrow or bullet) (2) **:** to cause a missile to be driven forth from (as a bow or gun) **:** DISCHARGE ⟨the sound of rifles being *shot* off⟩ **b :** to send forth with suddenness or intensity **:** DART ⟨*shot* at him a look of amazement⟩ **c :** to propel (as a ball or puck) toward a goal; *also* **:** to score by so doing ⟨~ a basket⟩ ⟨~ the winning goal⟩ **d :** PLAY ⟨~ a round of golf⟩ **2 a :** to strike with a missile esp.

from a bow or gun; *esp* : to wound or kill with a missile discharged from a firearm **b** (1) : to remove or destroy by use of firearms ⟨had his hand *shot* off⟩ ⟨*shot* out the light⟩ (2) : WRECK, EXPLODE **c** (1) : to practice the killing of (as game) with firearms esp. as a sport (2) : to hunt over ⟨~ a tract of woodland⟩ **3 a** : to push or slide (as the bolt of a door or a lock) into or out of a fastening **b** : to pass (a shuttle) through the warp threads in weaving **4 a** : to throw or cast suddenly or with force : FLING ⟨*shot* his rider over his head⟩ **b** : to discharge, dump, or empty esp. by overturning, upending, or directing into a slide **c** : to spend extravagantly : use up : EXHAUST **d** : to throw out (dice) : CAST; *also* : to place or offer (a bet) on the result of such casting ⟨~ five dollars⟩ **5 a** : to push or thrust forward : stick out : PROTRUDE ⟨lizards ~*ing* out their tongues⟩ **b** : to put forth in growing **6 a** : to utter (as words or sounds) rapidly or suddenly or with force **b** : to emit (as light, flame, or fumes) suddenly or rapidly **7 a** : to place, send, or bring into position abruptly **b** : to cause (as a boat) to move suddenly or swiftly forward **c** : to send or carry in haste or swiftly : DISPATCH **8** : to variegate as if by sprinkling color in streaks, flecks, or patches **9** : to pass swiftly along ⟨~*ing* rapids⟩ or by or past **10** : to plane (as the edge of a board) straight or true **11 a** : to set off : DETONATE, IGNITE **b** : to effect by blasting **12 a** : to take the altitude of **b** : to take a picture of : PHOTOGRAPH, FILM **13** : to give an injection to ~ *vi* **1 a** : to go or pass rapidly and precipitately ⟨sparks ~*ing* up⟩ ⟨his feet ~ out from under him⟩ **b** : to move ahead by force of momentum **c** : to stream out suddenly : SPURT **d** : to dart in or as if in rays from a source of light **e** : to dart with a piercing sensation **2 a** : to cause an engine or weapon to discharge a missile **b** : to use a firearm or bow esp. for sport (as in hunting) **3** : to carry when discharged ⟨guns that ~ many miles⟩ **4** : PROTRUDE, PROJECT **5 a** : to grow or sprout by or as if by putting forth shoots **b** : DEVELOP, MATURE **6 a** : to play by propelling a ball or other object in a particular way **b** : to drive the ball at goal or toward a green **7** : to cast dice **8** : to slide into or out of a fastening ⟨a bolt that ~*s* in either direction⟩ **9** : to photograph a scene esp. of a moving picture; *also* : to operate a camera or set cameras in operation : take a photograph — **shoot·er** *n* — **shoot at** *or* **shoot for** : to aim at : strive for — **shoot one's bolt** : to exhaust one's capabilities and resources — **shoot the works 1** : to venture all one's capital on one play **2** : to put forth all one's efforts

[2]**shoot** *n* **1** : a sending out of new growth or the growth sent out: as **a** : a stem or branch with its leaves and appendages esp. when not yet mature **b** : OFFSHOOT **c** : a similar formation of crystal **2 a** : an act of shooting (as with a bow or a firearm): (1) : SHOT (2) : the firing of a missile esp. by artillery **b** (1) : a hunting trip or party (2) : the right to shoot game in a particular area or land over which it is held **c** (1) : a shooting match ⟨skeet ~⟩ (2) : a round of shots in a shooting match **d** (1) : the action of shooting with a camera (2) : a launching of a rocket device or a guided missile esp. experimentally **3 a** : a motion or movement of rapid thrusting: as (1) : a sudden or rapid advance (2) [perh. by folk etymology fr. F *chute* — more at CHUTE] : a rush of water down a steep or rapid (3) : a momentary darting sensation : TWINGE (4) : THRUST 2b (5) : a falling of a detached mass of earth or ice (6) : the pace between strokes in rowing **b** : a bar of rays : BEAM ⟨a ~ of sunlight⟩ **4** [prob. by folk etymology fr. F *chute* — more at CHUTE] **a** : a place where a stream runs or descends swiftly **b** : any of various inclined channels or troughs through which something (as water, logs, or grain) is moved

syn BRANCH, BOUGH, LIMB: SHOOT applies to an outgrowth from any plant and stresses the actual growing of a young, undeveloped member; BRANCH stresses division and applies to any well-developed member whether growing from the trunk or a subdivision; BOUGH carries a weak implication of division and a strong suggestion of bearing foliage; LIMB applies to one of the divisions made by forking of the trunk esp. of a large tree

shooting gallery *n* : a range usu. covered and equipped with targets for practice with firearms

shooting iron *n* : FIREARM

shooting script *n* **1** : the final completely detailed version of a motion-picture script in which scenes are grouped in the order most convenient for shooting and without regard to plot sequence **2** : the final version of a television script used in the production of a program

shooting star *n* **1** : a visual meteor appearing as a temporary streak of light in the night sky **2** : a No. American perennial herb (*Dodecatheon meadia*) of the primrose family with entire oblong leaves and showy flowers — called also *American cowslip*

shooting stick *n* : a spiked stick with a top that opens into a seat

shoot-the-chutes \ˌshüt-t͟hə-'shüts\ *n pl but sing or pl in constr* : an amusement ride consisting of a steep incline down which toboggans or boats with flat bottoms slide usu. to continue across a body of water at the bottom

[1]**shop** \'shäp\ *n, often attrib* [ME *shoppe*, fr. OE *sceoppa* booth; akin to OHG *scopf* shed] **1** : a handicraft establishment : ATELIER **2 a** : a building or room stocked with merchandise for sale : STORE **b** *or* **shoppe** \'shäp\ : a small retail establishment or a department in a large one offering a specified line of goods or services **3** : FACTORY, MILL **4 a** : a school laboratory equipped for instruction in manual arts **b** : the art or science of working with tools and machinery **5 a** : a business establishment; *esp* : OFFICE **b** : SHOPTALK — **shop·keep·er** \-ˌkē-pər\ *n*

[2]**shop** *vi* **shopped**; **shop·ping 1 a** : to examine goods or services with intent to buy **b** : to probe a market in search of the best buy **2** : to make a search : HUNT

shop·lift·er \'shäp-ˌlif-tər\ *n* : a thief who steals merchandise on display in stores

shop·lift·ing \-tiŋ\ *n* : the stealing of goods on display in a store

shop·per \'shäp-ər\ *n* **1** : one that shops **2** : one whose occupation is shopping as an agent for customers or for an employer

shop steward *n* : a union member elected as the union representative of a shop or department in dealings with the management

shop·talk \'shäp-ˌtȯk\ *n* : the jargon or subject matter peculiar to an occupation or a special area of interest

shop·worn \-ˌwō(ə)rn, -ˌwȯ(ə)rn\ *adj* **1** : faded, soiled, or otherwise impaired by remaining too long in a store **2** : BEDRAGGLED, JADED

sho·ran \'shō(ə)r-ˌan, 'shȯ(ə)r-\ *n* [*short-range navigation*] : a system of short-range navigation in which two radar signals transmitted by an airplane are intercepted and rebroadcast to the airplane by two ground stations of known position are used to determine the position of the airplane

[1]**shore** \'shō(ə)r, 'shȯ(ə)r\ *n, often attrib* [ME, fr. (assumed) OE *scor;* akin to OE *scieran* to cut — more at SHEAR] : the land bordering a usu. large body of water; *specif* : COAST — **shore·line** \-ˌlīn\ *n*

[2]**shore** *vt* [ME *shoren;* akin to ON *skortha* to prop] **1** : to support by a shore : PROP **2** : to give support to : BRACE

[3]**shore** *n* : a prop for preventing sinking or sagging

shore·bird \-ˌbərd\ *n* : any of a suborder (Charadrii) of birds that frequent the seashore

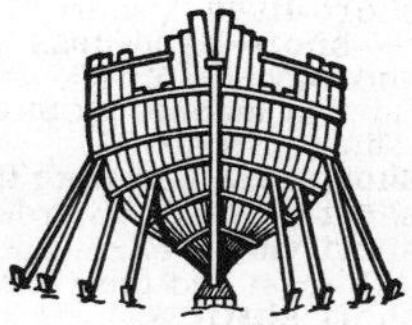

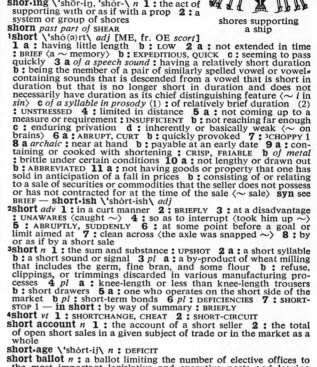

shores supporting a ship

shore dinner *n* : a usu. full course dinner consisting mainly of various seafoods

shore leave *n* : a leave of absence to go on shore granted to a sailor or naval officer

shore patrol *n* : a branch of a navy that exercises guard and police functions

shor·ing \'shōr-iŋ, 'shȯr-\ *n* **1** : the act of supporting with or as if with a prop **2** : a system or group of shores

shorn *past part of* SHEAR

[1]**short** \'shȯ(ə)rt\ *adj* [ME, fr. OE *scort*] **1 a** : having little length **b** : LOW **2 a** : not extended in time : BRIEF ⟨a ~ memory⟩ **b** : EXPEDITIOUS, QUICK **c** : seeming to pass quickly **3 a** *of a speech sound* : having a relatively short duration **b** : being the member of a pair of similarly spelled vowel or vowel-containing sounds that is descended from a vowel that is short in duration but that is no longer short in duration and does not necessarily have duration as its chief distinguishing feature ⟨~ *i* in *sin*⟩ **c** *of a syllable in prosody* (1) : of relatively brief duration (2) : UNSTRESSED **4** : limited in distance **5 a** : not coming up to a measure or requirement : INSUFFICIENT **b** : not reaching far enough **c** : enduring privation **d** : inherently or basically weak ⟨~ on brains⟩ **6 a** : ABRUPT, CURT **b** : quickly provoked **7** : [3]CHOPPY 1 **8 a** *archaic* : near at hand **b** : payable at an early date **9 a** : containing or cooked with shortening : CRISP, FRIABLE **b** *of metal* : brittle under certain conditions **10 a** : not lengthy or drawn out **b** : ABBREVIATED **11 a** : not having goods or property that one has sold in anticipation of a fall in prices **b** : consisting of or relating to a sale of securities or commodities that the seller does not possess or has not contracted for at the time of the sale ⟨~ sale⟩ **syn** see BRIEF — **short·ish** \'shȯrt-ish\ *adj*

[2]**short** *adv* **1** : in a curt manner **2** : BRIEFLY **3** : at a disadvantage : UNAWARES ⟨caught ~⟩ **4** : so as to interrupt ⟨took him up ~⟩ **5** : ABRUPTLY, SUDDENLY **6** : at some point before a goal or limit aimed at **7** : clean across ⟨the axle was snapped ~⟩ **8** : by or as if by a short sale

[3]**short** *n* **1** : the sum and substance : UPSHOT **2 a** : a short syllable **b** : a short sound or signal **3** *pl* **a** : a by-product of wheat milling that includes the germ, fine bran, and some flour **b** : refuse, clippings, or trimmings discarded in various manufacturing processes **4** *pl* **a** : knee-length or less than knee-length trousers **b** : short drawers **5 a** : one who operates on the short side of the market **b** *pl* : short-term bonds **6** *pl* : DEFICIENCIES **7** : SHORTSTOP 1 — **in short** : by way of summary : BRIEFLY

[4]**short** *vt* **1** : SHORTCHANGE, CHEAT **2** : SHORT-CIRCUIT

short account *n* **1** : the account of a short seller **2** : the total of open short sales in a given subject of trade or in the market as a whole

short·age \'shȯrt-ij\ *n* : DEFICIT

short ballot *n* : a ballot limiting the number of elective offices to the most important legislative and executive posts and leaving minor positions to be filled by appointment

short·bread \'shȯrt-ˌbred\ *n* : a thick cookie made of flour, sugar, and much shortening

short·cake \-ˌkāk\ *n* **1** : a crisp and often unsweetened biscuit or cookie **2** : a dessert made of usu. very short baking-powder-biscuit dough spread with sweetened fruit

short·change \-'chānj\ *vt* **1** : to give less than the correct amount of change to **2** : to deprive of something due : CHEAT — **short·chang·er** *n*

short circuit *n* : a connection of comparatively low resistance accidentally or intentionally made between points on a circuit between which the resistance is normally much greater

short-cir·cuit \'shȯrt-'sər-kət\ *vt* **1** : to apply a short circuit to or establish a short circuit in **2** : BYPASS **3** : FRUSTRATE, IMPEDE

short·com·ing \-ˌkəm-iŋ\ *n* : DEFICIENCY, DEFECT

short covering *n* : buying in securities or other property to close out a short sale

short·cut \-ˌkət\ *n* **1** : a route more direct than the one ordinarily taken **2** : a method of doing something more directly and quickly than by ordinary procedure

short-day \'shȯrt-ˌdā\ *adj* : responding to a short photoperiod — used of a plant

short division *n* : mathematical division in which the successive steps are performed without writing out the remainders

short·en \'shȯrt-ᵊn\ *vb* **short·en·ing** \'shȯrt-niŋ, -ᵊn-iŋ\ *vt* **1** : to make short or shorter **2 a** : to reduce in power or efficiency **b** *obs* : to deprive of effect **3** : to make crumbly ⟨~ pastry⟩ ~ *vi* : to become short or shorter — **short·en·er** \-nər, -ᵊn-ər\ *n*

syn SHORTEN, CURTAIL, ABBREVIATE, ABRIDGE, RETRENCH mean to reduce in extent. SHORTEN implies reduction in length or duration; CURTAIL adds an implication of cutting that in some way deprives of completeness or adequacy; ABBREVIATE implies a making shorter usually by omitting some part; ABRIDGE implies a reduction in compass or scope with retention of essential elements and a relative completeness in the result; RETRENCH suggests a reduction in extent or costs of something felt to be excessive

short·en·ing \'shȯrt-niŋ, -ᵊn-iŋ\ *n* **1** : the action or process of making or becoming short; *specif* : the dropping of the latter part of a word so as to produce a new and shorter word of the same meaning **2** : an edible fat used to shorten baked goods

short·hand \'shȯrt-ˌhand\ *n* **1** : a method of writing rapidly by substituting characters, abbreviations, or symbols for letters, words, or phrases : STENOGRAPHY **2** : a system or instance of rapid

or abbreviated communication — **shorthand** *adj*

short·hand·ed \'han-dəd\ *adj* **:** short of the regular or necessary number of people

short·horn \'shȯrt-ˌhȯ(ə)rn\ *n, often cap* **:** any of a breed of red, roan, or white beef cattle originating in the north of England and including good milk-producing strains from which the Milking Shorthorn breed has been evolved — called also *Durham*

short–horned grasshopper \ˌshȯrt-ˌhȯrn(d)-\ *n* **:** any of a family (Acrididae) of grasshoppers with short antennae

short line *n* **:** a transportation system (as a railroad) operating over a relatively short distance

short–lived \'shȯrt-'līvd, -'livd\ *adj* **:** not living or lasting long — **short–lived·ness** \-'līv(d)-nəs, -'liv(d)-\ *n*

short·ly \'shȯrt-lē\ *adv* **1 a :** in a few words **:** BRIEFLY **b :** in an abrupt manner **:** CURTLY **2 a :** in a short time **:** SOON **b :** at a short interval

short·ness \-nəs\ *n* **:** the quality or state of being short

short order *n* **:** an order for food that can be quickly cooked

short ribs *n pl* **:** a cut of beef consisting of rib ends between the rib roast and the plate

short shrift *n* **1 :** a brief respite from death **2 :** summary treatment

short sight *n* **:** MYOPIA

short·sight·ed \'shȯrt-'sīt-əd\ *adj* **1 :** NEARSIGHTED **2 :** lacking foresight — **short·sight·ed·ly** *adv* — **short·sight·ed·ness** *n*

short snort·er \-'snȯrt-ər\ *n* [*short snort* (quick drink)] **1 :** a member of an informal club for which one who has made a transoceanic flight is eligible **2 :** a piece of paper money endorsed by short snorters as a membership certificate for a new member

short–spo·ken \-'spō-kən\ *adj* **:** CURT

short·stop \'shȯrt-ˌstäp\ *n* **1 :** the player position in baseball for defending the infield area to the third-base side of second base **2 :** the player stationed in the shortstop position

short–stop \-ˌstäp\ *n* **:** an acid bath used to check photographic development of a negative or print

short story *n* **:** a brief invented prose narrative usu. dealing with a few characters and aiming at unity of effect and often concentrating on the creation of mood rather than plot

short–tem·pered \'shȯrt-'tem-pərd\ *adj* **:** having a quick temper

short–term \-'tərm\ *adj* **1 :** occurring over or involving a relatively short period of time **2 a :** of or relating to a financial transaction based on a term usu. of less than a year **b :** of or relating to capital assets held for less than six months

short·wave \'shȯrt-'wāv\ *n, often attrib* **1 :** a radio wave of 60-meter wavelength or less **2 :** a radio transmitter using shortwaves

short–wind·ed \-'win-dəd\ *adj* **1 :** affected with or characterized by shortness of breath **2 :** BRIEF, DISCONNECTED

Sho·sho·ne·an \shə-'shō-nē-ən\ *n* **:** a language family of the Uto-Aztecan phylum comprising the languages of most of the Uto-Aztecan peoples in the U. S.

Sho·sho·ni *also* **Sho·sho·ne** \shə-'shō-nē\ *n, pl* **Shoshoni** *or* **Shoshonis** *also* **Shoshone** *or* **Shoshones 1 :** a group of Shoshonean peoples in California, Colorado, Idaho, Nevada, Utah, and Wyoming **2 :** a member of the Shoshoni group of peoples

1**shot** \'shät\ *n* [ME, fr. OE *scot;* akin to ON *skot* shot, OHG *scuz,* OE *scēotan* to shoot — more at SHOOT] **1 a :** an action of shooting **b :** a directed propelling of a missile; *specif* **:** a directed discharge of a firearm **c :** a stroke or throw in a game **d :** BLAST **e :** a medical injection **2 a** *pl* **shot :** something propelled by shooting; *esp* **:** small lead or steel pellets esp. forming a charge for a shotgun **b :** a metal sphere of iron or brass that is put for distance **3 a :** the distance that a missile is or can be thrown **b :** RANGE, REACH **4 :** a charge to be paid **:** SCOT **5 :** one that shoots **:** MARKSMAN **6 a :** ATTEMPT, TRY **b :** GUESS, CONJECTURE **c :** CHANCE **7 :** a remark so directed as to have telling effect **8 a :** a single photographic exposure; *esp* **:** SNAPSHOT **b :** a single sequence of a motion picture or a television program shot by one camera without interruption **9 :** a charge of explosives **10 a :** a single drink of liquor **b :** a small amount applied at one time **:** DOSE

2**shot** *adj* **1 a** *of a fabric* **:** having contrasting and changeable color effects that react varyingly to dyes **:** IRIDESCENT **b :** suffused or streaked with a color ⟨hair ~ with gray⟩ **c :** PERMEATED ⟨~ through with wit⟩ **2 :** having the form of pellets resembling shot **3 :** reduced to a state of ruin, prostration, or uselessness

1**shot·gun** \'shät-ˌgən\ *n* **:** an often double-barreled smoothbore shoulder weapon for firing shot at short ranges

2**shotgun** *adj* **1 :** of, relating to, or using a shotgun **2 :** involving coercion **3 :** covering a wide field with hit-or-miss effectiveness

shotgun marriage *n* **:** a marriage forced or required because of pregnancy — called also *shotgun wedding*

shot hole *n* **1 :** a drilled hole in which a charge of dynamite is exploded **2 :** a hole made usu. by a boring insect

shot put *n* **:** a field event consisting in putting the shot for distance — **shot–put·ter** \'shät-ˌpu̇t-ər\ *n* — **shot–put·ting** \-iŋ\ *n*

shott *var of* CHOTT

shot·ten \'shät-ᵊn\ *adj* [ME *shotyn,* fr. pp. of *shuten* to shoot] **1 :** having ejected the spawn and so of inferior food value ⟨~ herring⟩ **2 :** WORTHLESS

should \shəd, (')shu̇d\ [ME *sholde,* fr. OE *sceolde* owed, was obliged to; akin to OHG *scolta* owed, was obliged to] *past of* SHALL **1** — used in auxiliary function to express condition ⟨if he ~ leave his father, his father would die —Gen 44:22 (RSV)⟩ **2** — used in auxiliary function to express obligation, propriety, or expediency ⟨'tis commanded I ~ do so —Shak.⟩ ⟨this is as it ~ be —H.L.Savage⟩ ⟨you ~ brush your teeth after each meal⟩ **3** — used in auxiliary function to express futurity from a point of view in the past ⟨realized that she ~ have to do most of her farm work before sunrise —Ellen Glasgow⟩ **4** — used in auxiliary function to express what is probable or expected ⟨with an early start, they ~ be here by noon⟩ **5** — used in auxiliary function to tone down a direct statement or request ⟨I ~ suggest that a guide to available materials is the first essential —L.D.Reddick⟩

1**shoul·der** \'shōl-dər\ *n, often attrib* [ME *sholder,* fr. OE *sculdor;* akin to OHG *scultra* shoulder, OE *sciell* shell — more at SHELL] **1 a :** the laterally projecting part of the human body formed of the bones and joints by which the arm is connected with the trunk and the muscles covering them **b :** the corresponding but usu. less projecting region of the body of a lower vertebrate **2 a :** the two shoulders and the upper part of the back — usu. used in pl. **b** *pl* **:** capacity for bearing a task or blame **3 :** a cut of meat including the upper joint of the foreleg and adjacent parts **4 :** the part of a garment at the wearer's shoulder **5 :** something resembling a human shoulder: as **a** (1) **:** the part of a hill or mountain near the top (2) **:** a lateral protrusion or extension of a hill or mountain **b :** the flat top of the body of a piece of printing type from which the bevel rises to join the face **c :** either edge of a roadway; *specif* **:** the part of a roadway outside of the traveled way

2**shoulder** *vb* **shoul·der·ing** \-d(ə-)riŋ\ *vt* **1 :** to push or thrust with the shoulder **:** JOSTLE **2 a :** to place or bear on the shoulder **b :** to assume the burden or responsibility of **~** *vi* **:** to push with the shoulders aggressively

shoulder belt *n* **:** an anchored belt worn across the upper torso and over the shoulders to hold a person steady in a seat esp. in case of an automobile collision — called also *shoulder harness*

shoulder blade *n* **:** SCAPULA — called also *shoulder bone*

shoulder board *n* **:** one of a pair of broad pieces of stiffened cloth worn on the shoulders of a military uniform and carrying insignia

shoulder girdle *n* **:** PECTORAL GIRDLE

shoulder knot *n* **1 :** an ornamental knot of ribbon or lace worn on the shoulder in the 17th and 18th centuries **2 :** a detachable ornament of braided wire cord worn on the shoulders of a uniform of ceremony by a commissioned officer

shoulder mark *n* **:** one of a pair of rectangular pieces of cloth worn parallel to the shoulder of some uniforms of U.S. Navy officers bearing insignia of rank and line or corps devices

shoulder patch *n* **:** a cloth patch bearing an identifying mark and worn on one sleeve of a uniform below the shoulder

should·est \'shu̇d-əst\ *archaic past 2d sing of* SHALL

shouldn't \'shu̇d-ᵊnt\ **:** should not

shouldst \shədst, (')shu̇dst, shətst, (')shu̇tst\ *archaic past 2d sing of* SHALL

1**shout** \'shau̇t\ *vb* [ME *shouten*] *vi* **:** to utter a sudden loud cry **~** *vt* **:** to utter in a loud voice — **shout·er** *n*

2**shout** *n* **:** a loud cry or call

shouting distance *n* **:** easy reach — usu. used with *within*

shout song *n* **:** a rhythmic religious song characterized by responsive singing between leader and congregation

1**shove** \'shəv\ *vb* [ME *shoven,* fr. OE *scūfan* to thrust away; akin to OHG *scioban* to push, OSlav *skubati* to tear] *vt* **1 :** to push along **2 :** to push or put in a rough, careless, or hasty manner **:** THRUST **3 :** to force by other than physical means **:** COMPEL **~** *vi* **1 :** to move by forcing a way ⟨~ off⟩ **2 a :** to move something by exerting force **b :** LEAVE **syn** see PUSH — **shov·er** *n*

2**shove** *n* **:** an act or instance of shoving

1**shov·el** \'shəv-əl\ *n* [ME, fr. OE *scofl;* akin to OHG *scūfla* shovel, OE *scūfan* to thrust away] **1 a :** a hand implement consisting of a broad scoop or a more or less hollowed out blade with a handle used to lift and throw material **b :** something that resembles a shovel **2 :** SHOVELFUL

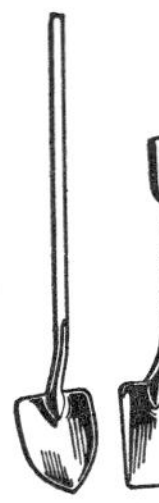

shovels 1a

2**shovel** *vb* **shov·eled** *or* **shov·elled; shov·el·ing** *or* **shov·el·ling** \-(ə-)liŋ\ *vt* **1 :** to take up and throw with a shovel **2 :** to dig or clean out with a shovel **3 :** to throw or convey roughly or in the mass as if with a shovel **~** *vi* **:** to use a shovel

shov·el·bill \'shəv-əl-ˌbil\ *n* **:** SHOVELER 2

shov·el·er *or* **shov·el·ler** \'shəv-(ə-)lər\ *n* **1 :** one that shovels **2 :** any of several river ducks (genus *Anas*) having a large and very broad bill

shov·el·ful \'shəv-əl-ˌfu̇l\ *n, pl* **shovelfuls** \-ˌfu̇lz\ *or* **shov·els·ful** \-əlz-ˌfu̇l\ **:** the amount held by a shovel

shovel hat *n* **:** a shallow-crowned hat with a wide brim curved up at the sides that is worn by some clergymen

shov·el·head \'shəv-əl-ˌhed\ *n* **:** any of several fishes with heads resembling a shovel; *esp* **:** a shark (*Sphyrna tiburo*) smaller than the related hammerhead and with narrower head

shov·el·man \-ˌman, -mən\ *n* **:** one who works with a shovel

shov·el·nose \-ˌnōz\ *n* **:** a shovel-nosed animal and esp. fish

shov·el–nosed \ˌshəv-əl-'nōzd\ *adj* **:** having a broad flat head, nose, or beak

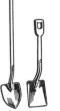

1**show** \'shō\ *vb* **showed** \'shōd\ **shown** \'shōn\ *or* **showed; show·ing** [ME *shewen, showen,* fr. OE *scēawian* to look, look at, see; akin to OHG *scouwōn* to look, look at, L *cavēre* to be on one's guard] *vt* **1 :** to cause or permit to be seen **:** EXHIBIT **2 :** to set out for sale **:** OFFER **3 :** to present as a public spectacle **:** PERFORM **4 :** to display for the notice of others **5 :** to reveal by one's condition, nature, or behavior **6 :** to give indication of by record **7 a :** to point out to someone **b :** CONDUCT, USHER **8 :** ACCORD, BESTOW **9 a :** to set forth **:** DECLARE **b :** ALLEGE, PLEAD — used esp. in law **10 a :** DEMONSTRATE, PROVE **b :** INFORM, INSTRUCT **~** *vi* **1 :** to be or come in view **:** be present or noticeable **2 a :** to appear in a particular way **:** have a particular quality **b :** SEEM, APPEAR **3 :** to give a theatrical performance **4 :** to finish third or at least third in a horse race

syn SHOW, MANIFEST, EVIDENCE, EVINCE, DEMONSTRATE mean to reveal something not plain. SHOW is the general term but may imply inference from acts, books, or words; MANIFEST implies a plainer, more immediate revelation; EVIDENCE suggests serving as proof of the actuality or existence of something; EVINCE implies a showing by outward marks or tokens; DEMONSTRATE implies showing by action or by display of feeling

syn SHOW, EXHIBIT, DISPLAY, EXPOSE, PARADE, FLAUNT mean to present so as to invite notice or attention. SHOW implies enabling another to see or examine; EXHIBIT applies to putting forward prominently or openly; DISPLAY stresses putting in position where one may see to advantage; EXPOSE suggests bringing from concealment and displaying; PARADE implies an ostentatious or arrogant displaying; FLAUNT suggests a shameless, boastful, often offensive parading

2**show** *n, often attrib* **1 :** a demonstrative display **2 a** *archaic* **:** outward appearance **b :** a false semblance **:** PRETENSE **c :** a more or less true appearance of something **:** SIGN **d :** an impressive display **e :** OSTENTATION **3 :** CHANCE **4 :** something exhibited esp. for wonder or ridicule **:** SPECTACLE **5 :** a large display or exhibition arranged to arouse interest or stimulate sales **6 a :** a theatrical presentation **b :** a radio or television program **c :** ENTERTAINMENT 3 **7 :** ENTERPRISE, AFFAIR **8 :** an indication of metal in a mine or of gas or oil in a well **9 :** third place at the finish of a horse race

show bill *n* **:** an advertising poster

show·boat \'shō-ˌbōt\ *n* **:** a river steamship containing a theater

and carrying a troupe of actors to give plays at river communities
showbread *var of* SHEWBREAD
show·case \'shō-,kās\ *n* **1 :** a glazed case, box, or cabinet to display and protect wares in a store or articles in a museum **2 :** a setting or framework for exhibiting something esp. at its best
show·down \-,daun\ *n* **1 :** the placing of poker hands faceup on the table to determine the winner of a pot **2 :** the final settlement of a contested issue or the test of strength by which it is settled
¹show·er \'shau̇(-ə)r\ *n* [ME *shour*, fr. OE *scūr*; akin to OHG *scūr* shower, L *caurus* northwest wind] **1 a :** a fall of rain of short duration **b :** a like fall of sleet, hail, or snow **2 :** something resembling a rain shower **3 :** a party given by friends who bring gifts often of a particular kind — **show·ery** \-ē\ *adj*
²shower *vi* **1 :** to rain or fall in or as if in a shower **2 :** to bathe in a shower bath ~ *vt* **1 :** to wet copiously (as with water) in a spray, fine stream, or drops **2 :** to give in abundance
³show·er \'shō(-ə)r\ *n* **:** one that shows **:** EXHIBITOR
shower bath *n* **:** a bath in which water is showered on the person; *also* **:** the apparatus that provides a shower bath
show·i·ly \'shō-ə-lē\ *adv* **:** in a showy manner
show·i·ness \'shō-ē-nəs\ *n* **:** the quality or state of being showy
show·ing *n* **1 :** an act of putting something on view **:** DISPLAY **2 :** PERFORMANCE, RECORD **3 a :** a statement or presentation of a case **b :** APPEARANCE, EVIDENCE
show·man \'shō-mən\ *n* **1 :** the producer of a play or other theatrical show **2 :** a person having a sense or knack for dramatization or visual effectiveness — **show·man·ship** \-,ship\ *n*
show–me \'shō-mē\ *adj* **:** insistent on proof or evidence **:** SKEPTICAL, INCREDULOUS
show off *vt* **:** to display proudly ~ *vi* **:** to seek to attract attention by conspicuous behavior
show–off \'shō-,ȯf\ *n* **1 :** the act of showing off **2 :** one that shows off
show·piece \-,pēs\ *n* **:** a prime or outstanding example used for exhibition
show·place \-,plās\ *n* **:** a place (as an estate or building) that is frequently exhibited or is regarded as an example of beauty or excellence
show·room \-,rüm, -,ru̇m\ *n* **:** a room where merchandise is exposed for sale or where samples are displayed
show up *vt* **:** to reveal the true nature of **:** EXPOSE ~ *vi* **:** ARRIVE
showy \'shō-ē\ *adj* **1 :** making an attractive show **:** STRIKING **2 :** marked by ostentation **:** GAUDY
syn SHOWY, PRETENTIOUS, OSTENTATIOUS, POMPOUS mean given to excessive outward display. SHOWY implies an imposing or striking appearance but usu. suggests cheapness or poor taste; PRETENTIOUS implies an appearance of importance not justified by the thing's value or the person's standing; OSTENTATIOUS stresses vainglorious display or parade; POMPOUS suggests an ostentatiousness prompted by love of ceremony or exaggerated sense of self-importance
shrap·nel \'shrap-nᵊl, *esp South* 'srap-\ *n, pl* **shrapnel** [Henry *Shrapnel* †1842 E artillery officer] **1 :** a projectile that consists of a case provided with a powder charge and a large number of usu. lead balls and is exploded in flight **2 :** bomb, mine, or shell fragments

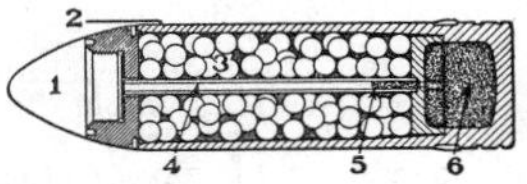

shrapnel: *1* combination fuze, time and percussion, *2* steel case, *3* shrapnel balls, *4* central tube, *5* guncotton, *6* loose powder

¹shred \'shred, *esp South* 'sred\ *n* [ME *shrede*, fr. OE *scrēade*; akin to OHG *scrōt* piece cut off, L *scrupus* sharp stone, OE *scieran* to cut — more at SHEAR] **:** a long narrow strip cut or torn off **:** PARTICLE, SCRAP
²shred *vb* **shred·ded; shred·ding** *vt* **1** *archaic* **:** to cut off **2 :** to cut or tear into shreds ~ *vi* **:** to break up into shreds — **shred·der** *n*
¹shrew \'shrü, *esp South* 'srü\ *n* [ME *shrewe* evil or scolding person, fr. OE *scrēawa* shrewmouse] **1 :** any of numerous small chiefly nocturnal mammals (family Soricidae) related to the moles and distinguished by a long pointed snout, very small eyes, and velvety fur **2 :** a vexatious, scolding, or brawling woman **:** SCOLD
²shrew *vt, obs* **:** CURSE
shrewd \'shrüd, *esp South* 'srüd\ *adj* [ME *shrewe* + *-ed*] **1** *archaic* **:** MISCHIEVOUS **2** *obs* **:** SHREWISH, ABUSIVE **3** *obs* **:** OMINOUS, DANGEROUS **4 a :** SEVERE, HARD ⟨~ knock⟩ **b :** BITING, PIERCING ⟨~ wind⟩ **5 a :** marked by cleverness, discernment, or sagacity **:** ASTUTE **b :** WILY, TRICKY — **shrewd·ly** *adv* — **shrewd·ness** *n*
syn SAGACIOUS, PERSPICACIOUS, ASTUTE: SHREWD implies practical, hardheaded cleverness and judgment and acute perception; SAGACIOUS suggests wisdom, penetration, and farsightedness; PERSPICACIOUS implies unusual power to see through and understand what is dark or hidden; ASTUTE suggests shrewdness, perspicacity, and diplomatic skill
shrew·ish \'shrü-ish, *esp South* 'srü-\ *adj* **:** ill-tempered **:** INTRACTABLE — **shrew·ish·ly** *adv* — **shrew·ish·ness** *n*
shrew·mouse \-,mau̇s\ *n* **:** SHREW 1
shri \'s(h)rē\ *var of* SRI
¹shriek \'shrēk, *esp South* 'srēk\ *vb* [prob. irreg. fr. ME *shriken* to shriek; akin to ME *scremen* to scream] *vi* **1 :** to utter a sharp shrill sound **2 :** to cry out in a high-pitched voice **:** SCREECH ~ *vt* **:** to utter with a shriek or sharply and shrilly
²shriek *n* **1 :** a shrill usu. wild or involuntary cry **2 :** a sound resembling a shriek
shriev·al \'shrē-vəl, *esp South* 'srē-\ *adj* [obs. *shrieve* sheriff, fr. ME *shirreve* — more at SHERIFF] **:** of or relating to a sheriff — **shriev·al·ty** \-tē\ *n*
shrieve \'shrēv, *esp South* 'srēv\ *archaic var of* SHRIVE
shrift \'shrift, *esp South* 'srift\ *n* [ME, fr. OE *scrift*, fr. *scrīfan* to shrive — more at SHRIVE] **1** *archaic* **a :** the act of shriving **:** CONFESSION **b :** a remission of sins pronounced by a priest in the sacrament of penance **2** *obs* **:** CONFESSIONAL
shrike \'shrīk, *esp South* 'srīk\ *n* [perh. fr. (assumed) ME *shrik*, fr. OE *scrīc* thrush; akin to ME *shriken* to shriek] **:** any of numerous usu. largely gray or brownish oscine birds ⟨family Laniidae⟩ that have a strong notched bill hooked at the tip, feed chiefly on insects, and often impale their prey on thorns
¹shrill \'shril, *esp South* 'sril\ *vb* [ME *shrillen*] *vi* **:** to utter or emit an acute, piercing sound ~ *vt* **:** SCREAM
²shrill *adj* **1 a :** having or emitting a sharp high-pitched tone or sound **:** PIERCING **b :** accompanied by sharp high-pitched sounds or cries **2 :** having a sharp or vivid effect on the senses ⟨~ light⟩ **3 :** INTEMPERATE, EXTRAVAGANT ⟨~ anger⟩ — **shrill** *adv* — **shrill·ness** *n* — **shril·ly** \'s(h)ril-lē\ *adv*
³shrill *n* **:** a shrill sound
¹shrimp \'shrimp, *esp South* 'srimp\ *n, pl* **shrimps** *also* **shrimp** [ME *shrimpe*; akin to ON *skorpna* to shrivel up, L *curvus* curved — more at CROWN] **1 :** any of numerous mostly small and marine decapod crustaceans (suborder Natantia) having a slender elongated body, compressed abdomen, long legs, and a long, spiny rostrum; *also* **:** a small crustacean (as an amphipod or a branchiopod) resembling the true shrimps **2 :** a very small or puny person or thing

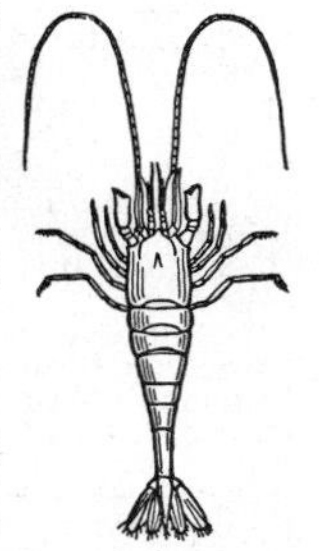
shrimp

²shrimp *vi* **:** to fish for or catch shrimps
shrimp pink *n* **:** a variable color averaging a deep pink
¹shrine \'shrīn, *esp South* 'srīn\ *n* [ME, fr. OE *scrīn*, fr. L *scrinium* case, chest] **1 a :** the reliquary or tomb of a saint **b :** a place in which devotion is paid to a saint or deity **:** SANCTUARY **c :** a niche containing a religious image **2 :** a place or object hallowed by its associations **3 :** something that enshrines
²shrine *vt* **:** ENSHRINE
¹shrink \'shriŋk, *esp South* 'sriŋk\ *vb* **shrank** \'s(h)raŋk\ *also* **shrunk** \'s(h)rəŋk\ **shrunk** *or* **shrunk·en** \'s(h)rəŋ-kən\ [ME *shrinken*, fr. OE *scrincan*; akin to MD *schrinken* to draw back, L *curvus* curved — more at CROWN] *vi* **1 :** to contract or curl up the body or part of it **:** HUDDLE, COWER **2 a :** to contract to a less extent or compass **b :** to become smaller or more compacted **c :** to lose substance or weight **d :** to lessen in value **:** DWINDLE **3 :** to draw back ~ *vt* **:** to cause to contract or shrink; *specif* **:** to compact (cloth) by causing to contract when subjected to washing, boiling, steaming, or other processes **syn** see CONTRACT, RECOIL — **shrink·able** \'s(h)riŋ-kə-bəl\ *adj* — **shrink·er** *n*
²shrink *n* **1 :** the act of shrinking **2 :** SHRINKAGE
shrink·age \'shriŋ-kij, *esp South* 'sriŋ-\ *n* **1 :** the act or process of shrinking **2 :** the loss in weight of livestock during shipment and in the process of preparing the meat for consumption **3 :** the amount lost by shrinkage
shrinking violet *n* **:** a bashful or retiring person; *esp* **:** one who shrinks from public recognition of his merit
shrive \'shrīv, *esp South* 'srīv\ *vb* **shrived** *or* **shrove** \'s(h)rōv\ **shriv·en** \'s(h)riv-ən\ *or* **shrived** [ME *shriven*, fr. OE *scrīfan* to shrive, prescribe; akin OHG *scrīban* to write; both fr. a prehistoric WGmc word borrowed fr. L *scribere* to write — more at SCRIBE] *vt* **1 :** to minister the sacrament of penance to **2 :** PARDON, PURGE ~ *vi* **:** to confess one's sins esp. to a priest
shriv·el \'shriv-əl, *esp South* 'sriv-\ *vb* **shriv·eled** *or* **shriv·elled; shriv·el·ing** *or* **shriv·el·ling** \-(ə-)liŋ\ [origin unknown] *vi* **1 :** to draw into wrinkles esp. with a loss of moisture **2 :** to become reduced to inanition, helplessness, or inefficiency ~ *vt* **:** to cause to shrivel **:** WITHER
¹shroff \'shräf, 'shrȯf, *esp South* 'sräf, 'srȯf\ *n* [Hindi *ṣarrāf*, fr. Ar] **:** a banker or money changer in the Far East; *esp* **:** one who tests and evaluates coin
²shroff *vt* **:** to sort (coins) into good and bad pieces
Shrop·shire \'shräp-,shi(ə)r, -shər, *esp US* -,shī(ə)r, *esp South* 'sräp-\ *n* [*Shropshire* county, England] **:** any of an English breed of dark-faced hornless mutton-type sheep that yield a heavy fleece
¹shroud \'shrau̇d, *esp South* 'srau̇d\ *n* [ME, fr. OE *scrūd*; akin to OE *screāde* shred — more at SHRED] **1 :** burial garment **:** WINDING-SHEET, CEREMENT **2** *obs* **:** SHELTER, PROTECTION **3 :** something that covers, screens, or guards **4 a :** one of the ropes leading usu. in pairs from a ship's mastheads to give lateral support to the masts **b :** one of the cords that suspend the harness of a parachute from the canopy
²shroud *vt* **1 a** *archaic* **:** to cover for protection **b** *obs* **:** CONCEAL **2 a :** to cut off from view **:** SCREEN **b :** to veil under another appearance **3 :** to dress for burial ~ *vi, archaic* **:** to take or seek shelter
shroud–laid \-,lād\ *adj, of a rope* **:** composed of four strands and laid right-handed with a heart or core
Shrove·tide \'shrōv-,tīd, *esp South* 'srōv-\ *n* [ME *schroftide*, fr. *schrof-* (fr. *shriven* to shrive) + *tide*] **:** the period usu. of three days immediately preceding Ash Wednesday
Shrove Tuesday *n* [ME *schroftewesday*, fr. *schrof-* (as in *schroftide*) + *tewesday* Tuesday] **:** the Tuesday before Ash Wednesday
¹shrub \'shrəb, *esp South* 'srəb\ *n* [ME *schrobbe*, fr. OE *scrybb* brushwood; akin to Norw *skrubbebær* dwarf cornel] **:** a low usu. several-stemmed woody plant
²shrub *n* [Ar *sharāb* beverage] **1 :** a beverage that consists of an alcoholic liquor, fruit juice, fruit rind, and sugar **2 :** a beverage made by adding acidulated fruit juice to iced water
shrub·bery \'shrəb-(ə-)rē, *esp South* 'srəb-\ *n* **:** a planting or growth of shrubs
shrub·by \'shrəb-ē, *esp South* 'srəb-\ *adj* **1 :** consisting of or covered with shrubs **2 :** resembling a shrub
¹shrug \'shrəg, *esp South* 'srəg\ *vb* **shrugged; shrug·ging** [ME *schruggen*] *vi* **:** to raise or draw in the shoulders esp. to express indifference or aversion ~ *vt* **:** to lift or contract (the shoulders) esp. to express lack of interest or dislike
²shrug *n* **1 :** an act of shrugging **2 :** a woman's small waist-length or shorter jacket
shrug off *vt* **1 :** to brush aside **:** MINIMIZE **2 :** to shake off **3 :** to remove (a garment) by wriggling out of it
¹shuck \'shək\ *n* [origin unknown] **1 :** SHELL, HUSK: as **a :** the outer covering of a nut or of Indian corn **b :** the shell of an oyster or clam **2 :** something of little value ⟨not worth ~*s*⟩
²shuck *vt* **1 :** to strip of shucks **2 :** to peel off — **shuck·er** *n*
¹shud·der \'shəd-ər\ *vi* **shud·der·ing** \-(ə-)riŋ\ [ME *shoddren*; akin to OHG *skutten* to shake, Lith *kuteti* to shake up] **1 :** to tremble convulsively **:** SHIVER **2 :** QUIVER

2shudder *n* **:** an act of shuddering **:** TREMOR — **shud·dery** \-(ə-)rē\ *adj*

1shuf·fle \'shəf-əl\ *vb* **shuf·fling** \-(ə-)liŋ\ [perh. irreg. fr. *1shove*] *vt* **1 :** to mix in a mass confusedly **:** JUMBLE **2 :** to put or thrust aside or under cover **3 a :** to manipulate (as a pack of cards) with the real or ostensible purpose of causing a later appearance in random **b :** to move about, back and forth, or from one place to another **:** SHIFT **4 a :** to move (as the feet) by sliding along or back and forth without lifting **b :** to perform (as a dance) with a dragging, sliding step **~** *vi* **1 :** to work into or out of trickily **:** WORM **2 :** to act or speak in a shifty or evasive manner **3 a :** to move or walk in a sliding, dragging manner without lifting the feet **b :** to dance in a lazy nonchalant manner with sliding and tapping motions of the feet **c :** to execute in a perfunctory or clumsy manner **4 :** to mix playing cards or counters by shuffling — **shuf·fler** \-(ə-)lər\ *n*

2shuffle *n* **1 :** an evasion of the issue **:** EQUIVOCATION **2 a :** an act of shuffling **b :** a right or turn to shuffle **c :** JUMBLE **3 a :** a dragging sliding movement; *specif* **:** a sliding or scraping step in dancing **b :** a dance characterized by such a step

shuf·fle·board \'shəf-əl-,bō(ə)rd, -,bȯ(ə)rd\ *n* [alter. of obs. E

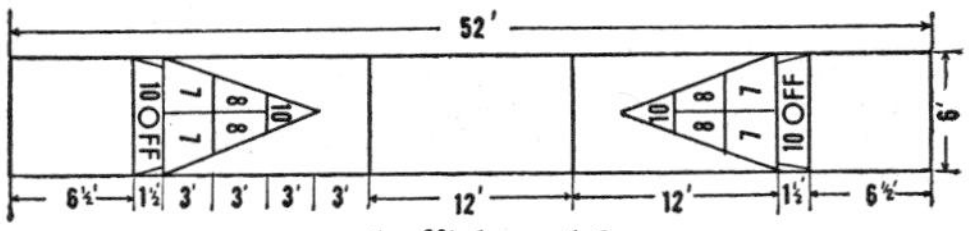

shuffleboard 2

shove-board] **1 :** a game in which players use long-handled cues to shove wooden disks into scoring beds of a diagram marked on a smooth surface **2 :** the diagram on which shuffleboard is played

shul \'shül\ *n* [Yiddish, fr. MHG *schuol*, lit., school] **:** SYNAGOGUE

shun \'shən\ *vt* **shunned; shun·ning** [ME *shunnen*, fr. OE *scunian*] **:** to avoid deliberately and esp. habitually **syn** see ESCAPE — **shun·ner** *n*

shun·pike \'shən-,pīk\ *n* **:** a side road used to avoid toll on a turnpike

1shunt \'shənt\ *vb* [ME *shunten* to flinch] *vt* **1 :** to turn off to one side **:** SHIFT; *specif* **:** to switch (as a train) from one track to another **2 :** to provide with or divert by means of an electrical shunt **~** *vi* **1 :** to move to the side **2 :** to travel back and forth — **shunt·er** *n*

2shunt *n* **:** a means or mechanism for turning or thrusting aside: as **a** *chiefly Brit* **:** a railroad switch **b :** a conductor joining two points in an electrical circuit so as to form a parallel or alternative path through which a portion of the current may pass (as for regulating the amount passing in the main circuit)

shunt winding *n* **:** a winding so arranged as to divide the armature current and lead a portion of it around the field-magnet coils — **shunt-wound** \'shənt-'waund\ *adj*

shush \'shəsh\ *n* [imit.] **:** a sibilant sound uttered to demand silence — **shush** *vt*

1shut \'shət\ *vb* **shut; shut·ting** [ME *shutten*, fr. OE *scyttan;* akin to OE *scēotan* to shoot — more at SHOOT] *vt* **1 a :** to move into position to close an opening ⟨~ the door⟩ **b :** to prevent passage to or from by closing doors or openings **:** CLOSE **c :** to forbid entrance into **:** BAR **2 :** to confine by or as if by enclosure ⟨~ him in the closet⟩ **3 :** to fasten with a lock or bolt **4 :** to close by bringing enclosing or covering parts together ⟨~ the eyes⟩ **5 :** to cause to cease or suspend operation **~** *vi* **:** to close itself or become closed

2shut *n* **1 :** the act or time of shutting **2 :** the line of union at a welded joint

shut·down \'shət-,daun\ *n* **:** the cessation or suspension of an activity (as work in a mine or factory)

shute *var of* CHUTE

shut-eye \'shət-,ī\ *n, slang* **:** SLEEP

shut-in \,shət-,in\ *adj* **1 :** confined to one's home or an institution by illness or incapacity **2 a :** BROODING, SECRETIVE **b :** WITHDRAWN — **shut-in** \'shət-,in\ *n*

shut·off \'shət-,ȯf\ *n* **1 :** something that shuts off **2 :** INTERRUPTION, STOPPAGE

shut out *vt* **1 :** to keep out **:** EXCLUDE **2 :** to prevent (an opponent) from scoring in a game or contest **3 :** to forestall the bidding of (bridge opponents) by making a high or preemptive bid

shut·out \'shət-,aut\ *n* **1 :** a game or contest in which one side fails to score **2 :** a preemptive bid in bridge

1shut·ter \'shət-ər\ *n, often attrib* **1 :** one that shuts **2 :** a usu. movable cover or screen for a window or door **3 :** a mechanical device of various forms attached to a camera to expose the film or plate by opening and closing an aperture **4 :** the movable louvers in a pipe organ by which the swell box is opened

2shutter *vt* **1 :** to close with or by shutters **2 :** to furnish with shutters

shut·ter·bug \'shət-ər-,bəg\ *n* **:** a photography enthusiast

1shut·tle \'shət-ᵊl\ *n, often attrib* [ME *shittle*, prob. fr. OE *scytel* bar, bolt; akin to ON *skutill* bolt, OE *scēotan* to shoot — more at SHOOT] **1 a :** a device used in weaving for passing or shooting the thread of the woof between the threads of the warp **b :** a spindle-shaped device holding the thread in tatting, knotting, or netting **c :** any of various sliding thread holders for the lower thread of a sewing machine that carry the lower thread through a loop of the upper thread to make a stitch **2 a :** a going back and forth regularly over a specified and often short route by a vehicle **b :** an established route used in a shuttle; *also* **:** a vehicle used in a shuttle

2shuttle *vb* **shut·tling** \'shət-liŋ, -ᵊl-iŋ\ **1 :** to move or travel back and forth frequently **2 :** to move by or as if by a shuttle

1shut·tle·cock \'shət-ᵊl-,käk\ *n* **:** a feathered cork that is struck with rackets and played back and forth (as in badminton)

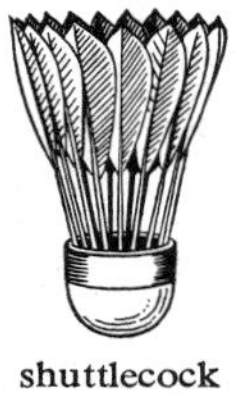
shuttlecock

2shuttlecock *vt* **:** to send or toss to and fro **:** BANDY

shut up *vt* **:** to cause (a person) to stop talking **~** *vi* **:** to cease writing or speaking

1shy \'shī\ *adj* **shi·er** *or* **shy·er** \'shī(-ə)r\ **shi·est** *or* **shy·est** \'shī-əst\ [ME *schey*, fr. OE *scēoh;* akin to OHG *sciuhen* to frighten off, OSlav *šćuti* to chase] **1 :** easily frightened **:** TIMID **2 :** disposed to avoid a person or thing **:** DISTRUSTFUL **3 :** hesitant in committing oneself **:** CHARY **4 :** marked by sensitive diffidence **:** BASHFUL **5 :** HIDDEN, SECLUDED **6 a :** very light **:** SCANT **b :** DEFICIENT, LACKING **7 :** DISREPUTABLE ⟨~ saloon⟩

syn BASHFUL, DIFFIDENT, MODEST, COY: SHY implies a timid reserve and a shrinking from familiarity or contact with others; BASHFUL implies a frightened or hesitant shyness characteristic of childhood and adolescence; DIFFIDENT stresses a distrust of one's own ability or opinion that causes hesitation in acting or speaking; MODEST suggests absence of undue confidence or conceit; COY implies an assumed or affected shyness

2shy *vi* **shied; shy·ing 1 :** to develop or show a sudden dislike or distaste **:** RECOIL ⟨*shied* from publicity⟩ **2 :** to start suddenly aside through fright or alarm

3shy *n, pl* **shies :** a sudden start aside (as of a horse)

4shy *vb* **shied; shy·ing** [perh. fr. *1shy*] **:** to throw with a jerk **:** FLING

5shy *n, pl* **shies 1 :** the act of shying **:** TOSS, THROW **2 :** a verbal fling **3 :** COCKSHY

Shy·lock \'shī-,läk\ *n* **1 :** a revengeful Jewish moneylender in Shakespeare's *The Merchant of Venice* **2 :** an extortionate creditor

shy·ly \'shī-lē\ *adv* **:** in a shy manner

shy·ness \-nəs\ *n* **:** the quality or state of being shy

shy·ster \'shī-stər\ *n* [prob. after *Scheuster fl*1840 Am attorney frequently rebuked in a New York court for pettifoggery] **:** one who is professionally unscrupulous esp. in the practice of law or politics **:** PETTIFOGGER

si \'sē\ *n* [It] **:** the 7th tone of the diatonic scale in solmization **:** TI

si·al·a·gog·ic \(,)sī-,al-ə-'gäj-ik\ *adj* [NL *sialagogus*, fr. Gk *sialon* saliva + *-agōgos* promoting the expulsion of; akin to L *spuere* to spit — more at SPEW, -AGOGUE] **:** promoting the flow of saliva — **si·al·a·gogue** \sī-'al-ə-,gäg\ *n*

si·a·mang \'sē-ə-,maŋ, sē-'am-əŋ\ *n* [Malay] **:** a black gibbon (*Symphalangus syndactylus*) of Sumatra that is the largest of the gibbons

1Si·a·mese \,sī-ə-'mēz, -'mēs\ *adj* [*Siam* (Thailand); in senses 2 & 3, fr. *Siamese twin*] **1 :** of, relating to, or characteristic of Thailand, the Thais, or their language **2 :** exhibiting great resemblance **:** very like **3** *not cap* **:** connecting two or more pipes or hose so as to permit discharge in a single stream

2Siamese *n, pl* **Siamese 1 :** THAI 1 **2 :** THAI 2

Siamese cat *n* **:** a slender blue-eyed short-haired domestic cat of a breed of oriental origin with pale fawn or gray body and darker ears, paws, tail, and face

Siamese twin *n* [fr. Chang †1874 and Eng †1874 congenitally united twins born in Siam] **1 :** one of a pair of congenitally united twins in man or lower animals **2 :** a double monster

1sib \'sib\ *adj* [ME, fr. OE *sibb*, fr. *sibb* kinship; akin to OHG *sippa* kinship, family, L *suus* one's own — more at SUICIDE] **:** related by blood **:** AKIN

2sib *n* **1 a :** KINDRED, RELATIVES **b :** a blood relation **:** KINSMAN **2 :** a brother or sister considered irrespective of sex; *broadly* **:** any plant or animal of a group sharing a corresponding degree of relation **3 :** a group of persons unilaterally descended from a real or supposed ancestor

Si·be·ri·an husky \(,)sī-,bir-ē-ən-\ *n* **:** any of a breed of medium-sized compact dogs developed as sled dogs in northeastern Siberia that in general resemble the larger Alaskan malamutes

1sib·i·lant \'sib-ə-lənt\ *adj* [L *sibilant-*, *sibilans*, prp. of *sibilare* to hiss, whistle, of imit. origin] **:** having, containing, or producing the sound of or a sound resembling that of the *s* or the *sh* in *sash* ⟨a ~ affricate⟩ ⟨a ~ snake⟩ — **sib·i·lant·ly** *adv*

2sibilant *n* **:** a sibilant speech sound (as English \s\, \z\, \sh\, \zh\, \ch(=tsh)\, or \j(=dzh)\)

sib·i·late \-,lāt\ *vb* [L *sibilatus*, pp. of *sibilare*] *vi* **1 :** HISS **2 :** to utter an initial sibilant **:** prefix an \s\-sound **~** *vt* **1 :** HISS **2 :** to pronounce with an initial sibilant **:** prefix an \s\-sound to — **sib·i·la·tion** \,sib-ə-'lā-shən\ *n*

sib·ling \'sib-liŋ\ *n* **:** SIB 2; *also* **:** one of two or more persons having one common parent

sib·yl \'sib-əl\ *n, often cap* [ME *sibile*, *sybylle*, fr. MF & L; MF *sibile*, fr. L *sibylla*, fr. Gk] **1 :** any of several prophetesses usu. accepted as 10 in number and credited to widely separate parts of the ancient world (as Babylonia, Egypt, Greece, and Italy) **2 a :** a female prophet **b :** FORTUNE-TELLER — **si·byl·ic** *or* **si·byl·lic** \sə-'bil-ik\ *adj* — **sib·yl·line** \'sib-ə-,līn, -,lēn\ *adj*

1sic \(')sik\ *chiefly Scot var of* SUCH

2sic *or* **sick** \'sik\ *vt* **sicced** *or* **sicked** \'sikt\ **sic·cing** *or* **sick·ing** [alter. of *seek*] **1 :** CHASE, ATTACK — usu. used as an imperative esp. to a dog ⟨~ 'em⟩ **2 :** to incite or urge to an attack, pursuit, or harassment **:** SET

3sic \'sik, 'sēk\ *adv* [L, so, thus — more at SO] **:** intentionally so written — used after a printed word or passage to indicate that it is intended exactly as printed or to indicate that it exactly reproduces an original ⟨said he seed [~] it all⟩

sic·ca·tive \'sik-ət-iv\ *n* [LL *siccativus* making dry, fr. L *siccatus*, pp. of *siccare* to dry, fr. *siccus* dry — more at SACK] **:** DRIER 2

sick \'sik\ *adj* [ME *sek*, *sik*, fr. OE *sēoc;* akin to OHG *sioh* sick, MIr *socht* depression] **1 a** (1) **:** affected with disease or ill health **:** AILING (2) **:** of, relating to, or intended for use in sickness ⟨~ pay⟩ ⟨a ~ ward⟩ **b :** NAUSEATED, QUEASY ⟨~ at one's stomach⟩ ⟨was ~ in the car⟩ **c :** MENSTRUATING **2 :** spiritually or morally unsound or corrupt **3 a :** sickened by strong emotion (as shame or fear) ⟨~ with fear⟩ ⟨worried ~⟩ **b :** SATIATED, SURFEITED ⟨~ of flattery⟩ **c :** DISGUSTED, CHAGRINED ⟨gossip that makes one ~⟩ **d :** depressed and longing for something ⟨~ for one's home⟩ **4 :** mentally or emotionally unsound or disordered **:** MORBID ⟨~ thoughts⟩ **5 :** lacking vigor **:** SICKLY: as **a :** badly outclassed ⟨looked ~ in the contest⟩ **b :** declining or inactive after a period of speculative activity ⟨grain futures were ~⟩ **c :** incapable of yielding a profitable crop esp. because of buildup of disease organisms ⟨clover-*sick* soils⟩

syn SICK, ILL mean not being in good health. SICK is the common term in American use but not in British use where ILL is preferred and SICK usu. restricted to mean violently nauseated

sick bay *n* **:** a compartment in a ship used as a dispensary and hospital; *broadly* **:** a place for the care of the sick or injured

sick·bed \'sik-,bed\ *n* **:** the bed upon which one lies sick

sick call *n* **1 :** a usu. daily formation at which individuals report as sick to the medical officer **2 :** the period during which sick call is held

sick·en \'sik-ən\ *vb* **sick·en·ing** \-(ə-)niŋ\ *vt* **1 :** to make sick

2 : to cause revulsion in as a result of weariness or satiety ~ *vi* **1 :** to become sick **2 :** to become weary or satiated ⟨~ of the rat race⟩

sick·en·er \'sik-(ə-)nər\ *n* **:** something that sickens

sick·en·ing *adj* **:** causing sickness **:** NAUSEATING — **sick·en·ing·ly** \-(ə-)niŋ-lē\ *adv*

sick·er \'sik-ər\ *adj* [ME *siker,* fr. OE *sicor;* akin to OHG *sichor* secure; both fr. a prehistoric WGmc word borrowed fr. L *securus* secure] *chiefly Scot* **:** SECURE, SAFE; *also* **:** DEPENDABLE — **sicker** *adv*

sick·er·ly \-lē\ *adv, chiefly Scot* **:** SICKER

sick headache *n* **:** MIGRAINE

sick·ish \'sik-ish\ *adj* **1** *archaic* **:** somewhat ill **:** SICKLY **2 :** somewhat nauseated **:** QUEASY **3 :** somewhat sickening ⟨a ~ odor⟩ — **sick·ish·ly** *adv* — **sick·ish·ness** *n*

sick·le \'sik-əl\ *n* [ME *sikel,* fr. OE *sicol;* akin to OHG *sichila* sickle; both fr. a prehistoric WGmc word borrowed fr. L *secula* sickle — more at SAW] **1 a :** an agricultural implement consisting of a curved metal blade with a short handle fitted on a tang **b :** the cutting mechanism (as of a reaper, combine, or mower) consisting of a bar with a series of cutting elements **2** *cap* **:** a group of six stars in the constellation Leo — **sickle** *adj*

sick leave *n* **1 :** an absence from work permitted because of illness **2 :** the number of days per year for which an employer agrees to pay employees who are sick

sick·le·bill \'sik-əl-,bil\ *n* **:** any of various birds (as a curlew or thrasher) with a strongly curved bill

sickle cell *n* **:** an abnormal red blood cell of crescent shape

sickle feather *n* **:** one of the long curved tail feathers of a cock

sick·li·ly \'sik-lə-lē\ *adv* **:** in a sickly manner

sick·li·ness \'sik-lē-nəs\ *n* **:** the quality or state of being sickly

1sick·ly \'sik-lē\ *adj* **1 :** somewhat unwell; *also* **:** habitually ailing **2 :** produced by or associated with sickness ⟨a ~ complexion⟩ ⟨a ~ appetite⟩ **3 :** producing or tending to disease **:** UNWHOLESOME ⟨a ~ climate⟩ **4 :** appearing as if sick: **a :** LANGUID, PALE ⟨a ~ flame⟩ **b :** WRETCHED, UNEASY ⟨a ~ smile⟩ **c :** lacking in vigor **:** WEAK ⟨a ~ plant⟩ ⟨~ beer⟩ **5 a :** tending to produce nausea ⟨a ~ odor⟩ **b :** MAWKISH — **sickly** *adv*

2sickly *vt* **:** to make sick or sickly

sick·ness \'sik-nəs\ *n* **1 :** ill health **:** ILLNESS **2 :** a specific disease **:** MALADY **3 :** NAUSEA, QUEASINESS

sick·room \'sik-,rüm, -,rủm\ *n* **:** a room in which a person is confined by sickness

sic pas·sim \'sik-'pas-əm, 'sēk-'päs-,im\ *adv* [L] **:** so throughout — used of a word or idea to be found throughout a book or a writer's work

sid·dur \'sid-,ủ(ə)r, 'sid-ər\ *n, pl* **sid·du·rim** \sə-'dủr-əm\ [MHeb *siddūr,* lit., order, arrangement] **:** a Jewish prayer book containing both Hebrew and Aramaic prayers used in the daily liturgy

1side \'sīd\ *n* [ME, fr. OE *sīde;* akin to OHG *sīta* side, OE *sīd* ample, wide, *sāwan* to sow — more at SOW] **1 :** the right or left part of the trunk of the body **2 :** a place, space, or direction with respect to a center or to a line of division (as of an aisle, river, or street) **3 :** a surface forming a border or face of an object **4 :** an outer portion of a thing considered as facing in a particular direction ⟨the upper ~ of a sphere⟩ **5 :** a slope or declivity of a hill or ridge **6 a :** a bounding line of a geometrical figure ⟨~ of a square⟩ **b :** one of the surfaces that delimit a solid; *esp* **:** one of the longer surfaces **c :** either surface of a thin object ⟨one ~ of a record⟩ ⟨right ~ of the cloth⟩ **7 :** the space beside one **8 :** the attitude or activity of one person or group with respect to another **:** PART **9 :** a body of partisans or contestants ⟨victory for neither ~⟩ **10 :** a line of descent traced through one's parent ⟨grandfather on his mother's ~⟩ **11 a :** an outer portion of something held to face in a particular direction **b :** an aspect or part of something held to be contrasted with some other aspect or part ⟨the better ~ of his nature⟩ **12 :** a position viewed as opposite to or contrasted with another ⟨two ~*s* to every question⟩ **13 :** one of the halves of the animal body on either side of the mesial plane **14 :** one longitudinal half of a hide **15** *Brit* **:** sideways spin imparted to a billiard ball **16 :** a sheet containing the lines and cues for a single theatrical role **syn** see PHASE — **on the side 1 :** in addition to the main portion **2 :** in addition to a principal occupation

2side *adj* **1 a :** of or relating to the side **b :** situated on the side ⟨~ window⟩ **2 a :** directed toward or from the side ⟨~ thrust⟩ ⟨~ wind⟩ **b :** INCIDENTAL, INDIRECT ⟨~ issue⟩ ⟨~ remark⟩ **c :** made on the side ⟨~ payment⟩ **d :** additional to the main portion ⟨~ order of french fries⟩

3side *vt* **1 :** to agree with **:** SUPPORT **2 :** to be side by side with **3 :** to set or put aside **:** clear away ⟨~ dishes⟩ **4 :** to furnish with sides or siding ⟨~ a house⟩ ~ *vi* **:** to take sides **:** join or form sides ⟨*sided* with the rebels⟩

4side *n* [obs. E *side* (proud, boastful)] **:** swaggering or arrogant manner **:** PRETENTIOUSNESS

side arm *n* **:** a weapon worn at the side or in the belt (as a sword, revolver, or bayonet)

side·arm \,sī-,därm\ *adj* **:** of, relating to, or constituting a baseball pitching style in which the arm is not raised above the shoulder and the ball is delivered with a sideways sweep of the arm between shoulder and hip ⟨~ delivery⟩ — **sidearm** \'sī-\ *adv*

side band *n* **:** the band of radio frequencies on either side of the carrier frequency produced by modulation

side·board \'sīd-,bō(ə)rd, -,bȯ(ə)rd\ *n* **:** a piece of dining-room furniture having compartments and shelves for holding articles of table service

side·burns \-,bərnz\ *n pl* [anagram of *burnsides*] **1 :** SIDE-WHISKERS; *esp* **:** short side-whiskers worn with a smooth chin **2 :** continuations of the hairline in front of the ears

side·car \-,kär\ *n* **1 :** a car attached to a motorcycle for a passenger seated abreast of the cyclist **2 :** a cocktail consisting of a liqueur with lemon juice and brandy

sid·ed \'sīd-əd\ *adj* **:** having sides often of a specified number or kind ⟨one-*sided*⟩ ⟨glass-*sided*⟩

side dish *n* **:** one of the foods subordinate to the main course

side effect *n* **:** a secondary and usu. adverse effect (as of a drug) ⟨toxic *side effects*⟩ — called also *side reaction*

side–glance \'sīd-,glan(t)s\ *n* **1 :** a glance directed to the side **2 :** a passing allusion **:** an indirect or slight reference

1side·hill \'sīd-,hil\ *n* **:** HILLSIDE ⟨horses grazing up the ~ —H.L. Davis⟩

2sidehill \,sīd-\ *adj* **:** used or located on or designed for a sidehill

side issue *n* **:** an issue apart from the main point

side·kick \'sīd-,kik\ *n* **:** a person closely associated with another as subordinate or partner

side·light \-,līt\ *n* **1 a :** light from the side **b :** incidental light or information **2 :** the red light on the port bow or the green light on the starboard bow carried by ships under way at night

side·line \-,līn\ *n* **1 :** a line at right angles to a goal line or end line and marking a side of a field of play for athletic games **2 a :** a line of goods sold in addition to one's principal line **b :** a business or activity pursued in addition to one's regular occupation **3 a :** the space immediately outside the lines along either side of an athletic field **b :** the standpoint of persons not immediately participating (as in an athletic contest)

side·lin·er \-,lī-nər\ *n* **:** one that remains on the sidelines during an activity **:** one that does not participate

1side·ling *or* **sid·ling** \'sīd-liŋ\ *adv* [ME *sidling,* fr. *1side* + *-ling*] **:** in a sidelong direction **:** SIDEWAYS

2sideling *or* **sidling** *adj* **1 :** directed toward one side **:** OBLIQUE **2 :** having an inclination **:** SLOPING ⟨~ ground⟩

1side·long \'sīd-,lȯŋ\ *adv* [alter. of *1sideling*] **1 :** OBLIQUELY, SIDEWAYS **2 :** on the side

2sidelong \,sīd-\ *adj* **1 :** lying or inclining to one side **:** SLANTING **2 a :** directed to one side ⟨~ looks⟩ **b :** indirect rather than straightforward

side·man \'sīd-,man\ *n* **:** a member of a band or orchestra and esp. a jazz or swing band or orchestra

side·piece \'sīd-,pēs\ *n* **:** a piece forming or contained in the side of something

sider- *or* **sidero-** *comb form* [MF, fr. L, fr. Gk *sidēr-, sidēro-,* fr. *sidēros*] **:** iron ⟨*sidero*lite⟩ ⟨*sidero*sis⟩

si·de·re·al \sī-'dir-ē-əl\ *adj* [L *sidereus,* fr. *sider-, sidus* star, constellation; akin to Lith *svidus* shining] **1 :** of or relating to stars or constellations **:** ASTRAL **2 :** expressed in relation to the heavens above

sidereal day *n* **:** the interval between two successive transits of the March equinox over the upper meridian of a place **:** 23 hours, 56 minutes, 4.09 seconds of mean solar time

sidereal hour *n* **:** the 24th part of a sidereal day

sidereal minute *n* **:** the 60th part of a sidereal hour

sidereal month *n* **:** the mean time of the moon's revolution in its orbit from a star back to the same star **:** 27 days, 7 hours, 43 minutes, 11.5 seconds of mean solar time

sidereal second *n* **:** the 60th part of a sidereal minute

sidereal time *n* **1 :** time based on the sidereal day **2 :** the hour angle of the March equinox at a place

sidereal year *n* **:** the time in which the earth completes one revolution in its orbit around the sun measured with respect to the fixed stars **:** 365 days, 6 hours, 9 minutes, and 9.54 seconds of solar time

1sid·er·ite \'sid-ə-,rīt\ *n* [G *siderit,* fr. Gk *sidēros* iron] **:** a native ferrous carbonate $FeCO_3$ that is a valuable iron ore

2siderite *n* [Gk *sidēros*] **:** a nickel-iron meteorite

sid·er·it·ic \,sid-ə-'rit-ik\ *adj* **:** of, relating to, or containing siderite

si·de·ro·lite \'sid-ə-rə-,līt, sī-'dir-ə-\ *n* **:** a stony iron meteorite

side·sad·dle \'sīd-,sad-ᵊl\ *n* **:** a saddle for women in which the rider sits with both legs on the same side of the horse — **sidesaddle** *adv*

side·show \-,shō\ *n* **1 :** a minor show offered in addition to a main exhibition (as of a circus) **2 :** an incidental diversion

side·slip \-,slip\ *vi* **1 :** to skid sideways — used esp. of an automobile **2 :** to slide sideways through the air in a downward direction in an airplane along an inclined lateral axis — **sideslip** *n*

side·spin \-,spin\ *n* [*1side* + *spin*] **:** a rotary motion that causes a ball to revolve horizontally

side·split·ting \-,split-iŋ\ *adj* **:** affecting the sides convulsively (as with laughter) ⟨a ~ yarn⟩

side step *n* **1 :** a step aside (as in boxing to avoid a blow) **2 :** a step taken sideways (as when climbing on skis)

side·step \'sīd-,step\ *vi* **1 :** to take a side step **2 :** to avoid an issue or decision ⟨men who know how to dodge, trim, and ~ —C. M.Fassett⟩ ~ *vt* **1 :** to move out of the way of **:** AVOID **2 :** BYPASS, EVADE **syn** see DODGE

side·stroke \-,strōk\ *n* **:** a swimming stroke in which the arms are worked forward and backward and the legs do a scissors kick

side·swipe \-,swīp\ *vt* **:** to strike with a glancing blow along the side ⟨*sideswiped* a parked car⟩ — **sideswipe** *n*

1side·track \-,trak\ *n* **1 :** SIDING **2 :** a position or condition of secondary importance to which one may be diverted

2sidetrack *vt* **1 :** to transfer to a railroad siding **2 a :** to turn aside from a purpose **:** DEFLECT **b :** to divert to a subordinate position; *also* **:** STULTIFY

side·walk \'sī-,dwȯk\ *n* **:** a walk for pedestrians at the side of a street

sidewalk superintendent *n* **:** a spectator at a building or demolition job

side·wall \'sī-,dwȯl\ *n* **1 :** a wall forming the side of something **2 :** the side of an automotive tire between the tread shoulder and the rim bead

side·ward \'sī-dwərd\ *or* **side·wards** \-dwərdz\ *adv* (*or adj*) **:** toward a side

side·way \'sī-,dwā\ *adv* (*or adj*) **:** SIDEWAYS

side·ways \-,dwāz\ *adv* (*or adj*) **1 :** from one side **2 :** with one side forward **3 :** obliquely or downward to one side; *also* **:** ASKANCE

side–wheel \,sīd-,hwēl, ,sī-,dwēl\ *adj* **:** of or constituting a steamer having a paddle wheel on each side

side–wheel·er \-ər\ *n* **:** a side-wheel steamer

side–whis·kers \'sīd-,hwis-kərz, 'sī-,dwis-\ *n pl* **:** whiskers on the side of the face usu. worn long

side·wind·er \'sī-,dwīn-dər\ *n* **1 :** a heavy swinging blow from the side **2 :** a small pale-colored desert rattlesnake (*Crotalus cerastes*) of the southwestern U.S. that moves by throwing the body forward in a series of loops

side·wise \ˈsī-ˌdwīz\ *adv* (*or adj*) : SIDEWAYS
sid·ing \ˈsīd-iŋ\ *n* **1** *archaic* : the taking of sides : PARTISANSHIP **2** : a short railroad track connected with the main track — called also *sidetrack* **3** : material (as boards or metal pieces) forming the exposed surface of outside walls of frame buildings
si·dle \ˈsīd-ᵊl\ *vb* **si·dling** \ˈsīd-liŋ, -ᵊl-iŋ\ [prob. back-formation fr. ²*sideling*] *vi* : to go or move with one side foremost esp. in a furtive advance ~ *vt* : to cause to move or turn sideways — **sidle** *n*
¹**siege** \ˈsēj\ *n* [ME *sege*, fr. OF, seat, blockade, fr. (assumed) VL *sedicum*, fr. *sedicare*, to settle, fr. L *sedēre* to sit — more at SIT] **1** *obs* : a seat of distinction : THRONE **2 a** : a military blockade of a city or fortified place to compel it to surrender **b** : a persistent attack (as of illness)
²**siege** *vt* : BESIEGE
Siege Perilous *n* : a seat at King Arthur's Round Table reserved for the knight destined to achieve the quest of the Holy Grail and fatal to any other occupying it
Sieg·fried \ˈsig-ˌfrēd, ˈsēg-\ *n* [G] : a hero in Germanic legend noted esp. for winning the hoard of the Nibelungs and for slaying a dragon
Siegfried line *n* [*Siegfried*, Germanic hero] : a line of German defensive fortifications facing the Maginot Line
si·en·na \sē-ˈen-ə\ *n* [It *terra di Siena*, lit., Siena earth, fr. *Siena*, Italy] : an earthy substance containing oxides of iron and usu. of manganese that is brownish yellow when raw and orange red or reddish brown when burnt and is used as a pigment
si·ero·zem \sē-ˌer-ə-ˈzhȯm\ *n* [Russ *serozem*, fr. *seryĭ* gray + *zemlya* earth] : any of a zonal group of soils brownish gray at the surface and lighter below, based in a carbonate or hardpan layer, and characteristic of temperate to cool arid regions
si·er·ra \sē-ˈer-ə\ *n* [Sp, lit., saw, fr. L *serra*] **1 a** : a range of mountains esp. with a serrated or irregular outline **b** : the country about a sierra **2** : any of various large fishes (genus *Scomberomorus*) that resemble mackerel (as a cero or Spanish mackerel)
Sierra — a communications code word for the letter *s*
si·er·ran \sē-ˈer-ən\ *adj* **1** : of or relating to a sierra ⟨~ foothills⟩ **2** *cap* : of or relating to the Sierra Nevada mountains of the western U.S.
Sierran *n* : a native or inhabitant of the region around the Sierra Nevada mountains
si·es·ta \sē-ˈes-tə\ *n* [Sp, fr. L *sexta* (*hora*) noon, lit., sixth hour — more at SEXT] : an afternoon nap or rest
sie·va bean \ˈsē-və-, ˈsiv-ē-\ *n* [origin unknown] : any of several small-seeded beans closely related to and sometimes classed as lima beans; *also* : the seed of a sieva bean
¹**sieve** \ˈsiv\ *n* [ME *sive*, fr. OE *sife*; akin to OHG *sib* sieve, Serb *sípiti* to drizzle] : a device with meshes or perforations through which finer particles of a mixture (as of ashes, flour, or sand) of various sizes are passed to separate them from coarser ones, through which the liquid is drained from liquid-containing material, or through which soft materials are forced for reduction to fine particles
²**sieve** *vb* : SIFT
sieve tube *n* : a tube consisting of an end to end series of thin-walled living cells characteristic of the phloem and held to function chiefly in translocation of organic solutes
sift \ˈsift\ *vb* [ME *siften*, fr. OE *siftan*; akin to OE *sife* sieve] *vt* **1 a** : to put through a sieve ⟨~ flour⟩ **b** : to separate or separate out by putting through a sieve **2 a** : to screen out the valuable or good : SELECT **b** : to study or investigate thoroughly : PROBE ~ *vi* **1** : to use a sieve **2** : SCREEN, SELECT — **sift·er** *n*
sift·ing *n* **1** : the act or process of sifting **2** *pl* : sifted material ⟨bran mixed with ~*s*⟩
sigh \ˈsī\ *vb* [ME *sihen*, alter. of *sichen*, fr. OE *sīcan*; akin to MD ver*siken* to sigh] *vi* **1** : to take a deep audible breath (as in weariness or grief) **2** : to make a sound like sighing ⟨wind ~*ing* in the branches⟩ **3** : GRIEVE, YEARN ⟨~*ing* for the days of his youth⟩ ~ *vt* **1** : to express by sighs **2** *archaic* : to utter sighs over : MOURN — **sigh** *n* — **sigh·er** \ˈsī(-ə)r\ *n*
¹**sight** \ˈsīt\ *n* [ME, fr. OE *gesiht* faculty or act of sight, thing seen; akin to OHG *gisiht* sight, OE *sēon* to see] **1** : something that is seen : SPECTACLE **2 a** : a thing regarded as worth seeing **b** : something ludicrous or disorderly in appearance **3** *chiefly dial* : a great number or quantity **4 a** : the process, power, or function of seeing; *specif* : the animal sense of which the end organ is the eye and by which the position, shape, and color of objects are perceived **b** : mental or spiritual perception **c** : mental view; *specif* : JUDGMENT **5 a** : the act of looking at or beholding **b** : INSPECTION, PERUSAL ⟨this letter is for your ~ only⟩ **c** : VIEW, GLIMPSE **d** : an observation to determine direction or position (as by a navigator) **6 a** : a perception of an object by the eye **b** : the range of vision **7** : presentation of a note or draft to the maker or draftee : DEMAND **8 a** : a device for guiding the eye (as in aiming a firearm or bomb) **b** : a device with a small aperture through which objects are to be seen and by which their direction is ascertained

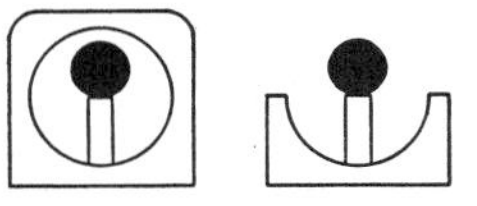

sight 8b: aiming patterns for peep sight and open sight

²**sight** *adj* **1** : based on recognition or comprehension without previous study **2** : payable on presentation
³**sight** *vt* **1** : to get or catch sight of **2** : to look at through or as if through a sight; *esp* : to test for straightness **3** : to aim by means of sights **4 a** : to equip with sights **b** : to adjust the sights of ~ *vi* **1** : to take aim **2** : to look carefully in a particular direction
sight draft *n* : a draft payable on presentation
sight·ed \ˈsīt-əd\ *adj* : having sight ⟨clear-*sighted*⟩
sight·less \-ləs\ *adj* **1** : lacking sight : BLIND **2** : INVISIBLE — **sight·less·ness** *n*
sight·li·ness \ˈsīt-lē-nəs\ *n* : the quality or state of being sightly
sight·ly \-lē\ *adj* **1** : pleasing to the sight : COMELY **2** : affording a fine view — **sightly** *adv*
sight–read \-ˌrēd\ *vb* [back-formation fr. *sight reader*] *vt* : to read (as a foreign language) or perform (music) without previous preparation or study ~ *vi* : to read at sight; *esp* : to play or sing music at sight — **sight reader** *n*
¹**sight–see·ing** \ˈsīt-ˌsē-iŋ\ *adj* : engaged in, devoted to, or used for seeing sights
²**sight–seeing** *n* : the act or pastime of seeing sights — **sight·se·er** \ˈsīt-ˌsē-ər, -ˌsi(-ə)r\ *n*
sight unseen *adv* : without inspection or appraisal
sig·il \ˈsij-əl, ˈsig-ˌil\ *n* [L *sigillum* — more at SEAL] **1** : SEAL, SIGNET **2** : a sign, word, or device of supposed occult power in astrology or magic
sig·ma \ˈsig-mə\ *n* [Gk] : the 18th letter of the Greek alphabet — symbol Σ or σ or ς
sig·mate \ˈsig-ˌmāt\ *adj* : having the shape or form of the Greek sigma or the letter S
sig·moid \-ˌmȯid\ *adj* [Gk *sigmoeidēs*, fr. *sigma*; fr. a common form of sigma shaped like the Roman letter C] **1 a** : curved like the letter C **b** : curved in two directions like the letter S **2** : of, relating to, or being the sigmoid flexure of the intestine — **sig·moi·dal·ly** \sig-ˈmȯid-ᵊl-ē\ *adv*
sigmoid flexure *n* **1** : an S-shaped curve **2** : the contracted and crooked part of the colon immediately above the rectum — called also *sigmoid colon*
¹**sign** \ˈsīn\ *n* [ME *signe*, fr. OF, fr. L *signum* mark, token, sign, image, seal; prob. akin to L *secare* to cut — more at SAW] **1 a** : a motion or gesture by which a thought is expressed or a command or wish made known **b** : SIGNAL 2a **c** : a fundamental linguistic unit that designates an object or relation or has a purely syntactic function **d** : one of a set of gestures used to represent language **2** : a mark having a conventional meaning and used in place of words or to represent a complex notion **3** : one of the 12 divisions of the zodiac **4 a** : a character (as a flat or sharp) used in musical notation; *specif* : SEGNO **b** : a character (as ÷, √‾‾, or ∫) indicating a mathematical operation; *also* : one of two characters + and — that form part of the symbol of a number and characterize it as positive or negative **5 a** : a lettered board or other display used to identify or advertise a place of business **b** : a posted command, warning, or direction **c** : SIGNBOARD **6 a** : something material or external that stands for or signifies something spiritual **b** : something that serves to indicate the presence or existence of something : TOKEN **c** : PRESAGE, PORTENT **d** : an objective evidence of plant or animal disease **7** : a remarkable event supposed to indicate the will of a deity : PRODIGY

syn SIGN, MARK, TOKEN, NOTE, SYMPTOM mean a sensible indication of what is not itself directly perceptible. SIGN applies to any indication to be perceived by the senses or the reason; MARK suggests something impressed on or inherently characteristic of a thing often in contrast to general outward appearance; TOKEN applies to something that serves as a proof of something intangible; NOTE suggests a distinguishing mark or characteristic; SYMPTOM suggests an outward indication of an inward change or condition as in the human body, a social group, or a mechanism

²**sign** *vb* [ME *signen*, fr. MF *signer*, fr. L *signare* to mark, sign, seal, fr. *signum*] *vt* **1 a** : to place a sign upon **b** : CROSS 2 **c** : to represent or indicate by a sign **2 a** : to affix a signature to : SUBSCRIBE **b** : to write down (one's name) **3** : to communicate by making a sign **4** : to engage or hire by securing the signature of on a contract of employment ~ *vi* **1** : to write one's name in token of assent, responsibility, or obligation **2** : to make a sign or signal — **sign·er** *n*
¹**sig·nal** \ˈsig-nᵊl\ *n* [ME, fr. MF, fr. ML *signale*, fr. LL, neut. of *signalis* of a sign, fr. L *signum*] **1** *archaic* : TOKEN, INDICATION **2 a** : an act, event, or watchword that has been agreed upon as the occasion of concerted action **b** : something that incites to action **3 a** : a sound or gesture made to give warning or command **b** : an object placed to convey notice or warning **4** : an object (as a flag on a pole) centered over a point so as to be observed from other positions in surveying **5 a** : an object used to transmit or convey information beyond the range of human voice **b** : the sound or image conveyed in telegraphy, telephony, radio, radar, or television **c** : a detectable physical quantity or impulse (as a voltage, current, or magnetic field strength) by which messages or information can be transmitted
²**signal** *vb* **sig·naled** *or* **sig·nalled**; **sig·nal·ing** *or* **sig·nal·ling** *vt* **1** : to notify by a signal **2 a** : to communicate by signals **b** : to constitute a characteristic feature of (a meaningful linguistic form) ~ *vi* : to make or send a signal — **sig·nal·er** *or* **sig·nal·ler** *n*
³**signal** *adj* [modif. of F *signalé*, pp. of *signaler* to distinguish, fr. OIt *segnalare* to signal, distinguish, fr. *segnale* signal, fr. ML *signale*] **1** : distinguished from the ordinary : OUTSTANDING ⟨~ achievement⟩ **2** : used in signaling ⟨~ beacon⟩ **syn** see NOTICEABLE
sig·nal·iza·tion \ˌsig-nᵊl-ə-ˈzā-shən\ *n* : the act of signalizing
sig·nal·ize \ˈsig-nᵊl-ˌīz\ *vt* [³*signal*] **1** : to make conspicuous : DISTINGUISH **2** : to point out carefully or distinctly **3** : to make signals to : SIGNAL; *also* : INDICATE **4** : to place traffic signals at or on ⟨~ an intersection⟩
sig·nal·ly \-nᵊl-ē\ *adv* : in a signal manner : NOTABLY
sig·nal·man \ˈsig-nᵊl-mən, -ˌman\ *n* : one who signals or works with signals
sig·nal·ment \-mənt\ *n* [F *signalement*, fr. *signaler*] : description by peculiar, appropriate, or characteristic marks; *specif* : the systematic description of a person for purposes of identification
sig·na·to·ry \ˈsig-nə-ˌtōr-ē, -ˌtȯr-\ *n* [L *signatorius* of sealing, fr. *signatus*, pp.] : a signer with another or others; *specif* : a government bound with others by a signed convention — **signatory** *adj*
sig·na·ture \ˈsig-nə-ˌchu̇(ə)r, -chər, -ˌt(y)u̇(ə)r\ *n* [MF or ML; MF, fr. ML *signatura*, fr. L *signatus*, pp. of *signare* to sign, seal] **1 a** : the name of a person written with his own hand **b** : the act of signing one's name **2** : a feature in the appearance or qualities of a natural object formerly held to indicate its utility in medicine **3 a** : a letter or figure placed usu. at the bottom of the first page on each sheet of printed pages (as of a book) as a direction to the binder in arranging and gathering the sheets **b** : the sheet itself which when folded becomes one unit of the book **4 a** : KEY SIGNATURE **b** : TIME SIGNATURE **5** : the part of a medical prescription which contains the directions to the patient **6** : a tune, musical number, or sound effect or in television a characteristic title or picture used to identify a program, entertainer, or orchestra
sign·board \ˈsīn-ˌbō(ə)rd, -ˌbȯ(ə)rd\ *n* : a board bearing a notice or sign
¹**sig·net** \ˈsig-nət\ *n* [ME, fr. MF, dim. of *signe* sign, seal] **1** : a seal used officially to give personal authority to a document in lieu of signature **2** : the impression made by or as if by a signet **3** : a small intaglio seal (as in a finger ring)
²**signet** *vt* : to stamp or authenticate with a signet

signet ring *n* **:** a finger ring engraved with a signet, seal, or monogram **:** SEAL RING

sig·ni·fi·able \'sig-nə-,fī-ə-bəl\ *adj* **:** capable of being represented by a sign or symbol

sig·nif·i·cance \sig-'nif-i-kən(t)s\ *n* **1 a :** something signified **b :** SUGGESTIVENESS **2 :** CONSEQUENCE **syn** see IMPORTANCE, MEANING

sig·nif·i·can·cy \-kən-sē\ *n* **:** SIGNIFICANCE

sig·nif·i·cant \-kənt\ *adj* [L *significant-, significans,* prp. of *significare* to signify] **1 :** having meaning; *esp* **:** SUGGESTIVE, EXPRESSIVE **2 :** suggesting or containing a disguised or special meaning **3 a :** IMPORTANT, WEIGHTY **b :** probably caused by something other than mere chance ⟨statistically ~ correlation between vitamin deficiency and disease⟩ **c :** essential to the determination of some larger element of a language **:** DISTINCTIVE ⟨the difference between the initial sounds of *keel* and *cool* is not ~ in English⟩ — **sig·nif·i·cant·ly** *adv*

significant figures *n pl* **:** figures of a number that end with the last figure to the right that is not zero or is a zero that is considered to be correct

sig·ni·fi·ca·tion \,sig-nə-fə-'kā-shən\ *n* **1 a :** the act or process of signifying by signs or other symbolic means **b :** a formal notification ⟨~ of a judicial decree⟩ **2 :** IMPORT **3** *chiefly dial* **:** IMPORTANCE, CONSEQUENCE **syn** see MEANING

sig·nif·i·ca·tive \sig-'nif-ə-,kāt-iv\ *adj* **1 :** INDICATIVE **2 :** SIGNIFICANT, SUGGESTIVE — **sig·nif·i·ca·tive·ly** *adv* — **sig·nif·i·ca·tive·ness** *n*

sig·nif·ics \sig-'nif-iks\ *n pl but sing or pl in constr* [*signify*] **:** SEMIOTIC, SEMANTICS

sig·ni·fi·er \'sig-nə-,fī(-ə)r\ *n* **:** one that signifies **:** SIGN

sig·ni·fy \'sig-nə-,fī\ *vb* [ME *signifien,* fr. OF *signifier,* fr. L *significare* to indicate, signify, fr. *signum* sign] *vt* **1 a :** MEAN, DENOTE **b :** IMPLY **2 :** to show esp. by a conventional token (as word, signal, or gesture) **~** *vi* **:** to have significance **:** MATTER

si·gnior *n* [It *signor*] **:** SIGNOR

sign language *n* **:** a system of hand gestures used for communication by the deaf or by people speaking different languages

sign manual *n, pl* **signs manual** ['*sign* + *manual,* adj.] **:** SIGNATURE; *specif* **:** the king's signature on a royal grant or charter placed at the top of the document

sign of aggregation : any of various conventional devices (as braces, brackets, parentheses, or vinculums) used in mathematics to indicate that two or more terms are to be treated as one quantity

sign off *vi* **:** to announce the end of a message, program, or broadcast and discontinue transmitting

sign of the cross : a gesture of the hand forming a cross esp. on forehead, shoulders, and breast to profess Christian faith or invoke divine protection or blessing

si·gnor \sēn-'yȯ(ə)r, -'yō(ə)r\ *n, pl* **signors** *or* **si·gno·ri** \sēn-'yōr-(,)ē, -'yȯr-\ [It *signore, signor,* fr. ML *senior* superior, lord — more at SENOR] **:** a usu. Italian man of rank or gentility — used as a title equivalent to *Mister*

si·gno·ra \sēn-'yōr-ə, -'yȯr-\ *n, pl* **signoras** *or* **si·gno·re** \-'yōr-(,)ā, -'yȯr-\ [It, fem. of *signore, signor*] **:** an Italian married woman usu. of rank or gentility — used as a title equivalent to *Mrs.*

si·gno·re \sēn-'yōr-(,)ā, -'yȯr-\ *n, pl* **si·gno·ri** \-'yōr-(,)ē, -'yȯr-\ [It] **:** SIGNOR

si·gno·ri·na \,sē-nyə-'rē-nə\ *n, pl* **signorinas** *or* **si·gno·ri·ne** \-(,)nā\ [It, fr. dim. of *signora*] **:** an unmarried Italian woman — used as a title equivalent to *Miss*

si·gno·ri·no \-(,)nō\ *n, pl* **si·gno·ri·ni** \-(,)nē\ [It, fr. dim. of *signore*] **:** a young Italian esp. of rank — used as a title equivalent to *Master*

si·gnory *or* **si·gniory** \'sē-nyə-rē\ *n* [ME *signorie,* fr. MF *seigneurie*] **:** SEIGNIORY

sign·post \'sīn-,pōst\ *n* **:** a post bearing a sign or signs; *specif* **:** a post (as at the fork of a road) with signs on it to direct travelers

Sig·urd \'sig-,u̇(ə)rd, 'sig-ərd\ *n* [ON *Sigurthr*] **:** a hero in Norse mythology who slays the dragon Fafnir

sike \'sīk\ *n* [ME, fr. OE *sīc;* akin to ON *sīk* sike, OE *sicerian* to trickle] *dial chiefly Brit* **:** a small stream; *esp* **:** one that dries up in summer **:** BROOK; *also* **:** DITCH

Sikh \'sēk\ *n* [Hindi, lit., disciple] **:** an adherent of a monotheistic religion of India founded about 1500 by a Hindu under Islamic influence and marked by rejection of idolatry and caste — **Sikh** *adj* — **Sikh·ism** \'sē-,kiz-əm\ *n*

si·lage \'sī-lij\ *n* [short for *ensilage*] **:** fodder converted into succulent feed for livestock through processes of anaerobic acid fermentation (as in a silo)

sild \'sil(d)\ *n, pl* **sild** *or* **silds** [Norw] **:** a young herring other than a brisling that is canned as a sardine in Norway

1si·lence \'sī-lən(t)s\ *n* [ME, fr. OF, fr. L *silentium,* fr. *silent-, silens*] **1 :** forbearance from speech or noise **:** MUTENESS — often used interjectionally **2 :** absence of sound or noise **:** STILLNESS **3 :** absence of mention: **a :** OBLIVION, OBSCURITY **b :** SECRECY

2silence *vt* **1 :** to compel or reduce to silence **:** STILL **2 :** to restrain from expression **:** SUPPRESS **3 :** to cause to cease hostile firing by return fire or bombing

si·lenc·er \-lən-sər\ *n* **:** one that silences: as **a :** *chiefly Brit* **:** the muffler of an internal-combustion engine **b :** a silencing device for small arms

si·lent \'sī-lənt\ *adj* [L *silent-, silens,* fr. prp. of *silēre* to be silent; akin to Goth ana*silan* to subside, L *sinere* to let go, lay — more at SITE] **1 :** making no utterance: **a :** MUTE, SPEECHLESS **b :** indisposed to speak **:** TACITURN **2 :** free from sound or noise **:** STILL **3 :** performed or borne without utterance **:** UNSPOKEN **4 a :** making no mention ⟨history is ~ about this man⟩ **b :** not mentioned **c :** taking no active part in the conduct of a business ⟨~ partner⟩ **5 :** UNPRONOUNCED ⟨~ *b* in *doubt*⟩ **6 :** lacking spoken dialogue ⟨~ drama⟩ — **si·lent·ly** *adv*

syn TACITURN, RETICENT, RESERVED, SECRETIVE: SILENT implies a habit of saying no more than is absolutely necessary; TACITURN suggests a temperamental disinclination to talk; RETICENT implies a reluctance to speak out or at length esp. about one's personal affairs; RESERVED suggests the restraining influence of caution or formality checking easy familiar talk; SECRETIVE implies an undue caution or reticence about ordinary matters

silent butler *n* **:** a receptacle with hinged lid for collecting table crumbs and the contents of ash trays

si·lents \'sī-lən(t)s\ *n pl* **:** motion pictures without spoken dialogue

si·le·nus \sī-'lē-nəs\ *n, pl* **si·le·ni** \-,nī\ [L, fr. Gk *silēnos,* fr. *Silēnos* foster father of Dionysus] **:** a minor woodland deity and companion of Dionysus in ancient Greek mythology with a horse's ears and tail

si·le·sia \sī-'lē-zh(ē-)ə, sə-, -sh(ē-)ə\ *n* [*Silesia,* former Prussian province] **1** *archaic* **:** a linen cloth of Silesian origin **2 :** a soft sturdy lightweight cotton twill

si·lex \'sī-,leks\ *n* [L *silic-, silex* flint, quartz — more at SHELL] **:** silica or a siliceous powder (as tripoli) esp. for use as a filler in paints or wood or as a dental material

Silex *trademark* — used for a vacuum coffee maker

1sil·hou·ette \,sil-ə-'wet\ *n* [F, fr. Étienne de *Silhouette* †1767 F controller general of finances; fr. his petty economies] **:** a representation of the outlines of an object filled in with black or some other uniform color **syn** see OUTLINE

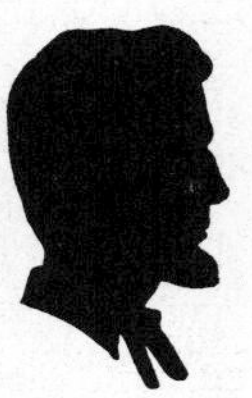

silhouette

2silhouette *vt* **:** to represent by a silhouette; *also* **:** to project upon a background like a silhouette

silic- *or* **silico-** *comb form* [*silicon*] **:** silicon ⟨*silicone*⟩

sil·i·ca \'sil-i-kə\ *n* [NL, fr. L *silic-, silex* flint, quartz] **:** silicon dioxide SiO_2 occurring in crystalline, amorphous, and impure forms (as in quartz, opal, and sand respectively)

silica gel *n* **:** colloidal silica resembling coarse white sand in appearance but possessing many fine pores and therefore extremely adsorbent

sil·i·cate \'sil-ə-,kāt, 'sil-i-kət\ *n* [*silicic (acid)*] **:** a salt or ester derived from a silicic acid

si·li·ceous *or* **si·li·cious** \sə-'lish-əs\ *adj* [L *siliceus* of flint, fr. *silic-, silex* flint, quartz] **:** of, relating to, or containing silica or a silicate ⟨~ limestone⟩

silici- *comb form* [NL *silica*] **:** silica ⟨*siliciferous*⟩

si·lic·ic \sə-'lis-ik\ *adj* [NL *silica* & NL *silicium* silicon (fr. *silica*)] **:** of, relating to, or derived from silica or silicon

silicic acid *n* **:** any of various weakly acid substances obtained as gelatinous masses by treating silicates with acids

sil·i·cic·o·lous \,sil-ə-'sik-ə-ləs\ *adj* **:** growing or thriving in siliceous soil ⟨~ plants⟩

sil·i·cide \'sil-ə-,sīd\ *n* [ISV] **:** a binary compound of silicon usu. with a more electropositive element or radical

sil·i·cif·er·ous \,sil-ə-'sif-(ə-)rəs\ *adj* **:** producing, containing, or united with silica

si·lic·i·fi·ca·tion \sə-,lis-ə-fə-'kā-shən\ *n* **:** the act or process of silicifying **:** the state of being silicified

silicified wood *n* **:** chalcedony in the form of petrified wood

si·lic·i·fy \sə-'lis-ə-,fī\ *vt* **:** to convert into or impregnate with silica **~** *vi* **:** to become silicified

sil·i·cle \'sil-i-kəl\ *n* [L *silicula,* dim. of *siliqua*] **:** a broad short silique

sil·i·con \'sil-i-kən, 'sil-ə-,kän\ *n* [NL *silica* + E *-on* (as in *carbon*)] **:** a tetravalent nonmetallic element that occurs combined as the most abundant element next to oxygen in the earth's crust and is used esp. in alloys — see ELEMENT table

sil·i·cone \'sil-ə-,kōn\ *n* [*silic-* + *-one*] **:** any of various polymeric organic silicon compounds obtained as oils, greases, or plastics and used esp. for water-resistant and heat-resistant lubricants, varnishes, binders, and electric insulators

silicone rubber *n* **:** rubber made from silicone elastomers and noted for its retention of flexibility, resilience, and tensile strength over a wide temperature range

sil·i·co·sis \,sil-ə-'kō-səs\ *n* [NL] **:** a condition of massive fibrosis of the lungs marked by shortness of breath and caused by prolonged inhalation of silica dusts — **sil·i·cot·ic** \-'kät-ik\ *adj or n*

si·lic·u·lose \sə-'lik-yə-,lōs\ *adj* [NL *siliculosus,* fr. *silicula*] **1 :** bearing silicles **2 :** of the form or appearance of a silicle

si·lique \sə-'lēk\ *n* [F, fr. NL *siliqua,* fr. L, pod, husk; akin to L *silic-, silex* flint — more at SHELL] **:** a narrow elongated two-valved usu. many-seeded capsule characteristic of the mustard family that opens by sutures at either margin and has two parietal placentas — **sil·i·quose** \'sil-ə-,kwōs\ *or* **sil·i·quous** \-kwəs\ *adj*

1silk \'silk\ *n, often attrib* [ME, fr. OE *seolc;* prob. of Baltic or Slav origin; akin to OPruss *silkas* silk, OSlav *shelkŭ*] **1 :** a fine continuous protein fiber produced by various insect larvae usu. for cocoons; *esp* **:** a lustrous tough elastic fiber produced by silkworms and used for textiles **2 :** thread, yarn, or fabric made from silk filaments **3 a :** a garment of silk **b** (1) **:** a distinctive silk gown worn by a King's or Queen's Counsel (2) **:** a King's or Queen's Counsel **c** *pl* **:** the colored cap and blouse of a jockey or harness horse driver made in the registered racing color of his stable **4 a :** a filament resembling silk (as that produced by a spider) **b :** silky material ⟨milkweed ~⟩; *esp* **:** the styles of an ear of Indian corn **5 :** PARACHUTE

2silk *vi, of corn* **:** to develop the silk

silk·aline *or* **silk·oline** \,sil-kə-'lēn\ *n* ['*silk* + *-oline* (as in *crinoline*)] **:** a soft light cotton fabric with a smooth lustrous finish like that of silk

silk cotton *n* **:** the silky or cottony covering of seeds of various silk-cotton trees; *esp* **:** KAPOK

silk–cotton tree *n* **:** any of various tropical trees (family Bombacaceae, the silk-cotton family) with palmate leaves and large fruits with the seeds enveloped by silk cotton; *esp* **:** CEIBA

silk·en \'sil-kən\ *adj* **1 :** made or consisting of silk **2 :** resembling silk: as **a :** SOFT, LUSTROUS **b** (1) **:** agreeably smooth **:** HARMONIOUS (2) **:** INGRATIATING **3 a :** dressed in silk ⟨~ ankles⟩ **b :** LUXURIOUS

silk floss *n* **:** KAPOK

silk grass *n* **:** any of several strong lustrous commercial fibers from bromeliads

silk hat *n* **:** a hat with a tall cylindrical crown and a silk-plush finish worn by men as a dress hat

silk·i·ly \'sil-kə-lē\ *adv* **:** in a silky manner

silk·i·ness \-kē-nəs\ *n* **:** the quality or state of being silky

silk oak *n* **:** any of various Australian timber trees (family Protaceae

and esp. genus *Grevillea*) with mottled wood used in cabinetmaking and veneering — called also *silky oak*
silk–screen process *n* **:** a stencil process in which coloring matter is forced onto the material to be printed through the meshes of a silk or organdy screen so prepared as to have pervious printing areas and impervious nonprinting areas
silk–stock·ing \'silk-'stäk-iŋ\ *adj* **1 :** fashionably dressed **:** LUXURIOUS ⟨a *silk-stocking* audience⟩ **2 :** ARISTOCRATIC, WEALTHY **3 :** of or relating to the American Federalist party
silk stocking *n* **1 :** a fashionably dressed person **2 :** an aristocratic or wealthy person **3 :** FEDERALIST 2
silk·weed \'sil-,kwēd\ *n* **1 :** MILKWEED **2 :** any of several smooth filamentous algae
silk·worm \'sil-,kwərm\ *n* **:** a moth larva that spins a large amount of strong silk in constructing its cocoon; *esp* **:** the rough wrinkled hairless yellowish caterpillar of an Asiatic moth (*Bombyx mori*)
silky \'sil-kē\ *adj* **1 a :** resembling or consisting of silk **b :** INGRATIATING **2 :** having or covered with fine soft hairs, plumes, or scales
sill \'sil\ *n* [ME *sille*, fr. OE *syll*; akin to OHG *swelli* beam, threshold, Gk *selis* crossbeam] **1 :** a horizontal piece (as a timber) that forms the lowest member or one of the lowest members of a framework or supporting structure: as **a :** the horizontal member at the base of a window **b :** the timber or stone at the foot of a door **:** THRESHOLD **2 :** a tabular body of igneous rock injected while molten between other rocks
sillabub *var of* SYLLABUB
sil·ler \'sil-ər\ *chiefly dial var of* SILVER
sil·li·ly \'sil-ə-lē\ *adv* **:** in a silly manner
sil·li·man·ite \'sil-ə-mə-,nīt\ *n* [Benjamin *Silliman* †1864 Am geologist] **:** a brown, grayish, or pale green mineral Al_2SiO_5 that consists of an aluminum silicate in orthorhombic crystals often occurring in fibrous or columnar forms
sil·li·ness \'sil-ē-nəs\ *n* **1 :** the quality or state of being silly **2 :** a silly practice
sil·ly \'sil-ē\ *adj* [ME *sely, silly* happy, innocent, pitiable, feeble, fr. (assumed) OE *sǣlig*, fr. OE *sǣl* happiness; akin to OHG *sālig* happy, L *solari* to console, Gk *hilaros* cheerful] **1** *archaic* **:** HELPLESS, WEAK **2 a :** RUSTIC, PLAIN **b** *obs* **:** lowly in station **:** HUMBLE **3 a :** weak in intellect **:** FOOLISH **b :** contrary to reason **:** ABSURD **c :** TRIFLING, FRIVOLOUS **syn** see SIMPLE — **silly** *n or adv*
silly season *n* **:** a period (as late summer) when newspapers must resort to minor or fantastic matters for lack of major news stories
si·lo \'sī-(,)lō\ *n* [Sp] **1 :** a trench, pit, or esp. a tall cylinder (as of wood or concrete) usu. sealed to exclude air and used for making and storing silage **2 :** a deep bin for storing material or for housing a missile underground
Si·lo·am \sī-'lō-əm, sə-, 'sī-,lōm\ *n* [Gk *Silōam*, fr. Heb *Shīlōaḥ*] **:** a pool of water near Jerusalem
si·lox·ane \sə-'läk-,sān\ *n* [*sil*icon + *ox*ygen + meth*ane*] **:** any of various compounds containing alternate silicon and oxygen atoms in either a linear or cyclic arrangement usu. with one or two organic groups attached to each silicon atom
1**silt** \'silt\ *n* [ME *cylte*, prob. of Scand origin; akin to Dan *sylt* salt marsh; akin to OHG *sulza* salt marsh, OE *sealt* salt] **1 :** loose sedimentary material with rock particles usu. 1/20 millimeter or less in diameter; *also* **:** soil containing 80 percent or more of such silt and less than 12 percent of clay **2 :** a deposit of sediment (as by a river) — **silty** \'sil-tē\ *adj*
2**silt** *vi* **:** to become choked or obstructed with silt ~ *vt* **:** to choke, cover, or obstruct with silt or mud — **silt·ation** \sil-'tā-shən\ *n*
Sil·u·res \'sil-yə-,rēz\ *n* [L] **:** a people of ancient Britain described by Tacitus as occupying chiefly southern Wales
Si·lu·ri·an \sī-'lu̇r-ē-ən, sə-\ *adj* [L *Silures*] **1 :** of or relating to the Silures or their place of habitation **2 :** of, relating to, or being a period of the Paleozoic era between the Ordovician and Devonian or the corresponding system of rocks marked by the beginning of coral-reef building and the appearance of some great crustaceans — **Silurian** *n*
sil·u·roid \'sil-yə-,rȯid\ *n* [deriv. of Gk *silouros*, a large river fish] **:** any of a suborder (Siluroidea) of fishes **:** CATFISH — **siluroid** *adj*
sil·va \'sil-və\ *n* [NL, fr. L, wood, forest] **1 :** the forest trees of a region or country **2 :** a description of or treatise on the trees of a region — **sil·van** \-vən\ *adj*
silvan *var of* SYLVAN
1**sil·ver** \'sil-vər\ *n* [ME, fr. OE *seolfor*; akin to OHG *silbar* silver] **1 :** a white metallic element that is sonorous, ductile, very malleable, capable of a high degree of polish, and chiefly univalent in compounds, and that has the highest thermal and electric conductivity of any substance — see ELEMENT table **2 :** silver as a commodity ⟨the value of ~ has risen⟩ **3 :** coin made of silver **4 a :** flatware used at table and made of sterling or plated silver **b :** hollow ware made of silver for table use **5 :** a nearly neutral slightly brownish medium gray
2**silver** *adj* **1 :** made of silver **2 :** resembling silver: as **a :** having a white lustrous sheen **b :** giving a soft resonant sound **c :** eloquently persuasive ⟨~ tongue⟩ **3 :** consisting of or yielding silver **4 :** of, relating to, or characteristic of silver ⟨~ legislation⟩ **5 :** advocating the use of silver as a standard of currency
3**silver** *vt* **sil·ver·ing** \'silv-(ə-)riŋ\ **1 a :** to cover with silver (as by electroplating) **b :** to coat with a substance (as a metal) resembling silver ⟨~ a glass with an amalgam⟩ **2 a :** to give a silvery luster to **b :** to make white like silver ⟨time had ~*ed* her hair⟩ — **sil·ver·er** \'sil-vər-ər\ *n*
silver age *n* **:** an historical period of achievement secondary to that of a golden age
silver bell *n* **:** a medium-sized tree (*Halesia carolina*) of the storax family of the southeastern U.S. cultivated for its bell-shaped white flowers
sil·ver·ber·ry \'sil-vər-,ber-ē\ *n* **:** a silvery No. American shrub (*Elaeagnus argentea*) related to the buffalo berry
silver bromide *n* **:** a compound AgBr that is extremely sensitive to light and is much used in the preparation of sensitive emulsion coatings for photographic materials
silver certificate *n* **:** a certificate issued against the deposit of silver coin that is legal tender for all public and private debts and for public charges, taxes, duties, and dues in the U.S. and its possessions
silver chloride *n* **:** a compound AgCl sensitive to light and used esp. for photographic materials
silver cord *n* [*The Silver Cord* (1926), play by Sidney Howard] **:** the emotional tie between mother and child
sil·ver·fish \'sil-vər-,fish\ *n* **1 :** any of various silvery fishes (as a tarpon or silversides) **2 :** any of various small wingless insects (order Thysanura); *esp* **:** one (*Lepisma saccharina*) found in houses and sometimes injurious to sized papers or starched clothes
silver fox *n* **:** a color phase of the common red fox in which the pelt is black tipped with white and which is a genetic variant that can breed true
sil·ver·i·ness \'silv-(ə-)rē-nəs\ *n* **:** the quality or state of being silvery
silver iodide *n* **:** a compound AgI that darkens on exposure to light and is used in photography, rainmaking, and medicine
silver–lace vine *n* **:** a twining Asiatic perennial (*Polygonum aubertii*) of the buckwheat family widely grown for its racemes of fragrant greenish flowers
silver lining *n* **1 :** a white edge on a cloud **2 :** a consoling or hopeful prospect
sil·ver·ly \'sil-vər-lē\ *adv* **:** with silvery appearance or sound
sil·vern \'sil-vərn\ *adj* **1 :** made of silver **2 :** resembling or characteristic of silver **:** SILVERY
silver nitrate *n* **:** an irritant compound $AgNO_3$ that in contact with organic matter turns black and is used as a chemical reagent, in photography, and in medicine esp. as an antiseptic
silver paper *n* **:** a metallic paper with a coating or lamination resembling silver — called also *tinfoil*
silver perch *n* **:** any of various somewhat silvery fishes that resemble perch: as **a :** WHITE PERCH 1 **b :** WHITE CRAPPIE
silver plate *n* **1 :** a plating of silver **2 :** domestic flatware and hollow ware of silver or of a silver-plated base metal
silver protein *n* **:** any of several colloidal light-sensitive preparations of silver and protein used in aqueous solution on mucous membranes as antiseptics
silver screen *n* **1 :** a motion-picture screen **2 :** MOTION PICTURES
sil·ver·sides \'sil-vər-,sīdz\ *n pl but sing or pl in constr* **1 :** any of various small fishes (family Atherinidae) with a silvery stripe along each side of the body **2 :** any of various freshwater minnows (as of the genus *Notropis*)
sil·ver·smith \-,smith\ *n* **:** an artisan who makes articles of silverware
silver spoon *n* **:** WEALTH; *esp* **:** inherited wealth ⟨born with a *silver spoon* in his mouth⟩
silver standard *n* **:** a monetary standard under which the currency unit is defined by a stated quantity of silver
Silver Star Medal *n* **:** a U.S. military decoration awarded for gallantry in action
sil·ver–tongued \,sil-vər-'təŋd\ *adj* **:** ELOQUENT
sil·ver·ware \'sil-vər-,wa(ə)r, -,we(ə)r\ *n* **:** SILVER PLATE, FLATWARE
sil·ver·weed \-,wēd\ *n* **:** any of various somewhat silvery plants; *esp* **:** a cinquefoil (as the European *Potentilla anserina*) with leaves silvery or white-tomentose beneath
sil·very \'silv-(ə-)rē\ *adj* **1 :** having the soft clear musical tone of silver **2 :** having the luster of silver **3 :** containing or consisting of silver
sil·vi·cal \'sil-vi-kəl\ *adj* **:** of or relating to silvics
sil·vic·o·lous \sil-'vik-ə-ləs\ *adj* [L *silvicola* inhabitant of a wood, fr. *silva* wood + *colere* to inhabit — more at WHEEL] **:** living in woodlands
sil·vics \'sil-viks\ *n pl but sing in constr* [NL *silva*] **:** the study of the life history, characteristics, and ecology of forest trees esp. in stands
sil·vi·cul·tur·al \,sil-və-'kəlch-(ə-)rəl\ *adj* **:** of or relating to silviculture — **sil·vi·cul·tur·al·ly** \-ē\ *adv*
sil·vi·cul·ture \'sil-və-,kəl-chər\ *n* [F, fr. L *silva, sylva* forest + *cultura* culture] **:** a phase of forestry dealing with the development and care of forests — **sil·vi·cul·tur·ist** \,sil-və-'kəlch-(ə-)rəst\ *n*
si·mar \si-'mär\ *n* [F *simarre*] **:** a loose robe for women
Sim·chas To·rah \,sim-kä-'stōr-ə, -'stȯr-\ *n* [Heb *śimḥath tōrāh* rejoicing of the Torah] **:** a Jewish holiday observed on the 23d of Tishri in celebration of the completion of the annual reading of the Torah
Sim·e·on \'sim-ē-ən\ *n* [LL, fr. Gk *Symeōn*, fr. Heb *Shim'ōn*] **1 :** a son of Jacob and ancestor of one of the tribes of Israel **2 :** a devout man of Jerusalem held to have uttered the Nunc Dimittis on seeing the infant Jesus in the temple
1**sim·i·an** \'sim-ē-ən\ *adj* [L *simia* ape, fr. *simus* snub-nosed, fr. Gk *simos*] **:** of, relating to, or resembling monkeys or apes
2**simian** *n* **:** MONKEY, APE
sim·i·lar \'sim-(ə-)lər\ *adj* [F *similaire*, fr. L *similis* like, similar — more at SAME] **1 :** marked by correspondence or resemblance **2 :** alike in substance or structure **:** IDENTICAL **3 :** not differing in shape but only in size or position ⟨~ triangles⟩ ⟨~ polygons⟩ — **sim·i·lar·ly** *adv*
syn SIMILAR, ALIKE, AKIN, ANALOGOUS, PARALLEL, HOMOGENEOUS, UNIFORM mean closely resembling each other. SIMILAR implies the possibility of being mistaken for each other; ALIKE implies having close resemblance even though obviously distinct; AKIN suggests essential rather than superficial likeness; ANALOGOUS applies to things susceptible of comparison even though belonging to different categories; PARALLEL suggests a marked likeness in the course or development of two things; HOMOGENEOUS implies likeness of a number of things in kind, sort, or class; UNIFORM implies lack of variance or variation in any instances of a number or group of things
sim·i·lar·i·ty \,sim-ə-'lar-ət-ē\ *n* **1 :** the quality or state of being similar **:** RESEMBLANCE **2 :** a comparable aspect **:** CORRESPONDENCE **syn** see LIKENESS
sim·i·le \'sim-ə-(,)lē\ *n* [L, comparison, fr. neut. of *similis*] **:** a figure of speech comparing two unlike things that is often introduced by *like* or *as* (as in *cheeks like roses*)
si·mil·i·tude \sə-'mil-ə-,t(y)üd\ *n* [ME, fr. MF, resemblance, likeness, fr. L *similitudo*, fr. *similis*] **1 a :** COUNTERPART, DOUBLE **b :** a visible likeness **:** IMAGE **2 :** an imaginative comparison **:** ALLEGORY **3 a :** RESEMBLANCE, CORRESPONDENCE **b :** a point of comparison **syn** see LIKENESS
sim·mer \'sim-ər\ *vb* **sim·mer·ing** \-(ə-)riŋ\ [alter. of E dial. *simper*, fr. ME *simperen*, of imit. origin] *vi* **1 :** to stew gently below or just at the boiling point **2 a :** to be in a state of incipient development **:** FERMENT **b :** to be in inward turmoil **:** SEETHE ~ *vt* **:** to cook slowly in a liquid just below the boiling point

sim·nel \'sim-nᵊl\ *n* [ME *simenel*, fr. OF, fr. L *simila* fine wheat flour] **1** : a bun or bread of fine wheat flour **2** *Brit* : a rich fruit cake sometimes coated with almond paste and baked for mid-Lent, Easter, and Christmas

si·mo·le·on \sə-'mō-lē-ən\ *n* [origin unknown] *slang* : DOLLAR

Si·mon \'sī-mən\ *n* [Gk *Simōn*, fr. Heb *Shim'ōn*] **1** : PETER — called also *Simon Peter* **2** : one of the twelve disciples of Jesus — called also *Simon the Zealot* **3** : a kinsman of Jesus **4** : a Samaritan sorcerer converted by the evangelist Philip — called also *Simon Ma·gus* \ˌsī-mən-'mā-gəs\

si·mo·ni·ac \sī-'mō-nē-ˌak, sə-\ *n* [ME, fr. MF or ML; MF *simoniaque*, fr. ML *simoniacus*, fr. LL *simonia* simony] : one who practices simony — **simoniac** *or* **si·mo·ni·a·cal** \ˌsī-mə-'nī-ə-kəl, ˌsim-ə-\ *adj* — **si·mo·ni·a·cal·ly** \-k(ə-)lē\ *adv*

si·mo·nize \'sī-mə-ˌnīz\ *vt* [fr. *Simoniz*, a trademark] : to polish with or as if with wax

Si·mon Le·gree \ˌsī-mən-lə-'grē\ *n* : a cruel slave dealer in Harriet B. Stowe's novel *Uncle Tom's Cabin*

si·mon–pure \ˌsī-mən-'pyu̇(ə)r\ *adj* [fr. *the real Simon Pure*, alluding to a character impersonated by another in the play *A Bold Stroke for a Wife* (1718) by Susanna Centlivre] : of untainted purity or integrity; *also* : pretentiously or hypocritically pure

si·mo·ny \'sī-mə-nē, 'sim-ə-\ *n* [LL *simonia*, fr. *Simon* Magus 1st cent. A.D. Samaritan sorcerer (Acts 8:9–24)] : the buying or selling of a church office

si·moom \sə-'müm, sī-\ *or* **si·moon** \-'mün\ *n* [Ar *samūm*] : a hot dry violent wind laden with dust from Asian and African deserts

sim·pa·ti·co \sim-'pät-i-ˌkō, -'pat-\ *adj* [It *simpatico* & Sp *simpático*, deriv. of L *sympathia* sympathy] : CONGENIAL, LIKABLE

¹**sim·per** \'sim-pər\ *vi* **sim·per·ing** \-p(ə-)riŋ\ [perh. of Scand origin; akin to Dan dial. *simper* affected, coy] : to smile in a silly manner — **sim·per·er** \-pər-ər\ *n*

²**simper** *n* : a silly smile

¹**sim·ple** \'sim-pəl\ *adj* **sim·pler** \-p(ə-)lər\ **sim·plest** \-p(ə-)ləst\ [ME, fr. OF, plain, uncomplicated, artless, fr. L *simplus*, *simplex*, lit., single; L *simplus* fr. *sem-*, *sim-* one + *-plus* multiplied by; L *simplic-*, *simplex* fr. *sem-*, *sim-* + *-plic-*, *-plex* -fold; akin to Gk di*plak-*, di*plax* double — more at SAME, DOUBLE] **1** : free from guile : INNOCENT **2 a** : free from vanity : MODEST **b** : PLAIN, UNADORNED **3** : of humble origin : COMMON ⟨~ farmer⟩ **4 a** : UNEDUCATED **b** (1) : mentally retarded : HALF-WITTED (2) : CREDULOUS **c** : NAIVE, UNSOPHISTICATED **5 a** : UNMIXED, SHEER ⟨~ honesty⟩ **b** : free of secondary complications ⟨a ~ fracture⟩ **c** : not compound or complex ⟨~ sentence⟩ ⟨~ word⟩ **d** : constituting a basic element : FUNDAMENTAL **e** : not compound ⟨~ eye⟩ **6** : free from elaboration or figuration ⟨~ harmony⟩ **7 a** (1) : not subdivided into branches ⟨~ stem⟩ (2) : MONOCARPELLARY (3) : developing from a single ovary ⟨~ fruit⟩ **b** : controlled by a single gene ⟨~ inherited characters⟩ **8** : having no limitation or restrictions : ABSOLUTE, UNCONDITIONAL ⟨~ obligation⟩ **9** : causing little difficulty : EASY, STRAIGHTFORWARD ⟨~ statement⟩ — **sim·ple·ness** \-pəl-nəs\ *n*

syn FOOLISH, SILLY, FATUOUS, ASININE: SIMPLE implies a degree of intelligence inadequate to cope with anything complex or involving mental effort; FOOLISH implies the character of being or seeming unable to use judgment, discretion, or good sense; SILLY suggests failure to act as a rational being esp. by ridiculous behavior; FATUOUS implies foolishness, inanity, and disregard of reality; ASININE suggests utter and contemptible failure to use normal rationality or perception **syn** see in addition EASY

²**simple** *n* **1 a** : a person of humble birth : COMMONER **b** (1) : a rude or credulous person : IGNORAMUS (2) : a mentally retarded person **2 a** : a medicinal plant **b** : a vegetable drug having only one ingredient **3** : one component of a complex; *specif* : an unanalyzable constituent

simple equation *n* : a linear equation

simple fraction *n* : a fraction having whole numbers for the numerator and denominator — compare COMPLEX FRACTION

simple honors *n pl* : three trump honors or three aces at a no-trump contract in bridge held by the same side

simple interest *n* : interest paid or computed on the original principal only of a loan or on the amount of an account often on the assumption that each day is ¹⁄₃₆₀ of a year

simple machine *n* : any of various elementary mechanisms having the elements of which all machines are composed and including the lever, the wheel and axle, the pulley, the inclined plane, the wedge, and the screw

sim·ple·mind·ed \ˌsim-pəl-'mīn-dəd\ *adj* : devoid of subtlety; *also* : FOOLISH — **sim·ple·mind·ed·ly** *adv* — **sim·ple·mind·ed·ness** *n*

simple motion *n* : a motion in a straight line, circle or circular arc, or helix

sim·ple·ton \'sim-pəl-tən\ *n* [¹*simple* + *-ton* (as in surnames such as *Washington*)] : a person lacking in common sense **syn** see FOOL

simple vow *n* : a public vow taken by a religious in the Roman Catholic Church under which retention of property by the individual is permitted and marriage though regarded as a sin is valid under canon law

¹**sim·plex** \'sim-ˌpleks\ *adj* [L *simplic-*, *simplex* — more at SIMPLE] **1** : SIMPLE, SINGLE **2** : allowing telecommunication in only one direction at a time ⟨~ system⟩

²**simplex** *n, pl* **sim·plex·es 1** *or pl* **sim·pli·ces** \-plə-ˌsēz\ *or* **sim·pli·cia** \sim-'plish-(ē-)ə\ : a simple word **2** : a spatial configuration determined by a number of points one more than the number of dimensions of the space

sim·pli·cial \sim-'plish-əl\ *adj* : of or relating to simplexes

sim·plici·den·tate \sim-ˌplis-ə-'den-ˌtāt\ *adj* [deriv. of L *simplic-*, *simplex* + *dentatus* toothed, fr. *dent-*, *dens* tooth] : RODENT 2

sim·plic·i·ty \sim-'plis-ət-ē, -'plis-tē\ *n* [ME *simplicite*, fr. MF *simplicité*, fr. L *simplicitat-*, *simplicitas*, fr. *simplic-*, *simplex*] **1** : the state of being simple or uncompounded **2 a** : lack of subtlety or penetration : INNOCENCE **b** : FOLLY, SILLINESS **3** : freedom from pretense or guile : CANDOR **4 a** : directness of expression : CLARITY **b** : restraint in ornamentation : PLAINNESS

sim·pli·fi·ca·tion \ˌsim-plə-fə-'kā-shən\ *n* : an act, process, or result of simplifying

sim·pli·fi·er \'sim-plə-ˌfī(-ə)r\ *n* : one that simplifies

sim·pli·fy \-ˌfī\ *vt* [F *simplifier*, fr. ML *simplificare*, fr. L *simplus* simple] : to make simple or simpler: as **a** : to reduce to basic essentials **b** : to diminish in scope or complexity : STREAMLINE **c** : to make more intelligible : CLARIFY

sim·plism \'sim-ˌpliz-əm\ *n* : OVERSIMPLIFICATION; *esp* : the reduction of a problem to a false simplicity by ignoring complicating factors — **sim·plis·tic** \sim-'plis-tik\ *adj* — **sim·plis·ti·cal·ly** \-ti-k(ə-)lē\ *adv*

sim·ply \'sim-plē, *for 1 also* -pə-lē\ *adv* **1 a** : without ambiguity : CLEARLY **b** : without embellishment : PLAINLY **c** : DIRECTLY, CANDIDLY **2 a** : MERELY, SOLELY **b** : LITERALLY, REALLY

simply ordered *adj* : having any two elements equal or asymetrically related and any three elements transitively related

sim·u·la·cre \'sim-yə-ˌlāk-ər, -ˌlak-\ *n* [ME, fr. MF, fr. L *simulacrum*] *archaic* : SIMULACRUM

sim·u·la·crum \ˌsim-yə-'lāk-rəm, -'lak-\ *n, pl* **sim·u·la·cra** \-rə\ *also* **simulacrums** [L, fr. *simulare*] **1** : IMAGE, REPRESENTATION **2** : an insubstantial form or semblance of something : SHADOW; *also* : TRACE

¹**sim·u·lar** \'sim-yə-lər, -ˌlär\ *n* [irreg. fr. L *simulare* to simulate] *archaic* : SIMULATOR

²**simular** *adj, archaic* : COUNTERFEIT, PRETENDED

sim·u·late \'sim-yə-ˌlāt\ *vt* [L *simulatus*, pp. of *simulare* to copy, represent, feign, fr. *similis* like — more at SAME] **1** : to give the appearance or effect of : FEIGN **2** : to make a simulation of **syn** see ASSUME — **sim·u·la·tive** \-ˌlāt-iv\ *adj*

simulated rank *n* : a civilian status equivalent to a military rank

sim·u·la·tion \ˌsim-yə-'lā-shən\ *n* **1** : the act or process of simulating : FEIGNING **2** : a sham object : COUNTERFEIT **3 a** : the representation of a system by a device (as a computer) that imitates the behavior of the system **b** : examination of a problem often not subject to direct experimentation by means of a simulating device

sim·u·la·tor \'sim-yə-ˌlāt-ər\ *n* : one that simulates; *specif* : a laboratory device that enables the operator to reproduce under test conditions phenomena likely to occur in actual performance

si·mul·cast \'sī-məl-ˌkast *also* 'sim-əl-\ *vb* [*simul*taneous broad*cast*] : to broadcast simultaneously by AM and FM radio or by radio and television — **simulcast** *n*

si·mul·ta·ne·ity \ˌsī-məl-tə-'nē-ət-ē *also* ˌsim-əl-\ *n* : the quality or state of being simultaneous

si·mul·ta·neous \-'tā-nē-əs, -nyəs\ *adj* [(assumed) ML *simultaneus*, fr. L *simul* at the same time — more at SAME] **1** : existing or occurring at the same time : COINCIDENT **2** : satisfied by the same values of the variables ⟨~ equations⟩ **syn** see CONTEMPORARY — **si·mul·ta·neous·ly** *adv* — **si·mul·ta·neous·ness** *n*

¹**sin** \'sin\ *n* [ME *sinne*, fr. OE *synn;* akin to OHG *sunta* sin] **1 a** : an offense against God **b** : MISDEED, FAULT **2 a** : transgression of the law of God **b** : a vitiated state of human nature in which the self is estranged from God **syn** see OFFENSE

²**sin** *vi* **sinned**; **sin·ning 1** : to commit a sin **2** : to commit an offense or fault

³**sin** \'sēn, 'sin\ *n* [Heb *śin*] : the 21st letter of the Hebrew alphabet — symbol שׂ

Sin·an·thro·pus \sī-'nan(t)-thrə-pəs, sə-; ˌsīn-ˌan-'thrō-, ˌsin-\ *n* [NL, fr. LL *Sinae*, pl., Chinese + Gk *anthrōpos* man — more at SINOLOGUE] : PEKING MAN

sin·a·pism \'sin-ə-ˌpiz-əm\ *n* [LL *sinapismus*, deriv. of Gk *sinapi* mustard] : MUSTARD PLASTER

¹**since** \(')sin(t)s\ *adv* [ME *sins*, contr. of *sithens*, fr. *sithen*, fr. OE *siththan*, fr. *sith tham* since that, fr. *sith* since + *tham*, dat. of *thæt* that; akin to OHG *sīd* since, L *serus* late, OE *sāwan* to sow] **1** : from a definite past time until now ⟨has stayed there ever ~⟩ **2** : before the present time : AGO ⟨long ~ dead⟩ **3** : after a time in the past : SUBSEQUENTLY ⟨has ~ become rich⟩

²**since** *prep* **1** : in the period after a specified time in the past ⟨improvements made ~ 1928⟩ **2** : continuously from a specified time in the past ⟨happy ~ then⟩

³**since** *conj* **1** : at a time or times in the past after or later than ⟨has held two jobs ~ he graduated⟩ **2** *obs* : WHEN **3** : from the time in the past when ⟨ever ~ he was a child⟩ **4** : in view of the fact that : BECAUSE ⟨~ it was raining he wore a hat⟩

sin·cere \sin-'si(ə)r, sən-\ *adj* [MF, fr. L *sincerus*] **1 a** : free of dissimulation : not hypocritical : HONEST ⟨a ~ friend⟩ ⟨~ interest⟩ **b** : free from adulteration : PURE ⟨~ doctrine⟩ ⟨~ wine⟩ **2** : marked by genuineness : TRUE — **sin·cere·ly** *adv* — **sin·cere·ness** *n*

syn SINCERE, WHOLEHEARTED, HEARTFELT, HEARTY, UNFEIGNED mean genuine in feeling. SINCERE stresses absence of hypocrisy, feigning, or any falsifying embellishment or exaggeration; WHOLEHEARTED suggests sincerity and earnest devotion without reservation or misgiving; HEARTFELT suggests depth of genuine feeling outwardly expressed; HEARTY suggests honesty, warmth, and exuberance in displaying feeling; UNFEIGNED stresses spontaneity and absence of pretense

sin·cer·i·ty \-'ser-ət-ē, -'sir-\ *n* : the quality or state of being sincere : honesty of mind : freedom from hypocrisy

sin·cip·i·tal \sin-'sip-ət-ᵊl\ *adj* : of or relating to the sinciput

sin·ci·put \'sin(t)-sə-(ˌ)pət\ *n, pl* **sinciputs** *or* **sin·cip·i·ta** \sin-'sip-ət-ə\ [L *sincipit-*, *sinciput*, fr. *semi-* + *caput* head — more at HEAD] **1** : FOREHEAD **2** : the upper half of the skull

Sind·bad the Sailor \'sin-ˌbad-\ *n* : a citizen of Baghdad whose adventures are narrated in the *Arabian Nights' Entertainments*

Sin·dhi \'sin-dē\ *n, pl* **Sindhi** *or* **Sindhis** [Ar *Sindi*] **1 a** : a mostly Muslim people of Sind **b** : a member of this people **2** : the Indic language of Sind

sine \'sīn\ *n* [ML *sinus*, fr. L, curve] : the trigonometric function that for an acute angle in a right triangle is the ratio of the side opposite the angle to the hypotenuse

si·ne·cure \'sī-ni-ˌkyu̇(ə)r, 'sin-i-\ *n* [ML *sine cura* without cure of souls] **1** : an ecclesiastical benefice without cure of souls **2** : an office or position that requires little or no work

sine curve *n* : the graph in rectangular coordinates of the equation $y = a \sin bx$ where a and b are constants

si·ne die \ˌsī-nē-'dī-ˌē, ˌsin-ē-'dē-ˌā\ *adv* [L, without day] : INDEFINITELY

si·ne qua non \ˌsin-ē-ˌkwä-'nōn, ˌsī-nē-ˌkwā-'nän\ *n* [LL, without which not] : an absolutely indispensable or essential thing

¹**sin·ew** \'sin-(ˌ)yü, -yə-w *also* 'sin-(ˌ)ü, -ə-w\ *n* [ME *sinewe*, fr. OE

seono; akin to OHG *senawa* sinew, L *saeta* bristle] **1 :** TENDON; *esp* **:** one dressed for use as a cord or thread **2** *obs* **:** NERVE **3 a :** solid resilient strength **:** POWER **b :** the chief supporting force **:** MAINSTAY — usu. used in pl.

²**sinew** *vt* **:** to strengthen as if with sinews

sine wave *n* **:** a wave form that represents periodic oscillations in which the amplitude of displacement at each point is proportional to the sine of the phase angle of the displacement and that is visualized as a sine curve

sin·ewy \'sin-yə-wē *also* 'sin-ə-\ *adj* **1 :** having sinews: **a :** TENDINOUS **b :** marked by strong or prominent sinews **2 :** strong and firm **:** TOUGH

sin·fo·nia \,sin-fə-'nē-ə, ,sim(p)-fə-\ *n, pl* **sin·fo·nie** \-'nē-,ā\ [It, fr. L *symphonia* symphony] **1 :** an orchestral musical composition found in 18th century opera **2 :** SYMPHONY 2a, 2c

sin·fo·niet·ta \,sin-fən-'yet-ə, -(,)fōn-\ *n* [It, dim. of *sinfonia*] **1 :** a symphony of less than standard length or for fewer instruments **2 :** a small symphony orchestra; *esp* **:** an orchestra of strings only

sin·ful \'sin-fəl\ *adj* **:** tainted with, marked by, or full of sin **:** WICKED — **sin·ful·ly** \-fə-lē\ *adv* — **sin·ful·ness** *n*

¹**sing** \'siŋ\ *vb* **sang** \'saŋ\ *or* **sung** \'səŋ\ **sung; sing·ing** \'siŋ-iŋ\ [ME *singen,* fr. OE *singan;* akin to OHG *singan* to sing, Gk *omphē* voice] *vi* **1 a :** to produce musical tones by means of the voice **b :** to utter words in musical tones and with musical inflections and modulations **c :** to deliver songs as a trained or professional singer **2 :** to make a shrill whining or whistling sound **3 a :** to relate or celebrate something in verse **b :** to compose poetry **4 :** to produce musical or harmonious sounds **5 :** BUZZ, RING **6 :** to make a cry **:** CALL **7 :** to give information or evidence ~ *vt* **1 :** to utter with musical inflections; *esp* **:** to interpret in musical tones produced by the voice **2 :** to relate or celebrate in verse **3 :** CHANT, INTONE **4 :** to bring or accompany to a place or state by singing ⟨~*s* the child to sleep⟩ — **sing·able** \'siŋ-ə-bəl\ *adj*

²**sing** *n* **:** a singing esp. in company

¹**singe** \'sinj\ *vt* **singed; singe·ing** \'sin-jiŋ\ [ME *sengen,* fr. OE *sengan;* akin to OHG bi*sengan* to singe, OSlav *isęčiti* to dry] **:** to burn (something) superficially or lightly **:** SCORCH; *specif* **:** to remove the hair, down, or fuzz from esp. by passing rapidly over a flame

²**singe** *n* **:** a slight burn **:** SCORCH

¹**sing·er** \'siŋ-ər\ *n* **:** one that sings

²**sing·er** \'sin-jə(r)\ *n* **:** one that singes

singing bird *n* **1 :** SONGBIRD 1 **2 :** a passerine bird

¹**sin·gle** \'siŋ-gəl\ *adj* [ME, fr. MF, fr. L *singulus* one only; akin to L *sem-* one — more at SAME] **1 a :** UNMARRIED **b :** of or relating to celibacy **2 :** LONE, SOLITARY **3 a** (1) **:** consisting of or having only one part, feature, or portion ⟨~ consonants⟩ (2) **:** consisting of one as opposed to or in contrast with many **:** UNIFORM ⟨~ standard⟩ (3) **:** consisting of only one in number ⟨holds to a ~ ideal⟩ **b :** having but one whorl of petals or ray flowers ⟨a ~ rose⟩ **4 a :** consisting of a separate unique whole **:** INDIVIDUAL ⟨each ~ citizen⟩ **b :** of, relating to, or involving only one person **5 a :** FRANK, HONEST ⟨a ~ devotion⟩ **b :** exclusively attentive ⟨an eye ~ to the truth⟩ **6 :** UNBROKEN, UNDIVIDED **7 :** man to man **8 :** having no equal or like **:** SINGULAR **9 :** designed for the use of one person or family only ⟨a ~ room⟩

syn SOLE, UNIQUE, SEPARATE, SOLITARY, PARTICULAR: SINGLE implies being unaccompanied by or unsupported by any other; SOLE applies to the only one that exists, acts, or receives action; UNIQUE applies to the only one of its kind or character in existence; SEPARATE stresses discreteness and disconnection from every other one; SOLITARY implies being both single and isolated; PARTICULAR implies numerical distinctness from other instances, examples, or members of a class

²**single** *n* **1 :** a separate individual person or thing **2 :** ONE-BASE HIT **3** *pl* **a :** a tennis match or similar game with one player on each side **b :** a golf match between two players

³**single** *vb* **sin·gling** \'siŋ-g(ə-)liŋ\ *vt* **1 :** to select or distinguish (a person or thing) from a number or group **2 a :** to advance (a base runner in baseball) by a one-base hit **b :** to bring about the scoring of (a run in baseball) by a one-base hit ~ *vi* **:** to make a one-base hit in baseball

sin·gle–breast·ed \,siŋ-gəl-'bres-təd\ *adj* **:** having a center closing with one row of buttons and no lap ⟨~ coat⟩

single combat *n* **:** combat between two persons

single entry *n* **:** a method of bookkeeping that recognizes only one side of a business transaction and usu. consists only of a record of cash and personal accounts with debtors and creditors

single file *n* **:** a line (as of persons) moving one behind another — **single file** \,siŋ-gəl-'fī(ə)l\ *adv*

¹**sin·gle–foot** \'siŋ-gəl-,fu̇t\ *n, pl* **single–foots :** ⁷RACK b

²**single–foot** *vi, of a horse* **:** to go at a rack — **sin·gle–foot·er** *n*

¹**sin·gle–hand·ed** \,siŋ-gəl-'han-dəd\ *adj* **1 :** managed or done by one person or with one on a side **2 :** working alone or unassisted by others — **sin·gle–hand·ed·ly** *adv* — **sin·gle–hand·ed·ness** *n*

²**single–handed** *adv* **:** SINGLE-HANDEDLY

sin·gle–heart·ed \-'härt-əd\ *adj* **:** characterized by sincerity and unity of purpose or dedication — **sin·gle–heart·ed·ly** *adv* — **sin·gle–heart·ed·ness** *n*

single knot *n* **:** OVERHAND KNOT

sin·gle–mind·ed \,siŋ-gəl-'mīn-dəd\ *adj* **1 :** GUILELESS, SINCERE **2 :** having one unifying purpose — **sin·gle–mind·ed·ly** *adv* — **sin·gle–mind·ed·ness** *n*

single–name paper *n* **:** a promissory note with no endorsement other than the signature of the maker

sin·gle·ness \'siŋ-gəl-nəs\ *n* **:** the quality or state of being single

sin·gle–phase \,siŋ-gəl-'fāz\ *adj* **:** of or relating to a circuit energized by a single alternating electromotive force

sin·gle–space \-'spās\ *vt* **:** to type or print with no blank lines between lines of copy

sin·gle·stick \'siŋ-gəl-,stik\ *n* **:** fighting or fencing with a one-handed wooden stick or sword; *also* **:** the weapon used

sin·gle·stick·er \,siŋ-gəl-'stik-ər\ *n* **:** a single-masted vessel **:** SLOOP, CUTTER

sin·glet \'siŋ-glət\ *n, chiefly Brit* **:** an athletic jersey **:** UNDERSHIRT

single tax *n* **:** a tax to be levied on a single object as the sole source of public revenue

sin·gle·ton \'siŋ-gəl-tən\ *n* [F, fr. E *single*] **1 :** a card that is the only one of its suit orig. held in a hand **2 :** an individual member or thing distinct from others grouped with it; *specif* **:** an offspring born singly

sin·gle–track \,siŋ-gəl-,trak\ *adj* **:** lacking intellectual range, receptiveness, or flexibility **:** ONE-TRACK

sin·gle·tree \'siŋ-gəl-(,)trē\ *n* **:** WHIFFLETREE

sin·gly \'siŋ-g(ə-)lē\ *adv* **1 :** by or with oneself **:** INDIVIDUALLY **2 :** SINGLE-HANDEDLY

¹**sing·song** \'siŋ-,sȯŋ\ *n* **1 :** verse with marked and regular rhythm and rhyme **:** a jingling song **2 :** a voice delivery characterized by a narrow range or monotonous pattern of pitch

²**singsong** *adj* **:** having a monotonous cadence or rhythm

sing·spiel \'siŋ-,spēl, 'ziŋ-,shpēl\ *n* [G, fr. *singen* to sing + *spiel* play] **:** a usu. comic dramatic musical work popular in Germany esp. in the latter part of the 18th century characterized by spoken dialogue interspersed with popular or folk songs

¹**sin·gu·lar** \'siŋ-gyə-lər\ *adj* [ME *singuler,* fr. MF, fr. L *singularis,* fr. *singulus* only one — more at SINGLE] **1 a :** of or relating to a separate person or thing **:** INDIVIDUAL **b :** of, relating to, or being a word form denoting one person, thing, or instance **c :** of or relating to a single instance or to something considered by itself **2 :** distinguished by superiority **:** EXCEPTIONAL **3 :** of unusual quality **:** UNIQUE **4 :** being at variance with others **:** DIFFERING **syn** see STRANGE — **sin·gu·lar·ly** *adv*

²**singular** *n* **1 :** the singular number, the inflectional form denoting it, or a word in that form **2 :** a singular term or proposition

sin·gu·lar·i·ty \,siŋ-gyə-'lar-ət-ē\ *n* **1 :** something that is singular; *esp* **:** a distinctive or eccentric quality **:** PECULIARITY **2 :** the quality or state of being singular

sin·gu·lar·ize \'siŋ-gyə-lə-,rīz\ *vt* **:** to make singular

singular point *n* **:** a point of the curve $f(x, y) = 0$ where both partial derivatives are zero

singular proposition *n* **:** a proposition having as its subject a proper noun or a descriptive phrase which applies only to one individual

Sin·ha·lese *or* **Sin·gha·lese** \,siŋ-gə-'lēz, ,sin-(h)ə-, -'lēs\ *n, pl* **Sinhalese** *or* **Singhalese** [Skt *Siṁhala* Ceylon] **1 a :** a people inhabiting the island of Ceylon and forming a major part of its population **b :** a member of this people **2 :** the Indic language of the Sinhalese people — **Sinhalese** *or* **Singhalese** *adj*

Si·ni·cism \'sī-nə-,siz-əm, 'sin-ə-\ *n* [ML *sinicus* Chinese, fr. LL *Sinae,* pl., Chinese — more at SINOLOGUE] **:** something (as a manner or custom) peculiar to the Chinese

si·ni·cize \-,sīz\ *vt, often cap* **:** to modify by Chinese influence

si·ni·fy \'sī-nə-,fī, 'sin-ə-\ *vt, often cap* [LL *Sinae,* pl., Chinese] **:** SINICIZE

sin·is·ter \'sin-əs-tər, *archaic* sə-'nis-\ *adj* [ME *sinistre,* fr. L *sinistr-, sinister* on the left side, unlucky, inauspicious] **1** *archaic* **:** UNFAVORABLE, UNLUCKY **2** *obs* **:** conveying misleading or detrimental opinion or advice **3** *archaic* **:** dishonestly underhanded **:** FRAUDULENT **4 :** singularly evil or productive of evil **:** BAD, CORRUPTIVE **5 a :** of, relating to, or situated to the left or on the left side of something ⟨bearing a bar ~⟩ **b :** of ill omen by reason of being on the left **6 :** presaging ill fortune or trouble **:** OMINOUS **7 :** accompanied by or leading to disaster or unfavorable developments — **sin·is·ter·ly** *adv* — **sin·is·ter·ness** *n*

syn SINISTER, BALEFUL, MALIGN mean seriously threatening evil or disaster. SINISTER applies to what threatens by appearance or reputation to be formidably troublesome or dangerous in some undisclosed way; BALEFUL imputes perniciousness or destructiveness to something whether working openly or covertly; MALIGN applies to what is inherently evil or harmful

si·nis·tral \'sin-əs-trəl, sə-'nis-\ *adj* **:** of, relating to, or inclined to the left: as **a :** LEFT-HANDED **b** *of a flatfish* **:** having the left side turned uppermost **c :** having whorls turning from the right toward the left as viewed with the apex toward the observer — **si·nis·tral·ly** \-trə-lē\ *adv*

sin·is·trorse \'sin-ə-,strȯ(ə)rs\ *also* **sin·is·tror·sal** \,sin-ə-'strȯr-səl\ *adj* [NL *sinistrorsus,* fr. L, toward the left side, fr. *sinistr-, sinister* + *versus,* pp. of *vertere* to turn — more at WORTH] **1** *of a plant* **:** twining spirally upward around an axis from right to left — compare DEXTRORSE **2 :** SINISTRAL c — **sin·is·trorse·ly** *also* **sin·is·tror·sal·ly** \-'strȯr-sə-lē\ *adv*

si·nis·trous \'sin-əs-trəs, sə-'nis-\ *adj* **:** SINISTER

Si·nit·ic \sī-'nit-ik, sə-\ *adj* [LL *Sinae,* pl., Chinese — more at SINOLOGUE] **:** of or relating to the Chinese, their language, or their culture

¹**sink** \'siŋk\ *vb* **sank** \'saŋk\ *or* **sunk** \'səŋk\ **sunk** *or* **sunk·en** \'səŋ-kən\ **sink·ing** [ME *sinken,* fr. OE *sincan;* akin to OHG *sinkan* to sink, Arm *ankanim* I fall] *vi* **1 a :** to become submerged **:** go to the bottom **:** SUBMERGE **b :** to become partly buried (as in mud) **c :** to become engulfed **2 a** (1) **:** to fall or drop to a lower place or level (2) **:** to flow at a lower depth or level (3) **:** to burn with lower intensity (4) **:** to fall to a lower pitch or volume ⟨his voice ~*s* to a whisper⟩ **b :** to subside gradually **:** SETTLE **c :** to disappear from view **d :** to slope gradually **:** DIP **3 a :** to soak or become absorbed **:** PENETRATE **b :** to become impressively known or felt ⟨the lesson had *sunk* in⟩ **4 :** to become deeply absorbed ⟨*sank* into reverie⟩ **5 a :** to go downward in quality, state, or condition **:** DEGENERATE, RETROGRESS **b :** to grow less in amount or worth **:** DECLINE **6 a :** to fall or drop slowly for lack of strength **:** COLLAPSE **b :** to become depressed **c :** to fail in health or strength ~ *vt* **1 a :** to cause to sink **b :** to force down esp. below the earth's surface **c :** to cause (something) to penetrate **2 a :** to cause (as a ship) to plunge to the bottom **b :** to place or force beneath the water **:** SUBMERGE **c :** to engage deeply the attention of **:** IMMERSE **3 a :** to dig or bore (a well or shaft) in the earth **:** EXCAVATE **b :** to form by cutting or excising ⟨~ words in stone⟩ **4 :** to cast down or bring to a low condition or state **:** OVERWHELM, DEFEAT **5 a :** to lower in standing or reputation **:** ABASE **b** *archaic* **:** DEGRADE **6 a** *archaic* **:** to cause to become dejected **b :** to weaken physically **:** DEBILITATE **7 a** *archaic* **:** to lessen in value or amount ⟨a great surplus ~*s* the prices⟩ **b :** to lower or soften (the voice) in speaking **8 :** to set aside **:** RESTRAIN, SUPPRESS **9 :** to pay off (as a debt) **:** LIQUIDATE **10 :** INVEST — **sink·able** \'siŋ-kə-bəl\ *adj*

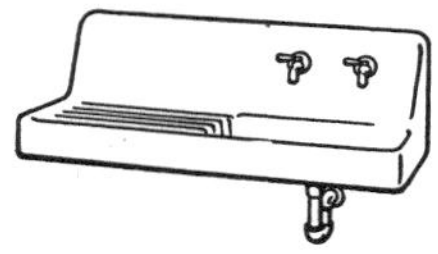

sink 1c

²**sink** *n* **1 a :** a pool or pit for the deposit of waste or sewage **:** CESSPOOL **b :** a ditch or tunnel for carrying off

sewage : SEWER **c** : a stationary basin connected with a drain and usu. a water supply for washing and drainage **2** : a place where vice, corruption, or evil collect **3** : SUMP **4 a** : a depression in the land surface; *esp* : one having a saline lake with no outlet **b** : a hollow in a limestone region communicating with a cavern or passage

sink·age \'siŋ-kij\ *n* **1** : the act, process, or degree of sinking **2** : SINKING, DEPRESSION **3** : the distance from the top line of a full page to the first line of sunk matter

sink·er \'siŋ-kər\ *n* **1** : one that sinks; *specif* : a weight for sinking a fishing line, seine, or sounding line **2** : DOUGHNUT

sink·hole \'siŋk-ˌhōl\ *n* : a hollow place or depression in which drainage collects

sinking fund *n* : a fund set up and accumulated by usu. regular deposits for paying off the principal of a debt when it falls due

sin·less \'sin-ləs\ *adj* : free from sin : IMPECCABLE, HOLY — **sin·less·ly** *adv* — **sin·less·ness** *n*

sin·ner \'sin-ər\ *n* **1** : one that sins **2** : REPROBATE, SCAMP

Sino- *comb form* [F, fr. LL *Sinae*] **1** : Chinese ⟨*Sino*phile⟩ **2** : Chinese and ⟨*Sino*-Tibetan⟩

si·no·log·i·cal \ˌsīn-ᵊl-'äj-i-kəl, ˌsin-\ *adj* : of, relating to, or characteristic of the Chinese culture, language, or literature

si·nol·o·gist \sī-'näl-ə-jəst, sə-\ *n* : SINOLOGUE

si·no·logue \'sīn-ᵊl-ˌòg, 'sin-, -ˌäg\ *n* [F, fr. LL *Sinae*, pl. Chinese (fr. Gk *Sinai*, fr. Ar *Sīn* China) + F *-logue*] : a specialist in sinology

si·nol·o·gy \sī-'näl-ə-jē, sə-\ *n* [prob. fr. F *sinologie*, fr. *sino-* + *-logie* -logy] : the study of the Chinese and esp. their language, literature, history, and culture

Si·no–Ti·bet·an \ˌsī-(ˌ)nō-tə-'bet-ᵊn, ˌsin-(ˌ)ō-\ *n* : a language group comprising Tibeto-Burman and Chinese

sin·syne \'sin-ˌsīn\ *adv* [ME (Sc) *sensyne*, fr. *sen* since (contr. of ME *sithen*) + *syne* since — more at SINCE, SYNE] *chiefly Scot* : since that time : AGO

¹sin·ter \'sint-ər\ *n* [G, fr. OHG *sintar* slag — more at CINDER] : a deposit formed by the evaporation of spring or lake water

²sinter *vt* **sin·ter·ing** \'sin-t(ə-)riŋ\ : to cause to become a coherent mass by heating without melting

sin·u·ate \'sin-yə-wət, -ˌwāt\ *adj* [L *sinuatus*, pp. of *sinuare* to bend, fr. *sinus* curve] : having the margin wavy with strong indentations ⟨~ leaves⟩ — **sin·u·ate** \-ˌwāt\ *vi* — **sin·u·ate·ly** \-wət-lē, -ˌwāt-\ *adv*

sin·u·os·i·ty \ˌsin-yə-'wäs-ət-ē\ *n* **1** : the quality or state of being sinuous **2** : something that is sinuous

sin·u·ous \'sin-yə-wəs\ *adj* [L *sinuosus*, fr. *sinus*] **1 a** : of a serpentine or wavy form : WINDING **b** : marked by strong lithe movements **2** : INTRICATE, COMPLEX **3** : SINUATE — **sin·u·ous·ly** *adv* — **sin·u·ous·ness** *n*

si·nus \'sī-nəs\ *n* [NL, fr. L, curve, fold, hollow] : CAVITY, HOLLOW: as **a** : a narrow elongated tract extending from a focus of suppuration and serving for the discharge of pus **b** (1) : a cavity in the substance of a bone of the skull that usu. communicates with the nostrils and contains air (2) : a channel for venous blood (3) : a dilatation in a bodily canal or vessel **c** : a cleft or indentation between adjoining lobes

si·nus·itis \ˌsī-nə-'sīt-əs\ *n* : inflammation of a sinus

si·nus·oid \'sī-nə-ˌsȯid\ *n* [ML *sinus* sine] : SINE CURVE — **si·nus·oi·dal** \ˌsī-nə-'sȯid-ᵊl\ *adj*

sinusoidal projection *n* : an equal-area map projection capable of showing the entire surface of the earth with all parallels as straight lines evenly spaced, the central meridian as one half the length of the equator, and all other meridians as curved lines

Si·on \'sī-ən\ *var of* ZION

Siou·an \'sü-ən\ *n* **1** : a language stock of central and eastern No. America **2 a** : a group of peoples speaking Siouan languages **b** : a member of these peoples

Sioux \'sü\ *n, pl* **Sioux** \'sü(z)\ [F, short for *Nadowessioux*, fr. Chippewa *Nadoweisiw*] **1** : DAKOTA **2** : SIOUAN

¹sip \'sip\ *vb* **sipped**; **sip·ping** [ME *sippen*; akin to LG *sippen* to sip] *vi* : to take a sip of something esp. repeatedly ~ *vt* **1** : to drink in small quantities **2** : to take sips from : TASTE — **sip·per** *n*

²sip *n* **1** : the act of sipping **2** : a small draft taken with the lips

¹si·phon \'sī-fən\ *n* [F *siphon*, fr. L *siphon-*, *sipho*, fr. Gk *siphōn*] **1 a** : a tube bent to form two legs of unequal length by which a liquid can be transferred to a lower level over an intermediate elevation by the pressure of the atmosphere in forcing the liquid up the shorter branch of the tube immersed in it while the excess of weight of the liquid in the longer branch when once filled causes a continuous flow **b** *usu* **syphon** : a bottle for holding aerated water that is driven out through a bent tube in its neck by the pressure of the gas when a valve in the tube is opened **2** : any of various tubular organs in animals and esp. mollusks or arthropods used for drawing in or ejecting fluids

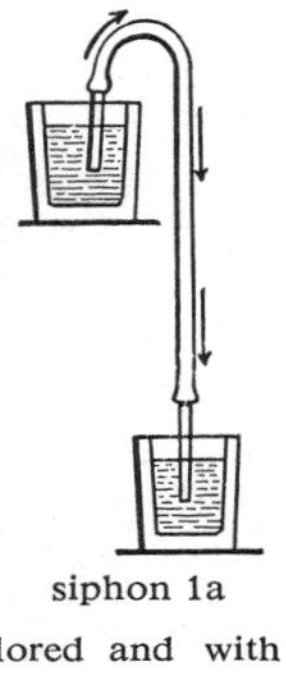

siphon 1a

²siphon *vb* **si·phon·ing** \'sīf-(ə-)niŋ\ *vt* : to convey, draw off, or empty by or as if by a siphon ~ *vi* : to pass by or as if by a siphon

si·pho·no·phore \sī-'fän-ə-ˌfō(ə)r, 'sī-fə-nə-, -ˌfȯ(ə)r\ *n* [deriv. of Gk *siphōn* + *pherein* to carry — more at BEAR] : any of an order (Siphonophora) of compound free-swimming or floating pelagic hydrozoans mostly delicate, transparent, and colored and with specialized zooids

si·pho·no·stele \sī-'fän-ə-ˌstēl, ˌsī-fə-nə-'stē-lē\ *n* : a stele consisting of vascular tissue surrounding a central core of pith parenchyma — **si·pho·no·ste·lic** \ˌsī-fə-nə-'stē-lik, (ˌ)sī-ˌfän-ə-\ *adj* — **si·pho·no·ste·ly** \'sī-fə-nə-ˌstē-lē, sī-'fän-ə-\ *n*

sip·pet \'sip-ət\ *n* [alter. of *sop*] : a small bit of toast or fried bread esp. for garnishing

sir \(')sər\ *n* [ME, fr. *sire*] **1 a** : a man of rank or position **b** : a man entitled to be addressed as *sir* — used as a title before the given name of a knight or baronet and formerly sometimes before the given name of a priest **2 a** — used as a usu. respectful form of address **b** *cap* — used as a conventional form of address in the salutation of a letter

sir·dar \'sər-ˌdär\ *n* [Hindi *sardār*, fr. Per] **1** : a person of high rank (as an hereditary noble, a chieftain, or a high military officer) esp. in India **2** : one holding a position of some responsibility in India: as **a** : FOREMAN **b** : TENANT FARMER

¹sire \'sī(ə)r\ *n* [ME, fr. OF, fr. L *senior* older — more at SENIOR] **1 a** : FATHER **b** *archaic* : male ancestor : FOREFATHER **c** : ORIGINATOR, AUTHOR **2 a** *archaic* : a man of rank or authority; *esp* : LORD — used formerly as a form of address and as a title **b** *obs* : an elderly man : SENIOR **3** : the male parent of an animal and esp. of a domestic animal

²sire *vt* **1** : BEGET, PROCREATE — used esp. of domestic animals **2** : to bring into being : ORIGINATE

¹si·ren \'sī-rən, *for 3 also* sī-'rēn\ *n* [ME, fr. MF & L; MF *sereine*, fr. LL *sirena*, fr. L *siren*, fr. Gk *seirēn*] **1** *often cap* : one of a group of creatures in Greek mythology having the heads and sometimes the breasts and arms of women but otherwise the forms of birds that lured mariners to destruction by their singing **2 a** : a woman who sings with bewitching sweetness **b** : a temptingly beautiful woman; *esp* : one who is insidiously seductive : TEMPTRESS **3 a** : an apparatus producing musical tones esp. in acoustical studies by the rapid interruption of a current of air, steam, or fluid by a perforated rotating disk **b** : a device often electrically operated for producing a penetrating warning sound ⟨ambulance ~⟩ ⟨air-raid ~⟩ **4 a** [NL, genus name, fr. L] : any of a genus (*Siren*) of eel-shaped amphibians with small forelimbs but neither hind legs nor pelvis and with permanent external gills as well as lungs **b** : SEA COW 1

²si·ren \'sī-rən\ *also* **si·re·nic** \sī-'ren-ik, -'rēn-\ *adj* : of or relating to a siren : ENTICING, BEWITCHING ⟨a ~ song⟩

si·re·ni·an \sī-'rē-nē-ən\ *n* [NL *Sirenia*, order name, fr. *Siren*] : any of an order (Sirenia) of aquatic herbivorous mammals including the manatee and dugong

siren song *n* : an alluring utterance or appeal; *esp* : one that is seductive or deceptive

Sir·i·us \'sir-ē-əs\ *n* [ME, fr. L, fr. Gk *Seirios*, lit., glowing] : a star of the constellation Canis Major constituting the brightest star in the heavens — called also *Dog Star*

sir·loin \'sər-ˌlȯin\ *n* [alter. of earlier *surloin*, modif. of MF *surlonge*, fr. *sur* over (fr. L *super*) + *loigne*, *longe* loin — more at OVER] : a cut of meat and esp. of beef from the part of the hindquarter just in front of the round

si·roc·co \sə-'räk-(ˌ)ō\ *n* [It, fr. Ar *sharq* east] **1 a** : a hot dust-laden wind from the Libyan deserts that blows on the northern Mediterranean coast chiefly in Italy, Malta, and Sicily **b** : a warm moist oppressive southeast wind in the same regions **2** : a hot or warm wind of cyclonic origin from an arid or heated region

sir·rah *also* **sir·ra** \'sir-ə\ *n* [alter. of *sir*] *obs* — used as a form of address implying inferiority and often used in anger or contempt

sir·ree *also* **sir·ee** \(ˌ)sər-'ē\ *n* [by alter.] : SIR — used as an emphatic form usu. after *yes* or *no*

sir–rev·er·ence \sə-'rev-(ə-)rən(t)s, -'rev-ərn(t)s\ *n* [prob. alter. of *save-reverence*, trans. of ML *salva reverentia* saving (your) reverence] *obs* — used as an expression of apology before a statement that might be taken as offensive

Sir Rog·er de Cov·er·ley \sə(r)-ˌräj-ərd-i-'kəv-ər-lē\ *n* [alter. (influenced by *Sir Roger de Coverley*, fictitious country gentleman appearing in many of the *Spectator* papers by Joseph Addison and Sir Richard Steele, fr. *roger of coverley*) of *roger of coverley*, prob. fr. *Roger* the name + *of* + *Coverley*, a fictitious place name] : an English country-dance performed in two straight lines by an indefinite number

sirup, **sirupy** *var of* SYRUP, SYRUPY

sir·vente \si(ə)r-'vänt, -'vent\ *or* **sir·ven·tes** \-'vent-əs\ *n, pl* **sir·ventes** \-'vänt, -'vän(t)s, -'vents, -'vent-əs\ [F, fr. Prov *sirventes*, lit., servant's song, fr. *sirvent* servant, fr. L *servient-*, *serviens*, prp. of *servire* to serve] : a usu. moral or religious song of the Provençal troubadours satirizing social vices

-sis \səs\ *n suffix, pl* **-ses** \ˌsēz\ [L, fr. Gk, fem. suffix of action] : process : action ⟨peristal*sis*⟩

si·sal \'sī-səl, -zəl\ *n* [MexSp, fr. *Sisal*, Yucatán, Mexico] **1 a** : a strong durable white fiber used for hard fiber cordage and for binder twine **b** : a widely cultivated West Indian agave (*Agave sisalana*) whose leaves yield sisal **2** : any of several fibers similar to true sisal

sis·kin \'sis-kən\ *n* [G dial. *sisschen*, dim. of MHG *zīse* siskin, of Slav origin; akin to Czech *čížek* siskin] : a small sharp-billed chiefly greenish and yellowish finch (*Spinus spinus*) of temperate Europe and Asia related to the goldfinch — compare RED SISKIN

sis·si·fied \'sis-i-ˌfīd\ *adj* : SISSY

sis·sy \'sis-ē\ *n* [*sis*, short for *sister*] : an effeminate man or boy; *also* : a timid or cowardly person — **sissy** *adj*

sis·ter \'sis-tər\ *n, often attrib* [ME *suster*, *sister*, partly fr. OE *sweostor* and partly of Scand origin; akin to ON *systir* sister; akin to L *soror* sister] **1 a** (1) : a female human being related to another person having the same parents (2) : HALF SISTER (3) : SISTER-IN-LAW **b** : a female of a lower animal in relation to another having a common parent **2** *often cap* **a** : a member of a religious sisterhood; *specif* : one of a Roman Catholic congregation under simple vows **b** : a female member of a Christian church **3 a** : a woman related to another by a common tie or interest **b** : one having similar characteristics to another ⟨~ ships⟩ **4** *chiefly Brit* : NURSE **5 a** : GIRL, WOMAN **b** : PERSON — usu. used in the phrase *weak sister*

sis·ter·hood \-ˌhu̇d\ *n* **1 a** : the state of being a sister **b** : sisterly relationship **2** : a community or society of sisters; *specif* : a society of women religious

sis·ter–in–law \'sis-t(ə-)rən-ˌlȯ, -tərn-ˌlȯ\ *n, pl* **sis·ters–in–law** \-tər-zən-\ **1** : the sister of one's spouse **2 a** : the wife of one's brother **b** : the wife of one's spouse's brother

sis·ter·ly \'sis-tər-lē\ *adj* : of, relating to, or having the characteristics of a sister — **sisterly** *adv*

Sis·tine \'sis-ˌtēn, sis-'\ *adj* [It *sistino*, fr. NL *sixtinus*, fr. *Sixtus*, name of some popes] **1** : of or relating to any of the popes named Sixtus **2** [fr. Pope *Sixtus* IV †1484] : of or relating to the Sistine chapel in the Vatican

sis·trum \'sis-trəm\ *n, pl* **sistrums** *or* **sis·tra** \-trə\ [ME, fr. L, fr. Gk *seistron*, fr. *seiein* to shake — more at SEISMIC] : an ancient Egyptian percussion instrument consisting of a thin metal frame with numerous metal rods or loops that jingle when shaken

Sis·y·phe·an \ˌsis-i-'fē-ən\ *or* **Si·syph·i·an** \sis-'if-ē-ən\ *adj* : of,

relating to, or suggestive of the labors of Sisyphus
Sis·y·phus \'sis-i-fəs\ *n* [L, fr. Gk *Sisyphos*] **:** a legendary king of Corinth condemned to roll a heavy stone up a steep hill in Hades only to have it roll down again as it nears the top

1sit \'sit\ *vb* **sat** \'sat\ **sit·ting** [ME *sitten*, fr. OE *sittan;* akin to OHG *sizzen* to sit, L *sedēre*, Gk *hezesthai* to sit, *hedra* seat] *vi* **1 a :** to rest upon the buttocks or haunches ⟨~ in a chair⟩ **b :** PERCH, ROOST **2 :** to occupy a place as a member of an official body ⟨~ in Congress⟩ **3 :** to hold a session **:** be in session for official business **4 :** to cover eggs for hatching **:** BROOD **5 a :** to take a position for having one's portrait painted or for being photographed **b :** to serve as a model **6** *archaic* **:** to have one's dwelling place **:** DWELL **7 a :** to lie or hang relative to a wearer ⟨the collar ~*s* awkwardly⟩ **b :** to be apt or suitable **c :** to affect one with a certain weight **8 :** to lie or rest in any condition **9 a :** to have a location ⟨house ~*s* well back from the road⟩ **b** *of wind* **:** to blow from a certain direction **10 :** to remain inactive or quiescent ⟨the car ~*s* in the garage⟩ **11 :** to take an examination **12 :** BABY-SIT **~** *vt* **1 :** to cause (oneself) to be seated ⟨*sat* him down to write a letter⟩ **2 :** to cause to be seated **:** place on or in a seat **3 :** to sit upon (eggs) **4 :** to keep one's seat upon ⟨~ a horse⟩ **5 :** to provide seats or seating room for ⟨car will ~ six people⟩ — **sit on 1 :** to hold deliberations concerning **2 :** REPRESS, SQUELCH **3 :** to delay action or decision concerning **:** SUPPRESS — **sit on one's hands 1 :** to withhold applause **2 :** to fail to take action — **sit pretty :** to be in a highly favorable situation — **sit tight 1 :** to maintain one's position without change **2 :** to remain quiet in or as if in hiding — **sit under :** to attend religious service under the instruction or ministrations of; *also* **:** to attend the classes or lectures of (a teacher)

2sit *n* **1 :** an act or period of sitting **2 :** the manner in which a garment fits

si·tar \sə-'tär, si-\ *n* [Hindi *sitār*] **:** a Hindu guitar with a long neck and a varying number of strings

sit–down \'sit-,daùn, 'sid-,aùn\ *n* **:** a cessation of work by employees while maintaining continuous occupation of place of employment as a protest and means toward forcing compliance with demands

1site \'sīt\ *n* [ME, place, position, fr. MF or L; MF, fr. L *situs*, fr. *situs*, pp. of *sinere* to leave, place, lay; akin to L *serere* to sow — more at SOW] **1 a :** the local position of building, town, monument, or similar work **b :** a space of ground occupied or to be occupied by a building **2 :** the place or scene of something

2site *vt* **:** to place on a site or in position **:** LOCATE

sith \(')sith\ *or* **sith·ence** \'sith-ən(t)s\ *or* **sith·ens** \-ənz\ *archaic var of* SINCE

sit–in \'sit-,in\ *n* **1 :** SIT-DOWN **2 :** an act of occupying seats in a racially segregated establishment in organized protest against discrimination

si·tol·o·gy \sī-'täl-ə-jē, sə-\ *n* [Gk *sitos* grain + ISV *-logy*] **:** the science of nutrition and dietetics

si·tos·ter·ol \sī-'täs-tə-,ròl, -,rōl\ *n* [Gk *sitos* grain + E *sterol*] **:** any of several sterols widespread esp. in plant products (as wheat germ or soy bean oil) used as a starting material for the synthesis of steroid hormones

sit·ter \'sit-ər\ *n* **:** one that sits; *specif* **:** BABY-SITTER

sit·ter–in \,sit-ə-'rin, 'sit-ə-,\ *n, pl* **sitters–in** *chiefly Brit* **:** BABY-SITTER

1sit·ting \'sit-iŋ\ *n* **1 :** an act of one that sits; *esp* **:** a single occasion of continuous sitting **2 a :** a brooding over eggs for hatching **b :** SETTING 6 **3 :** SESSION ⟨~ of the legislature⟩

2sitting *adj* **1 :** that is setting ⟨~ hen⟩ **2 :** occupying a judicial or legislative seat **:** being in office **3 :** easily hit or played ⟨~ target⟩ ⟨~ game in spades⟩ **4 a :** used in or for sitting ⟨a ~ position⟩ **b :** performed while sitting ⟨a ~ shot⟩

sitting duck *n* **:** an easy or defenseless target for attack or criticism or sharp practice

sitting room *n* **:** LIVING ROOM 1

1sit·u·ate \'sich-(ə-)wət, -ə-,wāt\ *adj* [ML *situatus*, pp. of *situare* to place, fr. L *situs*] **:** having its site **:** LOCATED

2sit·u·ate \'sich-ə-,wāt\ *vt* **:** to place in a site, situation, or category **:** LOCATE

sit·u·at·ed *adj* **1 :** LOCATED **2 :** CIRCUMSTANCED ⟨not rich but comfortably ~⟩

sit·u·a·tion \,sich-ə-'wā-shən\ *n* **1 a :** the way in which something is placed in relation to its surroundings **b :** SITE **c** *archaic* **:** LOCALITY **2** *archaic* **:** state of health **3 a :** position or place of employment **:** POST, JOB **b :** position in life **:** STATUS **4 a :** position with respect to conditions and circumstances ⟨military ~⟩ **b :** the sum total of internal and external stimuli that act upon an organism within a given time interval **5 a :** relative position or combination of circumstances at a certain moment ⟨the ~ seemed to call for a general retreat⟩ **b :** a critical, trying, or unusual state of affairs **:** PROBLEM **c :** a particular or striking complex of affairs at a stage in the action of a narrative or drama **syn** see POSITION, STATE — **sit·u·a·tion·al** \-shnəl, -shən-ᵊl\ *adj* — **sit·u·a·tion·al·ly** \-ē\ *adv*

si·tus \'sīt-əs\ *n, pl* **si·tus** \'sīt-əs, 'sī-,tüs\ [L — more at SITE] **:** the place where something exists or originates

sitz bath \'sits-\ *n* [part trans. of G *sitzbad*, fr. *sitz* act of sitting + *bad* bath] **:** a tub in which one bathes in a sitting posture; *also* **:** a bath so taken esp. therapeutically

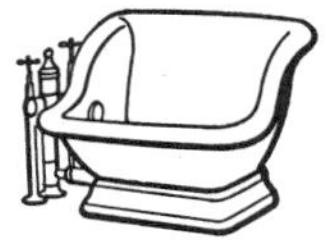
sitz bath

sitz·krieg \'sit-,skrēg, 'zit-\ *n* [G, fr. *sitz* + *krieg* war] **:** static or nonaggressive warfare

sitz·mark \'sit-,smärk, 'zit-\ *n* [part trans. of G *sitzmarke*, fr. *sitz* + *marke* mark] **:** a depression left in the snow by a skier falling backward

Si·va \'s(h)ē-və\ *n* [Skt *Śiva*] **:** a Hindu god who represents the principle of destruction in the Trimurti and is worshiped as the gracious creator and sustainer of the world in a major cult — **Si·va·ism** \-,iz-əm\ *n*

Si·va·ite \-,īt\ *or* **Si·vite** \'s(h)ē-,vīt\ *n* **:** SAIVA

Si·van \'siv-ən\ *n* [Heb *Sīwān*, fr. Akkadian *Simānu*] **:** the 9th month of the civil year or the 3d month of the ecclesiastical year in the Jewish calendar

Si·wash \'sī-,wòsh, -,wäsh\ *n* [*Siwash*, fictional college in stories by George Fitch] **:** a small usu. inland college that is notably provincial in outlook ⟨cheer for dear old *Siwash*⟩

six \'siks\ *n* [ME, fr. *six*, adj., fr. OE *siex;* akin to OHG *sehs* six, L *sex*, Gk *hex*] **1** — see NUMBER table **2 :** the sixth in a set or series ⟨the ~ of hearts⟩ **3 :** something having six units or members: as **a :** an ice hockey team **b :** a six-cylinder engine or automobile — **six** *adj or pron* — **at sixes and sevens :** in disorder **:** CONFUSED

six–by–six \,siks-bə-'siks\ *n* **:** a six-wheeled motor vehicle with six driving wheels

six–gun \'siks-,gən\ *n* **:** a 6-chambered revolver — called also *six-shoot·er* \'sik(s)-'shüt-ər\

six·mo \'sik-(,)smō\ *n* **:** the size of a piece of paper cut six from a sheet; *also* **:** a book, a page, or paper of this size — called also *sexto*

six–o–six *or* **606** \,sik-,sō-'siks\ *n* [fr. its having been the 606th compound tested and introduced by Paul Ehrlich] **:** ARSPHENAMINE

six–pack \'sik-,spak\ *n* **:** an open paperboard carton containing six bottles or cans (as of a beverage) and usu. having a handle for carrying

six·pence \'sik-spən(t)s, *US also* -,spen(t)s\ *n* **:** the sum of six pence; *also* **:** a coin representing six pence or half a shilling

six·pen·ny \-spə-nē, *US also* -,spen-ē\ *adj* **1 :** of the value of or costing sixpence **2 :** of trifling worth **:** CHEAP, TRASHY

sixpenny bit *n* **:** SIXPENCE

sixte \'sikst, 'sēkst\ *n* [F, lit., sixth, fr. L *sextus* — more at SEXT] **:** the sixth of the eight defensive positions in fencing

six·teen \(')sik-'stēn\ *n* [ME *sixtene*, fr. OE *sixtȳne*, fr. *sixtȳne*, adj.; akin to OE *tīen* ten] — see NUMBER table — **sixteen** *adj or pron* — **six·teenth** \-'stēn(t)th\ *adj* — **sixteenth** *n, pl* **six·teenths** \-'stēn(t)s, -'stēn(t)ths\

six·teen·mo \sik-'stēn-(,)mō\ *n* **:** the size of a piece of paper cut 16 from a sheet; *also* **:** a book, a page, or paper of this size — called also *sextodecimo*

sixteenth note *n* **:** a musical note with the time value of one sixteenth of a whole note

sixth \'siks(t)th, 'sikst\ *n, pl* **sixths** \'siks(ts), 'siks(t)ths\ **1** — see NUMBER table **2 a :** a musical interval embracing six diatonic degrees **b :** SUBMEDIANT **c :** the harmonic combination of two tones a sixth apart — **sixth** *adj or adv* — **sixth·ly** *adv*

sixth chord *n* **:** a musical chord consisting of a tone with its third and its sixth above and usu. being the first inversion of a triad

sixth sense *n* **:** a power of perception like but not one of the five senses **:** a keen intuitive power

six·ti·eth \'sik-stē-əth\ *n* — see NUMBER table — **sixtieth** *adj*

Six·tine \'sik-,stīn, -,stēn\ *var of* SISTINE

six·ty \'sik-stē\ *n* [ME, fr. *sixty*, adj., fr. OE *siextig*, n., group of sixty, fr. *siex* six + *-tig* group of ten — more at EIGHTY] **1** — see NUMBER table **2** *pl* **:** the numbers 60 to 69 inclusive; *specif* **:** the years 60 to 69 in a lifetime or century — **sixty** *adj or pron* — **like sixty :** with great speed, ease, or force ⟨run *like sixty*⟩

six·ty–fourth note \,sik-stē-'fōrth-, -'fòrth-\ *n* **:** a musical note with half the time value of a thirty-second note

six·ty–nine \-'nīn\ *n* **1** — see NUMBER table **2 :** SOIXANTE-NEUF — **sixty–nine** *adj or pron*

siz·able *or* **size·able** \'sī-zə-bəl\ *adj* **:** fairly large **:** CONSIDERABLE — **siz·able·ness** *n* — **siz·ably** \-blē\ *adv*

siz·ar *also* **siz·er** \'sī-zər\ *n* [*sizar* alter. of *sizer*, fr. 1*size*] **:** a student (as in the universities of Cambridge and Dublin) who receives orig. in return for acting as a servant to other students an allowance toward his college expenses

1size \'sīz\ *n* [ME *sise* assize, fr. MF, fr. OF, short for *assise* — more at ASSIZE] **1** *dial Brit* **:** ASSIZE 5a — usu. used in pl. **2** *archaic* **:** a fixed portion of food or drink **3 a :** physical magnitude, extent, or bulk **:** relative or proportionate dimensions **b :** BIGNESS **4 :** one of a series of graduated measures esp. of manufactured articles (as of clothing) conventionally identified by numbers or letters ⟨a ~ 7 hat⟩ ⟨a shoe of ~ 4A⟩ **5 :** character, quality, or status of a person or thing esp. with reference to importance, relative merit, or correspondence to needs **6 :** actual state of affairs **:** true condition ⟨that's about the ~ of it⟩

2size *vt* **1 :** to make a particular size **:** bring to proper or suitable size **2 :** to arrange, grade, or classify according to size or bulk **3 :** to form a judgment of — usu. used with *up* **~** *vi* **:** to equal in size or other particular characteristic **:** COMPARE — usu. used with *up* and often with *to* or *with*

3size *n* [ME *sise*] **:** any of various glutinous materials (as preparations of glue, flour, varnish, or resins) used for filling the pores in surfaces (as of paper, textiles, leather, or plaster) or in bookbinding for applying color or leaf to book edges or covers

4size *vt* **:** to cover, stiffen, or glaze with or as if with size

5size *adj* **:** SIZED — usu. used in combination

sized \'sīzd\ *adj* **1 :** having a specified size or bulk — usu. used in combination ⟨a small-*sized* house⟩ **2 :** arranged or adjusted according to size

siz·ing \'sī-ziŋ\ *n* **:** 3SIZE

1siz·zle \'siz-əl\ *vb* **siz·zling** \-(ə-)liŋ\ [perh. freq. of *siss* (to hiss)] *vt* **:** to burn up or sear with a hissing sound **~** *vi* **1 :** to make a hissing sound in or as if in burning or frying **2 :** to seethe with deep anger or resentment

2sizzle *n* **:** a hissing sound (as of something frying over a fire)

siz·zler \'siz-(ə-)lər\ *n* **:** one that sizzles; *esp* **:** SCORCHER

skald \'skòld, 'skäld\ *n* [ON *skāld* — more at SCOLD] **:** an ancient Scandinavian poet or historiographer; *broadly* **:** BARD — **skald·ic** \-ik\ *adj*

skat \'skät, 'skat\ *n* [G, modif. of It *scarto* discard, fr. *scartare* to discard, fr. *s-* (fr. L *ex-*) + *carta* card] **1 :** a three-handed card game **2 :** a widow of two cards in skat that may be used by the winner of the bid

1skate \'skāt\ *n, pl* **skates** *also* **skate** [ME *scate*, fr. ON *skata*] **:** any of numerous rays (as of the genus *Raja*) with the pectoral fins greatly developed giving the animal a rhomboidal shape

2skate *n* [modif. of D *schaats* stilt, skate, fr. (assumed) ONF *escache* stilt; akin to OF *eschace* stilt] **1 a :** a metallic runner that has a frame usu. shaped to fit the sole of a shoe to which it is attached and that is used for gliding on ice — called also *ice skate* **b :** ROLLER SKATE **2 :** a period of skating

3skate *vi* **1 :** to glide along on skates propelled by the alternate action of the legs **2 :** to slip or glide as if on skates **:** pass lightly

4skate *n* [prob. alter. of E dial. *skite* (an offensive person)] **1 :** a thin awkward-looking or decrepit horse **:** NAG **2 :** FELLOW

skat·er \'skāt-ər\ *n* **1 :** one that skates **2 :** WATER STRIDER

skat·ole \'skat-,ōl\ *n* [ISV, fr. Gk *skat-*, *skōr* excrement — more at SCAT-] **:** a foul-smelling compound C_9H_9N found in the intestines and feces, in civet, and in several plants or made synthetically and used in perfumes as a fixative

skean *or* **skene** \'skē(-ə)n\ *n* [IrGael *scian* & ScGael *sgian*] : DAGGER, DIRK

ske·dad·dle \ski-'dad-ᵊl\ *vi* **ske·dad·dling** \-'dad-liŋ, -ᵊl-iŋ\ [origin unknown] : to run away; *specif* : to flee in a panic

Skee–Ball \'skē-,bȯl\ *trademark* — used for an indoor target game in which several hard rubber balls are rolled up an incline into one of several concentric circular scoring troughs

skeet \'skēt\ *n* [modif. of ON *skjōta* to shoot — more at SHOOT] : trapshooting in which clay targets are thrown in such a way as to simulate the angles of flight found in wing shooting

1**skee·ter** \'skēt-ər\ *n* [by shortening & alter.] **1** : MOSQUITO **2** : a small iceboat equipped with a single sail

2**skeet·er** \'skēt-ər\ *n* : a skeet shooter

skeg \'skeg\ *also* **skag** \'skag\ *n* [D *scheg;* akin to OSlav *skokŭ* leap — more at SHAG] : the stern of the keel of a ship near the sternpost; *esp* : the part connecting the keel with the bottom of the rudderpost in a single-screw ship

skeigh \'skēk\ *adj* [perh. of Scand origin; akin to Sw *skygg* shy; akin to OE *scēoh* shy — more at SHY] *chiefly Scot* : proudly spirited : SKITTISH

1**skein** \'skān\ *n* [ME *skeyne*, fr. MF *escaigne*] **1** *or* **skean** *or* **skeane** \'skān\ : a loosely coiled length of yarn or thread wound on a reel **2** : something suggesting the twists or coils of a skein : TANGLE

2**skein** *vt* : to wind into skeins ⟨~ yarn⟩

skel·e·tal \'skel-ət-ᵊl\ *adj* : of, relating to, forming, or resembling a skeleton — **skel·e·tal·ly** \-ᵊl-ē\ *adv*

1**skel·e·ton** \'skel-ət-ᵊn\ *n* [NL, fr. Gk, neut. of *skeletos* dried up; akin to Gk *skellein* to dry up, *sklēros* hard, OE *scealdl* shallow] **1** : a usu. rigid supportive or protective structure or framework of an organism; *esp* : the bony or more or less cartilaginous framework supporting the soft tissues and protecting the internal organs of a vertebrate (as a fish or man) **2** : something reduced to its minimum form or essential parts **3** : an emaciated person or animal **4** : something forming a structural framework **5** : something shameful and kept secret (as in a family)

2**skeleton** *adj* : of, consisting of, or resembling a skeleton ⟨a ~ hand⟩ ⟨a ~ crew⟩ ⟨~ essays⟩

skel·e·ton·ize \-,īz\ *vt* : to produce in or reduce to skeleton form ⟨~ a leaf⟩ ⟨~ a news story⟩ ⟨~ a regiment⟩

skel·e·ton·iz·er \-,ī-zər\ *n* : one that skeletonizes; *specif* : any of various lepidopterous larvae that eat the parenchyma of leaves leaving the skeleton of veins

skeleton key *n* : a key with a large part of the bit filed away to enable it to open low quality locks as a master key

skel·lum \'skel-əm\ *n* [D *schelm*, fr. LG; akin to OHG *skelmo* person deserving death] *chiefly Scot* : SCOUNDREL, RASCAL

1**skelp** \'skelp\ *vb* **skelped** \'skelpt\ *also* **skel·pit** \'skel-pət\ **skelp·ing** [ME *skelpen*] *vt*, *dial Brit* : STRIKE, SLAP, BEAT ~ *vi* : to step lively : HUSTLE

2**skelp** *n*, *dial Brit* : a smart blow : SLAP

skel·ter \'skel-tər\ *vi* **skel·ter·ing** \-t(ə-)riŋ\ [fr. *-skelter* (in *helter-skelter*)] : SCURRY

Skel·ton·ic \skel-'tän-ik\ *adj* : of, relating to, or characteristic of the English poet John Skelton or his writings — **Skel·ton·i·cal** \-i-kəl\ *adj*

Skel·ton·ics \-iks\ *n pl* [John *Skelton*] : short verses of an irregular meter with two or three stresses sometimes in falling and sometimes in rising rhythm and usu. with rhymed couplets

skep \'skep\ *n* [ME *skeppe* basket, basketful, fr. OE *sceppe*, fr. ON *skeppa* bushel; akin to OE *scieppan* to form, create — more at SHAPE] : BEEHIVE; *esp* : a domed hive made of twisted straw

skep·sis \'skep-səs\ *n* [NL, fr. Gk *skepsis* examination, doubt, skeptical philosophy, fr. *skeptesthai*] : philosophic doubt as to the objective reality of phenomena; *broadly* : a skeptical outlook or attitude

skep·tic \'skep-tik\ *n* [L or Gk; L *scepticus*, fr. Gk *skeptikos*, fr. *skeptikos* thoughtful, fr. *skeptesthai* to look, consider — more at SPY] **1** : an adherent or advocate of skepticism **2** : a person disposed to skepticism esp. regarding religion or religious principles

skep·ti·cal \-ti-kəl\ *adj* : relating to, characteristic of, or marked by skepticism ⟨~ arguments⟩ ⟨a ~ listener⟩ — **skep·ti·cal·ly** \-k(ə-)lē\ *adv*

skep·ti·cism \'skep-tə-,siz-əm\ *n* **1 a** : the doctrine that true knowledge or knowledge in a particular area is uncertain **b** : the method of suspended judgment, systematic doubt, or criticism characteristic of skeptics **2** : an attitude or disposition toward doubt **3** : doubt concerning basic religious principles (as immortality, providence, revelation) **syn** see UNCERTAINTY

sker·ry \'sker-ē, 'skər-\ *n* [of Scand origin; akin to ON *sker* skerry and to ON *ey* island; akin to L *aqua* water — more at SCAR, ISLAND] : a rocky isle : REEF

1**sketch** \'skech\ *n* [D *schets*, fr. It *schizzo*, fr. *schizzare* to splash] **1 a** : a rough drawing representing the chief features of an object or scene and often made as a preliminary study **b** : a tentative draft (as for a literary work) **2** : a brief description (as of a person) or outline **3 a** : a short literary composition somewhat resembling the short story and the essay but intentionally slight in treatment, discursive in style, and familiar in tone **b** : a short instrumental composition usu. for piano **c** : a slight theatrical piece having a single scene; *esp* : a comic variety act **syn** see COMPENDIUM

2**sketch** *vt* : to make a sketch, rough draft, or outline of ~ *vi* : to draw or paint a sketch — **sketch·er** *n*

sketch·book \'skech-,bu̇k\ *n* : a book of or for sketches

sketch·i·ly \'skech-ə-lē\ *adv* : in a sketchy manner

sketch·i·ness \'skech-ē-nəs\ *n* : the quality or state of being sketchy

sketchy \'skech-ē\ *adj* **1** : of the nature of a sketch : roughly outlined **2** : wanting in completeness, clearness, or substance : SLIGHT, SUPERFICIAL

1**skew** \'skyü\ *vb* [ME *skewen* to escape, skew, fr. ONF *escuer* to shun, of Gmc origin; akin to OHG *sciuhen* to frighten off — more at SHY] *vi* **1** : to take an oblique course : SWERVE **2** : to look askance : SQUINT ~ *vt* **1** : to make, set, or cut on the skew **2** : to distort from a true value or symmetrical form ⟨~*ed* statistical data⟩

2**skew** *adj* **1** : set, placed, or running obliquely : SLANTING **2** : more developed on one side or in one direction than another : not symmetrical

3**skew** *n* : a deviation from a straight line : SLANT

skew arch *n* : an arch whose jambs are not at right angles with the face

skew·back \'skyü-,bak\ *n* : a course of masonry, a stone, or an iron plate having an inclined face against which the voussoirs of a segmental arch abut

skew·bald \-,bȯld\ *adj* [*skewed* (skewbald) + *bald*] *of an animal* : marked with spots and patches of white and some other color

skew distribution *n* : an unsymmetrical frequency distribution having the mode at a different value from the mean

1**skew·er** \'skyü-ər, 'skyu̇(-ə)r\ *n* [prob. alter. of *skiver*] **1** : a pin of wood or metal for fastening meat to keep it in form while roasting or to hold small pieces of meat and vegetables for broiling **2** : any of various things shaped or used like a meat skewer

2**skewer** *vt* : to fasten or pierce with or as if with a skewer

skew·ness \'skyü-nəs\ *n* : lack of straightness or symmetry : DISTORTION; *esp* : lack of symmetry in a frequency distribution

skew polygon *n* : a figure analagous to a polygon whose sides do not all lie in one and the same plane

1**ski** \'skē, *Brit also* 'shē\ *n*, *pl* **skis** *or* **ski** *also* **skiis** \'skēz, 'shēz\ [Norw, fr. ON *skīth* stick of wood, ski; akin to OHG *skīt* stick of wood, OE *scēadan* to divide — more at SHED] : one of a pair of narrow strips of wood, metal, or plastic curving upward in front that are used esp. for gliding over snow

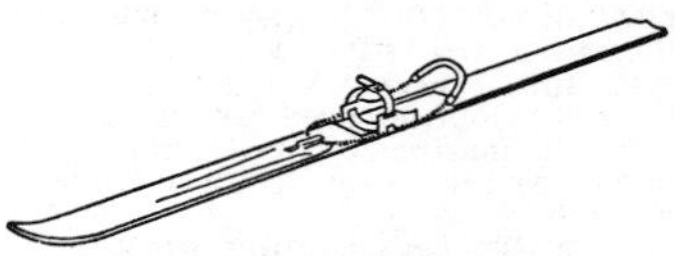

ski and binding

2**ski** *vi* **skied** \'skēd, 'shēd\ **ski·ing** : to glide on skis in travel or as a sport

skia- *comb form* [NL, fr. Gk *skia* — more at SCENE] : shadow ⟨*skia*graph⟩

skia·gram \'skī-ə-,gram\ *n* [ISV] **1** : a figure formed by shading in the outline of a shadow **2** : RADIOGRAPH

skia·graph \-,graf\ *n* : RADIOGRAPH

ski·ag·ra·phy \skī-'ag-rə-fē\ *n* [ISV] : the making of skiagrams

skia·scope \'skī-ə-,skōp\ *n* : a device for determining the refractive state of the eye from the movements of retinal lights and shadows — **ski·as·co·py** \skī-'as-kə-pē\ *n*

ski boot *n* : a rigid padded shoe usu. of leather or plastic that extends just above the ankle, is securely fastened to the foot (as with laces, buckles, or hinges), and is locked into position in a ski binding

1**skid** \'skid\ *n* [perh. of Scand origin; akin to ON *skīth* stick of wood] **1** : one of a group of objects (as planks or logs) used to support or elevate a structure or object **2** : a wooden fender hung over a ship's side to protect it in handling cargo **3** : a usu. iron shoe or clog attached to a chain and placed under a wheel to prevent its turning when descending a steep hill : DRAG **4** : a timber, bar, rail, pole, or log used in pairs or sets to form a slideway (as for an incline from a truck to the sidewalk) **5** : the act of skidding : SLIP, SIDESLIP **6** : a runner used as a member of the landing gear of an airplane or helicopter **7** *pl* : a route to defeat or downfall ⟨had made it big but was now on the ~*s*⟩ **8** : a low platform mounted (as on wheels) on which material is set for handling and moving

2**skid** *vb* **skid·ded**; **skid·ding** *vt* **1** : to apply a brake or skid to : slow or halt by a skid **2** : to haul along, slide, hoist, or store on skids ~ *vi* **1** : to slide without rotating (as a wheel held from turning while a vehicle moves onward) **2 a** : to fail to grip the roadway; *specif* : to slip sideways on the road **b** *of an airplane* : to slide sidewise away from the center of curvature when turning **c** : SLIDE, SLIP **3** : to fall rapidly, steeply, or far

skid·der \'skid-ər\ *n* : one that skids or uses a skid

skid·doo *or* **ski·doo** \skid-'ü\ *vi* [prob. alter. of *skedaddle*] : to go away : DEPART

skid fin *n* : a fore-and-aft vertical surface usu. placed above the upper wing of a biplane to provide lateral stability

skid road *n* **1** : a road along which logs are skidded **2 a** *West* : the part of a town frequented by loggers **b** : SKID ROW

skid row *n* [alter. of *skid road*] : a district of cheap saloons, flophouses, and employment agencies frequented by migrant workers, vagrants, and alcoholics

ski·er \'skē-ər, *Brit also* 'shē-\ *n* : one that skis

ski·ey *var of* SKYEY

skiff \'skif\ *n* [MF or OIt; MF *esquif*, fr. OIt *schifo*, of Gmc origin; akin to OE *scip* ship] **1** : a small light sailing ship **2** : a light rowboat **3** : a boat with centerboard and spritsail light enough to be rowed — called also *St. Lawrence skiff* **4** : a small fast powerboat

ski·ing *n* : the art or sport of sliding and jumping on skis

ski·jor·ing \'skē-,jȯr-iŋ, -,jȯr-\ *or* **ski·ör·ing** \-,(y)ər-\ *n* [modif. of Norw *skikjøring*, fr. *ski* + *kjøring* driving] : a winter sport in which a person wearing skis is drawn over snow or ice by a horse or vehicle

ski jump *n* : a jump made by a person wearing skis; *also* : a course or track esp. prepared for such jumping — **ski jump** *vi*

ski lift *n* : a power-driven conveyor for transporting skiers or sightseers up a long slope or mountainside

1**skill** \'skil\ *n* [ME *skil*, fr. ON, distinction, knowledge; akin to OE *scylian* to separate, *sciell* shell — more at SHELL] **1** *obs* : CAUSE, REASON **2** : the ability to use one's knowledge effectively and readily in execution or performance : technical expertness : PROFICIENCY, DEXTERITY **3** : a learned power of doing a thing competently : a developed aptitude or ability **syn** see ART

2**skill** *vi*, *archaic* : to make a difference : MATTER, AVAIL

skilled \'skild\ *adj* **1** : having skill : EXPERT, SKILLFUL **2** : of, relating to, or requiring workers or labor with skill and training in a particular occupation, craft, or trade ⟨~ labor⟩ **syn** see PROFICIENT

skil·let \'skil-ət\ *n* [ME *skelet*] **1** *chiefly Brit* : a small kettle or pot usu. having three or four often long feet and used for cooking on the hearth **2** : a frying pan

skill·ful *or* **skil·ful** \'skil-fəl\ *adj* **1** : possessed of or displaying skill : EXPERT ⟨~ debater⟩ **2** : accomplished with skill **syn** see PROFICIENT — **skill·ful·ly** \-fə-lē\ *adv* — **skill·ful·ness** *n*

skil·ling \'skil-iŋ, 'shil-\ *n* [Sw, Norw, & Dan, fr. ON *skillingr*, a gold coin; akin to OE *scilling* shilling] **1 :** any of various old Scandinavian units of value **2 :** any of the small coins representing one skilling

skill–less *or* **skil·less** \'skil-ləs\ *adj* **:** having no skill — **skill–less·ness** *n*

[1]**skim** \'skim\ *vb* **skimmed; skim·ming** [ME *skimmen*] *vt* **1 a :** to clear (a liquid) of scum or floating substance ⟨~ boiling syrup⟩ **b :** to remove (as film or scum) from the surface of a liquid **c :** to remove cream from by skimming **d :** to remove the best or most easily obtainable contents from **2 :** to read, study, or examine superficially and rapidly; *specif* **:** to glance through (as a book) for the chief ideas or the plot **3 :** to throw in a gliding path; *specif* **:** to throw so as to ricochet along the surface of water **4 :** to cover with or as if with a film, scum, or coat **5 :** to pass swiftly or lightly over ~ *vi* **1 a :** to pass lightly or hastily **:** glide or skip along, above, or near a surface **b :** to give a cursory glance or consideration **2 :** to become coated with a thin layer of film or scum **3 :** to put on a finishing coat of plaster

[2]**skim** *n* **1 :** a thin layer, coating, or film **2 :** the act of skimming **3 :** something skimmed; *specif* **:** SKIM MILK

[3]**skim** *adj* **1 :** SKIMMED **2 :** made of skim milk ⟨~ cheese⟩

skim·ble–skam·ble \,skim-bəl-'skam-bəl\ *adj* [redupl. of *scamble*] **:** RAMBLING, SENSELESS

skim·mer \'skim-ər\ *n* **1 :** one that skims; *specif* **:** a flat perforated scoop or spoon used for skimming **2 a :** any of several long-winged marine birds (genus *Rhynchops*) related to the terns **b :** WATER STRIDER **3 :** a usu. straw flat-crowned hat with a wide straight brim

skim milk *also* **skimmed milk** *n* **:** milk from which the cream has been taken

skim·ming *n* **:** that which is skimmed from a liquid

[1]**skimp** \'skimp\ *adj* [perh. alter. of *scrimp*] **:** SCANTY, MEAGER

[2]**skimp** *vt* **:** to give insufficient or barely sufficient attention or effort to or funds for **:** SCAMP ~ *vi* **:** to save by or as if by skimping **:** SCRIMP

skimp·i·ly \'skim-pə-lē\ *adv* **:** in a skimpy manner

skimp·i·ness \-pē-nəs\ *n* **:** the quality or state of being skimpy

skimpy \'skim-pē\ *adj* **:** deficient in supply or execution esp. through skimping **:** SCANTY

[1]**skin** \'skin\ *n, often attrib* [ME, fr. ON *skinn*; akin to OE *scinn* skin, MHG *schint* fruit peel, W *ysgythru* to cut] **1 a :** the integument of an animal and esp. a small animal or fur-bearer separated from the body whether green or dressed for use — compare HIDE **b :** a sheet of parchment or vellum made from a hide **c :** BOTTLE 1b **2 a :** the external limiting layer of an animal body esp. when forming a tough but flexible cover relatively impermeable from without while intact **b :** any of various outer or surface layers (as a rind, husk, or pellicle) ⟨a sausage ~⟩ **3 :** the life or physical well-being of a person ⟨made sure to save his ~⟩ **4 :** a sheathing or casing forming the outside surface of a structure (as a ship or airplane) — **skinned** \'skind\ *adj*

[2]**skin** *vb* **skinned; skin·ning** *vt* **1 a :** to cover with or as if with skin **b :** to heal over with skin **2 a :** to strip, scrape, or rub off an outer covering (as the skin or rind) of **b :** to strip or peel off **3 a :** to strip of money or property **:** FLEECE **b :** DEFEAT **c :** CENSURE, CASTIGATE **4 :** to urge on and direct the course of (as a draft animal) ~ *vi* **1 :** to become covered with or as if with skin **2 a :** to climb or descend ⟨~ up and down a rope⟩ **b :** to pass or get by with scant room to spare

skin–deep \'skin-'dēp\ *adj* **1 :** as deep as the skin **2 :** not thorough or lasting in impression **:** SUPERFICIAL

skin dive *vi* **:** to swim deep below the surface of water with a face mask and flippers and with or without a portable breathing device — **skin diver** *n*

skin effect *n* **:** an effect characteristic of current distribution in a conductor at high frequencies by virtue of which the current is greater near the surface of the conductor than in its interior

skin·flint \'skin-,flint\ *n* **:** a person who would save, gain, or extort money by any means **:** MISER, NIGGARD

skin·ful \-,fu̇l\ *n* **1 :** the contents of a skin bottle **2 :** a large or satisfying quantity esp. of liquor

skin game *n* **:** a swindling game or trick

skin graft *n* **:** a piece of skin transferred from a donor area to a place denuded (as by a burn) to grow new skin — **skin grafting** *n*

[1]**skink** \'skiŋk\ *vt* [ME *skinken*, fr. MD *schenken*; akin to OE *scencan* to pour out drink, *scanca* shank] *chiefly dial* **:** to draw, pour out, or serve (drink)

[2]**skink** *n* [L *scincus*, fr. Gk *skinkos*] **:** any of a family (Scincidae) of pleurodont lizards mostly small and with small scales

skink·er \'skiŋ-kər\ *n* **:** TAPSTER

skin·less \'skin-ləs\ *adj* **:** having no skin ⟨~ frankfurts⟩

skin·ner \'skin-ər\ *n* **1 a :** one that deals in skins, pelts, or hides **b :** one that removes, cures, or dresses skins **2 :** SHARPER **3 :** a driver of draft animals **:** TEAMSTER

skin·ni·ness \'skin-ē-nəs\ *n* **:** the quality or state of being skinny

skin·ny \'skin-ē\ *adj* **1 :** resembling skin **:** MEMBRANOUS **2 a :** lacking sufficient flesh **:** very thin **:** EMACIATED **b :** lacking usual or desirable bulk, quantity, qualities, or significance **syn** see LEAN

skin test *n* **:** a test (as a scratch test) performed on the skin and used in detecting allergic hypersensitivity

skin·tight \'skin-'tīt\ *adj* **:** closely fitted to the figure

[1]**skip** \'skip\ *vb* **skipped; skip·ping** [ME *skippen*, perh. of Scand origin; akin to Sw dial. *skopa* to hop] *vi* **1 a :** to move or proceed with leaps and bounds **:** CAPER **b :** to bound off one point after another **:** RICOCHET **2 :** to leave hurriedly or secretly **3 a :** to pass over or omit an interval, item, or step **b :** to omit a grade in school in advancing to the next **c :** MISFIRE 1 ~ *vt* **1 a :** to pass over without notice or mention **:** OMIT **b :** to pass by or leave out (a step in a progression or series) **2 a :** to cause to skip (a grade in school) **b :** to cause to bound or skim over a surface ⟨~ a stone across a pond⟩ **3 :** to leap over lightly and nimbly **4 a :** to depart from quickly and secretly **b :** to fail to attend ⟨~ the staff meeting⟩

[2]**skip** *n* **1 a :** a light bounding step **b :** a gait composed of alternating hops and steps **2 :** an act of omission or the thing omitted

[3]**skip** *n* [short for [2]*skipper*] **1 :** the captain of a side in a game (as curling or lawn bowling) who advises his men as to the play and controls the action **2 :** SKIPPER

[4]**skip** *vt* **skipped; skip·ping :** to act as skipper of

ski pants *n pl* **:** pants for skiing that are ribbed or close-fitted at the ankle

skip bomb *vt* **:** to attack by releasing delayed-action bombs from a low-flying airplane so as to skip along a land or water surface and strike a target

skip·jack \'skip-,jak\ *n, pl* **skipjacks** *or* **skipjack :** any of various fishes that jump above or play at the surface of the water (as bonito, tenpounder, or bluefish)

ski pole *n* **:** a metal-pointed pole or stick of steel or cane fitted with a strap for the hand at the top and an encircling disk set a little above the point and used as an aid in skiing — called also *ski stick*

[1]**skip·per** \'skip-ər\ *n* **1 :** any of various erratically active insects **2 :** one that skips **3 :** the Atlantic saury (*Scombresox saurus*) or a related fish that jumps freely above the water **4 :** any of numerous small stout-bodied lepidopterous insects (superfamily Hesperioidea) that differ from the typical butterflies in wing venation and the form of the antennae

[2]**skipper** *n* [ME, fr. MD *schipper*, fr. *schip* ship; akin to OE *scip* ship — more at SHIP] **1 :** the master of a ship; *esp* **:** the master of a fishing, small trading, or pleasure boat **2 :** the captain or first pilot of an airplane

[1]**skirl** \'skər(-ə)l, 'skir(ə)l\ *vb* [ME (Sc) *skrillen, skirlen*, of Scand origin; akin to OSw *skrælla* to rattle; akin to OE *scrallettan* to sound loudly] *vi, of a bagpipe* **:** to emit the high shrill tone of the chanter; *also* **:** to give forth music ~ *vt* **:** to play (music) on the bagpipe

[2]**skirl** *n* **:** a high shrill sound produced by the chanter of a bagpipe

[1]**skir·mish** \'skər-mish\ *n* [ME *skyrmissh*, alter. of *skarmish*, fr. MF *escarmouche*, fr. OIt *scaramuccia*, of Gmc origin; akin to OHG *skirmen* to defend] **1 :** a minor fight in war usu. incidental to larger movements **2 :** a brisk preliminary verbal conflict **syn** see ENCOUNTER

[2]**skirmish** *vi* **1 a :** to engage in a skirmish **b :** to engage in a minor or preliminary argument **2 :** to search about (as for supplies) **:** scout around — **skir·mish·er** *n*

[1]**skirr** \'skər\ *vb* [perh. alter. of [1]*scour*] *vi* **1 :** to leave hastily **:** FLEE ⟨birds ~*ed* off from the bushes —D.H.Lawrence⟩ **2 :** to run, fly, sail, or otherwise move rapidly ~ *vt* **1 :** to search about in ⟨~ the country round —Shak.⟩ **2 a :** to pass rapidly over **:** SKIM **b** *dial* **:** to cause to skim ⟨~ a stone⟩

[2]**skirr** *n* [prob. imit.] **:** WHIR, ROAR

[1]**skirt** \'skərt\ *n* [ME, fr. ON *skyrta* shirt, kirtle — more at SHIRT] **1 a** (1) **:** a free hanging part of an outer garment or undergarment extending from the waist down (2) **:** a separate free hanging outer garment or undergarment for women and girls covering the body from the waist down **b :** either of two usu. leather flaps on a saddle covering the bars on which the stirrups are hung **2 a :** the rim, periphery, or environs of an area **b** *pl* **:** the outlying parts of a town or city **:** OUTSKIRTS **3 :** a part or attachment serving as a rim, border, or edging **4** *slang* **:** GIRL, WOMAN

[2]**skirt** *vt* **1 :** to form or run along the border or edge of **:** BORDER **2 a :** to provide a skirt for ⟨a full-*skirted* coat⟩ **b :** to furnish a border or shield for **3 a :** to go or pass around or about; *specif* **:** to go around or keep away from in order to avoid danger or discovery **b :** to avoid because of difficulty or fear of controversy **c :** to evade or miss by a narrow margin ~ *vi* **:** to be, lie, or move along an edge, border, or margin

skirt·er \-ər\ *n* **:** one that skirts

skirt·ing \-iŋ\ *n* **1 :** something that skirts: as **a :** BORDER, EDGING **b** *Brit* **:** BASEBOARD **2 :** fabric (as wool) suitable for skirts

ski run *n* **:** a slope or trail suitable for skiing

ski suit *n* **:** a warm outfit for winter sports made in one-piece or two-piece style with a jacket top and pants usu. having ribbed cuffs

skit \'skit\ *n* [origin unknown] **1 :** a jeering or satirical remark **:** TAUNT **2 a :** a satirical or humorous story or sketch **b** (1) **:** a brief burlesque or comic sketch included in a dramatic performance (as a review) (2) **:** a short serious dramatic piece included in a review or given separately

ski tow *n* **1 :** a power-driven conveyor for pulling skiers to the top of a slope that consists usu. of an endless motor-driven moving rope which the skier grasps **2 :** SKI LIFT

skit·ter \'skit-ər\ *vb* [prob. freq. of E dial. *skite* to move quickly] *vi* **1 :** to glide or skip lightly or quickly along a surface **2 :** to twitch the hook of a fishing line through or along the surface of water ~ *vt* **:** to cause to skitter

skit·tish \'skit-ish\ *adj* [ME] **1 a :** lively or frisky in action **:** CAPRICIOUS **b :** FLUCTUATING, VARIABLE **2 :** easily frightened **:** RESTIVE — used chiefly of a horse **3 :** COY, BASHFUL — **skit·tish·ly** *adv* — **skit·tish·ness** *n*

skit·tle \'skit-ᵊl\ *n* [perh. of Scand origin; akin to ON *skutill* bolt — more at SHUTTLE] **1** *pl but sing in constr* **:** English ninepins played with a wooden disk or wooden ball to knock down pins **2 :** one of the pins used in skittles

skive \'skīv\ *vt* [of Scand origin; akin to ON *skīfa* to slice; akin to OE *scēadan* to divide — more at SHED] **:** to cut off (as leather or rubber) in thin layers or pieces **:** PARE

skiv·er \'skī-vər\ *n* **1 :** a thin soft leather made of the grain side of a split sheepskin, usu. tanned in sumac and dyed **2 :** one that skives something (as leather)

[1]**skiv·vy** \'skiv-ē\ *n* [origin unknown] *Brit* **:** a female domestic servant

[2]**skivvy** *n* [origin unknown] **:** underwear consisting of shorts and a collarless short-sleeved pullover of knitted cotton — usu. used in pl.

sklent \'sklent\ *vb* [ME *sclenten* to strike obliquely, alter. of *slenten* — more at SLANT] *vi* **1** *chiefly Scot* **:** to look askance **2** *chiefly Scot* **:** to cast aspersions ~ *vt, Scot* **:** to direct sideways **:** SLANT

skoal \'skōl\ *n* [Dan *skaal*, lit., cup; akin to ON *skāl* bowl — more at SCALE] **:** TOAST, HEALTH — often used interjectionally

skua \'skyü-ə\ *n* [NL, fr. Faeroese *skūgvur*; akin to ON *skūfr* tassel, skua, OE *scēaf* sheaf — more at SHEAF] **:** JAEGER 2; *esp* **:** a large No. Atlantic jaeger (*Catharacta skua*) — called also *great skua*

skul·dug·gery *or* **skull·dug·gery** \,skəl-'dəg-(ə-)rē\ *n* [origin unknown] **:** a devious device or trick; *also* **:** the habit or practice of deviousness

[1]**skulk** \'skəlk\ *vb* [ME *skulken*, of Scand origin; akin to Dan *skulke* to shirk, play truant] *vi* **1 :** to move in a stealthy or furtive manner **2 a :** to hide or conceal oneself often from cowardice

or fear or with sinister intent ⟨~*ing* in thickets⟩ **b** *chiefly Brit* **:** MALINGER **syn** see LURK — **skulk·er** *n*
2skulk *n* **1 :** SKULKER **2 :** a group of foxes
skull \'skəl\ *n* [ME *skulle,* of Scand origin; akin to Sw *skulle* skull] **1 :** the skeleton of the head of a vertebrate forming a bony or cartilaginous case that encloses and protects the brain and chief sense organs and supports the jaws **2 :** the seat of understanding or intelligence **:** MIND
skull and cross·bones \-'krȯs-,bōnz\ *n, pl* **skulls and crossbones :** a representation of a human skull over crossbones usu. used as a warning of danger to life
skull·cap \'skəl-,kap\ *n* **1 :** a close-fitting cap; *esp* **:** a light cap without brim for indoor wear **2 :** any of various mints (genus *Scutellaria*) having a calyx that when inverted resembles a helmet
skull practice *n* **:** a strategy class for an athletic team
1skunk \'skəŋk\ *n, pl* **skunks** *also* **skunk** [of Algonquian origin; akin to Abnaki *segākw* skunk] **1 a :** any of various common omnivorous black-and-white New World mammals (esp. genus *Mephitis*) related to the weasels and fitted with a pair of perineal glands from which an intensely malodorous secretion is ejected when the animal is startled **b :** any of various offensive-smelling Old World animals **2 :** an obnoxious person
2skunk *vt* **1 a :** DEFEAT; *esp* **:** to defeat by more than double the opponent's score (as in cribbage) **b :** to shut out in a game **2 :** to fail to pay; *also* **:** CHEAT
skunk cabbage *n* **:** an eastern No. American perennial herb (*Symplocarpus foetidus*) of the arum family that sends up in early spring a cowl-shaped brownish purple spathe having an unpleasant odor; *also* **:** a related plant (*Lysichiton camstschatcense*) of the Pacific coast region
1sky \'skī\ *n, pl* **skies** [ME, cloud, sky, fr. ON *sky̅* cloud; akin to OE *scēo* cloud, L *cutis* skin — more at HIDE] **1 :** the upper atmosphere that constitutes an apparent great vault or arch over the earth **:** FIRMAMENT **2 :** HEAVEN 2 **3 a :** weather in the upper atmosphere **b :** CLIMATE
2sky *vt* **skied** *or* **skyed; sky·ing 1** *chiefly Brit* **:** to throw or toss up **:** FLIP **2 :** to hang (as a painting) above the line of vision
sky blue *n* **:** a variable color averaging a pale to light blue
sky·borne \'skī-,bō(ə)rn, -,bȯ(ə)rn\ *adj* **:** AIRBORNE ⟨~ troops⟩
sky·cap \'skī-,kap\ *n* [1*sky* + *-cap* (as in *redcap*)] **:** one employed to carry hand luggage at an airport
sky·div·ing \-,dī-viŋ\ *n* **:** the sport of jumping from an airplane (as at an altitude of 6000 feet) and executing various body maneuvers before pulling the rip cord of a parachute
Skye terrier \'skī-\ *n* [*Skye,* island of the Inner Hebrides, Scotland] **:** any of a Scottish breed of terriers with a long head, a long low body, and short straight legs
sky·ey \'skī-ē\ *adj* **:** of or resembling the sky **:** ETHEREAL
sky-high \'skī-'hī\ *adv (or adj)* **1 a :** high into the air **b :** to a high level or degree **2 :** in an enthusiastic manner **3 :** to bits **:** APART **4 :** EXORBITANTLY
1sky·lark \'skī-,lärk\ *n* **1 :** a common largely brown Old World lark (*Alauda arvensis*) noted for its song esp. as uttered in vertical flight **2 :** any of various birds resembling the skylark
2skylark *vi* **1 :** to run up and down the rigging of a ship in sport **2 :** FROLIC, SPORT — **sky·lark·er** *n*
sky·light \'skī-,līt\ *n* **1 :** the diffused and reflected light of the sky **2 :** a glazed opening in a house roof or ship's deck to admit light

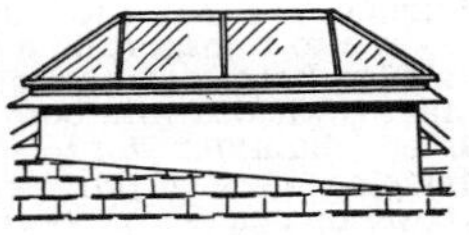
skylight 2

sky·line \-,līn\ *n* **1 :** the apparent juncture of earth and sky **:** HORIZON **2 :** an outline (as of buildings or a mountain range) against the background of the sky
sky·phos \'skī-,fäs, 'skē-,fȯs\ *var of* SCYPHUS
sky pilot *n* **:** CLERGYMAN; *specif* **:** CHAPLAIN
1sky·rock·et \'skī-,räk-ət\ *n* **:** 2ROCKET 1
2skyrocket *vi* **:** to shoot up abruptly ~ *vt* **1 :** to cause to rise or increase abruptly and rapidly **2 :** CATAPULT ⟨an invention ~*ed* him to affluence⟩
sky·sail \'skī-,sāl, -səl\ *n* **:** the sail above the royal
sky·scrap·er \-,skrā-pər\ *n* **:** a very tall building
sky·ward \-wərd\ *adv (or adj)* **1 :** toward the sky ⟨gaze ~⟩ **2 :** UPWARD
sky wave *n* **:** a radio wave that is propagated by means of the ionosphere
sky·way \'skī-,wā\ *n* **1 :** a route used by airplanes **:** AIR LANE **2 :** an elevated highway
sky·write \-,rīt\ *vb* [back-formation from *skywriting*] *vi* **:** to do skywriting ~ *vt* **:** to letter by skywriting — **sky·writ·er** *n*
sky·writ·ing \-,rīt-iŋ\ *n* **:** writing formed in the sky by means of a visible substance (as smoke) emitted from an airplane
1slab \'slab\ *n* [ME *slabbe*] **:** a thick plate or slice (as of stone, wood, or bread) **:** as **a :** the outside piece cut from a log in squaring it **b :** concrete pavement (as of a road); *specif* **:** a strip of concrete pavement laid as a single unjointed piece
2slab *vt* **slabbed; slab·bing 1 a :** to divide or form into slabs **b :** to remove an outer slab from (as a log) **2 :** to cover (as a roadbed or roof) with slabs **3 :** to put on thickly ⟨*slabbed* butter on the bread⟩
3slab *adj* [prob. of Scand origin; akin to obs. Dan *slab* slippery] *dial chiefly Eng* **:** THICK, VISCOUS
1slab·ber \'slab-ər\ *vb* **slab·ber·ing** \-(ə-)riŋ\ [prob. fr. D *slabberen,* freq. of *slabben* to slaver — more at SLAVER] **:** SLOBBER, DROOL
2slabber *n* **:** SLOBBER, SLAVER
slab-sid·ed \'slab-'sīd-əd\ *adj* **:** having flat sides; *also* **:** being tall or long and lank
1slack \'slak\ *adj* [ME *slak,* fr. OE *sleac;* akin to OHG *slah* slack, L *laxus* slack, loose, *languēre* to languish, Gk *lēgein* to stop] **1 :** not using due diligence, care, or dispatch **:** NEGLIGENT **2 a :** characterized by slowness, sluggishness, or lack of energy ⟨~ pace⟩ **b :** moderate in some quality; *esp* **:** moderately warm ⟨~ oven⟩ **c :** blowing or flowing at low speed ⟨~ tide⟩ **3 a :** not tight **:** not tense or taut **:** RELAXED ⟨~ rope⟩ **b :** lacking in firmness **:** WEAK, SOFT ⟨~ control⟩ **4 :** wanting in activity **:** DULL ⟨~ season⟩ **5 :** lacking in completeness, finish, or perfection **6 :** not watertight ⟨~ cooperage⟩ **syn** see NEGLIGENT — **slack·ly** *adv* — **slack·ness** *n*
2slack *vt* **1 a :** to be slack or negligent in performing or doing **b :** LESSEN, MODERATE **2 :** to release tension on **:** LOOSEN **3 a :** to cause to abate **b :** SLAKE 4 ~ *vi* **1 :** to be or become slack **2 :** to shirk or evade work or duty
3slack *n* **1 :** cessation in movement or flow **2 :** a part of something that hangs loose without strain ⟨take up the ~ of a rope⟩ **3** *pl* **:** trousers esp. for casual wear **4 :** a dull season or period **:** LULL
4slack *n* [ME *slak,* fr. ON *slakki*] *dial Eng* **:** a pass between hills **:** GLEN
5slack *n* [ME *sleck*] **:** the finest screenings of coal produced at a mine unusable as fuel unless cleaned
slack-baked \-'bākt\ *adj* **1 :** UNDERDONE **2 :** physically or mentally inferior **:** HALF-BAKED
slack·en \'slak-ən\ *vb* **slack·en·ing** \-(ə-)niŋ\ *vt* **1 :** to make less active **:** slow up **:** MODERATE, RETARD ⟨~ speed at a crossing⟩ **2 :** to make slack (as by lessening tension or firmness) **:** LOOSEN ⟨~ sail⟩ ~ *vi* **1 :** to become slack or slow or negligent **:** slow down **2 :** to become less active **:** SLACK **syn** see DELAY
slack·er \'slak-ər\ *n* **:** a person who shirks work or obligation; *esp* **:** one who evades military service in time of war
slack suit *n* **:** a man's or woman's suit for casual wear or lounging consisting of a pair of slacks and jacket top or sport shirt often of the same material and color
slack water *n* **:** the period at the turn of the tide when there is little or no horizontal motion of tidal water — called also *slack tide*
slag \'slag\ *n* [MLG *slagge*] **1 :** the dross or scoria of a metal **:** CINDER **2 :** the scoriaceous lava from a volcano
slain *past part of* SLAY
slake \'slāk, *vi 3 & vt 4 are also* 'slak\ *vb* [ME *slaken,* fr. OE *slacian,* fr. *sleac* slack] *vi* **1** *obs* **:** to slacken one's efforts **:** FLAG **2** *archaic* **:** to become less violent, intense, or severe **:** ABATE **3 :** to become slaked **:** CRUMBLE ⟨lime may ~ spontaneously in moist air⟩ ~ *vt* **1** *obs* **:** SLACK 2 **2 a** *obs* **:** to make less **:** DIMINISH **b** *archaic* **:** EASE, MITIGATE **c :** to lessen the force of **:** MODERATE **3 :** SATISFY, QUENCH **4 a :** to cause (as lime) to heat and crumble by treatment with water **:** HYDRATE **b :** to alter (as lime) by exposure to air with conversion at least in part to a carbonate
sla·lom \'släl-əm\ *n* [Norw, lit., sloping track] **:** skiing in a zigzag or wavy course between upright obstacles (as flags); *also* **:** a race against time over such a course
1slam \'slam\ *n* [origin unknown] **:** the winning of all or all but one of the tricks or points of a deal in a game of cards
2slam *n* [prob. of Scand origin; akin to Icel *slæma* to slam] **1 :** a heavy blow or impact **2 a :** a noisy violent closing **b :** a banging noise; *esp* **:** one made by the slam of a door **3 :** a cutting or violent criticism
3slam *vb* **slammed; slam·ming** *vt* **1 :** to strike or beat hard **:** KNOCK **2 :** to shut forcibly and noisily **:** BANG **3 :** to set or slap down violently or noisily **4 :** to criticize harshly ~ *vi* **1 :** to make a banging noise **2 :** to work or act noisily **3 :** to utter verbal abuse
slam-bang \'slam-'baŋ\ *adv (or adj)* **1 :** with noisy violence **2 :** HEADLONG, RECKLESSLY
1slan·der \'slan-dər\ *n* [ME *sclaundre, slaundre,* fr. OF *esclandre,* fr. LL *scandalum* stumbling block, offense — more at SCANDAL] **1 :** the utterance of false charges or misrepresentations which defame and damage another's reputation **2 :** a false and defamatory oral statement about a person — compare LIBEL — **slan·der·ous** \-d(ə-)rəs\ *adj* — **slan·der·ous·ly** *adv* — **slan·der·ous·ness** *n*
2slander *vt* **slan·der·ing** \-d(ə-)riŋ\ **:** to utter slander against **:** DEFAME **syn** see MALIGN — **slan·der·er** \-dər-ər\ *n*
1slang \'slaŋ\ *n* [origin unknown] **1 :** language peculiar to a particular group: as **a :** ARGOT **b :** JARGON 2 **2 :** an informal nonstandard vocabulary composed typically of coinages, arbitrarily changed words, and extravagant, forced, or facetious figures of speech **syn** see DIALECT — **slang** *adj* — **slang·i·ly** \'slaŋ-ə-lē\ *adv* — **slang·i·ness** \'slaŋ-ē-nəs\ *n* — **slangy** \'slaŋ-ē\ *adj*
2slang *vt* **1** *slang Brit* **:** CHEAT, SWINDLE **2** *chiefly Brit* **:** to abuse with harsh or coarse language ~ *vi* **:** to use slang or vulgar abuse
1slant \'slant\ *vb* [ME *slenten* to fall obliquely, of Scand origin; akin to Sw *slinta* to slide; akin to OE *slīdan* to slide] *vi* **:** to turn or incline from a right line or a level **:** SLOPE ~ *vt* **1 :** to give an oblique or sloping direction to **2 :** to interpret or present in line with a special interest or bias **:** ANGLE
2slant *n* **1 :** a slanting direction, line, or plane **:** SLOPE **2 a :** something that slants **b :** DIAGONAL 3 **3 a :** a peculiar or personal point of view, attitude, or opinion **b :** a slanting view **:** GLANCE — **slant** *adj* — **slant·ways** \-,wāz\ *adv* — **slant·wise** \-,wīz\ *adv (or adj)*
1slap \'slap\ *n* [ME *slop,* fr. MD; akin to MD *slippen* to slip] **1** *dial Brit* **:** a pass or notch between hills **2** *dial Brit* **:** OPENING, BREACH
2slap *n* [LG *slapp,* of imit. origin] **1 a :** a blow with the open hand **b :** a quick sharp blow **2 :** a noise like that of a slap; *specif* **:** a noise resulting from play or slackness between parts of a machine **3 :** REBUFF, INSULT
3slap *vt* **slapped; slap·ping 1 :** to strike with or as if with the open hand **2 :** to put, place, or throw with careless haste or force **3 :** to assail verbally **:** INSULT **syn** see STRIKE
4slap *adv* [prob. fr. LG *slapp,* fr. *slapp,* n.] **:** DIRECTLY, SMACK
slap·dash \'slap-'dash, -,dash\ *adv (or adj)* **:** in a slipshod manner **:** HAPHAZARD; *also* **:** HASTILY
slap down *vt* **1 :** to prohibit or restrain usu. abruptly and with censure from acting in a specified way **:** SQUELCH **2 :** to put an abrupt stop to **:** SUPPRESS
slap·hap·py \-,hap-ē\ *adj, slang* **:** PUNCH-DRUNK; *also* **:** RECKLESS
slap·jack \-,jak\ *n* [3*slap* + *-jack* (as in *flapjack*)] **1 :** GRIDDLE CAKE **2 :** a card game
slap·stick \'slap-,stik\ *n* **1 :** a device made of two flat pieces of wood fastened at one end so as to make a loud noise when used by an actor to strike a person **2 :** comedy stressing farce and horseplay — **slapstick** *adj*
1slash \'slash\ *vb* [ME *slaschen*] *vt* **1 :** to cut with rough sweeping strokes **2 :** CANE, LASH **3 :** to cut slits in (as a garment) so as

to reveal a color beneath **4 :** to criticize cuttingly **5 :** to reduce sharply **:** CUT ~ *vi* **:** to cut recklessly or savagely with or as if with an edged blade — **slash·er** *n*

2**slash** *n* **1 :** the act of slashing; *also* **:** a long cut or stroke made by slashing **2 :** an ornamental slit in a garment **3 :** an open tract in a forest strewn with debris (as from logging); *also* **:** the debris in such a tract

3**slash** *n* [prob. alter. of *plash* (marshy pool)] **:** a low swampy area often overgrown with brush

1**slash·ing** *n* **1 :** the act or process of slashing **2 :** an insert or underlayer of contrasting color revealed by a slash (as in a garment) **3 :** SLASH 3

2**slashing** *adj* **1 :** incisively satiric ⟨~ wit⟩ **2 :** DASHING, SPIRITED ⟨a ~ fellow⟩ **3 :** HUGE, IMMENSE **4 :** PELTING, DRIVING ⟨~ rain⟩ **5 :** VIVID, BRILLIANT — **slash·ing·ly** *adv*

slash pocket *n* **:** a pocket suspended on the wrong side of a garment from a finished slit on the right side that serves as its opening

1**slat** \\'slat\\ *n* [ME, slate, fr. MF *esclat* splinter, fr. OF, fr. *esclater* to burst, splinter] **1 :** a thin narrow flat strip esp. of wood or metal: as **a :** LATH **b :** LOUVER **c :** STAVE **d :** one of the thin flat members in the back of a ladder-back chair **2** *pl, slang* **a :** BUTTOCKS **b :** RIBS — **slat** *adj*

2**slat** *vt* **slat·ted; slat·ting :** to make or equip with slats

3**slat** *vt* **slat·ted; slat·ting** [prob. of Scand origin; akin to ON *sletta* to slap, throw] **1** *dial Eng* **:** to hurl or throw smartly **2** *dial Eng* **:** STRIKE, PUMMEL

1**slate** \\'slāt\\ *n* [ME, fr. MF *esclat* splinter] **1 :** a piece of construction material (as laminated rock) prepared as a shingle for roofing and siding **2 :** a dense fine-grained rock produced by the compression of clays, shales, and various other rocks so as to develop a characteristic cleavage **3 :** a tablet of material (as slate) used for writing on **4 a :** a record of deeds or events ⟨a clean ~⟩ **b :** a list of candidates for nomination or election **5 a :** a dark purplish gray **b :** any of various grays similar in color to common roofing slates — **slate** *adj* — **slate·like** \\-,līk\\ *adj*

2**slate** *vt* **1 :** to cover with slate or a slatelike substance ⟨~ a roof⟩ **2 :** to register, schedule, or designate for action or appointment

3**slate** *vt* [prob. alter. of 3*slat*] **1 :** to thrash or pummel severely **2** *chiefly Brit* **:** to criticize or censure severely **:** BERATE

slate black *n* **:** a nearly neutral slightly purplish black

slate blue *n* **:** a variable color averaging a grayish blue

slat·er \\'slāt-ər\\ *n* **1 :** one that slates **2 a :** WOOD LOUSE 1 **b :** any of various marine isopods — called also *sea slater*

slath·er \\'slath-ər\\ *vt* **slath·er·ing** \\-(ə-)riŋ\\ [*slather*, n. (a great quantity)] **1 a :** to spread thickly or lavishly **b :** to spread something thickly or lavishly on **2 :** to use or spend in a wasteful or lavish manner **:** SQUANDER — **slather** *n*

slat·ted \\'slat-əd\\ *adj* **:** having or made of slats

1**slat·tern** \\'slat-ərn\\ *n* [prob. fr. G *schlottern* to hang loosely, slouch; akin to D *slodderen* to hang loosely, *slodder* slut] **:** an untidy slovenly woman; *also* **:** SLUT, PROSTITUTE — **slattern** *adj* — **slat·tern·ly** \\-lē\\ *adj or adv*

2**slattern** *vt* **:** FRITTER, WASTE — usu. used with *away*

slat·tern·li·ness \\-lē-nəs\\ *n* **:** the quality or state of being slatternly

slaty \\'slāt-ē\\ *adj* **:** of, containing, or characteristic of slate; *also* **:** gray like slate

1**slaugh·ter** \\'slȯt-ər\\ *n* [ME, of Scand origin; akin to ON *slātra* to slaughter; akin to OE *sleaht* slaughter, *slēan* to slay — more at SLAY] **1 :** the act of killing; *specif* **:** the butchering of livestock for market **2 :** destruction of human lives in battle **:** CARNAGE

2**slaughter** *vt* **1 :** to kill (animals) for food **:** BUTCHER **2 a :** to kill in a bloody or violent manner **:** SLAY **b :** to kill in large numbers **:** MASSACRE — **slaugh·ter·er** \\-ər-ər\\ *n*

slaugh·ter·house \\'slȯt-ər-,haủs\\ *n* **:** an establishment where animals are butchered

slaugh·ter·ous \\'slȯt-ə-rəs\\ *adj* **:** of or relating to slaughter **:** MURDEROUS — **slaugh·ter·ous·ly** *adv*

Slav \\'slāv, 'slav\\ *n* [ME *Sclav*, fr. ML *Sclavus*, fr. LGk *Sklabos*, fr. *Sklabēnoi* Slavs, of Slav origin; akin to OSlav *Slověne*, a Slavic people in the area of Salonika] **:** a person speaking a Slavic language as his native tongue

1**slave** \\'slāv\\ *n* [ME *sclave*, fr. OF or ML; OF *esclave*, fr. ML *sclavus*, fr. *Sclavus* Slav; fr. the reduction to slavery of many Slavic peoples of central Europe] **1 :** a person held in servitude as the chattel of another **:** BONDMAN **2 :** a person who has lost control of himself and is dominated by something or someone ⟨a ~ to drink⟩ **3 :** a mechanical device that is directly responsive to another **4 :** DRUDGE, TOILER — **slave** *adj*

2**slave** *vt, archaic* **:** ENSLAVE ~ *vi* **1 :** to work like a slave **:** DRUDGE **2 :** to traffic in slaves

slave ant *n* **:** an ant enslaved by a slave-making ant

slave driver *n* **1 :** a supervisor of slaves at work **2 :** a harsh taskmaster

slave·hold·er \\'slāv-,hōl-dər\\ *n* **:** an owner of slaves — **slave·hold·ing** \\-diŋ\\ *adj or n*

slave-mak·ing ant \\'slāv-,mā-kiŋ-\\ *n* **:** an ant that attacks the colonies of ants of other species and carries off the larvae and pupae to be reared in its own nest as slaves

1**sla·ver** \\'slav-ər, 'slāv-, 'släv-\\ *vb* **sla·ver·ing** \\-(ə-)riŋ\\ [ME *slaveren*, of Scand origin; akin to ON *slafra* to slaver; akin to MD *slabben* to slaver, L *labi* to slip — more at SLEEP] *vi* **:** DROOL, SLOBBER ~ *vt, archaic* **:** to smear with or as if with saliva

2**slaver** *n* **:** saliva dribbling from the mouth

3**slav·er** \\'slā-vər\\ *n* **1 a :** a person engaged in the slave trade **b :** a ship used in the slave trade **2 :** WHITE SLAVER

slav·ery \\'slāv-(ə-)rē\\ *n* **1 :** DRUDGERY, TOIL **2 :** submission to a dominating influence **:** SUBSERVIENCE **3 a :** the state of being a slave **b :** the practice of slaveholding **syn** see SERVITUDE

slave state *n* **1 :** a state of the U.S. in which Negro slavery was legal until the Civil War **2 :** a nation subjected to totalitarian rule

slave trade *n* **:** traffic in slaves; *esp* **:** the buying and selling of Negroes for profit prior to the American Civil War

slav·ey \\'slā-vē\\ *n* **:** DRUDGE; *esp* **:** a maid of all work

1**Slav·ic** \\'slav-ik, 'släv-\\ *adj* **:** of, relating to, or characteristic of the Slavs or their languages

2**Slavic** *n* **:** a branch of the Indo-European language family containing Belorussian, Bulgarian, Czech, Polish, Serbo-Croatian, Slovene, Russian, and Ukrainian — see INDO-EUROPEAN LANGUAGES table

Slav·i·cist \\'slav-ə-səst, 'släv-\\ *or* **Slav·ist** \\'släv-əst, 'slav-\\ *n* **:** a specialist in the Slavic languages or literatures

slav·ish \\'slā-vish\\ *adj* **1 a :** of or characteristic of a slave **:** SERVILE **b** *archaic* **:** DESPICABLE, LOW **2** *archaic* **:** OPPRESSIVE, TYRANNICAL **3 :** copying obsequiously or without originality **:** IMITATIVE **syn** see SUBSERVIENT — **slav·ish·ly** *adv* — **slav·ish·ness** *n*

slav·oc·ra·cy \\slā-'väk-rə-sē\\ *n* **:** a powerful faction of slaveholders and advocates of slavery in the South before the Civil War

1**Sla·vo·ni·an** \\slə-'vō-nē-ən\\ *n* [*Slavonia*, region of southeast Europe, fr. ML *Sclavonia, Slavonia* land of the Slavs, fr. *Sclavus* Slav] **:** SLOVENE 1b

2**Slavonian** *adj* **1 :** SLOVENE **2** *archaic* **:** SLAVIC

1**Sla·von·ic** \\slə-'vän-ik\\ *adj* [NL *slavonicus*, fr. ML *Sclavonia, Slavonia* land of the Slavs] **:** SLAVIC

2**Slavonic** *n* **1 :** SLAVIC **2 :** OLD CHURCH SLAVONIC

Slav·o·phile \\'slav-ə-,fīl, 'släv-\\ *or* **Slav·o·phil** \\-,fil\\ *n* **:** an admirer of the Slavs **:** an advocate of Slavophilism

Slav·oph·i·lism \\sla-'väf-ə-,liz-əm, 'slav-ə-,fī-,liz-\\ *n* **:** advocacy of Slavic and specif. Russian culture over that of the West esp. as practiced among some members of the Russian intelligentsia in the middle 19th century

slaw \\'slȯ\\ *n* **:** COLESLAW

slay \\'slā\\ *vb* **slew** \\'slü\\ **slain** \\'slān\\ **slay·ing** [ME *slen*, fr. OE *slēan* to strike, slay; akin to OHG *slahan* to strike, MIr *slacain* I beat] *vt* **1 :** to put to death violently **:** KILL **2** *slang* **:** to affect overpoweringly **:** OVERWHELM ⟨~s the girls⟩ ~ *vi* **:** KILL, MURDER **syn** see KILL — **slay·er** *n*

1**sleave** \\'slēv\\ *vb* [(assumed) ME *sleven*, fr. OE *-slǣfan* to cut — more at SLIVER] *vt, obs* **:** to separate (silk thread) into filaments ~ *vi* **:** to separate into filaments

2**sleave** *n* **1** *obs* **:** FLOSS 1 **2 :** THREAD ⟨sleep that knits up the raveled ~ of care —Shak.⟩

sleave silk *n, obs* **:** floss silk that is easily separated into filaments for embroidery

slea·zi·ly \\'slē-zə-lē *also* 'slā-\\ *adv* **:** in a sleazy manner

slea·zi·ness \\-zē-nəs\\ *n* **:** the state or quality of being sleazy

slea·zy \\'slē-zē *also* 'slā-\\ *adj* [origin unknown] **1 a :** lacking firmness of texture **:** FLIMSY **b :** carelessly made of inferior materials **:** SHODDY **2 :** marked by cheapness of character or quality **syn** see LIMP

1**sled** \\'sled\\ *n* [ME *sledde*, fr. MD; akin to OE *slīdan* to slide] **1 :** a vehicle on runners for conveying loads esp. over snow or ice **:** SLEDGE **2 :** a sled used by children for coasting down snow-covered hills

2**sled** *vb* **sled·ded; sled·ding** *vt* **:** SLEDGE ~ *vi* **:** to ride on a sled or sleigh — **sled·der** *n*

sled·ding *n* **1 a :** the use of a sled **b :** the conditions under which one may use a sled **2 :** GOING 4

sled dog *n* **:** a dog trained to draw a sledge esp. in the Arctic regions — called also *sledge dog*

1**sledge** \\'slej\\ *n* [ME *slegge*, fr. OE *slecg;* akin to ON *sleggja* sledgehammer, OE *slēan* to strike — more at SLAY] **:** SLEDGEHAMMER

2**sledge** *vb* **:** SLEDGEHAMMER

3**sledge** *n* [D dial. *sleedse;* akin to MD *sledde* sled] **1** *Brit* **:** SLEIGH **2 :** a vehicle with low runners that is used for transporting loads esp. over snow or ice

4**sledge** *vi* **1** *Brit* **:** to ride in a sleigh **2 :** to travel with a sledge ~ *vt* **:** to transport on a sledge

1**sledge·ham·mer** \\-,ham-ər\\ *n* [1*sledge*] **:** a large heavy hammer that is wielded with both hands — **sledgehammer** *adj*

2**sledgehammer** *vb* **:** to strike with or as if with a sledgehammer

1**sleek** \\'slēk\\ *vb* [ME *sleken*, alter. of *sliken*] *vt* **1 :** SLICK **2 :** to cover up **:** gloss over ~ *vi* **:** SLICK

2**sleek** \\'slēk\\ *adj* [alter. of 2*slick*] **1 a :** smooth and glossy as if polished ⟨~ dark hair⟩ **b :** having a smooth well-groomed look ⟨~ cattle grazing⟩ **c :** healthy-looking **2 :** SLICK 3 **3 a :** having a prosperous air **:** THRIVING **b :** ELEGANT, STYLISH — **sleek·ly** *adv* — **sleek·ness** *n*

sleek·en \\'slē-kən\\ *vt* **sleek·en·ing** \\'slēk-(ə-)niŋ\\ **:** to make sleek

sleek·er \\'slē-kər\\ *n* **:** SLICKER

sleek·it \\'slē-kət\\ *adj* [Sc, fr. pp. of 1*sleek*] **1** *chiefly Scot* **:** SLEEK, SMOOTH **2** *chiefly Scot* **:** CRAFTY, DECEITFUL

1**sleep** \\'slēp\\ *n* [ME *slepe*, fr. OE *slǣp;* akin to OHG *slāf* sleep, L *labi* to slip, slide and perh. to Gk *lobos* pod, lobe] **1 :** the natural periodic suspension of consciousness during which the powers of the body are restored **2 :** a state resembling sleep: as **a :** a state of torpid inactivity **b :** DEATH; *also* **:** TRANCE, COMA **c :** the closing of leaves or petals esp. at night **3 a :** NIGHT **b :** a day's journey — **sleep·like** \\'slē-,plīk\\ *adj*

2**sleep** *vb* **slept** \\'slept\\ **sleep·ing** *vi* **1 :** to rest in a state of sleep **2 :** to be in a state (as of quiescence or death) resembling sleep **3 :** to have sexual relations ~ *vt* **1 :** to be slumbering in ⟨*slept* the sleep of the dead⟩ **2 :** to get rid of or spend in or by sleep **3 :** to provide sleeping accommodations for ⟨the boat ~s six⟩

sleep·er \\'slē-pər\\ *n* **1 :** one that sleeps **2 :** a piece of timber, stone, or steel on or near the ground to support a superstructure, keep railroad rails in place, or receive floor joists **:** STRINGPIECE **3 :** SLEEPING CAR **4 :** something unpromising or unnoticed that suddenly attains prominence or value: as **a :** a racehorse that wins unexpectedly after performing poorly **b :** an article of merchandise having a value that goes unrecognized for a time **5 :** a calf earmarked but not branded

sleep·i·ly \\'slē-pə-lē\\ *adv* **:** in a sleepy manner

sleep in *vi* **1 :** to sleep where one is employed ⟨two maids who *sleep in*⟩ **2 a :** OVERSLEEP **b :** to sleep late intentionally

sleep·i·ness \\-pē-nəs\\ *n* **:** the quality or state of being sleepy

sleeping bag *n* **:** a bag usu. waterproof and warmly lined or padded to sleep in outdoors

sleeping car *n* **:** a railroad passenger car having berths for sleeping

sleeping partner *n* **:** a silent partner whose connection with the business is not publicly known

sleeping porch *n* **:** a porch or room having open sides or many windows arranged to permit sleeping in the open air

sleeping sickness *n* **1 :** a serious disease found prevalent in much of tropical Africa, marked by fever, protracted lethargy, tremors, and loss of weight, caused by either of two trypanosomes (*Trypanosoma gambiense* and *T. rhodesiense*), and transmitted by tsetse flies

2 : any of various viral encephalitides or encephalomyelitides of which lethargy or somnolence is a prominent feature

sleep·less \'slē-pləs\ *adj* **1 :** not able to sleep **:** INSOMNIAC **2 :** affording no sleep **3 :** unceasingly active — **sleep·less·ly** *adv* — **sleep·less·ness** *n*

sleep out *vi* **1 :** to sleep outdoors **2 :** to go home at night from one's place of employment ⟨a cook who *sleeps out*⟩ **3 :** to sleep away from home

sleep·walk \'slēp-,wȯk\ *vi* [back-formation fr. *sleepwalker*] **:** to walk in one's sleep

sleep·walk·er \-,wȯ-kər\ *n* **:** one that walks in his sleep **:** SOMNAMBULIST — **sleep·walk·ing** \-kiŋ\ *n*

sleepy \'slē-pē\ *adj* **1 a :** ready to fall asleep **:** DROWSY **b :** of, relating to, or characteristic of sleep **2 :** sluggish as if from sleep **:** LETHARGIC; *also* **:** INACTIVE **3 :** sleep-inducing **:** SOPORIFIC

sleepy·head \-,hed\ *n* **:** a sleepy person

1sleet \'slēt\ *n* [ME *slete;* akin to MHG *slōz* hailstone, ME *sloor* mud — more at SLUR] **1 :** frozen or partly frozen rain **2 :** GLAZE 1 — **sleety** \-ē\ *adj*

2sleet *vi* **:** to shower sleet

sleeve \'slēv\ *n* [ME *sleve,* fr. OE *slīefe;* akin to OE *slēfan* to slip (clothes) on, *slūpan* to slip, OHG *sliofan,* L *lubricus* slippery] **1 a :** a part of a garment covering an arm **b :** SLEEVELET **2 :** a tubular machine part designed to fit over another part (as a hollow axle or a bushing) — **sleeved** \'slēvd\ *adj* — **sleeve·less** \'slēv-ləs\ *adj*

sleeve·let \'slēv-lət\ *n* **:** a covering for the forearm to protect clothing from wear or dirt

sleeve target *n* **:** a tubular cloth target towed by an airplane for use in air and ground antiaircraft gunnery practice

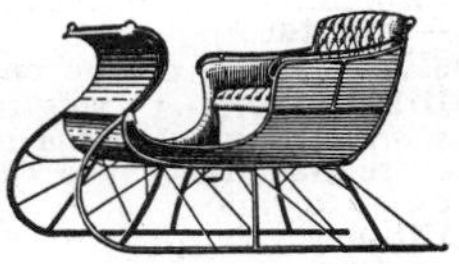

sleigh

1sleigh \'slā\ *n* [D *slee,* alter. of *slede;* akin to MD *sledde* sled] **:** a vehicle on runners used for transporting persons or goods on snow or ice

2sleigh *vi* **:** to drive or travel in a sleigh

sleigh bed *n* **:** a bed common esp. in the first half of the 19th century having a solid headboard and footboard that roll outward at the top

sleigh bell *n* **:** any of various bells commonly attached to a sleigh or to the harness of a horse drawing a sleigh: as **a :** CASCABEL 2 **b :** a hemispherical bell with an attached clapper often attached in series to a leather or metal strap fastened to a harness or sleigh

sleight \'slīt\ *n* [ME, fr. ON *slœgth,* fr. *slœgr* sly — more at SLY] **1 :** deceitful craftiness; *also* **:** STRATAGEM **2 :** DEXTERITY, SKILL

sleight of hand 1 a : skill and dexterity in juggling or conjuring tricks **b :** adroitness in deception **2 :** a conjuring or juggling trick requiring sleight of hand

slen·der \'slen-dər\ *adj* [ME *sclendre, slendre*] **1 a :** spare in frame or flesh; *esp* **:** gracefully slight **b :** small or narrow in circumference or width in proportion to length or height **2 :** limited or inadequate in amount **:** MEAGER **syn** see THIN — **slen·der·ly** *adv* — **slen·der·ness** *n*

slen·der·ize \-də-,rīz\ *vt* **:** to make slender

1sleuth \'slüth\ *n* [short for *sleuthhound*] **:** DETECTIVE

2sleuth *vi* **:** to act as a detective

sleuth·hound \-,hau̇nd\ *n* [ME, fr. *sleuth* track of an animal or person (fr. ON *slōth*) + *hound*] **1 :** a hound that tracks by scent; *specif* **:** BLOODHOUND **2 :** DETECTIVE

1slew *past of* SLAY

2slew \'slü\ *var of* SLOUGH

3slew *var of* SLUE

4slew \'slü\ *n* [IrGael *sluagh*] **:** a large number

1slice \'slīs\ *n* [ME, fr. MF *esclice* splinter, fr. OF, fr. *esclicier* to splinter, of Gmc origin; akin to OHG *slīzan* to tear apart — more at SLIT] **1 :** a thin flat piece cut from something **2 :** a spatula for spreading paint or ink **3 :** a serving knife with wedge-shaped blade ⟨fish ~⟩ **4 :** a flight of a ball (as in golf) that deviates from a straight course and curves to the right of a right-handed player and to the left of a left-handed player

2slice *vt* **1 :** to cut with or as if with a knife **2 :** to stir or spread with a slice **3 :** to hit (a ball) so that a slice results **~** *vi* **:** to slice something — **slic·er** *n*

slice bar *n* **:** a steel bar with a broad flat blade for chipping or scraping (as breaking up clinkers)

1slick \'slik\ *vb* [ME *sliken;* akin to OHG *slīhhan* to glide, Gk *leios* smooth] *vt* **:** to make sleek or smooth **~** *vi* **:** SPRUCE — usu. used with *up*

2slick *adj* **1 a :** having a smooth surface **:** SLIPPERY **b :** having surface plausibility **:** GLIB **c :** based on stereotype **:** TRITE **2 :** *archaic* **:** SLEEK 1 **3 a :** characterized by subtlety or nimble wit **:** CLEVER; *esp* **:** WILY **b :** DEFT, SKILLFUL **4 :** extremely good **:** FIRST-RATE — **slick·ly** *adv* — **slick·ness** *n*

3slick *adv* **:** in a slick manner

4slick *n* **1 a :** something that is smooth or slippery; *esp* **:** a smooth patch of water covered with a film of oil **b :** a film of oil **2 :** an implement for producing a slick surface: as **a :** a flat paddle usu. of steel for smoothing a sample of flour **b :** a foundry tool for smoothing the surface of a sand mold or unbaked core **3 :** a popular magazine printed on coated stock

slick–ear \'slik-,i(ə)r\ *n* **:** a range animal lacking an earmark

slick·en·side \'slik-ən-,sīd\ *n* [E dial. *slicken* smooth (alter. of E *2slick*) + E *side*] **:** a smooth striated polished surface produced on rock by friction — usu. used in pl.

slick·er \'slik-ər\ *n* **1** [*2slick*] **a :** OILSKIN; *broadly* **:** RAINCOAT **2** [*slick* (to defraud cleverly)] **a :** a clever crook **:** SWINDLER **b :** a city dweller esp. of natty appearance or sophisticated mannerisms

1slide \'slīd\ *vb* **slid** \'slid\ **slid·ing** \'slīd-iŋ\ [ME *sliden,* fr. OE *slīdan;* akin to MHG *slīten* to slide, Gk *leios* smooth — more at LIME] *vi* **1 a :** to move smoothly along a surface **:** SLIP **b :** to coast over snow or ice **2 a :** to slip or fall by loss of footing **b :** to change position or become dislocated **:** SHIFT **3 a :** to slither along the ground **:** CRAWL **b :** to stream along **:** FLOW **4 :** to take a natural course **:** DRIFT **5 a :** to pass unobtrusively **:** STEAL **b :** to pass by gradations **~** *vt* **1 a :** to cause to glide or slip **b :** to traverse in a sliding manner **2 :** to put surreptitiously — **slid·er** \'slīd-ər\ *n*

2slide *n* **1 a :** an act or instance of sliding **b** (1) **:** a musical grace of two or more small notes (2) **:** PORTAMENTO **2 :** a sliding part or mechanism: as **a :** a U-shaped section of tube in the trombone that is pushed out and in to produce the tones between the fundamental and its harmonics **b** (1) **:** a moving piece (as the ram of a punch press) that is guided by a part along which it slides (2) **:** a guiding surface (as a feeding mechanism) along which something slides **c :** SLIDING SEAT **3 a :** the descent of a mass of earth, rock, or snow down a hill or mountainside **b :** a dislocation in which one rock mass in a mining lode has slid on another **:** FAULT **4 a** (1) **:** a slippery surface for coasting (2) **:** a playground chute **b :** a channel or track on which something is slid **c :** a sloping trough down which objects are carried by gravity ⟨log ~⟩ **5 a :** a flat piece of glass on which an object is mounted for microscopic examination **b :** a photographic transparency on a small plate or film arranged for projection

slide fastener *n* **:** ZIPPER

slide rule *n* **:** an instrument consisting in its simple form of a ruler and a medial slide that are graduated with similar logarithmic scales labeled with the corresponding antilogarithms and used for rapid calculation

slide valve *n* **:** a valve that opens and closes a passageway by sliding over a port; *specif* **:** such a valve often used in steam engines for admitting steam to the piston and releasing it

slide·way \'slī-,dwā\ *n* **:** a way along which something slides

sliding board *n* **:** a playground slide

sliding scale *n* **1 :** a wage scale geared to the selling price of the product or to the cost-of-living index but usu. guaranteeing a minimum below which the wage will not fall **2 a :** a system for raising or lowering tariffs in accord with price changes **b :** a flexible scale (as of fees or subsidies) adjusted to the needs or income of individuals ⟨the *sliding scale* of medical fees⟩

sliding seat *n* **:** a rower's seat (as in a racing shell) that slides fore and aft — called also *slide*

1slight \'slīt\ *adj* [ME, smooth, slight, prob. fr. MD *slicht;* akin to OHG *slīhhan* to glide — more at SLICK] **1 a :** having a slim or delicate build **:** not stout or massive in body **b :** lacking in strength or substance **:** FLIMSY, FRAIL **c :** deficient in weight, solidity, or importance **:** TRIVIAL **2 :** small of its kind or in amount **:** SCANTY, MEAGER **syn** see THIN — **slight·ly** *adv* — **slight·ness** *n*

2slight *vt* **1 :** to treat as slight or unimportant **:** make light of **2 :** to treat with disdain or indifference **:** ignore discourteously **3 :** to perform or attend to carelessly and inadequately **4 :** 1SLUR 3 **syn** see NEGLECT

3slight *n* **1 :** an act or an instance of slighting **2 :** an instance of being slighted **:** a humiliating discourtesy

slight·ing *adj* **:** characterized by disregard or disrespect **:** DISPARAGING ⟨a ~ remark⟩ — **slight·ing·ly** \-iŋ-lē\ *adv*

sli·ly *var of* SLYLY

1slim \'slim\ *adj* **slim·mer; slim·mest** [D, bad, inferior, fr. MD *slimp* crooked, bad; akin to MHG *slimp* awry] **1 :** of small diameter or thickness in proportion to the height or length **:** SLENDER **2 a :** MEAN, WORTHLESS **b :** ADROIT, CRAFTY **3 a :** inferior in quality or amount **:** SLIGHT **b :** SCANTY, SMALL **syn** see THIN — **slim·ly** *adv* — **slim·ness** *n*

2slim *vb* **slimmed; slim·ming** *vt* **:** to make slender **~** *vi* **:** to become slender

1slime \'slīm\ *n* [ME, fr. OE *slīm;* akin to OHG *slīmen* to smooth, L *lima* file — more at LIME] **1 :** soft moist earth or clay; *esp* **:** viscous mud **2 :** a viscous or glutinous substance: as **a :** a mucous or mucoid secretion of various animals (as slugs and catfishes) **b :** a product of wet crushing consisting of ore ground so fine as to pass a 200-mesh screen

2slime *vt* **1 :** to smear or cover with slime **2 :** to remove slime from (as fish for canning) **3 :** to crush or grind (ore) to a slime **~** *vi* **:** to become slimy

slime mold *n* **:** any of a group (Myxomycetes or Mycetozoa) of organisms usu. held to be lower fungi but sometimes considered protozoan that exist vegetatively as mobile plasmodia and reproduce by spores

slim·i·ly \'slī-mə-lē\ *adv* **:** in a slimy manner

slim·i·ness \-mē-nəs\ *n* **:** the quality or state of being slimy

slim–jim \'slim-'jim\ *n* [*1slim* + *Jim,* nickname for *James*] **:** one that is notably slender

slim·ming *adj* **:** giving an effect of slenderness

slim·sy *or* **slimp·sy** \'slim-zē, 'slim(p)-sē\ *adj* [blend of *slim* and *flimsy*] **:** FLIMSY, FRAIL

slimy \'slī-mē\ *adj* **1 :** of, relating to, or resembling slime **:** VISCOUS; *also* **:** covered with or yielding slime **2 :** VILE, OFFENSIVE

1sling \'sliŋ\ *vt* **slung** \'sləŋ\ **sling·ing** \'sliŋ-iŋ\ [ME *slingen,* prob. fr. ON *slyngva* to hurl; akin to OE & OHG *slingan* to worm, twist, Lith *slinkti*] **1 :** to cast forcibly **:** FLING **2 :** to throw with a sling **syn** see THROW — **sling·er** \'sliŋ-ər\ *n*

2sling *n* **:** a slinging or hurling of or as if of a missile

3sling *n* **1 a :** an instrument for throwing stones that usu. consists of a short strap with strings fastened to its ends and is whirled round to discharge its missile by centrifugal force **b :** SLINGSHOT **2 a :** a usu. looped line (as of strap, chain, or rope) used to hoist, lower, or carry something; *esp* **:** a hanging bandage suspended from the neck to support an arm or hand **b :** a chain or rope attached to a lower yard at the middle and passing around a mast near the masthead to support a yard **c :** a chain hooked at the bow and stern of a boat for lowering or hoisting **d :** a device (as a rope net) for enclosing material to be hoisted by a tackle or crane

4sling *vt* **slung** \'sləŋ\ **sling·ing** \'sliŋ-iŋ\ **:** to place in a sling for hoisting or lowering

5sling *n* [origin unknown] **:** an alcoholic drink usu. made of whiskey, brandy, or esp. gin with plain or carbonated water, sugar, and sometimes bitters and often garnished with lemon or lime peel if cold or dusted with nutmeg if hot ⟨gin ~⟩ ⟨rum ~⟩

slinger ring *n* **:** a tubular ring fitted round the propeller hub of an airplane through which a spray of antifreeze solution is spread by centrifugal force over the propeller blades to prevent formation of ice

sling·shot \'sliŋ-,shät\ *n* **:** a forked stick with an elastic band attached for shooting small stones

1slink \'sliŋk\ *vb* **slunk** \'sləŋk\ **slink·ing** [ME *slinken,* fr. OE

slincan to creep; akin to OE *slingan* to worm, twist] *vi* **:** to go or move stealthily or furtively (as in fear or shame) **:** STEAL ~ *vt* **:** to give premature birth to — used esp. of a domestic animal ⟨a cow that ~s her calf⟩ **syn** see LURK

2**slink** *n* **1 a :** the young of an animal (as a calf) brought forth prematurely **b :** the flesh or skin of such a calf **2** *chiefly dial* **:** WEAKLING

3**slink** *adj* **1 :** born prematurely or abortively ⟨a ~ calf⟩ **2** *chiefly dial* **:** starved looking **:** THIN, SCRAWNY

slinky \'sliŋ-kē\ *adj* **1 :** characterized by slinking **:** stealthily quiet ⟨~ movements⟩ **2 :** sleek and sinuous in outline; *esp* **:** following the lines of the figure in a gracefully flowing manner ⟨a ~ evening gown⟩

1**slip** \'slip\ *vb* **slipped; slip·ping** [ME *slippen*, fr. MD or MLG; akin to Gk *olibros* slippery, *leios* smooth — more at LIME] *vi* **1 a :** to move with a smooth sliding motion **b :** to move quietly and cautiously **:** STEAL **c :** ELAPSE, PASS **2 a** (1) **:** to escape from memory or consciousness (2) **:** to become uttered through inadvertence **b :** to pass quickly or easily away **:** become lost ⟨let an opportunity ~⟩ **3 :** to fall into error or fault **:** LAPSE **4 a :** to slide out of place or away from a support or one's grasp **b :** to slide on or down a slippery surface ⟨~ on the stairs⟩ **c :** to flow smoothly **5 :** to get speedily into or out of clothing ⟨*slipped* into his coat⟩ **6 :** to fall off from a standard or accustomed level by degrees **:** DECLINE **7 :** SIDESLIP ~ *vt* **1 :** to cause to move easily and smoothly **:** SLIDE **2 a :** to get away from **:** ELUDE, EVADE ⟨*slipped* his pursuers⟩ **b :** to free oneself from ⟨dog *slipped* his collar⟩ **c :** to escape from (one's memory or notice) **3 :** CAST, SHED ⟨snake *slipped* its skin⟩ **4 :** to put on (a garment) hurriedly **5 a :** to let loose from a restraining leash or grasp **b :** to cause to slip open **:** RELEASE, UNDO ⟨~ a lock⟩ **c :** to let go of **d :** to disengage from (an anchor) instead of hauling **6 a :** to insert, place, or pass quietly or secretly **b :** to give or pay on the sly **7 :** SLINK, ABORT **8 :** DISLOCATE ⟨*slipped* his shoulder⟩ **9 :** to transfer (a stitch) from one needle to another without working a stitch **10 :** to avoid (a punch) by moving the body or head quickly to one side — **slip something over :** to foist something on another **:** get the better of another by trickery

2**slip** *n* **1 a :** a sloping ramp extending out into the water to serve as a place for landing or repairing ships **b :** a ship's berth between two piers **2 :** the act or an instance of departing secretly or hurriedly **3 a :** a mistake in judgment, policy, or procedure **:** BLUNDER **b :** a slight offense **:** MISSTEP **4 :** a leash so made that it can be quickly slipped **5 a :** the act or an instance of slipping down or out of place ⟨a ~ on the ice⟩ **:** a sudden mishap ⟨many a ~ between the cup and the lip⟩ **b :** a movement dislocating the parts of a rock mass or the result of such movement **c :** a fall from some level or standard **:** DECLINE ⟨~ in stock prices⟩ **6 a :** an undergarment made in dress length with shoulder straps **b :** PILLOWCASE **7 a :** one of several cricket fielders positioned on the off side of the wicketkeeper and behind point **b** *pl but sing in constr* **:** the part of the field in which the slips are placed **8 a :** the motion of the center of resistance of the float of a paddle wheel or the blade of an oar through the water horizontally; *also* **:** the difference between a ship's actual speed and the speed which it would have if the propeller worked in a solid **b :** retrograde movement of a belt on a pulley **c :** the amount of leakage past the piston of a pump or the impellers of a blower **9 :** a disposition or tendency to slip easily **10 :** SIDESLIP **syn** see ERROR

3**slip** *adj* **1 a :** operating by slipping ⟨~ bar⟩ **b :** DETACHABLE ⟨~ compartment⟩ **2 :** having a slipknot ⟨~ cord⟩ **3 :** capable of being released quickly ⟨~ bolt⟩

4**slip** *n* [ME *slippe*, prob. fr. MD or MLG, split, slit, flap] **1 a :** a small shoot or twig cut for planting or grafting **:** SCION **b :** DESCENDANT, OFFSPRING **2 a :** a long narrow strip of material **b :** a piece of paper used for a memorandum or record ⟨sales ~⟩ **3 :** a young and slender person ⟨~ of a girl⟩ **4 :** a long seat or narrow pew

5**slip** *vt* **slipped; slip·ping :** to take cuttings from (a plant) **:** divide into slips ⟨~ a geranium⟩

6**slip** *n* [ME *slyp* slime, fr. OE *slypa* slime paste; akin to OE *slūpan* to slip — more at SLEEVE] **1 :** a mixture of fine clay and water used in ceramic casting, for decoration, or as a cement for handles **:** SLURRY **2 :** enamel or glaze powdered and suspended in water

slip·case \'slip-ˌkās\ *n* **:** a protective container with one open end for books

slip·cov·er \'slip-ˌkəv-ər\ *n* **1 :** a cover that may be slipped off and on; *specif* **:** a removable protective covering for an article of furniture **2 :** a protective cover readily slipped on or off a book **:** JACKET

slipe \'slīp\ *vt* [ME *slypen*] **1** *dial Brit* **:** to remove an outer covering from **:** PEEL **2** *dial Brit* **:** to cut off **:** SLICE

slip·knot \'slip-ˌnät\ *n* **:** a knot that slips along the rope or line around which it is made; *esp* **:** one made by tying an overhand knot around the standing part of a rope

slip noose *n* **:** a noose with a slipknot

slip–on \'slip-ˌȯn, -ˌän\ *n* **:** an article of clothing that is easily slipped on or off: as **a :** a glove or shoe without fastenings **b :** a garment (as a girdle) that one steps into and pulls up **c :** PULLOVER

slip·over \-ˌō-vər\ *n* **:** a garment or cover that slips on and off easily; *specif* **:** a pullover sweater

slip·page \'slip-ij\ *n* **1 :** an act, instance, or process of slipping **2 :** a loss in transmission of power; *also* **:** the difference between theoretical and actual output (as of power)

slipped disk *n* **:** a protrusion of one of the cartilage disks between vertebrae with pressure on spinal nerves resulting in low back pain or sciatic pain

1**slip·per** \'slip-ər\ *adj* [ME] *chiefly dial* **:** SLIPPERY

2**slipper** *n* [ME, fr. *slippen* to slip] **:** a light low-cut shoe that is easily slipped on the foot and is worn for undress

slip·per·i·ness \'slip-(ə-)rē-nəs\ *n* **:** the quality or state of being slippery

slip·pery \'slip-(ə-)rē\ *adj* [alter. of ME *slipper*, fr. OE *slipor;* akin to MLG *slipper* slippery, *slippen* to slip] **1 a :** causing one to slide or fall **b :** tending to slip from the grasp **2 :** not firmly fixed **:** UNSTABLE **3 :** not to be trusted **:** TRICKY

slip·py \'slip-ē\ *adj* **:** SLIPPERY

slip ring *n* [2*slip*] **:** one of two or more continuous conducting rings from which the brushes take or to which they deliver current in a dynamo or motor

slip sheet *n* [1*slip*] **:** a sheet of paper placed between newly printed sheets to prevent offsetting

slip–sheet \'slip-ˌshēt\ *vt* **:** to interleave (as printed sheets) with slip sheets

slip·shod \'slip-'shäd\ *adj* [1*slip*] **1 :** wearing shoes or slippers that are loose **:** down at the heel **:** SHABBY ⟨~ shoes⟩ **2 :** CARELESS, SLOVENLY

slip·slop \'slip-ˌsläp\ *n* [redupl. of 2*slop*] **1** *archaic* **:** a watery food **:** SLOPS **2 :** shallow talk or writing **:** TWADDLE **3** [imit.] **:** a loose flapping sound — **slip–slop** *adj*

slip·sole \-ˌsōl\ *n* **1 :** a thin insole **2 :** a half sole inserted between the insole or welt and the outsole of a shoe to give additional height — called also *slip tap*

slip·stick \-ˌstik\ *n* **:** SLIDE RULE

slip stitch *n* **1 :** a concealed stitch for sewing folded edges (as hems) made by alternately running the needle inside the fold and picking up a thread or two from the body of the article **2 :** an unworked stitch; *esp* **:** a knitting stitch that is shifted from one needle to another without knitting in it

slip·stream \-ˌstrēm\ *n* **:** the stream of air driven aft by the propeller of an aircraft

slip up *vi* **:** to make a mistake **:** BLUNDER ⟨*slipped up* in his calculations⟩

slip·up \'slip-ˌəp\ *n* **1 :** MISTAKE **2 :** MISCHANCE

1**slit** \'slit\ *vt* **slit; slit·ting** [ME *slitten;* akin to MHG *slitzen* to slit, OHG *slīzan* to tear apart, OE *sciell* shell — more at SHELL] **1 a :** to make a slit in **:** SLASH **b :** to cut off or away **:** SEVER **c :** to form into a slit ⟨*slitted* his eyes⟩ **2 :** to cut into long narrow strips — **slit·ter** *n*

2**slit** *n* **:** a long narrow cut or opening — **slit** *adj*

slith·er \'slit͟h-ər\ *vb* **slith·er·ing** \-(ə-)riŋ\ [ME *slideren*, fr. OE *slidrian*, freq. of *slīdan* to slide] *vi* **1 :** to slide on or as if on a loose gravelly surface **2 :** to slip or slide like a snake ~ *vt* **:** to cause to slide

slith·ery \'slit͟h-(ə-)rē\ *adj* **:** having a slippery surface, texture, or quality

slit trench *n* **:** a narrow trench for shelter in battle from bomb and shell fragments

1**sli·ver** \'sliv-ər, *2 is usu* 'slīv-\ *n* [ME *slivere*, fr. *sliven* to slice off, fr. OE *-slīfan;* akin to OE *-slǣfan* to cut] **1 :** a long slender piece cut or torn off **:** SPLINTER **2 :** an untwisted strand or rope of textile fiber produced by a carding or combing machine and ready for drawing, roving, or spinning

2**sliv·er** \'sliv-ər\ *vb* **sliv·er·ing** \-(ə-)riŋ\ *vt* **:** to cut into slivers **:** SPLINTER ~ *vi* **:** to become split into slivers

sliv·o·vitz \'sliv-ə-ˌvits\ *n* [Serbo-Croatian *sljivovica*, fr. *sljiva*, *sliva* plum; akin to Russ *sliva* plum — more at LIVID] **:** a dry usu. colorless plum brandy made esp. in Hungary and the Balkan countries

slob \'släb\ *n* [Ir *slab*] **1 :** a heavy sludge of sea ice **2 :** a slovenly or boorish person

1**slob·ber** \'släb-ər\ *vb* **slob·ber·ing** \-(ə-)riŋ\ [ME *sloberen;* akin to LG *slubberen* to sip, Lith *lūpa* lip] *vi* **1 :** to let saliva dribble from the mouth **:** DROOL **2 :** to gush effusively ~ *vt* **:** to smear with or as if with dribbling saliva or food — **slob·ber·er** \-ər-ər\ *n*

2**slobber** *n* **1 :** spittle drooled from the mouth **2 :** driveling, sloppy, or incoherent utterance — **slob·bery** \'släb-(ə-)rē\ *adj*

sloe \'slō\ *n* [ME *slo*, fr. OE *slāh* — more at LIVID] **:** the small dark globose astringent fruit of the blackthorn; *also* **:** BLACKTHORN 1

sloe–eyed \'slō-'īd\ *adj* **1 :** having soft dark bluish or purplish black eyes **2 :** having slanted eyes

sloe gin *n* **:** a sweet reddish liqueur consisting of grain spirits flavored chiefly with sloes

1**slog** \'släg\ *vb* **slogged; slog·ging** [origin unknown] *vt* **:** to hit hard **:** BEAT ~ *vi* **1 :** to plod heavily **:** TRAMP **2 :** to work hard and steadily **:** PLUG — **slog·ger** *n*

2**slog** *n* **1 :** hard persistent work **2 :** a hard dogged march or tramp

slo·gan \'slō-gən\ *n* [alter. of earlier *slogorn*, fr. Gael *sluagh-ghairm* army cry] **1 a :** a war cry or gathering word esp. of a Scottish clan **b :** a word or phrase used to express a characteristic position or stand or a goal of endeavor **2 :** a brief striking phrase used in advertising or promotion

slo·gan·eer \ˌslō-gə-'ni(ə)r\ *n* **:** a coiner or user of slogans — **sloganeer** *vi*

slo·gan·ize \'slō-gə-ˌnīz\ *vt* **:** to express as a slogan

sloop \'slüp\ *n* [D *sloep*] **:** a fore-and-aft rigged boat with one mast and a single headsail jib

sloop of war 1 : a warship rigged as a ship, brig, or schooner mounting from 10 to 32 guns **2 :** a warship larger than a gunboat with guns on one deck only

1**slop** \'släp\ *n* [ME *sloppe*, prob. fr. MD *slop;* akin to OE *oferslop* slop] **1 :** a loose smock or overall **2** *pl* **:** short full breeches worn by men in the 16th century **3** *pl* **:** articles (as clothing) sold to sailors

2**slop** *n* [ME *sloppe*] **1 :** soft mud **:** SLUSH **2 :** thin tasteless drink or liquid food — usu. used in pl. **3 :** liquid spilled or splashed **4 a :** food waste fed to animals **:** GARBAGE **b :** excreted body waste — usu. used in pl.

3**slop** *vb* **slopped; slop·ping** *vt* **1 a :** to spill from a container **b :** to splash or spill liquid on **c :** to cause (a liquid) to splash **2 :** to dish out messily **3 :** to eat or drink greedily or noisily **4 :** to feed with slops ~ *vi* **1 :** to tramp in mud or slush **2 :** to become spilled or splashed **3 :** to be effusive **:** GUSH **4 :** to exceed a boundary or limit

slop basin *n, Brit* **:** a bowl for receiving the leavings of tea or coffee cups at table

slop chest *n* **:** a store of clothing and personal requisites (as tobacco) carried on merchant ships for issue to the crew usu. as a charge against their wages

slop chute *n* **:** a chute toward the rear of a ship for dumping garbage

1**slope** \'slōp\ *adj* [ME *slope*, adv., obliquely] **:** SLANTING, SLOPING

2**slope** *vi* **1 :** to take an oblique course **2 :** to lie or fall in a slant **:** INCLINE **3 :** GO, TRAVEL ~ *vt* **:** to cause to incline or slant — **slop·er** *n*

3**slope** *n* **1 :** ground that forms a natural or artificial incline **2 :** upward or downward slant or inclination or degree of slant **3 :** the part of a continent draining to a particular ocean **4 a :** the tangent

of the angle made by a straight line with the x-axis **b** : the slope of the line tangent to a plane curve at a point

slop jar *n* : a large pail used as a chamber pot or to receive waste water from a washbowl or the contents of chamber pots

slop pail *n* : a pail for toilet or household slops

slop·pi·ly \'släp-ə-lē\ *adv* : in a sloppy manner

slop·pi·ness \'släp-ē-nəs\ *n* : the quality or state of being sloppy

slop·py \'släp-ē\ *adj* **1 a** : wet so as to spatter easily : SLUSHY **b** : wet with or as if with something slopped over **2** : SLOVENLY, CARELESS **3** : disagreeably effusive

slop·work \'släp-,wərk\ *n* **1** : the manufacture of cheap ready-made clothing **2** : hasty slovenly work — **slop·work·er** \-,wər-kər\ *n*

1**slosh** \'släsh, 'slȯsh\ *n* [prob. blend of *slop* and *slush*] **1** : SLUSH **2** : the slap or splash of liquid

2**slosh** *vi* **1** : to flounder or splash through water, mud, or slush **2** : to move with a splashing motion ~ *vt* **1** : to splash about in liquid **2** : to splash (a liquid) about or on something **3** : to splash with liquid

1**slot** \'slät\ *n* [ME, the hollow running down the middle of the breast, fr. MF *esclot*] **1 a** : a long narrow opening or groove : SLIT, NOTCH **b** : a narrow passage or enclosure **c** : a passage through an airplane wing located usu. near the leading edge and formed between a main and an auxiliary airfoil for improving flow conditions over the wing so as to increase lift and delay stalling of the wing **2** : a place or position in an organization or sequence : NICHE

2**slot** *vt* **slot·ted**; **slot·ting** : to cut a slot in

3**slot** *n, pl* **slot** [MF *esclot* track] : the track of an animal (as a deer) : TRACK, TRAIL

sloth \'slȯth, 'slōth, 'släth\ *n, pl* **sloths** \'slȯths, 'slōths, 'släths, *or with* th\ [ME *slouthe*, fr. *slow*] **1** : disinclination to action or labor : INDOLENCE **2** : any of several slow-moving arboreal edentate mammals that inhabit tropical forests of So. and Central America, hang from the branches back downward, and feed on leaves, shoots, and fruits

sloth·ful \'slȯth-fəl, 'slōth-, 'släth-\ *adj* : inclined to sloth : INDOLENT **syn** see LAZY — **sloth·ful·ly** \-fə-lē\ *adv* — **sloth·ful·ness** *n*

slot machine *n* : a machine whose operation is begun by dropping a coin into a slot

1**slouch** \'slau̇ch\ *n* [origin unknown] **1 a** : an awkward fellow : LOUT **b** : a lazy or incompetent person **2** : a gait or posture characterized by ungainly stooping of head and shoulders or undue relaxation of body muscles

2**slouch** *vi* **1** : to walk with or assume a slouch **2** : DROOP ~ *vt* : to cause to droop — **slouch·er** *n*

slouch hat *n* : a soft usu. felt hat with a wide flexible brim

slouch·i·ly \'slau̇-chə-lē\ *adv* : in a slouchy manner ⟨~ dressed⟩

slouch·i·ness \-chē-nəs\ *n* : the quality or state of being slouchy

slouchy \'slau̇-chē\ *adj* : slouching esp. in gait or posture

1**slough** *n* [ME *slogh*, fr. OE *slōh*; akin to MHG *slouche* ditch] **1** \'slü, *chiefly Brit or by Americans vaguely familiar with this sense* 'slau̇\ **a** : a place of deep mud or mire **b** (1) : SWAMP (2) : an inlet from a river; *also* : BACKWATER (3) : a creek in a marsh or tide flat **2** \'slau̇ *also* 'slü\ : a state of moral degradation or spiritual dejection

2**slough** *vt* : to engulf in a slough ~ *vi* : to plod through mud : SLOG

3**slough** *or* **sluff** \'sləf\ *n* [ME *slughe*; akin to MHG *slūch* snake skin, Lith *šliaužti* to crawl] **1** : the cast-off skin of a snake **2** : a mass of dead tissue separating from an ulcer **3** : something that may be shed or cast off

4**slough** *or* **sluff** \'sləf\ *vi* **1 a** : to become shed or cast off **b** : to cast off one's skin **c** : to separate in the form of dead tissue from living tissue **2** : to crumble slowly and fall away ~ *vt* **1** : to cast off **2** : to get rid of or discard as irksome, objectionable, or disadvantageous; *esp* : to get rid of (a losing card) in bridge **syn** see DISCARD

slough of de·spond \,slau̇-əv-di-'spänd, ,slü-\ [fr. The *Slough of Despond*, deep bog into which Christian falls on the way from the City of Destruction and from which Help saves him in the allegory *Pilgrim's Progress* (1678) by John Bunyan] : a state of extreme depression

slough over \,sləf-\ *vt* : to treat as slight or unimportant ⟨*sloughed over* certain aspects of the plan⟩

sloughy \'slü-ē, 'slau̇- — *see* 1SLOUGH 1\ *adj* : full of sloughs : MIRY ⟨a ~ creek⟩

Slo·vak \'slō-,väk, -,vak\ *n* [Slovak *Slovák*] **1 a** : one of a Slavic people of eastern Czechoslovakia **b** : a member of this people **2** : the Slavic language of the Slovak people — **Slovak** *adj* — **Slo·va·ki·an** \slō-'väk-ē-ən, -'vak-\ *adj or n*

1**slov·en** \'sləv-ən\ *n* [ME *sloveyn* rascal, perh. fr. Flem *sloovin* woman of low character] : one habitually negligent of neatness or cleanliness esp. in dress or person

2**sloven** *adj* **1** : SLOVENLY **2** : UNCULTIVATED, UNDEVELOPED

Slo·vene \'slō-,vēn\ *n* [G, fr. Slovene *Sloven*] **1 a** : a member of a southern Slavic group of people usu. classed with the Serbs and Croats and living in Yugoslavia **b** : a native or inhabitant of Slovenia **2** : the language of the Slovenes — **Slovene** *adj* — **Slo·ve·nian** \slō-'vē-nē-ən, -nyən\ *adj or n*

slov·en·li·ness \'sləv-ən-lē-nəs\ *n* : the quality or state of being slovenly

slov·en·ly \-lē\ *adj* **1 a** : untidy esp. in dress or person **b** : lazily slipshod **2** : characteristic of a sloven — **slovenly** *adv*

1**slow** \'slō\ *adj* [ME, fr. OE *slāw*; akin to OHG *slēo* dull, Skt *srēvayati* he causes to fail] **1 a** : mentally dull : STUPID **b** : naturally inert or sluggish **2 a** : lacking in readiness, promptness, or willingness **b** : not hasty or precipitate **3 a** : moving, flowing, or proceeding without speed or at less than usual speed **b** : exhibiting or marked by retarded speed **c** : not acute **d** : LOW, GENTLE ⟨~ fire⟩ **4** : requiring a long time : GRADUAL **5** : having qualities that hinder or stop rapid progress or action **6 a** : registering behind or below what is correct **b** : less than the time indicated by another method of reckoning **c** : that is behind the time at a specified time or place **7** : lacking in life, animation, or gaiety : BORING — **slow·ly** *adv* — **slow·ness** *n*

2**slow** *adv* : SLOWLY

3**slow** *vt* : to make slow or slower : RETARD ~ *vi* : to go slower **syn** see DELAY

slow·down \'slō-,dau̇n\ *n* : a slowing down

slow-foot·ed \'slō-'fu̇t-əd\ *adj* : moving at a very slow pace : PLODDING — **slow-footed·ness** *n*

slow·ish \'slō-ish\ *adj* : somewhat slow ⟨a ~ reader⟩

slow match *n* : a match or fuse made so as to burn slowly and evenly and used for firing (as of blasting charges)

slow motion *n* : the action in a projected motion picture apparently taking place at a speed much slower than that of the photographed action

slow·poke \'slō-,pōk\ *n* : a very slow person

slow-wit·ted \-'wit-əd\ *adj* : mentally slow : DULL

slow·worm \'slō-,wərm\ *n* [ME *sloworm*, fr. OE *slāwyrm*, fr. *slā-* (akin to Sw *slå* earthworm) + *wyrm* worm] : BLINDWORM

sloyd \'slȯid\ *n* [Sw *slöjd* skill; akin to ON *slægth* cunning — more at SLEIGHT] : an orig. Swedish system of manual training using wood carving as a means of training in the use of tools

1**slub** \'sləb\ *vt* **slubbed**; **slub·bing** [back-formation fr. *slubbing*] : to draw out and twist (as slivers of wool) slightly

2**slub** *n* : SLUBBING

slub·ber \'sləb-ər\ *vt* **slub·ber·ing** \-(ə-)riŋ\ [prob. fr. obs. D *slubberen*] **1** *dial chiefly Eng* : STAIN, SULLY **2** : to perform in a slipshod fashion

slub·bing \'sləb-iŋ\ *n* [origin unknown] : slightly twisted roving

sludge \'sləj\ *n* [prob. alter. of *slush*] **1** : MUD, MIRE; *esp* : a muddy deposit (as on a riverbed) : OOZE **2** : a muddy or slushy mass, deposit, or sediment: as **a** : precipitated solid matter produced by water and sewage treatment processes **b** : muddy sediment in a steam boiler **c** : a precipitate or settling (as a mixture of impurities and acid) from a mineral oil **3** : new sea ice forming in thin detached crystals

sludgy \'sləj-ē\ *adj* : full of sludge

1**slue** \'slü\ *var of* SLOUGH

2**slue** \'slü\ *vb* [origin unknown] *vt* **1** : to turn (as a ship's spar) about a fixed point that is usu. the axis **2** : TWIST, VEER ~ *vi* **1** : to turn, twist, or swing about : PIVOT **2** : SKID

3**slue** *n* : position or inclination after sluing

4**slue** *var of* SLEW

1**slug** \'sləg\ *n* [ME *slugge*, of Scand origin; akin to Norw dial. *slugga* to walk sluggishly; akin to ME *sloor* mud — more at SLUR] **1** : SLUGGARD **2** : any of numerous chiefly terrestrial pulmonate gastropods (family Limacidae) found in most parts of the world where there is a reasonable supply of moisture and closely related to the land snails with a rudimentary shell often buried in the mantle or entirely absent **3** : a smooth soft larva of a sawfly or moth that creeps like a mollusk

2**slug** *n* [prob. fr. 1*slug*] **1** : a lump, disk, or cylinder of metal: as **a** (1) : a musket ball (2) : BULLET **b** : a piece of metal roughly shaped for subsequent processing **c** : a metal disk for insertion in a slot machine; *esp* : one used illegally instead of a coin **2 a** : a strip of metal thicker than a printer's lead **b** : a line of type cast as one piece **c** : a usu. temporary type line serving to instruct or identify **3** : a single drink of liquor : SHOT **4** : the gravitational unit of mass in the fps system to which a pound force can impart an acceleration of one foot per second per second

3**slug** *vt* **slugged**; **slug·ging** : to add a printer's slug to

4**slug** *n* [perh. fr. *slug* (to load with slugs)] : a heavy blow esp. with the fist

5**slug** *vt* **slugged**; **slug·ging** : to strike heavily with or as if with the fist or a bat

slug·abed \'sləg-ə-,bed\ *n* : one who stays in bed after his usual or obligated time of getting up

slug·fest \'sləg-,fest\ *n* : a fight marked by exchange of heavy blows

slug·gard \'sləg-ərd\ *n* [ME *sluggart*] : an habitually lazy person — **sluggard** *adj*

slug·gard·ly \-lē\ *adj* : lazily inactive

slug·gard·ness \-nəs\ *n* : the quality or state of being sluggardly : INDOLENCE

slug·ger \'sləg-ər\ *n* : one that strikes hard or with heavy blows: as **a** : a prizefighter who punches hard but has usu. little defensive skill **b** : a hard-hitting batter in baseball

slug·ging \'sləg-iŋ\ *n* : illegal use of the fist or forearm on an opponent in football

slug·gish \'sləg-ish\ *adj* **1** : averse to activity or exertion : INDOLENT; *also* : TORPID **2** : slow to respond to stimulation or treatment **3 a** : markedly slow in movement, flow, or growth **b** : economically inactive or slow — **slug·gish·ly** *adv* — **slug·gish·ness** *n*

1**sluice** \'slüs\ *n* [alter. of ME *scluse*, fr. MF *escluse*, fr. LL *exclusa*, fr. L, fem. of *exclusus*, pp. of *excludere* to exclude] **1 a** : an artificial passage for water (as in a millstream) fitted with a valve or gate for stopping or regulating flow **b** : a body of water pent up behind a floodgate **2** : a dock gate : FLOODGATE **3 a** : a stream flowing through a floodgate **b** : a channel to drain or carry off surplus water **4** : a long inclined trough usu. on the ground (as for floating logs); *specif* : such a contrivance paved usu. with riffles to hold quicksilver for catching gold

2**sluice** *vt* **1** : to draw off by or through a sluice **2 a** : to wash with or in water running through or from a sluice **b** : DRENCH, FLUSH **3** : to transport (as logs) in a sluice ~ *vi* : to pour as if from a sluice

sluice·way \'slüs-,swā\ *n* : an artificial channel into which water is let by a sluice

sluicy \'slü-sē\ *adj* : falling copiously or in streams : STREAMING ⟨~ sheets of rain⟩

1**slum** \'sləm\ *n* [origin unknown] : a highly congested area marked by deteriorated unsanitary buildings, poverty, and social disorganization

2**slum** *vi* **slummed**; **slum·ming** : to visit slums esp. out of curiosity or for pleasure — **slum·mer** *n*

1**slum·ber** \'sləm-bər\ *vi* **slum·ber·ing** \-b(ə-)riŋ\ [ME *slumberen*, freq. of *slumen* to doze, prob. fr. *slume* slumber, fr. OE *slūma*; akin to Lith *slugti* to diminish — more at SLUR] **1 a** : to sleep lightly : DOZE **b** : SLEEP **2 a** : to be in a torpid or slothful state **b** : to lie dormant or latent — **slum·ber·er** \-bər-ər\ *n*

²slumber *n* **1 a :** SLEEP **b :** light sleep **2 :** LETHARGY, TORPOR

slum·ber·ous *or* **slum·brous** \'sləm-b(ə-)rəs\ *adj* **1 :** SLEEPY, SOMNOLENT **2 :** inviting slumber **:** SOPORIFIC

slumber party *n* **:** an overnight gathering of teen-age girls usu. at one of their homes at which they dress in nightclothes but pass the night more in talking than sleeping

slum·bery \'sləm-b(ə-)rē\ *adj* **:** SLUMBEROUS

slum·gul·lion \'sləm-ˌgəl-yən, ˌsləm-'\ *n* [perh. fr. *slum* (slime) + E dial. *gullion* (mud, cesspool)] **:** a meat stew

slum·lord \'sləm-ˌlȯ(ə)rd\ *n* [¹*slum* + land*lord*] **:** a landlord who receives unusually large profits from substandard properties

¹**slump** \'sləmp\ *vi* [prob. of Scand origin; akin to Norw *slumpa* to fall; akin to L *labi* to slide — more at SLEEP] **1 a :** to fall or sink suddenly **b :** to drop or slide down suddenly **:** COLLAPSE **2 :** to assume a drooping posture or carriage **:** SLOUCH **3 :** to fall off **:** DECLINE

²**slump** *n* **:** a marked or sustained decline esp. in economic activity or prices

slung *past of* SLING

slung·shot \'sləŋ-ˌshät\ *n* **:** a striking weapon consisting of a small mass of metal or stone fixed on a flexible handle or strap **:** BLACKJACK

slunk *past of* SLINK

¹**slur** \'slər\ *vb* **slurred; slur·ring** [prob. fr. LG *slurrn* to shuffle; akin to ME *sloor* mud] *vt* **1 a :** to slide or slip over without due mention, consideration, or emphasis **b :** to perform hurriedly **:** SKIMP **2 :** to perform (successive tones of different pitch) in a smooth or connected manner **3 a :** to reduce, make a substitution for, or omit (sounds that would normally occur in an utterance) **b :** to utter with such reduction, substitution, or omission of sounds ~ *vi* **1** *dial chiefly Eng* **:** SLIP, SLIDE **2 :** DRAG, SHUFFLE

²**slur** *n* **1 a :** a curved line ⌣ or ⌢ connecting notes to be sung to the same syllable or performed without a break **b :** the combination of two or more slurred tones **2 :** a slurring manner of speech

³**slur** *vb* **slurred; slur·ring** [obs. E dial. *slur* thin mud, fr. ME *sloor;* akin to MHG *slier* mud, Lith *slugti* to diminish] *vt* **1 :** to cast aspersions upon **:** DISPARAGE **2 :** to make indistinct **:** OBSCURE ~ *vi* **:** to slip so as to cause a slur

⁴**slur** *n* **1 a :** ASPERSION, CALUMNY **b :** REPROACH, STIGMA **2 :** a blurred spot in printed matter **:** SMUDGE

slurp \'slərp\ *vb* [D *slurpen;* akin to MLG *slorpen* to slurp] **:** to eat or drink noisily or with a sucking sound — **slurp** *n*

slur·ry \'slər-ē, 'slə-rē\ *n* [ME *slory*] **:** a watery mixture of insoluble matter (as mud, lime, or plaster of paris)

¹**slush** \'sləsh\ *n* [perh. of Scand origin; akin to Norw *slusk* slush] **1 a :** partly melted or watery snow **b :** loose ice crystals formed during the early stages of freezing of salt water **2 a :** soft mud **:** MIRE **b :** grout made of portland cement, sand, and water **3 :** refuse grease and fat from cooking esp. on shipboard **4 :** a soft mixture of grease or oil and other materials for protecting the surface of metal parts against corrosion; *esp* **:** a mixture of white lead and lime for painting the bright parts of machines to preserve them from oxidation **5 :** paper pulp in water suspension **6 :** RUBBISH, DRIVEL

²**slush** *vt* **1 :** to wet, splash, or paint with slush **2 :** to fill in (as joints) with slush or grout ~ *vi* **1 :** to make one's way through slush **2 :** to make a splashing sound

slush fund *n* **1 :** a fund raised from the sale of refuse to obtain small luxuries or pleasures for a warship's crew **2 :** a fund for bribing public officials or carrying on corruptive propaganda

slush·i·ness \'sləsh-ē-nəs\ *n* **:** the quality or state of being slushy

slushy \'sləsh-ē\ *adj* **:** full of or marked by slush

slut \'slət\ *n* [ME *slutte*] **1 :** a slovenly woman **:** SLATTERN **2 a :** a lewd woman; *esp* **:** PROSTITUTE **b :** a saucy girl **:** MINX **3 :** BITCH 1 — **slut·tish** \'slət-ish\ *adj* — **slut·tish·ly** *adv* — **slut·tish·ness** *n*

sly \'slī\ *adj* **sli·er** *also* **sly·er** \'slī(-ə)r\ **sli·est** *also* **sly·est** \'slī-əst\ [ME *sli*, fr. ON *slægr;* akin to OE *slēan* to strike — more at SLAY] **1** *chiefly dial* **a :** CANNY, SHREWD **b :** displaying cleverness **:** INGENIOUS **2 a :** artfully cunning **:** CRAFTY **b :** SECRETIVE, FURTIVE **3 :** lightly mischievous **:** ROGUISH — **sly·ly** *adv* — **sly·ness** *n*

syn SLY, CUNNING, CRAFTY, TRICKY, FOXY, WILY, ARTFUL mean attaining one's ends by devious means. SLY implies lack of candor, furtiveness, and skill in concealing one's intentions and methods; CUNNING suggests the effective use of sometimes limited intelligence in evading or circumventing; CRAFTY implies clever cunning and subtlety of method; TRICKY may stress unscrupulous cunning; FOXY suggests shrewd and wary craftiness; WILY stresses astuteness in tricking or laying traps; ARTFUL suggests insinuating or ingratiating craftiness

— **on the sly :** FURTIVELY

sly·boots \-ˌbüts\ *n pl but sing in constr* **:** a sly tricky person; *esp* **:** one who is cunning or mischievous in an engaging, diverting way

slype \'slīp\ *n* [prob. fr. Flem *slijpe* place for slipping in and out] **:** a narrow passage; *specif* **:** one between the transept and chapter house or deanery in an English cathedral

¹**smack** \'smak\ *n* [ME, fr. OE *smæc;* akin to OHG *smac* taste, Lith *smaguriauti* to nibble] **1 :** characteristic taste or flavor; *also* **:** a perceptible taste or tincture **2 :** a small quantity **syn** see TASTE

²**smack** *vi* **1 :** to have a taste or flavor **2 :** to have a trace, vestige, or suggestion ⟨a proposal that ~*s* of treason⟩

³**smack** *vb* [akin to MD *smacken* to strike] *vt* **1 :** to close and open (lips) noisily and in rapid succession esp. in eating **2 a :** to kiss with or as if with a smack **b :** to strike so as to produce a smack ~ *vi* **:** to make or give a smack

⁴**smack** *n* **1 :** a quick sharp noise made by rapidly compressing and opening the lips **2 :** a loud kiss **:** BUSS **3 :** a sharp slap or blow

⁵**smack** *adv* **:** squarely and sharply **:** DIRECTLY

⁶**smack** *n* [D *smak* or LG *smack*] **:** a sailing ship (as a sloop or cutter) used chiefly in coasting and fishing

smack-dab \'smak-'dab\ *adv, dial* **:** SQUARELY, EXACTLY

smack·er \'smak-ər\ *n* **1 :** one that smacks **2** *slang* **:** DOLLAR

smack·ing \-iŋ\ *adj* **:** BRISK, LIVELY ⟨a ~ breeze⟩

¹**small** \'smȯl\ *adj* [ME *smal*, fr. OE *smæl;* akin to OHG *smal* small, L *malus* bad] **1 a :** having comparatively little size **b :** LOWERCASE **2 a :** minor in influence, power, or rank **b :** operating on a limited scale **3 :** lacking in strength **4 a :** measurably little (as in quantity, amount, value) **b :** made up of few or little units **5 a :** of little consequence **:** TRIVIAL, INSIGNIFICANT **b :** HUMBLE, MODEST **6 :** limited in degree **:** TRIFLING **7 a :** MEAN, PETTY **b :** HUMILIATED — **small·ness** *n*

syn SMALL, LITTLE, DIMINUTIVE, MINUTE, PETITE, TINY, MINIATURE, WEE mean noticeably below average in size. SMALL and LITTLE are often interchangeable, but SMALL applies more to relative size determined by capacity, value, number; LITTLE is more absolute in implication often carrying the idea of petiteness, pettiness, insignificance, immaturity; DIMINUTIVE implies abnormal smallness; MINUTE implies extreme smallness; PETITE applies chiefly to girls and women and implies marked but not abnormal smallness and trimness of figure; TINY is an informal equivalent to MINUTE; MINIATURE applies to an exactly proportioned reproduction on a very small scale; WEE is homely or dialect for DIMINUTIVE

²**small** *adv* **1 :** in or into small pieces **2 :** without force or loudness **3 :** in a small manner

³**small** *n* **1 :** a part smaller and esp. narrower than the remainder ⟨the ~ of the back⟩ **2 a** *pl* **:** small-sized products **b** *pl, Brit* **:** SMALLCLOTHES 1

smal·lage \'smȯ-lij\ *n* [alter. of ME *smalache*, fr. *smal* + *ache* wild celery, fr. OF, fr. L *apium*] **:** a strongly scented herb (*Apium graveolens*) that is the wild form of celery

small ale *n* **:** a weak ale brewed with little malt and little or no hops as a mild and cheap drink

small arm *n* **:** a firearm fired while held in the hands

small beer *n* **1 :** weak or inferior beer **2 :** something of small importance **:** TRIVIA

small capital *n* **:** a letter having the form of but smaller than a capital letter (as in THESE WORDS)

small change *n* **1 :** CHANGE 4c **2 :** something trifling or petty

small·clothes \'smȯl-ˌklō(th)z\ *n pl* **1 :** close-fitting knee breeches worn in the 18th century **2 :** small articles of clothing (as underclothing)

small-fry \-ˌfrī\ *adj* **1 :** MINOR, UNIMPORTANT **2 :** of or relating to children **:** CHILDISH

small game *n* **:** game birds and mammals not classed as big game

small hours *n pl* **:** the early morning hours

small intestine *n* **:** the anterior portion of the intestine that secretes digestive enzymes and through the wall of which digested nutrients pass into the blood and lymph

small·ish \'smȯ-lish\ *adj* **:** somewhat small

small-mind·ed \'smȯl-'mīn-dəd\ *adj* **1 :** having narrow interests, sympathies, or outlook **2 :** typical of a small-minded person — **small-mind·ed·ly** *adv* — **small-mind·ed·ness** *n*

small potato *n* **:** someone or something of trivial importance or worth — usu. used in pl. but sing. or pl. in constr.

small·pox \'smȯl-ˌpäks\ *n* **:** an acute contagious febrile virus disease characterized by skin eruption with pustules, sloughing, and scar formation

small-scale \-'skā(ə)l\ *adj* **1 :** small in scope; *esp* **:** small in output or operation **2** *of a map* **:** having a scale (as one inch to 25 miles) that permits plotting of comparatively little detail

small stores *n pl* **:** articles of clothing sold by a naval supply officer to naval personnel

small stuff *n* **:** small rope (as spun yarn or marline) usu. identified by the number of threads or yarns which it contains

small·sword \'smȯl-ˌsō(ə)rd, -ˌsȯ(ə)rd\ *n* **:** a light tapering sword for thrusting used chiefly in dueling and fencing

small talk *n* **:** light or casual conversation **:** CHITCHAT

small-time \'smȯl-'tīm\ *adj* **:** MINOR, INSIGNIFICANT — **small-tim·er** \-'tī-mər\ *n*

smalt \'smȯlt\ *n* [MF, fr. OIt *smalto*, of Gmc origin; akin to OHG *smelzan* to melt — more at SMELT] **:** a deep blue pigment used esp. as a ceramic color and prepared by fusing together silica, potash, and oxide of cobalt and grinding to powder the resultant glass

smalt·ite \'smȯl-ˌtīt\ *n* [alter. of *smaltine*, fr. F, fr. *smalt*] **:** a tin-white or gray isometric mineral of metallic luster that is essentially a compound of cobalt and nickel with arsenic

smal·to \'smäl-(ˌ)tō, 'smȯl-\ *n* [It, smalt, smalto] **:** colored glass or enamel or a piece of either used in mosaic work

sma·ragd \smə-'ragd, 'smar-igd\ *n* [ME *smaragde*, fr. L *smaragdus*] **:** EMERALD — **sma·rag·dine** \smə-'rag-dən\ *adj*

sma·rag·dite \smə-'rag-ˌdīt\ *n* [F, fr. L *smaragdus* emerald — more at EMERALD] **:** a green foliated amphibole

¹**smart** \'smärt\ *vi* [ME *smerten*, fr. OE *smeortan;* akin to OHG *smerzan* to pain, L *mordēre* to bite, Gk *marainein* to waste away] **1 :** to cause or be the cause or seat of a sharp poignant pain; *also* **:** to feel or have such a pain **2 :** to feel acutely remorseful **3 :** to endure sharp pain; *esp* **:** to pay a heavy or stinging penalty

²**smart** *adj* **1 :** making one smart **:** causing a sharp stinging **2 :** marked by often sharp forceful activity or vigorous strength **3 :** BRISK, SPIRITED **4 a :** mentally alert **:** BRIGHT **b :** sharp in scheming **:** SHREWD **5 a :** WITTY, CLEVER **b :** PERT, SAUCY **6 a :** NEAT, TRIM **b :** stylish or elegant in dress or appearance **c** (1) **:** SOPHISTICATED (2) **:** characteristic of or patronized by fashionable society — **smart·ly** *adv* — **smart·ness** *n*

³**smart** *adv* **:** SMARTLY

⁴**smart** *n* **1 :** a smarting pain; *esp* **:** a stinging local pain **2 :** poignant grief or remorse **3 :** an affectedly witty or fashionable person

smart al·eck \-ˌal-ik, -ˌel-\ *n* [*Aleck*, nickname for *Alexander*] **:** an offensively conceited and bumptious person — **smart-al·ecky** \-ˌal-ə-kē, -ˌel-\ *or* **smart-aleck** \-ik\ *adj*

smart·en \'smärt-ᵊn\ *vt* **smart·en·ing** \'smärt-niŋ, -ᵊn-iŋ\ **:** to make smart or smarter; *esp* **:** SPRUCE — usu. used with *up* ~ *vi* **:** to smarten oneself — used with *up*

¹**smart money** \-ˌmən-ē\ *n* **:** punitive damages awarded for gross misconduct

²**smart money** \-'mən-ē, -ˌmən-\ *n* **:** money ventured by one having inside information or much experience

smart set *n* **:** ultrafashionable society

smart·weed \'smärt-ˌwēd\ *n* **:** any of various knotgrasses (genus *Polygonum*) with strong acrid juice; *also* **:** a plant (as a nettle) that causes a burning sensation in contact with the skin

smarty *or* **smart·ie** \'smärt-ē\ *n* **:** SMART ALECK

smarty-pants \-ˌpan(t)s\ *n pl but sing in constr* **:** SMARTY

¹**smash** \'smash\ *vb* [perh. blend of *smack* and *mash*] *vt* **1 :** to

break in pieces by violence : SHATTER **2 a :** to drive or throw violently esp. with a shattering or battering effect; *also* : to effect in this way **b :** to hit (as a tennis ball) with a hard overhand stroke **3 :** to destroy utterly : WRECK ~ *vi* **1 :** to move or become propelled with violence or crashing effect **2 :** to become wrecked **3 :** to go to pieces suddenly under collision or pressure **4 :** to execute a smash (as in tennis) — **smash·er** *n*

2smash *n* **1 a :** a smashing blow or attack **b :** a hard overhand stroke in tennis or badminton **2 :** the condition of being smashed **3 a :** the action or sound of smashing; *esp* : a wreck due to collision : CRASH **b :** utter collapse : RUIN; *esp* : BANKRUPTCY **4 :** a fruit beverage made with crushed or squeezed fruit **5 :** a striking success : HIT

3smash *adv* : with a resounding crash

4smash *adj* : being a smash : OUTSTANDING ⟨~ hit⟩

smash·ing *adj* **1 :** CRUSHING, CRASHING **2 :** extraordinarily impressive or effective — **smash·ing·ly** \-iŋ-lē\ *adv*

smash·up \'smash-,əp\ *n* **1 :** a complete collapse **2 :** a collision of motor vehicles

1smat·ter \'smat-ər\ *vb* [ME *smateren*] *vt* **1 :** to speak with spotty or superficial knowledge ⟨~ French⟩ **2 :** to dabble in ~ *vi* : BABBLE, CHATTER — **smat·ter·er** \-ər-ər\ *n*

2smatter *n* : SMATTERING

smat·ter·ing \'smat-ə-riŋ\ *n* **1 :** superficial piecemeal knowledge **2 :** a small scattered number

smaze \'smāz\ *n* [*smoke* + *haze*] : a combination of haze and smoke similar to smog in appearance but less damp in consistency

1smear \'smi(ə)r\ *n* [ME *smere*, fr. OE *smeoru;* akin to OHG *smero* grease, Gk *smyris* emery, *myron* unguent] **1 a :** a viscous or sticky substance **b :** a spot made by or as if by an unctuous or adhesive substance **2 :** material smeared on a surface (as of a microscopic slide); *also* : a preparation made by smearing material on a surface ⟨vaginal ~⟩ **3 :** a usu. unsubstantiated charge or accusation against a person or organization

2smear *vt* **1 a :** to overspread with something unctuous, viscous, or adhesive : DAUB **b :** to spread over a surface **2 a :** to stain, smudge, or dirty by or as if by smearing **b :** SULLY, BESMIRCH; *specif* : to vilify by applying an odious epithet or by secretly and maliciously spreading gross charges and imputations **3 :** to obliterate, obscure, blur, blend, or wipe out by or as if by smearing — **smear·er** *n*

smear·case *or* **smier·case** \'smi(ə)r-,kās\ *n* [modif. of G *schmierkäse*, fr. *schmieren* to smear + *käse* cheese] *chiefly Midland* : COTTAGE CHEESE

smear word *n* : an epithet intended to smear a person or group

smeary \'smi(ə)r-ē\ *adj* **1 :** SMEARED **2 :** liable to cause smears

smeek \'smēk\ *n* [ME *smek*] *chiefly Scot* : SMOKE

1smell \'smel\ *vb* **smelled** \'smeld\ *or* **smelt** \'smelt\ **smell·ing** [ME *smellen;* akin to MD *smölen* to scorch, Russ *smalit'*] *vt* **1 :** to get the odor or scent of through stimuli affecting the olfactory nerves **2 :** to detect or become aware of as if by the sense of smell **3 :** to emit the odor of ~ *vi* **1 :** to exercise the sense of smell **2 a** (1) **:** to have an odor or scent (2) **:** to have a characteristic aura or atmosphere : SUGGEST **b** (1) **:** to have an offensive odor : STINK (2) **:** to appear evil, dishonest, or ugly — **smell·er** *n* — **smell a rat :** to have a suspicion of something wrong

2smell *n* **1 a :** the process, function, or power of smelling **b :** the special sense concerned with the perception of odor **2 :** the property of a thing that affects the olfactory organs : ODOR **3 :** a pervading quality : AURA **4 :** an act or instance of smelling

syn SMELL, SCENT, ODOR, AROMA mean the quality that makes a thing perceptible to the olfactory sense. SMELL implies solely the sensation without suggestion of quality or character; SCENT applies to the often delicate effluvium esp. from an animal source; ODOR implies a stronger or more readily distinguished scent or any smell; AROMA suggests a somewhat penetrating usu. pleasant odor

smelling salts *n pl but sing or pl in constr* : a usu. scented aromatic preparation of ammonium carbonate and ammonia water used as a stimulant and restorative

smelly \'smel-ē\ *adj* : having a smell; *esp* : MALODOROUS

1smelt \'smelt\ *n, pl* **smelts** *or* **smelt** [ME, fr. OE; akin to Norw *smelte* whiting] : any of various small salmonoid fishes (family Osmeridae and esp. genus *Osmerus*) that closely resemble the trouts in general structure, live along coasts and ascend rivers to spawn or are landlocked, and have delicate oily flesh with a distinctive odor and taste

2smelt *vt* [D or LG *smelten;* akin to OHG *smelzan* to melt, OE *meltan*] **1 :** to melt or fuse (as ore) often with an accompanying chemical change usu. to separate the metal **2 :** REFINE, REDUCE

smelt·er \'smel-tər\ *n* **1 a :** one that smelts; *specif* : a worker who smelts ore **b :** an owner of a smeltery **2** *or* **smelt·ery** \-t(ə-)rē\ : an establishment for smelting

smew \'smyü\ *n* [akin to MHG *smiehe* smew] : a merganser (*Mergus albellus*) of northern Europe and Asia with the male white-crested

smid·gen *or* **smid·geon** *or* **smid·gin** \'smij-ən\ *n* [prob. alter. of E dial *smitch* (soiling mark)] : a small amount : BIT

smi·lax \'smī-,laks\ *n* [L, bindweed, yew, fr. Gk] **1 :** GREENBRIER **2 :** a delicate greenhouse twining plant (*Asparagus asparagoides*) with ovate bright green cladophylls

1smile \'smī(ə)l\ *vb* [ME *smilen;* akin to OE *smerian* to laugh, L *mirari* to wonder, Skt *smayate* he smiles] *vi* **1 :** to have, produce, or exhibit a smile **2 a :** to look or regard with amusement or ridicule **b :** to be propitious **c :** to appear pleasant or agreeable ~ *vt* **1 :** to affect with or by smiling **2 :** to express by a smile — **smil·er** *n* — **smil·ing·ly** \'smī-liŋ-lē\ *adv*

2smile *n* **1 :** a change of facial expression involving a brightening of the eyes and an upward curving of the corners of the mouth that may express amusement, pleasure, affection, irony, or derision **2 :** a pleasant or encouraging appearance

smile·less \'smī(ə)l-ləs\ *adj* : exhibiting no smile : SOLEMN — **smile·less·ly** *adv*

smirch \'smərch\ *vt* [ME *smorchen*] **1 a :** to make dirty, stained, or discolored : SULLY **b :** to smear with something that stains or dirties **2 :** to bring discredit or disgrace on — **smirch** *n*

smirk \'smərk\ *vi* [ME *smirken*, fr. OE *smearcian* to smile; akin to OE *smerian* to laugh] : to smile in an affected manner : SIMPER — **smirk** *n*

smirky \'smər-kē\ *adj* : SMIRKING

smite \'smīt\ *vb* **smote** \'smōt\ **smit·ten** \'smit-ᵊn\ *or* **smote; smit·ing** \'smīt-iŋ\ [ME *smiten*, fr. OE *smītan;* akin to OHG bi*smīzan* to defile and perh. to L *mittere* to let go, send] *vt* **1 :** to strike sharply or heavily esp. with the hand **2 a :** to kill or severely injure by smiting **b :** to attack or afflict suddenly and injuriously ⟨*smitten* by disease⟩ **3 :** to cause to strike **4 :** to impress suddenly ~ *vi* : to deliver or deal a blow with or as if with the hand or something held **syn** see STRIKE — **smit·er** \'smīt-ər\ *n*

smith \'smith\ *n* [ME, fr. OE; akin to OHG *smid* smith, Gk *smilē* wood-carving knife] **1 :** a worker in metals : BLACKSMITH **2 :** MAKER ⟨gun*smith*⟩ ⟨tune*smith*⟩

smith·er·eens \,smith-ə-'rēnz\ *n pl* [IrGael *smidirīn*] : FRAGMENTS, BITS

smith·ery \'smith-(ə-)rē\ *n* **1 :** the work, art, or trade of a smith **2 :** SMITHY 1

smith·son·ite \'smith-sə-,nīt\ *n* [James *Smithson* †1829 Brit chemist] **1 :** a usu. white or nearly white native zinc carbonate $ZnCO_3$ **2 :** a mineral $Zn_4Si_2O_7OH.H_2O$ consisting of a zinc silicate and constituting an ore of zinc

smithy \'smith-ē *also* 'smith-\ *n* **1 :** the workshop of a smith **2 :** BLACKSMITH

1smock \'smäk\ *n* [ME *smok*, fr. OE *smoc;* akin to OHG *smocco* adornment] **1** *archaic* : a woman's undergarment; *esp* : CHEMISE **2 :** a light loose garment worn esp. for protection of clothing while working

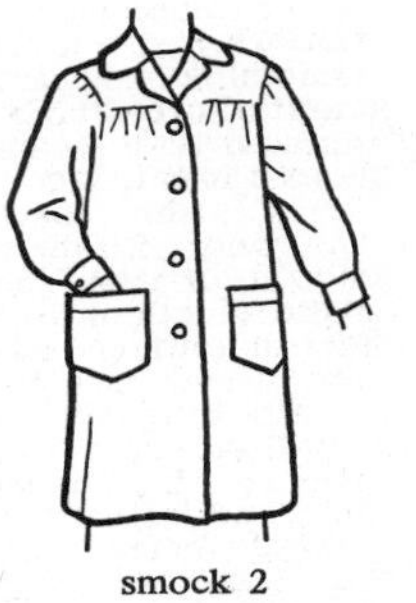

smock 2

2smock *vt* : to embroider or shirr with smocking

smock frock *n* : a loose outer garment worn by workmen esp. in Europe

smock·ing \'smäk-iŋ\ *n* : a decorative embroidery or shirring made by gathering cloth in regularly spaced round tucks

smog \'smäg *also* 'smȯg\ *n* [blend of *smoke* and *fog*] : a fog made heavier and darker by smoke and chemical fumes

smog·gy \-ē\ *adj* : characterized by or abounding in smog

smok·able *or* **smoke·able** \'smō-kə-bəl\ *adj* : fit for smoking

1smoke \'smōk\ *n* [ME, fr. OE *smoca;* akin to MHG *smouch* smoke, Gk *smychein* to smolder] **1 a :** the gaseous products of burning carbonaceous materials made visible by the presence of small particles of carbon **b :** a suspension of solid particles in a gas **2 a :** a mass or column of smoke **b :** SMUDGE **3 :** fume or vapor often resulting from the action of heat on moisture **4 :** visible or tangible evidence **5 :** something of little substance, permanence, or value **6 :** something that obscures **7 a :** something to smoke (as a cigarette) : TOBACCO **b :** an act or spell of smoking tobacco **8 a :** a pale blue **b :** any of the colors of smoke — **smoke·like** \'smō-,klīk\ *adj*

2smoke *vi* **1 a :** to emit or exhale smoke **b :** to emit excessive smoke **2** *archaic* : to undergo punishment : SUFFER **3 :** to spread or rise like smoke **4 :** to inhale and exhale the fumes of tobacco or something like tobacco ~ *vt* **1 a :** FUMIGATE **b :** to drive away by smoke **c :** to blacken or discolor with smoke **d :** to cure by exposure to smoke **e :** to stupefy (as bees) by smoke **2** *archaic* : SUSPECT **3 :** to inhale and exhale the smoke of **4** *archaic* : RIDICULE

smoke·chas·er \-,chā-sər\ *n* : a forest fire fighter; *esp* : one with light equipment that enables him to get to fires quickly

smoke–filled room \,smōk-,fil-'drüm\ *n* : a room (as in a hotel) in which a small group of politicians carry on negotiations

smoke·house \'smōk-,haüs\ *n* : a building where meat or fish is cured by means of dense smoke

smoke·jack \-,jak\ *n* : a contrivance for turning a spit by a fly or wheel moved by rising gases in a chimney

smoke jumper *n* : a forest fire fighter who parachutes to locations otherwise difficult to reach

smoke·less \'smō-kləs\ *adj* : producing or having little or no smoke

smokeless powder *n* : any of a class of propellants in various forms producing comparatively little smoke on explosion and consisting typically of gelatinized cellulose nitrates either alone or mixed

smoke out *vt* **1 :** to drive out by or as if by smoke **2 :** to bring to public view or knowledge

smoke·proof \'smōk-'prüf\ *adj* : impermeable to smoke; *specif* : designed to restrict the spread of smoke through a building ⟨~ partitions⟩

smok·er \'smō-kər\ *n* **1 :** one that smokes **2 :** a railroad car or compartment in which smoking is allowed **3 :** an informal social gathering for men

smoke screen *n* : a screen of smoke to hinder enemy observation of a military force, area, or activity

smoke·stack \'smōk-,stak\ *n* : a chimney or funnel through which smoke and gases are discharged

smoke tree *n* : either of two small shrubby trees (genus *Cotinus*) of the sumac family often grown for their large panicles of minute flowers suggesting a cloud of smoke

smok·i·ly \'smō-kə-lē\ *adv* : in a smoky manner

smok·i·ness \-kē-nəs\ *n* : the quality or state of being smoky

smoking jacket *n* : a man's soft jacket for wear at home

smoking lamp *n* : a lamp on a ship kept lighted during the hours when smoking is allowed

smoking room *n* : a room (as in a hotel or club) set apart for smokers

smoking–room *adj* : marked by indecency or obscenity : SMUTTY ⟨~ stories⟩

smoky \'smō-kē\ *adj* **1 :** emitting smoke esp. in large quantities **2 :** of the nature of or resembling smoke **3 a :** filled with smoke **b :** made dark or black by smoke

smoky quartz *n* : CAIRNGORM

1smol·der *or* **smoul·der** \'smōl-dər\ *n* [ME *smolder;* akin to ME *smellen* to smell] **1 :** SMOKE, SMUDGE **2 :** a smoldering fire

2smolder *or* **smoulder** *vi* **smol·der·ing** \-d(ə-)riŋ\ **1 a :** to burn and smoke without flame **b :** to waste away by slow combustion ⟨fire was ~*ing* in the grate⟩ — often used with *out* **2 :** to exist in a state of suppressed activity **3 :** to show suppressed anger, hate, or jealousy

ə abut; ᵊ kitten; ər further; a back; ā bake; ä cot, cart; aü out; ch chin; e less; ē easy; g gift; i trip; ī life
j joke; ŋ sing; ō flow; ȯ flaw; ȯi coin; th thin; th this; ü loot; u̇ foot; y yet; yü few; yu̇ furious; zh vision

smolt \'smōlt\ *n* [ME (Sc)] **:** a salmon or sea trout when it is about two years old and silvery and first descends to the sea
[1]**smooch** \'smüch\ *vt* [prob. alter. of *smutch*, vb.] **:** SMUDGE, SMEAR
[2]**smooch** *n* **:** SMUDGE, SMEAR — **smoochy** \'smü-chē\ *adj*
[3]**smooch** *vi* [alter. of *smouch* (to kiss loudly)] **:** KISS, PET
[4]**smooch** *n* **:** KISS
[1]**smooth** \'smüth\ *adj* [ME *smothe*, fr. OE *smōth;* akin to OS *smōthi* smooth] **1 a :** having a continuous even surface **b :** being without hair **c :** GLABROUS **d :** causing no resistance to sliding **2 :** free from obstructions or impediments ⟨broad ~ highways⟩ **3 :** even and uninterrupted in flow or flight **4 :** plausibly flattering **:** INGRATIATING **5 a :** SERENE, EQUABLE **b :** AMIABLE, COURTEOUS **6 :** sounded without the aspirate — used of a Greek vowel ⟨~ breathing⟩ **7 :** not sharp or acid **:** BLAND **syn** see EASY, LEVEL, SUAVE — **smooth** *adv* — **smooth·ly** *adv* — **smooth·ness** *n*
[2]**smooth** *vt* **1 :** to make smooth **2 a :** to free from what is harsh or disagreeable **:** POLISH **b :** SOOTHE **3 :** to minimize (as a fault) in order to allay anger or ill will **:** PALLIATE **4 :** to free from obstruction or difficulty **5 a :** to press flat **b :** to remove expression from (one's face) **:** COMPOSE **6 :** to cause to lie evenly and in order **:** PREEN ~ *vi* **:** to become smooth — **smooth·er** *n*
[3]**smooth** *n* **1 :** a smooth part **2 :** the act of smoothing **3 :** a smoothing implement
smooth·bore \-'bō(ə)r, -'bȯ(ə)r\ *adj, of a firearm* **:** having a smooth-surfaced bore — **smoothbore** \'smüth-,\ *n*
smooth breathing *n* **1 :** a mark ' placed over some initial vowels in Greek to show that they are not aspirated (as in ἄγειν pronounced \'ä-,gān\) **2 :** the sound indicated by a mark ' over a Greek vowel
smooth·en \'smü-thən\ *vb* **smooth·en·ing** \'smüth-(ə-)niŋ\ **:** to make smooth or become smooth
smooth hound *n* **:** a dogfish (as *Mustelus mustelus* of southern European waters) lacking a spine in front of the dorsal fin
smooth–tongued \'smüth-'təŋd\ *adj* **:** ingratiating in speech
smoothy *or* **smooth·ie** \'smü-thē\ *n* **1 a :** a person with polished manners **b :** one who behaves or performs with deftness, assurance, and easy competence; *esp* **:** a man with an ingratiating manner toward women **2 :** a smooth-tongued person
smor·gas·bord \'smȯr-gəs-,bȯ(ə)rd, -,bō(ə)rd\ *n* [Sw *smörgåsbord*, fr. *smörgås* open sandwich + *bord* table] **:** a luncheon or supper buffet offering a variety of foods and dishes (as hors d'oeuvres, hot and cold meats, smoked and pickled fish, cheeses, salads, and relishes)
smote *past of* SMITE
[1]**smoth·er** \'sməth-ər\ *n* [ME, alter. of *smorther*, fr. *smoren* to smother, fr. OE *smorian* to suffocate; akin to MD *smoren* to suffocate] **1 a :** thick stifling smoke or smudge **b :** a state of being stifled or suppressed **2 :** a dense cloud of fog, foam, spray, snow, or dust **3 :** a confused multitude of things **:** WELTER — **smoth·ery** \-(ə-)rē\ *adj*
[2]**smother** *vb* **smoth·er·ing** \-(ə-)riŋ\ *vt* **1 :** to overcome or kill with smoke or fumes **2 a :** to destroy the life of by depriving of air **b :** to overcome or discomfit through or as if through lack of air **c :** to suppress (a fire) by excluding oxygen **3 a :** to cause to smolder **b :** to suppress expression or knowledge of **c :** to stop or prevent the growth or activity of **d :** to cover thickly **:** BLANKET **e :** OVERCOME, VANQUISH **4 :** to cook in a covered pan or pot with little liquid over low heat ~ *vi* **:** to become smothered
[1]**smudge** \'sməj\ *vb* [ME *smogen*] *vt* **1 a :** to make a smudge on **b :** to soil as if by smudging **2 a :** to rub, daub, or wipe in a smeary manner **b :** to make indistinct **:** BLUR **3 :** to smoke or protect by means of a smudge ~ *vi* **1 :** to make a smudge **2 :** to become smudged
[2]**smudge** *n* **1 a :** a blurry spot or streak **b :** an immaterial stain **c :** an indistinct mass **:** BLUR **2 :** a smoldering mass placed on the windward side (as to repel insects or protect from frost) — **smudg·i·ly** \'sməj-ə-lē\ *adv* — **smudg·i·ness** \'sməj-ē-nəs\ *n* — **smudgy** \-ē\ *adj*
smug \'sməg\ *adj* **smug·ger; smug·gest** [prob. modif. of LG *smuck* neat, fr. MLG, fr. *smucken* to dress; akin to OE *smoc* smock] **1 :** trim or smart in dress **:** SPRUCE **2 :** scrupulously clean, neat, or correct **:** TIDY **3 :** highly self-satisfied **:** COMPLACENT — **smug·ly** *adv* — **smug·ness** *n*
smug·gle \'sməg-əl\ *vb* **smug·gling** \-(ə-)liŋ\ [LG *smuggeln* & D *smokkelen;* akin to OE *smoc* smock] *vt* **1 :** to import or export secretly contrary to the law and esp. without paying duties imposed by law **2 :** to convey or introduce surreptitiously ~ *vi* **:** to import or export anything in violation of the customs laws — **smug·gler** \'sməg-lər, *before* "*of*" *also* -ə-lər\ *n*
[1]**smut** \'smət\ *vb* **smut·ted; smut·ting** [prob. alter. of earlier *smot* to stain, fr. ME *smotten;* akin to MHG *smutzen* to stain] *vt* **1 :** to stain or taint with smut **2 :** to affect (a crop or plant) with smut ~ *vi* **:** to become affected by smut
[2]**smut** *n* **1 :** matter that soils or blackens; *specif* **:** a particle of soot **2 :** any of various destructive diseases esp. of cereal grasses caused by parasitic fungi (order Ustilaginales) and marked by transformation of plant organs into dark masses of spores; *also* **:** a fungus causing a smut **3 :** material treated obscenely or felt to be morally fouling
smutch \'sməch\ *n* [prob. irreg. fr. *smudge*] **:** a dark stain **:** SMUDGE — **smutch** *vt* — **smutchy** \-ē\ *adj*
smut·ti·ly \'smət-ᵊl-ē\ *adv* **:** in a smutty manner
smut·ti·ness \'smət-ē-nəs\ *n* **:** the quality or state of being smutty
smut·ty \'smət-ē\ *adj* **1 :** soiled or tainted with smut; *esp* **:** affected with smut fungus **2 :** OBSCENE, INDECENT **3 :** resembling smut in appearance **:** SOOTY
[1]**snack** \'snak\ *vi* [ME *snaken* to bite] **:** to eat a snack **:** LUNCH
[2]**snack** *n* **:** a light meal **:** LUNCH
snack bar *n* **:** a public eating place where snacks are served usu. at a counter
snack table *n* **:** a small portable table designed to hold food or drink for one person
snaf·fle \'snaf-əl\ *n* [origin unknown] **:** a simple jointed bit for a bridle — **snaffle** *vt* **snaf·fling** \-(ə-)liŋ\
sna·fu \sna-'fü\ *adj* [*s*ituation *n*ormal *a*ll *f*ouled *u*p] *slang* **:** snarled or stalled in confusion **:** AWRY — **snafu** *n* — **snafu** *vt*
[1]**snag** \'snag\ *n* [of Scand origin; akin to ON *snagi* clothes peg] **1 a :** a stub or stump remaining after a branch has been lopped or torn off **b :** a tree or branch embedded in a lake or stream bed and constituting a hazard to navigation **2 :** a rough sharp or jagged projecting part **:** PROTUBERANCE: as **a :** a projecting tooth; *also* **:** a stump of a tooth **b :** one of the secondary branches of an antler **3 :** a concealed or unexpected difficulty or obstacle **4 :** a jagged tear made by or as if by catching on a snag — **snag·gy** \'snag-ē\ *adj*
[2]**snag** *vt* **snagged; snag·ging 1 :** to hew, trim, or cut roughly or jaggedly **2 a :** to catch and usu. damage on or as if on a snag **b :** to halt or impede as if by catching on a snag **3 :** to clear (as water) of snags **4 :** to catch or obtain by quick action
snag·gle·tooth \'snag-əl-,tüth\ *n* [E dial. *snaggle* (irregularly shaped tooth) + E *tooth*] **:** an irregular, broken, or projecting tooth — **snag·gle·toothed** \,snag-əl-'tütht\ *adj*
snail \'snā(ə)l\ *n* [ME, fr. OE *snægl;* akin to OHG *snecko* snail, *snahhan* to creep, Lith *snākе* snail] **1 :** a gastropod mollusk esp. when having an external enclosing spiral shell **2 :** a slow-moving or sluggish person or thing — **snail·like** \'snā(ə)l-,līk\ *adj*
snail–paced \-'pāst\ *adj* **:** moving very slowly
[1]**snake** \'snāk\ *n* [ME, fr. OE *snaca;* akin to OE *snægl* snail] **1 :** any of numerous limbless scaled reptiles (suborder Serpentes or Ophidia) with a long tapering body and often salivary glands modified to produce venom which is injected through grooved or tubular fangs **2 :** a worthless or treacherous fellow
[2]**snake** *vt* **1 :** to wind (as one's way) in the manner of a snake **2 :** to move (as logs) by dragging **:** SKID ~ *vi* **:** to crawl or move silently, secretly, or sinuously
snake·bird \-,bərd\ *n* **:** any of several fish-eating birds (genus *Anhinga*) related to the cormorants but distinguished by a long slender neck and sharp-pointed bill
snake·bite \-,bīt\ *n* **:** the bite of a snake and esp. a venomous snake
snake charmer *n* **:** an entertainer who exhibits his professed power to charm or fascinate venomous snakes
snake dance *n* **1 :** a ceremonial dance in which snakes or their images are handled, invoked, or symbolically imitated by individual sinuous actions **2 :** a group progression in a single-file serpentine path (as in celebration of an athletic victory)
snake doctor *n* **1 :** HELLGRAMMITE **2 :** DRAGONFLY
snake fence *n* **:** WORM FENCE
snake in the grass 1 : a lurking or unsuspected danger **2 :** a secretly faithless friend
snake·like \'snā-,klīk\ *adj* **:** resembling a snake esp. in elongate tapering form
snake·mouth \'snāk-,mau̇th\ *n* **:** a bog orchid (*Pogonia ophioglossoides*) of eastern No. America and Japan with showy pink flowers
snake oil *n* **:** any of various substances or mixtures sold (as by a traveling medicine show) as medicine usu. without regard to their medical worth or properties
snake pit *n* **:** a place of chaotic disorder and distress; *esp* **:** a hospital for mental diseases
snake·root \'snā-,krüt\ *n* **:** any of numerous plants mostly with roots reputed to cure snakebites; *also* **:** the root of such a plant
snake·skin \'snāk-,skin\ *n* **:** leather prepared from the skin of a snake
snake·weed \'snā-,kwēd\ *n* **:** any of several plants associated with snakes (as in appearance, habitat, or use in treatment of snakebite)
snak·i·ly \'snā-kə-lē\ *adv* **:** in a snaky manner
snaky \'snā-kē\ *adj* **1 :** of, formed of, or entwined with snakes **2 :** SNAKELIKE, SERPENTINE **3 :** likened to a snake (as in slyness, treachery, venom, or spitefulness) **4 :** abounding in snakes
[1]**snap** \'snap\ *vb* **snapped; snap·ping** [D or LG *snappen;* akin to MHG *snappen* to snap] *vi* **1 a :** to make a sudden closing of the jaws **:** seize something sharply with the mouth ⟨fish *snapping* at the bait⟩ **b :** to grasp at something eagerly **:** make a pounce or snatch ⟨~ at any chance⟩ **2 :** to utter sharp biting words **:** bark out irritable or peevish retorts **3 a :** to break suddenly with a sharp sound ⟨the twig *snapped*⟩ **b :** to give way suddenly under strain **4 :** to make a sharp or crackling sound **5 :** to close or fit in place with an abrupt movement **6 :** to emit sparks or flashes **:** SPARKLE ⟨eyes *snapping* with fury⟩ ~ *vt* **1 :** to seize with or as if with a snap of the jaws **2 :** to capture or take possession of suddenly **3 a :** to retort to or interrupt curtly and irritably **b :** to utter curtly or abruptly **4 :** to break suddenly **:** break short or in two **5 a :** to cause to make a snapping sound ⟨~ his fingers⟩ ⟨~ a whip⟩ **b :** to put into or remove from a particular position by a sudden movement or with a snapping sound ⟨~ the lock shut⟩ **6 a :** to project with a snap **:** FILLIP **b :** to make or do without preparation or delay; *esp* **:** to fire (a projectile) without careful aim **c :** to put (a football) in play with a quick motion **d :** to take a snapshot of — **snap one's fingers at :** to treat with contempt or indifference
[2]**snap** *n* **1 :** an abrupt closing (as of the mouth in biting or of scissors in cutting); *esp* **:** a biting or snatching with the teeth or jaws **2 a** *obs* **:** a share of profits or booty **b :** a chance to make money easily or quickly; *specif* **:** an easy remunerative post or position **c :** something that is easy and presents no problems **:** CINCH **3 :** a small amount **:** BIT, MORSEL **4 a :** an act or instance of seizing abruptly **:** a sudden snatching at something **b :** a quick short movement **c :** a sudden sharp breaking **5 a :** a sound made by snapping something (as together, apart, into place, off) ⟨shut the book with a ~⟩ **b :** a brief sharp and usu. irritable speech or retort **6 :** a sudden interval of harsh weather ⟨cold ~⟩ **7 :** a catch or fastening that closes or locks with a click ⟨~ of a bracelet⟩ **8 :** a thin brittle cooky **9 :** SNAPSHOT **10 a :** the condition of being vigorous in body, mind, or spirit **:** ALERTNESS, ENERGY **b :** a pleasing invigorating quality **:** SMARTNESS, SNAPPINESS **11 :** an act or instance of snapping a football
[3]**snap** *adv* **:** with a snap **:** BRISKLY
[4]**snap** *adj* **1 :** done or carried through suddenly or without deliberation ⟨a ~ judgment⟩ **2 :** called or taken without prior warning ⟨calling ~ votes⟩ **3 :** shutting or fastening with a click or by means of a device that snaps ⟨~ lock⟩ **4 :** unusually easy or simple ⟨~ course⟩
snap back *vi* **:** to make a quick or vigorous recovery
snap·back \'snap-,bak\ *n* **1 :** a football snap **2 :** a sudden rebound or recovery
snap bean *n* **:** a bean grown primarily for its young pods usu. used broken in pieces as a cooked vegetable
snap–brim \'snap-,brim\ *n* **:** a hat usu. of felt with brim turned up in back and down in front and a dented crown
snap·drag·on \'snap-,drag-ən\ *n* **:** any of several garden plants (genus *Antirrhinum* and esp. *A. majus*) of the figwort family having

showy white, crimson, or yellow bilabiate flowers likened to the face of a dragon
snap fastener *n* **:** a metal fastener consisting essentially of a ball and a socket attached to opposed parts of an article and used to hold meeting edges together
snap·per \'snap-ər\ *n, pl* **snappers 1 a :** something that snaps **b** (1) **:** SNAPPING TURTLE (2) **:** CLICK BEETLE **2** *pl also* **snapper a :** any of numerous active carnivorous fishes (family Lutjanidae) of warm seas important as food and often as sport fishes **b :** any of several immature fishes (as the young of the bluefish) that resemble a snapper
snap·per–back \-,bak\ *n* **:** a football center
snap·pi·ly \'snap-ə-lē\ *adv* **:** in a snappy manner
snap·pi·ness \'snap-ē-nəs\ *n* **:** the quality or state of being snappy
snapping beetle *n* **:** CLICK BEETLE
snapping turtle *n* **:** any of several large edible American aquatic turtles (family Chelydridae) with powerful jaws and a strong musky odor
snap·pish \'snap-ish\ *adj* **1 a :** given to snapping irritable speech **:** IRASCIBLE **b :** arising from a harsh irascible nature **2 :** inclined to bite — **snap·pish·ly** *adv* — **snap·pish·ness** *n*
snap·py \'snap-ē\ *adj* **1 :** SNAPPISH **2 a :** BRISK, LIVELY **b :** briskly cold **c :** STYLISH, SMART **3 :** emitting a series of sharp quick reports **:** CRACKLING
snap roll *n* **:** a maneuver in which an airplane is made by quick movement of the controls to complete a full revolution about its longitudinal axis while maintaining an approximately level line of flight
snap·shoot \'snap-,shüt\ *vt* [back-formation fr. *snapshot*] **:** to take a snapshot of — **snap·shoot·er** *n*
snap shot *n* **:** a quick shot made without deliberately taking aim
snap·shot \'snap-,shät\ *n* **:** a casual photograph made by rapid exposure usu. with a small hand-held camera
1**snare** \'sna(ə)r, 'sne(ə)r\ *n* [ME, fr. OE *sneare*, fr. ON *snara;* akin to Gk *narkē* numbness, OHG *snuor* cord — more at NARROW] **1 a** (1) **:** a contrivance often consisting of a noose for entangling birds or mammals (2) **:** TRAP, GIN **b** (1) **:** something by which one is entangled, involved in difficulties, or impeded (2) **:** something deceptively attractive **:** LURE **2** [prob. fr. D *snaar*, lit., cord; akin to OHG *snuor*] **:** one of the catgut strings or metal spirals of a snare drum **3 :** a surgical instrument consisting usu. of a wire loop constricted by a mechanism in the handle and used for removing tissue masses (as tonsils)
2**snare** *vt* **1 a :** to capture by or as if by use of a snare **b :** to win or attain by artful or skillful maneuvers **2 :** to entangle as if in a snare **syn** see CATCH — **snar·er** *n*
snare drum *n* **:** a small double-headed drum with one or more snares stretched across its lower head
1**snarl** \'snär(ə)l\ *n* [ME *snarle*, prob. dim. of *snare*] **:** a tangle esp. of hairs or thread **:** KNOT; *also* **:** a tangled situation **:** COMPLICATION
2**snarl** *vt* **1 :** to cause to become knotted and intertwined **:** TANGLE **2 :** to make excessively complicated ~ *vi* **:** to become snarled — **snarl·er** *n*
3**snarl** *vb* [freq. of obs. E *snar* (to growl)] *vi* **1 :** to growl with a snapping or gnashing of teeth **2 :** to give vent to anger in surly language ~ *vt* **:** to utter or express with a snarl or by snarling — **snarl·er** *n*
4**snarl** *n* **:** a surly angry growl
1**snarly** \'snär-lē\ *adj* [1*snarl*] **:** full of tangles and snarls **:** TANGLED ⟨~ yarn⟩
2**snarly** *adj* [3*snarl*] **:** marked by ill nature **:** SURLY
snash \'snash\ *n* [origin unknown] *chiefly Scot* **:** INSOLENCE, ABUSE
1**snatch** \'snach\ *vb* [ME *snacchen* to give a sudden snap, seize; akin to MD *snacken* to snap at] *vi* **:** to attempt to seize something suddenly ~ *vt* **1 :** to grasp abruptly or hastily **2 :** to seize or grab suddenly without permission, ceremony, or right **syn** see TAKE — **snatch·er** *n*
2**snatch** *n* **1 a :** a snatching at or of something **b** *slang* **:** KIDNAPPING **2 :** a brief opportune period **3 :** something brief, fragmentary, or hurried
snatch block *n* **:** a block that can be opened on one side to receive the bight of a rope
snatchy \'snach-ē\ *adj* **:** done in or by snatches; *broadly* **:** marked by breaks in continuity ⟨a ~ conversation⟩
snath \'snath, 'sneth\ *or* **snathe** \'snāth, 'snāth\ *n* [ME *snede*, fr. OE *snǣd;* akin to OHG *snīdan* to cut, Czech *snět* branch] **:** the handle of a scythe
snaz·zy \'snaz-ē\ *adj* [origin unknown] **:** conspicuously or flashily attractive
1**sneak** \'snēk\ *vb* [akin to OE *snīcan* to sneak along, OHG *snahhan* to creep — more at SNAIL] *vi* **1 :** to go stealthily or furtively **:** SLINK **2 :** to behave in a furtive or servile manner ~ *vt* **:** to put, bring, or take in a furtive or artful manner ⟨~ a smoke⟩ **syn** see LURK
2**sneak** *n* **1 :** a person who acts in a stealthy, furtive, or shifty manner **2 a :** a stealthy or furtive move **b :** an unobserved departure or escape **3 :** SNEAKER 2 — usu. used in pl.
3**sneak** *adj* **1 :** carried on secretly **:** CLANDESTINE **2 :** occurring without warning **:** SURPRISE ⟨a ~ attack⟩
sneak·er \'snē-kər\ *n* **1 :** one that sneaks **2 :** a usu. canvas sports shoe with a pliable rubber sole — used usu. in pl.
sneak·i·ly \-kə-lē\ *adv* **:** in a sneaky manner
sneak·i·ness \-kē-nəs\ *n* **:** the quality or state of being sneaky
sneak·ing \-kiŋ\ *adj* **1 :** FURTIVE, UNDERHAND **2 :** MEAN, CONTEMPTIBLE **3 a :** not openly expressed as if something to be ashamed of ⟨a ~ sympathy⟩ **b :** that is a persistent conjecture ⟨a ~ suspicion⟩ — **sneak·ing·ly** \-kiŋ-lē\ *adv*
sneak preview *n* **:** a special advanced showing of a motion picture usu. announced but not named
sneak thief *n* **:** a thief who steals whatever he can reach without using violence or forcibly breaking into buildings
sneaky \'snē-kē\ *adj* **:** marked by stealth, furtiveness, or shiftiness
1**sneap** \'snēp\ *vt* [ME *snaipen*, prob. of Scand origin; akin to Icel *sneypa* to scold — more at SNUB] **1** *dial Eng* **:** CHIDE **2** *archaic* **:** to blast or blight with cold **:** NIP
2**sneap** *n, archaic* **:** REBUKE, SNUB
sneck \'snek\ *n* [ME *snekke*] *chiefly dial* **:** LATCH
1**sneer** \'sni(ə)r\ *vb* [prob. akin to MHG *snerren* to chatter, gossip — more at SNORE] *vi* **1 :** to smile or laugh with facial contortions that express scorn or contempt **2 :** to speak or write in a scornfully jeering manner ~ *vt* **:** to utter with a sneer **syn** see SCOFF — **sneer·er** *n*
2**sneer** *n* **:** the act of sneering **:** a sneering expression, remark, or saying
sneesh \'snēsh\ *n* [short for E dial. *sneeshing*, alter. of obs. E *sneezing*, fr. E, gerund of *sneeze*] *dial Brit* **:** SNUFF
1**sneeze** \'snēz\ *vi* [ME *snesen*, alter. of *fnesen*, fr. OE *fnēosan;* akin to MHG *pfnūsen* to snort, sneeze, Gk *pnein* to breathe] **:** to make a sudden violent spasmodic audible expiration of breath — **sneez·er** *n* — **sneeze at :** to treat lightly **:** DESPISE
2**sneeze** *n* **:** an act or fact of sneezing
sneeze·weed \'snēz-,wēd\ *n* **1 :** any of several composite plants; *esp* **:** a No. American yellow-flowered perennial herb (*Helenium autumnale*) the odor of which is said to cause sneezing **2 :** SNEEZEWORT
sneeze·wort \-,wərt, -,wȯ(ə)rt\ *n* **:** a strong-scented Eurasian composite perennial herb (*Achillea ptarmica*) resembling yarrow
sneezy \'snē-zē\ *adj* **:** given to or causing sneezing
1**snell** \'snel\ *adj* [ME, fr. OE; akin to OHG *snel* bold, agile] **1** *chiefly dial* **:** QUICK, ACUTE **2 :** KEEN, PIERCING ⟨a ~ wind⟩
2**snell** *n* [origin unknown] **:** a short line (as of gut) by which a fishhook is attached to a longer line
1**snick** \'snik\ *vt* [prob. fr. obs. *snick or snee* to engage in cut-and-thrust fighting — more at SNICKERSNEE] **:** to cut slightly **:** NICK
2**snick** *n* **:** a small cut **:** NICK
3**snick** *vb* [imit.] **:** CLICK
4**snick** *n* **:** a cutting or clicking noise
1**snick·er** \'snik-ər\ *or* **snig·ger** \'snig-ər\ *vi* **snick·er·ing** *or* **snig·ger·ing** \-(ə-)riŋ\ [imit.] **:** to laugh in a slight, covert, or partly suppressed manner **:** TITTER
2**snicker** *or* **snigger** *n* **:** an act or sound of snickering
snick·er·snee *or* **snick–a–snee** *or* **snick–or–snee** \'snik-ə(r)-,snē\ *n* [obs. *snick or snee* to engage in cut-and-thrust fighting, alter. of earlier *steake or snye*, fr. D *steken of snijden* to thrust or cut] **1** *archaic* **:** the act or practice of engaging in cut-and-thrust fighting with knives **2 :** a large knife or sword
snide \'snīd\ *adj* [origin unknown] **1 a :** COUNTERFEIT, SPURIOUS **b :** DISHONEST, CROOKED ⟨a ~ merchant⟩ **2 :** MEAN, LOW, CHEAP ⟨a ~ trick⟩ **3 :** slyly disparaging **:** INSINUATING ⟨~ remarks⟩
sniff \'snif\ *vb* [ME *sniffen*] *vi* **1 :** to draw air audibly up the nose **2 :** to show or express disdain or scorn ~ *vt* **1 :** to smell or take by inhalation through the nose **:** INHALE **2 :** to recognize or detect by or as if by smelling ⟨~ out trouble⟩ — **sniff** *n* — **sniff·er** *n*
sniff·i·ly \-ə-lē\ *adv* **:** in a sniffy manner **:** DISDAINFULLY
sniff·i·ness \-ē-nəs\ *n* **:** the quality or state of being sniffy
sniff·ish \'snif-ish\ *adj* **:** DISDAINFUL, SUPERCILIOUS — **sniff·ish·ly** *adv* — **sniff·ish·ness** *n*
1**snif·fle** \'snif-əl\ *vi* **snif·fling** \-(ə-)liŋ\ [freq. of *sniff*] **1 :** to sniff repeatedly **:** SNUFFLE **2 :** to speak with or as if with sniffling — **snif·fler** \-(ə-)lər\ *n*
2**sniffle** *n* **1 :** an act or sound of sniffling **2** *pl* **:** a head cold marked by nasal discharge
sniffy \'snif-ē\ *adj* **:** inclined to sniff haughtily **:** SUPERCILIOUS
snif·ter \'snif-tər\ *n* [E dial., sniff, snort, fr. ME *snifteren* to sniff, snort] **1 :** a small drink of distilled liquor **2 :** a large short-stemmed goblet with a bowl narrowing toward the top
snig·gle \'snig-əl\ *vb* **snig·gling** \-(ə-)liŋ\ [E dial. *snig* small eel, fr. ME *snygge*] *vi* **:** to fish for eels by thrusting a baited hook or needle into their hiding places ~ *vt* **:** to catch (an eel) by sniggling
1**snip** \'snip\ *n* [fr. or akin to D&LG *snip*] **1 a :** a small piece that is snipped off; *also* **:** FRAGMENT, BIT **b :** a cut or notch made by snipping **c :** an act or sound of snipping **2 :** a presumptuous or impertinent person **:** MINX
2**snip** *vb* **snipped; snip·ping** *vt* **:** to cut or cut off with or as if with shears or scissors; *specif* **:** to clip suddenly or by bits ~ *vi* **:** to make a short quick cut with or as if with shears or scissors — **snip·per** *n*
1**snipe** \'snīp\ *n, pl* **snipes** [ME, of Scand origin; akin to ON *snīpa* snipe; akin to OHG *snepfa* snipe] **1** *or pl* **snipe a :** any of several game birds (genus *Capella*) esp. of marshy areas that resemble the related woodcocks **b :** any of various usu. slender-billed related birds ⟨suborder Charadrii⟩ **2 :** a contemptible person
2**snipe** *vi* **1 :** to shoot or hunt snipe **2 a :** to shoot at exposed individuals of an enemy's forces esp. when not in action from a usu. concealed point of vantage **b :** to aim a carping or snide attack — **snip·er** *n*
snip·er·scope \'snī-pər-,skōp\ *n* **:** a snooperscope for use on a rifle or carbine
snip·per·snap·per \'snip-ər-,snap-ər\ *n* [origin unknown] **:** WHIPPERSNAPPER
snip·pet \'snip-ət\ *n* [1*snip*] **:** a small part, piece, or thing; *specif* **:** a brief quotable passage
snip·pety \-ət-ē\ *adj* **1 :** made up of snippets **2 :** SNIPPY
snip·pi·ness \'snip-ē-nəs\ *n* **:** the quality or state of being snippy
snip·py \'snip-ē\ *adj* [2*snip*] **1 :** SHORT-TEMPERED, SNAPPISH **2 :** unduly brief or curt **3 :** putting on airs **:** SNIFFY
snips \'snips\ *n pl but sing or pl in constr* **:** hand shears used esp. for cutting sheet metal
snip–snap \'snip-,snap\ *n* **:** clever quick repartee
snit \'snit\ *n* [origin unknown] **:** a state of agitation
snitch \'snich\ *vi* [origin unknown] **:** INFORM, TATTLE ~ *vt* [prob. alter. of *snatch*] **:** to take by stealth; *specif* **:** PILFER — **snitch·er** *n*
1**sniv·el** \'sniv-əl\ *vi* **sniv·eled** *or* **sniv·elled; sniv·el·ing** *or* **sniv·el·ling** \-(ə-)liŋ\ [ME *snivelen*, fr. (assumed) OE *snyflan;* akin to D *snuffelen* to snuffle, *snuffen* to sniff, Gk *nan* to flow — more at NOURISH] **1 :** to run at the nose **2 :** to snuff mucus up the nose audibly **:** SNUFFLE **3 :** to cry or whine with snuffling **4 :** to speak or act in a whining, sniffling, tearful, or weakly emotional manner — **sniv·el·er** \-(ə-)lər\ *n*
2**snivel** *n* **1** *pl, dial* **:** HEAD COLD **2 :** an act or instance of sniveling
snob \'snäb\ *n* [obs. *snob* member of the lower classes, fr. E dial.,

shoemaker] **1 :** one who blatantly imitates, fawningly admires, or vulgarly seeks association with those he regards as his superiors **2 a :** one who tends to rebuff the advances of those he regards as inferior **b :** one who has an offensive air of superiority in matters of knowledge or taste

snob appeal *n* **:** qualities in a product (as high price, rarity, or foreign origin) that appeal to the snobbery in a purchaser

snob·bery \'snäb-(ə-)rē\ *n* **:** snobbish conduct **:** SNOBBISHNESS

snob·bish \'snäb-ish\ *adj* **:** characteristic of or befitting a snob — **snob·bish·ly** *adv* — **snob·bish·ness** *n*

snob·bism \'snäb-ˌiz-əm\ *n* **:** SNOBBERY

snob·by \'snäb-ē\ *adj* **:** SNOBBISH

Sno–Cat \'snō-ˌkat\ *trademark* — used for a tracklaying vehicle designed for travel on snow

snol·ly·gos·ter \'snäl-ē-ˌgäs-tər\ *n* [prob. alter. of *snallygaster* (a mythical creature that preys on poultry and children)] **:** an unprincipled but shrewd person

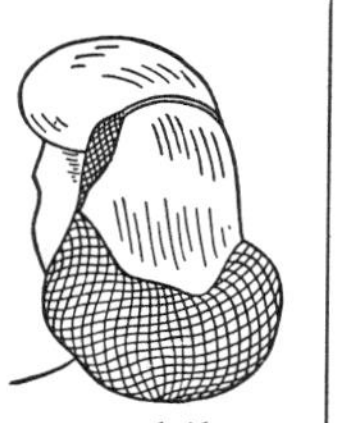
snood 1b

¹**snood** \'snüd\ *n* [(assumed) ME, fr. OE *snōd;* akin to OIr *snāth* thread, OE *nǣdle* needle] **1 a** *Scot* **:** a fillet or band for a woman's hair **b :** a net or fabric bag for confining a woman's hair pinned or tied on at the back of the head **2 :** SNELL

²**snood** *vt* **:** to secure with a snood

¹**snook** \'snu̇k, 'snük\ *n, pl* **snook** *or* **snooks** [D *snoek* pike, snook] **:** a large vigorous percoid sport and food fish (*Centropomus undecimalis*) of warm seas resembling a pike; *also* **:** any of various similar marine fishes

²**snook** *n* [origin unknown] **:** a gesture of derision consisting of a thumbing of the nose

snook·er \'snu̇k-ər\ *n* [origin unknown] **:** pool played with 15 red balls and 6 variously colored balls

¹**snoop** \'snüp\ *vi* [D *snoepen* to buy or eat on the sly; akin to D *snappen* to snap] **:** to look or pry in a sneaking or meddlesome manner

²**snoop** *or* **snoop·er** \'snü-pər\ *n* **:** one that snoops

snoop·er·scope \'snü-pər-ˌskōp\ *n* **:** a device utilizing infrared radiation for enabling a person to see an object obscured (as by darkness)

snoopy \'snü-pē\ *adj* **:** given to snooping esp. for personal information about others

snoot \'snüt\ *n* [ME *snute*] **1 a :** SNOUT **b :** NOSE **2 :** a grimace expressive of contempt **3 :** a snooty person

snoot·i·ly \'snüt-ᵊl-ē\ *adv* **:** in a snooty manner

snoot·i·ness \'snüt-ē-nəs\ *n* **:** the quality or state of being snooty

snooty \'snüt-ē\ *adj* **:** haughtily contemptuous **:** SNOBBISH

¹**snooze** \'snüz\ *vi* [origin unknown] **:** to take a nap **:** DOZE — **snoozer** *n*

²**snooze** *n* **:** a short sleep **:** NAP

snoo·zle \'snü-zəl\ *vb* **snoo·zling** \'snüz-(ə-)liŋ\ [perh. blend of *snooze* and *nuzzle*] *chiefly dial* **:** NUZZLE

¹**snore** \'snō(ə)r, 'snȯ(ə)r\ *vb* [ME *snoren;* akin to MLG *snorren* to drone, MHG *snerren* to chatter] *vi* **:** to breathe during sleep with a rough hoarse noise due to vibration of the soft palate **~** *vt* **:** to spend in snoring ⟨*snored* away the time⟩ — **snor·er** *n*

²**snore** *n* **:** an act or noise of snoring

¹**snor·kel** \'snȯr-kəl\ *n* [G *schnorchel*] **1 :** a tube housing air intake and exhaust pipes protrusible above the surface of the water for operating submerged submarines **2 :** any of various devices resembling a snorkel in function (as for an underwater swimmer)

²**snorkel** *vi* **snor·kel·ing** \-k(ə-)liŋ\ **:** to operate or swim submerged with only a snorkel above water

¹**snort** \'snȯ(ə)rt\ *vb* [ME *snorten*] *vi* **1 a :** to force air violently through the nose with a rough harsh sound **b :** to express scorn, anger, indignation, or surprise by a snort **2 :** to emit explosive sounds like or in the manner of a snort **~** *vt* **1 :** to utter with or express by a snort **2 :** to expel or emit with or as if with snorts

²**snort** *n* **1 :** an act or sound of snorting **2 :** a drink of usu. straight liquor taken in one draft

snort·er \'snȯrt-ər\ *n* **1 :** one that snorts **2 :** something that is extraordinary or prominent **:** HUMDINGER **3 :** SNORT 2

snout \'snau̇t\ *n* [ME *snute;* akin to G *schnauze* snout] **1 a :** a long projecting nose (as of a swine); *also* **:** an anterior prolongation of the head of various animals (as a weevil) **:** ROSTRUM **b :** the human nose esp. when large or grotesque **2 :** something resembling an animal's snout in position, function, or shape: as **a :** PROW **b :** NOZZLE — **snout·ed** \-əd\ *adj* — **snout·ish** \-ish\ *adj* — **snouty** \-ē\ *adj*

snout beetle *n* **:** any of a group (Rhynchophora) of beetles comprising the true weevils and usu. having the head produced into a snout or beak

¹**snow** \'snō\ *n, often attrib* [ME, fr. OE *snāw;* akin to OHG *snēo* snow, L *niv-, nix,* Gk *nipha* (acc.)] **1 a :** small tabular and columnar white crystals of frozen water formed directly from the water vapor of the air at a temperature of less than 32°F **b** (1) **:** a descent or shower of snow crystals (2) **:** a mass of fallen snow crystals **2 :** something resembling snow: as **a :** a dessert made of stiffly beaten whites of eggs, sugar, and fruit pulp **b :** any of various congealed or crystallized substances resembling snow in appearance **c** *slang* **:** COCAINE **d :** small transient light or dark spots on a television or radar screen

²**snow** *vi* **:** to fall in or as snow **~** *vt* **1 :** to cause to fall like or as snow **2 a :** to cover, shut in, or imprison with or as if with snow **b** *slang* **:** to deceive, persuade, or charm glibly **3 :** to whiten like snow ⟨hair *~ed* by age⟩

¹**snow·ball** \-ˌbȯl\ *n* **1 :** a round mass of snow pressed or rolled together **2 :** any of several cultivated shrubs (genus *Viburnum*) with clusters of white sterile flowers

²**snowball** *vt* **1 :** to throw snowballs at **2 :** to cause to increase or multiply at a rapidly accelerating rate **~** *vi* **1 :** to engage in throwing snowballs **2 :** to increase, accumulate, expand, or multiply at a rapidly accelerating rate

snow·bell \-ˌbel\ *n* **:** a shrubby storax (*Styrax grandifolia*) of the southeastern U.S. with showy clusters of fragrant white flowers

snow·ber·ry \-ˌber-ē\ *n* **:** any of several white-berried shrubs (esp. genus *Symphoricarpos* of the honeysuckle family); *esp* **:** a low-growing No. American shrub (*S. albus*) with pink flowers in small axillary clusters

snow·bird \-ˌbərd\ *n* **1 :** any of several small birds (as a junco or fieldfare) seen chiefly in winter **2** *slang* **:** a cocaine addict

snow–blind \-ˌblīnd\ *or* **snow–blind·ed** \-'blīn-dəd\ *adj* **:** affected with snow blindness

snow blindness *n* **:** inflammation and photophobia caused by exposure of the eyes to ultraviolet rays reflected from snow or ice

snow·blink \'snō-ˌbliŋk\ *n* **:** a white glare in the sky over a snowfield

snow boot *n* **:** a boot reaching to the ankle or above for wear in snow

snow·bound \'snō-'bau̇nd\ *adj* **:** shut in or blockaded by snow

snow–broth \-ˌbrȯth\ *n* **1 :** mixed snow and water **2 :** newly melted snow

snow·bush \-ˌbu̇sh\ *n* **:** any of several white-flowered shrubs; *esp* **:** a spreading western No. American shrub (*Ceanothus velutina*) of the buckthorn family with scented leaves and panicles of small flowers

snow·cap \-ˌkap\ *n* **:** a covering cap of snow (as on a mountain peak) — **snow·capped** \-'kapt\ *adj*

snow devil *n* **:** a column of fine snow blown upward from a surface by the wind

snow·drift \'snō-ˌdrift\ *n* **:** a bank of drifted snow

snow·drop \-ˌdräp\ *n* **1 :** a bulbous European herb (*Galanthus nivalis*) of the amaryllis family bearing nodding white flowers that often appear while the snow is on the ground **2 :** a common wood anemone (*Anemone quinquefolia*)

snow·fall \'snō-ˌfȯl\ *n* **:** a fall of snow; *specif* **:** the amount of snow that falls in a single storm or in a given period

snow·field \-ˌfēld\ *n* **:** a broad level expanse of snow; *esp* **:** a mass of perennial snow as at the head of a glacier

snow·flake \-ˌflāk\ *n* **1 :** a flake or crystal of snow **2 :** any of a genus (*Leucojum*) of bulbous plants of the amaryllis family; *esp* **:** one (*L. vernum*) resembling the snowdrop

snow·i·ly \'snō-ə-lē\ *adv* **:** in a snowy manner

snow·i·ness \'snō-ē-nəs\ *n* **:** the quality or state of being snowy

snow job *n, slang* **:** a long involved effort at persuasion or deception with a vast amount of information or fictitious exploits

snow leopard *n* **:** a showily marked large cat (*Felis uncia*) of upland central Asia with a long heavy pelt grayish white irregularly blotched with brownish black in summer and almost pure white in winter

snow lily *n* **:** a Rocky Mountain dogtooth violet (*Erythronium grandiflorum*) with showy yellow or white flowers

snow line *n* **:** the lower margin of a perennial snowfield

snow·man \'snō-ˌman, -'man\ *n* **:** snow shaped to resemble a person

snow·mo·bile \'snō-mō-ˌbēl\ *n* [¹*snow* + auto*mobile*] **:** any of various automotive vehicles for travel on snow

snow–on–the–mountain *n* **:** a spurge (*Euphorbia marginata*) of the western U.S. with showy white-bracted flower clusters grown as an ornamental

snow·pack \'snō-ˌpak\ *n* **:** packed snow that ordinarily melts slowly and yields water for irrigation or power during summer months

snow plant *n* **:** a fleshy bright-red saprophytic California herb (*Sarcodes sanguinea*) of the wintergreen family growing in coniferous woods at high altitudes and often appearing before the snow melts

snow·plow \'snō-ˌplau̇\ *n* **1 :** any of various devices used for clearing away snow **2 :** a stemming with both skis used for coming to a stop, slowing down, or descending slowly — **snowplow** *vi*

snow pudding *n* **:** a pudding made very fluffy and light by the addition of whipped egg whites and gelatin

snow·shed \'snō-ˌshed\ *n* **1 :** a shelter against snowslides **2 :** a watershed supplied largely by snowfalls

¹**snow·shoe** \-ˌshü\ *n* **:** a light oval wooden frame strengthened by two crosspieces, strung with thongs, and attached to the foot that is used to enable a person to walk on soft snow without sinking

²**snowshoe** *vi* **:** to travel on snowshoes

snow·slide \-ˌslīd\ *n* **:** an avalanche of snow

snow·suit \-ˌsüt\ *n* **:** a one-piece or two-piece lined garment worn by children

snow tire *n* **:** an automotive tire with a tread designed to give added traction on snow or ice

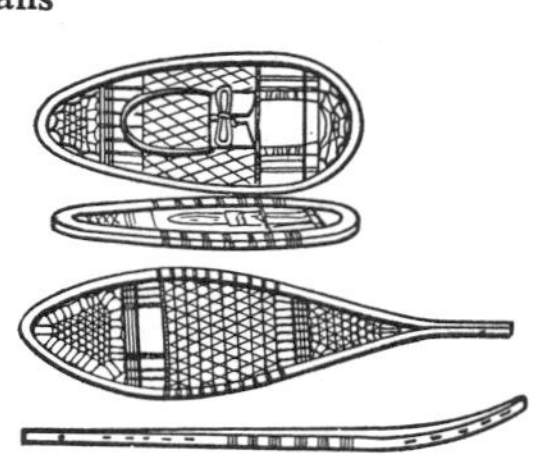
snowshoes

snow train *n* **:** a special train to a place suitable for winter sports

snow under *vt* **1 :** to overwhelm esp. in excess of capacity to absorb or deal with something **2 :** to defeat by a large margin

snow–white \'snō-'hwīt, -'wīt\ *adj* **:** white as snow

snowy \'snō-ē\ *adj* **1 a :** composed of snow or melted snow **b :** marked by or covered with snow **2 :** whitened by snow **:** SNOW-WHITE

¹**snub** \'snəb\ *vt* **snubbed; snub·bing** [ME *snubben,* of Scand origin; akin to ON *snubba* to scold; akin to Icel *sneypa* to scold] **1 :** to check or stop with a cutting retort **:** REBUKE **2 a :** to check (as a line) suddenly while running out esp. by turning around a fixed object (as a post); *also* **:** to check the motion of by snubbing a line **b :** SUPPRESS, RESTRAIN ⟨~ a vibration⟩ **3 :** to treat with contempt or neglect; *also* **:** to affect in a specified way by such treatment **4 :** to extinguish by stubbing ⟨~ out a cigarette⟩

²**snub** *n* **:** an act or an instance of snubbing; *esp* **:** REBUFF, SLIGHT

³**snub** *adj* **1 :** used in snubbing ⟨~ line⟩ **2** *or* **snubbed** \'snəbd\ **:** BLUNT, STUBBY — **snub·ness** *n*

snub·ber \'snəb-ər\ *n* **1 :** one that snubs **2 :** SHOCK ABSORBER

snub·bi·ness \'snəb-ē-nəs\ *n* **:** the quality or state of being snubby

snub·by \'snəb-ē\ *adj* **1 :** SNUB **2 :** SNUB-NOSED

snub–nosed \'snəb-'nōzd\ *adj* **:** having a stubby and usu. slightly turned-up nose

¹**snuff** \'snəf\ *n* [ME *snoffe*] **1 :** the charred part of a candlewick **2 a** *obs* **:** UMBRAGE, OFFENSE **b** *chiefly Scot* **:** HUFF

²**snuff** *vt* **1 :** to crop the snuff of (a candle) by pinching or by the use of snuffers so as to brighten the light **2 :** to extinguish by or as if by the use of snuffers

3**snuff** *vb* [akin to D *snuffen* to sniff, snuff — more at SNIVEL] *vt* **1 :** to draw forcibly through or into the nostrils **2 :** SCENT, SMELL **3 :** to sniff at in order to examine — used of an animal ~ *vi* **1 :** to inhale through the nose noisily and forcibly; *also* **:** to sniff or smell inquiringly **2** *obs* **:** to sniff loudly in or as if in disgust

4**snuff** *n* **:** the act of snuffing **:** SNIFF

5**snuff** *n* [D *snuf,* short for *snuftabak,* fr. *snuffen* to snuff + *tabak* tobacco] **1 :** a preparation of pulverized tobacco to be inhaled through the nostrils, chewed, or placed against the gums **2 :** the amount of snuff taken at one time — **up to snuff :** in good shape

snuff·box \'snəf-,bäks\ *n* **:** a small box for holding snuff usu. carried about the person

1**snuff·er** \'snəf-ər\ *n* **1 :** a device somewhat like a pair of scissors for cropping and holding the snuff of a candle — usu. used in pl. but sing. or pl. in constr. **2 :** a device for extinguishing candles

2**snuffer** *n* **:** one that snuffs or sniffs

1**snuf·fle** \'snəf-əl\ *vb* **snuf·fling** \-(ə-)liŋ\ [akin to D *snuffelen* to snuffle — more at SNIVEL] *vi* **1 :** to snuff or sniff usu. audibly and repeatedly **2 :** to breathe through an obstructed nose with a sniffing sound **3 :** to speak through or as if through the nose **:** WHINE ~ *vt* **:** to seek or test by or as if by repeated sniffs — **snuf·fler** \-(ə-)lər\ *n*

2**snuffle** *n* **1 a :** the act or fact of snuffling **b :** the sound made in snuffling **2 :** a nasal twang **3** *pl* **:** SNIFFLES

snuffy \'snəf-ē\ *adj* **1 :** resembling snuff **2 a :** addicted to the use of snuff **b :** DISAGREEABLE **3 :** soiled with snuff

1**snug** \'snəg\ *adj* **snug·ger; snug·gest** [perh. of Scand origin; akin to Sw *snygg* tidy; akin to ON *snöggr* shorn, bald, L *novacula* razor] **1 a** *of a ship* **:** manifesting seaworthiness **:** TAUT **b :** TRIM, NEAT **c :** fitting closely and comfortably ⟨a ~ coat⟩ **2 a :** enjoying or affording warm secure shelter or cover and opportunity for ease and contentment **b :** marked by cordiality and secure privacy **3 :** affording a degree of comfort and ease **4 :** SECRETED, CONCEALED — **snug** *adv* — **snug·ly** *adv* — **snug·ness** *n*

2**snug** *vb* **snugged; snug·ging** *vi* **:** SNUGGLE ~ *vt* **1 :** to cause to fit closely **2 :** to make snug **3 :** HIDE **4 :** to prepare (a ship) for a gale esp. by reducing sail, lowering topmasts, or lashing down movables

3**snug** *n, Brit* **:** a small private room in a pub

snug·gery \'snəg-(ə-)rē\ *n, chiefly Brit* **:** a snug cozy place; *esp* **:** a small room **:** DEN

snug·gle \'snəg-əl\ *vb* **snug·gling** \-(ə-)liŋ\ [freq. of 2*snug*] *vi* **:** to curl up comfortably or cozily **:** CUDDLE ~ *vt* **1 :** to draw close esp. for comfort or in affection **2 :** to make snug — **snuggle** *n*

1**so** \(')sō, *esp before adj or adv & "that"* sə\ *adv* [ME, fr. OE *swā;* akin to OHG *sō* so, L *sic* so, thus, *si* if, Gk *hōs* so, thus, L *suus* one's own — more at SUICIDE] **1 a :** in a manner or way that is indicated or suggested ⟨said he'd attend and did ~⟩ ⟨it ~ happened that all were wrong⟩ **b :** in the same manner or way **:** ALSO ⟨worked hard and ~ did she⟩ **c :** in the following manner **:** THUS ⟨for ~ the Lord said — Isa 18:4(AV)⟩ **d :** SUBSEQUENTLY, THEN ⟨and ~ home and to bed⟩ **2 a :** to an indicated or suggested extent or degree ⟨had never been ~ happy⟩ **b :** to a great extent or degree **:** VERY, EXTREMELY ⟨left her because he loved her ~⟩ **c :** to a definite but unspecified extent or degree ⟨can only do ~ much in a day⟩ **d :** most certainly **:** INDEED ⟨you did ~ do it⟩ **3 :** for a reason that has just been stated **:** THEREFORE ⟨the witness is biased and ~ unreliable⟩

2**so** \(')sō\ *conj* **1 a :** with the result that ⟨her diction is good, ~ every word is clear⟩ **b :** in order that ⟨be quiet ~ he can sleep⟩ **2 :** provided that **3 a :** for that reason **:** THEREFORE ⟨don't want to go, ~ I won't⟩ **b (1)** — used as an introductory particle ⟨~ here we are⟩ often to belittle a point under discussion ⟨~ what?⟩ **(2)** — used interjectionally to indicate awareness of a discovery ⟨~, that's who did it⟩ or surprised dissent

3**so** \'sō\ *adj* **1 :** conforming with actual facts **:** TRUE ⟨said things that were not ~⟩ **2 :** marked by a definite order ⟨his books are always just ~⟩

4**so** \,sō, 'sō\ *pron* **1 :** such as has been specified or suggested **:** the same ⟨became chairman and remained ~⟩ **2 :** something that approximates what has just been indicated ⟨I've known him 20 years or ~⟩

5**so** \'sō\ *var of* SOL

1**soak** \'sōk\ *vb* [ME *soken,* fr. OE *socian;* akin to OE *sūcan* to suck] *vi* **1 :** to remain steeping in water or other liquid **2 a :** to enter or pass through something by or as if by pores or interstices **:** PERMEATE **b :** to penetrate or affect the mind or feelings **3 :** to drink alcoholic beverages intemperately ~ *vt* **1 :** to permeate so as to wet, soften, or fill thoroughly **:** SATURATE **2 a :** to place in a liquid or other surrounding element to wet or as if to wet thoroughly **:** SUBMERGE **b :** to imbue fully **:** IMMERSE **3 a :** to extract by or as if by steeping ⟨~ the dirt out⟩ **b :** to levy an exorbitant charge against ⟨~*ed* the taxpayers⟩ **4 a :** to draw in by or as if by suction or absorption ⟨~*ed* up the sunshine⟩ **b :** to intoxicate (oneself) by drinking alcoholic beverages **5 :** to beat or punish severely — **soak·er** *n*

syn SOAK, SATURATE, DRENCH, STEEP, IMPREGNATE mean to subject to a liquid until thorough permeation is attained. SOAK implies usu. prolonged immersion as for softening or cleansing; SATURATE implies a resulting effect of complete absorption until no more liquid can be held; DRENCH implies a thorough wetting by something poured; STEEP suggests either the extraction of an essence (as of tea leaves) by the liquid or the imparting of a quality (as a color) to the thing immersed; IMPREGNATE implies a thorough interpenetration of one thing by another

2**soak** *n* **1 a :** the act or process of soaking **:** the state of being soaked **b :** the liquid in which something is soaked **:** STEEP **2 :** DRUNKARD **3** *slang* **:** 1PAWN 2

soak·age \'sō-kij\ *n* **1 :** liquid gained by absorption or lost by seepage **2 :** the act or process of soaking **:** the state of being soaked

so-and-so \'sō-ən-,sō\ *n* **1 :** an unnamed or unspecified person or thing **2 :** BASTARD 3

1**soap** \'sōp\ *n* [ME *sope,* fr. OE *sāpe;* akin to OHG *seifa* soap, L *sebum* tallow] **1 :** a cleansing and emulsifying agent made usu. by action of alkali on fat or fatty acids and consisting essentially of sodium or potassium salts of such acids **2 :** a salt of a fatty acid — **soap·mak·ing** \-,mā-kiŋ\ *n*

2**soap** *vt* **1 :** to rub soap over or into **2 :** to address in smooth or complimentary speech **:** FLATTER

soap·bark \-,bärk\ *n* **1 :** a Chilean tree (*Quillaja saponaria*) of the rose family with shining leaves and terminal white flowers; *also* **:** its saponin-rich bark used in cleaning and in emulsifying oils **2 :** any of several tropical American trees or leguminous shrubs (genus *Pithecolobium*) with saponaceous bark

soap·ber·ry \-,ber-ē\ *n* **:** any of a genus (*Sapindus* of the family Sapindaceae, the soapberry family) of chiefly tropical woody plants; *also* **:** the fruit of a soapberry and esp. of a tree (*S. saponaria*) that is saponin-rich and used as a soap substitute

soap·box \-,bäks\ *n* **1 a :** a small receptacle for a bar of soap **b :** a packing box used for shipping soap **2 :** an improvised platform used by a self-appointed, spontaneous, or informal orator — **soapbox** *adj*

Soap Box Derby *service mark* — used for a downhill race for children's homemade racing cars without pedals or motors

soap bubble *n* **:** a hollow iridescent globe formed by blowing a film of soapsuds from a pipe

soap·i·ly \'sō-pə-lē\ *adv* **:** in a smooth or slippery manner

soap·i·ness \-pē-nəs\ *n* **:** the quality or state of being soapy

soap·less \'sō-pləs\ *adj* **1 :** lacking soap **2 :** UNWASHED, DIRTY

soap opera *n* [fr. its frequently being sponsored by soap manufacturers] **:** a radio or television serial drama performed usu. on a daytime commercial program and chiefly characterized by stock domestic situations and often melodramatic or sentimental treatment

soap plant *n* **:** a plant having a part (as a root or fruit) that may be used in place of soap

soap·stone \'sōp-,stōn\ *n* **:** a soft stone having a soapy feel and composed essentially of talc, chlorite, and often some magnetite

soap·suds \-,sədz\ *n pl* **:** SUDS 1

soap·wort \-,wərt, -,wȯ(ə)rt\ *n* **:** a European perennial herb (*Saponaria officinalis*) of the pink family widely naturalized in the U.S. that has pink or white flowers and leaves detergent when bruised

soapy \'sō-pē\ *adj* **1 :** smeared with soap **:** LATHERED **2 :** containing or combined with soap or saponin **3 a :** resembling or having the qualities of soap **b :** UNCTUOUS, SUAVE

1**soar** \'sō(ə)r, 'sȯ(ə)r\ *vi* [ME *soren,* fr. MF *essorer* to air, soar, fr. (assumed) VL *exaurare* to air, fr. L *ex-* + *aura* air — more at AURA] **1 a :** to fly aloft or about **b (1) :** to sail or hover in the air often at a great height **:** GLIDE **(2)** *of a glider* **:** to fly without engine power and without loss of altitude **2 :** to go or move upward in position or status **:** RISE **3 :** to ascend to a higher or more exalted level **4 :** to rise to majestic stature **:** TOWER — **soar·er** *n*

2**soar** *n* **1 :** the range, distance, or height attained in soaring **2 :** the act of soaring **:** upward flight

1**sob** \'säb\ *vb* **sobbed; sob·bing** [ME *sobben*] *vi* **1 a :** to catch the breath audibly in a spasmodic contraction of the throat **b :** to cry or weep with such convulsive catching of the breath **2 :** to make a sound like that of a sob or sobbing ~ *vt* **1 :** to bring (as oneself) to a specified state by sobbing ⟨*sobbed* himself to sleep⟩ **2 :** to utter with sobs ⟨*sobbed* out her grief⟩

2**sob** *n* **1 :** an act of sobbing **2 :** a sound like that of a sob

1**so·ber** \'sō-bər\ *adj* **so·ber·er** \-bər-ər\ **so·ber·est** \-b(ə-)rəst\ [ME *sobre,* fr. MF, fr. L *sobrius;* akin to L *ebrius* drunk] **1 a :** sparing in the use of food and drink **:** ABSTEMIOUS **b :** not addicted to intoxicating drink **:** ABSTINENT **c :** not drunk **2 :** marked by sedate or gravely or earnestly thoughtful character or demeanor **:** SERIOUS, SOLEMN **3** *archaic* **:** UNHURRIED, CALM **4 :** marked by temperance, moderation, or seriousness **5 :** subdued in tone or color **6 :** showing no excessive or extreme qualities of fancy, emotion, or prejudice: as **a :** REALISTIC **b :** well balanced **:** RESTRAINED **c :** RATIONAL **syn** see SERIOUS — **so·ber·ly** \-bər-lē\ *adv* — **so·ber·ness** *n*

2**sober** *vb* **so·ber·ing** \-b(ə-)riŋ\ *vt* **:** to make sober ~ *vi* **:** to become sober

so·ber·ize \'sō-bə-,rīz\ *vt* **:** to make sober

so·ber·sid·ed \,sō-bər-'sīd-əd\ *adj* **:** of a grave or serious nature **:** EARNEST, SOLEMN

so·ber·sides \'sō-bər-,sīdz\ *n pl but sing or pl in constr* **:** one who is sobersided

so·bri·ety \sə-'brī-ət-ē, sō-\ *n* [ME *sobrietie,* fr. MF *sobrieté,* fr. L *sobrietat-, sobrietas,* fr. *sobrius*] **:** the quality or state of being sober

so·bri·quet \'sō-bri-,kā, -,ket, ,sō-bri-'\ *n* [F] **:** a fanciful name or epithet **:** NICKNAME

sob sister *n* **1 :** a journalist who specializes in writing or editing sob stories or other material of a sentimental type **2 :** a sentimental and often impractical person usu. engaged in good works

sob story *n* **:** a sentimental story or account designed chiefly to evoke sympathy or sadness

so·cage \'säk-ij, 'sōk-\ *or* **soc·cage** \'säk-\ *n* [ME, fr. *soc* soke] **:** a tenure of land by agricultural service fixed in amount and kind or by payment of money rent only and not burdened with any military service — **so·cag·er** \-ij-ər\ *n*

so-called \'sō-'kȯld\ *adj* **1 :** commonly named **:** popularly so termed ⟨the ~ pocket veto⟩ **2 :** falsely or improperly so named ⟨deceived by his ~ friend⟩

soc·cer \'säk-ər\ *n, often attrib* [by shortening & alter. fr. *association football*] **:** a football game with 11 players on a side in which a round ball is advanced by kicking or by propelling it with any part of the body except the hands and arms — called also *association football*

so·cia·bil·i·ty \,sō-shə-'bil-ət-ē\ *n* **:** the quality or state of being sociable **:** AFFABILITY; *also* **:** the act or an instance of being sociable

1**so·cia·ble** \'sō-shə-bəl\ *adj* [MF or L; MF, fr. L *sociabilis,* fr. *sociare* to join, associate, fr. *socius*] **1 :** inclined by nature to companionship with others of the same species **:** SOCIAL **2 a :** inclined to seek or enjoy companionship **:** AFFABLE, FRIENDLY **b :** conducive to friendliness or pleasant social relations **syn** see GRACIOUS — **so·cia·ble·ness** *n* — **so·cia·bly** \-blē\ *adv*

2**sociable** *n* **:** an informal gathering for sociability and frequently a special activity or interest

1**so·cial** \'sō-shəl\ *adj* [L *socialis,* fr. *socius* companion, ally, associate; akin to L *sequi* to follow — more at SUE] **1 :** involving

allies or confederates ⟨the *Social* War⟩ **2 a :** marked by or passed in pleasant companionship with one's friends or associates ⟨leads a very full ~ life⟩ **:** engaged in for sociability ⟨~ drinking⟩ **b :** SOCIABLE **c :** of, relating to, or designed for sociability ⟨a ~ club⟩ **3 a :** tending to form cooperative and interdependent relationships with one's fellows **:** GREGARIOUS ⟨man is a ~ being⟩ **b :** living and breeding in more or less organized communities **c** *of a plant* **:** tending to grow in groups or masses so as to form a pure stand **4 :** of or relating to human society, the interaction of the individual and the group, or the welfare of human beings as members of society ⟨~ institutions⟩ ⟨~ behavior⟩ ⟨~ legislation⟩ **5 a :** of, relating to, or based on rank or status in a particular society ⟨a member of his ~ set⟩ **b :** of, belonging to, or characteristic of the upper classes **c :** FORMAL

[2]**social** *n* **:** SOCIABLE

social climber *n* **:** one who attempts to gain a higher social position or acceptance in fashionable society

social contract *n* **:** an agreement among individuals forming an organized society or between the community and the ruler that defines and limits the rights and duties of each

social democracy *n* **:** a political movement advocating a gradual and peaceful transition from capitalism to socialism by democratic means — **social democrat** *n* — **social democratic** *adj*

social disease *n* **1 :** VENEREAL DISEASE **2 :** a disease (as tuberculosis) whose incidence is directly related to social and economic factors

social gospel *n* **1 :** the application of biblical teachings esp. of Jesus to social problems **2** *cap S&G* **:** a movement in American Protestant Christianity esp. in the first part of the 20th century to bring the social order into conformity with the teachings of Jesus

social insurance *n* **:** insurance under government operation or sponsorship against economic hazards and esp. unemployment that affect the public welfare

so·cial·ism \'sō-shə-,liz-əm\ *n* **1 :** any of various economic and political theories advocating collective or governmental ownership and administration of the means of production and distribution of goods **2 a :** a system of society or group living in which there is no private property **b :** a system or condition of society in which the means of production are owned and controlled by the state **3 :** a stage of society in Marxist theory transitional between capitalism and communism and distinguished by unequal distribution of goods and pay according to work done

[1]**so·cial·ist** \'sōsh-(ə-)ləst\ *n* **1 :** one who advocates or practices socialism **2** *cap* **:** a member of a socialist party or political group

[2]**socialist** *adj* **1 :** of, relating to, or promoting socialism ⟨~ theory⟩ ⟨a ~ state⟩ ⟨~ tendencies⟩ **2** *cap* **:** of, belonging to, or constituting a political party advocating socialism

so·cial·is·tic \,sō-shə-'lis-tik\ *adj* **:** of, relating to, or tending toward socialism — **so·cial·is·ti·cal·ly** \-ti-k(ə-)lē\ *adv*

so·cial·ite \'sō-shə-,līt\ *n* **:** a socially prominent person

so·ci·al·i·ty \,sō-shē-'al-ət-ē\ *n* **1 a :** SOCIABILITY **b :** an instance of social intercourse or sociability **2 :** the tendency to associate with one's fellows or to form social groups

so·cial·iza·tion \,sō-shə-lə-'zā-shən\ *n* **:** the act or process of socializing **:** the state of being socialized

so·cial·ize \'sō-shə-,līz\ *vt* **1 :** to make social; *esp* **:** to fit or train for a social environment **2 a :** to constitute on a socialistic basis ⟨~ industry⟩ **b :** to adapt to social needs or uses ⟨~ science⟩ **3 :** to organize group participation in ⟨~ a recitation⟩ **~** *vi* **:** to participate actively in a social group

socialized medicine *n* **:** administration by an organized group, a state, or a nation of medical and hospital services to suit the needs of all members of a class or all members of the population by funds derived esp. from assessments, philanthropy, or taxation

so·cial·iz·er \'sō-shə-,lī-zər\ *n* **:** one that socializes

so·cial·ly \'sōsh-(ə-)lē\ *adv* **1 :** in a social manner ⟨~ popular⟩ **2 :** with respect to society ⟨~ inferior⟩ **3 :** by society ⟨~ prescribed values⟩

so·cial–mind·ed \,sō-shəl-'mīn-dəd\ *adj* **:** having an interest in society; *specif* **:** actively interested in social welfare or the well-being of society as a whole

social science *n* **1 :** a branch of science that deals with the institutions and functioning of human society and with the interpersonal relationships of individuals as members of society **2 :** a science (as economics or political science) dealing with a particular phase or aspect of human society

social scientist *n* **:** a specialist in the social sciences

social secretary *n* **:** a personal secretary employed to handle social correspondence and appointments

social security *n* **1 :** the principle or practice of public provision (as through social insurance or assistance) for the economic security and social welfare of the individual and his family **2** *often cap* **:** a U.S. government program established in 1935 to include old-age and survivors insurance, contributions to state unemployment insurance, and old-age assistance

social service *n* **:** an activity designed to promote social welfare; *specif* **:** organized philanthropic assistance of the sick, destitute, or unfortunate **:** WELFARE WORK

social studies *n pl* **:** a part of a school or college curriculum concerned with the study of social relationships and the functioning of society and usu. made up of courses in history, government, economics, civics, sociology, geography, and anthropology

social welfare *n* **:** organized public or private social services for the assistance of disadvantaged classes or groups; *specif* **:** SOCIAL WORK

social work *n* **:** any of various professional services, activities, or methods concretely concerned with the investigation, treatment, and material aid of the economically underprivileged and socially maladjusted — **social worker** *n*

so·ci·etal \sə-'sī-ət-ᵊl\ *adj* **:** of or relating to society **:** SOCIAL ⟨~ forces⟩ — **so·ci·etal·ly** \-ᵊl-ē\ *adv*

[1]**so·ci·ety** \sə-'sī-ət-ē\ *n* [MF *societé*, fr. L *societat-, societas*, fr. *socius* companion — more at SOCIAL] **1 :** companionship or association with one's fellows **:** friendly or intimate intercourse **:** COMPANY **2 :** a voluntary association of individuals for common ends; *esp* **:** an organized group working together or periodically meeting because of common interests, beliefs, or profession **3 a :** an enduring and cooperating social group whose members have developed organized patterns of relationships through interaction with one another **b :** a community, nation, or broad grouping of people having common traditions, institutions, and collective activities and interests **4 a :** a part of a community that is a unit distinguishable by particular aims or standards of living or conduct **:** a social circle or a group of social circles having a clearly marked identity ⟨move in polite ~⟩ ⟨literary ~⟩ **b :** a part of the community that sets itself apart as a leisure class and that regards itself as the arbiter of fashion and manners **5 a** (1) **:** a unit assemblage of plants usu. of a single species or habit within an association (2) **:** ASSOCIATION 6 **b :** the progeny of a pair of insects when constituting a social unit (as a hive of bees); *broadly* **:** an interdependent system of organisms or biological units

[2]**society** *adj* **:** of, relating to, or characteristic of fashionable society

society verse *n* **:** VERS DE SOCIÉTÉ

So·cin·i·an \sə-'sin-ē-ən, sō-\ *n* [NL *socinianus*, fr. Faustus *Socinus* (Fausto Sozzini) †1604 It theologian] **:** an adherent of a 16th and 17th century theological movement denying the divinity of Christ and holding rationalistic views of sin and salvation — **Socinian** *adj* — **So·cin·i·an·ism** \-ē-ə-,niz-əm\ *n*

socio- *comb form* [F, fr. L *socius* companion] **1 :** society ⟨*sociography*⟩ **:** social ⟨*sociogram*⟩ **2 :** social and ⟨*sociopolitical*⟩ **3 :** sociological and ⟨*sociopsychiatric*⟩

so·cio·eco·nom·ic \,sō-sē-,ō-,ek-ə-'näm-ik, ,sō-shē-, -,ē-kə-\ *adj* **:** of, relating to, or involving a combination of social and economic factors

so·cio·log·ic \,sō-sē-ə-'läj-ik, ,sō-sh(ē-)ə-\ *adj* **1 :** of or relating to sociology or to the methodological approach of sociology **2 :** oriented or directed toward social needs and problems ⟨~ jurisprudence⟩ ⟨~ novels⟩ ⟨~ criticism⟩ — **so·cio·log·i·cal** \-i-kəl\ *adj* — **so·cio·log·i·cal·ly** \-k(ə-)lē\ *adv*

so·ci·ol·o·gist \,sō-sē-'äl-ə-jəst, -shē-\ *n* **:** a specialist in sociology

so·ci·ol·o·gy \-jē\ *n* [F *sociologie*, fr. *socio-* + *-logie* -logy] **1 :** the science of society, social institutions, and social relationships; *specif* **:** the systematic study of the development, structure, and function of human groups conceived as processes of interaction or as organized patterns of collective behavior **2 :** the scientific analysis of a social institution as a functioning whole and as it relates to the rest of society **3 :** SYNECOLOGY

so·ci·om·e·try \-'äm-ə-trē\ *n* [ISV] **:** the study and measurement of interpersonal relationships in a group of people

so·cio·po·lit·i·cal \,sō-sē-,ō-pə-'lit-i-kəl, ,sō-shē-\ *adj* **:** of, relating to, or involving a combination of social and political factors

[1]**sock** \'säk\ *n, pl* **socks** [ME *socke*, fr. OE *socc*, fr. L *soccus*] **1** *archaic* **:** a low shoe or slipper **2** *or pl* **sox** \'säks\ **:** a knitted or woven covering for the foot usu. extending above the ankle and sometimes to the knee **3 a :** a shoe worn by actors in Greek and Roman comedy **b :** comic drama **4 :** a receptacle for savings

[2]**sock** *vb* [prob. of Scand origin; akin to ON *sökkva* to cause to sink; akin to OE *sincan* to sink] *vt* **:** to hit, strike, or apply forcefully **~** *vi* **:** to deliver a blow **:** HIT

[3]**sock** *n* **:** a vigorous or violent blow **:** PUNCH

sock away *vt, slang* **:** to put away (money) as savings or investment

sock·dol·a·ger *or* **sock·dol·o·ger** \säk-'däl-i-jər\ *n* [perh. alter. of *doxology*] **1 :** something that settles a matter **:** a decisive blow or answer **:** FINISHER **2 :** something outstanding or exceptional

[1]**sock·et** \'säk-ət\ *n* [ME *soket*, fr. AF, dim. of OF *soc* plowshare, of Celt origin; akin to MIr *soc* plowshare, lit., snout of a hog; akin to OE *sugu* sow — more at SOW] **:** an opening or hollow that forms a holder for something ⟨an electric bulb ~⟩ ⟨the eye ~⟩

[2]**socket** *vt* **:** to provide with or support in or by a socket

sock·eye \'säk-,ī\ *n* [by folk etymology fr. Salish dial. *suk-kegh*] **:** a small but commercially important Pacific salmon (*Oncorhynchus nerka*) ascending rivers chiefly from the Columbia northward to spawn in spring — called also *red salmon*

so·cle \'säk-əl, sōklᵊ\ *n* [F, fr. It *zoccolo* sock, wooden shoe, fr. L *socculus*, dim. of *soccus* sock] **:** a projecting usu. molded member at the foot of a wall or pier or beneath the base of a column, pedestal, or superstructure

[1]**So·crat·ic** \sə-'krat-ik, sō-\ *adj* **:** of or relating to Socrates, his followers, or his philosophical method of systematic doubt and questioning of another to elicit a clear expression of something supposed to be implicitly known by all rational beings — **So·crat·i·cal·ly** \-i-k(ə-)lē\ *adv*

[2]**Socratic** *n* **:** a follower of Socrates

[1]**sod** \'säd\ *n, often attrib* [ME, fr. MD or MLG *sode*; akin to OFris *sātha* sod] **1 a :** TURF 1 **b :** the grass and forb covered surface of the ground ⟨*sod*breaking equipment⟩ **2 :** one's native land

[2]**sod** *vt* **sod·ded; sod·ding :** to cover with sod or turfs

[3]**sod** *n* [short for *sodomite*] **:** BUGGER

so·da \'sōd-ə\ *n* [It, barilla plant, soda, fr. (assumed) ML, barilla plant] **1 a :** SODIUM CARBONATE **b :** SODIUM BICARBONATE **c :** SODIUM HYDROXIDE **d :** sodium oxide Na_2O **e :** SODIUM — used in combination ⟨~ alum⟩ **2 a :** SODA WATER 2 **b :** a sweet drink consisting of soda water, flavoring, and often ice cream **3 :** the faro card that shows face up in the dealing box before play begins

soda ash *n* **:** commercial anhydrous sodium carbonate

soda biscuit *n* **1 :** a biscuit leavened with baking soda and sour milk or buttermilk **2 :** SODA CRACKER

soda cracker *n* **:** a cracker leavened with bicarbonate of soda and cream of tartar

soda fountain *n* **1 :** an apparatus with delivery tube and faucets for drawing soda water **2 :** the equipment and counter for the preparation and serving of sodas, sundaes, and ice cream

soda jerk \'sōd-ə-,jərk\ *n* **:** a counterman who dispenses carbonated drinks and ice cream at a soda fountain — called also *soda jerk·er* \-,jər-kər\

soda lime *n* **:** a mixture of sodium hydroxide and slaked lime used esp. to absorb moisture and gases

so·da·list \'sōd-ᵊl-əst, sō-'dal-\ *n* **:** a member of a sodality

so·da·lite \'sōd-ᵊl-,īt\ *n* [*soda*] **:** a transparent to translucent mineral $Na_4Al_3Si_3O_{12}Cl$ consisting of a sodium aluminum silicate with some chlorine that has a vitreous or greasy luster and is found in various igneous rocks

so·dal·i·ty \sō-'dal-ət-ē\ *n* [L *sodalitat-, sodalitas* comradeship, club, fr. *sodalis* comrade — more at ETHICAL] **1 :** BROTHERHOOD, COMMUNITY **2 :** an organized society or fellowship; *specif* **:** a devotional or charitable association of Roman Catholic laity

soda pop *n* **:** SODA WATER 2b

soda water *n* **1 :** a weak solution of sodium bicarbonate with some

acid added to cause effervescence **2 a :** a beverage consisting of water highly charged with carbonic acid gas **b :** a bottled soft drink consisting of such charged water with added flavoring and a sweet syrup

¹sod·den \'säd-ᵊn\ *adj* [ME *soden*, fr. pp. of *sethen* to seethe] **1** *archaic* **:** cooked by stewing **:** BOILED **2 a :** dull or expressionless esp. from or as if from continued indulgence in alcoholic beverages ⟨his ~ features⟩ **b :** TORPID, UNIMAGINATIVE ⟨~ minds⟩ **3 a :** heavy with moisture or water **:** SOAKED, SATURATED ⟨the ~ ground⟩ **b :** heavy or doughy because of imperfect cooking ⟨~ biscuits⟩ — **sod·den·ly** *adv* — **sod·den·ness** \-ᵊn-(n)əs\ *n*

²sodden *vb* **sod·den·ing** \'säd-niŋ, -ᵊn-iŋ\ *vt* **:** to make sodden ~ *vi* **:** to become soaked or saturated

sod·dy \'säd-ē\ *or* **sod house** *n* [¹*sod*] **:** a house built of turfs laid in horizontal layers

so·di·um \'sōd-ē-əm\ *n* [NL, fr. E *soda*] **:** a silver white soft waxy ductile element of the alkali metal group that occurs abundantly in nature in combined form and is very active chemically — see ELEMENT table

sodium benzoate *n* **:** a crystalline or granular salt C_6H_5COONa used chiefly as a food preservative

sodium bicarbonate *n* **:** a white crystalline weakly alkaline salt $NaHCO_3$ used esp. in baking powders, fire extinguishers, and medicine — called also *baking soda, saleratus*

sodium carbonate *n* **:** a sodium salt of carbonic acid used esp. in making soaps and chemicals, in water softening, in cleaning and bleaching, and in photography: as **a :** a hygroscopic crystalline anhydrous strongly alkaline salt Na_2CO_3 **b :** SAL SODA

sodium chlorate *n* **:** a colorless crystalline salt $NaClO_3$ used as an oxidizing agent and weed killer

sodium chloride *n* **:** SALT 1a

sodium cyanide *n* **:** a white deliquescent poisonous salt NaCN used esp. in electroplating, fumigating, and treating steel

sodium dichromate *n* **:** a red crystalline salt $Na_2Cr_2O_7$

sodium hydroxide *n* **:** a white brittle solid NaOH that is a strong caustic base used esp. in making soap, rayon, and paper and in bleaching

sodium hyposulfite *n* **1 :** SODIUM THIOSULFATE **2 :** a crystalline water-soluble salt $Na_2S_2O_4$ used esp. in dyeing and bleaching

sodium nitrate *n* **:** a deliquescent crystalline salt $NaNO_3$ found in crude form in Chile and used as a fertilizer and an oxidizing agent and in curing meat

sodium thiosulfate *n* **:** a hygroscopic crystalline salt $Na_2S_2O_3$ used esp. as a photographic fixing agent and a reducing or bleaching agent — called also *hypo, sodium hyposulfite*

sodium–vapor lamp *n* **:** an electric lamp that contains sodium vapor and electrodes between which a luminous discharge takes place and that is used esp. for lighting highways

Sod·om \'säd-əm\ *n* [*Sodom*, city of ancient Palestine destroyed by God for its wickedness (Gen 18:20, 21; 19:24–28)] **:** a place notorious for vice or corruption

sod·om·ite \'säd-ə-,mīt\ *n* **:** one who practices sodomy

sod·omy \'säd-ə-mē\ *n* [ME, fr. OF *sodomie*, fr. LL *Sodoma* Sodom; fr. the homosexual proclivities of the men of the city (Gen 19:1–11)] **:** carnal copulation with a member of the same sex or with an animal **:** noncoital carnal copulation with a member of the opposite sex

so·ev·er \sō-'ev-ər\ *adv* [*-soever* (as in *howsoever*)] **1 :** to any possible or known extent — used after an adjective preceded by *how* or a superlative preceded by *the* ⟨how fair ~ she may be⟩ ⟨the most selfish ~ in this world⟩ **2 :** of any or every kind that may be specified — used after a noun modified as by *any, no,* or *what* ⟨he gives no information ~⟩

so·fa \'sō-fə\ *n* [Ar *ṣuffah* long bench] **:** a long upholstered seat usu. with arms and a back and often convertible into a bed

sofa bed *n* **:** an upholstered sofa that can be made to serve as a double bed by lowering its hinged upholstered back to horizontal position

so·far \'sō-,fär\ *n* [*so*und *f*ixing *a*nd *r*anging] **:** a system for locating an underwater explosion at sea by triangulation based on the reception of the sound by three widely separated shore stations

sof·fit \'säf-ət\ *n* [F *soffite*, fr. It *soffitto*, fr. (assumed) VL *suffictus*, pp. of L *suffigere* to fasten underneath — more at SUFFIX] **:** the underside of a part or member of a building (as of an overhang or staircase); *esp* **:** the intrados of an arch

¹soft \'sȯft\ *adj* [ME, fr. OE *sōfte*, alter. of *sēfte;* akin to OHG *semfti* soft] **1 a :** pleasing or agreeable to the senses: bringing ease, comfort, or quiet ⟨the ~ influences of home⟩ **b** (1) **:** having a bland or mellow rather than a sharp or acid taste or flavor (2) **:** containing no alcohol — used of beverages **c** (1) **:** not bright or glaring **:** SUBDUED (2) **:** having or producing little contrast or a relatively short range of tones ⟨~ photographic print⟩ ⟨~ lighting⟩ **d** (1) **:** quiet in pitch or volume (2) **:** MELODIOUS **e** *of the eyes* **:** having a liquid or gentle appearance **f :** smooth or delicate in texture, grain, or fiber **g** (1) **:** balmy, mild, or clement in weather or temperature (2) **:** moving or falling with slight force or impact **:** not violent ⟨~ breezes⟩ **2 :** demanding little work or effort **:** EASY, IDLE ⟨a ~ job⟩ **3 a :** sounding as in *ace* and *gem* respectively — used of *c* and *g* or their sound **b** *of a consonant* **:** VOICED **c :** constituting a vowel before which there is a \y\ sound or a \y\-like modification of a consonant or constituting a consonant in whose articulation there is a \y\-like modification or which is followed by a \y\ sound (as in Russian) **4** *archaic* **:** moving in a leisurely manner **5 :** rising gradually ⟨a ~ slope⟩ **6 :** having curved or rounded outline **:** not harsh or jagged ⟨~ hills against the horizon⟩ **7 a :** marked by gentleness, kindness, or tenderness **b :** IMPRESSIONABLE, SUGGESTIBLE **c :** unduly susceptible to influence **:** COMPLIANT **d :** lacking firmness or strength of character **:** FEEBLE, UNMANLY **e :** amorously attracted **8 a :** lacking robust strength, stamina, or endurance esp. because of living in ease or luxury **b :** weak or deficient mentally **9 a :** yielding to physical pressure **b :** permitting someone or something to sink in **c :** COMPRESSIBLE, MALLEABLE **d :** lacking relatively or comparatively in hardness ⟨~ iron⟩ **10 :** deficient in or free from substances (as calcium and magnesium salts) that prevent lathering of soap ⟨~ water⟩ **11 :** having relatively low penetrating power ⟨~ X rays⟩ — **soft·ly** *adv* — **soft·ness** \'sȯf(t)-nəs\ *n*

syn SOFT, BLAND, MILD, GENTLE, LENIENT mean devoid of harshness, roughness, or intensity. SOFT implies a subduing of all that is vivid, intense or forceful until it is agreeably soothing; BLAND implies the absence of anything that might disturb, stimulate, or irritate; MILD and GENTLE stress moderation or restraint of force or intensity; LENIENT implies a relaxing or assuasive quality

²soft *n* **:** a soft object, material, or part ⟨the ~ of the thumb⟩

³soft *adv* **:** in a soft or gentle manner **:** SOFTLY

soft·ball \'sȯf(t)-,bȯl\ *n* **:** a team game of seven innings closely resembling baseball but played on a smaller diamond with a ball that is larger and softer than a baseball and that is pitched underhand; *also* **:** the ball used in this game

soft–bill \-,bil\ *n* **:** a bird with a weak bill adapted to feeding esp. on insects — compare HARD-BILL

soft–boiled \-'bȯi(ə)ld\ *adj* **1** *of an egg* **:** boiled to a soft consistency **2 :** SENTIMENTAL

soft coal *n* **:** BITUMINOUS COAL

soft·en \'sȯ-fən\ *vb* **soft·en·ing** \'sȯf-(ə-)niŋ\ *vt* **1 :** to make soft or softer **2 :** to weaken the military resistance or the morale of esp. by preliminary bombardment or other harassment — often used with *up* ~ *vi* **:** to become soft or softer — **soft·en·er** \'sȯf-(ə-)nər\ *n*

soft–finned \'sȯf(t)-'find\ *adj* **:** having fins in which the membrane is supported entirely or mostly by soft or articulated rays — used of higher teleost fishes; compare SPINY-FINNED

soft·head \'sȯft-,hed\ *n* **:** a silly or feebleminded person **:** SIMPLETON

soft·head·ed \-'hed-əd\ *adj* **:** having a weak, unrealistic, or uncritical mind **:** lacking judgment **:** IMPRACTICAL — **soft·head·ed·ly** *adv* — **soft·head·ed·ness** *n*

soft·heart·ed \-'härt-əd\ *adj* **:** emotionally responsive **:** SYMPATHETIC, TENDER — **soft·heart·ed·ly** *adv* — **soft·heart·ed·ness** *n*

soft palate *n* **:** the fold at the back of the hard palate that partially separates the mouth and pharynx

soft pedal *n* **1 :** a foot pedal on a piano that reduces the volume of sound **2 :** something that muffles, deadens, or reduces effect

soft–ped·al \'sȯf(t)-'ped-ᵊl\ *vt* **1 :** to use the soft pedal in playing **2 :** to play down **:** OBSCURE, MUFFLE

soft–rayed \'sȯf-'trād\ *adj* **1** *of a fin* **:** having soft articulated rays **2 :** SOFT-FINNED

soft rot *n* **:** a mushy, watery, or slimy decay of plants or their parts caused by bacteria or fungi

soft scale *n* **:** a scale insect more or less active in all stages

soft sell *n* **:** the use of suggestion or persuasion in selling rather than aggressive pressure

soft–shell \'sȯf(t)-,shel\ *or* **soft–shelled** \-'sheld\ *adj* **:** having a soft or fragile shell esp. as a result of recent shedding

soft–shelled turtle \,sȯf(t)-,shel(d)-\ *n* **:** any of numerous fiercely voracious aquatic turtles (family Trionychidae) with a flat shell covered with soft leathery skin instead of with horny plates

soft–shoe \'sȯf(t)-'shü\ *adj* **:** of or relating to tap dancing done in soft-soled shoes without metal taps

soft soap *n* **1 :** a semifluid soap **2 :** FLATTERY

soft–soap \'sȯf(t)-'sōp\ *vb* **:** to soothe or persuade with flattery or blarney — **soft–soap·er** \-'sō-pər\ *n*

soft–spo·ken \-'spō-kən\ *adj* **:** speaking softly **:** having a mild or gentle voice **:** SUAVE

soft·ware \'sȯf-,twa(ə)r, -,twe(ə)r\ *n* **:** the features of an apparatus that are not hardware ⟨the programs for a computer are ~⟩

soft wheat *n* **:** a wheat with soft starchy kernels high in starch but usu. low in gluten

¹soft·wood \'sȯf-,twu̇d\ *n* **1 :** the wood of a coniferous tree including both soft and hard woods **2 :** a tree that yields softwood

²softwood *adj* **1 :** having or made of softwood **2 :** consisting of immature still pliable tissue ⟨~ cuttings for propagating plants⟩

soft–wood·ed \'sȯf-'twu̇d-əd\ *adj* **1 :** having soft wood that is easy to work or finish **2 :** SOFTWOOD 1

softy *or* **soft·ie** \'sȯf-tē\ *n* [¹*soft*] **1 :** an excessively sentimental or susceptible person **2 :** a weak, effeminate, or foolish person

Sog·di·an \'säg-dē-ən\ *n* [L *Sogdiani*, pl., fr. pl. of *sogdianus* adj., Sogdian, fr. OPers *Sughuda* Sogdiana] **1 :** a native or inhabitant of Sogdiana **2 :** an Iranian language of the Sogdians — **Sogdian** *adj*

sog·gi·ly \'säg-ə-lē, 'sȯg-\ *adv* **:** in a soggy manner

sog·gi·ness \-ē-nəs\ *n* **:** the quality or state of being soggy

sog·gy \'säg-ē, 'sȯg-\ *adj* [E dial. *sog* (to soak)] **1 :** saturated or heavy with water or moisture: as **a :** WATERLOGGED, SOAKED ⟨a ~ lawn⟩ **b :** SODDEN **2 :** heavily dull ⟨~ prose⟩

soi–di·sant \,swäd-ē-'zäⁿ\ *adj* [F, lit., saying oneself] **:** SELF-STYLED, SO-CALLED — usu. used disparagingly ⟨a *soi-disant* artist⟩

soi·gné *or* **soi·gnée** \swän-'yā\ *adj* [F, fr. pp. of *soigner* to take care of, fr. ML *soniare*] **1 :** elegantly maintained **:** MODISH ⟨a ~ restaurant⟩ **2 :** WELL-GROOMED, SLEEK

¹soil \'sȯi(ə)l\ *vb* [ME *soilen*, fr. OF *soiller* to wallow, soil, fr. *soil* pigsty, prob. fr. L *suile*, fr. *sus* pig — more at SOW] *vt* **1 :** to stain or defile morally **:** CORRUPT, POLLUTE **2 :** to make unclean esp. superficially **:** DIRTY **3 :** to blacken or besmirch (as a person's reputation) **:** SULLY, DISGRACE ~ *vi* **:** to become soiled or dirty

²soil *n* **1 a :** SOILAGE 1, STAIN **b :** moral defilement **:** CORRUPTION **2 :** something that soils or pollutes: as **a :** foreign matter **:** REFUSE **b :** SEWAGE **c :** DUNG, EXCREMENT

³soil *n* [ME, fr. AF, fr. L *solium* seat; prob. akin to L *sedēre* to sit — more at SIT] **1 :** firm land **:** EARTH **2 :** the upper layer of earth that may be dug or plowed; *specif* **:** the loose surface material of the earth in which plants grow **3 :** COUNTRY, LAND **4 :** the agricultural life or calling **5 :** a medium in which something takes hold and develops

⁴soil *vt* [origin unknown] **:** to feed (livestock) in the barn or an enclosure with fresh grass or green food; *also* **:** to purge (livestock) by feeding on green food

soil·age \'sȯi-lij\ *n* **1** [¹*soil*] **:** the act of soiling **:** the condition of being soiled **2** [⁴*soil*] **:** green crops cut for feeding confined animals

soil conservation *n* **:** management of soil so as to obtain optimum yields while improving and protecting the soil

soil·less \'sȯi(ə)l-ləs\ *adj* **:** carried on without soil ⟨~ agriculture⟩

soil pipe *n* **:** a pipe for carrying off liquid wastes from toilets

soil·ure \'sȯil-yər\ *n* **1 :** the act of soiling **:** the condition of being soiled **2 :** STAIN, SMUDGE

soi·ree *or* **soi·rée** \swä-'rā\ *n* [F *soirée* evening period, evening party, fr. MF, fr. *soir* evening, fr. L *sero* at a late hour, fr. *serus* late — more at SINCE] **:** an evening party or reception

soixante-neuf \swȧ-säⁿt-nœf\ *n* [F, lit., sixty-nine] **:** simultaneous cunnilingus and fellatio **:** double fellatio **:** double cunnilingus

1so·journ \'sō-,jərn, sō-'\ *n* [ME *sojorn*, fr. OF, fr. *sojorner*] **:** a temporary stay

2sojourn *vi* [ME *sojornen*, fr. OF *sojorner*, fr. (assumed) VL *subdiurnare*, fr. L *sub* under, during + LL *diurnum* day — more at SUB-, JOURNEY] **:** to stay as a temporary resident **:** STOP ⟨~*ed* for a month at a resort⟩ — **so·journ·er** *n*

soke \'sōk\ *n* [ME *soc, soke*, fr. ML *soca*, fr. OE *sōcn* inquiry, jurisdiction; akin to OE *sēcan* to seek] **1 :** the right in Anglo-Saxon and early English law to hold court and do justice with the franchise to receive certain fees or fines arising from it **:** jurisdiction over a territory or over people **2 :** the district included in a soke jurisdiction or franchise

soke·man \'sōk-mən\ *n* **:** a man who is under the soke of another **:** a tenant by socage

1sol \'sōl\ *n* [ML *sol*, fr. the syllable sung to this note in a medieval hymn to St. John the Baptist] **:** the fifth tone of the diatonic scale in solmization

2sol \'säl, 'sȯl\ *n* [ME, fr. MF — more at SOU] **:** an old French coin equal to 12 deniers; *also* **:** a corresponding unit of value

3sol \'säl, 'sȯl\ *n, pl* **so·les** \'sō-(,)lās\ [AmerSp, fr. Sp, sun, fr. L] — see MONEY table

4sol \'säl, 'sȯl\ *n* [*-sol* (as in *hydrosol*), fr. *solution*] **:** a fluid colloidal system

Sol \'säl\ *n* [ME, fr. L] **1 :** SUN **2** *not cap* **:** GOLD — used in alchemy **3 :** the sun-god of the ancient Romans

sola *pl of* SOLUM

1so·lace \'säl-əs *also* 'sōl-\ *n* [ME *solas*, fr. OF, fr. L *solacium*, fr. *solari* to console — more at SILLY] **1 :** alleviation of grief or anxiety **2 :** a source of relief or consolation

2solace *vt* **1 :** to give solace to **:** CONSOLE **2 a :** to make cheerful **b :** AMUSE **3 :** ALLAY, SOOTHE **syn** see COMFORT — **so·lace·ment** \-ə-smənt\ *n* — **so·lac·er** *n*

so·lan goose \,sō-lən-\ *n* [ME *soland*, fr. ON *sūla* pillar, gannet + *önd* duck; akin to OE *sȳl* pillar and to OHG *anut* duck, L *anas*] **:** a very large white gannet (*Sula bassana* or *Moris bassana*) with black wing tips

so·la·nine *or* **so·la·nin** \'sō-lə-,nēn, -nən\ *n* [F *solanine*, fr. L *solanum* nightshade] **:** a bitter poisonous crystalline alkaloid $C_{45}H_{73}NO_{15}$ from several plants (as some potatoes or tomatoes) of the nightshade family

so·la·num \sə-'lān-əm, -'län-, -'lan-\ *n* [NL, genus name, fr. L, nightshade] **:** any of a genus (*Solanum*) of herbs, shrubs, or trees of the nightshade family

so·lar \'sō-lər\ *adj* [ME, fr. L *solaris*, fr. *sol* sun; akin to OE & ON *sōl* sun, Gk *hēlios*] **1 :** of, derived from, or relating to the sun esp. as affecting the earth **2 :** measured by the earth's course in relation to the sun ⟨~ time⟩ ⟨~ year⟩; *also* **:** relating to or reckoned by solar time **3 :** produced or operated by the action of the sun's light or heat; *also* **:** utilizing the sun's rays

solar battery *n* **:** a device of one or more units for converting the energy of sunlight into electrical energy

solar constant *n* **:** the quantity of radiant solar heat received normally at the outer layer of the earth's atmosphere and having an average value of about 1.94 gram calories per square centimeter per minute

solar flare *n* **:** a sudden temporary outburst of energy from a small area of the sun's surface

solar house *n* **:** a house equipped with glass areas and so planned as to utilize the sun's rays extensively in heating

so·lar·i·um \sō-'lar-ē-əm, sə-, -'ler-\ *n, pl* **so·lar·ia** \-ē-ə\ *also* **so·lar·i·ums** [L, fr. *sol*] **:** an apartment exposed to the sun (as for treatment of illness by administration of sunbaths)

so·lar·iza·tion \,sō-lə-rə-'zā-shən\ *n* **1 :** an act or process of solarizing **2 :** a reversal of gradation in a photographic image obtained by intense or continued exposure

so·lar·ize \'sō-lə-,rīz\ *vt* **1 a :** to expose to sunlight **b :** to affect by the action of the sun's rays **2 :** to subject (photographic materials) to solarization

solar plexus *n* **1 :** a nerve plexus in the abdomen behind the stomach and in front of the aorta and the crura of the diaphragm that contains several ganglia distributing nerve fibers to the viscera — called also *coeliac plexus* **2 :** the pit of the stomach

solar system *n* **:** the sun with the group of celestial bodies that are held by its attraction and revolve around it

sol·ate \'säl-,āt, 'sȯl-\ *vi* [*4sol*] **:** to change to a sol

so·la·ti·um \sō-'lā-shē-əm\ *n, pl* **so·la·tia** \-shē-ə\ [LL *solacium, solatium*, fr. L, solace] **:** a compensation given as solace for suffering, loss, or injured feelings

sold *past of* SELL

sol·dan \'säl-dən, 'sōl-\ *n* [ME, fr. MF, fr. Ar *sulṭān*] *archaic* **:** SULTAN; *esp* **:** the sultan of Egypt

1sol·der \'säd-ər, 'sȯd-\ *n* [ME *soudure*, fr. MF, fr. *souder* to solder, fr. L *solidare* to make solid, fr. *solidus* solid] **1 :** a metal or metallic alloy used when melted to join metallic surfaces; *esp* **:** an alloy of lead and tin so used **2 :** something that unites or cements

2solder *vb* **sol·der·ing** \-(ə-)riŋ\ *vt* **1 :** to unite or make whole by solder **2 :** to bring into or restore to firm union ~ *vi* **1 :** to use solder **2 :** to become united or repaired by or as if by solder — **sol·der·er** \-ər-ər\ *n*

1sol·dier \'sōl-jər\ *n* [ME *soudier*, fr. OF, fr. *soulde* pay, fr. LL *solidus* solidus] **1 a :** one engaged in military service **b :** an enlisted man or woman **c :** a skilled warrior **2 :** a militant leader, follower, or worker **3 a :** one of a caste of wingless sterile termites usu. differing from workers in larger size and head and long jaws **b :** one of a type of worker ants distinguished by exceptionally large head and jaws **c :** any of several showy fishes or shellfishes **4 :** SHIRKER, LOAFER — **sol·dier·ly** \-lē\ *adj or adv* — **sol·dier·ship** \-,ship\ *n*

2soldier *vi* **sol·dier·ing** \'sōlj-(ə-)riŋ\ **1 a :** to serve as a soldier **b :** to behave in a soldierly manner **2 :** to make a pretense of working while really loafing **:** MALINGER

sol·dier·ing *n* **:** the life, service, or practice of one who soldiers

soldier of fortune : one who follows a military career wherever there is promise of profit, adventure, or pleasure

soldiers' home *n* **:** an institution maintained (as by the federal or a state government) for the care and relief of military veterans

soldier's medal *n* **:** a U.S. military decoration awarded for heroism not involving combat

sol·diery \'sōlj-(ə-)rē\ *n* **1 a :** a body of soldiers **b :** SOLDIERS, MILITARY **2 :** the profession or technique of soldiering

sol·do \'sȯl-(,)dō\ *n, pl* **sol·di** \-(,)dē\ [It, fr. LL *solidus*] **:** an Italian 5-centesimi piece

1sole \'sōl\ *n* [ME, fr. MF, fr. L *solea* sandal; akin to L *solum* base, ground, soil] **1 a :** the undersurface of a foot **b :** the part of a shoe or other footwear on which the sole rests **2 :** the bottom or lower part of something or the base on which something rests — **soled** \'sōld\ *adj*

2sole *vt* **1 :** to furnish with a sole **2 :** to place the sole of (a golf club) on the ground

3sole *n* [ME, fr. MF, fr. L *solea* sandal, a flatfish] **:** a flatfish (family Soleidae) having a small mouth, small or rudimentary fins, and small eyes placed close together and including superior food fishes (as *Solea solea* of Europe); *also* **:** any of various mostly market flatfishes of other families

4sole *adj* [ME, alone, fr. MF *seul*, fr. L *solus*] **1 :** UNMARRIED — used chiefly of women **2 :** having no companion **:** SOLITARY **3 a :** having no sharer **b :** being the only one **4 :** functioning independently and without assistance or interference ⟨the ~ judge⟩ **5 :** belonging exclusively or otherwise limited to one usu. specified individual, unit, or group ⟨given ~ authority⟩ **syn** see SINGLE

so·le·cism \'säl-ə-,siz-əm, 'sō-lə-\ *n* [L *soloecismus*, fr. Gk *soloikismos*, fr. *soloikos* speaking incorrectly, lit., inhabitant of Soloi, fr. *Soloi*, city in ancient Cilicia where a substandard form of Attic was spoken] **1 :** an ungrammatical combination of words in a sentence; *also* **:** a minor blunder in speech **2 :** something deviating from the proper, normal, or accepted order **3 :** a breach of etiquette or decorum — **so·le·cis·tic** \,säl-ə-'sis-tik, ,sō-lə-\ *adj*

sole·ly \'sō(l)-lē\ *adv* **1 :** without another **:** SINGLY, ALONE **2 :** EXCLUSIVELY, ENTIRELY ⟨done ~ for money⟩

sol·emn \'säl-əm\ *adj* [ME *solemne*, fr. MF, fr. L *sollemnis* regularly appointed, solemn] **1 :** marked by the invocation of a religious sanction **2 :** marked by the observance of established form or ceremony; *specif* **:** celebrated with full liturgical ceremony **3 a :** awe-inspiring **:** SUBLIME **b :** highly serious **c :** SOMBER, GLOOMY **syn** see SERIOUS — **sol·emn·ly** *adv* — **sol·emn·ness** *n*

so·lem·ni·fy \sə-'lem-nə-,fī\ *vt* **:** to make solemn

so·lem·ni·ty \sə-'lem-nət-ē\ *n* **1 :** formal or ceremonious observance of an occasion or event **2 :** a solemn event or occasion **3 :** a solemn condition or quality (as of mien)

sol·em·ni·za·tion \,säl-əm-nə-'zā-shən\ *n* **:** an act of solemnizing **:** the state of being solemnized

sol·em·nize \'säl-əm-,nīz\ *vt* **1 :** to observe or honor with solemnity **2 :** to perform with pomp or ceremony; *esp* **:** to celebrate (a marriage) with religious rites **3 :** to make solemn **:** DIGNIFY

solemn mass *n, often cap S&M* **:** a mass celebrated with full ceremony including the use of incense and music by an officiating priest assisted by a deacon and subdeacon

solemn vow *n* **:** an absolute and irrevocable public vow taken by a religious in the Roman Catholic Church under which ownership of property by the individual is prohibited and marriage is invalid under canon law

sole·ness \'sōl-nəs\ *n* **:** the quality or state of being sole

so·le·no·glyph \sə-'lē-nə-,glif\ *n* [NL, deriv. of Gk *sōlēn* pipe channel + *glyphein* to carve — more at CLEAVE] **:** a venomous snake with tubular erectile fangs

so·le·noid \'sō-lə-,nȯid\ *n* [F *solénoïde*, fr. Gk *sōlēnoeidēs* pipe-shaped, fr. Gk *sōlēn* pipe — more at SYRINGE] **:** a coil of wire commonly in the form of a long cylinder that when carrying a current resembles a bar magnet so that a movable core is drawn into the coil when a current flows — **so·le·noi·dal** \,sō-lə-'nȯid-ᵊl\ *adj*

sole·plate \'sōl-,plāt\ *n* **:** the undersurface of a flatiron

sole·print \'sōl-,print\ *n* **:** a print of the sole of the foot; *esp* **:** one made in the manner of a fingerprint and used for the identification of an infant

soles *pl of* SOL

1sol-fa \(')sōl-'fä\ *n* **1 :** SOL-FA SYLLABLES **2 :** SOLMIZATION; *also* **:** an exercise thus sung **3 :** TONIC SOL-FA — **sol-fa·ist** \-'fä-(ə)st, -'fä-,ist\ *n*

2sol-fa *vi* **:** to sing the sol-fa syllables ~ *vt* **:** to sing (as a melody) to sol-fa syllables

sol-fa syllables *n pl* **:** the syllables *do, re, mi, fa, sol, la, ti* used in singing the tones of the scale

sol·fa·ta·ra \,sōl-fə-'tär-ə\ *n* [It, sulfur mine, fr. *solfo* sulfur, fr. L *sulfur*] **:** a volcanic area or vent that yields only hot vapors and gases in part sulfurous

sol·fège \säl-'fezh, -'fāzh\ *n* [F, fr. It *solfeggio*] **1 :** the application of the sol-fa syllables to a musical scale or to a melody **2 :** a singing exercise esp. using sol-fa syllables; *also* **:** practice in sight-singing using the sol-fa syllables

sol·feg·gio \säl-'fej-(,)ō, -'fej-ē-,ō\ *n* [It] **:** SOLFÈGE

sol·gel \'säl-,jel, 'sȯl-\ *adj* **:** involving alternation between sol and gel states

soli *pl of* SOLO

so·lic·it \sə-'lis-ət\ *vb* [ME *soliciten* to disturb, take charge of, fr. MF *solliciter*, fr. L *sollicitare* to disturb, fr. *sollicitus* anxious, fr. *sollus* whole (fr. Oscan; akin to Gk *holos* whole) + *citus*, pp. of *ciēre* to move — more at SAFE, HIGHT] *vt* **1 a :** to make petition to **:** ENTREAT **b :** to approach with a request or plea **2 :** to strongly urge (as one's cause) **3 a :** to entice or lure esp. into evil **b** *obs* **:** to attempt to seduce **c :** to accost (a man) for immoral purposes **4 :** to try to obtain by asking ~ *vi* **:** to make solicitation **:** IMPORTUNE **syn** see ASK, INVITE

so·lic·i·tant \sə-'lis-ət-ənt\ *n* **:** one who solicits

so·lic·i·ta·tion \sə-,lis-ə-'tā-shən\ *n* **1 :** the practice or act or an instance of soliciting; *esp* **:** ENTREATY, IMPORTUNITY **2 :** INCITEMENT, ALLUREMENT

so·lic·i·tor \sə-'lis-ət-ər, -'lis-tər\ *n* **1 :** one that solicits; *esp* **:** an agent that solicits (as contributions to charity) **2 :** a lawyer who advises clients, represents them in the lower courts, and prepares cases for barristers to try in higher courts **3 :** the chief law officer of a municipality, county, or government department — **syn** see LAWYER

solicitor general *n, pl* **solicitors general :** a law officer appointed primarily to assist an attorney general

so·lic·i·tor·ship \sə-ˈlis-ət-ər-ˌship, -ˈlis-tər-\ *n* **:** the position or status of a solicitor

so·lic·i·tous \sə-ˈlis-ət-əs, -ˈlis-təs\ *adj* **1 :** full of concern or fears **:** APPREHENSIVE **2 :** full of desire **:** EAGER **3 :** meticulously careful **4 :** manifesting or expressing solicitude — **so·lic·i·tous·ly** *adv* — **so·lic·i·tous·ness** *n*

so·lic·i·tude \sə-ˈlis-ə-ˌt(y)üd\ *n* **1 :** the state of being solicitous **:** ANXIETY; *also* **:** excessive care or attention **2 :** causes of care or concern — usu. used in pl. **syn** see CARE

¹sol·id \ˈsäl-əd\ *adj* [ME *solide*, fr. MF, fr. L *solidus;* akin to Gk *holos* whole — more at SAFE] **1 a :** having an interior filled with matter **b** (1) **:** printed with minimum space between lines (2) **:** joined without a hyphen ⟨a ~ compound⟩ **c :** not interrupted **2 :** having, involving, or dealing with three dimensions or with solids ⟨~ configuration⟩ **3 a :** not disintegrated **:** not loose or spongy **:** COMPACT **b :** neither gaseous nor liquid **4 :** of good substantial quality or kind ⟨~ comfort⟩: as **a :** SOUND ⟨~ reasons⟩ **b :** STURDY **c :** musically excellent **5 :** UNANIMOUS **6 a :** PRUDENT; *also* **:** well-established financially **b :** serious in purpose or character **7 :** of one substance or character: as **a :** entirely of one metal or containing the minimum of alloy necessary to impart hardness ⟨~ gold⟩ **b :** of a single color or tone **syn** see FIRM — **sol·id·ly** *adv* — **sol·id·ness** *n*

²solid *adv* **:** SOLIDLY; *also* **:** UNANIMOUSLY

³solid *n* **1 :** a geometrical figure or element (as a cube or sphere) having three dimensions **2 :** a substance that does not flow perceptibly under moderate stress **3 :** a solid substance or body

sol·i·da·go \ˌsäl-ə-ˈdā-(ˌ)gō, -ˈdäg-(ˌ)ō\ *n* [NL, genus name, fr. ML *soldago*, an herb reputed to heal wounds, fr. *soldare* to make whole, fr. L *solidare*, fr. *solidus* solid] **:** any of a genus (*Solidago*) of chiefly No. American composite herbs related to the asters that comprises the typical goldenrods

solid angle *n* **:** the three-dimensional angular spread at the vertex of a cone measured by the area intercepted by the cone on a unit sphere whose center is the vertex of the cone

sol·i·da·rism \ˈsäl-əd-ə-ˌriz-əm\ *n* [*solidar*ity + *-ism*] **1 :** SOLIDARITY **2 :** a sociological theory maintaining that the mutual interdependence of members of society offers a basis for a social organization based upon solidarity of interests — **sol·i·da·rist** \-rəst\ *n* — **sol·i·da·ris·tic** \ˌsäl-əd-ə-ˈris-tik\ *adj*

sol·i·dar·i·ty \ˌsäl-ə-ˈdar-ət-ē\ *n* [F *solidarité*, fr. *solidaire* characterized by solidarity, fr. L *solidum* whole sum, fr. neut. of *solidus* solid] **:** community of interests, objectives, or standards in a group **syn** see UNITY

solid geometry *n* **:** a branch of geometry that deals with figures of three-dimensional space

so·lid·i·fi·ca·tion \sə-ˌlid-ə-fə-ˈkā-shən\ *n* **:** an act or instance of solidifying **:** the condition of being solidified

so·lid·i·fy \sə-ˈlid-ə-ˌfī\ *vt* **:** to make solid, compact, or hard **~** *vi* **:** to become solid, compact, or hard

so·lid·i·ty \sə-ˈlid-ət-ē\ *n* **1 :** the quality or state of being solid **2 :** moral, mental, or financial soundness **3 :** something solid

sol·id–look·ing \ˌsäl-əd-ˈluk-iŋ\ *adj* **:** giving an impression of solid worth or substance ⟨~ well-fed citizens⟩

sol·id–state \ˌsäl-əd-ˌstāt\ *adj* **1 :** relating to the properties or structure of solids and esp. crystalline solids ⟨~ physics⟩ **2 :** not utilizing electron tubes ⟨a ~ stereo system⟩

sol·i·dus \ˈsäl-əd-əs\ *n, pl* **sol·i·di** \-ə-ˌdī, -ˌdē\ [ME, fr. LL, fr. L, solid] **1 :** an ancient Roman gold coin introduced by Constantine and used to the fall of the Byzantine Empire **2** [ML, shilling, fr. LL; fr. its use as a symbol for shillings] **:** DIAGONAL 3

so·lil·o·quist \sə-ˈlil-ə-kwəst\ *n* **:** one who soliloquizes

so·lil·o·quize \sə-ˈlil-ə-ˌkwīz\ *vi* **:** to utter a soliloquy **:** talk to oneself — **so·lil·o·quiz·er** *n*

so·lil·o·quy \sə-ˈlil-ə-kwē\ *n* [LL *soliloquium*, fr. L *solus* alone + *loqui* to speak] **1 :** the act of talking to oneself **2 :** a dramatic monologue that gives the illusion of being a series of unspoken reflections

so·lip·sism \ˈsō-ləp-ˌsiz-əm, ˈsäl-əp-\ *n* [L *solus* alone + *ipse* self] **:** a theory holding that the self can know nothing but its own modifications and that the self is the only existent thing — **so·lip·sist** \ˈsō-ləp-səst, ˈsäl-əp-, sə-ˈlip-\ *n* — **so·lip·sis·tic** \ˌsō-ləp-ˈsis-tik, ˌsäl-əp-\ *adj*

sol·i·taire \ˈsäl-ə-ˌta(ə)r, -ˌte(ə)r\ *n* [F, fr. *solitaire*, adj., solitary, fr. L *solitarius*] **1 :** a single gem (as a diamond) set alone **2 :** a card game played by one person alone

sol·i·tar·i·ly \ˌsäl-ə-ˈter-ə-lē\ *adv* **:** in a solitary manner

sol·i·tar·i·ness \ˈsäl-ə-ˌter-ē-nəs\ *n* **:** the quality or state of being solitary

¹sol·i·tary \ˈsäl-ə-ˌter-ē\ *adj* [ME, fr. L *solitarius*, fr. *solitas* aloneness, fr. *solus* alone] **1 a :** being, living, or going alone or without companions **b :** LONELY **2 :** UNFREQUENTED, DESOLATE **3 :** taken, passed, or performed without companions ⟨a ~ ramble⟩ **4 :** SINGLE, SOLE ⟨a ~ example⟩ **5 a :** occurring singly and not as part of a group or cluster ⟨flowers terminal and ~⟩ **b :** not gregarious, colonial, social, or compound ⟨~ bees⟩ **syn** see ALONE, SINGLE

²solitary *n* **1 :** one who lives or seeks to live a solitary life **:** RECLUSE **2 :** solitary confinement in prison

sol·i·tude \ˈsäl-ə-ˌt(y)üd\ *n* [ME, fr. MF, fr. L *solitudin-*, *solitudo*, fr. *solus*] **1 :** the quality or state of being alone or remote from society **:** SECLUSION **2 :** a lonely place (as a desert)

syn SOLITUDE, ISOLATION, SECLUSION mean the state of one who is alone. SOLITUDE may imply a condition of being apart from all human beings or of being cut off by wish or compulsion from friends and neighbors; ISOLATION stresses detachment from others often because of circumstances not under one's control; SECLUSION suggests a shutting away or keeping apart from others often connoting deliberate withdrawal from the world or retirement to a quiet life

sol·i·tu·di·nar·i·an \ˌsäl-ə-ˌt(y)üd-ᵊn-ˈer-ē-ən\ *n* [L *solitudin-*, *solitudo* + E *-arian*] **:** RECLUSE

sol·ler·et \ˌsäl-ə-ˈret\ *n* [F] **:** a flexible steel shoe forming part of a medieval suit of armor

sol·mi·za·tion \ˌsäl-mə-ˈzā-shən\ *n* [F *solmisation*, fr. *solmiser* to sol-fa, fr. *sol* (fr. ML) + *mi* (fr. ML) + *-iser* -ize] **:** the act, practice, or system of using syllables to denote the tones of a musical scale

¹so·lo \ˈsō-(ˌ)lō\ *n, pl* **solos** [It, fr. *solo* alone, fr. L *solus*] **1** *or pl* **so·li** \ˈsō-(ˌ)lē\ **a :** a musical composition for a single voice or instrument with or without accompaniment **b :** the featured part of a concerto or similar work **2 :** a performance in which the performer has no partner or associate **3 :** any of several card games in which each player plays without a partner against the others

²solo *adv* **:** without a companion **:** ALONE

³solo *vi* **so·loed; so·lo·ing** \-(ˌ)lō-iŋ, -lə-wiŋ\ **:** to perform by oneself; *esp* **:** to fly solo in an airplane

so·lo·ist \ˈsō-lə-wəst, -(ˌ)lō-əst\ *n* **:** one who performs a solo

Sol·o·mon \ˈsäl-ə-mən\ *n* [LL, fr. Heb *Shĕlōmōh*] **:** a son of David and 10th-century B.C. king of Israel noted for his wisdom

Solomon's seal *n* **1 :** an emblem consisting of two triangles forming a 6-pointed star and formerly used as an amulet esp. against fever **2 :** any of a genus (*Polygonatum*) of perennial herbs of the lily family with gnarled rhizomes

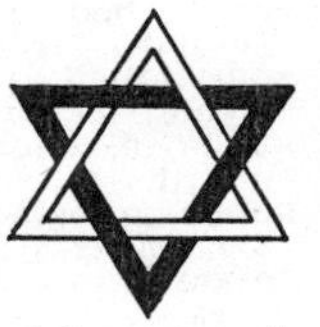
Solomon's seal

so·lon \ˈsō-lən, -ˌlän\ *n* [*Solon* †*ab*559B.C. Athenian lawgiver] **1 :** a wise and skillful lawgiver **2 :** a member of a legislative body

sol·on·chak \ˌsäl-ən-ˈchak\ *n* [Russ, salt marsh] **:** any of an intrazonal group of strongly saline usu. pale soils found esp. in poorly drained arid or semiarid areas

sol·o·netz \ˌsäl-ə-ˈnets\ *n* [Russ *solonets* salt not extracted by decoction] **:** any of an intrazonal group of dark hard alkaline soils evolved by leaching and alkalizing from solonchak — **sol·o·netz·ic** \-ˈnet-sik\ *adj*

so long \sō-ˈlȯŋ\ *interj* — used to express farewell

so long as *conj* **1 :** during and up to the end of the time that **:** WHILE **2 :** provided that

sol·stice \ˈsäl-stəs, ˈsōl-, ˈsȯl-\ *n* [ME, fr. OF, fr. L *solstitium*, fr. *sol* sun + *status*, pp. of *sistere* to come to a stop, cause to stand; akin to L *stare* to stand — more at SOLAR, STAND] **1 :** one of the two points on the ecliptic at which its distance from the celestial equator is greatest and which is reached by the sun each year about June 22d and December 22d **2 :** the time of the sun's passing a solstice which occurs on June 22d to begin summer in the northern hemisphere and on December 22d to begin winter in the northern hemisphere

sol·sti·tial \säl-ˈstish-əl, sōl-, sȯl-\ *adj* [L *solstitialis*, fr. *solstitium*] **1 :** of, relating to, or characteristic of a solstice and esp. the summer solstice **2 :** happening or appearing at or associated with a solstice

sol·u·bil·i·ty \ˌsäl-yə-ˈbil-ət-ē\ *n* **1 :** the quality or state of being soluble **2 :** the amount of a substance that will dissolve in a given amount of another substance

sol·u·bi·lize \ˈsäl-yə-bə-ˌlīz\ *vt* **:** to make soluble or increase the solubility of

sol·u·ble \ˈsäl-yə-bəl\ *adj* [ME, fr. MF, capable of being loosened or dissolved, fr. LL *solubilis*, fr. L *solvere* to loosen, dissolve — more at SOLVE] **1 a :** susceptible of being dissolved in or as if in a fluid **b :** EMULSIFIABLE, DISPERSIBLE ⟨a ~ oil⟩ **2 :** subject to being solved or explained — **sol·u·ble·ness** *n* — **sol·u·bly** \-blē\ *adv*

soluble glass *n* **:** WATER GLASS 4

so·lum \ˈsō-ləm\ *n, pl* **so·la** \-lə\ *or* **solums** [NL, fr. L, ground, soil] **:** the altered layer of soil above the parent material that includes the A- and B-horizons

so·lu·nar \sə-ˈlü-nər, sä-\ *adj* [alter. of *sol-lunar*] **:** resulting from the combined action of sun and moon; *esp* **:** of or relating to the effect of such action on biological systems

so·lus \ˈsō-ləs\ *adv* (*or adj*) [L] **:** ALONE — often used in stage directions

sol·ute \ˈsäl-ˌyüt, ˈsō-ˌlüt\ *n* [L *solutus*, pp.] **:** a dissolved substance

so·lu·tion \sə-ˈlü-shən\ *n* [ME, fr. MF, fr. L *solution-*, *solutio*, fr. *solutus*, pp. of *solvere* to loosen, solve] **1 a :** an action or process of solving a problem **b :** an answer to a problem **:** EXPLANATION; *specif* **:** a set of values of the variables that satisfies an equation **2 a :** an act or the process by which a solid, liquid, or gaseous substance is homogeneously mixed with a liquid or sometimes a gas or solid **b :** a typically liquid homogeneous mixture formed by this process **c :** the condition of being dissolved **d :** a liquid containing a dissolved substance **3 :** a bringing or coming to an end or into a state of discontinuity

So·lu·tre·an *or* **So·lu·tri·an** \sə-ˈlü-trē-ən\ *adj* [*Solutré*, village in France] **:** of or relating to an upper Paleolithic culture characterized by leaf-shaped finely flaked stone implements

solv·abil·i·ty \ˌsäl-və-ˈbil-ət-ē, ˌsȯl-\ *n* **:** the quality or state of being solvable

solv·able \ˈsäl-və-bəl, ˈsȯl-\ *adj* **:** susceptible of solution or of being solved, resolved, or explained

¹sol·vate \ˈsäl-ˌvāt, ˈsȯl-\ *n* [*solvent*] **:** a substance (as a hydrate) formed by chemical or physical combination of a solute and solvent

²solvate *vt* **:** to convert into a solvate **~** *vi* **:** to become or behave as a solvate — **sol·va·tion** \säl-ˈvā-shən, sȯl-\ *n*

Sol·vay process \ˈsäl-ˌvā-\ *n* [Ernest *Solvay* †1922 Belg chemist] **:** a process for making soda from common salt by passing carbon dioxide into ammoniacal brine resulting in precipitation of sodium bicarbonate which is then calcined to carbonate

solve \ˈsälv, ˈsȯlv\ *vt* [ME *solven* to loosen, fr. L *solvere* to loosen, solve, dissolve, fr. *sed-*, *se-* apart + *luere* to release] **1 :** to find a solution for **2 :** to pay (as a debt) in full — **solv·er** *n*

sol·ven·cy \ˈsäl-vən-sē, ˈsȯl-\ *n* **:** the quality or state of being solvent

¹sol·vent \-vənt\ *adj* [L *solvent-*, *solvens*, prp. of *solvere* to dissolve, pay] **1 :** able to pay all legal debts **2 :** that dissolves or can dissolve ⟨~ fluids⟩ ⟨~ action of water⟩ — **sol·vent·ly** *adv*

²solvent *n* **1 :** a usu. liquid substance capable of dissolving or dispersing one or more other substances **2 :** something that provides a solution

sol·vol·y·sis \säl-ˈväl-ə-səs, sȯl-\ *n* [NL, fr. E *solvent* + *-o-* + NL *-lysis*] **:** a chemical reaction (as hydrolysis) of a solvent and solute with the formation of new compounds — **sol·vo·lyt·ic** \ˌsäl-və-ˈlit-ik, ˌsȯl-\ *adj*

¹so·ma \ˈsō-mə\ *n* [Skt; akin to Av *haoma* haoma, Gk *hyein* to rain — more at SUCK] **:** an East Indian leafless vine (*Sarcostemma acidum*) of the milkweed family with a milky acid juice

²soma *n* [NL *somat-*, *soma*, fr. Gk *sōmat-*, *sōma* body] **:** all of an organism except the germ cells

So·ma·li \sō-ˈmäl-ē\ *n, pl* **Somali** *or* **Somalis** **1 a :** a tall dark Cushitic-speaking people of Somaliland apparently of mixed Mediterranean and negroid stock and almost universally Muslim

b : a member of this people **2 :** the Cushitic language of the Somali people
Somali shilling *n* — see MONEY table
so many *adj* **1 :** constituting an unspecified number **2 :** constituting a group or pack ⟨behaved like *so many* animals⟩
somat- *or* **somato-** *comb form* [NL, fr. Gk *sōmat-*, *sōmato-*, fr. *sōmat-*, *sōma* body; akin to L *tumēre* to swell — more at THUMB] **1 :** body ⟨*somato*logy⟩ **2 :** soma ⟨*somato*plasm⟩
so·mat·ic \sō-'mat-ik, sə-\ *adj* [Gk *sōmatikos*, fr. *sōmat-*, *sōma*] **1 :** of, relating to, or affecting the body esp. as distinguished from the germ plasm or the psyche ⟨~ cells⟩ **2 :** of or relating to the wall of the body **:** PARIETAL **3 :** MESOMORPHIC **syn** see BODILY — **so·mat·i·cal·ly** \-i-k(ə-)lē\ *adv*
somatic cell *n* **:** one of the cells of the body that compose the tissues, organs, and parts of that individual other than the germ cells
so·ma·to·gen·ic \,sō-mət-ə-'jen-ik\ *adj* **:** originating in, affecting, or acting through somatic cells — compare PSYCHOGENIC
so·ma·to·log·i·cal \,sō-mət-ᵊl-'äj-i-kəl\ *adj* **:** of or relating to somatology
so·ma·tol·o·gy \,sō-mə-'täl-ə-jē\ *n* [NL *somatologia*, fr. *somat-* + *-logia* -logy] **:** a branch of anthropology primarily concerned with the comparative study of human evolution, variation, and classification esp. through measurement and observation
so·ma·to·plasm \'sō-mət-ə-,plaz-əm, sō-'mat-\ *n* **1 :** protoplasm of somatic cells **2 :** somatic cells as distinguished from germ cells — **so·ma·to·plas·tic** \,sō-mət-ə-'plas-tik, sō-,mat-\ *adj*
so·ma·to·pleure \'sō-mət-ə-,plu̇(ə)r, sō-'mat-\ *n* [NL *somatopleura*, fr. *somat-* + Gk *pleura* side] **:** a complex layer in the embryo of a craniate vertebrate consisting of the outer of the two layers into which the lateral plate of the mesoderm splits together with the ectoderm that sheathes it externally and giving rise to the body wall — **so·ma·to·pleu·ric** \,sō-mət-ə-'plu̇r-ik, sō-,mat-\ *adj*
so·ma·to·type \'sō-mət-ə-,tīp, sō-'mat-\ *n* **:** body type **:** PHYSIQUE — **so·ma·to·typ·ic** \,sō-mət-ə-'tip-ik, sō-,mat-\ *adj* — **so·ma·to·typ·i·cal·ly** \-i-k(ə-)lē\ *adv*
som·ber *or* **som·bre** \'säm-bər *also* 'sȯm-\ *adj* [F *sombre*] **1 :** so shaded as to be dark and gloomy **2 a :** of a serious mien **:** GRAVE **b :** of a dismal or depressing character **:** MELANCHOLY **c :** conveying gloomy suggestions or ideas **3 :** of a dull or heavy cast or shade **:** dark colored — **som·ber·ly** *or* **som·bre·ly** *adv* — **som·ber·ness** *or* **som·bre·ness** *n*
som·bre·ro \səm-'bre(ə)r-(,)ō, säm-\ *n* [Sp] **:** a high-crowned hat of felt or straw with a very wide brim worn esp. in the Southwest and Mexico
som·brous \'säm-brəs, 'sȯm-\ *adj* [F *sombre*] **:** SOMBER
1**some** \'səm\ *adj* [ME *som*, adj. & pron., fr. OE *sum*; akin to OHG *sum* some, Gk *hamē* somehow, *homos* same — more at SAME] **1 :** being one unknown, undetermined, or unspecified unit or thing ⟨~ person knocked⟩ **2 a :** being one, a part, or an unspecified number of something (as a class or group) named or implied ⟨~ gems are hard⟩ **b :** being of an unspecified amount or number ⟨give me ~ water⟩ ⟨have ~ apples⟩ **3 :** IMPORTANT, STRIKING ⟨that was ~ party⟩ **4 :** being at least one and sometimes all of
2**some** \'səm\ *pron, sing or pl in constr* **1 :** some one person or thing among a number **2 :** one indeterminate quantity, portion, or number as distinguished from the rest **3 :** an indefinite additional amount ⟨ran a mile and then ~⟩
3**some** \'səm, ,səm\ *adv* **1 :** ABOUT ⟨~ eighty houses⟩ **2 :** SOMEWHAT ⟨felt ~ better⟩
1**-some** \səm; (t)-səm *after stressed-syllable* n\ *adj suffix* [ME *-som*, fr. OE *-sum*; akin to OHG *-sam* -some, OE *sum* some] **:** characterized by a (specified) thing, quality, state, or action ⟨awe*some*⟩ ⟨burden*some*⟩ ⟨cuddle*some*⟩ ⟨lone*some*⟩
2**-some** *n suffix* [ME (northern dial) *-sum*, fr. ME *sum*, pron., one, some] **:** group of (so many) members and esp. persons ⟨four*some*⟩
3**-some** \,sōm\ *n comb form* [NL *-somat-*, *-soma*, fr. Gk *sōmat-*, *sōma* — more at SOMAT-] **1 :** body ⟨chromo*some*⟩ **2 :** chromosome ⟨mono*some*⟩
1**some·body** \'səm-,bäd-ē, -bəd-\ *pron* **:** one or some person of no certain or known identity ⟨~ will come in⟩
2**somebody** *n* **:** a person of position or importance
some·day \'səm-,dā\ *adv* **:** at some future time
some·deal \'səm-,dēl\ *adv, archaic* **:** SOMEWHAT
some·how \'səm-,hau̇\ *adv* **:** in one way or another not known or designated **:** by some means
some·one \-(,)wən\ *pron* **:** some person **:** SOMEBODY
some·place \-,plās\ *adv* **:** SOMEWHERE
som·er·sault \'səm-ər-,sȯlt\ *n* [MF *sombresaut* leap, deriv. of L *super* over + *saltus* leap, fr. *saltus*, pp. of *salire* to jump — more at OVER, SALLY] **:** a leap or roll in which a person turns his heels over his head — **somersault** *vi*
som·er·set \-,set\ *n or vb* [by alter.] **:** SOMERSAULT
1**some·thing** \'səm(p)-thiŋ, *esp rapid or for 3* 'səmp-ᵊm\ *pron* **1 a :** some undetermined or unspecified thing **b :** some thing not remembered or immaterial ⟨the twelve ~ train⟩ **2 :** some definite but not specified thing ⟨~ to live for⟩ **3 :** a person or thing of consequence
2**something** *adv* **1 :** in some degree **:** SOMEWHAT **2 :** EXTREMELY ⟨swears ~ awful⟩
1**some·time** \'səm-,tīm\ *adv* **1** *archaic* **:** FORMERLY **2** *archaic* **:** OCCASIONALLY, SOMETIMES **3 :** at some time in the future ⟨I'll do it ~⟩ **4 :** at some not specified or definitely known point of time
2**sometime** *adj* **:** FORMER, LATE
1**some·times** \'səm-,tīmz *also* (,)səm-'\ *adv* **:** at times **:** now and then **:** OCCASIONALLY
2**sometimes** *adj, archaic* **:** FORMER
some·way \'səm-,wā\ *also* **some·ways** \-,wāz\ *adv* **:** in some way **:** SOMEHOW
1**some·what** \-,(h)wät, -,(h)wət, (,)səm-'\ *pron* **1 :** something (as an amount or degree) indefinite or unspecified **2 :** some unspecified or indeterminate thing **:** SOMETHING **3 :** one having a character, quality, or nature to some extent ⟨~ of a connoisseur⟩ **4 :** an important or noteworthy person or thing
2**somewhat** *adv* **:** in some degree or measure **:** SLIGHTLY
some·when \'səm-,(h)wen\ *adv* **:** SOMETIME
1**some·where** \-,(h)we(ə)r, -,(h)wa(ə)r, -(,)(h)wər\ *adv* **1 :** in, at, or to a place unknown or unspecified **2 :** APPROXIMATELY ⟨~ about nine o'clock⟩
2**somewhere** *n* **:** an undetermined or unnamed place
some·wheres \-,(h)we(ə)rz, -,(h)wa(ə)rz, -(,)(h)wərz\ *adv, chiefly dial* **:** SOMEWHERE
some·whith·er \-,(h)wit͟h-ər\ *adv* **:** to some place **:** SOMEWHERE
-so·mic \'sō-mik\ *adj comb form* [ISV 3*-some* + *-ic*] **:** having or being a body of chromosomes of which one or more but not all members exhibit (such) a degree of reduplication of chromosomes or genomes ⟨mono*somic*⟩
so·mite \'sō-,mīt\ *n* [ISV, fr. Gk *sōma* body — more at SOMAT-] **:** one of the longitudinal series of segments into which the body of many animals (as articulate animals and vertebrates) is divided **:** METAMERE — **so·mit·ic** \sō-'mit-ik\ *adj*
som·me·lier \,səm-əl-'yā\ *n, pl* **sommeliers** \-'yā(z)\ [F, fr. MF, court official charged with transportation of supplies, pack animal driver, fr. OProv *saumalier* pack animal driver, fr. *sauma* pack animal, load of a pack animal, fr. LL *sagma* packsaddle — more at SUMPTER] **:** a waiter in a restaurant who has charge of wines and their service **:** a wine steward
somnambul- *comb form* [NL, fr. *somnambulus* somnambulist, fr. L *somnus* sleep + *-ambulus* (as in *funambulus* funambulist) — more at SOMNOLENT] **:** somnambulist **:** somnambulism ⟨somnambul*ant*⟩
som·nam·bu·lant \säm-'nam-byə-lənt\ *adj* **:** walking or addicted to walking while asleep
som·nam·bu·lar \-lər\ *adj* **:** of, relating to, or characterized by somnambulism
som·nam·bu·late \-,lāt\ *vi* **:** to walk when asleep — **som·nam·bu·la·tion** \(,)säm-,nam-byə-'lā-shən\ *n* — **som·nam·bu·la·tor** \säm-'nam-byə-,lāt-ər\ *n*
som·nam·bu·lism \säm-'nam-byə-,liz-əm\ *n* **:** a sleep or somnolent state in which motor acts (as walking) are performed; *also* **:** actions characteristic of this state — **som·nam·bu·list** \-ləst\ *n* — **som·nam·bu·lis·tic** \(,)säm-,nam-byə-'lis-tik\ *adj* — **som·nam·bu·lis·ti·cal·ly** \-ti-k(ə-)lē\ *adv*
som·ni·fa·cient \,säm-nə-'fā-shənt\ *adj* [L *somnus* sleep + E *-facient*] **:** HYPNOTIC 1 — **somnifacient** *n*
som·nif·er·ous \säm-'nif-(ə-)rəs\ *adj* [L *somnifer* somniferous, fr. *somnus* + *-fer* -ferous] **:** SOPORIFIC — **som·nif·er·ous·ly** *adv*
som·nif·ic \-'nif-ik\ *adj* [L *somnificus*, fr. *somnus* + *-ficus* -fic] **:** SOMNIFEROUS
som·no·lence \'säm-nə-lən(t)s\ *also* **som·no·len·cy** \-lən-sē\ *n* **:** DROWSINESS, SLEEPINESS
som·no·lent \-lənt\ *adj* [ME *sompnolent*, fr. MF, fr. L *somnolentus*, fr. *somnus* sleep; akin to OE *swefn* sleep, Gk *hypnos*] **1 :** SOPORIFIC 1 **2 :** inclined to or heavy with sleep **:** DROWSY ⟨a ~ village⟩ — **som·no·lent·ly** *adv*
1**so much** *adv* **:** by the amount indicated or suggested ⟨if they lose their way, *so much* the better for us⟩
2**so much** *adj* **1 :** of an equal amount — often used as an intensive ⟨the house burned like *so much* paper⟩ **2 :** of an unspecified amount — often used as an intensive ⟨sounded like *so much* nonsense⟩
3**so much** *pron* **1 :** something (as an amount or price) unspecified or undetermined ⟨charge *so much* a mile⟩ **2 :** that is all that can be or is to be said or done now ⟨*so much* for the history of the case⟩
son \'sən\ *n* [ME *sone*, fr. OE *sunu*; akin to OHG *sun* son, Gk *hyios*] **1 a :** a male offspring of human beings **b :** a male adopted child **c :** a male descendant — usu. used in pl. **2** *cap* **:** the second person of the Trinity **3 :** a person closely associated with or deriving from a formative agent (as a nation, school, or race)
so·nance \'sō-nən(t)s\ *n* **:** SOUND
1**so·nant** \-nənt\ *adj* [L *sonant-*, *sonans*, prp. of *sonare* to sound — more at SOUND] **1** *of a speech sound* **:** VOICED **2** *of a consonant* **:** SYLLABIC
2**sonant** *n* **1 :** a voiced sound **2 :** a syllabic consonant
so·nar \'sō-,när\ *n* [*so*und *na*vigation *r*anging] **:** an apparatus that detects the presence and location of a submerged object (as a submarine) by means of sonic and supersonic waves reflected back to it from the object
so·nar·man \-mən, -,man\ *n* **:** an enlisted man in the navy who operates sonar equipment
so·na·ta \sə-'nät-ə\ *n* [It, fr. *sonare* to sound, fr. L] **:** an instrumental musical composition typically of three or four movements in contrasting forms and keys
sonata form *n* **:** a musical form consisting basically of an exposition, a development, and a recapitulation used esp. for the first movement of a sonata
son·a·ti·na \,sän-ə-'tē-nə\ *also* **son·a·tine** \-'tēn\ *n* [*sonatina* fr. It, dim. of *sonata*; *sonatine* fr. F, fr. It *sonatina*] **:** a short usu. simplified sonata
sonde \'sänd\ *n* [F, lit., sounding line — more at SOUND] **:** any of various devices for testing physical and meteorological conditions at high altitudes above the earth's surface
sone \'sōn\ *n* [ISV, fr. L *sonus* sound — more at SOUND] **:** a subjective unit of loudness for a given listener equal to the loudness of a 1000-cycle sound that has an intensity 40 decibels above the listener's own threshold
song \'sȯŋ\ *n* [ME, fr. OE *sang*; akin to OE *singan* to sing] **1 :** the act or art of singing **2 :** poetical composition **3 a :** a short musical composition of words and music **b :** a collection of such compositions **4 a :** a melody for a lyric poem or ballad **b :** a poem easily set to music **5 :** a habitual or characteristic manner or noisy reaction ⟨put up quite a ~⟩ **6 :** a small amount ⟨sold for a ~⟩ — **song·book** \-,bu̇k\ *n*
song and dance *n* **:** a statement or explanation interesting in itself but not necessarily true or pertinent
song·bird \'sȯŋ-,bərd\ *n* **1 a :** a bird that utters a succession of musical tones **b :** SINGING BIRD 2 **2 :** a female singer
song·fest \-,fest\ *n* **:** an informal session of group singing of popular or folk songs
song·ful \-fəl\ *adj* **:** given to singing **:** MELODIOUS — **song·ful·ly** \-fə-lē\ *adv* — **song·ful·ness** *n*
song·less \'sȯŋ-ləs\ *adj* **:** lacking in, incapable of, or not given to song — **song·less·ly** *adv*
song·smith \-,smith\ *n* **:** a composer of songs
song·ster \'sȯŋ(k)-stər\ *n* **1 :** one skilled in song **2 :** SONGBOOK — **song·stress** \-strəs\ *n*
song·writ·er \'sȯŋ-,rīt-ər\ *n* **:** a person who composes words or music or both esp. for popular songs
son·ic \'sän-ik\ *adj* [L *sonus* sound — more at SOUND] **1 :** having a frequency within the audibility range of the human ear — used of

waves and vibrations **2 :** utilizing, produced by, or relating to sound waves ⟨~ altimeter⟩ **3 :** of, relating to, or being the speed of sound in air that is about 741 miles per hour at sea level **4 :** capable of uttering sounds — **son·i·cal·ly** \-i-k(ə-)lē\ *adv*

sonic barrier *n* **:** a sudden large increase in aerodynamic drag that occurs as the speed of an aircraft approaches the speed of sound

sonic boom *n* **:** a sound resembling an explosion produced when a shock wave formed at the nose of an aircraft traveling at supersonic speed reaches the ground

sonic depth finder *n* **:** an instrument for determining the depth of a body of water or of an object below the surface by means of sound waves

son–in–law \'sən-ən-,lȯ\ *n, pl* **sons–in–law** \'sən-zən-\ **:** the husband of one's daughter

son·less \'sən-ləs\ *adj* **:** not possessing or never having had a son

son·ly \-lē\ *adj* **:** FILIAL

son·net \'sän-ət\ *n* [It *sonetto*, fr. OProv *sonet* little song, fr. *son* sound, song, fr. L *sonus* sound] **:** a fixed verse form of Italian origin consisting of fourteen lines that are typically five-foot iambics rhyming according to a prescribed scheme; *also* **:** a poem in this pattern

son·ne·teer \,sän-ə-'ti(ə)r\ *n* **1 :** a composer of sonnets **2 :** a minor or insignificant poet

son·net·ize \'sän-ət-,īz\ *vi* **:** to compose a sonnet ~ *vt* **:** to compose a sonnet on or to

sonnet sequence *n* **:** a series of sonnets often having a unifying theme

son·ny \'sən-ē\ *n* **:** a young boy — used chiefly as a term of address

so·no·buoy \'sō-nə-,bü-ē, 'sän-ə-, -,bȯi\ *n* [L *sonus* sound + E *-o-* + *buoy* — more at SOUND] **:** a buoy equipped for detecting underwater sounds and transmitting them by radio

so·no·rant \sə-'nōr-ənt, -'nȯr-; 'sän-ə-rənt\ *n* [*sonorous* + *-ant* (as in *resonant*)] **:** RESONANT

so·nor·i·ty \sə-'nȯr-ət-ē, -'när-\ *n* **1 :** the quality or state of being sonorous **:** RESONANCE **2 :** a sonorous tone or speech

so·no·rous \sə-'nōr-əs, -'nȯr-; 'sän-ə-rəs\ *adj* [L *sonorus;* akin to L *sonus* sound] **1 :** producing sound (as when struck) **2 :** full or loud in sound **:** RESONANT **3 :** imposing or impressive in effect or style **4 :** having a high or an indicated degree of sonority ⟨~ sounds like \ä\ and \ȯ\⟩ — **so·no·rous·ly** *adv* — **so·no·rous·ness** *n*

so·no·vox \'sō-nə-,väks, 'sän-ə-\ *n* [L *sonus* + *vox* voice — more at VOICE] **:** an electronic sound effects device held against the throat to give the effect of speech to recorded nonhuman sounds (as of a waterfall or train whistle) that are transmitted through the larynx and formed into words by the mouth

son·ship \'sən-,ship\ *n* **:** the relationship of son to father

sonsy *or* **sons·ie** \'sän(t)-sē\ *adj* [Sc *sons* health] **1** *chiefly dial* **:** BUXOM, COMELY **2** *chiefly dial* **:** GENIAL

soon \'sün, *esp NewEng* 'sůn\ *adv* [ME *soone*, fr. OE *sōna;* akin to OHG *sān* immediately] **1 a** *obs* **:** at once **:** IMMEDIATELY **b :** before long **:** without undue time lapse ⟨~ after sunrise⟩ **2 :** PROMPTLY, SPEEDILY ⟨as ~ as possible⟩ **3 :** before the usual time **4 :** READILY, WILLINGLY

soon·er \'sü-nər\ *n* [*sooner*, compar. of *soon*] **1 :** a person settling on land in the early West before its official opening to settlement in order to gain the prior claim allowed by law to the first settler after official opening **2** *cap* **:** a native or resident of Oklahoma — used as a nickname

[1]**soot** \'sůt, 'sət, 'süt\ *n* [ME, fr. OE *sōt;* akin to OIr *sūide* soot, OE *sittan* to sit] **:** a black substance formed by combustion or separated from fuel during combustion, rising in fine particles, and adhering to the sides of the chimney or pipe conveying the smoke; *esp* **:** the fine powder consisting chiefly of carbon that colors smoke

[2]**soot** *vt* **:** to coat or cover with soot

[1]**sooth** \'süth\ *adj* [ME, fr. OE *sōth;* akin to OHG *sand* true, Gk *eteos*, L *esse* to be] **1** *archaic* **:** TRUE **2** *archaic* **:** SOFT, SWEET

[2]**sooth** *n* **1** *archaic* **:** TRUTH, REALITY **2** *obs* **:** CAJOLERY, BLANDISHMENT

soothe \'süth\ *vb* [ME *sothen* to prove the truth, fr. OE *sōthian*, fr. *sōth*] *vt* **1** *obs* **:** to humor by complying **2 a :** to please by or as if by attention or concern **:** PLACATE **b :** RELIEVE, ALLEVIATE **3 :** to bring comfort, solace, or reassurance to ~ *vi* **:** to bring peace, composure, or quietude — **sooth·er** *n*

sooth·fast \'süth-,fast\ *adj* **1** *archaic* **:** TRUE **2** *archaic* **:** TRUTHFUL

sooth·ing \'sü-thiŋ\ *adj* **:** CALMING; *also* **:** having a sedative effect ⟨~ syrup⟩ — **sooth·ing·ly** \-thiŋ-lē\ *adv* — **sooth·ing·ness** *n*

sooth·ly \'süth-lē\ *adv, archaic* **:** in truth **:** TRULY

sooth·say \-,sā\ *vi* **:** to practice soothsaying — **sooth·say·er** *n*

sooth·say·ing \-,sā-iŋ\ *n* **1 :** the act of foretelling events **2 :** PREDICTION, PROPHECY

soot·i·ly \'sůt-ᵊl-ē, 'sət-, 'süt-\ *adv* **:** in a sooty manner

soot·i·ness \-ē-nəs\ *n* **:** the quality or state of being sooty

sooty \'sůt-ē, 'sət-, 'süt-\ *adj* **1 a :** of, relating to, or producing soot **b :** soiled with soot **2 :** of the color of soot

sooty mold *n* **:** a dark growth of fungus mycelium growing in insect honeydew on plants; *also* **:** a fungus producing such growth

[1]**sop** \'säp\ *n* [ME *soppe*, fr. OE *sopp;* akin to OE *sūpan* to swallow — more at SUP] **1** *chiefly dial* **:** a piece of food dipped or steeped in a liquid **2 :** a conciliatory or propitiatory bribe, gift, or advance

[2]**sop** *vt* **sopped; sop·ping 1 a :** to steep or dip in or as if in liquid **b :** to wet thoroughly **:** SOAK **2 :** to mop up (as water) **3 :** to give a bribe or conciliatory gift to

soph·ism \'säf-,iz-əm\ *n* **1 :** an argument correct in form or appearance but actually invalid; *esp* **:** one used to deceive **2 :** SOPHISTRY

soph·ist \'säf-əst\ *n* [L *sophista*, fr. Gk *sophistēs*, lit., expert, wise man, fr. *sophizesthai* to become wise, deceive, fr. *sophos* clever, wise] **1** *cap* **:** one of a class of ancient Greek teachers of rhetoric, philosophy, and the art of successful living prominent about the middle of the 5th century B.C. for their adroit subtle often specious reasoning **2 :** THINKER, PHILOSOPHER **3 :** a captious or fallacious reasoner

so·phis·tic \sä-'fis-tik, sə-\ *adj* **1 :** of or relating to sophists, sophistry, or the ancient Sophists ⟨~ rhetoric⟩ ⟨~ subtleties⟩ **2 :** plausible but fallacious ⟨~ reasoning⟩ — **so·phis·ti·cal** \-ti-kəl\ *adj* — **so·phis·ti·cal·ly** \-k(ə-)lē\ *adv*

[1]**so·phis·ti·cate** \sə-'fis-tə-,kāt\ *vt* [ME *sophisticaten*, fr. ML *sophisticatus*, pp. of *sophisticare*, fr. L *sophisticus* sophistic, fr. Gk *sophistikos*, fr. *sophistēs* sophist] **1 :** to alter deceptively; *esp* **:** ADULTERATE **2 :** to deprive of genuineness, naturalness, or simplicity; *esp* **:** to deprive of naïveté and make worldly-wise **:** DISILLUSION **3 :** to make complicated or complex **:** REFINE — **so·phis·ti·ca·tion** \-,fis-tə-'kā-shən\ *n*

[2]**so·phis·ti·cate** \-'fis-ti-kət, -tə-,kāt\ *n* **:** a sophisticated person

so·phis·ti·cat·ed \-tə-,kāt-əd\ *adj* [ML *sophisticatus*] **1 :** not in a natural, pure, or original state **:** ADULTERATED ⟨a ~ oil⟩ **2 :** deprived of native or original simplicity: as **a :** highly complicated **:** COMPLEX ⟨~ instruments⟩ **b :** WORLDLY-WISE, KNOWING ⟨a ~ adolescent⟩ **3 :** devoid of grossness **:** SUBTLE: as **a :** finely experienced and aware ⟨a ~ columnist⟩ **b :** intellectually appealing ⟨a ~ novel⟩ — **so·phis·ti·cat·ed·ly** *adv*

soph·ist·ry \'säf-ə-strē\ *n* **1 :** deceptively subtle reasoning or argumentation **2 :** SOPHISM 1

Soph·o·cle·an \,säf-ə-'klē-ən\ *adj* **:** of, relating to, or characteristic of Sophocles or his tragedies

soph·o·more \'säf-ᵊm-,ō(ə)r, -,ȯ(ə)r; 'säf-,mō(ə)r, -,mȯ(ə)r\ *n* [prob. fr. Gk *sophos* wise + *mōros* foolish — more at MORON] **:** a student in his second year at a college or secondary school

soph·o·mor·ic \,säf-ə-'mōr-ik, -'mȯr-, -'mär-\ *adj* **1 :** of, relating to, or characteristic of a sophomore **2 :** conceited and overconfident of knowledge but poorly informed and immature

so·phy \'sō-fē\ *n* [Per *Ṣafī*] *archaic* **:** a sovereign of Persia

-so·phy \sə-fē\ *n comb form* [ME *-sophie*, fr. OF, fr. L *-sophia*, fr. Gk, fr. *sophia* wisdom, fr. *sophos*] **:** knowledge **:** wisdom **:** science ⟨anthropo*sophy*⟩

so·pite \sō-'pīt\ *vt* [L *sopitus*, pp. of *sopire* to put to sleep, fr. *sopor*] **1 :** to put to sleep **:** LULL **2 :** to put an end to (as a claim) **:** SETTLE

so·por \'sō-pər, -,pȯ(ə)r\ *n* [L] **:** profound or lethargic sleep **:** STUPOR

so·po·rif·er·ous \,säp-ə-'rif-(ə-)rəs, ,sō-pə-\ *adj* [L *soporifer* soporiferous, fr. *sopor* + *-fer* -ferous] **:** SOPORIFIC — **so·po·rif·er·ous·ly** *adv* — **so·po·rif·er·ous·ness** *n*

[1]**so·po·rif·ic** \-'rif-ik\ *adj* [prob. fr. F *soporifique*, fr. L *sopor* deep sleep; akin to L *somnus* sleep — more at SOMNOLENT] **1 a :** causing or tending to cause sleep **b :** tending to dull awareness or alertness **2 :** of, relating to, or characterized by sleepiness or lethargy

[2]**soporific** *n* **:** a soporific agent; *specif* **:** HYPNOTIC 1

sop·ping \'säp-iŋ\ *adj* **:** wet through **:** SOAKING

sop·py \'säp-ē\ *adj* **1 :** soaked through **:** SATURATED **2 :** very wet

[1]**so·pra·no** \sə-'pran-(,)ō, -'prän-\ *n* [It, adj. & n., fr. *sopra* above, fr. L *supra;* akin to L *super* above — more at OVER] **1 :** the highest voice part in four-part mixed harmony **2 :** the highest singing voice **3 :** a singer with a soprano voice

[2]**soprano** *adj* **1 :** relating to the soprano voice or part **2 :** having a high range ⟨~ sax⟩

so·ra \'sōr-ə, 'sȯr-\ *n* [origin unknown] **:** a small short-billed No. American rail (*Porzana carolina*) common in marshes

[1]**sorb** \'sȯ(ə)rb\ *n* [F *sorbe* fruit of the service tree, fr. L *sorbum*] **1 :** any of several Old World trees related to the apples and pears (as a service or rowan tree) **2 :** the fruit of a sorb

[2]**sorb** *vt* [back-formation fr. *absorb* & *adsorb*] **:** to take up and hold by either adsorption or absorption

Sorb \'sȯ(ə)rb\ *n* [G *Sorbe*, fr. Sorbian *Serb*] **1 :** a member of a Slavic people whose present representatives are the Wends living in Saxony and Brandenburg **2 :** WENDISH — **Sor·bi·an** \'sȯr-bē-ən\ *adj or n*

sor·bate \'sȯ(ə)r-,bāt, 'sȯr-bət\ *n* **:** a sorbed substance

sor·bent \'sȯr-bənt\ *n* [L *sorbent-*, *sorbens*, prp. of *sorbēre* to suck up — more at ABSORB] **:** a substance that sorbs

sor·bic acid \,sȯr-bik-\ *n* [[1]*sorb*] **:** a crystalline acid $C_6H_8O_2$ obtained from the unripe fruits of the mountain ash or synthesized and used as a fungicide and food preservative

Sor·bon·ist \sȯr-'bän-əst\ *n* [F *sorboniste*, fr. *Sorbonne*] **:** a doctor of or student at the Sorbonne

sor·bose \'sȯ(ə)r-,bōs, -,bōz\ *n* [ISV *sorbitol* (an alcohol)] **:** a sweet crystalline unfermentable ketohexose sugar $C_6H_{12}O_6$ used esp. in making ascorbic acid

sor·cer·er \'sȯrs-(ə-)rər\ *n* **:** a person who practices sorcery **:** WIZARD — **sor·cer·ess** \-(ə-)rəs\ *n*

sor·cer·ous \'sȯrs-(ə-)rəs\ *adj* **:** of or relating to sorcery **:** MAGICAL

sor·cery \'sȯrs-(ə-)rē\ *n* [ME *sorcerie*, fr. OF, fr. *sorcier* sorcerer, fr. (assumed) VL *sortiarius*, fr. L *sort-*, *sors* chance, lot] **:** the use of power gained from the assistance or control of evil spirits esp. for divining **:** NECROMANCY

sor·did \'sȯrd-əd\ *adj* [L *sordidus*, fr. *sordes* dirt — more at SWART] **1 a :** DIRTY, FILTHY **b :** WRETCHED, SQUALID **2 :** marked by baseness or grossness **:** VILE ⟨~ motives⟩ **3 :** meanly avaricious **:** COVETOUS **4 :** of a dull or muddy color **syn** see MEAN — **sor·did·ly** *adv* — **sor·did·ness** *n*

sor·di·no \sȯr-'dē-(,)nō\ *n, pl* **sor·di·ni** \-(,)nē\ [It, fr. *sordo* silent, fr. L *surdus* — more at SURD] **:** [2]MUTE 3

[1]**sore** \'sō(ə)r, 'sȯ(ə)r\ *adj* [ME *sor*, fr. OE *sār;* akin to OHG *sēr* sore, L *saevus* fierce] **1 a :** causing pain or distress **b :** painfully sensitive **:** TENDER ⟨~ muscles⟩ **c :** hurt or inflamed so as to be or seem painful ⟨~ runny eyes⟩ ⟨a dog limping on a ~ leg⟩ **2 :** attended by difficulties, hardship, or exertion **3 :** ANGERED, VEXED — **sore·ly** *adv* — **sore·ness** *n*

[2]**sore** *n* **1 :** a localized sore spot on the body; *esp* **:** one (as an ulcer) with the tissues ruptured or abraded and usu. with infection **2 :** a source of pain or vexation **:** AFFLICTION

[3]**sore** *adv* **:** SORELY

sore·head \-,hed\ *n* **:** a person easily angered or disgruntled — **sorehead** *or* **sore·head·ed** \-'hed-əd\ *adj*

sore throat *n* **:** painful throat due to inflammation of the fauces and pharynx

sor·ghum \'sȯr-gəm\ *n* [NL, genus name, fr. It *sorgo*] **1 :** any of an economically important genus (*Sorghum*) of Old World tropical grasses similar to Indian corn in habit but with the spikelets in pairs on a hairy rachis; *esp* **:** a cultivated plant (as a grain sorghum or sorgo) derived from a common species (*S. vulgare*) **2 :** syrup from

the juice of a sorgo that resembles cane syrup but contains much invert sugar **3 :** something cloyingly sentimental

sor·go \'sȯ(ə)r-(,)gō\ *n* [It] **:** a sorghum cultivated primarily for its sweet juice and also widely used for fodder and silage — called also *sweet sorghum*

sor·i·cine \'sȯr-ə-,sīn, 'sär-, 'sōr-\ *adj* [L *soricinus*, fr. *soric-, sorex* shrew; akin to L *susurrus* hum — more at SWARM] **:** resembling a shrew ⟨~ bats⟩

so·ri·tes \sə-'rīt-(,)ēz\ *n, pl* **sorites** [L, fr. Gk *sōritēs*, fr. *sōros* heap — more at SORUS] **:** an abridged series of syllogisms in a series of propositions so arranged that the predicate of any one forms the subject of the next and the conclusion unites the subject of the first proposition with the predicate of the last

so·rop·ti·mist \sə-'räp-tə-məst\ *n* [blend of *sorority* and *optimist*] **:** a member of a club composed of professional women and women business executives associated primarily for service

so·ro·ral \sə-'rōr-əl, -'rȯr-\ *adj* [L *soror* sister — more at SISTER] **:** of, relating to, or characteristic of a sister **:** SISTERLY

so·ro·rate \sə-'rōr-ət, -'rȯr-\ *n* [L *soror* sister] **:** the marriage of one man with two or more sisters usu. successively and after the first wife has been found to be barren or after her death

so·ror·i·ty \sə-'rȯr-ət-ē, -'rär-\ *n* [ML *sororitas* sisterhood, fr. L *soror* sister] **:** a club of girls or women esp. at a college

so·rose \'sō(ə)r-,ōs, 'sȯ(ə)r-\ *adj* **:** bearing sori

sorp·tion \'sȯrp-shən\ *n* [back-formation fr. *absorption* & *adsorption*] **:** the process of sorbing **:** the state of being sorbed

[1]**sor·rel** \'sȯr-əl, 'sär-\ *n* [ME *sorelle*, fr. MF *sorel*, n. & adj., fr. *sor* reddish brown] **1 :** an animal (as a horse) of a sorrel color **2 :** a brownish orange to light brown

[2]**sorrel** *n* [ME *sorel*, fr. MF *surele*, fr. OF, fr. *sur* sour, of Gmc origin; akin to OHG *sūr* sour — more at SOUR] **:** any of various plants with sour juice: as **a :** [1]DOCK 1 **b :** WOOD SORREL

sorrel tree *n* **:** SOURWOOD

sor·ri·ly \'sär-ə-lē, 'sȯr-\ *adv* **:** in a sorry manner

sor·ri·ness \'sär-ē-nəs, 'sȯr-\ *n* **:** the quality or state of being sorry

[1]**sor·row** \'sär-(,)ō, 'sȯr-, -ə(-w)\ *n* [ME *sorow*, fr. OE *sorg*; akin to OHG *sorga* sorrow, OSlav *sraga* sickness] **1 a :** sadness or anguish due to loss (as of something loved) **b :** a cause of grief or sadness **2 :** CONTRITION, REPENTANCE **3 :** a display of grief or sadness

syn SORROW, GRIEF, ANGUISH, WOE, REGRET mean distress of mind. SORROW implies a sense of loss or a sense of guilt and remorse; GRIEF implies poignant sorrow for an immediate cause; ANGUISH suggests torturing grief or dread; WOE is deep or inconsolable grief or misery; REGRET implies pain caused by deep disappointment, fruitless longing, or unavailing remorse

[2]**sorrow** *vi* **:** to feel or express sorrow **:** GRIEVE — **sor·row·er** \-ə-wər\ *n*

sor·row·ful \-ō-fəl, -ə-fəl\ *adj* **1 :** full of or marked by sorrow **2 :** expressive of or inducing sorrow — **sor·row·ful·ly** \-fə-lē\ *adv* — **sor·row·ful·ness** *n*

sor·ry \'sär-ē, 'sȯr-\ *adj* [ME *sory*, fr. OE *sārig*, fr. *sār* sore] **1 :** feeling sorrow, regret, or penitence **2 :** MOURNFUL, SAD **3 :** inspiring sorrow, pity, scorn, or ridicule **:** WRETCHED **syn** see CONTEMPTIBLE

[1]**sort** \'sȯ(ə)rt\ *n* [ME, fr. MF *sorte*, prob. fr. ML *sort-, sors*, fr. L, chance, lot] **1 :** a group set up on the basis of any characteristic in common **:** CLASS, KIND **2 :** a number of things used together **:** SET, SUIT **3 a :** method or manner of acting **:** WAY, MANNER **b :** CHARACTER, NATURE ⟨people of an evil ~⟩ **4 a :** a letter or character that is one element of a font **b :** a character or piece of type that is not part of a regular font **syn** see TYPE — **after a sort :** in a rough or haphazard way — **of sorts** *or* **of a sort :** of an inconsequential or mediocre quality ⟨a poet *of sorts*⟩ — **out of sorts :** out of temper **:** VEXED, DISTURBED

[2]**sort** *vt* **1** *obs* **:** to select as of a certain sort **:** CHOOSE **2** *obs* **:** ALLOT **3 :** to put in a certain place or rank according to kind, class, or nature ⟨~ mail⟩ **:** arrange according to characteristics **:** CLASSIFY ⟨~ out colors⟩ **4** *chiefly Scot* **a :** to put to rights **:** put in order **b :** to put to rights morally by punishing or scolding **~** *vi* **1 :** to join or associate with others esp. of the same kind ⟨~ with thieves⟩ **2** *archaic* **:** SUIT, HARMONIZE, AGREE — **sort·able** \'sȯrt-ə-bəl\ *adj* — **sort·er** *n*

sor·tie \'sȯrt-ē, sȯr-'tē\ *n* [F, fr. MF, fr. *sortir* to escape] **1 :** a sudden issuing of troops from a defensive position against the enemy **:** SALLY **2 :** one mission or attack by a single plane — **sortie** *vi*

sor·ti·lege \'sȯrt-ᵊl-ij, -,ej\ *n* [ME, fr. ML *sortilegium*, fr. L *sortilegus* foretelling, fr. *sort-, sors* lot + *-i-* + *legere* to gather — more at LEGEND] **1 :** divination by lots **2 :** SORCERY, ENCHANTMENT

sor·ti·tion \sȯr-'tish-ən\ *n* [L *sortition-, sortitio*, fr. *sortitus*, pp. of *sortiri* to cast or draw lots, fr. *sort-, sors* lot] **:** the act or an instance of casting lots

sort of \,sȯrt-ə(v), -ər\ *adv* **:** to a moderate degree **:** RATHER

so·rus \'sōr-əs, 'sȯr-\ *n, pl* **so·ri** \'sō(ə)r-,ī, 'sȯ(ə)r-, -(,)ē\ [NL, fr. Gk *sōros* heap; akin to L *tumēre* to swell — more at THUMB] **:** a cluster of plant reproductive bodies (as sporangia on a fern frond, spores on the host plant of a fungus, or gemmae on a lichen thallus)

SOS \,es-(,)ō-'es, ,es-ə-'wes\ *n* **1 :** an internationally recognized signal of distress in radio code . . . – – – . . . used esp. by ships calling for help **2 :** a call or request for help or rescue

[1]**so–so** \'sō-'sō\ *adv* **:** TOLERABLY, PASSABLY

[2]**so–so** *adj* **:** neither very good nor very bad **:** MIDDLING

[1]**so·ste·nu·to** \,sō-stə-'nüt-(,)ō, ,sō-\ *adv (or adj)* [It, fr. pp. of *sostenere* to sustain, fr. L *sustinēre*] **:** SUSTAINED, PROLONGED — used as a direction in music

[2]**sostenuto** *n* **:** a movement or passage whose notes are markedly prolonged

sot \'sät\ *n* [ME, fool, fr. OE *sott*] **:** a habitual drunkard

so·te·ri·o·log·i·cal \sō-,tir-ē-ə-'läj-i-kəl\ *adj* **:** of or relating to soteriology

so·te·ri·ol·o·gy \sō-,tir-ē-'äl-ə-jē\ *n* [Gk *sōtērion* salvation (fr. *sōtēr* savior, fr. *sōzein* to save) + E *-logy*; akin to Gk *sōma* body — more at SOMAT-] **:** theology dealing with salvation esp. as effected by Jesus Christ

So·thic \'sō-thik, 'säth-ik\ *adj* **1 :** of, relating to, or named from Sothis **2 :** relating to the ancient Egyptian year of 365¼ days or to the Sothic cycle

Sothic cycle *n* **:** a cycle of 1460 Sothic years in the Egyptian calendar

So·this \'sō-thəs\ *n* [Gk *Sōthis*] **:** SIRIUS

so·tol \sō-'tōl\ *n* [AmerSp, fr. Nahuatl *tzotolli*] **:** a plant (genus *Dasylirion*) of the lily family of the southwestern U.S. and Mexico resembling a yucca

sot·ted \'sät-əd\ *adj* [ME, short for *assotted*, pp. of *assotten* to be a fool, fr. OF *assoter* to treat as a fool, fr. *a-* (fr. L *ad-*) + *sot* fool] **:** BESOTTED

sot·tish \'sät-ish\ *adj* **:** resembling a sot **:** STUPID; *also* **:** DRUNKEN — **sot·tish·ly** *adv* — **sot·tish·ness** *n*

sot·to vo·ce \,sät-ō-'vō-chē\ *adv (or adj)* [It *sottovoce*, lit., under the voice] **1 :** under the breath **:** in an undertone; *also* **:** PRIVATELY **2 :** very softly ⟨play the finale *sotto voce*⟩

sou \'sü\ *n, pl* **sous** \'süz\ [F, fr. OF *sol*, fr. LL *solidus* solidus] **1 :** [2]SOL **2 :** a 5-centime piece

sou·a·ri nut \sü-'är-ē-\ *n* [F *saouari* tree producing souari nuts, fr. Galibi *sawarra*] **:** the large edible oil-yielding seed of a So. American tree (genus *Caryocar* of the family Caryocaraceae, esp. *C. nuciferum*)

sou·bise \sü-'bēz\ *n* [F, fr. Charles de Rohan, Prince de *Soubise* †1787 F nobleman] **:** a white or brown sauce containing onions or onion purée

sou·brette \sü-'bret\ *n* [F, fr. Prov *soubreto*, fem. of *soubret* coy, fr. *soubra* to surmount, exceed, fr. L *superare* — more at SUPERABLE] **1 a :** a coquettish maid or frivolous young woman in comedies **b :** an actress who plays such a part **2 :** a soprano who sings supporting roles in comic opera

sou·bri·quet \'sō-, ,sō-\ *var of* SOBRIQUET

sou·chong \'sü-,chȯŋ, -,shȯŋ\ *n* [Chin (Pek) *hsiao³ chung³*, lit., small sort] **:** a large-leafed black tea esp. from China

[1]**souf·flé** \sü-'flā\ *n* [F, fr. *soufflé*, pp. of *souffler* to blow, puff up, fr. L *sufflare*, fr. *sub-* + *flare* to blow — more at BLOW] **:** an entrée or dessert made with a white sauce, egg yolks and stiffly whipped egg whites, seasonings, and added ingredients

[2]**soufflé** *or* **souf·fléed** \-'flād\ *adj* **:** puffed by or in cooking

sough \'saù, 'səf\ *vi* [ME *swoughen*, fr. OE *swōgan*; akin to Goth *gaswogjan* to groan, Lith *svagėti* to sound] **:** to make a moaning or sighing sound — **sough** *n*

sought *past of* SEEK

[1]**soul** \'sōl\ *n* [ME *soule*, fr. OE *sāwol*; akin to OHG *sēula* soul] **1 :** the immaterial essence, animating principle, or actuating cause of an individual life **2 a :** the spiritual principle embodied in human beings, all rational and spiritual beings, or the universe **b** *cap, Christian Science* **:** [2]GOD b **3 :** a person's total self **4 a :** an active or essential part **b :** moving spirit **:** LEADER **5 a :** man's moral and emotional nature **b :** the quality that arouses emotion and sentiment **c :** spiritual or moral force **:** FERVOR **6 :** PERSON **7 :** EXEMPLIFICATION, PERSONIFICATION **8 :** a quality that is essential to or characteristic of the cultural heritage of black Americans; *also* **:** the sum of such qualities

syn SOUL, SPIRIT mean an immaterial entity distinguishable from and superior to the body. SOUL is preferred when the emphasis is on the entity having functions, responsibilities, aspects, or a destiny, or when its connection with the body is in view; SPIRIT may stress an opposition or antagonism to the material or corporeal; it is preferred when the stress is on the quality, movement, or activity of that entity

[2]**soul** *adj* **:** having soul ⟨~ food⟩ ⟨~ music⟩

souled \'sōld\ *adj* **:** having a soul **:** possessing soul and feeling — usu. used in combination ⟨whole-*souled* repentance⟩

soul·ful \-fəl\ *adj* **:** full of or expressing feeling or emotion — **soul·ful·ly** \-fə-lē\ *adv* — **soul·ful·ness** *n*

soul·less \'sōl-ləs\ *adj* **:** having no soul or no greatness or nobleness of mind or feeling — **soul·less·ly** *adv*

soul mate *n* **:** one of two persons esp. of opposite sex temperamentally suited to each other **:** AFFINITY; *often* **:** a partner in an illicit relationship **:** LOVER, MISTRESS

soul–search·ing \'sōl-,sər-chiŋ\ *n* **:** examination of one's conscience esp. with regard to motives and values

sou mar·kee \,sü-(,)mär-'kē\ *n* [F *sou marqué*, lit., marked sou] **1 :** a small 18th century French coin issued for the colonies and formerly circulating in the West Indies and on the No. American mainland **2 :** something of little or no value **:** CONTINENTAL

[1]**sound** \'saùnd\ *adj* [ME, fr. OE *gesund*; akin to OHG *gisunt* healthy] **1 a :** free from injury or disease **:** ROBUST **b :** free from flaw, defect, or decay ⟨~ timber⟩ **2 :** SOLID, FIRM; *also* **:** STABLE **3 a :** free from error, fallacy, or misapprehension ⟨~ reasoning⟩ **b :** ACCURATE, PRECISE ⟨~ scholarship⟩ **c :** LEGAL, VALID **d :** agreeing with accepted views **:** ORTHODOX **4 a :** THOROUGH **b :** deep and undisturbed ⟨a ~ sleep⟩ **c :** HARD, SEVERE **5 :** showing good judgment or sense **syn** see HEALTHY, VALID — **sound·ly** \'saùn-(d)lē\ *adv* — **sound·ness** \'saùn(d)-nəs\ *n*

[2]**sound** *adv* **:** SOUNDLY ⟨~ asleep⟩

[3]**sound** *n* [ME *soun*, fr. OF *son*, fr. L *sonus*; akin to OE *swinn* melody, L *sonare* to sound, Skt *svanati* it sounds] **1 a :** the sensation perceived by the sense of hearing **b :** a particular auditory impression **:** NOISE, TONE **c :** mechanical radiant energy that is transmitted by longitudinal pressure waves in air or other material medium and is the objective cause of hearing **2 a :** a speech sound ⟨a peculiar *r-sound*⟩ **b :** value in terms of speech sounds ⟨*-cher* of *teacher* and *-ture* of *creature* have the same ~⟩ **3** *archaic* **:** RUMOR, FAME **4 a :** meaningless noise **b** *obs* **:** MEANING **c :** impression conveyed **:** IMPORT **5 :** hearing distance **:** EARSHOT **6 :** recorded auditory material

[4]**sound** *vi* **1 a :** to make a sound **b :** RESOUND **c :** to give a summons by sound **2 :** to make or convey an impression **:** SEEM ⟨~s incredible⟩ **~** *vt* **1 :** to cause to sound **2 :** to put into words **:** VOICE **3 a :** to make known **:** PROCLAIM **b :** to order, signal, or indicate by a sound **4 :** to examine by causing to emit sounds ⟨~ the lungs⟩ — **sound·able** \'saùn-də-bəl\ *adj*

[5]**sound** *n* [ME, fr. OE *sund* swimming, sea & ON *sund* swimming, strait; akin to OE *swimman* to swim] **1 a :** a long broad inlet of the ocean generally parallel to the coast **b :** a long passage of water connecting two larger bodies (as a sea with the ocean) or passing between a mainland and an island **2 :** the air bladder of a fish

[6]**sound** *vb* [ME *sounden*, fr. MF *sonder*, fr. *sonde* sounding line, prob. of Gmc origin; akin to OE *sundlīne* sounding line, *sund* sea] *vt* **1 :** to measure the depth of **:** FATHOM **2 :** to try to find out the views or intentions of **:** PROBE **3 :** to explore or examine (a body cavity) with a sound **~** *vi* **1 a :** to ascertain the depth of water esp. with a sounding line **b :** to look into or investigate the possibility **2 :** to dive down suddenly — used of a fish or whale

[7]**sound** *n* [F *sonde*, fr. MF, lit., sounding line] **:** an elongated instrument for exploring surgically body cavities

sound barrier n : SONIC BARRIER
sound·board \'saun(d)-,bō(ə)rd, -,bȯ(ə)rd\ n 1 : a thin resonant board (as the belly of a violin) so placed in an instrument as to reinforce its tones by sympathetic vibration 2 : SOUNDING BOARD 1a
sound bow n : the thick part of a bell against which the clapper strikes
sound box n 1 : a device in a phonograph using vibrating needle and thin diaphragm to convert phonograph record groove undulations into sound 2 : a hollow chamber in a musical instrument for increasing its sonority
sound camera n : a motion-picture camera equipped to record sound simultaneously with the picture on a single film
sound effects n pl : effects that are imitative of sounds called for in the script of a play, radio or television program, or motion picture and are produced by various means (as phonograph records, musical instruments, or mechanical devices)
sound·er \'saun-dər\ n : one that sounds; specif : a device for making soundings
¹**sound·ing** \'saun-diŋ\ n 1 a : measurement by sounding b : the depth so ascertained c pl : a place or part of a body of water where a hand sounding line will reach bottom 2 : measurement of atmospheric conditions at various heights 3 : a probe, test, or sampling of opinion or intention
²**sounding** adj 1 : RESONANT, SONOROUS 2 : HIGH-SOUNDING — **sound·ing·ly** \-liŋ-lē\ adv
sounding board n 1 a : a structure behind or over a pulpit, rostrum, or platform to give distinctness and sonority to sound uttered from it b : a device or agency that helps propagate opinions or utterances 2 : SOUNDBOARD 1
sounding line n : a line, wire, or cord weighted at one end for sounding
sounding rocket n : a rocket used to obtain information concerning atmospheric conditions at various altitudes
¹**sound·less** \'saun-(d)ləs\ adj [⁶sound] : incapable of being sounded : UNFATHOMABLE
²**soundless** adj [³sound] : making no sound : SILENT — **sound·less·ly** adv

sounding line : 1, 4, 6, 8, 9, 11, 12, 14, 16, 18, 19, 21, 22, 23, 24, deeps; 2, 3, 5, 7, 10, 13, 15, 17, 20, 25, marks

sound motion picture n : a motion picture accompanied by synchronized recorded sound
sound off vi 1 : to play three chords before and after marching up and down a line of troops during a ceremonial parade or formal guard mount 2 : to count cadence while marching 3 a : to speak up in a loud voice b : to voice one's opinions freely and vigorously
¹**sound·proof** \'saun(d)-'prüf\ adj : impervious to sound ⟨~ room⟩
²**soundproof** vt : to insulate so as to obstruct the passage of sound
sound track n : the area on a motion-picture film that carries the sound record
sound truck n : a truck equipped with a loudspeaker
sound wave n 1 : ³SOUND 1b 2 pl : longitudinal pressure waves in any material medium regardless of whether they constitute audible sound ⟨earthquake waves and ultrasonic waves are sometimes called sound waves⟩
¹**soup** \'süp\ n [F soupe sop, soup, of Gmc origin; akin to ON soppa soup, OE sopp sop] 1 : a liquid food esp. with a meat, fish, or vegetable stock as a base and often containing pieces of solid food 2 : something having or suggesting the consistency of soup (as a heavy fog or nitroglycerine) 3 : an unfortunate predicament ⟨in the ~⟩
²**soup** vt [E slang soup (dope injected into a racehorse to change its speed)] : to increase the power or efficiency of ⟨~ up an engine⟩ — **souped–up** \'süp-'təp\ adj
soup·çon \süp-'sōⁿ, 'süp-,sän\ n [F, lit., suspicion, fr. (assumed) VL suspection-, suspectio, fr. L suspectus, pp. of suspicere to suspect — more at SUSPECT] : a little bit : TRACE
soup kitchen n : an establishment dispensing soup, bread, and other minimum dietary essentials to the needy
soupy \'sü-pē\ adj 1 : having the consistency of soup 2 : densely foggy or cloudy
¹**sour** \'sau(ə)r\ adj [ME, fr. OE sūr; akin to OHG sūr sour, Lith suras salty] 1 : causing or characterized by the basic taste sensation produced chiefly by acids 2 a (1) : having the acid taste or smell of or as if of fermentation : TURNED ⟨~ milk⟩ (2) : of or relating to fermentation b : smelling or tasting of decay : RANCID, ROTTEN ⟨~ breath⟩ c (1) : BAD, WRONG ⟨a project gone ~⟩ (2) : DISENCHANTED, HOSTILE ⟨went ~ on Marxism⟩ 3 a : UNPLEASANT, DISTASTEFUL b : CROSS, ACID 4 : acid in reaction — used of soil 5 a : containing malodorous sulfur compounds — used esp. of petroleum products b : JARRING, POOR ⟨play a ~ note⟩ — **sour·ish** \'sau(ə)r-ish\ adj — **sour·ly** adv — **sour·ness** n
syn ACID, ACIDULOUS, TART: SOUR usu. applies to that which has lost its natural sweetness or freshness through fermentation or decay; ACID applies to what has a biting taste naturally or normally; ACIDULOUS implies a slight acidity; TART suggests a sharp but usu. agreeable acidity
²**sour** n 1 a : something sour b : the primary taste sensation produced by acid stimuli 2 : a cocktail made with spirituous liquor, lemon or lime juice, sugar, and sometimes soda water
³**sour** vi : to become sour ~ vt : to make sour
sour ball n : a spherical piece of hard candy having a tart flavor
source \'sō(ə)rs, 'sȯ(ə)rs\ n [ME sours, fr. MF sors, sourse, fr. OF, fr. pp. of sourdre to rise, spring forth, fr. L surgere — more at SURGE] 1 a : the point of origin of a stream of water : FOUNTAINHEAD b archaic : SPRING, FOUNT 2 a : a generative force : CAUSE b (1) : a point of origin (2) : one that initiates : AUTHOR; also : PROTOTYPE, MODEL (3) : one that supplies information 3 a : firsthand document or primary reference work syn see ORIGIN
source book n : a fundamental document or record (as of history, literature, art, or religion) upon which subsequent writings, compositions, opinions, beliefs, or practices are based; also : a collection of such documents

sour cherry n : a round-headed Eurasian tree (Prunus cerasus) widely grown for its bright red to almost black soft-fleshed acid fruits; also : its fruit
sour·dine \su̇(ə)r-'dēn\ n [F, fr. It sordina, fr. sordo silent, dull-sounding, deaf, fr. L surdus — more at SURD] : any of several obsolete musical instruments distinguished by their low or soft tone
sour·dough \'sau̇(ə)r-,dō\ n 1 : a leaven of dough in which fermentation is active 2 [fr. the use of sourdough for making bread in prospectors' camps] : a veteran inhabitant and esp. an old-time prospector of Alaska or northwestern Canada
sour grapes n pl [fr. the fable ascribed to Aesop of the fox who after finding himself unable to reach some grapes he had desired disparaged them as sour] : disparagement of something that has proven unattainable
sour gum n : any of several American trees (genus Nyssa); esp : a timber tree (N. sylvatica) of the eastern U.S. with blue-black fruits and close-grained grayish wood — called also black gum
sour mash n : grain mash for brewing or distilling whose initial acidity has been adjusted to optimum condition for yeast fermentation by mash from a previous run
sour orange n : a tree (Citrus aurantium) much used as an understock in grafting citrus; also : its bitter fruit
sour salt n : CITRIC ACID
sour·sop \'sau̇(ə)r-,säp\ n : a small tropical American tree (Annona muricata) of the custard-apple family; also : its large edible fruit with fleshy spines and a slightly acid fibrous pulp
sour·wood \-,wu̇d\ n : a small tree (Oxydendrum arboreum) of the heath family with white flowers and sour-tasting leaves
sou·sa·phone \'sü-zə-,fōn, 'sü-sə-\ n [John P. Sousa †1932 Am bandmaster and composer] : a large circular tuba with a flaring adjustable bell
¹**souse** \'saus\ vb [ME sousen, fr. MF souz, souce pickling solution, of Gmc origin; akin to OHG sulza brine, OE sealt salt] vt 1 : PICKLE 2 a : to plunge in liquid : IMMERSE b : DRENCH, SATURATE 3 : to make drunk : INEBRIATE ~ vi : to become immersed or drenched
²**souse** n 1 : something pickled; esp : seasoned and chopped pork trimmings, fish, or shellfish 2 : an act of sousing : WETTING 3 a : an habitual drunkard b : a drinking spree : BINGE
³**souse** n [ME souce, alter. of sours, fr. MF sourse, fr. sourdre to rise] obs : the start of a bird's flight or the stoop of a hawk intercepting it
⁴**souse** vi, archaic : to swoop down : PLUNGE ~ vt, archaic : to knock down by swooping upon
sou·tache \sü-'tash\ n [F, fr. It sottana, lit., undergarment, fr. fem. of sottano being underneath, fr. ML subtanus, fr. L subtus underneath; akin to L sub under — more at UP] : a narrow braid with herringbone pattern used as trimming
sou·tane \sü-'tän, -'tan\ n [F, fr. It sottana, lit., undergarment, fr. fem. of sottano being underneath, fr. ML subtanus, fr. L subtus underneath; akin to L sub under — more at UP] : a cassock with buttons down the front worn esp. by Roman Catholic secular clergy
sou·ter \'süt-ər\ n [ME, fr. OE sūtere, fr. L sutor, pp. of suere to sew — more at SEW] chiefly Scot : SHOEMAKER
¹**south** \'sau̇th\ adv [ME, fr. OE sūth; akin to OHG sund- south, OE sunne sun] 1 : to, toward, or in the south : SOUTHWARD
²**south** adj 1 : situated toward or at the south ⟨the ~ entrance⟩ 2 : coming from the south ⟨~ wind⟩
³**south** n 1 a : the direction of the south terrestrial pole : the direction to the right of one facing east b : the cardinal point directly opposite to north 2 cap : regions or countries lying to the south of a specified or implied point of orientation 3 : the right side of a church looking toward the altar from the nave
South African n : a native or inhabitant of the Republic of South Africa; esp : AFRIKANER — **South African** adj
south·bound \'sau̇th-,bau̇nd\ adj : traveling or headed south
south by east : a compass point that is one point east of due south : S11°15′E
south by west : a compass point that is one point west of due south : S11°15′W
South·down \'sau̇th-,dau̇n\ n [South Downs, range of hills in England] : any of an English breed of small medium-wooled hornless mutton-type sheep
¹**south·east** \sau̇-'thēst, naut (')sau̇-'ēst\ adv : to, toward, or in the southeast
²**southeast** n 1 a : the general direction between south and east b : the point midway between the cardinal points south and east 2 cap : regions or countries lying to the southeast of a specified or implied point of orientation
³**southeast** adj 1 : coming from the southeast ⟨~ wind⟩ 2 : situated toward or at the southeast ⟨~ corner⟩
southeast by east : a compass point that is one point east of due southeast : S56°15′E
southeast by south : a compass point that is one point south of due southeast : S33°45′E
south·east·er \sau̇-'thē-stər, sau̇-'ē-\ n : a storm, strong wind, or gale coming from the southeast
south·east·er·ly \-stər-lē\ adv (or adj) [²southeast + -erly (as in easterly)] 1 : from the southeast 2 : toward the southeast
south·east·ern \-stərn\ adj [²southeast + -ern (as in eastern)] 1 often cap : of, relating to, or characteristic of a region conventionally designated southeast 2 : lying toward or coming from the southeast — **south·east·ern·most** \-,mōst\ adj
South·east·ern·er \-stə(r)-nər\ n : a native or inhabitant of the Southeast; esp : a native or resident of the southeastern part of the U.S.
¹**south·east·ward** \sau̇-'thēs-twərd, sau̇-'ēs-\ adv (or adj) : toward the southeast
²**southeastward** n : SOUTHEAST
south·east·wards \-twərdz\ adv : SOUTHEASTWARD
south·er \'sau̇-thər\ n : a strong southerly wind
south·er·ly \'səth-ər-lē\ adv (or adj) [³south + -erly (as in easterly)] 1 : from the south 2 : toward the south
south·ern \'səth-ərn\ adj [ME southern, southren, fr. OE sūtherne; akin to OHG sundrōni southern, OE sūth south] 1 often cap : of, relating to, or characteristic of a region conventionally designated South 2 a : lying toward or to the south b : coming from the south — **south·ern·most** \-,mōst\ adj

Southern *n* **:** the dialect of English spoken in most of the Chesapeake Bay area, the coastal plain and the greater part of the upland plateau in Virginia, North Carolina, South Carolina, and Georgia, and the Gulf states at least as far west as the valley of the Brazos in Texas

Southern Cross *n* **:** four bright stars in the southern hemisphere, situated as if at the extremities of a Latin cross; *also* **:** the constellation of which the four stars above are the brightest

Southern Crown *n* **:** CORONA AUSTRALIS

Southern English *n* **1 :** the English spoken esp. by cultivated people native to or educated in the South of England **2 :** SOUTHERN

South·ern·er \ˈsəth-ə(r)-nər\ *n* **:** a native or inhabitant of the South; *esp* **:** a native or resident of the southern part of the U.S.

south·ern·ism \ˈsəth-ər-ˌniz-əm\ *n* **1 :** a locution or pronunciation characteristic of the southern U.S. **2 :** an attitude or trait characteristic of the South or Southerners esp. in the U.S.

southern lights *n pl* **:** AURORA AUSTRALIS

south·ern·ly \ˈsəth-ərn-lē\ *adj* **1 :** coming from the south **2 :** headed south

south·ern·wood \-ˌwu̇d\ *n* **:** a shrubby fragrant European wormwood (*Artemisia abrotanum*) with bitter foliage

south·ing \ˈsau̇-thiŋ, -thiŋ\ *n* **1 :** difference in latitude to the south from the last preceding point of reckoning **2 :** southerly progress

south·land \ˈsau̇th-ˌland, -lənd\ *n, often cap* **:** land in the south **:** the south of a country

south·paw \-(ˌ)pȯ\ *n* **:** LEFT-HANDER; *specif* **:** a left-handed baseball pitcher — **southpaw** *adj*

south pole *n* **1 a** *often cap S & P* **:** the southernmost point of the earth **b :** the zenith of the heavens as viewed from the south terrestrial pole **2** *of a magnet* **:** the pole that points toward the south

[1]**South·ron** \ˈsəth-rən\ *adj* [ME (Sc), fr. ME *southren*] *chiefly Scot* **:** SOUTHERN; *specif* **:** ENGLISH

[2]**Southron** *n* **:** SOUTHERNER: as **a** *chiefly Scot* **:** ENGLISHMAN **b** *chiefly South* **:** a native or inhabitant of the southern states of the U. S.

south–southeast *n* **:** a compass point two points east of due south **:** S22°30′E

south–southwest *n* **:** a compass point two points west of due south **:** S22°30′W

[1]**south·ward** \ˈsau̇th-wərd\ *adv (or adj)* **:** toward the south

[2]**southward** *n* **:** southward direction or part ⟨sail to the ~⟩

south·wards \-wərdz\ *adv* **:** SOUTHWARD

[1]**south·west** \sau̇th-ˈwest, *naut* (ˈ)sau̇-ˈwest\ *adv* **:** to, toward, or in the southwest

[2]**southwest** *n* **1 a :** the general direction between south and west **b :** the point of the compass midway between the cardinal points south and west **2** *cap* **:** regions or countries lying to the southwest of a specified or implied point of orientation **3 :** the southwest wind

[3]**southwest** *adj* **1 :** coming from the southwest ⟨a ~ wind⟩ **2 :** situated toward or at the southwest

southwest by south : a compass point that is one point south of due southwest **:** S33° 45′W

southwest by west : a compass point that is one point west of due southwest **:** S56° 15′W

south·west·er \sau̇(th)-ˈwes-tər\ *n* **:** a storm or gale from the southwest

south·west·er·ly \-tər-lē\ *adv (or adj)* [[2]*southwest* + *-erly* (as in *westerly*)] **1 :** from the southwest **2 :** toward the southwest

south·west·ern \-tərn\ *adj* [[2]*southwest* + *-ern* (as in *western*)] **1** *often cap* **:** of, relating to, or characteristic of a region conventionally designated Southwest **2 :** lying toward or coming from the southwest — **south·west·ern·most** \-ˌmōst\ *adj*

South·west·ern·er \-tə(r)-nər\ *n* **:** a native or inhabitant of the Southwest; *esp* **:** a native or resident of the southwestern U.S.

[1]**south·west·ward** \sau̇(th)-ˈwes-twərd\ *adv (or adj)* **:** toward the southwest

[2]**southwestward** *n* **:** SOUTHWEST

south·west·wards \-twərdz\ *adv* **:** SOUTHWESTWARD

sou·ve·nir \ˈsü-və-ˌni(ə)r, ˌsü-və-ˈ\ *n* [F, lit. act of remembering, fr. MF, fr. (*se*) *souvenir* to remember, fr. L *subvenire* to come up, come to mind] **:** something that serves as a reminder **:** MEMENTO

souvenir sheet *n* **:** a block or set of postage stamps or a single stamp printed on a single sheet of paper without gum or perforations and with margins containing lettering or design that identifies some notable event being commemorated

sou'·west·er \sau̇-ˈwes-tər\ *n* **1 :** SOUTHWESTER **2 a :** a long oilskin coat worn esp. at sea during stormy weather **b :** a waterproof hat with wide slanting brim longer in back than in front

[1]**sov·er·eign** *also* **sov·ran** \ˈsäv-(ə-)rən, ˈsäv-ərn, ˈsəv-\ *n* [ME *soverain*, fr. OF, fr. *soverain*, adj.] **1 a :** one possessing or held to possess sovereignty **b :** one that exercises supreme authority within a limited sphere **c :** an acknowledged leader **:** ARBITER **2 :** a gold coin of Great Britain containing 113 grains of fine gold

[2]**sovereign** *also* **sovran** *adj* [ME *soverain*, fr. MF, fr. OF, fr. (assumed) *VL superanus*, fr. L *super* over, above — more at OVER] **1 a :** possessed of supreme power ⟨~ ruler⟩ **b :** unlimited in extent **:** ABSOLUTE **c :** enjoying autonomy **:** INDEPENDENT ⟨a ~ state⟩ **2 a :** SUPREME, CHIEF ⟨~ virtue⟩ **b :** superlative in quality **:** EXCELLENT **c :** having generalized curative powers **:** POTENT ⟨~ remedy⟩ **d :** UNQUALIFIED, UNMITIGATED **e :** having undisputed ascendancy **:** PARAMOUNT **3 :** relating to, characteristic of, or befitting a sovereign **syn** see DOMINANT, FREE — **sov·er·eign·ly** *adv*

sov·er·eign·ty *also* **sov·ran·ty** \-tē\ *n* [ME *soverainte*, fr. MF *souveraineté*, fr. OF, fr. *soverain*] **1** *obs* **:** supreme excellence or an example of it ⟨of all complexions the cull'd ~ do meet . . . in her fair cheek —Shak.⟩ **2 a :** supreme power esp. over a body politic **:** DOMINION **b :** freedom from external control **:** AUTONOMY **3 :** one that is sovereign; *esp* **:** an autonomous state

so·vi·et \ˈsōv-ē-ˌet, ˈsäv-, -ē-ət\ *n* [Russ *sovet*] **1 :** an elected governmental council in a Communist country **2** *pl, cap* **a :** BOLSHEVIKS **b :** the people and esp. the political and military leaders of the U.S.S.R. — **soviet** *adj, often cap* — **so·vi·et·ism** \-ˌiz-əm\ *n, often cap*

so·vi·et·iza·tion \ˌsō-vē-ˌet-ə-ˈzā-shən, ˌsäv-, -ət-\ *n, often cap* **:** conversion to the Soviet system

so·vi·et·ize \-ˌīz\ *vt, often cap* **1 :** to bring under Soviet control **2 :** to force into conformity with Soviet cultural patterns or governmental policies

sov·khoz \säf-ˈkȯz, -ˈkȯs\ *n, pl* **sov·kho·zy** \-ˈkȯ-zē\ *or* **sov·khoz·es** [Russ, short for *sovetskoe khozyaĭstvo* soviet farm] **:** a state-owned farm of the U.S.S.R. paying wages to the workers — compare KOLKHOZ

[1]**sow** \ˈsau̇\ *n* [ME *sowe*, fr. OE *sugu*; akin to OE & OHG *sū* sow, L *sus* pig, swine, hog, Gk *hys*] **1 :** an adult female swine **2 a :** a channel that conducts molten metal to molds in a pig bed **b :** a mass of metal solidified in such a mold **:** INGOT

[2]**sow** \ˈsō\ *vb* **sowed; sown** \ˈsōn\ *or* **sowed; sow·ing** [ME *sowen*, fr. OE *sāwan*; akin to OHG *sāwen* to sow, L *serere*] *vi* **1 :** to plant seed for growth esp. by scattering **2 :** to set something in motion ~ *vt* **1 a :** to scatter (as seed) upon the earth for growth; *broadly* **:** PLANT 1a **b :** to strew with or as if with seed **c :** to introduce into a selected environment **:** IMPLANT **2 :** to set in motion **:** FOMENT ⟨~ suspicion⟩ **3 :** to spread abroad **:** DISPERSE

sow·bel·ly \ˈsau̇-ˌbel-ē\ *n* **:** fat salt pork or bacon

sow bug *n* **:** WOOD LOUSE 1

sow·ens \ˈsü-ənz, ˈsō-\ *n pl but sing or pl in constr* [ScGael *sūghan*] **:** porridge from oat husks and siftings

sow·er \ˈsō(-ə)r\ *n* **:** one that sows

sow thistle \ˈsau̇-\ *n* **:** any of a genus (*Sonchus*) of spiny weedy European composite herbs widely naturalized

sox *pl of* SOCK

soy \ˈsȯi\ *n* [Jap *shōyu*, fr. Chin (Cant) *shī-yaū*, lit., soybean oil] **1 :** an oriental brown liquid sauce made by subjecting beans (as soybeans) to long fermentation and to digestion in brine **2 :** SOYBEAN

soya \ˈsȯi-(y)ə\ *n* [D *soja*, fr. Jap *shōyu* soy] **:** SOYBEAN

soy·bean \ˈsȯi-ˈbēn, -ˌbēn\ *n* **:** a hairy annual Asiatic legume (*Glycine max*) widely grown for its oil-rich proteinaceous seeds and for forage and soil improvement; *also* **:** its seed

spa \ˈspä, ˈspȯ\ *n* [*Spa*, watering place in Belgium] **1 a :** a mineral spring **b :** a resort with mineral springs **2 :** a fashionable resort or hotel

[1]**space** \ˈspās\ *n, often attrib* [ME, fr. OF *espace*, fr. L *spatium* area, room, interval of space or time — more at SPEED] **1 :** a period of time; *also* **:** its duration **2 a :** a limited extent in one, two, or three dimensions **:** DISTANCE, AREA, VOLUME **b :** an extent set apart or available ⟨parking ~⟩ ⟨floor ~⟩ **3 :** one of the degrees between or above or below the lines of a musical staff **4 a :** a boundless three-dimensional extent in which objects and events occur and have relative position and direction **b :** physical space independent of what occupies it — called also *absolute space* **5 :** the region beyond the earth's atmosphere or beyond the solar system **6 a :** a blank area separating words or lines **b :** material used to produce such blank area; *specif* **:** a piece of type less than one en in width **7 :** a set of mathematical elements and esp. of abstractions of all the points on a line, in a plane, or in physical space **8 :** an interval in operation during which a telegraph key is not in contact **9 a :** LINAGE 1 **b :** broadcast time available esp. to advertisers **10 :** accommodations on a public vehicle

[2]**space** *vt* **:** to place at intervals or arrange with space between — often used with *out*

space charge *n* **:** an electric charge (as the electrons in the region near the filament of a vacuum tube) distributed throughout a three-dimensional region

space·craft \ˈspā-ˌskraft\ *n* **:** SPACESHIP

space·flight \ˈspās-ˌflīt\ *n* **:** flight beyond the earth's atmosphere

space heater *n* **:** a device for heating an enclosed space; *esp* **:** an often portable device that heats the space in which it is located and has no external heating ducts or connection to a chimney

space heating *n* **:** heating of spaces esp. for human comfort by any means (as fuel, electricity, or solar radiation) with the heater either within the space or external to it

space lattice *n* **:** the geometrical arrangement of the atoms in a crystal

space·less \ˈspā-sləs\ *adj* **1 :** having no limits **:** BOUNDLESS **2 :** occupying no space

space·man \ˈspā-ˌsman, -smən\ *n* **1 a :** one who travels outside the earth's atmosphere **b :** one engaged in any of various fields bearing on flight through outer space **2 :** a visitor to earth from outer space

space mark *n* **:** the symbol #

space medicine *n* **:** a branch of medicine that deals with the physiologic and biologic effects on the human body of rocket or jet flight beyond the earth's atmosphere

space·port \ˈspā-ˌspō(ə)rt, -ˌspȯ(ə)rt\ *n* **:** an installation for testing and launching rockets, missiles, and satellites

space·ship \ˈspās(h)-ˌship\ *n* **:** a vehicle designed to operate in free space outside the earth's atmosphere

space station *n* **:** a manned artificial satellite designed for a fixed orbit about the earth and to serve as a base (as for scientific observation) — called also *space platform*

space suit *n* **1 :** a suit with air supply and other provisions to make life in free space possible for its wearer **2 :** G SUIT

space–time \ˈspā-ˈstīm, ˈspā-ˌ\ *n* **1 :** a system of one temporal and three spatial coordinates by which any physical object or event can be located — called also *space-time continuum* **2 :** the whole or a portion of physical reality determinable by a four-dimensional coordinate system; *also* **:** the properties characteristic of such an order

space·ward \ˈspā-swərd\ *adv* **:** toward space

space writer *n* **:** a writer paid according to the space his matter fills in print

spa·cial *var of* SPATIAL

spac·ing *n* **1 :** an arrangement in space **2 a :** SPACE **b :** the distance between any two objects in a usu. regularly arranged series

spa·cious \ˈspā-shəs\ *adj* [ME, fr. MF *spacieux*, fr. L *spatiosus*, fr. *spatium* space, room] **1 :** vast or ample in extent **:** ROOMY ⟨a ~ residence⟩ **2 :** large or magnificent in scale **:** EXPANSIVE ⟨a more ~ and stimulating existence than the farm could offer —H.L.Mencken⟩ — **spa·cious·ly** *adv* — **spa·cious·ness** *n*

spac·is·tor \ˈspā-ˌsis-tər\ *n* [[1]*space* + *-istor* (as in *transistor*)] **:** a high frequency semiconductor amplifying device

spack·le \ˈspak-əl\ *vt* **spack·ling** \-(ə-)liŋ\ [*Spackle*] **:** to apply Spackle paste to

Spackle *trademark* — used for a powder mixed with water to form a paste and used as a filler for cracks in a surface before painting

[1]**spade** \'spād\ *n* [ME, fr. OE *spadu;* akin to Gk *spathē* blade of a sword or oar, OHG *spān* chip of wood — more at SPOON] **1 :** a digging implement adapted for being pushed into the ground with the foot **2 :** a spade-shaped instrument — **spade·ful** \-,fu̇l\ *n* — **call a spade a spade 1 :** to call a thing by its right name however coarse **2 :** to speak frankly

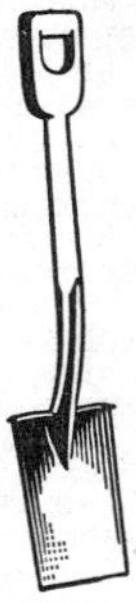
spade

[2]**spade** *vt* **:** to dig or pare off with a spade ~ *vi* **:** to use a spade — **spad·er** *n*

[3]**spade** *n* [It *spada* or Sp *espada* broad sword; both fr. L *spatha*, fr. Gk *spathē* blade] **:** a black figure ♠ on each playing card of one of the four suits; *also* **:** a card or the suit of cards marked with this figure

spade·fish \'spād-,fish\ *n* **1 :** a deep-bodied spiny-finned food fish (*Chaetodipterus faber*) found on the warmer western Atlantic **2 :** PADDLEFISH

spade·work \'spā-,dwərk\ *n* **1 :** work done with the spade **2 :** the hard plain preliminary drudgery in any undertaking

spa·dix \'spād-iks\ *n, pl* **spa·di·ces** \'spād-ə-,sēz, spā-'dī-(,)sēz\ [NL *spadic-, spadix*, fr. L, frond torn from a palm tree, fr. Gk *spadik-, spadix*, fr. *span* to draw, pull — more at SPAN] **:** a floral spike with a fleshy or succulent axis usu. enclosed in a spathe

spae \'spā\ *vt* [ME *span*, fr. ON *spā;* akin to OHG *spehōn* to watch, spy — more at SPY] *chiefly Scot* **:** FORETELL, PROPHESY

spa·ghet·ti \spə-'get-ē\ *n* [It, fr. pl. of *sphaghetto*, dim. of *spago* cord, string] **1 :** a dough made in solid strings of small diameter but larger than vermicelli **2 :** electrically insulating tubing typically of varnished cloth or of plastic for covering bare wire or holding insulated wires together

spa·gyr·ic \spə-'jir-ik\ *adj* [NL *spagiricus*] **:** ALCHEMIC

spa·hi \'spä-,hē\ *n* [MF, fr. Turk *sipahi*, fr. Per *sipāhī* cavalryman] **1 :** one of a corps of irregular Turkish cavalry **2 :** one of a corps of Algerian native cavalry in the French Army

spake \'spāk\ *archaic past of* SPEAK

[1]**spall** \'spȯl\ *n* [ME *spalle*] **:** a small fragment or chip esp. of stone

[2]**spall** *vt* **:** to break up or reduce by chipping with a hammer ~ *vi* **1 :** to break off chips, scales, or slabs **:** EXFOLIATE **2 :** to undergo spallation

spall·ation \spȯ-'lā-shən\ *n* [[2]*spall*] **:** a nuclear reaction in which light particles are ejected as the result of bombardment (as by high-energy protons)

spal·peen \spal-'pēn, spȯl-\ *n* [IrGael *spailpīn* migratory laborer, rascal] *chiefly Irish* **:** RASCAL

[1]**span** \'span\ *archaic past of* SPIN

[2]**span** *n* [ME, fr. OE *spann;* akin to OHG *spanna* span, MD *spannen* to stretch, hitch up, L *pendere* to weigh, Gk *span* to draw, pull] **1 :** the distance from the end of the thumb to the end of the little finger of a spread hand; *also* **:** an English unit of length equal to 9 inches **2 :** an extent, stretch, reach, or spread between two limits: as **a :** a limited space of time **b :** spread or extent between abutments or supports; *also* **:** the portion thus extended **3 :** the amount grasped in a single mental performance **4 :** the maximum distance laterally from tip to tip of an airplane

[3]**span** *vt* **spanned; span·ning 1 a :** to measure by or as if by the hand with fingers and thumb extended **b :** MEASURE **2 a :** to reach or extend across **b :** to place or construct a span over

[4]**span** *n* [D, fr. MD, fr. *spannen* to hitch up] **:** a pair of animals (as mules) usu. matched in looks and action and driven together

span·drel *or* **span·dril** \'span-drəl\ *n* [ME *spandrell*, fr. AF *spaundre*, fr. OF *espandre* to spread out — more at SPAWN] **1 :** the sometimes ornamented space between the right or left exterior curve of an arch and an enclosing right angle **2 :** the triangular space beneath the string of a stair

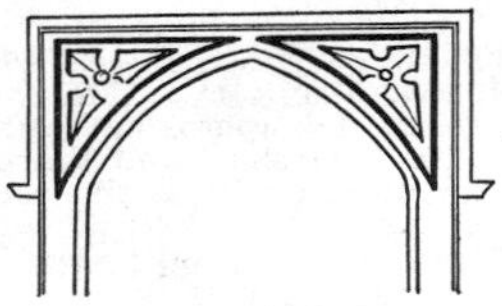
spandrels

spang \'spaŋ\ *adv* [Sc *spang* to leap, cast, bang] **1 :** COMPLETELY **2 :** EXACTLY, SQUARELY

[1]**span·gle** \'spaŋ-gəl\ *n* [ME *spangel*, dim. of *spang* shiny ornament, prob. of Scand origin; akin to ON *spöng* spangle; akin to OE *spang* buckle, MD *spannen* to stretch] **1 :** a small plate of shining metal or plastic used for ornamentation esp. on dresses **2 :** a small glittering object

[2]**spangle** *vb* **span·gling** \'spaŋ-g(ə-)liŋ\ *vt* **:** to set or sprinkle with or as if with spangles **:** adorn with small brilliant objects ~ *vi* **:** to glitter as if covered with spangles **:** SPARKLE

Span·iard \'span-yərd\ *n* [ME *Spaignard*, fr. MF *Espaignart*, fr. *Espaigne* Spain, fr. L *Hispania*] **:** a native or inhabitant of Spain

span·iel \'span-yəl *also* 'span-ᵊl\ *n* [ME *spaniell*, fr. MF *espaignol*, lit., Spaniard, fr. (assumed) VL *Hispaniolus*, fr. L *Hispania* Spain] **1 :** any of numerous small or medium-sized mostly short-legged dogs usu. having long wavy hair, feathered legs and tail, and large drooping ears **2 :** a servile person

Span·ish \'span-ish\ *n* [*Spanish*, adj., fr. ME *Spainish*, fr. *Spain*] **1 :** the Romance language of the largest part of Spain and of the countries colonized by Spaniards **2** *pl in constr* **:** the people of Spain — **Spanish** *adj*

Spanish American *n* **1 :** a native or inhabitant of one of the countries of America in which Spanish is the national language **2 :** a resident of the U.S. whose native language is Spanish and whose culture is of Spanish origin

Spanish bayonet *n* **:** any of several yuccas; *esp* **:** one (*Yucca aloifolia*) with a short trunk and rigid spine-tipped leaves

Spanish fly *n* **1 :** a green blister beetle (*Lytta vesicatoria*) of southern Europe **2 :** CANTHARIS 2

Spanish heel *n* **:** a high leather-covered wooden heel having a straight fore part

Spanish influenza *n* **:** pandemic influenza

Spanish mackerel *n* **:** any of various usu. large fishes (esp. genera *Scomberomorus* or *Trachurus*) chiefly of warm seas that resemble or are related to the common mackerel

Spanish moss *n* **:** an epiphytic plant (*Tillandsia usneoides*) of the pineapple family forming pendent tufts of grayish green filaments on trees in the southern U.S. and the West Indies

Spanish needles \'span-ish-, ,span-ish-'\ *n pl but sing or pl in constr* **:** a bur marigold (esp. *Bidens bipinnata*) of the eastern U.S.

Spanish omelet *n* **:** an omelet served with a sauce containing chopped green pepper, onion, and tomato

Spanish paprika *n* **1 :** PIMIENTO 1 **2 :** a paprika produced from pimientos usu. in Spain

Spanish rice *n* **:** rice cooked with onions, green pepper, and tomatoes

[1]**spank** \'spaŋk\ *vt* [imit.] **:** to strike esp. on the buttocks with the open hand — **spank** *n*

[2]**spank** *vi* [back-formation fr. *spanking*] **:** to move quickly, dashingly, or spiritedly

spank·er \'spaŋ-kər\ *n* [origin unknown] **1 :** the fore-and-aft sail on the mast nearest the stern of a square-rigged ship **2 :** the sail on the sternmost mast in a schooner of four or more masts

spank·ing \'spaŋ-kiŋ\ *adj* [origin unknown] **1 :** remarkable of its kind **2 :** being fresh and strong **:** BRISK

span·ner \'span-ər\ *n* [G, instrument for winding springs, fr. *spannen* to stretch; akin to MD *spannen* to stretch — more at SPAN] **1** *chiefly Brit* **:** WRENCH **2 :** a wrench that has a jaw or socket to fit a nut or head of a bolt, a pipe, or hose coupling; *esp* **:** one having a pin in its jaw to fit a hole or slot in an object

span–new \'span-'n(y)ü\ *adj* [ME, part trans. of ON *spānnȳr*, fr. *spānn* chip of wood + *nȳr* new] **:** BRAND-NEW

span·worm \'span-,wərm\ *n* [[3]*span*] **:** LOOPER 1

[1]**spar** \'spär\ *n* [ME *sparre;* akin to OE *spere* spear] **1 :** a stout pole **2 a :** a stout rounded wood or metal piece (as a mast, boom, gaff, or yard) used to support rigging **b** (1) **:** one of the main longitudinal members of the wing of an airplane that carry the ribs (2) **:** LONGERON

[2]**spar** *vi* **sparred; spar·ring** [prob. alter. of [2]*spur*] **1 :** to strike or fight with the feet or spurs like a gamecock **2 a :** BOX; *esp* **:** to gesture without landing a blow to draw one's opponent or create an opening **b :** to engage in a practice or exhibition bout of boxing **3 :** SKIRMISH, WRANGLE

[3]**spar** *n* **1 :** a movement of offense or defense in boxing **2 :** a sparring match or session

[4]**spar** *n* [LG; akin to OE *spærstān* gypsum, *spæren* of plaster] **:** any of various nonmetallic usu. cleavable and lustrous minerals

Spar \'spär\ *n* [*S*emper *Par*atus, motto of the U.S. Coast Guard, fr. NL, always ready] **:** a member of the women's reserve of the U.S. Coast Guard

spar·a·ble \'spar-ə-bəl\ *n* [alter. of earlier *sparrowbill*] **:** a small headless nail used by shoemakers to protect shoe soles against wear

[1]**spare** \'spa(ə)r, 'spe(ə)r\ *vb* [ME *sparen*, fr. OE *sparian;* akin to OHG *sparōn* to spare, OE *spær*, adj., spare] *vt* **1 :** to forbear to destroy, punish, or harm **2 :** to refrain from attacking or reprimanding with necessary or salutary severity **3 :** to relieve of the necessity of doing or undergoing something **:** EXEMPT **4 :** to refrain from **:** AVOID **5 :** to use frugally **6 a :** to give up as not strictly needed **b :** to have left over or as margin ⟨time to ~⟩ ~ *vi* **1 :** to be frugal **2 :** to refrain from doing harm **:** be lenient — **spar·er** *n*

[2]**spare** *adj* [ME, fr. OE *spær;* akin to OSlav *sporŭ* abundant, OE *spēd* prosperity — more at SPEED] **1 :** not being used; *esp* **:** held for emergency use **2 :** being over and above what is needed **:** SUPERFLUOUS **3 :** not liberal or profuse **:** SPARING **4 :** somewhat thin **5 :** not abundant or plentiful **:** SCANTY **syn** see LEAN, MEAGER — **spare·ly** *adv* — **spare·ness** *n*

[3]**spare** *n* **1 a :** a spare tire **b :** one duplicate kept in reserve **2 :** the knocking down of all 10 pins with the first 2 bowls of a frame in bowling

spare·able \'spar-ə-bəl, 'sper-\ *adj* **:** that can be spared

spare·ribs \'spa(ə)r-,(r)ibz, 'spe(ə)r-, -əbz\ *n pl* [by folk etymology fr. LG *ribbesper* pickled pork ribs roasted on a spit, fr. MLG, fr. *ribbe* rib + *sper* spear, spit] **:** a cut of pork ribs separated from the bacon strip

sparge \'spärj\ *vt* [prob. fr. MF *espargier*, fr. L *spargere* to scatter] **1 :** SPRINKLE, BESPATTER; *esp* **:** SPRAY **2 :** to agitate (a liquid) by means of compressed air or gas entering through a sparger — **sparge** *n* — **sparg·er** *n*

spar·id \'spar-əd, 'sper-\ *adj* [deriv. of Gk *sparos* gilthead — more at SPEAR] **:** of or relating to a family (Sparidae) of deep-bodied spiny-finned marine fishes including the porgies, scup, and sheepshead — **sparid** *n*

spar·ing \'spa(ə)r-iŋ, 'spe(ə)r-\ *adj* **1 :** tending to save; *esp* **:** FRUGAL **2 :** MEAGER, BARE — **spar·ing·ly** \-iŋ-lē\ *adv*

syn SPARING, FRUGAL, THRIFTY, ECONOMICAL mean careful in the use of one's money or resources. SPARING stresses abstention and restraint; FRUGAL implies simplicity in food, dress, ways of living; THRIFTY stresses good management and industry; ECONOMICAL stresses prudent management, lack of wastefulness, and use of things to their best advantage

[1]**spark** \'spärk\ *n* [ME *sparke*, fr. OE *spearca;* akin to MD *sparke* spark, L *spargere* to scatter, Gk *spargan* to swell] **1 a :** a small particle of a burning substance thrown out by a body in combustion or remaining when combustion is nearly completed **b :** a hot glowing particle struck from a larger mass; *esp* **:** one heated by friction ⟨produce a ~ by striking flint with steel⟩ **2 a :** a luminous disruptive electrical discharge of very short duration between two conductors separated by air or other gas **b :** the discharge in a spark plug **c :** the mechanism controlling the discharge in a spark plug **3 :** SPARKLE, FLASH **4 :** something that sets off a sudden force **5 :** a latent particle capable of growth or developing **:** GERM **6** *pl but sing in constr* **:** a radio operator on a ship

[2]**spark** *vb* [ME *sparken*, fr. *sparke*] *vi* **1 a :** to throw out sparks **b :** to flash or fall like sparks **2 :** to produce sparks; *specif* **:** to have the electric ignition working **3 :** to respond with enthusiasm ~ *vt* **1 :** to set off in a burst of activity **:** ACTIVATE **2 :** to stir to activity **:** INCITE — **spark·er** *n*

[3]**spark** *n* [perh. of Scand origin; akin to ON *sparkr* sprightly] **1 :** a foppish young man **:** GALLANT **2 :** LOVER, BEAU — **spark·ish** \'spär-kish\ *adj*

[4]**spark** *vb* **:** WOO, COURT — **spark·er** *n*

spark arrester *n* **:** a device for preventing the escape of sparks (as from a smokestack)

spark coil *n* **:** an induction coil for producing the spark for an internal-combustion engine
spark gap *n* **:** a space between two high-potential terminals (as of an induction coil) through which pass discharges of electricity; *also* **:** a device having a spark gap
sparking plug *n, Brit* **:** SPARK PLUG
[1]**spar·kle** \'spär-kəl\ *vi* **spar·kling** \-k(ə-)liŋ\ [ME *sparklen,* freq. of *sparken* to spark] **1 a :** to throw out sparks **b :** to shine as if throwing out sparks **:** GLISTEN **c :** to perform brilliantly **2 :** EFFERVESCE **3 :** to become lively or animated **syn** see FLASH
[2]**sparkle** *n* [ME, dim. of *sparke*] **1 :** a little spark **:** SCINTILLATION **2 :** the quality of sparkling **3 a :** ANIMATION, LIVELINESS **b :** EFFERVESCENCE
spar·kler \-k(ə-)lər\ *n* **:** one that sparkles: as **a :** DIAMOND **b :** a firework that throws off brilliant sparks on burning
spark plug *n* **1 :** a part that fits into the cylinder head of an internal-combustion engine and carries two electrodes separated by an air gap across which the current from the ignition system discharges to form the spark for combustion **2 :** one that initiates or gives impetus to an undertaking — **spark-plug** \'spärk-,pləg\ *vt*
spark transmitter *n* **:** a radio transmitter that utilizes the discharge of a condenser through a spark gap as a source of its alternating-current power
spar·ling \'spär-lən, -liŋ\ *n, pl* **sparling** *or* **sparlings** [ME *sperling,* fr. MF *esperling,* fr. MD *spierlinc,* fr. *spier* shoot, blade of grass] **:** a European smelt (*Osmerus eperlanus*)
spar·oid \'spa(ə)r-,öid, 'spe(ə)r-\ *adj or n* [deriv. of Gk *sparos* gilthead — more at SPEAR] **:** SPARID
sparring partner *n* **:** a pugilist's companion for practice in sparring during training
spar·row \'spar-(,)ō, -ə(-w)\ *n* [ME *sparow,* fr. OE *spearwa;* akin to OHG *sparo* sparrow, Gk *psar* starling] **1 :** any of several small dull singing birds (genus *Passer* of the family Ploceidae) related to the finches **2 :** any of various finches (as of the genera *Spezilla* or *Melospiza*) resembling the true sparrows
spar·row·grass \'spar-ə-,gras, -grəs\ *n* [by folk etymology fr. *asparagus*] *chiefly dial* **:** ASPARAGUS
sparrow hawk *n* **:** any of various small hawks or falcons (as the Old World *Accipiter nisus* or the No. American *Falco sparverius*)
sparse \'spärs\ *adj* [L *sparsus* spread out, fr. pp. of *spargere* to scatter — more at SPARK] **:** of few and scattered elements; *esp* **:** not thickly grown or settled **syn** see MEAGER — **sparse·ly** *adv* — **sparse·ness** *n* — **spar·si·ty** \'spär-sət-ē, -stē\ *n*
Spar·ta·cist \'spärt-ə-səst\ *n* [G *Spartakist,* fr. *Spartakusbund,* lit., league of Spartakus, a revolutionary organization, fr. *Spartakus,* pen name of Karl Liebknecht, its cofounder] **:** a member of a revolutionary political group organized in Germany in 1918 and advocating extreme socialistic doctrines
[1]**Spar·tan** \'spärt-ᵊn\ *n* **1 :** a native or inhabitant of ancient Sparta **2 :** a person of great courage and fortitude — **Spar·tan·ism** \-,iz-əm\ *n*
[2]**Spartan** *adj* **1 :** of or relating to Sparta in ancient Greece **2 a :** marked by strict self-discipline and avoidance of comfort and luxury **b :** LACONIC **c :** undaunted by pain or danger
spar·te·ine \'spärt-ē-ən, 'spär-,tēn\ *n* [L *spartum* esparto, broom + ISV *-eine* — more at ESPARTO] **:** a liquid alkaloid $C_{15}H_{26}N_2$ extracted from the common broom
spar varnish *n* [[1]*spar*] **:** an exterior waterproof varnish
spasm \'spaz-əm\ *n* [ME *spasme,* fr. MF, fr. L *spasmus,* fr. Gk *spasmos,* fr. *span* to draw, pull — more at SPAN] **1 :** an involuntary and abnormal muscular contraction **2 :** a sudden violent and temporary effort or emotion
spas·mod·ic \spaz-'mäd-ik\ *adj* [NL *spasmodicus,* fr. Gk *spasmōdēs,* fr. *spasmos*] **1 a :** relating to or affected or characterized by spasm **b :** resembling a spasm esp. in sudden violence ⟨a ~ jerk⟩ **2 :** acting or proceeding fitfully **:** INTERMITTENT **3 :** subject to outbursts of emotional excitement **:** EXCITABLE **syn** see FITFUL — **spas·mod·i·cal** \-i-kəl\ *adj* — **spas·mod·i·cal·ly** \-k(ə-)lē\ *adv*
[1]**spas·tic** \'spas-tik\ *adj* [L *spasticus,* fr. Gk *spastikos* drawing in, fr. *span*] **1 :** of, relating to, or characterized by spasm ⟨~ colon⟩ **2 :** suffering from spastic paralysis ⟨~ child⟩ — **spas·ti·cal·ly** \-ti-k(ə-)lē\ *adv* — **spas·tic·i·ty** \spa-'stis-ət-ē\ *n*
[2]**spastic** *n* **:** one suffering from spastic paralysis
spastic paralysis *n* **:** paralysis with tonic spasm of the muscles affected and increased tendon reflexes — compare CEREBRAL PALSY
[1]**spat** *past of* SPIT
[2]**spat** \'spat\ *n, pl* **spat** *or* **spats** [origin unknown] **:** a young oyster or other bivalve — usu. used collectively
[3]**spat** *n* [short for *spatterdash* (legging)] **:** a cloth or leather gaiter covering the instep and ankle — usu. used in pl.
[4]**spat** *n* [prob. imit.] **1 :** a brief petty quarrel **2** *chiefly dial* **:** SLAP **3 :** a sound like that of rain falling in large drops ⟨~ of bullets⟩ **syn** see QUARREL
[5]**spat** *vb* **spat·ted; spat·ting** *vt, chiefly dial* **:** SLAP ~ *vi* **1 :** to quarrel pettily or briefly **2 :** to strike with a sound like that of rain falling in large drops
spate \'spāt\ *n* [ME] **1 :** FRESHET, FLOOD **2 a :** a large number or amount **b :** a sudden or strong outburst **:** RUSH
spa·tha·ceous \spā-'thā-shəs\ *adj* **:** having or resembling a spathe
spathe \'spāth\ *n* [NL *spatha,* fr. L, broad sword — more at SPADE] **:** a sheathing bract or pair of bracts enclosing an inflorescence and esp. a spadix on the same axis (as in the calla) — **spathed** \'spāthd\ *adj* — **spa·those** \'spā-,thōs\ *adj*
spath·ic \'spath-ik\ *adj* [G *spath, spat* spar; akin to OHG *spān* chip — more at SPOON] **:** resembling spar **:** FOLIATED
spath·u·late \'spath-yə-lət\ *adj* [LL *spathula, spatula* spatula] **:** SPATULATE ⟨~ petals of a flower⟩
spa·tial \'spā-shəl\ *adj* [L *spatium* space — more at SPEED] **:** relating to, occupying, or of the nature of space — **spa·ti·al·i·ty** \,spā-shē-'al-ət-ē\ *n* — **spa·tial·ly** \'spāsh-(ə-)lē\ *adv*
spa·tio·tem·po·ral \,spā-shē-(,)ō-'tem-p(ə-)rəl\ *adj* [L *spatium* + *tempor-, tempus* time — more at TEMPORAL] **1 :** having both spatial and temporal qualities **2 :** of or relating to space-time — **spa·tio·tem·po·ral·ly** \-ē\ *adv*
[1]**spat·ter** \'spat-ər\ *vb* [akin to Flem *spetteren* to spatter] *vt* **1 :** to splash with or as if with a liquid; *also* **:** to soil in this way **2 :** to scatter by splashing **3 :** to injure by aspersion **:** DEFAME ~ *vi* **:** to spurt forth in scattered drops
[2]**spatter** *n* **1 a :** the act or process of spattering **:** the state of being spattered **b :** the noise of spattering **2 a :** a drop or splash spattered on something or a spot or stain due to spattering **b :** a small number **:** SPRINKLE
spat·ter·dock \-,däk\ *n* **:** a common yellow No. American water lily (*Nuphar advenum*) or other plant of the same genus
spat·u·la \'spach-(ə-)lə\ *n* [LL, spoon, spatula — more at EPAULET] **:** a flat thin usu. metal implement used esp. for spreading or mixing soft substances, scooping, or lifting

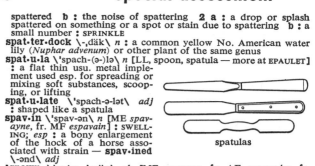

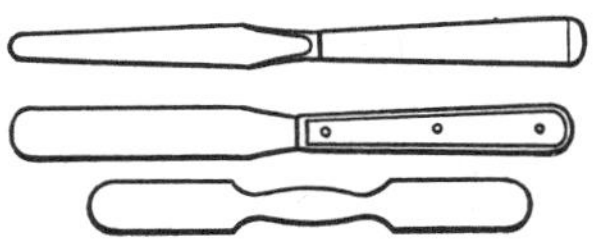
spatulas

spat·u·late \'spach-ə-lət\ *adj* **:** shaped like a spatula
spav·in \'spav-ən\ *n* [ME *spavayne,* fr. MF *espavain*] **:** SWELLING; *esp* **:** a bony enlargement of the hock of a horse associated with strain — **spav·ined** \-ənd\ *adj*
[1]**spawn** \'spȯn, 'spän\ *vb* [ME *spawnen,* fr. AF *espaundre,* fr. OF *espandre* to spread out, expand — more at EXPAND] *vt* **1 a :** to produce or deposit (eggs) — used of an aquatic animal **b :** to induce (fish) to spawn **c :** to plant with mushroom spawn **2 :** to bring forth **:** GENERATE ~ *vi* **1 :** to deposit spawn **2 :** to produce young esp. in large numbers — **spawn·er** *n*
[2]**spawn** *n* **1 :** the eggs of aquatic animals (as fishes or oysters) that lay many small eggs **2 :** PRODUCT, OFFSPRING; *also* **:** numerous issue **3 :** the seed, germ, or source of something **4 :** mycelium esp. prepared (as in bricks) for propagating mushrooms
spay \'spā, *substand* 'spād\ *vt* **spayed** \'spād, *substand* 'spād-əd\ **spay·ing** \'spā-iŋ, *substand* 'spād-iŋ\ [ME *spayen,* fr. MF *espeer* to cut with a sword, fr. OF, fr. *espee* sword, fr. L *spatha* sword — more at SPADE] **:** to remove the ovaries of (a female animal)
speak \'spēk\ *vb* **spoke** \'spōk\ **spo·ken** \'spō-kən\ **speak·ing** [ME *speken,* fr. OE *sprecan, specan;* akin to OHG *sprehhan* to speak, Gk *spharageisthai* to crackle] *vi* **1 a :** to utter words or articulate sounds with the ordinary voice **:** TALK **b** (1) **:** to express opinions (2) **:** to extend a greeting **c** (1) **:** to express oneself before a group (2) **:** to address one's remarks ⟨~ to the issue⟩ **2 a :** to make a written statement **b :** to express oneself **c :** to serve as spokesman **3 a :** to express feelings by other than verbal means **b :** SIGNAL **c :** to be interesting or attractive **:** APPEAL **4 :** to make a request **:** ASK **5 :** to make a characteristic or natural sound **6 a :** TESTIFY **b :** to be indicative or suggestive ~ *vt* **1 a** (1) **:** to utter by speaking voice (2) **:** to give a recitation of **:** DECLAIM **b :** to express orally **:** DECLARE **c :** ADDRESS, ACCOST; *esp* **:** HAIL **2 :** to make known in writing **:** STATE **3 :** to use or be able to use in speaking ⟨~s Spanish⟩ **4 :** to indicate by other than verbal means **:** REVEAL, SUGGEST **5** *archaic* **:** DESCRIBE, DEPICT — **speak·able** \'spē-kə-bəl\ *adj*

syn TALK, CONVERSE: SPEAK may apply to any utterance ranging from the least to the most coherent; TALK implies a listener or interlocutor and less formality; CONVERSE implies an interchange of opinions and ideas in talk

speak·easy \'spē-,kē-zē\ *n* **:** a place where alcoholic drinks are illegally sold
speak·er \'spē-kər\ *n* **1 a :** one that speaks **b :** one who makes a public speech **c :** one who acts as a spokesman **2 :** the presiding officer of a deliberative assembly ⟨*Speaker* of the House of Representatives⟩ **3 :** LOUDSPEAKER — **speak·er·ship** \-,ship\ *n*
speak·ing \'spē-kiŋ\ *adj* **1 :** highly significant or expressive **:** ELOQUENT **2 :** STRIKING, FAITHFUL
speaking tube *n* **:** a pipe through which conversation may be conducted (as between different parts of a building)
spean \'spēn\ *vt* [MD *spenen*] *chiefly Scot* **:** WEAN
[1]**spear** \'spi(ə)r\ *n* [ME *spere,* fr. OE; akin to OHG *sper* spear, L *sparus,* Gk *sparos* gilthead] **1 :** a thrusting or throwing weapon with long shaft and sharp head or blade **2 :** a sharp-pointed instrument with barbs used in spearing fish **3 :** SPEARMAN — **spear·er** *n*
[2]**spear** *adj* [[1]*spear*] **:** PATERNAL, MALE ⟨the ~ side of the family⟩ — compare DISTAFF
[3]**spear** *vt* **1 :** to pierce or strike with or as if with a spear **2 :** to catch (as a baseball) with a sudden thrust of the arm ~ *vi* **:** to thrust with or as if with a spear
[4]**spear** *n* [alter. of [1]*spire*] **:** a usu. young blade, shoot, or sprout (as of grass)
[5]**spear** *vi, of a plant* **:** to thrust upward a spear
[1]**spear·fish** \'spi(ə)r-,fish\ *n* **:** any of several large powerful pelagic fishes (genus *Tetrapturus*) related to the marlins and sailfishes
[2]**spearfish** *vi* **:** to fish with a spear
[1]**spear·head** \-,hed\ *n* **1 :** the sharp-pointed head of a spear **2 :** a leading element, force, or influence
[2]**spearhead** *vt* **:** to serve as leader or leading element of ⟨~ the attack⟩
spear·man \'spi(ə)r-mən\ *n* **:** one armed with a spear
spear·mint \-,mint, -mənt\ *n* **:** a common mint (*Mentha spicata*) grown for flavoring and esp. for its aromatic oil
spear·wort \-,wərt, -,wȯ(ə)rt\ *n* **:** any of several crowfoots with spear-shaped leaves (esp. *Ranunculus flammula*)
spe·cial \'spesh-əl\ *adj* [ME, fr. OF or L; OF *especial,* fr. L *specialis* individual, particular, fr. *species* species] **1 :** distinguished by some unusual quality **2 a :** PECULIAR, UNIQUE **b :** of, relating to, or constituting a species **:** SPECIFIC **3 :** ADDITIONAL, EXTRA **4 :** designed for a particular purpose or occasion — **special** *n* — **spe·cial·ly** \-(ə-)lē\ *adv*

syn SPECIAL, ESPECIAL, SPECIFIC, PARTICULAR, INDIVIDUAL, RESPECTIVE, CONCRETE mean of or belonging to one only. SPECIAL stresses having a quality, character, identity, or use of its own; ESPECIAL may add implications of preeminence or preference; SPECIFIC implies a quality or character distinguishing a kind or a species; PARTICULAR implies a distinguishing mark of an individual; INDIVIDUAL implies unequivocal reference to one of a class or group; RESPECTIVE implies reference to each one of several in the order named; CONCRETE suggests individuality and actuality of existence or experience

special act *n* **:** a legislative act applying only to particular persons or to a particular area
special assessment *n* **:** a specific tax levied on private property to

meet the cost of public improvements that enhance the value of the property

special delivery *n* **:** expedited messenger delivery of mail matter for an extra fee

special handling *n* **:** the handling of parcel-post or fourth-class mail as first-class but not as special-delivery matter for an extra postal fee

special interest *n* **:** a person or group having an interest in a particular part of the economy and receiving or seeking special advantages therein often to the detriment of the general public

spe·cial·ism \'spesh-ə-ˌliz-əm\ *n* **1 :** specialization in an occupation or branch of learning **2 :** a field of specialization **:** SPECIALTY

spe·cial·ist \'spesh-(ə-)ləst\ *n* **1 :** one who devotes himself to a special occupation or branch of learning **2 :** any of six enlisted ranks in the army corresponding to the ranks of corporal through sergeant major — **specialist** *or* **spe·cial·is·tic** \ˌspesh-ə-'lis-tik\ *adj*

spe·ci·al·i·ty \ˌspesh-ē-'al-ət-ē\ *n* **1 :** a special mark or quality **2 :** a special object or class of objects **3 a :** a special aptitude or skill **b :** a particular occupation or branch of learning

spe·cial·iza·tion \ˌspesh-(ə-)lə-'zā-shən\ *n* **1 :** a making or becoming specialized **2 a :** structural adaptation of a body part to a particular function or of an organism for life in a particular environment **b :** a body part or an organism adapted by specialization

spe·cial·ize \'spesh-ə-ˌlīz\ *vt* **1 :** to make particular mention of **:** PARTICULARIZE **2 :** to apply or direct to a specific end or use ~ *vi* **1 :** to concentrate one's efforts in a special activity or field **2 :** to undergo specialization; *esp* **:** to change adaptively

special jury *n* **:** a jury chosen by the court upon request from a list of better educated or presumably more intelligent prospective jurors for a case involving complicated issues of fact or serious felonies — called also *blue-ribbon jury*

special pleading *n* **1 :** the allegation of special or new matter to avoid the effect of matter pleaded by the opposite side and admitted, as distinguished from a direct denial of the matter pleaded **2 :** misleading argument that presents one point or phase as if it covered the entire question at issue

special privilege *n* **:** a privilege granted esp. by a law or constitution to an individual or group to the exclusion of others and in derogation of common right

special session *n* **:** an extraordinary session of a legislative body or a court

spe·cial·ty \'spesh-əl-tē\ *n* [ME *specialte*, fr. MF *especialté*, fr. LL *specialitat-, specialitas*, fr. L *specialis* special] **1 :** a distinctive mark or quality **2 a :** a special object or class of objects: as (1) **:** a legal agreement embodied in a sealed instrument (2) **:** a product of a special kind or of special excellence **b :** the state of being special, distinctive, or peculiar **3 :** something in which one specializes

spe·ci·ate \'spē-s(h)ē-ˌāt\ *vi* [back-formation fr. *speciation*, fr. *species*] **:** to differentiate into new biological species — **spe·ci·a·tion** \ˌspē-s(h)ē-'ā-shən\ *n* — **spe·ci·a·tion·al** \-shnəl, -shən-ᵊl\ *adj*

spe·cie \'spē-shē, -sē\ *n* [fr. *in specie*, fr. L, in kind] **:** money in coin — **in specie :** in the same or like form or kind; *also* **:** in coin

1**spe·cies** \'spē-(ˌ)shēz, -(ˌ)sēz\ *n, pl* **species** [L, appearance, kind, species — more at SPY] **1 a :** a class of individuals having common attributes and designated by a common name; *specif* **:** a logical division of a genus or more comprehensive class **b :** KIND, SORT **c** (1) **:** a category of biological classification ranking immediately below the genus or subgenus, comprising related organisms or populations potentially capable of interbreeding, and being designated by a binomial that consists of the name of its genus followed by a Latin or latinized uncapitalized noun or adjective agreeing grammatically with the genus name (2) **:** an individual or kind belonging to such a species **d :** a particular kind of atomic nucleus or atom **2 :** the consecrated eucharistic elements; *specif* **:** the accidents of the eucharistic bread and wine as distinguished in Roman Catholicism from their substance **3 a :** a mental image; *also* **:** a sensible object **b :** an object of thought correlative with a natural object

2**species** *adj* **:** belonging to a biological species as distinguished from a horticultural variety ⟨a ~ rose⟩

spec·i·fi·able \'spes-ə-ˌfī-ə-bəl\ *adj* **:** capable of being specified

1**spe·cif·ic** \spi-'sif-ik\ *adj* [LL *specificus*, fr. L *species*] **1 :** constituting or falling into a named category **2 :** characteristic of or peculiar to something: as **a :** exerting a distinctive influence on a body part or on a particular disease ⟨a ~ antibody⟩ **b** *of a disease* **:** caused by a particular pathogen **3 :** ACCURATE, PRECISE **4 :** of, relating to, or constituting a species and esp. a biologic species **5 :** being any of various arbitrary physical constants and esp. one relating a quantitative attribute to unit mass, volume, or area **syn** see EXPLICIT, SPECIAL — **spe·cif·i·cal** \-i-kəl\ *adj* — **spe·cif·i·cal·ly** \-k(ə-)lē\ *adv* — **spec·i·fic·i·ty** \ˌspes-ə-'fis-ət-ē\ *n*

2**specific** *n* **1 a :** something peculiarly adapted to a purpose or use **b :** a drug or remedy having a specific mitigating effect on a disease **2 a :** a characteristic quality or trait **b :** DETAILS, PARTICULARS **c** *pl* **:** SPECIFICATION 2a **syn** see REMEDY

spec·i·fi·ca·tion \ˌspes-(ə-)fə-'kā-shən\ *n* **1 :** the act or process of specifying **2 a :** a detailed precise presentation of something or of a plan or proposal for something — usu. used in pl. **b :** a statement of legal particulars (as of charges or of contract terms); *also* **:** a single item of such statement **c :** a written description of an invention for which a patent is sought

specific character *n* **:** a character distinguishing one species from another or from every other species of the same genus

specific epithet *n* **:** the Latin or latinized noun or adjective that follows the genus name in a taxonomic binomial

specific gravity *n* **:** the ratio of the density of a substance to the density of a substance (as pure water or hydrogen) taken as a standard when both densities are obtained by weighing in air

specific heat *n* **1 :** the ratio of the quantity of heat required to raise the temperature of a body one degree to that required to raise the temperature of an equal mass of water one degree **2 :** the heat in calories required to raise the temperature of one gram of a substance one degree centigrade

specific performance *n* **1 :** the performance of a legal contract strictly or substantially according to its terms **2 :** an equitable remedy enjoining specific performance

spec·i·fi·er \'spes-ə-ˌfī(-ə)r\ *n* **:** one that specifies

spec·i·fy \'spes-ə-ˌfī\ *vt* [ME *specifien*, fr. OF *specifier*, fr. LL *specificare*, fr. *specificus*] **1 :** to name or state explicitly or in detail **2 :** to include as an item in a specification

spec·i·men \'spes-(ə-)mən\ *n* [L, fr. *specere* to look at, look] **1 :** an item or part typical of a group or whole **:** SAMPLE **2 :** LOT, SORT ⟨a tough ~⟩ **syn** see INSTANCE

spe·ci·os·i·ty \ˌspē-shē-'äs-ət-ē\ *n* **:** SPECIOUSNESS

spe·cious \'spē-shəs\ *adj* [ME, fr. L *speciosus* beautiful, plausible, fr. *species*] **1** *obs* **:** SHOWY **2 :** having deceptive attraction or allure **3 :** having a false look of truth or genuineness **:** SOPHISTICAL **syn** see PLAUSIBLE — **spe·cious·ly** *adv* — **spe·cious·ness** *n*

1**speck** \'spek\ *n* [ME *specke*, fr. OE *specca*] **1 :** a small discoloration or spot esp. from stain or decay **2 :** BIT, PARTICLE **3 :** something marked or marred with specks

2**speck** *vt* **:** to produce specks on or in

1**speck·le** \'spek-əl\ *n* [ME; akin to OE *specca*] **:** a little speck

2**speckle** *vt* **speck·ling** \-(ə-)liŋ\ **1 :** to mark with speckles **2 :** to be distributed in or on like speckles

specs \'speks\ *n pl* **1** [contr. of *spectacles*] **:** GLASS 2b(2) **2** [by contr.] **:** SPECIFICATIONS

spec·ta·cle \'spek-ti-kəl; *oftenest for 2, 3* -ˌtik-əl\ *n* [ME, fr. MF, fr. L *spectaculum*, fr. *spectare* to watch, fr. *spectus*, pp. of *specere* to look, look at — more at SPY] **1 a :** something exhibited to view as unusual, notable, or entertaining; *esp* **:** an eye-catching or dramatic public display **b :** an object of curiosity or contempt **2** *pl* **:** GLASS 2b(2) **3 :** any of various things felt to resemble a pair of glasses

spec·ta·cled \-ti-kəld, -ˌtik-əld\ *adj* **1 :** having or wearing spectacles **2 :** having markings suggesting a pair of spectacles

1**spec·tac·u·lar** \spek-'tak-yə-lər, spək-\ *adj* [L *spectaculum*] **:** of, relating to, or constituting a spectacle — **spec·tac·u·lar·ly** *adv*

2**spectacular** *n* **:** something spectacular (as an elaborate television show)

spec·tate \'spek-ˌtāt\ *vi* [back formation fr. *spectator*] **:** to be present as a spectator (as at a sports event)

spec·ta·tor \'spek-ˌtāt-ər, spek-'\ *n* [L, fr. *spectatus*, pp. of *spectare* to watch] **:** one who looks on or watches **:** ONLOOKER — **spectator** *adj* — **spec·ta·tress** \spek-'tā-trəs\ *n*

spec·ter *or* **spec·tre** \'spek-tər\ *n* [F *spectre*, fr. L *spectrum* appearance, specter, fr. *specere* to look, look at — more at SPY] **1 :** a visible disembodied spirit **:** GHOST **2 :** something that haunts or perturbs the mind **:** PHANTASM

spec·tral \'spek-trəl\ *adj* **1 :** of, relating to, or suggesting a specter **:** GHOSTLY **2 :** of, relating to, or made by a spectrum — **spec·tral·i·ty** \spek-'tral-ət-ē\ *n* — **spec·tral·ly** \'spek-trə-lē\ *adv* — **spec·tral·ness** \'spek-trəl-nəs\ *n*

spectral line *n* **:** one of a series of linear images of the narrow slit of a spectrograph or similar instrument corresponding to a component of the spectrum of the radiation emitted by a particular source

spectro- *comb form* **1** [NL *spectrum*] **:** spectrum ⟨*spectro*scope⟩ **2** [*spectroscope*] **:** combined with a spectroscope ⟨*spectro*polarimeter⟩

spec·tro·gram \'spek-t(r)ə-ˌgram\ *n* [ISV] **:** a photograph or diagram of a spectrum

spec·tro·graph \-ˌgraf\ *n* [ISV] **:** an apparatus for dispersing radiation into a spectrum and photographing or mapping the spectrum — **spec·tro·graph·ic** \ˌspek-t(r)ə-'graf-ik\ *adj* — **spec·tro·graph·i·cal·ly** \-i-k(ə-)lē\ *adv*

spec·tro·he·lio·gram \ˌspek-(ˌ)trō-'hē-lē-ə-ˌgram\ *n* **:** a photograph of the sun that is made by monochromatic light and shows the sun's faculae and prominences

spec·tro·he·lio·graph \-ˌgraf\ *n* [ISV] **:** an apparatus for making spectroheliograms

spec·tro·he·lio·scope \-ˌskōp\ *n* [ISV] **1 :** SPECTROHELIOGRAPH **2 :** an instrument similar to a spectroheliograph used for visual as distinguished from photographic observations

spec·trom·e·ter \spek-'träm-ət-ər\ *n* [ISV] **1 :** an instrument used in determining the index of refraction **2 :** a spectroscope fitted for measurements of the spectra observed with it — **spec·tro·met·ric** \ˌspek-trə-'me-trik\ *adj* — **spec·trom·e·try** \spek-'träm-ə-trē\ *n*

spec·tro·pho·tom·e·ter \ˌspek-(ˌ)trō-fə-'täm-ət-ər\ *n* [ISV] **:** a photometer for measuring the relative intensities of the light in different parts of a spectrum — **spec·tro·pho·to·met·ric** \ˌspek-trə-ˌfōt-ə-'me-trik\ *adj* — **spec·tro·pho·tom·e·try** \ˌspek-(ˌ)trō-fə-'täm-ə-trē\ *n*

spec·tro·scope \'spek-trə-ˌskōp\ *n* [ISV] **:** any of various instruments for forming and examining optical spectra — **spec·tro·scop·ic** \ˌspek-trə-'skäp-ik\ *adj* — **spec·tro·scop·i·cal·ly** \-i-k(ə-)lē\ *adv* — **spec·tros·co·pist** \spek-'träs-kə-pəst\ *n* — **spec·tros·co·py** \-pē\ *n*

spec·trum \'spek-trəm\ *n, pl* **spec·tra** \-trə\ *or* **spectrums** [NL, fr. L, appearance — more at SPECTER] **1 :** an array of the components of an emission or wave separated and arranged in the order of some varying characteristic (as wavelength, mass, or energy): as **a :** a series of images formed when a beam of radiant energy is subjected to dispersion and brought to focus so that the component waves are arranged in the order of their wavelengths (as when a beam of sunlight that is refracted and dispersed by a prism forms a display of colors) **b :** ELECTROMAGNETIC SPECTRUM **c :** RADIO SPECTRUM **2 :** a continuous sequence or range

spec·u·lar \'spek-yə-lər\ *adj* [L *specularis* of a mirror, fr. *speculum*] **:** of, relating to, or having the qualities of a mirror; *esp* **:** conducted with the aid of a medical speculum — **spec·u·lar·ly** *adv*

spec·u·late \'spek-yə-ˌlāt\ *vi* [L *speculatus*, pp. of *speculari* to spy out, examine, fr. *specula* watchtower, fr. *specere* to look, look at] **1 a :** to meditate on or ponder a subject **:** REFLECT **b :** to review something idly or casually and often inconclusively **2 :** to assume a business risk in hope of gain; *esp* **:** to buy or sell in expectation of profiting from market fluctuations **syn** see THINK — **spec·u·la·tion** \ˌspek-yə-'lā-shən\ *n* — **spec·u·la·tive** \'spek-yə-ˌlāt-iv, -lət-\ *adj* — **spec·u·la·tor** \-ˌlāt-ər\ *n*

spec·u·lum \'spek-yə-ləm\ *n, pl* **spec·u·la** \-lə\ *also* **speculums** [L, mirror, fr. *specere*] **1 :** a tubular instrument inserted into a body passage for inspection or medication **2 a :** an ancient mirror

usu. of bronze or silver **b :** a reflector in an optical instrument **3 :** a medieval compendium of all knowledge **4 :** a drawing or table showing the relative positions of all the planets **5 :** a patch of color on the secondaries of most ducks and some other birds

speech \'spēch\ *n* [ME *speche,* fr. OE *sprǣc, spǣc;* akin to OE *sprecan* to speak — more at SPEAK] **1 a :** the communication or expression of thoughts in spoken words **b :** exchange of spoken words **:** CONVERSATION **2 a :** something that is spoken **:** UTTERANCE **b :** a public discourse **:** ADDRESS **3 a :** LANGUAGE, DIALECT **b :** an individual manner or style of speaking **4 :** the power of expressing or communicating thoughts by speaking

speech community *n* **:** a group of people sharing characteristic patterns of vocabulary, grammar, and pronunciation

speech·ify \'spē-chə-,fī\ *vi* **:** to make a speech **:** HARANGUE

speech·less \'spēch-ləs\ *adj* **1 :** unable to speak **:** DUMB **2 :** not speaking **:** SILENT **3 :** unexpressed in words **:** UNSPOKEN — **speech·less·ly** *adv* — **speech·less·ness** *n*

1**speed** \'spēd\ *n* [ME *spede,* fr. OE *spēd;* akin to OHG *spuot* prosperity, speed, L *spes* hope, *spatium* space] **1** *archaic* **:** prosperity in an undertaking **:** SUCCESS **2 a :** the act or state of moving swiftly **:** SWIFTNESS **b :** rate of motion **:** VELOCITY **c :** MOMENTUM **3 :** swiftness or rate of performance or action **:** QUICKNESS **4 a :** the sensitivity of a photographic film, plate, or paper expressed numerically **b :** the light gathering power of a lens or optical system expressed as relative aperture **c :** the time during which a camera shutter is open **5 :** a transmission gear in automotive vehicles **6 :** a synthetic drug used esp. as a stimulant for the central nervous system **syn** see HASTE

2**speed** *vb* **sped** \'sped\ *or* **speed·ed; speed·ing** *vi* **1 a :** to prosper in an undertaking **b :** to get along **:** FARE **2 a :** to make haste **b :** to go or drive at excessive or illegal speed **3 :** to move, work, or take place faster **:** ACCELERATE ⟨the heart ~s up⟩ ~ *vt* **1 a** *archaic* **:** to cause or help to prosper **:** AID **b :** to further the success of **2 a :** to cause to move quickly **:** HASTEN **b :** to wish Godspeed to **c :** to increase the speed of **:** ACCELERATE ⟨~*ed* up the engine⟩ **3 :** to send out **:** DISCHARGE ⟨~ an arrow⟩ — **speed·er** *n* — **speed·ster** \-stər\ *n*

3**speed** *adj* **:** of or relating to speed

speed·boat \'spēd-,bōt\ *n* **:** a fast launch or motorboat

speed·boat·ing \-iŋ\ *n* **:** the act, art, or sport of managing a speedboat

speed·i·ly \'spēd-ᵊl-ē\ *adv* **:** in a speedy manner

speed·i·ness \'spēd-ē-nəs\ *n* **:** the quality or state of being speedy

speed·light \-,līt\ *n* **:** STROBOTRON

speed limit *n* **:** the maximum speed permitted by law in a given area under specified circumstances

speed·om·e·ter \spi-'däm-ət-ər\ *n* **1 :** an instrument for indicating speed **:** TACHOMETER **2 :** an instrument for indicating distance traversed as well as speed of travel; *also* **:** ODOMETER

speed trap *n* **:** a stretch of road policed by concealed officers or devices against speeding

speed·up \'spē-,dəp\ *n* **:** an employer's demand for accelerated output without increased pay

speed·way \'spē-,dwā\ *n* **1 :** a public road on which fast driving is allowed; *specif* **:** EXPRESSWAY **2 :** a racecourse for automobiles or motorcycles

speed·well \'spē-,dwel\ *n* **:** any of a genus (*Veronica*) of herbs of the figwort family; *esp* **:** a perennial European herb (*V. officinalis*) with small bluish flowers

speedy \'spēd-ē\ *adj* **:** rapid in motion **:** QUICK, SWIFT

speel \'spē(ə)l\ *vb* [origin unknown] **:** CLIMB

speer *or* **speir** \'spi(ə)r\ *vb* [ME (Sc) *speren,* fr. OE *spyrian* to seek after; akin to OE *spor* spoor] *chiefly Scot* **:** ASK, INQUIRE

speiss \'spīs\ *n* [G *speise,* lit., food, fr. (assumed) VL *spesa,* fr. LL *expensa* expense] **:** a mixture of impure metallic arsenides produced as a regulus in smelting certain ores

spe·le·o·log·i·cal \,spē-lē-ə-'läj-i-kəl, ,spel-ē-\ *adj* **:** of or relating to speleology

spe·le·ol·o·gist \-'äl-ə-jəst\ *n* **:** a specialist in speleology

spe·le·ol·o·gy \-jē\ *n* [L *speleum* cave (fr. Gk *spēlaion*) + ISV *-o-* + *-logy*] **:** the scientific study or exploration of caves

1**spell** \'spel\ *n* [ME, talk, tale, fr. OE; akin to OHG *spel* talk, tale, Gk *apeilē* boast] **1 a :** a spoken word or form of words believed to have magic power **:** INCANTATION **b :** a state of enchantment **2 :** a strong compelling influence or attraction

2**spell** *vt* **:** to put under a spell **:** BEWITCH

3**spell** *vb* **spelled** \'speld, 'spelt\ **spell·ing** [ME *spellen,* fr. OF *espeller,* of Gmc origin; akin to OE *spell* talk] *vt* **1 :** to read slowly and with difficulty **2 a :** to find out by study **:** DISCOVER **b :** COMPREHEND, UNDERSTAND **3 a :** to name the letters of in order; *also* **:** to write or print the letters of in order **b :** to make up (a word) **:** FORM **4 :** MEAN, SIGNIFY ~ *vi* **:** to form words with letters

4**spell** *vb* **spelled** \'speld\ **spell·ing** [ME *spelen,* fr. OE *spelian;* akin to OE *spala* substitute] *vt* **1 :** to take the place of for a time **:** RELIEVE **2 :** to allow an interval of rest to **:** REST ~ *vi* **1 :** to work in turns **2 :** to rest from work or activity for a time

5**spell** *n* **1 a** *archaic* **:** a shift of workers **b :** one's turn at work **2 a :** a period spent in a job or occupation **b** *chiefly Austral* **:** a period of rest from work, activity, or use **3 a :** an indeterminate period of time **b :** a stretch of a specified type of weather **4 :** a period of bodily or mental distress or disorder ⟨a ~ of coughing⟩ ⟨fainting ~s⟩

spell·bind \'spel-,bīnd\ *vt* [back-formation fr. *spellbound*] **:** to bind or hold by a spell or charm **:** FASCINATE

spell·bind·er \-,bīn-dər\ *n* **:** a speaker of compelling eloquence

spell·bound \-'baůnd\ *adj* **:** ENTRANCED, FASCINATED

spell down *vt* **:** to defeat in a spelling match

spell·er \'spel-ər\ *n* **1 :** one who spells words **2 :** a book with exercises for teaching spelling

spell·ing *n* **:** the forming of words from letters according to accepted usage **:** ORTHOGRAPHY; *also* **:** the letters composing a word

spell out *vt* **:** to make plain

1**spelt** \'spelt\ *n* [ME, fr. OE, fr. LL *spelta,* of Gmc origin; akin to MHG *spelte* split piece of wood, OHG *spaltan* to split — more at SPILL] **:** a wheat (*Triticum spelta*) with lax spikes and spikelets containing two light red kernels — called also *speltz*

2**spelt** \'spelt\ *chiefly Brit past of* SPELL

spel·ter \'spel-tər\ *n* [prob. alter. of MD *speauter*] **:** ZINC; *esp* **:** zinc cast in slabs for commercial use

spe·lunk·er \spi-'ləŋ-kər, 'spē-,\ *n* [L *spelunca* cave, fr. Gk *spēlynx;* akin to Gk *spēlaion* cave] **:** one who makes a hobby of exploring and studying caves

spe·lunk·ing \-kiŋ\ *n* **:** the hobby or practice of exploring caves

spence \'spen(t)s\ *n* [ME, fr. MF *despense,* fr. ML *dispensa,* fr. L, fem. of *dispensus,* pp. of *dispendere* to weigh out — more at DISPENSE] *dial Brit* **:** PANTRY

1**spen·cer** \'spen(t)-sər\ *n* [George John, 2d earl *Spencer* †1834 E politician] **:** a short waist-length jacket

2**spencer** *n* [prob. fr. the name *Spencer*] **:** a trysail abaft the foremast or mainmast

1**Spen·ce·ri·an** \spen-'sir-ē-ən\ *adj* **:** of or relating to Herbert Spencer or Spencerianism

2**Spencerian** *adj* [Platt R. *Spencer* †1864 Am calligrapher] **:** of or relating to a form of slanting handwriting

Spen·ce·ri·an·ism \-ē-ə-,niz-əm\ *n* **:** the synthetic philosophy of Herbert Spencer that has as its central idea the mechanistic evolution of the cosmos from relative simplicity to relative complexity

spend \'spend\ *vb* **spent** \'spent\ **spend·ing** [ME *spenden,* fr. OE & OF; OE *spendan,* fr. L *expendere* to expend; OF *despendre,* fr. L *dispendere* to weigh out — more at DISPENSE] *vt* **1 :** to use up or pay out **:** EXPEND **2 a :** to wear out **:** EXHAUST **b :** to consume wastefully **:** SQUANDER **3 :** to cause or permit to elapse **:** PASS **4 :** to give up **:** SACRIFICE ~ *vi* **1 :** to expend or waste wealth or strength **2 :** to become expended or consumed — **spend·er** *n*

spend·able \'spen-də-bəl\ *adj* **:** available for spending

spending money *n* **:** POCKET MONEY

spend·thrift \'spen(d)-,thrift\ *n* **:** one who spends improvidently or wastefully — **spendthrift** *adj*

Spen·gle·ri·an \s(h)peŋ-'(g)lir-ē-ən\ *adj* **:** of or relating to the theory of world history developed by Oswald Spengler that all major cultures undergo similar cyclical developments from birth to maturity to decay — **Spenglerian** *n*

Spen·se·ri·an \spen-'sir-ē-ən\ *adj* **:** of or relating to the poet Spenser or his works

Spenserian sonnet *n* [Edmund *Spenser* †1599 E poet] **:** a sonnet consisting of three interlocked quatrains and a couplet with a rhyme scheme *abab, bcbc, cdcd, ee*

Spenserian stanza *n* **:** a stanza consisting of eight verses of iambic pentameter and an alexandrine with a rhyme scheme *ababbcbcc*

spent \'spent\ *adj* [ME, fr. pp. of *spenden* to spend] **1 :** used up **:** CONSUMED **2 :** drained of energy or effectiveness **:** EXHAUSTED **3 :** exhausted of spawn or sperm

sperm \'spərm\ *n, pl* **sperm** *or* **sperms** [ME, fr. MF *esperme,* fr. LL *spermat-, sperma,* fr. Gk; akin to Gk *speirein* to sow — more at SPROUT] **1 a :** the male fecundating fluid **:** SEMEN **b :** a male gamete **2 :** a product of the sperm whale

sperm- *or* **spermo-** *or* **sperma-** *or* **spermi-** *comb form* [Gk *sperm-, spermo-,* fr. *sperma*] **:** seed **:** germ **:** sperm ⟨*spermo*phile⟩ ⟨*sperma*theca⟩ ⟨*sperm*ary⟩ ⟨*spermi*cidal⟩

sper·ma·ce·ti \,spər-mə-'sēt-ē, -'set-\ *n* [ME *sperma cete,* fr. ML *sperma ceti* whale sperm] **:** a waxy solid obtained from the oil of cetaceans and esp. sperm whale and used in ointments, cosmetics, and candles

sper·ma·go·ni·um \,spər-mə-'gō-nē-əm\ *n, pl* **sper·ma·go·nia** \-nē-ə\ [NL] **:** a flask-shaped or depressed receptacle in which spermatia are produced in some fungi and lichens

sper·ma·ry \'spərm-(ə-)rē\ *n* [NL *spermarium,* fr. Gk *sperma*] **:** an organ in which male gametes are developed

spermat- *or* **spermato-** *comb form* [MF, fr. LL, fr. Gk, fr. *spermat-, sperma* sperm] **:** seed **:** spermatozoon ⟨*spermat*id⟩ ⟨*spermato*cyte⟩

sper·ma·the·ca \,spər-mə-'thē-kə\ *n* [NL] **:** a sac for sperm storage in the female reproductive tract of many lower animals — **sper·ma·the·cal** \-kəl\ *adj*

sper·ma·tial \(,)spər-'mā-sh(ē-)əl\ *adj* **:** of, relating to, or being a spermatium

sper·mat·ic \(,)spər-'mat-ik\ *adj* **1 :** relating to sperm or a spermary **2 :** resembling, carrying, or full of sperm

spermatic cord *n* **:** a cord that suspends the testis within the scrotum and contains the vas deferens and vessels and nerves of the testis

sper·ma·tid \'spər-mət-əd\ *n* **:** one of the cells formed by division of the secondary spermatocytes that differentiate into spermatozoa

sper·ma·ti·um \(,)spər-'mā-shē-əm\ *n, pl* **sper·ma·tia** \-shē-ə\ [NL, fr. Gk *spermation,* dim. of *spermat-, sperma*] **:** a nonmotile cell functioning or held to function as a male gamete in some lower plants

sper·ma·to·ci·dal \(,)spər-,mat-ə-'sīd-ᵊl, ,spər-mət-\ *or* **sper·mi·ci·dal** \,spər-mə-'sīd-ᵊl\ *adj* **:** able or used to kill sperm — **sper·ma·to·cide** \(,)spər-'mat-ə-,sīd, 'spər-mət-\ *n*

sper·ma·to·cyte \(,)spər-'mat-ə-,sīt, 'spər-mət-\ *n* **:** a cell giving rise to sperm cells; *esp* **:** a cell of the last generation or next to the last generation preceding the spermatozoon

sper·ma·to·gen·e·sis \,spər-mət-ə-'jen-ə-səs, (,)spər-,mat-\ *n* [NL] **:** the process of male gamete formation including meiosis and transformation of the four resulting spermatids into spermatozoa — **sper·ma·to·ge·net·ic** \(,)spər-,mat-ə-jə-'net-ik, ,spər-mət-ō-\ *adj*

sper·ma·to·go·ni·al \,spər-mət-ə-'gō-nē-əl, (,)spər-,mat-\ *adj* **:** of, relating to, or producing spermatogonia

sper·ma·to·go·ni·um \-nē-əm\ *n, pl* **sper·ma·to·go·nia** \-nē-ə\ [NL] **:** a primitive male germ cell

sper·ma·to·phore \(,)spər-'mat-ə-,fō(ə)r, 'spər-mət-, -,fȯ(ə)r\ *n* [ISV] **:** a capsule, packet, or mass enclosing spermatozoa extruded by the male and conveyed to the female in the insemination of various lower animals

sper·ma·to·phyte \-,fīt\ *n* [deriv. of NL *spermat-* + Gk *phyton* plant — more at PHYT-] **:** any of a group (Spermatophyta) of higher plants comprising those that produce seeds and including the gymnosperms and angiosperms — **sper·ma·to·phyt·ic** \(,)spər-,mat-ə-'fit-ik, ,spər-mət-\ *adj*

sper·ma·to·zo·al \,spər-mət-ə-'zō-əl, (,)spər-,mat-\ *adj* **:** of or relating to spermatozoa

sper·ma·to·zo·id \-'zō-əd\ *n* [ISV, fr. NL *spermatozoa*] **:** a male gamete of a plant motile by anterior cilia and usu. produced in an antheridium

sper·ma·to·zo·on \-'zō-,än, -'zō-ən\ *n, pl* **sper·ma·to·zoa** \-'zō-ə\ [NL] **1 :** a motile male gamete of an animal usu. with rounded or elongate head and a long posterior flagellum **2 :** SPERMATOZOID

sperm·ine \'spər-,mēn\ *n* **:** a crystalline aliphatic base $C_{10}H_{26}N_4$ found esp. in semen and in yeast

sper·mio·gen·e·sis \ˌspər-mē-ō-ˈjen-ə-səs\ *n* [NL, fr. *spermium* spermatozoon + *-o-* + L *genesis*] **1 :** transformation of a spermatid into a spermatozoon **2 :** SPERMATOGENESIS
sperm oil *n* **:** a pale yellow oil from the sperm whale
sper·mo·phile \ˈspər-mə-ˌfīl\ *n* [deriv. of Gk *sperma* sperm + *philos* loving] **:** any of various burrowing rodents (as of the genus *Citellus*) that are related to the squirrels and live in colonies esp. in open areas, often damage crops, and include vectors of plague
sperm whale \ˈspərm-\ *n* [short for *spermaceti whale*] **:** a large toothed whale (*Physeter catodon*) with a large closed cavity in the head containing a fluid mixture of spermaceti and oil
-sper·my \ˌspər-mē\ *n comb form* [Gk *sperma* seed, sperm] **:** state of exhibiting or resulting from (such) a fertilization ⟨agamo*spermy*⟩
sper·ry·lite \ˈsper-i-ˌlīt\ *n* [Francis L. *Sperry*, 19th cent. Can chemist + E *-lite*] **:** a mineral $PtAs_2$ consisting of a platinum arsenide occurring near Sudbury, Ontario, in grains and minute isometric crystals of a tin-white color
spes·sar·tite \ˈspes-ər-ˌtīt\ *also* **spes·sar·tine** \-ˌtēn\ *n* [F, fr. *Spessart* mountain range, Germany] **:** a manganese aluminum garnet usu. containing iron, magnesium, or other elements in minor amounts
1**spew** \ˈspyü\ *vb* [ME *spewen*, fr. OE *spīwan*; akin to OHG *spīwan* to spit, L *spuere*, Gk *ptyein*] *vi* **1 :** VOMIT **2 :** to come in a flood or gush **3 :** to ooze forth **:** EXUDE ~ *vt* **1 :** VOMIT **2 :** to cast forth with vigor or violence — **spew·er** *n*
2**spew** *n* **1 :** matter that is vomited **:** VOMIT **2 :** material that exudes or is extruded
sphag·nic·o·lous \sfag-ˈnik-ə-ləs\ *adj* **:** inhabiting or growing in sphagnum ⟨~ rotifers⟩
sphag·nous \ˈsfag-nəs\ *adj* **:** of, relating to, or abounding in sphagnum
sphag·num \ˈsfag-nəm\ *n* [NL, genus name, fr. L *sphagnos*, a moss, fr. Gk] **1 :** any of a large genus (*Sphagnum*, coextensive with the order Sphagnales) of atypical mosses that grow only in wet acid areas where their remains become compacted with other plant debris to form peat **2 :** a mass of sphagnum plants
sphal·er·ite \ˈsfal-ə-ˌrīt\ *n* [G *sphalerit*, fr. Gk *sphaleros* deceitful, fr. *sphallein* to cause to fall — more at SPILL] **:** a widely distributed ore of zinc composed essentially of zinc sulfide ZnS
sphene \ˈsfēn\ *n* [F *sphène*, fr. Gk *sphēn* wedge — more at SPOON] **:** a mineral $CaTiSiO_5$ that is a silicate of calcium and titanium and often contains other elements
sphen·odon \ˈsfē-nə-ˌdän, ˈsfen-ə-\ *n* [NL, deriv. of Gk *sphēn* wedge + *odōn* tooth — more at TOOTH] **:** TUATARA — **sphen·odont** \-ˌdänt\ *adj*
1**sphe·noid** \ˈsfē-ˌnȯid\ *or* **sphe·noi·dal** \sfi-ˈnȯid-ᵊl\ *adj* [NL *sphenoides*, fr. Gk *sphēnoeidēs* wedge-shaped, fr. *sphēn* wedge] **1 :** of, relating to, or being a winged compound bone of the base of the cranium **2** *usu sphenoidal* **:** wedge-shaped
2**sphenoid** *n* **:** a sphenoid bone
spher·al \ˈsfir-əl\ *adj* **1 :** SPHERICAL **2 :** SYMMETRICAL, HARMONIOUS
1**sphere** \ˈsfi(ə)r\ *n* [ME *spere* globe, celestial sphere, fr. MF *espere*, fr. L *sphaera*, fr. Gk *sphaira*, lit., ball] **1 a** (1) **:** the apparent surface of the heavens of which half forms the dome of the visible sky (2) **:** one of the concentric and eccentric revolving spherical transparent shells in which according to ancient astronomy stars, sun, planets, and moon are set **b :** a globe depicting such a sphere; *broadly* **:** GLOBE a **2 a :** a globular body **:** BALL **b :** PLANET, STAR **c :** a surface all points of which are equally distant from a center — see VOLUME table **3 :** natural, normal, or proper place; *esp* **:** social order or rank **4 a** *obs* **:** ORBIT **b :** a field or range of influence or significance **:** PROVINCE — **spher·ic** \ˈsfi(ə)r-ik, ˈsfer-\ *adj* — **sphe·ric·i·ty** \sfir-ˈis-ət-ē\ *n*
2**sphere** *vt* **1 :** to place in a sphere or among the spheres **:** ENSPHERE **2 :** to form into a sphere
sphere of influence : a territorial area within which the political influence or the interests of one nation are held to be more or less paramount
spher·i·cal \ˈsfir-i-kəl, ˈsfer-\ *adj* **1 :** having the form of a sphere or of one of its segments **2 :** relating to or dealing with a sphere or its properties — **spher·i·cal·ly** \-k(ə-)lē\ *adv*
spherical aberration *n* **:** aberration caused by the spherical form of a lens or mirror that gives different foci for central and marginal rays
spherical angle *n* **:** the angle between two intersecting arcs of great circles of a sphere measured by the plane angle formed by the tangents to the arcs at the point of intersection
spherical coordinate *n* **:** one of the two coordinates of a plane polar coordinate system or the angle between the plane and a fixed plane containing a reference line
spherical excess *n* **:** the amount by which the sum of the three angles of a spherical triangle exceeds two right angles
spherical geometry *n* **:** the geometry of figures on a sphere
spherical polygon *n* **:** a figure analogous to a plane polygon that is formed on a sphere by arcs of great circles
spherical triangle *n* **:** a spherical polygon of three sides
spherical trigonometry *n* **:** trigonometry applied to spherical triangles and polygons
1**spher·ics** \ˈsfi(ə)r-iks, ˈsfer-\ *n pl but sing in constr* **1 :** SPHERICAL GEOMETRY **2 :** SPHERICAL TRIGONOMETRY
2**spherics** *var of* SFERICS
spher·oid \ˈsfi(ə)r-ˌȯid, ˈsfe(ə)r-\ *n* **:** a figure resembling a sphere; *esp* **:** an ellipsoid of revolution
sphe·roi·dal \sfir-ˈȯid-ᵊl\ *also* **spher·oid** \ˈsfi(ə)r-ˌȯid, ˈsfe(ə)r-\ *adj* **:** having the form of a spheroid — **sphe·roi·dal·ly** \sfir-ˈȯid-ᵊl-ē\ *adv*
sphe·rom·e·ter \sfir-ˈäm-ət-ər\ *n* [ISV] **:** an instrument for measuring the curvature of a surface
spher·ule \ˈsfi(ə)r-(ˌ)(y)ü(ə)l, ˈsfe(ə)r-\ *n* **:** a little sphere or spherical body
spher·u·lite \ˈsfir-(y)ə-ˌlīt, ˈsfer-\ *n* **:** a usu. spherical crystalline body of radiating crystal fibers found in vitreous volcanic rocks — **spher·u·lit·ic** \ˌsfir-(y)ə-ˈlit-ik, ˌsfer-\ *adj*
sphery \ˈsfi(ə)r-ē\ *adj* **1 :** SPHERICAL, STARLIKE **2 :** of or relating to the spheres
sphinc·ter \ˈsfiŋ(k)-tər\ *n* [LL, fr. Gk *sphinktēr*, lit., band; akin to L *spatium* space — more at SPEED] **:** an annular muscle surrounding and able to contract or close a bodily opening — **sphinc·ter·al** \-t(ə-)rəl\ *adj*
sphin·gid \ˈsfin-jəd\ *n* [deriv. of Gk *sphing-*, *sphinx* sphinx] **:** HAWKMOTH
sphinx \ˈsfiŋ(k)s\ *n, pl* **sphinx·es** *or* **sphin·ges** \ˈsfin-ˌjēz\ [L, fr. Gk; akin to Gk *sphinktēr* sphincter] **1 a :** an enigmatic monster in ancient Greek mythology having typically a lion's body, wings, and the head and bust of a woman **b :** a person enigmatic like the sphinx of ancient Greece **2 :** an ancient Egyptian image in the form of a recumbent lion having a man's head, a ram's head, or a hawk's head **3 :** HAWKMOTH
sphra·gis·tic \sfrə-ˈjis-tik\ *adj* [LGk *sphragistikos*, fr. Gk *sphragizein* to close with a seal, fr. *sphragis* seal] **:** of or relating to a seal or signet
sphra·gis·tics \-tiks\ *n pl but sing or pl in constr* **:** the science of seals and signets
sphyg·mo·graph \ˈsfig-mə-ˌgraf\ *n* [Gk *sphygmos* pulse + ISV *-graph*] **:** an instrument that records graphically the movements or character of the pulse — **sphyg·mo·graph·ic** \ˌsfig-mə-ˈgraf-ik\ *adj* — **sphyg·mog·ra·phy** \sfig-ˈmäg-rə-fē\ *n*
sphyg·mo·ma·nom·e·ter \ˌsfig-(ˌ)mō-mə-ˈnäm-ət-ər\ *n* [Gk *sphygmos* pulse + ISV *manometer*; akin to Gk *asphyxia* stopping of the pulse — more at ASPHYXIA] **:** an instrument for measuring blood pressure and esp. arterial blood pressure — **sphyg·mo·mano·met·ric** \-ˌman-ə-ˈme-trik\ *adj* — **sphyg·mo·mano·met·ri·cal·ly** \-tri-k(ə-)lē\ *adv* — **sphyg·mo·ma·nom·e·try** \-mə-ˈnäm-ə-trē\ *n*
sphyg·mom·e·ter \sfig-ˈmäm-ət-ər\ *n* [Gk *sphygmos* + ISV *-meter*] **:** SPHYGMOGRAPH
spi·ca \ˈspī-kə\ *n, pl* **spi·cae** \-ˌkē\ *or* **spicas** [L, spike of grain — more at SPIKE] **:** a spiral reverse plain or plaster bandage used to immobilize a limb esp. at a joint
Spi·ca \ˈspī-kə\ *n* [L, lit., spike of grain] **:** a star of the first magnitude in the constellation Virgo
spi·cate \ˈspī-ˌkāt\ *adj* [L *spicatus*, pp. of *spicare* to arrange in the shape of heads of grain, fr. *spica*] **:** POINTED, SPIKED; *specif* **:** arranged in the form of a spike ⟨a ~ inflorescence⟩
1**spic·ca·to** \spi-ˈkät-(ˌ)ō\ *adj* [It, pp. of *spiccare* to detach] **:** performed with springing bow — used as a direction in music for stringed instruments
2**spiccato** *n* **:** a spiccato technique, performance, or passage
1**spice** \ˈspīs\ *n* [ME, fr. OF *espice*, fr. LL *species* spices, fr. L, species] **1 :** any of various aromatic vegetable products (as pepper or nutmeg) used to season or flavor foods **2 a** *archaic* **:** a small portion, quantity, or admixture **:** DASH **b :** something that gives zest or relish **3 :** a pungent or fragrant odor **:** PERFUME
2**spice** *vt* **:** to season with spices
spice·ber·ry \ˈspīs-ˌber-ē\ *n* **:** any of several spicy plants; *esp* **:** WINTERGREEN 2
spice box *n* **:** a box holding or designed to hold spices; *esp* **:** a box fitted with smaller boxes for holding spices
spice·bush \-ˌbu̇sh\ *n* **1 :** an aromatic shrub (*Lindera benzoin*) of the laurel family **2 :** a tall upright strawberry shrub (*Calycanthus occidentalis*) with slightly fragrant brown flowers
spic·ery \ˈspīs-(ə-)rē\ *n* **1 :** SPICES **2** *archaic* **:** a repository of spices **3 :** a spicy quality
spi·ci·form \ˈspī-kə-ˌfȯrm, -sə-\ *adj* [prob. fr. (assumed) NL *spiciformis*, fr. L *spica* head of grain + *-formis* -form — more at SPIKE] **:** shaped like a spike ⟨~ panicle⟩
spic·i·ly \ˈspī-sə-lē\ *adv* **:** in a spicy manner **:** PUNGENTLY
spic·i·ness \-sē-nəs\ *n* **:** the quality of being spicy
spick-and-span *or* **spic-and-span** \ˌspik-ən-ˈspan\ *adj* [short for *spick-and-span-new*, fr. obs E *spick* (spike) + E *and* + *span-new* (brand-new)] **1 :** FRESH, BRAND-NEW **2 :** spotlessly clean **:** SPRUCE
spic·u·la \ˈspik-yə-lə\ *n, pl* **spic·u·lae** \-yə-ˌlē, -ˌlī\ [NL, fr. ML, arrowhead, alter. of L *spiculum*, dim. of *spica*] **:** SPICULE, PRICKLE — **spic·u·lar** \-lər\ *adj*
spic·u·late \ˈspik-yə-lət, -ˌlāt\ *adj* **:** covered with or having spicules — **spic·u·la·tion** \ˌspik-yə-ˈlā-shən\ *n*
spic·ule \ˈspik-(ˌ)yü(ə)l\ *n* [NL *spicula* & L *spiculum*] **:** a minute slender pointed usu. hard body; *esp* **:** one of the minute calcareous or siliceous bodies that support the tissues of various invertebrates — **spic·u·lif·er·ous** \ˌspik-yu̇-ˈlif-(ə-)rəs\ *adj*
spic·u·lum \ˈspik-yə-ləm\ *n, pl* **spic·u·la** \-lə\ [L, small sharp organ, arrowhead] **:** an organ having the form of a spicule; *broadly* **:** SPICULE
spicy \ˈspī-sē\ *adj* **1 :** having the quality, flavor, or fragrance of spice **2 :** producing or abounding in spices **3 :** SPIRITED, ZESTFUL **4 :** PIQUANT, RACY; *esp* **:** somewhat scandalous or salacious
spi·der \ˈspīd-ər\ *n* [ME, alter. of *spithre*; akin to OE *spinnan* to spin] **1 :** any of an order (Araneida) of arachnids having a body with two main divisions, four pairs of walking legs, and two or more pairs of abdominal spinnerets for spinning threads of silk used in making cocoons for their eggs, nests for themselves, or webs for entangling their prey **2 :** a cast-iron frying pan orig. made with short feet to stand among coals on the hearth **3 :** any of various devices consisting of a frame or skeleton with radiating arm or members
spider crab *n* **:** any of numerous crabs (esp. family Majidae) with extremely long legs and nearly triangular bodies which they often cover with kelp
spider mite *n* **:** RED SPIDER
spider monkey *n* **:** any of a genus (*Ateles*) of New World monkeys with long slender limbs, the thumb absent or rudimentary, and a very long prehensile tail
spider phaeton *n* **:** a very high light carriage with a covered seat in front and a footman's seat behind
spi·der·wort \ˈspīd-ər-ˌwərt, -ˌwȯ(ə)rt\ *n* **:** any of a genus (*Tradescantia* of the family Commelinaceae) of monocotyledonous plants with ephemeral usu. blue or violet flowers
spi·dery \ˈspīd-ə-rē\ *adj* **1 a :** resembling a spider **b :** resembling a spider web **2 :** infested with spiders
spie·gel·ei·sen \ˈspē-gə-ˌlīz-ᵊn\ *also* **spie·gel** \ˈspē-gəl\ *n* [G *spiegeleisen*, fr. *spiegel* mirror + *eisen* iron] **:** a variety of pig iron

containing 15 to 30 percent manganese and 4.5 to 6.5 percent carbon

1**spiel** \'spē(ə)l\ *vb* [G *spielen* to play, fr. OHG *spilōn;* akin to OE *spilian* to revel] *vi* **1 :** to play music **2 :** to talk volubly or extravagantly ~ *vt* **:** to utter, express, or describe volubly or extravagantly — **spiel·er** *n*

2**spiel** *n* **:** a voluble line of often extravagant talk **:** PITCH

1**spi·er** \'spī(-ə)r\ *n* **:** SPY

2**spier** \'spi(ə)r\ *chiefly Scot var of* SPEER

spiffy \'spif-ē\ *adj* [E dial. *spiff* dandified] **:** fine looking **:** SMART

spig·ot \'spig-ət, 'spik-ət\ *n* [ME] **1 :** a pin or peg used to stop the vent in a cask **2 :** the plug of a faucet or cock **3 :** FAUCET

1**spike** \'spīk\ *n* [ME, prob. fr. MD; akin to L *spina* thorn — more at SPINE] **1 :** a very large nail **2 a :** one of a row of pointed irons placed (as on the top of a wall) to prevent passage **b** (1) **:** one of several metal projections set in the sole and heel of a shoe to improve traction (2) **:** a shoe having spikes attached to the sole or heel **3 :** something resembling a spike: as **a :** a young mackerel not over six inches long **b :** an unbranched antler of a young deer **4 :** a spike-heeled shoe **5 a :** the pointed element in a graph or tracing **b :** an unusually high and sharply defined maximum (as of amplitude in a wave train)

2**spike** *vt* **1 :** to fasten or furnish with spikes **2 a :** to disable (a muzzle-loading cannon) temporarily by driving a spike into the vent **b :** to suppress or block completely **3 :** to pierce or impale with or on a spike **4 :** to add alcohol or liquor to (a drink)

3**spike** *n* [ME *spik* head of grain, fr. L *spica;* akin to L *spina* thorn] **1 :** an ear of grain **2 :** an elongated inflorescence similar to a raceme but having the flowers sessile on the main axis

spiked \'spīkt, 'spī-kəd\ *adj* **1 a :** bearing ears **b :** having a spiky inflorescence ⟨~ flowers⟩ **2 :** SPIKY

spike heel *n* **:** a very high tapering heel used on women's shoes

spike lavender \'spīk-\ *n* [alter. of E dial. *spick* (lavender)] **:** a European mint (*Lavandula latifolia*) related to true lavender

spike·let \'spī-klət\ *n* **:** a small or secondary spike; *specif* **:** one of the small few-flowered bracted spikes that make up the compound inflorescence of a grass or sedge

spike·like \'spī-,klīk\ *adj* **:** resembling a spike

spike·nard \'spīk-,närd\ *n* [ME, fr. MF or ML; MF *spicanarde,* fr. ML *spica nardi,* lit., spike of nard] **1 a :** a fragrant ointment of the ancients **b :** an East Indian aromatic plant (*Nardostachys jatamansi*) of the valerian family from which the above is believed to have been derived **2 :** an American herb (*Aralia racemosa*) of the ginseng family with aromatic root and panicled umbels

spike–tooth harrow \,spīk-,tüth-\ *n* **:** a harrow with straight steel teeth set in horizontal bars

spiky \'spī-kē\ *adj* **:** having a sharp projecting point

1**spile** \'spī(ə)l\ *n* [prob. fr. D *spijl* stake; akin to L *spina* thorn — more at SPINE] **1 :** PILE **2 :** a small plug used to stop the vent of a cask **:** BUNG **3 :** a spout inserted in a tree to draw off sap

2**spile** *vt* **1 a :** to plug with a spile **b :** to draw off through a spile **2 :** to supply with a spile

spil·ing \'spī-liŋ\ *n* **:** a set of piles **:** PILING

1**spill** \'spil\ *vb* **spilled** \'spild, 'spilt\ *also* **spilt** \'spilt\ **spill·ing** [ME *spillen,* fr. OE *spillan;* akin to OHG *spaltan* to split, L *spolia* spoils, Gk *sphallein* to cause to fall] *vt* **1 a** *archaic* **:** KILL, DESTROY **b :** to cause (blood) to flow **2 :** to cause or allow accidentally or unintentionally to fall, flow, or run out so as to be lost or wasted **3 :** to relieve (a sail) from the pressure of the wind so as to reef or furl it; *also* **:** to relieve the pressure of (wind) on a sail by coming about or by adjusting it with lines **4 :** to throw off or out ⟨a horse ~*ed* him⟩ **5 :** to let out **:** DIVULGE ~ *vi* **1 a :** to flow, run, or fall out, over, or off and become wasted or lost **b :** to cause or allow something to spill **2 :** to fall from one's place — **spill·able** \'spil-ə-bəl\ *adj*

2**spill** *n* **1 :** an act or instance of spilling; *specif* **:** a fall from a horse or vehicle or an erect position **2 :** something spilled **3 :** SPILLWAY

3**spill** *n* [ME *spille*] **1 :** a wooden splinter **2 :** a slender piece: as **a :** a metallic rod or pin **b** (1) **:** a small roll or twist of paper or slip of wood for lighting a fire (2) **:** a roll or cone of paper serving as a container **c :** a peg or pin for plugging a hole **:** SPILE

spill·age \'spil-ij\ *n* **1 :** the act or process of spilling **2 :** the quantity that spills

spil·li·kin \'spil-i-kən\ *n* [prob. alter. of obs. D *spelleken* small peg] **:** JACKSTRAW

spill·way \'spil-,wā\ *n* **:** a passage for surplus water to run over or around a dam or similar obstruction

spi·lo·site \'spī-lə-,sīt\ *n* [G *spilosit,* fr. Gk *spilos* spot] **:** a spotted schistose rock produced by contact metamorphism of clay slate usu. by diabase

spilth \'spilth\ *n* **1 :** an act or instance of spilling **2 a :** something spilled **b :** REFUSE, RUBBISH

1**spin** \'spin\ *vb* **spun** \'spən\ **spin·ning** [ME *spinnen,* fr. OE *spinnan;* akin to OHG *spinnan* to spin, L *sponte* voluntarily, Gk *span* to draw — more at SPAN] *vi* **1 :** to draw out and twist fiber into yarn or thread **2 :** to form a thread by extruding a viscous rapidly hardening fluid — used of a spider or insect **3 a :** to revolve rapidly **:** GYRATE **b :** to be in a whirl **:** REEL **4 :** to move swiftly on wheels or in a vehicle **5 :** to fish with spinning bait **:** TROLL **6 a** *of an airplane* **:** to fall in a spin **b :** to spiral rapidly downward ~ *vt* **1 a :** to draw out and twist into yarns or threads **b :** to produce by drawing out and twisting a fibrous material **2 :** to form (as a web or cocoon) by spinning **3 a :** to draw out slowly **:** PROTRACT **b :** to evolve, express, or fabricate by processes of mind or imagination ⟨~ a yarn⟩ **4 :** to cause to whirl **:** TWIRL **5 :** to throw off by or as if by centrifugal force **6 :** to shape into threadlike form in manufacture; *also* **:** to manufacture by a whirling process

2**spin** *n* **1 a :** the act of spinning or twirling something **b :** the whirling motion imparted by spinning **c :** an excursion in a vehicle esp. on wheels **2 a :** an aerial maneuver or flight condition consisting of a combination of roll and yaw with the longitudinal axis of the airplane inclined steeply downward **b :** a plunging descent or downward spiral **c :** a state of mental confusion

spin·ach \'spin-ich\ *n* [MF *espinache, espinage,* fr. OSp *espinaca,* fr. Ar *isfānākh,* fr. Per] **1 :** a potherb (*Spinacia oleracea*) of the goosefoot family cultivated for its edible leaves **2 a :** something unwanted, insubstantial, or spurious **b :** an untidy overgrowth

1**spi·nal** \'spīn-ᵊl\ *adj* **1 :** of, relating to, or situated near the backbone **2 :** of, relating to, or affecting the spinal cord **3 :** of, relating to, or resembling a spine

2**spinal** *n* **:** a spinal anesthetic

spinal canal *n* **:** a canal that lodges the spinal cord and is formed by the arches on the dorsal side of the vertebrae

spinal column *n* **:** the axial skeleton of the trunk and tail of a vertebrate consisting of an articulated series of vertebrae and protecting the spinal cord — called also *backbone*

spinal cord *n* **:** the longitudinal cord of nervous tissue extending from the brain along the back in the spinal canal

spi·nal·ly \'spīn-ᵊl-ē\ *adv* **:** with respect to or along the spine

1**spin·dle** \'spin-dᵊl\ *n* [ME *spindel,* fr. OE *spinel;* akin to OE *spinnan* to spin] **1 a :** a round stick with tapered ends used to form and twist the yarn in hand spinning **b :** the long slender pin by which the thread is twisted in a spinning wheel **c :** any of the various rods or pins holding a bobbin in a spinning frame or other textile machine **d :** the pin in a loom shuttle **2 :** something shaped like a spindle (as a spindle-shaped achromatic figure along which the chromosomes are distributed during mitosis) **3 a :** the bar or shaft usu. of square section that carries the knobs and actuates the latch or bolt of a lock **b** (1) **:** a turned often decorative piece (2) **:** NEWEL **c** (1) **:** a revolving piece esp. if less in size than a shaft (2) **:** a horizontal or vertical axle revolving on pin or pivot ends (3) **:** a rod attached to a valve to move or guide it **d :** the part of an axle on which a vehicle wheel turns

2**spindle** *vb* **spin·dling** \-(d)liŋ, -(d)lən, -dᵊl-iŋ, -dᵊl-ən\ *vi* **1 :** to shoot or grow into a long slender stalk **2 :** to grow to stalk or stem rather than to flower or fruit ~ *vt* **:** to impale, thrust, or perforate on the spike of a spindle file

spin·dle–legged \,spin-dᵊl-'(l)eg(-ə)d, -'(l)āg(-ə)d\ *adj* **:** having long slender legs

spin·dle–shanked \-'shaŋ(k)t\ *adj* **:** SPINDLE-LEGGED

spindle tree *n* **:** any of a genus (*Euonymus*) of the staff-tree family of often cultivated shrubs or trees with hard wood

spin·dling \'spin-(d)liŋ, -(d)lən, -dᵊl-iŋ, -dᵊl-ən\ *adj* **:** SPINDLY

spin·dly \'spin-(d)lē, -dᵊl-ē\ *adj* **1 :** of a tall thin appearance that often suggests physical weakness **2 :** frail or flimsy in appearance or structure

spin·drift \'spin-,drift\ *n* [alter. of Sc *speendrift,* fr. *speen* to drive before a strong wind + E *drift*] **:** sea spray **:** SPOONDRIFT

spine \'spīn\ *n* [ME, thorn, spinal column, fr. L *spina;* akin to Latvian *spina* twig] **1 a :** SPINAL COLUMN **b :** something resembling a spinal column or constituting a central axis or chief support **c :** the backbone of a book **2 :** a stiff pointed plant process; *esp* **:** one that is a modified leaf or leaf part **3 :** a sharp rigid process on an animal: as **a :** SPICULE **b :** a stiff unsegmented fin ray of a fish **c :** a pointed prominence on a bone

spi·nel *or* **spi·nelle** \spə-'nel\ *n* [It *spinella,* dim. of *spina* thorn, fr. L] **1 :** a hard crystalline mineral $MgAl_2O_4$ consisting of an oxide of magnesium and aluminum that varies from colorless to ruby-red to black and is used as a gem **2 :** any of a group of minerals that are essentially oxides of magnesium, ferrous iron, zinc, or manganese

spine·less \'spīn-ləs\ *adj* **1 :** free from spines, thorns, or prickles **2 a :** having no spinal column **:** INVERTEBRATE **b :** lacking strength of character **:** WEAK — **spine·less·ly** *adv* — **spine·less·ness** *n*

spi·nes·cent \spī-'nes-ᵊnt\ *adj* [NL *spinescent-, spinescens,* fr. LL, prp. of *spinescere* to become thorny, fr. L *spina*] **:** SPINY; *also* **:** tending toward spininess

spin·et \'spin-ət\ *n* [It *spinetta*] **1 :** a small harpsichord similar to the virginal **2 a :** a compactly built small upright piano **b :** a small electronic organ

spi·ni·fex \'spī-nə-,feks\ *n* [NL, genus name, fr. L *spina* + *facere* to make — more at DO] **:** any of several Australian grasses (genera *Spinifex* or *Triodia*) with spiny seeds or stiff sharp leaves

spin·i·ness \'spī-nē-nəs\ *n* **:** the quality or state of being spiny

spin·na·ker \'spin-i-kər\ *n* [prob. irreg. fr. *Sphinx,* yacht that carried such a sail] **:** a large triangular sail set on a long light pole and used when running before the wind

spin·ner \'spin-ər\ *n* **1 :** one that spins **2 :** a fisherman's lure consisting of a spoon, blade, or set of wings that revolves when drawn through the water **3 :** a bowled cricket ball to which spin has been imparted **4 :** a conical sheet metal fairing which is attached to an airplane propeller boss and revolves with it **5 :** a movable arrow that is spun on its dial to indicate the number or kind of moves a player may make in a board game

spin·ner·et \,spin-ə-'ret\ *n* **1 :** an organ (as of a spider or caterpillar) for producing threads of silk from the secretion of silk glands **2** *or* **spin·ner·ette :** a small metal plate, thimble, or cap with fine holes through which a cellulose or chemical solution is forced in the spinning of rayon, nylon, and other man-made filaments

spinner play *n* **:** a football play in which the ballcarrier spins around in an attempt to deceive opposing players

spin·ney \'spin-ē\ *n* [MF *espinaye* thorny thicket, fr. *espine* thorn, fr. L *spina*] *Brit* **:** a small wood with undergrowth **:** COPSE

spinning frame *n* **:** a machine that draws, twists, and winds yarn

spinning jen·ny \-,jen-ē\ *n* [*Jenny,* nickname for *Jane*] **:** an early multiple-spindle machine for spinning wool or cotton

spinning wheel *n* **:** a small domestic hand-driven or foot-driven machine for spinning yarn or thread in which a wheel drives a single spindle

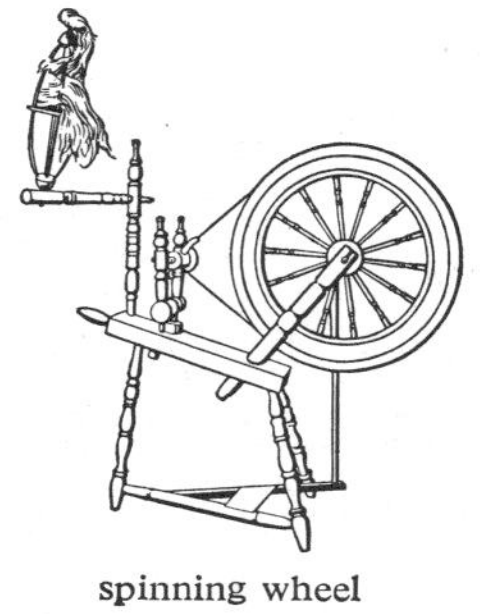

spinning wheel

spin–off \'spin-,ȯf\ *n* **1 :** the distribution by a business to its stockholders of particular assets and esp. of stock of another company **2 :** a useful by-product ⟨household products that are ~*s* from missile research⟩

spin·or \'spin-ər, -,ȯ(ə)r\ *n* [1*spin*] **:** a vector whose components are complex numbers in a two-dimensional or four-dimensional space and which is used esp. in the mathematics of the theory of relativity

spi·nose \'spī-,nōs\ *adj* **:** SPINY 1 — **spi·nose·ly** *adv*

spi·nos·i·ty \spī-'näs-ət-ē\ *n* **1 :** the quality or state of being spinose **2 :** something that is nettlesome or difficult

spi·nous \'spī-nəs\ *adj* **1 :** difficult or unpleasant to handle or meet **:** THORNY ⟨a ~ humor⟩ **2 :** SPINY 1, 3
spinous process *n* **:** SPINE 3; *esp* **:** the median spiny dorsal process of the neural arch of a vertebra
Spi·no·zism \spin-'ō-,ziz-əm\ *n* **:** the philosophy of Spinoza who taught that reality is one substance with an infinite number of attributes of which only thought and extension are capable of being apprehended by the human mind — **Spi·no·zist** \-zəst\ *n*
spin·ster \'spin(t)-stər\ *n* **1 :** a woman whose occupation is to spin **2 a** *archaic* **:** an unmarried woman of gentle family **b :** an unmarried woman **3 :** a woman past the common age for marrying or one who seems unlikely to marry — **spin·ster·hood** \-,hu̇d\ *n* — **spin·ster·ish** \-st(ə-)rish\ *adj*
spin·thari·scope \spin-'thar-ə-,skōp\ *n* [Gk *spintharis* spark + E *-scope*] **:** an instrument consisting of a fluorescent screen and a magnifying lens system for visual detection of alpha rays
spin the bottle *n* **1 :** the game spin the plate when played with a bottle **2 :** a method of choosing a performer (as a partner in a kissing game) according to whom the mouth of a bottle points to when it stops spinning
spin the plate *n* **:** a game in which something round (as a plate) is spun on edge and the name of a player is called upon which the named player must catch the spinning object before it falls or pay a forfeit — called also *spin the platter*
spi·nule \'spī-(,)nyü(ə)l\ *n* [L *spinula*, dim. of *spina* thorn — more at SPINE] **:** a minute spine — **spi·nu·lose** \'spī-nyə-,lōs\ *adj*
spiny \'spī-nē\ *adj* **1 :** covered or armed with spines; *broadly* **:** bearing spines, prickles, or thorns **2 :** abounding with difficulties, obstacles, or annoyances **:** THORNY **3 :** slender and pointed like a spine
spiny anteater *n* **:** ECHIDNA
spiny–finned \,spī-nē-'find\ *adj* **:** having fins with one or more stiff unbranched rays without transverse segmentation — used of acanthopterygian fishes; compare SOFT-FINNED
spiny lobster *n* **:** an edible crustacean (family Palinuridae) distinguished from the true lobster by the simple unenlarged first pair of legs and spiny carapace
spiny–rayed \,spī-ne-'rād\ *adj* **1** *of a fin* **:** having stiff unarticulated rays **2 :** SPINY-FINNED
spi·ra·cle \'spī-ri-kəl, 'spir-i-\ *n* [L *spiraculum*, fr. *spirare* to breathe — more at SPIRIT] **1 :** a breathing hole **:** VENT **2 :** a breathing orifice: as **a :** BLOWHOLE 2 **b :** an external tracheal aperture of a terrestrial arthropod that in an insect is usu. one of a series of small apertures located along each side of the thorax and abdomen — **spi·rac·u·lar** \spī-'rak-yə-lər, spə-\ *adj*
[1]**spi·ral** \'spī-rəl\ *adj* [ML *spiralis*, fr. L *spira* coil] **1 a :** winding around a center or pole and gradually receding from or approaching it ⟨~ curve⟩ **b :** HELICAL **2 :** advancing to higher levels through a series of cyclical movements — **spi·ral·ly** \-rə-lē\ *adv*
[2]**spiral** *n* **1 a :** the path of a point in a plane moving around an axis while continuously receding from or approaching it **b :** a three-dimensional curve (as a helix) with one or more turns about an axis **2 :** a single turn or coil in a spiral object **3 a :** something having a spiral form **b** (1) **:** a spiral flight (2) **:** a kick or pass in which a football rotates on its long axis while moving through the air **4 :** a continuously spreading and accelerating increase or decrease ⟨wage ~⟩
[3]**spiral** *vb* **spi·raled** *or* **spi·ralled; spi·ral·ing** *or* **spi·ral·ling** *vi* **:** to move in a spiral course ~ *vt* **1 :** to form into a spiral **2 :** to cause to spiral
spiral galaxy *n* **:** a galaxy exhibiting a central nucleus or barred structure from which extend concentrations of matter forming curved arms — called also *spiral nebula*
spiral spring *n* **:** a spring consisting of a wire coiled usu. in a flat spiral or in a helix
spi·rant \'spī-rənt\ *n* [ISV, fr. L *spirant-*, *spirans*, prp. of *spirare*] **:** a consonant (as \f\, \s\, \sh\) uttered with decided friction of the breath against some part of the oral passage **:** FRICATIVE — **spirant** *adj*
[1]**spire** \'spī(ə)r\ *n* [ME, fr. OE *spīr;* akin to MD *spier* blade of grass, L *spina* thorn — more at SPINE] **1 :** a slender tapering blade or stalk (as of grass) **2 :** the upper tapering part of something (as a tree or antler) **:** PINNACLE **3 a :** a tapering roof or analogous pyramidal construction surmounting a tower **b :** STEEPLE
[2]**spire** *vi* **:** to shoot up like a spire
[3]**spire** *n* [L *spira* coil, fr. Gk *speira;* akin to Gk *sparton* rope, esparto, Lith *springti* to choke in swallowing] **1 a :** SPIRAL **b :** COIL **2 :** the upper part of a spiral mollusk shell
[4]**spire** *vi* **:** to rise upward in a spiral
spi·rea *or* **spi·raea** \spī-'rē-ə\ *n* [NL *Spiraea*, genus name, fr. L, a plant, fr. Gk *speiraia*] **1 :** any of a genus (*Spiraea*) of shrubs of the rose family with small perfect white or pink flowers in dense racemes, corymbs, cymes, or panicles **2 :** any of several garden plants resembling spireas; *esp* **:** a shrub (*Astilbe japonica*) of the saxifrage family
[1]**spired** \'spī(ə)rd\ *adj* **1 :** having a spire ⟨a ~ church⟩ **2 :** tapering usu. to a sharp point
[2]**spired** \'spī(ə)rd\ *adj* **:** having a spire **:** SPIRAL ⟨~ shell⟩
spi·reme \'spī(ə)r-,ēm\ *n* [G *spirem*, fr. Gk *speirama*, *speirēma* convolution, fr. *speirasthai* to be coiled, fr. *speira*] **:** a continuous thread observed in fixed preparations of the prophase of mitosis that appears to be a strand of chromatin but is generally held to be an artifact
spi·rif·er·ous \spī-'rif-(ə-)rəs\ *adj* [prob. fr. NL *spirifer*, fr. L *spira* + *-i-* + *-fer* -ferous] **1 :** having a spiral part or organ **2 :** SPIRED
spi·ril·lum \spī-'ril-əm\ *n, pl* **spi·ril·la** \-'ril-ə\ [NL, genus name, fr. dim. of L *spira* coil] **:** any of a genus (*Spirillum*) of long curved flagellate bacteria; *broadly* **:** a spiral filamentous bacterium (as a spirochete)
[1]**spir·it** \'spir-ət\ *n* [ME, fr. OF or L; OF, fr. L *spiritus*, lit., breath; akin to L *spirare* to blow, breathe, ON *fīsa* to break wind] **1 :** an animating or vital principle held to give life to physical organisms **2 a :** a supernatural being (as an apparition or sprite) **b :** a supernatural incorporeal rational being or personality held to be able to become visible at will; *esp* **:** one held to be hostile to mankind **c :** a supernatural being held to be able to enter into and possess a person **d :** an incorporeal or immaterial being **e :** GHOST **3** *cap* **:** HOLY SPIRIT **4 :** SOUL 3 **5 a :** temper or disposition of mind ⟨in good ~*s*⟩ **b :** mental vigor or animation **:** VIVACITY **6 :** the immaterial intelligent or sentient part of a person **7 a :** the activating or essential principle influencing a person **b :** an inclination, impulse, or tendency of a specified kind **8 a :** a special attitude or frame of mind **b :** the feeling, quality, or disposition characterizing something ⟨undertaken in a ~ of fun⟩ **9 :** a lively or brisk quality in a person or his actions **10 :** a person having a character or disposition of a specified nature **11 :** a mental disposition characterized by firmness or assertiveness **:** ARDOR, METTLE **12 a :** DISTILLATE 1: as (1) **:** the liquid containing ethyl alcohol and water that is distilled from an alcoholic liquid or mash — often used in pl. (2) **:** any of various volatile liquids obtained by distillation or cracking (as of petroleum, shale, or wood) — often used in pl. (3) **:** ALCOHOL 1 **b :** a usu. volatile organic solvent (as an alcohol, ester, or hydrocarbon) **13 a :** prevailing tone or tendency ⟨~ of the age⟩ **b :** general intent or real meaning ⟨~ of the law⟩ **14 :** an alcoholic solution of a volatile substance ⟨~ of camphor⟩ **15** *cap, Christian Science* **:** [2]GOD b **syn** see COURAGE, SOUL
[2]**spirit** *vt* **1 :** to infuse with spirit; *esp* **:** ANIMATE, ENCOURAGE **2 a :** to carry off usu. secretly or mysteriously **b :** to convey in a secret or mysterious way
spir·it·ed \'spir-ət-əd\ *adj* **:** full of energy, animation, or courage — **spir·it·ed·ly** *adv* — **spir·it·ed·ness** *n*
spirit gum *n* **:** a solution (as of gum arabic in ether) used esp. for attaching false hair to the skin
spir·it·ism \'spir-ət-,iz-əm\ *n* **:** SPIRITUALISM 2a — **spir·it·ist** \-ət-əst\ *n* — **spir·it·is·tic** \,spir-ət-'is-tik\ *adj*
spirit lamp *n* **:** a lamp in which a volatile liquid fuel (as alcohol) is burned
spir·it·less \'spir-ət-ləs\ *adj* **:** lacking animation, cheerfulness, or courage — **spir·it·less·ly** *adv* — **spir·it·less·ness** *n*
spirit level *n* **:** LEVEL 1
spirit of hartshorn *or* **spirits of hartshorn :** AMMONIA WATER
spir·i·to·so \,spir-ə-'tō-(,)sō, -(,)zō\ *adj* [It, fr. *spirito* spirit, fr. L *spiritus*] **:** ANIMATED — used as a direction in music
spir·it·ous \'spir-ət-əs\ *adj, archaic* **:** PURE, REFINED
spirit rapping *n* **:** an alleged form of communication with the spirits of the dead by raps
spirits of turpentine *or* **spirit of turpentine :** TURPENTINE 2a
spirits of wine *or* **spirit of wine :** rectified spirit **:** ALCOHOL 1
[1]**spir·i·tu·al** \'spir-ich-(ə-)wəl, -ich-əl\ *adj* [ME, fr. MF & LL; MF *spirituel*, fr. LL *spiritualis*, fr. L, of breathing, of wind, fr. *spiritus*] **1 :** of, relating to, or consisting of spirit **:** INCORPOREAL **2 a :** of or relating to sacred matters ⟨~ songs⟩ **b :** ecclesiastical rather than lay or temporal ⟨lords ~⟩ **3 :** spiritually akin or related ⟨~ home⟩ ⟨~ heir⟩ **4 a :** of or relating to ghosts or similar supernatural beings **b :** SPIRITUALISTIC — **spir·i·tu·al·ly** \-ē\ *adv* — **spir·i·tu·al·ness** *n*
[2]**spiritual** *n* **1** *pl* **:** things of a spiritual, ecclesiastical, or religious nature **2 :** a Negro religious song esp. of the southern U.S. usu. of a deeply emotional character
spiritual bouquet *n* **:** an offering by a Roman Catholic of a number of devotional acts undertaken on behalf of a person on special occasions (as name days or anniversaries) or of someone recently deceased esp. as an expression of sympathy
spir·i·tu·al·ism \'spir-ich-(ə-)wə-,liz-əm, -ich-ə-,liz-\ *n* **1 :** the view that spirit is a prime element of reality **2 a :** a belief that departed spirits hold intercourse with the living usu. through a medium (as by rapping or trances) **b** *cap* **:** a movement comprising religious organizations emphasizing spiritualism — **spir·i·tu·al·ist** \-ləst\ *n, often cap* — **spir·i·tu·al·is·tic** \,spir-ich-(ə-)wə-'lis-tik, -ich-ə-'lis-\ *adj*
spir·i·tu·al·i·ty \,spir-ich-ə-'wal-ət-ē\ *n* **1 :** something that in ecclesiastical law belongs to the church or to a cleric as such **2 :** CLERGY **3 :** sensitivity or attachment to religious values **4 :** the quality or state of being spiritual
spir·i·tu·al·iza·tion \,spir-ich-(ə-)wə-lə-'zā-shən, -ich-ə-lə-\ *n* **:** the action of spiritualizing **:** the state of being spiritualized
spir·i·tu·al·ize \'spir-ich-(ə-)wə-,līz, -ich-ə-,līz\ *vt* **1 :** to make spiritual; *esp* **:** to purify from the corrupting influences of the world **2 :** to give a spiritual meaning to or understand in a spiritual sense
spir·i·tu·al·ty \'spir-ich-(ə-)wəl-tē, -ich-əl-\ *n* [ME *spiritualte*, fr. MF *spiritualté*, fr. ML *spiritualitat-*, *spiritualitas*, fr. LL *spiritualis* spiritual] **:** SPIRITUALITY 1, 2
spi·ri·tu·el *or* **spi·ri·tu·elle** \,spir-i-chə-'wel, spē-rē-tw(ʸ)el\ *adj* [*spirituel* fr. F, lit., spiritual; *spirituelle* fr. F, fem. of *spirituel*] **:** having or marked by a refined and esp. sprightly or witty nature
spir·i·tu·os·i·ty \,spir-ich-ə-'wäs-ət-ē\ *n* **:** the quality or state of being spirituous ⟨~ of wines and liquors⟩
spir·i·tu·ous \'spir-ich-(ə-)wəs, -ich-əs, 'spir-ət-əs\ *adj* [prob. fr. F *spiritueux*, fr. L *spiritus* spirit] **:** containing or impregnated with alcohol obtained by distillation ⟨~ liquors⟩
spirit writing *n* **:** automatic writing held to be produced under the influence of spirits
spiro- *comb form* [ISV, fr. L *spirare* to breathe — more at SPIRIT] **:** respiration ⟨*spiro*graph⟩
spi·ro·chae·ta \,spī-rə-'kēt-ə\ *n, pl* **spi·ro·chae·tae** \-'kēt-(,)ē\ [NL] **:** SPIROCHETE
spi·ro·chet·al \,spī-rə-'kēt-ᵊl\ *adj* **:** caused by spirochetes ⟨~ jaundice⟩
spi·ro·chete *or* **spi·ro·chaete** \'spī-rə-,kēt\ *n* [NL *Spirochaeta*, genus of bacteria, fr. L *spira* coil + Gk *chaitē* long hair — more at SPIRE, CHAETA] **:** any of an order (Spirochaetales) of slender spirally undulating bacteria including those causing syphilis and relapsing fever
spi·ro·chet·osis \,spī-rə-,kēt-'ō-səs\ *n* **:** infection with or a disease caused by spirochetes
spi·ro·graph \'spī-rə-,graf\ *n* [ISV] **:** an instrument recording respiratory movements — **spi·ro·graph·ic** \,spī-rə-'graf-ik\ *adj*
spi·ro·gy·ra \,spī-rə-'jī-rə\ *n* [NL, genus name, fr. Gk *speira* coil + *gyros* ring, circle — more at SPIRE, COWER] **:** any of a genus (*Spirogyra*) of freshwater green algae with spiral chlorophyll bands
spi·rom·e·ter \spī-'räm-ət-ər\ *n* [ISV] **:** an instrument for measuring the air entering and leaving the lungs — **spi·ro·met·ric** \,spī-rə-'me-trik\ *adj* — **spi·rom·e·try** \spī-'räm-ə-trē\ *n*

spirt *var of* SPURT
spi·ru·la \'spir-(y)ə-lə, 'spīr-\ *n* [NL, genus name, fr. dim. of L *spira* coil] **:** any of a genus (*Spirula*) of small dibranchiate cephalopods having a many-chambered shell in a flat spiral
spiry \'spī(ə)r-ē\ *adj* **:** resembling a spire; *esp* **:** being tall, slender, and tapering
[1]**spit** \'spit\ *n* [ME, fr. OE *spitu;* akin to L *spina* thorn, spine] **1 :** a slender pointed rod for holding meat over a fire **2 :** a small point of land esp. of sand or gravel running into a body of water
[2]**spit** *vt* **spit·ted; spit·ting :** to fix on or as if on a spit **:** IMPALE
[3]**spit** *vb* **spit** *or* **spat** \'spat\ **spit·ting** [ME *spitten,* fr. OE *spittan,* of imit. origin] *vt* **1 a :** to eject (as saliva) from the mouth **:** EXPECTORATE **b** (1) **:** to express by or as if by spitting (2) **:** to utter with a spitting sound or scornful expression **c :** to emit as if by spitting; *specif* **:** to emit (precipitation) in driving particles or in flurries ⟨~ rain⟩ **2 :** to set to burning ⟨~ a fuse⟩ ~ *vi* **1 a** (1) **:** to eject saliva as in aversion or contempt (2) **:** to exhibit contempt **b :** to eject saliva from the mouth **:** EXPECTORATE **2 :** to rain or snow slightly or in flurries **3 :** to make a noise suggesting expectoration **:** SPUTTER — **spit·ter** *n*
[4]**spit** *n* **1 a** (1) **:** SPITTLE, SALIVA (2) **:** the act or an instance of spitting **b** (1) **:** a frothy secretion exuded by spittlebugs (2) **:** SPITTLEBUG **2 :** perfect likeness **3 :** a sprinkle of rain or flurry of snow
spit·al *or* **spit·tle** \'spit-ᵊl\ *n* [ME *spitel,* modif. of ML *hospitale* — more at HOSPITAL] **:** LAZARETTO, HOSPITAL
spit and polish *n* [fr. the practice of polishing objects such as shoes by spitting on them and then rubbing them with a cloth] **:** extreme attention to cleanliness, orderliness, smartness of appearance, and ceremonial esp. at the expense of operational efficiency
spit·ball \'spit-,bȯl\ *n* **1 :** paper chewed and rolled into a ball to be thrown as a missile **2 :** a baseball pitch delivered after the ball has been moistened with saliva or sweat
spit curl *n* [prob. fr. its being sometimes plastered down with saliva] **:** a spiral curl that is usu. plastered on the forehead, temple, or cheek
[1]**spite** \'spīt\ *n* [ME, short for *despite*] **1 :** petty ill will or hatred with the disposition to irritate, annoy, or thwart **2 :** an instance of spite **:** GRUDGE **syn** see MALICE — **in spite of :** in defiance or contempt of **:** NOTWITHSTANDING
[2]**spite** *vt* **1 :** to treat maliciously (as by shaming or thwarting) **2 a :** to fill with spite **b :** ANNOY
spite·ful \-fəl\ *adj* **:** filled with or showing spite **:** MALICIOUS — **spite·ful·ly** \-fə-lē\ *adv* — **spite·ful·ness** *n*
spit·fire \'spit-,fī(ə)r\ *n* **:** a quick-tempered or highly emotional person
spit·tle \'spit-ᵊl\ *n* [ME *spetil,* fr. OE *spǣtl;* akin to OE *spittan*] **1 :** SALIVA **2 :** SPIT 1b(1)
spit·tle·bug \-,bəg\ *n* **:** any of numerous leaping homopterous insects (family Cercopidae) whose larvae secrete froth
spittle insect *n* **:** SPITTLEBUG
spit·toon \spi-'tün, spə-\ *n* [[4]*spit* + *-oon* (as in *balloon*)] **:** a receptacle for spit — called also *cuspidor*
spitz \'spits\ *n* [G, fr. *spitz* pointed; akin to OE *spitu* spit; fr. the shape of its ears and muzzle] **:** any of several stocky heavy-coated dogs of northern origin with erect ears and a heavily furred tail tightly recurved over the back; *esp* **:** a medium-sized white dog descended from Pomeranian ancestors and often held to form a separate breed
spiv \'spiv\ *n* [alter. of E dial. *spiff* flashy dresser, fr. *spiff* dandified] **1** *Brit* **:** one who lives by his wits without working **2** *Brit* **:** SLACKER
splanch·nic \'splaŋk-nik\ *adj* [NL *splanchnicus,* fr. Gk *splanchnikos,* fr. *splanchna,* pl., viscera; akin to Gk *splēn* spleen] **:** of or relating to the viscera **:** VISCERAL
[1]**splash** \'splash\ *vb* [alter. of *plash*] *vi* **1 a :** to strike and dash about a liquid or semiliquid substance **b :** to move in or into a liquid or semiliquid substance and cause it to spatter **2 a** (1) **:** to become spattered about (2) **:** to spread or scatter in the manner of splashed liquid **b :** to fall, strike, or move with a splashing sound ~ *vt* **1 a** (1) **:** to dash a liquid or thinly viscous substance upon or against (2) **:** to soil or stain with splashed liquid **b :** to mark or overlay with patches of contrasting color or texture **c :** to display prominently **2 a :** to cause (a liquid or thinly viscous substance) to spatter about esp. with force **b :** to scatter in the manner of a splashed liquid — **splash·er** *n*
[2]**splash** *n* **1 a** (1) **:** splashed liquid or semiliquid substance; *also* **:** impounded water released suddenly (2) **:** a spot or daub from or as if from splashed liquid **b :** a colored patch **:** BLOTCH **2 a :** the action of splashing **b :** a short plunge **3 :** a sound produced by or as if by a liquid falling, moving, being hurled, or oscillating **4 a :** a vivid impression created esp. by ostentatious activity or appearance **b :** ostentatious display — **splashy** \'splash-ē\ *adj*
splash·board \'splash-,bō(ə)rd, -,bȯ(ə)rd\ *n* **1 a :** DASHBOARD 1 **b :** a panel to protect against splashes **2 :** a plank used to close a sluice or spillway of a dam
splash down *vi* **:** to land a manned spacecraft in the ocean
splash·down \'splash-,daủn\ *n* **:** the landing of a manned spacecraft in the ocean
splash guard *n* **:** a flap suspended behind a rear wheel to prevent tire splash from muddying windshields of following vehicles
splash·i·ly \'splash-ə-lē\ *adv* **:** in a splashy manner
splash·i·ness \'splash-ē-nəs\ *n* **:** the quality or state of being splashy
splat \'splat\ *n* [obs. *splat* (to spread flat)] **:** a single flat thin often ornamental member of a back of a chair
splat·ter \'splat-ər\ *vb* [prob. blend of *splash* and *spatter*] **:** SPATTER — **splatter** *n*
[1]**splay** \'splā\ *vb* [ME *splayen,* short for *displayen* — more at DISPLAY] *vt* **1 :** to spread out **2 :** to make (as the jamb of a door) oblique **:** BEVEL ~ *vi* **1 :** to become splayed **2 :** SLOPE, SLANT
[2]**splay** *n* **1 :** a slope or bevel esp. of the sides of a door or window **2 :** SPREAD, EXPANSION
[3]**splay** *adj* **1 :** turned outward **2 :** AWKWARD, UNGAINLY
splay·foot \'splā-,fủt, -'fủt\ *n* **:** a foot abnormally flattened and spread out; *specif* **:** FLATFOOT — **splayfoot** *or* **splay·foot·ed** \-'fủt-əd\ *adj*
spleen \'splēn\ *n* [ME *splen,* fr. MF or L; MF *esplen,* fr. L *splen,* fr. Gk *splēn;* akin to L *lien* spleen] **1 :** a highly vascular ductless organ near the stomach or intestine of most vertebrates concerned with final destruction of blood cells, storage of blood, and production of lymphocytes **2** *obs* **:** the seat of emotions or passions **3** *archaic* **:** MELANCHOLY **4 :** ANGER, MALICE **5** *obs* **:** a sudden impulse or whim **:** CAPRICE **syn** see MALICE
spleen·ful \-fəl\ *adj* **:** full of or affected with spleen **:** SPLENETIC
spleen·wort \-,wərt, -,wȯ(ə)rt\ *n* **:** any of a genus (*Asplenium*) of ferns having linear or oblong sori borne obliquely on the upper side of a veinlet
spleeny \'splē-nē\ *adj* **1 :** full of or displaying spleen **2** *NewEng* **:** peevish and irritable with hypochondriac inclinations
splen- *or* **spleno-** *comb form* [L, fr. Gk *splēn-, splēno-,* fr. *splēn*] **:** spleen ⟨*splen*ectomy⟩ ⟨*spleno*megaly⟩
splen·dent \'splen-dənt\ *adj* [ME, fr. LL *splendent-, splendens,* fr. L, prp. of *splendēre*] **1 :** SHINING, GLOSSY **2 :** ILLUSTRIOUS, BRILLIANT
splen·did \'splen-dəd\ *adj* [L *splendidus,* fr. *splendēre* to shine; akin to Gk *splēdos* ashes, Skt *sphuliṅga* spark] **1 :** possessing or displaying splendor: as **a :** SHINING, BRILLIANT **b :** SHOWY, MAGNIFICENT **2 :** ILLUSTRIOUS, GRAND, GLORIOUS **3 :** EXCELLENT — **splen·did·ly** *adv* — **splen·did·ness** *n*
syn SPLENDID, RESPLENDENT, GORGEOUS, GLORIOUS, SUBLIME, SUPERB mean extraordinarily or transcendently impressive. SPLENDID implies outshining the usual or customary; RESPLENDENT suggests a glowing or blazing splendor; GORGEOUS implies a rich splendor esp. in display of color; GLORIOUS suggests radiance that heightens beauty or distinction; SUBLIME implies an exaltation or elevation almost beyond human comprehension; SUPERB suggests a magnificence or excellence reaching the highest conceivable degree
splen·dif·er·ous \splen-'dif-(ə-)rəs\ *adj* [*splendor* + *-i-* + *-ferous*] **1 :** SPLENDID **2 :** deceptively splendid — **splen·dif·er·ous·ly** *adv* — **splen·dif·er·ous·ness** *n*
splen·dor *or chiefly Brit* **splen·dour** \'splen-dər\ *n* [ME *splendure,* fr. AF *splendur,* fr. L *splendor,* fr. *splendēre*] **1 a :** great brightness or luster **:** BRILLIANCY **b :** MAGNIFICENCE, POMP **2 :** something splendid — **splen·dor·ous** *also* **splen·drous** \-d(ə-)rəs\ *adj*
sple·nec·to·my \spli-'nek-tə-mē\ *n* [ISV] **:** surgical removal of the spleen
sple·net·ic \spli-'net-ik, *archaic* 'splen-ə-(,)tik\ *adj* [LL *spleneticus,* fr. L *splen* spleen] **1 :** SPLENIC **2** *archaic* **:** given to melancholy **3 :** marked by bad temper, malevolence, or spite **syn** see IRASCIBLE — **splenetic** *n* — **sple·net·i·cal·ly** \spli-'net-i-k(ə-)lē\ *adv*
sple·nic \'splē-nik, 'splen-ik\ *adj* [L *splenicus,* fr. Gk *splēnikos,* fr. *splēn* spleen] **:** of, relating to, or located in the spleen
sple·ni·us \'splē-nē-əs\ *n, pl* **sple·nii** \-nē-,ī\ [NL, fr. L *splenium* plaster, compress, fr. Gk *splēnion,* fr. *splēn*] **:** a flat oblique muscle of each side of the back of the neck
sple·no·meg·a·ly \,splē-nō-'meg-ə-lē\ *n* [ISV *splen-* + Gk *megal-, megas* large — more at MUCH] **:** enlargement of the spleen
spleu·chan \'splük-ən, 'splük-\ *n* [ScGael *spliūcan* & IrGael *spliūchān*] *Scot & Irish* **:** a pouch esp. for tobacco or money
[1]**splice** \'splīs\ *vt* [obs. D *splissen;* akin to MD *splitten* to split] **1 a :** to unite (as two ropes) by interweaving the strands **b :** to unite (as spars, timbers, rails) by lapping two ends together or by applying a piece that laps upon two ends and making fast **2 :** to unite in marriage **:** MARRY — **splic·er** *n*
[2]**splice** *n* **1 :** a joining or joint made by splicing **2 :** MARRIAGE, WEDDING

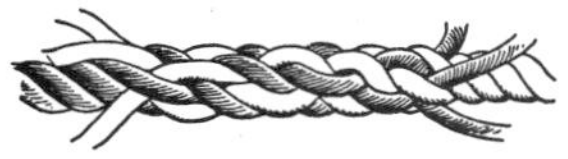

splice

spline \'splīn\ *n* [origin unknown] **1 :** a thin wood or metal strip used in building construction **2 :** a key that is fixed to one of two connected mechanical parts and fits into a keyway in the other; *also* **:** a keyway for such a key
[1]**splint** \'splint\ *or* **splent** \'splent\ *n, often attrib* [ME, fr. MLG *splinte, splente;* akin to OHG *spaltan* to split — more at SPILL] **1 :** a small plate or strip of metal **2 a :** a thin strip of wood interwoven with others in caning **b :** SPLINTER **c :** material or a device used to protect and immobilize a body part (as a broken arm) **3 :** a bony enlargement on the upper part of the cannon bone of a horse usu. on the inside of the leg
[2]**splint** *vt* **1 :** to support and immobilize (as a broken bone) with a splint **2 :** to brace with or as if with splints
splint bone *n* **:** one of the slender rudimentary metacarpal or metatarsal bones on either side of the cannon bone in the limbs of the horse and related animals
[1]**splin·ter** \'splint-ər\ *n* [ME, fr. MD; akin to MLG *splinte* splint] **1 :** a thin piece split or rent off lengthwise **:** SLIVER **2 :** a group or faction broken away from a parent body — **splin·tery** \'splint-ə-rē, 'splin-trē\ *adj*
[2]**splinter** *vb* **splin·ter·ing** \'splint-ə-riŋ, 'splin-triŋ\ *vt* **1 :** to split or rend into long thin pieces **:** SHIVER **2 :** to split into fragments, parts, or factions ~ *vi* **:** to become splintered
[1]**split** \'split\ *vb* **split; split·ting** [D *splitten,* fr. MD; akin to OHG *spaltan* to split — more at SPILL] *vt* **1 a :** to divide lengthwise usu. along a grain or seam or by layers **b :** to affect as if by cleaving or forcing apart **2 a** (1) **:** to tear or rend apart **:** BURST (2) **:** to subject (an atom or atomic nucleus) to artificial disintegration esp. by fission **b :** to affect as if by breaking up or tearing apart **:** SHATTER **3 :** to divide into parts or portions: as **a :** to divide between persons **:** SHARE **b :** to divide into factions, parties, or groups **c :** to mark (a ballot) or cast or register (a vote) so as to vote for candidates of different parties **d** (1) **:** to divide or break down (a chemical compound) into constituents ⟨~ a fat into glycerol and fatty acids⟩ (2) **:** to remove by such separation ⟨~ off carbon dioxide⟩ **e :** to divide (stock) by issuing a larger number of shares to existing shareholders usu. without increase in total par value **4 :** to separate (the parts of a whole) by interposing something ⟨~ an infinitive⟩ ~ *vi* **1 a :** to become split lengthwise or into layers **b :** to break apart **:** BURST **2 a :** to become divided up or separated off ⟨~ into factions⟩ **b :** to sever relations or connections **3 :** to apportion shares **syn** see TEAR — **split·ter** *n* — **split hairs :** to make oversubtle or trivial distinctions
[2]**split** *n* **1 a :** a narrow break made by or as if by splitting **b :** a position of bowling pins left standing with space for pins between them **2 :** a piece split off or made thin by splitting **3 a :** a division into or between divergent or antagonistic elements or forces **b :** a faction formed in this way **4 a :** the act or process of splitting **b :** a lowering oneself to the floor or leaping into the air with legs extended at right angles to the trunk **5 :** a product of division by or as if by splitting **6 :** a bottle of half the size of the usual small bottle for a drink **7 :** a sweet composed of sliced fruit (as banana), ice cream, nuts, and syrups

[3]split *adj* **1 :** DIVIDED, FRACTURED **2 :** prepared for use by splitting ⟨~ bamboo⟩ ⟨~ hides⟩ **3 :** HETEROZYGOUS
split decision *n* **:** a decision in a boxing match reflecting a division of opinion among the referee and judges
split infinitive *n* **:** an infinitive with *to* having a modifier between the *to* and the verbal (as in "to really start")
split–lev•el \'split-'lev-əl\ *adj* **:** divided vertically so that the floor level of rooms in one part is approximately midway between the levels of two successive stories in an adjoining part ⟨*split-level* house⟩ — **split–level** \-ˌlev-əl\ *n*
split pea *n* **:** a dried hulled pea in which the cotyledons usu. split apart
split personality *n* **:** a personality structure composed of two or more internally consistent groups of behavior tendencies and attitudes each acting independently of and apparently dissociated from the other
split rail *n* **:** a fence rail split from a log
split second *n* **:** a fractional part of a second **:** FLASH ⟨happened in a *split second*⟩
split shift *n* **:** a shift of working hours divided into two or more working periods at times (as morning and evening) separated by more than normal periods of time off (as for lunch or rest)
split T formation *n* **:** a variation of the football T formation in which the quarterback either moves along the line of scrimmage with the ball or keeps or pitches the ball out
split ticket *n* **:** a ballot cast by a voter who votes for candidates of more than one party
splore \'splō(ə)r, 'splȯ(ə)r\ *n* [origin unknown] **1** *Scot* **:** FROLIC, CAROUSAL **2** *Scot* **:** COMMOTION
splotch \'spläch\ *n* [perh. blend of *spot* and *blotch*] **:** BLOTCH, SPOT — **splotch** *vt* — **splotchy** \'spläch-ē\ *adj*
[1]splurge \'splərj\ *n* [perh. blend of *splash* and *surge*] **:** an ostentatious demonstration or effort
[2]splurge *vi* **1 :** to make a splurge **2 :** to indulge oneself extravagantly ~ *vt* **:** to spend extravagantly or ostentatiously
[1]splut•ter \'splət-ər\ *n* [prob. alter. of *sputter*] **1 :** a confused noise (as of hasty speaking) **2 :** a splashing or sputtering sound
[2]splutter *vi* **1 :** to make a noise as if spitting **2 :** to speak hastily and confusedly ~ *vt* **:** to utter hastily or confusedly **:** STAMMER — **splut•ter•er** \'splət-ər-ər\ *n*
splut•tery \'splət-ə-rē\ *adj* **:** marked by spluttering
Spode \'spōd\ *n* [Josiah *Spode* †1827 E potter] **:** a fine pottery or porcelain made at the works of Josiah Spode at Stoke in Staffordshire, England
spod•u•mene \'späj-ə-ˌmēn\ *n* [prob. fr. F *spodumène*, fr. G *spodumen*, fr. Gk *spodoumenos*, prp. of *spodousthai* to be burnt to ashes, fr. *spodos* ashes] **:** a white to yellowish, purplish, or emerald-green monoclinic mineral $LiAlSi_2O_6$ that is a lithium aluminum silicate and occurs in prismatic crystals often of great size
[1]spoil \'spȯi(ə)l\ *n* [ME *spoile*, fr. MF *espoille*, fr. L *spolia*, pl. of *spolium* — more at SPILL] **1 a :** plunder taken from an enemy in war or a victim in robbery **:** LOOT **b :** public offices made the property of a successful party — usu. used in pl. **c :** something gained by special effort — usu. used in pl. **2 a :** PLUNDERING, SPOLIATION **b :** the act of damaging **:** HARM, IMPAIRMENT **3 :** an object of plundering **:** PREY **4 :** earth and rock excavated or dredged **5 :** an object damaged or flawed in the making
syn SPOIL, PILLAGE, PLUNDER, BOOTY, PRIZE, LOOT mean something taken from another by force or craft. SPOIL, more commonly SPOILS, applies to what belongs by right or custom to the victor in war or political contest; PILLAGE stresses more open violence or lawlessness; PLUNDER applies to what is taken not only in war but in robbery, banditry, grafting, or swindling; BOOTY implies plunder to be shared among confederates; PRIZE applies to spoils captured on the high seas or territorial waters of the enemy; LOOT is a contemptuous term for plunder and applies esp. to what is taken from victims of a catastrophe
[2]spoil *vb* **spoiled** \'spȯi(ə)ld, 'spȯi(ə)lt\ *or* **spoilt** \'spȯi(ə)lt\ **spoil•ing** [ME *spoilen*, fr. MF *espoillier*, fr. L *spoliare*, fr. *spolium*] *vt* **1 a :** DESPOIL, STRIP **b :** PILLAGE, ROB **2** *archaic* **:** to seize by force **3 a :** to damage seriously **:** RUIN ⟨a crop ~*ed* by floods⟩ **b :** impair the quality or effect of ⟨a quarrel ~*ed* the celebration⟩ **4 a :** to impair the disposition or character of by overindulgence or excessive praise **b :** to pamper excessively **:** CODDLE ~ *vi* **1 :** to practice plunder and robbery **2 :** to become corrupted or tainted **3 :** to have an eager desire ⟨~*ing* for a fight⟩ **syn** see DECAY, INDULGE
spoil•able \'spȯi-lə-bəl\ *adj* **:** capable of spoiling or of being spoiled
spoil•age \'spȯi-lij\ *n* **1 :** the act or process of spoiling **2 :** something spoiled or wasted **3 :** loss by spoilage
spoil•er \-lər\ *n* **1 :** one that spoils **2 :** a long narrow plate along the upper surface of an airplane wing that may be raised for reducing lift and increasing drag
spoils•man \'spȯi(ə)lz-mən\ *n* **:** one who serves a party for a share of the spoils; *also* **:** one who sanctions such practice
spoil•sport \'spȯi(ə)l-ˌspō(ə)rt, -ˌspȯ(ə)rt\ *n* **:** one who spoils the sport or pleasure of others
spoils system *n* **:** a practice of regarding public offices and their emoluments as plunder to be distributed to members of the victorious party
[1]spoke *past & archaic past part of* SPEAK
[2]spoke \'spōk\ *n* [ME, fr. OE *spāca;* akin to MD *spike* spike] **1 a :** one of the small radiating bars inserted in the hub of a wheel to support the rim **b :** something resembling the spoke of a wheel **2 :** a rung of a ladder **3 :** one of the projecting handles of a steering wheel of a boat
[3]spoke *vt* **:** to furnish with or as if with spokes
spo•ken \'spō-kən\ *adj* **1 a :** delivered by word of mouth **:** ORAL **b :** used in speaking **:** UTTERED ⟨the ~ word⟩ **2 :** characterized by speaking in (such) a manner — used in combination ⟨*soft-spoken*⟩ ⟨*plainspoken*⟩
spoke•shave \'spōk-ˌshāv\ *n* [[2]*spoke*] **:** a drawing knife or small transverse plane with end handles for planing convex or concave surfaces

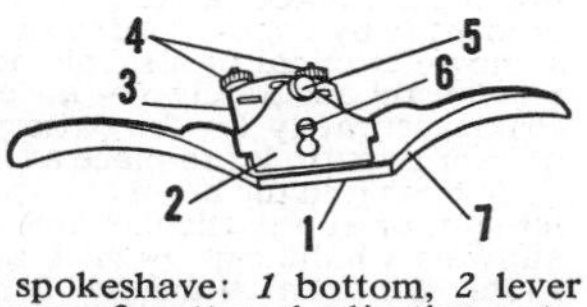

spokeshave: *1* bottom, *2* lever cap, *3* cutter, *4* adjusting nuts, *5* lever cap thumbscrew, *6* lever cap screw, *7* frame and handles

spokes•man \'spōk-smən\ *n* [prob. irreg. fr. *spoke*, obs. pp. of *speak*] **:** one who speaks as the representative of another or others — **spokes•wom•an** \-ˌswu̇m-ən\ *n*
spo•li•ate \'spō-lē-ˌāt\ [L *spoliatus*, pp.] *vt* **:** DESPOIL
spo•li•a•tion \ˌspō-lē-'ā-shən\ *n* [ME, fr. L *spoliation-*, *spoliatio*, fr. *spoliatus*, pp. of *spoliare* to plunder — more at SPOIL] **1 :** the act of plundering; *specif* **:** the state of having been plundered esp. in war **2 :** the act of injuring esp. beyond reclaim — **spo•li•a•tor** \'spō-lē-ˌāt-ər\ *n*
spon•da•ic \spän-'dā-ik\ *adj* [F or LL; F *spondaïque*, fr. LL *spondiacus*, *spondaicus*, fr. Gk *spondeiakos*, fr. *spondeios*] **:** of, relating to, or consisting of spondees — **spondaic** *n*
spon•dee \'spän-ˌdē\ *n* [ME *sponde*, fr.MF or L; MF *spondee*, fr. L *spondeum*, fr. Gk *spondeios*, fr. *spondeios* of a libation, fr. *spondē* libation; fr. its use in music accompanying libations — more at SPOUSE] **:** a metrical foot consisting of two long or stressed syllables
spon•dy•li•tis \ˌspän-də-'līt-əs\ *n* [NL, fr. Gk *sphondylos*, *spondylos* vertebra, lit., whorl; akin to Gk *sphadazein* to jerk, *sphendonē* sling] **:** inflammation of the vertebrae
[1]sponge \'spənj\ *n* [ME, fr. OE, fr. L *spongia*, fr. Gk] **1 a** (1) **:** an elastic porous mass of interlacing horny fibers that forms the internal skeleton of various marine animals (phylum Porifera) and is able when wetted to absorb water (2) **:** a piece of this material (as for scrubbing and cleaning) (3) **:** a porous rubber or cellulose product similarly used **b :** any of a phylum (Porifera) of lowly aquatic animals that are essentially double-walled cell colonies and permanently attached as adults **2 a** *archaic* **:** something that effaces or blots out existing impressions, memories, or emotions **b** *obs* **:** a process or method of cancelling or wiping off indebtedness without making payment **3 :** a pad (as of folded gauze) used in surgery and medicine (as to remove discharges or apply medication) **4 :** one who lives upon others **:** SPONGER **5 a :** raised dough **b :** a whipped dessert usu. containing whites of eggs or gelatin **c :** a metal (as platinum) obtained in porous form usu. by reduction without fusion ⟨titanium ~⟩ **d :** the egg mass of a crab
[2]sponge *vt* **1 :** to cleanse, wipe, or moisten with or as if with a sponge **2 :** to erase or destroy with or as if with a sponge **3 :** to get by sponging on another **4 :** to absorb with or as if with or in the manner of a sponge ~ *vi* **1 :** to absorb, soak up, or imbibe like a sponge **2 :** to get something from or live on another by imposing on hospitality or good nature **3 :** to dive or dredge for sponges — **spong•er** *n*
sponge cake *n* **:** a cake made without shortening
sponge cloth *n* **:** any of various soft porous fabrics esp. in a loose honeycomb weave
sponge rubber *n* **:** cellular rubber resembling a natural sponge in structure used for cushions,vibration dampeners, weather stripping, and gaskets
spon•gin \'spən-jən\ *n* [G, fr. L *spongia* sponge] **:** a scleroprotein that is the chief constituent of flexible fibers in sponge skeletons
spong•i•ness \'spən-jē-nəs\ *n* **:** the quality or state of being spongy
spongy \'spən-jē\ *adj* **1 :** resembling a sponge: **a :** soft and full of cavities ⟨~ ice⟩ **b :** elastic, porous, and absorbent **2 :** not firm or solid **3 :** moist and soft like a sponge full of water ⟨~ moor⟩
spon•son \'spän(t)-sən\ *n* [prob. by shortening & alter. fr. *expansion*] **1 a :** a projection (as a gun platform) from the side of a ship or a tank **b :** an air chamber along a canoe to increase stability and buoyancy **2 :** a light air-filled structure protruding from the hull of a seaplane to steady it on water
[1]spon•sor \'spän(t)-sər\ *n* [LL, fr. L, guarantor, surety, fr. *sponsus*, pp. of *spondēre* to promise — more at SPOUSE] **1 :** one who presents a candidate for baptism or confirmation and undertakes responsibility for his religious education or spiritual welfare **2 :** one who assumes responsibility for some other person or thing **3 :** a business firm who pays a broadcaster and the performer for a radio or television program that allots some time to advertising its products — **spon•so•ri•al** \spän-'sōr-ē-əl, -'sȯr-\ *adj* — **spon•sor•ship** \'spän(t)-sər-ˌship\ *n*
[2]sponsor *vt* **spon•sor•ing** \'spän(t)s-(ə-)riŋ\ **:** to be or stand sponsor for
spon•ta•ne•ity \ˌspänt-ən-'ē-ət-ē, ˌspänt-ᵊn-, -'ā-ət-\ *n* **1 :** the quality or state of being spontaneous **2 :** voluntary or undetermined action or movement; *also* **:** its source
spon•ta•ne•ous \spän-'tā-nē-əs\ *adj* [LL *spontaneus*, fr. L *sponte* of one's free will, voluntarily — more at SPIN] **1 :** arising without external constraint or stimulus **:** VOLUNTARY **2 :** arising from a momentary impulse **3 :** controlled and directed internally **:** SELF-ACTING ⟨~ movement characteristic of living things⟩ **4 :** produced without being planted or without human labor **:** INDIGENOUS **5 :** developing without apparent external influence, force, cause, or treatment ⟨~ recovery⟩ **6 :** not apparently contrived or manipulated **:** NATURAL — **spon•ta•ne•ous•ly** *adv* — **spon•ta•ne•ous•ness** *n*
syn SPONTANEOUS, IMPULSIVE, INSTINCTIVE, AUTOMATIC, MECHANICAL mean acting or activated without deliberation. SPONTANEOUS further implies lack of prompting and connotes naturalness; IMPULSIVE implies acting under stress of emotion or spirit of the moment; INSTINCTIVE stresses spontaneous action involving neither judgment nor will; AUTOMATIC and MECHANICAL apply to action seeming to engage neither the mind nor the emotions and connotes uniformity and predictability of response
spontaneous combustion *n* **:** self-ignition of combustible material through chemical action (as oxidation) of its constituents
spontaneous generation *n* **:** ABIOGENESIS
spon•toon \spän-'tün\ *n* [F *sponton*, fr. It *spuntone*, fr. *punta* sharp point, fr. (assumed) VL *puncta* — more at POINT] **:** a short pike formerly borne by subordinate officers of infantry
[1]spoof \'spüf\ *vt* [*Spoof*, a hoaxing game invented by Arthur Roberts †1933 E comedian] **1 :** DECEIVE, HOAX **2 :** to make good-natured fun of
[2]spoof *n* **1 :** HOAX, DECEPTION **2 :** a light humorous parody
[1]spook \'spük\ *n* [D; akin to MLG *spōk* ghost] **:** GHOST, SPECTER — **spook•ish** \'spü-kish\ *adj*
[2]spook *vt* **1 :** HAUNT 3 **2 :** to make frightened or frantic **:** SCARE; *esp* **:** to startle into violent activity (as stampeding) ⟨~ a horse⟩ ~ *vi* **:** to become spooked ⟨cattle ~*ing* at shadows⟩

spook·i·ness \ˈspü-kē-nəs\ *n* : the quality or state of being spooky
spooky \ˈspü-kē\ *adj* **1** : relating to, resembling, or suggesting spooks ⟨~ houses⟩ **2** : NERVOUS, SKITTISH ⟨a ~ horse⟩
spool \ˈspül\ *n* [ME *spole*, fr. MF or MD; MF *espole*, fr. MD *spoele;* akin to OHG *spuola* spool] **1 a** : a cylindrical device which has a rim or ridge at each end and an axial hole for a pin or spindle and on which thread, wire, or tape is wound **b** : something like a spool **2** : material or the amount of material wound on a spool — **spool** *vb*
1spoon \ˈspün\ *n* [ME, fr. OE *spōn* splinter, chip; akin to OHG *spān* splinter, chip, Gk *sphēn* wedge] **1** : an eating or cooking implement consisting of a small shallow bowl with a handle **2** : something that resembles a spoon in shape (as a usu. metal or shell fishing lure) **3** : a wooden golf club with more loft than a brassie — called also *number three wood*
2spoon *vt* **1** : to take up and usu. transfer in a spoon **2** : to propel (a ball) by a weak lifting stroke ~ *vi* **1** [prob. fr. the Welsh custom of an engaged man's presenting his fiancée with a spoon] : to make love by caressing, kissing, and talking amorously : NECK **2** : to spoon a ball
spoon·bill \ˈspün-ˌbil\ *n* **1** : any of several wading birds (family Plataleidae) related to the ibises that have the bill greatly expanded and flattened at the tip **2** : any of several broad-billed ducks (as the shoveler)
spoonbill cat *n* : PADDLEFISH
spoon–billed \ˈspün-ˈbild\ *adj* : having the bill or snout expanded and spatulate at the end
spoon bread *n*, *chiefly South & Midland* : soft bread made of cornmeal with or without rice and hominy mixed with milk, eggs, shortening, and leavening to a consistency that it must be served with a spoon
spoon·drift \ˈspün-ˌdrift\ *n* [alter. of Sc *speendrift* — more at SPINDRIFT] : spray blown from waves during a gale at sea : SPINDRIFT
spoo·ner·ism \ˈspü-nə-ˌriz-əm\ *n* [William A. *Spooner* †1930 E clergyman and educator] : a transposition of usu. initial sounds of two or more words (as in *tons of soil* for *sons of toil*)
spoon–feed \ˈspün-ˌfēd\ *vt* **1** : to feed by means of a spoon **2 a** : to present (information) so completely as to preclude independent thought **b** : to present information to in this manner
spoon·ful \ˈspün-ˌfu̇l\ *n*, *pl* **spoonfuls** \-ˌfu̇lz\ *or* **spoons·ful** \ˈspünz-ˌfu̇l\ : the amount a spoon contains; *specif* : TEASPOONFUL
spoony *or* **spoon·ey** \ˈspü-nē\ *adj* **spoon·i·er**; **spoon·i·est** [E slang *spoon* (simpleton)] **1** : SILLY, FOOLISH; *esp* : unduly sentimental **2** : sentimentally in love
1spoor \ˈspu̇(ə)r, ˈspō(ə)r, ˈspȯ(ə)r\ *n* [Afrik, fr. MD; akin to OE *spor* footprint, spoor, *spurnan* to kick — more at SPURN] : a track or trail esp. of a wild animal
2spoor *vt* : to track by a spoor ~ *vi* : to track something by its spoor
spor- *or* **spori-** *or* **sporo-** *comb form* [NL *spora*] : seed : spore ⟨*sporo*cyst⟩ ⟨*spor*angium⟩ ⟨*spori*cidal⟩
spo·rad·ic \spə-ˈrad-ik\ *adj* [ML *sporadicus*, fr. Gk *sporadikos*, fr. *sporadēn* here and there, fr. *sporad-*, *sporas* scattered; akin to Gk *speirein* to sow] : occurring occasionally, singly, or in scattered instances : SEPARATE, ISOLATED ⟨~ case of disease⟩ **syn** see INFREQUENT — **spo·rad·i·cal·ly** \-i-k(ə-)lē\ *adv*
sporadic E layer *n* : a layer of ionization occurring irregularly within the E region of the ionosphere
spo·ran·gial \spə-ˈran-j(ē-)əl\ *adj* : of, relating to, or made up of sporangia
spo·ran·gio·phore \spə-ˈran-jē-ə-ˌfō(ə)r, -ˌfȯ(ə)r\ *n* : a stalk or receptacle bearing sporangia
spo·ran·gi·um \spə-ˈran-jē-əm\ *n*, *pl* **spo·ran·gia** \-jē-ə\ [NL, fr. *spor-* + Gk *angeion* vessel — more at ANGI-] : a case within which usu. asexual spores are produced whether a cell (as in bacteria or algae) producing spores endogenously or a complex structure (as in a fern)
1spore \ˈspō(ə)r, ˈspȯ(ə)r\ *n* [NL *spora* seed, spore, fr. Gk, act of sowing, seed, fr. *speirein* to sow — more at SPROUT] : a primitive usu. unicellular resistant or reproductive body produced by plants and some invertebrates and capable of development into a new individual in some cases unlike the parent either directly or after fusion with another spore — **spored** \ˈspō(ə)rd, ˈspȯ(ə)rd\ *adj*
2spore *vi* : to produce or reproduce by spores
spore case *n* : a case containing spores : SPORANGIUM
spore fruit *n* : a specialized structure (as an ascocarp) that produces spores : FRUITING BODY
spo·ri·ci·dal \ˌspōr-ə-ˈsīd-ᵊl, ˌspȯr-\ *adj* : tending to kill spores — **spo·ri·cide** \ˈspōr-ə-ˌsīd, ˈspȯr-\ *n*
spo·rif·er·ous \spə-ˈrif-(ə-)rəs; spōr-ˈif-, spȯr-\ *adj* : bearing or producing spores
spo·ro·carp \ˈspōr-ə-ˌkärp, ˈspȯr-\ *n* [ISV *spor-* + Gk *karpos* fruit — more at HARVEST] : a structure (as in red algae, fungi, or mosses) in or on which spores are produced
spo·ro·cyst \-ˌsist\ *n* [ISV] **1** : a unicellular resting cell (as in slime molds and algae) that may give rise to asexual spores **2 a** : a case or cyst secreted by some sporozoans preliminary to sporogony; *also* : a sporozoan encysted in such a case **b** : a saccular body that is the first asexual reproductive form of a digenetic trematode and buds off cells from its inner surface which develop into rediae — **spo·ro·cys·tic** \ˌspōr-ə-ˈsis-tik, ˌspȯr-\ *adj*
spo·ro·gen·e·sis \ˌspōr-ə-ˈjen-ə-səs, ˌspȯr-\ *n* [NL] **1** : reproduction by spores **2** : spore formation — **spo·ro·gen·ic** \-ˈjen-ik\ *adj* — **spo·rog·e·nous** \spə-ˈräj-ə-nəs\ *adj*
spo·rog·e·ny \spə-ˈräj-ə-nē\ *n* : SPOROGENESIS
spo·ro·go·ni·um \ˌspōr-ə-ˈgō-nē-əm, ˌspȯr-\ *n*, *pl* **spo·ro·go·nia** \-nē-ə\ [NL, fr. *spor-* + *-gonium* (as in *archegonium*)] : the sporophyte of a moss or liverwort consisting typically of a stalk bearing a capsule in which spores are produced and remaining permanently attached to the gametophyte
spo·rog·o·ny \spə-ˈräg-ə-nē\ *n* [ISV] : reproduction by spores; *specif* : spore formation in a sporozoan by encystment and subsequent division of a zygote
spo·ro·phore \ˈspōr-ə-ˌfō(ə)r, ˈspȯr-ə-ˌfȯ(ə)r\ *n* [ISV] : the part (as a spore fruit of a fungus or the placenta of a seed plant) of a sporophyte that develops spores — **spo·ro·phor·ic** \ˌspōr-ə-ˈfȯr-ik, ˌspȯr-, -ˈfär-\ *adj*
spo·ro·phyll \ˈspōr-ə-ˌfil, ˈspȯr-\ *n* [ISV] : a leaf often modified in form and structure that develops sporangia — **spo·ro·phyl·la·ry** \ˌspōr-ə-ˈfil-ə-rē, ˌspȯr-\ *adj*
spo·ro·phyte \ˈspōr-ə-ˌfīt, ˈspȯr-\ *n* [ISV] : the individual or generation of a plant exhibiting alternation of generations that bears asexual spores — **spo·ro·phyt·ic** \ˌspōr-ə-ˈfit-ik, ˌspȯr-\ *adj*
-spo·rous \ˈspōr-əs, ˈspȯr-; s-pə-rəs\ *adj comb form* [NL *spora* spore] : having (such or so many) spores ⟨homo*sporous*⟩
spo·ro·zo·an \ˌspōr-ə-ˈzō-ən, ˌspȯr-\ *n* [NL *Sporozoa*, class name, fr. *spor-* + *-zoa*] : any of a large class (Sporozoa) of strictly parasitic protozoans that have a complicated life cycle usu. involving both asexual and sexual generations often in different hosts and include important pathogens (as malaria parasites, coccidia, and piroplasms) — **spo·ro·zo·al** \-ˈzō-əl\ *adj* — **sporozoan** *adj*
spo·ro·zo·ite \-ˈzō-ˌīt\ *n* [NL *Sporozoa* + ISV *-ite*] : a usu. motile infective form of some sporozoans that is a product of sporogony and initiates an asexual cycle in the new host
spor·ran \ˈspȯr-ən, ˈspär-\ *n* [ScGael *sporan*] : a pouch of skin with the hair or fur on that is worn in front of the kilt by Highlanders in full dress
1sport \ˈspō(ə)rt, ˈspȯ(ə)rt\ *vb* [ME *sporten* to divert, disport, short for *disporten*] *vt* **1** : to make usu. ostentatious display of : show off ⟨~ a new hat⟩ **2** [*2sport*] : to put forth as a sport or bud variation ~ *vi* **1 a** : to amuse oneself : FROLIC **b** : to engage in a sport **2 a** : to mock or ridicule something **b** : to speak or act jestingly : TRIFLE **3** [*2sport*] : to deviate or vary abruptly from type (as by bud variation) : MUTATE
2sport *n* **1 a** : a source of diversion : RECREATION **b** : sexual play **c** (1) : physical activity engaged in for pleasure (2) : a particular activity (as hunting or an athletic game) so engaged in **2 a** : PLEASANTRY, JEST **b** : MOCKERY, DERISION **3 a** : something tossed or driven about in or as if in play **b** : LAUGHINGSTOCK **4 a** : SPORTSMAN: **b** : a person living up to the ideals of sportsmanship **c** : a companionable person **5** : an individual exhibiting a sudden deviation from type beyond the normal limits of individual variation usu. as a result of mutation esp. of somatic tissue **syn** see FUN
3sport *or* **sports** *adj* : of, relating to, or suitable for sports ⟨~ coats⟩
sport fish *n* : a fish important for the sport it affords anglers
sport·ful \ˈspōrt-fəl, ˈspȯrt-\ *adj* **1 a** : ENTERTAINING, DIVERTING **b** : PLAYFUL, FROLICSOME **2** : done in sport — **sport·ful·ly** \-fə-lē\ *adv* — **sport·ful·ness** *n*
sport·i·ly \ˈspōrt-ᵊl-ē, ˈspȯrt-\ *adv* : in a sporty manner
sport·i·ness \-ē-nəs\ *n* : the quality or state of being sporty
sport·ing \ˈspōrt-iŋ, ˈspȯrt-\ *adj* **1 a** : used or suitable for sport **b** : marked by or calling for sportsmanship **c** : involving such risk as a sports contender may expect to take or encounter ⟨a ~ chance⟩ **2** : of or relating to dissipation and esp. gambling **3** : tending to mutate freely
sport·ive \-iv\ *adj* **1 a** : FROLICSOME, PLAYFUL **b** : ARDENT, WANTON **2** : relating to sports and esp. field sports — **sport·ive·ly** *adv* — **sport·ive·ness** *n*
sports car *also* **sport car** *n* : a low fast usu. two-seat open automobile
sports·cast \ˈspō(ə)rt-ˌskast, ˈspȯ(ə)rt-\ *n* [*sport* + broad*cast*] : a radio or television broadcast of a sports event or of information about sports — **sports·cast·er** \-ˌskas-tər\ *n*
sport shirt *n* : a soft shirt for casual wear with open neck
sports·man \ˈspō(ə)rt-smən, ˈspȯ(ə)rt-\ *n* **1** : one who engages in the sports and esp. in field sports **2** : a person who is fair and generous and a good loser and a graceful winner — **sports·man·like** \-ˌlīk\ *adj* — **sports·man·ly** \-lē\ *adj* — **sports·wom·an** \-ˌswu̇m-ən\ *n*
sports·man·ship \-ˌship\ *n* : conduct becoming to a sportsman (as fairness, courteous relations, and graceful acceptance of results)
sports·wear \ˈspō(ə)rt-ˌswa(ə)r, ˈspȯ(ə)rt-, -ˌswe(ə)r\ *n* : clothing suitable for recreation
sports·writ·er \ˈspō(ə)rts-ˌrīt-ər, ˈspȯ(ə)rts-\ *n* : one who writes about sports esp. for a newspaper
sporty \ˈspōrt-ē, ˈspȯrt-\ *adj* **1** : characteristic of a sport or sportsman : SPORTSMANLIKE **2 a** : notably gay or dissipated : FAST **b** : FLASHY, SHOWY **3** : capable of giving good sport ⟨a ~ boat⟩
spor·u·late \ˈspōr-yə-ˌlāt, ˈspȯr-\ *vi* [back-formation fr. *sporulation*] : to undergo sporulation
spor·u·la·tion \ˌspōr-yə-ˈlā-shən, ˌspȯr-\ *n* [ISV, fr. NL *sporula*, dim. of *spora* spore] : the formation of spores; *esp* : division into many small spores (as after encystment) — **spor·u·la·tive** \ˈspōr-yə-ˌlāt-iv, ˈspȯr-\ *adj*
-spo·ry \ˌspōr-ē, ˌspȯr-; s-pə-rē\ *n comb form* [*-sporous* + *-y*] : quality or state of having (such) spores ⟨homo*spory*⟩
1spot \ˈspät\ *n* [ME; akin to MD *spotte* stain, speck, ON *spotti* small piece] **1** : a taint on character or reputation : FAULT **2 a** : a small area visibly different (as in color, finish, or material) from the surrounding area **b** : such a spot constituting a disfigurement or blemish (as from soiling or disease) **c** : a conventionalized design used on playing cards to distinguish suits and indicate values **3** : an object having a specified number of spots or a specified numeral on its surface **4** : a small quantity or amount **5 a** : a particular place or area **b** : a small extent of space **6** : a small croaker (*Leiostomus xanthurus*) of the Atlantic coast with a black spot behind the shoulders **7 a** : a particular position (as in an organization or a hierarchy) **b** : a place on an entertainment program **8** : a position usu. of difficulty or embarrassment **9** : a brief announcement or advertisement broadcast between scheduled radio or television programs — **on the spot** *or* **upon the spot** **1** : at once : IMMEDIATELY **2** : at the place of action **3 a** : in a responsible or accountable position **b** : in difficulty or danger
2spot *vb* **spot·ted**; **spot·ting** *vt* **1** : to stain the character or reputation of : DISGRACE **2** : to mark in or with a spot : STAIN **3** : to locate or identify by a spot **4 a** : to single out : IDENTIFY; *specif* : to note as a known criminal or a suspicious person **b** : DETECT, NOTICE **c** (1) : to locate accurately ⟨~ an enemy position⟩ (2) : to cause to strike accurately ⟨~ the battery's fire⟩ **5 a** : to lie at intervals in or over : STUD **b** : to place at intervals or in a desired spot **c** : to fix in or as if in the beam of a spotlight **d** : to schedule in a particular spot or at a particular time **6** : to remove a spot from **7** : to allow as a handicap ~ *vi* **1** : to become stained or discolored in spots **2** : to cause a spot **3** : to act as a spotter; *esp* : to locate targets — **spot·ta·ble** \ˈspät-ə-bəl\ *adj*
3spot *adj* **1 a** : being, originating, or done on the spot or in a few spots ⟨~ coverage of the news⟩ **b** : available for immediate delivery after sale ⟨~ commodities⟩ **c** (1) : paid out upon delivery ⟨~ cash⟩ (2) : involving immediate cash payment ⟨~ transaction⟩ **d** (1) : broadcast between scheduled programs ⟨~ announcements⟩

(2) **:** originating in a local station for a national advertiser **2 :** made at random or restricted to a few places or instances ⟨~ check⟩; *also* **:** selected at random or as a sample

spot–check \'spät-ˌchek\ *vt* **:** to sample or investigate quickly or at random **~** *vi* **:** to make a spot check

spot·less \'spät-ləs\ *adj* **:** having no spot: **a :** free from impurity **:** IMMACULATE ⟨~ kitchens⟩ **b :** PURE, UNBLEMISHED ⟨~ reputation⟩ — **spot·less·ly** *adv* — **spot·less·ness** *n*

[1]**spot·light** \'spät-ˌlīt\ *n* **1 a :** a projected spot of light used to illuminate brilliantly a person, object, or group on a stage **b :** conspicuous public notice **2 a :** a light designed to direct a narrow intense beam of light on a small area **b :** something that illuminates brilliantly

[2]**spotlight** *vt* **:** to illuminate with or as if with a spotlight

spot pass *n* **:** a pass (as in football) made to a predetermined spot usu. well down the field or court rather than directly to a player

spot·ted \'spät-əd\ *adj* **1 :** marked with spots **2 :** SULLIED, TARNISHED **3 :** characterized by the appearance of spots

spotted adder *n* **1 :** MILK SNAKE **2 :** HOGNOSE SNAKE

spotted fever *n* **:** any of various eruptive fevers: as **a :** TYPHUS **b :** ROCKY MOUNTAIN SPOTTED FEVER

spot·ter \'spät-ər\ *n* **1 :** one that makes or applies a spot (as for identification) **2 :** one that looks or keeps watch: as **a :** one that locates enemy targets **b :** a civilian who watches for approaching airplanes **3 :** one that removes spots **4 :** one that places something on or in a desired spot

spot test *n* **1 :** a test conducted on the spot to yield immediate results **2 :** a test limited to a few key or sample points or a relatively small percentage of random spots

spot·ti·ly \'spät-ᵊl-ē\ *adv* **:** in a spotty manner

spot·ti·ness \'spät-ē-nəs\ *n* **:** the quality or state of being spotty

spot·ty \'spät-ē\ *adj* **1 :** marked with spots **:** SPOTTED **2 :** lacking uniformity esp. in quality **:** UNEVEN ⟨~ attendance⟩

spou·sal \'spau̇-zəl, -səl\ *n* [ME *spousaille*, fr. MF *espousailles* espousal] **:** NUPTIALS — usu. used in pl. — **spousal** *adj*

[1]**spouse** \'spau̇s *also* 'spau̇z\ *n* [ME, fr. OF *espous* (masc.) & *espouse* (fem.), fr. L *sponsus* betrothed man, groom & *sponsa* betrothed woman, bride, fr. *sponsus*, pp. of *spondēre* to promise, betroth; akin to Gk *spendein* to make a libation, promise, *spondē* libation (pl., treaty)] **:** married person **:** HUSBAND, WIFE

[2]**spouse** \'spau̇z, 'spau̇s\ *vt, archaic* **:** ESPOUSE, WED

[1]**spout** \'spau̇t\ *vb* [ME *spouten;* akin to MD *spoiten* to spout, OE *spīwan* to spew] *vt* **1 :** to eject (as liquid) in a stream **2 a :** to speak or utter readily, volubly, and at length **b :** DECLAIM **~** *vi* **1 :** to issue with force or in a jet **:** SPURT **2 :** to eject material (as liquid) in a jet **3 :** DECLAIM — **spout·er** *n*

[2]**spout** *n* **1 :** a pipe or conductor through which a liquid is discharged or conveyed in a stream: as **a :** a pipe for carrying rainwater from a roof **b :** a projecting tube or lip from which water issues **2 :** a discharge or jet of liquid from or as if from a pipe; *esp* **:** WATERSPOUT **3** *archaic* **:** PAWNSHOP

sprach·ge·fühl \'shpräk-kə-ˌfu̅e̅l\ *n* [G, fr. *sprache* language + *gefühl* feeling] **1 :** sensibility to conformance with or divergence from the established usage of a language **2 :** a feeling for what is linguistically effective or appropriate

sprag \'sprag\ *n* [perh. of Scand origin; akin to Sw dial. *spragge* branch] **:** a pointed stake or steel bar let down from a halted vehicle (as a wagon) to prevent it from rolling

[1]**sprain** \'sprān\ *n* [origin unknown] **1 :** a sudden or violent twist or wrench of a joint with stretching or tearing of ligaments **2 :** a sprained condition

[2]**sprain** *vt* **:** to subject to sprain

sprat \'sprat\ *n* [alter. of ME *sprot*, fr. OE *sprott*] **1 :** a small European herring (*Clupea sprattus*) closely related to the common herring; *also* **:** a small or young herring or similar fish (as an anchovy) **2 :** a young, small, or insignificant person

sprawl \'sprȯl\ *vb* [ME *sprawlen*, fr. OE *sprēawlian*] *vi* **1 a** *archaic* **:** to lie thrashing or tossing about **b :** to creep or clamber awkwardly **2 :** to lie or sit with arms and legs spread out **3 :** to spread irregularly **:** STRAGGLE **~** *vt* **:** to cause to spread out carelessly or awkwardly — **sprawl** *n*

[1]**spray** \'sprā\ *n* [ME] **1 a :** a usu. flowering branch or shoot **b :** a decorative arrangement of flowers and foliage (as on a dress or coffin) **2 :** something resembling a spray

[2]**spray** *n* [obs. E *spray* (to sprinkle), fr. MD *sprayen;* akin to Gk *speirein* to scatter — more at SPROUT] **1 :** water flying in small drops or particles blown from waves or thrown up by a waterfall **2 a :** a jet of vapor or finely divided liquid dispersed (as by an atomizer or sprayer) usu. for its medical, insecticidal, or deodorant property **b :** a device (as an atomizer or sprayer) by which a spray is dispersed or applied ⟨paint ~*s*⟩ **c :** an application of a spray or by spraying

[3]**spray** *vt* **1 :** to disperse or apply as a spray **2 :** to project spray on or into **~** *vi* **1 :** to break up into spray **2 :** to disperse or apply a spray — **spray·er** *n*

spray gun *n* **:** an apparatus resembling a gun for applying a substance (as paint or insecticide) in the form of a spray

[1]**spread** \'spred\ *vb* **spread; spread·ing** [ME *spreden*, fr. OE *sprǣdan;* akin to OHG *spreiten* to spread, OE *-sprūtan* to sprout — more at SPROUT] *vt* **1 a :** to open or expand over a larger area ⟨~ out the map⟩ **b :** to stretch out **:** EXTEND **2 a :** SCATTER, STREW **b :** to distribute over a period or among a group **c :** to apply on a surface ⟨~ butter on bread⟩ **d** (1) **:** to cover or overlay with (2) *archaic* **:** to cover completely **e** (1) **:** to prepare or furnish for dining **:** SET ⟨~ the table⟩ (2) **:** SERVE **3 a :** to make widely known ⟨~ the news⟩ **b :** to extend the range or incidence of ⟨~ a disease⟩ **c :** DIFFUSE, EMIT **4 :** to push apart by weight or force **~** *vi* **1 a :** to become dispersed, distributed, or scattered **b :** to become known or disseminated ⟨panic ~ rapidly⟩ **2 :** to grow in length or breadth **:** EXPAND **3 :** to move apart (as from pressure or weight) **:** SEPARATE

[2]**spread** *n* **1 a :** the act or process of spreading **b :** extent of spreading **2 :** something spread out: as **a :** a surface area **:** EXPANSE **b** *West* **:** RANCH **c** (1) **:** a prominent display in a periodical (2) **:** two facing pages (as of a newspaper) usu. with matter running across the fold; *also* **:** the matter occupying these pages **3 :** something spread on or over a surface: as **a :** a food to be spread on bread or crackers **b :** a sumptuous meal **:** FEAST **c :** a cloth cover for a table or bed **4 :** distance between two points **:** GAP

spread eagle *n* **1 :** a representation of an eagle with wings raised and legs extended **2 :** something resembling or suggestive of a spread eagle; *specif* **:** a skating figure executed with the skates heel to heel in a straight line

[1]**spread–ea·gle** \'spred-ˌē-gəl\ *vb* **spread–ea·gling** \-ˌē-g(ə-)liŋ\ *vi* **1 :** to execute a spread eagle (as in skating) **2 :** to stand or move with arms and legs stretched out **:** SPRAWL **~** *vt* **1 :** to stretch out into the position of a spread eagle **2 :** to spread over **:** STRADDLE

[2]**spread–eagle** *adj* **:** marked by bombast and boastful exaggeration esp. of the greatness of the U.S.

spread·er \'spred-ər\ *n* **:** one that spreads: as **a :** an implement for scattering material **b :** a small knife for spreading butter **c :** WETTING AGENT **d :** a device (as a bar) holding two linear elements (as lines, guys, rails) apart and usu. taut

spread formation *n* **:** a double or triple wing offensive formation in football in which the ends are spread three to five yards outside the tackles, the tailback plays seven to eight yards behind the line, and the other three backs are in flanking position close to the line

spreading factor *n* **:** HYALURONIDASE

spree \'sprē\ *n* [perh. alter. of Sc *spreath* cattle raid, foray, fr. ScGael *sprēidh* cattle, fr. L *praeda* booty — more at PREY] **:** an unrestrained indulgence in or outburst of activity ⟨buying ~⟩; *esp* **:** BINGE, CAROUSAL

sprent \'sprent\ *adj* [fr. pp. of obs. *sprenge* (to sprinkle)] *archaic* **:** SPRINKLED

[1]**sprig** \'sprig\ *n* [ME *sprigge*] **1 :** a small shoot **:** TWIG **2 a :** HEIR **b :** YOUTH **3 :** an ornament resembling a sprig, stemmed flower, or leaf **4 :** a small headless nail **:** BRAD

[2]**sprig** *vt* **sprigged; sprig·ging 1 :** to drive sprigs or brads into **2 :** to mark or adorn with the representation of plant sprigs

spright·ful \'sprīt-fəl\ *adj* [obs. *spright*] **:** full of life or spirit **:** SPRIGHTLY — **spright·ful·ly** \-fə-lē\ *adv* — **spright·ful·ness** *n*

spright·li·ness \'sprīt-lē-nəs\ *n* **:** the quality or state of being sprightly

spright·ly \-lē\ *adj* [obs. *spright* (sprite), alter. of *sprite*] **:** marked by a gay lightness and vivacity **:** SPIRITED **syn** see LIVELY

sprig·tail \'sprig-ˌtāl\ *n* **:** any of several birds with pointed tails; *esp* **:** PINTAIL a

[1]**spring** \'spriŋ\ *vb* **sprang** \'spraŋ\ *or* **sprung** \'sprəŋ\ **sprung; spring·ing** \'spriŋ-iŋ\ [ME *springen*, fr. OE *springan;* akin to OHG *springan* to jump, Gk *sperchesthai* to hasten] *vi* **1 a** (1) **:** DART, SHOOT (2) **:** to be resilient or elastic; *also* **:** to move by elastic force ⟨the lid *sprang* shut⟩ **b :** to become warped **2 :** to issue with speed and force or as a stream **3 a :** to grow as a plant **b :** to issue by birth or descent **c :** to come into being **:** ARISE **d** *archaic* **:** DAWN **e :** to begin to blow — used with *up* **4 a :** to make a leap or series of leaps **b :** to leap or jump up suddenly **5 :** to stretch out in height **:** RISE **~** *vt* **1 :** to cause to spring **2 a :** to undergo or bring about the splitting or cracking of ⟨wind *sprang* the mast⟩ **b :** to undergo the opening of (a leak) **3 a :** to cause to operate suddenly ⟨~ a trap⟩ **b :** to apply or insert by bending **c :** to bend by force **4 :** to leap over **5 :** to produce or disclose suddenly or unexpectedly **6 :** to make lame **:** STRAIN **7** *slang* **:** to release or cause to be released from confinement or custody

syn SPRING, ARISE, RISE, ORIGINATE, DERIVE, FLOW, ISSUE, EMANATE, PROCEED, STEM mean to come up or out of something into existence. SPRING implies rapid or sudden emerging; ARISE and RISE may both convey the fact of coming into existence or notice but RISE often stresses gradual growth or ascent; ORIGINATE implies a definite source or starting point; DERIVE implies a prior existence in another form; FLOW adds to SPRING a suggestion of abundance or ease of inception; ISSUE suggests emerging from confinement through an outlet; EMANATE applies to the coming of something immaterial (as a principle or thought) from a source; PROCEED stresses place of origin, derivation, parentage, or logical cause; STEM implies originating by dividing or branching off from something as an outgrowth or subordinate development

[2]**spring** *n* **1 a :** a source of supply; *esp* **:** a source of water issuing from the ground **b :** an ultimate source esp. of action or motion **2 :** a time or season of growth or development; *specif* **:** the season between winter and summer comprising in the northern hemisphere usu. the months of March, April, and May or as reckoned astronomically extending from the March equinox to the June solstice **3 :** an elastic body or device that recovers its original shape when released after being distorted **4 a :** the act or an instance of leaping up or forward **:** BOUND **b** (1) **:** capacity for springing **:** RESILIENCE (2) **:** BOUNCE, ENERGY **5 :** the point or plane at which an arch or vault curve springs from its impost **syn** see MOTIVE

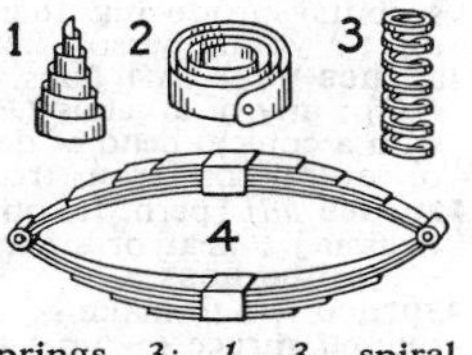

springs 3: *1*, *3*, spiral springs, *2* coil spring, *4* elliptic leaf spring

[3]**spring** *vt* **sprung** \'sprəŋ\ **sprung; spring·ing** \'spriŋ-iŋ\ **:** to fit with springs

spring·ald \'spriŋ-əld\ *or* **spring·al** \-əl\ *n* [prob. fr. ME, a kind of catapult, fr. MF *espringale*] **:** a young man **:** STRIPLING

spring beauty *n* **:** any of a genus (*Claytonia*) of plants of the purslane family; *esp* **:** one (*C. virginica*) that sends up in early spring a 2-leaved stem bearing delicate pink flowers

spring·board \'spriŋ-ˌbō(ə)rd, -ˌbȯ(ə)rd\ *n* **1 :** a flexible board usu. secured at one end and used for gymnastic stunts or diving **2 :** a point of departure

spring·bok \'spriŋ-ˌbäk\ *n, pl* **springbok** *or* **springboks** [Afrik, fr. *spring* to jump + *bok* male goat] **:** a swift and graceful southern African gazelle (*Antidorcas euchore*) noted for its habit of springing lightly and suddenly into the air

spring–clean·ing \'spriŋ-'klē-niŋ\ *n* [[2]*spring*] **:** the act or process of doing a thorough cleaning of a place

springe \'sprinj\ *n* [ME *sprenge, springe;* akin to OE *springan* to spring] **1 :** a noose fastened to an elastic body to catch small game **2 :** SNARE, TRAP

spring·er \'spriŋ-ər\ *n* **1 :** a stone or other solid laid at the impost of an arch **2 :** one that springs **3 :** a cow nearly ready to calve

springer spaniel *n* **:** a medium-sized largely white sporting dog of

either an English or a Welsh breed used chiefly for finding and flushing small game
spring fever *n* : a lazy or restless feeling often associated with the onset of spring
Spring·field \'spriŋ-ˌfēld\ *n* [*Springfield*, Mass.] : a .30 caliber bolt-operated rifle adopted by the U.S. army in 1903
spring·halt \'spriŋ-ˌhȯlt\ *n* [by alter.] : STRINGHALT
spring·head \-ˌhed\ *n* : FOUNTAINHEAD
spring·house \-ˌhau̇s\ *n* : a small building over a spring used for cool storage (as of dairy products or meat)
spring·i·ly \'spriŋ-ə-lē\ *adv* : in a springy manner
spring·i·ness \'spriŋ-ē-nəs\ *n* : the quality or state of being springy
spring·ing \'spriŋ-iŋ\ *n* : the usu. horizontal line from which an arch springs
spring·let \'spriŋ-lət\ *n* : a little spring : STREAMLET
spring peeper *n* : a small brown tree toad (*Hyla crucifer*) of the eastern U.S. and Canada with a shrill piping call
spring·tail \'spriŋ-ˌtāl\ *n* : any of an order (Collembola) of small primitive wingless arthropods related to or classed among the insects
spring·tide \-ˌtīd\ *n* : SPRINGTIME
spring tide *n* : a tide of greater-than-average range around the times of new and full moon
spring·time \'spriŋ-ˌtīm\ *n* **1** : the season of spring **2** : YOUTH **3** : an early or flourishing stage of development
spring wagon *n* : a light wagon equipped with springs
spring·wood \'spriŋ-ˌwu̇d\ *n* : the softer more porous portion of an annual ring of wood that develops early in the growing season — compare SUMMERWOOD
springy \'spriŋ-ē\ *adj* **1** : abounding with springs : SPONGY **2** : having an elastic quality : RESILIENT **syn** see ELASTIC
1**sprin·kle** \'spriŋ-kəl\ *vb* **sprin·kling** \-k(ə-)liŋ\ [ME *sprenklen, sprinclen;* akin to MHG *spreckel, sprenkel* spot, OE *spearca* spark] *vt* **1** : to scatter in drops or particles **2 a** : to scatter over **b** : to scatter at intervals in or among : DOT **c** : to wet lightly ~ *vi* **1** : to scatter a liquid in fine drops **2** : to rain lightly in scattered drops — **sprin·kler** \-k(ə-)lər\ *n*
2**sprinkle** *n* **1** : the act or an instance of sprinkling; *specif* : a light rain **2** : SPRINKLING
sprinkler system *n* : a system for protection against fire in which pipes are distributed for conveying water or other extinguishing fluid to outlets
sprin·kling \'spriŋ-kliŋ\ *n* **1** : a limited quantity or amount : MODICUM **2** : a small quantity falling in scattered drops **3** : a small number distributed at random : SCATTERING
1**sprint** \'sprint\ *vi* [of Scand origin; akin to Sw dial. *sprinta* to jump, hop; akin to OHG *sprinzan* to jump up, Gk *spyrthizein*] : to run at top speed esp. for a short distance — **sprint·er** *n*
2**sprint** *n* **1** : the act or an instance of sprinting **2 a** : DASH 6b **b** : a burst of speed
sprit \'sprit\ *n* [ME *spret, sprit*, fr. OE *sprēot* pole, spear; akin to OE *-sprūtan* to sprout] : a spar that crosses a fore-and-aft sail diagonally
sprite \'sprīt\ *n* [ME *sprit*, fr. OF *esprit*, fr. L *spiritus* spirit] **1 a** *archaic* : SOUL **b** : a disembodied spirit : GHOST **2 a** : ELF, FAIRY **b** : an elfish person
sprit·sail \'sprit-ˌsāl, -səl\ *n* : a sail extended by a sprit
sprock·et \'spräk-ət\ *n* [origin unknown] : a tooth or projection (as on a wheel) shaped so as to engage with a chain
sprocket wheel *n* : a wheel with cogs or sprockets to engage with the links of a chain
1**sprout** \'sprau̇t\ *vb* [ME *sprouten*, fr. OE *-sprūtan;* akin to OHG *spriozan* to sprout, Gk *speirein* to scatter, sow] *vi* **1** : to send out new growth **2** : to grow rapidly or greatly : BURGEON ~ *vt* : to cause to grow : BEAR
2**sprout** *n* **1 a** : SHOOT 1a; *esp* : a young shoot (as from a seed or root) **b** *pl* : edible shoots esp. of a crucifer or a plant (as brussels sprouts) producing them **2** : something resembling a sprout; *esp* : a young person : SCION
1**spruce** \'sprüs\ *n* [obs. *Spruce* Prussia, fr. ME, alter. of *Pruce*, fr. OF] : any of a genus (*Picea*) of evergreen trees of the pine family with a conical head of dense foliage and soft light wood; *also* : any of several coniferous trees (as Douglas fir) of similar habit
2**spruce** *adj* [perh. fr. obs. E *Spruce leather* leather imported from Prussia] : neat or smart in appearance : TRIM — **spruce·ly** *adv* — **spruce·ness** *n*
3**spruce** *vt* : to make spruce — often used with *up* ~ *vi* : to make oneself spruce ⟨~ up a bit⟩
spruce beer *n* : a beverage flavored with spruce; *esp* : one made from spruce twigs and leaves boiled with molasses or sugar and fermented with yeast
spruce pine *n* : a tree (as some pines and spruces or the common eastern hemlock) of the pine family with light, soft, or weak wood
sprucy \'sprü-sē\ *adj* : SPRUCE
1**sprue** \'sprü\ *n* [D *spruw;* akin to MLG *sprūwe*, a kind of tumor] : a chronic disease marked esp. by fatty diarrhea and deficiency symptoms
2**sprue** *n* [origin unknown] **1** : the hole through which metal or plastic is poured into the gate and thence into a mold **2** : the waste piece cast in a sprue
sprung *past of* SPRING
sprung rhythm *n* : a poetic rhythm designed to approximate the natural rhythm of speech and characterized by the frequent juxtaposition of single accented syllables and the occurrence of mixed types of feet
spry \'sprī\ *adj* **spri·er** *or* **spry·er** \'sprī(-ə)r\ **spri·est** *or* **spry·est** \'sprī-əst\ [perh. of Scand origin; akin to Sw dial *sprygg* spry] : vigorously active : BRISK **syn** see AGILE — **spry·ly** *adv* — **spry·ness** *n*
1**spud** \'spəd\ *n* [ME *spudde* dagger] **1** : a tool or device (as for digging, lifting, or cutting) combining the characteristics of spade and chisel **2** : POTATO
2**spud** *vb* **spud·ded; spud·ding** : to dig with a spud
1**spume** \'spyüm\ *n* [ME, fr. MF, fr. L *spuma* — more at FOAM] : frothy matter on liquids : FOAM, SCUM — **spu·mous** \'spyü-məs\ *adj* — **spumy** \-mē\ *adj*
2**spume** *vi* : FROTH, FOAM
spu·mo·ni *or* **spu·mo·ne** \spu̇-'mō-nē\ *n* [It *spumone*, aug. of *spuma* foam, fr. L] : ice cream in layers of different colors, flavors, and textures often with candied fruits and nuts
spun *past of* SPIN
spun glass *n* **1** : FIBER GLASS **2** : blown glass that has slender threads of glass incorporated in it
1**spunk** \'spəŋk\ *n* [ScGael *spong* sponge, tinder, fr. L *spongia* sponge] **1 a** : a woody tinder : PUNK **b** : any of various fungi used as tinder **2** : METTLE, SPIRIT
2**spunk** *vi, dial* : KINDLE
spunk·ie \'spəŋ-kē\ *n* **1** *Scot* : IGNIS FATUUS **2** *Scot* : LIQUOR, SPIRITS
spunk·i·ly \'spəŋ-kə-lē\ *adv* : in a spunky manner
spunk·i·ness \-kē-nəs\ *n* : the quality or state of being spunky
spunky \'spəŋ-kē\ *adj* : full of spunk : SPIRITED
spun rayon *n* : a rayon-staple yarn or fabric
spun sugar *n* : sugar boiled to long threads and gathered up and shaped or heaped on a stick as a candy
spun yarn *n* **1** : a textile yarn spun from staple-length fiber **2** : a small rope or stuff formed of two or more rope yarns loosely twisted and used for seizings esp. on board ship
1**spur** \'spər\ *n* [ME *spure*, fr. OE *spura;* akin to OE *spurnan* to kick — more at SPURN] **1 a** : a pointed device secured to a rider's heel and used to urge the horse **b** [ME *spores* knighthood] *pl* : recognition and reward for achievement **2** : a goad to action : STIMULUS **3** : something projecting like or suggesting a spur: as **a** : a projecting root or branch of a tree **b** (1) : a stiff sharp spine (as on the wings or legs of a bird or insect); *esp* : one on a cock's leg (2) : a gaff for a gamecock **c** : a hollow projecting appendage of a corolla or calyx (as in larkspur or columbine) **d** : CLIMBING IRON **4** : a ridge or lesser elevation that extends laterally from a mountain or mountain range **5** : a short wooden brace of a post **6** : a reinforcing buttress of masonry in a fortification **syn** see MOTIVE — **on the spur of the moment** : on hasty impulse
2**spur** *vb* **spurred; spur·ring** *vt* **1** : to urge (a horse) on with spurs **2** : to incite to action or accelerated growth or development : STIMULATE **3** : to put spurs on ~ *vi* : to spur one's horse on
spurge \'spərj\ *n* [ME, fr. MF, purge, spurge, fr. *espurgier* to purge, fr. L *expurgare* — more at EXPURGATE] : any of various mostly shrubby plants (family Euphorbiaceae, the spurge family, and esp. genus *Euphorbia*) with a bitter milky juice
spur gear *n* : a gear wheel with radial teeth parallel to its axis — called also *spur wheel*
spurge laurel *n* : a low Eurasian shrub (*Daphne laureola*) with oblong evergreen leaves and axillary racemes of yellowish flowers
spu·ri·ous \'spyu̇r-ē-əs\ *adj* [LL & L; LL *spurius* false, fr. L, of illegitimate birth, fr. *spurius*, n., bastard] **1** : of illegitimate birth : BASTARD **2 a** : FALSE, COUNTERFEIT **b** : superficially like but morphologically unlike ⟨a ~ fruit⟩ **3** : FORGED, FRAUDULENT — **spu·ri·ous·ly** *adv* — **spu·ri·ous·ness** *n*
1**spurn** \'spərn\ *vb* [ME *spurnen*, fr. OE *spurnan;* akin to OHG *spurnan* to kick, L *spernere* to spurn, Gk *spairein* to quiver] *vi* **1** *obs* **a** : STUMBLE **b** : KICK **2** : to reject something disdainfully — usu. used with *at* ⟨~ at danger⟩ ~ *vt* **1** : to tread sharply or heavily upon : TRAMPLE **2** : to reject with disdain or contempt : SCORN **syn** see DECLINE — **spurn·er** *n*
2**spurn** *n* **1 a** : KICK **b** *obs* : STUMBLE **2 a** : disdainful rejection **b** : contemptuous treatment
spur-of-the-moment *adj* : occurring or developing without premeditation : hastily extemporized
spurred \'spərd\ *adj* **1** : wearing spurs **2** : having one or more spurs ⟨a ~ violet⟩
spur·ri·er \'spər-ē-ər, 'spə-rē-\ *n* : one who makes spurs
spur·ry *or* **spur·rey** \'spər-ē, 'spə-rē\ *n* [D *spurrie*, fr. ML *spergula*] : a small white-flowered European weed (*Spergula arvensis*) of the pink family with whorled filiform leaves; *also* : any of several related and similar herbs
1**spurt** \'spərt\ *n* [origin unknown] **1** : a short period of time : MOMENT **2 a** : a sudden brief burst of effort or activity **b** : a sharp or sudden increase in business activity
2**spurt** *vi* : to make a spurt
3**spurt** *vb* [perh. akin to MHG *spürzen* to spit, OE *-sprūtan* to sprout — more at SPROUT] *vi* : to gush forth : SPOUT ~ *vt* : to expel in a stream or jet : SQUIRT
4**spurt** *n* : a sudden gush : JET
spur·tle \'spərt-ᵊl\ *n* [origin unknown] *chiefly Scot* : a wooden stick for stirring porridge
spur track *n* : a track that diverges from a main line
spur-winged \'spər-'wiŋd\ *adj* : having one or more horny spurs on the bend of the wings
sput·nik \'spu̇t-nik, 'spət-, 'spüt-, -ˌnik\ *n* [Russ, lit., traveling companion, fr. *s, so* with + *put'* path; akin to Gk *hama* together and to Skt *patha* way — more at SAME, FIND] : SATELLITE 2b
1**sput·ter** \'spət-ər\ *vb* [akin to D *sputteren* to sputter, OE *-sprūtan* to sprout] *vt* **1** : to spit or squirt from the mouth with explosive sounds : SPLUTTER **2** : to utter hastily or explosively in confusion or excitement ~ *vi* **1** : to spit or squirt particles of food or saliva noisily from the mouth **2** : to speak, reply, or ejaculate explosively or confusedly in anger or excitement **3 a** : to make explosive popping sounds **b** : to come to a sputtering stop — **sput·ter·er** \-ər-ər\ *n*
2**sputter** *n* **1** : confused and excited speech or discussion **2** : the act or sound of sputtering
spu·tum \'sp(y)üt-əm\ *n, pl* **spu·ta** \-ə\ [L, fr. neut. of *sputus*, pp. of *spuere* to spit — more at SPEW] : expectorated matter made up of saliva and often discharges from the respiratory passages
1**spy** \'spī\ *vb* **spied; spy·ing** [ME *spien*, fr. OF *espier*, of Gmc origin; akin to OHG *spehōn* to spy; akin to L *specere* to look, look at, *species* appearance, species, Gk *skeptesthai* & *skopein* to watch, look at, consider] *vt* **1** : to watch secretly usu. for hostile purposes : SCOUT **2** : to catch sight of : SEE **3** : to search or look for intensively ~ *vi* **1** : to observe or search for something : LOOK **2** : to watch secretly as a spy
2**spy** *n, pl* **spies** **1** : one that spies: **a** : one who keeps secret watch on a person or thing to obtain information **b** : one who acts in a clandestine manner or on false pretenses to obtain information in the zone of operations of a belligerent with the intention of communicating it to the hostile party **2** : an act of spying
spy·glass \-ˌglas\ *n* : a small telescope
squab \'skwäb\ *n, pl* **squabs** [prob. of Scand origin; akin to Sw dial. *skvabb* anything soft and thick] **1** *or pl* **squab** : a fledgling

bird; *specif* **:** a fledgling pigeon about four weeks old **2 :** a short fat person **3 a :** COUCH **b :** a cushion for a chair or couch — **squab** *adj*

1**squab·ble** \'skwäb-əl\ *n* [prob. of Scand origin; akin to Sw dial. *skvabbel* dispute] **:** a noisy altercation or quarrel usu. over trifles **:** WRANGLE **syn** see QUARREL

2**squabble** *vb* **squab·bling** \-(ə-)liŋ\ *vi* **:** to quarrel noisily and to no purpose **:** WRANGLE ~ *vt* **:** to disarrange (set type) so that the letters or lines need readjustment — compare 3PI — **squab·bler** \-(ə-)lər\ *n*

1**squad** \'skwäd\ *n* [MF *esquade*, fr. OSp & OIt; OSp *escuadra* & OIt *squadra* derivs. of (assumed) VL *exquadrare* to make square — more at SQUARE] **1 :** a small organized group of military personnel; *esp* **:** a tactical unit that can be easily directed in the field **2 :** a small group engaged in a common effort or occupation ⟨a football ~⟩ ⟨a police ~⟩

2**squad** *vt* **squad·ded; squad·ding :** to arrange in squads

squad car *n* **:** a police automobile connected by shortwave radiophone with headquarters — called also *cruiser, prowl car*

squad·ron \'skwäd-rən\ *n* [It *squadrone*, aug. of *squadra* squad] **:** a unit of military organization: **a :** a cavalry unit higher than a troop and lower than a regiment **b :** a naval unit consisting of two or more divisions and sometimes additional vessels **c** (1) **:** a unit of the U.S. Air Force higher than a flight and lower than a group (2) **:** a military flight formation

squad room *n* **1 :** a room in a barracks used to billet soldiers **2 :** a room in a police station where members of the force assemble (as for roll call or the assignment of duties)

squa·lene \'skwā-ˌlēn\ *n* [ISV, fr. L *squalus*, a sea fish] **:** an acyclic hydrocarbon $C_{30}H_{50}$ that is found esp. in shark-liver oils and is a precursor of cholesterol

squal·id \'skwäl-əd\ *adj* [L *squalidus* — more at SQUALOR] **1 :** marked by filthiness and degradation from neglect or poverty **2 :** morally debased **:** SORDID **syn** see DIRTY — **squal·id·ly** *adv* — **squal·id·ness** *n*

1**squall** \'skwȯl\ *vb* [of Scand origin; akin to ON *skval* useless chatter] **:** to cry out raucously **:** SCREAM — **squall·er** *n*

2**squall** *n* **:** a raucous cry

3**squall** *n* [prob. of Scand origin; akin to Sw *skval* rushing water] **1 :** a sudden violent wind often with rain or snow **2 :** a short-lived commotion

4**squall** *vi* **:** to blow a squall

squally \'skwȯ-lē\ *adj* **1 :** marked by squalls **2 :** GUSTY

squa·loid \'skwā-ˌlȯid\ *adj* [NL *Squalus*, genus of sharks, fr. L *squalus*, a sea fish] **:** being or resembling a typical shark

squa·lor \'skwäl-ər *also* 'skwāl-\ *n* [L; akin to L *squalidus* squalid, *squama* scale] **:** the quality or state of being squalid

squam- *or* **squamo-** *comb form* [NL, fr. L *squama*] **:** scale **:** squama ⟨*squam*ation⟩

squa·ma \'skwā-mə, 'skwä-\ *n, pl* **squa·mae** \'skwā-ˌmē, 'skwä-ˌmī\ [L] **:** SCALE **:** a structure resembling a scale

squa·mate \-ˌmāt\ *adj* **:** SCALY

squa·ma·tion \skwə-'mā-shən\ *n* **1 :** the state of being scaly **2 :** the arrangement of scales on an animal

1**squa·mo·sal** \skwə-'mō-səl, -zəl\ *adj* **1 :** SQUAMOUS **2 :** of, relating to, or being a membrane bone of the skull of many vertebrates corresponding to the squamous portion of the temporal bone of man

2**squamosal** *n* **:** a squamosal bone

squa·mose \'skwā-ˌmōs, 'skwä-\ *adj* **:** SQUAMOUS — **squa·mose·ly** *adv* — **squa·mose·ness** *n*

squa·mous \-məs\ *adj* [L *squamosus*, fr. *squama* scale] **1 :** covered with or consisting of scales **:** SCALY **2 :** of, relating to, or being the anterior upper portion of the temporal bone of man and various mammals — **squa·mous·ly** *adv*

squa·mu·lose \-myə-ˌlōs\ *adj* [L *squamula*, dim. of *squama*] **:** minutely squamous

1**squan·der** \'skwän-dər\ *vb* **squan·der·ing** \-d(ə-)riŋ\ [origin unknown] *vt* **1 :** SCATTER **2 :** to spend extravagantly or foolishly **:** DISSIPATE ~ *vi* **1 :** to spend wastefully **2 :** SCATTER — **squan·der·er** \-dər-ər, -drər\ *n*

2**squander** *n* **:** an act of squandering

1**square** \'skwa(ə)r, 'skwe(ə)r\ *n* [ME, fr. MF *esquarre*, fr. (assumed) VL *exquadra*, fr. *exquadrare* to square, fr. L *ex-* + *quadrare* to square — more at QUADRATE] **1 :** an instrument having at least one right angle and two straight edges used to lay out or test right angles **2 :** a rectangle with all four sides equal **3 :** any of the quadrilateral spaces marked out on a board for playing games **4 :** the product of a number multiplied by itself **5 a :** an open place or area formed at the meeting of two or more streets **b :** BLOCK 6c **6 :** a solid object or piece approximating a cube or having a square as its largest face **7 :** an unopened cotton flower with its enclosing bracts **8 :** a person who is overly conventional or conservative in taste or way of life — **on the square 1 :** at right angles **2 :** in a fair open manner **:** HONESTLY — **out of square :** not at an exact right angle

2**square** *adj* **1 a :** having four equal sides and four right angles **b :** forming a right angle ⟨~ corner⟩ **2 :** raised to the second power **3 a :** being approximately square ⟨~ cabinet⟩ **b :** of a shape suggesting strength and solidity ⟨~ jaw⟩ ⟨~ shoulders⟩ **c :** rectangular and equilateral in section ⟨~ tower⟩ **4 a :** converted from a linear unit into a square unit having the same length of side **:** SQUARED ⟨~ foot⟩ — see MEASURE table, METRIC SYSTEM table **b :** being of a specified length in each of two equal dimensions ⟨10 feet ~⟩ **5 a :** exactly adjusted **:** well made **b :** JUST, FAIR **c :** leaving no balance **:** SETTLED **d :** EVEN, TIED **e :** SUBSTANTIAL, SATISFYING ⟨~ meal⟩ **f** *slang* **:** having unsophisticated or conservative tastes **6 :** set at right angles with the mast and keel — used of the yards of a square-rigged ship — **square·ly** *adv* — **square·ness** *n*

3**square** *vt* **1 a :** to make square or rectangular ⟨~ a building stone⟩ **b :** to test for deviation from a right angle, straight line, or plane surface **2 :** to bring to a right angle ⟨*squared* his shoulders⟩ **3 a :** to multiply (a number) by itself **:** raise to the second power **b :** to find a square equal in area to ⟨~ a circle⟩ **4 :** to compare with a standard **:** TEST **5 a :** BALANCE, SETTLE ⟨~ an account⟩ **b :** to even the score of **6 :** to mark off into squares **7 a :** to set right **:** bring into agreement **b :** BRIBE, FIX ~ *vi* **1 :** AGREE, MATCH **2 :** to settle matters; *esp* **:** to pay the bill **3 :** to take a fighting stance **syn** see AGREE

4**square** *adv* **1 :** STRAIGHTFORWARDLY, HONESTLY **2 :** so as to face or be face to face; *also* **:** at right angles **3 :** with nothing intervening **:** DIRECTLY **4 :** FIRMLY, SOLIDLY **5 :** in a square shape ⟨cut a diamond ~⟩

square away *vi* **1 :** to square the yards so as to sail before the wind **2 :** to put everything in order or in readiness **3 :** to take up a fighting stance ~ *vt* **:** to put in order or readiness

square dance *n* **:** a dance for four couples who form a hollow square — **square dancing** *n*

squared circle *n* **:** a boxing ring

square deal *n* **:** an honest and fair transaction or trade

square knot *n* **:** a knot made of two reverse half-knots and typically used to join the ends of two cords

square measure *n* **:** a unit or system of units for measuring area — see MEASURE table, METRIC SYSTEM table

square of opposition : a square figure on which may be demonstrated the four logical oppositions by contrariety, subcontrariety, subalternation, and contradiction

squar·er \'skwar-ər, 'skwer-\ *n* **:** a workman who squares timber or stone

square rig *n* **:** a sailing-ship rig in which the sails are bent to the yards carried athwart the mast and trimmed with braces — **square-rigged** \'skwa(ə)r-'rigd, 'skwe(ə)r-\ *adj* — **square-rig·ger** \-'rig-ər\ *n*

square root *n* **:** a factor of a number that when squared gives the number ⟨the *square root* of 9 is ± 3⟩

square sail \-ˌsāl, -səl\ *n* **:** a 4-sided sail extended on a yard suspended at the middle from a mast

square shooter *n* **:** a just or honest person

square-shoul·dered \'skwa(ə)r-'shōl-dərd, 'skwe(ə)r-\ *adj* **:** having the shoulders high and well braced back

square-toed \-'tōd\ *adj* **1 :** having the toe square ⟨~ boots⟩ **2 :** OLD-FASHIONED, CONSERVATIVE — **square-toed·ness** *n*

squar·ish \'skwa(ə)r-ish, 'skwe(ə)r-\ *adj* **:** somewhat square in form or appearance — **squar·ish·ly** *adv*

squar·rose \'skwär-ˌōs, 'skwa(ə)r-\ *adj* [L *squarrosus* scurfy; akin to OSlav *skvrŭna* filth] **:** rough with divergent scales or processes; *esp* **:** having stiff spreading bracts ⟨a ~ involucre⟩ — **squar·rose·ly** *adv*

1**squash** \'skwäsh, 'skwȯsh\ *vb* [MF *esquasser*, fr. (assumed) VL *exquassare*, fr. L *ex-* + *quassare* to shake — more at QUASH] *vt* **1 :** to press or beat into a pulp or a flat mass **:** CRUSH **2 :** to put down **:** SUPPRESS ⟨~ a revolt⟩ ~ *vi* **1 :** to flatten out under pressure or impact **2 :** to proceed with a splashing or squelching sound **3 :** SQUEEZE, PRESS ⟨four of us ~*ed* into the seat⟩ — **squash·er** *n*

2**squash** *n* **1** *obs* **:** something soft and easily crushed **2 :** the sudden fall of a heavy soft body or the sound of such a fall **3 :** a squelching sound made by walking on oozy ground or in water-soaked boots **4 :** a crushed mass **5** *Brit* **:** a drink of the sweetened juice of a citrus fruit usu. with added soda water **6 :** SQUASH RACQUETS

3**squash** *adv* **:** with a squash or a squashing sound

4**squash** *n, pl* **squash·es** *or* **squash** [by shortening & alter. fr. earlier *isquoutersquash*, fr. Natick & Narraganset *askútasquash*] **:** any of various fruits of plants (genus *Cucurbita*) of the gourd family widely cultivated as vegetables and for livestock feed; *also* **:** a vine or other plant that bears squashes

squash bug *n* **:** a large black American bug (*Anasa tristis* of the family Coreidae) injurious to squash vines

squash·i·ly \'skwäsh-ə-lē, 'skwȯsh-\ *adv* **:** in a squashy manner

squash·i·ness \-ē-nəs\ *n* **:** the quality of being squashy

squash racquets *n pl but sing in constr* **:** a game played in a 4-wall court with a racket and a rubber ball

squash tennis *n* **:** a racket game resembling squash racquets played with an inflated ball the size of a tennis ball

squashy \'skwäsh-ē, 'skwȯsh-\ *adj* **1 :** easily squashed **2 :** softly wet **:** BOGGY **3 :** soft because overripe ⟨~ melons⟩

1**squat** \'skwät\ *vb* **squat·ted; squat·ting** [ME *squatten*, fr. MF *esquatir*, fr. *es-* ex- (fr. L *ex-*) + *quatir* to press, fr. (assumed) VL *coactire* to press together, fr. L *coactus*, pp. of *cogere* to drive together — more at COGENT] *vt* **1 :** to cause (oneself) to crouch or sit on the ground **2 :** to occupy as a squatter ~ *vi* **1 :** CROUCH, COWER ⟨*squatting* hare⟩ **2 :** to sit on one's haunches or heels **3 :** to become a squatter

2**squat** *n* **1 a :** the act of squatting **b :** the posture of one that squats **2 :** a place where one squats; *esp* **:** the lair of a small animal ⟨~ of a hare⟩

3**squat** *adj* **squat·ter; squat·test 1 :** sitting with the haunches close above the heels **2 :** low to the ground; *also* **:** short and thick — **squat·ly** *adv* — **squat·ness** *n*

1**squat·ter** \'skwät-ər\ *vi* [prob. of Scand origin; akin to Dan *skvatte* to sprinkle] **:** to go along through or as if through water

2**squatter** *n* **:** one that squats: as **a :** one that settles on land without right or title or payment of rent **b :** one that settles on public land under government regulation with the purpose of acquiring title

squatter sovereignty *n* **:** POPULAR SOVEREIGNTY

squat·ty \'skwät-ē\ *adj* **:** low to the ground; *also* **:** DUMPY, THICKSET

squaw \'skwȯ\ *n* [of Algonquian origin; akin to Natick *squàas* woman] **1 :** an American Indian woman **2 :** WOMAN, WIFE — usu. used disparagingly

squaw·fish \-ˌfish\ *n* **1 :** any of several large cyprinid fishes (genus *Ptychocheilus*) of western No. America **2 :** a common surf fish (*Taeniotoca lateralis*) of the Pacific coast of No. America

1**squawk** \'skwȯk\ *vi* [prob. blend of *squall* and *squeak*] **1 :** to utter a harsh abrupt scream **2 :** to complain or protest loudly or vehemently — **squawk·er** *n*

2**squawk** *n* **1 :** a harsh abrupt scream **2 :** a noisy complaint

squawk box *n* **:** an intercom speaker

squaw man *n* **:** a white man married to an Indian woman and usu. living as one of her tribe

squaw·root \'skwȯ-ˌrüt, -ˌrůt\ *n* **:** a No. American scaly herb

(*Conopholis americana*) of the broomrape family parasitic on oak and hemlock roots

1squeak \'skwēk\ *vb* [ME *squeken*] *vi* **1 :** to utter or make a short shrill cry or noise **2 :** SQUEAL 2a **3 :** to pass, succeed, or win by a narrow margin ⟨just ~*ed* by⟩ ~ *vt* **:** to utter in a shrill piping tone

2squeak *n* **1 :** a sharp shrill cry or sound **2 :** ESCAPE ⟨a close ~⟩ — **squeak·er** *n* — **squeaky** \'skwē-kē\ *adj*

1squeal \'skwē(ə)l\ *vb* [ME *squelen*] *vi* **1 :** to make a shrill cry or noise **2 a :** to turn informer **b :** COMPLAIN, PROTEST ~ *vt* **:** to utter or express with or as if with a squeal — **squeal·er** *n*

2squeal *n* **:** a shrill sharp cry or noise

squea·mish \'skwē-mish\ *adj* [ME *squaymisch*, modif. of AF *escoymous*] **1 a :** easily nauseated **:** QUEASY **b :** affected with nausea **:** NAUSEATED **2 a :** easily shocked **:** PRUDISH **b :** excessively fastidious or scrupulous in conduct or belief **c :** easily offended or disgusted **syn** see NICE — **squea·mish·ly** *adv* — **squea·mish·ness** *n*

1squee·gee \'skwē-ˌjē\ *n* [prob. imit.] **:** a blade of leather or rubber set on a handle and used for spreading, pushing, or wiping liquid material on, across, or off a surface (as a window); *also* **:** a smaller similar device or a small rubber roller with handle used by a photographer or lithographer

2squeegee *vt* **squee·geed; squee·gee·ing :** to smooth, wipe, or treat with a squeegee

1squeeze \'skwēz\ *vb* [alter. of obs. E *quease*, fr. ME *queysen*, fr. OE *cwȳsan;* akin to Icel *kveisa* stomach cramps] *vt* **1 a :** to exert pressure esp. on opposite sides of **:** COMPRESS **b :** to extract or emit under pressure **c :** to force or thrust by compression **2 a** (1) **:** to get by extortion (2) **:** to deprive by extortion **b :** to cause economic hardship to **c :** to reduce the amount of ⟨~*s* profits⟩ **3 :** to crowd into a limited area **4 :** to gain or win by a narrow margin **5 :** to constrain (another player) to discard in bridge so as to unguard a suit **6 :** to score by means of a squeeze play ~ *vi* **1 :** to give way before pressure **2 :** to exert pressure; *also* **:** to practice extortion or oppression **3 :** to force one's way ⟨~ through a door⟩ **4 :** to pass, win, or get by narrowly — **squeez·er** *n* — **squeeze the shorts :** to force short sellers to cover at higher prices

2squeeze *n* **1 a :** an act or instance of squeezing **:** COMPRESSION **b :** HANDCLASP; *also* **:** EMBRACE **2 a :** a quantity squeezed out from something ⟨a ~ of lemon⟩ **b :** a group crowded together **:** CROWD **3 a :** the commission taken by an oriental servant **b :** a profit taken by an oriental official or middleman on goods or transactions **:** GRAFT **4 :** any of various financial pressures caused by narrowing margins or by shortages **5 :** a forced discard in bridge

squeeze bottle *n* **:** a bottle of flexible plastic that dispenses its contents by being pressed

squeeze play *n* **1 :** a baseball play in which a batter attempts to score a runner from third base by bunting **2 :** the exertion of pressure in order to extort a concession or gain a goal **:** SQUEEZE

squeg \'skweg\ *vi* **squegged; squeg·ging** [back-formation fr. *squegger* (tube in which the valve oscillates)] **:** to oscillate in a highly irregular fashion — used of an electronic system

1squelch \'skwelch\ *n* [imit.] **1 :** a sound of or as if of semiliquid matter under suction ⟨the ~ of mud⟩ **2 :** the act of suppressing; *esp* **:** a retort that silences an opponent

2squelch *vt* **1 a :** to fall or stamp on so as to crush **b** (1) **:** to completely suppress **:** QUELL (2) **:** SILENCE **2 :** to emit or move with a sucking sound ~ *vi* **1 :** to emit a sucking sound like that of an object being withdrawn from mire **2 :** to splash through water, slush, or mire — **squelch·er** *n*

sque·teague \skwi-'tēg\ *n, pl* **squeteague** [Narraganset *pesukwiteaug*, pl.] **:** GRAY TROUT; *also* **:** any of various other weakfishes

1squib \'skwib\ *n* [origin unknown] **1 a :** a small firecracker **b :** a broken firecracker the powder in which burns with a fizz **2 a :** a short humorous or satiric writing or speech **b :** a short carelessly written piece **:** SCRIBBLE

2squib *vb* **squibbed; squib·bing** *vi* **1 :** to speak, write, or publish squibs **2 :** to fire a squib ~ *vt* **1 a :** to utter in an offhand manner **b :** to make squibs against **:** LAMPOON **2 :** to shoot off **:** FIRE

1squid \'skwid\ *n, pl* **squid** *or* **squids** [origin unknown] **:** any of numerous 10-armed cephalopods (esp. of the genera *Loligo* and *Ommastrephes*) having a long tapered body, a caudal fin on each side, and usu. a slender internal chitinous support

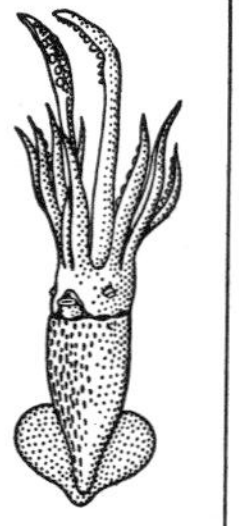

squid

2squid *vi* **squid·ded; squid·ding :** to fish with or for squid

squiffed \'skwift\ *or* **squif·fy** \'skwif-ē\ *adj* [origin unknown] **:** INTOXICATED, DRUNK

1squig·gle \'skwig-əl\ *vb* **squig·gling** \-(ə-)liŋ\ [blend of *squirm* and *wriggle*] *vi* **1 :** SQUIRM, WRIGGLE **2 :** to write or paint hastily **:** SCRIBBLE ~ *vt* **1 :** SCRIBBLE **2 :** to form or cause to form in squiggles

2squiggle *n* **:** a short wavy twist or line **:** CURLICUE; *esp* **:** an illegible scrawl

squil·gee \'skwē-ˌjē, 'skwil-ˌjē\ *var of* SQUEEGEE

squill \'skwil\ *n* [ME, fr. L *squilla* sea onion, fr. Gk *skilla*] **1 a :** a Mediterranean bulbous herb (*Urginea maritima*) of the lily family **b** (1) *usu pl* **:** its dried sliced bulb scales used as an expectorant, cardiac stimulant, and diuretic (2) **:** the bulb of a red-bulbed form of squill used in rat poison **2 :** SCILLA **3** [NL *Squilla*] **:** SQUILLA

squil·la \'skwil-ə\ *n, pl* **squillas** *or* **squil·lae** \'skwil-ˌē, -ˌī\ [NL, genus name, fr. L, squill, prawn] **:** any of various stomatopod crustaceans (esp. genus *Squilla*) that burrow in mud or beneath stones in shallow water along the seashore

1squinch \'skwinch\ *n* [alter. of earlier *scunch* (back part of the side of an opening)] **:** a support (as an arch, lintel, or corbeling) carried across the corner of a room under a superimposed mass

2squinch *vb* [prob. blend of *squint* and *pinch*] *vt* **1 :** to screw up (the eyes or face) **:** SQUINT **2 :** to cause to crouch down or draw together ~ *vi* **1 :** FLINCH **2 :** to crouch down or draw together **3 :** SQUINT

1squin·ny \'skwin-ē\ *vb* [prob. fr. obs. E *squin* asquint, fr. ME *skuin*] **:** SQUINT

2squinny *n* **:** SQUINT — **squinny** *adj*

1squint \'skwint\ *adj* [short for *asquint*] **1** *of an eye* **:** looking or tending to look obliquely or askance (as with envy, disdain, or distrust) **2** *of the eyes* **:** not having the visual axes parallel **:** CROSSED

2squint *vi* **1 a :** to have an indirect bearing, reference, or aim **b :** to deviate from a true line **2 a :** to look in a squint-eyed manner **b :** to be cross-eyed **c :** to look or peer with eyes partly closed ~ *vt* **:** to cause (an eye) to squint — **squint·er** *n* — **squint·ing·ly** \-iŋ-lē\ *adv*

3squint *n* **1 :** STRABISMUS **2 :** an instance of squinting **3 :** HAGIOSCOPE — **squinty** \'skwint-ē\ *adj*

squint–eyed \'skwint-'īd\ *adj* **1 :** having eyes that squint; *specif* **:** CROSS-EYED **2 :** looking askance (as in envy or malice)

squinting construction *n* **:** an ambiguous grammatical construction that contains a word or phrase (as *often* in "getting dressed often is a nuisance") interpretable as modifying either what precedes or what follows

1squire \'skwī(ə)r\ *n* [ME *squier*, fr. OF *esquier* — more at ESQUIRE] **1 :** a shield bearer or armor-bearer of a knight **2 a :** a male attendant on a great personage **b :** a man devotedly attending a lady **:** GALLANT **3 a :** a member of the British gentry ranking below a knight and above a gentleman **b :** an owner of a country estate; *esp* **:** the principal landowner in a village or district **c** (1) **:** JUSTICE OF THE PEACE (2) **:** LAWYER (3) **:** JUDGE

2squire *vt* **:** to attend as a squire **:** ESCORT

squire·ar·chy *or* **squir·ar·chy** \'skwī(ə)r-ˌär-kē\ *n* **1 :** the gentry or landed-proprietor class **2 :** government by a landed gentry

squir·ish \'skwī(ə)r-ish\ *adj* **:** of, relating to, or having the characteristics of a squire

squirm \'skwərm\ *vi* [perh. imit.] **:** to twist about like an eel or a worm **syn** see WRITHE — **squirm** *n* — **squirmy** \'skwər-mē\ *adj*

squir·rel \'skwər(-ə)l, 'skwə-rəl, *chiefly Brit* 'skwir-əl\ *n, pl* **squirrels** *also* **squirrel** [ME *squirel*, fr. MF *esquireul*, fr. (assumed) VL *scuriolus*, dim. of *scurius*, alter. of L *sciurus*, fr. Gk *skiouros*, fr. *skia* shadow + *oura* tail; akin to OHG *ars* buttocks, OIr *err* tail — more at SHINE] **1 :** any of various small or medium-sized rodents (family Sciuridae): as **a :** any of numerous New or Old World arboreal forms having a long bushy tail and strong hind legs **b :** any of numerous burrowing forms including the chipmunks and spermophiles — called also *ground squirrel* **2 :** the fur of a squirrel

squirrel cage *n* **1 :** a cage for a small animal (as a squirrel) that contains a rotatable cylinder for exercising **2 :** something resembling a squirrel cage in construction or in senseless repetitiveness

squirrel corn *n* **:** a No. American herb (*Dicentra canadensis*) of the fumitory family with much-divided leaves and a scapose raceme of cream-colored flowers

squir·rel·ly \'skwər(-ə)-lē, 'skwə-rə-\ *adj* **:** extremely odd **:** CRAZY

squirrel rifle *n* [fr. its being suitable only for small game] **:** a small-bore rifle — called also *squirrel gun*

1squirt \'skwərt\ *vb* [ME *squirten;* akin to LG *swirtjen* to squirt] *vi* **:** to eject liquid in a thin spurt ~ *vt* **:** to cause to squirt — **squirt·er** *n*

2squirt *n* **1 a :** an instrument (as a syringe) for squirting a liquid **b :** a small quick stream **:** JET **c :** the action of squirting **2 :** an impudent youngster

squirting cucumber *n* **:** a Mediterranean plant (*Ecballium elaterium*) of the gourd family with oblong fruit that bursts from the peduncle when ripe and forcibly ejects the seeds

squish \'skwish\ *vb* [alter. of *squash*] *vt* **1 :** SQUASH **2 :** SQUELCH, SUCK ~ *vi* **:** SQUELCH, SUCK — **squish** *n*

squishy \-ē\ *adj* **:** being soft, yielding, and damp

sri \'s(h)rē\ *n* [Skt *śrī*, lit., majesty, holiness akin to Gk *kreiōn* ruler, master] — used as a conventional title of respect when addressing or speaking of a distinguished Indian

-st — see -EST

1stab \'stab\ *n* [ME *stabbe*] **1 :** a wound produced by a pointed weapon **2 :** a thrust of a pointed weapon **3 :** EFFORT, TRY

2stab *vb* **stabbed; stab·bing** *vt* **1 :** to wound or pierce by the thrust of a pointed weapon **2 :** THRUST, DRIVE ~ *vi* **:** to thrust or give a wound with or as if with a pointed weapon — **stab·ber** *n*

1sta·bile \'stā-ˌbīl, -ˌbil\ *adj* [L *stabilis* — more at STABLE] **1 :** not moving **:** STATIONARY, STABLE **2 :** not fluctuating **3 :** resistant to chemical change

2sta·bile \-ˌbēl\ *n* **:** a stable abstract sculpture or construction typically made of sheet metal, wire, and wood — compare MOBILE

sta·bil·i·ty \stə-'bil-ət-ē\ *n* **1 :** the quality, state, or degree of being stable: as **a :** the strength to stand or endure **:** FIRMNESS **b :** the property of a body that causes it when disturbed from a condition of equilibrium or steady motion to develop forces or moments that restore the original condition **c :** resistance to chemical change or to physical disintegration **2 :** a vow binding a monk for life to one monastery

sta·bi·li·za·tion \ˌstā-b(ə-)lə-'zā-shən\ *n* **:** the act or process of stabilizing or the state of being stabilized

sta·bi·lize \'stā-bə-ˌlīz\ *vt* **1 :** to make stable, steadfast, or firm **2 :** to hold steady: as **a :** to maintain the stability of (as an airplane) by means of a stabilizer **b :** to limit fluctuations of (as prices) **c :** to establish a minimum price for ~ *vi* **:** to become stable, firm, or steadfast

sta·bi·liz·er \-ˌlī-zər\ *n* **:** one that stabilizes something: as **a :** a substance added to another substance (as an explosive or plastic) or to a system (as an emulsion) to prevent or retard an unwanted alteration of physical state **b :** a gyroscope device to keep ships steady in a heavy sea **c :** an airfoil providing stability for an airplane; *specif* **:** the fixed horizontal member of the tail assembly

1sta·ble \'stā-bəl\ *n* [ME, fr. OF *estable*, fr. L *stabulum*, fr. *stare* to stand — more at STAND] **1 :** a building in which domestic animals are sheltered and fed; *esp* **:** such a building having stalls or compartments ⟨horse ~⟩ **2 a :** the racehorses of one owner **b :** a group of athletes (as boxers) under one management — **sta·ble·man** \-mən, -ˌman\ *n*

2stable *vb* **sta·bling** \-b(ə-)liŋ\ *vt* **:** to put or keep in a stable ~ *vi* **:** to dwell in or as if in a stable

3stable *adj* **sta·bler** \-b(ə-)lər\ **sta·blest** \-b(ə-)ləst\ [ME, fr. OF *estable*, fr. L *stabilis*, fr. *stare* to stand] **1 a :** firmly established **:** FIXED, STEADFAST **b :** not changing or fluctuating **:** UNVARYING **c :** ENDURING, PERMANENT **2 :** steady in purpose **:** CONSTANT **3 a** (1) **:** placed so as to resist forces tending to cause motion or change of motion (2) **:** designed so as to develop forces that restore the original condition when disturbed from a condition of equilibrium or steady motion **b** (1) **:** not readily altering in chemical

makeup or physical state ⟨~ emulsions⟩ (2) **:** not spontaneously radioactive **syn** see LASTING — **sta·bly** \-b(ə-)lē\ *adv*

sta·ble·ness \-bəl-nəs\ *n* **:** STABILITY

sta·bler \-b(ə-)lər\ *n* **:** one that keeps a stable

sta·bling *n* **:** accommodation for animals in a building; *also* **:** the building for this

stab·lish \'stab-lish\ *vb* [by shortening] *archaic* **:** ESTABLISH — **stab·lish·ment** \-mənt\ *n, archaic*

stac·ca·to \stə-'kät-(,)ō\ *adj* [It, fr. pp. of *staccare* to detach, deriv. of OF *destachier* — more at DETACH] **1 a :** cut short or apart in performing **:** DISCONNECTED ⟨~ notes⟩ **b :** marked by short clear-cut playing or singing of tones or chords ⟨a ~ style⟩ **2 :** ABRUPT, DISJOINTED — **staccato** *adv* — **staccato** *n*

staccato mark *n* **:** a pointed vertical stroke or a dot placed over or under a musical note to be produced staccato

[1]**stack** \'stak\ *n* [ME *stak*, fr. ON *stakkr;* akin to OE *staca* stake] **1 :** a large usu. conical pile (as of hay) left standing in the field for storage **2 a :** an orderly pile or heap **b :** a large quantity or number **3 :** an English unit of measure esp. for firewood that is equal to 108 cubic feet **4 a :** a number of flues embodied in one structure rising above a roof **b :** a vertical pipe (as to carry off smoke) **c :** the exhaust pipe of an internal-combustion engine **5 :** a pyramid of three rifles interlocked **6 :** a structure of bookshelves for compact storage of books — usu. used in pl. **7 :** a pile of chips sold to or won by a poker player

[2]**stack** *vt* **1 :** to arrange in a stack **:** PILE **2 :** to arrange secretly for cheating ⟨the cards were *~ed* against him⟩ **3 :** to assign (an airplane) by radio to a particular altitude and position within a group circling before landing **~** *vi* **:** to form a stack — **stack·er** *n*

stack up *vi* **1 :** to add up **:** TOTAL **2 :** to measure up **:** COMPARE — usu. used with *against*

stac·te \'stak-tē\ *n* [L, fr. Gk *staktē*, fr. fem. of *staktos* oozing out in drops, fr. *stazein* to drip — more at STAGNATE] **:** a sweet spice used by the ancient Jews in preparing incense

stad·dle \'stad-ᵊl\ *n* [ME *stathel* base, support, fr. OE *stathol;* akin to OE *stede* place — more at STEAD] **1 :** a base (as of piling) for a stack of hay or straw **2 :** any supporting framework

stade \'stād\ *n* [MF *estade*, fr. L *stadium*] **:** STADIUM 1a

sta·dia \'stād-ē-ə\ *n* [It, prob. fr. L, pl. of *stadium*] **:** a surveying method for determination of distances and differences of elevation by means of a telescopic instrument having two horizontal lines through which the marks on a graduated rod are observed; *also* **:** the instrument or rod

sta·di·um \'stād-ē-əm\ *n, pl* **sta·dia** \-ē-ə\ *or* **sta·di·ums** [ME, fr. L, fr. Gk *stadion*, alter. of *spadion*, fr. *span* to pull — more at SPAN] **1 a :** any of various ancient Greek units of length ranging in value from 607 to 738 English feet **b :** an ancient Roman unit of length equal to 606.95 English feet **2 a :** a course for footraces in ancient Greece orig. one stadium in length **b :** a tiered structure with seats for spectators surrounding an ancient Greek running track **c** *pl usu stadiums* **:** a large usu. unroofed building with tiers of seats for spectators at sports events **3** [NL, fr. L] **:** a stage in a life history; *esp* **:** one between successive molts

stadt·hold·er \'stat-,hōl-dər\ *n* [part trans. of D *stadhouder*, fr. *stad* place + *houder* holder] **1 a :** a viceroy in a province of the Netherlands **b :** a chief executive officer of the United Provinces of the Netherlands **2 :** a viceroy or lieutenant governor of a region outside the Netherlands — **stadt·hold·er·ate** \-də-rət\ *n* — **stadt·hold·er·ship** \-dər-,ship\ *n*

[1]**staff** \'staf\ *n, pl* **staffs** *or* **staves** \'stavz, 'stāvz\ [ME *staf*, fr. OE *stæf;* akin to OHG *stab* staff, *stampfōn* to stamp — more at STAMP] **1 a :** a long stick carried in the hand for support in walking **b :** a supporting rod: as (1) *archaic* **:** SHAFT 1a(1) (2) **:** a crosspiece in a ladder or chair **:** RUNG (3) **:** FLAGSTAFF (4) **:** a pivoted arbor **c :** CLUB, CUDGEL **2 a :** CROSIER **b :** a rod carried as a symbol of office or authority **3 :** the horizontal lines with their spaces on which music is written — called also *stave* **4 :** any of various graduated sticks or rules used for measuring **:** ROD **5** *pl staffs* **a :** the officers chiefly responsible for the internal operations of an institution or business **b :** a group of officers appointed to assist a civil executive or commanding officer **c :** military or naval officers not eligible for operational command **d :** the personnel who assist a director in carrying out an assigned task — **staff** *adj*

[2]**staff** *vt* **:** to supply with a staff or with workers

[3]**staff** *n* [prob. fr. G *staffieren* to trim] **:** a building material having a plaster of Paris base and used in exterior wall coverings of temporary buildings

staff·er \'staf-ər\ *n* **:** a member of a staff; *specif* **:** a newspaper reporter or editor

staff officer *n* **:** a commissioned officer assigned to a military commander's staff

staff of life : a staple of diet; *esp* **:** BREAD

Staf·ford·shire terrier \,staf-ərd-,shi(ə)r-, -shər-\ *n* [*Staffordshire*, England] **:** BULLTERRIER

staff sergeant *n* **:** a noncommissioned officer ranking in the army above a sergeant and below a sergeant first class, in the air force above an airman first class and below a technical sergeant, and in the marine corps above a sergeant and below a gunnery sergeant

staff tree *n* **:** any of a genus (*Celastrus* of the family Celastraceae, the staff-tree family) of mostly twining shrubby plants including the common bittersweet

[1]**stag** \'stag\ *n, pl* **stags** [ME *stagge*, fr. OE *stagga;* akin to ON *andarsteggi* drake, OE *stingan* to sting] **1** *or pl* **stag :** an adult male red deer; *broadly* **:** the male of various deer (esp. genus *Cervus*) **2** *chiefly Scot* **:** a young horse; *esp* **:** a young unbroken stallion **3 :** a male animal castrated after maturity **4 :** a young adult male domestic fowl **5 a :** a social gathering of men only **b :** a man who attends a dance or party unaccompanied by a woman

[2]**stag** *vb* **stagged; stag·ging** [*stag* (informer)] *vt, Brit* **:** to spy on **~** *vi* **1** *Brit* **:** to turn informer **2 :** to attend a dance or party without a woman companion

[3]**stag** *adj* **1 a :** restricted to men ⟨a ~ party⟩ **b :** intended or suitable for a gathering of men only ⟨~ movies⟩ **2 :** unaccompanied by someone of the opposite sex ⟨~ women⟩ — **stag** *adv*

stag beetle *n* **:** any of numerous mostly large lamellicorn beetles (family Lucanidae) having males with long and often branched mandibles suggesting the antlers of a stag

[1]**stage** \'stāj\ *n* [ME, fr. OF *estage*, fr. (assumed) VL *staticum*, fr. L *stare* to stand — more at STAND] **1 a :** one of a series of positions or stations one above the other **:** STEP **b :** the height of the surface of a river above an arbitrary zero point **2 a** (1) **:** a raised platform (2) **:** the part of a theater between the proscenium and the rear wall including the acting area, wings, and storage space **b :** a center of attention or scene of action **3 a :** a scaffold for workmen **b :** the small platform of a microscope on which an object is placed for examination **4 a :** a place of rest formerly provided for those traveling by stagecoach **:** STATION **b :** the distance between two stopping places on a road **c :** STAGECOACH **5 a :** a period or step in a process, activity, or development **b :** one passing through a (specified) stage **6 :** an element or part in a complex electronic contrivance; *specif* **:** a single tube with its associated components in an amplifier **7 :** a propulsion unit of a rocket with its own fuel and container — **on the stage :** in or into the acting profession

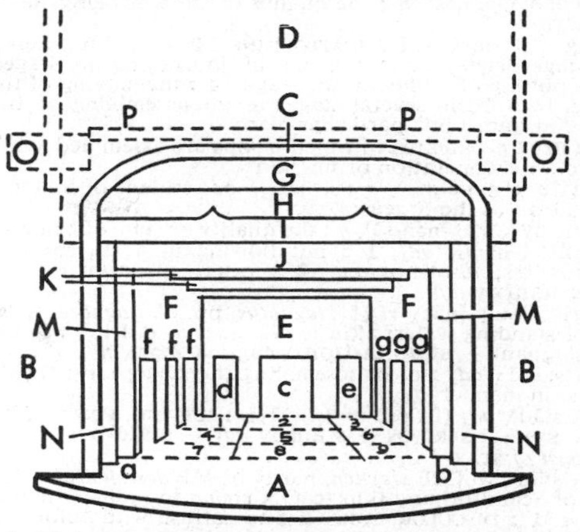

stage 2a(2): proscenium, *A;* wings, *B,B;* proscenium arch, *C;* flies, *D;* back flat, *E;* flats, *F,F;* asbestos curtain, *G;* grand drape, *H;* act drop, *I;* teaser, *J;* borders, *K,K;* returns, *M,M;* tormentors, *N,N;* fly gallery, *O,O;* bridge, *P,P; 1* up right center; *2* up center; *3* up left center; *4* right center; *5* center; *6* left center; *7* down right center; *8* down center; *9* down left center; *a* right first entrance; *b* left first entrance; *c* center entrance; *d* right center entrance; *e* left center entrance; *f,f,f,* right side entrances; *g,g,g,* left side entrances

[2]**stage** *vt* **1 :** to produce on the stage **2 :** to produce for public view ⟨~ a track meet⟩

stage·coach \-,kōch\ *n* **:** a horse-drawn passenger and mail coach running on a regular schedule between established stops

stage·craft \-,kraft\ *n* **:** the effective management of theatrical devices or techniques

stage direction *n* **:** a description or direction (as to describe a character or setting or to indicate a piece of stage business) written or printed in a play

stage director *n* **1 :** DIRECTOR c **2 :** STAGE MANAGER

stage fright *n* **:** nervousness felt at appearing before an audience

stage·hand \'stāj-,hand\ *n* **:** a stage worker who handles scenery, properties, or lights

stage–man·age \-,man-ij\ *vt* [back-formation fr. *stage manager*] **1 a :** to arrange or exhibit with an eye to effect **b :** to arrange or direct from behind the scenes **2 :** to act as stage manager for

stage manager *n* **:** one who supervises the physical aspects of a stage production, assists the director during rehearsals, and is in complete charge of the stage during a performance

stag·er \'stā-jər\ *n* **:** an experienced person **:** VETERAN ⟨old ~⟩

stage set *n* **:** an arrangement of scenery and properties for a particular scene in a play

stage·struck \'stāj-,strək\ *adj* **:** fascinated by the stage; *esp* **:** seized by a passionate desire to become an actor

stage whisper *n* **1 :** a loud whisper by an actor that is audible to the spectators but is supposed for dramatic effect not to be heard by one or more of the actors **2 :** an audible whisper

[1]**stag·ger** \'stag-ər\ *vb* **stag·ger·ing** \-(ə-)riŋ\ [alter. of earlier *stacker*, fr. ME *stakeren*, fr. ON *stakra*, freq. of *staka* to push; akin to OE *staca* stake] *vi* **1 a :** to reel from side to side **:** TOTTER **b :** to move on unsteadily **2 :** to rock violently **:** SHAKE ⟨the ship *~ed*⟩ **3 :** to waver in purpose or action **:** HESITATE **~** *vt* **1 :** to cause to doubt or hesitate **:** PERPLEX **2 :** to cause to reel or totter **3 :** to arrange in any of various zigzags, alternations, or overlappings of position or time ⟨~ work shifts⟩ ⟨~ teeth on a cutter⟩ **4 :** to adjust (as the wings of a biplane) so that the leading edge of one wing projects beyond the leading edge of another wing — **stag·ger·er** \-ər-ər\ *n*

[2]**stagger** *n* **1** *pl but sing or pl in constr* **:** an abnormal condition of domestic mammals and birds associated with damage to the central nervous system and marked by incoordination and a reeling unsteady gait **2 :** a reeling or unsteady gait or stance **3 :** the amount by which the leading edge of an upper wing of a biplane is advanced over that of a lower expressed as percentage of gap

[3]**stagger** *adj* **:** marked by an alternating or overlapping arrangement

stag·ger·bush \'stag-ər-,bu̇sh\ *n* **:** a shrubby heath (*Lyonia mariana*) of the eastern U.S. that is poisonous to livestock

stag·ger·ing *adj* **:** serving to stagger **:** ASTONISHING, OVERWHELMING — **stag·ger·ing·ly** \'stag-(ə-)riŋ-lē\ *adv*

stag·gery \'stag-(ə-)rē\ *adj* **:** UNSTEADY

stag·gy \'stag-ē\ *adj* **:** having the appearance of a mature male — used of a female or castrated male

stag·hound \'stag-,hau̇nd\ *n* **:** a hound formerly used in hunting the stag and other large animals; *specif* **:** a large heavy hound resembling the English foxhound

stag·i·ly \'stā-jə-lē\ *adv* **:** in a stagy manner **:** THEATRICALLY
stag·i·ness \-jē-nəs\ *n* **:** the quality or state of being stagy **:** THEATRICALITY
stag·ing \'stā-jiŋ\ *n* **1 :** SCAFFOLDING **2 a :** the business of running stagecoaches **b :** the act of journeying in stagecoaches **3 :** the putting of a play on the stage **4 :** the moving of troops or matériel forward in several stages or the assembling of troops or matériel in transit in a particular place
staging area *n* **:** an area in which troops are assembled and readied prior to a new operation or mission
Stag·i·rite \'staj-ə-,rīt\ *n* **:** a native or resident of Stagira ⟨Aristotle, known as the *Stagirite*⟩
stag·nan·cy \'stag-nən-sē\ *n* **:** the quality or state of being stagnant
stag·nant \-nənt\ *adj* **1 :** not flowing in a current or stream **:** MOTIONLESS; *also* **:** STALE **2 :** DULL, INACTIVE ⟨~ business⟩ — **stag·nant·ly** *adv*
stag·nate \'stag-,nāt\ *vi* [L *stagnatus*, pp. of *stagnare*, fr. *stagnum* body of standing water; akin to Gk *stazein* to drip] **:** to be or become stagnant — **stag·na·tion** \stag-'nā-shən\ *n*
stagy \'stā-jē\ *adj* **:** of or resembling the stage; *esp* **:** theatrical or artificial in manner
1**staid** \'stād\ *adj* [fr. pp. of 3*stay*] **1 :** SETTLED, FIXED **2 :** GRAVE, SEDATE **syn** see SERIOUS — **staid·ly** *adv* — **staid·ness** *n*
2**staid** *past of* STAY
1**stain** \'stān\ *vb* [ME *steynen*, partly fr. MF *desteindre* to discolor & partly of Scand origin; akin to ON *steina* to paint — more at DISTAIN] *vt* **1 :** DISCOLOR, SOIL **2 :** to suffuse with color **3 a :** to taint with guilt, vice, or corruption **b :** to bring reproach on **4 :** to color (as wood, glass, or cloth) by processes affecting chemically or otherwise the material itself ~ *vi* **:** to receive a stain — **stain·able** \'stā-nə-bəl\ *adj*
2**stain** *n* **1 a :** a soiled or discolored spot **b :** a natural spot of color contrasting with the ground **2 :** a taint of guilt **:** STIGMA **3 a :** a preparation (as of dye or pigment) used in staining; *esp* **:** one capable of penetrating the pores of wood **b :** a dye or mixture of dyes used in microscopy to make visible minute and transparent structures, to differentiate tissue elements, or to produce specific chemical reactions — **stain·less** \'stān-ləs\ *adj* — **stain·less·ly** *adv*
stained *adj* **1 :** discolored with stains ⟨a ~ and tattered jacket⟩ **2 :** colored with stain ⟨a bookcase ~ and waxed⟩
stained glass *n* **:** glass colored or stained for use in windows: **a :** glass colored throughout by metallic oxides fused into it **b :** white glass cased with colored glass **c :** white glass into whose surface the pigments have been burned
stain·er \'stā-nər\ *n* **:** one that stains: as **a :** a worker who applies a coloring or finishing stain to wood or leather **b :** a pigment used merely to give color to a paint as distinguished from the base **c :** an insect that stains the material on which it feeds
stainless steel *n* **:** a chromium alloy steel practically immune to rusting and ordinary corrosion
stair \'sta(ə)r, 'ste(ə)r\ *n* [ME *steir*, fr. OE *stǣger;* akin to OE & OHG *stīgan* to rise, Gk *steichein* to walk] **1 :** a series of steps or flights of steps for passing from one level to another — often used in pl. but sing. or pl. in constr. ⟨a narrow private ~*s* to connect the upper and lower rooms —Lewis Mumford⟩ **2 :** any one step of a stairway
stair·case \-,kās\ *n* **1 :** the structure containing a stairway **2 :** a flight of stairs with the supporting framework, casing, and balusters
stair·way \-,wā\ *n* **:** one or more flights of stairs usu. with landings to pass from one level to another
stair·well \-,wel\ *n* **:** a vertical shaft around which stairs are located
staithe \'stāth, 'stāth\ *n* [ME *stathe*, of Scand origin; akin to ON *stöth* staithe] *dial Eng* **:** a wharf for transshipment esp. of coal (as from railroad cars into ships)
1**stake** \'stāk\ *n* [ME, fr. OE *staca;* akin to MLG *stake* stake, L *tignum* beam] **1 :** a pointed piece of wood or other material driven or to be driven into the ground as a marker or support **2 a :** a post to which a person is bound for execution by burning **b :** execution by burning at a stake **3 a :** something that is staked for gain or loss **b :** the prize in a contest **c :** an interest or share in a commercial venture **4 :** a Mormon territorial jurisdiction comprising a group of wards **5 :** an upright stick at the side or end of a vehicle to retain the load **6 :** GRUBSTAKE — **at stake :** at issue **:** in jeopardy
2**stake** *vt* **1 :** to mark the limits of by stakes **2 :** to tether to a stake **3 :** BET, HAZARD **4 :** to fasten up or support (as plants) with stakes **5 :** to back financially **6 :** GRUBSTAKE
stake body *n* **:** an open motortruck body consisting of a platform with stakes inserted along the outside edges to retain a load
stake driver *n* **:** the common American bittern
stake·hold·er \-,hōl-dər\ *n* **:** a person entrusted with the stakes of two or more bettors
stake race *n* **:** a horse race in which the money stake or prize offered is the total contributed by the nominators
stake truck *n* **:** a truck having a stake body
Sta·kha·nov·ite \stə-'kän-ə-,vīt\ *n* [Alexei G. *Stakhanov* b1905 Russ miner] **:** a Soviet industrial worker awarded recognition and special privileges for output beyond production norms
sta·lac·tite \stə-'lak-,tīt\ *n* [NL *stalactites*, fr. Gk *stalaktos* dripping, fr. *stalassein* to let drip — more at STALE] **:** a deposit of calcium carbonate (as calcite) resembling an icicle hanging from the roof or sides of a cavern — **sta·lac·tit·ic** \,stal-,ak-'tit-ik, stə-,lak-\ *adj*
sta·lag \'stäl-,äg\ *n* [G, short for *stammlager* base camp, fr. *stamm* base + *lager* camp] **:** a German prison camp for noncommissioned officers or enlisted men
sta·lag·mite \stə-'lag-,mīt\ *n* [NL *stalagmites*, fr. Gk *stalagma* drop or *stalagmos* dripping; akin to Gk *stalassein* to let drip] **:** a deposit of calcium carbonate like an inverted stalactite formed on the floor of a cave by the drip of calcareous water — **sta·lag·mit·ic** \,stal-,ag-'mit-ik, stə-,lag-\ *adj*
1**stale** \'stā(ə)l\ *adj* [ME, aged (of ale); akin to MD *stel* stale] **1 :** tasteless or unpalatable from age **2 :** tedious from familiarity **3 :** impaired in legal force or effect by reason of laches or being allowed to rest without use, action, or demand ⟨a ~ affidavit⟩ ⟨a ~ debt⟩ **4 :** impaired in vigor or effectiveness — **stale·ly** \'stā(ə)l-lē\ *adv* — **stale·ness** *n*
2**stale** *vt* **1 :** to make stale **2** *archaic* **:** to make common **:** CHEAPEN ~ *vi* **:** to become stale
3**stale** *n* [ME; akin to MLG *stal* horse urine, Gk *stalassein* to let drip] **:** urine of a domestic animal (as a horse)
4**stale** *vi* **:** URINATE — used chiefly of camels and horses
1**stale·mate** \'stā(ə)l-,māt\ *n* [obs. E *stale* (stalemate) + E *mate*] **1 :** a drawing position in chess in which only the king can move and although not in check can move only into check **2 :** a drawn contest **:** DEADLOCK
2**stalemate** *vt* **:** to bring into a stalemate
Sta·lin·ism \'stäl-ə-,niz-əm, 'stal-\ *n* **:** the political, economic, and social principles and policies associated with Stalin; *esp* **:** the theory and practice of communism developed by Stalin from Marxism-Leninism and characterized esp. by rigid authoritarianism, widespread use of terror, and often by emphasis on Russian nationalism — **Sta·lin·ist** \-nəst\ *n or adj* — **Stalinize** *vt* — **Stalinoid** *n or adj*
1**stalk** \'stȯk\ *vb* [ME *stalken*, fr. OE *bestealcian;* akin to OE *stealc* lofty, *stelan* to steal — more at STEAL] *vi* **1** *obs* **:** to walk cautiously or furtively **:** STEAL **2 :** to pursue quarry or prey stealthily **3 :** to walk stiffly or haughtily ~ *vt* **1 :** to pursue by stalking **2 :** to go through (an area) in search of prey or quarry ⟨~ the woods for deer⟩ — **stalk·er** *n*
2**stalk** *n* **1 :** the act of stalking **2 :** a stalking gait
3**stalk** *n* [ME *stalke;* akin to OE *stealc* lofty] **1 a :** the main stem of an herbaceous plant often with its dependent parts **b :** a part of a plant (as a petiole, stipe, or peduncle) that supports another **2 :** a slender upright object or supporting or connecting part; *esp* **:** PEDUNCLE ⟨the ~ of a crinoid⟩ — **stalked** \'stȯkt\ *adj* — **stalk·less** \'stȯ-kləs\ *adj* — **stalky** \'stȯ-kē\ *adj*
stalk–eyed \'stȯ-'kīd\ *adj* **:** having the eyes raised on stalks — used chiefly of crustaceans
stalk·ing–horse \'stȯ-kiŋ-,hȯ(ə)rs\ *n* **1 :** a horse or a figure like a horse behind which a hunter stalks game **2 :** something used to mask a purpose **3 :** a candidate put forward to divide the opposition or to conceal someone's real candidacy
1**stall** \'stȯl\ *n* [ME, fr. OE *steall;* akin to OHG *stal* place, stall, L *locus* (OL *stlocus*) place, Gk *stellein* to set up, place, send] **1 a :** a compartment for a domestic animal in a stable or barn **b :** a space marked off for parking a motor vehicle **2 a :** a seat in the chancel of a church with back and sides wholly or partly enclosed **b :** a church pew **c** *Brit* **:** a front orchestra seat in a theater **3 :** a booth, stand, or counter at which articles are displayed for sale **4 :** a protective sheath for a finger or toe **:** COT **5 :** a small compartment ⟨a shower ~⟩
2**stall** *vt* **1 a :** to put into or keep in a stall **b** *archaic* **:** to fatten by stall-feeding **2** *obs* **:** to install in office **3 a :** to bring to a standstill **:** BLOCK; *esp* **:** MIRE **b :** to cause (an engine) to stop usu. inadvertently **c :** to cause (an airplane or airfoil) to go into a stall ~ *vi* **1 :** to come to a standstill (as from mired wheels or engine failure) **2 :** to experience a stall in flying
3**stall** *n* **:** the condition of an airfoil or airplane operating so that there is a flow breakdown and loss of lift with a tendency to drop
4**stall** *n* [alter. of *stale* (lure)] **:** a ruse to deceive or delay
5**stall** *vi* **:** to play for time **:** DELAY ~ *vt* **:** to hold off, divert, or delay by evasion or deception
stall–feed \-,fēd\ *vt* **:** to feed in a stall esp. so as to fatten ⟨~ an ox⟩
stal·lion \'stal-yən\ *n* [ME *stalion*, fr. MF *estalon*, of Gmc origin; akin to OHG *stal* stall] **:** a male horse not castrated; *also* **:** a male kept primarily as a stud
1**stal·wart** \'stȯl-wərt\ *adj* [ME, alter. of *stalworth*, fr. OE *stǣlwierthe* serviceable] **1 :** STOUT, STURDY **2 :** VALIANT, RESOLUTE **syn** see STRONG — **stal·wart·ly** *adv* — **stal·wart·ness** *n*
2**stalwart** *n* **1 :** a stalwart person **2 :** an unwavering partisan (as in politics)
stal·worth \'stȯl-wərth\ *archaic var of* STALWART
sta·men \'stā-mən\ *n, pl* **stamens** *also* **sta·mi·na** \'stā-mə-nə, 'stam-ə-\ [L, warp, thread; akin to Gk *stēmōn* thread, *histanai* to cause to stand — more at STAND] **:** a microsporophyll of a seed plant; *specif* **:** the organ of a flower that produces the male gamete, consists of an anther and a filament, and is morphologically a spore-bearing leaf
stamin- *or* **stamini-** *comb form* [L *stamin-*, *stamen*] **:** stamen ⟨*stamin*ody⟩ ⟨*stamini*ferous⟩
stam·i·na \'stam-ə-nə\ *n* [L, pl. of *stamen* warp, thread of life spun by the Fates] **:** STAYING POWER, ENDURANCE
stam·i·nal *adj* **1** \'stam-ən-ᵊl\ **:** of, relating to, or constituting stamina **2** \'stā-mən-ᵊl, 'stam-ən-\ **:** of, relating to, or consisting of a stamen
sta·mi·nate \'stā-mə-nət, 'stam-ə-, -,nāt\ *adj* **1 :** having or producing stamens **2** *of a diclinous flower* **:** having stamens but no pistils
sta·mi·no·di·um \,stā-mə-'nōd-ē-əm, ,stam-ə-\ *n, pl* **sta·mi·no·dia** \-ē-ə\ [NL, fr. *stamin-* + *-odium* thing resembling, fr. Gk *-ōdēs* like] **:** an abortive or sterile stamen
sta·mi·no·dy \'stā-mə-,nōd-ē, 'stam-ə-\ *n* [*stamin-* + Gk *-ōdēs* like] **:** the metamorphosis of other floral organs into stamens
stam·mel \'stam-əl\ *n* [prob. fr. *stamin*] **1** *obs* **:** a coarse woolen clothing fabric usu. dyed red and used sometimes for undershirts of penitents **2** *or* **stam·mel·col·or** \-,kəl-ər\ **:** the bright red color of stammel
1**stam·mer** \'stam-ər\ *vb* **stam·mer·ing** \-(ə-)riŋ\ [ME *stameren*, fr. OE *stamerian;* akin to OHG *stamalōn* to stammer, Lith *stumti* to push] *vi* **:** to make involuntary stops and repetitions in speaking **:** HALT — compare STUTTER ~ *vt* **:** to utter with involuntary stops or repetitions — **stam·mer·er** \-ər-ər\ *n*
syn STAMMER, STUTTER mean to speak stumblingly. STAMMER more often implies a temporary inhibition through fear, embarrassment, or shock; STUTTER suggests a habitual defect of speech organs or nerves but may imply a merely temporary effect of haste or excitement
2**stammer** *n* **:** an act or instance of stammering
1**stamp** \'stamp; *vt2a & vi2 are also* 'stämp *or* 'stȯmp\ *vb* [ME *stampen;* akin to OHG *stampfōn* to stamp, L *temnere* to despise, Gk *stembein* to shake up] *vt* **1 :** to pound or crush with a pestle or a heavy instrument **2 a** (1) **:** to strike or beat forcibly with the bottom of the foot (2) **:** to bring down (the foot) forcibly **b :** to extinguish or destroy by or as if by stamping with the foot **3 a :** IMPRESS, IMPRINT ⟨~ "paid" on the bill⟩ **b :** to attach a stamp to ⟨~ a letter⟩ **4 :** to cut out, bend, or form with a stamp or die

5 : CHARACTERIZE ~ *vi* **1** : POUND **2** : to strike or thrust the foot forcibly or noisily downward

[2]**stamp** *n* **1** : a device or instrument for stamping **2** : the impression or mark made by stamping or imprinting **3 a** : a distinctive character, indication, or mark **b** : a lasting imprint **4** : the act of stamping **5** : a stamped or printed paper affixed in evidence that a tax has been paid; *also* : POSTAGE STAMP

[1]**stam·pede** \stam-ˈpēd\ *n* [AmerSp *estampida*, fr. Sp, crash, fr. *estampar* to stamp, of Gmc origin; akin to OHG *stampfōn* to stamp] **1** : a wild headlong rush or flight of frightened animals **2** : a mass movement of people at a common impulse

[2]**stampede** *vt* **1** : to cause to run away in headlong panic **2** : to cause (a group of people) to act on mass impulse ~ *vi* **1** : to flee headlong in panic **2** : to act on mass impulse

stamp·er \ˈstam-pər, ˈstäm-, ˈstȯm-; *compare* [1]STAMP\ *n* : one that stamps: as **a** : a worker who performs an industrial stamping operation **b** : an implement for pounding or stamping **c** : any of various stamping machines

stamping ground \ˈstamp-, ˈstämp-, ˈstȯmp-\ *n* : a favorite or habitual resort

stamp mill \ˈstamp-\ *or* **stamping mill** \ˈstam-piŋ-\ *n* : a mill in which ore is crushed with stamps; *also* : a machine for stamping ore — called also *quartz battery*

stamp tax *n* : a tax collected by means of a stamp purchased and affixed (as to a deck of playing cards); *specif* : such a tax on a document (as a deed or promissory note) — called also *stamp duty*

stance \ˈstan(t)s\ *n* [MF *estance* position, posture, stay, fr. (assumed) VL *stantia*, fr. L *stant-*, *stans*, prp. of *stare* to stand] **1** *chiefly Scot* **a** : STATION **b** : SITE **2 a** : a mode of standing or being placed : POSTURE **b** : intellectual or emotional attitude **3 a** : the position of the feet of a golfer or batter preparatory to making a swing **b** : the position of both body and feet from which an athlete starts or operates

[1]**stanch** \ˈstȯnch, ˈstänch\ *vt* [ME *staunchen*, fr. MF *estancher*, fr. (assumed) VL *stanticare*, fr. L *stant-*, *stans*, prp.] **1** : to check or stop the flowing of; *also* : to stop the flow of blood from (a wound) **2** *archaic* : ALLAY, EXTINGUISH **3 a** : to stop or check in its course **b** : to make watertight — **stanch·er** *n*

[2]**stanch** *var of* STAUNCH

[1]**stan·chion** \ˈstan-chən, *2 is often* -chəl\ *n* [ME *stanchon*, fr. MF *estanchon*, fr. OF, aug. of *estance* stay, prop] **1** : an upright bar, post, or support **2** : a device that fits loosely around a cow's neck and limits forward and backward motion (as in a stall)

[2]**stanchion** *vt* **stan·chion·ing** \ˈstanch-(ə-)niŋ, -(ə-)liŋ\ **1 a** : to provide with stanchions **b** : to support or brace with or as if with a stanchion **2** : to secure (as a cow) by a stanchion

[1]**stand** \ˈstand\ *vb* **stood** \ˈstu̇d\ **stand·ing** [ME *standen*, fr. OE *standan*; akin to OHG *stantan*, *stān* to stand, L *stare*, Gk *histanai* to cause to stand, set, *histasthai* to stand, be standing] *vi* **1 a** : to support oneself on the feet in an erect position **b** : to be a (specified) height when fully erect **c** : to rise to an erect position **2 a** : to take up or maintain a specified position or posture ⟨~ aside⟩ **b** : to maintain one's position **3 a** : to be firm and steadfast in support or opposition **b** : to be in a particular state or situation ⟨~*s* accused⟩ **4** : to hold a course at sea **5** *obs* : HESITATE **6** : to have or maintain a relative position in or as if in a graded scale ⟨~*s* first in his class⟩ **7** *chiefly Brit* : to be a candidate : RUN **8 a** : to rest or remain upright on a base or lower end **b** : to occupy a place or location **9 a** : to remain stationary or inactive ⟨the car *stood* in the garage for a week⟩ ⟨rainwater ~*ing* in stagnant pools⟩ **b** : to gather slowly and remain ⟨tears ~*ing* in her eyes⟩ **10** : AGREE, ACCORD — used chiefly in the expression *it stands to reason* **11 a** : to exist in a definite written or printed form ⟨copy a passage exactly as it ~*s*⟩ **b** : to remain valid or efficacious ⟨the order given last week still ~*s*⟩ **12** *of a male animal* : to be available as a sire — used esp. of horses ~ *vt* **1 a** : to endure or undergo successfully **b** : TOLERATE, BEAR **2** : to remain firm in the face of **3** : to submit to ⟨~ trial⟩ **4 a** : to perform the duty of ⟨~ guard⟩ **b** : to participate in (a military formation) **5** : to pay for ⟨~ drinks⟩ **6** : to set upright **syn** see BEAR — **stand·er** *n* — **stand a chance** : to have a chance — **stand by** : to remain loyal or faithful to : DEFEND — **stand for 1** : to be a symbol for : REPRESENT **2** : to put up with : PERMIT — **stand on 1** : to depend upon **2** : to insist on — **stand one's ground** : to maintain one's position — **stand pat 1** : to play one's hand as dealt in draw poker without drawing **2** : to oppose or resist change

[2]**stand** *n* **1** : an act of stopping or staying in one place **2 a** : a halt for defense or resistance **b** : a defensive effort of some duration or degree of success ⟨goal-line ~⟩ **c** (1) : a stop made to give a performance (2) : a town where such a stop is made **3 a** : a place or post where one stands **b** : a position esp. with respect to an issue **4 a** : the place taken by a witness for testifying in court **b** : a section of the tiered seats for spectators of an outdoor sport or spectacle; *also* : the occupants of such seats — usu. used in pl. **c** : a raised platform serving as a point of vantage (as for a speaker) **5 a** : a small often open-air structure for a small retail business **b** : a site fit for business opportunity **6** : a place where a passenger vehicle stops or parks **7** : [1]HIVE 2 **8** : a frame on or in which something may be placed for support **9** : a group of plants growing in a continuous area **10** : a standing posture

[1]**stan·dard** \ˈstan-dərd\ *n* [ME, fr. MF *estandard* rallying point, standard, of Gmc origin; akin to OE *standan* to stand and to OE *ord* point — more at ODD] **1** : a conspicuous object (as a banner) formerly used at the top of a pole to mark a rallying point esp. in battle or to serve as an emblem **2 a** : a long narrow tapering flag that is personal to an individual or corporation and bears heraldic devices **b** : the personal flag of the head of a state or of a member of a royal family **c** : an organization flag carried by a mounted or motorized military unit **d** : BANNER **3** : something established by authority, custom, or general consent as a model or example : CRITERION **4** : something set up and established by authority as a rule for the measure of quantity, weight, extent, value, or quality **5 a** : the fineness and legally fixed weight of the metal used in coins **b** : the basis of value in a monetary system **6** : a structure built for or serving as a base or support **7** : a plant grown with an erect main stem so that it forms or resembles a tree; *also* : a fruit tree grafted on a stock that does not induce dwarfing **8 a** : the large upper posterior petal of some flowers **b** : one of the three inner usu. erect and incurved petals of an iris

syn STANDARD, CRITERION, GAUGE, YARDSTICK, TOUCHSTONE denote a means of determining what a thing should be. STANDARD applies to any definite rule, principle, or measure established by authority; CRITERION may apply to anything used as a test of quality whether formulated as a rule or principle or not; GAUGE applies to a means of testing a particular dimension (as thickness, depth, diameter) or figuratively a particular quality or aspect; YARDSTICK is an informal substitute for CRITERION that suggests quantity more often than quality; TOUCHSTONE suggests a simple test of the authenticity or value of something intangible

[2]**standard** *adj* **1 a** : constituting or conforming to a standard established by law or custom ⟨~ weight⟩ ⟨~ silver⟩ ⟨window of ~ width⟩ **b** : sound and usable but of inferior quality ⟨~ beef⟩ **2** : regularly and widely used **3** : having recognized and permanent value ⟨~ reference work⟩ **4** : substantially uniform and well-established by usage in the speech and writing of the educated and widely recognized as acceptable

stan·dard–bear·er \-ˌbar-ər, -ˌber-\ *n* **1** : one that bears a standard or banner **2** : the leader of an organization or movement

stan·dard·bred \-ˌbred\ *n* : any of an American breed of light trotting and pacing horses bred for speed and noted for endurance

standard candle *n* : CANDLE 3

standard deviation *n* : the square root of the arithmetic mean of the squares of the deviation from the arithmetic mean of a frequency distribution

Standard English *n* : the English that with respect to spelling, grammar, pronunciation, and vocabulary is substantially uniform though not devoid of regional differences, that is well established by usage in the formal and informal speech and writing of the educated, and that is widely recognized as acceptable wherever English is spoken and understood

standard error *n* : the standard deviation of a sample of a normal frequency distribution that equals the standard deviation of the distribution divided by the square root of the size of the sample

standard gauge *n* : a railroad gauge of 4 feet 8½ inches

stan·dard·iza·tion \ˌstan-dərd-ə-ˈzā-shən\ *n* : the act, process, or result of standardizing

stan·dard·ize \ˈstan-dər-ˌdīz\ *vt* **1** : to compare with a standard **2** : to bring into conformity with a standard

standard of living *or* **standard of life** : a minimum of necessities, comforts, or luxuries that is essential to maintaining a person or group in customary or proper status or circumstances

standard position *n* : the position of an angle with its vertex at the origin of a rectangular coordinate system and its initial side coinciding with the positive x-axis

standard time *n* : the time of a region or country that is established by law or general usage as civil time; *specif* : the mean solar time of a meridian that is a multiple of 15° arbitrarily applied to a local

STANDARD TIME IN 50 PLACES THROUGHOUT THE WORLD WHEN IT IS 12:00 NOON IN NEW YORK

CITY	TIME	CITY	TIME
[1]Amsterdam, Netherlands	6:00 P.M.	Montreal, Que.	12:00 NOON
Anchorage, Alaska	7:00 A.M.	[1]Moscow, U.S.S.R.	8:00 P.M.
Bangkok, Thailand	12:00 MIDNIGHT	Ottawa, Ont.	12:00 NOON
Berlin, Germany	6:00 P.M.	[1]Paris, France	6:00 P.M.
Bombay, India	10:30 P.M.	Peking, China	1:00 A.M. next day
[1]Brussels, Belgium	6:00 P.M.	Perth, Australia	1:00 A.M. next day
Buenos Aires, Argentina	1:00 P.M.	Rio de Janeiro, Brazil	2:00 P.M.
Calcutta, India	10:30 P.M.	Rome, Italy	6:00 P.M.
Cape Town, So. Africa	7:00 P.M.	Saint John's, Nfld.	1:30 P.M.
Chicago, Ill.	11:00 A.M.	Salt Lake City, Utah	10:00 A.M.
Delhi, India	10:30 P.M.	San Francisco, Calif.	9:00 A.M.
Denver, Colo.	10:00 A.M.	San Juan, Puerto Rico	1:00 P.M.
Djakarta, Indonesia	12:00 MIDNIGHT	Santiago, Chile	1:00 P.M.
Halifax, N.S.	1:00 P.M.	Shanghai, China	1:00 A.M. next day
Hong Kong	1:00 A.M. next day	Singapore	12:30 A.M. next day
Honolulu, Hawaii	7:00 A.M.	Stockholm, Sweden	6:00 P.M.
Istanbul, Turkey	7:00 P.M.	Sydney, Australia	3:00 A.M. next day
Juneau, Alaska	9:00 A.M.	Tehran, Iran	8:30 P.M.
Karachi, Pakistan	10:00 P.M.	Tokyo, Japan	2:00 A.M. next day
London, England	5:00 P.M.	Toronto, Ont.	12:00 NOON
Los Angeles, Calif.	9:00 A.M.	Vancouver, B.C.	9:00 A.M.
[1]Madrid, Spain	6:00 P.M.	[1]Vladivostok, U.S.S.R.	3:00 A.M. next day
Manila, Philippines	1:00 A.M. next day	Washington, D.C.	12:00 NOON
Mexico City, Mexico	11:00 A.M.	Wellington, New Zealand	5:00 A.M. next day
[1]Montevideo, Uruguay	2:00 P.M.	Winnipeg, Man.	11:00 A.M.

[1]Time in France, Spain, Netherlands, Belgium, Uruguay, and the U.S.S.R. is one hour in advance of the standard meridians.

area or to one of the 24 time zones and designated as a number of hours earlier or later than Greenwich time
stand·away \ˌstan-də-ˌwā\ *adj* : standing out from the body ⟨~ skirt⟩
stand by *vi* **1** : to be present; *also* : to remain apart or aloof **2** : to be or to get ready to act
stand·by \ˈstan(d)-ˌbī\ *n* **1 a** : one to be relied upon esp. in emergencies **b** : a favorite or reliable choice or resource **2** : one that is held in reserve ready for use : SUBSTITUTE
stand down *vi* : to leave the witness stand
stand·ee \stan-ˈdē\ *n* : one who occupies standing room
stand in *vi* : to act as a stand-in — **stand in with** : to be in a specially favored position with
stand–in \ˈstan-ˌdin\ *n* **1** : someone employed to stand in an actor's place until lights and camera are ready **2** : SUBSTITUTE
1**stand·ing** *adj* **1** : upright on the feet or base : ERECT **2 a** : not being used or operated **b** : not flowing : STAGNANT **3 a** : remaining at the same level, degree, or amount for an indeterminate period ⟨~ offer⟩ **b** : continuing in existence or use indefinitely ⟨~ problem⟩ **4** : established by law or custom **5** : not movable **6** : done from a standing position ⟨~ jump⟩
2**standing** *n* **1 a** : a place to stand in : LOCATION **b** : a position from which one may assert or enforce legal rights and duties **2 a** : length of service or experience esp. as determining rank, pay, or privilege **b** : position or condition in society or in a profession; *esp* : good reputation **c** : position relative to a standard of achievement or to achievements of competitors **3** : maintenance of position or condition : DURATION
standing army *n* : a permanent army of paid soldiers
standing committee *n* : a permanent committee esp. of a legislative body
standing order *n* : an instruction or prescribed procedure in force permanently or until specifically changed or canceled; *esp* : any of the rules for the guidance and government of parliamentary procedure which endure through successive sessions until vacated or repealed
standing room *n* : space for standing; *esp* : accommodation available for spectators or passengers after all seats are filled
standing wave *n* : a single-frequency mode of vibration of a body or physical system in which the amplitude varies from place to place, is constantly zero at fixed points, and has maxima at other points
stan·dish \ˈstan-dish\ *n* [origin unknown] : a stand for writing materials : INKSTAND
stand off *vi* **1** : to stay at a distance in social intercourse **2** : to sail away from the shore ~ *vt* **1** : to keep from advancing : REPEL **2** : to put off : STALL
1**stand·off** \ˈstan-ˌdȯf\ *adj* **1** : STANDOFFISH **2** : used for holding something at a distance from a surface ⟨~ insulator⟩
2**standoff** *n* **1** : the act of standing off **2 a** : a counterbalancing effect **b** : TIE, DRAW, DEADLOCK
stand·off·ish \stan-ˈdȯ-fish\ *adj* : lacking cordiality
stand oil *n* : a thickened drying oil; *esp* : linseed oil heated to about 600° F
stand out *vi* **1 a** : to appear as if in relief : PROJECT **b** : to be prominent or conspicuous **2** : to steer away from shore **3** : to be stubborn in resolution or resistance
stand·out \ˈstan-ˌdau̇t\ *n* : one that is prominent or conspicuous esp. because of excellence
stand·pat \ˈstan(d)-ˌpat\ *adj* [*stand pat*] : stubbornly conservative
stand·pat·ter \-ˌpat-ər, -ˈpat-\ *n* : one that resists or opposes change
stand·pipe \-ˌpīp\ *n* : a high vertical pipe or reservoir for water used to secure a uniform pressure
stand·point \-ˌpȯint\ *n* : a position from which objects or principles are viewed and according to which they are compared and judged
stand·still \-ˌstil\ *n* : a state characterized by absence of motion or of progress : STOP
stand up *vi* : to remain sound and intact ~ *vt* : to fail to keep an appointment with — **stand up for** : to defend against attack or criticism — **stand up to 1** : to meet fairly and fully **2** : to defend oneself against
stand–up \ˈstan-ˌdəp\ *adj* **1 a** : ERECT, UPRIGHT **b** *of a collar* : stiffened to stay upright without folding over **2** : performed in or requiring a standing position
stane \ˈstān\ *Scot var of* STONE
Stan·ford–Bi·net test \ˌstan-fərd-bi-ˈnā-\ *or* **Stanford revision** *n* [*Stanford* University, Calif.] : an intelligence test prepared at Stanford University as a revision of the Binet-Simon scale and commonly employed with children
1**stang** \ˈstaŋ\ *vt* [ME *stangen*, fr. ON *stanga* to prick; akin to ON *stinga* to sting] *chiefly Scot* : STING
2**stang** *n, chiefly Scot* : PANG
stan·hope \ˈstan-əp\ *n* [Fitzroy *Stanhope* †1864 Brit clergyman] : a gig, buggy, or light phaeton typically having a high seat and closed back
1**stank** *past of* STINK
2**stank** \ˈstaŋk\ *n* [ME, fr. OF *estanc*] **1** *dial Brit* **a** : POND, POOL **b** : a ditch containing water **2** *Brit* : a small dam : WEIR
stan·na·ry \ˈstan-ə-rē\ *n* [ML *stannaria* tin mine, fr. LL *stannum* tin] : one of the regions in England containing tinworks — usu. used in pl.
stan·nic \ˈstan-ik\ *adj* [prob. fr. F *stannique*, fr. LL *stannum* tin, fr. L, an alloy of silver and lead, prob. of Celt origin; akin to Corn *stēn* tin] : of, relating to, or containing tin esp. with a valence of four
stan·nite \ˈstan-ˌīt\ *n* [LL *stannum* tin] : a mineral Cu_2FeSnS consisting of a steel-gray or iron-black sulfide of copper, iron, and tin, of a metallic luster occurring in granular masses
stan·nous \ˈstan-əs\ *adj* [ISV, fr. LL *stannum*] : of, relating to, or containing tin esp. when bivalent
stan·za \ˈstan-zə\ *n* [It, stay, abode, room, stanza, fr. (assumed) VL *stantia* stay — more at STANCE] : a division of a poem consisting of a series of lines arranged together in a usu. recurring pattern of meter and rhyme : STROPHE — **stan·za·ic** \stan-ˈzā-ik\ *adj*
sta·pe·di·al \stā-ˈpēd-ē-əl, stə-\ *adj* : of, relating to, or located near the stapes
sta·pe·lia \stə-ˈpēl-yə\ *n* [NL, genus name, fr. J. B. van *Stapel* †1636 D botanist] : any of a genus (*Stapelia*) of African plants of the milkweed family with succulent leafless toothed stems like cactus joints and showy but putrid-smelling flowers
sta·pes \ˈstā-ˌpēz\ *n, pl* **stapes** *or* **sta·pe·des** \ˈstā-pə-ˌdēz\ [NL *staped-*, *stapes*, fr. ML, stirrup, alter. of LL *stapia*] : the innermost ossicle of the ear of mammals
staph \ˈstaf\ *n* : STAPHYLOCOCCUS
staph·y·lo·coc·cal \ˌstaf-ə-lō-ˈkäk-əl\ *adj* : of, relating to, or being a staphylococcus
staph·y·lo·coc·cic \-ˈkäk-(s)ik\ *adj* : caused by a staphylococcus
staph·y·lo·coc·cus \-ˈkäk-əs\ *n, pl* **staph·y·lo·coc·ci** \-ˈkäk-ˌ(s)ī, -(ˌ)(s)ē\ [NL, genus name, fr. Gk *staphylē* bunch of grapes + NL *-coccus*; akin to OE *stæf* staff] : any of various nonmotile gram-positive spherical bacteria (esp. genus *Staphylococcus*) that occur singly, in pairs or tetrads, or in irregular clusters and include parasites of skin and mucous membranes
1**sta·ple** \ˈstā-pəl\ *n* [ME *stapel* post, staple, fr. OE *stapol* post; akin to MD *stapel* step, heap, emporium, OE *steppan* to step] **1** : a U-shaped metal loop both ends of which are driven into a surface to hold the hook, hasp, or bolt of a lock, secure a rope, or fix a wire in place **2** : a small U-shaped wire both ends of which are driven through layers of thin and easily penetrable material (as paper) and usu. clinched to hold the layers together

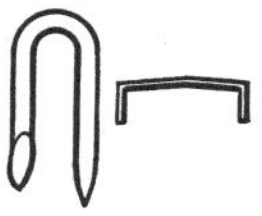

staples

2**staple** *vt* **sta·pling** \-p(ə-)liŋ\ : to provide with or secure by staples
3**staple** *n* [ME, fr. MD *stapel* emporium] **1** : a town used as a center for the sale or exportation of commodities in bulk **2** : a place of supply : SOURCE **3** : a chief commodity or production of a place **4 a** : a commodity for which the demand is constant **b** : something having widespread and constant use or appeal **c** : the sustaining or principal element : SUBSTANCE **5** : RAW MATERIAL **6 a** : textile fiber (as wool or rayon) of relatively short length that when spun and twisted forms a yarn rather than a filament **b** : the length of a piece of such textile fiber
4**staple** *adj* **1** : used, needed, or enjoyed constantly usu. by many individuals **2** : produced regularly or in large quantities **3** : PRINCIPAL, CHIEF ⟨~ crop⟩
1**sta·pler** \ˈstā-p(ə-)lər\ *n* : one that deals in staple goods or in staple fiber
2**stapler** *n* : one that inserts staples; *esp* : a small usu. hand-operated device for inserting the wire staples that bind papers together
1**star** \ˈstär\ *n* [ME *sterre*, fr. OE *steorra*; akin to OHG *sterno* star, L *stella*, Gk *astēr*, *astron*] **1 a** : any natural luminous body visible in the sky esp. at night **b** : a self-luminous gaseous celestial body of great mass whose shape is usu. spheroidal and whose size may be as small as the earth or larger than the earth's orbit **2 a** (1) : a planet or a configuration of the planets that is held in astrology to influence one's destiny or fortune — usu. used in pl. (2) : a waxing or waning fortune or fame **b** *obs* : DESTINY **3 a** : a conventional figure with five or more points that represents a star; *esp* : ASTERISK **b** : an often star-shaped ornament or medal worn as a badge of honor, authority, or rank or as the insignia of an order **4** : something resembling a star **5 a** : the principal member of a theatrical or operatic company who usu. plays the chief roles **b** : a highly publicized theatrical or motion-picture performer **c** : an outstandingly talented performer — **star·less** \-ləs\ *adj* — **star·like** \-ˌlīk\ *adj*
2**star** *vb* **starred**; **star·ring** *vt* **1** : to sprinkle or adorn with stars **2 a** : to mark with a star as being preeminent **b** : to mark with an asterisk **3** : to present in the role of a star ~ *vi* **1** : to play the most prominent or important role **2** : to perform outstandingly
3**star** *adj* **1** : of, relating to, or being a star **2** : being of outstanding excellence : PREEMINENT
star apple *n* : a tropical American tree (*Chrysophyllum cainito*) of the sapodilla family grown in warm regions for ornament or fruit; *also* : its apple-shaped edible fruit
1**star·board** \ˈstär-bərd\ *n* [ME *sterbord*, fr. OE *stēorbord*, fr. *stēor-* steering oar + *bord* ship's side — more at STEER, BOARD] : the right side of a ship or airplane looking forward — compare PORT
2**starboard** *vt* : to turn or put (a helm or rudder) to the right
3**starboard** *adj* : of, relating to, or situated to starboard
1**starch** \ˈstärch\ *vt* [ME *sterchen*, prob. fr. (assumed) OE *stercan* to stiffen; akin to OE *stearc* stiff — more at STARK] : to stiffen with or as if with starch
2**starch** *n* **1** : a white odorless tasteless granular or powdery complex carbohydrate $(C_6H_{10}O_5)_x$ that is the chief storage form of carbohydrate in plants, is an important foodstuff, and is used also in adhesives and sizes, in laundering, and in pharmacy and medicine **2** : a stiff formal manner : FORMALITY **3** : resolute vigor
star–cham·ber \ˈstär-ˈchām-bər\ *adj* [*Star Chamber*, a court existing in England from the 15th century until 1641] : characterized by secrecy and often irresponsibly arbitrary and oppressive
starch·i·ness \ˈstär-chē-nəs\ *n* : the quality or state of being starchy
starchy \ˈstär-chē\ *adj* **1** : containing, consisting of, or resembling starch **2** : consisting of or marked by formality or stiffness
star–crossed \ˈstär-ˌkrȯst\ *adj* : not favored by the stars : ILL-FATED
star·dom \ˈstärd-əm\ *n* **1** : the status or position of a star **2** : a body of stars
star·dust \ˈstär-ˌdəst\ *n* : a feeling or impression of romance, magic, or ethereality
1**stare** \ˈsta(ə)r, ˈste(ə)r\ *vb* [ME *staren*, fr. OE *starian*; akin to OHG *starēn* to stare, L *strenuus* strenuous, Gk *stereos* solid, Lith *starinti* to stiffen] *vi* **1** : to look fixedly often with wide-open eyes **2** : to show oneself conspicuously **3** *of hair* : to stand on end : BRISTLE; *also* : to appear rough and lusterless ~ *vt* **1** : to have an effect upon by staring **2** : to look at with a searching or earnest gaze **syn** see GAZE — **star·er** *n*
2**stare** *n* : the act or an instance of staring
sta·re de·ci·sis \ˌstar-ē-di-ˈsī-səs, ˌster-\ *n* [L, to stand by decided matters] : a doctrine or policy of following rules or principles laid down in previous judicial decisions unless they contravene the ordinary principles of justice
stare down *vt* : to cause to waver or submit by or as if by staring
sta·rets \ˈstär-(y)əts\ *n, pl* **star·tsy** \ˈstärt-sē\ [Russ, lit., old man, fr. *staryĭ* old — more at STOUR] : a spiritual director or re-

ligious teacher and counselor in the Eastern Orthodox Church **:** a spiritual advisor who is not necessarily a priest, who is recognized for his piety, and who is turned to by monks or members of the laity for spiritual guidance

star facet *n* **:** one of the eight small triangular facets which abut on the table in the bezel of a brilliant

star·fish \'stär-,fish\ *n* **:** any of a class (Asteroidea) of echinoderms having a body of usu. five radially disposed arms about a central disk and feeding largely on mollusks (as oysters)

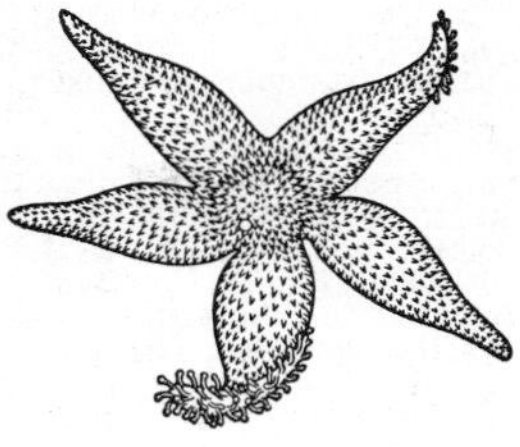
starfish

star·flow·er \-,flau̇(-ə)r\ *n* **:** any of several plants having star-shaped pentamerous flowers: as **a :** STAR-OF-BETHLEHEM **b :** any of a genus (*Trientalis*, esp. *T. americana*) of plants of the primrose family

star·gaze \-,gāz\ *vi* [back-formation fr. *stargazer*] **:** to gaze at or as if at stars

star·gaz·er \-,gā-zər\ *n* **1 :** one that gazes at the stars: as **a :** ASTROLOGER **b :** ASTRONOMER **2 :** any of several marine percoid fishes (family Uranoscopidae) with the eyes on top of the head

star·gaz·ing *n* **1 :** the act or practice of a stargazer **2 :** ABSENT-MINDEDNESS, DAYDREAMING

star grass *n* **:** any of various grassy plants with stellate flowers or arrangement of leaves; *esp* **:** any of a genus (*Hypoxis*) of herbs of the amaryllis family

1stark \'stärk\ *adj* [ME, stiff, strong, fr. OE *stearc;* akin to OHG *starc* strong, Lith *starinti* to stiffen — more at STARE] **1 :** STRONG, ROBUST **2 a :** rigid in or as if in death **b :** UNBENDING, STRICT **3 :** SHEER, UTTER **4 a :** BARREN, DESOLATE **b** (1) **:** having few or no ornaments **:** BARE (2) **:** HARSH **5 :** sharply delineated **syn** see STIFF — **stark·ly** *adv* — **stark·ness** *n*

2stark *adv* **1 :** STARKLY **2 :** WHOLLY, ABSOLUTELY

star·let \'stär-lət\ *n* **1 :** a little star **2 :** a young movie actress being coached and publicized for starring roles

star·light \-,līt\ *n* **:** the light given by the stars

1star·ling \'stär-liŋ\ *n* [ME, fr. OE *stærlinc*, fr. *stær* starling + *-ling*, *-linc* -ling; akin to OHG *stara* starling, L *sturnus*] **:** any of a family (Sturnidae, esp. genus *Sturnus*) of usu. dark gregarious passerine birds; *esp* **:** a dark brown or in summer glossy greenish black European bird (*S. vulgaris*) naturalized and often a pest in the U.S., Australia, and New Zealand

2starling *n* [prob. alter. of ME *stadeling*, fr. ME *stathel* foundation, support — more at STADDLE] **:** a protecting structure of piles driven close together around a pier of a bridge

star·lit \'stär-,lit\ *adj* **:** lighted by the stars

star of Beth·le·hem \-'beth-li-,hem, -lē-(h)əm\ **:** a star held to have guided the Magi to the infant Jesus in Bethlehem

star-of-Bethlehem *n* **:** any of a genus (*Ornithogalum*) of plants of the lily family; *esp* **:** one (*O. umbellatum*) with greenish flowers that is naturalized in the eastern U.S.

Star of Da·vid \-'dā-vəd\ **:** MAGEN DAVID

star route *n* [so called fr. the asterisk used to designate such routes in postal publications] **:** a mail-delivery route in a rural or thinly populated area served by a private carrier under contract who takes mail from one post office to another or from a railroad station to a post office and usu. also delivers mail to private mailboxes along the route

star·ry \'stär-ē\ *adj* **1 a :** adorned or studded with stars **b :** of, relating to, or consisting of the stars **:** STELLAR **c :** shining like stars **:** SPARKLING **d :** having parts arranged like the rays of a star **:** STELLATE **2 :** as high as or seemingly as high as the stars

star·ry-eyed \,stär-ē-'īd\ *adj* **:** regarding an object or a prospect in an overly favorable light; *specif* **:** VISIONARY

Stars and Bars *n pl but sing in constr* **:** the first flag of the Confederate States of America having three bars of red, white, and red respectively and a blue union with white stars in a circle representing the seceded states

Stars and Stripes *n pl but sing in constr* **:** the flag of the United States having 13 alternately red and white horizontal stripes and a blue union with white stars representing the states

star sapphire *n* **:** a sapphire that when cut with a convex surface and polished exhibits asterism

star shell *n* **1 :** a shell that on bursting releases a shower of brilliant stars and is used for signaling **2 :** a shell with an illuminating projectile

star-span·gled \'stär-,spaŋ-gəld\ *adj* **:** studded with stars

Star-Spangled Banner *n* **:** STARS AND STRIPES

1start \'stärt\ *vb* [ME *sterten;* akin to MHG *sterzen* to stand up stiffly, move quickly, Lith *starinti* to stiffen — more at STARE] *vi* **1 a :** to move suddenly and violently **:** JUMP **b :** to react with a sudden brief involuntary movement **2 a :** to issue with sudden force **b :** to come into being, activity, or operation **:** BEGIN **3 :** to protrude or seem to protrude **4 :** to become loosened or forced out of place **5 a :** to begin a course or journey **b :** to range from a specified initial point **6 :** to be a participant in a game or contest ~ *vt* **1 :** to cause to leave a place of concealment **:** FLUSH **2** *archaic* **:** STARTLE, ALARM **3 :** to bring up for consideration or discussion **4 :** to bring into being **5 :** to cause to become loosened or displaced **6 :** to begin the use or employment of **7 a :** to cause to move, act, or operate ⟨~ the motor⟩ **b :** to cause to enter a game or contest **c :** to care for during early stages **8 :** to perform the first stages or actions of **syn** see BEGIN

2start *n* **1 a :** a sudden involuntary bodily movement or reaction **b :** a brief and sudden action or movement **c :** a sudden capricious impulse or outburst **2 :** a beginning of movement, activity, or development **3 :** a lead or handicap at the beginning of a race or competition **4 :** a place of beginning **5 :** the act or an instance of being a competitor in a race or a member of a starting lineup in a game

start·er \'stärt-ər\ *n* **1 :** one who initiates or sets going: as **a :** an official who gives the signal to begin a race **b :** one who dispatches vehicles **2 a :** one that enters a competition **b :** one that begins to engage in an activity or process **3 :** one that causes something to begin operating: as **a :** SELF-STARTER **b :** material containing microorganisms used to induce a desired fermentation **4 :** something that is the beginning of a process, activity, or series

star thistle *n* **:** any of several knapweeds; *esp* **:** a widely naturalized spiny European weed (*Centaurea calcitrapa*) with purple flowers

1star·tle \'stärt-ᵊl\ *vb* **star·tling** \'stärt-liŋ, -ᵊl-iŋ\ [ME *stertlen*, freq. of *sterten* to start] *vi* **:** to move or jump suddenly (as in surprise or alarm) ~ *vt* **1 :** to frighten suddenly and usu. not seriously **2 :** to cause to start

2startle *n* **:** a sudden mild shock as of surprise or alarm **:** START

star·tling *adj* **:** causing a momentary fright, surprise, or astonishment — **star·tling·ly** \'stärt-liŋ-lē, -ᵊl-iŋ-\ *adv*

star turn *n, chiefly Brit* **:** the featured skit or number in a theatrical production; *broadly* **:** the most widely publicized person or item in a group

star·va·tion \stär-'vā-shən\ *n* **:** the act or an instance of starving **:** the state of being starved

starvation wages *n* **:** wages insufficient to provide the ordinary necessities of life

starve \'stärv\ *vb* [ME *sterven* to die, fr. OE *steorfan;* akin to OHG *sterban* to die, Lith *starinti* to stiffen — more at STARE] *vi* **1 a :** to perish from lack of food **b :** to suffer extreme hunger **2** *archaic* **a :** to die of cold **b :** to suffer greatly from cold **3 :** to suffer or perish from deprivation ~ *vt* **1 a :** to kill with hunger **b :** to deprive of nourishment **c :** to cause to capitulate by or as if by depriving of nourishment **2 :** to destroy by or cause to suffer from deprivation **3** *archaic* **:** to kill with cold

starve·ling \-liŋ\ *n* **:** one that is thin from or as if from lack of nutriment

1stash \'stash\ *vt* [origin unknown] **1** *chiefly Brit* **:** STOP, QUIT **2 :** to store in a usu. secret place for future use

2stash *n* **1 :** hiding place **:** CACHE **2 :** something stored or hidden away

sta·sis \'stā-səs, 'stas-əs\ *n, pl* **sta·ses** \'stā-,sēz, 'stas-,ēz\ [NL, fr. Gk, act or condition of standing, stopping, fr. *histasthai* to stand — more at STAND] **1 :** a slowing or stoppage of the normal flow of body fluids: as **a :** slowing of the current of circulating blood **b :** reduced motility of the intestines with retention of feces **2 :** a state of static balance or equilibrium among opposing tendencies or forces **:** STAGNATION

-sta·sis \'stā-səs, 'stas-əs, s-tə-səs\ *n comb form, pl* **-sta·ses** \'stā-,sēz, 'stas-,ēz, s-tə-,sēz\ [NL, fr. Gk *stasis* standing, stopping] **1 :** stoppage **:** slowing ⟨hemo*stasis*⟩ ⟨bacterio*stasis*⟩ **2 :** stable state ⟨homeo*stasis*⟩

-stat \,stat\ *n comb form* [NL *-stata*, fr. Gk *-statēs* one that stops or steadies, fr. *histanai* to cause to stand — more at STAND] **1 :** stabilizing agent or device ⟨gyro*stat*⟩ ⟨thermo*stat*⟩ **2 :** instrument for reflecting (something specified) constantly in one direction ⟨helio*stat*⟩ **3 :** agent causing inhibition of growth without destruction ⟨bacterio*stat*⟩

stat·able *or* **state·able** \'stāt-ə-bəl\ *adj* **:** capable of being stated

1state \'stāt\ *n, often attrib* [ME *stat*, fr. OF & L; OF *estat*, fr. L *status*, fr. *status*, pp. of *stare* to stand — more at STAND] **1 a :** mode or condition of being ⟨water in the gaseous ~⟩ ⟨~ of readiness⟩ **b** (1) **:** condition of mind or temperament ⟨in a highly nervous ~⟩ (2) **:** a condition of abnormal tension or excitement **2 a :** social position; *esp* **:** high rank **b** (1) **:** elaborate or luxurious style of living (2) **:** formal dignity **:** POMP — usu. used with *in* **3 a :** a body of persons constituting a special class in a society **:** ESTATE 3 **b** *pl* **:** the members or representatives of the governing classes assembled in a legislative body **c** *obs* **:** a person of high rank (as a noble) **4 a :** a politically organized body of people usu. occupying a definite territory; *esp* **:** one that is sovereign **b :** the political organization of such a body of people **5 :** the operations or concerns of the government of a country **6 :** one of the constituent units of a nation having a federal government ⟨the United *States* of America⟩ **7 :** the territory of a state

syn CONDITION, SITUATION, STATUS: STATE may imply a mode of existence but usu. implies the sum of the qualities involved in a thing's existence at a particular time and place; CONDITION more distinctly implies the influence of immediate or temporary circumstances; SITUATION applies to a juncture of circumstances in which a thing is placed rather than to its own state or character; STATUS implies one's state as determined for legal administration or social consideration

2state *vt* **1 :** to set by regulation or authority **2 :** to express the particulars of esp. in words **:** REPORT; *broadly* **:** to express in words

state aid *n* **:** public monies appropriated by a state government for the partial support or improvement of a public local institution (as a library, hospital, or educational institution)

State attorney *or* **State's attorney** *n* **:** a legal officer appointed to represent a state in the courts **:** PROSECUTING ATTORNEY

state bank *n* **:** a bank chartered by and operating under the laws of a state of the U.S.

state capitalism *n* **:** an economic system in which private capitalism is modified by a varying degree of government ownership and control

state church *n, often cap S&C* **:** ESTABLISHED CHURCH

state college *n* **:** a college that is financially supported by a state government, often specializes in a branch of technical or professional education, and often forms part of the state university

state·craft \'stāt-,kraft\ *n* **:** the art of conducting state affairs **:** STATESMANSHIP

stat·ed \'stāt-əd\ *adj* **1 :** ESTABLISHED, REGULAR **2 :** set down explicitly **:** DECLARED — **stat·ed·ly** *adv*

stated clerk *n* **:** an executive officer of a Presbyterian general assembly, synod, or presbytery ranking below the moderator

State flower *n* **:** a flowering plant selected as the floral emblem of a state of the U.S.

state guard *n* **:** a military force organized for use within a state in time of war or when the National Guard has been called into federal service

state·hood \'stāt-,hu̇d\ *n* **:** the condition of being a state; *esp* **:** the condition or status of one of the states of the U.S.

state·house \-,hau̇s\ *n* **:** the building in which a state legislature sits

state·less \'stāt-ləs\ *adj* **1 :** having no state **2 :** lacking the status of a national — **state·less·ness** *n*

state·li·ness \-lē-nəs\ *n* **:** the quality or state of being stately

state·ly \'stāt-lē\ *adj* **1 a :** HAUGHTY, UNAPPROACHABLE **b :** marked by lofty or imposing dignity **2 :** impressive in size or proportions **syn** see GRAND — **stately** *adv*

state medicine *n* **:** administration and control by the national government of medical and hospital services provided to the whole population and paid for out of funds raised by taxation

state·ment \'stāt-mənt\ *n* **1 :** the act or process of stating or presenting orally or on paper **2 :** something stated: as **a :** a report of facts or opinions **b :** a single declaration or remark **:** ASSERTION **3 :** PROPOSITION 2a **4 :** the enunciation of a theme in a musical composition **5 :** a summary of a financial account showing the balance due

state of war **1 a :** a state of actual armed hostilities regardless of a formal declaration of war **b :** a legal state created and ended by official declaration regardless of actual armed hostilities and usu. characterized by operation of the rules of war **2 :** the period of time during which a state of war is in effect

state prison *n* **:** a prison maintained by a state of the U.S. for the imprisonment of persons convicted of the more serious crimes

sta·ter \'stāt-ər, stä-'te(ə)r\ *n* [ME, fr. LL, fr. Gk *statēr*, lit., a unit of weight, fr. *histanai* to cause to stand, weigh — more at STAND] **:** an ancient gold or silver coin of the Greek city-states of any of numerous standards

state·room \'stāt-,rüm, -,ru̇m\ *n* **1 :** CABIN 1a **2 :** a private room on a railroad car with one or more berths and a toilet

state's evidence *n, often cap S* **1 :** one who gives evidence for the prosecution in U.S. state or federal criminal proceedings **2 :** evidence for the prosecution in a criminal proceeding

States General *n pl* **1 :** the assembly of the three orders of clergy, nobility, and third estate in France before the Revolution **2 :** the legislature of the Netherlands from the 15th century to 1796

[1]**state·side** \'stāt-,sīd\ *adj* [*(United) States* + *side*] **:** being in, going to, coming from, or characteristic of the 48 conterminous states of the U. S.

[2]**stateside** *adv* **:** in or to the continental U.S.

states·man \'stāt-smən\ *n* **1 :** one versed in the principles or art of government; *esp* **:** one actively engaged in conducting the business of a government or in shaping its policies **2 :** one who exercises political leadership wisely and without narrow partisanship in the general interest — **states·man·like** \-,līk\ *adj* — **states·man·ly** \-lē\ *adj* — **states·man·ship** \-,ship\ *n*

state socialism *n* **:** an economic system in which limited socialist objectives have been achieved by gradual political action

states' right·er \'stāts-'rīt-ər\ *n* **:** one who advocates strict interpretation of the U. S. constitutional guarantee of states' rights and is opposed to the exercise of federal authority in matters (as education or racial relations) that he regards as the exclusive concern of the several states

states' rights *n pl* **:** all rights not vested by the Constitution of the U.S. in the federal government nor forbidden by it to the separate states

state university *n* **:** a university maintained and administered by one of the states of the U.S. as part of the state public educational system

[1]**stat·ic** \'stat-ik\ *adj* [NL *staticus*, fr. Gk *statikos* causing to stand, skilled in weighing, fr. *histanai* to cause to stand, weigh — more at STAND] **1 :** exerting force by reason of weight alone without motion **2 :** of or relating to bodies at rest or forces in equilibrium **3 :** showing little change **4 a :** characterized by a lack of movement, animation, or progression **b :** producing an effect of repose or quiescence **5 a :** STATIONARY **b** *of water* **:** stored in a tank but not under pressure **6 :** of, relating to, or producing stationary charges of electricity **:** ELECTROSTATIC **7 :** of, relating to, or caused by radio static — **stat·i·cal** \-i-kəl\ *adj* — **stat·i·cal·ly** \-i-k(ə-)lē\ *adv*

[2]**static** *n* [*static electricity*] **:** disturbing effects produced in a radio or television receiver by atmospheric or various other electrical disturbances; *also* **:** the electrical disturbances producing these effects

stat·i·ce \'stat-ə-(,)sē\ *n* [NL, genus of herbs, fr. L, an astringent plant, fr. Gk *statikē*, fr. fem. of *statikos* causing to stand, astringent] **:** SEA LAVENDER, THRIFT

static line *n* **:** a cord attached to a parachute pack and to an airplane to open the parachute after a jumper clears the plane

stat·ics \'stat-iks\ *n pl but sing or pl in constr* **:** a branch of mechanics dealing with the relations of forces that produce equilibrium among material bodies

static tube *n* **:** a tube used for indicating static as distinct from impact pressure in a stream of fluid

[1]**sta·tion** \'stā-shən\ *n, often attrib* [ME *stacioun*, fr. MF *station*, fr. L *station-*, *statio*, fr. *status*, pp. of *stare* to stand — more at STAND] **1 :** the place or position in which something or someone stands or is assigned to stand or remain **2 :** the act or manner of standing **:** POSTURE **3 :** a stopping place: as **a** (1) **:** a regular stopping place in a transportation route (2) **:** the building connected with such a stopping place **:** DEPOT 3 **b :** one of the stations of the cross **4 :** a post or sphere of duty or occupation; *specif, Austral* **:** RANCH **5 :** STANDING, RANK ⟨a woman of high ~⟩ **6 :** a place for specialized observation and study of scientific phenomena **7 :** a place established to provide a public service: as **a :** FIRE STATION **b :** a branch post office **8 a :** a complete assemblage of radio or television equipment for transmitting or receiving **b :** the place in which such a station is located

[2]**station** *vt* **sta·tion·ing** \'stā-sh(ə-)niŋ\ **:** to assign to or set in a station or position **:** POST

sta·tion·al \'stā-shnəl, -shən-ᵊl\ *adj* **:** of or relating to an ecclesiastical station

sta·tion·ary \'stā-shə-,ner-ē\ *adj* **1 :** fixed in a station, course, or mode **:** IMMOBILE **2 :** unchanging in condition

stationary engine *n* **:** a steam engine permanently placed

stationary engineer *n* **:** one who operates stationary engines and related equipment

stationary front *n* **:** the boundary between two air masses neither of which is replacing the other

stationary wave *n* **:** STANDING WAVE — called also *stationary vibration*

station break *n* **:** a pause in a radio or television broadcast for announcement of the identity of the network or station; *also* **:** an announcement during this pause

sta·tio·ner \'stā-sh(ə-)nər\ *n* [ME *stacionner*, fr. ML *stationarius*, fr. *station-*, *statio* shop, fr. L, station] **1** *archaic* **a :** BOOKSELLER **b :** PUBLISHER **2 :** one that sells stationery

sta·tio·nery \'stā-shə-,ner-ē\ *n* [*stationer*] **1 :** materials (as paper, pens, and ink) for writing or typing **2 :** letter paper usu. accompanied with matching envelopes

station house *n* **:** a house at a post or station; *specif* **:** a police station

sta·tion·mas·ter \'stā-shən-,mas-tər\ *n* **:** an official in charge of the operation of a railroad station

stations of the cross *often cap S&C* **1 :** a series of usu. 14 images or pictures esp. in a church that represent the stages of Christ's passion **2 :** a devotion involving commemorative meditation before the stations of the cross

station wagon *n* **:** an automobile that has an interior longer than a sedan's, has one or more rear seats readily lifted out or folded to facilitate light trucking, has no separate luggage compartment, and often has a tailgate

stat·ism \'stāt-,iz-əm\ *n* **:** concentration of economic controls and planning in the hands of a highly centralized government

stat·ist \'stāt-əst\ *n* **:** an advocate of statism — **statist** *adj*

sta·tis·tic \stə-'tis-tik\ *n* [back-formation fr. *statistics*] **1 :** a single term or datum in a collection of statistics **2 :** ESTIMATE 3b

sta·tis·ti·cal \-ti-kəl\ *adj* **:** of, relating to, or dealing with statistics — **sta·tis·ti·cal·ly** \-k(ə-)lē\ *adv*

stat·is·ti·cian \,stat-ə-'stish-ən\ *n* **:** one versed in or engaged in compiling statistics

sta·tis·tics \stə-'tis-tiks\ *n pl but sing or pl in constr* [G *statistik* study of political facts and figures, fr. NL *statisticus* of politics, fr. L *status* state] **1 :** a branch of mathematics dealing with the collection, analysis, interpretation, and presentation of masses of numerical data **2 :** a collection of quantitative data

stato- *comb form* [ISV, fr. Gk *statos* stationary, fr. *histasthai* to stand — more at STAND] **1 :** resting ⟨*stato*blast⟩ **2 :** equilibrium ⟨*stato*cyst⟩

stato·blast \'stat-ə-,blast\ *n* [ISV] **1 :** a bud in a freshwater bryozoan that overwinters in a chitinous envelope and develops into a new individual in spring **2 :** GEMMULE

stato·cyst \-,sist\ *n* [ISV] **:** an organ of equilibrium occurring esp. among invertebrate animals and consisting usu. of a fluid-filled vesicle in which are suspended calcareous particles

stat·ol·a·try \stāt-'äl-ə-trē\ *n* **:** advocacy of a highly centralized and all-powerful national government

stato·lith \'stat-ᵊl-,ith\ *n* [ISV] **:** the calcareous body in a statocyst — **stato·lith·ic** \,stat-ᵊl-'ith-ik\ *adj*

sta·tor \'stāt-ər\ *n* [NL, fr. L, one that stands, fr. *status*, pp. of *stare* to stand — more at STAND] **:** a stationary part in a machine in or about which a rotor revolves

stato·scope \'stat-ə-,skōp\ *n* [ISV] **1 :** a sensitive aneroid barometer for recording small changes in atmospheric pressure **2 :** an instrument for indicating small changes in the altitude of an airplane

[1]**stat·u·ary** \'stach-ə-,wer-ē\ *n* **1 a :** a branch of sculpture treating of figures in the round **b :** a collection of statues **2 :** SCULPTOR

[2]**statuary** *adj* **:** of, relating to, or suitable for statues

stat·ue \'stach-(,)ü, 'stach-ə-w\ *n* [ME, fr. MF, fr. L *statua*, fr. *statuere* to set up — more at STATUTE] **:** a likeness (as of a person or animal) sculptured or modeled in a solid substance

Statue of Liberty : a large copper statue of a woman holding a torch aloft in her right hand located on Liberty Island in New York harbor

stat·u·esque \,stach-ə-'wesk\ *adj* **:** resembling a statue esp. in well-proportioned or massive dignity — **stat·u·esque·ly** *adv* — **stat·u·esque·ness** *n*

stat·u·ette \,stach-ə-'wet\ *n* **:** a small statue

stat·ure \'stach-ər\ *n* [ME, fr. OF, fr. L *statura*, fr. *status*, pp. of *stare* to stand — more at STAND] **1 :** natural height (as of a person) in an upright position **2 :** quality or status gained by growth, development, or achievement **syn** see HEIGHT

sta·tus \'stāt-əs, 'stat-\ *n, often attrib* [L — more at STATE] **1 :** the condition of a person or thing in the eyes of the law; *broadly* **:** CONDITION **2 a :** position or rank in relation to others ⟨the ~ of a father⟩ **b :** relative rank in a hierarchy of prestige; *esp* **:** high prestige **3 :** state of affairs **:** SITUATION **syn** see STATE

sta·tus quo \,stāt-ə-'skwō, ,stat-\ *n* [L, state in which] **:** the existing state of affairs

stat·ut·able \'stach-ət-ə-bəl\ *adj* **:** made, regulated, or imposed by or in conformity to statute **:** STATUTORY

stat·ute \'stach-(,)üt, -ət\ *n, often attrib* [ME, fr. OF *statut*, fr. LL *statutum* law, regulation, fr. L, neut. of *statutus*, pp. of *statuere* to set up, station, fr. *status* position, condition, state] **1 :** a law enacted by the legislative branch of a government **2 :** an act of a corporation or of its founder intended as a permanent rule **3 :** an international instrument setting up an agency and regulating its scope or authority

statute book *n* **:** the whole body of legislation of a given jurisdiction whether or not published as a whole — usu. used in pl.

statute mile *n* **:** MILE a

statute of limitations : a statute assigning a certain time after which rights cannot be enforced by legal action

stat·u·to·ry \'stach-ə-,tōr-ē, -,tȯr-\ *adj* **1 :** of or relating to statutes **2 :** enacted, created, or regulated by statute

statutory offense *n* **:** a crime created by statute; *esp* **:** STATUTORY RAPE

statutory rape *n* **:** sexual intercourse with a female below the statutory age of consent

[1]**staunch** *var of* STANCH

[2]**staunch** \'stȯnch, 'stänch\ *adj* [ME, fr. MF *estanche*, fem. of *estanc*, fr. OF, fr. *estancher* to stanch] **1 a :** WATERTIGHT, SOUND **b :** strongly built **:** SUBSTANTIAL **2 :** steadfast in loyalty or principle **syn** see FAITHFUL — **staunch·ly** *adv* — **staunch·ness** *n*

stau·ro·lite \'stȯr-ə-,līt\ *n* [F, fr. Gk *stauros* cross + F *-lite* — more at STEER] **:** a mineral $(Fe,Mg)_2Al_9Si_4O_{23}(OH)$ consisting of basic iron aluminum silicate in prismatic orthorhombic crystals often twinned so as to resemble a cross — **stau·ro·lit·ic** \,stȯr-ə-'lit-ik\ *adj*

[1]**stave** \'stāv\ *n* [back-formation fr. *staves*] **1 :** a wooden stick **:** [1]STAFF 1, 2 **2 :** any of the narrow strips of wood or narrow iron

plates placed edge to edge to form the sides, covering, or lining of a vessel (as a barrel) or structure **3 :** 2RUNG 3b **4 :** STANZA **5 :** 1STAFF 3

2stave *vb* **staved** *or* **stove** \ˈstōv\ **stav·ing** *vt* **1 :** to break in the staves of (a cask) **2 :** to smash a hole in ⟨~ in a boat⟩; *also* **:** to crush or break inward ⟨*staved* in several ribs⟩ **3 :** to drive or thrust away ~ *vi* **1 :** to become stove in — used of a boat or ship **2 :** to walk or move rapidly

stave off *vt* **:** to ward or fend off

staves *pl of* STAFF

staves·acre \ˈstāv-ˌzā-kər\ *n* [ME *staphisagre*, fr. ML *staphis agria*, fr. Gk, lit., wild raisin] **:** a Eurasian larkspur (*Delphinium staphisagria*); *also* **:** its violently emetic and cathartic seeds

1stay \ˈstā\ *n* [ME, fr. OE *stæg;* akin to ON *stag* stay, OE *stēle* steel] **1 :** a large strong rope usu. of wire used to support a mast **2 :** a guy rope — **in stays :** in process of going about from one tack to another

2stay *vt* **1 :** to fasten (as a smokestack) with or as if with stays **2 :** to incline (a mast) forward, aft, or to one side by the stays ~ *vi* **:** to go about **:** TACK

3stay *vb* **stayed** \ˈstād\ *or* **staid** \ˈstād\ **stay·ing** [ME *stayen*, fr. MF *ester* to stand, stay, fr. L *stare* — more at STAND] *vi* **1 :** to stop going forward **:** PAUSE **2 :** to stop doing something **:** CEASE **3 a :** to continue in a place or condition **:** REMAIN **b :** to have powers of endurance **4 :** to stand firm **5 :** to take up residence **:** LODGE **6 :** to keep even in a contest or rivalry ⟨~ with the leaders⟩ **7 :** to call a poker bet without raising **8** *obs* **:** to be in waiting or attendance ~ *vt* **1 :** to wait for **:** AWAIT **2 :** to last out (as a race) **3 :** to remain during ⟨~*ed* the whole time⟩ **4 :** to hold from proceeding **:** CHECK ⟨~ an execution⟩ **5 :** to check the course of (a disease or an evil influence) **:** HALT **6 a :** ALLAY, PACIFY **b :** to quiet the hunger of temporarily

syn STAY, REMAIN, WAIT, ABIDE, TARRY, LINGER mean to continue in a place. STAY often implies the status of a guest or visitor; REMAIN suggests a continuing after others have left or departed; WAIT implies a staying in expectation or readiness; ABIDE may apply either to continuing in a residence or waiting patiently for an outcome; TARRY suggests failing to proceed when it is time to do so; LINGER implies a tarrying because of disinclination to depart **syn** see in addition DEFER

4stay *n* **1 a :** the action of halting **:** the state of being stopped **b :** a stopping or suspension of procedure or execution by judicial or executive order **2** *obs* **:** MODERATION, SELF-CONTROL **3 :** a residence or sojourn in a place **4 :** capacity for endurance

5stay *n* [MF *estaie*, of Gmc origin; akin to OHG *stān* to stand — more at STAND] **1 :** something that serves as a prop **:** SUPPORT **2 :** a corset stiffened with bones — usu. used in pl.

6stay *vt* **1 :** to provide physical or moral support for **:** SUSTAIN **2 :** to fix on as a foundation

stay-at-home \ˌstā-ət-ˌhōm\ *adj* **:** remaining habitually in one's residence, locality, or country — **stay-at-home** \ˈstā-\ *n*

stay·er \ˈstā-ər\ *n* **:** one that stays; *esp* **:** one that upholds or supports

staying power *n* **:** capacity for endurance **:** STAMINA

stay-in strike \ˈstā-ˌin-\ *n* **:** a slowdown or stoppage of work intended to bring pressure on an employer and concerted by workers who remain in their work place — compare SIT-DOWN

stay·sail \ˈstā-ˌsāl, -səl\ *n* **:** a fore-and-aft sail hoisted on a stay

1stead \ˈsted\ *n* [ME *stede*, fr. OE; akin to OHG *stat* place, *stān* to stand] **1** *obs* **:** LOCALITY, PLACE **2 :** ADVANTAGE, SERVICE — used chiefly in the phrase *to stand one in good stead* **3 :** the office, place, or function ordinarily occupied or carried out by someone or something else

2stead *vt* **:** to be of avail to **:** HELP

stead·fast \ˈsted-ˌfast *also* -fəst\ *adj* **1 a :** firmly fixed in place **b :** not subject to change **2 :** firm in belief, determination, or adherence **:** LOYAL **syn** see FAITHFUL — **stead·fast·ly** *adv* — **stead·fast·ness** \-ˌfas(t)-nəs, -fəs(t)-\ *n*

stead·i·er \ˈsted-ē-ər\ *n* **:** one that steadies

stead·i·ly \ˈsted-ᵊl-ē\ *adv* **:** in a steady manner

stead·i·ness \ˈsted-ē-nəs\ *n* **:** the quality or state of being steady

stead·ing \ˈsted-ᵊn, ˈsted-, -iŋ\ *n* [ME *steding*, fr. *stede* place, farm] **1 :** a small farm **2** *chiefly Scot* **:** the service buildings or area of a farm

1steady \ˈsted-ē\ *adj* [1stead] **1 a :** firm in position **:** FIXED **b :** direct or sure in movement **:** UNFALTERING **c :** keeping nearly upright in a seaway ⟨~ ship⟩ **2 a (1) :** REGULAR, UNIFORM **(2) :** not changed, replaced, or interrupted **b :** not fluctuating or varying widely **3 a :** not easily moved or upset **:** RESOLUTE **b (1) :** constant in feeling, principle, purpose, or attachment **(2) :** consistent in behavior **:** DEPENDABLE **c :** not given to dissipation **:** SOBER

syn STEADY, EVEN, EQUABLE mean not varying throughout its course or extent. STEADY implies lack of fluctuation or interruption of movement; EVEN suggests a lack of variation in quality or character; EQUABLE implies lack of extremes or of sudden sharp changes

2steady *vt* **:** to make or keep steady ~ *vi* **:** to become steady

3steady *adv* **1 :** in a steady manner **:** STEADILY **2 :** on the course set — used as a direction to the helmsman of a ship

4steady *n* **:** one that is steady; *specif* **:** a boyfriend or girl friend with whom one goes steady

steak \ˈstāk\ *n* [ME *steke*, fr. ON *steik;* akin to ON *steikja* to roast on a stake, *stik* stick, stake — more at STICK] **1 a :** a slice of meat cut from a fleshy part of a beef carcass and usu. cooked or to be cooked by broiling **b :** a similar slice of a specified meat other than beef **c :** a cross-section slice of a large fish **2 :** ground beef prepared for cooking or for serving

steak knife *n* **:** a table knife having a steel blade often with a serrated edge

1steal \ˈstē(ə)l\ *vb* **stole** \ˈstōl\ **sto·len** \ˈstō-lən\ **steal·ing** [ME *stelen*, fr. OE *stelan;* akin to OHG *stelan* to steal] *vi* **1 :** to take the property of another **2 :** to come or go secretly, unobtrusively, gradually, or unexpectedly **3 :** to steal a base ~ *vt* **1 a :** to take or appropriate without right or leave and with intent to keep or make use of wrongfully **b :** to take away by force or unjust means **c :** to take secretly or without permission **d :** to appropriate entirely to oneself or beyond one's proper share ⟨~ the show⟩ **2 a :** to move, convey, or introduce secretly **:** SMUGGLE **b :** to accomplish in a concealed or unobserved manner **3 a :** to seize, gain, or win by trickery, skill, or daring ⟨a basketball player adept at ~*ing* the ball from his opponents⟩ **b** *of a base runner* **:** to gain (a base) by running without the aid of a hit or an error — **steal·er** *n*

syn STEAL, PILFER, FILCH, PURLOIN mean to take from another without right or without detection. STEAL may apply to any surreptitious taking of anything tangible or intangible; PILFER implies stealing repeatedly in small amounts; FILCH adds a suggestion of snatching quickly and surreptitiously; PURLOIN stresses removing or carrying off for one's own use or purposes

2steal *n* **1 :** the act or an instance of stealing **2 :** a fraudulent or questionable political deal **3 :** BARGAIN 2

1steal·ing *n* **:** the act of one who steals

2stealing *adj* **:** THIEVING

stealth \ˈstelth\ *n* [ME *stelthe;* akin to OE *stelan* to steal] **1 a** *archaic* **:** THEFT **b** *obs* **:** something stolen **2 :** the act or action of going or proceeding furtively, secretly, or imperceptibly **3 :** FURTIVENESS, SLYNESS

stealth·i·ly \ˈstel-thə-lē\ *adv* **:** in a stealthy manner

stealth·i·ness \-thē-nəs\ *n* **:** the quality or state of being stealthy

stealthy \ˈstel-thē\ *adj* **1 :** slow, deliberate, and secret in action or character **2 :** intended to escape observation **:** FURTIVE **syn** see SECRET

1steam \ˈstēm\ *n, often attrib* [ME *stem*, fr. OE *stēam;* akin to D *stoom* steam] **1 :** a vapor arising from some heated substance **2 a :** the invisible vapor into which water is converted when heated to the boiling point **b :** the mist formed by the condensation on cooling of water vapor **3 a :** water vapor kept under pressure so as to supply energy for heating, cooking, or mechanical work; *also* **:** the power so generated **b :** driving force **:** POWER **c :** emotional tension **4 a :** STEAMER 2a **b :** travel by or a trip in a steamer

2steam *vi* **1 :** to rise or pass off as vapor **2 :** to give off steam or vapor **3 :** to move or travel by or as if by the agency of steam **4 :** to be angry **:** BOIL ~ *vt* **1 :** to give out as fumes **:** EXHALE **2 :** to expose to the action of steam (as for softening or cooking)

steam·boat \-ˌbōt\ *n* **:** a boat propelled by steam power

steamboat Gothic *n* [fr. its use in homes of retired steamboat captains in imitation of the style of river steamboats] **:** an elaborately ornamental architectural style used in homes built in the middle 19th century in the Ohio and Mississippi river valleys

steam boiler *n* **:** a boiler for producing steam

steam chest *n* **:** the chamber from which steam is distributed to a cylinder of a steam engine

steam engine *n* **:** an engine driven or worked by steam; *specif* **:** a reciprocating engine having a piston driven in a closed cylinder by steam

steam·er \ˈstē-mər\ *n* **1 :** a vessel in which articles are subjected to steam **2 a :** a ship propelled by steam **b :** an engine, machine, or vehicle operated or propelled by steam **3 :** one that steams

steamer rug *n* **:** a warm covering for the lap and feet esp. of a person sitting on a ship's deck

steamer trunk *n* **:** a trunk suitable for use in a stateroom of a steamer; *esp* **:** a shallow trunk that may be stowed beneath a berth

steam fitter *n* **:** one that installs or repairs steam pipes or other equipment for heating, ventilating, or refrigerating systems — **steam fitting** *n*

steam heating *n* **:** a system of heating (as for a building) in which steam generated in a boiler is piped to radiators

steam·i·ly \ˈstē-mə-lē\ *adv* **:** in a steamy manner

steam·i·ness \-mē-nəs\ *n* **:** the quality or state of being steamy

steam iron *n* **:** a pressing iron with a compartment holding water that is converted to steam by the iron's heat and emitted through the soleplate onto the fabric being pressed

1steam·roll·er \ˈstēm-ˈrō-lər\ *n* **1 :** a steam-driven road roller **2 :** a crushing force esp. when ruthlessly applied to overcome opposition

2steamroller *also* **steam·roll** \-ˈrōl\ *vt* **1 :** to crush with a steamroller **2 a :** to overwhelm or coerce by greatly superior force **b :** to exert crushing force or pressure with respect to ~ *vi* **:** to move or proceed with irresistible force

steam·ship \ˈstēm-ˌship\ *n* **:** STEAMER 2a

steam shovel *n* **:** a power shovel operated by steam

steam table *n* **:** a table having openings to hold containers of cooked food over steam or hot water circulating beneath them

steam turbine *n* **:** a turbine that is driven by the pressure of steam discharged at high velocity against the turbine vanes

steam up *vt* **:** to make angry or excited **:** AROUSE

steamy \ˈstē-mē\ *adj* **:** consisting of, characterized by, or full of steam

ste·ap·sin \stē-ˈap-sən\ *n* [Gk *stear* fat + E *-psin* (as in *pepsin*)] **:** the lipase in pancreatic juice

stea·rate \ˈstē-ə-ˌrāt, ˈsti(-ə)r-ˌāt\ *n* **:** a salt or ester of stearic acid

ste·a·ric \stē-ˈar-ik, ˈsti(ə)r-ik\ *adj* [F *stéarique*, fr. Gk *stear*] **:** of, relating to, obtained from, or resembling stearin or tallow

stearic acid *n* **:** a white crystalline fatty acid $C_{18}H_{36}O_2$ obtained by saponifying tallow or other hard fats containing stearin; *also* **:** a commercial mixture of stearic and palmitic acids

stea·rin \ˈstē-ə-rən, ˈsti(-ə)r-ən\ *n* [F *stéarine*, fr. Gk *stear*] **1 :** an ester of glycerol and stearic acid **2** *also* **stea·rine** *same or* ˈstē-ə-ˌrēn, ˈsti(-ə)r-ˌēn\ **:** the solid portion of a fat **3** *usu* **stearine :** commercial stearic acid

steat- *or* **steato-** *comb form* [Gk, fr. *steat-*, *stear* — more at STONE] **:** fat ⟨*steato*lysis⟩

ste·atite \ˈstē-ə-ˌtīt\ *n* [L *steatitis*, a precious stone, fr. Gk, fr. *steat-*] **1 :** a massive talc having a grayish green or brown color **:** SOAPSTONE **2 :** an electrically insulating porcelain composed largely of steatite — **ste·atit·ic** \ˌstē-ə-ˈtit-ik\ *adj*

ste·atol·y·sis \ˌstē-ə-ˈtäl-ə-səs\ *n* [NL] **:** breakdown of neutral fats into glycerol and free fatty acids

ste·ato·py·gia \ˌstē-ət-ō-ˈpij-ē-ə, -ˈpī-jē-\ *n* [NL, fr. *steat-* + Gk *pygē* rump, buttocks; akin to Latvian *pauga* cushion, Gk *physan* to blow — more at FOG] **:** an excessive development of fat on the buttocks esp. of females that is common among the Hottentots and some Negro peoples — **ste·ato·pyg·ic** \-ˈpij-ik\ *or* **ste·ato·py·gous** \-ˈpī-gəs\ *adj*

ste·ator·rhea \ˌstē-ət-ə-'rē-ə\ *n* [NL] **:** an excess of fat in the stools
stedfast *var of* STEADFAST
steed \'stēd\ *n* [ME *stede*, fr. OE *stēda* stallion; akin to OE *stōd* stud — more at STUD] **:** HORSE; *esp* **:** a spirited horse for state or war
steek \'stēk\ *vb* [ME *steken* to pierce, fix, enclose; akin to OE *stician* to pierce — more at STICK] *chiefly Scot* **:** SHUT, CLOSE
1**steel** \'stē(ə)l\ *n* [ME *stele*, fr. OE *stȳle*, *stēle*; akin to OHG *stahal* steel, Skt *stakati* he resists] **1 :** commercial iron that contains carbon in any amount up to about 1.7 percent as an essential alloying constituent, is malleable when under suitable conditions, and is distinguished from cast iron by its malleability and lower carbon content **2 :** an instrument or implement of or characteristically of steel: as **a :** a thrusting or cutting weapon **b :** an instrument (as a fluted round rod with a handle) for sharpening knives **c :** a piece of steel for striking sparks from flint **d :** a strip of steel used for stiffening **3 :** a quality characteristic of steel **4 a :** the steel manufacturing industry **b** *pl* **:** shares of stock in steel companies
2**steel** *vt* **1 :** to overlay, point, or edge with steel **2 a :** to cause to resemble steel **b :** to fill with resolution or determination
3**steel** *adj* **1 :** made of steel **2 :** of or relating to the production of steel **3 :** resembling steel
steel band *n* **:** a band orig. developed in Trinidad and composed of tuned percussion instruments cut out of oil barrels
steel blue *n* **1 :** a variable color averaging a grayish blue **2 :** any of the blue colors assumed by steel at various temperatures in tempering
steel engraving *n* **1 :** the art or process of engraving on steel **2 :** an impression taken from an engraved steel plate
steel guitar *n* **:** HAWAIIAN GUITAR
steel·head \'stē(ə)l-ˌhed\ *n* **:** a large-sized western No. American silvery anadromous trout usu. held to be a race of the rainbow trout (*Salmo gairdneri*)
steel·i·ness \'stē-lē-nəs\ *n* **:** the quality or state of being steely
steel wool *n* **:** an abrasive material composed of long fine steel shavings and used esp. for scouring and burnishing
steel·work \'stē(ə)l-ˌwərk\ *n* **1 :** work in steel **2** *pl but sing or pl in constr* **:** an establishment where steel is made
steel·work·er \-ˌwər-kər\ *n* **:** one that works in steel and esp. in the manufacturing of it
steely \'stē-lē\ *adj* **1 :** made of steel **2 :** resembling steel
steel·yard \'stē(ə)l-ˌyärd, 'stil-yərd\ *n* [prob. fr. 3*steel* + *yard* (rod)] **:** a balance in which the object is suspended from the shorter arm of a lever and the weight of the object found by moving a counterpoise along the longer arm to produce equilibrium

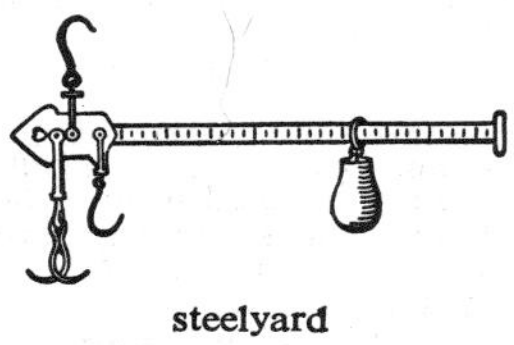
steelyard

steen·bok \'stēn-ˌbäk, 'stān-\ *or* **stein·bok** \'stīn-\ *n* [Afrik *steenbok*; akin to OE *stānbucca* ibex; both fr. a prehistoric WGmc compound whose elements are represented respectively by OE *stān* stone and OE *bucca* buck] **:** any of a genus (*Raphicerus*) of small plains antelopes of southern and eastern Africa
1**steep** \'stēp\ *adj* [ME *stepe*, fr. OE *stēap* high, steep, deep; akin to MHG *stief* steep, ON *staup* lump, knoll, cup] **1 :** LOFTY, HIGH — used chiefly of a sea **2 :** making a large angle with the plane of the horizon **:** PRECIPITOUS **3 a :** mounting or falling precipitously **b :** being or characterized by a very rapid decline or increase **4 :** difficult to accept, meet, or perform **:** EXCESSIVE — **steep·ly** *adv* — **steep·ness** *n*
syn ABRUPT, PRECIPITOUS, SHEER: STEEP implies such sharpness of pitch that ascent or descent is very difficult; ABRUPT implies a sharper pitch and a sudden break in the level; PRECIPITOUS applies to an incline approaching the vertical; SHEER suggests an unbroken perpendicular expanse
2**steep** *n* **:** a precipitous place
3**steep** *vb* [ME *stepen*; akin to Sw *stöpa* to steep, and prob. to ON *staup* cup] *vt* **1 :** to soak in a liquid at a temperature under the boiling point (as for softening, bleaching, or extracting a flavor) **2 :** BATHE, WET **3 :** to saturate with or subject thoroughly to (some strong or pervading influence) ~ *vi* **:** to undergo the process of soaking in a liquid **syn** see SOAK — **steep·er** *n*
4**steep** *n* **1 :** the state or process of being steeped **2 :** a bath or solution in which something is steeped **3 :** a tank in which a material is steeped
steep·en \'stē-pən, 'stēp-ᵊm\ *vb* **steep·en·ing** \'stēp-(ə-)niŋ\ *vt* **:** to make steeper ~ *vi* **:** to become steeper
stee·ple \'stē-pəl\ *n* [ME *stepel*, fr. OE *stēpel* tower; akin to OE *stēap* steep] **:** a tall structure usu. having a small spire at the top and surmounting a church tower; *broadly* **:** the whole of a church tower
stee·ple·bush \-ˌbu̇sh\ *n* **:** HARDHACK
stee·ple·chase \-ˌchās\ *n* [fr. the use of church steeples as landmarks to guide the riders] **:** a race across country by horsemen; *also* **:** a race over a course obstructed by obstacles (as hedges, walls, or hurdles) — **stee·ple·chas·er** \-ˌchā-sər\ *n*
stee·ple·jack \-ˌjak\ *n* **:** one whose work is building smokestacks, towers, or steeples or climbing up the outside of such structures to paint and make repairs
1**steer** \'sti(ə)r\ *n* [ME, fr. OE *stēor* young ox; akin to OHG *stior* young ox, Skt *sthavira*, *sthūra* stout, thick, broad] **1 :** a male bovine animal castrated before sexual maturity **2 :** a usu. young ox
2**steer** *vb* [ME *steren*, fr. OE *stīeran*; akin to OE *stēor-* steering oar, Gk *stauros* stake, cross, *stylos* pillar, Skt *sthavira*, *sthūra* stout, thick, L *stare* to stand — more at STAND] *vt* **1 :** to direct the course of; *specif* **:** to guide by mechanical means (as a rudder) **2 :** to set and hold to (a course) ~ *vi* **1 :** to direct the course (as of a ship or automobile) **2 :** to pursue a course of action **3 :** to be subject to guidance or direction ⟨an automobile that ~*s* well⟩ **syn** see GUIDE — **steer·able** \'stir-ə-bəl\ *adj* — **steer·er** *n* — **steer clear :** to keep entirely away — often used with *of*
3**steer** *n* **:** a hint as to procedure **:** TIP
4**steer** *dial Brit var of* STIR
steer·age \'sti(ə)r-ij\ *n* **1 :** the act or practice of steering; *broadly* **:** DIRECTION **2** [fr. its orig. being located near the rudder] **:** a section in a passenger ship for passengers paying the lowest fares and given inferior accommodations
steer·age·way \-ˌwā\ *n* **:** a rate of motion sufficient to make a ship or boat answer the helm
steering committee *n* **:** a managing or directing committee; *specif* **:** a committee that determines the order in which business will be taken up in a U.S. legislative body
steering gear *n* **:** a mechanism by which something is steered
steering wheel *n* **:** a handwheel by means of which one steers
steers·man \'sti(ə)rz-mən\ *n* **:** one who steers **:** HELMSMAN
1**steeve** \'stēv\ *vt* [ME *steven*, prob. fr. Sp *estibar* or Pg *estivar* to pack tightly, fr. L *stipare* to press together — more at STIFF] **:** to stow esp. in a ship's hold
2**steeve** *vb* [origin unknown] *vi, of a bowsprit* **:** to incline upward at an angle with the horizon or the line of the keel ~ *vt* **:** to set (a bowsprit) at an upward inclination
3**steeve** *n* **:** the angle that a bowsprit makes with the horizon or with the keel
stego·sau·rus \ˌsteg-ə-'sȯr-əs\ *n* [NL, genus name, fr. Gk *stegos* roof + *sauros* lizard — more at THATCH, SAURIA] **:** any of a genus (*Stegosaurus*) of large armored dinosaurs of the Upper Jurassic rocks of Colorado and Wyoming
stein \'stīn\ *n* [prob. fr. G *steingut* stoneware, fr. *stein* stone + *gut* goods] **:** an earthenware mug esp. for beer commonly holding about a pint; *also* **:** the quantity of beer that a stein holds
ste·la \'stē-lə\ *or* **ste·le** \'stē-lē\ *n, pl* **ste·lae** \-(ˌ)lē\ [L & Gk; L *stela*, fr. Gk *stēlē*; akin to Gk *stellein* to set up — more at STALL] **:** a usu. carved or inscribed stone slab or pillar used for commemorative purposes
ste·lar \'stē-lər\ *adj* **:** of, relating to, or constituting a stele
stele \'stē(ə)l, 'stē-lē\ *n* [NL, fr. Gk *stēlē* stela, pillar] **:** the usu. cylindrical central vascular portion of the axis of a vascular plant
stel·lar \'stel-ər\ *adj* [LL *stellaris*, fr. L *stella* star — more at STAR] **1 a :** of or relating to the stars **:** ASTRAL **b :** composed of stars **2 :** of or relating to a theatrical or film star **3 a :** LEADING, PRINCIPAL **b :** OUTSTANDING
stel·late \'stel-ˌāt\ *adj* **:** resembling a star (as in shape) **:** RADIATED ⟨a ~ leaf⟩ — **stel·late·ly** *adv*
stel·li·form \'stel-ə-ˌfȯrm\ *adj* [NL *stelliformis*, fr. L *stella* + *-iformis* -iform] **:** shaped like a star
stel·li·fy \-ˌfī\ *vt* [ME *stellifien*, fr. MF *stellifier*, fr. ML *stellificare*, fr. L *stella* star] **:** to turn into a star **:** place among the stars
stel·lu·lar \'stel-yə-lər\ *adj* [LL *stellula*, dim. of L *stella*] **1 :** having the shape of a small star **2 :** radiating like a star
1**stem** \'stem\ *n* [ME, fr. OE *stefn*, *stemn* stem of a plant or ship; OE *stefn* akin to OE *stæf* staff; OE *stemn* akin to OE *standan* to stand] **1 a :** the main trunk of a tree or other plant; *specif* **:** a primary plant axis that develops buds and shoots instead of roots **b :** a plant part (as a branch, petiole, or stipe) that supports another (as a leaf or fruit) **c :** a bunch of bananas **d :** the bow or prow of a ship **2 :** a line of ancestry **:** STOCK; *esp* **:** a fundamental line from which others have arisen **3 :** the part of an inflected word that remains unchanged except by phonetic changes or variations throughout an inflection **4 :** something felt to resemble a plant stem: as **a :** a main or heavy stroke of a letter; *also* **:** BODY 7 **b :** the short perpendicular line extending from the head of a musical note **c :** the part of a tobacco pipe from the bowl outward **d :** the cylindrical support of a piece of stemware (as a goblet) **e :** a shaft of a watch — **from stem to stern :** THROUGHOUT, THOROUGHLY
2**stem** *vt* **stemmed; stem·ming 1 :** to make headway against (as an adverse tide, current, or wind) **2 :** to check or progress against (something adverse) ⟨*stemming* the angry crowd⟩ — **stem·mer** *n*
3**stem** *vb* **stemmed; stem·ming** *vi* **:** to have or trace an origin or development **:** DERIVE ~ *vt* **1 :** to remove the stem from **2 :** to make stems for **syn** see SPRING — **stem·mer** *n*
4**stem** *vb* **stemmed; stem·ming** [ME *stemmen* to dam up, fr. ON *stemma*; akin to OE *stamerian* to stammer] *vt* **1 :** to stop, check, or restrain by or as if by damming **2 :** to turn (skis) in stemming ~ *vi* **1 :** to restrain or check oneself; *also* **:** to become checked or stanched **2 :** to retard oneself by forcing the heel of one ski or of both skis outward from the line of progress
5**stem** *n* **1 :** CHECK, DAM **2 :** an act or instance of stemming on skis
stem·less \-ləs\ *adj* **:** having no stem **:** ACAULESCENT
stem·ma \'stem-ə\ *n, pl* **stem·ma·ta** \-ət-ə\ [L, wreath, pedigree (fr. the wreaths placed on ancestral images), fr. Gk, wreath, fr. *stephein* to crown, enwreath] **1 :** a scroll (as among the ancient Romans) containing a list of family names with indication of genealogical relations **2 :** a tree showing the relationships of the manuscripts of a literary work
1**stemmed** \'stemd\ *adj* **:** having a stem
2**stemmed** *adj* **:** having the stem removed ⟨~ berries⟩
stem·my \'stem-ē\ *adj* **:** abounding in stems ⟨~ hay⟩
stem·son \'stem(p)-sən\ *n* [*stem* + *-son* (as in *keelson*)] **:** a piece of curved timber bolted to the stem, keelson, and apron in a ship's frame near the bow
stem turn *n* **:** a skiing turn executed by stemming an outside ski
stem·ware \'stem-ˌwa(ə)r, -ˌwe(ə)r\ *n* **:** glass hollow ware mounted on a stem
stem–wind·er \-'wīn-dər\ *n* **1 :** a stem-winding watch **2 :** one that is first-rate of its kind
stem–wind·ing \-diŋ\ *adj* **:** wound by an inside mechanism turned by the knurled knob at the outside end of the stem
Sten \'sten\ *n* [Major *S*heppard, 20th cent. E army officer + Mr. *T*urpin, 20th cent. E civil servant + *En*gland] **:** a light simple 9-millimeter British submachine carbine
sten- *or* **steno-** *comb form* [Gk, fr. *stenos*] **:** close **:** narrow **:** little ⟨*steno*bathic⟩
stench \'stench\ *n* [ME, fr. OE *stenc*; akin to OE *stincan* to emit a smell — more at STINK] **:** STINK
stench·ful \-fəl\ *adj* **:** full of disagreeable smells
stenchy \'sten-chē\ *adj* **:** having a stench
1**sten·cil** \'sten(t)-səl\ *n* [ME *stanselen* to ornament with sparkling colors, fr. MF *estanceler*, fr. *estancele* spark, fr. (assumed) VL *stincilla*, fr. L *scintilla*] **1 :** an impervious material (as a sheet of paper, thin wax, or woven fabric) perforated with lettering or a design through which a substance (as ink, paint, or metallic powder) is forced onto a surface to be printed **2 :** a pattern,

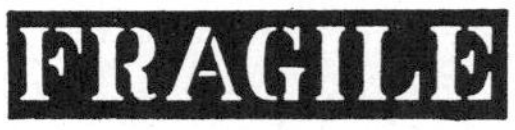

stencil 1

design, or print produced by means of a stencil **3** : a printing process that uses a stencil

2**stencil** *vt* **sten·ciled** *or* **sten·cilled; sten·cil·ing** *or* **sten·cil·ling** \-s(ə-)liŋ\ **1** : to produce by stencil **2** : to mark or paint with a stencil — **sten·cil·er** *or* **sten·cil·ler** \-s(ə-)lər\ *n*

sten·cil·ize \-sə-ˌlīz\ *vt* **1** : STENCIL 2 **2** : to cut into a stencil

stencil paper *n* : strong tissue paper impregnated or coated (as with paraffin) for stencils

steno \ˈsten-(ˌ)ō\ *n* : STENOGRAPHER

steno·bath·ic \ˌsten-ə-ˈbath-ik\ *adj* [*sten-* + Gk *bathos* depth — more at BATH-] *of a pelagic organism* : living within narrow limits of depth

steno·graph \ˈsten-ə-ˌgraf\ *vt* [back-formation fr. *stenographer*] : to write or report in stenographic characters

ste·nog·ra·pher \stə-ˈnäg-rə-fər\ *n* **1** : a writer of shorthand **2** : one employed chiefly to take and transcribe dictation

steno·graph·ic \ˌsten-ə-ˈgraf-ik\ *adj* : of, relating to, or using stenography — **steno·graph·i·cal·ly** \-i-k(ə-)lē\ *adv*

ste·nog·ra·phy \stə-ˈnäg-rə-fē\ *n* **1** : the art or process of writing in shorthand **2** : shorthand esp. written from dictation or oral discourse **3** : the making of shorthand notes and subsequent transcription of them

steno·ha·line \ˌsten-ō-ˈhā-ˌlīn, -ˈhal-ˌīn\ *adj* [ISV *sten-* + Gk *halinos* of salt, fr. *hals* salt — more at SALT] *of an aquatic organism* : unable to withstand wide variation in salinity of the surrounding water

ste·noph·a·gous \ste-ˈnäf-ə-gəs\ *adj* [ISV] : eating few kinds of foods ⟨~ insects⟩

ste·nosed \stə-ˈnōst, -ˈnōzd\ *adj* [fr. pp. of *stenose* (to affect with stenosis)] : affected with stenosis

ste·no·sis \stə-ˈnō-səs\ *n* [NL, fr. Gk *stenōsis* act of narrowing, fr. *stenoun* to narrow, fr. *stenos* narrow] : a narrowing or constriction of the diameter of bodily passage or orifice — **ste·not·ic** \-ˈnät-ik\ *adj*

steno·therm \ˈsten-ə-ˌthərm\ *n* [back-formation fr. *stenothermal*] : an organism only slightly resistant to change in temperature — **steno·ther·mal** \ˌsten-ə-ˈthər-məl\ *adj* — **steno·ther·my** \ˈsten-ə-ˌthər-mē\ *n*

steno·top·ic \ˌsten-ə-ˈtäp-ik\ *adj* [prob. fr. G *stenotop* stenotopic, fr. *sten-* + Gk *topos* place — more at TOPIC] : having a narrow range of adaptability to changes in environmental conditions

steno·type \ˈsten-ə-ˌtīp\ *n* [*steno-* (as in *stenography*) + *type*] : a small machine somewhat like a typewriter used to record speech by means of phonograms — **stenotype** *vt* — **steno·typ·ist** \-ˌtī-pəst\ *n*

sten·tor \ˈsten-ˌtȯ(ə)r, ˈstent-ər\ *n* [L, fr. Gk *Stentōr*] **1** *cap* : a Greek herald in the Trojan War noted for his loud voice **2** : a person having a loud voice

sten·to·ri·an \sten-ˈtōr-ē-ən, -ˈtȯr-\ *adj* : extremely loud

sten·to·ro·phon·ic \ˌstent-ə-rə-ˈfän-ik\ *adj* [NL *stentorophonicus*, fr. Gk *Stentōr* Stentor + *-o-* + *phōnē* voice — more at BAN] : speaking or sounding very loud : STENTORIAN

1**step** \ˈstep\ *n* [ME, fr. OE *stæpe*; akin to OHG *stapfo* step, *stampfōn* to stamp] **1** : a rest for the foot in ascending or descending: as **a** : STAIR **b** : a ladder rung **2 a** (1) : an advance or movement made by raising the foot and bringing it down elsewhere (2) : a combination of foot or foot and body movements constituting a unit or a repeated pattern (3) : manner of walking : STRIDE **b** : FOOTPRINT **c** : the sound of a footstep **3 a** : the space passed over in one step **b** : a short distance **c** : the height of one stair **4** *pl* : COURSE, WAY **5 a** : a degree, grade, or rank in a scale **b** : a stage in a process **6** : a frame on a ship designed to receive an upright shaft; *esp* : a block supporting the heel of a mast **7** : an action, proceeding, or measure often occurring as one in a series **8** : pace with another **9** : a steplike offset or part usu. occurring in a series **10** : a musical scale degree — **step·like** \-ˌlīk\ *adj* — **stepped** \ˈstept\ *adj*

2**step** *vb* **stepped; step·ping** *vi* **1 a** : to move by raising the foot and bringing it down elsewhere or by moving each foot in succession **b** : DANCE **2 a** : to go on foot : WALK **b** *obs* : ADVANCE, PROCEED **c** : DEPART **d** : to move briskly **3** : to press down with the foot **4** : to come as if at a single step ~ *vt* **1** : to take by moving the feet in succession ⟨~ three paces⟩ **2 a** : to move (the foot) in any direction : SET **b** : to traverse on foot **3** : to go through the steps of : PERFORM **4** : to erect by fixing the lower end in a step **5** : to measure by steps ⟨~ off 50 yards⟩ **6 a** : to provide with steps **b** : to make steps in ⟨~ a key⟩ **7** : to construct or arrange in or as if in steps

step- *comb form* [ME, fr. OE *stēop-*; akin to OHG *stiof-* step-] : related by virtue of a remarriage (as of a parent) and not by blood ⟨*step*parent⟩ ⟨*step*sister⟩

step·broth·er \ˈstep-ˌbrəth-ər\ *n* : a son of one's stepparent by a former marriage

step-by-step \ˌstep-bə-ˈstep\ *adj* : marked by successive degrees usu. of limited extent : GRADUAL

step·child \ˈstep-ˌchīld\ *n* : a child of one's wife or husband by a former marriage

step-cline \ˈstep-ˌklīn\ *n* : an irregular or interrupted cline

step·daugh·ter \ˈstep-ˌdȯt-ər\ *n* : a daughter of one's wife or husband by a former marriage

step down *vt* : to lower the voltage of (a current) by means of a transformer

step-down \ˈstep-ˌdau̇n\ *n* : a decrease or reduction in size or amount ⟨a ~ in dosage⟩

step·fa·ther \ˈstep-ˌfäth-ər\ *n* : the husband of one's mother by a subsequent marriage

step in *vi* **1** : to make a brief informal visit **2** : to enter into an affair or dispute often without invitation, permission, or welcome

1**step-in** \ˈstep-ˌin\ *adj* : put on by being stepped into ⟨~ clothing⟩

2**step-in** *n* : an article of step-in clothing; *esp, pl* : a woman's brief panties

step·lad·der \ˈstep-ˌlad-ər\ *n* : a portable set of steps with a hinged frame for steadying

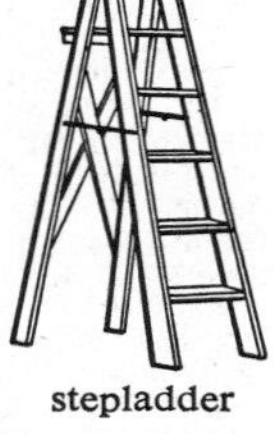

stepladder

step·moth·er \-ˌməth-ər\ *n* : the wife of one's father by a subsequent marriage

step out *vi* **1** : to go away from a place usu. for a short distance and for a short time **2** : to go or march at a vigorous or increased pace **3** : DIE **4** : to lead an active social life **5** : to be unfaithful — usu. used with *on*

step·par·ent \ˈstep-ˌpar-ənt, -ˌper-\ *n* : the husband or wife of one's mother or father by a subsequent marriage

steppe \ˈstep\ *n* [Russ *step'*] **1** : one of the vast usu. level and treeless tracts in southeastern Europe or Asia **2** : arid land with xerophilous vegetation found usu. in regions of extreme temperature range and loess soil

stepped-up \ˈstep-ˈtəp\ *adj* : ACCELERATED, INTENSIFIED

step·per \ˈstep-ər\ *n* : one that steps (as a fast horse or a dancer)

step·ping-off place \ˌstep-iŋ-ˈȯf-\ *n* **1** : the outbound end of a transportation line **2** : a place from which one departs for unknown territory

step·ping-stone \ˈstep-iŋ-ˌstōn\ *n* **1** : a stone on which to step (as in crossing a stream) **2** : a means of progress or advancement

step rocket *n* : a multistage rocket whose sections are fired successively

step·sis·ter \ˈstep-ˌsis-tər\ *n* : a daughter of one's stepparent by a former marriage

step·son \-ˌsən\ *n* : a son of one's husband or wife by a former marriage

step stool *n* : a stool with one or two steps that often fold away beneath the seat

step turn *n* : a skiing turn executed in a downhill traverse by lifting the upper ski from the ground, placing it in the desired direction, weighting it, and bringing the other ski parallel

step up *vt* **1** : to increase the voltage of (a current) by means of a transformer **2** : to increase, augment, or advance by one or more steps ~ *vi* **1** : to come forward **2** : to undergo an increase **3** : to receive a promotion — **step-up** \ˈstep-ˌəp\ *adj*

step-up \ˈstep-ˌəp\ *n* : an increase or advance in size or amount

step·wise \-ˌwīz\ *adj* **1** : marked by steps : GRADUAL **2** : moving by step to adjacent musical tones

-ster \stər\ *n comb form* [ME, fr. OE *-estre* female agent; akin to MD *-ster*] **1** : one that does or handles or operates ⟨spin*ster*⟩ ⟨tap*ster*⟩ ⟨team*ster*⟩ **2** : one that makes or uses ⟨song*ster*⟩ ⟨pun*ster*⟩ **3** : one that is associated with or participates in ⟨game*ster*⟩ ⟨gang*ster*⟩ **4** : one that is ⟨young*ster*⟩

ster·co·ra·ceous \ˌstər-kə-ˈrā-shəs\ *adj* [L *stercor-*, *stercus* excrement; akin to MHG *drec* filth] : relating to, being, or containing dung

ster·co·ric·o·lous \-ˈrik-ə-ləs\ *adj* [L *stercor-*, *stercus* excrement + E *-i-* + *-colous*] : living in dung

ster·cov·o·rous \ˌstər-ˈkäv-ə-rəs\ *adj* [L *stercus* excrement + E *-o-* + *-vorous*] : SCATOPHAGOUS ⟨~ insects⟩

stere \ˈsti(ə)r, ˈste(ə)r\ *n* [F *stère*, fr. Gk *stereos*] — see METRIC SYSTEM table

stere- *or* **stereo-** *comb form* [NL, fr. Gk, fr. *stereos* solid — more at STARE] **1** : solid : solid body ⟨*stereo*taxis⟩ **2 a** : stereoscopic ⟨*stere*opsis⟩ **b** : having or dealing with three dimensions of space ⟨*stereo*chemistry⟩

1**ste·reo** \ˈster-ē-ˌō, ˈstir-\ *n* **1** : STEREOTYPE **2** [short for *stereoscopy*] **a** : a stereoscopic method, system, or effect **b** : a stereoscopic photograph **3** [short for *stereophonic*] **a** : stereophonic reproduction **b** : a stereophonic sound system

2**stereo** *adj* **1 a** : STEREOSCOPIC **b** : STEREOTYPED **2** : STEREOPHONIC

ste·reo·bate \ˈster-ē-ə-ˌbāt, ˈstir-\ *n* [F or L; F *stéréobate*, fr. L *stereobata* foundation, fr. Gk *stereobatēs*, fr. *stere-* + *bainein* to go — more at COME] : a substructure of masonry visible above the ground level

ste·reo·chem·is·try \ˌster-ē-ō-ˈkem-ə-strē, ˌstir-\ *n* [ISV] : a branch of chemistry that deals with the spatial arrangement of atoms and groups in molecules

ste·reo·gram \ˈster-ē-ə-ˌgram, ˈstir-\ *n* [ISV] **1** : a diagram or picture representing objects with an impression of solidity or relief **2** : STEREOGRAPH

ste·reo·graph \-ˌgraf\ *n* [ISV] : a pair of stereoscopic pictures or a picture composed of two superposed stereoscopic images that gives a three-dimensional effect when viewed with a stereoscope or special spectacles — **stereograph** *vb*

ste·reo·graph·ic \ˌster-ē-ə-ˈgraf-ik, ˌstir-\ *adj* : made or done according to stereography — **ste·reo·graph·i·cal·ly** \-i-k(ə-)lē\ *adv*

ste·re·og·ra·phy \ˌster-ē-ˈäg-rə-fē, ˌstir-\ *n* **1** : the art, process, or technique of delineating the forms of solid bodies on a plane **2** : stereoscopic photography

ste·reo·iso·mer \ˌster-ē-ō-ˈī-sə-mər, ˌstir-\ *n* [ISV] : any isomer in an example of stereoisomerism

ste·reo·iso·mer·ic \-ˌī-sə-ˈmer-ik\ *adj* : of, relating to, or exhibiting stereoisomerism

ste·reo·isom·er·ism \-(ˌ)ī-ˈsäm-ə-ˌriz-əm\ *n* : isomerism in which atoms are linked in the same order but differ in their spatial arrangement

ste·reo·met·ric \ˌster-ē-ō-ˈme-trik, ˌstir-\ *adj* [NL *stereometricus*, fr. Gk *stereometrikos*, fr. *stereometria* measurement of solids, fr. *stere-* + *-metria* -metry] : having or representing a simple readily measurable solid form

ste·reo·mi·cro·scope \-ˈmī-krə-ˌskōp\ *n* : a microscope having a set of optics for each eye to make an object appear in three dimensions

ste·reo·pho·nic \-ē-ə-ˈfän-ik *also* -ˈfō-nik\ *adj* [ISV] : giving, relating to, or constituting a three-dimensional effect of auditory perspective — **ste·reo·pho·ny** \ˌster-ē-ˈäf-ə-nē, ˌstir-; ˈster-ē-ə-ˌfō-nē, ˈstir-\ *n*

ste·reo·pho·tog·ra·phy \ˌster-ē-ō-fə-ˈtäg-rə-fē, ˌstir-\ *n* [ISV] : stereoscopic photography

ste·re·op·sis \ˌster-ē-ˈäp-səs, ˌstir-\ *n* [NL] : stereoscopic vision

ste·re·op·ti·con \-ˈäp-ti-kən\ *n* [NL, fr. *stere-* + Gk *optikon*, neut. of *optikos* optic] : a projector for transparent slides often made double so as to produce dissolving views

ste·reo·scope \ˈster-ē-ə-ˌskōp, ˈstir-\ *n* : an optical instrument with two eyeglasses for helping the observer to combine the images of two pictures taken from points of view a little way apart and thus to get the effect of solidity or depth

ste·reo·scop·ic \ˌster-ē-ə-ˈskäp-ik, ˌstir-\ *adj* **1 :** of or relating to stereoscopy or the stereoscope **2 :** characterized by stereoscopy ⟨~ vision⟩ — **ste·reo·scop·i·cal·ly** \-i-k(ə-)lē\ *adv*

ste·re·os·co·py \ˌster-ē-ˈäs-kə-pē, ˌstir-; ˈster-ē-ə-ˌskō-pē, ˈstir-\ *n* [ISV] **1 :** a science that deals with stereoscopic effects and methods **2 :** the seeing of objects in three dimensions

ste·reo·tax·is \ˌster-ē-ə-ˈtak-səs, ˌstir-\ *n* [NL] **:** a taxis in which contact esp. with a solid body is the directive factor

ste·re·ot·o·my \-ē-ˈät-ə-mē\ *n* [F *stéréotomie*, fr. *stéré-* stere- + *-tomie* -tomy] **:** the art or technique of cutting solids; *esp* **:** the art of stonecutting

ste·re·ot·ro·pism \ˌster-ē-ˈä-trə-ˌpiz-əm, ˌstir-\ *n* [ISV] **:** a tropism in which contact esp. with a solid or a rigid surface is the orienting factor

1**ste·reo·type** \ˈster-ē-ə-ˌtīp, ˈstir-\ *n* [F *stéréotype*, fr. *stéré-* stere- + *type*] **1 :** a plate made by molding a matrix of a printing surface and making from this a cast in type metal **2 :** something conforming to a fixed or general pattern; *esp* **:** a standardized mental picture held in common by members of a group and representing an oversimplified opinion, affective attitude, or uncritical judgment (as of a person, a race, an issue, or an event)

2**stereotype** *vt* **1 :** to make a stereotype from **2 a :** to repeat without variation **b :** to develop a mental stereotype about — **ste·reo·typ·er** *n*

ste·reo·typed *adj* **:** lacking originality or individuality ⟨~ thinking⟩ **syn** see TRITE

ste·reo·ty·py \-ē-ə-ˌtī-pē\ *n* **1 :** the art or process of making or of printing from stereotype plates **2 :** frequent almost mechanical repetition of the same posture, movement, or form of speech (as in schizophrenia)

ste·ric \ˈster-ik, ˈsti(ə)r-\ *adj* [ISV *stere-* + *-ic*] **:** relating to the arrangement of atoms in space **:** SPATIAL — **ste·ri·cal·ly** \ˈster-i-k(ə-)lē, ˈstir-\ *adv*

ster·ile \ˈster-əl, *chiefly Brit* -ˌīl\ *adj* [L *sterilis*; akin to Goth *stairo* sterile, Gk *steira*] **1 a :** failing to produce or incapable of producing offspring ⟨a ~ hybrid⟩ **b :** failing to bear or incapable of producing fruit or spores **c :** incapable of germinating ⟨~ spores⟩ **d** *of a flower* **:** neither perfect nor pistillate **2 a :** unproductive of vegetation ⟨a ~ arid region⟩ **b :** deficient in ideas or originality **c :** free from living organisms and esp. microorganisms — **ste·ril·i·ty** \stə-ˈril-ət-ē\ *n*

syn STERILE, BARREN, IMPOTENT, UNFRUITFUL, INFERTILE mean lacking the power to produce offspring or bear fruit. STERILE implies inability as through an organic defect; BARREN stresses lack of issue or return for effort expended; IMPOTENT implies lack of ability to perform the act of procreation; UNFRUITFUL is less forceful than BARREN and applies more often to land or to efforts that bring forth nothing worthwhile; INFERTILE stresses the fact of sterility without suggesting the cause

ster·il·iza·tion \ˌster-ə-lə-ˈzā-shən\ *n* **:** the act or process of sterilizing

ster·il·ize \ˈster-ə-ˌlīz\ *vt* **:** to make sterile: as **a :** to cause (land) to become unfruitful **b (1) :** to deprive of the power of reproducing **(2) :** to make incapable of germination **c :** to make powerless or useless **d :** to free from living microorganisms — **ster·il·iz·er** *n*

ster·let \ˈstər-lət\ *n* [Russ *sterlyad'*] **:** a small sturgeon (*Acipenser ruthenus*) found in the Caspian sea and its rivers and esteemed for its flavor and its caviar

1**ster·ling** \ˈstər-liŋ\ *n* [ME] **1 :** British money **2 :** sterling silver or articles of it

2**sterling** *adj* **1 a :** of, relating to, or calculated in terms of British sterling **b :** payable in sterling **2 a** *of silver* **:** having a fixed standard of purity usu. defined legally as represented by an alloy of 925 parts of silver with 75 parts of copper **b :** made of sterling silver **3 :** conforming to the highest standard — **ster·ling·ly** \-liŋ-lē\ *adv* — **ster·ling·ness** *n*

sterling area *n* **:** a group of countries whose currencies are tied to the British pound sterling — called also *sterling bloc*

1**stern** \ˈstərn\ *adj* [ME *sterne*, fr. OE *styrne*; akin to OE *starian* to stare] **1 a :** having a definite hardness or severity of nature or manner **:** AUSTERE **b :** expressive of severe displeasure **:** HARSH **2 :** forbidding or gloomy in appearance **3 :** INEXORABLE ⟨~ necessity⟩ **4 :** STURDY, STOUT ⟨a ~ resolve⟩ **syn** see SEVERE — **stern·ly** *adv* — **stern·ness** \ˈstərn-nəs\ *n*

2**stern** *n* [ME, rudder, prob. of Scand origin; akin to ON *stjōrn* act of steering; akin to OE *stīeran* to steer — more at STEER] **1 :** the rear end of a boat **2 :** a hinder or rear part

ster·nal \ˈstərn-ᵊl\ *adj* **:** of or relating to the sternum

stern chase *n* **:** a chase in which a pursuing ship follows in the path of another

stern chaser *n* **:** a gun so placed as to be able to fire astern at a ship in chase

stern·fore·most \ˈstərn-ˈfō(ə)r-ˌmōst, -ˈfȯ(ə)r-\ *adv* **:** with the stern in advance **:** BACKWARD

stern·most \ˈstərn-ˌmōst\ *adj* **:** farthest astern

ster·no·cos·tal \ˌstər-(ˌ)nō-ˈkäst-ᵊl\ *adj* [NL *stern*um + E *-o-* + *costal*] **:** of, relating to, or situated between the sternum and ribs

stern·post \ˈstərn-ˌpōst\ *n* **:** the principal member at the stern of a ship extending from keel to deck

stern·son \ˈstərn(t)-sən\ *n* [*stern* + keel*son*] **:** the end of a keelson to which the sternpost is bolted

ster·num \ˈstər-nəm\ *n, pl* **sternums** *or* **ster·na** \-nə\ [NL, fr. Gk *sternon* chest, breastbone; akin to OHG *stirna* forehead, L *sternere* to spread out — more at STREW] **:** a compound ventral bone or cartilage connecting the ribs or the shoulder girdle or both — called also *breastbone*

ster·nu·ta·tion \ˌstər-nyə-ˈtā-shən\ *n* [L *sternutation-*, *sternutatio*, fr. *sternutatus*, pp. of *sternutare* to sneeze, fr. *sternutus*, pp. of *sternuere* to sneeze; akin to Gk *ptarnysthai* to sneeze] **:** the act, fact, or noise of sneezing — **ster·nu·ta·to·ry** \ˌstər-ˈn(y)üt-ə-ˌtōr-ē, -ˌtȯr-\ *or* **ster·nu·ta·tive** \ˌstər-ˈn(y)üt-ət-iv, ˈstər-nyə-ˌtāt-\ *adj*

ster·nu·ta·tor \ˈstər-nyə-ˌtāt-ər\ *n* **:** an agent that induces sneezing and often lacrimation and vomiting

stern·ward \ˈstərn-wərd\ *or* **stern·wards** \-wərdz\ *adv* (*or adj*) **:** AFT, ASTERN

stern·way \ˈstərn-ˌwā\ *n* **:** movement of a ship backward or with stern foremost

stern–wheel·er \-ˈhwē-lər, -ˈwē-\ *n* **:** a paddle-wheel steamer having a stern wheel instead of side wheels

ste·roid \ˈsti(ə)r-ˌȯid, ˈste(ə)r-\ *n* **:** any of numerous compounds containing the carbon ring system of the sterols and including the sterols and various hormones and glycosides — **steroid** *or* **ste·roi·dal** \stə-ˈrȯid-ᵊl\ *adj*

ste·rol \ˈsti(ə)r-ˌȯl, ˈste(ə)r-, -ˌōl\ *n* [ISV, fr. *-sterol* (as in *cholesterol*)] **:** any of various solid cyclic alcohols (as cholesterol) widely distributed in animal and plant lipides

ster·tor \ˈstərt-ər\ *n* [NL, fr. L *stertere* to snore; akin to *sternuere* to sneeze] **:** the act or fact of producing a snoring sound **:** SNORING

ster·to·rous \-ə-rəs\ *adj* **:** characterized by a harsh snoring or gasping sound — **ster·to·rous·ly** *adv* — **ster·to·rous·ness** *n*

stet \ˈstet\ *vt* **stet·ted; stet·ting** [L, let it stand, fr. *stare* to stand — more at STAND] **:** to annotate with the word *stet* or otherwise mark to nullify a previous order to delete or omit (a word or passage) from a manuscript or printer's proof

stetho·scope \ˈsteth-ə-ˌskōp, ˈsteth-\ *n* [F *stéthoscope*, fr. Gk *stēthos* chest + F *-scope*] **:** an instrument used to detect and study sounds produced in the body — **stetho·scop·ic** \ˌsteth-ə-ˈskäp-ik, ˌsteth-\ *or* **stetho·scop·i·cal** \-i-kəl\ *adj* — **stetho·scop·i·cal·ly** \-k(ə-)lē\ *adv* — **ste·tho·sco·py** \ste-ˈthäs-kə-pē, ˈsteth-ə-ˌskō-pē\ *n*

ste·ve·dore \ˈstē-və-ˌdō(ə)r, -ˌdȯ(ə)r\ *n* [Sp *estibador*, fr. *estibar* to pack, fr. L *stipare* to press together — more at STIFF] **:** one who works at or is responsible for unloading a ship in port — **stevedore** *vb*

stevedore knot *or* **stevedore's knot** *n* **:** a stopper knot similar to a figure eight knot but with one or more extra turns

1**stew** \ˈst(y)ü\ *n* [ME *stu*, fr. MF *estuve*, fr. (assumed) VL *extufa*, fr. *extufare* to stew] **1** *obs* **:** a utensil used for boiling **2 :** a hot bath **3 a :** BROTHEL **b :** a district of brothels — usu. used in pl. **4 a :** food prepared by stewing; *esp* **:** fish or meat usu. with vegetables prepared in this way **b (1) :** a heterogeneous mixture **(2) :** a state of heat and congestion **5 :** a state of excitement, worry, or confusion

2**stew** *vt* **:** to boil slowly or with simmering heat **~** *vi* **1 :** to become cooked by stewing **2 :** to swelter esp. from confinement in a hot or stuffy atmosphere **3 :** to become agitated or worried **:** FRET

1**stew·ard** \ˈst(y)ü-ərd, ˈst(y)ů(-ə)rd\ *n* [ME, fr. OE *stīweard*, fr. *stī* hall, sty + *weard* ward] **1 :** one employed in a large household or estate to manage domestic concerns including supervision of servants, collection of rents, and keeping of accounts **2 :** SHOP STEWARD **3 :** a finance officer **4 a :** an employee on a ship, airplane, bus, or train who manages the provisioning of food and otherwise attends passengers **b :** one appointed to supervise the provision and distribution of food and drink in an institution **5 :** one who actively directs affairs **:** MANAGER — **stew·ard·ess** \-əs\ *n* — **stew·ard·ship** \-ˌship\ *n*

2**steward** *vt* **:** to act as a steward for **:** MANAGE **~** *vi* **:** to perform the duties of a steward

stew·pan \ˈst(y)ü-ˌpan\ *n* **:** a saucepan used for stewing

sthen·ic \ˈsthen-ik\ *adj* [NL *sthenicus*, fr. Gk *sthenos* strength] **1 :** notably or excessively vigorous or energetic ⟨~ fever⟩ ⟨~ emotions⟩ **2 :** PYKNIC

stib·ine \ˈstib-ˌēn\ *n* [ISV, fr. L *stibium*] **:** a colorless poisonous flammable gas SbH_3 of antimony and hydrogen with a disagreeable odor

stib·nite \ˈstib-ˌnīt\ *n* [alter. of obs. E *stibine* stibnite, fr. F, fr. L *stibium* antimony, fr. Gk *stibi*, fr. Egypt *stm*] **:** a mineral Sb_2S_3 consisting of antimony trisulfide occurring in orthorhombic lead-gray crystals of metallic luster and also massive

sticho·myth·ia \ˌstik-ə-ˈmith-ē-ə\ *n* [Gk, fr. *stichomythein* to speak dialogue in alternate lines, fr. *stichos* row, verse + *mythos* tale, myth; akin to Gk *steichein* to walk, go — more at STAIR] **:** dialogue esp. of altercation or dispute delivered in alternating lines (as in classical Greek drama) — **sticho·myth·ic** \-ˈmith-ik\ *adj*

1**stick** \ˈstik\ *n* [ME *stik*, fr. OE *sticca*; akin to ON *stik* stick, OE *stician* to stick] **1 :** a woody piece or part of a tree or shrub: as **a :** a usu. dry or dead severed shoot, twig, or slender branch **b :** a cut or broken branch or piece of wood gathered for fuel or construction material **2 :** a long slender piece of wood: as **a (1) :** a club or staff used as a weapon **(2) :** something suitable for use in compelling **b :** WALKING STICK **c :** any implement used for striking or propelling an object in a game **d :** a baton symbolizing an office or dignity; *also* **:** a person entitled to bear such a baton **3 :** a piece of the materials composing something (as a building) **4 :** any of various implements resembling a stick in shape, origin, or use: as **a (1) :** COMPOSING STICK **(2) :** STICKFUL **b :** an airplane lever operating the elevators and ailerons **c :** the gearshift lever of an automobile **5 a :** PERSON, CHAP **b :** a dull, inert, stiff, or spiritless person **6** *pl* **:** wooded or rural districts ⟨a hick from the ~*s*⟩ **7 :** an herbaceous stalk resembling a woody stick ⟨celery ~*s*⟩ **8 :** MAST; *also* **:** YARD **9 :** a piece of furniture **10 :** a number of bombs arranged for release from a bombing plane in a series across a target

2**stick** *vt* **1 :** to arrange (lumber) in stacks **2 :** to provide a stick as a support for **3 :** to set (type) in a composing stick **:** COMPOSE

3**stick** *vb* **stuck** \ˈstək\ **stuck; stick·ing** [ME *stikken*, fr. OE *stician*; akin to OHG *sticken* to prick, L *in*stigare to urge on, goad, Gk *stizein* to tattoo] *vt* **1 a :** to pierce with something pointed **:** STAB **b :** to kill by piercing **2 :** to push or thrust so as or as if to pierce **3 a :** to fasten by thrusting in **b :** IMPALE **c :** PUSH, THRUST **4 :** to put or set in a specified place or position **5 :** to furnish with things fastened on by or as if by piercing **6 :** to attach by or as if by causing to adhere to a surface **7 a :** to compel to pay esp. by trickery **b :** OVERCHARGE **8 a :** to halt the movement or action of **b :** BAFFLE, STUMP **9 a :** CHEAT, DEFRAUD **b :** to saddle with something disadvantageous or disagreeable **~** *vi* **1 :** to hold to something firmly by or as if by adhesion: **a :** to become fixed in place by means of a pointed end **b :** to become fast by or as if by miring or by gluing or plastering ⟨*stuck* in the mud⟩ **2 a :** to remain in a place, situation, or environment **b :** to hold fast or adhere resolutely **:** CLING **c :** to remain effective **d :** to keep close in a chase or competition **3 :** to become blocked, wedged, or jammed **4 a :** BALK, SCRUPLE **b :** to find oneself baffled **c :** to be unable to proceed **5 :** PROJECT, PROTRUDE

syn STICK, ADHERE, COHERE, CLING, CLEAVE mean to become closely attached. STICK implies attachment by affixing or by being glued together; ADHERE implies a growing together or figuratively a deliberate accepting; COHERE suggests a sticking together of parts so that they form a unified mass; CLING implies attachment by hanging on with arms or tendrils; CLEAVE stresses strength of attachment

[4]**stick** *n* **1 :** a thrust with a pointed instrument **:** STAB **2 a :** DELAY, STOP **b :** IMPEDIMENT **3 :** adhesive quality or substance

stick·abil·i·ty \ˌstik-ə-ˈbil-ət-ē\ *n* [[3]*stick* + *ability*] **:** ability to endure or persevere

stick around *vi* **:** to stay or wait about **:** LINGER

stick·er \ˈstik-ər\ *n* **1 :** one that pierces with a point **2 a :** one that adheres or causes adhesion **b :** a slip of paper with gummed back that when moistened adheres to a surface

stick·ful \ˈstik-ˌfu̇l\ *n* **:** as much set type as fills a composing stick

stick·i·ly \ˈstik-ə-lē\ *adv* **:** in a sticky manner

stick·i·ness \ˈstik-ē-nəs\ *n* **:** the quality or state of being sticky

sticking plaster *n* **:** an adhesive plaster esp. for closing superficial wounds

stick insect *n* **:** any of various usu. wingless insects (esp. family Phasmatidae) with a long round body resembling a stick

stick–in–the–mud \ˈstik-ən-t͟hə-ˌməd\ *n* **:** one who is slow, old-fashioned, or unprogressive; *esp* **:** an old fogy

stick·it \ˈstik-ət\ *adj* [Sc, fr. pp. of E [3]*stick*] **1** *Scot* **:** UNFINISHED **2** *chiefly Scot* **:** having failed esp. in an intended profession

stick·le \ˈstik-əl\ *vi* **stick·ling** \-(ə-)liŋ\ [ME *stightlen*, freq. of *stighten* to arrange, fr. OE *stihtan;* akin to OE *stǣger* stair — more at STAIR] **1 :** to contend esp. stubbornly and usu. on insufficient grounds **2 :** to feel scruples **:** SCRUPLE

stick·le·back \ˈstik-əl-ˌbak\ *n* [ME *stykylbak*, fr. OE *sticel* goad + ME *bak* back; akin to OE *stician* to stick] **:** any of numerous small scaleless fishes (family Gasterosteidae) having two or more free spines in front of the dorsal fin

stick·ler \ˈstik-(ə-)lər\ *n* **1 :** one who insists on exactness or completeness in the observance of something ⟨~ for obedience⟩ **2 :** POSER, STICKER

stick·man \ˈstik-ˌman, -mən\ *n* **:** one who handles a stick: as **a :** one who supervises the play at a dice table, calls the decisions, and retrieves the dice **b :** a player in any of various games (as lacrosse) played with a stick

stick out *vi* **1 a :** to jut out **:** PROJECT **b :** to be prominent or conspicuous **2 a :** to be persistent (as in a demand or an opinion) **b :** STRIKE **~** *vt* **:** to endure to the end — often used with *it*

stick·pin \ˈstik-ˌpin\ *n* **:** an ornamental pin worn in a necktie

stick·seed \-ˌsēd\ *n* **:** any of a genus (*Lappula*) of weedy herbs of the borage family with bristly adhesive fruit

stick·tight \-ˌtīt\ *n* **1 :** BUR MARIGOLD **2 :** STICKSEED

stick–to–it·ive·ness \stik-ˈtü-ət-iv-nəs\ *n* [fr. the phrase *stick to it*] **:** dogged perseverance **:** TENACITY

stick up *vt* **:** to rob at the point of a gun — **stick·up** \ˈstik-ˌəp\ *n*

stick·weed \ˈstik-ˌwēd\ *n* **:** any of several plants with adhesive seeds: as **a :** an annual ragweed (*Ambrosia artemisiifolia*) with finely divided foliage **b :** AGRIMONY **c :** a beggar's-lice (*Lappula virginica*)

stick·work \-ˌwərk\ *n* **1 :** the use (as in lacrosse) of one's stick in offensive and defensive techniques **2 :** batting ability in baseball

sticky \ˈstik-ē\ *adj* **1 a :** ADHESIVE **b** (1) **:** GLUEY, VISCOUS (2) **:** coated with a sticky substance **2 :** HUMID, MUGGY; *also* **:** CLAMMY **3 :** tending to stick ⟨~ valve⟩ **4 a :** DISAGREEABLE, PAINFUL **b :** AWKWARD, STIFF

[1]**stiff** \ˈstif\ *adj* [ME *stif*, fr. OE *stīf;* akin to MD *stijf* stiff, L *stipare* to press together, Gk *steibein* to tread on] **1 a :** not easily bent **:** RIGID **b :** lacking in suppleness ⟨~ muscles⟩ **c :** impeded in movement — used of a mechanism **d :** DRUNK **2 a :** FIRM, RESOLUTE **b :** STUBBORN, UNYIELDING **c :** PROUD **d** (1) **:** marked by reserve or decorum **:** FORMAL (2) **:** lacking in ease or grace **:** STILTED **3 :** hard fought **:** PUGNACIOUS, SHARP **4 a** (1) **:** exerting great force **:** STRONG ⟨~ wind⟩ (2) **:** FORCEFUL, VIGOROUS **b :** POTENT ⟨a ~ dose⟩ **5 :** of a dense or glutinous consistency **:** THICK **6 a :** HARSH, SEVERE ⟨a ~ penalty⟩ **b :** ARDUOUS, RUGGED ⟨~ terrain⟩ **7 :** not easily heeled over by an external force (as the wind) ⟨a ~ ship⟩ **8 :** EXPENSIVE, STEEP ⟨paid a ~ duty⟩ — **stiff·ly** *adv* — **stiff·ness** *n*

syn STIFF, RIGID, INFLEXIBLE, TENSE, STARK mean impossible to bend. STIFF may apply to any degree of this condition; RIGID applies to something so stiff that it cannot be bent without breaking; INFLEXIBLE stresses lack of suppleness or pliability; TENSE suggests a straining or stretching to a point where elasticity is lost; STARK implies a stiffness associated with loss of life or warmth

[2]**stiff** *adv* **1 :** STIFFLY **2 :** to an extreme degree **:** INTENSELY ⟨bored ~⟩

[3]**stiff** *n* **1 :** CORPSE **2 a :** BUM, TRAMP **b :** LABORER, HAND

[1]**stiff–arm** \ˈstif-ˌärm\ *vb* **:** STRAIGHT-ARM

[2]**stiff–arm** *n* **:** STRAIGHT-ARM

stiff·en \ˈstif-ən\ *vb* **stiff·en·ing** \-(ə-)niŋ\ **:** to make or become stiff or stiffer — **stiff·en·er** \-(ə-)nər\ *n*

stiff·ish \-ish\ *adj* **:** moderately stiff

stiff–necked \ˈstif-ˈnekt\ *adj* **1 :** HAUGHTY, STUBBORN **2 :** STILTED

[1]**sti·fle** \ˈstī-fəl\ *n* [ME] **:** the joint next above the hock in the hind leg of a quadruped (as a horse) corresponding to the knee in man

[2]**stifle** *vb* **sti·fling** \-f(ə-)liŋ\ [alter. of ME *stuflen*] *vt* **1 a :** to kill by depriving of oxygen **:** SUFFOCATE **b** (1) **:** SMOTHER (2) **:** MUFFLE **2 a :** to cut off (as the voice or breath) **b :** to withhold from circulation or expression **:** REPRESS ⟨~ his anger⟩ **c :** DETER, DISCOURAGE **~** *vi* **:** to become suffocated by or as if by lack of oxygen **:** SMOTHER — **sti·fler** \-f(ə-)lər\ *n* — **sti·fling** *adj* — **sti·fling·ly** \-f(ə-)liŋ-lē\ *adv*

stig·ma \ˈstig-mə\ *n, pl* **stig·ma·ta** \stig-ˈmät-ə, ˈstig-mət-ə\ *or* **stigmas** [L *stigmat-, stigma* mark, brand, fr. Gk, fr. *stizein* to tattoo — more at STICK] **1 a** *archaic* **:** a scar left by a hot iron **:** BRAND **b :** a mark of shame or discredit **:** STAIN **c :** an identifying mark or characteristic; *specif* **:** a specific diagnostic sign of a disease **2 a stigmata** *pl* **:** bodily marks or pains resembling the wounds of the crucified Christ and sometimes accompanying religious ecstasy **b :** PETECHIA **3 a :** a small spot, scar, or opening on a plant or animal **b :** the part of the pistil of a flower which receives the pollen grains and on which they germinate — **stig·mal** \ˈstig-məl\ *adj*

stig·mas·ter·ol \stig-ˈmas-tə-ˌrȯl, -ˌrōl\ *n* [NL Physo*stigma* (genus including the Calabar bean) + ISV *sterol*] **:** a crystalline sterol $C_{29}H_{47}OH$ obtained esp. from the oils of Calabar beans and soybeans

[1]**stig·mat·ic** \stig-ˈmat-ik\ *adj* **1 :** having or conveying a social stigma **2 :** of or relating to supernatural stigmata **3 :** ANASTIGMATIC — used esp. of a bundle of light rays intersecting at a single point — **stig·mat·i·cal·ly** \-i-k(ə-)lē\ *adv*

[2]**stigmatic** *n* **:** one marked with stigmata

stig·ma·tism \ˈstig-mə-ˌtiz-əm\ *n* [L *stigmat-, stigma*] **:** the condition of an optical system (as a lens) in which rays of light from a single point converge in a single focal point — compare ASTIGMATISM

stig·ma·tist \ˈstig-mət-əst, stig-ˈmät-\ *n* **:** STIGMATIC

stig·ma·ti·za·tion \ˌstig-mət-ə-ˈzā-shən\ *n* **:** an act or instance of stigmatizing

stig·ma·tize \ˈstig-mə-ˌtīz\ *vt* **1 a** *archaic* **:** BRAND **b :** to describe or identify in opprobrious terms **2 :** to mark with stigmata

stil·bene \ˈstil-ˌbēn\ *n* [ISV, fr. Gk *stilbein* to glitter] **:** an aromatic hydrocarbon $C_{14}H_{12}$ used as a phosphor and in making dyes

stil·bes·trol \stil-ˈbes-ˌtrȯl, -ˌtrōl\ *n* [*stilbene* + *estrus*] **1 :** a crystalline synthetic derivative $C_{14}H_{12}O_2$ of stilbene with little estrogenic activity **2 :** DIETHYLSTILBESTROL

stil·bite \ˈstil-ˌbīt\ *n* [F, fr. Gk *stilbein*] **:** a mineral $NaCa_2Al_5Si_{13}O_{36}.14H_2O$ consisting of a hydrous silicate of aluminum, calcium, and sodium often occurring in sheaflike aggregations of crystals

[1]**stile** \ˈstī(ə)l\ *n* [ME, fr. OE *stigel;* akin to OE *stǣger* stair — more at STAIR] **:** a step or set of steps for passing over a fence or wall; *also* **:** TURNSTILE

[2]**stile** *n* [prob. fr. D *stijl* post] **:** one of the vertical members in a frame or panel into which the secondary members are fitted

sti·let·to \stə-ˈlet-(ˌ)ō\ *n, pl* **stilettos** *or* **stilettoes** [It, dim. of *stilo* stylus, dagger, fr. L *stilus* stylus — more at STYLE] **1 :** a slender dagger with a blade thick in proportion to its breadth **2 :** a pointed instrument for piercing holes for eyelets or embroidery

[1]**still** \ˈstil\ *adj* [ME *stille*, fr. OE; akin to OHG *stilli* still, OE *steall* stall] **1 a :** MOTIONLESS **b** *archaic* **:** SEDENTARY **c :** not carbonated ⟨~ wine⟩ **d :** of, relating to, or being a static photograph as contrasted with a motion picture **2 a :** uttering no sound **:** QUIET **b :** SUBDUED, MUTED **3 a :** CALM, TRANQUIL **b :** free from noise or turbulence **:** PEACEFUL — **still·ness** *n*

[2]**still** *vt* **1 a :** ALLAY, CALM **b :** SETTLE **2 :** to arrest the motion of **:** ASSUAGE **3 :** SILENCE **~** *vi* **:** to become motionless or silent **:** QUIET

[3]**still** *adv* **1 :** without motion ⟨sit ~⟩ **2** *archaic* **a :** ALWAYS, CONTINUALLY **b :** PROGRESSIVELY, INCREASINGLY **3 —** used as a function word to indicate the continuance of an action or condition ⟨~ lived there⟩ ⟨drink it while it's ~ hot⟩ ⟨will ~ be rich⟩ **4 :** in spite of that **:** NEVERTHELESS ⟨those who take the greatest care ~ make mistakes⟩ ⟨the book is not perfect; ~, it is very good⟩ **5 a :** EVEN 2c ⟨a ~ more difficult problem⟩ **b :** YET 1a

[4]**still** *n* **1 :** QUIET, SILENCE **2 :** a static photograph; *specif* **:** a photograph of actors or scenes of a motion picture for publicity or documentary purposes

[5]**still** *vb* [ME *stillen*, short for *distillen* to distill] **:** DISTILL

[6]**still** *n* **1 :** DISTILLERY **2 :** apparatus used in distillation comprising either the chamber in which the vaporization is carried out or the entire equipment

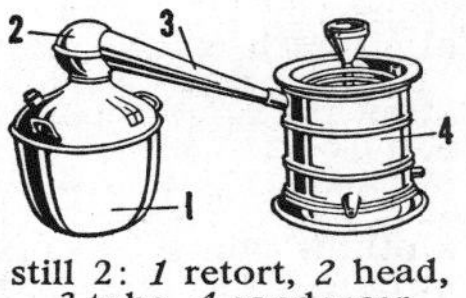

still 2: *1* retort, *2* head, *3* tube, *4* condenser

still alarm *n* **:** a fire alarm transmitted (as by telephone call) without sounding the signal apparatus

still·birth \ˈstil-ˌbərth, -ˈbərth\ *n* **:** the birth of a dead fetus

still·born \-ˈbȯ(ə)rn\ *adj* **1 :** dead at birth **2 :** failing from the start **:** ABORTIVE — **stillborn** \-ˌbȯ(ə)rn\ *n*

still hunt *n* **:** a quiet pursuing or ambushing of game — **still–hunt** \ˈstil-ˌhənt\ *vb*

still life *n, pl* **still lifes 1 :** a picture consisting predominantly of inanimate objects **2 :** the category of graphic arts concerned with inanimate subject matter

still·man \ˈstil-mən\ *n* **1 :** one who owns or operates a still **:** DISTILLER **2 :** one who tends distillation equipment (as in an oil refinery)

still water *n* **:** a part of a stream where the gradient is so gentle that no current is visible

[1]**stil·ly** \ˈstil-lē\ *adv* **:** CALMLY, QUIETLY

[2]**stilly** \ˈstil-ē\ *adj* **:** STILL

[1]**stilt** \ˈstilt\ *n* [ME *stilte;* akin to OHG *stelza* stilt, OE *steall* position, stall — more at STALL] **1 a :** one of two poles each with a rest or strap for the foot used to elevate the wearer above the ground in walking **b :** a pile or post serving as one of the supports of a structure above ground or water level **2** *pl also* **stilt :** any of various notably long-legged three-toed limicoline birds (genera *Himantopus* and *Cladorhynchus*) related to the avocets that frequent inland ponds and marshes and nest in small colonies

[2]**stilt** *vt* **:** to raise on or as if on stilts

stilt·ed \ˈstil-təd\ *adj* **1 :** having the springing higher than the apparent level of the impost ⟨~ arch⟩ **2 a :** POMPOUS, LOFTY **b :** FORMAL, STIFF ⟨~ diction⟩ — **stilt·ed·ly** *adv* — **stilt·ed·ness** *n*

Stil·ton \ˈstilt-ᵊn\ *n* [*Stilton*, Huntingdonshire, England] **:** a blue-veined cheese with wrinkled rind made of whole cows' milk enriched with cream

stime \ˈstīm\ *n* [ME (northern dial.)] *chiefly Scot & Irish* **:** GLIMMER; *also* **:** GLIMPSE

stim·u·lant \ˈstim-yə-lənt\ *n* **1 :** an agent (as a drug) that produces a temporary increase of the functional activity or efficiency of an organism or any of its parts **2 :** STIMULUS **3 :** an alcoholic beverage — **stimu·lant** *adj*

stim·u·late \-ˌlāt\ *vb* [L *stimulatus*, pp. of *stimulare*, fr. *stimulus* goad; akin to L *stilus* stake, stylus — more at STYLE] *vt* **1 :** to excite to activity or growth or to greater activity **:** ANIMATE, AROUSE **2 a :** to function as a physiological stimulus to **b :** to arouse or affect by a stimulant (as a drug) **~** *vi* **:** to act as a stimulant or stimulus **syn** see PROVOKE — **stim·u·la·tion** \ˌstim-yə-ˈlā-shən\ *n* — **stim·u·la·tive** \ˈstim-yə-ˌlāt-iv\ *adj* — **stim·u·la·tor** \-ˌlāt-ər\ *n* — **stim·u·la·to·ry** \-lə-ˌtōr-ē, -ˌtȯr-\ *adj*

stim·u·lus \ˈstim-yə-ləs\ *n, pl* **stim·u·li** \-ˌlī, -ˌlē\ [L] **:** something that rouses or incites to activity: as **a :** STIMULANT 1 **b :** an agent (as an environmental change) that directly influences the activity

of living protoplasm (as by exciting a sensory organ or evoking muscular contraction or glandular secretion)

[1]**sting** \'stiŋ\ *vb* **stung** \'stəŋ\ **sting·ing** \'stiŋ-iŋ\ [ME *stingen*, fr. OE *stingan*; akin to ON *stinga* to sting, Gk *stachys* spike of grain, *stochos* target, aim] *vt* **1 :** to prick painfully: as **a :** to pierce or wound with a poisonous or irritating process **b :** to affect with sharp quick pain or smart ⟨hail *stung* their faces⟩ **2 :** to cause to suffer acutely ⟨*stung* with remorse⟩ **3 :** OVERCHARGE, CHEAT ~ *vi* **1 :** to use a sting **2 :** to feel a keen burning pain or smart

[2]**sting** *n* **1 a :** the act of stinging; *specif* **:** the thrust of a stinger into the flesh **b :** a wound or pain caused by or as if by stinging **2 :** STINGER 2 **3 :** a stinging element, force, or quality

sting·a·ree \'stiŋ-ə-rē *also* 'stiŋ-rē\ *n* [by alter.] **:** STINGRAY

sting·er \'stiŋ-ər\ *n* **1 :** one that stings; *specif* **:** a sharp blow or remark **2 :** a sharp organ (as of a bee, scorpion, or stingray) of offense and defense usu. connected with a poison gland or otherwise adapted to wound by piercing and inoculating a poisonous secretion **3 :** a cocktail of equal parts of white crème de menthe and brandy

stin·gi·ly \'stin-jə-lē\ *adv* **:** in a stingy manner

stin·gi·ness \-jē-nəs\ *n* **:** the quality or state of being stingy

sting·ing hair \,stiŋ-iŋ-\ *n* **:** a glandular hair (as of a nettle) whose base secretes a stinging fluid

sting·less \'stiŋ-ləs\ *adj* **:** having no sting or stinger

sting·ray \-,rā *also* -rē\ *n* **:** any of numerous rays (as of the family Dasyatidae) with one or more large sharp barbed dorsal spines near the base of the whiplike tail capable of inflicting severe wounds

[1]**stin·gy** \'stin-jē\ *adj* [prob. fr. (assumed) E dial. *stinge*, n., sting; akin to OE *stingan* to sting] **1 :** not generous or liberal **:** sparing or scant in giving or spending **2 :** meanly scanty or small **:** MEAGER ⟨~ portion⟩

syn CLOSE, NIGGARDLY, PARSIMONIOUS, PENURIOUS, MISERLY: STINGY implies a marked lack of generosity; CLOSE suggests keeping a tight grip on one's money and possessions; NIGGARDLY implies giving or spending the very smallest amount possible; PARSIMONIOUS suggests a frugality so extreme as to lead to stinginess; PENURIOUS implies niggardliness that gives an appearance of actual poverty; MISERLY suggests a sordid avariciousness and a morbid pleasure in hoarding

[2]**stingy** \'stiŋ-ē\ *adj* **:** able to sting

[1]**stink** \'stiŋk\ *vi* **stank** \'staŋk\ *or* **stunk** \'stəŋk\ **stunk; stink·ing** [ME *stinken*, fr. OE *stincan*; akin to OHG *stinkan* to emit a smell] **1 :** to emit a strong offensive odor **2 :** to be offensive; *also* **:** to be in bad repute **3 :** to possess something to an offensive degree **4 :** to be extremely bad in quality — **stinky** \'stiŋ-kē\ *adj*

[2]**stink** *n* **1 :** a strong offensive odor **:** STENCH **2 :** a public outcry against something offensive

stink·ard \'stiŋ-kərd\ *n* **:** a mean or contemptible person

stink·bug \'stiŋk-,bəg\ *n* **:** any of various true bugs (order Hemiptera) that emit a disagreeable odor

stink·er \'stiŋ-kər\ *n* **1 a :** one that stinks **b :** an offensive or contemptible person **c :** something of very poor quality **2 :** any of several large petrels of an offensive odor **3** *slang* **:** something extremely difficult ⟨the examination was a real ~⟩

stink·horn \'stiŋk-,hȯ(ə)rn\ *n* **:** an ill-smelling fungus (order Phallales, esp. *Phallus impudicus*)

stink·ing *adj* **1 :** offensive to the smell **:** RANK **2** *slang* **:** offensively drunk **syn** see MALODOROUS — **stink·ing·ly** \'stiŋ-kiŋ-lē\ *adv*

stink·ing rog·er \,stiŋ-kiŋ-'räj-ər, -kən-\ *n* [fr. the name *Roger*] **:** any of various fetid plants (as a figwort or henbane)

stinking smut *n* **:** [2]BUNT

stink·pot \'stiŋk-,pät\ *n* **:** an earthen jar charged with materials of an offensive and suffocating smell formerly sometimes thrown upon an enemy's deck

stink·stone \'stiŋk-,stōn\ *n* **:** a stone that emits a fetid smell on being struck or rubbed owing to decomposition of organic matter

stink·weed \'stiŋk-,kwēd\ *n* **:** any of various strong-scented or fetid plants (as a jimsonweed)

stink·wood \-,kwu̇d\ *n* **1 :** any of several trees with a wood of unpleasant odor; *esp* **:** a southern African tree (*Ocotia bullata*) of the laurel family yielding a valued cabinet wood **2 :** the wood of a stinkwood

[1]**stint** \'stint\ *vb* [ME *stinten*, fr. OE *styntan* to blunt, dull; akin to ON *stuttr* scant, L *tundere* to beat, OE *stocc* stock] *vt* **1** *archaic* **:** to put an end to **:** STOP **2 a :** to restrain within certain limits **:** CONFINE **b :** to restrict with respect to a share or allowance **3 :** to assign a task to (a person) ~ *vi* **1** *archaic* **:** STOP, DESIST **2 :** to be sparing or frugal — **stint·er** *n*

[2]**stint** *n* **1 :** RESTRAINT, LIMITATION **2 :** a definite quantity of work assigned **syn** see TASK

[3]**stint** *n, pl* **stints** *also* **stint** [ME *stynte*] **:** any of several small sandpipers

stipe \'stīp\ *n* [NL *stipes*, fr. L, tree trunk; akin to L *stipare* to press together — more at STIFF] **:** a usu. short plant stalk: as **a :** the stem supporting the cap of a fungus **b :** the like part connecting the holdfast and blade of a frondose alga **c :** the petiole of a fern frond **d :** a prolongation of the receptacle beneath the ovary of a seed plant — **stiped** \'stīpt\ *adj*

sti·pel \'stī-pəl, stī-'pel\ *n* [NL *stipella*, dim. of *stipula* stipule] **:** the stipule of a leaflet — **sti·pel·late** \stī-'pel-ət, 'stī-pə-,lāt\ *adj*

sti·pend \'stī-,pend, -pənd\ *n* [alter. of ME *stipendy*, fr. L *stipendium*, fr. *stip-*, *stips* gift + *pendere* to weigh, pay — more at PENDANT] **:** a fixed sum of money paid periodically for services or to defray expenses **syn** see WAGE

[1]**sti·pen·di·ary** \stī-'pen-dē-,er-ē\ *adj* **1 :** receiving or compensated by wages or salary ⟨a ~ curate⟩ **2 :** of or relating to a stipend

[2]**stipendiary** *n* **:** one who receives a stipend

sti·pes \'stī-,pēz\ *n, pl* **stip·i·tes** \'stip-ə-,tēz\ [NL *stipit-*, *stipes*, fr. L, tree trunk; akin to L *stipare* to press together — more at STIFF] **:** PEDUNCLE; *esp* **:** the second basal segment of a maxilla of an insect or crustacean — **stip·i·tate** \'stip-ə-,tāt\ *adj*

[1]**stip·ple** \'stip-əl\ *vt* **stip·pling** \-(ə-)liŋ\ [D *stippelen* to spot, dot; akin to L *stipare* to press together] **1 :** to engrave by means of dots and flicks — compare LINE ENGRAVING **2 a :** to make (as in paint or ink) by small short touches that together produce an even or softly graded shadow **b :** to apply (as paint) by repeated small touches **3 :** SPECKLE, FLECK — **stip·pler** \-(ə-)lər\ *n*

[2]**stipple** *n* **:** production of gradation of light and shade in graphic art by stippling small points, larger dots, or longer strokes; *also* **:** an effect produced by or as if by stippling

stip·u·lar \'stip-yə-lər\ *adj* **:** of, resembling, or provided with stipules ⟨~ glands⟩

[1]**stip·u·late** \'stip-yə-,lāt\ *vb* [L *stipulatus*, pp. of *stipulari* to demand some term in an agreement] *vi* **1 :** to make an agreement or covenant to do or forbear something **:** CONTRACT **2 :** to demand an express term in an agreement — used with *for* ~ *vt* **1 :** to specify as a condition or requirement of an agreement or offer **2 :** to give a guarantee of **:** PROMISE — **stip·u·la·tor** \-,lāt-ər\ *n*

[2]**stip·u·late** \-lət\ *adj* **:** having stipules

stip·u·la·tion \,stip-yə-'lā-shən\ *n* **1 :** an act of stipulating **2 :** something stipulated; *esp* **:** a condition, requirement, or item specified in an instrument — **stip·u·la·to·ry** \'stip-yə-lə-,tōr-ē, -,tȯr-\ *adj*

stip·ule \'stip-(,)yü(ə)l\ *n* [NL *stipula*, fr. L, stalk; akin to L *stipes* tree trunk] **:** either of a pair of appendages borne at the base of the leaf in many plants — **stip·uled** \-,yü(ə)ld\ *adj*

[1]**stir** \'stər\ *vb* **stirred; stir·ring** [ME *stiren*, fr. OE *styrian*; akin to MHG *stürn* to incite] *vt* **1 a :** to cause an esp. slight movement or change of position of **b :** to disturb the quiet of **:** AGITATE **2 a :** to disturb the relative position of the particles or parts of esp. by a continued circular movement **b :** to mix by or as if by stirring **3 :** BESTIR, EXERT **4 :** to bring into notice or debate **:** RAISE **5 a :** INCITE **b :** QUICKEN **c :** to call forth (as a memory) **:** EVOKE **d :** PROVOKE ~ *vi* **1 a :** to make a slight movement **b :** to begin to move (as in rousing) **2 :** to begin to be active **3 :** to be active or busy **4 :** to pass an implement through a substance with a circular movement **5 :** to be able to be stirred — **stir·rer** *n*

[2]**stir** *n* **1 a :** a state of disturbance, agitation, or activity **b :** widespread notice and discussion **:** IMPRESSION **2 :** a slight movement **3 :** a stirring movement

syn STIR, BUSTLE, FLURRY, POTHER, FUSS, ADO mean excitement or agitation accompanying an action or event. STIR suggests brisk and restless movement of a crowd; BUSTLE implies a noisy, obtrusive, often self-important activity; FLURRY suggests nervous agitation and undue haste; POTHER and FUSS imply fidgety, needless activity; ADO suggests fussy activity and waste of energy

[3]**stir** *n* [origin unknown] *slang* **:** PRISON

stir·about \'stər-ə-,bau̇t\ *n* **:** a porridge of oatmeal or cornmeal boiled in water or milk and stirred

stirk \'stərk\ *n* [ME, fr. OE *stirc*; akin to L *sterilis* sterile] *Brit* **:** a young bull or cow esp. between one and two years old

stirp \'stərp\ *n* [L *stirp-*, *stirps* — more at TORPID] **:** a line descending from a common ancestor **:** STOCK, LINEAGE

stirps \'sti(ə)rps, 'stərps\ *n, pl* **stir·pes** \'sti(ə)r-,pās, 'stər-(,)pēz\ [L, lit., stem, stock — more at TORPID] **1 :** a branch of a family or the person from whom it is descended **2 a :** a group of animals equivalent to a superfamily **b :** a race or fixed variety of plants

stir·ring *adj* **1 :** ACTIVE, BUSTLING **2 :** ROUSING, INSPIRING

stir·rup \'stər-əp *also* 'stə-rəp, 'stir-əp\ *n* [ME *stirop*, fr. OE *stigrāp*; akin to OHG *stegareif* stirrup; both fr. a prehistoric NGmc-WGmc compound whose first element is akin to OHG *stīgan* to go up and whose second element is represented by OE *rāp* rope — more at STAIR] **1 :** a ring made horizontal in one part for receiving the foot of a rider, attached by a strap to a saddle, and used to aid in mounting and as a support while riding **2 :** a piece resembling a stirrup (as a support or clamp in carpentry and machinery) **3 :** a rope secured to a yard and attached to a thimble in its lower end for supporting a footrope

stirrup cup *n* **1 :** a cup of drink (as wine) taken by a rider about to depart **2 :** a farewell cup

stirrup leather *n* **:** the strap suspending a stirrup

stirrup pump *n* **:** a portable hand pump held in position by a foot bracket and used for throwing a jet or spray of liquid

[1]**stitch** \'stich\ *n* [ME *stiche*, fr. OE *stice*; akin to OE *stician* to stick] **1 :** a local sharp and sudden pain esp. in the side **2 a :** one in-and-out movement of a threaded needle in sewing, embroidering, or suturing **b :** a portion of thread left in the material after one stitch **3 :** a least part esp. of clothing **4 :** a single loop of thread or yarn around an implement (as a knitting needle or crochet hook) **5 :** a series of stitches **6 :** a method of stitching — **in stitches :** in a state of uncontrollable laughter

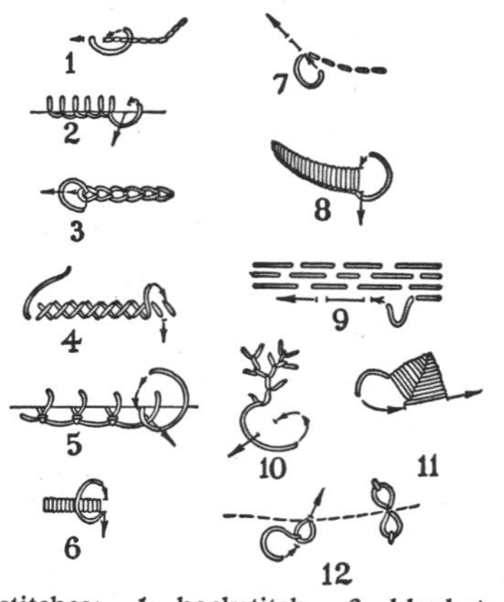

stitches: *1* backstitch, *2* blanket stitch, *3* chain stitch, *4* cross-stitch, *5* knot stitch, *6* overcast stitch, *7* running stitch, *8* buttonhole stitch, *9* darning stitch, *10* featherstitch, *11* fishbone stitch, *12* loop stitch

[2]**stitch** *vt* **1 a :** to fasten, join, or close with or as if with stitches **b :** to make, mend, or decorate with or as if with stitches **2 :** to unite by means of staples ~ *vi* **:** to do needlework **:** SEW — **stitch·er** *n*

stitch·wort \-,wərt, -,wȯ(ə)rt\ *n* **:** any of several chickweeds (genus *Stellaria*)

stithy \'stith-ē, 'stith-\ *n* [ME, fr. ON *stethi*; akin to OE *stede* stead] **1 :** ANVIL **2 :** SMITHY

sti·ver \'stī-vər\ *n* [D *stuiver*] **1 a :** a unit of value of the Netherlands equal to 1/20 gulden **b :** a coin representing one stiver **2 :** something of little value

stoa \'stō-ə\ *n* [Gk; akin to Gk *stylos* pillar — more at STEER] **:** an ancient Greek portico usu. walled at the back with a front colonnade to afford a sheltered promenade

stoat \'stōt\ *n, pl* **stoats** *also* **stoat** [ME *stote*] **:** ERMINE 1a; *broadly* **:** any weasel with a black-tipped tail — used esp. of the animal when in the brown summer coat

stob \'stäb\ *n* [ME, stump; akin to ME *stubb* stub] *chiefly dial* **:** STAKE, POST

stoc·ca·do \stə-'käd-(,)ō\ *n* [OIt *stoccata*] *archaic* **:** a thrust with a rapier

sto·chas·tic \stō-'kas-tik\ *adj* [Gk *stochastikos* skillful in aiming,

fr. *stochazesthai* to aim at, guess at, fr. *stochos* target, aim, guess — more at STING] **:** RANDOM ⟨~ variable⟩; *specif* **:** involving a variate at each moment of time ⟨~ process⟩

1stock \'stäk\ *n* [ME *stok*, fr. OE *stocc;* akin to OHG *stoc* stick, MIr *tūag* bow] **1 a :** STUMP **b** *archaic* **:** a log or block of wood **c** (1) **:** something without life or consciousness (2) **:** a dull, stupid, or lifeless person **2 :** a supporting framework or structure: as **a** *pl* **:** the frame or timbers holding a ship during construction **b** *pl* **:** a timber frame with holes to contain the feet or feet and hands of an offender undergoing public punishment — compare PILLORY **c** (1) **:** the wooden part by which a rifle or shotgun is held during firing (2) **:** the butt of an implement (as a whip or fishing rod) (3) **:** BITSTOCK, BRACE **d** (1) **:** a long beam on a field gun forming the third support point in firing (2) **:** the beam of a plow to which handles, share, colter, and moldboard are secured **3 a :** the main stem of a plant **:** TRUNK **b** (1) **:** a plant or plant part united with a scion in grafting and supplying mostly underground parts to a graft (2) **:** a plant from which slips or cuttings are taken **4 :** the crosspiece of an anchor **5 a :** the original (as a man, race, or language) from which others derive **:** SOURCE **b** (1) **:** the descendants of one individual **:** FAMILY, LINEAGE (2) **:** a compound organism — compare CLONE **c :** an infraspecific group usu. having unity of descent **d** (1) **:** a related group of languages (2) **:** a language family **6 a** (1) **:** the equipment, materials, or supplies of an establishment (2) **:** LIVESTOCK **b :** a store or supply accumulated; *esp* **:** the inventory of goods of a merchant or manufacturer **7 :** the capital that a firm employs in the conduct of business: as **a** (1) **:** the debt due from a government or private company or corporation to individuals for money loaned at interest and not divided into shares (2) **:** a security representing such a debt or fund — usu. used in pl. **b** (1) **:** the proprietorship element in a corporation divided into shares giving to the owners an interest in its assets and earnings and usu. voting power (2) **:** a share of such stock (3) **:** a security representing such a share **8 :** any of a genus (*Matthiola*) of herbs or subshrubs of the mustard family with racemes of usu. sweet-scented flowers **9 :** a wide band or scarf worn about the neck esp. by some clergymen **10 a :** liquid in which meat, fish, or vegetables are simmered used as a basis for soup, stew, gravy, or sauce **b :** raw material from which something is manufactured **c :** the portion of a pack of cards not distributed to the players at the beginning of a game **11 a** (1) **:** the act of estimating or evaluating (2) **:** the estimation in which someone or something is held **b :** confidence or faith placed in someone or something **12 :** the production and presentation of plays by a stock company

2stock *vt* **1 :** to make (a domestic animal) pregnant **2 :** to fit to or with a stock **3 :** to provide with stock or a stock **:** SUPPLY **4 :** to procure or keep a stock of **5 :** to graze (livestock) on land ~ *vi* **1 :** to send out new shoots **2 :** to put in stock or supplies ⟨~ up on supplies⟩

3stock *adv* **:** COMPLETELY — used in combination ⟨stood *stock*-still⟩

4stock *adj* **1 a :** kept regularly in stock ⟨comes in ~ sizes⟩ ⟨a ~ model⟩ **b :** commonly used or brought forward **:** STANDARD ⟨the ~ answer⟩ **2 a :** kept for breeding purposes **:** BROOD ⟨a ~ mare⟩ **b :** devoted to the breeding and rearing of livestock ⟨~ farm⟩ **c :** used or intended for livestock ⟨~ train⟩ **3 :** of or relating to a stock company

1stock·ade \stä-'kād\ *n* [Sp *estacada*, fr. *estaca* stake, pale, of Gmc origin; akin to OE *staca* stake] **1 :** a line of stout posts set firmly to form a defense **2 a :** an enclosure or pen made with posts and stakes **b :** an enclosure in which prisoners are kept

2stockade *vt* **:** to fortify or surround with a stockade

stock·bro·ker \'stäk-,brō-kər\ *n* **:** one that deals in or executes orders to buy and sell securities — **stock·brok·ing** \-,brō-kiŋ\ *or* **stock·bro·ker·age** \-k(ə-)rij\ *n*

stock car *n* **1 :** an automotive vehicle of a model and type kept in stock for regular sales **2 :** a racing car having the basic chassis of a commercially produced assembly-line model

stock certificate *n* **:** an instrument evidencing ownership of one or more shares of the capital stock of a corporation

stock clerk *n* **:** one that receives and handles merchandise and supplies in a stock room

stock company *n* **1 :** a corporation or joint-stock company of which the capital is represented by stock **2 :** a theatrical company attached to a repertory theater; *esp* **:** one without outstanding stars

stock dividend *n* **1 :** the payment by a corporation of a dividend in the form of additional shares of its own stock **2 :** the stock distributed in a stock dividend

stock exchange *n* **1 :** a place where security trading is conducted on an organized system **2 :** an association of people organized to provide an auction market among themselves for the purchase and sale of securities

stock·fish \'stäk-,fish\ *n* [ME *stokfish*, fr. MD *stocvisch*, fr. *stoc* stick + *visch* fish] **:** fish (as cod, haddock, or hake) dried hard in the open air without salt

stock·hold·er \-,hōl-dər\ *n* **:** an owner of stocks **:** SHAREHOLDER

stock·i·ly \'stäk-ə-lē\ *adv* **:** in a stocky manner ⟨a ~ built man⟩

stock·i·nette *or* **stock·i·net** \,stäk-ə-'net\ *n* [alter. of earlier *stocking net*] **:** a soft elastic usu. cotton fabric used esp. for bandages and infants' wear

stock·ing \'stäk-iŋ\ *n* **1 a :** a usu. knit close-fitting covering for the foot and leg **b :** SOCK **2 :** something resembling a stocking; *esp* **:** a ring of distinctive color on the lower part of the leg of an animal

stocking cap *n* **:** a long knitted cone-shaped cap with a tassel or pompon worn esp. for winter sports or play

stock–in–trade \,stäk-ən-'trād\ *n* **1 :** the equipment necessary to or used in a trade or business **2 :** something held to resemble the standard equipment of a tradesman or business

stock·ish \'stäk-ish\ *adj* **:** like a stock **:** STUPID

stock·job·ber \'stäk-,jäb-ər\ *n* **:** STOCKBROKER; *esp* **:** one held to be unscrupulous or to deal in stocks of doubtful worth — **stock·job·bing** \-,jäb-iŋ\ *n*

stock·man \-mən, -,man\ *n* **:** one occupied as an owner or worker in the raising of livestock (as cattle or sheep)

stock market *n* **1 :** STOCK EXCHANGE 1 **2 a :** a market for particular stocks **b :** the market for stocks throughout a country

stock·pile \'stäk-,pīl\ *n* **:** a storage pile; *specif* **:** a reserve supply of something essential (as processed food or a raw material) accumulated within a country for use during a shortage — **stockpile** *vb*

stock·pot \-,pät\ *n* **1 :** a pot in which soup stock is prepared **2 :** a receptacle containing a mixture of materials

stock·proof \-'prüf\ *adj* **:** proof against livestock

stock·room \-,rüm, -,rům\ *n* **1 :** a storage place for supplies or goods used in a business **2 :** a room (as in a hotel) where commercial travelers may exhibit their goods

stock split *n* **:** a division of corporate stock by the issuance to existing shareholders of a specified number of new shares for each outstanding share

stocky \'stäk-ē\ *adj* **:** compact, sturdy, and relatively thick in build

stock·yard \'stäk-,yärd\ *n* **:** a yard for stock; *specif* **:** one in which cattle, sheep, swine, or horses are kept temporarily for slaughter, market, or shipping

stodge \'stäj\ *vt* [origin unknown] **:** to stuff full esp. with food

stodg·i·ly \'stäj-ə-lē\ *adv* **:** in a stodgy manner

stodg·i·ness \'stäj-ē-nəs\ *n* **:** the quality or state of being stodgy

stodgy \'stäj-ē\ *adj* [*stodge* (thick filling food), fr. *stodge*, v.] **1 :** having a thick gluey consistency **:** HEAVY ⟨~ bread⟩ **2 :** moving in a slow plodding way esp. as a result of physical bulkiness **3 :** lacking lightness or wit **:** DULL, PEDANTIC ⟨a ~ book⟩ **4 :** having no excitement or interest **:** PROSAIC **5 :** extremely old-fashioned **:** HIDEBOUND **6 a :** DRAB **b :** DOWDY

sto·gie *or* **sto·gy** \'stō-gē\ *n* [*Conestoga*, Pa.] **1 :** a stout coarse shoe **:** BROGAN **2 :** an inexpensive slender cylindrical cigar

1sto·ic \'stō-ik\ *n* [ME, fr. L *stoicus*, fr. Gk *stōikos*, lit., of the portico, fr. *Stoa* (*Poikilē*) the Painted Portico, portico at Athens where Zeno taught] **1** *cap* **:** a member of a school of philosophy founded by Zeno of Citium about 300 B.C. holding that the wise man should be free from passion, unmoved by joy or grief, and submissive to natural law **2 :** one apparently or professedly indifferent to pleasure or pain

2stoic *adj* **1** *cap* **:** of, relating to, or resembling the Stoics or their doctrines ⟨*Stoic* logic⟩ **2 :** not affected by passion or feeling; *esp* **:** manifesting indifference to pain **syn** see IMPASSIVE — **sto·ical** \-i-kəl\ *adj* — **sto·ical·ly** \-k(ə-)lē\ *adv*

stoi·chio·met·ric \,stȯi-kē-ō-'me-trik\ *adj* **:** of, relating to, used in, or marked by stoichiometry — **stoi·chio·met·ri·cal·ly** \-trik(ə-)lē\ *adv*

stoi·chi·om·e·try \,stȯi-kē-'äm-ə-trē\ *n* [Gk *stoicheion* element + E *-metry;* akin to Gk *stichos* row, *steichein* to walk, go — more at STAIR] **1 :** a branch of science that deals with the application of the laws of definite proportions and of the conservation of matter and energy to chemical activity **2 :** quantitative chemical properties and composition

sto·icism \'stō-ə-,siz-əm\ *n* **1** *cap* **:** the philosophy of the Stoics **2 :** indifference to pleasure or pain **:** IMPASSIVENESS

stoke \'stōk\ *vb* [D *stoken;* akin to MD *stuken* to push] *vt* **1 :** to stir up or tend (as a fire) **:** supply with fuel **2 :** to feed abundantly ~ *vi* **:** to stir up a fire **:** tend the fires of furnaces **:** supply a furnace with fuel

stoke·hold \-,hōld\ *n* **1 :** one of the spaces in front of the boilers of a ship from which the furnaces are fed **2 :** a room containing a ship's boilers — called also *fireroom*

stoke·hole \-,hōl\ *n* **1 :** the mouth to the grate of a furnace **2 :** STOKEHOLD

stok·er \'stō-kər\ *n* **1 :** one employed to tend a furnace and supply it with fuel; *specif* **:** one that tends a marine steam boiler **2 :** a machine for feeding a fire

stoke·sia \stō-'kē-zh(ē-)ə, 'stōk-sē-ə\ *n* [NL, genus name, fr. Jonathan *Stokes* †1831 E botanist] **:** a perennial composite herb (*Stokesia laevis*) of the southern U.S. often grown for its large showy heads of blue flowers — called also *Stokes' aster* \,stōks-(əz-)\

1stole *past of* STEAL

2stole \'stōl\ *n* [ME, fr. OE, fr. L *stola*, fr. Gk *stolē* equipment, robe, fr. *stellein* to set up, make ready — more at STALL] **1 :** a long loose garment **:** ROBE **2 :** an ecclesiastical vestment consisting of a long narrow band worn around the neck by bishops and priests and over the left shoulder by deacons **3 :** a long wide scarf or similar covering worn by women usu. across the shoulders

stoled \'stōld\ *adj* **:** having or wearing a stole

stolen *past part of* STEAL

stol·id \'stäl-əd\ *adj* [L *stolidus* dull, stupid; akin to OHG *stal* place — more at STALL] **:** having or expressing little or no sensibility **:** not easily aroused or excited **:** UNEMOTIONAL **syn** see IMPASSIVE — **sto·lid·i·ty** \stä-'lid-ət-ē, stə-\ *n* — **stol·id·ly** \'stäl-əd-lē\ *adv*

stol·len \'s(h)tō-lən, 's(h)tȯ-; 'stəl-ə(n)\ *n, pl* **stollen** *or* **stollens** [G] **:** a sweet yeast bread containing fruit and nuts

sto·lon \'stō-lən, -,län\ *n* [NL *stolon-*, *stolo*, fr. L, branch, sucker; akin to Arm *steɫn* branch, OHG *stal* place — more at STALL] **1 :** a horizontal branch from the base of a plant that produces new plants from buds at its tip or nodes (as in the strawberry) — called also *runner* **2 :** an extension of the body wall (as of a hydrozoan) that develops buds giving rise to new zooids which usu. remain united by the stolon — **sto·lon·ate** \-lə-,nāt\ *adj*

sto·lon·if·er·ous \,stō-lə-'nif-(ə-)rəs\ *adj* **:** bearing or developing stolons — **sto·lon·if·er·ous·ly** *adv*

stom- *or* **stomo-** *comb form* [Gk & NL *stoma*] **:** mouth **:** stoma ⟨*stom*odaeum⟩

sto·ma \'stō-mə\ *n, pl* **sto·ma·ta** \-mət-ə\ *also* **stomas** [NL *stomat-*, *stoma*, fr. Gk] **:** any small opening (as in a lower animal or in the epidermis of a plant) like a mouth in form or function

1stom·ach \'stəm-ək, -ik\ *n, often attrib* [ME *stomak*, fr. MF *estomac*, fr. L *stomachus* gullet, esophagus, stomach, fr. Gk *stomachos*, fr. *stoma* mouth; akin to MBret *staffu* mouth, Av *staman-*] **1 a :** a dilatation of the alimentary canal of a vertebrate communicating anteriorly with the esophagus and posteriorly with the duodenum **b :** an analogous cavity in an invertebrate animal **c :** the part of the body that contains the stomach **:** BELLY, ABDOMEN **2 a :** desire for food caused by hunger **:** APPETITE **b :** INCLINATION, DESIRE **3** *obs* **a :** SPIRIT, VALOR **b :** PRIDE **c :** SPLEEN, RESENTMENT

2stomach *vt* **1** *archaic* **:** to take offense at **2 :** to bear without overt reaction or resentment **:** put up with **:** BROOK

stom·ach·ache \-,āk\ *n* **:** pain in or in the region of the stomach

stom·ach·er \'stəm-i-kər, -i-chər\ *n* **:** the center front section of a waist or underwaist or a usu. heavily embroidered or jeweled

separate piece for the center front of a bodice worn by men or women in the 15th and 16th centuries and by women later
sto·mach·ic \stə-'mak-ik\ *adj* **1 :** of or relating to the stomach ⟨~ vessels⟩ **2 :** strengthening or stimulating to the stomach — **stomachic** *n* — **sto·mach·i·cal·ly** \-i-k(ə-)lē\ *adv*
stom·achy \'stəm-ək-ē, -ik-\ *adj* **1** *dial Brit* **:** IRASCIBLE, IRRITABLE **2 :** having a large stomach
sto·mal \'stō-məl\ *adj* **:** STOMATAL
stomat- *or* **stomato-** *comb form* [NL, fr. Gk, fr. *stomat-, stoma*] **:** mouth **:** stoma ⟨*stomat*itis⟩ ⟨*stomato*logy⟩
sto·ma·tal \'stōm-ət-ᵊl, 'stäm-\ *adj* **:** of, relating to, or constituting a stoma ⟨~ openings⟩
sto·mat·ic \stō-'mat-ik\ *adj* **:** relating to or constituting a stoma
sto·ma·ti·tis \ˌstō-mə-'tīt-əs\ *n* [NL] **:** any of numerous inflammatory diseases of the mouth
sto·ma·tol·o·gy \ˌstō-mə-'täl-ə-jē\ *n* [ISV] **:** a branch of medical science dealing with the mouth and its disorders
sto·mato·pod \stō-'mat-ə-ˌpäd\ *n* [NL *Stomatopoda*, order name, fr. *stomat-* + *-poda*] **:** any of an order (Stomatopoda) of marine crustaceans including the squillas and having gills on the abdominal appendages — **stomatopod** *adj*
sto·ma·tous \'stōm-ət-əs, 'stäm-\ *adj* **:** having stomata or a stoma
sto·mo·dae·al *or* **sto·mo·de·al** \ˌstō-mə-'dē-əl\ *adj* **:** of, relating to, or derived from a stomodaeum
sto·mo·dae·um *or* **sto·mo·de·um** \-'dē-əm\ *n, pl* **sto·mo·daea** \-'dē-ə\ *also* **sto·mo·dae·ums** *or* **sto·mo·dea** \-'dē-ə\ *also* **sto·mo·de·ums** [NL, fr. *stom-* + Gk *hodaios* being on the way, fr. *hodos* way — more at CEDE] **:** the anterior ectodermal part of the alimentary canal or tract
¹stomp \'stämp, 'stȯmp\ *vb* **:** STAMP
²stomp *n* **1 :** STAMP 4 **2 :** a jazz dance characterized by heavy stamping
-s·to·my \s-tə-mē\ *n comb form* [ISV, fr. Gk *stoma* mouth, opening] **:** surgical operation establishing a usu. permanent opening into (such) a part ⟨entero*stomy*⟩
¹stone \'stōn\ *n* [ME, fr. OE *stān;* akin to OHG *stein* stone, Gk *stear* hard fat] **1 :** a concretion of earthy or mineral matter: **a** (1) **:** such a concretion of indeterminate size or shape (2) **:** ROCK **b :** a piece of rock for a specified function: as (1) **:** a building block (2) **:** a paving block (3) **:** a precious stone **:** GEM (4) **:** GRAVESTONE (5) **:** GRINDSTONE (6) **:** WHETSTONE (7) **:** a stand or table with a smooth flat top on which to impose or set type (8) **:** a surface upon which a drawing, text, or design to be lithographed is drawn or transferred **c :** CALCULUS 1 **2 :** something resembling a small stone: as **a** *archaic* **:** TESTIS **b** (1) **:** the hard central portion of a drupaceous fruit (as a peach) (2) **:** a hard stony seed (as of a date) **3 :** *pl usu* **stone :** any of various units of weight; *esp* **:** an official British unit equal to 14 pounds
²stone *vt* **1 :** to hurl stones at; *esp* **:** to pelt to death with stones **2** *obs* **:** to make hard or insensitive to feeling **3 :** to face, pave, or fortify with stones **4 :** to remove the stones or seeds of (a fruit) **5 a :** to rub, scour, or polish (as leather, dies, or machined metal) with a stone **b :** to sharpen with a whetstone — **ston·er** *n*
³stone *adj* **:** of, relating to, or made of stone
Stone Age *n* **:** the first known period of prehistoric human culture characterized by the use of stone tools
stone–blind \'stōn-'blīnd\ *adj* **:** totally blind — **stone–blind·ness** \-'blīn(d)-nəs\ *n*
stone–broke \-'brōk\ *adj* **:** completely broke **:** lacking funds
stone·chat \-ˌchat\ *n* **:** a common European singing bird (*Saxicola torquata*); *also* **:** any of various related birds (genus *Saxicola*)
stone·crop \-ˌkräp\ *n* **1 :** SEDUM; *esp* **:** a mossy evergreen creeping sedum (*Sedum acre*) with pungent fleshy leaves **2 :** any of various plants of the orpine family related to the sedums
stone·cut·ter \-ˌkət-ər\ *n* **1 :** one that cuts, carves, or dresses stone **2 :** a machine for dressing stone — **stone·cut·ting** \-ˌkət-iŋ\ *n*
stone–deaf \-'def\ *adj* **:** totally deaf — **stone–deaf·ness** *n*
stone·fish \'stōn-ˌfish\ *n* **:** any of several small spiny venomous scorpion fishes (esp. genus *Synanceja*) common about coral reefs of the tropical Indo-Pacific
stone fly *n* **:** an insect (order Plecoptera) with aquatic gilled carnivorous nymphs and adults used by anglers for bait
stone fruit *n* **:** a fruit with a stony endocarp **:** DRUPE
stone–ground \'stōn-'grau̇nd\ *adj* **:** ground in a buhrstone mill ⟨~ flour⟩
stone lily *n* **:** a fossil crinoid
stone·ma·son \'stōn-ˌmās-ᵊn\ *n* **:** a mason who builds with stone — **stone·ma·son·ry** \-rē\ *n*
stone parsley *n* **:** a slender herb (*Sison amomum*) of the carrot family with aromatic seeds used as a condiment
stone roller *n* **1 :** an American sucker (*Hypentelium nigricans*) **2 :** a common American cyprinid fish (*Campostoma anomalum*)
stone wall *n* **1** *chiefly North* **:** a fence made of stones; *esp* **:** one built of rough stones without mortar to enclose a field **2 :** an immovable block or obstruction (as in public affairs)
stone·wall \'stōn-'wȯl\ *vi, chiefly Brit* **:** to engage in obstructive parliamentary debate or delaying tactics **:** FILIBUSTER — **stone·wall·er** *n*
stone·ware \-ˌwa(ə)r, -ˌwe(ə)r\ *n* **:** an opaque pottery that is high-fired, well vitrified, and nonporous, that may be glazed, unglazed, or salt-glazed, and that is commonly made from a single clay
stone·work \-ˌwərk\ *n* **1 :** a structure or part built of stone **:** MASONRY **2 :** the shaping, preparation, or setting of stone
stone·wort \-ˌwərt, -ˌwȯ(ə)rt\ *n* **:** any of a family (Characeae) of freshwater green algae resembling the horsetails and often encrusted with calcareous deposits
ston·i·ly \'stōn-ᵊl-ē\ *adv* **:** in a stony manner
ston·i·ness \'stō-nē-nəs\ *n* **:** the quality or state of being stony
stony *also* **ston·ey** \'stō-nē\ *adj* **ston·i·er; ston·i·est 1 :** abounding in or having the nature of stone **:** ROCKY **2 a :** insensitive to pity or human feeling **:** HARDHEARTED, OBDURATE **b :** manifesting no movement or reaction **:** DUMB, EXPRESSIONLESS **c :** PETRIFYING **3** *archaic* **:** consisting of or made of stones **4 :** STONE-BROKE
stony·heart·ed \ˌstō-nē-'härt-əd\ *adj* **:** UNFEELING, CRUEL — **stony·heart·ed·ness** *n*
stood *past of* STAND
¹stooge \'stüj\ *n* [origin unknown] **1 :** an actor who carries on repartee that allows a principal comedian to make humorous sallies **:** STRAIGHT MAN **2 a :** one who plays a subordinate or compliant role to a principal **b :** PUPPET 4a **3 :** STOOL PIGEON
²stooge *vi* **:** to act as a stooge
¹stool \'stül\ *n* [ME, fr. OE *stōl;* akin to OHG *stuol* chair, OSlav *stolŭ* seat, throne, OE *standan* to stand] **1 a :** a seat without back or arms supported by three or four legs or by a central pedestal **b :** a low bench or portable support for the feet or knees **:** FOOTSTOOL **2 :** a seat used as a symbol of office or authority; *also* **:** CHIEFTAINCY **3 a :** a seat used while defecating or urinating **b :** a discharge of fecal matter **4 a :** a stump or group of stumps of a tree esp. when producing suckers **b :** a plant crown from which shoots grow out **c :** a shoot or growth from a stool
²stool *vi* **:** to throw out shoots in the manner of a stool
stool·ie \'stü-lē\ *n* **:** STOOL PIGEON
stool pigeon *n* [prob. fr. the early practice of fastening the decoy bird to a stool] **1 :** a pigeon used as a decoy to draw others within a net **2 :** a person acting as a decoy or informer; *esp* **:** a spy sent into a group to report (as to the police) on its activities
¹stoop \'stüp\ *vb* [ME *stoupen*, fr. OE *stūpian;* akin to OE *stēap* steep, deep — more at STEEP] *vi* **1 a :** to bend the body forward and downward sometimes simultaneously bending the knees **b :** to stand or walk with a temporary or habitual forward inclination of the head, body, or shoulders **2 :** YIELD, SUBMIT **3 a :** to descend from a superior rank, dignity, or status **b :** to lower oneself morally **4 a** *archaic* **:** to move down from a height **:** ALIGHT **b :** to fly or dive down swiftly usu. to attack prey **~** *vt* **1 :** DEBASE, DEGRADE **2 :** to bend (a part of the body) forward and downward
syn STOOP, CONDESCEND, DEIGN mean to descend from one's level to do something. STOOP may imply a descent in dignity or from a relatively high moral plane to a much lower one; CONDESCEND implies a stooping by one of high rank or position to accommodate himself to intercourse with his social inferiors; DEIGN suggests a reluctant condescension of one in a haughty mood; CONDESCEND and DEIGN are applied chiefly in irony or mild derision
²stoop *n* **1 a :** an act of bending the body forward **b :** a temporary or habitual forward bend of the back and shoulders **2 :** the descent of a bird esp. on its prey **3 :** a lowering of oneself **:** CONDESCENSION, CONCESSION
³stoop *n* [D *stoep;* akin to OE *stæpe* step — more at STEP] **:** a porch, platform, entrance stairway, or small veranda at a house door
¹stop \'stäp\ *vb* **stopped; stop·ping** [ME *stoppen*, fr. OE *-stoppian;* akin to OHG *stopfōn* to stop, stuff; both fr. a prehistoric WGmc word borrowed fr. (assumed) VL *stuppare* to stop with tow, fr. L *stuppa* tow, fr. Gk *styppē*] *vt* **1 a :** to close by filling or obstructing **b :** to hinder or prevent the passage of **2 a :** to close up or block off (an opening) **:** PLUG **b :** to make impassable **:** CHOKE, OBSTRUCT **c :** to cover over or fill in (a hole or crevice) **3 a :** to cause to give up or change a course of action **b :** to hold back **:** RESTRAIN, PREVENT **4 a :** to cause to cease **:** CHECK, SUPPRESS **b :** DISCONTINUE **5 a :** to deduct or withhold (a sum due) **b :** to instruct one's bank not to honor or pay **6 a :** to arrest the progress or motion of **:** cause to halt **:** INTERCEPT **b :** PARRY **c :** to check by means of a weapon **:** bring down **:** KILL **d :** to beat in a prizefight by a knockout; *broadly* **:** DEFEAT **e :** BAFFLE, NONPLUS **7 :** to regulate the pitch of (as a violin string) by pressing with the finger or (as a wind instrument) by closing one or more finger holes or by thrusting the hand or a mute into the bell **8 :** to hold an honor card and enough protecting cards to be able to block (a bridge suit) before an opponent can run off many tricks **~** *vi* **1 a :** to cease activity or operation **b :** to come to an end esp. suddenly **:** CLOSE, FINISH **2 a :** to cease to move on **:** HALT **b :** PAUSE, HESITATE **3 a :** to break one's journey **:** STAY **b** *chiefly Brit* **:** REMAIN **c :** to make a brief call **:** drop in **4 :** to become choked **:** CLOG
syn CEASE, QUIT, DISCONTINUE, DESIST: STOP applies primarily to a suspending or interfering with what is moving, operating, or progressing; CEASE applies to what is thought of as having existence and may add an implication of gradualness; QUIT may suggest either finality or abruptness in stopping or ceasing; DISCONTINUE applies to the stopping of an accustomed activity or practice; DESIST implies forbearance or restraint as the motive for stopping
²stop *n* **1 a :** CESSATION, END **b :** a pause or breaking off in speech **2 a** (1) **:** a graduated set of organ pipes of like kind and tone quality (2) **:** a corresponding set of vibrators or reeds of a reed organ (3) **:** STOP KNOB **b :** a means of regulating the pitch of a musical instrument **3 a :** something that impedes, obstructs, or brings to a halt **:** IMPEDIMENT, OBSTACLE **b :** the aperture of a camera lens; *also* **:** a marking of a series (as of f-numbers) on a camera for indicating settings of the diaphragm **c :** a drain plug **:** STOPPER **4 :** a device for arresting or limiting motion **5 :** the act of stopping **:** the state of being stopped **:** CHECK **6 a :** a halt in a journey **:** STAY **b :** a stopping place **7 a** *chiefly Brit* **:** any of several punctuation marks **b** — used in telegrams and cables to indicate a period **c :** a pause or break in a verse that marks the end of a grammatical unit **8 a :** an order stopping payment (as of a check or note) by a bank **b :** STOP ORDER **9 :** a consonant in the articulation of which there is a stage (as in the *p* of *apt* or the *g* of *tiger*) when the breath passage is completely closed **10 :** a depression in the face of an animal at the junction of forehead and foreface
³stop *adj* **:** serving to stop **:** designed to stop ⟨~ line⟩ ⟨~ signal⟩ ⟨~ valve⟩
stop bath *n* **:** SHORT-STOP
stop·cock \-ˌkäk\ *n* **:** a cock for stopping or regulating flow (as through a pipe)

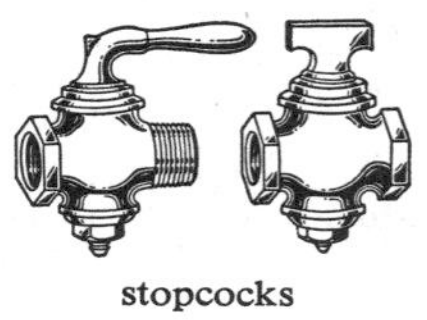

stopcocks

stop down *vt* **:** to reduce the effective aperture of (a lens) by means of a diaphragm
¹stope \'stōp\ *n* [prob. fr. LG *stope*, lit., step; akin to OE *stæpe* step — more at STEP] **:** a usu. steplike excavation underground for the removal of ore
²stope *vi* **:** to mine by means of a stope **~** *vt* **:** to extract (ore) from a stope
stop·gap \'stäp-ˌgap\ *n* **:** something that serves as a temporary expedient **:** MAKESHIFT
stop knob *n* **:** one of the handles by which an organist draws or shuts off a particular stop
stop·light \'stäp-ˌlīt\ *n* **1 :** a light on the rear of a motor vehicle that is illuminated when the driver presses the brake pedal **2 :** TRAFFIC SIGNAL

stop order *or* **stop–loss order** \'stäp-,lȯs-\ *n* **:** an order to a broker to buy or sell at the market when the price of a security advances or declines to a designated level

stop·over \'stäp-,ō-vər\ *n* **1 :** a stop at an intermediate point in one's journey **2 :** a stopping place on a journey

stop·page \'stäp-ij\ *n* **:** the act of stopping **:** the state of being stopped **:** HALT, OBSTRUCTION

stop payment *n* **:** a depositor's order to a bank to refuse to honor a specified check drawn by him

1stop·per \'stäp-ər\ *n* **1 :** one that brings to a halt or causes to stop operating or functioning **:** CHECK **2 :** one that closes, shuts, or fills up; *specif* **:** something (as a bung or cork) used to plug an opening

2stopper *vt* **stop·per·ing** \-(ə-)riŋ\ **:** to close or secure with or as if with a stopper

stopper knot *n* **:** a knot used to prevent a rope from passing through a hole or opening

1stop·ple \'stäp-əl\ *n* [ME *stoppell,* fr. *stoppen* to stop] **:** something that closes an aperture **:** STOPPER, PLUG

2stopple *vt* **stop·pling** \-(ə-)liŋ\ **:** to close the mouth of with or as if with a stopple **:** STOPPER

stop street *n* **:** a street on which a vehicle must stop just before entering a through street

stop·watch \'stäp-,wäch\ *n* **:** a watch having a hand that can be started or stopped at will for exact timing (as of a race)

stor·able \'stōr-ə-bəl, 'stȯr-\ *adj* **:** that may be stored ⟨~ commodities⟩ — **storable** *n*

stor·age \'stōr-ij, 'stȯr-\ *n, often attrib* **1 a :** space or a place for storing **b :** an amount stored **2 a :** the act of storing **:** the state of being stored; *specif* **:** the safekeeping of goods in a warehouse or other depository **b :** the price charged for keeping goods in a storehouse **3 :** the production by means of electric energy of chemical reactions that when allowed to reverse themselves generate electricity again without serious loss

storage cell *n* **:** a cell or connected group of cells that converts chemical energy into electrical energy by reversible chemical reactions and that may be recharged by passing a current through it in the direction opposite to that of its discharge — called also *storage battery*

sto·rax \'stō(ə)r-,aks, 'stȯ(ə)r-\ *n* [ME, fr. LL, alter. of L *styrax,* fr. Gk] **1 :** a resin from trees (genus *Styrax,* esp. *S. officinalis*) formerly used for incense **2 :** a fragrant balsam from trees (genus *Liquidambar,* esp. the Asiatic *L. orientalis*) of the witch-hazel family **3 :** any of a genus (*Styrax* of the family Styracaceae, the storax family) of trees or shrubs with usu. hairy leaves and flowers in drooping racemes — compare BENZOIN

1store \'stō(ə)r, 'stȯ(ə)r\ *vt* [ME *storen,* fr. OF *estorer* to construct, restore, store, fr. L *instaurare* to renew, restore, fr. *in-* + *-staurare* (akin to Gk *stauros* stake) — more at STEER] **1 :** FURNISH, SUPPLY; *esp* **:** to stock against a future time ⟨~ a ship with provisions⟩ **2 :** to lay away **:** ACCUMULATE ⟨~ vegetables for winter use⟩ **3 :** to leave or deposit in a place (as a warehouse) for preservation or disposal **4 :** to provide storage room for **:** HOLD

2store *n* **1 a :** something that is stored or kept for future use **b** *pl* **:** articles (as of food) accumulated for some specific object and drawn upon as needed **:** STOCK, SUPPLIES **c :** something that is accumulated **:** a source from which things may be drawn as needed **:** a reserve fund **2 :** STORAGE **3 :** something that is highly valued or greatly relied upon **:** TREASURE ⟨set great ~ by tradition⟩ **4 :** a large quantity, supply, or number **:** ABUNDANCE **5 :** STOREHOUSE, WAREHOUSE **6 :** a business establishment where usu. diversified goods are kept for retail sale ⟨grocery ~⟩ ⟨furniture ~⟩ — compare SHOP — **in store :** in a state of accumulation **:** in readiness for use

3store *adj* **1** *or* **stores :** of, relating to, kept in, or used for a store ⟨~ barge⟩ **2 :** purchased from a store as opposed to natural or homemade **:** MANUFACTURED, READY-MADE ⟨~ clothes⟩ ⟨~ bread⟩ ⟨~ teeth⟩

store·house \'stō(ə)r-,hau̇s, 'stȯ(ə)r-\ *n* **1 :** a building for storing goods (as provisions) **:** MAGAZINE, WAREHOUSE **2 :** an abundant supply or source **:** REPOSITORY

store·keep·er \-,kē-pər\ *n* **1 :** one that has charge of supplies (as military stores) **2 :** one that operates a retail store

store·room \-,rüm, -,ru̇m\ *n* **1 :** a room or space for the storing of goods or supplies **2 :** STOREHOUSE 2

store·wide \-'wīd\ *adj* **:** including all or most merchandise in a store ⟨a ~ sale⟩

1sto·ried \'stōr-ēd, 'stȯr-\ *adj* **1 :** decorated with designs representing scenes from story or history ⟨a ~ frieze⟩ ⟨a ~ tapestry⟩ **2 :** having an interesting history **:** celebrated in story or history ⟨a ~ castle⟩

2storied *or* **sto·reyed** *adj* **:** having stories ⟨a two-*storied* house⟩

stork \'stȯ(ə)rk\ *n* [ME, fr. OE *storc;* akin to OHG *storah* stork, OE *stearc* stiff — more at STARK] **:** any of various large mostly Old World wading birds (family Ciconiidae) with long stout bills that are related to the ibises and herons

stork's–bill \'stȯ(ə)rks-,bil\ *n* **:** any of several plants of the geranium family with elongate beaked fruits; *esp* **:** PELARGONIUM

1storm \'stȯ(ə)rm\ *n, often attrib* [ME, fr. OE; akin to OHG *sturm* storm, OE *styrian* to stir] **1 a :** a disturbance of the atmosphere attended by wind and usu. by rain, snow, hail, sleet, or thunder and lightning **b :** a heavy fall of rain, snow, or hail **c :** wind having a speed of 64 to 72 miles per hour **d :** a serious disturbance of any element of nature **2 :** a disturbed or agitated state **:** a sudden or violent commotion **3 a :** PAROXYSM, CRISIS **b :** a sudden heavy influx or onset **4 :** a heavy discharge of objects (as missiles) or actions (as blows) **5 :** a tumultuous outburst **6 :** a violent assault on a defended position

2storm *vi* **1 a :** to blow with violence **b :** to rain, hail, snow, or sleet **2 :** to attack by storm ⟨~*ed* ashore at zero hour⟩ **3 :** to be in or to exhibit a violent passion **:** RAGE ⟨~*ing* at the unusual delay⟩ **4 :** to rush about or move impetuously, violently, or angrily ⟨the mob ~*ed* through the streets⟩ ~ *vt* **:** to attack, take, or win over by storm ⟨~ a fort⟩ **syn** see ATTACK

storm and stress *n, often cap both Ss* **:** STURM UND DRANG

storm boat *n* **:** a light fast craft used to transport attacking troops across streams

storm·bound \'stȯ(ə)rm-,bau̇nd\ *adj* **:** cut off from outside communication by a storm or its effects **:** stopped or delayed by storms ⟨~ ports⟩ ⟨~ travelers⟩

storm door *n* **:** an additional door placed outside an ordinary outside door for protection against severe weather

storm·i·ly \'stȯr-mə-lē\ *adv* **:** in a stormy manner

storm·i·ness \-mē-nəs\ *n* **:** the quality or state of being stormy

storm petrel *n* **:** any of various small petrels; *esp* **:** a small sooty black white-marked petrel (*Hydrobates pelagicus*) frequenting the north Atlantic and Mediterranean — called also *stormy petrel*

storm trooper *n* **1 :** a member of a private Nazi army notorious for aggressiveness, violence, and brutality **2 :** one held to resemble a Nazi storm trooper

storm window *n* **:** a sash placed outside an ordinary window as a protection against severe weather — called also *storm sash*

stormy \'stȯr-mē\ *adj* **1 :** relating to, characterized by, or indicative of a storm **:** TEMPESTUOUS ⟨a ~ day⟩ ⟨a ~ autumn⟩ **2 :** marked by turmoil or fury **:** PASSIONATE, TURBULENT ⟨a ~ life⟩ ⟨a ~ conference⟩

stormy petrel *n* **1 :** STORM PETREL **2 :** one fond of strife **:** a harbinger of trouble

1sto·ry \'stōr-ē, 'stȯr-\ *n* [ME *storie,* fr. OF *estorie,* fr. L *historia*] **1** *archaic* **:** HISTORY 1,3 **2 a :** an account of incidents or events **b :** a statement regarding the facts pertinent to a situation in question **c :** ANECDOTE; *esp* **:** an amusing one **3 a :** a fictional narrative shorter than a novel; *specif* **:** SHORT STORY **b :** the intrigue or plot of a narrative or dramatic work **4 :** a widely circulated rumor **5 :** LIE, FALSEHOOD **6 :** LEGEND, ROMANCE **7 :** a news article or broadcast — **sto·ry·writ·er** \-,rīt-ər\ *n*

2story *vt* **1** *archaic* **:** to narrate or describe in story **2 :** to adorn with a story or a scene from history

3story *or* **sto·rey** *n* [ME *storie,* fr. ML *historia* picture, story of a building, fr. L, history, tale; prob. fr. pictures adorning the windows of medieval buildings] **1 :** a set of rooms on one floor level of a building **2 :** a horizontal division of a building's exterior not necessarily corresponding exactly with the stories within

sto·ry·book \-,bu̇k\ *n* **:** a book of stories ⟨~*s* for children⟩

sto·ry·tell·er \-,tel-ər\ *n* **:** a teller of stories — **sto·ry·tell·ing** \-,tel-iŋ\ *adj or n*

stoss \'stäs, 's(h)tōs\ *adj* [G *stoss-,* fr. *stossen* to push; akin to L *tundere* to beat — more at STINT] **:** facing toward the direction from which an overriding glacier impinges ⟨the ~ slope of a hill⟩

sto·tin·ka \stō-'tiŋ-kə\ *n, pl* **sto·tin·ki** \-kē\ [Bulg] — see LEV at MONEY table

stound \'stau̇nd, 'stünd\ *n* [ME, fr. OE *stund;* akin to OHG *stunta* time, hour, OE *standan* to stand] *archaic* **:** TIME, WHILE

stoup \'stüp\ *n* [ME *stowp,* prob. of Scand origin; akin to ON *staup* cup — more at STEEP] **1 :** a container for beverages: as **a :** a large glass **b :** TANKARD **c :** FLAGON **2 :** a basin at the entrance of a Roman Catholic church for holy water

1stour \'stu̇(ə)r\ *adj* [ME *stor,* fr. OE *stōr;* akin to OHG *stuori* large, Russ *staryĭ* old, OE *standan* to stand] **1** *chiefly Scot* **:** STRONG, HARDY **2** *chiefly Scot* **:** STERN, HARSH

2stour *n* [ME, fr. OF *estour,* of Gmc origin; akin to OHG *sturm* storm, battle] **1 a** *archaic* **:** BATTLE, CONFLICT **b** *dial Brit* **:** TUMULT, UPROAR **2** *chiefly Scot* **:** DUST, POWDER

1stout \'stau̇t\ *adj* [ME, fr. OF *estout,* of Gmc origin; akin to OHG *stolz* proud] **1 :** strong of character: as **a :** BRAVE, BOLD **b :** FIRM, DETERMINED; *also* **:** OBSTINATE, UNCOMPROMISING **2 :** physically or materially strong: **a :** STURDY, VIGOROUS **b :** STAUNCH, ENDURING **c :** SOLID, SUBSTANTIAL **3 :** FORCEFUL ⟨a ~ attack⟩; *also* **:** VIOLENT ⟨a ~ wind⟩ **4 :** bulky in body **:** THICKSET **syn** see STRONG — **stout·ly** *adv* — **stout·ness** *n*

2stout *n* **1 :** a heavy-bodied brew that is darker and sweeter than porter and is made with roasted malt and a relatively high percentage of hops **2 a :** a fat person **b :** a clothing size designed for the large figure

stout·en \'stau̇t-ᵊn\ *vb* **stout·en·ing** \'stau̇t-niŋ, -ᵊn-iŋ\ *vt* **:** to make stout ⟨~ a resolve⟩ ~ *vi* **:** to become stout ⟨she's ~*ed* lately⟩

stout·heart·ed \'stau̇t-'härt-əd\ *adj* **:** having a stout heart or spirit: **a :** COURAGEOUS **b :** STUBBORN — **stout·heart·ed·ly** *adv* — **stout·heart·ed·ness** *n*

stout·ish \'stau̇t-ish\ *adj* **:** somewhat stout

1stove \'stōv\ *n, often attrib* [ME, fr. MD or MLG, heated room, steam room; akin to OHG *stuba* heated room, steam room; both fr. a prehistoric WGmc-NGmc word borrowed fr. (assumed) VL *extufa,* deriv. of L *ex-* + Gk *typhein* to smoke — more at DEAF] **1 a :** a portable or fixed apparatus that burns fuel or uses electricity to provide heat (as for cooking or heating) **b :** a device that generates heat for special purposes (as for heating tools or heating air for a hot blast) **c :** KILN **2** *chiefly Brit* **:** a hothouse esp. for the cultivation of tropical exotics; *broadly* **:** GREENHOUSE

2stove *past of* STAVE

stove·pipe \'stōv-,pīp\ *n* **1 :** pipe of large diameter usu. of sheet steel used as a stove chimney or to connect a stove with a flue **2 :** a very tall silk hat

sto·ver \'stō-vər\ *n* [ME, modif. of AF *estovers* necessary supplies, fr. OF *estoveir* to be necessary, fr. L *est opus* there is need] **1** *chiefly dial Eng* **:** FODDER **2 :** mature cured stalks of grain from which the ears have been removed used as feed for livestock

stow \'stō\ *vt* [ME *stowen* to place, fr. *stowe* place, fr. OE *stōw;* akin to OFris *stō* place, Gk *stylos* pillar — more at STEER] **1 :** HOUSE, LODGE **2 a :** to put away **:** STORE **b** *obs* **:** to lock up for safekeeping **:** CONFINE **3 a :** to dispose in an orderly fashion **:** ARRANGE, PACK **b :** LOAD **4** *slang* **:** to put aside **:** STOP **5 a** *archaic* **:** CROWD **b :** to cram in (food)

stow·age \-ij\ *n* **1 a :** an act or process of stowing **b :** goods in storage or to be stowed **2 a :** storage capacity **b :** a place or receptacle for storage **3 :** STORAGE

stow away *vi* **:** to secrete oneself aboard a vehicle as a means of obtaining transportation

stow·away \'stō-ə-,wā\ *n* **:** an unregistered passenger **:** one who stows away

stra·bis·mic \strə-'biz-mik\ *adj* **:** of, relating to, or affected with strabismus

stra·bis·mus \-məs\ *n* [NL, fr. Gk *strabismos* condition of squinting, fr. *strabizein* to squint, fr. *strabos* squint-eyed; akin to Gk *strephein* to twist — more at STROPHE] **:** inability of one eye to attain

ə abut; ᵊ kitten; ər further; a back; ā bake; ä cot, cart; au̇ out; ch chin; e less; ē easy; g gift; i trip; ī life
j joke; ŋ sing; ō flow; ȯ flaw; ȯi coin; th thin; t͟h this; ü loot; u̇ foot; y yet; yü few; yu̇ furious; zh vision

binocular vision with the other because of imbalance of the muscles of the eyeball — called also *squint*

1strad·dle \'strad-ᵊl\ *vb* **strad·dling** \'strad-liŋ, -ᵊl-iŋ\ [irreg. fr. *stride*] *vi* **1 :** to part the legs wide **:** stand, sit, or walk with the legs wide apart; *esp* **:** to sit astride **2 :** to spread out irregularly **:** SPRAWL **3 :** to be noncommittal **:** favor or seem to favor two apparently opposite sides **4 :** to buy in one market and sell short in another ~ *vt* **1 :** to stand, sit, or be astride of **2 :** to be noncommittal in regard to ⟨~ an issue⟩ — **strad·dler** \-lər, -ᵊl-ər\ *n*

2straddle *n* **1 :** the act or position of one who straddles **2 :** a noncommittal or equivocal position **3 a :** an option giving the holder the double privilege of a put and a call **b :** the state of being long in one market and short in another

strafe \'strāf, *esp Brit* 'sträf\ *vt* [G *Gott strafe England* God punish England, slogan of the Germans in World War I] **:** to rake (as ground troops) with fire at close range and esp. with machine-gun fire from low-flying aircraft — **strafe** *n* — **straf·er** *n*

1strag·gle \'strag-əl\ *vi* **strag·gling** \-(ə-)liŋ\ [ME *straglen*] **1 :** to wander from the direct course or way **:** ROVE, STRAY **2 :** to trail off from others of its kind **:** spread out irregularly or scatteringly — **strag·gler** \-(ə-)lər\ *n*

2straggle *n* **:** a straggling body or arrangement (as of persons or objects)

strag·gly \-(ə-)lē\ *adj* **:** spread out or scattered irregularly **:** STRAGGLING

1straight \'strāt\ *adj* [ME *streght, straight,* fr. pp. of *strecchen* to stretch] **1 a :** free from curves, bends, angles, or irregularities ⟨~ hair⟩ ⟨~ timber⟩ ⟨~ stream⟩ **b :** generated by a point moving continuously in the same direction and expressed by a linear equation ⟨~ line⟩ ⟨~ segment of a curve⟩ **2 :** DIRECT, UNINTERRUPTED: as **a :** lying along or holding to a direct or proper course or method ⟨the ~*er* path there⟩ ⟨~ thinker⟩ **b :** CANDID, FRANK ⟨~ speech⟩ ⟨a ~ answer⟩ **c :** coming directly from a trustworthy source ⟨a ~ tip on the horses⟩ **d :** having the elements in an order ⟨the ~ sequence of events⟩ **e :** having the cylinders arranged in a single straight line ⟨a ~ eight-cylinder engine⟩ **f :** UPRIGHT, VERTICAL **3 a :** JUST, VIRTUOUS ⟨~ dealing⟩ **b :** properly ordered or arranged ⟨set the kitchen ~⟩ **c :** free from extraneous matter **:** UNMIXED ⟨writes ~ humor⟩ **d :** marked by no exceptions or deviations in one's support of a principle or party ⟨a ~ Republican⟩ ⟨a ~ ballot⟩ **e :** having a fixed price for each regardless of the number sold ⟨cigars 10 cents ~⟩ **f :** not deviating from the general norm or prescribed pattern ⟨a ~ part⟩ — **straight·ly** *adv* — **straight·ness** *n*

2straight *adv* **:** in a straight manner

3straight *vt, chiefly Scot* **:** STRAIGHTEN

4straight *n* **1 :** something that is straight: as **a :** a straight line or arrangement **b :** STRAIGHTAWAY; *esp* **:** HOMESTRETCH **c :** a true or honest report or course **2 a :** a sequence (as of shots, strokes, or moves) resulting in a perfect score in a game or contest **b :** first place at the finish of a horse race **:** WIN — compare PLACE, SHOW **3 :** a combination of five cards in sequence in a poker hand

straight angle *n* **:** an angle whose sides lie in opposite directions from the vertex in the same straight line and that equals two right angles

straight–arm \'strāt-,ärm\ *vt* **:** to ward off (an opponent) with the arm held straight — **straight–arm** *n*

1straight·away \'strāt-ə-,wā\ *adj* **1 :** proceeding in a straight line **:** continuous in direction **:** STRAIGHTFORWARD **2 :** IMMEDIATE

2straightaway *n* **:** a straight course: as **a :** the straight part of a closed racecourse **:** STRETCH **b :** a straight and unimpeded stretch of road or way

3straight·away \,strāt-ə-'wā\ *adv* **:** without hesitation or delay **:** IMMEDIATELY

straight chain *n* **:** an open chain of atoms having no side chains

straight·edge \'strāt-,ej\ *n* **:** a bar or piece of wood, metal, or plastic with a straight edge for testing straight lines and surfaces or drawing straight lines

straight·en \'strāt-ᵊn\ *vb* **straight·en·ing** \'strāt-niŋ, -ᵊn-iŋ\ **:** to make or become straight — **straight·en·er** \-nər, -ᵊn-ər\ *n*

straight face *n* **:** a face giving no evidence of emotion and esp. of merriment — **straight–faced** \'strāt-'fāst\ *adj*

1straight·for·ward \(')strāt-'fȯr-wərd\ *also* **straight·for·wards** \-wərdz\ *adv* **:** in a straightforward manner

2straightforward *adj* **1 :** proceeding in a straight course or manner **:** DIRECT, UNDEVIATING **2 a :** OUTSPOKEN, CANDID **b :** CLEAR-CUT, PRECISE — **straight·for·ward·ly** *adv* — **straight·for·ward·ness** *n*

straight·ish \'strāt-ish\ *adj* **:** somewhat straight

straight–line \,strāt-,līn\ *adj* **1 :** being a mechanical linkage or equivalent device designed to produce or copy motion in a straight line **2 :** having the principal parts arranged in a straight line ⟨a ~ compressor having the steam and air cylinders in a straight line⟩ **3 :** marked by a uniform spread and esp. in equal segments over a given term ⟨~ amortization⟩ ⟨~ depreciation⟩

straight man *n* **:** an entertainer who feeds lines to a comedian

straight off *adv* **:** IMMEDIATELY

straight–out \'strāt-,au̇t\ *adj* **1 :** FORTHRIGHT, BLUNT **2 :** OUTRIGHT, THOROUGHGOING

straight razor *n* **:** a razor with a rigid steel cutting blade hinged to a case that forms a handle when the razor is open for use

straight ticket *n* **:** a ballot cast for all the candidates of one party

1straight·way \'strāt-'wā, -,wā\ *adv* **1 :** in a direct course **:** DIRECTLY **2 :** IMMEDIATELY, FORTHWITH

2straight·way \-,wā\ *adj* **:** having or affording a straight way

1strain \'strān\ *n* [ME *streen* progeny, lineage, fr. OE *strēon* gain, acquisition; akin to OHG *gistriuni* gain, L *struere* to heap up — more at STRUCTURE] **1 a :** LINEAGE, ANCESTRY **b :** a group of presumed common ancestry with clear-cut physiological but usu. not morphological distinctions ⟨a high-yielding ~ of winter wheat⟩; *broadly* **:** a specified infraspecific group (as a stock, line, or ecotype) **c :** KIND, SORT **2 a :** inherited or inherent character, quality, or disposition ⟨a ~ of madness in the family⟩ **b :** TRACE, STREAK ⟨a ~ of fanaticism⟩ **3 a :** TUNE, AIR **b :** a passage of verbal or musical expression **c :** a stream or outburst of forceful or impassioned speech **4 a :** the tenor, pervading note, burden, or tone of an utterance (as a song or speech) or of a course of action or conduct **b :** MOOD, TEMPER

2strain *vb* [ME *strainen,* fr. MF *estraindre,* fr. L *stringere* to bind or draw tight, press together; akin to Gk *strang-, stranx* drop squeezed out, *strangalē* halter] *vt* **1 a :** to draw tight **:** cause to clasp firmly **b :** to stretch to maximum extension and tautness **2 a :** to exert (as oneself) to the utmost **b :** to injure by overuse, misuse, or excessive pressure ⟨~*ed* his heart by overwork⟩ **c :** to cause a change of form or size in (a body) by application of external force **3 :** to squeeze or clasp tightly: as **a :** HUG **b :** CONSTRICT **4 a :** FILTER **b :** to remove by straining ⟨~ lumps out of the gravy⟩ **5 :** to stretch beyond a proper limit **6** *obs* **:** to squeeze out **:** EXTORT ~ *vi* **1 a :** to make violent efforts **:** STRIVE **b :** to sustain a strain, wrench, or distortion **2 :** to pass through or as if through a strainer ⟨the liquid ~*s* readily⟩ **3 :** to make great difficulty or resistance **:** BALK

3strain *n* **1 :** an act of straining or the condition of being strained: as **a :** excessive physical or mental tension **b :** excessive or difficult exertion or labor **c :** bodily injury from excessive tension, effort, or use ⟨heart ~⟩; *esp* **:** one resulting from a wrench or twist and involving undue stretching of muscles or ligaments ⟨back ~⟩ **d :** deformation of a material body under the action of applied forces **2 :** an unusual reach, degree, or intensity **:** PITCH **3** *archaic* **:** a strained interpretation of something said or written

strain·er \'strā-nər\ *n* **:** one that strains: as **a :** a device (as a screen, sieve, or filter) to retain solid pieces while a liquid passes through **b :** any of various devices for stretching or tightening something

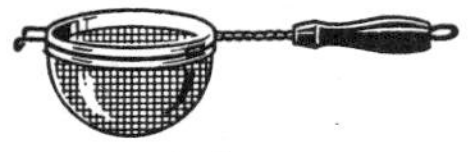

strainer a

strain·om·e·ter \strā-'näm-ət-ər\ *n* **:** EXTENSOMETER

1strait \'strāt\ *adj* [ME, fr. OF *estreit,* fr. L *strictus* strait, strict — more at STRICT] **1** *archaic* **a :** NARROW **b :** RESTRICTED **c :** closely fitting **:** CONSTRICTED, TIGHT **2** *archaic* **:** STRICT, RIGOROUS **3 a :** DISTRESSFUL, DIFFICULT **b :** LIMITED, STRAITENED — **strait·ly** *adv* — **strait·ness** *n*

2strait *adv, obs* **:** CLOSELY, TIGHTLY

3strait *n* **1 a** *archaic* **:** a narrow space or passage **b :** a comparatively narrow passageway connecting two large bodies of water — often used in pl. but sing. in constr. **c :** ISTHMUS **2 :** a situation of perplexity or distress **:** DIFFICULTY, NEED — often used in pl.
syn see JUNCTURE

strait·en \'strāt-ᵊn\ *vt* **strait·en·ing** \'strāt-niŋ, -ᵊn-iŋ\ **1 a :** to make strait or narrow **b :** to hem in **:** squeeze together **:** CONFINE **2** *archaic* **:** to restrict in freedom or scope **:** HAMPER **3 :** to subject to distress, privation, or deficiency ⟨found himself in ~*ed* circumstances⟩

1strait·jack·et *or* **straight·jack·et** \'strāt-,jak-ət\ *n* **1 :** a cover or overgarment of strong material (as canvas) used to bind the body and esp. the arms closely in restraining a violent prisoner or patient **2 :** something that restricts or confines like a straitjacket

2straitjacket *or* **straightjacket** *vt* **:** to confine in or as if in a straitjacket

strait·laced *or* **straight·laced** \'strāt-'lāst\ *adj* **1 :** wearing or having a bodice or stays tightly laced **2 :** excessively strict in manners, morals, or opinion — **strait·laced·ly** \-'lāst-lē, -'lā-səd-lē\ *adv* — **strait·laced·ness** \-'lās(t)-nəs, -'lā-səd-nəs\ *n*

Straits dollar \'strāts-\ *n* [*Straits* Settlements, former British crown colony] **:** a dollar formerly issued by British Malaya and used in much of southern and eastern Asia and the East Indies

strake \'strāk\ *n* [ME; akin to OE *streccan* to stretch — more at STRETCH] **1 :** a continuous band of hull planking or plates on a ship; *also* **:** the width of such a band **2 :** STREAK, STRIPE

stram·ash \'stram-ish\ *n* [prob. imit.] *chiefly Scot* **1 :** DISTURBANCE, RACKET **2 :** CRASH, SMASHUP

stra·mo·ni·um \strə-'mō-nē-əm\ *n* [NL] **1 :** THORN APPLE 2 **2 :** the dried leaves of the thorn apple used in medicine similarly to belladonna esp. in asthma

1strand \'strand\ *n* [ME, fr. OE; akin to ON *strönd* strand, L *sternere* to spread out — more at STREW] **:** the land bordering a body of water **:** SHORE, BEACH

2strand *vt* **1 :** to run, drive, or cause to drift onto a strand **:** run aground **:** BEACH **2 :** to leave in a strange or an unfavorable place esp. without funds or means to depart ~ *vi* **:** to become stranded

3strand *n* [ME *stronde, strande*] *Scot & dial Eng* **1 :** STREAM **2 :** SEA

4strand *n* [ME *strond*] **1 a :** fibers or filaments twisted, plaited, or laid parallel to form a unit for further twisting or plaiting into yarn, thread, rope, or cordage **b :** one of the wires twisted together or laid parallel to form a wire rope or cable **2 :** an element (as a yarn or thread) of a woven or plaited material **3 :** an elongated or twisted and plaited body resembling a rope ⟨a ~ of pearls⟩ **4 :** one of the elements interwoven in a complex whole ⟨the ~*s* of a legal argument⟩

5strand *vt* **1 :** to break a strand of (a rope) accidentally **2 a :** to form (as a rope) from strands **b :** to play out, twist, or arrange in a strand

strand·er \'stran-dər\ *n* **:** a machine that makes strands into cable or rope

strand·line \'stran-,(d)līn\ *n* **:** SHORELINE; *esp* **:** a shoreline above the present water level

strange \'strānj\ *adj* [ME, fr. OF *estrange,* fr. L *extraneus,* lit., external, fr. *extra* outside — more at EXTRA-] **1 a** *archaic* **:** of, relating to, or characteristic of another country **:** FOREIGN, ALIEN **b :** not native to or naturally belonging in a place **:** of external origin, kind, or character **2 a :** not before known, heard, or seen **:** NEW, UNFAMILIAR **b :** exciting wonder or awe **:** strikingly uncommon or unnatural **:** EXTRAORDINARY, QUEER **3 :** discouraging familiarities **:** RESERVED, DISTANT **4 :** UNACCUSTOMED, UNVERSED — **strange·ly** *adv* — **strange·ness** *n*

syn SINGULAR, UNIQUE, PECULIAR, ECCENTRIC, ERRATIC, ODD, QUEER, QUAINT, OUTLANDISH: STRANGE stresses unfamiliarity and may apply to the foreign, the unnatural, the unaccountable; SINGULAR suggests individuality or puzzling strangeness; UNIQUE implies singularity and the fact of being without a known parallel; PECULIAR implies a marked distinctiveness; ECCENTRIC suggests a wide divergence from the usual or normal esp. in behavior; ERRATIC stresses a capricious and unpredictable wandering or deviating; ODD applies to a departure from the regular or expected; QUEER suggests a dubious sometimes sinister oddness; QUAINT suggests an old-fashioned but pleasant oddness; OUTLANDISH applies to what is uncouth, bizarre, or barbaric

1strang·er \'strān-jər\ *n* [ME, fr. MF *estrangier* foreign, foreigner, fr. *estrange*] **1 :** one who is strange: as **a** (1) **:** FOREIGNER (2) **:** a resident alien **b :** one in the house of another as a guest, visitor, or intruder **c :** a person or thing that is unknown or with whom one is unacquainted **d :** one who does not belong to or is kept from the activities of a group **e :** one not privy or party to an act, contract,

or title : a mere intruder or intermeddler **2** : one ignorant of or unacquainted with someone or something

2**stranger** *adj* : of, relating to, or being a stranger : FOREIGN, ALIEN

3**stranger** *vt, obs* : ESTRANGE, ALIENATE

strange woman *n* [fr. the use of the expression in Prov 5:3 (AV)] : PROSTITUTE

stran·gle \ˈstraŋ-gəl\ *vb* **stran·gling** \-g(ə-)liŋ\ [ME *stranglen*, fr. MF *estrangler*, fr. L *strangulare*, fr. Gk *strangalan*, fr. *strangalē* halter — more at STRAIN] *vt* **1 a** : to choke to death by compressing the throat with or as if with a hand or rope : THROTTLE **b** : to obstruct seriously or fatally the normal breathing of : SMOTHER **c** : STIFLE **2** : to suppress or hinder the rise, expression, or growth of : choke off ~ *vi* **1** : to become strangled **2** : to die from or as if from interference with breathing — **stran·gler** \-g(ə-)lər\ *n*

stran·gle·hold \ˈstraŋ-gəl-ˌhōld\ *n* **1** : an illegal wrestling hold by which one's opponent is choked **2** : a force or influence that chokes or suppresses freedom of movement or expression

stran·gles \ˈstraŋ-gəlz\ *n pl but sing or pl in constr* [pl. of obs. *strangle* (act of strangling)] : an infectious febrile disease of horses caused by a bacterium (*Streptococcus equi*) and marked by inflammation and congestion of mucous membranes

stran·gu·late \ˈstraŋ-gyə-ˌlāt\ *vb* [L *strangulatus*, pp. of *strangulare*] *vt* : STRANGLE, CONSTRICT ~ *vi* : to become constricted so as to stop circulation ⟨the hernia will ~ and become necrotic⟩

stran·gu·la·tion \ˌstraŋ-gyə-ˈlā-shən\ *n* **1** : the action or process of strangling : the state of being strangled **2** : inordinate compression or constriction of a bodily tube or part that causes a suspension of breathing, circulation, or the passage of contents

stran·gu·ry \ˈstraŋ-gyə-rē\ *n* [ME, fr. L *stranguria*, fr. Gk *strangouria*, fr. *strang-*, *stranx* drop squeezed out + *ourein* to urinate, fr. *ouron* urine — more at STRAIN, URINE] : a slow and painful discharge of urine drop by drop

1**strap** \ˈstrap\ *n, often attrib* [alter. of *strop*, fr. ME, band or loop of leather or rope, fr. OE, thong for securing an oar; akin to MHG *strupfe* strap; all fr. a prehistoric WGmc word borrowed fr. L *struppus*, fr. Gk *strophos* twisted band; akin to Gk *strephein* to twist — more at STROPHE] **1** : a band, plate, or loop of metal for binding objects together or for clamping an object in position **2 a** : a narrow usu. flat strip or thong of a flexible material and esp. leather used variously (as for securing, holding together, or wrapping) **b** : something made of a strap forming a loop ⟨boot ~⟩ **c** : a strip of leather used for flogging **d** : STROP **3** : a shoe fastened with a usu. buckled strap **4** *Irish* : TROLLOP — **strap·less** \-ləs\ *adj*

2**strap** *vt* **strapped; strap·ping** **1 a** (1) : to secure with or attach by means of a strap (2) : to support (as a sprained joint) with overlapping strips of adhesive plaster **b** : BIND, CONSTRICT **2** : to beat or punish with a strap **3** : STROP

strap·hang·er \-ˌhaŋ-ər\ *n* : a passenger in a subway, streetcar, bus, or train who clings for support while standing to one of the short straps or similar devices running along the aisle

strap·less \-ləs\ *adj* : having no strap; *specif* : made or worn without shoulder straps ⟨~ evening gown⟩

strap·pa·do \strə-ˈpād-(ˌ)ō, -ˈpäd-\ *n* [modif. of It *strappata*, lit., sharp pull] : a former punishment or torture consisting of hoisting the subject by a rope and letting him fall to the length of the rope; *also* : a machine used in the infliction of this torture

strap·per \ˈstrap-ər\ *n* : one that is unusually large or robust

strap·ping \ˈstrap-iŋ\ *adj* : having a vigorously sturdy constitution : ROBUST

strass \ˈstras\ *n* [F *stras*, *strass*] : PASTE 3

strat·a·gem \ˈstrat-ə-jəm, -ˌjem\ *n* [It *stratagemma*, fr. L *strategema*, fr. Gk *stratēgēma*, fr. *stratēgein* to be a general, maneuver, fr. *stratēgos* general, fr. *stratos* army (akin to L *stratus*, pp. of *sternere* to spread out) + *agein* to lead — more at STRATUM, AGENT] **1 a** : an artifice or trick in war for deceiving and outwitting the enemy **b** : a cleverly contrived trick or scheme for gaining an end **2** : skill in ruses or trickery **syn** see TRICK

stra·te·gic \strə-ˈtē-jik\ *adj* **1** : of, relating to, or marked by strategy ⟨~ value of the position⟩ ⟨a ~ retreat⟩ **2 a** : necessary to or important in the initiation, conduct, or completion of a strategic plan **b** : required for the conduct of war ⟨~ materials⟩ **c** : of great importance within an integrated whole or to a planned effect ⟨emphasized ~ points⟩ **3** : designed or trained to strike an enemy at the sources of his military, economic, or political power ⟨~ bomber⟩ — **stra·te·gi·cal** \-ji-kəl\ *adj* — **stra·te·gi·cal·ly** \-k(ə-)lē\ *adv*

strat·e·gist \ˈstrat-ə-jəst\ *n* : one skilled in strategy

strat·e·gy \-jē\ *n* [Gk *stratēgia* generalship, fr. *stratēgos*] **1 a** (1) : the science and art of employing the political, economic, psychological, and military forces of a nation or group of nations to afford the maximum support to adopted policies in peace or war (2) : the science and art of military command exercised to meet the enemy in combat under advantageous conditions — compare TACTICS **b** : a variety of or instance of the use of strategy **2 a** : a careful plan or method : a clever stratagem **b** : the art of devising or employing plans or stratagems toward a goal

strath \ˈstrath\ *n* [ScGael *srath*] : a flat wide river valley or the low-lying grassland along it

strath·spey \strath-ˈspā\ *n* [*Strath Spey* district of Scotland] : a Scottish dance that is similar to but slower than the reel; *also* : the music for this dance

strati- *comb form* [NL *stratum*] : stratum ⟨*strati*form⟩ ⟨*stratigraphy*⟩

stra·tic·u·late \strə-ˈtik-yə-lət, stra-\ *adj* [(assumed) NL *straticulum*, dim. of *stratum*] : characterized by thin parallel strata

strat·i·fi·ca·tion \ˌstrat-ə-fə-ˈkā-shən\ *n* : the act or process of stratifying or state of being stratified : a stratified formation

strat·i·form \ˈstrat-ə-ˌfȯrm\ *adj* : having a stratified formation

strat·i·fy \ˈstrat-ə-ˌfī\ *vb* [NL *stratificare*, fr. *stratum* + L *-ificare* -ify] *vt* **1 a** : to form, deposit, or arrange in strata **b** (1) : to divide or arrange into classes, castes, or social strata (2) : to divide into a series of graded statuses **2** : to store (seeds) in layers alternating with moisture-holding material (as earth or peat) ~ *vi* : to become arranged in strata

stra·tig·ra·pher \strə-ˈtig-rə-fər, stə-\ *n* : a geologist who specializes in stratigraphy

strati·graph·ic \ˌstrat-ə-ˈgraf-ik\ *adj* : of, relating to, or determined by stratigraphy

stra·tig·ra·phy \strə-ˈtig-rə-fē, stə-\ *n* [ISV] **1** : the arrangement of strata **2** : geology that deals with the origin, composition, distribution, and succession of strata

strato- *comb form* [NL *stratus*] : stratus and ⟨*strato*cumulus⟩

stra·toc·ra·cy \strə-ˈtäk-rə-sē\ *n* [Gk *stratos* army — more at STRATAGEM] : a military government : government based on an army

stra·to·cu·mu·lus \ˌstrāt-(ˌ)ō-ˈkyü-myə-ləs, ˌstrat-\ *n* [NL] : stratified cumulus consisting of large balls or rolls of dark cloud which often cover the whole sky esp. in winter

strato·sphere \ˈstrat-ə-ˌsfi(ə)r\ *n* [F *stratosphère*, fr. NL *stratum* + *-o-* + F *sphère* sphere, fr. L *sphaera*] : an upper portion of the atmosphere above seven miles more or less depending on latitude, season, and weather in which temperature changes but little with altitude and clouds of water are rare — **strato·spher·ic** \ˌstrat-ə-ˈsfi(ə)r-ik, -ˈsfer-\ *adj*

stra·tum \ˈstrāt-əm, ˈstrat-\ *n, pl* **stra·ta** \ˈstrāt-ə, ˈstrat-\ [NL, fr. L, spread, bed, fr. neut. of *stratus*, pp. of *sternere* to spread out — more at STREW] **1** : a bed or layer artificially made **2 a** : a sheetlike mass of sedimentary rock or earth of one kind lying between beds of other kinds **b** : a region of the sea or atmosphere that is analogous to a stratum of the earth **c** : a layer of tissue ⟨deep ~ of the skin⟩ **d** : a layer in which archaeological material (as artifacts, skeletons, and dwelling remains) is found on excavation **3 a** : a part of a historical or sociological series representing a period or a stage of development **b** : a socioeconomic level of society comprised of persons of the same or similar status esp. with regard to education or culture **4** : one of the sets considered as an integrated whole that make up an ordered, layered, or superimposed group of sets ⟨a statistical sampling of various population *strata*⟩

stra·tus \ˈstrāt-əs, ˈstrat-\ *n, pl* **stra·ti** \ˈstrāt-ˌī, ˈstrat-\ [NL, fr. L, pp. of *sternere*] : a cloud form of greater horizontal extension and comparatively lower altitude (2000 to 7000 feet) than the cumulostratus or cirrostratus

stra·vage *or* **stra·vaig** \strə-ˈvāg\ *vi* [prob. by shortening and alter. fr. *extravagate*] *chiefly Scot* : ROAM

1**straw** \ˈstrȯ\ *n* [ME, fr. OE *strēaw*; akin to OHG *strō* straw, OE *strewian* to strew] **1 a** : stalks of grain after threshing; *broadly* : dry stalky plant residue used like grain straw (as for bedding or packing) **b** : a natural or artificial heavy fiber used for weaving, plaiting, or braiding **2** : a dry coarse stem esp. of a cereal grass **3 a** (1) : something of small worth or significance (2) : something too insubstantial to provide support or help in a desperate situation (3) : a slight fact that is an indication of a coming event **b** : CHAFF 2 **4 a** : something made of straw **b** : a prepared tube originally cut from a wheat straw for sucking up a beverage — **strawy** \ˈstrȯ(-)i\ *adj*

2**straw** *adj* **1** : made of straw ⟨~ rug⟩ **2** : of, relating to, or used for straw ⟨~ barn⟩ **3** : of the color of straw **4** : of little or no value : WORTHLESS **5** : of, relating to, resembling, or being a man of straw **6** : of, relating to, or concerned with the discovery of preferences by means of a straw vote

straw·ber·ry \ˈstrȯ-ˌber-ē, -b(ə-)rē\ *n, often attrib* [fr. the appearance of the achenes on the surface] : the juicy edible usu. red fruit of a plant (genus *Fragaria*) of the rose family that is technically an enlarged pulpy receptacle bearing numerous achenes; *also* : a plant whose fruits are strawberries

strawberry bush *n* : a No. American euonymus (*Euonymus americanus*) with crimson pods and seeds with a scarlet aril; *also* : 2WAHOO a

strawberry mark *n* : a usu. red and elevated birthmark that is a small vascular tumor

strawberry roan *n* : a roan horse with a decidedly red ground color

strawberry shrub *n* : any of a genus (*Calycanthus* of the family Calycanthaceae, the strawberry-shrub family) of shrubs with fragrant brownish red flowers

strawberry tomato *n* : GROUND-CHERRY 2; *esp* : a stout hairy annual herb (*Physalis pruinosa*) of eastern No. America with sweet globular yellow fruits

strawberry tree *n* **1** : a European evergreen tree (*Arbutus unedo*) of the heath family with racemose white flowers and fruits like strawberries **2** : STRAWBERRY BUSH

straw·board \ˈstrȯ-ˌbō(ə)rd, -ˌbȯ(ə)rd\ *n* : board made of straw pulp and used esp. for packing

straw boss *n* **1** : an assistant to a foreman in charge of supervising and expediting the work of a small gang of workmen **2** : a member of a group of workers who supervises the work of the others in addition to doing his own job

straw·flow·er \ˈstrȯ-ˌflau̇(-ə)r\ *n* : any of several everlasting flowers

straw·hat theater \ˌstrȯ-ˌhat-\ *n* [fr. the former fashion of wearing straw hats in summer] : a summer theater

straw man *n* **1** : a weak or imaginary opposition (as an argument or adversary) set up only to be easily confuted **2** : a person set up to serve as a cover for a usu. questionable transaction

straw vote *n* : an unofficial vote (as taken at a chance gathering) to indicate the relative strength of opposing candidates or issues

straw wine *n* : a sweet dessert wine produced from grapes partially dried in the sun often on straw before fermentation

straw·worm \ˈstrȯ-ˌwərm\ *n* **1** : CADDISWORM **2** : any of several larval chalcid flies that injure the straw of wheat and other grains

straw yellow *n* : a pale yellow

1**stray** \ˈstrā\ *vi* [ME *straien*, fr. MF *estraier*, fr. (assumed) VL *extragare*, fr. L *extra-* outside + *vagari* to wander — more at EXTRA-, VAGARY] **1** : to wander from company, restraint, or proper limits : ROAM **2 a** : to wander from a direct course or at random : DEVIATE, MEANDER **b** : ERR, SIN — **stray·er** *n*

2**stray** *n* [ME, fr. OF *estraié*, pp. of *estraier*] **1 a** : a domestic animal wandering at large or lost **b** : a person or thing that strays : a detached individual : STRAGGLER, WAIF **2** [ME, fr. *straien* to stray] *archaic* : the act of going astray **3** : a disturbing electrical effect in radio reception not produced by a transmitting station **4** : an unexpected formation encountered in drilling an oil or gas well

3**stray** *adj* **1** : having strayed : WANDERING ⟨a ~ cow⟩ ⟨~ survivors⟩ **2** : occurring at random or as detached individuals : SCATTERED, OCCASIONAL ⟨a few ~ hairs⟩ ⟨~ remarks⟩

1**streak** \ˈstrēk\ *n* [ME *streke*, fr. OE *strica*; akin to OHG *strich*

line, L *striga* row — more at STRIKE] **1 :** a line or mark of a different color or texture from the ground **:** STRIPE **2 a :** the color of the fine powder of a mineral obtained by scratching or rubbing against a hard white surface and constituting an important distinguishing character **b :** inoculum implanted in a line on a solid medium **3 a :** a narrow band of light **b :** a lightning bolt **4 a :** a slight admixture **:** TRACE **b :** a brief run (as of luck) **c :** a consecutive series ⟨winning ~⟩ **5 :** a narrow layer (as of ore)

2**streak** *vt* **:** to make streaks on or in **:** STRIATE ~ *vi* **:** to move swiftly **:** RUSH

streaked \'strēkt, 'strē-kəd\ *adj* **1 :** marked with stripes or linear discolorations **2 :** physically or mentally disturbed **:** UPSET

streak·i·ness \'strē-kē-nəs\ *n* **:** the quality or state of being streaky

streaky \'strē-kē\ *adj* **1 :** marked with streaks **2 :** APPREHENSIVE **3 :** VARIABLE, UNRELIABLE

1**stream** \'strēm\ *n* [ME *streme*, fr. OE *strēam;* akin to OHG *stroum* stream, Gk *rhein* to flow, Skt *sarati* it flows — more at SERUM] **1 :** a body of running water (as a river or brook) flowing on the earth; *also* **:** any body of flowing fluid (as water or gas) **2 a :** a steady succession **b :** a constantly renewed supply **c :** a continuous moving procession **3 :** an unbroken flow (as of gas or particles of matter) **4 :** a ray or beam of light **5 :** a dominant attitude, group, or line of development — **on stream :** in or into production

2**stream** *vi* **1 a :** to flow in or as if in a stream **b :** to leave a bright trail **2 a :** to exude a bodily fluid profusely **b :** to become saturated **3 :** to trail out at full length **4 :** to pour in large numbers ~ *vt* **1 :** to cause to flow **:** EXUDE **2 :** to display fully extended

stream·er \'strē-mər\ *n* **1 a :** a flag that streams in the wind; *esp* **:** PENNANT **b :** any long narrow wavy strip like or suggesting a banner floating in the wind **c :** BANNER 2 **2 a :** a long gauzy extension of the solar corona visible only during a total solar eclipse **b** *pl* **:** AURORA BOREALIS

stream·ing *n* **:** an act or instance of flowing; *specif* **:** CYCLOSIS

stream·let \'strēm-lət\ *n* **:** a small stream

1**stream·line** \'strēm-,līn, -'līn\ *n* **1 :** the path of a fluid particle relative to a solid body past which the fluid is moving in smooth flow without turbulence **2 a :** a contour designed to minimize resistance to motion through a fluid (as air) **b :** a fluid or smooth line designed as if for decreasing air resistance

2**streamline** *vt* **1 :** to design or construct with a streamline **2 :** to bring up to date **:** MODERNIZE **3 a :** ORGANIZE **b :** to make simpler or more efficient

stream·lined \-,līnd, -'līnd\ *adj* **1 a :** contoured to reduce resistance to motion through a fluid (as air) **b :** stripped of nonessentials **:** SIMPLIFIED, COMPACT **c :** effectively integrated **:** ORGANIZED **2 :** having fluid lines **3 :** MODERNIZED **4 :** of or relating to streamline flow

streamline flow *n* **:** an uninterrupted flow (as of air) past a solid body in which the direction at every point remains unchanged with the passage of time

stream·lin·er \'strēm-'lī-nər\ *n* **:** one that is streamlined; *esp* **:** a streamlined train

stream of consciousness 1 : individual conscious experience considered as a series of processes or experiences continuously moving forward in time **2 :** a usu. extended representation in monologue of a fictional character's sequence of thought and feeling

streek \'strēk\ *vt* [ME (northern dial.) *streken;* akin to OE *streccan* to stretch] **1** *chiefly Scot* **:** STRETCH, EXTEND **2** *chiefly Scot* **:** to lay out (a dead body)

1**street** \'strēt\ *n* [ME *strete*, fr. OE *strǣt;* akin to OHG *strāza* street; both fr. a prehistoric WGmc word borrowed fr. LL *strata* paved road, fr. L, fem. of *stratus*, pp. of *sternere* to spread out — more at STREW] **1 a :** a thoroughfare esp. in a city, town, or village usu. including sidewalks and being wider than an alley or lane **b :** the part of a street reserved for vehicles **c :** a thoroughfare with abutting property **2 :** the people occupying property on a street **3 :** a promising line of development **4** *cap* **:** a district (as Wall Street or Fleet Street) identified with a particular profession

2**street** *adj* **1 a :** suitable for wear on the street **b :** not touching the ground — used of a woman's dress **2 :** caused by a street virus ⟨~ distemper⟩

street arab \-'ar-əb, -'ā-,rab\ *n, often cap A* **:** a homeless vagabond and esp. an outcast boy or girl in the streets of a city **:** GAMIN

street·car \'strēt-,kär\ *n* **:** a vehicle on rails used primarily for transporting passengers and typically operating on city streets

street railway *n* **:** a line operating streetcars or buses

street virus *n* **:** virulent or natural virus (as of rabies) as distinguished from virus attenuated in the laboratory

street·walk·er \'strēt-,wȯ-kər\ *n* **:** PROSTITUTE — **street·walk·ing** \-kiŋ\ *n*

strength \'streŋ(k)th\ *n, pl* **strengths** \'streŋ(k)s, 'streŋ(k)ths\ [ME *strengthe*, fr. OE *strengthu;* akin to OHG *strengi* strong — more at STRONG] **1 :** the quality or state of being strong **:** capacity for exertion or endurance **2 :** power to resist force **:** SOLIDITY, TOUGHNESS **3 :** power of resisting attack **:** IMPREGNABILITY **4 :** legal, logical, or moral force **5 a :** degree of potency of effect or of concentration **b :** intensity of light, color, sound, or odor **c :** vigor of expression **6 :** force as measured in numbers **:** effective numbers of any body or organization ⟨army at full ~⟩ **7 :** one regarded as embodying or affording force or firmness **:** SUPPORT **8 :** maintenance of or a rising tendency in a price level **:** firmness of prices **syn** see POWER

strength·en \'streŋ(k)-thən\ *vb* **strength·en·ing** \'streŋ(k)th-(ə-)niŋ\ *vt* **:** to make stronger ~ *vi* **:** to become stronger — **strength·en·er** \'streŋ(k)th-(ə-)nər\ *n*

strength·less \'streŋ(k)th-ləs\ *adj* [ME *strentheles*, fr. *strenthe* strength + *-les* -less] **:** having no strength — **strength·less·ness** *n*

stren·u·os·i·ty \,stren-yə-'wäs-ət-ē\ *n* **:** the quality or state of being strenuous

stren·u·ous \'stren-yə-wəs\ *adj* [L *strenuus* — more at STARE] **1 a :** vigorously active **:** ENERGETIC **b :** FERVENT, ZEALOUS **2 :** marked by or calling for energy or stamina **:** ARDUOUS **syn** see VIGOROUS — **stren·u·ous·ly** *adv* — **stren·u·ous·ness** *n*

strep \'strep\ *adj* **:** STREPTOCOCCAL

strep throat *n* **:** SEPTIC SORE THROAT

strepto- *comb form* [NL, fr. Gk, fr. *streptos* twisted, fr. *strephein* to twist — more at STROPHE] **1 :** twisted **:** twisted chain ⟨*strepto*coccus⟩ **2 :** streptococcus ⟨*strepto*kinase⟩

strep·to·ba·cil·lus \,strep-(,)tō-bə-'sil-əs\ *n* [NL] **:** any of various bacilli in which the individual cells are joined in a chain

strep·to·coc·cal \,strep-tə-'käk-əl\ *or* **strep·to·coc·cic** \-'käk-(s)ik\ *adj* **:** of, relating to, or caused by streptococci ⟨a ~ sore throat⟩ ⟨~ organisms⟩

strep·to·coc·cus \-'käk-əs\ *n, pl* **strep·to·coc·ci** \-'käk-,(s)ī, -'käk-(,)(s)ē\ [NL, genus name] **:** any of a genus (*Streptococcus*) of nonmotile chiefly parasitic gram-positive bacteria that divide only in one plane, occur in pairs or chains but not in packets, and include important pathogens of man and domestic animals; *broadly* **:** any coccus occurring in chains

strep·to·ki·nase \-'kīn-,ās, -'kin-, -,āz\ *n* **:** a proteolytic enzyme from hemolytic streptococci active in promoting dissolution of blood clots

strep·to·ly·sin \strep-'täl-ə-sən, ,strep-tə-'līs-ᵊn\ *n* **:** an antigenic hemolysin produced by streptococci

strep·to·my·ces \,strep-tə-'mī-,sēz\ *n, pl* **streptomyces** *or* **strep·to·my·cetes** \-'mī-,sēts, -(,)mī-'; -(,)mī-'sēt-(,)ēz\ [NL, fr. *strepto-* + Gk *mykēs* fungus; akin to L *mucus* mucus] **:** any of a genus (*Streptomyces*) of mostly soil actinomycetes including some that form antibiotics as by-products of their metabolism

strep·to·my·cin \,strep-tə-'mīs-ᵊn\ *n* **:** an antibiotic organic base $C_{21}H_{39}H_7O_{12}$ produced by a soil actinomycete (*Streptomyces griseus*), active against many bacteria, and used esp. in the treatment of infections (as tuberculosis) by gram-negative bacteria

strep·to·thri·cin \-'thrīs-ᵊn, -'thris-\ *n* [NL *Streptothric-*, *Streptothrix*, genus of bacteria, fr. *strepto-* + Gk *trich-*, *thrix* hair — more at TRICH-] **:** a basic antibiotic produced by a soil actinomycete (*Streptomyces lavendulae*) and active against bacteria and to some degree against fungi

1**stress** \'stres\ *n* [ME *stresse* stress, distress, fr. *destresse* — more at DISTRESS] **1 :** constraining force or influence: as **a :** mutual force or action between contiguous surfaces of bodies caused by external force (as tension or shear); *specif* **:** the intensity of this mutual force commonly expressed in pounds per square inch **b :** a physical, chemical, or emotional factor that causes bodily or mental tension and may be a factor in disease causation **c :** a state resulting from a stress; *esp* **:** one of bodily or mental tension resulting from factors that tend to alter an existent equilibrium **2 :** EMPHASIS, WEIGHT ⟨lay ~ on a point⟩ **3** *archaic* **:** intense effort or exertion **4 :** intensity of utterance given to a speech sound, syllable, or word producing relative loudness **5 a :** relative force or prominence of sound in verse **b :** a syllable having relative force or prominence **6 :** ACCENT 6a, 6b(2)

2**stress** *vt* **1 :** to subject to phonetic stress **:** ACCENT **2 :** to subject to physical stress **3 :** to lay stress on **:** EMPHASIZE

stress·ful \-fəl\ *adj* **:** full of or subject to stress — **stress·ful·ly** \-fə-lē\ *adv*

stress·less \-ləs\ *adj* **:** having no stress **:** UNACCENTED — **stress·less·ness** *n*

stress–verse \'stres-,vərs\ *n* **:** verse whose rhythm is produced by recurrence of stresses without regard to number of syllables or any fixed distribution of unstressed elements

1**stretch** \'strech\ *vb* [ME *strecchen*, fr. OE *streccan;* akin to OHG *strecchan* to stretch, OE *starian* to stare] *vt* **1 :** to extend (as one's limbs or body) in a reclining position **2 :** to reach out **:** EXTEND ⟨~*ed* forth his arm⟩ **3 :** to extend in length **4 :** to fell with or as if with a blow **5 :** to cause the limbs of (a person) to be pulled esp. in torture **6 :** to draw up (one's body) from a cramped, stooping, or relaxed position **7 :** to pull taut **8 a :** to enlarge or distend esp. by force **b :** STRAIN **9 :** to cause to reach or continue ⟨~ a wire between two posts⟩ **10 :** to extend often unduly the scope or meaning of ~ *vi* **1 a :** to become extended in length or breadth or both **:** SPREAD **b :** to extend over a continuous period **2 :** to become extended without breaking **3 a :** to extend one's body or limbs **b :** to lie down at full length — **stretch·abil·i·ty** \,strech-ə-'bil-ət-ē\ *n* — **stretch·able** \'strech-ə-bəl\ *adj*

2**stretch** *n* **1 a :** an exercise of something (as the understanding) beyond ordinary or normal limits **b :** an extension of the scope or application of something **2 :** the extent to which something may be stretched **3 :** the act of stretching or the state of being stretched **4 a :** an extent in length or area **b :** a continuous period of time **5 :** a walk to relieve fatigue **6 :** a term of imprisonment **7 a :** either of the straight sides of a racecourse **b :** a final stage **8 :** the capacity for being stretched **:** ELASTICITY

3**stretch** *adj* **:** easily stretched **:** ELASTIC ⟨~ hosiery⟩

stretch·er \'strech-ər\ *n* **1 :** one that stretches; *esp* **:** a device or machine for stretching or expanding something **2 a :** a brick or stone laid with its length parallel to the face of the wall **b :** a timber or rod used esp. when horizontal as a tie in framed work **3 :** a litter (as of canvas) for carrying a disabled or dead person **4 :** a rod or bar extending between two legs of a chair or table

stretch·er–bear·er \-,bar-ər, -,ber-\ *n* **:** one who carries one end of a stretcher

stretch–out \'strech-,au̇t\ *n* **:** a system of industrial operation in which workers are required to do extra work and esp. to operate more machines than formerly either with slight or with no additional pay

stret·to \'stret-(,)ō, 'strāt-\ *also* **stret·ta** \-ə\ *n, pl* **stret·ti** \-(,)ē\ *or* **strettos** [*stretto* fr. It, lit., narrow, close; *stretta* fr. It, fr. fem. of *stretto*] **1 a :** the overlapping of answer with subject in a musical fugue **b :** the part of a fugue characterized by this overlapping **2 :** a concluding passage performed in a quicker tempo

strew \'strü\ *vt* **strewed; strewed** *or* **strewn** \'strün\ **strew·ing** [ME *strewen*, *strowen*, fr. OE *strewian*, *strēowian;* akin to OHG *strewen* to strew, L *sternere* to spread out, Gk *stornynai*] **1 :** to spread by scattering **2 :** to cover by or as if by scattering something over or on **3 :** to become dispersed over **4 :** to spread abroad **:** DISSEMINATE

strew·ment \'strü-mənt\ *n, archaic* **:** something (as flowers) strewed or designed for strewing

stria \'strī-ə\ *n, pl* **stri·ae** \'strī-,ē\ [L, furrow, channel — more at STRIKE] **1 :** a minute groove or channel **2 :** a narrow line or band (as of color) esp. when one of a series of parallel grooves or lines

1**stri·ate** \'strī-ət, -,āt\ *adj* **:** STRIATED

2**stri·ate** \-,āt\ *vt* **:** to mark with striae

stri·at·ed \'strī-,āt-əd\ *adj* **:** marked with striae

stri·a·tion \strī-'ā-shən\ *n* **1 a :** the fact or state of being striated **b :** arrangement of striae **2 :** STRIA

strick \'strik\ *n* [ME *stric*, *strik*, prob. of LG or D origin; akin to MLG *strik* rope, MD *stric*] **:** a bunch of hackled flax, jute, or hemp

strick·en \'strik-ən\ *adj* [fr. pp. of *strike*] **1 :** having the contents leveled off even with the top ⟨a ~ measure of grain⟩ **2 :** hit or wounded by or as if by a missile **3 a :** afflicted with disease, misfortune, or sorrow **b :** INCAPACITATED

¹strick·le \'strik-əl\ *n* [ME *strikell;* akin to OE *strīcan* to stroke — more at STRIKE] **1 :** an instrument for leveling off measures of grain **2 :** an instrument for whetting scythes **3 :** a foundry tool for smoothing the surface of a core or mold

²strickle *vt* **strick·ling** \-(ə-)liŋ\ **:** to smooth or form with a strickle

strict \'strikt\ *adj* [L *strictus,* fr. pp. of *stringere* to bind tight — more at STRAIN] **1 :** permitting no evasion or escape ⟨under ~ orders⟩ **2 a :** inflexibly maintained or adhered to **:** COMPLETE ⟨~ secrecy⟩ **b** (1) **:** rigorously conforming to principle or a norm ⟨a ~ Catholic⟩ (2) **:** severe in discipline **3** *archaic* **:** NARROW, TIGHT; *also* **:** INTIMATE **4 :** EXACT, PRECISE **5 :** of narrow erect habit of growth ⟨a ~ inflorescence⟩ **syn** see RIGID — **strict·ly** \'strik-(t)lē\ *adv* — **strict·ness** \'strik(t)-nəs\ *n*

stric·ture \'strik-chər\ *n* [ME, fr. LL *strictura,* fr. L *strictus,* pp. of *stringere* to bind tight] **1 :** an abnormal narrowing of a bodily passage; *also* **:** the narrowed part **2 :** something that closely restrains or limits **:** RESTRICTION **3 :** an adverse criticism **:** CENSURE **syn** see ANIMADVERSION

¹stride \'strīd\ *vb* **strode** \'strōd\ **strid·den** \'strid-ᵊn\ **strid·ing** \'strīd-iŋ\ [ME *striden,* fr. OE *strīdan;* akin to MLG *striden* to straddle, OE *starian* to stare] *vi* **1 :** to stand astride **2 :** to move with or as if with long steps **3 :** to take a very long step ~ *vt* **1 :** BESTRIDE, STRADDLE **2 :** to step over **3 :** to move over or along with or as if with long measured steps — **strid·er** \'strīd-ər\ *n*

²stride *n* **1 :** a long step **2 :** an act of striding **3 :** a stage of progress **:** ADVANCE **4 a :** a cycle of locomotor movements (as of a horse) completed when the feet regain the initial relative positions; *also* **:** the distance traversed in a stride **b :** the most effective natural pace **5 :** a manner of striding

stri·den·cy \'strīd-ᵊn-sē\ *n* **:** the quality or state of being strident

stri·dent \'strīd-ᵊnt\ *adj* [L *strident-, stridens,* prp. of *stridere, stridēre* to make a harsh noise; akin to Gk & L *strix* owl] **:** harsh sounding **:** GRATING; *also* **:** SHRILL **syn** see VOCIFEROUS — **stri·dent·ly** *adv*

stri·dor \'strīd-ər, 'strī-,dȯ(ə)r\ *n* [L, fr. *stridere, stridēre*] **1 :** a harsh, shrill, or creaking noise **2 :** a harsh vibrating sound heard during expiration in obstruction of the air passages

strid·u·late \'strij-ə-,lāt\ *vi* [back-formation fr. *stridulation*] **:** to make a shrill creaking noise by rubbing together special bodily structures — used esp. of male insects (as crickets or grasshoppers) — **strid·u·la·tion** \,strij-ə-'lā-shən\ *n* — **strid·u·la·to·ry** \'strij-ə-lə-,tōr-ē, -,tȯr-\ *adj*

strid·u·lous \'strij-ə-ləs\ *adj* [L *stridulus,* fr. *stridere, stridēre*] **:** making a shrill creaking sound — **strid·u·lous·ly** *adv*

strife \'strīf\ *n* [ME *strif,* fr. OF *estrif*] **1 a :** bitter sometimes violent conflict or dissension ⟨political ~⟩ **b :** an act of contention **:** FIGHT, STRUGGLE **2 :** exertion or contention for superiority **3** *archaic* **:** earnest endeavor **syn** see DISCORD

strife·less \'strī-fləs\ *adj* **:** free from strife

strig·il \'strij-əl\ *n* [L *strigilis;* akin to L *stringere* to touch lightly — more at STRIKE] **:** an instrument used by ancient Greeks and Romans for scraping the skin esp. after the bath

strig·il·lose \'strij-ə-,lōs\ *adj* [NL *strigilla,* dim. of *striga* bristle] **:** finely strigose

stri·gose \'strī-,gōs\ *adj* [NL *strigosus,* fr. *striga* bristle, fr. L, furrow] **1 :** having appressed bristles or scales ⟨a ~ leaf⟩ **2 :** marked with fine closely set grooves

¹strike \'strīk\ *vb* **struck** \'strək\ **struck** *also* **strick·en** \'strik-ən\ **strik·ing** \'strī-kiŋ\ [ME *striken,* fr. OE *strīcan* to stroke, go; akin to OHG *strīhhan* to stroke, L *stringere* to touch lightly, *striga, stria* furrow] *vi* **1 :** to take a course **:** GO **2 :** to deliver or aim a blow or thrust **:** HIT **3 :** CONTACT, COLLIDE **4 :** DELETE, CANCEL **5 :** to lower a flag usu. in surrender **6 a :** to become indicated by a clock, bell, or chime **b :** to make known the time by sounding **7 :** PIERCE, PENETRATE **8 a :** to engage in battle **b :** to make a military attack **9 :** to become ignited **10 :** to discover something **11 a :** to pull on a fishing rod in order to set the hook **b** *of a fish* **:** to seize the bait **12 :** DART, SHOOT **13 a** *of a plant cutting* **:** to take root **b** *of a seed* **:** GERMINATE **14 :** to make an impression **15 :** to stop work in order to force an employer to comply with demands **16 :** to make a beginning **17 :** to thrust oneself forward **18 :** to work diligently **:** STRIVE ~ *vt* **1 a :** to strike at **:** HIT **b :** to drive or remove by or as if by a blow **c :** to attack or seize with a sharp blow (as of fangs or claws) ⟨*struck* by a snake⟩ **d :** INFLICT **e :** to produce by or as if by a blow or stroke **f :** to separate by a sharp blow ⟨~ off flints⟩ **2 a :** to haul down **:** LOWER **b :** to dismantle and take away **c :** to strike the tents of (a camp) **3 :** to afflict suddenly **4 a :** to engage in (a battle) **:** FIGHT **b :** to make a military attack on **5 :** DELETE, CANCEL **6 a :** to penetrate painfully **:** PIERCE **b :** to cause to penetrate **c :** to send down or out **7 a :** to level (as a measure of grain) by scraping off what is above the rim **b :** STRICKLE **8 :** to indicate by sounding **9 a** (1) **:** to bring into forceful contact (2) **:** to shake (hands) in confirming an agreement (3) **:** to thrust suddenly **b :** to come into contact or collision with **c** *of light* **:** to fall on **d** *of a sound* **:** to become audible to **10 a :** to affect with a mental or emotional state or a strong emotion **b :** to affect a person with (a strong emotion) **c :** to cause to become by or as if by a sudden blow ⟨*struck* him dead⟩ **11 a :** to produce by stamping **b** (1) **:** to produce (as fire) by or as if by striking (2) **:** to cause to ignite by friction **12 :** to make and ratify the terms of ⟨~ a bargain⟩ **13 a :** to play by stroking keys or strings **b :** to produce by or as if by playing an instrument **14 a :** to hook (a fish) by a sharp pull on the line **b** *of a fish* **:** to snatch at (a bait) **15 a** (1) **:** to occur to (2) **:** to appear to **b :** to appear remarkable to **:** IMPRESS **16 :** BEWITCH **17 :** to arrive at by computation ⟨~ a balance⟩ **18 a :** to come to **:** ATTAIN **b :** to come upon **:** DISCOVER **19 :** to engage in a strike against (an employer) **20 :** to take on **:** ASSUME ⟨~ a pose⟩ **21 a :** to place (a plant cutting) in a medium for growth and rooting **b :** to so propagate (a plant) **22 :** to make one's way along **23 :** to cause (an arc) to form (as between electrodes of an arc lamp) **24** *of an insect* **:** to oviposit on or in

syn HIT, SMITE, SLAP, SWAT, PUNCH: STRIKE implies aiming and dealing a blow usu. with moderate to heavy force with the hand or with a weapon or tool; HIT more often stresses the impact of the blow or the reaching of the target aimed at; SMITE suggests greater force or emphasis than HIT; SLAP implies striking with the open hand; SWAT implies a slapping or striking hard with a fairly light implement; PUNCH implies hitting with the closed fist

²strike *n* **1 :** STRICKLE **2 :** an act or instance of striking **3 a :** a work stoppage by a body of workers to enforce compliance with demands made on an employer **b :** a temporary stoppage of activities in protest against an act or condition **4 :** the direction of the line of intersection of a horizontal plane with an uptilted geological stratum **5 a :** a pull on a fishing rod to strike a fish **b :** a pull on a line by a fish in striking **6 :** a stroke of good luck; *esp* **:** a discovery of a valuable mineral deposit **7 a :** a pitched ball that is in the strike zone or is swung at and is not hit fair **b :** DISADVANTAGE, HANDICAP **8 :** an act or instance of knocking down all the bowling pins with the first bowl **9 :** establishment of roots and plant growth **10 :** cutaneous myiasis (as of sheep) ⟨body ~⟩ **11 a :** a military attack; *esp* **:** an air attack on a single objective **b :** a group of airplanes taking part in such an attack

strike·bound \'strīk-,baund\ *adj* **:** subjected to a strike

strike·break·er \'strīk-,brā-kər\ *n* **:** one hired to replace a striking worker

strike·break·ing \-kiŋ\ *n* **:** action designed to break up a strike

strike·less \'strī-kləs\ *adj* **:** marked by the absence of strikes

strike off *vt* **1 :** to produce in an effortless manner **2 :** to depict clearly and exactly

strike out *vt* **:** to retire (a baseball batter) by a strikeout ~ *vi* **1 :** to enter upon a course of action **2 :** to set out vigorously **3 :** to make an out in baseball by a strikeout

strike·out \'strī-,kaut\ *n* **:** an out in baseball resulting from a batter's being charged with three strikes

strike·over \'strī-,kō-vər\ *n* **:** an act or instance of striking a typewriter character on a spot already occupied by another character

strik·er \'strī-kər\ *n* **1 :** one that strikes: as **a :** a player in any of several games who strikes **b :** the hammer of the striking mechanism of a clock or watch **c :** BLACKSMITH **d :** a worker on strike **2 :** an enlisted man working for a petty officer's rate

strike up *vi* **:** to begin to sing or play or to be sung or played ⟨a march *struck up* and the parade began⟩ ~ *vt* **1 :** to cause to begin singing or playing ⟨*strike up* the band⟩ **2 :** to cause to begin ⟨*strike up* a conversation⟩

strike zone *n* **:** the area (as between the armpits and tops of the knees of a batter in his natural stance) over home plate through which a pitched baseball must pass to be called a strike

strik·ing \'strī-kiŋ\ *adj* **:** REMARKABLE, SURPRISING **syn** see NOTICEABLE — **strik·ing·ly** \-kiŋ-lē\ *adv*

¹string \'striŋ\ *n* [ME, fr. OE *streng;* akin to L *stringere* to bind tight — more at STRAIN] **1 :** a small cord (as used to bind, fasten, or tie) **2 a** *archaic* **:** a cord (as a tendon or ligament) of an animal body **b :** a plant fiber (as a leaf vein) **3 a :** the gut or wire cord of a musical instrument **b** *pl* (1) **:** the stringed instruments of an orchestra (2) **:** the players of such instruments **4 a :** a group of objects threaded on a string **b :** a series of things arranged in or as if in a line **c :** the animals and esp. horses belonging to or used by one individual **5 a :** a means of recourse **:** EXPEDIENT **b :** a group of players ranked according to skill or proficiency **6 :** SUCCESSION, SEQUENCE **7 a :** one of the inclined sides of a stair supporting the treads and risers **b :** STRINGCOURSE **8 a :** BALKLINE **b :** the action of lagging for break in billiards **9 :** LINE 13 **10** *pl* **a :** contingent conditions or obligations **b :** CONTROL, DOMINATION

²string *vb* **strung** \'strəŋ\ **string·ing** \'striŋ-iŋ\ *vt* **1 a :** to equip with strings **b :** to tune the strings of **2 :** to make tense **3 a :** to thread on or as if on a string **b :** to thread with objects **c :** to tie, hang, or fasten with string **4 :** to hang by the neck **5 :** to remove the strings of ⟨~ beans⟩ **6 a :** to extend or stretch like a string ⟨~ wires from tree to tree⟩ **b :** to set out in a line or series **7 :** FOOL, HOAX ~ *vi* **1 :** to move, progress, or lie in a string **2 :** to form into strings **3 :** LAG 3

string along *vi* **:** to go along **:** AGREE ~ *vt* **1 :** to keep dangling or waiting **2 :** DECEIVE, FOOL

string bass *n* **:** DOUBLE BASS

string bean *n* **1 :** SNAP BEAN **2 :** a very tall thin person

string·board \'striŋ-,bō(ə)rd, -,bȯ(ə)rd\ *n* **:** a board or built-up facing used in stair building to cover the ends of the steps and hide the true string

string·course \-,kō(ə)rs, -,kȯ(ə)rs\ *n* **:** a horizontal band (as of bricks) in a building forming a part of the design

stringed \'striŋd\ *adj* **1 :** having strings **2 :** produced by strings

stringed instrument *n* **:** a musical instrument (as a violin, harp, or piano) sounded by plucking or striking or by drawing a bow across tense strings

strin·gen·cy \'strin-jən-sē\ *n* **:** the quality or state of being stringent

strin·gen·do \strin-'jen-(,)dō\ *adv* [It, verbal of *stringere* to press, fr. L, to bind tight] **:** with quickening of tempo (as to a climax) — used as a direction in music

strin·gent \'strin-jənt\ *adj* [L *stringent-, stringens,* prp. of *stringere* to bind tight] **1 :** TIGHT, CONSTRICTED **2 :** marked by rigor, strictness, or severity esp. with regard to rule or standard **3 :** marked by money scarcity and credit strictness **syn** see RIGID — **strin·gent·ly** *adv*

string·er \'striŋ-ər\ *n* **1 :** one that strings **2 a :** a long horizontal timber to connect uprights in a frame or to support a floor **b :** STRING 7a **c :** a tie in a truss **3 a :** a longitudinal member extending from bent to bent of a railroad bridge and carrying the track **b :** a longitudinal member (as in an airplane fuselage or wing) to reinforce the skin **4 :** one estimated to be of specified excellence or quality or efficiency — usu. used in combination ⟨first-*stringer*⟩ ⟨second-*stringer*⟩

string·halt \'striŋ-,hȯlt\ *n* **:** a lameness in the hind legs of a horse caused by muscular spasms — **string·halt·ed** \-,hȯl-təd\ *adj*

string·hold·er \-,hōl-dər\ *n* **:** TAILPIECE 2

string·i·ness \'striŋ-ē-nəs\ *n* **:** the quality or state of being stringy

string·ing \'striŋ-iŋ\ *n* **:** the gut, silk, or nylon with which a racket is strung

string·less \'striŋ-ləs\ *adj* **:** having no strings

string line *n* **:** BALKLINE 1

string·piece \'striŋ-,pēs\ *n* **:** the heavy squared timber lying along the top of the piles forming a dock front or timber pier

string quartet *n* **1 :** a quartet of performers on stringed instru-

ments usu. including a first and second violin, a viola, and a cello **2 :** a composition for string quartet

string tie *n* **:** a narrow necktie

stringy \'striŋ-ē\ *adj* **1 a :** containing, consisting of, or resembling fibrous matter or a string **b :** lean and sinewy in build **:** WIRY **2 :** capable of being drawn out to form a string **:** ROPY ⟨a ~ precipitate⟩

stri·o·late \'strī-ə-,lāt\ *or* **stri·o·lat·ed** \-,lāt-əd\ *adj* [NL *striola*, dim. of *stria*] **:** minutely striate

1strip \'strip\ *vb* **stripped** \'stript\ *also* **stript; strip·ping** [ME *strippen*, fr. OE *-strīpan;* akin to OHG *stroufen* to strip] *vt* **1 a :** to remove clothing, covering, or surface matter from **b :** to remove (as clothing) from a person **2 :** to divest of honors, privileges, or functions **3 a :** to remove extraneous or superficial matter from ⟨a prose style *stripped* to the bones⟩ **b :** to remove furniture, equipment, or accessories from ⟨~ a ship for action⟩ **4 :** PLUNDER, SPOIL **5 :** to make bare or clear (as by cutting or grazing) **6 :** DISMANTLE, DISASSEMBLE **7 :** to finish a milking of by pressing the last available milk from the teats ⟨~ a cow⟩ **8 :** to remove cured leaves from the stalks of (tobacco) or the midrib from (tobacco leaves) **9 :** to tear or damage the screw thread of (a bolt or nut) **10 :** to separate (components) from a mixture or solution **~** *vi* **1 :** to take off clothes **2 :** PEEL *vi* 1; *specif* **:** to perform a striptease

2strip *n* [perh. fr. MLG *strippe* strap] **1 :** a long narrow piece or area **2 :** AIRSTRIP

strip–crop \'strip-,kräp\ *vt* **:** to practice strip-cropping on **~** *vi* **:** to practice strip-cropping

strip–crop·ping *n* **:** the growing of a cultivated crop (as corn) in strips alternating with strips of a sod-forming crop (as hay) arranged to follow an approximate contour of the land and minimize erosion

1stripe \'strīp\ *n* [ME; akin to MD *stripe*] **:** a stroke or blow with a rod or lash

2stripe *n* [prob. fr. MD; akin to OE *strica* streak — more at STREAK] **1 a :** a line or long narrow section differing in color or texture from parts adjoining **b** (1) **:** a textile design consisting of lines or bands against a plain background (2) **:** a fabric with a striped design **2 a :** a piece of braid (as on the sleeve) to indicate military rank or length of service **b :** CHEVRON **3 :** a distinct variety or sort **:** TYPE

3stripe *vt* **:** to make stripes on or variegate with stripes

striped \'strīpt, 'strī-pəd\ *adj* **:** having stripes or streaks

striped bass *n* **:** any of several percoid fishes (family Serranidae); *esp* **:** a large anadromous sea bass (*Roccus saxatilis*) of the Atlantic coast of the U. S. highly esteemed for sport and food

stripe·less \'strī-pləs\ *adj* **:** having no stripes

strip·er \'strī-pər\ *n* **:** one that wears stripes (as on a sleeve) to indicate rank or length of service

strip·film \'strip-,film\ *n* **:** FILMSTRIP

strip·ing *n* **1 :** the act or process of marking with stripes **2 a :** the stripes marked or painted on something **b :** a design of stripes

strip·ling \'strip-liŋ\ *n* [ME] **:** an adolescent boy

strip·per \'strip-ər\ *n* **1 :** one that strips **2 :** STRIPTEASER

strip·tease \'strip-,tēz\ *n* **:** a burlesque act in which a female performer removes her clothing piece by piece in view of the audience — **strip·teas·er** \-,tē-zər\ *n*

stripy \'strī-pē\ *adj* **:** marked by stripes or streaks

strive \'strīv\ *vi* **strove** \'strōv\ *also* **strived** \'strīvd\ **striv·en** \'striv-ən\ *or* **strived; striv·ing** \'strī-viŋ\ [ME *striven*, fr. OF *estriver*, of Gmc origin; akin to MHG *streben* to endeavor, OE *strīdan* to stride] **1 :** to struggle in opposition **:** CONTEND **2 :** to devote serious effort or energy **:** ENDEAVOR **syn** see ATTEMPT — **striv·er** \'strī-vər\ *n*

strobe \'strōb\ *n* [by shortening & alter.] **1 :** STROBOSCOPE **2 :** STROBOTRON ⟨~ photograph⟩

stro·bi·la \strō-'bī-lə\ *n, pl* **stro·bi·lae** \-(,)lē\ [NL, fr. Gk *strobilē* plug of lint shaped like a pinecone, fr. *strobilos* pinecone] **:** a linear series of similar animal structures (as the segmented body of a tapeworm) produced by budding — **stro·bi·lar** \-lər\ *adj* — **stro·bi·la·tion** \,strō-,bī-'lā-shən, -bə-; ,sträb-ə-\ *or* **stro·bi·li·za·tion** \(,)strō-,bī-lə-'zā-shən\ *n*

stro·bile \'sträb-,īl, 'strōb-, -əl\ *also* **stro·bil** \-əl\ *n* [NL *strobilus*] **1 :** STROBILUS **2 :** a spike with persistent overlapping bracts that resembles a cone and is the pistillate inflorescence of the hop — **stro·bi·lif·er·ous** \,sträb-,ī-'lif-(ə-)rəs, ,sträb-ə-, ,strōb-\ *adj*

stro·bi·lus \strō-'bī-ləs\ *n, pl* **stro·bi·li** \-,lī\ [NL, fr. LL, pinecone, fr. Gk *strobilos* twisted object, top, pinecone, fr. *strobos* action of whirling — more at STROPHE] **1 a :** an aggregation of sporophylls resembling a cone (as in the club mosses and horsetails) **b :** the cone of a gymnosperm **2 :** STROBILE 2 **3 :** STROBILA

stro·bo·scope \'strō-bə-,skōp\ *n* [Gk *strobos* + ISV *-scope*] **:** an instrument for determining speeds of rotation or frequencies of vibration made in the form of a revolving disk with holes around the edge through which an object is viewed or a rapidly flashing light that illuminates an object intermittently or a cardboard disk with marks to be viewed under intermittent light

stro·bo·scop·ic \,strō-bə-'skäp-ik\ *adj* **:** of, utilizing, or relating to a stroboscope or a strobotron — **stro·bo·scop·i·cal·ly** \-i-k(ə-)lē\ *adv*

stro·bo·tron \'strō-bə-,trän\ *n* [*strobo*scope + *-tron*] **:** a gas-filled electron tube with a cold cathode used esp. as a source of bright flashes of light for a stroboscope

strode *past of* STRIDE

stro·ga·noff \'strȯ-gə-,nȯf, -,nȯv\ *adj* [Count Paul *Stroganoff* 19th cent. Russ diplomat] **:** sliced thin and cooked in a sauce of consommé, sour cream, mustard, onion, and condiments — used postpositively ⟨beef ~⟩

1stroke \'strōk\ *vt* [ME *stroken*, fr. OE *strācian;* akin to OHG *strīhhan* to stroke — more at STRIKE] **:** to rub gently in one direction; *also* **:** CARESS — **strok·er** *n*

2stroke *n* **1 :** the act of striking; *esp* **:** a blow with a weapon or implement **2 :** a single unbroken movement; *esp* **:** one of a series of repeated or to-and-fro movements **3 :** a striking of the ball in a game (as tennis); *specif* **:** a striking or attempt to strike the ball that constitutes the scoring unit in golf **4 :** a sudden action or process producing an impact ⟨~ of lightning⟩ or unexpected result ⟨~ of luck⟩ **5 :** APOPLEXY **6 a :** one of a series of propelling beats or movements against a resisting medium **b :** an oarsman who sets the tempo for a crew **7 a :** a vigorous or energetic effort **b :** a delicate or clever touch in a narrative, description, or construction **8 :** HEARTBEAT **9 :** the movement or the distance of the movement in either direction of a mechanical part (as a piston rod) having a reciprocating motion **10 :** the sound of a bell being struck **11** [1*stroke*] **:** an act of stroking or caressing **12 a :** a mark or dash made by a single movement of an implement **b :** one of the lines of a letter of the alphabet

3stroke *vt* **1 a :** to mark with a short line ⟨~ the *t*'s⟩ **b :** to cancel by drawing a line through ⟨*stroked* out his name⟩ **2 :** to set the stroke for (a rowing crew); *also* **:** to set the stroke for the crew of (a rowing boat) **3 :** HIT; *esp* **:** to propel (a ball) with a controlled swinging blow

stroll \'strōl\ *vb* [prob. fr. G dial. *strollen*] *vi* **1 :** to walk in a leisurely or idle manner **:** RAMBLE **2 :** to go from place to place in search of occupation or profit **~** *vt* **:** to walk at leisure along or about — **stroll** *n*

stroll·er \'strō-lər\ *n* **1 :** one that strolls **2 a :** VAGRANT, TRAMP **b :** an itinerant actor **3 :** a carriage designed as a chair in which a baby may be pushed

stro·ma \'strō-mə\ *n, pl* **stro·ma·ta** \-mət-ə\ [NL *stromat-*, *stroma*, fr. L, bed covering, fr. Gk *strōmat-*, *strōma*, fr. *stornynai* to spread out — more at STREW] **1 a :** the supporting framework of an animal organ typically consisting of connective tissue **b :** the spongy protoplasmic framework of some cells (as a red blood cell) **2 :** a compact mass of fungous hyphae producing perithecia or pycnidia — **stro·mal** \-məl\ *adj* — **stro·ma·tal** \-mət-ᵊl\ *adj* — **stro·mat·ic** \strō-'mat-ik\ *adj*

stro·mey·er·ite \'strō-,mī-(ə-),rīt\ *n* [G *stromeyerit*, fr. Friedrich *Strohmeyer* †1835 G chemist] **:** a steel-gray mineral CuAgS consisting of silver copper sulfide of metallic luster

strong \'strȯŋ\ *adj* **stron·ger** \'strȯŋ-gər\ **stron·gest** \'strȯŋ-gəst\ [ME, fr. OE *strang;* akin to OHG *strengi* strong, L *stringere* to bind tight — more at STRAIN] **1 :** having or marked by great physical power **:** ROBUST **2 :** having moral or intellectual power **3 :** having great resources (as of wealth) **4 :** of a specified number ⟨an army ten thousand ~⟩ **5 :** effective or efficient esp. in a specified direction **6 :** FORCEFUL, COGENT **7 :** not mild or weak **:** INTENSE: as **a :** rich in some active agent (as a flavor or extract) ⟨~ beer⟩ **b** *of a color* **:** high in chroma **c :** ionizing freely in solution ⟨~ acids and bases⟩ **d :** magnifying by refracting greatly ⟨~ lens⟩ **8** *obs* **:** FLAGRANT **9 :** moving with rapidity or force ⟨~ wind⟩ **10 :** ARDENT, ZEALOUS **11 a :** not easily injured **:** SOLID **b :** not easily subdued or taken ⟨a ~ fort⟩ **12 :** well-established **:** FIRM **13 :** having an offensive or intense odor or flavor **:** RANK **14 :** tending to steady or higher prices ⟨a ~ market⟩ **15 :** of, relating to, or constituting a verb or verb conjugation that forms the past tense by a change in the root vowel and the past participle usu. by the addition of *-en* with or without change of the root vowel (as *strive, strove, striven* or *drink, drank, drunk*) — **strong** *adv* — **strong·ly** \'strȯŋ-lē\ *adv*

syn STRONG, STOUT, STURDY, STALWART, TOUGH, TENACIOUS mean showing power to resist or to endure. STRONG may imply power derived from muscular vigor, large size, structural soundness, intellectual or spiritual resources; STOUT suggests an ability to endure stress, pain, or hard use without giving way; STURDY implies strength derived from vigorous growth, determination of spirit, solidity of construction; STALWART suggests an unshakable dependability and connotes great physical strength; TOUGH implies great firmness and resiliency; TENACIOUS suggests strength in seizing, retaining, clinging to, or holding together

1strong–arm \'strȯŋ-'ärm\ *adj* **:** having or using undue force **:** VIOLENT ⟨~ methods⟩

2strong–arm *vt* **1 :** to use force upon **:** ASSAULT **2 :** to rob by violence

strong·box \-,bäks\ *n* **:** a strongly made chest or case for money or valuables

strong breeze *n* **:** wind having a speed of 25 to 31 miles per hour

strong drink *n* **:** intoxicating liquor

strong gale *n* **:** wind having a speed of 47 to 54 miles per hour

strong·hold \'strȯŋ-,hōld\ *n* **1 :** a fortified place **:** FORTRESS **2 :** a place dominated by a particular group

strong·ish \'strȯŋ-ish\ *adj* **:** somewhat strong ⟨~ wind⟩

strong–mind·ed \-'mīn-dəd\ *adj* **:** having a vigorous mind; *esp* **:** marked by independence of thought and judgment — **strong-mind·ed·ly** *adv* — **strong–mind·ed·ness** *n*

strong room *n* **:** a room for money or valuables specially constructed to be fireproof and burglar-proof

strong suit *n* **1 :** a long suit containing high cards **2 :** something in which one excels **:** FORTE

stron·gyle \'strän-,jīl, -jəl\ *n* [deriv. of Gk *strongylos* round, compact; akin to L *stringere* to bind tight — more at STRAIN] **:** any of various roundworms (family Strongylidae) related to the hookworms and mostly parasitic in the alimentary tract and tissues of the horse

stron·gy·lo·sis \,strän-jə-'lō-səs\ *n* [NL] **:** infestation with or disease caused by strongyles

stron·tia \'strän-ch(ē-)ə, 'stränt-ē-ə\ *n* [NL, fr. obs. E *strontian*, fr. *Strontian*, village in Scotland] **1 :** a white solid monoxide SrO of strontium resembling lime and baryta **2 :** strontium hydroxide $Sr(OH)_2$

stron·tian \'strän-ch(ē-)ən, 'stränt-ē-ən\ *n* [*Strontian*, village in Scotland] **:** STRONTIUM

stron·tian·ite \-,īt\ *n* **:** a mineral $SrCO_3$ consisting of strontium carbonate and occurring in various forms and colors

stron·tic \'stränt-ik\ *adj* **:** of or relating to strontium

stron·tium \'strän-ch(ē-)əm, 'stränt-ē-əm\ *n* [NL, fr. *strontia*] **:** a soft malleable ductile bivalent metallic element of the alkaline-earth group occurring only in combination and used esp. in crimson fireworks — see ELEMENT table

strontium 90 *n* **:** a heavy radioactive isotope of strontium having the mass number 90 that is present in the fallout from nuclear explosions and is hazardous because assimilable by the animal body — called also *radiostrontium*

1strop \'sträp\ *n* [ME — more at STRAP] **:** STRAP: **a :** a short rope with its ends spliced to form a circle **b :** a usu. leather band for sharpening a razor

2strop *vt* **stropped; strop·ping :** to sharpen (a razor) on a strop

stro·phan·thin \strō-'fan(t)-thən\ *n* [ISV, fr. NL *Strophanthus* (genus of tropical trees or vines)] **:** any of several glycosides or mixtures of glycosides from African plants (genera *Strophanthus* and *Acocanthera*) of the dogbane family; *esp* **:** a bitter toxic

glycoside $C_{36}H_{54}O_{14}$ from a woody vine (*Strophanthus kombé*) used similarly to digitalis

stro·phe \'strō-fē, -ˌfē\ *n* [Gk *strophē*, lit., act of turning, fr. *strephein* to turn, twist; akin to Gk *strobos* action of whirling] **1 :** the movement of the classical Greek chorus while turning from one side to the other of the orchestra **2 a :** a rhythmic system composed of two or more lines repeated as a unit; *esp* **:** such a unit recurring in a series of strophic units **b :** STANZA **c :** the part of a Greek choral ode sung during the strophe of the dance — **stro·phic** \'sträf-ik, 'strō-fik\ *adj*

stroud \'strau̇d\ *n* [prob. fr. *Stroud*, England] **1** *also* **stroud·ing** \-iŋ\ **:** a coarse woolen cloth formerly used in trade with No. American Indians **2 :** a blanket or garment of stroud

strove *past & chiefly dial past part of* STRIVE

strow \'strō\ *vt* **strowed; strown** \'strōn\ *or* **strowed; strow·ing** [ME *strowen* — more at STREW] *archaic* **:** SCATTER

stroy \'strȯi\ *vb* [ME *stroyen*, short for *destroyen*] *obs* **:** DESTROY

struck \'strək\ *adj* **:** closed or affected by a labor strike ⟨a ~ factory⟩ ⟨a ~ employer⟩

struc·tur·al \'strək-chə-rəl, 'strək-shrəl\ *adj* **1 a :** of, relating to, or affecting structure ⟨~ stability⟩ **b :** used in building structures ⟨~ clay⟩ **c :** involved in or caused by structure esp. of the economy ⟨~ unemployment⟩ **2 :** of or relating to the physical makeup of a plant or animal body **3 :** of, relating to, or resulting from the effects of folding or faulting of the earth's crust **:** TECTONIC **4 :** concerned with or relating to structure rather than history or comparison ⟨~ linguistics⟩ — **struc·tur·al·ly** \-ē\ *adv*

structural formula *n* **:** an expanded molecular formula showing the arrangement within the molecule of atoms and of bonds

structural iron *n* **:** iron worked or cast in structural shapes

struc·tur·al·iza·tion \ˌstrək-chə-rə-lə-'zā-shən, ˌstrək-shrə-lə-\ *n* **:** the process of structuralizing or becoming structuralized

struc·tur·al·ize \'strək-chə-rə-ˌlīz, 'strək-shrə-ˌlīz\ *vt* **:** to embody in or incorporate into a structure

structural steel *n* **1 :** rolled steel in structural shapes **2 :** steel suitable for structural shapes

1struc·ture \'strək-chər\ *n* [ME, fr. L *structura*, fr. *structus*, pp. of *struere* to heap up, build; akin to L *sternere* to spread out — more at STREW] **1 :** the action of building **:** CONSTRUCTION **2 a :** something constructed **b :** something made up of interdependent parts in a definite pattern of organization **3 :** manner of construction **:** MAKEUP **4 a :** the arrangement of particles or parts in a substance or body ⟨soil ~⟩ ⟨the ~ of a plant⟩ ⟨molecular ~⟩ **b :** interrelation of parts as dominated by the general character of the whole ⟨economic ~⟩ **5 a :** the elements of an entity or the position of such elements in their relationships to each other **b** (1) **:** the composition of conscious experience with its elements and their combinations (2) **:** GESTALT

2structure *vt* **struc·tur·ing** \'strək-chə-riŋ, 'strək-shriŋ\ **1 :** to form into a structure **:** ORGANIZE **2 :** BUILD, CONSTRUCT

struc·ture·less \'strək-chər-ləs\ *adj* **:** lacking structure; *esp* **:** devoid of cells ⟨a ~ membrane⟩ — **struc·ture·less·ness** *n*

stru·del \'s(h)trüd-ᵊl\ *n* [G, lit., whirlpool] **:** a sheet of paper-thin dough rolled up with filling and baked

1strug·gle \'strəg-əl\ *vi* **strug·gling** \-(ə-)liŋ\ [ME *struglen*] **1 :** to make violent strenuous efforts against opposition **:** STRIVE **2 :** to proceed with difficulty or with great effort — **strug·gler** \-(ə-)lər\ *n*

2struggle *n* **1 :** a violent effort or exertion **2 :** CONTEST, STRIFE

strum \'strəm\ *vb* **strummed; strum·ming** [imit.] *vt* **:** to brush the fingers lightly over the strings of (a stringed instrument) in playing ⟨~ a guitar⟩; *also* **:** THRUM **~** *vi* **:** to strum a stringed instrument — **strum** *n* — **strum·mer** *n*

stru·ma \'strü-mə\ *n, pl* **stru·mae** \-(ˌ)mē, -ˌmī\ *or* **strumas** **1** [L — more at STRUT] **a** *archaic* **:** SCROFULA **b :** GOITER **2** [NL, fr. L] **:** a swelling at the base of the capsule in many mosses — **stru·mose** \-ˌmōs\ *adj* — **stru·mous** \-məs\ *adj*

strum·pet \'strəm-pət\ *n* [ME] **:** PROSTITUTE, HARLOT

strung past of STRING

1strunt \'strənt\ *vi* [by alter.] *Scot* **:** STRUT

2strunt *n* [origin unknown] *Scot* **:** LIQUOR

1strut \'strət\ *vb* **strut·ted; strut·ting** [ME *strouten*, fr. OE *strūtian* to exert oneself; akin to L *struma* goiter, OE *starian* to stare] *vi* **1 :** to become turgid **:** SWELL **2 :** to walk with a lofty proud gait; *esp* **:** SWAGGER **~** *vt* **:** to parade (as clothes) with a show of pride — **strut·ter** *n*

2strut *n* **1 :** a structural piece designed to resist pressure in the direction of its length ⟨a ~ supporting a rafter⟩ ⟨an airplane landing-gear ~⟩ **2 :** a pompous step or walk

3strut *vt* **strut·ted; strut·ting :** to provide, stiffen, support, or hold apart with or as if with a strut

stru·thi·ous \'strü-thē-əs, -t͟hē-\ *adj* [LL *struthio* ostrich, irreg. fr. Gk *strouthos*] **:** of or relating to the ostriches and related birds **:** RATITE

strych·nia \'strik-nē-ə\ *n* [NL, fr. *Strychnos*] **:** STRYCHNINE — **strych·nic** \-nik\ *adj*

strych·nine \'strik-ˌnīn, -nən, -ˌnēn\ *n* [F, fr. NL *Strychnos*, genus name, fr. L, nightshade, fr. Gk] **:** a bitter poisonous alkaloid $C_{21}H_{22}N_2O_2$ obtained from nux vomica and related plants (genus *Strychnos*) and used as an economic poison (as for rodents) and medicinally as a tonic and stimulant for the central nervous system

strych·nin·ism \-ˌiz-əm\ *n* **:** chronic strychnine poisoning

Stu·art \'st(y)ü-ərt, 'st(y)u̇(-ə)rt\ *n* **:** a member or supporter of the British house of Stuart — **Stuart** *adj*

1stub \'stəb\ *n* [ME *stubb*, fr. OE *stybb*; akin to Gk *stypos* stem, *typtein* to beat — more at TYPE] **1 a :** STUMP 2 **b :** a short piece remaining on a stem or trunk where a branch has been lost **2 :** something made or worn to a short or blunt shape; *esp* **:** a pen with a short blunt nib **3 :** a short blunt part left after a larger part has been broken off or used up ⟨pencil ~⟩ **4 :** something cut short or stunted **5 a :** a small part of a leaf (as of a checkbook) attached to the backbone for memoranda of the contents of the part torn away **b :** the part of a ticket returned to the user

2stub *vt* **stubbed; stub·bing 1 a :** to grub up by the roots **b :** to clear (land) by grubbing out rooted growth **c :** to hew or cut down (a tree) close to the ground **2 :** to extinguish (as a cigarette) by crushing **3 :** to strike (one's foot or toe) against an object

stub·ble \'stəb-əl\ *n, often attrib* [ME *stuble*, fr. OF *estuble*, fr. L *stupula* stalk, straw, alter. of *stipula* — more at STIPULE] **1 :** the basal part of herbaceous plants and esp. cereal grasses remaining attached to the soil after harvest **2 :** a rough surface or growth resembling stubble; *esp* **:** a short growth of beard

stubble mulch *n* **:** a lightly tilled mulch of plant residue used to prevent erosion, conserve moisture, and add organic matter to the soil

stub·bly \'stəb-(ə-)lē\ *adj* **1 :** covered with stubble ⟨~ fields⟩ **2 :** resembling stubble ⟨a ~ beard⟩

stub·born \'stəb-ərn\ *adj* [ME *stuborn*] **1 :** RESOLUTE, UNYIELDING **2 :** OBSTINATE **3 :** performed or carried on in an unyielding, obstinate, or persistent manner ⟨~ strife⟩ **4 :** difficult to handle, manage, or treat **:** REFRACTORY **syn** see OBSTINATE — **stub·born·ly** *adv* — **stub·born·ness** \-ərn-nəs\ *n*

stub·by \'stəb-ē\ *adj* **1 a :** resembling a stub **:** being short and thick ⟨~ fingers⟩ **b :** being short and thickset **:** SQUAT **c :** being short, broad, or blunt (as from use or wear) **2 :** abounding with stubs **:** BRISTLY

1stuc·co \'stək-(ˌ)ō\ *n, pl* **stuccos** *or* **stuccoes** [It, of Gmc origin; akin to OHG *stucki* piece, crust, OE *stocc* stock] **1 a :** a material usu. made of portland cement, sand, and a small percentage of lime and applied in a plastic state to form a hard covering for exterior walls **b :** a fine plaster used in decoration and ornamentation of interior walls **2 :** STUCCOWORK

2stucco *vt* **stuc·coed; stuc·co·ing :** to coat or decorate with stucco

stuc·co·work \'stək-ō-ˌwərk\ *n* **:** work done in stucco

stuck *past of* STICK

stuck-up \'stək-'əp\ *adj* **:** being self-important and supercilious **:** CONCEITED

1stud \'stəd\ *n, often attrib* [ME *stod*, fr. OE *stōd*; akin to OE *standan* to stand] **1 a :** a group of animals and esp. horses kept primarily for breeding **b :** a place (as a farm) where such a stud is kept **2 :** STUDHORSE; *broadly* **:** a male animal kept for breeding — **at stud :** for breeding as a stud ⟨retired racers standing *at stud*⟩

2stud *n* [ME *stode*, fr. OE *studu*; akin to OE *stōw* place — more at STOW] **1 a :** one of the smaller uprights in the framing of the walls of a building to which sheathing, paneling, or laths are fastened **:** SCANTLING **b :** the height of a room **2 a :** a boss, rivet, or nail with a large head used (as on a shield or belt) for ornament or protection **b :** a solid button with a shank or eye on the back inserted through an eyelet in a garment as a fastener or ornament **3 :** any of various infixed pieces (as a rod or pin) projecting from a machine and serving chiefly as a support or axis

3stud *vt* **stud·ded; stud·ding 1 :** to furnish (a building or wall) with studs **2 :** to adorn, cover, or protect with studs **3 :** to set (a place or thing) with a number of prominent objects ⟨water *studded* with islands⟩

stud·book \'stəd-ˌbu̇k\ *n* **:** an official record (as in a book) of the pedigree of purebred animals (as horses or dogs)

stud·ding \'stəd-iŋ\ *n* **1 :** material for studs **2 :** STUDS

stud·ding sail \'stəd-iŋ-ˌsāl, 'stən(t)-səl\ *n* [origin unknown] **:** a light sail set at the side of a principal square sail of a ship in free winds

stu·dent \'st(y)üd-ᵊnt, *oftenest in South* -ənt\ *n* [ME, fr. L *student-*, *studens*, fr. prp. of *studēre* to study — more at STUDY] **1 :** LEARNER, SCHOLAR; *esp* **:** one who attends a school **2 :** one who studies **:** an attentive and systematic observer ⟨a ~ of life⟩ **syn** see SCHOLAR

student government *n* **:** the organization and management of student life, activities, or discipline by various student organizations in a school or college

student lamp *n* **:** a desk reading lamp with a tubular shaft, one or two arms for a shaded light, and originally an oil reservoir

stu·dent·ship \'st(y)üd-ᵊnt-ˌship, -ənt-\ *n* **1 :** the state of being a student **2** *Brit* **:** a grant for university study

student teacher *n* **:** a student who is engaged in practice teaching

stud·horse \'stəd-ˌhȯ(ə)rs\ *n* **:** a stallion kept esp. for breeding

stud·ied \'stəd-ēd\ *adj* **1 :** KNOWLEDGEABLE, LEARNED **2 :** carefully considered or prepared **:** THOUGHTFUL **3 :** produced or marked by conscious design or premeditation ⟨~ indifference⟩ — **stud·ied·ly** *adv* — **stud·ied·ness** *n*

stu·dio \'st(y)üd-ē-ˌō\ *n* [It, lit., study, fr. L *studium*] **1 a :** the working place of a painter, sculptor, or photographer **b :** a place for the study of an art (as dancing, singing, or acting) **2 :** a place where motion pictures are made **3 :** a place maintained and equipped for the transmission of radio or television programs

studio couch *n* **:** an upholstered usu. backless couch that can be made to serve as a double bed by sliding from underneath it the frame of a single cot

stu·di·ous \'st(y)üd-ē-əs\ *adj* **1 :** given to study **2 a :** of, relating to, or concerned with study **b :** favorable to study **3 a :** diligent or earnest in intent **b :** marked by purposefulness or diligence **c :** deliberately planned **:** STUDIED — **stu·di·ous·ly** *adv* — **stu·di·ous·ness** *n*

stud poker *n* ['stud] **:** poker in which each player is dealt his first card facedown and his other four cards faceup with a round of betting taking place after each of the last four rounds

stud·work \'stəd-ˌwərk\ *n* **:** work supported, strengthened, held together, or ornamented by studs

1study \'stəd-ē\ *n* [ME *studie*, fr. OF *estudie*, fr. L *studium*; akin to L *studēre* to study] **1 :** a state of contemplation **:** REVERIE **2 a :** application of the mental faculties to the acquisition of knowledge **b :** such application in a particular field or to a specific subject **c :** a careful examination or analysis of a phenomenon, development, or question; *also* **:** a paper in which such a study is published **3 :** a building or room devoted to study or literary pursuits **4 :** PURPOSE, INTENT **5 a :** a branch or department of learning **:** SUBJECT **b :** the activity or work of a student **c :** an object of study **d :** something attracting close attention or examination **6 :** a literary or artistic production intended as a preliminary outline or an experimental interpretation of specific features or characteristics **7 :** a musical composition devoted entirely to a problem of technique

2study *vi* **1 a :** to engage in study **b :** to undertake formal study of a subject **2** *dial* **:** MEDITATE, REFLECT **3 :** ENDEAVOR, TRY **~** *vt* **1 :** to read in detail esp. with the intention of learning **2 :** to

engage in the study of ⟨~ biology⟩ ⟨~ medicine⟩ **3 :** PLOT, DESIGN **4 :** to consider attentively or in detail **syn** see CONSIDER

study hall *n* **1 :** a room in a school set aside for study **2 :** a period in a student's day set aside for study and homework

[1]**stuff** \'stəf\ *n* [ME, fr. MF *estoffe*, fr. OF, fr. *estoffer* to equip, stock] **1 :** materials, supplies, or equipment used in various activities: as **a** *obs* **:** military baggage **b :** bullets or shells fired from a gun **:** PROJECTILES **c :** PERSONAL PROPERTY, POSSESSIONS **2 :** material to be manufactured, wrought, or used in construction **3 :** a finished textile suitable for clothing; *esp* **:** wool or worsted material **4 a :** literary or artistic production **b :** writing, discourse, or ideas of little value **:** RUBBISH **5 a :** an aggregate of matter ⟨volcanic rock is curious ~⟩ **b :** matter of a particular kind often unspecified ⟨sold tons of the ~⟩; *esp* **:** something (as a drug or food) consumed by man **6 a :** fundamental material **:** SUBSTANCE ⟨~ of greatness⟩ ⟨~ of manhood⟩ **b :** subject matter **7 a :** actions or talk in specific circumstances **b :** special knowledge or capability **8 a :** spin imparted to a thrown or hit ball to make it curve or change course **b :** speed and esp. variety of pitches or curves of a baseball pitcher

[2]**stuff** *vt* **1 a :** to fill by packing things in **:** CRAM **b :** to fill (as one's stomach) to fullness **:** SURFEIT **c :** to prepare (meat or vegetables) by filling or lining with a seasoned mixture **d :** to fill (as a cushion) with a soft material or padding **e :** to fill out the skin of (an animal) for mounting **f :** to fill (a hole) by packing in material **:** stop up **:** PLUG **2 :** to fill with ideas or information **3 :** to choke up or block (the nasal passages) **4 a :** to insert snugly or tightly **:** TUCK **b :** to cause to enter or fill **:** THRUST, PRESS **5 :** to impregnate (leather) for softening and preserving **6 :** to fill (a ballot box) with fraudulent votes **~** *vi* **:** to eat gluttonously **:** GORGE — **stuff·er** *n*

stuffed shirt *n* **:** a smug conceited inflexibly conservative usu. pompous person

stuff·i·ly \'stəf-ə-lē\ *adv* **:** in a stuffy manner

stuff·i·ness \'stəf-ē-nəs\ *n* **:** the quality or state of being stuffy

stuff·ing \'stəf-iŋ\ *n* **:** material used to stuff; *esp* **:** a seasoning mixture used to stuff meat, vegetables, eggs, or poultry

stuffing box *n* **:** a device to prevent leakage along a moving part (as a piston rod) passing through a hole in a vessel (as a cylinder) containing steam, water, or oil consisting of a box or chamber made by enlarging the hole and a gland to compress the contained packing

stuff·less \'stəf-ləs\ *adj* **:** lacking stuff or substance

stuffy \'stəf-ē\ *adj* **1 :** SULLEN, ILL-HUMORED **2 a :** oppressive to the breathing **:** CLOSE **b :** stuffed or choked up **3 :** DULL, STODGY **4 :** narrowly inflexible in standards of conduct **:** SELF-RIGHTEOUS

stull \'stəl\ *n* [perh. modif. of G *stollen* post, support] **1 :** a round timber used to support the sides or back of a mine **2 :** one of a series of props wedged between the walls of a stope to hold up a platform

stul·ti·fi·ca·tion \ˌstəl-tə-fə-'kā-shən\ *n* **:** the act or process of stultifying **:** the state of being stultified

stul·ti·fy \'stəl-tə-ˌfī\ *vt* [LL *stultificare* to make foolish, fr. L *stultus* foolish; akin to L *stolidus* stolid] **1 :** to allege or prove to be of unsound mind and not responsible **2 a :** to cause to appear or be stupid, foolish, or absurdly illogical **b :** to impair, invalidate, or reduce to futility esp. through debasing or repressive influences

[1]**stum** \'stəm\ *vt* **stummed; stum·ming** [D *stommen*, fr. *stom*, n.] *archaic* **:** to renew (wine) by mixing with must and reviving fermentation

[2]**stum** *n* [D *stom*] **:** unfermented or partly fermented grape juice; *esp* **:** must in which fermentation has been artificially arrested

stum·ble \'stəm-bəl\ *vb* **stum·bling** \-b(ə-)liŋ\ [ME *stumblen*, prob. of Scand origin; akin to Norw dial. *stumle* to stumble; akin to OE *stamerian* to stammer] *vi* **1 a :** to fall into sin or waywardness **b :** to make an error **:** BLUNDER **c :** to come to a block to belief **2 :** to trip in walking or running **3 a :** to walk unsteadily or clumsily **b :** to speak or act in a hesitant or faltering manner **4 a :** to come unexpectedly **:** MEET ⟨~ onto the truth⟩ **b :** to fall or move carelessly **~** *vt* **1 :** to cause to stumble **:** TRIP **2 :** CONFOUND, PERPLEX — **stumble** *n* — **stum·bler** \-b(ə-)lər\ *n* — **stum·bling·ly** \-bliŋ-lē\ *adv*

stum·ble·bum \'stəm-bəl-ˌbəm\ *n* **:** a punch-drunk, clumsy, or inept boxer

stumbling block \'stəm-bliŋ-\ *n* **1 :** an impediment to belief or understanding **:** PERPLEXITY **2 :** an obstacle to progress

[1]**stump** \'stəmp\ *n* [ME *stumpe;* akin to OHG *stumpf* stump, ME *stampen* to stamp] **1 a :** the basal portion of a bodily part remaining after the rest is removed **b :** a rudimentary or vestigial bodily part **2 :** the part of a tree remaining attached to the root after the trunk is cut **3 :** a remaining part **:** STUB **4 :** a place or occasion for political public speaking

[2]**stump** *vt* **1 :** to reduce to a stump **:** TRIM, LOP **2 a :** CHALLENGE, DARE **b :** PERPLEX, CONFOUND **3 :** to clear (land) of stumps **4 :** to travel over (a region) making political speeches or supporting a cause **5 a :** to walk over heavily or clumsily **b :** STUB 3 **~** *vi* **1 :** to walk heavily or noisily **2 :** to go about making political speeches or supporting a cause — **stump·er** *n*

[3]**stump** *n* [F or Flem; F *estompe*, fr. Flem *stomp*, lit., stub, fr. MD; akin to OHG *stumpf* stump] **:** a short thick roll of leather or paper cut to a point and used for shading a crayon or pencil drawing by rubbing

[4]**stump** *vt* **:** to tone or treat (a crayon drawing) with a stump

stump·age \'stəm-pij\ *n* **:** the value of standing timber; *also* **:** uncut timber itself or the right to cut it

stump speaking *n* **:** speaking addressed to the general public esp. during a political campaign

stumpy \'stəm-pē\ *adj* **1 :** full of stumps **2 :** being short and thick **:** STUBBY

stun \'stən\ *vt* **stunned; stun·ning** [ME *stunen*, modif. of OF *estoner* — more at ASTONISH] **1 :** to make senseless or dizzy by or as if by a blow **2 :** to bewilder with noise **:** DAZE **3 :** to overcome esp. with astonishment or disbelief **:** STUPEFY — **stun** *n*

stung *past of* STING

stunk *past of* STINK

stun·ner \'stən-ər\ *n* **:** one that stuns; *esp* **:** an unusually attractive person

stun·ning \'stən-iŋ\ *adj* **:** strikingly beautiful or attractive — **stun·ning·ly** \-iŋ-lē\ *adv*

stun·sail *or* **stun·s'l** \'stən(t)-səl\ *n* [by contr.] **:** STUDDING SAIL

[1]**stunt** \'stənt\ *vt* [E dial. *stunt* stubborn, stunted, abrupt, prob. of Scand origin; akin to ON *stuttr* scant — more at STINT] **:** to hinder the normal growth of **:** DWARF, CHECK

[2]**stunt** *n* **1 :** a stunting or stunted thing **2 :** a plant disease in which dwarfing occurs

[3]**stunt** *n* [prob. alter. of *stump* (challenge)] **:** an unusual or difficult feat performed or undertaken chiefly to gain attention or publicity

[4]**stunt** *vi* **:** to perform stunts

stunt·ed·ness \'stənt-əd-nəs\ *n* **:** the quality or state of being stunted

stu·pa \'stü-pə\ *n* [Skt *stūpa*] **:** a hemispherical or cylindrical mound or tower serving as a Buddhist shrine

stupe \'st(y)üp\ *n* [ME, fr. L *stuppa* coarse part of flax, tow, fr. Gk *styppē*] **:** a hot wet often medicated cloth applied externally (as to stimulate circulation)

stu·pe·fa·cient \ˌst(y)ü-pə-'fā-shənt\ *adj* [L *stupefacient-, stupefaciens*, prp. of *stupefacere* to stupefy] **:** bringing about a stupor **:** STUPEFYING, NARCOTIC — **stupefacient** *n*

stu·pe·fac·tion \-'fak-shən\ *n* [NL *stupefaction-, stupefactio*, fr. L *stupefactus*, pp. of *stupefacere*] **:** the act of stupefying **:** the state of being stupefied

stu·pe·fi·er \'st(y)ü-pə-ˌfī(-ə)r\ *n* **:** one that stupefies

stu·pe·fy \-ˌfī\ *vt* [MF *stupefier*, modif. of L *stupefacere*, fr. *stupēre* to be astonished + *facere* to make, do — more at DO] **1 :** to make stupid, dull, or insensible **:** BENUMB **2 :** ASTONISH

stu·pen·dous \st(y)ü-'pen-dəs\ *adj* [L *stupendus*, gerundive of *stupēre*] **1 :** causing astonishment or wonder **:** AWESOME, MARVELOUS **2 :** of amazing size or greatness **:** PRODIGIOUS **syn** see MONSTROUS — **stu·pen·dous·ly** *adv* — **stu·pen·dous·ness** *n*

[1]**stu·pid** \'st(y)ü-pəd\ *adj* [MF *stupide*, fr. L *stupidus*, fr. *stupēre* to be benumbed, be astonished; akin to Gk *typtein* to beat — more at TYPE] **1 a :** slow of mind **:** OBTUSE **b :** UNTHINKING, IRRATIONAL **c :** lacking intelligence or reason **:** BRUTISH **2 a :** dulled in feeling or sensation **:** TORPID **b :** incapable of feeling or sensation **:** INANIMATE **3 :** marked by or resulting from dullness **:** SENSELESS **4 :** DREARY, BORING — **stu·pid·ly** *adv* — **stu·pid·ness** *n*

syn STUPID, DULL, DENSE, CRASS, DUMB mean lacking in power to absorb ideas or impressions. STUPID implies a slow-witted or dazed state of mind that may be either congenital or temporary; DULL suggests a slow or sluggish mind such as results from disease, depression, or shock; DENSE implies a thickheaded imperviousness to ideas; CRASS suggests a grossness of mind precluding discrimination or delicacy; DUMB applies to an exasperating obtuseness or lack of comprehension

[2]**stupid** *n* **:** a stupid person

stu·pid·i·ty \st(y)ü-'pid-ət-ē\ *n* **1 :** the quality or state of being stupid **2 :** a stupid idea or act

stu·por \'st(y)ü-pər\ *n* [ME, fr. L, fr. *stupēre*] **1 :** a condition characterized by great diminution or suspension of sense or feeling ⟨drunken ~⟩ **2 :** a state of extreme apathy or torpor resulting often from stress or shock **syn** see LETHARGY — **stu·por·ous** \-p(ə-)rəs\ *adj*

stur·di·ly \'stərd-ᵊl-ē\ *adv* **:** in a sturdy manner

stur·di·ness \'stərd-ē-nəs\ *n* **:** the quality or state of being sturdy

stur·dy \'stərd-ē\ *adj* [ME, brave, stubborn, fr. OF *estourdi* stunned, fr. pp. of *estourdir* to stun, fr. (assumed) VL *exturdire* to be dizzy as a thrush that is drunk from eating grapes, fr. L *ex-* + *turdus* thrush — more at THRUSH] **1 a :** firmly built or constituted **:** STOUT **b :** HARDY **c :** sound in design or execution **:** SUBSTANTIAL **2 a :** marked by or reflecting physical strength or vigor **:** ROBUST **b :** FIRM, RESOLUTE **syn** see STRONG

stur·geon \'stər-jən\ *n* [ME, fr. OF *estourjon*, of Gmc origin; akin to OE *styria* sturgeon] **:** any of various usu. large elongate ganoid fishes (as of the genus *Acipenser*) widely distributed in the north temperate zone and valued for their flesh and esp. for their roe which is made into caviar

Sturm und Drang \ˌshtu̇r-mu̇nt-'dräŋ, -mənt-\ *n* [G, fr. *Sturm und Drang* (*Storm and Stress*), drama by Friedrich von Klinger] **:** a late 18th century German literary movement marked by a revolt against the French Enlightenment and German imitation of it

sturt \'stərt\ *n* [ME, contention, alter. of *strut;* akin to OE *strūtian* to exert oneself — more at STRUT] *chiefly Scot* **:** DISTURBANCE — **sturt** *vb*

stut·ter \'stət-ər\ *vb* [freq. of E dial. *stut* to stutter, fr. ME *stutten;* akin to D *stotteren* to stutter, L *tundere* to beat — more at STINT] *vi* **:** to speak with spasmodic repetition as a result of excitement or impediment **~** *vt* **:** to say, speak, or sound with or as if with a stutter **syn** see STAMMER — **stutter** *n* — **stut·ter·er** \-ər-ər\ *n*

[1]**sty** \'stī\ *n, pl* **sties** *also* **styes** [ME, fr. OE *stig;* akin to ON *-stī* sty] **1 :** a pen or enclosed housing for swine **2 :** a filthy, low, or vicious place

[2]**sty** *vb* **stied; sty·ing** *vt* **:** to lodge or keep in or as if in a sty **~** *vi* **:** to live in a sty

[3]**sty** *or* **stye** \'stī\ *n, pl* **sties** *or* **styes** [short for obs. E *styan*, fr. (assumed) ME, alter. of OE *stīgend*, fr. *stīgan* to go up, rise — more at STAIR] **:** an inflamed swelling of a sebaceous gland at the margin of an eyelid

sty·gian \'stij-(ē-)ən\ *adj, often cap* **1 :** of or relating to the river Styx **2 a :** INFERNAL, GLOOMY **b :** INVIOLABLE

[1]**styl-** *or* **stylo-** *comb form* [L, fr. Gk, fr. *stylos* — more at STEER] **:** pillar ⟨*stylo*lite⟩

[2]**styl-** *or* **styli-** *or* **stylo-** *comb form* [L *stilus* stake, stalk — more at STYLE] **:** style **:** styloid process ⟨*styl*ate⟩ ⟨*styli*ferous⟩ ⟨*stylo*graphic⟩

sty·lar \'stī-lər\ *adj* **:** of, relating to, or resembling a style **:** STYLIFORM

-sty·lar \'stī-lər\ *adj comb form* [Gk *stylos* pillar — more at STEER] **:** having (such or so many) pillars **:** having (such) columniation ⟨amphi*stylar*⟩

sty·late \'stī(ə)l-ˌāt\ *adj* **:** bearing or resembling a style or stylet ⟨~ insects⟩

[1]**style** \'stī(ə)l\ *n* [ME *stile, style*, fr. L *stilus* stake, stylus, style of writing; akin to OE *stician* to stick] **1 a :** an instrument used by the ancients in writing on waxed tablets **b** (1) **:** the shadow-producing pin of a sundial (2) **:** PEN (3) **:** STYLET (4) **:** GRAVER (5) **:** a phonograph needle **c :** a filiform prolongation of a plant ovary bearing a stigma at its apex **d :** a slender bristle or other elongated process on an animal **2 a :** mode of expressing thought in language; *esp* **:** a manner of expression characteristic of an individual, period, school, or nation ⟨classic ~⟩ **b :** manner or tone assumed in discourse **c :** the custom or plan followed in spelling,

capitalization, punctuation, and typographic arrangement and display **3 :** mode of address **:** TITLE **4 a** (1) **:** manner or method of acting or performing esp. as sanctioned by some standard (2) **:** a distinctive or characteristic manner **b :** a fashionable luxurious mode of life ⟨lived in ~⟩ **c :** overall excellence, skill, or grace in performance, manner, or appearance **syn** see FASHION

²**style** *vt* **1 :** to designate by an identifying term **:** NAME ⟨~*s* himself scientist⟩ **2 a :** to cause to conform to a customary style **b :** to design and make in accord with the prevailing mode — **styl·er** *n*

style·book \ˈstī(ə)l-ˌbu̇k\ *n* **:** a book explaining, describing, or illustrating the prevailing, accepted, or authorized style

style·less \ˈstī(ə)l-ləs\ *adj* **:** lacking in style

sty·let \ˈstī-lət\ *n* [F, fr. MF *stilet* stiletto, fr. OIt *stiletto*] **1 :** a slender surgical probe **2 a :** STYLE 1c **b :** STYLE 1d **3 :** STILETTO

sty·lif·er·ous \stī-ˈlif-(ə-)rəs\ *adj* **:** bearing one or more styles

sty·li·form \ˈstī-lə-ˌfȯrm\ *adj* [NL *stiliformis*, fr. L *stilus* + *-formis* -form] **:** resembling a style **:** bristle-shaped

styl·ish \ˈstī-lish\ *adj* **:** having style; *esp* **:** conforming to current fashion — **styl·ish·ly** *adv* — **styl·ish·ness** *n*

styl·ist \ˈstī-ləst\ *n* **1 :** a master or model of style; *esp* **:** a writer or speaker eminent in matters of style **2 :** one who develops, designs, or advises on styles — **sty·lis·tic** \stī-ˈlis-tik\ *also* **sty·lis·ti·cal** \-ti-kəl\ *adj* — **sty·lis·ti·cal·ly** \-ti-k(ə-)lē\ *adv*

sty·lis·tics \stī-ˈlis-tiks\ *n pl but sing or pl in constr* **1 :** an aspect of literary study that emphasizes the analysis of various elements of style (as metaphor and diction) **2 :** the study of the devices in a language that produce expressive value (as rhetorical figures and syntactical patterns)

sty·lite \ˈstī(ə)l-ˌīt\ *n* [LGk *stylitēs*, fr. Gk *stylos* pillar — more at STEER] **:** a Christian ascetic living atop a pillar — **sty·lit·ic** \stī-ˈlit-ik\ *adj* — **sty·lit·ism** \ˈstī(ə)l-ˌīt-ˌiz-əm\ *n*

styl·iza·tion \ˌstī-lə-ˈzā-shən\ *n* **1 :** the quality or state of being stylized **2 :** an act or instance of stylizing

styl·ize \ˈstī(ə)l-ˌīz\ *vt* **:** to conform to a style **:** CONVENTIONALIZE; *specif* **:** to represent or design according to a style or stylistic pattern rather than according to nature — **styl·iz·er** *n*

sty·lo·bate \ˈstī-lə-ˌbāt\ *n* [L *stylobates*, fr. Gk *stylobatēs*, fr. *stylos* pillar + *bainein* to walk, go — more at COME] **:** a continuous flat coping or pavement on which a row of architectural columns is supported

sty·lo·graph \-ˌgraf\ *n* **:** a stylographic pen

sty·lo·graph·ic \ˌstī-lə-ˈgraf-ik\ *adj* **1 :** of or relating to stylography **2 :** of, relating to, or being a fountain pen that has a fine point fitted with a needle which by pressure of the point on a surface is pushed back to release the flow of ink — **sty·lo·graph·i·cal** \-i-kəl\ *adj* — **sty·lo·graph·i·cal·ly** \-i-k(ə-)lē\ *adv*

sty·log·ra·phy \stī-ˈläg-rə-fē\ *n* **:** a mode of writing or tracing lines by means of a style or similar instrument

sty·loid \ˈstī(ə)l-ˌȯid\ *adj* **:** resembling a style **:** STYLIFORM — used esp. of slender pointed skeletal processes (as on the temporal bone or ulna)

sty·lo·lite \ˈstī-lə-ˌlīt\ *n* [ISV] **:** a small longitudinally grooved column of the same material as the rock in which it occurs

sty·lo·po·di·um \ˌstī-lə-ˈpōd-ē-əm\ *n*, *pl* **sty·lo·po·dia** \-ē-ə\ [NL, fr. ²*styl-* + Gk *podion* small foot, base — more at PEW] **:** a disk-shaped or conical expansion at the base of the style in plants of the carrot family

-sty·lous \ˈstī-ləs\ *adj comb form* [¹*style*] **:** having (such or so many) floral styles ⟨mono*stylous*⟩

sty·lus \ˈstī-ləs\ *n*, *pl* **sty·li** \ˈstī(ə)l-ˌī\ *also* **sty·lus·es** \ˈstī-lə-səz\ [in sense 1, fr. NL, alter. of L *stilus* stake, stylus; in other senses, modif. of L *stilus* — more at STYLE] **1 a :** STYLE 1c **b :** STYLE 1d **2 :** an instrument for writing or marking: as **a :** a hard-pointed pen-shaped instrument for marking on stencils used in a reproducing machine **b** (1) **:** NEEDLE 3c (2) **:** a cutting tool used to produce an original record groove during disc recording

¹**sty·mie** \ˈstī-mē\ *n* [perh. fr. Sc *stymie* person with poor eyesight] **1 :** a condition existing on a golf putting green when the ball nearer the hole lies in the line of play of another ball **2 :** a thoroughly distressing and thwarting situation

²**stymie** *vt* **sty·mied; sty·mie·ing :** BLOCK, CHECK

styp·tic \ˈstip-tik\ *adj* [ME *stiptik*, fr. L *stypticus*, fr. Gk *styptikos*, fr. *styphein* to contract] **:** tending to contract or bind **:** ASTRINGENT; *esp* **:** tending to check bleeding ⟨~ effect of cold⟩ — **styptic** *n* — **styp·tic·i·ty** \stip-ˈtis-ət-ē\ *n*

sty·rax \ˈstī(ə)r-ˌaks\ *n* [L *styrax*] **:** STORAX

sty·rene \ˈstī(ə)r-ˌēn\ *n* [ISV, fr. L *styrax*] **:** a fragrant liquid unsaturated hydrocarbon $C_6H_5CH{=}CH_2$ used chiefly in making synthetic rubber, resins, and plastics and in improving drying oils

Styx \ˈstiks\ *n* [*Styg-*, *Styx*, fr. Gk] **:** the chief river of the lower world in Greek mythology

su·abil·i·ty \ˌsü-ə-ˈbil-ət-ē\ *n* **:** the quality or state of being suable

su·able \ˈsü-ə-bəl\ *adj* **:** liable to be sued in court — **su·ably** \-blē\ *adv*

sua·sion \ˈswā-zhən\ *n* [ME, fr. L *suasion-*, *suasio*, fr. *suasus*, pp. of *suadēre* to urge, persuade; akin to L *suavis*] **:** the act of influencing or persuading — **sua·sive** \ˈswā-siv, -ziv\ *adj* — **sua·sive·ly** *adv* — **sua·sive·ness** *n*

suave \ˈswäv\ *adj* [MF, pleasant, sweet, fr. L *suavis* — more at SWEET] **:** POLISHED, URBANE; *also* **:** SMOOTH — **suave·ly** *adv* — **suave·ness** *n* — **sua·vi·ty** \ˈswäv-ət-ē\ *n*

syn SUAVE, URBANE, DIPLOMATIC, BLAND, SMOOTH, POLITIC mean ingratiatingly tactful and well-mannered. SUAVE suggests a specific ability to encourage easy and frictionless dealings with others; URBANE implies high cultivation and poise coming from wide social experience; DIPLOMATIC stresses an ability to deal with ticklish situations tactfully; BLAND emphasizes mildness of manner and absence of irritating qualities; SMOOTH suggests often a deliberately assumed suavity; POLITIC implies shrewd as well as tactful and suave handling of people

¹**sub** \ˈsəb\ *adj* **:** SUBORDINATE, SECONDARY ⟨a ~ theme in a musical composition⟩

²**sub** *n* **:** SUBSTITUTE

³**sub** *vb* **subbed; sub·bing** *vi* **:** to act as a substitute ~ *vt* **:** to apply a substratum to (as a photographic film)

⁴**sub** *n* **:** SUBMARINE

⁵**sub** *n* [short for *substratum*] **:** a photographic substratum

sub- *prefix* [ME, fr. L, under, below, secretly, from below, up, near, fr. *sub* under, close to — more at UP] **1 :** under **:** beneath **:** below ⟨*sub*soil⟩ ⟨*sub*aqueous⟩ **2 a :** subordinate **:** secondary **:** next lower than or inferior to ⟨*sub*station⟩ ⟨*sub*topic⟩ ⟨*sub*species⟩ **b :** subordinate portion of **:** subdivision of ⟨*sub*committee⟩; *also* **:** with repetition (as of a process) so as to form, stress, or deal with subordinate parts or relations ⟨*sub*let⟩ ⟨*sub*contract⟩ **3 a :** less than completely, perfectly, or normally **:** somewhat ⟨*sub*dominant⟩ ⟨*sub*ovate⟩ ⟨*sub*clinical⟩ **b** (1) **:** containing less than the usual or normal amount of (such) an element or radical ⟨*sub*oxide⟩ (2) **:** basic — in names of salts ⟨*sub*acetate⟩ **4 a :** almost **:** nearly ⟨*sub*erect⟩ **b :** falling nearly in the category of and often adjoining **:** bordering upon ⟨*sub*arctic⟩

sub·ac·e·tate \ˌsəb-ˈas-ə-ˌtāt, ˈsəb-\ *n* **:** a basic acetate

sub·ac·id \-ˈas-əd\ *adj* [L *subacidus*, fr. *sub-* + *acidus* acid] **1 :** moderately acid ⟨~ fruit juices⟩ **2 :** rather tart ⟨~ prose⟩ — **sub·ac·id·ly** *adv* — **sub·ac·id·ness** *n*

sub·acute \ˌsəb-ə-ˈkyüt\ *adj* **:** moderately acute ⟨a ~ angle⟩ ⟨a ~ flower petal⟩ ⟨large ~ spines on some sea urchins⟩ ⟨~ inflammation⟩ — **sub·acute·ly** *adv*

sub·adult \ˌsəb-ə-ˈdəlt; ˌsəb-ˈad-ˌəlt, ˈsəb-\ *n* **:** an individual that has passed through the juvenile period but not yet attained typical adult characteristics

sub·aer·i·al \ˌsəb-ˈar-ē-əl, ˈsəb-, -ˈer-; ˌsəb-(ˌ)ā-ˈir-ē-əl\ *adj* **:** situated or occurring on or immediately adjacent to the surface of the earth ⟨~ erosion⟩ ⟨~ roots⟩ — **sub·aer·i·al·ly** \-ē-ə-lē\ *adv*

sub·agen·cy \ˌsəb-ˈā-jən-sē, ˈsəb-ˌ\ *n* **:** a subordinate agency

sub·agent \ˈsəb-ˌā-jənt\ *n* **:** a subordinate agent; *specif* **:** a person employed by an agent to assist him in transacting the affairs of his principal

su·bah·dar *or* **su·ba·dar** \ˌsü-bə-ˈdär\ *n* [Per *ṣūbadār*] **1 :** a governor of a province **2 :** the chief native officer of a native company in the former British Indian army

sub·al·pine \ˌsəb-ˈal-ˌpīn, ˈsəb-\ *adj* **1 :** of or relating to the region about the foot and lower slopes of the Alps **2** *cap* **:** of, relating to, or growing on high upland slopes

¹**sub·al·tern** \sə-ˈbȯl-tərn, *esp Brit* ˈsəb-əl-tərn\ *adj* [LL *subalternus*, fr. L *sub-* + *alternus* alternate, fr. *alter* other (of two) — more at ALTER] **1 :** ranked below **:** SUBORDINATE **2 :** particular with reference to a related universal proposition

²**subaltern** *n* **1 :** a person holding a subordinate position **2 :** SUBALTERNATE

¹**sub·al·ter·nate** *adj* **1** \sə-ˈbȯl-tər-nət\ **:** inferior in quality or status **2** \ˌsəb-ˈȯl-tər-nət, ˈsəb-, -ˈal-\ [*sub-* + *alternate*] **:** nearly alternate but with a tendency to become opposite — used of plant parts — **sub·al·ter·nate·ly** *adv*

²**sub·al·ter·nate** \sə-ˈbȯl-tər-nət\ *n* **:** a particular proposition that follows immediately from a universal

sub·al·ter·na·tion \sə-ˌbȯl-tər-ˈnā-shən\ *n* **1 :** the quality or state of being subalternate **:** SUBORDINATION **2 :** the relation of a subalternate to a universal

sub·api·cal \ˌsəb-ˈap-i-kəl, -ˈā-pi-, ˈsəb-\ *adj* **:** situated below or near an apex — **sub·api·cal·ly** \-k(ə-)lē\ *adv*

sub·aquat·ic \ˌsəb-ə-ˈkwät-ik, -ˈkwat-\ *adj* [ISV] **:** somewhat aquatic ⟨a marginal ~ flora⟩

sub·aque·ous \ˌsəb-ˈā-kwē-əs, ˈsəb-, -ˈak-wē-\ *adj* **1 :** being under the surface of water **2 :** formed or taking place in or under water

sub·arc·tic \-ˈärk-tik, -ˈärt-ik\ *adj* [ISV] **:** of, relating to, or being regions immediately outside of the arctic circle or regions similar to these in climate or conditions of life

sub·ar·ea \ˈsəb-ˌar-ē-ə, -ˌer-\ *n* **:** a subdivision of an area

sub·as·sem·bler \ˌsəb-ə-ˈsem-b(ə-)lər\ *n* **:** a worker that puts together subassemblies in the process of manufacture

sub·as·sem·bly \ˌsəb-ə-ˈsem-blē\ *n* **:** an assembled unit designed to be incorporated with other units in a finished product

sub·at·mo·spher·ic \ˌsəb-ˌat-mə-ˈsfi(ə)r-ik, ˈsəb-, -ˈsfer-\ *adj* **:** less or lower than that of the atmosphere ⟨~ temperatures⟩

sub·atom·ic \ˌsəb-ə-ˈtäm-ik\ *adj* **:** of or relating to the inside of the atom or particles smaller than atoms

sub·au·di·tion \ˌsəb-(ˌ)ȯ-ˈdish-ən\ *n* [LL *subaudition-*, *subauditio*, fr. *subauditus*, pp. of *subaudire* to understand, fr. L *sub-* + *audire* to hear — more at AUDIBLE] **:** the act of understanding or supplying something not expressed; *also* **:** the ideas supplied

sub·av·er·age \ˌsəb-ˈav-(ə-)rij, ˈsəb-\ *adj* **:** of a lower level or quality than some norm ⟨~ minds⟩ ⟨~ education⟩

sub·base \ˈsəb-ˌbās\ *n* **:** the lowermost part of a base; *specif* **:** the lowest member horizontally of an architectural base or of a baseboard or pedestal

sub·base·ment \ˈsəb-ˌbā-smənt\ *n* **:** a basement located below the true basement of a building

sub·bass \ˈsəb-ˈbās, -ˌbās\ *n* **:** a pipe-organ stop used usu. in a pedal organ

sub·bing \ˈsəb-iŋ\ *n* [fr. gerund of ³*sub*] **1 :** the act of working as a substitute **2** [⁵*sub*] **:** SUBSTRATUM e

sub·cal·i·ber \ˌsəb-ˈkal-ə-bər, ˈsəb-\ *adj* **1 :** smaller than the caliber of a gun ⟨a ~ projectile⟩ **2 :** of or relating to the firing of a subcaliber projectile

sub·car·ti·lag·i·nous \ˌsəb-ˌkärt-ᵊl-ˈaj-ə-nəs\ *adj* [MF *subcartilagineux*, fr. *sub-* (fr. L) + *cartilagineux* cartilaginous] **1 :** partially cartilaginous **2 :** situated under a cartilage

sub·ce·les·tial \ˌsəb-sə-ˈles(h)-chəl\ *adj* **:** situated beneath the heavens; *specif* **:** MUNDANE

sub·cen·tral \ˌsəb-ˈsen-trəl, ˈsəb-\ *adj* **1 :** located under a center **2 :** not quite central — **sub·cen·tral·ly** \-trə-lē\ *adv*

sub·chas·er \ˈsəb-ˌchā-sər\ *n* **:** SUBMARINE CHASER

sub·chlo·ride \ˌsəb-ˈklō(ə)r-ˌīd, ˈsəb-, -ˈklȯ(ə)r-\ *n* [ISV] **1 :** a binary chloride containing a relatively small proportion of chlorine **2 :** a basic chloride

sub·class \ˈsəb-ˌklas\ *n* **:** a primary division of a class: as **a :** a biological taxonomic category below a class and above an order **b :** SUBSET

¹**sub·cla·vi·an** \ˌsəb-ˈklā-vē-ən\ *adj* [NL *subclavius*, fr. *sub-* + *clavicula* clavicle] **1 :** located under the clavicle **2 :** of or relating to a subclavian part (as an artery, vein, or nerve)

²**subclavian** *n* **:** a subclavian part

subclavian artery *n* **:** the proximal part of the main artery of the arm or forelimb

subclavian vein *n* **:** the proximal part of the main vein of the arm or forelimb
sub·cli·max \ˌsəb-ˈklī-ˌmaks, ˈsəb-\ *n* **:** a stage or community in an ecological succession immediately preceding a climax; *esp* **:** one held in relative stability through edaphic or biotic influences or by fire
sub·clin·i·cal \-ˈklin-i-kəl\ *adj* **:** only slightly abnormal and not detectable by the usual clinical tests ⟨a ~ infection⟩ — **sub·clin·i·cal·ly** \-k(ə-)lē\ *adv*
sub·col·le·giate \ˌsəb-kə-ˈlē-j(ē-)ət\ *or* **sub·col·lege** \ˌsəb-ˈkäl-ij, ˈsəb-\ *adj* **:** offered to or adapted to the needs of students not intending or inadequately prepared to attend college ⟨studies of ~ grade⟩
sub·com·mit·tee \ˈsəb-kə-ˌmit-ē, ˌsəb-kə-ˈ\ *n* **:** a subdivision of a committee usu. organized for a specific purpose
[1]**sub·con·scious** \ˌsəb-ˈkän-chəs, ˈsəb-\ *adj* **1 :** existing in the mind but not immediately available to consciousness **2 :** imperfectly conscious ⟨a ~ state⟩ — **sub·con·scious·ly** *adv* — **sub·con·scious·ness** *n*
[2]**subconscious** *n* **:** the mental activities just below the threshold of consciousness
sub·con·ti·nent \ˈsəb-ˈkänt-ᵊn-ənt, -ˈkänt-nənt, -ˌkänt-\ *n* **1 :** a landmass (as Greenland) of great size but smaller than any of the usu. recognized continents **2 :** a vast subdivision of a continent — **sub·con·ti·nen·tal** \ˌsəb-ˌkänt-ᵊn-ˈent-ᵊl\ *adj*
[1]**sub·con·tract** \ˌsəb-ˈkän-ˌtrakt, ˈsəb-; ˌsəb-kən-ˈ\ *vt* **1 :** to engage a third party to perform under a subcontract all or part of (work included in an original contract) **2 :** to undertake (work) under a subcontract ~ *vi* **:** to let out or undertake work under a subcontract
[2]**sub·con·tract** \ˈsəb-ˈkän-ˌtrakt, -ˌkän-\ *n* **:** a contract between a party to an original contract and a third party; *esp* **:** one to provide all or a specified part of the work or materials required in the original contract
sub·con·trac·tor \ˌsəb-ˈkän-ˌtrak-tər, ˈsəb-; ˌsəb-kən-ˈ\ *n* **:** an individual or business firm contracting to perform part or all of another's contract
sub·con·tra·oc·tave \ˌsəb-ˌkän-trə-ˈäk-tiv, ˈsəb-, -təv, -ˌtāv\ *n* **:** the musical octave that begins on the fourth C below middle C
sub·con·tra·ri·ety \ˌsəb-ˌkän-trə-ˈrī-ət-ē\ *n* **:** the relation existing between subcontrary propositions in logic
[1]**sub·con·trary** \ˌsəb-ˈkän-ˌtrer-ē, ˈsəb-\ *adj* [LL *subcontrarius*, fr. L *sub-* + *contrarius* contrary — more at CONTRARY] **:** being one of two subcontraries
[2]**subcontrary** *n* **:** a proposition so related to another that both may be true but both cannot be false
sub·cool \-ˈkül\ *vt* **:** SUPERCOOL
sub·cor·date \-ˈkȯ(ə)r-ˌdāt\ *adj* **:** incompletely cordate ⟨a ~ leaf⟩
sub·cor·tex \ˌsəb-ˈkȯr-ˌteks, ˈsəb-\ *n* [NL] **:** the parts of the brain immediately beneath the cerebral cortex — **sub·cor·ti·cal** \-ˈkȯrt-i-kəl\ *adj*
sub·crit·i·cal \-ˈkrit-i-kəl\ *adj* **1 :** less or lower than critical **2 a :** of insufficient size to sustain a chain reaction ⟨~ mass of fissionable material⟩ **b :** constituting or designed for use with fissionable material of subcritical mass ⟨a ~ reactor⟩
sub·cul·ture \ˈsəb-ˌkəl-chər\ *n* **1 :** a culture (as of bacteria) derived from another culture; *also* **:** an act or instance of producing a subculture **2 :** an ethnic, regional, economic, or social group exhibiting characteristic patterns of behavior sufficient to distinguish it from others within an embracing culture or society ⟨a criminal ~⟩
sub·cu·ta·ne·ous \ˌsəb-kyu̇-ˈtā-nē-əs\ *adj* [LL *subcutaneus*, fr. L *sub-* + *cutis* skin — more at HIDE] **:** being, living, used, or made under the skin ⟨a ~ needle⟩ ⟨~ parasite⟩ — **sub·cu·ta·ne·ous·ly** *adv*
sub·cu·tis \ˌsəb-ˈkyüt-əs, ˈsəb-\ *n* [NL, fr. LL, beneath the skin, fr. L *sub-* + *cutis*] **:** the deeper part of the dermis
sub·dea·con \-ˈdē-kən\ *n* [ME *subdecon*, fr. LL *subdiaconus*, fr. L *sub-* + LL *diaconus* deacon] **:** a cleric ranking below a deacon: as **a :** a candidate for the Roman Catholic priesthood admitted to the lowest of the major orders and acting as an officer at high mass **b :** a deacon or priest performing the liturgical duties of a subdeacon — **sub·di·ac·o·nal** \ˌsəb-(ˌ)dī-ˈak-ən-ᵊl\ *adj* — **sub·di·ac·o·nate** \-ˈak-ə-nət\ *n*
sub·deb \ˈsəb-ˌdeb\ *n* **:** SUBDEBUTANTE
sub·deb·u·tante \ˌsəb-ˈdeb-yu̇-ˌtänt, ˈsəb-\ *n* **:** a young girl who is about to become a society debutante; *broadly* **:** a girl in her middle teens ⟨~ styles⟩
sub·den·tate \ˌsəb-ˈden-ˌtāt, ˈsəb-\ *adj* **:** partially or imperfectly dentate ⟨leaves with margins ~⟩
sub·de·pot \-ˈdep-(ˌ)ō *also* -ˈdē-(ˌ)pō\ *n* **:** a military depot that operates under the jurisdiction of another depot and usu. performs only specified depot functions
sub·di·vid·able \ˌsəb-də-ˈvīd-ə-bəl, ˈsəb-də-ˌ\ *adj* **:** capable of being further divided **:** suitable for subdividing
sub·di·vide \ˌsəb-də-ˈvīd, ˈsəb-də-ˌ\ *vb* [ME *subdividen*, fr. LL *subdividere*, fr. L *sub-* + *dividere* to divide] *vt* **1 :** to divide the parts of into more parts **2 :** to divide into several parts; *esp* **:** to divide (a tract of land) into building lots ~ *vi* **:** to separate or become separated into subdivisions — **sub·di·vid·er** *n* — **sub·di·vi·sion** \ˌsəb-də-ˈvizh-ən, ˈsəb-də-ˌ\ *n* — **sub·di·vi·sion·al** \ˌsəb-də-ˈvizh-nəl, -ən-ᵊl\ *adj*
sub·dom·i·nant \ˌsəb-ˈdäm-(ə-)nənt, ˈsəb-\ *n* **:** something dominant to an inferior or partial degree: as **a :** the fourth musical degree of the major or minor scale (as F in the scale of C) **b :** an ecologically important life-form subordinate in influence to the dominants of a community — **subdominant** *adj*
sub·duct \səb-ˈdəkt\ *vb* [L *subductus*, pp. of *subducere* to withdraw, fr. *sub-* + *ducere* to draw — more at TOW] **:** SUBTRACT, DEDUCT — **sub·duc·tion** \-ˈdək-shən\ *n*
sub·due \səb-ˈd(y)ü\ *vt* [ME *sodewen*, *subduen* (influenced in form and meaning by L *subdere* to subject), fr. MF *soduire* to seduce (influenced in meaning by L *seducere* to seduce), fr. L *subducere* to withdraw] **1 :** to conquer and bring into subjection **:** VANQUISH **2 :** to bring under control esp. by an exertion of the will **:** CURB **3 :** to bring under cultivation **4 :** to reduce the intensity or degree of **syn** see CONQUER — **sub·du·er** *n*
sub·en·try \ˈsəb-ˌen-trē\ *n* **:** an entry made under a more general entry
su·ber \ˈsü-bər\ *n* [L, cork tree, cork] **:** corky plant tissue **:** PHELLEM — **su·be·re·ous** \sü-ˈbir-ē-əs\ *or* **su·ber·ic** \-ˈber-ik\ *adj*
sub·erect \ˌsəb-i-ˈrekt\ *adj* **:** standing or growing in a nearly erect position ⟨a ~ shrub⟩
suberic acid *n* [F *subérique*, fr. L *suber*] **:** a dicarboxylic acid $C_8H_{14}O_4$ from cork or various fatty oils or acids
su·ber·in \ˈsü-bə-rən\ *n* [F *subérine*, fr. L *suber*] **:** a complex fatty substance that is the basis of cork
su·ber·iza·tion \ˌsü-bə-rə-ˈzā-shən\ *n* **:** conversion of the cell walls into corky tissue by infiltration with suberin
su·ber·ize \ˈsü-bə-ˌrīz\ *vt* **:** to cause suberization of
su·ber·ose \ˈsü-bə-ˌrōs\ *also* **su·ber·ous** \-rəs\ *adj* **:** having a corky texture **:** SUBERIZED
sub·es·sen·tial \ˌsəb-ə-ˈsen-chəl\ *adj* **:** important but not absolutely essential
sub·fam·i·ly \ˈsəb-ˌfam-(ə-)lē\ *n* [ISV] **:** a taxonomic category next below a family
sub·fix \ˈsəb-ˌfiks\ *n* [*sub-* + *-fix* (as in *prefix*)] **:** a subscript sign, letter, or character
sub·fos·sil \ˈsəb-ˌfäs-əl\ *adj* [ISV] **:** of less than typical fossil age but partially fossilized — **subfossil** *n*
sub·freez·ing \ˈsəb-ˈfrē-ziŋ\ *adj* **:** lower than is required to produce freezing
sub·fusc \ˌsəb-ˈfəsk, ˈsəb-ˌ\ *adj* [L *subfuscus* brownish, dusky, fr. *sub-* + *fuscus* dark brown — more at DUSK] **:** having little of brightness or appeal **:** DRAB, DUSKY
sub·ge·nus \ˈsəb-ˌjē-nəs\ *n* [NL] **:** a category in biological taxonomy below a genus and above a species
sub·gla·cial \ˌsəb-ˈglā-shəl, ˈsəb-\ *adj* **:** of or relating to the bottom of a glacier or the area immediately underlying a glacier — **sub·gla·cial·ly** \-shə-lē\ *adv*
sub·grade \ˈsəb-ˌgrād\ *n* **:** a surface of earth or rock leveled off to receive a foundation (as of a road)
sub·group \-ˌgrüp\ *n* **1 :** a subordinate group usu. of individuals sharing some common differential quality **2 :** a subset of a mathematical group
sub·head \-ˌhed\ *n* **1 :** any of the heads under which each of the main divisions of a subject may be subdivided **2 :** a subordinate caption or title
sub·hu·man \ˌsəb-ˈhyü-mən, ˈsəb-, -ˈyü-\ *adj* **:** less than human
sub·in·dex \ˌsəb-ˈin-ˌdeks, ˈsəb-\ *n* **1 :** a mathematical subscript **2 :** an index to a division of a main classification
sub·in·feu·date \ˌsəb-in-ˈfyü-ˌdāt\ *also* **sub·in·feud** \-ˈfyüd\ *vt* [back-formation fr. *subinfeudation*] **:** to make subinfeudation of
sub·in·feu·da·tion \ˌsəb-ˌin-fyü-ˈdā-shən\ *n* [*sub-* + *infeudation* (enfeoffment)] **:** the granting of feudal lands by a vassal lord to another to hold as vassal of himself rather than of his own superior; *also* **:** the relation or tenure of a vassal so holding land — **sub·in·feu·da·to·ry** \ˌsəb-in-ˈfyüd-ə-ˌtōr-ē, -ˌtȯr-\ *adj*
sub·in·ter·val \ˌsəb-ˈint-ər-vəl, ˈsəb-\ *n* **:** an interval that is a subdivision of a larger or major interval (as in music or mathematics)
sub·ir·ri·gate \ˌsəb-ˈir-ə-ˌgāt, ˈsəb-\ *vt* **:** to water from beneath (as by the periodic rise of a water table); *also* **:** to irrigate below the surface (as by a system of underground porous pipes) — **sub·ir·ri·ga·tion** \ˌsəb-ˌir-ə-ˈgā-shən\ *n*
su·bi·to \ˈsü-bi-ˌtō\ *adv* [It, fr. L, suddenly, fr. *subitus* sudden — more at SUDDEN] **:** IMMEDIATELY, SUDDENLY — used as a direction in music
sub·ja·cen·cy \ˌsəb-ˈjās-ᵊn-sē\ *n* **:** the quality or state of being subjacent
sub·ja·cent \-ᵊnt\ *adj* [L *subjacent-*, *subjacens*, prp. of *subjacēre* to lie under, fr. *sub-* + *jacēre* to lie — more at ADJACENT] **:** lying under or below; *also* **:** lower than though not directly below ⟨hills and ~ valleys⟩ — **sub·ja·cent·ly** *adv*
[1]**sub·ject** \ˈsəb-jikt\ *n* [ME, fr. MF, fr. L *subjectus* one under authority & *subjectum* subject of a proposition, fr. masc. & neut. respectively of *subjectus*, pp. of *subicere* to subject, lit., to throw under, fr. *sub-* + *jacere* to throw — more at JET] **1 :** one that is placed under authority or control: as **a :** VASSAL **b** (1) **:** one subject to a monarch and governed by his law (2) **:** one who lives in the territory of, enjoys the protection of, and owes allegiance to a sovereign power or state **2 a :** that of which a quality, attribute, or relation may be affirmed or in which it may inhere **b :** SUBSTRATUM; *esp* **:** material or essential substance **c :** the mind, ego, or agent of whatever sort that sustains or assumes the form of thought or consciousness **3 a :** a department of knowledge or learning **b :** MOTIVE, CAUSE **c** (1) **:** one that is acted upon (2) **:** an individual whose reactions or responses are studied (3) **:** a dead body for anatomical study and dissection **d** (1) **:** something concerning which something is said or done (2) **:** something represented or indicated in a work of art **e** (1) **:** the term of a logical proposition that denotes the entity of which something is affirmed or denied; *also* **:** the entity denoted (2) **:** a word or word group denoting that of which something is predicated **f :** the principal melodic phrase on which a musical composition or movement is based **syn** see CITIZEN
[2]**subject** *adj* **1 :** owing obedience or allegiance to the power or dominion of another **2 a :** EXPOSED, LIABLE **b :** PRONE, DISPOSED **3 :** CONDITIONED, CONTINGENT **syn** see LIABLE
[3]**sub·ject** \səb-ˈjekt\ *vt* **1 a :** to bring under control or dominion **:** SUBJUGATE **b :** to make (as oneself) amenable to the discipline and control of a superior **2 a :** to make liable **:** PREDISPOSE **b :** to make accountable **:** SUBMIT **3 :** to cause to undergo or submit to **:** EXPOSE — **sub·jec·tion** \-ˈjek-shən\ *n*
[1]**sub·jec·tive** \(ˌ)səb-ˈjek-tiv\ *adj* **1 :** of, relating to, or constituting a subject: as **a** *obs* **:** of, relating to, or characteristic of one that is subject esp. in lack of freedom of action or in submissiveness **b :** being, resembling, or relating to a grammatical subject; *esp* **:** NOMINATIVE **2 a :** of or relating to the essential being supporting attributes or relations **:** SUBSTANTIAL **b** (1) **:** relating to or determined by the mind as the subject of experience (2) **:** characteristic of or belonging to reality as perceived rather than as independent of mind **:** PHENOMENAL **c :** relating to or being experience or knowledge as conditioned by personal mental characteristics or states **3 a :** peculiar to a particular individual **:** PERSONAL ⟨a ~ impression⟩ ⟨~ judgments⟩ **b :** arising from conditions within the brain or sense organs and not directly caused by external stimuli ⟨~ sensations⟩ **c :** arising out of or identified by means of one's awareness of his own states and processes ⟨a ~ symptom of disease⟩ **d :** lacking in reality or substance **:** ILLUSORY — **sub·jec·tive·ly** *adv* — **sub·jec·tive·ness** *n* — **sub·jec·tiv·i·ty** \-ˌjek-ˈtiv-ət-ē\ *n*

2subjective *n* **:** something that is subjective; *also* **:** NOMINATIVE

subjective complement *n* **:** a grammatical complement relating to the subject of an intransitive verb ⟨in "he had fallen sick" *sick* is a *subjective complement*⟩

sub·jec·tiv·ism \-'jek-tiv-,iz-əm\ *n* **1 a :** a theory that limits knowledge to conscious states and elements **b :** a theory that stresses the subjective elements in experience **2 a :** a doctrine that the supreme good is a subjective experience or feeling (as pleasure) **b :** a doctrine that individual feeling or apprehension is the ultimate criterion of the good and the right — **sub·jec·tiv·ist** \-əst\ *n* — **sub·jec·tiv·is·tic** \-,jek-tiv-'is-tik\ *adj*

subject matter *n* **:** matter presented for consideration in discussion, thought, or study

sub·join \(,)səb-'jȯin\ *vt* [MF *subjoindre*, fr. L *subjungere*, to join beneath, add, fr. *sub-* + *jungere* to join — more at YOKE] **:** ANNEX, APPEND

sub ju·di·ce \(')sủb-'yüd-i-,kā, 'səb-'jüd-ə-(,)sē\ *adv* [L] **:** before a judge or court **:** not yet decided

sub·ju·gate \'səb-ji-,gāt\ *vt* [ME *subjugaten*, fr. L *subjugatus*, pp. of *subjugare*, lit., to bring under the yoke, fr. *sub-* + *jugum* yoke — more at YOKE] **1 :** to force to submit to control and governance **:** MASTER **2 :** to bring into servitude **:** ENSLAVE — **sub·ju·ga·tion** \,səb-ji-'gā-shən\ *n* — **sub·ju·ga·tor** \'səb-ji-,gāt-ər\ *n*

sub·junc·tion \(,)səb-'jəŋ(k)-shən\ *n* **1 :** an act of subjoining or the state of being subjoined **2 :** something subjoined

sub·junc·tive \səb-'jəŋ(k)-tiv\ *adj* [LL *subjunctivus*, fr. L *subjunctus*, pp. of *subjungere* to join beneath, subordinate] **:** of, relating to, or constituting a verb form or set of verb forms that represents a denoted act or state not as fact but as contingent or possible or viewed emotionally (as with doubt or desire) ⟨the ~ mood⟩ — **subjunctive** *n*

sub·king·dom \'səb-,kiŋ-dəm\ *n* **:** a primary division of a taxonomic kingdom

sub·late \,səb-'lāt\ *vt* [L *sublatus* (pp. of *tollere* to take away, lift up), fr. *sub-* up + *latus*, pp. of *ferre* to carry — more at SUB-, TOLERATE, BEAR] **1 a :** NEGATE, DENY **b :** CANCEL, ELIMINATE **2 :** to cancel but also preserve and elevate (an element in a dialectic process) as a partial element in a synthesis — **sub·la·tion** \-'lā-shən\ *n*

sub·lease \'səb-'lēs\ *n* **:** a lease by a tenant or lessee of part or all of leased premises to another person for a shorter term than his own and under which he retains some right or interest under the original lease — **sublease** *vb* — **sub·les·see** \,səb-(,)le-'sē\ *n* — **sub·les·sor** \-'sȯ(ə)r\ *n*

sub·let \'səb-'let\ *vt* **1 a :** to lease or rent all or part of (a leased or rented property) to another person **b :** to lease or rent all or part of (a leased or rented property) from the original lessee or tenant **2 :** SUBCONTRACT 1 — **sublet** *n*

1sub·li·mate \'səb-lə-,māt\ *vt* [ML *sublimatus*, pp. of *sublimare*] **1 a :** SUBLIME 1 **b** *archaic* **:** to improve or refine as if by subliming **2 :** to direct the energy of (an impulse) from its primitive aim to one that is ethically or culturally higher — **sub·li·ma·tion** \,səb-lə-'mā-shən\ *n*

2sub·li·mate \'səb-lə-,māt, -mət\ *n* **:** a chemical product obtained by sublimation

1sub·lime \sə-'blīm\ *vb* [ME *sublimen*, fr. MF *sublimer*, fr. ML *sublimare* to refine, sublime, fr. L, to elevate, fr. *sublimis*] *vt* **1 :** to cause to pass from the solid to the vapor state by heating and again condense to solid form **2** [F *sublimer*, fr. L *sublimare*] **a** (1) **:** to elevate or exalt esp. in dignity or honor (2) **:** to render finer (as in purity or excellence) **b :** to convert (something inferior) into something of higher worth ~ *vi* **:** to pass directly from the solid to the vapor state — **sub·lim·er** *n*

2sublime *adj* [L *sublimis*, lit., to or in a high position, fr. *sub* under, up to + *limen* threshold, lintel — more at UP, LIMB] **1 a :** lofty, grand, or exalted in thought, expression, or manner **b :** of outstanding spiritual, intellectual, or moral worth **c :** inspiring awe **:** SOLEMN **2 a** *archaic* **:** high in place **b** *obs* **:** lofty of mien **:** HAUGHTY **c** *cap* **:** SUPREME — used in a style of address (as to former Turkish sovereigns) **syn** see SPLENDID — **sub·lime·ly** *adv* — **sub·lime·ness** *n*

sub·li·mi·nal \(,)səb-'lim-ən-ᵊl, 'səb-, -'lī-mən-\ *adj* [*sub-* + L *limin-*, *limen* threshold] **1 :** inadequate to produce a sensation or a perception **2 :** existing or functioning outside the area of conscious awareness ⟨the ~ mind⟩ ⟨~ techniques in advertising⟩ — **sub·li·mi·nal·ly** \-ē\ *adv*

sub·lim·i·ty \sə-'blim-ət-ē\ *n* **1 :** something sublime or exalted **2 :** the quality or state of being sublime

sub·lin·gual \,səb-'liŋ-gwəl, 'səb-\ *adj* [NL *sublingualis* fr. L *sub-* + *lingua* tongue — more at TONGUE] **:** situated or occurring under the tongue

sub·lu·nar \-'lü-nər\ *adj* **:** SUBLUNARY

sub·lu·na·ry \-nə-rē; 'səb-lü-,ner-ē\ *adj* [modif. of LL *sublunaris*, fr. L *sub-* + *luna* moon — more at LUNAR] **:** situated beneath the moon **:** TERRESTRIAL

sub·ma·chine gun \,səb-mə-'shēn-,gən\ *n* **:** a lightweight automatic or semiautomatic portable firearm fired from the shoulder or hip

sub·mar·gin·al \,səb-'märj-nəl, 'səb-, -ən-ᵊl\ *adj* **1 :** adjacent to a margin or a marginal part or structure **2 :** falling below a necessary minimum — **sub·mar·gin·al·ly** \-ē\ *adv*

1sub·ma·rine \'səb-mə-,rēn, ,səb-mə-'\ *adj* **:** being, acting, or growing under water esp. in the sea ⟨~ plants⟩

2submarine *n* **:** something (as an explosive mine) that functions or operates underwater; *specif* **:** a warship designed for undersea operations

3submarine *vt* **:** to make an attack upon or to sink by means of a submarine

submarine chaser *n* **:** a boat fitted to operate offensively against submarines

sub·ma·ri·ner \'səb-mə-,rē-nər, ,səb-mə-' *also* ,səb-'mar-ə-\ *n* **:** a crewman of a submarine

sub·max·il·la \,səb-,mak-'sil-ə\ *n*, *pl* **sub·max·il·lae** \-'sil-(,)ē, -,ī\ *also* **submaxillas** [NL] **:** the lower jaw or inferior maxillary bone; *specif* **:** the human mandible

1sub·max·il·lary \,səb-'mak-sə-,ler-ē, 'səb-, *chiefly Brit* ,səb-(,)mak-'sil-ə-rē\ *adj* **1 :** of, relating to, or situated below the lower jaw **2 :** of, relating to, or associated with the submaxillary salivary gland of either side

2submaxillary *n* **:** a submaxillary part (as an artery or bone)

sub·me·di·ant \-'mēd-ē-ənt\ *n* **:** the sixth tone above or the third below the tonic

sub·merge \səb-'mərj\ *vb* [L *submergere*, fr. *sub-* + *mergere* to plunge — more at MERGE] *vt* **1 :** to put under water **2 :** to cover or overflow with water **:** INUNDATE ⟨*submerged* the town⟩ **3 :** to lose sight of **:** OBSCURE ~ *vi* **:** to go under water — **sub·mer·gence** \-'mər-jən(t)s\ *n* — **sub·merg·ible** \-jə-bəl\ *adj*

sub·merged *adj* **1 :** SUBMERSED b **2 :** sunk in poverty and misery **3 :** HIDDEN, CRYPTIC ⟨a ~ gene effect⟩

sub·merse \səb-'mərs\ *vt* [L *submersus*, pp. of *submergere*] **:** SUBMERGE — **sub·mer·sion** \-'mər-zhən, -shən\ *n*

sub·mersed *adj* **:** SUBMERGED: as **a :** covered with water **b :** growing or adapted to grow under water

1sub·mers·ible \səb-'mər-sə-bəl\ *adj* **:** SUBMERGIBLE

2submersible *n* **:** a boat capable of submerging **:** SUBMARINE

sub·mi·cro·scop·ic \,səb-,mī-krə-'skäp-ik\ *adj* [ISV] **:** too small to be seen in an ordinary light microscope

sub·min·ia·ture \,səb-'min-ē-ə-,chủ(ə)r, -'min-i-,chủ(ə)r, -'min-yə-,-chər, -,t(y)ủ(ə)r\ *adj* [ISV] **:** very small — used esp. of a very compact assembly of electronic equipment

sub·miss \səb-'mis\ *adj* [L *submissus*, fr. pp. of *submittere*] **1** *archaic* **:** SUBMISSIVE, HUMBLE **2** *archaic* **:** low in tone **:** SUBDUED

sub·mis·sion \səb-'mish-ən\ *n* [ME, fr. MF, fr. L *submission-*, *submissio* act of lowering, fr. *submissus*, pp. of *submittere*] **1 a :** a legal agreement to submit to the decision of arbitrators **b :** an act of submitting something (as for consideration, inspection, or comment) **2 :** the condition of being submissive, humble, or compliant **3 :** an act of submitting to the authority or control of another

sub·mis·sive \-'mis-iv\ *adj* **:** submitting to others **:** YIELDING — **sub·mis·sive·ly** *adv* — **sub·mis·sive·ness** *n*

sub·mit \səb-'mit\ *vb* **sub·mit·ted**; **sub·mit·ting** [ME *submitten*, fr. L *submittere* to lower, submit, fr. *sub-* + *mittere* to send — more at SMITE] *vt* **1 a :** to yield to governance or authority **b :** to subject to a regime, condition, or practice ⟨the metal was *submitted* to analysis⟩ **2 a :** to commit to the discretion or judgment of another **b :** to make available **:** OFFER **c :** to put forward as an opinion **:** AFFIRM ⟨we ~ that the charge is not proved⟩ ~ *vi* **1 a :** to yield oneself to the authority or will of another **b :** to yield oneself as subject (as to surgery) **2 :** to defer to the opinion or authority of another **syn** see YIELD

sub·mon·tane \,səb-'män-,tān, 'səb-; ,səb-(,)män-'tān\ *adj* [LL *submontanus* lying under a mountain, fr. L *sub-* + *mont-*, *mons* mountain — more MOUNT] **:** situated at the foot or near the base of a mountain or mountains — **sub·mon·tane·ly** *adv*

sub·mul·ti·ple \,səb-'məl-tə-pəl, 'səb-\ *n* **:** an exact divisor of a number ⟨8 is a ~ of 72⟩

1sub·nor·mal \-'nȯr-məl\ *adj* [ISV] **:** less than normal — **sub·nor·mal·i·ty** \,səb-(,)nȯr-'mal-ət-ē\ *n* — **sub·nor·mal·ly** \,səb-'nȯr-mə-lē, 'səb-\ *adv*

2subnormal *n* **:** one who is below normal; *esp* **:** a person of subnormal intelligence

sub·oce·an·ic \,səb-,ō-shē-'an-ik\ *adj* **:** situated, taking place, or formed beneath the ocean or the bottom of the ocean ⟨~ light⟩ ⟨~ oil resources⟩

sub·oc·u·lar \,səb-'äk-yə-lər, 'səb-\ *adj* [LL *subocularis*, fr. L *sub-* + *oculus* eye — more at EYE] **:** situated below the eye

sub·op·po·site \,səb-'äp-ə-zət, 'səb-, -'äp-sət\ *adj* **:** nearly opposite ⟨leaves ~⟩

sub·or·bic·u·lar \,səb-(,)ȯr-'bik-yə-lər\ *adj* [ISV] **:** approximately circular

sub·or·bit·al \,səb-'ȯr-bət-ᵊl, 'səb-\ *adj* **1 :** situated beneath the orbit of the eye; *also* **:** SUBOCULAR **2 :** not being in orbit

sub·or·der \'səb-,ȯrd-ər\ *n* **:** a subdivision of an order ⟨a soil ~⟩; *esp* **:** a taxonomic category ranking between an order and a family

1sub·or·di·nate \sə-'bȯrd-ᵊn-ət, -'bȯrd-nət\ *adj* [ME *subordinat*, fr. ML *subordinatus*, pp. of *subordinare* to subordinate, fr. L *sub-* + *ordinare* to order — more at ORDAIN] **1 :** placed in a lower class or rank **:** INFERIOR **2 :** submissive to or controlled by authority **3 a :** of, relating to, or constituting a clause that functions as a noun, adjective, or adverb **b :** grammatically subordinating — **sub·or·di·nate·ly** *adv* — **sub·or·di·nate·ness** *n*

2subordinate *n* **:** one that is subordinate

3sub·or·di·nate \sə-'bȯrd-ᵊn-,āt\ *vt* **1 :** to place in a lower order or class **2 :** to make subject or subservient **:** SUBDUE — **sub·or·di·na·tion** \-,bȯrd-ᵊn-'ā-shən\ *n* — **sub·or·di·na·tive** \-'bȯrd-ᵊn-,āt-iv\ *adj*

sub·orn \sə-'bȯ(ə)rn\ *vt* [MF *suborner*, fr. L *subornare*, fr. *sub-* secretly + *ornare* to furnish, equip — more at ORNATE] **1 :** to induce secretly to do an unlawful thing **:** INSTIGATE **2 :** to induce to commit perjury; *also* **:** to obtain (perjured testimony) from a witness — **sub·orn·er** *n*

sub·or·na·tion \,səb-(,)ȯr-'nā-shən\ *n* **:** the procuring (as by bribes or persuasion) of an improper or unlawful act; *esp* **:** the crime of procuring perjury

sub·ovate \,səb-'ō-,vāt, 'səb-\ *adj* **:** approximately ovate

sub·ox·ide \-'äk-,sīd\ *n* [ISV] **:** an oxide containing a relatively small proportion of oxygen

sub·phy·lum \'səb-,fī-ləm\ *n* [NL] **:** a primary division of a phylum

sub·plot \'səb-,plät\ *n* **:** a subordinate plot in fiction or drama

1sub·poe·na \sə-'pē-nə, *substand* -nē\ *n* [ME *suppena*, fr. L *sub poena* under penalty] **:** a writ commanding a person designated in it to attend court under a penalty for failure

2subpoena *vt* **:** to serve or summon with a writ of subpoena

subpoena ad tes·ti·fi·can·dum \-,ad-,tes-tə-fə-'kan-dəm\ *n* [NL, under penalty to give testimony] **:** a writ commanding a person to appear in court for testifying as a witness

subpoena du·ces te·cum \-,dü-,kā-'stā-,kủm\ *n* [NL, under penalty you shall bring with you] **:** a writ commanding a person to produce in court certain designated documents or other evidence

sub·prin·ci·pal \,səb-'prin(t)-s(ə-)pəl, 'səb-, -sə-bəl\ *n* **1 :** an

assistant principal (as of a school) **2 :** a secondary or bracing rafter **3 :** an open diapason subbass in a pipe organ

sub·re·gion \ˈsəb-ˌrē-jən\ *n* [ISV] **:** a subdivision of a region; *esp* **:** one of the primary divisions of a biogeographic region — **sub·re·gion·al** \-ˌrēj-nəl, -ən-ᵊl\ *adj*

sub·rep·tion \(ˌ)səb-ˈrep-shən\ *n* [LL *subreption-, subreptio,* fr. L, act of stealing, fr. *subreptus,* pp. of *subripere, surripere* to take away secretly — more at SURREPTITIOUS] **:** a deliberate misrepresentation; *also* **:** an inference drawn from it — **sub·rep·ti·tious** \ˌsəb-ˌrep-ˈtish-əs\ *adj* — **sub·rep·ti·tious·ly** *adv*

sub·ro·gate \ˈsəb-rō-ˌgāt\ *vt* [L *subrogatus,* pp. of *subrogare, surrogare* — more at SURROGATE] **:** to put in the place of another **:** SUBSTITUTE

sub·ro·ga·tion \ˌsəb-rō-ˈgā-shən\ *n* **:** the substitution of one for another as a creditor so that the new creditor succeeds to the former's rights

sub ro·sa \ˌsəb-ˈrō-zə\ *adv* [NL, lit., under the rose; fr. the ancient custom of hanging a rose over the council table to indicate that all present were sworn to secrecy] **:** in confidence **:** SECRETLY

sub·rou·tine \ˌsəb-(ˌ)rü-ˈtēn\ *n* [ISV] **:** a subordinate routine; *esp* **:** a usu. coded specific instruction by which a digital computer is guided to perform a precisely defined mathematical or logical operation

sub·sa·line \ˌsəb-ˈsā-ˌlēn, ˈsəb-, -ˌlīn\ *adj* **:** somewhat salty

sub·sat·u·rat·ed \ˌsəb-ˈsach-ə-ˌrāt-əd, ˈsəb-\ *adj* **:** nearly but not fully saturated — **sub·sat·u·ra·tion** \ˌsəb-ˌsach-ə-ˈrā-shən\ *n*

sub·scap·u·lar \ˌsəb-ˈskap-yə-lər, ˈsəb-\ *adj* [NL *subscapularis,* fr. L *sub-* + *scapula*] **:** situated under the scapula; *also* **:** of or relating to the ventral or in man the anterior surface of the scapula

sub·scribe \səb-ˈskrīb\ *vb* [ME *subscriben,* fr. L *subscribere,* lit., to write beneath, fr. *sub-* + *scribere* to write — more at SCRIBE] *vt* **1 :** to write (one's name) underneath **:** SIGN **2 a :** to sign with one's own hand in token of consent or obligation by writing one's name beneath **b :** to attest by signing **c :** to pledge (a gift or contribution) by writing one's name with the amount **3 :** to assent to **:** SUPPORT ~ *vi* **1 :** to sign one's name to a letter or other document **2 a :** to give consent to something written by signing **b :** to set one's name to a paper in token of promise to give something; *also* **:** to give something in accordance with such a promise **c :** to place an order by signing ⟨~ to a magazine⟩ ⟨~ for stock⟩ **3 :** to feel favorably disposed **:** APPROVE ⟨anyone would ~ to your sentiments⟩ **syn** see ASSENT — **sub·scrib·er** *n*

sub·script \ˈsəb-ˌskript\ *n* [L *subscriptus,* pp. of *subscribere*] **:** a distinguishing symbol or letter written immediately below or below and to the right or left of another character — **subscript** *adj*

sub·scrip·tion \səb-ˈskrip-shən\ *n* [ME *subscripcioun* signature, fr. L *subscription-, subscriptio,* fr. *subscriptus,* pp. of *subscribere*] **1 a :** the acceptance (as of ecclesiastical articles of faith) attested by the signing of one's name **b :** the act of signing one's name **2 :** something that is subscribed: as **a :** an autograph signature; *also* **:** a paper to which a signature is attached **b :** a sum subscribed **c :** a purchase by signed order

sub·se·quence \ˈsəb-sə-ˌkwen(t)s, -si-kwən(t)s\ *n* **:** the quality or state of being subsequent; *also* **:** a subsequent event

sub·se·quent \-kwənt, -ˌkwent\ *adj* [ME, fr. L *subsequent-, subsequens,* prp. of *subsequi* to follow close, fr. *sub-* near + *sequi* to follow — more at SUB-, SUE] **:** following in time, order, or place **:** SUCCEEDING — **subsequent** *n* — **sub·se·quent·ly** \-ˌkwent-lē, -kwənt-\ *adv* — **sub·se·quent·ness** \-ˌkwent-, -kwənt-\ *n*

sub·sere \ˈsəb-ˌsi(ə)r\ *n* **:** a secondary succession arising after an ecological climax community has been interrupted (as by fire or human agency)

sub·serve \səb-ˈsərv\ *vt* [L *subservire* to serve, be subservient, fr. *sub-* + *servire* to serve] **1 :** to serve as an instrument or means of **2 :** to promote the welfare or purposes of

sub·ser·vi·ence \səb-ˈsər-vē-ən(t)s\ *also* **sub·ser·vi·en·cy** \-ən-sē\ *n* **1 :** a subservient or subordinate place or function **2 :** obsequious servility

sub·ser·vi·ent \-ənt\ *adj* [L *subservient-, subserviens,* prp. of *subservire*] **1 :** useful in an inferior capacity **:** SUBORDINATE **2 :** serving to promote some end **3 :** obsequiously servile **:** TRUCKLING — **sub·ser·vi·ent·ly** *adv*

syn SERVILE, SLAVISH, MENIAL, OBSEQUIOUS: SUBSERVIENT applies to the cringing manner of one very conscious of a subordinate position; SERVILE suggests the mean or fawning behavior of a slave; SLAVISH suggests abject or debased servility; MENIAL stresses the degradation associated with working solely at the bidding of and for the benefit of others; OBSEQUIOUS implies fawning or sycophantic compliance and exaggerated deference of manner

sub·set \ˈsəb-ˌset\ *n* **:** a mathematical set each of whose elements is an element of an inclusive set

sub·shrub \-ˌshrəb, *esp South* -ˌsrəb\ *n* **1 :** a perennial plant having woody stems except for the terminal part of the new growth which is killed back annually **2 :** UNDERSHRUB 2 — **sub·shrub·by** \-ē\ *adj*

sub·side \səb-ˈsīd\ *vi* [L *subsidere,* fr. *sub-* + *sidere* to sit down, sink; akin to L *sedēre* to sit — more at SIT] **1 :** to sink or fall to the bottom **:** SETTLE **2 :** to tend downward **:** DESCEND; *esp* **:** to flatten out so as to form a depression **3 :** to let oneself settle down **:** SINK ⟨*subsided* into a chair⟩ **4 :** to become tranquil ⟨the sea ~*s*⟩ **syn** see ABATE — **sub·si·dence** \səb-ˈsīd-ᵊn(t)s, ˈsəb-səd-ən(t)s\ *n*

sub·sid·i·ar·i·ly \(ˌ)səb-ˌsid-ē-ˈer-ə-lē\ *adv* **:** in a subsidiary manner

¹**sub·sid·iary** \səb-ˈsid-ē-ˌer-ē, -ˈsid-ə-rē\ *adj* [L *subsidiarius,* fr. *subsidium* reserve troops] **1 a :** furnishing aid or support **:** AUXILIARY **b :** of secondary importance **:** TRIBUTARY **2 :** of, relating to, or constituting a subsidy

²**subsidiary** *n* **:** one that is subsidiary; *esp* **:** a company wholly controlled by another

sub·si·di·za·tion \ˌsəb-səd-ə-ˈzā-shən, -zəd-\ *n* **:** the act of subsidizing

sub·si·dize \ˈsəb-sə-ˌdīz, -zə-\ *vt* **:** to furnish with a subsidy: as **a :** to purchase the assistance of by payment of a subsidy **b :** to aid or promote (as a private enterprise) with public money ⟨~ a steamship line⟩ — **sub·si·diz·er** *n*

sub·si·dy \ˈsəb-səd-ē, -zəd-\ *n* [ME, fr. L *subsidium* reserve troops, support, assistance, fr. *sub-* near + *sedēre* to sit — more at SUB-] **:** a grant or gift of money: as **a :** a sum of money formerly granted by the British Parliament to the crown and raised by special taxation **b :** money granted by one state to another **c :** a grant by a government to a private person or company to assist an enterprise deemed advantageous to the public

sub·sist \səb-ˈsist\ *vb* [LL *subsistere* to exist, fr. L, to come to a halt, remain, fr. *sub-* + *sistere* to come to a stand; akin to L *stare* to stand — more at STAND] *vi* **1 :** to have existence **:** BE; *often* **:** PERSIST, CONTINUE **2 :** to receive maintenance (as food and clothing) **:** LIVE **3 a :** to hold true **b :** to be logically conceivable as the subject of true statements ~ *vt* **:** to support with provisions **:** MAINTAIN

sub·sis·tence \səb-ˈsis-tən(t)s\ *n* [ME, fr. LL *subsistentia,* fr. *subsistent-, subsistens,* prp. of *subsistere*] **1 a** (1) **:** real being **:** EXISTENCE (2) **:** CONTINUATION, PERSISTENCE (3) **:** INHERENCY ⟨~ of a quality in a body⟩ **b :** something by which an individual is what it is **c :** the character possessed by whatever is logically conceivable **2 :** means of subsisting: as **a :** the minimum (as of food and shelter) necessary to support life **b :** a source or means of obtaining the necessities of life — **sub·sis·tent** \-tənt\ *adj*

¹**sub·soil** \ˈsəb-ˌsȯil\ *n* **:** the stratum of weathered material that underlies the surface soil

²**subsoil** *vt* **:** to turn, break, or stir the subsoil of — **sub·soil·er** *n*

sub·so·lar \ˌsəb-ˈsō-lər, ˈsəb-\ *adj* **:** having the sun in the zenith; *specif* **:** situated between the tropics

sub·son·ic \-ˈsän-ik\ *adj* [ISV] **1 :** of, relating to, or being a speed less than that of sound in air **2 :** moving, capable of moving, or utilizing air currents moving at a subsonic speed **3 :** INFRASONIC 1

sub·space \ˈsəb-ˌspās\ *n* **:** a space each of whose points is contained in a given space but which does not itself contain all the points of the given space

sub spe·cie ae·ter·ni·ta·tis \su̇b-ˈspek-ē-ˌā-ˌī-ˌter-nə-ˈtät-əs\ *adv* [NL, lit., under the aspect of eternity] **:** in its essential or universal form or nature

sub·spe·cies \ˈsəb-ˌspē-shēz, -sēz\ *n* [NL] **:** a subdivision of a species: as **a :** a taxonomic category that ranks immediately below a species and designates a morphologically distinguishable and geographically isolated group whose members interbreed successfully with those of other subspecies of the same species where their ranges overlap **b :** a named subdivision (as a race or variety) of a taxonomic species — **sub·spe·cif·ic** \ˌsəb-spi-ˈsif-ik\ *adj*

sub·stance \ˈsəb-stən(t)s\ *n* [ME, fr. OF, fr. L *substantia,* fr. *substant-, substans,* prp. of *substare* to stand under, fr. *sub-* + *stare* to stand — more at STAND] **1 a :** essential nature **:** ESSENCE **b :** a fundamental or characteristic part or quality **c** *Christian Science* **:** SPIRIT 15 **2 a :** ultimate reality that underlies all outward manifestations and change **b :** the real subject of predication **c :** FORM **d :** an individual compounded of matter and form **3 a :** physical material from which something is made or which has discrete existence **b :** matter of particular or definite chemical constitution **4 :** material possessions **:** PROPERTY

sub·stan·dard \ˌsəb-ˈstan-dərd, ˈsəb-\ *adj* **:** deviating from or falling short of a standard or norm: as **a :** of a quality lower than that prescribed by law ⟨~ canned goods⟩ **b :** conforming to a pattern of linguistic usage existing within a speech community but not that of the prestige group in that community — compare NONSTANDARD **c :** constituting a greater than normal risk to an insurer

sub·stan·tial \səb-ˈstan-chəl\ *adj* **1 a :** consisting of or relating to substance **b :** REAL, TRUE **c :** IMPORTANT, ESSENTIAL **2 :** ample to satisfy and nourish **:** FULL **3 :** possessed of means **:** WELL-TO-DO **4 :** firmly constructed **:** STURDY **5 :** being that specified to a large degree or in the main ⟨a ~ victory⟩ — **substantial** *n* — **sub·stan·ti·al·i·ty** \-ˌstan-chē-ˈal-ət-ē\ *n* — **sub·stan·tial·ly** \-ˈstanch-(ə-)lē\ *adv* — **sub·stan·tial·ness** \-ˈstan-chəl-nəs\ *n*

sub·stan·ti·ate \səb-ˈstan-chē-ˌāt\ *vt* **1 :** to impart substance to **2 :** to put into concrete form **:** EMBODY **3 :** to establish by proof or competent evidence **:** VERIFY ⟨~ a charge⟩ **syn** see CONFIRM — **sub·stan·ti·a·tion** \-ˌstan-chē-ˈā-shən\ *n* — **sub·stan·ti·a·tive** \-ˈstan-chē-ˌāt-iv\ *adj*

sub·stan·ti·val \ˌsəb-stən-ˈtī-vəl\ *adj* **:** of, relating to, or serving as a substantive — **sub·stan·ti·val·ly** \-və-lē\ *adv*

¹**sub·stan·tive** \ˈsəb-stən-tiv\ *n* [ME *substantif,* fr. MF, fr. *substantif,* adj., having or expressing substance, fr. LL *substantivus*] **:** NOUN; *broadly* **:** a word or word group functioning syntactically as a noun — **sub·stan·tiv·ize** \-stənt-iv-ˌīz\ *vt*

²**sub·stan·tive** \ˈsəb-stən-tiv; *except 2c & 3 also* səb-ˈstant-iv\ *adj* [ME, fr. LL *substantivus* having substance, fr. L *substantia*] **1 :** being a totally independent entity **2 a :** real rather than apparent **:** FIRM; *also* **:** ENDURING, PERMANENT **b :** of the nature of substance **:** ESSENTIAL **c :** betokening or expressing existence ⟨the ~ verb is the verb *to be*⟩ **3 a :** having the nature or function of a grammatical substantive ⟨a ~ phrase⟩ **b :** relating to or having the character of a noun or pronominal term in logic **4 :** considerable in amount or numbers **:** SUBSTANTIAL **5 :** creating and defining rights and duties ⟨~ law⟩ — **sub·stan·tive·ly** *adv* — **sub·stan·tive·ness** *n*

substantive right *n* **:** a right (as of life, liberty, property, or reputation) held to exist for its own sake and to constitute part of the normal legal order of society

sub·sta·tion \ˈsəb-ˌstā-shən\ *n* **1 :** a subsidiary station in which electric current is transformed **2 :** a branch post office

sub·stit·u·ent \səb-ˈstich-(ə-)wənt\ *n* [L *substituent-, substituens,* prp. of *substituere*] **:** an atom or group substituted for another or entering a molecule in place of some other part — **substituent** *adj*

sub·sti·tut·able \ˈsəb-stə-ˌt(y)üt-ə-bəl\ *adj* **:** capable of being substituted

¹**sub·sti·tute** \ˈsəb-stə-ˌt(y)üt\ *n* [ME, fr. L *substitutus,* pp. of *substituere* to put in place of, fr. *sub-* + *statuere* to set up, place — more at STATUTE] **1 :** a person or thing that takes the place of another **2 :** a word that replaces another word, phrase, or clause in a context — **substitute** *adj*

²**substitute** *vt* **1 :** to put in the place of another **:** EXCHANGE **2 :** REPLACE ~ *vi* **:** to serve as a substitute — **sub·sti·tu·tion** \ˌsəb-stə-ˈt(y)ü-shən\ *n* — **sub·sti·tu·tion·al** \-shnəl, -shən-ᵊl\ *adj* — **sub·sti·tu·tion·al·ly** \-ē\ *adv* — **sub·sti·tu·tion·ary** \-shə-ˌner-ē\ *adj*

sub·sti·tu·tive \ˈsəb-stə-ˌt(y)üt-iv\ *adj* **:** serving or suitable as a substitute — **sub·sti·tu·tive·ly** *adv*

sub·strate \ˈsəb-ˌstrāt\ *n* [ML *substratum*] **1 :** SUBSTRATUM **2 :** the base on which an organism lives ⟨the soil is the ~ of most seed plants⟩ **3 :** a substance acted upon (as by an enzyme)

sub·strato·sphere \ˌsəb-ˈstrat-ə-ˌsfi(ə)r, ˈsəb-\ *n* [ISV] **:** the region

of the atmosphere just below the stratosphere — **sub·strato·spher·ic** \-ˌstrat-ə-'sfi(ə)r-ik, -'sfer-\ *adj*

sub·stra·tum \'səb-ˌstrāt-əm, -ˌstrat-, 'səb-'\ *n, pl* **sub·stra·ta** \-ə\ [ML, fr. L, neut. of *substratus*, pp. of *substernere* to spread under, fr. *sub-* + *sternere* to spread — more at STREW] **:** an underlying support **:** FOUNDATION: as **a :** substance that is a permanent subject of qualities or phenomena **b :** the material of which something is made and from which it derives its special qualities **c :** a layer beneath the surface soil; *specif* **:** SUBSOIL **d :** SUBSTRATE 2, 3 **e :** a thin coating (as of hardened gelatin) on the support of a photographic film or plate to facilitate the adhesion of the sensitive emulsion

sub·struc·tion \'səb-ˌstrək-shən\ *n* [L *substruction-, substructio*, fr. *substructus*, pp. of *substruere* to build beneath, fr. *sub-* + *struere* to build — more at STRUCTURE] **:** the underlying or supporting part of a fabrication (as a building or dam) **:** SUBSTRUCTURE — **sub·struc·tion·al** \-'strək-shnəl, -shən-ᵊl\ *adj*

sub·struc·ture \'səb-ˌstrək-chər\ *n* [*sub- + structure*] **:** UNDER-CARRIAGE, GROUNDWORK

sub·sume \səb-'süm\ *vt* [NL *subsumere*, fr. L *sub-* + *sumere* to take up — more at CONSUME] **:** to classify within a larger category or under a general principle ⟨~ an individual under a species⟩

sub·sump·tion \səb-'səm(p)-shən\ *n* [NL *subsumption-, subsumptio*, fr. *subsumptus*, pp. of *subsumere*] **1 :** MINOR PREMISE **2 :** something that is subsumed **3 :** the act or process of subsuming **4 :** the condition of something that is subsumed

sub·sur·face \'səb-ˌsər-fəs\ *n* **:** earth material (as rock) near but not exposed at the surface of the ground — **subsurface** *adj*

sub·teen \'səb-'tēn\ *n* **:** one of less than teen age; *esp* **:** a girl under 13 years of age for whom clothing in sizes 8–14 is designed

sub·tem·per·ate \ˌsəb-'tem-p(ə-)rət, 'səb-\ *adj* **:** less than typically temperate ⟨a ~ climate⟩; *also* **:** of or relating to the colder parts of the temperate zones

sub·ten·an·cy \-'ten-ən-sē\ *n* **:** the state of being a subtenant

sub·ten·ant \-'ten-ənt\ *n* **:** one who rents from a tenant **:** SUB-LESSEE

sub·tend \səb-'tend\ *vt* [L *subtendere* to stretch beneath, fr. *sub-* + *tendere* to stretch — more at THIN] **1 a :** to be opposite to ⟨a hypotenuse ~s a right angle⟩ **b :** to extend under and mark off or enclose ⟨a chord ~s an arc⟩ **2 :** to underlie so as to include

sub·ter·fuge \'səb-tər-ˌfyüj\ *n* [LL *subterfugium*, fr. L *subterfugere* to escape, evade, fr. *subter-* secretly (fr. *subter* underneath) + *fugere* to flee; akin to L *sub* under — more at UP, FUGITIVE] **:** deception by artifice or stratagem in order to conceal, escape, or evade **syn** see DECEPTION

sub·ter·ra·nean \ˌsəb-tə-'rā-nē-ən, -nyən\ *or* **sub·ter·ra·neous** \-nē-əs, -nyəs\ *adj* [L *subterraneus*, fr. *sub* under + *terra* earth — more at UP, TERRACE] **1 :** being, lying, or operating under the surface of the earth **2 :** existing or working in secret **:** HIDDEN — **sub·ter·ra·nean·ly** *adv*

sub·te·tan·ic \ˌsəb-te-'tan-ik\ *adj* **:** approaching tetany or tetanus esp. in form or degree of contraction

sub·thresh·old \ˌsəb-'thresh-ˌ(h)ōld\ *adj* **:** inadequate to produce a response ⟨~ dosage⟩

sub·tile \'sət-ᵊl, 'səb-t ᵊl\ *adj* **sub·til·er** \'sət-lər, -ᵊl-ər; 'səb-tə-lər\ **sub·til·est** \'sət-ləst, -ᵊl-əst; 'səb-tə-ləst\ [ME, fr. L *subtilis*] **1 :** SUBTLE, ELUSIVE ⟨a ~ aroma⟩ **2 :** CUNNING, CRAFTY — **sub·tile·ly** \'sət-lē, -ᵊl-(l)ē; 'səb-tə-lē\ *adv* — **sub·tile·ness** \'sət-ᵊl-nəs, 'səb-tᵊl-\ *n*

sub·til·iza·tion \ˌsət-ᵊl-ə-'zā-shən, ˌsəb-tə-lə-\ *n* **:** an act of subtilizing; *also* **:** something subtilized

sub·til·ize \'sət-ᵊl-ˌīz, 'səb-tə-ˌlīz\ *vt* **:** to make subtile ~ *vi* **:** to act or think subtly

sub·til·ty \'sət-ᵊl-tē, 'səb-tᵊl-\ *n* **:** SUBTLETY

¹sub·ti·tle \'səb-ˌtīt-ᵊl\ *n* **1 :** a secondary or explanatory title **2 :** a printed statement or fragment of dialogue appearing on the screen between the scenes of a silent motion picture or appearing as a translation at the bottom of the screen during the scenes

²subtitle *vt* **:** to give a subtitle to

sub·tle \'sət-ᵊl\ *adj* **sub·tler** \'sət-lər, -ᵊl-ər\ **sub·tlest** \'sət-ləst, -ᵊl-əst\ [ME *sutil, sotil*, fr. OF *soutil*, fr. L *subtilis*, lit., finely woven, fr. *sub-* + *tela* web; akin to L *texere* to weave — more at TECHNICAL] **1 :** DELICATE, REFINED **2 :** mentally acute **:** KEEN **3 a :** highly skillful **:** EXPERT **b :** cunningly made or contrived **:** INGENIOUS **4 :** ARTFUL, CRAFTY ⟨a ~ rogue⟩ **5 :** operating insidiously ⟨~ poisons⟩ — **sub·tle·ness** \'sət-ᵊl-nəs\ *n* — **sub·tly** \'sət-lē, -ᵊl-(l)ē\ *adv*

sub·tle·ty \'sət-ᵊl-tē\ *n* [ME *sutilte*, fr. OF *sutilté*, fr. L *subtilitat-, subtilitas*, fr. *subtilis*] **1 :** the quality or state of being subtle: as **a :** TENUOUSNESS **b :** acuteness of mind **2 :** something subtle; *esp* **:** a fine distinction

sub·ton·ic \ˌsəb-'tän-ik, 'səb-\ *n* **:** the seventh degree of the musical scale **:** LEADING TONE

sub·tract \səb-'trakt\ *vb* [L *subtractus*, pp. of *subtrahere* to draw from beneath, withdraw, fr. *sub-* + *trahere* to draw — more at DRAW] *vt* **:** to take away by deducting ⟨~ 5 from 9⟩ ~ *vi* **:** to perform a subtraction — **sub·tract·er** *n*

sub·trac·tion \səb-'trak-shən\ *n* **1 :** an act or instance of subtracting **2 :** the withdrawing or withholding from one of a right to which he is entitled **3 :** the operation of deducting one number from another

sub·trac·tive \-'trak-tiv\ *adj* **1 :** tending to subtract **2 :** constituting or involving subtraction ⟨a ~ error in spelling⟩ ⟨a ~ correction⟩

sub·tra·hend \'səb-trə-ˌhend\ *n* [L *subtrahendus*, gerundive of *subtrahere*] **:** a number that is to be subtracted from a minuend

sub·trop·i·cal \ˌsəb-'träp-i-kəl, 'səb-\ *also* **sub·trop·ic** \-ik\ *adj* [ISV] **:** of, relating to, or being the regions bordering on the tropical zone

sub·trop·ics \-iks\ *n pl* **:** subtropical regions

su·bu·late \'sü-byə-lət\ *adj* [NL *subulatus*, fr. L *subula* awl; akin to OHG *siula* awl, L *suere* to sew — more at SEW] **:** linear and tapering to a fine point ⟨a ~ leaf⟩

sub·um·brel·la \ˌsəb-(ˌ)əm-'brel-ə\ *n* **:** the concave undersurface of a jellyfish

sub·urb \'səb-ˌərb\ *n* [ME, fr. L *suburbium*, fr. *sub-* near + *urbs* city — more at SUB-] **1 a :** an outlying part of a city or town **b :** a smaller community adjacent to a city **2** *pl* **:** the near vicinity **:** ENVIRONS — **sub·ur·ban** \sə-'bər-bən\ *adj or n*

sub·ur·ban·ite \sə-'bər-bə-ˌnīt\ *n* **:** a dweller in the suburbs

sub·ur·bia \-bē-ə\ *n* [NL, fr. E *suburb* + L *-ia* -y] **:** the suburbs of a city; *also* **:** suburbanites as a class

sub·ven·tion \səb-'ven-chən\ *n* [LL *subvention-, subventio* assistance, fr. L *subventus*, pp. of *subvenire* to come up, come to the rescue, fr. *sub-* up + *venire* to come — more at SUB-, COME] **:** the provision of assistance or financial support: as **a :** ENDOWMENT **b :** a subsidy from a government or foundation — **sub·ven·tion·ary** \-chə-ˌner-ē\ *adj*

sub·ver·sion \səb-'vər-zhən, -shən\ *n* [ME, fr. MF, fr. LL *subversion-, subversio*, fr. L *subversus*, pp. of *subvertere*] **1 :** the act of subverting **:** the state of being subverted **:** OVERTHROW **2** *obs* **:** a cause of overthrow or destruction — **sub·ver·sion·ary** \-zhə-ˌner-ē, -shə-\ *adj* — **sub·ver·sive** \-'vər-siv, -ziv\ *adj or n* — **sub·ver·sive·ly** *adv* — **sub·ver·sive·ness** *n*

sub·vert \səb-'vərt\ *vt* [ME *subverten*, fr. MF *subvertir*, fr. L *subvertere*, lit., to turn from beneath, fr. *sub-* + *vertere* to turn — more at WORTH] **1 :** to overturn or overthrow from the foundation **:** RUIN **2 :** to pervert or corrupt by an undermining of morals, allegiance, or faith — **sub·vert·er** *n*

sub·way \'səb-ˌwā\ *n* **:** an underground way: as **a :** a passage under a street (as for pedestrians, power cables, or water or gas mains) **b :** a usu. electric underground railway **c :** UNDERPASS

suc·ce·da·ne·ous \ˌsək-sə-'dā-nē-əs\ *adj* **:** serving as a succedaneum **:** SUBSTITUTED

suc·ce·da·ne·um \-nē-əm\ *n, pl* **suc·ce·da·nea** \-nē-ə\ [NL, fr. L, neut. of *succedaneus* substituted, fr. *succedere* to follow after] **:** SUBSTITUTE

suc·ce·dent \sək-'sēd-ᵊnt\ *adj* [L *succedent-, succedens*, prp. of *succedere*] **:** SUCCEEDING, SUBSEQUENT

suc·ceed \sək-'sēd\ *vb* [ME *succeden*, fr. L *succedere* to go up, follow after, succeed, fr. *sub-* near + *cedere* to go — more at SUB-, CEDE] *vi* **1 a :** to come next after another in or in possession of an estate; *specif* **:** to inherit sovereignty **b :** to follow after another in order **2 a :** to turn out well **b :** to attain a desired object or end **:** be successful **3** *obs* **:** to devolve upon a person by inheritance ~ *vt* **1 :** to follow in sequence and esp. immediately **2 :** to come after as heir or successor **syn** see FOLLOW — **suc·ceed·er** *n*

suc·cès d'es·time \sək-ˌsā-des-'tēm, (ˌ)sük-\ *n* [F, lit., success of esteem] **:** the reception accorded a work of art that wins critical respect but not popular success

suc·cess \sək-'ses\ *n* [L *successus*, fr. *successus*, pp. of *succedere*] **1** *obs* **:** OUTCOME, RESULT **2 a :** degree or measure of succeeding **b :** a favorable termination of a venture; *specif* **:** the attainment of wealth, favor, or eminence **3 :** one that succeeds

suc·cess·ful \-fəl\ *adj* **1 :** resulting or terminating in success **2 :** gaining or having gained success — **suc·cess·ful·ly** \-fə-lē\ *adv* — **suc·cess·ful·ness** *n*

suc·ces·sion \sək-'sesh-ən\ *n* [ME, fr. MF or L; MF, fr. L *succession-, successio*, fr. *successus*, pp.] **1 a :** the order in which or the conditions under which one person after another succeeds to a property, dignity, title, or throne **b :** the right of a person or line to succeed **c :** the line having such a right **2 a :** the act or process of following in order **:** SEQUENCE **b** (1) **:** the act or process of one person's taking the place of another in the enjoyment of or liability for his rights or duties or both (2) **:** the act or process of a person's becoming beneficially entitled to a property or property interest of a deceased person **3 a :** a number of persons or things that follow each other in sequence **b :** a group, type, or series that succeeds or displaces another — **suc·ces·sion·al** \-'sesh-nəl, -ən-ᵊl\ *adj* — **suc·ces·sion·al·ly** \-ē\ *adv*

succession duty *n, chiefly Brit* **:** an inheritance tax

suc·ces·sive \sək-'ses-iv\ *adj* **1 :** following in succession or serial order **:** following each other without interruption **2 :** characterized by or produced in succession **syn** see CONSECUTIVE — **suc·ces·sive·ly** *adv* — **suc·ces·sive·ness** *n*

suc·ces·sor \sək-'ses-ər\ *n* [ME *successour*, fr. OF, fr. L *successor*, fr. *successus*, pp.] **:** one that follows; *esp* **:** one who succeeds to a throne, title, estate, or office

suc·ci·nate \'sək-sə-ˌnāt\ *n* **:** a salt or ester of succinic acid

suc·cinct \(ˌ)sək-'siŋ(k)t, sə-'siŋ(k)t\ *adj* [ME, fr. L *succinctus*, pp. of *succingere* to gird from below, tuck up, fr. *sub-* + *cingere* to gird — more at CINCTURE] **1** *archaic* **a :** GIRDED **b :** close-fitting **2 :** compressed into a narrow compass **:** TERSE, CURT **syn** see CONCISE — **suc·cinct·ly** \-'siŋ(k)-tlē, -'siŋ-klē\ *adv* — **suc·cinct·ness** \-'siŋt-nəs, -'siŋk-nəs\ *n*

suc·cin·ic acid \(ˌ)sək-ˌsin-ik-\ *n* [F *succinique*, fr. L *succinum* amber] **:** a crystalline dicarboxylic acid $C_4H_6O_4$ found widely in nature and active in biological energy-yielding reactions

¹suc·cor \'sək-ər\ *n* [ME *succur*, taken as sing., fr. earlier *sucurs*, fr. OF *sucors*, fr. ML *succursus*, fr. L *succursus*, pp. of *succurrere* to run up, run to help, fr. *sub-* up + *currere* to run — more at CURRENT] **1 :** RELIEF; *also* **:** AID, HELP **2 :** something that furnishes relief

²succor *vt* **suc·cor·ing** \'sək-(ə-)riŋ\ **:** to go to the aid of (one in want or distress) **:** RELIEVE — **suc·cor·er** \'sək-ər-ər\ *n*

suc·co·ry \'sək-(ə-)rē\ *n* [alter. of ME *cicoree*] **:** CHICORY

suc·co·tash \'sək-ə-ˌtash\ *n* [of Algonquian origin; akin to Narraganset *msəkwataš* succotash] **:** lima or shell beans and green corn cooked together

suc·cu·ba \'sək-yə-bə\ *n, pl* **suc·cu·bae** \-ˌbē, -ˌbī\ [LL, prostitute] **:** SUCCUBUS

suc·cu·bus \-bəs\ *n, pl* **suc·cu·bi** \-ˌbī, -ˌbē\ [ME, fr. ML, alter. of LL *succuba* prostitute, fr. L *succubare* to lie under, fr. *sub-* + *cubare* to lie, recline — more at HIP] **:** a demon assuming female form to have sexual intercourse with men in their sleep — compare INCUBUS

suc·cu·lence \'sək-yə-lən(t)s\ *n* **1 :** the state of being succulent **2 :** succulent feed

¹suc·cu·lent \-lənt\ *adj* [L *suculentus*, fr. *sucus* juice, sap; akin to L *sugere* to suck — more at SUCK] **1 a :** full of juice **:** JUICY **b** *of a plant* **:** having fleshy tissues designed to conserve moisture **2 :** full of vitality, freshness, or richness — **suc·cu·lent·ly** *adv*

²succulent *n* **:** a succulent plant (as a cactus)

suc·cumb \sə-'kəm\ *vi* [F & L; F *succomber*, fr. L *succumbere*, fr. *sub-* + *-cumbere* to lie down; akin to L *cubare* to lie — more at HIP]

1 : to yield to superior strength or force or overpowering appeal or desire 2 : to cease to exist : DIE **syn** see YIELD

suc·cus·sa·to·ry \sə-'kəs-ə-,tōr-ē, -,tȯr-\ *adj* : characterized by up-and-down vibrations of short amplitude — used of an earthquake

suc·cus·sion \sə-'kəsh-ən\ *n* [L *succussion-*, *succussio*, fr. *succussus*, pp. of *succutere* to fling up, fr. *sub-* up + *quatere* to shake — more at SUB-, QUASH] : the action or process of shaking or the state of being shaken esp. with violence

¹**such** \(')səch, (,)sich\ *adj* [ME, fr. OE *swilc;* akin to OHG *sulīh* such; both fr. a prehistoric Gmc compound whose constituents are respectively represented by OE *swā* so and by OE *gelīc* like — more at SO, LIKE] **1 a** : of a kind or character to be indicated or suggested ⟨bag ~ as a doctor carries⟩ **b** : having a quality to a degree to be indicated ⟨his excitement was ~ that he shouted⟩ **2 a** : having a quality already or just specified ⟨deeply moved by ~ acts of kindness⟩ **b** : of the character, quality, or extent previously indicated or implied **3** : of so extreme a degree or quality ⟨never heard ~ a hubbub⟩ **4** : MEDIOCRE **5** : of the same class, type, or sort : SIMILAR ⟨established twenty ~ clinics throughout the state⟩ **6** : not specified

²**such** *pron* **1** : such a person or thing or such persons or things **2** : someone or something stated, implied, or exemplified ⟨~ was the result⟩ **3** : one of the same kind ⟨tin and glass and ~⟩ — **as such** : intrinsically considered : in itself ⟨*as such* the gift was worth little⟩

³**such** *adv* **1 a** : to such a degree : SO ⟨~ tall buildings⟩ ⟨~ a fine person⟩ **b** : ESPECIALLY, VERY ⟨hasn't been in ~ good spirits lately⟩ **2** : in such a way

¹**such·like** \'səch-,līk\ *adj* : of like kind : SIMILAR

²**suchlike** *pron* : someone or something of the same sort : a similar person or thing

¹**suck** \'sək\ *vb* [ME *souken*, fr. OE *sūcan;* akin to OHG *sūgan* to suck, L *sugere*, Gk *hyein* to rain] *vt* **1 a** (1) : to draw (liquid and esp. mother's milk) into the mouth (2) : to draw or remove by application of the tongue, lips, or mouth (3) : to draw by or as if by suction, absorption, inhalation : to gather or exhaust a supply of **2 a** : to draw liquid from by motion of the mouth ⟨~ an orange⟩; *specif* : to suck milk from (a breast or udder) **b** : to consume by or as if by licking or sucking ⟨~ a lollipop⟩ ~ *vi* **1** : to draw milk from a breast or udder **2** : to draw something in by or as if by a vacuum **3** : to become sucked so as to make a sound or motion ⟨his pipe ~*ed* hollowly —Walter Machen⟩ ⟨flanks ~*ed* in and out, the long nose resting on his paws —Virginia Woolf⟩ **4** : to act in an obsequious manner ⟨when they want votes . . . the candidates come ~*ing* around —W.G.Hardy⟩

²**suck** *n* **1** : the act of sucking **2** : a sucking movement or force

¹**suck·er** \'sək-ər\ *n* **1 a** : one that sucks esp. a breast or udder : SUCKLING **b** : a device for creating or regulating suction (as a piston or valve in a pump) **c** : a pipe or tube through which something is drawn by suction **d** (1) : an organ in various animals for adhering or holding (2) : a mouth (as of a leech) adapted for sucking or adhering **2** : a shoot from the roots or lower part of the stem of a plant **3** : any of numerous freshwater fishes (family Catostomidae) closely related to the carps **4** : LOLLIPOP **5 a** : a person easily cheated or deceived **b** : a person irresistibly attracted by a specific type of object

²**sucker** *vb* **suck·er·ing** \'sək-(ə-)riŋ\ *vt* : to remove suckers from ~ *vi* : to send out suckers

suck·fish \'sək-,fish\ *n* : REMORA

suck·ing *adj* : not yet weaned; *broadly* : very young

sucking louse *n* : any of an order (Anoplura) of wingless insects comprising the true lice with mouthparts adapted to sucking body fluids

suck·le \'sək-əl\ *vt* **suck·ling** \-(ə-)liŋ\ [prob. back-formation fr. *suckling*] **1** : to give suck to **2** : to nurse at or from : SUCK

suck·ling \'sək-liŋ\ *n* : a young unweaned mammal

su·crase \'sü-,krās, -,krāz\ *n* [ISV, fr. F *sucre* sugar — more at SUGAR] : INVERTASE

su·crate \'sü-,krāt\ *n* : a metallic derivative of sucrose

su·cre \'sü-(,)krā\ *n* [Sp, fr. Antonio José de *Sucre* †1830 So. American liberator] — see MONEY table

su·crose \'sü-,krōs, -,krōz\ *n* [ISV, fr. F *sucre* sugar] : a sweet crystalline dextrorotatory nonreducing disaccharide sugar $C_{12}H_{22}O_{11}$ that occurs naturally in most land plants and is the sugar obtained from sugarcane or sugar beets

suc·tion \'sək-shən\ *n* [LL *suction-*, *suctio*, fr. L *suctus*, pp. of *sugere* to suck — more at SUCK] **1** : the act or process of sucking **2 a** : the act or process of exerting a force upon a solid, liquid, or gaseous body by reason of reduced air pressure over part of its surface **b** : force so exerted **3** : a device (as a pipe or fitting) used in a machine that operates by suction

suction pump *n* : a common pump in which the liquid to be raised is pushed by atmospheric pressure into the partial vacuum under a retreating valved piston on the upstroke and reflux is prevented by a check valve in the pipe

suction stop *n* : a voice stop in the formation of which air behind the articulation is rarefied with consequent inrush of air when articulation is broken

suc·to·ri·al \,sək-'tōr-ē-əl, -'tȯr-\ *adj* [NL *suctorius*, fr. L *suctus*, pp.] **1** : adapted for sucking; *esp* : serving to draw up fluid or to adhere by suction ⟨~ mouths⟩ **2 a** : provided with suctorial organs ⟨a ~ fish⟩ **b** : living by sucking the blood or juices of animals or plants

Su·dan grass \sü-'dan-, -'dän-\ *n* [the *Sudan*, region in Africa] : a vigorous tall-growing annual grass (*Sorghum vulgare sudanensis*) widely grown for hay and fodder

Su·dan·ic \sü-'dan-ik\ *n* [the *Sudan*] : the languages neither Bantu nor Hamitic spoken in a belt extending from Senegal to southern Sudan — **Sudanic** *adj*

su·da·to·ri·um \,süd-ə-'tōr-ē-əm, -'tȯr-\ *n, pl* **su·da·to·ria** \-ē-ə\ [L, fr. *sudatus*, pp. of *sudare* to sweat — more at SWEAT] : a sweat room in a bath

su·da·to·ry \'süd-ə-,tōr-ē, -,tȯr-\ *n* : SUDATORIUM

sudd \'səd\ *n* [Ar, lit., obstruction] : floating vegetable matter that forms obstructive masses in the upper White Nile

¹**sud·den** \'səd-ᵊn\ *adj* [ME *sodain*, fr. MF, fr. L *subitaneus*, fr. *subitus* sudden, fr. pp. of *subire* to come up, fr. *sub-* up + *ire* to go — more at SUB-, ISSUE] **1 a** : happening or coming unexpectedly ⟨~ shower⟩ **b** : changing angle or character all at once : PRECIPITOUS, ABRUPT **2** : marked by or manifesting hastiness : RASH **3** : made or brought about in a short time : PROMPT ⟨~ cure⟩ **syn** see PRECIPITATE — **sud·den·ly** *adv* — **sud·den·ness** \'səd-ᵊn-(n)əs\ *n*

²**sudden** *n, obs* : an unexpected occurrence : EMERGENCY — **all of a sudden** *or* **on a sudden** : sooner than was expected : at once : SUDDENLY

sudden death *n* **1** : unexpected death that is instantaneous or occurs within minutes from any cause other than violence ⟨*sudden death* following coronary occlusion⟩ **2 a** : a single full game played to break a tie **b** : a period of play to break a tie that terminates the moment one side scores

su·do·rif·er·ous \,süd-ə-'rif-(ə-)rəs\ *adj* [LL *sudorifer*, fr. L *sudor* sweat + *-ifer* -iferous — more at SWEAT] : producing or conveying sweat ⟨~ glands⟩ ⟨a ~ duct⟩

su·do·rif·ic \-'rif-ik\ *adj* [NL *sudorificus*, fr. L *sudor*] : causing or inducing sweat : DIAPHORETIC ⟨~ herbs⟩ — **sudorific** *n*

Su·dra \'s(h)ü-drə\ *n* [Skt *śūdra*] : a Hindu of a lower caste traditionally assigned to menial occupations — **Sudra** *adj*

¹**suds** \'sədz\ *n pl but sing or pl in constr* [prob. fr. MD *sudse* marsh; akin to OE *sēothan* to seethe — more at SEETHE] **1** : soapy water esp. when frothy; *also* : the lather or froth on soapy water **2** *slang* : BEER

²**suds** *vt* : to wash in suds ~ *vi* : to form suds

sudsy \'səd-zē\ *adj* : full of suds : FROTHY, FOAMY

sue \'sü\ *vb* [ME *suen*, fr. OF *suivre*, fr. (assumed) VL *sequere*, fr. L *sequi* to follow, come or go after; akin to Gk *hepesthai* to follow] *vt* **1** *obs* : to make petition to or for : SOLICIT **2** : to pay court or suit to : WOO **3 a** : to seek justice or right from (a person) by legal process; *specif* : to bring an action against **b** : to proceed with and follow up (a legal action) to proper termination ~ *vi* **1** : to make a request or application : PLEAD — usu. used with *for* or *to* **2** : to pay court : WOO **3** : to take legal proceedings in court — **su·er** *n*

suede *or* **suède** \'swād\ *n* [F *gants de Suède* Swedish gloves] **1** : leather with a napped surface **2** : a fabric finished with a nap to simulate suede

su·et \'sü-ət\ *n* [ME *sewet*, fr. (assumed) AF, dim. of AF *sue*, fr. L *sebum* tallow, suet — more at SOAP] : the hard fat about the kidneys and loins in beef and mutton that yields tallow

suf·fer \'səf-ər\ *vb* **suf·fer·ing** \-(ə-)riŋ\ [ME *suffren*, fr. OF *souffrir*, fr. (assumed) VL *sufferire*, fr. L *sufferre*, fr. *sub-* up + *ferre* to bear — more at SUB-, BEAR] *vt* **1 a** : to submit to or be forced to endure ⟨~ martyrdom⟩ **b** : to feel keenly : labor under ⟨~ thirst⟩ **2** : UNDERGO, EXPERIENCE **3** : to bear up under : ENDURE — used chiefly in negative statements ⟨not able to ~ pain⟩ **4** : ALLOW, TOLERATE ~ *vi* **1** : to endure death, pain, or distress **2** : to sustain loss or damage **3** : to be subject to disability or handicap **syn** see BEAR — **suf·fer·able** \'səf-(ə-)rə-bəl\ *adj* — **suf·fer·able·ness** *n* — **suf·fer·ably** \-blē\ *adv* — **suf·fer·er** \'səf-ər-ər, 'səf-rər\ *n*

suf·fer·ance \'səf-(ə-)rən(t)s\ *n* **1** : patient endurance : LONGSUFFERING **2** : PAIN, MISERY **3** : consent or sanction implied by a lack of interference or failure to enforce a prohibition **4** : power or ability to withstand : ENDURANCE ⟨it is beyond ~⟩

suf·fer·ing *n* **1** : the state or experience of one that suffers **2** : PAIN **syn** see DISTRESS — **suf·fer·ing·ly** \-(ə-)riŋ-lē\ *adv*

suf·fice \sə-'fīs *also* -'fīz\ *vb* [ME *sufficen*, fr. MF *suffis-*, stem of *suffire*, fr. L *sufficere*, lit., to put under, fr. *sub-* + *facere* to make, do — more at DO] *vi* **1** : to meet or satisfy a need : be sufficient **2** : to be competent or capable ~ *vt* : to be enough for — **suf·fic·er** *n*

suf·fi·cien·cy \sə-'fish-ən-sē\ *n* **1** : sufficient means to meet one's needs : COMPETENCY; *also* : a modest but adequate scale of living **2** : the quality or state of being sufficient : ADEQUACY

suf·fi·cient \sə-'fish-ənt\ *adj* [ME, fr. L *sufficient-*, *sufficiens*, fr. prp. of *sufficere*] **1** : enough to meet the needs of a situation or a proposed end **2** *archaic* : QUALIFIED, COMPETENT — **suf·fi·cient·ly** *adv*

syn ENOUGH, ADEQUATE, COMPETENT: SUFFICIENT suggests a close meeting of a need; ENOUGH is less exact in suggestion than SUFFICIENT; ADEQUATE may imply barely meeting a requirement; COMPETENT suggests measuring up to all requirements without question or being adequately adapted to an end

sufficient condition *n* : a proposition whose validity is sufficient evidence that a second is valid

¹**suf·fix** \'səf-,iks\ *n* [NL *suffixum*, fr. L, neut. of *suffixus*, pp. of *suffigere* to fasten underneath, fr. *sub-* + *figere* to fasten — more at DIKE] **1** : an affix occurring at the end of a word, base, or phrase **2** : SUBINDEX 1 — **suf·fix·al** \'səf-,ik-səl, (,)sə-'fik-səl\ *adj*

²**suf·fix** \'səf-,iks, (,)sə-'fiks\ *vt* : to attach as a suffix — **suf·fix·ation** \,səf-,ik-'sā-shən\ *n*

suf·fo·cate \'səf-ə-,kāt\ *vb* [L *suffocatus*, pp. of *suffocare* to choke, stifle, fr. *sub-* + *fauces* throat] *vt* **1 a** : to stop the respiration of (as by strangling or asphyxiation) **b** : to deprive of oxygen **2 a** : to make uncomfortable by want of cool fresh air **b** : to impede or stop the development of ~ *vi* : to become suffocated: **a** : to die from being unable to breathe **b** : to be uncomfortable through lack of air **c** : to become checked in development — **suf·fo·cat·ing·ly** \-,kāt-iŋ-lē\ *adv* — **suf·fo·ca·tion** \,səf-ə-'kā-shən\ *n* — **suf·fo·ca·tive** \'səf-ə-,kāt-iv\ *adj*

Suf·folk \'səf-ək, -,ōk\ *n* [*Suffolk*, England] **1** : any of a breed of black-faced hornless English sheep producing excellent mutton **2** : any of an English breed of chestnut-colored draft horses

¹**suf·fra·gan** \'səf-ri-gən, 'səf-ri-jən\ *n* [ME, fr. MF, fr. ML *suffraganeus*, fr. *suffragium* support, prayer] **1** : a diocesan bishop (as in the Roman Catholic Church and the Church of England) subordinate to a metropolitan **2** : an Anglican or Episcopal bishop assisting a diocesan bishop and not having the right of succession

²**suffragan** *adj* **1** : of or being a suffragan **2** : subordinate to a metropolitan or archiepiscopal see

suf·frage \'səf-rij, *substand* -ə-rij\ *n* [in sense 1, fr. ME, fr. MF, fr. ML *suffragium*, fr. L, vote, political support; in other senses, fr. L *suffragium*] **1** : an intercessory prayer : SUPPLICATION **2** : a vote given in deciding a controverted question or in the choice of a person for an office or trust **3** : the right of voting in political matters or the exercise of such right : FRANCHISE

suf·frag·ette \,səf-ri-'jet\ *n* : a woman who advocates suffrage for her sex

suf·frag·ist \'səf-ri-jəst\ *n* : one who advocates extension of suffrage esp. to women

suf·fru·tes·cent \ˌsəf-(ˌ)rü-ˈtes-ᵊnt\ *adj* [NL *suffrutescent-, suffrutescens*, fr. L *sub-* + NL *frutescent-, frutescens* frutescent] *of a plant or stem* **:** having a somewhat woody base that does not die down each year

suf·fru·ti·cose \ˌsəf-ˈrüt-i-ˌkōs\ *adj* [NL *suffruticosus*, fr. L *sub-* + *fruticosus* fruticose] **:** woody and perennial at the base but remaining herbaceous above ⟨a low ~ perennial⟩

suf·fuse \sə-ˈfyüz\ *vt* [L *suffusus*, pp. of *suffundere*, lit., to pour beneath, fr. *sub-* + *fundere* to pour — more at FOUND] **:** to spread over or through in the manner of fluid or light **:** FLUSH, FILL **syn** see INFUSE — **suf·fu·sion** \-ˈfyü-zhən\ *n* — **suf·fu·sive** \-ˈfyü-siv, -ziv\ *adj*

Su·fi \ˈsü-(ˌ)fē\ *n* [Ar *ṣūfīy*, lit., (man) of wool] **:** a Muslim mystic — **Sufi** *adj* — **Su·fic** \-fik\ *adj* — **Su·fism** \-ˌfiz-əm\ *n*

¹**sug·ar** \ˈshu̇g-ər\ *n* [ME *sucre*, fr. MF, fr. ML *zuccarum*, fr. OIt *zucchero*, fr. Ar *sukkar*, fr. Per *shakar*, fr. Skt *śarkarā*; akin to Skt *śarkara* pebble] **1 a :** a sweet crystallizable material that consists wholly or essentially of sucrose, is colorless or white when pure tending to brown when less refined, is obtained commercially from sugarcane or sugar beet and less extensively from sorghum, maples, and palms, and is nutritionally important as a source of dietary carbohydrate and as a sweetener and preservative of other foods **b :** any of various water-soluble compounds that vary widely in sweetness and comprise the oligosaccharides including sucrose **2 :** a unit (as a spoonful, cube, or lump) of sugar ⟨how many ~*s* in your tea⟩ **3 :** a sugar bowl

²**sugar** *vb* **sug·ar·ing** \ˈshu̇g-(ə-)riŋ\ *vt* **1 :** to make palatable or attractive **:** SWEETEN **2 :** to sprinkle or mix with sugar ~ *vi* **1 :** to form sugar **2 :** to become granular **:** GRANULATE

sugar apple *n* **:** the fruit of the sweetsop

sugar beet *n* **:** a white-rooted beet grown for the sugar in its roots

sug·ar·ber·ry \ˈshu̇g-ər-ˌber-ē\ *n* **1 :** a hackberry with sweet edible fruits **2 :** JUNEBERRY

sugar bush *n* **:** a woods in which sugar maples predominate

sug·ar·cane \ˈshu̇g-ər-ˌkān\ *n* **:** a stout tall perennial grass (*Saccharum officinarum*) with a large terminal panicle widely grown in warm regions as a source of sugar

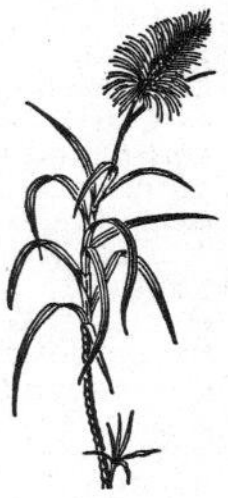

sugarcane

sug·ar·coat \ˌshu̇g-ər-ˈkōt\ *vt* **1 :** to coat with sugar **2 :** to make superficially attractive or palatable

sug·ar·house \ˈshu̇g-ər-ˌhau̇s\ *n* **:** a building where sugar is made or refined; *specif* **:** a shed where maple sap is boiled and maple syrup and maple sugar are made

sugaring off *n* **1 :** the act or process of converting maple syrup into sugar **2 :** a party held at the time of sugaring off

sug·ar·loaf \ˈshu̇g-ər-ˌlōf\ *n* **1 :** refined sugar molded into a cone **2 :** a hill or mountain shaped like a sugarloaf — **sugar-loaf** *adj*

sugar maple *n* **:** a maple with a sweet sap; *specif* **:** one (*Acer saccharum*) of eastern No. America with 3- to 5-lobed leaves, hard close-grained wood much used for cabinetwork, and sap that is the chief source of maple sugar

sugar of lead : LEAD ACETATE

sugar orchard *n, chiefly NewEng* **:** SUGAR BUSH

sug·ar·plum \ˈshu̇g-ər-ˌpləm\ *n* **1 :** a small candy in a ball or disk **:** SWEETMEAT **2 :** JUNEBERRY

sug·ary \ˈshu̇g-(ə-)rē\ *adj* **1 :** containing, resembling, or tasting of sugar **2 a :** ostentatiously sweet **:** HONEYED **b :** cloyingly sweet **:** SENTIMENTAL

sug·gest \sə(g)-ˈjest\ *vt* [L *suggestus*, pp. of *suggerere* to put under, furnish, suggest, fr. *sub-* + *gerere* to carry — more at CAST] **1 a** *obs* **:** to seek to influence **:** SEDUCE **b :** to call forth **:** EVOKE **c :** to imply as a possibility **:** INTIMATE **d :** to propose as desirable or fitting ⟨~ a stroll⟩ **e :** to offer for consideration or as a hypothesis **2 a :** to call to mind by thought or association **b :** to serve as a motive or inspiration for — **sug·gest·er** *n*

syn SUGGEST, IMPLY, HINT, INTIMATE, INSINUATE mean to convey an idea indirectly. SUGGEST stresses putting into the mind by association of ideas; IMPLY is close to SUGGEST but may indicate that the unexpressed idea is more definitely or logically related to the expressed; HINT implies the use of slight or remote suggestion with a minimum of overt statement; INTIMATE stresses delicacy of suggestion without connoting any lack of candor; INSINUATE applies to the conveying of a usu. unpleasant or depreciatory idea in a sly, underhanded manner

sug·gest·ibil·i·ty \sə(g)-ˌjes-tə-ˈbil-ət-ē\ *n* **:** the quality or state of being suggestible

sug·gest·ible \sə(g)-ˈjes-tə-bəl\ *adj* **:** easily influenced by suggestion

sug·ges·tion \sə(g)-ˈjes(h)-chən\ *n* **1 a :** the act or process of suggesting **b :** something suggested **2 a :** the process by which one thought leads to another esp. through association of ideas **b :** a means or process of influencing attitudes and behavior hypnotically **3 :** a slight indication **:** TRACE

sug·ges·tive \sə(g)-ˈjes-tiv\ *adj* **1 a :** giving a suggestion **:** INDICATIVE **b :** full of suggestions **:** PROVOCATIVE ⟨~ commentary⟩ **c :** stirring mental associations **:** EVOCATIVE **2 :** suggesting or tending to suggest something improper or indecent **:** RISQUÉ — **sug·ges·tive·ly** *adv* — **sug·ges·tive·ness** *n*

sui·ci·dal \ˌsü-ə-ˈsīd-ᵊl\ *adj* **1 :** relating to or of the nature of suicide **2 :** marked by an impulse to commit suicide **3 :** dangerous esp. to life — **sui·ci·dal·ly** \-ᵊl-ē\ *adv*

¹**sui·cide** \ˈsü-ə-ˌsīd\ *n* [L *sui* (gen.) of oneself + E *-cide*; akin to OE & OHG *sīn* his, L *suus* one's own, Skt *sva* oneself, one's own] **1 a :** the act or an instance of taking one's own life voluntarily and intentionally esp. by a person of years of discretion and of sound mind **b :** ruin of one's own interests **2 :** one that commits or attempts suicide

²**suicide** *vi* **:** to commit suicide ~ *vt* **:** to put (as oneself) to death **:** KILL

sui ge·ner·is \ˌsü-ˌī-ˈjen-ə-rəs; ˌsü-ē-ˈjen-, -ˈgen-\ *adj* [L, of its own kind] **:** constituting a class alone **:** UNIQUE, PECULIAR

sui ju·ris \ˌsü-ˌī-ˈju̇r-əs, ˌsü-ē-ˈyu̇r-\ *adj* [L, of one's own right] **:** having full legal rights or capacity

su·int \ˈsü-ənt, ˈswint\ *n* [F, fr. MF, fr. *suer* to sweat, fr. L *sudare* — more at SWEAT] **:** dried perspiration of sheep deposited in the wool and found rich in potassium salts

¹**suit** \ˈsüt\ *n* [ME *siute* act of following, retinue, sequence, set,

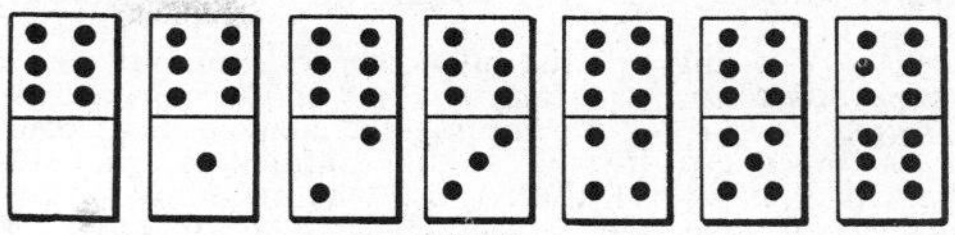

suit 6b

fr. OF, act of following, retinue, fr. *suir* to follow, fr. (assumed) VL *sequitus*, pp. of *sequere* to follow — more at SUE] **1** *archaic* **:** SUITE 1 **2 a :** recourse or appeal to a feudal superior for justice or redress **b :** an action or process in a court for the recovery of a right or claim **3 :** an act or instance of suing or seeking by entreaty **:** APPEAL; *specif* **:** COURTSHIP **4 :** SUITE 2 — used chiefly of armor, sails, and counters in games **5 :** a set of garments: as **a :** an outer costume of two or more pieces **b :** a costume to be worn for a special purpose or under particular conditions ⟨gym ~⟩ ⟨space ~⟩ **6 a :** all the cards in a pack bearing the same pip **b :** all the dominoes bearing the same number

²**suit** *vi* **1 :** ACCORD, AGREE ⟨position ~*s* with his abilities⟩ **2 :** to be appropriate or satisfactory ~ *vt* **1 :** to outfit with clothes **:** DRESS **2 :** ACCOMMODATE, ADAPT ⟨~ the action to the word⟩ **3 a :** to be proper for **:** BEFIT **b :** to be becoming to **4 :** to meet the needs or desires of **:** PLEASE ⟨~*s* me fine⟩

suit·abil·i·ty \ˌsüt-ə-ˈbil-ət-ē\ *n* **:** the quality or state of being suitable

suit·able \ˈsüt-ə-bəl\ *adj* **1** *obs* **:** MATCHING, SIMILAR **2 a :** adapted to a use or purpose **:** FIT **b :** satisfying propriety **:** PROPER **c :** ABLE, QUALIFIED **syn** see FIT — **suit·able·ness** *n* — **suit·ably** \-blē\ *adv*

suit·case \ˈsüt-ˌkās\ *n* **:** TRAVELING BAG; *esp* **:** a rigid flat rectangular one

suite \ˈswēt, *2c is also* ˈsüt\ *n* [F, alter. of OF *siute* — more at SUIT] **1 :** RETINUE; *esp* **:** the personal staff accompanying a ruler, diplomat, or dignitary on official business **2 :** a group of things forming a unit or constituting a collection **:** SET: as **a :** a group of rooms occupied as a unit **:** APARTMENT **b** (1) **:** a 17th and 18th century instrumental musical form consisting of a series of dances in the same or related keys (2) **:** a modern instrumental composition free in its character and number of movements (3) **:** a long orchestral concert arrangement in suite form of material drawn from a longer work (as a ballet) **c :** a set of matched furniture for a room

suit·ing \ˈsüt-iŋ\ *n* **:** fabric for suits

suit·or \ˈsüt-ər\ *n* [ME, follower, pleader, fr. AF, fr. L *secutor* follower, fr. *secutus*, pp. of *sequi* to follow — more at SUE] **1 :** one that petitions or entreats **:** PLEADER **2 :** a party to a suit at law **3 :** one who courts a woman or seeks to marry her

su·ki·ya·ki \skē-ˈ(y)äk-ē; ˌsu̇k-ē-ˈ, ˌsük-\ *n* [Jap] **:** meat, soybean curd, onions, and other vegetables cooked in soy sauce, sake, and sugar

Suk·koth \ˈsu̇k-ˌōt(h), -ˌōs, -əs\ *n* [Heb *sukkōth*, pl. of *sukkāh* thicket] **:** a Jewish harvest festival beginning on the 15th of Tishri and commemorating the temporary shelter of the Jews during their wandering in the wilderness

sul·cate \ˈsəl-ˌkāt\ *also* **sul·cat·ed** \-ˌkāt-əd\ *adj* [L *sulcatus*, pp. of *sulcare* to furrow, fr. *sulcus*] **:** scored with usu. longitudinal furrows **:** GROOVED

sul·cus \ˈsəl-kəs\ *n, pl* **sul·ci** \-ˌkī, -ˌkē\ [L; akin to OE *sulh* plow, Gk *holkos* furrow, *helkein* to pull] **:** FURROW, GROOVE; *esp* **:** a shallow furrow on the surface of the brain separating adjacent convolutions

sulf- *or* **sulfo-** *or* **sulph-** *or* **sulpho-** *comb form* [F *sulf-, sulfo-*, fr. L *sulfur*] **:** sulfur **:** containing sulfur ⟨*sulf*ochloride⟩ ⟨*sulf*onium⟩

sul·fa \ˈsəl-fə\ *adj* [short for *sulfanilamide*] **1 :** related chemically to sulfanilamide **2 :** of, relating to, or containing sulfa drugs ⟨~ therapy⟩

sulfa drug *n* **:** any of various synthetic organic bacteria-inhibiting drugs that are sulfonamides closely related chemically to sulfanilamide

sul·fa·nil·amide \ˌsəl-fə-ˈnil-ə-ˌmīd, -məd\ *n* [*sulfanil*ic + *amide*] **:** a crystalline sulfonamide $C_6H_8N_2O_2S$ that is the amide of sulfanilic acid and the parent compound of most of the sulfa drugs

sul·fa·nil·ic acid \ˌsəl-fə-ˌnil-ik-\ *n* [ISV *sulf-* + *anil*ine + *-ic*] **:** a crystalline acid $C_6H_7NO_3S$ obtained from aniline and used esp. in making dyes

sulf·ar·se·nide \ˌsəl-ˈfärs-ᵊn-ˌīd\ *n* **:** a compound that is both a sulfide and an arsenide

¹**sul·fate** \ˈsəl-ˌfāt\ *n* [F, fr. L *sulfur*] **:** a salt or ester of sulfuric acid

²**sulfate** *vt* **1 :** to treat or combine with sulfuric acid, a sulfate, or a related agent; *also* **:** to convert into a sulfate **2 :** to form a deposit of a whitish scale of lead sulfate on (the plates of a storage battery) ~ *vi* **:** to become sulfated

sul·fide *or* **sul·phide** \ˈsəl-ˌfīd\ *n* **:** a compound of sulfur analogous to an oxide or ether with sulfur in place of oxygen **:** a salt or ester of hydrogen sulfide

sul·fi·nyl \ˈsəl-fə-ˌnil\ *n* [*sulfin*ic acid (RSO_2H) + *-yl*] **:** the bivalent group or radical >SO

sul·fite *or* **sul·phite** \ˈsəl-ˌfīt\ *n* [F *sulfite*, alter. of *sulfate*] **:** a salt or ester of sulfurous acid — **sul·fit·ic** \ˌsəl-ˈfit-ik\ *adj*

sulfon- *comb form* [ISV *sulfonic*] **1 :** sulfonic ⟨*sulfon*amide⟩ **2 :** sulfonyl ⟨*sulfon*methane⟩

sul·fon·amide \ˌsəl-ˈfän-ə-ˌmīd, -ˈfōn-, -məd\ *n* **:** the amide (as sulfanilamide) of a sulfonic acid; *also* **:** SULFA DRUG

¹**sul·fo·nate** \ˈsəl-fə-ˌnāt\ *n* **:** a salt or ester of a sulfonic acid

²**sulfonate** *vt* **:** to introduce the sulfonic group into **:** convert into a sulfonic acid

sul·fone \ˈsəl-ˌfōn\ *n* **:** any of various compounds containing the sulfonyl group doubly united by its sulfur usu. with carbon

sul·fon·ic \ˌsəl-ˈfän-ik, -ˈfōn-\ *adj* **:** of, relating to, being, or derived from the univalent acid group $-SO_3H$

sulfonic acid *n* **:** any of numerous acids that contain the sulfonic group and may be derived from sulfuric acid by replacement of a

hydroxyl group by either an inorganic anion or a univalent organic radical
sul·fo·ni·um \ˌsəl-ˈfō-nē-əm\ *n* [NL, fr. *sulf-* + ammonium] **:** a univalent radical or cation SH_3 analogous to oxonium
sul·fon·meth·ane \ˌsəl-ˌfōn-ˈmeth-ˌān\ *n* **:** a crystalline hypnotic sulfone $C_5H_{10}O_4S_2$
sul·fo·nyl \ˈsəl-fə-ˌnil\ *n* **:** the bivalent group or radical $>SO_2$
1**sul·fur** *or* **sul·phur** \ˈsəl-fər\ *n* [ME *sulphur* brimstone, fr. L *sulpur, sulphur, sulfur*] **1 :** a nonmetallic element that occurs either free or combined esp. in sulfides and sulfates, is a constituent of proteins, exists in several allotropic forms including yellow orthorhombic crystals, resembles oxygen chemically but is less active and more acidic, and is used esp. in the chemical and paper industries, in rubber vulcanization, and in medicine for treating skin diseases — see ELEMENT table **2 :** something that suggests sulfur
2**sulfur** *vt* **sul·fur·ing** \-f(ə-)riŋ\ **:** to treat with sulfur or a sulfur compound
sulfur dioxide *n* **:** a heavy pungent gas SO_2 easily condensed to a colorless liquid and used esp. in making sulfuric acid, in bleaching, as a preservative, and as a refrigerant
sul·fu·re·ous \ˌsəl-ˈfyu̇r-ē-əs\ *adj* **:** SULFUROUS — **sul·fu·re·ous·ly** *adv* — **sul·fu·re·ous·ness** *n*
1**sul·fu·ret** \ˈsəl-f(y)ə-ˌret\ *n* [NL *sulfuretum*, fr. L *sulfur*] **:** SULFIDE
2**sulfuret** *vt* **sul·fu·ret·ed** *or* **sul·fu·ret·ted; sul·fu·ret·ing** *or* **sul·fu·ret·ting :** to combine or impregnate with sulfur
sul·fu·ric *or* **sul·phu·ric** \ˌsəl-ˈfyu̇(ə)r-ik\ *adj* **:** of, relating to, or containing sulfur esp. in a higher valence ⟨~ esters⟩
sulfuric acid *n* **:** a heavy corrosive oily dibasic strong acid H_2SO_4 that is colorless when pure and is a vigorous oxidizing and dehydrating agent — called also *oil of vitriol*
sul·fu·rize \ˈsəl-f(y)ə-ˌrīz\ *vt* **:** SULFUR
sul·fu·rous *or* **sul·phu·rous** \ˈsəl-f(y)ə-rəs, *also esp for 1* ˌsəl-ˈfyu̇r-əs\ *adj* **1 a :** resembling or emanating from sulfur and esp. burning sulfur **b :** of, relating to, or containing sulfur esp. in a lower valence ⟨~ esters⟩ **2 a :** of, relating to, or dealing with the fire of hell **:** INFERNAL **b :** SCATHING, VIRULENT **c :** PROFANE, BLASPHEMOUS — **sul·fu·rous·ly** *adv* — **sul·fu·rous·ness** *n*
sulfurous acid *n* **:** a weak unstable dibasic acid H_2SO_3 known in solution and through its salts and used as a reducing and bleaching agent
sul·fu·ryl \ˈsəl-f(y)ə-ˌril\ *n* [ISV] **:** SULFONYL — used esp. in names of inorganic compounds
1**sulk** \ˈsəlk\ *vi* [back-formation fr. *sulky*] **:** to be moodily silent
2**sulk** *n* **1 :** the state of one sulking — often used in pl. ⟨had a case of the ~*s*⟩ **2 :** a sulky mood or spell ⟨in a ~⟩
sulk·i·ly \ˈsəl-kə-lē\ *adv* **:** in a sulky manner
sulk·i·ness \-kē-nəs\ *n* **:** the state of being sulky
1**sulky** \ˈsəl-kē\ *adj* [prob. alter. of obs. *sulke* (sluggish)] **1 :** sulking or given to spells of sulking **2 :** having wheels and usu. a seat for the driver ⟨~ plow⟩ **syn** see SULLEN
2**sulky** *n* [prob. fr. 1*sulky*] **:** a light 2-wheeled vehicle having a seat for the driver only and usu. no body
sul·lage \ˈsəl-ij\ *n* [prob. fr. MF *soiller, souiller* to soil — more at SOIL] **1 :** REFUSE, SEWAGE **2 :** mud deposited by water **:** SILT **3 :** scoria on molten metal in the ladle
sul·len \ˈsəl-ən\ *adj* [ME *solain* sullen, solitary, prob. fr. (assumed) MF, fr. L *solus* alone] **1 a :** gloomily or resentfully silent or repressed **b :** suggesting a sullen state **:** LOWERING **2 :** dull or somber in sound or color **3 :** DISMAL, GLOOMY **4 :** moving sluggishly — **sul·len·ly** *adv* — **sul·len·ness** \ˈsəl-ən-nəs\ *n*
syn GLUM, MOROSE, SURLY, SULKY, CRABBED, SATURNINE, GLOOMY: SULLEN implies a silent ill humor and a refusal to be sociable; GLUM suggests a silent dispiritedness; MOROSE adds to GLUM an element of bitterness or misanthropy; SURLY implies gruffness and sullenness of speech or manner; SULKY suggests childish resentment expressed in peevish sullenness; CRABBED applies to a forbidding morose harshness of manner; SATURNINE describes a heavy forbidding aspect or suggests a bitter disposition; GLOOMY implies a depression in mood making for seeming sullenness or glumness
1**sul·ly** \ˈsəl-ē\ *vt* [prob. fr. MF *soiller* to soil] **:** to make soiled or tarnished **:** DEFILE
2**sully** *n, archaic* **:** SOIL, STAIN
sulph- *or* **sulpho-** — see SULF-
sulphur butterfly *n* **:** any of numerous butterflies (family Pieridae) having the wings usu. yellow or orange with a black border
sulphur yellow *n* **:** a variable color averaging a brilliant greenish yellow
sul·tan \ˈsəlt-ᵊn *also* su̇l-ˈtän, ˌsəl-ˈtan\ *n* [MF, fr. Ar *sulṭān*] **:** a king or sovereign esp. of a Muslim state
sul·ta·na \ˌsəl-ˈtan-ə, su̇l-ˈtän-\ *n* [It, fem. of *sultano* sultan, fr. Ar *sulṭān*] **1 :** a female member of a sultan's family; *esp* **:** a sultan's wife **2 a :** a pale yellow seedless grape grown for raisins and wine **b :** the raisin of this grape
sul·tan·ate \ˈsəlt-ᵊn-ˌāt; su̇l-ˈtän-ət, ˌsəl-ˈtan-\ *n* **1 :** the office, dignity, or power of a sultan **2 :** a state or country governed by a sultan
sul·tan·ess \ˈsəlt-ᵊn-əs\ *n, archaic* **:** SULTANA
sul·tri·ly \ˈsəl-trə-lē\ *adv* **:** in a sultry manner
sul·tri·ness \-trē-nəs\ *n* **:** the quality or state of being sultry
sul·try \ˈsəl-trē\ *adj* [obs. E *sulter* to swelter, alter. of E *swelter*] **1 a :** very hot and humid **:** SWELTERING **b :** burning hot **:** TORRID **2 a :** hot with passion or anger **b :** exciting or capable of exciting strong sexual desire **:** VOLUPTUOUS ⟨~ glances⟩
1**sum** \ˈsəm\ *n* [ME *summe*, fr. OF, fr. L *summa*, fr. fem. of *summus* highest; akin to L *super* over — more at OVER] **1 :** an indefinite or specified amount of money **2 :** the whole amount **:** AGGREGATE **3 :** the utmost degree **:** HEIGHT **4 a :** EPITOME, SUMMARY **b :** GIST **5 a** (1) **:** the result of adding numbers ⟨~ of 5 and 7 is 12⟩ (2) **:** the limit of the sum of the first *n* terms of an infinite series as *n* increases indefinitely **b :** numbers to be added; *broadly* **:** a problem in arithmetic **c** (1) **:** DISJUNCTION 2 (2) **:** the set of all elements belonging to one or both of two sets
syn AMOUNT, AGGREGATE, TOTAL, WHOLE, NUMBER, QUANTITY: SUM indicates the result of simple addition of numbers or of particulars; AMOUNT implies the result of cumulative or combinative processes; AGGREGATE stresses the notion of distinct individuals being grouped together; TOTAL and WHOLE stress the completeness or inclusiveness of a putting together; NUMBER applies to an aggregate of countable units; QUANTITY applies to things measurable in bulk
2**sum** *vt* **summed; sum·ming 1 :** to calculate the sum of **:** COUNT **2 :** SUMMARIZE — usu. used with *up* ~ *vi* **:** to reach a sum **:** AMOUNT
su·mac *or* **su·mach** \ˈs(h)ü-ˌmak\ *n* [ME *sumac*, fr. MF, fr. Ar *summāq*] **1 :** any of a genus (*Rhus* of the family Anacardiaceae, the sumac family) of trees, shrubs, and woody vines with dioecious flowers and drupaceous fruits and in some cases foliage poisonous to the touch — used esp. of innocuous members of the genus; compare POISON IVY, POISON OAK **2 :** a material used in tanning and dyeing that consists of dried powdered leaves and flowers of various sumacs
Su·me·ri·an \su̇-ˈmer-ē-ən, -ˈmir-\ *n* **1 :** a native of Sumer **2 :** the language of the Sumerians surviving as a literary language after the rise of Akkadian — **Sumerian** *adj*
sum·ma \ˈsu̇m-ə, ˈsüm-, ˈsəm-\ *n, pl* **sum·mae** \ˈsu̇m-ˌī, ˈsüm-, -ˌā; ˈsəm-ˌē, -ˌī\ [ML, fr. L, sum] **:** a comprehensive treatise; *esp* **:** one by a scholastic philosopher
sum·ma cum lau·de \ˌsu̇m-ə-(ˌ)ku̇m-ˈlau̇d-ə, ˌsüm-, -ˈlau̇d-ē; ˌsəm-ə-ˌkəm-ˈlȯd-ē\ *adv (or adj)* [L, with highest praise] **:** with highest academic distinction ⟨graduated *summa cum laude*⟩
sum·ma·ri·ly \(ˌ)sə-ˈmer-ə-lē, ˈsəm-(ə-)rə-lē\ *adv* **:** in a summary manner or form
sum·ma·ri·za·tion \ˌsəm-(ə-)rə-ˈzā-shən\ *n* **1 :** the act of summarizing **2 :** SUMMARY
sum·ma·rize \ˈsəm-ə-ˌrīz\ *vt* **:** to tell in or reduce to a summary ~ *vi* **:** to make a summary — **sum·ma·riz·er** *n*
1**sum·ma·ry** \ˈsəm-ə-rē *also* ˈsəm-rē\ *adj* [ME, fr. ML *summarius*, fr. L *summa* sum] **1 :** COMPREHENSIVE; *esp* **:** summarizing concisely **2 a :** done without delay or formality ⟨~ vengeance⟩ **b :** of or relating to a proceeding without usual legal formalities used for the speedy and peremptory disposition of minor matters **syn** see CONCISE
2**summary** *n* **:** an abstract, abridgment, or compendium esp. of a preceding discourse **:** RECAPITULATION
sum·ma·tion \(ˌ)sə-ˈmā-shən\ *n* **1 :** the act or process of forming a sum **:** ADDITION **2 :** SUM, TOTAL **3 :** cumulative action or effect esp. of individually subliminal stimuli **4 :** a final part of an argument reviewing points made and expressing conclusions — **sum·ma·tion·al** \-shnəl, -shən-ᵊl\ *adj*
1**sum·mer** \ˈsəm-ər\ *n* [ME *sumer*, fr. OE *sumor*; akin to OHG & ON *sumer* summer, Skt *samā* year, season] **1 :** the season between spring and autumn comprising in the northern hemisphere usu. the months of June, July, and August or as reckoned astronomically extending from the June solstice to the September equinox **2 :** the warmer half of the year **3 :** YEAR **4 :** a period of fulfillment
2**summer** *vb* **sum·mer·ing** \ˈsəm-(ə-)riŋ\ *vi* **:** to pass the summer ~ *vt* **:** to keep or carry through the summer; *esp* **:** to provide with pasture during the summer
3**summer** *n* [ME, packhorse, beam, fr. MF *somier*, fr. (assumed) VL *sagmarius*, fr. LL *sagma* packsaddle, fr. Gk] **:** a large horizontal beam or stone used esp. in building: as **a :** the lintel of a door or window **b :** a stone forming the cap of a pier (as to support a lintel or arch)
summer cypress *n* **:** a densely branched Eurasian herb (*Kochia scoparia*) of the goosefoot family grown for its foliage which turns red in autumn
sum·mer·house \ˈsəm-ər-ˌhau̇s\ *n* **:** a rustic covered structure in a garden or park to provide a cool shady retreat in summer
summer kitchen *n* **:** a small building or shed adjacent to a house and used as a kitchen in warm weather
sum·mer·sault *var of* SOMERSAULT
summer school *n* **:** a school or school session conducted in summer enabling students to accelerate progress toward a degree, to make up credits lost through absence or failure, or to round out professional education
summer squash *n* **:** any of various garden squashes derived from a variety (*Cucurbita pepo melopepo*) and used as a vegetable while immature and before hardening of the seeds and rind
sum·mer·time \ˈsəm-ər-ˌtīm\ *n* **:** the summer season or a period like summer
summer time *n, chiefly Brit* **:** DAYLIGHT SAVING TIME
sum·mer·wood \-ˌwu̇d\ *n* **:** the harder less porous portion of an annual ring of wood that develops late in the growing season — compare SPRINGWOOD
sum·mery \ˈsəm-(ə-)rē\ *adj* **:** of, resembling, or fit for summer
sum·mit \ˈsəm-ət\ *n* [ME *somete*, fr. MF, fr. OF, dim. of *sum* top, fr. L *summum*, neut. of *summus* highest — more at SUM] **1 :** TOP, APEX; *esp* **:** the highest point **:** PEAK **2 :** the highest degree **:** PINNACLE **3 :** the highest level of officials; *esp* **:** the level of heads of government
syn SUMMIT, PEAK, PINNACLE, CLIMAX, APEX, ACME, CULMINATION, MERIDIAN, ZENITH mean the highest point attained or attainable. SUMMIT implies the topmost level attainable; PEAK suggests the highest among other high points; PINNACLE suggests a dizzying and often insecure height; CLIMAX implies the highest point in an ascending series; APEX implies the point where all ascending lines converge; ACME implies a level of quality representing the perfection of a thing; CULMINATION suggests the outcome of a growth or development representing an attained objective; MERIDIAN implies the stage at which a living and growing thing reaches its fullest development and vigor; ZENITH adds to MERIDIAN implications of luster and distinction
sum·mon \ˈsəm-ən\ *vt* **sum·mon·ing** \-(ə-)niŋ\ [ME *somonen*, fr. OF *somondre*, fr. (assumed) VL *summonere*, alter. of L *summonēre* to remind secretly, fr. *sub-* secretly + *monēre* to warn — more at SUB-, MIND] **1 :** to issue a call to convene **:** CONVOKE **2 :** to command by service of a summons to appear in court **3 :** to call upon for specified action ⟨~ one to be in readiness⟩ **4 :** to bid to come **:** send for ⟨~ a physician⟩ **5 :** to call forth **:** EVOKE — **sum·mon·er** \-(ə-)nər\ *n*
syn SUMMON, CALL, CITE, CONVOKE, CONVENE, MUSTER mean to demand the presence of. SUMMON specif. implies the exercise of authority; CALL may be used less formally for SUMMON; CITE implies a summoning to court usu. to answer a charge; CONVOKE implies a summons to assemble for deliberative or legislative purposes; CONVENE is somewhat less formal than CONVOKE; MUSTER suggests a calling up or calling out of troops or a ship's company as for action, inspection, or parade and may connote a gathering of strength or courage
1**sum·mons** \ˈsəm-ənz\ *n, pl* **sum·mon·ses** [ME *somouns*, fr. OF *somonse*, fr. pp. of *somondre*] **1 :** the act of summoning; *esp* **:** a call by authority to appear at a place named or to attend to some duty **2 :** a warning or citation to appear in court: as **a :** a written

notification to be served on a person warning him to appear in court at a day specified to answer to the plaintiff **b :** a subpoena to appear as a witness **3 :** a call, signal, or knock that summons

2summons *vt* **:** SUMMON 2

sum·mum bo·num \,sùm-əm-'bō-nəm, ,sùm-,ùm-, -,süm-; ,səm-(,)əm-\ *n* [L] **:** the supreme good from which all others are derived

summum ge·nus \-'gen-əs, -'gā-nəs; -'jē-nəs\ *n, pl* **sum·ma ge·nera** \,sùm-ə-'gen-ə-rə, ,süm-, -'gān-; ,səm-ə-'jen-ə-rə\ [NL, lit., highest genus] **:** a logical genus that cannot be classed as a species of a higher genus

su·mo \'sü-(,)mō\ *n* [Jap *sumō*] **:** a Japanese form of wrestling in which a contestant loses the match if he is forced out of the ring or if any part of his body except his feet touches the ground

sump \'səmp\ *n* [ME *sompe* swamp — more at SWAMP] **1 :** a pit or reservoir serving as a drain or receptacle for liquids: as **a :** CESSPOOL **b :** a pit at the lowest point in a circulating or drainage system (as the oil-circulating system of an internal-combustion engine) **c** *chiefly Brit* **:** OIL PAN **2** *Brit* **:** CRANKCASE **3** [G *sumpf*, lit., marsh, fr. MHG — more at SWAMP] **a :** the lowest part of a mine shaft into which water drains **b :** an excavation ahead of regular work in driving a mine tunnel or sinking a mine shaft

sump pump *n* **:** a pump to remove accumulations of liquid from a sump pit

sump·ter \'səm(p)-tər\ *n* [short for *sumpter horse*, fr. ME *sumpter* driver of a packhorse, fr. MF *sometier*, fr. (assumed) VL *sagmatarius*, fr. LL *sagmat-*, *sagma* packsaddle, fr. Gk] **:** a pack animal

sump·tu·ary \'səm(p)-chə-,wer-ē\ *adj* [L *sumptuarius*, fr. *sumptus* expense, fr. *sumptus*, pp. of *sumere* to take, spend — more at CONSUME] **1 :** designed to regulate personal expenditures and esp. to prevent extravagance and luxury ⟨~ laws⟩ **2 :** designed to regulate habits on moral or religious grounds ⟨~ laws⟩ ⟨~ tax⟩

sump·tu·ous \'səm(p)-ch(ə-w)əs, 'səm(p)sh-wəs\ *adj* **:** involving large outlay or expense **:** LAVISH ⟨~ banquet⟩ **syn** see LUXURIOUS — **sump·tu·ous·ly** *adv* — **sump·tu·ous·ness** *n*

sum total *n* **1 :** a total arrived at through the counting of sums **2 :** TOTALITY

1sun \'sən\ *n* [ME *sunne*, fr. OE; akin to OHG *sunna* sun, L *sol* — more at SOLAR] **1 a :** the luminous celestial body around which the earth and other planets revolve, from which they receive heat and light, and which has a mean distance from earth of 93,000,000 miles, a linear diameter of 864,000 miles, a mass 332,000 times greater than earth, and a mean density about one fourth that of earth **b :** a celestial body like the sun **2 :** the heat or light radiated from the sun **3 :** one resembling the sun usu. in brilliance **4 :** the rising or setting of the sun ⟨from ~ to ~⟩ **5 :** GLORY, SPLENDOR — **in the sun :** in the public eye

2sun *vb* **sunned; sun·ning** *vt* **:** to expose to or as if to the rays of the sun ~ *vi* **:** to sun oneself

sun·baked \'sən-,bākt\ *adj* **1 :** baked by exposure to sunshine ⟨~ bricks⟩ **2 :** heated, parched, or compacted esp. by excessive sunlight

sun·bath \'sən-,bath, -,bàth\ *n* **:** exposure to sunlight or a sunlamp

sun·bathe \-,bāth\ *vi* [back-formation fr. *sunbather*] **:** to take a sunbath — **sun·bath·er** \-,bā-thər\ *n*

sun·beam \-,bēm\ *n* **:** a ray of sunlight

sun·bird \-,bərd\ *n* **1 :** any of numerous small brilliantly colored singing birds (family Nectariniidae) of the tropical Old World somewhat resembling hummingbirds **2 :** SUN-GREBE

sun·bon·net \-,bän-ət\ *n* **:** a woman's bonnet worn for protection from the sun usu. with a free extension at the back resembling a small cape

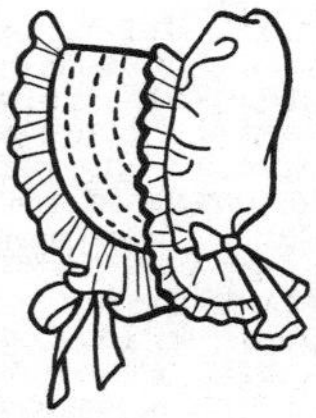

sunbonnet

sun·bow \-,bō\ *n* **:** an arch resembling a rainbow made by the sun shining through vapor or mist

1sun·burn \-,bərn\ *vb* [back-formation fr. *sunburned*, fr. *sun* + *burned*] *vt* **:** to burn or discolor by the sun ~ *vi* **:** to become sunburned

2sunburn *n* **:** inflammation of the skin caused by overexposure to sunlight

sun·burst \-,bərst\ *n* **1 :** a flash of sunlight esp. through a break in clouds **2 :** a jeweled brooch representing a sun surrounded by rays

sun·dae \'sən-dē\ *n* [prob. alter. of *Sunday*] **:** ice cream served with topping (as crushed fruit, syrups, nuts)

sun dance *n* **:** a solo or group solstice rite of American Indians

1Sun·day \'sən-dē\ *n* [ME, fr. OE *sunnandæg;* akin to OHG *sunnūntag* Sunday; both fr. a prehistoric WGmc-NGmc compound whose components are represented by OE *sunne* sun and by OE *dæg* day] **:** the first day of the week **:** the Christian analogue of the Jewish Sabbath — **Sun·days** \-dēz\ *adv*

2Sunday *adj* **1 :** of, relating to, or associated with Sunday **2 :** BEST ⟨*Sunday* suit⟩ **3 :** AMATEUR, DILETTANTE ⟨*Sunday* painters⟩

3Sunday *vi* **:** to spend Sunday ⟨was *Sundaying* in the country⟩

Sun·day–go–to–meet·ing \-,gōt-ə-'mēt-iŋ\ *adj* **:** appropriate for Sunday churchgoing

Sunday punch *n* **:** a blow in boxing intended to knock out an opponent

Sunday school *n* **:** a school held on Sunday for religious education; *also* **:** the teachers and pupils of such a school

sun deck *n* **1 :** the usu. upper deck of a ship exposed to the most sun **2 :** a roof or terrace used for sunning

sun·der \'sən-dər\ *vt* **sun·der·ing** \-d(ə-)riŋ\ [ME *sunderen*, fr. OE ge*sundrian, syndrian;* akin to OHG *suntarōn* to sunder, L *sine* without] **:** to break apart or in two **:** sever with violence **syn** see SEPARATE

sun·dew \'sən-(,)d(y)ü\ *n* **:** any of a genus (*Drosera* of the family Droseraceae, the sundew family) of bog-inhabiting insectivorous herbs having viscid glands on the leaves

sun·di·al \-,dī(-ə)l\ *n* **:** an instrument to show the time of day by the shadow of a gnomon on a usu. horizontal plate or on a cylindrical surface

sun disk *n* **:** an ancient Near Eastern symbol consisting of a disk with conventionalized wings emblematic of the sun-god (as Ra in Egypt)

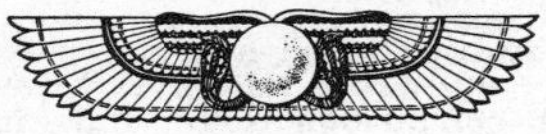

sun disk

sun dog *n* **1 :** PARHELION **2 :** a small nearly round halo on the parhelic circle most frequently just outside the halo of 22 degrees

sun·down \'sən-,daùn\ *n* **:** SUNSET 2

sun·down·er \-,daù-nər\ *n, Austral* **:** HOBO, TRAMP

sun·dries \'sən-drēz\ *n pl* [1*sundry*] **:** miscellaneous articles, details, or items of inconsiderable size or amount individually

sun·drops \'sən-,dräps\ *n pl but sing or pl in constr* **:** any of several day-flowering herbs (genus *Oenothera*) — compare EVENING PRIMROSE

1sun·dry \'sən-drē\ *adj* [ME, different for each, fr. OE *syndrig;* akin to OHG *suntarīg* sundry, L *sine* without — more at SUNDER] **:** MISCELLANEOUS, SEVERAL, VARIOUS

2sundry *pron, pl in constr* **:** an indeterminate number

sun·fast \'sən-,fast\ *adj* **:** resistant to fading by sunlight ⟨~ dyes⟩

sun·fish \-,fish\ *n* **1 :** a large marine plectognath fish (*Mola mola*) having high dorsal and anal fins and a body nearly oval in outline due to a sharply truncated posterior extremity and attaining a length of 10 feet and a weight in excess of 2 tons **2 :** any of numerous American percoid freshwater fishes (family Centrarchidae) usu. with a deep compressed body and metallic luster

sun·flow·er \-,flaù(-ə)r\ *n* **:** any of a genus (*Helianthus*) of composite plants with large yellow-rayed flower heads bearing seeds that serve as stock food and yield an edible oil

sung *past of* SING

Sung \'sùŋ\ *n* [Chin (Pek) *Sung*4] **:** a Chinese dynasty dated A.D. 960–1280 and marked by cultural refinement and achievements in philosophy, literature, and art

sun·glass·es \'sən-,glas-əz\ *n pl* **:** glasses to protect the eyes from the sun

sun·glow \-,glō\ *n* **:** a brownish yellow or rosy flush often seen in the sky before sunrise or after sunset due to solar rays scattered or diffracted from particles in the lower and upper air

sung mass *n* **:** a modification of high mass sung without a deacon or subdeacon by the celebrant and choir or congregation

sun–god \'sən-,gäd\ *n* **:** a god that represents or is the personification of the sun in various religions

sun–grebe \'sən-,grēb\ *n* **:** any of several tropical American and African birds (family Heliornithidae) related to the cranes and herons — called also *sun bittern*

sunk *past of* SINK

sunk·en \'səŋ-kən\ *adj* [fr. pp. of *sink*] **1 :** SUBMERGED; *esp* **:** at the bottom of a body of water **2 a :** HOLLOW, RECESSED **b :** lying in a depression ⟨~ garden⟩ **c :** settled below the normal level **d :** constructed below the normal floor level ⟨~ living room⟩

sunk fence *n* **:** a ditch with a retaining wall used to divide lands without defacing a landscape — called also *ha-ha*

sun·lamp \'sən-,lamp\ *n* **:** an electric lamp designed to emit radiation of wavelengths from ultraviolet to infrared and used esp. for therapeutic purposes

sun·less \'sən-ləs\ *adj* **:** lacking sunshine **:** CHEERLESS, DARK

sun·light \-,līt\ *n* **:** the light of the sun **:** SUNSHINE

sun·lit \-,lit\ *adj* **:** lighted by or as if by the sun

sunn \'sən\ *n* [Hindi *san*, fr. Skt *śaṇa*] **:** an East Indian leguminous plant (*Crotalaria juncea*) with slender branches, simple leaves, and yellow flowers; *also* **:** its valuable fiber resembling hemp and lighter and stronger than jute

sun·na \'sùn-ə, 'sən-\ *n, often cap* [Ar *sunnah*] **:** the body of Islamic custom and practice based on Muhammad's words and deeds

Sun·ni \-ē\ *n* [Ar *sunnīy*] **1 :** the Muslims of the branch of Islam that adheres to the orthodox tradition and acknowledges the first four caliphs as rightful successors of Muhammad — compare SHIA **2 :** SUNNITE — **Sunni** *adj*

sun·ni·ly \'sən-ᵊl-ē\ *adv* **:** in a sunny manner

sun·ni·ness \'sən-ē-nəs\ *n* **:** the quality or state of being sunny

Sun·nism \'sùn-,iz-əm, 'sən-\ *n* **:** the religious system or distinctive tenets of the Sunni

Sun·nite \-,īt\ *n* **:** a Sunni Muslim

sun·ny \'sən-ē\ *adj* **1 :** marked by brilliant sunlight **2 :** MERRY, OPTIMISTIC **3 :** exposed to, brightened, or warmed by the sun

sun·ny–side up \,sən-ē-,sīd-'əp\ *adj, of an egg* **:** fried on one side only

sun parlor *n* **:** a glass enclosed porch or living room with a sunny exposure — called also *sun porch, sun-room*

sun·rise \'sən-,rīz\ *n* **1 :** the apparent rising of the sun above the horizon; *also* **:** the accompanying atmospheric effects **2 :** the time when the upper limb of the sun appears above the sensible horizon as a result of the diurnal rotation of the earth

sun·set \-,set\ *n* **1 :** the apparent descent of the sun below the horizon; *also* **:** the accompanying atmospheric effects **2 :** the time when the upper limb of the sun disappears below the sensible horizon as a result of the diurnal rotation of the earth **3 :** a period of decline; *esp* **:** old age

sun·shade \-,shād\ *n* **:** something used as a protection from the sun's rays: as **a :** PARASOL **b :** AWNING

sun·shine \-,shīn\ *n* **1 a :** the sun's light or direct rays **b :** the warmth and light given by the sun's rays **c :** a spot or surface on which the sun's light shines **2 :** something that radiates warmth, cheer, or happiness — **sun·shiny** \-,shī-nē\ *adj*

sun·spot \-,spät\ *n* **:** one of the dark spots that appear from time to time on the sun's surface consisting commonly of a blue-black umbra with a surrounding penumbra of lighter shade and usu. visible only with the telescope

sun·stroke \-,strōk\ *n* **:** heatstroke caused by direct exposure to the sun

sun·struck \-,strək\ *adj* **:** affected or touched by the sun

sun·suit \-,süt\ *n* **:** an abbreviated playsuit worn usu. for sunbathing and play

sun·tan \-,tan\ *n, often attrib* **:** a browning of the skin from exposure to the rays of the sun

sun·up \-,əp\ *n* **:** SUNRISE

1sun·ward \-wərd\ *or* **sun·wards** \-wərdz\ *adv* **:** toward the sun

2sunward *adj* **:** facing the sun

sun·wise \-,wīz\ *adv* **:** CLOCKWISE

1sup \'səp\ *vb* **supped; sup·ping** [ME *suppen*, fr. OE *sūpan, suppan;* akin to OHG *sūfan* to drink, sip, OE *sūcan* to suck — more at SUCK] *vt* **:** to take or drink in swallows or gulps ~ *vi, chiefly dial* **:** to take

food and esp. liquid food into the mouth a little at a time either by drinking or with a spoon
²**sup** *n* **:** a mouthful esp. of liquor or broth **:** SIP; *also* **:** a small quantity of liquid ⟨a ~ of tea⟩
³**sup** *vi* **supped; sup·ping** [ME *soupen, suppen*, fr. OF *souper*, fr. *soupe* sop, soup — more at SOUP] **1 :** to eat the evening meal **2 :** to make one's supper — used with *on* or *off* ⟨~ on roast beef⟩
¹**su·per** \'sü-pər\ *n* **1** [by shortening] **a :** SUPERNUMERARY; *esp* **:** a supernumerary actor **b :** SUPERINTENDENT, SUPERVISOR **2** [short for obs. *superhive*] **:** a removable upper story of a beehive **3** [³*super*] **:** a superfine grade or extra large size **4** [origin unknown] **:** a thin loosely woven open-meshed starched cotton fabric used esp. for reinforcing books
²**super** *vt* **su·per·ing** \-p(ə-)riŋ\ **:** to reinforce (as a book backbone) with super
³**super** *adj* [short for *superfine*] **1 :** SUPERFINE **2 :** very large or powerful **:** GREAT **3 :** EXCESSIVE, EXTREME **4 :** INCLUSIVE, COMPREHENSIVE — **super** *adv*
super- *prefix* [L, over, above, in addition, fr. *super* over, above, on top of — more at OVER] **1 a** (1) **:** over and above **:** higher in quantity, quality, or degree than **:** more than ⟨*super*human⟩ (2) **:** in addition **:** extra ⟨*super*tax⟩ **b** (1) **:** exceeding or so as to exceed a norm ⟨*super*heat⟩ (2) **:** in excessive degree or intensity ⟨*super*subtle⟩ **c :** surpassing all or most others of its kind ⟨*super*highway⟩ **2 a :** situated or placed above, on, or at the top of ⟨*super*lunary⟩; *specif* **:** situated on the dorsal side of **b :** next above or higher ⟨*super*tonic⟩ **3 :** having the (specified) ingredient present in a large or unusually large proportion ⟨*super*phosphate⟩ **4 :** constituting a more inclusive category than that specified ⟨*super*family⟩ **5 :** superior in status, title, or position ⟨*super*state⟩
su·per·a·ble \'sü-p(ə-)rə-bəl\ *adj* [L *superabilis*, fr. *superare* to surmount — more at INSUPERABLE] **:** capable of being overcome or conquered **:** SURMOUNTABLE — **su·per·a·ble·ness** *n* — **su·per·a·bly** \-blē\ *adv*
su·per·abound \,sü-pə-rə-'baund\ *vi* [ME *superabounden*, fr. LL *superabundare*, fr. L *super-* + *abundare* to abound] **:** to abound or prevail in greater measure or to excess
su·per·abun·dance \-'bən-dən(t)s\ *n* **:** the quality or state of being superabundant
su·per·abun·dant \-dənt\ *adj* [ME, fr. LL *superabundant-, superabundans*, fr. prp. of *superabundare*] **:** more than ample **:** EXCESSIVE — **su·per·abun·dant·ly** *adv*
su·per·add \,sü-pə-'rad\ *vt* [ME *superadden*, fr. L *superaddere*, fr. *super-* + *addere* to add] **:** to add over and above something or in extra or superfluous amount — **su·per·ad·di·tion** \-pə-rə-'dish-ən\ *n*
su·per·al·tern \,sü-pə-'ròl-tərn\ *n* [*super-* + *-altern* (as in *subaltern*)] **:** a universal proposition in traditional logic that is a ground for the immediate inference of a corresponding subaltern nate
su·per·an·nu·ate \,sü-pə-'ran-yə-,wāt\ *vb* [back-formation fr. *superannuated*] *vt* **1 :** to make, declare, or prove obsolete or out-of-date **2 :** to retire and pension because of age or infirmity ~ *vi* **:** to become retired or antiquated — **su·per·an·nu·a·tion** \-,ran-yə-'wā-shən\ *n*
su·per·an·nu·at·ed *adj* [ML *superannuatus*, pp. of *superannuari* to be too old, fr. L *super-* + *annus* year — more at ANNUAL] **:** rated no longer fully or passably efficient in one's job because of age **:** incapacitated or disqualified for active duty by advanced age
su·perb \sù-'pərb\ *adj* [L *superbus* excellent, proud, fr. *super* above + *-bus* (akin to OE *bēon* to be) — more at OVER, BE] **1 :** MAJESTIC, NOBLE **2 :** RICH, SUMPTUOUS **3 :** of supreme excellence or beauty **syn** see SPLENDID — **su·perb·ly** *adv* — **su·perb·ness** *n*
¹**su·per·cal·en·der** \'sü-pər-,kal-ən-dər\ *n* **:** a calender stack of highly polished rolls used to give an extra finish to paper
²**supercalender** *vt* **:** to process (paper) in a supercalender
su·per·car·go \,sü-pər-'kär-(,)gō, 'sü-pər-,\ *n* [Sp *sobrecargo*, fr. *sobre-* over (fr. L *super-*) + *cargo*] **:** an officer in a merchant ship in charge of the commercial concerns of the voyage
su·per·charge \'sü-pər-,chärj\ *vt* **1 :** to supply a charge to the intake of (as an engine) at a pressure higher than that of the surrounding atmosphere **2 :** PRESSURIZE 1
su·per·charg·er \-,chär-jər\ *n* **:** a device (as a blower or compressor) for pressurizing the cabin of an airplane or for increasing the volume air charge of an internal-combustion engine over that which would normally be drawn in through the pumping action of the pistons

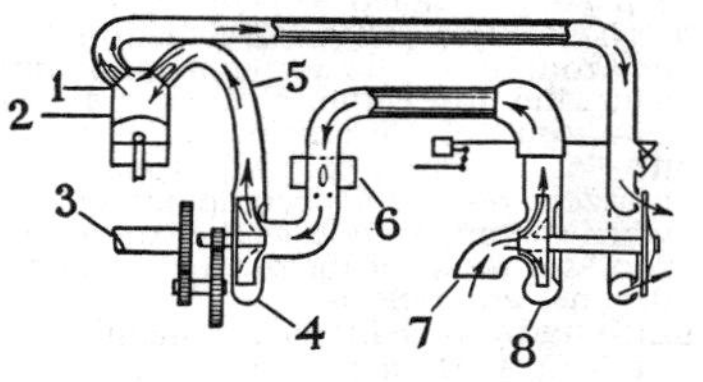

supercharger (simplified combination of internal centrifugal and external exhaust-driven types): *1* exhaust valve, *2* cylinder, *3* crankshaft, *4* internal supercharger, *5* intake pipe, *6* carburetor, *7* air intake, *8* turbosupercharger

su·per·cil·i·ary \,sü-pər-'sil-ē-,er-ē\ *adj* [NL *superciliaris*, fr. L *supercilium*] **:** of, relating to, or adjoining the eyebrow **:** SUPRAORBITAL — **superciliary** *n*
su·per·cil·ious \-'sil-ē-əs, -'sil-yəs\ *adj* [L *superciliosus*, fr. *supercilium* eyebrow, haughtiness, fr. *super-* + *-cilium* (akin to *celare* to hide) — more at HELL] **:** haughtily contemptuous **syn** see PROUD — **su·per·cil·ious·ly** *adv* — **su·per·cil·ious·ness** *n*
su·per·class \'sü-pər-,klas\ *n* **:** a category in taxonomy ranking between a phylum or division and a class
su·per·con·duc·tive \,sü-pər-kən-'dək-tiv\ *adj* **:** exhibiting superconductivity
su·per·con·duc·tiv·i·ty \-,kän-,dək-'tiv-ət-ē, -kən-\ *n* **:** an almost complete disappearance of electrical resistance in various metals at temperatures near absolute zero — **su·per·con·duc·tor** \-kən-'dək-tər\ *n*
su·per·cool \,sü-pər-'kül\ *vt* **:** to cool below the freezing point without solidification or crystallization
su·per·dom·i·nant \-'däm-(ə-)nənt\ *n* **:** SUBMEDIANT
su·per·ego \,sü-pə-'rē-(,)gō *also* -'reg-(,)ō\ *n* **:** a major sector of the psyche that is only partly conscious and that aids in character formation by reflecting parental conscience and the rules of society
su·per·el·e·vate \,sü-pə-'rel-ə-,vāt\ *vt* **:** BANK 1c
su·per·el·e·va·tion \-,rel-ə-'vā-shən\ *n* **:** the vertical distance between the heights of inner and outer edges of highway pavement or railroad rails
su·per·em·i·nence \-'rem-ə-nən(t)s\ *n* **:** the quality or state of being supereminent
su·per·em·i·nent \-nənt\ *adj* [LL *supereminent-, supereminens*, fr. L, prp. of *supereminēre* to stand out above, fr. *super-* + *eminēre* to stand out — more at EMINENT] **:** extremely high, distinguished, or conspicuous — **su·per·em·i·nent·ly** *adv*
su·per·em·pir·i·cal \,sü-pə-rim-'pir-i-kəl, -(,)rem-\ *adj* **:** experienced or experiencing by more than empirical means **:** TRANSCENDENT, TRANSCENDENTAL
su·per·er·o·ga·tion \,sü-pə-,rer-ə-'gā-shən\ *n* [ML *supererogation-, supererogatio*, fr. *supererogatus*, pp. of *supererogare* to perform beyond the call of duty, fr. LL, to expend in addition, fr. L *super-* + *erogare* to expend public funds after asking the consent of the people, fr. *e-* + *rogare* to ask — more at RIGHT] **:** the act of performing more than is required by duty, obligation, or need
su·per·erog·a·to·ry \,sü-pə-ri-'räg-ə-,tōr-ē, -,tòr-\ *adj* **1 :** observed or performed to an extent not enjoined or required **2 :** SUPERFLUOUS, NONESSENTIAL
syn SUPEREROGATORY, GRATUITOUS, UNCALLED-FOR, WANTON mean done without need or compulsion or warrant. SUPEREROGATORY implies a giving above what is required by rule and may suggest adding something not needed or not wanted; GRATUITOUS usu. applies to something offensive or unpleasant given or done without provocation; UNCALLED-FOR adds to GRATUITOUS implication of impertinence or logical absurdity; WANTON implies not only a lack of provocation but a malicious or sportive motive
su·per·fam·i·ly \'sü-pər-,fam-(ə-)lē\ *n* **:** a category of taxonomic classification ranking next above a family
su·per·fe·cun·da·tion \,sü-pər-,fek-ən-'dā-shən, -,fē-kən-\ *n* **1 :** successive fertilization of two or more ova from the same ovulation esp. by different sires **2 :** fertilization at one time of a number of ova excessive for the species
su·per·fe·ta·tion \-fē-'tā-shən\ *n* [ML *superfetation-, superfetatio*, fr. L *superfetatus*, pp. of *superfetare* to conceive while already pregnant, fr. *super-* + *fetus* act of bearing young, offspring — more at FETUS] **1 :** successive fertilization of two or more ova of different ovulations resulting in the presence of embryos of unlike ages in the same uterus **2 :** fertilization of an ovule by two or more kinds of pollen **3 :** a progressive accumulation or accretion reaching an extreme or excessive degree
su·per·fi·cial \,sü-pər-'fish-əl\ *adj* [ME, fr. LL *superficialis*, fr. L *superficies*] **1 a** (1) **:** of or relating to a surface (2) **:** lying on, not penetrating below, or affecting only the surface **b** *of a unit of measure* **:** SQUARE ⟨~ foot⟩ **2 a :** concerned only with the obvious or apparent **:** SHALLOW **b :** lying on the surface **:** EXTERNAL **c :** presenting only an appearance without substance or significance — **su·per·fi·cial·ly** \-'fish-(ə-)lē\ *adv* — **su·per·fi·cial·ness** \-'fish-əl-nəs\ *n*
syn SUPERFICIAL, SHALLOW, CURSORY mean lacking in depth or solidity. SUPERFICIAL implies a concern only with surface aspects; SHALLOW is more generally derogatory in implying lack of depth in knowledge, reasoning, emotions, or character; CURSORY suggests a lack of thoroughness or a neglect of details
su·per·fi·ci·al·i·ty \-,fish-ē-'al-ət-ē\ *n* **:** the quality or state of being superficial; *also* **:** something superficial
su·per·fi·cies \-'fish-(,)ēz, -ē-,ēz\ *n, pl* **superficies** [L, surface, fr. *super-* + *facies* face, aspect — more at FACE] **1 :** a surface of a body or a region of space **2 :** the external aspects or appearance of a thing
su·per·fine \,sü-pər-'fīn\ *adj* **1 :** overly refined or nice **2 :** extremely fine **3 :** of high quality or grade
su·per·fix \'sü-pər-,fiks\ *n* [*super-* + *-fix* (as in *prefix*)] **:** a recurrent predictable pattern of stress that characterizes small stretches of speech whose constituents are parallel in relationship
su·per·flu·id \,sü-pər-'flü-əd\ *n* **:** matter in a unique state characterized by extraordinarily large thermal conductivity and capillarity — **su·per·flu·id·i·ty** \-(,)flü-'id-ət-ē\ *n*
su·per·flu·ity \,sü-pər-'flü-ət-ē\ *n* [ME *superfluitee*, fr. MF *superfluité*, fr. LL *superfluitat-, superfluitas*, fr. L *superfluus*] **1 a :** EXCESS, OVERSUPPLY **b :** something unnecessary or more than enough **2 :** immoderate or luxurious living, habits, or desires **:** EXTRAVAGANCE **syn** see EXCESS
su·per·flu·ous \sù-'pər-flə-wəs\ *adj* [ME, fr. L *superfluus*, lit., running over, fr. *superfluere* to overflow, fr. *super-* + *fluere* to flow — more at FLUID] **1 :** exceeding what is sufficient or necessary **:** EXTRA **2** *obs* **:** WASTEFUL, EXTRAVAGANT — **su·per·flu·ous·ly** *adv* — **su·per·flu·ous·ness** *n*
su·per·gal·axy \'sü-pər-,gal-ək-sē\ *n* **:** a large cluster of galaxies
¹**su·per·heat** \,sü-pər-'hēt\ *vt* **1 a :** to heat (a liquid) above the boiling point without converting into vapor **b :** to heat (a vapor not in contact with its own liquid) so as to cause to remain free from suspended liquid droplets ⟨~*ed* steam⟩ **2 :** OVERHEAT — **su·per·heat·er** *n*
²**su·per·heat** \'sü-pər-,hēt, ,sü-pər-'\ *n* **:** the extra heat imparted to a vapor in superheating it from a dry and saturated condition; *also* **:** the corresponding rise of temperature
¹**su·per·het·ero·dyne** \,sü-pər-'het-ə-rə-,dīn, -'he-trə-\ *adj* [*supersonic* + *heterodyne*] **:** of or relating to a form of beat reception in which beats are produced of a frequency above audibility but below that of the received signals and the current of the beat frequency is then rectified, amplified, and finally rectified again so as to reproduce the sound
²**superheterodyne** *n* **:** a radio set for superheterodyne reception
su·per·high frequency \,sü-pər-,hī-\ *n* **:** a radio frequency in the next to the highest range of the radio spectrum — see RADIO FREQUENCY table
su·per·high·way \,sü-pər-'hī-,wā\ *n* **:** a broad arterial highway (as an expressway or turnpike) designed for high-speed traffic
su·per·hu·man \,sü-pər-'hyü-mən, -'yü-\ *adj* **1 :** being above the human **:** DIVINE ⟨~ beings⟩ ⟨~ agency⟩ **2 :** exceeding normal human power, size, or capability **:** HERCULEAN ⟨~ effort⟩ — **su·per·hu·man·i·ty** \-hyü-'man-ət-ē, -yü-\ *n* — **su·per·hu·man·ly** *adv* — **su·per·hu·man·ness** \-mən-nəs\ *n*
su·per·im·pos·able \,sü-pə-rim-'pō-zə-bəl\ *adj* **:** capable of being superimposed
su·per·im·pose \,sü-pə-rim-'pōz\ *vt* **:** to place or lay over or above something — **su·per·im·po·si·tion** \-,rim-pə-'zish-ən\ *n*
su·per·in·cum·bent \-rin-'kəm-bənt\ *adj* [L *superincumbent-*,

superincumbens, *prp.* of *superincumbere* to lie on top of, fr. *super-* + *incumbere* to lie down on — more at INCUMBENT] : lying or resting on something else — **su·per·in·cum·bent·ly** *adv*

su·per·in·di·vid·u·al \ˌsü-pə-ˌrin-də-'vij-(ə-)wəl, -'vij-əl\ *adj* : of, relating to, or being an organism, entity, or complex of more than individual complexity or nature

su·per·in·duce \ˌsü-pə-rin-'d(y)üs\ *vt* [L *superinducere*, fr. *super-* + *inducere* to lead in — more at INDUCE] **1** : to introduce as an addition over or above something already existing **2** : to bring on : INDUCE — **su·per·in·duc·tion** \-'dək-shən\ *n*

su·per·in·tend \ˌsü-p(ə-)rin-'tend, ˌsü-pərin-\ *vt* [LL *superintendere*, fr. L *super-* + *intendere* to attend, direct attention to — more at INTEND] : to have or exercise the charge and oversight of : DIRECT

su·per·in·ten·dence \-'ten-dən(t)s\ *n* : the act or function of superintending or directing : SUPERVISION

su·per·in·ten·den·cy \-dən-sē\ *n* : the office, post, or jurisdiction of a superintendent; *also* : SUPERINTENDENCE

su·per·in·ten·dent \-dənt\ *n* [ML *superintendent-, superintendens*, fr. LL, prp. of *superintendere*] : one who has executive oversight and charge — **superintendent** *adj*

¹**su·pe·ri·or** \sù-'pir-ē-ər\ *adj* [ME, fr. MF *superieur*, fr. L *superior*, compar. of *superus* upper, fr. *super* over, above — more at OVER] **1** : situated higher up : UPPER **2** : of higher rank, quality, or importance **3** : courageously or serenely indifferent (as to something painful, disheartening, or demoralizing) **4 a** : greater in quantity or numbers **b** : excellent of its kind : BETTER **5** : SUPERSCRIPT **6 a** *of an animal structure* : situated above or anterior or dorsal to another and esp. a corresponding part (a ~ artery) **b** *of a plant structure* : situated above or near the top of another part: as (1) *of a calyx* : attached to and apparently arising from the ovary (2) *of an ovary* : free from the calyx or other floral envelope **7** : more comprehensive (a genus is ~ to a species) **8** : affecting or assuming an air of superiority : SUPERCILIOUS

²**superior** *n* **1** : one who is above another in rank, station, or office; *esp* : the head of a religious house or order **2** : one that surpasses another in quality or merit

superior conjunction *n* : a conjunction in which a lesser or secondary celestial body passes farther from the observer than the primary body around which it revolves (*superior conjunction* of Venus to the sun)

superior court *n* **1** : a court of general jurisdiction intermediate between the inferior courts (as a justice of the peace court) and the higher appellate courts **2** : a court with juries having original jurisdiction

superior general *n*, *pl* **superiors general** : the superior of a religious order or congregation

su·pe·ri·or·i·ty \sù-ˌpir-ē-'ȯr-ət-ē, -ˌsü-, -'är-\ *n* : the quality or state of being superior; *also* : a superior characteristic

superiority complex *n* **1** : an exaggerated opinion of oneself **2** : an excessive striving for or pretense of superiority to compensate for supposed inferiority

su·pe·ri·or·ly \sù-'pir-ē-ər-lē\ *adv* : in a higher or better manner or degree; *also* : SUPERCILIOUSLY

superior planet *n* : a planet whose orbit lies outside that of the earth

su·per·ja·cent \ˌsü-pər-'jās-ᵊnt\ *adj* [L *superjacent-, superjacens*, prp. of *superjacēre* to lie over or upon, fr. *super-* + *jacēre* to lie; akin to L *jacere* to throw — more at JET] : lying above or upon : OVERLYING (~ rocks)

¹**su·per·la·tive** \sù-'pər-lət-iv\ *adj* [ME *superlatif*, fr. MF, fr. LL *superlativus*, fr. L *superlatus* (pp. of *superferre* to carry over, raise high), fr. *super-* + *latus*, pp. of *ferre* to carry — more at TOLERATE, BEAR] **1** : of, relating to, or constituting the degree of grammatical comparison that denotes an extreme or unsurpassed level or extent **2** : surpassing all others : SUPREME **3** : EXAGGERATED, EXCESSIVE — **su·per·la·tive·ly** *adv* — **su·per·la·tive·ness** *n*

²**superlative** *n* **1 a** : the superlative degree of comparison in a language **b** : a superlative form of an adjective or adverb **2** : the superlative or utmost degree of something : ACME **3** : a superlative person or thing

su·per·lin·er \'sü-pər-ˌlī-nər\ *n* : a fast luxurious passenger liner of great size

su·per·lu·na·ry \ˌsü-pər-'lü-nə-rē\ *also* **su·per·lu·nar** \-nər\ *adj* [L *super-* + *luna* moon — more at LUNAR] : being above the moon : CELESTIAL

su·per·man \'sü-pər-ˌman\ *n* **1** : a superior man that according to Nietzsche has learned to forgo fleeting pleasures and attain happiness and dominance through the exercise of creative power **2** : a person of extraordinary or superhuman power or achievements

su·per·mar·ket \-ˌmär-kət\ *n* : a self-service retail market selling foods and household merchandise

su·per·nal \sù-'pərn-ᵊl\ *adj* [ME, fr. MF, fr. L *supernus*, fr. *super* over, above — more at OVER] **1** : being or coming from on high : HEAVENLY **2** : located in or belonging to the sky — **su·per·nal·ly** \-ᵊl-ē\ *adv*

su·per·na·tant \ˌsü-pər-'nāt-ᵊnt\ *adj* [L *supernatant-, supernatans*, prp. of *supernatare* to float, fr. *super-* + *natare* to swim — more at NATANT] : floating on the surface — **supernatant** *n*

su·per·nat·u·ral \ˌsü-pər-'nach-(ə-)rəl\ *adj* [ML *supernaturalis*, fr. L *super-* + *natura* nature] **1** : of or relating to an order of existence beyond the visible observable universe; *esp* : of or relating to God or a god, demigod, spirit, or infernal being **2** : attributed to a ghost or spirit : EERIE — **supernatural** *n* — **su·per·nat·u·ral·ly** \-'nach-(ə-)rə-lē, -'nach-ər-lē\ *adv* — **su·per·nat·u·ral·ness** \-'nach-(ə-)rəl-nəs\ *n*

su·per·nat·u·ral·ism \-'nach-(ə-)rə-ˌliz-əm\ *n* **1** : the quality or state of being supernatural **2** : belief in a supernatural power and order of existence — **su·per·nat·u·ral·ist** \-ləst\ *n or adj* — **su·per·nat·u·ral·is·tic** \-ˌnach-(ə-)rə-'lis-tik\ *adj*

su·per·nor·mal \ˌsü-pər-'nȯr-məl\ *adj* **1** : exceeding the normal or average **2** : being beyond natural human powers : PARANORMAL — **su·per·nor·mal·i·ty** \-(ˌ)nȯr-'mal-ət-ē\ *n* — **su·per·nor·mal·ly** \-'nȯr-mə-lē\ *adv*

su·per·no·va \ˌsü-pər-'nō-və\ *n* [NL] : one of the rarely observed nova outbursts in which the maximum intrinsic luminosity may reach 100 million times that of the sun

¹**su·per·nu·mer·ary** \ˌsü-pər-'n(y)ü-mə-ˌrer-ē, -'n(y)üm-(ə-)rē\ *adj* [LL *supernumerarius*, fr. L *super-* + *numerus* number — more at NIMBLE] **1** : exceeding the stated or prescribed number **2** : exceeding what is necessary, required, or desired : SUPERFLUOUS **3** : more numerous

²**supernumerary** *n* **1** : a supernumerary person or thing **2** : an actor employed to play a walk-on (as in a mob scene or spectacle)

su·per·or·der \'sü-pər-ˌȯrd-ər\ *n* : a taxonomic category between an order and a class or a subclass

su·per·or·di·nate \ˌsü-pə-'rȯrd-nət, -ᵊn-ət, -ᵊn-ˌāt\ *adj* [*super-* + *-ordinate* (as in *subordinate*)] : superior in rank, class, or status

su·per·phos·phate \ˌsü-pər-'fäs-ˌfāt\ *n* **1** : an acid phosphate **2** : a soluble mixture of phosphates used as fertilizer and made from insoluble mineral phosphates by treatment with sulfuric acid

su·per·phys·i·cal \-'fiz-i-kəl\ *adj* : being above or beyond the physical world or explanation on physical principles

su·per·pos·able \ˌsü-pər-'pō-zə-bəl\ *adj* : capable of being completely superposed

su·per·pose \-'pōz\ *vt* [prob. fr. F *superposer*, back-formation fr. *superposition*, fr. LL *superposition-, superpositio*, fr. L *superpositus*, pp. of *superponere* to superpose, fr. *super-* + *ponere* to place — more at POSITION] **1** : to place or lay over or above whether in or not in contact : SUPERIMPOSE **2** : to lay (a geometric figure) upon another so as to make all like parts coincide — **su·per·po·si·tion** \-pə-'zish-ən\ *n*

su·per·posed \-'pōzd\ *adj* : growing or situated vertically over another part or organ

su·per·pow·er \'sü-pər-ˌpau̇(-ə)r\ *n* **1** : excessive or superior power **2 a** : an extremely powerful nation; *specif* : one of a very few dominant states in an era when the world is divided politically into these states and their satellites **b** : an international governing body able to enforce its will upon the most powerful states — **su·per·pow·ered** \-ˌpau̇(-ə)rd\ *adj*

su·per·sat·u·rate \ˌsü-pər-'sach-ə-ˌrāt\ *vt* : to add to beyond saturation — **su·per·sat·u·ra·tion** \-ˌsach-ə-'rā-shən\ *n*

su·per·scribe \'sü-pər-ˌskrīb, ˌsü-pər-'\ *vt* [L *superscribere*, fr. *super-* + *scribere* to write — more at SCRIBE] **1** : to write or engrave on the top or outside **2** : to write (as a name or address) on the outside or cover of : ADDRESS

su·per·script \'sü-pər-ˌskript\ *n* [L *superscriptus*, pp. of *superscribere*] : a distinguishing symbol or letter written immediately above or above and to the right or left of another character — **superscript** *adj*

su·per·scrip·tion \ˌsü-pər-'skrip-shən\ *n* [ME, fr. MF, fr. LL *superscription-, superscriptio*, fr. L *superscriptus*] **1** : the act of superscribing **2** : something written or engraved on the surface of, outside, or above something else : INSCRIPTION; *also* : ADDRESS

su·per·sede \ˌsü-pər-'sēd\ *vt* [MF *superseder* to refrain from, fr. L *supersedēre* to be superior to, refrain from, fr. *super-* + *sedēre* to sit — more at SIT] **1 a** : to cause to be set aside **b** : to force out of use as inferior **2** : to take the place, room, or position of : REPLACE **3** : to displace in favor of another : SUPPLANT **syn** see REPLACE — **su·per·sed·er** *n*

su·per·se·de·as \-'sēd-ē-əs\ *n*, *pl* **supersedeas** [ME, fr. L, you shall refrain, fr. *supersedēre*] **1** : a common-law writ commanding a stay of legal proceedings issued under various conditions and esp. to stay an officer from proceeding under another writ **2** : an order staying proceedings of an inferior court

su·per·se·dure \-'sē-jər\ *n* : the act or process of superseding; *specif* : the replacement of an old or inferior queen bee by a young or superior queen

su·per·sen·si·ble \ˌsü-pər-'sen(t)-sə-bəl\ *adj* : being above or beyond that which is apparent to the senses : SPIRITUAL

su·per·sen·si·tive \-'sen(t)-sət-iv, -'sen(t)-stiv\ *adj* **1** : HYPERSENSITIVE **2** : specially treated to increase sensitivity (a ~ photographic emulsion) — **su·per·sen·si·tive·ness** *n*

su·per·sen·so·ry \-'sen(t)s-(ə-)rē\ *adj* : SUPERSENSIBLE

su·per·ser·vice·able \-'sər-və-sə-bəl\ *adj* : offering unwanted services : OFFICIOUS

su·per·ses·sion \ˌsü-pər-'sesh-ən\ *n* [ML *supersession-, supersessio*, fr. L *supersessus*, pp. of *supersedēre*] : the act of superseding : the state of being superseded : SUPERSEDURE — **su·per·ses·sive** \-'ses-iv\ *adj*

¹**su·per·son·ic** \-'sän-ik\ *adj* [L *super-* + *sonus* sound — more at SOUND] **1** : having a frequency above the human ear's audibility limit of about 20,000 cycles per second — used of waves and vibrations; compare SONIC **2** : utilizing, produced by, or relating to supersonic waves or vibrations **3** : of, being, or relating to speeds from one to five times the speed of sound in air — compare SONIC **4** : moving, capable of moving, or utilizing air currents moving at supersonic speed — **su·per·son·i·cal·ly** \-i-k(ə-)lē\ *adv*

²**supersonic** *n* : a supersonic wave or frequency

su·per·son·ics \-'sän-iks\ *n pl but sing in constr* : the science of supersonic phenomena

su·per·sti·tion \ˌsü-pər-'stish-ən\ *n* [ME *supersticion*, fr. MF, fr. L *superstition-, superstitio*, fr. *superstit-, superstes* standing over (as witness or survivor), fr. *super-* + *stare* to stand — more at STAND] **1** : a belief or practice resulting from ignorance, fear of the unknown, or trust in magic or chance **2** : an irrational abject attitude of mind toward the supernatural, nature, or God resulting from superstitious beliefs or fears

su·per·sti·tious \-'stish-əs\ *adj* : of, relating to, or manifesting superstition — **su·per·sti·tious·ly** *adv* — **su·per·sti·tious·ness** *n*

su·per·stra·tum \'sü-pər-ˌstrāt-əm, -ˌstrat-\ *n* [*super-* + *-stratum* (as in *substratum*)] : an overlying stratum or layer

su·per·struc·ture \-ˌstrək-chər\ *n* [L *superstructus*, pp. of *superstruere* to build on or over, fr. *super-* + *struere* to build — more at STRUCTURE] **1** : a structure built as a vertical extension of something else: as **a** : all of a building above the basement **b** : the structural part of a ship above the main deck **c** : the ties, rails, and fastenings of a railroad track in distinction from the roadbed **2** : an entity, concept, or complex based on a more fundamental one; *specif* : legal, financial, political, and other institutions that are in Marxist theory erected upon the economic base

su·per·sub·stan·tial \ˌsü-pər-səb-'stan-chəl\ *adj* [LL *supersubstantialis*, fr. L *super-* + *substantia* substance] : being above material substance : of a transcending substance

su·per·sub·tle \-'səb-ᵊl\ *adj* : extremely or excessively subtle — **su·per·sub·tle·ty** \-tē\ *n*

su·per·tank·er \-ˌtaŋ-kər\ *n* **:** an exceptionally large and fast tanker
su·per·tax \-ˌtaks\ *n* **1 :** SURTAX **2 :** a graduated income tax imposed in the United Kingdom in addition to the normal income tax
su·per·ton·ic \ˌsü-pər-ˈtän-ik\ *n* **:** the second tone of the musical scale
su·per·vene \ˌsü-pər-ˈvēn\ *vi* [L *supervenire*, fr. *super-* + *venire* to come — more at COME] **:** to take place as an additional, adventitious, or unlooked-for development **syn** see FOLLOW — **su·per·ven·tion** \-ˈven-chən\ *n*
su·per·ve·nience \-ˈvē-nyən(t)s\ *n* **:** the condition of being supervenient
su·per·ve·nient \-nyənt\ *adj* [L *supervenient-*, *superveniens*, prp. of *supervenire*] **:** coming or occurring as something additional, extraneous, or unexpected
su·per·vise \ˈsü-pər-ˌvīz\ *vt* [ML *supervisus*, pp. of *supervidēre*, fr. L *super-* + *vidēre* to see — more at WIT] **:** SUPERINTEND, OVERSEE — **su·per·vi·sion** \ˌsü-pər-ˈvizh-ən\ *n*
su·per·vi·sor \ˈsü-pər-ˌvī-zər\ *n* **:** an administrative officer in charge of any of various business, government, or school units or operations — **su·per·vi·so·ry** \ˌsü-pər-ˈvīz-(ə-)rē\ *adj*
su·pi·nate \ˈsü-pə-ˌnāt\ *vb* [L *supinatus*, pp. of *supinare* to lay backward or on the back, fr. *supinus*] *vt* **:** to cause to assume a position of supination ~ *vi* **:** to assume a position of supination
su·pi·na·tion \ˌsü-pə-ˈnā-shən\ *n* **1 :** rotation of the forearm and hand or sometimes of other joints (as the shoulder, hip, or knee) backward and away from the midline of the body **2 :** the position resulting from supination with the palm of the hand directed forward and the thumb away from the body
su·pi·na·tor \ˈsü-pə-ˌnāt-ər\ *n* [NL, fr. L *supinatus*, pp.] **:** a muscle that produces the motion of supination
¹su·pine \sü-ˈpīn\ *adj* [L *supinus*; akin to L *sub* under, up to — more at UP] **1 a :** lying on the back or with the face upward **b :** marked by supination **2 :** manifesting mental or moral slackness **:** ABJECT **3** *archaic* **:** leaning or sloping backward **syn** see INACTIVE, PRONE — **su·pine·ly** *adv* — **su·pine·ness** \-ˈpīn-nəs\ *n*
²su·pine \ˈsü-ˌpīn\ *n* [ME *supyn*, fr. LL *supinum*, fr. L, neut. of *supinus*, adj.] **1 :** a Latin verbal noun having an accusative of purpose in *-um* and an ablative of specification in *-u* **2 :** an English infinitive with *to*
sup·per \ˈsəp-ər\ *n* [ME, fr. OF *souper*, fr. *souper* to sup — more at SUP] **1 :** the evening meal when dinner is taken at midday **2 :** a light meal served late in the evening ⟨had ~ after the theater⟩
sup·plant \sə-ˈplant\ *vt* [ME *supplanten*, fr. MF *supplanter*, fr. L *supplantare* to overthrow by tripping up, fr. *sub-* + *planta* sole of the foot — more at PLACE] **1 :** to supersede (another) esp. by force or treachery **2 a** (1) *obs* **:** UPROOT (2) **:** to eradicate and supply a substitute for ⟨efforts to ~ the vernacular⟩ **b :** to take the place of and serve as a substitute for esp. by reason of superior excellence or power **syn** see REPLACE — **sup·plan·ta·tion** \ˌsə-ˌplan-ˈtā-shən\ *n* — **sup·plant·er** \sə-ˈplant-ər\ *n*
¹sup·ple \ˈsəp-əl *also* ˈsüp-\ *adj* **sup·pler** \-(ə-)lər\ **sup·plest** \-(ə-)ləst\ [ME *souple*, fr. OF, fr. L *supplic-*, *supplex* submissive, suppliant, lit., bending under, fr. *sub-* + *plic-* (akin to *plicare* to fold) — more at PLY] **1 a :** compliant often to the point of obsequiousness **b :** readily adaptable or responsive to new situations **2 a :** capable of being bent or folded without creases, cracks, or breaks **:** PLIANT ⟨~ leather⟩ **b :** able to perform bending or twisting movements with ease and grace **:** LIMBER ⟨~ legs of a dancer⟩ **syn** see ELASTIC — **sup·ple·ly** \-ə(l)-lē\ *or* **sup·ply** \-(ə-)lē\ *adv* — **sup·ple·ness** \-əl-nəs\ *n*
²supple *vb* **sup·pling** \-(ə-)liŋ\ *vt* **1 :** to make pacific or complaisant **2 :** to alleviate with a salve **3 :** to make flexible or pliant ~ *vi* **:** to become soft and pliant
sup·ple·jack \-əl-ˌjak\ *n* **:** any of various woody climbers having tough pliant stems; *esp* **:** a southern U.S. vine (*Berchemia scandens*) of the buckthorn family
¹sup·ple·ment \ˈsəp-lə-mənt\ *n* [ME, fr. L *supplementum*, fr. *supplēre* to fill up, complete — more at SUPPLY] **1 :** something that completes or makes an addition **2 :** a continuation of a book or periodical containing corrections or additions **3 :** the amount by which an arc or an angle falls short of 180 degrees — **sup·ple·men·tal** \ˌsəp-lə-ˈment-ᵊl\ *adj*
²sup·ple·ment \ˈsəp-lə-ˌment\ *vt* **:** to add to **:** COMPLETE — **sup·ple·men·ta·tion** \ˌsəp-lə-ˌmen-ˈtā-shən, -mən-\ *n*
sup·ple·men·ta·ry \ˌsəp-lə-ˈment-ə-rē, -ˈmen-trē\ *adj* **:** added as a supplement **:** ADDITIONAL
supplementary angles *n pl* **:** two angles whose sum is 180 degrees
sup·ple·tion \sə-ˈplē-shən\ *n* [ML *suppletion-*, *suppletio* act of supplementing, fr. L *suppletus*, pp. of *supplēre*] **:** the occurrence of phonemically unrelated allomorphs of the same morpheme (as *go*, past tense *went* or plural ending *-es* in *boxes*, *-en* in *oxen*) — **sup·ple·tive** \sə-ˈplēt-iv, ˈsəp-lət-\ *adj*
sup·ple·to·ry \sə-ˈplēt-ə-rē; ˈsəp-lə-ˌtōr-ē, -ˌtȯr-\ *adj* [L *suppletus*, pp.] **:** supplying deficiencies **:** SUPPLEMENTARY
sup·pli·ance \ˈsəp-lē-ən(t)s\ *n* **:** SUPPLICATION, ENTREATY
¹sup·pli·ant \-ənt\ *n* [ME, fr. MF, fr. prp. of *supplier* to supplicate, fr. L *supplicare*] **:** one who supplicates
²suppliant *adj* [MF, prp.] **:** BESEECHING, IMPLORING — **sup·pli·ant·ly** *adv*
¹sup·pli·cant \ˈsəp-li-kənt\ *adj* **:** asking submissively **:** ENTREATING — **sup·pli·cant·ly** *adv*
²supplicant *n* **:** SUPPLIANT
sup·pli·cate \ˈsəp-lə-ˌkāt\ *vb* [ME *supplicaten*, fr. L *supplicatus*, pp. of *supplicare*, fr. *supplic-*, *supplex* suppliant — more at SUPPLE] *vi* **:** to make a humble entreaty; *esp* **:** to pray to God ~ *vt* **1 :** to ask humbly and earnestly of **2 :** to ask for earnestly and humbly **syn** see BEG — **sup·pli·ca·tion** \ˌsəp-lə-ˈkā-shən\ *n*
sup·pli·ca·to·ry \ˈsəp-li-kə-ˌtōr-ē, -ˌtȯr-\ *adj* **:** expressing supplication **:** BESEECHING
sup·pli·er \sə-ˈplī(-ə)r\ *n* **:** one that supplies
¹sup·ply \sə-ˈplī\ *vb* [ME *supplien*, fr. MF *soupleier*, fr. L *supplēre* to fill up, supplement, supply, fr. *sub-* up + *plēre* to fill — more at SUB-, FULL] *vt* **1 :** to add as a supplement **2 a :** to provide for **:** SATISFY **b :** to provide or furnish with **:** AFFORD **c :** to satisfy the needs or wishes of **3 a :** to substitute for another in; *specif* **:** to serve as a supply in (a church or pulpit) **b :** to serve instead of **:** REPLACE ~ *vi* **:** to serve as a supply
²supply *n* **1** *obs* **:** ASSISTANCE, SUCCOR **2 a** *obs* **:** REINFORCEMENTS — often used in pl. **b :** a clergyman filling a vacant pulpit temporarily **c :** the quantity or amount (as of a commodity) needed or available **d :** PROVISIONS, STORES — usu. used in pl. **3 :** the act or process of filling a want or need **:** PROVISION **4 :** the quantities of goods or services offered for sale at a particular time or at one price **5 :** something that maintains or constitutes a supply
¹sup·port \sə-ˈpō(ə)rt, -ˈpȯ(ə)rt\ *vt* [ME *supporten*, fr. MF *supporter*, fr. LL *supportare*, fr. L, to carry, fr. *sub-* + *portare* to carry — more at FARE] **1 :** to endure bravely or quietly **:** BEAR **2 a** (1) **:** to promote the interests or cause of (2) **:** to uphold or defend as valid or right **:** ADVOCATE (3) **:** to argue or vote for **b** (1) **:** ASSIST, HELP (2) **:** to act with (a star actor) (3) **:** to bid in bridge so as to show support for **c :** SUBSTANTIATE, VERIFY **3 :** to pay the costs of **:** MAINTAIN **4 a :** to hold up or serve as a foundation or prop for **b :** to maintain (a price) at a high level by purchases or loans; *also* **:** to maintain the price of by purchases or loans **5 :** to keep from fainting, yielding, or losing courage **:** COMFORT **6 :** to keep (something) going
syn SUPPORT, UPHOLD, ADVOCATE, BACK, CHAMPION means to favor actively one that meets opposition. SUPPORT is least explicit about the nature of the assistance given; UPHOLD implies extended support given to something attacked or challenged; ADVOCATE stresses urging or pleading; BACK suggests supporting by lending assistance to one failing or falling; CHAMPION suggests publicly defending one unjustly attacked or too weak to advocate his own cause
²support *n* **1 :** the act or process of supporting **:** the condition of being supported **2 :** one that supports
sup·port·able \sə-ˈpōrt-ə-bəl, -ˈpȯrt-\ *adj* **:** capable of being supported — **sup·port·able·ness** *n* — **sup·port·ably** \-blē\ *adv*
sup·port·er *n* **:** one that supports or acts as a support: as **a :** ADHERENT, PARTISAN **b :** GARTER 1 **c :** one of two figures (as of men or animals) placed one on each side of an escutcheon and exterior to it
supporting distance *n* **:** the distance beyond which one military unit cannot come to the aid of another before it is defeated
sup·port·ive \sə-ˈpōrt-iv, -ˈpȯrt-\ *adj* **:** furnishing or intended to furnish support
support mission *n* **:** an air attack in close support of ground forces against enemy ground forces
sup·pos·able \sə-ˈpō-zə-bəl\ *adj* **:** capable of being supposed **:** CONCEIVABLE — **sup·pos·ably** \-blē\ *adv*
sup·pos·al \-ˈpō-zəl\ *n* **1 :** the act or process of supposing **2 :** HYPOTHESIS, SUPPOSITION
sup·pose \sə-ˈpōz, *oftenest after "I"* ˈspōz\ *vb* [ME *supposen*, fr. MF *supposer*, fr. ML *supponere* (perf. indic. *supposui*), fr. L, to put under, substitute, fr. *sub-* + *ponere* to put — more at POSITION] *vt* **1 a :** to lay down tentatively as a hypothesis or assumption **b** (1) **:** to hold as an opinion **:** BELIEVE (2) **:** to think probable or in keeping with the facts **2 a :** CONCEIVE, IMAGINE **b :** to have a suspicion of **3 :** PRESUPPOSE ~ *vi* **:** CONJECTURE, OPINE
sup·posed \sə-ˈpōzd\ *adj* **:** BELIEVED; *also* **:** mistakenly believed **:** IMAGINED — **sup·pos·ed·ly** \-ˈpō-zəd-lē\ *adv*
sup·pos·ing \sə-ˈpō-ziŋ\ *conj* **:** if by way of hypothesis **:** on the assumption that
sup·po·si·tion \ˌsəp-ə-ˈzish-ən\ *n* [ME, fr. LL *supposition-*, *suppositio*, fr. L, act of placing beneath, fr. *suppositus*, pp. of *supponere*] **1 :** something that is supposed **:** HYPOTHESIS **2 :** the act of supposing — **sup·po·si·tion·al** \-ˈzish-nəl, -ən-ᵊl\ *adj* — **sup·po·si·tion·al·ly** \-ē\ *adv*
sup·po·si·tious \-ˈzish-əs\ *adj* [by contr.] **:** SUPPOSITITIOUS
sup·pos·i·ti·tious \sə-ˌpäz-ə-ˈtish-əs\ *adj* [L *supposititicius*, fr. *suppositus*, pp. of *supponere* to substitute] **1 a :** fraudulently substituted **:** SPURIOUS **b** *of a child* (1) **:** falsely presented as a genuine heir (2) **:** ILLEGITIMATE **2** [influenced in meaning by *supposition*] **:** of the nature of a supposition **:** HYPOTHETICAL — **sup·pos·i·ti·tious·ly** *adv* — **sup·pos·i·ti·tious·ness** *n*
sup·pos·i·tive \sə-ˈpäz-ət-iv, -ˈpäz-tiv\ *adj* **:** characterized by, involving, or implying supposition — **sup·pos·i·tive·ly** *adv*
sup·pos·i·to·ry \sə-ˈpäz-ə-ˌtōr-ē, -ˌtȯr-\ *n* [ML *suppositorium*, fr. LL, neut. of *suppositorius* placed beneath, fr. L *suppositus*, pp. of *supponere* to put under] **:** an easily fusible usu. medicated and cone-shaped or cylindrical preparation for insertion into a tubular bodily cavity (as the rectum)
sup·press \sə-ˈpres\ *vt* [ME *suppressen*, fr. L *suppressus*, pp. of *supprimere*, fr. *sub-* + *premere* to press — more at PRESS] **1 :** to put down by authority or force **:** SUBDUE **2 :** to keep from public knowledge: as **a :** to keep secret **b :** to stop or prohibit the publication or revelation of **3 a :** to exclude from consciousness **b :** to keep from giving vent to **:** CHECK **4** *obs* **:** to press down **5 a :** to restrain from a usual course or action **:** ARREST ⟨~ a cough⟩ **b :** to inhibit the growth or development of **:** STUNT **syn** see CRUSH — **sup·press·ible** \-ə-bəl\ *adj* — **sup·pres·sor** \-ˈpres-ər\ *n*
sup·pres·sion \sə-ˈpresh-ən\ *n* **1 :** an act or instance of suppressing **:** the state of being suppressed **2 :** the conscious intentional exclusion from consciousness of a thought or feeling
sup·pres·sive \-ˈpres-iv\ *adj* **:** tending or serving to suppress
sup·pu·rate \ˈsəp-yə-ˌrāt\ *vi* [L *suppuratus*, pp. of *suppurare*, fr. *sub-* + *pur-*, *pus* pus — more at FOUL] **:** to form or discharge pus
sup·pu·ra·tion \ˌsəp-yə-ˈrā-shən\ *n* **:** the act or process of suppurating — **sup·pu·ra·tive** \ˈsəp-yə-ˌrāt-iv\ *adj*
su·pra \ˈsü-prə, -ˌprä\ *adv* [L] **:** ABOVE **:** earlier in this writing
supra- *prefix* [L, fr. *supra* above, beyond, earlier; akin to L *super* over — more at OVER] **1 :** SUPER- 2a ⟨*supra*orbital⟩ **2 :** transcending ⟨*supra*molecular⟩
su·pra·li·mi·nal \ˌsü-prə-ˈlim-ən-ᵊl, -ˌprä-, -ˈlī-mən-\ *adj* [*supra-* + L *limin-*, *limen* threshold — more at LIMB] **1 :** existing above the threshold of consciousness **:** CONSCIOUS **2** *of a stimulus* **:** adequate to evoke or be distinguishable as a sensation — **su·pra·li·mi·nal·ly** \-ᵊl-ē\ *adv*
su·pra·mo·lec·u·lar \-mə-ˈlek-yə-lər\ *adj* **:** more complex than a molecule; *also* **:** composed of many molecules
su·pra·na·tion·al \-ˈnash-nəl, -ən-ᵊl\ *adj* **:** transcending national boundaries or authority
su·pra·or·bit·al \-ˈȯr-bət-ᵊl\ *adj* [NL *supraorbitalis*, fr. L *supra-* + ML *orbita* orbit] **:** situated or occurring above the orbit of the eye
su·pra·or·ga·nism \-ˈȯr-gə-ˌniz-əm\ *n* **:** an organized society (as of a social insect) that functions as an organic whole
su·pra·pro·test \-ˈprō-ˌtest\ *n* [modif. of It *sopra protesto* upon protest] **:** an acceptance or payment of a bill by a third person for

the honor of the drawer after protest for nonacceptance or non-payment by the drawee

¹**su·pra·re·nal** \-'rēn-°l\ *adj* [NL *suprarenalis*, fr. L *supra-* + *renes* kidneys] : situated above or anterior to the kidneys; *specif* : ADRENAL

²**suprarenal** *n* : a suprarenal part; *esp* : ADRENAL GLAND

suprarenal gland *n* : ADRENAL GLAND

su·prem·a·cist \su̇-'prem-ə-səst\ *n* : an advocate or adherent of group supremacy ⟨a white ~⟩

su·prem·a·cy \su̇-'prem-ə-sē\ *n* [*supreme* + *-acy* (as in *primacy*)] : the quality or state of being supreme; *also* : supreme authority or power

syn SUPREMACY, ASCENDANCY mean the position of being first (as in rank, power, or influence). SUPREMACY implies superiority over all others; ASCENDANCY may imply supremacy but involves necessarily only the idea of domination over one other

su·preme \su̇-'prēm\ *adj* [L *supremus*, superl. of *superus* upper — more at SUPERIOR] 1 : highest in rank or authority 2 : highest in degree or quality 3 : ULTIMATE, FINAL ⟨~ sacrifice⟩ — **su·preme·ly** *adv* — **su·preme·ness** *n*

Supreme Being *n* : ²GOD

supreme court *n* 1 : the highest judicial tribunal in a political unit (as a nation or state) 2 : a court of original jurisdiction in New York state that is subordinate to a final court of appeals

sur- *prefix* [ME, fr. OF, fr. L *super-*] 1 : over : SUPER- ⟨*surprint*⟩ ⟨*surtax*⟩ 2 : above : up ⟨*surbase*⟩

su·ra \'su̇r-ə, 'su̇-rə\ *n* [Ar *sūrah*, lit., row] : one of the sections of the Koran

su·rah \'su̇r-ə\ *n* [prob. alter. of *surat* (a cotton produced in Surat, India)] : a soft twilled fabric of silk or rayon

sur·base \'sər-ˌbās\ *n* : a molding just above the base of a wall, pedestal, or podium

sur·based \-ˌbāst\ *adj* [F *surbaissé*] 1 : having the curve center below the springing line of imposts ⟨~ arch⟩ 2 : having a surbase

¹**sur·cease** \(ˌ)sər-'sēs, 'sər-ˌ\ *vb* [ME *sursesen, surcesen*, fr. MF *sursis*, pp. of *surseoir*, fr. L *supersedēre* — more at SUPERSEDE] *vi* : to desist from action; *also* : to come to an end : CEASE ~ *vt* : to put an end to : DISCONTINUE

²**sur·cease** \'sər-ˌsēs, (ˌ)sər-'\ *n* : CESSATION; *esp* : a temporary respite or end

¹**sur·charge** \'sər-ˌchärj\ *vt* [ME *surchargen*, fr. MF *surchargier*, fr. *sur-* + *chargier* to charge] 1 a : OVERCHARGE b : to charge an extra fee c : to show an omission in (an account) for which credit ought to have been given 2 *Brit* : OVERSTOCK 3 : OVERBURDEN, OVERLOAD 4 a : to mark a new denomination figure or a surcharge on (a stamp) b : OVERPRINT ⟨~ a stamp⟩ ⟨~ a banknote⟩

²**surcharge** *n* 1 a : an additional tax, cost, or impost b : an extra fare ⟨a sleeping car ~⟩ c : an instance of surcharging an account 2 : an excessive load or burden 3 : the action of surcharging : the state of being surcharged 4 a (1) : an overprint on a stamp; *specif* : one that alters the denomination (2) : a stamp bearing such an overprint b : an overprint on a currency note

sur·cin·gle \'sər-ˌsiŋ-gəl\ *n* [ME *sursengle*, fr. MF *surcengle*, fr. *sur-* + *cengle* girdle, fr. L *cingulum* — more at CINGULUM] 1 : a belt, band, or girth passing around the body of a horse to bind a saddle or pack fast to the horse's back 2 : the girdle or cincture of a cassock

sur·coat \'sər-ˌkōt\ *n* [ME *surcote*, fr. MF, fr. *sur-* + *cote* coat] : an outer coat or cloak; *specif* : a tunic worn over armor

sur·cu·lose \'sər-kyə-ˌlōs\ *adj* [L *surculosus*, fr. *surculus* sucker, dim. of *surus* branch, stake; akin to OE *swēor* pillar] : producing basal shoots

¹**surd** \'sərd\ *adj* [L *surdus* deaf, silent, stupid; akin to L *susurrus* hum — more at SWARM] 1 : IRRATIONAL 2 : VOICELESS — used of speech sounds

²**surd** *n* 1 a : an irrational root (as $\sqrt{3}$) b : IRRATIONAL 2 2 : a surd speech sound

¹**sure** \'shu̇(ə)r, *esp South* 'shō(ə)r\ *adj* [ME, fr. MF *sur*, fr. L *securus* secure] 1 *obs* : safe from danger or harm 2 : firmly established : STEADFAST 3 : RELIABLE, TRUSTWORTHY 4 : ASSURED, CONFIDENT 5 : admitting of no doubt : CERTAIN 6 a : bound to happen : INEVITABLE ⟨~ disaster⟩ b : DESTINED, BOUND ⟨he is ~ to win⟩ — **sure·ness** *n*

syn SURE, CERTAIN, POSITIVE, COCKSURE mean having no doubt of one's opinion or conclusion. SURE usu. stresses the subjective or intuitive feeling of assurance; CERTAIN may apply to a basing of a conclusion or conviction on definite grounds or indubitable evidence; POSITIVE intensifies sureness or certainty and may imply opiniated conviction or forceful expression of it; COCKSURE implies presumptuous or careless positiveness

²**sure** *adv* : SURELY

sure·fire \-'fī(ə)r\ *adj* : certain to get results : DEPENDABLE

sure·foot·ed \-'fu̇t-əd\ *adj* : not liable to stumble or fall — **sure·foot·ed·ness** *n*

sure·ly \'shu̇(ə)r-lē, *esp South* 'shō(ə)r-\ *adv* 1 : in a sure manner: a *archaic* : SAFELY b (1) : with assurance : CONFIDENTLY (2) : without doubt 2 : INDEED, REALLY — often used as an intensive

sure·ty \'shu̇r-ət-ē, 'shu̇(ə)rt-ē\ *n* [ME *surte*, fr. MF *surté*, fr. L *securitat-, securitas* security, fr. *securus*] 1 : the state of being sure: as a : sure knowledge : CERTAINTY b : confident manner or behavior : ASSURANCE 2 a : a pledge or other formal engagement given for the fulfillment of an undertaking : GUARANTEE b : ground or confidence of security 3 a : a sponsor at baptism b : one who has become legally liable for the debt, default, or failure in duty (as appearance in court) of another — **sure·ty·ship** \-ˌship\ *n*

surety bond *n* : a bond guaranteeing performance of a contract or obligation

¹**surf** \'sərf\ *n* [origin unknown] 1 : the swell of the sea that breaks upon the shore 2 : the foam, splash, and sound of breaking waves

²**surf** *vi* : to ride the surf (as on a surfboard) — **surf·er** *n*

¹**sur·face** \'sər-fəs\ *n* [F, fr. *sur-* + *face*] 1 : the exterior or upper boundary of an object or body 2 : a plane or curved two-dimensional locus of points ⟨as the boundary of a three-dimensional region⟩ ⟨plane ~⟩ ⟨~ of a sphere⟩ 3 : the external or superficial aspect of something 4 : a complete airfoil used for sustentation or control or to increase stability — **surface** *adj*

²**surface** *vt* 1 : to give a surface to: as a : to plane or make smooth

b : to apply the surface layer to 2 : to bring to the surface ~ *vi* 1 : to work on or at the surface 2 : to come to the surface — **sur·fac·er** *n*

sur·face-ac·tive \'sər-fə-ˌsak-tiv\ *adj* : altering the properties and esp. lowering the tension at the surface of contact between phases ⟨soaps, wetting agents, and other ~ substances⟩

surface color *n* 1 : the color ascribed to an opaque substance or object 2 : a color extending no farther than the surface

surface of revolution *n* : a surface formed by the revolution of a plane curve about a line in its plane

surface plate *n* : a precision-dressed steel or iron surface used as a standard of flatness

surface tension *n* : a condition that exists at the free surface of a body (as a liquid) by reason of intermolecular forces about the individual surface molecules and is manifested by properties resembling those of an elastic skin under tension

sur·fac·ing *n* : material forming or used to form a surface

surf·bird \'sərf-ˌbərd\ *n* : a shorebird (*Aphriza virgata*) of the Pacific coasts of America that is related to the turnstones and has the tail blackish at the tip and white at the base

surf·board \-ˌbō(ə)rd, -ˌbȯ(ə)rd\ *n* : a long narrow buoyant board used in the sport of riding the surf — **surfboard** *vi* — **surf·board·er** *n*

surf·boat \-ˌbōt\ *n* : a boat for use in heavy surf

surf caster *n* : one that engages in surf casting

surf casting *n* : the technique or act of casting artificial or natural bait into the open ocean or in a bay where waves break on a beach

surf clam *n* : any of various typically rather large surf-dwelling edible clams (family Mactridae)

¹**sur·feit** \'sər-fət\ *n* [ME *surfait*, fr. MF, fr. *surfaire* to overdo, fr. *sur-* + *faire* to do, fr. L *facere* — more at DO] 1 : an overabundant supply : EXCESS 2 : an intemperate or immoderate indulgence in something (as food or drink) 3 : disgust caused by excess : SATIETY

²**surfeit** *vt* : to feed, supply, or give to surfeit : CLOY ~ *vi, archaic* : to indulge to satiety in any gratification (as of the appetite or senses) syn see SATIATE — **sur·feit·er** *n*

surf fish *n* : any of a family (Embiotocidae) of small or medium-sized viviparous fishes of shallow water along the Pacific coast of No. America; *also* : any of several croakers of the same region

sur·fi·cial \ˌsər-'fish-əl\ *adj* [*surface* + *-icial* (as in *superficial*)] : of or relating to a surface

surf-rid·ing \'sər-ˌfrīd-iŋ\ *n* : the sport of riding the surf on a surfboard

¹**surge** \'sərj\ *vb* [MF *sourge-*, stem of *sourdre* to rise, surge, fr. L *surgere* to go straight up, rise, fr. *sub-* up + *regere* to lead straight — more at SUB-, RIGHT] *vi* 1 : to rise and fall actively : TOSS 2 : to rise and move in waves or billows : SWELL 3 : to slip around a windlass, capstan, or bitts — used esp. of a rope 4 : to rise suddenly to an excessive or abnormal value — used esp. of current or voltage ~ *vt* : to let go or slacken gradually (as a rope) ⟨~ a hawser to prevent its parting⟩

²**surge** *n* 1 : a swelling, rolling, or sweeping forward like that of a wave or series of waves 2 a : a large wave or billow : SWELL b : a series of such swells or billows 3 : the tapered part of a windlass barrel or a capstan 4 a : a movement (as a slipping or slackening) of a rope or cable b : a sudden jerk or strain caused by such a movement 5 : a transient sudden rise of current in an electrical circuit

sur·geon \'sər-jən\ *n* [ME *surgien*, fr. AF, fr. OF *cirurgien*, fr. *cirurgie* surgery] : a medical specialist who practices surgery

sur·geon·cy \-sē\ *n, Brit* : the office or position of a surgeon

surgeon general *n, pl* **surgeons general** : the chief medical officer of a branch of the armed services or of a federal or state public health service

surgeon's knot *n* : any of several knots used in tying ligatures or stitches

sur·gery \'sərj-(ə-)rē\ *n* [ME *surgerie*, fr. OF *cirurgie, surgerie*, fr. L *chirurgia*, fr. Gk *cheirourgia*, fr. *cheirourgos* surgeon, fr. *cheirourgein* working with the hand, fr. *cheir* hand + *ergon* work — more at CHIR-, WORK] 1 : a branch of medicine concerned with diseases and conditions requiring or amenable to operative or manual procedures 2 a *Brit* : a physician's or dentist's office b : a room or area where surgery is performed 3 a : the work done by a surgeon b : OPERATION

sur·gi·cal \'sər-ji-kəl\ *adj* [*surgeon* + *-ical*] 1 a : of or relating to surgeons or surgery ⟨~ skills⟩ ⟨a ~ operation⟩ b : used in or in connection with surgery ⟨~ implements⟩ ⟨a ~ stocking⟩ 2 : following or resulting from surgery ⟨~ fevers⟩ — **sur·gi·cal·ly** \-k(ə-)lē\ *adv*

su·ri·cate \'su̇r-ə-ˌkāt\ *n* [F *surikate*] : a burrowing grayish black-handed social mammal (*Suricata tetradactyla*) of southern Africa related to the mongooses but with only four toes

sur·li·ly \'sər-lə-lē\ *adv* : in a surly manner

sur·li·ness \'sər-lē-nəs\ *n* : the quality or state of being surly

sur·ly \'sər-lē\ *adj* [alter. of ME *sirly* lordly, imperious, fr. *sir*] 1 *obs* : ARROGANT, IMPERIOUS 2 : HARSH, RUDE 3 : MENACING, THREATENING syn see SULLEN — **surly** *adv*

¹**sur·mise** \sər-'mīz\ *vt* [ME *surmisen* to accuse, fr. MF *surmis*, pp. of *surmetre*, fr. L *supermittere* to throw on, fr. *super-* + *mittere* to send — more at SMITE] : to imagine or infer on slight grounds : GUESS syn see CONJECTURE

²**sur·mise** \sər-'mīz, 'sər-ˌ\ *n* : a thought or idea based on scanty evidence : CONJECTURE

sur·mount \sər-'maunt\ *vt* [ME *surmounten*, fr. MF *surmonter*, fr. *sur-* + *monter* to mount] 1 *obs* : to surpass in quality or attainment : EXCEL 2 : to rise superior to : OVERCOME ⟨~ an obstacle⟩ 3 : to get to the top of : CLIMB 4 : to stand or lie at the top of : CROWN — **sur·mount·able** \-ə-bəl\ *adj*

sur·mul·let \ˌsər-'məl-ət, 'sər-ˌ\ *n, pl* **surmullets** *also* **surmullet** [F *surmulet*] : MULLET 2

¹**sur·name** \'sər-ˌnām\ *n* 1 : an added name derived from occupation or other circumstance : NICKNAME 2 : the name borne in common by members of a family

²**surname** *vt* : to give a surname to

sur·pass \sər-'pas\ *vt* [MF *surpasser*, fr. *sur-* + *passer* to pass] 1 : to become better, greater, or stronger than : EXCEED 2 : to go

beyond **3 :** to transcend the reach, capacity, or powers of **syn** see EXCEED — **sur·pass·able** \-ə-bəl\ *adj*

sur·pass·ing *adj* **:** of a very high degree — **sur·pass·ing·ly** \-iŋ-lē\ *adv*

sur·plice \'sər-pləs\ *n* [ME *surplis,* fr. OF *surpliz,* fr. ML *superpellicium,* fr. *super-* + *pellicium* coat of skins, fr. L, neut. of *pellicius* made of skins, fr. *pellis* skin — more at FELL] **:** a loose white outer vestment of knee length with large open sleeves that is worn at service by some clergymen

sur·plus \'sər-(,)pləs\ *n* [ME, fr. MF, fr. ML *superplus,* fr. L *super-* + *plus* more — more at PLUS] **1 a :** the amount that remains when use or need is satisfied **b :** an excess of receipts over disbursements **2 :** the excess of a corporation's net worth over the par or stated value of its capital stock — **surplus** *adj*

sur·plus·age \'sər-(,)pləs-ij\ *n* **1 :** SURPLUS 1a **2 a :** excessive or nonesssential matter **b :** matter introduced in legal pleading which is not necessary or relevant to the case **syn** see EXCESS

surplus value *n* **:** the difference in Marxist theory between the value of work done or of commodities produced by labor and the usu. subsistence wages paid by the employer

[1]**sur·print** \'sər-,print\ *vt* **:** OVERPRINT

[2]**surprint** *n* **:** OVERPRINT

sur·pris·al \sə(r)-'prī-zəl\ *n* **:** the action of surprising **:** the state of being surprised

[1]**sur·prise** \sə(r)-'prīz\ *n* [ME, fr. MF, fr. *surprendre* to take over, surprise, fr. *sur-* + *prendre* to take — more at PRIZE] **1 a :** an attack made without warning **b :** a taking unawares **2 :** something that surprises **3 :** the state of being surprised **:** ASTONISHMENT

[2]**surprise** *also* **sur·prize** *vt* **1 :** to attack unexpectedly; *also* **:** to capture by an unexpected attack **2 a :** to take unawares **b :** to detect or elicit by a taking unawares **3 :** to strike with wonder or amazement because unexpected — **sur·pris·er** *n*

syn SURPRISE, ASTONISH, ASTOUND, AMAZE, FLABBERGAST mean to impress forcibly through unexpectedness. SURPRISE differs from the other words in applying specifically to events causing an effect by taking unawares rather than by being essentially startling in quality; ASTONISH implies surprising so greatly as to seem incredible: ASTOUND stresses the shock of astonishment; AMAZE suggests an effect of bewilderment; FLABBERGAST may suggest thorough astonishment and bewilderment or dismay

sur·pris·ing *adj* **:** ASTONISHING, AMAZING — **sur·pris·ing·ly** \-'prī-ziŋ-lē\ *adv*

sur·ra \'sùr-ə\ *n* [Marathi *sūra* wheezing sound] **:** a severe Old World febrile and hemorrhagic disease of domestic animals that is caused by a protozoan (*Trypanosoma evansi*)

sur·re·al \sə-'rē(-ə)l\ *adj* [back-formation fr. *surrealism*] **:** having the intense irrational reality of a dream; *also* **:** SURREALISTIC

sur·re·al·ism \sə-'rē(-ə)-,liz-əm\ *n* [F *surréalisme,* fr. *sur-* + *réalisme* realism] **:** the principles, ideals, or practice of producing fantastic or incongruous imagery in art or literature by means of unnatural juxtapositions and combinations — **sur·re·al·ist** \-ləst\ *n or adj* — **sur·re·al·is·tic** \-,rē(-ə)-'lis-tik\ *adj* — **sur·re·al·is·ti·cal·ly** \-ti-k(ə-)lē\ *adv*

sur·re·but·ter \,sər-(r)i-'bət-ər\ *or* **sur·re·but·tal** \-'bət-ᵊl\ *n* **:** the reply in common law pleading of a plaintiff to a defendant's rebutter

sur·re·join·der \-(r)i-'jòin-dər\ *n* **:** the answer in common law pleading of a plaintiff to a defendant's rejoinder

[1]**sur·ren·der** \sə-'ren-dər\ *vb* **sur·ren·der·ing** \-d(ə-)riŋ\ [ME *surrenderen,* fr. MF *surrendre* fr. *sur-* + *rendre* to give back, yield — more at RENDER] *vt* **1 a :** to yield to the power, control, or possession of another upon compulsion or demand ⟨~*ed* the fort⟩ **b :** to give up completely or agree to forgo esp. in favor of another **2 a :** to give (oneself) up into the power of another esp. as a prisoner **b :** to give (oneself) over to something (as an influence or course of action) **~** *vi* **:** to give oneself up into the power of another **:** YIELD **syn** see RELINQUISH

[2]**surrender** *n* **1 a :** the action of yielding one's person or giving up the possession of something into the power of another **b :** the relinquishment by a patentee of his rights or claims under a patent **c :** the delivery of a principal into lawful custody by his bail or of a fugitive from justice by one government to another — called also *surrender by bail* **d :** the voluntary cancellation of the legal liability of an insurance company by the insured and beneficiary for a consideration **2 :** an instance of surrendering

sur·rep·ti·tious \,sər-əp-'tish-əs, ,sə-rəp-, sə-,rep-\ *adj* [ME, fr. L *surrepticius,* fr. *surreptus,* pp. of *surripere* to snatch secretly, fr. *sub-* + *rapere* to seize — more at RAPID] **1 :** done, made, or acquired by stealth **:** CLANDESTINE **2 :** acting or doing something clandestinely **:** STEALTHY **syn** see SECRET — **sur·rep·ti·tious·ly** *adv* — **sur·rep·ti·tious·ness** *n*

sur·rey \'sər-ē, 'sə-rē\ *n* [*Surrey,* county of England] **:** a four-wheel two-seated horse-drawn pleasure carriage

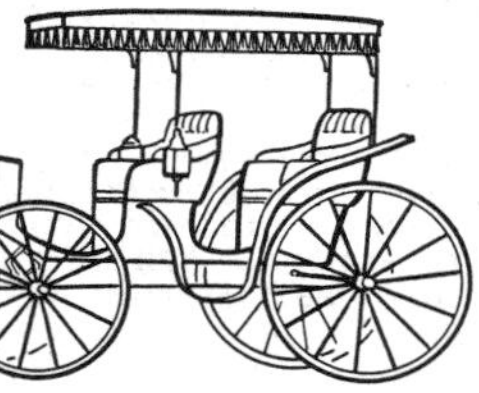

surrey

[1]**sur·ro·gate** \'sər-ə-,gāt, 'sə-rə-\ *vt* [L *surrogatus,* pp. of *surrogare* to choose in place of another, substitute, fr. *sub-* + *rogare* to ask — more at RIGHT] **:** to put in the place of another: **a :** to appoint as successor, deputy, or substitute for oneself **b :** SUBSTITUTE

[2]**sur·ro·gate** \-,gāt, -gət\ *n* **1 a :** a person appointed to act in place of another **:** DEPUTY **b :** a local judicial officer in New York and some other states who has jurisdiction over the probate of wills, the settlement of estates, and the appointment and supervision of guardians **2 :** something that serves as a substitute

[1]**sur·round** \sə-'raùnd\ *vt* [ME *surrounden* to overflow, fr. MF *suronder,* fr. LL *superundare,* fr. L *super-* + *unda* wave — more at WATER] **1 :** to enclose on all sides **:** ENCOMPASS **2 :** to ring about **:** ENCIRCLE **3 :** to enclose so as to cut off communication or retreat; *also* **:** INVEST

[2]**surround** *n* **:** something (as a border or edging) that surrounds

sur·round·ings \sə-'raùn-diŋz\ *n pl* **:** the circumstances, conditions, or objects by which one is surrounded **:** ENVIRONMENT

sur·roy·al \'sər-,ròi(-ə)l\ *n* [ME *surryal,* fr. *sur-* + *royal* royal antler] — see ANTLER illustration

sur·sum cor·da \,sù(ə)r-səm-'kòrd-ə, -'kò(ə)r-,dä\ *n* [LL, (lift) up (your) hearts] **1** *often cap S&C* **:** a versicle exhorting to thanksgiving to God **2 :** something inspiriting

sur·tax \'sər-,taks\ *n* **1 :** an extra tax or charge **2 :** a graduated income tax in addition to the normal income tax imposed on the amount by which one's net income exceeds a specified sum

sur·tout \(,)sər-'tü\ *n* [F, fr. *sur* over (fr. L *super*) + *tout* all, fr. L *totus* whole — more at OVER] **:** a man's long close-fitting overcoat

sur·veil·lance \sər-'vā-lən(t)s, -'vāl-yən(t)s\ *n* [F, fr. *surveiller* to watch over, fr. *sur-* + *veiller* to watch, fr. L *vigilare,* fr. *vigil* watchful — more at VIGIL] **:** close watch kept over a person or group (as by a detective); *also* **:** SUPERVISION

sur·veil·lant \-lənt, -yənt\ *n* **:** one that exercises surveillance

[1]**sur·vey** \sər-'vā, 'sər-,\ *vb* [ME *surveyen,* fr. MF *surveeir* to look over, fr. *sur-* + *veeir* to see — more at VIEW] *vt* **1 a :** to examine as to condition, situation, or value **:** APPRAISE **b :** to make a survey of **2 :** to determine and delineate the form, extent, and position of (as a tract of land) by taking linear and angular measurements and by applying the principles of geometry and trigonometry **3 :** to view comprehensively **4 :** INSPECT, SCRUTINIZE **~** *vi* **:** to make a survey

[2]**sur·vey** \'sər-,vā, sər-'\ *n* **:** the act or an instance of surveying; *also* **:** something that is surveyed **syn** see COMPENDIUM

sur·vey·ing \sər-'vā-iŋ\ *n* **:** a branch of applied mathematics that teaches the art of making surveys

sur·vey·or \sər-'vā-ər\ *n* **:** one that surveys; *esp* **:** one that practices the art of surveying land

surveyor's level *n* **:** a level consisting of a telescope and a spirit level mounted on a tripod and revolving on a vertical axis

surveyor's measure *n* **:** a system of measurement having the surveyor's chain as a unit and used in land surveying

sur·viv·al \sər-'vī-vəl\ *n* **1 :** a living or continuing longer than another person or thing **2 :** one that survives

survival of the fittest : NATURAL SELECTION

survival value *n* **:** utility in the struggle for existence

sur·viv·ance \sər-'vī-vən(t)s\ *n* **:** SURVIVAL

sur·vive \sər-'vīv\ *vb* [ME *surviven,* fr. MF *survivre* to outlive, fr. L *supervivere,* fr. *super-* + *vivere* to live] *vi* **:** to remain alive or in existence **:** live on **~** *vt* **1 :** to remain alive after the death of ⟨his son *survived* him⟩ **2 :** to continue to exist or live after (as a time or event) **syn** see OUTLIVE — **sur·vi·vor** \-'vī-vər\ *n*

sur·viv·er \-'vī-vər\ *n, archaic* **:** SURVIVOR

sur·vi·vor·ship \-'vī-vər-,ship\ *n* **1 :** the legal right of the survivor of persons having joint interests in property (as an estate) to take the interest of the dying person **2 :** the state of being a survivor

sus·cep·ti·bil·i·ty \sə-,sep-tə-'bil-ət-ē\ *n* **1 :** the quality or state of being susceptible; *esp* **:** lack of ability to resist some extraneous agent (as a pathogen or drug) **:** SENSITIVITY **2 a :** a susceptible temperament or constitution **b** *pl* **:** FEELINGS, SENSIBILITIES **3 a :** the ratio of the magnetization in a substance to the corresponding magnetizing force **b :** the ratio of the electric polarization to the electric intensity in a polarized dielectric

sus·cep·ti·ble \sə-'sep-tə-bəl\ *adj* [LL *susceptibilis,* fr. L *susceptus,* pp. of *suscipere* to take up, admit, fr. *sub-, sus-* up + *capere* to take — more at SUB-, HEAVE] **1 :** capable of submitting to an action, process, or operation ⟨a theory ~ to proof⟩ **2 :** open, subject, or unresistant to some stimulus, influence, or agency **3 :** IMPRESSIONABLE, RESPONSIVE **syn** see LIABLE — **sus·cep·ti·ble·ness** *n* — **sus·cep·ti·bly** \-blē\ *adv*

sus·cep·tive \-tiv\ *adj* **1 :** RECEPTIVE **2 :** SUSCEPTIBLE — **sus·cep·tive·ness** *n* — **sus·cep·tiv·i·ty** \sə-,sep-'tiv-ət-ē\ *n*

su·slik \'sü-slik\ *n* [Russ] **1 :** any of several rather large short-tailed ground squirrels (genus *Citellus*) of eastern Europe or northern Asia **2 :** the mottled grayish black fur of a suslik

[1]**sus·pect** \'səs-,pekt, sə-'spekt\ *adj* [ME, fr. MF, fr. L *suspectus,* fr. pp. of *suspicere*] **:** regarded with suspicion **:** SUSPECTED

[2]**sus·pect** \'səs-,pekt\ *n* **:** one who is suspected

[3]**sus·pect** \sə-'spekt\ *vb* [ME *suspecten,* fr. L *suspectare,* fr. *suspectus,* pp. of *suspicere* to look up at, regard with awe, suspect, fr. *sub-, sus-* up, secretly + *specere* to look at] *vt* **1 :** to have doubts of **:** DISTRUST **2 :** to imagine (one) to be guilty or culpable on slight evidence or without proof **3 :** to imagine to be or be true, likely, or probable **~** *vi* **:** to imagine something true or likely

sus·pend \sə-'spend\ *vb* [ME *suspenden,* fr. OF *suspendre* to hang up, interrupt, fr. L *suspendere,* fr. *sub-, sus-* up + *pendere* to cause to hang, weigh — more at PENDANT] *vt* **1 :** to debar temporarily from any privilege, office, or function ⟨~ a student from school⟩ **2 a :** to cause to stop temporarily ⟨~ bus service⟩ **b :** to set aside or make temporarily inoperative ⟨~ the rules during the holiday⟩ **3 :** to defer till later on specified conditions ⟨~ sentence on a convicted man⟩ **4 :** to hold in an undetermined or undecided state awaiting fuller information ⟨~ judgment⟩ **5 a :** HANG; *esp* **:** to hang so as to be free on all sides except at the point of support ⟨~ a ball by a thread⟩ **b :** to maintain from falling or sinking by some invisible support (as buoyancy) ⟨dust ~*ed* in the air⟩ **6 a :** to keep fixed or lost (as in wonder or contemplation) **b :** to keep waiting in suspense or indecision **7 :** to hold (a musical note) over into the following chord **~** *vi* **1 :** to cease temporarily from operation **2 :** to stop payment or fail to meet obligations **3 :** HANG **syn** see DEFER, EXCLUDE

suspended animation *n* **:** temporary suspension of the vital functions

sus·pend·er \sə-'spen-dər\ *n* **1 :** one that suspends **2 :** a device by which something may be suspended: as **a :** one of two supporting bands worn across the shoulders to support trousers, skirt, or belt — usu. used in pl. and often with *pair* ⟨a pair of ~*s*⟩ **b** *Brit* **:** GARTER

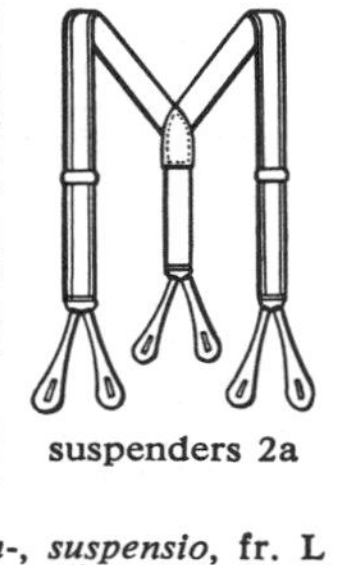

suspenders 2a

sus·pense \sə-'spen(t)s\ *n* [ME, fr. MF, fr. *suspendre*] **1 :** the state of being suspended **:** SUSPENSION **2 :** mental uncertainty **:** ANXIETY **3 :** the state or character of being undecided or doubtful **:** INDECISIVENESS — **sus·pense·ful** \-fəl\ *adj*

suspense account *n* **:** an account for the temporary entry of charges or credits or esp. of doubtful accounts receivable pending determination of their ultimate disposition

sus·pen·sion \sə-'spen-chən\ *n* [LL *suspension-, suspensio,* fr. L *suspensus,* pp. of *suspendere*] **1 :** the act of suspending **:** the state

or period of being suspended: as **a :** temporary removal from office or privileges **b :** temporary withholding (as of belief or decision) **c :** temporary abrogation of a law or rule **d** (1) **:** the holding over of one or more musical tones of a chord into the following chord and producing a momentary discord and suspending the concord which the ear expects; *specif* **:** such a dissonance which resolves downward (2) **:** the tone thus held over **e :** stoppage of payment of business obligations **:** FAILURE **f :** a rhetorical device whereby the principal idea is deferred to the end of a sentence or longer unit **2 a :** the act of hanging **:** the state of being hung **b** (1) **:** the state of a substance when its particles are mixed with but undissolved in a fluid or solid (2) **:** a substance in this state (3) **:** a system consisting of a solid dispersed in a solid, liquid, or gas usu. in particles of larger than colloidal size — compare EMULSION **3 :** something suspended **4 a :** a device by which something (as a magnetic needle) is suspended **b :** the system of devices (as springs) supporting the upper part of a vehicle on the axles **c :** the act, process, or manner in which the pendulum or torsion balance of a timepiece is suspended

suspension bridge *n* **:** a bridge that has its roadway suspended from two or more cables usu. passing over towers and securely anchored at the ends

suspension points *n pl* **:** usu. three spaced periods used to mark an omission of a word or word group from a written context

sus·pen·sive \sə-'spen(t)-siv\ *adj* **1 :** stopping temporarily **:** SUSPENDING **2 :** characterized by suspense, suspended judgment, or indecisiveness **3 :** characterized by suspension — **sus·pen·sive·ly** *adv*

sus·pen·soid \sə-'spen(t)-ˌsȯid\ *n* [ISV *suspens*ion + coll*oid*] **1 :** a colloidal system in which the dispersed particles are solid **2 :** a lyophobic sol (as a gold sol)

sus·pen·sor \sə-'spen(t)-sər\ *n* **:** a suspending part or structure; *esp* **:** a cellular support of a plant embryo or zygospore

1sus·pen·so·ry \sə-'spen(t)s-(ə-)rē\ *adj* **1 :** SUSPENDED; *also* **:** fitted or serving to suspend **2 :** temporarily leaving undetermined **:** SUSPENSIVE 1

2suspensory *n* **:** something that suspends or holds up; *esp* **:** a fabric supporter for the scrotum

suspensory ligament *n* **1 :** an annular fibrous membrane holding the lens of the eye in place **2 :** the falciform ligament of the liver

1sus·pi·cion \sə-'spish-ən\ *n* [ME, fr. L *suspicion-, suspicio,* fr. *suspicere* to suspect — more at SUSPECT] **1 :** the act or an instance of suspecting something wrong without proof or on slight evidence **:** MISTRUST **2 :** a slight touch or trace **:** SUGGESTION ⟨just a ~ of garlic⟩ **syn** see UNCERTAINTY

2suspicion *vt* **sus·pi·cion·ing** \-(ə-)niŋ\ *chiefly substand* **:** SUSPECT

sus·pi·cious \sə-'spish-əs\ *adj* **1 :** tending to arouse suspicion **:** QUESTIONABLE **2 :** disposed to suspect **:** DISTRUSTFUL **3 :** indicative of suspicion ⟨a ~ glance⟩ — **sus·pi·cious·ly** *adv* — **sus·pi·cious·ness** *n*

sus·pi·ra·tion \ˌsəs-pə-'rā-shən, -(ˌ)pir-'ā-\ *n* **:** a long deep breath **:** SIGH

sus·pire \sə-'spī(ə)r\ *vi* [ME *suspiren,* fr. L *suspirare,* fr. *sub-* + *spirare* to breathe — more at SPIRIT] **:** SIGH

Sus·sex spaniel \ˌsəs-ik(s)-\ *n* [*Sussex,* county of England] **:** any of a British breed of short-legged short-necked long-bodied spaniels with a flat or slightly wavy golden liver-colored coat

sus·tain \sə-'stān\ *vt* [ME *sustenen,* fr. OF *sustenir,* fr. L *sustinēre* to hold up, sustain, fr. *sub-, sus-* up + *tenēre* to hold — more at SUB-, THIN] **1 :** to give support or relief to **2 :** to supply with sustenance **:** NOURISH **3 :** to keep up **:** PROLONG **4 :** to support the weight of **:** PROP; *also* **:** to carry or withstand (a weight or pressure) **5 :** to buoy up **6 :** to bear up under **:** ENDURE **7 a :** to support as true, legal, or just **b :** to allow or admit as valid ⟨the court ~*ed* the motion⟩ **8 :** to support by adequate proof **:** CONFIRM — **sus·tain·able** \-'stā-nə-bəl\ *adj* — **sus·tain·er** *n*

sustaining program *n* **:** a radio or television program that is paid for by a station or network and has no commercial sponsor

sus·te·nance \'səs-tə-nən(t)s\ *n* [ME, fr. OF, fr. *sustenir*] **1 a :** means of support, maintenance, or subsistence **:** LIVING **b :** FOOD, PROVISIONS; *also* **:** NOURISHMENT **2 a :** the act of sustaining or the state of being sustained **b :** a supplying or being supplied with the necessaries of life **3 :** something that gives support, endurance, or strength

sus·ten·tac·u·lar \ˌsəs-tən-'tak-yə-lər, -ˌten-\ *adj* [NL *sustentaculum* supporting part, fr. L, prop, fr. *sustentare*] **:** serving to support or sustain

sus·ten·ta·tion \-'tā-shən\ *n* [ME, fr. MF, fr. L *sustentation-, sustentatio* act of holding up, fr. *sustentatus,* pp. of *sustentare* to hold up, fr. *sustentus,* pp. of *sustinēre*] **1 :** the act of sustaining **:** the state of being sustained: as **a :** MAINTENANCE, UPKEEP **b :** PRESERVATION, CONSERVATION **c :** maintenance of life, growth, or morale **d :** provision with sustenance **2 :** something that sustains **:** SUPPORT — **sus·ten·ta·tive** \'səs-tən-ˌtāt-iv, sə-'stent-ət-\ *adj*

sus·ten·tion \sə-'sten-chən\ *n* [*sustain*] **:** SUSTENTATION

Su·su \'sü-(ˌ)sü\ *n, pl* **Susu** *or* **Susus 1 a :** a West African people of the Sudan and Guinea republics and the area along the northern border of Sierra Leone **b :** a member of this people **2 :** the language of the Susu people

su·sur·rant \sü-'sər-ənt, -'sə-rənt\ *adj* **:** WHISPERING, MURMURING

su·sur·ra·tion \ˌsü-sə-'rā-shən\ *n* **:** WHISPERING, MURMUR

su·sur·rous \sü-'sər-əs, -'sə-rəs\ *adj* **:** full of whispering sounds **:** RUSTLING

su·sur·rus \sü-'sər-əs, -'sə-rəs\ *n* [L, hum, whisper — more at SWARM] **:** a whispering or rustling sound

sut·ler \'sət-lər\ *n* [obs. D *soeteler,* fr. LG *suteler* sloppy worker, camp cook; akin to OE *besūtian* to dirty, Gk *hyein* to rain — more at SUCK] **:** a provisioner to an army post often established in a shop on the post

su·tra \'sü-trə\ *n* [Skt *sūtra* thread, string of precepts, sutra; akin to L *suere* to sew — more at SEW] **1 :** a precept summarizing Vedic teaching **2 :** a discourse of the Buddha **3 :** a collection of sutras

sut·tee \(ˌ)sə-'tē, 'sə-ˌtē\ *n* [Skt *satī* wife who performs suttee, lit., good woman, fr. fem. of *sat* true, good; akin to OE *sōth* true — more at SOOTH] **:** the act or custom of a Hindu widow willingly cremating herself or being cremated on the funeral pile of her husband as an indication of her devotion to him; *also* **:** a woman cremated in this way

su·tur·al \'süch-(ə-)rəl\ *adj* **:** of, relating to, or situated in a suture — **su·tur·al·ly** \-ē\ *adv*

1su·ture \'sü-chər\ *n* [MF & L; MF, fr. L *sutura* seam, suture, fr. *sutus,* pp. of *suere* to sew — more at SEW] **1 a :** a strand or fiber used to sew parts of the living body **b :** a stitch made with a suture **c :** the act or process of sewing with sutures **2 a :** a uniting of parts **b :** the seam or seamlike line along which two things or parts are sewed or united **3 a :** the line of union in an immovable articulation (as between the bones of the skull); *also* **:** such an articulation **b :** a furrow at the junction of adjacent bodily parts; *esp* **:** a line of dehiscence (as on a fruit)

2suture *vt* **su·tur·ing** \'süch-(ə-)riŋ\ **:** to unite, close, or secure with sutures ⟨~ a wound⟩

su·zer·ain \'süz-(ə-)rən, -ə-ˌrān\ *n* [F, fr. (assumed) MF *suserain,* fr. MF *sus* up (fr. L *sursum,* fr. *sub-* up + *versum* -ward, fr. neut. of *versus,* pp. of *vertere* to turn) + *-erain* (as in *soverain* sovereign) — more at WORTH] **1 :** a superior feudal lord to whom fealty is due **:** OVERLORD **2 :** a dominant state controlling the foreign relations of a vassal state but allowing it sovereign authority in its internal affairs

su·zer·ain·ty \-tē\ *n* [F *suzeraineté,* fr. MF *susereneté,* fr. (assumed) MF *suserain*] **:** the dominion of a suzerain **:** OVERLORDSHIP

svelte \'sfelt\ *adj* [F, fr. It *svelto,* fr. pp. of *svellere* to pluck out, modif. of L *evellere,* fr. *e-* + *vellere* to pluck — more at VULNERABLE] **1 a :** SLENDER, LITHE **b :** having clean lines **:** SLEEK **2 :** URBANE, SUAVE — **svelte·ly** *adv* — **svelte·ness** *n*

Sven·ga·li \sfen-'gäl-ē\ *n* [*Svengali,* maleficent hypnotist in the novel *Trilby* (1894) by George du Maurier] **:** one who attempts usu. with evil intentions to persuade or force another to do his bidding

1swab \'swäb\ *n* [prob. fr. obs. D *swabbe;* akin to LG *swabber* mop] **1 a :** MOP; *esp* **:** a yarn mop **b** (1) **:** a wad of absorbent material usu. wound around one end of a small stick and used for applying medication or for removing material from an area (2) **:** a specimen taken with a swab **c :** a sponge attached to a long handle, for cleaning the bore of a firearm **2 a :** a useless or contemptible person **b :** SAILOR, GOB

2swab *vt* **swabbed; swab·bing** [back-formation fr. *swabber*] **:** to use a swab on **:** MOP

swab·ber \'swäb-ər\ *n* [akin to LG *swabber* mop, ME *swabben* to sway] **1 :** one that swabs **2 :** SWAB 2a

swab·bie *also* **swab·by** \-ē\ *n, slang* **:** SWAB 2b

swad·dle \'swäd-ᵊl\ *vt* **swad·dled; swad·dling** \'swäd-liŋ, -ᵊl-iŋ\ [ME *swadelen, swathelen,* prob. alter. of *swedelen, swethelen,* fr. *swethel* swaddling band, fr. OE; akin to OE *swathian* to swathe] **1 a :** to wrap (an infant) with swaddling clothes **b :** SWATHE, ENVELOP **2 :** RESTRAIN, RESTRICT

swaddling clothes *n pl* **1 :** narrow strips of cloth wrapped around an infant to restrict movement **2 :** limitations or restrictions imposed upon the immature or inexperienced

1swag \'swag\ *vi* **swagged; swag·ging** [prob. of Scand origin; akin to ON *sveggja* to cause to sway; akin to OHG *swingan* to swing] **1 :** SWAY, LURCH **2 :** SAG

2swag *n* **1 :** SWAY **2 a :** something hanging in a curve between two points **:** FESTOON **b :** a suspended cluster (as of evergreen branches) **3 a :** goods acquired by unlawful means **:** LOOT **b :** SPOILS, PROFITS **4 :** a depression in the earth **5** *chiefly Austral* **:** a pack of personal belongings

1swage \'swāj, 'swej\ *n* [ME, ornamental border, fr. MF *souage*] **:** a tool used by workers in metals for shaping their work by holding it on the work, or the work on it and striking with a hammer or sledge

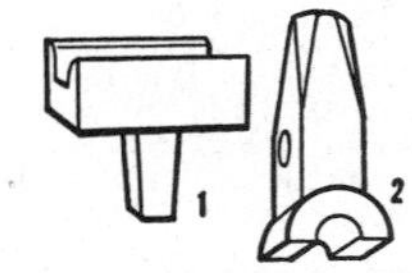

swage: *1* bottom, *2* top

2swage *vt* **:** to shape by means of a swage

swage block *n* **:** a perforated cast-iron or steel block with grooved sides that is used in heading bolts and swaging bars of various sizes by hand

1swag·ger \'swag-ər\ *vb* **swag·ger·ing** \-(ə-)riŋ\ [prob. fr. *swag* + *-er* (as in *chatter*)] *vi* **1 :** to conduct oneself in an arrogant or superciliously pompous manner; *esp* **:** to walk with an air of overbearing self-confidence **2 :** BOAST, BRAG ~ *vt* **:** to force by argument or threat **:** BULLY — **swag·ger·er** \-ər-ər\ *n* — **swag·ger·ing·ly** \-(ə-)riŋ-lē\ *adv*

2swagger *n* **1 a :** an act or instance of swaggering **b :** arrogant or conceitedly self-assured behavior **c :** ostentatious display or bravado **2 :** a self-confident outlook **:** COCKINESS

3swagger *adj* **:** marked by elegance or showiness **:** POSH

swagger stick *n* **:** a short light stick usu. covered with leather and tipped with metal at each end

swag·man \'swag-mən\ *n, chiefly Austral* **:** VAGRANT; *esp* **:** one who carries a swag when traveling

Swa·hi·li \swä-'hē-lē\ *n, pl* **Swahili** *or* **Swahilis** [Ar *sawāḥil,* pl. of *sāḥil* coast] **1 a :** a Bantu-speaking people of Zanzibar and the adjacent coast **b :** a member of this people **2 :** a Bantu language that is a trade and governmental language over much of East Africa and in the Congo

swain \'swān\ *n* [ME *swein* boy, servant, fr. ON *sveinn;* akin to OE *swān* swain, L *suus* one's own — more at SUICIDE] **1 :** RUSTIC, PEASANT; *specif* **:** SHEPHERD **2 :** a male admirer or suitor — **swain·ish** \'swā-nish\ *adj* — **swain·ish·ness** *n*

swale \'swā(ə)l\ *n* [ME, shade, prob. of Scand origin; akin to ON *svalr* cool; akin to OE *swelan* to burn — more at SWELTER] **:** a low-lying stretch of land (as a small meadow, swamp, or marshy heavily vegetated depression)

1swal·low \'swäl-(ˌ)ō, -ə(-w)\ *n* [ME *swalowe,* fr. OE *swealwe;* akin to OHG *swalawa* swallow, Russ *solovei* nightingale] **1 :** any of numerous small long-winged passerine birds (family Hirundinidae) that are noted for their graceful flight and regular migrations, have a short bill with a wide gape, small weak feet, and often a deeply forked tail, occur in all parts of the world except New Zealand and polar regions, and feed on insects caught on the wing **2 :** any of several swifts that superficially resemble swallows

[2]swallow *vb* [ME *swalowen*, fr. OE *swelgan*; akin to OHG *swelgan* to swallow] *vt* **1 :** to take through the mouth and esophagus into the stomach **2 :** to envelop or take in as if by swallowing **:** ABSORB **3 :** to accept without question, protest, or resentment **4 :** to take back **:** RETRACT **5 :** to keep from expressing or showing **:** REPRESS **6 :** to utter (as words) indistinctly ~ *vi* **1 :** to receive something into the body through the mouth and esophagus **2 :** to perform the action characteristic of swallowing something esp. under emotional stress — **swal·low·er** \ˈswäl-ə-wər\ *n*

[3]swallow *n* **1 :** the passage connecting the mouth to the stomach **2 :** a capacity for swallowing **3 a :** an act of swallowing **b :** an amount that can be swallowed at one time **4 :** an aperture in a block on a ship between the sheave and frame through which the rope reeves

swal·low·tail \ˈswäl-ō-ˌtāl, -ə-\ *n* **1 :** a deeply forked and tapering tail (as of a swallow) **2 :** TAILCOAT **3 :** any of various large butterflies (esp. genus *Papilio*) with the border of the hind wing produced into a process resembling a tail — **swal·low–tailed** \ˌswäl-ō-ˈtāld, -ə-\ *adj*

swal·low·wort \ˈswäl-ō-ˌwərt, -ə-, -ˌwȯ(ə)rt\ *n* **1 :** CELANDINE 1 **2 :** any of several plants of the milkweed family: as **a :** SOMA **b :** a European twining vine (*Cynanchum nigrum*) whose root has been used as an emetic, cathartic, and diuretic

swam *past of* SWIM

swa·mi \ˈswäm-ē\ *n* [Hindi *svāmī*, fr. Skt *svāmin* owner, lord, fr. *sva* one's own] **1 :** a Hindu ascetic or religious teacher; *specif* **:** a senior member of a religious order — used as a title **2 :** PUNDIT

[1]swamp \ˈswämp, ˈswȯmp\ *n, often attrib* [alter. of ME *sompe*, fr. MD *somp* morass; akin to MHG *sumpf* marsh, Gk *somphos* spongy] **1 :** wet spongy land saturated and sometimes partially or intermittently covered with water **2 :** a tract of swamp — **swampy** \ˈswäm-pē, ˈswȯm-\ *adj*

[2]swamp *vt* **1 :** to submerge with or as if with water **:** INUNDATE **2 :** to open by removing underbrush and debris ~ *vi* **:** to become submerged

swamp buggy *n* **:** a vehicle used to negotiate swampy terrain: as **a :** an amphibious tractor **b :** a flat-bottomed boat driven by an airplane propeller

swamp·er \ˈswäm-pər, ˈswȯm-\ *n* **1 :** an inhabitant of swampy terrain **2 :** a general assistant **:** HELPER

swamp·i·ness \ˈswäm-pē-nəs, ˈswȯm-\ *n* **:** the quality or state of being swampy

swamp·land \-ˌpland\ *n* **:** SWAMP

[1]swan \ˈswän\ *n, pl* **swans** *often attrib* [ME, fr. OE; akin to MHG *swan*, L *sonus* sound — more at SOUND] **1** *pl also* **swan :** any of various heavy-bodied long-necked mostly pure white aquatic birds (family Anatidae) related to but larger than the geese that walk awkwardly, fly strongly when once started, and are graceful swimmers **2 :** a person or thing suggesting a swan because of its grace, whiteness, or fabled power of melody when dying **3** *cap* **:** the constellation Cygnus

[2]swan *vi* **swanned; swanning :** to wander idly **:** DALLY

[3]swan *vi* **swanned; swan·ning** [perh. euphemism for *swear*] *dial* **:** DECLARE, SWEAR

swan boat *n* **:** a small boat usu. for children or sightseers pedaled by an operator who sits aft in a large model of a swan

swan dive *n* **:** a front dive executed with the head back, back arched, and arms spread sideways and then brought together above the head to form a straight line with the body as the diver enters the water

swan·herd \ˈswän-ˌhərd\ *n* **:** one that tends swans

[1]swank \ˈswaŋk\ *adj* [MLG or MD *swanc* supple; akin to OHG *swingan* to swing] *Scot* **:** full of life or energy **:** ACTIVE

[2]swank *vi* [perh. fr. MHG *swanken* to sway; akin to MD *swanc* supple] **:** to show off **:** SWAGGER

[3]swank *n* **1 :** PRETENTIOUSNESS, SWAGGER **2 :** ELEGANCE

[4]swank *or* **swanky** \ˈswaŋ-kē\ *adj* **1 :** characterized by showy display **:** OSTENTATIOUS **2 :** fashionably elegant **:** SMART — **swank·i·ly** \-kə-lē\ *adv* — **swank·i·ness** \-kē-nəs\ *n*

swan·nery \ˈswän-(ə-)rē\ *n* **:** a place where swans are bred or kept

swans·down \ˈswänz-ˌdau̇n\ *n* **1 :** the soft downy feathers of the swan often used as trimming on articles of dress **2 :** a heavy cotton flannel with a thick nap on the face made with sateen weave

swan·skin \ˈswän-ˌskin\ *n* **1 :** the skin of a swan with the down or feathers on it **2 :** any of various fabrics resembling flannel and having a soft nap or surface

swan song *n* **1 :** a song formerly thought to be uttered by a dying swan **2 :** a farewell appearance or final act or pronouncement

[1]swap \ˈswäp\ *vb* **swapped; swap·ping** [ME *swappen* to strike; fr. the practice of striking hands in closing a business deal] *vt* **:** to give in exchange **:** BARTER ~ *vi* **:** to make an exchange

[2]swap *n* **:** EXCHANGE, TRADE

swa·raj \swə-ˈräj\ *n* [Skt *svarāj* self-ruling, fr. *sva* one's self + *rājya* rule — more at SUICIDE, RAJ] **:** Indian national or local self-government — **swa·raj·ist** \-əst\ *n*

sward \ˈswȯ(ə)rd\ *n* [ME, fr. OE *sweard, swearth* skin, rind; akin to MHG *swart* skin, hide, L *operire* to cover — more at WEIR] **:** the grassy surface of land **:** TURF

swarf \ˈswȯ(ə)rf\ *n* [of Scand origin; akin to ON *svarf* file dust; akin to OE *sweorfan* to file away — more at SWERVE] **:** fine metallic particles removed by a cutting or grinding tool

[1]swarm \ˈswȯ(ə)rm\ *n* [ME, fr. OE *swearm*; akin to OHG *swaram* swarm and prob. to L *susurrus* hum] **1 :** a great number of honeybees emigrating together from a hive in company with a queen to start a new colony elsewhere; *also* **:** a colony of honeybees settled in a hive **2 a :** an extremely large number massed together and usu. in motion **b :** an aggregation of free-floating or free-swimming unicellular organisms — usu. used of zoospores

[2]swarm *vi* **1 a :** to form and depart from a hive in a swarm **b :** to escape in a swarm (as from a sporangium) **2 a :** to move or assemble in a crowd **:** THRONG **b :** to hover about in the manner of a bee in a swarm **3 :** to contain a swarm **:** TEEM ~ *vt* **:** to fill with a swarm — **swarm·er** *n*

[3]swarm *vb* [origin unknown] **:** to climb with the hands and feet; *specif* **:** SHIN ⟨~ up a pole⟩

swarm spore *n* **:** any of various minute motile sexual or asexual spores; *esp* **:** ZOOSPORE

swart \ˈswȯ(ə)rt\ *adj* [ME, fr. OE *sweart*; akin to OHG *swarz* black, L *sordes* dirt] **1 a :** SWARTHY **b** *archaic* **:** producing a swarthy complexion **2 :** BANEFUL, MALIGNANT — **swart·ness** *n*

[1]swarth \ˈswȯ(ə)rth\ *n* [ME, fr. OE *swearth* skin] **:** SWARD

[2]swarth *n* **:** SWATH 1b

[3]swarth *adj* [alter. of *swart*] **:** SWARTHY

swarth·i·ness \ˈswȯr-thē-nəs, -thē-\ *n* **:** the quality or state of being swarthy

swarthy \ˈswȯr-thē, -thē\ *adj* [alter. of obs. *swarty*, fr. *swart*] **:** being of a dark color, complexion, or cast **syn** see DUSKY

Swart·kranz ape–man \ˈsfärt-ˌkrän(t)s-\ *n* [*Swartkranz*, region in So. Africa] **:** an australopithecine (*Homo erectus capensis*) with a distinctly human jaw and teeth

[1]swash \ˈswäsh, ˈswȯsh\ *n* [prob. imit.] **1 a :** a body of splashing water **b :** a narrow channel of water lying within a sandbank or between a sandbank and the shore **2 :** a dashing of water against or upon something **3 :** a bar over which the sea washes **4 :** SWAGGER

[2]swash *vi* **1 :** BLUSTER, SWAGGER **2 :** to make violent noisy movements **3 :** to move with a splashing sound ~ *vt* **:** to cause to splash

[3]swash *adj* [obs. E *swash* slanting] **:** having one or more strokes ending in an extended flourish ⟨the ~ letters *ARPN*⟩

swash·buck·le \-ˌbək-əl\ *vi* [back-formation fr. *swashbuckler*] **:** to play the swashbuckler

swash·buck·ler \-ˌbək-lər\ *n* [[2]*swash* + *buckler*] **1 :** a boasting soldier or blustering daredevil **:** BRAVO **2 :** a novel or drama dealing with a swashbuckler

swash·buck·ling \-ˌbək-(ə-)liŋ\ *adj* [*swashbuckler*] **1 :** acting in the manner of a swashbuckler **2 :** characteristic of, marked by, or done by swashbucklers

swash·er \ˈswäsh-ər, ˈswȯsh-\ *n* **:** SWASHBUCKLER

swas·ti·ka \ˈswäs-ti-kə *also* swä-ˈstē-\ *n* [Skt *svastika*, fr. *svasti* welfare, fr. *su-* well + *asti* he is] **:** a symbol or ornament in the form of a Greek cross with the ends of the arms extended at right angles all in the same rotary direction

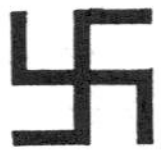

swastika

[1]swat \ˈswät\ *vb* **swat·ted; swat·ting** [E dial., to squat, alter. of E *squat*] **:** to hit with a quick hard blow **syn** see STRIKE — **swat·ter** *n*

[2]swat *n* **1 :** a powerful or crushing blow **2 :** a long hit in baseball; *esp* **:** HOME RUN

swatch \ˈswäch\ *n* [origin unknown] **1 a :** a sample piece (as of fabric) or a collection of samples **b :** a characteristic specimen **2 :** PATCH **3 :** a small collection

swath \ˈswäth, ˈswȯth\ *or* **swathe** \ˈswäth, ˈswȯth, ˈswāth\ *n* [ME, fr. OE *swæth* footstep, trace; akin to MHG *swade* swath] **1 a :** the sweep of a scythe or a machine in mowing or the path cut in one course **b :** a row of cut grain or grass left by a scythe or mowing machine **2 :** a long broad strip or belt **3 :** a stroke of or as if of a scythe **4 :** a space devastated as if by a scythe

[1]swathe \ˈswäth, ˈswȯth, ˈswāth\ *vt* [ME *swathen*, fr. OE *swathian*; akin to ON *svatha* to swathe, Lith *svaigti* to become dizzy] **1 :** to bind, wrap, or swaddle with or as if with a bandage **2 :** ENVELOP — **swath·er** *n*

[2]swathe \ˈswäth, ˈswȯth, ˈswāth\ *or* **swath** \ˈswäth, ˈswäth, ˈswȯth, ˈswȯth\ *n* **1 :** a band used in swathing **2 :** an enveloping medium

swathing clothes *n pl* [ME] *obs* **:** SWADDLING CLOTHES

swats \ˈswäts\ *n pl* [prob. fr. OE *swātan*, pl., beer] *Scot* **:** DRINK; *esp* **:** new ale

[1]sway \ˈswā\ *vb* [alter. of earlier *swey* to fall, swoon, fr. ME *sweyen*, prob. of Scand origin; akin to ON *sveigja* to sway; akin to OE *swathian* to swathe] *vi* **1 a :** to swing slowly and rhythmically back and forth from a base or pivot **b :** to move gently from an upright to a leaning position **2 :** to hold sway **:** act as ruler or governor **3 :** to fluctuate or veer between one point, position, or opinion and another ~ *vt* **1 a :** to cause to sway **:** set to swinging, rocking, or oscillating **b :** to cause to bend downward to one side **c :** to cause to turn aside **:** DEFLECT, DIVERT **2** *archaic* **a :** WIELD **b :** GOVERN, RULE **3 a :** to cause to vacillate **b :** to exert a guiding or controlling influence upon **4 :** to hoist in place ⟨~ up a mast⟩ **syn** see AFFECT, SWING — **sway·er** *n*

[2]sway *n* **1 :** the action or an instance of swaying or of being swayed **:** an oscillating, fluctuating, or sweeping motion **2 :** an inclination or deflection caused by or as if by swaying **3 a :** a preponderating force or pressure **:** a controlling influence **b :** sovereign power **:** DOMINION **c :** the ability to exercise influence or authority **:** DOMINANCE **syn** see POWER

sway·back \ˈswā-ˈbak\ *n* **1 :** an abnormally hollow condition or sagging of the back found esp. in horses **2 :** a sagging back — **sway·backed** \-ˈbakt\ *adj*

Swa·zi \ˈswäz-ē\ *n, pl* **Swazi** *or* **Swazis 1 a :** a Bantu people of Swaziland **b :** a member of this people **2 :** a Bantu language of the Swazi people

swear \ˈswa(ə)r, ˈswe(ə)r\ *vb* **swore** \ˈswō(ə)r, ˈswȯ(ə)r\ **sworn** \ˈswō(ə)rn, ˈswȯ(ə)rn\ **swear·ing** [ME *sweren*, fr. OE *swerian*; akin to OHG *swerien* to swear, Russ *svara* altercation] *vt* **1 :** to utter or take solemnly (an oath) **2 a :** to assert as true or promise under oath **b :** to assert or promise emphatically or earnestly **3 a :** to put to an oath **:** administer an oath to **b :** to bind by an oath **4** *obs* **:** to invoke the name of (a sacred being) in an oath **5 :** to bring into a specified state by swearing ⟨*swore* his life away⟩ ~ *vi* **1 :** to take an oath **2 :** to use profane or obscene language **:** CURSE — **swear·er** *n* — **swear by 1 :** to take an oath by ⟨*swear by* Apollo⟩ **2 :** to be sure of the existence of **:** be barely positive of — used in the phrase *enough to swear by* **3 :** to place great confidence in — **swear for :** to answer for **:** GUARANTEE — **swear off :** to vow to abstain from **:** RENOUNCE

swear in *vt* **:** to induct into office by administration of an oath

swear out *vt* **:** to procure (a warrant for arrest) by making a sworn accusation

swear·word \ˈswa(ə)r-ˌwərd, ˈswe(ə)r-\ *n* **:** a profane or obscene oath or word

[1]sweat \ˈswet\ *vb* **sweat** *or* **sweat·ed; sweat·ing** [ME *sweten*, fr. OE *swǣtan*, fr. *swāt* sweat; akin to OHG *sweiz* sweat, L *sudor* sweat, *sudare* to sweat] *vi* **1 a :** to excrete moisture in visible quantities through the openings of the sweat glands **:** PERSPIRE **b :** to labor so as to cause perspiration **:** work hard **2 a :** to emit or exude moisture ⟨cheese ~*s* in ripening⟩ **b :** to gather surface moisture in beads as a result of condensation ⟨stones ~ at night⟩ **c** (1) **:** FERMENT (2) **:** PUTREFY **3 :** to undergo anxiety or mental or emotional distress **4 :** to become exuded through pores or a porous surface **:** OOZE ~ *vt* **1 :** to emit or seem to emit from pores **:** EXUDE **2 :** to manipulate or produce by hard work or drudgery

3 : to get rid of or lose (weight) by or as if by sweating or being sweated 4 : to make wet with perspiration 5 a : to cause to excrete moisture from the skin b : to drive hard : OVERWORK c : to exact work from at low wages and under unfair or unhealthful conditions d *slang* : to give the third degree to 6 : to cause to exude or lose moisture; *esp* : to subject to fermentation (as tobacco leaves) 7 a : to extract something valuable from by unfair or dishonest means : FLEECE b : to remove particles of metal from (a coin) by abrasion 8 a : to heat (as solder) so as to melt and cause to run esp. between surfaces to unite them; *also* : to unite by such means ⟨~ a pipe joint⟩ b : to heat so as to extract an easily fusible constituent ⟨~ bismuth ore⟩ c : to apply heat to : STEAM — **sweat blood** : to work or worry intensely

2sweat *n* 1 : hard work : DRUDGERY 2 : the fluid excreted from the sweat glands of the skin : PERSPIRATION 3 : moisture issuing from or gathering in drops on a surface 4 a : the condition of one sweating or sweated b : a spell of sweating 5 : a state of anxiety or impatience — **sweaty** \ˈswet-ē\ *adj*

sweat·band \ˈswet-ˌband\ *n* 1 : a usu. leather band lining the inner edge of a hat or cap to prevent sweat damage 2 : a band of material tied around the head to absorb sweat

sweat·box \-ˌbäks\ *n* 1 : a device for sweating something (as hides in tanning or dried figs) 2 : a place in which one is made to sweat; *esp* : a narrow box in which a prisoner is placed for punishment

sweat·ed *adj* : of, subjected to, or produced under a sweating system ⟨~ labor⟩ ⟨~ goods⟩

sweat·er \ˈswet-ər\ *n* 1 : one that sweats or causes sweating 2 : a knitted or crocheted jacket or pullover

sweater girl *n* : a girl with a shapely bust

sweat gland *n* : a simple tubular gland of the skin that secretes perspiration, in man is widely distributed in nearly all parts of the skin, and consists typically of an epithelial tube extending spirally from a minute pore on the surface of the skin into the dermis or subcutaneous tissues where it ends in a convoluted tuft

sweat·i·ly \ˈswet-ᵊl-ē\ *adv* : in a sweaty manner

sweat·i·ness \ˈswet-ē-nəs\ *n* : the quality or state of being sweaty

sweating sickness *n* : an epidemic febrile disease characterized by profuse sweating and early high mortality

sweat out *vt* 1 : to endure or wait through the course of 2 : to work one's way painfully through or to

sweat pants *n pl* : pants having a drawstring waist and elastic cuffs at the ankle that are worn esp. by athletes in warming up

sweat shirt *n* : a loose collarless long-sleeved pullover of heavy cotton jersey

sweat·shop \ˈswet-ˌshäp\ *n* : a usu. small manufacturing establishment employing workers under unfair and unsanitary conditions

swede \ˈswēd\ *n* [LG or obs. D] 1 *cap* a : a native or inhabitant of Sweden b : a person of Swedish descent 2 : RUTABAGA

Swe·den·bor·gian \ˌswēd-ᵊn-ˈbȯr-j(ē-)ən, -ˈbȯr-gē-ən\ *adj* : of, relating to, or characteristic of Emanuel Swedenborg or the Church of the New Jerusalem based on his teachings — **Swedenborgian** *n* — **Swe·den·bor·gian·ism** \-ˌiz-əm\ *n*

Swed·ish \ˈswēd-ish\ *n* 1 : the North Germanic language spoken in Sweden and a part of Finland 2 *pl in constr* : the people of Sweden — **Swedish** *adj*

Swedish massage *n* : massage with Swedish movements

Swedish movements *n pl* : a system of active and passive exercise of muscles and joints

Swedish turnip *n* : RUTABAGA

swee·ny \ˈswē-nē, ˈswin-ē\ *n* [by folk etymology fr. PaG *schwinne*] : a muscular atrophy of a horse esp. in the shoulder

1sweep \ˈswēp\ *vb* **swept** \ˈswept\ **sweep·ing** [ME *swepen*; akin to OE *swāpan* to sweep — more at SWOOP] *vt* 1 a : to remove from a surface with or as if with a broom or brush b : to remove or take with a single continuous forceful action c : to drive or carry along with irresistible force 2 a : to clean with or as if with a broom or brush b : to clear by repeated and forcible action c : to move across or along swiftly, violently, or overwhelmingly d : to win an overwhelming victory in or on ⟨~ the elections⟩ 3 : to touch in passing with a swift continuous movement 4 : to trace the outline of (a curve) 5 : to cover the entire range of ~ *vi* 1 a : to clean a surface with or as if with a broom b : to move swiftly, forcefully, or devastatingly 2 : to go with stately or sweeping movements 3 : to move or extend in a wide curve or range — **sweep·er** *n*

2sweep *n* 1 : something that sweeps or works with a sweeping motion: as a : a long pole or timber pivoted on a tall post and used to raise and lower a bucket in a well b : a triangular cultivator blade that cuts off weeds under the soil surface c : a windmill sail 2 a : an instance of sweeping; *specif* : a clearing out or away with or as if with a broom b : the removal from the table in one play in casino of all the cards by pairing or combining c : an overwhelming victory d : a winning of all the contests or prizes in a competition 3 a : a movement of great range and force b : a curving or circular course or line c : the compass of a sweeping movement : SCOPE d : a broad extent 4 : CHIMNEY SWEEP 5 : SWEEPSTAKES

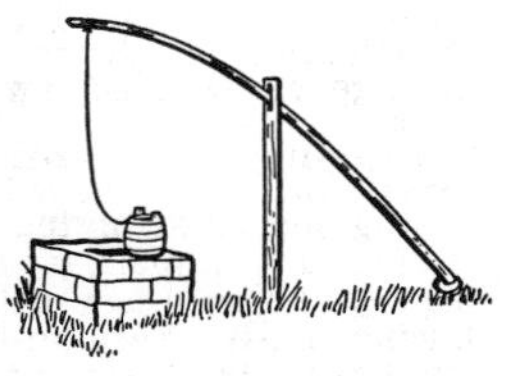

sweep 1a

sweep·back \ˈswēp-ˌbak\ *n* : the backward slant of an airplane wing in which the outer portion of the wing is downstream from the inner portion

sweep hand *n* : SWEEP-SECOND

1sweep·ing *n* 1 : the act or action of one that sweeps ⟨gave the room a good ~⟩ 2 *pl* : things collected by sweeping : REFUSE

2sweeping *adj* 1 a : moving or extending in a wide curve or over a wide area b : having a curving line or form 2 a : EXTENSIVE ⟨~ reforms⟩ b : WHOLESALE ⟨~ generalizations⟩ **syn** see INDISCRIMINATE — **sweep·ing·ly** \ˈswē-piŋ-lē\ *adv* — **sweep·ing·ness** *n*

sweep–sec·ond \ˈswēp-ˌsek-ənd, -ənt\ *n* : a hand marking seconds on a timepiece mounted concentrically with the other hands and read on the minute dial

sweep·stakes \-ˌstāks\ *n pl but sing or pl in constr, also* **sweep·stake** \-ˌstāk\ [ME *swepestake* one who wins all the stakes in a game, fr. *swepen* to sweep + *stake*] 1 a : a race or contest in which the entire prize may be awarded to the winner; *specif* : a horse race in which the stakes are made up at least in part of the entry fees or other money contributed by the owners of the horses b : CONTEST, COMPETITION 2 : any of various lotteries

sweepy \ˈswē-pē\ *adj* : sweeping in motion, line, or force

1sweet \ˈswēt\ *adj* [ME *swete*, fr. OE *swēte*; akin to OHG *suozi* sweet, L *suavis*, Gk *hēdys*] 1 a (1) : pleasing to the taste (2) : being or inducing the one of the four basic taste sensations that is typically induced by disaccharides and is mediated esp. by receptors in taste buds at the front of the tongue b (1) *of a beverage* : containing a sweetening ingredient : not dry (2) *of wine* : retaining a portion of natural sugar 2 a : pleasing to the mind or feelings : AGREEABLE — often used as a generalized term of approval b : marked by gentle good humor or kindliness c : FRAGRANT d (1) : delicately pleasing to the ear or eye (2) : played in a straightforward melodic style ⟨~ jazz⟩ e : CLOYING, SACCHARINE 3 : much loved : DEAR 4 a : not sour, rancid, decaying, or stale : WHOLESOME ⟨~ milk⟩ b : not salt or salted : FRESH ⟨~ water⟩ c *of land* : free from excessive acidity d : free from noxious gases and odors e : free from excess of acid, sulfur, or corrosive salts 5 : FINE, GREAT — used as an intensive — **sweet·ly** *adv* — **sweet·ness** *n* — **sweet on** : in love with

2sweet *adv* : SWEETLY

3sweet *n* 1 : something that is sweet to the taste: as a : a food (as a candy or preserve) having a high sugar content ⟨fill up on ~s⟩ b *Brit* : DESSERT c *Brit* : hard candy 2 : a sweet taste sensation 3 : a pleasant or gratifying experience, possession, or state 4 : DARLING 5 a *archaic* : FRAGRANCE b *pl, archaic* : things having a sweet smell

sweet alyssum *n* : a perennial European herb (*Lobularia maritima*) of the mustard family having clusters of small fragrant usu. white flowers

sweet–and–sour \ˌswēt-ᵊn-ˈsau̇(ə)r\ *adj* : seasoned with sugar and vinegar or lemon juice

sweet bay *n* 1 : LAUREL 1 2 : an American magnolia (*Magnolia virginiana*) abundant along the Atlantic coast and in the southern states that has glaucous leaves and rather small globose fragrant white flowers

sweet·bread \ˈswēt-ˌbred\ *n* : the thymus of a young animal (as a calf) used for food

sweet·bri·er \-ˌbrī(-ə)r\ *n* : an Old World rose (esp. *Rosa eglanteria*) with stout recurved prickles and white to deep rosy pink single flowers — called also *eglantine*

sweet cherry *n* : a white-flowered Eurasian cherry (*Prunus avium*) widely grown for its large sweet-flavored fruits; *also* : its fruit

sweet chocolate *n* : chocolate that contains added sugar

sweet clover *n* : any of a genus (*Melilotus*) of erect legumes widely grown for soil improvement or hay

sweet corn *n* : an Indian corn (esp. *Zea mays saccharata*) with kernels containing a high percentage of sugar and adapted for table use when in the milk stage

sweet·en \ˈswēt-ᵊn\ *vb* **sweet·en·ing** \ˈswēt-niŋ, -ᵊn-iŋ\ *vt* 1 : to make sweet 2 : to soften the mood or attitude of 3 : to make less painful or trying 4 : to free from a harmful or undesirable quality or substance 5 : to make more valuable or attractive: as a : to add poker chips to (a pot not won on the previous deal) prior to another deal b : to place additional securities as collateral for (a loan) ~ *vi* : to become sweet — **sweet·en·er** \ˈswēt-nər, -ᵊn-ər\ *n*

sweet·en·ing *n* 1 : the act or process of making sweet 2 : something that sweetens

sweet fern *n* 1 : any of several ferns (genus *Dryopteris*) 2 : a small No. American shrub (*Comptonia peregrina*) of the wax-myrtle family with sweet-scented or aromatic leaves

sweet flag *n* : a perennial marsh herb (*Acorus calamus*) of the arum family with long leaves and a pungent rootstock

sweet·heart \ˈswēt-ˌhärt\ *n* 1 : DARLING 2 : one who is loved : LOVER

sweetheart neckline *n* : a neckline for women's clothing that is high in back and low in front where it is scalloped to resemble the top of a heart

sweet·ie \ˈswēt-ē\ *n* 1 *pl, Brit* : SWEET 1a 2 : SWEETHEART

sweetie pie *n* : SWEETHEART

sweet·ing \ˈswēt-iŋ\ *n* 1 *archaic* : SWEETHEART 2 : a sweet apple

sweet·ish \-ish\ *adj* 1 : somewhat sweet 2 : unpleasantly sweet — **sweet·ish·ly** *adv*

sweet marjoram *n* : an aromatic European herb (*Majorana hortensis*) with dense spikelike flower clusters

sweet·meat \ˈswēt-ˌmēt\ *n* : a food rich in sugar: as a : a candied or crystallized fruit b : CANDY, CONFECTION

sweet oil *n* : a mild edible oil (as olive oil)

sweet pea *n* : a garden plant (*Lathyrus odoratus*) having slender climbing stems and large fragrant flowers

sweet pepper *n* : a large mild thick-walled capsicum fruit; *also* : a pepper plant bearing this fruit

sweet potato *n* 1 : a tropical vine (*Ipomoea batatas*) related to the morning glory with variously shaped leaves and purplish flowers; *also* : its large thick sweet and mealy tuberous root that is cooked and eaten as a vegetable 2 : OCARINA

sweet·shop \ˈswēt-ˌshäp\ *n, chiefly Brit* : a candy store

sweet·sop \-ˌsäp\ *n* : a tropical American tree (*Annona squamosa*) of the custard-apple family; *also* : its edible sweet pulpy fruit with thick green scaly rind and shining black seeds

sweet sorghum *n* : SORGO

sweet–talk \ˈswēt-ˌtȯk\ *vt* : BLANDISH, COAX ~ *vi* : to use flattery

sweet tooth *n* : a craving or fondness for sweet food

sweet wil·liam \swēt-ˈwil-yəm\ *n, often cap W* [fr. the name *William*] : a widely cultivated Eurasian pink (*Dianthus barbatus*) with small white to deep red or purple flowers often showily spotted, banded, or mottled and borne in flat bracteate heads on erect stalks

1swell \ˈswel\ *vb* **swelled** *or* **swol·len** \ˈswō-lən, *esp before vowels or in poetry* ˈswōln\ **swell·ing** [ME *swellen*, fr. OE *swellan*; akin to OHG *swellan* to swell] *vi* 1 a : to expand abnormally; *specif* : to puff up by internal pressure or growth b : to increase in size, number, or intensity c : to form a bulge or rounded elevation 2 a : to become filled with pride and arrogance b : to behave or speak in a pompous, blustering, or self-important manner c : to play the swell 3 : to become distended with emotion ~ *vt*

1 **:** to affect with a powerful or expansive emotion **2 :** to increase the size, number, or intensity of **syn** see EXPAND

2swell *n* **1 a :** the condition of being protuberant **b :** a rounded elevation **2 :** a long often massive crestless wave or succession of waves continuing beyond or after its cause (as a gale) **3 a :** the act or process of swelling **b** (1) **:** a gradual increase and decrease of the loudness of a musical sound; *also* **:** a sign <> indicating a swell (2) **:** a device used in an organ for governing loudness **4 a** *archaic* **:** an impressive, pompous, or fashionable air or display **b :** a person dressed in the height of fashion **c :** a person of high social position or outstanding competence

3swell *adj* **1 a :** STYLISH **b :** socially prominent **2 :** EXCELLENT — used as a generalized term of enthusiasm

swell box *n* **:** a chamber in an organ containing a set of pipes and having shutters that open or shut to regulate the volume of tone

swell–but·ted \\'bət-əd\\ *adj, of a tree* **:** greatly enlarged at the base

swelled head *n* **:** an exaggerated opinion of oneself **:** SELF-CONCEIT — **swelled–head·ed** \\'sweld-'hed-əd\\ *adj* — **swelled–head·ed·ness** *n*

swell·fish \\'swel-,fish\\ *n* **:** GLOBEFISH

swell·head \\-,hed\\ *n* **:** one who has a swelled head **:** a conceited person — **swell·head·ed** \\-'hed-əd\\ *adj* — **swell·head·ed·ness** *n*

swell·ing \\'swel-iŋ\\ *n* **1 :** something that is swollen; *specif* **:** an abnormal bodily protuberance or localized enlargement **2 :** the condition of being swollen

1swel·ter \\'swel-tər\\ *vb* **swel·ter·ing** \\-t(ə-)riŋ\\ [ME *sweltren*, freq. of *swelten* to die, be overcome by heat, fr. OE *sweltan* to die; akin to OHG *swelzan* to burn up and prob. to OE *swelan* to burn] *vi* **:** to suffer, sweat, or be faint from heat ∼ *vt* **1 :** to oppress with heat **2** *archaic* **:** EXUDE ⟨∼*ed* venom —Shak.⟩

2swelter *n* **1 :** a state of oppressive heat **2 :** WELTER **3 :** an excited or overwrought state of mind **:** SWEAT ⟨in a ∼⟩

swel·ter·ing *adj* **:** oppressively hot — **swel·ter·ing·ly** \\-t(ə-)riŋ-lē\\ *adv*

swept \\'swept\\ *adj* [*swept*, pp. of *sweep*] **:** slanted backward ⟨∼ airplane wing⟩

swept–back \\'swep(t)-'bak\\ *adj* **:** possessing sweepback

1swerve \\'swərv\\ *vb* [ME *swerven*, fr. OE *sweorfan* to wipe, file away; akin to OHG *swerban* to wipe off, Gk *syrein* to drag] *vi* **:** to turn aside abruptly from a straight line or course **:** DEVIATE ∼ *vt* **:** to cause to turn aside or deviate

syn SWERVE, VEER, DEVIATE, DEPART, DIGRESS, DIVERGE mean to turn aside from a straight course. SWERVE may suggest a physical, mental, or moral turning away from a given course, often with abruptness; VEER implies a large change in direction; DEVIATE implies a turning from a customary or prescribed course; DEPART suggests a deviation from a traditional or conventional course or type; DIGRESS applies to a departing from the subject of one's discourse; DIVERGE may equal DEPART but usu. suggests a branching of a main path into two or more leading in different directions

2swerve *n* **:** an act or instance of swerving

swev·en \\'swev-ən\\ *n* [ME, fr. OE *swefn* sleep, dream, vision — more at SOMNOLENT] *archaic* **:** DREAM, VISION

1swift \\'swift\\ *adj* [ME, fr. OE; akin to OE *swīfan* to revolve — more at SWIVEL] **1 :** moving or capable of moving with great speed **2 :** occurring suddenly or within a very short time **3 :** quick to respond **:** READY **syn** see FAST — **swift·ly** *adv* — **swift·ness** \\'swif(t)-nəs\\ *n*

2swift *adv* **:** SWIFTLY ⟨*swift*-flowing⟩

3swift *n* **1 :** any of several lizards (esp. of the genus *Sceloporus*) that run swiftly **2 a :** a reel for winding yarn or thread **b :** one of the large cylinders that carry forward the material in a carding machine; *also* **:** a similar cylinder in other machines **3 :** any of numerous small plainly colored birds (family Apodidae) that are related to the hummingbirds and goatsuckers but superficially much resemble swallows

1swig \\'swig\\ *n* [origin unknown] **:** a quantity drunk at one time **:** DRAFT

2swig *vb* **swigged; swig·ging** *vt* **:** to drink in long drafts ∼ *vi* **:** to take a swig **:** DRINK — **swig·ger** *n*

1swill \\'swil\\ *vb* [ME *swilen*, fr. OE *swillan*] *vt* **1 :** WASH, DRENCH **2 :** to drink great drafts of **:** GUZZLE **3 :** to feed (as a pig) with swill ∼ *vi* **1 :** to drink or eat freely, greedily, or to excess **2 :** SWASH — **swill·er** *n*

2swill *n* **1 a :** a semiliquid food for animals (as swine) composed of edible refuse mixed with water or skimmed or sour milk **b :** GARBAGE **2 :** something suggestive of slop or garbage **:** REFUSE **3 :** a draft of liquor

1swim \\'swim\\ *vb* **swam** \\'swam *also* 'swäm\\ **swum** \\'swəm\\ **swim·ming** [ME *swimmen*, fr. OE *swimman;* akin to OHG *swimman* to swim] *vi* **1 :** to propel oneself in water by natural means (as movements of the limbs, fins, or tail) **2 :** to move with a motion like that of swimming **:** GLIDE **3 a :** to float on a liquid **:** not sink **b :** to surmount difficulties **:** not go under **4 :** to become immersed or flooded with or as if with a liquid ⟨the meat ∼*s* in gravy⟩ **5 :** to have a floating or reeling appearance or sensation ∼ *vt* **1 a :** to cross by propelling oneself through water ⟨∼ a stream⟩ **b :** to execute in swimming **2 :** to cause to swim or float — **swim·mer** *n*

2swim *n* **1 :** a smooth gliding motion **2 :** an act or period of swimming **3 :** a temporary dizziness or unconsciousness **4 a :** an area frequented by fish **b :** the main current of activity ⟨be in the ∼⟩

swim bladder *n* **:** the air bladder of a fish

swim fin *n* **:** FLIPPER 1b

swim·ma·ble \\'swim-ə-bəl\\ *adj* **:** that can be swum

swim·mer·et *also* **swim·mer·ette** \\,swim-ə-'ret\\ *n* **:** one of a series of small unspecialized appendages under the abdomen of many crustaceans that are best developed in some decapods and are used in some cases for swimming but usu. for carrying eggs

swimmer's itch *n* **:** a severe urticarial reaction to the presence in the skin of schistosomes not normally parasitic in man

swim·mi·ly \\'swim-ə-lē\\ *adv* **:** in a swimmy manner

swim·mi·ness \\'swim-ē-nəs\\ *n* **:** the quality or state of being swimmy

swim·ming *adj* **1 :** that swims **2 :** adapted to or used in or for swimming

swim·ming·ly \\-iŋ-lē\\ *adv* **:** very well **:** SPLENDIDLY

swim·my \\'swim-ē\\ *adj* **1 :** verging on, causing, or affected by dizziness or giddiness **2** *of vision* **:** BLURRED, UNSTEADY

swim·suit \\'swim-,süt\\ *n* **:** a suit for swimming or bathing

1swin·dle \\'swin-dᵊl\\ *vb* **swin·dling** \\-(d)liŋ, -dᵊl-iŋ\\ [back-formation fr. *swindler*, fr. G *schwindler* giddy person, fr. *schwindeln* to be dizzy, fr. OHG *swintilōn*, freq. of *swintan* to diminish, vanish; akin to OE *swindan* to vanish, OIr *a-sennad* finally] *vi* **:** to obtain money or property by fraud or deceit ∼ *vt* **1 :** to take money or property from by fraud or deceit **2 :** to get by fraud or deceit **syn** see CHEAT — **swin·dler** \\-(d)lər, -dᵊl-ər\\ *n*

2swindle *n* **:** an act or instance of swindling **:** FRAUD

swine \\'swīn\\ *n, pl* **swine** [ME, fr. OE *swīn;* akin to OHG *swīn* swine, L *sus* — more at SOW] **1 :** any of various stout-bodied short-legged omnivorous mammals (family Suidae) with a thick bristly skin and a long mobile snout; *esp* **:** a domesticated member of the species (*Sus scrofa*) that includes the European wild boar — usu. used collectively **2 :** a contemptible person

swine·herd \\-,hərd\\ *n* **:** one who tends swine

1swing \\'swiŋ\\ *vb* **swung** \\'swəŋ\\ **swing·ing** \\'swiŋ-iŋ\\ [ME *swingen* to beat, fling, hurl, rush, fr. OE *swingan* to beat, fling oneself, rush; akin to OHG *swingan* to fling, rush] *vt* **1 a :** to wield with a sweep or flourish ⟨∼ an axe⟩ **b :** to cause to sway to and fro **c** (1) **:** to cause to turn on an axis (2) **:** to cause to face or move in another direction **2 :** to suspend so as to permit swaying or turning **3 :** to convey by suspension **4 a** (1) **:** to influence decisively ⟨∼ a lot of votes⟩ (2) **:** to bring around by influence **b :** to handle successfully **:** MANAGE **5 :** to play or sing (as a melody) in the style of swing music ∼ *vi* **1 :** to move freely to and fro esp. in suspension from an overhead support **2 a :** to die by hanging **b :** to hang freely from a support **3 :** to move in or describe a circle or arc: **a :** to turn on a hinge or pivot **b :** to turn in place **c :** to convey oneself by grasping a fixed support ⟨∼ aboard the train⟩ **4 a :** to have a steady pulsing rhythm **b :** to play or sing with a lively compelling rhythm; *specif* **:** to play swing music **5 :** to shift or fluctuate from one condition, form, position, or object of attention or favor to another **6 a :** to move along rhythmically **b :** to start up in a smooth vigorous manner **7 :** to hit or aim at something with a sweeping arm movement **8 :** to be lively and up-to-date — **swing·able** \\'swiŋ-ə-bəl\\ *adj* — **swing·ably** \\-blē\\ *adv*

syn SWING, WAVE, FLOURISH, BRANDISH, THRASH mean to wield or cause to move to and fro or up and down. SWING implies regularity or periodicity of movement; WAVE usu. implies smooth or continuous motion; FLOURISH suggests vigorous, ostentatious, graceful movement; BRANDISH implies threatening or menacing motion; THRASH suggests vigorous, abrupt, violent movement

syn SWING, SWAY, OSCILLATE, VIBRATE, FLUCTUATE, WAVER, UNDULATE mean to move from one direction to its opposite. SWING implies a movement of something attached at one end or one side; SWAY implies a slow swinging or teetering movement; OSCILLATE stresses a usu. rapid alternation of direction; VIBRATE suggests the rapid oscillation of an elastic body under stress or impact; FLUCTUATE suggests constant irregular changes of level, intensity, or value; WAVER stresses irregular motion suggestive of reeling or tottering; UNDULATE suggests a gentle rise and fall as of a fairly calm sea

2swing *n* **1 :** an act or instance of swinging **:** swinging movement: as **a** (1) **:** a stroke or blow delivered with a sweeping arm movement (2) **:** a sweeping or rhythmic movement of the body or a bodily part (3) **:** a dance figure in which two dancers revolve with joined arms or hands (4) **:** jazz dancing in moderate tempo with a lilting syncopation **b** (1) **:** the regular movement of a freely suspended object (as a pendulum) along an arc and back (2) **:** back and forth sweep ⟨the ∼ of the tides⟩ **c** (1) **:** steady pulsing rhythm (as in poetry or music) (2) **:** a steady vigorous movement characterizing an activity or creative work **d** (1) **:** a trend toward a high or low point in a fluctuating cycle (as of business activity) (2) **:** an often periodic shift from one condition, form, position, or object of attention or favor to another **2 a :** liberty of action **:** free scope **b** (1) **:** the driving power of something swung or hurled (2) **:** steady vigorous advance **:** driving speed ⟨a train approaching at full ∼⟩ **3 :** the progression of an activity, process, or phase of existence ⟨the work is in full ∼⟩ **4 :** the arc or range through which something swings **5 :** something that swings freely from or on a support; *esp* **:** a seat suspended by a rope or chains for swinging to and fro on for pleasure **6 a :** a curving course or outline **b :** a course from and back to a point **:** a circular tour **7 :** music (as for a dance band) characterized by a lively insistent rhythm, a basic melody often submerged in improvisation, and a collective use of syncopated rhythms — **swing** *adj*

1swinge \\'swinj\\ *vt* **swinged; swinge·ing** [ME *swengen* to shake, fr. OE *swengan;* akin to OE *swingan*] *chiefly dial* **:** BEAT, SCOURGE

2swinge *vt* **swinged; swinge·ing** [alter. of *singe*] *dial* **:** SINGE, SCORCH

1swinge·ing *or* **swing·ing** \\'swin-jiŋ\\ *adj* [fr. prp. of 1*swinge*] *chiefly Brit* **:** superlative in size, amount, or character

2swingeing *or* **swinging** *adv, chiefly Brit* **:** SUPERLATIVELY, VERY

1swing·er \\'swiŋ-ər\\ *n* **:** one that swings

2swing·er \\'swin-jər\\ *n* [1*swinge*] **:** WHOPPER

1swing·ing·ly \\'swin-jiŋ-lē\\ *adv, chiefly Brit* **:** SWINGEING

2swing·ing·ly \\'swiŋ-iŋ-lē\\ *adv* **:** in a swinging manner **:** with a swinging movement

swin·gle·tree \\'swiŋ-gəl-(,)trē\\ *n* [*swingle* (cudgel) + *tree*] **:** WHIFFLETREE

swing shift *n* **:** the work shift between the day and night shifts (as from 4 P.M. to midnight)

swingy \\'swiŋ-ē\\ *adj* **:** marked by swing

swin·ish \\'swī-nish\\ *adj* **:** of, suggesting, or befitting swine **:** BEASTLY — **swin·ish·ly** *adv* — **swin·ish·ness** *n*

1swink \\'swiŋk\\ *vi* [ME *swinken*, fr. OE *swincan;* akin to OHG *swingan* to rush — more at SWING] *archaic* **:** TOIL, SLAVE

2swink *n, archaic* **:** LABOR, DRUDGERY

1swipe \\'swīp\\ *n* [prob. alter. of *sweep*] **1 :** a strong sweeping blow **2 :** one who takes care of horses **:** GROOM

2swipe *vi* **:** to strike with a sweeping motion ∼ *vt* **1 :** to strike or wipe with a sweeping motion **2 :** SNATCH, PILFER

swipes \\'swīps\\ *n pl* [origin unknown] *Brit* **:** poor, thin, or spoiled beer; *also* **:** BEER

1swirl \\'swər(-ə)l\\ *n* [ME (Sc)] **1 a :** a whirling mass or motion **:** EDDY **b :** whirling confusion **2 :** a twisting shape or mark

2swirl *vi* **1 a :** to move with an eddying or whirling motion **b :** to pass in whirling confusion **2 :** to have a twist or convolution ∼ *vt* **:** to cause to swirl — **swirl·ing·ly** \\'swər-liŋ-lē\\ *adv*

swirly \\'swər-lē\\ *adj* **1** *Scot* **:** KNOTTED, TWISTED **2 :** SWIRLING

¹**swish** \'swish\ vb [imit.] : to move, cut, or strike with a swish — **swish·er** n — **swish·ing·ly** \-iŋ-lē\ adv

²**swish** n 1 a : a prolonged hissing sound (as of a whip cutting the air) b : a light sweeping or brushing sound (as of a full silk skirt in motion) 2 : a swishing movement

³**swish** adj [origin unknown] : SMART, FASHIONABLE

swishy \'swish-ē\ adj : producing a swishing sound

¹**Swiss** \'swis\ n [MF Suisse, fr. MHG Swīzer, fr. Swīz Switzerland] 1 pl **Swiss** a : a native or inhabitant of Switzerland b : one that is of Swiss descent 2 often not cap : any of various fine sheer fabrics of cotton made in Switzerland; esp : DOTTED SWISS 3 : a hard cheese characterized by elastic texture, mild nutlike flavor, and large holes that form during ripening

²**Swiss** adj : of, relating to, or characteristic of Switzerland or the Swiss

Swiss steak n : a slice of round steak pounded with flour, browned in fat, and smothered in vegetables and seasonings

¹**switch** \'swich\ n [perh. fr. MD swijch twig] 1 : a slender flexible whip, rod, or twig 2 : an act of switching: as a : a blow with a switch b : a shift from one to another 3 : a tuft of long hairs at the end of the tail of an animal (as a cow) 4 a : a device made usu. of two movable rails and necessary connections and designed to turn a locomotive or train from one track to another b : a railroad siding 5 : a device for making, breaking, or changing the connections in an electrical circuit 6 : a heavy strand of hair used in addition to a person's own hair for some coiffures

²**switch** vt 1 : to strike or beat with or as if with a switch 2 : WHISK, LASH 3 (1) : to turn from one railroad track to another : SHUNT (2) : to move (cars) to different positions on the same track within terminal areas b : to make a shift in or exchange of 4 a : to shift to another electrical circuit by means of a switch b : to operate an electrical switch so as to turn off or on ~ vi 1 : to lash from side to side 2 : to make a shift or exchange — **switch·er** n

switch·back \'swich-,bak\ n : a zigzag road in a mountainous region; specif : an arrangement of zigzag railroad tracks for surmounting the grade of a steep hill

switch·blade knife \,swich-,blād-\ n : a pocketknife having the blade spring-operated so that pressure on a release catch causes it to fly open

switch·board \'swich-,bō(ə)rd, -,bo(ə)rd\ n : an apparatus consisting of a panel or a frame on which are mounted insulated switching, measuring, controlling, and protective devices with connections so arranged that a number of circuits may be connected, combined, controlled, measured, and protected

switch cane n : an important forage grass (Arundinaria tecta) of moist locations esp. in the southern U. S.

switch·er·oo \,swich-ə-'rü\ n [alter. of switch] slang : a surprising variation : REVERSAL

switch-hit·ter \'swich-'hit-ər\ n : a baseball player who can bat either left-handed or right-handed

switch knife n : SWITCHBLADE KNIFE

switch·man \'swich-mən\ n : one who attends a switch (as in a railroad yard)

switch·yard \-,yärd\ n : a place where railroad cars are switched from one track to another and trains are made up

swith \'swith\ adv [ME, strongly, quickly, fr. OE swīthe strongly, fr. swīth strong; akin to OE gesund sound — more at SOUND] chiefly dial : INSTANTLY, QUICKLY

¹**swith·er** \'swith-ər\ vi [origin unknown] dial chiefly Brit : DOUBT, WAVER, HESITATE

²**swither** n, dial chiefly Brit : DOUBT, AGITATION

Swit·zer \'swit-sər\ n [MHG Swīzer] : SWISS

¹**swiv·el** \'swiv-əl\ n [ME; akin to OE swīfan to revolve, ON sveigja to sway — more at SWAY] : a device joining two parts so that one or both can pivot freely (as on a bolt or pin)

²**swivel** vb **swiv·eled** or **swiv·elled**; **swiv·el·ing** or **swiv·el·ling** \-(ə-)liŋ\ : to turn on or as if on a swivel

swivel chair n : a chair that swivels on its base

swiv·et \'swiv-ət\ n [origin unknown] : a state of extreme agitation : TIZZY (in a ~)

¹**swiz·zle** \'swiz-əl\ n [origin unknown] : a cocktail consisting of a spirituous liquor, lime or lemon juice, bitters, and sugar churned in ice in a pitcher until the surface is frothed

²**swizzle** vb **swiz·zling** \-(ə-)liŋ\ vi : to drink esp. to excess : GUZZLE ~ vt : to mix or stir with or as if with a swizzle stick — **swiz·zler** \-(ə-)lər\ n

swizzle stick n : a stick used to stir mixed drinks

swob var of SWAB

swollen past part of SWELL

¹**swoon** \'swün\ vi [ME swounen] 1 a : FAINT b : to become enraptured 2 : FLOAT, FADE — **swoon·er** n — **swoon·ing·ly** \'swü-niŋ-lē\ adv

²**swoon** n 1 a : a partial or total loss of consciousness b : DAZE, RAPTURE 2 : a languorous drift

¹**swoop** \'swüp\ vb [alter. of ME swopen to sweep, fr. OE swāpan; akin to ON svatha to swathe — more at SWATHE] vi : to move with a sweep; specif : to make a sudden attack ~ vt : to carry off abruptly : SWEEP — **swoop·er** n

²**swoop** n : an act or instance of swooping

swoop·stake \-,stāk\ adv [fr. alter. of sweepstake] obs : INDISCRIMINATELY

¹**swoosh** \'swüsh, 'swùsh\ vb [imit.] vi 1 : to make or move with a rushing sound 2 : GUSH, SWIRL ~ vt : to discharge or transport with a rushing sound

²**swoosh** n : an act or instance of swooshing

swop var of SWAP

sword \'sō(ə)rd, 'so(ə)rd\ n, often attrib [ME, fr. OE sweord; akin to OHG swert sword, Av xvara wound] 1 : a weapon (as a cutlass, rapier) with a long blade for cutting or thrusting often used as a symbol of honor or authority 2 a : an agency or instrument of destruction or combat b : the use of force (as in war) 3 : coercive power 4 : something that resembles a sword — **sword·like** \-,līk\ adj — **at swords' points** : mutually antagonistic

sword cane n : a cane concealing a sword or dagger blade

sword dance n 1 : a dance executed by men holding swords in a ring 2 : a dance performed over or around swords — **sword dancer** n

sword fern n : any of several ferns with long narrow more or less sword-shaped fronds

sword·fish \'sō(ə)rd-,fish, 'so(ə)rd-\ n : a very large oceanic food fish (Xiphias gladius) having a long swordlike beak formed by the bones of the upper jaw

sword grass n : any of various grasses or sedges having leaves with a sharp or toothed edge

sword knot n : an ornamental cord or tassel tied to the hilt of a sword

sword·play \-,plā\ n 1 : the art or skill of wielding a sword esp. in fencing 2 : an exhibition of swordplay — **sword·play·er** n

swords·man \'sō(ə)rdz-mən, 'so(ə)rdz-\ n 1 : one skilled in swordplay; esp : a saber fencer 2 archaic : a soldier armed with a sword

swords·man·ship \-,ship\ n : SWORDPLAY

sword·tail \'sō(ə)rd-,tāl, 'so(ə)rd-\ n : a small brightly marked Central American topminnow (Xiphophorus helleri) often kept in the tropical aquarium and bred in many colors

swore past of SWEAR

sworn past part of SWEAR

¹**swot** \'swät\ n [alter. of sweat] Brit : GRIND 2b

²**swot** vi **swot·ted**; **swot·ting** Brit : GRIND 4

¹**swound** \'swaùnd, 'swünd\ n [ME, alter. of swoun swoon, fr. swounen to swoon] archaic : SWOON 1a

²**swound** vi, archaic : SWOON

swum past part of SWIM

swung past of SWING

swung dash n : a character ~ used in printing to conserve space by representing part or all of a previously spelled out word

Syb·a·rite \'sib-ə-,rīt\ n 1 : a native or resident of the ancient city of Sybaris 2 [fr. the notorious luxury of the Sybarites] often not cap : VOLUPTUARY, SENSUALIST — **Syb·a·rit·ic** \,sib-ə-'rit-ik\ adj — **Syb·a·rit·i·cal·ly** \-i-k(ə-)lē\ adv — **Syb·a·rit·ism** \'sib-ə-,rīt-,iz-əm\ n

syc·a·mine \'sik-ə-,mīn, -mən\ n [L sycaminus, fr. Gk sykaminos, of Sem origin; akin to Heb shiqmāh mulberry tree, sycamore] : MULBERRY 1

syc·a·more \'sik-ə-,mō(ə)r, -,mo(ə)r\ n [ME sicamour, fr. MF sicamor, fr. L sycomorus, fr. Gk sykomoros, prob. modif. of a Sem word akin to Heb shiqmāh sycamore] 1 : a tree (Ficus sycomorus) of Egypt and Asia Minor that is the sycamore of Scripture, is useful as a shade tree, and has sweet and edible fruit similar but inferior to the common fig 2 : a Eurasian maple (Acer pseudo-platanus) with long racemes of showy yellow flowers that is widely planted as a shade tree 3 : ²PLANE; esp : a very large spreading tree (Platanus occidentalis) of eastern and central No. America with 3- to 5-lobed broadly ovate leaves

syce \'sīs\ n [Hindi sā'is, fr. Ar] : an attendant esp. in India

sy·cee \'sī-,sē\ n [Chin (Cant) saì sz, lit., fine silk] : silver money formerly used in China and made in the form of ingots measured by weight and usu. stamped

sy·co·ni·um \sī-'kō-nē-əm\ n, pl **sy·co·nia** \-nē-ə\ [NL, fr. Gk sykon fig + NL -ium] : a collective fleshy fruit in which the ovaries are borne within an enlarged succulent concave or hollow receptacle

syc·o·phan·cy \'sik-ə-fən-sē\ n : obsequious flattery : TOADYING; also : the character or behavior of a sycophant

syc·o·phant \-fənt\ n [L sycophanta informer, swindler, sycophant, fr. Gk sykophantēs informer] : a servile self-seeking flatterer : PARASITE — **sycophant** adj — **syc·o·phan·tic** \,sik-ə-'fant-ik\ adj — **syc·o·phan·ti·cal·ly** \-i-k(ə-)lē\ adv

syc·o·phant·ish \,sik-ə-'fant-ish; 'sik-ə-,fant-ish, -fənt-\ adj : SYCOPHANTIC — **syc·o·phant·ish·ly** adv

syc·o·phant·ism \'sik-ə-fənt-,iz-əm\ n : SYCOPHANCY

syc·o·phant·ly \'sik-ə-fənt-lē\ adv : SYCOPHANTICALLY

sy·co·sis \sī-'kō-səs\ n [NL, fr. Gk sykōsis, fr. sykon fig] : a chronic inflammatory disorder of the hair follicles marked by papules, pustules, and tubercles with crusting

sy·e·nite \'sī-ə-,nīt\ n [L Syenites (lapis) stone of Syene, fr. Syene, ancient city in Egypt] : an igneous rock composed chiefly of feldspar — **sy·e·nit·ic** \,sī-ə-'nit-ik\ adj

syl·la·bar·i·um \,sil-ə-'ber-ē-əm\ n, pl **syl·la·bar·ia** \-ē-ə\ [NL] : SYLLABARY

syl·la·bary \'sil-ə-,ber-ē\ n [NL syllabarium, fr. L syllaba syllable] : a table or listing of syllables; specif : a series or set of written characters each one of which is used to represent a syllable

¹**syl·lab·ic** \sə-'lab-ik\ adj [LL syllabicus, fr. Gk syllabikos, fr. syllabē syllable] 1 : of, relating to, or denoting syllables (~ accent) 2 : constituting a syllable or the nucleus of a syllable: a of a consonant : not accompanied in the same syllable by a vowel (\n\ is ~ in \bāt°nē\ botany, nonsyllabic in \bätnē\) b of a vowel : having vowel quality more prominent than that of another vowel in the syllable (the first vowel of a falling diphthong, as \o\ in \oi\, is ~) 3 : characterized by distinct enunciation or separation of syllables 4 : of, relating to, or constituting a type of verse distinguished primarily by count of syllables rather than by rhythmical arrangement of accents or quantities — **syl·lab·i·cal·ly** \-i-k(ə-)lē\ adv

²**syllabic** n : a syllabic character or sound

syl·lab·i·ca·tion \sə-,lab-ə-'kā-shən\ n : the act, process, or method of forming or dividing words into syllables

syl·la·bic·i·ty \,sil-ə-'bis-ət-ē\ n : the state of being or the power of forming a syllable

syl·lab·i·fi·ca·tion \sə-,lab-ə-fə-'kā-shən\ n : SYLLABICATION

syl·lab·i·fy \sə-'lab-ə-,fī\ vt [L syllaba syllable] : to form or divide into syllables

¹**syl·la·ble** \'sil-ə-bəl\ n [ME, fr. MF sillabe, fr. L syllaba, fr. Gk syllabē, fr. syllambanein to gather together, fr. syn- + lambanein to take — more at LATCH] 1 : a unit of spoken language that is next bigger than a speech sound and consists of one or more vowel sounds alone or of a syllabic consonant alone or of either with one or more consonant sounds preceding or following 2 : one or more letters (as syl, la, and ble) in a word (as syl·la·ble) usu. set off from the rest of the word by a centered dot or a hyphen and

roughly corresponding to the syllables of spoken language and treated as helps to pronunciation or as guides to hyphenation at the end of a line **3 :** the smallest conceivable expression or unit of something **4 :** SOL-FA SYLLABLES

2**syllable** *vt* **syl·la·bling** \-b(ə-)liŋ\ **1 :** to give a number or arrangement of syllables to (a word or verse) **2 :** to express or utter in or as if in syllables

syl·la·bub \'sil-ə-,bəb\ *n* [origin unknown] **1 :** a drink or dessert made by curdling milk or cream with wine or other acid **2 :** a dessert of sweetened milk or cream beaten to a froth and flavored with wine or liquor

syl·la·bus \-bəs\ *n, pl* **syl·la·bi** \-,bī, -,bē\ *or* **syl·la·bus·es** [LL, alter. of L *sillybus* label for a book, fr. Gk *sillybos*] **1 :** a summary outline of a discourse, treatise, or course of study or of examination requirements **2 :** HEADNOTE **syn** see COMPENDIUM

syl·lep·sis \sə-'lep-səs\ *n, pl* **syl·lep·ses** \-'lep-,sēz\ [L, fr. Gk *syllēpsis*, fr. *syllambanein*] **:** the use of a word to modify or govern syntactically two or sometimes more words with only one of which it formally agrees in gender, number, or case — **syl·lep·tic** \-'lep-tik\ *adj*

syl·lo·gism \'sil-ə-,jiz-əm\ *n* [ME *silogisme*, fr. MF, fr. L *syllogismus*, fr. Gk *syllogismos*, fr. *syllogizesthai* to syllogize, fr. *syn-* + *logizesthai* to calculate, fr. *logos* reckoning, word — more at LEGEND] **1 :** a deductive scheme of a formal argument consisting of a major and a minor premise and a conclusion (as in "every virtue is laudable; kindness is a virtue; therefore kindness is laudable") **2 :** deductive reasoning **3 :** a subtle, specious, or crafty argument — **syl·lo·gis·tic** \,sil-ə-'jis-tik\ *adj* — **syl·lo·gis·ti·cal** \-ti-kəl\ *adj* — **syl·lo·gis·ti·cal·ly** \-ti-k(ə-)lē\ *adv*

syl·lo·gist \'sil-ə-jəst\ *n* **:** one who applies or is skilled in syllogistic reasoning

syl·lo·gize \'sil-ə-,jīz\ *vb* [ME *sylogysen*, fr. LL *syllogizare*, fr. Gk *syllogizesthai*] *vi* **:** to reason by means of syllogisms **~** *vt* **:** to deduce by syllogism

sylph \'silf\ *n* [NL *sylphus*] **1 :** an elemental being in the theory of Paracelsus inhabiting air **2 :** a slender graceful woman or girl — **sylph·like** \'sil-,flīk\ *adj*

sylph·id \'sil-fəd\ *n* **:** a young or diminutive sylph

sylva, sylviculture *var of* **:** SILVA, SILVICULTURE

1**syl·van** \'sil-vən\ *adj* [ML *silvanus*, *sylvanus*, fr. L *silva*, *sylva* wood] **1 a :** living or located in the woods or forest **b :** of, relating to, or characteristic of the woods or forest **2 a :** made, shaped, or formed of woods or trees **b :** abounding in woods, groves, or trees **:** WOODED

2**sylvan** *n* **:** one that frequents groves or woods

syl·va·nite \'sil-və-,nīt\ *n* [F *sylvanite*, fr. NL *sylvanium* tellurium, fr. *Transylvania*, region in Romania] **:** a mineral $(Au,Ag)Te_2$ consisting of a gold silver telluride and often occurring in crystals resembling written characters

syl·vat·ic \sil-'vat-ik\ *adj* [L *silvaticus* of the woods, wild — more at SAVAGE] **:** occurring in or affecting wild animals

syl·vite \'sil-,vīt\ *also* **syl·vine** \-,vēn\ *n* [F *sylvine*, fr. NL *sal digestivus Sylvii* digestive salt of Sylvius] **:** a mineral KCl consisting of potassium chloride and occurring in colorless cubes or crystalline masses

sym- — see SYN-

sym·bi·on \'sim-,bī-,än, -bē-\ *n* [NL, fr. Gk *symbiōn* (prp. of *symbioun*) or fr. Gk *symbion*, neut. of *symbios*] **:** SYMBIONT — **sym·bi·on·ic** \,sim-,bī-'än-ik, -bē-\ *adj*

sym·bi·ont \'sim-,bī-,änt, -bē-\ *n* [prob. fr. G, modif. of Gk *symbiount-*, *symbiōn*, prp. of *symbioun*] **:** an organism living in symbiosis; *esp* **:** the smaller member of a symbiotic pair — called also *symbiote* — **sym·bi·on·tic** \,sim-,bī-'änt-ik, -bē-\ *adj*

sym·bi·o·sis \,sim-,bī-'ō-səs, -bē-\ *n* [NL, fr. G *symbiose*, fr. Gk *symbiōsis* state of living together, fr. *symbioun* to live together, fr. *symbios* living together, fr. *sym-* + *bios* life — more at QUICK] **1 :** the living together in more or less intimate association or close union of two dissimilar organisms **2 :** the intimate living together of two dissimilar organisms in a mutually beneficial relationship; *esp* **:** MUTUALISM — **sym·bi·ot·ic** \-'ät-ik\ *adj* — **sym·bi·ot·i·cal·ly** \-i-k(ə-)lē\ *adv*

1**sym·bol** \'sim-bəl\ *n* [in sense 1, fr. LL *symbolum*, fr. LGk *symbolon*, fr. Gk, token, sign; in other senses fr. L *symbolus*, *symbolum* token, sign, symbol, fr. Gk, lit., token of identity verified by comparing its other half, fr. *symballein* to throw together, compare, fr. *syn-* + *ballein* to throw — more at DEVIL] **1 :** a creedal form **2 :** something that stands for or suggests something else by reason of relationship, association, convention, or accidental resemblance; *esp* **:** a visible sign of something invisible **3 :** an arbitrary or conventional sign used in writing or printing relating to a particular field to represent operations, quantities, elements, relations, or qualities **4 :** an object or act that represents a repressed complex through unconscious association **5 :** an act, sound, or object having cultural significance and the capacity to excite or objectify a response

2**symbol** *vb* **sym·boled** *or* **sym·bolled; sym·bol·ing** *or* **sym·bol·ling :** SYMBOLIZE

sym·bol·ic \sim-'bäl-ik\ *adj* **1 :** of, relating to, or constituting a symbol **2 a :** using, employing, or exhibiting a symbol **b :** consisting of or proceeding by means of symbols **3 :** characterized by or terminating in symbols ⟨~ thinking⟩ **4 :** characterized by symbolism ⟨~ dance⟩ — **sym·bol·i·cal** \-i-kəl\ *adj* — **sym·bol·i·cal·ly** \-k(ə-)lē\ *adv*

symbolic logic *n* **:** a science of developing and representing logical principles by means of symbols so as to provide an exact canon of deduction based on primitives, postulates, and rules for combining and transforming the primitives

sym·bol·ism \'sim-bə-,liz-əm\ *n* **1 :** the art or practice of using symbols esp. by investing things with a symbolic meaning or by expressing the invisible or intangible by means of visible or sensuous representations: as **a :** the use of conventional or traditional signs in the representation of divine beings and spirits **b :** artistic imitation or invention that is a method of revealing or suggesting immaterial, ideal, or otherwise intangible truth or states **2 :** a system of symbols or representations

sym·bol·ist \-ləst\ *n* **1 :** one who employs symbols or symbolism **2 :** one skilled in the interpretation or explication of symbols **3 :** one of a group of writers and artists in France after 1880 reacting against realism, concerning themselves with general truths instead of actualities, exalting the metaphysical and the mysterious, and aiming to unify and blend the arts and the functions of the senses — **symbolist** *or* **sym·bol·is·tic** \,sim-bə-'lis-tik\ *adj*

sym·bol·iza·tion \,sim-bə-lə-'zā-shən\ *n* **1 :** an act or instance of symbolizing **2 :** man's capacity to develop a system of meaningful symbols

sym·bol·ize \'sim-bə-,līz\ *vi* **:** to use symbols or symbolism **~** *vt* **1 :** to serve as a symbol of **2 :** to represent, express, or identify by a symbol — **sym·bol·iz·er** *n*

sym·bol·o·gy \sim-'bäl-ə-jē\ *n* [*symbol* + *-logy*] **1 :** the art of expression by symbols **2 :** the study or interpretation of symbols

sym·met·al·lism \(')sim-'(m)et-ᵊl-,iz-əm\ *n* [*syn-* + *-metallism* (as in *bimetallism*)] **:** a system of coinage in which the unit of currency consists of a particular weight of an amalgam of two or more metals (as gold and silver)

sym·met·ri·cal \sə-'me-tri-kəl\ *or* **sym·met·ric** \-trik\ *adj* **1 :** having, involving, or exhibiting symmetry **2 :** having corresponding points whose connecting lines are bisected by a given point or perpendicularly bisected by a given line or plane ⟨~ curves⟩ **3 :** being such that the terms may be interchanged without altering the value, character, or truth ⟨~ equations⟩ **4 a :** capable of division by a longitudinal plane into similar halves ⟨~ plant parts⟩ **b :** having the same number of members in each whorl of floral leaves ⟨~ flowers⟩ **5 :** affecting corresponding parts simultaneously and similarly ⟨~ rash⟩ **6 :** exhibiting symmetry in a structural formula; *esp* **:** being a derivative with groups substituted symmetrically in the molecule — **sym·met·ri·cal·ly** \-tri-k(ə-)lē\ *adv* — **sym·met·ri·cal·ness** \-kəl-nəs\ *n*

sym·me·tri·za·tion \,sim-ə-trə-'zā-shən\ *n* **:** the action of making symmetrical

sym·me·trize \'sim-ə-,trīz\ *vt* **:** to make symmetrical

sym·me·try \'sim-ə-trē\ *n* [L *symmetria*, fr. Gk, fr. *symmetros* symmetrical, fr. *syn-* + *metron* measure — more at MEASURE] **1 :** balanced proportions; *also* **:** beauty of form arising from balanced proportions **2 :** the property of being symmetrical; *esp* **:** correspondence in size, shape, and relative position of parts on opposite sides of a dividing line or median plane or about a center or axis

sym·pa·thec·to·my \,sim-pə-'thek-tə-mē\ *n* [ISV *sympath-* (fr. 2*sympathetic*) + *-ectomy*] **:** surgical interruption of sympathetic nerve pathways

1**sym·pa·thet·ic** \,sim-pə-'thet-ik\ *adj* [NL *sympatheticus*, fr. L *sympathia* sympathy] **1 :** existing or operating through an affinity, interdependence, or mutual association **2 a :** not discordant or antagonistic **b :** appropriate to one's mood, inclinations, or disposition **c :** marked by kindly or pleased appreciation **3 :** given to, marked by, or arising from sympathy, compassion, friendliness, and sensitivity to others' emotions **4 :** favorably inclined **:** APPROVING **5 :** showing empathy **6 a :** of or relating to the sympathetic nervous system **b :** mediated by or acting on the sympathetic nerves **7 :** relating to musical tones produced by means of sympathetic vibration or so tuned as to sound by sympathetic vibration **syn** see CONSONANT — **sym·pa·thet·i·cal·ly** \-i-k(ə-)lē\ *adv*

2**sympathetic** *n* **:** a sympathetic structure

sympathetic nervous system *n* **1** *archaic* **:** AUTONOMIC NERVOUS SYSTEM **2 :** the part of the autonomic nervous system that contains chiefly adrenergic fibers and tends to depress secretion, decrease the tone and contractility of smooth muscle, and cause the contraction of blood vessels

sympathetic strike *n* **:** SYMPATHY STRIKE

sympathetic vibration *n* **:** a vibration produced in one body by the vibrations of exactly the same period in a neighboring body

sym·pa·thin \'sim-pə-thən\ *n* [ISV, fr. 2*sympathetic*] **:** a substance that is secreted by sympathetic nerve endings and acts as a chemical mediator

sym·pa·thize \'sim-pə-,thīz\ *vi* **1 :** to react or respond in sympathy **2 :** to be in keeping, accord, or harmony **3 a :** to share in suffering or grief **:** COMMISERATE **b :** to express such sympathy **4 :** to be in sympathy intellectually — **sym·pa·thiz·er** *n*

sym·pa·tho·lyt·ic \,sim-pə-thō-'lit-ik\ *adj* [ISV *sympath*etic + *-o-* + *-lytic*] **:** tending to oppose the physiological results of sympathetic nervous activity or of sympathomimetic drugs

sym·pa·tho·mi·met·ic \,sim-pə-thō-mə-'met-ik, -thō-(,)mī-\ *adj* [ISV *sympath*etic + *-o-* + *mimetic*] **:** simulating sympathetic nervous action in physiological effect

sym·pa·thy \'sim-pə-thē\ *n* [L *sympathia*, fr. Gk *sympatheia*, fr. *sympathēs* having common feelings, sympathetic, fr. *syn-* + *pathos* feelings emotion, experience — more at PATHOS] **1 a :** an affinity, association, or relationship between persons or things wherein whatever affects one similarly affects the other **b :** mutual or parallel susceptibility or a condition brought about by it **c :** unity or harmony in action or effect **2 a :** inclination to think or feel alike **:** emotional or intellectual accord **b :** feeling of loyalty **:** tendency to favor or support ⟨republican *sympathies*⟩ **3 a :** the act or capacity of entering into or sharing the feelings or interests of another **b :** the feeling or mental state brought about by such sensitivity ⟨have ~ for the poor⟩ ⟨seek ~ from a friend⟩ **4 :** the correlation existing between bodies capable of communicating their vibrational energy to one another through some medium **syn** see ATTRACTION, PITY

sympathy strike *n* **:** a strike in which the strikers have no direct grievance against their own employer but attempt to support or aid usu. another group of workers on strike

sym·pat·ric \sim-'pa-trik\ *adj* [*syn-* + Gk *patra* fatherland, fr. *patēr* father — more at FATHER] **:** occurring in the same area; *specif* **:** occupying the same range without loss of identity from interbreeding ⟨~ species⟩ — **sym·pat·ri·cal·ly** \-tri-k(ə-)lē\ *adv* — **sym·pat·ry** \'sim-,pa-trē\ *n*

sym·pet·al·ous \(')sim-'pet-ᵊl-əs\ *adj* **:** GAMOPETALOUS — **sym·pet·aly** \-ᵊl-ē, 'sim-,\ *n*

sym·phon·ic \sim-'fän-ik\ *adj* **1 :** HARMONIOUS, SYMPHONIOUS **2 :** relating to or characteristic of a symphony or symphony orchestra **3 :** suggestive of a symphony — **sym·phon·i·cal·ly** \-i-k(ə-)lē\ *adv*

symphonic poem *n* **:** an extended programmatic composition for symphony orchestra usu. freer in form than a symphony

sym·pho·ni·ous \sim-'fō-nē-əs\ *adj* **:** agreeing esp. in sound **:** ACCORDANT — **sym·pho·ni·ous·ly** *adv*

sym·pho·nist \'sim(p)-fə-nəst\ *n* **:** a composer of symphonies

sym·pho·ny \-nē\ *n* [ME *symphonie*, fr. OF, fr. L *symphonia*, fr.

Gk *symphōnia*, fr. *symphōnos* concordant in sound, fr. *syn-* + *phōnē* voice, sound — more at BAN] **1** : consonance of sounds **2 a** : RITORNELLO 1 **b** : SINFONIA 1 **c** (1) : a usu. long and complex sonata for symphony orchestra (2) : something resembling such a symphony in complexity or variety **3** : a symphony orchestra concert

symphony orchestra *n* : a large orchestra of winds, strings, and percussion that plays symphonic works

sym·phy·se·al \,sim(p)-fə-'sē-əl\ *also* **sym·phys·i·al** \sim-'fiz-ē-əl\ *adj* [Gk *symphyse-*, *symphysis* symphysis] : of, relating to, or constituting a symphysis

sym·phy·sis \'sim(p)-fə-səs\ *n*, *pl* **sym·phy·ses** \-fə-,sēz\ [NL, fr. Gk, state of growing together, fr. *symphyesthai* to grow together, fr. *syn-* + *phyein* to make grow, bring forth — more at BE] **1** : an immovable or more or less movable articulation of various bones in the median plane of the body **2** : an articulation in which the bony surfaces are connected by pads of fibrous cartilage without a synovial membrane

sym·po·di·al \sim-'pōd-ē-əl\ *adj* [NL *sympodium* apparent main axis formed from secondary axes, fr. Gk *syn-* + *podion* base — more at -PODIUM] : having or involving the formation of an apparent main axis from successive secondary axes — **sym·po·di·al·ly** \-ə-lē\ *adv*

sym·po·si·arch \sim-'pō-zē-ärk\ *n* [Gk *symposiarchos*, fr. *symposion* symposium + *archos* -arch] : one who presides over a symposium

sym·po·si·ast \sim-'pō-zē-,ast, -əst\ *n* [Gk *symposiazein* to take part in a symposium, fr. *symposion*] **1** : BANQUETER **2** : one who contributes to a symposium

sym·po·sium \sim-'pō-zē-əm *also* -zh(ē-)əm\ *n*, *pl* **sym·po·sia** \-zē-ə, -zh(ē-)ə\ *or* **symposiums** [L, fr. Gk *symposion*, fr. *sympinein* to drink together, fr. *syn-* + *pinein* to drink — more at POTABLE] **1 a** : a drinking party esp. following a banquet **b** : a social gathering at which there is free interchange of ideas **2 a** : a meeting at which several speakers deliver short addresses on a topic or on related topics **b** : a collection of opinions on a subject; *esp* : one published by a periodical **c** : DISCUSSION

symp·tom \'sim(p)-təm\ *n* [LL *symptomat-*, *symptoma*, fr. Gk *symptōmat-*, *symptōma* happening, attribute, symptom, fr. *sympiptein* to happen, fr. *syn-* + *piptein* to fall — more at FEATHER] **1** : subjective evidence of disease or physical disturbance **2 a** : something that indicates the existence of something else **b** : a slight indication : TRACE **syn** see SIGN

symp·tom·at·ic \,sim(p)-tə-'mat-ik\ *adj* **1 a** : being a symptom of a disease **b** : having the characteristics of a particular disease but arising from another cause **2** : concerned with or affecting symptoms **3** : CHARACTERISTIC, INDICATIVE — **symp·tom·at·i·cal·ly** \-i-k(ə-)lē\ *adv*

symp·tom·atol·o·gy \,sim(p)-tə-mə-'täl-ə-jē\ *n* **1** : a branch of medical science concerned with symptoms of diseases **2** : the symptom complex of a disease

symp·tom·less \'sim(p)-təm-ləs\ *adj* : exhibiting no symptoms

syn- *or* **sym-** *prefix* [ME, fr. OF, fr. L, fr. Gk, fr. *syn* with, together with] **1** : with : along with : together \synclinal\ \sympetalous\ **2** : at the same time \synesthesia\

syn·ae·re·sis *var of* SYNERESIS

syn·aes·the·sia, syn·aes·thet·ic *var of* SYNESTHESIA, SYNESTHETIC

syn·aes·the·sis \,sin-əs-'thē-səs\ *n* [Gk *synaisthēsis* joint perception, fr. *synaisthanesthai* to perceive simultaneously, fr. *syn-* + *aisthanesthai* to perceive — more at AUDIBLE] : harmony of different or opposing impulses produced by a work of art

syn·a·gog·al \sin-i-'gäg-əl\ *adj* : of, relating to, or performed in a synagogue

syn·a·gogue *or* **syn·a·gog** \'sin-i-,gäg\ *n* [ME *synagoge*, fr. OF, fr. LL *synagoga*, fr. Gk *synagōgē* assembly, synagogue, fr. *synagein* to bring together, fr. *syn-* + *agein* to lead — more at AGENT] **1** : a Jewish congregation **2** : the house of worship and communal center of a Jewish congregation

syn·a·loe·pha *or* **syn·a·le·pha** \sin-ə-'lē-fə\ *n* [NL, fr. Gk *synaloiphē*, fr. *synaleiphein* to clog up, coalesce, unite two syllables into one, fr. *syn-* + *aleiphein* to anoint, besmear] : the reduction to one syllable of two vowels of adjacent syllables (as in *th' army*, for *the army*)

¹syn·apse \'sin-,aps, sə-'naps\ *n* [NL *synapsis*, fr. Gk, juncture, fr. *synaptein* to fasten together, fr. *syn-* + *haptein* to fasten] : the point at which a nervous impulse passes from one neuron to another

²synapse *vi* : to form a synapse or come together in synapsis

syn·ap·sis \sə-'nap-səs\ *n* [NL, fr. Gk, juncture] **1** : the process of association of homologous chromosomes with chiasma formation characteristic of the first meiotic prophase and the mechanism for crossing-over **2** : SYNAPSE — **syn·ap·tic** \-'nap-tik\ *adj*

syn·ar·thro·di·al \,sin-(,)är-'thrōd-ē-əl\ *adj* [NL *synarthrodia* synarthrosis] : of, relating to, or being a synarthrosis — **syn·ar·thro·di·al·ly** \-ē-ə-lē\ *adv*

syn·ar·thro·sis \-'thrō-səs\ *n* [Gk *synarthrōsis*, fr. *syn-* + *arthrōsis* arthrosis] : an immovable articulation in which the bones are united by intervening fibrous connective tissues

¹sync \'siŋk\ *n* : SYNCHRONIZATION, SYNCHRONISM — **sync** *adj*

²sync *vb* **synced** \'siŋ(k)t\ **sync·ing** \'siŋ-kiŋ\ : SYNCHRONIZE

syn·car·pous \(')sin-'kär-pəs\ *adj* : having the carpels of the gynoecium united in a compound ovary — **syn·car·py** \'sin-,kär-pē\ *n*

¹syn·chro \'siŋ-(,)krō, 'sin-\ *n* [*synchronous*] : SELSYN

²synchro *adj* [*synchro-*] : adapted to synchronization; *specif* : SYNCHROMESH

synchro- *comb form* [*synchronized* & *synchronous*] : synchronized : synchronous \synchroflash\ \synchromesh\

syn·chro–cy·clo·tron \,siŋ-(,)krō-'sī-klə-,trän, ,sin-\ *n* : a modified cyclotron that achieves greater energies for the charged particles by compensating for the variation in mass that the particles experience with increasing velocity

syn·chro·flash \'siŋ-krō-,flash, 'sin-\ *adj* : employing or produced with a mechanism that fires a flash lamp the instant the camera shutter opens

syn·chro·mesh \-,mesh\ *adj* : designed for effecting synchronized shifting of gears — **synchromesh** *n*

syn·chro·nal \'siŋ-krən-°l, 'sin-\ *adj* : SYNCHRONOUS

syn·chron·ic \sin-'krän-ik, siŋ-\ *adj* **1** : SYNCHRONOUS **2 a** : DESCRIPTIVE 4 \~ linguistics\ **b** : concerned with the complex of events existing in a limited time period and ignoring historical antecedents — **syn·chron·i·cal** \-i-kəl\ *adj* — **syn·chron·i·cal·ly** \-k(ə-)lē\ *adv*

syn·chro·nism \'siŋ-krə-,niz-əm, 'sin-\ *n* **1** : the quality or state of being synchronous : SIMULTANEOUSNESS **2** : chronological arrangement of historical events and personages so as to indicate coincidence or coexistence; *also* : a table showing such concurrences — **syn·chro·nis·tic** \,siŋ-krə-'nis-tik, ,sin-\ *adj*

syn·chro·ni·za·tion \,siŋ-krə-nə-'zā-shən, ,sin-\ *n* : the act or result of synchronizing

syn·chro·nize \'siŋ-krə-,nīz, 'sin-\ *vi* : to happen at the same time ~ *vt* **1** : to represent or arrange (events) to indicate coincidence or coexistence **2** : to make synchronous in operation **3** : to make (motion picture sound) exactly simultaneous with the action — **syn·chro·niz·er** *n*

syn·chro·nous \'siŋ-krə-nəs, 'sin-\ *adj* [LL *synchronos*, fr. Gk, fr. *syn-* + *chronos* time] **1** : happening, existing, or arising at the same time **2** : recurring or operating at exactly the same periods **3** : involving or indicating synchronism **4** : having the same period; *also* : having the same period and phase **syn** see CONTEMPORARY — **syn·chro·nous·ly** *adv* — **syn·chro·nous·ness** *n*

synchronous motor *n* : an electric motor having a speed strictly proportional to the frequency of the operating current

syn·chro·ny \'siŋ-krə-nē, 'sin-\ *n* : synchronistic occurrence, arrangement, or treatment

syn·chro·scope \-,skōp\ *n* : any of several devices for showing whether two associated machines or moving parts are operating in synchronism with each other

syn·chro·tron \'siŋ-k(r)ə-,trän, 'sin-\ *n* : an apparatus for imparting very high speeds to charged particles by means of a combination of a high-frequency electric field and a low-frequency magnetic field

syn·cli·nal \sin-'klīn-°l, 'siŋ-\ *adj* [Gk *syn-* + *klinein* to lean — more at LEAN] **1** : inclined down from opposite directions so as to meet **2** : having or relating to a folded rock structure in which the sides dip toward a common line or plane

syn·cline \'sin-,klīn\ *n* [back-formation fr. *synclinal*] : a trough of stratified rock in which the beds dip toward each other from either side — compare ANTICLINE

syn·co·pal \'siŋ-kə-pəl, 'sin-\ *adj* : of, relating to, or characterized by syncope

syn·co·pate \'siŋ-kə-,pāt, 'sin-\ *vt* **1 a** : to shorten or produce by syncope \~ *suppose* to *s'pose*\ **b** : to omit (a sound or letter) in the interior of a word \~ to cut short : CLIP, ABBREVIATE **2** : to modify or affect (musical rhythm) by syncopation — **syn·co·pa·tor** \-,pāt-ər\ *n*

syn·co·pat·ed *adj* **1** : marked by or exhibiting syncopation \~ *rhythm*\ **2** : cut short : ABBREVIATED

syn·co·pa·tion \,siŋ-kə-'pā-shən, ,sin-\ *n* **1** : a temporary displacement of the regular metrical accent in music caused typically by stressing the weak beat **2** : a syncopated rhythm, passage, or dance step — **syn·co·pa·tive** \'siŋ-kə-,pāt-iv, 'sin-\ *adj*

syncopation

syn·co·pe \'siŋ-kə-(,)pē, 'sin-\ *n* [LL, fr. Gk *synkopē*, lit., cutting short, fr. *synkoptein* to cut short, fr. *syn-* + *koptein* to cut — more at CAPON] **1** : a partial or complete temporary suspension of respiration and circulation due to cerebral ischemia : FAINT **2** : the loss of one or more sounds or letters in the interior of a word (as in *fo'c's'le* for *forecastle*)

syn·cret·ic \sin-'kret-ik, siŋ-\ *adj* : characterized or brought about by syncretism : SYNCRETISTIC

syn·cre·tism \'siŋ-krə-,tiz-əm, 'sin-\ *n* [NL *syncretismus*, fr. Gk *synkrētismos* federation of Cretan cities, fr. *syn-* + *Krēt-*, *Krēs* Cretan] **1** : the combination of different forms of belief or practice **2** : the fusion of two or more orig. different inflectional forms — **syn·cre·tist** \-təst\ *n or adj* — **syn·cre·tis·tic** \,siŋ-krə-'tis-tik, ,sin-\ *adj*

syn·cy·tial \sin-'sish-əl\ *adj* : of, relating to, or constituting syncytium \~ *tissue*\

syn·cy·tium \sin-'sish-(ē-)əm\ *n*, *pl* **syn·cy·tia** \-(ē-)ə\ [NL, fr. *syn-* + *cyt-*] **1** : a multinucleate mass of protoplasm resulting from fusion of cells **2** : COENOCYTE 1

¹syn·dac·tyl *or* **syn·dac·tyle** \sin-'dak-t°l\ *adj* [F *syndactyle*, fr. Gk *syn-* + *daktylos* finger] : having two or more digits wholly or partly united — **syn·dac·ty·lism** \-'dak-tə-,liz-əm\ *n*

²syndactyl *or* **syndactyle** *n* : a syndactyl bird or mammal

syn·de·sis \'sin-də-səs\ *n* [NL, fr. Gk, action of binding together, fr. *syndein* to bind together — more at ASYNDETON] : SYNAPSIS

syn·des·mo·sis \,sin-,dez-'mō-səs, -,des-\ *n* [NL, fr. Gk *syndesmos* fastening, ligament, fr. *syndein*] : an articulation in which the contiguous surfaces of the bones are rough and are bound together by a ligament — **syn·des·mot·ic** \-'mät-ik\ *adj*

syn·det·ic \sin-'det-ik\ *adj* [Gk *syndetikos*, fr. *syndein*] : CONNECTING, CONNECTIVE \~ *pronoun*\ : marked by a conjunctive \~ *relative clause*\ — **syn·det·i·cal·ly** \-i-k(ə-)lē\ *adv*

syn·dic \'sin-dik\ *n* [F, fr. LL *syndicus* representative of a corporation, fr. Gk *syndikos* assistant at law, advocate, representative of a state, fr. *syn-* + *dikē* judgment, case at law — more at DICTION] **1** : a municipal magistrate in some countries **2** : an agent of a university or other corporation

syn·di·cal \-di-kəl\ *adj* **1** : of or relating to a syndic or to a committee that assumes the powers of a syndic **2** : of or relating to syndicalism

syn·di·cal·ism \'sin-di-kə-,liz-əm\ *n* [F *syndicalisme*, fr. *chambre syndicale* trade union] **1** : a revolutionary doctrine by which workers seize control of the economy and the government by the general strike and other direct means **2** : a system of economic organization in which industries are owned and managed by the

workers **3 :** a theory of government based on functional rather than territorial representation — **syn·di·cal·ist** \-ləst\ *adj or n*

1syn·di·cate \'sin-di-kət\ *n* [F *syndicat*, fr. *syndic*] **1 a :** the office or jurisdiction of a syndic **b :** a council or body of syndics **2 :** an association of persons officially authorized to undertake some duty or negotiate some business **3 a :** a group of persons or concerns who combine to carry out a particular transaction **b :** CARTEL 2 **c :** a loose association of racketeers in control of organized crime **4 :** a business concern that sells materials for publication in a number of newspapers or periodicals simultaneously **5 :** a group of newspapers under one management **syn** see MONOPOLY

2syn·di·cate \'sin-də-ˌkāt\ *vt* **1 :** to subject to or manage as a syndicate **2 :** to sell (as a cartoon) to a syndicate or for publication in many newspapers or periodicals at once ~ *vi* **:** to unite to form a syndicate — **syn·di·ca·tion** \ˌsin-də-'kā-shən\ *n* — **syn·di·ca·tor** \'sin-də-ˌkāt-ər\ *n*

syn·drome \'sin-ˌdrōm *also* -drəm\ *n* [NL, fr. Gk *syndromē* combination, syndrome, fr. *syn-* + *dramein* to run — more at DROMEDARY] **:** a group of signs and symptoms that occur together and characterize a particular abnormality — **syn·dro·mic** \sin-'drō-mik, -'dräm-ik\ *adj*

1syne \(')sīn\ *adv* [ME (northern), prob. fr. ON *sīthan;* akin to OE *siththan* since — more at SINCE] *chiefly Scot* **:** since then **:** AGO

2syne *conj, Scot* **:** SINCE

3syne *prep, Scot* **:** SINCE

syn·ec·do·che \sə-'nek-də-(ˌ)kē\ *n* [L, fr. Gk *synekdochē*, fr. *syn-* + *ekdochē* sense, interpretation, fr. *ekdechesthai* to receive, understand, fr. *ex* from + *dechesthai* to receive; akin to Gk *dokein* to seem good — more at EX-, DECENT] **:** a figure of speech by which a part is put for the whole (as *fifty sail* for *fifty ships*), the whole for a part (as *the smiling year* for *spring*), the species for the genus (as *cutthroat* for *assassin*), the genus for the species (as *a creature* for *a man*), or the name of the material for the thing made (as *willow* for *bat*) — **syn·ec·doch·ic** \ˌsin-ˌek-'däk-ik\ *adj* — **syn·ec·doch·i·cal** \-'däk-i-kəl\ *adj* — **syn·ec·doch·i·cal·ly** \-i-k(ə-)lē\ *adv*

syn·eco·log·ic \ˌsin-ˌek-ə-'läj-ik, -ˌē-kə-\ *adj* **:** of, relating to, or involving synecology — **syn·eco·log·i·cal** \-'läj-i-kəl\ *adj* — **syn·eco·log·i·cal·ly** \-k(ə-)lē\ *adv*

syn·ecol·o·gy \ˌsin-i-'käl-ə-jē\ *n* [G *synökologie*, fr. *syn* + *ökologie* ecology] **:** a branch of ecology that deals with the structure, development, and distribution of ecological communities

syn·eph·rine \sə-'nef-ˌrēn, -rən\ *n* [*syn-* + epin*ephrine*] **:** a crystalline sympathomimetic amine $C_9H_{13}NO_2$

syn·ere·sis \sə-'ner-ə-səs, -'nir-, *esp for 2* ˌsin-ə-'rē-\ *n* [LL *synaeresis*, fr. Gk *synairesis*, fr. *synairein* to contract, fr. *syn-* + *hairein* to take] **1 a :** the union into one syllable of two vowels ordinarily separated in pronunciation (as \'sēst\ for \'sē-əst\ *seest*) **b :** SYNIZESIS 1 **2 :** the separation of liquid from a gel caused by contraction

syn·er·get·ic \ˌsin-ər-'jet-ik\ *adj* [Gk *synergētikos*, fr. *synergein* to work with, cooperate, fr. *synergos* working together, fr. *syn-* + *ergon* work — more at WORK] **:** SYNERGIC

syn·er·gic \sə-'nər-jik\ *adj* **:** working together **:** COOPERATING — **syn·er·gi·cal·ly** \-ji-k(ə-)lē\ *adv*

syn·er·gid \sə-'nər-jəd, 'sin-ər-\ *n* [NL *synergida*, fr. Gk *synergos* working together] **:** one of two small cells lying near the micropyle of the embryo sac of a seed plant

syn·er·gism \'sin-ər-ˌjiz-əm\ *n* [NL *synergismus*, fr. Gk *synergos*] **:** cooperative action of discrete agencies such that the total effect is greater than the sum of the effects taken independently — **syn·er·gist** \-jəst\ *n*

syn·er·gis·tic \ˌsin-ər-'jis-tik\ *adj* **1 :** having the capacity to act in synergism ⟨~ drug⟩ ⟨~ muscle⟩ **2 :** of, relating to, or resembling synergism ⟨a ~ reaction⟩ ⟨a ~ effect⟩ — **syn·er·gis·ti·cal·ly** \-ti-k(ə-)lē\ *adv*

syn·er·gy \'sin-ər-jē\ *n* [NL *synergia*, fr. Gk *synergos* working together] **:** combined action or operation (as of muscles); *specif* **:** SYNERGISM

syn·e·sis \'sin-ə-səs\ *n* [NL, fr. Gk, understanding, sense, fr. *synienai* to bring together, understand, fr. *syn-* + *hienai* to send — more at JET] **:** a grammatical construction in which agreement or reference is according to sense rather than strict syntax (as *anyone* and *them* in "if anyone calls, tell them I am out")

syn·es·the·sia \ˌsin-əs-'thē-zh(ē-)ə\ *n* [NL, fr. *syn-* + *-esthesia* (as in *anesthesia*)] **:** a concomitant sensation; *esp* **:** a subjective sensation or image of a sense (as of color) other than the one (as of sound) being stimulated — **syn·es·thet·ic** \-'thet-ik\ *adj*

syn·gam·ic \sin-'gam-ik, siŋ-\ *adj* **:** of or relating to sexual reproduction

syn·ga·my \'siŋ-gə-mē\ *n* [ISV] **:** sexual reproduction by union of gametes

syn·gen·e·sis \sin-'jen-ə-səs\ *n* [NL] **1 :** sexual reproduction; *specif* **:** derivation of the zygote from both paternal and maternal substance **2 :** community of origin; *also* **:** blood relationship — **syn·ge·net·ic** \ˌsin-jə-'net-ik\ *adj*

syn·gna·thous \'siŋ-nə-thəs, sin-'nā-\ *adj* **:** having the jaws drawn out into a tubular snout

syn·i·ze·sis \ˌsin-ə-'zē-səs\ *n* [LL, fr. Gk *synizēsis*, fr. *synizein* to sit down together, collapse, blend, fr. *syn-* + *hizein* to sit down; akin to L *sidere* to sit down — more at SUBSIDE] **1 :** contraction of two syllables into one by uniting in pronunciation two adjacent vowels **2 a :** the massing of the chromatin of the nucleus preceding the maturation division **b :** SYNAPSIS

syn·kary·on \sin-'kar-ē-ˌän, -ē-ən\ *n* [NL, fr. Gk *syn-* + *karyon* nut — more at CAREEN] **:** a cell nucleus formed by the fusion of two preexisting nuclei — **syn·kary·on·ic** \ˌsin-ˌkar-ē-'än-ik\ *adj*

syn·od \'sin-əd\ *n* [LL *synodus*, fr. LGk *synodos*, fr. Gk, meeting, assembly, fr. *syn-* + *hodos* way, journey — more at CEDE] **:** COUNCIL: as **a :** the governing assembly of an Episcopal province **b :** a Presbyterian governing body ranking between the presbytery and the general assembly **c :** a regional or national organization of Lutheran congregations — **syn·od·al** \-əd-ᵊl\ *adj*

syn·od·i·cal \sə-'näd-i-kəl\ *or* **syn·od·ic** \-ik\ *adj* **1 :** SYNODAL **2** [Gk *synodikos*, fr. *synodos* meeting, conjunction] **:** relating to conjunction; *esp* **:** relating to the period between two successive conjunctions of the same celestial bodies

syn·oe·cious \sə-'nē-shəs\ *adj* [*syn-* + *-oecious* (as in *dioecious*)] **1 :** exhibiting monoecism **2 :** exhibiting or relating to synoecy — **syn·oe·cious·ly** *adv* — **syn·oe·cious·ness** *n*

syn·oe·cy \sə-'nē-sē, 'sin-ˌē-\ *n* [Gk *synoikia* community, fr. *synoikos* dwelling together, fr. *syn-* + *oikos* house — more at VICINITY] **1 :** commensalism in which the guests are indifferently tolerated by their hosts **2 :** association between two species benefiting the one without harm to the other

syn·oi·cous \sə-'nȯi-kəs\ *adj* [Gk *synoikos* dwelling together] **:** having archegonia and antheridia in the same involucre

syn·onym \'sin-ə-ˌnim\ *n* [ME *sinonyme*, fr. L *synonymum*, fr. Gk *synōnymon*, fr. neut. of *synōnymos* synonymous, fr. *syn-* + *onyma* name — more at NAME] **1 :** one of two or more words or expressions of the same language that have the same or nearly the same meaning in some or all senses **2 :** a symbolic or figurative name **:** METONYM **3 :** a taxonomic name rejected as being incorrectly applied or incorrect in form — **syn·onym·ic** \ˌsin-ə-'nim-ik\ *or* **syn·onym·i·cal** \-i-kəl\ *adj* — **syn·onym·i·ty** \-'nim-ət-ē\ *n*

syn·on·y·mist \sə-'nän-ə-məst\ *n* **:** one who lists, studies, or discriminates synonyms

syn·on·y·mize \sə-'nän-ə-ˌmīz\ *vt* **1 a :** to give or analyze the synonyms of (a word) **b :** to provide (as a dictionary) with synonymies **2 :** to demonstrate (a taxonomic name) to be a synonym

syn·on·y·mous \-məs\ *adj* **:** having the character of a synonym; *also* **:** alike in meaning or significance — **syn·on·y·mous·ly** *adv*

syn·on·y·my \-mē\ *n* **1 a :** the study or discrimination of synonyms **b :** a list or collection of synonyms often defined and discriminated from each other **2 :** the scientific names that have been used in different publications to designate a taxonomic group (as a species); *also* **:** a list of these **3 :** the quality or state of being synonymous

syn·op·sis \sə-'näp-səs\ *n, pl* **syn·op·ses** \-ˌsēz\ [LL, fr. Gk, lit., comprehensive view, fr. *synopsesthai* to be going to see together, fr. *syn-* + *opsesthai* to be going to see — more at OPTIC] **1 :** a condensed statement or outline (as of a narrative or treatise) **:** ABSTRACT **2 :** the abbreviated conjugation of a verb in one person only **syn** see ABRIDGMENT

syn·op·size \-ˌsīz\ *vt* **1 :** to make a synopsis of **2 :** EPITOMIZE

syn·op·tic \sə-'näp-tik\ *adj* [Gk *synoptikos*, fr. *synopsesthai*] **1 :** affording a general view of a whole **2 :** manifesting or characterized by comprehensiveness or breadth of view **3 :** presenting or taking the same or common view; *specif, often cap* **:** of or relating to the first three Gospels of the New Testament **4 :** relating to or displaying atmospheric and weather conditions as they exist simultaneously over a broad area — **syn·op·ti·cal** \-ti-kəl\ *adj* — **syn·op·ti·cal·ly** \-k(ə-)lē\ *adv*

syn·os·to·sis \ˌsin-(ˌ)äs-'tō-səs\ *n* [NL] **:** union of two or more separate bones to form a single bone — **syn·os·tot·ic** \-'tät-ik\ *adj*

syn·o·via \sə-'nō-vē-ə\ *n* [NL] **:** a transparent viscid lubricating fluid secreted by a membrane of an articulation, bursa, or tendon sheath — **syn·o·vi·al** \-vē-əl\ *adj*

syn·o·vi·tis \ˌsin-ə-'vīt-əs\ *n* **:** inflammation of a synovial membrane

syn·sep·al·ous \(')sin-'sep-ə-ləs\ *adj* **:** GAMOSEPALOUS

syn·tac·tic \sin-'tak-tik\ *adj* [NL *syntacticus*, fr. Gk *syntaktikos* arranging together, fr. *syntassein*] **:** of, relating to, or according to the rules of syntax or syntactics — **syn·tac·ti·cal** \-ti-kəl\ *adj* — **syn·tac·ti·cal·ly** \-k(ə-)lē\ *adv*

syn·tac·tics \-tiks\ *n pl but sing or pl in constr* **:** a branch of semiotic that deals with the formal relations between signs or expressions in abstraction from their signification and their interpreters

syn·tax \'sin-ˌtaks\ *n* [F or LL; F *syntaxe*, fr. LL *syntaxis*, fr. Gk, fr. *syntassein* to arrange together, fr. *syn-* + *tassein* to arrange — more at TACTICS] **1 :** connected or orderly system or arrangement **2 a :** the way in which words are put together to form phrases, clauses, or sentences **b :** the part of grammar dealing with this **3 :** syntactics esp. as dealing with the formal properties of languages or calculi

syn·the·sis \'sin(t)-thə-səs\ *n, pl* **syn·the·ses** \-thə-ˌsēz\ [Gk, fr. *syntithenai* to put together, fr. *syn-* + *tithenai* to put, place — more at DO] **1 a :** the composition or combination of parts or elements so as to form a whole **b :** the production of a substance by the union of elements or simpler chemical compounds or by the degradation of a complex compound **c :** the combining of often diverse conceptions into a coherent whole; *also* **:** the complex so formed **2 a :** deductive reasoning **b :** the dialectic combination of thesis and antithesis into a higher stage of truth — **syn·the·sist** \-səst\ *n*

syn·the·size \-ˌsīz\ *vt* **1 :** to combine or produce by synthesis **2 :** to make a synthesis of ~ *vi* **:** to make a synthesis — **syn·the·siz·er** *n*

1syn·thet·ic \sin-'thet-ik\ *adj* [Gk *synthetikos* of composition, component, fr. *syntithenai* to put together] **1 :** relating to or involving synthesis **2 a :** attributing to a subject a predicate that is not part of the meaning of that subject **b :** EMPIRICAL **c :** not resulting in a contradiction upon being negated **3** *of a language* **:** characterized by frequent and systematic use of inflected grammatical forms **4 a :** produced artificially **:** MAN-MADE ⟨~ dyes⟩ ⟨~ drugs⟩ ⟨~ silk⟩ **b :** devised, arranged, or fabricated for special situations to imitate or replace usual realities **c :** FACTITIOUS, BOGUS **syn** see ARTIFICIAL — **syn·thet·i·cal** \-i-kəl\ *adj* — **syn·thet·i·cal·ly** \-k(ə-)lē\ *adv*

2synthetic *n* **:** a product of chemical synthesis

synthetic resin *n* **:** RESIN 2

synthetic rubber *n* **:** RUBBER 2b

syn·the·tize \'sin(t)-thə-ˌtīz\ *vt* [*1synthetic* + *-ize*] **:** SYNTHESIZE

syn·ton·ic \sin-'tän-ik\ *adj* [Gk *syntonos* being in harmony, fr. *syn-* + *tonos* tone] **:** normally responsive and adaptive to the social or interpersonal environment — **syn·ton·i·cal·ly** \-i-k(ə-)lē\ *adv*

syphil- *or* **syphilo-** *comb form* [NL, fr. *syphilis*] **:** syphilis ⟨*syphilol*ogy⟩ ⟨*syphil*oma⟩

syph·i·lis \'sif-(ə-)ləs\ *n* [NL, fr. *Syphilus*, hero of the poem *Syphilis sive Morbus Gallicus* (*Syphilis or the French disease*) (1530) by Girolamo Fracastoro] **:** a chronic contagious usu. venereal and often congenital disease caused by a spirochete (*Treponema pallidum*) and characterized by a clinical course in three stages continued over many years — **syph·i·lit·ic** \ˌsif-ə-'lit-ik\ *adj or n*

syph·i·lol·o·gist \ˌsif-ə-'läl-ə-jəst\ *n* **:** a physician who specializes in the diagnosis and treatment of syphilis

syph·i·lol·o·gy \-jē\ *n* **:** a branch of medicine that deals with syphilis

syph·i·lo·ma \ˌsif-ə-'lō-mə\ *n* [NL] **:** a syphilitic tumor **:** GUMMA — **syph·i·lo·ma·tous** \-'läm-ət-əs, -'lōm-\ *adj*

sy·phon *var of* SIPHON

sy·ren *chiefly Brit var of* SIREN

Sy·rette \sə-'ret\ *trademark* — used for a small collapsible tube fitted with a hypodermic needle for injecting a single dose of a medicinal agent

Syr·i·ac \'sir-ē-,ak\ *n* [L *syriacus* Syrian, fr. Gk *syriakos*, fr. *Syria*, ancient country in Asia] **1** : a literary language based on an eastern Aramaic dialect and used as the literary and liturgical language by several eastern Christian churches **2** : Aramaic spoken by Christian communities — **Syriac** *adj*

sy·rin·ga \sə-'riŋ-gə\ *n* [NL, genus name, fr. Gk *syring-, syrinx* panpipe] : PHILADELPHUS

¹sy·ringe \sə-'rinj *also* 'sir-(,)inj\ *n* [ME *syring*, fr. ML *syringa*, fr. LL, injection, fr. Gk *syring-, syrinx* panpipe, tube; akin to Gk *sōlēn* pipe, Skt *tūṇava* flute] : a device used to inject fluids into or withdraw them from the body or its cavities; *esp* : a gravity device consisting of a reservoir fitted with a long rubber tube ending with an exchangeable nozzle that is used for irrigation of the vagina or bowel

syringe

²syringe *vt* : to irrigate or spray with or as if with a syringe

sy·rin·ge·al \sə-'riŋ-gē-əl, -'rin-jē-\ *adj* : of or relating to the syrinx ⟨∼ muscles⟩

sy·rin·go·my·elia \sə-,riŋ-gō-(,)mī-'ē-lē-ə\ *n* [NL, fr. Gk *syring-, syrinx* tube, fistula + NL *-myelia*] : a chronic progressive disease of the spinal cord associated with sensory disturbances, muscle atrophy, and spasticity — **sy·rin·go·my·el·ic** \-'el-ik\ *adj*

syr·inx \'sir-iŋ(k)s\ *n, pl* **sy·rin·ges** \sə-'rin-,gēz, -'rin-,jēz\ *or* **syr·inx·es 1** [LL, fr. Gk, panpipe] **2** [NL, fr. Gk, panpipe] : the vocal organ of birds that is a special modification of the lower part of the trachea or of the bronchi or of both

syr·phus fly \'sər-fəs-, 'sir-\ *n* [NL *Syrphus*, genus of flies, fr. Gk *syrphos* gnat] : any of numerous dipterous flies (family Syrphidae) that frequent flowers and sometimes have larvae that prey on plant lice

syr·up \'sər-əp, 'sir-əp, 'sə-rəp\ *n* [ME *sirup*, fr. MF *sirop*, fr. ML *syrupus*, fr. Ar *sharāb*] **1 a** : a thick sticky solution of sugar and water often flavored or medicated **b** : the concentrated juice of a fruit or plant **2** : cloying sweetness or sentimentality — **syr·upy** \-ē\ *adj*

sys·sar·co·sis \,sis-(,)är-'kō-səs\ *n* [NL, fr. Gk *syssarkōsis* condition of being overgrown with flesh, fr. *syssarkousthai* to be overgrown with flesh, fr. *syn-* + *sark-, sarx* flesh — more at SARCASM] : the junction of two or more bones by means of attached muscles

sys·tal·tic \sis-'tȯl-tik, -'tal-\ *adj* [Gk *systaltos*, (assumed) verbal of *systellein* to contract — more at SYSTOLE] : marked by regular contraction and dilatation : PULSING

sys·tem \'sis-təm\ *n* [LL *systemat-, systema*, fr. Gk *systēmat-, systēma*, fr. *synistanai* to combine, fr. *syn-* + *histanai* to cause to stand — more at STAND] **1** : a regularly interacting or interdependent group of items forming a unified whole ⟨number ∼⟩: as **a (1)** : a group of interacting bodies under the influence of related forces ⟨gravitational ∼⟩ **(2)** : an assemblage of substances that is in or tends to equilibrium ⟨thermodynamic ∼⟩ **b** : a group of body organs that together perform one or more vital functions ⟨digestive ∼⟩ **(2)** : the body considered as a functional unit **c** : a group of related natural objects or forces ⟨river ∼⟩ **d** : a group of devices or artificial objects or an organization forming a network esp. for distributing something or serving a common purpose ⟨telephone ∼⟩ ⟨heating ∼⟩ ⟨park ∼⟩ ⟨highway ∼⟩ **e** : a major division of rocks usu. larger than a series and including all formed during a period or era **f** : a form of social, economic, or political organization or practice ⟨capitalist ∼⟩ **2** : an organized set of doctrines, ideas, or principles usu. intended to explain the arrangement or working of a systematic whole ⟨Newtonian ∼ of mechanics⟩ **3 a** : an organized or established procedure : METHOD ⟨touch ∼ of typing⟩ **b** : a manner of classifying, symbolizing, or schematizing ⟨taxonomic ∼⟩ ⟨decimal ∼⟩ ⟨∼ of musical notation⟩ **4** : harmonious arrangement or pattern : ORDER ⟨bring ∼ out of confusion —Ellen Glasgow⟩ **syn** *see* METHOD

sys·tem·at·ic \,sis-tə-'mat-ik\ *adj* [LL *systematicus*, fr. Gk *systēmatikos*, fr. *systēmat-, systēma*] **1** : relating to or consisting of a system ⟨∼ error⟩ ⟨∼ thought⟩ **2** : presented or formulated as a system : SYSTEMATIZED **3 a** : methodical in procedure or plan ⟨∼ investigation⟩ ⟨∼ scholar⟩ **b** : marked by thoroughness and regularity ⟨∼ efforts⟩ **4** : of, relating to, or concerned with classification; *specif* : TAXONOMIC — **sys·tem·at·i·cal** \-i-kəl\ *adj* — **sys·tem·at·i·cal·ly** \-i-k(ə-)lē\ *adv* — **sys·tem·at·ic·ness** \-ik-nəs\ *n*

sys·tem·at·ics \-'mat-iks\ *n pl but sing in constr* **1** : the science of classification **2** : a system of classification; *also* : the classification and study of organisms with regard to their natural relationships : TAXONOMY

systematic theology *n* : a branch of theology that attempts to reduce all religious truth to statements forming a self-consistent and organized whole

sys·tem·atism \'sis-tə-mə-,tiz-əm, sis-'tem-ə-\ *n* : the practice of forming intellectual systems

sys·tem·atist \'sis-tə-mət-əst, sis-'tem-ət-\ *n* **1** : a maker or follower of a system **2** : TAXONOMIST

sys·tem·ati·za·tion \,sis-tə-mət-ə-'zā-shən, -,mat-; sis-,tem-ət-ə-\ *n* : the act or practice of systematizing

sys·tem·atize \'sis-tə-mə-,tīz\ *vt* : to make into a system : arrange methodically **syn** *see* ORDER — **sys·tem·atiz·er** *n*

sys·tem·ic \sis-'tem-ik\ *adj* : of, relating to, or common to a system; *specif* : affecting the body generally — **sys·tem·i·cal·ly** \-i-k(ə-)lē\ *adv*

systemic insecticide *n* : a substance harmless to a plant or higher animal into whose blood or sap stream it is absorbed but destructive to sucking arthropods

sys·tem·iza·tion \,sis-tə-mə-'zā-shən\ *n* : SYSTEMATIZATION

sys·tem·ize \'sis-tə-,mīz\ *vt* : SYSTEMATIZE

sys·tem·less \-təm-ləs\ *adj* : devoid of system, order, or structure

systems analysis *n* : the act, process, or profession of studying an activity (as a procedure, a business, or a physiological function) typically by mathematical means in order to determine its desired or essential end and how this may most efficiently be attained — **systems analyst** *n*

sys·to·le \'sis-tə-(,)lē\ *n* [Gk *systolē*, fr. *systellein* to contract, fr. *syn-* + *stellein* to send — more at STALL] : a rhythmically recurrent contraction; *esp* : the contraction of the heart by which the blood is forced onward and the circulation kept up — **sys·tol·ic** \sis-'täl-ik\ *adj*

sy·zy·gial \sə-'zij-(ē-)əl\ *adj* : of or relating to a syzygy

syz·y·gy \'siz-ə-jē\ *n* [LL *syzygia* conjunction, fr. Gk, fr. *syzygos* yoked together, fr. *syn-* + *zygon* yoke — more at YOKE] : the nearly straight-line configuration of three celestial bodies (as the sun, moon, and earth during a solar or lunar eclipse) in a gravitational system

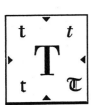

t \'tē\ *n, often cap, often attrib* **1 a :** the 20th letter of the English alphabet **b :** a graphic representation of this letter **c :** a speech counterpart of orthographic *t* **2 :** a graphic device for reproducing the letter *t* **3 :** one designated *t* esp. as the 19th or when j is used for the 10th the 20th in order or class **4 :** something shaped like the letter T — **to a T** [short for *to a tittle*] **:** to perfection ⟨suits me *to a T*⟩

't \t\ *pron* **:** IT ⟨*'t*will do⟩

ta \'tä\ *n* [baby talk] *dial Brit* **:** THANKS

Taal \'täl\ *n* [Afrik, fr. D, language; akin to OE *talu* talk — more at TALE] **:** AFRIKAANS — usu. used with *the*

¹tab \'tab\ *n, often attrib* [origin unknown] **1 a :** a short projecting device (as a flap or loop): as (1) **:** a small hand grip (2) **:** a projection from a card used as an aid in filing **b :** a small insert, addition, or remnant ⟨license plate ~⟩ **c :** APPENDAGE, EXTENSION; *esp* **:** one of a series of small pendants forming a decorative border or edge of a garment **d :** a small auxiliary airfoil hinged to a control surface (as a trailing edge) to help stabilize an airplane in flight **2** [partly short for *¹table;* partly fr. sense 1] **a :** close surveillance **:** WATCH ⟨keep ~s on him⟩ **b :** a creditor's statement **:** BILL, CHECK **3** [by shortening] **a :** TABLOID **b :** TABULATOR **c :** TABLET

²tab *vt* **tabbed; tab·bing 1 :** to furnish or ornament with tabs **2 :** to single out **:** DESIGNATE **3 :** TABULATE

ta·ba·nid \tə-'bā-nəd, -'ban-əd\ *n* [deriv. of L *tabanus* horsefly] **:** any of various large biting flies (family Tabanidae) comprising the horseflies — **tabanid** *adj*

tab·ard \'tab-ərd\ *n* [ME, fr. OF *tabart*] **1 :** a tunic worn by a knight over his armor and emblazoned with his arms **2 :** a herald's official cape or coat emblazoned with his lord's arms

Ta·bas·co \tə-'bas-(,)kō\ *trademark* — used for a pungent condiment sauce made from capsicum berries

¹tab·by \'tab-ē\ *n* [F *tabis*, fr. ML *attabi*, fr. Ar *'attābī*, fr. Al-*'Attābiya*, quarter in Baghdad] **1 a** *archaic* **:** a plain silk taffeta esp. with moiré finish **b :** a plain weave fabric **2** [*²tabby*] **a :** a domestic cat with a striped and mottled coat **b :** a domestic cat; *esp* **:** a female cat **3 a :** a prying woman **b** *chiefly Brit* **:** SPINSTER 3

²tabby *adj* **1 :** relating to or made of tabby **2 :** striped and mottled with darker color **:** BRINDLED ⟨~ cat⟩

¹tab·er·na·cle \'tab-ər-,nak-əl\ *n* [ME, fr. OF, fr. LL *tabernaculum*, fr. L, tent, dim. of *taberna* hut — more at TAVERN] **1 a** *often cap* **:** a tent sanctuary used by the Israelites during the Exodus **b** (1) **:** a dwelling place (2) *archaic* **:** the body as the temporary abode of the soul **c** *archaic* **:** a temporary shelter **:** TENT **2 :** a receptacle for the consecrated elements of the Eucharist; *esp* **:** an ornamental locked box fixed to the middle of the altar and used for reserving the host **3 :** a house of worship; *specif* **:** a building or shelter used for evangelistic services — **tab·er·nac·u·lar** \,tab-ər-'nak-yə-lər\ *adj*

²tabernacle *vi* **tab·er·na·cling** \-,nak-(ə-)liŋ\ **:** to take up temporary residence; *esp*: to inhabit a physical body

ta·bes \'tā-,bēz\ *n, pl* **tabes** [L — more at THAW] **:** wasting accompanying a chronic disease — **ta·bet·ic** \tə-'bet-ik\ *adj or n*

ta·bes dor·sa·lis \-dòr-'sal-əs, -'säl-, -'säl-\ *n* [NL, dorsal tabes] **:** a syphilitic disorder of the nervous system marked by wasting, pain, incoordination of voluntary movements and reflexes, and disorders of sensation, nutrition, and vision

tab·la·ture \'tab-lə-,chu̇(ə)r, -chər, -,t(y)u̇(ə)r\ *n* [MF, fr. ML *tabulatus* tablet, fr. L *tabula*] **:** an instrumental notation indicating the string, fret, key, or finger to be used instead of the tone to be sounded

¹ta·ble \'tā-bəl\ *n, often attrib* [ME, fr. OE *tabule* & OF *table;* both fr. L *tabula* board, tablet, list] **1 :** TABLET 1a **2 a** *pl* **:** BACKGAMMON **b :** one of the two leaves of a backgammon board or either half of a leaf **3 a :** a piece of furniture consisting of a smooth flat slab fixed on legs **b** (1) **:** a supply or source of food **:** BOARD (2) **:** an act or instance of assembling to eat **:** MEAL **c** (1) **:** a group of people assembled at or as if at a table (2) **:** a legislative or negotiating session **4 :** STRINGCOURSE **5 a :** a systematic arrangement of data usu. in rows and columns for ready reference **b :** a condensed enumeration **:** LIST **6 a :** the upper flat surface of a precious stone **b** (1) **:** TABLELAND (2) **:** a horizontal stratum

²table *vt* **ta·bling** \-b(ə-)liŋ\ **1 :** TABULATE **2 a** *Brit* **:** to place on the agenda **b :** to remove (a parliamentary motion) from consideration indefinitely **c :** to put on a table

tab·leau \'tab-,lō, ta-'blō\ *n, pl* **tab·leaux** \-,lōz, -'blōz\ *also* **tableaus** [F, fr. MF *tablel*, dim. of *table*] **1 :** a graphic description or representation **:** PICTURE **2 :** a striking or artistic grouping **3 :** a static depiction of a scene usu. presented on a stage by costumed participants

tableau curtain *n* **:** a stage curtain that opens in the center and has its sections drawn upward as well as to the side in order to produce a draped effect

ta·ble·cloth \'tā-bəl-,klòth\ *n* **:** a covering spread over a dining table before the places are set

ta·ble d'hôte \,täb-əl-'dōt, ,tab-\ *n* [F, lit., host's table] **1 :** a meal served to all guests at a stated hour and fixed price **2 :** a complete meal of several courses offered at a fixed price — compare A LA CARTE

ta·ble–hop \'tā-bəl-,häp\ *vi* **:** to move from table to table (as in a restaurant) visiting with friends — **ta·ble–hop·per** *n*

ta·ble·land \-bə(l)-,land\ *n* **:** a broad level elevated area **:** PLATEAU

table linen *n* **:** linen (as tablecloths and napkins) for the table

table salt *n* **:** salt for use at the table and in cooking; *esp* **:** SALT 1a

ta·ble·spoon \'tā-bəl-,spün\ *n* **1 :** a large spoon used for serving **2 :** TABLESPOONFUL

ta·ble·spoon·ful \,tā-bəl-'spün-,fu̇l, 'tā-bəl-,\ *n, pl* **tablespoonfuls** \-,fu̇lz\ *or* **ta·ble·spoons·ful** \-'spünz-,fu̇l, -,spünz-\ **1 :** enough to fill a tablespoon **2 :** a unit of measure used esp. in cookery equal to 4 fluidrams

tab·let \'tab-lət\ *n* [ME *tablett*, fr. MF *tablete*, dim. of *table*] **1 a :** a flat slab or plaque suited for or bearing an inscription **b :** a thin slab or one of a set of portable sheets used for writing **c :** a collection of sheets of paper glued together at one edge **2 a :** a compressed or molded block of a solid material **:** CAKE **b :** a small mass of medicated material usu. in the shape of a disk or flat square

table talk *n* **:** informal conversation at or as if at a dining table

table tennis *n* **:** a table game resembling lawn tennis played with wooden paddles and a small hollow plastic ball

ta·ble·top \'tā-bəl-,täp\ *n* **1 :** the top of a table **2 :** a photograph of small objects or a miniature scene arranged on a table — **tabletop** *adj*

ta·ble·ware \'tā-bəl-,wa(ə)r, -,we(ə)r\ *n* **:** utensils (as of china, glass, or silver) for table use

table wine *n* **:** a still wine of not more than 14 percent alcohol by volume usu. served with food

¹tab·loid \'tab-,lòid\ *adj* [fr. *Tabloid*, a trademark] **:** compressed or condensed into small scope ⟨~ criticism⟩

²tabloid *n* **1 :** a newspaper about half the page size of an ordinary newspaper containing news in condensed form and much photographic matter **2 :** DIGEST, SUMMARY

¹ta·boo *or* **ta·bu** \tə-'bü, ta-\ *adj* [Tongan *tabu*] **1 :** set apart as charged with a dangerous supernatural power and forbidden to profane use or contact **2 a :** banned on grounds of morality or taste ⟨a list of ~ songs⟩ **b :** banned as constituting a risk ⟨milk from tubercular cows is ~⟩

²taboo *or* **tabu** *n* **1 :** a prohibition instituted for the protecton of a cultural group against supernatural reprisal **2 :** a prohibition imposed by social usage or as a protective measure **3 :** belief in or observance of taboos

³taboo *or* **tabu** *vt* **1 :** to exclude from profane use or contact as sacrosanct esp. by marking with a ritualistic symbol **2 :** to avoid or ban as taboo

¹ta·bor *also* **ta·bour** \'tā-bər\ *n* [ME, fr. OF] **:** a small drum with one head of soft calfskin used to accompany a pipe or fife played by the same person

²tabor *also* **tabour** *vi, dial* **:** to beat on or as if on a drum

ta·bor·er *also* **ta·bour·er** \-bər-ər\ *n* **:** one that plays on the tabor

tab·o·ret *or* **tab·ou·ret** \,tab-ə-'ret, -'rā\ *n* [F *tabouret*, lit., small drum, fr. MF, dim. of *tabor, tabour* drum] **1 :** a cylindrical seat or stool without arms or back **2 :** a small portable stand

tab·o·rin \'tab-ə-rən\ *also* **tab·o·rine** \,tab-ə-'rēn\ *n* [MF *tabourin*, fr. OF *tabor*] **:** TABRET

ta·bret \'tab-rət, 'tā-brət\ *n* [ME *taberet*, fr. *tabor*] **:** a small tabor

tab·u·lar \'tab-yə-lər\ *adj* [L *tabularis* of boards, fr. *tabula* board, tablet] **1 :** having a flat surface **:** LAMINAR **2 a :** of, relating to, or arranged in a table; *specif* **:** set up in rows and columns **b :** computed by means of a table — **tab·u·lar·ly** *adv*

ta·bu·la ra·sa \,tab-yə-lə-'räz-ə, -'räs-\ *n, pl* **ta·bu·lae ra·sae** \-,lī-'räz-,ī, -'räs-\ [L] **:** the mind in its hypothetical primary blank or empty state before receiving outside impressions

tab·u·late \'tab-yə-,lāt\ *vt* [L *tabula* tablet] **:** to put into tabular form — **tab·u·la·tion** \,tab-yə-'lā-shən\ *n*

tab·u·la·tor \'tab-yə-,lāt-ər\ *n* **:** one that tabulates: as **a :** a business machine that sorts and selects information from marked or perforated cards **b :** a device on a typewriter or biller for arranging data in columns

tac·a·ma·hac \'tak-ə-mə-,hak\ *n* [Sp *tacamahaca*, fr. Nahuatl *tecamaca*] **1 :** any of several aromatic oleoresins used in ointments and plasters and for incense **2 :** a tree yielding tacamahac; *esp* **:** a No. American poplar (*Populus balsamifera*) with resin-coated buds — called also *balsam poplar*

tace \'tas, 'tās\ *var of* TASSE

ta·cet \'täk-,et, 'täch-,et\ *v imper* [L, lit., (it) is silent, fr. *tacēre* to be silent — more at TACIT] **:** be silent — used as a direction in music

tache *or* **tach** \'tach\ *n* [ME, fr. MF *tache* nail, of Gmc origin; akin to MD *tac* sharp point — more at TACK] **:** BUCKLE, CLASP

tach·i·na fly \,tak-ə-nə-\ *n* [NL *Tachina*, genus of flies, fr. Gk *tachinos* fleet, fr. *tachos* speed; akin to Gk *tachys* swift] **:** any of numerous bristly usu. grayish or black flies comprising a family (Tachinidae) and having parasitic larvae important in the biological control of pest insects

ta·chis·to·scope \tə-'kis-tə-,skōp\ *n* [Gk *tachistos* (superl. of *tachys* swift) + ISV *-scope*] **:** an apparatus for the brief exposure of visual stimuli

ta·chom·e·ter \ta-'käm-ət-ər, tə-\ *n* [Gk *tachos* speed + E *-meter*] **:** a device for indicating speed of rotation

tachy- *comb form* [Gk, fr. *tachys*] **:** rapid **:** accelerated ⟨*tachy*cardia⟩

tachy·car·dia \,tak-i-'kärd-ē-ə\ *n* [NL] **:** relatively rapid heart action

tachy·graph·ic \-'graf-ik\ *adj* **:** of or relating to tachygraphy — **tachy·graph·i·cal** \-i-kəl\ *adj*

ta·chyg·ra·phy \ta-'kig-rə-fē, tə-\ *n* [Gk *tachygraphos* stenographer, fr. *tachy-* + *graphein* to write — more at CARVE] **1 :** the art or practice of rapid writing **:** STENOGRAPHY; *esp* **:** the shorthand of the ancient Greeks and Romans **2 a :** cursive writing **b :** the abbreviated form of Greek and Latin used in the Middle Ages

tachy·lyte *also* **tachy·lite** \'tak-ə-,līt\ *n* [G *tachylyt*, fr. Gk *tachy-* + *lyein* to dissolve — more at LOSE] **:** black glassy basalt

ta·chym·e·ter \ta-'kim-ət-ər, tə-\ *n* [ISV] **:** a surveying instrument (as a transit) for determining quickly the distances, bearings, and elevations of distant objects

tac·it \'tas-ət\ *adj* [F or L; F *tacite*, fr. L *tacitus* silent, fr. pp. of *tacēre* to be silent; akin to OHG *dagēn* to be silent] **1 :** expressed or carried on without words or speech **2 a :** implied or indicated but not actually expressed ⟨~ consent⟩ **b** (1) **:** arising without express contract or agreement (2) **:** arising by operation of law ⟨~ mortgage⟩ — **tac·it·ly** *adv* — **tac·it·ness** *n*

tac·i·turn \'tas-ə-,tərn\ *adj* [F or L; F *taciturne*, fr. L *taciturnus*, fr. *tacitus*] **:** temperamentally disinclined to talk **syn** see SILENT — **tac·i·tur·ni·ty** \,tas-ə-'tər-nət-ē\ *n*

¹tack \'tak\ *n, often attrib* [ME *tak* something that attaches; akin to MD *tac* sharp point] **1 :** a small short sharp-pointed nail usu. having a broad flat head **2 a :** a rope to hold in place the forward lower corner of a course on a sailing ship **b :** a rope for hauling the outer lower corner of a studding sail to the end of the boom **c :** the lower forward corner of a fore-and-aft sail **d :** the corner of a sail to which a tack is fastened **3 a :** the direction of a ship with respect to the trim of her sails ⟨starboard ~⟩ **b :** the run of a sailing ship on one tack **c :** a change when close-hauled from the starboard to the port tack or vice versa **d :** a zigzag movement on land **e :** a course or method of action; *esp* **:** one sharply divergent from that previously followed **4 :** any of various usu. temporary stitches **5 :** ADHESIVENESS, STICKINESS **6 :** stable gear

²tack *vt* **1 :** ATTACH; *esp* **:** to fasten or affix with tacks **2 :** to join in a slight or hasty manner **3 a :** to add as a supplement **b :** to add (a rider) to a parliamentary bill **4 :** to change the direction of

(a sailing ship) when sailing close-hauled by putting the helm alee and shifting the sails ~ *vi* **1 a :** to tack a sailing ship **b** *of a sailing ship* **:** to move in a different direction by a tack **2 a :** to follow a zigzag course **b :** to modify one's policy or an attitude abruptly — **tack·er** *n*

3**tack** *n* [origin unknown] **:** STUFF; *esp* **:** FOODSTUFF

tack board *n* **:** a usu. cork board for tacking up notices and display materials

tack·i·ness \'tak-ē-nəs\ *n* **:** the quality or state of being tacky

1**tack·le** \'tak-əl, *naut often* 'tāk-\ *n, often attrib* [ME *takel;* akin to MD *takel* ship's rigging] **1 :** a set of the equipment used in a particular activity **:** GEAR ⟨fishing ~⟩ **2 a :** a ship's rigging **b :** an assemblage of ropes and pulleys arranged to gain mechanical advantage for hoisting and pulling **3 a :** the act or an instance of tackling **b :** one of two players on each side of the center and between guard and end in a football line

2**tackle** *vb* **tack·ling** \-(ə-)liŋ\ *vt* **1 :** to attach or secure with or as if with tackle **2 a :** to seize, take hold of, or grapple with esp. with the intention of stopping or subduing **b :** to seize and throw down or stop (an opposing player with the ball) in football **3 :** to set about dealing with ~ *vi* **:** to tackle an opposing player in football — **tack·ler** \-(ə-)lər\ *n*

tack·ling \'tak-liŋ, *naut often* 'tāk-\ *n* **:** GEAR, TACKLE

1**tacky** \'tak-ē\ *adj* [2*tack*] **:** barely sticky to the touch **:** ADHESIVE ⟨~ varnish⟩

2**tacky** *adj* [*tacky* (a low-class person)] **1 a :** characteristic of or suitable for a low-class person **b :** SHABBY, SEEDY **2 a :** marked by lack of style or good taste **:** DOWDY **b :** marked by cheap showiness **:** GAUDY

tacky party *n* **:** a party at which the guests wear tacky clothes and prizes are awarded for the tackiest costume

ta·co \'täk-(,)ō\ *n, pl* **tacos** \-(,)ōz, -(,)ōs\ [MexSp] **:** a sandwich made of a tortilla rolled up with or folded over a filling

tac·o·nite \'tak-ə-,nīt\ *n* [*Taconic* mountain range, U.S.] **:** a flintlike rock high enough in iron content to become commercially valuable as an ore

tact \'takt\ *n* [F, sense of touch, fr. L *tactus,* fr. *tactus,* pp. of *tangere* to touch — more at TANGENT] **1 :** sensitive mental or aesthetic perception **2 :** a keen sense of what to do or say in order to maintain good relations with others or avoid offense

syn ADDRESS, POISE, SAVOIR FAIRE: TACT implies delicate and sympathetic perception of what is fit or considerate in dealing with others; ADDRESS implies dexterity and grace in coping with new or difficult social situations or with strangers; POISE stresses self-possession in meeting embarrassing or upsetting situations; SAVOIR FAIRE implies knowledge of the proper thing to say or do under all circumstances

tact·ful \'takt-fəl\ *adj* **:** having or showing tact — **tact·ful·ly** \-fə-lē\ *adv* — **tact·ful·ness** *n*

1**tac·tic** \'tak-tik\ *adj* [NL *tacticus,* fr. Gk *taktikos*] **1 :** of or relating to arrangement or order **2** [Gk *taktikos*] **:** of, relating to, or showing biological taxis

2**tactic** *n* [NL *tactica,* fr. Gk *taktikē,* fr. fem. of *taktikos*] **1 :** a method of employing forces in combat **2 :** a device for accomplishing an end

-tac·tic \'tak-tik\ *adj comb form* [Gk *taktikos*] **1 :** of, relating to, or having (such) an arrangement or pattern ⟨para*tactic*⟩ **2 :** showing orientation or movement directed by a (specified) force or agent ⟨geo*tactic*⟩

tac·ti·cal \'tak-ti-kəl\ *adj* **1 :** of or relating to combat tactics: as **a :** involving actions or means of less magnitude or at a shorter distance from a base of operations than those of strategy **b** *of an air force* **:** of, relating to, or designed for air attack in close support of friendly ground forces **2 a :** of or relating to tactics: as (1) **:** of or relating to small-scale actions serving a larger purpose (2) **:** made or carried out with only a limited or immediate end in view **b :** adroit in planning or maneuvering to accomplish a purpose — **tac·ti·cal·ly** \-k(ə-)lē\ *adv*

tac·ti·cian \tak-'tish-ən\ *n* **:** one versed in tactics

tac·tics \'tak-tiks\ *n pl but sing or pl in constr* [NL *tactica,* pl., fr. Gk *taktika,* fr. neut. pl. of *taktikos* of order, of tactics, fit for arranging, fr. *tassein* to arrange, place in battle formation; akin to Lith *patogus* comfortable] **1 a :** the science and art of disposing and maneuvering forces in combat **b :** the art or skill of employing available means to accomplish an end **2 :** a system or mode of procedure **3 :** the study of the grammatical relations within a language including morphology and syntax

tac·tile \'tak-tᵊl, -,tīl\ *adj* [F or L; F, fr. L *tactilis,* fr. *tactus,* pp. of *tangere* to touch — more at TANGENT] **1 :** perceptible by the touch **:** TANGIBLE **2 :** of or relating to the sense of touch — **tac·til·i·ty** \tak-'til-ət-ē\ *n*

tactile corpuscle *n* **:** an end organ of touch

tac·tion \'tak-shən\ *n* [L *taction-, tactio,* fr. *tactus,* pp.] **:** TOUCH, CONTACT

tact·less \'takt-ləs\ *adj* **:** marked by lack of tact — **tact·less·ly** *adv* — **tact·less·ness** *n*

tac·tu·al \'tak-chə-wəl\ *adj* [L *tactus* sense of touch — more at TACT] **:** TACTILE — **tac·tu·al·ly** \-wə-lē\ *adv*

tad \'tad\ *n* [prob. fr. E dial., toad, fr. ME *tode* — more at TOAD] **:** BOY

tad·pole \'tad-,pōl\ *n* [ME *taddepol,* fr. *tode* toad + *polle* head — more at POLL] **:** a larval amphibian; *specif* **:** a frog or toad larva that has a rounded body with a long fin-bordered tail and external gills soon replaced by internal gills and undergoes a metamorphosis in which adult structures are attained

tae·di·um vi·tae \,tīd-ē-əm-'wē-,tī, -ē-,u̇m-; ,tēd-ē-əm-'vīt-ē\ *n* [L] **:** weariness or loathing of life

tael \'tā(ə)l\ *n* [Pg, fr. Malay *tahil*] **1 :** any of various units of weight of eastern Asia; *esp* **:** LIANG **2 :** any of various Chinese units of value based on the value of a tael weight of silver

tae·nia \'tē-nē-ə\ *n, pl* **tae·ni·ae** \-nē-,ē\ *or* **taenias** [L, fr. Gk *tainia;* akin to Gk *teinein* to stretch — more at THIN] **1 :** an ancient Greek fillet **2 :** a band on a Doric order separating the frieze from the architrave **3** [NL, fr. L, fillet, band] **:** a band of nervous tissue or muscle **4 :** TAPEWORM

tae·nia·cide *also* **te·nia·cide** \'tē-nē-ə-,sīd\ *n* **:** an agent that destroys tapeworms

tae·ni·a·sis \tē-'nī-ə-səs\ *n* [NL, fr. L *taenia* tapeworm] **:** infestation with or disease caused by tapeworms

taf·fe·ta \'taf-ət-ə\ *n* [ME, fr. MF *taffetas,* fr. OIt *taffettà,* fr. Turk *tafta,* fr. Per *tāftah* woven] **:** a crisp plain-woven lustrous fabric of various fibers used esp. for women's clothing

taffeta weave *n* **:** PLAIN WEAVE

taf·fe·tized \'taf-ə-,tīzd\ *adj, of cloth* **:** having a crisp finish

taff·rail \'taf-rəl, -,rāl\ *n* [modif. of D *tafereel,* fr. MD, picture, fr. OF *tablel* — more at TABLEAU] **1 :** the upper part of the stern of a wooden ship **2 :** a rail around the stern of a ship

taf·fy \'taf-ē\ *n* [origin unknown] **1 :** a candy usu. of molasses or brown sugar boiled and pulled until porous and light-colored **2 :** insincere flattery

taffy pull *n* **:** a social gathering at which taffy is made

taf·ia \'taf-ē-ə\ *n* [F, fr. West Indian Creole, alter. of *ratafia*] **:** a rum made esp. from distilled sugarcane juice in the West Indies

1**tag** \'tag\ *n* [ME *tagge,* prob. of Scand origin; akin to Sw *tagg* barb] **1 :** a loose hanging piece of cloth **:** TATTER **2 :** a metal or plastic binding on an end of a shoelace **3 :** a piece of hanging or attached material; *specif* **:** a loop, knot, or tassel on a garment **4 a** (1) **:** a brief quotation used for rhetorical emphasis or sententious effect (2) **:** a hackneyed saying **:** CLICHÉ **b :** a recurrent or characteristic verbal expression **5 a :** a cardboard, plastic, or metal marker used for identification or classification **b :** a descriptive or identifying epithet **6 :** a small piece of tinsel or other bright material around the shank of the hook at the end of the body of an artificial fly **7 :** a detached fragmentary piece **:** VESTIGE

2**tag** *vb* **tagged; tag·ging** *vt* **1 :** to provide or mark with or as if with a tag: as **a :** to supply with an identifying marker **b :** to provide with a name or epithet **:** IDENTIFY **c :** to put a ticket on for a traffic violation **2 :** to attach as an addition **:** APPEND **3 :** to follow closely and persistently **4 :** to hold responsible for something; *esp* **:** to charge with violating the law **5 :** LABEL 2 ~ *vi* **:** to keep close

3**tag** *n* [origin unknown] **1 :** a game in which one player chases others and tries to make one of them it by touching him **2 :** an act or instance of tagging a runner in baseball

4**tag** *vt* **tagged; tag·ging 1 a :** to touch in or as if in a game of tag **b :** to put out (a runner in baseball) by a touch with the ball or the gloved hand containing the ball **2 :** to hit solidly **:** STRIKE **3 :** SELECT

Ta·ga·log \tə-'gäl-əg, -,ȯg\ *n, pl* **Tagalog** *or* **Tagalogs** [Tag] **1 a :** a people of central Luzon **b :** a member of this people **2 :** an Austronesian language of the Tagalog people that is the official national language of the Republic of the Philippines

tag·along \'tag-ə-,lȯŋ\ *n* **:** one that persistently and often annoyingly follows the lead of another

tag·board \'tag-,bō(ə)rd, -,bȯ(ə)rd\ *n* **:** strong cardboard used esp. for making shipping tags

tag day *n* **:** a day on which contributions are solicited (as for a charity) and small tags are given in return

tag end *n* **1 :** the last part **2 :** a miscellaneous or random fragment

tag line *n* **1 :** a final line (as in a play or joke); *esp* **:** one that serves to clarify a point or create a dramatic effect **2 :** a reiterated phrase identified with an individual, group, or product **:** SLOGAN

tag, rag, and bobtail *or* **tagrag and bobtail** *n* **:** RABBLE

tag up *vi* **:** to touch a base in baseball before running after a fly ball is caught

Ta·hi·tian \tə-'hē-shən *also* -'hēt-ē-ən\ *n* **1 :** a native or inhabitant of Tahiti **2 :** the Polynesian language of the Tahitians — **Tahitian** *adj*

tah·sil·dar \tə-'sēl-,där\ *n* [Hindi *taḥsīldār*] **:** a revenue officer in India

Tai \'tī\ *n, pl* **Tai :** a widespread group of peoples in south China and southeast Asia associated ethnically with valley paddy-rice culture

tai·ga \tī-'gä\ *n* [Russ *taĭga*] **:** swampy coniferous forest of Siberia beginning where the tundra ends; *also* **:** similar northern forest of Europe and No. America

1**tail** \'tā(ə)l\ *n, often attrib* [ME, fr. OE *tægel;* akin to OHG *zagal* tail, OIr *dúal* lock of hair] **1 :** the rear end or a process or prolongation of the rear end of the body of an animal **2 :** something resembling an animal's tail (as the luminous train of a comet) in shape or position **3 :** RETINUE **4** *pl* **a :** TAILCOAT **b :** full evening dress for men **5 :** the back, last, lower, or inferior part of something; *esp* **:** the reverse of a coin **6 :** a spy (as a detective) who follows someone **7 :** a group of lines of verse added to a recognized prosodic form **8 :** the blank space at the bottom of a page **9 :** the rear part of an airplane consisting of horizontal and vertical stabilizing surfaces with attached control surfaces **10 :** the trail of a fugitive in flight ⟨posse on his ~⟩ — **tailed** \'tā(ə)ld\ *adj* — **tail·less** \'tā(ə)l-ləs\ *adj* — **tail·like** \-,līk\ *adj*

2**tail** *vt* **1 a :** to fasten by or at the tail, stern, or rear **b :** to connect end to end **2 :** 3DOCK 1 **3 a :** to make or furnish with a tail **b :** to follow or be drawn behind like a tail **4 :** to fasten an end of (a tile, brick, or timber) into a wall or other support **5 :** to follow for purposes of surveillance ~ *vi* **1 :** to form or move in a straggling line **2 :** to grow progressively smaller, fainter, or more scattered **:** SUBSIDE **3 :** to hold by the end — used of a timber, tile, or brick built into a support **4 :** to swing or lie with the stern in a named direction — used of a ship at anchor **5 :** 2TAG 3

3**tail** *adj* [ME *taille,* fr. AF *taylé,* fr. OF *taillié,* pp. of *taillier* to cut, limit — more at TAILOR] **:** limited as to tenure **:** ENTAILED

4**tail** *n* **:** ENTAIL 1a

tail·back \'tā(ə)l-,bak\ *n* **:** the offensive football back farthest from the line of scrimmage

tail·board \-,bō(ə)rd, -,bȯ(ə)rd\ *n* **:** the tail gate esp. of a wagon

tail·bone \-'bōn, -,bōn\ *n* **1 :** a caudal vertebra **2 :** COCCYX

tail·coat \-'kōt\ *n* **:** a coat with tails; *esp* **:** a man's full-dress coat with two long tapering skirts at the back

tail covert *n* **:** one of the coverts of the tail quills

tailed sonnet *n* **:** a sonnet augmented by additional systematically arranged lines

tail end *n* **1 :** RUMP, BUTTOCKS **2 :** the hindmost end ⟨the *tail end* of the line⟩ **3 :** the concluding period

tail·er \'tā-lər\ *n* **:** one that tails; *specif* **:** SHADOW 10b

tail fin *n* **1 :** the terminal fin of a fish **2 :** FIN 2b(3)

1tail·gate \'tā(ə)l-ˌgāt\ *n* **1 :** a board or gate at the rear of a vehicle that can be removed or let down for loading **2** [fr. the custom of seating trombonists at the rear of trucks carrying jazz bands in parades] **:** a jazz trombone style marked by much use of slides to and from long sustained tones

2tailgate \'tā(ə)l-ˌgāt\ *vi* **:** to drive dangerously close to another vehicle

tail·ing \'tā-liŋ\ *n* **1** *pl* **:** refuse material separated as residue in the preparation of various products (as grain or ores) **2 :** the part of a projecting stone or brick inserted in a wall

tail lamp *n* **:** TAILLIGHT

taille \'tä-yə, 'tā(ə)l\ *n* [F, fr. OF, fr. *taillier* to cut, tax] **:** a tax formerly levied by a French king or seigneur on his subjects or on lands held of him

tail·light \'tā(ə)l-ˌlīt\ *n* **:** a usu. red warning light mounted at the rear of a vehicle

1tai·lor \'tā-lər\ *n* [ME *taillour*, fr. OF *tailleur*, fr. *taillier* to cut, fr. LL *taliare*, fr. L *talea* twig, cutting; akin to Gk *tēlis* fenugreek] **:** one whose occupation is making or altering men's or women's outer garments — **tai·lor·ess** \-lə-rəs\ *n*

2tailor *vi* **:** to do the work of a tailor **~** *vt* **1 a :** to make or fashion as the work of a tailor **b :** to make or adapt to suit a special need or purpose **2 :** to fit with clothes **3 :** to style (as women's garments) with trim straight lines and finished handwork like that of a tailor's work on men's garments

tai·lor·bird \'tā-lər-ˌbərd\ *n* **:** any of numerous Asiatic, East Indian, and African warblers (family Sylviidae) that stitch leaves together to support and hide their nests

tai·lored \'tā-lərd\ *adj* **1 :** made by a tailor **2 :** fashioned or fitted to resemble a tailor's work **3 :** CUSTOM-MADE **4 a :** having the look of one fitted by a custom tailor **b :** appearing well cared for

tail·or·ing *n* **1 a :** the business or occupation of a tailor **b :** the work or workmanship of a tailor **2 :** the making or adapting of something to suit a particular purpose

tai·lor–made \ˌtā-lər-'mād\ *adj* **1 a :** made by a tailor or with a tailor's care and style **b :** finely trim in fit and simple in line, ornament and finish — used of women's garments **c :** appearing like one turned out by a good tailor **2 :** made or fitted esp. to a particular use or purpose **3** *of a cigarette* **:** factory-made rather than hand-rolled

tailor's chalk *n* **:** a thin flat piece of hard chalk or soapstone used by tailors and sewers to make temporary marks on cloth

tail·piece \'tā(ə)l-ˌpēs\ *n* **1 :** a piece added at the end **:** APPENDAGE **2 :** a triangular piece from which the strings of a stringed instrument are stretched to the pegs **3 :** a short beam or rafter tailed in a wall and supported by a header **4 :** an ornament placed below the text matter of a page (as at the end of a chapter)

tail pipe *n* **1 :** the pipe discharging the exhaust gases from the muffler of an automotive engine **2 :** the part of a jet engine that carries the exhaust gases rearward and discharges them through a nozzle

tail plane *n* **:** the horizontal tail surfaces of an airplane including the stabilizer and the elevator

tail·race \'tā(ə)l-ˌrās\ *n* **1 :** a lower millrace **2 :** the channel in which mine tailings are floated off

tail·spin \-ˌspin\ *n* **1 :** SPIN 2a **2 :** a collapse into depression or confusion **:** DEMORALIZATION

tail·stock \-ˌstäk\ *n* **:** the adjustable or sliding head of a lathe containing the dead center

tail wind *n* **:** a wind having the same general direction as the course of a moving airplane or ship

Tai·no \'tī-(ˌ)nō\ *n, pl* **Taino** *or* **Tainos** [Sp] **1 a :** an extinct aboriginal Arawakan people of the Greater Antilles and the Bahamas **b :** a member of this people **2 :** the language of the Taino people

1taint \'tānt\ *vb* [ME *tainten* to color & *taynten* to attaint; ME *tainten*, fr. AF *teinter*, fr. MF *teint*, pp. of *teindre*, fr. L *tingere*; ME *taynten*, fr. MF *ataint*, pp. of *ataindre* — more at TINGE, ATTAIN] *vt* **1 :** to touch or affect slightly with something bad **2 :** to affect with putrefaction **:** ROT **3 :** to contaminate morally **:** CORRUPT **~** *vi* **1** *obs* **:** to become weak ⟨cannot ~ with fear —Shak.⟩ **2** *archaic* **:** to become affected with putrefaction **:** ROT **syn** see CONTAMINATE

2taint *n* **1 :** SPOT, BLEMISH **2 :** a contaminating influence — **taint·less** \-ləs\ *adj*

Tai·ping \'tī-'piŋ\ *n* [Chin (Pek) *t'ai⁴ ping²* peaceful] **:** a Chinese insurgent taking part in a rebellion (1848–65) against the Manchu dynasty

Ta·jik \tä-'jik, tə-, -'jēk\ *n* **:** a member of a people of Iranian blood and speech who resemble Europeans and are dispersed among the populations of Afghanistan and Turkestan

Ta·jiki \-'jik-ē, -'jē-kē\ *n* **:** the Iranian language of the Tajik people

1take \'tāk\ *vb* **took** \'tu̇k\ **tak·en** \'tā-kən\ **tak·ing** [ME *taken*, fr. OE *tacan*, fr. ON *taka*; akin to MD *taken* to take] *vt* **1 :** to get into one's hands or into one's possession, power, or control: as **a :** to seize or capture physically **b :** to get possession of (as fish or game) by killing or capturing **c :** to move against (as an opponent's piece in chess or a card) and remove from play **:** WIN **d :** CONFISCATE **e :** to catch (a batted ball) in baseball or cricket ⟨~ it on the fly⟩ **2 :** GRASP, GRIP ⟨~ the ax by the handle⟩ **3 a :** to catch or attack through the effect of a sudden force or influence ⟨*taken* with a fit of laughing⟩ ⟨*taken* ill⟩ **b :** to catch or come upon in a particular situation or action ⟨tried to ~ him napping⟩ **c :** to strike or hit in or on a specified part ⟨*took* the boy a smart box on the ear⟩ **d :** to gain the approval or liking of **:** CAPTIVATE, DELIGHT **4 a :** to receive into one's body (as by eating, drinking, or inhaling) ⟨~ a glass of water⟩ ⟨~ one tablet after each meal⟩ **b :** to expose oneself to (as sun or air) for pleasure or physical benefit **c :** to partake of **:** EAT **5 a :** to bring or receive into a relation or connection ⟨reduced to *taking* lodgers⟩ ⟨time he *took* a wife⟩ **b :** to copulate with **6 :** to transfer into one's own keeping: **a :** APPROPRIATE **b** (1) **:** to obtain or secure for use (as by lease or contract) ⟨~ a box at the opera⟩ (2) **:** BUY ⟨I'll ~ this hat⟩ **7 a :** ASSUME ⟨gods often *took* the likeness of a human being⟩ ⟨~ the veil⟩ **b :** to charge oneself with (as a duty, obligation, or task) **:** UNDERTAKE ⟨~ office⟩ ⟨~ a role⟩ **c :** to subject oneself to **:** bind oneself by ⟨~ a vow⟩ **d :** to impose upon oneself ⟨~ the trouble to do good work⟩ **e :** to adopt as one's own **:** align or ally oneself with **f :** to adopt or advance as one's fundamental point of argument or defense ⟨a point well *taken*⟩ **g :** to arrogate to oneself ⟨~ the credit⟩ **h :** to have or assume as a proper part of or accompaniment to itself ⟨transitive verbs ~ an object⟩ **8 a :** to secure by winning in competition ⟨*took* first place⟩ **b :** DEFEAT **9 :** to pick out **:** CHOOSE, SELECT **10 :** to adopt, choose, or avail oneself of for use: as **a :** to have recourse to as an instrument for doing something ⟨~ a scythe to the weeds⟩ **b :** to use as a means of transportation or progression ⟨*took* a freighter to Europe⟩ **c :** to have recourse to for safety or refuge ⟨~ shelter⟩ **d** (1) **:** to proceed to occupy ⟨~ a seat in the rear⟩ (2) **:** NEED, REQUIRE **11 a :** to obtain by deriving from a source **:** DRAW ⟨~*s* its title from the name of the hero⟩ **:** BORROW **b** (1) **:** to obtain as the result of a special procedure **:** ASCERTAIN ⟨~ the temperature⟩ ⟨~ a census⟩ (2) **:** to get in writing **:** write down ⟨~ notes⟩ ⟨~ an inventory⟩ (3) **:** to get by drawing or painting or by photography; *esp* **:** PHOTOGRAPH ⟨~ a snapshot⟩ (4) **:** to get by transference from one surface to another ⟨~ a proof⟩ ⟨~ fingerprints⟩ **12 :** to receive or accept whether willingly or reluctantly ⟨~ a bribe⟩ ⟨~ a bet⟩: as **a :** to receive when bestowed or tendered ⟨~ an honorary doctorate⟩ **b** (1) **:** to submit to **:** ENDURE, UNDERGO ⟨*took* his punishment like a man⟩ (2) **:** WITHSTAND ⟨~*s* a punch well⟩ **c** (1) **:** to accept as true **:** BELIEVE (2) **:** FOLLOW ⟨~ a suggestion⟩ (3) **:** to accept with the mind in a specified way ⟨~ things as they come⟩ **d :** to indulge in and enjoy ⟨was *taking* his ease on the porch⟩ **e :** to receive or accept as a return (as in payment, compensation, or reparation) **f :** to refrain from hitting at (a pitched ball) **13 a** (1) **:** to let in **:** ADMIT ⟨the boat was ~*ing* water fast⟩ (2) **:** ACCOMMODATE **b :** to be affected injuriously by (as a disease) **:** CONTRACT ⟨~ cold⟩ **:** be seized by ⟨~ a fit⟩ **c :** to absorb or become impregnated with (as dye) **:** be affected by (as polish) **14 a :** APPREHEND, UNDERSTAND ⟨slow to ~ his meaning⟩ **b :** CONSIDER, SUPPOSE ⟨~ it as settled⟩ **c :** to accept or reckon as being or as equal to ⟨*taking* a stride at 30 inches⟩ **d :** FEEL, EXPERIENCE ⟨~ pleasure⟩ **15 :** to lead, carry, or cause to go along to another place ⟨this bus will ~ you into town⟩ ⟨~ the dishes to the kitchen⟩ **16 a :** to remove or obtain by removing **:** ABSTRACT ⟨~ eggs from a nest⟩ **b :** to remove by death **:** cause to die ⟨*taken* in his prime⟩ **c :** SUBTRACT ⟨~ two from four⟩ **17 :** to undertake and make, do, or perform ⟨~ a walk⟩ ⟨~ aim⟩ ⟨~ legal action⟩ **18 a :** to deal with ⟨~ first things first⟩ **b :** to consider or view in a particular relation ⟨*taking* one thing with another⟩ **c :** to apply oneself to the study of ⟨~ music lessons⟩ **19 :** CHEAT, SWINDLE **~** *vi* **1 :** to obtain possession: as **a :** CAPTURE **b :** to receive property under law as one's own **2 :** to lay hold **:** CATCH, HOLD **3 :** to establish a take esp. by uniting or growing ⟨90 percent of the grafts ~⟩ **4 a :** to betake oneself **:** set out **:** GO ⟨~ across a field⟩ **b** *chiefly dial* — used as an intensifier or redundantly with a following verb ⟨*took* and swung at the ball⟩ **5 a :** to take effect **:** ACT, OPERATE **b :** to show the natural or intended effect ⟨dry fuel ~*s* readily⟩ **6 :** CHARM, CAPTIVATE: **a :** to exert a spell **b :** to prove attractive **:** win popular favor **7 :** DETRACT ⟨irritations that *took* from their general satisfaction⟩ **8 a :** to be seized or attacked in a specified way **:** BECOME ⟨*took* sick⟩ **b :** to be capable of being moved in a specified way ⟨table ~*s* apart for packing⟩ **c :** to adhere or become absorbed ⟨ink that ~*s* well on cloth⟩ **d :** to admit of being photographed — **tak·er** *n*

syn SEIZE, GRASP, CLUTCH, SNATCH, GRAB: TAKE is a general term applicable to any manner of getting something into one's possession or control; SEIZE implies a sudden and forcible movement in getting hold of something tangible or an apprehending of something fleeting or elusive when intangible; GRASP stresses a laying hold so as to have firmly in possession; CLUTCH suggests avidity or anxiety in seizing or grasping and may imply less success in holding; SNATCH suggests more suddenness or quickness but less force than SEIZE; GRAB implies more roughness or rudeness than SNATCH **syn** see in addition RECEIVE

— **take account of :** to take into account — **take advantage of 1 :** to use to advantage **:** profit by **2 :** to impose upon **:** EXPLOIT — **take after 1 :** to take as an example **:** FOLLOW **2 :** to resemble in features, build, character, or disposition — **take amiss :** to impute a wrong motive or a bad meaning or intention to **:** take offense at — **take apart 1 :** DISASSEMBLE, DISMANTLE **2 :** to analyze or dissect esp. in order to discover or reveal a weakness, flaw, or fallacy **3 :** to treat roughly or harshly **:** tear into — **take care :** to be careful **:** exercise caution or prudence **:** be watchful — **take care of :** to attend to or provide for the needs, operation, or treatment of — **take effect 1 :** to become operative **2 :** to produce a result as expected or intended **:** be effective — **take five** *or* **take ten :** to take a five or ten minute intermission **:** take a short break — **take for :** to suppose to be; *esp* **:** to suppose mistakenly to be — **take for granted 1 :** to assume as true, real, or expected **2 :** to value too lightly — **take heart :** to gain courage or confidence — **take hold 1 :** GRASP, GRIP, SEIZE **2 :** to become attached or established **:** take effect — **take in vain :** to use (a name) profanely or without proper respect — **take issue :** to take up the opposite side — **take part :** JOIN, PARTICIPATE, SHARE — **take place :** HAPPEN, OCCUR — **take root 1 :** to become rooted **2 :** to become fixed or established — **take shape :** to assume a definite or distinctive form — **take stock :** INVENTORY, ASSESS — **take the cake :** to carry off the prize **:** rank first — **take the count 1** *of a boxer* **:** to be counted out **2 :** to go down in defeat — **take the field 1 :** to go upon the playing field **2 :** to enter upon a military campaign — **take the floor :** to rise (as in a meeting or a legislative assembly) to make a formal address — **take to 1 :** to take in hand **:** take care of **2 :** to betake oneself to ⟨*take to* the woods⟩ **3 :** to apply or devote oneself to (as a practice, habit, or occupation) ⟨*take to* begging⟩ **4 :** to adapt oneself to **:** respond to ⟨*takes to* water like a duck⟩ **5 :** to conceive a liking for — **take to task :** to call to account for a shortcoming **:** REPROVE

2take *n* **1 :** an act or the action of taking (as by seizing, accepting, or otherwise coming into possession): as **a :** the action of killing, capturing, or catching (as game or fish) **b** (1) **:** the uninterrupted photographing or televising of a scene (2) **:** the making of a sound recording **2 :** something that is taken: **a :** the amount of money received (as from a business venture, sale, or admission charge) **:** PROCEEDS, RECEIPTS, INCOME **b :** SHARE, CUT **c :** the number or quantity (as of animals, fish, or pelts) taken at one time **:** CATCH, HAUL **d** (1) **:** a scene filmed or televised at one time without stopping the camera (2) **:** a sound recording made during a single recording period; *often* **:** a trial recording **3 a :** a local or systemic reaction indicative of successful vaccination against smallpox **b :** a successful union (as of a graft) **4 :** mental response or reaction ⟨delayed ~⟩ — compare DOUBLE TAKE

take back *vt* **:** RETRACT, WITHDRAW ⟨would neither apologize nor *take back* what he had said⟩

take down *vt* **1 a :** to pull to pieces **b :** DISASSEMBLE **2 :** to lower the spirit or vanity of **:** HUMBLE **3 a :** to write down **b :** to record by mechanical means **~** *vi* **1 :** to become seized or attacked esp. by illness **2 :** to admit of being taken down

[1]**take·down** \'tāk-,dau̇n\ *adj* **:** constructed so as to be readily taken apart ⟨~ rifle⟩

[2]**takedown** *n* **1 :** the action or an act of taking down: as **a :** the action of humiliating **b :** the action of taking apart **c :** the act of bringing one's opponent in amateur wrestling under control to the mat from a standing position **2 :** something (as a rifle or shotgun) having takedown construction

take–home pay \'tāk-,hōm-\ *n* **:** the part of gross salary or wages after deductions (as of income-tax withholding, retirement insurance payments, or union dues)

take in *vt* **1 :** to draw into a smaller compass ⟨*take in* a slack line⟩: **a :** FURL **b :** to make (a garment) smaller by enlarging seams or tucks **2 a :** to receive as a guest or inmate **b :** to give shelter to **3 :** to receive (work) into one's house to be done for pay ⟨*take in* washing⟩ **4 :** to encompass within its limits **:** COMPRISE, INCLUDE **5 :** ATTEND ⟨*take in* a movie⟩ **6 :** to receive into the mind **:** PERCEIVE, COMPREHEND **7 :** to impose upon **:** CHEAT, DECEIVE

take–in \'tā-,kin\ *n* **:** an act of taking in esp. by cheating

take off *vt* **1 :** REMOVE **2 a :** RELEASE ⟨*take* the brake *off*⟩ **b :** WITHDRAW **c :** to take or allow as a discount **3 :** to omit or withhold from service owed or from time being spent (as at one's occupation) ⟨*took* two weeks *off* in August⟩ **4 :** to take the life of **5 a :** to copy from an original **:** REPRODUCE **b :** to make a likeness of **:** PORTRAY **c :** MIMIC **~** *vi* **1 :** to take away **:** DETRACT **2 a :** to start off or away **:** set out ⟨*took off* without delay⟩ **b** (1) **:** to branch off (as from a main stream or stem) (2) **:** STEM **c :** to begin a leap or spring **d :** to leave the surface **:** begin flight

take·off \'tā-,kȯf\ *n, often attrib* **1 :** an imitation esp. in the way of caricature **2 a :** a rise or leap from a surface in making a jump or flight or an ascent in an aircraft or in the launching of a rocket **b :** an action of starting out or setting out **3 a :** a spot at which one takes off **b :** a starting point **:** point of departure **4 :** an action of removing something **5 :** the action of estimating or measuring an amount of material needed **6 :** a mechanism for transmission of the power of an engine or vehicle to operate some other mechanism

take on *vt* **1 a :** to begin to perform or deal with **:** UNDERTAKE **b :** to engage with as an opponent **2 a :** ENGAGE, HIRE **b :** to accept in a relationship ⟨*taking* me *on* as a client⟩ **3 :** to assume or acquire (as an appearance or quality) as or as if one's own **~** *vi* **1 :** to show one's feelings esp. of grief or anger in a demonstrative way **2 :** to behave in a proud or haughty manner

take out *vt* **1 a** (1) **:** DEDUCT, SEPARATE (2) **:** EXCEPT, OMIT (3) **:** WITHDRAW, WITHHOLD **b :** to draw out by cleansing **c :** to find release for **:** EXPEND **d :** ELIMINATE **2 :** to conduct or escort into the open or to a public entertainment **3 :** to take as an equivalent in another form ⟨*took* the debt *out* in goods⟩ **4 a :** to obtain from the proper authority ⟨*take out* a charter⟩ **b :** to arrange for (insurance) **5 :** to overcall (a bridge partner) in a suit different from his **~** *vi* **:** to start on a course **:** set out — **take it out on :** to expend (as anger, vexation, frustration) in harassment of

take·out \'tā-,kau̇t\ *n* **:** the action or an act of taking out; *specif* **:** a bridge bid that takes a partner out of a bid, double, or redouble

take over *vt* **:** to assume control or possession of or responsibility for **~** *vi* **1 :** to assume control or possession **2 :** to become dominant ⟨saw a new point of view *taking over* —W.H.Hale⟩

take–over \'tā-,kō-vər\ *n* **:** the action or an act of taking over

take up *vt* **1 a :** to pick up **:** LIFT **b :** to remove by lifting or pulling up **2 a :** to begin to occupy (land) **b :** to buy up **c :** to pay the amount of (as a loan) **d :** COLLECT **3 :** to accept or adopt for the purpose of assisting **4 a :** to take or accept (as a belief, idea, or practice) as one's own **b :** ASSUME ⟨*take up* a hostile attitude⟩ **5 a :** to enter upon (as a business, profession, or subject of study) **b :** to proceed to deal with **6 :** REBUKE, REPRIMAND **7 :** to establish oneself in **8 :** to occupy (as space, time, or attention) entirely or exclusively **:** fill up **9 :** to pull up or pull in so as to tighten or to shorten **10 :** ARREST, SEIZE **11 :** to respond favorably to (as a bet, challenge, or proposal) **12 :** to begin again or take over from another **~** *vi* **1 :** to make a beginning where another has left off **2 :** to become shortened **:** draw together **:** SHRINK — **take up with 1 :** to become interested or absorbed in **2 :** to begin to associate with **:** CONSORT

take–up \'tā-,kəp\ *n* **1 :** the action of taking up (as by gathering, contraction, absorption, or adjustment) **2 :** UPTAKE 2 **3 :** any of various devices for tightening or drawing in

ta·kin \'täk-,ēn\ *n* [Mishmi] **:** a large heavily built goat antelope (*Budorcas taxicolor*) of Tibet

[1]**tak·ing** \'tā-kiŋ\ *n* **1 :** SEIZURE **2 a** *chiefly Scot* **:** an unhappy state **:** PLIGHT **b :** a state of violent agitation and distress **3 a** *pl* **:** receipts esp. of money **b :** a take of fish or animals

[2]**taking** *adj* **1 :** ATTRACTIVE, CAPTIVATING **2 :** CONTAGIOUS

ta·lar·ia \tə-'lar-ē-ə, -'ler-\ *n pl* [L, fr. neut. pl. of *talaris* of the ankles, fr. *talus* ankle, heel] **:** the winged shoes of the god Mercury

Tal·bot \'tȯl-bət, 'tal-\ *n* [prob. fr. *Talbot*, name of a Norman family in England] **:** a large heavy mostly white hound with pendulous ears and drooping flews held to be ancestral to the bloodhound

talc \'talk\ *n* [MF *talc* mica, fr. ML *talk*, fr. Ar *ṭalq*] **:** a soft mineral $Mg_3Si_4O_{10}(OH)_2$ consisting of a basic magnesium silicate that is usu. whitish, greenish, or grayish with a soapy feel and occurs in foliated, granular, or fibrous masses (hardness 1, sp. gr. 2.6–2.9)

talcky \'tal-kē\ *adj* [irreg. fr. *talc*] **:** TALCOSE

talc·ose \'tal-,kōs\ *adj* **:** of, relating to, or containing talc

tal·cum powder \'tal-kəm-\ *n* [ML *talcum* mica, alter. of earlier *talk*] **1 :** powdered talc **2 :** a toilet powder composed of perfumed talc or talc and a mild antiseptic

tale \'tā(ə)l\ *n* [ME, fr. OE *talu;* akin to ON *tala* talk, and prob. to L *dolus* guile, deceit, Gk *dolos*] **1** *obs* **:** DISCOURSE, TALK **2 a :** a relation of a series of events or facts **:** ACCOUNT **b** (1) **:** an improper report of a private or confidential matter (2) **:** a libelous report or piece of gossip **3 a :** a usu. imaginative narrative of an event **:** STORY **b :** an intentionally untrue relation **:** FALSEHOOD **4 a :** COUNT, TALLY **b :** a number of things taken together **:** TOTAL

tale·bear·er \-,bar-ər, -,ber-\ *n* **:** one that spreads gossip, scandal, or idle rumors **:** GOSSIP — **tale·bear·ing** \-iŋ\ *adj or n*

tal·ent \'tal-ənt\ *n* [ME, fr. OE *talente*, fr. L *talenta*, pl. of *talentum* unit of weight or money, fr. Gk *talanton;* akin to L *tollere* to lift up; in senses 2–5, fr. the parable of the talents in Mt 25:14–30 — more at TOLERATE] **1 a :** any of several ancient units of weight (as a unit of Palestine and Syria equal to 3000 shekels or a Greek unit equal to 6000 drachmas) **b :** a unit of value equal to the value of a talent of gold or silver **2** *archaic* **:** a characteristic feature, aptitude, or disposition of a person or animal **3 :** the natural endowments of a person **4 a :** a special often creative or artistic aptitude **b :** general intelligence or mental power **:** ABILITY **5 :** a person of talent or a group of persons of talent in a field or activity **syn** see GIFT — **tal·ent·ed** \-ən-təd\ *adj*

talent scout *n* **:** a person engaged in discovering and recruiting people of talent for a specialized field or activity

talent show *n* **:** a show consisting of a series of individual performances (as singing) by amateurs who may be selected for special recognition as performing talent

ta·ler \'täl-ər\ *n* [G — more at DOLLAR] **:** any of numerous silver coins issued by various German states from the 15th to the 19th centuries

tales·man \'tā(ə)lz-mən, 'tā-lēz-\ *n* [ME *tales* talesmen, fr. ML *tales de circumstantibus* such (persons) of the bystanders; fr. the wording of the writ summoning them] **:** a person added to a jury usu. from among bystanders to make up a deficiency in the available number of jurors

tale–tell·er \'tā(ə)l-,tel-ər\ *n* **1 :** one who tells tales or stories **2 :** TALEBEARER — **tale–tell·ing** \-iŋ\ *adj or n*

tali *pl of* TALUS

tali·grade \'tal-ə-,grād\ *adj* [L *talus* ankle + E *-i-* + *-grade*] **:** bearing the weight on the outer side of the foot in walking

tali·pes \'tal-ə-,pēz\ *n* [NL, fr. L *talus* ankle + *pes* foot — more at FOOT] **:** CLUBFOOT

tal·i·pot \'tal-ə-,pät\ *n* [Bengali *tālipōt* palm leaf] **1 :** a tall showy fan-leaved palm (*Corypha umbraculifera*) of Ceylon, the Philippines, and the Malabar coast bearing a crown of huge leaves used as umbrellas and fans and cut into strips for writing paper **2 :** a starch obtained from the talipot palm

tal·is·man \'tal-ə-smən, -əz-mən\ *n* [F *talisman* or Sp *talismán* or It *talismano*, fr. Ar *ṭilsam*, fr. MGk *telesma*, fr. Gk, consecration, fr. *telein* to initiate into the mysteries, complete, fr. *telos* end — more at WHEEL] **1 :** an object bearing a sign or character engraved under astrological influences and thought to act as a charm to avert evil and bring good fortune **2 :** something producing apparently magical or miraculous effects **syn** see FETISH — **tal·is·man·ic** \,tal-ə-'sman-ik, -əz-'man-\ *adj* — **tal·is·man·i·cal·ly** \-i-k(ə-)lē\ *adv*

[1]**talk** \'tȯk\ *vb* [ME *talken;* akin to OE *talu* tale] *vt* **1 :** to deliver or express in speech **:** UTTER **2 :** to make the subject of conversation or discourse **:** DISCUSS ⟨~ business⟩ **3 :** to influence, affect, or cause by talking ⟨~*ed* them into agreeing⟩ **4 :** to use (a language) for conversing or communicating **:** SPEAK **~** *vi* **1 a :** to express or exchange ideas by means of spoken words **:** CONVERSE **b :** to convey information or communicate in any way (as with signs or sounds) **2 a :** to use speech **:** SPEAK **b :** to speak idly **:** PRATE **3 a :** GOSSIP **b :** to reveal secret or confidential information **4 :** to give a talk **:** LECTURE **syn** see SPEAK — **talk·er** *n* — **talk back :** to answer impertinently — **talk turkey :** to speak frankly or bluntly

[2]**talk** *n* **1 :** the act or an instance of talking **:** SPEECH **2 :** a way of speaking **:** LANGUAGE **3 :** pointless or fruitless discussion **:** VERBIAGE **4 :** a formal discussion, negotiation, or exchange of views **:** CONFERENCE **5 a :** MENTION, REPORT **b :** RUMOR, GOSSIP **6 :** the topic of interested comment, conversation, or gossip **7 a :** ADDRESS, LECTURE **b :** written analysis or discussion presented in an informal or conversational manner **8 :** communicative sounds or signs resembling or functioning as talk ⟨bird ~⟩

talk·ative \'tȯ-kət-iv\ *adj* **:** given to talking — **talk·ative·ly** *adv* — **talk·ative·ness** *n*

syn TALKATIVE, LOQUACIOUS, GARRULOUS, VOLUBLE mean given to talk or talking. TALKATIVE may imply a readiness to engage in talk or a disposition to enjoy conversation; LOQUACIOUS suggests the power of expressing oneself articulately, fluently, or glibly; GARRULOUS implies prosy, rambling, or tedious loquacity; VOLUBLE suggests a free, easy, and unending loquacity

talk down *vt* **1 :** to overcome or silence by argument or by loud talking **2 :** to disparage or belittle by talking **~** *vi* **:** to speak in a condescending or oversimplified fashion on the assumption that the listener is ignorant of the matter involved

talk·ie \'tȯ-kē\ *n* [*talk* + *movie*] **:** a motion picture with synchronized sound effects

talking book *n* **:** a phonograph recording of a reading of a book or magazine designed chiefly for the use of the blind

talking machine *n* **:** PHONOGRAPH

talking point *n* **:** something that lends support for an argument or proposal

talk·ing–to \'tȯ-kiŋ-,tü\ *n* **:** REPRIMAND, ADMONITION

talk out *vt* **:** to clarify or settle by oral discussion ⟨*talk out* their differences⟩

talk over *vt* **:** to review or consider in conversation **:** DISCUSS

talk up *vt* **:** to discuss favorably **:** ADVOCATE

talky \'tȯ-kē\ *adj* **1 :** given to talking **:** TALKATIVE **2 :** containing too much talk

tall \'tȯl\ *adj* [ME, prob. fr. OE *getæl* quick, ready; akin to OHG *gizal* quick, OE *talu* tale] **1** *obs* **:** BRAVE, COURAGEOUS **2 a :** high in stature **b :** of a specified height ⟨five feet ~⟩ **3 a :** of considerable height **:** LOFTY **b :** long from bottom to top ⟨a ~ book⟩ **c :** of a higher growing variety or species of plant **4 a :** large or formidable in amount, extent, or degree ⟨~ order to fill⟩ **b :** GRANDILOQUENT, HIGH-FLOWN ⟨~ talk⟩ **c :** INCREDIBLE, IMPROBABLE ⟨~ story⟩ **syn** see HIGH — **tall** *adv* — **tall·ness** *n*

tal·lage \'tal-ij\ *n* [ME *taillage, tallage*, fr. OF *taillage*, fr. *taillier* to cut, limit, tax — more at TAILOR] **1 :** a toll, fee, or render paid by a feudal tenant to his lord **2 :** an impost or due levied by a lord upon his tenants

tall·boy \'tȯl-,bȯi\ *n* **1 a :** HIGHBOY **b :** a double chest of drawers with the lower section having short feet and the upper being slightly smaller than the lower **2** *Brit* **:** CLOTHESPRESS

tall·ish \'tȯ-lish\ *adj* **:** rather tall
tal·lith \'täl-əs, 'tal-, -ət(h)\ *n, pl* **tal·li·thim** \ˌtäl-ə-'sēm, -'t(h)ēm\ [Heb *ṭallīth* cover, cloak] **:** a shawl with fringed corners traditionally worn over the head or shoulders by Jewish men during morning prayers
tall oil \'täl-, 'tȯl-\ *n* [part trans. of G *tallöl*, part trans. of Sw *tallolja*, fr. *tall* pine + *olja* oil] **:** a resinous by-product from the manufacture of chemical wood pulp used esp. in making soaps, coatings, and oils
1**tal·low** \'tal-(ˌ)ō, -ə(-w)\ *n, often attrib* [ME *talgh, talow;* akin to MD *talch* tallow] **:** the white nearly tasteless solid rendered fat of cattle and sheep used chiefly in soap, margarine, candles, and lubricants — **tal·lowy** \'tal-ə-wē\ *adj*
2**tallow** *vt* **:** to grease or smear with tallow
1**tal·ly** \'tal-ē\ *n* [ME *talye*, fr. ML *talea, tallia* fr. L *talea* twig, cutting — more at TAILOR] **1 :** a device for visibly recording or accounting esp. business transactions: as **a :** a wooden rod notched with marks representing numbers and split lengthwise through the notches so that each of two parties may have a record of a transaction and of the amount due or paid **b :** any of various bookkeeping forms or sheets **c :** a mechanical counter held in the hand and operated with a button or lever **2 a :** a reckoning or recorded account **b :** a score or point made (as in a game) **3 a :** a part that corresponds to an opposite or companion member **:** COMPLEMENT **b :** CORRESPONDENCE, AGREEMENT **4 a :** a usu. specified number or lot taken as a whole **b :** a number or division used as a unit of computation **c :** the last of a specified unit or number
2**tally** *vt* **1 a :** to mark on or as if on a tally **:** TABULATE **b :** to list or check off (as a cargo) by items **c :** to register (as a score) in a contest **2 :** to make a count of **:** RECKON **3 :** to cause to correspond ~ *vi* **1 a :** to make a tally by or as if by tabulating **b :** to register a point in a contest **:** SCORE **2 :** CORRESPOND, MATCH
tal·ly·ho \ˌtal-ē-'hō\ *n, pl* **tallyhos** [prob. fr. F *taïaut*, a cry used to excite hounds in deer hunting] **1 :** a call of a huntsman at sight of the fox **2** [*Tally-ho*, name of a coach formerly plying between London and Birmingham] **:** a four-in-hand coach
tal·ly·man \'tal-ē-mən\ *n* **1** *Brit* **:** one who sells goods on the installment plan **2 :** one who tallies, checks, or keeps an account or record (as of receipt of goods)
Tal·mud \'täl-ˌmu̇d, 'tal-məd\ *n* [LHeb *talmūdh*, lit., instruction] **:** the authoritative body of Jewish tradition comprising the Mishnah and Gemara — **tal·mu·dic** \tal-'m(y)üd-ik, -'məd-; täl-'mu̇d-\ *also* **tal·mu·di·cal** \-i-kəl\ *adj, often cap* — **tal·mud·ism** \'täl-ˌmu̇d-ˌiz-əm, 'tal-məd-\ *n, often cap* — **tal·mud·ist** \-əst\ *n, often cap*
tal·on \'tal-ən\ *n* [ME, fr. MF, heel, spur, fr. (assumed) VL *talon-, talo*, fr. L *talus* ankle, anklebone] **1 a :** the claw of an animal and esp. of a bird of prey **b :** a finger or hand of a human being **2 :** a part or object shaped like or suggestive of a heel or claw: as **a :** an ogee molding **b :** the shoulder of the bolt of a lock on which the key acts to shoot the bolt **3 a :** cards laid aside in a pile in solitaire **b :** STOCK 10c — **tal·oned** \-ənd\ *adj*
1**ta·lus** \'tā-ləs, ta-'lü\ *n* [F, fr. L *talutium* slope indicating presence of gold under the soil] **1 :** a slope formed esp. by an accumulation of rock debris **2 :** rock debris at the base of a cliff
2**ta·lus** \'tā-ləs\ *n, pl* **ta·li** \'tā-ˌlī\ [NL, fr. L] **1 :** the astragalus of man bearing the weight of the body and with the tibia and fibula forming the ankle joint **2 :** the entire ankle
tam \'tam\ *n* **:** TAM-O'-SHANTER
tam·able *or* **tame·able** \'tā-mə-bəl\ *adj* **:** capable of being tamed
ta·ma·le \tə-'mäl-ē\ *n* [MexSp *tamales*, pl. of *tamal* tamale, fr. Nahuatl *tamalli*] **:** ground meat seasoned usu. with chili, rolled in cornmeal dough, wrapped in corn husks, and steamed
ta·man·dua \tə-ˌman-də-'wä\ *n* [Pg *tamanduá*, fr. Tupi] **:** an arboreal anteater (*Tamandua tetradactyla*) of Central and So. America
tam·a·rack \'tam-ə-ˌrak\ *n* [origin unknown] **1 :** any of several American larches; *esp* **:** a larch (*Larix laricina*) of northern U.S., Canada, and Alaska **2 :** the wood of a tamarack
tam·a·rau \ˌtam-ə-'rau̇\ *n* [Tag *tamaráw*] **:** a small dark sturdily built buffalo (*Bubalus mindorensis*) native to the Philippine island of Mindoro
tam·a·rin \'tam-ə-rən, -ˌran\ *n* [F, fr. Galibi] **:** any of numerous small So. American marmosets (genus *Leontocebus*) with silky fur and long tail
tam·a·rind \'tam-ə-rənd, -ˌrind\ *n* [Sp & Pg *tamarindo*, fr. Ar *tamr hindī*, lit., Indian date] **:** a tropical leguminous tree (*Tamarindus indica*) with hard yellowish wood, pinnate leaves, and red-striped yellow flowers; *also* **:** its fruit which has an acid pulp used for preserves or in a cooling laxative drink
tam·a·risk \'tam-ə-ˌrisk\ *n* [ME *tamarisc*, fr. LL *tamariscus*, fr. L *tamaric-, tamarix*] **:** any of a genus (*Tamarix* of the family Tamaricaceae, the tamarisk family) of chiefly desert shrubs and trees having narrow entire leaves and flowers with five stamens and a one-celled ovary
1**tam·bour** \'tam-ˌbu̇(ə)r, tam-'\ *n* [F, drum, fr. Ar *ṭanbūr*, modif. of Per *tabīr*] **1 :** 1DRUM 1 **2 a :** an embroidery frame; *esp* **:** a set of two interlocking hoops between which cloth is stretched before stitching **b :** embroidery made on a tambour frame **3 :** a shallow metallic cup or drum with a thin elastic membrane supporting a writing lever used to transmit and register slight motions (as arterial pulsations) **4 :** a rolling top or front (as of a desk) of narrow strips of wood glued on canvas
2**tambour** *vt* **:** to embroider (cloth) with tambour ~ *vi* **:** to work at a tambour frame — **tam·bour·er** *n*
tam·bou·rine \ˌtam-bə-'rēn\ *n* [MF *tambourin*, dim. of *tambour*] **:** a small drum; *esp* **:** a shallow one-headed drum with loose metallic disks at the sides played by shaking, striking with the hand, or rubbing with the thumb

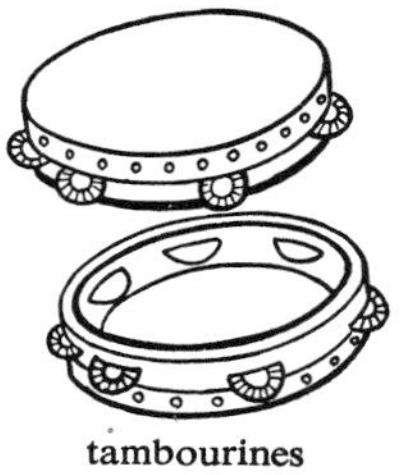
tambourines

1**tame** \'tām\ *adj* [ME, fr. OE *tam;* akin to OHG *zam* tame, L *domare* to tame, Gk *damnanai*] **1 :** reduced from a state of native wildness esp. so as to be tractable and useful to man **:** DOMESTICATED **2 :** made docile and submissive **:** SUBDUED **3 :** lacking spirit, zest, or interest **:** INSIPID — **tame·ly** *adv* — **tame·ness** *n*
2**tame** *vt* **1 a :** to reduce from a wild to a domestic state **b :** to subject to cultivation **2 :** HUMBLE, SUBDUE **3 :** to tone down **:** SOFTEN ~ *vi* **:** to become tame — **tam·er** *n*
tame·less \'tām-ləs\ *adj* **:** not tamed or tamable
Tam·il \'tam-əl\ *n* **1 :** a Dravidian language of Madras state and of northern and eastern Ceylon **2 :** a Tamil-speaking person or a descendant of Tamil-speaking ancestors
Tam·ma·ny \'tam-ə-nē\ *adj* [*Tammany Hall*, headquarters of the Tammany Society, political organization in New York City] **:** of, relating to, or constituting a group or organization exercising or seeking municipal political control by methods often associated with corruption and bossism — **Tam·ma·ny·ism** \-ˌiz-əm\ *n*
Tam·muz \'täm-ˌu̇z\ *n* [Heb *Tammūz*] **:** the 10th month of the civil year or the 4th month of the ecclesiastical year in the Jewish calendar
Tam o' Shan·ter *n* **1** \ˌtam-ə-'shant-ər\ **:** the hero of Burns's poem *Tam o' Shanter* **2** *usu* **tam–o'–shanter** \'tam-ə-ˌ\ **:** a woolen cap of Scottish origin with a tight headband, wide flat circular crown, and usu. a pompon in the center
1**tamp** \'tamp\ *vt* [prob. back-formation fr. obs. *tampion, tampin* (plug), fr. ME, fr. MF *tapon, tampon*, fr. (assumed) OF *taper* to plug, of Gmc origin; akin to OE *tæppa* tap] **1 :** to fill up (a drill hole) above a blasting charge with material (as sand) **2 :** to drive in or down by a succession of light or medium blows **:** COMPACT ⟨~ wet concrete⟩ — **tamp·er** *n*
2**tamp** *n* **:** a tool for tamping
tam·pala \tam-ə-'pal-ə\ *n* [native name in India] **:** an annual amaranth (*Amaranthus tricolor*) cultivated as a potherb
tam·per \'tam-pər\ *vb* **tam·per·ing** \-p(ə-)riŋ\ [prob. fr. MF *temprer* to temper, mix, meddle — more at TEMPER] **1 :** to carry on underhand or improper negotiations (as by bribery) **2 a :** to interfere so as to weaken or change for the worse **b :** to try foolish or dangerous experiments **:** MEDDLE ~ *vt* **:** to alter for an improper purpose or in an improper way — **tam·per·er** \-pər-ər\ *n*
tam·pi·on \'tam-pē-ən, 'täm-\ *n* [obs. *tampion, tampin* plug — more at TAMP] **:** a wooden plug or a metal or canvas cover for the muzzle of a gun
1**tam·pon** \'tam-ˌpän\ *n* [F, lit., plug — more at TAMP] **:** a plug (as of cotton) introduced into a cavity usu. to arrest hemorrhage or absorb secretions
2**tampon** *vt* **:** to plug with a tampon
tam–tam \'tam-ˌtam, 'täm-ˌtäm\ *n* [Hindi *ṭamṭam*] **1 :** TOM-TOM **2 :** GONG; *esp* **:** one of a tuned set in a gamelan orchestra
1**tan** \'tan\ *vb* **tanned; tan·ning** [ME *tannen*, fr. MF *tanner*, fr. ML *tannare*, fr. *tanum, tannum* tanbark] *vt* **1 :** to convert (hide) into leather by treatment with an infusion of tannin-rich bark or other agent of similar effect **2 :** to make brown or tan esp. by exposure to the sun **3 :** THRASH, WHIP ~ *vi* **:** to get or become tanned
2**tan** *n* [F, fr. OF, fr. ML *tanum*] **1 :** TANBARK 1 **2 :** a tanning material or its active agent (as tannin) **3 :** a brown color imparted to the skin by exposure to the sun or weather **4 :** a variable color averaging a light yellowish brown
3**tan** *adj* **1 :** of, relating to, or used for tan or tanning **2 :** of the color tan
tan·a·ger \'tan-i-jər\ *n* [NL *tanagra*, fr. Pg *tangará*, fr. Tupi] **:** any of numerous American passerine birds (family Thraupidae) having brightly colored males, being mainly unmusical, and chiefly inhabiting woodlands
tan·bark \'tan-ˌbärk\ *n* **1 :** a bark rich in tannin bruised or cut into small pieces and used in tanning **2 :** a surface (as a circus ring) covered with spent tanbark
1**tan·dem** \'tan-dəm\ *n* [L, at last, at length (taken to mean "lengthwise"), fr. *tam* so; akin to OE *thæt* that] **1 a** (1) **:** a 2-seated carriage drawn by horses harnessed one before the other (2) **:** a team so harnessed **b :** a vehicle having close-coupled pairs of axles **2 :** a group of two or more arranged one behind the other or used or acting in conjunction
2**tandem** *adv* (*or adj*) **:** one after or behind another
tandem bicycle *n* **:** a bicycle for two or more persons sitting tandem
tandem cart *n* **:** a 2-wheeled vehicle having seats back to back with the front one somewhat elevated
1**tang** \'taŋ\ *n* [ME, of Scand origin; akin to ON *tangi* point of land, tang] **1 :** a projecting shank, prong, fang, or tongue (as on a knife, file, or sword) to connect with the handle **2 a :** a sharp distinctive often lingering flavor **b :** a pungent odor **3 a :** a faint suggestion **:** TRACE **b :** a distinguishing characteristic that sets apart or gives a special individuality **syn** see TASTE — **tanged** \'taŋd\ *adj*
2**tang** *vt* **1 :** to furnish with a tang **2 :** to affect with or as if with a tang
3**tang** *n* [of Scand origin; akin to Dan & Norw *tang* seaweed] **:** any of various large coarse seaweeds (esp. genus *Fucus*)
4**tang** *vb* [imit.] **:** CLANG, RING
5**tang** *n* **:** a sharp twanging sound
Tang \'täŋ\ *n* [Chin (Pek) *t'ang²*] **:** a Chinese dynasty dated A.D. 618–907 and marked by wide contacts with other cultures and by the development of printing and the flourishing of poetry and art
tan·ge·lo \'tan-jə-ˌlō\ *n* [blend of *tangerine* and *pomelo*] **:** a hybrid between a tangerine or mandarin orange and either a grapefruit or pomelo; *also* **:** its fruit
tan·gen·cy \'tan-jən-sē\ *n* **:** the quality or state of being tangent
1**tan·gent** \-jənt\ *adj* [L *tangent-, tangens*, prp. of *tangere* to touch; akin to OE *thaccian* to touch gently, stroke] **1 a :** so meeting a curve or surface that all points of intersection in an interval are coincident ⟨straight line ~ to a curve⟩ **b** (1) **:** having a common tangent line at a point ⟨~ curves⟩ (2) **:** having a common tangent plane at a point ⟨~ surfaces⟩ **2 :** diverging from an original purpose or course **:** IRRELEVANT ⟨~ remarks⟩
2**tangent** *n* [NL *tangent-, tangens*, fr. *linea tangens* tangent line] **1 :** the trigonometric function that for an acute angle in a right triangle is the ratio of the side opposite to the side adjacent **2 a :** a tangent line; *specif* **:** a straight line that is the limiting position of a secant of a curve through a fixed point and a variable point on the curve as the variable point approaches the fixed point **b :** the part of a tangent to a plane curve between the point of tangency and the x-axis **3 :** an abrupt change of course **:** DIGRESSION **4 :** a small upright flat-ended metal pin at the inner end of a clavichord key that strikes the string to produce the tone **5 :** a straight section of a road or railroad

tan·gen·tial \tan-'jen-chəl\ *adj* **1 :** of, relating to, or of the nature of a tangent **2 :** acting along or lying in a tangent ⟨~ forces⟩ **3 :** DIVERGENT, DIGRESSIVE ⟨~ comment⟩ — **tan·gen·tial·ly** \-'jench-(ə-)lē\ *adv*

tangent plane *n* **:** the plane through a point of a surface that contains the tangent lines to all the curves on the surface through the same point

tan·ger·ine \'tan-jə-,rēn, ,tan-jə-'\ *n* [F *Tanger* Tangier, Morocco] **1 a :** any of various mandarins with deep orange to almost scarlet skin and pulp grown in the U.S. and southern Africa; *broadly* **:** MANDARIN 3b **b :** a tree producing tangerines **2 :** a moderate to strong reddish orange

tan·gi·bil·i·ty \,tan-jə-'bil-ət-ē\ *n* **:** the quality or state of being tangible

1**tan·gi·ble** \'tan-jə-bəl\ *adj* [LL *tangibilis*, fr. L *tangere* to touch] **1 a :** capable of being perceived esp. by the sense of touch **:** PALPABLE **b :** substantially real **:** MATERIAL **2 :** capable of being precisely realized by the mind **3 :** capable of being appraised at an actual or approximate value ⟨~ assets⟩ **syn** see PERCEPTIBLE — **tan·gi·ble·ness** *n* — **tan·gi·bly** \-blē\ *adv*

2**tangible** *n* **:** something tangible; *esp* **:** a tangible asset

1**tan·gle** \'taŋ-gəl\ *vb* **tan·gling** \-g(ə-)liŋ\ [ME *tangilen*, prob. of Scand origin; akin to Sw dial. *taggla* to tangle] *vt* **1 :** to involve so as to hamper, obstruct, or embarrass **2 :** to seize and hold in or as if in a snare **:** ENTRAP **3 :** to unite or knit together in intricate confusion ~ *vi* **1 :** to become involved in argument or altercation **2 :** to become entangled

2**tangle** *n* **1 :** a tangled twisted mass (as of vines) confusedly interwoven **:** SNARL **2 a :** a complicated or confused state or condition **b :** a state of perplexity or complete bewilderment **3 :** DISPUTE, ARGUMENT

3**tangle** *n* [of Scand origin; akin to ON *thöngull* tangle, *thang* kelp] **:** a large seaweed

tan·gled \'taŋ-gəld\ *adj* **1 :** existing in or giving the appearance of a state of utter disorder **:** thickly intertwined **2 :** very involved ⟨~ regulations⟩

tan·gle·ment \-gəl-mənt\ *n* **:** ENTANGLEMENT

tan·gly \'taŋ-g(ə-)lē\ *adj* **:** full of tangles or knots **:** INTRICATE

1**tan·go** \'taŋ-(,)gō\ *n, pl* **tangos** [AmerSp] **:** a ballroom dance of Spanish-American origin in ¼ time and marked by posturing, frequent pointing positions, and a variety of steps

2**tango** *vi* **:** to dance the tango

Tango — a communications code word for the letter *t*

tangy \'taŋ-ē\ *adj* **:** having or suggestive of a tang

1**tank** \'taŋk\ *n* [Pg *tanque*, alter. of *estanque*, fr. *estancar* to stanch, fr. (assumed) VL *stanticare* — more at STANCH] **1** *dial* **:** POND, POOL; *esp* **:** one built as a water supply **2 :** a usu. large receptacle for holding, transporting, or storing liquids **3 :** an enclosed heavily armed and armored combat vehicle supported, driven, and steered by caterpillar treads **4 :** a prison cell or enclosure used esp. for receiving prisoners

2**tank** *vt* **:** to place, store, or treat in a tank

tan·ka \'täŋ-kə\ *n* [Jap] **:** a Japanese fixed form of verse consisting of five lines the first and third of which have five syllables and the others seven

tank·age \'taŋ-kij\ *n* **1 :** the capacity or contents of a tank **2 :** dried animal residues usu. freed from the fat and gelatin and used as fertilizer and feedstuff **3 a :** the act or process of putting or storing in tanks **b :** fees charged for storage in tanks

tan·kard \'taŋ-kərd\ *n* [ME] **:** a tall one-handled drinking vessel; *esp* **:** a silver or pewter mug with a lid

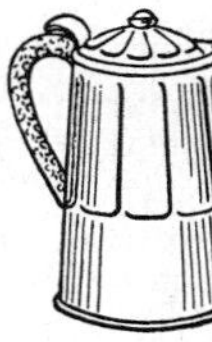

tankard

tank destroyer *n* **:** a highly mobile lightly armored vehicle usu. on a half-track or a tank chassis and mounting a cannon

tank·er \'taŋ-kər\ *n* **1 a :** a cargo boat fitted with tanks for carrying liquid in bulk **b :** a vehicle on which a tank is mounted to carry liquids; *also* **:** a cargo airplane for transporting fuel **2 :** a member of a military tank crew

tank farm *n* **:** an area with tanks for storage of oil

tank town *n* **1 :** a town at which trains stop for water **2 :** a small town

tank trailer *n* **:** a truck-drawn trailer equipped as a tanker

tan·nage \'tan-ij\ *n* **:** the act, process, or result of tanning

tan·nate \'tan-,āt\ *n* [F, fr. *tannin*] **:** a compound (as a salt) of a tannin

1**tan·ner** \'tan-ər\ *n* **:** one that tans hides

2**tanner** *n* [origin unknown] *Brit* **:** SIXPENCE

tan·nery \'tan-(ə-)rē\ *n* **:** a place where tanning is carried on

Tann·häu·ser \'tän-,hȯi-zər\ *n* [G] **:** a German knight and minnesinger noted in legend for his stay with Venus in the Venusberg cavern and his subsequent repentance

tan·nic \'tan-ik\ *adj* [F *tannique*, fr. *tannin*] **:** of, resembling, or derived from tan or a tannin

tannic acid *n* **:** TANNIN 1

tan·nin \'tan-ən\ *n* [F, fr. *tanner* to tan] **1 :** any of various soluble astringent complex phenolic substances of plant origin used in tanning, dyeing, and the making of ink and in medicine **2 :** a substance that has a tanning effect

tan·ning *n* **1 :** the art or process by which a skin is tanned **2 :** a browning of the skin by exposure to sun **3 :** WHIPPING, FLOGGING

tan·nish \'tan-ish\ *adj* **:** somewhat tan

Ta·no·an \'tän-ə-wən\ *n* [*Tano*, a group of former pueblos in New Mexico] **:** a language family of New Mexico — **Tanoan** *adj*

tan·sy \'tan-zē\ *n* [ME *tanesey*, fr. OF *tanesie*, fr. ML *athanasia*, fr. Gk, immortality, fr. *athanatos* immortal, fr. *a-* + *thanatos* death — more at THANATOS] **:** any of a genus (*Tanacetum*) of composite herbs; *esp* **:** one (*T. vulgare*) with aromatic odor and very bitter taste

tansy ragwort *n* **:** a common ragwort (*Senecio jacobaea*) with yellow flower heads that in some areas is an aggressive weed and toxic to cattle

tan·ta·late \'tant-ᵊl-,āt\ *n* **:** a salt of a tantalic acid

tan·tal·ic \tan-'tal-ik\ *adj* **:** of, relating to, or derived from tantalum; *esp* **:** being one of the weak acids derived from tantalum pentoxide and known chiefly in salts

tan·ta·lite \'tant-ᵊl-,īt\ *n* **:** a mineral $(Fe\,Mn)(Ta\,Cb)_2O_6$ consisting of a heavy iron-black oxide of iron, manganese, tantalum, and columbium

tan·ta·lize \'tant-ᵊl-,īz\ *vb* [*Tantalus*] **:** to tease or torment by or as if by presenting something desirable to the view but continually keeping it out of reach **syn** see WORRY — **tan·ta·liz·er** *n*

tan·ta·liz·ing *adj* **:** possessing a quality that arouses or stimulates desire or interest **:** mockingly or teasingly out of reach — **tan·ta·liz·ing·ly** \-,ī-ziŋ-lē\ *adv*

tan·ta·lum \'tant-ᵊl-əm\ *n* [NL, fr. L *Tantalus*; fr. its inability to absorb acid] **:** a hard ductile gray-white acid-resisting metallic element of the vanadium family found combined in rare minerals (as tantalite and columbite) — see ELEMENT table

tan·ta·lus \'tant-ᵊl-əs\ *n* [L, fr. Gk *Tantalos*] **1** *cap* **:** a wealthy king and son of Zeus punished in the lower world by being condemned to stand in water up to the chin and beneath fruit-laden branches with water and fruit receding at each attempt to drink or eat **2 :** a locked case or cellarette with contents visible but not obtainable without a key

tan·ta·mount \'tant-ə-,maůnt\ *adj* [obs. *tantamount*, n. (equivalent), fr. AF *tant amunter* to amount to as much] **:** equivalent in value, significance, or effect

tan·ta·ra \tan-'tar-ə, -'tär-\ *n* [L *taratantara*, of imit. origin] **:** the blare of a trumpet or horn

1**tan·tivy** \tan-'tiv-ē\ *adv* (*or adj*) [origin unknown] **:** at a gallop **:** HEADLONG

2**tantivy** *n* **:** a rapid gallop or ride **:** headlong rush

tan·tra \'tən-trə, 'tan-\ *n, often cap* [Skt, lit., warp, fr. *tanoti* he stretches, weaves; akin to Gk *teinein* to stretch — more at THIN] **:** one of the later Hindu or Buddhist scriptures marked by mysticism and magic and used esp. in the worship of Shakti — **tan·tric** \-trik\ *adj, often cap* — **Tan·trism** \-,triz-əm\ *n* — **Tan·trist** \-trəst\ *n*

tan·trum \'tan-trəm\ *n* [origin unknown] **:** a fit of bad temper

tan·yard \'tan-,yärd\ *n* **:** the section or part of a tannery housing tanning vats

Tao \'taů, 'daů\ *n* [Chin (Pek) tao^4, lit., way] **1 :** the ultimate principle of the universe in Taoism **2** *often not cap* **:** the path of virtuous conduct in Confucianism

Tao·ism \-,iz-əm\ *n* [*tao*] **1 :** a Chinese mystical philosophy traditionally founded by Lao-tzu in the 6th century B.C. that teaches conformity to the Tao by unassertive action and simplicity **2 :** a religion developed from Taoist philosophy and folk and Buddhist religion and concerned with obtaining long life and good fortune often by magical means — **Tao·ist** \-əst\ *adj or n* — **Tao·is·tic** \taů-'is-tik, daů-\ *adj*

1**tap** \'tap\ *n* [ME *tappe*, fr. OE *tæppa*; akin to OHG *zapho* tap] **1 a :** a plug for a hole (as in a cask) **:** SPIGOT **b :** a device consisting of a spout and valve attached to the end of a pipe to control the flow of a fluid **:** COCK **2 a :** liquor drawn through a tap **b :** the procedure of removing fluid (as from a body cavity) **3 :** a tool for forming an internal screw thread **4 :** an intermediate point in an electric circuit where a connection may be made **5 :** the action or an instance of wiretapping — **on tap 1 :** ready to be drawn ⟨ale *on tap*⟩ **2 :** broached or furnished with a tap **3 :** on hand **:** AVAILABLE

2**tap** *vt* **tapped; tap·ping 1 :** to let out or cause to flow by piercing or by drawing a plug from the containing vessel **2 a :** to pierce so as to let out or draw off a fluid **b :** to draw from or upon; *specif* **:** to cut in on (a telephone or telegraph wire) to get information or to cut in (an electrical circuit) on another circuit **3 :** to form a female screw in by means of a tap **4 :** to get money from as a loan or gift **5 :** to connect (a street gas or water main) with a local supply — **tap·per** *n*

3**tap** *vb* **tapped; tap·ping** [ME *tappen*, fr. MF *taper* to strike with the flat of the hand, of Gmc origin; akin to MHG *tāpe* paw, blow dealt with the paw] *vt* **1 :** to strike lightly esp. with a slight sound **2 :** to give a light blow with **3 :** to bring about by repeated light blows **4 :** to repair by putting a tap on **5 :** SELECT, DESIGNATE; *specif* **:** to elect to membership (as in a fraternity) ~ *vi* **1 :** to strike a light audible blow **:** RAP **2 :** to walk with light audible steps **3 :** TAP-DANCE — **tap·per** *n*

4**tap** *n* **1 a :** a light usu. audible blow; *also* **:** its sound **b :** one of several usu. rapid drumbeats on a snare drum **2 :** HALF SOLE **3 :** a small metal plate for the sole or heel of a shoe (as for tap dancing)

ta·pa \'täp-ə, 'tap-\ *n* [Marquesan & Tahitian] **1 :** the bark of the paper mulberry or of an Hawaiian tree (*Pipturus albidus*) **2 :** a coarse cloth made in the Pacific islands from the pounded bark of the paper mulberry, breadfruit, and other plants and usu. decorated with geometric patterns

tap dance *n* **:** a step dance tapped out audibly with the feet — **tap–dance** \'tap-,dan(t)s\ *vi* — **tap dancer** *n* — **tap dancing** *n*

1**tape** \'tāp\ *n* [ME, fr. OE *tæppe*] **1 :** a narrow woven fabric **2 :** a string stretched breast-high above the finishing line of a race **3 :** a narrow flexible strip or band; *specif* **:** MAGNETIC TAPE

2**tape** *vt* **1 :** to fasten, tie, bind, cover, or support with tape **2 :** to measure with a tape measure **3 :** to record on magnetic tape ~ *vi* **:** MEASURE

tape grass *n* **:** a submerged aquatic plant (*Vallisneria spiralis* of the family Vallisneriaceae) with long ribbonlike leaves

tape·line \'tā-,plīn\ *n* **:** TAPE MEASURE

tape measure *n* **:** a narrow strip (as of a limp cloth or steel tape) marked off in units (as inches or centimeters) for measuring

1**ta·per** \'tā-pər\ *n* [ME, fr. OE *tapor*, *taper*] **1 a :** a long waxed wick used esp. for lighting lamps, pipes, or fires **b :** a feeble light **2 a :** a tapering form or figure **b :** gradual diminution of thickness, diameter, or width in an elongated object **c :** a gradual decrease

2**taper** *adj* **1 :** regularly narrowed toward a point **2 :** GRADUATED ⟨~ freight rates⟩

3**taper** *vb* **ta·per·ing** \'tā-p(ə-)riŋ\ **1 :** to make or become gradually smaller toward one end **2 :** to diminish gradually

4**tap·er** \'tā-pər\ *n* **:** one that applies tape (as to seal, label, protect, decorate, or strengthen) by hand or by machine

tape–re·cord \,tā-pri-'kȯ(ə)rd\ *vt* [back-formation fr. *tape*

recording] : to make a recording of on magnetic tape — **tape recorder** *n* — **tape recording** *n*

ta·per·er \'tā-pər-ər\ *n* : one who bears a taper in a religious procession

taper off *vi* **1** : TAPER **2** : to stop gradually ~ *vt* : to make or cause to taper

tap·es·tried \'tap-ə-strēd\ *adj* **1** : covered or decorated with or as if with tapestry **2** : woven or depicted in tapestry

tap·es·try \-strē\ *n* [ME *tapistry*, modif. of MF *tapisserie*, fr. *tapisser* to carpet, cover with tapestry, fr. OF *tapis* carpet, fr. Gk *tapēs* rug, carpet] **1** : a heavy handwoven reversible textile used for hangings, curtains, and upholstery and characterized by complicated pictorial designs **2** : a nonreversible imitation of tapestry used chiefly for upholstery **3** : embroidery on canvas resembling woven tapestry

tapestry carpet *n* : a carpet in which the designs are printed in colors on the threads before the fabric is woven

ta·pe·tum \tə-'pēt-əm\ *n, pl* **ta·pe·ta** \-'pēt-ə\ [NL, fr. L *tapete* carpet, tapestry, fr. Gk *tapēt-*, *tapēs* rug, carpet] **1** : a layer of nutritive cells that invests the sporogenous tissue in the sporangium of higher plants **2** : any of various membranous layers or areas esp. of the choroid coat and retina of the eye

tape·worm \'tāp-,wərm\ *n* : any of numerous cestode worms (as of the genus *Taenia*) parasitic when adult in the intestine of man or other vertebrates

tap·hole \'tap-,hōl\ *n* : a hole for a tap; *specif* : a hole at or near the bottom of a furnace or ladle through which molten metal, matte, or slag can be tapped

tap·i·o·ca \,tap-ē-'ō-kə\ *n* [Sp & Pg, fr. Tupi *typyóca*] : a usu. granular preparation of cassava starch used esp. in puddings and as a thickening in liquid foods

ta·pir \'tā-pər; tə-'pi(ə)r, 'tā-,\ *n, pl* **tapir** *or* **tapirs** [Tupi *tapiira*] : any of several large inoffensive chiefly nocturnal ungulates (family Tapiridae) of tropical America, Malaya, and Sumatra related to the horses and rhinoceroses

ta·pis \ta-'pē, 'ta-,\ *n* [MF — more at TAPESTRY] *obs* : tapestry or similar material used for hangings and floor and table coverings — **on the tapis** : under consideration

tap·pet \'tap-ət\ *n* [irreg. fr. 3*tap*] : a lever or projection moved by some other piece (as a cam) or intended to tap or touch something else to cause a particular motion (as in forms of internal-combustion-engine valve gear)

tap·ping *n* : the act, process, or means by which something is tapped

tap·pit hen \'tap-ət-\ *n* [Sc *tappit*, alter. of E *topped*] **1** *Scot* : a crested hen **2** *Scot* : a drinking vessel with a knob on the lid

tap·room \'tap-,rüm, -,ru̇m\ *n* : BARROOM

tap·root \-,rüt, -,ru̇t\ *n* [1*tap*] **1** : a primary root that grows vertically downward and gives off small lateral roots **2** : one that has a deep central position in a line of growth or development

taps \'taps\ *n pl but sing or pl in constr* [prob. alter. of earlier *taptoo* tattoo — more at TATTOO] : the last bugle call at night blown as a signal that lights are to be put out; *also* : a similar call blown at military funerals and memorial services

tap·sal–tee·rie \,tap-səl-'tē-rē\ *adv* [by alter.] *Scot* : TOPSY-TURVY

tap·ster \'tap-stər\ *n* : one employed to dispense liquors in a barroom

1tar \'tär\ *n* [ME *terr*, *tarr*, fr. OE *teoru*; akin to OE *trēow* tree — more at TREE] **1** : a dark brown or black bituminous usu. odorous viscous liquid obtained by destructive distillation of organic material (as wood, coal, or peat) **2** [short for *tarpaulin*] : SEAMAN, SAILOR ⟨salt ~*s*⟩

2tar *vt* **tarred**; **tar·ring** : to smear with or as if with tar

3tar *or* **tarre** \'tär\ *vt* **tarred**; **tar·ring**; **tars** *or* **tarres** [ME *terren*, *tarren*, fr. OE *tyrwan*] : to urge to action : INCITE — usu. used with *on*

Tara·ca·hi·tian \,tar-ə-kə-'hē-shən\ *adj* [*Tara*humara (a Mexican people) + *Cahita* (a Mexican people)] : of, relating to, or constituting a language family of the Uto-Aztecan phylum

tar·a·did·dle *or* **tar·ra·did·dle** \,tar-ə-'did-ᵊl, 'tar-ə-,\ *n* [origin unknown] **1** : a minor falsehood : FIB **2** : pretentious nonsense

tar·an·tel·la \,tar-ən-'tel-ə\ *n* [It, fr. *Taranto*, Italy] : a vivacious folk dance of southern Italy in 6/8 time

tar·an·tism \'tar-ən-,tiz-əm\ *n* [NL *tarantismus*, fr. *Taranto*, Italy] : a dancing mania or malady of late medieval Europe

ta·ran·tu·la \tə-'ranch-(ə-)lə, -'rant-ᵊl-ə\ *n, pl* **ta·ran·tu·las** *also* **ta·ran·tu·lae** \-'ran-chə-,lē, -'rant-ᵊl-,ē\ [ML, fr. OIt *tarantola*, fr. *Taranto*] **1** : a European wolf spider (*Lycosa tarentula*) popularly held to be the cause of tarantism **2** : any of various large hairy spiders (family Theraphosidae) that are typically rather sluggish and though capable of biting sharply are not significantly poisonous to man

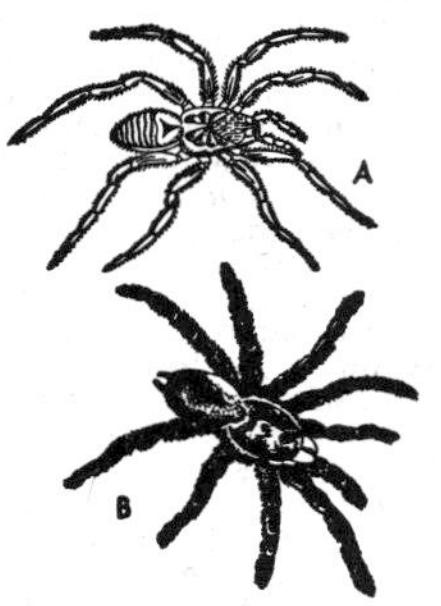

tarantulas: *A* European, *B* American

ta·rax·a·cum \tə-'rak-si-kəm\ *n* [NL, genus name, fr. Ar *ṭarakhshaqūn* wild chicory] : the dried rhizome and roots of the dandelion (*Taraxacum officinale*) used as a diuretic, a tonic, and an aperient

tar·boosh *also* **tar·bush** \tär-'büsh\ *n* [Ar *ṭarbūsh*] : a red hat similar to the fez used alone or as part of a turban and worn esp. by Muslim men

tar·brush \'tär-,brəsh\ *n* : a brush for applying tar

tar·di·grade \'tärd-ə-,grād\ *n* [deriv. of L *tardigradus* slow-moving, fr. *tardus* slow + *gradi* to step, go — more at GRADE] : any of a division (Tardigrada) of microscopic arthropods with four pairs of legs that live usu. in water or damp moss — **tardigrade** *adj*

tar·di·ly \'tärd-ᵊl-ē\ *adv* : LATE

tar·di·ness \'tärd-ē-nəs\ *n* : the quality or state of being tardy

tar·do \'tärd-(,)ō\ *adj* [It, fr. L *tardus*] : SLOW — used as a direction in music

tar·dy \'tärd-ē\ *adj* [alter. of earlier *tardif*, fr. MF, fr. (assumed) VL *tardivus*, fr. L *tardus*] **1** : moving slowly : SLUGGISH **2** : LATE; *also* : DILATORY

1tare \'ta(ə)r, 'te(ə)r\ *n* [ME] **1 a** : the seed of a vetch **b** : any of several vetches (esp. *Vicia sativa* and *V. hirsuta*) **2** *pl* : a weed of grainfields usu. held to be the darnel **3** *pl* : an undesirable element

2tare *n* [ME, fr. MF, fr. OIt *tara*, fr. Ar *ṭarḥa*, lit., that which is removed] **1** : a deduction from the gross weight of a substance and its container made in allowance for the weight of the container **2** : COUNTERWEIGHT; *esp* : an empty vessel similar to a container used to counterpoise change in weight of the container due to conditions (as temperature or moisture)

3tare *vt* : to ascertain or mark the tare of; *esp* : to weigh so as to determine the tare

targe \'tärj\ *n* [ME, fr. OF] *archaic* : a light shield

1tar·get \'tär-gət\ *n* [ME, fr. MF *targette*, dim. of *targe* light shield, of Gmc origin; akin to ON *targa* shield] **1** : a small round shield : BUCKLER **2 a** : a mark to shoot at **b** : a target marked by shots fired at it **c** : something fired at **3 a** : an object of ridicule or criticism **b** : something to be affected by an action or development **c** : a goal to be achieved **4 a** : a railroad day signal that is attached to a switch stand and indicates whether the switch is open or closed **b** : a sliding sight on a surveyor's leveling rod **5 a** : the metallic surface usu. of platinum or tungsten upon which the stream of cathode rays within an X-ray tube is focused and from which the X rays are emitted **b** : a body or surface bombarded with nuclear particles or electrons; *specif* : the fluorescent material on which the desired visual effects in electronic devices (as in radar and television) are produced

2target *vt* : to make a target of; *esp* : to set as a goal

target date *n* : the date set for an event or for the completion of a project, goal, or quota

Tar·gum \'tär-,gu̇m, -,güm\ *n* [LHeb *targūm*, fr. Aram, translation] : an Aramaic translation or paraphrase of a portion of the Old Testament

Tar·heel \'tär-,hēl\ *n* : a native or resident of North Carolina — used as a nickname

1tar·iff \'tar-əf\ *n* [It *tariffa*, fr. Ar *ta'rīf* notification] **1 a** : a schedule of duties imposed by a government on imported or in some countries exported goods **b** : a duty or rate of duty imposed in such a schedule **2** : a schedule of rates or charges of a business or public utility

2tariff *vt* : to subject to a tariff

tar·la·tan \'tär-lət-ᵊn\ *n* [F *tarlatane*] : a sheer cotton fabric in open plain weave usu. heavily sized

tar·mac \'tär-,mak\ *n* [fr. *Tarmac*, a trademark] : a tarmacadam road, apron, or runway

Tarmac *trademark* — used for a bituminous binder for roads

tar·mac·ad·am \,tär-mə-'kad-əm\ *n* **1** : a pavement constructed by spraying or pouring a tar binder over courses of crushed stone in situ and then rolling **2** : a material of tar and aggregates mixed in a plant and shaped on the roadway

tarn \'tärn\ *n* [ME *terne*, of Scand origin; akin to ON *tjörn* small lake; akin to OE *teran* to tear] : a small steep-banked mountain lake or pool

tar·nish \'tär-nish\ *vb* [MF *terniss-*, stem of *ternir*] *vt* **1** : to dull or destroy the luster of by or as if by air, dust, or dirt : SOIL, STAIN **2 a** : to detract from the good quality of : VITIATE **b** : to bring disgrace on : SULLY ~ *vi* : to become tarnished — **tarnish** *n* — **tar·nish·able** \-ə-bəl\ *adj*

ta·ro \'tär-(,)ō, 'tar-, 'ter-\ *n* [Tahitian & Maori] : a plant (*Colocasia esculenta*) of the arum family grown throughout the tropics for its edible starchy tuberous rootstocks and in temperate regions for ornament; *also* : its rootstock

tarp \'tärp\ *n* : TARPAULIN

tar paper *n* : a heavy paper coated or impregnated with tar for use esp. in building

tar·pau·lin \tär-'pȯ-lən, 'tär-pə-\ *n* [prob. fr. 1*tar* + -*palling*, -*pauling* (fr. *pall*)] **1** : waterproofed canvas or other material used for protecting goods, vehicles, athletic fields, or other exposed objects **2** : SAILOR

Tar·pe·ian \tär-'pē-(y)ən\ *adj* [L *tarpeius*] : of, relating to, or being a cliff of the Capitoline hill in Rome used in ancient times for hurling condemned criminals to their deaths

tar·pon \'tär-pən\ *n, pl* **tarpon** *or* **tarpons** [origin unknown] : a large silvery elongate isospondylous marine fish (*Tarpon atlanticus*) common off the coast of Florida that reaches a length of about six feet and is a noted sport fish

tar·ra·gon \'tar-ə-,gän, -gən\ *n* [MF *targon*, fr. ML *tarchon*, fr. Ar *ṭarkhūn*] : a small European perennial wormwood (*Artemisia dracunculus*) grown for its pungent aromatic foliage used in making pickles and vinegar; *also* : its foliage

tar·ri·ance \'tar-ē-ən(t)s\ *n* : the act or an instance of tarrying

1tar·ry \'tar-ē\ *vi* [ME *tarien*] **1** : to delay or be tardy : LINGER **2** : to abide or stay in or at a place : SOJOURN **syn** see STAY

2tarry *n* : STAY, SOJOURN

3tar·ry \'tär-ē\ *adj* : of, resembling, or covered with tar

1tar·sal \'tär-səl\ *adj* **1** : of or relating to the tarsus **2** : being or relating to plates of dense connective tissue that serve to stiffen the eyelids

2tarsal *n* : a tarsal part (as a bone or cartilage)

tar·si·er \'tär-sē-,ā, -sē-ər\ *n* [F, fr. *tarse* tarsus, fr. NL *tarsus*] : any of several small nocturnal arboreal East Indian mammals (genus *Tarsius*) related to the lemurs

tar·so·meta·tar·sus \,tär-(,)sō-'met-ə-,tär-səs\ *n* [NL, fr. *tarsus* + -*o-* + *metatarsus*] : the large compound bone of the tarsus of a bird; *also* : the segment of the limb it supports

tar·sus \'tär-səs\ *n, pl* **tar·si** \-,sī, -,sē\ [NL, fr. Gk *tarsos* wickerwork mat, flat of the foot, ankle, edge of the eyelid; akin to Gk *tersesthai* to become dry — more at THIRST] **1** : the part of the foot of a vertebrate between the metatarsus and the leg; *also* : the small bones that support this part of the limb **2** : TARSOMETATARSUS **3** : the distal part of the limb of an arthropod **4** : the tarsal plate of the eyelid

1tart \'tärt\ *adj* [ME, fr. OE *teart* sharp, severe; akin to MHG *traz* spite] **1** : agreeably sharp to the taste : pleasantly acid **2** : BITING, CAUSTIC **syn** see SOUR — **tart·ly** *adv* — **tart·ness** *n*

2tart *n* [ME *tarte*, fr. MF] **1** : a small pie or pastry shell containing jelly, custard, or fruit **2** : PROSTITUTE

1tar·tan \'tärt-ᵊn\ *n* [prob. fr. MF *tiretaine* linsey-woolsey] **1** : a plaid textile design of Scottish origin consisting of stripes of varying width and color against a solid ground and usu. patterned to designate a distinctive clan **2 a** : a twilled woolen fabric with

tartan design **b** : any fabric with tartan design **3** : a garment of tartan design

²**tar·tan** \'tärt-ᵊn, tär-'tan\ *n* [F *tartane*, fr. It *tartana*] : a Mediterranean coasting vessel with one mast carrying a large lateen sail

¹**tar·tar** \'tärt-ər\ *n* [ME, fr. ML *tartarum*] **1** : a substance consisting essentially of cream of tartar found in the juice of grapes and deposited in wine casks together with yeast and other suspended matters as a pale or dark reddish crust or sediment; *esp* : a recrystallized product yielding cream of tartar on further purification **2** : an incrustation on the teeth consisting of salivary secretion, food residue, and various salts (as calcium carbonate or phosphate)

²**tartar** *n* [ME *Tartre*, fr. MF *Tartare*, prob. fr. ML *Tartarus*, modif. of Per *Tātār* — more at TATAR] **1** *cap* : a native or inhabitant of Tatary **2** *cap* : TATAR 2 **3** *often cap* : a person of irritable or violent temper **4** : an unexpectedly formidable person — **Tartar** *adj* — **Tar·tar·i·an** \tär-'tar-ē-ən, -'ter-\ *adj*

Tar·tar·e·an \tär-'tar-ē-ən, -'ter-\ *adj* [L *tartareus*, fr. Gk *tartareios*, fr. *Tartaros*] : of, relating to, or resembling Tartarus : INFERNAL

tartar emetic *n* : a poisonous efflorescent crystalline salt $KSbOC_4H_4O_6.\frac{1}{2}H_2O$ of sweetish metallic taste that is used in dyeing as a mordant and in medicine esp. in the treatment of amebiasis

tar·tar·ic \tär-'tar-ik\ *adj* : relating to, derived from, or resembling tartar or tartaric acid

tartaric acid *n* : a strong dicarboxylic acid $C_4H_6O_6$ of plant origin that occurs in four optically isomeric crystalline forms, is usu. obtained from tartar, and is used esp. in food and medicines, in photography, and in making salts and esters

tar·tar·ous \'tärt-ə-rəs\ *adj* : containing, consisting of, or resembling tartar; *also* : derived from tartar

tar·tar sauce *or* **tar·tare sauce** \,tärt-ər-\ *n* [F *sauce tartare*] : mayonnaise with chopped pickles, olives, capers, and parsley

Tar·ta·rus \'tärt-ə-rəs\ *n* [L, fr. Gk *Tartaros*] : the infernal regions of ancient classical mythology

tart·ish \'tärt-ish\ *adj* : somewhat tart — **tart·ish·ly** *adv*

tart·let \'tärt-lət\ *n* : a small tart

tar·trate \'tär-,trāt\ *n* [ISV, fr. F *tartre* tartar, fr. ML *tartarum*] : a salt or ester of tartaric acid

tar·trat·ed \-,trāt-əd\ *adj* **1** : containing or derived from tartar **2** : combined with tartaric acid

tar·tuffe \tär-'tu̇f, -'tüf\ *n* [F *Tartufe*] **1** *cap* : a religious hypocrite and protagonist in Molière's play *Tartuffe* **2** : HYPOCRITE

Tar·via \'tär-vē-ə\ *trademark* — used for a viscid surfacing and binding material for roads

Tar·zan \'tärz-ᵊn, 'tär-,zan\ *n* [*Tarzan*, hero of adventure stories by Edgar Rice Burroughs] : a strong agile person of heroic proportions and bearing

¹**task** \'task\ *n* [ME *taske*, fr. ONF *tasque*, fr. ML *tasca* tax or service imposed by a feudal superior, fr. *taxare* to tax] **1 a** : a usu. assigned piece of work often to be finished within a certain time **b** : something hard or unpleasant that has to be done **c** : DUTY, FUNCTION **2** : REPRIMAND — used in the expressions *to take, call, or bring to task*

syn TASK, DUTY, JOB, CHORE, STINT, ASSIGNMENT mean a piece of work to be done. TASK implies work imposed by a teacher or employer or by circumstance; DUTY implies an obligation to perform or responsibility for performance; JOB applies to a piece of work voluntarily performed; it may sometimes suggest difficulty or importance; CHORE implies a minor routine activity necessary for maintaining a home or farm or enterprise; STINT implies a carefully allotted or measured quantity of assigned work or service; ASSIGNMENT implies a definite limited task assigned by one in authority

²**task** *vt* **1** *obs* : TAX **2** : to assign a task to **3** : to oppress with great labor : BURDEN

task force *n* : a temporary grouping esp. of armed forces units under one leader for the purpose of accomplishing a definite objective

task·mas·ter \'task-,mas-tər\ *n* : one that imposes a task or burdens another with labor — **task·mis·tress** \-,mis-trəs\ *n*

task·work \'tas-,kwərk\ *n* **1** : PIECEWORK **2** : hard work

Tas·ma·nian devil \(,)taz-,mā-nē-ən-, -nyən-\ *n* : a powerful carnivorous burrowing Tasmanian marsupial (*Sarcophilus ursinus*)

Tasmanian wolf *n* : a carnivorous marsupial (*Thylacinus cynocephalus*) formerly common in Australia but now limited to the remoter parts of Tasmania that somewhat resembles a dog

tasse \'tas\ *n* [perh. fr. MF *tasse* purse, pouch] : one of a series of overlapping metal plates in a suit of armor that form a short skirt over the body below the waist

¹**tas·sel** \'tas-əl, *oftenest of corn* 'täs-, 'tȯs-\ *n* [ME, clasp, tassel, fr. OF, fr. (assumed) VL *tassellus*, fr. L *taxillus* small die; akin to L *talus* anklebone, die] **1** : a pendent ornament made by laying parallel a bunch of cords of even length and fastening them at one end **2** : something resembling a tassel; *esp* : the terminal male inflorescence of some plants and esp. Indian corn

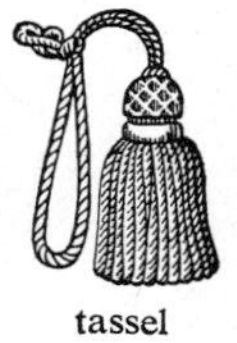

tassel

²**tassel** *vb* **tas·seled** *or* **tas·selled**; **tas·sel·ing** *or* **tas·sel·ling** \-(ə-)liŋ\ *vt* : to adorn with tassels ~ *vi* : to put forth tassel inflorescences

¹**taste** \'tāst\ *vb* [ME *tasten* to touch, test, taste, fr. OF *taster*, fr. (assumed) VL *taxitare*, freq. of L *taxare* to touch — more at TAX] *vt* **1** : EXPERIENCE, UNDERGO **2** : to ascertain the flavor of by taking a little into the mouth **3 a** : to eat or drink esp. in small quantities **b** : to experience slightly **4** : to perceive or recognize as if by the sense of taste **5** *archaic* : APPRECIATE, ENJOY ~ *vi* **1** : to eat or drink a little **2** : to test the flavor of something by taking a small part into the mouth **3** : to have perception, experience, or enjoyment : PARTAKE **4** : to have a specific flavor

²**taste** *n* **1** *obs* : TEST **2 a** *obs* : the act of tasting **b** : a small amount tasted **c** : a small amount : BIT; *esp* : a sample of experience **3** : the one of the special senses that perceives and distinguishes the sweet, sour, bitter, or salty quality of a dissolved substance and is mediated by taste buds on the tongue **4** : the objective sweet, sour, bitter, or salty quality of a dissolved substance as perceived by the sense of taste **5 a** : a sensation produced by the stimulation of the sense of taste usu. together with that of touch and smell : FLAVOR **b** : the distinctive quality of an experience **6** : individual preference : INCLINATION **7 a** : critical judgment, discernment, or appreciation **b** : manner or aesthetic quality indicative of such discernment or appreciation

syn TASTE, SAPIDITY, FLAVOR, SAVOR, TANG, RELISH, SMACK mean that property of a substance that makes it perceptible to the gustatory sense. TASTE merely indicates the property; SAPIDITY implies a highly perceptible taste as opposed to blandness; FLAVOR suggests both taste and smell acting together; SAVOR suggests delicate or pervasive flavor appealing to a sensitive palate; TANG implies a sharp, penetrating savor; RELISH stresses the peculiar flavor of a thing; SMACK suggests a taste imparted by something added to a thing; RELISH and SMACK both strongly connote enjoyment

syn TASTE, PALATE RELISH, GUSTO, ZEST mean a liking for something that gives pleasure. TASTE implies a specific liking or interest natural or acquired; PALATE implies a liking dependent on pleasurable sensation; RELISH suggests a capability for keen gratification; GUSTO implies a hearty relish that goes with vitality or high spirits; ZEST implies eagerness and avidity for doing, making, encountering, experiencing

taste bud *n* : an end organ mediating the sensation of taste and lying chiefly in the epithelium of the tongue

taste·ful \'tāst-fəl\ *adj* : having, exhibiting, or conforming to good taste — **taste·ful·ly** \-fə-lē\ *adv* — **taste·ful·ness** *n*

taste·less \'tāst-ləs\ *adj* **1 a** : having no taste : INSIPID ⟨~ vegetables⟩ **b** : DULL, UNINTERESTING **2** : not having or exhibiting good taste — **taste·less·ly** *adv* — **taste·less·ness** *n*

tast·er \'tā-stər\ *n* **1** one that tastes; *esp* : one that tests (as tea) by tasting **2** : a device for tasting or sampling; *esp* : a shallow metal cup used in testing wine

tast·i·ly \'tā-stə-lē\ *adv* : in a tasteful or tasty manner

tast·i·ness \'tā-stē-nəs\ *n* : the quality or state of being tasty

tasty \'tā-stē\ *adj* **1** : pleasing to the taste : SAVORY **2** : TASTEFUL

tat \'tat\ *vb* **tat·ted**; **tat·ting** [back-formation fr. *tatting*] *vi* : to work at tatting ~ *vt* : to make by tatting

Ta·tar \'tät-ər\ *n* [Per *Tātār*, of Turkic origin; akin to Turk *Tatar*] **1** : a member of any of numerous chiefly Turkic peoples found mainly in the Tatar republic of the U.S.S.R., the north Caucasus, Crimea, and parts of Siberia **2** : the Turkic language of any of the Tatar peoples

ta·ter \'tāt-ər\ *n* [by shortening & alter.] *dial* : POTATO

¹**tat·ter** \'tat-ər\ *n* [ME, of Scand origin; akin to ON *tötturr* tatter; akin to OHG *zotta* matted hair, tuft] **1** : a part torn and left hanging : SHRED **2** *pl* : tattered clothing : RAGS

²**tatter** *vb* : to make or become ragged

tat·ter·de·ma·lion \,tat-ərd-i-'māl-yən, -'mal-, -ē-ən\ *n* [origin unknown] : a person dressed in ragged clothing : RAGAMUFFIN

tat·tered \'tat-ərd\ *adj* **1** : wearing ragged clothes ⟨a ~ barefoot boy⟩ **2** : torn in shreds : RAGGED ⟨~ flag⟩ **3 a** : broken down : DILAPIDATED **b** : DISRUPTED, SHATTERED

tat·ter·sall \'tat-ər-,sȯl, -səl\ *n* [*Tattersall's* horse market, London, England] **1** : a pattern of colored lines forming squares of solid background **2** : a fabric woven or printed in a tattersall pattern

tat·ting \'tat-iŋ\ *n* [origin unknown] **1** : a delicate handmade lace formed usu. by looping and knotting with a single cotton thread and a small shuttle **2** : the act or process of making tatting

¹**tat·tle** \'tat-ᵊl\ *vb* **tat·tling** \'tat-liŋ, -ᵊl-iŋ\ [MD *tatelen*; akin to ME *tateren* to tattle] *vi* **1** : CHATTER PRATE **2** : to tell secrets : BLAB ~ *vt* : to utter or disclose in gossip or chatter

²**tattle** *n* **1** : idle talk : CHATTER **2** : GOSSIP, TALEBEARING

tat·tler \'tat-lər, -ᵊl-ər\ *n* **1** : TATTLETALE **2** : any of various slender long-legged shorebirds (as the willet, yellowlegs, and redshank) with a loud and frequent call

tat·tle·tale \'tat-ᵊl-,tāl\ *n* : one that tattles : INFORMER

tattletale gray *n* : a grayish white

¹**tat·too** \ta-'tü\ *n* [alter. of earlier *taptoo*, fr. D *taptoe*, fr. the phrase *tap toe!* taps shut!] **1 a** : a call sounded shortly before taps as notice to go to quarters **b** : outdoor military exercise given by troops as evening entertainment **2** : a rapid rhythmic rapping

²**tattoo** *vt* : to beat or rap rhythmically on : drum on ~ *vi* : to give a series of rhythmic taps

³**tattoo** *n* [Tahitian *tatau*] **1** : the act of tattooing : the fact of being tattooed **2** : an indelible mark or figure fixed upon the body by insertion of pigment under the skin or by production of scars

⁴**tattoo** *vt* **1** : to mark or color (the skin) with tattoos **2** : to mark the skin with (a tattoo) ⟨~*ed* a flag on his chest⟩ — **tat·too·er** *n*

tau \'tau̇, 'tȯ\ *n* [Gk, of Sem origin; akin to Heb *tāw* taw] : the 19th letter of the Greek alphabet — symbol T or τ

tau cross *n* — see CROSS illustration

taught *past of* TEACH

¹**taunt** \'tȯnt, 'tänt\ *vt* [perh. fr. MF *tenter* to try, tempt — more at TEMPT] : to reproach or challenge in a mocking or insulting manner : jeer at **syn** see RIDICULE — **taunt·er** *n* — **taunt·ing·ly** \-iŋ-lē\ *adv*

²**taunt** *n* **1** : a sarcastic challenge or insult **2** *archaic* : an object of reproach

³**taunt** *adj* [origin unknown] : very tall — used of a mast

taupe \'tōp\ *n* [F, lit., mole, fr. L *talpa*] : a brownish gray

¹**tau·rine** \'tȯr-,īn\ *adj* [L *taurinus*, fr. *taurus* bull; akin to Gk *tauros* bull, MIr *tarb*] **1** : of or relating to a bull : BOVINE **2** : of or relating to the common ox (*Bos taurus*) as distinguished from the zebu (*B. indicus*)

²**tau·rine** \'tȯr-,ēn\ *n* [ISV, fr. L *taurus*; fr. its having been discovered in ox bile] : a colorless crystalline compound $C_2H_7NO_3S$ of neutral reaction found in the juices of muscle esp. in invertebrates and obtained as a cleavage product of taurocholic acid

tau·ro·cho·lic \,tȯr-ə-'kō-lik, -'käl-ik\ *adj* [L *taurus* + ISV *-o-* + *cholic* (*acid*)] : of, relating to, or being a deliquescent acid $C_{26}H_{45}NO_7S$ occurring as the sodium salt in the bile of man, the ox, and various carnivores

Tau·rus \'tȯr-əs\ *n* [ME, fr. L (gen. *Tauri*), lit., bull] **1** : a zodiacal constellation that contains the Pleiades and Hyades and is represented pictorially by a bull's forequarters **2** : the 2d sign of the zodiac

¹**taut** \'tȯt\ *adj* [ME *tought*] **1 a** : tightly drawn : not slack **b** : HIGH-STRUNG, TENSE **2 a** : kept in proper order or condition

⟨a ~ ship⟩ **b :** not loose or flabby **:** FIRM **syn** see TIGHT — **taut·ly** *adv* — **taut·ness** *n*

2taut \'tåt\ *vt* [origin unknown] *Scot* **:** MAT, TANGLE

taut- *or* **tauto-** *comb form* [LL, fr. Gk, fr. *tauto* the same, contr. of *to auto*] **:** same ⟨*tauto*merism⟩ ⟨*taut*onym⟩

taut·en \'tȯt-ᵊn\ *vb* **taut·en·ing** \'tȯt-niŋ, -ᵊn-iŋ\ **:** to make or become taut

tau·tog \'tȯ-,tȯg, -,täg, tȯ-'\ *n* [Narraganset *tautauog*, pl.] **:** an edible fish (*Tautoga onitis*) of the wrasse family found along the Atlantic coast of the U. S. — called also *blackfish*

tau·to·log·i·cal \,tȯt-ᵊl-'äj-i-kəl\ *adj* **:** TAUTOLOGOUS — **tau·to·log·i·cal·ly** \-k(ə-)lē\ *adv*

tau·tol·o·gous \tȯ-'täl-ə-gəs\ *adj* [Gk *tautologos*, fr. *taut-* + *legein* to speak — more at LEGEND] **1 :** involving rhetorical tautology **2 :** true by virtue of its logical form alone **:** ANALYTIC — **tau·tol·o·gous·ly** *adv*

tau·tol·o·gy \tȯ-'täl-ə-jē\ *n* [LL *tautologia*, fr. Gk, fr. *tautologos*] **1 a :** needless repetition of an idea, statement, or word **b :** an instance of such repetition **2 :** a tautologous statement

tau·to·mer \'tȯt-ə-mər\ *n* [ISV] **:** one of the forms of a tautomeric compound

tau·to·mer·ic \,tȯt-ə-'mer-ik\ *adj* **:** of, relating to, or marked by tautomerism

tau·tom·er·ism \tȯ-'täm-ə-,riz-əm\ *n* **:** isomerism in which the isomers change into one another with great ease so that they ordinarily exist together in equilibrium

taut·onym \'tȯt-ə-,nim\ *n* [*taut-* + *-onym*] **:** a taxonomic binomial in which the generic name and specific epithet are alike and which is common in zoology esp. to designate a typical form but is forbidden to botany under the International Code of Botanical Nomenclature — **taut·onym·ic** \,tȯt-ə-'nim-ik\ *or* **tau·ton·y·mous** \tȯ-'tän-ə-məs\ *adj* — **tau·ton·y·my** \-mē\ *n*

tav·ern \'tav-ərn\ *n* [ME *taverne*, fr. OF, fr. L *taberna*, lit., shed, hut, shop, fr. *trabs* beam] **1 :** an establishment where alcoholic liquors are sold to be drunk on the premises **2 :** INN

tav·ern·er \'tav-ə(r)-nər\ *n* **:** one who keeps a tavern

1taw \'tȯ\ *vt* [ME *tawen* to prepare for use, fr. OE *tawian;* akin to L *bonus* good] **:** to tan (skin) with alum or salt

2taw *n* [origin unknown] **1 a :** a marble used as a shooter **b :** RINGTAW **2 :** the line from which players shoot at marbles **3 :** a square-dance partner

3taw *vi* **:** to shoot a marble

4taw \'täf, 'tȯf, 'täv, 'tȯv\ *n* [Heb *tāw*, lit., mark, cross] **:** the 23d letter of the Hebrew alphabet — symbol ת

taw·dri·ly \'tȯd-rə-lē, 'täd-\ *adv* **:** in a tawdry manner

taw·dri·ness \'tȯd-rē-nəs, 'täd-\ *n* **:** the quality or state of being tawdry

1taw·dry \-rē\ *n* [*tawdry lace* (a tie of lace for the neck), fr. *St. Audrey* (St. Etheldreda) †679 queen of Northumbria] **:** cheap showy finery

2tawdry *adj* **:** cheap and gaudy in appearance and quality **syn** see GAUDY

taw·ie \'tȯ-ē\ *adj* [prob. fr. 1*taw*] *Scot* **:** TRACTABLE

taw·ni·ness \'tȯ-nē-nəs, 'tän-ē-\ *n* **:** the quality or state of being tawny

1taw·ny \'tȯ-nē, 'tän-ē\ *adj* [ME, fr. MF *tanné*, pp. of *tanner* to tan] **:** of the color tawny **syn** see DUSKY

2tawny *n* **:** a brownish orange to light brown that is slightly redder than sorrel

taw·pie \'tȯ-pē\ *n* [of Scand origin; akin to Norw *tåpe* simpleton] *chiefly Scot* **:** a foolish or awkward young person

taws \'tȯz\ *n pl but sing or pl in constr* [prob. fr. pl. of obs. *taw* (tawed leather)] *Brit* **:** a leather strap slit into strips at the end

1tax \'taks\ *vt* [ME *taxen* to estimate, assess, tax, fr. MF *taxer*, fr. ML *taxare*, fr. L, to feel, estimate, censure, freq. of *tangere* to touch — more at TANGENT] **1 :** to assess or determine judicially the amount of (costs in a court action) **2 :** to levy a tax on **3** *obs* **:** to enter in a list **4 :** CHARGE, ACCUSE; *also* **:** CENSURE **5 :** to place under onerous and rigorous demands — **tax·abil·i·ty** \,tak-sə-'bil-ət-ē\ *n* — **tax·able** \'tak-sə-bəl\ *adj* — **tax·er** *n*

2tax *n* **1 a :** a usu. pecuniary charge imposed by authority upon persons or property for public purposes **b :** a sum levied on members of an organization to defray expenses **2 :** a heavy charge

tax- *or* **taxo-** *also* **taxi-** *comb form* [Gk *taxi-*, fr. *taxis*] **:** arrangement ⟨*tax*eme⟩ ⟨*taxi*dermy⟩

taxa *pl of* TAXON

tax·a·tion \tak-'sā-shən\ *n* **1 :** the action of taxing; *esp* **:** the imposition of taxes **2 :** revenue obtained from taxes

tax·eme \'tak-,sēm\ *n* [*tax-*] **:** a minimum grammatical feature of selection, order, stress, pitch, or phonetic modification — **tax·e·mic** \tak-'sē-mik\ *adj*

tax evasion *n* **:** deliberate failure to pay taxes usu. by falsely reporting taxable income or property

tax–ex·empt \,tak-sig-'zem(p)t\ *adj* **1 :** exempted from a tax **2 :** bearing interest that is free from federal or state income tax

1taxi \'tak-sē\ *n, pl* **tax·is** \-sēz\ *also* **tax·ies :** TAXICAB; *also* **:** a similarly operated boat or airplane

2taxi *vb* **tax·ied; taxi·ing** *or* **taxy·ing; tax·is** *or* **tax·ies** *vi* **1 :** to ride in a taxicab **2 a** *of an airplane* **:** to go at low speed along the surface of the ground or water (as when maneuvering into position for takeoff or parking) **b :** to operate an airplane on the ground under its own power ~ *vt* **1 :** to transport by taxi **2 :** to cause (an airplane) to taxi

taxi·cab \'tak-sē-,kab\ *n* [*taxi*meter *cab*] **:** an automobile that carries passengers for a fare usu. determined by the distance traveled

taxi dancer *n* **:** a girl employed by a dance hall, café, or cabaret to dance with patrons who pay a certain amount for each dance

tax·i·der·mic \,tak-sə-'dər-mik\ *adj* **:** of or relating to taxidermy

taxi·der·mist \'tak-sə-,dər-məst\ *n* **:** one who practices taxidermy

taxi·der·my \-mē\ *n* [*tax-* + *derm-* + *-y*] **:** the art of preparing, stuffing, and mounting the skins of animals and esp. vertebrates

taxi·man \'tak-sē-mən\ *n, chiefly Brit* **:** the operator of a taxi

taxi·me·ter \'tak-sē-,mēt-ər\ *n* [F *taximètre*, modif. of G *taxameter*, fr. ML *taxa* tax, charge (fr. *taxare* to tax) + *-meter*] **:** an instrument for use in a hired vehicle (as a taxicab) for automatically showing the fare due

tax·ing *adj* **:** ONEROUS, WEARING

tax·is \'tak-səs\ *n, pl* **tax·es** \'tak-,sēz\ [Gk, lit., arrangement, order, fr. *tassein* to arrange — more at TACTICS] **1 :** the manual restoration of a displaced body part; *specif* **:** manual reduction of a hernia **2 a :** reflex translational or orientational movement by a freely motile and usu. simple organism in relation to a source of stimulation (as a light or a temperature or chemical gradient) **b :** a reflex reaction involving such movement

-tax·is \'tak-səs\ *n comb form, pl* **-tax·es** \'tak-,sēz\ [NL, fr. Gk, fr. *taxis*] **1 :** arrangement **:** order ⟨homo*taxis*⟩ **2 :** taxis (sense 2) ⟨chemo*taxis*⟩

taxi stand *n* **:** a place where taxis may park awaiting hire **:** CABSTAND

tax·ite \'tak-,sīt\ *n* [G *taxit*, fr. Gk *taxis*] **:** volcanic rock of clastic or schlieric appearance — **tax·it·ic** \tak-'sit-ik\ *adj*

taxi·way \'tak-sē-,wā\ *n* **:** a usu. paved strip for taxiing (as from the terminal to a runway) at an airport

tax·on \'tak-,sän\ *n, pl* **taxa** \-sə\ *also* **tax·ons** [ISV, back-formation fr. *taxonomy*] **1 :** a taxonomic group or entity **2 :** the name applied to a taxonomic group in a formal system of nomenclature

tax·o·nom·ic \,tak-sə-'näm-ik\ *adj* **:** of or relating to taxonomy — **tax·o·nom·i·cal·ly** \-i-k(ə-)lē\ *adv*

tax·on·o·mist \tak-'sän-ə-məst\ *n* **:** a specialist in taxonomy

tax·on·o·my \-mē\ *n* [F *taxonomie*, fr. *tax-* + *-nomie* -nomy] **1 :** the study of the general principles of scientific classification **:** SYSTEMATICS **2 :** CLASSIFICATION; *specif* **:** orderly classification of plants and animals according to their presumed natural relationships

tax·pay·er \'tak-,spā-ər\ *n* **:** one that pays or is liable to pay a tax

tax stamp *n* **:** a stamp marked on or affixed to a taxable item as evidence that the tax has been paid

tax·us \'tak-səs\ *n, pl* **tax·us** \-səs\ [NL, genus comprising the yews, fr. L, yew] **:** YEW 1a

taz·za \'tät-sə\ *n* [It, cup, fr. Ar *ṭassah*] **:** a shallow cup or vase on a pedestal

TB \(')tē-'bē\ *n* [*TB* (abbr. for *tubercle bacillus*)] **:** TUBERCULOSIS

T–bar lift \,tē-,bär-\ *n* **:** a ski lift in which two skiers at a time lean against a bar suspended in the center

T–bone \'tē-,bōn\ *n* **:** a small beefsteak from the thin end of the short loin containing a T-shaped bone and a small piece of tenderloin

tea \'tē\ *n* [Chin (Amoy) *t'e*] **1 a :** a shrub (*Camellia sinensis* of the family Theaceae, the tea family) cultivated esp. in China, Japan, and the East Indies **b :** the leaves, leaf buds, and internodes of this plant used in preparing a beverage after curing by immediate withering and firing or by firing after fermenting and oxidizing or after partial oxidizing — called also respectively *green tea, black tea, oolong* **2 :** an aromatic beverage prepared from tea leaves by infusion with boiling water **3 :** any of numerous other plants more or less like tea; *also* **:** an infusion from their leaves used medicinally or as a beverage **4 a :** refreshments usu. including tea with bread and butter sandwiches, crackers, or cookies served in late afternoon **b :** a reception at which tea is served

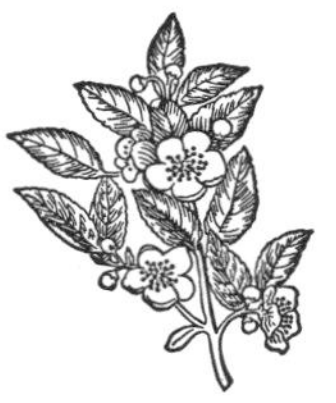

branch of tea plant in flower

tea bag *n* **:** a cloth or filter paper bag holding enough tea for an individual serving

tea ball *n* **:** a perforated metal ball for making tea in cups or in a teapot

tea·ber·ry \'tē-,ber-ē\ *n* [fr. the use of its leaves as a substitute for tea] **:** CHECKERBERRY

tea biscuit *n, Brit* **:** CRACKER, COOKIE

tea·board \'tē-,bō(ə)rd, -,bȯ(ə)rd\ *n* **:** a tray for serving tea

tea·bowl \-,bōl\ *n* **:** a teacup having no handle

tea cake *n* **1** *Brit* **:** a light flat cake **2 :** COOKIE

tea cart *n* **:** TEA WAGON

teach \'tēch\ *vb* **taught** \'tȯt\ **teach·ing** [ME *techen* to show, instruct, fr. OE *tǣcan;* akin to OE *tācn* sign — more at TOKEN] *vt* **1 a :** to cause to know a subject **b :** to cause to know how **c :** to accustom to some action or attitude **d :** to make to know the disagreeable consequences of some action **2 :** to guide the studies of **3 :** to impart the knowledge of ⟨~ algebra⟩ **4 a :** to instruct by precept, example, or experience **b :** to seek to make known and accepted ~ *vi* **:** to provide instruction **:** act as a teacher
syn INSTRUCT, EDUCATE, TRAIN, DISCIPLINE, SCHOOL: TEACH applies to any manner of imparting information or skill so that others may learn; INSTRUCT suggests methodical or formal teaching; EDUCATE implies attempting to bring out latent capabilities; TRAIN stresses instruction and drill with a specific end in view; DISCIPLINE implies subordinating to a master for the sake of controlling; SCHOOL implies training or disciplining esp. in what is hard to master or to bear

teach·abil·i·ty \,tē-chə-'bil-ət-ē\ *n* **1 :** suitability for use in teaching **2 :** ability to learn by instruction

teach·able \'tē-chə-bəl\ *adj* **:** capable of being taught; *esp* **:** apt and willing to learn — **teach·able·ness** *n* — **teach·ably** \-blē\ *adv*

teach·er \'tē-chər\ *n* **1 :** one that teaches; *esp* **:** one whose occupation is to instruct **2 :** a Mormon ranking above a deacon in the Aaronic priesthood

teachers college *n* **:** a college for the training of teachers usu. offering a full four-year course and granting a bachelor's degree

teach·er·ship \'tē-chər-,ship\ *n* **:** a teaching position

teach–in \'tē-,chin\ *n* [*teach* + *-in* (as in *sit-in*)] **:** an extended meeting esp. of college students and faculty members for lectures, debates, and discussions on U.S. foreign policy

teach·ing *n* **1 :** the act, practice, or profession of a teacher **2 :** something taught; *esp* **:** DOCTRINE

teaching fellow *n* **:** a resident student at a graduate school who holds a fellowship that involves teaching or laboratory duties

teaching machine *n* **:** any of various mechanical devices for presenting a program of instructional material

tea·cup \'tē-,kəp\ *n* **:** a cup usu. of less than 8-ounce capacity used with a saucer for hot beverages

tea·cup·ful \-,fu̇l\ *n, pl* **teacupfuls** \-,fu̇lz\ *or* **tea·cups·ful** \-,kəps-,fu̇l\ **:** as much as a teacup can hold

tea dance *n* **:** a dance held in the late afternoon

tea garden *n* **1 :** a public garden where tea and other refreshments are served **2 :** a tea plantation

tea gown *n* **:** a semiformal gown of fine materials in graceful flowing lines worn esp. for afternoon entertaining at home

tea·house \ˈtē-ˌhau̇s\ *n* **:** a public house or restaurant where tea and light refreshments are sold

teak \ˈtēk\ *n* [Pg *teca,* fr. Malayalam *tēkka*] **:** a tall East Indian timber tree (*Tectona grandis*) of the vervain family; *also* **:** its hard yellowish brown wood used esp. for shipbuilding

tea·ket·tle \ˈtē-ˌket-ᵊl, -ˌkit-\ *n* **:** a covered kettle with a handle and spout for boiling water

teak·wood \ˈtē-ˌkwu̇d\ *n* **:** TEAK

teal \ˈtē(ə)l\ *n, pl* **teal** *or* **teals** [ME *tele;* akin to MD *teling* teal] **:** any of several small short-necked river ducks (esp. genus *Anas*) of Europe and America

teal blue *n* **:** a variable color averaging a dark greenish blue

¹**team** \ˈtēm\ *n* [ME *teme,* fr. OE *tēam* offspring, lineage, group of draft animals; akin to OE *tēon* to draw, pull — more at TOW] **1** *obs* **:** LINEAGE, RACE **2 :** a group of animals: as **a :** a brood esp. of young pigs or ducks **b :** a matched group of animals for exhibition **3 a :** two or more draft animals harnessed to the same vehicle or implement; *also* **:** these with their harness and attached vehicle **b :** a draft animal often with harness and vehicle **c :** a drawn vehicle (as a wagon) **4 :** a number of persons associated together in work or activity: as **a :** a group on one side in a match **b :** CREW, GANG

²**team** *vt* **1 :** to yoke or join in a team **2 :** to convey or haul with a team ~ *vi* **1 :** to drive a team or motor-truck **2 :** to form a team ⟨~ up together⟩

³**team** *adj* **:** of or performed by a team

tea maker *n* **:** a covered spoon with perforations for holding tea used in brewing tea in a cup

team·mate \ˈtēm-ˌmāt\ *n* **:** a fellow member of a team

team·ster \ˈtēm(p)-stər\ *n* **:** one who drives a team or motortruck esp. as an occupation

team·work \ˈtēm-ˌwərk\ *n* **:** work done by a number of associates each doing a part but all subordinating personal prominence to the efficiency of the whole

tea party *n* **1 :** an afternoon social gathering at which tea is served **2** [fr. the Boston Tea Party, name facetiously applied to the occasion in 1773 when a group of citizens threw a shipment of tea into Boston harbor in protest against the tax on imports] **:** an exciting disturbance or proceeding

tea·pot \ˈtē-ˌpät\ *n* **:** a vessel with a spout in which tea is brewed and from which it is served

tea·poy \-ˌpȯi\ *n* [Hindi *tipāī*] **1 :** a 3-legged ornamental stand **2 :** a stand for a tea service

¹**tear** \ˈti(ə)r\ *n* [ME, fr. OE *tæhher, tēar;* akin to OHG *zahar* tear, L *dacruma, lacrima,* Gk *dakry*] **1 a :** a drop of clear saline fluid secreted by the lacrimal gland and diffused between the eye and eyelids to moisten the parts and facilitate their motion **b** *pl* **:** a secretion of profuse tears that overflow the eyelids and dampen the face **2** *pl* **:** an act of weeping or grieving **3 :** a transparent drop of fluid or hardened fluid matter (as resin) — **teary** \ˈti(ə)r-ē\ *adj*

²**tear** *vi* **:** to shed tears

³**tear** \ˈta(ə)r, ˈte(ə)r\ *vb* **tore** \ˈtō(ə)r, ˈtȯ(ə)r\ **torn** \ˈtō(ə)rn, ˈtȯ(ə)rn\ **tear·ing** [ME *teren,* fr. OE *teran;* akin to OHG *zeran* to destroy, Gk *derein* to skin] *vt* **1 :** to separate parts of or pull apart by force **:** REND; *also* **:** LACERATE ⟨~ the skin⟩ **2 :** to divide or disrupt by the pull of contrary forces ⟨a mind *torn* with doubts⟩ **3 :** to remove by force **:** WRENCH **4 :** to make or effect by or as if by tearing ⟨~ a hole in the wall⟩ ~ *vi* **1 :** to separate on being pulled **:** REND **2 :** to move or act with violence, haste, or force — **tear·er** *n*

syn TEAR, RIP, REND, SPLIT, CLEAVE, RIVE mean to separate forcibly. TEAR implies pulling apart by main force and leaving jagged edges; RIP implies a pulling apart in one rapid uninterrupted motion often along a seam or joint; REND is rhetorical and implies very violent or ruthless severing or sundering; SPLIT suggests a forceful but often precise separating in the direction of grain or layers; CLEAVE implies very forceful splitting or cutting with a blow; RIVE suggests action rougher and more violent than split or cleave

⁴**tear** \ˈta(ə)r, ˈte(ə)r\ *n* **1 a :** the act of tearing **b :** damage from being torn; *esp* **:** a hole or flaw made by tearing **:** RENT **2 a :** a tearing pace **:** HURRY **b :** SPREE ⟨go on a ~⟩

tear around *vi* **1 :** to go about in excited or angry haste **2 :** to lead a wild or disorderly life

tear away *vt* **:** to remove (as oneself) reluctantly

tear down *vt* **1 a :** to cause to decompose or disintegrate **:** DESTROY **b :** VILIFY, DENIGRATE **2 :** to take apart **:** DISASSEMBLE

tear·down \ˈta(ə)r-ˌdau̇n, ˈte(ə)r-\ *n* **:** DISASSEMBLY

tear·drop \ˈti(ə)r-ˌdräp\ *n* **1 :** ¹TEAR 1a **2 :** something shaped like a dropping tear; *specif* **:** a pendent gem on an earring or necklace

tear·ful \ˈti(ə)r-fəl\ *adj* **:** flowing with, accompanied by, or causing tears — **tear·ful·ly** \-fə-lē\ *adv* — **tear·ful·ness** *n*

tear gas *n* **:** a solid, liquid, or gaseous substance that on dispersion in the atmosphere blinds the eyes with tears and is used chiefly in dispelling mobs

tear·jerk·er \ˈti(ə)r-ˌjər-kər\ *n* **:** an extravagantly pathetic story, play, film, or broadcast — **tear–jerk·ing** \-kiŋ\ *adj*

tear·less \-ləs\ *adj* **:** free from tears — **tear·less·ly** *adv*

tear off *vt* **:** to compose rapidly

tea·room \ˈtē-ˌrüm, -ˌru̇m\ *n* **:** a small restaurant with service and decor designed primarily for a feminine clientele

tea rose *n* **:** any of numerous tender or half-hardy hybrid garden bush roses descended chiefly from a Chinese rose (*Rosa odorata*) and valued esp. for their abundant large usu. tea-scented blossoms — compare HYBRID TEA ROSE

tear sheet *n* **:** a sheet torn from a publication usu. to prove insertion of an advertisement to an advertiser

tear·stain \ˈti(ə)r-ˌstān\ *n* **:** a spot or streak left by tears — **tear-stained** \-ˌstānd\ *adj*

tear strip *n* **:** the scored band in a can or added narrow ribbon in a wrapper or on a fiber box that provides an easy and defined way of opening

tear tape *n* **:** a strong tape glued to the inside of a shipping container with one end protruding so that the container is readily opened by pulling out the tape

tear up *vt* **:** to damage, remove, or effect an opening in

¹**tease** \ˈtēz\ *vt* [ME *tesen,* fr. OE *tǣsan;* akin to OHG *zeisan* to tease] **1 a :** to disentangle and lay parallel by combing or carding ⟨~ wool⟩ **b :** TEASEL **2 :** to tear in pieces; *esp* **:** to shred (a tissue or specimen) for microscopic examination **3 a :** to annoy persistently **:** HARASS **b :** TANTALIZE **c :** to goad to anger, resentment, or confusion esp. in sport **:** TORMENT **d :** to annoy with petty persistent requests **:** PESTER; *also* **:** to obtain by repeated coaxing **e :** to persuade to acquiesce esp. by persistent small efforts **:** COAX **4 :** to comb (hair) by taking hold of a strand and pushing the short hairs toward the scalp with the comb **syn** see WORRY — **teas·er** *n* — **teas·ing·ly** \ˈtē-ziŋ-lē\ *adv*

²**tease** *n* **1 :** the act of teasing **:** the state of being teased **2 :** one that teases

¹**tea·sel** *or* **tea·zel** *or* **tea·zle** \ˈtē-zəl\ *n* [ME *tesel,* fr. OE *tǣsel;* akin to OE *tǣsan* to tease] **1 :** any of a genus (*Dipsacus* of the family Dipsacaceae, the teasel family) of Old World prickly herbs; *esp* **:** one (*D. fullonum*) with flower heads covered with stiff hooked bracts — called also *fuller's teasel* **2 a :** a flower head of the fuller's teasel used when dried to raise a nap on woolen cloth **b :** a wire substitute for the fuller's teasel

²**teasel** *vt* **tea·seled** *or* **tea·selled; tea·sel·ing** *or* **tea·sel·ling** \ˈtēz-(ə-)liŋ\ **:** to nap (cloth) with teasels

tease out *vt* **:** to obtain by disentangling or freeing with a pointed instrument

tea service *n* **:** a set of china or metalware for service at table: **a :** a set of china consisting usu. of a teapot, sugar bowl, creamer, and plates, cups, and saucers **b :** a set of metalware consisting usu. of a teapot, sugar bowl, creamer, and waste bowl, kettle, and tray

tea set *n* **1 :** TEA SERVICE **2 :** a china set consisting of teapot, sugar bowl, creamer, cups and saucers, and dessert plates

tea shop *n* **1** *chiefly Brit* **:** TEAROOM **2** *Brit* **:** LUNCHROOM, RESTAURANT

tea·spoon \ˈtē-ˌspün, -ˈspün\ *n* **:** a small spoon used esp. for eating soft foods and stirring beverages and holding one third of a tablespoon

tea·spoon·ful \-ˌfu̇l\ *n, pl* **teaspoonfuls** \-ˌfu̇lz\ *or* **tea·spoons·ful** \-ˌspünz-ˌfu̇l, -ˈspünz-\ **1 :** as much as a teaspoon can hold **2 :** a unit of measure equal to 1⅓ fluidrams

teat \ˈtit, ˈtēt\ *n* [ME *tete,* fr. OF, of Gmc origin; akin to OE *tit* teat, MHG *zitze*] **1 :** the protuberance through which milk is drawn from an udder or breast **:** NIPPLE **2 :** a small projection or a nib (as on a mechanical part)

tea table *n* **:** a table used or spread for tea; *specif* **:** a small table for serving afternoon tea

teat·ed \ˈtit-əd, ˈtēt-\ *adj* **:** having teats

tea·time \ˈtē-ˌtīm\ *n* **:** the customary time for tea **:** late afternoon or early evening

tea towel *n* **:** DISH TOWEL

tea tray *n* **:** a tray that accommodates a tea service

tea wagon *n* **:** a small table on wheels used in serving tea and light refreshments

Te·bet \tā-ˈvāt(h), ˈtā-ˌves\ *n* [Heb *Ṭēbhēth*] **:** the 4th month of the civil year or the 10th month of the ecclesiastical year in the Jewish calendar

teched \ˈtecht\ *adj* [alter. of *touched*] **:** somewhat deranged

tech·ne·tium \tek-ˈnē-sh(ē-)əm\ *n* [NL, fr. Gk *technētos* artificial, fr. *technasthai* to devise by art, fr. *technē*] **:** a metallic element obtained by bombarding molybdenum with deuterons or neutrons and in the fission of uranium — see ELEMENT table

¹**tech·nic** \ˈtek-nik\ *adj* [Gk *technikos*] **:** TECHNICAL

²**tech·nic** \ˈtek-nik, *for 1 also* tek-ˈnēk\ *n* **1 :** TECHNIQUE 1 **2** *pl but sing or pl in constr* **:** TECHNOLOGY 2a

tech·ni·cal \ˈtek-ni-kəl\ *adj* [Gk *technikos* of art, skillful, fr. *technē* art, craft, skill; akin to Gk *tektōn* builder, carpenter, L *texere* to weave, OHG *dahs* badger] **1 a :** having special usu. practical knowledge esp. of a mechanical or scientific subject **b :** marked by or characteristic of specialization **2 :** of or relating to a particular subject; *esp* **:** of or relating to a practical subject organized on scientific principles **3 a :** according to a strict legal interpretation **b :** LEGAL 6 **4 :** of or relating to technique **5 :** of, relating to, or produced by commercial processes ⟨~ sulfuric acid⟩ **6 :** resulting chiefly from internal market factors rather than external influences ⟨~ reaction⟩ — **tech·ni·cal·ly** \-k(ə-)lē\ *adv* — **tech·ni·cal·ness** \-kəl-nəs\ *n*

tech·ni·cal·i·ty \ˌtek-nə-ˈkal-ət-ē\ *n* **1 :** the quality or state of being technical **2 :** something technical; *esp* **:** a detail meaningful only to a specialist

tech·ni·cal·iza·tion \ˌtek-ni-kə-lə-ˈzā-shən\ *n* **:** the action of making technical

technical knockout *n* **:** a knockout ruled by the referee when a boxer is unable or is declared to be unable (as because of injury) to continue the fight

technical sergeant *n* **:** a noncommissioned officer in the air force ranking above a staff sergeant and below a master sergeant

tech·ni·cian \tek-ˈnish-ən\ *n* **1 :** a specialist in the technical details of a subject or occupation **2 :** one who has acquired the technique of an art or other area of specialization

tech·nique \tek-ˈnēk\ *n* [F, fr. *technique* technical, fr. Gk *technikos*] **1 :** the manner in which technical details are treated (as by a writer) or basic physical movements are used (as by a dancer); *also* **:** ability to treat such details or use such movements **2 a :** technical methods esp. in scientific research **b :** a method of accomplishing a desired aim

techno- *comb form* [Gk, fr. *technē*] **1 :** art **:** craft ⟨*techno*graphy⟩ **2 :** technical **:** technological ⟨*techno*cracy⟩

tech·noc·ra·cy \tek-ˈnäk-rə-sē\ *n* **:** government by technicians; *specif* **:** management of society by technical experts — **tech·no·crat** \ˈtek-nə-ˌkrat\ *n* — **tech·no·crat·ic** \ˌtek-nə-ˈkrat-ik\ *adj*

tech·no·log·i·cal \ˌtek-nə-ˈläj-i-kəl\ *or* **tech·no·log·ic** \-ˈläj-ik\ *adj* **1 :** of, relating to, or characterized by technology ⟨~ advance⟩ **2 :** resulting from improvement in technical processes that increases productivity of machines and eliminates manual operations or operations done by older machines ⟨~ unemployment⟩ — **tech·no·log·i·cal·ly** \-i-k(ə-)lē\ *adv*

tech·nol·o·gist \tek-ˈnäl-ə-jəst\ *n* **:** a specialist in technology

tech·nol·o·gy \-jē\ *n* [Gk *technologia* systematic treatment of an art, fr. *techno-* + *-logia* -logy] **1 :** technical language **2 a :** applied science **b :** a technical method of achieving a practical purpose **3 :** the totality of the means employed to provide objects necessary for human sustenance and comfort

techy *var of* TETCHY

tec·ton·ic \tek-'tän-ik\ *adj* [LL *tectonicus*, fr. Gk *tektonikos* of a builder, fr. *tektōn* builder — more at TECHNICAL] **:** STRUCTURAL, CONSTRUCTIONAL: as **a :** ARCHITECTURAL **b :** of or relating to the deformation of the earth's crust, the forces involved in or producing such deformation, and the resulting forms

tec·ton·ics \-iks\ *n pl but sing or pl in constr* **1 :** the science or art of construction (as of a building) **2 a :** a branch of geology concerned with structure esp. with folding and faulting **b :** DIASTROPHISM

tec·trix \'tek-triks\ *n, pl* **tec·tri·ces** \'tek-trə-,sēz, tek-'trī-(,)\ [NL *tectric-*, *tectrix*, fem. of L *tector* one that covers, fr. *tectus*, pp. of *tegere* to cover — more at THATCH] **:** COVERT 2

ted \'ted\ *vt* **ted·ded; ted·ding** [(assumed) ME *tedden;* akin to Gk *daiesthai* to divide, distribute — more at TIDE] **:** to spread or turn from the swath and scatter (as new-mown grass) for drying

ted·der \'ted-ər\ *n* **:** one that teds; *specif* **:** a machine for stirring and spreading hay to hasten drying and curing

ted·dy bear \'ted-ē-, , ,ted-ē-'\ *n* [*Teddy*, nickname of Theodore Roosevelt †1919 26th U.S. president; fr. a cartoon depicting the president sparing the life of a bear cub while hunting] **:** a stuffed toy bear

Te De·um \(')tā-'dā-əm, (')tē-'dē-\ *n, pl* **Te Deums** [ME, fr. LL *te deum laudamus* thee, God, we praise; fr. the opening words of the hymn] **:** an ancient liturgical hymn of praise to God

te·dious \'tēd-ē-əs, 'tē-jəs\ *adj* [ME, fr. LL *taediosus*, fr. L *taedium*] **:** tiresome because of length or dullness **:** BORING — **te·dious·ly** *adv* — **te·dious·ness** *n*

te·di·um \'tēd-ē-əm\ *n* [L *taedium* disgust, irksomeness, fr. *taedēre* to disgust, weary] **:** the quality or state of being tedious **:** TEDIOUSNESS; *also* **:** BOREDOM

1tee \'tē\ *n* [ME] **1 :** the letter *t* **2 :** something shaped like a capital T — **to a tee :** PRECISELY, EXACTLY

2tee *n* [of unknown origin] **1 a :** a small mound or a peg on which a golf ball is placed before the beginning of play on a hole **b :** a device for holding a football in position for kicking **2 :** the area from which a golf ball is struck at the beginning of play on a hole

3tee *vt* **teed; tee·ing :** to place (a ball) on a tee — often used with *up*

1teem \'tēm\ *vb* [ME *temen*, fr. OE *tīeman, tǣman;* akin to OE *tēam* offspring — more at TEAM] *vt, archaic* **:** to bring forth **:** give birth to **:** PRODUCE ~ *vi* **1** *obs* **:** to become pregnant **:** CONCEIVE **2 a :** to become filled to overflowing **:** ABOUND ⟨lakes ~ with fish⟩ **b :** to be present in large quantity

2teem *vt* [ME *temen*, fr. ON *tœma;* akin to OE *tōm* empty] *archaic* **:** EMPTY, POUR

1teen \'tēn\ *n* [ME *tene*, fr. OE *tēona*, injury, grief; akin to ON *tjōn* loss, damage] *archaic* **:** MISERY, AFFLICTION

2teen *adj* **:** TEEN-AGE

teen–age \'tē-,nāj\ *or* **teen–aged** \-,nājd\ *adj* **:** of, being, or relating to people in their teens

teen–ag·er \-,nā-jər\ *n* **:** a person in his teens

teen·er \'tē-nər\ *n* **:** TEEN-AGER

teens \'tēnz\ *n pl* [-*teen* (as in *thirteen*)] **1 :** the numbers 13 to 19 inclusive; *specif* **:** the years 13 to 19 in a lifetime or century **2 :** TEEN-AGERS

tee·ny \'tē-nē\ *adj* [by alter.] **:** TINY

teeny·bop·per \'tē-nē-,bäp-ər\ *n* [2*teen* + -*y* + *bopper*] **1 :** a teen-aged girl **2 :** a young teen-ager who emulates the older hippies

tee off *vi* **1 :** to drive from a tee **2 :** BEGIN, START **3 :** to hit hard — often used with *on* **4 :** to make an angry denunciation — often used with *on*

tee·pee *var of* TEPEE

tee shirt *var of* T-SHIRT

tee·ter \'tēt-ər\ *vi* [ME *titeren* to totter, reel; akin to OHG *zittarōn* to shiver, Gk *dramein* to run] **1 a :** to move unsteadily **:** WOBBLE **b :** WAVER, VACILLATE **2 :** SEESAW — **teeter** *n*

tee·ter·board \-,bō(ə)rd, -,bȯ(ə)rd\ *n* **1 :** SEESAW 2b **2 :** a board placed on a raised support in such a way that a person standing on one end of the board is thrown into the air if another person jumps on the opposite end

teeth *pl of* TOOTH

teethe \'tēth\ *vi* [back-formation fr. *teething*] **:** to cut one's teeth **:** grow teeth

teeth·ing \'tē-thiŋ\ *n* [*teeth*] **1 :** the first growth of teeth **2 :** the phenomena accompanying growth of teeth through the gums

teething ring *n* **:** a usu. rubber or plastic ring for a teething infant to bite on

teeth·ridge \'tēth-,rij\ *n* **:** the inner surface of the gums of the upper front teeth

tee·to·tal \'tē-'tōt-ᵊl, -,tōt-\ *adj* [total + *total* (abstinence)] **1 :** of, relating to, or practicing teetotalism **2 :** TOTAL, COMPLETE —**teetotal** *vi* — **tee·to·tal·er** *or* **tee·to·tal·ler** \-'tōt-ᵊl-ər\ *n* — **tee·to·tal·ly** \-'tōt-ᵊl-ē, -,tōt-\ *adv*

tee·to·tal·ism \-'tōt-ᵊl-,iz-əm\ *n* **:** the principle or practice of complete abstinence from alcoholic drinks — **tee·to·tal·ist** \-ᵊl-əst\ *n*

tee·to·tum \'tē-'tōt-əm\ *n* [1*tee* + L *totum* all, fr. neut. of *totus* whole; fr. the letter *T* inscribed on one side as an abbr. of *totum* (take) all] **:** a small top usu. inscribed with letters

teg·men \'teg-mən\ *n, pl* **teg·mi·na** \-mə-nə\ [NL *tegmin-*, *tegmen*, fr. L, covering, fr. *tegere* to cover — more at THATCH] **:** a superficial layer or cover usu. of a plant or animal part

teg·men·tum \teg-'ment-əm\ *or* **teg·u·men·tum** \,teg-yə-\ *n, pl* **teg·men·ta** *or* **teg·u·men·ta** \-'ment-ə\ [NL, fr. L, fr. *tegere*] **:** COVERING, TEGMEN

teg·u·lar \'teg-yə-lər\ *adj* [L *tegula* tile, fr. *tegere*] **:** of, relating to, or resembling a tile; *also* **:** arranged like tiles — **teg·u·lar·ly** *adv*

teg·u·ment \'teg-yə-mənt\ *n* [ME, fr. L *tegumentum*] **:** INTEGUMENT — **teg·u·men·ta·ry** \,teg-yə-'ment-ə-rē, -'men-trē\ *adj*

teil tree \'tē(ə)l-\ *n* [F dial. *teil*, fr. OF, fr. L *tilia*] **:** LINDEN 1a

tek·tite \'tek-,tīt\ *n* [ISV, fr. Gk *tēktos* molten, fr. *tēkein* to melt — more at THAW] **:** a glassy body of probably meteoritic origin and of rounded but indefinite shape found esp. in Czechoslovakia, Indonesia, and Australia

tel- *or* **telo-** *comb form* [ISV, fr. Gk *telos* — more at WHEEL] **:** end ⟨*tel*angiectasia⟩

tel·a·mon \'tel-ə-,män\ *n, pl* **tel·a·mo·nes** \,tel-ə-'mō-(,)nēz\ [L, fr. Gk *telamōn* bearer, supporter; akin to Gk *tlēnai* to bear — more at TOLERATE] **:** a male figure used like a caryatid as a supporting column or pilaster

tel·an·gi·ec·ta·sia \,tel-,an-jē-,ek-'tā-zh(ē-)ə\ *or* **tel·an·gi·ec·ta·sis** \-'ek-tə-səs\ *n* [NL, fr. *tel-* + *angi-* + *ectasia, ectasis* ectasis] **:** an abnormal dilatation of capillary vessels and arterioles that often forms an angioma — **tel·an·gi·ec·tat·ic** \-,ek-'tat-ik\ *adj*

Tel·Au·to·graph \te-'lȯt-ə-,graf\ *trademark* — used for a facsimile telegraph for reproducing graphic matter by means of a transmitter in which the motions of a pencil are reproduced by a receiving pen controlled by electromagnetic devices

tele \'tel-ē\ *n* **:** TELEVISION

tele- *or* **tel-** *comb form* [NL, fr. Gk *tēle-*, *tēl-*, fr. *tēle* far off — more at PALE-] **1 :** distant **:** at a distance **:** over a distance ⟨*tele*gram⟩ ⟨*tel*esthesia⟩ **2 a :** telegraph ⟨*tele*typewriter⟩ **b :** television ⟨*tele*cast⟩ **c :** telephoto ⟨*tel*elens⟩ **d :** telecommunication ⟨*tele*man⟩

tele·cam·era \'tel-i-,kam-(ə-)rə\ *n* **:** a television camera

tele·cast \'tel-i-,kast\ *vb* **telecast** *also* **tele·cast·ed; tele·cast·ing** [*tele-* + broad*cast*] **:** to broadcast by television — **telecast** *n* — **tele·cast·er** *n*

tele·com·mu·ni·ca·tion \,tel-i-kə-,myü-nə-'kā-shən\ *n* [ISV] **1 :** communication at a distance (as by cable, radio, telegraph, telephone, or television) **2 :** a science that deals with telecommunication ⟨study ~⟩ — usu. used in pl.

tele·course \'tel-i-,kō(ə)rs, -,kȯ(ə)rs\ *n* **:** a course of study conducted over television

te·le·du \'tel-ə-,dü, tə-'led-(,)ü\ *n* [Malay *tĕledu*] **:** a small short-tailed blackish brown carnivorous mammal (*Mydaus meliceps*) of the mountains of Java and Sumatra that like the related skunk secretes and expels offensive fluid

tele·film \'tel-ə-,film\ *n* **:** a motion picture produced for televising

tele·ge·nic \,tel-ə-'jen-ik, -'jē-nik\ *adj* **:** suitable for television broadcast — **tele·ge·ni·cal·ly** \-i-k(ə-)lē, -ni-\ *adv*

te·leg·o·ny \tə-'leg-ə-nē\ *n* [ISV] **:** the supposed carrying over of the influence of a sire to the offspring of subsequent matings of the dam with other males

1tele·gram \'tel-ə-,gram, *South also* -grəm\ *n* **:** a telegraphic dispatch

2tele·gram \-,gram\ *vb* **tele·grammed; tele·gram·ming :** TELEGRAPH

1tele·graph \-,graf\ *n* [F *télégraphe*, fr. *télé-* tele- (fr. Gk *tēle-*) + *-graphe* -graph] **1 :** an apparatus for communication at a distance by coded signals; *esp* **:** an apparatus, system, or process for communication at a distance by electric transmission over wire **2 :** TELEGRAM

2telegraph *vt* **1 a :** to send or communicate by or as if by telegraph **b :** to send a telegram to **c :** to send by means of a telegraphic order **2 :** to make known by signs esp. unknowingly and in advance ⟨~ a punch⟩ — **te·leg·ra·pher** \tə-'leg-rə-fər\ *n* — **te·leg·ra·phist** \-fəst\ *n*

tele·graph·ic \,tel-ə-'graf-ik\ *adj* **1 :** of or relating to the telegraph **2 :** CONCISE, TERSE — **tele·graph·i·cal·ly** \-i-k(ə-)lē\ *adv*

te·leg·ra·phone \tə-'leg-rə-,fōn\ *n* [Dan *telegrafon*, fr. ISV *tele-* + *-graph* + *-phone*] **:** an early magnetic recorder

telegraph plant *n* **:** an East Indian tick trefoil (*Desmodium gyrans*) whose lateral leaflets jerk up and down like the arms of a semaphore and also rotate on their axes

te·leg·ra·phy \tə-'leg-rə-fē\ *n* **:** the use or operation of a telegraph apparatus or system for transmitting or receiving communications

tele·ki·ne·sis \,tel-i-kə-'nē-səs, -(,)kī-\ *n* [NL, fr. Gk *tēle-* + *kinēsis* motion — more at -KINESIS] **:** the apparent production of motion in objects (as by a spiritualistic medium) without contact or other physical means — **tele·ki·net·ic** \-'net-ik\ *adj*

tele·lens \'tel-i-,lenz\ *n* **:** a telephoto lens

Te·lem·a·chus \tə-'lem-ə-kəs\ *n* [L, fr. Gk *Tēlemachos*] **:** a son of Odysseus and Penelope who after failing to find his father returns home to Ithaca in time to help slay Penelope's suitors

tele·man \'tel-ē-,man\ *n* [*tele-* + *man*] **:** a petty officer in the navy who performs clerical, coding, and communications duties

tel·e·mark \'tel-ə-,märk\ *n, often cap* [Norw, fr. *Telemark*, region in Norway] **:** a turn in which the ski that is to be on the outside of the turn is advanced considerably ahead of the other ski and then turned inward at a steadily widening angle until the actual turn

1tele·me·ter \'tel-ə-,mēt-ər\ *n* [ISV] **1 :** an instrument for measuring the distance of an object from an observer **2 :** an electrical apparatus for measuring a quantity (as pressure, radiation intensity, speed, or temperature), transmitting the result esp. by radio to a distant station, and there indicating or recording the quantity measured — **tele·met·ric** \,tel-ə-'me-trik\ *adj* — **tele·met·ri·cal·ly** \-tri-k(ə-)lē\ *adv* — **te·lem·e·try** \tə-'lem-ə-trē\ *n*

2telemeter *vt* **:** to transmit (the measurement of a quantity) by telemeter ⟨data ~*ed* from a rocket⟩ ~ *vi* **:** to telemeter the measurement of a quantity ⟨a ~*ing* device⟩

tel·en·ce·phal·ic \,tel-,en(t)-sə-'fal-ik\ *adj* **:** of or relating to the telencephalon

tel·en·ceph·a·lon \,tel-en-'sef-ə-,län, -lən\ *n* [NL, fr. *tel-* + *encephalon*] **:** the anterior subdivision of the forebrain comprising the cerebral hemispheres and associated structures

te·le·o·log·i·cal \,tel-ē-ə-'läj-i-kəl, ,tē-lē-\ *or* **te·le·o·log·ic** \-'läj-ik\ *adj* **:** exhibiting or relating to design or purpose esp. in nature ⟨~ argument for God's existence⟩ — **te·le·o·log·i·cal·ly** \-i-k(ə-)lē\ *adv*

te·le·ol·o·gist \-'äl-ə-jəst\ *n* **:** a specialist or believer in teleology

te·le·ol·o·gy \-jē\ *n* [NL *teleologia*, fr. Gk *tele-*, *telos* end, purpose + *-logia* -logy — more at WHEEL] **1 a :** the study of evidences of design in nature **b :** a doctrine (as vitalism) that ends are immanent in nature **c :** a doctrine explaining phenomena by final causes **2 :** the fact or character attributed to nature or natural processes of being directed toward an end or shaped by a purpose **3 :** use of design or purpose as an explanation of natural phenomena

te·le·ost \'tel-ē-,äst, 'tē-lē-\ *n* [deriv. of Gk *teleios* complete, perfect (fr. *telos* end) + *osteon* bone — more at OSSEOUS] **:** any of a group (Teleostei or Teleostomi) of fishes comprising the fishes with a bony rather than a cartilaginous skeleton and including all jawed fishes with the exception of the elasmobranchs and sometimes of the ganoids and dipnoans — **teleost** *adj* — **te·le·os·te·an** \,tel-ē-'äs-tē-ən, ,tē-lē-\ *adj or n*

tel·eo·stome \'tel-ē-ə-,stōm, 'tē-lē-\ *n* [deriv. of Gk *teleios* + *stoma* mouth — more at STOMACH] **:** TELEOST

tele·path·ic \,tel-ə-'path-ik\ *adj* **:** of, relating to, or communicated by telepathy — **tele·path·i·cal·ly** \-i-k(ə-)lē\ *adv*

te·lep·a·thy \tə-'lep-ə-thē\ *n* **:** apparent communication from one mind to another otherwise than through the channels of sense

¹**tele·phone** \ˈtel-ə-ˌfōn\ *n* **:** an instrument for reproducing sounds at a distance; *specif* **:** one in which sound is converted into electrical impulses for transmission by wire

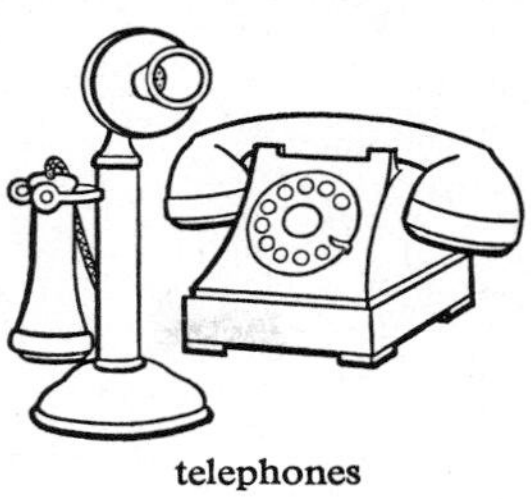
telephones

²**telephone** *vi* **:** to communicate by telephone ~ *vt* **1 :** to send by telephone **2 :** to speak to by telephone — **tele·phon·er** *n*

telephone book *n* **:** a book listing names, addresses, and telephone numbers of telephone subscribers — called also *telephone directory*

telephone booth *n* **:** an enclosure within which one may stand or sit while calling a number over the telephone

telephone receiver *n* **:** a device (as in a telephone) for converting electric impulses or varying current into sound

tele·phon·ic \ˌtel-ə-ˈfän-ik\ *adj* **1 :** conveying sound to a distance **2 :** of, relating to, or conveyed by telephone — **tele·phon·i·cal·ly** \-i-k(ə-)lē\ *adv*

te·le·pho·nist \ˈtel-ə-ˌfō-nəst, tə-ˈlef-ə-\ *n, Brit* **:** a telephone switchboard operator

te·le·pho·ny \tə-ˈlef-ə-nē, ˈtel-ə-ˌfō-\ *n* **:** the use or operation of an apparatus for transmission of sounds between widely removed points with or without connecting wires

¹**tele·pho·to** \ˌtel-ə-ˈfōt-(ˌ)ō\ *adj* **:** TELEPHOTOGRAPHIC ⟨a ~ effect⟩; *specif* **:** being a camera lens system designed to give a usu. large image of a distant object

²**telephoto** *n* **:** a telephoto lens

Telephoto *trademark* — used for an apparatus for transmitting photographs electrically or for a photograph so transmitted

tele·pho·to·graph·ic \-ˌfōt-ə-ˈgraf-ik\ *adj* **:** of, relating to, or being the process of telephotography

tele·pho·tog·ra·phy \-fə-ˈtäg-rə-fē\ *n* [ISV] **1 :** FACSIMILE 2 **2 :** the photography of distant objects usu. by a camera provided with a telephoto lens or mounted in place of the eyepiece of a telescope

tele·play \ˈtel-ə-ˌplā\ *n* **:** a play written for television

tele·print·er \-ˌprint-ər\ *n* **:** TELETYPEWRITER

Tele·Promp·Ter \-ˌpräm(p)-tər\ *trademark* — used for a device for unrolling a magnified script in front of a speaker on television

tel·er·an \ˈtel-ə-ˌran\ *n* [*tele*vision-*ra*dar *n*avigation] **:** a system of aerial navigation that utilizes a combination of television and radar for the guidance of airplanes

¹**tele·scope** \ˈtel-ə-ˌskōp\ *n* [NL *telescopium*, fr. Gk *tēleskopos* farseeing, fr. *tēle-* tele- + *skopein* to look — more at SPY] **1 :** a usu. tubular optical instrument for viewing distant objects by means of the refraction of light rays through a lens or the reflection of light rays by a concave mirror — compare REFLECTOR, REFRACTOR **2 :** any of various tubular magnifying optical instruments **3 :** RADIO TELESCOPE

²**telescope** *vi* **1 :** to slide or pass one within another like the cylindrical sections of a hand telescope **2 :** to force a way into or enter another lengthwise as the result of collision **3 :** to become telescoped ~ *vt* **1 :** to cause to telescope **2 :** COMPRESS, CONDENSE

telescope box *n* **:** a two-piece box in which the sides of one part fit over those of the other

tele·scop·ic \ˌtel-ə-ˈskäp-ik\ *adj* **1 a :** of, with, or relating to a telescope **b :** suitable for seeing or magnifying distant objects **2 :** seen or discoverable only by a telescope ⟨~ stars⟩ **3 :** able to discern objects at a distance **:** FARSEEING **4 :** having parts that telescope — **tele·scop·i·cal·ly** \-i-k(ə-)lē\ *adv*

tel·es·the·sia \ˌtel-əs-ˈthē-zh(ē-)ə\ *n* [NL, fr. *tele-* + *esthesia*] **:** an impression supposedly received at a distance without the normal operation of the organs of sense — **tel·es·thet·ic** \-ˈthet-ik\ *adj*

tele·ther·mo·scope \ˌtel-ə-ˈthər-mə-ˌskōp\ *n* **:** an apparatus for indicating the temperature at a distant point (as by a thermoelectric circuit and a galvanometer)

tele·thon \ˈtel-ə-ˌthän\ *n* [*tele-* + *-thon* (as in *marathon*)] **:** a long television program usu. to solicit funds for a charity

tele·tran·scrip·tion \ˌtel-ə-ˌtran(t)s-ˈkrip-shən\ *n* **:** KINESCOPE 2

Tele·type \ˈtel-ə-ˌtīp\ *trademark* **1** — used for a teletypewriter **2 :** a message sent by a Teletype machine

Tele·type·set·ter \-ˈtīp-ˌset-ər\ *trademark* — used for a telegraphic apparatus for the automatic operation of a keyboard typesetting machine

tele·type·writ·er \-ˈtī-ˌprīt-ər\ *n* **:** a printing telegraph that records like a typewriter and is capable of being used over most telephonic communications systems

tele·typ·ist \ˈtel-ə-ˌtī-pəst\ *n* **:** one that operates a teletypewriter

te·leu·to·spore \tə-ˈlüt-ə-ˌspō(ə)r, -ˌspȯ(ə)r\ *n* [Gk *teleutē* end + ISV *spore*; akin to Gk *telos* end — more at WHEEL] **:** TELIOSPORE — **te·leu·to·spor·ic** \tə-ˌlüt-ə-ˈspōr-ik, -ˈspȯr-\ *adj*

tele·view \ˈtel-ə-ˌvyü\ *vi* **:** to observe or watch by means of a television receiver — **tele·view·er** *n*

tele·vise \ˈtel-ə-ˌvīz\ *vb* [back-formation fr. *television*] *vt* **:** to pick up and usu. to broadcast (as a baseball game) by television ~ *vi* **:** to broadcast by television

tele·vi·sion \ˈtel-ə-ˌvizh-ən *also* ˌtel-ə-ˈ\ *n* [F *télévision*, fr. *télé-* tele- (fr. Gk *tēle-*) + *vision*] **1 :** an electronic system of transmitting transient images of fixed or moving objects together with sound over a wire or through space by apparatus that converts light and sound into electrical waves and reconverts them into visible light rays and audible sound **2 :** a television receiving set **3 a :** the television broadcasting industry **b :** television as a medium of communication — **tele·vi·sion·al·ly** \ˌtel-ə-ˈvizh-nə-lē, -ˈvizh-ən-ᵊl-ē\ *adv* — **tele·vi·sion·ary** \-ˈvizh-ə-ˌner-ē\ *adj*

television tube *n* **:** KINESCOPE 1

tele·vi·sor \ˈtel-ə-ˌvī-zər\ *n* **1 :** a transmitting or receiving apparatus for television **2 a :** a television broadcaster **b :** one that uses a television receiver

tele·vi·su·al \ˌtel-ə-ˈvizh-(ə-)wəl, -ˈvizh-əl\ *adj* **1 :** of or relating to television **2 :** TELEGENIC

te·li·al \ˈtē-lē-əl\ *adj* **:** of or relating to a telium

te·lic \ˈtel-ik, ˈtē-lik\ *adj* [Gk *telikos*, fr. *telos* end — more at WHEEL] **:** tending toward an end **:** PURPOSIVE — **te·li·cal·ly** \ˈtel-i-k(ə-)lē, ˈtē-li-\ *adv*

te·lio·spore \ˈtē-lē-ə-ˌspō(ə)r, -ˌspȯ(ə)r\ *n* [Gk *teleios* complete (fr. *telos* end) + E *spore*] **:** a thick-walled chlamydospore forming the final stage in the life cycle of a rust fungus and after nuclear fusion giving rise to the basidium — **te·lio·spor·ic** \ˌtē-lē-ə-ˈspōr-ik, -ˈspȯr-\ *adj*

te·li·um \ˈtē-lē-əm\ *n, pl* **te·lia** \-lē-ə\ [NL, fr. Gk *teleios* complete] **:** a teliospore-containing sorus or pustule on the host plant of a rust fungus

tell \ˈtel\ *vb* **told** \ˈtōld\ **tell·ing** [ME *tellen*, fr. OE *tellan;* akin to OHG *zellen* to count, tell, OE *talu* tale] *vt* **1 :** COUNT, ENUMERATE **2 a :** to relate in detail **:** NARRATE **b :** SAY, UTTER **3 a :** to make known, DIVULGE, REVEAL **b :** to express in words **4 a :** to report to **:** INFORM **b :** to assure emphatically ⟨he did not do it, I ~ you⟩ **5 :** ORDER, DIRECT ⟨*told* her to wait⟩ **6 :** to ascertain by observing **:** find out ~ *vi* **1 :** to give an account **2 :** to act as a talebearer **:** INFORM **3 :** to take effect **:** have a marked effect **4 :** to serve as evidence or indication **syn** see REVEAL

tell·er \ˈtel-ər\ *n* **1 :** one that relates or communicates **2 :** one that reckons or counts: as **a :** one appointed to count votes **b :** a member of a bank's staff concerned with the direct handling of money received or paid out

tell·ing \ˈtel-iŋ\ *adj* **1 :** producing a marked effect **:** EFFECTIVE **2 :** REVEALING, EXPRESSIVE **syn** see VALID — **tell·ing·ly** \-iŋ-lē\ *adv*

tell off *vt* **1 :** to number and set apart; *esp* **:** to detail for special duty **2 :** REPRIMAND, SCOLD

tell·tale \ˈtel-ˌtāl\ *n* **1 a :** TALEBEARER, INFORMER **b :** an outward sign **:** INDICATION **2 :** a device for indicating or recording something: as **a :** a device for keeping a check on employees; *esp* **:** TIME CLOCK **b :** a device that shows the position of the helm or rudder **c :** a strip of metal on the front wall of a racquets or squash court to a height of from 2 to 2½ feet above the ground over which the ball must be hit **d :** a railroad warning device (as a row of long strips over tracks approaching a low overhead bridge) — **telltale** *adj*

tellur- *or* **telluro-** *comb form* [L *tellur-*, *tellus* — more at THILL] **1 :** earth ⟨*tellur*ian⟩ **2** [NL *tellurium*] **:** tellurium ⟨*tellur*ic⟩

¹**tel·lu·ri·an** \tə-ˈlu̇r-ē-ən, te-\ *adj* **:** of, relating to, or characteristic of the earth

²**tellurian** *n* **:** a dweller on the earth

³**tellurian** *or* **tel·lu·ri·on** \-ē-ən, -ē-ˌän\ *n* [NL *tellurion*, fr. L *tellur-*, *tellus*] **:** an apparatus to illustrate the causation of day and night by the rotation of the earth on its axis and the dependence of the seasons on the sun's declination

tel·lu·ric \tə-ˈlu̇(ə)r-ik, te-\ *adj* **1 :** of, relating to, or containing tellurium esp. with a higher valence than in tellurous compounds **2 :** TERRESTRIAL

tel·lu·ride \ˈtel-yə-ˌrīd\ *n* [ISV] **:** a binary compound of tellurium usu. with a more electropositive element or radical

tel·lu·rite \-ˌrīt\ *n* **1 :** a salt of tellurous acid **2 :** a mineral TeO_2 that consists of tellurium dioxide and occurs sparingly in tufts of white or yellowish crystals

tel·lu·ri·um \tə-ˈlu̇r-ē-əm, te-\ *n* [NL, fr. L *tellur-*, *tellus* earth] **:** a semimetallic element related to selenium and sulfur that occurs in a silvery white brittle crystalline form of metallic luster, in a dark amorphous form, or combined with metals — see ELEMENT table

tel·lu·rous \ˈtel-yə-rəs; tə-ˈlu̇r-əs, te-\ *adj* [ISV] **:** of, relating to, or containing tellurium esp. with a lower valence than in telluric compounds

tel·ly \ˈtel-ē\ *n* [by shortening & alter.] *chiefly Brit* **:** TELEVISION

telo- — see TEL-

te·lome \ˈtē-ˌlōm\ *n* [ISV *tel-* + *-ome*] **:** a basic structural unit of the vascular plant consisting typically of a terminal branchlet with distal sporangium and vascular supply — **te·lo·mic** \tē-ˈlōm-ik, -ˈläm-\ *adj*

te·lo·phase \ˈtē-lə-ˌfāz, ˈtel-ə-\ *n* [ISV] **:** the final stage of mitosis in which the new nuclei are differentiated — **te·lo·pha·sic** \ˌtē-lə-ˈfā-zik, ˌtel-ə-\ *adj*

tel·pher \ˈtel-fər\ *n* [irreg. fr. Gk *tēle-* tele- + *pherein* to bear — more at BEAR] **:** a light car suspended from and running on aerial cables; *esp* **:** one propelled by electricity

tel·pher·age \-f(ə-)rij\ *n* **:** an electric transportation system; *esp* **:** one using telphers

tel·son \ˈtel-sən\ *n* [NL, fr. Gk, end of a plowed field; prob. akin to Gk *telos* end] **:** the terminal segment of the body of an arthropod or segmented worm; *esp* **:** that of a crustacean forming the middle lobe of the tail

Tel·u·gu \ˈtel-ə-ˌgü\ *n, pl* **Telugu** *or* **Telugus 1 a :** the largest group of people in Andhra Pradesh, India **b :** a member of this people **2 :** the Dravidian language of the Telugu people

tem·blor \ˈtem-blər; ˈtem-ˌblȯ(ə)r, -ˌblō(ə)r, tem-ˈ\ *n* [Sp, lit., trembling, fr. *temblar* to tremble, fr. ML *tremulare* — more at TREMBLE] **:** EARTHQUAKE

tem·er·ar·i·ous \ˌtem-ə-ˈrar-ē-əs, -ˈrer-\ *adj* [L *temerarius*, fr. *temere*] **:** marked by temerity **:** rashly or presumptuously daring **:** RECKLESS, BRASH — **tem·er·ar·i·ous·ly** *adv*

te·mer·i·ty \tə-ˈmer-ət-ē\ *n* [ME *temeryte*, fr. L *temeritas*, fr. *temere* at random, rashly; akin to OHG *demar* darkness, L *tenebrae*, Skt *tamas*] **:** unreasonable or foolhardy contempt of danger or opposition **:** RASHNESS, RECKLESSNESS

syn AUDACITY, HARDIHOOD, EFFRONTERY, NERVE, CHEEK, GALL: TEMERITY suggests boldness arising from rashness and contempt of danger; AUDACITY implies a disregard of restraints commonly imposed by convention or prudence; HARDIHOOD suggests firmness in daring and defiance; EFFRONTERY implies shameless, insolent disregard of propriety or courtesy; NERVE, CHEEK, GALL are informal equivalents for EFFRONTERY

¹**tem·per** \ˈtem-pər\ *vb* **tem·per·ing** \-p(ə-)riŋ\ [ME *temperen*, fr. OE & OF; OE *temprian* & OF *temprer*, fr. L *temperare* to moderate, mix, temper; prob. akin to L *tempor-*, *tempus* time — more at TEMPORAL] *vt* **1 :** to dilute or soften by the addition of something else **:** MODERATE, SEASON ⟨~ justice with mercy⟩ **2** *archaic* **a :** to exercise control over **:** GOVERN, RESTRAIN **b :** to cause to be well disposed **:** MOLLIFY **3 :** to bring to a suitable state by mixing in or adding a usu. liquid ingredient: as **a :** to mix (clay) with water and knead to a uniform texture **b :** to mix oil with (colors) in making

paint ready for use **4 a** (1) **:** to soften (hardened steel or cast iron) by reheating at a lower temperature (2) **:** to harden (steel) by reheating and cooling in oil **b :** to anneal or toughen (glass) by a process of gradually heating and cooling **5 :** to make stronger and more resilient through hardship **:** TOUGHEN ⟨troops ~*ed* in battle⟩ **6 a :** to put in tune with something **:** ATTUNE **b :** to adjust the pitch of (a note, chord, or instrument) to a temperament ~ *vi* **:** to produce satisfactory temper (as in a metal) — **tem·per·able** \-p(ə-)rə-bəl\ *adj* — **tem·per·er** \-pər-ər\ *n*

2temper *n* **1 a** *archaic* **:** a suitable proportion or balance of qualities **:** a middle state between extremes **:** MEAN, MEDIUM **b** *archaic* **:** CHARACTER, QUALITY **c :** characteristic tone **:** TREND, TENDENCY **d :** high quality of mind or spirit **:** COURAGE, METTLE **2 :** the state of a substance with respect to certain desired qualities (as hardness, elasticity, or workability): as **a** (1) **:** the degree of hardness or resiliency given steel by tempering (2) **:** the color of steel after tempering **b :** the feel and relative solidity of leather **3 :** a substance added to or mixed with something else to modify the properties of the latter: as **a :** any of various mixtures of metals added to another metal in making an alloy **b :** the carbon content of steel that affects its hardening properties **4 a :** a characteristic cast of mind or state of feeling **:** DISPOSITION **b :** calmness of mind **:** COMPOSURE, EQUANIMITY **c :** state of feeling or frame of mind at a particular time **:** HUMOR, MOOD **d :** heat of mind or emotion **:** proneness to anger **:** PASSION **syn** see DISPOSITION, MOOD

tem·pera *also* **tem·po·ra** \'tem-pə-rə\ *n, often attrib* [It *tempera*, lit., temper, fr. *temperare* to temper, fr. L] **:** a process of painting in which an albuminous or colloidal medium is employed as a vehicle instead of oil

tem·per·a·ment \'tem-p(ə-)rə-mənt, -pər-mənt\ *n* [ME, fr. L *temperamentum*, fr. *temperare* to mix, temper] **1** *obs* **a :** constitution of a substance, body, or organism with respect to the mixture or balance of its elements, qualities, or parts **:** MAKEUP **b :** COMPLEXION 1b **2 a :** the peculiar or distinguishing mental or physical character determined by the relative proportions of the humors according to medieval physiology **b :** characteristic or habitual inclination or mode of emotional response ⟨nervous ~⟩ **c :** extremely high sensibility; *esp* **:** excessive sensitiveness or irritability **3** *obs* **a :** CLIMATE **b :** TEMPERATURE 3 **4 a :** the act or process of tempering or modifying **:** ADJUSTMENT, COMPROMISE **b :** middle course **:** MEAN **5 :** the process of slightly modifying the musical intervals of the pure scale to produce a set of 12 equally spaced tones to the octave enabling a keyboard instrument to play in all keys **syn** see DISPOSITION

tem·per·a·men·tal \,tem-p(ə-)rə-'ment-ᵊl\ *adj* **1 :** of, relating to, or arising from temperament **:** CONSTITUTIONAL ⟨~ peculiarities⟩ **2 a :** marked by excessive sensitivity and impulsive changes of mood **:** HIGH-STRUNG, EXCITABLE ⟨a ~ opera singer⟩ **b :** UNPREDICTABLE, CAPRICIOUS — **tem·per·a·men·tal·ly** \-ᵊl-ē\ *adv*

tem·per·ance \'tem-p(ə-)rən(t)s, -pərn(t)s\ *n, often attrib* [ME, fr. L *temperantia*, fr. *temperant-, temperans*, prp. of *temperare* to moderate, be moderate] **1 a :** moderation in action, thought, or feeling **:** RESTRAINT **b :** habitual moderation in the indulgence of the appetites or passions **:** SELF-CONTROL; *specif* **:** moderation in or abstinence from the use of intoxicating drink **:** SOBRIETY **2** *obs* **:** TEMPERATENESS

tem·per·ate \'tem-p(ə-)rət\ *adj* [ME *temperat*, fr. L *temperatus*, fr. pp. of *temperare*] **1 :** marked by moderation: as **a :** keeping or held within limits **:** not extreme or excessive **:** MILD **b :** moderate in indulgence of appetite or desire **c :** moderate in the use of intoxicating liquors **d :** marked by an absence or avoidance of extravagance, violence, or extreme partisanship **:** RESTRAINED **2 a :** having a moderate climate **b :** found in or associated with a moderate climate ⟨~ insects⟩ **syn** see MODERATE — **tem·per·ate·ly** *adv* — **tem·per·ate·ness** *n*

temperate zone *n, often cap T&Z* **:** the area or region between the tropic of Cancer and the arctic circle or between the tropic of Capricorn and the antarctic circle

tem·per·a·ture \'tem-pər-,chu̇(ə)r, -p(ə-)rə-, -chər, -,t(y)u̇(ə)r; 'temp-(ə-)chər\ *n, often attrib* **1** *obs* **:** TEMPERATENESS **2** *archaic* **a :** COMPLEXION 1 **b :** TEMPERAMENT 2b **3 a :** degree of hotness or coldness measured on a definite scale — compare THERMOMETER **b :** the degree of heat that is natural to the body of a living being **c :** abnormally high body heat **:** feverish condition **d :** INTENSITY

temperature gradient *n* **:** the rate of change of temperature with displacement in a given direction (as with increase of height)

tem·pered \'tem-pərd\ *adj* **1 a :** having the elements mixed in satisfying proportions **:** TEMPERATE **b :** qualified, lessened, or diluted by the mixture or influence of an additional ingredient **:** MODERATED **2 :** treated by tempering **3 :** having a specified temper ⟨short-*tempered*⟩ **4 :** conformed to esp. equal temperament — used of a musical interval, intonation, semitone, or scale

1tem·pest \'tem-pəst\ *n* [ME, fr. OF *tempeste*, fr. (assumed) VL *tempesta*, alter. of L *tempestas* season, weather, storm, fr. *tempus* time — more at TEMPORAL] **1 :** an extensive violent wind; *esp* **:** one accompanied by rain, hail, or snow **:** a furious storm **2 :** a violent commotion **:** TUMULT, UPROAR

2tempest *vt* **:** to raise a tempest in or around

tem·pes·tu·ous \tem-'pes(h)-chə-wəs\ *adj* [LL *tempestuosus*, fr. OL *tempestus* season, weather, storm, fr. *tempus*] **:** of, involving, or resembling a tempest **:** TURBULENT, STORMY — **tem·pes·tu·ous·ly** *adv* — **tem·pes·tu·ous·ness** *n*

Tem·plar \'tem-plər\ *n* [ME *templer*, fr. OF *templier*, fr. ML *templarius*, fr. L *templum* temple] **1 :** a knight of a religious military order established in 1118 in Jerusalem for the protection of pilgrims and the Holy Sepulcher **2** *not cap* **:** a barrister or student of law in London **3 :** KNIGHT TEMPLAR 2

tem·plate *or* **tem·plet** \'tem-plət\ *n* [prob. fr. F *templet*, dim. of *temple* temple of a loom] **1 :** a short piece placed horizontally in a wall under a beam to distribute its weight or pressure (as over a door or window frame) **2 a :** a gauge, pattern, or mold (as a thin plate or board) used as a guide to the form of a piece being made **b :** OVERLAY 2d

1tem·ple \'tem-pəl\ *n, often attrib* [ME, fr. OE & OF; OE *tempel* & OF *temple*, fr. L *templum* space marked out for observation of auguries, temple; prob. akin to L *tempus* time] **1 :** an edifice for the worship of a deity **2** *often cap* **:** one of three successive national sanctuaries in ancient Jerusalem **3 :** a building for Mormon sacred ordinances **4 :** a Reform or Conservative synagogue **5 :** a local lodge of any of various fraternal orders or the building housing it **6 :** a place devoted to a special or exalted purpose — **tem·pled** \-pəld\ *adj*

2temple *n* [ME, fr. MF, fr. (assumed) VL *tempula*, alter. of L *tempora* (pl.) temples; prob akin to L *tempor-, tempus* time] **:** the flattened space on each side of the forehead of man and some other mammals

3temple *n* [ME *tempylle*, fr. MF *temple*, prob. fr. L *templum* temple, small timber] **:** a device in a loom for keeping the web stretched transversely

tem·po \'tem-(,)pō\ *n, pl* **tem·pi** \-(,)pē\ *or* **tempos** [It, lit., time, fr. L *tempus*] **1 :** the rate of speed of a musical piece or passage indicated by one of a series of directions (as largo, presto, or allegro) and often by an exact metronome marking **2 :** rate of motion or activity **:** PACE **3 :** a turn to move in chess in relation to one's opponent's turns

1tem·po·ral \'tem-p(ə-)rəl\ *adj* [ME, fr. L *temporalis*, fr. *tempor-, tempus* time; akin to Lith *tempti* to stretch, and prob. to L *tendere* to stretch — more at THIN] **1 a :** of or relating to time — compare ETERNAL **b :** of or relating to earthly life **c :** of or relating to lay or secular concerns **2 :** of or relating to grammatical tense or a distinction of time — **tem·po·ral·ly** \-ē\ *adv*

2temporal *adj* [MF, fr. LL *temporalis*, fr. L *tempora* temples] **:** of or relating to the temples or the sides of the skull behind the orbits

temporal bone *n* **:** a compound bone of the side of the human skull

tem·po·ral·i·ty \,tem-pə-'ral-ət-ē\ *n* **1 a :** civil or political as distinguished from spiritual or ecclesiastical power or authority **b :** an ecclesiastical property or revenue — often used in pl. **2 :** the quality or state of being temporal

tem·po·ral·ize \'tem-p(ə-)rə-,līz\ *vt* **1 :** to place or define in time relations **2 :** SECULARIZE

tem·po·rar·i·ly \,tem-pə-'rer-ə-lē\ *adv* **:** during a limited time **:** BRIEFLY

tem·po·rar·i·ness \'tem-pə-,rer-ē-nəs\ *n* **:** the quality or state of being temporary

tem·po·rary \-,rer-ē\ *adj* [L *temporarius*, fr. *tempor-, tempus* time] **:** lasting for a time only **:** IMPERMANENT, TRANSITORY

temporary duty *n* **:** temporary military service away from one's unit

tem·po·ri·za·tion \,tem-pə-rə-'zā-shən\ *n* **:** the act, policy, or practice of temporizing

tem·po·rize \'tem-pə-,rīz\ *vi* [MF *temporiser*, fr. ML *temporizare* to pass the time, fr. L *tempor-, tempus*] **1 :** to act to suit the time or occasion **:** yield to current or dominant opinion **:** COMPROMISE, TRIM **2 :** to draw out negotiations so as to gain time — **tem·po·riz·er** *n*

tempt \'tem(p)t\ *vt* [ME *tempten*, fr. OF *tempter, tenter*, fr. L *temptare, tentare* to feel, try, tempt; akin to L *tendere* to stretch — more at THIN] **1 :** to entice to do wrong by promise of pleasure or gain **:** allure into evil **:** SEDUCE **2 a** *obs* **:** to make trial of **:** TEST **b :** to try presumptuously **:** PROVOKE **c :** to risk the dangers of **3 :** to induce to do something **:** INCITE, PERSUADE **syn** see LURE — **tempt·able** \'tem(p)-tə-bəl\ *adj*

temp·ta·tion \tem(p)-'tā-shən\ *n* **1 :** the act of tempting or the state of being tempted esp. to evil **:** ENTICEMENT **2 :** something tempting **:** a cause or occasion of enticement

tempt·er \'tem(p)-tər\ *n* **:** one that tempts or entices — **tempt·ress** \-trəs\ *n*

tempt·ing *adj* **:** ENTICING — **tempt·ing·ly** \'tem(p)-tiŋ-lē\ *adv*

ten \'ten\ *n* [ME, fr. OE *tīene*, fr. *tīen*, adj., ten; akin to OHG *zehan* ten, L *decem*, Gk *deka*] **1** — see NUMBER table **2 :** the tenth in a set or series ⟨the ~ of hearts⟩ **3 :** something having ten units or members **4 :** a ten-dollar bill **5 :** the number occupying the position two to the left of the decimal point in the arabic notation — **ten** *adj or pron*

ten·a·bil·i·ty \,ten-ə-'bil-ət-ē *also chiefly Brit* ,tē-nə-\ *n* **:** the quality or state of being tenable

ten·a·ble \'ten-ə-bəl *also chiefly Brit* 'tē-nə-\ *adj* [F, fr. OF, fr. *tenir* to hold, fr. L *tenēre* — more at THIN] **:** capable of being held, maintained, or defended **:** DEFENSIBLE, REASONABLE — **ten·a·ble·ness** *n* — **ten·a·bly** \-blē\ *adv*

ten·ace \'ten-,ās, te-'nās, 'ten-əs\ *n* [modif. of Sp *tenaza*, lit., forceps, prob. fr. L *tenacia*, neut. pl. of *tenax*] **:** a combination in one hand (as in bridge) of two high or relatively high cards (as ace and queen) once separated in rank

te·na·cious \tə-'nā-shəs\ *adj* [L *tenac-, tenax* tending to hold fast, fr. *tenēre* to hold] **1 a :** not easily pulled apart **:** COHESIVE, TOUGH ⟨a ~ metal⟩ **b :** tending to adhere to another substance **:** STICKY ⟨~ burs⟩ **2 a :** holding fast or tending to hold fast **:** PERSISTENT, STUBBORN ⟨~ of his rights⟩ **b :** RETENTIVE ⟨a ~ memory⟩ **syn** see STRONG — **te·na·cious·ly** *adv* — **te·na·cious·ness** *n*

te·nac·i·ty \tə-'nas-ət-ē\ *n* **:** the quality or state of being tenacious **syn** see COURAGE

te·nac·u·lum \tə-'nak-yə-ləm\ *n, pl* **te·nac·u·la** \-lə\ *or* **tenaculums** [NL, fr. LL, instrument for holding, fr. L *tenēre*] **1 :** a slender sharp-pointed hook attached to a handle and used mainly in surgery for seizing and holding parts (as arteries) **2 :** an adhesive animal structure

ten·an·cy \'ten-ən-sē\ *n* **:** a holding of an estate or a mode of holding an estate **:** the temporary possession or occupancy of something (as a house) that belongs to another; *also* **:** the period of a tenant's occupancy or possession

1ten·ant \'ten-ənt\ *n* [ME, fr. MF, fr. prp. of *tenir* to hold] **1 a :** one who holds or possesses real estate or sometimes personal property (as an annuity) by any kind of right **b :** one who has the occupation or temporary possession of lands or tenements of another; *specif* **:** one who rents or leases (as a house) from a landlord **2 :** DWELLER, OCCUPANT

2tenant *vt* **:** to hold or occupy as a tenant **:** INHABIT — **ten·ant·able** \-ən-tə-bəl\ *adj*

tenant farmer *n* **:** a farmer who works land owned by another and pays rent either in cash or in shares of produce

ten·ant·less \'ten-ənt-ləs\ *adj* **:** having no tenants **:** UNOCCUPIED

ten·ant·ry \'ten-ən-trē\ *n* **1 :** TENANCY **2 :** the body of tenants

ten–cent store \ten-'sent-\ *n* **:** FIVE-AND-TEN

tench \'tench\ *n, pl* **tench** *or* **tench·es** [ME, fr. MF *tenche*, fr. LL *tinca*] **:** a Eurasian freshwater fish (*Tinca tinca*) related to the dace and noted for its ability to survive outside water

Ten Commandments *n pl* **:** the commandments of God given to Moses on Mount Sinai

1tend \'tend\ *vb* [ME *tenden*, short for *attenden* to attend] *vi* **1** *archaic* **:** to give ear **:** LISTEN **2 :** to pay attention **:** apply oneself ⟨~ to your own affairs⟩ **3 :** to act as an attendant **:** SERVE **4** *obs* **:** AWAIT ~ *vt* **1** *archaic* **:** to attend as a servant **2 a :** to apply

oneself to the care of : watch over **b** : to have or take charge of as a caretaker or overseer **c** : CULTIVATE, FOSTER **d** : to manage the operations of : MIND ⟨~ a store⟩

2**tend** *vb* [ME *tenden*, fr. MF *tendre* to stretch, tend, fr. L *tendere* — more at THIN] *vi* **1** : to move, direct, or develop one's course in a particular direction **2** : to exhibit an inclination or tendency : CONDUCE ~ *vt* : to stand by (as a rope) in readiness to prevent fouling or other mischance

ten·dance \'ten-dən(t)s\ *n* [short for *attendance*] **1** : watchful care : ATTENDANCE, MINISTRATION **2** *archaic* : persons in attendance : RETINUE

ten·den·cy \'ten-dən-sē\ *n* [ML *tendentia*, fr. L *tendent-, tendens*, prp. of *tendere*] **1 a** (1) : direction or approach toward a place, object, effect, or limit (2) : BIAS, INCLINATION **b** : a proneness to a particular kind of thought or action : PROPENSITY **2 a** : the purposeful trend of something written or said : AIM **b** : deliberate but indirect advocacy

syn TENDENCY, TREND, DRIFT, TENOR, CURRENT mean movement in a particular direction. TENDENCY implies a driving force sending a person or thing in a given direction; TREND implies a direction maintained in spite of minor irregularities or windings and more subject to change than TENDENCY; DRIFT suggests a tendency influenced by wind or current, or it may apply to an underlying inferred meaning; TENOR is close to the latter sense of DRIFT but suggests more clarity or definiteness; CURRENT implies a clearly defined but not necessarily unalterable direction or tendency

ten·den·tious *also* **ten·den·cious** \ten-'den-chəs\ *adj* : marked by a tendency in favor of a particular point of view : BIASED — **ten·den·tious·ly** *adv* — **ten·den·tious·ness** *n*

1**ten·der** \'ten-dər\ *adj* [ME, fr. OF *tendre*, fr. L *tener*] **1 a** : having a soft or yielding texture : easily broken, cut, or damaged : DELICATE, FRAGILE ⟨~ feet⟩ **b** : easily chewed : SUCCULENT **2 a** : physically weak : not able to endure hardship **b** : IMMATURE, YOUNG ⟨children of ~ years⟩ **c** : incapable of resisting cold **3** : marked by, responding to, or expressing the softer emotions : FOND, LOVING ⟨a ~ lover⟩ **4 a** : showing care : CONSIDERATE, SOLICITOUS **b** : highly susceptible to impressions or emotions : IMPRESSIONABLE ⟨a ~ conscience⟩ **5 a** : appropriate or conducive to a delicate or sensitive constitution or character : GENTLE, MILD ⟨~ breeding⟩ ⟨~ irony⟩ **b** : delicate or soft in quality or tone **6** *obs* : DEAR, PRECIOUS **7 a** : sensitive to touch or palpation **b** : sensitive to injury or insult : TOUCHY **c** : demanding careful and sensitive handling : TICKLISH **d** *of a ship* : inclined to heel over easily under sail — **ten·der·ly** *adv* — **ten·der·ness** *n*

2**tender** *vb* **ten·der·ing** \-d(ə-)riŋ\ *vt* **1** : to make tender : SOFTEN, WEAKEN **2** *archaic* : to regard or treat with tenderness ~ *vi* : to become tender

3**tender** *n* [1*tender*] *obs* : CONSIDERATION, REGARD

4**tend·er** \'ten-dər\ *n* : one that tends or takes care: as **a** (1) : a ship employed to attend other ships (as to supply provisions) (2) : a boat or small steamer for communication between shore and a larger ship (3) : a warship that provides logistic support **b** : a vehicle attached to a locomotive for carrying a supply of fuel and water

5**ten·der** *n* [MF *tendre* to stretch, stretch out, offer — more at TEND] **1** : an unconditional offer of money or service in satisfaction of a debt or obligation made to save a penalty or forfeiture for nonpayment or nonperformance **2** : an offer or proposal made for acceptance; *specif* : an offer of a bid for a contract **3** : something that may be offered in payment; *specif* : MONEY

6**ten·der** *vt* **ten·der·ing** \-d(ə-)riŋ\ **1** : to make a tender of ⟨~ the amount of rent⟩ **2** : to present for acceptance : PROFFER ⟨~*ed* his resignation⟩

ten·der·foot \'ten-dər-,fu̇t\ *n, pl* **ten·der·feet** \-,fēt\ *also* **ten·der·foots** \-,fu̇ts\ *often attrib* **1** : a newcomer in a comparatively rough or newly settled region; *esp* : one not hardened to frontier or outdoor life **2** : an inexperienced beginner : NEOPHYTE

ten·der·heart·ed \,ten-dər-'härt-əd\ *adj* : easily moved to love, pity, or sorrow : COMPASSIONATE, IMPRESSIONABLE — **ten·der·heart·ed·ly** *adv* — **ten·der·heart·ed·ness** *n*

ten·der–heft·ed \-'hef-təd\ *adj* [1*tender* + *heft*, alter. of *haft* handle] *archaic* : TENDERHEARTED

ten·der·iza·tion \,ten-d(ə-)rə-'zā-shən\ *n* : the process of tenderizing

ten·der·ize \'ten-də-,rīz\ *vt* : to make (meat or meat products) tender by applying a process or substance that breaks down connective tissue — **ten·der·iz·er** *n*

ten·der·loin \'ten-dər-,lȯin\ *n* **1** : a strip of tender meat consisting of a large internal muscle of the loin on each side of the vertebral column : a fillet of beef or pork **2** [fr. its making possible a luxurious diet for a corrupt policeman] : a district of a city largely devoted to vice and other forms of lawbreaking that encourage political or police corruption

ten·der–mind·ed \,ten-dər-'mīn-dəd\ *adj* : marked by idealism, optimism, and dogmatism; *esp* : reluctant to test assumptions by facts — compare TOUGH-MINDED

ten·di·nous \'ten-də-nəs\ *adj* [NL *tendinosus*, fr. *tendin-, tendo* tendon, alter. of ML *tendon-, tendo*] **1** : of, relating to, or resembling a tendon **2** : consisting of tendons : SINEWY

ten·don \'ten-dən\ *n* [ML *tendon-, tendo*, fr. L *tendere* to stretch — more at THIN] : a tough cord or band of dense white fibrous connective tissue that unites a muscle with some other part and transmits the force which the muscle exerts

ten·dresse \täⁿ-dres\ *n* [F, fr. MF, fr. *tendre* tender] : tender feeling : FONDNESS

ten·dril \'ten-drəl\ *n* [perh. modif. of MF *tendron*, alter. of *tendon*, lit., tendon, fr. ML *tendon-, tendo*] **1** : a leaf, stipule, or stem modified into a slender spirally coiling sensitive organ serving to attach a plant to its support **2** : something resembling a tendril — **ten·driled** *or* **ten·drilled** \-drəld\ *adj* — **ten·dril·ly** \-drə-lē\ *adj* — **ten·dril·ous** \-drə-ləs\ *adj*

Ten·e·brae \'ten-ə-,brā, -,brī, -,brē\ *n pl but sing or pl in constr* [ML, fr. L, darkness] : the office of matins and lauds for the last three days of Holy Week commemorating the sufferings and death of Christ with a progressive extinguishing of candles

ten·e·brif·ic \,ten-ə-'brif-ik\ *adj* [L *tenebrae* darkness] **1** : GLOOMY **2** : causing gloom or darkness

te·neb·ri·ous \tə-'neb-rē-əs\ *adj* [by alter.] : TENEBROUS

ten·e·brous \'ten-ə-brəs\ *adj* [ME, fr. MF *tenebreus*, fr. L *tenebrosus*, fr. *tenebrae*] : shut off from the light : GLOOMY, OBSCURE

1080 *also* **ten-eighty** \te-'nāt-ē\ *n* [fr. its laboratory serial number] : a poisonous substance that is chemically sodium fluoroacetate $C_2H_2FNaO_2$ and is used as a rodenticide

ten·e·ment \'ten-ə-mənt\ *n* [ME, fr. MF, fr. ML *tenementum*, fr. L *tenēre* to hold — more at THIN] **1** : land or any of various forms of incorporeal property treated like land that is held by a person of another : HOLDING **2 a** : a house used as a dwelling : RESIDENCE **b** : APARTMENT, FLAT **c** : TENEMENT HOUSE **3** : DWELLING

ten·e·men·ta·ry \,ten-ə-'ment-ə-rē, -'men-trē\ *adj* : consisting of tenements

tenement house *n* : APARTMENT BUILDING; *esp* : one meeting minimum standards of sanitation, safety, and comfort and housing poorer families

te·nes·mus \tə-'nez-məs\ *n* [L, fr. Gk *teinesmos*, fr. *teinein* to stretch, strain — more at THIN] : a distressing but ineffectual urge to evacuate the rectum or bladder

te·net \'ten-ət *also* 'tē-nət\ *n* [L, he holds, fr. *tenēre* to hold] : a principle, belief, or doctrine generally held to be true; *esp* : one held in common by members of an organization, group, movement, or profession **syn** see DOCTRINE

ten·fold \'ten-,fōld, -'fōld\ *adj* **1** : having 10 units or members **2** : being 10 times as great or as many — **ten·fold** \-'fōld\ *adv*

te·nia *var of* TAENIA

te·ni·a·sis *var of* TAENIASIS

Ten·nes·see walking horse \,ten-ə-,sē-\ *n* [*Tennessee*, state of U.S.] : any of an American breed of large easy-gaited saddle horses largely of Standardbred and Morgan ancestry — called also *Tennessee walker*

ten·nis \'ten-əs\ *n, often attrib* [ME *tenetz, tenys*] **1** : COURT TENNIS **2** : a typically outdoor game that is played with rackets and a light elastic ball by two players or pairs of players on a level court divided by a low net

tennis shoe *n* : SNEAKER

Ten·ny·so·ni·an \,ten-ə-'sō-nē-ən\ *adj* : of, relating to, or characteristic of the poet Tennyson or his writings

1**ten·on** \'ten-ən\ *n* [ME, fr. OF, fr. *tenir* to hold — more at TENABLE] : a projecting member in a piece of wood or other material for insertion into a mortise to make a joint

2**tenon** *vt* **1** : to unite by a tenon **2** : to cut or fit for insertion in a mortise

1**ten·or** *or chiefly Brit* **ten·our** \'ten-ər\ *n* [ME, fr. OF, fr. L *tenor* uninterrupted course, fr. *tenēre* to hold — more at THIN] **1 a** : the general drift of something spoken or written : PURPORT **b** : an exact copy of a writing : TRANSCRIPT **c** : the subject of a metaphor **2 a** (1) : the melodic line usu. forming the cantus firmus in medieval music (2) : the voice part next to the lowest in 4-part harmony **b** : the highest natural adult male voice **c** : one that performs a tenor part **3** : a continuance in a course, movement, or activity : TREND **syn** see TENDENCY

2**tenor** *adj* **1** : of or relating to the tenor in music **2** : close in range to a tenor voice ⟨~ sax⟩

te·no·syn·o·vi·tis \,ten-ō-,sin-ə-'vīt-əs, ,tē-nō-\ *n* [NL, fr. Gk *tenōn* tendon + NL *synovitis*; akin to Gk *teinein* to stretch — more at THIN] : inflammation of a tendon sheath

ten·pen·ny \,ten-,pen-ē, *Brit* -pə-nē-\ *adj* : amounting to, worth, or costing ten pennies

tenpenny nail *n* [fr. its original price per hundred] : a nail 3 inches long

ten·pin \'ten-,pin\ *n* **1** : a bottle-shaped bowling pin 15 inches high **2** *pl but sing in constr* : a bowling game using 10 tenpins and a large ball 27 inches in circumference and allowing each player to bowl 2 balls in each of 10 frames

ten·pound·er \'ten-'pau̇n-dər\ *n* : a large silvery food and sport fish (*Elops saurus*) that resembles somewhat a herring but is related to the tarpon

ten·rec \'ten-,rek, 'tän-\ *n* [F, fr. Malagasy *tàndraka*] : any of numerous small often spiny insectivorous mammals (family Tenrecidae) of Madagascar

1**tense** \'ten(t)s\ *n* [ME *tens* time, tense, fr. MF, fr. L *tempus* — more at TEMPORAL] **1** : a distinction of form in a verb to express distinctions of time **2 a** : a set of inflectional forms of a verb that express distinctions of time **b** : a particular inflectional form of a verb expressing a specific time distinction

2**tense** *adj* [L *tensus*, fr. pp. of *tendere* to stretch — more at THIN] **1** : stretched tight : made taut : RIGID **2 a** : feeling or showing nervous tension : HIGH-STRUNG, JITTERY **b** : marked by strain or suspense **3** *of a speech sound* : produced with the muscles involved in a relatively tense state ⟨the vowels \ē\ and \ü\ in contrast with the vowels \i\ and \u̇\ are ~⟩ **syn** see STIFF, TIGHT — **tense·ly** *adv* — **tense·ness** *n*

3**tense** *vt* : to make tense ~ *vi* : to become tense

ten·sile \'ten(t)-səl, 'ten-,sīl\ *adj* **1** : capable of tension : DUCTILE **2** : of or relating to tension — **ten·sil·i·ty** \ten-'sil-ət-ē\ *n*

tensile strength *n* : the greatest longitudinal stress (as pounds per square inch) a substance can bear without tearing apart

ten·sim·e·ter \ten-'sim-ət-ər\ *n* [*tension* + *-meter*] : an instrument for measuring gas or vapor pressure

ten·si·om·e·ter \,ten(t)-sē-'äm-ət-ər\ *n* [*tension*] **1** *or* **ten·som·e·ter** \ten-'säm-\ [2*tense*] : a device for measuring tension (as of fabric, yarn, or structural material) **2** : an instrument for determining the moisture content of soil

Tensiometer *trademark* — used for an instrument for measuring the surface tension of liquids

1**ten·sion** \'ten-chən\ *n, often attrib* [MF or L; MF, fr. L *tension-, tensio*, fr. *tensus*, pp.] **1 a** : the act or action of stretching or the condition or degree of being stretched to stiffness : TAUTNESS **b** : STRESS 1b **2 a** : either of two balancing forces causing or tending to cause extension **b** : the stress resulting from the elongation of an elastic body **c** *archaic* : PRESSURE **3 a** : a state of psychic unrest often with signs of physiological stress **b** : a state of latent hostility or opposition between individuals or groups **c** : a balance maintained in an artistic work between opposing forces or elements **4** : POTENTIAL **5** : a device to produce a desired tension (as in a loom) — **ten·sion·al** \'tench-nəl, -ən-ᵊl\ *adj*

[2]tension *vt* **ten·sion·ing** \'tench-(ə-)niŋ\ : to subject to tension
ten·sion·less \'ten-chən-ləs\ *adj* : free from tension
ten·si·ty \'ten(t)-sət-ē\ *n* : TENSENESS
ten·sive \'ten(t)-siv\ *adj* : of, relating to, or causing tension
ten·sor \'ten(t)-sər, 'ten-ˌsȯ(ə)r\ *n* [NL, fr. L *tensus*, pp.] **1** : a muscle that stretches a part **2** : a generalization of the concept of vector that consists of a set of components usu. having a double row of indices that are functions of the coordinate system and have invariant properties under transformation of the coordinate system — **ten·so·ri·al** \ten-'sōr-ē-əl, -'sȯr-\ *adj*
ten–strike \'ten-ˌstrīk\ *n* **1** : a strike in tenpins **2** : a highly successful stroke or achievement
[1]**tent** \'tent\ *n*, *often attrib* [ME *tente*, fr. OF, fr. L *tenta*, fem. of *tentus*, pp. of *tendere* to stretch — more at THIN] **1** : a collapsible shelter of canvas or other material stretched and sustained by poles and used for camping outdoors or as a temporary building **2** : DWELLING **3** : something that resembles a tent or that serves as a shelter; *esp* : a canopy or enclosure placed over the head and shoulders to retain vapors or oxygen during medical administration
[2]**tent** *vi* **1** : to reside for the time being : LODGE **2** : to live in a tent ~ *vt* **1** : to cover with or as if with a tent **2** : to lodge in tents
[3]**tent** *vt* [ME *tenten*, fr. *tent* attention, short for *attent*, fr. OF *attente*, fr. *attendre* to attend] *chiefly Scot* : to attend to : WATCH, TEND
ten·ta·cle \'tent-i-kəl\ *n* [NL *tentaculum* fr. L *tentare* to feel, touch — more at TEMPT] **1** : any of various elongate flexible usu. tactile or prehensile processes borne by animals chiefly on the head or about the mouth **2 a** : something that acts like a tentacle in grasping or feeling out **b** : a sensitive hair or emergence on a plant (as the sundew) — **ten·ta·cled** \-kəld\ *adj* — **ten·tac·u·lar** \ten-'tak-yə-lər\ *adj*
tent·age \'tent-ij\ *n* : a collection of tents : tent equipment
ten·ta·tive \'tent-ət-iv\ *adj* [ML *tentativus*, fr. L *tentatus*, pp. of *tentare* to feel, try — more at TEMPT] **1** : of the nature of an experiment or hypothesis : not final : PROVISIONAL, TEMPORARY ⟨~ plans⟩ **2** : HESITANT, UNCERTAIN ⟨a ~ smile⟩ — **tentative** *n* — **ten·ta·tive·ly** *adv* — **ten·ta·tive·ness** *n*
tent caterpillar *n* : any of several destructive gregarious caterpillars (esp. *Malacosoma americanum*) that construct on trees large silken webs
tent·ed \'tent-əd\ *adj* **1** : covered with a tent or tents **2** : shaped like a tent
[1]**ten·ter** \'tent-ər\ *n* [ME *teyntur*, *tentowre*] **1** : a frame or endless track with hooks or clips along two sides that is used for drying and stretching cloth **2** *archaic* : TENTERHOOK
[2]**tenter** *vt* : to hang or stretch on or as if on a tenter
ten·ter·hook \'tent-ər-ˌhu̇k\ *n* : a sharp hooked nail used esp. for fastening cloth on a tenter — **on tenterhooks** : in a state of uneasiness, strain, or suspense
tenth \'ten(t)th\ *n*, *pl* **tenths** \'ten(t)s, 'ten(t)ths\ — see NUMBER table — **tenth** *adj or adv*
tenth–rate \'ten(t)-'thrāt\ *adj* : most inferior : of the lowest character or quality
tent·less \'tent-ləs\ *adj* : having no tent : SHELTERLESS
tent·mak·er \'tent-ˌmā-kər\ *n* : one that makes tents
tent stitch *n* : a short stitch slanting to the right that is used in embroidery and canvas work to form even lines of solid background
tenty *also* **tent·ie** \'tent-ē\ *adj* [[3]*tent*] *Scot* : ATTENTIVE, WATCHFUL
ten·u·is \'ten-yə-wəs\ *n*, *pl* **ten·u·es** \-yə-ˌwēz, -ˌwās\ [ML, fr. L, thin, slight] : one of the stops κ, π, τ in Greek
te·nu·i·ty \te-'n(y)ü-ət-ē, tə-\ *n* [L *tenuitas*, fr. *tenuis* thin, tenuous] **1** : lack of substance or strength **2** : SLENDERNESS, THINNESS **3** : rarefied quality or state : RARITY
ten·u·ous \'ten-yə-wəs\ *adj* [L *tenuis* thin, slight, tenuous — more at THIN] **1** : not dense : RARE ⟨a ~ fluid⟩ **2** : not thick : SLENDER ⟨a ~ rope⟩ **3** : having little substance or strength : FLIMSY, WEAK ⟨~ influences⟩ ⟨a ~ hold on reality⟩ **syn** see THIN — **ten·u·ous·ly** *adv* — **ten·u·ous·ness** *n*
ten·ure \'ten-yər, -ˌyu̇(ə)r\ *n* [ME, fr. OF *teneüre*, *tenure*, fr. ML *tenitura*, fr. (assumed) VL *tenitus*, pp. of L *tenēre* to hold — more at THIN] **1** : the act, right, manner, or term of holding something (as a landed property, a position, or an office) **2** : GRASP, HOLD — **ten·ur·ial** \te-'nyu̇r-ē-əl\ *adj* — **ten·ur·ial·ly** \-ə-lē\ *adv*
te·nu·to \tā-'nüt-(ˌ)ō\ *adv* (*or adj*) [It, fr. pp. of *tenere* to hold, fr. L *tenēre*] : in a manner so as to hold a tone or chord firmly to its full value — used as a direction in music
te·o·cal·li \ˌtē-ə-'kal-ē, ˌtā-ə-'käl-\ *n* [Nahuatl, fr. *teotl* god + *calli* house] : an ancient temple of Mexico or Central America usu. built upon the summit of a truncated pyramidal mound; *also* : the mound itself
te·o·sin·te \ˌtā-ə-'sint-ē\ *n* [MexSp, fr. Nahuatl *teocentli*, fr. *teotl* god + *centli* ear of corn] : a large annual fodder grass (*Euchlaena mexicana*) of Mexico and Central America closely related to and possibly ancestral to maize
te·pee \'tē-(ˌ)pē\ *n* [Dakota *tipi*, fr. *ti* to dwell + *pi* to use for] : an American Indian conical tent usu. of skins used esp. by the Plains peoples

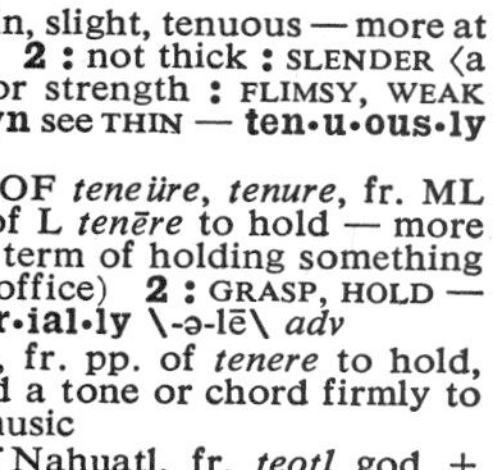
tepee

tep·id \'tep-əd\ *adj* [L *tepidus*, fr. *tepēre* to be moderately warm; akin to Skt *tapati* it gives out heat, OIr *tess* heat] **1** : moderately warm : LUKEWARM ⟨a ~ bath⟩ **2** : marked by an absence of enthusiasm or conviction : HALF-HEARTED ⟨a ~ interest⟩ — **te·pid·i·ty** \tə-'pid-ət-ē, te-\ *n* — **tep·id·ly** \'tep-əd-lē\ *adv* — **tep·id·ness** *n*
te·qui·la \tə-'kē-lə\ *n* [Sp, fr. *Tequila*, district of Mexico] **1** : a Mexican century plant (*Agave tequilana*) much cultivated as a source of mescal **2** : a Mexican liquor made by redistilling mescal
ter- *comb form* [L, fr. *ter*; akin to Gk & Skt *tris* three times, L *tres* three — more at THREE] : three times : threefold : three ⟨*ter*centenary⟩
te·rai \tə-'rī\ *n* [*Tarai*, lowland belt of India] : a wide-brimmed double felt sun hat worn esp. in subtropical regions
ter·aph \'ter-əf\ *n*, *pl* **ter·a·phim** \'ter-ə-ˌfim\ [Heb *tĕrāphīm* (pl. in form but sing. in meaning)] : an image of a Semitic household god
ter·a·to·log·i·cal \ˌter-ət-ᵊl-'äj-i-kəl\ *adj* **1** : abnormal in growth or structure **2** : of or relating to teratology
ter·a·tol·o·gy \ˌter-ə-'täl-ə-jē\ *n* [Gk *terat-*, *teras* marvel, monster + ISV *-logy*; akin to Lith *keras* enchantment] : the study of malformations, monstrosities, or serious deviations from the normal type in organisms
ter·a·to·ma \ˌter-ə-'tō-mə\ *n* [NL, fr. Gk *terat-*, *teras* monster] : a tumor made up of a heterogeneous mixture of tissues — **ter·a·to·ma·tous** \-'täm-ət-əs, -'tōm-\ *adj*
ter·bi·um \'tər-bē-əm\ *n* [NL, fr. *Ytterby*, Sweden] : a usu. trivalent metallic element of the rare-earth group — see ELEMENT table
terbium metal *n* : any of several rare-earth metals separable as a group from other metals and including terbium, europium, gadolinium, and sometimes dysprosium
terce \'tərs\ *n* [ME, third — more at TIERCE] *often cap* : the third of the canonical hours
ter·cel \'tər-səl\ *var of* TIERCEL
ter·cen·te·na·ry \ˌtər-(ˌ)sen-'ten-ə-rē, (')tər-'sent-ᵊn-ˌer-ē\ *n* : a 300th anniversary or its celebration — **tercentenary** *adj*
ter·cen·ten·ni·al \ˌtər-(ˌ)sen-'ten-ē-əl\ *adj or n* : TERCENTENARY
ter·cet \'tər-sət\ *n* [It *terzetto*, fr. dim. of *terzo* third, fr. L *tertius* — more at THIRD] : a unit or group of three lines of verse: **a** : one of the 3-line stanzas linked by rhyme in terza rima **b** : one of the two groups of three lines forming the sestet in an Italian sonnet
ter·e·bene \'ter-ə-ˌbēn\ *n* [F *térébène*, fr. *térébinthe* terebinth] : a mixture of terpenes from oil of turpentine
te·re·bic \tə-'reb-ik, -'rēb-\ *adj* [L *terebinthus* terebinth] : of, relating to, or constituting a white crystalline acid $C_7H_{10}O_4$ obtained esp. by the oxidation of oil of turpentine
ter·e·binth \'ter-ə-ˌbin(t)th\ *n* [ME *terebynt*, fr. MF *terebinthe*, fr. L *terebinthus* — more at TURPENTINE] : a small European tree (*Pistacia terebinthus*) of the sumac family yielding Chian turpentine
ter·e·bin·thine \ˌter-ə-'bin(t)-thən, -'bin-ˌthīn\ *adj* [L *terebinthinus* of the terebinth] : consisting of or resembling turpentine
te·re·do \tə-'rēd-(ˌ)ō, -'rād-\ *n*, *pl* **teredos** *or* **te·red·i·nes** \-'red-ᵊn-ˌēz\ [L *teredin-*, *teredo*, fr. Gk *terēdōn*; akin to Gk *tetrainein* to bore — more at THROW] : SHIPWORM
te·rete \tə-'rēt, te-\ *adj* [L *teret-*, *teres* well turned, rounded; akin to L *terere* to rub — more at THROW] : approximately cylindrical but usu. tapering at both ends ⟨a ~ seed pod⟩
Te·reus \'tē-ˌrüs, 'tir-ē-əs\ *n* [L, fr. Gk *Tēreus*] : the husband of Procne and brother-in-law of Philomela
ter·gal \'tər-gəl\ *adj* : relating to a tergum; *specif* : DORSAL
ter·gi·ver·sate \'tər-ji-(ˌ)vər-ˌsāt, ˌtər-ji-'; (ˌ)tər-'jiv-ər-\ *vi* [L *tergiversatus*, pp. of *tergiversari* to turn the back, shuffle, fr. *tergum* back + *versare* to turn, fr. *versus*, pp. of *vertere* to turn — more at WORTH] **1** : to become a renegade : APOSTATIZE **2** : to use subterfuges : EQUIVOCATE — **ter·gi·ver·sa·tor** \-ˌsāt-ər\ *n*
ter·gi·ver·sa·tion \ˌtər-ji-(ˌ)vər-'sā-shən, (ˌ)tər-ˌjiv-ər-\ *n* **1** : desertion of a cause, party, or faith **2** : evasion of straightforward action or clear-cut statement : EQUIVOCATION
ter·gum \'tər-gəm\ *n*, *pl* **ter·ga** \-gə\ [L] : the back of an animal
[1]**term** \'tərm\ *n* [ME *terme* boundary, end, fr. OF, fr. L *terminus*; akin to Gk *termōn* boundary, end, Skt *tarati* he crosses over — more at THROUGH] **1** : END, TERMINATION **2 a** : a limited or definite extent of time; *esp* : the time for which something lasts : DURATION, TENURE **b** : parturition at the normal period **3** : a fixed period of time: as **a** : one for which an estate is granted **b** : one during which a court is in session **4** : division in a school year during which instruction is regularly given to students **5 a** : a unitary or compound expression connected with another by a plus or minus sign **b** : an element of a fraction or proportion or of a series or sequence **6** : one of the three substantive elements of a syllogism **7 a** : a word or expression that has a precise meaning in some uses or is peculiar to a science, art, profession, or subject ⟨legal ~⟩ **b** *pl* : diction of a specified kind **8** *pl* : provisions stated or offered for acceptance and determining the nature and scope of the agreement **9** *pl* **a** : mutual relationship : FOOTING **b** : AGREEMENT, CONCORD **10** : a boundary post or stone; *esp* : a quadrangular pillar often tapering downward and adorned with a head or upper body — **in terms of** : with respect to
[2]**term** *vt* : to apply a term to : CALL, NAME
[1]**ter·ma·gant** \'tər-mə-gənt\ *n* [ME] **1** *cap* : a legendary Muslim deity represented in early English drama as a boisterous character **2** : an overbearing or nagging woman : SHREW
[2]**termagant** *adj* : TUMULTUOUS, TURBULENT — **ter·ma·gant·ly** *adv*
term·er \'tər-mər\ *n* : a person serving for a specified term (as in prison) ⟨first ~⟩
ter·mi·na·ble \'tərm-(ə-)nə-bəl\ *adj* [ME, fr. *terminen* to terminate, fr. OF *terminer*, fr. L *terminare*] : capable of being terminated — **ter·mi·na·ble·ness** *n* — **ter·mi·na·bly** \-blē\ *adv*
[1]**ter·mi·nal** \'tərm-nəl, -ən-ᵊl\ *adj* [L *terminalis*, fr. *terminus*] **1 a** : of or relating to an end, extremity, boundary, or terminus ⟨~ pillar⟩ **b** : growing at the end of a branch or stem ⟨~ bud⟩ **2** : of, relating to, or occurring in a term or each term **3 a** : occurring at or constituting the end of a period or series : CONCLUDING **b** : limited but complete **syn** see LAST — **ter·mi·nal·ly** \-ē\ *adv*
[2]**terminal** *n* **1** : a part that forms the end : EXTREMITY, TERMINATION **2** : a terminating usu. ornamental detail : FINIAL **3** : a device attached to the end of a wire or cable or to an electrical apparatus for convenience in making connections **4 a** : either end of a carrier line (as a railroad, trucking or shipping line, or airline) with classifying yards, dock and lighterage facilities, management offices, storage sheds, and freight and passenger stations **b** : a freight or passenger station that is central to a considerable area or serves as a junction at any point with other lines **c** : a town or city at the end of a carrier line : TERMINUS
terminal leave *n* : a final leave consisting of accumulated unused leave granted to a member of the armed forces just prior to his separation or discharge from service
[1]**ter·mi·nate** \'tər-mə-ˌnāt\ *vb* [L *terminatus*, pp. of *terminare*, fr. *terminus*] *vt* **1 a** : to bring to an end : CLOSE **b** : to form the conclusion of **2** : to serve as a limit to in space ~ *vi* **1** : to extend only to a limit (as a point or line); *esp* : to reach a terminus **2** : to come to an end in time **3** : to form an ending **syn** see CLOSE
[2]**ter·mi·nate** \-nət\ *adj* **1** : coming to an end or capable of ending **2** : indicating an action as a whole

ter·mi·na·tion \ˌtər-mə-ˈnā-shən\ *n* **1 :** end in time or existence **:** CONCLUSION ⟨~ of life⟩ **2 :** a limit in space or extent **:** BOUND **3 :** the last part of a word **:** SUFFIX; *esp* **:** an inflectional ending **4 :** the act of terminating **5 :** OUTCOME, RESULT **syn** see END — **ter·mi·na·tion·al** \-shnəl, -shən-ᵊl\ *adj*

ter·mi·na·tive \ˈtər-mə-ˌnāt-iv\ *adj* **:** tending or serving to terminate **:** DETERMINING — **ter·mi·na·tive·ly** *adv*

ter·mi·na·tor \-ˌnāt-ər\ *n* **1 :** one that terminates **2 :** the dividing line between the illuminated and the unilluminated part of the moon's or a planet's disk

ter·mi·no·log·i·cal \ˌtərm-nə-ˈläj-i-kəl, -ən-ᵊl-ˈäj-\ *adj* **:** of or relating to terminology — **ter·mi·no·log·i·cal·ly** \-k(ə-)lē\ *adv*

ter·mi·nol·o·gy \ˌtər-mə-ˈnäl-ə-jē\ *n* [ML *terminus* term, expression (fr. L, boundary, limit) + E *-o-* + *-logy*] **1 :** the technical or special terms or expressions used in a business, art, science, or special subject **2 :** nomenclature as a field of study

term insurance *n* **:** insurance for a specified period providing for no payment to the insured except upon losses during the period and becoming void upon its expiration

ter·mi·nus \ˈtər-mə-nəs\ *n, pl* **ter·mi·ni** \-ˌnī, -ˌnē\ *or* **ter·mi·nus·es** [L, boundary, end — more at TERM] **1 :** final goal **:** finishing point **2 :** a post or stone marking a boundary **3 a :** either end of a transportation line or travel route **b :** the station or the town or city at such a place **:** TERMINAL **4 :** EXTREMITY, TIP ⟨~ of a glacier⟩ **syn** see END

terminus ad quem \-ˌäd-ˈkwem\ *n* [NL, lit., limit to which] **:** a final limiting point in time

terminus a quo \-ˌäk-ˈwō\ *n* [NL, lit., limit from which] **1 :** a point of origin **2 :** the first of two limiting points in time

ter·mite \ˈtər-ˌmīt\ *n* [NL *Termit-, Termes,* genus of termites, fr. LL, a worm that eats wood, alter. of L *tarmit-, tarmes;* akin to Gk *tetrainein* to bore — more at THROW] **:** any of numerous pale-colored soft-bodied social insects (order Isoptera) that live in colonies consisting of winged sexual forms, wingless sterile workers, and often soldiers, feed on wood, and include some which are very destructive to wooden structures and trees — called also *white ant*

term·less \ˈtərm-ləs\ *adj* **1 :** BOUNDLESS, UNENDING **2 :** UNCONDITIONED, UNCONDITIONAL

term paper *n* **:** a major written assignment in a school or college course representative of a student's achievement during a term

term·time \ˈtərm-ˌtīm\ *n* **:** the time during an academic or legal term

tern \ˈtərn\ *n* [of Scand origin; akin to Dan *terne* tern] **:** any of numerous sea gulls (*Sterna* and related genera) that are smaller and slenderer in body and bill than typical gulls with narrower wings, often forked tails, black cap, and white body

ter·na·ry \ˈtər-nə-rē\ *adj* [ME, fr. L *ternarius,* fr. *terni* three each; akin to L *tres* three — more at THREE] **1 a :** of, relating to, or proceeding by threes **b :** having three elements, parts, or divisions **:** THREEFOLD **c :** arranged in threes ⟨~ petals⟩ **2 :** using three as the base ⟨~ logarithm⟩ **3 :** consisting of an alloy of three elements **4 :** containing or relating to three different elements, atoms, radicals, or groups ⟨sulfuric acid is a ~ acid⟩ **5 :** third in order or rank

ter·nate \ˈtər-ˌnāt, -nət\ *adj* [NL *ternatus,* fr. ML, pp. of *ternare* to treble, fr. L *terni*] **:** arranged in threes or in subdivisions so arranged ⟨a ~ leaf⟩ — **ter·nate·ly** *adv*

terne \ˈtərn\ *also* **terne·plate** \-ˌplāt\ *n* [prob. fr. F *terne* dull, fr. MF, fr. *ternir* to tarnish] **:** sheet iron or steel coated with an alloy of about 4 parts lead to 1 part tin

ter·pene \ˈtər-ˌpēn\ *n* [ISV *terp-* (fr. G *terpentin* turpentine, fr. ML *terbentina*) + *-ene* — more at TURPENTINE] **:** any of various isomeric hydrocarbons $C_{10}H_{16}$ found present in essential oils esp. from conifers and used esp. as solvents and in organic synthesis; *broadly* **:** any of numerous hydrocarbons $(C_5H_8)_n$ found esp. in essential oils, resins, and balsams — **ter·pe·nic** \ˌtər-ˈpē-nik, -ˈpen-ik\ *adj* — **ter·pe·noid** \ˈtər-pə-ˌnȯid\ *adj or n*

ter·pin·e·ol \ˌtər-ˈpin-ē-ˌȯl, -ˌōl\ *n* [ISV, fr. *terpine* ($C_{10}H_{18}(OH)_2$) **:** any of three fragrant isomeric alcohols $C_{10}H_{17}OH$ found in essential oils or made artificially and used esp. in perfume or as solvents

Terp·sich·o·re \ˌtərp-ˈsik-ə-(ˌ)rē\ *n* [L, fr. Gk *Terpsichorē*] **:** the Greek Muse of dancing and choral song

terp·si·cho·re·an \ˌtərp-(ˌ)sik-ə-ˈrē-ən; -sə-ˈkōr-ē-, -ˈkȯr-\ *adj* **:** of or relating to dancing

ter·ra al·ba \ˌter-ə-ˈal-bə, -ˈȯl-\ *n* [NL, lit., white earth] **:** any of several white mineral substances: as **a :** gypsum ground for a pigment **b :** kaolin used esp. as an adulterant of paints **c :** MAGNESIA 1

1**ter·race** \ˈter-əs\ *n* [MF, pile of earth, platform, terrace, fr. OProv *terrassa,* fr. *terra* earth, fr. L, earth, land; akin to L *torrēre* to parch — more at THIRST] **1 a :** a colonnaded porch or promenade **b :** a flat roof or open platform **:** BALCONY, DECK **c :** a relatively level paved or planted area adjoining a building **2 :** a raised embankment with the top leveled **3 :** a level ordinarily narrow plain usu. with steep front bordering a river, lake, or sea **4 a :** a row of houses or apartments on raised ground or a sloping site **b :** a group of row houses **c :** a strip of park in the middle of a street usu. planted with trees or shrubs **d :** a street usu. taking its name from the presence of a terrace

2**terrace** *vt* **:** to make into a terrace or supply with terraces

ter·rac·er \ˈter-ə-sər\ *n* **:** a machine used for constructing terraces or wide channels for surface drainage

ter·ra-cot·ta \ˌter-ə-ˈkät-ə\ *n, pl* **terra-cottas** [It *terra cotta,* lit., baked earth] **1 :** a glazed or unglazed fired clay used for statuettes and vases and architectural purposes (as roofing, facing, and relief ornamentation) **2 :** a brownish orange

terra fir·ma \-ˈfər-mə\ *n* [NL, lit., solid land] **:** dry land **:** solid ground

ter·rain \tə-ˈrān, te-\ *n* [F, land, ground, fr. L *terrenum,* fr. neut. of *terrenus* of earth — more at TERRENE] **1 a** (1) **:** a geographical area **:** REGION (2) **:** a piece of earth **:** GROUND **b :** the physical features of a tract of land **:** TOPOGRAPHY **2 :** TERRANE 1 **3 :** ENVIRONMENT, MILIEU

ter·ra in·cog·ni·ta \ˈter-ə-ˌin-ˌkäg-ˈnēt-ə, -in-ˈkäg-nət-ə\ *n, pl* **ter·rae in·cog·ni·tae** \ˈte(ə)r-ˌī-ˌin-ˌkäg-ˈnē-ˌtī, -in-ˈkäg-nə-ˌtī\ [L] **:** unknown territory **:** an unexplored country or field of knowledge

Ter·ra·my·cin \ˌter-ə-ˈmīs-ᵊn\ *trademark* — used for oxytetracycline

ter·rane \tə-ˈrān, te-\ *n* [alter. of *terrain*] **1 :** the area or surface over which a particular rock or group of rocks is prevalent **2 :** TERRAIN 1a

ter·ra·pin \ˈter-ə-pən, ˈtar-\ *n* [of Algonquian origin; akin to Delaware *torope* turtle] **:** any of various edible No. American turtles (family Testudinidae) living in fresh or brackish water

ter·raque·ous \te-ˈrā-kwē-əs, tə-, -ˈrak-wē-\ *adj* [L *terra* land + E *aqueous*] **:** consisting of land and water

ter·rar·i·um \tə-ˈrar-ē-əm, -ˈrer-\ *n, pl* **ter·rar·ia** \-ē-ə\ *or* **ter·rar·i·ums** [NL, fr. L *terra* + *-arium* (as in *aquarium*)] **:** a vivarium without standing water

ter·raz·zo \tə-ˈraz-(ˌ)ō, -ˈrät-(ˌ)sō\ *n* [It, lit., terrace, perh. fr. OProv *terrassa*] **:** a mosaic flooring made by embedding small pieces of marble or granite in mortar and polishing

ter·rene \te-ˈrēn, tə-; ˈte(ə)r-ˌēn\ *adj* [ME, fr. L *terrenus* of earth, fr. *terra* earth] **:** MUNDANE, EARTHLY — **terrene** *n*

ter·re·plein \ˈter-ə-ˌplān\ *n* [MF, fr. OIt *terrapieno,* fr. ML *terraplenum,* fr. *terra plenus* filled with earth] **:** the level space behind a parapet where guns are mounted

ter·res·tri·al \tə-ˈres-t(r)ē-əl, -ˈres(h)-chəl\ *adj* [ME, fr. L *terrestris,* fr. *terra* earth — more at TERRACE] **1 a :** of or relating to the earth or its inhabitants ⟨~ magnetism⟩ **b :** mundane in scope or character **:** PROSAIC **2 a :** of or relating to land as distinct from air or water ⟨~ transportation⟩ **b** (1) **:** living on or in or growing from land ⟨~ plants⟩ ⟨~ birds⟩ (2) **:** of or relating to terrestrial organisms ⟨~ habits⟩ **syn** see EARTHLY — **terrestrial** *n* — **ter·res·tri·al·ly** \-ē\ *adv*

ter·ret \ˈter-ət\ *n* [ME *teret,* alter. of *toret,* fr. MF, fr. OF, dim. of *tour* circuit, ring — more at TURN] **:** one of the rings on the top of a harness pad through which the reins pass

ter·ri·ble \ˈter-ə-bəl\ *adj* [ME, fr. MF, fr. L *terribilis,* fr. *terrēre* to frighten — more at TERROR] **1 a :** exciting terror **:** TERRIFYING **b :** AWESOME, IMPOSING **c :** DIFFICULT **2 :** EXTREME, GREAT **3 a :** strongly repulsive **:** OBNOXIOUS **b :** tending to appall **:** APPALLING, DREADFUL **4 :** of very poor quality **syn** see FEARFUL — **ter·ri·ble·ness** *n* — **ter·ri·bly** \-blē\ *adv*

ter·ric·o·lous \te-ˈrik-ə-ləs, tə-\ *adj* [L *terricola* earth dweller, fr. *terra* earth + *colere* to inhabit — more at WHEEL] **:** living on or in the ground

ter·ri·er \ˈter-ē-ər\ *n* [F (*chien*) *terrier,* lit., earth dog, fr. *terrier* of earth, fr. ML *terrarius,* fr. L *terra*] **:** any of various usu. small dogs orig. used by hunters to dig for small furred game and engage the quarry underground or drive it out

ter·rif·ic \tə-ˈrif-ik\ *adj* [L *terrificus,* fr. *terrēre* to frighten] **1 a :** exciting fear or awe **:** TERRIBLE **b :** very bad **:** FRIGHTFUL **2 :** EXTRAORDINARY, ASTOUNDING ⟨~ speed⟩ **3 :** unusually fine **:** MAGNIFICENT **syn** see FEARFUL — **ter·rif·i·cal·ly** \-i-k(ə-)lē\ *adv*

ter·ri·fy \ˈter-ə-ˌfī\ *vt* [L *terrificare,* fr. *terrificus*] **1 :** to fill with terror **2 a :** to drive or impel by menacing **b :** DETER, INTIMIDATE — **ter·ri·fy·ing·ly** \-iŋ-lē\ *adv*

ter·rig·e·nous \te-ˈrij-ə-nəs, tə-\ *adj* [L *terrigena* earthborn, fr. *terra* earth + *gignere* to beget — more at KIN] **:** formed by the erosive action of rivers, tides, and currents ⟨~ sediment⟩

1**ter·ri·to·ri·al** \ˌter-ə-ˈtōr-ē-əl, -ˈtȯr-\ *adj* **1 a :** NEARBY, LOCAL **b :** serving outlying areas **:** REGIONAL **2 a :** of or relating to a territory **b :** of or relating to private property **3 a :** of or relating to an assigned or preempted area **b :** exhibiting territoriality ⟨~ birds⟩ — **ter·ri·to·ri·al·ly** \-ē-ə-lē\ *adv*

2**territorial** *n* **:** a member of a territorial military unit

ter·ri·to·ri·al·ism \-ē-ə-ˌliz-əm\ *n* **1 :** LANDLORDISM **2 :** the principle established in 1555 requiring the inhabitants of a territory of the Holy Roman Empire to conform to the religion of their ruler or to emigrate **3** *often cap* **:** a theory or movement proposing an autonomous territory for the Jews — **ter·ri·to·ri·al·ist** \-ləst\ *n*

ter·ri·to·ri·al·i·ty \-ˌtōr-ē-ˈal-ət-ē, -ˌtȯr-\ *n* **1 :** territorial status **2 a :** persistent attachment to a specific territory **b :** the pattern of behavior associated with the defense of a male animal's territory

ter·ri·to·ri·al·iza·tion \-ē-ə-lə-ˈzā-shən\ *n* **:** the act or process of organizing into territories

ter·ri·to·ri·al·ize \-ˈtōr-ē-ə-ˌlīz, -ˈtȯr-\ *vt* **:** to organize on a territorial basis

territorial waters *n pl* **:** the waters under the sovereign jurisdiction of a nation or state including both marginal sea and inland waters

ter·ri·to·ry \ˈter-ə-ˌtōr-ē, -ˌtȯr-\ *n* [ME, fr. L *territorium,* lit., land around a town, prob. fr. *terra* land + *-torium* (as in *praetorium*) — more at TERRACE] **1 a :** a geographical area belonging to or under the jurisdiction of a governmental authority **b :** an administrative subdivision of a country **c :** a part of the U.S. not included within any state but organized with a separate legislature **d :** a geographical area (as a colonial possession) dependent upon an external government but having some degree of autonomy — compare TRUST TERRITORY **2 a :** an indeterminate geographical area **b :** a field of knowledge or interest **3 a :** an assigned area; *esp* **:** one in which a salesman or distributor operates **b :** an area usu. including the nesting or denning site and a variable foraging range that is preempted and defended by a male bird or mammal

ter·ror \ˈter-ər\ *n* [ME, fr. MF *terreur,* fr. L *terror,* fr. *terrēre* to frighten; akin to Gk *trein* to be afraid, flee, *tremein* to tremble — more at TREMBLE] **1 a :** a state of intense fear **b :** TERRIBLENESS **2 a :** one that inspires fear **:** SCOURGE **b :** a frightening aspect **c :** a cause of anxiety **:** WORRY **d :** an appalling person or thing; *esp* **:** BRAT **3 :** REIGN OF TERROR **syn** see FEAR

ter·ror·ism \ˈter-ər-ˌiz-əm\ *n* **:** the systematic use of terror esp. as a means of coercion — **ter·ror·ist** \-ər-əst\ *adj or n* — **ter·ror·is·tic** \ˌter-ər-ˈis-tik\ *adj*

ter·ror·iza·tion \ˌter-ər-ə-ˈzā-shən\ *n* **:** the act or process of terrorizing

ter·ror·ize \ˈter-ər-ˌīz\ *vt* **1 :** to fill with terror or anxiety **:** SCARE **2 :** to coerce by threat or violence

ter·ror·less \ˈter-ər-ləs\ *adj* **:** holding no terrors

ter·ry \ˈter-ē\ *n* [perh. modif. of F *tiré,* pp. of *tirer* to draw — more at TIRADE] **:** the loop forming the pile in uncut pile fabrics; *also* **:** an absorbent fabric with such loops

terse \ˈtərs\ *adj* [L *tersus* clean, neat, fr. pp. of *tergēre* to wipe off; akin to Gk *trōgein* to gnaw, L *terere* to rub — more at THROW]

1 : smoothly elegant : POLISHED, REFINED 2 : devoid of superfluity : SUCCINCT **syn** see CONCISE — **terse·ly** *adv* — **terse·ness** *n*
ter·tial \'tər-shəl\ *adj* [L *tertius* third; fr. the fact that flight feathers form the third row of feathers] : of, relating to, or being flight feathers on the basal joint of a bird's wing — **tertial** *n*
1**ter·tian** \'tər-shən\ *adj* [ME *tercian*, fr. L *tertianus*, lit., of the third, fr. *tertius* third — more at THIRD] : recurring at approximately 48-hour intervals — used of malaria
2**tertian** *n* : a tertian fever; *specif* : malaria caused by a malaria parasite (*Plasmodium vivax*) and marked by recurrence of paroxysms at 48-hour intervals — called also *vi·vax malaria* \,vī-,vaks-\
1**ter·ti·ary** \'tər-shē-,er-ē\ *n* 1 [ML *tertiarius*, fr. L, of a third] : a member of a monastic third order esp. of lay people 2 : a tertial feather 3 *cap* : the Tertiary period or system of rocks
2**tertiary** *adj* [L *tertiarius* of or containing a third, fr. *tertius* third] 1 a : of 3d rank, importance, or value b : of, relating to, or constituting the 3d strongest of the three or four degrees of stress recognized by most linguists ⟨the 3d syllable of *basketball team* carries ~ stress⟩ 2 *cap* : of, relating to, or being the first period of the Cenozoic era or the corresponding system of rocks marked by the formation of high mountains (as the Alps, Caucasus, and Himalayas) and the dominance of mammals on land 3 : characterized by replacement in the 3d degree : resulting from the substitution of three atoms or groups ⟨a ~ salt⟩ 4 : occurring in or being a 3d stage
tertiary color *n* : a color produced by mixing two secondary colors
ter·ti·um quid \,tər-shē-əm-'kwid, ,tərt-ē-\ *n* [LL, lit., third something] 1 : something that escapes a division into two groups supposed to be exhaustive 2 : a 3d party of ambiguous status
ter·va·lent \,tər-'vā-lənt, 'tər-\ *adj* : TRIVALENT
ter·za ri·ma \,tert-sə-'rē-mə\ *n* [It, lit., third rhyme] : a verse form consisting of tercets usu. in iambic pentameter with an interlaced rhyme scheme (as *aba*, *bcb*, *cdc*) in English poetry
tes·sel·late \'tes-ə-,lāt\ *vt* [LL *tessellatus*, pp. of *tessellare* to pave with tesserae, fr. L *tessella*, dim. of *tessera*] : to form into or adorn with mosaic
tes·sel·lat·ed \-,lāt-əd\ *adj* : having a checkered appearance : MOTTLED, RETICULATED
tes·sel·la·tion \,tes-ə-'lā-shən\ *n* 1 : an act of tessellating : the state of being tessellated 2 : a careful juxtaposition of elements into a coherent pattern : MOSAIC
tes·sera \'tes-(ə-)rə\ *n, pl* **tes·ser·ae** \-ə-,rē, -,rī\ [L; prob. deriv. of Gk *tessares* four; fr. its having four corners — more at FOUR] 1 : a small tablet (as of wood, bone, or ivory) used by the ancient Romans as a ticket, tally, voucher, or means of identification 2 : a small piece (as of marble, glass, or tile) used in mosaic work
tes·si·tu·ra \,tes-ə-'tu̇r-ə\ *n* [It, lit., texture, fr. L *textura*] : the average pitch within the most often used range of a melody or voice
1**test** \'test\ *n* [ME, vessel in which metals were assayed, cupel, fr. MF, fr. L *testum* earthen vessel; akin to L *testa* earthen pot, shell, *texere* to weave — more at TECHNICAL] 1 a *chiefly Brit* : CUPEL b (1) : a critical examination, observation, or evaluation : TRIAL (2) : a basis for evaluation : CRITERION c : an ordeal or oath required as proof of conformity with a set of beliefs 2 a : a means of testing: as (1) : a procedure, reaction, or reagent used to identify or characterize a substance or constituent (2) : a series of questions or exercises or other means of measuring the skill, knowledge, intelligence, capacities, or aptitudes of an individual or group b : a positive result in such a test
2**test** *vt* 1 : to put to test or proof : TRY 2 : to require a doctrinal oath of ~ *vi* 1 a : to undergo a test b : to achieve a rating on the basis of tests 2 : to apply a test as a means of analysis or diagnosis — used with *for* ⟨~ for mechanical aptitude⟩ — **test·able** \'tes-tə-bəl\ *adj*
3**test** *n* [L *testa* shell] : an external hard or firm covering (as a shell) of many invertebrates
tes·ta \'tes-tə\ *n, pl* **tes·tae** \-,tē, -,tī\ [NL, fr. L, shell] : the hard external coating or integument of a seed
tes·ta·cean \te-'stā-shən\ *n* [deriv. of L *testaceus*] : any of an order (Testacea) of shelled rhizopods
tes·ta·ceous \-shəs\ *adj* [L *testaceus*, fr. *testa* shell, earthen pot, brick] 1 a : having a shell ⟨a ~ protozoan⟩ b : consisting of shell or calcareous material 2 : of any of the several light colors of bricks
tes·ta·cy \'tes-tə-sē\ *n* : the state or circumstance of being testate
tes·ta·ment \'tes-tə-mənt\ *n* [ME, fr. LL & L; LL *testamentum* covenant with God, holy scripture, fr. L, last will, fr. *testari* to be a witness, call to witness, make a will, fr. *testis* witness; akin to L *tres* three & to L *stare* to stand; fr. the witness's standing by as a third party in a litigation — more at THREE, STAND] 1 a *archaic* : a covenant between God and man b *cap* (1) : either of two main divisions of the Bible (2) : NEW TESTAMENT 2 a : a tangible proof or tribute b : an expression of conviction : CREDO 3 a : an act by which a person determines the disposition of his property after his death b : WILL — **tes·ta·men·ta·ry** \,tes-tə-'ment-ə-rē, -'men-trē\ *adj*
1**tes·tate** \'tes-,tāt, -tət\ *adj* [ME, fr. L *testatus*, pp. of *testari* to make a will] : having left a will ⟨a person dying ~⟩
2**tes·tate** \-,tāt\ *adj* [3*test* or *testa*] : having a firm external covering and esp. a test or testa
tes·ta·tor \'tes-,tāt-ər, te-'stāt-\ *n* [ME *testatour*, fr. AF, fr. LL *testator*, fr. L *testatus*, pp.] : a person who leaves a will or testament in force at his death — **tes·ta·trix** \te-'stā-triks\ *n*
test case *n* 1 : a representative case whose outcome is likely to serve as a precedent 2 : a proceeding brought by agreement or on an understanding of the parties to obtain a decision as to the constitutionality of a statute
test·ed *adj* : subjected to or qualified through testing ⟨time-*tested* principles⟩ ⟨tuberculin-*tested* cattle⟩
1**tes·ter** \'tēs-tər, 'tes-\ *n* [ME, fr. MF *testiere* headpiece, head covering, fr. *teste* head, fr. LL *testa* skull, fr. L, shell — more at TEST] : the canopy over a bed, pulpit, or altar
2**tes·ter** \'tes-tər\ *n* [modif. of MF *testart*, fr. *teston*] : TESTON b
3**test·er** \'tes-tər\ *n* : one that tests
tes·ti·cle \'tes-ti-kəl\ *n* [ME *testicule*, fr. L *testiculus*, dim. of *testis*] : TESTIS — **tes·tic·u·lar** \te-'stik-yə-lər\ *adj*
tes·tic·u·late \te-'stik-yə-lət\ *adj* [NL *testiculatus*, fr. L *testiculus*] : ovate and solid like a testis ⟨a ~ root⟩
tes·ti·fi·er \'tes-tə-,fī(-ə)r\ *n* : one that testifies : WITNESS
tes·ti·fy \'tes-tə-,fī\ *vb* [ME *testifien*, fr. L *testificari*, fr. *testis* witness] *vi* 1 a : to make a statement based on personal knowledge or belief : bear witness b : to serve as evidence or proof 2 : to express a personal conviction 3 : to make a solemn declaration under oath for the purpose of establishing a fact (as in a court) ~ *vt* 1 a : to bear witness to : ATTEST b : to serve as evidence of : PROVE 2 *archaic* a : to make known (a personal conviction) : PROFESS b : to give evidence of : SHOW 3 : to declare under oath before a tribunal or officially constituted public body
tes·ti·ly \'tes-tə-lē\ *adv* : in a testy manner
1**tes·ti·mo·ni·al** \,tes-tə-'mō-nē-əl\ *adj* 1 : of, relating to, or constituting testimony 2 : expressive of appreciation or esteem ⟨~ dinner⟩
2**testimonial** *n* 1 : EVIDENCE, TESTIMONY 2 a : a statement testifying to benefits received b : a character reference : letter of recommendation 3 : an expression of appreciation : TRIBUTE
tes·ti·mo·ny \'tes-tə-,mō-nē\ *n* [ME, fr. LL & L; LL *testimonium* Decalogue, fr. L, evidence, witness, fr. *testis* witness — more at TESTAMENT] 1 a : the tablets inscribed with the Mosaic law or the ark containing them b : a divine decree attested in the Scriptures 2 a : firsthand authentication of a fact : EVIDENCE b : an outward sign : SYMBOL c : a solemn declaration usu. made orally by a witness under oath in response to interrogation by a lawyer or authorized public official 3 a : an open acknowledgment : PROFESSION b : a public profession of religious experience
tes·ti·ness \'tes-tē-nəs\ *n* : the quality or state of being testy
tes·tis \'tes-təs\ *n, pl* **tes·tes** \'tes-,tēz\ [L, witness, testis] : a male reproductive gland
test match *n* 1 : any of a series of championship cricket matches played between teams representing Australia and England 2 : a championship game or series (as of cricket) played between teams representing different countries
tes·ton \'tes-,tän\ *or* **tes·toon** \te-'stün\ *n* [MF, fr. OIt *testone*, aug. of *testa* head, fr. LL, skull — more at TESTER] : any of several old European coins: as a : a French silver coin of the 16th century worth between 10 and 14½ sous b : a shilling of Henry VIII of England decreasing in value to ninepence and then to sixpence in Shakespeare's time
tes·tos·ter·one \te-'stäs-tə-,rōn\ *n* [*testis* + *-o-* + *sterol* + *-one*] : a crystalline androgenic hydroxy steroid ketone $C_{19}H_{28}O_2$ obtained esp. from the testes of bulls or synthetically and used in medicine usu. as an ester
test paper *n* : paper saturated with a reagent that changes color in testing for various substances
test pilot *n* : a pilot who specializes in putting new or experimental airplanes through maneuvers designed to test them (as for strength) by producing strains in excess of normal
test tube *n* : a usu. plain tube of thin glass closed at one end and used esp. in chemistry and biology
test–tube \,tes-,t(y)üb\ *adj* : produced by artificial insemination ⟨~ babies⟩
1**tes·tu·di·nate** \te-'st(y)üd-ᵊn-ət\ *adj* [deriv. of L *testudin-*, *testudo* tortoise shell] : CHELONIAN
2**testudinate** *n* : 2TURTLE
tes·tu·do \te-'st(y)üd-(,)ō\ *n* [L *testudin-*, *testudo*, lit., tortoise, tortoise shell; akin to L *testa* shell — more at TEST] : a cover of overlapping shields or a shed wheeled up to a wall used to protect an attacking force by the ancient Romans
tes·ty \'tes-tē\ *adj* [ME *testif*, fr. AF, headstrong, fr. OF *teste* head — more at TESTER] 1 : easily annoyed : IRRITABLE 2 : marked by impatience or ill humor : EXASPERATED ⟨~ remark⟩ **syn** see IRASCIBLE
tet·a·nal \'tet-ᵊn-əl\ *adj* : relating to or derived from tetanus ⟨~ antitoxin⟩
te·tan·ic \te-'tan-ik\ *adj* : of, relating to, being, or tending to produce tetanus or tetany — **te·tan·i·cal·ly** \-i-k(ə-)lē\ *adv*
tet·a·nize \'tet-ᵊn-,īz\ *vt* : to induce tetanus in ⟨~ a muscle⟩
tet·a·nus \'tet-ᵊn-əs, 'tet-nəs\ *n* [ME, fr. L, fr. Gk *tetanos*, fr. *tetanos* stretched, rigid; akin to Gk *teinein* to stretch — more at THIN] 1 a : an acute infectious disease characterized by tonic spasm of voluntary muscles esp. of the jaw and caused by the specific toxin of a bacillus (*Clostridium tetani*) which is usu. introduced through a wound b : the bacterium that causes tetanus 2 : prolonged contraction of a muscle resulting from rapidly repeated motor impulses
tet·a·ny \'tet-ᵊn-ē, 'tet-nē\ *n* [ISV, fr. L *tetanus*] : a condition of physiologic mineral imbalance marked by tonic spasm of muscles and associated usu. with deficient parathyroid secretion
te·tar·to·he·dral \tə-,tärt-ō-'hē-drəl\ *adj* [Gk *tetartos* fourth; akin to Gk *tettares* four — more at FOUR] *of a crystal* : having one fourth the number of planes required by complete symmetry — compare HOLOHEDRAL
tetched *var of* TECHED
tetchy \'tech-ē\ *adj* [perh. fr. obs. *tetch* (habit)] : irritably or peevishly sensitive : TOUCHY
1**tête–à–tête** \,tāt-ə-'tāt, -ə-'tā\ *adv* [F, lit., head to head] : face to face : PRIVATELY
2**tête–à–tête** *n* 1 : a private conversation between two persons 2 : a short piece of furniture (as a sofa) intended to seat two persons esp. facing each other
3**tête–à–tête** *adj* : being face to face : PRIVATE
tête–bêche \'tāt-'bāsh\ *adj* [F, n., pair of inverted stamps, fr. *tête* head + *-bêche*, alter. of MF *bechevet* head against foot] : of or relating to a pair of stamps inverted in relation to one another either through a printing error or intentionally
teth \'tāt(h), 'tās\ *n* [Heb *ṭēth*] : the 9th letter of the Hebrew alphabet — symbol ט
1**teth·er** \'teth-ər\ *n* [ME *tethir*, prob. of Scand origin; akin to ON *tjōthr* tether; akin to OHG *zeotar* pole of a wagon] 1 : something (as a rope or chain) by which an animal is fastened so that it can range only within a set radius 2 : the limit of one's strength or resources : SCOPE ⟨the end of his ~⟩
2**tether** *vt* **teth·er·ing** \-(ə-)riŋ\ : to fasten or restrain by or as if by a tether
teth·er·ball \'teth-ər-,bȯl\ *n* : a game which is played by two contestants with rackets and a ball suspended by a string from an upright pole and in which the object of each contestant is to wrap the string around the pole by striking the ball in a direction opposite to the other

Te·thys \'tē-thəs\ *n* [L, fr. Gk *Tēthys*] **:** a Titaness and wife of Oceanus

tet·ra \'te-trə\ *n* [by shortening fr. NL *Tetragonopterus*, former genus name, fr. LL *tetragonum* quadrangle + Gk *pteron* wing — more at TETRAGONAL, FEATHER] **:** any of numerous small brightly colored So. American characin fishes often bred in the tropical aquarium

tetra- *or* **tetr-** *comb form* [ME, fr. L, fr. Gk; akin to Gk *tettares* four — more at FOUR] **1 :** four **:** having four **:** having four parts ⟨*tetra*tomic⟩ **2 :** containing four atoms, radicals, or groups (of a specified kind) ⟨*tetra*basic⟩ ⟨*tetr*acid⟩

tet·ra·ba·sic \,te-trə-'bā-sik\ *adj* [ISV] **1 :** having four hydrogen atoms capable of replacement by basic atoms or radicals **2 :** containing four atoms of a univalent metal or their equivalent **3 :** having four basic hydroxyl groups **:** able to react with four molecules of a monoacid — **tet·ra·ba·sic·i·ty** \-bā-'sis-ət-ē\ *n*

tet·ra·branch \'te-trə-,braŋk\ *n* [deriv. of Gk *tetra-* + *branchion* gill — more at BRANCHIA] **:** NAUTILOID — **tetrabranch** *or* **tet·ra·bran·chi·ate** \,te-trə-'braŋ-kē-ət\ *adj*

tet·ra·chlo·ride \,te-trə-'klō(ə)r-,īd, -'klȯ(ə)r-\ *n* **:** a chloride containing four atoms of chlorine

tet·ra·chord \'te-trə-,kȯ(ə)rd\ *n* [Gk *tetrachordon*, fr. neut. of *tetrachordos* of four strings, fr. *tetra-* + *chordē* string — more at YARN] **:** a diatonic series of four tones with an interval of a perfect fourth between the first and last

te·trac·id\te-'tras-əd\ *adj* **1 :** able to react with four molecules of a monoacid or two of a diacid to form a salt or ester **2 :** having four hydrogen atoms replaceable by basic atoms or radicals

tet·ra·cy·cline \,te-trə-'sī-,klēn\ *n* [ISV, fr. *tetracyclic* (containing four fused rings in the molecular structure)] **:** a yellow crystalline broad-spectrum antibiotic $C_{22}H_{24}N_2O_8$ produced by a soil actinomycete (*Streptomyces viridifaciens*) or synthetically

tet·rad \'te-,trad\ *n* [Gk *tetrad-*, *tetras*, fr. *tetra-*] **:** a group or arrangement of four: as **a :** a tetravalent element, atom, or radical **b :** a group of four cells arranged usu. in the form of a tetrahedron and produced by the successive divisions of a mother cell **c :** an arrangement of chromosomes by fours in the first meiotic prophase due to precocious longitudinal splitting of paired chromosomes — **te·trad·ic** \te-'trad-ik\ *adj*

te·trad·y·mite \te-'trad-ə-,mīt\ *n* [LGk *tetradymos* fourfold, fr. Gk *tetra-* + *-dymos* (as in *didymos* didymous); fr. its occurrence in compound twin crystals] **:** a pale steel-gray mineral Bi_2Te_2S consisting essentially of a telluride and sulfide of bismuth and having a metallic luster

tet·ra·dy·na·mous \,te-trə-'dī-nə-məs\ *adj* [ISV *tetra-* + Gk *dynamis* power — more at DYNAMIC] **:** having six stamens four of which are longer than the others

tet·ra·eth·yl \,te-trə-'eth-əl\ *adj* [ISV] **:** containing four ethyl groups in the molecule

tetraethyl lead *n* **:** a heavy oily poisonous liquid $Pb(C_2H_5)_4$ used as an antiknock agent

tet·ra·flu·o·ride \,te-trə-'flu̇(-ə)r-,īd\ *n* **:** a fluoride containing four atoms of fluorine

te·trag·o·nal \te-'trag-ən-ᵊl\ *adj* [LL *tetragonalis*, fr. *tetragonum* quadrangle, fr. Gk *tetragōnon*, fr. neut. of *tetragōnos* tetragonal, fr. *tetra-* + *gōnia* angle — more at -GON] **1 :** having four angles and four sides **2 :** of, relating to, or characteristic of the tetragonal system — **te·trag·o·nal·ly** \-ᵊl-ē\ *adv* — **te·trag·o·nal·ness** *n*

tetragonal system *n* **:** a crystal system characterized by three axes at right angles of which only the two lateral axes are equal

tet·ra·gram·ma·ton \,te-trə-'gram-ə-,tän\ *n* [ME, fr. Gk, fr. neut. of *tetragrammatos* having four letters, fr. *tetra-* + *grammat-*, *gramma* letter — more at GRAM] **:** the four Hebrew letters usu. transliterated YHWH or JHVH that form a biblical proper name of God — compare YAHWEH

tet·ra·gy·nous \,te-trə-'jī-nəs, -'gī-; te-'traj-ə-nəs\ *adj* **:** having four pistils or carpels

tet·ra·he·dral \,te-trə-'hē-drəl\ *adj* **1 :** relating to, forming, or having the form of a tetrahedron **2 :** having four faces ⟨~ angle⟩ — **tet·ra·he·dral·ly** \-drə-lē\ *adv*

tet·ra·he·drite \-,drīt\ *n* [G *tetraëdrit*, fr. LGk *tetraedros* having four faces] **:** a fine-grained gray mineral $(Cu,Fe)_{12}Sb_4S_{13}$ that consists essentially of a sulfide of copper, iron, and antimony and often other elements, occurs in tetrahedral crystals and also massive, and is often a valuable ore of silver

tet·ra·he·dron \,te-trə-'hē-drən\ *n, pl* **tetrahedrons** *or* **tet·ra·he·dra** \-drə\ [NL, fr. LGk *tetraedron*, neut. of *tetraedros* having four faces, fr. Gk *tetra-* + *hedra* seat, face — more at SIT] **:** a polyhedron of four faces

tet·ra·hy·drate \-'hī-drət, -,drāt\ *n* **:** a chemical compound with four molecules of water — **tet·ra·hy·drat·ed** \-,drāt-əd\ *adj*

tet·ra·hy·droxy \-(,)hī-'dräk-sē\ *adj* [*tetra-* + *hydroxyl*] **:** containing four hydroxyl groups in the molecule

te·tral·o·gy \te-'träl-ə-jē, -'tral-\ *n* [Gk *tetralogia*, fr. *tetra-* + *-logia* -logy] **1 :** a group of four dramatic pieces represented consecutively on the Attic stage at the Dionysiac festival **2 :** a series of four connected works (as operas or novels)

tet·ra·mer \'te-trə-mər\ *n* **:** a polymer formed from four molecules of a monomer

te·tram·er·ous \te-'tram-ə-rəs\ *adj* [NL *tetramerus*, fr. Gk *tetramerēs*, fr. *tetra-* + *meros* part — more at MERIT] **:** having or characterized by the presence of four parts: **a** *of a flower* **:** having the parts arranged in sets or multiples of four — often written *4-merous* **b :** having four or apparently only four joints in each tarsus ⟨~ beetles⟩

te·tram·e·ter \te-'tram-ət-ər\ *n* [Gk *tetrametron*, fr. neut. of *tetrametros* having four measures, fr. *tetra-* + *metron* measure — more at MEASURE] **:** a verse consisting either of four dipodies (as in classical iambic, trochaic, and anapestic verse) or four feet (as in modern English verse)

te·tran·drous \te-'t(r)an-drəs\ *adj* [ISV] **:** having four stamens

tet·ra·pet·al·ous \,te-trə-'pet-ᵊl-əs\ *adj* [NL *tetrapetalus*, fr. *tetra-* + *petalum* petal] **:** having four petals

[1]**tet·ra·ploid** \'te-trə-,plȯid\ *adj* [ISV] **:** fourfold in appearance or arrangement; *specif* **:** having or being a chromosome number four times the monoploid number ⟨a ~ cell⟩ — **tet·ra·ploi·dic** \,te-trə-'plȯid-ik\ *adj* — **tet·ra·ploi·dy** \'te-trə-,plȯid-ē\ *n*

[2]**tetraploid** *n* **:** a tetraploid individual

te·trap·ter·ous \te-'trap-tə-rəs\ *adj* [Gk *tetrapteros*, fr. *tetra-* + *pteron* wing — more at FEATHER] **:** having four wings

te·trarch \'te-,trärk, 'tē-\ *n* [ME, fr. L *tetrarcha*, fr. Gk *tetrarchēs*, fr. *tetra-* + *-archēs* -arch] **1 :** a governor of the fourth part of a province **2 :** a subordinate prince — **te·trar·chic** \te-'trär-kik, tē-\ *adj*

te·trar·chy \'te-,trär-kē, 'tē-\ *n* **:** four persons ruling jointly

tet·ra·spore \'te-trə-,spō(ə)r, -,spȯ(ə)r\ *n* [ISV] **:** one of the haploid asexual spores developed meiotically in the red algae usu. in groups of four — **tet·ra·spor·ic** \,te-trə-'spōr-ik, -'spȯr-\ *or* **te·tra·spo·rous** \,te-trə-'spōr-əs, -'spȯr-; te-'tras-pə-rəs\ *adj*

te·tras·ti·chous \te-'tras-ti-kəs\ *adj* [Gk *tetrastichos* of four rows, fr. *tetra-* + *stichos* row, verse — more at DISTICH] **:** four-ranked — used esp. of flowers arranged in a spike in four vertical rows

tet·ra·tom·ic \,te-trə-'täm-ik\ *adj* [ISV] **1 :** consisting of four atoms **:** having four atoms in the molecule **2 :** having four replaceable atoms or radicals

tet·ra·va·lent \,te-trə-'vā-lənt\ *adj* [ISV] **1 :** having a valence of four **2 :** QUADRUPLE — used of homologous chromosomes in synapsis

tet·rode \'te-,trōd\ *n* **:** a vacuum tube with four electrodes, a cathode, an anode, a control grid, and an additional grid or other electrode

te·trox·ide \te-'träk-,sīd\ *n* [ISV] **:** a compound of an element or radical with four atoms of oxygen

tet·ryl \'te-trəl\ *n* [ISV] **:** a pale yellow crystalline explosive $C_7H_5N_5O_8$ used esp. as a detonator

tet·ter \'tet-ər\ *n* [ME *teter*, fr. OE; akin to OE *teran* to tear] **:** any of various vesicular skin diseases (as ringworm, eczema, and herpes)

Teu·ton \'t(y)üt-ᵊn\ *n* [L *Teutoni*, pl.] **1 :** a member of an ancient prob. Germanic or Celtic people **2 :** a member of a people speaking a language of the Germanic branch of the Indo-European language family; *esp* **:** GERMAN

[1]**Teu·ton·ic** \t(y)ü-'tän-ik\ *adj* **:** of, relating to, or characteristic of the Teutons — **Teu·ton·i·cal·ly** \-i-k(ə-)lē\ *adv*

[2]**Teutonic** *n* **:** GERMANIC

Teu·ton·ism \'t(y)üt-ᵊn-,iz-əm\ *n* **:** GERMANISM

Teu·ton·ist \-ᵊn-əst\ *n* **:** GERMANIST

teu·ton·ize \-ᵊn-,īz\ *vt, often cap* **:** GERMANIZE

tex·as \'tek-səs, -siz\ *n* [*Texas*, state of U.S.; fr. the naming of cabins on Mississippi steamboats after states, the officers' cabins being the largest] **:** a structure on the awning deck of a steamer containing the officers' cabins and having the pilothouse in front or on top

Texas fever *n* [*Texas*, state of U.S.] **:** an infectious disease of cattle transmitted by the cattle tick and caused by a protozoan (*Babesia bigemina*) that multiplies in the blood and destroys the red blood cells

Texas Independence Day *n* **:** March 2 observed as the anniversary of the declaration of independence of Texas from Mexico in 1836 and also as the birthday of Sam Houston

texas leaguer *n* [*Texas League*, a baseball minor league] **:** a fly in baseball that falls too far out to be caught by an infielder and too close in to be caught by an outfielder

Texas Ranger *n* **:** a member of a mounted police force in Texas

Texas tower *n* [fr. the resemblance to Texas offshore oil derricks] **:** a radar-equipped platform supported on caissons sunk in the ocean floor

text \'tekst\ *n* [ME, fr. MF *texte*, fr. ML *textus*, fr. L, texture, context, fr. *textus*, pp. of *texere* to weave — more at TECHNICAL] **1 a** (1) **:** the original written or printed words and form of a literary work (2) **:** an edited or emended copy of an original work **b :** a work containing such text **2 a :** the main body of printed or written matter on a page **b :** the principal part of a book exclusive of front and back matter **c :** the printed score of a musical composition **3 a** (1) **:** a verse or passage of Scriptures chosen esp. for the subject of a sermon or for authoritative support (as for a doctrine) (2) **:** a passage from an authoritative source providing an introduction or basis (as for a speech) **b :** a source of information or authority **c :** TEXTBOOK **4 :** a type suitable for printing running text **5 :** THEME, TOPIC **6 :** the words of something (as a poem) set to music

text·book \'teks(t)-,bu̇k\ *n* **:** a book used in the study of a subject: as **a :** one containing a presentation of the principles of a subject **b :** a literary work relevant to the study of a subject

text·book·ish \-ish\ *adj* **:** of, relating to, or having the characteristics of a textbook

text edition *n* **:** an edition prepared for use esp. in schools and colleges — compare TRADE EDITION

text hand *n* **:** a style of handwriting marked by use of large letters

tex·tile \'tek-,stīl, 'teks-tᵊl\ *n, often attrib* [L, fr. neut. of *textilis* woven, fr. *textus*, pp. of *texere*] **1 :** CLOTH 1a; *esp* **:** a woven or knit cloth **2 :** a fiber, filament, or yarn used in making cloth

tex·tu·al \'teks-chə(-wə)l\ *adj* [ME, fr. ML *textus* text] **:** of, relating to, or based on a text — **tex·tu·al·ly** \-ē\ *adv*

textual critic *n* **:** a practitioner of textual criticism

textual criticism *n* **1 :** the study of a literary work that aims to establish the original text **2 :** a critical study of literature emphasizing a close reading and analysis of the text

[1]**tex·tu·ary** \'teks-chə-,wer-ē\ *n* [ML *textus*] **:** one who is well informed on the Bible or in biblical scholarship

[2]**textuary** *adj* **:** TEXTUAL

tex·tur·al \'teks-chə-rəl\ *adj* **:** of, relating to, or marked by texture

[1]**tex·ture** \'teks-chər\ *n* [L *textura*, fr. *textus*, pp. of *texere* to weave — more at TECHNICAL] **1 a :** something composed of closely interwoven elements; *specif* **:** a woven cloth **b :** the structure formed by the threads of a fabric **2 a :** essential part **:** SUBSTANCE **b :** identifying quality **:** CHARACTER **3 :** the disposition or manner of union of the particles of a body or substance **4 a :** basic scheme or structure **:** FABRIC **b :** overall structure **:** BODY

[2]**texture** *vt* **:** to give a particular texture to

tex·tus re·cep·tus \,tek-stəs-ri-'sep-təs\ *n* [NL, lit., received text] **:** the generally accepted text of a literary work (as the Greek New Testament)

T formation *n* **:** an offensive football formation in which the full-

back lines up behind the center and quarterback and one halfback is stationed on each side of the fullback

1-th — see -ETH

2-th *or* **-eth** *adj suffix* [ME *-the, -te,* fr. OE *-tha, -ta;* akin to OHG *-do* -th, L *-tus,* Gk *-tos,* Skt *-tha*] — used in forming ordinal numbers ⟨hundred*th*⟩ ⟨forti*eth*⟩

3-th *n suffix* [ME, fr. OE; akin to OHG *-ida,* suffix forming abstract nouns, L *-ta,* Gk *-tē,* Skt *-tā*] **1 :** act or process ⟨spil*th*⟩ **2 :** state or condition ⟨dear*th*⟩

Thai \'tī\ *n* **1 :** a native or inhabitant of Thailand or one of his descendants **2 :** the official language of Thailand **3 :** a group of languages including Thai held by some to belong to the Sino-Tibetan language group

thal·am·en·ceph·a·lon \ˌthal-ə-ˌmen-'sef-ə-ˌlän, -lən\ *n* [NL, fr. *thalamus* + *encephalon*] **:** DIENCEPHALON

tha·lam·ic \thə-'lam-ik\ *adj* **:** of, relating to, or involving the thalamus — **tha·lam·i·cal·ly** \-i-k(ə-)lē\ *adv*

thal·a·mus \'thal-ə-məs\ *n, pl* **thal·a·mi** \-ˌmī, -ˌmē\ [NL, fr. Gk *thalamos* chamber] **1 :** the largest subdivision of the diencephalon consisting chiefly of an ovoid mass of nuclei in each lateral wall of the third ventricle **2 :** RECEPTACLE 2b

tha·las·sic \thə-'las-ik\ *adj* [F *thalassique,* fr. Gk *thalassa* sea] **1 :** of or relating to the sea or ocean **2 :** of or relating to seas or gulfs as distinguished from oceans

thal·as·soc·ra·cy \ˌthal-ə-'säk-rə-sē\ *n* [Gk *thalassokratia,* fr. *thalassa* + *-kratia* -cracy] **:** maritime supremacy

tha·las·so·crat \thə-'las-ə-ˌkrat\ *n* **:** one who has maritime supremacy

tha·ler \'täl-ər\ *var of* TALER

Tha·lia \thə-'lī-ə\ *n* [L, fr. Gk *Thaleia*] **1 :** the Greek Muse of comedy and pastoral poetry **2 :** one of the three Graces

thall- *or* **thallo-** *comb form* [NL, fr. Gk, fr. *thallos* — more at THALLUS] **1 a :** a young shoot ⟨*thall*ium⟩ **b :** thallus ⟨*Thallo*phyta⟩ **2 :** thallium ⟨*thall*ic⟩

thal·lic \'thal-ik\ *adj* **:** of, relating to, or containing thallium esp. when trivalent

thal·li·um \'thal-ē-əm\ *n* [NL; so called from the bright green line in its spectrum] **:** a sparsely but widely distributed poisonous metallic element resembling lead in physical properties — see ELEMENT table

thal·log·e·nous \tha-'läj-ə-nəs\ *adj* **:** increasing by growth otherwise than from an apical growing point

thal·loid \'thal-ˌȯid\ *adj* **:** of, relating to, resembling, or consisting of a thallus

thal·lo·phyte \'thal-ə-ˌfīt\ *n* [deriv. of Gk *thallos* + *phyton* plant — more at PHYT-] **:** any of a primary division (Thallophyta) of the plant kingdom comprising plants with single-celled sex organs or with many-celled sex organs of which all cells give rise to gametes, including the algae, fungi, and lichens, and usu. held to be a heterogeneous assemblage — **thal·lo·phyt·ic** \ˌthal-ə-'fit-ik\ *adj*

thal·lous \'thal-əs\ *adj* **:** of, relating to, or containing thallium when univalent

thal·lus \'thal-əs\ *n, pl* **thal·li** \'thal-ˌī, -ˌē\ *or* **thal·lus·es** [NL, fr. Gk *thallos,* fr. *thallein* to sprout; akin to Alb *dal* I come forth] **:** a plant body that is characteristic of thallophytes, lacks differentiation into distinct members (as stem, leaves, and roots), and does not grow from an apical point

1than \thən, (')than\ *conj* [ME *than, then* then, than — more at THEN] **1 a** — used as a function word to indicate the second member or the member taken as point of departure in a comparison expressive of inequality; used with comparative adjectives and comparative adverbs ⟨older ~ I am⟩ ⟨easier said ~ done⟩ **b** — used as a function word to indicate difference of kind, manner, or identity; used esp. with some adjectives and adverbs that express diversity ⟨anywhere else ~ at home⟩ **2 :** rather than — usu. used only after *prefer, preferable,* and *preferably* **3 :** other than **4 :** WHEN — used esp. after *scarcely* and *hardly*

2than *prep* **:** in comparison with ⟨is older ~ me⟩

Than·a·tos \'than-ə-ˌtäs\ *n* [Gk, death; akin to Skt *adhvanīt* it vanished, L *fumus* smoke] **:** instinctual desire for death

thane \'thān\ *n* [ME *theyn,* fr. OE *thegn;* akin to OHG *thegan* thane, Gk *tiktein* to bear, beget] **1 :** a free retainer of an Anglo-Saxon lord; *esp* **:** one resembling a feudal baron by holding lands of and performing military service for the king **2 :** a Scottish feudal lord

thane·ship \-ˌship\ *n* **:** the office or position of a thane

1thank \'thaŋk\ *n* [ME, fr. OE *thanc* thought, gratitude; akin to OHG *dank* gratitude, L *tongēre* to know] **1** *pl* **:** kindly or grateful thoughts **:** GRATITUDE **2 :** an expression of gratitude — usu. used in pl. ⟨return ~*s* before the meal⟩; often used in an utterance containing no verb and serving as a courteous and somewhat informal expression of gratitude ⟨many ~*s*⟩

2thank *vt* **1 :** to express gratitude to ⟨~*ed* her for the present⟩ — used in the phrase *thank you* usu. without a subject to politely express gratitude ⟨~ you for the loan⟩ **2 :** to hold responsible

thank·er \'thaŋ-kər\ *n* **:** one that thanks

thank·ful \'thaŋk-fəl\ *adj* **1 :** conscious of benefit received **2 :** expressive of thanks ⟨~ service⟩ **3 :** well pleased **:** GLAD **syn** see GRATEFUL — **thank·ful·ly** \-fə-lē\ *adv* — **thank·ful·ness** *n*

thank·less \'thaŋ-kləs\ *adj* **1 :** not expressing or feeling gratitude **:** UNGRATEFUL **2 :** not likely to obtain thanks **:** UNAPPRECIATED — **thank·less·ly** *adv* — **thank·less·ness** *n*

thanks·giv·ing \thaŋ(k)s-'giv-iŋ\ *n* **1 :** the act of giving thanks **2 :** a prayer expressing gratitude **3 a :** a public acknowledgment or celebration of divine goodness **b** *cap* **:** THANKSGIVING DAY

Thanksgiving Day *n* **:** a day appointed for giving thanks for divine goodness: as **a :** the fourth Thursday in November observed as a legal holiday in the U.S. **b :** the second Monday in October observed as a legal holiday in Canada

thank·wor·thy \'thaŋ-ˌkwər-thē\ *adj* **:** worthy of thanks or gratitude **:** MERITORIOUS

thank-you-ma'am \'thaŋk-yü-ˌmam, -(y)ē-\ *n* [prob. fr. its causing a nodding of the head] **:** a bump or depression in a road

1that \(')that\ *pron, pl* **those** \(')thōz\ [ME, fr. OE *thæt,* neut. demonstrative pron. & definite article; akin to OHG *daz,* neuter demonstrative pron. & definite article, Gk *to,* L *istud* neut. demonstrative pron.] **1 a :** the person, thing, or idea indicated, mentioned, or understood from the situation ⟨~ is my father⟩ **b :** the time, action, or event just mentioned ⟨after ~ he went to bed⟩ **c :** the kind or thing specified as follows ⟨the purest water is ~ produced by distillation⟩ **d :** one or a group of the indicated kind ⟨~'*s* a fox — wily and destructive⟩ **2 a :** the one farther away or less immediately under observation or discussion ⟨*those* are maples and these elms⟩ **b :** the former one **3 a** — used as a function word after *and* to indicate emphatic repetition of the idea expressed by a previous word or phrase not necessarily a noun or noun equivalent ⟨he was helpful, and ~ to an unusual degree⟩ **b** — used as a function word immediately before or after a word group consisting of a verbal auxiliary or a form of the verb *be* preceded by *there* or a personal pronoun subject to indicate emphatic repetition of the idea expressed by a previous verb or predicate noun or predicate adjective ⟨is he capable? He is ~⟩ **4 a :** the one **:** the thing **:** the kind **:** SOMETHING, ANYTHING ⟨the truth of ~ which is true⟩ ⟨the senses are ~ whereby we experience the world⟩ ⟨what's ~ you say⟩ **b** *pl* **:** some persons ⟨*those* who think the time has come⟩ — **all that :** everything of the kind indicated ⟨tact, discretion, and *all that*⟩ — **at that 1 :** in spite of what has been said or implied **2 :** in addition **:** BESIDES

2that *adj, pl* **those 1 a :** being the person, thing, or idea specified, mentioned, or understood **b :** so great a **:** SUCH **2 :** the farther away or less immediately under observation or discussion ⟨this chair or ~ one⟩

3that \thət, (ˌ)that\ *conj* **1 a** (1) — used as a function word to introduce a noun clause used esp. as the subject or object of a verb or as a predicate nominative ⟨said ~ he was afraid⟩ (2) — used as a function word to introduce a subordinate clause anticipated by the expletive *it* occurring as subject of the verb *be* followed by an adverb or adverbial phrase logically modifying the verb of the clause introduced by *that* ⟨it was there ~ I first met her⟩ (3) — used as a function word to introduce a subordinate clause that is joined as complement or modifier to a noun or adjective or is in apposition with a noun ⟨we are certain ~ this is true⟩ ⟨the certainty ~ this is true⟩ ⟨the fact ~ you are here⟩ (4) — used as a function word to introduce a subordinate clause modifying an adverb or adverbial expression ⟨will go anywhere ~ he is invited⟩ **b** — used as a function word to introduce an exclamatory clause expressing a strong emotion esp. of surprise, sorrow, or indignation ⟨~ it should come to this!⟩ **2 a** — used as a function word to introduce a subordinate clause expressing purpose, result, or cause ⟨worked so hard ~ he became exhausted⟩ **b** — used as a function word to introduce an exclamatory clause expressing a wish ⟨oh, ~ he would come⟩ **3** — used as a function word after a subordinating conjunction without modifying its meaning ⟨now ~ we have the facts, let's decide⟩ ⟨if ~ thy bent of love be honorable —Shak.⟩

4that \thət, (ˌ)that\ *pron* **1** — used as a function word to introduce a relative clause and to serve as a substitute within that clause for the substantive modified by that clause ⟨the house ~ Jack built⟩ **2 a :** at which **:** in which **:** on which **:** by which **:** with which **:** to which ⟨each year ~ the lectures are given⟩ **b :** according to what **:** to the extent of what — used after a negative ⟨has never been here ~ I know of⟩ **3 a** *archaic* **:** that which **b** *obs* **:** the person who

5that \'that\ *adv* **:** to such an extent ⟨a nail about ~ long⟩

1thatch \'thach\ *vt* [ME *thecchen,* fr. OE *theccan* to cover; akin to OHG *decchen* to cover, L *tegere,* Gk *stegein* to cover, *stegos* roof, Skt *sthagati* he covers] **:** to cover with or as if with thatch — **thatch·er** *n*

2thatch *n* **:** a plant material (as straw) used as a sheltering cover esp. of a house; *also* **:** a sheltering cover (as a house roof) made of such material

thau·ma·turge \'thȯ-mə-ˌtərj\ *n* [F, fr. NL *thaumaturgus,* fr. Gk *thaumatourgos* working miracles, fr. *thaumat-, thauma* miracle + *ergon* work — more at THEATER, WORK] **:** THAUMATURGIST

thau·ma·tur·gic \ˌthȯ-mə-'tər-jik\ *adj* **1 :** performing miracles **2 :** of, relating to, or dependent on thaumaturgy

thau·ma·tur·gist \'thȯ-mə-ˌtər-jəst\ *n* **:** a performer of miracles; *esp* **:** MAGICIAN

thau·ma·tur·gy \-jē\ *n* **:** the performance of miracles; *specif* **:** MAGIC

1thaw \'thȯ\ *vb* [ME *thawen,* fr. OE *thawian;* akin to OHG *douwen* to thaw, Gk *tēkein* to melt, L *tabes* wasting disease] *vt* **:** to cause to thaw ~ *vi* **1 a :** to go from a frozen to a liquid state **:** MELT **b :** to become free of the effect (as stiffness or numbness) of cold as a result of being warmed **2 :** to be warm enough to melt ice and snow — used with *it* of the weather **3 :** to abandon aloofness, reserve, or hostility **:** UNBEND **4 :** to become mobile, active, or susceptible to change

2thaw *n* **1 :** the action, fact, or process of thawing **2 :** a warmth of weather sufficient to thaw ice

1the \thə (*before consonant & esp South sometimes vowel sounds*), thē (*before vowel sounds*); *1k is often* 'thē\ *definite article* [ME, fr. OE *thē,* masc. demonstrative pron. & definite article, alter. (influenced by oblique cases — as *thæs,* gen. — & neut., *thæt*) of *sē;* akin to Gk *ho,* masc. demonstrative pron. &. definite article — more at THAT] **1 a** — used as a function word to indicate that a following noun or noun equivalent refers to someone or something previously mentioned or clearly understood from the context or the situation ⟨put ~ cat out⟩ or to indicate that a following noun or noun equivalent refers to someone or something that is unique or exists as only one at a time ⟨~ Lord⟩ **b** — used as a function word before nouns that designate natural phenomena or points of the compass ⟨~ night is cold⟩ **c** — used as a function word before a title or a class name to designate the particular holder of that title or the particular member of that class that is most familiar ⟨~ President⟩ **d** — used as a function word before a noun denoting time to indicate reference to what is present or immediate or is under consideration ⟨in ~ future⟩ **e** — used as a function word before names of some parts of the body or of the clothing as an equivalent of a possessive adjective ⟨how's ~ arm today⟩ **f** — used as a function word before the name of a branch of human endeavor or proficiency ⟨~ law⟩ **g** (1) **:** in, to, or for each ⟨a dollar ~ bottle⟩ (2) **:** EACH, EVERY ⟨eighty crackers to ~ box⟩ (3) — used as a function word in prepositional phrases to indicate that the noun in the phrase serves as a basis for computation ⟨sold by ~ dozen⟩ **h** — used as a function word before the proper name of a ship or a well-known building ⟨~ Mayflower⟩ **i** — used as a function word before the plural form of a numeral that is a multiple of ten to denote a particular decade of a century or of a person's life ⟨life in ~ twenties⟩ **j** — used as a function word before the name of a commodity or any familiar appurtenance of daily life to indicate reference to the individual thing, part, or supply thought of as at hand ⟨talked on ~ telephone⟩ **k** — used as a function word to designate one of a class as the best, most

typical, or most worth singling out ⟨this is ~ life⟩ **1 :** ENOUGH ⟨didn't have ~ time to write⟩ **2 a** (1) — used as a function word with a noun modified by an adjective or by an attributive noun to limit the application of the modified noun to that specified by the adjective or by the attributive noun ⟨~ right answer⟩ ⟨Peter ~ Great⟩ (2) — used as a function word before an absolute adjective ⟨nothing but ~ best⟩ **b** — used as a function word before a noun to limit its application to that specified by a succeeding element in the sentence ⟨~ poet Wordsworth⟩ ⟨~ days of our youth⟩ **3 a** — used as a function word before a singular noun to indicate that the noun is to be understood generically ⟨courtesy distinguishes ~ gentleman⟩ ⟨good for ~ soul⟩ **b** — used as a function word before a singular substantivized adjective to indicate an abstract idea ⟨an essay on ~ sublime⟩ **4** — used as a function word before a noun or a plural substantivized adjective to indicate reference to a group as a whole ⟨~ elite⟩

²**the** *adv* [ME, fr. OE *thȳ* by that, instrumental of *thæt* that] **1 :** than before **:** than otherwise — used before a comparative ⟨none ~ wiser for attending⟩ **2 a :** to what extent ⟨~ sooner the better⟩ **b :** to that extent ⟨the sooner ~ better⟩ **3 :** beyond all others ⟨calls this ~ best⟩

the- *or* **theo-** *comb form* [ME *theo-*, fr. L, fr. Gk *the-*, *theo-*, fr. *theos*] **:** god **:** God ⟨*the*ism⟩ ⟨*theo*centric⟩

the·ater *or* **the·atre** \'thē-ət-ər, 'thi-\ *n* [ME *theatre*, fr. MF, fr. L *theatrum*, fr. Gk *theatron*, fr. *theasthai* to view, fr. *thea* act of seeing; akin to Gk *thauma* miracle] **1 a :** an outdoor structure for dramatic performances or spectacles in ancient Greece and Rome **b :** a building for dramatic performances **c :** a building or area for showing motion pictures **2 a :** a place rising by steps or gradations **b :** a room often with rising tiers of seats for lectures, surgical demonstrations, or other assemblies **3 :** a place of enactment of significant events or action **4 a :** dramatic literature or performance **b :** dramatic effectiveness

the·ater·go·er \-ˌgō(-ə)r\ *n* **:** a person who frequently goes to the theater

the·ater·go·ing \-ˌgō-iŋ, -ˌgȯ(-)iŋ\ *n* **:** attendance at the theater

theater–in–the–round *n* **:** ARENA THEATER

The·atine \'thē-ə-ˌtīn, -ˌtēn\ *n* [NL *Theatinus*, fr. L *Teatinus* inhabitant of Chieti, fr. *Teate* Chieti, Italy] **:** a priest of the Order of Clerks Regular established in 1524 in Italy to reform morality and combat Lutheranism — **Theatine** *adj*

¹**the·at·ri·cal** \thē-'a-tri-kəl\ *adj* **1 :** of or relating to the theater or the presentation of plays ⟨~ costume⟩ **2 :** marked by pretense or artificiality of emotion **3 a :** HISTRIONIC ⟨~ gesture⟩ **b :** marked by extravagant display or exhibitionism **:** SHOWY ⟨~ acceptance speech⟩ **syn** see DRAMATIC — **the·at·ri·cal·ism** \-kə-ˌliz-əm\ *n* — **the·at·ri·cal·i·ty** \-ˌa-trə-'kal-ət-ē\ *n* — **the·at·ri·cal·ly** \-'a-tri-k(ə-)lē\ *adv*

²**theatrical** *n* **1** *pl* **a :** the performance of plays ⟨amateur ~*s*⟩ **b :** DRAMATICS **2 :** a professional actor

the·at·ri·cal·ize \thē-'a-tri-kə-ˌlīz\ *vt* **1 :** to adapt to the theater **:** DRAMATIZE **2 :** to display in showy fashion

the·at·rics \thē-'a-triks\ *n pl* **1 :** THEATRICAL 1 **2 :** staged or contrived effects

the·ca \'thē-kə\ *n*, *pl* **the·cae** \'thē-ˌsē, -ˌkē\ [NL, fr. L, cover — more at TICK] **1 :** SAC, CAPSULE, SPORE CASE **2 :** an enveloping sheath or case of an animal or animal part — **the·cal** \'thē-kəl\ *or* **the·cate** \-ˌkāt\ *adj*

-the·ci·um \'thē-s(h)ē-əm\ *n comb form*, *pl* **-the·cia** \-s(h)ē-ə\ [NL, fr. Gk *thēkion*, dim. of *thēkē* case — more at TICK] **:** small containing structure ⟨endo*thecium*⟩

thé dan·sant \tā-dänⁿ-säⁿ\ *n*, *pl* **thés dansants** *same*\ [F] **:** TEA DANCE

thee \(')thē\ *pron*, *objective case of* THOU **1 a :** ¹THOU **b** — used by Friends esp. among themselves in contexts where the nominative case form is to be expected **2** *archaic* **:** THYSELF

thee·lin \'thē-(ə-)lən\ *n* [irreg. fr. Gk *thēlys* female — more at FEMININE] **:** ESTRONE

thee·lol \-(ə-)ˌlȯl, -ˌlōl\ *n* [ISV, fr. *theelin*] **:** ESTRIOL

theft \'theft\ *n* [ME *thiefthe*, fr. OE *thīefth;* akin to OE *thēof* thief] **1 a :** the act of stealing; *specif* **:** LARCENY **b :** an unlawful taking (as by embezzlement or burglary) of property **2** *obs* **:** something stolen

thegn \'thān\ *n* [OE — more at THANE] **:** THANE 1

thegn·ly \-lē\ *adj* **:** of, relating to, or befitting a thegn

the·ine \'thē-ən\ *n* [NL *theina*, fr. *thea* tea, fr. Chin (Amoy) *t'e*] **:** CAFFEINE

their \thər, (ˌ)the(ə)r, (ˌ)tha(ə)r\ *adj* [ME, fr. *their*, pron., fr. ON *theirra*, gen. pl. demonstrative & personal pron.; akin to OE *thæt* that] **1 :** of or relating to them or themselves esp. as possessors ⟨~ furniture⟩, agents ⟨~ verses⟩, or objects of an action ⟨~ being seen⟩ **2 :** his or her **:** HIS, HER, ITS — used with an indefinite singular antecedent ⟨anyone in ~ senses —W.H.Auden⟩

theirs \'the(ə)rz, 'tha(ə)rz\ *pron*, *sing or pl in constr* **1 :** their one **:** their ones — used without a following noun as a pronoun equivalent in meaning to the adjective *their* **2 :** his or hers **:** HIS, HERS — used with an indefinite singular antecedent ⟨I will do my part if everybody else will do ~⟩

the·ism \'thē-ˌiz-əm\ *n* **:** belief in the existence of a god or gods; *specif* **:** belief in the existence of one God viewed as the creative source of man and the world who transcends yet is immanent in the world — **the·ist** \-əst\ *n or adj* — **the·is·tic** \thē-'is-tik\ *adj* — **the·is·ti·cal** \-ti-kəl\ *adj* — **the·is·ti·cal·ly** \-k(ə-)lē\ *adv*

-theism *n comb form* [MF *-théisme*, fr. Gk *theos* god] **:** belief in (such) a god or (such or so many) gods ⟨mono*theism*⟩

-theist *n comb form* **:** believer in (such) a god or (such or so many) gods ⟨pan*theist*⟩

them \(th)əm, (')them, *after* p, b, v, f *also* ᵊm\ *pron*, *objective case of* THEY

the·mat·ic \thi-'mat-ik\ *adj* [Gk *thematikos*, fr. *themat-*, *thema* theme] **1 a :** of or relating to the stem of a word **b** *of a vowel* **:** being the last part of a word stem before an inflectional ending **2 :** of, relating to, or constituting a theme — **the·mat·i·cal·ly** \-i-k(ə-)lē\ *adv*

theme \'thēm\ *n* [ME *teme*, *theme*, fr. OF & L; OF *teme*, fr. L *thema*, fr. Gk, lit., something laid down, fr. *tithenai* to place — more at DO] **1 :** a subject or topic of discourse or of artistic representation **2 :** STEM 3 **3 :** a written exercise **:** COMPOSITION **4 :** a melodic subject of a musical composition or movement

theme song *n* **1 :** a melody recurring so often in a musical play that it characterizes the production or one of its characters **2 :** SIGNATURE 6

them·selves \thəm-'selvz, them-\ *pron pl* **1 :** those identical ones that are they — compare THEY 1a; used reflexively, for emphasis, or in absolute constructions ⟨nations that govern ~⟩ ⟨they ~ were present⟩ ⟨~ busy, they disliked idleness in others⟩ **2 :** their normal, healthy, or sane condition or selves **3 :** himself or herself **:** HIMSELF, HERSELF — used with an indefinite singular antecedent ⟨nobody can call ~ oppressed —Leonard Wibberley⟩

¹**then** \(')then\ *adv* [ME *than*, *then* then, than, fr. OE *thonne*, *thænne;* akin to OHG *denne* then, than, OE *thæt* that] **1 :** at that time **2 :** soon after that ⟨walked to the door, ~ turned⟩ **3 a :** following next after in order **b :** in addition **:** BESIDES **4 a :** in that case **b :** according to that ⟨your mind is made up, ~⟩ **c :** as it appears ⟨the cause, ~, is established⟩ **d :** as a necessary consequence

²**then** \'then\ *n* **:** that time

³**then** \'then\ *adj* **:** existing or acting at or belonging to the time mentioned ⟨the ~ king⟩

the·nar \'thē-ˌnär, -nər\ *n* [NL, fr. Gk — more at DEN] **1 :** the ball of the thumb **2 :** PALM 2; *also* **:** ¹SOLE 1a — **thenar** *adj*

thence \'then(t)s *also* 'then(t)s\ *adv* [ME *thannes*, fr. *thanne* from that place, fr. OE *thanon;* akin to OHG *thanan* from that place, OE *thænne* then — more at THEN] **1 :** from that place **2** *archaic* **:** from that time **:** THENCEFORTH **3 :** from that fact or circumstance **:** THEREFROM

thence·forth \-ˌfō(ə)rth, -ˌfȯ(ə)rth\ *adv* **:** from that time forward **:** THEREAFTER

thence·for·ward \then(t)s-'fȯr-wərd *also* then(t)s-\ *also* **thence·for·wards** \-wərdz\ *adv* **:** onward from that place or time **:** THENCEFORTH

theo- — see THE-

theo·bro·mine \ˌthē-ə-'brō-ˌmēn, -mən\ *n* [NL *Theobroma*, genus of trees, fr. *the-* + Gk *brōma* food, fr. *bibrōskein* to devour — more at VORACIOUS] **:** a bitter weakly basic crystalline compound $C_7H_8N_4O_2$ found esp. in cacao beans and chocolate and closely related to caffeine

theo·cen·tric \-'sen-trik\ *adj* **:** having God as the central interest and ultimate concern — **theo·cen·tric·i·ty** \-ˌsen-'tris-ət-ē\ *n* — **theo·cen·trism** \-'sen-ˌtriz-əm\ *n*

the·oc·ra·cy \thē-'äk-rə-sē\ *n* [Gk *theokratia*, fr. *the-* + *-kratia* -cracy] **1 :** government of a state by immediate divine guidance or by officials regarded as divinely guided **2 :** a state governed by a theocracy — **theo·crat** \'thē-ə-ˌkrat\ *n* — **theo·crat·ic** \ˌthē-ə-'krat-ik\ *also* **theo·crat·i·cal** \-i-kəl\ *adj* — **theo·crat·i·cal·ly** \-k(ə-)lē\ *adv*

the·od·i·cy \thē-'äd-ə-sē\ *n* [modif. of F *théodicée*, fr. *théo-* the- (fr. L *theo-*) + Gk *dikē* judgment, right — more at DICTION] **:** defense of God's goodness and omnipotence in view of the existence of evil

the·od·o·lite \thē-'äd-ᵊl-ˌīt\ *n* [NL *theodolitus*] **:** a surveyor's instrument for measuring horizontal and usu. also vertical angles — **the·od·o·lit·ic** \-ˌäd-ᵊl-'it-ik\ *adj*

theo·gon·ic \ˌthē-ə-'gän-ik\ *adj* **:** of or relating to theogony

the·og·o·ny \thē-'äg-ə-nē\ *n* [Gk *theogonia*, fr. *the-* + *-gonia* -gony] **:** an account of the origin and descent of the gods

theo·lo·gian \ˌthē-ə-'lō-jən\ *n* **:** a specialist in theology

theo·log·i·cal \-'läj-i-kəl\ *also* **theo·log·ic** \-ik\ *adj* **1 :** of or relating to theology **2 :** preparing for a religious vocation — **theo·log·i·cal·ly** \-i-k(ə-)lē\ *adv*

theological virtue *n* **:** one of the three spiritual graces faith, hope, and charity held to perfect the natural virtues

the·ol·o·gize \thē-'äl-ə-ˌjīz\ *vi* **:** to theorize theologically ~ *vt* **:** to make theological — **the·ol·o·giz·er** *n*

theo·logue *or* **theo·log** \'thē-ə-ˌlȯg, -ˌläg\ *n* [L *theologus* theologian, fr. Gk *theologos*, fr. *the-* + *legein* to speak — more at LEGEND] **:** a theological student or specialist

the·ol·o·gy \thē-'äl-ə-jē\ *n* [ME *theologie*, fr. L *theologia*, fr. Gk, fr. *the-* + *-logia* -logy] **1 :** rational interpretation of religious faith, practice, and experience; *specif* **:** a branch of systematic theology dealing with God and his relation to the world **2 a :** a theological theory or system **b :** a distinctive body of theological opinion **3 :** a usu. four-year course of specialized religious training in a Roman Catholic major seminary

the·on·o·mous \thē-'än-ə-məs\ *adj* [*the-* + *-nomous* (as in *autonomous*)] **:** governed by God — **the·on·o·mous·ly** *adv*

the·on·o·my \-mē\ *n* [G *theonomie*, fr. *theo-* the- (fr. L) + *-nomie* -nomy] **:** the state of being theonomous

theo·phan·ic \ˌthē-ə-'fan-ik\ *adj* **:** relating to, characterized by, or constituting a theophany

the·oph·a·ny \thē-'äf-ə-nē\ *n* [ML *theophania*, fr. LGk *theophaneia*, fr. Gk *the-* + *-phaneia* (as in *epiphaneia* appearance) — more at EPIPHANY] **:** a visible manifestation of a deity

theo·phyl·line \ˌthē-ə-'fil-ˌēn\ *n* [ISV *theo*bromine + *phyll-* + *-ine*] **:** a feebly basic bitter crystalline compound $C_7H_8N_4O_2$ from tea leaves that is isomeric with theobromine

the·or·bo \thē-'ȯr-(ˌ)bō\ *n* [modif. of It *tiorba*] **:** a 17th century musical instrument like a large lute but having two necks

the·o·rem \'thē-ə-rəm, 'thi(-ə)r-əm\ *n* [LL *theorema*, fr. Gk *theōrēma*, fr. *theōrein* to look at, fr. *theōros* spectator, fr. *thea* act of seeing — more at THEATER] **1 :** a formula, proposition, or statement in mathematics or logic deduced or to be deduced from other formulas or propositions **2 :** an idea accepted or proposed as a demonstrable truth often as a part of a general theory **:** PROPOSITION ⟨the ~ that the best defense is offense⟩ — **the·o·rem·at·ic** \ˌthē-ə-rə-'mat-ik, ˌthi(-ə)r-ə-\ *adj*

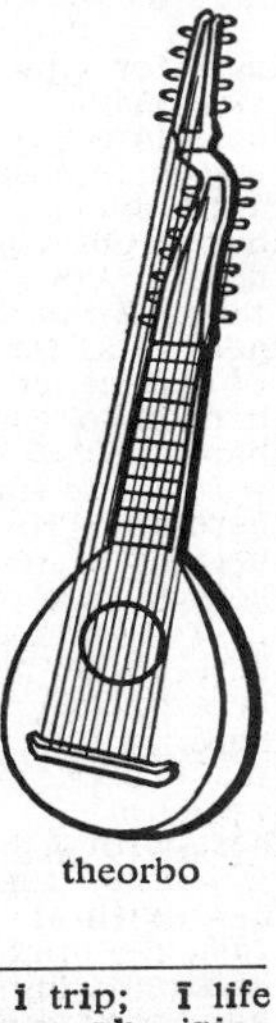

theorbo

the·o·ret·i·cal \ˌthē-ə-ˈret-i-kəl, ˌthi(-ə)r-ˈet-\ *also* **the·o·ret·ic** \-ik\ *adj* [LL *theoreticus*, fr. Gk *theōrētikos*, fr. *theōrein*] **1 a :** relating to or having the character of theory : ABSTRACT **b :** confined to theory or speculation : SPECULATIVE ⟨~ mechanics⟩ **2 :** given to or skilled in theorizing **3 :** existing only in theory : HYPOTHETICAL — **the·o·ret·i·cal·ly** \-i-k(ə-)lē\ *adv*

the·o·re·ti·cian \ˌthē-ə-rə-ˈtish-ən, ˌthi(-ə)r-ə-\ *n* : THEORIST

the·o·rist \ˈthē-ə-rəst, ˈthi(-ə)r-əst\ *n* **:** a person that theorizes

the·o·ri·za·tion \ˌthē-ə-rə-ˈzā-shən, ˌthi(-ə)r-ə-\ *n* **:** an act or product of theorizing

the·o·rize \ˈthē-ə-ˌrīz\ *vi* **:** to form a theory : SPECULATE — **the·o·riz·er** *n*

the·o·ry \ˈthē-ə-rē, ˈthi(-ə)r-ē\ *n* [LL *theoria*, fr. Gk *theōria*, fr. *theōrein*] **1 :** the analysis of a set of facts in their relation to one another **2 :** the general or abstract principles of a body of fact, a science, or an art ⟨music ~⟩ — compare PRACTICE **3 :** a plausible or scientifically acceptable general principle or body of principles offered to explain phenomena ⟨wave ~ of light⟩ **4 a :** a hypothesis assumed for the sake of argument or investigation **b :** SUPPOSITION, CONJECTURE **c :** a body of theorems presenting a concise systematic view of a subject ⟨~ of equations⟩ **5 :** abstract thought : SPECULATION **syn** see HYPOTHESIS

theory of games : the analysis of a situation involving conflicting interests (as in business or military strategy) in terms of gains and losses among opposing players

theo·soph·i·cal \ˌthē-ə-ˈsäf-i-kəl\ *adj* **:** of or relating to theosophy — **theo·soph·i·cal·ly** \-i-k(ə-)lē\ *adv*

the·os·o·phist \thē-ˈäs-ə-fəst\ *n* **1 :** an adherent of theosophy **2** *cap* **:** a member of a theosophical society

the·os·o·phy \-fē\ *n* [ML *theosophia*, fr. LGk, fr. Gk *the-* + *sophia* wisdom — more at -SOPHY] **1 :** belief about God and the world held to be based on mystical insight **2** *often cap* **:** the beliefs of a modern movement originating in the U.S. in 1875 and following chiefly Buddhist and Brahmanic theories esp. of pantheistic evolution and reincarnation

ther·a·peu·sis \ˌther-ə-ˈpyü-səs\ *n, pl* **ther·a·peu·ses** \-ˈpyü-ˌsēz\ [NL, fr. Gk, treatment, fr. *therapeuein*] **:** THERAPEUTICS

ther·a·peu·tic \ˌther-ə-ˈpyüt-ik\ *adj* [Gk *therapeutikos*, fr. *therapeuein* to attend, treat, fr. *theraps* attendant] **:** of or relating to the treatment of disease or disorders by remedial agents or methods : MEDICINAL ⟨~ diet⟩ ⟨~ approach to criminality⟩ — **ther·a·peu·ti·cal·ly** \-i-k(ə-)lē\ *adv*

ther·a·peu·tics \-iks\ *n pl but sing or pl in constr* **:** a branch of medical science dealing with the application of remedies for diseases

ther·a·peu·tist \-ˈpyüt-əst\ *n* **:** one skilled in therapeutics

ther·a·pist \ˈther-ə-pəst\ *n* **:** one specializing in therapy; *esp* **:** a person trained in methods (as occupational or physical) of treatment and rehabilitation other than the use of drugs or surgery ⟨a speech ~⟩

ther·a·py \-pē\ *n* [NL *therapia*, fr. Gk *therapeia*, fr. *therapeuein*] **:** therapeutic treatment: as **a :** remedial treatment of bodily disorder **b :** PSYCHOTHERAPY **c :** an agency (as treatment) designed or serving to bring about social adjustment

Ther·a·va·da \ˌther-ə-ˈväd-ə\ *n* [Pali *theravāda*, lit., doctrine of the elders] **:** HINAYANA

¹there \ˈtha(ə)r, ˈthe(ə)r\ *adv* [ME, fr. OE *thǣr;* akin to OHG *dār* there, OE *thæt* that] **1 :** in or at that place ⟨stand over ~⟩ — often used interjectionally **2 :** to or into that place : THITHER **3 :** at that point or stage **4 :** in that matter, respect, or relation **5 —** used interjectionally to express satisfaction, approval, soothing, or defiance

²there \(ˌ)tha(ə)r, (ˌ)the(ə)r, *1 is also* thər\ *pron* **1 —** used as a function word to introduce a sentence or clause esp. when the subject follows the verb ⟨~ shall come a time⟩ **2 —** used as an indefinite substitute for a name ⟨hi ~⟩

³there *like* ¹\ *n* **1 :** that place or position **2 :** that point ⟨you take it from ~⟩

⁴there *like* ¹\ *adj* **—** used for emphasis esp. after a demonstrative pronoun or a noun modified by a demonstrative adjective ⟨those men ~ can tell you⟩

there·abouts *or* **there·about** \ˌthar-ə-ˈbaüt(s), ˈthar-ə-ˌ, ˌther-ə-ˈbaüt(s), ˈther-ə-ˌ\ *adv* **1 :** near that place or time **2 :** near that number, degree, or quantity

there·af·ter \tha-ˈraf-tər, the-\ *adv* **1 :** after that **2** *archaic* **:** accordingly : ACCORDINGLY

there·at \-ˈrat\ *adv* **1 :** at that place **2 :** at that occurrence : on that account

there·by \tha(ə)r-ˈbī, the(ə)r-, ˈtha(ə)r-ˌ, ˈthe(ə)r-ˌ\ *adv* **1 :** by that : by that means **2 :** connected with or with reference to that

there·for \tha(ə)r-ˈfȯ(ə)r, the(ə)r-\ *adv* **:** for or in return for that ⟨issued bonds ~⟩

there·fore \ˈtha(ə)r-ˌfō(ə)r, ˈthe(ə)r-, -ˌfȯ(ə)r\ *adv* **1 a :** for that reason : CONSEQUENTLY **b :** because of that **c :** on that ground **2 :** to that end

there·from \tha(ə)r-ˈfrəm, the(ə)r-, -ˈfräm\ *adv* **:** from that or it

there·in \tha-ˈrin, the-\ *adv* **1 :** in or into that place, time, or thing **2 :** in that particular or respect

there·in·af·ter \ˌthar-in-ˈaf-tər, ˌther-\ *adv* **:** in the following part of that matter (as writing, document, or speech)

there·in·to \tha-ˈrin-(ˌ)tü, the-\ *adv, archaic* **:** into that or it

there·of \-ˈrəv, -ˈräv\ *adv* **1 :** of that or it **2 :** from that cause or particular : THEREFROM

there·on \-ˈrȯn, -ˈrän\ *adv* **1 :** on that **2** *archaic* **:** THEREUPON

there·to \tha(ə)r-ˈtü, the(ə)r-\ *adv* **:** to that

there·to·fore \ˈtha(ə)rt-ə-ˌfō(ə)r, ˈthe(ə)rt-, -ˌfȯ(ə)r; ˌthart-ə-ˈ, ˌthert-\ *adv* **:** up to that time

there·un·der \tha-ˈrən-dər, the-\ *adv* **:** under that

there·un·to \-ˈrən-(ˌ)tü; ˌthar-ən-ˈtü, ˌther-\ *adv, archaic* **:** THERETO

there·upon \ˈthar-ə-ˌpȯn, ˈther-, -ˌpän; ˌthar-ə-ˈ, ˌther-\ *adv* **1 :** on that matter : THEREON **2 :** THEREFORE **3 :** immediately after that : at once

there·with \tha(ə)r-ˈwith, the(ə)r-, -ˈwith\ *adv* **1 :** with that **2** *archaic* **:** THEREUPON, FORTHWITH

there·with·al \ˈtha(ə)r-with-ˌȯl, ˈthe(ə)r-, -with-\ *adv* **1** *archaic* **:** BESIDES **2 :** THEREWITH

the·ri·ac \ˈthir-ē-ˌak\ *n* **1 :** THERIACA **2 :** CURE-ALL

the·ri·a·ca \thir-ˈī-ə-kə\ *n* [NL, fr. L, antidote against poison — more at TREACLE] **:** a mixture of many drugs and honey formerly held to be an antidote to poison — **the·ri·a·cal** \-kəl\ *adj*

the·rio·mor·phic \ˌthir-ē-ō-ˈmȯr-fik\ *adj* [Gk *thēriomorphos*, fr. *thērion* beast + *morphē* form — more at TREACLE] **:** having an animal form ⟨~ gods⟩

-the·ri·um \ˈthir-ē-əm\ *n comb form* [NL, fr. Gk *thērion*] **:** beast : animal — in generic names of extinct mammalian forms ⟨Mega*therium*⟩

therm \ˈthərm\ *n* [Gk *thermē* heat; akin to Gk *thermos* hot — more at WARM] **:** any of several units of quantity of heat: as **a :** CALORIE 1b **b :** CALORIE 1a **c :** 1000 kilogram calories **d :** 100,000 British thermal units

therm- *or* **thermo-** *comb form* [Gk, fr. *thermē*] **1 :** heat ⟨*therm*ion⟩ ⟨*thermo*stat⟩ **2 :** thermoelectric ⟨*thermo*pile⟩

-therm \ˌthərm\ *n comb form* [Gk *thermē* heat] **:** animal having a (specified) body temperature ⟨ecto*therm*⟩

ther·mae \ˈthər-ˌmē, -ˌmī\ *n pl* [L, fr. Gk *thermai*, fr. pl. of *thermē* heat] **:** a public bathing establishment esp. in ancient Greece or Rome

¹ther·mal \ˈthər-məl\ *adj* [Gk *thermē*] **:** of, relating to, or caused by heat : WARM, HOT — **ther·mal·ly** \-mə-lē\ *adv*

²thermal *n* **:** a rising body of warm air

thermal barrier *n* **:** a limit to unlimited increase in airplane or rocket speeds imposed by aerodynamic heating

thermal spring *n* **:** a spring whose water issues at a temperature higher than the mean temperature of the locality where the spring is situated

ther·mic \ˈthər-mik\ *adj* : THERMAL ⟨~ energy⟩ — **ther·mi·cal·ly** \-mi-k(ə-)lē\ *adv*

therm·ion \ˈthər-ˌmī-ən, -ˌmī-ˌän\ *n* [ISV *therm-* + *ion*] **:** an electrically charged particle emitted by an incandescent substance — **therm·ion·ic** \ˌthər-(ˌ)mī-ˈän-ik\ *adj*

thermionic current *n* **:** an electric current due to the directed movements of thermions

therm·ion·ics \ˌthər-(ˌ)mī-ˈän-iks\ *n pl but sing in constr* **:** physics dealing with thermionic phenomena

thermionic tube *n* **:** an electron tube in which electron emission is produced by the heating of an electrode

therm·is·tor \ˈthər-ˌmis-tər\ *n* [*therm*al res*istor*] **:** an electrical resistor made of a material whose resistance varies sharply in a known manner with the temperature

Ther·mit \ˈthər-mət, -ˌmit\ *trademark* — used for a mixture of aluminum powder and iron oxide that when ignited evolves a great deal of heat and is used in welding and in incendiary bombs

ther·mo·co·ag·u·la·tion \ˌthər-(ˌ)mō-kō-ˌag-yə-ˈlā-shən\ *n* **:** surgical coagulation of tissue by the application of heat

ther·mo·cou·ple \ˈthər-mə-ˌkəp-əl\ *n* **:** a thermoelectric couple used to measure temperature differences

ther·mo·du·ric \ˌthər-mō-ˈd(y)u̇(ə)r-ik\ *adj* [*therm-* + L *durare* to last — more at DURING] **:** able to survive high temperatures; *specif* **:** able to survive pasteurization — used of microorganisms

ther·mo·dy·nam·ic \ˌthər-mə-(ˌ)dī-ˈnam-ik\ *adj* **1 :** of or relating to thermodynamics **2 :** being an aggregation of atoms, molecules, colloidal particles, or larger bodies that constitute an isolated group — **ther·mo·dy·nam·i·cal·ly** \-i-k(ə-)lē\ *adv*

ther·mo·dy·nam·ics \-iks\ *n pl but sing or pl in constr* **1 :** physics that deals with the mechanical action or relations of heat **2 :** thermodynamic processes and phenomena

ther·mo·elec·tric \ˌthər-mō-i-ˈlek-trik\ *adj* **:** of or relating to phenomena involving relations between the temperature and the electrical condition in a metal or in contacting metals

thermoelectric couple *n* **:** a union of two conductors (as bars or wires of dissimilar metals joined at their extremities) for producing a thermoelectric current

ther·mo·elec·tric·i·ty \ˌthər-mō-i-ˌlek-ˈtris-ət-ē, -ˈtris-tē\ *n* **:** electricity produced by the direct action of heat (as by the unequal heating of a circuit composed of two dissimilar metals)

ther·mo·elec·tron \-i-ˈlek-ˌträn\ *n* **:** an electron released in thermionic emission

ther·mo·el·e·ment \-ˈel-ə-mənt\ *n* [*thermo*couple + *element*] **:** a device for measuring small currents consisting of a wire heating element and a thermocouple in electrical contact with it

ther·mo·gram \ˈthər-mə-ˌgram\ *n* **:** the record made by a thermograph

¹ther·mo·graph \-ˌgraf\ *n* [ISV] **:** a self-recording thermometer

²thermograph *vt* **:** to produce by thermography ⟨a ~*ed* business card⟩ — **ther·mog·ra·pher** \(ˌ)thər-ˈmäg-rə-fər\ *n* — **ther·mo·graph·ic** \ˌthər-mə-ˈgraf-ik\ *adj*

ther·mog·ra·phy \(ˌ)thər-ˈmäg-rə-fē\ *n* **:** a raised-printing process in which matter printed by letterpress is dusted with powder and heated to make the lettering rise

ther·mo·junc·tion \ˌthər-mō-ˈjəŋ(k)-shən\ *n* **:** a junction of two dissimilar conductors used to produce a thermoelectric current

ther·mo·la·bile \-ˈlā-ˌbīl, -bəl\ *adj* [ISV] **:** unstable when heated; *specif* **:** subject to loss of characteristic properties on being heated to or above 55°C ⟨many immune bodies, enzymes, and vitamins are ~⟩ — **ther·mo·la·bil·i·ty** \-lā-ˈbil-ət-ē\ *n*

ther·mol·y·sis \(ˌ)thər-ˈmäl-ə-səs\ *n* [NL] **:** the dissipation of heat from the living body — **ther·mo·lyt·ic** \ˌthər-mə-ˈlit-ik\ *adj*

ther·mom·e·ter \thə(r)-ˈmäm-ət-ər\ *n* [F *thermomètre*, fr. Gk. *thermē* heat + F *-o-* + *-mètre* -meter — more at THERM] **:** an instrument for determining temperature consisting typically of a glass bulb attached to a fine tube of glass with a numbered scale and containing a liquid (as mercury or

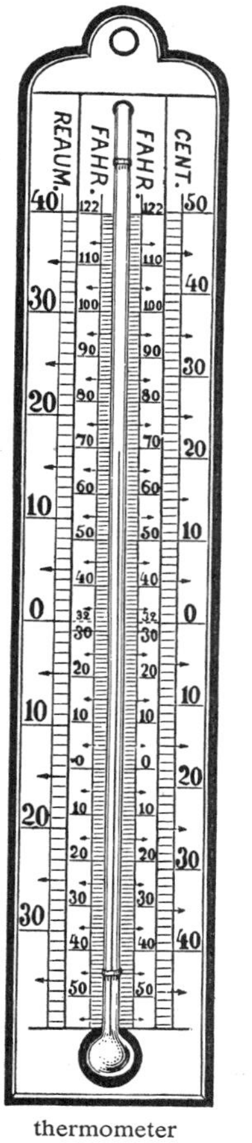

thermometer

colored alcohol) that is sealed in and rises and falls with changes of temperature — **ther·mo·met·ric** \,thər-mə-'me-trik\ adj — **ther·mo·met·ri·cal·ly** \-tri-k(ə-)lē\ adv

ther·mom·e·try \thə(r)-'mäm-ə-trē\ n [ISV] : the measurement of temperature

ther·mo·nu·cle·ar \,thər-mō-'n(y)ü-klē-ər\ adj [ISV] **1** : of or relating to the transformations in the nucleus of atoms of low atomic weight (as hydrogen) that require a very high temperature for their inception (as in the hydrogen bomb or in the sun) ⟨~ reaction⟩ ⟨~ weapon⟩ **2** : of, utilizing, or relating to a thermonuclear bomb ⟨~ war⟩ ⟨~ attack⟩

ther·mo·pe·ri·od·ism \,thər-mō-'pir-ē-ə-,diz-əm\ or **ther·mo·pe·ri·o·dic·i·ty** \-,pir-ē-ə-'dis-ət-ē-\ n : the sum of the responses of an organism to appropriately fluctuating temperatures

ther·mo·phile \'thər-mə-,fīl\ n : an organism growing at a high temperature — **thermophile** or **ther·mo·phil·ic** \,thər-mə-'fil-ik\ adj

ther·mo·pile \'thər-mə-,pīl\ n : an apparatus consisting of a number of thermoelectric couples combined so as to multiply the effect and used for generating electric currents or for determining intensities of radiation

ther·mo·plas·tic \,thər-mə-'plas-tik\ adj : having the property of softening or fusing when heated and of hardening again when cooled ⟨~ synthetic resins⟩ — **thermoplastic** n — **ther·mo·plas·tic·i·ty** \-,plas-'tis-ət-ē\ n

ther·mo·reg·u·la·tion \,thər-mō-,reg-yə-'lā-shən\ n [ISV] : the maintenance or regulation of temperature; specif : the maintenance of a particular temperature of the living body — **ther·mo·reg·u·la·to·ry** \-'reg-yə-lə-,tōr-ē, -,tor-\ adj

ther·mo·reg·u·la·tor \-'reg-yə-,lāt-ər\ n [ISV] : a device for the regulation of temperature : THERMOSTAT

ther·mos \'thər-məs\ n [fr. Thermos, a trademark] : VACUUM BOTTLE

ther·mo·scope \'thər-mə-,skōp\ n [NL thermoscopium, fr. therm- + -scopium -scope] : an instrument for indicating changes of temperature by the accompanying changes in volume of a material (as a gas)

ther·mo·set·ting \'thər-mō-,set-iŋ\ adj : having the property of becoming permanently rigid when heated or cured ⟨a ~ resin⟩

ther·mo·sta·bil·i·ty \,thər-mō-stə-'bil-ət-ē\ n : thermostable state

ther·mo·sta·ble \-'stā-bəl\ adj : stable when heated; specif : retaining characteristic properties on being moderately heated — compare THERMOLABILE

¹ther·mo·stat \'thər-mə-,stat\ n : an automatic device for regulating (as by the supply of gas or electricity to a heating apparatus) temperature; also : a similar device for actuating fire alarms or for controlling automatic sprinklers — **ther·mo·stat·ic** \,thər-mə-'stat-ik\ adj — **ther·mo·stat·i·cal·ly** \-i-k(ə-)lē\ adv

²thermostat vt **ther·mo·stat·ed** or **ther·mo·stat·ted**; **ther·mo·stat·ing** or **ther·mo·stat·ting** : to provide with or control by a thermostat

ther·mo·tac·tic \,thər-mə-'tak-tik\ adj : of, relating to, or exhibiting thermotaxis

ther·mo·tax·is \-'tak-səs\ n [NL] **1** : a taxis in which a temperature gradient constitutes the directive factor **2** : the regulation of body temperature

ther·mo·trop·ic \-'träp-ik\ adj [ISV] : of, relating to, or exhibiting thermotropism

ther·mot·ro·pism \(,)thər-'mä-trə-,piz-əm\ n [ISV] : a tropism in which a temperature gradient determines the orientation

-ther·my \,thər-mē\ n comb form [NL -thermia, fr. Gk thermē heat — more at THERM] **1** : state of heat ⟨homoiothermy⟩ **2** : generation of heat ⟨diathermy⟩

Ther·si·tes \(,)thər-'sīt-(,)ēz\ n [L, fr. Gk Thersitēs] : an ugly abusive Greek in the Trojan War

the·sau·rus \thi-'sor-əs\ n, pl **the·sau·ri** \-'so(ə)r-,ī, -,ē\ or **the·sau·rus·es** \-'sor-ə-səz\ [NL, fr. L, treasure, collection, fr. Gk thēsauros] **1** : a book of words or of information about a particular field or set of concepts; specif : a dictionary of synonyms **2** : TREASURY, STOREHOUSE

these pl of THIS

The·seus \'thē-,süs, -sē-əs\ n [L, fr. Gk Thēseus] : a Greek hero held to have slain Procrustes and the Minotaur and to have conquered the Amazons and married their queen

the·sis \'thē-səs, Brit esp for 4 'thes-is\ n, pl **the·ses** \'thē-,sēz\ [L, fr. Gk, lit., act of laying down, fr. tithenai to put, lay down — more at DO] **1 a** : a position or proposition that a person (as a candidate for scholastic honors) advances and offers to maintain by argument **b** : a proposition to be proved or one advanced without proof : HYPOTHESIS **2** : the first and least adequate stage of dialectic — compare SYNTHESIS **3** : a dissertation embodying results of original research and esp. substantiating a specific view; esp : one written by a candidate for an academic degree **4** [LL & Gk; LL, lowering of the voice, fr. Gk, downbeat, more important part of foot, lit., act of laying down] **a** (1) : the unstressed part of a poetic foot esp. in accentual verse (2) : the longer part of a poetic foot esp. in quantitative verse **b** : the accented part of a musical measure : DOWNBEAT — compare ARSIS

¹thes·pi·an \'thes-pē-ən\ adj **1** cap : of or relating to Thespis **2** often cap [fr. the tradition that Thespis was the originator of the actor's role] : relating to the drama : DRAMATIC

²thespian n : ACTOR

the·ta \'thāt-ə, 'thēt-\ n [Gk thēta, of Sem origin; akin to Heb ṭēth teth] : the 8th letter of the Greek alphabet — symbol Θ or θ

thet·ic \'thet-ik, 'thēt-\ adj [Gk thetikos of a proposition, fr. tithenai to lay down] : constituting or beginning with a poetic thesis — **thet·i·cal·ly** \-i-k(ə-)lē\ adv

The·tis \'thēt-əs\ n [L, fr. Gk] : a Nereid and mother of Achilles

the·ur·gic \thē-'ər-jik\ adj : of or relating to theurgy : MAGICAL — **the·ur·gi·cal** \-ji-kəl\ adj

the·ur·gist \'thē-,ər-jəst\ n : WONDER-WORKER, MAGICIAN

the·ur·gy \'thē-,ər-jē\ n [LL theurgia, fr. LGk theourgia, fr. theourgos miracle worker, fr. Gk the- + ergon work — more at WORK] : the art or science of compelling or persuading a god or beneficent or supernatural power to do or refrain from doing something

thew \'th(y)ü\ n [ME, personal quality, virtue, fr. OE thēaw; akin

to OHG kathau discipline] **1** : MUSCLE, SINEW — usu. used in pl. **2 a** : muscular power or development **b** : STRENGTH

they \(')thā\ pron, pl in constr [ME, fr. ON their, masc. pl. demonstrative & personal pron.; akin to OE thæt that] **1 a** : those ones — used as 3d person pronoun serving as the plural of he, she, or it or referring to a group of two or more individuals not all of the same sex ⟨~ dance well⟩ **b** : ¹HE **2** — used with an indefinite singular antecedent **2** : ¹PEOPLE 1a ⟨as lazy as ~ come⟩

they'd \(,)thād\ : they had : they would

they'll \(,)thā(ə)l, thel\ : they will : they shall

they're \thər, (,)the(ə)r, ,tha-ər\ : they are

they've \(,)thāv\ : they have

thi- or **thio-** comb form [ISV, fr. Gk thei-, theio-, fr. theion] : sulfur ⟨thiamin⟩ ⟨thiophosphate⟩

thi·am·i·nase \thī-'am-ə-,nās, 'thī-ə-mə-, -,nāz\ n [ISV] : an enzyme that promotes the destruction of thiamine

thi·a·mine \'thī-ə-,mēn, -mən\ or **thi·a·min** \-mən\ n [thiamine alter. of thiamin, fr. thi- + -amin (as in vitamin)] : a vitamin ($C_{12}H_{17}N_4OS)Cl$ of the B complex that is essential to normal metabolism and nerve function and is widespread in plants and animals — called also vitamin B_1

thi·a·zine \'thī-ə-,zēn\ n [ISV] : any of various compounds characterized by a ring composed of four carbon atoms, one sulfur atom, and one nitrogen atom

thi·a·zole \'thī-ə-,zōl\ n [ISV] : a colorless basic liquid C_3H_3NS consisting of a five-membered ring and having an odor like pyridine; also : any of its various derivatives

¹thick \'thik\ adj [ME thikke, fr. OE thicce; akin to OHG dicki thick, OIr tiug] **1 a** : having or being of relatively great depth or extent from one surface to its opposite ⟨~ plank⟩ **b** : heavily built : THICKSET **2 a** : close-packed : DENSE ⟨~ forest⟩ **b** : occurring in large numbers : NUMEROUS **c** : viscous in consistency ⟨~ syrup⟩ **d** : SULTRY, STUFFY **e** : marked by haze, fog, or mist ⟨~ weather⟩ **f** : impenetrable to the eye : PROFOUND ⟨~ darkness⟩ **g** : extremely intense ⟨~ silence⟩ **3** : measuring in thickness ⟨12 inches ~⟩ **4 a** : imperfectly articulated : INDISTINCT ⟨~ speech⟩ **b** : PRONOUNCED ⟨~ French accent⟩ **c** : producing inarticulate speech ⟨~ tongue⟩ **5** : OBTUSE, STUPID **6** : associated on close terms : INTIMATE **7** : exceeding bounds of propriety or fitness : EXCESSIVE **syn** see CLOSE — **thick·ish** \-ish\ adj — **thick·ly** adv

²thick n **1** : the most crowded or active part **2** : the part of greatest thickness

³thick adv : THICKLY

thick and thin n : every difficulty and obstacle — used esp. in the phrase through thick and thin

thick·en \'thik-ən\ vb **thick·en·ing** \-(ə-)niŋ\ vt **1 a** : to make thick, dense, or viscous in consistency **b** : to make close or compact **2** : to add to the depth or diameter of **3** : to make inarticulate : BLUR ⟨alcohol ~ed his speech⟩ ~ vi **1 a** : to become dense ⟨the mist ~ed⟩ **b** : to become concentrated in numbers, mass, or frequency **2** : to grow blurred or obscure **3** : to grow broader or bulkier **4** : to grow complicated or keen ⟨the plot ~s⟩ — **thick·en·er** \-(ə-)nər\ n

thick·en·ing n **1** : the act of making or becoming thick **2** : something used to thicken (as flour in a gravy) **3** : a thickened part or place

thick·et \'thik-ət\ n [(assumed) ME thikket, fr. OE thiccet, fr. thicce thick] **1** : a dense growth of shrubbery or small trees : COPPICE **2** : something resembling a thicket in density or impenetrability : TANGLE — **thick·ety** \-ē\ adj

thick·et·ed \'thik-ət-əd\ adj : dotted or covered with thickets ⟨~ hills⟩

thick·head·ed \'thik-'hed-əd\ adj **1** : having a thick head **2** : STUPID

thick·ness \-nəs\ n **1** : the quality or state of being thick **2** : the smallest of three dimensions ⟨length, width, and ~⟩ **3 a** : viscous consistency **b** : the condition of being smoky, foul, or foggy **4** : the thick part of something **5** : CONCENTRATION, DENSITY **6** : DULLNESS, STUPIDITY **7** : LAYER, PLY, SHEET ⟨a single ~ of canvas⟩

thick·set \'thik-'set\ adj **1** : closely placed; also : growing thickly **2** : having a thick body : BURLY

thick-skinned \'thik-'skind\ adj **1** : having a thick skin : PACHYDERMATOUS **2** : CALLOUS, INSENSITIVE

thick-wit·ted \-'wit-əd\ adj : dull or slow of mind : STUPID

thief \'thēf\ n, pl **thieves** \'thēvz\ [ME theef, fr. OE thēof; akin to OHG diob thief, Lith tupėti to crouch] : one that steals esp. stealthily or secretly; also : one who commits theft or larceny

thieve \'thēv\ vb [fr. thief] : STEAL, ROB

thiev·ery \'thēv-(ə-)rē\ n : the act or practice or an instance of stealing : THEFT

thiev·ish \'thē-vish\ adj **1** : given to stealing **2** : of, relating to, or characteristic of a thief — **thiev·ish·ly** adv — **thiev·ish·ness** n

thigh \'thī\ n [ME, fr. OE thēoh; akin to OHG dioh thigh, L tumēre to swell — more at THUMB] **1 a** : the proximal segment of the vertebrate hind limb extending from the hip to the knee and supported by a single large bone **b** : the segment of the leg immediately distal to the thigh in a bird or in a quadruped in which the true thigh is obscured **c** : the femur of an insect **2** : something resembling or covering a thigh

thigh·bone \-'bōn, -,bōn\ n : FEMUR

thig·mo·tax·is \,thig-mə-'tak-səs\ n [NL, fr. Gk thigma touch (fr. thinganein to touch) + NL -taxis; akin to L fingere to shape — more at DOUGH] : STEREOTAXIS

thig·mot·ro·pism \thig-'mä-trə-,piz-əm\ n [Gk thigma + ISV -o- + -tropism] : STEREOTROPISM

thill \'thil\ n [ME thille, perh. fr. OE, plank; akin to OHG dili plank, L tellus earth] : the shaft of a vehicle

thim·ble \'thim-bəl\ n [ME thymbyl, prob. alter. of OE thȳmel thumbstall, fr. thūma thumb] **1** : a cap or cover used in sewing to protect the finger when pushing the needle **2** : a thimble-shaped cup, appendage, or fixture: as **a** : a grooved ring of thin metal used to fit in a spliced loop in a rope as protection from chafing **b** : a fixed or movable ring, tube, or lining in a hole

thim·ble·ber·ry \-,ber-ē\ n : any of several American raspberries or blackberries (esp. Rubus occidentalis, R. parviflorus, and R. argutus) having thimble-shaped fruit

---

ə abut; ᵊ kitten; ər further; a back; ā bake; ä cot, cart; au̇ out; ch chin; e less; ē easy; g gift; i trip; ī life
j joke; ŋ sing; ō flow; ȯ flaw; ȯi coin; th thin; th̲ this; ü loot; u̇ foot; y yet; yü few; yu̇ furious; zh vision

thim·ble·ful \-ˌfu̇l\ *n* **1 :** as much as a thimble will hold **2 :** a very small quantity

¹thim·ble·rig \-ˌrig\ *n* **1 :** a swindling trick in which a small ball or pea is quickly shifted from under one to another of three small cups to fool the spectator guessing its location **2 :** THIMBLERIGGER

²thimblerig *vt* **1 :** to swindle by thimblerig **2 :** to cheat by trickery — **thim·ble·rig·ger** *n*

thim·ble·weed \-ˌwēd\ *n* **1 :** RUDBECKIA **2 :** any of various anemones

thi·mer·o·sal \thī-ˈmer-ə-ˌsal\ *n* [prob. fr. *thi-* + *mercury* + *-o-* + *sal*icylate] **:** a crystalline organic mercurial $C_9H_9HgNaO_2S$ used as an antiseptic and germicide

¹thin \ˈthin\ *adj* **thin·ner; thin·nest** [ME *thinne*, fr. OE *thynne;* akin to OHG *dunni* thin, L *tenuis* thin, *tenēre* to hold, *tendere* to stretch, Gk *teinein*] **1 a :** having little extent from one surface to its opposite ⟨∼ paper⟩ **b :** measuring little in cross section or diameter ⟨∼ rope⟩ **2 :** not dense in arrangement or distribution ⟨∼ hair⟩ **3 :** not well fleshed **:** LEAN **4 a :** more fluid or rarefied than normal ⟨∼ air⟩ **b :** having less than the usual number **:** SCANTY ⟨∼ attendance⟩ **c :** few in number **:** SCARCE **d :** scantily supplied **e :** characterized by a paucity of bids or offerings ⟨∼ market⟩ **5 :** lacking substance or strength ⟨∼ broth⟩ **6 a :** FLIMSY, UNCONVINCING ⟨∼ excuse⟩ **b :** not up to expectations **7 :** somewhat feeble, shrill, and lacking in resonance ⟨∼ voice⟩ **8 :** lacking in intensity or brilliance ⟨∼ light⟩ **9 :** ready to give way **10 :** lacking sufficient photographic density or contrast — **thin·ly** *adv* — **thin·ness** \ˈthin-nəs\ *n* — **thin·nish** \ˈthin-ish\ *adj*

syn THIN, SLENDER, SLIM, SLIGHT, TENUOUS mean not thick, broad, abundant, or dense. THIN implies comparatively little extension between surfaces or in diameter, or it may imply lack of substance, richness, or abundance; SLENDER implies leanness or spareness often with grace and good proportion; SLIM applies to slenderness that suggests fragility or scantiness; SLIGHT implies smallness as well as thinness; TENUOUS implies extreme thinness, sheerness, or lack of substance and firmness

²thin *adv* **thin·ner; thin·nest :** THINLY — used esp. in combinations ⟨*thin*-clad⟩

³thin *vb* **thinned; thin·ning** *vt* **:** to make thin or thinner: **a :** to reduce in thickness or depth **:** ATTENUATE **b :** to make less dense or viscous **c :** DILUTE, WEAKEN **d :** to cause to lose flesh **e :** to reduce in number or bulk ∼ *vi* **1 :** to become thin or thinner **2 :** to become weak

¹thine \(ˈ)t͟hīn\ *adj* [ME *thin*, fr. OE *thīn*] *archaic* **:** THY — used esp. before a word beginning with a vowel or *h*

²thine \ˈt͟hīn\ *pron, sing or pl in constr* [ME *thin*, fr. OE *thīn*, fr. *thīn* thy — more at THY] **:** thy one **:** thy ones — used without a following noun as a pronoun equivalent in meaning to the adjective *thy;* used archaically esp. in biblical or poetic language and still surviving in the speech of Friends esp. among themselves

thing \ˈthiŋ\ *n* [ME, fr. OE, thing, assembly; akin to OHG *ding* thing, assembly, Goth *theihs* time] **1 a :** a matter of concern **:** AFFAIR ⟨many ∼*s* to do⟩ **b** *pl* **:** state of affairs in general or within a specified or implied sphere ⟨∼*s* are improving⟩ **c :** a particular state of affairs **:** SITUATION ⟨look at this ∼ another way⟩ **d :** EVENT, CIRCUMSTANCE ⟨that shooting was a terrible ∼⟩ **2 a :** DEED, ACT, ACCOMPLISHMENT ⟨do great ∼*s*⟩ **b :** a product of work or activity ⟨likes to build ∼*s*⟩ **c :** the aim of effort or activity ⟨the ∼ is to get well⟩ **3 a :** a separate and distinct individual quality, fact, idea, or usu. entity **b :** the concrete entity as distinguished from its appearances **c :** a spatial entity **d :** an inanimate object distinguished from a living being **4 a** *pl* **:** POSSESSIONS, EFFECTS ⟨pack your ∼*s*⟩ **b :** whatever may be possessed or owned or be the object of a right **c :** an article of clothing ⟨not a ∼ to wear⟩ **d** *pl* **:** equipment or utensils esp. for a particular purpose ⟨bring the tea ∼*s*⟩ **5 :** an object or entity not precisely designated or capable of being designated ⟨use this ∼⟩ **6 a :** DETAIL, POINT ⟨checks every little ∼⟩ **b :** a material or substance of a specified kind ⟨avoid starchy ∼*s*⟩ **7 a :** a spoken or written observation or point **b :** IDEA, NOTION ⟨says the first ∼ he thinks of⟩ **c :** a piece of news or information ⟨couldn't get a ∼ out of him⟩ **8 :** INDIVIDUAL; *esp* **:** PERSON **9 :** the proper or fashionable way of behaving, talking, or dressing — used with *the* **10 :** a mild obsession or phobia ⟨has a ∼ about driving⟩

thing·ama·jig *or* **thing·um·a·jig** \ˈthiŋ-ə-mə-ˌjig\ *n* [alter. of earlier *thingum*, fr. *thing*] **:** something that is hard to classify or whose name is unknown or forgotten — called also *thingamabob*

thing-in-itself *n, pl* **things-in-themselves :** NOUMENON

thing·ness \ˈthiŋ-nəs\ *n* **:** the quality or state of objective existence or reality

thing·um·my \ˈthiŋ-ə-mē\ *n* [alter. of earlier *thingum*] **:** THINGAMAJIG

¹think \ˈthiŋk\ *vb* **thought** \ˈthȯt\ **think·ing** [ME *thenken*, fr. OE *thencan;* akin to OHG *denken* to think, L *tongēre* to know — more at THANK] *vt* **1 :** to form or have in the mind **2 :** INTEND, PLAN ⟨*thought* to return early⟩ **3 a :** to have as an opinion **:** BELIEVE ⟨∼ it's so⟩ **b :** to regard as **:** CONSIDER ⟨∼ the rule unfair⟩ **4 a :** to reflect on **:** PONDER ⟨∼ the matter over⟩ **b :** to determine by reflecting ⟨∼ what to do next⟩ **5 :** to call to mind **:** REMEMBER ⟨never ∼ to ask⟩ **6 :** to devise by thinking **7 :** EXPECT ⟨*thought* to find him home⟩ **8 a :** to center one's thoughts on ⟨talks and ∼*s* business⟩ **b :** to form a mental picture of **9 :** to subject to the processes of logical thought ⟨∼ things out⟩ ∼ *vi* **1 a :** to exercise the powers of judgment, conception, or inference **:** REASON **b :** to have in or call to mind a thought **2 a :** to have the mind engaged in reflection **:** MEDITATE **b :** to consider the suitability ⟨*thought* of him for president⟩ **3 :** to have a view or opinion **:** REGARD ⟨∼*s* of himself as a poet⟩ **4 :** to have concern ⟨∼ of just yourself⟩ **5 :** EXPECT, SUSPECT — **think·er** *n*

syn THINK, CONCEIVE, IMAGINE, FANCY, REALIZE, ENVISAGE, ENVISION mean to form an idea of. THINK implies the entrance of an idea into one's mind with or without deliberate consideration or reflection; CONCEIVE suggests the forming and bringing forth and usu. developing of an idea, plan, design; IMAGINE stresses a visualization; FANCY suggests an imagining often unrestrained by factual reality; REALIZE stresses a grasping of the significance of what is conceived or imagined; ENVISAGE and ENVISION imply a conceiving or imagining that is esp. clear or detailed

syn THINK, COGITATE, REFLECT, REASON, SPECULATE, DELIBERATE mean to use one's powers of conception, judgment, or inference. THINK is general and may apply to any mental activity, but used alone often suggests attainment of clear ideas or conclusions; COGITATE implies deep or intent thinking; REFLECT suggests unhurried consideration of something recalled to the mind; REASON stresses consecutive logical thinking; SPECULATE implies reasoning about things theoretical or problematic; DELIBERATE suggests slow or careful reasoning before forming an opinion or reaching a conclusion or decision

²think *n* **:** an act of thinking ⟨has another ∼ coming⟩

³think *adj* **:** of or relating to thinking

think·able \ˈthiŋ-kə-bəl\ *adj* **1 :** capable of being thought about **2 :** conceivably possible — **think·able·ness** *n* — **think·ably** \-blē\ *adv*

¹think·ing *n* **1 :** the action of using one's mind to produce thoughts **2 a :** OPINION, JUDGMENT **b :** THOUGHT

²thinking *adj* **:** marked by use of the intellect **:** RATIONAL — **think·ing·ly** \ˈthiŋ-kiŋ-lē\ *adv* — **think·ing·ness** *n*

thinking cap *n* **:** a state or mood in which one thinks

think piece *n* **:** a news article consisting chiefly of background material and personal opinion and analysis

thin·ner \ˈthin-ər\ *n* **:** one that thins; *specif* **:** a volatile liquid (as turpentine) used esp. to thin paint

thin-skinned \ˈthin-ˈskind\ *adj* **1 :** having a thin skin or rind **2 :** unduly susceptible to criticism or insult **:** TOUCHY

thio- — see THI-

thio·ace·tic acid \ˌthī-(ˌ)ō-ə-ˌsēt-ik-\ *n* [ISV] **:** a pungent liquid acid CH_3COSH made by heating acetic acid with a phosphorus sulfide and used as a chemical reagent

thio acid \ˈthī-(ˌ)ō-\ *n* [ISV, fr. *thi-*] **:** an acid in which oxygen is partly or wholly replaced by sulfur

thio·car·ba·mide \ˌthī-ō-ˈkär-bə-ˌmīd, -(ˌ)kär-ˈbam-ˌīd\ *n* [ISV] **:** THIOUREA

thio·cy·a·nate \-ˈsī-ə-ˌnāt, -nət\ *n* [ISV] **:** a salt or ester of thiocyanic acid

thio·cy·an·ic \ˌthī-ō-(ˌ)sī-ˈan-ik\ *adj* [ISV] **:** of, relating to, or being a colorless unstable liquid acid HSCN of strong odor

Thi·o·kol \ˈthī-ə-ˌkȯl, -ˌkōl\ *trademark* — used for any of a series of polysulfide rubbers or closely related liquid polymers or water-dispersed latices

thion- *comb form* [ISV, fr. Gk *theion*] **:** sulfur ⟨*thion*ic⟩

thi·o·nate \ˈthī-ə-ˌnāt\ *n* [ISV] **:** a salt or ester of a thionic acid

thi·on·ic \thī-ˈän-ik\ *adj* [ISV] **:** relating to or containing sulfur

thionic acid *n* **:** any of various unstable acids of the general formula $H_2S_xO_6$

thi·o·nyl \ˈthī-ə-ˌnil\ *n* [ISV] **:** the bivalent radical or cation >SO of sulfurous acid

thio·pen·tal \ˌthī-ō-ˈpen-ˌtal, -ˌtȯl\ *n* [*thio-* + *pento*barbi*tal*] **:** a barbiturate $C_{11}H_{18}N_2O_2S$ used as sodium thiopental in intravenous anesthesia and psychotherapy

thio·phene \ˈthī-ə-ˌfēn\ *n* [ISV *thi-* + *phene* (benzene)] **:** a heterocyclic liquid C_4H_4S from coal tar that resembles benzene

thio·phos·phate \ˌthī-ō-ˈfäs-ˌfāt\ *n* [ISV] **:** a salt or ester of a thiophosphoric acid

thio·phos·pho·ric acid \-ˌfäs-ˌfȯr-ik-, -ˌfär-; -ˌfäs-f(ə-)rik-\ *n* **:** an acid derived from a phosphoric acid by replacement of one or more atoms of oxygen with sulfur

thio·sul·fate \-ˈsəl-ˌfāt\ *n* [ISV] **:** a salt or ester of thiosulfuric acid

thio·sul·fu·ric \-ˌsəl-ˈfyu̇(ə)r-ik\ *adj* **:** of, relating to, or being an unstable acid $H_2S_2O_3$ derived from sulfuric acid by replacement of one oxygen atom by sulfur and known only in solution or in salts and esters

thio·ura·cil \ˌthī-ō-ˈyu̇r-ə-ˌsil\ *n* [ISV *thi-* + *uracil*] **:** a bitter crystalline compound $C_4H_4N_2OS$ that depresses the function of the thyroid gland

thio·urea \-yu̇-ˈrē-ə *also* -ˈyu̇r-ē-ə\ *n* [NL, fr. *thi-* + *urea*] **:** a colorless crystalline bitter compound $CS(NH_2)_2$ analogous to and resembling urea that is used esp. as a photographic and organic chemical reagent

thir \t͟hər, (ˈ)t͟hi(ə)r, (ˈ)t͟hu̇(ə)r\ *pron* [ME (northern), perh. irreg. fr. ME *this*] *dial Brit* **:** THESE

thi·ram \ˈthī-ˌram\ *n* [prob. by alter. fr. *thiuram* (the chemical radical NH_2CS)] **:** a compound $C_6H_{12}N_2S_4$ used as a fungicide and seed disinfectant

¹third \ˈthərd\ *adj* [ME *thridde, thirde*, fr. OE *thridda, thirdda;* akin to L *tertius* third, Gk *tritos, treis* three — more at THREE] **1 a** — see NUMBER table **b** (1) **:** being next to the second in place or time ⟨∼ in line⟩ (2) **:** ranking next to the second of a grade or degree in authority or precedence ⟨∼ mate⟩ **c :** being a type of grammatical declension or conjugation conventionally placed third in a sequential arrangement **d :** being the forward speed or gear next higher than second in an automotive vehicle **2 a :** being one of three equal parts into which anything is divisible **b :** being the last in each group of three in a series ⟨take out every ∼ card⟩ — **third** *or* **third·ly** *adv*

²third *n* **1** — see NUMBER table **2 :** one of three equal parts of something **3 a :** a musical interval embracing three diatonic degrees **b :** a tone at this interval; *specif* **:** MEDIANT **c :** the harmonic combination of two tones a third apart **4 :** the third gear or speed of an automotive vehicle **5 :** one ranking next below second in authority or precedence

third base *n* **1 :** the base that must be touched third by a base runner in baseball **2 :** the player position for defending the area around third base

third class *n* **1 :** the third and usu. next below second class in a classification **2 :** the least expensive class of accommodations (as on a passenger ship) **3 a :** a class of U.S. mail comprising printed matter exclusive of regularly issued periodicals and merchandise less than 16 ounces in weight and not sealed against inspection **b :** a similar class of Canadian mail with different weight limits

third-class \ˈthərd-ˈklas\ *adj* **:** of or relating to a class, rank, or grade next below the second; *specif* **:** of or relating to a grade of travel accommodation inferior to second-class — **third-class** *adv*

third degree *n* **:** the subjection of a prisoner to mental or physical torture to wring a confession from him

third-degree burn *n* **:** a burn characterized by destruction of the skin through the depth of the derma and possibly into underlying tissues, loss of fluid, and sometimes shock

third dimension *n* **1 :** thickness, depth, or apparent thickness or depth when a quality that confers solidity on an object **2 :** a quality that confers reality or lifelikeness — **third-di·men·sion·al** \ˌthərd-də-ˈmench-nəl, -(ˌ)dī-, -ən-ᵊl\ *adj*

third estate *n* **:** the third of the traditional political orders; *specif* **:** the commons

third force *n* **:** a grouping (as of political parties or international powers) intermediate between two opposing political forces
third house *n* **:** a legislative lobby
third order *n, often cap T & O* **1 :** an organization composed of lay people living in secular society under a religious rule and directed by a religious order **2 :** a congregation esp. of teaching or nursing sisters affiliated with a religious order
third party *n* **1 :** a person other than the principals ⟨a *third party* to a divorce proceeding⟩ **2 a :** a major political party operating over a limited period of time in addition to two other major parties in a nation or state normally characterized by a two-party system **b :** MINOR PARTY
third person *n* **1 a :** a set of linguistic forms (as verb forms, pronouns, and inflectional affixes) referring to someone or something that is neither the speaker or writer of the utterance in which they occur nor the one to whom that utterance is addressed **b :** a linguistic form belonging to such a set **2 :** reference of a linguistic form to someone or something that is neither the speaker or writer of the utterance in which it occurs nor the one to whom that utterance is addressed
third rail *n* **:** a metal rail through which electric current is led to the motors of an electric locomotive
third-rate \'thər-'drāt\ *adj* **:** of third quality or value; *specif* **:** worse than second-rate — **third-rat·er** \-'drāt-ər\ *n*
third reading *n* **:** the final stage of the consideration of a legislative bill before a vote on its final disposition
third ventricle *n* **:** the median unpaired ventricle of the brain bounded by parts of the telencephalon and diencephalon
third world *n, often cap T&W* **:** a group of nations especially in Africa and Asia that are not aligned with either the Communist or the non-Communist blocs
[1]**thirl** \'thər(-ə)l\ *n* [ME, fr. OE *thyrel*, fr. *thurh* through — more at THROUGH] *dial* **:** HOLE, PERFORATION, OPENING
[2]**thirl** *vt* **1** *dial Brit* **:** PIERCE, PERFORATE **2** *dial Brit* **:** THRILL
[1]**thirst** \'thərst\ *n* [ME, fr. OE *thurst;* akin to OHG *durst* thirst, L *torrēre* to dry, parch, Gk *tersesthai* to become dry] **1 a :** a sensation of dryness in the mouth and throat associated with a desire for liquids; *also* **:** the bodily condition (as of dehydration) that induces this sensation **b :** a desire or need to drink **2 :** an ardent desire **:** CRAVING, LONGING
[2]**thirst** *vi* **1 :** to feel thirsty **:** suffer thirst **2 :** to have a vehement desire **:** CRAVE **syn** see LONG — **thirst·er** *n*
thirst·i·ly \'thər-stə-lē\ *adv* **:** with or on account of thirst
thirst·i·ness \-stē-nəs\ *n* **:** the quality or state of being thirsty
thirsty \'thər-stē\ *adj* **1 a :** feeling thirst **b :** deficient in moisture **:** PARCHED ⟨~ land⟩ **c :** highly absorbent ⟨~ towels⟩ **2 :** having a strong desire **:** AVID ⟨~ for knowledge⟩
thir·teen \,thər(t)-'tēn, 'thər(t)-\ *n* [ME *thrittene*, fr. *thrittene*, adj., fr. OE *thrēotīne;* akin to OE *tīen* ten — more at TEN] — see NUMBER table — **thirteen** *adj or pron* — **thir·teenth** \-'tēn(t)th\ *adj* — **thirteenth** *n, pl* **thir·teenths** \-'tēn(t)s, -'tēn(t)ths\
thir·ti·eth \'thərt-ē-əth\ *n* — see NUMBER table — **thirtieth** *adj*
thir·ty \'thərt-ē\ *n* [ME *thritty*, fr. *thritty*, adj., fr. OE *thrītig*, fr. *thrītig* group of 30, fr. *thrīe* three + *-tig* group of ten — more at EIGHTY] **1** — see NUMBER table **2** *pl* **:** the numbers 30 to 39; *specif* **:** the years 30 to 39 in a lifetime or century **3 a :** a mark or sign of completion ⟨"Thank you, Mr. President" the traditional ~ closing press conferences —*Ethyl News*⟩ **b :** END, CONCLUSION ⟨had ~ written on their earthly life —*Trade Compositor*⟩ **4 :** the second point scored by a side in a game of tennis **5 :** a 30 caliber machine gun — usu. written .30 — **thirty** *adj or pron*
thir·ty-eight \,thərt-ē-'āt\ *n* **1** — see NUMBER table **2 :** a 38 caliber pistol — usu. written .38 — **thirty-eight** *adj or pron*
thir·ty-sec·ond note \-'sek-ən-,nōt\ *n* **:** a musical note with a 3-flagged stem having the time value of one thirty-second of a whole note
thir·ty-three \,thərt-ē-'thrē\ *n* **1** — see NUMBER table **2 :** a microgroove phonograph record designed to be played at 33⅓ revolutions per minute — usu. written 33 — **thirty-three** *adj or pron*
thir·ty-two \-'tü\ *n* **1** — see NUMBER table **2 :** a 32 caliber pistol — usu. written .32 — **thirty-two** *adj or pron*
thir·ty-two·mo \-(,)mō\ *n* **:** the size of a piece of paper cut 32 from a sheet; *also* **:** a book, a page, or paper of this size
[1]**this** \(')t͟his, t͟həs\ *pron, pl* **these** \(')t͟hēz\ [ME, pron. & adj., fr. OE *thes* (masc.), *this* (neut.); akin to OHG *dese* this; akin to OE *thæt* that] **1 a** (1) **:** the person, thing, or idea present or near in place, time, or thought, or just mentioned ⟨*these* are my hands⟩ (2) **:** what is stated in the following or not yet completed phrase, clause, or discourse **b :** this time or place ⟨expected to return before ~⟩ **2 a :** the one nearer or more immediately under observation or discussion ⟨~ is iron and that is tin⟩ **b :** LATTER
[2]**this** *adj, pl* **these** **1 a :** being the person, thing, or idea present or near in place, time, or thought, or just mentioned ⟨~ book is mine⟩ ⟨early ~ morning⟩ **b :** constituting the immediately following part of the present discourse **c :** constituting the immediate past or future ⟨friends all *these* years⟩ **d :** being one not previously mentioned **2 a :** the nearer at hand or more immediately under observation or discussion ⟨~ car or that one⟩ **b :** a certain **:** ONE, SOME ⟨~ way and that⟩
[3]**this** \'t͟his\ *adv* **:** to the degree or extent indicated by something immediately present ⟨didn't expect to wait ~ long⟩
This·be \'thiz-bē\ *n* [L, fr. Gk *Thisbē*] **:** a legendary young woman of Babylon loved by Pyramus
this·tle \'this-əl\ *n* [ME *thistel*, fr. OE; akin to OHG *distill* thistle] **:** any of various prickly composite plants (esp. genera *Carduus, Circium*, and *Onopordon*) with often showy heads of mostly tubular flowers; *also* **:** any of various other prickly plants — **this·tly** \'this-(ə-)lē\ *adj*
this·tle·down \'this-əl-,daùn\ *n* **:** the pappus from the ripe flower head of a thistle
[1]**thith·er** \'thit͟h-ər *also* 'thit͟h-\ *adv* [ME, fr. OE *thider;* akin to ON *thathra* there, OE *thæt* that] **:** to that place **:** THERE
[2]**thither** *adj* **:** being on the other and farther side **:** more remote
thith·er·to \-,tü; ,thit͟h-ər-', ,thit͟h-\ *adv* **:** until that time
thith·er·ward \'thit͟h-ər-wərd, 'thit͟h-\ *also* **thith·er·wards** \-wərdz\ *adv* **:** toward that place **:** THITHER
tho *var of* THOUGH
[1]**thole** \'thōl\ *vb* [ME *tholen*, fr. OE *tholian*] *chiefly dial* **:** ENDURE
[2]**thole** *n* [ME *tholle*, fr. OE *thol;* akin to Gk *tylos* knob, callus, L *tumēre* to swell — more at THUMB] **1 :** PEG, PIN **2 :** a pin set in pairs in the gunwale of a boat in place of oarlocks
thole·pin \'thōl-,pin\ *n* **:** a thole for an oar
Thom·as \'täm-əs\ *n* [Gk *Thōmas*, fr. Heb *t'ōm* twin] **:** an apostle who demanded proof of Christ's resurrection
Tho·mism \'tō-,miz-əm\ *n* [prob. fr. (assumed) NL *thomismus*, fr. St. *Thomas* Aquinas] **:** the scholastic philosophical and theological system of St. Thomas Aquinas — **Tho·mist** \-məst\ *n or adj* — **Tho·mis·tic** \tō-'mis-tik\ *adj*
Thomp·son submachine gun \'täm(p)-sən-\ *n* [John T. *Thompson* †1940 Am army officer] **:** a portable automatic weapon with a magazine or drum feed and a pistol grip and buttstock for firing from the shoulder
thong \'thȯŋ\ *n* [ME, fr. OE *thwong;* akin ON *thvengr* thong, Av *thwązjaiti* he is distressed] **:** a strip of leather or hide
Thor \'thȯ(ə)r\ *n* [ON *Thōrr*] **:** the god of thunder in Norse mythology represented as armed with a hammer
tho·rac·ic \thə-'ras-ik\ *adj* **:** of, relating to, located within, or involving the thorax
thoracic duct *n* **:** the main trunk of the system of lymphatic vessels lying along the front of the spinal column and opening into the left subclavian vein
tho·ra·cot·o·my \,thōr-ə-'kät-ə-mē, ,thȯr-\ *n* [L *thorac-, thorax* + ISV *-tomy*] **:** surgical incision of the chest wall
tho·rax \'thō(ə)r-,aks, 'thȯ(ə)r-\ *n, pl* **tho·rax·es** *or* **tho·ra·ces** \thə-'rā-,sēz, thō-, 'thōr-ə-,sēz, 'thȯr-\ [ME, fr. L *thorac-, thorax* breastplate, thorax, fr. Gk *thōrak-, thōrax*] **1 :** the part of the body of man and other mammals between the neck and the abdomen; *also* **:** its cavity in which the heart and lungs lie **2 :** the middle of the three chief divisions of the body of an insect
tho·ria \'thōr-ē-ə, 'thȯr-\ *n* [NL, fr. *thorium* + *-a* (as in *magnesia*)] **:** a refractory powdery white oxide of thorium ThO_2 used esp. in gas mantles, crucibles and refractories, and optical glass
tho·ri·a·nite \-ē-ə-,nīt\ *n* [irreg. fr. *thoria*] **:** a strongly radioactive mineral ThO_2 that is an oxide of thorium and often contains rare-earth metals
tho·ric \'thȯr-ik, 'thär-, 'thōr-\ *adj* **:** of, relating to, or containing thorium
tho·rite \'thō(ə)r-,īt, 'thȯ(ə)r-\ *n* [Sw *thorit*, fr. NL *thorium*] **:** a rare mineral $ThSiO_4$ that is a brown to black or sometimes orange-yellow thorium silicate resembling zircon
tho·ri·um \'thōr-ē-əm, 'thȯr-\ *n* [NL, fr. ON *Thōrr* Thor] **:** a radioactive tetravalent metallic element that occurs combined in minerals and is usu. associated with rare earths — see ELEMENT table
thorn \'thȯ(ə)rn\ *n, often attrib* [ME, fr. OE; akin to OHG *dorn* thorn, Skt *tṛṇa* grass, blade of grass] **1 :** a woody plant bearing a sharp impeding process (as briers, prickles, or spines); *esp* **:** any of a genus (*Crataegus*) of the rose family **2 a :** a sharp rigid process on a plant; *specif* **:** a short, indurated, sharp-pointed, and leafless branch **b :** any of various sharp spinose structures on an animal **3 :** something that causes distress or irritation **4 :** the runic letter þ used in Old English and Middle English for either of the sounds of Modern English *th* (as in *thin, then*) — **thorned** \'thȯ(ə)rnd\ *adj* — **thorn·less** \'thȯ(ə)rn-ləs\ *adj*
thorn apple *n* **1 :** the fruit of a hawthorn **2 :** JIMSONWEED; *also* **:** any plant of the same genus
thorn·back \'thȯ(ə)rn-,bak\ *n* **1 :** any of various rays having spines on the back **2 :** a large European spider crab (*Maja squinado*)
thorn·bush \-,bu̇sh\ *n* **1 :** any of various spiny or thorny shrubs or small trees **2 :** a low growth of thorny shrubs esp. of dry tropical regions
thorn·i·ness \'thȯr-nē-nəs\ *n* **:** the quality or state of being thorny
thorn·like \'thȯ(ə)rn-,līk\ *adj* **:** resembling a thorn esp. in sharpness
thorny \'thȯr-nē\ *adj* **1 :** full of thorns **2 :** full of difficulties or controversial points **:** TICKLISH ⟨~ problem⟩
thoro *nonstand var of* THOROUGH
tho·ron \'thō(ə)r-,än, 'thȯ(ə)r-\ *n* [NL, fr. *thorium*] **:** a gaseous radioactive element formed from thorium and isotopic with radon
[1]**thor·ough** \'thər-(,)ō, -ə(-w); 'thə-(,)rō, -rə(-w)\ *prep* [ME *thorow*, fr. OE *thurh, thuruh*, prep. & adv.] *archaic* **:** THROUGH
[2]**thorough** *adv, archaic* **:** THROUGH
[3]**thorough** *adj* **1 :** carried through to completion **:** EXHAUSTIVE ⟨~ search⟩ **2 a :** marked by full detail ⟨~ description⟩ **b :** careful about detail **:** PAINSTAKING ⟨~ scholar⟩ **c :** complete in all respects ⟨~ pleasure⟩ **d :** having full mastery (as of an art) ⟨~ musician⟩ **3 :** passing through — **thor·ough·ly** *adv* — **thor·ough·ness** *n*
thorough bass *n* **:** the representation of chords by figures under the bass notes; *also* **:** the technique of writing or reading this
thor·ough·brace \'thər-ə-,brās, 'thə-rə-\ *n* **:** one of several leather straps supporting the body of a carriage and serving as springs
[1]**thor·ough·bred** \-,bred\ *adj* **1 :** thoroughly trained or skilled **2 :** bred from the best blood through a long line **:** PUREBRED ⟨~ dogs⟩ **3 a** *cap* **:** of, relating to, or being a member of the Thoroughbred breed of horses **b** (1) **:** having characteristics resembling those of a Thoroughbred **:** ELEGANT (2) **:** FIRST-CLASS
[2]**thoroughbred** *n* **1** *cap* **:** any of an English breed of light speedy horses kept chiefly for racing and originating from crosses between English mares of uncertain ancestry and Arabian stallions **2 :** a purebred or pedigreed animal **3 :** one that has characteristics resembling those of a Thoroughbred
thor·ough·fare \-,fa(ə)r, -,fe(ə)r\ *n* **1 :** a way or place for passage: as **a :** a street open at both ends **b :** a main road **2 a :** PASSAGE, TRANSIT **b :** the conditions necessary for passing through
thor·ough·go·ing \,thər-ə-'gō-iŋ, ,thə-rə-, -'gȯ(-)iŋ\ *adj* **:** marked by thoroughness or zeal
thor·ough-paced \-'pāst\ *adj* **1 :** thoroughly trained **:** ACCOMPLISHED **2 :** THOROUGH, COMPLETE
thor·ough·pin \'thər-ə-,pin, 'thə-rə-\ *n* **:** a synovial dilatation just above the hock of a horse on both sides of the leg and slightly anterior to the hamstring tendon that is often associated with lameness
thor·ough·wort \-,wərt, -,wȯ(ə)rt\ *n* **:** BONESET
thorp \'thȯ(ə)rp\ *n* [ME, fr. OE; akin to OHG *dorf* village, L *trabs* beam, roof] *archaic* **:** VILLAGE, HAMLET

those [ME, fr. *those* these, fr. OE *thās*, pl. of *thes* this — more at THIS] *pl of* THAT

1**thou** \(')thau̇\ *pron* [ME, fr. OE *thū*; akin to OHG *dū* thou, L *tu*, Gk *sy*] **:** the one addressed ⟨~ shalt have no other gods before me —Exod 20:3 (AV)⟩ — used by Friends as the universal form of address to one person

2**thou** \'thau̇\ *vt* **:** to address as *thou*

3**thou** \'thau̇\ *n, pl* **thou** *or* **thous** \'thau̇z\ [short for *thousand*] **:** a thousand of something (as dollars)

1**though** \'thō\ *adv* [ME, adv. & conj., of Scand origin; akin to ON *thō* nevertheless; akin to OE *thēah* nevertheless, OHG *doh*] **:** HOWEVER, NEVERTHELESS ⟨continued to eat at the hotel ~ —Sloan Wilson⟩

2**though** \(,)thō\ *conj* **1 :** in spite of the fact that **:** WHILE ⟨~ they know the war is lost, they continue to fight —Bruce Bliven⟩ **2 :** in spite of the possibility that **:** even if ⟨~ they all may fail, they all will try⟩

1**thought** *past of* THINK

2**thought** \'thȯt\ *n* [ME, fr. OE *thōht*; akin to OE *thencan* to think — more at THINK] **1 a :** the action or process of thinking **:** COGITATION **b :** serious consideration **:** REGARD **c :** RECOLLECTION **2 a :** reasoning power **b :** the power to imagine **:** CONCEPTION **3 :** something that is thought: as **a :** an individual act or product of thinking **b :** INTENTION, PLAN **c :** OPINION, BELIEF **d :** the intellectual product or the organized views and principles of a period, place, group, or individual **4 :** a slight amount **:** BIT **syn** see IDEA

thought·ful \'thȯt-fəl\ *adj* **1 a :** absorbed in thought **:** MEDITATIVE **b :** characterized by careful reasoned thinking **2 :** MINDFUL, HEEDFUL; *specif* **:** mindful of others — **thought·ful·ly** \-fə-lē\ *adv* — **thought·ful·ness** *n*

syn THOUGHTFUL, CONSIDERATE, ATTENTIVE mean mindful of others. THOUGHTFUL implies unselfish concern and ability to anticipate another's needs; CONSIDERATE implies concern for the feelings of others; ATTENTIVE suggests repeated acts of kindness or courtesy

thought·less \'thȯt-ləs\ *adj* **1 a :** insufficiently alert **:** CARELESS **b :** RECKLESS, RASH **2 :** devoid of thought **:** INSENSATE **3 :** lacking concern for others **:** INCONSIDERATE — **thought·less·ly** *adv* — **thought·less·ness** *n*

thought–out \-,au̇t\ *adj* **:** produced or arrived at through careful and thorough consideration

thought·way \-,wā\ *n* **:** a way of thinking that is characteristic of a particular group, time, or culture

thou·sand \'thau̇z-ᵊn(d)\ *n, pl* **thousands** *or* **thousand** [ME, fr. OE *thūsend*; akin to OHG *dūsunt* thousand; both fr. a prehistoric Gmc compound whose constituents are respectively akin to Russ *tys*yacha thousand, Skt *tavas* strong, L *tumēre* to swell and to OE *hund* hundred — more at THUMB] **1** — see NUMBER table **2 a :** the numerable quantity symbolized by the arabic numerals 1000 **b :** the letter M **3 :** the number occupying the position four to the left of the decimal point in the Arabic notation **4 :** a very large number ⟨had a ~ things to do⟩ — **thousand** *adj* — **thou·sandth** \-ᵊn(t)th\ *adj* — **thousandth** *n, pl* **thousandths** \-ᵊn(t)s, -ᵊn(t)ths\

thou·sand–head·ed kale \,thau̇z-ᵊn-,hed-əd-\ *n* **:** a tall branched leafy kale (*Brassica oleracea fruticosa*) used as green feed for livestock

Thousand Island dressing *n* [prob. fr. *Thousand Islands*, islands in the St. Lawrence river] **:** mayonnaise with various added seasonings and flavorings

thou·sand–leg·ger \,thau̇z-ᵊn-'leg-ər, -'lāg-\ *n* **:** MILLIPEDE

Thra·cian \'thrā-shən\ *n* **1 :** a native or inhabitant of Thrace **2 :** the language of the Thracians generally assumed to be Indo-European — **Thracian** *adj*

Thra·co–Il·lyr·i·an \,thrā-(,)kō-il-'ir-ē-ən\ *adj* **:** of, relating to, or constituting a supposed subfamily of Indo-European languages comprising Thracian, Illyrian, and Albanian

Thra·co–Phry·gian \-'frij-(ē-)ən\ *adj* **:** of, relating to, or constituting a tentative branch of the Indo-European language family to which are sometimes assigned various languages of the Balkans and Asia Minor

1**thrall** \'thrȯl\ *n* [ME *thral*, fr. OE *thrǣl*, fr. ON *thræll*] **1 a :** a servant slave **:** BONDMAN; *also* **:** SERF **b :** a person in moral or mental servitude **2 :** the condition of a thrall **:** SLAVERY — **thrall** *adj*

2**thrall** *vt, archaic* **:** ENTHRALL, ENSLAVE

thrall·dom *or* **thral·dom** \-dəm\ *n* **:** the condition of a thrall **:** SLAVERY

1**thrash** \'thrash\ *vb* [alter. of *thresh*] *vt* **1 :** to separate the seeds of from the husks and straw by beating **:** THRESH 1 **2 :** to beat soundly with or as if with a stick or whip **:** FLOG; *also* **:** DEFEAT **3 :** to swing, beat, or strike in the manner of a rapidly moving flail ⟨~*ing* his arms⟩ **4 a :** to go over again and again ⟨~ the matter over inconclusively⟩ **b :** to hammer out **:** FORGE ⟨~ out a plan⟩ ~ *vi* **1 :** THRESH 1 **2 :** to deal blows or strokes like one using a flail or whip **3 :** to move or stir about violently **:** toss about ⟨~ in bed with a fever⟩ **syn** see SWING

2**thrash** *n* **:** an act of thrashing esp. in swimming the crawl or the backstroke

1**thrash·er** \'thrash-ər\ *n* **:** one that thrashes or threshes

2**thrash·er** \'thrash-ər\ *n* [prob. alter. of *thrush*] **:** any of numerous long-tailed American singing birds (family Mimidae and esp. genus *Toxostoma*) that resemble thrushes and include notable singers and mimics

thra·son·i·cal \thrā-'sän-i-kəl, thrə-\ *adj* [L *Thrason-*, *Thraso* Thraso, braggart soldier in the comedy *Eunuchus* by Terence] **:** of, relating to, like, or characteristic of Thraso **:** BRAGGING, BOASTFUL — **thra·son·i·cal·ly** \-k(ə-)lē\ *adv*

1**thraw** \'thrȯ\ *vb* [ME *thrawen*, fr. OE *thrāwan*] *vt* **1** *chiefly Scot* **:** to cause to twist or turn **2** *chiefly Scot* **:** CROSS, THWART ~ *vi* **1** *chiefly Scot* **:** TWIST, TURN **2** *chiefly Scot* **:** to be in disagreement

2**thraw** *n* **1** *chiefly Scot* **:** TWIST, TURN **2** *chiefly Scot* **:** ill humor **:** ANGER

thra·wart \'thrȧ-wərt\ *adj* [ME (Sc), alter. of ME *fraward*, *froward* froward] **1** *chiefly Scot* **:** STUBBORN, PERVERSE **2** *Scot* **:** CROOKED, TWISTED

thrawn \'thrȧn\ *adj* [ME (Sc) *thrawin*, fr. pp. of ME *thrawen*] *chiefly Scot* **:** UNPLEASING: as **a :** PERVERSE, RECALCITRANT **b :** CROOKED, MISSHAPEN — **thrawn·ly** *adv, chiefly Scot*

1**thread** \'thred\ *n* [ME *thred*, fr. OE *thrǣd*; akin to OHG *drāt* wire, OE *thrāwan* to cause to twist or turn — more at THROW] **1 a :** a filament, a group of filaments twisted together, or a filamentous length formed by spinning and twisting short textile fibers into a continuous strand **b :** a piece of thread **2 a :** any of various natural filaments ⟨the ~*s* of a spider web⟩ **b :** a slender stream **c :** a streak of light or color **d :** SCREW THREAD **3 :** something felt to resemble a textile thread: as **a :** a train of thought **b :** a continuing element ⟨a ~ of poetry marked all his writing⟩ **4 :** a tenuous or feeble support — **thread·like** \-,līk\ *adj*

2**thread** *vt* **1 a :** to pass a thread through the eye of (a needle) **b :** to arrange a thread, yarn, or lead-in piece in working position for use in (a machine) **2 a :** to pass through in the manner of a thread ⟨a ~ a pipe with wire⟩ **b :** to make one's way through or between ⟨~*ing* narrow alleys⟩ **3 :** to put together on or as if on a thread **:** STRING ⟨~ beads⟩ **4 :** to interweave with or as if with threads **:** INTERSPERSE ⟨dark hair ~*ed* with silver⟩ **5 :** to form a screw thread on or in ~ *vi* **1 :** to thread or wind a way ⟨~*ing* through narrow passages⟩ **2 :** to form a thread when poured from a spoon — **thread·er** *n*

thread·bare \'thred-,ba(ə)r, -,be(ə)r\ *adj* **1 :** having the nap worn off so that the thread shows **:** SHABBY **2 :** HACKNEYED **syn** see TRITE — **thread·bare·ness** *n*

thread·fin \-,fin\ *n* **:** any of a family (Polynemidae) of fishes related to the mullets and having filamentous rays on the lower part of the pectoral fin

thread·i·ness \-ē-nəs\ *n* **:** the quality or state of being thready

thread·less \'thred-ləs\ *adj* **:** lacking a thread ⟨a ~ connection between pipes⟩

thread·worm \'thred-,wərm\ *n* **:** a long slender nematode worm

thready \-ē\ *adj* **1 :** consisting of or bearing fibers or filaments ⟨a ~ bark⟩ **2 a :** resembling a thread **:** FILAMENTOUS **b :** tending to form or draw out into strands **:** ROPY **3 :** lacking in fullness, body, or vigor **:** THIN ⟨a ~ voice⟩ ⟨a ~ pulse⟩

threap \'thrēp\ *vt* [ME *threpen*, fr. OE *thrēapian*] **1** *chiefly Scot* **:** SCOLD, CHIDE **2** *chiefly Scot* **:** to maintain persistently

1**threat** \'thret\ *n* [ME *thret* coercion, threat, fr. OE *thrēat* coercion; akin to MHG *drōz* annoyance, L *trudere* to push, thrust] **1 :** an expression of intention to inflict evil, injury, or damage **2 :** something that threatens

2**threat** *vb, archaic* **:** THREATEN

threat·en \'thret-ᵊn\ *vb* **threat·en·ing** \'thret-niŋ, -ᵊn-iŋ\ *vt* **1 :** to utter threats against **2 a :** to give signs or warning of **:** PORTEND **b :** to hang over as a threat **:** MENACE ~ *vi* **1 :** to utter threats **2 :** to portend evil — **threat·en·ing·ly** \'thret-niŋ-lē, -ᵊn-iŋ-\ *adv*

syn THREATEN, MENACE mean to forecast danger or evil. THREATEN may imply an impersonal warning of trouble, punishment, or retribution; MENACE implies alarming by a definitely hostile aspect or character

threat·en·er \'thret-nər, -ᵊn-ər\ *n* **:** one that threatens

three \'thrē\ *n* [ME, fr. *three*, adj., fr. OE *thrīe* (masc.), *thrēo* (fem. & neut.); akin to OHG *drī* three, L *tres*, Gk *treis*] **1** — see NUMBER table **2 :** the third in a set or series ⟨the ~ of hearts⟩ **3 :** something having three units or members — **three** *adj or pron*

three–base hit \,thrē-,bās-\ *n* **:** a base hit that enables a batter to reach third base safely — called also *three-bag·ger* \'thrē-'bag-ər\

three–card monte \,thrē-,kärd-\ *n* **:** a gambling game in which the dealer shows three cards and then shuffles and throws them face down before anyone who wishes to pick out a particular card

three–col·or \'thrē-'kəl-ər\ *adj* **:** being or relating to a printing or photographic process wherein three primary colors are used to reproduce all the colors of the subject

3–D \'thrē-'dē\ *n* [*D*, abbr. of *dimensional*] **:** the three-dimensional form or a picture produced in it

three–deck·er \'thrē-'dek-ər\ *n* **1 a :** a warship carrying guns on three decks **b :** a cargo or passenger ship with three full decks **2 :** anything made with three floors, tiers, or layers; *esp* **:** a sandwich made of three slices of bread and two fillings

three–di·men·sion·al \,thrēd-ə-'mench-nəl, ,thrēd-ī-, -ən-ᵊl\ *adj* **1 :** of or relating to three dimensions **2 :** giving the illusion of depth or varying distances — used of a pictorial representation esp. when this illusion is enhanced by stereoscopic means

three·fold \'thrē-,fōld\ *adj* **1 :** having three units or members **:** TRIPLE **2 :** being three times as great or as many — **three·fold** \-'fōld\ *adv*

three–gait·ed \-'gāt-əd\ *adj, of a horse* **:** trained to use the walk, trot, and canter

three–hand·ed \-'han-dəd\ *adj* **:** played or to be played by three players ⟨~ bridge⟩

Three Hours *n* **:** a service of devotion between noon and three o'clock on Good Friday

three–legged \'thrē-'leg(ə)d, -'lāg(ə)d\ *adj* **:** having three legs ⟨a ~ stool⟩

three–mile limit \,thrē-,mīl-\ *n* **:** the limit of the marginal sea of three miles included in the territorial waters of a state

three·pence \'thrip-ən(t)s, 'thrəp-, 'threp-, -ᵊm(p)s, *US also* 'thrē-,pen(t)s\ *n, pl* **threepence** *or* **three·penc·es** **1 :** the sum of three usu. British pennies **2 :** a coin worth three pennies

three·pen·ny \'thrip-(ə-)nē, 'thrəp-, 'threp-, *US also* 'thrē-,pen-ē\ *adj* **1 :** costing or worth threepence **2 :** worth little **:** POOR

three–phase \'thrē-'fāz\ *adj* **:** of, relating to, or operating by means of a combination of three circuits energized by alternating electromotive forces that differ in phase by one third of a cycle

three–piece \-'pēs\ *adj* **:** consisting of or made in three pieces

three–ply \-'plī\ *adj* **:** consisting of three distinct strands, veneers, or interwoven layers

three–point landing \,thrē-,pȯint-\ *n* **:** an airplane landing in which the two main wheels of the landing gear and the tail wheel or skid or nose wheel touch the ground simultaneously

three–quar·ter \'thrē-'kwȯ(r)t-ər\ *n* **1 :** a three-quarter length portrait **2 :** a three-quarter face portrait — **three–quarter** *adj*

three–quarter binding *n* **:** a bookbinding in which the material of the back extends upon the boards for one third of their width

three–ring circus \,thrē-,riŋ-\ *n* **1 :** a circus with simultaneous performances in three rings **2 :** something confusing, engrossing, or entertaining

three R's *n pl* [fr. the facetiously used phrase *reading, 'riting, and 'rithmetic*] **:** the fundamentals taught in elementary school; *esp* **:** reading, writing, and arithmetic

three·score \'thrē-'skō(ə)r, -'skȯ(ə)r\ *adj* **:** being three times twenty **:** SIXTY

three·some \'thrē-səm\ *n* **1 :** a group of three persons or things

: TRIO **2** : a golf match in which one person plays his ball against the ball of two others playing each stroke alternately
three–square \-'skwa(ə)r, -'skwe(ə)r\ *adj* : having an equilateral triangular cross section — used esp. of a file
three–val·ued \-'val-(,)yüd\ *adj* : possessing three truth-values ⟨~ logic⟩
threm·ma·tol·o·gy \,threm-ə-'täl-ə-jē\ *n* [Gk *thremmat-, thremma* nursling + E *-o-* + *-logy;* akin to Gk *trephein* to nourish — more at ATROPHY] : the science of breeding animals and plants under domestication
thre·node \'thrē-,nōd, 'thren-,ōd\ *n* : THRENODY — **thre·nod·ic** \thri-'näd-ik\ *adj* — **thren·o·dist** \'thren-əd-əst\ *n*
thren·o·dy \'thren-əd-ē\ *n* [Gk *thrēnōidia,* fr. *thrēnos* dirge + *aeidein* to sing; akin to Skt *dhraṇati* it sounds — more at ODE] : a song of lamentation for the dead : ELEGY
thre·o·nine \'thrē-ə-,nēn\ *n* [prob. fr. *threonic acid* ($C_4H_8O_5$)] : a colorless crystalline amino acid $C_4H_9NO_3$ held essential to normal nutrition
thresh \'thrash, 'thresh\ *vb* [ME *thresshen,* fr. OE *threscan;* akin to OHG *dreskan* to thresh, L *terere* to rub — more at THROW] *vt* **1** : to separate seed from (a harvested plant) mechanically; *also* : to separate (seed) in this way **2 a** : to go over again and again ⟨~ the matter over⟩ **b** : to hammer out : FORGE ⟨~ out a plan⟩ **3** : to strike repeatedly : THRASH ~ *vi* **1** : to thresh grain **2** : to strike with or as if with a flail or whip **3** : to toss about
thresh·er *n* **1** : one that threshes **2** : a large nearly cosmopolitan shark (*Alopias vulpinus*) having a greatly elongated curved upper lobe of its tail with which it is said to thresh the water to round up the fish on which it feeds — called also *fox shark*
threshing machine *n* : a machine for separating grain or seeds from straw
thresh·old \'thresh-,(h)ōld\ *n* [ME *thresshold,* fr. OE *threscwald;* akin to ON *threskjǫldr* threshold, OE *threscan* to thresh] **1** : the plank, stone, or piece of timber that lies under a door : SILL **2 a** : GATE, DOOR **b** (1) : END, BOUNDARY; *specif* : the end of a runway (2) : the place or point of entering or beginning : OUTSET **3** : the point at which a physiological or psychological effect begins to be produced ⟨~ of consciousness⟩ ⟨a high renal clearance ~⟩
threw *past of* THROW
thrice \'thrīs\ *adv* [ME *thrie, thries,* fr. OE *thriga;* akin to OFris *thria* three times, OE *thrīe* three] **1** : three times **2 a** : in a threefold manner or degree **b** : to a high degree
thrift \'thrift\ *n, often attrib* [ME, fr. ON, prosperity, fr. *thrīfask* to thrive] **1** : healthy and vigorous growth **2** : careful management esp. of money : FRUGALITY **3** *chiefly Scot* : gainful occupation : EMPLOYMENT **4** : any of a genus (*Armeria*) of the plumbago family of tufted acaulescent herbs; *esp* : a scapose herb (*A. maritima*) with pink or white flower heads
thrift·i·ly \'thrif-tə-lē\ *adv* : in a thrifty manner
thrift·i·ness \-tē-nəs\ *n* : the quality or state of being thrifty
thrift·less \'thrift-ləs\ *adj* **1** : lacking usefulness or worth **2** : wasteful of money or resources : IMPROVIDENT — **thrift·less·ness** *n*
thrifty \'thrif-tē\ *adj* **1** : thriving by industry and frugality : PROSPEROUS **2** : growing vigorously **3** : practicing economy and good management : PROVIDENT **syn** see SPARING
thrill \'thril\ *vb* [ME *thirlen, thrillen* to pierce, fr. OE *thyrlian,* fr. *thyrel* hole, fr. *thurh* through — more at THROUGH] *vt* **1 a** : to cause to experience a sudden sharp feeling of excitement **b** : to cause to have a shivering or tingling sensation **2** : to cause to vibrate or tremble perceptibly ~ *vi* **1** : to move or pass so as to cause thrills **2** : to become thrilled: **a** : to experience a sudden sharp excitement **b** : TINGLE, THROB **3** : TREMBLE, VIBRATE — **thrill** *n* — **thrill·er** *n*
thrips \'thrips\ *n, pl* **thrips** [L, woodworm, fr. Gk] : any of an order (Thysanoptera) of small to minute sucking insects most of which feed often destructively on plant juices
thrive \'thrīv\ *vi* **throve** \'thrōv\ *or* **thrived**; **thriv·en** \'thriv-ən\ *also* **thrived**; **thriv·ing** \'thrī-viŋ\ [ME *thriven,* fr. ON *thrīfask,* prob. reflexive of *thrīfa* to grasp] **1** : to grow vigorously : FLOURISH **2** : to gain in wealth or possessions : PROSPER **3** : to progress toward or realize a goal — **thriv·er** \'thrī-vər\ *n*
thriv·ing *adj* : characterized by prosperity — **thriv·ing·ly** \'thrī-viŋ-lē\ *adv*
thro \(')thrü\ *prep, archaic* : THROUGH
1throat \'thrōt\ *n* [ME *throte,* fr. OE; akin to OHG *drozza* throat] **1 a** (1) : the part of the neck in front of the spinal column (2) : the passage through it to the stomach and lungs **b** (1) : VOICE (2) : the seat of the voice **2** : something resembling the throat esp. in being an entrance, a passageway, a constriction, or a narrowed part: as **a** : the orifice of a tubular organ esp. of a plant **b** : the opening in the vamp of a shoe at the instep **c** : the part of a tennis racket between the head and the handle — **throat·ed** \-əd\ *adj*
2throat *vt* **1** : to utter in the throat : MUTTER **2** : to sing or enunciate in a throaty voice
throat·i·ly \'thrōt-ᵊl-ē\ *adv* : in a throaty manner or tone
throat·i·ness \'thrōt-ē-nəs\ *n* : the quality or state of being throaty
throat·latch \-,lach\ *n* **1** : a strap of a bridle or halter passing under a horse's throat **2** : the part of a horse's throat around which the throatlatch passes
throaty \'thrōt-ē\ *adj* **1** : uttered or produced from low in the throat ⟨a ~ voice⟩ **2** : heavy, thick, and deep as if from the throat ⟨~ notes of a horn⟩
1throb \'thräb\ *vi* **throbbed**; **throb·bing** [ME *throbben,* prob. of imit. origin] **1** : to pulsate or pound with abnormal force or rapidity : PALPITATE **2** : to beat or vibrate rhythmically — **throb·ber** *n*
2throb *n* : BEAT, PULSE
throe \'thrō\ *n* [ME *thrawe, throwe,* fr. OE *thrawu, thrēa* threat, pang; akin to OHG *drawa* threat, Gk *trauma* wound, *tetrainein* to bore — more at THROW] **1** : PANG, SPASM ⟨death ~*s*⟩ ⟨~*s* of childbirth⟩ **2** *pl* : a hard or painful struggle
thromb- *or* **thrombo-** *comb form* [Gk *thrombos* clot] : blood clot : clotting of blood ⟨*thrombin*⟩ ⟨*thrombo*-plastic⟩
throm·base \'thräm-,bās, -,bāz\ *n* [ISV] : THROMBIN
throm·bin \-bən\ *n* [ISV] : a proteolytic enzyme that is formed from prothrombin and facilitates the clotting of blood by promoting conversion of fibrinogen to fibrin
throm·bo·cyte \-bə-,sīt\ *n* [ISV] : BLOOD PLATELET; *also* : an invertebrate cell with similar function — **throm·bo·cyt·ic** \,thräm-bə-'sit-ik\ *adj*
throm·bo·em·bo·lism \,thräm-(,)bō-'em-bə-,liz-əm\ *n* : the blocking of a blood vessel by an embolus that has broken away from a thrombus at its site of formation
throm·bo·gen \'thräm-bə-jən\ *n* [ISV] : PROTHROMBIN
throm·bo·ki·nase \,thräm-bō-'kī-,nās, -'kin-, -,nāz\ *n* [ISV] : THROMBOPLASTIN
throm·bo·phle·bi·tis \-(,)bō-fli-'bīt-əs\ *n* [NL] : inflammation of a vein with formation of a thrombus
throm·bo·plas·tic \-bō-'plas-tik\ *adj* [ISV] **1** : initiating or accelerating the clotting of blood **2** : of, relating to, or being thromboplastin — **throm·bo·plas·ti·cal·ly** \-ti-k(ə-)lē\ *adv*
throm·bo·plas·tin \-'plas-tən\ *n* [ISV, fr. *thromboplastic*] : a complex protein substance found esp. in blood platelets that functions in the clotting of blood
throm·bo·sis \thräm-'bō-səs, thrəm-\ *n* [NL, fr. Gk *thrombōsis* clotting, deriv. of *thrombos* clot] : the formation or presence of a blood clot within a blood vessel during life — **throm·bot·ic** \-'bät-ik\ *adj*
throm·bus \'thräm-bəs\ *n, pl* **throm·bi** \-,bī, -,bē\ [NL, fr. Gk *thrombos* clot] : a clot of blood formed within a blood vessel and remaining attached to its place of origin — compare EMBOLUS
1throne \'thrōn\ *n* [ME *trone, throne,* fr. OF *trone,* fr. L *thronus,* fr. Gk *thronos* — more at FIRM] **1 a** : the chair of state of a king, prince, or bishop **b** : the seat of a deity or devil **2** : royal or sometimes episcopal power and dignity : SOVEREIGNTY **3** *pl* : a high order of angels
2throne *vt* **1** : to seat on a throne **2** : to invest with kingly rank or power ~ *vi* : to sit on a throne or hold kingly power
throne room *n* : a formal audience room containing the throne of a sovereign
1throng \'thrȯŋ\ *n* [ME *thrang, throng,* fr. OE *thrang, gethrang;* akin to OE *thringan* to press, crowd, OHG *dringan,* Lith *trenkti* to jolt] **1 a** : a multitude of assembled persons **b** : a large number : HOST **2 a** : a crowding together of many persons **b** : pressure of business **syn** see CROWD
2throng *vt* **throng·ing** \'thrȯŋ-iŋ\ **1** : to crowd upon : PRESS **2** : to crowd into : PACK ~ *vi* : to crowd together in great numbers
thros·tle \'thräs-əl\ *n* [ME, fr. OE — more at THRUSH] **1** : 1THRUSH 1 **2 a** : an outmoded frame for spinning cotton from roving **b** *Brit* : a worsted spinning frame
1throt·tle \'thrät-ᵊl\ *vb* **throt·tling** \'thrät-liŋ, -ᵊl-iŋ\ [ME *throtlen,* fr. *throte* throat] *vt* **1 a** (1) : to compress the throat of : CHOKE (2) : to kill by such action **b** : to prevent or check expression or activity of : SUPPRESS **2 a** : to obstruct the flow of (as steam to an engine) by a throttle valve **b** : to reduce the speed of (as an engine) by such means ~ *vi* : CHOKE — **throt·tler** \-lər, -ᵊl-ər\ *n*
2throttle *n* [perh. alter. of E dial. *thropple* (throat)] **1 a** : THROAT 1 **b** : TRACHEA 1 **2 a** : the valve controlling the volume of vaporized fuel charge delivered to the cylinders of an internal-combustion engine **b** : the lever controlling this valve
throt·tle·hold \'thrät-ᵊl-,hōld\ *n* : a vicious, strangling, or stultifying control
1through *also* **thru** \(')thrü\ *prep* [ME *thurh, thruh, through,* fr. OE *thurh;* akin to OHG *durh* through, L *trans* across, beyond, Skt *tarati* he crosses over] **1 a** (1) : in at one side or point and out at another esp. the opposite side of ⟨drove a nail ~ the board⟩ ⟨a path ~ the woods⟩ (2) : by way of ⟨left ~ the window⟩ (3) — used as a function word to indicate passage between or among separate units ⟨a highway ~ the trees⟩ (4) : without stopping for : PAST ⟨drove ~ a red light⟩ **b** — used as a function word to indicate passage into and out of a treatment, handling, or process ⟨has already passed ~ his hands⟩ **2 a** : by means of : by the agency of **b** : because of ⟨failed ~ ignorance⟩ **3 a** : over the whole surface or extent of **b** — used as a function word to indicate movement within a large expanse ⟨flew ~ the air⟩ or exposure to a specified set of conditions ⟨put her ~ hell⟩ **4 a** : during the entire period of **b** : from the beginning to the end of **c** : to and including ⟨Monday ~ Friday⟩ **5 a** — used as a function word to indicate completion or exhaustion ⟨got ~ the book⟩ ⟨went ~ a fortune in a year⟩ **b** — used as a function word to indicate acceptance or approval esp. by an official body ⟨got the bill ~ the legislature⟩
2through *also* **thru** \'thrü\ *adv* **1** : from one end or side to the other **2 a** : from beginning to end **b** : to completion, conclusion, or accomplishment ⟨see it ~⟩ **3** : to the core : COMPLETELY **4** : into the open : OUT ⟨break ~⟩
3through *also* **thru** \'thrü\ *adj* **1 a** : extending from one surface to another ⟨a ~ mortise⟩ **b** : admitting free or continuous passage : DIRECT ⟨a ~ road⟩ **2 a** (1) : going from point of origin to destination without change or reshipment ⟨~ train⟩ (2) : of or relating to such movement ⟨a ~ ticket⟩ **b** : initiated at and destined for points outside a local zone ⟨~ traffic⟩ **3 a** : arrived at completion or accomplishment ⟨he is ~ with the job⟩ **b** : WASHED-UP, FINISHED ⟨you're ~ — that was your last chance⟩
through·ith·er *or* **through·oth·er** \'thrü-(ə-)t͟hər\ *adv* [1*through* + *other*] *chiefly Scot* : in confusion : PROMISCUOUSLY
through·ly \'thrü-lē\ *adv, archaic* : THOROUGHLY
1through·out \thrü-'au̇t\ *adv* **1** : in or to every part : EVERYWHERE **2** : during the whole time or action : from beginning to end
2throughout *prep* **1** : all the way from one end to the other of : in or to every part of **2** : during the whole course or period of
through street *n* : a street on which the through movement of traffic is given preference
throughway *var of* THRUWAY
throve *past of* THRIVE
1throw \'thrō\ *vb* **threw** \'thrü\ **thrown** \'thrōn\ **throw·ing** [ME *thrawen, throwen* to cause to twist, throw, fr. OE *thrāwan* to cause to twist or turn; akin to OHG *drāen* to turn, L *terere* to rub, Gk *tetrainein* to bore, pierce] *vt* **1 a** : to propel through the air by a forward motion of the hand and arm ⟨~ a baseball⟩ **b** : to propel through the air in any manner **2 a** : to cause to fall ⟨*threw* his opponent⟩ **b** : to cause to fall off : UNSEAT ⟨the horse *threw* his rider⟩ **3** : to fling precipitately or violently : DASH **4 a** (1) : to put in some position or condition (2) : to put on or off hastily or carelessly ⟨*threw* on a coat⟩ **b** : to bring to bear : EXERT ⟨*threw*

all his influence into the boy's defense› **5 :** to form or shape on a potter's wheel **6 :** to deliver (a blow) in or as if in boxing **7 :** to twist two or more filaments of into a thread or yarn **8 a :** to make a cast of (dice) **b :** to make (a cast) at dice **9 :** to give up **:** ABANDON **10 :** to send forth **:** PROJECT ‹the setting sun *threw* long shadows› **11 :** to make (oneself) dependent **:** commit (oneself) for help, support, or protection ‹*threw* himself on the mercy of the court› **12 :** to bring forth **:** PRODUCE ‹~*s* a good crop› ‹*threw* large litters› **13 :** to lose intentionally ‹~ a game› **14 :** to move (a lever) so as to connect or disconnect parts of a clutch or switch; *also* **:** to make or break (a connection) with a lever ~ *vi* **:** CAST, HURL — **throw·er** \'thrō(-ə)r\ *n*

syn CAST, TOSS, FLING, HURL, PITCH, SLING: THROW is general and interchangeable with the other terms but may specifically imply a distinctive motion with bent arm; CAST usu. implies lightness in the thing thrown and sometimes a scattering; TOSS suggests a light or careless or aimless throwing and may imply an upward motion; FLING stresses a violent throwing; HURL implies power as in throwing a massive weight; PITCH suggests throwing carefully at a target; SLING stresses either the use of whirling momentum in throwing or directness of aim

²throw *n* **1 a :** an act of throwing, hurling, or flinging **b** (1) **:** an act of throwing dice (2) **:** the number thrown with a cast of dice **c :** a method of throwing an opponent in wrestling or judo **2 :** the distance a missile may be thrown **3 :** an undertaking involving chance or danger **4 :** the amount of vertical displacement produced by a geological fault **5 a :** the extreme movement given to a pivoted or reciprocating piece by a cam, crank, or eccentric **:** STROKE **b :** the length of the radius of a crank or the virtual crank radius of an eccentric or cam **6 a :** a light coverlet **b :** a woman's scarf or light wrap

throw away *vt* **1 a :** to get rid of as worthless or unnecessary **b :** DISCARD 1b **2 a :** to use in a foolish or wasteful manner **:** SQUANDER **b :** to fail to take advantage of **:** WASTE **3 :** to make (as a line in a play) unemphatic by casual delivery

throw·away \'thrō-ə-,wā\ *n* **:** a free handbill or circular

throw back *vt* **1 :** to delay the progress or advance of **:** CHECK **2 :** to cause to rely **:** make dependent **3 :** REFLECT ~ *vi* **:** to revert to an earlier type or phase

throw·back \'thrō-,bak\ *n* **1 :** reversion to an earlier type or phase **:** ATAVISM **2 :** an instance or product of atavistic reversion

throw down *vt* **1 :** to cause to fall **:** OVERTHROW **2 :** PRECIPITATE **3 :** to cast off **:** DISCARD

throw in *vt* **1 :** to add as a gratuity or supplement **2 :** to introduce or interject in the course of something **:** CONTRIBUTE **3 :** DISTRIBUTE 3b ~ *vi* **:** to enter into association or partnership **:** JOIN

throw off *vt* **1 a :** to free oneself from **b :** to cast off often in a hurried or vigorous manner **c :** to shake off **:** DIVERT **2 :** to give off **:** EMIT **3 :** to produce in an offhand manner **4 a :** to cause to depart from an expected or desired course **b :** to cause to make a mistake **:** MISLEAD ~ *vi* **1 :** to begin hunting **2 :** to make derogatory comments

throw out *vt* **1 a :** to remove from a place, office, or employment usu. in a sudden or unexpected manner **b :** to get rid of as worthless or unnecessary **2 :** to give expression to **:** UTTER **3 :** to dismiss from acceptance or consideration **:** REJECT **4 :** to make visible or manifest **:** DISPLAY **5 :** to leave behind **:** OUTDISTANCE **6 :** to give forth from within **:** EMIT **7 a :** to send out **b :** to cause to project **:** EXTEND **8 :** to put out **:** CONFUSE **9 :** to cause to stand out **:** make prominent **10 :** to make a throw that enables a teammate in baseball to put out (a base runner) **11 :** DISENGAGE ‹*throw out* the clutch›

throw over *vt* **1 :** to forsake despite bonds of attachment or duty **2 :** to refuse to accept **:** REJECT

throw rug *n* **:** SCATTER RUG

throw·ster \'thrō-stər\ *n* **:** one who throws silk or synthetic filaments

throw up *vt* **1 :** to raise quickly **2 :** to give up **:** QUIT **3 :** to build hurriedly **4 :** VOMIT **5 :** to bring forth **6 :** to cause to stand out **7 :** to mention repeatedly by way of reproach ~ *vi* **:** VOMIT

¹thrum \'thrəm\ *n* [ME, fr. OE *-thrum* (in *tungethrum* ligament of the tongue); akin to OHG *drum* fragment, L *terminus* boundary, end — more at TERM] **1 a** (1) **:** a fringe of warp threads left on the loom after the cloth has been removed (2) **:** one of these warp threads **b :** a tuft or short piece of rope yarn used in thrumming canvas — usu. used in pl. **c :** BIT, PARTICLE **2 :** a hair, fiber, or threadlike leaf on a plant; *also* **:** a tuft or fringe of such structures — **thrum** *adj*

²thrum *vt* **thrummed; thrum·ming 1 :** to furnish with thrums **:** FRINGE **2 :** to insert short pieces of rope yarn or spun yarn in (a piece of canvas) to make a rough surface or a mat which can be wrapped about rigging to prevent chafing

³thrum *vb* **thrummed; thrum·ming** [imit.] *vi* **1 :** to play or pluck a stringed instrument idly **:** STRUM **2 :** to sound with a monotonous hum ~ *vt* **1 :** to play (as a stringed instrument) in an idle or relaxed manner ‹~ a guitar› **2 :** to recite tiresomely or monotonously

⁴thrum *n* **:** the monotonous sound of thrumming

¹thrush \'thrəsh\ *n* [ME *thrusche*, fr. OE *thrysce;* akin to OE *throstle* thrush, OHG *droscala*, L *turdus*] **1 :** any of numerous small or medium-sized passerine birds (family Turdidae) that are mostly of a plain color often with spotted underparts and include many excellent singers **2 :** a bird felt to resemble a thrush

²thrush *n* [prob. of Scand origin; akin to Dan & Norw *trøske* thrush] **1 :** a fungal disease seen esp. in infants and marked by white patches in the oral cavity **2 :** a suppurative disorder of the feet in various animals

¹thrust \'thrəst\ *vb* **thrust; thrust·ing** [ME *thrusten, thristen*, fr. ON *thrȳsta*] *vt* **1 :** to push or drive with force **:** SHOVE **2 :** to cause to enter or pierce something by or as if by pushing **3 :** EXTEND, SPREAD **4 :** STAB, PIERCE **5 :** INTERJECT, INTERPOLATE **6 :** to press, force, or impose the acceptance of upon someone ~ *vi* **1 a :** to force an entrance or passage **b :** to push forward **:** press onward **c :** to push upward **:** PROJECT **2 :** to make a thrust, stab, or lunge with or as if with a pointed weapon **syn** see PUSH — **thrust·er** *n*

²thrust *n* **1 a :** a push or lunge with a pointed weapon **b** (1) **:** a verbal attack (2) **:** a military assault **2 a :** a strong continued pressure **b :** the sideways force or pressure of one part of a structure against another part (as of an arch against an abutment) **c** (1) **:** the force exerted endwise through a propeller shaft to give forward motion (2) **:** the forward directed reaction force produced by a high-speed jet of fluid discharged rearward from a nozzle (as in a jet airplane or a rocket) **d :** a nearly horizontal geological fault **3 a :** a forward or upward push **b :** a movement (as by a group of people) in a specified direction

thru·way \'thrü-,wā\ *n* **:** EXPRESSWAY

¹thud \'thəd\ *vi* **thud·ded; thud·ding** [prob. fr. ME *thudden* to thrust, fr. OE *thyddan*] **:** to move or strike so as to make a thud

²thud *n* **1 :** BLOW **2 :** a dull sound **:** THUMP

thug \'thəg\ *n* [Hindi *ṭhag*, lit., thief, fr. Skt *sthaga* rogue, fr. *sthagati* he covers, conceals — more at THATCH] **:** a brutal ruffian or assassin — **thug·gery** \-(ə-)rē\ *n* — **thug·gish** \-ish\ *adj*

thug·gee \'thəg-,ē\ *n* [Hindi *ṭhagī* robbery, fr. *ṭhag*] **:** the practice of murder and robbery by thugs

thu·ja \'th(y)ü-jə\ *n* [NL *Thuja*, genus name, fr. ML *thuia*, a cedar, fr. Gk *thyia*] **:** any of a genus (*Thuja*) of evergreen shrubs and trees of the pine family; *esp* **:** ARBORVITAE

thuja oil *n* **:** a fragrant essential oil from arborvitae

Thu·le \'th(y)ü-lē\ *n* [L *Thule, Thyle*, fr. Gk *Thoulē, Thylē*] **:** the northernmost part of the habitable ancient world

thu·li·um \'th(y)ü-lē-əm\ *n* [NL, fr. L *Thule*] **:** a trivalent metallic element of the rare-earth group — see ELEMENT table

¹thumb \'thəm\ *n* [ME *thoume, thoumbe*, fr. OE *thūma;* akin to OHG *thūmo* thumb, L *tumēre* to swell, Gk *sōs* safe, whole] **1 :** the first digit of the human hand opposable to the other fingers; *also* **:** the corresponding digit in lower animals **2 :** the part of a glove or mitten that covers the thumb **3 :** a convex molding **:** OVOLO

²thumb *vt* **1 a :** to leaf through (pages) with the thumb **:** TURN **b :** to soil or wear by or as if by repeated thumbing **2 :** to request or obtain (a ride) in a passing automobile by signaling with the thumb — **thumb one's nose :** to place the thumb at one's nose and extend the fingers as a gesture of scorn or defiance

thumb·hole \'thəm-,hōl\ *n* **1 :** an opening in which to insert the thumb **2 :** a hole in a wind musical instrument opened or closed by the thumb

thumb index *n* **:** an index consisting of rounded thumb notches cut symmetrically on the fore edge of a book and tabs denoting the letters (as in a dictionary) or sections referred to

¹thumb·nail \'thəm-,nāl, -'nā(ə)l\ *n* **:** the nail of the thumb

²thumb·nail \,thəm-,nāl\ *adj* **:** BRIEF, CONCISE ‹~ sketch›

thumb·print \'thəm-,print\ *n* **:** an impression made by the thumb; *esp* **:** a print made by the inside of the first joint

thumb·screw \'thəm-,skrü\ *n* **1 :** a screw having a flat-sided or knurled head so that it may be turned by the thumb and forefinger **2 :** an instrument of torture for compressing the thumb by a screw

thumb·tack \-,tak\ *n* **:** a tack with a broad flat head for pressing into a board with the thumb

¹thump \'thəmp\ *vb* [imit.] *vt* **1 :** to strike or beat with or as if with something thick or heavy so as to cause a dull sound **2 :** POUND, KNOCK **3 :** CUDGEL, THRASH ~ *vi* **:** to inflict or emit a thump

²thump *n* **:** a blow or knock with or as if with something blunt or heavy; *also* **:** the sound made by such a blow

thump·ing *adj* [*thumping*, prp. of ¹*thump*] **:** impressively large, great, or excellent ‹a ~ majority›

¹thun·der \'thən-dər\ *n* [ME *thoner, thunder*, fr. OE *thunor;* akin to OHG *thonar* thunder, L *tonare* to thunder] **1 a :** the sound that follows a flash of lightning and is caused by sudden expansion of the air in the path of the electrical discharge **b** *archaic* **:** a discharge of lightning **:** THUNDERBOLT **2 :** a loud utterance or threat **3 :** BANG, RUMBLE

²thunder *vb* **thun·der·ing** \-d(ə-)riŋ\ *vi* **1 a :** to produce thunder — usu. used impersonally ‹it ~*ed*› **b :** to give forth a sound likened to thunder ‹horses ~*ed* down the road› **2 :** ROAR, SHOUT ~ *vt* **1 :** to utter loudly **:** ROAR **2 :** to strike with a sound likened to thunder — **thun·der·er** \-dər-ər\ *n*

thun·der·bird \'thən-dər-,bərd\ *n* **:** a mythical bird believed by American Indians to cause lightning and thunder

thun·der·bolt \-,bōlt\ *n* **1 a :** a single discharge of lightning with the accompanying thunder **b :** an imaginary elongated mass cast as a missile to earth in the lightning flash **2 a :** a person or thing likened to lightning in suddenness, effectiveness, or destructive power **b :** vehement threatening or censure **:** FULMINATION

thun·der·clap \-,klap\ *n* **1 :** a clap of thunder **2 :** something sharp, loud, or sudden like a clap of thunder

thun·der·cloud \-,klau̇d\ *n* **:** a cloud charged with electricity and producing lightning and thunder

thun·der–gust \-,gəst\ *n* **:** a thunderstorm with wind

thun·der·head \-,hed\ *n* **:** a rounded mass of cumulus cloud often appearing before a thunderstorm

thun·der·ing *adj* [*thundering*, prp. of ²*thunder*] **:** awesomely great, intense, or unusual — **thun·der·ing·ly** \-d(ə-)riŋ-lē\ *adv*

thun·der·ous \'thən-d(ə-)rəs\ *adj* **:** producing thunder; *also* **:** making or accompanied by a noise like thunder — **thun·der·ous·ly** *adv*

thun·der·peal \'thən-dər-,pēl\ *n* **:** THUNDERCLAP

thun·der·show·er \-,shau̇(-ə)r\ *n* **:** a shower accompanied by lightning and thunder

thun·der·stick \-,stik\ *n* **:** BULL-ROARER

thun·der·stone \-,stōn\ *n* **1** *archaic* **:** THUNDERBOLT 1b **2 :** any of various stones (as a meteorite) believed to be a thunderbolt

thun·der·storm \-,stȯ(ə)rm\ *n* **:** a storm accompanied by lightning and thunder

thun·der·strike \-,strīk\ *vt* **1** *archaic* **:** to strike, blast, or injure by or as if by lightning **2 :** to strike dumb **:** ASTONISH ‹he was *thunderstruck* at the insolence›

thun·der·stroke \-,strōk\ *n* **:** a stroke of or as if of lightning with the attendant thunder

thu·ri·ble \'th(y)u̇r-ə-bəl, 'thər-\ *n* [ME *turrible*, fr. MF *thurible*, fr. L *thuribulum*, fr. *thur-, thus* incense, fr. Gk *thyos* incense, sacrifice, fr. *thyein* to sacrifice — more at THYME] **:** CENSER

thu·ri·fer \-ə-fər\ *n* [NL, fr. L *thurifer*, adj., incense-burning, fr. *thur-, thus* + *-ifer* -iferous] **:** one who carries a censer in a liturgical service

Thu·rin·gian \th(y)u̇-'rin-j(ē-)ən\ *n* **1 :** a member of an ancient Germanic people whose kingdom was overthrown by the Franks in the 6th century **2 :** a native or inhabitant of Thuringia — **Thuringian** *adj*

thurl \ˈthər(-ə)l\ *n* [perh. fr. E dial., gaunt] **:** the hip joint in cattle

Thurs·day \ˈthərz-dē\ *n* [ME, fr. OE *thursdæg*, fr. ON *thōrsdagr;* akin to OE *thunresdæg* Thursday, OHG *Donares tag;* all fr. a prehistoric NGmc-WGmc compound whose components are represented by OHG *Donar*, Germanic god of the sky (fr. *thonar, donar* thunder) and by OHG *tag* day — more at THUNDER, DAY] **:** the fifth day of the week — **Thurs·days** \-dēz\ *adv*

thus \ˈt͟həs\ *adv* [ME, fr. OE; akin to MD *dus* thus, OE *thæt*, neut. demonstrative pron. — more at THAT] **1 :** in this or that manner or way **2 :** to this degree or extent **:** so **3 :** because of this or that **:** HENCE **4 :** as an example

[1]thwack \ˈthwak\ *vt* [imit.] **:** to strike with or as if with something flat or heavy **:** WHACK

[2]thwack *n* **:** a heavy blow **:** WHACK

[1]thwart \ˈthwȯ(ə)rt, *naut often* ˈthȯ(ə)rt\ *adv* [ME *thwert*, fr. ON *thvert*, fr. neut. of *thverr* transverse, oblique; akin to OHG *dwerah* transverse, oblique, L *torquēre* to twist — more at TORTURE] **:** ATHWART

[2]thwart *adj* **:** situated or placed across something else **:** TRANSVERSE — **thwart·ly** *adv*

[3]thwart *vt* **1 a :** OPPOSE, BAFFLE **b :** BLOCK, DEFEAT **2 :** to pass through or across **syn** see FRUSTRATE — **thwart·er** *n*

[4]thwart *n* **:** a rower's seat extending athwart a boat

thwart·wise \-ˌwīz\ *adv (or adj)* **:** CROSSWISE

thy \(ˌ)t͟hī\ *adj* [ME *thin, thy*, fr. OE *thīn*, gen. of *thū* thou — more at THOU] *archaic* **:** of or relating to thee or thyself esp. as possessor or agent or as object of an action — used sometimes by Friends esp. among themselves

Thy·es·te·an \thī-ˈes-tē-ən\ *adj* **1 :** of or relating to Thyestes **2 :** CANNIBAL

Thy·es·tes \-(ˌ)tēz\ *n* [L, fr. Gk *Thyestēs*] **:** a son of Pelops held in Greek legend to have eaten unwittingly the flesh of his sons

thy·la·cine \ˈthī-lə-ˌsīn\ *n* [NL *Thylacinus*, genus of marsupials, fr. Gk *thylakos* sack, pouch] **:** TASMANIAN WOLF

[1]thym- *or* **thymo-** *comb form* [ISV, fr. L *thymum*] **:** thyme ⟨*thym*ol⟩

[2]thym- *or* **thymo-** *comb form* [NL *thymus*] **:** thymus ⟨*thym*ic⟩ ⟨*thymo*nucleic acid⟩

thyme \ˈtīm *also* ˈthīm\ *n* [ME, fr. MF *thym*, fr. L *thymum*, fr. Gk *thymon*, fr. *thyein* to make a burnt offering, sacrifice; akin to L *fumus* smoke — more at FUME] **:** any of a genus (*Thymus*) of mints with small pungent aromatic leaves; *esp* **:** a garden herb (*T. vulgaris*) used in seasoning and formerly in medicine

-thy·mia \ˈthī-mē-ə\ *n comb form* [NL, fr. Gk, fr. *thymos* mind — more at FUME] **:** condition of mind and will ⟨schizo*thymia*⟩

[1]thym·ic \ˈtī-mik, ˈthī-\ *adj* [ISV] **:** relating to or derived from thyme ⟨~ acid⟩

[2]thy·mic \ˈthī-mik\ *adj* **:** of or relating to the thymus

thy·mol \ˈthī-ˌmȯl, -ˌmōl\ *n* [ISV] **:** a crystalline phenol $C_{10}H_{14}O$ of aromatic odor and antiseptic properties found in thyme oil or made synthetically and used as a fungicide and preservative

thy·mo·nu·cle·ic acid \ˌthī-mō-n(y)u̇-ˌklē-ik-, -ˌklā-\ *n* [ISV] **:** DEOXYRIBONUCLEIC ACID

thy·mus \ˈthī-məs\ *n* [NL, fr. Gk *thymos* warty excrescence, thymus] **:** a glandular structure of largely lymphoid tissue and uncertain function that is present in the young of most vertebrates typically in the upper anterior chest or at the base of the neck and tends to disappear or become rudimentary in the adult

thymy *or* **thym·ey** \ˈtī-mē *also* ˈthī-\ *adj* **:** abounding in or fragrant with thyme

thyr- *or* **thyro-** *comb form* [*thyroid*] **:** thyroid ⟨*thyro*toxicosis⟩ ⟨*thyr*oxine⟩

thy·ra·tron \ˈthī-rə-ˌträn\ *n* [fr. *Thyratron*, a trademark] **:** a gas-filled 3-element hot-cathode electron tube in which the grid controls only the start of a continuous current

[1]thy·roid \ˈthī(ə)r-ˌȯid\ *adj* [NL *thyroides*, fr. Gk *thyreoeidēs* shield-shaped, thyroid, fr. *thyreos* shield shaped like a door, fr. *thyra* door — more at DOOR] **1 a :** of, relating to, or being a large endocrine of craniate vertebrates lying at the base of the neck and producing an iodine-containing hormone that affects esp. growth, development, and metabolic rate **b :** suggestive of a disordered thyroid ⟨a ~ personality⟩ **2 :** of, relating to, or being the chief cartilage of the larynx

[2]thyroid *n* **1 :** a thyroid gland or cartilage; *also* **:** a part (as an artery or nerve) associated with either of these **2 :** a preparation of mammalian thyroid gland used in treating thyroid disorders

thy·roid·ec·to·my \ˌthī-ˌrȯi-ˈdek-tə-mē\ *n* **:** surgical removal of thyroid gland tissue

thy·ro·tox·i·co·sis \ˌthī-(ˌ)rō-ˌtäk-sə-ˈkō-səs\ *n* [NL] **:** HYPERTHYROIDISM

thy·ro·tro·phin \thī-ˈrä-trə-fən, ˌthī-rə-ˈtrō-\ *or* **thy·ro·tro·pin** \-pən\ *n* [*thyrotrophic, thyrotropic* (influencing the activity of the thyroid gland)] **:** an anterior pituitary secretion that regulates the formation and secretion of thyroid hormone

thy·rox·ine *or* **thy·rox·in** \thī-ˈräk-ˌsēn, -sən\ *n* [ISV] **:** the active principle $C_{15}H_{11}I_4NO_4$ of the thyroid gland used to treat thyroid disorders

thyrse \ˈthərs\ *n* [NL *thyrsus*] **:** an inflorescence (as in the lilac and horse chestnut) in which the main axis is racemose and the secondary and later axes are cymose

thyr·soid \ˈthər-ˌsȯid\ *adj* **:** having somewhat the form of a thyrse ⟨a ~ panicle⟩

thyr·sus \ˈthər-səs\ *n, pl* **thyr·si** \-ˌsī, -ˌsē\ [L, fr. Gk *thyrsos*] **1 :** a staff surmounted by a pine cone or by a bunch of vine or ivy leaves with grapes or berries that is an attribute of Bacchus and of satyrs and others engaging in bacchic rites **2** [NL, fr. L] **:** THYRSE

thy·sa·nop·ter·an \ˌthī-sə-ˈnäp-tə-rən\ *n* [deriv. of Gk *thysanos* tassel + *pteron* wing — more at FEATHER] **:** any of an order (Thysanoptera) of winged insects comprising the thrips — **thysanopteran** *adj* — **thy·sa·nop·ter·ous** \-rəs\ *adj*

thy·sa·nu·ran \ˌthī-sə-ˈn(y)u̇r-ən\ *n* [deriv. of Gk *thysanos* tassel + *oura* tail — more at SQUIRREL] **:** any of an order (Thysanura) of wingless insects having projecting caudal bristles and comprising the bristletails — **thysanuran** *adj* — **thy·sa·nu·rous** \-ˈn(y)u̇r-əs\ *adj*

thy·self \t͟hī-ˈself\ *pron, archaic* **:** YOURSELF — used sometimes by Friends esp. among themselves

[1]ti \ˈtē\ *n* [Tahitian, Marquesan, Samoan, & Maori] **:** any of several Asiatic and Pacific trees or shrubs (genus *Cordyline*) of the lily family with leaves in terminal tufts

[2]ti *n* [alter. of *si*] **:** the seventh tone of the diatonic scale in solmization

ti·ara \tē-ˈar-ə, -ˈer-, -ˈär-\ *n* [L, royal Persian headdress, fr. Gk] **1 :** the pope's triple crown **2 :** a decorative jeweled or flowered headband or semicircle for formal wear by women

Ti·bet·an \tə-ˈbet-ᵊn\ *n* **1 a :** a member of the Mongoloid native race of Tibet modified in the west and south by intermixture with Indian peoples and in the east with Chinese **b :** a native or inhabitant of Tibet **2 :** the Tibeto-Burman language of the Tibetan people — **Tibetan** *adj*

Tibetan terrier *n* **:** any of a breed of terriers resembling Old English sheepdogs but having a curled well-feathered tail

Ti·beto-Bur·man \tə-ˌbet-ō-ˈbər-mən\ *n* **1 :** a language family of Asia by some included in Sino-Tibetan **2 :** a member of a people speaking a Tibeto-Burman language

tib·ia \ˈtib-ē-ə\ *n, pl* **tib·i·ae** \-ē-ˌē, -ē-ˌī\ *also* **tib·i·as** [L] **1 a :** the inner and usu. larger of the two bones of the vertebrate hind limb between the knee and ankle **b :** the fourth joint of the leg of an insect between the femur and tarsus **2 :** an ancient flute orig. fashioned from an animal's leg bone — **tib·i·al** \-ē-əl\ *adj*

tic \ˈtik\ *n* [F] **:** local and habitual spasmodic motion of particular muscles esp. of the face **:** TWITCHING

ti·cal \ti-ˈkäl, ˈtik-əl\ *n, pl* **ticals** *or* **tical** [Thai, fr. Malay *tikal*, a monetary unit] **:** BAHT

tic dou·lou·reux \ˈtik-ˌdü-lə-ˈrü, -ˈrə(r)\ *n* [F, painful twitch] **:** TRIGEMINAL NEURALGIA

[1]tick \ˈtik\ *n* [ME *tyke, teke;* akin to MHG *zeche* tick, Arm *tiz*] **1 :** any of numerous bloodsucking arachnids that form a superfamily (Ixodoidea of the order Acarina), are larger than the related mites, attach themselves to warm-blooded vertebrates to feed, and include important vectors of infectious diseases **2 :** any of various usu. wingless parasitic dipterous insects — compare SHEEP KED

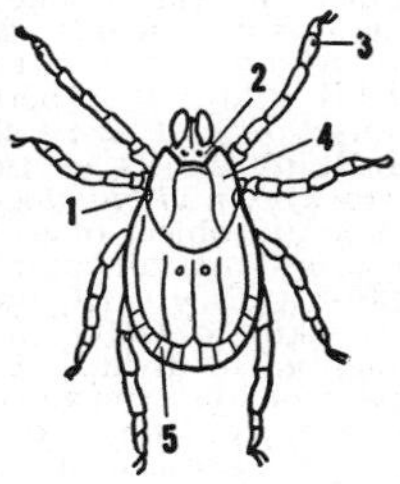

tick 2: *1* ocellus, *2* capitulum, *3* sense organ of tarsus, *4* shield, *5* festoon

[2]tick *n* [ME *tek;* akin to MHG *zic* light push] **1 a :** a light rhythmic audible tap or beat; *also* **:** a series of such ticks **b** *chiefly Brit* **:** the time taken by the tick of a clock **:** MOMENT **2 :** a small spot or mark; *esp* **:** one used to direct attention to something, to check an item on a list, or to represent a point on a scale

[3]tick *vi* **1 :** to make the sound of a tick or a series of ticks **2 :** to operate as a functioning mechanism **:** RUN ⟨tried to understand what made him ~⟩ ~ *vt* **1 :** to mark with a written tick **:** CHECK **2 :** to mark, count, or announce by or as if by ticking beats ⟨a meter ~*ing* off his cab fare⟩

[4]tick *n* [ME *tike*, prob. fr. MD; akin to OHG *ziahha* tick; both fr. a prehistoric WGmc word borrowed fr. L *theca* cover, fr. Gk *thēkē* case; akin to Gk *tithenai* to place — more at DO] **1 :** the fabric case of a mattress, pillow, or bolster; *also* **:** a mattress consisting of a tick and its filling **2 :** TICKING

[5]tick *n* [short for [1]*ticket*] **:** CREDIT, TRUST; *also* **:** a credit account ⟨bought on ~⟩

ticked \ˈtikt\ *adj* **1 :** marked with ticks **:** FLECKED **2** *of a hair* **:** banded with two or more colors

tick·er \ˈtik-ər\ *n* **:** something that ticks or produces a ticking sound: as **a :** WATCH **b :** a telegraphic receiving instrument that automatically prints off stock quotations or news on a paper ribbon **c** *slang* **:** HEART

ticker tape *n* **:** the paper ribbon on which a telegraphic ticker prints off its information

[1]tick·et \ˈtik-ət\ *n* [obs. F *etiquet* (now *étiquette*), fr. MF *estiquet*, fr. *estiquier* to attach, fr. MD *steken* to stick; akin to OHG *sticken* to prick — more at STICK] **1 a :** a document that serves as a certificate, license, or permit; *esp* **:** a mariner's or airman's certificate **b :** TAG, LABEL **2 :** a summons or warning issued to a traffic offender **3 :** a certificate or token showing that a fare or admission fee has been paid **4 :** SLATE 4b **5 :** a slip or card recording a transaction or undertaking or giving instructions

[2]ticket *vt* **1 :** to attach a ticket to **:** LABEL; *also* **:** DESIGNATE **2 :** to furnish with a ticket **:** BOOK

ticket agency *n* **:** an agency selling transportation or theater and entertainment tickets

ticket agent *n* **:** one who acts as an agent of a transportation company to sell tickets for travel by train, boat, airplane, or bus; *also* **:** one who sells theater and entertainment tickets

ticket office *n* **:** an office of a transportation company, theatrical or entertainment enterprise, or ticket agency where tickets are sold and reservations made

tick·et-of-leave \ˌtik-ət-ə(v)-ˈlēv\ *n, pl* **tickets-of-leave** \-ət-sə(v)-\ **:** a license or permit formerly given in the United Kingdom and the British Commonwealth to a convict under imprisonment to go at large and to labor for himself subject to certain specific conditions

tick fever *n* **1 :** a febrile disease (as Rocky Mountain spotted fever) transmitted by the bites of ticks **2 :** TEXAS FEVER

tick·icide \ˈtik-ə-ˌsīd\ *n* **:** an agent used to kill ticks

[1]tick·ing \ˈtik-iŋ\ *n* [[4]*tick*] **:** a strong linen or cotton fabric used in upholstering and as a mattress covering

[2]ticking *n* [[2]*tick*] **:** ticked marking on a bird or mammal or on individual hairs

[1]tick·le \ˈtik-əl\ *vb* **tick·ling** \-(ə-)liŋ\ [ME *tikelen;* akin to OE *tinclian* to tickle] *vi* **1 :** to have a tingling or prickling sensation ⟨my back ~*s*⟩ **2 :** to excite the surface nerves to prickle ~ *vt* **1 a :** to excite or stir up agreeably **:** PLEASE **b :** to provoke to laughter or merriment **:** AMUSE **2 :** to touch (as a body part) lightly so as to excite the surface nerves and cause uneasiness, laughter, or spasmodic movements **syn** see PLEASE

[2]tickle *n* **1 :** something that tickles **2 :** a tickling sensation **3 :** the act of tickling

tick·ler \-(ə-)lər\ *n* **1 :** a person or device that tickles **2 :** a

device for jogging the memory; *specif* : a file that serves as a reminder and is arranged to bring matters to timely attention
tickler coil *n* : a small coil connected in series with the plate circuit of an electron tube and inductively coupled with its grid circuit to return a part of the amplified signal for repeated amplification
tick·lish \'tik-(ə-)lish\ *adj* **1** : sensitive to tickling **2 a** : TOUCHY, OVERSENSITIVE **b** : easily overturned : UNSTABLE ⟨a canoe is ~ to handle⟩ **3** : requiring delicate handling : CRITICAL ⟨a ~ subject⟩ — **tick·lish·ly** *adv* — **tick·lish·ness** *n*
tick·seed \'tik-,sēd\ *n* [¹*tick*] **1** : COREOPSIS **2** : TICK TREFOIL
tick·tack *or* **tic·tac** \'tik-,tak\ *n* [imit.] **1** : a ticking or tapping beat like that of a clock or watch **2** : a contrivance used by children to tap on a window from a distance
tick·tack·toe *also* **tic–tac–toe** \,tik-,tak-'tō\ *n* [*tic-tac-toe* (former game in which players with eyes shut brought a pencil down on a slate marked with numbers and scored the number hit)] : a game in which two players alternately put crosses and ciphers in compartments of a figure formed by two vertical lines crossing two horizontal lines and each tries to get a row of three crosses or three ciphers before the opponent does
tick·tock \'tik-'täk, -,täk\ *n* [imit.] : the ticking sound of a clock
tick trefoil *n* [¹*tick*] : any of various leguminous plants (genus *Desmodium*) with trifoliolate leaves and rough sticky loments
tid·al \'tīd-ᵊl\ *adj* **1** : of or relating to tides : periodically rising and falling or flowing and ebbing ⟨~ waters⟩ **2** : dependent (as to the time of arrival or departure) upon the state of the tide ⟨~ steamer⟩ — **tid·al·ly** \-ᵊl-ē\ *adv*
tidal wave *n* **1 a** : an unusually high sea wave that sometimes follows an earthquake **b** : an unusual rise of water alongshore due to strong winds **2** : something overwhelming (as a sweeping majority vote or an irresistible impulse)
tid·bit \'tid-,bit\ *n* [perh. fr. *tit-* (as in *titmouse*) + *bit*] **1** : a choice morsel of food **2** : a choice or pleasing bit (as of news)
tid·dle·dy·winks *or* **tid·dly·winks** \'tid-ᵊl-(d)ē-,wiŋ(k)s, 'tid-lē-,wiŋ(k)s\ *n pl but sing in constr* [prob. fr. E dial. *tiddly* little] : a game the object of which is to snap small disks from a flat surface into a small container
¹tide \'tīd\ *n* [ME, time, fr. OE *tīd;* akin to OHG *zīt* time, Gk *daiesthai* to divide] **1 a** *obs* : a space of time : PERIOD **b** : a fit or opportune time : OPPORTUNITY **c** : an ecclesiastical anniversary or festival or its season **2 a** (1) : the alternate rising and falling of the surface of the ocean and of water bodies (as gulfs and bays) connected with the ocean that occurs twice a day and is caused by the gravitational attraction of the sun and moon occurring unequally on different parts of the earth (2) : a less marked rising and falling of an inland body of water **b** : FLOOD TIDE **3** : something that fluctuates like the tides of the sea : VICISSITUDE **4 a** : a flowing stream : CURRENT **b** : the waters of the ocean **c** : the overflow of a flooding stream : FLOODWATERS

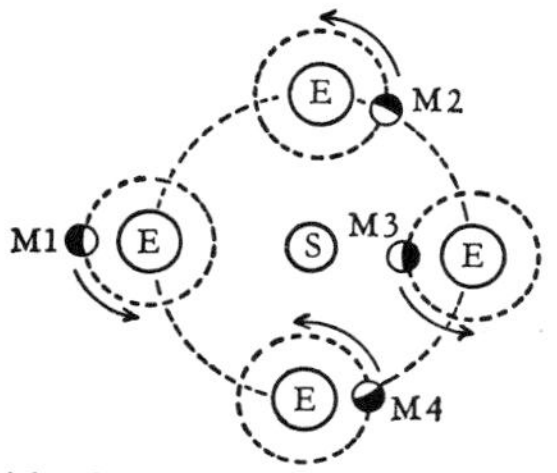

tides 2a(1): M1 and M3 position of moon at spring tides; M2 and M4 moon at neap tide

²tide *vi* **1** : to flow as or in a tide : SURGE **2** : to drift with the tide esp. in navigating a ship into or out of an anchorage, harbor, or river ~ *vt* **1 a** : to cause to float with the tide **b** : to enable to surmount or endure a difficulty — used with *over* ⟨the gift *tided* him over⟩ ⟨money to ~ him over the emergency⟩ **2** : to proceed along (one's way) by taking advantage of tides
³tide *vi* [ME *tiden*, fr. OE *tīdan;* akin to MD *tiden* to go, come, OE *tīd* time] *archaic* : BETIDE, BEFALL
tide·land \-,land, -lənd\ *n* **1** : land overflowed during flood tide **2** : land underlying the ocean and lying beyond the low-water limit of the tide but being within the territorial waters of a nation — often used in pl.
tide·less \-ləs\ *adj* : having no tides ⟨a ~ sea⟩
tide·mark \-,märk\ *n* **1 a** : a high-water or sometimes low-water mark left by tidal water or a flood **b** : a mark placed to indicate this point **2** : the point to which something has attained or below which it has receded
tide table *n* : a table that indicates the height of the tide at one place at different times of day throughout one year
tide·wait·er \'tī-,dwāt-ər\ *n* : a customs inspector working on the docks or aboard ships
tide·wa·ter \'tī-,dwȯt-ər, -,dwät-\ *n* **1** : water overflowing land at flood tide; *also* : water affected by the ebb and flow of the tide **2** : low-lying coastal land
tide·way \'tī-,dwā\ *n* : a channel in which the tide runs
ti·di·ly \'tīd-ᵊl-ē\ *adv* : in a tidy manner
ti·di·ness \'tīd-ē-nəs\ *n* : the quality or state of being tidy
tid·ing \'tīd-iŋ\ *n* [ME, fr. OE *tīdung*, fr. *tīdan* to betide] : a piece of news — usu. used in pl. ⟨good ~*s*⟩
¹ti·dy \'tīd-ē\ *adj* [ME, fr. *tide* time] **1** : properly filled out : PLUMP **2** : ADEQUATE, SATISFACTORY; *also* : DECENT, FAIR **3 a** : neat and orderly in appearance or habits : well ordered and cared for **b** : METHODICAL, PRECISE ⟨~ mind⟩ **4** : LARGE, SUBSTANTIAL ⟨a ~ price⟩ **syn** see NEAT
²tidy *vt* : to put in order ⟨~ up a room⟩ ~ *vi* : to make things tidy ⟨~*ing* up after supper⟩
³tidy *n* **1** : a piece of fancywork used to protect the back, arms, or headrest of a chair or sofa from wear or soil **2** : a receptacle for sewing materials or odds and ends
ti·dy·tips \'tīd-ē-,tips\ *n pl but sing or pl in constr* : an annual California composite herb (*Layia platyglossa*) having yellow-rayed flower heads often tipped with white
¹tie \'tī\ *n* [ME *teg, tye*, fr. OE *tēag;* akin to ON *taug* rope, OE *tēon* to pull — more at TOW] **1 a** : a line, ribbon, or cord used for fastening, uniting, or drawing something closed; *esp* : SHOELACE **b** (1) : a structural element (as a rod or angle iron) holding two pieces together : a tension member in a construction (2) : one of the transverse supports to which railroad rails are fastened to keep them to line **2** : something that serves as a connecting link: as **a** : a moral or legal obligation to someone or something typically constituting a restraining power, influence, or duty **b** : a bond of kinship or affection **3** : a curved line that joins two musical notes indicating the same pitch used to denote a single tone sustained through the time value of the two **4 a** : an equality in number (as of votes or scores) **b** : equality in a contest; *also* : a contest that ends in a draw **5** : a method or style of tying or knotting **6** : something that is knotted or is to be knotted when worn: as **a** : NECKTIE **b** : a low laced shoe : OXFORD
²tie *vb* **tied; ty·ing** \'tī-iŋ\ *or* **tie·ing** *vt* **1 a** : to fasten, attach, or close by means of a tie **b** : to form a knot or bow in ⟨~ your scarf⟩ **c** : to make by tying constituent elements ⟨*tied* a wreath⟩ ⟨~ a fishing fly⟩ **2 a** : to unite in marriage **b** : to unite (musical notes) by a tie **c** : to join electrically (two power systems) **3** : to restrain from independence or freedom of action or choice : constrain by or as if by authority, influence, agreement, or obligation **4 a** : to make or have an equal score with in a contest **b** : to come up with something equal to : EQUAL ~ *vi* : to make a tie: as **a** : to make a bond or connection **b** : to make an equal score **c** : ATTACH **d** : to close by means of a tie — **tie into** : to attack with vigor
tie·back \'tī-,bak\ *n* **1** : a decorative strip or device of cloth, cord, or metal for draping a curtain to the side of a window **2** : a curtain with a tieback — usu. used in pl.
tie in *vt* : to bring into connection with something relevant: as **a** : to make the final connection of ⟨*tied in* the new branch pipeline⟩ **b** : to coordinate in such a manner as to produce balance and unity ⟨the illustrations were cleverly *tied in* with the text⟩ **c** : to use as a tie-in esp. in advertising ~ *vi* : to become tied in
tie–in \'tī-,in\ *n* : something that ties in, relates, or connects
tie·mann·ite \'tē-mə-,nīt\ *n* [G *tiemannit*, fr. W. *Tiemann*, 19th cent. G scientist who discovered it] : a mineral HgSe that consists of mercuric selenide and occurs in dark gray or nearly black masses of metallic luster
tie·pin \'tī-,pin\ *n* : an ornamental straight pin that has usu. a jeweled head and a sheath for the point and is used to hold the ends of a necktie in place
¹tier \'ti(ə)r\ *n* [MF *tire* rank] : a row, rank, or layer of articles; *esp* : one of two or more rows arranged one above another
²tier *vt* : to place or arrange in tiers ~ *vi* : to rise in tiers
¹tierce \'ti(ə)rs\ *var of* TERCE
²tierce *n* [ME *terce, tierce*, fr. MF, fr. fem. of *terz*, adj., third, fr. L *tertius* — more at THIRD] **1** *obs* : THIRD 1 **2** : any of various units of liquid capacity equal to ⅓ pipe; *esp* : a unit equal to 42 gallons **3** : a sequence of three playing cards of the same suit **4** : the third of the eight defensive positions in fencing
tier·cel \'ti(ə)r-səl\ *n* [ME *tercel*, fr. MF, fr. (assumed) VL *tertiolus*, fr. dim. of L *tertius* third] : a male hawk
tiered \'ti(ə)rd\ *adj* : having or arranged in tiers, rows, or layers — used chiefly in combination ⟨triple-*tiered*⟩
tier table *n* : a small table or stand with two or more usu. round tops arranged one above another
tie silk *n* : a silk fabric of firm resilient pliable texture used for neckties and for blouses and accessories
tie tack *n* : an ornamented pin whose point holds a necktie to a shirt and fits into a receiving button or snap underneath
tie up *vt* **1** : to attach, fasten, or bind securely; *also* : to wrap up and fasten **2 a** : to connect closely : JOIN **b** : to cause to be linked so as to depend on something **3 a** : to place or invest in such a manner as to make unavailable for other purposes **b** : to restrain from operation or progress ⟨traffic was *tied up* for miles⟩ ~ *vi* **1** : DOCK ⟨the ferry *ties up* at the south slip⟩ **2** : to assume a definite relationship ⟨this *ties up* with what you were told before⟩
tie–up \'tī-,əp\ *n* **1 a** : a mooring place for a boat **b** : a cow stable; *also* : a space for a single cow in a stable **2** : a suspension of traffic or business (as by a strike or lockout or a mechanical breakdown) **3** : CONNECTION, ASSOCIATION ⟨a helpful financial ~⟩
¹tiff \'tif\ *n* [origin unknown] : a petty quarrel **syn** see QUARREL
²tiff *vi* : to have a minor quarrel
tif·fa·ny \'tif-ə-nē\ *n* [prob. fr. obs. F *tiphanie* Epiphany, fr. LL *theophania*, fr. LGk, deriv. of Gk *theos* god + *phainein* to show] **1** : a sheer silk gauze formerly used for clothing and trimmings **2** : a plain-weave open-mesh cotton fabric (as cheesecloth)
¹tif·fin \'tif-ən\ *n* [prob. alter. of *tiffing*, gerund of obs. E *tiff* (to eat between meals)] : a midday meal : LUNCHEON
²tiffin *vi* : to take tiffin : LUNCH
ti·ger \'tī-gər\ *n, pl* **tigers** [ME *tigre*, fr. OE *tiger* & OF *tigre*, both fr. L *tigris*, fr. Gk, of Iranian origin; akin to Av *tighra-* pointed; akin to Gk *stizein* to tattoo — more at STICK] **1** *pl also* **tiger a** : a large Asiatic carnivorous mammal (*Felis tigris*) of the cat family having a tawny coat transversely striped with black **b** : any of several large wildcats (as the jaguar or cougar) **c** : a domestic cat with striped pattern **d** *Austral* : TASMANIAN WOLF **e** : any of several strong vigorous aggressive fishes **2 a** : a representation of a tiger as the emblem of an organization **b** *often cap* : any of several organizations having a tiger as emblem **3** : a fierce and bloodthirsty person or quality ⟨aroused the ~ in him⟩ **4** *Brit* : a groom in livery; *esp* : a young or small groom **5** : a yell often of the word *tiger* that ends a round of cheering
tiger beetle *n* : any of numerous active carnivorous beetles (family Cicindelidae) having larvae that tunnel in the soil
tiger cat *n* **1** : any of various wildcats (as the serval, ocelot, or margay) of moderate size and variegated coloration **2** : a striped or sometimes blotched tabby cat
ti·ger·eye \'tī-gə-,rī\ *also* **ti·ger's–eye** \-gər-,zī\ *n* : a usu. yellow-brown chatoyant stone that is much used for ornament and is a silicified crocidolite
ti·ger·ish \'tī-g(ə-)rish\ *adj* : of, relating to, or resembling a tiger — **ti·ger·ish·ly** *adv* — **ti·ger·ish·ness** *n*
ti·ger·like \'tī-gər-,līk\ *adj* : having the ways or appearance of a tiger
tiger lily *n* : a common Asiatic garden lily (*Lilium tigrinum*) having nodding orange-colored flowers densely spotted with black; *also* : any of various lilies with similar flowers
tiger moth *n* : any of a family (Arctiidae) of stout-bodied moths usu. with broad striped or spotted wings
¹tight \'tīt\ *adj* [ME, alter. of *thight*, of Scand origin; akin to ON *thēttr* tight; akin to MHG *dīhte* thick, Skt *tanakti* it causes to coagulate] **1** : of firm compact texture **2** : so close in structure as not to permit passage of a liquid or gas or light ⟨a ~ roof⟩ **3 a** : fixed very firmly in place ⟨loosen a ~ jar cover⟩ **b** : not slack or loose : TAUT ⟨~ drumhead⟩ ⟨~ knot⟩ **c** : fitting usu. too closely (as for comfort) ⟨~ shoe⟩ **4** : set close together : COMPACT ⟨~ defensive formation⟩ **5 a** : CAPABLE, ALERT, READY **b** (1) : trim

and tidy in dress (2) : neat and orderly in arrangement or design : SNUG **6** : difficult to get through or out of : TRYING, EXACTING ⟨in a ~ corner⟩ **7 a** : firm in control ⟨kept a ~ hand on all his affairs⟩ **b** : STINGY, MISERLY **8** : evenly contested : CLOSE ⟨~ tennis match⟩ **9** : packed or compressed to the limit : entirely full ⟨~ bale⟩ **10** : INTOXICATED, DRUNK **11 a** : highly condensed ⟨~ literary style⟩ **b** : closely spaced ⟨a ~ line of print⟩ **12 a** : scantily supplied or obtainable in proportion to demand ⟨~ money⟩ **b** : characterized by such a scarcity ⟨~ labor market⟩ **13** *of lumber* : sound and free from checks ⟨logs with ~ hearts⟩ — **tight·ly** *adv* — **tight·ness** *n*

syn TIGHT, TAUT, TENSE mean drawn or stretched to the limit. TIGHT commonly implies close constriction effecting immobility or impenetrability; TAUT suggests the pulling of a rope or fabric until there is no give or slack; TENSE adds to TAUT the idea of strain inhibiting normal functioning **syn** see in addition DRUNK

²**tight** *adv* **1** : TIGHTLY, FIRMLY, HARD ⟨door was shut ~⟩ **2** : SOUNDLY ⟨sleep ~⟩

tight·en \'tīt-ᵊn\ *vb* **tight·en·ing** \'tīt-niŋ, -ᵊn-iŋ\ *vt* : to make tight or tighter ~ *vi* : to become tight or tighter — **tight·en·er** \-nər, -ᵊn-ər\ *n*

tight·fist·ed \'tīt-'fis-təd\ *adj* : MISERLY, STINGY **syn** see STINGY

tight–lipped \-'lipt\ *adj* **1** : having the lips closed tight (as in determination) **2** : TACITURN **syn** see SILENT

tight–mouthed \-'mau̇t͟hd, -'mau̇tht\ *adj* : CLOSEMOUTHED

tight·rope \'tīt-,rōp\ *n* : a rope or wire stretched taut for acrobats to perform on

tights \'tīts\ *n pl* : skintight garments covering the body from the neck down or from the waist down

tight·wad \'tīt-,wäd\ *n* : a close or miserly person

tight·wire \-,wī(ə)r\ *n* : a tightrope made of wire

ti·gon \'tī-gən\ *n* [*tiger* + *lion*] : a hybrid between a male tiger and a female lion

ti·gress \'tī-grəs\ *n* : a female tiger; *also* : a tigerish woman

Ti·gri·nya \tə-'grē-nyə\ *n* : a Semitic language of northern Ethiopia

tike *var of* TYKE

ti·ki \'tē-kē\ *n* [Maori & Marquesan] **1** *cap* : the creator of mankind in Polynesian myth **2** : a wood or stone image of a Polynesian supernatural power

til \'til\ *n* [Hindi, fr. Skt *tila*] : SESAME

til·bury \'til-,ber-ē, -b(ə-)rē\ *n* [*Tilbury*, 19th cent. E coach builder] : a light two-wheeled carriage : GIG

til·de \'til-də\ *n* [Sp, fr. L *titulus* sign, title] **1** : a mark ~ placed esp. over the letter *n* (as in Spanish *señor* sir) to denote the sound \nʸ\ or over vowels (as in Portuguese *irmã* sister) to indicate nasality **2** : the mark ~ used in logic and mathematics to indicate negation

¹**tile** \'tī(ə)l\ *n* [ME, fr. OE *tigele;* akin to ON *tigl* tile; both fr. a prehistoric WGmc-NGmc word borrowed fr. L *tegula* tile; akin to L *tegere* to cover — more at THATCH] **1** *pl* **tiles** *or* **tile a** : a flat or curved piece of fired clay, stone, or concrete used esp. for roofs, floors, or walls and often for ornamental work **b** : a hollow or a semicircular and open earthenware or concrete piece used in constructing a drain **c** : a hollow building unit made of burned clay or shale or of gypsum **2** : TILING **3** : HAT; *esp* : a high silk hat **4** : a thin piece of resilient material (as an asphalt composition, cork, linoleum, or rubber) used esp. for covering floors or walls

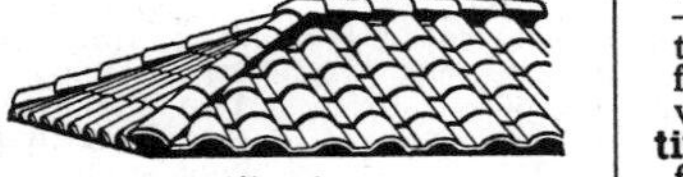

tiles 1a

²**tile** *vt* **1** : to cover with tiles **2** : to install drainage tile in — **til·er** *n*

tile·fish \'tī(ə)l-,fish\ *n* [*tile-* modif. of NL *Lopholatilus*, genus name] : a large violet percoid food fish (*Lopholatilus chamaeleonticeps*) of deep waters with a fleshy appendage on the head and large round yellow spots

til·ing \'tī-liŋ\ *n* **1** : the act of one who tiles **2 a** : TILES **b** : a surface of tiles

¹**till** \tᵊl, təl, (,)til\ *prep* [ME, fr. OE *til;* akin to ON *til* to, till, OE *til* good] **1** *chiefly Scot* : TO **2** : UNTIL

²**till** *conj* : UNTIL

³**till** \'til\ *vt* [ME *tilien, tillen*, fr. OE *tilian;* akin to OE *til* good, suitable, OHG *zil* goal] : to work by plowing, sowing, and raising crops from : CULTIVATE — **till·able** \-ə-bəl\ *adj*

⁴**till** \'til\ *n* [AF *tylle*] **1** : a box, drawer, or tray in a cabinet or chest used esp. for valuables **2** : a money drawer in a store or bank

⁵**till** \'til\ *n* [origin unknown] : unstratified glacial drift consisting of clay, sand, gravel and boulders intermingled

till·age \'til-ij\ *n* **1** : the operation of tilling land **2** : cultivated land

til·land·sia \tə-'lan(d)-zē-ə\ *n* [NL, genus name, fr. Elias *Tillands* †1693 Finn botanist] : any of a very large genus (*Tillandsia*) of chiefly epiphytic plants of the pineapple family native to tropical and subtropical America

¹**till·er** \'til-ər\ *n* : one that tills : CULTIVATOR

²**til·ler** \'til-ər\ *n* [ME *tiler* stock of a crossbow, fr. MF *telier*, lit., beam of a loom, fr. ML *telarium*, fr. L *tela* web — more at TOIL] : a lever used to turn the rudder of a boat from side to side

³**til·ler** *n* [fr. (assumed) ME, fr. OE *telgor, telgra* twig, shoot; akin to OHG *zelga* twig, Gk *daidalos* ingeniously formed — more at CONDOLE] : SPROUT, STALK; *esp* : one from the base of a plant or from the axils of its lower leaves

⁴**tiller** *vi* **til·ler·ing** \'til-(ə-)riŋ\ *of a plant* : to put forth tillers

til·ler·man \'til-ər-mən\ *n* : one in charge of a tiller

¹**tilt** \'tilt\ *vb* [ME *tulten, tilten;* akin to Sw *tulta* to waddle] *vt* **1** : to cause to slope : INCLINE **2 a** : to point or thrust in or as if in a tilt ⟨~ a lance⟩ **b** : to charge against ⟨~ an adversary⟩ ~ *vi* **1** : to move or shift so as to lean or incline : SLANT **2 a** : to engage in a combat with lances : JOUST **b** : to make an impetuous attack ⟨~ at wrongs⟩ — **tilt·er** *n*

²**tilt** *n* **1 a** : a military exercise on horseback in which two combatants charging with lances or similar weapons try to unhorse each other : JOUST **b** : a tournament of tilts **2 a** : a verbal contest between disputants : CONTENTION **b** : SPEED — used in the phrase *at full tilt* **3 a** : the act of tilting : the state or position of being tilted **b** : a sloping surface **4** : any of various sports resembling or suggesting tilting with lances; *esp* : a water sport in which the contestants stand on logs or in canoes or boats and thrust with poles — **tilt** *adj*

³**tilt** *n* [ME *teld, telte* tent, canopy, fr. OE *teld;* akin to OHG *zelt* tent] : a canopy for a wagon, boat, or stall

⁴**tilt** *vt* : to cover or provide with a tilt

tilth \'tilth\ *n* [ME, fr. OE, fr. *tilian* to till] **1** : cultivation of the soil **2** : cultivated land : TILLAGE **3** : the state of being tilled

tilt·me·ter \'tilt-,mēt-ər\ *n* : an instrument to measure the tilting of the earth's surface

tilt·yard \'tilt-,yärd\ *n* : a yard or place for tilting

tim·bal \'tim-bəl\ *n* [F *timbale*, fr. MF, alter. of *tamballe*, modif. of OSp *atabal*, fr. Ar *aṭ-ṭabl* the drum] : KETTLEDRUM

tim·bale \'tim-bəl\ *n* [F, lit., kettledrum] **1** : a creamy mixture (as of chicken, lobster, cheese, or fish) cooked in a drum-shaped mold **2** : a small pastry shell filled with a cooked timbale mixture

¹**tim·ber** \'tim-bər\ *n* [ME, fr. OE, building, wood; akin to OHG *zimbar* room, wood, L *domus* house, Gk *demein* to build] **1** : growing trees or their wood ⟨standing ~⟩ **2** : wood suitable for building or for carpentry **3** : MATERIAL, STUFF **4 a** : a large squared or dressed piece of wood ready for use or forming part of a structure **b** *Brit* : ²LUMBER 2a **c** : a curving frame branching outward from the keel of a ship and bending upward in a vertical direction that is usu. composed of several pieces united : RIB — **timber** *adj* — **tim·ber·man** \-mən, -,man\ *n*

²**timber** *vt* **tim·ber·ing** \-b(ə-)riŋ\ : to frame, cover, or support with timbers

tim·ber·doo·dle \,tim-bər-'düd-ᵊl\ *n* [¹*timber* + *doodle* (cock)] : the American woodcock

tim·bered \'tim-bərd\ *adj* **1 a** : furnished with, made of, or covered with timber **b** : having walls framed by exposed timbers **2** : having a specified structure or constitution **3** : covered with growing timber : WOODED

tim·ber·head \'tim-bər-,hed\ *n* **1** : the top end of a ship's timber used above the gunwale (as for belaying ropes) **2** : a bollard bolted to the deck where the end of a timber would come

timber hitch *n* : a knot used to secure a line to a log or spar

tim·ber·ing \'tim-b(ə-)riŋ\ *n* : a set of timbers : TIMBERWORK

tim·ber·land \-bər-,land\ *n* : wooded land esp. with marketable timber

tim·ber·line \-,līn\ *n* : the upper limit of arboreal growth in mountains or high latitudes

timber right *n* : ownership of standing timber without ownership of the land

tim·ber·work \'tim-bər-,wərk\ *n* : a timber construction

tim·bre \'tam-bər, 'tim-\ *n* [F, fr. MF, bell struck by a hammer, fr. OF, drum, fr. MGk *tymbanon* kettledrum, fr. Gk *tympanon* — more at TYMPANUM] : the quality given to a sound by its overtones: as **a** : the resonance by which the ear recognizes and identifies a voiced speech sound **b** : the tone distinctive of a singing voice or a musical instrument

tim·brel \'tim-brəl\ *n* [dim. of obs. E *timbre* tambourine, fr. ME, fr. OF, drum] : a small hand drum or tambourine — **tim·brelled** \-brəld\ *adj*

¹**time** \'tīm\ *n* [ME, fr. OE *tīma;* akin to ON *tīmi* time, OE *tīd* — more at TIDE] **1 a** : the measured or measurable period during which an action, process, or condition exists or continues : DURATION **b** : LEISURE ⟨~ for reading⟩ **2** : the point or period when something occurs : OCCASION **3** : an appointed, fixed, or customary moment or hour for something to happen, begin, or end **4 a** : an historical period : AGE **b** : a division of geologic chronology **c** : conditions at present or at some specified period ⟨~*s* are hard⟩ ⟨move with the ~*s*⟩ **d** : the present time ⟨issues of the ~⟩ **5 a** : LIFETIME **b** : a period of apprenticeship **c** : a term of military service **d** : a prison sentence **6** : SEASON **7 a** : rate of speed : TEMPO **b** : the grouping of the beats of music : RHYTHM **8 a** : a moment, hour, day, or year as indicated by a clock or calendar ⟨what ~ is it⟩ **b** : any of various systems (as sidereal or solar) of reckoning time **9 a** : one of a series of recurring instances or repeated actions ⟨you've been told many ~*s*⟩ **b** *pl* : multiplied instances ⟨five ~*s* greater⟩ **c** : TURN ⟨three ~*s* at bat⟩ **10** : finite as contrasted with infinite duration **11** : a person's experience during a specified period or on a particular occasion ⟨a good ~⟩ **12 a** : the hours or days occupied by one's work ⟨make up ~⟩ **b** : an hourly pay rate ⟨straight ~⟩ **c** : wages paid at discharge or resignation ⟨pick up your ~ and get out⟩ **13 a** : the playing time of a game **b** : TIME-OUT **syn** see OPPORTUNITY

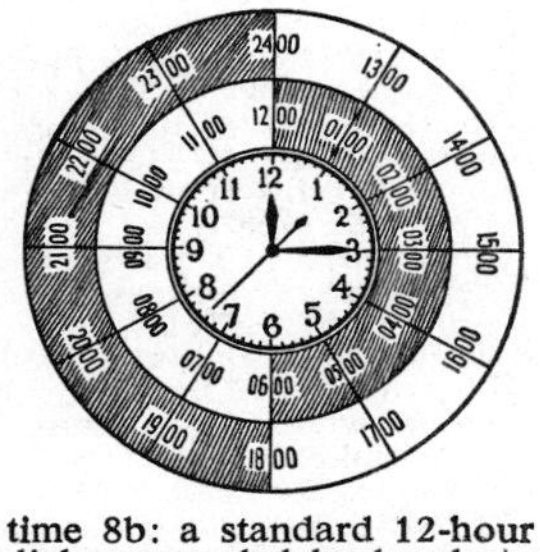

time 8b: a standard 12-hour dial surrounded by bands to show equivalent 24-hour time

²**time** *vt* **1 a** : to arrange or set the time of : SCHEDULE **b** : to regulate (a watch) to keep correct time **2** : to set the tempo, speed, or duration of **3** : to cause to keep time with something **4** : to determine or record the time, duration, or rate of **5** : to dispose (as a mechanical part) so that an action occurs at a desired instant or in a desired way ~ *vi* : to keep or beat time : move in time

³**time** *adj* **1 a** : of or relating to time **b** : recording time **2** : timed to ignite or explode at a specific moment ⟨~ charge⟩ **3 a** : payable on a specified future day or a certain length of time after presentation for acceptance **b** : based on installment payments ⟨~ sale⟩

time and a half *n* : payment of a worker (as for overtime or holiday work) at one and a half times his regular wage rate

time bill *n* : a bill of exchange payable at a definite future time

time capsule *n* : a container holding historical records or objects representative of current culture that is deposited (as in a cornerstone) for preservation until discovery by some future age

time card *n* : a card used with a time clock to record an employee's starting and quitting times each day or on each job

time chart *n* : a chart showing the standard times in various parts of the world with reference to a specified time at a specified place

time clock *n* : a clock that stamps an employee's starting and quitting times on his time card

time–con·sum·ing \'tīm-kən-'sü-miŋ\ *adj* **1** : using or taking up a great deal of time ⟨~ chores⟩ **2** : wasteful of time ⟨~ tactics⟩

timed \'tīmd\ *adj* **1** : made to occur at or in a set time ⟨a ~ explosion⟩ **2** : done or taking place at a time of a specified sort ⟨an ill-*timed* arrival⟩

time deposit *n* : a bank deposit payable a specified number of days after deposit or upon advance notice to the bank

time draft *n* : a draft payable a specified number of days after date of the draft or presentation to the drawee

time exposure *n* : exposure of a photographic film for a definite time usu. of more than one half second; *also* : a photograph taken by such exposure

time–hon·ored \'tī-,män-ərd\ *adj* : honored because of age or long usage

time immemorial *n* **1** : a time antedating a period legally fixed as the basis for a custom or right **2** : time so long past as to be indefinite in history or tradition — called also *time out of mind*

time·keep·er \'tīm-,kē-pər\ *n* **1** : TIMEPIECE **2** : a clerk who keeps records of the time worked by employees **3** : one appointed to mark and announce the time in an athletic game or contest — **time·keep·ing** \-piŋ\ *n*

time killer *n* **1** : a person with time on his hands **2** : something that passes the time : DIVERSION

time–lapse \-,laps\ *adj* : of, relating to, or constituting a motion picture made so that when projected a slow action (as the opening of a flower bud) appears to be speeded up

time·less \'tīm-ləs\ *adj* **1** *archaic* : PREMATURE, UNTIMELY **2 a** : having no beginning or end : UNENDING **b** : not restricted to a particular time or date : DATELESS **3** : not affected by time : AGELESS — **time·less·ly** *adv* — **time·less·ness** *n*

time·li·ness \-lē-nəs\ *n* : the quality or state of being timely

time loan *n* : a loan with a definite maturity date

time lock *n* : a lock controlled by clockwork to prevent its being opened before a set time

1**time·ly** \'tīm-lē\ *adv* **1** *archaic* : EARLY, SOON **2** : in time : OPPORTUNELY

2**timely** *adj* **1** : coming early or at the right time : OPPORTUNE **2** : appropriate or adapted to the times or the occasion ⟨a ~ book⟩ **syn** see SEASONABLE

time money *n* : money loaned or available to be loaned for a specified period of time

time note *n* : a note payable at a specified time

time·ous \'tī-məs\ *adj* : TIMELY — **time·ous·ly** *adv*

time–out \'tī-'maůt\ *n* : a suspension of play in an athletic game

time·piece \'tīm-,pēs\ *n* : a device (as a clock or watch) to measure or show progress of time

time·pleas·er \-,plē-zər\ *n, obs* : TIMESERVER

tim·er \'tī-mər\ *n* : one that times: as **a** : TIMEPIECE; *esp* : a stopwatch for timing races **b** : TIMEKEEPER **c** : a device in the ignition system of an internal-combustion engine that causes the spark to be produced in the cylinder at the correct time **d** : a device (as a clock) that indicates by a sound the end of an interval of time or that starts or stops a device at predetermined times

times \,tīmz, təmz\ *prep* : multiplied by ⟨two ~ two is four⟩

time–sav·er \'tīm-,sā-vər\ *n* : something that saves time

time·sav·ing \-viŋ\ *adj* : intended or serving to expedite something

time·serv·er \-,sər-vər\ *n* : a person obsequious to the manners of his time or to his superiors — **time·serv·ing** \-viŋ\ *adj or n*

time–shar·ing \-,she(ə)r-iŋ, -,sha(ə)r-\ *n* : simultaneous access to a computer by many users whose programs are interspersed and processed rapidly

time sheet *n* **1** : a sheet for recording the time of arrival and departure of workers and for recording the amount of time spent on each job **2** : a sheet for summarizing hours worked by each worker during a pay period

time signature *n* : a fractional sign placed just after the key signature whose denominator indicates the kind of note (as a quarter note) taken as the time unit for the beat and whose numerator indicates the number of these to the measure

time·ta·ble \'tīm-,tā-bəl\ *n* **1** : a table of departure and arrival times of trains, buses, or airplanes **2** : a schedule showing a planned order or sequence

time·work \-,wərk\ *n* : work paid for at a standard rate for the hour or the day — **time·work·er** *n*

time·worn \-,wō(ə)rn, -,wȯ(ə)rn\ *adj* **1** : worn or impaired by time **2 a** : AGE-OLD, ANCIENT **b** : HACKNEYED, STALE ⟨a ~ joke⟩

time zone *n* : a geographical region within which the same standard time is used

tim·id \'tim-əd\ *adj* [L *timidus*, fr. *timēre* to fear] : lacking in courage or self-confidence : FEARFUL — **ti·mid·i·ty** \tə-'mid-ət-ē\ *n* — **tim·id·ly** \'tim-əd-lē\ *adv* — **tim·id·ness** *n*

syn TIMOROUS: TIMID implies fearfulness of venturing into the unknown or the uncertain; TIMOROUS implies a habitual domination by fear and a shrinking from decision or independence of action

tim·ing *n* **1** : selection for maximum effect of the precise moment for beginning or doing something **2** : observation and recording (as by a stopwatch) of the elapsed time of an act, action, or process

ti·moc·ra·cy \tī-'mäk-rə-sē\ *n* [MF *tymocracie*, fr. ML *timocratia*, fr. Gk *timokratia*, fr. *timē* price, value, honor + *-kratia* -cracy — more at PAIN] **1** : government based on wealth **2** : government based on love of honor — **ti·mo·crat·ic** \,tī-mə-'krat-ik\ *adj* — **ti·mo·crat·i·cal** \-i-kəl\ *adj*

tim·o·rous \'tim-(ə-)rəs\ *adj* [ME, fr. MF *timoureus*, fr. ML *timorosus*, fr. L *timor* fear, fr. *timēre* to fear] **1** : of a timid disposition : AFRAID **2** : expressing or suggesting timidity ⟨a ~ bearing⟩ **syn** see TIMID — **tim·o·rous·ly** *adv* — **tim·o·rous·ness** *n*

tim·o·thy \'tim-ə-thē\ *n* [prob. after *Timothy* Hanson, 18th cent. Am farmer said to have introduced it from New England to the southern states] : a European grass (*Phleum pratense*) with long cylindrical spikes widely grown for hay

Tim·o·thy \'tim-ə-thē\ *n* [L *Timotheus*, fr. Gk *Timotheos*] : a disciple of the apostle Paul

tim·pa·ni \'tim-pə-nē\ *n pl but sing or pl in constr* [It, pl. of *timpano* kettledrum, fr. L *tympanum* drum — more at TYMPANUM] : a set of two or three kettledrums played by one performer in an orchestra or band — **tim·pa·nist** \-nəst\ *n*

1**tin** \'tin\ *n, often attrib* [ME, fr. OE; akin to OHG *zin* tin] **1** : a soft faintly bluish white lustrous low-melting crystalline metallic element that is malleable and ductile at ordinary temperatures and that is used as a protective coating in tinfoil and in soft solders and alloys — see ELEMENT table **2 a** : a box, can, pan, vessel, or a sheet made of tinplate **b** : a vacuum-sealed can holding food

2**tin** *vt* **tinned; tin·ning** **1** : to cover or plate with tin or a tin alloy **2** *chiefly Brit* : to put up or pack in tins : CAN

tin·a·mou \'tin-ə-,mü\ *n* [F, fr. Galibi *tinamu*] : any of a family (Tinamidae) of So. American game birds resembling gallinaceous birds in habits but related to the ratite birds

tin·cal \'tiŋ-kəl\ *n* [Malay *tingkal*] : crude native borax

tin can *n, slang* : DESTROYER 2

1**tinct** \'tiŋ(k)t\ *adj* [L *tinctus*, pp.] : TINGED, TINTED

2**tinct** *n* : TINCTURE, TINGE

tinc·to·ri·al \tiŋk-'tōr-ē-əl, -'tȯr-\ *adj* [L *tinctorius*, fr. *tinctus*, pp.] : of or relating to colors or to dyeing or staining; *also* : imparting color — **tinc·to·ri·al·ly** \-ē-ə-lē\ *adv*

1**tinc·ture** \'tiŋ(k)-chər\ *n* [ME, fr. L *tinctura* act of dyeing, fr. *tinctus*, pp. of *tingere* to tinge] **1 a** : a substance that colors, dyes, or stains **b** : COLOR, TINT **2 a** : a characteristic quality : CAST **b** : a slight admixture : TRACE **3** *obs* : an active principle or extract **4** : a heraldic metal, color, or fur **5** : a solution of a medicinal substance in an alcoholic menstruum

2**tincture** *vt* **tinc·tur·ing** \'tiŋ(k)-chə-riŋ, -shriŋ\ **1** : to tint or stain with a color : TINGE **2** : to infuse or instill with a property or entity : IMPREGNATE

tin·der \'tin-dər\ *n* [ME, fr. OE *tynder;* akin to OHG *zuntra* tinder, OE *tendan* to kindle] : a very flammable substance adaptable for use as kindling — **tin·dery** \-d(ə-)rē\ *adj*

tin·der·box \'tin-dər-,bäks\ *n* **1 a** : a metal box for holding tinder and usu. a flint and steel for striking a spark **b** : a highly inflammable object or place **2** : one that is a potential source of sudden strife or conflict

1**tine** \'tīn\ *n* [ME *tind*, fr. OE; akin to OHG *zint* point, tine] **1** : slender pointed projecting part : PRONG **2** : a pointed branch of an antler

2**tine** *vb* **tined** \'tīnd\ *or* **tint** \'tint\ **tin·ing** \'tī-niŋ\ [ME *tinen*, of Scand origin; akin to ON *tȳna* to lose, destroy; akin to ON *tjōn* injury — more at TEEN] *vt, dial Brit* : LOSE ~ *vi, dial Brit* : to become lost

tin·ea \'tin-ē-ə\ *n* [ME, fr. ML, fr. L, worm, moth] : any of several fungous diseases of the skin; *esp* : RINGWORM — **tin·e·al** \-ē-əl\ *adj*

tin fish *n, slang* : TORPEDO

tin·foil \'tin-,fȯil\ *n* **1** : a thin metal sheeting usu. of aluminum or tin-lead alloy **2** : SILVER PAPER

1**ting** \'tiŋ\ *vb* [ME *tingen*, of imit. origin] *vt* : to cause to make a ting ~ *vi* : to sound with a ting

2**ting** *n* : a high-pitched sound (as made by a light stroke on a glass)

1**tinge** \'tinj\ *vt* **tinged; tinge·ing** *or* **ting·ing** \'tin-jiŋ\ [ME *tingen*, fr. L *tingere* to dip, moisten, tinge; akin to OHG *dunkōn* to dip, Gk *tengein* to moisten] **1 a** : to color with a slight shade or stain : TINT **b** : to affect or modify with a slight odor or taste **2** : to affect or modify in character

2**tinge** *n* **1** : a slight staining or suffusing shade or color **2** : an affective or modifying property or influence : TOUCH **syn** see COLOR

tin·gle \'tiŋ-gəl\ *vi* **tin·gling** \-g(ə-)liŋ\ [ME *tinglen*, alter. of *tinklen* to tinkle, tingle] **1 a** : to feel a ringing, stinging, prickling, or thrilling sensation **b** : to cause such a sensation **2** : TINKLE — **tingle** *n*

tin hat *n* : a metal helmet

tin·horn \'tin-,hȯ(ə)rn\ *n* : a pretentious or boastful person

ti·ni·ly \'tīn-ᵊl-ē\ *adv* : in the manner of something tiny

ti·ni·ness \'tī-nē-nəs\ *n* : the quality or state of being tiny

1**tin·ker** \'tiŋ-kər\ *n* [ME *tinkere*] **1 a** : a usu. itinerant mender of household utensils **b** : an unskillful mender : BUNGLER **2** : any of several small fishes; *esp* : a young mackerel

2**tinker** *vb* **tin·ker·ing** \-k(ə-)riŋ\ *vi* : to work in the manner of a tinker; *esp* : to repair or adjust something in an unskilled or experimental manner ~ *vt* : to repair, adjust, or experiment with — **tin·ker·er** \-kər-ər\ *n*

tinker's damn *or* **tinker's dam** *n* [prob. fr. the tinkers' reputation for blasphemy] : something absolutely worthless

1**tin·kle** \'tiŋ-kəl\ *vb* **tin·kling** \-k(ə-)liŋ\ [ME *tinklen*, freq. of *tinken* to tinkle, of imit. origin] *vi* : to make or emit a tinkle ~ *vt* **1** : to sound or make known (the time) by a tinkle **2 a** : to cause to make a tinkle **b** : to produce by tinkling ⟨~ a tune⟩

2**tinkle** *n* **1** : a series of short high ringing or clinking sounds **2** : a jingling effect in repetitious verse or empty prose

tin·kly \'tiŋ-k(ə-)lē\ *adj* : TINKLING

tin·man \'tin-mən\ *n* : TINSMITH

tin·ner \'tin-ər\ *n* **1** : a tin miner **2** : TINSMITH

tin·ni·ly \'tin-ᵊl-ē\ *adv* : in a tinny manner : with a tinny sound

tin·ni·ness \'tin-ē-nəs\ *n* : the quality or state of being tinny

tin·ni·tus \'tin-ə-təs *also* tə-'nīt-əs, tə-'nēt-\ *n* [L, ringing, tinnitus, fr. *tinnitus*, pp. of *tinnire* to ring, of imit. origin] : a sensation of noise (as a ringing or roaring) that is purely subjective

tin·ny \'tin-ē\ *adj* **1** : of, abounding in, or yielding tin **2** : resembling tin: **a** : LIGHT, CHEAP **b** : thin in tone ⟨a ~ voice⟩

Tin Pan Alley *n* : a district occupied chiefly by composers or publishers of popular music; *also* : the body of such composers or publishers

tin·plate \'tin-'plāt\ *n* : thin sheet iron or steel coated with tin

tin–plate *vt* : to plate or coat (as a metal sheet) with tin

1**tin·sel** \'tin(t)-səl *also* 'tin-zəl\ *n* [MF *estincelle, etincelle* spark, glitter, spangle — more at STENCIL] **1** : a thread, strip, or sheet of metal, paper, or plastic used to produce a glittering and sparkling appearance in fabrics, yarns, or decorations **2** : something superficially attractive or glamorous but of little real worth

2**tinsel** *adj* **1** : made of or covered with tinsel **2** : cheaply gaudy : TAWDRY

3**tinsel** *vt* **tin·seled** *or* **tin·selled; tin·sel·ing** *or* **tin·sel·ling** \'tin(t)-s(ə-)liŋ, 'tin-zə-liŋ\ **1** : to interweave, overlay, or adorn with or as if with tinsel **2** : to impart a specious brightness to

tin·sel·ly \'tin(t)-s(ə-)lē, 'tin-zə-lē\ *adj* : TINSELED

tin·smith \'tin-,smith\ *n* : a worker who makes or repairs things of metal (as tin)

tin spirit *n* : a solution of various tin compounds used as a mordant

tin·stone \'tin-,stōn\ *n* : CASSITERITE

1tint \'tint\ *n* [alter. of earlier *tinct*, fr. L *tinctus* act of dyeing, fr. *tinctus*, pp. of *tingere* to tinge] **1 a :** a usu. slight or pale coloration **:** HUE **b :** any of various lighter or darker shades of a color **:** TINGE **2 :** a variation of a color produced by adding white to it and characterized by a low saturation with relatively high lightness **3 :** a usu. slight modifying quality or characteristic **4 :** a shaded effect in engraving produced by fine parallel lines close together **5 :** a panel of light color serving as background **6 :** dye for the hair **syn** see COLOR — **tint·er** *n*

2tint *vt* **:** to impart or apply a tint to **:** COLOR

tint·ing *n* **1 :** the act or process of one that tints **2 :** the engraved or colored tint produced by tinting

tin·tin·nab·u·lary \ˌtin-tə-'nab-yə-ˌler-ē\ *adj* [L *tintinnabulum* bell] **:** of, relating to, or characterized by bells or their sounds

tin·tin·nab·u·la·tion \ˌtin-tə-ˌnab-yə-'lā-shən\ *n* [L *tintinnabulum* bell, fr. *tintinnare* to ring, jingle, of imit. origin] **1 :** the ringing or sounding of bells **2 :** a jingling or tinkling sound as if of bells

tint·less \'tint-ləs\ *adj* **:** having no tints **:** lacking color

tin·type \'tin-ˌtīp\ *n* **:** FERROTYPE 1

tin·ware \-ˌwa(ə)r, -ˌwe(ə)r\ *n* **:** articles made of tinplate

tin·work \-ˌwərk\ *n* **1 :** work in tin **2** *pl but sing or pl in constr* **:** an establishment where tin is smelted, rolled, or otherwise worked

ti·ny \'tī-nē\ *adj* [alter. of ME *tine*] **:** very small or diminutive **:** MINUTE **syn** see SMALL

1tip \'tip\ *n* [ME; akin to MHG *zipf* tip, OE *tæppa* tap — more at TAP] **1 :** the usu. pointed end of something **2 :** a small piece or part serving as an end, cap, or point — **tipped** \'tipt\ *adj*

2tip *vt* **tipped; tip·ping 1 a :** to furnish with a tip **b (1) :** to cover or adorn the tip of **(2) :** to blend (furs) for improved appearance by brushing the tips of the hair with dye **2 :** to affix (an insert) in a book — often used with *in* **3 :** to remove the ends of ⟨~ raspberries⟩

3tip *vb* **tipped; tip·ping** [ME *tipen*] *vt* **1 :** OVERTURN, UPSET **2 :** CANT, TILT ~ *vi* **1 :** to become tipped **:** TOPPLE **2 :** LEAN, SLANT

4tip *n* **1 :** the act or an instance of tipping **:** TILT **2 :** a place for depositing something (as rubbish) by tipping or dumping

5tip *vb* **tipped; tip·ping** [akin to LG *tippen* to tap] *vt* **1 :** to strike lightly **:** TAP **2 :** to hit (a baseball) a glancing blow with the edge of the bat ~ *vi* **:** TIPTOE

6tip *vb* **tipped; tip·ping** [perh. fr. *5tip*] *vt* **1 :** GIVE, PRESENT **2 :** to give a gratuity to ~ *vi* **:** to bestow a gratuity

7tip *n* **:** a gift or small sum of money tendered for a service performed or anticipated **:** GRATUITY

8tip *n* [perh. fr. *6tip*] **1 :** an item of expert or authoritative information **2 :** a piece of advance or confidential information given by one thought to have access to special or inside sources

9tip *vt* **tipped; tip·ping 1 :** to impart a piece of information or advice about or to **2 :** to mention as a prospective winner or profitable investment — **tip one's hand :** to declare one's intentions or reveal one's resources ⟨the Justice Department wouldn't *tip its hand* by saying what its next move . . . would be —*Newsweek*⟩

tip·cart \'tip-ˌkärt\ *n* **:** a cart whose body can be tipped on the frame to empty its contents

tip·cat \-ˌkat\ *n* [*5tip*] **:** a game in which one player using a bat strikes lightly a tapered wooden peg and as it flies up strikes it again to drive it as far as possible while fielders try to recover it; *also* **:** the peg used in this game

ti·pi \'tē-(ˌ)pē\ *var of* TEPEE

tip–off \'tip-ˌȯf\ *n* [*9tip*] **:** WARNING, TIP

tip·per \'tip-ər\ *n* **:** one that tips

tip·pet \'tip-ət\ *n* [ME *tipet*] **1 :** a long hanging end of cloth attached to a sleeve, cap, or hood **2 :** a shoulder cape of fur or cloth often with hanging ends **3 :** a long black scarf worn over the robe by Anglican and Episcopal clergymen

1tip·ple \'tip-əl\ *vb* **tip·pling** \-(ə-)liŋ\ [back-formation fr. obs. *tippler* (barkeeper)] *vt* **:** to drink (intoxicating liquor) esp. continuously in small amounts ~ *vi* **:** to drink intoxicating liquor esp. by habit or to excess — **tip·pler** \-(ə-)lər\ *n*

2tipple *n* **:** an intoxicating beverage **:** DRINK

3tipple *n* [E dial. *tipple* to tip over, freq. of E *tip*] **1 :** an apparatus by which loaded cars are emptied by tipping **2 :** the place where tipping is done; *specif* **:** a coal-screening plant

tip·si·ly \'tip-sə-lē\ *adv* **:** in a tipsy manner **:** UNSTEADILY

tip·si·ness \-sē-nəs\ *n* **:** the quality or state of being tipsy

tip·staff \'tip-ˌstaf\ *n, pl* **tip·staves** \-ˌstavz, -ˌstāvz\ [obs. *tip-staff* (staff tipped with metal)] **:** an officer (as a constable or bailiff) who bears a staff

tip·ster \'tip-stər\ *n* **:** one who gives or sells tips esp. for gambling or speculation

tip·stock \'tip-ˌstäk\ *n* [*1tip*] **:** the detachable or movable forepart of a gunstock that lies beneath the barrel and forms a hold for the left hand

tip·sy \'tip-sē\ *adj* [*3tip* + *-sy* (as in *tricksy*)] **1 :** unsteady, staggering, or foolish from the effects of alcohol **:** FUDDLED **2 :** UNSTEADY, ASKEW ⟨a ~ angle⟩ **syn** see DRUNK

1tip·toe \'tip-ˌtō, -'tō\ *n* **:** the tip of a toe; *also* **:** the ends of the toes — **on tiptoe :** AROUSED, ALERT

2tiptoe *adv* **:** on or as if on tiptoe

3tiptoe *adj* **1 :** standing or walking on or as if on tiptoe **2 :** CAUTIOUS, STEALTHY

4tiptoe *vi* **:** to stand, raise oneself, or walk or proceed on or as if on tiptoe

1tip–top \'tip-'täp, -ˌtäp\ *n* [*1tip* + *top*] **:** the highest point **:** SUMMIT

2tip–top *adj* **:** EXCELLENT, FIRST-RATE

3tip–top *adv* **:** very well

ti·rade \tī-'rād, 'tī(ə)r-ˌād\ *n* [F, shot, tirade, fr. MF, fr. OIt *tirata*, fr. *tirare* to draw, shoot; akin to Sp & Pg *tirar* to draw, shoot, OF *tirer*] **:** a protracted speech usu. marked by intemperate, vituperative, or harshly censorious language

1tire \'tī(ə)r\ *vb* [ME *tyren*, fr. OE *tēorian, tӯrian*] *vi* **:** to become weary ~ *vt* **1 :** to exhaust or greatly decrease the physical strength of **:** FATIGUE **2 :** to wear out the patience of **:** bore completely

syn TIRE, WEARY, FATIGUE, EXHAUST, JADE, FAG mean to make or become unable or unwilling to continue. TIRE implies a draining of one's strength or patience; WEARY stresses tiring until one is unable to endure more of the same thing; FATIGUE suggests causing great lassitude through excessive strain or undue effort; EXHAUST implies complete draining of strength by hard exertion; JADE suggests the loss of all freshness and eagerness; FAG implies a drooping with fatigue

2tire *n* [ME, short for *attire*] **1** *obs* **:** ATTIRE **2 :** a woman's headband or hair ornament

3tire *vt* **1** *obs* **:** ATTIRE **2 :** to dress (the hair)

4tire *n* [ME, prob. fr. *2tire*] **1 :** a metal hoop forming the tread of a wheel **2 a :** a continuous solid or pneumatic rubber cushion encircling a wheel usu. consisting when pneumatic of an external rubber-and-fabric covering containing and protecting from injury an air-filled inner tube **b :** the external rubber-and-fabric covering of a pneumatic tire

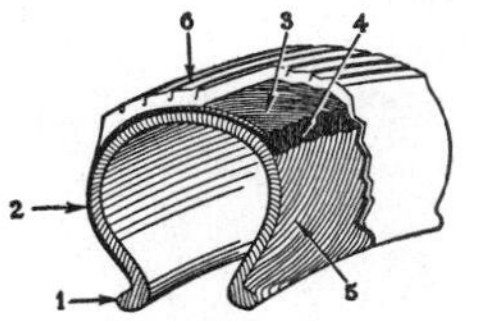

cross-section cutaway of fabric tire 2a: *1* bead, *2* sidewall, *3* breaker strip, *4* cushion, *5* carcass, *6* tread

tired \'tī(ə)rd\ *adj* **1 :** FATIGUED, WEARY **2 :** HACKNEYED — **tired·ly** *adv* — **tired·ness** *n*

tire·less \'tī(ə)r-ləs\ *adj* **:** UNTIRING, INDEFATIGABLE — **tire·less·ly** *adv* — **tire·less·ness** *n*

Ti·re·si·as \tī-'rē-sē-əs, -zē-\ *n* [L, fr. Gk *Teiresias*] **:** a blind Theban soothsayer given knowledge of future events and of the language of birds by Athena

tire·some \'tī(ə)r-səm\ *adj* **:** WEARISOME, TEDIOUS — **tire·some·ly** *adv* — **tire·some·ness** *n*

tire·wom·an \-ˌwu̇m-ən\ *n* [*2tire*] **:** a lady's maid

tir·ing–house \'tī-riŋ-ˌhau̇s\ *n* [*3tire*] **:** a section of a theater reserved for the actors and used esp. for dressing and preparing for stage entrances

tir·ing–room \'tī-riŋ-ˌrüm, -ˌru̇m\ *n* [*3tire*] **:** a dressing room esp. in a theater

tirl \'tərl\ *vb* [alter. of *1trill*] *vi, chiefly Scot* **:** to make a rattling sound (as with a door latch) ~ *vt, chiefly Scot* **:** TWIRL

tiro *var of* TYRO

ti·sane \ti-'zan, -'zän\ *n* [ME, fr. MF, fr. L *ptisana*, fr. Gk *ptisanē*, lit., crushed barley] **:** an infusion (as of dried leaves or flowers) used as a beverage or for mildly medicinal effects

Tish·ah–b'Ab \'tish-ə-ˌbäv, -ˌbȯv\ *n* [Heb *tish'āh bĕ Ābh* ninth in Ab] **:** a Jewish holiday observed with fasting on the 9th of Ab in commemoration of the destruction of the temples at Jerusalem

Tish·ri \'tish-rē\ *n* [Heb *tishrī*] **:** the 1st month of the civil year or the 7th month of the ecclesiastical year in the Jewish calendar

tis·sue \'tish-(ˌ)ü, 'tish-ə-w, *chiefly Brit* 'tis-(ˌ)yü\ *n* [ME *tissu*, a rich fabric, fr. OF, fr. pp. of *tistre* to weave, fr. L *texere* — more at TECHNICAL] **1 a :** a fine lightweight often sheer fabric **b :** MESH, NETWORK, WEB ⟨a ~ of lies⟩ **2 :** a piece of soft absorbent tissue paper used esp. as a handkerchief or for removing cosmetics **3 :** an aggregate of cells usu. of a particular kind together with their intercellular substance that form one of the structural materials of a plant or an animal

tissue paper *n* **:** a thin gauzy paper used variously (as to protect engravings in books or to wrap delicate articles)

1tit \'tit\ *n* [ME, fr. OE] **:** TEAT

2tit *n* [*tit-* (as in *titmouse*)] **:** a small or inferior horse

3tit *n* **:** TITMOUSE; *broadly* **:** any of various small plump often long-tailed birds

ti·tan \'tīt-ᵊn\ *n* [Gk] **1** *cap* **:** one of a family of giants and children of Uranus and Gaea overthrown by the Olympian gods **2 :** one gigantic in size or power

Titan *adj* **:** TITANIC

titan- *or* **titano-** *comb form* [NL *titanium*] **:** titanium ⟨*titan*ate⟩

ti·ta·nate \'tīt-ᵊn-ˌāt\ *n* **1 :** any of various multiple oxides of titanium dioxide with other metallic oxides **2 :** a titanium ester

ti·tan·ess \'tīt-ᵊn-əs\ *n, often cap* **:** a female titan

Ti·ta·nia \tə-'tān-yə, -'tän-; tī-'tān-\ *n* **:** the wife of Oberon and queen of the fairies in Shakespeare's *A Midsummer Night's Dream*

1ti·tan·ic \tī-'tan-ik *also* tə-\ *adj* **1** *cap* **:** of, relating to, or resembling the Titans **2 :** of great magnitude, force, or power **:** COLOSSAL

2ti·ta·nic \tī-'tan-ik, tə-, -'tā-nik\ *adj* **:** of, relating to, or containing titanium esp. when tetravalent

titanic acid *n* **:** any of various amorphous weakly acid substances that are hydrates of titanium dioxide

ti·tan·i·cal·ly \tī-'tan-i-k(ə-)lē *also* tə-\ *adv* **:** in a titanic manner

ti·ta·nif·er·ous \ˌtīt-ᵊn-'if-(ə-)rəs, tə-ˌtā-'nif-\ *adj* **:** containing or yielding titanium

ti·tan·ism \'tīt-ᵊn-ˌiz-əm\ *n, often cap* **:** spirit characteristic of a Titan; *esp* **:** defiance of and revolt against social or artistic conventions

ti·ta·ni·um \tī-'tā-nē-əm, tə- *also* -'tan-ē-\ *n* [NL, fr. Gk *Titan*] **:** a silvery gray light strong metallic element found combined in ilmenite and rutile and used in alloys (as steel) — see ELEMENT table

titanium dioxide *n* **:** an oxide TiO_2 of titanium found esp. in rutile or ilmenite and used esp. as a pigment

titanium white *n* **:** titanium dioxide used as a pigment

ti·tano·saur \tī-'tan-ə-ˌsȯ(ə)r\ *n* [NL *Titanosaurus*, genus of dinosaurs, fr. Gk *Titan* + *-o-* + *saurus* lizard — more at SAURIAN] **:** any of a genus (*Titanosaurus*) of large herbivorous Cretaceous dinosaurs mostly of the southern hemisphere

ti·ta·nous \tī-'tan-əs, tə-, -'tān-; 'tīt-ᵊn-\ *adj* [ISV] **:** of, relating to, or derived from titanium esp. when trivalent

tit·bit \'tit-ˌbit\ *var of* TIDBIT

ti·ter *or* **ti·tre** \'tīt-ər\ *n* [F *titre* title, proportion of gold or silver in a coin, fr. OF *title* inscription, title] **:** the strength of a solution or the concentration of a substance in solution as determined by titration

tit for tat \ˌtit-fər-'tat\ [alter. of earlier *tip for tap*, fr. *tip* (blow) + *for* + *tap*] **:** an equivalent given in return (as for an injury) **:** RETALIATION

tith·able \'tī-t͟hə-bəl\ *adj* **:** subject or liable to payment of tithes

1tithe \'tīt͟h\ *vb* [ME *tithen*, fr. OE *teogothian*, fr. *teogotha* tenth] *vt*

1 : to pay or give a tenth part of esp. for the support of the church **2 :** to levy a tithe on ~ *vi* **:** to pay tithe — **tith·er** *n*

[2]tithe *n* [ME, fr. OE *teogotha* tenth; akin to MLG *tegede* tenth; both fr. a prehistoric WGmc derivative of the word represented by OE *tīen* ten — more at TEN] **1 :** a tenth part paid in kind or money as a voluntary contribution or as a tax esp. for the support of a religious establishment **2 :** the obligation represented by individual tithes — usu. used without article **3 a :** TENTH **b :** a small part **4 :** a small tax or levy

tith·ing \'tī-thiŋ\ *n* [ME, fr. OE *tēothung*, fr. *teogothian*, *tēothian* to tithe, take one tenth] **:** a small administrative division preserved in parts of England apparently orig. consisting of ten men with their families

Ti·tho·nus \tə-'thō-nəs\ *n* [L, fr. Gk *Tithōnos*] **:** a son of Laomedon granted immortality but not immortal youth by the gods and finally transformed into a grasshopper

[1]ti·ti \'tī-ˌtī, 'tīt-ˌī\ *n* [prob. fr. Timucua] **:** a tree (*Cliftonia monophylla* of the family Cyrillaceae) of the southern U.S. with glossy leaves and racemes of fragrant white flowers; *also* **:** any of several trees of a related genus (*Cyrilla*)

[2]ti·ti \ti-'tē\ *n* [Sp *tití*, fr. Aymara *titi*, lit., little cat] **:** any of various small So. American monkeys (genus *Callicebus*) resembling squirrel monkeys

ti·tian \'tish-ən\ *adj, often cap* [*Titian* †1576 It painter] **:** of a brownish orange color

tit·il·late \'tit-ᵊl-ˌāt\ *vt* [L *titillatus*, pp. of *titillare*] **1 :** TICKLE **2 :** to excite pleasurably — **tit·il·la·tion** \ˌtit-ᵊl-'ā-shən\ *n* — **tit·il·la·tive** \'tit-ᵊl-ˌāt-iv\ *adj*

tit·i·vate *or* **tit·ti·vate** \'tit-ə-ˌvāt\ *vb* [perh. fr. [1]*tidy* + *-vate* (as in *renovate*)] **:** to dress up **:** spruce up **:** SMARTEN — **tit·i·va·tion** \ˌtit-ə-'vā-shən\ *n*

tit·lark \'tit-ˌlärk\ *n* [*tit-* (as in *titmouse*) + *lark*] **:** PIPIT

[1]ti·tle \'tīt-ᵊl\ *n* [ME, fr. OF, fr. L *titulus* inscription, title] **1 a** *obs* **:** INSCRIPTION **b :** written material introduced into a motion picture or television program to give credits, explain an action, or represent dialogue **2 a :** the union of all the elements constituting legal ownership **b :** something that constitutes a legally just cause of exclusive possession ⟨a good ~⟩ **c :** the instrument (as a deed) that is evidence of a right **3 a :** something that justifies or substantiates a claim **b :** an alleged or recognized right **4 a :** a descriptive or general heading (as of a chapter in a book) **b :** the heading which names an act or statute **c :** the heading of a legal action or proceeding **5 a :** the distinguishing name of a written, printed, or filmed production **b :** a similar distinguishing name of a musical composition or a work of art **6 :** a descriptive name **:** APPELLATION **7 :** a division of an instrument, book, or bill; *esp* **:** one larger than a section or article **8 a :** an appellation of dignity, honor, distinction, or preeminence attached to a person or family by virtue of rank, office, precedent, privilege, attainment, or lands **b :** a person holding a title esp. of nobility **9 :** a literary work as distinguished from a particular copy **10 :** CHAMPIONSHIP 1 ⟨won the batting ~⟩

[2]title *vt* **ti·tling** \'tīt-liŋ, -ᵊl-iŋ\ **:** to designate or call by a title **:** TERM, STYLE

ti·tled \'tīt-ᵊld\ *adj* **:** having a title esp. of nobility

title deed *n* **:** the deed constituting the evidence of a person's legal ownership

ti·tle·hold·er \'tīt-ᵊl-ˌhōl-dər\ *n* **:** one that holds a title; *specif* **:** CHAMPION

title page *n* **:** a page of a book bearing the title and usu. the names of the author and publisher and the place and sometimes date of publication

ti·tlist \'tīt-ᵊl-əst, 'tīt-ləst\ *n* **:** TITLEHOLDER

tit·mouse \'tit-ˌmau̇s\ *n, pl* **tit·mice** \-ˌmīs\ [ME *titmose* fr. (assumed) ME *tit* any small object or creature + ME *mose* titmouse, fr. OE *māse*; akin to OHG *meisa* titmouse] **:** any of numerous small arboreal and insectivorous passerine birds (family Paridae and esp. genus *Parus*) related to the nuthatches but longer tailed

Ti·to·ism \'tēt-(ˌ)ō-ˌiz-əm\ *n* **:** the political, economic, and social policies associated with Tito; *specif* **:** nationalistic policies and practices followed by a communist state or group independently of and often in opposition to the U.S.S.R.

ti·trat·able \'tī-ˌtrāt-ə-bəl\ *adj* **:** capable of being titrated ⟨~ acidity⟩

ti·trate \'tī-ˌtrāt\ *vb* [*titer*] *vt* **:** to subject to titration ~ *vi* **:** to perform titration

ti·tra·tion \tī-'trā-shən\ *n* **:** a method or the process of determining the strength of a solution or the concentration of a substance in solution in terms of the smallest amount of a reagent of known concentration required to bring about a given effect in reaction with a known volume of the test solution

ti·tri·met·ric \ˌtī-trə-'me-trik\ *adj* [*titration* + *-i-* + *-metric*] **:** determined by titration — **ti·tri·met·ri·cal·ly** \-tri-k(ə-)lē\ *adv*

tit–tat–toe \ˌti-ˌta(t)-'tō\ *var of* TICKTACKTOE

tit·ter \'tit-ər\ *vi* [imit.] **1 :** to give vent to laughter one is seeking to suppress **2 :** to laugh in a nervous or affected manner esp. at a high pitch — **titter** *n*

tit·tie \'tit-ē\ *n* [prob. baby talk alter. of *sister*] *chiefly Scot* **:** SISTER

tit·tle \'tit-ᵊl\ *n* [ME *titel*, fr. ML *titulus*, fr. L, title] **1 :** a point or small sign used as a diacritical mark in writing or printing **2 :** a very small part

tit·tle–tat·tle \'tit-ᵊl-ˌtat-ᵊl\ *n* [redupl. of [2]*tattle*] **:** GOSSIP, PRATTLE — **tittle–tattle** *vi*

[1]tit·tup \'tit-əp\ *n* [imit. of the sound of a horse's hooves] **:** lively, gay, or restless behavior **:** PRANCE, CAPER

[2]tittup *vi* **tit·tupped** *or* **tit·tuped**; **tit·tup·ping** *or* **tit·tup·ing :** to move in a lively manner often with an exaggerated or affected action

[1]tit·u·lar \'tich-(ə-)lər\ *adj* [L *titulus* title] **1 a :** existing in title only **:** NOMINAL **b :** having the title and usu. the honors belonging to an office or dignity without the duties, functions, or responsibilities **2 :** bearing a title **3 :** of, relating to, or constituting a title — **tit·u·lar·ly** *adv*

[2]titular *n* **:** a person holding a title

titular bishop *n* **:** a Roman Catholic bishop with the title of but without jurisdiction in a defunct see (as in former Christian lands now under Muslim control)

Tiu \'tē-(ˌ)ü\ *n* [OE *Tīw* — more at DEITY] **:** a god of the sky and of war in Germanic mythology

tiz·zy \'tiz-ē\ *n* [origin unknown] **:** a highly excited and distracted state of mind

Tlin·git \'tliŋ-(g)ət, 'tliŋ-kət\ *n, pl* **Tlingit** *or* **Tlingits 1 a :** a group of Indian peoples of the islands and coast of southern Alaska **b :** a member of any of these peoples **2 :** a language stock of the Na-dene phylum

T–man \'tē-ˌman\ *n* [*T*reasury *man*] **:** a special agent of the U.S. Treasury Department

tme·sis \(tə-)'mē-səs\ *n* [LL, fr. Gk *tmēsis* act of cutting, fr. *temnein* to cut — more at TOME] **:** separation of parts of a compound word by the intervention of one or more words (as *what place soever* for *whatsoever place*)

TNT \ˌtē-ˌen-'tē\ *n* [*trinitrotoluene*] **:** TRINITROTOLUENE

[1]to \tə(-w), (ˈ)tü\ *prep* [ME, fr. OE *tō*; akin to OHG *zuo* to, L *donec* as long as, until] **1 a —** used as a function word to indicate movement or an action or condition suggestive of movement toward a place, person, or thing reached ⟨drove ~ the city⟩ ⟨went back ~ his original idea⟩ or a place, person, or thing not reached or not fully reached ⟨turned his back ~ the door⟩ **b —** used as a function word to indicate direction ⟨a mile ~ the south⟩ ⟨a tendency ~ silliness⟩ **c —** used as a function word to indicate contact or proximity **d (1) :** close against **:** ON ⟨applied polish ~ the table⟩ **(2) :** before and straight at esp. in defiance ⟨tell him ~ his teeth —Shak.⟩ **e (1) —** used as a function word to indicate the place or point that is the far limit ⟨100 miles ~ the nearest town⟩ **(2) —** used as a function word to indicate the limit of extent ⟨stripped ~ the waist⟩ **f —** used as a function word to indicate relative position ⟨perpendicular ~ the floor⟩ **2 a —** used as a function word to indicate purpose, intention, tendency, result, or end **b :** for the purpose of **:** FOR ⟨came ~ our aid⟩ **c :** in honor of **:** with all good wishes for ⟨drink ~ his health⟩ **d —** used as a function word to indicate the result of an action or a process ⟨broken all ~ pieces⟩ ⟨go ~ seed⟩ **(2) :** with the result of ⟨~ their surprise, the train left on time⟩ **e —** used as a function word to indicate a determined condition or end ⟨sentenced ~ death⟩ **f —** used as a function word to indicate the object of a right or claim ⟨title ~ the property⟩ **3 a —** used as a function word to indicate position or relation in time **b :** BEFORE ⟨five minutes ~ five⟩ **c :** TILL ⟨from eight ~ five⟩ **4 a —** used as a function word to indicate addition, attachment, connection, belonging ⟨the key ~ the door⟩, possession, accompaniment, or response **b :** to the accompaniment of ⟨sang ~ his guitar⟩ **c :** in response or reaction to ⟨comes ~ his call⟩ **5 —** used as a function word **(1)** to indicate the extent or degree (as of completeness or accuracy) ⟨loyal ~ a man⟩ or the extent and result (as of an action or a condition) ⟨beaten ~ death⟩ **(2)** to indicate the last or an intermediate point of a series ⟨moderate ~ cool temperatures⟩ **6 a —** used as a function word **(1)** to indicate a relation to one that serves as a standard **(2)** to indicate similarity, correspondence, dissimilarity, or proportion ⟨compared him ~ a god⟩ **b :** in comparison with ⟨inferior ~ earlier works⟩ **c (1) —** used as a function word to indicate agreement or conformity ⟨add salt ~ taste⟩ **(2) :** according to ⟨~ my knowledge⟩ **d —** used as a function word to indicate a proportion in terms of numbers or quantities ⟨400 ~ the box⟩ **7 a —** used as a function word **(1)** to indicate the application of an adjective or a noun ⟨agreeable ~ everyone⟩ ⟨attitude ~ friends⟩ **(2)** to indicate the relation of a verb to its complement or to a complementary element ⟨refers ~ the traditions⟩ ⟨refers him ~ the traditions⟩ **(3)** to indicate the receiver of an action or the one for which something is done or exists ⟨spoke ~ his father⟩ ⟨gives a dollar ~ the man⟩ ⟨the total effect was a gain ~ reading —Joseph Trenaman⟩ and often used with a reflexive pronoun to indicate exclusiveness (as of possession) or separateness ⟨had the house ~ themselves⟩ ⟨thought ~ himself⟩ **b :** in the opinion of ⟨~ him it seems unnecessary⟩ **c :** at the hands of **:** through the agency of ⟨falls ~ his opponent's blows⟩ **8 —** used as a function word to indicate that the following verb is an infinitive ⟨wants ~ go⟩ ⟨something ~ do⟩ and often used by itself at the end of a clause in place of an infinitive suggested by the preceding context ⟨knows more than he seems ~⟩ ⟨don't want ~⟩

[2]to \'tü\ *adv* **1 a —** used as a function word to indicate direction toward ⟨feathers wrong end ~⟩ ⟨run ~ and fro⟩ **b :** close to the wind ⟨the gale having gone over, we came ~ —R.H.Dana⟩ **2 a :** into contact esp. with the frame of a door or a window ⟨the door snapped ~⟩ **b —** used as a function word to indicate physical application or attachment ⟨set ~ his seal⟩ **3 —** used as a function word to indicate application or attention ⟨were hungry and fell ~ with a vengeance⟩ **4 :** to a state of consciousness or awareness ⟨brings her ~ with smelling salts⟩ **5 :** at hand **:** BY ⟨get to see 'em close ~ —Richard Llewellyn⟩

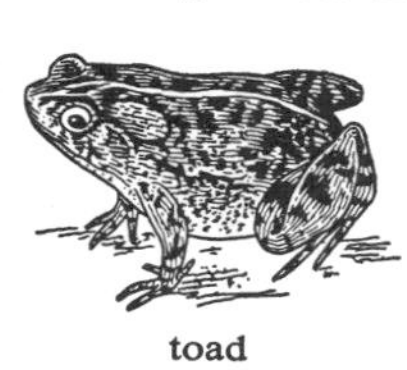
toad

toad \'tōd\ *n, often attrib* [ME *tode*, fr. OE *tāde*, *tādige*] **1 :** any of numerous tailless leaping amphibians (esp. family Bufonidae) that as compared with the related frogs are generally more terrestrial in habit though returning to water to lay their eggs, squatter and shorter in build and with weaker hind limbs, and rough, dry, and warty rather than smooth and moist of skin **2 :** a contemptible person or thing

toad·eat·er \-ˌēt-ər\ *n* **:** TOADY

toad·fish \-ˌfish\ *n* **:** any of various marine fishes (family Batrachoididae) with jugular pelvic fins, a large thick head, a wide mouth, and scaleless slimy skin

toad·flax \-ˌflaks\ *n* **:** a common European perennial herb (*Linaria vulgaris*) of the figwort family having showy yellow and orange flowers and being a naturalized weed in much of No. America; *also* **:** any of numerous plants related or similar

toad spit *n* **:** CUCKOO SPIT 1 — called also *toad spittle*

toad·stone \'tōd-ˌstōn\ *n* **:** a stone or similar object held to have formed in the head or body of a toad and formerly often worn as a charm or antidote to poison

toad·stool \-ˌstül\ *n* **:** a fungus having an umbrella-shaped pileus **:** MUSHROOM; *esp* **:** a poisonous or inedible one as distinguished from an edible mushroom

[1]toady \'tōd-ē\ *n* **:** one who flatters in the hope of gaining favors **:** SYCOPHANT

[2]toady *vi* **:** to behave as a toady **:** engage in sycophancy **syn** see FAWN — **toady·ism** \-ˌiz-əm\ *n*

to–and–fro \ˌtü-ən-'frō\ *adj* **:** forward and backward ⟨~ motion⟩ ⟨~ visiting⟩

1**toast** \'tōst\ *vb* [ME *tosten*, fr. MF *toster*, fr. LL *tostare* to roast, fr. L *tostus*, pp. of *torrēre* to dry, parch — more at THIRST] *vt* **1 :** to make (as bread) crisp, hot, and brown by heat **2 :** to warm thoroughly ~ *vi* **:** to become toasted; *esp* **:** to warm thoroughly

2**toast** *n* **1 a :** sliced bread browned on both sides by heat **b :** food prepared with toasted or recooked bread **2** [fr. the use of pieces of spiced toast to flavor drinks] **a :** a person whose health is drunk or something in honor of which persons drink **b :** a highly admired person **3** [3*toast*] **:** an act of proposing or of drinking in honor of a toast

3**toast** *vt* [2*toast*] **:** to propose or drink to as a toast

toast·er \'tō-stər\ *n* **:** one that toasts; *esp* **:** an electrical appliance for toasting

toast·mas·ter \'tōs(t)-ˌmas-tər\ *n* **:** one that presides at a banquet and introduces the after-dinner speakers — **toast·mis·tress** \-ˌmis-trəs\ *n*

to·bac·co \tə-'bak-(ˌ)ō, -'bak-ə(-w)\ *n, pl* **tobaccos** [Sp *tabaco*, prob. fr. Taino, roll of tobacco leaves smoked by the Indians of the Antilles at the time of Columbus] **1 :** any of a genus (*Nicotiana*) of chiefly American plants of the nightshade family with viscid foliage and tubular flowers; *esp* **:** a tall erect annual So. American herb (*N. tabacum*) cultivated for its leaves **2 :** the leaves of cultivated tobacco prepared for use in smoking or chewing or as snuff **3 :** manufactured products of tobacco (as cigars or cigarettes); *also* **:** smoking as a practice

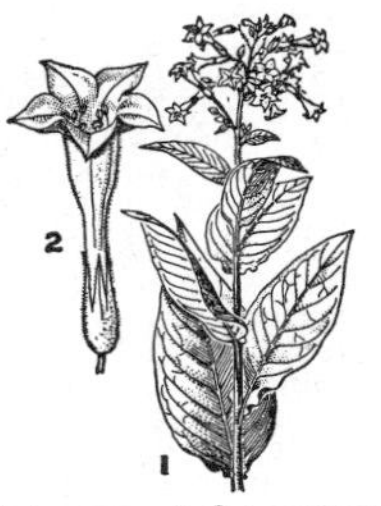

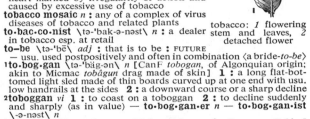

tobacco: *1* flowering stem and leaves, *2* detached flower

tobacco heart *n* **:** a functional disorder of the heart marked by irregularity of action and caused by excessive use of tobacco

tobacco mosaic *n* **:** any of a complex of virus diseases of tobacco and related plants

to·bac·co·nist \tə-'bak-ə-nəst\ *n* **:** a dealer in tobacco esp. at retail

to–be \tə-'bē\ *adj* **:** that is to be **:** FUTURE — usu. used postpositively and often in combination ⟨a bride-*to-be*⟩

1**to·bog·gan** \tə-'bäg-ən\ *n* [CanF *tobogan*, of Algonquian origin; akin to Micmac *tobâgun* drag made of skin] **1 :** a long flat-bottomed light sled made of thin boards curved up at one end with usu. low handrails at the sides **2 :** a downward course or a sharp decline

2**toboggan** *vi* **1 :** to coast on a toboggan **2 :** to decline suddenly and sharply (as in value) — **to·bog·gan·er** *n* — **to·bog·gan·ist** \-ə-nəst\ *n*

to·by \'tō-bē\ *n, often cap* [*Toby*, nickname fr. the name *Tobias*] **:** a small jug, pitcher, or mug generally used for ale and shaped somewhat like a stout man with a cocked hat for the brim

toc·ca·ta \tə-'kät-ə\ *n* [It, fr. *toccare* to touch, fr. (assumed) VL] **:** a brilliant musical composition usu. for organ or harpsichord in a free style

To·char·i·an \tō-'kar-ē-ən, -'ker-, -'kär-\ *n* [L *Tochari* (pl.), fr. Gk *Tocharoi*] **1 :** a member of a people of presumably European origin dwelling in central Asia during the first millennium of the Christian era **2 a :** a language of central Asia known from documents from the seventh century A.D. **b :** a branch of the Indo-European language family containing Tocharian

Tocharian A *n* **:** the eastern dialect of Tocharian

Tocharian B *n* **:** the western dialect of Tocharian

toch·er \'täk-ər\ *n* [ScGael *tochar*] *chiefly Scot* **:** marriage portion **:** DOT

to·col·o·gy \tō-'käl-ə-jē\ *n* [Gk *tokos* childbirth (fr. *tiktein* to give birth to, beget) + E *-logy* — more at THANE] **:** OBSTETRICS

to·coph·er·ol \tō-'käf-ə-ˌrȯl, -ˌrōl\ *n* [ISV, deriv. of Gk *tokos* childbirth, offspring + *pherein* to carry, bear — more at BEAR] **:** any of several fat-soluble oily phenolic compounds with varying degrees of antioxidant vitamin E activity; *esp* **:** one $C_{29}H_{50}O_2$ of high vitamin E potency obtained from germ oils or by synthesis — called also *alpha-tocopherol*

toc·sin \'täk-sən\ *n* [MF *toquassen*, fr. OProv *tocasenh*, fr. *tocar* to touch, ring a bell (fr. assumed VL *toccare*) + *senh* sign, bell, fr. ML & L *signum;* ML, bell, fr. LL, ringing of a bell, fr. L, mark, sign — more at TOUCH, SIGN] **1 :** an alarm bell or the ringing of it **2 :** a warning signal

1**tod** \'täd\ *n* [ME] *chiefly Scot* **:** FOX

2**tod** *n* [ME *todd, todde;* prob. akin to OHG *zotta* tuft of hair] **1 :** any of various units of weight for wool; *esp* **:** one equal to 28 pounds **2** *Brit* **:** a bushy clump (as of ivy)

1**to·day** \tə-'dā\ *adv* **1 :** on or for this day **2 :** at the present time **:** NOWADAYS

2**today** *n* **:** the present day, time, or age

tod·dle \'täd-ᵊl\ *vi* **tod·dling** \'täd-liŋ, -ᵊl-iŋ\ [origin unknown] **:** to walk with short tottering steps in the manner of a young child — **toddle** *n* — **tod·dler** \-lər, -ᵊl-ər\ *n*

tod·dy \'täd-ē\ *n* [Hindi *tāṛī* juice of the palmyra palm, fr. *tāṛ* palmyra palm, fr. Skt *tāla*] **1 :** the fresh or fermented sap of various chiefly East Indian palms **2 :** a hot drink consisting of an alcoholic liquor, water, sugar, and spices

to–do \tə-'dü\ *n* **:** BUSTLE, STIR

to·dy \'tōd-ē\ *n* [modif. of F *todier*, fr. L *todus*, a small bird] **:** any of several tiny nonpasserine insectivorous West Indian birds (genus *Todus*) closely related to the kingfishers

1**toe** \'tō\ *n* [ME *to*, fr. OE *tā;* akin to OHG *zēha* toe, L *digitus* finger] **1 a** (1) **:** one of the terminal members of a vertebrate's foot (2) **:** the fore end of a foot or hoof **b :** a terminal segment of a limb of an invertebrate **c :** the forepart of something worn on the foot **2 :** a part that by its position or form is felt to resemble a toe: as **a :** a journal or pivot supported in a bearing **b :** a lateral projection at one end or between the ends of a piece (as a rod or bolt) by which it is moved

2**toe** *vb* **toed; toe·ing** *vt* **1 :** to furnish with a toe **2 :** to touch, reach, or drive with the toe **3 :** to drive (as a nail) slantingly; *also* **:** to clinch or fasten by or with nails or rods so driven ~ *vi* **1 :** TIPTOE **2 :** to stand, walk, or be placed so that the toes assume an indicated position or direction — **toe the line :** to conform rigorously to a rule or standard

toe box *n* **:** a piece of leather or other material placed between the toe cap and lining of a shoe and treated with a substance (as a gum) that hardens after the shoe is lasted permanently

toe cap *n* **:** a piece of leather covering the toe of a shoe and reinforcing or decorating it

toe crack *n* **:** a sand crack in the front wall of a horse's hoof

toed \'tōd\ *adj* [1*toe*] **1 :** having a toe or such or so many toes — used esp. in combination ⟨five-*toed*⟩ **2** [fr. pp. of 2*toe*] **:** driven obliquely ⟨a ~ nail⟩; *also* **:** secured by diagonal or oblique nailing

toe dance *n* **:** a dance executed on the tips of the toes — **toe–dance** \'tō-ˌdan(t)s\ *vi* — **toe dancer** *n*

toe·hold \'tō-ˌhōld\ *n* **1 a :** a hold or place of support for the toes (as in climbing) **b** (1) **:** a means of progressing (as in surmounting barriers) (2) **:** a slight footing **2 :** a wrestling hold in which the aggressor bends or twists his opponent's foot

toe–in \'tō-ˌin\ *n* **1 :** CAMBER 3 **2 :** adjustment of the front wheels of an automotive vehicle so that they are closer together at the front than at the back

toe·less \'tō-ləs\ *adj* **:** lacking a toe ⟨a ~ shoe⟩

1**toe·nail** \'tō-ˌnāl, -'nā(ə)l\ *n* **:** a nail of a toe

2**toenail** *vt* **:** to fasten by toed nails **:** TOE

toe·piece \'tō-ˌpēs\ *n* **:** a piece designed to form a toe (as of a shoe) or cover the toes of the foot

toe·plate \-ˌplāt\ *n* **:** a metal tab attached to the toe of a shoe (as to prevent wear due to heavy use)

toff \'täf\ *n* [prob. alter. of *tuft* (titled college student)] *chiefly Brit* **:** DANDY, SWELL

tof·fee *or* **tof·fy** \'täf-ē\ *n* [alter. of *taffy*] **:** candy of brittle but tender texture made by boiling sugar and butter together

toft \'tȯft, 'täft\ *n* [ME, fr. OE, fr. ON *topt*] *Brit* **:** a site for a dwelling and its outbuildings; *also* **:** an entire holding comprising a homestead and additional land

tog \'täg *also* 'tȯg\ *vt* **togged; tog·ging :** to put togs on **:** DRESS

to·ga \'tō-gə\ *n* [L; akin to L *tegere* to cover — more at THATCH] **:** the loose outer garment worn in public by citizens of ancient Rome; *also* **:** a similar loose wrap or a professional, official, or academic gown — **to·gaed** \-gəd\ *adj*

to·ga vi·ri·lis \ˌtō-gə-və-'rē-ləs, -wə-\ *n, pl* **to·gae vi·ri·les** \'tō-ˌgī-və-'rē-ˌlās, -wə-\ [L, men's toga] **:** the white toga of manhood assumed by boys of ancient Rome at the end of their fourteenth year

to·geth·er \tə-'geth-ər\ *adv* [ME *togedere*, fr. OE *togædere*, fr. *tō* to + *gædere* together; akin to MHG *gater* together, OE *gaderian* to gather] **1 a :** in or into one place, mass, collection, or group **b :** in a body **:** as a group **2 a :** in or into contact (as connection, collision, or union) ⟨mix ~⟩ ⟨rush ~⟩ **b :** in or into association or relationship **3 a :** at one time **:** COINCIDENTALLY **b :** in succession **:** without intermission **4 a :** by combined action **:** JOINTLY **b :** in or into agreement or harmony **5 a :** MUTUALLY, RECIPROCALLY — used pleonastically and as an intensive after certain verbs ⟨join ~⟩ ⟨add ~⟩ **b :** as a unit **:** in the aggregate — **to·geth·er·ness** *n*

tog·gery \'täg-(ə-)rē *also* 'tȯg-\ *n* **:** CLOTHING

1**tog·gle** \'täg-əl\ *n* [origin unknown] **1 :** a piece or device for holding or securing: as **a :** a pin inserted in a nautical knot to make it more secure or easier to slip **b :** any crosspiece attached to the end of or to a loop in something (as a chain, rope, line, strap, or belt) usu. to prevent slipping, to serve in twisting or tightening, or to hold something attached **2 :** a device having a toggle joint

2**toggle** *vt* **tog·gling** \-(ə-)liŋ\ **1 :** to fasten with or as if with a toggle **2 :** to furnish with a toggle **3 :** to release (a bomb) from an airplane by a toggle switch

toggle joint *n* **:** a device consisting of two bars jointed together end to end but not in line so that when a force is applied to the knee tending to straighten the arrangement the parts abutting or jointed to the ends of the bars will receive an endwise pressure

toggle switch *n* **:** an electric switch depending on a toggle joint with a spring to open or close the circuit when the projecting lever is pushed through a small arc

togs \'tägz *also* 'tȯgz\ *n pl* [pl. of E slang *tog* (coat), short for obs. E cant *togeman, togman*] **:** CLOTHING; *esp* **:** a set of clothes and accessories for a specified use ⟨riding ~*s*⟩

1**toil** \'tȯi(ə)l\ *n* [ME *toile*, fr. AF *toyl*, fr. OF *toeil* battle, confusion, fr. *toeillier*] **1** *archaic* **a :** STRUGGLE, BATTLE **b :** laborious effort **2 :** long strenuous fatiguing labor **:** DRUDGERY **syn** see WORK

2**toil** *vb* [ME *toilen* to argue, struggle, fr. AF *toiller*, fr. OF *toeillier* to stir, disturb, dispute, fr. L *tudiculare* to crush, grind, fr. *tudicula* machine for crushing olives, dim. of *tudes* hammer; akin to L *tundere* to beat] *vi* **1 :** to work hard and long **:** LABOR **2 :** to proceed with laborious effort **:** PLOD ~ *vt* **1** *archaic* **:** OVERWORK **2** *archaic* **:** to get or accomplish with great effort — **toil·er** *n*

3**toil** *n* [MF *toile* cloth, net, fr. L *tela* web, fr. *texere* to weave, construct] **1 :** a net to trap game **2 :** something by which one is held fast or inextricably involved **:** SNARE, TRAP — usu. used in pl.

toile \'twäl\ *n* [F, linen, cloth] **1 :** any of many plain or simple twill weave fabrics; *esp* **:** LINEN — usu. used in combination **2 :** a muslin model of a garment

toile de Jouy \ˌtwäl-dəzh-'wē\ *n* [F, lit., cloth of Jouy, fr. *Jouy*-en-Josar, France] **:** an 18th century French scenic pattern usu. printed on cotton, linen, or silk in one color on a light ground; *broadly* **:** any similar printed fabric

1**toi·let** \'tȯi-lət\ *n* [MF *toilette* cloth put over the shoulders while dressing the hair or shaving, dim. of *toile* cloth] **1** *archaic* **:** DRESSING TABLE **2 :** the act or process of dressing and grooming oneself **3 a** (1) **:** BATHROOM, LAVATORY 2 (2) **:** PRIVY **b :** a fixture for defecation and urination; *esp* **:** WATER CLOSET **4 :** cleansing in preparation for or in association with a medical or surgical procedure

2**toilet** *vi* **1 :** to dress and groom oneself **2 :** to use the toilet ~ *vt* **1 :** DRESS, GARB **2 :** to see to the toileting of (a child)

toilet paper *n* **:** a thin soft sanitary absorbent paper for bathroom use chiefly after evacuation

toilet powder *n* **:** a fine powder usu. with soothing or antiseptic ingredients for sprinkling or rubbing (as after bathing) over the skin

toi·let·ry \'tȯi-lə-trē\ *n* **:** an article or preparation used in making one's toilet — usu. used in pl.

toilet soap *n* **:** a mild soap that is made from fatty materials of high quality and that is often perfumed and colored and stabilized with preservatives

toi·lette \twä-ˈlet\ *n* [F, fr. MF] **1 :** TOILET 2 **2 a :** formal or fashionable attire or style of dressing **b :** a particular costume or outfit

toilet water *n* **:** a perfumed largely alcoholic liquid for use in or after a bath or as a skin freshener

toil·ful \ˈtȯi(ə)l-fəl\ *adj* **:** marked by or demanding toil **:** LABORIOUS — **toil·ful·ly** \-fə-lē\ *adv*

toil·some \-səm\ *adj* **:** attended with toil or fatigue **:** LABORIOUS — **toil·some·ly** *adv* — **toil·some·ness** *n*

toil·worn \-ˌwō(ə)rn, -ˌwȯ(ə)rn\ *adj* **:** showing the effects of or worn out with toil

To·kay \tō-ˈkā\ *n* **1 :** a sweet usu. dark gold dessert wine made near Tokaj, Hungary **2 :** a blend of Angelica, port, and sherry

[1]**to·ken** \ˈtō-kən\ *n* [ME, fr. OE *tācen*, *tācn* sign, token; akin to OHG *zeihhan* sign, Gk *deiknynai* to show — more at DICTION] **1 :** an outward sign ⟨~*s* of his grief⟩ **2 a :** SYMBOL, EMBLEM ⟨a white flag is a ~ of surrender⟩ **b :** an instance of a linguistic expression **3 :** a distinguishing feature **:** CHARACTERISTIC **4 a :** SOUVENIR, KEEPSAKE **b :** a small part representing the whole **:** INDICATION **c :** something given or shown as a guarantee (as of authority, right, or identity) **5 a :** a piece resembling a coin issued as money by some person or body other than a de jure government **b :** a piece resembling a coin issued for use (as for fare on a bus) by a particular group on specified terms **syn** see SIGN

[2]**token** *adj* **1 :** done or given as a token esp. in partial fulfillment of an obligation or engagement **2 a :** SIMULATED **b :** MINIMAL, PERFUNCTORY ⟨~ resistance⟩ ⟨~ integration⟩

to·ken·ism \ˈtō-kə-ˌniz-əm\ *n* **:** the policy or practice of making only a token effort (as to end racial segregation)

token money *n* **1 :** money of regular government issue (as paper currency or coins) having a greater face value than intrinsic value **2 :** a medium of exchange consisting of privately issued tokens

token payment *n* **:** a small payment made upon a debt and intended by the payer merely to acknowledge the existence of the obligation

To·khar·i·an *var of* TOCHARIAN

to·ko·no·ma \ˌtō-kə-ˈnō-mə\ *n* [Jap] **:** a niche or recess opening from the living room of a Japanese house in which a kakemono may be hung

tol- *or* **tolu-** *comb form* [ISV, fr. *tolu*] **1 :** tolu ⟨*tolu*ol⟩ **2 :** toluene ⟨*tolu*ic⟩ ⟨*tol*yl⟩ **:** toluic ⟨*tolu*ate⟩

to·la \ˈtō-lə, tō-ˈlä\ *n* [Hindi *tolā*, fr. Skt *tulā* weight; akin to L *tollere* to lift up] **:** a unit of weight of India equal to 180 grains troy or 0.4114 ounce

tol·booth \ˈtō(l)-ˌbüth, ˈtäl-, ˈtȯl-\ *n* [ME *tolbothe*, *tollbothe* tollbooth, town hall, jail] **1** *Scot* **:** a town or market hall **2** *Scot* **:** JAIL, PRISON

tol·bu·ta·mide \täl-ˈbyüt-ə-ˌmīd\ *n* [*tol-* + *but-* + *amide*] **:** a sulfonamide $C_{12}H_{18}N_2O_3S$ that lowers blood sugar level and is used in the treatment of diabetes

told *past of* TELL

tole \ˈtōl\ *n* [F *tôle* sheet metal (esp. iron), fr. F dial. (Bordeaux area), table, slab, fr. L *tabula* board, tablet] **:** sheet metal and esp. tinplate for use in domestic and ornamental wares in which it is usu. japanned or painted and often elaborately decorated; *also* **:** the finished material or ware made from it ⟨a ~ tray⟩

To·le·do \tə-ˈlēd-(ˌ)ō\ *n* **:** a finely tempered sword of a kind made in Toledo, Spain

tol·er·a·bil·i·ty \ˌtäl-(ə-)rə-ˈbil-ət-ē\ *n* **:** the quality or state of being tolerable

tol·er·a·ble \ˈtäl-(ə-)rə-bəl, ˈtäl-ər-bəl\ *adj* **1 :** capable of being borne or endured **2 :** moderately good or agreeable **:** PASSABLE — **tol·er·a·bly** \-blē\ *adv*

tol·er·ance \ˈtäl(-ə)-rən(t)s\ *n* **1 a :** relative capacity to endure or adapt physiologically to an unfavorable environmental factor **b :** the maximum amount of a pesticide residue that may lawfully remain on or in food **2 a :** sympathy or indulgence for beliefs or practices differing from or conflicting with one's own **b :** the act of allowing something **:** TOLERATION **3 :** the allowable deviation from a standard; *specif* **:** the range of variation permitted in maintaining a specified dimension in machining a piece

tol·er·ant \-rənt\ *adj* **1 :** inclined to tolerate; *esp* **:** FORBEARING **2 :** exhibiting environmental tolerance — **tol·er·ant·ly** *adv*

tol·er·ate \ˈtäl-ə-ˌrāt\ *vt* [L *toleratus*, pp. of *tolerare* to endure, put up with; akin to OE *tholian* to bear, L *tollere* to lift up, *latus* carried (suppletive pp. of *ferre*), Gk *tlēnai* to bear] **1 :** to endure or resist the action of (as a drug) without grave or lasting injury **2 :** to suffer to be or to be done without prohibition, hindrance, or contradiction **syn** see BEAR — **tol·er·a·tive** \-ˌrāt-iv\ *adj* — **tol·er·a·tor** \-ˌrāt-ər\ *n*

tol·er·a·tion \ˌtäl-ə-ˈrā-shən\ *n* **1 a :** the act or practice of tolerating something **b :** a government policy of permitting forms of religious belief and worship not officially established **2 :** TOLERANCE 1b

tol·i·dine \ˈtäl-ə-ˌdēn\ *n* [ISV] **:** any of several isomeric aromatic diamines $C_{14}H_{16}N_2$ that are homologues of benzidine used esp. as dye intermediates

[1]**toll** \ˈtōl\ *n* [ME, fr. OE; akin to ON *tollr* toll; both fr. a prehistoric WGmc-NGmc word borrowed fr. (assumed) VL *tolonium*, alter. of LL *telonium* customhouse, fr. Gk *telōnion*, fr. *telōnēs* collector of tolls, fr. *telos* tax, toll; akin to Gk *tlēnai* to bear] **1 :** a tax or fee paid for some liberty or privilege (as of passing over a highway or bridge) **2 :** compensation for services rendered: as **a :** a charge for transportation **b :** a charge for a long-distance telephone call **3 :** a grievous or ruinous price; *esp* **:** cost in life or health ⟨fever had taken a heavy ~ of her —L. C. Douglas⟩

[2]**toll** *vi* **:** to take or levy toll ~ *vt* **1 a :** to exact part of as a toll **b :** to take as toll **2 :** to exact a toll from (someone)

[3]**toll** *or* **tole** \ˈtōl\ *vt* [ME *tollen*, *tolen*; akin to OE *talu* talk, narrative — more at TALE] **1 :** ALLURE, ENTICE **2 a :** to entice (game) to approach **b :** to attract (fish) with scattered bait **c :** to lead or attract (domestic animals) to a desired point

[4]**toll** *vb* [ME *tollen*, perh. fr. *tollen* to entice] *vt* **1 a :** to give signal or announcement of **:** SOUND **b :** to announce by tolling **c :** to call to or from a place or occasion **2 :** to sound (a bell) by tolling ~ *vi* **1 :** to sound with slow measured strokes **2 :** to toll a bell

[5]**toll** *n* **:** the sound of a tolling bell

toll·booth \ˈtōl-ˌbüth\ *n* [ME *tolbothe*, *tollbothe* tollbooth, town hall, jail, fr. *tol*, *toll* toll + *bothe* booth] **:** a booth where tolls are paid

toll call *n* **:** a long-distance telephone call at charges above a local rate

toll·gate \ˈtōl-ˌgāt\ *n* **:** a point where vehicles pause to pay toll

toll·house \-ˌhau̇s\ *n* **:** a house or booth where tolls are taken

toll·man \-mən\ *n* **:** a collector of tolls (as on a highway or bridge)

Tol·tec \ˈtōl-ˌtek, ˈtäl-\ *n* [Sp *tolteca*, of AmerInd origin] **:** a member of a Nahuatlan people of central and southern Mexico — **Tol·tec·an** \-ən\ *adj*

tolu *n* [Sp *tolú*, fr. Santiago de *Tolú*, Colombia] **:** BALSAM OF TOLU

tol·u·ate \ˈtäl-yə-ˌwāt\ *n* [ISV] **:** a salt or ester of a toluic acid

tol·u·ene \-ˌwēn\ *n* [ISV] **:** a liquid aromatic hydrocarbon C_7H_8 that resembles benzene but is less volatile, flammable, and toxic, is produced commercially from light oils from coke-oven gas and coal tar and from petroleum, and is used as a solvent, in organic synthesis, and as an antiknock agent for gasoline — called also *methylbenzene*

to·lu·ic \tə-ˈlü-ik\ *adj* [ISV] **:** of, relating to, or being any of four isomeric acids $C_8H_8O_2$ derived from toluene

to·lu·idine \tə-ˈlü-ə-ˌdēn\ *n* [ISV] **:** any of three isomeric amino derivatives of toluene C_7H_9N analogous to aniline that are used as dye intermediates

toluidine blue *n* **:** a basic thiazine dye used as a biological stain and in medicine to treat hemorrhage

tol·u·ol \ˈtäl-yə-ˌwȯl, -ˌwōl\ *n* **:** toluene esp. of commercial grade

tol·yl \ˈtäl-əl\ *n* [ISV] **:** any of three univalent radicals $CH_3C_6H_4$— derived from toluene

tom \ˈtäm\ *n* [*Tom*, nickname for *Thomas*] **:** the male of various animals ⟨a ~ swan⟩: as **a :** TOMCAT **b :** a male turkey

[1]**tom·a·hawk** \ˈtäm-i-ˌhȯk\ *n* [*tomahack* (in some Algonquian language of Virginia)] **:** a light ax used as a missile and as a hand weapon by No. American Indians

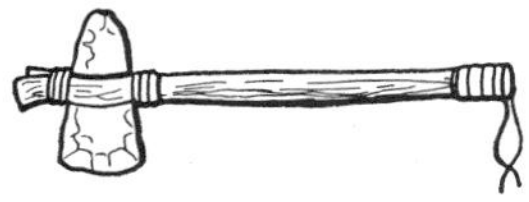
tomahawk

[2]**tomahawk** *vt* **:** to cut, strike, or kill with a tomahawk

tom·al·ley \tä-ˈmal-ē, ˈtäm-ˌal-ē\ *n* [of Cariban origin; akin to Galibi *tumali* sauce of lobster livers] **:** the liver of the lobster

Tom and Jer·ry \ˌtäm-ən-ˈjer-ē\ *n* [Corinthian *Tom* & *Jerry* Hawthorne, characters in *Life in London* (1821) by Pierce Egan] **:** a hot sweetened drink of rum, water, and spices (as cinnamon) mixed with an egg beaten separately

to·ma·to \tə-ˈmāt-(ˌ)ō, -ə(-w), -ˈmät-\ *n*, *pl* **tomatoes** [alter. of earlier *tomate*, fr. Sp, fr. Nahuatl *tomatl*] **1 :** any of a genus (*Lycopersicon*) of So. American herbs of the nightshade family; *esp* **:** a perennial plant (*L. esculentum*) widely cultivated for its edible fruits **2 :** the usu. large rounded and red or yellow pulpy berry of a tomato

[1]**tomb** \ˈtüm\ *n* [ME *tombe*, fr. AF *tumbe*, fr. LL *tumba* sepulchral mound, fr. Gk *tymbos;* akin to L *tumēre* to be swollen — more at THUMB] **1 a :** GRAVE **b :** a place of interment **2 :** a house, chamber, or vault resembling a tomb in form or appearance

[2]**tomb** *vt* **:** BURY, ENTOMB

tom·bac \ˈtäm-ˌbak\ *n* [F, fr. D *tombak*, fr. Malay *tĕmbaga* copper] **:** an alloy consisting essentially of copper and zinc and sometimes arsenic and used esp. for cheap jewelry and gilding

tomb·less \ˈtüm-ləs\ *adj* **:** having no tomb

tom·bo·lo \ˈtōm-bə-ˌlō, ˈtäm-\ *n* [It] **:** a sand or gravel bar connecting an island with the mainland or another island

tom·boy \ˈtäm-ˌbȯi\ *n* **:** a girl of boyish behavior **:** HOYDEN — **tom·boy·ish** \-ish\ *adj* — **tom·boy·ish·ness** *n*

tomb·stone \ˈtüm-ˌstōn\ *n* **:** GRAVESTONE

tom·cat \ˈtäm-ˌkat\ *n* **:** a male cat

tom·cod \-ˌkäd\ *n* **1 :** any of several small fishes (genus *Microgadus*) resembling the related common codfish **2 :** any of several croakers of the Pacific coast

Tom Col·lins \ˈtäm-ˈkäl-ənz\ *n* [fr. the name *Tom Collins*] **:** a collins with a base of gin

Tom, Dick, and Har·ry \ˌtäm-ˌdik-ən-ˈhar-ē\ *n* **:** persons taken at random **:** the common run of humanity **:** EVERYBODY, EVERYONE

tome \ˈtōm\ *n* [MF or L; MF, fr. L *tomus*, fr. Gk *tomos* section, roll of papyrus, tome, fr. *temnein* to cut; akin to L *tondēre* to shear, Gk *tendein* to gnaw] **1 :** a volume forming part of a larger work **2 :** BOOK; *esp* **:** a large or scholarly one

-tome \ˌtōm\ *n comb form* [Gk *tomos*] **:** part **:** segment ⟨myo*tome*⟩

to·men·tose \tō-ˈmen-ˌtōs, ˈtō-mən-\ *adj* [NL *tomentosus*, fr. L *tomentum*] **:** covered with densely matted hairs ⟨a ~ leaf⟩

to·men·tu·lose \tō-ˈmen-chə-ˌlōs\ *adj* [NL *tomentulosus*, dim. of *tomentosus*] **:** minutely or slightly tomentose

to·men·tum \tō-ˈment-əm\ *n*, *pl* **to·men·ta** \-ə\ [NL, fr. L, cushion stuffing; akin to L *tumēre* to be swollen — more at THUMB] **:** pubescence composed of densely matted woolly hairs

[1]**tom·fool** \ˈtäm-ˈfül\ *n* **:** a great fool **:** BLOCKHEAD

[2]**tom·fool** \-ˌfül\ *adj* **:** extremely foolish, stupid, or doltish

tom·fool·ery \täm-ˈfül-(ə-)rē\ *n* **:** foolish trifling **:** NONSENSE

Tom·my \ˈtäm-ē\ *n* [*Thomas* Atkins, name used as model in official army forms] **:** a British soldier — called also *Tommy At·kins* \ˌtäm-ē-ˈat-kənz\

tom·my gun \ˈtäm-ē-ˌgən\ *n* [by shortening & alter.] **:** THOMPSON SUBMACHINE GUN; *broadly* **:** SUBMACHINE GUN

tommy–gun *vt* **:** to shoot with a tommy gun

tom·my·rot \ˈtäm-ē-ˌrät\ *n* [E dial. *tommy* fool + E *rot*] **:** rank foolishness or nonsense

to·mog·ra·phy \tō-ˈmäg-rə-fē\ *n* [Gk *tomos* section + ISV *-graphy* — more at TOME] **:** a diagnostic technique using X-ray photographs in which the shadows of structures before and behind the section under scrutiny do not show

[1]**to·mor·row** \tə-ˈmär-(ˌ)ō, -ˈmȯr-, -ə(-w)\ *adv* [ME *to morgen*, fr. OE *tō morgen*, fr. *tō* to + *morgen* morrow, morning — more at MORN] **:** on or for the day after today

[2]**tomorrow** *n* **1 :** the day after the present **2 :** FUTURE 1a

tom·pi·on \ˈtäm-pē-ən\ *var of* TAMPION

Tom Thumb \ˈtäm-ˈthəm\ *n* **:** a legendary English dwarf

tom·tit \(ˈ)täm-ˈtit\ *n* [prob. short for *tomtitmouse*, fr. the name *Tom* + *titmouse*] **:** any of various small active birds

tom–tom \ˈtäm-ˌtäm, ˈtəm-ˌtəm\ *n* [Hindi *ṭamṭam*] **1 :** a small-headed drum commonly beaten with the hands **2 :** a monotonous beating, rhythm, or rhythmical sound

-t·o·my \t-ə-mē\ *n comb form* [NL *-tomia*, fr. Gk, fr. *-tomos* that

cuts, fr. *temnein* to cut — more at TOME] **:** incision **:** section ⟨lapar*otomy*⟩

1ton \'tən\ *n, pl* **tons** *also* **ton** [ME *tunne* unit of weight or capacity — more at TUN] **1 :** any of various units of weight: **a** — see MEASURE table **b :** METRIC TON **2 a :** a unit of internal capacity for ships equal to 100 cubic feet — called also *register ton* **b :** a unit approximately equal to the volume of a long ton weight of seawater used in reckoning the displacement of ships and equal to 35 cubic feet — called also *displacement ton* **c :** a unit of volume for cargo freight usu. reckoned at 40 cubic feet — called also *freight ton, measurement ton* **3 :** a great quantity **:** LOT — used chiefly in pl.

2ton \'tō^{n}\ *n* [F, lit., tone, fr. L *tonus*] **1 :** the prevailing fashion **:** VOGUE **2 :** SMARTNESS, STYLE

ton·al \'tōn-ᵊl\ *adj* **1 :** of or relating to tone, tonality, or tonicity **2 :** having tonality — **ton·al·ly** \-ᵊl-ē\ *adv*

to·nal·i·ty \tō-'nal-ət-ē\ *n* **1 :** tonal quality **2 a :** KEY 8 **b :** the organization of all the tones and chords of a piece of music in relation to a tonic **3 :** the arrangement or interrelation of the tones of a picture

1tone \'tōn\ *n* [ME, fr. L *tonus* tension, tone, fr Gk *tonos*, lit., act of stretching; akin to Gk *teinein* to stretch — more at THIN] **1 :** vocal or musical sound; *esp* **:** sound quality **2 a :** a sound of definite pitch and vibration **b :** WHOLE STEP **3 :** accent or inflection expressive of a mood or emotion **4 :** the pitch of a word often used to express differences of meaning **5 :** a particular pitch or change of pitch constituting an element in the intonation of a phrase or sentence ⟨high ~⟩ ⟨low ~⟩ ⟨mid ~⟩ ⟨low-rising ~⟩ ⟨falling ~⟩ **6 :** style or manner of expression in speaking or writing **7 a** (1) **:** color quality or value (2) **:** a tint or shade of color **b :** the color that appreciably modifies a hue or white or black ⟨gray walls of greenish ~⟩ **8 :** the effect in painting of light and shade together with color **9 a :** the state of a living body or of any of its organs or parts in which the functions are healthy and performed with due vigor **b :** normal tension or responsiveness to stimuli; *specif* **:** TONUS **10 a :** healthy elasticity **:** RESILIENCY **b :** general character, quality, or trend ⟨a city's low moral ~⟩ **c :** frame of mind **:** MOOD

2tone *vt* **1 :** INTONE **2 :** to give a particular intonation or inflection to **3 a :** to impart tone to **:** STRENGTHEN ⟨medicine to ~ up the system⟩ **b :** to soften in color, appearance, or sound **:** MELLOW **c :** to change the normal silver image of (as a photographic print) into a colored image ~ *vi* **1 :** to assume a pleasing color quality or tint **2 :** to blend or harmonize in color — **ton·er** *n*

tone arm *n* **:** the movable part of a phonograph that carries the pickup and permits the needle to follow the record groove

tone–deaf \'tōn-,def\ *adj* **:** relatively insensitive to differences in musical pitch

tone language *n* **:** a language (as Chinese, Sudanic, or Bantu) in which variations in tone are regularly used to distinguish words of different meaning that otherwise would sound alike

tone·less \'tōn-ləs\ *adj* **:** lacking in tone, modulation, or expression — **tone·less·ly** *adv* — **tone·less·ness** *n*

to·neme \'tō-,nēm\ *n* **:** a phoneme consisting of a specific intonation in a tone language — **to·ne·mic** \tō-'nē-mik\ *adj*

tone poem *n* **:** SYMPHONIC POEM — **tone poet** *n*

to·net·ic \tō-'net-ik\ *adj* **1 :** relating to linguistic tones or to tone languages **2 :** dealing with or expressing intonation ⟨~ notation⟩ — **to·net·i·cal·ly** \-i-k(ə-)lē\ *adv*

to·net·ics \-iks\ *n pl but sing in constr* **:** the use or study of linguistic tones

1tong \'täŋ, 'tȯŋ\ *vt* **:** to take, gather, hold, or handle with tongs ~ *vi* **:** to use tongs esp. in taking or gathering something — **tong·er** \'täŋ-ər, 'tȯŋ-\ *n*

2tong *n* [Chin (Cant) *t'ong* hall] **:** a secret society or fraternal organization esp. of Chinese in the U.S. formerly notorious for gang warfare

ton·ga \'täŋ-gə\ *n* [Hindi *tāṅgā*] **:** a light 2-wheeled vehicle for two or four persons drawn by one horse and common in India

tongs \'täŋz, 'tȯŋz\ *n pl but sing or pl in constr* [ME *tonges*, pl. of *tonge*, fr. OE *tang*; akin to OHG *zanga* tongs, Gk *daknein* to bite] **:** any of numerous grasping devices consisting commonly of two pieces joined at one end by a pivot or hinged like scissors

1tongue \'təŋ\ *n* [ME *tunge*, fr. OE; akin to OHG *zunga* tongue, L *lingua*] **1 a :** a fleshy movable process of the floor of the mouths of most vertebrates that bears sensory end organs and small glands and functions esp. in taking and swallowing food and in man as a speech organ **b :** an analogous part of various invertebrate animals **2 :** the flesh of a tongue (as of the ox or sheep) used as food **3 :** the power of communication through speech **4 a :** LANGUAGE; *esp* **:** a spoken language **b :** manner or quality of utterance with respect to tone or sound, the sense of what is expressed, or the intention of the speaker **c** (1) **:** ecstatic usu. unintelligible utterance accompanying religious excitation (2) **:** the charismatic gift of ecstatic speech **d :** the cry of or as if of a hound pursuing or in sight of game — used esp. in the phrase *to give tongue* **5 :** a long narrow strip of land projecting into a body of water **6 :** something resembling an animal's tongue in being elongated and fastened at one end only: as **a :** a movable pin in a buckle **b :** a metal ball suspended inside a bell so as to strike against the sides as the bell is swung **c :** the pole of a vehicle **d :** the flap under the lacing or buckles of a shoe at the throat of the vamp **7 a :** the rib on one edge of a board that fits into a corresponding groove in an edge of another board to make a flush joint **b :** FEATHER 4 — **tongue·like** \-,līk\ *adj*

2tongue *vt* **tongu·ing** \'təŋ-iŋ\ **1** *archaic* **:** SCOLD **2 :** to touch or lick with or as if with the tongue **3 a :** to cut a tongue on ⟨~ a board⟩ **b :** to join (as boards) by means of a tongue and groove **4 :** to articulate (notes) by tonguing ~ *vi* **1 :** to project in a tongue **2 :** to articulate notes on a wind instrument

tongue and groove *n* **:** a joint made by a tongue on one edge of a board fitting into a corresponding groove on the edge of another board

tongue in cheek *adv (or adj)* **:** with insincerity, irony, or whimsical exaggeration

tongue–lash \'təŋ-,lash\ *vb* [back-formation fr. *tongue-lashing*] **:** CHIDE, REPROVE — **tongue–lash·ing** *n*

tongue·less \'təŋ-ləs\ *adj* **1 :** having no tongue **2 :** lacking power of speech **:** MUTE

1tongue–tie \'təŋ-,tī\ *vt* [back-formation fr. *tongue-tied*] **:** to deprive of speech or the power of distinct articulation

2tongue–tie *n* **:** limited mobility of the tongue due to shortness of its frenum

tongue–tied \-,tīd\ *adj* **1 :** affected with tongue-tie **2 :** unable to speak freely (as from shyness)

tongue twister *n* **:** a word, phrase, or sentence difficult to articulate because of a succession of similar consonantal sounds (as in "twin-screw steel cruiser")

tongu·ing *n* **:** an attack on or articulation of a note on a wind instrument by the use of the tongue

-to·nia \'tō-nē-ə\ *n comb form* [NL, fr. *tonus*] **:** condition or degree of tonus ⟨myo*tonia*⟩

1ton·ic \'tän-ik\ *adj* [Gk *tonikos*, fr. *tonos* tension, tone] **1 a :** relating to or characterized by tension **b :** producing or adapted to produce healthy muscular condition and reaction **c :** characterized by tonus ⟨~ contraction of muscle⟩; *also* **:** marked by prolonged muscular contraction ⟨~ convulsions⟩ **2 a :** increasing or restoring physical or mental tone **:** INVIGORATING **b :** yielding a tonic substance **3 :** relating to or based on the first tone of a scale ⟨~ harmony⟩ **4 a :** VOICED 2 **b** *of a syllable* **:** bearing a principal stress or accent **5 :** of or relating to speech tones or to languages using them to distinguish words otherwise identical — **ton·i·cal·ly** \'tän-i-kə-lē\ *adv*

2tonic *n* **1 a :** an agent (as a drug) that increases body tone **b :** something that invigorates, restores, refreshes, or stimulates **c :** a liquid preparation for the scalp **2 :** the first degree of a major or minor scale **3 :** a voiced sound

tonic accent *n* **1 :** relative phonetic prominence (as from greater stress or higher pitch) of a spoken syllable or word **2 :** accent depending on pitch rather than stress

to·nic·i·ty \tō-'nis-ət-ē\ *n* **1 :** the property of possessing tone; *esp* **:** healthy vigor of body or mind **2 :** muscular tonus

tonic sol-fa *n* **:** a system of solmization based on key relationships that replaces the normal notation with sol-fa syllables or their initials

1to·night \tə-'nīt\ *adv* **:** on this present night or the night following this present day

2tonight *n* **:** the present or the coming night

ton·ka bean \'täŋ-kə-\ *n* [prob. fr. Tupi *tonka*] **:** the seed of any of several leguminous trees (genus *Dipteryx*) that contains coumarin and is used in perfumes and as a flavor; *also* **:** a tree bearing such seed

ton·nage \'tən-ij\ *n* **1** [ME, fr. MF, fr. OF *tonne* tun — more at TUNNEL] **:** a duty formerly levied on every tun of wine imported into England **2 a :** a duty or impost on vessels based on cargo capacity **b :** a duty on goods per ton transported **3 :** ships in terms of the total number of tons registered or carried or of their carrying capacity **4 a :** the cubical content of a merchant ship in units of 100 cubic feet **b :** the displacement of a warship **5 :** total weight in tons shipped, carried, or mined

ton·neau \tə-'nō, tä-\ *n* [F, lit., tun, fr. OF *tonel* — more at TUNNEL] **1 :** the rear seating compartment of an automobile **2 :** a shape of watch case or dial resembling a barrel in profile

ton·ner \'tən-ər\ *n* **:** an object (as a ship) having tonnage — usu. used in combination ⟨a thousand-*tonner*⟩

to·nom·e·ter \tō-'näm-ət-ər\ *n* [Gk *tonos* tone + E *-meter*] **1 :** an instrument or device for determining the exact pitch or the vibration rate of tones **2 :** an instrument for measuring tension (as of the eyeball) or pressure (as of blood or a gas) **3 :** a device for measuring vapor pressure — **to·no·met·ric** \,tō-nə-'me-trik\ *adj* — **to·nom·e·try** \tō-'näm-ə-trē\ *n*

ton·sil \'tän(t)-səl\ *n* [L *tonsillae*, pl., tonsils] **:** either of a pair of prominent masses of lymphoid tissue that lie one on each side of the throat between the anterior and posterior pillars of the fauces; *also* **:** any of various similar masses of lymphoid tissue — **ton·sil·lar** \'tän(t)-s(ə-)lər\ *adj*

tonsill- *or* **tonsillo-** *comb form* [L *tonsillae*] **:** tonsil ⟨*tonsill*ectomy⟩ ⟨*tonsillo*tomy⟩

ton·sil·lec·to·my \,tän(t)-sə-'lek-tə-mē\ *n* **:** the surgical removal of the tonsils

ton·sil·li·tis \-'līt-əs\ *n* [NL] **:** inflammation of the tonsils

ton·sil·lot·o·my \-'lät-ə-mē\ *n* **:** incision of a tonsil; *also* **:** partial or total tonsillectomy

ton·so·ri·al \tän-'sōr-ē-əl, -'sȯr-\ *adj* [L *tonsorius*, fr. *tonsus*, pp.] **:** of or relating to a barber or his work ⟨~ parlor⟩

1ton·sure \'tän-chər\ *n* [ME, fr. ML *tonsura*, fr. L, act of shearing, fr. *tonsus*, pp. of *tondēre* to shear — more at TOME] **1 :** the Roman Catholic or Eastern rite of admission to the clerical state by the clipping or shaving of the head **2 :** the shaven crown or patch worn by monks and other clerics **3 :** a bald spot resembling a tonsure

2tonsure *vt* **ton·sur·ing** \'tänch-(ə-)riŋ\ **:** to shave the head of; *esp* **:** to confer the tonsure upon

ton·tine \'tän-,tēn, tän-'\ *n* [F, fr. Lorenzo *Tonti* †1695 It banker] **:** a financial arrangement (as an insurance policy) whereby a group of participants share various advantages on such terms that upon the death or default of any member his advantages are distributed among the remaining members until on the death of all but one the whole goes to him or on the expiration of an agreed period the whole goes to those remaining; *also* **:** the share or right of each individual

to·nus \'tō-nəs\ *n* [NL, fr. L, tension, tone] **:** TONE 9a; *esp* **:** a state of partial contraction characteristic of normal muscle

too \(')tü\ *adv* [ME, fr. OE *tō* to, too — more at TO] **1 :** ALSO, BESIDES ⟨sell the house and furniture ~⟩ **2 a :** EXCESSIVELY **b :** to such a degree as to be regrettable **c :** VERY

took *past of* TAKE

1tool \'tül\ *n* [ME, fr. OE *tōl*; akin to OE *tawian* to prepare for use — more at TAW] **1 a :** an instrument (as a hammer) used or worked by hand **:** IMPLEMENT **b** (1) **:** the cutting or shaping part in a machine or machine tool (2) **:** a machine for shaping metal **:** MACHINE TOOL **2 a :** an instrument or apparatus used in performing an operation or necessary in the practice of a vocation or profession ⟨a scholar's books are ~*s*⟩ **b :** a means to an end **3 :** one who is used or manipulated by another **:** DUPE **syn** see IMPLEMENT

2tool *vt* **1 :** DRIVE **2 :** to shape, form, or finish with a tool; *specif*

: to letter or ornament (as a book cover) by means of hand tools **3 :** to equip (as a plant or industry) with tools, machines, and instruments for production ~ *vi* **1 :** DRIVE, RIDE **2 :** to use tools **3 :** to equip a plant or industry with the machines, tools, and instruments required for production

tool•box \'tül-,bäks\ *n* **:** a chest for tools

tool engineering *n* **:** a branch of engineering in industry whose function is to plan the processes of manufacture, develop the tools and machines, and integrate the facilities required for producing particular products with minimal expenditure of time, labor, and materials

tool•head \'tül-,hed\ *n* **:** a part of a machine in which a tool or toolholder is clamped and which is provided with adjustments to bring the tool into the desired position

tool•hold•er \-,hōl-dər\ *n* **:** a short steel bar having a shank at one end to fit into the toolhead of a machine and a clamp at the other end to hold small interchangeable cutting bits

tool•house \-,haus\ *n* **:** a building (as in a garden) for storing tools — called also *tool•shed* \-,shed\

tool•mak•er \'tül-,mā-kər\ *n* **:** a machinist who specializes in the construction, repair, maintenance, and calibration of the tools, jigs, fixtures, and instruments of a machine shop

tool•mak•ing \-kiŋ\ *n* **:** the act, process, or art of making tools

tool•room \'tül-,rüm, -,rum\ *n* **:** a room where tools are kept; *esp* **:** a room in a machine shop in which tools are made, stored, or loaned out to the workmen

tool subject *n* **:** a subject studied to gain competence in a skill used in other subjects

toom \'tüm\ *adj* [ME, fr. OE *tōm* — more at TEEM] *chiefly Scot* **:** EMPTY

toon \'tün\ *n* [Hindi *tūn*, fr. Skt *tunna*] **:** an East Indian and Australian tree (*Cedrela toona*) of the mahogany family with fragrant dark red wood and flowers that yield a dye; *also* **:** its wood

1**toot** \'tüt\ *vb* [prob. imit.] *vi* **1 a :** to sound a short blast ⟨horn ~*ed*⟩ **b :** to sound a note or call suggesting the short blast of a wind instrument **2 :** to blow or sound a horn or other instrument esp. so as to produce short blasts ~ *vt* **:** to cause to sound ⟨~ a whistle⟩ — **toot•er** *n*

2**toot** *n* **:** a short blast (as on a horn); *also* **:** a sound resembling such blast

3**toot** *n* [Sc *toot* to drink heavily] **:** a drinking bout **:** SPREE

1**tooth** \'tüth\ *n, pl* **teeth** \'tēth\ [ME, fr. OE *tōth*; akin to OHG *zand* tooth, L *dent-, dens*, Gk *odont-, odous*] **1 a :** one of the hard bony appendages that are borne on the jaws or in many of the lower vertebrates on other bones in the walls of the mouth or pharynx and serve esp. for the prehension and mastication of food and as weapons of offense and defense **b :** any of various usu. hard and sharp processes esp. about the mouth of an invertebrate **2 :** TASTE, LIKING **3 :** a projection resembling or suggesting the tooth of an animal in shape, arrangement, or action ⟨saw ~⟩: as **a :** one of the regular projections on the circumference or sometimes the face of a wheel that engage with corresponding projections on another wheel esp. to transmit force **:** COG **b :** a small sharp-pointed marginal lobe or process on a plant **4 a :** something that injures, tortures, devours, or destroys **b** *pl* **:** effective means of enforcement **5 :** a roughness of surface produced by mechanical or artificial means — **tooth•like** \-,līk\ *adj*

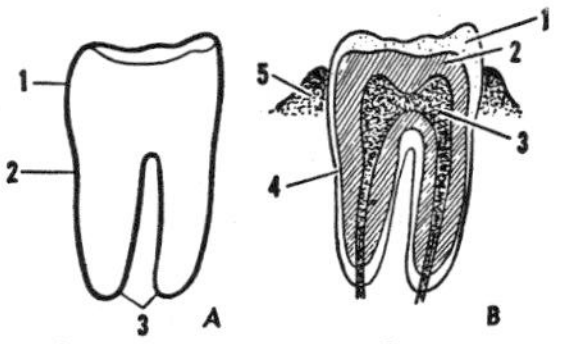

teeth 1a: *A* outside of a molar: *1* crown, *2* neck, *3* roots; *B* cross section of a molar: *1* enamel, *2* dentin, *3* pulp chamber, *4* cementum, *5* gum

2**tooth** \'tüth, 'tüth\ *vt* **:** to furnish with teeth; *specif* **:** INDENT, JAG ⟨~ a saw⟩

tooth•ache \'tü-,thāk\ *n* **:** pain in or about a tooth

tooth and nail *adv* **:** with every available means **:** all out ⟨fight *tooth and nail*⟩

tooth–billed \'tüth-,bild\ *adj* **:** having a notched bill

tooth•brush \-,brəsh\ *n* **:** a brush for cleaning the teeth

toothed \'tütht, *uncompounded also* 'tü-thəd\ *adj* **:** provided with teeth or such or so many teeth

toothed whale \'tütht-, ,tü-thəd-\ *n* **:** any of various whales (suborder Odontoceti) with numerous simple conical teeth

tooth•i•ly \'tü-thə-lē\ *adv* **:** in a toothy manner

tooth•less \'tüth-ləs\ *adj* **:** having no teeth

tooth•paste \-,pāst\ *n* **:** a paste dentifrice

tooth•pick \-,pik\ *n* **:** a pointed instrument (as a small flat tapering splinter) used for clearing the teeth of substances lodged between them

tooth powder *n* **:** a dentifrice in powder form

tooth shell *n* **:** any of a class (Scaphopoda) of marine mollusks with a tapering tubular shell; *also* **:** this shell

tooth•some \'tüth-səm\ *adj* **1 :** pleasing to the taste **:** DELICIOUS **2 :** ATTRACTIVE, LUSCIOUS — **tooth•some•ly** *adv* — **tooth•some•ness** *n*

tooth•wort \-,wərt, -,wo(ə)rt\ *n* **1 :** a European parasitic plant (*Lathraea squamaria*) of the broomrape family having a rootstock covered with tooth-shaped scales **2 :** any of various cresses (genus *Dentaria*) including several cultivated for their showy flowers

toothy \'tü-thē\ *adj* **:** having or showing prominent teeth ⟨~ grin⟩

too•tle \'tüt-ᵊl\ *vb* **too•tling** \'tüt-liŋ, -ᵊl-iŋ\ [freq. of 1*toot*] *vi* **:** to toot gently, repeatedly, or continuously ~ *vt* **:** to toot continuously on — **tootle** *n* — **too•tler** \'tüt-lər, -ᵊl-ər\ *n*

1**top** \'täp\ *n* [ME, fr. OE; akin to OHG *zopf* tip, tuft of hair] **1 a** (1) **:** the highest point, level, or part of something **:** SUMMIT, CROWN (2) **:** the head or top of the head — used esp. in the phrase *top to toe* (3) **:** the head of a plant and esp. one with edible roots ⟨beet ~*s*⟩ **b** (1) **:** the highest or uppermost region or part (2) **:** the upper end, edge, or surface **2 :** a fitted, integral, or attached part or unit serving as an upper piece, lid, or covering **3 a :** a platform surrounding the head of a lower mast that serves to spread the topmast rigging, strengthen the mast, and furnish a standing place for men aloft **b :** a comparable part of the superstructure; *esp* **:** such a part on a warship used as a fire-control station or antiaircraft gun platform **4 :** the highest degree or pitch conceivable or attained **:** ACME, PINNACLE **5 a** (1) **:** the highest position (as in rank or achievement) (2) **:** a person or thing at the top **b** *pl* **:** aces and kings in a hand or the three highest honors in a suit **6 :** the choicest part **:** CREAM, PICK **7 :** a forward spin given to a ball (as in golf, tennis, or billiards) by striking it on or near the top or above the center; *also* **:** the stroke so given — **topped** \'täpt\ *adj*

2**top** *vb* **topped; top•ping** *vt* **1 :** to remove or cut the top of: as **a :** to shorten or remove the top of (a plant) **b :** PINCH 1b **c :** to remove the most volatile parts from (as crude petroleum) **2 a :** to cover with a top or on the top **:** provide, form, or serve as a top **:** CROWN, CAP **b :** to supply with a decorative or protective finish **3 a :** to be or become higher than **:** OVERTOP ⟨~*s* the previous record⟩ **b :** to be superior to **:** EXCEL, SURPASS **c :** to gain ascendancy over **:** DOMINATE **4 a :** to rise to, reach, or be at the top of **b :** to go over the top of **:** CLEAR, SURMOUNT **5 :** to strike (a golf ball) above the center; *also* **:** to make (as a stroke) by hitting the ball in this way ~ *vi* **:** to make an end, finish, or conclusion ⟨a trail *topping* out on a mesa —J.F.Dobie⟩

3**top** *adj* **:** of, relating to, or at the top **:** HIGHEST, UPPERMOST

4**top** *n* [ME, fr. OE] **:** a commonly cylindrical or conoidal toy that has a tapering usu. steel-shod point on which it is made to spin

top- *or* **topo-** *comb form* [ME, fr. LL, fr. Gk, fr. *topos* — more at TOPIC] **:** place **:** locality ⟨*topo*logy⟩ ⟨*top*onymy⟩

to•paz \'tō-,paz\ *n* [ME *topace*, fr. OF, fr. L *topazus*, fr. Gk *topazos*] **1 a :** a mineral Al_2SiO_4(F,OH) consisting of a silicate of aluminum and usu. occurring in white orthorhombic translucent or transparent crystals or in white translucent masses **b :** a usu. yellow, reddish, or pink transparent mineral topaz used as a gem **c :** a yellow sapphire **d :** a yellow quartz **2 :** either of two large brilliantly colored So. American hummingbirds (*Topaza pella* and *T. pyra*)

top billing *n* **1 :** the position at the top of a theatrical bill usu. featuring the star's name **2 :** prominent emphasis, featuring, or advertising

top boot *n* **:** a high boot often with light-colored leather bands around the upper part

top•coat \'täp-,kōt\ *n* **:** a lightweight overcoat

top•cross \-,kros\ *n* **:** a cross between a superior or purebred male and inferior female stock to improve the average quality of the progeny; *also* **:** the product of such a cross

top dog *n* **:** a person or group in a position of authority esp. through victory in a hard-fought competition

top drawer *n* **:** the highest level of society, authority, or excellence

top–dress \'täp-,dres\ *vt* **:** to apply material to (as land or a road) without working it in; *esp* **:** to scatter fertilizer over (land)

1**tope** \'tōp\ *vi* [obs. E *tope* (interj. used to wish good health before drinking)] **:** to drink intoxicating liquor to excess **:** drink hard

2**tope** *n* [origin unknown] **:** a small cosmopolitan shark (*Galeorhinus galeus*) with a liver very rich in vitamin A

3**tope** *n* [Hindi *top*, prob. fr. Skt *stūpa*] **:** a round cupola-topped Buddhist shrine **:** STUPA

to•pee *or* **to•pi** \tō-'pē, 'tō-(,)pē\ *n* [Hindi *ṭopī*] **:** a lightweight helmet-shaped hat made of pith or cork

top•er \'tō-pər\ *n* **:** one that topes; *esp* **:** DRUNKARD

top flight *n* **:** the highest level of achievement, excellence, or eminence **:** TOP DRAWER — **top•flight** \'täp-'flīt\ *adj*

top•ful *or* **top•full** \'täp-'ful\ *adj* **:** BRIMFUL

1**top•gal•lant** \(')täp-'gal-ənt, tə-'gal-\ *adj* [1*top* + *gallant*, adj.] **1 :** of, relating to, or being a part next above the topmast and below the royal mast ⟨~ sail⟩ ⟨~ mast⟩ **2 :** raised above the adjoining portions ⟨~ rail⟩

2**topgallant** *n* **1 :** a topgallant mast or sail **2 :** the topmost point

top–ham•per \'täp-'ham-pər\ *n* **1 :** matter or weight (as spars or rigging) in the upper part of a ship **2 :** unnecessary cumbersome matter

top hat *n* **:** a man's tall-crowned hat usu. of beaver or silk

top–heavy \'täp-,hev-ē\ *adj* **1 :** having the top part too heavy for the lower part **:** lacking in stability **2 :** OVERCAPITALIZED

To•phet \'tō-fət\ *n* [ME, shrine south of ancient Jerusalem where human sacrifices were performed to Moloch (Jer 7:31), Gehenna, fr. Heb *tōpheth*] **:** GEHENNA, HELL

top–hole \'täp-'hōl\ *adj, chiefly Brit* **:** EXCELLENT, FIRST-CLASS

to•phus \'tō-fəs\ *n, pl* **to•phi** \'tō-,fī, -,fē\ [L, tufa] **:** a deposit of urates in tissues (as cartilage) characteristic of gout

1**to•pi•ary** \'tō-pē-,er-ē\ *adj* [L *topiarius*, fr. *topia* ornamental gardening, irreg. fr. Gk *topos* place] **:** of, relating to, or being the practice or art of training, cutting, and trimming trees or shrubs into odd or ornamental shapes; *also* **:** characterized by such work

2**topiary** *n* **:** topiary art or gardening; *also* **:** a topiary garden

top•ic \'täp-ik\ *n* [L *Topica* Topics (work by Aristotle), fr. Gk *Topika*, fr. *topika*, neut. pl. of *topikos* of a place, of a commonplace, fr. *topos* place, commonplace; akin to OE *thafian* to agree] **1 a :** one of the general forms of argument employed in probable reasoning **b :** ARGUMENT, REASON **2 a :** a heading in an outlined argument or exposition **b :** the subject of a discourse or a section of it **:** THEME

top•i•cal \-i-kəl\ *adj* **1 a :** of or relating to a place **b :** local or designed for local application ⟨a ~ remedy⟩ ⟨a ~ anesthetic⟩ **2 a :** of, relating to, or arranged by topics ⟨set down in ~ form⟩ **b :** referring to the topics of the day or place ⟨~ allusions⟩ — **top•i•cal•ly** \-k(ə-)lē\ *adv*

top•i•cal•i•ty \,täp-ə-'kal-ət-ē\ *n* **1 :** the quality or state of being topical **2 :** an item of merely topical interest

topic sentence *n* **:** a sentence that states the main thought of a paragraph or of a larger unit of discourse and is usu. placed at or near the beginning

top•kick \'täp-'kik\ *n* **:** FIRST SERGEANT 1

top•knot \-,nät\ *n* **1 :** an ornament (as a knot of ribbons or a pompon) forming a headdress or worn as part of a coiffure **2 :** a crest of feathers or hair on the top of the head

top•less \-ləs\ *adj* **1 :** being without a top **2** *archaic* **:** so high as to reach up beyond sight ⟨and burnt the ~ towers of Ilium —Christopher Marlowe⟩ **3 a :** wearing no clothing on the upper body **b :** featuring topless waitresses or entertainers

top lift *n* **:** the bottom layer of a heel

top•loft•i•ness \'täp-,lof-tē-nəs\ *n* **:** the quality or state of being toplofty

top•lofty \-tē\ *also* **top•loft•i•cal** \täp-'lof-ti-kəl\ *adj* [prob. fr. the phrase *top loft*] **:** very superior in air or attitude **:** HAUGHTY

top·mast \'täp-,mast, -məst\ *n* **:** the mast that is next above the lower mast and topmost in a fore-and-aft rig

top milk *n* **:** the upper layer of milk in a container enriched by whatever cream has risen

top·min·now \'täp-,min-(,)ō, -ə(-w)\ *n* **:** any of numerous small viviparous surface-feeding fishes constituting a family (Poeciliidae)

top·most \'täp-,mōst\ *adj* **:** highest of all **:** UPPERMOST

top–notch \-'näch\ *adj* **:** of the highest quality **:** FIRST-RATE — **top·notch** *n* — **top·notch·er** \-'näch-ər\ *n*

to·pog·ra·pher \tə-'päg-rə-fər\ *n* **:** one skilled in topography

to·po·graph·ic \,täp-ə-'graf-ik, ,tō-pə-\ *adj* **:** TOPOGRAPHICAL 1

to·po·graph·i·cal \-i-kəl\ *adj* **1 :** of, relating to, or concerned with topography ⟨~ engineer⟩ **2 :** of, relating to, or concerned with the artistic representation of a particular locality ⟨a ~ poem⟩ ⟨~ painting⟩ — **to·po·graph·i·cal·ly** \-k(ə-)lē\ *adv*

to·pog·ra·phy \tə-'päg-rə-fē\ *n* [ME *topographie*, fr. LL *topographia*, fr. Gk, fr. *topographein* to describe a place, fr. *topos* place + *graphein* to write — more at CARVE] **1 a :** the art or practice of graphic delineation in detail usu. on maps or charts of natural and man-made features of a place or region esp. in a way to show their relative positions and elevations **b :** topographical surveying **2 a :** the configuration of a surface including its relief and the position of its natural and man-made features **b :** the physical or natural features of an object or entity and their structural relationships

to·po·log·i·cal \,täp-ə-'läj-i-kəl, ,tō-pə-\ *adj* **1 :** of or relating to topology **2 :** being or involving properties unaltered under a one-to-one continuous transformation ⟨continuity and connectedness are ~ properties⟩ — **to·po·log·i·cal·ly** \-k(ə-)lē\ *adv*

topological transformation *n* **:** HOMEOMORPHISM

to·pol·o·gist \tə-'päl-ə-jəst, tō-\ *n* **:** a student of or specialist in topology

to·pol·o·gy \-jē\ *n* [ISV] **1 :** topographical study of a particular place; *specif* **:** the history of a region as indicated by its topography **2 :** the anatomy of a particular region of the body **3 :** a branch of mathematics that investigates the properties of a geometric configuration (as a point set) that are unaltered if the configuration is subjected to a one-to-one continuous transformation in both directions

top·onym \'täp-ə-,nim, 'tō-pə-\ *n* [ISV, back-formation fr. *toponymy*] **:** PLACE-NAME

top·onym·ic \,täp-ə-'nim-ik, ,tō-pə-\ *adj* **:** of or relating to toponyms or toponymy — **top·onym·i·cal** \-i-kəl\ *adj*

top·on·y·my \tə-'pän-ə-mē, tō-\ *n* [ISV, fr. *top-* + Gk *onyma*, *onoma* name — more at NAME] **1 :** the place-names of a region or language or the esp. etymological study of them **2 :** the nomenclature of regional anatomy

top·per \'täp-ər\ *n* **1 :** one that puts on or takes off tops **2 :** one that is at or on the top **3 a :** SILK HAT **b :** OPERA HAT **4 :** something (as a joke) that caps everything preceding **5 :** a woman's usu. short and loose-fitting lightweight outer coat

¹**top·ping** \'täp-iŋ\ *n* **1 :** something that forms a top: as **a :** GARNISH **b :** a flavorful addition (as of sauce or nuts) served on top of a dessert **c :** a finishing layer of mortar on concrete **2 :** the action of one that tops **3 :** something removed by topping

²**topping** *adj* **1 :** highest in rank or eminence **2** *NewEng* **:** PROUD **3** *chiefly Brit* **:** EXCELLENT

top·ple \'täp-əl\ *vb* **top·pling** \-(ə-)liŋ\ [freq. of ²*top*] *vi* **1 :** to fall from or as if from being top-heavy **2 :** to be or seem unsteady **:** TOTTER ~ *vt* **1 :** to cause to topple **:** OVERTURN **2 :** OVERTHROW

top round *n* **:** meat (as steak) from the inner part of a round of beef

tops \'täps\ *adj* **:** topmost in quality, ability, popularity, or eminence — used predicatively

top·sail \'täp-,sāl, -səl\ *also* **top·s'l** \-səl\ *n* **1 :** the sail next above the lowermost sail on a mast in a square-rigged ship **2 :** the sail set above and sometimes on the gaff in a fore-and-aft rigged ship

top secret *adj* **:** demanding inviolate secrecy among top officials or a select few

top sergeant *n* **:** FIRST SERGEANT 1

¹**top·side** \'täp-'sīd\ *n, often attrib* **1** *pl* **:** the top portion of the outer surface of a ship on each side above the waterline **2 :** the highest level of authority

²**topside** *adv* **1** *also* **top·sides** \-'sīdz\ **:** on deck **2 :** to or on the top or surface **3 :** in a position of authority

top·soil \'täp-,sȯil\ *n* **:** surface soil usu. including the average plow depth or the A-horizon

top spin *n* [¹*top*] **:** a rotary motion imparted to a ball that causes it to rotate forward in the direction of its flight

top·stitch \'täp-,stich\ *vt* **:** to make a line of stitching on the outside of (a garment) close to a seam

top·stone \'täp-,stōn\ *n* **:** CAPSTONE

top·sy–tur·vi·ly \,täp-sē-'tər-və-lē\ *adv* **:** in a topsy-turvy manner

top·sy–tur·vi·ness \-vē-nəs\ *n* **:** the quality or state of being topsy-turvy

¹**top·sy–tur·vy** \,täp-sē-'tər-vē\ *adv* [prob. deriv. of *tops* (pl. of ¹*top*) + obs. E *terve* (to turn upside down)] **1 :** with the top or head downward **:** upside down **2 :** in utter confusion or disorder

²**topsy–turvy** *adj* **:** turned topsy-turvy **:** totally disordered

³**topsy–turvy** *n* **:** TOPSY-TURVINESS — **top·sy–tur·vy·dom** \-vēd-əm\ *n*

top·work \'täp-,wərk\ *vt* **:** to graft scions of another variety on the main branches of (as fruit trees) usu. to obtain more desirable fruit

toque \'tōk\ *n* [MF, soft hat with a narrow brim worn esp. in the 16th cent., fr. OSp *toca* headdress] **1 :** a woman's small hat without a brim made in any of various soft close-fitting shapes **2 :** TUQUE

tor \'tȯ(ə)r\ *n* [ME, fr. OE *torr*] **:** a high craggy hill

To·rah \'tōr-ə, 'tȯr-\ *n* [Heb *tōrāh*] **1 :** LAW 2b **2 :** the body of divine knowledge and law found in the Jewish scriptures and oral tradition **3 :** a leather or parchment scroll of the Pentateuch used in a synagogue for liturgical purposes

torch \'tȯ(ə)rch\ *n, often attrib* [ME *torche*, fr. OF, bundle of twisted straw or tow, torch, fr. (assumed) VL *torca;* akin to L *torquēre* to twist — more at TORTURE] **1 :** a burning stick of resinous wood or twist of tow used to give light and usu. carried in the hand **:** FLAMBEAU **2 :** something (as wisdom or knowledge) likened to a torch as giving light or guidance **3 :** any of various portable devices for emitting an unusually hot flame — compare BLOWTORCH **4** *chiefly Brit* **:** FLASHLIGHT — **torch·bear·er** \-,bar-ər, -,ber-\ *n* — **torch·light** \-,līt\ *n*

tor·chon \'tȯr-,shän\ *n* [F, duster, fr. OF, bundle of twisted straw, fr. *torche*] **:** a coarse bobbin or machine-made lace made with fan-shaped designs forming a scalloped edge

torch singer *n* **:** a singer of torch songs

torch song *n* **:** a popular sentimental song of unrequited love

torch·wood \'tȯrch-,wu̇d\ *n* **1 :** a notably resinous or oily wood suitable for torches **2 a :** any of a genus (*Amyris*) usu. placed in the rue family of tropical American trees and shrubs having fragrant resinous streaky yellowish brown wood that is hard and heavy **b :** the wood of a torchwood

tore *past of* TEAR

to·re·ador \'tȯr-ē-ə-,dȯ(ə)r, 'tōr-, 'tär-\ *n* [Sp, fr. *toreado*, pp. of *torear* to fight bulls, fr. *toro* bull, fr. L *taurus* — more at TAURINE] **:** BULLFIGHTER, TORERO

to·re·ro \tə-'re(ə)r-(,)ō\ *n* [Sp, fr. LL *taurarius*, fr. L *taurus* bull] **:** BULLFIGHTER

to·reu·tic \tə-'rüt-ik\ *adj* [Gk *toreutikos*, fr. *toreuein* to bore through, chase, fr. *toreus* boring tool; akin to Gk *tetrainein* to bore — more at THROW] **:** of or relating to work wrought in metal esp. by embossing or chasing

to·reu·tics \-iks\ *n pl but sing in constr* **:** the art or process of making toreutic work

tori *pl of* TORUS

to·ric \'tōr-ik, 'tȯr-\ *adj* **:** of, relating to, or shaped like a torus or segment of a torus

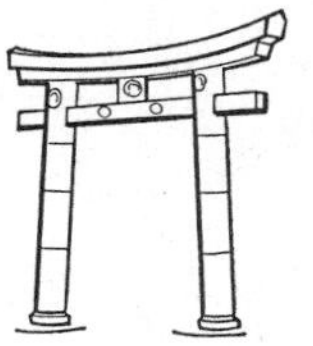
torii

to·rii \'tōr-ē-,ē, 'tȯr-\ *n, pl* **torii** [Jap] **:** a Japanese gateway of light construction commonly built at the approach to a Shinto temple

¹**tor·ment** \'tȯr-,ment\ *n* [ME, fr. OF, fr. L *tormentum* torture, fr. *torquēre* to twist — more at TORTURE] **1 :** the infliction of torture (as by rack or wheel) **2 :** extreme pain or anguish of body or mind **:** AGONY **3 :** a source of vexation or pain

²**tor·ment** \tȯr-'ment, 'tȯr-,\ *vt* **1 a :** to cause severe suffering of body or mind to **:** AFFLICT, DISTRESS **b :** to stir up **:** AGITATE ⟨~*ed* seas⟩ **c :** to cause worry or vexation to **:** HARASS **2 :** DISTORT, TWIST **syn** see AFFLICT

tor·men·til \'tȯr-mən-,til\ *n* [ME *turmentill*, fr. ML *tormentilla*, fr. L *tormentum;* fr. its use in allaying pain] **:** a yellow-flowered Eurasian potentilla (*Potentilla tormentilla*) with a root used in tanning and dyeing

tor·men·tor *also* **tor·ment·er** \tȯr-'ment-ər, 'tȯr-,\ *n* **1 :** one that torments **2 :** a fixed curtain or flat on each side of a theater stage that prevents the audience from seeing into the wings **3 :** a screen covered to prevent echo during the taking of motion-picture scenes

torn *past part of* TEAR

tor·na·dic \tȯr-'nād-ik, -'nad-\ *adj* **:** relating to, characteristic of, or constituting a tornado

tor·na·do \tȯr-'nād-(,)ō\ *n, pl* **tornadoes** *or* **tornados** [modif. of Sp *tronada* thunderstorm, fr. *tronar* to thunder, fr. L *tonare* — more at THUNDER] **1** *archaic* **:** a tropical thunderstorm **2 a :** a squall accompanying a thunderstorm in Africa **b :** a violent destructive whirling wind accompanied by a funnel-shaped cloud that progresses in a narrow path over the land **3 :** a violent or destructive windstorm **:** WHIRLWIND

tor·nil·lo \tȯr-'nē-(,)(y)ō, -'nil-(,)ō\ *n, pl* **tornillos** [Sp, lit., small lathe, screw, dim. of *torno* lathe, fr. L *tornus* — more at TURN] **:** SCREW BEAN 1

to·roid \'tō(ə)r-,ȯid, 'tȯ(ə)r-\ *n* [NL *torus*] **1 :** a surface generated by a plane closed curve rotated about a line in its plane that does not intersect the curve **2 :** a body whose surface has the form of a toroid

to·roi·dal \tō-'rȯid-ᵊl\ *adj* **:** of, relating to, or shaped like a torus or toroid **:** doughnut-shaped ⟨a ~ resistance coil⟩ — **to·roi·dal·ly** \-ᵊl-ē\ *adv*

to·rose \'tō(ə)r-,ōs, 'tȯ(ə)r-\ *adj* [L *torosus*, fr. *torus* protuberance, bulge] **:** KNOBBED; *esp, of a plant part* **:** cylindrical with alternate swellings and contractions

¹**tor·pe·do** \tȯr-'pēd-(,)ō\ *n, pl* **torpedoes** [L, lit., stiffness, numbness, fr. *torpēre* to be stiff or numb] **1 :** ELECTRIC RAY **2 :** an engine or machine for destroying ships by blowing them up: as **a :** a submarine mine **b :** a dirigible self-propelling cigar-shaped submarine projectile filled with an explosive charge that is projected from a ship often designed for the purpose against another at a distance **3 a :** a charge of explosive enclosed in a container or case **b :** a small firework that explodes when thrown against a hard object **4 :** a professional gunman or assassin

²**torpedo** *vt* **tor·pe·do·ing** \-'pēd-ə-wiŋ\ **1 :** to hit or sink (a ship) with a naval torpedo **:** strike or destroy by torpedo **2 :** to destroy or nullify altogether **:** WRECK ⟨~ a plan⟩

torpedo boat *n* **:** a boat designed for firing torpedoes; *specif* **:** a small very fast thinly plated boat with one or more torpedo tubes

torpedo–boat destroyer *n* **:** a large, swift, and powerfully armed torpedo boat orig. intended principally for the destruction of torpedo boats but later used also as a formidable torpedo boat

torpedo tube *n* **:** a tube fixed near the waterline through which a torpedo is fired

tor·pid \'tȯr-pəd\ *adj* [L *torpidus*, fr. *torpēre* to be stiff or numb; akin to L *stirps* trunk, stock, lineage, OE *starian* to stare — more at STARE] **1 a :** having lost motion or the power of exertion or feeling **:** DORMANT, NUMB **b :** sluggish in functioning or acting ⟨a ~ frog⟩ ⟨a ~ mind⟩ **2 :** lacking in energy or vigor **:** APATHETIC, DULL — **tor·pid·i·ty** \tȯr-'pid-ət-ē\ *n* — **tor·pid·ly** \'tȯr-pəd-lē\ *adv*

tor·por \'tȯr-pər\ *n* [L, fr. *torpēre*] **1 :** a state of mental and motor inactivity with partial or total insensibility **:** extreme sluggishness or stagnation of function **2 :** DULLNESS, APATHY **syn** see LETHARGY

tor·quate \'tȯr-,kwāt\ *adj* [L *torquatus*, lit., wearing a torque, fr. *torques*] **:** having a ring esp. of color around the neck

¹**torque** \'tȯ(ə)rk\ *n* [F, fr. L *torques*, fr. *torquēre* to twist — more at TORTURE] **:** a usu. metal collar or neck chain worn by the ancient Gauls, Germans, and Britons

2**torque** *n* [L *torquēre* to twist] **:** something that produces or tends to produce rotation or torsion and whose effectiveness is measured by the product of the force and the perpendicular distance from the line of action of the force to the axis of rotation; *broadly* **:** a turning or twisting force

torque converter *n* **:** a device for transmitting and amplifying torque esp. by hydraulic means

torr \'tȯ(ə)r\ *n, pl* **torr** [Evangelista *Torricelli* †1647 It inventor of the barometer] **:** a unit of pressure equal to 1⁄760 of an atmosphere

1**tor·rent** \'tȯr-ənt, 'tär-\ *n* [F, fr. L *torrent-, torrens*, fr. *torrent-, torrens* burning, seething, rushing, fr. prp. of *torrēre* to parch, burn — more at THIRST] **1 :** a violent stream of a liquid (as water or lava) **2 :** a raging flood **:** a tumultuous outpouring **:** FLUX, RUSH

2**torrent** *adj* **:** TORRENTIAL

tor·ren·tial \tȯ-'ren-chəl, tə-\ *adj* **1 a :** relating to or having the character of a torrent ⟨~ rains⟩ **b :** caused by or resulting from action of rapid streams ⟨~ gravel⟩ **2 :** resembling a torrent in violence or rapidity of flow — **tor·ren·tial·ly** \-'rench-(ə-)lē\ *adv*

tor·rid \'tȯr-əd, 'tär-\ *adj* [L *torridus*, fr. *torrēre*] **1 a :** parched with heat esp. of the sun **:** HOT ⟨~ sands⟩ **b :** giving off intense heat **:** SCORCHING **2 :** ARDENT, PASSIONATE ⟨~ love letters⟩ — **tor·rid·i·ty** \tȯ-'rid-ət-ē\ *n* — **tor·rid·ly** \'tȯr-əd-lē, 'tär-\ *adv* — **tor·rid·ness** *n*

torrid zone *n* **:** the belt of the earth between the tropics over which the sun is vertical at some period of the year

tor·sade \tȯr-'säd, -'sād\ *n* [F, fr. obs. F *tors* twisted, fr. LL *torsus*] **:** a twisted cord or ribbon used esp. as a hat ornament

tor·sion \'tȯr-shən\ *n* [LL *torsus*, pp. of L *torquēre* to twist] **1 :** the twisting or wrenching of a body by the exertion of forces tending to turn one end or part about a longitudinal axis while the other is held fast or turned in the opposite direction; *also* **:** the state of being twisted **2 :** the reactive torque that an elastic solid exerts by reason of being under torsion — **tor·sion·al** \'tȯr-shnəl, -shən-ᵊl\ *adj* — **tor·sion·al·ly** \-ē\ *adv*

torsion balance *n* **:** an instrument used to measure minute forces (as electrostatic or magnetic attraction and repulsion) by the torsion of a wire or filament

tor·so \'tȯr-(,)sō\ *n, pl* **torsos** *or* **tor·si** \'tȯr-,sē\ [It, lit., stalk, fr. L *thyrsus* stalk, thyrsus] **1 :** the trunk of a sculptured representation of a human body; *esp* **:** the trunk of a statue whose head and limbs are mutilated **2 :** something that is mutilated or left unfinished **3 :** the human trunk

tort \'tȯ(ə)rt\ *n* [ME, fr. MF, fr. ML *tortum*, fr. L, neut. of *tortus* twisted, fr. pp. of *torquēre*] **:** a wrongful act for which a civil action will lie except one involving a breach of contract

torte \'tȯrt-ə, 'tȯ(ə)rt\ *n, pl* **tor·ten** \'tȯrt-ᵊn\ *or* **tortes** [G, prob. fr. It *torta*, fr. LL, round loaf of bread] **:** a cake made of many eggs, sugar, and often grated nuts or dry bread crumbs and usu. covered with a rich frosting

tor·tel·li·ni \,tȯrt-ᵊl-'ē-nē\ *n* [It] **:** a noodle dough cut in rounds, filled with savory fillings, and boiled

tor·ti·col·lis \,tȯrt-ə-'käl-əs\ *n* [NL, fr. L *tortus* twisted + *-i-* + *collum* neck] **:** a more-or-less fixed twisting of the neck resulting in an abnormal carriage of the head — called also *wryneck*

tor·ti·lla \tȯr-'tē-(y)ə\ *n* [AmerSp, dim. of Sp *torta* cake, fr. LL, round loaf of bread] **:** a round thin cake of unleavened cornmeal bread usu. eaten hot with a topping or filling of ground meat or cheese

tor·tious \'tȯr-shəs\ *adj* **:** implying or involving tort — **tor·tious·ly** *adv*

tor·toise \'tȯrt-əs\ *n* [ME *tortu, tortuce*, fr. MF *tortue*] **1 :** any of an order (Testudinata) of reptiles **:** TURTLE; *esp* **:** a land turtle **2 :** someone or something regarded as slow or laggard

tortoise beetle *n* **:** any of a family (Chrysomelidae) of small tortoise-shaped beetles with larvae that feed on leaves

tor·toise·shell \'tȯrt-ə-,shel, -əs(h)-,shel\ *n* **1 :** the mottled horny substance of the shell of some turtles (as the hawksbill turtle) used in inlaying and in making various ornamental articles **2 :** any of several showy butterflies (genus *Nymphalis*)

tor·to·ni \tȯr-'tō-nē\ *n* [prob. fr. *Tortoni*, 19th cent. It restaurateur in Paris] **:** ice cream made of heavy cream sometimes with minced almonds, chopped maraschino cherries, or various flavoring ingredients

tor·tri·cid \'tȯr-trə-səd\ *adj* [NL *Tortric-, Tortrix*] **:** of or relating to a family (Tortricidae) of small stout-bodied moths many of whose larvae feed in fruits — **tortricid** *n*

tor·trix \'tȯr-triks\ *n* [NL *Tortric-, Tortrix*, genus of moths, fr. L *tortus*, pp. of *torquēre* to twist; fr. the habit of twisting or rolling leaves to make a nest] **:** a tortricid moth

tor·tu·os·i·ty \,tȯr-chə-'wäs-ət-ē\ *n* **1 :** the quality or state of being tortuous **2 :** something winding or twisted **:** a crooked place or part **:** BEND, SINUOSITY

tor·tu·ous \'tȯrch-(ə-)wəs\ *adj* [ME, fr. MF *tortueux*, fr. L *tortuosus*, fr. *tortus* twist, fr. *tortus*, pp. of *torquēre*] **1 :** marked by repeated twists, bends, or turns **:** WINDING **2 a :** marked by devious or indirect tactics **:** CROOKED, TRICKY **b :** CIRCUITOUS, INVOLVED — **tor·tu·ous·ly** *adv* — **tor·tu·ous·ness** *n*

1**tor·ture** \'tȯr-chər\ *n* [F, fr. LL *tortura*, fr. L *tortus*, pp. of *torquēre* to twist; akin to OHG *drāhsil* turner, Gk *atraktos* spindle] **1 :** the infliction of intense pain (as from burning, crushing, or wounding) to punish, coerce, or afford sadistic pleasure **2 a :** anguish of body or mind **:** AGONY **b :** something that causes agony or pain **3 :** distortion or overrefinement of a meaning or an argument **:** STRAINING

2**torture** *vt* **tor·tur·ing** \'tȯrch-(ə-)riŋ\ **1 :** to punish or coerce by inflicting excruciating pain **2 :** to cause intense suffering to **:** TORMENT **3 :** to twist or wrench out of shape **:** DISTORT, WARP **syn** see AFFLICT — **tor·tur·er** \'tȯr-chər-ər\ *n*

tor·tur·ous \'tȯrch-(ə-)rəs\ *adj* **:** causing torture **:** cruelly painful — **tor·tur·ous·ly** *adv*

tor·u·la \'tȯr-(y)ə-lə, 'tär-\ *n, pl* **tor·u·lae** \-,lē, -,lī\ *also* **torulas** [NL, fr. L *torus* protuberance] **:** any of various yeasts or similar fungi that lack sexual spores, do not produce alcoholic fermentations, and are typically acid formers

tor·u·lose \-,lōs\ *adj* [NL *torulosus*, dim. of L *torosus* torose] **:** somewhat torose

to·rus \'tōr-əs, 'tȯr-\ *n, pl* **to·ri** \'tō(ə)r-,ī, 'tȯ(ə)r-, -,ē\ [NL, fr. L, protuberance, bulge, torus molding] **1 :** a smooth rounded anatomical protuberance **2 :** a large molding of convex profile commonly occurring as the lowest molding in the base of a column **3 :** RECEPTACLE 2b **4 :** a doughnut-shaped surface generated by a circle rotated about an axis in its plane that does not intersect the circle; *broadly* **:** TOROID

To·ry \'tōr-ē, 'tȯr-\ *n* [IrGael *tōraidhe* pursued man, robber, fr. MIr *tōir* pursuit] **1 :** an Irish papist or royalist outlaw chiefly of the 17th century **2** *obs* **:** MARAUDER **3 a :** a member or supporter of a major British political group of the 18th and early 19th centuries favoring at first the Stuarts and later royal authority and the established church and seeking to preserve the traditional political structure and defeat parliamentary reform — compare WHIG **b :** CONSERVATIVE 1b **4 :** an American upholding the cause of the British Crown against the supporters of colonial independence during the American Revolution **:** LOYALIST **5** *often not cap* **:** an extreme conservative esp. in political and economic principles — **Tory** *adj*

Tory Democracy *n* **:** a political philosophy advocating preservation of established institutions and traditional principles combined with political democracy and a social and economic program designed to benefit the common man

To·ry·ism \'tōr-ē-,iz-əm, 'tȯr-\ *n* **:** the principles and practices of or associated with Tories

tory–rory *adj* [origin unknown] *obs* **:** UPROARIOUS, ROISTERING

tosh \'täsh\ *n* [origin unknown] **:** sheer nonsense **:** BOSH, TWADDLE

1**toss** \'tȯs, 'täs\ *vb* [prob. of Scand origin; akin to Sw dial. *tossa* to spread, scatter] *vt* **1 a :** to fling or heave continuously about, to and fro, or up and down ⟨a ship *~ed* by waves⟩ **b :** BANDY 2c **c :** to mix lightly until well coated with a dressing ⟨~ a salad⟩ **2 :** to make uneasy **:** stir up **:** DISTURB **3 a :** to throw with a quick, light, or careless motion or with a sudden jerk ⟨~ a ball around⟩ **b :** to throw up in the air ⟨*~ed* by a bull⟩ **c :** 2MATCH 5a **4 a :** to fling or lift with a sudden motion ⟨*~es* her head angrily⟩ **b :** to tilt suddenly so as to empty by drinking ⟨*~ed* his glass⟩ **5 :** to accomplish, provide, or dispose of readily or easily ⟨~ off a few verses⟩ ~ *vi* **1 a :** to move restlessly or turbulently; *esp* **:** to twist and turn repeatedly ⟨*~ed* sleeplessly all night⟩ **b :** to move with a quick or spirited gesture **:** FLOUNCE **2 :** to decide an issue by flipping a coin **syn** see THROW — **toss·er** *n*

2**toss** *n* **1 :** the state or fact of being tossed **2 :** an act or instance of tossing: as **a :** an abrupt tilting or upward fling **b :** a deciding by chance and esp. by flipping a coin **c :** THROW, PITCH

toss·pot \-,pät\ *n* **:** DRUNKARD, SOT

toss–up \-,əp\ *n* **1 :** TOSS 2b **2 :** an even chance

1**tot** \'tät\ *n* [origin unknown] **1 :** a small child **:** TODDLER **2 :** a small drink or allowance of liquor **:** SHOT

2**tot** *vb* **tot·ted; tot·ting** [*tot.*, abbr. of *total*] *vt* **:** to add together **:** SUMMARIZE, TOTAL ~ *vi* **:** ADD

1**to·tal** \'tōt-ᵊl\ *adj* [ME, fr. MF, fr. ML *totalis*, fr. L *totus* whole, entire] **1 :** comprising or constituting a whole **:** ENTIRE ⟨~ amount⟩ **2 :** COMPLETE, UTTER ⟨a ~ failure⟩ **3 :** concentrating all available personnel and resources on a single objective **:** ALL-OUT, THOROUGHGOING **syn** see WHOLE

2**total** *n* **1 :** a product of addition **:** SUM **2 :** an entire quantity **:** AMOUNT **syn** see SUM

3**total** *adv* **:** TOTALLY

4**total** *vt* **to·taled** *or* **to·talled; to·tal·ing** *or* **to·tal·ling** **1 :** to add up **:** COMPUTE **2 :** to amount to **:** NUMBER

total depravity *n* **:** a state of corruption due to original sin held in Calvinism to infect every part of man's nature and to make the natural man unable to know or obey God

total eclipse *n* **:** an eclipse in which one celestial body is completely obscured by the shadow or body of another

to·tal·ism \'tōt-ᵊl-,iz-əm\ *n* **:** TOTALITARIANISM — **to·tal·is·tic** \,tōt-ᵊl-'is-tik\ *adj*

to·tal·i·tar·i·an \(,)tō-,tal-ə-'ter-ē-ən\ *adj* [*total* + *-itarian* (as in *authoritarian*)] **1 a :** of or relating to centralized control by an autocratic leader or hierarchy **:** AUTHORITARIAN, DICTATORIAL; *esp* **:** DESPOTIC **b :** of or relating to a political regime based on subordination of the individual to the state and strict control of all aspects of the life and productive capacity of the nation esp. by coercive measures (as censorship and terrorism) **2 a :** advocating or characteristic of totalitarianism **b :** completely regulated by the state esp. as an aid to national mobilization in an emergency **c :** exercising autocratic powers **:** tending toward monopoly — **totalitarian** *n* — **to·tal·i·tar·i·an·ism** \-ē-ə-,niz-əm\ *n* — **to·tal·i·tar·i·an·ize** \-,nīz\ *vt*

to·tal·i·ty \tō-'tal-ət-ē\ *n* **1 :** an aggregate amount **:** SUM, WHOLE **2 :** the quality or state of being total **:** ENTIRETY, WHOLENESS

to·tal·iza·tor *or* **to·tal·isa·tor** \'tōt-ᵊl-ə-,zāt-ər\ *n* **:** a pari-mutuel machine

to·tal·ize \'tōt-ᵊl-,īz\ *vt* **1 :** to add up **:** TOTAL **2 :** to express as a whole **:** SUMMARIZE

to·tal·iz·er \-,ī-zər\ *n* **:** one that totalizes; *specif* **:** a pari-mutuel machine

to·tal·ly \'tōt-ᵊl-ē\ *adv* **1 :** in a total manner **:** WHOLLY **2 :** as a whole **:** in toto

total utility *n* **:** the degree of utility of an economic good (as an article or service) considered as a whole — compare MARGINAL UTILITY

to·ta·quine \'tōt-ə-,kwīn, -,k(w)ēn, -k(w)ən\ *or* **to·ta·qui·na** \,tōt-ə-'kwī-nə, -'k(w)ē-\ *n* [NL *totaquina*, fr. ML *totalis* total + Sp *quina* cinchona; fr. its containing all the alkaloids of cinchona bark — more at QUININE] **:** an antimalarial drug containing quinine and other alkaloids extracted from American cinchona bark

1**tote** \'tōt\ *vt* [origin unknown] **1 :** to carry by hand **:** bear on the person **:** LUG, PACK **2 :** HAUL, CONVEY

2**tote** *n, often attrib* **:** BURDEN, LOAD

3**tote** *vb* [E dial. *tote*, n. (total)] **:** TOT, TOTAL

4**tote** *n* [short for *totalizator*] **:** a pari-mutuel machine

to·tem \'tōt-əm\ *n, often attrib* [Ojibwa *ototeman* his totem] **1 a :** an object (as an animal or plant) serving as the emblem of a family or clan and often as a reminder of its ancestry; *also* **:** a usu. carved or painted representation of such an object **b :** a family or clan identified by a common totemic object **2 :** something that serves as an emblem or revered symbol — **to·tem·ic** \tō-'tem-ik\ *adj*

to·tem·ism \'tōt-ə-,miz-əm\ *n* **1 :** belief in kinship with or a mystical relationship between a group or an individual and a totem **2 :** a system of social organization based on totemic affiliations

to·tem·ist \-ə-məst\ *n* **:** a practitioner of or specialist in totemism

to·tem·is·tic \ˌtōt-ə-ˈmis-tik\ *adj* **:** of or relating to totemists or totemism **:** TOTEMIC

to·tem·ite \ˈtōt-ə-ˌmīt\ *n* **:** TOTEMIST

totem pole *n* **1 :** a pole or pillar carved and painted with a series of totemic symbols representing family lineage that is erected before the houses of some Indian tribes of the northwest coast of No. America **2 :** an order of rank **:** HIERARCHY

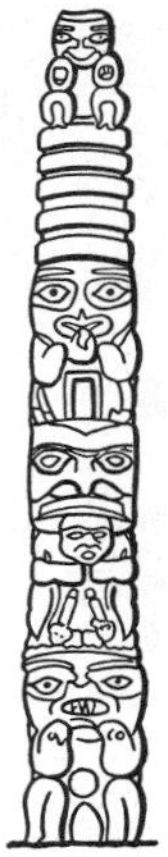
totem pole

tot·er \ˈtōt-ər\ *n* **:** one that totes

tote road *n* **:** a road for hauling supplies esp. into a lumber camp

toth·er *or* **t'oth·er** \ˈtət͟h-ər\ *pron or adj* [ME *tother*, alter. (resulting from incorrect division of *thet other* the other, fr. *thet* the — fr. OE *thæt* — + *other*) of *other* — more at THAT] *chiefly dial* **:** the other

toti- *comb form* [L *totus* whole, entire] **:** whole **:** wholly ⟨*toti*palmate⟩

to·ti·pal·mate \ˌtōt-ə-ˈpal-ˌmāt, -ˈpä(l)m-ˌāt\ *adj* **:** having all four toes united by a web ⟨pelicans are ∼⟩ — **to·ti·pal·ma·tion** \-ˌpal-ˈmā-shən, -ˌpä(l)m-ˈā-\ *n*

to·ti·po·ten·cy \tō-ˈtip-ət-ən-sē, ˌtōt-ə-ˈpōt-ᵊn-\ *n* **:** ability to generate or regenerate a whole organism from a part

to·ti·po·tent \-ənt, -ᵊnt\ *adj* **:** capable of development along any of the lines inherently possible to its kind ⟨a mesenchyme cell is ∼⟩

¹**tot·ter** \ˈtät-ər\ *vi* [ME *toteren*] **1 a :** to tremble or rock as if about to fall **:** SWAY **b :** to become unstable **:** threaten to collapse **2 :** to move unsteadily **:** STAGGER, WOBBLE — **tot·tery** \-ə-rē\ *adj*

²**totter** *n* **:** an unsteady gait **:** WOBBLE

tot·ter·ing *adj* **1 a :** being in an unstable condition ⟨a ∼ building⟩ **b :** walking unsteadily **2 :** lacking firmness or stability **:** INSECURE ⟨a ∼ regime⟩ — **tot·ter·ing·ly** \-ə-riŋ-lē\ *adv*

tot·ty \ˈtät-ē\ *adj* [ME *toty*] *archaic* **:** DAZED, FUDDLED

Toua·reg *var of* TUAREG

tou·can \ˈtü-ˌkan, -ˌkän, tü-ˈ\ *n* [F, fr. Pg *tucano*, fr. Tupi] **:** any of a family (Ramphastidae) of fruit-eating birds of tropical America with brilliant coloring and a very large but light and thin-walled beak

¹**touch** \ˈtəch\ *vb* [ME *touchen*, fr. OF *tuchier*, fr. (assumed) VL *toccare* to knock, strike a bell, touch, of imit. origin] *vt* **1 :** to bring a bodily part into contact with esp. so as to perceive through the tactile sense **:** PALPATE **2 :** to strike or push lightly esp. with the hand or foot or an implement **3 :** to lay hands upon (one afflicted with scrofula) — compare KING'S EVIL **4** *archaic* **a :** to play on (a stringed instrument) **b :** to perform (a melody) by playing or singing **5 a :** to take into the hands or mouth ⟨never ∼*es* alcohol⟩ **b :** to put hands upon in any way or degree ⟨don't ∼ anything before the police come⟩; *esp* **:** to commit violence upon ⟨swears he never ∼*ed* the child⟩ **6 :** to concern oneself with **7 :** to induce to give or lend ⟨∼*ed* him for ten dollars⟩ **8 :** to cause to be briefly in contact or conjunction with something ⟨∼*ed* his spurs to his horse⟩ **9 a** (1) **:** to meet without overlapping or penetrating **:** ADJOIN (2) **:** to get to **:** REACH ⟨the speedometer needle ∼*ed* 80⟩ **b :** to be tangent to **c :** to rival in quality or value ⟨nothing can ∼ that cloth for durability⟩ **10 :** to speak or tell of esp. in passing **11 :** to affect the interest of **:** CONCERN **12 a :** to leave a mark or impression on **b :** to harm slightly by or as if by contact **:** TAINT, BLEMISH ⟨fruit ∼*ed* by frost⟩ ⟨a horse ∼*ed* in the wind⟩ **c :** to give a delicate tint, line, or expression to ⟨a smile ∼*ed* her lips⟩ **13 :** to draw or delineate with light strokes **14 a :** to hurt the feelings of **:** WOUND **b :** to move to sympathetic feeling ⟨∼*ed* by the loyalty of his friends⟩ ∼ *vi* **1 a :** to feel something with a body part (as the hand or foot) **b :** to lay hand or finger on a person to cure disease (as scrofula) **2 :** to be in contact **3 :** to come close **:** VERGE ⟨his actions ∼ on treason⟩ **4 :** to have a bearing **:** RELATE — used with *on* or *upon* **5 a :** to make a brief or incidental stop on shore during a trip by water ⟨∼*ed* at several ports⟩ **b :** to treat a topic in a brief or casual manner — used with *on* or *upon* ⟨∼*ed* upon many points⟩ **syn** see AFFECT — **touch·able** \-ə-bəl\ *adj* — **touch·er** *n*

²**touch** *n* **1 :** a light stroke, tap, or push **2 :** the act or fact of touching **3 :** the special sense by which pressure or traction exerted on the skin or mucous membrane is perceived **4 :** mental or moral sensitiveness, responsiveness, or tact **5 :** a specified sensation conveyed through the tactile receptors **:** FEEL ⟨the velvety ∼ of a fabric⟩ **6 a :** the act of rubbing gold or silver on a touchstone to test its quality **b :** TEST, TRIAL **7 a :** a visible effect **:** MARK **b :** WEAKNESS, DEFECT **8 :** something slight of its kind: as **a :** a light attack ⟨∼ of fever⟩ **b :** a small quantity **:** TRACE ⟨∼ of spring in the air⟩ **c :** a transient emotion ⟨momentary ∼ of compunction⟩ **9 a** *archaic* **:** the playing of an instrument (as a lute or piano) with the fingers; *also* **:** musical notes or strains so produced **b :** a manner or method of touching or striking esp. the keys of a keyboard instrument **c :** particular action of a keyboard instrument with reference to the resistance of its keys to pressure ⟨piano with a stiff ∼⟩ **10 :** a set of changes in change ringing less than the total number possible or less than a peal **11 :** a delicate stroke in creating or improving an artistic composition **12 :** distinctive manner or method ⟨the ∼ of a master⟩ **13 :** a characteristic or distinguishing trait or quality **14** *slang* **:** an act of soliciting or getting a gift or loan **15 :** the state or fact of being in contact or communication **16 :** the area outside of the sidelines in soccer or outside of and including the touchlines in rugby

touch and go *n* **1 :** rapid movement from point to point **2 :** a highly uncertain or precarious situation

touch·back \ˈtəch-ˌbak\ *n* **:** an act or instance in football of being in possession of the ball behind one's own goal line when the ball is declared dead after crossing the goal line as the result of an impetus given by an opponent

touch down *vt* **:** to place (the ball in rugby) by hand on the ground on or over an opponent's goal line in scoring a try or behind one's own goal line as a defensive measure ∼ *vi, of an airplane* **:** LAND

touch·down \ˈtəch-ˌdau̇n\ *n* **1 :** the act of touching a football to the ground behind an opponent's goal; *specif* **:** the act of scoring six points in American football by being lawfully in possession of the ball on, above, or behind an opponent's goal line when the ball is declared dead **2 :** the act or moment of touching down with an airplane

tou·ché \tü-ˈshā\ *interj* [F, fr. pp. of *toucher* to touch, fr. OF *tuchier*] — used to acknowledge a hit in fencing or the success of an argument

touched \ˈtəcht\ *adj* **1 :** emotionally stirred **2 :** slightly unbalanced mentally

touch football *n* **:** football played informally and chiefly characterized by the substitution of touching for tackling

touch·hole \ˈtəch-ˌhōl\ *n* **:** the vent in old-time cannons or firearms through which the charge was ignited

touch·i·ly \ˈtəch-ə-lē\ *adv* **:** in a touchy manner

touch·i·ness \ˈtəch-ē-nəs\ *n* **:** the quality or state of being touchy

¹**touch·ing** *prep* **:** in reference to **:** CONCERNING

²**touching** *adj* **:** capable of stirring emotions **:** PATHETIC **syn** see MOVING — **touch·ing·ly** \-iŋ-lē\ *adv*

touch·line \ˈtəch-ˌlīn\ *n* **:** either of the lines that bound the sides of the field of play in rugby and soccer

touch·mark \-ˌmärk\ *n* **:** an identifying maker's mark impressed on pewter

touch–me–not \ˈtəch-mē-ˌnät\ *n* **1 :** JEWELWEED **2 :** SQUIRTING CUCUMBER

touch off *vt* **1 :** to describe or characterize to a nicety **2 a :** to cause to explode by or as if by touching with fire **b :** to release or initiate with sudden violence ⟨*touched off* a new wave of violence⟩

touch·stone \ˈtəch-ˌstōn\ *n* **1 :** a black siliceous stone related to flint and formerly used to test the purity of gold and silver by the streak left on the stone when rubbed by the metal **2 :** a test or criterion for determining the quality or genuineness of a thing **syn** see STANDARD

touch system *n* **:** a method of typewriting that assigns a particular finger to each key and makes it possible to type without looking at the keyboard

touch–type \ˈtəch-ˌtīp\ *vb* **:** to type by the touch system

touch up *vt* **1 :** to improve or perfect by small additional strokes or alterations **2 :** to stimulate by or as if by a flick of a whip

touch·wood \ˈtəch-ˌwu̇d\ *n* **:** ³PUNK

touchy \ˈtəch-ē\ *adj* **1 :** marked by readiness to take offense on slight provocation **2 a** *of a body part* **:** acutely sensitive or irritable **b** *of a chemical* **:** highly explosive or inflammable **3 :** calling for tact, care, or caution in treatment ⟨a ∼ subject among the members of his family⟩ **syn** see IRASCIBLE

¹**tough** \ˈtəf\ *adj* [ME, fr. OE *tōh*; akin to OHG *zāhi* tough] **1 a :** strong or firm in texture but flexible and not brittle **b :** not easily chewed **2 :** GLUTINOUS, STICKY **3 :** characterized by severity or uncompromising determination ⟨∼ and inflexible foreign policy —*New Statesman & Nation*⟩ **4 :** capable of enduring strain, hardship, or severe labor **5 :** very hard to influence **:** STUBBORN **6 :** extremely difficult to cope with **7 :** stubbornly fought ⟨∼ contest⟩ **8 :** ROWDYISH, RUFFIANLY **9 :** marked by absence of softness or sentimentality **syn** see STRONG — **tough·ly** *adv* — **tough·ness** *n*

²**tough** *n* **:** a tough person; *esp* **:** ROWDY

tough·en \ˈtəf-ən\ *vb* **tough·en·ing** \-(ə-)niŋ\ *vt* **:** to make tough ∼ *vi* **:** to become tough

tough·ie *also* **toughy** \ˈtəf-ē\ *n* **:** one that is tough: as **a :** a loud rough rowdy person **b :** a difficult problem

tough–mind·ed \ˈtəf-ˈmīn-dəd\ *adj* **:** realistic or unsentimental in temper or habitual point of view

tou·pee \tü-ˈpā\ *n* [F *toupet* forelock, fr. OF, dim. of *top*, *toup*, of Gmc origin; akin to OHG *zopf* tuft of hair — more at TOP] **1 :** a curl or lock of hair made into a topknot on a periwig or natural hairdress; *also* **:** a periwig with such a topknot **2 :** a small wig or section of false hair worn to cover a bald spot

¹**tour** \ˈtu̇(ə)r, *1 is also* ˈtau̇(ə)r\ *n* [ME, fr. MF, fr. OF *tourn*, *tour* lathe, circuit, turn — more at TURN] **1 :** one's turn in an orderly schedule **:** SHIFT **2 a :** a journey for business, pleasure, or education in which one returns to the starting point **b :** a brief turn **:** ROUND

²**tour** *vi* **:** to make a tour ∼ *vt* **1 :** to make a tour of **2 :** to present (as a theatrical production) on a tour

tou·ra·co \ˈtu̇r-ə-ˌkō\ *n, pl* **touracos** [native name in western Africa] **:** any of a family (Musophagidae) of African birds related to the cuckoos

tour·bil·lion \tu̇r-ˈbil-yən\ *or* **tour·bil·lon** \tür-bē-(y)ōⁿ\ *n* [MF *tourbillon*, fr. L *turbin-*, *turbo* — more at TURBINE] **1 :** WHIRLWIND **2 :** a vortex esp. of a whirlwind or whirlpool **3 :** a firework having a spiral flight

tour de force \ˌtu̇(ə)rd-ə-ˈfō(ə)rs, -ˈfȯ(ə)rs\ *n, pl* **tours de force** *same*\ [F] **:** a feat of strength, skill, or ingenuity

touring car *n* **:** an open automobile with two cross seats, usu. four doors, and a folding top — called also *phaeton*, *tour·er* \ˈtu̇r-ər\

tour·ism \ˈtu̇(ə)r-ˌiz-əm\ *n* **1 :** the practice of traveling for recreation **2 :** the guidance or management of tourists **3 a :** the promotion or encouragement of touring **b :** the accommodation of tourists

tour·ist \ˈtu̇r-əst\ *n* **:** one that makes a tour for pleasure or culture — **tourist** *adj*

tourist card *n* **:** a citizenship identity card issued to a tourist usu. for a stated period of time in lieu of a passport or a visa

tourist class *n* **:** economy accommodation on a ship, airplane, or train

tourist court *n* **:** MOTEL

tourist home *n* **:** a house in which rooms are available for rent to transients

tour·ma·line \ˈtu̇r-mə-lən, -ˌlēn\ *n* [Sinhalese *toramalli* carnelian] **:** a mineral of variable color $(Na,Ca)(Li,Mg,Fe,Al)(Al,Fe)_6B_3Si_6O_{27}(O,OH,F)_4$ that consists of a complex silicate and makes a gem of great beauty when transparent and cut

tour·na·ment \ˈtu̇r-nə-mənt, ˈtər-\ *n* [ME *tornement*, fr. OF *torneiement*, fr. *torneier*] **1 a :** a knightly sport of the middle ages between mounted combatants armed with blunted lances or swords and divided into two parties contesting for a prize or favor bestowed by the lady of the tournament **b :** the whole series of knightly sports, jousts, and tilts occurring at one time and place **2 :** a championship series of games or athletic contests

¹**tour·ney** \ˈtu̇(-ə)r-nē, ˈtər-\ *vi* [ME *tourneyen*, fr. MF *torneier*, fr.

OF, fr. *torn, tourn* lathe, circuit] : to perform in a tournament
²**tourney** *n* : TOURNAMENT
tour·ni·quet \'tu̇r-ni-kət, 'tər-\ *n* [F, turnstile, tourniquet, fr. *tourner* to turn, fr. OF *torner* — more at TURN] : a device (as a bandage twisted tight with a stick) to arrest bleeding
¹**touse** \'tau̇z, 'tüz\ *vt* [ME *-tousen;* akin to OHG *zirzūsōn* to pull to pieces] : RUMPLE, TOUSLE
²**touse** *n* : a noisy disturbance
¹**tou·sle** \'tau̇-zəl\ *vt* **tou·sling** \'tau̇z-(ə-)liŋ\ [ME *touselen,* freq. of *-tousen*] : DISHEVEL, RUMPLE
²**tou·sle** \'tau̇-zəl, *1 is also* 'tü-\ *n* **1** *Scot* : rough dalliance : TUSSLE **2** : a tangled mass
¹**tout** \'tau̇t\ *vb* [ME *tuten* to peer; akin to OE *tōtian* to stick out, Norw *tyte*] *vi* **1** : to canvass for customers **2 a** *chiefly Brit* : to spy on racehorse trials or stable secrets for betting purposes **b** : to give a tip or solicit bets on a racehorse ~ *vt* **1** : to spy on : WATCH **2 a** *Brit* : to spy out information about (as a racing stable or horse) **b** : to give a tip or solicit bets on (a racehorse) **3** : to solicit or peddle importunately
²**tout** *n* : one who touts: as **a** : one who solicits custom **b** *chiefly Brit* : one who spies out racing information for betting purposes **c** : one who gives tips or solicits bets on a racehorse
³**tout** \'tau̇t, 'tüt\ *vt* [alter. of ¹*toot*] : to praise or publicize loudly : BALLYHOO
tout·er \'tau̇t-ər\ *n* : TOUT
to·va·rich *or* **to·va·rish** \tə-'vär-ish(ch)\ *n* [Russ *tovarishch*] : COMRADE
¹**tow** \'tō\ *vt* [ME *towen,* fr. OE *togian;* akin to OE *tēon* to draw, pull, OHG *ziohan* to draw, pull, L *ducere* to draw, lead] : to draw or pull along behind : HAUL
²**tow** *n* **1** : a rope or chain for towing **2 a** : the act or an instance of towing **b** : the fact or state of being towed **3** : something towed (as a boat or car)
³**tow** *n* [ME, fr. OE *tow-* spinning; akin to ON *tō* tuft of wool for spinning, OE *tawian* to prepare for use — more at TAW] **1** : short broken fiber from flax, hemp, or jute that is used for yarn, twine, or stuffing **2** : yarn or cloth made of tow
⁴**tow** *n* [ME (Sc), prob. fr. OE *toh-* (in *tohlīne* towline); akin to OE *togian* to tow] *chiefly Scot & dial Eng* : ROPE
tow·age \'tō-ij\ *n* **1** : the act of towing **2** : the price paid for towing
¹**to·ward** \'tō(-ə)rd, 'tȯ(-ə)rd\ *adj* [ME *toward,* fr. OE *tōweard* facing, imminent, fr. *tō,* prep., to + *-weard* -ward] **1** *also* **to·wards** \'tō(-ə)rdz, 'tȯ(-ə)rdz\ [ME *towardes,* fr. OE *tōweardes,* prep., toward, fr. *tōweard,* adj.] **a** : coming soon : IMMINENT **b** : happening at the moment : AFOOT **2 a** *obs* : quick to learn : APT **b** : FAVORING, PROPITIOUS ⟨a ~ breeze⟩
²**to·ward** *or* **to·wards** \(')tō(-ə)rd(z), (')tȯ(-ə)rd(z), tə-'wȯrd(z), (')twȯrd(z), (')twōrd(z)\ *prep* **1** : in the direction of ⟨driving ~ town⟩ **2 a** : along a course leading to ⟨a long stride ~ disarmament⟩ **b** : in relation to ⟨an attitude ~ life⟩ **3 a** : at a point in the direction of : NEAR ⟨a cottage somewhere up ~ the lake⟩ **b** : in such a position as to face ⟨his back was ~ me⟩ **4** : not long before ⟨~ the end of the afternoon⟩ **5 a** : in the way of help or assistance in ⟨did all he could ~ raising campaign funds⟩ **b** : for the partial payment of ⟨proceeds go ~ the establishment of a scholarship⟩
to·ward·li·ness \'tōrd-lē-nəs, 'tȯrd-\ *n, archaic* **1** : the quality or state of being toward or towardly
to·ward·ly \'tō(-ə)rd-lē, 'tȯ(-ə)rd-\ *adj* **1** *archaic* : FAVORABLE, PROPITIOUS **2** : developing favorably : PROMISING **3** : PLEASANT, AFFABLE — **towardly** *adv*
tow·boat \'tō-,bōt\ *n* **1** : TUGBOAT **2** : a compact shallow-draft boat with squared bow and towing knees for pushing tows of barges on inland waterways
tow car *n* : WRECKER 2b — called also *tow truck*
¹**tow·el** \'tau̇(-ə)l\ *n* [ME *towaille,* fr. OF *toaille,* of Gmc origin; akin to OHG *dwahila* towel; akin to OHG *dwahan* to wash, OPruss *twaxtan* bath cloth] : an absorbent cloth or paper for wiping or drying
²**towel** *vb* **tow·eled** *or* **tow·elled; tow·el·ing** *or* **tow·el·ling** *vt* : to rub or dry with a towel ~ *vi* : to use a towel
tow·el·ing *or* **tow·el·ling** \'tau̇-(ə-)liŋ\ *n* : a cotton or linen fabric often used for making towels
¹**tow·er** \'tau̇(-ə)r\ *n, often attrib* [ME *tour, tor,* fr. OE *torr* & OF *tor, tur,* both fr. L *turris,* fr. Gk *tyrsis*] **1** : a building or structure typically higher than its diameter and high relative to its surroundings that may stand apart (as a campanile), or be attached (as a church belfry) to a larger structure, and that may be of skeleton framework (as an observation or transmission tower) **2** : a towering citadel : FORTRESS — **tow·ered** \'tau̇(-ə)rd\ *adj*
²**tower** *vi* : to reach or rise to a great height : SOAR; *also* : OVERSHADOW
tower house *n* : a medieval fortified castle (as in Scotland)
tow·er·ing *adj* **1 a** : rising to a great height : IMPOSING ⟨~ pines⟩ **b** : impressively great : SURPASSING **2** : reaching a high point of intensity : OVERWHELMING ⟨a ~ rage⟩ **3** : going beyond proper bounds : OVERWEENING ⟨~ ambitions⟩
tower wagon *n* : a wagon or motor truck with a high adjustable platform on which workmen can stand
tow·head \'tō-,hed\ *n* : a person having soft whitish hair — **tow·head·ed** \-'hed-əd\ *adj*
to·whee \tō-'(h)ē, -'(h)wē; 'tō-,hē, 'tō-(,)ē\ *n* [imit.] : any of numerous American finches (genera *Pipilo* and *Chlorura*); *esp* : a common finch (*P. erythrophthalmus*) of eastern No. America having the male black, white, and rufous — called also *chewink*
towing basin *n* : a tank of water in which models of ship or seaplane hulls or floats are tested — called also *towing tank*
to wit \tə-'wit\ *adv* [ME *to witen,* lit., to know — more at WIT] : that is to say : NAMELY
tow·line \'tō-,līn\ *n* : a line used in towing
tow·mond \'tō-,mänd\ *n* [ME *towlmonyth,* fr. OE *twelf mōnath,* fr. *twelf* twelve + *mōnath* month] *Scot* : TWELVEMONTH, YEAR
town \'tau̇n\ *n* [ME, fr. OE *tūn* enclosure, village, town; akin to OHG *zūn* enclosure, OIr *dūn* fortress] **1** *dial Eng* : a cluster or aggregation of houses recognized as a distinct place with a place-name : HAMLET **2 a** : a compactly settled area as distinguished from surrounding rural territory **b** : a compactly settled area usu. larger than a village but smaller than a city **c** : a large densely populated urban area : CITY **d** : an English village having a periodic fair or market **3** : a neighboring city, capital city, or metropolis **4** : the city or urban life as contrasted with the country **5** : a New England territorial and political unit usu. containing both rural and unincorporated urban areas under a single town government — called also *township; also* : a New England community governed by a town meeting — **town** *adj*
town car *n* : a 4-door automobile with a permanently enclosed passenger compartment in the rear separated from the driver's compartment by a sliding glass partition
town clerk *n* : a public officer charged with recording the official proceedings and vital statistics of a town
town crier *n* : a town officer who makes proclamations
town·ee \tau̇-'nē\ *n* : TOWNSMAN
town hall *n* : a public building used for town-government offices and meetings
town house *n* : a house in town; *specif* : the city residence of one having a countryseat or having a chief residence elsewhere
town manager *n* : a New England town official having the status and functions of a city manager
town meeting *n* : a meeting of inhabitants or taxpayers constituting the legislative authority of a town
towns·folk \'tau̇nz-,fōk\ *n pl* : TOWNSPEOPLE
town·ship \'tau̇n-,ship\ *n* **1** : an ancient unit of administration in England identical in area with or a division of a parish **2 a** : TOWN 5 **b** : a unit of local government in some northeastern and north central states usu. having a chief administrative officer or board **c** : an unorganized subdivision of the county in Maine, New Hampshire, and Vermont **d** : an electoral and administrative district of the county in the southern U.S. **3** : a division of territory in surveys of U.S. public land containing 36 sections or 36 square miles
towns·man \'tau̇nz-mən\ *n* **1 a** : a native or resident of a town or city **b** : an urban or urbane person **2** : a fellow citizen of a town
towns·peo·ple \-,pē-pəl\ *n pl* **1** : the inhabitants of a town or city : TOWNSMEN **2** : town-dwelling or town-bred persons
towns·wom·an \-,wu̇m-ən\ *n* **1** : a woman native or resident of a town or city **2** : a woman born or residing in the same town or city as another
town·wear \'tau̇n-,wa(ə)r, -,we(ə)r\ *n* : apparel (as of dark color or tailored style) that is suitable for wear in the city or to business
towny \'tau̇-nē\ *n* : TOWNSMAN
tow·path \'tō-,path, -,pȧth\ *or* **towing path** *n* : a path (as along a canal) traveled by men or animals towing boats
tow·rope \-,rōp\ *n* : a line used in towing
tow sack \'tō-'sak\ *n* [³*tow*] *Midland & South* : GUNNYSACK
tox- *or* **toxo-** *comb form* [LL, fr. L *toxicum* poison] : poisonous : poison ⟨*tox*emia⟩ ⟨*Toxo*plasma⟩
tox·al·bu·min \,täk-,sal-'byü-mən\ *n* [ISV] : any of various toxic substances of protein nature
tox·a·phene \'täk-sə-,fēn\ *n* [fr. *Toxaphene,* a trademark] : a chlorinated camphene insecticide
tox·emia \täk-'sē-mē-ə\ *n* [NL] : an abnormal condition associated with the presence of toxic substances in the blood — **tox·emic** \-mik\ *adj*
tox·ic \'täk-sik\ *adj* [LL *toxicus,* fr. L *toxicum* poison, fr. Gk *toxikon* arrow poison, fr. neut. of *toxikos* of a bow, fr. *toxon* bow, arrow] **1** : of, relating to, or caused by a poison or toxin **2** : POISONOUS — **tox·ic·i·ty** \täk-'sis-ət-ē\ *n*
toxic- *or* **toxico-** *comb form* [NL, fr. L *toxicum*] : poison ⟨*toxicology*⟩ ⟨*toxicosis*⟩
tox·i·cant \'täk-si-kənt\ *n* [ML *toxicant-, toxicans,* prp. of *toxicare* to poison, fr. L *toxicum*] : a toxic agent; *esp* : one for insect control that kills rather than repels — **toxicant** *adj*
tox·i·co·gen·ic \,täk-si-kō-'jen-ik\ *adj* : producing toxic products ⟨~ bacteria⟩
tox·i·co·log·ic \-kə-'läj-ik\ *adj* : of or relating to toxicology or toxins — **tox·i·co·log·i·cal·ly** \-i-k(ə-)lē\ *adv*
tox·i·col·o·gist \,täk-sə-'käl-ə-jəst\ *n* : a specialist in toxicology
tox·i·col·o·gy \-jē\ *n* : a science that deals with poisons and their effect and with the problems involved (as clinical, industrial, or legal)
tox·i·co·sis \,täk-sə-'kō-səs\ *n* [NL] : a pathological condition caused by the action of a poison or toxin
tox·in \'täk-sən\ *n* [ISV] : a colloidal proteinaceous poisonous substance that is a specific product of the metabolic activities of a living organism and is usu. very unstable, notably toxic when introduced into the tissues, and typically capable of inducing antibody formation
tox·in–an·ti·tox·in \'täk-sə-'nant-i-,täk-sən\ *n* : a mixture of toxin and antitoxin used esp. formerly in immunizing against a disease (as diphtheria) for which they are specific
tox·oid \'täk-,sȯid\ *n* [ISV] : a toxin of a pathogenic organism treated so as to destroy its toxicity but leave it capable of inducing the formation of antibodies on injection
tox·oph·i·lite \täk-'säf-ə-,līt\ *n* [Gk *toxon* bow, arrow + *philos* dear, loving] : one fond of or expert at archery — **toxophilite** *adj* — **tox·oph·i·ly** \-lē\ *n*
toxo·plas·mo·sis \,täk-sə-,plaz-'mō-səs\ *n* [NL, fr. *Toxoplasma,* genus name, fr. *tox-* + *plasma*] : infection of man, other mammals, or birds with disease caused by microorganisms (genus *Toxoplasma*) that invade the tissues and may seriously damage the central nervous system esp. of infants
¹**toy** \'tȯi\ *n* [ME *toye* dalliance] **1** *obs* **a** : amorous dalliance : FLIRTING **b** : PASTIME, SPORT; *also* : a sportive or amusing act : ANTIC **2 a** : something paltry or trifling **b** : a literary or musical trifle or diversion **c** : TRINKET, BAUBLE **3** : something for a child to play with **4** : something diminutive; *esp* : a diminutive animal (as of a small breed or variety) **5** : something that can be toyed with **6** *Scot* : a headdress of linen or woolen hanging down over the shoulders and formerly worn by old women of the lower classes — **toy** *adj* — **toy·like** \'tȯi-,līk\ *adj*
²**toy** *vi* **1** : to engage in flirtation : DALLY **2** : to amuse oneself as if with a toy : PLAY **syn** see TRIFLE — **toy·er** \'tȯi(-ə)r\ *n*
toy Man·ches·ter \-'man-,ches-tər, -chə-stər\ *n* [*Manchester,* England] : any of an English breed of small long-legged black-and-tan terriers with erect ears
toy·on \'tȯi-,än\ *n* [AmerSp *tollon*] : an ornamental evergreen shrub (*Photinia arbutifolia*) of the rose family of the No. American Pacific coast having white flowers succeeded by persistent bright red berries

tra·be·at·ed \'trā-bē-,āt-əd\ *adj* [L *trabes* beam] **:** designed or constructed of horizontal beams or lintels — **tra·be·ation** \,trā-bē-'ā-shən\ *n*

tra·bec·u·la \trə-'bek-yə-lə\ *n, pl* **tra·bec·u·lae** \-,lē, -,lī\ *also* **trabeculas** [NL, fr. L, little beam, dim. of *trabs, trabes* beam — more at THORP] **1 :** a small bar, rod, bundle of fibers, or septal membrane in the framework of a body organ or part **2 :** a fold, ridge, or bar projecting into or extending from a plant part; *esp* **:** a row of cells bridging an intercellular space — **tra·bec·u·lar** \-lər\ *adj* — **tra·bec·u·late** \-lət\ *adj*

1**trace** \'trās\ *n* [ME, fr. MF, fr. *tracier* to trace] **1** *archaic* **:** a course or path that one follows **:** ROAD **2 a :** a mark or line left by something that has passed; *also* **:** FOOTPRINT **b :** a path beaten by or as if by feet **:** TRAIL **3 :** a sign or evidence of some past thing **:** VESTIGE; *esp* **:** ENGRAM **4 :** something traced or drawn (as a traced or lightly marked line): as **a :** the marking made by a recording instrument (as a seismograph or kymograph) **b :** the ground plan of a military installation or position either on a map or on the ground **5 a :** the intersection of a line or plane with a plane **b :** the usu. bright line or spot that moves across the screen of a cathode-ray tube; *also* **:** the path taken by such a line or spot **6 :** a minute and often barely detectable amount or indication; *esp* **:** an amount of a chemical constituent not quantitatively determined because of minuteness

syn TRACE, VESTIGE, TRACK mean a perceptible sign made by something that has passed. TRACE may suggest any line, mark, or discernible effect; VESTIGE applies to a tangible reminder such as a fragment or remnant of what is past and gone; TRACK implies a continuous line that can be followed

2**trace** *vb* [ME *tracen*, fr. MF *tracier*, fr. (assumed) VL *tractiare* to drag, draw, fr. L *tractus*, pp. of *trahere* to pull, draw — more at DRAW] *vt* **1 a :** DELINEATE, SKETCH **b :** to form (as letters or figures) carefully or painstakingly **c :** to copy (as a drawing) by following the lines or letters as seen through a transparent superimposed sheet **d :** to impress or imprint (as a design or pattern) with a tracer **e :** to record a tracing of in the form of a curved, wavy, or broken line ⟨~ the heart action⟩ **f :** to adorn with linear ornamentation (as tracery or chasing) **2** *archaic* **:** to travel over **:** TRAVERSE **3 a :** to follow the footprints, track, or trail of **b :** to follow or study out in detail or step by step **c :** to discover by going backward over the evidence step by step **d :** to discover signs, evidence, or remains of **4 :** to lay out the trace of (a military installation) ~ *vi* **1 :** to make one's way; *esp* **:** to follow a track or trail **2 :** to be traceable historically ⟨a family that ~s to the Norman conquest⟩

3**trace** *n* [ME *trais*, pl., traces, fr. MF, pl. of *trait* pull, draft, trace — more at TRAIT] **1 :** either of two straps, chains, or lines of a harness for attaching a horse to something (as a vehicle) to be drawn **2 :** LEADER 1e(2) **3 :** one or more vascular bundles supplying a leaf or twig **4 :** a connecting bar or rod pivoted at each end to another piece and used for transmitting motion

trace·able \'trā-sə-bəl\ *adj* **:** capable of being traced — **trace·able·ness** *n* — **trace·ably** \-blē\ *adv*

trace element *n* **:** a chemical element used by organisms in minute quantities and held essential to their physiology

trace·less \'trā-sləs\ *adj* **:** having or leaving no trace — **trace·less·ly** *adv*

trac·er \'trā-sər\ *n* **1 a :** a person who traces missing persons or property and esp. goods lost in transit **b :** an inquiry sent out in tracing a shipment lost in transit **2 :** a draftsman who traces designs, patterns, or markings **3 :** a device (as a stylus) used in tracing **4 a :** ammunition containing a chemical composition to mark the flight of projectiles by a trail of smoke or fire **b :** a substance and esp. a labeled element or atom used to trace the course of a chemical or biological process

trac·ery \'trās-(ə-)rē\ *n* **1 :** architectural ornamental work with branching lines; *esp* **:** decorative openwork in the head of a Gothic window **2 :** a decorative interlacing of lines suggestive of Gothic tracery

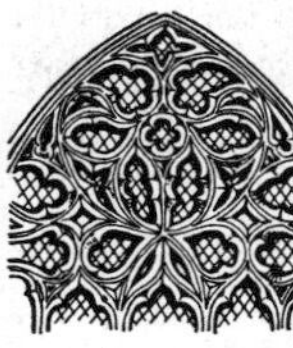
tracery

trache- *or* **tracheo-** *comb form* [NL, fr. ML *trachea*] **1 :** trachea ⟨*trache*itis⟩ ⟨*tracheo*tomy⟩ **2 :** tracheal and ⟨*tracheo*bronchial⟩

tra·chea \'trā-kē-ə\ *n, pl* **tra·che·ae** \-kē-,ē, -kē-,ī\ *also* **tra·che·as** [ME, fr. ML, fr. LL *trachia*, fr. Gk *tracheia* (*artēria*) rough (artery), fr. fem. of *trachys* rough; akin to Gk *thrassein* to trouble — more at DARK] **1 :** the main trunk of the system of tubes by which air passes to and from the lungs in vertebrates **2** [NL, fr. ML] **:** a xylem element or series of elements felt to resemble an animal trachea **3** [NL] **:** one of the air-conveying tubules forming the respiratory system of most insects and many other arthropods

tra·che·al \-kē-əl\ *adj* **:** of, relating to, or resembling a trachea or tracheae

tra·che·ary \'trā-kē-,er-ē\ *adj* **1 :** breathing by means of tracheae **2 :** TRACHEAL

tra·che·ate \-kē-,āt, -ət\ *adj* **:** having tracheae as breathing organs

tra·cheid \'trā-kē-əd, -,kēd\ *n* [ISV] **:** a long tubular cell that is peculiar to xylem and functions in conduction and support with tapering closed ends and thickened lignified walls — **tra·che·idal** \trā-'kē-əd-ᵊl\ *adj*

tra·che·itis \,trā-kē-'īt-əs\ *n* [NL] **:** inflammation of the trachea

tra·cheo·bron·chi·al \,trā-kē-ō-'bräŋ-kē-əl\ *adj* **:** of or relating to both trachea and bronchi ⟨~ lesions⟩

tra·cheo·phyte \'trā-kē-ə-,fīt\ *n* [NL *Tracheophyta*, fr. *trache-* + Gk *phyton* plant; akin to Gk *phyein* to bring forth — more at BE] **:** any of a division (Tracheophyta) comprising green plants with a vascular system that contains tracheids or tracheary elements and including ferns and related plants and the seed plants

tra·che·ot·o·my \,trā-kē-'ät-ə-mē\ *n* **:** the surgical operation of cutting into the trachea esp. through the skin

tra·chle \'trak-əl\ *vt* [perh. fr. Flem *tragelen* to walk with difficulty, drag; akin to OHG *trāgi* sluggish, Lith *drižti* to become tired] **1** *Scot* **:** BEDRAGGLE, SOIL **2** *Scot* **:** to tire by overwork

tra·cho·ma \trə-'kō-mə\ *n* [NL, fr. Gk *trachōma*, fr. *trachys*] **:** a chronic contagious conjunctivitis marked by inflammatory granulations on the conjunctival surfaces and caused by a rickettsia (*Chlamydia trachomatis*) — **tra·cho·ma·tous** \trə-'käm-ət-əs, -'kōm-\ *adj*

tra·chy·sper·mous \,trak-i-'spər-məs, ,trā-ki-\ *adj* [deriv. of Gk *trachys* + Gk *sperma* seed, sperm] **:** rough-seeded

tra·chyte \'trak-,īt, 'trā-,kīt\ *n* [F, fr. Gk *trachys*] **:** a usu. light-colored volcanic rock consisting chiefly of potash feldspar

tra·chyt·ic \trə-'kit-ik\ *adj* **:** of or relating to a texture of igneous rocks in which lath-shaped feldspar crystals are in almost parallel lines

trac·ing *n* **1 :** the act of one that traces **2 :** something that is traced: as **a :** a copy made on a superimposed transparent sheet **b :** a graphic record of a movement made instrumentally

1**track** \'trak\ *n* [ME *trak*, fr. MF *trac*, perh. of Gmc origin; akin to MD *tracken, trecken* to pull, haul — more at TREK] **1 a :** detectable evidence (as the wake of a ship, a line of footprints, or a wheel rut) that something has passed **b :** a path made by repeated footfalls **:** TRAIL **c** (1) **:** a course laid out esp. for racing (2) **:** the parallel rails of a railroad **2 :** VESTIGE, TRACE **3 a :** the course along which something moves **b :** the projection on the earth's surface of the path along which an airplane has actually flown **4 a :** a sequence of events **:** a train of ideas **:** SUCCESSION **b :** awareness of a fact or progression ⟨keep ~⟩ ⟨lose ~⟩ **5 a :** the width of a wheeled vehicle from wheel to wheel and usu. from the outside of the rims **b :** the tread of an automobile tire **c :** either of two endless metal belts on which a tracklaying vehicle travels **6 :** track-and-field sports; *esp* **:** those performed on a racing track **syn** see TRACE

2**track** *vt* **1 :** to follow the tracks or traces of **:** TRAIL **2 a :** to follow by vestiges **:** TRACE **b :** to observe or plot the moving path of (as a target or missile) with an instrument (as a telescope) **3 :** to pass over **:** TRAVERSE **4 a :** to make tracks upon **b :** to carry (as mud) on the feet and deposit ~ *vi* **1 a** *of a pair of wheels* (1) **:** to maintain a constant distance apart on the straightaway (2) **:** to fit a track or rails **b** *of a rear wheel of a vehicle* **:** to accurately follow the corresponding fore wheel on a straightaway **2 :** to leave tracks (as on a floor) — **track·er** *n*

track·age \-ij\ *n* **1 :** lines of railway track **2 a :** a right to use the tracks of another road **b :** the charge for such right

track–and–field \,trak-ən-'fē(ə)ld\ *adj* **:** of or relating to a sport performed on a racing track or on the adjacent field

track·lay·er \'trak-,lā-ər, -,le(-ə)r\ *n* **:** a tracklaying vehicle

track·lay·ing \-,lā-iŋ\ *adj* **:** of, relating to, or being a vehicle that travels on two endless metal belts

track·less \'trak-ləs\ *adj* **:** having no track **:** UNTROD — **track·less·ly** *adv* — **track·less·ness** *n*

trackless trolley *n* **:** TROLLEYBUS

track·walk·er \'trak-,wȯ-kər\ *n* **:** a worker employed to walk over and inspect a section of railroad tracks

1**tract** \'trakt\ *n, often cap* [ME *tracte*, fr. ML *tractus*, fr. L, action of drawing, extension; fr. its being sung without a break by one voice] **:** verses of Scripture sung or recited in the Mass on penitential days from Septuagesima to Holy Saturday, on ember days, and at requiems

2**tract** *n* [ME, modif. of L *tractatus* treatise] **:** a pamphlet or leaflet of political or religious propaganda

3**tract** *n* [L *tractus* action of drawing, extension, fr. *tractus*, pp. of *trahere* to pull, draw — more at DRAW] **1** *archaic* **:** extent or lapse of time **2 :** an area either large or small: as **a :** an indefinite stretch of land **b :** a defined area of land **3 :** a system of body parts or organs that collectively serve some special purpose ⟨the digestive ~⟩

trac·ta·bil·i·ty \,trak-tə-'bil-ət-ē\ *n* **:** the quality or state of being tractable

trac·ta·ble \'trak-tə-bəl\ *adj* [L *tractabilis*, fr. *tractare* to handle, treat] **1 :** capable of being easily led, taught, or controlled **:** DOCILE ⟨~ horse⟩ **2 :** easily handled, managed, or wrought **:** MALLEABLE **syn** see OBEDIENT — **trac·ta·ble·ness** *n* — **trac·ta·bly** \-blē\ *adv*

Trac·tar·i·an \trak-'ter-ē-ən\ *n* [fr. the fact that the Oxford movement was expounded in a series of pamphlets called *Tracts for the Times*] **:** a promoter or supporter of the Oxford movement esp. in its beginnings — **Tractarian** *adj* — **Trac·tar·i·an·ism** \-ē-ə-,niz-əm\ *n*

trac·tate \'trak-,tāt\ *n* [L *tractatus*, fr. *tractatus*, pp. of *tractare* to draw out, handle, treat — more at TREAT] **:** TREATISE, DISSERTATION

trac·tile \'trak-tᵊl, -,tīl\ *adj* [L *tractus*, pp. of *trahere*] **:** capable of being drawn out in length **:** TENSILE, DUCTILE — **trac·til·i·ty** \trak-'til-ət-ē\ *n*

trac·tion \'trak-shən\ *n* [ML *traction-, tractio*, fr. L *tractus*, pp.] **1 :** the act of drawing **:** the state of being drawn; *also* **:** the force exerted in drawing **2 :** the drawing of a vehicle by motive power; *also* **:** the motive power employed **3 :** the adhesive friction of a body on a surface on which it moves (as of a wheel on a rail) — **trac·tion·al** \-shnəl, -shən-ᵊl\ *adj*

traction engine *n* **1 :** a locomotive for drawing vehicles on highways or in the fields **2 :** a railway locomotive

trac·tive \'trak-tiv\ *adj* [L *tractus*, pp.] **1 :** serving to draw **2 :** TRACTIONAL

trac·tor \'trak-tər\ *n* [NL, fr. L *tractus*, pp.] **1 :** TRACTION ENGINE 1 **2 a :** a 4-wheeled or Caterpillar-tread rider-controlled automotive vehicle used esp. for drawing implements (as agricultural) or for bearing and propelling such implements **b :** a smaller 2-wheeled apparatus controlled through handlebars by a walking operator **c :** a truck with short chassis and no body used in combination with a trailer for the highway hauling of freight — called also *truck tractor* **3 :** an airplane having the propeller forward of the main supporting surfaces

1**trade** \'trād\ *n* [ME, fr. MLG; akin to OHG *trata* track, course, OE *tredan* to tread] **1 a** *obs* **:** a path traversed **:** WAY **b** *archaic* **:** a track or trail left by a man or animal **:** TREAD 1 **2 :** a customary course of action **:** PRACTICE **3 a :** the business or work in which one engages regularly **:** OCCUPATION **b :** an occupation requiring manual or mechanical skill **:** CRAFT **c :** the persons engaged in an occupation, business, or industry **4 a** *obs* **:** dealings between persons or groups **:** INTERCOURSE **b :** the business of buying and selling or bartering commodities **:** COMMERCE; *also* **:** TRAFFIC, MARKET **5 a :** an act or instance of trading **:** TRANSACTION; *also* **:** an exchange of property usu. without use of money **b :** a firm's cus-

tomers : CLIENTELE **c** : the concerns engaged in a business or industry

[2]**trade** *vt* **1** *archaic* : to do business with **2 a** : to give in exchange for another commodity : BARTER; *also* : to make an exchange of **b** : to buy and sell (as stock) regularly ~ *vi* **1** *obs* : to have dealings : NEGOTIATE **2 a** : to engage in the exchange, purchase, or sale of goods **b** : to make one's purchases : SHOP ⟨~*s* at his store⟩ **3** : to give one thing in exchange for another

[3]**trade** *adj* **1** : of, relating to, or used in trade **2 a** : intended for or limited to persons in a business or industry ⟨a ~ journal⟩ **b** : serving others in the same business rather than the ultimate user or consumer ⟨a ~ printing house⟩ **3** *also* **trades** : of, composed of, or representing the trades or trade unions ⟨a ~ club⟩ **4** : of or associated with a trade wind ⟨the ~ belts⟩

trade acceptance *n* : a time draft or bill of exchange for the amount of a specific purchase drawn by the seller on the buyer, bearing the buyer's acceptance, and often noting the place of payment (as a bank)

trade agreement *n* **1** : an international agreement on conditions of trade in goods and services **2** : an agreement resulting from collective bargaining

trade book *n* **1** : a book intended for general readership **2** : TRADE EDITION

trade discount *n* : a deduction from the list price of goods allowed by a manufacturer or wholesaler to a merchant

trade dollar *n* : a U. S. silver dollar weighing 420 grains .900 fine issued 1875–85 for use in Oriental trade

trade edition *n* : an edition in a standard format intended for general distribution — compare TEXT EDITION

trade in *vt* : to turn in as payment or part payment for a purchase or bill ⟨*trade* an old car *in* for a new one⟩

trade–in \ˈtrā-ˌdin\ *n* : an item of merchandise (as an automobile or refrigerator) taken as payment or part payment for a purchase

trade–last \ˈtrād-ˌlast\ *n* : a complimentary remark by a third person that a hearer offers to repeat to the person complimented if he will first report a compliment made about the hearer

[1]**trade·mark** \-ˌmärk\ *n* : a device (as a word) pointing distinctly to the origin or ownership of merchandise to which it is applied and legally reserved to the exclusive use of the owner as maker or seller

[2]**trademark** *vt* : to secure trademark rights for : register the trademark of

trade name *n* **1 a** : the name used for an article among traders **b** : an arbitrarily adopted name that is given by a manufacturer or merchant to an article or service to distinguish it as produced or sold by him and that may be used and protected as a trademark **2** : the name or style under which a concern does business

trad·er \ˈtrād-ər\ *n* **1** : a person whose business is buying and selling or barter : MERCHANT **2** : a ship engaged in the coastal or foreign trade

trade route *n* **1** : a route followed by traders (as in caravans) **2** : one of the sea lanes ordinarily used by merchant ships

trad·es·can·tia \ˌtrad-ə-ˈskan-ch(ē-)ə\ *n* [NL, genus name, fr. John *Tradescant* †1638 E traveler and gardener] : any of a genus (*Tradescantia* of the family Commelinaceae) of American herbs : SPIDERWORT

trade school *n* : a secondary school teaching the skilled trades

trade secret *n* : a formula, process, or device used in a business that is not published or divulged and that thereby gives an advantage over competitors

trades·folk \ˈtrādz-ˌfōk\ *n pl* : people in trade; *specif* : TRADESMEN

trades·man \ˈtrādz-mən\ *n* **1** : one who runs a retail store : SHOPKEEPER **2** : a workman in a skilled trade : CRAFTSMAN

trades·peo·ple \-ˌpē-pəl\ *n pl* : TRADESMEN 1

trade union *also* **trades union** *n* : LABOR UNION — **trade unionism** *n* — **trade unionist** *n*

tra·dev·man \trə-ˈdev-mən, ˈtrā-,\ *n* [*tra*ining *dev*ices *man*] : a petty officer in charge of naval training equipment

trade wind *n* : a wind blowing almost constantly in one direction; *esp* : a wind blowing almost continually toward the equator from the northeast in the belt between the northern horse latitudes and the doldrums and from the southeast in the belt between the southern horse latitudes and the doldrums

trading post *n* **1** : a station of a trader or trading company established in a sparsely settled region where trade in products of local origin (as furs) is carried on **2** : [6]POST 3b

trading stamp *n* : a printed stamp of value given as a premium to a retail customer to be accumulated and redeemed in merchandise

tra·di·tion \trə-ˈdish-ən\ *n* [ME *tradicioun*, fr. MF & L; MF *tradition*, fr. L *tradition-, traditio* action of handing over, tradition — more at TREASON] **1** : the handing down of information, beliefs, and customs by word of mouth or by example from one generation to another without written instruction **2** : an inherited pattern of thought or action (as a religious doctrine or practice or a social custom) **3** : cultural continuity in social attitudes and institutions — **tra·di·tion·al** \-ˈdish-nəl, -ən-ᵊl\ *adj* — **tra·di·tion·al·ly** \-ē\ *adv*

tra·di·tion·al·ism \-ˈdish-nə-ˌliz-əm, -ən-ᵊl-ˌiz-\ *n* **1** : the doctrines or practices of those who follow or accept tradition **2** : the beliefs of those opposed to modernism, liberalism, or radicalism — **tra·di·tion·al·ist** \-nə-ləst, -ən-ᵊl-əst\ *n or adj* — **tra·di·tion·al·is·tic** \-ˌdish-nə-ˈlis-tik, -ən-ᵊl-ˈis-\ *adj*

tra·di·tion·al·ize \trə-ˈdish-nə-ˌlīz, -ən-ᵊl-ˌīz\ *vt* : to make traditional

tra·di·tion·ary \trə-ˈdish-ə-ˌner-ē\ *adj* : TRADITIONAL

tra·di·tion·less \trə-ˈdish-ən-ləs\ *adj* : having no traditions

trad·i·tor \ˈtrad-ət-ər\ *n, pl* **trad·i·to·res** \ˌtrad-ə-ˈtōr-(ˌ)ēz, -ˈtȯr-\ [ME *traditour*, fr. L *traditor* — more at TRAITOR] **1** *obs* : TRAITOR **2** : a Christian surrendering the Scriptures, the sacred vessels, or the names of fellow Christians under Roman persecution

tra·duce \trə-ˈd(y)üs\ *vt* [L *traducere* to lead across, transfer, degrade, fr. *tra-, trans-* trans- + *ducere* to lead — more at TOW] **1** : to lower or disgrace the reputation of : DEFAME **2** : VIOLATE, BETRAY **syn** see MALIGN — **tra·duc·er** *n*

tra·duce·ment \-ˈd(y)ü-smənt\ *n* : an act of traducing

[1]**traf·fic** \ˈtraf-ik\ *n* [MF *trafique*, fr. OIt *traffico*, fr. *trafficare* to traffic] **1 a** : import and export trade **b** : the business of bartering or buying and selling **2** : INTERCOURSE, BUSINESS **3** *archaic* : GOODS, WARES **4 a** : the movement (as of vehicles or pedestrians) through an area or along a route **b** : the vehicles or pedestrians moving along a route **c** : the information or signals transmitted over a communications system : MESSAGES **5 a** : the passengers or cargo carried by a transportation system **b** : the business of transporting passengers or freight **syn** see BUSINESS

[2]**traffic** *vi* **traf·ficked; traf·fick·ing** : to carry on traffic — **traf·fick·er** *n*

traffic circle *n* : ROTARY 2

traffic court *n* : a minor court for disposition of petty prosecutions for violations of statutes, ordinances, and local regulations governing the use of highways and motor vehicles

traffic engineering *n* : engineering dealing with the design of streets and control of traffic

traffic island *n* : a paved or planted island in a roadway designed to guide the flow of traffic

traffic signal *n* : a usu. electrically operated signal (as a system of colored lights) for controlling traffic — called also *traffic light*

trag·a·canth \ˈtraj-ə-ˌkan(t)th, ˈtrag-, -kən(t)th; ˈtrag-ə-ˌsan(t)th\ *n* [MF *tragacanthe*, fr. L *tragacantha*, fr. Gk *tragakantha*, fr. *tragos* goat + *akantha* thorn — more at ACANTH-] : a gum obtained from various Asiatic or East European leguminous plants (genus *Astragalus*, esp. *A. gummifer*) that swells in water and is used in the arts and in pharmacy; *also* : a plant yielding this

tra·ge·di·an \trə-ˈjēd-ē-ən\ *n* **1** : a writer of tragedies **2** : an actor specializing in tragic roles

tra·ge·di·enne \trə-ˌjēd-ē-ˈen\ *n* [F *tragédienne*, fr. MF, fr. *tragedie*] : an actress who plays tragic roles

trag·e·dy \ˈtraj-əd-ē\ *n* [ME *tragedie*, fr. MF, fr. L *tragoedia*, fr. Gk *tragōidia*, fr. *tragos* goat + *aeidein* to sing; prob. fr. the satyrs represented by the original chorus; akin to Gk *trōgein* to gnaw — more at TERSE, ODE] **1 a** : a medieval narrative poem or tale typically describing the downfall of a great man **b** : a serious drama typically describing a conflict between the protagonist and a superior force (as destiny) and having a sorrowful or disastrous conclusion that excites pity or terror **c** : the literary genre of tragic dramas **2 a** : a disastrous event : CALAMITY **b** : MISFORTUNE **3** : tragic quality or element

trag·ic \ˈtraj-ik\ *adj* [L *tragicus*, fr. Gk *tragikos*, irreg. fr. *tragōidia* tragedy] **1** : of, marked by, or expressive of tragedy **2 a** : dealing with or treated in tragedy ⟨the ~ hero⟩ **b** : appropriate to or typical of tragedy **3 a** : DEPLORABLE, LAMENTABLE **b** : marked by a sense of tragedy

trag·i·cal \ˈtraj-i-kəl\ *adj* : TRAGIC — **trag·i·cal·ly** \-k(ə-)lē\ *adv* — **trag·i·cal·ness** \-kəl-nəs\ *n*

tragic flaw *n* : a flaw in the character of the hero of a tragedy that brings about his downfall

tragi·com·e·dy \ˌtraj-i-ˈkäm-əd-ē\ *n* [MF *tragicomedie*, fr. OIt *tragicomedia*, fr. OSp, fr. L *tragicomoedia*, fr. *tragicus* + *comoedia* comedy] : a drama or a situation blending tragic and comic elements — **tragi·com·ic** \-ˈkäm-ik\ *or* **tragi·com·i·cal** \-i-kəl\ *adj*

trago·pan \ˈtrag-ə-ˌpan\ *n* [NL, genus name, fr. L, an Ethiopian bird, fr. Gk, fr. *tragos* goat + *Pan* Pan] : any of several brilliantly colored Asiatic pheasants (genus *Tragopan*) having the back and breast usu. covered with white or buff ocelli

tra·gus \ˈtrā-gəs\ *n, pl* **tra·gi** \-ˌgī, -ˌjī\ [NL, fr. Gk *tragos*, a part of the ear, lit., goat] : the prominence in front of the external opening of the ear

[1]**trail** \ˈtrā(ə)l\ *vb* [ME *trailen*, fr. MF *trailler* to tow, fr. (assumed) VL *tragulare*, fr. L *tragula* sledge, dragnet] *vi* **1 a** : to hang down so as to drag along or sweep the ground **b** : to extend over a surface in a loose or straggling manner **c** : to grow to such length as to droop over the ground **2 a** : to walk or proceed draggingly, heavily, or wearily : PLOD, TRUDGE **b** : to lag behind : do poorly in relation to others **3** : to move, flow, or extend slowly in thin streams ⟨smoke ~*ing* from chimneys⟩ **4 a** : to extend in an erratic or uneven course or line : STRAGGLE **b** : DWINDLE ⟨voice ~*ing* off⟩ **5** : to follow a trail : track game ~ *vt* **1 a** : to draw or drag loosely along a surface : allow to sweep the ground **b** : HAUL, TOW **2 a** : to drag heavily or wearily (as a limb or the body) **b** : to carry or bring along as an addition, burden, or encumbrance **c** : to draw along in one's wake **3 a** : to follow upon the scent or trace of : TRACK **b** : to follow in the footsteps of : PURSUE **c** : to follow along behind **d** : to lag behind (as competitor) **syn** see CHASE

[2]**trail** *n* **1** : something that trails or is trailed : as **a** : a trailing plant **b** : the train of a gown **c** : a trailing arrangement (as of flowers) : SPRAY **d** : the part of a gun carriage that rests on the ground when the piece is unlimbered **2 a** : something that follows or moves along as if being drawn along : TRAIN **b** (1) : the streak produced by a meteor (2) : a continuous line produced photographically by permitting the image of a celestial body (as a star) to move over the plate **c** : a chain of consequences : AFTERMATH **3 a** : a trace or mark left by something that has passed or been drawn along : SCENT, TRACK ⟨a ~ of blood⟩ **b** (1) : a track made by passage through a wilderness : a beaten path (2) : a marked path through a forest or mountainous region

trail·blaz·er \-ˌblā-zər\ *n* **1** : one that blazes a trail to guide others : PATHFINDER **2** : PIONEER

trail·blaz·ing \-ziŋ\ *adj* : making or pointing a new way

trail·er \ˈtrā-lər\ *n* **1** : one that trails **2** : a trailing plant **3 a** : a highway or industrial-plant vehicle designed to be hauled (as by a tractor) **b** : a highway vehicle designed to serve wherever parked as a dwelling or as a place of business

trailer camp *n* : an area where house trailers are congregated — called also *trailer court, trailer park*

trail·er·ite \ˈtrā-lə-ˌrīt\ *n* : a person living or accustomed to live in a trailer

trailing arbutus *n* : an arbutus (*Epigaea repens*)

trailing edge *n* : the rearmost edge of an airfoil

[1]**train** \ˈtrān\ *n* [ME *traine*, fr. MF, fr. OF, fr. *traïr* to betray, fr. L *tradere* — more at TRAITOR] *obs* : SCHEME, TRICK

[2]**train** *n* [ME, fr. MF, fr. OF, fr. *trainer* to draw, drag] **1** : a part of a gown that trails behind the wearer **2 a** : RETINUE, SUITE **b** : a moving file of persons, vehicles, or animals **3** : the vehicles, men, and sometimes animals that furnish supply, maintenance, and evacuation services to a combat unit **4 a** : order designed to lead to some result **b** : a connected series ⟨~ of thought⟩ **c** : accompanying circumstances : AFTERMATH **5** : a line of gunpowder laid to lead fire to a charge **6** : a series of moving machine parts (as gears) for transmitting and modifying motion **7 a** : a connected line of railroad cars with or without a locomotive **b** : an automotive tractor with one or more trailer units

[3]train *vb* [ME *trainen*, fr. MF *trainer*, fr. OF, fr. (assumed) VL *traginare;* akin to L *trahere* to draw — more at DRAW] *vt* **1 :** TRAIL, DRAG **2 :** to direct the growth of (a plant) usu. by bending, pruning, and tying **3 a :** to form by instruction, discipline, or drill **b :** to teach so as to be fitted, qualified, or proficient **4 :** to make prepared (as by exercise) for a test of skill **5 :** to aim at an object **:** bring to bear ~ *vi* **1 :** to undergo instruction, discipline, or drill **2 :** to go by train **syn** see TEACH — **train·able** \ˈtrā-nə-bəl\ *adj* — **train·ee** \trā-ˈnē\ *n* — **train·er** \ˈtrā-nər\ *n*

train·band \ˈtrān-ˌband\ *n* [alter. of *trained band*] **:** a 17th or 18th century militia company in England or America

train·bear·er \ˈtrān-ˌbar-ər, -ˌber-\ *n* **:** an attendant who holds up (as on a ceremonial occasion) the train of a robe or gown

train dispatcher *n* **:** a railroad employee who directs the movement of trains within a division and coordinates their movement from one division to another

train·ing *n* **1 :** the act, process, or method of one who trains **2 :** the state of being trained

training college *n, Brit* **:** TEACHERS COLLEGE

training school *n* **1 :** a school preparing students for a particular occupation **2 :** a correctional institution for the custody and reeducation of juvenile delinquents

training table *n* **:** a table where men under an athletic training regimen eat meals planned to help in their conditioning

train·load \ˈtrān-ˈlōd\ *n* **:** the full freight or passenger capacity of a railroad train

train·man \ˈtrān-mən, -ˌman\ *n* **:** a member of a train crew supervised by a conductor

train oil \ˈtrān-\ *n* [obs. *train* (train oil), fr. ME *trane*, fr. MD *trane* or MLG *trān*] **:** oil from a marine animal (as a whale)

train·sick \ˈtrān-ˌsik\ *adj* **:** affected with motion sickness induced by riding on a train — **train sickness** *n*

traipse \ˈtrāps\ *vb* [origin unknown] *vi* **:** to walk or tramp about **:** GAD ~ *vt* **:** TRAMP, WALK — **traipse** *n*

trait \ˈtrāt, *Brit usu* ˈtrā\ *n* [MF, lit., act of drawing, fr. L *tractus* — more at TRACT] **1 a :** a stroke of or as of a pencil **b :** TOUCH, TRACE **2 :** a distinguishing quality (as of personal character) **:** PECULIARITY

trai·tor \ˈtrāt-ər\ *n* [ME *traitre*, fr. OF, fr. L *traditor*, fr. *traditus*, pp. of *tradere* to hand over, deliver, betray, fr. *trans-*, *tra-* trans- + *dare* to give — more at DATE] **1 :** one who betrays another's trust or is false to an obligation or duty **2 :** one who commits treason — **trai·tress** \ˈtrā-trəs, ˈtrāt-ə-rəs\ *n*

trai·tor·ous \ˈtrāt-ə-rəs, ˈtrā-trəs\ *adj* **1 :** guilty or capable of treason **2 :** constituting treason **syn** see FAITHLESS — **trai·tor·ous·ly** *adv*

tra·ject \trə-ˈjekt\ *vt* [L *trajectus*, pp.] **:** TRANSMIT — **tra·jec·tion** \-ˈjek-shən\ *n*

tra·jec·to·ry \trə-ˈjek-t(ə-)rē\ *n* [NL *trajectoria*, fr. fem. of *trajectorius* of passing, fr. L *trajectus*, pp. of *traicere* to cause to cross, cross, fr. *trans-*, *tra-* trans- + *jacere* to throw — more at JET] **:** the curve that a body (as a planet or comet in its orbit, a projectile in passing from muzzle to first point of impact, or a rocket) describes in space

[1]tram \ˈtram\ *n* [F *trame* weft, tram] **:** a loosely twisted silk yarn usu. used for the weft of a fabric

[2]tram *n* [E dial., shaft of a wheelbarrow, prob. fr. LG *traam*, lit., beam] **1 :** any of various vehicles: as **a :** a boxlike wagon running on a railway (as in a mine) **b** *chiefly Brit* **:** STREETCAR **c :** a carrier that travels on an overhead cable or rails **2 a** *pl, chiefly Brit* **:** a streetcar line **b :** TRAMROAD

[3]tram *vt* **trammed; tram·ming :** to haul in a tram or over a tramway

tram·car \ˈtram-ˌkär\ *n* **1** *chiefly Brit* **:** STREETCAR **2 :** [2]TRAM 1a

tram·line \-ˌlīn\ *n, Brit* **:** a streetcar line

[1]tram·mel \ˈtram-əl\ *n* [ME *tramayle*, a kind of net, fr. MF *tremail*, fr. LL *tremaculum*, fr. L *tres* three + *macula* mesh, spot — more at THREE] **1 :** a net for catching birds or fish; *esp* **:** one having three layers with the middle one finer-meshed and slack so that fish passing through carry some of the center net through the coarser opposite net and are trapped **2 :** a shackle used for making a horse amble **3 :** something impeding activity, progress, or freedom **:** RESTRAINT — usu. used in pl. **4 :** an adjustable pothook for a fireplace crane **5 a :** an instrument for drawing ellipses **b :** a compass for drawing large circles that consists of a beam with two sliding parts — usu. used in pl. **c :** any of various gauges used for aligning or adjusting machine parts

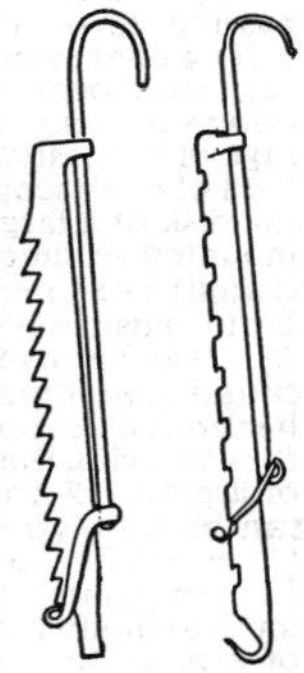

trammels 4

[2]trammel *vt* **tram·meled** *or* **tram·melled; tram·mel·ing** *or* **tram·mel·ling** \ˈtram-(ə-)liŋ\ **1 :** to catch or hold in or as if in a net **:** ENMESH **2 :** to prevent or impede the free play of **:** CONFINE **syn** see HAMPER

[1]tra·mon·tane \trə-ˈmän-ˌtān, ˌtram-ən-ˈ\ *adj* [It *tramontano*, fr. L *transmontanus*, fr. *trans-* + *mont-, mons* mountain — more at MOUNT] **1 :** TRANSALPINE **2 :** lying on or coming from the other side of the mountains

[2]tramontane *n* **:** one dwelling in a tramontane region; *broadly* **:** FOREIGNER

[1]tramp \ˈtramp, *vi 1 & vt 1 are also* ˈträmp, ˈtrȯmp\ *vb* [ME *trampen;* akin to MLG *trampen* to stamp, OE *treppan* to tread — more at TRAP] *vi* **1 :** to walk, tread, or step esp. heavily **2 a :** to travel about on foot **:** HIKE **b :** to journey as a tramp ~ *vt* **1 :** to tread on forcibly and repeatedly **:** TRAMPLE **2 :** to travel or wander through on foot — **tramp·er** *n*

[2]tramp \ˈtramp, *3, 4 are also* ˈträmp, ˈtrȯmp\ *n* **1 a :** a foot traveler **b :** a begging or thieving vagrant **c :** PROSTITUTE **2 :** a walking trip **:** HIKE **3 :** the succession of sounds made by the beating of feet on a road, pavement, or floor **4 :** an iron plate to protect the sole of a shoe **5 :** a ship not making regular trips but taking cargo when and where it offers and to any port

tram·ple \ˈtram-pəl\ *vb* **tram·pling** \-p(ə-)liŋ\ [ME *tramplen*, freq. of *trampen* to tramp] *vi* **1 :** TRAMP; *esp* **:** to tread heavily so as to bruise, crush, or injure **2 a :** to inflict injury or destruction **b :** to act contemptuously or ruthlessly ~ *vt* **:** to press down, crush, or injure by or as if by treading **:** STAMP — **trample** *n* — **tram·pler** \-p(ə-)lər\ *n*

tram·po·line \ˌtram-pə-ˈlēn, ˈtram-pə-ˌ\ *n* [Sp *trampolín*, fr. It *trampolino*, of Gmc origin; akin to MLG *trampen* to stamp] **:** a resilient canvas sheet or web supported by springs in a metal frame used as a springboard in tumbling — **tram·po·lin·er** \-ər\ *n* — **tram·po·lin·ist** \-əst\ *n*

tram·road \ˈtram-ˌrōd\ *n* **:** a roadway for trams consisting of parallel tracks made of usu. metal-faced wooden beams, stone blocks, metal plates, or rails; *specif* **:** a railway in a mine

tram·way \ˈtram-ˌwā\ *n* **:** a way for trams: as **a :** TRAMROAD **b** *Brit* **:** a streetcar line

[1]trance \ˈtran(t)s\ *n* [ME, fr. MF *transe*, fr. *transir* to pass away, swoon, fr. L *transire* to pass, pass away — more at TRANSIENT] **1 :** a state of partly suspended animation or inability to function **:** STUPOR **2 :** a somnolent state (as of deep hypnosis) **3 :** a state of profound abstraction or absorption **:** ECSTASY

[2]trance *vt* **:** ENTRANCE, ENRAPTURE

[3]trance *n* [perh. by shortening & alter. fr. *transit*] *chiefly Scot* **:** PASSAGE, PASSAGEWAY

tran·gam \ˈtraŋ-gəm\ *n* [origin unknown] *archaic* **:** TRINKET, GIMCRACK

tran·quil \ˈtraŋ-kwəl, ˈtran-\ *adj* [L *tranquillus*] **1 a :** free from agitation **:** SERENE **b :** free from disturbance or turmoil **:** QUIET **2 :** STEADY, STABLE **syn** see CALM — **tran·quil·ly** \-kwə-lē\ *adv* — **tran·quil·ness** *n*

tran·quil·ize *or* **tran·quil·lize** \-kwə-ˌlīz\ *vt* **:** to make tranquil or calm **:** PACIFY; *esp* **:** to relieve of mental tension and anxiety by means of drugs ~ *vi* **:** to become tranquil **:** RELAX 2

tran·quil·iz·er \-ˌlī-zər\ *n* **:** one that tranquilizes; *esp* **:** a drug used to reduce anxiety and tension without impairing mental alertness

tran·quil·li·ty *or* **tran·quil·i·ty** \tran-ˈkwil-ət-ē, traŋ-\ *n* **:** the quality or state of being tranquil

trans \ˈtran(t)s, ˈtranz\ *adj* [*trans-*] **:** having various atoms or groups on opposite sides of the molecule

trans- *prefix* [L *trans-*, *tra-* across, beyond, through, so as to change, fr. *trans* across, beyond — more at THROUGH] **1 :** on or to the other side of **:** across **:** beyond ⟨*trans*atlantic⟩ **2 :** beyond (a specified chemical element) in the periodic table ⟨*trans*uranium⟩ **3 :** through ⟨*trans*cutaneous⟩ **4 :** so or such as to change or transfer ⟨*trans*literate⟩ ⟨*trans*location⟩ ⟨*trans*amination⟩ ⟨*trans*ship⟩

trans·act \tran(t)s-ˈakt, tranz-\ *vb* [L *transactus*, pp. of *transigere* to drive through, complete, transact, fr. *trans-* + *agere* to drive, do] *vi* **:** to carry on business **:** NEGOTIATE ~ *vt* **:** to carry out **:** PERFORM; *esp* **:** to carry on **:** CONDUCT — **trans·ac·tor** \-ˈak-tər\ *n*

trans·ac·tion \-ˈak-shən\ *n* **1 :** an act, process, or instance of transacting **2 a :** something transacted; *esp* **:** a business deal **b** *pl* **:** the often published record of the meeting of a society or association **:** PROCEEDINGS — **trans·ac·tion·al** \-shnəl, -shən-ᵊl\ *adj*

trans·al·pine \tran(t)s-ˈal-ˌpīn, tranz-\ *adj* [L *transalpinus*, fr. *trans-* + *Alpes* the Alps] **1 :** situated on the farther side of the Alps **2 :** of, relating to, or characteristic of the region or peoples beyond the Alps — **transalpine** *n*

trans·am·i·nase \-ˈam-ə-ˌnās, -ˌnāz\ *n* **:** an enzyme promoting transamination

trans·am·i·na·tion \ˌtran(t)s-ˌam-ə-ˈnā-shən, ˌtranz-\ *n* **:** a reversible oxidation-reduction reaction in which an amino group is transferred typically from an alpha-amino acid to the carbonyl carbon atom of an alpha-keto acid

trans·at·lan·tic \ˌtran(t)s-ət-ˈlant-ik, ˌtranz-\ *adj* **:** extending across or situated beyond the Atlantic ocean

trans·ceiv·er \tran(t)s-ˈē-vər, tranz-\ *n* [*trans*mitter + *receiver*] **:** a radio transmitter-receiver that uses many of the same components for both transmission and reception

tran·scend \tran(t)s-ˈend\ *vb* [L *transcendere* to climb across, transcend, fr. *trans-* + *scandere* to climb — more at SCAN] *vt* **1 a :** to rise above or go beyond the limits of **:** EXCEED **b :** to be prior to, beyond, and above (the universe or material existence) **2 :** SURPASS ~ *vi* **:** EXCEL, SURPASS **syn** see EXCEED

tran·scen·dence \-ˈen-dən(t)s\ *n* **:** the quality or state of being transcendent

tran·scen·den·cy \-dən-sē\ *n* **:** TRANSCENDENCE

tran·scen·dent \-dənt\ *adj* [L *transcendent-*, *transcendens*, prp. of *transcendere*] **1 a :** exceeding usual limits **:** SURPASSING **b :** extending or lying beyond the limits of ordinary experience **c** *Kantianism* **:** being beyond the limits of all possible experience and knowledge **2 :** transcending the universe or material existence — **tran·scen·dent·ly** *adv*

tran·scen·den·tal \ˌtran(t)s-ˌen-ˈdent-ᵊl, -ən-\ *adj* **1** *Kantianism* **a :** of or relating to experience as determined by the mind's makeup **b :** transcending experience but not human knowledge **2 :** TRANSCENDENT 1a **3 a :** incapable of being the root of an algebraic equation with rational coefficients ⟨π is a ~ number⟩ **b :** being, involving, or representing a function (as sin x, log x, e^x) that cannot be expressed by a finite number of algebraic operations ⟨~ curves⟩ **4 a :** TRANSCENDENT 1b **b :** SUPERNATURAL **c :** ABSTRUSE, ABSTRACT **d :** of or relating to transcendentalism — **tran·scen·den·tal·ly** \-ᵊl-ē\ *adv*

tran·scen·den·tal·ism \-ᵊl-ˌiz-əm\ *n* **1 :** a philosophy that emphasizes the a priori conditions of knowledge and experience or the unknowable character of ultimate reality or that emphasizes the transcendent as the fundamental reality **2 :** a philosophy that asserts the primacy of the spiritual and transcendental over the material and empirical — **tran·scen·den·tal·ist** \-ᵊl-əst\ *adj or n*

trans·con·ti·nen·tal \ˌtran(t)s-ˌkänt-ᵊn-ˈent-ᵊl\ *adj* **1 :** extending or going across a continent ⟨~ railroad⟩ **2 :** situated on the farther side of a continent

tran·scribe \tran(t)s-ˈkrīb\ *vt* [L *transcribere*, fr. *trans-* + *scribere* to write — more at SCRIBE] **1 a :** to make a written copy of **b :** to make a copy of (dictated or recorded matter) in longhand or on a typewriter **c :** to paraphrase in writing **d :** to write down **:** RECORD **2 a :** to represent (speech sounds) by means of phonetic symbols **b :** TRANSLATE 2a **c :** to transfer (data) from one recording form to another **d :** to record (as on magnetic tape) for later broadcast **3 :** to make a musical transcription of **4 :** to broadcast by electrical transcription — **tran·scrib·er** *n*

tran·script \ˈtran(t)s-ˌkript\ *n* [ME, fr. ML *transcriptum*, fr. L, neut. of *transcriptus*, pp. of *transcribere*] **1 a :** a written, printed, or typed copy **b :** an official or legal and often published copy; *specif* **:** an official copy of a student's educational record **2 :** a usu. artistic rendering (as of experience)

tran·scrip·tion \tran(t)s-ˈkrip-shən\ *n* **1 :** an act, process, or instance of transcribing **2 :** COPY, TRANSCRIPT: as **a :** an arrangement of a musical composition for some instrument or voice other than the original **b :** ELECTRICAL TRANSCRIPTION — **tran·scrip·tion·al** \-shnəl, -shən-ᵊl\ *adj* — **tran·scrip·tion·al·ly** \-ē\ *adv*

trans·cu·ta·ne·ous \ˌtran(t)s-kyu̇-ˈtā-nē-əs\ *adj* **:** passing or entering through the skin ⟨~ infection⟩ ⟨~ inoculation⟩

trans·duc·er \tran(t)s-ˈd(y)ü-sər, tranz-\ *n* [L *transducere* to lead across, fr. *trans-* + *ducere* to lead — more at TOW] **:** a device that is actuated by power from one system and supplies power in any other form to a second system (as a telephone receiver that is actuated by electric power and supplies acoustic power to the surrounding air)

trans·duc·tion \-ˈdək-shən\ *n* [L *transductus*, pp. of *transducere*] **:** the transfer of genetic determinants from one microorganism to another by a filterable agent

tran·sect \tran(t)s-ˈekt\ *vt* [*trans-* + *-sect*] **:** to cut transversely — **tran·sec·tion** \-ˈek-shən\ *n*

tran·sept \ˈtran(t)s-ˌept\ *n* [NL *transeptum*, fr. L *trans-* + *septum*, *saeptum* enclosure, wall — more at SEPTUM] **:** the part of a cruciform church that crosses at right angles to the greatest length between the nave and the apse or choir; *also* **:** either of the projecting ends of a transept — **tran·sep·tal** \tran(t)s-ˈep-tᵊl\ *adj*

1**trans·fer** \tran(t)s-ˈfər, ˈtran(t)s-ˌ\ *vb* **trans·ferred; trans·fer·ring** [ME *transferren*, fr. L *transferre*, fr. *trans-* + *ferre* to carry — more at BEAR] *vt* **1 a :** to convey from one person, place, or situation to another **:** TRANSPORT **b :** to cause to pass from one to another **:** TRANSMIT **c :** TRANSFORM, CHANGE **2 :** to make over the possession or control of **:** CONVEY **3 :** to print or otherwise copy from one surface to another by contact ~ *vi* **1 :** to move to a different place, region, or situation; *specif* **:** to withdraw from one educational institution to enroll at another **2 :** to change from one vehicle or transportation line to another — **trans·fer·able** \-ə-bəl\ *adj* — **trans·fer·al** \-əl\ *n* — **trans·fer·rer** \-ər\ *n*

2**trans·fer** \ˈtran(t)s-ˌfər\ *n* **1 a :** conveyance of right, title, or interest in real or personal property from one person to another **b :** removal or acquisition of property by mere delivery with intent to transfer title **2 :** an act, process, or instance of transferring **:** TRANSFERENCE **3 :** one that transfers or is transferred; *specif* **:** a graphic image transferred by contact from one surface to another **4 :** a place where a transfer is made (as of trains to ferries or as where one form of power is changed to another) **5 :** a ticket entitling a passenger on a public conveyance to continue his journey on another route

trans·fer·ase \ˈtran(t)s-(ˌ)fər-ˌās, -ˌāz\ *n* **:** an enzyme that promotes transfer of a group from one molecule to another

trans·fer·ee \ˌtran(t)s-(ˌ)fər-ˈē\ *n* **1 :** a person to whom a conveyance is made **2 :** one transferred

trans·fer·ence \tran(t)s-ˈfər-ən(t)s, ˈtran(t)s-(ˌ)\ *n* **1 :** an act, process, or instance of transferring **:** TRANSFER **2 :** the redirection of feelings and desires and esp. of those unconsciously retained from childhood toward a new object (as a psychoanalyst conducting therapy) — **trans·fer·en·tial** \ˌtran(t)s-fə-ˈren-chəl\ *adj*

trans·fer·or \tran(t)s-ˈfər-ər\ *n* **:** one that conveys a title, right, or property

transfer payment *n* **:** a public expenditure made for a purpose (as veterans' benefits or unemployment compensation) other than procuring goods or services — usu. used in pl.

trans·fer·rin \tran(t)s-ˈfer-ən\ *n* [*trans-* + L *ferrum* iron] **:** a beta globulin in blood plasma capable of combining with ferric ions and transporting iron in the body

trans·fig·u·ra·tion \(ˌ)tran(t)s-ˌfig-(y)ə-ˈrā-shən\ *n* **1 a :** a change in form or appearance **:** METAMORPHOSIS **b :** an exalting, glorifying, or spiritual change **2** *cap* **:** a feast observed in some branches of the Christian church on August 6 in commemoration of the supernatural change in the appearance of Jesus on the mountain

trans·fig·ure \tran(t)s-ˈfig-yər, *esp Brit* -ˈfig-ər\ *vt* [ME *transfiguren*, fr. L *transfigurare*, fr. *trans-* + *figurare* to shape, fashion, fr. *figura* figure] **1 :** to change the form or appearance of **:** METAMORPHOSE **2 :** EXALT, GLORIFY **syn** see TRANSFORM

trans·fi·nite \(ˈ)tran(t)s-ˈfī-ˌnīt\ *adj* [G *transfinit*, fr. *trans-* (fr. L) + *finit* finite, fr. L *finitus*] **:** extending or lying beyond the finite

transfinite cardinal *n* **:** the cardinal number of a set that has as many elements as or more elements than the set of natural numbers

transfinite ordinal *n* **:** the ordinal number of an ordered set containing an infinite number of elements

trans·fix \tran(t)s-ˈfiks\ *vt* [L *transfixus*, pp. of *transfigere*, fr. *trans-* + *figere* to fasten, pierce — more at DIKE] **1 :** to pierce through with or as if with a pointed weapon **:** IMPALE **2 :** to hold motionless by or as if by piercing — **trans·fix·ion** \-ˈfik-shən\ *n*

1**trans·form** \tran(t)s-ˈfȯ(ə)rm\ *vb* [ME *transformen*, fr. L *transformare*, fr. *trans-* + *formare* to form, fr. *forma* form] *vt* **1 a :** to change in composition or structure **b :** to change the outward form or appearance of **c :** to change in character or condition **:** CONVERT **2 :** to subject to mathematical transformation **3 :** to change (a current) in potential (as from high voltage to low) or in type (as from alternating to direct) ~ *vi* **:** to become transformed **:** CHANGE — **trans·for·ma·tive** \-ˈfȯr-mət-iv\ *adj*

syn TRANSFORM, METAMORPHOSE, TRANSMUTE, CONVERT, TRANSMOGRIFY, TRANSFIGURE mean to change a thing into a different thing. TRANSFORM implies a major change in form, nature, or function; METAMORPHOSE suggests a change induced supernaturally or magically or as if by magic; TRANSMUTE implies transforming into a higher element or thing; CONVERT implies a change fitting something for a new or different use or function; TRANSMOGRIFY suggests a grotesque or preposterous metamorphosis; TRANSFIGURE implies a change that exalts or glorifies

2**trans·form** \ˈtran(t)s-ˌfȯrm\ *n* **1 :** a mathematical element obtained from another by transformation **2 :** TRANSFORMATION 3

trans·form·able \tran(t)s-ˈfȯr-mə-bəl\ *adj* **:** capable of being transformed

trans·for·ma·tion \ˌtran(t)s-fər-ˈmā-shən, -ˌfȯr-\ *n* **1 :** an act, process, or instance of transforming or being transformed **2 :** false hair esp. as worn by a woman **3 a :** the operation of changing (as by rotation or mapping) one configuration or expression into another in accordance with a mathematical rule **b :** the formula that effects such a change

trans·form·er \tran(t)s-ˈfȯr-mər\ *n* **:** one that transforms; *specif* **:** a device employing the principle of mutual induction to convert variations of current in a primary circuit into variations of voltage and current in a secondary circuit

trans·fuse \tran(t)s-ˈfyüz\ *vt* [ME *transfusen*, fr. L *transfusus*, pp. of *transfundere*, fr. *trans-* + *fundere* to pour — more at FOUND] **1 a :** to cause to pass from one to another **:** TRANSMIT **b :** to diffuse into or through **:** PERMEATE **2 a :** to transfer (as blood or saline) into a vein of a man or animal **b :** to subject (a patient) to transfusion — **trans·fus·ible** *or* **trans·fus·able** \-ˈfyü-zə-bəl\ *adj*

trans·fu·sion \tran(t)s-ˈfyü-zhən\ *n* **:** an act, process, or instance of transfusing; *esp* **:** the act or an instance of transfusing fluid into a vein or artery

trans·gress \tran(t)s-ˈgres, tranz-\ *vb* [F *transgresser*, fr. L *transgressus*, pp. of *transgredi* to step beyond or across, fr. *trans-* + *gradi* to step — more at GRADE] *vt* **1 :** to go beyond limits set or prescribed by **:** VIOLATE ⟨~ the divine law⟩ **2 :** to pass beyond or go over (a limit or boundary) ~ *vi* **1 :** to violate a command or law **:** SIN **2 :** to go beyond a boundary or limit — **trans·gres·sive** \-ˈgres-iv\ *adj* — **trans·gres·sor** \-ˈgres-ər\ *n*

trans·gres·sion \-ˈgresh-ən\ *n* **:** an act, process, or instance of transgressing; *specif* **:** infringement or violation of a law, command, or duty **syn** see BREACH

tran·ship *var of* TRANSSHIP

trans·hu·mance \tran(t)s-ˈ(h)yü-mən(t)s, tranz-\ *n* [F, fr. *transhumer* to practice transhumance, fr. Sp *trashumar*, fr. *tras-* trans- (fr. L *trans-*) + L *humus* earth — more at HUMBLE] **:** seasonal movement of livestock and esp. sheep between mountain and lowland pastures either under the care of herders or in company with the owners — **trans·hu·mant** \-mənt\ *adj or n*

tran·sience \ˈtranch-ən(t)s; ˈtranz-ē-ən(t)s, ˈtran(t)s-ē-, ˈtranch-ē-; ˈtranzh-ən(t)s, ˈtranj-\ *n* **:** the quality or state of being transient

tran·sien·cy \-ən-sē\ *n* **:** TRANSIENCE

1**tran·sient** \-ənt\ *adj* [L *transeunt-*, *transiens*, prp. of *transire* to go across, pass, fr. *trans-* + *ire* to go] **1 a :** passing esp. quickly into and out of existence **:** TRANSITORY **b :** passing through or by a place with only a brief stay or sojourn **2 :** affecting something or producing results beyond itself — **tran·sient·ly** *adv*

syn TRANSITORY, EPHEMERAL, MOMENTARY, FUGITIVE, FLEETING, EVANESCENT: TRANSIENT applies to what is short in duration and passes quickly; TRANSITORY suggests the inevitability of changing, ending, or dying out; EPHEMERAL implies striking brevity of life or duration; MOMENTARY suggests coming and going quickly and being therefore merely a brief interruption of a more enduring state; FUGITIVE and FLEETING imply passing so quickly as to make apprehending difficult; EVANESCENT suggests vanishing almost as it comes and may connote an airy or fragile quality

2**transient** *n* **1 :** one that is transient: as **a :** a transient guest **b :** a person traveling about usu. in search of work **2 a :** a temporary oscillation that occurs in a circuit because of a sudden change of voltage or of load **b :** a transient current or voltage

trans·il·lu·mi·nate \ˌtran(t)s-ə-ˈlü-mə-ˌnāt, ˌtranz-\ *vt* **:** to cause light to pass through; *specif* **:** to pass light through (a body part) for medical examination — **trans·il·lu·mi·na·tion** \-ˌlü-mə-ˈnā-shən\ *n*

tran·sis·tor \tranz-ˈis-tər, tran(t)s-\ *n* [1*trans*fer + re*sistor*; fr. its transferring an electrical signal across a resistor] **1 :** an electronic device similar to the electron tube in use (as amplification and rectification) consisting of a small block of a semiconductor (as germanium) that has at least three electrodes **2 :** a transistorized radio

tran·sis·tor·ize \-tə-ˌrīz\ *vt* **:** to equip (a device) with transistors

1**tran·sit** \ˈtran(t)s-ət, ˈtranz-\ *n* [L *transitus*, fr. *transitus*, pp. of *transire* to go across, pass] **1 a :** an act, process, or instance of passing through or over **:** PASSAGE **b :** CHANGE, TRANSITION **c** (1) **:** conveyance of persons or things from one place to another (2) **:** usu. local transportation esp. of people by public conveyance; *also* **:** vehicles or a system engaged in such transportation **2 a :** passage of a celestial body over the meridian of a place or through the field of a telescope **b :** passage of a smaller body (as Venus) across the disk of a larger (as the sun) **3 :** a theodolite with the telescope mounted so that it can be transited

2**transit** *vi* **:** to make a transit ~ *vt* **1 a :** to pass over or through **b :** to cause to pass over or through **2 :** to pass across **3 :** to turn (a telescope) over about the horizontal transverse axis in surveying

transit instrument *n* **1 :** a telescope mounted at right angles to a horizontal east-west axis and used with a clock and chronograph for observing the time of transit of a celestial body over the meridian of a place **2 :** TRANSIT 3

tran·si·tion \tran(t)s-ˈish-ən, tranz-, *chiefly Brit* tran(t)s-ˈizh-\ *n* [L *transition-*, *transitio*, fr. *transitus*, pp. of *transire*] **1 :** passage from one state, stage, place, or subject to another **:** CHANGE **2 a :** a musical modulation **b :** a musical passage leading from one section of a piece to another — **tran·si·tion·al** \-ˈish-nəl, -ˈizh-, -ən-ᵊl\ *adj* — **tran·si·tion·al·ly** \-ē\ *adv*

tran·si·tive \ˈtran(t)s-ət-iv, ˈtranz-; ˈtran(t)s-tiv\ *adj* [LL *transitivus*, fr. L *transitus*, pp. of *transire*] **1 :** characterized by having or containing a direct object ⟨a ~ verb⟩ ⟨a ~ construction⟩ **2 :** so relating items that if the first is related to the second and the second is to a third then the first is so related to the third ⟨equality is a ~ relation⟩ **3 :** TRANSITIONAL — **tran·si·tive·ly** *adv* — **tran·si·tive·ness** *n* — **tran·si·tiv·i·ty** \ˌtran(t)s-ə-ˈtiv-ət-ē, ˌtranz-\ *n*

tran·si·to·ri·ly \ˌtran(t)s-ə-ˈtōr-ə-lē, ˌtranz-, -ˈtȯr-\ *adv* **:** in a transitory manner **:** TEMPORARILY

tran·si·to·ri·ness \ˈtran(t)s-ə-ˌtōr-ē-nəs, ˈtranz-, -ˌtȯr-\ *n* **:** the quality or state of being transitory

tran·si·to·ry \-ē\ *adj* [ME *transitorie*, fr. MF *transitoire*, fr. LL *transitorius*, fr. L, of or allowing passage, fr. *transitus*, pp. of *transire*] **1 :** EVANESCENT, TRANSIENT **2 :** of brief duration **:** TEMPORARY **syn** see TRANSIENT

trans·lat·abil·i·ty \(ˌ)tran(t)s-ˌlāt-ə-ˈbil-ət-ē, (ˌ)tranz-\ *n* **:** the quality or state of being translatable

trans·lat·able \tran(t)s-ˈlāt-ə-bəl, tranz-\ *adj* **:** capable of being translated

trans·late \-ˈlāt\ *vb* [L *translatus* (pp. of *transferre* to transfer, translate), fr. *trans-* + *latus*, pp. of *ferre* to carry — more at TOLERATE, BEAR] *vt* **1 a :** to bear or change from one place, state, form,

or appearance to another : TRANSFER, TRANSFORM **b** : to convey to heaven or to a nontemporal condition without death **c** : to transfer (a bishop) from one see to another **2 a** : to turn into one's own or another language **b** : to transfer or turn from one set of symbols into another : TRANSCRIBE **c** : PARAPHRASE, EXPLAIN **3** : ENRAPTURE **4** : to change the spatial coordinates of without rotation ~ *vi* : to practice translation or make a translation; *also* : to admit of translation — **trans·la·tor** \-ˈlāt-ər\ *n*

trans·la·tion \-ˈlā-shən\ *n* : an act, process, or instance of translating: as **a** : a rendering from one language into another; *also* : the product of such a rendering **b** : CONVERSION **c (1)** : a shift movement of a configuration to new coordinates parallel with the old **(2)** : uniform motion of a body in a straight line — **trans·la·tion·al** \-shnəl, -shən-ᵊl\ *adj*

trans·la·tive \tran(t)s-ˈlāt-iv, tranz-\ *adj* **1** : of, relating to, or involving removal or transference from one person or place to another **2** : of, relating to, or serving to translate from one language or system into another

trans·lit·er·ate \tran(t)s-ˈlit-ə-ˌrāt, tranz-\ *vt* [*trans-* + L *littera* letter] : to represent or spell in the characters of another alphabet — **trans·lit·er·a·tion** \ˌtran(t)s-ˌlit-ə-ˈrā-shən, ˌtranz-\ *n*

trans·lo·cate \ˈtran(t)s-lō-ˌkāt, ˈtranz-, (ˈ)tran(t)s-ˈ, (ˈ)tranz-ˈ\ *vt* [prob. back-formation fr. *translocation*] : to transfer (as food materials or products of metabolism) from one location to another in the plant body

trans·lo·ca·tion \ˌtran(t)s-(ˌ)lō-ˈkā-shən, ˌtranz-\ *n* : a change of location : DISPLACEMENT: as **a** : the conduction of soluble material from one part of a plant to another **b** : the exchange of parts between nonhomologous chromosomes

trans·lu·cence \tran(t)s-ˈlüs-ᵊn(t)s, tranz-\ *or* **trans·lu·cen·cy** \-ᵊn-sē\ *n* : the quality or state of being translucent

trans·lu·cent \-ᵊnt\ *adj* [L *translucent-, translucens*, prp. of *translucēre* to shine through, fr. *trans-* + *lucēre* to shine — more at LIGHT] **1** : shining or glowing through : LUMINOUS **2 a** : TRANSPARENT **b** : readily perceptible : LUCID **3** : admitting and diffusing light so that objects beyond cannot be clearly distinguished : partly transparent **syn** see CLEAR — **trans·lu·cent·ly** *adv*

trans·lu·cid \-ˈlü-səd\ *adj* [L *translucidus*, fr. *translucēre*] : TRANSLUCENT 3

trans·ma·rine \ˌtran(t)s-mə-ˈrēn, ˌtranz-\ *adj* [L *transmarinus*, fr. *trans-* + *mare* sea — more at MARINE] **1** : being or coming from beyond or across the sea ⟨a ~ people⟩ **2** : passing over or extending across the sea

trans·mi·grate \(ˈ)tran(t)s-ˈmī-ˌgrāt, (ˈ)tranz-, ˈtran(t)s-ˌ, ˈtranz-ˌ\ *vi* [L *transmigratus*, pp. of *transmigrare* to migrate to another place, fr. *trans-* + *migrare* to migrate] **1** : to pass at death from one body or being to another **2** : MIGRATE — **trans·mi·gra·tion** \ˌtran(t)s-(ˌ)mī-ˈgrā-shən, ˌtranz-\ *n* — **trans·mi·gra·tor** \(ˈ)tran(t)s-ˈmī-ˌgrāt-ər, (ˈ)tranz-, ˈtran(t)s-ˌ, ˈtranz-ˌ\ *n* — **trans·mi·gra·to·ry** \tran(t)s-ˈmī-grə-ˌtōr-ē, tranz-, -ˌtȯr-\ *adj*

trans·mis·si·bil·i·ty \ˌtran(t)s-ˌmis-ə-ˈbil-ət-ē, ˌtranz-\ *n* : the quality or state of being transmissible

trans·mis·si·ble \tran(t)s-ˈmis-ə-bəl, tranz-\ *adj* : capable of being transmitted

trans·mis·sion \-ˈmish-ən\ *n* [L *transmission-, transmissio*, fr. *transmissus*, pp. of *transmittere* to transmit] **1** : an act, process, or instance of transmitting **2** : the passage of radio waves in the space between transmitting and receiving stations; *also* : the act or process of transmitting by radio or television **3** : the gear including the change gear and the propeller shaft by which power is transmitted from an automobile engine to the live axle **4** : something transmitted — **trans·mis·sive** \-ˈmis-iv\ *adj* — **trans·mis·siv·i·ty** \ˌtran(t)s-(ˌ)mis-ˈiv-ət-ē, ˌtranz-\ *n*

trans·mit \tran(t)s-ˈmit, tranz-\ *vb* **trans·mit·ted; trans·mit·ting** [ME *transmitten*, fr. L *transmittere*, fr. *trans-* + *mittere* to send — more at SMITE] *vt* **1 a** : to send or transfer from one person or place to another : FORWARD **b** : to cause or allow to spread : as **(1)** : to convey by or as if by inheritance or heredity **(2)** : to convey (infection) abroad or to another **2 a (1)** : to cause (as light or force) to pass or be conveyed through space or a medium **(2)** : to admit the passage of ⟨glass ~s light⟩ **b** : to send out (a signal) either by radio waves or over a wire ~ *vi* : to send out a signal either by radio waves or over a wire — **trans·mit·ta·ble** \-ˈmit-ə-bəl\ *adj* — **trans·mit·tal** \-ˈmit-ᵊl\ *n*

trans·mit·tance \-ˈmit-ᵊn(t)s\ *n* **1** : TRANSMISSION **2** : the fraction of radiant energy that having entered a layer of absorbing matter reaches its farther boundary

trans·mit·tan·cy \-ᵊn-sē\ *n* **1** : the ratio of the transmittance of a solution of a material to that of an equal thickness of the solvent **2** : TRANSMITTANCE 2

trans·mit·ter \-ˈmit-ər\ *n* : one that transmits: as **a (1)** : a part on a telephone into which one speaks and which contains a mechanism for converting sound waves into equivalent electric waves **(2)** : the portion of a telegraph instrument by which the message is sent **b** : a radio or television transmitting set

trans·mog·ri·fi·ca·tion \ˌtran(t)s-ˌmäg-rə-fə-ˈkā-shən, tranz-\ *n* : an act, process, or instance of transmogrifying

trans·mog·ri·fy \tran(t)s-ˈmäg-rə-ˌfī, tranz-\ *vt* [origin unknown] : to change or alter often with grotesque or humorous effect **syn** see TRANSFORM

trans·mon·tane \(ˈ)tran(t)s-ˈmän-ˌtān, (ˈ)tranz-; ˌtran(t)s-(ˌ)män-ˈ, ˌtranz-\ *adj* [L *transmontanus*] : TRAMONTANE

trans·mut·able \tran(t)s-ˈmyüt-ə-bəl, tranz-\ *adj* : capable of being transmuted

trans·mu·ta·tion \ˌtran(t)s-myü-ˈtā-shən, ˌtranz-\ *n* : an act or instance of transmuting or being transmuted: as **a** : the conversion of base metals into gold or silver **b** : the conversion of one element or nuclide into another either naturally or artificially — **trans·mut·ative** \tran(t)s-ˈmyüt-ət-iv, tranz-\ *adj*

trans·mute \tran(t)s-ˈmyüt, tranz-\ *vb* [ME *transmuten*, fr. L *transmutare*, fr. *trans-* + *mutare* to change — more at MISS] *vt* **1** : to change or alter in form, appearance, or nature : CONVERT **2** : to subject (as an element or base metal) to transmutation ~ *vi* : to undergo transmutation **syn** see TRANSFORM

trans·na·tion·al \(ˈ)tran(t)s-ˈnash-nəl, (ˈ)tranz-, -ən-ᵊl\ *adj* : extending beyond national boundaries

trans·nat·u·ral \-ˈnach-(ə-)rəl\ *adj* : being above or beyond nature : SUPERNATURAL

trans·oce·an·ic \ˌtran(t)s-ˌō-shē-ˈan-ik, ˌtranz-\ *adj* **1** : lying or dwelling beyond the ocean **2** : crossing or extending across the ocean

tran·som \ˈtran(t)-səm\ *n* [ME *traunsom*, prob. fr. L *transtrum*, fr. *trans* across — more at THROUGH] **1** : a transverse piece in a structure : CROSSPIECE: as **a** : LINTEL **b** : a horizontal crossbar in a window, over a door, or between a door and a window or fanlight above it **c** : the horizontal bar or member of a cross or gallows **d** : any of several transverse timbers or beams secured to the sternpost of a boat **2** : a window above a door or other window built on and commonly hinged to a transom

tran·son·ic *also* **trans–son·ic** \tran(t)s-ˈsän-ik, tran-ˈsän-\ *adj* [*trans-* + *-sonic* (as in *supersonic*)] **1** : being or relating to a speed approximating the speed of sound in air which is a speed of about 1087 feet per second or about 738 miles per hour at sea level — often used of aeronautical speeds between 600 and 900 miles per hour **2** : moving, capable of moving, or utilizing air currents moving at a transonic speed

trans·pa·cif·ic \ˌtran(t)s-pə-ˈsif-ik\ *adj* : crossing or extending across or situated beyond the Pacific ocean

trans·par·ence \tran(t)s-ˈpar-ən(t)s, -ˈper-\ *n* : TRANSPARENCY 1

trans·par·en·cy \-ən-sē\ *n* **1** : the quality or state of being transparent **2** : something transparent: as **a** : a picture or design on glass, thin cloth, paper, or film viewed by light shining through it or by projection **b** : a framework covered with thin cloth or paper bearing a device for public display (as for advertisement) and lighted from within

trans·par·ent \-ənt\ *adj* [ME, fr. ML *transparent-, transparens*, prp. of *transparēre* to show through, fr. L *trans-* + *parēre* to show oneself — more at APPEAR] **1 a (1)** : having the property of transmitting light without appreciable scattering so that bodies lying beyond are entirely visible : PELLUCID **(2)** : pervious to any specified form of radiation (as X rays or ultraviolet light) **b** : SHEER, DIAPHANOUS **2 a** : FRANK, GUILELESS **b** : easily detected or seen through : OBVIOUS **c** : readily understood : CLEAR **syn** see CLEAR — **trans·par·ent·ly** *adv* — **trans·par·ent·ness** *n*

trans·per·son·al \(ˈ)tran(t)s-ˈpərs-nəl, -ən-ᵊl\ *adj* : extending beyond the personal or individual

tran·spic·u·ous \tran(t)s-ˈpik-yə-wəs\ *adj* [NL *transpicuus*, fr. L *transpicere* to look through, fr. *trans-* + *specere* to look, see — more at SPY] : TRANSPARENT

trans·pierce \tran(t)s-ˈpi(ə)rs\ *vt* [MF *transpercer*, fr. OF, fr. *trans-* (fr. L) + *percer* to pierce] : to pierce through : PENETRATE

tran·spi·ra·tion \ˌtran(t)s-pə-ˈrā-shən\ *n* : an act or instance of transpiring: as **a** : the passage of fluid through an animal membrane in the form of a vapor; *also* : material so transpired **b** : the emission of watery vapor from the surface of plant parts (as leaves)

tran·spire \tran(t)s-ˈpī(ə)r\ *vb* [MF *transpirer*, fr. L *trans-* + *spirare* to breathe — more at SPIRIT] *vt* : to cause (a fluid) to pass through a tissue or substance or its pores or interstices; *esp* : to excrete (as water) in the form of a vapor through a living membrane (as the skin) ~ *vi* **1** : to give off vaporous material **2** : to pass in the form of a vapor from a living body **3 a** : to become known or apparent : DEVELOP **b** : to be revealed : come to light **4** : to come to pass : OCCUR **syn** see HAPPEN

trans·pla·cen·tal \ˌtran(t)s-plə-ˈsent-ᵊl\ *adj* [ISV] : passing through or occurring by way of the placenta ⟨~ immunization⟩

1**trans·plant** \tran(t)s-ˈplant\ *vb* [ME *transplaunten*, fr. LL *transplantare*, fr. L *trans-* + *plantare* to plant] *vt* **1** : to lift and reset (a plant) in another soil or situation **2** : to remove from one place and settle or introduce elsewhere : TRANSPORT **3** : to transfer (an organ or tissue) from one part or individual to another ~ *vi* : to admit of being transplanted — **trans·plant·able** \-ə-bəl\ *adj* — **trans·plan·ta·tion** \ˌtran(t)s-ˌplan-ˈtā-shən\ *n* — **trans·plant·er** \tran(t)s-ˈplant-ər\ *n*

2**trans·plant** \ˈtran(t)s-ˌplant\ *n* **1** : the act or process of transplanting **2** : something transplanted

trans·po·lar \(ˈ)tran(t)s-ˈpō-lər\ *adj* : going or extending across either of the polar regions

tran·spon·der \tran(t)s-ˈpän-dər\ *n* [*trans*mitter + res*ponder*] : a radio or radar set that upon receiving a designated signal emits a radio signal of its own

trans·pon·tine \tran(t)s-ˈpän-ˌtīn\ *adj* [*trans-* + L *pont-, pons* bridge — more at FIND] **1** : situated on the other side of a bridge **2** : characteristic of London south of the Thames

1**trans·port** \tran(t)s-ˈpō(ə)rt, -ˈpȯ(ə)rt\ *vt* [ME *transporten*, fr. MF or L; MF *transporter*, fr. L *transportare*, fr. *trans-* + *portare* to carry — more at FARE] **1** : to convey from one place to another : CARRY **2** : ENRAPTURE ⟨~*ed* with delight⟩ **3** : to send to a penal colony overseas **syn** see BANISH, CARRY — **trans·port·abil·i·ty** \ˌtran(t)s-ˌpōrt-ə-ˈbil-ət-ē, -ˌpȯrt-\ *n* — **trans·port·able** \tran(t)s-ˈpōrt-ə-bəl, -ˈpȯrt-\ *adj* — **trans·port·er** *n*

2**trans·port** \ˈtran(t)s-ˌpō(ə)rt, -ˌpȯ(ə)rt\ *n, often attrib* **1** : act of transporting : TRANSPORTATION **2** : strong or intensely pleasurable emotion : ECSTASY, RAPTURE ⟨~*s* of joy⟩ **3 a** : a ship for carrying soldiers or military equipment **b** : a vehicle (as a truck or plane) used to transport persons or goods **c** : a system of public conveyance : TRANSIT **4** : a transported convict **syn** see ECSTASY

trans·por·ta·tion \ˌtran(t)s-pər-ˈtā-shən\ *n* **1** : an act, process, or instance of transporting or being transported **2** : banishment to a penal colony **3 a** : means of conveyance or travel from one place to another **b** : public conveyance of passengers or goods esp. as a commercial enterprise — **trans·por·ta·tion·al** \-shnəl, -shən-ᵊl\ *adj*

trans·pos·able \tran(t)s-ˈpō-zə-bəl\ *adj* : capable of being transposed or interchanged

trans·pose \tran(t)s-ˈpōz\ *vt* [ME *transposen*, fr. MF *transposer*, fr. L *transponere* (perf. indic. *transposui*) to change the position of, fr. *trans-* + *ponere* to put, place — more at POSITION] **1** : TRANSFORM, TRANSMUTE **2** : TRANSLATE **3** : to transfer from one place or period to another : SHIFT **4** : to change the relative place or normal order of : alter the sequence of ⟨~ letters to change the spelling⟩ **5** : to write or perform (a musical composition) in a different key **6** : to bring (a term) from one side of an algebraic equation to the other with change of sign **syn** see REVERSE — **trans·po·si·tion** \ˌtran(t)s-pə-ˈzish-ən\ *n* — **trans·po·si·tion·al** \-ˈzish-nəl, -ᵊn-əl\ *adj*

trans·shape \tran(ch)-'shāp, tran(t)s-\ *vt* **:** to change into another shape **:** TRANSFORM
trans·ship \tran(ch)-'ship, tran(t)s-\ *vb* **:** to transfer for further transportation from one ship or conveyance to another — **trans·ship·ment** \-mənt\ *n*
tran·sub·stan·ti·ate \ˌtran(t)s-əb-'stan-chē-ˌāt\ *vb* [ML *transubstantiatus*, pp. of *transubstantiare*, fr. L *trans-* + *substantia* substance] *vt* **1 :** to change into another substance **:** TRANSMUTE **2 :** to effect transubstantiation in (sacramental bread and wine) ~ *vi* **:** to undergo transubstantiation
tran·sub·stan·ti·a·tion \-ˌstan-chē-'ā-shən\ *n* **1 :** an act or instance of transubstantiating or being transubstantiated **2 :** the change in the eucharistic elements at their consecration in the mass from the substance of bread and wine to the substance of the body and blood of Christ with only the accidents (as taste, color, shape, and smell) of the bread and wine remaining
tran·sud·ate \tran(t)s-'(y)üd-ət, tranz-, -ˌāt; 'tran(t)s-(y)ü-ˌdāt, 'tranz-\ *n* **:** a product of transudation
tran·su·da·tion \ˌtran(t)s-(ˌ)(y)ü-'dā-shən, ˌtranz-\ *n* **1 :** the act or process of transuding or being transuded **2 :** TRANSUDATE
tran·sude \tran(t)s-'(y)üd, tranz-\ *vb* [NL *transudare*, fr. L *trans-* + *sudare* to sweat — more at SWEAT] *vi* **:** to pass through a membrane or permeable substance **:** EXUDE ~ *vt* **:** to permit passage of **:** EXUDE
trans·ura·ni·um \ˌtran-shə-'rā-nē-əm, ˌtran-zhə-, ˌtran(t)s-yü-, ˌtranz-yü-\ *or* **trans·uran·ic** \-'ran-ik, -'rā-nik\ *adj* **:** having an atomic number greater than that of uranium
trans·val·u·ate \(')tran(t)s-'val-yə-ˌwāt, (')tranz-\ *vt* [back-formation fr. *transvaluation*] **:** TRANSVALUE
trans·val·u·a·tion \ˌtran(t)s-ˌval-yə-'wā-shən, ˌtranz-\ *n* **:** the act or process of transvaluing
trans·val·ue \tran(t)s-'val-(ˌ)yü, tranz-, -'val-yə-w\ *vt* **:** to reevaluate esp. on a basis that repudiates accepted standards
1**trans·ver·sal** \tran(t)s-'vər-səl, tranz-\ *adj* **:** TRANSVERSE ⟨~ line⟩ — **trans·ver·sal·ly** \-sə-lē\ *adv*
2**transversal** *n* **:** a line that intersects a system of lines
1**trans·verse** \tran(t)s-'vərs, tranz-, 'tran(t)s-, 'tranz-,\ *adj* [L *transversus*, fr. pp. of *transvertere* to turn across, fr. *trans-* + *vertere* to turn — more at WORTH] **:** extended or lying across — **trans·verse·ly** *adv*
2**trans·verse** \'tran(t)s-ˌvərs, 'tranz-\ *n* **:** something transverse (as a piece, muscle, or part)
transverse colon *n* **:** the middle portion of the colon that extends across the abdominal cavity
transverse process *n* **:** a lateral process of a vertebra
trans·ves·tism \tran(t)s-'ves-ˌtiz-əm, tranz-\ *n* [G *transvestismus*, fr. L *trans-* + *vestire* to clothe — more at VEST] **:** adoption of the dress and often behavior of the opposite sex — **trans·ves·tite** \-ˌtīt\ *adj or n*
1**trap** \'trap\ *n* [ME, fr. OE *treppe* & OF *trape* (of Gmc origin); akin to MD *trappe* trap, stair, OE *treppan* to tread, Skt *dravati* he runs] **1 :** a device for taking game or other animals; *esp* **:** one that holds by springing shut suddenly **2 :** something by which one is caught or stopped unawares **3 a :** a device for hurling clay pigeons into the air **b :** a hazard on a golf course consisting of a depression containing sand **4 :** a light usu. one-horse carriage with springs **5 :** any of various devices for preventing passage of something often while allowing other matter to proceed; *specif* **:** a device for drains or sewers consisting of a bend or partitioned chamber in which the liquid forms a seal to prevent the passage of sewer gas **6 :** a percussion instrument — usu. used in pl.
2**trap** *vb* **trapped; trap·ping** *vt* **1 a :** to catch or take in or as if in a trap **:** ENSNARE **b :** to place in a restricted position **:** CONFINE **2 :** to provide or set (a place) with traps **3 a :** STOP, HOLD **b :** to separate out (as water from steam) ~ *vi* **:** to set traps for animals esp. as a business **syn** see CATCH — **trap·per** *n*
3**trap** *vt* **trapped; trap·ping** [ME *trappen*, fr. *trappe* cloth, modif. of MF *drap* — more at DRAB] **:** to adorn with or as if with trappings
4**trap** *also* **trap·rock** \'trap-'räk\ *n* [Sw *trapp*, fr. *trappa* stair, fr. MLG *trappe;* akin to MD *trappe* stair] **:** any of various dark-colored fine-grained igneous rocks (as basalt or amygdaloid) used esp. in road making
trap·door \'trap-'dō(ə)r, -'dȯ(ə)r\ *n* **:** a lifting or sliding door covering an opening in a roof, ceiling, or floor
tra·peze \tra-'pēz *also* trə-\ *n* [F *trapèze*, fr. NL *trapezium*] **:** a gymnastic or acrobatic apparatus consisting of a short horizontal bar suspended by two parallel ropes
tra·pez·ist \-'pē-zəst\ *n* **:** a performer on the trapeze
tra·pe·zi·um \trə-'pē-zē-əm\ *n, pl* **tra·pe·zi·ums** *or* **tra·pe·zia** \-zē-ə\ [NL, fr. Gk *trapezion*, lit., small table, dim. of *trapeza* table, fr. *tra-* four (akin to *tettares* four) + *peza* foot; akin to Gk *pod-*, *pous* foot — more at FOUR, FOOT] **1 a :** a quadrilateral having no two sides parallel **b** *Brit* **:** TRAPEZOID 1b **2 :** a bone in the wrist at the base of the thumb

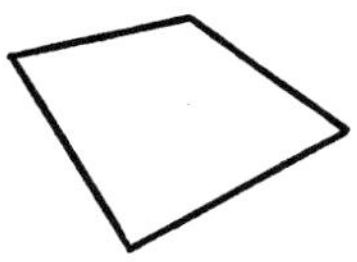
trapezium 1a

tra·pe·zi·us \-zē-əs\ *n* [NL, fr. *trapezium;* fr. the pair on the back forming together the figure of a trapezium] **:** a large flat triangular superficial muscle of each side of the back
tra·pe·zo·he·dron \trə-ˌpē-zō-'hē-drən, ˌtrap-ə-\ *n, pl* **trape·zohedrons** *or* **tra·pe·zo·he·dra** \-drə\ [NL, fr. *trapezium* + *-o-* + *-hedron*] **:** a crystalline form whose faces are trapeziums
trap·e·zoid \'trap-ə-ˌzȯid\ *n* [NL *trapezoïdes*, fr. Gk *trapezoeidēs* trapezium-shaped, fr. *trapeza* table] **1 a** *Brit* **:** TRAPEZIUM 1a **b :** a quadrilateral having only two sides parallel **2 :** a bone in the wrist at the base of the forefinger — **trap·e·zoi·dal** \ˌtrap-ə-'zȯid-ᵊl\ *adj*
trap·nest \'trap-ˌnest\ *n* **:** a nest equipped with a hinged door designed to trap and confine a hen so that individual egg production may be determined — **trapnest** *vt*
trap·ping \'trap-iŋ\ *n* [ME, fr. gerund of *trappen* to adorn] **1 :** CAPARISON 1 — usu. used in pl. **2** *pl* **:** outward decoration or dress **:** ORNAMENTS
Trap·pist \'trap-əst\ *n* [F *trappiste*, fr. La *Trappe*, France] **:** a member of a reformed branch of the Roman Catholic Cistercian Order established in 1664 at the monastery of La Trappe in Normandy — **Trappist** *adj*
traps \'traps\ *n pl* [ME *trappe* cloth — more at TRAP] **:** personal belongings **:** LUGGAGE

trap·shoot·er \'trap-ˌshüt-ər\ *n* **:** one who engages in trapshooting
trap·shoot·ing \'trap-ˌshüt-iŋ\ *n* **:** shooting at clay pigeons sprung into the air from a trap
tra·pun·to \trə-'pün-(ˌ)tō\ *n, pl* **trapuntos** [It] **:** a decorative quilted design in high relief worked through at least two layers of cloth by outlining the design in running stitch and padding it from the underside
trash \'trash\ *n* [of Scand origin; akin to Norw *trask* trash; akin to OE *teran* to tear] **1 :** something worth little or nothing: as **a :** JUNK, RUBBISH **b** (1) **:** empty talk **:** NONSENSE (2) **:** inferior or worthless artistic matter **2 :** something in a crumbled or broken condition or mass; *esp* **:** debris from pruning or processing plant material **3 :** a worthless person; *also* **:** such persons as a group **:** RIFFRAFF
trash farming *n* **:** a method of cultivation in which the soil is loosened by methods that leave vegetational residues (as stubble) on or near the surface to check erosion and serve as a mulch
trash·i·ness \'trash-ē-nəs\ *n* **:** the quality or state of being trashy
trashy \'trash-ē\ *adj* **:** resembling trash **:** WORTHLESS
trass \'tras\ *n* [D] **:** a light-colored volcanic tuff resembling pozzolana in composition sometimes ground for use in a hydraulic cement
trat·to·ria \ˌträt-ə-'rē-ə\ *n* [It] **:** an eating house **:** RESTAURANT
trau·ma \'trau̇-mə, 'trȯ-\ *n, pl* **trau·ma·ta** \-mət-ə\ *or* **traumas** [Gk *traumat-*, *trauma* wound — more at THROE] **1 a :** an injury (as a wound) to living tissue caused by an extrinsic agent ⟨surgical ~⟩ **b :** a disordered psychic or behavioral state resulting from mental or emotional stress or physical injury **2 :** an agent, force, or mechanism that causes trauma — **trau·mat·ic** \trə-'mat-ik, trȯ-, trau̇-\ *adj* — **trau·mat·i·cal·ly** \-i-k(ə-)lē\ *adv*
trau·ma·tism \'trau̇-mə-ˌtiz-əm, 'trȯ-\ *n* **:** the development or occurrence of trauma; *also* **:** TRAUMA
trau·ma·tize \-ˌtīz\ *vt* **:** to inflict a trauma upon
1**tra·vail** \trə-'vā(ə)l, 'trav-ˌāl\ *n* [ME, fr. OF, fr. *travaillier* to torture, travail, fr. (assumed) VL *tripaliare* to torture, fr. *tripalium* instrument of torture, fr. L *tripalis* having three stakes, fr. *tri-* + *palus* stake — more at POLE] **1 a :** work esp. of a painful or laborious nature **:** TOIL **b :** a piece of work **:** TASK **c :** AGONY, TORMENT **2 :** LABOR, PARTURITION **syn** see WORK
2**travail** *like* 1; *in prayer-book communion service usu* 'trav-ˌāl\ *vi* [ME *travailen*, fr. OF *travaillier*] **1 :** to labor hard **:** TOIL **2 :** LABOR 3
trave \'trāv\ *n* [ME, fr. MF, beam, fr. L *trabs* — more at THORP] **1 :** a traverse beam **2 :** a division or bay (as in a ceiling) made by or as if by traverse beams
1**trav·el** \'trav-əl\ *vb* **trav·eled** *or* **trav·elled; trav·el·ing** *or* **trav·el·ling** \-(ə-)liŋ\ [ME *travailen* to travail, journey, fr. OF *travaillier*] *vi* **1 a :** to go on or as if on a trip or tour **:** JOURNEY **b** (1) **:** to go as if by traveling **:** PASS (2) **:** ASSOCIATE **c :** to go from place to place as a salesman or business agent **2 a :** to move or advance from one place to another **b :** to undergo transportation **c :** to move in a given direction or path or through a given distance ~ *vt* **1 :** to journey through or over **:** TRAVERSE **2 :** to traverse (a specified distance) **3 :** to cover as a commercial traveler
2**travel** *n* **1 a :** the act of traveling **:** PASSAGE **b :** JOURNEY, TRIP — often used in pl. **2** *pl* **:** an account of one's travels **3 :** the number traveling **:** TRAFFIC **4 a :** MOVEMENT, PROGRESSION **b :** the motion of a piece of machinery; *esp* **:** reciprocating motion
travel agency *n* **:** an agency engaged in selling, arranging, or furnishing information about personal transportation or travel — called also *travel bureau*
travel agent *n* **:** a person engaged in selling or arranging personal transportation, tours, or trips
trav·eled *or* **trav·elled** \'trav-əld\ *adj* **:** experienced in travel
trav·el·er *or* **trav·el·ler** \'trav-(ə-)lər\ *n* **1 :** one that travels: as **a :** one that goes on a trip or journey **b :** TRAVELING SALESMAN **2 a :** an iron ring sliding along a rope, bar, or rod of a ship **b :** a rod on the deck on which such a ring slides **3 :** any of various devices for transporting laterally
traveler's check *n* **:** a draft issued by a bank or express company payable on presentation by any correspondent of the issuer
traveling bag *n* **:** a bag carried by hand and designed to hold a traveler's clothing and personal articles
traveling case *n* **:** a usu. stiff and box-shaped traveling bag
traveling fellowship *n* **:** a fellowship whose terms permit or direct the holder to travel or go abroad for study or research
traveling salesman *n* **:** a traveling representative of a business concern who solicits orders
trav·el·ogue *also* **trav·el·og** \'trav-ə-ˌlȯg, -ˌläg\ *n* [*travel* + *-logue*] **:** a usu. illustrated lecture on travel
tra·vers·able \trə-'vər-sə-bəl *also* tra-', 'tra-(ˌ)\ *adj* **:** capable of being traversed
tra·vers·al \-səl\ *n* **:** the act or an instance of traversing
1**tra·verse** \'tra-vərs *also* -ˌvərs, *esp for 6 & 8 also* trə-', tra-'\ *n* [ME *travers*, fr. MF *traverse*, fr. *traverser* to cross, fr. LL *transversare*, fr. L *transversus*, pp. of *transvertere* — more at TRANSVERSE] **1 :** something that crosses or lies across **2 :** OBSTACLE, ADVERSITY **3 :** a formal denial of a matter of fact alleged by the opposite party in a legal pleading **4 a :** a compartment or recess formed by a partition, curtain, or screen **b :** a gallery or loft of communication from side to side in a large building **5 :** a route or way across or over (as a zigzag course) **6 :** the act or an instance of traversing **:** CROSSING **7 :** a protective projecting wall or bank of earth in a trench **8 a :** a lateral movement (as of the saddle of a lathe carriage); *also* **:** a device for imparting such movement **b :** the lateral movement of a gun about a pivot or on a carriage to change direction of fire **9 :** a line surveyed across a plot of ground
2**tra·verse** \trə-'vərs *also* tra-', 'tra-(ˌ)\ *vt* **1 a :** to go against or act in opposition to **:** OPPOSE, THWART **b :** to deny (as an allegation of fact or an indictment) formally at law **2 :** to pass through **:** PENETRATE **3 a :** to go or travel across or over **b :** to move along or through **4 :** to make a study of **:** EXAMINE **5 :** to lie or extend across **:** CROSS ⟨bridge ~s a rivulet⟩ **6 a :** to move to and fro over or along **b :** to ascend, descend, or cross (a slope or gap) at an angle **c :** to move (a gun) to right or left on a pivot **7 :** to make or carry out a traverse survey of ~ *vi* **1 :** to move back and forth or from side to side **2 :** to move or turn laterally **:** SWIVEL **3 :** to slide one's blade in fencing toward the opponent's hilt **4 :** to climb or ski at an angle or in a zigzag course **5 :** to make a traverse survey — **tra·vers·er** *n*
3**tra·verse** \'tra-(ˌ)vərs, trə-', tra-'\ *adj* **:** lying across **:** TRANSVERSE
trav·erse jury \'trav-ərs-\ *n* **:** PETIT JURY

trav·er·tine *also* **trav·er·tin** \'trav-ər-ˌtēn, -tən\ *n* [F *travertin*] **:** a mineral consisting of a massive usu. layered calcium carbonate (as aragonite or calcite) formed by deposition from spring waters or esp. from hot springs

1trav·es·ty \'trav-ə-stē\ *n* [obs. E *travesty*, disguised, parodied, fr. F *travesti*, pp. of *travestir* to disguise, fr. It *travestire*, fr. *tra-* across (fr. L *trans-*) + *vestire* to dress, fr. L, fr. *vestis* garment — more at WEAR] **1 :** a burlesque and usu. grotesque translation or imitation **2 :** an inferior imitation or likeness ⟨a ~ of justice⟩ **syn** see CARICATURE

2travesty *vt* **:** to make a travesty of **:** PARODY

tra·vois \trə-'vȯi, 'trav-ˌȯi\ *also* **tra·voise** \-'vȯiz, -ˌȯiz\ *n, pl* **tra·vois** \-'vȯiz, -ˌȯiz\ *also* **tra·vois·es** \-'vȯi-zəz, -ˌȯi-zəz\ [CanF *travois*] **:** a primitive vehicle used by Plains Indians consisting of two trailing poles serving as shafts and bearing a platform or net for the load

1trawl \'trȯl\ *vb* [prob. fr. obs. D *tragelen*] *vi* **1 :** to fish with a trawl **2 :** TROLL 2 ~ *vt* **:** to catch (fish) with a trawl — **trawl·er** *n*

2trawl *n* **1 :** a large conical net dragged along the sea bottom in gathering fish or other marine life **2 :** SETLINE

tray \'trā\ *n* [ME, fr. OE *trīg, trēg;* akin to OE *trēow* tree — more at TREE] **:** an open receptacle with flat bottom and low rim for holding, carrying, or exhibiting articles

treach·er·ous \'trech-(ə-)rəs\ *adj* **1 :** characterized by or manifesting treachery **:** PERFIDIOUS **2 a :** likely to betray trust **:** UNRELIABLE ⟨a ~ memory⟩ **b :** providing insecure footing or support ⟨~ quicksand⟩ **c :** marked by hidden dangers, hazards, or perils **syn** see FAITHLESS — **treach·er·ous·ly** *adv* — **treach·er·ous·ness** *n*

treach·ery \'trech-(ə-)rē\ *n* [ME *trecherie*, fr. OF, fr. *trechier* to deceive] **1 :** violation of allegiance or of faith and confidence **:** TREASON **2 :** an act of perfidy or treason

trea·cle \'trē-kəl\ *n* [ME *triacle*, fr. MF, fr. L *theriaca*, fr. Gk *thēriakē* antidote against a poisonous bite, fr. fem. of *thēriakos* of a wild animal, fr. *thērion* wild animal, dim. of *thēr* wild animal — more at FIERCE] **1 :** a medicinal compound formerly in wide use as a remedy against poison **2** *chiefly Brit* **:** MOLASSES **3 :** something (as a tone of voice) heavily sweet and cloying — **trea·cly** \-k(ə-)lē\ *adj*

1tread \'tred\ *vb* **trod** \'träd\ **trod·den** \'träd-ᵊn\ *or* **trod; tread·ing** [ME *treden*, fr. OE *tredan;* akin to OHG *tretan* to tread] *vt* **1 a :** to step or walk on or over **b :** to walk along **:** FOLLOW **2 a :** to beat or press with the feet **:** TRAMPLE **b :** to subdue or repress as if by trampling **:** CRUSH **3 :** to copulate with — used of a male bird **4 a :** to form by treading **:** BEAT ⟨~ a path⟩ **b :** to execute by stepping or dancing ⟨~ a measure⟩ ~ *vi* **1 :** to move on foot **:** WALK **2 a :** to set foot **b :** to put one's foot **:** STEP **3 :** COPULATE 1 — **tread·er** *n* — **tread water :** to keep the body nearly upright in the water and the head above water by a treading motion of the feet usu. aided by the hands

2tread *n* **1 :** a mark made by or as if by treading **2 a** (1) **:** the action of treading (2) **:** an act or instance of treading **:** STEP **b :** manner of stepping **c :** the sound of treading **3 :** CHALAZA 1 **4 a** (1) **:** the part of a sole that touches the ground (2) **:** the part of a wheel that bears on a road or rail; *esp* **:** the thickened face of an automobile tire **b :** the design on a tread **5 :** the distance between the points of contact with the ground of the two front wheels or the two rear wheels of a vehicle **6 a :** the upper horizontal part of a step **b :** the width of such a tread

trea·dle \'tred-ᵊl\ *n* [ME *tredel* step of a stair, fr. OE, fr. *tredan*] **1 :** a swiveling or lever device pressed by the foot to drive a machine **2 :** CHALAZA 1 — **treadle** *vi* **trea·dling** \'tred-liŋ, -ᵊl-iŋ\

tread·mill \'tred-ˌmil\ *n* **1 a :** a mill worked by persons treading on steps on the periphery of a wide wheel having a horizontal axis and used formerly in prison discipline **b :** a mill worked by an animal treading an endless belt **2 :** a wearisome routine

trea·son \'trēz-ᵊn\ *n* [ME *tresoun*, fr. OF *traison*, fr. ML *tradition-, traditio*, fr. L, act of handing over, fr. *traditus*, pp. of *tradere* to hand over, betray — more at TRAITOR] **1 :** the betrayal of a trust **:** PERFIDY, TREACHERY **2 :** the offense of attempting by overt acts to overthrow the government of the state to which the offender owes allegiance or to kill or personally injure the sovereign or his family **syn** see SEDITION

trea·son·able \'trēz-nə-bəl, -ᵊn-ə-bəl\ *adj* **:** relating to, consisting of, or involving treason — **trea·son·ably** \-blē\ *adv*

trea·son·ous \'trēz-nəs, -ᵊn-əs\ *adj* **:** TREASONABLE

trea·sur·able \'trezh-(ə-)rə-bəl, 'trāzh-\ *adj* **:** worthy of being treasured **:** PRECIOUS

1trea·sure \'trezh-ər, 'trāzh-\ *n* [ME *tresor*, fr. OF, fr. L *thesaurus*, fr. Gk *thēsauros*] **1 a** (1) **:** wealth (as money, jewels, or precious metals) stored up (2) **:** RICHES **b :** a store of money in reserve **2 :** something of great worth or value **3 :** a collection of precious things

2treasure *vt* **trea·sur·ing** \-(ə-)riŋ\ **1 :** to collect and store up (something of value) for future use **:** HOARD **2 :** to hold or keep as precious **:** CHERISH **syn** see APPRECIATE

treasure hunt *n* **:** a game in which each player or team tries to be first to find whatever has been hidden

trea·sur·er \'trezh-rər, 'trezh-ər-ər, 'trāzh-\ *n* **1 :** one having official charge of treasure; *esp* **:** a guardian of a collection of treasures **:** CURATOR **2 :** an officer entrusted with the receipt, care, and disbursement of funds: as **a :** a governmental officer charged with receiving, keeping, and disbursing public revenues **b :** the executive financial officer of a club, society, or business corporation — **trea·sur·er·ship** \-ˌship\ *n*

treasure trove \-ˌtrōv\ *n* [AF *tresor trové*, lit., found treasure] **1 :** treasure that anyone finds; *specif* **:** gold or silver in the form of money, plate, or bullion which is found hidden and whose ownership is not known **2 :** a valuable or productive discovery

trea·sury \'trezh-(ə-)rē, 'trāzh-\ *n* **1 a :** a place in which stores of wealth are kept **b :** the place of deposit and disbursement of collected funds; *esp* **:** one where public revenues are deposited, kept, and disbursed **c :** funds kept in such a depository **2** *obs* **:** TREASURE **3** *cap* **:** a governmental department in charge of finances and esp. the collection, management, and expenditure of public revenues **4** *cap* **:** a government security (as a note or bill) issued by the Treasury

treasury note *n* **:** a currency note issued by the U.S. Treasury in payment for silver bullion purchased under the Sherman Silver Purchase Act of 1890

treasury of merits : the superabundant satisfaction of Christ for men's sins and the excess of merit of the saints to eternal life forming a store held in Roman Catholic theology to be effective to the salvation of others and to be available for dispensation through indulgences — called also *treasury of the Church, treasury of the saints*

treasury stock *n* **:** issued stock reacquired by a corporation and held as an asset

1treat \'trēt\ *vb* [ME *treten*, fr. OF *traitier*, fr. L *tractare* to handle, deal with, fr. *tractus*, pp. of *trahere* to draw — more at DRAW] *vi* **1 :** to discuss terms of accommodation or settlement **:** NEGOTIATE **2 :** to deal with a matter esp. in writing **:** DISCOURSE — usu. used with *of* **3 :** to bear the expense of another's entertainment ~ *vt* **1 a :** to deal with in speech or writing **:** EXPOUND **b :** to present or represent artistically **c :** to deal with **:** HANDLE **2 a :** to bear oneself toward **:** USE ⟨~ a horse cruelly⟩ **b :** to regard and deal with in a specified manner — usu. used with *as* **3 a :** to provide with free food, drink, or entertainment **b :** to provide with enjoyment or gratification **4 :** to care for or deal with medically or surgically ⟨~ a disease⟩ **5 :** to act upon with some agent esp. to improve or alter ⟨~ a metal with acid⟩ — **treat·able** \-ə-bəl\ *adj* — **treat·er** *n*

2treat *n* **1 :** an entertainment given without expense to those invited **2 :** an esp. unexpected source of joy, delight, or amusement

trea·tise \'trēt-əs *also* -əz\ *n* [ME *tretis*, fr. AF *tretiz*, fr. OF *traitier* to treat] **1 :** a systematic exposition or argument in writing including a methodical discussion of the facts and principles involved and conclusions reached **2** *obs* **:** ACCOUNT, TALE

treat·ment \'trēt-mənt\ *n* **1 :** the act or manner or an instance of treating someone or something **:** HANDLING, USAGE **2 :** a substance or technique used in treating

trea·ty \'trēt-ē\ *n* [ME *tretee*, fr. MF *traité*, fr. ML *tractatus*, fr. L handling, treatment, fr. *tractatus*, pp. of *tractare* to treat] **1 :** the action of treating and esp. of negotiating **2 a :** an agreement or arrangement made by negotiation: (1) **:** PRIVATE TREATY (2) **:** a contract in writing between two or more political authorities (as states or sovereigns) formally signed by representatives duly authorized and usu. ratified by the lawmaking authority of the state **b :** a document in which such a contract is set down

treaty port *n* **:** one of a number of ports and inland cities in China, Japan, and Korea formerly open by treaty to foreign commerce

1tre·ble \'treb-əl\ *n* [ME, perh. fr. MF, trio, fr. *treble*, adj.] **1 a :** the highest of the four voice parts in vocal music **:** SOPRANO **b :** a singer or instrument taking this part **c :** a high-pitched or shrill voice, tone, or sound **d :** the upper half of the musical pitch range **e :** the higher portion of the audio frequency range in sound recording and broadcasting **2 :** something treble in construction, uses, amount, number, or value

2treble *adj* [ME, fr. MF, fr. L *triplus* — more at TRIPLE] **1 a :** having three parts **:** THREEFOLD **b :** triple in number or amount **2 a :** relating to or having the range of a musical treble ⟨~ voice⟩ **b :** high-pitched **:** SHRILL **c :** of, relating to, or having the range of treble in sound recording and broadcasting ⟨~ frequencies⟩ — **tre·bly** \'treb-(ə-)lē\ *adv*

3treble *vb* **tre·bling** \-(ə-)liŋ\ *vt* **:** to increase threefold ~ *vi* **1 :** to sing treble **2 :** to grow to three times the size, amount, or number

treble clef *n* [fr. its use for the notation of treble parts] **1 :** a clef that places G above middle C on the second line of the staff **2 :** TREBLE STAFF

treble staff *n* **:** the musical staff carrying the treble clef

treb·u·chet \ˌtreb-(y)ə-'shet, -'chet\ *or* **treb·uc·ket** \ˌtreb-ə-'ket\ *n* [ME *trebochet*, fr. MF *trebuchet*] **:** a medieval military engine for hurling missiles with great force

tre·cen·to \trā-'chen-(ˌ)tō\ *n, pl* **trecentos** [It, lit., three hundred, fr. L *tres* three + *centum* hundred — more at THREE, HUNDRED] **:** the 14th century; *specif* **:** the 14th century in Italian literature and art

tre·de·cil·lion \ˌtrēd-i-'sil-yən\ *n, often attrib* [L *tredecim* thirteen (fr. *tres* three + *decem* ten) + E *-illion* (as in *million*) — more at THREE, TEN] — see NUMBER table

1tree \'trē\ *n, often attrib* [ME, fr. OE *trēow;* akin to ON *trē* tree, Gk *drys*, Skt *dāru* wood] **1 a :** a woody perennial plant having a single usu. elongate main stem generally with few or no branches on its lower part **b :** a shrub or herb of arborescent form ⟨rose ~*s*⟩ ⟨a banana ~⟩ **2 a** (1) **:** a piece of wood (as a post or pole) usu. adapted to a particular use or forming part of a structure or implement (2) *archaic* **:** the cross on which Jesus was crucified **b** *archaic* **:** GALLOWS **3 :** something in the form of or felt to resemble a tree: as **a :** a diagram that depicts a branching from an original stem ⟨genealogical ~⟩ **b :** an arborescent aggregation of crystals **c :** a much-branched system of channels esp. in an animal body ⟨the vascular ~⟩ — **tree·less** \-ləs\ *adj*

2tree *vt* **treed; tree·ing 1 a :** to drive to or up a tree ⟨*treed* by a bull⟩ ⟨dogs ~*ing* game⟩ **b :** to bring to bay **:** CORNER **2 :** to furnish or fit with a tree

tree farm *n* **:** an area of forest land managed to ensure continuous commercial production

tree fern *n* **:** a fern (chiefly of families Cyatheaceae and Marattiaceae) of arborescent habit with a woody caudex

tree heath *n* **:** a shrubby heath (*Erica arborea*) of the Mediterranean and Caucasian region cultivated for its nearly globular white flowers

tree·hop·per \'trē-ˌhäp-ər\ *n* **:** any of numerous small leaping homopterous insects (family Membracidae) living on a sap from branches and twigs

tree house *n* **:** a structure (as a playhouse) built among the branches of a tree

tree line *n* **:** TIMBERLINE

tree·nail *also* **tre·nail** \'trē-ˌnāl, 'tren-ᵊl, 'trən-ᵊl\ *n* **:** a wooden peg made usu. of dry compressed timber so as to swell in its hole when moistened

tree of heaven : an Asiatic ailanthus (*Ailanthus glandulosa*) widely grown as a shade and ornamental tree

tree shrew *n* **:** any of a family (Tupaiidae) of arboreal insectivorous mammals sometimes held to be true insectivores and sometimes primitive primates

tree surgeon *n* **:** a specialist in tree surgery
tree surgery *n* **:** operative treatment of diseased trees esp. for control of decay; *broadly* **:** practices forming part of the professional care of specimen or shade trees
tree toad *n* **:** any of numerous tailless amphibians of arboreal habits (esp. family Hylidae) — called also *tree frog*
tree·top \'trē-,täp\ *n* **1 :** the topmost part of a tree **2** *pl* **:** the height or line marked by the tops of a group of trees
tref \'trāf\ *adj* [Yiddish *treyfe, treyf,* fr. Heb *ṭĕrēphāh* animal torn by wild beasts] **:** ritually unclean according to Jewish law
tre·foil \'trē-,fȯil, 'tref-,ȯil\ *n* [ME, fr. MF *trefeuil,* fr. L *trifolium,* fr. *tri-* + *folium* leaf] **1 a :** CLOVER; *broadly* **:** any of several trifoliolate leguminous herbs **b :** a trifoliolate leaf **2 :** an ornament or symbol in the form of a stylized trifoliolate leaf
tre·ha·lose \tri-'häl-,ōs, -,ōz\ *n* [ISV *trehala* (a sweet substance constituting the pupal covering of a beetle)] **:** a crystalline disaccharide sugar $C_{12}H_{22}O_{11}$ stored instead of starch by many fungi
treil·lage \tre-'yäzh\ *n* [F, fr. MF, fr. *treille* vine arbor, fr. L *trichila*] **:** latticework for vines **:** TRELLIS
1**trek** \'trek\ *n* [Afrik, fr. MD *treck* pull, haul, fr. *trecken*] **1** *chiefly southern Africa* **:** a journey by ox wagon; *esp* **:** an organized migration by a group of settlers **2 :** a trip or movement esp. when involving difficulties or complex organization
2**trek** *vi* **trekked; trek·king** [Afrik, fr. MD *trecken* to pull, haul, migrate; akin to OHG *trechan* to pull] **1** *chiefly southern Africa* **a :** to travel by ox wagon **b :** to migrate by ox wagon or in a train of such **2 :** to make one's way arduously — **trek·ker** *n*
1**trel·lis** \'trel-əs\ *n* [ME *trelis,* fr. MF *treliz* fabric of coarse weave, trellis, fr. (assumed) VL *trilicius* woven with triple thread, fr. L *tri-* + *liceum* thread] **1 :** a frame of latticework **2 :** a construction of latticework **3 :** an arrangement that forms a lattice

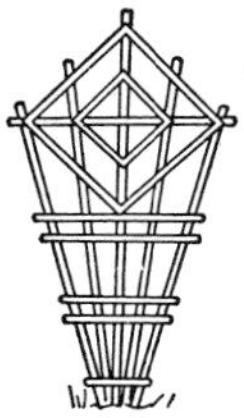
trellis 1

2**trellis** *vt* **1 :** to provide with a trellis; *esp* **:** to train (as a vine) on a trellis **2 :** to cross or interlace on or through **:** INTERWEAVE
trel·lised \'trel-əst\ *adj* **:** having or furnished with a trellis
trel·lis·work \'trel-ə-,swərk\ *n* **:** LATTICEWORK
trem·a·tode \'trem-ə-,tōd\ *n* [deriv. of Gk *trēmatōdēs* pierced with holes, fr. *trēmat-, trēma* hole, fr. *tetrainein* to bore — more at THROW] **:** any of a class (Trematoda) of parasitic flatworms including the flukes — **trematode** *adj*
1**trem·ble** \'trem-bəl\ *vi* **trem·bling** \-b(ə-)liŋ\ [ME *tremblen,* fr. MF *trembler,* fr. ML *tremulare,* fr. L *tremulus* tremulous, fr. *tremere* to tremble; akin to Gk *tremein* to tremble] **1 :** to shake involuntarily (as with fear or cold) **:** SHIVER **2 :** to move, sound, pass, or come to pass as if shaken or tremulous **3 :** to be affected with fear or doubt — **trem·bler** \-b(ə-)lər\ *n*
2**tremble** *n* **1 :** a fit or spell of involuntary shaking or quivering **2 :** a tremor or series of tremors **3** *pl but sing in constr* **:** severe poisoning of livestock and esp. cattle by a toxic alcohol present in a snakeroot and rayless goldenrod
trem·bly \'trem-b(ə-)lē\ *adj* **:** TREMBLING, TREMULOUS
tre·men·dous \tri-'men-dəs\ *adj* [L *tremendus,* fr. gerundive of *tremere*] **1 :** such as may excite trembling or arouse dread, awe, or terror **:** DREADFUL **2 :** astonishing by reason of extreme size, power, greatness, or excellence **syn** see MONSTROUS — **tre·men·dous·ly** *adv* — **tre·men·dous·ness** *n*
1**trem·o·lant** \'trem-ə-lənt\ *n* [It *tremolante,* fr. *tremolante* tremulant, fr. ML *tremulant-, tremulans*] **1 :** an organ pipe producing a tremolant tone **2 :** a device to impart a vibration causing a tremolant sound
2**tremolant** *adj* **:** marked by tremolo
trem·o·lite \'trem-ə-,līt\ *n* [F *trémolite,* fr. *Tremola,* valley in Switzerland] **:** a white or gray mineral $Ca_2Mg_5Si_8O_{22}(OH)_2$ of the amphibole group that is a calcium magnesium silicate
trem·o·lo \'trem-ə-,lō\ *n, pl* **tremolos** [It, fr. *tremolo* tremulous, fr. L *tremulus*] **1 a :** the rapid reiteration of a musical tone or of alternating tones to produce a tremulous effect **b :** a perceptible rapid variation of pitch in the voice esp. in singing similar to the vibrato of a stringed instrument **2 :** a mechanical device in an organ for causing a tremulous effect
trem·or \'trem-ər\ *n* [ME *tremour,* fr. MF, fr. L *tremor,* fr. *tremere*] **1 :** a trembling or shaking usu. from weakness or disease **2 :** a quivering or vibratory motion **3 a :** a feeling of uncertainty or insecurity **b :** a cause of such a feeling
trem·u·lant \'trem-yə-lənt\ *adj* [ML *tremulant-, tremulans,* prp. of *tremulare*] **:** TREMULOUS, TREMBLING
trem·u·lous \-ləs\ *adj* [L *tremulus*] **1 :** characterized by or affected with trembling or tremors **2 :** affected with timidity **:** TIMOROUS **3 :** such as is caused by a tremulous state **4 :** exceedingly sensitive — **trem·u·lous·ly** *adv* — **trem·u·lous·ness** *n*
1**trench** \'trench\ *n* [ME *trenche* track cut through a wood, fr. MF, act of cutting, fr. *trenchier* to cut] **:** a long cut in the ground or a similar depression in an ocean floor **:** DITCH; *specif* **:** one used for military defense often with the excavated dirt thrown up in front
2**trench** *vt* **1 :** to make a cut in **:** CARVE **2 a :** to protect with or as if with a trench **b :** to cut a trench in **:** DITCH ~ *vi* **1 :** to come close **:** VERGE **2 :** to dig a trench
tren·chan·cy \'tren-chən-sē\ *n* **:** the quality of being trenchant
tren·chant \-chənt\ *adj* [ME, fr. MF, prp. of *trenchier*] **1** *archaic* **:** KEEN, SHARP **2 :** vigorously effective; *specif* **:** CAUSTIC **3 a :** sharply perceptive **:** PENETRATING **b :** CLEAR-CUT, DISTINCT **syn** see INCISIVE — **tren·chant·ly** *adv*
trench coat *n* **1 :** a waterproof overcoat with a removable lining designed for wear in trenches **2 :** a loose double-breasted raincoat with deep pockets, belt, and straps on the shoulders
trenched \'trencht\ *adj* **1 :** furrowed or drained by trenches **2 :** provided with protective trenches
1**tren·cher** \'tren-chər\ *n* [ME, fr. MF *trencheoir,* fr. *trenchier* to cut] **:** a wooden platter for serving food
2**trencher** *adj* **1 :** of or relating to a trencher or to meals **2** *archaic* **:** PARASITIC, SYCOPHANTIC
3**trench·er** \'tren-chər\ *n* [2*trench*] **:** one that digs trenches
tren·cher·man \'tren-chər-mən\ *n* **1 :** a hearty eater **2** *archaic* **:** HANGER-ON, SPONGER
trench fever *n* **:** a rickettsial disease marked by fever and pain in muscles, bones, and joints and transmitted by the body louse
trench foot *n* **:** a painful foot disorder resembling frostbite and resulting from exposure to cold and wet
trench knife *n* **:** a knife with a strong double-edged 8-inch blade suited for hand-to-hand fighting
trench mouth *n* **1 :** VINCENT'S ANGINA **2 :** VINCENT'S INFECTION
1**trend** \'trend\ *vi* [ME *trenden* to turn, revolve, fr. OE *trendan;* akin to MHG *trendel* disk, spinning top, OE *teran* to tear — more at TEAR] **1 a :** to extend in a general direction **b :** to veer in a new direction **:** BEND **2 a :** to show a tendency **:** INCLINE **b :** to become deflected **:** SHIFT
2**trend** *n* **1 :** direction of movement **:** FLOW **2 a :** a prevailing tendency or inclination **:** DRIFT **b :** a general movement **:** SWING **c :** a current style or preference **:** VOGUE **d :** a line of development **:** APPROACH **syn** see TENDENCY
trente–et–qua·rante \,tränt-,ā-kə-'ränt\ *n* [F *trente et quarante,* lit., thirty and forty] **:** ROUGE ET NOIR
1**tre·pan** \tri-'pan\ *n* [ME *trepane,* fr. ML *trepanum,* fr. Gk *trypanon* auger, fr. *trypan* to bore, fr. *trypa* hole; akin to Gk *tetrainein* to pierce — more at THROW] **1 :** TREPHINE **2 :** a heavy tool used in boring mine shafts
2**trepan** *vt* **tre·panned; tre·pan·ning** **1 :** to use a trephine on (the skull) **2 :** to remove a disk or cylindrical core from (as with a saw) — **tre·pa·na·tion** \,trep-ə-'nā-shən, tri-,pan-'ā-\ *n*
3**trepan** *n* [origin unknown] **1** *archaic* **:** TRICKSTER **2** *archaic* **:** a deceptive device **:** SNARE
4**trepan** *vt* **tre·panned; tre·pan·ning** *archaic* **:** ENTRAP, LURE
tre·pang \tri-'paŋ\ *n* [Malay *tĕripang*] **:** any of several large sea cucumbers (esp. genera *Actinopyga* and *Holothuria*) that are taken mostly in northern Australia and the East Indies, boiled, dried, and used esp. by the Chinese for making soup — called also *bêche-de-mer*
treph·i·na·tion \,tref-ə-'nā-shən\ *n* **:** an act or instance of perforating the skull with a surgical instrument
1**tre·phine** \'trē-,fīn\ *n* [F *tréphine,* fr. obs. E *trefine, trafine,* fr. L *tres fines* three ends, fr. *tres* three + *fines,* pl. of *finis* end — more at THREE] **:** a surgical instrument for cutting out circular sections (as of bone or corneal tissue)
2**trephine** *vt* **:** to operate on with or extract by means of a trephine
trep·id \'trep-əd\ *adj* [L *trepidus*] **:** TIMOROUS
trep·i·dant \'trep-əd-ənt\ *adj* [L *trepidant-, trepidans,* prp. of *trepidare*] **:** TIMID, TREMBLING
trep·i·da·tion \,trep-ə-'dā-shən\ *n* [L *trepidation-, trepidatio,* fr. *trepidatus,* pp. of *trepidare* to tremble, fr. *trepidus* agitated; akin to OE *thrafian* to urge, push, Gk *trapein* to press grapes] **1** *archaic* **:** a tremulous motion **:** TREMOR **2 :** nervous agitation **:** APPREHENSION **syn** see FEAR
trepo·ne·ma \,trep-ə-'nē-mə\ *n, pl* **trepo·ne·ma·ta** \-mət-ə\ *or* **treponemas** [NL, genus name, deriv. of Gk *trepein* to turn + *nēma* thread, fr. *nēn* to spin — more at TROPE, NEEDLE] **:** any of a genus (*Treponema*) of spirochetes that parasitize man and other warm-blooded animals and include organisms causing syphilis and yaws — **trepo·ne·mal** \-məl\ *or* **trepo·ne·ma·tous** \-'nem-ət-əs, -'nēm-\ *adj*
1**tres·pass** \'tres-pəs, -,pas\ *n* [ME *trespas,* fr. OF, crossing, trespass, fr. *trespasser* to go across] **1 a :** a violation of moral or social ethics **:** TRANSGRESSION; *esp* **:** SIN **b :** an unwarranted infringement **2 a** (1) **:** an unlawful act committed on the person, property, or rights of another (2) **:** the action for injuries done by such an act **b :** the tort of wrongful entry on real property
2**trespass** *same;* -,pas *more often than for* 1\ *vi* [ME *trespassen,* fr. MF *trespasser,* fr. OF, lit., to go across, fr. *tres* across (fr. L *trans*) + *passer* to pass — more at THROUGH, PASS] **1 a :** ERR, SIN **b :** to make an unwarranted or uninvited incursion **2 :** to commit a trespass; *esp* **:** to enter unlawfully upon the land of another — **tres·pass·er** *n*
syn ENCROACH, ENTRENCH, INFRINGE, INVADE: TRESPASS implies an unwarranted, unlawful, or offensive intrusion; ENCROACH suggests gradual or stealthy entrance upon another's territory or usurpation of his rights or possessions; ENTRENCH suggests establishing and maintaining oneself in a position of advantage or profit at the expense of others; INFRINGE implies an encroachment clearly violating a right or prerogative; INVADE implies a hostile and injurious entry into the territory or sphere of another
tress \'tres\ *n* [ME *tresse,* fr. OF *trece*] **1** *archaic* **:** a plait of hair **:** BRAID **2 :** a long lock of hair; *esp* **:** the long unbound hair of a woman — usu. used in pl.
tressed \'trest\ *adj* **1 :** BRAIDED, PLAITED **2 :** having tresses — usu. used in combination ⟨golden-*tressed*⟩
tres–tine \'tres-,tīn\ *n* [prob. fr. L *tres* three + E *tine*] **:** ROYAL ANTLER
tres·tle *or* **tres·sel** \'tres-əl, 'trəs-\ *n* [ME *trestel,* fr. MF, modif. of (assumed) VL *transtellum,* fr. L *transtillum,* dim. of *transtrum* traverse beam, transom — more at TRANSOM] **1 :** HORSE 2b **2 :** a braced frame serving as a support (as for a table top) **3 :** a braced framework of timbers, piles, or steelwork for carrying a road or railroad over a depression
tres·tle·tree \-(,)trē\ *n* **:** one of a pair of timber crosspieces fixed fore and aft on the masthead to support the crosstrees, top, and fid of the mast — usu. used in pl.
tres·tle·work \-,wərk\ *n* **:** a system of connected trestles supporting a structure (as a bridge)
trews \'trüz\ *n pl* [ScGael *triubhas*] **1 :** tight-fitting trousers usu. of tartan **2 :** close-cut tartan shorts worn under the kilt in Highland dress
trey \'trā\ *n* [ME *treye, treis,* fr. MF *treie, treis,* fr. L *tres* three] **1 :** the side of a die or domino that has three spots **2 :** a card numbered three or having three main pips
tri- *comb form* [ME, fr. L (fr. *tri-, tres*) & Gk, fr. *tri-, treis* — more at THREE] **1 :** three ⟨*tri*costate⟩ **:** having three elements or parts ⟨*tri*graph⟩ **2 :** into three ⟨*tri*sect⟩ **3 :** thrice ⟨*tri*weekly⟩ **:** every third ⟨*tri*monthly⟩
tri·able \'trī-ə-bəl\ *adj* **:** liable or subject to judicial or quasi-judicial examination or trial ⟨a case ~ without a jury⟩ — **tri·able·ness** *n*
1**tri·ac·id** \(')trī-'as-əd\ *adj* [ISV] **1 :** able to react with three molecules of a monobasic acid or one of a triacid to form a salt or ester — used esp. of bases **2 :** containing three hydrogen atoms replaceable by basic atoms or radicals — used esp. of acid salts
2**triacid** *n* **:** an acid having three acid hydrogen atoms

tri·ad \'trī-ˌad, -əd\ *n* [L *triad-, trias,* fr. Gk, fr. *treis* three] **1 :** a union or group of three esp. of three closely related persons, beings, or things **:** TRINITY **2 :** a chord of three tones consisting of a root with its third and fifth and constituting the harmonic basis of tonal music — called also *common chord* — **tri·ad·ic** \trī-'ad-ik\ *adj* — **tri·ad·i·cal·ly** \-i-k(ə-)lē\ *adv*

1**tri·al** \'trī(-ə)l\ *n* [AF, fr. *trier* to try] **1 :** the action or process of trying or putting to the proof **:** TEST **2 :** the formal examination before a competent tribunal of the matter in issue in a civil or criminal cause in order to determine such issue **3 :** a test of faith, patience, or stamina by suffering or temptation; *broadly* **:** a source of vexation or annoyance **4 :** a tryout or experiment to test quality, value, or usefulness **5 :** ATTEMPT, EFFORT

2**trial** *adj* **1 :** of, relating to, or used in a trial **2 :** made or done as a test or experiment **3 :** used or tried out in a test or experiment

trial and error *n* **:** a finding out of the best way to reach a desired result or a correct solution by trying out one or more ways or means and by noting and eliminating errors or causes of failure; *also* **:** the trying of this and that until something succeeds

trial balance *n* **:** a list of the debit and credit balances of accounts in a double-entry ledger at a given date prepared primarily to test their equality

trial balloon *n* **1 :** a balloon sent up to test air currents and wind velocity **2 :** a project or scheme tentatively announced in order to test public opinion

trial examiner *n* **:** a person appointed to hold hearings and to investigate and report facts sometimes with recommendations to an administrative or quasi-judicial agency or tribunal

trial jury *n* **:** a jury impaneled to try a cause **:** PETIT JURY

trial lawyer *n* **:** a lawyer who engages chiefly in the trial of cases before courts of original jurisdiction

trial run *n* **:** a testing exercise **:** EXPERIMENT

tri·an·gle \'trī-ˌaŋ-gəl\ *n* [ME, fr. L *triangulum,* fr. neut. of *triangulus* triangular, fr. *tri-* + *angulus* angle] **1 :** a polygon having three sides **2 a :** a musical percussion instrument made of a rod of steel bent into the form of a triangle open at one angle **b :** a drafting instrument consisting of a thin flat right-angled triangle of wood or plastic with acute angles of 45 degrees or of 30 degrees and 60 degrees **3 :** a situation involving the love of two persons of one sex for one of the opposite sex with the resulting complications ⟨the eternal ~⟩

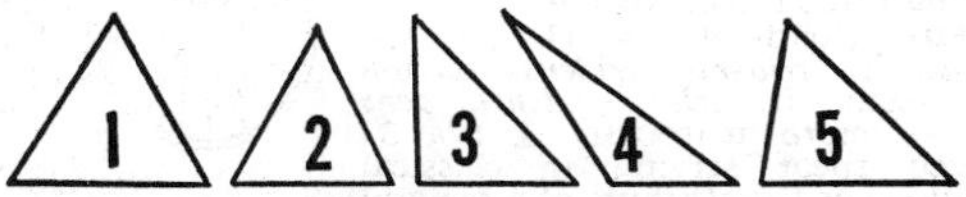

triangles: *1* equilateral, *2* isosceles, *3* right-angled, *4* obtuse, *5* scalene

tri·an·gu·lar \trī-'aŋ-gyə-lər\ *adj* [LL *triangularis,* fr. L *triangulum*] **1 a :** of, relating to, or having the form of a triangle ⟨~ plot of land⟩ **b :** having a triangular base or principal surface ⟨~ table⟩ ⟨~ pyramid⟩ **2 a** (1) **:** of, relating to, or involving three elements (2) *of a military group* **:** based primarily on three units ⟨~ division⟩ **b :** of or relating to a love triangle ⟨a ~ love affair⟩ — **tri·an·gu·lar·i·ty** \(ˌ)trī-ˌaŋ-gyə-'lar-ət-ē\ *n* — **tri·an·gu·lar·ly** \trī-'aŋ-gyə-lər-lē\ *adv*

1**tri·an·gu·late** \trī-'aŋ-gyə-lət\ *adj* [ML *triangulatus,* pp. of *triangulare* to make triangles, fr. L *triangulum*] **:** consisting of or marked with triangles — **tri·an·gu·late·ly** *adv*

2**tri·an·gu·late** \-ˌlāt\ *vt* **1 a :** to divide into triangles **b :** to give triangular form to **2 :** to survey, map, or determine by triangulation

tri·an·gu·la·tion \(ˌ)trī-ˌaŋ-gyə-'lā-shən\ *n* **:** the measurement of the elements necessary to determine the network of triangles into which any part of the earth's surface is divided in surveying; *broadly* **:** any similar trigonometric operation for finding a position or location by means of bearings from two fixed points a known distance apart

tri·ar·chy \'trī-ˌär-kē\ *n* [Gk *triarchia,* fr. *tri-* + *-archia* -archy] **1 :** government by three persons **:** TRIUMVIRATE **2 :** a country under three rulers

Tri·as·sic \trī-'as-ik\ *adj* [ISV, fr. L *trias* triad; fr. the three subdivisions of the European Triassic — more at TRIAD] **:** of, relating to, or being the earliest period of the Mesozoic era or the corresponding system of rocks — **Triassic** *n*

tri·at·ic stay \(ˌ)trī-ˌat-ik-\ *n* [origin unknown] **:** a stay running horizontally between the heads of the foremast and mainmast

tri·atom·ic \ˌtrī-ə-'täm-ik\ *adj* [ISV] **1 :** having three atoms in the molecule **2 :** having three replaceable atoms or radicals

tri·ax·i·al \(')trī-'ak-sē-əl\ *adj* [ISV] **:** having or involving three axes

tri·azine \'trī-ə-ˌzēn, trī-'az-ˌēn\ *n* [ISV] **:** any of three compounds $C_3H_3N_3$ containing a ring composed of three carbon and three nitrogen atoms; *also* **:** any of various derivatives of these

tri·azole \'trī-ə-ˌzōl, trī-'az-ˌōl\ *n* [ISV] **:** any of four compounds $C_2H_3N_3$ containing a ring composed of two carbon atoms and three nitrogen atoms; *also* **:** any of various derivatives of these — **tri·azol·ic** \ˌtrī-ə-'zäl-ik\ *adj*

trib·al \'trī-bəl\ *adj* **:** of, relating to, or characteristic of a tribe ⟨~ customs⟩ — **trib·al·ly** \-bə-lē\ *adv*

trib·al·ism \-bə-ˌliz-əm\ *n* **1 :** tribal consciousness and loyalty; *esp* **:** exaltation of the tribe above other groups **2 :** strong ingroup loyalty

tri·ba·sic \(')trī-'bā-sik\ *adj* **1 :** having three hydrogen atoms capable of replacement by basic atoms or radicals — used of acids **2 :** containing three atoms of a univalent metal or their equivalent **3 :** having three basic hydroxyl groups and able to react with three molecules of a monobasic acid — used of bases and basic salts — **tri·ba·sic·i·ty** \ˌtrī-bā-'sis-ət-ē\ *n*

tribe \'trīb\ *n* [ME, fr. L *tribus,* a division of the Roman people, tribe] **1 a :** a social group comprising numerous families, clans, or generations together with slaves, dependents, or adopted strangers **b :** a political division of the Roman people orig. representing one of the three primitive tribes of ancient Rome **c :** PHYLE **2 :** a group of persons having a common character, occupation, or interest **3 a :** a category of taxonomic classification sometimes equivalent to or ranking just below a suborder or ranking below a subfamily; *also* **:** a natural group irrespective of taxonomic rank ⟨the cat ~⟩ ⟨rose ~⟩ **b :** a group of closely related animals or strains within a breed

tribes·man \'trībz-mən\ *n* **:** a member of a tribe

tribo- *comb form* [F, fr. Gk *tribein* to rub; akin to L *terere* to rub — more at THROW] **:** friction ⟨*tribo*luminescence⟩

tri·bo·elec·tric \ˌtrī-bō-i-'lek-trik, ˌtrib-ō-\ *adj* **:** of, relating to, or marked by triboelectricity

tri·bo·elec·tric·i·ty \-i-ˌlek-'tris-ət-ē, -'tris-tē\ *n* **:** a charge of electricity generated by friction (as by rubbing glass with silk)

tri·bo·lu·mi·nes·cence \-ˌlü-mə-'nes-ᵊn(t)s\ *n* [ISV] **:** luminescence due to friction — **tri·bo·lu·mi·nes·cent** \-ᵊnt\ *adj*

tri·bo·phys·ics \'trī-bō-ˌfiz-iks, 'trib-ō-\ *n pl but sing or pl in constr* **:** the physics of friction

tri·brach \'trī-ˌbrak\ *n* [L *tribrachys,* fr. Gk, having three short syllables, fr. *tri-* + *brachys* short — more at BRIEF] **:** a metrical foot of three short syllables of which two belong to the thesis and one to the arsis — **tri·brach·ic** \trī-'brak-ik\ *adj*

tri·bro·mide \(')trī-'brō-ˌmīd\ *n* **:** a compound of an element or radical with three atoms of bromine

tri·bro·mo·eth·a·nol \ˌtrī-ˌbrō-mō-'eth-ə-ˌnȯl, -ˌnōl\ *n* **:** a bromine derivative CBr_3CH_2OH of ethyl alcohol used as a basal anesthetic

trib·u·late \'trib-yə-ˌlāt\ *vt* [LL *tribulatus,* pp. of *tribulare* to oppress, afflict] **:** to cause to endure tribulation

trib·u·la·tion \ˌtrib-yə-'lā-shən\ *n* [ME *tribulacion,* fr. OF, fr. L *tribulation-, tribulatio,* fr. *tribulatus,* pp. of *tribulare* to press, oppress, fr. *tribulum* threshing sledge, fr. *terere* to rub — more at THROW] **:** distress or suffering resulting from oppression or persecution; *also* **:** a trying experience

tri·bu·nal \trī-'byün-ᵊl, trib-'yün-\ *n* [L, platform for magistrates, fr. *tribunus* tribune] **1 :** the seat of a judge **:** TRIBUNE **2 :** a court or forum of justice **3 :** something that decides or determines

tri·bu·nate \'trib-yə-ˌnāt, trib-'yü-nət\ *n* **:** TRIBUNESHIP

1**tri·bune** \'trib-ˌyün, trib-'yün\ *n* [ME, fr. L *tribunus,* fr. *tribus* tribe] **1 :** a Roman official under the monarchy and the republic with the function of protecting the plebeian citizen from arbitrary action by the patrician magistrates **2 :** a defender of the people — **tri·bune·ship** \-ˌship\ *n*

2**tribune** *n* [F, fr. It *tribuna,* fr. L *tribunal*] **:** a dais or platform from which an assembly is addressed

1**trib·u·tary** \'trib-yə-ˌter-ē\ *adj* **1 :** paying tribute to another to acknowledge submission, to obtain protection, or to purchase peace **:** SUBJECT **2 :** paid or owed as tribute **3 :** channeling supplies into something more inclusive **:** CONTRIBUTORY

2**tributary** *n* **1 :** a ruler or state that pays tribute to a conqueror **2 :** a stream feeding a larger stream or a lake

trib·ute \'trib-(ˌ)yüt, -yət\ *n* [ME *tribut,* fr. L *tributum,* fr. neut. of *tributus,* pp. of *tribuere* to allot, bestow, grant, pay, fr. *tribus* tribe] **1 a :** a payment by one ruler or nation to another in acknowledgment of submission or as the price of protection; *also* **:** the tax levied for such a payment **b** (1) **:** an excessive tax, rental, or tariff imposed by a government, sovereign, lord, or landlord (2) **:** an exorbitant charge levied by a person or group having the power of coercion **c :** the liability to pay tribute **2 :** something given or contributed voluntarily as due or deserved **:** a gift or service showing respect, gratitude, or affection ⟨floral ~⟩; *specif* **:** PRAISE, CREDIT **syn** see ENCOMIUM

tri·car·box·yl·ic \ˌtrī-ˌkär-ˌbäk-'sil-ik\ *adj* **:** containing three carboxyl groups in the molecule

tri·car·pel·lary \(')trī-'kär-pə-ˌler-ē\ *adj* **:** having or made up of three usu. fused carpels

1**trice** \'trīs\ *vt* [ME *trisen, tricen* to pull, trice, fr. MD *trisen* to hoist] **:** to haul up or in and lash or secure (as a sail) with a small rope

2**trice** *n* [ME *trise,* lit., pull, fr. *trisen*] **:** a brief space of time **:** INSTANT — used chiefly in the phrase *in a trice*

tri·ceps \'trī-ˌseps\ *n, pl* **tri·ceps·es** *also* **triceps** [NL *tricipit-, triceps,* fr. L, three-headed, fr. *tri-* + *capit-, caput* head — more at HEAD] **:** a muscle that arises from three heads; *esp* **:** the great extensor muscle along the back of the upper arm

-trices *pl of* -TRIX

trich- *or* **tricho-** *comb form* [NL, fr. Gk, fr. *trich-, thrix* hair; akin to MIr *gairbdriuch* bristle] **:** hair **:** filament ⟨*tricho*gyne⟩

tri·chi·a·sis \trik-'ī-ə-səs\ *n* [LL, fr. Gk, fr. *trich* + *-iasis*] **:** a turning inward of the eyelashes often causing irritation of the eyeball

tri·chi·na \trik-'ī-nə\ *n, pl* **tri·chi·nae** \-(ˌ)nē\ *also* **trichinas** [NL, fr. Gk *trichinos* made of hair, fr. *trich-, thrix* hair] **1 :** a small slender nematode worm (*Trichinella spiralis*) that in the larval state is parasitic in the voluntary muscles of flesh-eating mammals (as man and hog) **2 :** TRICHINOSIS — **tri·chi·nal** \-'īn-ᵊl\ *adj*

trich·i·nize \'trik-ə-ˌnīz\ *vt* **:** to infest with trichinae

trich·i·no·sis \ˌtrik-ə-'nō-səs\ *n* [NL] **:** infestation with or disease caused by trichinae and marked esp. by muscular pain, dyspnea, fever, and edema

tri·chi·nous \trik-'ī-nəs, 'trik-ə-\ *adj* [ISV] **1 :** infested with trichinae ⟨~ meat⟩ **2 :** of, relating to, or involving trichinae or trichinosis ⟨~ infection⟩

trich·ite \'trik-ˌīt\ *n* [G *trichit,* fr. Gk *trich-, thrix* hair] **:** a minute acicular body — **tri·chit·ic** \trik-'it-ik\ *adj*

tri·chlo·ride \(')trī-'klō(ə)r-ˌīd, -'klȯ(ə)r-\ *n* [ISV] **:** a compound of an element or radical with three atoms of chlorine

tri·chlo·ro·ace·tic acid \ˌtrī-ˌklōr-ə-wə-ˌsēt-ik-, -ˌklȯr-\ *n* [ISV] **:** a strong vesicant pungent acid CCl_3COOH used in weed control and in medicine as a caustic and astringent

tricho·cyst \'trik-ə-ˌsist\ *n* **:** any of the minute lassoing or stinging organs on the body of protozoans — **tricho·cys·tic** \ˌtrik-ə-'sis-tik\ *adj*

tricho·gyne \'trik-ə-ˌjīn, -ˌgīn\ *n* [ISV] **:** a prolonged terminal receptive portion of an archicarp or of a similar reproductive structure in a red alga — **tricho·gy·ni·al** \ˌtrik-ə-'jin-ē-əl, -'gī-nē-\ *or* **tricho·gy·nic** \-jin-ik, -'gī-nik\ *adj*

tri·choid \'trik-ˌȯid, 'trī-ˌkȯid\ *adj* [Gk *trichoeidēs,* fr. *trich-, thrix*] **:** resembling a hair **:** CAPILLARY

tri·chome \'trik-,ōm, 'trī-,kōm\ *n* [G *trichom*, fr. Gk *trichōma* growth of hair, fr. *trichoun* to cover with hair, fr. *trich-*, *thrix* hair — more at TRICH-] **:** a filamentous outgrowth; *esp* **:** an epidermal hair structure on a plant — **tri·cho·mic** \trik-'äm-ik, -'ōm-; trī-'käm-, -'kōm-\ *adj*

tricho·mo·nad \,trik-ə-'män-,ad, -'mō-,nad\ *n* [NL *Trichomonad-*, *Trichomonas*, genus name, fr. *trich-* + LL *monad-*, *monas* monad] **:** any of a genus (*Trichomonas*) of flagellated protozoans parasitic in many animals including man — **trichomonad** *or* **tricho·mo·na·dal** \-'män-əd-ᵊl, -'mō-nəd-\ *or* **tricho·mo·nal** \-'män-ᵊl, -'mōn-\ *adj*

tricho·mo·ni·a·sis \,trik-ə-mə-'nī-ə-səs\ *n* [NL, fr. *Trichomonas* + *-iasis*] **:** infection with or disease caused by trichomonads: as **a :** a human vaginitis characterized by a persistent discharge **b :** a venereal disease of domestic cattle marked by abortion and sterility **c :** one or more diseases of various birds resembling blackhead

tri·chop·ter·an \trik-'äp-tə-rən\ *n* [deriv. of Gk *trich-*, *thrix* hair + *pteron* wing — more at FEATHER] **:** any of an order (Trichoptera) of insects consisting of the caddis flies — **trichopteran** *or* **tri·chop·ter·ous** \-rəs\ *adj*

tri·chot·o·mous \trī-'kät-ə-məs\ *adj* [LGk *trichotomein* to trisect, fr. Gk *tricha* in three (fr. *treis* three) + *-tomein* (akin to *temnein* to cut) — more at THREE, TOME] **:** divided or dividing into three parts or into threes **:** THREE-FOLD ⟨~ branching⟩ — **tri·chot·o·mous·ly** *adv*

tri·chot·o·my \-mē\ *n* **:** division into three parts, elements, or classes

-tri·chous \tri-kəs\ *adj comb form* [Gk *-trichos*, fr. *trich-*, *thrix* hair — more at TRICH-] **:** having (such) hair **:** -haired ⟨peri*trichous*⟩

tri·chro·mat \'trī-krō-,mat, (')trī-'\ *n* [back-formation fr. *trichromatic*] **:** a person with normal color vision requiring that three primary colors be mixed in order to match the spectrum as he sees it

tri·chro·mat·ic \,trī-krō-'mat-ik\ *adj* **1 :** of, relating to, or consisting of three colors **2 :** relating to or exhibiting trichromatism

tri·chro·ma·tism \(')trī-'krō-mə-,tiz-əm\ *n* **1 :** the quality or state of being trichromatic **:** the use of three colors (as in photography) **2 :** vision in which all of the fundamental colors are perceived though not necessarily with equal facility

trich·u·ri·a·sis \,trik-yə-'rī-ə-səs\ *n, pl* **trich·u·ri·a·ses** \-ə-,sēz\ [NL, fr. *Trichuris*, genus of worms] **:** infestation with or disease caused by whipworms (genus *Trichuris*)

1**trick** \'trik\ *n* [ME *trik*, fr. ONF *trique*, fr. *trikier* to deceive, cheat] **1 a :** a crafty procedure or practice meant to deceive or defraud **b :** a mischievous act **:** PRANK **c :** an indiscreet or childish action **d :** a deceptive, dexterous, or ingenious feat designed to puzzle or amuse ⟨a juggler's ~*s*⟩ **2 a :** an habitual peculiarity of behavior or manner ⟨a horse with the ~ of shying⟩ **b :** a characteristic and identifying feature ⟨a ~ of speech⟩ **c :** an optical illusion ⟨a mere ~ of the light⟩ **3 a :** a quick or artful way of getting a result **:** KNACK **b :** a technical device (as of an art or craft) ⟨the ~*s* of stage technique⟩ **4 :** the cards played in one round of a card game often used as a scoring unit **5 a :** a turn of duty at the helm usu. lasting for two hours **b :** SHIFT 4b(1) **c :** a trip taken as part of one's employment **6 :** an attractive child or pretty young woman ⟨cute little ~⟩

syn TRICK, RUSE, STRATAGEM, MANEUVER, ARTIFICE, WILE, FEINT mean an indirect means to gain an end. TRICK may imply deception, roguishness, illusion, and either an evil or harmless end; RUSE stresses an attempt to mislead by a false impression; STRATAGEM implies a ruse used to entrap, outwit, circumvent, or surprise an opponent or enemy; MANEUVER suggests adroit and skillful avoidance of difficulty; ARTIFICE implies ingenious contrivance or invention; WILE suggests an attempt to entrap or deceive with false allurements; FEINT implies a diversion or distraction of attention away from one's real intent

2**trick** *adj* **1 :** of or relating to or involving tricks or trickery ⟨~ photography⟩ ⟨~ dice⟩ **2 :** TRIG **3 a :** somewhat defective and unreliable ⟨a ~ lock⟩ **b :** inclined to give way unexpectedly ⟨a ~ knee⟩

3**trick** *vt* **1 :** to deceive by cunning or artifice **:** CHEAT **2 :** to dress or adorn fancifully or ornately **:** ORNAMENT ⟨~*ed* out in a gaudy uniform⟩ **syn** see DUPE

trick·er \'trik-ər\ *n* **:** one that tricks **:** TRICKSTER

trick·ery \'trik-(ə-)rē\ *n* **:** deception or fraud by tricks and stratagems **syn** see DECEPTION

trick·i·ly \'trik-ə-lē\ *adv* **:** in a tricky manner

trick·i·ness \'trik-ē-nəs\ *n* **:** the quality or state of being tricky

trick·ish \'trik-ish\ *adj* **:** given to or characterized by tricks or trickery **:** TRICKY — **trick·ish·ly** *adv* — **trick·ish·ness** *n*

1**trick·le** \'trik-əl\ *vi* **trick·ling** \-(ə-)liŋ\ [ME *triklen*] **1 :** to run or fall in drops **2 :** to flow in a thin gentle stream

2**trickle** *n* **:** a drip or stream that trickles

trick·let \'trik-lət\ *n* **:** a thin stream

trick or treat *n* **:** the children's Halloween practice of asking for goodies from door to door under threat of playing tricks on householders who refuse

tricks·i·ness \'trik-sē-nəs\ *n* **:** the quality or state of being tricksy

trick·ster \'trik-stər\ *n* **:** one who tricks or cheats

tricksy \'trik-sē\ *adj* [*tricks*, pl. of *trick*] **1** *archaic* **:** smartly attired **:** SPRUCE **2 :** full of tricks **:** PRANKISH **3 a** *archaic* **:** having the craftiness of a trickster **:** DECEPTIVE **b :** difficult to cope with or handle **:** TRYING ⟨a ~ job⟩

tricky \'trik-ē\ *adj* **1 :** of or characteristic of a trickster **2 :** requiring skill, knack, or caution **:** DELICATE **3 :** TRICK 3 **syn** see SLY

tri·clin·ic \(')trī-'klin-ik\ *adj* [ISV] **:** having three unequal axes intersecting at oblique angles — used esp. of a crystal

tri·clin·i·um \trī-'klin-ē-əm\ *n, pl* **tri·clin·ia** \-ē-ə\ [L, fr. Gk *triklinion*, fr. *tri-* + *klinein* to lean, recline — more at LEAN] **1 :** a couch used by ancient Romans for reclining at meals, extending round three sides of a table, and usu. divided into three parts **2 :** a dining room furnished with a triclinium

tric·o·lette \,trik-ə-'let\ *n* [*tricot* + *-lette* (as in *flannelette*)] **:** a usu. silk or rayon knitted fabric used esp. for women's clothing

1**tri·col·or** \'trī-,kəl-ər, *esp Brit* 'trik-ə-lər\ *n* [F *tricolore*, fr. *tricolore* three-colored, fr. LL *tricolor*, fr. L *tri-* + *color*] **:** a flag of three colors ⟨the French ~⟩

2**tricolor** *adj* [F *tricolore*] **1** *or* **tri·col·ored** \'trī-kəl-ərd\ **:** having or using three colors **2 :** of, relating to, or characteristic of a tricolor or a nation whose flag is a tricolor; *often* **:** FRENCH

tri·corn \'trī-,kȯ(ə)rn\ *adj* [L *tricornis*] **:** having three horns or corners

tri·corne *or* **tri·corn** \'trī-,kȯ(ə)rn\ *n* [F *tricorne*, fr. *tricorne* three-cornered, fr. L *tricornis*, fr. *tri-* + *cornu* horn — more at HORN] **:** COCKED HAT 1

tri·cor·nered \'trī-'kȯ(r)-nərd\ *adj* **:** having three corners

tri·cos·tate \(')trī-'käs-,tāt\ *adj* [ISV] **:** having three costae

tri·cot \'trē-(,)kō, 'trī-kət\ *n* [F, fr. *tricoter* to knit] **1 :** a plain warp-knitted fabric of nylon, wool, rayon, silk, or cotton used in clothing (as underwear) **2 :** a twilled clothing fabric of wool with fine warp ribs or of wool and cotton with fine weft ribs

tri·co·tine \,trik-ə-'tēn, ,trē-kə-\ *n* [F, fr. *tricot*] **:** a sturdy suiting woven of tightly twisted yarns in a steep double twill

tri·cot·y·le·don·ous \,trī-,kät-ᵊl-'ēd-nəs, -ᵊn-əs\ *adj* **:** having three cotyledons ⟨a ~ seedling⟩

tri·crot·ic \(')trī-'krät-ik\ *adj* [Gk *trikrotos* having a triple beat, fr. *tri-* + *krotein* to clap, beat; akin to OE *hrindan* to thrust] **:** of or relating to tricrotism

tri·cro·tism \'trī-krə-,tiz-əm\ *n* **:** a condition of the arterial pulse in which there is a triple beat

tric·trac \'trik-,trak\ *n* [F, of imit. origin; fr. the sound made by the pegs] **:** a variety of backgammon formerly played with pegs

1**tri·cus·pid** \(')trī-'kəs-pəd\ *adj* [L *tricuspid-*, *tricuspis*, fr. *tri-* + *cuspid-*, *cuspis* point] **:** having three cusps

2**tricuspid** *n* **:** a tricuspid anatomical structure; *esp* **:** a tooth having three cusps

tri·cus·pi·date \-pə-,dāt\ *adj* **:** cuspidate with three points **:** TRICUSPID

tricuspid valve *n* **:** a valve of three flaps that prevents reflux of blood from the right ventricle to the right auricle

tri·cy·cle \'trī-,sik-əl\ *n* [F, fr. *tri-* + Gk *kyklos* wheel — more at WHEEL] **:** a 3-wheeled vehicle propelled by pedals, hand levers, or a motor

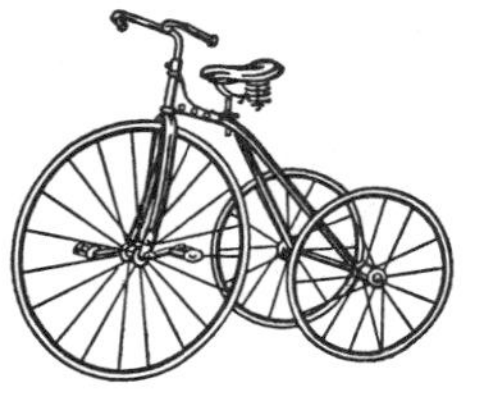
tricycle

tri·cy·clic \(')trī-'sī-klik, -'sik-lik\ *adj* [*tri* + *cyclic*] **:** containing three usu. fused rings in the molecular structure

tri·dac·tyl \(')trī-'dak-tᵊl\ *or* **tri·dac·ty·lous** \-tə-ləs\ *adj* [Gk *tridaktylos*, fr. *tri-* + *daktylos* finger, toe] **:** having three fingers or toes

1**tri·dent** \'trīd-ᵊnt\ *n* [L *trident-*, *tridens*, fr. *trident-* *tridens* having three teeth, fr. *tri-* + *dent-*, *dens* tooth — more at TOOTH] **1 :** a 3-pronged spear serving in classical mythology as the attribute of a sea-god **2 :** a 3-pronged spear used by ancient Roman retiarii **3 :** a 3-pronged fish spear

2**trident** *adj* [L *trident-*, *tridens*] **:** having three teeth, processes, or points

tri·den·tate \(')trī-'den-,tāt\ *adj* [NL *tridentatus*, fr. *tri-* + L *dentatus* dentate] **:** having three teeth, processes, or points ⟨a ~ leaf⟩

Tri·den·tine \trī-'dent-ᵊn, -'den-,tēn\ *adj* [NL *Tridentinus*, fr. L *Tridentum* Trent] **:** of or relating to Trent, Italy, or to a Roman Catholic church council held there from 1545 to 1563

tri·di·men·sion·al \,trīd-ə-'mench-nəl, ,trīd-(,)ī-, -ən-ᵊl\ *adj* [ISV] **:** of, relating to, or concerned with three dimensions ⟨~ space⟩ ⟨a ~ motion-picture technique⟩ — **tri·di·men·sion·al·i·ty** \-,men-chə-'nal-ət-ē\ *n*

trid·u·um \'trij-ə-wəm, 'trid-yə-\ *n* [L, fr. *tri-* + *-duum* (akin to *dies* day) — more at DEITY] **:** a period of three days of prayer usu. preceding a Roman Catholic feast

tried \'trīd\ *adj* [ME, fr. pp. of *trien* to try, test] **1 :** found good, faithful, or trustworthy through experience or testing ⟨a ~ recipe⟩ **2 :** subjected to trials or distress ⟨a kind but much-*tried* father⟩

tri·ene \'trī-,ēn\ *n* **:** a chemical compound containing three double bonds

tri·en·ni·al \(')trī-'en-ē-əl\ *adj* **1 :** consisting of or lasting for three years **2 :** occurring or being done every three years — **triennial** *n* — **tri·en·ni·al·ly** \-ē-ə-lē\ *adv*

tri·en·ni·um \trī-'en-ē-əm\ *n, pl* **trienniums** *or* **tri·en·nia** \-ē-ə\ [L, fr. *tri-* + *annus* year — more at ANNUAL] **:** a period of three years

tri·er \'trī(-ə)r\ *n* **:** someone or something that tries

tri·er·arch \'trī(-ə)-,rärk\ *n* [L *trierarchus*, fr. Gk *triērarchos*, fr. *triērēs* trireme (fr. *tri-* + *-ērēs* — akin to L *rēmus* oar) + *-archos* -arch — more at ROW] **1 :** the commander of a trireme **2 :** an Athenian citizen who had to fit out a trireme for the public service

tri·er·ar·chy \-,rär-kē\ *n* **:** the ancient Athenian plan whereby individual citizens furnished and maintained triremes as part of their civic duty

tri·eth·yl \(')trī-'eth-əl\ *adj* [ISV] **:** containing three ethyl groups in the molecule

tri·fa·cial \-'fā-shəl\ *adj or n* [ISV] **:** TRIGEMINAL

tri·fid \'trī-,fid, -fəd\ *adj* [L *trifidus* split into three, fr. *tri-* + *findere* to split — more at BITE] **:** being deeply and narrowly tridentate

1**tri·fle** \'trī-fəl\ *n* [ME *trufle*, *trifle*, fr. OF *trufe*, *trufle* mockery] **1 :** something of little value or importance; *esp* **:** an insignificant amount (as of money) **2 :** a dessert of sponge cake spread with jam or jelly, sprinkled with crumbled macaroons, soaked in wine, and served with custard and whipped cream **3 :** a pewter of moderate hardness used esp. for small utensils

2**trifle** *vb* **tri·fling** \-f(ə-)liŋ\ [ME *truflen*, *triflen*, fr. OF *trufer*, *trufler* to mock, trick] *vi* **1 a :** to talk in a jesting or mocking manner or with intent to delude or mislead **b :** to act heedlessly or frivolously **:** PLAY **2 :** to waste time **:** DALLY **3 :** to handle something idly **:** TOY ~ *vt* **:** to spend or waste in trifling or on trifles ⟨~ away money⟩ — **tri·fler** \-f(ə-)lər\ *n*

syn TRIFLE, TOY, DALLY, FLIRT, COQUET mean to deal with or act toward without serious purpose. TRIFLE may imply playfulness, unconcern, indulgent contempt; TOY implies acting without full attention or serious exertion of one's powers; DALLY suggests indulging in thoughts or plans merely as an amusement; FLIRT implies an interest or attention that soon passes to another object; COQUET implies attracting interest or admiration without serious intention

tri·fling \'trī-fliŋ\ *adj* **:** lacking in significance or solid worth: as

a : FRIVOLOUS ⟨~ talk⟩ **b :** TRIVIAL ⟨a ~ gift⟩ **c** *chiefly dial* **:** LAZY, SHIFTLESS ⟨a ~ fellow⟩

1**tri·fo·cal** \(ˈ)trī-ˈfō-kəl\ *adj* **:** having three focal lengths

2**trifocal** *n* **1 :** a trifocal glass or lens **2** *pl* **:** eyeglasses with trifocal lenses

tri·fo·li·ate \(ˈ)trī-ˈfō-lē-ət\ *adj* **1** *or* **tri·fo·li·at·ed** \-lē-ˌāt-əd\ **:** having three leaves ⟨a ~ plant⟩ **2 :** TRIFOLIOLATE

trifoliate orange *n* **:** a hardy deciduous Chinese orange (*Poncirus trifoliata*) with trifoliolate leaves widely grown for ornament and esp. as a stock for budding other oranges

tri·fo·li·o·late \(ˈ)trī-ˈfō-lē-ə-ˌlāt\ *adj* [ISV] **:** having three leaflets ⟨a ~ leaf⟩

tri·fo·li·um \trī-ˈfō-lē-əm\ *n* [NL, genus name, fr. L, trefoil — more at TREFOIL] **:** any of a genus (*Trifolium*) of leguminous herbs comprising the typical clovers

tri·fo·ri·um \trī-ˈfōr-ē-əm, -ˈfȯr-\ *n, pl* **tri·fo·ria** \-ē-ə\ [ML] **:** a gallery forming an upper story to the aisle of a church and typically an arcaded story between the nave arches and clerestory

tri·form \ˈtrī-ˌfȯrm\ *adj* [L *triformis*, fr. *tri-* + *forma* form] **:** having a triple form or nature

tri·fur·cate \(ˈ)trī-ˈfər-kət, -ˌkāt; ˈtrī-(ˌ)fər-ˌkāt\ *adj* [L *trifurcus*, fr. *tri-* + *furca* fork] **:** having three branches or forks **:** TRICHOTOMOUS — **tri·fur·cate** \ˈtrī-(ˌ)fər-ˌkāt, trī-ˈfər-\ *vi* — **tri·fur·ca·tion** \ˌtrī-(ˌ)fər-ˈkā-shən\ *n*

1**trig** \ˈtrig\ *adj* [ME, trusty, nimble, of Scand origin; akin to ON *tryggr* faithful; akin to OE *trēowe* faithful — more at TRUE] **1 :** stylishly trim **:** SMART **2 :** extremely precise **:** PRIM **3** *dial chiefly Brit* **:** FIRM, VIGOROUS **syn** see NEAT

2**trig** *vt* **trigged; trig·ging** *dial chiefly Brit* **:** to put in order **:** TIDY — usu. used with *up*

3**trig** *vt* **trigged; trig·ging** [perh. of Scand origin; akin to ON *tryggja* to make firm, *tryggr* faithful] *chiefly dial* **:** to restrain from moving or shifting: as **a :** to stop or slow (a wheel) usu. by placing a wedge or block under it **b :** to support with props or wedges

4**trig** *n, chiefly dial* **:** a stone or block used as a support in trigging

5**trig** *n* **:** TRIGONOMETRY

tri·gem·i·nal \trī-ˈjem-ən-ᵊl\ *adj* [NL *trigeminus* trigeminal nerve, fr. L, threefold, fr. *tri-* + *geminus* twin] **:** of, relating to, or being a pair of large mixed nerves that are the fifth cranial nerves and supply motor and sensory fibers mostly to the face — **trigeminal** *n*

trigeminal neuralgia *n* **:** an intense paroxysmal neuralgia involving one or more branches of the trigeminal nerve

1**trig·ger** \ˈtrig-ər\ *n* [alter. of earlier *tricker*, fr. D *trekker*, fr. MD *trecker* one that pulls, fr. *trecken* to pull — more at TREK] **1 :** a piece (as a lever) connected with a catch or detent as a means of releasing it; *esp* **:** the part of the action moved by the finger to fire a gun **2 :** a stimulus that initiates a physiological or pathological process — **trigger** *adj* — **trig·gered** \ˈtrig-ərd\ *adj*

2**trigger** *vb* **trig·ger·ing** \ˈtrig-(ə-)riŋ\ *vt* **1 :** to fire by pulling a mechanical trigger ⟨~ a rifle⟩; *broadly* **:** to cause the explosion of ⟨~ a missile with a proximity fuze⟩ **2 :** to initiate, actuate, or set off as if by pulling a trigger **~** *vi* **:** to release a mechanical trigger

trig·ger·fish \ˈtrig-ər-ˌfish\ *n* **:** any of numerous deep-bodied plectognath fishes (as of the genus *Balistes*) of warm seas having an anterior dorsal fin with two or three stout erectile spines

trig·ger–hap·py \-ˌhap-ē\ *adj* **1 :** irresponsible in the use of firearms; *esp* **:** inclined to shoot before clearly identifying the target **2 a :** inclined to be irresponsible in matters that might precipitate war **b :** aggressively belligerent in attitude

trig·ger·man \-mən, -ˌman\ *n* **:** a gunman who shoots the victim in a gang murder; *also* **:** a gangster's personal bodyguard

tri·glyph \ˈtrī-ˌglif\ *n* [L *triglyphus*, fr. Gk *triglyphos*, fr. *tri-* + *glyphein* to carve — more at CLEAVE] **:** a slightly projecting rectangular tablet in a Doric frieze with two vertical channels of V section and two corresponding chamfers or half channels on the vertical sides — **tri·glyph·ic** \trī-ˈglif-ik\ *or* **tri·glyph·i·cal** \-i-kəl\ *adj*

tri·gon \ˈtrī-ˌgän\ *n* [L *trigonum*, fr. Gk *trigōnon*, fr. neut. of *trigōnos* triangular, fr. *tri-* + *gōnia* angle — more at -GON] **1 :** TRIANGLE **2 a :** TRIPLICITY 1 **b :** TRINE 2 **3 :** an ancient triangular harp

trig·o·no·met·ric \ˌtrig-ə-nə-ˈme-trik\ *adj* **:** of, relating to, or in accordance with trigonometry — **trig·o·no·met·ri·cal** \-tri-kəl\ *adj* — **trig·o·no·met·ri·cal·ly** \-k(ə-)lē\ *adv*

trigonometric function *n* **:** a function (as sine, cosine, tangent, cotangent, secant, or cosecant) of an arc or angle most simply expressed in terms of the ratios of pairs of sides of a right-angled triangle; *also* **:** the inverse of such a function — called also *circular function*

trig·o·nom·e·try \ˌtrig-ə-ˈnäm-ə-trē\ *n* [NL *trigonometria*, fr. Gk *trigōnon* + *-metria* -metry] **:** the study of the properties of triangles and trigonometric functions and of their applications

tri·go·nous \ˈtrig-ə-nəs, trī-ˈgō-\ *adj* [L *trigonus* triangular, fr. Gk *trigōnos*] **:** triangular in cross section

tri·graph \ˈtrī-ˌgraf\ *n* **1 :** three letters spelling a single consonant, vowel, or diphthong ⟨*eau* of *beau* is a ~⟩ **2 :** a cluster of three successive letters ⟨THE is a high frequency ~⟩ — **tri·graph·ic** \(ˈ)trī-ˈgraf-ik\ *adj*

tri·he·dral \(ˈ)trī-ˈhē-drəl\ *adj* **1 :** having three faces ⟨~ angle⟩ **2 :** of or relating to a trihedral angle — **trihedral** *n*

tri·hy·drate \-ˈhī-ˌdrāt\ *n* **:** a chemical compound with three molecules of water — **tri·hy·drat·ed** \-ˌdrāt-əd\ *adj*

tri·hy·droxy \ˌtrī-(ˌ)hī-ˈdräk-sē\ *adj* [ISV *tri-* + *hydroxyl*] **:** containing three hydroxyl groups in the molecule

tri·io·do·thy·ro·nine \ˌtrī-ˌī-əd-ō-ˈthī-rə-ˌnēn\ *n* [*tri-* + *iod-* + *thyronine* (an amino acid of which thyroxine is a derivative)] **:** an iodine-containing amino acid $C_{15}H_{12}I_3NO_4$ believed to be formed from thyroxine by loss of one iodine atom per molecule and used esp. in the treatment of hypothyroidism

tri·ju·gate \ˈtrī-jə-ˌgāt, (ˈ)trī-ˈjü-gət\ *adj* [ISV, fr. L *trijugus* threefold, fr. *tri-* + *jungere* to join — more at YOKE] **:** having three pairs of leaflets ⟨a ~ leaf⟩

tri·lat·er·al \(ˈ)trī-ˈlat-ə-rəl, -ˈla-trəl\ *adj* [L *trilaterus*, fr. *tri-* + *later-*, *latus* side] **:** having three sides ⟨a triangle is ~⟩ — **tri·lat·er·al·i·ty** \ˌtrī-ˌlat-ə-ˈral-ət-ē\ *n* — **tri·lat·er·al·ly** \(ˈ)trī-ˈlat-ə-rə-lē, -ˈla-trə-\ *adv*

tril·by \ˈtril-bē\ *n* [fr. the fact that such a hat was worn in the London stage version of *Trilby*, novel by George du Maurier] *chiefly Brit* **:** a soft felt hat with indented crown

tri·lin·ear \(ˈ)trī-ˈlin-ē-ər\ *adj* **:** of, relating to, or involving three lines

tri·lin·gual \(ˈ)trī-ˈliŋ-gwəl\ *adj* **:** consisting of, having, or expressed in three languages; *also* **:** familiar with or able to use three languages — **tri·lin·gual·ly** \-gwə-lē\ *adv*

1**tri·lit·er·al** \(ˈ)trī-ˈlit-ə-rəl, -ˈli-trəl\ *adj* [*tri-* + L *litera* letter] **:** consisting of three letters and esp. of three consonants ⟨~ roots in Semitic languages⟩ — **tri·lit·er·al·ism** \-ˌiz-əm\ *n*

2**triliteral** *n* **:** a root or word that is triliteral

1**trill** \ˈtril\ *vb* [ME *trillen*, prob. of Scand origin; akin to Sw *trilla* to roll; akin to MD *trillen* to vibrate] *vi* **1 :** TWIRL, REVOLVE **2 :** to flow in a small stream or in drops **:** TRICKLE **~** *vt* **:** to cause to flow in a small stream

2**trill** *n* [It *trillo*, fr. *trillare* to trill, prob. fr. D *trillen* to vibrate; akin to MD *trappe* step, trap] **1 a :** the alternation of two musical tones a scale degree apart — called also *shake* **b :** VIBRATO **c :** a rapid reiteration of the same tone esp. on a percussion instrument **2 :** a sound felt to resemble a musical trill **:** WARBLE **3 a :** the rapid vibration of one speech organ against another (as of the tip of the tongue against the teethridge) **b :** a speech sound so made

3**trill** *vt* **:** to utter as or with a trill ⟨~ the *r*⟩ **~** *vi* **:** to play or sing with a trill **:** QUAVER — **trill·er** *n*

tril·lion \ˈtril-yən\ *n* [F, fr. *tri-* + *-illion* (as in *million*)] **1** — see NUMBER table **2 :** a very large number — **trillion** *adj* — **tril·lionth** \-yən(t)th\ *adj* — **trillionth** *n, pl* **tril·lionths** \-yən(t)s, -yən(t)ths\

tril·li·um \ˈtril-ē-əm\ *n* [NL, genus name, fr. *tri-*; fr. its three leaves] **:** any of a genus (*Trillium*) of herbs of the lily family with short rootstocks and an erect stem bearing a whorl of three leaves and a large solitary flower

tri·lo·bate \(ˈ)trī-ˈlō-ˌbāt\ *or* **tri·lo·bat·ed** \-ˌbāt-əd\ *or* **tri·lobed** \ˈtrī-ˈlōbd\ *adj* **:** having three lobes ⟨a ~ leaf⟩ — **tri·lo·ba·tion** \ˌtrī-lō-ˈbā-shən\ *n*

tri·lo·bite \ˈtrī-lə-ˌbīt\ *n* [deriv. of Gk *trilobos* three-lobed, fr. *tri-* + *lobos* lobe] **:** any of numerous extinct Paleozoic marine arthropods (group Trilobita) having the segments of the body divided by furrows on the dorsal surface into three lobes — **tri·lo·bit·ic** \ˌtrī-lə-ˈbit-ik\ *adj*

tri·loc·u·lar \(ˈ)trī-ˈläk-yə-lər\ *or* **tri·loc·u·late** \-lət\ *adj* [ISV] **:** having three cells or cavities

tril·o·gy \ˈtril-ə-jē\ *n* [Gk *trilogia*, fr. *tri-* + *-logia* -logy] **:** a series of three dramas or sometimes three literary or musical compositions that although each is in one sense complete are closely related and develop a single theme

1**trim** \ˈtrim\ *vb* **trimmed; trim·ming** [(assumed) ME *trimmen* to prepare, put in order, fr. OE *trymian*, *trymman* to strengthen, arrange, fr. *trum* strong, firm; akin to Skt *dāru* wood — more at TREE] *vt* **1 a :** to embellish with ribbons, lace, or ornaments **:** ADORN **b :** to arrange a display of goods in (a shop window) **2 a** (1) **:** to administer a beating to **:** THRASH (2) **:** to defeat resoundingly ⟨*trimmed* him at chess⟩ **b :** CHEAT, SWINDLE **3 a :** to make trim and neat esp. by cutting or clipping **b :** to free of excess or extraneous matter by or as if by cutting ⟨~ a tree⟩ ⟨~ a budget⟩ **c :** to remove by or as if by cutting **4 a** (1) **:** to cause (a ship or boat) to assume a desirable position in the water by arrangement of ballast, cargo, or passengers (2) **:** to adjust (as an airplane, blimp, or submarine) for horizontal movement or for motion upward or downward **b :** to adjust (as a sail) to a desired position ⟨~ cargo⟩ **~** *vi* **1 a :** to maintain neutrality between opposing parties or to favor each equally **b :** to change one's views for reasons of expediency **2 :** to assume or cause a boat to assume a desired position in the water ⟨a boat that ~s badly⟩

2**trim** *adj* **trim·mer; trim·mest 1** *obs* **:** EXCELLENT, FINE; *also* **:** PLEASANT **2** *archaic* **:** suitably adjusted, equipped, or prepared for service or use **3 :** exhibiting neatness, good order, or compactness of line or structure ⟨~ houses⟩ ⟨~ figure⟩ **syn** see NEAT — **trim·ly** *adv* — **trim·ness** *n*

3**trim** *adv* **:** TRIMLY

4**trim** *n* **1 a :** the readiness of a ship for sailing **b :** the readiness of a person or thing for action or use **:** FITNESS **2 a :** one's clothing or appearance **b :** material used for ornament or trimming **c :** the lighter woodwork in the finish of a building esp. around openings **d :** the interior furnishings of an automobile **e :** WINDOW DRESSING **3 a :** the position of a ship or boat esp. with reference to the horizontal; *also* **:** the difference between the draft of a ship forward and that aft **b :** the relation between the plane of a sail and the direction of the ship **c :** the buoyancy status of a submarine **d :** the attitude of a lighter-than-air craft relative to a fore-and-aft horizontal plane **e :** the attitude with respect to wind axes at which an airplane will continue in level flight with free controls **4 :** something that is trimmed off or cut out

tri·mer \ˈtrī-mər\ *n* [ISV] **:** a polymer formed from three molecules of a monomer — **tri·mer·ic** \trī-ˈmer-ik\ *adj*

trim·er·ous \ˈtrim-ə-rəs\ *adj* [NL *trimerus*, fr. Gk *tri-* + *meros* part — more at MERIT] **:** having the parts in threes — used of a flower and often written *3-merous*

tri·mes·ter \(ˈ)trī-ˈmes-tər, ˈtrī-ˌ\ *n* [F *trimestre*, fr. L *trimestris* of three months, fr. *tri-* + *mensis* month — more at MOON] **1 :** a period of three or about three months **2 :** one of three terms into which the academic year is sometimes divided — **tri·mes·tral** \trī-ˈmes-trəl\ *adj* — **tri·mes·tri·al** \-trē-əl\ *adj*

trim·e·ter \ˈtrim-ət-ər\ *n* [L *trimetrus*, fr. Gk *trimetros* having three measures, fr. *tri-* + *metron* measure — more at MEASURE] **:** a verse consisting of either three dipodies (as in classical iambic, trochaic, and anapestic verse) or three feet (as in modern English verse)

tri·metha·di·one \ˌtrī-ˌmeth-ə-ˈdī-ˌōn\ *n* [irreg. fr. *tri-* + *methyl* + *-dione* (compound containing two carbonyl groups)] **:** a crystalline drug $C_6H_9NO_3$ used in the treatment of epilepsy

tri·met·ro·gon \trī-ˈme-trə-ˌgän\ *n* [*tri-* + Gk *metron* measure + E *-gon*] **:** a system of aerial mapping involving the use of sets of one vertical and two oblique aerial photographs taken simultaneously over the area being mapped

trim·mer \ˈtrim-ər\ *n* **1 a :** one that trims articles; *esp* **:** one that stows coal or freight on a ship so as to distribute the weight properly **b :** an instrument or machine with which trimming is done **2 :** a beam that receives the end of a header in floor framing

3 : a person who will modify his policy, position, or opinions out of expediency

trim·ming *n* **1 :** the act of one who trims **2 a :** a decorative accessory or additional item that serves to finish or complete ⟨~*s* for a hat⟩ **b :** an additional garnishing that is not essential but adds to the interest or attractiveness of a main item ⟨turkey and all the ~*s*⟩

tri·mo·lec·u·lar \ˌtrī-mə-ˈlek-yə-lər\ *adj* **:** of, relating to, or formed from three molecules

tri·month·ly \(ˈ)trī-ˈmən(t)th-lē\ *adj* **:** occurring every three months

tri·morph \ˈtrī-ˌmȯrf\ *n* [ISV, back-formation fr. *trimorphous*] **:** any of the three crystalline forms of a trimorphous substance

tri·mor·phic \(ˈ)trī-ˈmȯr-fik\ *or* **tri·mor·phous** \-fəs\ *adj* [Gk *trimorphos* having three forms, fr. *tri-* + *-morphos* -morphous] **:** occurring in or having three distinct forms — **tri·mor·phism** \-ˌfiz-əm\ *n*

tri·mo·tor \ˈtrī-ˌmōt-ər\ *n* **:** an airplane powered by three engines

trim size *n* **:** the actual size (as of a book page) after excess material required in production has been cut off

Tri·mur·ti \tri-ˈmu̇(ə)rt-ē\ *n* [Skt *-trimūrti*, fr. *trimūrti* having three forms, fr. *tri-* + *mūrti* body, form] **:** the great triad of Hindu gods comprising Brahma, Vishnu, and Siva

tri·nal \ˈtrīn-ᵊl\ *adj* [LL *trinalis*, fr. L *trini* three each — more at TRINE] **:** THREEFOLD

tri·na·ry \ˈtrī-nə-rē\ *adj* [LL *trinarius*, fr. L *trini* three each] **:** TERNARY

[1]**trin·dle** \ˈtrin-(d)ᵊl\ *n* [ME *trindel*, fr. OE *trendel*, *tryndel* circle, ring — more at TRUNDLE] *dial Eng* **:** a round or circular object; *specif* **:** the wheel of a wheelbarrow

[2]**trindle** *vi*, *dial* **:** ROLL, TRUNDLE

[1]**trine** \ˈtrīn\ *adj* [ME, fr. MF *trin*, fr. L *trinus*, back-formation fr. *trini* three each; akin to L *tres* three — more at THREE] **1 :** THREEFOLD, TRIPLE **2 :** of, relating to, or being the favorable astrological aspect of two heavenly bodies 120 degrees apart

[2]**trine** *n* **1 a :** a group of three **:** TRIAD **b** *cap* **:** TRINITY **2 :** the trine astrological aspect of two heavenly bodies

trine immersion *n* **:** the practice of immersing a candidate for baptism three times in the names in turn of the Trinity

trin·i·tar·i·an \ˌtrin-ə-ˈter-ē-ən\ *adj* **1** *cap* **:** of or relating to the Trinity, the doctrine of the Trinity, or adherents to that doctrine **2 :** having three parts or aspects **:** THREEFOLD

Trinitarian *n* **:** one who subscribes to the doctrine of the Trinity — **Trin·i·tar·i·an·ism** \-ē-ə-ˌniz-əm\ *n*

tri·ni·tro·cre·sol \ˌtrī-ˌnī-trō-ˈkrē-ˌsȯl, -ˌsōl\ *n* [ISV] **:** a high explosive $C_7H_5N_3O_7$ similar to picric acid

tri·ni·tro·glyc·er·in \-ˈglis-(ə-)rən\ *n* **:** NITROGLYCERIN

tri·ni·tro·tol·u·ene \-ˈtäl-yə-ˌwēn\ *n* [ISV] **:** a flammable toxic derivative $CH_3C_6H_2(NO_2)_3$ of toluene obtained by nitrating toluene and used as a high explosive and in chemical synthesis — called also *TNT*

Trin·i·ty \ˈtrin-ət-ē\ *n* [ME *trinite*, fr. OF *trinité*, fr. LL *trinitat-*, *trinitas* state of being threefold, fr. L *trinus* trine] **1 :** the unity of Father, Son, and Holy Spirit as three persons in one Godhead **2** *not cap* **:** any union of three in one **:** TRIAD **3 :** the Sunday after Whitsunday observed as a feast in honor of the Trinity

Trin·i·ty·tide \-ˌtīd\ *n* **:** the season of the church year between Trinity Sunday and Advent

[1]**trin·ket** \ˈtriŋ-kət\ *n* [perh. fr. ME *trenket* small knife, fr. ONF *trenquet*] **1 :** a small article of equipment **2 :** a small ornament (as a jewel or ring) **3 :** a thing of little value **:** TRIFLE

[2]**trinket** *vi* [perh. fr. [1]*trinket*] **:** to deal clandestinely **:** INTRIGUE — **trin·ket·er** *n*

trin·ket·ry \-kə-trē\ *n* **:** small items of personal ornament

trin·kums \ˈtriŋ-kəmz\ *n pl* [alter. of *trinkets*] **:** TRINKETS, FRIPPERY

[1]**tri·no·mi·al** \trī-ˈnō-mē-əl\ *n* [*tri-* + *-nomial* (as in *binomial*)] **1 :** a polynomial of three terms **2 :** a trinomial name

[2]**trinomial** *adj* **1 :** consisting of three mathematical terms **2 :** of, relating to, or being biological taxa of three terms of which the first designates the genus, the second the species, and the third the subspecies or variety

trio \ˈtrē-(ˌ)ō\ *n* [F, fr. It, fr. *tri-* (fr. L)] **1 a :** a musical composition for three voice parts or three instruments **b :** the secondary or episodic division of a minuet or scherzo, a march, or of various dance forms **2 :** the performers of a musical or dance trio **3 :** a group or set of three

tri·ode \ˈtrī-ˌōd\ *n* **:** an electron tube with an anode, a cathode, and a controlling grid

tri·oe·cious \(ˈ)trī-ˈē-shəs\ *adj* [deriv. of Gk *tri-* + *oikos* house — more at VICINITY] **:** having staminate, pistillate, and hermaphrodite flowers on different plants — **tri·oe·cious·ly** *adv*

tri·ol \ˈtrī-ˌȯl, -ˌōl\ *n* **:** a chemical compound containing three hydroxyl groups

tri·o·let \ˌtrē-ə-ˈlā, ˈtrī-ə-lət\ *n* [F] **:** a poem or stanza of eight lines in which the first line is repeated as the fourth and seventh and the second line as the eighth with a rhyme scheme of *ABaAabAB*

tri·ose \ˈtrī-ˌōs, -ˌōz\ *n* [ISV] **:** either of two simple sugars $C_3H_6O_3$ containing three carbon atoms

tri·ox·ide \(ˈ)trī-ˈäk-ˌsīd\ *n* [ISV] **:** an oxide containing three atoms of oxygen

[1]**trip** \ˈtrip\ *vb* **tripped; trip·ping** [ME *trippen*, fr. MF *triper*, of Gmc origin; akin to OE *treppan* to tread — more at TRAP] *vi* **1 a :** to dance, skip, or caper with light quick steps **b :** to walk with light quick steps **2 :** to catch the foot against something so as to stumble **3 :** to make a mistake or false step (as in morality, propriety, or accuracy) **:** SLIP **4 :** to stumble in articulation when speaking **5 :** to make a journey **6 :** to run past the pallet of an escapement without previously locking — used of a tooth of the escapement wheel of a watch **7 a :** to actuate a mechanism **b :** to become operative **8 :** to turn on (as with LSD) ~ *vt* **1 a :** to cause to stumble **b :** to cause to fail **:** OBSTRUCT **2 :** to detect in a misstep, fault, or blunder; *also* **:** EXPOSE **3** *archaic* **:** to perform (as a dance) lightly or nimbly **4 :** to raise (an anchor) from the bottom so that it hangs free **5 a :** to pull (a yard) into a perpendicular position for lowering **b :** to hoist (a topmast) far enough to enable the fid to be withdrawn preparatory to housing or lowering **6 :** to release or operate (a mechanism) esp. by releasing a catch or detent

[2]**trip** *n* **1 :** a stroke or catch by which a wrestler is made to lose footing **2 a :** VOYAGE, JOURNEY **b :** a single round or tour on a business errand **3 :** ERROR, MISSTEP **4 :** a quick light step **5 :** a false step **:** STUMBLE **6 a :** the action of tripping mechanically **b** (1) **:** a device for tripping a mechanism (as a catch or detent) (2) **:** TUP 2 **7 :** an intense visionary experience undergone by a person who has turned on (as with LSD)

tri·pack \ˈtrī-ˌpak\ *n* **:** a combination of three superposed films each sensitive to a different primary color for simultaneous exposure in one camera

tri·par·tite \(ˈ)trī-ˈpär-ˌtīt\ *adj* [ME, fr. L *tripartitus*, fr. *tri-* + *partitus* partite] **1 :** divided into or composed of three parts **2 :** having three corresponding parts or copies **3 :** made between or involving three parties ⟨a ~ treaty⟩ — **tri·par·tite·ly** *adv*

tri·par·ti·tion \ˌtrī-(ˌ)pär-ˈtish-ən\ *n* **:** a division by threes or into three parts; *also* **:** the taking of a third part

tripe \ˈtrīp\ *n* [ME, fr. OF] **1 :** stomach tissue of a ruminant and esp. of the ox for use as a food: **a :** that of the rumen wall — called also *plain tripe* **b :** that of the reticulum wall — called also *honeycomb tripe* **2 :** something poor, worthless, or offensive **:** TRASH

tri·pet·al·ous \(ˈ)trī-ˈpet-ᵊl-əs\ *adj* **:** having three petals

trip-ham·mer \ˈtrip-ˌham-ər\ *n* **:** a massive power hammer having a helve that is tripped and allowed to fall by cam or lever action

tri·phe·nyl·meth·ane \ˌtrī-ˌfen-ᵊl-ˈmeth-ˌān, -ˌfēn-\ *n* [ISV] **:** a crystalline hydrocarbon $CH(C_6H_5)_3$ that is the parent compound of many dyes

[1]**tri·phib·i·an** \(ˈ)trī-ˈfib-ē-ən\ *n* [*tri-* + *-phibian* (as in *amphibian*)] **1 :** a triphibian commander **2 :** a triphibian airplane

[2]**triphibian** *adj* **1 a :** adept at war alike on land, at sea, and in the air **b :** designed for or equipped to operate from land, water, snow, or ice as well as in the air ⟨a ~ airplane⟩ **2 :** TRIPHIBIOUS 1 ⟨a ~ military operation⟩

tri·phib·i·ous \-ē-əs\ *adj* [*tri-* + *-phibious* (as in *amphibious*)] **1 :** employing, involving, or constituted by land, naval, and air forces and often including airborne troops in coordinated attack ⟨~ operations⟩ **2 :** TRIPHIBIAN 1 ⟨~ marines⟩

triph·thong \ˈtrif-ˌthȯŋ, ˈtrip-\ *n* [*tri-* + *-phthong* (as in *diphthong*)] **1 :** a speech item consisting of three successive sounds **2 :** TRIGRAPH — **triph·thon·gal** \trif-ˈthȯŋ-(g)əl, trip-\ *adj*

triph·y·lite \ˈtrif-ə-ˌlīt\ *also* **triph·y·line** \-ˌlēn\ *n* [G *triphylin*, fr. Gk *tri-* + *phylon* tribe, race — more at PHYL-] **:** a grayish green or bluish mineral that consists of a phosphate of lithium, iron, and manganese and is commonly massive

tri·pin·nate \(ˈ)trī-ˈpin-ˌāt\ *adj* **:** bipinnate with each division pinnate — **tri·pin·nate·ly** *adv*

tri·plane \ˈtrī-ˌplān\ *n* **:** an airplane with three main supporting surfaces superposed

[1]**tri·ple** \ˈtrip-əl\ *vb* **tri·pling** \-(ə-)liŋ\ [ME *triplen*, fr. LL *triplare*, fr. L *triplus*, adj.] *vt* **1 :** to make three times as great or as many **2 a :** to advance (a base runner in baseball) by a three-base hit **b :** to bring about the scoring of (a run in baseball) by a three-base hit ~ *vi* **1 :** to become three times as great or as numerous **2 :** to make a three-base hit in baseball

[2]**triple** *n* [ME, fr. L *triplus*, adj.] **1 a :** a triple sum, quantity, or number **b :** a combination, group, or series of three **2 :** THREE-BASE HIT

[3]**triple** *adj* [MF or L; MF, fr. L *triplus*, fr. *tri-* + *-plus* multiplied by — more at DOUBLE] **1 :** having three units or members **2 :** being three times as great or as many **3 :** having a threefold relation or character **4 :** three times repeated **:** TREBLE **5 :** marked by three beats per musical measure ⟨~ meter⟩ **6 a :** having units of three components ⟨~ feet⟩ **b** *of rhyme* **:** involving correspondence of three syllables (as in *unfortunate-importunate*)

triple counterpoint *n* **:** three-part musical counterpoint so written that any part may be transposed above or below any other

tri·ple-nerved \ˌtrip-əl-ˈnərvd\ *adj*, *of a leaf* **:** having a prominent vein on each side of the midrib above the base

triple play *n* **:** a play in baseball by which three base runners are put out

tri·ple-space \ˌtrip-əl-ˈspās\ *vt* **:** to type (copy) leaving two blank lines between lines of copy ~ *vi* **:** to type on every third line

trip·let \ˈtrip-lət\ *n* [[2]*triple*] **1 :** a unit of three lines of verse **2 :** a combination, set, or group of three **3 :** one of three children or offspring born at one birth **4 :** a group of three musical notes or tones performed in the time of two of the same value

tri·ple·tail \ˈtrip-əl-ˌtāl\ *n* **:** a large edible marine percoid fish (*Lobotes surinamensis*) of the warm western Atlantic in which the long dorsal and anal fins extend backward and with the caudal fin appear like a 3-lobed tail

triple threat *n* **:** a football player adept at running, kicking, and forward passing

tri·ple-tongue \ˌtrip-əl-ˈtəŋ\ *vi* **:** to articulate the notes of triplets in fast tempo on a wind instrument by using the tongue positions for *t*, *k*, *t* for each successive triplet

[1]**tri·plex** \ˈtrip-ˌleks, ˈtrī-ˌpleks\ *adj* [L, fr. *tri-* + *-plex* -fold — more at SIMPLE] **:** THREEFOLD, TRIPLE

[2]**triplex** *n* **:** something (as a building or apartment) that is triplex

[1]**trip·li·cate** \ˈtrip-li-kət\ *adj* [ME, fr. L *triplicatus*, pp. of *triplicare* to triple, fr. *triplic-*, *triplex* threefold] **1 :** repeated three times **2 :** THIRD ⟨file the ~ copy⟩ — **triplicate** *n*

[2]**trip·li·cate** \-lə-ˌkāt\ *vt* **1 :** TRIPLE **2 :** to provide in triplicate

trip·li·ca·tion \ˌtrip-lə-ˈkā-shən\ *n* **:** the action of tripling, making threefold, or adding three together; *also* **:** something that is triplicated or threefold

tri·plic·i·ty \trip-ˈlis-ət-ē, trī-ˈplis-\ *n* [ME *triplicite*, fr. LL *triplicitas* condition of being threefold, fr. L *triplic-*, *triplex*] **1 :** one of the groups of three signs each distant 120 degrees from the other two into which the signs of the zodiac are divided — called also *trigon* **2 :** the quality or state of being triple or threefold

trip·lite \ˈtrip-ˌlīt\ *n* [G *triplit*, fr. L *triplus* triple; fr. its threefold cleavage] **:** a dark brown monoclinic mineral that consists of a basic phosphate of iron, manganese, magnesium, and calcium

trip·lo·blas·tic \ˌtrip-lō-ˈblas-tik\ *adj* [L *triplus* + E *-o-* + *-blastic*] **:** having three primary germ layers

trip·loid \ˈtrip-ˌlȯid\ *adj* [ISV, fr. L *triplus* triple] **:** having or being a chromosome number three times the monoploid number — **triploid** *n* — **trip·loi·dy** \-ˌlȯid-ē\ *n*

tri·ply \ˈtrip-(ə-)lē\ *adv* **:** in a triple degree, amount, or manner

tri·pod \ˈtrī-ˌpäd\ *n* [L *tripod-*, *tripus*, fr. Gk *tripod-*, *tripous*, fr. *tripod-*, *tripous* three-footed, fr. *tri-* + *pod-*, *pous* foot — more at FOOT] **1 :** a vessel (as a caldron) resting on three legs **2 :** a stool, table, or altar with three legs **3 :** a three-legged stand (as for a camera) — **tripod** *or* **tri·po·dal** \ˈtrip-əd-ᵊl, ˈtrī-ˌpäd-\ *adj*

trip·o·li \'trip-ə-lē\ *n* [F, fr. *Tripoli*, region of Africa] **1 :** an earth consisting of very friable soft schistose deposits of silica and including diatomite and kieselguhr **2 :** an earth consisting of friable dustlike silica not of diatomaceous origin

tri·pos \'trī-,päs\ *n* [modif. of L *tripus*] **1** *archaic* **:** TRIPOD **2** [fr. the three-legged stool occupied by a participant in a disputation at the degree ceremonies] **:** a final honors examination at Cambridge university orig. in mathematics

trip·per \'trip-ər\ *n* **1 a** *chiefly Brit* **:** one that takes a trip **:** EXCURSIONIST **b :** an extra employee on a street railway employed by the trip **2 :** a tripping device (as for operating a signal on a railroad)

trip·pet \'trip-ət\ *n* [ME *tripet* tipcat peg, fr. *trippen* to trip] **:** a cam, wiper, or projecting piece that strikes another piece at definite times

trip·ping·ly \'trip-iŋ-lē\ *adv* **:** NIMBLY; *also* **:** FLUENTLY

trip·tane \'trip-,tān\ *n* [irreg. fr. *tri-* + *butane*] **:** a liquid hydrocarbon C_7H_{16} of high antiknock properties used esp. in aviation gasolines to increase their power

trip·tych \'trip-(,)tik\ *n* [Gk *triptychos* having three folds, fr. *tri-* + *ptychē* fold] **1 :** an ancient Roman writing tablet with three waxed leaves hinged together **2 :** a picture or carving in three panels side by side; *esp* **:** an altarpiece with a central panel and two flanking panels half its size that fold over it

tri·que·trous \trī-'kwē-trəs, -'kwe-\ *adj* [L *triquetrus* three-cornered, fr. *tri-*] **:** having three acute angles **:** TRIANGULAR ⟨~ stems⟩

tri·ra·di·ate \(')trī-'rād-ē-ət, -ē-,āt\ *adj* **:** having three rays or radiating branches — **triradiate** *n* — **tri·ra·di·ate·ly** *adv*

tri·reme \'trī-,rēm\ *n* [L *triremis*, fr. *tri-* + *remus* oar — more at ROW] **:** an ancient galley having three banks of oars

tri·sac·cha·ride \(')trī-'sak-ə-,rīd\ *n* [ISV] **:** any sugar that yields on complete hydrolysis three monosaccharide molecules

tri·sect \'trī-,sekt, trī-'\ *vt* **:** to divide into three usu. equal parts — **tri·sec·tion** \'trī-,sek-shən, trī-'\ *n* — **tri·sec·tor** \'trī-,sek-tər, trī-'\ *n*

tri·sep·tate \(')trī-'sep-,tāt\ *adj* **:** having three septa

tri·skel·i·on \trī-'skel-ē-ən, tris-'kel-\ *or* **tri·skele** \'trī-,skēl, 'tris-,kēl\ *n* [*triskelion*, fr. NL, fr. Gk *triskelēs* three-legged, fr. *tri-* + *skelos* leg; *triskele* fr. Gk *triskelēs*] **:** a figure composed of three usu. curved or bent branches radiating from a center

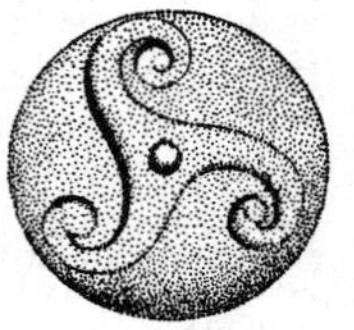
triskelion

tris·mus \'triz-məs\ *n* [NL, fr. Gk *trismos* gnashing (of teeth), fr. *trizein* to squeak, gnash; akin to L *stridēre* to creak — more at STRIDENT] **:** spasm of the muscles of mastication **:** LOCKJAW

tris·oc·ta·he·dron \,tris-,äk-tə-'hē-drən\ *n* [Gk *tris* thrice (akin to *treis* three) + E *octahedron* — more at THREE] **:** a solid (as a crystal) having 24 congruent faces meeting on the edges of a regular octahedron

tri·so·di·um \,trī-,sōd-ē-əm\ *adj* **:** containing three atoms of sodium in the molecule

tri·so·mic \(')trī-'sō-mik\ *adj* **:** having one or a few chromosomes triploid in an otherwise diploid set — **trisomic** *or* **tri·some** \'trī-,sōm\ *n* — **tri·so·my** \-,sō-mē\ *n*

Tris·tan \'tris-tən, -,tän, -,tan\ *n* **:** TRISTRAM

triste \'trēst\ *adj* [F, fr. L *tristis*] **:** SAD, MOURNFUL; *also* **:** WISTFUL

trist·ful \'trist-fəl\ *adj* [ME *trist* sad, fr. MF *triste*] **:** SAD, MELANCHOLY — **trist·ful·ly** \-fə-lē\ *adv* — **trist·ful·ness** *n*

Tris·tram \'tris-t(r)əm\ *n* [ME *Tristrem*, fr. AF *Tristan*, fr. OW *Trystan*] **:** a hero of medieval romance held to have drunk a love potion and ultimately to have died with the Irish princess Isolde and in some legends to have married Isolde the daughter of the king of Brittany

tri·sty·lous \(')trī-'stī-ləs\ *adj* **:** having three styles ⟨~ flowers⟩ — **tri·sty·ly** \'trī-,stī-lē\ *n*

tri·sub·sti·tut·ed \'trī-'səb-stə-,t(y)üt-əd\ *adj* **:** having three substituent atoms or groups in the molecule

tri·sul·fide \(')trī-'səl-,fīd\ *n* **:** a compound of an element or radical with three atoms of sulfur

tri·syl·lab·ic \,trī-sə-'lab-ik\ *adj* [L *trisyllabus*, fr. Gk *trisyllabos*, fr. *tri-* + *syllabē* syllable] **:** having three syllables ⟨a ~ word⟩ — **tri·syl·lab·i·cal·ly** \-i-k(ə-)lē\ *adv*

tri·syl·la·ble \'trī-,sil-ə-bəl, (')trī-'\ *n* **:** a word of three syllables

trite \'trīt\ *adj* [L *tritus*, fr. pp. of *terere* to rub, wear away — more at THROW] **:** hackneyed from much use **:** STALE — **trite·ly** *adv* — **trite·ness** *n*

syn TRITE, HACKNEYED, STEREOTYPED, THREADBARE mean lacking the freshness that evokes attention or interest. TRITE applies to a once effective phrase or idea spoiled from long familiarity; HACKNEYED stresses being worn out by overuse so as to become dull and meaningless; STEREOTYPED implies falling invariably into the same pattern or form; THREADBARE applies to what has been used until its possibilities of interest have been totally exhausted

tri·the·ism \'trī-thē-,iz-əm\ *n* **:** a belief in three gods; *specif* **:** the doctrine that the Father, Son, and Holy Spirit are three distinct Gods — **tri·the·ist** \-(,)thē-əst\ *n or adj* — **tri·the·is·tic** \,trī-thē-'is-tik\ *adj* — **tri·the·is·ti·cal** \-'is-ti-kəl\ *adj*

tri·thing \'trī-thiŋ\ *n* [ME, alter. of (assumed) OE *thrithing*, *thriding*] *archaic* **:** [1]RIDING 1

tri·ti·at·ed \'trit-ē-,āt-əd, 'trish-ē-\ *adj* **:** containing tritium

tri·ti·um \'trit-ē-əm, 'trish-ē-\ *n* [NL, fr. Gk *tritos* third — more at THIRD] **:** a radioactive isotope of hydrogen with atoms of three times the mass of ordinary light hydrogen atoms

trit·o·ma \'trit-ə-mə\ *n* [NL, genus name, fr. Gk *tritomos* cut thrice, fr. *tri-* + *temnein* to cut; fr. their trimerous flowers — more at TOME] **:** any of a genus (*Kniphofia*) of African herbs of the lily family that are often grown for their spikes of showy red or yellow flowers

[1]**tri·ton** \'trīt-ᵊn\ *n* [L, fr. Gk *Tritōn*] **1** *cap* **:** a son of Poseidon and Amphitrite described as a demigod of the sea with the lower part of his body like that of a fish **2** [NL, genus name, fr. L *Triton*] **a :** any of various large marine gastropod mollusks (esp. family Cymatiidae) with a heavy elongated conical shell; *also* **:** this shell **b :** any of various aquatic salamanders **:** NEWT, EFT

[2]**tri·ton** \'trī-,tän\ *n* [*trit*ium + *-on*] **:** the nucleus of tritium

tri·tone \'trī-,tōn\ *n* [Gk *tritonon*, fr. *tri-* + *tonos* tone] **:** a musical interval of three whole steps

trit·u·ra·ble \'trich-(ə-)rə-bəl\ *adj* **:** capable of being triturated

[1]**trit·u·rate** \'trich-ə-,rāt\ *vt* [LL *trituratus*, pp. of *triturare* to thresh, fr. L *tritura* act of rubbing, threshing, fr. *tritus*, pp. of *terere* to rub — more at THROW] **1 :** CRUSH, GRIND **2 :** to pulverize and comminute thoroughly by rubbing or grinding — **trit·u·ra·tor** \-,rāt-ər\ *n*

[2]**trit·u·rate** \-rət\ *n* **:** a triturated substance **:** TRITURATION 2

trit·u·ra·tion \,trich-ə-'rā-shən\ *n* **1 :** the act or process of triturating or state of being triturated **:** COMMINUTION **2 :** a triturated powder; *esp* **:** one made by triturating a substance with lactose as a diluent

[1]**tri·umph** \'trī-əm(p)f\ *n*, *pl* **tri·umphs** \-əm(p)fs, -əm(p)s\ [ME *triumphe*, fr. MF, fr. L *triumphus*] **1 :** an ancient Roman ceremonial honoring a general for a decisive victory over a foreign enemy **2 :** the joy or exultation of victory or success **3 :** a military victory or conquest; *also* **:** a success of any sort **syn** see VICTORY

[2]**triumph** *vi* **1 a :** to receive the honor of a triumph **b :** to celebrate victory or success boastfully or exultingly **2 :** to obtain victory **:** PREVAIL

tri·um·phal \trī-'əm(p)-fəl\ *adj* **:** of, relating to, or used in a triumph

tri·um·phant \trī-'əm(p)-fənt\ *adj* **1 :** CONQUERING, VICTORIOUS **2** *archaic* **:** TRIUMPHAL **3 :** rejoicing for or celebrating victory **:** EXULTANT — **tri·um·phant·ly** *adv*

tri·um·vir \trī-'əm-vər\ *n*, *pl* **triumvirs** *also* **tri·um·vi·ri** \-və-,rī, -,rē\ [L, back-formation fr. *triumviri*, pl., commission of three men, fr. *trium virum* of three men] **:** one of a commission or ruling body of three — **tri·um·vi·ral** \-və-rəl\ *adj*

tri·um·vi·rate \-və-rət\ *n* **1 :** the office or government of triumvirs **2 :** a body of triumvirs **3 :** a group or association of three

[1]**tri·une** \'trī-,(y)ün\ *n* [L *tri-* + *unus* one — more at ONE] **:** TRINITY

[2]**triune** *adj* **:** three in one; *esp* **:** of or relating to the Trinity ⟨the ~ God⟩

tri·va·lence \(')trī-'vā-lən(t)s\ *or* **tri·va·len·cy** \-lən-sē\ *n* **:** the quality or state of being trivalent

tri·va·lent \-lənt\ *adj* [ISV] **1 :** having a valence of three **2 :** TRIPLE — used of homologous chromosomes

tri·valve \'trī-,valv\ *adj* **:** having three valves

triv·et \'triv-ət\ *n* [ME *trevet*, fr. OE *trefet*, prob. modif. of LL *triped-*, *tripes*, fr. L, three-footed, fr. *tri-* + *ped-*, *pes* foot — more at FOOT] **1 :** a three-legged stand **:** TRIPOD **2 :** a metal stand with short feet for use under a hot dish at table

triv·ia \'triv-ē-ə\ *n pl but sing or pl in constr* [NL, back-formation fr. L *trivialis* trivial] **:** unimportant matters **:** TRIFLES

triv·i·al \'triv-ē-əl\ *adj* [L *trivialis* found everywhere, commonplace, trivial, fr. *trivium* crossroads, fr. *tri-* + *via* way — more at VIA] **1 :** COMMONPLACE, ORDINARY **2 :** of little worth or importance **:** INSIGNIFICANT — **triv·i·al·ly** \-ə-lē\ *adv*

triv·i·al·i·ty \,triv-ē-'al-ət-ē\ *n* **1 :** the quality or state of being trivial **2 :** something trivial **:** TRIFLE

triv·i·al·iza·tion \,triv-ē-ə-lə-'zā-shən\ *n* **:** the act, process, or result of trivializing ⟨the ~ of education⟩

triv·i·al·ize \'triv-ē-ə-,līz\ *vt* **:** to make trivial **:** reduce to triviality

trivial name *n* **1 :** SPECIFIC EPITHET **2 :** a common or vernacular name of an organism or chemical

triv·i·um \'triv-ē-əm\ *n*, *pl* **triv·ia** \-ē-ə\ [ML, fr. L, meeting of three ways, crossroads] **:** the three liberal arts of grammar, rhetoric, and logic forming the elementary division of the seven liberal arts in medieval schools — compare QUADRIVIUM

[1]**tri·week·ly** \(')trī-'wē-klē\ *adj* **1 :** occurring or appearing three times a week **2 :** occurring or appearing every three weeks — **triweekly** *adv*

[2]**triweekly** *n* **:** a triweekly publication

-trix \(,)triks\ *n suffix*, *pl* **-tri·ces** \trə-,sēz, 'trī-(,)sēz\ *or* **-trix·es** \(,)trik-səz\ [ME, fr. L, fem. of *-tor*, suffix denoting an agent, fr. *-tus*, pp. ending + *-or* — more at -ED] **1 :** female that does or is associated with a (specified) thing ⟨avia*trix*⟩ **2 :** geometric line, point, or surface ⟨genera*trix*⟩

tro·car *also* **tro·char** \'trō-,kär\ *n* [F *trocart*, fr. *trois* three (fr. L *tres*) + *carre* side of a sword blade, fr. *carrer* to make square, fr. L *quadrare* — more at THREE, QUADRATE] **:** a sharp-pointed instrument fitted with a cannula and used esp. to insert the cannula into a body cavity as a drainage outlet

tro·cha·ic \trō-'kā-ik\ *adj* [MF *trochaïque*, fr. L *trochaicus*, fr. Gk *trochaikos*, fr. *trochaios* trochee] **:** of, relating to, or consisting of trochees — **trochaic** *n*

tro·chal \'trō-kəl, 'träk-əl\ *adj* [Gk *trochos* wheel] **:** resembling a wheel

tro·chan·ter \trō-'kant-ər\ *n* [Gk *trochantēr;* akin to Gk *trechein* to run] **1 :** a rough prominence at the upper part of the femur of many vertebrates **2 :** the second segment counting from the base of the leg of an insect — **tro·chan·ter·al** \-ə-rəl\ *or* **tro·chan·ter·ic** \,trō-,kan-'ter-ik\ *adj*

tro·che \'trō-kē, *Brit also* 'trōsh\ *n* [alter. of earlier *trochisk*, fr. LL *trochiscus*, fr. Gk *trochiskos*, fr. dim. of *trochos* wheel] **:** a usu. circular medicinal tablet or lozenge; *esp* **:** one used as a demulcent

tro·chee \'trō-(,)kē\ *n* [F *trochée*, fr. L *trochaeus*, fr. Gk *trochaios*, fr. *trochaios* running, fr. *trochē* run, course, fr. *trechein* to run; akin to Gk *trochos* wheel, OIr *droch*] **:** a metrical foot consisting of one long syllable followed by one short syllable or of one stressed syllable followed by one unstressed syllable (as in *apple*) — compare IAMB

troch·el·minth \'träk-əl-,min(t)th, trō-'kel-\ *n* [deriv. of Gk *trochos* wheel + *helminth-*, *helmis* worm] **:** any of a phylum (Trochelminthes) of invertebrates including the rotifers

troch·i·lus \'träk-ə-ləs\ *n*, *pl* **troch·i·li** \-,lī, -,lē\ [NL, genus name, fr. Gk *trochilos* crocodile bird; akin to Gk *trechein* to run] **1 :** CROCODILE BIRD **2 :** any of several Old World warblers **3 :** HUMMINGBIRD

troch·lea \'träk-lē-ə\ *n* [NL, fr. L, block of pulleys, fr. Gk *trochileia;* akin to Gk *trechein* to run] **:** an anatomical structure felt to resemble a pulley; *esp* **:** the articular surface on the medial condyle of the humerus that articulates with the ulna

troch·le·ar \-ər\ *adj* **1 :** of, relating to, or being a trochlea **2 :** round and narrow in the middle like the wheel of a pulley ⟨a ~ plant embryo⟩

1**tro·choid** \'trō-,kȯid, 'träk-,ȯid\ *n* [Gk *trochoeidēs* like a wheel, fr. *trochos* wheel] **:** the curve generated by a point on the radius of a circle as the circle rolls on a fixed straight line — **tro·choi·dal** \trō-'kȯid-ᵊl, trä-\ *adj*

2**trochoid** *adj* [Gk *trochoeidēs* like a wheel] **:** admitting of rotation on a longitudinal axis ⟨a ~ joint⟩

trocho·phore \'träk-ə-,fō(ə)r, -,fȯ(ə)r\ *n* [deriv. of Gk *trochos* wheel + *pherein* to carry — more at BEAR] **:** a free-swimming ciliate larva typical of marine annelid worms but occurring in several invertebrate groups

trod *past of* TREAD

trodden *past part of* TREAD

trof·fer \'träf-ər, 'trȯf-\ *n* [perh. by alter. fr. *trough*] **:** an inverted trough serving as a support and reflector usu. for a fluorescent lighting unit

trog·lo·dyte \'träg-lə-,dīt\ *n* [L *troglodytae*, pl., fr. Gk *trōglodytai*, fr. *trōglē* hole, cave + *dyein* to enter; akin to Gk *trōgein* to gnaw] **1 :** a member of a primitive people dwelling in caves **2 :** a person felt to resemble a troglodyte; *esp* **:** an unsocial seclusive person **3 :** an anthropoid ape — **trog·lo·dyt·ic** \,träg-lə-'dit-ik\ *adj*

tro·gon \'trō-,gän\ *n* [NL, genus name, fr. Gk *trōgōn*, prp. of *trōgein* to gnaw] **:** any of numerous nonpasserine tropical birds (family Trogonidae) with brilliant lustrous plumage

troi·ka \'trȯi-kə\ *n* [Russ *troĭka*, fr. *troe* three; akin to OE *thrīe* three] **1 :** a Russian vehicle drawn by three horses abreast; *also* **:** a team for such a vehicle **2 :** a group of three closely related persons or things

Troi·lus \'trȯi-ləs, 'trō-ə-ləs\ *n* [ME, fr. L, fr. Gk *Trōïlos*] **:** a son of Priam and lover of Cressida

troilus butterfly *n* **:** a large American showy black butterfly (*Papilio troilus*) with yellow marginal spots on the front wings and blue on the rear

Tro·jan \'trō-jən\ *n* [ME, fr. L *trojanus* of Troy, fr. *Troia, Troja* Troy, fr. Gk *Trōïa*] **1 :** a native or inhabitant of Troy **2 :** one who shows pluck, endurance, or determined energy **3 :** a gay, irresponsible, or disreputable companion — **Trojan** *adj*

Trojan horse *n* **1 :** a large hollow wooden horse filled with Greek soldiers and introduced within the walls of Troy by a stratagem during the Trojan War **2 :** someone or something intended to undermine or subvert from within

Trojan War *n* **:** a 10-year war between the Greeks and Trojans brought on by the abduction of Helen by Paris and ended with the destruction of Troy

1**troll** \'trōl\ *vb* [ME *trollen*] *vt* **1 :** to cause to move round and round **:** ROLL **2 a :** to sing the parts of (as a round or catch) in succession **b :** to sing loudly **c :** to celebrate in song **3 :** to speak or recite in a rolling voice **4** *obs* **:** to move rapidly **:** WAG **5 a :** to angle for with a hook and line drawn through the water **b :** to angle in ⟨~ lakes⟩ **c :** to pull through the water in angling ⟨~ a lure⟩ ~ *vi* **1 :** to move around **:** RAMBLE **2 :** to fish esp. by trolling a hook **3 :** to sing or play in a jovial manner **4 :** to speak rapidly — **troll·er** *n*

2**troll** *n* **1 :** a lure or a line with its lure and hook used in trolling **2 :** a song sung in parts successively **:** ROUND

3**troll** *n* [Norw *troll* & Dan *trold*, fr. ON *troll* giant, demon; akin to MHG *trolle* monster, OE *treppan* to tread — more at TRAP] **:** a fabled dwarf or giant of Teutonic folklore inhabiting caves or hills

1**trol·ley** *or* **trol·ly** \'träl-ē\ *n, pl* **trolleys** *or* **trollies** [prob. fr. 1*troll*] **1** *dial Eng* **:** a cart of any of various kinds **2 a :** a current collector operating in connection with a trolley wire **b :** an electric car **3 :** a wheeled carriage running on an overhead rail or track (as of a parcel railway in a store)

2**trolley** *or* **trolly** *vb* **trol·leyed** *or* **trol·lied; trol·ley·ing** *or* **trol·ly·ing** *vt* **:** to convey by a trolley ~ *vi* **:** to ride on a trolley

trol·ley·bus \'träl-ē-,bəs\ *n* **:** a bus electrically propelled by power from two overhead wires and similar in appearance to a motor bus

trolley car *n* **:** a public conveyance for passengers that runs on tracks with motive power derived through a trolley

trol·lop \'träl-əp\ *n* [prob. irreg. fr. G dial. *trolle*, fr. MHG *trulle* prostitute — more at TRULL] **1 :** a slovenly woman **:** SLATTERN **2 :** a loose woman **:** WANTON

Trol·lo·pi·an \trä-'lō-pē-ən\ *adj* **:** of, relating to, or characteristic of the novelist Anthony Trollope or his writings

trom·bi·di·a·sis \,träm-bə-'dī-ə-səs\ *n* [NL, fr. *Trombidium*, genus of mites] **:** infestation with chiggers

trom·bone \träm-'bōn, (,)trəm-', 'träm-,\ *n* [It, aug. of *tromba* trumpet, of Gmc origin; akin to OHG *trumba, trumpa* trumpet] **:** a brass wind instrument that has a cupped mouthpiece, that consists of a long cylindrical metal tube bent twice upon itself and ending in a bell and that has a movable slide with which to vary the pitch — **trom·bon·ist** \-əst\ *n*

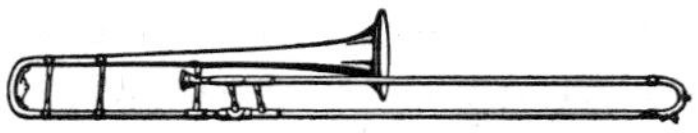

trombone

trom·mel \'träm-əl\ *n* [G, drum, fr. MHG *trummel*, dim. of *trumme* drum] **:** a screen used esp. for screening or sizing rock, ore, or coal

-tron \,trän\ *n suffix* [Gk, suffix denoting an instrument; akin to OE *-thor*, suffix denoting an instrument, L *-trum*] **1 :** vacuum tube ⟨magne*tron*⟩ **2 :** device for the manipulation of subatomic particles ⟨cyclo*tron*⟩

tro·na \'trō-nə\ *n* [Sw] **:** a gray-white or yellowish white monoclinic mineral $Na_3H(CO_3)_2.2H_2O$ consisting of a hydrous acid sodium carbonate

trone \'trōn\ *n* [AF] *chiefly Scot* **:** a weighing machine for heavy wares

1**troop** \'trüp\ *n* [MF *trope, troupe* company, herd, of Gmc origin; akin to OE *thorp, throp* village — more at THORP] **1 a :** a group of soldiers **b :** a cavalry unit corresponding to an infantry company **c :** armed forces **:** SOLDIERS — usu. used in pl. **2 :** a collection of people or things **:** COMPANY **3 :** a flock of mammals or birds **4 :** a unit of boy or girl scouts under a leader

2**troop** *vi* **1 :** to move or gather in crowds **2 :** to consort in company **:** ASSOCIATE **3 :** to move in large numbers **:** THRONG

troop carrier *n* **:** a transport airplane used to carry troops

troop·er \'trü-pər\ *n* **1 a** (1) **:** an enlisted cavalryman (2) **:** the horse of a cavalryman **b :** PARATROOPER **2 a :** a mounted policeman **b :** a private of state police

troop·ship \'trüp-,ship\ *n* **:** a ship for carrying troops **:** TRANSPORT

troost·ite \'trü-,stīt, 'trō-\ *n* [Gerard *Troost* †1850 Am geologist] **:** a variety of willemite occurring in large reddish crystals in which the zinc is partly replaced by manganese

trop- *or* **tropo-** *comb form* [ISV, fr. Gk *tropos*] **1 :** turn **:** turning **:** change ⟨*tropo*sphere⟩ **2 :** tropism ⟨*trop*ic⟩

tro·pae·o·lum \trō-'pē-ə-ləm\ *n* [NL, genus name, dim. of L *tropaeum* trophy — more at TROPHY] **:** any of a genus (*Tropaeolum*) of tropical American diffuse or climbing pungent herbs having lobed or dissected peltate leaves and showy flowers and including the nasturtium

trope \'trōp\ *n* [L *tropus*, fr. Gk *tropos* turn, way, manner, style, trope, fr. *trepein* to turn; akin to L *trepit* he turns] **1 :** the use of a word or expression in a figurative sense **:** FIGURE OF SPEECH **2 :** a phrase or verse added as an embellishment or interpolation to the sung parts of the mass in the medieval period

troph- *or* **tropho-** *comb form* [F, fr. Gk, fr. *trophē* nourishment] **:** nutritive ⟨*tropho*plasm⟩

tro·phic \'träf-ik, 'trō-fik\ *adj* [F *trophique*, fr. Gk *trophikos*, fr. *trophē* nourishment, fr. *trephein* to nourish — more at ATROPHY] **1 :** of or relating to nutrition **:** NUTRITIONAL ⟨~ disorders⟩ **2 :** 3TROPIC — **tro·phi·cal·ly** \-(ə-)lē\ *adv*

-tro·phic \'träf-ik, 'trō-fik\ *adj comb form* [NL *-trophia* -trophy] **1 a :** of, relating to, or characterized by (such) nutrition ⟨ecto*trophic*⟩ **b :** requiring or utilizing (such) a kind of nutrition ⟨poly*trophic*⟩ **2 :** -TROPIC ⟨lipo*trophic*⟩

tro·pho·blast \'träf-ə-,blast, 'trō-fə-\ *n* [ISV] **:** a layer of ectoderm that forms the outer surface of the blastodermic vesicle of many mammals and functions in the nutrition and implantation of the embryo — **tro·pho·blas·tic** \,träf-ə-'blas-tik, ,trō-fə-\ *adj*

tro·pho·plasm \'träf-ə-,plaz-əm, 'trō-fə-\ *n* [ISV] **:** relatively unspecialized protoplasm held to be nutritive as distinguished from highly active differentiated protoplasm — **tro·pho·plas·mat·ic** \,träf-ə-,plaz-'mat-ik, ,trō-fə-\ *adj* — **tro·pho·plas·mic** \-'plaz-mik\ *adj*

tro·pho·zo·ite \,träf-ə-'zō-,īt, ,trō-fə-\ *n* **:** a vegetative protozoan as distinguished from a reproductive or resting form

1**tro·phy** \'trō-fē\ *n* [MF *trophee*, fr. L *tropaeum, trophaeum*, fr. Gk *tropaion*, fr. neut. of *tropaios* of a turning, of a rout, fr. *tropē* turn, rout, fr. *trepein* to turn — more at TROPE] **1 a :** a memorial of an ancient Greek or Roman victory raised on the field of battle or in case of a naval victory on the nearest land **b :** a representation of such a memorial (as on a medal); *also* **:** an architectural ornament representing a group of military weapons **2 :** something gained or given in victory or conquest esp. when preserved or mounted as a memorial

2**trophy** *vt* **:** to honor or adorn with a trophy

-tro·phy \trə-fē\ *n comb form* [NL *-trophia*, fr. Gk, fr. *-trophos* nourishing, fr. *trephein*] **:** nutrition **:** nurture **:** growth ⟨hyper*trophy*⟩

1**trop·ic** \'träp-ik\ *n* [ME *tropik*, fr. L *tropicus* of the solstice, fr. Gk *tropikos*, fr. *tropē* turn] **1 :** either of the two small circles of the celestial sphere on each side of and parallel to the equator at a distance of 23½ degrees which the sun reaches at its greatest declination north or south **2 a :** either of the two parallels of terrestrial latitude corresponding to the celestial tropics — compare TROPIC OF CANCER, TROPIC OF CAPRICORN **b** *pl, often cap* **:** the region lying between these parallels of latitude

2**tropic** *adj* **:** of, relating to, or occurring in the tropics **:** TROPICAL

3**tropic** *adj* [*trop-*] **1 :** of, relating to, or characteristic of tropism or of a tropism **2** *of a hormone* **:** influencing the activity of a specified gland

-tropic \'träp-ik, *in some words also* 'trō-pik\ *adj comb form* [F *-tropique*, fr. Gk *-tropos* -tropous] **1:** turning, changing, or tending to turn or change in a (specified) manner or in response to a (specified) stimulus ⟨geo*tropic*⟩ **2 :** attracted to or acting upon (something specified) ⟨neuro*tropic*⟩

trop·i·cal *adj* **1** \'träp-i-kəl\ **a :** of, located in, or used in the tropics **b** *of a sign of the zodiac* **:** beginning at one of the tropics **2** \'trō-pi-kəl, 'träp-i-\ [L *tropicus*, fr. Gk *tropikos*, fr. *tropos* trope] **:** FIGURATIVE, METAPHORICAL — **trop·i·cal·ly** \-k(ə-)lē\ *adv*

tropical aquarium *n* **:** an aquarium kept at a uniform warmth and used esp. for tropical fish

tropical cyclone *n* **:** a cyclone in the tropics characterized by winds rotating at the rate of 75 miles an hour or more

tropical fish *n* **:** any of various small usu. showy fishes of exotic origin often kept in the tropical aquarium

tropical storm *n* **:** a tropical cyclone with strong winds of less than hurricane intensity

tropic bird *n* **:** any of several web-footed birds (genus *Phaëthon*) related to the gannets, found chiefly in tropical seas often far from land, and marked by mostly white satiny plumage with a little black, a greatly elongated central pair of tail feathers, and a bright-colored bill

tropic of Cancer [fr. the sign of the zodiac which its celestial projection intersects] **:** the parallel of latitude that is 23½ degrees north of the equator and is the northernmost latitude reached by the overhead sun

tropic of Capricorn [fr. the sign of the zodiac which its celestial projection intersects] **:** the parallel of latitude 23½ degrees south of the equator that is the southernmost latitude reached by the overhead sun

tro·pism \'trō-,piz-əm, 'träp-,iz-\ *n* [ISV *-tropism*] **1 a :** involuntary orientation by an organism or one of its parts that involves turning or curving and is a positive or negative response to a source of stimulation **b :** a reflex reaction involving such movement **2 :** an innate tendency to react in a definite manner to stimuli — **tro·pis·tic** \trō-'pis-tik, trä-\ *adj*

-tro·pism \trə-,piz-əm\ *n comb form* [ISV, fr. *trop-*] **:** tropism ⟨helio*tropism*⟩

tro·po·log·i·cal \,trō-pə-'läj-i-kəl, ,träp-ə-\ *also* **tro·po·log·ic** \-ik\ *adj* **1 :** characterized or varied by tropes **:** FIGURATIVE **2 :** of, relating to, or involving tropology; *also* **:** MORAL — **tro·po·log·i·cal·ly** \-i-k(ə-)lē\ *adv*

tro·pol·o·gy \trō-'päl-ə-jē\ *n* [LL *tropologia*, fr. LGk, fr. Gk *tropos* trope + *-logia* -logy] **1 :** a figurative mode of speech or writing **2 :** a mode of biblical interpretation stressing moral metaphor

tro·po·pause \'trō-pə-,pȯz, 'träp-ə-\ *n* [ISV *tropo*sphere + *pause*] **:** the region at the top of the troposphere
tro·poph·i·lous \trō-'päf-ə-ləs\ *adj* **:** physiologically adjusted to or thriving in an environment that undergoes marked periodic changes esp. in temperature, moisture, or light
tro·po·sphere \'trō-pə-,sfi(ə)r, 'träp-ə-\ *n* [ISV] **:** the portion of the atmosphere which is below the stratosphere, which extends outward about 7 to 10 miles from the earth's surface, and in which generally temperature decreases rapidly with altitude, clouds form, and convection is active — **tro·po·spher·ic** \,trō-pə-'sfi(ə)r-ik, ,träp-ə-, -'sfer-\ *adj*
-tro·pous \trə-pəs\ *adj comb form* [Gk *-tropos*, fr. *trepein* to turn — more at TROPE] **:** turning or curving in (such) a way **:** exhibiting (such) a tropism ⟨ana*tropous*⟩
-tro·py \trə-pē\ *n comb form* [F *-tropie*, fr. Gk *-tropia*, fr. *-tropos*] **:** condition of turning or curving in (such) a way or of exhibiting (such) a tropism ⟨en*tropy*⟩
1**trot** \'trät\ *n* [ME, fr. MF, fr. *troter* to trot, of Gmc origin; akin to OHG *trottōn* to tread, OE *tredan*] **1 a** (1) **:** a moderately fast gait of a quadruped (as a horse) in which the legs move in diagonal pairs (2) **:** a jogging gait of man that falls between a walk and a run **b :** a ride on horseback **2 a :** a small child **b :** an old woman **3 :** a literal translation for student use
2**trot** *vb* **trot·ted; trot·ting** *vi* **1 :** to ride, drive, or proceed at a trot **2 :** to proceed briskly **:** HURRY ~ *vt* **1 :** to cause to go at a trot **2 :** to traverse at a trot
3**trot** *n* **:** TROTLINE; *also* **:** one of the short lines with hooks that are attached to it at intervals
1**troth** \'trȯth, 'träth, 'trōth\ *n* [ME *trouth*, fr. OE *trēowth* — more at TRUTH] **1 :** loyal or pledged faithfulness **:** FIDELITY **2 :** one's pledged word; *also* **:** BETROTHAL
2**troth** \'träth, 'trȯth, 'trōth\ *vt* **:** PLEDGE, BETROTH
1**troth·plight** \'trȯth-,plīt, 'träth-, 'trōth-\ *n, archaic* **:** BETROTHAL
2**trothplight** *vt, archaic* **:** BETROTH
trot·line \'trät-,līn\ *n* [prob. fr. 2*trot*] **:** SETLINE; *esp* **:** a comparatively short setline used near shore or along streams
Trots·ky·ism \'trät-skē-,iz-əm, 'trȯt-\ *n* **:** the political, economic, and social principles advocated by Trotsky; *esp* **:** the theory and practice of communism developed by or associated with Trotsky and usu. including adherence to the concept of worldwide revolution as opposed to socialism in one country — **Trots·ky·ist** *n or adj* — **Trots·ky·ite** *n or adj*
trot·ter \'trät-ər\ *n* **1 :** one that trots; *specif* **:** a standardbred horse trained for harness racing **2 :** a pig's foot used as food
tro·tyl \'trōt-ᵊl\ *n* [*trinitrotol*uene + *-yl*] **:** TRINITROTOLUENE
trou·ba·dour \'trü-bə-,dō(ə)r, -,dȯ(ə)r, -,dü(ə)r\ *n* [F, fr. OProv *trobador*, fr. *trobar* to compose, prob. fr. (assumed) VL *tropare*, fr. L *tropus* trope] **:** one of a class of lyric poets and poet-musicians often of knightly rank flourishing from the 11th to the end of the 13th century chiefly in Provence, the south of France, and the north of Italy
1**trou·ble** \'trəb-əl\ *vb* **trou·bling** \'trəb-(ə-)liŋ\ [ME *troublen*, fr. OF *tourbler*, *troubler*, fr. (assumed) VL *turbulare*, alter. of L *turbidare*, fr. *turbidus* turbid, troubled] *vt* **1 a :** to agitate mentally or spiritually **:** WORRY, DISTURB **b** (1) *archaic* **:** MISTREAT, OPPRESS (2) **:** to produce physical disorder in **:** AFFLICT ⟨*troubled* with deafness⟩ **c :** to put to exertion or inconvenience **2 :** to put into confused motion ⟨wind *troubled* the sea⟩ ~ *vi* **1 :** to become mentally agitated **:** WORRY **2 :** to make an effort **:** be at pains — **trou·bler** \-(ə-)lər\ *n*
2**trouble** *n* **1 a :** the quality or state of being troubled **:** MISFORTUNE ⟨help people in ~⟩ **b :** an instance of distress, annoyance, or perturbation **2 a :** civil disorder or agitation ⟨labor ~⟩ **b :** EXERTION, PAINS ⟨took the ~ to call⟩ **c** (1) **:** a condition of physical distress (2) **:** DISEASE, AILMENT (3) **:** MALFUNCTION ⟨engine ~⟩ ⟨~ with the plumbing⟩ **d :** a personal characteristic that is a handicap or a source of distress **syn** see EFFORT
trou·ble·mak·er \'trəb-əl-,mā-kər\ *n* **:** a person who consciously or unconsciously causes friction
trou·ble·shoot·er \-,shüt-ər\ *n* **1 :** a skilled workman employed to locate trouble and make repairs in machinery and technical equipment **2 :** a man expert in resolving diplomatic, political, or other human disputes or obstructions
trou·ble·some \-səm\ *adj* **1 :** giving trouble or anxiety **:** VEXATIOUS **2** *archaic* **:** characterized by disturbance **:** TURBULENT **3** *archaic* **:** AFFLICTED, DISTRESSED **4 :** DIFFICULT, BURDENSOME — **trou·ble·some·ly** *adv* — **trou·ble·some·ness** *n*
trou·blous \'trəb-(ə-)ləs\ *adj* **1 :** full of trouble **:** AFFLICTED; *also* **:** AGITATED, STORMY **2 :** causing trouble **:** TURBULENT — **trou·blous·ly** *adv* — **trou·blous·ness** *n*
trou–de–loup \,trüd-ᵊl-'ü\ *n, pl* **trous–de–loup** \,trüd-ᵊl-'ü(z)\ [F, lit., wolf's hole] **:** a sloping pit with a pointed stake in the middle to form one of a group constructed as obstacles to the movements of an enemy — usu. used in pl.
trough \'trȯf, *by bakers often* 'trō\ *n, pl* **troughs** \'trȯfs, 'trȯvz, 'trōz\ [ME, fr. OE *trog*; akin to OE *trēow* tree, wood — more at TREE] **1 a :** a long shallow often V-shaped receptacle for the drinking water or feed of domestic animals **b :** any of various domestic or industrial containers **2 a :** a conduit, drain, or channel for water; *esp* **:** a gutter along the eaves **b :** a long and narrow or shallow channel or depression (as between waves or hills) **3 :** the minimum point of a complete cycle of a periodic function: as **a :** an elongated area of low barometric pressure **b :** the low point in a business cycle
trounce \'traun(t)s\ *vt* [origin unknown] **:** to thrash or punish severely: as **a :** FLOG, CUDGEL **b :** to defeat decisively
1**troupe** \'trüp\ *n* [F, fr. MF — more at TROOP] **:** COMPANY, TROOP; *esp* **:** a group of performers on the stage
2**troupe** *vi* **:** to travel in a troupe; *also* **:** to perform as a member of a theatrical troupe — **troup·er** *n*
trou·pi·al \'trü-pē-əl\ *n* [F *troupiale*, fr. *troupe*; fr. its living in flocks] **:** any of a family (Icteridae) of birds including the American blackbirds, grackles, and orioles; *specif* **:** one of the large showy orioles (as *Icterus icterus*) of Central and So. America
trou·ser \'trau̇-zər\ *adj* **:** of, relating to, or designed for trousers ⟨~ pockets⟩
trou·sers \'trau̇-zərz\ *n pl* [alter. of earlier *trouse*, fr. ScGael *triubhas*] **1 :** an outer garment extending from the waist to the ankle or sometimes only to the knee, covering each leg separately, and worn typically by men and boys **2 :** baggy pantaloons worn by both sexes in the Near East
trous·seau \'trü-(,)sō, trü-'\ *n, pl* **trous·seaux** \-(,)sō(z), -'sōz\ *or* **trousseaus** [F, fr. OF, dim. of *trousse* bundle, fr. *trousser* to truss] **:** the personal outfit of a bride usu. including clothes, accessories, and household linens
trout \'trau̇t\ *n, pl* **trout** *also* **trouts** [ME, fr. OE *trūht*, fr. LL *trocta*, *tructa*, a fish with sharp teeth, fr. Gk *trōktēs*, lit., gnawer, fr. *trōgein* to gnaw — more at TERSE] **1 :** any of various fishes (family Salmonidae) mostly smaller than the typical salmons, restricted to cool clear fresh waters, and highly regarded as table and angling fish: **a :** any of various Old or New World fishes (genus *Salmo*) some of which are anadromous **b :** any of various No. American fishes (genera *Salvelinus* or *Cristivomer*) **:** CHAR **2 :** any of various fishes felt to resemble the true trouts
trout lily *n* [prob. fr. its speckled leaves] **:** DOGTOOTH VIOLET
trout–perch \'trau̇t-,pərch\ *n* **:** a small freshwater fish (*Percopsis omiscomaycus*) of the central and eastern U.S.
trouty \'trau̇t-ē\ *adj* **:** containing or likely to contain abundant trout
trou·vère \trü-'ve(ə)r\ *n* [F, fr. OF *troveor*, *troverre*, fr. *trover* to compose, find, fr. (assumed) VL *tropare* — more at TROUBADOUR] **:** one of a school of poets flourishing in northern France from the 11th to the 14th centuries and producing typically the chansons de geste
trove \'trōv\ *n* [short for *treasure trove*] **1 :** DISCOVERY, FIND **2 :** a valuable collection **:** TREASURE; *also* **:** HAUL
tro·ver \'trō-vər\ *n* [MF *trover* to find] **:** a common law action to recover the value of goods wrongfully converted by another to his own use
trow \'trō\ *vb* [ME *trowen*, fr. OE *trēowan*; akin to OE *trēowe* faithful, true — more at TRUE] **1** *obs* **:** BELIEVE, TRUST **2** *archaic* **:** THINK, SUPPOSE
1**trow·el** \'trau̇(-ə)l\ *n* [ME *truel*, fr. MF *truelle*, fr. LL *truella*, fr. L *trulla*, dim. of *trua* ladle; akin to L *turbare* to disturb — more at TURBID] **:** any of various hand tools used to apply, spread, shape, or smooth loose or plastic material; *also* **:** a scoop-shaped or flat-bladed garden tool for taking up and setting small plants
2**trowel** *vt* **trow·eled** *or* **trow·elled; trow·el·ing** *or* **trow·el·ling :** to smooth, mix, or apply with or as if with a trowel — **trow·el·er** \'trau̇-(ə-)lər\ *n*

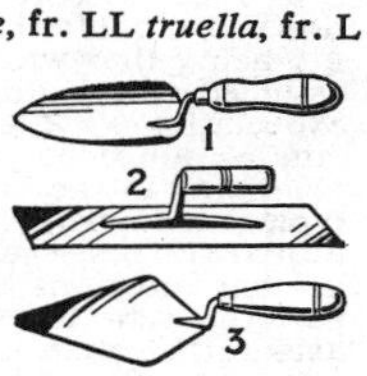

trowels: *1* gardener's, *2* plasterer's, *3* bricklayer's

trow·sers *n pl* **:** TROUSERS 1
troy \'trȯi\ *adj* [ME *troye*, fr. *Troyes*, France] **:** expressed in troy weight
troy weight *n* **:** a series of units of weight based on a pound of 12 ounces and the ounce of 20 pennyweights or 480 grains — see MEASURE table
tru·an·cy \'trü-ən-sē\ *n* **:** an act or instance of playing truant **:** the state of being truant
1**tru·ant** \'trü-ənt\ *n* [ME, vagabond, idler, fr. OF, vagrant, of Celt origin; akin to ScGael *truaghan* wretch] **:** one who shirks duty; *esp* **:** one who stays out of school without permission
2**truant** *adj* **:** being, resembling, or characteristic of a truant
3**truant** *vi* **:** to idle away time esp. while shirking some duty **:** play truant
truant officer *n* **:** one employed by a public-school system to investigate the continued absences of pupils
tru·ant·ry \'trü-ən-trē\ *n* **:** TRUANCY
1**truce** \'trüs\ *n* [ME *trewes*, pl. of *trewe* agreement, fr. OE *trēow* fidelity; akin to OE *trēowe* faithful — more at TRUE] **1 :** a suspension of fighting esp. of considerable duration by agreement of opposing forces **:** ARMISTICE, CEASE-FIRE **2 :** a respite esp. from a disagreeable or painful state or action
2**truce** *vi* **:** to make a truce ~ *vt* **:** to end with a truce
1**truck** \'trək\ *vb* [ME *trukken*, fr. OF *troquer*] *vt* **1 :** to give in exchange **:** SWAP **2 :** to barter or dispose of by barter ~ *vi* **1 :** to exchange commodities **:** BARTER **2 :** to negotiate or traffic esp. in an underhanded way **:** have dealings
2**truck** *n* **1 :** BARTER **2 :** commodities appropriate for barter or for small trade **3 :** close association **:** DEALINGS **4 :** payment of wages in goods instead of cash **5 :** vegetables grown for market **6 :** heterogeneous small articles often of little value; *also* **:** RUBBISH
3**truck** *n* [prob. fr. L *trochus* iron hoop, fr. Gk *trochos* wheel — more at TROCHEE] **1 :** a small wheel; *specif* **:** a small strong wheel for a gun carriage **2 :** a small wooden cap at the top of a flagstaff or masthead usu. having holes for reeving flag or signal halyards **3 :** a wheeled vehicle for moving heavy articles: as **a :** a strong horse-drawn or automotive vehicle for hauling; *also* **:** an automotive vehicle equipped with a swivel for hauling a trailer **b :** a small barrow consisting of a rectangular frame having at one end a pair of handles and at the other end a pair of small heavy wheels and a projecting edge to slide under a load — called also *hand truck* **c :** a small heavy rectangular frame supported on four wheels for moving heavy objects **d :** a small flat-topped car pushed or pulled by hand **e :** a shelved stand mounted on casters **4 a** *Brit* **:** an open railroad freight car **b :** a swiveling carriage consisting of a frame with one or more pairs of wheels and springs to carry and guide one end of a locomotive or a railroad car in turning sharp curves
4**truck** *vt* **:** to load or transport on a truck ~ *vi* **1 :** to transport goods by truck **2 :** to be employed in driving a truck
truck·age \'trək-ij\ *n* **1 :** money paid for conveyance on a truck **2 :** conveyance by truck
1**truck·er** \'trək-ər\ *n* **1 :** one that barters **2** *Scot* **:** PEDDLER
2**trucker** *n* **1 :** one whose business is transporting goods by truck **2 :** a truck driver
truck farm *n* **:** a farm devoted to the production of vegetables for the market — **truck farmer** *n*
truck·ing *n* **:** the process or business of transporting goods on trucks
1**truck·le** \'trək-əl\ *n* [ME *trocle*, fr. L *trochlea* block of pulleys — more at TROCHLEA] **:** a small wheel **:** PULLEY, CASTER
2**truckle** *vi* **truck·ling** \-(ə-)liŋ\ [fr. the lower position of the truckle bed] **:** to act in a subservient manner **:** bend obsequiously **:** SUBMIT ⟨~ to a conqueror⟩ **syn** see FAWN

ə abut; ᵊ kitten; ər further; a back; ā bake; ä cot, cart; au̇ out; ch chin; e less; ē easy; g gift; i trip; ī life
j joke; ŋ sing; ō flow; ȯ flaw; ȯi coin; th thin; t͟h this; ü loot; u̇ foot; y yet; yü few; yu̇ furious; zh vision

truckle bed *n* : TRUNDLE BED
truck·ler \'trək-(ə-)lər\ *n* : one that truckles
truck·line \'trək-ˌlīn\ *n* : a carrier using trucks and related freight vehicles
truck·load \-'lōd\ *n* **1** : a load that fills a truck **2** : the minimum weight required for shipping at truckload rates
truck·man \-mən\ *n* **1** : TRUCKER **2** : any of the members of a fire department unit that operates a ladder truck
truck·mas·ter \-ˌmas-tər\ *n, archaic* : an officer in charge of trade with Indians esp. among the early settlers
truck system *n* : the system of paying wages in goods instead of cash
truck trail·er *n* **1** \'trək-ˌtrā-lər\ : a nonautomotive freight vehicle to be drawn by a motortruck **2** *usu* **truck–trailer** \-'trā-lər\ : a combination of a truck trailer and its motortruck
tru·cu·lence \'trək-yə-lən(t)s *also* 'trük-\ *also* **tru·cu·len·cy** \-lən-sē\ *n* : the quality or state of being truculent
tru·cu·lent \-lənt\ *adj* [L *truculentus*, fr. *truc-*, *trux* fierce] **1** : feeling or displaying ferocity : CRUEL, FIERCE, SAVAGE **2** : DEADLY, DESTRUCTIVE **3** : scathingly harsh : VITRIOLIC, VITUPERATIVE **4** : aggressively self-assertive : BELLIGERENT, PUGNACIOUS — **tru·cu·lent·ly** *adv*
1trudge \'trəj\ *vb* [origin unknown] *vi* : to walk or march steadily and usu. laboriously ~ *vt* : to trudge along or over
2trudge *n* : a long tiring walk : TRAMP
trud·gen stroke \'trəj-ən-\ *n* [John *Trudgen*, 19th cent. E swimmer] : a swimming stroke in which a double overarm motion is combined with a scissors kick
trudg·er \'trəj-ər\ *n* : one that trudges
1true \'trü\ *adj* [ME *trewe*, fr. OE *trēowe* faithful; akin to OHG *gitriuwi* faithful, Skt *dāruṇa* hard, *dāru* wood — more at TREE] **1 a** : STEADFAST, LOYAL **b** : HONEST, JUST **c** *archaic* : TRUTHFUL **2 a** (1) : in accordance with the actual state of affairs ⟨~ description⟩ (2) : conformable to an essential reality **b** : IDEAL, ESSENTIAL **c** : being that which is the case rather than what is manifest or assumed ⟨the ~ dimension of the problem⟩ **d** : CONSISTENT ⟨~ to expectations⟩ **3 a** : properly so called ⟨~ love⟩ ⟨the ~ faith⟩ ⟨the ~ stomach⟩ **b** (1) : possessing the basic characters of and belonging to the same natural group as ⟨a whale is a ~ but not a typical mammal⟩ (2) : TYPICAL ⟨the ~ cats⟩ **4** : LEGITIMATE, RIGHTFUL ⟨our ~ and lawful king⟩ **5 a** : that is fitted or formed or that functions accurately **b** : comformable to a standard or pattern : ACCURATE **6** : determined with reference to the earth's axis rather than the magnetic poles ⟨~ north⟩ **7** : logically necessary **8** : NARROW, STRICT ⟨in the *truest* sense⟩ **9** : corrected for error **syn** see REAL
2true *n* **1** : TRUTH, REALITY — usu. used with *the* **2** : the quality or state of being accurate (as in alignment or adjustment) — used in the phrases *in true* and *out of true*
3true *vt* **trued; true·ing** *also* **tru·ing** : to make level, square, or concentric ⟨~ up an engine cylinder⟩
4true *adv* [ME *trewe*, fr. *trewe*, adj., true] **1** : TRUTHFULLY **2 a** : ACCURATELY ⟨the bullet flew straight and ~⟩ **b** : without variation from type ⟨breed ~⟩
true bill *n* : a bill of indictment endorsed by a grand jury as warranting prosecution of the accused
true blue *n* [fr. the old association of blue with constancy] : one who is true-blue
true–blue \'trü-'blü\ *adj* : marked by unswerving loyalty (as to a party) : highly faithful
true·born \-ˌbȯ(ə)rn\ *adj* : genuinely such by birth ⟨a ~ Englishman —Shak.⟩
true–false test \'trü-'fȯls-\ *n* : a test consisting of a series of statements to be marked as true or false
true·heart·ed \'trü-'härt-əd\ *adj* : FAITHFUL, STEADFAST, LOYAL — **true·heart·ed·ness** *n*
true–life \ˌtrü-ˌlīf\ *adj* : true to life ⟨a *true-life* story⟩
true·love \'trü-ˌləv\ *n* : one truly beloved or loving : SWEETHEART
true lover's knot *n* : a complicated ornamental knot not readily untying and emblematic of mutual love — called also *truelove knot*
true·ness \'trü-nəs\ *n* : the quality or state of being true
true·pen·ny \'trü-ˌpen-ē\ *n* : an honest or trusty person
true rib *n* : one of the ribs having costal cartilages connected directly with the sternum and in man constituting the first seven pairs
truf·fle \'trəf-əl, 'trüf-\ *n* [modif. of MF *truffe*, fr. OProv *trufa*, fr. (assumed) VL *tufera*, alter. of L *tuber* — more at TUBER] : the usu. dark and rugose edible subterranean fruiting body of European fungi (genus *Tuber*); *also* : one of the fungi
truf·fled \-əld\ *adj* : cooked, stuffed, or garnished with truffles
tru·ism \'trü-ˌiz-əm\ *n* : an undoubted or self-evident truth; *esp* : one too obvious or unimportant for mention — **tru·is·tic** \trü-'is-tik\ *adj*
trull \'trəl\ *n* [obs. G *trulle*, fr. MHG; akin to ON *troll* giant, demon — more at TROLL] : PROSTITUTE, STRUMPET
tru·ly \'trü-lē\ *adv* **1** : SINCERELY — often used as a complimentary close after *yours* **2** : TRUTHFULLY **3** : ACCURATELY **4 a** : INDEED — often used as an intensive ⟨~, she is fair⟩ or interjectionally to express astonishment or doubt **b** : GENUINELY **5** : PROPERLY, RIGHTFULLY
1trump \'trəmp\ *n* [ME *trompe*, fr. OF] **1 a** : TRUMPET **b** *chiefly Scot* : JEW'S HARP **2** : a sound of or as if of trumpeting
2trump *n* [alter. of 1*triumph*] **1 a** : a card of a suit any of whose cards will win over a card that is not a trump **b** : the suit whose cards are trumps for a particular hand — often used in pl. **2** : an influential factor or final resource **3** : a dependable and exemplary person
3trump *vt* **1** : to take with a trump ⟨~ a trick⟩ **2** : to get the better of : OUTDO ~ *vi* : to play a trump
trumped–up \'trəm(p)-'təp\ *adj* : fraudulently concocted : SPURIOUS ⟨~ charges⟩
trum·pery \'trəm-p(ə-)rē\ *n* [ME *tromperie* deceit, fr. MF, fr. *tromper* to deceive] **1 a** : trivial or useless articles : things of no value : RUBBISH, JUNK **b** : worthless nonsense **2** *archaic* : tawdry finery — **trumpery** *adj*

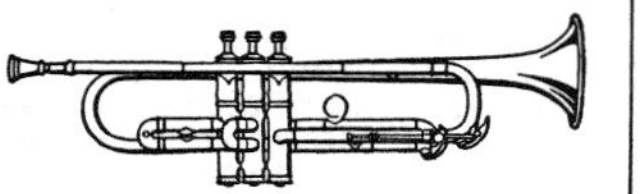
trumpet 1

1trum·pet \'trəm-pət\ *n* [ME *trompette*, fr MF, fr OF *trompe* trump] **1 a** : a wind instrument consisting of a long cylindrical metal tube commonly once or twice curved and ending in a bell **b** : a metal wind instrument (as the cornet) similar in shape and method of tone production to the trumpet **2** : a trumpet player **3** : something that resembles a trumpet or its tonal quality: as **a** : an 8-foot pipe-organ reed stop with a penetrating tone **b** : a funnel-shaped instrument (as a megaphone or a diaphragm horn) for collecting, directing, or intensifying sound **c** (1) : a stentorian voice (2) : a penetrating cry (as of an elephant)
2trumpet *vi* **1** : to blow a trumpet **2** : to make a sound suggestive of that of a trumpet ~ *vt* : to sound or proclaim on or as if on a trumpet
trumpet creeper *n* : a No. American woody vine (*Campsis radicans* of the family Bignoniaceae, the trumpet-creeper family) having pinnate leaves and large red trumpet-shaped flowers — called also *trumpet vine*
trum·pet·er \'trəm-pət-ər\ *n* **1 a** : a trumpet player; *specif* : one that gives signals with a trumpet **b** : one that praises or advocates : EULOGIST, SPOKESMAN **2 a** : any of several large gregarious long-legged long-necked So. American birds (genus *Psophia*) related to the cranes and often kept to protect poultry **b** : a rare pure white No. American wild swan (*Olor buccinator*) noted for its sonorous voice **c** : any of an Asiatic breed of pigeons with a rounded crest and heavily feathered feet **3** : any of several Australian and New Zealand marine spiny-finned food fishes (family Latrididae)
trumpet flower *n* **1** : a plant having trumpet-shaped flowers: as **a** : TRUMPET CREEPER **b** : an American honeysuckle (*Lonicera sempervirens*) with coral-red or orange flowers — called also *trumpet honeysuckle* **c** : DATURA **2** : the flower of a trumpet flower
trum·pet·like \'trəm-pət-ˌlīk\ *adj* : resembling a trumpet in shape or sound
trum·pet·weed \-ˌwēd\ *n* : any of several weedy herbs (esp. genus *Eupatorium*)
trump up *vt* **1** : to concoct esp. with intent to deceive : FABRICATE, INVENT **2** *archaic* : to cite as support for an action or claim : ALLEGE
1trun·cate \'trəŋ-ˌkāt, 'trən-\ *vt* [L *truncatus*, pp. of *truncare*, fr. *truncus* trunk] **1** : to shorten by or as if by cutting off : LOP **2** : to replace (an edge or corner of a crystal) by a plane — **trun·ca·tion** \ˌtrəŋ-'kā-shən, ˌtrən-\ *n*
2trun·cate \'trəŋ-ˌkāt, 'trən-\ *adj* **1** : having the end square or even ⟨a ~ leaf⟩ **2** : lacking an apex — used of a spiral shell
trun·cat·ed \-ˌkāt-əd\ *adj* **1** : having the apex replaced by a plane section and esp. by one parallel to the base ⟨~ cone⟩ **2 a** : cut short : CURTAILED **b** : lacking an expected or normal element (as a syllable) at beginning or end : CATALECTIC **3** : TRUNCATE 1
1trun·cheon \'trən-chən\ *n* [ME *tronchoun*, fr. MF *tronchon*, fr. (assumed) VL *truncion-*, *truncio*, fr. L *truncus* trunk] **1** : a shattered spear or lance **2 a** *obs* : CLUB, BLUDGEON **b** : BATON 2 **c** : a policeman's billy
2truncheon *vt, archaic* : to beat with a truncheon
1trun·dle \'trən-dᵊl\ *n* [alter. of earlier *trendle*, fr. ME, circle, ring, wheel, fr. OE *trendel*; akin to OE *trendan* to revolve — more at TREND] **1 a** : a small wheel or roller **b** : CIRCLET, HOOP **2** : LANTERN PINION; *also* : any of its bars
2trundle *vb* **trun·dling** \-(d)liŋ, -dᵊl-iŋ\ *vt* **1 a** : to propel by causing to rotate : ROLL **b** *archaic* : to cause to revolve : SPIN **2** : to transport in a wheeled vehicle : HAUL, WHEEL ~ *vi* **1** : to progress by revolving **2** : to move on or as if on wheels : ROLL — **trun·dler** \-(d)lər, -dᵊl-ər\ *n*
trundle bed *n* : a low bed usu. on casters that can be slid under a higher bed — called also *truckle bed*
trun·dle–tail \'trən-dᵊl-ˌtāl\ *n, archaic* : a curly-tailed dog : MONGREL
trunk \'trəŋk\ *n, often attrib* [ME *tronke* box, trunk, fr. MF *tronc*, fr. L *truncus* trunk, torso] **1 a** : the main stem of a tree apart from limbs and roots : BOLE **b** (1) : the human or animal body apart from the head and appendages : TORSO (2) : the thorax of an insect **c** : the central part of anything **2 a** (1) : a large rigid piece of luggage used usu. for transporting clothing and personal effects (2) : the luggage compartment of an automobile **b** (1) : a superstructure over a ship's hatches usu. level with the poop deck (2) : the part of the cabin of a boat projecting above the deck (3) : the housing for a centerboard or rudder **3** : PROBOSCIS; *esp* : the long muscular proboscis of the elephant **4** *pl* : men's shorts worn chiefly for sports **5 a** : a usu. major channel or passage : DUCT **b** : a circuit between two telephone exchanges for making connections between subscribers
trunk·fish \'trəŋk-ˌfish\ *n* : any of numerous small bright-colored fishes (family Ostraciontidae) of tropical seas with the body and head enclosed in a bony carapace
trunk hose \'trəŋk-\ *n pl* [prob. fr. obs. E *trunk* (to truncate)] : short full breeches reaching about halfway down the thigh worn chiefly in the late 16th and early 17th centuries
trunk line *n* **1** : a system handling long-distance through traffic **2 a** : a main supply channel **b** : a direct link
trun·nel \'trən-ᵊl\ *var of* TREENAIL
trun·nion \'trən-yən\ *n* [F *trognon* core, stump] : PIN, PIVOT; *esp* : either of two opposite gudgeons on which a cannon is swiveled
1truss \'trəs\ *vt* [ME *trussen*, fr. OF *trousser*] **1 a** : to secure tightly : BIND **b** : to arrange for cooking by binding close the wings or legs of (a fowl) **2** : to support, strengthen, or stiffen by a truss — **truss·er** *n*
2truss *n* **1** : an iron band around a lower mast **2 a** : BRACKET 1 **b** : an assemblage of members (as beams) forming a rigid framework **3** : a device worn to hold a hernia in place **4** : a compact flower or fruit cluster
truss bridge *n* : a bridge supported mainly by trusses
truss·ing \'trəs-iŋ\ *n* **1** : the members forming a truss **2** : the trusses and framework of a structure
1trust \'trəst\ *n* [ME, prob. of Scand origin; akin to ON *traust* trust; akin to OE *trēowe* faithful — more at TRUE] **1 a** : assured reliance on the character, ability, strength, or truth of someone or something **b** : one in which confidence is placed **2 a** : dependence on something future or contingent : HOPE **b** : reliance on future payment for property (as merchandise) delivered : CREDIT **3 a** : a property interest held by one person for the benefit of another **b** : a combination of firms or corporations formed by a legal agreement; *esp* : one that reduces or threatens to reduce competition **4** *archaic* : TRUSTWORTHINESS **5 a** (1) : a charge or duty imposed in faith or confidence or as a condition of some relationship (2)

: something committed or entrusted to one to be used or cared for in the interest of another **b :** responsible charge or office **c :** CARE, CUSTODY ⟨child committed to his ~⟩ **syn** see MONOPOLY — **in trust :** in the care or possession of a trustee

²**trust** *vi* **1 a :** to place confidence : DEPEND ⟨~ in God⟩ ⟨~ to luck⟩ **b :** to be confident : HOPE **2 :** to sell or deliver on credit ~ *vt* **1 a :** to commit or place in one's care or keeping : ENTRUST **b :** to permit to stay or go or to do something without fear or misgiving **2 a :** to rely on the truthfulness or accuracy of : BELIEVE **b :** to place confidence in : rely on **c :** to hope or expect confidently ⟨~*ed* to find oil on the land⟩ **3 :** to extend credit to **syn** see RELY — **trust·er** *n*

trust account *n* **:** an account opened with a trust company under which a living or testamentary trust is set up

trust·bust·er \'trəs(t)-,bəs-tər\ *n* [¹*trust* + *buster*] **:** one who seeks to break up business trusts; *specif* **:** a federal official who prosecutes trusts under the antitrust laws — **trust-bust·ing** \-tiŋ\ *n*

trust company *n* **:** a corporation and esp. a bank organized to perform fiduciary functions

¹**trust·ee** \,trəs-'tē\ *n* **1 a :** one to whom something is entrusted **b :** a country charged with the supervision of a trust territory **2 a :** a person to whom property is legally committed in trust **b :** one held to a fiduciary duty similar to that of a trustee

²**trustee** *vb* **trust·eed; trust·ee·ing** *vt* **:** to commit to the care of a trustee ~ *vi* **:** to serve as trustee

trust·ee·ship \-,ship\ *n* **1 :** the office or function of a trustee **2 :** supervisory control by one or more countries over a trust territory

trust·ful \'trəst-fəl\ *adj* **:** full of trust : CONFIDING — **trust·ful·ly** \-fə-lē\ *adv* — **trust·ful·ness** *n*

trust fund *n* **:** money, securities, or similar property settled or held in trust

trust·i·ness \'trəs-tē-nəs\ *n* **:** the quality or state of being trusty

trust·less \'trəst-ləs\ *adj* **1 :** not deserving of trust : FAITHLESS **2 :** DISTRUSTFUL

trust territory *n* **:** a non-self-governing territory placed under an administrative authority by the Trusteeship Council of the United Nations

trust·wor·thi·ly \'trəs-,twər-t͟hə-lē\ *adv* **:** in a trustworthy manner

trust·wor·thi·ness \'trəs-,twər-t͟hē-nəs\ *n* **:** the quality or state of being trustworthy

trust·wor·thy \-t͟hē\ *adj* **:** worthy of confidence : DEPENDABLE

¹**trusty** \'trəs-tē\ *adj* **:** TRUSTWORTHY, DEPENDABLE

²**trusty** \'trəs-tē *also* ,trəs-'tē\ *n* **:** a trusty or trusted person; *specif* **:** a convict considered trustworthy and allowed special privileges

truth \'trüth\ *n, pl* **truths** \'trüt͟hz, 'trüths\ [ME *trouthe*, fr. OE *trēowth* fidelity; akin to OE *trēowe* faithful — more at TRUE] **1 a** *archaic* **:** FIDELITY, CONSTANCY **b :** TRUTHFULNESS, HONESTY **2 a (1) :** the state of being the case : FACT **(2) :** the body of real things, events, and facts : ACTUALITY **(3)** *often cap* **:** a transcendent fundamental or spiritual reality **b :** a judgment, proposition, or idea that is true or accepted as true ⟨~*s* of thermodynamics⟩ **c :** the body of true statements and propositions **3 a :** agreement with fact or among true facts or propositions **b** *chiefly Brit* **:** TRUE 2 **c :** fidelity to an original or to a standard **4** *cap, Christian Science* **:** GOD

syn VERACITY, VERITY, VERISIMILITUDE: TRUTH may apply to an ideal abstraction conforming to a universal or generalized reality or it may represent a quality of statements, acts, or feelings of adhering to reality and avoiding error or falsehood; VERACITY implies rigid and unfailing observance of truth; VERITY suggests the quality of a thing that is exactly what it purports to be or is in complete accord with the facts; VERISIMILITUDE implies the quality of an artistic or literary representation that causes one to accept it as true to life or to human experience

— **in truth :** in accordance with fact : ACTUALLY

truth·ful \'trüth-fəl\ *adj* **:** telling or disposed to tell the truth — **truth·ful·ly** \-fə-lē\ *adv* — **truth·ful·ness** *n*

truth serum *n* **:** a hypnotic or anesthetic held to induce a subject under questioning to talk freely

¹**try** \'trī\ *vb* **tried; try·ing** [ME *trien*, fr. AF *trier*, fr. OF, to pick out, sift] *vt* **1 a :** to examine or investigate judicially **b (1) :** to conduct the trial of **(2) :** to participate as counsel in the judicial examination of **2 a :** to put to test or trial **b :** to test to the limit or breaking point ⟨~ one's patience⟩ **c :** DEMONSTRATE, PROVE **3 a** *obs* **:** PURIFY, REFINE **b :** to melt down and procure in a pure state : RENDER ⟨~ out whale oil from blubber⟩ **4 :** to fit or finish with accuracy **5 :** to make an attempt at — often used with an infinitive ~ *vi* **:** to make an attempt **syn** see AFFLICT, ATTEMPT — **try conclusions :** to test one's skill or strength against opposition

²**try** *n, pl* **tries :** an experimental trial : ATTEMPT

try for point : an attempt made after scoring a touchdown in football to kick a goal so as to score an additional point or to again carry the ball across the opponents' goal line or complete a forward pass in the opponents' end zone so as to score two additional points

try·ing \'trī-iŋ\ *adj* **:** severely straining the powers of endurance — **try·ing·ly** \-iŋ-lē\ *adv*

try·ma \'trī-mə\ *n* [NL, fr. Gk, hole; akin to Gk *tetrainein* to bore — more at THROW] **:** a drupe (as of the hickory) in which the epicarp and mesocarp separate as a fleshy or leathery rind from the hard 2-valved endocarp

try on *vt* **1 :** to put on (a garment) in order to test its fit **2 :** to use or test experimentally — **try-on** \'trī-,ȯn, -,än\ *n*

try·out \'trī-,au̇t\ *n* **:** an experimental performance or demonstration: as **a :** a test of the ability (as of an athlete or actor) to fill a part or meet standards **b :** a performance of a play prior to its official opening to determine response and discover weaknesses

try·pa·no·some \trip-'an-ə-,sōm, 'trip-ə-nə-\ *n* [NL *Trypanosoma*, genus name, fr. Gk *trypanon* auger + NL *-soma* -some — more at TREPAN] **:** any of a genus (*Trypanosoma*) of parasitic flagellate protozoans infesting the blood of various vertebrates including man usu. being transmitted by the bite of an insect, and including some that cause serious disease (as sleeping sickness)

try·pa·no·so·mi·a·sis \trip-,an-ə-sə-'mī-ə-səs, ,trip-ə-nō-\ *n* **:** infection with or disease caused by trypanosomes

tryp·ars·amide \trip-'är-sə-,mīd\ *n* [fr. *Tryparsamide*, a trademark] **:** an organic arsenical $C_8H_{10}AsN_2O_4Na.\frac{1}{2}H_2O$ used in the treatment of African sleeping sickness and syphilis

try-pot \'trī-,pät\ *n* **:** a metallic pot used on a whaler or on shore to render blubber

tryp·sin \'trip-sən\ *n* [Gk *tryein* to wear down + ISV *-psin* (as in *pepsin*); akin to L *terere* to rub — more at THROW] **:** a proteolytic enzyme from pancreatic juice active in an alkaline medium; *also* **:** any of several similar enzymes — **tryp·tic** \'trip-tik\ *adj*

tryp·sin·o·gen \trip-'sin-ə-jən\ *n* [ISV] **:** the inactive precursor of trypsin present in the pancreas

tryp·to·phan \'trip-tə-,fan\ *or* **tryp·to·phane** \-,fān\ *n* [ISV *tryptic* + *-o-* + *-phane*] **:** a crystalline amino acid $C_{11}H_{12}N_2O_2$ obtained esp. from casein and fibrin that is essential to animal life

try·sail \'trī-,sāl, -səl\ *n* [obs. *at try* (lying to)] **:** a fore-and-aft sail bent to a gaff and hoisted on a lower mast or a small mast close abaft

try square *n* **:** an instrument used for laying off right angles and testing whether work is square

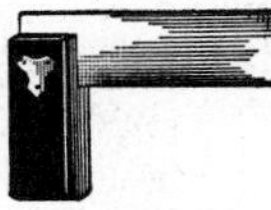

try square

tryst \'trist, 'trīst\ *n* [ME, fr. OF *triste* watch post, prob. of Scand origin; akin to ON *traust* trust] **1 :** an agreement (as between lovers) to meet **2 :** an appointed meeting or meeting place

try·works \'trī-,wərks\ *n pl* **:** a brick furnace in which try-pots are placed; *also* **:** the furnace with the pots

tsa·de \'(t)säd-ə, -ē\ *n* [Heb *ṣādhē*] **:** the 18th letter of the Hebrew alphabet — symbol צ or ץ

tsar \'zär, 'tsär\ *var of* CZAR

tset·se \'(t)set-sē, 'tet-, '(t)sēt-, 'tēt-\ *n, pl* **tsetse** *or* **tsetses** [Afrik, fr. Tswana *tsêtsê*] **:** any of several two-winged flies (genus *Glossina*) that occur in Africa south of the Sahara desert and include vectors of human and animal trypanosomes

Tshi \'chwē, 'twē, 'chē\ *var of* TWI

Tshi·lu·ba \chi-'lü-bə\ *n* **:** one of the major trade languages of Congo esp. in the southern part

T-shirt \'tē-,shərt\ *n* **1 :** a collarless short-sleeved cotton undershirt for men **2 :** a cotton or wool jersey outer shirt of similar design

T square *n* **:** a ruler with a crosspiece or head at one end used in making parallel lines

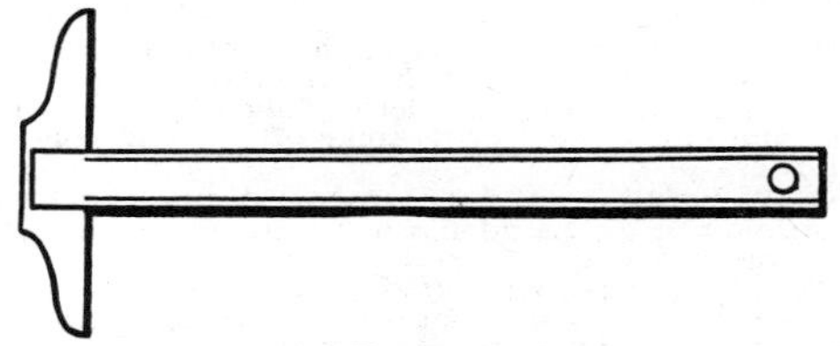

T square

tsu·na·mi \(t)sü-'näm-ē\ *n* [Jap] **:** a great sea wave produced by submarine earth movement or volcanic eruption — **tsu·na·mic** \-ik\ *adj*

tsu·tsu·ga·mu·shi disease \,(t)süt-sə-gə-'mü-shē-\ *n* [Jap *tsutsugamushi* scrub typhus mite, fr. *tsutsuga* sickness + *mushi* insect] **:** an acute febrile rickettsial disease resembling louse-borne typhus that is widespread in the western Pacific area and is transmitted by larval mites — called also *scrub typhus*

Tua·reg \'twä-,reg\ *n, pl* **Tuareg** *or* **Tuaregs** [Ar *Tawāriq*] **:** one of the dominant nomads of the central and western Sahara and along the Middle Niger from Timbuktu to Nigeria who have preserved their Hamitic speech but have adopted the Muslim religion

tu·a·ta·ra \,tü-ə-'tär-ə\ *n* [Maori *tuatàra*] **:** a large spiny quadrupedal reptile (*Sphenodon punctatum*) of islands off the coast of New Zealand that is the only surviving rhynchocephalian

¹**tub** \'təb\ *n* [ME *tubbe*, fr. MD; akin to MLG *tubbe* tub] **1 :** a wide low vessel orig. formed with wooden staves, round bottom, and hoops **2 :** an old or slow boat **3 :** BATHTUB; *also* **:** BATH **4 :** the amount that a tub will hold

²**tub** *vb* **tubbed; tub·bing** *vt* **1 :** to wash or bathe in a tub **2 :** to put or store in a tub ~ *vi* **1 :** BATHE **2 :** to undergo washing — **tub·ba·ble** \'təb-ə-bəl\ *adj* — **tub·ber** *n*

tu·ba \'t(y)ü-bə\ *n* [It, fr. L, trumpet] **1 :** a large low-pitched brass wind instrument; *esp* **:** one with a conical bore and cup-shaped mouthpiece **2 :** a powerful organ reed stop of 8-foot pitch

tub·al \'t(y)ü-bəl\ *adj* **:** of, relating to, or involving a tube and esp. a fallopian tube

tu·bate \'t(y)ü-,bāt\ *adj* **:** having or forming a tube : TUBULAR

tub·by \'təb-ē\ *adj* **:** PUDGY, FAT

tube \'t(y)üb\ *n* [F, fr. L *tubus;* akin to L *tuba* trumpet] **1 a :** a hollow elongated cylinder; *esp* **:** one to convey fluids **b (1) :** a slender channel within a plant or animal body : DUCT **(2) :** the narrow basal portion of a gamopetalous corolla or a gamosepalous calyx **2 :** any of various usu. cylindrical structures or devices: as **a :** a round metal container from which a paste is dispensed by squeezing **b :** TUNNEL **c :** the basically cylindrical part connecting the mouthpiece and bell of a wind instrument **3 :** an airtight tube of rubber placed inside the casing of a pneumatic tire to hold air under pressure **4 :** ELECTRON TUBE **5 :** VACUUM TUBE — **tubed** \'t(y)übd\ *adj* — **tube·like** \'t(y)ü-,blīk\ *adj*

tube foot *n* **:** one of the small flexible tubular processes of most echinoderms that are extensions of the water-vascular system used esp. in locomotion and grasping

tube·less \'t(y)ü-bləs\ *adj* **:** lacking a tube; *specif* **:** being a pneumatic tire that does not depend on an inner tube for airtightness

tu·ber \'t(y)ü-bər\ *n* [L, lump, tuber, truffle; akin to L *tumēre* to swell — more at THUMB] **1 a :** a short fleshy usu. underground stem bearing minute scale leaves each with a bud in its axil potentially able to produce a new plant — compare BULB, CORM **b :** a fleshy root or rhizome resembling a tuber **2 :** an anatomical prominence : TUBEROSITY

tu·ber·cle \'t(y)ü-bər-kəl\ *n* [L *tuberculum*, dim. of *tuber*] **1 :** a small knobby prominence or excrescence esp. on a plant or animal **:** NODULE: as **a :** an eminence near the head of a rib that articulates with the transverse process of a vertebra **b :** any of several prominences in the central nervous system **c :** NODULE b **2 :** a small abnormal discrete lump in the substance of an organ or in the skin; *esp* **:** the specific lesion of tuberculosis

tubercle bacillus *n* **:** a bacterium (*Mycobacterium tuberculosis*) that is the cause of tuberculosis

tu·ber·cled \'t(y)ü-bər-kəld\ *adj* **:** TUBERCULATE

tubercul- *or* **tuberculo-** *comb form* [NL, fr. L *tuberculum*] **1 :** tubercle ⟨*tubercul*ar⟩ **2 :** tubercle bacillus ⟨*tubercul*in⟩ **3 :** tuberculosis ⟨*tubercul*oid⟩

[1]**tu·ber·cu·lar** \t(y)ù-'bər-kyə-lər\ *adj* **1 :** relating to, resembling, or constituting a tubercle **:** TUBERCULATE **2 :** characterized by tubercular lesions ⟨~ leprosy⟩ **3 a :** of, relating to, or affected with tuberculosis **:** TUBERCULOUS **b :** caused by the tubercle bacillus ⟨~ meningitis⟩ — **tu·ber·cu·lar·ly** *adv*

[2]**tubercular** *n* **:** a person with tuberculosis

tu·ber·cu·late \t(y)ù-'bər-kyə-lət\ *or* **tu·ber·cu·lat·ed** \-,lāt-əd\ *adj* **1 :** having a tubercle **:** characterized by or beset with tubercles **2 :** TUBERCULAR — **tu·ber·cu·late·ly** *adv* — **tu·ber·cu·la·tion** \-,bər-kyə-'lā-shən\ *n*

tu·ber·cu·lin \t(y)ù-'bər-kyə-lən\ *n* [ISV] **:** a sterile liquid containing the growth products of or specific substances extracted from the tubercle bacillus and used in the diagnosis of tuberculosis esp. in children and cattle

tuberculin test *n* **:** a test for hypersensitivity to tuberculin as an indication of past or present tubercular infection

tu·ber·cu·loid \-,lȯid\ *adj* [ISV] **:** resembling tuberculosis esp. in the presence of tubercles ⟨~ leprosy⟩

tu·ber·cu·lo·sis \t(y)ù-,bər-kyə-'lō-sis\ *n* [NL] **:** a highly variable communicable disease of man and some other vertebrates caused by the tubercle bacillus and characterized by toxic symptoms or allergic manifestations which in man primarily affect the lungs

tu·ber·cu·lo·tox·in \t(y)ù-'bər-kyə-lō-,täk-sən\ *n* **:** a toxic substance from the tubercle bacillus

tu·ber·cu·lous \t(y)ù-'bər-kyə-ləs\ *adj* **1 :** TUBERCULAR 1, TUBERCULATE **2 a :** constituting or affected with tuberculosis ⟨a ~ process⟩ **b :** caused by or resulting from the presence or products of the tubercle bacillus ⟨~ peritonitis⟩ — **tu·ber·cu·lous·ly** *adv*

tube·rose \'t(y)ü-,brōz (*by folk etymology*), *also* -bə-,rōz, -bə-,rōs\ *n* [NL *tuberosa*, specific epithet, fr. L, fem. of *tuberosus* tuberous, fr. *tuber*] **:** a Mexican bulbous herb (*Polianthes tuberosa*) of the amaryllis family cultivated for its spike of fragrant white single or double flowers

tu·ber·os·i·ty \,t(y)ü-bə-'räs-ət-ē\ *n* **:** an obtuse prominence; *esp* **:** a large prominence on a bone usu. serving for the attachment of muscles or ligaments

tu·ber·ous \'t(y)ü-b(ə-)rəs\ *adj* **1 :** consisting of, bearing, or resembling a tuber **2 :** of, relating to, or being a plant tuber or tuberous root of a plant — **tu·ber·ous·ly** *adv*

tuberous root *n* **:** a thick fleshy storage root like a tuber but lacking buds or scale leaves — **tu·ber·ous–root·ed** \,t(y)ü-b(ə-)rəs-'rüt-əd, -'rút-\ *adj*

tu·bi·fex \'t(y)ü-bə-,feks\ *n, pl* **tubifex** *or* **tu·bi·fex·es** [NL, genus name, fr. L *tubus* tube + *facere* to make — more at DO] **:** any of a genus (*Tubifex*) of slender reddish oligochaete worms living in tubes in fresh or brackish water and being widely used as food for aquarium fish

tub·ing \'t(y)ü-biŋ\ *n* **1 :** material in the form of a tube; *also* **:** a length or piece of tube **2 :** a series or system of tubes

tu·bu·lar \'t(y)ü-byə-lər\ *adj* **1 a :** having the form of or consisting of a tube **:** FISTULOUS **b :** made or provided with tubes **2 :** of, relating to, or sounding as if produced through tubes — **tu·bu·lar·i·ty** \,t(y)ü-byə-'lar-ət-ē\ *n* — **tu·bu·lar·ly** *adv*

tubular floret *n* **:** DISK FLOWER

tu·bule \'t(y)ü-(,)byü(ə)l\ *n* [L *tubulus*, dim. of *tubus*] **:** a small tube; *esp* **:** a slender elongated anatomical channel

tubuli- *comb form* [NL, fr. L *tubulus*] **:** tubule **:** tubular ⟨*tubuli*florous⟩

tu·bu·lif·er·ous \,t(y)ü-byə-'lif-(ə-)rəs\ *adj* [NL *tubulifer*, fr. *tubuli-* + *-fer* -ferous] **:** having or made up of tubules

tu·bu·li·flo·ral \,t(y)ü-byə-lə-'flōr-əl, -'flȯr-\ *adj* [ISV *tubuli-* + L *flor-, flos* flower — more at BLOW] **:** having tubular flowers

tu·bu·li·flo·rous \-'flōr-əs, -'flȯr-\ *adj* [ISV *tubuli-* + L *flor-, flos*] **:** having all the flowers with tubular corollas — used esp. of a composite plant

tu·bu·lous \'t(y)ü-byə-ləs\ *adj* **:** having the form of a tube or containing tubular elements — **tu·bu·lous·ly** *adv*

tu·bu·lure \'t(y)ü-byə-,lù(ə)r\ *n* [F, fr. *tubule*, fr. L *tubulus* tubule] **:** a short tubular opening (as at the top of a retort)

tu·chun \'dü-'jüen\ *n* [Chin (Pek) *tu*[1] *chün*[1]] **1 :** a Chinese military governor (as of a province) **2 :** a Chinese warlord

[1]**tuck** \'tək\ *vb* [ME *tuken* to pull up sharply, scold, fr. OE *tūcian* to ill-treat; akin to OE *togian* to pull — more at TOW] *vt* **1 a :** to pull up into a fold **b :** to make a tuck in **2 :** to put into a snug often concealing or isolating place ⟨cottage ~*ed* away in the hill⟩ **3 a :** to push in the loose end of so as to hold tightly ⟨~ in your shirt⟩ **b :** to cover by tucking in bedclothes **4 :** to put into a tuck position ~ *vi* **1 :** to draw together into tucks or folds **2 :** to fit snugly

[2]**tuck** *n* **1 :** a fold stitched into cloth to shorten, decorate, or control fullness **2 :** the part of a vessel where the ends of the lower planks meet under the stern **3 a :** an act or instance of tucking **b :** something tucked or to be tucked in **4 :** a body position (as in diving) in which the knees are bent, the thighs drawn tightly to the chest, and the hands clasped around the shins

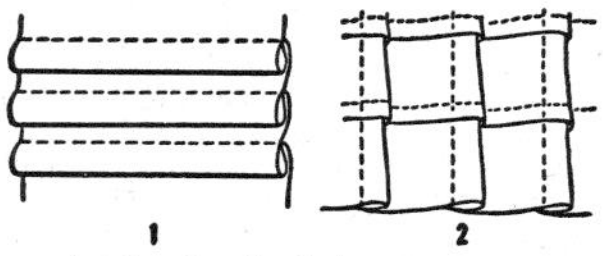

tucks 1: *1* plain, *2* cross

[3]**tuck** *n* [obs. E *tuk* (to beat the drum)] **:** a sound of or as if of a drumbeat

[4]**tuck** *n* [MF *estoc*, fr. OF, tree trunk, sword point, of Gmc origin; akin to OE *stocc* stump of a tree — more at STOCK] *archaic* **:** RAPIER

[5]**tuck** *n* [prob. fr. [2]*tuck*] **:** VIGOR, ENERGY

tuck·a·hoe \'tək-ə-,hō\ *n* [*tockawhoughe* (in some Algonquian language of Virginia)] **1 :** either of two American arums (*Peltandra virginica* and *Orantium aquaticum*) with rootstocks used as food by the Indians **2 :** the large edible sclerotium of a subterranean fungus (*Poria cocos*) — called also *Indian bread*

[1]**tuck·er** \'tək-ər\ *n* **1 :** one that tucks **2 :** a piece of lace or cloth in the neckline of a dress

[2]**tucker** *vt* **tuck·er·ing** \'tək-(ə-)riŋ\ [obs. E *tuck* (to reproach) + *-er* (as in [1]*batter*)] **:** EXHAUST

tuck·er–bag \'tək-ər-,bag\ *n* [Austral slang *tucker* (food, rations)] *chiefly Austral* **:** a bag used esp. by travelers in the bush to hold food

tuck·et \'tək-ət\ *n* [prob. fr. obs. E *tuk* (to beat the drum, sound the trumpet)] **:** a fanfare on a trumpet

tuck–point \-,pȯint\ *vt* **:** to finish (the mortar joints between bricks or stones) with a narrow ridge of putty or fine lime mortar

tuck–shop \-,shäp\ *n* [Brit slang *tuck* (food, confectionery)] *Brit* **:** a confectioner's shop **:** CONFECTIONERY

-tude \,t(y)üd\ *n suffix* [MF or L; MF, fr. L *-tudin-, -tudo*] **:** -NESS ⟨finitude⟩

Tu·dor \'t(y)üd-ər\ *adj* **1 :** of or relating to the English royal family reigning from 1485 to 1603 **2 :** of, relating to, or characteristic of the Tudor period

Tudor arch *n* — see ARCH illustration

Tues·day \'t(y)üz-dē\ *n* [ME *tiwesday*, fr. OE *tīwesdæg;* akin to OHG *zīostag* Tuesday; both fr. a prehistoric WGmc-NGmc compound whose components are represented by OE *Tīw*, god of war and by OE *dæg* day — more at DEITY] **:** the third day of the week — **Tues·days** \-dēz\ *adv*

tu·fa \'t(y)ü-fə\ *n* [It *tufo*, fr. L *tophus*] **1 :** TUFF **2 :** a porous rock formed as a deposit from springs or streams — **tu·fa·ceous** \t(y)ü-'fā-shəs\ *adj*

tuff \'təf\ *n* [MF *tuf*, fr. OIt *tufo* tufa] **:** a rock composed of the finer kinds of volcanic detritus — **tuff·aceous** \,tə-'fā-shəs\ *adj*

tuf·fet \'təf-ət\ *n* [alter. of [1]*tuft*] **1 :** TUFT 1a **2 :** a low seat

[1]**tuft** \'təft\ *n* [ME, modif. of MF *tufe*] **1 a :** a small cluster of elongated flexible outgrowths attached or close together at the base and free at the opposite ends; *esp* **:** a growing bunch of grasses or close-set plants **b :** a bunch of soft fluffy threads cut off short and used as ornament **2 :** CLUMP, CLUSTER **3 :** MOUND — **tufty** \'təf-tē\ *adj*

[2]**tuft** *vt* **1 :** to provide or adorn with a tuft **2 :** to make (as a mattress) firm by stitching at intervals and sewing on tufts ~ *vi* **:** to form into or grow in tufts — **tuft·er** *n*

[1]**tug** \'təg\ *vb* **tugged; tug·ging** [ME *tuggen;* akin to OE *togian* to pull — more at TOW] *vi* **1 :** to pull hard **2 :** to struggle in opposition **:** CONTEND **3 :** to exert oneself laboriously **:** LABOR ~ *vt* **1 :** to pull or strain hard at **2 a :** to move by pulling hard **:** HAUL **b :** to carry with difficulty **:** LUG **3 :** to tow with a tugboat **syn** see PULL — **tug·ger** *n*

[2]**tug** *n* **1 a :** [3]TRACE 1 **b :** a short leather strap or loop **c :** a rope or chain used for pulling **2 a :** an act or instance of tugging **:** PULL **b :** a strong pulling force **3 a :** a straining effort **b :** a struggle between two people or opposite forces **4 :** TUGBOAT

tug·boat \'təg-,bōt\ *n* **:** a strongly built powerful boat used for towing and pushing — called also *towboat*

tug–of–war \,təg-ə(v)-'wȯ(ə)r\ *n, pl* **tugs–of–war** **1 :** a struggle for supremacy **2 :** an athletic contest in which two teams pull against each other at opposite ends of a rope

tui \'tü-ē\ *n* [Maori] **:** a predominantly glossy black New Zealand honey eater (*Prosthemadera novaeseelandiae*) with white markings on throat, neck, and wings that is a notable mimic and often kept as a cage bird — called also *parson bird*

tuille \'twē(ə)l\ *n* [ME *toile*, fr. MF *tuille* tile, fr. L *tegula* — more at TILE] **:** one of the hinged plates before the thigh in plate armor

tu·ition \t(y)ù-'ish-ən\ *n* [ME *tuicioun* protection, fr. OF *tuicion*, fr. L *tuition-, tuitio*, fr. *tuitus*, pp. of *tueri* to look at] **1** *archaic* **:** CUSTODY, GUARDIANSHIP **2 :** the act or profession of teaching **:** INSTRUCTION **3 :** the price of or payment for instruction — **tu·ition·al** \-'ish-nəl, -ən-ᵊl\ *adj*

tu·la·re·mia \,t(y)ü-lə-'rē-mē-ə\ *n* [NL, fr. *Tulare* county, Calif.] **:** an infectious disease of rodents, man, and some domestic animals caused by a bacterium (*Pasteurella tularensis*), transmitted esp. by the bites of insects, and in man marked by symptoms (as fever) of toxemia — **tu·la·re·mic** \-mik\ *adj*

tu·le \'tü-lē\ *n* [Sp, fr. Nahuatl *tullin*] **:** either of two large bulrushes (*Scirpus lacustris* and *S. acutus*) growing on overflowed land in the southwestern U.S.

tu·lip \'t(y)ü-ləp\ *n* [NL *Tulipa*, fr. Turk *tülbend* turban] **:** any of a genus (*Tulipa*) of Eurasian bulbous herbs of the lily family with linear or broadly lanceolate leaves widely grown for their showy flowers; *also* **:** the flower or bulb of a tulip

tulip tree *n* **:** a tall No. American timber tree (*Liriodendron tulipifera*) of the magnolia family having large greenish yellow tulip-shaped flowers and soft white wood used esp. for cabinetwork and woodenware; *also* **:** any of various trees with tulip-shaped flowers

tu·lip·wood \-,wu̇d\ *n* **1 :** wood of the No. American tulip tree **:** WHITEWOOD **2 :** any of several showily striped or variegated woods; *also* **:** a tree yielding such wood

tulle \'tül\ *n* [F, fr. *Tulle*, France] **:** a sheer often stiffened silk, rayon, or nylon net used chiefly for veils, evening dresses, or ballet costumes

tul·li·bee \'təl-ə-,bē\ *n* [CanF *toulibi*] **:** any of several whitefishes of central and northern No. America; *esp* **:** a common cisco (*Leucichthys artedi*) that is a commercially important food fish

[1]**tum·ble** \'təm-bəl\ *vb* **tum·bling** \-b(ə-)liŋ\ [ME *tumblen*, freq. of *tumben* to dance, fr. OE *tumbian;* akin to OHG *tūmōn* to reel] *vi* **1 a :** to perform gymnastic feats of rolling and turning **b :** to turn end over end in falling or flight **2 a :** to fall suddenly and helplessly **b :** to suffer a sudden downfall, overthrow, or defeat **c :** to decline suddenly and sharply (as in price) **:** DROP **d :** to fall into ruin **:** COLLAPSE **3 :** to roll over and over or to and fro **:** TOSS **4 :** to issue forth hurriedly and confusedly **5 :** to come by chance **:** STUMBLE **6 :** to come to understand **:** catch on ~ *vt* **1 :** to cause to tumble (as by pushing, tossing, or toppling) **2 a :** to throw together in a confused mass **b :** RUMPLE, DISORDER **3 :** to whirl (objects or material) in a tumbling barrel (as in drying clothes)

[2]**tumble** *n* **1 a :** a random collection **:** HEAP **b :** a disorderly state **2 :** an act or instance of tumbling

tum·ble·bug \'təm-bəl-,bəg\ *n* **:** any of various scarabaeid beetles (esp. genera *Scarabaeus, Canthon, Copris,* or *Phanaeus*) that form

balls of dung which they bury in the ground and in which they lay their eggs

tum·ble·down \ˌtəm-bəl-ˌdau̇n\ *adj* **:** DILAPIDATED, RAMSHACKLE

tum·bler \ˈtəm-blər\ *n* **1 :** one that tumbles: as **a :** one that performs gymnastic feats **:** ACROBAT **b :** any of various domestic pigeons that tumble or somersault backward in flight or on the ground **2 :** a drinking glass without foot or stem and orig. with pointed or convex base **3 a :** a movable obstruction in a lock (as a lever, latch, wheel, slide, or pin) that must be adjusted to a particular position (as by a key) before the bolt can be thrown **b :** a piece on which the mainspring acts in a gunlock **c** (1) **:** a projecting piece on a revolving shaft or rockshaft for actuating another piece (2) **:** the movable part of a reversing or speed-changing gear **4 :** a device or mechanism for tumbling (as a revolving cage in which clothes are dried) **5 :** a worker that operates a tumbler

tum·ble·weed \ˈtəm-bəl-ˌwēd\ *n* **:** a plant that breaks away from its roots in the autumn and is driven about by the wind as a light rolling mass

1**tum·bling** \ˈtəm-b(ə-)liŋ\ *n* **:** the skill, practice, or sport of executing gymnastic tumbles

2**tumbling** *adj* **:** tipped or slanted out of the vertical — used esp. of a cattle brand

tumbling barrel *n* **:** a revolving cask in which objects or materials undergo a process (as polishing, coating, or drying) by being whirled about

tumbling verse *n* **:** an early modern English type of verse having four stresses but no prevailing type of foot and no regular number of syllables

tum·brel *or* **tum·bril** \ˈtəm-brəl\ *n* [ME *tombrel*, fr. OF *tumberel* tipcart, fr. *tomber* to tumble, of Gmc origin; akin to OHG *tūmōn* to reel — more at TUMBLE] **1 :** a farm tipcart **2 :** a vehicle carrying condemned persons (as political prisoners during the French Revolution) to a place of execution

tu·me·fac·tion \ˌt(y)ü-mə-ˈfak-shən, ˈt(y)ü-mə-ˌ\ *n* [MF, fr. L *tumefactus*, pp. of *tumefacere* to cause to swell, fr. *tumēre* to swell + *facere* to make, do — more at THUMB, DO] **:** an action or process of swelling or becoming tumorous or the resultant state or lesion — **tu·me·fac·tive** \-tiv\ *adj* — **tu·me·fied** \ˈt(y)ü-mə-ˌfīd\ *adj*

tu·mes·cence \t(y)ü-ˈmes-ᵊn(t)s\ *n* **:** the quality or state of being tumescent; *esp* **:** readiness for sexual activity marked esp. by vascular congestion of the sex organs

tu·mes·cent \-ᵊnt\ *adj* [L *tumescent-, tumescens*, prp. of *tumescere* to swell up, fr. *tumēre* to swell] **:** somewhat swollen ⟨~ tissue⟩

tu·mid \ˈt(y)ü-məd\ *adj* [L *tumidus*, fr. *tumēre*] **1 :** marked by swelling **:** SWOLLEN, ENLARGED **2 :** BULGING, PROTUBERANT **3 :** BOMBASTIC, TURGID **syn** see INFLATED — **tu·mid·i·ty** \t(y)ü-ˈmid-ət-ē\ *n* — **tu·mid·ly** \ˈt(y)ü-məd-lē\ *adv*

tum·my \ˈtəm-ē\ *n* [baby-talk for *stomach*] **:** STOMACH 1c

tu·mor *or chiefly Brit* **tu·mour** \ˈt(y)ü-mər\ *n* [L *tumor*, fr. *tumēre*] **1 :** a swollen or distended part **2 :** an abnormal mass of tissue that is not inflammatory, arises without obvious cause from cells of preexistent tissue, and possesses no physiologic function — **tu·mor·like** \-ˌlīk\ *adj* — **tu·mor·ous** \ˈt(y)üm-(ə-)rəs\ *adj*

tump \ˈtəmp\ *n* [origin unknown] **1** *chiefly dial Eng* **:** MOUND, HUMMOCK **2 :** a clump of vegetation

tump·line \ˈtəm-ˌplīn\ *n* [*tump*, of Algonquian origin; akin to Abnaki *mádûmbî* pack strap] **:** a sling formed by a strap slung over the forehead or chest used for carrying a pack on the back or in hauling loads

tu·mult \ˈt(y)ü-ˌməlt\ *n* [ME *tumulte*, fr. MF, fr. L *tumultus*; akin to Skt *tumula* noisy, L *tumēre*] **1 a :** disorderly agitation or milling about of a crowd usu. with uproar and confusion of voices **:** COMMOTION **b :** a turbulent uprising **:** RIOT **2 :** HUBBUB, DIN **3 a :** violent agitation of mind or feelings **b :** a violent outburst

tu·mul·tu·ary \t(y)u̇-ˈməl-chə-ˌwer-ē\ *adj* **:** attended or marked by tumult, riot, lawlessness, confusion, or impetuosity

tu·mul·tu·ous \t(y)u̇-ˈməlch-(ə-)wəs, -ˈməl-chəs\ *adj* **1 :** marked by tumult **2 :** tending or disposed to cause or incite a tumult **3 :** marked by violent or overwhelming turbulence or upheaval — **tu·mul·tu·ous·ly** *adv* — **tu·mul·tu·ous·ness** *n*

tu·mu·lus \ˈt(y)ü-myə-ləs\ *n, pl* **tu·mu·li** \-ˌlī, -ˌlē\ [L; akin to L *tumēre* to swell — more at THUMB] **:** an artificial hillock or mound (as over a grave); *esp* **:** an ancient grave **:** BARROW

tun \ˈtən\ *n* [ME *tunne*, fr. OE] **1 :** a large cask esp. for wine **2 :** any of various units of liquid capacity; *esp* **:** one equal to 252 wine gallons

1**tu·na** \ˈtü-nə\ *n* [Sp, fr. Taino] **1 :** any of various flat-jointed prickly pears (genus *Opuntia*); *esp* **:** one (*O. tuna*) common in tropical America **2 :** the edible fruit of a tuna

2**tu·na** \ˈt(y)ü-nə\ *n, pl* **tuna** *or* **tunas** [Amer Sp, alter. of Sp *atún*, modif. of Ar *tūn*, fr. L *thunnus*, fr. Gk *thynnos*] **1 a :** any of numerous large vigorous scombroid fishes including forms highly esteemed for sport and food; *esp* **:** ALBACORE **b :** any of various related but usu. smaller fishes; *esp* **:** BONITO **2 :** the flesh of a tuna esp. when canned for use as food

tun·able *also* **tune·able** \ˈt(y)ü-nə-bəl\ *adj* **1** *archaic* **a :** TUNEFUL **b :** sounding in tune **:** CONCORDANT **2 :** capable of being tuned — **tun·able·ness** *n* — **tun·ably** \-blē\ *adv*

tun·dra \ˈtən-drə, ˈtün-\ *n* [Russ, of Finno-Ugric origin; akin to Lapp *tundar* hill] **:** a level or undulating treeless plain characteristic of arctic and subarctic regions

1**tune** \ˈt(y)ün\ *n* [ME, alter. of *tone*] **1 a** *archaic* **:** quality of sound **:** TONE **b :** manner of utterance **:** INTONATION; *specif* **:** phonetic modulation **:** general attitude **:** APPROACH **c** *archaic* **:** a frame of mind **:** MOOD **2 a :** an easily remembered melody **b :** a dominant theme **3 a :** correct musical pitch or consonance **b :** harmonious relationship **:** AGREEMENT **4 :** AMOUNT, EXTENT ⟨custom-made to the ~ of $40 or $50 apiece —*Amer. Fabrics*⟩

2**tune** *vi* **1 :** to become attuned **2 :** to adjust a radio or television receiver to respond to waves of a particular frequency ~ *vt* **1 :** to adjust in musical pitch **2 a :** to bring into harmony **:** ATTUNE **b :** to adjust for precise functioning **3 a :** to adjust (a radio or television receiver) to respond to waves of a particular frequency — often used with *in* **b :** to establish radio contact with ⟨~ in a directional beacon⟩

tune·ful \ˈt(y)ün-fəl\ *adj* **:** MELODIOUS, MUSICAL — **tune·ful·ly** \-fə-lē\ *adv* — **tune·ful·ness** *n*

tune·less \-ləs\ *adj* **1 :** not tuneful **2 :** not producing music

tun·er \ˈt(y)ü-nər\ *n* **1 :** one that tunes ⟨piano ~⟩ **2 :** something used for tuning; *specif* **:** the part of a receiving set consisting of the circuit used to adjust resonance

tune–up \ˈt(y)ü-ˌnəp\ *n* **1 :** a general adjustment to insure operation at peak efficiency **2 :** a preliminary trial **:** WARM-UP

tung oil \ˈtəŋ-\ *n* [part trans. of Chin (Pek) *yu2 t'ung2*] **:** a pale yellow pungent drying oil from the seeds of tung trees, and used chiefly in quick-drying varnishes and paints and as a waterproofing agent

tungst- *or* **tungsto-** *comb form* [ISV, fr. *tungsten*] **:** tungsten ⟨*tungst*ate⟩

tung·state \ˈtəŋ(k)-ˌstāt\ *n* **:** a salt or ester of tungstic acid

tung·sten \ˈtəŋ(k)-stən\ *n* [Sw, fr. *tung* heavy + *sten* stone] **:** a gray-white heavy high-melting ductile hard polyvalent metallic element that resembles chromium and molybdenum in many of its properties and is used esp. for electrical purposes and in hardening alloys (as steel) — called also *wolfram;* see ELEMENT table

tung·stic \-stik\ *adj* [ISV] **:** of, relating to, or containing tungsten esp. with a valence of six

tungstic acid *n* **:** a yellow crystalline powder WO_3 that is the trioxide of tungsten; *also* **:** an acid (as H_2WO_4) derived from this

tung·stite \ˈtəŋ(k)-ˌstīt\ *n* **:** a mineral $WO_3.H_2O$(?) consisting of a hydrous tungsten trioxide and occurring in yellow or yellowish green pulverulent masses

tung tree \ˈtəŋ-\ *n* [Chin (Pek) *t'ung2*] **:** any of several trees (genus *Aleurites*) of the spurge family whose seeds yield a poisonous fixed drying oil; *esp* **:** a Chinese tree (*A. fordii*) widely grown in warm regions

Tun·gus \tu̇ŋ-ˈgüz, tən-\ *n, pl* **Tungus** *or* **Tun·gus·es** [Russ, one of the Tungus] **1 a :** a Mongoloid people widely spread over eastern Siberia **b :** a member of this people **2 :** the Tungusic languages of the Tungus peoples

Tun·gu·sic \-ˈgü-zik\ *n* **:** a subfamily of Altaic languages spoken in Manchuria and northward — **Tungusic** *adj*

tu·nic \ˈt(y)ü-nik\ *n* [L *tunica*, of Sem origin; akin to Heb *kuttōneth* coat] **1 a :** a simple slip-on garment made with or without sleeves and usu. knee-length or longer, belted at the waist, and worn as an under or outer garment by men and women of ancient Greece and Rome **b :** SURCOAT **2 :** a natural integument ⟨the ~ of a seed⟩ **3 :** a long usu. plain close-fitting jacket with high collar worn esp. as part of a uniform **4 :** TUNICLE **5 a :** a short overskirt **b :** a hip-length or longer blouse or jacket

tu·ni·ca \ˈt(y)ü-ni-kə\ *n, pl* **tu·ni·cae** \-nə-ˌkē, -ˌkī, -ˌsē\ [L, tunic, membrane] **:** an enveloping membrane or layer of body tissue

1**tu·ni·cate** \ˈt(y)ü-ni-kət, -nə-ˌkāt\ *also* **tu·ni·cat·ed** \-nə-ˌkāt-əd\ *adj* **1 a :** having or covered with a tunic or tunica **b :** having, arranged in, or made up of concentric layers ⟨a ~ bulb⟩ **2 :** of or relating to the tunicates

2**tunicate** *n* [deriv. of L *tunica* membrane] **:** any of a subphylum (Tunicata) of lowly marine chordates with a reduced nervous system and an outer cuticular covering

tu·ni·cle \ˈt(y)ü-ni-kəl\ *n* [ME, fr. L *tunicula*, dim. of *tunica*] **:** a short vestment worn by a subdeacon over the alb during mass and by a bishop under the dalmatic at pontifical ceremonies

tuning fork *n* **:** a 2-pronged metal implement that gives a fixed tone when struck and is useful for tuning musical instruments and ascertaining standard pitch

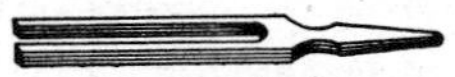
tuning fork

tuning pipe *n* **:** PITCH PIPE; *specif* **:** one of a set of pitch pipes used esp. for tuning stringed musical instruments

1**tun·nel** \ˈtən-ᵊl\ *n* [ME *tonel* tube-shaped net, fr. MF, tun, fr. OF, fr. *tonne* tun, fr. ML *tunna*, of Celt origin; akin to MIr *tonn* skin, hide; akin to L *tondēre* to shear — more at TOME] **1 :** a hollow conduit or recess **:** TUBE, WELL **2 a :** a covered passageway; *specif* **:** a horizontal passageway through or under an obstruction **b :** a subterranean gallery (as in a mine) **c :** BURROW — **tun·nel·like** \-ᵊl-ˌ(l)īk\ *adj*

2**tunnel** *vb* **tun·neled** *or* **tun·nelled; tun·nel·ing** *or* **tun·nel·ling** \ˈtən-liŋ, -ᵊl-iŋ\ *vt* **:** to make a tunnel or similar opening through or under ~ *vi* **:** to make or use a tunnel — **tun·nel·er** \ˈtən-lər, -ᵊl-ər\ *n*

tun·ny \ˈtən-ē\ *n, pl* **tunnies** *also* **tunny** [modif. of MF *thon* or OIt *tonno*; both fr. OProv *ton*, fr. L *thunnus*, fr. Gk *thynnos*] **:** TUNA; *esp* **:** BLUEFIN

1**tup** \ˈtəp\ *n* [ME *tupe*] **1** *chiefly Brit* **:** RAM 1 **2 :** a heavy metal body (as the weight of a pendulum)

2**tup** *vt* **tupped; tup·ping** *chiefly Brit* **:** to copulate with (a ewe) **:** COVER

tu·pe·lo \ˈt(y)ü-pə-ˌlō\ *n* [Creek *ito opilwa* swamp tree] **:** any of a genus (*Nyssa*) of mostly No. American trees having simple styles and 1-locular ovaries; *also* **:** the pale soft easily worked wood

Tu·pi \tü-ˈpē, ˈtü-ˌ\ *n, pl* **Tupi** *or* **Tupis** **1 a :** a group of Tupi-Guaranian peoples of Brazil living esp. in the Amazon valley **b :** a member of any of these peoples **2 :** the language of the Tupi people

Tu·pi·an \tü-ˈpē-ən, ˈtü-pē-\ *adj* **:** of, relating to, or constituting the Tupi or other Tupi-Guaranian peoples or their languages

Tu·pi–Gua·ra·ni \tü-ˌpē-ˌgwär-ə-ˈnē, ˈtü-ˌpē-\ *n* **1 a :** a So. American people spread over an area from eastern Brazil to the Peruvian Andes and from the Guianas to Uruguay **b :** a member of this people **2 :** TUPI-GUARANIAN

Tupi–Gua·ra·ni·an \-ˈnē-ən\ *n* **:** a language stock widely distributed in tropical So. America

tup·pence *var of* TWOPENCE

tuque \ˈt(y)ük\ *n* [CanF, fr. F *toque* — more at TOQUE] **:** a warm knitted stocking cap; *esp* **:** a close-fitting pointed cap made by folding one of the closed ends of a tapered tubular knitted piece up into the other

tu quo·que \ˈt(y)ü-ˈk(w)ō-kwē\ *n* [L, you also] **:** a retort charging an adversary with being or doing what he criticizes in others

Tu·ra·ni·an \t(y)u̇-ˈrā-nē-ən\ *n* [Per *Tūrān* Turkestan, the region north of the Amu Darya] **1 :** a member of any of the peoples of Ural-Altaic stock **2 :** the total body of various language families of Asia — **Turanian** *adj*

ə abut; ᵊ kitten; ər further; a back; ā bake; ä cot, cart; au̇ out; ch chin; e less; ē easy; g gift; i trip; ī life
j joke; ŋ sing; ō flow; ȯ flaw; ȯi coin; th thin; t͟h this; ü loot; u̇ foot; y yet; yü few; yu̇ furious; zh vision

tur·ban \'tər-bən\ *n* [MF *turbant*, fr. It *turbante*, fr. Turk *tülbend*, fr. Per *dulband*] **1 :** a headdress worn chiefly in countries of the eastern Mediterranean and southern Asia esp. by Muslims and made of a cap around which is wound a long cloth **2 :** a headdress resembling a Muslim turban; *specif* **:** a woman's close-fitting hat without a brim — **tur·baned** *or* **tur·banned** \-bənd\ *adj*

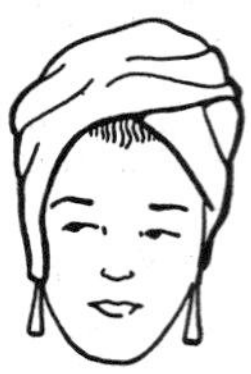
turban 2

tur·ba·ry \'tər-bə-rē\ *n* [ME, fr. ML *turbaria*, fr. *turba* turf, peat, of Gmc origin; akin to OE *turf*] **:** the ground where turf or peat may be dug **:** a peat bog

tur·bel·lar·i·an \,tər-bə-'ler-ē-ən, -'lar-\ *n* [deriv. of L *turbellae* (pl.) bustle, stir, dim. of *turba* confusion, crowd; fr. the tiny eddies created in water by the cilia] **:** any of a class (Turbellaria) of mostly aquatic and free-living flatworms; *esp* **:** PLANARIAN — **turbellarian** *adj*

tur·bid \'tər-bəd\ *adj* [L *turbidus* confused, turbid, fr. *turba* confusion, crowd; akin to OHG *dweran* to stir, L *turbare* to throw into disorder, disturb, Gk *tyrbē* confusion] **1 a :** thick or opaque with roiled sediment ⟨~ stream⟩ **b :** heavy with smoke or mist **:** DENSE **2 :** CONFUSED, MUDDLED ⟨~ thought⟩ — **tur·bid·i·ty** \,tər-'bid-ət-ē\ *n* — **tur·bid·ly** \'tər-bəd-lē\ *adv* — **tur·bid·ness** *n*

syn TURBID, MUDDY, ROILY mean clouded with stirred-up sediment. TURBID implies disturbance of sediment causing a darkening, obscuring, or confusing of what was or should be clear; MUDDY suggests the presence of mud or impurities causing discoloring, obscuring, or contamination; ROILY implies both turbidness and continuing agitation

tur·bi·dim·e·ter \,tər-bə-'dim-ət-ər\ *n* [ISV *turbidity* + *-meter*] **1 :** an instrument for measuring and comparing the turbidity of liquids by viewing light through them and determining how much light is cut off **2 :** NEPHELOMETER — **tur·bi·di·met·ric** \,tər-bəd-ə-'me-trik, ,tər-,bid-ə-\ *adj* — **tur·bi·di·met·ri·cal·ly** \-tri-k(ə-)lē\ *adv* — **tur·bi·dim·e·try** \,tər-bə-'dim-ə-trē\ *n*

[1]**tur·bi·nal** \'tər-bən-ᵊl\ *adj* [L *turbin-*, *turbo* top, whirlwind, whirl] **:** of, relating to, or being one of usu. several thin plicated membrane-covered bony or cartilaginous plates on the walls of the nasal chambers

[2]**turbinal** *n* **:** a turbinal bone or cartilage

tur·bi·nate \-bə-nət, -,nāt\ *adj* [L *turbinatus* shaped like a top, fr. *turbin-*, *turbo*] **1 :** spiral with whorls decreasing rapidly from base to apex ⟨~ gastropod shell⟩ **2 :** shaped like a top or an inverted cone ⟨~ seed capsule⟩ **3 :** TURBINAL — **tur·bi·nat·ed** \-,nāt-əd\ *adj*

tur·bine \'tər-bən, -,bīn\ *n* [F, fr. L *turbin-*, *turbo* top, whirlwind, whirl; akin to L *turbare* to disturb] **:** a rotary engine actuated by the reaction or impulse or both of a current of fluid (as water or steam) subject to pressure and usu. made with a series of curved vanes on a central rotating spindle

tur·bit \'tər-bət\ *n* [origin unknown] **:** a pigeon of a fancy breed having a short crested head, short beak, frilled breast, and mostly white plumage

tur·bo \'tər-(,)bō\ *n* [*turbo-*] **1 :** TURBINE **2** [by shortening] **:** TURBOSUPERCHARGER

turbo- *comb form* [*turbine*] **1 :** coupled directly to a driving turbine ⟨*turbo*fan⟩ **2 :** consisting of or incorporating a turbine ⟨*turbo*jet engine⟩

tur·bo·car \'tər-bō-,kär\ *n* **:** an automotive vehicle propelled by a gas turbine

tur·bo·charg·er \-(,)bō-,chär-jər\ *n* **:** a centrifugal blower driven by exhaust gas turbines and used to supercharge an engine

tur·bo·fan \-bō-,fan\ *n* **1 :** a fan that is directly connected to and driven by a turbine and is used to supply air for cooling, ventilation, or combustion **2 :** a jet engine having a turbofan

tur·bo·jet \-,jet\ *n* **:** an airplane powered by turbojet engines

turbojet engine *n* **:** an airplane propulsion system in which the power developed by a turbine is used to drive a compressor that supplies air to a burner and hot gases from the burner pass through the turbine and thence to a rearward-directed thrust-producing exhaust nozzle

tur·bo·prop \'tər-bō-,präp\ *n* **1 :** TURBO-PROPELLER ENGINE **2 :** an airplane powered by turbo-propeller engines

tur·bo–pro·pel·ler engine \,tər-(,)bō-prə-'pel-ər-\ *n* **:** a jet engine having a turbine-driven propeller and designed to produce thrust principally by means of a propeller although additional thrust is usu. obtained from the hot exhaust gases which issue in a jet

tur·bo·prop–jet engine \,tər-bō-'präp-,jet-\ *n* **:** TURBO-PROPELLER ENGINE

tur·bo·ram·jet engine \-'ram-,jet-\ *n* **:** a jet engine consisting essentially of a turbojet engine with provisions for burning additional fuel in the tail pipe or the portion of the engine to the rear of the turbine and thus making it possible to obtain higher gas temperatures in the exhaust jet than can be tolerated by the turbine blades

tur·bo·su·per·charged \,tər-(,)bō-'sü-pər-,chärjd\ *adj* **:** equipped with a turbosupercharger

tur·bo·su·per·charg·er \-,chär-jər\ *n* **:** a turbine compressor driven by hot exhaust gases of an airplane engine for feeding rarefied air at high altitudes into the carburetor of the engine at sea-level pressure so as to increase engine power

tur·bot \'tər-bət\ *n, pl* **turbot** *also* **turbots** [ME, fr. OF *tourbot*] **:** a large brownish European flatfish (*Psetta maxima*) highly esteemed as a food fish; *also* **:** any of various other flatfishes resembling this fish

tur·bu·la·tor \'tər-byə-,lāt-ər\ *n* **:** a device for causing turbulence of fluids

tur·bu·lence \'tər-byə-lən(t)s\ *n* **:** the quality or state of being turbulent: as **a :** wild commotion **b :** irregular atmospheric motion esp. when characterized by up and down currents **c :** departure in a fluid from a smooth flow

tur·bu·len·cy \-lən-sē\ *n, archaic* **:** TURBULENCE

tur·bu·lent \-lənt\ *adj* [L *turbulentus*, fr. *turba* confusion, crowd] **1 :** causing unrest, violence, or disturbance **2 :** characterized by agitation or tumult **:** TEMPESTUOUS — **tur·bu·lent·ly** *adv*

turbulent flow *n* **:** a fluid flow in which the velocity at a given point varies erratically in magnitude and direction

Tur·co- *or* **Tur·ko-** \'tər-(,)kō\ *comb form* [*Turco-* fr. ML *Turcus* Turk; *Turko-* fr. *Turk*] **1 :** Turkic **:** Turkish **:** Turk ⟨*Turco*phil⟩ **2 :** Turkish and ⟨*Turco*-Greek⟩

tu·reen \tə-'rēn, tyu̇-\ *n* [F *terrine*, fr. MF, fr. fem. of *terrin* of earth, fr. (assumed) VL *terrinus*, fr. L *terra* earth — more at TERRACE] **1 :** a deep bowl from which foods (as soup) are served at table **2 :** CASSEROLE 2

[1]**turf** \'tərf\ *n, pl* **turfs** \'tərfs\ *or* **turves** \'tərvz\ *often attrib* [ME, fr. OE; akin to OHG *zurba* turf, Skt *darbha* tuft of grass] **1 :** the upper stratum of soil bound by grass and plant roots into a thick mat; *also* **:** a piece of this **:** SOD **2 a :** PEAT **b :** a piece of peat dried for fuel **3 a :** a track or course for horse racing **b :** the sport or business of horse racing — **turfy** \'tər-fē\ *adj*

[2]**turf** *vt* **:** to cover with turf

turf·man \-mən\ *n* **:** a devotee of horse racing; *esp* **:** one who owns and races horses

tur·ges·cence \,tər-'jes-ᵊn(t)s\ *n* **:** the quality or state of being turgescent or pompous

tur·ges·cent \-ᵊnt\ *adj* [L *turgescent-*, *turgescens*, prp. of *turgescere* to swell, inchoative of *turgēre* to be swollen] **:** becoming turgid, distended, or inflated **:** SWELLING

tur·gid \'tər-jəd\ *adj* [L *turgidus*, fr. *turgēre* to be swollen] **1 :** being in a state of distension **:** SWOLLEN, TUMID ⟨~ limbs⟩; *esp* **:** exhibiting turgor **2 :** excessively embellished in style or language **:** BOMBASTIC, POMPOUS **syn** see INFLATED — **tur·gid·i·ty** \,tər-'jid-ət-ē\ *n* — **tur·gid·ly** \'tər-jəd-lē\ *adv* — **tur·gid·ness** *n*

tur·gor \'tər-gər, -,gȯ(ə)r\ *n* [LL, turgidity, swelling, fr. L *turgēre*] **:** the normal state of turgidity and tension in living cells; *esp* **:** the distension of the protoplasmic layer and wall of a plant cell by the fluid contents

Turk \'tərk\ *n* [ME, fr. MF or Turk; MF *Turc*, fr. ML or Turk; ML *Turcus*, fr. Turk *Türk*] **1 :** a member of any of numerous Asian peoples speaking Turkic languages who live in the region ranging from the Adriatic to the Okhotsk **2 :** a native or inhabitant of Turkey **3** *archaic* **:** one who is cruel or tyrannical **4 :** MUSLIM; *specif* **:** a Muslim subject of the Turkish sultan **5 :** a Turkish horse; *specif* **:** a Turkish strain of Arab and crossbred horses

tur·key \'tər-kē\ *n* [*Turkey*, country in western Asia and southeastern Europe; fr. confusion with the guinea fowl, supposed to be imported from Turkish territory] **1 :** either of two large American gallinaceous birds (*Meleagris gallopavo* and *Agriocharis ocellata*) of which the first is of wide range in No. America and is domesticated in most parts of the world **2 :** FAILURE, FLOP

turkey buzzard *n* **:** an American vulture (*Cathartes aura*) common in So. and Central America and in the southern U.S.

tur·key–cock \'tər-kē-,käk\ *n* **:** a male turkey — called also *turkey-gob·bler* \,tər-kē-'gäb-lər\

Tur·key red \,tər-kē-\ *n* [*Turkey*] **:** a brilliant durable red produced on cotton by means of alizarin in connection with an aluminum mordant and fatty matter

turkey shoot \'tər-kē-\ *n* **:** a contest of marksmanship with a gun at a moving target and with a turkey for a prize

turkey trot \'tər-kē-\ *n* [*turkey*] **:** a ragtime dance danced with the feet well apart and with a rise on the ball of the foot followed by a drop upon the heel

Tur·ki \'tər-,kē, 'tu̇(ə)r-\ *adj* [Per *turkī*, fr. *Turk* Turk, fr. Turk *Türk*] **1 :** of or relating to the peoples of Turkic speech **2 :** of or relating to any central Asian Turkic language particularly of the eastern group — **Turki** *n*

Turk·ic \'tər-kik\ *adj* **1 a :** of, relating to, or constituting a subfamily of Altaic languages including Turkish **b :** of or relating to the peoples speaking Turkic **2 :** TURKISH 1 — **Turkic** *n*

[1]**Turk·ish** \'tər-kish\ *adj* **1 :** of, relating to, or characteristic of Turkey, the Turks, or Turkish **2 :** TURKIC 1a

[2]**Turkish** *n* **:** the Turkic language of the Republic of Turkey

Turkish bath *n* **:** a bath in which the bather passes through a series of steam rooms of increasing temperature and then receives a rubdown, massage, and cold shower

Turkish coffee *n* **:** a sweetened decoction of pulverized coffee

Turkish delight *n* **:** a jellylike or gummy confection usu. cut in cubes and dusted with sugar — called also *Turkish paste*

Turkish tobacco *n* **:** a very aromatic tobacco of small leaf size grown chiefly in Turkey and Greece and adjoining territories and used esp. in cigarettes

Turkish towel *n* **:** a towel made of cotton terry cloth

Turk·ism \'tər-,kiz-əm\ *n* **:** the customs, beliefs, institutions, and principles of the Turks

Tur·ko·man *or* **Tur·co·man** \'tər-kə-mən\ *n, pl* **Turkomans** *or* **Turcomans** [ML *Turcomannus*, fr. Per *Turkmān*, fr. *turkmān* resembling a Turk, fr. *Turk*] **:** a member of a group of peoples of East Turkic stock living chiefly in the Turkmen, Uzbek, and Kazakh republics of the U.S.S.R.

Turk's head *n* **:** a turban-shaped knot worked on a rope with a piece of small line

tur·mer·ic \'tərm-(ə-)rik, 'tüm-\ *n* [modif. of MF *terre merite* saffron, fr. ML *terra merita*, lit., deserving or deserved earth] **1 :** an East Indian herb (*Curcuma longa*) of the ginger family; *also* **:** its aromatic rootstock powdered for use as a condiment, yellow dye, or stimulant **2 :** any of several plants resembling turmeric: as **a :** BLOODROOT **b :** GOLDENSEAL

tur·moil \'tər-,mȯil\ *n* [origin unknown] **:** an utterly confused or extremely agitated state or condition

[1]**turn** \'tərn\ *vb* [ME *turnen;* partly fr. OE *tyrnan* & *turnian* to turn, fr. ML *tornare*, fr. L, to turn on a lathe, fr. *tornus* lathe, fr. Gk *tornos;* partly fr. OF *torner*, *tourner* to turn, fr. ML *tornare;* akin to L *terere* to rub — more at THROW] *vt* **1 a :** to cause to move around an axis or a center **:** make rotate or revolve ⟨~ a wheel⟩ ⟨~ a crank⟩ **b** (1) **:** to cause to move around so as to effect a desired end (as of locking, opening, or shutting) ⟨~ a key⟩ (2) **:** to affect or alter the functioning of (as a mechanical device) by such movement ⟨~*ed* the lamp down⟩ **c :** to execute or perform by rotating or revolving ⟨~ handsprings⟩ **d :** to twist out of line or shape **:** WRENCH ⟨~*ing* his ankle painfully⟩ **2 a** (1) **:** to cause to change position by moving through an arc of a circle ⟨~*ed* his chair to the fire⟩ (2) **:** to cause to move around a center so as to show another side of ⟨~ a page of a book⟩ (3) **:** to cause (as a scale) to move so as to register weight (4) **:** to cause to move or stir in any way ⟨~ a finger to help⟩ **b :** to revolve mentally **:** think over **:** PONDER **3 a :** to reverse the sides or surfaces of **:** INVERT ⟨~ pancakes⟩: (1) **:** to dig or plow so as to bring the lower soil to the surface (2) **:** to make (as a garment) over by reversing the material and resewing ⟨~ a collar⟩ (3) **:** to invert feet up and face down (as a character, rule, or slug) in setting type **b :** to reverse or upset the order or disposition of ⟨everything ~*ed* topsy-turvy⟩ **c :** to disturb or upset the mental balance of

: DERANGE, UNSETTLE ⟨a mind ~*ed* by grief⟩ ⟨success had not ~*ed* his head⟩ **d :** to cause (the stomach) to revolt **e :** to set in another esp. contrary direction **4 a :** to bend or change the course of **:** DIVERT **b :** to cause to retreat ⟨used fire hoses to ~ the mob⟩ **c :** to alter the drift, tendency, or expected result of **d :** to bend a course around or about **:** ROUND ⟨~*ed* the corner at full speed⟩ **e :** to pass or go beyond (as an amount, age, or time) ⟨clock had just ~*ed* ten⟩ **5 a** (1) **:** to direct or point (as the face) in a specified way or direction (2) **:** to present by a change in direction or position ⟨~*ing* his back to his guests⟩ **b :** to bring to bear (as by aiming, pointing, or focusing) **:** TRAIN ⟨~*ed* his light into the dark doorway⟩ **c :** to direct (as the attention or mind) toward or away from something **d :** to induce or influence (a person) to change his way of life **e :** to direct the employment of **:** APPLY, DEVOTE **f** (1) **:** to cause to rebound or recoil ⟨~*s* their argument against them⟩ (2) **:** to make antagonistic **:** PREJUDICE ⟨~ a child against its mother⟩ **g** (1) **:** to cause to go in a particular direction ⟨~*ed* his steps homeward⟩ (2) **:** DRIVE, SEND ⟨~ cows to pasture⟩ ⟨officers were ~*ed* adrift by the mutineers⟩ ⟨~*ing* hunters off his land⟩ (3) **:** to convey or direct into or out of a receptacle by inverting **6 a** (1) **:** to make acid or sour **:** CURDLE, FERMENT (2) **:** to change the color of (as foliage) **b** (1) **:** CONVERT, TRANSFORM ⟨~ defeat into victory⟩ (2) **:** TRANSLATE, PARAPHRASE **c :** to cause to become of a specified nature or appearance ⟨~*ed* him into a fiend⟩ ⟨illness ~*ed* his hair white⟩ **d :** to exchange for something else ⟨~ coins into paper money⟩ **7 a :** to shape esp. in a rounded form by applying a cutting tool while revolving in a lathe **b :** to give a rounded form to by any means ⟨~ the heel of a sock⟩ **c :** to shape or mold artistically, gracefully, or neatly ⟨well ~*ed* ankles⟩ ⟨a knack for ~*ing* a phrase⟩ **8 :** to make a fold, bend, or curve in: **a :** to form by bending ⟨~ a lead pipe⟩ **b :** to cause (the edge of a blade) to bend back or over **:** BLUNT, DULL **9 a :** to keep (as money or goods) moving; *specif* **:** to dispose of (a stock) to make room for another **b :** to gain by passing in trade ⟨~*ing* a quick profit⟩ **~** *vi* **1 a :** to move around on an axis or through an arc of a circle **:** ROTATE **b :** to become giddy or dizzy **:** REEL ⟨heights always made his head ~⟩ **c** (1) **:** HINGE (2) **:** to have a center (as of interest) in something specified **2 a :** to direct one's course **b** (1) **:** to reverse a course or direction (2) **:** to have a reactive usu. adverse effect **:** RECOIL **c :** to take a different course or direction ⟨~*ed* toward home⟩ ⟨main road ~*s* sharp right⟩ **3 a :** to change position so as to face another way **b :** to face toward or away from someone or something **c :** to change one's attitude or reverse one's course of action to one of opposition or hostility ⟨felt the world had ~*ed* against him⟩ ⟨~*ed* upon them with ferocity⟩ **d :** to make a sudden violent assault esp. without evident cause ⟨dogs ~*ing* on their owners⟩ **4 a :** to direct one's attention or thoughts to or away from someone or something **b** (1) **:** to change one's religion (2) **:** to go over to another side or party **:** DEFECT **c :** to betake oneself (as for information, help, or support) **:** have recourse **:** REFER, RESORT **d :** to direct one's efforts or interests **:** devote or apply oneself ⟨~*ed* to the study of the law⟩ **5 a :** to become changed, altered, or transformed: as (1) *archaic* **:** to become different (2) **:** to change color ⟨the leaves have ~*ed*⟩ (3) **:** to become sour, rancid, or tainted ⟨the milk had ~*ed*⟩ (4) **:** to be variable or inconstant (5) **:** to become mentally unbalanced **:** become deranged **b** (1) **:** to pass from one state to another **:** CHANGE ⟨water had ~*ed* to ice⟩ (2) **:** GROW ⟨hair had ~*ed* gray⟩ ⟨weather ~*ed* bad⟩ (3) **:** to become someone or something specified by change from another state **:** change into ⟨~ traitor⟩ ⟨doctors ~*ed* authors⟩ **6 :** to become curved or bent (as from pressure); *esp* **:** to become blunted by bending ⟨edge of the knife had ~*ed*⟩ **7 :** to operate a lathe **8** *of merchandise* **:** to be stocked and disposed of **:** change hands **syn** see CURVE — **turn a hair :** to give a sign of discomposure or disturbance — used in negative constructions ⟨never *turned a hair*⟩ — **turn color 1 :** to become of a different color **2 a :** BLUSH, FLUSH **b :** to grow pale — **turn loose 1 a :** to set free **b :** to free from all restraints **2 :** to fire off **:** DISCHARGE **3 :** to open fire — **turn one's coat :** to go over to the opposite party — **turn one's hand** *or* **turn a hand 1 :** to engage in manual work **2 :** to set to work **:** apply oneself — **turn one's stomach :** to disgust completely **:** NAUSEATE, SICKEN — **turn tail :** to run away — **turn the scale 1 :** to register weight ⟨hand baggage *turned the scale* at 60 pounds⟩ **2 :** to decide or determine something doubtful **:** prove decisive — **turn the tables** [fr. *turn the tables* to reverse the relative positions as in a board game] **:** to bring about a reversal of the relative conditions or fortunes of two contending persons or parties — **turn the trick :** to bring about the desired result or effect — **turn turtle :** CAPSIZE, OVERTURN

²**turn** *n* [ME; partly fr. OF *tourn, tour* lathe, circuit, turn (partly fr. L *tornus* lathe; partly fr. OF *torner, tourner* to turn); partly fr. ME *turnen* to turn] **1 a :** the action or an act of turning about a center or axis **:** REVOLUTION, ROTATION **b** (1) **:** any of various rotating or pivoting movements in dancing (2) **:** a swing by a gymnast of less than a circle around a bar **2 a :** the action or an act of giving or taking a different direction **:** change of course or posture ⟨illegal left ~⟩: as (1) **:** a drill maneuver in which troops in mass formation change direction without preserving alignment (2) **:** any of various shifts of direction in skiing (3) **:** an interruption of a curve in figure skating **b :** DEFLECTION, DEVIATION **c :** the action or an act of turning so as to face in the opposite direction **:** reversal of posture or course ⟨an about ~⟩ ⟨~ of the tide⟩ **d :** a change effected by turning over to another side ⟨~ of the cards⟩ **e :** a place at which something turns, turns off, or turns back **:** BEND, CURVE **3 a :** an act of walking briefly around or out and back ⟨a short ~ through the garden⟩ **b :** a short trip out and back or round about **4** *archaic* **:** STRATAGEM, TRICK **5 :** an act or deed affecting another esp. when incidental or unexpected ⟨one good ~ deserves another⟩ **6 a :** a period of action or activity **:** GO, SPELL; *specif* **:** a bout of wrestling **b :** a place, time, or opportunity accorded an individual or unit of a series in simple succession or in a scheduled order ⟨waiting his ~ in a doctor's office⟩ **c :** a period or tour of duty **:** SHIFT **d :** a short act as for a variety show **e** (1) **:** an event in any gambling game after which bets are settled (2) **:** the order of the last three cards in faro — used in the phrase *call the turn* **7 :** something that revolves around a center: as **a** (1) **:** LATHE (2) **:** a catch or latch for a cupboard or cabinet door operated by turning a handle **b :** a musical ornament consisting of a group of four or more notes that wind about the principal note by including the notes next above and next below **8 :** a special purpose or requirement — used chiefly in the phrase *serve one's turn* **9 a :** an act of changing **:** ALTERATION, MODIFICATION ⟨a nasty ~ in the weather⟩ **b :** a change in tendency, trend, or drift ⟨hoped for a ~ in his luck⟩ ⟨a ~ for the better⟩ **c :** the time when something changes its direction or its course ⟨~ of the year⟩ **10 a :** distinctive quality or character **b** (1) **:** a skillful fashioning of language or arrangement of words (2) **:** a particular form of expression or peculiarity of phrasing **c :** the shape or mold in which something is fashioned **:** CAST **11 a :** the state or manner of being coiled or twisted **b :** a single round (as of rope passed about an object or of wire wound on a core) **12 :** natural or special ability or aptitude **:** BENT, INCLINATION ⟨a ~ for logic⟩ ⟨an optimistic ~ of mind⟩ **13 :** a special twist, construction, or interpretation ⟨gave the old yarn a new ~⟩ **14 a :** a disordering spell or attack (as of illness, faintness, or dizziness) **b :** a nervous start or shock **15 a :** a complete transaction involving a purchase and sale of securities; *also* **:** a profit from such a transaction **b :** TURNOVER 7b **16 :** something turned or to be turned: as **a :** a character or slug inverted in setting type **b :** a piece of type placed bottom up — **at every turn :** on every occasion **:** CONSTANTLY, CONTINUALLY — **by turns :** one after another in regular succession **:** ALTERNATELY, SUCCESSIVELY — **in turn :** in due order of succession **:** SUCCESSIVELY, ALTERNATELY — **on the turn :** at the point of turning ⟨tide is *on the turn*⟩ — **out of turn 1 :** not in due order of succession ⟨play *out of turn*⟩ **2 :** at a wrong time or place **:** IMPRUDENTLY, UNWISELY ⟨talking *out of turn*⟩ — **to a turn :** to perfection **:** precisely right **:** PERFECTLY

turn·about \'tər-nə-,bau̇t\ *n* **1 a :** a change or reversal of direction, trend, policy, or role **b :** a changing from one allegiance to another **c :** TURNCOAT, RENEGADE **2 :** MERRY-GO-ROUND

turn·around \-ə-,rau̇nd\ *n* **1 :** a space permitting the turning around of a vehicle **2 :** TURNABOUT 1b

turn away *vt* **1 :** DEFLECT, AVERT **2 a :** to send away **:** REJECT, DISMISS **b :** REPEL **c :** to refuse admittance or acceptance to **~** *vi* **:** to start to go away **:** DEPART

turn back *vi* **1 a :** to stop going forward **b :** to go in the reverse direction **2 :** to refer to an earlier time or place **~** *vt* **1 :** to drive back or away **2 :** to stop the advance of **3 :** to fold back

turn·buck·le \'tərn-,bək-əl\ *n* **:** a link with a screw thread at one end and a swivel at the other or a right-and-left screw link used for tightening a rod or stay

turn·coat \-,kōt\ *n* **:** one who forsakes his party or principles; *specif* **:** TRAITOR

turn down *vi* **:** to be capable of being folded or doubled down ⟨collar *turns down*⟩ **~** *vt* **1 :** to fold or double down **2 :** to turn upside down **:** INVERT **3 :** to reduce in height or intensity by turning a control ⟨*turn down* the lights⟩ **4 :** DECLINE, REJECT

¹**turn·down** \,tərn-,dau̇n\ *adj* **:** capable of being turned down; *esp* **:** worn turned down ⟨~ collar⟩

²**turn·down** \'tərn-,dau̇n\ *n* **1 :** REJECTION **2 :** something turned down **3 :** DOWNTURN

¹**turn·er** \'tər-nər\ *n* **:** one that turns or is used for turning ⟨cake ~⟩; *specif* **:** one that forms articles with a lathe

²**tur·ner** \'tər-nər, 'tu̇(ə)r-\ *n* [G, fr. *turnen* to perform gymnastic exercises, fr. OHG *turnēn* to turn, fr. ML *tornare* — more at TURN] **:** a member of a turnverein **:** GYMNAST

turn·ery \'tər-nə-rē\ *n* **:** the work, products, or shop of a turner

turn in *vt* **1 :** to deliver up **:** hand over **2 :** inform on **:** BETRAY **3 :** to give an account of oneself respecting ⟨*turn in* a good job⟩ **~** *vi* **1 :** to turn from a road or path so as to enter **2 :** to go to bed

turn–in \'tər-,nin\ *n* **:** something that turns in or is turned in

turn·ing *n* **1 :** the act or course of one that turns **2 :** a place of a change in direction **3 :** a forming by use of a lathe **:** TURNERY

turning chisel *n* **:** a chisel used for shaping or finishing work in a lathe

turning point *n* **:** a point at which a significant change occurs

tur·nip \'tər-nəp\ *n, often attrib* [prob. fr. ¹*turn* + E dial. *neep* (turnip); fr. the well-rounded root] **1 :** either of two biennial herbs of the mustard family with thick roots eaten as a vegetable or fed to stock: **a :** one (*Brassica rapa*) with hairy leaves and usu. flattened roots **b :** RUTABAGA **2 :** a large pocket watch

tur·nix \'tər-niks\ *n* [NL, short for L *coturnix* quail] **:** any of a genus (*Turnix*) of small mostly solitary three-toed birds of southern Europe, Asia, and northern Africa related to the plovers **:** BUTTON QUAIL

turn·key \'tərn-,kē\ *n* **:** one who has charge of a prison's keys

turn off *vt* **1 a :** DISMISS, DISCHARGE **b :** to dispose of **:** SELL **2 :** DEFLECT, EVADE **3 :** PRODUCE, ACCOMPLISH **4 :** to shut off or stop the flow of by or as if by turning a control **5 :** HANG 1b **6 a :** to remove (material) by the process of turning **b :** to shape or produce by turning **7 :** to cause to lose interest **:** BORE **~** *vi* **1 :** to deviate from a straight course or from a main road ⟨*turn off* into a side road⟩ **2 a** *Brit* **:** to turn bad **:** SPOIL **b :** to change to a specified state **:** BECOME

turn·off \'tər-,nȯf\ *n* **1 :** a turning off **2 :** a place where one turns off; *esp* **:** an exit ramp on a turnpike

turn on *vt* **1 :** to cause to flow or operate by or as if by turning a control ⟨*turn* the water *on* full⟩ **2 a :** to cause to undergo an intense visionary experience by taking a drug **b :** to move pleasurably **:** STIMULATE **~** *vi* **:** to undergo an intense visionary experience by taking a drug; *broadly* **:** to get high

turn out *vt* **1 a :** EXPEL, EVICT **b :** to put (as a horse) to pasture **2 a :** to turn inside out ⟨*turning out* his pockets⟩ **b :** to empty the contents of esp. for cleaning or rearranging; *also* **:** CLEAN **3 :** to produce by or as if by machine **:** make with rapidity or regularity **4 :** to equip, dress, or finish in a careful or elaborate way **5 :** to put out (a light) by turning a switch **6 :** to call (as the guard or a company) out from rest or shelter and into formation **~** *vi* **1 a :** to come or go out from home in answer to a summons **b :** to get out of bed **2 :** to prove to be in the result or end **:** END

turn·out \'tər-,nau̇t\ *n* **1 :** an act of turning out **2** *chiefly Brit* **a :** STRIKE 3a **b :** STRIKER d **3 :** a gathering of people for a special purpose **4 a :** a widened space in a highway for vehicles to pass or park **b :** a railroad siding **5 :** a clearing out and cleaning **6 a :** a coach or carriage together with the horses, harness, and at-

tendants **b** : EQUIPMENT, RIG **c** : manner of dress : GETUP **7** : net quantity of produce yielded

turn over *vt* **1** : to turn from an upright position : OVERTURN **2** : to search (as clothes or papers) by lifting or moving one by one **3** : to think over : meditate on **4** : to read or examine (as a book) slowly or idly **5** : DELIVER, SURRENDER **6 a** : to receive and dispose of (a stock of merchandise) **b** : to do business to the amount of ⟨*turning over* $1000 a week⟩ ~ *vi* **1** : UPSET, CAPSIZE **2** : ROTATE **3 a** *of one's stomach* : to heave with nausea **b** *of one's heart* : to seem to leap or lurch convulsively with sudden fright

¹**turn·over** \'tər-,nō-vər\ *n* **1** : an act or result of turning over : UPSET **2** : a turning from one side, place, or direction to its opposite : SHIFT, REVERSAL **3** : a reorganization with a view to a shift in personnel : SHAKE-UP **4** : something that is turned over **5** : a filled pastry made by turning half of the crust over the other half **6** : the amount of business done; *esp* : the volume of shares traded on a stock exchange **7 a** : movement (as of goods or people) into, through, and out of a place **b** : a cycle of purchase, sale, and replacement of a stock of goods; *also* : the ratio of sales for a stated period to average inventory **c** : the number of persons hired within a period to replace those leaving or dropped from a working force; *also* : the ratio of this number to the number in the average force maintained

²**turn·over** \,tər-,nō-vər\ *adj* : capable of being turned over : TURNDOWN

turn·pike \'tərn-,pīk\ *n* [ME *turnepike* revolving frame bearing spikes and serving as a barrier, fr. *turnen* to turn + *pike*] **1** : a toll bar : TOLLGATE **2 a** : a toll road or one formerly maintained as such; *esp* : a toll expressway **b** : a main road; *esp* : a paved highway with crowned surface

turn·sole \'tərn-,sōl\ *n* [ME *turnesole*, fr. MF *tournesol*, fr. OIt *tornasole*, fr. *tornare* to turn (fr. ML) + *sole* sun, fr. L *sol* — more at SOLAR] **1** : any of several plants whose flowers or stems are supposed to turn with the sun: as **a** : HELIOTROPE **b** : SUNFLOWER **2** : a European herb (*Chrozophora tinctoria*) of the spurge family with juice that is turned blue by ammonia; *also* : a purple dye obtained from it

turn·spit \-,spit\ *n* **1 a** : one that turns a spit; *specif* : a small dog formerly used in a treadmill to turn a spit **b** : a roasting jack **2** : a rotatable spit

turn·stile \-,stīl\ *n* **1** : a post with four arms pivoted on the top set in a passageway so that persons can pass through but cattle cannot **2** : a similar device set in an entrance for controlling or counting the persons entering

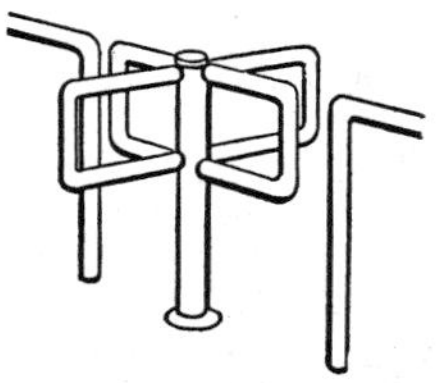

turnstile 2

turn·stone \-,stōn\ *n* [fr. a habit of turning over stones to find food] : any of various widely distributed migratory shorebirds (genus *Arenaria*) resembling the related plovers and sandpipers; *esp* : a widely distributed bird (*A. interpres*) having the upper surfaces variegated with black and chestnut and a black breast

turn·ta·ble \-,tā-bəl\ *n* **1** : a revolvable platform: as **a** : a platform with a track for turning wheeled vehicles **b** : LAZY SUSAN **c** : a rotating platform that carries a phonograph record **2** : a machine that reproduces speech or music from records and transcriptions for radiobroadcasting

turn to \'tərn-'tü\ *vi* : to apply oneself to work : act vigorously

turn up *vt* **1** : FIND, DISCOVER **2** : to raise or increase by turning a control **3** *Brit* **a** : to look up (as a word or fact) in a book **b** : to refer to or consult (a book) **4 a** : to bring to a supine position **b** : KILL **5** : to turn (a card) face upward **6** : to reach a rotational speed of : develop power to the extent of ⟨engine *turns up* 101 horsepower⟩ ~ *vi* **1** : to appear or come to light unexpectedly or after being lost **2 a** : to turn out to be ⟨*turned up* missing at roll call⟩ : become evident ⟨name is always *turning up* in the newspapers⟩ **b** : to arrive or show up at an appointed or expected time or place ⟨*turned up* half an hour late⟩ **3** : to happen or occur unexpectedly ⟨something always *turned up* to prevent their meeting⟩ **4** *of a ship* : TACK *vi* 1b — **turn up one's nose** : to show scorn or disdain

¹**turn·up** \'tər-,nəp\ *n* : something that is turned up

²**turn·up** \,tər-,nəp\ *adj* **1** : turned up ⟨~ nose⟩ **2** : made or fitted to be turned up ⟨~ collar⟩

turn·ver·ein \'tərn-və-,rīn, 'tu̇(ə)rn-\ *n* [G, fr. *turnen* to perform gymnastic exercises + *verein* club] : an athletic club

¹**tur·pen·tine** \'tər-pən-,tīn, 'tərp-ᵊm-\ *n* [ME *terbentyne*, *turpentyne*, fr. MF & ML; MF *terbentine*, *tourbentine*, fr. ML *terbentina*, fr. L *terebinthina*, fem. of *terebinthinus* of terebinth, fr. *terebinthus* terebinth, fr. Gk *terebinthos*] **1 a** : a yellow to brown semifluid oleoresin obtained as an exudate from the terebinth — called also *Chi·an turpentine* \,kī-ən-\ **b** : an oleoresin obtained from various conifers (as some pines and firs) **2 a** : an essential oil obtained from turpentines by distillation and used esp. as a solvent and thinner — called also *gum turpentine*, *oil of turpentine* **b** : a similar oil obtained by distillation or carbonization of pine-wood — called also *wood turpentine* — **tur·pen·tin·ic** \,tər-pən-'tin-ik, ,tərp-ᵊm-\ *or* **tur·pen·tin·ous** \-'tī-nəs\ *adj*

²**turpentine** *vt* **1** : to apply turpentine to **2** : to extract turpentine from (pine trees) ~ *vi* : to collect or make turpentine

tur·pi·tude \'tər-pə-,t(y)üd\ *n* [MF, fr. L *turpitudo*, fr. *turpis* vile, base] : inherent baseness : DEPRAVITY ⟨moral ~⟩; *also* : a base act

turps \'tərps\ *n pl but sing in constr* [by shortening & alter.] : TURPENTINE

tur·quoise *also* **tur·quois** \'tər-,k(w)ȯiz\ *n* [ME *turkeis*, *turcas*, fr. MF *turquoyse*, fr. fem. of *turquoys* Turkish, fr. OF, fr. *Turc* Turk] **1** : a mineral $CuAl_6(PO_4)_4(OH)_8.5H_2O$ consisting of a blue, bluish green, or greenish gray hydrous basic copper aluminum phosphate that takes a high polish and changes sometimes to a green tint but when sky blue is valued as a gem **2** : a variable color averaging a light greenish blue

turquoise blue *n* : a variable color averaging a light greenish blue that is paler and slightly bluer than average turquoise

turquoise green *n* : a variable color averaging a light bluish green

tur·ret \'tər-ət, 'tə-rət, 'tu̇r-ət\ *n* [ME *touret*, fr. MF *torete*, *tourete*, fr. OF, dim. of *tor*, *tur* tower — more at TOWER] **1** : a little tower; *specif* : an ornamental structure at an angle of a larger structure **2 a** : a pivoted and revolvable holder in a machine tool **b** : a monitor on a fire truck or on the deck of a fireboat **c** : a photographic or television camera device holding several lenses **3 a** : a tall building usu. moved on wheels and formerly used for carrying soldiers and equipment for breaching or scaling a wall **b** (1) : a gunner's fixed or movable enclosure in an airplane (2) : a revolving structure on a warship protecting the breech portion of a gun (3) : the upper structure of a tank rotatable for swinging the gun mounted within it

tur·ret·ed \-əd\ *adj* **1** : furnished with or as if with turrets **2** *of a mollusk shell* : having whorls forming a high conical spiral

¹**tur·tle** \'tərt-ᵊl\ *n* [ME, fr. OE *turtla*, fr. L *turtur*, of imit. origin] *archaic* : TURTLEDOVE

²**turtle** *n*, *pl* **turtles** *also* **turtle** *often attrib* [prob. by folk etymology fr. F *tortue*, prob. fr. (assumed) VL *tartaruca*, fr. LL *tartarucha*, fem. of *tartaruchus* of Tartarus, fr. Gk *tartarouchos*, fr. *Tartaros* Tartarus] : any of an order (Testudinata) of land, freshwater, and marine reptiles with a toothless horny beak and a bony shell which encloses the trunk and into which the head, limbs, and tail usu. may be withdrawn

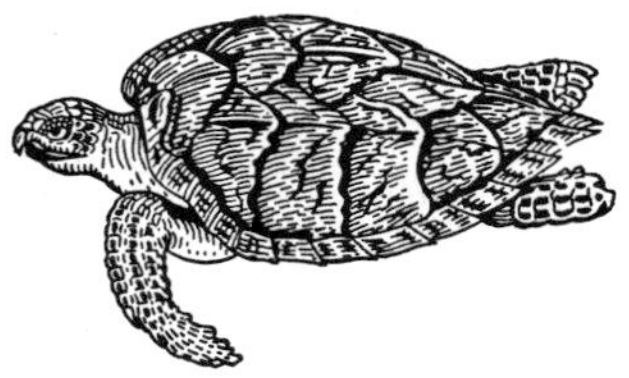

hawksbill turtle

³**turtle** *vi* **tur·tling** \'tərt-liŋ, -ᵊl-iŋ\ : to catch turtles esp. as an occupation

tur·tle·back \'tərt-ᵊl-,bak\ *n* : a raised convex surface — **turtle-back** *or* **tur·tle-backed** \,tərt-ᵊl-'bakt\ *adj*

tur·tle·dove \'tərt-ᵊl-,dəv\ *n* : any of several small wild pigeons esp. of an Old World genus (*Streptopelia*) noted for plaintive cooing

tur·tle·head \-,hed\ *n* : any of a genus (*Chelone*) of perennial herbs of the figwort family with spikes of showy white or purple flowers

tur·tle·neck \-,nek\ *n* : a high close-fitting turnover collar used esp. for sweaters; *also* : a sweater with a turtleneck

turves *pl of* TURF

¹**Tus·can** \'təs-kən\ *n* [ME, fr. L *tuscanus*, adj., Etruscan, fr. *Tusci* Etruscans] **1** : a native or inhabitant of Tuscany **2 a** : the Italian language spoken in Tuscany **b** : the standard literary dialect of Italian

²**Tuscan** *adj* **1** : of, relating to, or characteristic of Tuscany, the Tuscans, or Tuscan **2** : of or relating to one of the five classical orders of architecture that is of Roman origin and plain in style

Tus·ca·ro·ra \,təs-kə-'rōr-ə, -'rȯr-\ *n*, *pl* **Tuscarora** *or* **Tuscaroras** [Tuscarora *Skă-rū-rĕⁿ*, lit., Indian hemp gatherers] **1 a** : an Iroquoian people of No. Carolina and later of New York and Ontario **b** : a member of this people **2** : the language of the Tuscarora people

tu·sche \'tu̇sh-ə\ *n* [G, back-formation fr. *tuschen* to lay on color, fr. F *toucher*, lit., to touch] : a substance constituted like lithographic ink and used in lithography for drawing and painting and in etching and silk-screen process as a resist

¹**tush** \'təsh\ *n* [ME *tusch*, fr. OE *tūsc*; akin to OFris *tusk* tooth, OE *tōth* tooth] : a long pointed tooth : TUSK; *esp* : a horse's canine — **tushed** \'təsht\ *adj*

²**tush** *interj* [ME *tussch*] — used to express disdain or reproach

¹**tusk** \'təsk\ *n* [ME, alter. of *tux*, fr. OE *tūx*; akin to OE *tūsc* tush] **1** : an elongated greatly enlarged tooth that projects when the mouth is closed and serves for digging food or as a weapon; *broadly* : a long protruding tooth **2** : one of the small projections on a tusk tenon — **tusked** \'təskt\ *adj* — **tusk·like** \'təs-,klīk\ *adj*

²**tusk** *vt* : to dig up with a tusk; *also* : to gash with a tusk

tusk·er \'təs-kər\ *n* : an animal with tusks; *specif* : a male elephant with two normally developed tusks

tusk tenon *n* : a tenon strengthened by one or more smaller tenons underneath forming a steplike outline

tus·sah \'təs-ə, -,ȯ\ *or* **tus·sore** \'təs-,ō(ə)r, -,ȯ(ə)r, (,)təs-'\ *n* [Hindi *tasar*] : an Oriental silkworm that is the larva of a moth (*Antheraea paphia* of the family Saturniidae) and that produces a brownish silk; *also* : this silk or a fabric made of it

tus·sive \'təs-iv\ *adj* [L *tussis* cough] : of, relating to, or involved in coughing

¹**tus·sle** \'təs-əl\ *vi* **tus·sling** \-(ə-)liŋ\ [ME *tussillen*, freq. of ME *-tusen*, *-tousen* to tousle — more at TOUSE] : to struggle roughly : SCUFFLE

²**tussle** *n* **1** : a physical contest or struggle : SCUFFLE **2** : a rough argument, controversy, or struggle against difficult odds

tus·sock \'təs-ək\ *n* [origin unknown] : a compact tuft esp. of grass or sedge; *also* : a hummock in marsh bound together by plant roots — **tus·socky** \-ə-kē\ *adj*

tussock grass *n* : a grass or sedge that typically grows in tussocks

tussock moth *n* : any of numerous dull-colored moths (esp. family Lymantriidae) that commonly have wingless females

tut *a t-sound made by suction rather than explosion; often read as* 'tət\ *or* **tut-tut** *interj* [origin unknown] — used to express disapproval or disbelief

tu·tee \t(y)ü-'tē\ *n* : one who is being tutored

tu·te·lage \'t(y)üt-ᵊl-ij\ *n* [L *tutela* protection, guardian, fr. *tutus*, pp. of *tueri* to look at, guard] **1** : an act of guarding or protecting : GUARDIANSHIP **2** : the state of being under a guardian or tutor; *also* : the right or power of a tutor over his pupil **3 a** : instruction esp. of an individual **b** : a guiding influence

tu·te·lar \-ᵊl-ər\ *adj* : TUTELARY

¹**tu·te·lary** \'t(y)üt-ᵊl-,er-ē\ *adj* **1** : having the guardianship of a person or a thing ⟨~ goddess⟩ **2** : of or relating to a guardian ⟨~ authority⟩

²**tutelary** *n* : a tutelary power (as a deity)

¹**tu·tor** \'t(y)üt-ər\ *n* [ME, fr. MF & L; MF *tuteur*, fr. L *tutor*, fr. *tutus*, pp. of *tueri*] : a person charged with the instruction and guidance of another: as **a** : a private teacher **b** : a university officer serving as adviser to undergraduates assigned to him **c** : a teacher esp. in a British university ranking below an instructor

²**tutor** *vt* **1** : to have the guardianship, tutelage, or care of **2** : to teach or guide usu. individually in a special subject or for a particular purpose : COACH ~ *vi* **1** : to do the work of a tutor **2** : to receive instruction esp. privately

tu·tor·age \'t(y)üt-ə-rij\ *n* **:** the office, function, or work of a tutor
tu·tor·ess \'t(y)üt-ə-rəs\ *n* **:** a female tutor
1**tu·to·ri·al** \t(y)ü-'tōr-ē-əl, -'tòr-\ *adj* **:** of, relating to, or involving a tutor
2**tutorial** *n* **:** a class conducted by a tutor for one student or a small number of students
tu·tor·ship \'t(y)üt-ər-,ship\ *n* **1 :** the office, function, or practice of a tutor **2 :** TUTELAGE 3
tu·toy·er \tūē-twà-yā\ *vt* [F, to address with the pronoun *tu* ("thou"), fr. MF, fr. *tu* thou, fr. L — more at THOU] **:** to address familiarly
1**tut·ti** \'tüt-ē, 'tůt-; 'tü-,tē, 'tů-\ *adj (or adv)* [It, masc. pl. of *tutto* all] **:** ALL — used as a direction in music for voices or instruments to perform together
2**tutti** *n* **:** a passage or section performed by all the performers
tut·ti-frut·ti \,tüt-ē-'früt-ē\ *n* [It *tutti frutti*, lit., all fruits] **:** a confection or ice cream containing chopped usu. candied fruits
tut·ty \'tət-ē\ *n* [ME *tutie*, fr. MF, fr. Ar *tūtiyā'*, fr. Per, fr. Skt *tuttha*] **:** a crude zinc oxide obtained from the flues of smelting furnaces
tu·tu \'tü-(,)tü\ *n* [F, fr. (baby talk) *cucu, tutu* backside, alter. of *cul* — more at CULET] **:** a very short projecting skirt worn by a ballerina
tu-whit tu-whoo \tə-,(h)wit-tə-'(h)wü\ *n* [imit.] **:** the cry of an owl
tux \'təks\ *n* **:** TUXEDO
tux·e·do \,tək-'sēd-(,)ō\ *n* [*Tuxedo* Park, N. Y.] **1 :** a single-breasted or double-breasted usu. black or blackish blue jacket **2 :** semiformal evening clothes for men
tu·yere \twē-'e(ə)r\ *n* [F *tuyère*, fr. MF, fr. *tuyau* pipe] **:** a nozzle through which an air blast is delivered to a forge or blast furnace
twa \'twà\ *or* **twae** \'twà, 'twē\ *Scot var of* TWO
1**twad·dle** \'twäd-ᵊl\ *n* [prob. alter. of E dial. *twattle* (idle talk)] **1 :** silly idle talk **:** DRIVEL **2 :** TWADDLER
2**twaddle** *vb* **twad·dling** \'twäd-liŋ, -ᵊl-iŋ\ **:** PRATE, BABBLE — **twad·dler** \-lər, -ᵊl-ər\ *n*
1**twain** \'twān\ *adj* [ME, fr. OE *twēgen* — more at TWO] *archaic* **:** TWO
2**twain** *pron* **:** TWO ⟨mark ~⟩
3**twain** *n* **1 :** TWO **2 :** COUPLE, PAIR
1**twang** \'twaŋ\ *n* [imit.] **1 :** a harsh quick ringing sound like that of a plucked bowstring **2 a :** nasal speech or resonance **b :** the characteristic speech of a region, locality, or group of people **3 a :** an act of plucking **b :** PANG, TWINGE — **twangy** \'twaŋ-ē\ *adj*
2**twang** *vi* **twang·ing** \'twaŋ-iŋ\ **1 :** to sound with a twang ⟨the bowstring ~*ed*⟩ **2 :** to speak or sound with a nasal intonation **3 :** to throb or twitch with pain or tension ~ *vt* **1 :** to cause to sound with a twang **2 :** to utter or pronounce with a nasal twang **3 :** to pluck the string of ⟨~*ed* his bow⟩
3**twang** *n* [alter. of *tang*] **1 :** a persisting flavor, taste, or odor **:** TANG **2 :** SUGGESTION, TRACE
tway·blade \'twā-,blād\ *n* [E dial. *tway* (two)] **:** any of several orchids (esp. genera *Listera* or *Liparis*) having a pair of leaves
1**tweak** \'twēk\ *vb* [ME *twikken*, fr. OE *twiccian* to pluck — more at TWITCH] *vt* **1 :** to pinch and pull with a sudden jerk and twist **:** TWITCH **2 :** to pinch the nose of ⟨~ a baby⟩ ~ *vi* **:** TWITCH
2**tweak** *n* **1 :** an act of tweaking **:** PINCH **2 :** AGITATION, DISTRESS
tweed \'twēd\ *n* [alter. of Sc *tweel* twill, fr. ME *twyll*] **1 :** a rough woolen fabric made usu. in twill weaves and used esp. for suits and coats **2** *pl* **:** tweed clothing; *specif* **:** a tweed suit
tweed·ed \'twēd-əd\ *adj* **:** wearing tweeds
tweed·i·ness \'twēd-ē-nəs\ *n* **:** the quality or state of being tweedy
Twee·dle·dum and Twee·dle·dee \,twēd-ᵊl-'dəm-ən-,twēd-ᵊl-'dē\ *n* [E *tweedle* (to chirp) + *dum* (imit. of a low musical note) & *dee* (imit. of a high musical note)] **:** two individuals or groups that are practically indistinguishable
tweedy \'twēd-ē\ *adj* **1 :** of or resembling tweed **2 a :** given to wearing tweeds **b :** informal or suggestive of the outdoors in taste or habits
tween \(')twēn\ *prep* [ME *twene*, short for *betwene*] **:** BETWEEN
1**tweet** \'twēt\ *n* [imit.] **:** a chirping note
2**tweet** *vb* **:** CHIRP
tweet·er \'twēt-ər\ *n* **:** a small loudspeaker responsive only to the higher acoustic frequencies and reproducing sounds of high pitch
tweeze \'twēz\ *vt* [back-formation fr. *tweezers*] **:** to pluck or remove with tweezers
tweez·er \'twē-zər\ *n* **:** TWEEZERS
tweez·ers \-zərz\ *n pl but sing or pl in constr* [obs. E *tweeze*, n. (etui), short for obs. E *etweese*, fr. pl. of obs. E *etwee*, fr. F *étui*] **:** any of various small metal instruments that are usu. held between the thumb and forefinger, are used for plucking, holding, or manipulating, and consist of two legs joined at one end
twelfth \'twelfth, 'twelft\ *n, pl* **twelfths** — see NUMBER table — **twelfth** *adj*
Twelfth Day *n* **:** EPIPHANY
Twelfth Night *n* **1 :** the eve preceding Epiphany **2 :** the evening of Epiphany
twelve \'twelv\ *n* [ME, fr. *twelve*, adj., fr. OE *twelf;* akin to OHG *zwelif* twelve; both fr. a prehistoric Gmc compound whose first element is represented by OE *twā* two, and whose second element is represented by OE *-leofan* (in *endleofan* eleven) — more at TWO, ELEVEN] **1** — see NUMBER table **2** *cap* **:** the twelve original disciples of Jesus **3 :** the 12th in a set or series **4 :** something having 12 units or members **5** *pl* **:** TWELVEMO — **twelve** *adj or pron*
twelve·mo \'twelv-(,)mō\ *n* **:** the size of a piece of paper cut 12 from a sheet; *also* **:** a book, a page, or paper of this size — called also *duodecimo*
twelve·month \-,mən(t)th\ *n* **:** YEAR
twelve-tone \-'tōn\ *adj* **:** of or relating to music based on the 12 chromatic tones used in an arbitrary but fixed order without regard for traditional tonality
twen·ti·eth \'twent-ē-əth\ *n* — see NUMBER table — **twentieth** *adj*
twen·ty \'twent-ē\ *n* [ME, fr. *twenty*, adj., fr. OE *twēntig*, n., group of 20, fr. *twēn-* (akin to OE *twā* two) + *-tig* group of 10 — more at TWO, EIGHTY] **1** — see NUMBER table **2** *pl* **:** the numbers 20 to 29 inclusive; *specif* **:** the years 20 to 29 in a lifetime or century **3 :** a twenty-dollar bill — **twenty** *adj or pron*
twen·ty-four·mo \,twent-ē-'fō(ə)r-(,)mō, -'fò(ə)r-\ *n* **:** the size of a piece of paper cut 24 from a sheet; *also* **:** a book, a page, or paper of this size
twen·ty-one \,twent-ē-'wən\ *n* **1** — see NUMBER table **2** *or* **21** [trans. of F *vingt-et-un*] **:** a card game the object of which is to be dealt cards having a higher count than those of the dealer up to but not exceeding 21 — called also *blackjack, vingt-et-un* — **twenty-one** *adj or pron*
twenty-twenty *or* **20/20** \,twent-ē-'twent-ē\ *adj, of the human eye* **:** having normal visual acuity
twen·ty-two \,twent-ē-'tü\ *n* **1** — see NUMBER table **2 :** a 22-caliber rifle or pistol — usu. written .22 — **twenty-two** *adj or pron*
twerp \'twərp\ *n* [origin unknown] **:** a silly, insignificant, or contemptible person
Twi \'chwē, 'twē, 'chē\ *n* **1 :** a dialect of Akan **2 :** a literary language based on the Twi dialect and used by the Akan-speaking peoples (as the Ashanti)
twi- *prefix* [ME, fr. OE; akin to OHG *zwi-* twi-, L *bi-*, Gk *di-*, OE *twā* two] **:** two **:** double **:** doubly **:** twice ⟨*twi*light⟩
twice \'twīs\ *adv* [ME *twiges, twies*, fr. OE *twiga;* akin to OE *twi-*] **1 :** on two occasions ⟨~ absent⟩ **2 :** two times **:** in doubled quantity or degree ⟨~ two is four⟩
twice-born \-'bò(ə)rn\ *adj* **1 :** born a second time **2 :** having undergone a definite experience of fundamental moral and spiritual renewal **:** REGENERATE **3 :** of or forming one of the three upper Hindu caste groups in which boys undergo an initiation symbolizing spiritual birth
twice-laid \'twī-'slād\ *adj* **:** made from the ends of rope and strands of used rope ⟨*twice-laid* rope⟩
twice-told \,twī-,stōld\ *adj* **1 :** narrated twice **2 :** HACKNEYED, TRITE — used chiefly in the phrase *a twice-told tale*
1**twid·dle** \'twid-ᵊl\ *vb* **twid·dling** \'twid-liŋ, -ᵊl-iŋ\ [origin unknown] *vi* **1 :** to be busy with trifles; *also* **:** to play negligently with something **:** FIDDLE **2 :** to turn or jounce lightly **:** JIGGLE ~ *vt* **:** to rotate lightly or idly **:** TWIRL ⟨~ one's thumbs⟩
2**twiddle** *n* **:** TURN, TWIST
1**twig** \'twig\ *n* [ME *twigge*, fr. OE; akin to OHG *zwīg* twig, OE *twā* two] **:** a small shoot or branch — **twigged** \'twigd\ *adj* — **twig·gy** \'twig-ē\ *adj*
2**twig** *vb* **twigged; twig·ging** [perh. fr. ScGael *twig* I understand] *vt* **1 :** NOTICE, OBSERVE **2 :** to understand the meaning of **:** COMPREHEND ~ *vi* **:** NOTICE, UNDERSTAND
3**twig** *n* [origin unknown] *Brit* **:** FASHION, STYLE
twig pruner *n* **:** any of numerous small beetles whose larvae bore in twigs of trees and cut them off
twi·light \'twī-,līt\ *n, often attrib* **1 :** the light from the sky between full night and sunrise or between sunset and full night produced by diffusion of sunlight through the atmosphere and its dust **2 :** a state of imperfect clarity **:** a period of decline
Twilight of the Gods : RAGNAROK
twilight sleep *n* **:** a state produced by injection of morphine and scopolamine in which awareness and memory of pain is dulled or effaced
twi·lit \'twī-,lit\ *adj* [*twi*light + *lit*] **:** lighted by or as if by twilight
1**twill** \'twil\ *n* [ME *twyll*, fr. OE *twilic* having a double thread, modif. of L *bilic-, bilix*, fr. *bi-* + *licium* thread] **1 :** a fabric with a twill weave **2 :** a textile weave in which the filling threads pass over one and under two or more warp threads to give an appearance of diagonal lines
2**twill** *vt* **:** to make (cloth) with a twill weave
twilled \'twild\ *adj* **:** made with a twill weave
1**twin** \'twin\ *adj* [ME, fr. OE *twinn* twofold, two by two; akin to ON *tvinnr* two by two, OE *twā* two] **1 :** born with one other or as a pair at one birth ⟨~ brother⟩ ⟨~ girls⟩ **2 a :** made up of two similar, related, or connected members or parts **:** DOUBLE **b :** paired in a close or necessary relationship **:** MATCHING **c :** having or consisting of two identical units **d :** being one of a pair ⟨~ city⟩
2**twin** *n* **1 :** either of two offspring produced at a birth **2 :** one of two persons or things closely related to or resembling each other **3 :** a compound crystal composed of two or more crystals or parts of crystals of the same kind that are grown together in a specific manner

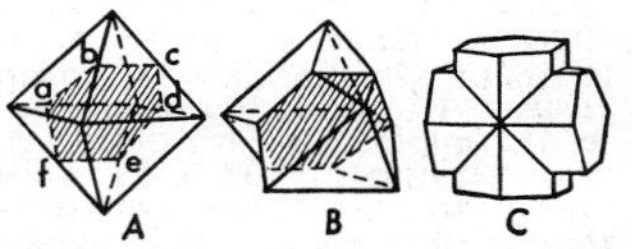

twins 3: *A* octahedron showing twinning plane, *a b c d e f; B* contact twin; *C* penetration twin

3**twin** *vb* **twinned; twin·ning** *vt* **1 :** to bring together in close association **:** COUPLE **2 :** DUPLICATE, MATCH ~ *vi* **1 :** to bring forth twins **2 :** to grow as a twin crystal
twin·ber·ry \'twin-,ber-ē\ *n* **1 :** a shrubby No. American honeysuckle (*Lonicera involucrata*) with purple involucrate flowers **2 :** PARTRIDGEBERRY
twin bill *n* **:** DOUBLEHEADER
twin·born \'twin-'bò(ə)rn\ *adj* **:** born at the same birth
1**twine** \'twīn\ *n* [ME *twin*, fr. OE *twīn;* akin to MD *twijn* twine, OE *twā* two] **1 :** a strong string of two or more strands twisted together **2 :** a twined or interlaced part or object **3 :** an act of twining, interlacing, or embracing — **twiny** \'twī-nē\ *adj*
2**twine** *vt* **1 :** to twist together; *also* **:** to form by twisting **:** WEAVE **2 a :** INTERLACE **b :** to cause to encircle or enfold another **:** WRAP **c :** to cause to be encircled ~ *vi* **1 :** to coil about a support **2 :** to stretch or move in a sinuous manner **:** MEANDER ⟨river ~*s* through the valley⟩ — **twin·er** *n*
twin·flow·er \'twin-,flaů(-ə)r\ *n* **:** either of two low prostrate subshrubs (*Linnaea borealis* of northern Europe and Asia and *L. americana* of northern No. America) of the honeysuckle family with opposite leaves and fragrant usu. pink flowers in pairs
1**twinge** \'twinj\ *vb* **twinged; twing·ing** *or* **twinge·ing** [ME *twengen*, fr. OE *twengan*] *vt* **1** *dial* **:** PLUCK, TWEAK **2 :** to affect with a sharp pain **:** PRICK ~ *vi* **:** to feel a sudden sharp local pain
2**twinge** *n* **1 :** a sudden sharp stab of pain **2 :** a moral or emotional pang

twi–night \'twī-ˌnīt\ *adj* [*twi*light + *night*] **:** of or relating to a baseball doubleheader in which the first game is played in the late afternoon and the second continues into the evening

1**twin·kle** \'twiŋ-kəl\ *vb* **twin·kling** \-k(ə-)liŋ\ [ME *twinklen*, fr. OE *twinclian;* akin to MHG *zwinken* to blink] *vi* **1 :** to shine with a flickering or sparkling light **:** SCINTILLATE **2 a :** to flutter the eyelids **b :** to appear bright with merriment or other usu. happy feeling ⟨his eyes *twinkled*⟩ **3 :** to flutter or flit rapidly **~** *vt* **1 :** to cause to shine with fluctuating light **2 :** to flicker or flirt rapidly — **twin·kler** \-k(ə-)lər\ *n*

2**twinkle** *n* **1 :** a wink of the eyelids **2 :** the instant's duration of a wink **:** TWINKLING **3 :** an intermittent radiance **:** FLICKER **4 :** a rapid flashing motion **:** FLIRT — **twin·kly** \-k(ə-)lē\ *adj*

twin·kling \'twiŋ-k(ə-)liŋ, *for 1b* -kliŋ\ *n* **1 a :** a winking of the eye **b :** the time required for a wink **:** INSTANT **2 :** SCINTILLATION

twin–screw \'twin-'skrü\ *adj* **:** having a right-handed and a left-handed propeller screw parallel to each other on each side of the plane of the keel

1**twirl** \'twər(-ə)l\ *vb* [perh. of Scand origin; akin to Norw dial. *tvirla* to twirl; akin to OHG *dweran* to stir — more at TURBID] *vi* **1 :** to revolve rapidly **:** SPIN **2 :** to pitch in a baseball game **~** *vt* **1 :** to cause to rotate rapidly **:** WHIRL **2 :** PITCH 2a — **twirl·er** \'twər-lər\ *n*

2**twirl** *n* **1 :** an act of twirling **2 :** COIL, WHORL — **twirly** \'twər-lē\ *adj*

twirp *var of* TWERP

1**twist** \'twist\ *vb* [ME *twisten*, fr. OE *-twist* rope; akin to MD *twist* quarrel, twine, OE *twā* two] *vt* **1 a :** to unite by winding one thread, strand, or wire around another **b :** PLAIT, WREATHE **c :** ENTWINE, INTERLACE **2 :** TWINE, COIL **3 a :** to wring or wrench so as to dislocate or distort; *esp* **:** SPRAIN ⟨*~ed* my ankle⟩ **b :** to alter the meaning of **:** PERVERT ⟨*~ed* the facts⟩ **c :** CONTORT ⟨*~ed* his face into a grin⟩ **d :** to pull off, turn, or break by torsion **e :** to cause to move with a turning motion **f :** to form into a spiral shape **g :** to cause to become deformed **:** WARP **h :** to make (one's way) in a winding or devious manner to a destination or objective **~** *vi* **1 :** to follow a winding course **:** SNAKE **2 a :** to turn or change shape under torsion **b :** to assume a spiral shape **c :** SQUIRM, WRITHE **3** *of a ball* **:** to rotate while taking a curving path or direction **4 :** to turn around **syn** see CURVE

2**twist** *n* **1 :** something formed by twisting or winding: as **a :** a thread, yarn, or cord formed by twisting two or more strands together **b :** a strong tightly twisted sewing silk **c :** a baked piece of twisted dough **d :** tobacco leaves twisted into a thick roll **2 :** the fleshing between the hind legs esp. of cattle or sheep **3 a :** an act of twisting **:** the state of being twisted **b :** a dance performed with strenuous gyrations esp. of the hips **c :** the spin given the ball in any of various games (as baseball) **d :** a spiral turn or curve **e** (1) **:** torque or torsional stress applied to a body (as a rod or shaft) (2) **:** torsional strain (3) **:** the angle through which a thing is twisted **4 a :** a turning aside **:** DEFLECTION **b :** ECCENTRICITY, IDIOSYNCRASY **c :** a distortion of meaning or sense **:** PERVERSION **5 a :** an unexpected turn or development **b :** DEVICE, TRICK **c :** a variant approach or method **:** GIMMICK **6** *slang* **:** GIRL, WOMAN; *esp* **:** FLOOZY — **twisty** \'twis-tē\ *adv*

twist drill *n* **:** a drill having deep helical grooves extending from the point to the smooth portion of the shank

twist·er \'twis-tər\ *n* **1 :** one that twists; *esp* **:** a ball with a forward and spinning motion **2 :** a tornado, waterspout, or dust devil in which the rotatory ascending movement of a column of air is esp. apparent

1**twit** \'twit\ *vt* **twit·ted; twit·ting** [ME *atwiten* to reproach, fr. OE *ætwītan*, fr. *æt* at + *wītan* to reproach; akin to OHG *wīzan* to punish, OE *witan* to know] **1 :** to subject to light ridicule or reproach **:** RALLY **2 :** to make fun of as a fault **syn** see RIDICULE

2**twit** *n* **:** an act of twitting **:** TAUNT

3**twit** *n* [imit.] **:** TWITTER, CHIRP

1**twitch** \'twich\ *vb* [ME *twicchen;* akin to OE *twiccian* to pluck, OHG *gizwickan* to pinch] *vt* **:** to move or pull with a sudden motion **:** JERK **~** *vi* **1 :** PULL, PLUCK ⟨*~ed* at my sleeve⟩ **2 a :** to move jerkily **:** QUIVER **b :** to ache with a twinge — **twitch·er** *n*

2**twitch** *n* **1 :** an act of twitching; *esp* **:** a short sudden pull or jerk **2 :** PANG, TWINGE **3 a :** a short spastic contraction of the muscle fibers **b :** a slight jerk of a body part — **twitchy** \'twich-ē\ *adj*

3**twitch** *n* [alter. of *quitch*] **:** a couch grass (*Agropyron repens*)

1**twit·ter** \'twit-ər\ *vb* [ME *twiteren;* akin to OHG *zwizzirōn* to twitter] *vi* **1 :** to utter successive chirping noises **2 a :** to talk in a chattering fashion **b :** GIGGLE, TITTER **3 :** to tremble with agitation **:** FLUTTER **~** *vt* **1 :** to chirp out **2 :** to shake rapidly back and forth **:** FLUTTER — **twit·ter·er** \-ər-ər\ *n*

2**twitter** *n* **1 :** a trembling agitation **:** QUIVER **2 :** the chirping of birds **3 a :** a light chattering **:** GABBLE **b :** a light silly laugh **:** GIGGLE — **twit·tery** \'twit-ə-rē\ *adj*

twixt \(')twikst\ *prep* [ME *twix*, short for *betwix*, *betwixt*] **:** BETWEEN

two \'tü\ *n* [ME *twa*, *two*, adj., fr. OE *twā* (fem. & neut.); akin to OE *twēgen* two (masc.), *tū* (neut.), OHG *zwēne*, L *duo*, Gk *dyo*] **1** — see NUMBER table **2 :** the second in a set or series ⟨the **~** of hearts⟩ **3 :** a 2-dollar bill **4 :** something having two units or members — **two** *adj or pron*

two–base hit \ˌtü-ˌbās-\ *n* **:** a base hit enabling a batter to reach second base safely **:** DOUBLE — called also *two-bag·ger* \'tü-'bag-ər\

two–bit \ˌtü-ˌbit\ *adj* **1 :** of the value of two bits **2 :** PETTY, SMALL-TIME

two bits *n pl but sing or pl in constr* **1 :** the value of a quarter of a dollar **2 :** something of small worth or importance

1**two–by–four** \ˌtü-bə-'fō(ə)r, -'fȯ(ə)r\ *adj* **1 :** measuring two units (as inches) by four **2 :** SMALL, CRAMPED

2**two–by–four** *n* **:** a piece of lumber approximately 2 by 4 inches as sawed and usu. 1⅝ by 3⅝ inches if dressed

two–cycle *adj*, *of an internal-combustion engine* **:** having a two-stroke cycle

two–dimensional *adj* **1 :** having two dimensions **2 :** lacking depth of characterization ⟨**~** fiction⟩

two–faced \'tü-'fāst\ *adj* **1 :** having two faces **2 :** DOUBLE-DEALING, FALSE — **two–faced·ly** \-'fā-səd-lē, -'fāst-lē\ *adv*

two–fist·ed \-'fis-təd\ *adj* **:** VIRILE, VIGOROUS

two·fold \'tü-ˌfōld, -'fōld\ *adj* **1 :** having two units or members **2 :** being twice as great or as many — **two·fold** \-'fōld\ *adv*

2, 4–D \ˌtü-ˌfōr-'dē, -ˌfȯr-\ *n* **:** a white crystalline compound $C_8H_6Cl_2O_3$ used as a weed killer

2, 4, 5–T \-ˌfīv-'tē\ *n* **:** an irritant compound $Cl_3C_8H_5O_3$ used in brush and weed control

two–hand·ed \'tü-'han-dəd\ *adj* **1 :** used with both hands **2 :** requiring two persons ⟨a **~** saw⟩ **3 :** STOUT, STRONG **4 :** having or efficient with two hands

two·pence \'təp-ən(t)s, -ᵊm(p)s, *US also* 'tü-ˌpen(t)s\ *n*, *pl* **two·pence** *or* **two·penc·es :** the sum of two pence

two·pen·ny \'təp-(ə-)nē, *US also* 'tü-ˌpen-ē\ *adj* **:** of the value of or costing twopence

two–phase *adj* **:** DIPHASE

two–ply *adj* **1 :** woven as a double cloth **2 :** consisting of two strands or thicknesses

two–sid·ed \'tü-'sīd-əd\ *adj* **1 :** having two sides **:** BILATERAL **2 :** HYPOCRITICAL

two·some \'tü-səm\ *n* **1 :** a group of two persons or things **:** COUPLE **2 :** a golf single

two–star *adj* **:** being or having the rank of major general or rear admiral

two–step \'tü-ˌstep\ *n* **1 :** a ballroom dance executed with a sliding step-close-step in march or polka time **2 :** a piece of music for the two-step — **two–step** *vi*

two–time \'tü-ˌtīm\ *vt* **1 :** to betray (a spouse or lover) by secret lovemaking with another **2 :** DOUBLE-CROSS

two–way *adj* **1 :** being a cock or valve that will connect a pipe or channel with either of two others **2 :** moving or allowing movement in either direction **3 a :** involving or allowing an exchange between two individuals or groups; *specif* **:** designed for both sending and receiving messages ⟨**~** radio⟩ **b :** involving mutual responsibility or reciprocal relationships **4 :** involving two participants **5 :** usable in either of two manners ⟨**~** collar⟩

two–winged \'tü-'wiŋd\ *adj* **:** having one pair of wings **:** DIPTEROUS

two–winged fly *n* **:** any of a large order (Diptera) of winged or rarely wingless insects having segmented often headless, eyeless, and legless larvae and including the true flies (as the housefly), mosquitoes, gnats, and related forms with the anterior wings functional and the posterior reduced to balancers

-ty *n suffix* [ME *-te*, fr. OF *-té*, fr. L *-tat-*, *-tas* — more at -ITY] **:** quality **:** condition **:** degree ⟨apriori*ty*⟩

Ty·burn \'tī-bərn\ *n* **:** a former place of public execution in London

ty·coon \tī-'kün\ *n* [Jap *taikun*, fr. Chin (Pek) *ta*^{4} great + *chün*^{1} ruler] **1 :** SHOGUN **2 a :** a businessman of exceptional wealth and power **b :** a masterful leader (as in politics)

Ty·deus \'tī-ˌd(y)üs, 'tīd-ē-əs\ *n* [L, fr. Gk] **:** one of the Seven against Thebes

tying *pres part of* TIE

tyke \'tīk\ *n* [ME *tyke*, fr. ON *tīk* bitch] **1 :** DOG, CUR **2 a :** a clumsy, churlish, or eccentric person **b :** a small child

tymbal *var of* TIMBAL

tym·pan \'tim-pən\ *n* [in sense 1, fr. ME, fr. OE *timpana*, fr. L *tympanum;* in other senses, fr. ML & L *tympanum*] **1 :** DRUM **2 :** a sheet (as of paper or cloth) placed between the impression surface of a press and the paper to be printed **3 :** an architectural panel **:** TYMPANUM

tympani *n pl but sing or pl in constr* [by alter.] **:** TIMPANI

tym·pan·ic \tim-'pan-ik\ *adj* [L & NL *tympanum*] **1 :** of, relating to, or being a tympanum **2 :** resembling a drum

tympanic bone *n* **:** a bone of the mammalian skull enclosing part of the middle ear and supporting the tympanic membrane

tympanic membrane *n* **:** a thin membrane closing externally the cavity of the middle ear — called also *eardrum*

tym·pa·nist \'tim-pə-nəst\ *n* **:** a member of an orchestra who plays the kettledrums

tym·pa·ni·tes \ˌtim-pə-'nīt-ēz\ *n* [ME, fr. LL, fr. Gk *tympanitēs*, fr. *tympanon*] **:** a distension of the abdomen caused by accumulation of gas in the intestinal tract or peritoneal cavity — **tym·pa·nit·ic** \-'nit-ik\ *adj*

tym·pa·num \'tim-pə-nəm\ *n*, *pl* **tym·pa·na** \-nə\ *also* **tym·panums** [ML & L; ML, eardrum, fr. L, drum, architectural panel, fr. Gk *tympanon* drum, kettledrum; akin to Gk *typtein* to beat] **1 a** (1) **:** TYMPANIC MEMBRANE (2) **:** the middle ear **b :** a thin tense membrane covering an organ of hearing of an insect **c :** a membranous resonator in a sound-producing organ **2 a :** the recessed usu. triangular face of a pediment within the frame made by the upper and lower cornices **b :** the space within an arch and above a lintel or a subordinate arch **3 :** TYMPAN 1 **4 :** the diaphragm of a telephone

tym·pa·ny \-nē\ *n* [ML *tympanias*, fr. Gk, fr. *tympanon*] **1 a :** TYMPANITES **b :** resonance on percussion **2 :** BOMBAST, TURGIDITY

tyne *var of* TINE

typ·able *or* **type·able** \'tī-pə-bəl\ *adj* **:** that may be typed

typ·al \'tī-pəl\ *adj* **1 :** of or relating to or belonging to a type **2 :** serving as a type **:** TYPICAL

1**type** \'tīp\ *n*, *often attrib* [LL *typus*, fr. L & Gk; L *typus* image, fr. Gk *typos* blow, impression, model, fr. *typtein* to strike, beat; akin to L *stuprum* defilement] **1 a :** a person or thing (as in the Old Testament) believed to foreshadow another (as in the New Testament) **b :** one having qualities of a higher category **:** MODEL **c :** a lower taxonomic category selected as a standard of reference for a higher category; *also* **:** a specimen or series of specimens on which a taxonomic species or subspecies is actually based **2 :** a distinctive mark or sign **3 a :** a rectangular block typically of metal or wood bearing a relief character from which an inked print is made **b :** a collection of such blocks **c :** TYPEFACE **d :** printed letters **4 a :** qualities common to a number of individuals that distinguish them as an

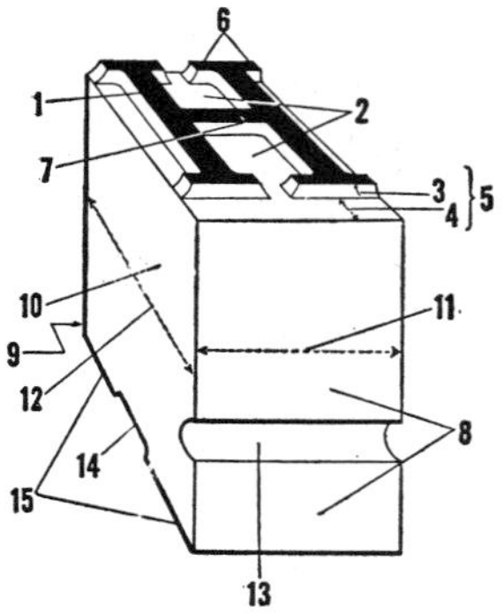

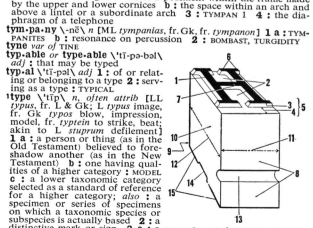

type 3a: *1* face, *2* counters, *3* bevel, *4* shoulder, *5* beard, *6* serifs, *7* crossbar, *8* belly, *9* back, *10* body, *11* set size, *12* point size, *13* nick, *14* groove, *15* feet

identifiable class: as (1) **:** the morphological, physiological, or ecological characters by which relationship between organisms may be recognized (2) **:** the form common to all instances of a word **b :** a typical and often superior specimen **c :** a particular kind, class, or group: as (1) **:** a taxonomic category essentially equivalent to a division or phylum (2) **:** a group distinguishable on physiologic or serological bases (3) **:** one of a hierarchy of mutually exclusive classes in logic suggested to avoid paradoxes **d :** something distinguishable as a variety **:** SORT

syn KIND, SORT, NATURE, DESCRIPTION, CHARACTER: TYPE may suggest strong and clearly marked similarity throughout the items included so that each is typical of the group; KIND and SORT imply a group with less explicit resemblances; KIND may suggest natural grouping; SORT often suggests some disparagement; NATURE may imply inherent, essential resemblance rather than obvious or superficial likenesses; DESCRIPTION implies a group marked by agreement in all details belonging to a type as described or defined; CHARACTER implies a group marked by distinctive likenesses peculiar to the type

TYPE

The following table shows the old names and the sizes of type; the black squares show the sizes of the corresponding em quad, and the numbers refer to the nearest equivalent in the American point system.

Name	Specimen	Em quad	Point
Diamond	abcdefghijklmnopqrstuvwxyz	■	4½
Pearl	abcdefghijklmnopqrstuvwxyz	■	5
Agate	abcdefghijklmnopqrstuvwx	■	5½
Nonpareil	abcdefghijklmnopqrstuvw	■	6
Minion	abcdefghijklmnopqrstu	■	7
Brevier	abcdefghijklmnopqrstu	■	8
Bourgeois	abcdefghijklmnopqrs	■	9
Long Primer	abcdefghijklmnopqr	■	10
Small Pica	abcdefghijklmnop	■	11
Pica	abcdefghijklmn	■	12
English	abcdefghijklm	■	14
Columbian	abcdefghijk	■	16
Great Primer	abcdefghij	■	18

²type *vt* **1 :** to represent beforehand as a type **:** PREFIGURE **2 :** to produce a copy of; *also* **:** REPRESENT, TYPIFY **3 :** TYPEWRITE **4 :** to identify as belonging to a type: as **a :** to determine the natural type of (as a blood sample) **b :** TYPECAST ~ *vi* **:** TYPEWRITE

type·case \'tīp-ˌkās\ *n* **:** ²CASE 3

type·cast \'tīp-ˌkast\ *vt* **1 :** to cast (an actor) in a part calling for the same characteristics as those possessed by the actor himself **2 :** to cast (an actor) repeatedly in the same type of role

type·face \-ˌfās\ *n* **1 :** the face of printing type; *also* **:** its printed impression **2 :** all type of a single design

type·found·er \-ˌfaùn-dər\ *n* **:** one engaged in the design and production of metal printing type for hand composition — **type·found·ing** \-diŋ\ *n* — **type·found·ry** \-drē\ *n*

type genus *n* **:** the genus of a taxonomic family or subfamily from which the name of the family or subfamily is formed

type-high \'tīp-ˈhī\ *adj (or adv)* **:** having the same foot-to-face height as printing type

type metal *n* **:** an alloy that consists essentially of lead, antimony, and tin and is used in making printing type

type·script \'tīp-ˌskript\ *n* [*type* + manu*script*] **:** typewritten matter

type·set \-ˌset\ *vt* **:** to set in type **:** COMPOSE ⟨~ a story⟩

type·set·ter \-ˌset-ər\ *n* **:** one (as a compositor) that sets type — **type·set·ting** \-ˌset-iŋ\ *adj or n*

type species *n* **:** the species of a genus with which the generic name is permanently associated

type specimen *n* **:** a specimen or individual designated as type of a species or lesser group and serving as the final criteron of the characteristics of that group

type·write \'tī-ˌprīt\ *vb* **:** to write with a typewriter

type·writ·er \-ˌprīt-ər\ *n* **1 :** a machine for writing in characters similar to those produced by printer's type by means of keyboard-operated types striking through an inked ribbon **2 :** TYPIST

type·writ·ing \-ˌprīt-iŋ\ *n* **1 :** the act or study of or skill in using a typewriter **2 :** the printing done with a typewriter

keyboard of a typewriter

Ty·phoe·an \tī-ˈfē-ən\ *adj* **:** of, relating to, or resembling Typhoeus

Ty·pho·eus \-ˈfō-ˌyüs\ *n* [L, fr. Gk *Typhōeus*] **:** a monster in Greek mythology having a hundred heads, fiery eyes, and a terrifying voice

¹ty·phoid \'tī-ˌfóid, (')tī-ˈ\ *adj* [NL *typhus*] **1 :** of, relating to, or suggestive of typhus **2** [²*typhoid*] **:** of, relating to, or constituting typhoid

²typhoid *n* **1 :** a communicable disease marked esp. by fever, diarrhea, prostration, headache, and intestinal inflammation and caused by a bacterium (*Salmonella typhosa*) — called also *typhoid fever* **2 :** a disease of domestic animals resembling human typhus or typhoid

Ty·phon \'tī-ˌfän\ *n* [L, fr. Gk *Typhōn*] **:** a monster in classical mythology and father of Cerberus, the Chimera, and the Sphinx

ty·phoon \tī-ˈfün\ *n* [alter. (influenced by Chin — Cant — *taaî fung* typhoon, fr. *taaî* great + *fung* wind) of earlier *touffon*, fr. Ar *ṭūfān* hurricane, fr. Gk *typhōn* whirlwind; akin to Gk *typhein* to smoke] **:** a tropical cyclone occurring in the region of the Philippines or the China sea

ty·phous \'tī-fəs\ *adj* **:** of, relating to, or resembling typhus

ty·phus \'tī-fəs\ *n* [NL, fr. Gk *typhos* fever; akin to Gk *typhein* to smoke — more at DEAF] **:** a human febrile disease; *esp* **:** a severe disease marked by high fever, stupor alternating with delirium, intense headache, and a dark red rash, caused by a rickettsia (*Rickettsia prowazekii*), and transmitted esp. by body lice

typ·ic \'tip-ik\ *adj* **:** TYPICAL

typ·i·cal \'tip-i-kəl\ *adj* **1 :** constituting or having the nature of a type **:** SYMBOLIC **2 a :** combining or exhibiting the essential characteristics of a group ⟨a ~ suburban house⟩ **b :** conforming to a type ⟨a specimen ~ of the species⟩ syn see REGULAR — **typ·i·cal·ly** \-k(ə-)lē\ *adv* — **typ·i·cal·ness** \-kəl-nəs\ *n*

typ·i·cal·i·ty \ˌtip-ə-ˈkal-ət-ē\ *n* **:** TYPICALNESS

typ·i·fi·ca·tion \ˌtip-ə-fə-ˈkā-shən\ *n* **:** the act of typifying

typ·i·fy \'tip-ə-ˌfī\ *vt* **1 :** to represent by an image, form, model, or resemblance **:** PREFIGURE **2 :** to embody the essential or salient characteristics of

typ·ist \'tī-pəst\ *n* **:** one who typewrites

ty·po \'tī-(ˌ)pō\ *n* [short for *typographical* (*error*)] **:** a typographical error

ty·po·graph \'tī-pə-ˌgraf\ *vt* **:** to produce (stamps) by letterpress

ty·pog·ra·pher \tī-ˈpäg-rə-fər\ *n* **1 :** COMPOSITOR **2 :** PRINTER **3 :** a specialist in the choice and arrangement of type matter

ty·po·graph·ic \ˌtī-pə-ˈgraf-ik\ *adj* **:** of, relating to, or occurring or used in typography — **ty·po·graph·i·cal** \-i-kəl\ *adj* — **ty·po·graph·i·cal·ly** \-i-k(ə-)lē\ *adv*

ty·pog·ra·phy \tī-ˈpäg-rə-fē\ *n* [ML *typographia*, fr. Gk *typos* impression, cast + -*graphia* -graphy — more at TYPE] **1 :** LETTERPRESS **2 :** the art of letterpress printing **3 :** the style, arrangement, or appearance of letterpress matter

ty·po·log·i·cal \ˌtī-pə-ˈläj-i-kəl\ *also* **ty·po·log·ic** \-ik\ *adj* **:** of or relating to typology or types — **ty·po·log·i·cal·ly** \-i-k(ə-)lē\ *adv*

ty·pol·o·gist \tī-ˈpäl-ə-jəst\ *n* **:** a student of or expert in typology

ty·pol·o·gy \-jē\ *n* **1 :** a doctrine of types **2 :** study of or analysis or classification based on types

ty·poth·e·tae \tī-ˈpäth-ə-ˌtē\ *n pl but sing in constr* [NL, lit., typesetters, deriv. of Gk *typos* impression + *tithenai* to place, set — more at DO] **:** an association of master printers

typy *or* **typ·ey** \'tī-pē\ *adj* **:** characterized by strict conformance to type; *also* **:** exhibiting superior bodily conformation

Tyr \'ti(ə)r\ *n* [ON *Tȳr* — more at DEITY] **:** a war-god and son of Odin in Norse mythology

ty·ra·mine \'tī-rə-ˌmēn\ *n* [ISV *tyrosine* + *amine*] **:** a phenolic amine $C_8H_{11}NO$ of sympathomimetic action derived from tyrosine

ty·ran·ni·cal \tə-ˈran-i-kəl, tī-\ *also* **ty·ran·nic** \-ik\ *adj* [L *tyrannicus*, fr. Gk *tyrannikos*, fr. *tyrannos* tyrant] **1 :** of, relating to, or characteristic of a tyrant or tyranny **:** given to oppressive, unjust, or arbitrary behavior or control **:** DESPOTIC — **ty·ran·ni·cal·ly** \-i-k(ə-)lē\ *adv* — **ty·ran·ni·cal·ness** \-kəl-nəs\ *n*

ty·ran·ni·cide \tə-ˈran-ə-ˌsīd, tī-\ *n* [in sense 1, fr. F, fr. L *tyrannicidium*, fr. *tyrannus* + -*i* + -*cidium* -cide (killing); in sense 2, fr. F, fr. L *tyrannicida*, fr. *tyrannus* + -*i* + -*cida* -cide (killer)] **1 :** the act of killing a tyrant **2 :** the killer of a tyrant

tyr·an·nize \'tir-ə-ˌnīz\ *vi* **:** to exercise arbitrary power ~ *vt* **:** to treat tyrannically **:** OPPRESS — **tyr·an·niz·er** *n*

ty·ran·no·saur \tə-ˈran-ə-ˌsó(ə)r, tī-\ *n* [NL *Tyrannosaurus*, genus name, deriv. of Gk *tyrannos* tyrant + *sauros* lizard — more at SAURIAN] **:** a very large bipedal carnivorous dinosaur (*Tyrannosaurus rex*) of the Upper Cretaceous of No. America

ty·ran·no·sau·rus \tə-ˌran-ə-ˈsór-əs, (ˌ)tī-\ *n* [NL] **:** TYRANNOSAUR

tyr·an·nous \'tir-ə-nəs\ *adj* **:** marked by tyranny; *esp* **:** unjustly severe — **tyr·an·nous·ly** *adv*

tyr·an·ny \'tir-ə-nē\ *n* [ME *tyrannie*, fr. MF, fr. ML *tyrannia*, fr. L *tyrannus* tyrant] **1 a :** a government in which absolute power is vested in a single ruler; *esp* **:** one characteristic of an ancient Greek city-state **b :** the office, authority, and administration of such a ruler **2 :** arbitrary and despotic government; *esp* **:** rigorous, cruel, and oppressive government **3 :** a severe condition or effect **:** RIGOR **4 :** a tyrannical act

ty·rant \'tī-rənt\ *n* [ME *tirant*, fr. OF *tyran*, *tyrant*, fr. L *tyrannus*, fr. Gk *tyrannos*] **1 a :** an absolute ruler unrestrained by law or constitution **b :** a usurper of sovereignty **2 a :** a ruler who exercises absolute power oppressively or brutally **b :** one resembling such a tyrant in the harsh use of authority or power

tyrant flycatcher *n* **:** any of various large American flycatchers (family Tyrannidae)

tyre *chiefly Brit var of* TIRE

Tyr·i·an purple \ˌtir-ē-ən-\ *n* [*Tyre*, maritime city of ancient Phoenicia] **:** a crimson or purple dye related to the indigo class, obtained by the ancient Greeks and Romans from gastropod mollusks and now made synthetically

ty·ro \'tī-(ə)r-(ˌ)ō\ *n* [ML, fr L *tiro* young soldier, tyro] **:** a beginner in learning **:** NOVICE syn see AMATEUR

ty·ro·ci·dine *or* **ty·ro·ci·din** \ˌtī-rə-ˈsīd-ᵊn\ *n* [*tyrosine* + -*cide* + -*ine*] **:** a basic polypeptide antibiotic produced by a soil bacillus (*Bacillus brevis*)

ty·ro·si·nase \'tī-rə-sən-ˌās, tī-ˈräs-ᵊn-, -ˌāz\ *n* **:** an enzyme that promotes the oxidation of phenols (as tyrosine) and is widespread in plants and animals

ty·ro·sine \'tī-rə-ˌsēn\ *n* [ISV, irreg. fr. Gk *tyros* cheese — more at BUTTER] **:** a phenolic amino acid $C_9H_{11}NO_3$ obtained by hydrolysis of proteins

tzar \'zär, 'tsär\ *var of* CZAR

tzi·gane \tsē-ˈgän\ *n* [F, fr. Hung *cigány*] **:** GYPSY — **tzigane** *adj*

ə abut; ᵊ kitten; ər further; a back; ā bake; ä cot, cart; aù out; ch chin; e less; ē easy; g gift; i trip; ī life
j joke; ŋ sing; ō flow; ò flaw; òi coin; th thin; ᵗh this; ü loot; ù foot; y yet; yü few; yù furious; zh vision

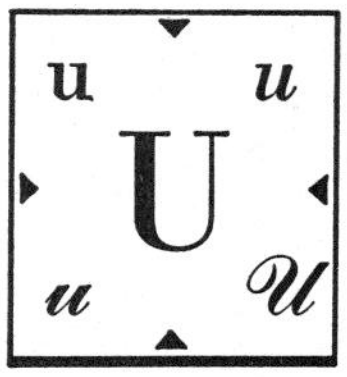

u \'yü\ *n, often cap, often attrib* **1 a :** the 21st letter of the English alphabet **b :** a graphic representation of this letter **c :** a speech counterpart of orthographic *u* **2 :** a graphic device for reproducing the letter *u* **3 :** one designated *u* esp. as the 20th or when *j* is used for the 10th the 21st in order or class **4 :** something shaped like the letter U

Uban·gi \(y)ü-'baŋ-(g)ē\ *n* [*Ubangi-Shari*, territory in French Equatorial Africa] **:** a woman of the district of Kyabé village in Africa with lips pierced and distended to unusual dimensions with wooden disks

ubiq·ui·tous \yü-'bik-wət-əs\ *adj* **:** existing or being everywhere at the same time **syn** see OMNIPRESENT — **ubiq·ui·tous·ly** *adv* — **ubiq·ui·tous·ness** *n*

ubiq·ui·ty \-wət-ē\ *n* [L *ubique* everywhere, fr. *ubi* where + *-que*, enclitic generalizing particle; akin to L *quis* who and to L *-que* and — more at WHO, SESQUI-] **:** presence everywhere or in many places esp. simultaneously **:** OMNIPRESENCE

ubi su·pra \,ü-bē-'sü-prə, -,prä\ *adv* [L, where above] **:** where above mentioned

U-boat \'yü-'bōt\ *n* [trans. of G *u-boot*, short for *unterseeboot*, lit., undersea boat] **:** a German submarine

ud·der \'əd-ər\ *n* [ME, fr. OE *ūder;* akin to OHG *ūtar* udder, L *uber*, Gk *outhar*, Skt *ūdhar*] **1 :** a large pendulous organ consisting of two or more mammary glands enclosed in a common envelope and each provided with a single nipple **2 :** a mammary gland

¹Uga·rit·ic \,(y)ü-gə-'rit-ik\ *adj* **:** of, relating to, or characteristic of the ancient city of Ugarit, its inhabitants, or Ugaritic

²Ugaritic *n* **:** the Semitic language of ancient Ugarit closely related to Phoenician and Hebrew

ugh *often read as* 'əg *or* 'ək\ *interj* — used to indicate the sound of a cough or grunt or to express disgust or horror

ug·li·fy \'əg-li-,fī\ *vt* **:** to make ugly

ug·li·ly \-lə-lē\ *adv* **:** in an ugly manner

ug·li·ness \-lē-nəs\ *n* **1 :** the quality or state of being ugly **2 :** an ugly thing or characteristic

ug·ly \'əg-lē\ *adj* [ME, fr. ON *uggligr*, fr. *uggr* fear; akin to ON *ugga* to fear] **1 :** FRIGHTFUL, DIRE **2 a :** offensive to the sight **:** HIDEOUS **b :** offensive or unpleasing to any sense **3 :** morally offensive or objectionable **:** REPULSIVE **4 a :** likely to cause inconvenience or discomfort **:** TROUBLESOME **b :** THREATENING **c :** SURLY, QUARRELSOME

ugly duckling *n* [*The Ugly Duckling*, story by Hans Christian Andersen] **:** an unpromising child or thing actually capable of developing into a person or thing worthy of attention or respect

Ugri·an \'(y)ü-grē-ən\ *n* [ORuss *Ugre* Hungarians] **:** a member of the eastern division of the Finno-Ugric peoples — **Ugrian** *adj*

Ugric \-grik\ *adj* **:** of, relating to, or characteristic of the languages of the Ugrians

ug·some \'əg-səm\ *adj* [ME, fr. *uggen* to fear, inspire fear, fr. ON *ugga* to fear] *archaic* **:** FRIGHTFUL, LOATHSOME

uh·lan \'ü-,län, ü-'; '(y)ü-lən\ *n* [G] **:** one of a body of Prussian light cavalry orig. modeled on Tatar lancers

Ui·ghur *or* **Ui·gur** \'wē-,gu̇(ə)r\ *n* [Uighur *Uighur*] **1 :** a member of a Turkic people powerful in Mongolia and eastern Turkestan between the 8th and 12th centuries A.D. who constitute a majority of the population of Chinese Turkestan **2 :** the Turkic language of the Uighur — **Uighur** *or* **Uigur** *adj*

uin·ta·ite *also* **uin·tah·ite** \yu̇-'int-ə-,īt\ *n* [*Uinta, Uintah*, mountains in Utah] **:** a black lustrous asphalt occurring esp. in Utah

Uit·land·er \'āt-,lan-dər\ *n* [Afrik] **:** FOREIGNER; *esp* **:** a British resident in the former republics of the Transvaal and Orange Free State

ukase \yü-'kās, -'kāz, 'yü-,; ü-'käz\ *n* [F & Russ; F, fr. Russ *ukaz*, fr. *ukazat'* to show, order; akin to OSlav *u-* away, L *au-*, Skt *ava-* and to OSlav *kazati* to show] **1 :** a proclamation by a Russian emperor or government having the force of law **2 :** EDICT

Ukrai·ni·an \yü-'krā-nē-ən\ *n* **1 :** a native or inhabitant of the Ukraine **2 :** the Slavic language of the Ukrainian people — **Ukrainian** *adj*

uku·le·le \,yü-kə-'lā-lē *also* ,ü-\ *n* [Hawaiian *'ukulele*, fr. *'uku* small person + *lele* jumping] **:** a small guitar of Portuguese origin popularized in Hawaii in the 1880s and strung typically with four strings

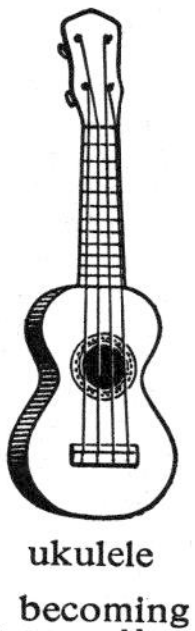
ukulele

ula·ma *or* **ule·ma** \,ü-lə-'mä\ *n* [Ar, Turk & Per; Turk & Per *'ulemā*, fr. Ar *'ulamā*] **1** *pl* **:** the body of mullahs **2 :** MULLAH

-u·lar \(y)ə-lər\ *adj suffix* [L *-ularis*, fr. *-ulus, -ula, -ulum* -ule + *-aris* -ar] **:** of, relating to, or resembling ⟨val*vular*⟩

¹ul·cer \'əl-sər\ *n* [ME, fr. L *ulcer-, ulcus;* akin to Gk *helkos* wound] **1 :** a break in skin or mucous membrane with loss of surface tissue, disintegration and necrosis of epithelial tissue, and often pus **2 :** something that festers and corrupts like an open sore

²ulcer *vb* **ul·cer·ing** \'əls-(ə-)riŋ\ **:** ULCERATE

ul·cer·ate \'əl-sə-,rāt\ *vt* **:** to affect with or as if with an ulcer ~ *vi* **:** to undergo ulceration

ul·cer·ation \,əl-sə-'rā-shən\ *n* **1 :** the process of becoming ulcerated **:** the state of being ulcerated **2 :** ULCER — **ul·cer·ative** \'əl-sə-,rāt-iv, 'əls-(ə-)rət-\ *adj*

ul·cer·ous \'əls-(ə-)rəs\ *adj* **1 :** being or marked by an ulceration ⟨~ lesions⟩ **2 :** affected with an ulcer **:** ULCERATED

-ule \(,)(y)ü(ə)l\ *n suffix* [F & L; F, fr. L *-ulus*, masc. dim. suffix, *-ula*, fem. dim. suffix, *-ulum*, neut. dim. suffix] **:** little one ⟨duct*ule*⟩

-u·lent \(y)ə-lənt\ *adj suffix* [L *-ulentus*] **:** that abounds in (a specified thing) ⟨floc*culent*⟩

ul·lage \'əl-ij\ *n* [ME *ulage*, fr. MF *eullage* act of filling a cask, fr. *eullier* to fill a cask, fr. OF *ouil* eye, bunghole, fr. L *oculus* eye] **:** the amount that a container (as a cask) lacks of being full

ul·na \'əl-nə\ *n, pl* **ul·nae** \'əl-,nē, -,nī\ *or* **ulnas** [NL, fr. L, elbow — more at ELL] **:** the inner of the two bones of the forearm or corresponding part of the forelimb of vertebrates above fishes — **ul·nad** \-,nad\ *adv* — **ul·nar** \-nər\ *adj*

-u·lose \(y)ə-,lōs, -,lōz\ *n suffix* [levulose] **:** ketose sugar ⟨hept*ulose*⟩

ulot·ri·chous \yü-'lä-tri-kəs\ *adj* [deriv. of Gk *oulotrich-, oulothrix*, fr. *oulos* curly + *trich-, thrix* hair; akin to Gk *eilyein* to roll — more at VOLUBLE, TRICH-] **:** having woolly or crisp hair — **ulot·ri·chy** \-trə-kē\ *n*

-u·lous \(y)ə-ləs\ *adj suffix* [L *-ulus*, dim. suffix] **:** being slightly or minutely (such) ⟨hirsu*tulous*⟩

ul·ster \'əl-stər\ *n* [*Ulster*, Ireland] **:** a long loose overcoat of Irish origin made of frieze or other heavy material

ul·te·ri·or \,əl-'tir-ē-ər\ *adj* [L, farther, further, compar. of (assumed) L *ulter* situated beyond, fr. *uls* beyond; akin to L *ollus, ille*, that one, OIr *indoll* beyond] **1 a :** FURTHER, FUTURE **b :** more distant **:** REMOTER **c :** situated on the farther side **:** THITHER **2 :** HIDDEN, LATENT ⟨~ motives⟩ — **ul·te·ri·or·ly** *adv*

ul·ti·ma \'əl-tə-mə\ *n* [L, fem. of *ultimus* last] **:** the last syllable of a word

ul·ti·ma·cy \'əl-tə-mə-sē\ *n* **1 :** the quality or state of being ultimate **2 :** ULTIMATE, FUNDAMENTAL

ul·ti·ma ra·tio \,ùl-tə-mə-'rät-ē-,ō\ *n* [NL] **:** the final argument; *also* **:** the last resort (as force)

¹ul·ti·mate \'əl-tə-mət\ *adj* [ML *ultimatus* last, final, fr. LL, pp. of *ultimare* to come to an end, be last, fr. L *ultimus* farthest, last, final, superl. of (assumed) L *ulter* situated beyond — more at ULTERIOR] **1 a :** most remote in space or time **:** FARTHEST **b :** last in a progression **:** FINAL **c :** EVENTUAL **d :** EXTREME, UTMOST **2 :** finally reckoned **3 a :** BASIC, FUNDAMENTAL **b :** incapable of further analysis, division, or separation **:** ELEMENTAL **4 :** MAXIMUM **syn** see LAST — **ul·ti·mate·ly** *adv* — **ul·ti·mate·ness** *n*

²ultimate *n* **1 :** something ultimate; *esp* **:** FUNDAMENTAL **2 :** ACME

ul·ti·ma Thu·le \,əl-tə-mə-'th(y)ü-lē\ *n* [L, farthest Thule] **:** THULE

ul·ti·ma·tum \,əl-tə-'māt-əm, -'mät-\ *n, pl* **ultimatums** *or* **ul·ti·ma·ta** \-ə\ [NL, fr. ML, neut. of *ultimatus* final] **:** a final proposition, condition, or demand; *esp* **:** one whose rejection will end negotiations and cause a resort to force or other direct action

ul·ti·mo \'əl-tə-,mō\ *adj* [L *ultimo mense* in the last month] **:** of or occurring in the month preceding the present

ul·ti·mo·gen·i·ture \,əl-tə-mō-'jen-ə-,chu̇(ə)r, -i-chər, -ə-,t(y)u̇(ə)r\ *n* [L *ultimus* last + E *-o-* + *-geniture* (as in *primogeniture*)] **:** a system of inheritance by which the youngest son succeeds to the estate

¹ul·tra \'əl-trə\ *adj* [*ultra-*] **:** going beyond others or beyond due limit **:** EXTREME

²ultra *n* [*ultra-*] **:** EXTREMIST

ultra- *prefix* [L, fr. *ultra* beyond, adv. & prep., fr. (assumed) L *ulter* situated beyond — more at ULTERIOR] **1 :** beyond in space **:** on the other side **:** TRANS- ⟨*ultra*violet⟩ **2 :** beyond the range or limits of **:** transcending **:** SUPER- ⟨*ultra*microscopic⟩ **3 :** beyond what is ordinary, proper, or moderate **:** excessively ⟨*ultra*modern⟩

ul·tra·cen·trif·u·gal \,əl-trə-(,)sen-'trif-yə-gəl, -'trif-i-gəl\ *adj* **:** of, relating to, or obtained by means of an ultracentrifuge

ul·tra·cen·trif·u·ga·tion \-(,)sen-,trif-(y)ə-'gā-shən, -(,)sän-\ *n* **:** processing in an ultracentrifuge

¹ul·tra·cen·tri·fuge \-'sen-trə-,fyüj, -'sän-\ *n* **:** a high-speed centrifuge able to sediment colloidal and other small particles and used esp. in determining sizes of such particles and molecular weights of large molecules

²ultracentrifuge *vt* **:** to subject to an ultracentrifuge

ul·tra·con·ser·va·tive \-kən-'sər-vət-iv\ *adj* **:** extremely conservative

ul·tra·fash·ion·able \-'fash-(ə-)nə-bəl\ *adj* **:** extremely fashionable

ul·tra·high frequency \,əl-trə-,hī-\ *n* **:** a radio frequency in the second from the highest range of the radio spectrum — see RADIO FREQUENCY table

ul·tra·ism \'əl-trə-,iz-əm\ *n* **1 :** the principles of those who advocate extreme measures (as radicalism) **2 :** an instance or example of radicalism — **ul·tra·ist** \-trə-əst\ *adj or n* — **ul·tra·is·tic** \,əl-trə-'is-tik\ *adj*

¹ul·tra·ma·rine \,əl-trə-mə-'rēn\ *n* [ML *ultramarinus* coming from beyond the sea] **1 a** (1) **:** a blue pigment prepared by powdering lapis lazuli (2) **:** a similar pigment prepared from kaolin, soda ash, sulfur, and charcoal **b :** any of several related pigments **2 :** a vivid blue

²ultramarine *adj* [ML *ultramarinus*, fr. L *ultra-* + *mare* sea — more at MARINE] **:** situated beyond the sea

ul·tra·mi·cro \,əl-trə-'mī-(,)krō\ *adj* **:** being or dealing with something smaller than micro

ul·tra·mi·cro·chem·is·try \-,mī-krō-'kem-ə-strē\ *n* **:** chemistry dealing with very minute quantities of substances

ul·tra·mi·cro·scope \,əl-trə-'mī-krə-,skōp\ *n* [back-formation fr. *ultramicroscopic*] **:** an apparatus for making visible by scattered light particles too small to be perceived by the ordinary microscope

ul·tra·mi·cro·scop·ic \-,mī-krə-'skäp-ik\ *adj* [ISV] **1 :** too small to be seen with an ordinary microscope **2 :** of or relating to an ultramicroscope

ul·tra·mod·ern \,əl-trə-'mäd-ərn\ *adj* **:** extreme or excessively modern in idea, style, or tendency — **ul·tra·mod·ern·ist** \-ər-nəst\ *n*

ul·tra·mon·tane \-'män-,tān, -,män-'\ *adj* [ML *ultramontanus*, fr. L *ultra-* + *mont-, mons* mountain — more at MOUNT] **1 :** of or relating to countries or peoples beyond the mountains (as the Alps) **2 :** favoring greater or absolute supremacy of papal over national or diocesan authority in the Roman Catholic Church — **ultramontane** *n, often cap* — **ul·tra·mon·tan·ism** \-'mänt-ᵊn-,iz-əm\ *n*

ul·tra·mun·dane \,əl-trə-'mən-,dān, -,mən-'\ *adj* [L *ultramundanus*, fr. *ultra* beyond + *mundus* world — more at ULTRA-] **:** situated beyond the world or beyond the limits of the solar system

ul·tra·na·tion·al·ism \-'nash-nə-,liz-əm, -ən-ᵊl-,iz-\ *n* **:** great or excessive devotion to or advocacy of national interests and rights esp. as opposed to international considerations — **ul·tra·na·tion·al·ist** \-nə-ləst, -ən-ᵊl-əst\ *adj or n*

ul·tra·red \,əl-trə-'red\ *adj* **:** INFRARED

ul·tra·short \-'shȯ(ə)rt\ *adj* **:** very short; *esp* **:** having a wavelength below 10 meters

¹ul·tra·son·ic \-'sän-ik\ *adj* **:** SUPERSONIC

²ultrasonic *n* **:** an ultrasonic wave or frequency

ul·tra·son·ics \-iks\ *n pl but sing in constr* **:** SUPERSONICS

ul·tra·sound \-'saund\ *n* **:** vibrations of the same physical nature as sound but with frequencies above the range of human hearing

ul·tra·struc·ture \'əl-trə-,strək-chər\ *n* **:** the invisible ultimate physiochemical organization of protoplasm

ul·tra·vi·o·let \,əl-trə-'vī-ə-lət\ *adj* **1 :** situated beyond the visible spectrum at its violet end — used of radiation having a wavelength

shorter than wavelengths of visible light and longer than those of X rays **2 :** relating to, producing, or employing ultraviolet radiation — **ultraviolet** *n*

ultraviolet light *n* **:** ultraviolet radiation

ul·tra vi·res \ˌəl-trə-ˈvī-(ˌ)rēz\ *adv* (*or adj*) [NL, lit., beyond power] **:** beyond the scope or in excess of legal power or authority

ul·tra·vi·rus \ˈəl-trə-ˌvī-rəs\ *n* [NL] **:** an ultramicroscopic or filterable virus — called also *ul·tra·mi·crobe* \-ˌmī-ˌkrōb\, *ul·tra·mi·cro·or·ga·nism* \-krō-ˌȯr-gə-ˌniz-əm\

ulu·lant \ˈəl-yə-lənt, ˈ(y)ül-yə-\ *adj* **:** HOWLING, WAILING

ulu·late \-ˌlāt\ *vi* [L *ululatus*, pp. of *ululare*, of imit. origin] **:** HOWL, WAIL — **ulu·la·tion** \ˌəl-yə-ˈlā-shən, ˌ(y)ül-yə-\ *n*

Ulys·ses \yu̇-ˈlis-(ˌ)ēz\ *n* [L, modif. of Gk *Odysseus*] **:** ODYSSEUS

um·bel \ˈəm-bəl\ *n* [NL *umbella*, fr. L, umbrella] **:** a racemose inflorescence typical of the carrot family in which the axis is very much contracted so that the pedicels appear to spring from the same point to form a flat or rounded flower cluster — **um·beled** *or* **um·belled** \-bəld\ *adj* — **um·bel·lar** \ˈəm-bə-lər, ˌəm-ˈbel-ər\ *adj*

um·bel·late \ˈəm-bə-ˌlāt, ˌəm-ˈbel-ət\ *also* **um·bel·lat·ed** \ˈəm-bə-ˌlāt-əd\ *adj* **1 :** bearing, consisting of, or arranged in umbels **2 :** resembling an umbel in form — **um·bel·late·ly** *adv*

um·bel·lif·er·ous \ˌəm-bə-ˈlif-(ə-)rəs\ *adj* [NL *umbellifer*, fr. *umbella* umbel + L *-fer* -ferous] **:** producing umbels

um·bel·lu·late \ˌəm-ˈbel-yə-lət\ *adj* **:** arranged in umbellules

um·bel·lule \ˈəm-bəl-ˌ(y)ü(ə)l, ˌəm-ˈbel-(ˌ)yü(ə)l\ *n* [NL *umbellula*, dim. of *umbella*] **:** a secondary umbel in a compound umbel

[1]**um·ber** \ˈəm-bər\ *n* [ME *umbre*, fr. MF, fr. L *umbra* shade, shadow, grayling] **:** a European grayling (*Thymallus thymallus*)

[2]**umber** *n* [prob. fr. obs. E, shade, color, fr. ME *umbre* shade, shadow, fr. MF, fr. L *umbra* — more at UMBRAGE] **1 :** a brown earth darker in color than ocher and sienna because of its content of manganese and iron oxides that is highly valued as a permanent pigment either in the raw or burnt state **2 a :** a moderate to dark yellowish brown **b :** a moderate brown

[3]**umber** *adj* **:** of, relating to, or having the characteristics of umber; *specif* **:** of the color of umber

[4]**umber** *vt* **um·ber·ing** \-b(ə-)riŋ\ **:** to stain umber **:** DARKEN

um·bil·i·cal \ˌəm-ˈbil-i-kəl\ *adj* **1 :** of, relating to, or used at the navel **2 :** of or relating to the central region of the abdomen

umbilical cord *n* **1 :** a cord arising from the navel that connects the fetus with the placenta; *also* **:** YOLK STALK **2 :** a servicing cable that is detached from a rocket vehicle at launching

um·bil·i·cate \ˌəm-ˈbil-i-kət\ *or* **um·bil·i·cat·ed** \-ə-ˌkāt-əd\ *adj* **1 :** depressed like a navel **2 :** having an umbilicus — **um·bil·i·ca·tion** \ˌəm-ˌbil-ə-ˈkā-shən\ *n*

um·bi·li·cus \ˌəm-ˈbil-i-kəs, ˌəm-bə-ˈlī-\ *n, pl* **um·bi·li·ci** \-ˈbil-ə-ˌkī, -ˌkē, -ˌsī; -ˈlī-ˌkī, -ˌsī\ *or* **um·bi·li·cus·es** [L — more at NAVEL] **1 a :** a small depression in the abdominal wall at the point of attachment of the umbilical cord to the embryo **b :** any of several morphological depressions; *esp* **:** HILUM 1a **2 :** a central point **:** CORE, HEART

um·bles \ˈəm-bəlz\ *n pl* [ME, alter. of *nombles*, fr. MF, pl. of *nomble* fillet of beef, pork loin, modif. of L *lumbulus*, dim. of *lumbus* loin — more at LOIN] **:** the entrails of an animal and esp. of a deer used as food

um·bo \ˈəm-(ˌ)bō\ *n, pl* **um·bo·nes** \ˌəm-ˈbō-(ˌ)nēz\ *or* **umbos** [L; akin to L *umbilicus* — more at NAVEL] **1 :** the boss of a shield **2 :** a rounded elevation: as **a :** an elevation in the tympanic membrane of the ear **b :** one of the lateral prominences just above the hinge of a bivalve shell — **um·bo·nal** \ˈəm-bən-ᵊl, ˌəm-ˈbōn-\ *also* **um·bon·ic** \ˌəm-ˈbän-ik\ *adj* — **um·bo·nate** \ˈəm-bə-ˌnāt\ *adj*

um·bra \ˈəm-brə\ *n, pl* **umbras** *or* **um·brae** \-(ˌ)brē, -ˌbrī\ [L] **1 :** a shaded area **2 a :** a conical shadow excluding all light from a given source; *specif* **:** the conical part of the shadow of a celestial body excluding all light from the primary source **b** (1) **:** PENUMBRA 2 (2) **:** the central dark part of a sunspot

um·brage \ˈəm-brij\ *n* [ME, fr. MF, fr. L *umbraticum*, neut. of *umbraticus* of shade, fr. *umbratus*, pp. of *umbrare* to shade, fr. *umbra* shade, shadow; akin to Lith *unksna* shadow] **1 :** SHADE, SHADOW **2 :** shady branches **:** FOLIAGE **3 a :** an indistinct indication **:** vague suggestion **:** HINT **b :** a reason for doubt **:** SUSPICION **4 :** DISPLEASURE, RESENTMENT ⟨take ~ at a remark⟩ **syn** see OFFENSE

um·bra·geous \ˌəm-ˈbrā-jəs\ *adj* **1 a :** providing shade **:** SHADY **b** (1) **:** SHADED (2) **:** filled with shadows **2 :** inclined to take offense easily — **um·bra·geous·ly** *adv* — **um·bra·geous·ness** *n*

[1]**um·brel·la** \ˌəm-ˈbrel-ə, *esp South* ˈəm-ˌ\ *n* [It *ombrella*, modif. of L *umbella*, dim. of *umbra*] **1 :** a small circular canopy with hinged ribs radiating from a center pole for protection against weather **2 :** the bell-shaped or saucer-shaped largely gelatinous structure that forms the chief part of the body of most jellyfishes **3 a :** a defensive formation of planes maintained over surface operations or a landmass **b :** a heavy barrage

umbrella

[2]**umbrella** *adj* **:** taking in many individuals or groups **:** all-embracing

[3]**umbrella** *vt* **:** to protect, cover, or provide with an umbrella

umbrella bird *n* **:** any of several tropical American birds (genus *Cephalopterus* and esp. *C. ornatus*) related to the tyrant flycatchers and noted for the black male with a radiating crest curving forward over the head

umbrella leaf *n* **:** a No. American herb (*Diphylleia cymosa*) of the barberry family with two large peltate stem leaves or a solitary lobed basal one

umbrella plant *n* **:** an African sedge (*Cyperus alternifolius*) with large terminal whorls of slender leaves that is often grown as an ornamental

umbrella tree *n* **1 :** an American magnolia (*Magnolia tripetala*) having large leaves clustered at the ends of the branches **2 :** any of various trees or shrubs resembling an umbrella esp. in the arrangement of leaves or the shape of the crown

Um·bri·an \ˈəm-brē-ən\ *n* **1 a :** a member of a people of ancient Italy occupying Umbria **b :** a native or inhabitant of the Italian province of Umbria **2 :** the Italic language of ancient Umbria — **Umbrian** *adj*

umi·ak \ˈü-mē-ˌak\ *n* [Esk] **:** an open Eskimo boat made of a wooden frame covered with hide and usu. propelled with broad paddles

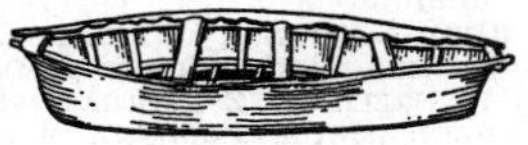

umiak

[1]**um·laut** \ˈu̇m-ˌlau̇t, ˈüm-\ *n* [G, fr. *um-* around + *laut* sound] **1 a :** the change of a vowel caused by partial assimilation to a succeeding sound; *esp* **:** the fronting or raising of a back or low vowel (as *a, o,* or *u*) caused by an *i* or *j* orig. standing in the following syllable but usu. lost or altered **b :** a vowel resulting from such partial assimilation **2 :** a diacritical mark ¨ placed esp. over a German vowel to indicate umlaut

[2]**umlaut** *vt* **1 :** to produce by umlaut **2 :** to write or print an umlaut over

um·pir·age \ˈəm-ˌpī(ə)r-ij\ *n* **1 :** the office or authority of an umpire **2 a :** an act or instance of umpiring **b :** a decision of an umpire

[1]**um·pire** \ˈəm-ˌpī(ə)r\ *n* [ME *oumpere*, alter. (resulting fr. incorrect division of *a noumpere*) of *noumpere*, fr. MF *nomper* not equal, not paired, fr. *non-* + *per* equal, fr. L *par*] **1 :** one having authority to decide finally a controversy or question between parties: as **a :** one appointed to decide between arbitrators who have disagreed **b :** an impartial third party chosen to arbitrate disputes arising under the terms of a labor agreement **2 :** an official in a sport who rules on plays **3 :** a military officer who evaluates maneuvers

[2]**umpire** *vt* **:** to supervise or decide as umpire **~** *vi* **:** to act as umpire

ump·teen \ˈəm(p)-ˈtēn, ˌəm(p)-\ *adj* [blend of *umpty* (such and such) + *-teen* (as in *thirteen*)] **:** very many **:** indefinitely numerous — **ump·teenth** \-ˈtēn(t)th\ *adj*

[1]**un-** \ˌən, ˈən *before* ˈ-stressed syll, ˌən *before* ˌ-stressed syll, ˌən *before unstressed syll*\ *prefix* [ME, fr. OE; akin to OHG *un-* un-, L *in-*, Gk *a-, an-*, OE *ne* not — more at NO] **1 :** not **:** IN-, NON- — in adjectives formed from adjectives ⟨*un*strenuous⟩ ⟨*un*skilled⟩ or participles ⟨*un*dressed⟩, in nouns formed from nouns ⟨*un*ostentation⟩, and rarely in verbs formed from verbs ⟨*un*be⟩; sometimes in words that have a meaning that merely negates that of the base word and are thereby distinguished from words that prefix *in-* or a variant of it (as *im-*) to the same base word and have a meaning positively opposite to that of the base word ⟨*un*artistic⟩ ⟨*un*moral⟩ **2 :** opposite of **:** contrary to — in adjectives formed from adjectives ⟨*un*constitutional⟩ ⟨*un*graceful⟩ ⟨*un*mannered⟩ or participles ⟨*un*believing⟩, and in nouns formed from nouns ⟨*un*rest⟩

[2]**un-** *prefix* [ME, fr. OE *un-, on-*, alter. of *and-* against — more at ANTE-] **1 a :** do the opposite of **:** reverse (a specified action) **:** DE- 1a, DIS- 1a — in verbs formed from verbs ⟨*un*bend⟩ ⟨*un*dress⟩ ⟨*un*fold⟩ **b :** cause to cease to — in verbs formed from verbs ⟨*un*be⟩ **2 a :** deprive of **:** remove (a specified thing) from **:** remove — in verbs formed from nouns ⟨*un*frock⟩ ⟨*un*sex⟩ **b :** release from **:** free from — in verbs formed from nouns ⟨*un*hand⟩ **c :** remove from **:** extract from **:** bring out of — in verbs formed from nouns ⟨*un*bosom⟩ **d :** cause to cease to be — in verbs formed from nouns ⟨*un*man⟩ **3 :** completely ⟨*un*loose⟩

un·abashed \ˌən-ə-ˈbasht\ *adj* **:** not abashed — **un·abashed·ly** \-ˈbasht-lē, -ˈbash-əd-lē\ *adv*

un·abat·ed \ˌən-ə-ˈbāt-əd\ *adj* **:** not abated **:** at full strength or force — **un·abat·ed·ly** *adv*

un·able \ˌən-ˈā-bəl, ˈən-\ *adj* **1 :** not able **:** INCAPABLE **2 a :** UNQUALIFIED, INCOMPETENT, INEFFICIENT **b :** IMPOTENT, HELPLESS

un·abridged \ˌən-ə-ˈbrijd\ *adj* **1 :** not abridged **:** COMPLETE **2 :** complete of its class **:** not based on one larger ⟨an ~ dictionary⟩

un·ac·com·mo·dat·ed \ˌən-ə-ˈkäm-ə-ˌdāt-əd\ *adj* **:** not accommodated **:** UNPROVIDED

un·ac·com·pa·nied \ˌən-ə-ˈkəmp-(ə-)nēd\ *adj* **:** not accompanied; *specif* **:** being without instrumental accompaniment

un·ac·count·able \ˌən-ə-ˈkau̇nt-ə-bəl\ *adj* **1 :** not to be accounted for **:** INEXPLICABLE, STRANGE, MYSTERIOUS **2 :** not to be called to account **:** not responsible — **un·ac·count·ably** \-blē\ *adv*

un·ac·count·ed \-ˈkau̇nt-əd\ *adj* **:** not accounted **:** UNEXPLAINED — often used with *for*

un·ac·cus·tomed \ˌən-ə-ˈkəs-təmd\ *adj* **1 :** not customary **:** not usual or common **2 :** not habituated — usu. used with *to*

una cor·da \ˌü-nə-ˈkȯr-ˌdä\ *adv* (*or adj*) [It, lit., one string] **:** with soft pedal depressed — used as a direction in piano music

una corda pedal *n* **:** SOFT PEDAL

un·adorned \ˌən-ə-ˈdȯ(ə)rnd\ *adj* **:** not adorned **:** lacking embellishment or decoration **:** BARE, PLAIN, SIMPLE

un·adul·ter·at·ed \ˌən-ə-ˈdəl-tə-ˌrāt-əd\ *adj* **:** PURE, UNMIXED — **un·adul·ter·at·ed·ly** *adv*

un·ad·vised \ˌən-əd-ˈvīzd\ *adj* **1 :** done without due consideration **:** RASH **2 :** not prudent — **un·ad·vis·ed·ly** \-ˈvī-zəd-lē\ *adv*

un·af·fect·ed \ˌən-ə-ˈfek-təd\ *adj* **1 :** not influenced or changed mentally, physically, or chemically **2 :** free from affectation **:** GENUINE — **un·af·fect·ed·ly** *adv* — **un·af·fect·ed·ness** *n*

un·aligned \ˌən-ᵊl-ˈīnd\ *adj* **:** not associated with any one of competing international blocs ⟨~ nations⟩

un·al·loyed \ˌən-ᵊl-ˈȯid\ *adj* **:** not alloyed **:** UNMIXED, UNQUALIFIED, PURE ⟨~ metals⟩ ⟨~ happiness⟩

un·al·ter·able \ˌən-ˈȯl-t(ə-)rə-bəl, ˈən-\ *adj* **:** not capable of being altered or changed ⟨~ resolve⟩ ⟨~ hatred⟩ — **un·al·ter·able·ness** *n* — **un·al·ter·ably** \-blē\ *adv*

See *un-* and 2d element	**unaccentuated**	**unaccountability**	**unadapted**	**unaesthetic**	**unaired**
unabbreviated	**unacceptable**	**unaccredited**	**unadjusted**	**unaffiliated**	**unalienable**
unabsolved	**unaccepted**	**unacknowledged**	**unadmirable**	**unafraid**	**unalike**
unabsorbable	**unacclimated**	**unacquainted**	**unadvantageous**	**unaged**	**unallied**
unabsorbed	**unacclimatized**	**unactable**	**unadventurous**	**unaggressive**	**unallowable**
unacademic	**unaccommodating**	**unacted**	**unadvertised**	**unaided**	**unalterability**
unaccented	**unaccomplished**	**unadaptable**	**unadvisable**	**unaimed**	**unaltered**

un–Amer·i·can \ˌən-ə-ˈmer-ə-kən\ *adj* : not American : not characteristic of or consistent with American customs, principles, or traditions

un·an·chor \ˌən-ˈaŋ-kər, ˈən-\ *vt* : to loosen from an anchor

un·aneled \ˌən-ə-ˈnē(ə)ld\ *adj, archaic* : not having received extreme unction

una·nim·i·ty \ˌyü-nə-ˈnim-ət-ē\ *n* : the quality or state of being unanimous

unan·i·mous \yu̇-ˈnan-ə-məs\ *adj* [L *unanimus*, fr. *unus* one + *animus* mind — more at ONE, ANIMATE] **1** : being of one mind : AGREEING **2** : formed with or indicating unanimity : having the agreement and consent of all — **unan·i·mous·ly** *adv*

un·an·swer·able \ˌən-ˈan(t)s-(ə-)rə-bəl, ˈən-\ *adj* : not answerable; esp : IRREFUTABLE

un·ap·peal·able \ˌən-ə-ˈpē-lə-bəl\ *adj* : not appealable : not subject to appeal

un·ap·peal·ing \-ˈpē-liŋ\ *adj* : not appealing : UNATTRACTIVE

un·ap·peas·able \-ˈpē-zə-bəl\ *adj* : not to be appeased : IMPLACABLE — **un·ap·peas·ably** \-blē\ *adv*

un·apt \ˌən-ˈapt, ˈən-\ *adj* **1** : UNSUITABLE, INAPPROPRIATE **2** : not accustomed and not likely **3** : INAPT, DULL, BACKWARD — **un·apt·ly** \-ˈap-(t)lē\ *adv* — **un·apt·ness** \-ˈap(t)-nəs\ *n*

un·arm \ˌən-ˈärm, ˈən-\ *vt* : DISARM

un·armed \-ˈärmd\ *adj* **1** : not armed or armored **2** : having no hard and sharp projections (as spines, spurs, or claws)

un·ar·mored scale \ˌən-ˌär-mərd-\ *n* : any of various scale insects usu. lacking a substantial waxy covering; *esp* : COCCID

un·asked \ˌən-ˈas(k)t, ˈən-\ *adj* **1** : not being asked : UNINVITED **2** : not asked for ⟨~ advice⟩

un·as·sail·able \ˌən-ə-ˈsā-lə-bəl\ *adj* : not assailable : not liable to doubt, attack, or question — **un·as·sail·ably** \-blē\ *adv*

un·as·ser·tive \ˌən-ə-ˈsərt-iv\ *adj* : not assertive : MODEST, SHY

un·as·sum·ing \-ˈsü-miŋ\ *adj* : not assuming : not arrogant or presuming : MODEST, RETIRING — **un·as·sum·ing·ness** *n*

un·at·tached \ˌən-ə-ˈtacht\ *adj* **1 a** : not assigned or committed (as to a particular task, organization, or person); *specif* : not married or engaged **b** : not seized as security for a legal judgment **2** : not joined or united ⟨~ polyps⟩

un·avail·able energy \ˌən-ə-ˌvā-lə-bəl-\ *n* : energy that is incapable of doing work under existing conditions

un·avoid·able \ˌən-ə-ˈvȯid-ə-bəl\ *adj* : not avoidable : INEVITABLE — **un·avoid·ably** \-blē\ *adv*

¹un·aware \-ˈwa(ə)r, -ˈwe(ə)r\ *adv* : UNAWARES

²unaware *adj* : not aware : IGNORANT — **un·aware·ness** *n*

un·awares \-ˈwa(ə)rz, -ˈwe(ə)rz\ *adv* [*un-* + *aware* + *-s*, adv. suffix, fr. ME, fr. *-s*, gen. sing. ending of nouns — more at -s] **1** : without design, attention, preparation, or premeditation **2** : without warning : SUDDENLY, UNEXPECTEDLY

un·backed \ˌən-ˈbakt, ˈən-\ *adj* **1** : never mounted by a rider : not broken **2** : not supported **3** : having no back

un·bal·ance \ˌən-ˈbal-ən(t)s, ˈən-\ *vt* : to put out of balance; *specif* : to derange mentally

un·bal·anced \-ən(t)st\ *adj* **1** : not in equilibrium **2** : mentally disordered or deranged **3** : not brought to an equality of debit and credit ⟨an ~ account⟩

un·bal·last·ed \-ˈbal-ə-stəd\ *adj* : not furnished with or steadied by ballast : UNSTEADY

un·bar \ˌən-ˈbär, ˈən-\ *vt* : to remove a bar from : UNBOLT, OPEN

un·barred \-ˈbärd\ *adj* **1** : not secured by a bar : UNLOCKED **2** : not marked with bars

un·bat·ed \-ˈbāt-əd\ *adj* **1** : UNABATED **2** *archaic* : not blunted

un·be \-ˈbē\ *vi, archaic* : to lack or cease to have being

un·bear·able \ˌən-ˈbar-ə-bəl, ˈən-, -ˈber-\ *adj* : not bearable : UNENDURABLE — **un·bear·ably** \-blē\ *adv*

un·beat·able \-ˈbēt-ə-bəl\ *adj* : not capable of being defeated

un·beat·en \-ˈbēt-ᵊn\ *adj* **1** : not pounded **2** : UNTROD **3** : UNDEFEATED

un·be·com·ing \ˌən-bi-ˈkəm-iŋ\ *adj* : not becoming : UNSUITABLE, IMPROPER **syn** see INDECOROUS — **un·be·com·ing·ly** \-iŋ-lē\ *adv* — **un·be·com·ing·ness** *n*

un·be·known \ˌən-bi-ˈnōn\ *or* **un·be·knownst** \-ˈnōn(t)st\ *adj* [¹*un-* + obs. E *beknown* (known)] : happening without one's knowledge : UNKNOWN — usu. used with *to*

un·be·lief \ˌən-bə-ˈlēf\ *n* : incredulity or skepticism esp. in matters of religious faith

syn DISBELIEF, INCREDULITY: UNBELIEF stresses absence of belief esp. but not always in religion or divine revelation; DISBELIEF stresses a positive rejection of what is asserted or stated; INCREDULITY suggests a disposition to refuse belief or acceptance

un·be·liev·able \-ˈlē-və-bəl\ *adj* : surpassing belief : INCREDIBLE — **un·be·liev·ably** \-blē\ *adv*

un·be·liev·er \-ˈlē-vər\ *n* **1** : one that does not believe : an incredulous person : DOUBTER, SKEPTIC **2** : one that does not believe in a particular religious faith : INFIDEL **syn** see ATHEIST

un·be·liev·ing \-ˈlē-viŋ\ *adj* : marked by unbelief — **un·be·liev·ing·ly** \-viŋ-lē\ *adv*

un·bend \ˌən-ˈbend, ˈən-\ *vt* **1** : to free from flexure : make or allow to become straight ⟨~ a bow⟩ **2** : to cause (as the mind) to relax **3 a** : to unfasten (as a sail) from a spar or stay **b** : to cast loose or untie (as a rope) ~ *vi* **1** : to relax one's severity, stiffness, or austerity **2** : to cease to be bent : become straight or relaxed

¹un·bend·ing \ˌən-ˈben-diŋ, ˈən-\ *adj* **1** : not bending : UNYIELDING, INFLEXIBLE **2** : cool, aloof, or unsocial in manner or mien

²unbending *adj* : that unbends : given to relaxation

un·be·seem·ing \ˌən-bi-ˈsē-miŋ\ *adj* : not befitting : UNBECOMING

un·bi·ased \ˌən-ˈbī-əst, ˈən-\ *adj* : free from bias ⟨~ estimate⟩; *esp* : UNPREJUDICED, IMPARTIAL **syn** see FAIR

un·bid·den \-ˈbid-ᵊn\ *also* **un·bid** \-ˈbid\ *adj* : not bidden : UNASKED, UNINVITED

un·bind \-ˈbīnd\ *vt* **1** : to remove a band from : free from fastenings : UNTIE, UNFASTEN, LOOSE **2** : to set free : RELEASE

un·bit·ted \ˌən-ˈbit-əd, ˈən-\ *adj* : UNBRIDLED, UNCONTROLLED

un·blenched \-ˈblencht\ *adj* : not disconcerted : UNDAUNTED

un·blessed *also* **un·blest** \-ˈblest\ *adj* **1** : not blessed **2** : EVIL

un·blush·ing \-ˈbləsh-iŋ\ *adj* **1** : not blushing **2** : SHAMELESS, UNABASHED — **un·blush·ing·ly** \-iŋ-lē\ *adv*

un·bod·ied \-ˈbäd-ēd\ *adj* **1** : having no body : INCORPOREAL; *also* : DISEMBODIED **2** : FORMLESS

un·bolt \ˌən-ˈbōlt, ˈən-\ *vt* : to open or unfasten by withdrawing a bolt

¹un·bolt·ed \-ˈbōl-təd\ *adj* : not sifted ⟨~ flour⟩; *also* : COARSE

²unbolted *adj* : not fastened by bolts

un·bon·net \ˌən-ˈbän-ət, ˈən-\ *vi* : to remove one's bonnet esp. as a mark of respect ~ *vt* : to take a bonnet from

un·bon·net·ed \-ət-əd\ *adj* : BAREHEADED

un·born \ˌən-ˈbȯ(ə)rn, ˈən-\ *adj* **1** : not born : not brought into life; *broadly* : still to appear : FUTURE **2** : existing without birth

un·bo·som \-ˈbu̇z-əm, -ˈbüz-\ *vt* **1** : to give expression to : DISCLOSE, REVEAL **2** : to disclose the thoughts or feelings of (oneself) ~ *vi* : to unbosom oneself

un·bound \-ˈbau̇nd\ *adj* : not bound: as **a** (1) : not fastened (2) : not confined **b** : not having the leaves fastened together ⟨an ~ book⟩ **c** : not held in chemical or physical combination

un·bound·ed \-ˈbau̇n-dəd\ *adj* **1** : having no limit **2** : UNCONTROLLED, UNRESTRAINED

un·bowed \ˌən-ˈbau̇d, ˈən-\ *adj* **1** : not bowed down **2** : UNSUBDUED

un·brace \-ˈbrās\ *vt* **1** : to free or detach by or as if by untying or removing a brace or bond **2** : ENFEEBLE, WEAKEN

un·braid \-ˈbrād\ *vt* : to separate the strands of : UNRAVEL

un·branched \-ˈbrancht\ *adj* **1** : having no branches ⟨a straight ~ trunk⟩ **2** : not divided into branches ⟨a leaf with ~ veins⟩

un·bred \-ˈbred\ *adj* **1** *obs* : ILL-BRED **2** : UNTAUGHT, UNTRAINED **3** : not bred : never having been bred ⟨an ~ heifer⟩

un·bri·dle \ˌən-ˈbrīd-ᵊl, ˈən-\ *vt* : to free or loose from a bridle; *broadly* : to set loose : free from restraint

un·bri·dled \-ˈbrīd-ᵊld\ *adj* **1** : not confined by a bridle **2** : UNRESTRAINED, UNGOVERNED

un·broke \-ˈbrōk\ *adj* : UNBROKEN

un·bro·ken \-ˈbrō-kən\ *adj* : not broken: as **a** : not violated **b** : WHOLE, INTACT **c** : UNSUBDUED, UNTAMED; *esp* : not trained for service or use ⟨~ colts⟩ **d** : UNINTERRUPTED **e** : UNPLOWED **f** : not disorganized ⟨advanced in ~ ranks⟩

un·buck·le \-ˈbək-əl\ *vt* : to loose the buckle of : UNFASTEN ~ *vi* **1** : to loosen buckles **2** : RELAX

un·build \ˌən-ˈbild, ˈən-\ *vt* : to pull down : DEMOLISH, RAZE

un·built \-ˈbilt\ *adj* **1** : not built : not yet constructed **2** : not built on ⟨an ~ plot⟩

un·bur·den \-ˈbərd-ᵊn\ *vt* **1** : to free or relieve from a burden **2** : to relieve oneself of (as cares, fears, or worries) : cast off

un·but·ton \-ˈbət-ᵊn\ *vt* **1** : to loose the buttons of **2** : to open as if by loosing buttons; *specif* : to open the hatches or apertures of (an armored vehicle) ~ *vi* : to undo buttons

un·but·toned \-ˈbət-ᵊnd\ *adj* **1 a** : not buttoned **b** : not provided with buttons **2** : not under constraint

un·cage \-ˈkāj\ *vt* : to release from or as if from a cage

un·called–for \ˌən-ˈkȯl(d)-ˌfȯ(ə)r, ˈən-\ *adj* **1** : not called for or needed : UNNECESSARY **2** : being without cause or occasion : GRATUITOUS ⟨an ~ display of temper⟩ **syn** see SUPEREROGATORY

un·can·ny \ˌən-ˈkan-ē, ˈən-\ *adj* **1 a** : seeming to have a supernatural character or origin : EERIE, MYSTERIOUS **b** : being beyond what is normal or expected : suggesting superhuman or supernatural powers ⟨an ~ sense of direction⟩ **2** *chiefly Scot* : PUNISHING, SEVERE **3** *chiefly Scot* : DANGEROUS **syn** see WEIRD

un·cap \-ˈkap\ *vt* : to remove a cap or covering from

un·caused \-ˈkȯzd\ *adj* : having no antecedent cause

un·ceas·ing \-ˈsē-siŋ\ *adj* : never ceasing : CONTINUOUS, INCESSANT — **un·ceas·ing·ly** \-ˈsē-siŋ-lē\ *adv*

un·cer·e·mo·ni·ous \ˌən-ˌser-ə-ˈmō-nē-əs\ *adj* **1** : not ceremonious : INFORMAL **2** : ABRUPT ⟨an ~ dismissal⟩ — **un·cer·e·mo·ni·ous·ly** *adv* — **un·cer·e·mo·ni·ous·ness** *n*

un·cer·tain \ˌən-ˈsərt-ᵊn, ˈən-\ *adj* **1** : INDETERMINATE **2** : not certain to occur : INDEFINITE, PROBLEMATICAL **3** : not reliable : UNTRUSTWORTHY **4 a** : not known beyond doubt : DUBIOUS **b** : not having certain knowledge : DOUBTFUL **c** : not clearly identified or defined **5** : not constant : VARIABLE, FITFUL — **un·cer·tain·ly** *adv* — **un·cer·tain·ness** \-ᵊn-(n)əs\ *n*

un·cer·tain·ty \-ᵊn-tē\ *n* **1** : the quality or state of being uncertain : DOUBT **2** : something that is uncertain

syn UNCERTAINTY, DOUBT, DUBIETY, DUBIOSITY, SKEPTICISM, SUSPICION, MISTRUST mean lack of sureness about someone or something. UNCERTAINTY may imply a falling short of certainty or an almost complete lack of definite knowledge esp. about an outcome or result; DOUBT suggests both uncertainty and inability to make a decision; DUBIETY stresses a wavering between conclusions; DUBIOSITY suggests vagueness or mental confusion; SKEPTICISM implies unwillingness to believe without conclusive evidence; SUSPICION stresses lack of faith in the truth, reality, fairness, or

See *un-* and 2d element

unambiguous
unambitious
unamiable
unanalyzable
unanimated
unannounced
unanswered
unanticipated
unapologetic
unappalled
unapparent
unappeased
unappetizing
unappreciated
unappreciative
unapproachable
unapproached
unappropriated
unapproved
unarmored
unarrested
unartistic
unashamed
unaspirated
unaspiring
unassailed
unassisted
unassociated
unastronomical
unattainable
unattempted
unattended
unattested
unattractive
unauspicious
unauthentic
unauthenticated
unauthenticity
unauthorized
unavailable
unavailing
unavowed
unawakened
unawed
unbaked
unbandage
unbaptized
unbeautiful
unbefitting
unblamable
unblamed
unbleached
unblemished
unblenching
unblinking
unborrowed
unbought
unbracketed
unbranded
unbreakable
unbridgeable
unbridged
unbrotherly
unbruised
unbrushed
unbudging
unburdened
unburied
unburned
unburnished
unburnt
uncalled
uncanceled
uncannily
uncanonical
uncapitalized
uncared-for
uncaring
uncastrated
uncataloged
uncaught
uncensored
uncensured

reliability of something or someone; MISTRUST implies a genuine doubt based upon suspicion
uncertainty principle *n* **:** a principle in quantum mechanics: it is impossible to assert in terms of the ordinary conventions of geometrical position and of motion that a particle (as an electron) is at the same time at a specified point and moving with a specified velocity
un·chain \ˌən-'chān, 'ən-\ *vt* **:** to free by removing a chain **:** set loose
un·chancy \-'chan(t)-sē\ *adj* **1** *chiefly Scot* **:** ILL-FATED **2** *chiefly Scot* **:** DANGEROUS
unchange *vt, obs* **:** ACQUIT
un·change·able \-'chān-jə-bəl\ *adj* **:** not changing or to be changed **:** IMMUTABLE — **un·change·able·ness** *n* — **un·change·ably** \-blē\ *adv*
un·charged \ˌən-'chärjd, 'ən-\ *adj* **:** not charged; *specif* **:** having no electric charge
un·char·i·ta·ble \ˌən-'char-ət-ə-bəl, 'ən-\ *adj* **:** lacking in charity **:** severe in judging **:** CENSORIOUS — **un·char·i·ta·ble·ness** *n* — **un·char·i·ta·bly** \-blē\ *adv*
un·chart·ed \-'chärt-əd\ *adj* **:** not recorded or plotted on a map, chart, or plan **:** UNKNOWN
un·chaste \-'chāst\ *adj* **:** not chaste **:** lacking in chastity — **un·chaste·ly** *adv* — **un·chaste·ness** \-'chās(t)-nəs\ *n* — **un·chas·ti·ty** \-'chas-tət-ē\ *n*
un·chris·tian \ˌən-'kris(h)-chən, 'ən-\ *adj* **1 :** not of the Christian faith **2 a :** contrary to the Christian spirit or character **b :** BARBAROUS, UNCIVILIZED
un·church \-'chərch\ *vt* **1 :** EXCOMMUNICATE **2 :** to deprive of a church or of status as a church
un·churched \-'chərcht\ *adj* **:** not belonging to or connected with a church
unci *pl of* UNCUS
1un·cial \'ən-chəl, 'ən(t)-sē-əl\ *adj* [L *uncialis* inch-high, fr. *uncia* twelfth part, ounce, inch] **:** written in the style or size of uncials — **un·cial·ly** \-ē\ *adv*
2uncial *n* **1 :** a handwriting used esp. in Greek and Latin manuscripts of the 4th to the 8th centuries A.D. and made with somewhat rounded separated majuscules but having cursive forms for some letters **2 :** an uncial letter

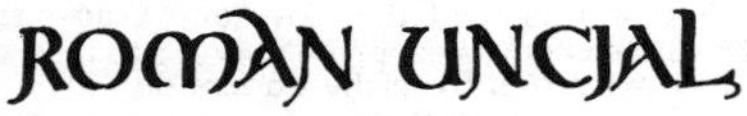

uncials

1un·ci·form \'ən(t)-sə-ˌfȯrm\ *adj* [NL *unciformis*, fr. L *uncus* hook + *-formis* -form — more at ANGLE] **:** hook-shaped **:** UNCINATE
2unciform *n* [NL *unciforme*, fr. neut. of *unciformis*] **:** HAMATUM
un·ci·nar·ia \ˌən(t)-sə-'nar-ē-ə, -'ner-\ *n* [NL, fr. L *uncinus* hook] **:** HOOKWORM
un·ci·na·ri·a·sis \ˌən-ˌsin-ə-'rī-ə-səs\ *n* [NL] **:** ANCYLOSTOMIASIS
un·ci·nate \'ən(t)-sə-ˌnāt\ *adj* **:** bent at the tip like a hook **:** HOOKED
un·ci·nus \ˌən-'sī-nəs\ *n, pl* **un·ci·ni** \-'sī-ˌnī\ [NL, fr. L, hook, fr. *uncus* — more at ANGLE] **:** a small uncinate structure or process
un·cir·cum·cised \ˌən-'sər-kəm-ˌsīzd, 'ən-\ *adj* **1 :** not circumcised **2 :** HEATHEN — **un·cir·cum·ci·sion** \ˌən-ˌsər-kəm-'sizh-ən\ *n*
un·civ·il \ˌən-'siv-əl, 'ən-\ *adj* **1 :** not civilized **:** BARBAROUS **2 :** lacking in courtesy **:** ILL-MANNERED, IMPOLITE **3 :** not conducive to civic harmony and welfare
un·civ·i·lized \-'siv-ə-ˌlīzd\ *adj* **1 :** not civilized **:** BARBAROUS **2 :** remote from civilization **:** WILD
un·clasp \-'klasp\ *vt* **1 :** to open the clasp of **2 :** to open or cause to be opened (as a clenched hand) ~ *vi* **:** to loosen a hold
un·clas·si·fied \-'klas-ə-ˌfīd\ *adj* **1 :** not placed or belonging in a class **2 :** not subject to a security classification
un·cle \'əŋ-kəl\ *n* [ME, fr. OF, fr. L *avunculus* mother's brother; akin to OE *ēam* uncle, OIr *aue* grandson, L *avus* grandfather] **1 a :** the brother of one's father or mother **b :** the husband of one's aunt **2 :** one who helps, advises, or encourages **3** *slang* **:** PAWNBROKER
un·clean \ˌən-'klēn, 'ən-\ *adj* **1 :** morally or spiritually impure **2 :** infected with a harmful supernatural contagion; *also* **:** prohibited by ritual law for use or contact **3 :** DIRTY, FILTHY **4 :** lacking in clarity and precision of conception or execution — **un·clean·ness** \-'klēn-nəs\ *n*
1un·clean·ly \-'klen-lē\ *adj* **:** morally or physically unclean
2un·clean·ly \-'klēn-lē\ *adv* **:** in an unclean manner
un·clench \-'klench\ *vt* **1 :** to open from a clenched position **2 :** to release from a grip ~ *vi* **:** to become unclasped or relaxed
Un·cle Sam \ˌəŋ-kəl-'sam\ *n* [expansion of *U.S.*, abbr. of *United States*] **1 :** the U.S. government personified **2 :** the American nation or people
Uncle Tom \-'täm\ *n* **1 :** a pious and faithful elderly Negro slave in the novel *Uncle Tom's Cabin* by Harriet Beecher Stowe **2 :** a subservient Negro
un·clinch \ˌən-'klinch, 'ən-\ *vt* **:** UNCLENCH
un·cloak \-'klōk\ *vt* **1 :** to remove a cloak or cover from **2 :** REVEAL, UNMASK ~ *vi* **:** to take off a cloak
un·close \-'klōz\ *vt* **1 :** OPEN **2 :** DISCLOSE, REVEAL ~ *vi* **:** to become opened
un·clothe \-'klōt͟h\ *vt* **1 :** to strip of clothes **2 :** DIVEST, UNCOVER
1un·co \'əŋ-(ˌ)kō, -kə\ *adj* [ME (Sc) *unkow*, alter. of ME *uncouth*] **1** *chiefly Scot* **a :** STRANGE, UNKNOWN **b :** UNCANNY, WEIRD **2** *chiefly Scot* **:** EXTRAORDINARY
2unco *adv* **:** EXTREMELY, REMARKABLY, UNCOMMONLY
3unco *n* **1** *pl, chiefly Scot* **:** NEWS, TIDINGS **2** *chiefly Scot* **:** STRANGER

un·coil \ˌən-'kȯi(ə)l, 'ən-\ *vt* **:** to release from a coiled state **:** UNWIND ~ *vi* **:** to become uncoiled
un·coined \-'kȯind\ *adj* **1 :** not minted ⟨~ metal⟩ **2 :** not fabricated **:** NATURAL
un·com·fort·able \ˌən-'kəm(p)(f)-tə-bəl, 'ən-, -'kəm(p)-fərt-ə-\ *adj* **1 :** causing discomfort ⟨an ~ chair⟩ **2 :** feeling discomfort **:** UNEASY — **un·com·fort·ably** \-blē\ *adv*
un·com·mit·ted \ˌən-kə-'mit-əd\ *adj* **:** not committed; *specif* **:** not pledged to a particular belief, allegiance, or program
un·com·mon \ˌən-'käm-ən, 'ən-\ *adj* **1 :** not ordinarily encountered **:** UNUSUAL **2 :** REMARKABLE, EXCEPTIONAL **syn** see INFREQUENT — **un·com·mon·ly** *adv* — **un·com·mon·ness** \-ən-nəs\ *n*
un·com·mu·ni·ca·tive \ˌən-kə-'myü-nə-ˌkāt-iv, -ni-kət-\ *adj* **:** not disposed to talk or impart information **:** RESERVED
un·com·pli·men·ta·ry \ˌən-ˌkäm-plə-'ment-ə-rē, -'men-trē\ *adj* **:** not complimentary **:** DEROGATORY
un·com·pro·mis·ing \ˌən-'käm-prə-ˌmī-ziŋ, 'ən-\ *adj* **:** not making or accepting a compromise **:** making no concessions **:** INFLEXIBLE, UNYIELDING — **un·com·pro·mis·ing·ly** \-ziŋ-lē\ *adv*
un·con·cern \ˌən-kən-'sərn\ *n* **1 :** lack of care or interest **:** INDIFFERENCE **2 :** freedom from excessive concern or anxiety
un·con·cerned \-'sərnd\ *adj* **1 :** lacking care, interest, or feeling **2 :** not anxious or solicitous **:** easy in mind **syn** see INDIFFERENT — **un·con·cerned·ly** \-'sər-nəd-lē, -'sərn-dlē\ *adv* — **un·con·cerned·ness** \-'sər-nəd-nəs, -'sərn(d)-nəs\ *n*
un·con·di·tion·al \ˌən-kən-'dish-nəl, -'dish-ən-ᵊl\ *adj* **:** not limited **:** ABSOLUTE — **un·con·di·tion·al·ly** \-ē\ *adv*
un·con·di·tioned \-'dish-ənd\ *adj* **1 :** not subject to conditions **2 :** not dependent on conditioning or learning **:** NATURAL
un·con·form·able \-'fȯr-mə-bəl\ *adj* **1 :** not conforming **2 :** exhibiting geological unconformity — **un·con·form·ably** \-blē\ *adv*
un·con·for·mi·ty \-'fȯr-mət-ē\ *n* **1** *archaic* **:** lack of conformity **2 a :** lack of continuity in deposition between rock strata in contact corresponding to a period of nondeposition, weathering, or erosion **b :** the surface of contact between unconformable strata
un·con·quer·able \ˌən-'käŋ-k(ə-)rə-bəl, 'ən-\ *adj* **1 :** incapable of being conquered **:** INDOMITABLE **2 :** incapable of being surmounted
un·con·scio·na·ble \-'känch-(ə-)nə-bəl\ *adj* **1 :** not guided or controlled by conscience **:** UNSCRUPULOUS ⟨an ~ villain⟩ **2 a :** EXCESSIVE, UNREASONABLE **b :** shockingly unfair or unjust **:** OUTRAGEOUS — **un·con·scio·na·bly** \-blē\ *adv*
1un·con·scious \ˌən-'kän-chəs, 'ən-\ *adj* **1 a :** not knowing or perceiving **:** not aware **b :** free from self-awareness **2 a :** not possessing mind or consciousness ⟨~ matter⟩ **b (1) :** not marked by conscious thought, sensation, or feeling **(2) :** of or relating to the unconscious **c :** having no consciousness for the time being ⟨was ~ for three days⟩ **3 :** not consciously held or deliberately planned or carried out **:** not consciously directed or realized ⟨~ bias⟩ — **un·con·scious·ly** *adv* — **un·con·scious·ness** *n*
2unconscious *n* **:** the greater part of the psychic apparatus not ordinarily available to consciousness and manifested in overt behavior (as slips of the tongue or dissociated acts) or in dreams
un·con·sid·ered \ˌən-kən-'sid-ərd\ *adj* **1 :** not considered or worth consideration **2 :** not resulting from consideration
un·con·sti·tu·tion·al \ˌən-ˌkän(t)-stə-'t(y)üsh-nəl, -ən-ᵊl\ *adj* **:** not according to or consistent with the constitution of a state or society — **un·con·sti·tu·tion·al·i·ty** \-ˌt(y)ü-shə-'nal-ət-ē\ *n* — **un·con·sti·tu·tion·al·ly** \-'t(y)üsh-nə-lē, -ən-ᵊl-ē\ *adv*
un·con·trol·la·ble \ˌən-kən-'trō-lə-bəl\ *adj* **1** *archaic* **:** free from control by a superior power **:** ABSOLUTE **2 :** incapable of being controlled **:** UNGOVERNABLE — **un·con·trol·la·bly** \-blē\ *adv*
un·con·ven·tion·al \ˌən-kən-'vench-nəl, -ən-ᵊl\ *adj* **:** not conventional **:** not bound by or in accordance with convention **:** being out of the ordinary — **un·con·ven·tion·al·i·ty** \-ˌven-chə-'nal-ət-ē\ *n* — **un·con·ven·tion·al·ly** \-'vench-nə-lē, -ən-ᵊl-ē\ *adv*
un·cork \ˌən-'kȯ(ə)rk, 'ən-\ *vt* **1 :** to draw a cork from **2 a :** to release from a sealed or pent-up state ⟨~ a surprise⟩ **b :** to let go **:** RELEASE ⟨~ a wild pitch⟩
un·count·ed \-'kau̇nt-əd\ *adj* **1 :** not counted **2 :** INNUMERABLE
un·cou·ple \-'kəp-əl\ *vt* **1 :** to release (dogs) from a couple **2 :** DETACH, DISCONNECT ⟨~ railroad cars⟩
un·couth \-'küth\ *adj* [ME, fr. OE *uncūth*, fr. *un-* + *cūth* familiar, known; akin to OHG *kund* known, OE *can* know — more at CAN] **1 a** *archaic* **:** not known or not familiar to one **:** seldom experienced **:** UNCOMMON, RARE **b** *obs* **:** MYSTERIOUS, UNCANNY **2 a :** strange or clumsy in shape or appearance **:** OUTLANDISH **b :** lacking in polish and grace **c :** awkward and uncultivated in appearance, manner, or behavior — **un·couth·ly** *adv* — **un·couth·ness** *n*
un·cov·er \ˌən-'kəv-ər, 'ən-\ *vt* **1 :** to make known **:** bring to light **:** DISCLOSE, REVEAL **2 :** to expose to view by removing some covering **3 a :** to take the cover from **b :** to remove the hat from **4 :** to deprive of protection ~ *vi* **1 :** to remove a cover or covering **2 :** to take off the hat as a token of respect
un·cov·ered \-ərd\ *adj* **1 :** not supplied with a covering **2 a :** not covered by insurance or included in a social insurance or welfare program **b :** not covered by collateral ⟨an ~ note⟩
un·cre·at·ed \ˌən-krē-'āt-əd\ *adj* **1 :** not existing by creation **:** ETERNAL, SELF-EXISTENT **2 :** not yet created
un·crit·i·cal \ˌən-'krit-i-kəl, 'ən-\ *adj* **1 :** not critical **:** lacking in discrimination **2 :** showing lack or improper use of critical standards or procedures — **un·crit·i·cal·ly** \-k(ə-)lē\ *adv*
un·cross \ˌən-'krȯs, 'ən-\ *vt* **:** to change from a crossed position
un·crown \-'krau̇n\ *vt* **:** to take the crown from **:** DEPOSE, DETHRONE

See *un-* and 2d element
unchallenged
unchanged
unchanging
unchaperoned
uncharacteristic
unchary
unchastened
unchecked
unchivalrous
unchristened
unciliated
unclad
unclaimed
unclassifiable
uncleaned
uncleanliness
uncleanness
unclear
uncleared
unclothed
unclouded
uncluttered
uncoated
uncocked
uncoiled
uncollected
uncollectible
uncolored
uncombed
uncombined
uncomely
uncomforted
uncompanionable
uncompensated
uncomplaining
uncompleted
uncomplicated
uncompounded
uncomprehended
uncomprehending
uncomprehensible
unconcealed
unconfined
unconfirmed
uncongealed
uncongenial
unconnected
unconquered
unconscientious
unconsecrated
unconsolidated
unconstrained
unconsumed
uncontaminated
uncontested
uncontradicted
uncontrolled
unconverted
unconvinced
unconvincing
uncooked
uncooperative
uncoordinated
uncordial
uncorked
uncorrected
uncorroborated
uncorrupted
uncountable
uncourteous
uncredited
uncrippled
uncropped
uncrossed
uncrowded
uncrowned

un·crys·tal·lized \-'kris-tə-,līzd\ *adj* : not crystallized; *specif* : not finally or definitely formed

unc·tion \'əŋ(k)-shən\ *n* [ME *unctioun*, fr. L *unction-*, *unctio*, fr. *unctus*, pp. of *unguere* to anoint — more at OINTMENT] **1** : the act of anointing as a rite of consecration or healing **2** : something used for anointing : OINTMENT, UNGUENT **3 a** : religious or spiritual fervor or the expression of such fervor **b** : exaggerated, assumed, or superficial earnestness of language or manner : UNCTUOUSNESS

unc·tu·ous \'əŋ(k)-chə(-wə)s, 'əŋ(k)sh-wəs\ *adj* [ME, fr. MF or ML; MF *unctueux*, fr. ML *unctuosus*, irreg. fr. L *unctum* ointment, fr. neut. of *unctus*, pp.] **1 a** : FATTY, OILY **b** : smooth and greasy in texture or appearance **2 a** : rich in organic matter and easily workable ⟨~ soil⟩ **b** : PLASTIC ⟨fine ~ clay⟩ **3** : full of unction; *esp* : revealing or marked by a smug, ingratiating, and false earnestness or spirituality — **unc·tu·ous·ly** *adv* — **unc·tu·ous·ness** *n*

un·curl \,ən-'kər(-ə)l, 'ən-\ *vi* : to become straightened out from a curled or coiled position ~ *vt* : to straighten the curls of : UNROLL

un·cus \'əŋ-kəs\ *n, pl* **un·ci** \'əŋ-,kī, -,kē; 'ən-,sī\ [NL, fr. L, hook — more at ANGLE] : a hooked anatomical part or process

un·cut \,ən-'kət, 'ən-\ *adj* **1** : not cut down or cut into **2** : not shaped by cutting ⟨an ~ diamond⟩ **3** *of a book* : not having the folds of the leaves slit **4** : not abridged or curtailed

un·daunt·ed \-'dȯnt-əd, -'dänt-\ *adj* : courageous with an undiminished resolution — **un·daunt·ed·ly** *adv*

undec- *comb form* [L *undecim*, fr. *unus* one + *decem* ten — more at ONE, TEN] : eleven ⟨*undec*illion⟩

un·de·ceive \,ən-di-'sēv\ *vt* : to free from deception or illusion

un·de·cil·lion \,ən-di-'sil-yən\ *n, often attrib* [*undec-* + *-illion* (as in *million*)] — see NUMBER table

un·dec·y·le·nic acid \,ən-,des-ə-,len-ik-, -,lēn-\ *n* [*undecylene* ($C_{11}H_{22}$)] : an acid $C_{11}H_{20}O_2$ found in perspiration, obtained commercially from castor oil, and used in the treatment of fungous infections of the skin

un·deed·ed \,ən-'dēd-əd, 'ən-\ *adj, obs* : not exploited in deeds

un·de·mon·stra·tive \,ən-di-'män(t)-strət-iv\ *adj* : restrained in expression of feeling : RESERVED — **un·de·mon·stra·tive·ly** *adv* — **un·de·mon·stra·tive·ness** *n*

un·de·ni·able \-'nī-ə-bəl\ *adj* **1** : plainly true : INCONTESTABLE **2** : unquestionably excellent or genuine ⟨an applicant with ~ references⟩ — **un·de·ni·able·ness** *n* — **un·de·ni·ably** \-blē\ *adv*

1**un·der** \'ən-dər\ *adv* [ME, adv. & prep., fr. OE; akin to OHG *untar* under, L *inferus* situated beneath, lower, *infra* below, Skt *adha*] **1** : in or into a position below or beneath something **2** : below some quantity or limit **3** : in or into a condition of subjection, subordination, or unconsciousness **4** : so as to be covered

2**un·der** \,ən-dər, 'ən-\ *prep* **1** : below and in such a position as to be overhung, surmounted, covered, protected, or concealed by ⟨~ sunny skies⟩ ⟨swims ~ water⟩ ⟨~ separate cover⟩ **2 a** (1) : subject to the authority, guidance, or instruction of ⟨served ~ the general⟩ (2) : attested or warranted by ⟨issued ~ the royal seal⟩ **b** : controlled, limited, weighed upon, or oppressed by ⟨~ quarantine⟩ ⟨collapsed ~ the strain⟩ **c** : receiving or undergoing the action or effect of ⟨~ ether⟩ **3 a** : within the group or designation of ⟨~ this heading⟩ **b** : bearing or assuming outwardly esp. for the sake of concealment ⟨~ a false name⟩ **4 a** : inferior or subordinate to (as in size, amount, or rank) ⟨all weights ~ 12 ounces⟩ **b** : inferior to the standard or required degree of ⟨~ legal age⟩

3**under** \'ən-dər\ *adj* **1 a** : lying or placed below, beneath, or on the ventral side ⟨~ parts⟩ — often used in combination ⟨gnawed his *under*lip⟩ **b** : facing or protruding downward **2** : lower in rank or authority : SUBORDINATE **3** : lower than usual, proper, or desired in amount, quality, or degree ⟨~ dose of medicine⟩

un·der·achiev·er \,ən-də-rə-'chē-vər\ *n* : a student who fails to achieve his scholastic potential

un·der·act \,ən-də-'rakt\ *vt* **1** : to perform (a dramatic part) with less than the requisite skill or vigor **2** : to perform with restraint for greater dramatic impact or personal force ~ *vi* : to perform feebly or with restraint

un·der·age \,ən-də-'rāj\ *adj* : of less than mature or legal age

1**un·der·arm** \,ən-də-,rärm\ *adj* **1** : placed under or on the underside of the arm ⟨~ seams⟩ **2** : UNDERHAND — **un·der·arm** \'ən-\ *n*

2**un·der·arm** \,ən-də-'rärm\ *adv* : UNDERHAND

un·der·bel·ly \'ən-dər-,bel-ē\ *n* : the under surface of a body or mass; *esp* : a vulnerable area

un·der·bid \,ən-dər-'bid\ *vt* **1** : to bid less than (a competing bidder) **2** : to bid (a hand of cards) at less than the strength of the hand warrants ~ *vi* : to bid too low — **un·der·bid·der** *n*

un·der·body \'ən-dər-,bäd-ē\ *n* : the lower part of an animal's body : UNDERPARTS

un·der·bred \,ən-dər-'bred\ *adj* **1** : marked by lack of good breeding : ILL-BRED **2** : of inferior or mixed breed ⟨~ dog⟩

un·der·brush \'ən-dər-,brəsh\ *n* : shrubs, bushes, or small trees growing beneath large trees in a wood or forest : BRUSH

un·der·car·riage \'ən-dər-,kar-ij\ *n* **1** : a supporting framework (as of an automobile) **2** : the landing gear of an airplane

un·der·charge \,ən-dər-'chärj\ *vt* : to charge (as a person) too little — **undercharge** \'ən-dər-,\ *n*

un·der·class·man \,ən-dər-'klas-mən\ *n* : a member of the freshman or sophomore class in a school or college

un·der·clothes \'ən-dər-,klō(th)z\ *n pl* : UNDERWEAR

un·der·cloth·ing \-,klō-thiŋ\ *n* : UNDERWEAR

un·der·coat \-,kōt\ *n* **1** : a coat or jacket formerly worn under another **2** : a growth of short hair or fur partly concealed by a longer growth ⟨a dog's ~⟩ **3** : a coat of paint under another **4** *dial* : PETTICOAT

un·der·coat·ing \-,kōt-iŋ\ *n* : a waterproof coating applied to the undersurfaces of a vehicle

un·der·col·ored \,ən-dər-'kəl-ərd\ *adj* : having less color than needed or proper

un·der·cool \-'kül\ *vt* : SUPERCOOL

un·der·cov·er \-'kəv-ər\ *adj* : acting or executed in secret; *specif* : employed or engaged in spying or secret investigation ⟨~ agent⟩

un·der·croft \'ən-dər-,krȯft\ *n* [ME, fr. *under* + *crofte* crypt, fr. MD, fr. ML *crupta*, fr. L *crypta*] : a subterranean room; *esp* : a vaulted chamber under a church : CRYPT

un·der·cur·rent \-,kər-ənt, -,kə-rənt\ *n* **1** : a current below the upper currents or surface **2** : a hidden tendency (as of opinion) often contrary to the one publicly shown — **undercurrent** *adj*

1**un·der·cut** \,ən-dər-'kət\ *vt* **1** : to cut away the underpart of ⟨~ a vein of ore⟩ **2** : to cut away material from the under side of (an object) so as to leave an overhanging portion in relief **3** : to offer to sell at lower prices than or to work for lower wages than (a competitor) **4** : to cut obliquely into (a tree) below the main cut and on the side toward which the tree will fall **5** : to strike (the ball) in golf, tennis, or hockey obliquely downward so as to give a backspin or elevation to the shot ~ *vi* : to perform the action of cutting away beneath

2**un·der·cut** \'ən-dər-,kət\ *n* **1** : the action or result of cutting away from the underside of anything **2** *Brit* : TENDERLOIN 1 **3** : a notch cut before felling in the base of a tree to determine the direction of falling and to prevent splitting **4** : a cut in tennis made with an underhand stroke

un·der·de·vel·oped \,ən-dərd-i-'vel-əpt\ *adj* **1** : not normally or adequately developed ⟨~ muscles⟩ **2** : failing to realize a potential economic level of industrial production and standard of living (as from lack of capital)

un·der·do \,ən-dər-'dü\ *vt* : to do less thoroughly than one can; *esp* : to cook (as meat) rare

un·der·dog \'ən-dər-,dȯg\ *n* **1** : a loser or predicted loser in a struggle or contest **2** : a victim of injustice or persecution

un·der·done \,ən-dər-'dən\ *adj* : not thoroughly cooked : RARE

un·der·draw·ers \'ən-dər-,drȯ(-ə)rz\ *n pl* : an article of underwear covering the lower body and the legs ⟨calf-length ~⟩

un·der·es·ti·mate \,ən-də-'res-tə-,māt\ *vt* **1** : to estimate as being less than the actual size, quantity, or number **2** : to place too low a value on : UNDERRATE — **un·der·es·ti·mate** \-mət\ *n* — **un·der·es·ti·ma·tion** \-,res-tə-'mā-shən\ *n*

un·der·ex·pose \,ən-də-rik-'spōz\ *vt* : to expose (as film) for less time than is needed — **un·der·ex·po·sure** \-'spō-zhər\ *n*

un·der·feed \,ən-dər-'fēd\ *vt* **1** : to feed with too little food **2** : to feed with fuel from the underside

un·der·foot \-'fu̇t\ *adv* **1** : under the foot esp. against the ground **2** : below, at, or before one's feet **3** : in the way

un·der·fur \'ən-dər-,fər\ *n* : the thick soft fur lying beneath the longer and coarser hair of a mammal — compare UNDERCOAT 2

un·der·gar·ment \-,gär-mənt\ *n* : a garment to be worn under another

un·der·gird \,ən-dər-'gərd\ *vt* **1** : to make secure underneath **2** : to brace up : STRENGTHEN

un·der·glaze \,ən-dər-,glāz\ *adj* **1** : applied before the glaze is put on **2** : suitable for applying under the glaze

un·der·go \,ən-dər-'gō\ *vt* **1** *obs* : UNDERTAKE **2** *obs* : to partake of **3** : to submit to : ENDURE **4** : to pass through : EXPERIENCE

un·der·grad·u·ate \,ən-dər-'graj-(ə-)wət, -ə-,wāt\ *n* : a student at a college or university who has not taken a first degree

1**un·der·ground** \,ən-dər-'grau̇nd\ *adv* **1** : beneath the surface of the earth **2** : in or into hiding or secret operation

2**un·der·ground** \'ən-dər-,grau̇nd\ *adj* **1** : being, growing, operating, or situated below the surface of the ground **2 a** : conducted by secret means **b** (1) : existing outside the establishment ⟨an ~ parish⟩ ⟨an ~ literary reputation⟩ (2) : produced or published outside the establishment esp. by the avant-garde ⟨~ movies⟩ ⟨~ newspapers⟩; *also* : of or relating to the avant-garde underground ⟨~ moviemaker⟩ ⟨an ~ theater⟩

3**underground** \'ən-dər-,\ *n* **1** : a subterranean space or channel **2** : an underground city railway system **3 a** : a movement or group organized in strict secrecy among citizens esp. in an occupied country for maintaining communications, popular solidarity, and concerted resistive action pending liberation **b** : a clandestine conspiratorial organization set up for revolutionary or other disruptive purposes esp. against a civil order **c** : an unofficial, unsanctioned, or illegal but informal movement or group; *esp* : one that is avant-garde

Underground Railroad *n* : a system of cooperation among active antislavery people in the U.S. before 1863 by which fugitive slaves were secretly helped to reach the North or Canada

un·der·growth \'ən-dər-,grōth\ *n* : low growth on the floor of a forest including seedlings and saplings, shrubs, and herbs

1**un·der·hand** \'ən-dər-,hand\ *adv* **1 a** : in a clandestine manner **b** *archaic* : QUIETLY **2** : with the target seen below the left hand **3** : with an underhand motion ⟨bowl ~⟩ ⟨pitch ~⟩

2**underhand** *adj* **1** : aimed so that the target is seen below the left hand ⟨~ shooting at long range⟩ **2** : marked by secrecy, chicanery, and deception : not honest and aboveboard : SLY **3** : done so as to evade notice **4** : performed with the hand kept below the level of the shoulder ⟨~ pass in football⟩ **syn** see SECRET

1**un·der·hand·ed** \,ən-dər-'han-dəd\ *adj* (*or adv*) : UNDERHAND — **un·der·hand·ed·ly** *adv* — **un·der·hand·ed·ness** *n*

2**underhanded** *adj* : insufficiently provided with workers

un·der·hung \,ən-dər-'həŋ\ *adj* **1 a** *of a lower jaw* : projecting beyond the upper jaw **b** : having such a jaw **2** : UNDERSLUNG

un·der·laid \-'lād\ *adj* **1** : laid or placed underneath **2** : having something laid or lying underneath

1**un·der·lay** \-'lā\ *vt* **1** : to cover, line, or traverse the bottom of : give support to on the underside or below **2** : to raise or support by something laid under

2**un·der·lay** \'ən-dər-,lā\ *n* : something that is laid under

un·der·let \,ən-dər-'let\ *vt* **1** : to let below the real value **2** : SUBLET

un·der·lie \-'lī\ *vt* **1** : to be subject or amenable to ⟨~ a challenge⟩ **2** : to lie or be situated under **3** : to be at the basis of : form the foundation of : SUPPORT ⟨ideas *underlying* the revolution⟩ **4** : to exist as a claim or security superior and prior to (another)

1**un·der·line** \'ən-dər-,līn, ,ən-dər-'\ *vt* **1** : to mark (a word) with a line underneath **2** : to put emphasis upon : STRESS

2**un·der·line** \'ən-dər-,līn\ *n* **1** : a horizontal line placed underneath something **2** : the outline of an animal's underbody

See *un-* and 2d element
uncultivable
uncultivated
uncultured
uncurbed
uncured
uncurious
uncurrent
uncurtained
undamaged
undamped
undated
undazzled
undecided
undecipherable
undecked
undeclared
undeclinable
undecorated
undefeated
undefended
undefiled
undefinable
undefined
undelayed
undeliverable
undemanding
undemocratic
undenominational
undependable

un·der·ling \'ən-dər-liŋ\ *n* **:** one who is under the orders of another **:** SUBORDINATE, INFERIOR
un·der·lip \ˌən-dər-'lip\ *n* **:** the lower lip
un·der·ly·ing \ˌən-dər-ˌlī-iŋ\ *adj* **1 :** lying beneath **:** FUNDAMENTAL **2 :** evident only on close inspection **:** IMPLICIT **3 :** anterior and prior in claim ⟨~ mortgage⟩
un·der·mine \ˌən-dər-'mīn\ *vt* **1 :** to excavate the earth beneath **:** form a mine under **:** SAP **2 :** to wash away supporting material from under **3 :** to subvert or weaken insidiously or secretly **4 :** to weaken or ruin by degrees **syn** see WEAKEN
un·der·most \'ən-dər-ˌmōst\ *adj* **:** lowest in relative position — **undermost** *adv*
¹un·der·neath \ˌən-dər-'nēth\ *prep* [ME *undernethe*, prep. & adv., fr. OE *underneothan*, fr. *under* + *neothan* below — more at BENEATH] **1 :** directly beneath or close under esp. so as to be hidden **2 :** under subjection to **3 :** under the guise or appearance of
²underneath *adv* **1 :** under or below an object or a surface **:** BENEATH **2 :** on the lower side
un·der·nour·ished \ˌən-dər-'nər-isht, -'nə-risht\ *adj* **:** supplied with less than the minimum amount of the foods essential for sound health and growth — **un·der·nour·ish·ment** \-'nər-ish-mənt, -'nə-rish-\ *n*
un·der·pants \'ən-dər-ˌpan(t)s\ *n pl* **:** DRAWERS
un·der·part \-ˌpärt\ *n* **1 :** a part lying on the lower side esp. of a bird or mammal **2 :** a subordinate or auxiliary part or role
un·der·pass \-ˌpas\ *n* **:** a crossing of two highways or of a highway and pedestrian path or railroad at different levels where clearance to traffic on the upper level is obtained by depressing (as with a tunnel) the lower level; *also* **:** the lower level of such a crossing
un·der·pin \ˌən-dər-'pin\ *vt* **1 :** to form part of, strengthen, or replace the foundation of ⟨~ a structure⟩ ⟨~ a sagging building⟩ **2 :** SUPPORT, SUBSTANTIATE ⟨~ a thesis with evidence⟩
un·der·pin·ning \'ən-dər-ˌpin-iŋ\ *n* **1 :** the material and construction (as a foundation) used for support of a structure **2 :** SUPPORT, PROP **3 :** a person's legs — usu. used in pl.
un·der·play \ˌən-dər-'plā\ *vt* **1 :** to play a card lower than (a held high card) **2 :** to act or present (as a role or a scene) with restraint **:** play down **~** *vi* **:** to play a role with subdued force
un·der·plot \'ən-dər-ˌplät\ *n* **:** a dramatic plot that is subordinate to the main action
un·der·priv·i·leged \ˌən-dər-'priv-(ə-)lijd\ *adj* **:** deprived through social or economic condition of some of the fundamental rights of all members of a civilized society **:** POOR
un·der·pro·duc·tion \-prə-'dək-shən\ *n* **:** the production of less than enough to satisfy the demand or of less than the usual supply
un·der·proof \ˌən-dər-'prüf\ *adj* **:** containing less alcohol than proof spirit
un·der·rate \ˌən-də(r)-'rāt\ *vt* **:** to rate too low **:** UNDERVALUE
un·der·ripe \-'rīp\ *adj* **:** insufficiently ripe
¹un·der·run \-'rən\ *vt* **1 :** to pass or extend under **2 :** to pass along under in order to examine (a cable)
²un·der·run \'ən-də(r)-ˌrən\ *n* **:** the amount by which something produced (as a cut of lumber) falls below an estimate
un·der·score \'ən-dər-ˌskō(ə)r, -ˌskȯ(ə)r\ *vt* **1 :** to draw a line under **:** UNDERLINE **2 :** EMPHASIZE — **underscore** *n*
¹un·der·sea \ˌən-dər-ˌsē\ *adj* **1 :** being or carried on under the sea or under the surface of the sea ⟨~ fighting⟩ **2 :** designed for use under the surface of the sea ⟨~ fleet⟩
²un·der·sea \ˌən-dər-'sē\ *or* **un·der·seas** \-'sēz\ *adv* **:** under the sea **:** beneath the surface of the sea ⟨photographs taken ~⟩
un·der·sec·re·tary \ˌən-dər-'sek-rə-ˌter-ē\ *n* **:** a secretary immediately subordinate to a principal secretary ⟨~ of state⟩
un·der·sell \ˌən-dər-'sel\ *vt* **:** to sell articles cheaper than
un·der·sexed \-'sekst\ *adj* **:** characterized by a subnormal degree of sexual desire
un·der·shirt \'ən-dər-ˌshərt\ *n* **:** a collarless undergarment with or without sleeves
un·der·shoot \ˌən-dər-'shüt\ *vt* **1 :** to shoot short of or below (a target) **2 :** to fall short of (a runway) in landing an airplane
un·der·shot \ˌən-dər-ˌshät\ *adj* **1 :** having the lower incisor teeth or lower jaw projecting beyond the upper when the mouth is closed **2 :** moved by water passing beneath ⟨~ wheel⟩
un·der·shrub \'ən-dər-ˌshrəb, *esp South* -ˌsrəb\ *n* **1 :** SUBSHRUB 1 **2 :** a small low-growing shrub — **un·der·shrub·by** *adj*
un·der·side \'ən-dər-ˌsīd, ˌən-dər-'\ *n* **:** the side or surface lying underneath
un·der·signed \'ən-dər-ˌsīnd\ *n, pl* **undersigned :** one who signs his name at the end of a document ⟨the ~ testifies⟩ ⟨the ~ all agree⟩
un·der·sized \ˌən-dər-'sīzd\ *also* **un·der·size** \-'sīz\ *adj* **:** of a size less than is common, proper, normal, or average ⟨~ trout⟩
un·der·skirt \'ən-dər-ˌskərt\ *n* **:** a skirt worn under an outer skirt; *esp* **:** PETTICOAT
un·der·slung \ˌən-dər-'sləŋ\ *adj* **1 a** *of a vehicle frame* **:** suspended so as to extend below the axles **b :** having a low center of gravity **2 :** UNDERSHOT 1
un·der·song \'ən-dər-ˌsȯŋ\ *n* **:** a subordinate melody or part
un·der·spin \-ˌspin\ *n* **:** BACKSPIN
un·der·stand \ˌən-dər-'stand\ *vb* **un·der·stood** \-'stu̇d\ **un·der·stand·ing** [ME *understanden*, fr. OE *understandan*, fr. *under* + *standan* to stand] *vt* **1 a :** to grasp the meaning of **:** COMPREHEND ⟨~ Russian⟩ ⟨~ a message in code⟩ **b :** to grasp the reasonableness of ⟨his behavior is hard to ~⟩ **c :** to have thorough or technical acquaintance with or expertness in the practice of ⟨~ finance⟩ **d :** to be thoroughly familiar with the character and propensities of ⟨~*s* children⟩ **2 :** to accept as a fact or truth or regard as plausible without utter certainty ⟨~ that he is returning from abroad⟩ **3 :** to interpret in one of a number of possible ways **4 :** to supply in thought as though expressed ⟨"to be married" is commonly *understood* after the word *engaged*⟩ **~** *vi* **1 :** to have understanding **:** have the power of comprehension **2 :** to achieve a grasp of the nature, significance, or explanation of something **3 :** to believe or infer something to be the case **4 :** to show a sympathetic or tolerant attitude toward something — **un·der·stand·abil·i·ty** \-ˌstan-də-'bil-ət-ē\ *n* — **un·der·stand·able** \-'stan-də-bəl\ *adj* — **un·der·stand·ably** \-blē\ *adv*

syn UNDERSTAND, COMPREHEND, APPRECIATE mean to have a clear or complete idea of. UNDERSTAND may differ from COMPREHEND in implying a result whereas COMPREHEND stresses the mental process of arriving at a result ⟨he *understood* the instructions without *comprehending* their purpose⟩ APPRECIATE implies a just estimation of a thing's value ⟨failed to *appreciate* the risks involved⟩
¹un·der·stand·ing \ˌən-dər-'stan-diŋ\ *n* **1 a :** DISCERNMENT, INSIGHT **b :** an act or result of interpreting **2 a :** the power of comprehending; *specif* **:** the capacity to apprehend general relations of particulars **b :** the power to make experience intelligible by applying concepts and categories **3 a :** friendly or harmonious relationship **b :** an agreement of opinion or feeling **:** adjustment of differences **c :** a mutual agreement not formally entered into but in some degree binding on each side
²understanding *adj* **1** *archaic* **:** KNOWING, INTELLIGENT **2 :** endowed with understanding **:** TOLERANT, SYMPATHETIC — **un·der·stand·ing·ly** \-'stan-diŋ-lē\ *adv*
un·der·state \ˌən-dər-'stāt\ *vt* **1 :** to represent as less than is the case **2 :** to state with restraint esp. for greater effect — **un·der·state·ment** \-mənt\ *n*
un·der·stood \ˌən-dər-'stu̇d\ *adj* **1 :** fully apprehended **2 :** agreed upon **3 :** IMPLICIT
un·der·sto·ry \'ən-dər-ˌstōr-ē, -ˌstȯr-\ *n* **:** the plants of a forest undergrowth; *broadly* **:** any underlying layer of low vegetation
un·der·strap·per \-ˌstrap-ər\ *n* [³*under* + *strapper* (one who harnesses horses)] **:** a petty agent or subordinate **:** UNDERLING
¹un·der·study \-ˌstəd-ē, ˌən-dər-'\ *vi* **:** to study another actor's part in order to be his substitute in an emergency **~** *vt* **:** to prepare (as a part) as understudy; *also* **:** to prepare as understudy to (as an actor)
²un·der·study \'ən-dər-ˌstəd-ē\ *n* **:** one who stands prepared to act another's part or take over another's duties
¹un·der·sur·face \-ˌsər-fəs\ *n* **:** UNDERSIDE
²undersurface *adj* **:** existing or moving below the surface
un·der·take \ˌən-dər-'tāk\ *vt* **1 :** to take in hand **:** enter upon **:** set about **:** ATTEMPT **2 :** to put oneself under obligation to perform **:** CONTRACT, COVENANT **3 :** GUARANTEE, PROMISE **4 :** to accept as a charge **~** *vi, archaic* **:** to give surety or assume responsibility
un·der·tak·er \ˌən-dər-'tā-kər, *2 is* 'ən-dər-ˌ\ *n* **1 :** one that undertakes **:** one that takes the risk and management of business **:** ENTREPRENEUR **2 :** one whose business is to prepare the dead for burial and to arrange and manage funerals **3 :** an Englishman taking over forfeited lands in Ireland in the 16th and 17th centuries
un·der·tak·ing \'ən-dər-ˌtā-kiŋ\ *n* **1 :** the act of one who undertakes or engages in a project or business; *specif* **:** the business of an undertaker **2 :** something undertaken **3 :** PLEDGE, GUARANTEE
un·der·ten·ant \'ən-dər-ˌten-ənt\ *n* **:** one who holds lands or tenements by a sublease
un·der–the–count·er \ˌən-dər-t͟hə-'kau̇nt-ər\ *adj* [fr. the hiding of illicit wares under the counter of stores where they are sold] **:** UNLAWFUL, ILLICIT ⟨~ sale of drugs⟩
un·der·tone \'ən-dər-ˌtōn\ *n* **1 :** a low or subdued utterance or accompanying sound **2 a :** an emotional quality underlying the surface of an utterance or action **b :** the underlying tendency of a market **3 :** a subdued color: as **a :** a color seen through and modifying another color **b :** the color of the light transmitted (as by a paint or varnish film)
un·der·tow \-ˌtō\ *n* **:** the current beneath the surface that sets seaward or along the beach when waves are breaking upon the shore
un·der·trick \-ˌtrik\ *n* **:** one of the tricks by which a declarer in bridge falls short of making his contract
un·der·val·u·a·tion \ˌən-dər-ˌval-yə-'wā-shən\ *n* **1 :** the act of undervaluing **2 :** a value under the real worth
un·der·val·ue \-'val-(ˌ)yü, -yə-w\ *vt* **1 :** to value, rate, or estimate below the real worth **2 :** to esteem lightly **:** DEPRECIATE
un·der·waist \'ən-dər-ˌwāst\ *n* **:** a waist for wear under another garment; *specif* **:** WAIST 3c
un·der·wa·ter \ˌən-dər-ˌwȯt-ər, -ˌwät-\ *adj* **1 :** lying, growing, worn, or operating below the surface of the water **2 :** being below the waterline of a ship — **un·der·wa·ter** \-'wȯt-, -'wät-\ *adv*
under way *adv* [prob. fr. D *onderweg*, fr. MD *onderwegen*, lit., under or among the ways] **1 :** in motion **:** not at anchor or aground **2 :** into motion from a standstill **3 :** in progress **:** AFOOT ⟨preparations were *under way*⟩
un·der·way \ˌən-dər-ˌwā\ *adj* **:** occurring, performed, or used while traveling or in motion ⟨~ refueling⟩
un·der·wear \'ən-dər-ˌwa(ə)r, -ˌwe(ə)r\ *n* **:** a garment worn next to the skin and under other clothing
under weigh *adv* [by folk etymology] **:** under way
¹un·der·weight \ˌən-dər-'wāt\ *n* **:** weight below normal, average, or requisite weight
²underweight *adj* **:** weighing less than the normal or requisite amount
¹un·der·wing \'ən-dər-ˌwiŋ\ *n* **:** one of the posterior wings of an insect
²underwing *adj* **:** placed or growing underneath the wing ⟨~ coverts⟩
un·der·wood \'ən-dər-ˌwu̇d\ *n* **:** UNDERGROWTH, UNDERBRUSH
un·der·wool \-ˌwu̇l\ *n* **:** short woolly underfur
un·der·world \-ˌwərld\ *n* **1** *archaic* **:** EARTH **2 :** the place of departed souls **:** HADES **3 :** the side of the earth opposite to one **4 :** a social sphere below the level of ordinary life; *esp* **:** the world of organized crime
un·der·write \'ən-də(r)-ˌrīt, ˌən-də(r)-'\ *vt* **1 :** to write under or at the end of something else **2 :** to set one's name to (an insurance policy) for the purpose of thereby becoming answerable for a designated loss or damage on consideration of receiving a premium percent **:** insure on life or property; *also* **:** to assume (a sum or risk) by way of insurance **3 :** to subscribe to **:** agree to **4 a :** to agree to purchase (a security issue) usu. on a fixed date at a fixed price with a view to public distribution **b :** to guarantee financial support of **~** *vi* **:** to carry on the business of an underwriter
un·der·writ·er \'ən-də(r)-ˌrīt-ər\ *n* **1 :** one that underwrites **:** GUARANTOR **2 a :** one that underwrites a policy of insurance **b :** one who selects risks to be solicited or rates the acceptability of risks solicited **3 :** one that underwrites a security issue

un·de·sign·ing \ˌən-di-ˈzī-niŋ\ *adj* **:** having no artful, ulterior, or fraudulent purpose **:** SINCERE, ARTLESS

un·de·sir·abil·i·ty \ˌən-di-ˌzī-rə-ˈbil-ət-ē\ *n* **:** the quality or state of being undesirable

¹**un·de·sir·able** \-ˈzī-rə-bəl\ *adj* **:** not desirable **:** UNWANTED — **un·de·sir·able·ness** *n* — **un·de·sir·ably** \-blē\ *adv*

²**undesirable** *n* **:** one that is undesirable

un·de·vi·at·ing \ˌən-ˈdē-vē-ˌāt-iŋ, ˈən-\ *adj* **:** keeping a true course **:** UNSWERVING — **un·de·vi·at·ing·ly** \-iŋ-lē\ *adv*

un·dies \ˈən-dēz\ *n pl* [by shortening & alter.] **:** UNDERWEAR; *esp* **:** women's underwear

un·dine \ˌən-ˈdēn, ˈən-ˌ\ *n* [NL *undina*, fr. L *unda* wave — more at WATER] **:** an elemental being in the theory of Paracelsus inhabiting water **:** WATER NYMPH

un·di·rect·ed \ˌən-də-ˈrek-təd, -ˌdī-\ *adj* **:** not directed ⟨~ efforts⟩

un·dis·so·ci·at·ed \ˌən-dis-ˈō-s(h)ē-ˌāt-əd\ *adj* **:** not electrolytically dissociated

un·do \ˌən-ˈdü, ˈən-\ *vt* **1 :** to open or loose by releasing a fastening (as a lock) **:** UNTIE **2 :** to make of no effect or as if not done **:** make null **:** REVERSE **3 a :** to ruin the worldly means, reputation, or hopes of **b :** to disturb the composure of **:** UPSET **c :** SEDUCE ~ *vi* **:** to come open or apart — **un·do·er** *n*

un·do·ing \-ˈdü-iŋ\ *n* **1 :** LOOSING, UNFASTENING **2 :** RUIN; *also* **:** a cause of ruin **3 :** ANNULMENT, REVERSAL

un·dou·ble \ˌən-ˈdəb-əl, ˈən-\ *vb* **:** UNFOLD, UNCLENCH

un·doubt·ed \-ˈdaůt-əd\ *adj* **:** not doubted **:** GENUINE, UNDISPUTED — **un·doubt·ed·ly** *adv*

un·drape \ˌən-ˈdrāp, ˈən-\ *vt* **:** to strip of drapery **:** UNVEIL

un·draw \-ˈdrȯ\ *vt* **:** to draw aside (as a curtain) **:** OPEN

¹**un·dress** \-ˈdres\ *vt* **1 :** to remove the clothes or covering of **:** DIVEST, STRIP **2 :** EXPOSE ~ *vi* **:** to take off one's clothes **:** DISROBE

²**undress** *n* **1 :** informal dress: as **a :** a loose robe or dressing gown **b :** ordinary dress — compare FULL DRESS **2 :** NUDITY

un·due \-ˈd(y)ü\ *adj* **1 :** not due **:** not yet payable **2 a :** INAPPROPRIATE, UNSUITABLE **b :** exceeding or violating propriety or fitness

un·du·lant \ˈən-jə-lənt, ˈən-d(y)ə-\ *adj* **:** UNDULATING

undulant fever *n* **:** a persistent human brucellosis marked by remittent fever, pain and swelling in the joints, and great weakness and contracted by contact with infected domestic animals or consumption of their products

¹**un·du·late** \-lət, -ˌlāt\ *or* **un·du·lat·ed** \-ˌlāt-əd\ *adj* [L *undulatus*, fr. (assumed) L *undula*, dim. of L *unda* wave — more at WATER] **:** having a wavy surface, margin, or markings

²**un·du·late** \-ˌlāt\ *vb* [LL *undula* small wave, fr. (assumed) L] *vi* **1 :** to form or move in waves **:** FLUCTUATE **2 :** to rise and fall in volume, pitch, or cadence **3 :** to present a wavy appearance ~ *vt* **:** to move or cause to move in wavy, sinuous, or flowing manner **syn** see SWING

un·du·la·tion \ˌən-jə-ˈlā-shən, ˌən-d(y)ə-\ *n* **1 a :** a rising and falling in waves **b :** a wavelike motion to and fro in a fluid or elastic medium propagated continuously among its particles but with little or no permanent translation of the particles in the direction of the propagation **:** VIBRATION **2 :** the pulsation caused by the vibrating together of two tones not quite in unison **3 :** a wavy appearance, outline, or form **:** WAVINESS

un·du·la·to·ry \ˈən-jə-lə-ˌtōr-ē, ˈən-d(y)ə-, -ˌtȯr-\ *adj* **:** of or relating to undulation **:** moving in or resembling waves **:** UNDULATING

undulatory theory *n* **:** a theory in physics: light is transmitted from luminous bodies to the eye and other objects by an undulatory movement — called also *wave theory*

un·du·ly \ˌən-ˈd(y)ü-lē, ˈən-\ *adv* **:** in an undue manner; *esp* **:** EXCESSIVELY

un·du·ti·ful \-ˈd(y)üt-i-fəl\ *adj* **:** not dutiful — **un·du·ti·ful·ly** \-fə-lē\ *adv* — **un·du·ti·ful·ness** *n*

un·dy·ing \-ˈdī-iŋ\ *adj* **:** not dying **:** IMMORTAL, PERPETUAL

un·earned \-ˈərnd\ *adj* **:** not gained by labor, service, or skill ⟨~ income⟩ ⟨~ runs⟩

unearned increment *n* **:** an increase in the value of property (as land) that is due to no labor or expenditure of the owner but to natural causes (as the increase of population) that create an increased demand for it

un·earth \ˌən-ˈərth, ˈən-\ *vt* **1 :** to dig up out of the earth **:** EXHUME, DISINTER ⟨~ a hidden treasure⟩ **2 :** to bring to light **:** UNCOVER, DISCOVER ⟨~ a plot⟩ **syn** see DISCOVER

un·earth·li·ness \-lē-nəs\ *n* **:** the quality or state of being unearthly

un·earth·ly \-lē\ *adj* **:** not earthly: as **a :** not terrestrial **b :** PRETERNATURAL, SUPERNATURAL **c :** WEIRD, EERIE **d :** SPIRITUAL, IDEAL ⟨~ love⟩ **e :** FANTASTIC, PREPOSTEROUS

un·eas·i·ly \ˌən-ˈēz-(ə-)lē, ˈən-\ *adv* **:** in an uneasy manner

un·eas·i·ness \-ˈē-zē-nəs\ *n* **:** the quality or state of being uneasy

¹**un·easy** \-ˈē-zē\ *adj* **1** *archaic* **:** causing physical or mental discomfort **2** *archaic* **:** DIFFICULT **3 :** AWKWARD, EMBARRASSED **4 :** WORRIED, APPREHENSIVE **5 :** RESTLESS, UNQUIET **6 :** UNSTABLE

²**uneasy** *adv* **:** UNEASILY

un·em·ploy·able \ˌən-im-ˈplȯi-ə-bəl\ *adj* **:** not acceptable for employment — **unemployable** *n*

un·em·ployed \-ˈplȯid\ *adj* **:** not employed: **a :** not being used **b :** not engaged in a gainful occupation **c :** not invested

un·em·ploy·ment \-ˈplȯi-mənt\ *n* **:** the state of being unemployed

¹**un·equal** \ˌən-ˈē-kwəl, ˈən-\ *adj* **1 a :** not of the same measurement, quantity, or number as another **b :** not like or not the same as another in degree, worth, or status **2 :** not uniform **:** VARIABLE, UNEVEN **3 a :** badly balanced or matched **b :** contracted between unequals ⟨~ marriages⟩ **c** *archaic* **:** not equable **4** *archaic* **:** not equitable **:** UNJUST **5 :** INADEQUATE, INSUFFICIENT ⟨timber ~ to the strain⟩ — **un·equal·ly** \-kwə-lē\ *adv*

²**unequal** *n* **:** one that is not equal to another

³**unequal** *adv, archaic* **:** UNEQUALLY ⟨~ match'd —Shak.⟩

un·equaled \-kwəld\ *adj* **:** not equaled **:** UNPARALLELED

un·equiv·o·cal \ˌən-i-ˈkwiv-ə-kəl\ *adj* **:** leaving no doubt **:** CLEAR, UNAMBIGUOUS — **un·equiv·o·cal·ly** \-k(ə-)lē\ *adv*

un·err·ing \ˌən-ˈe(ə)r-iŋ, ˌən-ˈər-, ˈən-\ *adj* **:** committing no error **:** FAULTLESS, UNFAILING — **un·err·ing·ly** \-iŋ-lē\ *adv*

un·es·sen·tial \ˌən-ə-ˈsen-chəl\ *adj* **1 :** not essential **:** DISPENSABLE, UNIMPORTANT **2** *archaic* **:** void of essence **:** INSUBSTANTIAL

un·even \ˌən-ˈē-vən, ˈən-\ *adj* **1 a** *archaic* **:** UNEQUAL 1a **b :** ODD 3a **2 a :** not even **:** not level or smooth **:** RUGGED, RAGGED ⟨large ~ teeth⟩ ⟨~ handwriting⟩ **b :** varying from the straight or parallel **c :** not uniform **:** IRREGULAR ⟨~ combustion⟩ **d :** varying in quality ⟨an ~ performance⟩ **syn** see ROUGH — **un·even·ly** *adv* — **un·even·ness** \-vən-nəs\ *n*

un·event·ful \ˌən-i-ˈvent-fəl\ *adj* **:** marked by no noteworthy or untoward incidents **:** PLACID — **un·event·ful·ly** \-fə-lē\ *adv*

un·ex·am·pled \ˌən-ig-ˈzam-pəld\ *adj* **:** having no example or parallel **:** UNPRECEDENTED

un·ex·cep·tion·able \ˌən-ik-ˈsep-sh(ə-)nə-bəl\ *adj* [*un-* + obs. *exception* (to take exception, object)] **:** not open to objection or criticism **:** beyond reproach **:** UNIMPEACHABLE — **un·ex·cep·tion·able·ness** *n* — **un·ex·cep·tion·ably** \-blē\ *adv*

un·ex·pect·ed \ˌən-ik-ˈspek-təd\ *adj* **:** not expected **:** UNFORESEEN — **un·ex·pect·ed·ly** *adv* — **un·ex·pect·ed·ness** *n*

un·ex·pres·sive \-ˈspres-iv\ *adj* **1 :** INEXPRESSIVE **2** *obs* **:** INEFFABLE

un·fad·able \ˌən-ˈfād-ə-bəl, ˈən-\ *adj* **1 :** not subject to fading **:** FAST **2 :** incapable of being forgotten

un·fail·ing \ˌən-ˈfā-liŋ, ˈən-\ *adj* **:** not failing or liable to fail: **a :** UNFLAGGING **b :** EVERLASTING, INEXHAUSTIBLE **c :** INFALLIBLE — **un·fail·ing·ly** \-liŋ-lē\ *adv* — **un·fail·ing·ness** *n*

un·fair \-ˈfa(ə)r, -ˈfe(ə)r\ *adj* **1 :** marked by injustice, partiality, or deception **:** UNJUST, DISHONEST **2 :** not equitable in business dealings — **un·fair·ly** *adv* — **un·fair·ness** *n*

un·faith \-ˈfāth\ *n* **:** absence of faith **:** DISBELIEF

un·faith·ful \-ˈfāth-fəl\ *adj* **:** not faithful: **a :** not adhering to vows, allegiance, or duty **:** DISLOYAL **b :** not faithful to marriage vows **c** *archaic* **:** wanting in good faith **:** DISHONEST **d :** INACCURATE, UNTRUSTWORTHY — **un·faith·ful·ly** \-fə-lē\ *adv* — **un·faith·ful·ness** *n*

un·fa·mil·iar \ˌən-fə-ˈmil-yər\ *adj* **:** not familiar: **a :** not well known **:** STRANGE ⟨an ~ place⟩ **b :** not well acquainted ⟨~ with the subject⟩ — **un·fa·mil·iar·i·ty** \-ˌmil-ˈyar-ət-ē, -ˌmil-ē-ˈ(y)ar-\ *n* — **un·fa·mil·iar·ly** \-ˈmil-yər-lē\ *adv*

un·fas·ten \ˌən-ˈfas-ᵊn, ˈən-\ *vt* **:** to make loose: **a :** UNPIN, UNBUCKLE **b :** UNDO **c :** DETACH

un·fa·thered \-ˈfāth-ərd\ *adj* **1 :** having no father **:** ILLEGITIMATE, BASTARD **2 :** having no known origin ⟨~ slanders⟩

un·fa·vor·able \-ˈfāv-(ə-)rə-bəl, -ˈfā-vər-bəl\ *adj* **1 :** OPPOSED, CONTRARY **2 :** not propitious **:** DISADVANTAGEOUS **3 :** not pleasing — **un·fa·vor·able·ness** *n* — **un·fa·vor·ably** \-blē\ *adv*

un·feath·ered \-ˈfeth-ərd\ *adj* **:** UNFLEDGED

un·feel·ing \-ˈfē-liŋ\ *adj* **1 :** devoid of feeling **:** INSENSATE **2 :** HARDHEARTED, CRUEL — **un·feel·ing·ly** \-liŋ-lē\ *adv* — **un·feel·ing·ness** *n*

un·feigned \ˌən-ˈfānd, ˈən-\ *adj* **:** not counterfeit **:** not hypocritical **:** GENUINE **syn** see SINCERE — **un·feigned·ly** \-ˈfā-nəd-lē, -ˈfān-dlē\ *adv*

un·fet·ter \-ˈfet-ər\ *vt* **1 :** to free from fetters **2 :** LIBERATE

un·fil·ial \-ˈfil-ē-əl, -ˈfil-yəl\ *adj* **:** not observing the obligations of a child to a parent **:** UNDUTIFUL

un·fin·ished \-ˈfin-isht\ *adj* **:** not finished: **a :** not brought to an end or to the desired final state **b :** subjected to no other processes (as bleaching or dyeing) after coming from the loom

¹**un·fit** \-ˈfit\ *adj* **:** not fit: **a :** not adapted to a purpose **:** UNSUITABLE **b :** INCAPABLE, INCOMPETENT **c :** physically or mentally unsound — **un·fit·ly** *adv* — **un·fit·ness** *n*

²**unfit** *vt* **:** to make unfit **:** DISABLE, DISQUALIFY

un·fix \ˌən-ˈfiks, ˈən-\ *vt* **1 :** to loosen from a fastening **:** DETACH, DISENGAGE **2 :** to make unstable **:** UNSETTLE

un·flap·pa·ble \-ˈflap-ə-bəl\ *adj* [¹*un-* + *flap* (state of excitement) + *-able*] **:** not easily upset or panicked **:** unusually calm

un·fledged \-ˈflejd\ *adj* **1 :** not feathered **:** not ready for flight **2 :** IMMATURE, CALLOW

un·flinch·ing \-ˈflin-chiŋ\ *adj* **:** not flinching or shrinking **:** STEADFAST — **un·flinch·ing·ly** \-chiŋ-lē\ *adv*

un·fold \-ˈfōld\ *vt* **1 a :** to open the folds of **:** spread or straighten out **:** EXPAND **b :** to remove (as a package) from the folds **:** UN-

See *un-* and 2d element
undeserved
undeserving
undesired
undetachable
undetected
undeterminable
undetermined
undeterred
undeveloped
undifferentiated
undigested
undignified
undiluted
undiminished
undimmed
undiplomatic
undiscerning
undischarged
undisciplined
undisclosed
undiscoverable
undiscovered
undiscriminating
undisguised
undismayed
undisputed
undissolved
undistinguished
undistributed
undisturbed
undiversified
undivided
undivulged
undogmatic
undomestic
undomesticated
undone
undoubled
undoubting
undrained
undramatic
undreamed
undreamt
undressed
undrinkable
undulled
undyed
uneager
unease
uneatable
uneaten
uneconomic
unedifying
uneducable
uneducated
unembarrassed
unembellished
unemotional
unemphatic
unenclosed
unencumbered
unending
unendorsed
unendurable
unenduring
unenforceable
unenforced
unengaged
unenjoyable
unenlarged
unenlightened
unenrolled
unenterprising
unentertaining
unenthusiastic
unenviable
unenvied
unenvious
unequipped
unescapable
unethical
unexaggerated
unexamined
unexcelled
unexceptional
unexchangeable
unexcited
unexciting
unexecuted
unexhausted
unexpanded
unexpended
unexpired
unexplainable
unexplained
unexploded
unexplored
unexposed
unexpressed
unexpurgated
unextended
unextinguished
unfading
unfaltering
unfashionable
unfastened
unfathomable
unfathomed
unfeasible
unfed
unfeminine
unfenced
unfermentable
unfermented
unfertilized
unfilled
unfired
unfitted
unfitting
unflagging
unflattering
unflavored
unflexed

WRAP **2** : to open to the view : REVEAL; *esp* : to make clear by gradual disclosure and often by recital ~ *vi* **1 a** : to open from a folded state : open out **b** : BLOSSOM **c** : DEVELOP **2** : to open out gradually to the view or understanding

un·for·get·ta·ble \,ən-fər-'get-ə-bəl\ *adj* : incapable of being forgotten : MEMORABLE — **un·for·get·ta·bly** \-blē\ *adv*

un·formed \,ən-'fȯ(ə)rmd, 'ən-\ *adj* : not arranged in regular shape, order, or relations **a** : UNDEVELOPED, IMMATURE **b** : INCHOATE, AMORPHOUS

¹un·for·tu·nate \-'fȯrch-(ə-)nət\ *adj* **1 a** : not favored by fortune : UNSUCCESSFUL, UNLUCKY **b** : marked or accompanied by or resulting in misfortune **2 a** : UNSUITABLE, INFELICITOUS **b** : DEPLORABLE — **un·for·tu·nate·ly** *adv*

²unfortunate *n* : an unfortunate person; *specif* : a social outcast

un·found·ed \,ən-'faún-dəd, 'ən-\ *adj* **1** *obs* : BOTTOMLESS **2** : lacking a sound basis : GROUNDLESS, ILLUSIVE

un·fre·quent·ed \,ən-frē-'kwent-əd; ,ən-'frē-kwənt-, 'ən-\ *adj* : not often visited or traveled over

un·friend·ed \,ən-'fren-dəd, 'ən-\ *adj* : having no friends : not befriended

un·friend·li·ness \-'fren-(d)lē-nəs\ *n* : the quality or state of being unfriendly : HOSTILITY

un·friend·ly \-'fren-(d)lē\ *adj* : not friendly: **a** : UNSYMPATHETIC, HOSTILE **b** : INHOSPITABLE, UNFAVORABLE

un·frock \-'fräk\ *vt* **1** : to divest of a frock **2** : to deprive (as a priest) of the right to exercise the functions of office

un·fruit·ful \-'früt-fəl\ *adj* : not fruitful: **a** : not producing offspring : INFERTILE, BARREN **b** : UNPROFITABLE *syn* see STERILE — **un·fruit·ful·ly** \-fə-lē\ *adv* — **un·fruit·ful·ness** *n*

un·fund·ed \,ən-'fən-dəd, 'ən-\ *adj* : not funded : FLOATING ⟨an ~ debt⟩

un·furl \-'fər(-ə)l\ *vt* **1** : to release from a furled state **2** : to open to the view ~ *vi* : to become visible or known

un·gain·li·ness \-'gān-lē-nəs\ *n* : the quality or state of being ungainly

un·gain·ly \-lē\ *adj* **1 a** : lacking in smoothness or dexterity : CLUMSY **b** : UNWIELDY **2** : COARSE, CRUDE

un·gen·er·ous \,ən-'jen-(ə-)rəs\ *adj* : not generous: **a** : PETTY, MEAN **b** : lacking in largess : STINGY — **un·gen·er·ous·ly** *adv*

un·gird \,ən-'gərd, 'ən-\ *vt* : to divest of a restraining band or girdle : UNBIND

un·girt \-'gərt\ *adj* **1** : having the belt or girdle off or loose **2** : LOOSE, SLACK

un·glue \-'glü\ *vt* : to disjoin by or as if by dissolving an adhesive

un·god·li·ness \-'gäd-lē-nəs *also* -'gȯd-\ *n* : the quality or state of being ungodly : WICKEDNESS

un·god·ly \-lē\ *adj* **1 a** : IMPIOUS, IRRELIGIOUS **b** : SINFUL, WICKED **2** : OUTRAGEOUS

un·got·ten \-'gät-ⁿn\ *or* **un·got** \-'gät\ *adj* **1** *obs* : not begotten **2** : not obtained

un·gov·ern·able \,ən-'gəv-ər-nə-bəl, 'ən-\ *adj* : not capable of being governed, guided, or restrained *syn* see UNRULY

un·grace·ful \-'grās-fəl\ *adj* : not graceful : AWKWARD, INELEGANT — **un·grace·ful·ly** \-fə-lē\ *adv* — **un·grace·ful·ness** *n*

un·gra·cious \-'grā-shəs\ *adj* **1** *archaic* : WICKED **2** : not courteous : RUDE **3** : not pleasing : DISAGREEABLE — **un·gra·cious·ly** *adv* — **un·gra·cious·ness** *n*

un·grate·ful \-'grāt-fəl\ *adj* **1** : showing no gratitude : making a poor return : THANKLESS **2** : DISAGREEABLE, REPELLENT — **un·grate·ful·ly** \-fə-lē\ *adv* — **un·grate·ful·ness** *n*

un·gual \'əŋ-gwəl, -gyü-wəl\ *adj* [L *unguis* nail, claw, hoof — more at NAIL] : of, relating to, or resembling a nail, claw, or hoof

un·guard \,ən-'gärd, 'ən-\ *vt* [back-formation fr. *unguarded*] : to leave unprotected

un·guard·ed \-'gärd-əd\ *adj* **1** : vulnerable to attack : UNPROTECTED **2** : free from guile or wariness : DIRECT, INCAUTIOUS — **un·guard·ed·ly** *adv*

un·guent \'əŋ-gwənt, 'ən-; 'ən-jənt\ *n* [L *unguentum* — more at OINTMENT] : a soothing or healing salve : OINTMENT

¹un·guic·u·late \,ən-'gwik-yə-lət, ,əŋ-\ *adj* [NL *unguiculatus*, fr. L *unguiculus*, dim. of *unguis*] : having nails or claws : CLAWED

²unguiculate *n* : a mammal having claws or nails as distinguished from an ungulate or cetacean

un·guis \'əŋ-gwəs, 'ən-\ *n, pl* **un·gues** \-,gwēz\ [L] **1** : a nail, claw, or hoof esp. on a digit of a vertebrate **2** : a narrow pointed base of a petal

¹un·gu·late \'əŋ-gyə-lət, 'ən-\ *adj* [LL *ungulatus*, fr. L *ungula* hoof, fr. *unguis* nail, hoof] **1** : having hoofs **2** : of or relating to the ungulates

²ungulate *n* [deriv. of L *ungula*] : any of a group (Ungulata) consisting of the hoofed mammals and including the ruminants, swine, horses, tapirs, rhinoceroses, elephants, and coneys of which most are herbivorous and many horned

un·hair \,ən-'ha(ə)r, 'ən-, -'he(ə)r\ *vt* **1** *archaic* : to deprive of hair **2** : to remove the guard hairs from ⟨~ a pelt⟩ ~ *vi* : to lose the hair

un·hal·low \-'hal-(,)ō, -'hal-ə-(w)\ *vt, archaic* : to make profane

un·hal·lowed \-(,)ōd, -əd\ *adj* **1** : UNCONSECRATED, UNHOLY **2 a** : IMPIOUS, PROFANE **b** : IMMORAL

un·hand \,ən-'hand, 'ən-\ *vt* : to remove the hand from : let go

un·hand·some \-'han(t)-səm\ *adj* : not handsome: as **a** : not beautiful : HOMELY **b** : UNBECOMING, UNSEEMLY **c** : lacking in courtesy or taste : RUDE — **un·hand·some·ly** *adv*

un·handy \-'han-dē\ *adj* **1** : hard to handle : INCONVENIENT **2** : lacking in skill or dexterity : AWKWARD

un·hap·pi·ly \-'hap-ə-lē\ *adv* : in an unhappy manner

un·hap·pi·ness \-'hap-i-nəs\ *n* : the quality or state of being unhappy

un·hap·py \-'hap-ē\ *adj* **1** : not fortunate : UNLUCKY **2** : not cheerful or glad : SAD, WRETCHED **3 a** : causing or subject to misfortune : INAUSPICIOUS **b** : INFELICITOUS, INAPPROPRIATE

un·har·ness \-'här-nəs\ *vt* : to divest of harness

un·health·i·ly \-'hel-thə-lē\ *adv* : in an unhealthy manner

un·health·i·ness \-thē-nəs\ *n* : the quality or state of being unhealthy

un·healthy \-thē\ *adj* **1** : not conducive to health ⟨an ~ climate⟩ **2** : not in good health : SICKLY, DISEASED **3 a** : RISKY, UNSOUND **b** : BAD, INJURIOUS **c** : morally contaminated : CORRUPT, UNWHOLESOME

un·heard \,ən-'hərd, 'ən-\ *adj* **1 a** : not perceived by the ear **b** : not given a hearing **2** *archaic* : UNHEARD-OF

un·heard–of \-,əv, -,äv\ *adj* : previously unknown : UNPRECEDENTED

un·hinge \,ən-'hinj, 'ən-\ *vt* **1** : to remove (as a door) from the hinges **2** : to make unstable : UNSETTLE, DISRUPT

un·hitch \-'hich\ *vt* : to free from or as if from being hitched

un·ho·li·ness \-'hō-lē-nəs\ *n* : the quality or state of being unholy

un·ho·ly \-'hō-lē\ *adj* **1 a** : IMPIOUS **b** : WICKED **2** : SHOCKING, OUTRAGEOUS

un·hood \,ən-'húd, 'ən-\ *vt* : to remove a hood or covering from

un·hook \-'húk\ *vt* **1** : to remove from a hook **2** : to unfasten by disengaging a hook

un·hoped \-'hōpt\ *adj, archaic* : not hoped or expected

un·horse \-'hȯ(ə)rs\ *vt* : to dislodge from or as if from a horse

un·hou·seled \-'haú-zəld\ *adj, archaic* : not having received the Eucharist

un·hur·ried \-'hər-ēd, -'hə-rēd\ *adj* : not hurried : LEISURELY

uni- *prefix* [ME, fr. MF, fr. L, fr. *unus* — more at ONE] : one : single ⟨*unicellular*⟩

Uni·ate *or* **Uni·at** \'(y)ü-nē-,at\ *n* [Russ *uniyat*] : a Christian of an Eastern rite submitting to the pope and differing from the Latin church in liturgy and discipline — **Uniate** *adj*

uni·ax·i·al \,yü-nē-'ak-sē-əl\ *adj* **1** : having only one axis **2** : of or relating to only one axis — **uni·ax·i·al·ly** \-sē-ə-lē\ *adv*

uni·cam·er·al \,yü-ni-'kam-(ə-)rəl\ *adj* : having or consisting of a single legislative chamber — **uni·cam·er·al·ly** \-ē\ *adv*

uni·cel·lu·lar \-'sel-yə-lər\ *adj* : having or consisting of a single cell — **uni·cel·lu·lar·i·ty** \-,sel-yə-'lar-ət-ē\ *n*

uni·corn \'yü-nə-,kȯ(ə)rn\ *n* [ME *unicorne*, fr. OF, fr. LL *unicornis*, fr. L, having one horn, fr. *uni-* + *cornu* horn — more at HORN] : a fabulous animal generally depicted with the body and head of a horse, the hind legs of a stag, the tail of a lion, and a single horn in the middle of the forehead

uni·cy·cle \'yü-ni-,sī-kəl\ *n* [*uni-* + *-cycle* (as in *tricycle*)] : any of various vehicles that have a single wheel and are propelled usu. by pedals or applied draft — **uni·cy·clist** \-,sī-k(ə-)ləst\ *n*

uni·di·rec·tion·al \,yü-ni-də-'rek-shnəl, -(,)dī-, -shən-ᵊl\ *adj* : having, involving, moving, or responsive in a single direction

unidirectional current *n* : DIRECT CURRENT

uni·fac·to·ri·al \,yü-ni-,fak-'tōr-ē-əl, -'tȯr-\ *adj* : relating to or controlled by a single gene

uni·fi·able \'yü-nə-,fī-ə-bəl\ *adj* : capable of being unified

uni·fi·ca·tion \,yü-nə-fə-'kā-shən\ *n* : the act, process, or result of unifying : the state of being unified

uni·fi·er \'yü-nə-,fī(-ə)r\ *n* : one that unifies

uni·fi·lar \,yü-ni-'fī-lər\ *adj* : having or involving use of only one thread, wire, or fiber

uni·fo·li·ate \-'fō-lē-ət\ *adj* **1** : having only one leaf **2** : UNIFOLIOLATE

uni·fo·li·o·late \-'fō-lē-ə-,lāt\ *adj, of a leaf* : compound but having only a single leaflet and distinguishable from a simple leaf by the basal joint

¹uni·form \'yü-nə-,form\ *adj* [MF *uniforme*, fr. L *uniformis*, fr. *uni-* + *-formis* -form] **1** : having always the same form, manner, or degree : not varying or variable **2** : of the same form with others : conforming to one rule or mode : CONSONANT **3** : presenting an undiversified appearance of surface, pattern, or color **4** : consistent in conduct or opinion *syn* see SIMILAR — **uni·form·ly** \'yü-nə-,form-lē, ,yü-nə-'\ *adv* — **uni·form·ness** \'yü-nə-,form-nəs\ *n*

²uniform *vt* **1** : to bring into uniformity **2** : to clothe with a uniform

³uniform *n* : dress of a distinctive design or fashion worn by members of a particular group and serving as a means of identification

Uniform — a communications code word for the letter *u*

uni·for·mi·tar·i·an \,yü-nə-,for-mə-'ter-ē-ən\ *n* : a believer in uniformitarianism : an advocate of uniformity — **uniformitarian** *adj*

uni·for·mi·tar·i·an·ism \-ē-ə-,niz-əm\ *n* : a geological doctrine that existing processes acting in the same manner as at present are sufficient to account for all geological changes

uni·for·mi·ty \,yü-nə-'fȯr-mət-ē\ *n* : the quality or state or an instance of being uniform

uni·fy \'yü-nə-,fī\ *vt* [LL *unificare*, fr. L *uni-* + *-ficare* -fy] : to make into a unit or a coherent whole : UNITE

uni·ju·gate \yú-'nij-ə-,gāt, ,yü-ni-'jü-gət\ *adj* : having but one pair of leaflets — used of a pinnate leaf

uni·lat·er·al \,yü-ni-'lat-ə-rəl, -'la-trəl\ *adj* **1 a** : of, relating to, or affecting one side of a subject : ONE-SIDED **b** : constituting or relating to a contract or engagement by which an express obliga-

See un- and 2d element	unframed	ungifted	unhampered	unhealthful	unhonored
unforced	unfree	unglazed	unhandiness	unheeded	unhoped-for
unforeseeable	unfrozen	ungoverned	unhanged	unheeding	unhoused
unforeseen	unfulfilled	ungraded	unhardened	unheralded	unhurt
unforgivable	unfurnished	ungrammatical	unharmed	unheroic	unhygienic
unforgiving	ungallant	ungrounded	unharmonious	unheroical	unideal
unforked	ungarnished	ungrudging	unharnessed	unhesitating	unidentified
unformulated	ungathered	unguided	unhatched	unhindered	unidiomatic
unfortified	ungentle	unhackneyed			

tion to do or forbear is imposed on but one party **2 :** produced or arranged on or directed toward one side ⟨a ~ raceme⟩ **3 :** tracing descent through either the maternal or paternal line only **4 :** having only one side — **uni·lat·er·al·ly** \-ē\ *adv*

uni·lin·ear \-'lin-ē-ər\ *adj* **:** developing in or involving a series of stages usu. from the primitive to the more advanced

uni·loc·u·lar \-'läk-yə-lər\ *adj* **:** containing a single cavity

un·im·peach·able \,ən-im-'pē-chə-bəl\ *adj* **:** not impeachable **:** not to be called in question **:** not liable to accusation **:** IRREPROACHABLE, BLAMELESS — **un·im·peach·ably** \-blē\ *adv*

1un·im·proved \-'prüvd\ *adj, obs* **:** UNREPROVED

2unimproved *adj* **:** not improved: as **a :** not tilled, built upon, or otherwise improved for use ⟨~ land⟩ **b :** not used or employed advantageously **c :** not selectively bred for better quality or productiveness

un·in·hib·it·ed \,ən-in-'hib-ət-əd\ *adj* **:** free from inhibition; *esp* **:** boisterously informal — **un·in·hib·it·ed·ly** *adv*

un·in·tel·li·gence \-'tel-ə-jən(t)s\ *n* **:** the quality or state of being unintelligent

un·in·tel·li·gent \-jənt\ *adj* **:** lacking intelligence **:** UNWISE, IGNORANT — **un·in·tel·li·gent·ly** *adv*

un·in·tel·li·gi·ble \-'tel-ə-jə-bəl\ *adj* **:** not intelligible **:** OBSCURE — **un·in·tel·li·gi·ble·ness** *n* — **un·in·tel·li·gi·bly** \-blē\ *adv*

un·in·ten·tion·al \,ən-in-'tench-nəl, -'ten-chən-ᵊl\ *adj* **:** not intentional — **un·in·ten·tion·al·ly** \-ē\ *adv*

un·in·ter·est·ed \,ən-'in-trəs-təd, 'ən-; -'int-ə-rəs-, -ə-,res, -ərs-; -'in-,tres-\ *adj* **:** not interested: as **a :** having no interest and esp. no property interest in **b :** not having the mind or feelings engaged

un·in·ter·rupt·ed \,ən-,int-ə-'rəp-təd\ *adj* **:** not interrupted **:** CONTINUOUS — **un·in·ter·rupt·ed·ly** *adv* — **un·in·ter·rupt·ed·ness** *n*

uni·nu·cle·ate \,yü-ni-'n(y)ü-klē-ət\ *also* **uni·nu·cle·ar** \-klē-ər\ *adj* **:** having a single nucleus

1union \'yü-nyən\ *n* [ME, fr. MF, fr. LL *union-*, *unio* oneness, union, fr. L *unus* one — more at ONE] **1 a :** an act or instance of uniting or joining two or more things into one: as (1) **:** the formation of a single political unit from two or more separate and independent units (2) **:** a uniting in marriage; *also* **:** SEXUAL INTERCOURSE (3) **:** the growing together of severed parts **b :** a unified condition **:** COMBINATION, JUNCTION **2 :** something that is made one **:** something formed by a combining or coalition of parts or members: as **a :** a confederation of independent individuals (as nations or persons) for some common purpose **b :** a political unit constituting an organic whole formed usu. from previously independent units (as England and Scotland in 1707) which have surrendered their principal powers to the government of the whole or a newly created government (as the U. S. in 1789) **c** *cap* **:** an organization on a college or university campus providing recreational, social, cultural, and sometimes dining facilities; *also* **:** the building housing it **d :** SUM 5c(2) **3 a :** a device emblematic of the union of two or more sovereignties borne on a national flag typically in the upper inner corner or constituting the whole design of the flag **b :** the upper inner corner of a flag **4 :** any of various devices for connecting parts (as of a machine); *esp* **:** a coupling for pipes or pipes and fittings **syn** see UNITY

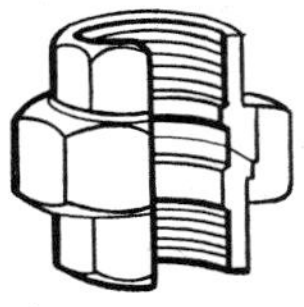

pipe union, cut-away

2union *adj* **:** of, relating to, dealing with, or constituting a union

union card *n* **:** a card certifying personal membership in good standing in a labor union

union·ism \'yü-nyə-,niz-əm\ *n* **:** the principle or policy of forming or adhering to a union: as **a** *cap* **:** adherence to the policy of a firm federal union between the states of the United States esp. during the Civil War period **b :** the principles, theory, or system of trade unions — **union·ist** \-nyə-nəst\ *n, often cap*

union·iza·tion \,yü-nyə-nə-'zā-shən\ *n* **1 :** the quality or state of being unionized **2 :** the act of unionizing

union·ize \'yü-nyə-,nīz\ *vt* **:** to cause to become a member of or subject to the rules of a labor union **:** form into a labor union

union jack *n, often cap U&J* **:** a jack consisting of the union of a national ensign

union shop *n* **:** an establishment in which the employer by agreement is free to hire nonmembers as well as members of the union but retains nonmembers on the payroll only on condition of their becoming members of the union within a specified time

union suit *n* **:** an undergarment with shirt and drawers in one piece

uni·pa·ren·tal \,yü-ni-pə-'rent-ᵊl\ *adj* **:** having or involving a single parent; *esp* **:** PARTHENOGENETIC — **uni·pa·ren·tal·ly** \-ᵊl-ē\ *adv*

unip·a·rous \yü-'nip-ə-rəs\ *adj* **1 a :** producing but one egg or offspring at a time **b :** having produced but one offspring **2 :** producing but one axis at each branching ⟨a ~ cyme⟩

uni·pla·nar \,yü-ni-'plā-nər, -,när\ *adj* **:** lying or occurring in one plane **:** PLANAR

uni·pod \'yü-nə-,päd\ *n* [*uni-* + *-pod* (as in *tripod*)] **:** a one-legged support (as for a camera)

uni·po·lar \,yü-ni-'pō-lər\ *adj* **1 :** having, produced by, or acting by a single magnetic or electrical pole **2 :** having but one process ⟨~ ganglion cells⟩ — **uni·po·lar·i·ty** \-pō-'lar-ət-ē, -pə-\ *n*

uni·po·tent \yü-'nip-ət-ənt, ,yü-ni-'pōt-\ *adj* **:** capable of developing only in one direction or to one end product ⟨~ cells⟩

unique \yù-'nēk\ *adj* [F, fr. L *unicus*, fr. *unus* one — more at ONE] **1 :** SINGLE, SOLE **2 :** being without a like or equal **:** UNEQUALED **3 :** very rare or uncommon **:** very unusual **syn** see SINGLE, STRANGE — **unique·ly** *adv* — **unique·ness** *n*

uni·ra·mous \,yü-ni-'rā-məs\ *or* **uni·ra·mose** \-,mōs\ *adj* **:** UNBRANCHED

uni·sex·u·al \-'seksh-(ə-)wəl, -'sek-shəl\ *adj* **:** of, relating to, or restricted to one sex: **a :** male or female but not hermaphroditic **b :** DICLINOUS ⟨a ~ flower⟩ — **uni·sex·u·al·i·ty** \-,sek-shə-'wal-ət-ē\ *n* — **uni·sex·u·al·ly** \-'seksh-(ə-)wə-lē, -'sek-shə-lē\ *adv*

uni·son \'yü-nə-sən, -nə-zən\ *n* [MF, fr. ML *unisonus* having the same sound, fr. L *uni-* + *sonus* sound — more at SOUND] **1 a :** identity in musical pitch; *specif* **:** the interval of a perfect prime **b :** the state of being so tuned or sounded **c :** the writing, playing, or singing of parts in a musical passage at the same pitch or in octaves **2 :** a harmonious agreement or union **:** CONCORD — **unison** *adj*

unis·o·nous \yü-'nis-ᵊn-əs\ *also* **unis·o·nal** \-ᵊn-əl\ *or* **unis·o·nant** \-ᵊn-ənt\ *adj* **:** being in unison **:** sounded alike in pitch

unit \'yü-nət\ *n* [back-formation fr. *unity*] **1 a** (1) **:** the first and least natural number **:** ONE (2) **:** a single quantity regarded as a whole in calculation **b :** the number occupying the position immediately to the left of the decimal point in the Arabic system of numerals **2 :** a determinate quantity (as of length, time, heat, value, or housing) adopted as a standard of measurement: as **a :** an amount of work (as 120 hours in a completed course) used in education in calculating student credits **b :** an amount of a biologically active agent (as a drug or antigen) required to produce a specific result under strictly controlled conditions **3 a :** a single thing or person or group that is a constituent of a whole **b :** a part of a military establishment that has a prescribed organization (as of personnel and materiel) **c :** a piece or complex of apparatus serving to perform one particular function **d :** a part of a school course focusing on a central theme and making use of resources from numerous subject areas and the pupils' own experience — **unit** *adj*

unit·age \'yü-nət-ij\ *n* **1 :** specification of the amount constituting a unit **2 :** amount in units

uni·tar·i·an \,yü-nə-'ter-ē-ən\ *n* [NL *unitarius*, fr. LL *unitus*, pp.] **1 a** *often cap* **:** one who believes that the deity exists only in one person **b** *cap* **:** a member of a denomination that stresses individual freedom of belief, the free use of reason in religion, a united world community, and liberal social action **2 :** an advocate of unity or a unitary system — **unitarian** *adj, often cap* — **uni·tar·i·an·ism** \-ē-ə-,niz-əm\ *n, often cap*

uni·tary \'yü-nə-,ter-ē\ *adj* **1 a :** of or relating to a unit **b :** based on or characterized by unity or units **2 :** having the character of a unit **:** UNDIVIDED, WHOLE

unit character *n* **:** a natural character inherited on an all or none basis; *esp* **:** one dependent on the presence or absence of a single gene

1unite \yù-'nīt\ *vb* [ME *uniten*, fr. LL *unitus*, pp. of *unire*, fr. L *unus* one — more at ONE] *vt* **1 a :** to put together to form a single unit **b :** to cause to adhere **c :** to link by a legal or moral bond **2 :** to possess (as qualities) in combination ~ *vi* **1 a :** to become one or as if one **b :** to become combined by or as if by adhesion or mixture **2 :** to act in concert **syn** see JOIN — **unit·er** *n*

2unite \'yü-,nīt\ *n* [obs. *unite* (united), fr. ME *unit*, fr. LL *unitus*, pp.] **:** an old British gold 20-shilling piece issued first by James I in 1604 for the newly united England and Scotland — called also *Jacobus*

unit·ed \yù-'nīt-əd, *esp South* 'yü-,\ *adj* **1 :** made one **:** COMBINED **2 :** relating to or produced by joint action **3 :** being in agreement **:** HARMONIOUS — **unit·ed·ly** *adv*

United Nations Day *n* **:** October 24 observed in commemoration of the founding of the United Nations

United States *n pl but sing or pl in constr* **:** a federation of states esp. when forming a nation in a usu. specified territory ⟨advocating a *United States* of Europe⟩

unit factor *n* **:** a gene that controls the inheritance of a unit character — compare POLYGENE

uni·tive \'yü-nət-iv, yù-'nīt-\ *adj* **:** characterized by or tending to produce union

unit·ize \'yü-nət-,īz\ *vt* **:** to convert into a unit

unit magnetic pole *n* **:** a magnetic pole that will repel an equal and like pole at a distance of one centimeter in a vacuum with a force of one dyne

unit rule *n* **:** a rule that may be adopted by a delegation to a Democratic national convention under which its entire vote is cast as a unit as determined by a majority vote

uni·ty \'yü-nət-ē\ *n* [ME *unite*, fr. OF *unité*, fr. L *unitat-*, *unitas*, fr. *unus* one] **1 a :** the quality or state of not being multiple **:** ONENESS **b** (1) **:** a definite amount taken as one or for which 1 is made to stand in calculation in a table of natural sines ⟨the radius of the circle is regarded as ~⟩ (2) **:** a number multiplication by which leaves any element of a system unchanged **2 a :** a condition of harmony **:** ACCORD **b :** continuity without deviation or change (as in purpose or action) **3 a :** the quality or state of being made one **:** UNIFICATION **b :** a combination or ordering of parts in a literary or artistic production that constitutes a whole or promotes an undivided total effect; *also* **:** the singleness of effect or symmetry and consistency of style and character secured **4 :** a totality of related parts **:** an entity that is a complex or systematic whole **5 :** any of three principles of dramatic structure derived by French classicists from Aristotle's *Poetics* and requiring a play to have a single action represented as occurring in one place and within one day **6** *cap* **:** a 20th century American religious movement for health and prosperity formerly affiliated with New Thought but closer to orthodox Christianity

syn SOLIDARITY, INTEGRITY, UNION: UNITY implies oneness esp. of what is varied and diverse in its elements or parts; SOLIDARITY implies a unity in a group or class that enables it to manifest its strength and exert its influence as one; INTEGRITY implies unity that indicates interdependence of the parts and completeness and perfection of the whole; UNION implies a thorough integration and harmonious cooperation of the parts

1uni·va·lent \,yü-ni-'vā-lənt\ *adj* [ISV] **1 :** having a chemical valence of one **2** *of a chromosome* **:** lacking a synaptic mate

2univalent *n* **:** a univalent chromosome

1uni·valve \'yü-ni-,valv\ *adj* **:** having or consisting of one valve

2univalve *n* **1 :** a mollusk with a univalve shell; *esp* **:** GASTROPOD **2 :** a mollusk shell consisting of one piece

1uni·ver·sal \,yü-nə-'vər-səl\ *adj* **1 :** including or covering all or a whole collectively or distributively without limit or exception **2 a :** present or occurring everywhere **b :** existent or operative everywhere or under all conditions ⟨~ cultural patterns⟩ **3 a :** em-

See *un-* and 2d element
unilluminated
unimaginable
unimaginative
unimpaired
unimpassioned
unimpeded
unimportance
unimportant
unimposing
unimpressible
unimpressionable
unimpressive
unincorporated
uninfected
uninflammable
uninflected
uninfluenced
uninformed
uninhabitable
uninhabited
uninitiated
uninjured
uninspired
uninspiring
uninstructed
uninsulated
unintelligibility
unintended
uninteresting
unintermitted
unintermittent
uninventive
uninvested
uninvited
uninviting

bracing a major part or the greatest portion ⟨a ~ state⟩ ⟨~ practices⟩ ⟨food is a ~ need⟩ **b :** comprehensively broad and versatile ⟨a ~ genius⟩ **4 a :** affirming or denying something of all members of a class ⟨~ affirmative⟩ or of all values of a variable ⟨~ quantifier⟩ **b :** denoting every member of a class ⟨~ term⟩ **5 :** adapted or adjustable to meet varied requirements (as of use, shape, or size) ⟨a ~ gear cutter⟩ — **uni·ver·sal·ly** \-s(ə-)lē\ *adv* — **uni·ver·sal·ness** \-səl-nəs\ *n*

syn UNIVERSAL, GENERAL, GENERIC mean of or relating to all or the whole. UNIVERSAL implies reference to every one without exception in the class, category, or genus considered; GENERAL implies reference to all or nearly all ⟨the theory has met *general* but not *universal* acceptance⟩ GENERIC implies reference to every member of a genus ⟨*generic* likenesses between all dogs⟩

²universal *n* **1 a :** a universal proposition in logic **b :** a predicable of traditional logic **c :** a general concept or term or something in reality to which it corresponds **:** ESSENCE **2 a :** a mode of behavior existing in all cultures **b :** a culture trait characteristic of all normal adult members of a particular society

uni·ver·sal·ism \-sə-,liz-əm\ *n* **1** *often cap* **a :** a theological doctrine that all men will eventually be saved **b :** the principles and practices of a liberal Christian denomination founded in the 18th century to uphold belief in universal salvation and now united with Unitarianism **2 :** UNIVERSALITY **3 :** a social relationship in which behavior is determined by an impersonal code or standard — **uni·ver·sal·ist** \-s(ə-)ləst\ *n or adj, often cap*

uni·ver·sal·i·ty \,yü-nə-(,)vər-'sal-ət-ē\ *n* **1 :** the quality or state of being universal **2 :** universal comprehensiveness in range **:** unrestricted versatility or power of adaptation or comprehension

uni·ver·sal·iza·tion \,yü-nə-,vər-s(ə-)lə-'zā-shən\ *n* **:** the quality or state of being universalized

uni·ver·sal·ize \-'vər-sə-,līz\ *vt* **:** to make universal **:** GENERALIZE

universal joint *n* **:** a shaft coupling capable of transmitting rotation from one shaft to another not collinear with it — called also *universal coupling*

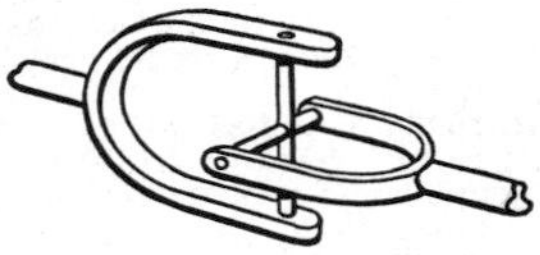

single universal joint

uni·verse \'yü-nə-,vərs\ *n* [L *universum*, fr. neut. of *universus* entire, whole, fr. *uni-* + *versus* turned toward, fr. pp. of *vertere* to turn — more at WORTH] **1 :** the whole body of things and phenomena observed or postulated **:** COSMOS **2 a :** a systematic whole held to arise by and persist through the direct intervention of divine power **b :** the world of human experience **c (1) :** MILKY WAY GALAXY **(2) :** an aggregate of stars comparable to the Milky Way galaxy **3 :** a distinct field or province of thought or reality that forms a closed system or self-inclusive and independent organization **4 :** POPULATION 4 **syn** see EARTH

universe of discourse : an inclusive class of entities that is tacitly implied or explicitly delineated as the subject of a statement, discourse, or theory

uni·ver·si·ty \,yü-nə-'vər-sət-ē, -'vər-stē\ *n, often attrib* [ME *universite*, fr. OF *université*, fr. ML *universitat-, universitas*, fr. L *universus*] **:** an institution of higher learning providing facilities for teaching and research and authorized to grant academic degrees; *specif* **:** one made up of an undergraduate division which confers bachelor's degrees and a graduate division which comprises a graduate school and professional schools each of which may confer master's degrees and doctorates

univ·o·cal \yü-'niv-ə-kəl\ *adj* [LL *univocus*, fr. L *uni-* + *voc-, vox* voice — more at VOICE] **:** having one meaning only — **univ·o·cal·ly** \-k(ə-)lē\ *adv*

un·just \,ən-'jəst, 'ən-\ *adj* **1 :** characterized by injustice **:** deficient in justice and fairness **:** WRONGFUL **2** *archaic* **:** DISHONEST, FAITHLESS — **un·just·ly** *adv* — **un·just·ness** \-'jəs(t)-nəs\ *n*

un·kempt \-'kem(p)t\ *adj* [*un-* + *kempt* (combed, neat)] **1 a :** not combed ⟨~ hair⟩ **b :** deficient in order or neatness of person **:** DISHEVELED **2 :** ROUGH, UNPOLISHED

un·kenned \-'kend\ *adj, chiefly dial* **:** UNKNOWN, STRANGE

un·ken·nel \-'ken-ᵊl\ *vt* **1 a :** to drive (as a fox) from a hiding place or den **b :** to free (dogs) from a kennel **2 :** UNCOVER

un·kind \,ən-'kīnd, 'ən-\ *adj* **:** deficient in kindness or sympathy **:** HARSH, CRUEL — **un·kind·ness** \-'kīn(d)-nəs\ *n*

un·kind·li·ness \-'kīn-(d)lē-nəs\ *n* **:** the quality or state of being unkindly

¹un·kind·ly \-'kīn-(d)lē\ *adj* **:** UNKIND

²unkindly *adv* **:** in an unkind manner

un·knit \,ən-'nit, 'ən-\ *vb* **:** UNDO, UNRAVEL

un·know·able \,ən-'nō-ə-bəl, 'ən-\ *adj* **:** not knowable; *esp* **:** lying beyond the limits of human experience or understanding

un·know·ing \,ən-'nō-iŋ, 'ən-\ *adj* **:** not knowing — **un·know·ing·ly** \-iŋ-lē\ *adv*

¹un·known \,ən-'nōn, 'ən-\ *adj* **:** not known; *also* **:** having an unknown value ⟨~ quantity⟩

²unknown *n* **:** something that is unknown and usu. to be discovered; *specif* **:** a symbol in a mathematical equation representing an unknown quantity and often being one of the last letters of the alphabet

Unknown Soldier *n* **:** an unidentified soldier whose body is selected to receive national honors as a representative of all of the same nation who died in a war and esp. in one of the world wars

un·lace \,ən-'lās, 'ən-\ *vt* **1 a :** to loose by undoing a lacing **b :** to unloose the dress of **2** *obs* **:** UNDO, DISGRACE

un·lade \-'lād\ *vt* **1 :** to take the load or cargo from **2 :** DISCHARGE, UNLOAD ~ *vi* **:** to discharge cargo

un·lash \-'lash\ *vt* **:** to untie the lashing of **:** LOOSE, UNDO

un·latch \-'lach\ *vt* **:** to open or loose by lifting the latch ~ *vi* **:** to become loosed or opened

un·law·ful \,ən-'lȯ-fəl, 'ən-\ *adj* **1 :** not lawful **2 :** IRREGULAR — **un·law·ful·ly** \-f(ə-)lē\ *adv* — **un·law·ful·ness** \-fəl-nəs\ *n*

un·lay \-'lā\ *vt* **:** to untwist the strands of (as a rope) ~ *vi* **:** UNTWIST

un·lead·ed \-'led-əd\ *adj* **1 :** stripped of lead **2 :** not having leads between the lines in printing

un·learn \-'lərn\ *vt* **:** to put out of one's knowledge or memory

un·learned \-'lər-nəd *for 1, 2,* -'lərnd *for 3*\ *adj* **1 :** possessing little or no learning or education **:** UNTAUGHT **2 :** characterized by or revealing ignorance **3 :** not gained by study or training **syn** see IGNORANT

un·leash \,ən-'lēsh, 'ən-\ *vt* **:** to free from or as if from a leash

¹un·less \ən-,les, ,ən-, *in some contexts* ᵊn-, ᵊm-, *or* ᵊŋ-\ *conj* [ME *unlesse*, alter. of *onlesse*, fr. *on* + *lesse* less] **1 :** under any other circumstance than that **:** except on the condition that **2 :** without the accompanying circumstance or condition that **:** but that **:** BUT

²unless *prep* **:** except possibly **:** EXCEPT

un·let·tered \,ən-'let-ərd, 'ən-\ *adj* **1 a :** not educated **b :** ILLITERATE **2 :** not marked with letters **syn** see IGNORANT

un·licked \-'likt\ *adj* **:** not licked dry **:** lacking proper form or shape

¹un·like \-'līk\ *prep* **:** not like: as **a :** different from **b :** not characteristic of **c :** in a different manner from

²unlike *adj* **:** not like: as **a :** marked by dissimilarity **:** DIFFERENT **b :** UNEQUAL — **un·like·ness** *n*

un·like·li·hood \-'lī-klē-,hu̇d\ *n* **:** IMPROBABILITY

un·like·li·ness \-'lī-klē-nəs\ *n* **:** UNLIKELIHOOD

un·like·ly \-'lī-klē\ *adj* **1 :** not likely **:** IMPROBABLE **2 :** likely to fail **:** UNPROMISING

un·lim·ber \,ən-'lim-bər, 'ən-\ *vt* **1 :** to detach the limber from and so make ready ⟨~ a gun for action⟩ **2 :** to prepare for action ~ *vi* **:** to perform the task of preparing something for action

un·lim·it·ed \-'lim-ət-əd\ *adj* **1 :** lacking any controls **2 :** BOUNDLESS, INFINITE **3 :** not bounded by exceptions **:** UNDEFINED

un·link \-'liŋk\ *vt* **:** to unfasten the links of **:** SEPARATE, DISCONNECT

un·list·ed \-'lis-təd\ *adj* **1 :** not appearing upon a list **2 :** of or relating to a stock or bond not listed on an organized securities exchange

un·live \-'liv\ *vt* **:** to live down **:** ANNUL, REVERSE

un·load \,ən-'lōd, 'ən-\ *vt* **1 a (1) :** to take off **:** DELIVER **(2) :** to take the cargo from **b :** to give outlet to **:** pour forth **2 :** to relieve of something burdensome, unwanted, or oppressive **3 :** to draw the charge from ⟨~*ed* the gun⟩ **4 :** to sell esp. in large quantities **:** DUMP ~ *vi* **:** to perform the act of unloading — **un·load·er** *n*

un·lock \-'läk\ *vt* **1 :** to unfasten the lock of **2 :** OPEN, UNDO **3 :** to cause to open **4 :** to furnish a key to **:** DISCLOSE ~ *vi* **:** to become unfastened or freed from restraints

un·looked–for \-'lu̇kt-,fȯ(ə)r\ *adj* **:** not observed or foreseen

un·loose \,ən-'lüs, 'ən-\ *vt* **1 :** to relax the strain of ⟨~ a grip⟩ **2 :** to release from or as if from restraints **:** set free **3 :** UNTIE

un·loos·en \-'lüs-ᵊn\ *vt* **:** UNLOOSE

un·love·li·ness \-'ləv-lē-nəs\ *n* **:** the quality or state of being unlovely

un·love·ly \-'ləv-lē\ *adj* **:** possessing qualities that inspire dislike **:** DISAGREEABLE, UNPLEASANT

un·luck·i·ly \-'lək-ə-lē\ *adv* **:** in an unlucky manner

un·luck·i·ness \-'lək-ē-nəs\ *n* **:** the quality or state of being unlucky

un·lucky \-'lək-ē\ *adj* **1 :** marked by adversity or failure **2 :** likely to bring misfortune **:** INAUSPICIOUS **3 :** producing dissatisfaction **:** REGRETTABLE

un·make \,ən-'māk, 'ən-\ *vt* **1 :** to cause to disappear **:** DESTROY **2 :** to deprive of rank or office **:** DEPOSE **3 :** to deprive of essential characteristics **:** change the nature of

un·man \-'man\ *vt* **1 :** to deprive of courage, strength, or vigor **2 :** CASTRATE, EMASCULATE **syn** see UNNERVE

un·man·li·ness \-'man-lē-nəs\ *n* **:** the quality or state of being unmanly

un·man·ly \-'man-lē\ *adj* **:** not manly: as **a :** being of weak character **:** COWARDLY **b :** EFFEMINATE

un·manned \-'mand\ *adj* **1 :** having no men aboard ⟨~ airplanes⟩ **2** *obs* **:** not trained ⟨an ~ hawk⟩

un·man·nered \-'man-ərd\ *adj* **1 :** marked by a lack of good manners **:** RUDE **2 :** UNAFFECTED — **un·man·nered·ly** *adv*

un·man·ner·li·ness \-'man-ər-lē-nəs\ *n* **:** the quality or state of being unmannerly

¹un·man·ner·ly \-'man-ər-lē\ *adv* **:** in an unmannerly fashion

²unmannerly *adj* **:** not mannerly **:** DISCOURTEOUS

un·mask \,ən-'mask, 'ən-\ *vt* **1 :** to remove a mask from **2 :** to reveal the true nature of **:** EXPOSE ~ *vi* **:** to remove one's mask

un·mean·ing \-'mē-niŋ\ *adj* **1 :** lacking intelligence **:** VAPID **2 :** having no meaning **:** SENSELESS

un·meant \-'ment\ *adj* **:** not meant **:** UNINTENTIONAL

un·meet \-'mēt\ *adj* **:** not meet **:** UNSUITABLE, IMPROPER

¹un·men·tion·able \-'mench-(ə-)nə-bəl\ *adj* **:** not mentionable **:** UNSPEAKABLE

²unmentionable *n* **:** one that is not to be mentioned or discussed: as **a** *pl* **:** TROUSERS **b** *pl* **:** UNDERWEAR

un·mer·ci·ful \-'mər-si-fəl\ *adj* **1 :** not merciful **:** MERCILESS **2 :** EXCESSIVE — **un·mer·ci·ful·ly** \-f(ə-)lē\ *adv*

un·mind·ful \-'mīn(d)-fəl\ *adj* **:** not mindful **:** CARELESS, UNAWARE **syn** see FORGETFUL

un·mis·tak·able \,ən-mə-'stā-kə-bəl\ *adj* **:** not capable of being mistaken or misunderstood **:** CLEAR — **un·mis·tak·ably** \-blē\ *adv*

See *un-* and 2d element	**unlaid**	**unlivable**	**unmanageable**	**unmeasured**	**unmerited**
unjointed	**unlamented**	**unlobed**	**unmanufactured**	**unmechanical**	**unmethodical**
unjustifiable	**unleavened**	**unlovable**	**unmarked**	**unmeditated**	**unmetrical**
unjustified	**unlicensed**	**unloved**	**unmarketable**	**unmelodious**	**unmilitary**
unkept	**unlighted**	**unloving**	**unmarried**	**unmelted**	**unmilled**
unknowledgeable	**unlikable**	**unmagnified**	**unmastered**	**unmentioned**	**unmingled**
unlabored	**unlined**	**unmailable**	**unmatched**	**unmerchantable**	**unmitigable**
unladylike	**unlit**	**unmalleable**	**unmeasurable**		

un·mit·i·gat·ed \ˌən-ˈmit-ə-ˌgāt-əd, ˈən-\ *adj* **1 :** not made less severe or intense : UNRELIEVED **2 :** not qualified : DOWNRIGHT, ABSOLUTE — **un·mit·i·gat·ed·ly** *adv*

un·moor \-ˈmu̇(ə)r\ *vt* **:** to loose from or as if from moorings ~ *vi* **:** to cast off moorings

un·mor·al \-ˈmȯr-əl, -ˈmär-\ *adj* **:** having no moral perception or quality : AMORAL — **un·mo·ral·i·ty** \ˌən-mə-ˈral-ət-ē, -mȯ-\ *n*

un·muf·fle \ˌən-ˈməf-əl, ˈən-\ *vt* **:** to free from something that muffles

un·muz·zle \-ˈməz-əl\ *vt* **:** to remove a muzzle from

un·my·elin·at·ed \-ˈmī-ə-lə-ˌnāt-əd\ *adj* **:** lacking a myelin sheath

un·nail \ˌən-ˈnā(ə)l, ˈən-\ *vt* **:** to unfasten by removing nails

un·nat·u·ral \ˌən-ˈnach-(ə-)rəl, ˈən-\ *adj* **1 :** not being in accordance with nature or consistent with a normal course of events **2 a :** not being in accordance with normal feelings or behavior : PERVERSE, ABNORMAL **b :** ARTIFICIAL, CONTRIVED **c :** STRANGE, IRREGULAR **syn** see IRREGULAR — **un·nat·u·ral·ly** \-ˈnach-(ə-)rə-lē, -ˈnach-ər-lē\ *adv* — **un·nat·u·ral·ness** \-ˈnach-(ə-)rəl-nəs\ *n*

un·nec·es·sar·i·ly \ˌən-ˌnes-ə-ˈser-ə-lē\ *adv* **:** not by necessity **:** to an unnecessary degree

un·nec·es·sary \ˌən-ˈnes-ə-ˌser-ē, ˈən-\ *adj* **:** not necessary

un·nerve \ˌən-ˈnərv, ˈən-\ *vt* **1 :** to deprive of courage, strength, or steadiness **2 :** to cause to become nervous : UPSET

syn UNNERVE, ENERVATE, UNMAN, EMASCULATE mean to deprive of vigor. UNNERVE implies marked often temporary loss of courage, self-control, or power to act; ENERVATE suggests a gradual physical or moral weakening (as through luxury or indolence) until one is too feeble to make an effort; UNMAN implies a loss of manly vigor, fortitude, or spirit; EMASCULATE stresses a depriving of characteristic force by removing something essential

un·num·bered \ˌən-ˈnəm-bərd, ˈən-\ *adj* **1 :** INNUMERABLE **2 :** not having an identifying number ⟨~ page⟩

un·ob·tru·sive \ˌən-əb-ˈtrü-siv, -ziv\ *adj* **:** not obtrusive **:** not blatant or aggressive : INCONSPICUOUS — **un·ob·tru·sive·ly** *adv* — **un·ob·tru·sive·ness** *n*

un·oc·cu·pied \ˌən-ˈäk-yə-ˌpīd, ˈən-\ *adj* **1 :** not busy : UNEMPLOYED **2 :** not occupied : EMPTY

un·of·fi·cial \ˌən-ə-ˈfish-əl\ *adj* **:** not official — **un·of·fi·cial·ly** \-ˈfish-(ə-)lē\ *adv*

un·or·ga·nized \ˌən-ˈȯr-gə-ˌnīzd, ˈən-\ *adj* **1 a :** not brought into a coherent or well-ordered whole **b :** not belonging to a labor union **2 :** not having the characteristics of a living organism

un·or·tho·dox \-ˈȯr-thə-ˌdäks\ *adj* **:** not orthodox

un·pack \ˌən-ˈpak, ˈən-\ *vt* **1 a :** to remove the contents of ⟨~ a trunk⟩ **b :** UNBURDEN, REVEAL **2 :** to remove or undo from packing or a container ~ *vi* **:** to engage in unpacking a container

un·paired \-ˈpa(ə)rd, -ˈpe(ə)rd\ *adj* **1 :** not paired; *esp* **:** not matched or mated **2 :** situated in the median plane of the body ⟨an ~ fin⟩

un·par·al·leled \-ˈpar-ə-ˌleld, -ləld\ *adj* **:** having no parallel; *esp* **:** having no equal or match : UNSURPASSED

un·par·lia·men·ta·ry \ˌən-ˌpär-lə-ˈment-ə-rē, -ˌpärl-yə-, -ˈmen-trē\ *adj* **:** contrary to the practice of parliamentary bodies

un·peg \ˌən-ˈpeg, ˈən-\ *vt* **:** to remove a peg from : UNFASTEN

un·peo·ple \-ˈpē-pəl\ *vt* **:** DEPOPULATE

un·per·fect \-ˈpər-fikt\ *adj* **1 :** IMPERFECT **2** *obs* **:** poorly trained

un·pile \ˌən-ˈpī(ə)l, ˈən-\ *vt* **:** to take or disentangle from a pile

un·pin \-ˈpin\ *vt* **1 :** to remove a pin from **2 a :** UNFASTEN **b :** LOOSEN, FREE

un·pleas·ant \ˌən-ˈplez-ᵊnt, ˈən-\ *adj* **:** not pleasant **:** not amiable or agreeable : DISPLEASING ⟨~ odors⟩ — **un·pleas·ant·ly** *adv*

un·pleas·ant·ness *n* **1 :** the quality or state of being unpleasant **2 :** an unpleasant situation, experience, or event

un·plumbed \-ˈpləmd\ *adj* **1 :** not tested with a plumb line **2 a :** not measured with a plumb **b :** not explored in depth, intensity, or significance

un·po·lit·i·cal \ˌən-pə-ˈlit-i-kəl\ *adj* **:** not interested or engaged in politics ⟨an ~ person⟩

un·pop·u·lar \ˌən-ˈpäp-yə-lər, ˈən-\ *adj* **:** not popular **:** viewed or received unfavorably by the public — **un·pop·u·lar·i·ty** \ˌən-ˌpäp-yə-ˈlar-ət-ē\ *n*

un·prec·e·dent·ed \ˌən-ˈpres-ə-ˌdent-əd, ˈən-\ *adj* **:** having no precedent : NOVEL, UNEXAMPLED — **un·prec·e·dent·ed·ly** *adv*

un·pre·dict·abil·i·ty \ˌən-pri-ˌdik-tə-ˈbil-ət-ē\ *n* **:** the quality or state of being unpredictable

un·pre·dict·able \-ˈdik-tə-bəl\ *adj* **:** not predictable — **un·pre·dict·ably** \-blē\ *adv*

un·preg·nant \ˌən-ˈpreg-nənt, ˈən-\ *adj*, *obs* **:** INAPT

un·prej·u·diced \-ˈprej-əd-əst\ *adj* **:** not prejudiced **:** free from undue bias, warp, or prepossession : IMPARTIAL

un·pre·ten·tious \ˌən-pri-ˈten-chəs\ *adj* **:** free from ostentation, elegance, or affectation : MODEST ⟨~ homes⟩ — **un·pre·ten·tious·ly** *adv* — **un·pre·ten·tious·ness** *n*

un·prin·ci·pled \ˌən-ˈprin(t)-s(ə-)pəld, ˈən-, -sə-bəld\ *adj* **:** lacking moral principles : UNSCRUPULOUS

un·print·able \-ˈprint-ə-bəl\ *adj* **:** unfit to be printed

un·pro·fessed \ˌən-prə-ˈfest\ *adj* **:** not professed ⟨an ~ aim⟩

un·pro·fes·sion·al \-ˈfesh-nəl, -ən-ᵊl\ *adj* **1 :** not belonging to a particular profession ⟨an ~ architect⟩ **2 :** not befitting a member of a profession ⟨~ language⟩ — **un·pro·fes·sion·al·ly** \-ē\ *adv*

un·prof·it·able \ˌən-ˈpräf-ət-ə-bəl, ˈən-, -ˈpräf-tə-bəl\ *adj* **:** not profitable : USELESS, VAIN — **un·prof·it·able·ness** *n* — **un·prof·it·ably** \-blē\ *adv*

un·prom·is·ing \-ˈpräm-ə-siŋ\ *adj* **:** appearing unlikely to prove worthwhile or result favorably — **un·prom·is·ing·ly** \-siŋ-lē\ *adv*

un·qual·i·fied \ˌən-ˈkwäl-ə-ˌfīd, ˈən-\ *adj* **1 :** not fit **:** not having requisite qualifications **2 :** not modified or restricted by reservations ⟨an ~ denial⟩ — **un·qual·i·fied·ly** \-ˌfī(-ə)d-lē\ *adv*

un·ques·tion·able \-ˈkwes(h)-chə-nə-bəl, *rapid* -ˈkwesh-nə-\ *adj* **1 :** acknowledged as beyond question or doubt ⟨~ authority⟩ **2 :** not questionable : INDISPUTABLE ⟨~ evidence⟩ — **un·ques·tion·ably** \-blē\ *adv*

un·ques·tion·ing \-ˈkwes(h)-chə-niŋ\ *adj* **:** not questioning **:** accepting without examination or hesitation ⟨~ obedience⟩ — **un·ques·tion·ing·ly** \-niŋ-lē\ *adv*

un·qui·et \-ˈkwī-ət\ *adj* **1 :** not quiet : AGITATED, TURBULENT **2 :** physically, emotionally, or mentally restless : UNEASY — **un·qui·et·ly** *adv* — **un·qui·et·ness** *n*

un·quote \ˈən-ˌkwōt *also* -ˌkōt\ *vi* **:** to inform a hearer or reader that the matter preceding is quoted

un·rav·el \ˌən-ˈrav-əl, ˈən-\ *vt* **1 :** to disengage or separate the threads of : DISENTANGLE **2 :** to resolve the intricacy, complexity, or obscurity of **:** clear up ~ *vi* **:** to become unraveled

un·read \-ˈred\ *adj* **1 :** not read **:** left unexamined **2 :** lacking the experience or the benefits of reading ⟨~ in political science⟩

un·read·i·ness \-ˈred-ē-nəs\ *n* **:** the quality or state of being unready

un·ready \-ˈred-ē\ *adj* **:** not ready : UNPREPARED

un·re·al \-ˈrē(-ə)l, -ˈri(-ə)l\ *adj* **:** lacking in reality, substance, or genuineness : ARTIFICIAL, ILLUSORY

un·re·al·is·tic \ˌən-ˌrē-(ə-)ˈlis-tik\ *adj* **:** not realistic **:** inappropriate to reality or fact — **un·re·al·is·ti·cal·ly** \-ti-k(ə-)lē\ *adv*

un·re·al·i·ty \ˌən-rē-ˈal-ət-ē\ *n* **1 a :** the quality or state of being unreal : NONEXISTENCE **b :** something unreal, insubstantial, or visionary : FIGMENT **2 :** ineptitude in dealing with reality

un·rea·son \ˌən-ˈrēz-ᵊn, ˈən-ˈrēz-\ *n* **:** the absence of reason or sanity : IRRATIONALITY, MADNESS

un·rea·son·able \-ˈrēz-nə-bəl, -ᵊn-ə-\ *adj* **1 a :** not governed by or acting according to reason **b :** not conformable to reason **2 :** exceeding the bounds of reason or moderation **syn** see IRRATIONAL — **un·rea·son·able·ness** *n* — **un·rea·son·ably** \-blē\ *adv*

un·rea·son·ing \-ˈrēz-niŋ, -ᵊn-iŋ\ *adj* **:** not reasoning; *esp* **:** swayed by emotion that is uncontrolled by reason or judgment — **un·rea·son·ing·ly** \-ˈrēz-niŋ-lē, -ᵊn-iŋ-\ *adv*

un·re·con·struct·ed \ˌən-ˌrē-kən-ˈstrək-təd\ *adj* **:** not reconciled to some political, economic, or social change; *esp* **:** holding stubbornly to principles, beliefs, or views that are or are held to be outmoded

un·reel \ˌən-ˈrē(ə)l, ˈən-\ *vt* **:** to unwind from or as if from a reel ~ *vi* **:** to become unwound

un·reeve \-ˈrēv\ *vt* **:** to withdraw (a rope) from an opening (as a ship's block or thimble)

un·re·gen·er·ate \ˌən-ri-ˈjen-(ə-)rət\ *also* **un·re·gen·er·at·ed** \-ˈjen-ə-ˌrāt-əd\ *adj* **1 :** not regenerated **2 :** not reformed : UNRECONSTRUCTED

un·re·lent·ing \-ˈlent-iŋ\ *adj* **1 :** not softening or yielding in determination : HARD, STERN **2 :** not letting up or weakening in vigor or pace — **un·re·lent·ing·ly** \-iŋ-lē\ *adv*

un·re·mit·ting \-ˈmit-iŋ\ *adj* **:** not remitting : CONSTANT, INCESSANT — **un·re·mit·ting·ly** \-iŋ-lē\ *adv*

un·re·serve \-ˈzərv\ *n* **:** absence of reserve : FRANKNESS

un·re·served \-ˈzərvd\ *adj* **1 :** not limited or partial : ENTIRE, UNQUALIFIED **2 :** not cautious or reticent : FRANK, OPEN — **un·re·serv·ed·ly** \-ˈzər-vəd-lē\ *adv* — **un·re·served·ness** \-ˈzər-vəd-nəs, -ˈzərv(d)-nəs\ *n*

un·re·spon·sive \ˌən-ri-ˈspän(t)-siv\ *adj* **:** not responsive — **un·re·spon·sive·ly** *adv* — **un·re·spon·sive·ness** *n*

un·rest \ˌən-ˈrest, ˈən-\ *n* **:** want of rest **:** a disturbed or uneasy state : TURMOIL

un·re·strained \ˌən-ri-ˈstrānd\ *adj* **1 :** not restrained : IMMODER-

See *un-* and 2d element

unmixed
unmodified
unmodulated
unmolested
unmortgaged
unmotivated
unmounted
unmovable
unmoved
unmoving
unmusical
unnameable
unnamed
unnaturalized
unnavigable
unneighborly
unnoticeable
unnoticed
unobjectionable
unobliging
unobscured
unobservant
unobserved
unobserving
unobstructed
unobtainable
unopen
unopened
unopposed
unordered
unoriginal
unostentatious
unowned
unoxygenated
unpaid
unpalatable
unpardonable
unpardoned
unparenthesized
unpartisan
unpartitioned
unpasteurized
unpastoral
unpatient
unpatriotic
unpaved
unpedigreed
unperceivable
unperceived
unperceiving
unperceptive
unperformed
unperplex
unpersuadable
unpersuasive
unperturbed
unphilosophic
unphilosophical
unphonetic
unpitied
unpitying
unplaced
unplanned
unplanted
unplayable
unpleasing
unpledged
unplowed
unpoetic
unpoetical
unpointed
unpolarized
unpolished
unpolled
unpolluted
unpolymerized
unposed
unpossessing
unpowered
unpractical
unpracticed
unpremeditated
unprepared
unprepossessing
unprescribed
unpresentable
unpressed
unpretending
unpretty
unprevailing
unpreventable
unprinted
unprivileged
unprocessed
unproductive
unprogressive
unprohibited
unprompted
unpronounceable
unpronounced
unpropitious
unproportionate
unproportioned
unprosperous
unprotected
unprotesting
unproved
unproven
unprovided
unprovoked
unpruned
unpublished
unpunctual
unpunished
unpurchasable
unpure
unquenchable
unquenched
unquestioned
unraised
unransomed
unratified
unravished
unreadable
unrealizable
unrealized
unreasoned
unrecognized
unrecompensed
unreconcilable
unreconciled
unrecorded
unredeemed
unrefined
unreflecting
unreflective
unreformable
unreformed
unregarded
unregimented
unregistered
unregulated
unrehearsed
unrelated
unrelaxed
unrelaxing
unreliability
unreliable
unrelieved
unreligious
unremarkable
unremembered
unremitted
unremunerated
unremunerative
unrenowned
unrent
unrepaid
unrepaired
unrepealed
unrepentant
unreported
unrepresentative
unrepresented
unrepressed
unreproved
unrequited
unresistant
unresisted
unresisting
unresolved
unrestful

ATE, UNCONTROLLED **2** : free of constraint : SPONTANEOUS — **un·re·strain·ed·ly** \-'strā-nəd-lē\ *adv*

un·rid·dle \ˌən-'rid-ᵊl, 'ən-\ *vt* : to read the riddle of : SOLVE

un·rig \-'rig\ *vt* : to strip of rigging ⟨~ a ship⟩

un·righ·teous \-'rī-chəs\ *adj* **1** : not righteous : SINFUL, WICKED **2** : UNJUST, UNMERITED — **un·righ·teous·ly** *adv* — **un·righ·teous·ness** *n*

un·rip \-'rip\ *vt* **1** : to rip or slit up : cut or tear open **2** : REVEAL

un·ripe \-'rīp\ *adj* **1** : not ripe : IMMATURE **2** : UNREADY, UNSEASONABLE — **un·ripe·ness** *n*

un·ri·valed *or* **un·ri·valled** \ˌən-'rī-vəld, 'ən-\ *adj* : having no rival : INCOMPARABLE, SUPREME

un·robe \-'rōb\ *vb* : DISROBE, UNDRESS

un·roll \-'rōl\ *vt* **1** : to unwind a roll of : open out : UNCOIL **2** : to spread out like a scroll for reading or inspection : UNFOLD, REVEAL ~ *vi* : to be unrolled : UNWIND

un·roof \-'rüf, -'ruf\ *vt* : to strip off the roof or covering of

un·root \-'rüt, -'rut\ *vt* : to tear up by the roots : UPROOT

un·round \ˌən-'raund, 'ən-\ *vt* **1** : to spread (the lips) laterally ⟨necessary to ~ the lips in pronouncing \ē\⟩ **2** : to pronounce (a sound) without lip rounding or with decreased lip rounding — **un·round·ed** *adj*

un·ruf·fled \-'rəf-əld\ *adj* **1** : not upset or agitated **2** : not ruffled : SMOOTH ⟨~ water⟩ **syn** see COOL

un·rul·i·ness \-'rü-lē-nəs\ *n* : the quality or state of being unruly

un·ruly \-'rü-lē\ *adj* [ME *unreuly*, fr. *un-* + *reuly* disciplined, fr. *reule* rule] : not readily ruled, disciplined, or managed : TURBULENT **syn** UNGOVERNABLE, INTRACTABLE, REFRACTORY, RECALCITRANT, WILLFUL, HEADSTRONG: UNRULY suggests a lack of or incapacity for discipline; UNGOVERNABLE implies not being subdued or restrained or an escape from guidance or control; INTRACTABLE suggests stubborn resistance to guidance or control; REFRACTORY stresses resistance to attempts to manage or to mold; RECALCITRANT suggests determined resistance to or defiance of authority; WILLFUL implies obstinate and often capricious self-will; HEADSTRONG suggests self-will impatient of restraint, advice, or suggestion

un·sad·dle \ˌən-'sad-ᵊl, 'ən-\ *vt* **1** : to take the saddle from **2** : to throw from the saddle ~ *vi* : to remove the saddle from a horse

un·safe·ty \-'sāf-tē\ *n* : want of safety : INSECURITY

un·sat·u·rate \-'sach-(ə-)rət\ *n* : an unsaturated chemical compound

un·sat·u·rat·ed \-'sach-ə-ˌrāt-əd\ *adj* : not saturated: as **a** : capable of absorbing or dissolving more of something ⟨an ~ solution⟩ **b** : able to form products by chemical addition; *esp* : containing double or triple bonds between carbon atoms

un·saved \-'sāvd\ *adj* : not saved; *esp* : not rescued from eternal punishment

un·sa·vory \ˌən-'sāv-(ə-)rē, 'ən-\ *adj* **1** : INSIPID, TASTELESS **2** : unpleasant to taste or smell : DISAGREEABLE, DISTASTEFUL **3** : morally offensive

un·say \-'sā, *South also* -'se\ *vt* : to make as if not said : RECANT, RECALL, RETRACT

un·scathed \ˌən-'skā<u>th</u>d, 'ən-\ *adj* : wholly unharmed : not injured

un·schooled \-'sküld\ *adj* **1** : not schooled : UNTAUGHT, UNTRAINED **2** : not artificial : NATURAL ⟨~ talent⟩

un·sci·en·tif·ic \ˌən-ˌsī-ən-'tif-ik\ *adj* : not scientific: as **a** : not used in scientific work **b** : not according with the principles and methods of science **c** : not showing scientific knowledge or familiarity with scientific methods — **un·sci·en·tif·i·cal·ly** \-i-k(ə-)lē\ *adv*

un·scram·ble \ˌən-'skram-bəl, 'ən-\ *vt* **1** : to separate (as a conglomeration or tangle) into original components : RESOLVE, CLARIFY **2** : to restore (as a radio message) to intelligible form

un·screw \-'skrü\ *vt* **1** : to draw the screws from **2** : to loosen or withdraw by turning ~ *vi* : to become or admit of being unscrewed

un·scru·pu·lous \-'skrü-pyə-ləs\ *adj* : not scrupulous : UNPRINCIPLED — **un·scru·pu·lous·ly** *adv* — **un·scru·pu·lous·ness** *n*

un·seal \-'sē(ə)l\ *vt* : to break or remove the seal of : OPEN

un·seam \-'sēm, 'ən-\ *vt* : to open the seams of

un·search·able \-'sər-chə-bəl\ *adj* : not to be searched or explored : INSCRUTABLE — **un·search·ably** \-blē\ *adv*

un·sea·son·able \-'sēz-ᵊn-ə-bəl, -'sēz-ᵊn-ə-\ *adj* **1** : occurring out of the proper season : UNTIMELY, INAPPROPRIATE **2** : not being in season **3 a** : not normal for the season of the year **b** : marked by unseasonable weather — **un·sea·son·able·ness** *n* — **un·sea·son·ably** \-blē\ *adv*

un·seat \-'sēt\ *vt* **1** : to dislodge from one's seat esp. on horseback **2** : to dislodge from a place or position; *specif* : to remove from political office

¹**un·seem·ly** \ˌən-'sēm-lē, 'ən-\ *adj* : not seemly: as **a** : not according with established standards of good form or taste ⟨~ bickering⟩ **b** : not suitable for time or place : INAPPROPRIATE, UNSEASONABLE **syn** see INDECOROUS

²**unseemly** *adv* : in an unseemly manner

un·seen \-'sēn\ *adj* **1** : not seen or perceived : INVISIBLE **2** : SIGHT ⟨an ~ translation⟩

un·seg·re·gat·ed \-'seg-ri-ˌgāt-əd\ *adj* : not segregated; *esp* : free from racial segregation

un·self·ish \-'sel-fish\ *adj* : not selfish : GENEROUS — **un·self·ish·ly** *adv* — **un·self·ish·ness** *n*

un·set \-'set\ *adj* : not set: as **a** : not fixed in a setting : UNMOUNTED **b** : not firmed or solidified ⟨~ concrete⟩

un·set·tle \ˌən-'set-ᵊl, 'ən-\ *vt* **1** : to loosen or move from a settled state or condition : make unstable : DISTURB, DISORDER **2** : to perturb or agitate mentally or emotionally : DISCOMPOSE ~ *vi* : to become unsettled

un·set·tled \-'set-ᵊld\ *adj* : not settled: as **a** (1) : not calm or tranquil : DISTURBED ⟨~ political conditions⟩ (2) : INCONSTANT, VARIABLE ⟨~ weather⟩ **b** (1) : not decided or determined : DOUBTFUL ⟨an ~ state of mind⟩ (2) : not resolved or worked out : UNDECIDED ⟨an ~ question⟩ **c** : characterized by irregularity ⟨an ~ life⟩ **d** : not inhabited or populated ⟨~ land⟩ **e** : mentally unbalanced **f** (1) : not disposed of according to law ⟨an ~ estate⟩ (2) : not paid or discharged ⟨~ debts⟩ — **un·set·tled·ness** \-ᵊl(d)-nəs\ *n*

un·sew \-'sō\ *vt* : to undo the sewing of

un·sex \-'seks\ *vt* **1** : to deprive of sex or sexual power **2** : to remove the qualities typical of one's sex

un·shack·le \-'shak-əl\ *vt* : to loose from shackles

un·shaped \-'shāpt\ *adj* : not shaped : not perfectly shaped : RUDE

un·shap·en \-'shā-pən\ *adj* [ME, fr. *un-* + *shapen*, pp. of *shapen* to shape] : UNSHAPED

un·sheathe \ˌən-'shē<u>th</u>, 'ən-\ *vt* : to draw from or as if from a sheath or scabbard

un·ship \-'ship\ *vt* **1** : to take out of a ship : DISCHARGE, UNLOAD **2** : to remove (as an oar or tiller) from position : DETACH ~ *vi* : to become or admit of being detached or removed

un·shod \-'shäd\ *adj* : not wearing shoes

un·sight \-'sīt\ *adj* : not sighted or examined

un·sight·ly \-'sīt-lē\ *adj* : not pleasing to the sight : not comely

un·skilled \ˌən-'skild, 'ən-\ *adj* **1** : not skilled; *specif* : not skilled in a specified branch of work : lacking technical training **2** : not requiring skill **3** : marked by lack of skill

un·skill·ful \-'skil-fəl\ *adj* : not skillful : lacking in skill or proficiency — **un·skill·ful·ly** \-fə-lē\ *adv* — **un·skill·ful·ness** *n*

un·sling \-'sliŋ\ *vt* **1** : to remove from being slung **2** : to take off the slings of esp. aboard ship : release from slings

un·snap \-'snap\ *vt* : to loosen or free by or as if by undoing a snap

un·snarl \-'snär(-ə)l\ *vt* : to disentangle a snarl in

un·so·cia·bil·i·ty \ˌən-ˌsō-shə-'bil-ət-ē\ *n* : the quality or state of being unsociable

un·so·cia·ble \ˌən-'sō-shə-bəl, 'ən-\ *adj* **1** : having or showing a disinclination for society or conversation : SOLITARY, RESERVED **2** : not conducive to sociability — **un·so·cia·ble·ness** *n* — **un·so·cia·bly** \-blē\ *adv*

un·so·cial \-'sō-shəl\ *adj* **1** : not social : not seeking or given to association **2** : ANTISOCIAL — **un·so·cial·ly** \-'sōsh-(ə-)lē\ *adv*

un·so·phis·ti·cat·ed \ˌən(t)-sə-'fis-tə-ˌkāt-əd\ *adj* : not sophisticated: as **a** : not changed or corrupted : GENUINE **b** (1) : not worldly-wise : lacking sophistication : ARTLESS, INGENUOUS (2) : lacking adornment or complexity of structure : PLAIN, SIMPLE **syn** see NATURAL

un·so·phis·ti·ca·tion \-ˌfis-tə-'kā-shən\ *n* : a lack of or freedom from sophistication

un·sought \ˌən-'sot, 'ən-\ *adj* : not sought: as **a** : not searched for or sought out **b** : not acquired by effort **c** : not asked for

un·sound \-'saund\ *adj* : not sound: as **a** : not healthy or whole **b** : not mentally normal : not wholly sane **c** : not firmly made, placed, or fixed **d** : not valid or true : INVALID, SPECIOUS — **un·sound·ly** \-'saun-(d)lē\ *adv* — **un·sound·ness** \-'saun(d)-nəs\ *n*

un·spar·ing \-'spa(ə)r-iŋ, -'spe(ə)r-\ *adj* **1** : not merciful or forbearing : HARD, RUTHLESS **2** : not frugal : LIBERAL, PROFUSE — **un·spar·ing·ly** \-iŋ-lē\ *adv*

un·speak \-'spēk\ *vt, obs* : UNSAY

un·speak·able \-'spē-kə-bəl\ *adj* **1 a** : incapable of being expressed in words : UNUTTERABLE **b** : inexpressibly bad **2** : that may not or cannot be spoken — **un·speak·ably** \-blē\ *adv*

un·sphere \ˌən-'sfi(ə)r, 'ən-\ *vt* : to remove (as a planet) from a sphere

un·spot·ted \-'spät-əd\ *adj* : not spotted : free from spot or stain; *esp* : free from moral stain

un·sprung \-'sprəŋ\ *adj* : not sprung; *esp* : not equipped with springs

un·sta·ble \-'stā-bəl\ *adj* : not stable : not firm or fixed : not constant: as **a** : FLUCTUATING, IRREGULAR **b** : FICKLE, VACILLATING **c** : UNSTEADY **d** : readily decomposing or changing otherwise in chemical composition or biological activity **e** : characterized by inability to control the emotions **syn** see INCONSTANT — **un·sta·ble·ness** *n* — **un·sta·bly** \-b(ə-)lē\ *adv*

un·state \-'stāt\ *vt* : to deprive of state, dignity, or rank

¹**un·steady** \ˌən-'sted-ē, 'ən-\ *vt* : to make unsteady

²**unsteady** *adj* : not steady: as **a** : not firm or solid : not fixed in

See *un-* and 2d element				
unrestraint	unruled	unscented	unseparated	unshrinking	unsorted
unrestricted	unsafe	unscheduled	unserved	unshut	unsounded
unretentive	unsaid	unscholarly	unserviceable	unsifted	unsoured
unretracted	unsaintly	unscorched	unsettlement	unsigned	unsown
unreturnable	unsalable	unscreened	unsexual	unsingable	unspecialized
unrevealed	unsalaried	unscriptural	unshaded	unsinkable	unspecific
unrevenged	unsalted	unsealed	unshadowed	unsized	unspecified
unrevoked	unsanctified	unseasoned	unshakable	unslacked	unspent
unrewarded	unsanctioned	unseaworthy	unshaken	unslaked	unspiritual
unrewarding	unsanitary	unseconded	unshapely	unsmiling	unsplit
unrhymed	unsaponified	unsecured	unshared	unsnuffed	unspoiled
unrhythmic	unsated	unseeded	unsharp	unsoiled	unspoken
unrhythmical	unsatiated	unseeing	unshaved	unsoiled	unsportsmanlike
unrightful	unsatisfactory	unseemliness	unshaven	unsold	unspun
unrinsed	unsatisfied	unsegmented	unshed	unsoldierly	unsquared
unripened	unsatisfying	unselected	unsheltered	unsolicited	unstained
unromantic	unscaled	unselfconscious	unshielded	unsolicitous	unstatesmanlike
unroofed	unscanned	unsensitive	unshorn	unsold	unsteadily
	unscarred	unsentimental	unshrinkable	unsolvable	unsteadiness
				unsolved	

position : UNSTABLE **b** : marked by change or fluctuation : CHANGEABLE **c** : not uniform or even : IRREGULAR
un·step \-ˈstep\ *vt* : to remove (a mast) from a step
un·stick \-ˈstik\ *vt* : to release from being stuck or bound
un·stop \-ˈstäp\ *vt* **1** : to free from an obstruction : OPEN **2** : to remove a stopper from
un·strap \-ˈstrap\ *vt* : to remove or loose a strap from
un·stressed \ˌən-ˈstrest, ˈən-\ *adj* : not stressed; *specif* : not bearing a stress or accent
un·string \-ˈstriŋ\ *vt* **1** : to loosen or remove the strings of **2** : to remove from a string **3** : to make weak, disordered, or unstable
un·stud·ied \-ˈstəd-ēd\ *adj* : not studied: as **a** : not acquired by study **b** : not forced : not done or planned for effect : UNLABORED
un·sub·stan·tial \ˌən(t)-səb-ˈstan-chəl\ *adj* : lacking substance, firmness, or strength — **un·sub·stan·ti·al·i·ty** \-ˌstan-chē-ˈal-ət-ē\ *n* — **un·sub·stan·tial·ly** \-ˈstanch-(ə-)lē\ *adv*
un·suc·cess \ˌən(t)-sək-ˈses\ *n* : lack of success : FAILURE
un·suc·cess·ful \-fəl\ *adj* : not successful : not meeting with or producing success — **un·suc·cess·ful·ly** \-fə-lē\ *adv*
un·suit·able \ˌən-ˈsüt-ə-bəl, ˈən-\ *adj* : not suitable or fitting : UNBECOMING, INAPPROPRIATE — **un·suit·ably** \-blē\ *adv*
un·sung \-ˈsəŋ\ *adj* **1** : not sung **2** : not celebrated in song or verse
un·swathe \ˌən-ˈswäth, -ˈswȯth, -ˈswāth, ˈən-\ *vt* : to free from something that swathes
un·swear \-ˈswa(ə)r, -ˈswe(ə)r\ *vi* : to unsay or retract something sworn ~ *vt* : to recant or recall (as an oath) esp. by a second oath
un·sym·met·ri·cal \ˌən(t)-sə-ˈme-tri-kəl\ *adj* : ASYMMETRIC — **un·sym·met·ri·cal·ly** \-k(ə-)lē\ *adv*
un·tan·gle \ˌən-ˈtaŋ-gəl, ˈən-\ *vt* : DISENTANGLE, RESOLVE **syn** see EXTRICATE
un·taught \-ˈtȯt\ *adj* **1** : not instructed or trained : IGNORANT **2** : NATURAL, SPONTANEOUS
un·teach \-ˈtēch\ *vt* **1** : to cause to unlearn something **2** : to teach the contrary of
un·ten·a·ble \-ˈten-ə-bəl\ *adj* **1** : not able to be defended **2** : not able to be occupied
un·tent·ed \-ˈtent-əd\ *adj* [[1]*un-* + obs. E *tented*, pp. of *tent* (to probe)] : not probed or dressed ⟨the ~ woundings of a father's curse —Shak.⟩
un·teth·er \-ˈteth-ər\ *vt* : to free from a tether
un·think \-ˈthiŋk\ *vi* : to terminate or reverse a thought process ~ *vt* : to put out of mind
un·think·able \-ˈthiŋ-kə-bəl\ *adj* **1** : not conceivable by the mind **2** : contrary to what is reasonable or probable : INCREDIBLE
un·think·ing \-ˈthiŋ-kiŋ\ *adj* **1** : not taking thought : HEEDLESS, UNMINDFUL **2** : not indicating thought or reflection **3** : not having the power of thought — **un·think·ing·ly** \-kiŋ-lē\ *adv*
un·thread \ˌən-ˈthred, ˈən-\ *vt* **1** : to draw or take out a thread from **2** : to loosen the threads or connections of **3** : to make one's way through ⟨~ a maze⟩
un·throne \-ˈthrōn\ *vt* : to remove from or as if from a throne
un·ti·dy \-ˈtīd-ē\ *adj* **1** : not neat : CARELESS, SLOVENLY **2 a** : not neatly organized or carried out **b** : conducive to a lack of neatness
un·tie \-ˈtī\ *vt* **1** : to free from something that ties, fastens, or restrains : UNBIND **2 a** : to disengage the knotted parts of **b** : DISENTANGLE, RESOLVE ~ *vi* : to become loosened or unbound
[1]un·til \ən-ˌtil, -tᵊl, -ˌtel, ˌən-, *in some contexts* ᵊn-, ᵊm-, *or* ᵊŋ-\ *prep* [ME, fr. *un-* unto, until (akin to OE *oth* to, until, OHG *unt* unto, until, OE *ende* end) + *til, till* till] **1** *chiefly Scot* : TO **2** — used as a function word to indicate continuance (as of an action or condition) to a specified time ⟨stayed ~ morning⟩ **3** : BEFORE ⟨not available ~ tomorrow⟩
[2]until *conj* **1** : up to the time that ⟨play continued ~ it got dark⟩ **2** : before the time that ⟨never able to relax ~ he took up fishing⟩ **3** : to the point or degree that ⟨ran ~ he was breathless⟩
un·time·li·ness \ˌən-ˈtīm-lē-nəs, ˈən-\ *n* : the quality or state of being untimely
[1]un·time·ly \-lē\ *adv* **1** : at an inopportune time : UNSEASONABLY **2** : PREMATURELY
[2]untimely *adj* **1** : occurring or done before the due, natural, or proper time : too early : PREMATURE ⟨~ death⟩ **2** : INOPPORTUNE, UNSEASONABLE ⟨an ~ joke⟩ ⟨~ frost⟩
un·time·ous \ˌən-ˈtī-məs, ˈən-\ *adj, chiefly Scot* : UNTIMELY
un·ti·tled \-ˈtīt-ᵊld\ *adj* **1** : having no title or right to rule **2** : not named ⟨an ~ novel⟩ **3** : not called by a title ⟨~ nobility⟩
un·to \ˌən-tə(-w), ˈən-(ˌ)tü\ *prep* [ME, fr. *un-* unto, until + *to*] : TO
un·told \ˌən-ˈtōld, ˈən-\ *adj* **1** : too great or numerous to count : INCALCULABLE, VAST **2 a** : not related **b** : kept secret
un·touch·abil·i·ty \ˌən-ˌtəch-ə-ˈbil-ət-ē\ *n* : the quality or state of being untouchable
[1]un·touch·able \ˌən-ˈtəch-ə-bəl, ˈən-\ *adj* **1 a** : forbidden to the touch **b** : exempt from criticism or control **2** : lying beyond the reach **3** : disagreeable or defiling to the touch
[2]untouchable *n* : one that is untouchable; *specif* : a member of a large formerly segregated hereditary group in India having in traditional Hindu belief the quality of defiling by contact a member of a higher caste
un·to·ward \ˌən-ˈtō(-ə)rd, ˈən-, -ˈtȯ(-ə)rd\ *adj* **1 a** : difficult to guide, manage, or work with : UNRULY, INTRACTABLE **b** *archaic* : AWKWARD, UNGRACEFUL **2 a** : marked by trouble or unhappiness : UNLUCKY **b** : not favoring : ADVERSE, UNPROPITIOUS — **un·to·ward·ly** *adv* — **un·to·ward·ness** *n*
un·tread \-ˈtred\ *vt* : to tread back : RETRACE
un·tried \-ˈtrīd\ *adj* **1** : not tested or proved by experience or trial **2** : not tried in court
un·true \-ˈtrü\ *adj* **1** : not faithful : DISLOYAL **2** : not according with a standard of correctness : not level or exact **3** : not according with the facts : FALSE — **un·tru·ly** \-ˈtrü-lē\ *adv*
un·truss \-ˈtrəs\ *vt* **1** *archaic* : UNTIE, UNFASTEN — used in the phrase *untruss one's points* **2** *archaic* : UNDRESS ~ *vi, archaic* : to unfasten or take off one's clothes and esp. one's breeches
un·truth \ˌən-ˈtrüth, ˈən-\ *n* **1** *archaic* : DISLOYALTY **2** : lack of truthfulness : FALSITY **3** : something that is untrue : FALSEHOOD
un·truth·ful \-ˈtrüth-fəl\ *adj* : not containing or telling the truth : FALSE, INACCURATE ⟨~ report⟩ **syn** see DISHONEST — **un·truth·ful·ly** \-fə-lē\ *adv* — **un·truth·ful·ness** *n*
un·tuck \-ˈtək\ *vt* : to release from a tuck or from being tucked up
un·tune \-ˈt(y)ün\ *vt* **1** : to put out of tune **2** : DISARRANGE, DISCOMPOSE
un·tu·tored \-ˈt(y)üt-ərd\ *adj* **1 a** : having no formal learning or training : UNTAUGHT **b** : NAÏVE, UNSOPHISTICATED **2** : not produced or developed by instruction **syn** see IGNORANT
un·twine \-ˈtwīn\ *vt* **1** : to unwind the twisted or tangled parts of : DISENTANGLE **2** : to remove by unwinding ~ *vi* : to become disentangled or unwound
un·twist \ˌən-ˈtwist, ˈən-\ *vt* : to separate the twisted parts of : UNTWINE ~ *vi* : to become untwined
un·used \-ˈyüzd, *in the phrase "unused to" usually* -ˈyüs(t)\ *adj* **1** : not habituated : UNACCUSTOMED **2** : not used: as **a** : FRESH, NEW **b** : not put to use : IDLE **c** : not consumed : ACCRUED
un·usu·al \-ˈyüzh-(ə-)wəl, -ˈyü-zhəl\ *adj* : not usual : UNCOMMON, RARE — **un·usu·al·ly** \-ē\ *adv* — **un·usu·al·ness** *n*
un·ut·ter·able \ˌən-ˈət-ə-rə-bəl, ˈən-\ *adj* : being beyond the powers of description : INEXPRESSIBLE — **un·ut·ter·ably** \-blē\ *adv*
un·val·ued \-ˈval-(ˌ)yüd\ *adj* **1** *obs* : INVALUABLE **2 a** : not important or prized : DISREGARDED **b** : not appraised
un·var·nished \-ˈvär-nisht\ *adj* **1 a** : not adorned or glossed : PLAIN, STRAIGHTFORWARD **b** : ARTLESS, FRANK **2** : not coated with or as if with varnish : CRUDE, UNFINISHED
un·veil \ˌən-ˈvā(ə)l, ˈən-\ *vt* **1** : to remove a veil or covering from **2** : DIVULGE, REVEAL ~ *vi* : to throw off a veil or protective cloak
un·vo·cal \-ˈvō-kəl\ *adj* : not eloquent or outspoken : INARTICULATE; *esp* : UNMUSICAL
un·voice \-ˈvȯis\ *vt* : DEVOICE
un·voiced \-ˈvȯist\ *adj* **1** : not verbally expressed **2** : VOICELESS 2
un·war·rant·able \-ˈwȯr-ənt-ə-bəl, -ˈwär-\ *adj* : not justifiable : INEXCUSABLE — **un·war·rant·ably** \-blē\ *adv*
un·wary \ˌən-ˈwa(ə)r-ē, ˈən-, -ˈwe(ə)r-\ *adj* : not alert : easily fooled or surprised : HEEDLESS, GULLIBLE
[1]un·washed \-ˈwȯsht, -ˈwäsht\ *adj* **1** : not cleaned with or as if with soap and water **2** : IGNORANT, PLEBEIAN
[2]unwashed *n* : an ignorant or underprivileged group : RABBLE
un·wea·ried \ˌən-ˈwi(ə)r-ēd, ˈən-\ *adj* : not tired or jaded : FRESH
un·weave \-ˈwēv\ *vt* : DISENTANGLE, RAVEL
un·weet·ing \-ˈwēt-iŋ\ *adj, archaic* : UNWITTING — **un·weet·ing·ly** \-iŋ-lē\ *adv, archaic*
un·well \-ˈwel\ *adj* **1** : being in poor health : AILING, SICK **2** : afflicted with the menses
un·whole·some \-ˈhōl-səm\ *adj* **1** : detrimental to physical, mental, or moral well-being : UNHEALTHY ⟨~ food⟩ ⟨~ pastimes⟩ **2 a** : CORRUPT, UNSOUND **b** : offensive to the senses : LOATHSOME
un·wield·i·ness \-ˈwēl-dē-nəs\ *n* : the quality or state of being unwieldy
un·wieldy \-ˈwē(ə)l-dē\ *adj* **1** : AWKWARD, CLUMSY **2** : not easily managed or handled esp. because of bulk or weight : CUMBERSOME
un·willed \ˌən-ˈwild, ˈən-\ *adj* : not willed : INVOLUNTARY
un·will·ing \-ˈwil-iŋ\ *adj* : not willing: **a** : LOATH, RELUCTANT, AVERSE **b** : done or given reluctantly — **un·will·ing·ly** \-iŋ-lē\ *adv* — **un·will·ing·ness** *n*
un·wind \-ˈwīnd\ *vt* **1 a** : to cause to uncoil : wind off : UNROLL **b** : to free from or as if from a binding or wrapping **c** : to release from tension : RELAX **2** *archaic* : RETRACE ~ *vi* **1** : to become uncoiled or disentangled **2** : to become released from tension
un·wis·dom \-ˈwiz-dəm\ *n* : lack of wisdom : FOOLISHNESS, FOLLY
un·wise \-ˈwīz\ *adj* : lacking wisdom or good sense : FOOLISH, IMPRUDENT, INJUDICIOUS — **un·wise·ly** *adv*
un·wish \-ˈwish\ *vt* **1** : to revoke as a wish **2** *obs* : to wish away
un·wit·ting \ˌən-ˈwit-iŋ, ˈən-\ *adj* **1** : not intended : INADVERTENT **2** : not knowing : UNAWARE — **un·wit·ting·ly** \-iŋ-lē\ *adv*
un·wont·ed \-ˈwȯnt-əd, -ˈwōnt-, -ˈwənt-\ *adj* **1** : being out of the ordinary : RARE, UNUSUAL **2** *archaic* : not accustomed by experience — **un·wont·ed·ly** *adv* — **un·wont·ed·ness** *n*

See *un-* and 2d element
unsterilized
unstinted
unstinting
unstopped
unstrained
unstratified
unstriped
unstructured
unstrung
unstuck
unsubdued
unsubstantiated
unsuggestive
unsuited
unsullied
unsupportable
unsupported
unsuppressed
unsure
unsurpassable
unsurpassed
unsusceptible
unsuspected
unsuspecting
unsuspicious
unsustained
unswayed
unsweetened
unswerving
unsworn
unsympathetic
unsympathizing
unsystematic
unsystematical
unsystematized
untactful
untainted
untalented
untalked-of
untamable
untamed
untanned
untapped
untarnished
untaxed
unteachable
untechnical
untempered
untenanted
untended
unterrified
untested
unthanked
unthankful
unthatched
unthawed
untheatrical
unthoughtful
unthought-of
unthreaded
unthrifty
untidily
untidiness
untillable
untilled
untired
untiring
untouched
untraceable
untracked
untrained
untrammeled
untransferable
untranslatable
untranslated
untraveled
untraversed
untreated
untrimmed
untrod
untrodden
untroubled
untrustworthy
untufted
untunable
untwisted
untypical
unusable
unuttered
unvaried
unvarying
unveiled
unventilated
unveracious
unverifiable
unverified
unversed
unvexed
unvisited
unvulcanized
unwalled
unwanted
unwarily
unwariness
unwarlike
unwarranted
unwatched
unwatered
unwavering
unweaned
unwearable
unwearying
unweathered
unwed
unwedded
unweeded
unwelcome
unwelded
unwept
unwifely
unwinking
unwished
unwitnessed
unwomanly
unwon

un·world·li·ness \-'wərl-(d)lē-nəs\ *n* : the quality or state of being unworldly

un·world·ly \-'wər(-ə)l-dlē, -'wərl-lē\ *adj* **1** : not of this world : UNEARTHLY; *specif* : SPIRITUAL **2 a** : not wise in the ways of the world : NAÏVE **b** : not swayed by mundane considerations

un·worn \-'wō(ə)rn, -'wȯ(ə)rn\ *adj* **1** : unimpaired by use : not worn away **2 a** : not jaded : FRESH, ORIGINAL **b** : not worn : NEW

un·wor·thi·ly \,ən-'wər-t͟hə-lē, 'ən-\ *adv* : in an unworthy manner

un·wor·thi·ness \-t͟hē-nəs\ *n* : the quality or state of being unworthy

un·wor·thy \-t͟hē\ *adj* **1 a** : lacking in excellence or value : POOR, WORTHLESS **b** : BASE, DISHONORABLE **2** : not meritorious : UNDESERVING **3** : not corresponding to desert : UNMERITED

un·wrap \,ən-'rap, 'ən-\ *vt* : to remove the wrapping from : DISCLOSE

un·wreathe \-'rēt͟h\ *vt* : UNCOIL, UNTWIST

un·writ·ten \-'rit-ᵊn\ *adj* **1** : not reduced to writing : ORAL, TRADITIONAL **2** : containing no writing : BLANK

unwritten constitution *n* : a constitution not embodied in a single document but based chiefly on custom and precedent as expressed in statutes and judicial decisions

unwritten law *n* : law based chiefly on custom rather than legislative enactments

un·yield·ing \,ən-'yē(ə)l-diŋ, 'ən-\ *adj* **1** : characterized by lack of softness or flexibility **2** : characterized by firmness or obduracy

un·yoke \-'yōk\ *vt* **1** : to free from a yoke or harness **2** : to take apart : DISJOIN ~ *vi* **1** *archaic* : to unharness a draft animal **2** *archaic* : to cease from work

un·zip \-'zip\ *vt* : to zip open ~ *vi* : to open by means of a zipper

1up \'əp\ *adv* [partly fr. ME *up* upward, fr. OE *ūp*; partly fr. ME *uppe* on high, fr. OE; both akin to OHG *ūf* up, L *sub* under, Gk *hypo* under, *hyper* over — more at OVER] **1 a** (1) : in or into a higher position or level; *specif* : away from the center of the earth ⟨lift ~ your eyes⟩ (2) : from beneath the ground or water to the surface (3) : from below the horizon (4) : UPSTREAM (5) : in or into an upright position ⟨sit ~⟩; *specif* : out of bed **b** : upward from the ground or surface so as to detach ⟨pull ~ a daisy⟩ **c** : so as to expose a particular surface **2** : with greater intensity ⟨speak ~⟩ **3 a** : in or into a better or more advanced state **b** : in or into a state of greater intensity or excitement **c** : in a continual sequence ⟨from third grade ~⟩ **4 a** (1) : into existence, evidence, prominence, or prevalence ⟨the money will turn ~⟩ (2) : into operation or practical form **b** : into consideration or attention ⟨bring ~ for discussion⟩ **5** : into possession or custody **6 a** : ENTIRELY, COMPLETELY **b** — used as a function word for emphasis ⟨clean ~ the house⟩ **7 a** : in or into storage : BY ⟨lay ~ supplies⟩ **b** : in or into a state of closure or confinement ⟨button ~⟩ **8 a** : so as to arrive or approach **b** : in a direction conventionally the opposite of down: (1) : to windward (2) : NORTHWARD (3) : to or at the top (4) : to or at the rear of a theatrical stage **c** : so as to be even with, overtake, find, or arrive at **9** : in or into parts **10** : to a stop — usu. used with *draw, bring, fetch,* or *pull* **11 a** : in advance ⟨one ~ on his opponent⟩ **b** : for each side ⟨the score is 15 ~⟩

2up *adj* **1 a** : risen above the horizon ⟨the sun is ~⟩ **b** : STANDING **c** : being out of bed **d** : relatively high ⟨the river is ~⟩ ⟨was well ~ in his class⟩ **e** : RAISED, LIFTED ⟨windows are ~⟩ **f** : BUILT **g** : having the face upward **h** : mounted on a horse ⟨a new jockey ~⟩ **i** : grown above a surface ⟨the corn is ~⟩ **j** (1) : moving, inclining, or directed upward ⟨the ~ escalator⟩ (2) : bound in a direction regarded as up **2 a** : marked by agitation, excitement, or activity **b** : being above a former or normal level (as of quantity or intensity) ⟨attendance is ~⟩ ⟨the wind is ~⟩ **c** : exerting enough power (as for operation) ⟨sail when steam is ~⟩ **d** : READY; *specif* : highly prepared **e** : going on : taking place ⟨find out what is ~⟩ **3** : COMPLETED, OVER ⟨your time is ~⟩ **4 a** : risen from a lower position ⟨men ~ from the ranks⟩ **b** : being at the same level or point ⟨did not feel ~ to par⟩ **c** (1) : well informed : ABREAST ⟨~ on the news⟩ (2) : being on schedule ⟨~ on his homework⟩ **d** : being ahead of one's opponent **5 a** : presented for or undergoing consideration ⟨contract ~ for negotiation⟩; *specif* : charged before a court ⟨~ for robbery⟩ **b** : BET, WAGERED — **up to 1** : capable of performing or dealing with ⟨feels *up to* her role⟩ **2** : engaged in ⟨what is he *up to*⟩ **3** : being the responsibility of ⟨it's *up to* me⟩

3up *vb* **upped** *or in vi 1* **up**; **upped**; **up·ping**; **ups** *or in vi 1* **up** *vi* **1** : to act abruptly or surprisingly — usu. followed by *and* and another verb **2 a** : to rise from a lying or sitting position **b** : to move upward : ASCEND ~ *vt* **1** : RAISE, LIFT **2 a** : to advance to a higher level: (1) : INCREASE (2) : PROMOTE 1a **b** : RAISE 8d, 8e

4up \(,)əp, 'əp\ *prep* **1 a** : to, toward, or at a higher point of **b** : up into or in the ⟨went ~ attic⟩ **2** : in a direction regarded as being toward or near the upper end or part of: as **a** : toward or near a point closer to the source or beginning of ⟨sail ~ the river⟩ **b** : toward, near, to, or in the inner part or interior of ⟨~ country⟩ **3** : in the direction opposite to : AGAINST ⟨~ the wind⟩

5up \'əp\ *n* **1** : one in a high or advantageous position **2** : an upward slope **3** : a period or state of prosperity or success

up–and–down \,əp-ᵊm-'dau̇n, ,əp-ən-\ *adj* **1** : marked by alternate upward and downward movement, action, or surface **2** : PERPENDICULAR

Upa·ni·shad \ü-'pan-ə-,shad, 'ü-pə-ni-shəd\ *n* [Skt *upaniṣad*] : one of a class of Vedic treatises dealing with broad philosophic problems

upas \'yü-pəs\ *n* [Malay *pohon upas* poison tree] **1 a** : a tall Asiatic and East Indian tree (*Antiaris toxicaria*) of the mulberry family with a latex that contains poisonous glucosides used as an arrow poison **b** : a shrub or tree (*Strychnos tieuté* of the family Loganiaceae) of the same region also yielding an arrow poison **2** : a poisonous concentrate of the juice or latex of a upas **3** : a poisonous or harmful influence or institution

1up·beat \'əp-,bēt\ *n* : an unaccented beat in a musical measure; *specif* : the last beat of the measure

2upbeat *adj* : OPTIMISTIC, CHEERFUL

up–bow \'əp-,bō\ *n* : a stroke in playing a bowed instrument (as a violin) made toward the heel of the bow

up·braid \,əp-'brād\ *vt* [ME *upbreyden*, fr. OE *ūpbregdan*] **1** : to criticize severely : find fault with **2** : to reproach severely : scold vehemently **syn** see SCOLD — **up·braid·er** *n*

up·bring·ing \'əp-,briŋ-iŋ\ *n* : the process of bringing up and training

up·build \,əp-'bild\ *vt* : to build up — **up·build·er** *n*

up·cast \'əp-,kast\ *n* **1** : a ventilating shaft up which air passes after circulation **2** : something cast up —**upcast** *adj*

up·chuck \'əp-,chək\ *vb* : VOMIT

up·com·ing \,əp-,kəm-iŋ\ *adj* : FORTHCOMING, APPROACHING

1up–coun·try \,əp-,kən-trē\ *adj* : of, relating to, or characteristic of the interior of a country or a region

2up–coun·try \,əp-'kən-trē\ *adv* : to or in the interior of a country

3up–coun·try \'əp-,kən-trē\ *n* : the interior of a country

up·date \,əp-'dāt\ *vt* : to bring up to date

up·do \'əp-(,)dü\ *n* [*up*swept hair*do*] : an upswept hairdo

up·draft \'əp-,draft, -,dra̱ft\ *n* : an upward movement of gas (as air)

up·end \,ə-'pend\ *vt* : to set or stand on end ~ *vi* : to rise on an end

1up·grade \'əp-,grād\ *n* : an upward grade

2up·grade \'əp-,grād, ,əp-'\ *vt* : to raise the grade of: as **a** : to improve (livestock) by use of purebred sires **b** : to advance to a job requiring a higher level of skill esp. as part of a training program **c** : to substitute (a product of lower quality) for a product of higher quality and price

up·growth \'əp-,grōth\ *n* : the process of growing upward : DEVELOPMENT; *also* : a product or result of this

up·heav·al \,əp-'hē-vəl, (,)ə-'pē-\ *n* **1** : the action or an instance of upheaving esp. of part of the earth's crust **2** : an instance of violent agitation or change

up·heave \,əp-'hēv, (,)ə-'pēv\ *vt* : to heave up : LIFT ~ *vi* : to move upward — **up·heav·er** *n*

1up·hill \'əp-,hil\ *n* : rising ground : ASCENT

2up·hill \-'hil\ *adv* **1** : upward on a hill or incline **2** : against difficulties

3up·hill \-,hil\ *adj* **1** : situated on elevated ground **2** : going up : ASCENDING **3** : DIFFICULT, LABORIOUS

up·hold \(,)əp-'hōld\ *vt* **up·held** \-'held\ **up·hold·ing** **1 a** : to give support to **b** : to support against an opponent **2 a** : to keep elevated **b** : to lift up **syn** see SUPPORT — **up·hold·er** *n*

up·hol·ster \(,)ə-'pōl-stər, (,)ə-'pōl-\ *vt* **up·hol·ster·ing** \-st(ə-)riŋ\ [back-formation fr. *upholstery*] : to furnish with or as if with upholstery — **up·hol·ster·er** \-stər-ər, -strər\ *n*

up·hol·stery \-st(ə-)rē\ *n* [ME *upholdester* upholsterer, fr. *upholden* to uphold, fr. *up* + *holden* to hold] : materials (as fabric, padding, and springs) used to make a soft covering esp. for a seat

up·keep \'əp-,kēp\ *n* **1** : the act or cost of maintaining in good condition : MAINTENANCE **2** : the state of being maintained

up·land \'əp-lənd, -,land\ *n* **1** : high land esp. far from the sea : PLATEAU **2** : ground elevated above the lowlands along rivers or between hills — **upland** *adj*

upland cotton *n, often cap U* : any of various usu. short-staple cottons cultivated esp. in the U.S.

upland plover *n* : a large sandpiper (*Bartramia longicauda*) of eastern No. America that frequents fields and uplands

1up·lift \(,)əp-'lift\ *vt* **1** : to lift up : ELEVATE **2** : to improve the condition of esp. spiritually, socially, or intellectually ~ *vi* : RISE — **up·lift·er** *n*

2up·lift \'əp-,lift\ *n, often attrib* : an act, process, or result of uplifting: as **a** : the uplifting of a part of the earth's surface **b** : a bettering of condition esp. spiritually, emotionally, or culturally **c** (1) : influences intended to uplift (2) : a social movement to improve esp. morally or culturally **d** : a brassiere designed to hold the breasts up

up·most \'əp-,mōst\ *adj* : UPPERMOST

1up·on \ə-'pȯn, -'pän, -(,)pən\ *prep* : ON

2up·on \ə-'pȯn, -'pän\ *adv* **1** *obs* : on it : on one **2** *obs* : THEREON

1up·per \'əp-ər\ *adj* **1** : higher in physical position, rank, or order **2** : constituting the branch of a bicameral legislature that is usu. smaller and more restricted in membership and possesses greater traditional prestige than the lower house **3 a** : constituting a stratum relatively near the earth's surface **b** *cap* : being a later epoch or series of the period or series named ⟨*Upper* Carboniferous⟩ **4** : EARLIER **5** : NORTHERN

2upper *n* : one that is upper: as **a** : the parts of a shoe or boot above the sole **b** : an upper tooth or denture **c** : an upper berth

upper case *n* : a type case containing capitals and usu. small capitals, fractions, symbols, and accents

1up·per·case \,əp-ər-'kās\ *adj* : CAPITAL

2uppercase *n* : capital letters

3uppercase *vt* : to print or set in capital letters

up·per–class \,əp-ər-'klas\ *adj* : of, relating to, or characteristic of a class regarded as socially superior or to the junior and senior classes in a college or high school

up·per·class·man \-mən\ *n* : a junior or senior in a college or high school

upper crust *n* : the highest social class or group

up·per·cut \'əp-ər-,kət\ *n* : a swinging blow (as in boxing) directed upward with a bent arm — **uppercut** *vb*

upper hand *n* : MASTERY, ADVANTAGE

up·per·most \'əp-ər-,mōst\ *adv* : in or into the highest or most prominent position — **uppermost** *adj*

up·pish \'əp-ish\ *adj* : UPPITY — **up·pish·ly** *adv* — **up·pish·ness** *n*

up·pi·ty \'əp-ət-ē\ *adj* [prob. fr. *up* + *-ity* (as in *persnickity*, var. of *persnickety*)] : ARROGANT, PRESUMPTUOUS — **up·pi·ty·ness** *n*

up·raise \(,)ə-'prāz\ *vt* : to raise or lift up : ELEVATE

up·rear \(,)ə-'pri(ə)r\ *vt* **1** : to lift up **2** : ERECT ~ *vi* : RISE

1up·right \'əp-,rīt\ *adj* **1 a** : PERPENDICULAR, VERTICAL **b** : erect in carriage or posture **c** : having the main axis or a main part perpendicular ⟨~ freezer⟩ **2** : morally correct — **up·right·ly** *adv* — **up·right·ness** *n*

syn HONEST, JUST, CONSCIENTIOUS, SCRUPULOUS, HONORABLE: UPRIGHT implies a strict adherence to moral principles; HONEST stresses adherence to such virtues as truthfulness, candor, fairness; JUST is archaic for UPRIGHT and HONEST; CONSCIENTIOUS and SCRUPULOUS imply an active moral sense governing all one's

See *un-* and 2d element	unwooded	unworked	unworried	unwounded	unwrinkled
	unworkable	unworkmanlike	unwound	unwoven	unwrought

actions; HONORABLE suggests a firm holding to codes of right behavior and the guidance of a high sense of honor and duty

2**upright** *n* **1 :** the state of being upright **:** PERPENDICULAR ⟨a pillar out of ~⟩ **2 :** something upright

upright piano *n* **:** a piano whose strings run vertically

1**up·rise** \ˌə-ˈprīz\ *vi* **up·rose** \-ˈprōz\ **up·ris·en** \-ˈpriz-ᵊn\ **up·ris·ing** \-ˈprī-ziŋ\ **1 a :** to rise to a higher position **b** (1) **:** to stand up (2) **:** to get out of bed **c :** to come into view esp. from below the horizon **2 :** to rise up in sound — **up·ris·er** *n*

2**up·rise** \ˈəp-ˌrīz\ *n* **1 :** an act or instance of uprising **2 :** an upward slope

up·ris·ing \ˈəp-ˌrī-ziŋ\ *n* **:** an act or instance of rising up; *esp* **:** INSURRECTION, REVOLT **syn** see REBELLION

up·roar \ˈəp-ˌrō(ə)r, -ˌrȯ(ə)r\ *n* [by folk etymology fr. D *oproer*, fr. MD, fr. *op* up + *roer* motion; akin to OE *ūp* up and to OE *hrēran* to stir] **:** a state of commotion, excitement, or violent disturbance

up·roar·i·ous \ˌə-ˈprōr-ē-əs, -ˈprȯr-\ *adj* **1 :** marked by uproar **2 :** very noisy and full **3 :** extremely funny — **up·roar·i·ous·ly** *adv* — **up·roar·i·ous·ness** *n*

up·root \(ˌ)ə-ˈprüt, -ˈpru̇t\ *vt* **1 :** to pull up by the roots **2 :** to remove as if by pulling up **3 :** to displace from a country or traditional habitat **syn** see EXTERMINATE — **up·root·er** *n*

ups and downs *n pl* **:** alternating rise and fall esp. in fortune

1**up·set** \(ˌ)əp-ˈset\ *vb* **upset; up·set·ting** *vt* **1 :** to thicken and shorten (as a heated bar of iron) by hammering on the end **:** SWAGE **2 :** to force out of the usual upright, level, or proper position **:** OVERTURN **3 a :** to disturb the poise of **b :** to throw into disorder **c :** INVALIDATE **d :** to defeat unexpectedly **4 :** to cause a physical disorder in; *specif* **:** to make somewhat ill ~ *vi* **:** to become overturned **syn** see DISCOMPOSE — **up·set·ter** *n*

2**up·set** \ˈəp-ˌset\ *n* **1 :** an act of overturning **:** OVERTURN **2 a** (1) **:** an act of throwing into disorder **:** DERANGEMENT (2) **:** a state of disorder **:** CONFUSION **b :** an unexpected defeat **3 a :** a minor physical disorder ⟨a stomach ~⟩ **b :** an emotional disturbance **4 a :** a part of a rod (as the head on a bolt) that is upset **b :** the expansion of a bullet on striking **5 :** a swage used in upsetting

up·set price \ˈəp-ˌset-\ *n* **:** the minimum price set for property offered at auction or public sale

up·shot \ˈəp-ˌshät\ *n* **:** final result **:** OUTCOME

up·side \ˈəp-ˌsīd\ *n* **:** the upper side or part

up·side down \ˌəp-ˌsīd-ˈdau̇n\ *adv* [alter. of ME *up so doun*, fr. *up* + *so* + *doun* down] **1 :** in such a way that the upper and the lower parts are reversed in position **2 :** in or into great disorder — **upside–down** *adj*

upside–down cake *n* **:** a cake baked with its batter over an arrangement of fruit and served fruit side up

up·si·lon \ˈyüp-sə-ˌlän, ˈəp-, -lən, *Brit usu* yüp-ˈsī-lən\ *n* [MGk *y psilon*, lit., simple *y*; fr. the desire to distinguish it from *oi*, which was pronounced the same in later Greek] **:** the 20th letter of the Greek alphabet — symbol Υ or υ

up·spring \ˌəp-ˈspriŋ\ *vi* **1 :** to spring up **2 :** to come into being — **up·spring** \ˈəp-ˌspriŋ\ *n, archaic*

1**up·stage** \ˈəp-ˈstāj\ *adv* **:** toward or at the rear of a theatrical stage

2**upstage** *adj* **1 :** of or relating to the rear of a stage **2 :** HAUGHTY

3**up·stage** \ˌəp-ˈstāj\ *vt* **1 :** to force (an actor) to face away from the audience by staying upstage **2 :** to steal the show from **3 :** to treat snobbishly

1**up·stairs** \ˈəp-ˈsta(ə)rz, -ˈste(ə)rz\ *adv* **1 :** up the stairs **:** to or on a higher floor **2 :** to or at a high altitude or higher position

2**up·stairs** \-ˌsta(ə)rz, -ˌste(ə)rz\ *adj* **1 a :** situated above the stairs esp. on an upper floor **b :** of or relating to the upper floors ⟨~ maid⟩ **2 :** higher level

3**up·stairs** \ˈəp-ˈ, ˈəp-ˌ\ *n pl but sing or pl in constr* **:** the part of a building above the ground floor

up·stand·ing \ˌəp-ˈstan-diŋ, ˈəp-ˌ\ *adj* **1 :** ERECT **2 :** marked by integrity **:** STRAIGHTFORWARD — **up·stand·ing·ness** *n*

1**up·start** \ˌəp-ˈstärt\ *vi* **:** to jump up suddenly

2**up·start** \ˈəp-ˌstärt\ *n* **:** one that has risen suddenly (as from a low position to wealth or power) **:** PARVENU; *esp* **:** one that claims more personal importance than he warrants — **up·start** \ˌəp-ˌ\ *adj*

1**up·state** \ˈəp-ˌstāt\ *adj* **:** of, relating to, or characteristic of a part of a state away from and esp. to the north of a large city

2**upstate** *n* **:** an upstate region — **up·stat·er** \-ˈstāt-ər\ *n*

up·stream \ˈəp-ˈstrēm\ *adv* **:** at or toward the source of a stream — **upstream** *adj*

up·stroke \ˈəp-ˌstrōk\ *n* **:** an upward stroke esp. of a pen

up·surge \ˈəp-ˌsərj\ *n* **:** a rapid or sudden rise

1**up·sweep** \ˈəp-ˌswēp\ *vi* **:** to sweep upward

2**upsweep** *n* **:** an upward sweep; *esp* **:** a hairdo in which the hair is brushed up to the top of the head

up·swept \ˈəp-ˌswept\ *adj* **:** swept upward; *specif* **:** brushed up to the top of the head ⟨~ hairdo⟩

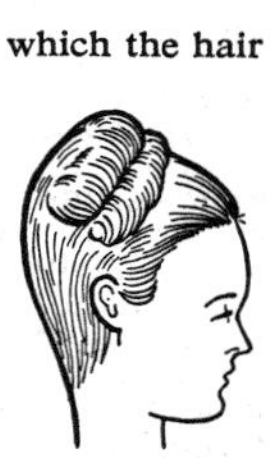
upsweep

up·swing \ˈəp-ˌswiŋ\ *n* **:** an upward swing; *esp* **:** a marked increase (as in activity)

up·take \ˈəp-ˌtāk\ *n* [Sc *uptake* to understand] **1 :** UNDERSTANDING, COMPREHENSION **2 :** a flue leading upward **3 :** an act or instance of absorbing and incorporating esp. into a living organism

up·throw \ˈəp-ˌthrō\ *n* **:** an upward displacement (as of a rock stratum) **:** UPHEAVAL

up·thrust \ˈəp-ˌthrəst\ *n* **:** an upward thrust; *specif* **:** an uplift of part of the earth's crust

up·tight \ˈəp-ˈtīt\ *adj* **1 :** being in financial difficulties **2 a :** being tense, nervous, or uneasy **b :** ANGRY, INDIGNANT **c :** rigidly conventional

up·tilt \ˌəp-ˈtilt\ *vt* **:** to tilt upward

up to *prep* **1 :** as far as a designated part or place ⟨sank *up to* his hips⟩ **2 :** to or in fulfillment of ⟨write *up to* the standard⟩ **3 a :** to the limit of ⟨guesses ran *up to* 1000⟩ **b :** as many or as much as ⟨carry *up to* 10 tons⟩ **4 :** UNTIL

up–to–date \ˌəp-tə-ˈdāt\ *adj* **1 :** extending to the present **2 :** abreast of the times — **up–to–date·ly** *adv* — **up–to–date·ness** *n*

up·town \ˈəp-ˈtau̇n\ *adv* **:** toward, to, or in the upper part of a town — **up·town** \-ˌtau̇n\ *adj*

up·trend \ˈəp-ˌtrend\ *n* **:** a tendency upward

1**up·turn** \ˈəp-ˌtərn, ˌəp-ˈ\ *vt* **1 :** to turn up or over **2 :** to direct upward ~ *vi* **:** to turn upward

2**up·turn** \ˈəp-ˌtərn\ *n* **:** an upward turn esp. toward higher prices

1**up·ward** \ˈəp-wərd\ *or* **up·wards** \-wərdz\ *adv* **1 a :** in a direction from lower to higher **b :** toward the source or interior **c :** in a higher position **d :** in the upper parts **:** toward the head **:** ABOVE **2 :** toward a higher or better condition or level **3 a :** indefinitely more or higher **b :** toward a greater amount or higher number, degree, or rate **4 :** toward or into later years

2**upward** *adj* **1 :** directed toward or situated in a higher place or level **:** ASCENDING **2 :** rising to a higher pitch — **up·ward·ly** *adv* — **up·ward·ness** *n*

upwards of *also* **upward of** *adv* **:** more than **:** in excess of

up·well \ˌəp-ˈwel\ *vi* **:** to well up; *specif* **:** to move or flow upward

up·wind \ˈəp-ˈwind\ *adv (or adj)* **:** in the direction from which the wind is blowing

1**ur-** *or* **uro-** *comb form* [NL, fr. Gk *our-*, *ouro-*, fr. *ouron* urine — more at URINE] **1 :** urine ⟨*ur*ic⟩ **2 :** urinary tract ⟨*uro*logy⟩ **3 :** urinal and ⟨*uro*genital⟩ **4 :** urea ⟨*ur*acil⟩

2**ur-** *or* **uro-** *comb form* [NL, fr. Gk *our-*, *ouro-*, fr. *oura* tail — more at SQUIRREL] **:** tail ⟨*uro*chord⟩

ura·cil \ˈyu̇r-ə-ˌsil\ *n* [ISV 1*ur-* + acetic + *-il* (substance relating to)] **:** a heterocyclic compound $C_4H_4N_2O_2$ that is a breakdown product of nucleic acids and a growth factor for some microorganisms

urae·mia *var of* UREMIA

urae·us \yu̇-ˈrē-əs\ *n, pl* **uraei** \-ˈrē-ˌī\ [NL, fr. LGk *ouraios*, a snake] **:** a representation of the sacred asp (*Naja haje*) on the headdress of ancient Egyptian rulers serving as a symbol of sovereignty

Ural–Al·ta·ic \ˌyu̇r-ə-(ˌ)lal-ˈtā-ik\ *n* **1 :** a postulated language group comprising the Uralic and Altaic languages **2 :** a language type showing agglutination and vowel harmony and occurring esp. in languages of Eurasia — **Ural–Altaic** *adj*

Ura·li·an \yu̇-ˈrā-lē-ən, -ˈral-ē-\ *adj* **1 :** of or relating to the Ural mountains **2 :** of, relating to, or constituting the Finno-Ugric or the Finno-Ugric and Samoyed languages

1**Ural·ic** \yu̇-ˈral-ik\ *adj* **:** URALIAN

2**Uralic** *n* **:** a language family comprising the Finno-Ugric and Samoyed languages

ural·ite \ˈyu̇r-ə-ˌlīt\ *n* [G *uralit*, fr. *Ural* mountains] **:** a usu. fibrous and dark green amphibole resulting from alteration of pyroxene — **ural·it·ic** \ˌyu̇r-ə-ˈlit-ik\ *adj*

1**uran-** *or* **urano-** *comb form* [L, fr. Gk *ouran-*, *ourano-*, fr. *ouranos*] **:** sky **:** heaven ⟨*uran*ic⟩ ⟨*urano*metry⟩

2**uran-** *or* **urano-** *comb form* [F, fr. NL *uranium*] **:** uranium ⟨*uran*yl⟩

Ura·nia \yu̇-ˈrā-nē-ə, -nyə\ *n* [L, fr. Gk *Ourania*] **:** the Greek Muse of astronomy

ura·nic \yu̇-ˈran-ik, -ˈrā-nik\ *adj* [ISV] **:** of, relating to, or containing uranium esp. with a valence higher than in uranous compounds

ura·nide \ˈyu̇r-ə-ˌnīd\ *n* **1 :** URANIUM **2 :** a transuranium element

ura·ni·nite \yu̇-ˈrā-nə-ˌnīt\ *n* [G *uranin* uraninite (fr. NL *uranium*) + E *-ite*] **:** a mineral UO_2 that is a black octahedral or cubic oxide of uranium, that contains thorium, the cerium and yttrium metals, and lead, that often when heated yields a gas consisting chiefly of helium, and that is the chief ore of uranium

ura·ni·um \yu̇-ˈrā-nē-əm\ *n, often attrib* [NL, fr. *Uranus*] **:** a silvery heavy radioactive polyvalent metallic element that is found esp. in pitchblende and uraninite and exists naturally as a mixture of three isotopes of mass number 234, 235, and 238 in the proportions of 0.006 percent, 0.71 percent, and 99.28 percent respectively — see ELEMENT table

uranium 238 *n* **:** an isotope of uranium of mass number 238 that absorbs fast neutrons to form a uranium isotope of mass number 239 which then decays through neptunium to form plutonium of mass number 239

uranium 235 *n* **:** a light isotope of uranium of mass number 235 that is physically separable from natural uranium, that when bombarded with slow neutrons undergoes rapid fission into smaller atoms with the release of neutrons and atomic energy, and that is used in power plants and atom bombs

ura·no·graph·ic \ˌyu̇r-ə-nō-ˈgraf-ik, yu̇-ˌran-ə-\ *adj* **:** of or relating to uranography — **ura·no·graph·i·cal** \-i-kəl\ *adj*

ura·nog·ra·phy \ˌyu̇r-ə-ˈnäg-rə-fē\ *n* [Gk *ouranographia* description of the heavens, fr. *ouran-* uran- + *-graphia* -graphy] **1 :** a science dealing with the description of the heavens and the celestial bodies **2 :** the construction of celestial representations (as maps)

ura·no·log·i·cal \ˌyu̇r-ə-nō-ˈläj-i-kəl, yu̇-ˌran-ᵊl-ˈäj-\ *adj* **:** of or relating to uranology

ura·nol·o·gy \ˌyu̇r-ə-ˈnäl-ə-jē\ *n* **1 :** ASTRONOMY **2 :** a treatise on the heavens and the celestial bodies

ura·nom·e·try \-ˈnäm-ə-trē\ *n* [NL *uranometria*, fr. *uran-* + *-metria* -metry] **1 :** a chart or catalog of celestial bodies and esp. of visible fixed stars **2 :** the measurement of the heavens

ura·nous \yu̇-ˈrā-nəs, ˈyu̇r-ə-\ *adj* **:** of, relating to, or containing uranium esp. with a lower valence than in uranic compounds

Ura·nus \ˈyu̇r-ə-nəs, yu̇-ˈrā-\ *n* [LL, fr. Gk *Ouranos*] **1 :** heaven personified as a god in Greek mythology and father of the Titans **2 :** the planet seventh in order from the sun — see PLANET table

ura·nyl \ˈyu̇r-ə-ˌnil, yu̇-ˈrān-ᵊl\ *n* [ISV] **:** a bivalent radical UO_2 formed by uranium trioxide in acid solution

urate \ˈyu̇(ə)r-ˌāt\ *n* [F, fr. *urique* uric, fr. E *uric*] **:** a salt of uric acid — **urat·ic** \yu̇-ˈrat-ik\ *adj*

ur·ban \ˈər-bən\ *adj* [L *urbanus*, fr. *urbs* city] **:** of, relating to, characteristic of, or constituting a city

ur·bane \ˌər-ˈbān\ *adj* [L *urbanus*] **:** notably polite or finished in manner **:** POLISHED **syn** see SUAVE — **ur·bane·ly** *adv*

ur·ban·ism \ˈər-bə-ˌniz-əm\ *n* **1 :** the characteristic way of life of city dwellers **2 :** the study of the physical needs of urban societies **3 :** URBANIZATION — **ur·ban·ist** \-nəst\ *n* — **ur·ban·is·tic** \ˌər-bə-ˈnis-tik\ *adj* — **ur·ban·is·ti·cal·ly** \-ti-k(ə-)lē\ *adv*

ur·ban·ite \ˈər-bə-ˌnīt\ *n* **:** one living in a city

ur·ban·i·ty \ˌər-ˈban-ət-ē\ *n* **1 :** the quality or state of being urbane **2** *pl* **:** urbane acts or conduct

ur·ban·iza·tion \ˌər-bə-nə-ˈzā-shən\ *n* **:** the quality or state of being or becoming urbanized

ur·ban·ize \ˈər-bə-ˌnīz\ *vt* **1 :** to cause to take on urban characteristics ⟨*urbanized* areas⟩ **2 :** to impart an urban way of life to

ur·bi·cul·ture \ˈər-bə-ˌkəl-chər\ *n* [L *urb-*, *urbs* city + E *-i-* + *culture*] **:** practices and problems peculiar to cities or to urban life

ur·ce·o·late \ˌər-ˈsē-ə-lət, ˈər-sē-ə-ˌlāt\ *adj* [NL *urceolatus*, fr. L *urceolus*, dim. of *urceus* pitcher] **:** shaped like an urn

ur·chin \ˈər-chən\ *n* [ME, fr. MF *herichon*, fr. L *ericius*, fr. *er;* akin to Gk *chēr* hedgehog, L *horrēre* to bristle, tremble] **1 :** HEDGEHOG **2 :** a pert or roguish youngster **3 :** SEA URCHIN
urd \ˈu̇(ə)rd, ˈərd\ *n* [Hindi] **:** an annual bean (*Phaseolus mungo*) widely grown in warm regions for its edible blackish seed, for green manure, or for forage — called also *black gram*
Ur·du \ˈu̇(ə)r-(ˌ)dü, ˈər-\ *n* [Hindi *urdū-zabān*, lit., camp language] **:** an Indic language that is an official literary language of Pakistan and is widely used in India
-ure *n suffix* [ME, fr. OF, fr. L *-ura*] **1 :** act **:** process **:** being ⟨expos*ure*⟩ **2 :** office **:** function; *also* **:** body performing (such) a function ⟨legislat*ure*⟩
urea \yu̇-ˈrē-ə\ *n* [NL, fr. F *urée*, fr. *urine*] **:** a soluble weakly basic nitrogenous compound $CO(NH_2)_2$ that is the chief solid component of mammalian urine and an end product of protein decomposition, is synthesized from carbon dioxide and ammonia, and is used esp. in synthesis (as of resins and plastics) and in fertilizers and animal rations — **ure·al** \-ˈrē-əl\ *adj* — **ure·ic** \-ˈrē-ik\ *adj*
urea–formaldehyde resin *n* **:** a thermosetting synthetic resin made by condensing urea with formaldehyde
ure·ase \ˈyu̇r-ē-ˌās, -ˌāz\ *n* **:** an enzyme that promotes the hydrolysis of urea
ure·din·i·al \ˌyu̇r-ə-ˈdin-ē-əl\ *adj* **:** of, relating to, or being a uredinium
ure·din·i·um \-ē-əm\ *n, pl* **ure·din·ia** \-ē-ə\ [NL, fr. L *uredin-*, *uredo* burning, blight, fr. *urere* to burn — more at EMBER] **:** a crowded usu. brownish mass of hyphae and spores of a rust fungus forming pustules that rupture the host's cuticle
ure·di·nous \yu̇-ˈred-ᵊn-əs, -ˈrēd-\ *adj* [deriv. of L *uredin-*, *uredo*] **:** of or relating to an order (Uredinales) of fungi comprising the rusts
ure·dio·spore \yu̇-ˈrēd-ē-ə-ˌspō(ə)r, -ˌspȯ(ə)r\ *or* **ure·do·spore** \-ˈrēd-ə-\ *n* [NL *uredium* + E *-o-* + *spore*] **:** one of the thin-walled spores that are produced in repeated crops by the uredinial hyphae of rust fungi, spread the fungus vegetatively, and follow the aecial spores
ure·di·um \yu̇-ˈrēd-ē-əm\ *n, pl* **ure·dia** \-ē-ə\ [NL, fr. *uredo*] **:** UREDINIUM
ure·do \yu̇-ˈrēd-(ˌ)ō\ *n* [NL, fr. L, burning, blight] **:** UREDOSTAGE
ure·do·stage \-ˈrēd-ō-ˌstāj\ *n* **:** the uredinial stage of a rust
ure·ide \ˈyu̇r-ē-ˌīd\ *n* **:** a cyclic or acyclic acyl derivative of urea
ure·mia \yu̇-ˈrē-mē-ə\ *n* [NL] **:** accumulation in the blood usu. in severe kidney disease of constituents normally eliminated in the urine producing a severe toxic condition — **ure·mic** \-mik\ *adj*
ure·ter \ˈyu̇r-ət-ər\ *n* [NL, fr. Gk *ourētēr*, fr. *ourein* to urinate — more at URINE] **:** a duct that carries away the urine from a kidney to the bladder or cloaca — **ure·ter·al** \yu̇-ˈrēt-ə-rəl\ *or* **ure·ter·ic** \ˌyu̇r-ə-ˈter-ik\ *adj*
ure·thane \ˈyu̇r-ə-ˌthān\ *or* **ure·than** \-ˌthan\ *n* [F *uréthane*, fr. *ur-* + *éth-* eth- + *-ane*] **1 :** a crystalline compound $C_3H_7NO_2$ used esp. as a solvent and medicinally as a palliative for leukemias **2 :** an ester of carbamic acid other than the ethyl ester
urethr- *or* **urethro-** *comb form* [NL, fr. LL *urethra*] **:** urethra ⟨*urethr*itis⟩ ⟨*urethro*scope⟩
ure·thra \yu̇-ˈrē-thrə\ *n, pl* **urethras** *or* **ure·thrae** \-(ˌ)thrē\ [LL, fr. Gk *ourēthra*, fr. *ourein* to urinate] **:** the canal that in most mammals carries off the urine from the bladder and in the male serves also as a genital duct — **ure·thral** \-thrəl\ *adj*
ure·thri·tis \ˌyu̇r-i-ˈthrīt-əs\ *n* [NL] **:** inflammation of the urethra
ure·thro·scope \yu̇-ˈrē-thrə-ˌskōp\ *n* [ISV] **:** an instrument for viewing the interior of the urethra — **ure·thro·scop·ic** \-ˌrē-thrə-ˈskäp-ik\ *adj*
¹**urge** \ˈərj\ *vb* [L *urgēre*] *vt* **1 :** to present, advocate, or demand earnestly or pressingly **2 :** to prosecute vigorously **3 a :** to make solicitations to **b :** to serve as a motive or reason for **4 :** to force or impel in an indicated direction or into motion or greater speed **5 :** STIMULATE, PROVOKE ~ *vi* **:** to declare, advance, or press earnestly a statement, argument, charge, or claim — **urg·er** *n*
²**urge** *n* **1 :** the act or process of urging **2 :** a force or impulse that urges; *esp* **:** a continuing impulse toward an activity or goal
ur·gen·cy \ˈər-jən-sē\ *n* **1 :** the quality or state of being urgent **:** INSISTENCE **2 :** a force or impulse that impels or constrains **:** URGE
ur·gent \ˈər-jənt\ *adj* [ME, fr. MF, fr. L *urgent-*, *urgens*, prp. of *urgēre*] **1 a :** calling for immediate attention **:** PRESSING ⟨~ appeals⟩ **b :** conveying a sense of urgency **2 :** urging insistently **:** IMPORTUNATE **syn** see PRESSING — **ur·gent·ly** *adv*
-ur·gy \(ˌ)ər-jē\ *n comb form* [NL *-urgia*, fr. Gk *-ourgia*, fr. *-ourgos* working, fr. *-o-* + *ergon* work] **:** technique or art of dealing or working with (such) a product, matter, or tool ⟨chem*urgy*⟩
-uria \ˈ(y)u̇r-ē-ə\ *n comb form* [NL, fr. Gk *-ouria*, fr. *ouron* urine — more at URINE] **1 :** presence of (a specified substance) in urine ⟨album*inuria*⟩ **2 :** condition of having (such) urine ⟨poly*uria*⟩; *esp* **:** abnormal or diseased condition marked by the presence of (a specified substance) ⟨py*uria*⟩
uric \ˈyu̇(ə)r-ik\ *adj* **:** of, relating to, or found in urine
uric acid *n* **:** a white odorless and tasteless nearly insoluble diacid $C_5H_4N_4O_3$ present in small quantity in urine
uri·cos·uric \ˌyu̇r-i(ˌ)kōs-ˈ(y)u̇(ə)r-ik\ *adj* [irreg. fr. *uric*] **:** relating to or promoting the excretion of uric acid in the urine
uri·dine \ˈyu̇r-ə-ˌdēn\ *n* [ISV] **:** a crystalline nucleoside $C_9H_{12}N_2O_6$ derived by hydrolysis from nucleic acids that is important in carbohydrate metabolism
Uri·el \ˈyu̇r-ē-əl\ *n* [Heb *Ūrī'ēl*] **:** one of the archangels
Urim and Thum·mim \ˌ(y)u̇r-ə-mən-ˈthəm-əm, ˌu̇(ə)r-ˌē-mən-ˈtu̇m-ˌēm\ *n pl* [part trans. of Heb *ūrīm wĕthummīm*] **:** sacred lots used in early times by the Hebrews
urin- *or* **urino-** *comb form* [ME, fr. OF, fr. L, fr. *urina* urine] **:** ¹UR- ⟨*urino*genital⟩ ⟨*urin*ary⟩
uri·nal \ˈyu̇r-ən-ᵊl\ *n* [ME, fr. OF, fr. LL, fr. L *urina*] **1 :** a vessel for receiving urine **2 :** a building or enclosure with facilities for urinating; *also* **:** a fixture used for urinating
uri·nal·y·sis \ˌyu̇r-ə-ˈnal-ə-səs\ *n* [NL, irreg. fr. *urin-* + *analysis*] **:** chemical analysis of urine
uri·nary \ˈyu̇r-ə-ˌner-ē\ *adj* **1 :** relating to, occurring in, or constituting the organs concerned with the formation and discharge of urine **2 :** of, relating to, or for urine **3 :** excreted as or in urine
urinary bladder *n* **:** a membranous sac in many vertebrates serving for the temporary retention of urine and discharging by the urethra
uri·nate \ˈyu̇r-ə-ˌnāt\ *vi* **:** to discharge urine **:** MICTURATE — **uri·na·tion** \ˌyu̇r-ə-ˈnā-shən\ *n*
urine \ˈyu̇r-ən\ *n* [ME, fr. MF, fr. L *urina;* akin to Gk *ouron* urine, *ourein* to urinate, OE *wæter* water] **:** the chief excretory product of the vertebrate being secreted by the kidney as liquid or semisolid matter rich in end products of protein metabolism, salts, and pigments and in man forming a clear amber usu. slightly acid fluid — **urin·ous** \ˈyu̇r-ə-nəs\ *adj*
uri·nif·er·ous tubule \ˌyu̇r-ə-ˌnif-(ə-)rəs-\ *n* **:** a vertebrate nephron
uri·no·gen·i·tal \ˌyu̇r-ə-nō-ˈjen-ə-tᵊl\ *adj* **:** UROGENITAL
uri·nom·e·ter \ˌyu̇r-ə-ˈnäm-ət-ər\ *n* [ISV] **:** a small hydrometer for determining the specific gravity of urine — **uri·no·met·ric** \-nō-ˈme-trik\ *adj* — **uri·nom·e·try** \-ˈnäm-ə-trē\ *n*
urn \ˈərn\ *n* [ME *urne*, fr. L *urna*] **1 :** a vessel of various forms that is typically a vase on a pedestal and that is used esp. for preserving the ashes of the dead after cremation **2 :** a closed vessel usu. with a spigot for serving a hot beverage ⟨coffee ~⟩
uro- — see UR-
uro·chord \ˈyu̇r-ə-ˌkȯ(ə)rd\ *n* **1 :** the notochord of larval ascidians and some adult tunicates **2 :** TUNICATE — **uro·chor·dal** \ˌyu̇r-ə-ˈkȯrd-ᵊl\ *adj* — **uro·chor·date** \-ˈkȯrd-ət, -ˈkȯ(ə)r-ˌdāt\ *adj or n*
uro·chrome \ˈyu̇r-ə-ˌkrōm\ *n* **:** a yellow pigment to which the color of normal urine is principally due
uro·dele \ˈyu̇r-ə-ˌdēl\ *n* [F *urodèle*, deriv. of Gk *oura* tail + *dēlos* evident, showing — more at SQUIRREL] **:** any of an order (Caudata) of amphibians (as newts) with a tail throughout life — **urodele** *adj*
uro·gen·i·tal \ˌyu̇r-ō-ˈjen-ə-tᵊl\ *adj* [ISV] **:** of, relating to, or being the organs or functions of excretion and reproduction
uro·lith \ˈyu̇r-ə-ˌlith\ *n* [ISV] **:** a calculus in the urinary tract — **uro·lith·ic** \ˌyu̇r-ə-ˈlith-ik\ *adj*
uro·log·ic \ˌyu̇r-ə-ˈläj-ik\ *adj* **:** of or relating to the urinary tract or to urology — **uro·log·i·cal** \-i-kəl\ *adj*
urol·o·gist \yu̇-ˈräl-ə-jəst\ *n* **:** a physician who specializes in urology
urol·o·gy \-jē\ *n* **:** a branch of medicine dealing with the urinary or urogenital tract
-u·ron·ic \(y)u̇-ˈrän-ik\ *adj suffix* [Gk *ouron* urine] **:** connected with urine — in names of certain aldehyde-acids derived from sugars or compounds of such acids ⟨hyal*uronic*⟩
uro·pod \ˈyu̇r-ə-ˌpäd\ *n* [ISV ²*ur-* + Gk *pod-*, *pous* foot — more at FOOT] **:** either of the flattened lateral appendages of the last abdominal segment of a crustacean; *broadly* **:** an abdominal appendage of a crustacean — **urop·o·dal** \yu̇-ˈräp-əd-ᵊl\ *or* **urop·o·dous** \-əd-əs\ *adj*
¹**uro·pyg·i·al** \ˌyu̇r-ə-ˈpij-ē-əl\ *adj* **:** of or relating to the uropygium
²**uropygial** *n* **:** a tail feather
uropygial gland *n* **:** a large gland opening on the back at the base of the tail feathers in most birds and secreting an oily fluid which the bird uses in preening its feathers
uro·pyg·i·um \ˌyu̇r-ə-ˈpij-ē-əm\ *n* [NL, fr. Gk *ouropygion*, fr. *ouro-* ²ur- + *pygē* rump] **:** the fleshy and bony prominence at the posterior extremity of a bird's body that supports the tail feathers
-urous \ˈ(y)u̇r-əs\ *adj comb form* [NL *-urus*, fr. Gk *-ouros*, fr. *oura* tail — more at SQUIRREL] **:** -tailed ⟨an*urous*⟩
Ur·sa Ma·jor \ˌər-sə-ˈmā-jər\ *n* [L (gen. *Ursae Majoris*), lit., greater bear] **:** the most conspicuous of the northern constellations that is situated near the north pole of the heavens and contains the stars forming the Big Dipper two of which are in a line indicating the direction of the North Star — called also *Great Bear*
Ursa Mi·nor \-ˈmī-nər\ *n* [L (gen. *Ursae Minoris*), lit., lesser bear] **:** the constellation including the north pole of the heavens and the stars that form the Little Dipper with the North Star at the tip of the handle — called also *Little Bear*
ur·si·form \ˈər-sə-ˌfȯrm\ *adj* [L *ursus* bear + E *-iform*] **:** resembling a bear
ur·sine \ˈər-ˌsīn\ *adj* [L *ursinus*, fr. *ursus* bear — more at ARCTIC] **:** of, relating to, or resembling a bear or the bear family (Ursidae)
Ur·spra·che \ˈu̇(ə)r-ˌshpräk-ə\ *n* [G, fr. *ur-* primitive + *sprache* language] **:** a parent language; *esp* **:** one reconstructed from the evidence of later languages
Ur·su·line \ˈər-sə-lən, -ˌlīn, -ˌlēn\ *n* [NL *ursulinus*, fr. *Ursula* St. Ursula, legendary Christian martyr] **:** a member of a teaching order of nuns founded in Italy about 1537 — **Ursuline** *adj*
ur·ti·cant \ˈərt-i-kənt\ *adj* **:** producing itching or stinging
ur·ti·car·ia \ˌərt-ə-ˈkar-ē-ə, -ˈker-\ *n* [NL, fr. L *urtica* nettle] **:** an allergic disorder marked by raised edematous patches of skin or mucous membrane and usu. intense itching and caused by contact with a specific precipitating factor either externally or internally (as by a food, drug, or inhalant) — **ur·ti·car·i·al** \-ē-əl\ *adj*
ur·ti·cate \ˈərt-ə-ˌkāt\ *vi* [ML *urticatus*, pp. of *urticare* to sting, fr. L *urtica*] **:** to produce wheals or itching; *esp* **:** to induce urticaria — **ur·ti·ca·tion** \ˌərt-ə-ˈkā-shən\ *n*
urus \ˈyu̇r-əs\ *n* [L, of Gmc origin; akin to OHG *ūro* urus] **:** an extinct large long-horned wild ox (*Bos primigenius*) of the German forests held to be a wild ancestor of domestic cattle
uru·shi·ol \(y)u̇-ˈrü-shē-ˌȯl, -ˌōl\ *n* [ISV, fr. Jap *urushi* lacquer] **:** an oily toxic irritant principle present in poison ivy and some related plants (genus *Rhus*) and in oriental lacquers derived from such plants that consists of one or more phenolic compounds with unsaturated side chains of 15 carbon atoms
us \(ˈ)əs\ *pron* [ME, fr. OE *ūs;* akin to OHG *uns* us, L *nos*] *objective case of* WE
us·abil·i·ty \ˌyü-zə-ˈbil-ət-ē\ *n* **:** the quality or state of being usable
us·able *also* **use·able** \ˈyü-zə-bəl\ *adj* **1 :** capable of being used **2 :** convenient and practicable for use — **us·able·ness** *n* — **us·ably** \-blē\ *adv*
us·age \ˈyü-sij, -zij\ *n* **1 a :** customary practice or procedure **b :** a uniform certain reasonable lawful practice existing in a particular locality or occupation and binding persons entering into transactions chiefly on the basis of presumed familiarity **c :** the way in which words and phrases are actually used (as in a particular form or sense) in a language community **2 a :** the action or mode of using **b :** manner of treating **syn** see HABIT
us·ance \ˈyüz-ᵊn(t)s\ *n* **1 :** USAGE 1a **2 :** USE, EMPLOYMENT **3 a** *obs* **:** USURY **b :** INTEREST **4 :** the time allowed by custom for

payment of a bill of exchange in foreign commerce

1**use** \'yüs\ *n* [ME *us*, fr. OF, fr. L *usus*, fr. *usus*, pp. of *uti* to use] **1 a :** the act or practice of employing something **:** EMPLOYMENT, APPLICATION ⟨put knowledge to ~⟩ **b :** the fact or state of being used ⟨a dish in daily ~⟩ **c :** a method or manner of employing or applying something **:** USAGE **2 a** (1) **:** habitual or customary practice (2) **:** an individual habit or group custom **b :** a liturgical form or observance; *esp* **:** a liturgy having modifications peculiar to a local church or religious order **3 a :** the privilege or benefit of using something **b :** the ability or power to use something (as a limb or faculty) **c :** the legal enjoyment of property that consists in its employment, occupation, exercise, or practice **4 a :** a particular service or end **:** OBJECT, FUNCTION **b :** the quality of being suitable for employment **:** USEFULNESS, UTILITY **c :** the occasion or need to employ **5 a :** the benefit in law of one or more persons; *specif* **:** the benefit or profit of property established in one other than the legal possessor **b :** a legal arrangement by which such benefits and profits are so established **6 :** ESTEEM, LIKING ⟨had no ~ for modern art⟩ **syn** see HABIT

2**use** \'yüz\ *vb* **used** \'yüzd, *in the phrase "used to" usually* 'yüs(t)\ **us·ing** \'yü-ziŋ\ *vt* **1 :** ACCUSTOM, HABITUATE, INURE **2 :** to put into action or service **:** avail oneself of **:** EMPLOY **3 :** to consume or take (as liquor or drugs) regularly **4 :** to carry out a purpose or action by means of **:** UTILIZE **5 :** to expend or consume by putting to use **6 :** to behave toward **:** act with regard to **:** TREAT ⟨*used* the prisoners cruelly⟩ ~ *vi* **1 :** to be in the habit or custom of doing something **2** — used in the past with *to* to indicate a former fact or state ⟨claims winters *used* to be harder⟩

syn EMPLOY, UTILIZE: USE implies availing oneself of as a means or instrument to an end; EMPLOY suggests the use of a person or thing that is available because idle, inactive, or disengaged; UTILIZE may suggest the discovery of a new, profitable, or practical use for something

used \'yüzd, *in the phrase "used to" usually* 'yüs(t)\ *adj* **1 :** employed in accomplishing something **2 :** that has endured use; *specif* **:** SECONDHAND **3 :** ACCUSTOMED, HABITUATED

use·ful \'yüs-fəl\ *adj* **:** capable of being put to use **:** SERVICEABLE; *esp* **:** having utility — **use·ful·ly** \-fə-lē\ *adv* — **use·ful·ness** *n*

use·less \'yü-sləs\ *adj* **:** having or being of no use **: a :** INEFFECTUAL **b :** UNSERVICEABLE — **use·less·ly** *adv* — **use·less·ness** *n*

1**us·er** \'yü-zər\ *n* **:** one that uses

2**user** *n* **:** the actual exercise or enjoyment of a right

use up *vt* **1 :** to leave nothing of as a result of continued expenditure **:** consume completely ⟨*used up* his supplies⟩ **2 :** to leave no capacity of force or use in **:** exhaust of strength

Ushas \'ü-shəs\ *n* [Skt *Uṣas*] **:** the Vedic goddess of the dawn

1**ush·er** \'əsh-ər\ *n* [ME *ussher*, fr. MF *ussier*, fr. (assumed) VL *ustiarius* doorkeeper, fr. L *ostium*, *ustium* door, mouth of a river; akin to L *or-*, *os* mouth — more at ORAL] **1 a :** an officer or servant who has the care of the door of a court, hall, or chamber **b :** an officer who walks before a person of rank **c :** one who escorts persons to seats (as in a theater) **2** *archaic* **:** an assistant teacher

2**usher** *vt* **ush·er·ing** \'əsh-(ə-)riŋ\ **1 :** to conduct to a place **2 :** to precede as an usher, forerunner, or harbinger **3 :** INAUGURATE, INTRODUCE ⟨~ in a new era⟩

us·que·baugh \'əs-kwi-,bȯ\ *n* [IrGael *uisce beathadh*] *Irish & Scot* **:** WHISKEY

usu·al \'yüzh-(ə-)wəl, 'yü-zhəl\ *adj* [LL *usualis*, fr. L *usus* use] **1 :** accordant with usage, custom, or habit **:** NORMAL **2 :** commonly or ordinarily used **3 :** found in ordinary practice or in the ordinary course of events **:** ORDINARY — **usu·al·ly** \-ē\ *adv* — **usu·al·ness** *n*

syn CUSTOMARY, HABITUAL, WONTED, ACCUSTOMED: USUAL stresses the absence of strangeness or unexpectedness; CUSTOMARY applies to what accords with the practices, conventions, or usages of an individual or community; HABITUAL suggests a practice settled or established by much repetition; WONTED closely approximates HABITUAL or CUSTOMARY; ACCUSTOMED is less emphatic than WONTED or HABITUAL in suggesting fixed habit or invariable custom

usu·fruct \'yü-zə-,frəkt\ *n* [L *ususfructus*, fr. *usus et fructus* use and enjoyment] **1 :** the legal right of using and enjoying the fruits or profits of something belonging to another **2 :** the right to use or enjoy something

1**usu·fruc·tu·ary** \,yü-zə-'frək-chə-,wer-ē\ *n* **1 :** one having the usufruct of property **2 :** one having the use or enjoyment of something

2**usufructuary** *adj* **:** of, relating to, or having the character of a usufruct

usu·rer \'yü-zhər-ər, 'yüzh-rər\ *n* **:** one that lends money esp. at an exorbitant rate

usu·ri·ous \yu̇-'zhu̇r-ē-əs\ *adj* **1 :** practicing usury **2 :** involving usury **:** of the character of usury — **usu·ri·ous·ly** *adv* — **usu·ri·ous·ness** *n*

usurp \yu̇-'sərp, -'zərp\ *vb* [ME *usurpen*, fr. MF *usurper*, fr. L *usurpare*, lit., to take possession of by use, fr. *usu* (abl. of *usus* use) + *rapere* to seize — more at RAPID] *vt* **:** to seize and hold (as office, place, powers) in possession by force or without right ⟨~ a throne⟩ ~ *vi* **:** to seize or exercise authority or possession wrongfully **syn** see APPROPRIATE — **usur·pa·tion** \,yü-sər-'pā-shən, ,yü-zər-\ *n* — **usurp·er** \yu̇-'sər-pər, -'zər-\ *n*

usu·ry \'yüzh-(ə-)rē\ *n* [ME, fr. ML *usuria*, alter. of L *usura*, fr. *usus*, pp. of *uti* to use] **1** *archaic* **:** INTEREST **2 :** the lending of money with an interest charge for its use **3 :** an unconscionable or exorbitant rate or amount of interest; *specif* **:** interest in excess of a legal rate charged to a borrower for the use of money

ut \'ət, 'üt, 'u̇t\ *n* [ME, first note in the diatonic scale, fr. ML, fr. the syllable sung to this note in a medieval hymn to St. John the Baptist] **:** the musical tone *C* in the French fixed-do system replaced in solmization by *do*

Ute \'yüt\ *n, pl* **Ute** *or* **Utes** [Ute *Yuta*] **1 :** a group of Shoshonean peoples of Colorado, Utah, and New Mexico **2 :** a member of any of the Ute peoples

uten·sil \yu̇-'ten(t)-səl, 'yü-,\ *n* [ME, vessels for domestic use, fr. MF *utensile*, fr. L *utensilia*, fr. neut. pl. of *utensilis* useful, fr. *uti* to use] **1 :** an instrument or vessel used in a household and esp. a kitchen **2 :** a useful tool or implement **syn** see IMPLEMENT

uter·ine \'yüt-ə-rən, -,rīn\ *adj* [ME, fr. LL *uterinus*, fr. L *uterus*] **1 :** born of the same mother but by a different father **2 :** of, relating to, or affecting the uterus

uter·us \'yüt-ə-rəs, 'yü-trəs\ *n, pl* **uteri** \-,rī, -,rē, -,trī, -,trē\ [L] **1 :** an organ of the female mammal for containing and usu. for nourishing the young during development previous to birth — called also *womb* **2 :** an analogous structure in some lower animals in which eggs or young develop

Uther \'yü-thər\ *n* **:** a legendary king of Britain and father of Arthur — called also *Uther Pendragon*

utile \'yüt-ᵊl, 'yü-,tīl\ *adj* [MF, fr. L *utilis*] **:** USEFUL

1**util·i·tar·i·an** \yu̇-,til-ə-'ter-ē-ən, ,yü-\ *n* **:** an advocate or adherent of utilitarianism

2**utilitarian** *adj* **1 :** of or relating to or advocating utilitarianism **2 :** marked by utilitarian views or practices **3 a :** of, relating to, or aiming at utility **b :** exhibiting or preferring mere utility

util·i·tar·i·an·ism \-ē-ə-,niz-əm\ *n* **1 :** a doctrine that the useful is the good and that the determining consideration of right conduct should be the usefulness of its consequences; *specif* **:** a theory that the aim of action is the largest possible balance of pleasure over pain or the greatest happiness of the greatest number **2 :** utilitarian character, spirit, or quality

1**util·i·ty** \yu̇-'til-ət-ē\ *n* [ME *utilite*, fr. MF *utilité*, fr. L *utilitat-*, *utilitas*, fr. *utilis* useful, fr. *uti* to use] **1 :** the quality or state of being useful **:** USEFULNESS **2 :** something useful or designed for use **3 a :** PUBLIC UTILITY **b** (1) **:** a service provided by a public utility (as light, power, or water) (2) **:** equipment or a piece of equipment to provide such service or a similar service

2**utility** *adj* **1 :** capable of serving as a substitute in various roles or positions ⟨~ infielder⟩ **2 a :** kept for the production of a useful product rather than for show or as pets **b :** being of a usable but inferior grade ⟨~ beef⟩ **3 :** serving primarily for utility rather than beauty **:** UTILITARIAN **4 :** designed for general use

uti·liz·able \'yüt-ᵊl-,ī-zə-bəl\ *adj* **:** capable of being utilized

uti·li·za·tion \,yüt-ᵊl-ə-'zā-shən\ *n* **:** the action of utilizing **:** the state of being utilized

uti·lize \'yüt-ᵊl-,īz\ *vt* [F *utiliser*, fr. *utile*] **:** to make use of **:** convert to use **syn** see USE — **uti·liz·er** *n*

ut·most \'ət-,mōst\ *adj* [ME, alter. of *utmest*, fr. OE *ūtmest*, superl. adj., fr. *ūt* out, adv. — more at OUT] **1 :** situated at the farthest or most distant point **:** EXTREME **2 :** of the greatest or highest degree, quantity, number, or amount — **utmost** *n*

Uto-Az·tec·an \,yü-(,)tō-'az-,tek-ən\ *n* [*Ute* + *-o-* + *Aztec*] **:** a language phylum comprising the Nahuatlan, Taracahitian, Piman, and Shoshonean families — **Uto-Aztecan** *adj*

uto·pia \yu̇-'tō-pē-ə\ *n* [*Utopia*, imaginary and ideal country in *Utopia* (1516) by Sir Thomas More, fr. Gk *ou* not, no + *topos* place] **1 :** an imaginary and indefinitely remote place **2** *often cap* **:** a place of ideal perfection esp. in laws, government, and social conditions **3 :** an impractical scheme for social improvement

1**uto·pi·an** \-pē-ən\ *adj, often cap* **1 :** of, relating to, or having the characteristics of a utopia; *specif* **:** having impossibly ideal conditions esp. of social organization **2 :** proposing or advocating impractically ideal social and political schemes **3 :** impossibly ideal **:** VISIONARY **4 :** believing in, advocating, or having the characteristics of utopian socialism

2**utopian** *n* **1 :** one that believes in the perfectibility of human society **2 :** one that proposes or advocates utopian schemes

uto·pi·an·ism \-pē-ə-,niz-əm\ *n* **1 :** a utopian idea or theory **2** *often cap* **:** the body of ideas, views, or aims of a utopian

utopian socialism *n* **:** socialism based on a belief that social ownership of the means of production can be achieved by voluntary and peaceful surrender of their holdings by propertied groups

uto·pism \'yüt-ə-,piz-əm, yu̇-'tō-\ *n* **:** UTOPIANISM 2 — **uto·pist** \-pəst\ *n* — **uto·pis·tic** \,yüt-ə-'pis-tik, ,yü-,tō-, yu̇-,tō-\ *adj*

utri·cle \'yü-tri-kəl\ *n* [L *utriculus*, dim. of *uter* leather bag] **:** any of various small pouches or saccate parts of an animal or plant body: as **a :** the part of the membranous labyrinth of the ear into which the semicircular canals open **b :** a small one-celled usu. indehiscent one-seeded or few-seeded achene with thin membranous pericarp

utric·u·lar \yu̇-'trik-yə-lər\ *adj* **:** of, relating to, resembling, or containing a utricle

utric·u·lar·ia \yu̇-,trik-yə-'lar-ē-ə, -'ler-\ *n* [NL, genus name, fr. L *utriculus*] **:** a bladderwort (genus *Utricularia*)

utric·u·lus \yu̇-'trik-yə-ləs\ *n* [L, small bag] **:** UTRICLE; *esp* **:** that of the ear

1**ut·ter** \'ət-ər\ *adj* [ME, remote, fr. OE *ūtera* outer, compar. adj. fr. *ūt* out, adv. — more at OUT] **:** ABSOLUTE, TOTAL — **ut·ter·ly** *adv*

2**utter** *vt* [ME *uttren*, fr. *utter* outside, adv., fr. OE *ūtor*, compar. of *ūt* out] **1** *obs* **:** to offer for sale **2 a :** to send forth as a sound **b :** to give utterance to **:** PRONOUNCE, SPEAK **c :** to give public expression to **:** express in words **3 :** to put (as currency) into circulation **4 :** to put forth or out **:** DISCHARGE **syn** see EXPRESS — **ut·ter·able** \'ət-ə-rə-bəl\ *adj* — **ut·ter·er** \'ət-ər-ər\ *n*

1**ut·ter·ance** \'ət-ə-rən(t)s, 'ə-trən(t)s\ *n* [ME *uttraunce*, modif. of MF *outrance*] **:** the last extremity **:** BITTER END

2**utterance** *n* **1 :** something uttered; *esp* **:** an oral or written statement **:** a stated or published expression **2 :** vocal expression **:** SPEECH **3 :** power, style, or manner of speaking

ut·ter·most \'ət-ər-,mōst\ *adj* [ME, alter. of *uttermest*, fr. 1*utter* + *-mest* (as in *utmest* utmost)] **:** EXTREME, UTMOST — **uttermost** *n*

uva·rov·ite \yu̇-'vär-ə-,vīt, ü-\ *n* [G *uwarowit*, fr. Count Sergei S. *Uvarov* †1855 Russ statesman] **:** an emerald green calcium-chromium garnet $Ca_3Cr_2(SiO_4)_3$

uvea \'yü-vē-ə\ *n* [ML, fr. L *uva* grape] **:** the posterior pigmented layer of the iris; *also* **:** the iris and ciliary body together with the choroid coat — **uve·al** \-vē-əl\ *adj* — **uve·ous** \-vē-əs\ *adj*

uve·itis \,yü-vē-'īt-əs\ *n* **:** inflammation of the uvea of the eye

uvu·la \'yü-vyə-lə\ *n, pl* **uvulas** *or* **uvu·lae** \-,lē, -,lī\ [ML, dim. of L *uva* grape, uvula; akin to OE *īw* yew] **:** the pendent fleshy lobe in the middle of the posterior border of the soft palate

uvu·lar \-lər\ *adj* **:** of or relating to the uvula ⟨~ glands⟩; *specif* **:** produced with the aid of the uvula — **uvu·lar·ly** *adv*

ux·o·ri·al \,ək-'sōr-ē-əl, -'sȯr-; ,əg-'zōr-, -'zȯr-\ *adj* [L *uxorius*] **:** of, relating to, or characteristic of a wife

ux·or·i·cide \,ək-'sȯr-ə-,sīd, -'sär-; ,əg-'zȯr-, -'zär-\ *n* **1** [ML *uxoricidium*, fr. L *uxor* wife + *-i-* + *-cidium* -cide] **:** murder of a wife by her husband **2** [L *uxor* + E *-i-* + *-cide*] **:** a wife murderer

ux·o·ri·ous \,ək-'sōr-ē-əs, -'sȯr-; ,əg-'zōr-, -'zȯr-\ *adj* [L *uxorius* uxorious, uxorial, fr. *uxor* wife] **:** excessively fond of or submissive to a wife — **ux·o·ri·ous·ly** *adv* — **ux·o·ri·ous·ness** *n*

Uz·bek \'u̇z-,bek, 'əz-\ *or* **Uz·beg** \-,beg\ *n* **1 :** a member of a Turkic people of Turkestan and esp. of the Uzbek Republic of the U.S.S.R. **2 :** the Turkic language of the Uzbek people

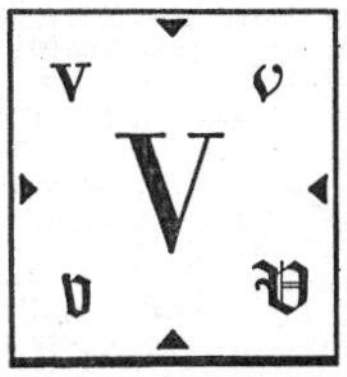

v \'vē\ *n, often cap, often attrib* **1 a :** the 22d letter of the English alphabet **b :** a graphic representation of this letter **c :** a speech counterpart of orthographic *v* **2 :** FIVE **3 :** a graphic device for reproducing the letter *v* **4 :** one designated *v* esp. as the 21st or when j is used for the 10th the 22d in order or class **5 :** something shaped like the letter V

va·can·cy \'vā-kən-sē\ *n* **1** *archaic* **:** an interval of leisure **2 :** physical or mental inactivity or relaxation **:** IDLENESS **3 a :** a vacating of an office, post, or piece of property **b :** the time such office or property is vacant **4 :** a vacant office, post, or tenancy **5 :** empty space **6 :** the state of being vacant **:** VACUITY

va·cant \-kənt\ *adj* [ME, fr. OF, fr. L *vacant-, vacans,* prp. of *vacare* to be empty, be free — more at VACUUM] **1 :** not occupied by an incumbent, possessor, or officer ⟨~ office⟩ ⟨~ throne⟩ **2 :** being without content or occupant ⟨~ seat in a bus⟩ ⟨~ room⟩ **3 :** free from activity or work **:** DISENGAGED ⟨~ hours⟩ **4 a :** STUPID, FOOLISH ⟨~ mind⟩ **b :** EXPRESSIONLESS ⟨~ face⟩ **c :** marked by a respite from reflection or care **5 :** not lived in ⟨~ house⟩ **6 a :** not put to use ⟨~ land⟩ **b :** having no heir or claimant **:** ABANDONED ⟨~ estate⟩ **syn** see EMPTY — **va·cant·ly** *adv* — **va·cant·ness** *n*

va·cate \'vā-,kāt, vā-'\ *vb* [L *vacatus,* pp. of *vacare*] *vt* **1 :** to make legally void **:** ANNUL **2 a :** to deprive of an incumbent or occupant **b :** to give up the incumbency or occupancy of ~ *vi* **:** to vacate an office, post, or tenancy

[1]**va·ca·tion** \vā-'kā-shən, və-\ *n, often attrib* [ME *vacacioun,* fr. MF *vacation,* fr. L *vacation-, vacatio* freedom, exemption, fr. *vacatus*] **1 :** a respite or a time of respite from something **:** INTERMISSION **2 a :** a scheduled period during which activity (as of a court or school) is suspended **b :** a period of exemption from work granted to an employee for rest and relaxation **3 :** a period spent away from home or business in travel or recreation ⟨had a restful ~ at the beach⟩ **4 :** an act or an instance of vacating

[2]**vacation** *vi* **va·ca·tion·ing** \-sh(ə-)niŋ\ **:** to take or spend a vacation

va·ca·tion·er \-sh(ə-)nər\ *n* **:** VACATIONIST

va·ca·tion·ist \-sh(ə-)nəst\ *n* **:** a person taking a vacation

va·ca·tion·land \-shən-,land\ *n* **:** an area with recreational attractions and facilities for vacationists

vac·ci·nal \'vak-sən-ᵊl, vak-'sēn-\ *adj* **:** of or relating to vaccine or vaccination

[1]**vac·ci·nate** \'vak-sə-,nāt\ *vt* **1 :** to inoculate (a person) with cowpox virus in order to produce immunity to smallpox **2 :** to administer a vaccine to usu. by injection ~ *vi* **:** to perform or practice vaccination — **vac·ci·na·tor** \'vak-sə-,nāt-ər\ *n*

[2]**vac·ci·nate** \'vak-sə-,nāt, -nət\ *n* **:** a vaccinated individual

vac·ci·na·tion \,vak-sə-'nā-shən\ *n* **1 :** the act of vaccinating **2 :** the scar left by vaccinating

[1]**vac·cine** \vak-'sēn, 'vak-,\ *adj* [L *vaccinus* of or from cows, fr. *vacca* cow; akin to Skt *vaśā* cow] **1 :** of, relating to, or derived from cows; *esp* **:** derived from cows infected with cowpox or inoculated with its virus ⟨~ lymph⟩ **2** [NL *vaccinus,* fr. L] **:** of or relating to vaccinia or vaccination ⟨a ~ pustule⟩

[2]**vaccine** *n* **1 :** matter or a preparation containing the virus of cowpox in a form used for vaccination **2 :** a preparation of killed microorganisms, living attenuated organisms, or living fully virulent organisms that is administered to produce or artificially increase immunity to a particular disease

vac·cin·ia \vak-'sin-ē-ə\ *n, often attrib* [NL, fr. *vaccinus*] **:** COWPOX — **vac·cin·i·al** \-ē-əl\ *adj*

vac·il·lant \'vas-ə-lənt\ *adj* **:** VACILLATING, UNCERTAIN

vac·il·late \'vas-ə-,lāt\ *vi* [L *vacillatus,* pp. of *vacillare* to sway, waver — more at PREVARICATE] **1 a :** to sway through lack of equilibrium **b :** FLUCTUATE, OSCILLATE **2 :** to waver in mind, will, or feeling **:** hesitate in choice of opinions or courses **syn** see HESITATE — **vac·il·la·tor** \'vas-ə-,lāt-ər\ *n*

vac·il·lat·ing·ly \'vas-ə-,lāt-iŋ-lē\ *adv* **:** in a vacillating manner

vac·il·la·tion \,vas-ə-'lā-shən\ *n* **1 :** an act or instance of vacillating **2 :** IRRESOLUTION, CHANGEABLENESS

vac·il·la·to·ry \'vas-(ə-)lə-,tōr-ē, -,tȯr-\ *adj* **:** VACILLATING

va·cu·ity \va-'kyü-ət-ē, və-\ *n* [L *vacuitas,* fr. *vacuus* empty] **1 :** an empty space **2 :** the state, fact, or quality of being vacuous **3 :** a vacuous or inane thing

vac·u·o·lar \,vak-yə-'wō-lər\ *adj* **:** of, relating to, or being a vacuole

vac·u·o·late \'vak-yə-(,)wō-,lāt\ *or* **vac·u·o·lat·ed** \-,lāt-əd\ *adj* **:** containing one or more vacuoles

vac·u·o·la·tion \,vak-yə-(,)wō-'lā-shən\ *n* **:** the development or formation of vacuoles

vac·u·ole \'vak-yə-,wōl\ *n* [F, lit., small vacuum, fr. L *vacuum*] **1 :** a small cavity or space in the tissues of an organism containing air or fluid **2 :** a cavity or vesicle in the protoplasm of a cell containing fluid

vac·u·ous \'vak-yə-wəs\ *adj* [L *vacuus*] **1 :** EMPTY **2 :** marked by lack of ideas or intelligence **:** STUPID, INANE ⟨~ mind⟩ ⟨~ expression⟩ **3 :** devoid of serious occupation **:** IDLE **syn** see EMPTY — **vac·u·ous·ly** *adv* — **vac·u·ous·ness** *n*

[1]**vac·u·um** \'vak-yə(-wə)m, -(,)yüm\ *n, pl* **vac·u·ums** *or* **vac·ua** \-yə-wə\ [L, fr. neut. of *vacuus* empty; akin to L *vacare* to be empty] **1 :** emptiness of space **2 a :** a space absolutely devoid of matter **b :** a space partially exhausted (as to the highest degree possible) by artificial means (as an air pump) **c :** a degree of rarefaction below atmospheric pressure **:** negative pressure **3 a :** a vacant space **:** VOID **b :** a state of isolation from outside influences **4 :** a device creating or utilizing a partial vacuum

[2]**vacuum** *adj* **1 :** of, containing, producing, or utilizing a partial vacuum **2 :** of or relating to a vacuum device or system

[3]**vacuum** *vt* **:** to use a vacuum device (as a cleaner) upon

vacuum bottle *n* **:** a cylindrical container with a vacuum between an inner and an outer wall used to keep liquids either hot or cold for considerable periods

vacuum cleaner *n* **:** an electrical appliance for cleaning (as floors, carpets, tapestry, or upholstered work) by suction

vacuum gauge *n* **:** a gauge indicating degree of negative pressure

vac·u·um·ize \'vak-yə-(wə-),mīz\ *vt* **1 :** to produce a vacuum in **2 :** to clean, dry, or pack by a vacuum mechanism or in a vacuum container

vac·u·um–packed \,vak-yə(-wə)m-'pakt, -(,)yüm-\ *adj* **:** having much of the air removed before being hermetically sealed

vacuum pan *n* **:** a tank with a vacuum pump for rapid evaporation and condensation (as of sugar syrup) by boiling at a low temperature

vacuum pump *n* **1 :** PULSOMETER **2 :** a pump for exhausting gas from an enclosed space

vacuum tube *n* **:** an electron tube evacuated to a high degree of vacuum

va·de me·cum \,vād-ē-'mē-kəm, ,väd-\ *n, pl* **vade mecums** [L, go with me] **1 :** a book for ready reference **:** MANUAL **2 :** something regularly carried about by a person

va·dose \'vā-,dōs\ *adj* [L *vadosus* shallow, fr. *vadum,* n., shallow, ford; akin to L *vadere* to go — more at WADE] **:** of, relating to, or being water or solutions in the earth's crust above the permanent groundwater level

vag- *or* **vago-** *comb form* [ISV, fr. NL *vagus*] **:** vagus nerve ⟨*vag*al⟩ ⟨*vago*tomy⟩

[1]**vag·a·bond** \'vag-ə-,bänd\ *adj* [ME, fr. MF, fr. L *vagabundus,* fr. *vagari* to wander] **1 :** moving from place to place without a fixed home **:** WANDERING **2 a :** of, relating to, or characteristic of a wanderer **b :** leading an unsettled, irresponsible, or disreputable life

[2]**vagabond** *n* **:** one leading a vagabond life; *specif* **:** TRAMP — **vag·a·bond·ism** \-,bän-,diz-əm\ *n*

[3]**vagabond** *vi* **:** to wander in the manner of a vagabond **:** roam about

vag·a·bond·age \-,bän-dij\ *n* **1 :** the act, condition, or practice of a vagabond **:** the state or habit of wandering about **2 :** VAGABONDS

vag·a·bond·ish \-dish\ *adj* **:** of, relating to, or characteristic of a vagabond

va·gal \'vā-gəl\ *adj* [ISV] **:** of, relating to, mediated by, or being the vagus nerve

va·gar·i·ous \vā-'ger-ē-əs, və-, -'gar-\ *adj* **:** marked by vagaries **:** CAPRICIOUS, WHIMSICAL — **va·gar·i·ous·ly** *adv*

va·ga·ry \'vā-gə-rē; və-'ge(ə)r-ē, -'ga(ə)r-, vā-'\ *n* [prob. fr. L *vagari* to wander; akin to L *vagus* wandering — more at PREVARICATE] **:** an eccentric or unpredictable manifestation, action, or notion **syn** see CAPRICE

vag·ile \'vaj-əl, -,īl\ *adj* [ISV, fr. L *vagus* wandering] **:** free to move about — **va·gil·i·ty** \və-'jil-ət-ē\ *n*

va·gi·na \və-'jī-nə\ *n, pl* **va·gi·nae** \-'jī-(,)nē\ *or* **vaginas** [L, lit., sheath] **1 :** a canal that leads from the uterus to the external orifice of the genital canal **2 :** SHEATH; *specif* **:** the expanded or ensheathing part of the base of a leaf

vag·i·nal \'vaj-ən-ᵊl\ *adj* **1 :** THECAL **2 :** of, relating to, or affecting the genital vagina

vag·i·nate \'vaj-ə-,nāt\ *or* **vag·i·nat·ed** \-,nāt-əd\ *adj* **:** invested with or as if with a sheath

vag·i·nic·o·lous \,vaj-ə-'nik-ə-ləs\ *adj* [L *vagina* sheath + E *-colous*] **:** secreting and inhabiting a theca

vag·i·ni·tis \,vaj-ə-'nīt-əs\ *n* **:** inflammation of the vagina or of a sheath (as a tendon sheath)

va·go·de·pres·sor \,vā-(,)gō-di-'pres-ər\ *adj* **:** depressing to the vagus nerve — used chiefly of a drug

va·got·o·my \vā-'gät-ə-mē\ *n* [ISV] **:** surgical division of the vagus nerve

va·go·to·nia \,vā-gə-'tō-nē-ə\ *n* [NL] **:** excessive excitability of the vagus nerve resulting typically in vasomotor instability, constipation, and sweating — **va·go·ton·ic** \-'tän-ik\ *adj*

va·go·trop·ic \-'träp-ik\ *adj* **:** acting selectively upon the vagus nerve ⟨~ drugs⟩

va·gran·cy \'vā-grən-sē\ *n* **1 :** VAGARY **2 :** the state or action of being vagrant **3 :** the offense of being a vagrant

[1]**va·grant** \'vā-grənt\ *n* [ME *vagraunt,* prob. modif. of MF *waucrant, wacrant* wandering, fr. OF, fr. prp. of *waucrer, wacrer* to roll, wander, of Gmc origin; akin to OE *wealcan* to roll — more at WALK] **1 a :** one who has no established residence and wanders idly from place to place without lawful or visible means of support **b :** one (as a common prostitute or drunkard) whose conduct constitutes statutory vagrancy **2 :** WANDERER, ROVER

[2]**vagrant** *adj* **1 :** wandering about from place to place usu. with no means of support **2 a :** having a fleeting, wayward, or inconstant quality **b :** having no fixed course **:** RANDOM — **va·grant·ly** *adv*

va·grom \'vā-grəm\ *adj* **:** VAGRANT

vague \'vāg\ *adj* [MF, fr. L *vagus,* lit., wandering] **1 a :** not clearly expressed **:** stated in indefinite terms ⟨~ accusation⟩ **b :** not having a precise meaning ⟨~ term of abuse⟩ **2 a :** not clearly defined, grasped, or understood **:** INDISTINCT ⟨~ idea⟩ **b :** not clearly felt or sensed **:** somewhat subconscious ⟨a ~ longing⟩ **3 :** not thinking or expressing one's thoughts clearly or precisely ⟨~ about dates and places⟩ **4 :** not sharply outlined **:** HAZY **syn** see OBSCURE — **vague·ly** *adv*

vague·ness \-nəs\ *n* **1 :** the quality or state of being vague **2 :** something that is vague

va·gus \'vā-gəs\ *n, pl* **va·gi** \'vā-,gī, -,jī\ [NL *vagus nervus,* lit., wandering nerve] **:** either of the tenth pair of cranial nerves arising from the medulla and supplying chiefly the viscera esp. with autonomic sensory and motor fibers

[1]**vail** \'vā(ə)l\ *vb* [ME *vailen,* fr. OF *vaill-,* stem of *valoir* to be of worth, fr. L *valēre* to be strong — more at WIELD] *archaic* **:** AVAIL

[2]**vail** *vt* [ME *valen,* partly fr. MF *valer* (short for *avaler* to let fall) & partly short for ME *avalen* to let fall, fr. MF *avaler,* fr. OF, fr. *aval* downward, fr. *a* to (fr. L *ad*) + *val* valley — more at AT] **:** to lower often as a sign of respect or submission

vain \'vān\ *adj* [ME, fr. OF, fr. L *vanus* empty, vain — more at WANE] **1 :** having no real value **:** IDLE, WORTHLESS **2 :** FRUITLESS, UNSUCCESSFUL **3 :** FOOLISH, SILLY **4 :** having or showing undue or excessive pride in one's appearance or achievements **:** CONCEITED — **vain·ly** *adv* — **vain·ness** \'vān-nəs\ *n*

syn VAIN, NUGATORY, OTIOSE, IDLE, EMPTY, HOLLOW mean being without worth or significance. VAIN implies either absolute or

ə abut; ᵊ kitten; ər further; a back; ā bake; ä cot, cart; aù out; ch chin; e less; ē easy; g gift; i trip; ī life
j joke; ŋ sing; ō flow; ȯ flaw; ȯi coin; th thin; th this; ü loot; ù foot; y yet; yü few; yù furious; zh vision

relative absence of value; NUGATORY suggests triviality or inoperativeness; OTIOSE suggests a lack of excuse for being as serving no purpose and being an encumbrance or superfluity; IDLE suggests being incapable of worthwhile use or effect; EMPTY and HOLLOW suggest a deceiving lack of real substance or soundness or genuineness **syn** see in addition FUTILE, PROUD
— **in vain** *adv* **1 :** to no end **:** without success or result **2 :** in an irreverent or blasphemous manner

vain·glo·ri·ous \(')vān-'glōr-ē-əs, -'glȯr-\ *adj* **:** marked by vainglory **:** BOASTFUL **syn** see PROUD — **vain·glo·ri·ous·ly** *adv* — **vain·glo·ri·ous·ness** *n*

vain·glo·ry \'vān-,glōr-ē, -,glȯr-, (')vān-'\ *n* **1 :** excessive or ostentatious pride esp. in one's achievements **2 :** vain display or show **:** VANITY

vair \'va(ə)r, 've(ə)r\ *n* [ME *veir*, fr. OF *vair*, fr. *vair*, adj., variegated, fr. L *varius* variegated, various] **:** the bluish gray and white fur of a squirrel prized for ornament in medieval times

Vaish·na·va \'vīsh-nə-və\ *n* [Skt *vaiṣṇava* of Vishnu, fr. *Viṣṇu* Vishnu] **:** a worshiper of Vishnu — **Vaishnava** *adj* — **Vaish·na·vism** \-nə-,viz-əm\ *n*

Vais·ya \'vīsh-(y)ə\ *n* [Skt *vaiśya*, fr. *viś* settlement; akin to Gk *oikos* house — more at VICINITY] **:** a Hindu of an upper caste traditionally assigned to commercial and agricultural occupations

va·lance \'val-ən(t)s, 'vāl-\ *n* [ME *vallance*, perh. fr. *Valence*, France] **1 :** a drapery hung along the edge of a bed, table, altar, canopy, or shelf **2 :** a short drapery or wood or metal frame used as a decorative heading to conceal the top of curtains and fixtures — **va·lanced** \-ən(t)st\ *adj*

[1]**vale** \'vā(ə)l\ *n* [ME, fr. OF *val*, fr. L *valles*, *vallis*; akin to L *volvere* to roll — more at VOLUBLE] **:** VALLEY, DALE

[2]**va·le** \'väl-(,)ā, 'wäl-\ *n* [L, farewell, interj., fr. 2d sing. imper. of *valēre* to be strong, be well — more at WIELD] **:** a salutation of leave-taking

vale·dic·tion \,val-ə-'dik-shən\ *n* [L *valedictus*, pp. of *valedicere* to say farewell, fr. *vale* farewell + *dicere* to say — more at DICTION] **:** an act or utterance of leave-taking **:** FAREWELL

vale·dic·to·ri·an \,val-ə-,dik-'tōr-ē-ən, -'tȯr-\ *n* **:** the student usu. of the highest rank in a graduating class who delivers the valedictory oration at the commencement exercises

[1]**vale·dic·to·ry** \-'dik-t(ə-)rē\ *adj* [L *valedictus*] **:** of or relating to leave-taking **:** FAREWELL; *esp* **:** given at a leave-taking ceremony (as school commencement exercises)

[2]**valedictory** *n* **:** a valedictory oration or statement

va·lence \'vā-lən(t)s\ *n* [LL *valentia* power, capacity, fr. L *valent-*, *valens*, prp. of *valēre* to be strong] **1 a :** the degree of combining power of an element or radical as shown by the number of atomic weights of a univalent element (as hydrogen) with which the atomic weight of the element or the partial molecular weight of the radical will combine or for which it can be substituted or with which it can be compared **b :** a unit of valence ⟨the four ~*s* of carbon⟩ **2 :** relative capacity to unite, react, or interact (as with antigens or a biological substrate)

Va·len·ci·ennes \və-,len(t)-sē-'en(z), ,val-ən-sē-\ *n* [*Valenciennes*, France] **:** a fine bobbin lace

-va·lent \'vā-lənt\ *adj comb form* [ISV, fr. L *valent-*, *valens*] **:** having a (specified) valence or valences ⟨bi*valent*⟩ ⟨multi*valent*⟩

val·en·tine \'val-ən-,tīn\ *n* **1 :** a sweetheart chosen or complimented on St. Valentine's Day **2 a :** a gift or greeting sent or given esp. to a sweetheart on St. Valentine's Day **b :** an ornamental greeting of a mock sentimental or comic character sent often anonymously on this day

Valentine Day *or* **Valentine's Day** *n* **:** SAINT VALENTINE'S DAY

val·er·ate \'val-ə-,rāt\ *n* **:** a salt or ester of valeric acid

va·le·ri·an \və-'lir-ē-ən\ *n* [ME, fr. MF or ML; MF *valeriane*, fr. ML *valeriana*, prob. fr. fem. of *valerianus* of Valeria, fr. *Valeria*, Roman province formerly part of Pannonia] **1 :** any of a genus (*Valeriana* of the family Valerianaceae, the valerian family) of perennial herbs many of which possess medicinal properties **2 :** a drug consisting of the dried rootstock and roots of the garden heliotrope (*V. officinalis*) formerly used as a carminative and sedative

va·le·ric acid \və-,lir-ik-, -,ler-\ *also* **va·le·ri·an·ic acid** \-,lir-ē-,an-ik-\ *n* [*valerian*; fr. its occurrence in the root of valerian] **:** any of four isomeric fatty acids C_4H_9COOH or a mixture of these; *esp* **:** a liquid acid of disagreeable odor obtained from valerian or made synthetically and used in organic synthesis

[1]**va·let** \'val-ət, va-'lā, 'val-(,)ā\ *n* [MF *vaslet*, *varlet*, *valet* young nobleman, page, domestic servant, fr. (assumed) ML *vassellittus*, dim. of ML *vassus* servant — more at VASSAL] **1 :** a man's male servant who performs personal services (as taking care of clothing) **2 :** an employee (as of a hotel) who performs personal services for guests

[2]**valet** *vt* **:** to serve as a valet

va·let de cham·bre \va-,lād-ə-'shäⁿbrᵊ, ,val-(,)ād-\ *n, pl* **va·lets de chambre** *same*\ [F, lit., chamber valet] **:** VALET 1

val·e·tu·di·nar·i·an \,val-ə-,t(y)üd-ᵊn-'er-ē-ən\ *n* [L *valetudinarius* sickly, infirm, fr. *valetudin-*, *valetudo* state of health, sickness, fr. *valēre* to be strong, be well] **:** a person of a weak or sickly constitution; *esp* **:** one whose chief concern is his invalidism — **valetudinarian** *adj*

val·e·tu·di·nar·i·an·ism \-ē-ə-,niz-əm\ *n* **:** the condition or state of mind of a valetudinarian

[1]**val·e·tu·di·nary** \-'t(y)üd-ᵊn-,er-ē\ *adj* [L *valetudinarius*] **:** VALETUDINARIAN

[2]**valetudinary** *n* **:** VALETUDINARIAN

val·gus \'val-gəs\ *adj* [NL, fr. L, bowlegged — more at WALK] **:** turned abnormally outward **:** TWISTED — used esp. of the lower extremities — **valgus** *n*

Val·hal·la \val-'hal-ə, väl-'häl-\ *n* [G & ON; G *Walhalla*, fr. ON *Valhöll*, lit., hall of the slain, fr. *valr* the slain + *höll* hall; akin to OE *wæl* slaughter, the slain, OIr *fuil* blood, and to OE *heall* hall] **:** the hall of Odin into which the souls of heroes slain in battle are received

val·iance \'val-yən(t)s\ *n* **:** VALOR

val·ian·cy \-yən-sē\ *n* **:** VALOR

[1]**val·iant** \-yənt\ *adj* [ME *valiaunt*, fr. MF *vaillant*, fr. OF, fr. prp. of *valoir* to be of worth, fr. L *valēre* to be strong — more at WIELD] **:** possessing or exhibiting valor **:** STOUTHEARTED — **val·iant·ly** *adv* — **val·iant·ness** *n*

[2]**valiant** *n* **:** a valiant person

val·id \'val-əd\ *adj* [MF or ML; MF *valide*, fr. ML *validus*, fr. L strong, fr. *valēre*] **1 :** having legal efficacy or force; *esp* **:** executed with the proper legal authority and formalities ⟨a ~ contract⟩ **2 a :** well grounded **:** SOUND ⟨a ~ argument⟩ **b** (1) **:** having a conclusion correctly derived from premises ⟨~ argument⟩ (2) **:** correctly derived from premises ⟨~ inference⟩ **3 :** EFFECTIVE, EFFICACIOUS ⟨~ methods⟩ — **val·id·ly** *adv* — **val·id·ness** *n*

syn VALID, SOUND, COGENT, CONVINCING, TELLING mean having such force as to compel acceptance. VALID implies being supported by objective truth or generally accepted authority; SOUND implies being based on flawless reasoning and on solid grounds; COGENT may stress weight of sound argument or evidence or the lucidness of the presentation of an argument; CONVINCING stresses having the power of overcoming doubt, opposition, or reluctance; TELLING suggests having the power of producing quickly the desired effect of an argument, phrase, or word

val·i·date \'val-ə-,dāt\ *vt* **1 a :** to make legally valid **b :** to grant official sanction to by marking **c :** to confirm the validity of (an election); *also* **:** to declare (a person) elected **2 :** VERIFY, SUBSTANTIATE **syn** see CONFIRM

val·i·da·tion \,val-ə-'dā-shən\ *n* **:** an act, process, or instance of validating; *specif* **:** the process of determining the degree of validity of a measuring device

va·lid·i·ty \və-'lid-ət-ē\ *n* **:** the quality or state of being valid

va·line \'val-,ēn, 'vā-,lēn\ *n* [ISV, fr. *valeric* (*acid*)] **:** a crystalline essential amino acid $C_5H_{11}NO_2$ that occurs esp. in fibrous proteins

va·lise \və-'lēs\ *n* [F, fr. It *valigia*] **:** TRAVELING BAG

Val·ky·rie \val-'kir-ē, -'kī(ə)r-, 'val-,\ *n* [G & ON; G *walküre*, fr. ON *valkyrja*, lit., chooser of the slain; akin to OE *wælcyrige* witch; both fr. a prehistoric WGmc-NGmc compound whose first constituent is represented by ON *valr* the slain and whose second constituent is akin to OE *cēosan* to choose — more at CHOOSE] **:** one of the maidens of Odin who choose the heroes to be slain in battle and conduct them to Valhalla

val·late \'val-,āt\ *adj* [L *vallatus*, pp. of *vallare* to surround with a wall, fr. *vallum* wall, rampart — more at WALL] **:** having a raised edge surrounding a depression

val·la·tion \va-'lā-shən\ *n* [LL *vallation-*, *vallatio*, fr. L *vallatus*] *archaic* **:** an earthwork wall **:** RAMPART

val·lec·u·la \va-'lek-yə-lə\ *n, pl* **val·lec·u·lae** \-yə-,lē, -,lī\ [NL, fr. LL, little valley, dim. of L *valles* valley — more at VALE] **:** an anatomical groove, channel, or depression; *esp* **:** one between the base of the tongue and the epiglottis

val·lec·u·lar \-yə-lər\ *adj* **:** of or relating to a vallecula

val·lec·u·late \-lət\ *adj* **:** having valleculae

val·ley \'val-ē\ *n, often attrib* [ME *valey*, fr. OF *valee*, fr. *val* valley — more at VALE] **1 a :** an elongate depression of the earth's surface usu. between ranges of hills or mountains **b :** an area drained by a river and its tributaries **2 a :** HOLLOW, DEPRESSION **b :** the place of meeting of two slopes of a roof that form on the plan a reentrant angle

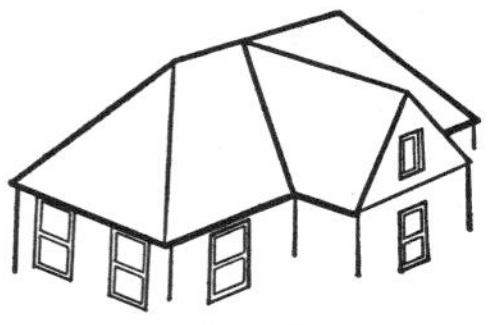
valley 2b

Va·lois \'val-,wä\ *adj* [*Valois*, French royal house] **:** of or relating to a French royal family furnishing the rulers of France from 1328 to 1589

va·lo·nia \və-'lō-nē-ə, -nyə\ *n* [It *vallonia*, fr. MGk *balanidia*, pl. of *balanidion*, dim. of Gk *balanos* acorn — more at GLAND] **:** dried acorn cups esp. from a Eurasian evergreen oak (*Quercus aegilops*) used in tanning or dressing leather

val·or \'val-ər\ *n* [ME, fr. MF *valour*, fr ML *valor* value, valor, fr. L *valēre* to be strong] **:** strength of mind or spirit that enables a man to encounter danger with firmness **:** personal bravery **syn** see HEROISM

val·o·ri·za·tion \,val-ə-rə-'zā-shən\ *n* [Pg *valorização*, fr. *valorizare* to valorize, fr. *valor* value, price, fr. ML] **:** the support of commodity prices by any of various forms of government subsidy

val·o·rize \'val-ə-,rīz\ *vt* **:** to set the price of (a commodity) by valorization

val·or·ous \'val-ə-rəs\ *adj* **1 :** possessing or exhibiting valor **:** BRAVE ⟨~ men⟩ **2 :** characterized by or performed with valor ⟨~ feats⟩ — **val·or·ous·ly** *adv*

valse \vàls\ *n* [F, fr. G *walzer*] **:** WALTZ; *specif* **:** a concert waltz

[1]**valu·able** \'val-yə-(wə-)bəl\ *adj* **1 a :** having monetary value **b :** worth a good price **2 a :** having value **b :** of great use or service **syn** see COSTLY — **valu·able·ness** *n* — **valu·ably** \-blē\ *adv*

[2]**valuable** *n* **:** a usu. personal possession (as a jewel) of relatively great monetary value

valuable consideration *n* **:** an equivalent or compensation having value that is given for something acquired or promised and that may consist either in a benefit accruing to one party or a loss falling upon the other

val·u·ate \'val-yə-,wāt\ *vt* **:** to place a value on **:** APPRAISE — **val·u·a·tor** \-,wāt-ər\ *n*

val·u·a·tion \,val-yə-'wā-shən\ *n* **1 :** the act or process of valuing; *specif* **:** appraisal of property **2 :** the estimated or determined market value of a thing **3 :** judgment or appreciation of worth or character

val·u·a·tion·al \-shnəl, -shən-ᵊl\ *adj* **:** of or relating to valuation — **val·u·a·tion·al·ly** \-ē\ *adv*

val·u·a·tor \'val-yə-,wāt-ər\ *n* **:** one that valuates; *specif* **:** APPRAISER

[1]**val·ue** \'val-(,)yü, -yə-w\ *n, often attrib* [ME, fr. MF, fr. (assumed) VL *valuta*, fr. fem. of *valutus*, pp. of L *valēre* to be worth, be strong] **1 :** a fair return or equivalent in goods, services, or money for something exchanged **2 :** the monetary worth of something **:** marketable price **3 :** relative worth, utility, or importance **:** degree of excellence **4 a :** a numerical quantity assigned or computed **b :** precise signification ⟨~ of a word⟩ **5 :** the relative duration of a musical note **6 a :** relative lightness or darkness of a color **:** LUMINOSITY **b :** the relation of one part in a picture to another with respect to lightness and darkness **7 :** something intrinsically valuable or desirable **8 :** DENOMINATION 4 **9 :** the distinctive character or quality of a speech sound **syn** see WORTH — **val·ued** \-(,)yüd\ *adj*

[2]**value** *vt* **1 a :** to estimate or assign the monetary worth of **:** APPRAISE ⟨~ a necklace⟩ **b :** to rate or scale in usefulness, importance, or general worth **:** EVALUATE **2 :** to consider or rate highly **:** PRIZE,

ESTEEM ⟨*valued* friendship⟩ **syn** see APPRECIATE, ESTIMATE — **val·u·er** \-yə-wər\ *n*

val·ue·less \'val-yü-ləs\ *adj* **:** of no value **:** WORTHLESS — **val·ue·less·ness** *n*

va·lu·ta \və-'lüt-ə, -'lü-(,)tä\ *n* [It, value, fr. (assumed) VL *valuta*] **1 :** the agreed or exchange value of a currency **2 :** foreign exchange in usable form

val·vate \'val-,vāt\ *adj* **:** having valves or parts resembling a valve: **a :** meeting at the edges without overlapping in the bud ⟨~ leaves⟩ **b :** opening as if by doors or valves ⟨~ capsules⟩ ⟨~ anthers⟩

valve \'valv\ *n, often attrib* [L *valva*; akin to L *volvere* to roll — more at VOLUBLE] **1** *archaic* **:** a leaf of a folding or double door **2** [NL *valva*, fr. L] **:** a structure esp. in a vein or lymphatic that closes temporarily a passage or orifice or permits movement of fluid in one direction only **3 a :** any of numerous mechanical devices by which the flow of liquid, gas (as air), or loose material in bulk may be started, stopped, or regulated by a movable part that opens, shuts, or partially obstructs one or more ports or passageways; *also* **:** the movable part of such a device **b :** a device in a brass wind instrument for quickly varying the tube length in order to change the fundamental tone by some definite interval **c** *chiefly Brit* **:** ELECTRON TUBE **4** [NL *valva*, fr. L] **:** one of the distinct and usu. movably articulated pieces of which the shell of lamellibranch mollusks, brachiopods, barnacles, and some other shell-bearing animals consists **5** [NL *valva*, fr. L] **a :** one of the segments or pieces into which a dehiscing capsule or legume separates **b :** the portion of various anthers (as of the barberry) resembling a lid **c :** one of the two encasing membranes of a diatom — **valved** \'valvd\ *adj*

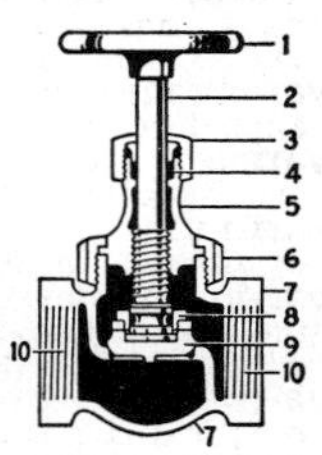

globe valve in section: *1* handwheel, *2* stem, *3* stuffing nut, *4* stuffing box, *5* bonnet, *6* bonnet ring, *7, 7* body, *8* locknut, *9* disk, *10, 10* pipe ends

valve–in–head engine \,val-vən-,hed-\ *n* **:** an internal-combustion engine in which both inlet and exhaust valves are located in the cylinder head

valve·less \'valv-ləs\ *adj* **:** having no valves

val·vif·er·ous \val-'vif-(ə-)rəs\ *adj* **:** having valves

val·vu·la \'val-vyə-lə\ *n, pl* **valvu·lae** \-,lē, -,lī\ [NL] **:** a small valve or fold

val·vu·lar \'val-vyə-lər\ *adj* **1 :** resembling or functioning as a valve; *also* **:** opening by valves **2 :** of or relating to a valve esp. of the heart

val·vule \'val-(,)vyü(ə)l\ *n* [NL *valvula*, dim. of *valva*] **:** a small valve or valvular structure

val·vu·li·tis \,val-vyə-'līt-əs\ *n* **:** inflammation of a valve esp. of the heart

va·moose \va-'müs, və-\ *vi* [Sp *vamos* let us go, suppletive 1st pl. imper. (fr. L *vadere* to go) of *ir* to go, fr. L *ire* — more at WADE, ISSUE] *slang* **:** to depart quickly **:** DECAMP

[1]**vamp** \'vamp\ *n* [ME *vampe* sock, fr. OF *avantpié*, fr. *avant-* fore- + *pié* foot, fr. L *ped-*, *pes* — more at VANGUARD, FOOT] **:** the part of a shoe upper or boot upper covering esp. the forepart of the foot and sometimes also extending forward over the toe or backward to the back seam of the upper

[2]**vamp** *vt* **1 a :** to provide (a shoe) with a new vamp **b :** to piece (something old) with a new part **:** PATCH ⟨~ up old sermons⟩ **2 :** INVENT, FABRICATE ⟨~ up an excuse⟩ — **vamp·er** *n*

[3]**vamp** *n* [short for *vampire*] **:** a woman who uses her charm or wiles to seduce and exploit men

[4]**vamp** *vt* **:** to practice seductive wiles on

vam·pire \'vam-,pī(ə)r\ *n* [F, fr. G *vampir*, of Slav origin; akin to Serb *vampir* vampire] **1 :** the body of a dead person believed to come from the grave at night and suck the blood of persons asleep **2 a :** one who lives by preying on others **b :** a woman who exploits and ruins her lover **3 :** any of various bats reputed to feed on blood: as **a :** any of several large So. and Central American insectivorous bats **b :** any of various So. American bats (genera *Desmodus* and *Diphylla* of the family Desmodontidae) structurally adapted for subsisting on blood and dangerous to man and domestic animals esp. as vectors of equine trypanosomiasis and of rabies **c :** a large insectivorous or frugivorous Old World bat (as a fruit bat)

vam·pir·ism \-,pī(ə)r-,iz-əm\ *n* **1 :** belief in vampires **2 :** the actions of a vampire

[1]**van** \'van\ *n* [ME, fr. MF, fr. L *vannus* — more at WINNOW] **1** *dial Eng* **:** a winnowing device (as a fan) **2 :** WING 1a

[2]**van** *n* [by shortening] **:** VANGUARD

[3]**van** *n* [short for *caravan*] **1 :** a usu. enclosed wagon or motortruck used for transportation of goods or animals **2** *chiefly Brit* **:** an enclosed railroad freight or baggage car

van·a·date \'van-ə-,dāt\ *n* **:** a salt or ester of vanadic acid

va·na·dic \və-'nād-ik, -'nad-\ *adj* **:** of, relating to, or containing vanadium esp. with a higher valence than in vanadous compounds

vanadic acid *n* **:** any of various acids that are hydrates of vanadium pentoxide or are known esp. in the form of salts and esters

va·na·di·nite \və-'nād-ᵊn-,īt, ,van-ə-'dēn-\ *n* [G *vanadinit*, fr. *vanadin* vanadium, fr. NL *vanadium*] **:** a mineral consisting of a lead vanadate and chloride and occurring in yellowish, brownish, or ruby-red hexagonal crystals

va·na·di·um \və-'nād-ē-əm\ *n* [NL, fr. ON *Vanadīs* Freya] **:** a grayish malleable ductile polyvalent metallic element found combined in minerals and used esp. to form alloys (as vanadium steel) — see ELEMENT table

va·na·dous \və-'nād-əs, 'van-əd-\ *adj* **:** of, relating to, or containing vanadium esp. with a lower valence than in vanadic compounds

Van Al·len radiation belt \va-'nal-ən-, və-\ *n* [James A. *Van Allen* b1914 Am physicist] **:** a belt of intense ionizing radiation that surrounds the earth in the outer atmosphere

va·nas·pa·ti \və-'nəs-pət-ē\ *n* [Skt, forest tree, soma plant, lit., lord of the forest, fr. *vana* forest + *pati* lord] **:** a hydrogenated vegetable fat used as a butter substitute in India

van·da \'van-də\ *n* [NL, genus name, fr. Hindi *vandā* mistletoe, fr. Skt, a parasitic plant] **:** any of a large genus (*Vanda*) of Indo-Malayan epiphytic orchids often grown for their loose racemes of showy flowers

van·dal \'van-dᵊl\ *n* [L *Vandalii* (pl.), of Gmc origin] **1** *cap* **:** one of a Germanic people anciently dwelling south of the Baltic between the Vistula and the Oder, overrunning Gaul, Spain, and northern Africa in the 4th and 5th centuries A.D., and in 455 sacking Rome **2 :** one who willfully or ignorantly destroys, damages, or defaces property belonging to another or to the public — **vandal** *adj, often cap* — **Van·dal·ic** \van-'dal-ik\ *adj*

van·dal·ism \'van-dᵊl-,iz-əm\ *n* **:** willful or malicious destruction or defacement of public or private property

van·dal·is·tic \,van-dᵊl-'is-tik\ *adj* **:** of, relating to, or perpetrating vandalism

van·dal·ize \'van-dᵊl-,īz\ *vt* **:** to subject to vandalism **:** DAMAGE

Van de Graaff generator \,van-də-,graf-\ *n* [Robert J. *Van de Graaff* †1967 Am physicist] **:** ELECTROSTATIC GENERATOR

Van·dyke \van-'dīk, vən-\ *n* [Sir Anthony *Vandyke* †1641 Flem painter] **1 a :** a wide collar with a deeply indented edge **b :** one of several V-shaped points forming a decorative edging **c :** a border of such points **2 :** a trim pointed beard — **van·dyked** \-'dīkt\ *adj*

Vandyke brown *n* [fr. its use by the painter Vandyke] **:** a natural brown-black pigment of organic matter obtained from bog earth or peat or lignite deposits; *also* **:** any of various synthetic brown pigments

vane \'vān\ *n* [ME (southern dial.), fr. OE *fana* banner; akin to OHG *fano* cloth, L *pannus* cloth, rag] **1 a :** a movable device attached to an elevated object (as a spire) for showing the direction of the wind **b :** one that is changeable or inconstant **2 :** a thin flat or curved object that is rotated about an axis by a flow of fluid or that rotates to cause a fluid to flow or that redirects a flow of fluid ⟨the ~s of a windmill⟩ **3 :** the web or flat expanded part of a feather **4 :** a feather fastened to the shaft near the nock of an arrow **5 a :** the target of a leveling rod **b :** one of the sights of a compass or quadrant — **vaned** \'vānd\ *adj*

van·guard \'van-,gärd\ *n* [ME *vantgard*, fr. MF *avant-garde*, fr. OF, fr. *avant-* fore- (fr. *avant* before, fr. L *abante*) + *garde* guard — more at ADVANCE] **1 :** the troops moving at the head of an army **2 :** the forefront of an action or movement

va·nil·la \və-'nil-ə, -'nel-\ *n* [NL, genus name, fr. Sp. *vainilla* vanilla (plant and fruit), dim. of *vaina* sheath, fr. L *vagina* sheath, vagina] **1 :** any of a genus (*Vanilla*) of tropical American climbing orchids **2 :** the long capsular fruit of a vanilla (esp. *Vanilla planifolia*) that is an important article of commerce for the flavoring extract that it yields; *also* **:** this extract

va·nil·lic \-'nil-ik\ *adj* **:** of or derived from vanilla or vanillin

va·nil·lin \'van-ᵊl-ən, və-'nil-ən\ *n* **:** a crystalline phenolic aldehyde $C_8H_8O_3$ that is the chief fragrant component of vanilla and is used in flavoring and in perfumery

Va·nir \'vän-,i(ə)r\ *n pl* [ON] **:** a race of gods in Norse mythology

van·ish \'van-ish\ *vi* [ME *vanisshen*, fr. MF *evaniss-*, stem of *evanir*, fr. (assumed) VL *exvanire*, alter. of L *evanescere* to dissipate like vapor, vanish, fr. *e-* + *vanescere* to vanish, fr. *vanus* empty] **1 a :** to pass quickly from sight **:** DISAPPEAR **b :** to pass completely from existence **2 :** to assume the value zero — **van·ish·er** *n*

vanishing cream *n* **:** a cosmetic preparation less oily than cold cream that is used chiefly as a foundation for face powder

vanishing point *n* **1 :** a point at which a group of receding parallel lines seems to meet when represented in linear perspective **2 :** a point at which something disappears or ceases to exist

van·i·ty \'van-ət-ē\ *n* [ME *vanite*, fr. OF *vanité* fr. L *vanitat-*, *vanitas* quality of being empty or vain, fr. *vanus* empty, vain — more at WANE] **1 :** something that is vain **2 :** the quality or fact of being vain: as **a :** WORTHLESSNESS, EMPTINESS **b :** FUTILITY **c :** inflated pride in oneself or one's appearance **:** CONCEIT **3 :** a fashionable trifle or knicknack **4 a :** [3]COMPACT 1 **b :** a small case or handbag for toilet articles used by women **5 :** DRESSING TABLE

vanity fair *n, often cap V&F* [*Vanity-Fair*, a fair held in the frivolous town of Vanity in *Pilgrim's Progress* (1678)] **:** a place of busy pride and empty ostentation

van·quish \'vaŋ-kwish, 'van-\ *vt* [ME *venquissen* fr. MF *venquis*, preterit of *veintre* to conquer, fr. L *vincere* — more at VICTOR] **1 :** to overcome in battle **:** subdue completely **2 :** to defeat in a conflict or contest **3 :** to gain mastery over (an emotion, passion, or temptation) **syn** see CONQUER — **van·quish·er** *n*

van·quish·able \-kwish-ə-bəl\ *adj* **:** capable of being vanquished

van·tage \'vant-ij\ *n* [ME, fr. AF, fr. MF *avantage* — more at ADVANTAGE] **1** *archaic* **:** BENEFIT, GAIN **2 :** superiority in a contest **3 :** a position giving a strategic advantage, commanding perspective, or comprehensive view **4 :** ADVANTAGE 4 — **to the vantage** *archaic* **:** in addition

[1]**van·ward** \'van-wərd\ *adj* **:** located in the vanguard **:** ADVANCED

[2]**vanward** *adv* **:** to or toward the vanguard **:** FOREWARD

va·pid \'vap-əd 'vā-pəd\ *adj* [L *vapidus* flat tasting; akin to L *vappa* vapid wine and prob. to L *vapor* steam] **:** lacking liveliness, tang, briskness, or force **:** FLAT, UNINTERESTING ⟨~ remark⟩ ⟨~ smile⟩ **syn** see INSIPID — **va·pid·ly** \'vap-əd-lē, 'vā-pəd-\ *adv* — **va·pid·ness** *n*

va·pid·i·ty \va-'pid-ət-ē, vā-\ *n* **1 :** the quality or state of being vapid **2 :** something vapid ⟨the *vapidities* of everyday conversation⟩

[1]**va·por** \'vā-pər\ *n* [ME *vapour*, fr. MF *vapeur*, fr. L *vapor* steam, vapor — more at COVET] **1 :** diffused matter (as smoke or fog) suspended floating in the air and impairing its transparency **2 a :** a substance in the gaseous state as distinguished from the liquid or solid state **b :** a substance (as gasoline, alcohol, mercury, or benzoin) vaporized for industrial, therapeutic or military uses; *also* **:** a mixture (as the explosive mixture in an internal-combustion engine) of such a vapor with air **3 a :** something unsubstantial or transitory **:** PHANTASM **b :** a foolish or fanciful idea **4** *pl* **a** *archaic* **:** exhalations of bodily organs (as the stomach) held to affect the physical or mental condition **b :** a depressed or hysterical nervous condition

[2]**vapor** *vi* **va·por·ing** \-p(ə-)riŋ\ **1 a :** to rise or pass off in vapor **b :** to emit vapor **2 :** to indulge in bragging, blustering, or idle talk — **va·por·er** \-pər-ər\ *n*

va·por·if·ic \,vā-pə-'rif-ik\ *adj* **:** producing vapor **:** tending to pass

or to cause to pass into vapor : VAPOROUS
va·por·ing \ˈvā-p(ə-)riŋ\ *n* : the act or speech of one that vapors; *specif* : an idle, extravagant, or high-flown expression or speech — usu. used in pl.
va·por·ish \ˈvā-p(ə-)rish\ *adj* **1** : resembling or suggestive of vapor **2** : given to fits of depression or hysteria — **va·por·ish·ness** *n*
va·por·iz·able \-pə-ˌrī-zə-bəl\ *adj* : capable of being vaporized
va·por·iza·tion \ˌvā-p(ə-)rə-ˈzā-shən\ *n* : the act or process of vaporizing : the state of being vaporized
va·por·ize \ˈvā-pə-ˌrīz\ *vt* **1** : to convert (as by the application of heat or by spraying) into vapor **2** : to cause to become ethereal or dissipated ~ *vi* **1** : to become vaporized **2** : VAPOR 2
va·por·iz·er \-ˌrī-zər\ *n* : one that vaporizes: as **a** : ATOMIZER **b** : an apparatus for vaporizing a heavy oil (as petroleum) for the explosive charge of an internal-combustion engine; *also* : a simple form of carburetor **c** : a device for converting a medicated liquid into a vapor for inhalation
vapor lock *n* : partial or complete interruption of fuel flow in an internal-combustion engine caused by the formation of bubbles of vapor in the fuel-feeding system
va·por·ous \ˈvā-p(ə-)rəs\ *adj* **1** : consisting or characteristic of vapor **2** : producing vapors : VOLATILE **3** : containing or obscured by vapors : MISTY **4 a** : ETHEREAL, UNSUBSTANTIAL **b** : consisting of or indulging in high flown expressions — **va·por·ous·ly** *adv* — **va·por·ous·ness** *n*
vapor pressure *n* : the pressure exerted by a vapor that is in equilibrium with its solid or liquid form — called also *vapor tension*
vapor trail *n* : CONTRAIL
va·pory \ˈvā-p(ə-)rē\ *adj* : VAPOROUS, VAGUE
va·que·ro \vä-ˈke(ə)r-(ˌ)ō\ *n, pl* **vaqueros** [Sp — more at BUCKAROO] : HERDSMAN, COWBOY
va·ra \ˈvär-ə\ *n* [Sp & Pg, lit., pole, fr. L, forked pole, fr. fem. of *varus* bent, crooked — more at PREVARICATE] **1** : any of various Spanish, Portuguese, and Latin American units of length equal to between 31 and 34 inches **2** : a Texas unit of length equal to 33.33 inches
vari- *or* **vario-** *comb form* [L *varius* — more at VARIOUS] : varied : diverse ⟨*vari*form⟩ ⟨*vario*coupler⟩
var·ia \ˈver-ē-ə, ˈvar-\ *n pl* [NL, fr. L, neut. pl. of *varius* various] : MISCELLANY; *esp* : a literary miscellany
vari·abil·i·ty \ˌver-ē-ə-ˈbil-ət-ē, ˌvar-\ *n* : the quality or fact of being variable
[1]**vari·able** \ˈver-ē-ə-bəl, ˈvar-\ *adj* **1 a** : able or apt to vary : CHANGEABLE ⟨~ winds⟩ **b** : FICKLE, INCONSTANT **2** : characterized by variations **3** : having the characteristics of a variable **4** : not true to type : ABERRANT — used of a biological group or character — **vari·able·ness** *n* — **vari·ably** \-blē\ *adv*
[2]**variable** *n* **1** : something that is variable **2 a** : a quantity that may assume any one of a set of values **b** : a symbol representing a variable
variable cost *n* : cost that fluctuates directly with changes in output
variable star *n* : a star whose brightness changes usu. in more or less regular periods
vari·ance \ˈver-ē-ən(t)s, ˈvar-\ *n* **1** : the fact, quality, or state of being variable or variant : DIFFERENCE, DEVIATION ⟨yearly ~ in crops⟩ **2** : the fact or state of being in disagreement : DISSENSION, DISPUTE **3** : a disagreement between two parts of the same legal proceeding that must be consonant **4** : a license to do some act contrary to the usual rule ⟨a zoning ~⟩ **5** : the square of the standard deviation **syn** see DISCORD — **at variance** : not in harmony or agreement
[1]**vari·ant** \ˈver-ē-ənt, ˈvar-\ *adj* **1** *obs* : VARIABLE **2** : manifesting variety, deviation, or disagreement **3** : varying usu. slightly from the standard form ⟨~ readings⟩
[2]**variant** *n* : one of two or more persons or things exhibiting usu. slight differences: as **a** : one that exhibits variation from a type or norm **b** : one of two or more different spellings or pronunciations of the same word
vari·ate \ˈver-ē-ˌāt, ˈvar-\ *n* : a variable that may take on any of the values of a specified set with a specified probability
vari·a·tion \ˌver-ē-ˈā-shən, ˌvar-\ *n* **1 a** : the act or process of varying : the state or fact of being varied **b** : an instance of varying **c** : the extent to which or range in which a thing varies **2** : DECLINATION 6 **3** : a change in the mean motion or mean orbit of a celestial body **4 a** : a change of algebraic sign between successive terms of a sequence **b** : a measure of the change in a variable or function **5** : the repetition of a musical theme with modifications in rhythm, tune, harmony, or key **6 a** : divergence in qualities of an organism or biotype from those typical or usual to its group **b** : an individual or group exhibiting variation **7 a** : a solo dance in classic ballet **b** : a repetition in modern ballet of a movement sequence with changes
vari·a·tion·al \-shnəl, -shən-ᵊl\ *adj* : of, relating to, or characterized by variation — **vari·a·tion·al·ly** \-ē\ *adv*
vari·a·tive \ˈver-ē-ˌāt-iv, ˈvar-\ *adj* : of, relating to, or showing variation
var·i·cel·la \ˌvar-ə-ˈsel-ə\ *n* [NL, irreg. dim. of *variola*] : CHICKEN POX — **var·i·cel·lar** \-ˈsel-ər\ *adj*
var·i·co·cele \ˈvar-ə-kō-ˌsēl\ *n* [NL, fr. L *varic-*, *varix* + *-o-* + *-cele*] : a varicose enlargement of the veins of the spermatic cord
vari·col·ored \ˈver-i-ˌkəl-ərd, ˈvar-\ *adj* : having various colors : VARIEGATED ⟨~ marble⟩
var·i·cose \ˈvar-ə-ˌkōs\ *adj* [L *varicosus* full of dilated veins, fr. *varic-*, *varix* dilated vein] **1 a** *also* **var·i·cosed** \-ˌkōst, -ˌkōzd\ : abnormally swollen or dilated ⟨~ veins⟩ **b** : causing abnormal swelling ⟨~ stasis⟩ **2** : of, relating to, or exhibiting varices ⟨~ mollusks⟩
var·i·cos·i·ty \ˌvar-ə-ˈkäs-ət-ē\ *n* **1** : the quality or state of being varicose **2** : VARIX
var·ied \ˈve(ə)r-ēd, ˈva(ə)r-\ *adj* **1** : CHANGED, ALTERED **2** : having numerous forms or types : DIVERSE **3** : VARIEGATED — **var·ied·ly** *adv*
var·ie·gate \ˈver-ē-ə-ˌgāt, ˈver-i-ˌgāt, ˈvar-\ *vt* [L *variegatus*, pp. of *variegare*, fr. *varius* various + *-egare* (akin to L *agere* to drive) — more at AGENT] **1** : to diversify in external appearance esp. with different colors : DAPPLE **2** : to enliven by variety — **var·ie·ga·tor** \-ˌgāt-ər\ *n*
var·ie·gat·ed \-ˌgāt-əd\ *adj* : VARIED; *esp* : having discrete markings of different colors
var·ie·ga·tion \ˌver-ē-ə-ˈgā-shən, ˌver-i-ˈgā-, ˌvar-\ *n* : the act of variegating : the state of being variegated; *esp* : diversity of colors
vari·er \ˈver-ē-ər, ˈvar-\ *n* : one that varies
va·ri·etal \və-ˈrī-ət-ᵊl\ *adj* : of, relating to, or characterizing a variety ⟨~ name⟩; *also* : being a variety in distinction from an individual or species — **va·ri·etal·ly** \-ᵊl-ē\ *adv*
va·ri·ety \və-ˈrī-ət-ē\ *n* [MF or L; MF *varieté*, fr. L *varietat-*, *varietas*, fr. *varius* various] **1** : the quality or state of having different forms or types **2** : a number or collection of different things esp. of a particular class : ASSORTMENT **3 a** : something differing from others of the same general kind **b** : any of various groups of plants or animals of less than specific rank **4** : entertainment consisting of successive unrelated performances (as songs, dances, skits, acrobatic feats, and trained animal acts)
variety meat *n* : an edible part (as liver or tongue) of a slaughter animal other than skeletal muscle
variety store *n* : a retail establishment dealing in a large variety of merchandise esp. of low unit value
vari·form \ˈver-ə-ˌfȯrm, ˈvar-\ *adj* : having various forms : varied or different in form
var·io·cou·pler \ˈver-ē-ō-ˌkəp-lər, ˈvar-\ *n* : an inductive coupler the mutual inductance of which is adjustable by moving one coil with respect to the other
va·ri·o·la \ˌver-ē-ˈō-lə, ˌvar-; və-ˈrī-ə-lə\ *n* [NL, fr. ML, pustule, pox, fr. LL, pustule] : any of several virus diseases (as smallpox or cowpox) marked by a pustular eruption
va·ri·o·lar \-lər\ *adj* : VARIOLOUS
var·i·o·lite \ˈver-ē-ə-ˌlīt, ˈvar-\ *n* [prob. fr. NL *variolites*, fr. ML *variola*] : a basic rock embedded with whitish spherules
va·ri·o·loid \ˌver-ē-ˈō-ˌlȯid, ˌvar-; və-ˈrī-ə-ˌlȯid\ *n* [NL *variola*] : a modified mild form of smallpox occurring in persons who have been vaccinated or who have had smallpox
va·ri·o·lous \ˌver-ē-ˈō-ləs, ˌvar-; və-ˈrī-ə-ləs\ *adj* : of or relating to smallpox
var·i·om·e·ter \ˌver-ē-ˈäm-ət-ər, ˌvar-\ *n* : VARIOCOUPLER
[1]**var·i·o·rum** \ˌver-ē-ˈōr-əm, ˌvar-, -ˈȯr-\ *n* [L *variorum* of various persons (gen. pl. masc. of *varius*), in the phrase *cum notis variorum* with the notes of various persons] **1** : an edition or text esp. of a classical author with notes by different persons **2** : an edition of a publication containing variant readings of the text
[2]**variorum** *adj* **1** : relating to or being an edition or text containing notes by different persons **2** : drawn or derived from various sources ⟨~ illustrations⟩
var·i·ous \ˈver-ē-əs, ˈvar-\ *adj* [L *varius*; prob. akin to L *varus* bent, crooked — more at PREVARICATE] **1** *archaic* : VARIABLE, INCONSTANT **2** : VARICOLORED ⟨birds of ~ plumage⟩ **3 a** : of differing kinds : MULTIFARIOUS **b** : UNLIKE ⟨animals as ~ as the jaguar and the sloth⟩ **4** : having a number of different aspects ⟨~ genius⟩ **5** : of an indefinite number greater than one ⟨stop at ~ towns⟩ **6** : INDIVIDUAL, SEPARATE ⟨refunds to the ~ club members⟩ **syn** see DIFFERENT — **var·i·ous·ly** *adv* — **var·i·ous·ness** *n*
vari·sized \ˈver-i-ˌsīzd, ˈvar-\ *adj* : of various sizes
va·ris·tor \va-ˈris-tər, ve-\ *n* [*vari-* + *resistor*] : an electrical resistor whose resistance depends on the applied voltage
var·ix \ˈvar-iks\ *n, pl* **var·i·ces** \ˈvar-ə-ˌsēz\ [L *varic-*, *varix*] **1** : an abnormally dilated and lengthened vein, artery, or lymph vessel; *esp* : a varicose vein **2** : one of the prominent ridges across each whorl of a gastropod shell
var·let \ˈvär-lət\ *n* [ME, fr. MF *vaslet*, *varlet* young nobleman, page — more at VALET] **1** *archaic* **a** : ATTENDANT, MENIAL **b** : a knight's page **2** : a low fellow
var·let·ry \-lə-trē\ *n, archaic* : a group of menials : RABBLE
var·mint \ˈvär-mənt\ *n* [alter. of *vermin*] **1** *dial* : a wild animal or bird considered a pest **2** : a contemptible person : RASCAL; *broadly* : PERSON, FELLOW
[1]**var·nish** \ˈvär-nish\ *n* [ME *vernisch*, fr. MF *vernis*, fr. OIt or ML; OIt *vernice*, fr. ML *veronic-*, *veronix* sandarac (resin)] **1 a** : a liquid preparation that when spread upon a surface dries forming a hard lustrous typically transparent coating **b** : the covering or glaze given by the application of varnish **c** : something that suggests varnish by its gloss **2** : outside show : GLOSS **3** *chiefly Brit* : a lacquer or enamel nail polish — **var·nishy** \-ni-shē\ *adj*
[2]**varnish** *vt* **1** : to apply varnish to **2** : to cover or conceal with something that gives a fair appearance : GLOSS 1 **3** : ADORN, EMBELLISH — **var·nish·er** \-nish-ər\ *n*
varnish tree *n* : any of various trees yielding a milky juice from which in some cases varnish or lacquer is prepared; *esp* : a Japanese sumac (*Rhus verniciflua*)
var·si·ty \ˈvär-sət-ē, -stē\ *n, often attrib* [by shortening & alter. fr. *university*] **1** *chiefly Brit* : UNIVERSITY **2** : a first team representing a university, college, school, or club
Var·u·na \ˈvar-ə-nə\ *n* [Skt *Varuṇa*] : the divine guardian of cosmic order in Vedic Hinduism
var·us \ˈvar-əs, ˈver-\ *adj* [NL, fr. L, bent, knock-kneed] : turned abnormally inward — used esp. of the lower extremities
varve \ˈvärv\ *n* [Sw *varv* turn, layer; akin to OE *hweorfan* to turn — more at WHARF] : a pair of layers of alternately finer and coarser silt or clay believed to comprise an annual cycle of deposition in a body of still water
vary \ˈve(ə)r-ē, ˈva(ə)r-\ *vb* [ME *varien*, fr. MF or L: MF *varier*, fr. L *variare*, fr. *varius* various] *vt* **1 a** : to make a partial change in : make different in some attribute or characteristic **b** : to make differences between items in : DIVERSIFY **2** : to present under new aspects ⟨~ the rhythm and harmonic treatment⟩ ~ *vi* **1** : to exhibit or undergo change ⟨a constantly ~*ing* sky⟩ **2** : DEVIATE, DEPART **3** : to take on successive values ⟨*y varies* inversely with *x*⟩ **4** : to exhibit divergence in structural or physiological characters from those typical or usual in the group **syn** see CHANGE — **vary·ing·ly** \-iŋ-lē\ *adv*
varying hare *n* : any of several hares having white fur in winter
vas \ˈvas\ *n, pl* **va·sa** \ˈvā-zə *also* -sə\ [NL, fr. L, vessel] : an anatomical vessel : DUCT — **va·sal** \-zəl *also* -səl\ *adj*
vas- *or* **vaso-** *comb form* [NL, fr. L *vas*] **1** : vessel: as **a** : blood vessel ⟨*vaso*motor⟩ **b** : vas deferens ⟨*vas*ectomy⟩ **2** : vascular and ⟨*vaso*vagal⟩ **3** : vasomotor ⟨*vaso*inhibitor⟩
vas·cu·lar \ˈvas-kyə-lər\ *adj* [NL *vascularis*, fr. L *vasculum* small vessel, dim. of *vas*] **1** : of or relating to a channel for the conveyance of a body fluid (as blood or sap) or to a system of such channels; *also* : supplied with or made up of such channels and esp.

blood vessels ⟨a ~ tumor⟩ ⟨a ~ system⟩ **2 :** marked by vigor and ardor **:** SPIRITED, PASSIONATE

vascular bundle *n* **:** a unit of the vascular system of a higher plant consisting usu. of vessels and sieve tubes together with parenchyma cells and fibers

vascular cylinder *n* **:** STELE

vas·cu·lar·i·ty \\ˌvas-kyə-ˈlar-ət-ē\\ *n* **:** the quality or state of being vascular

vascular plant *n* **:** a plant having a specialized conducting system that includes xylem and phloem **:** TRACHEOPHYTE

vascular ray *n* **:** a ray of cambial origin that in the stele of many vascular plants separates the vascular bundles

vascular tissue *n* **:** plant tissue concerned mainly with conduction; *esp* **:** the specialized tissue of higher plants consisting essentially of phloem and xylem and forming a continuous system throughout the body

vas·cu·lum \\ˈvas-kyə-ləm\\ *n, pl* **vas·cu·la** \\-lə\\ [NL, fr. L, small vessel] **:** a usu. metal and commonly cylindrical or flattened covered box used in collecting plants

vas de·fer·ens \\ˈvas-ˈdef-ə-rənz, -ˌrenz\\ *n, pl* **va·sa de·fer·en·tia** \\ˌvas-ə-ˌdef-ə-ˈren-ch(ē-)ə, ˌvās-, ˌvāz-\\ [NL, lit., deferent vessel] **:** a spermatic duct esp. of a higher vertebrate forming in man a small thick-walled tube about two feet long greatly convoluted in its proximal portion

vase \\ˈvās, ˈvāz, *esp Brit* ˈväz\\ *n* [F, fr. L *vas;* akin to Umbrian *vasor* vessels] **:** a usu. round vessel of greater depth than width used chiefly for ornament or for flowers

va·sec·to·my \\vas-ˈek-tə-mē, vā-zek-\\ *n* [ISV] **:** surgical excision of the vas deferens usu. to induce permanent sterility

Vas·e·line \\ˈvas-ə-ˌlēn, ˌvas-ə-ˈ\\ *trademark* — used for petrolatum

va·si·form \\ˈvās-ə-ˌfȯrm, ˈvāz- *also* (ˈ*tube*ˈ) ˈvas-\\ *adj* [NL *vasiformis*, fr. L *vas* + *-iformis* -iform] **:** having the form of a hollow tube or a vase

va·so·con·stric·tion \\ˌvā-zō-kən-ˈstrik-shən *also* -sō-\\ *n* [ISV] **:** narrowing of the lumen of blood vessels esp. as a result of vasomotor action

va·so·con·stric·tive \\-ˈstrik-tiv\\ *adj* **:** inducing vasoconstriction

va·so·con·stric·tor \\-tər\\ *n* **:** an agent (as a sympathetic nerve fiber or a drug) that induces or initiates vasoconstriction

va·so·di·la·ta·tion \\-ˌdil-ə-ˈtā-shən, -ˌdī-lə-\\ *or* **va·so·di·la·tion** \\-(ˌ)dī-ˈlā-shən, -də-\\ *n* [ISV] **:** widening of the lumen of blood vessels

va·so·di·la·tor \\-(ˌ)dī-ˈlāt-ər, -ˈdī-ˌlāt-, -də-ˈlāt-\\ *n* **:** an agent (as a parasympathetic nerve fiber or a drug) that induces or initiates vasodilation

va·so·in·hib·i·tor \\-in-ˈhib-ət-ər\\ *n* **:** an agent (as a drug) that depresses or inhibits vasomotor and esp. vasoconstrictor activity — **va·so·in·hib·i·to·ry** \\-ˈhib-ə-ˌtōr-ē, -ˌtȯr-\\ *adj*

va·so·mo·tor \\-ˈmōt-ər\\ *adj* [ISV] **:** of, relating to, or being nerves or centers controlling the size of blood vessels

va·so·pres·sin \\-ˈpres-ᵊn\\ *n* [fr. *Vasopressin*, a trademark] **:** a polypeptide hormone secreted by the posterior lobe of the pituitary that increases blood pressure and decreases urine flow

va·so·pres·sor \\-ˈpres-ər\\ *adj* **:** causing a rise in blood pressure by exerting a vasoconstrictor effect — **vasopressor** *n*

va·so·spasm \\ˈvā-zō-ˌspaz-əm *also* -sō-\\ *n* [ISV] **:** sharp and often persistent contraction of a blood vessel reducing its caliber and blood flow — **va·so·spas·tic** \\ˌvā-zō-ˈspas-tik *also* -sō-\\ *adj*

va·so·va·gal \\ˌvā-zō-ˈvā-gəl *also* -sō-\\ *adj* **:** of, relating to, or involving both vascular and vagal factors

vas·sal \\ˈvas-əl\\ *n* [ME, fr. MF, fr. ML *vassallus*, fr. *vassus* servant, vassal, of Celt origin; akin to W *gwas* boy, servant] **1 :** a person under the protection of another who is his feudal lord and to whom he has vowed homage and fealty **:** a feudal tenant **2 :** one in a subservient or subordinate position — **vassal** *adj*

vas·sal·age \\-ə-lij\\ *n* **1 :** the state of being a vassal **2 :** the homage, fealty, or services due from a vassal **3 :** a territory held in political dependence

¹**vast** \\ˈvast\\ *adj* [L *vastus;* akin to OIr *fot* length] **:** very great in size, amount, degree, intensity, or esp. in extent **syn** see ENORMOUS — **vast·ly** *adv* — **vast·ness** \\ˈvas(t)-nəs\\ *n*

²**vast** *n* **:** a boundless space **:** IMMENSITY

vas·ti·tude \\ˈvas-tə-ˌt(y)üd\\ *n* **:** vastness

vas·ti·ty \\ˈvas-tət-ē\\ *n* **:** VASTITUDE

vasty \\ˈvas-tē\\ *adj* **:** VAST, IMMENSE ⟨call spirits from the ~ deep — Shak.⟩

¹**vat** \\ˈvat\\ *n* [ME *fat, vat*, fr. OE *fæt;* akin to OHG *vaz* vessel, Lith *puodas* pot] **1 :** a large vessel (as a cistern, tub, or barrel) esp. for holding liquors in an immature state or preparations for dyeing or tanning **2 :** a liquor containing a dye converted into a soluble reduced colorless or weakly colored form that on textile material steeped in the liquor and exposed to the air is converted by oxidation to the original insoluble dye and precipitated in the fiber

²**vat** *vt* **vat·ted; vat·ting :** to put into or treat in a vat

vat dye *n* **:** a water-insoluble generally fast dye used in the form of a vat liquor — called also *vat color*

vat-dyed \\ˈvat-ˈdīd\\ *adj* **:** dyed with one or more vat dyes

vat·ic \\ˈvat-ik\\ *adj* [L *vates* seer, prophet; akin to OE *wōth* poetry, OHG *wuot* madness, OIr *fāith* seer, poet] **:** PROPHETIC, ORACULAR

Vat·i·can \\ˈvat-i-kən\\ *n* [L *Vaticanus* Vatican Hill (in Rome)] **1 :** the papal headquarters in Rome **2 :** the papal government — **Vatican** *adj*

va·tic·i·nal \\və-ˈtis-ᵊn-əl, va-\\ *adj* [L *vaticinus*, fr. *vaticinari*] **:** PROPHETIC

va·tic·i·nate \\-ᵊn-ˌāt\\ *vb* [L *vaticinatus*, pp. of *vaticinari*, fr. *vates* + *-cinari* (akin to L *canere* to sing) — more at CHANT] **:** PROPHESY, PREDICT

va·tic·i·na·tion \\-ˌtis-ᵊn-ˈā-shən\\ *n* **1 :** something foretold **:** PREDICTION **2 :** the act of prophesying

va·tic·i·na·tor \\-ˈtis-ᵊn-ˌāt-ər\\ *n* **:** PROPHET

vaude·ville \\ˈvȯd-(ə-)vəl, ˈvōd-, ˈväd-, -(ə-)ˌvil\\ *n* [F, fr. MF, popular satirical song, alter. of *vaudevire*, fr. *vau-de-Vire* valley of Vire, fr. *vau, val* valley + *de* from, of (fr. L) + *Vire*, town in northwest France where such songs were composed — more at VALE, DE-] **1 :** a light often comic theatrical piece frequently combining pantomime, dialogue, dancing, and song **2 :** stage entertainment consisting of various unrelated acts (as performing animals, acrobats, comedians, dancers, or singers)

¹**vaude·vil·lian** \\ˌvȯd-(ə-)ˈvil-yən, ˌvōd-, ˌväd-\\ *n* **:** a vaudeville writer, actor, singer, or performer

²**vaudevillian** *adj* **:** of, relating to, or characteristic of vaudeville

Vau·dois \\vō-ˈdwä\\ *n pl* [MF, fr. ML *Valdenses*] **:** WALDENSES

¹**vault** \\ˈvȯlt\\ *n* [ME *voute*, fr. MF, fr. (assumed) VL *volvita* turn, vault, prob. fr. *volvitare*] **1 a :** an arched structure of masonry usu. forming a ceiling or roof **b :** something (as the sky) resembling a vault **c :** an arched or dome-shaped anatomical structure **2 a :** a space covered by an arched structure; *esp* **:** an underground passage or room **b :** an underground storage compartment **c :** a room or compartment for the safekeeping of valuables **3 a :** a burial chamber **b :** a prefabricated container usu. of metal or concrete into which a casket is placed at burial

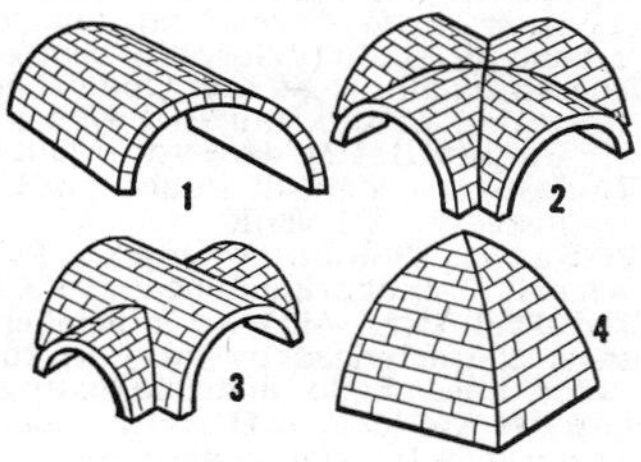

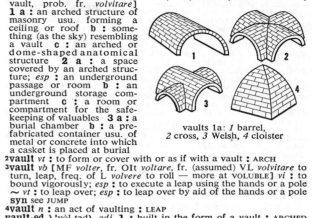

vaults 1a: *1* barrel, *2* cross, *3* Welsh, *4* cloister

²**vault** *vt* **:** to form or cover with or as if with a vault **:** ARCH

³**vault** *vb* [MF *volter*, fr. OIt *voltare*, fr. (assumed) VL *volvitare* to turn, leap, freq. of L *volvere* to roll — more at VOLUBLE] *vi* **:** to bound vigorously; *esp* **:** to execute a leap using the hands or a pole ~ *vt* **:** to leap over; *esp* **:** to leap over by aid of the hands or a pole **syn** see JUMP

⁴**vault** *n* **:** an act of vaulting **:** LEAP

vault·ed \\ˈvȯl-təd\\ *adj* **1 :** built in the form of a vault **:** ARCHED **2 :** covered with a vault

vault·er \\-tər\\ *n* **:** one that vaults; *esp* **:** POLE-VAULTER

¹**vault·ing** \\-tiŋ\\ *n* **:** vaulted construction

²**vaulting** *adj* **1 :** reaching or stretching for the heights **2 :** designed for use in vaulting or in gymnastic exercises ⟨a ~ block⟩

vaulty \\ˈvȯl-tē\\ *adj* **:** resembling a vault

¹**vaunt** \\ˈvȯnt, ˈvänt\\ *vb* [ME *vaunten*, fr. MF *vanter*, fr. LL *vanitare*, fr. L *vanitas* vanity] *vi* **:** to make a vain display of one's own worth or attainments **:** BRAG ~ *vt* **:** to boast of **syn** see BOAST — **vaunt·er** *n* — **vaunt·ing·ly** \\-iŋ-lē\\ *adv*

²**vaunt** *n* **1 :** a vainglorious display of what one is or has or has done **2 :** a bragging assertive speech

vaunt-cou·ri·er \\-ˈku̇r-ē-ər, -ˈkər-ē-, -ˈkə-rē-\\ *n* [MF *avant-courrier*, lit., advance courier] **1** *obs* **:** a member of an advance guard of a body of troops **2 :** one sent in advance **:** FORERUNNER

vaunt·ful \\-fəl\\ *adj* **:** BOASTFUL, VAINGLORIOUS

vaunty \\ˈvȯnt-ē, ˈvänt-\\ *adj, Scot* **:** BOASTFUL, PROUD, VAIN

vav *var of* WAW

vav·a·sor *or* **vav·a·sour** \\ˈvav-ə-ˌsȯ(ə)r, -ˌsō(ə)r\\ *n* [ME *vavasour*, fr. OF *vavassor*, prob. fr. ML *vassus vassorum* vassal of vassals] **:** a feudal tenant ranking directly below a peer or baron

va·ward \\ˈvau̇-ˌ(w)ȯ(ə)rd\\ *n* [ME *vauntwarde, vaward*, fr. ONF *avantwarde*, fr. *avant* before (fr. L *abante*) + *warde* guard, fr. *warder* to guard — more at ADVANCE, REWARD] **:** the foremost part **:** FOREFRONT

V-day \\ˈvē-ˌdā\\ *n* [victory *day*] **:** a day of victory

've \\v, əv\\ *vb* [by contr.] **:** HAVE ⟨we've been there⟩

Ve·adar \\ˈvā-ˌä-ˌdär\\ *n* [Heb *wĕ-Ādhār*, lit., and Adar (i.e., the second Adar)] **:** the intercalary month of the Jewish calendar following Adar in leap years

¹**veal** \\ˈvē(ə)l\\ *n, often attrib* [ME *veel*, fr. MF, fr. L *vitellus* small calf, dim. of *vitulus* calf — more at WETHER] **1 :** CALF; *esp* **:** VEALER **2 :** the flesh of a young calf

²**veal** *vt* **:** to kill and dress for veal

veal·er \\ˈvē-lər\\ *n* **:** a calf grown for or suitable for veal

vealy \\ˈvē-lē\\ *adj* **:** resembling or suggesting veal or a calf; *esp* **:** IMMATURE

vec·to·graph \\ˈvek-tə-ˌgraf\\ *n* [*vector* + *-graph*] **:** a picture composed of two superposed stereoscopic images that give a three-dimensional effect when viewed through polarizing spectacles — **vec·to·graph·ic** \\ˌvek-tə-ˈgraf-ik\\ *adj*

¹**vec·tor** \\ˈvek-tər\\ *n* [NL, fr. L, carrier, fr. *vectus*, pp. of *vehere* to carry — more at WAY] **1 a :** a quantity that has magnitude, direction, and sense and that is commonly represented by a directed line segment whose length represents the magnitude and whose orientation in space represents the direction **b :** a course or compass direction esp. of an airplane **2 :** an organism (as an insect) that transmits a pathogen **3 :** DRIVE 6 — **vec·to·ri·al** \\vek-ˈtōr-ē-əl, -ˈtȯr-\\ *adj*

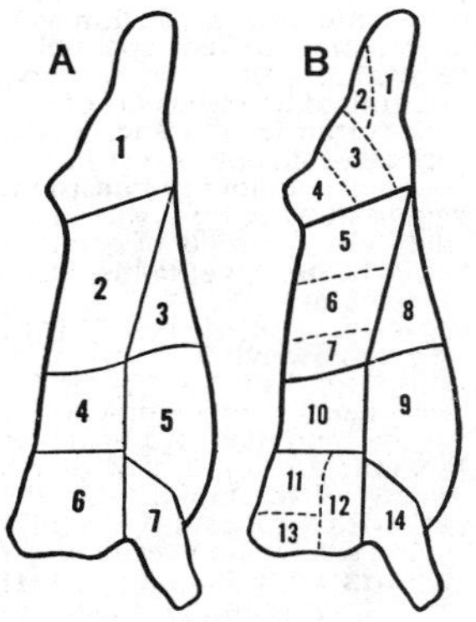

veal 2: *A* wholesale cuts: *1* leg, *2* loin, *3* flank, *4* rib, *5* breast, *6* shoulder, *7* shank; *B* retail cuts: *1* hind shank, *2* heel of round, *3* round, *4* rump roast, *5* sirloin steak, *6* loin chops, *7* kidney chops, *8* flank, *9* breast, *10* rib roast, *11* blade steak, *12* arm steak, *13* shoulder roast, *14* fore shank

²**vector** *vt* **vec·tor·ing** \\-t(ə-)riŋ\\ **:** to guide (as an airplane, its pilot, or a missile) in flight by means of a radioed vector

vector product *n* **:** a vector *c* whose length is the product of the lengths of two vectors *a* and *b* and the sine of their included angle, whose direction is perpendicular to their plane, and whose sense is that of a right-handed screw with axis *c* when *a* is rotated into *b*

vector sum *n* **:** the sum of a number of vectors that for the sum of

two vectors is geometrically represented by the diagonal of a parallelogram whose sides represent the two vectors being added

Ve·da \'vād-ə\ *n* [Skt, lit., knowledge; akin to Gk *eidenai* to know — more at WIT] **:** any of a primary class of Hindu sacred writings; *specif* **:** any of four canonical collections of hymns, prayers, and liturgical formulas

ve·da·lia \və-'dāl-yə\ *n* [NL] **:** an Australian ladybug (*Rodolia cardinalis*) introduced to many countries to control scale insects

Ve·dan·ta \vā-'dänt-ə, və-, -'dant-\ *n* [Skt *Vedānta*, lit., end of the Veda, fr. *Veda* + *anta* end; akin to OE *ende* end] **:** an orthodox system of Hindu philosophy developing esp. in a qualified monism the speculations of the Upanishads on ultimate reality and the liberation of the soul — **Ve·dan·tism** \-'dän-,tiz-əm, -'dan-\ *n* — **Ve·dan·tist** \-'dänt-əst, -'dant-\ *n*

Ve·dan·tic \-'dänt-ik, -'dant-\ *adj* **1 :** of or relating to the Vedanta philosophy **2 :** VEDIC

Ved·da *or* **Ved·dah** \'ved-ə\ *n* [Sinhalese *vedda* hunter] **:** one of a small dark aboriginal people of Ceylon

Ved·doid \'ved-,òid\ *n* **:** a member of an ancient race of southern Asia characterized by wavy to curly hair, chocolate-brown skin color, linear build, and fine features — **Veddoid** *adj*

ve·dette \vi-'det\ *n* [F, fr. It *vedetta*, alter. of *veletta*, prob. fr. Sp *vela* watch, fr. *velar* to keep watch, fr. L *vigilare* to wake, watch, fr. *vigil* awake] **:** a mounted sentinel stationed in advance of pickets

Ve·dic \'vād-ik\ *adj* **:** of or relating to the Vedas, the language in which they are written, or Hindu history and culture between 2000 B.C. and 500 B.C.

vee \'vē\ *n* **:** the letter *v*

veep \'vēp\ *n* [fr. *v. p.* (abbr. for *vice-president*)] **:** VICE-PRESIDENT

¹**veer** \'vi(ə)r\ *vt* [ME *veren*, of LG or D origin; akin to MD *vieren* to slacken, MLG *vīren*] **:** to let or pay out (as a rope or anchor chain)

²**veer** *vb* [MF *virer*, prob. of Celt origin; akin to OIr *fiar* oblique; akin to OE *wīr* wire] *vi* **1 :** to change direction or course **2** *of the wind* **:** to shift in a clockwise direction **3 :** to wear ship **~** *vt* **:** to direct to a different course; *specif* **:** WEAR 7 **syn** see SWERVE — **veer·ing·ly** \-iŋ-lē\ *adv*

³**veer** *n* **:** a change in course or direction

vee·ry \'vi(ə)r-ē\ *n* [perh. imit. of one of its notes] **:** a thrush (*Hylocichla fuscescens*) common in the eastern U.S.

Ve·ga \'vē-gə, 'vā-\ *n* [NL, fr. Ar (*al-Nasr*) *al-Wāqi'*, lit., the falling (vulture)] **:** a star of the first magnitude that is the brightest in the constellation Lyra

veg·an \'vej-ən, -,an\ *n* [by contr. fr. *vegetarian*] **:** an extreme vegetarian **:** one that consumes no animal food or dairy products — **veg·an·ism** \'vej-ə-,niz-əm\ *n*

¹**veg·e·ta·ble** \'vej-tə-bəl, 'vej-ət-ə-\ *adj* [ME, fr. ML *vegetabilis* vegetative, fr. *vegetare* to grow, fr. L, to animate, fr. *vegetus* lively, fr. *vegēre* to rouse, excite — more at WAKE] **1 a :** of, relating to, constituting, or growing like plants **b :** consisting of plants **:** VEGETATIONAL **2 :** made or obtained from plants or plant products ⟨~ silk⟩ **3 :** resembling or suggesting a plant (as in monotony of existence)

²**vegetable** *n* **1 :** PLANT 1b **2 :** a usu. herbaceous plant grown for an edible part which is usu. eaten with the principal part of a meal; *also* **:** such edible part **3 :** a human being having a dull or merely physical existence

vegetable butter *n* **1 :** a vegetable fat that resembles butter or lard esp. in consistency **2 :** AVOCADO

vegetable ivory *n* **1 :** the hard white opaque endosperm of the ivory nut that takes a high polish and is used as a substitute for ivory **2 :** IVORY NUT

vegetable marrow *n* **:** any of various smooth-skinned elongated summer squashes with creamy white to deep green skins

vegetable oil *n* **:** an oil of plant origin; *esp* **:** a fatty oil from seeds or fruits

vegetable plate *n* **:** a main course without meat consisting of several vegetables cooked separately and served on one plate

vegetable silk *n* **:** a cottony fibrous material obtained from the coating of tree seeds (as of a Brazilian tree, *Chorisia speciosa*, of the silk-cotton family) and used esp. for stuffing cushions

vegetable tallow *n* **:** a fatty substance obtained from plants that resembles tallow in consistency

vegetable wax *n* **:** a wax of plant origin secreted commonly in thin flakes by the walls of epidermal cells

veg·e·ta·bly \'vej-tə-blē, 'vej-ət-ə-\ *adv* **:** in the manner of or like a vegetable

veg·e·tal \'vej-ət-ᵊl\ *adj* [ML *vegetare* to grow] **1 :** VEGETABLE **2 :** VEGETATIVE

¹**veg·e·tar·i·an** \,vej-ə-'ter-ē-ən\ *n* [²*vegetable* + *-arian*] **1 :** one who believes in or practices living solely upon vegetables, fruits, grains, and nuts **2 :** HERBIVORE

²**vegetarian** *adj* **1 :** of or relating to vegetarians **2 :** consisting wholly of vegetables ⟨a ~ diet⟩

veg·e·tar·i·an·ism \-ē-ə-,niz-əm\ *n* **:** the theory or practice of living solely upon vegetables, fruits, grains, and nuts

veg·e·tate \'vej-ə-,tāt\ *vb* [ML *vegetatus*, pp. of *vegetare* to grow] *vi* **1 a :** to grow in the manner of a plant; *also* **:** to grow exuberantly or with proliferation of fleshy or warty outgrowths **b :** to produce vegetation **2 :** to lead a passive existence without exertion of body or mind **~** *vt* **:** to establish vegetation in or on

veg·e·ta·tion \,vej-ə-'tā-shən\ *n* **1 :** the act or process of vegetating **2 :** inert existence **3 :** plant life or total plant cover (as of an area) **4 :** an abnormal outgrowth upon a body part — **veg·e·ta·tion·al** \-shnəl, -shən-ᵊl\ *adj*

veg·e·ta·tive \'vej-ə-,tāt-iv\ *adj* **1 a** (1) **:** growing or having the power of growing (2) **:** of, relating to, or engaged in nutritive and growth functions as contrasted with reproductive functions ⟨a ~ nucleus⟩ **b :** promoting plant growth ⟨the ~ properties of soil⟩ **c :** of, relating to, or involving propagation by nonsexual processes or methods **2 :** VEGETATIONAL ⟨~ cover⟩ **3 :** of or relating to the division of nature comprising the plant kingdom **4 :** affecting, arising from, or relating to involuntary bodily functions **5 :** VEGETABLE 3 — **veg·e·ta·tive·ly** *adv* — **veg·e·ta·tive·ness** *n*

ve·gete \və-'jēt\ *adj* [L *vegetus* — more at VEGETABLE] *archaic* **:** LIVELY, HEALTHY

veg·e·tive \'vej-ət-iv\ *adj* [ML *vegetare* to grow] **:** VEGETABLE, VEGETATIVE

ve·he·mence \'vē-ə-mən(t)s\ *n* **:** the quality or state of being vehement **:** INTENSITY, VIOLENCE

ve·he·ment \-mənt\ *adj* [MF, fr. L *vehement-*, *vehemens*; akin to L *vehere*] **1 :** marked by the exertion of great force or energy **:** STRONG **2 :** marked by strong feeling or forcible expression **:** PASSIONATE, EMPHATIC **3 :** strong in effect **:** INTENSE — **ve·he·ment·ly** *adv*

ve·hi·cle \'vē-,(h)ik-əl\ *n, often attrib* [F *véhicule*, fr. L *vehiculum* carriage, conveyance, fr. *vehere* to carry — more at WAY] **1 a :** an inert medium in which a medicinally active agent is administered **b :** any of various other media acting usu. as solvents, carriers, or binders for active ingredients or pigments **2 :** an agent of transmission **:** CARRIER **3 :** a medium through which something is expressed, achieved, or displayed **4 :** a means of carrying or transporting something **:** CONVEYANCE: as **a :** MOTOR VEHICLE **b :** a piece of mechanized equipment

ve·hic·u·lar \vē-'hik-yə-lər\ *adj* **1 a :** of, relating to, or designed for vehicles and esp. motor vehicles **b :** transported by vehicle **2 :** serving as a vehicle

V-eight \'vē-'āt\ *n* **:** an internal-combustion engine having two banks of four cylinders each with the banks at an angle to each other; *also* **:** an automobile having such an engine

¹**veil** \'vā(ə)l\ *n* [ME *veile*, fr. ONF, fr. L *vela*, pl. of *velum* veil] **1 a** (1) **:** a length of cloth worn by women as a covering for the head and shoulders and often also in eastern countries the face; *specif* **:** the outer covering of a nun's headdress (2) **:** the cloistered life of a nun **b :** a length of veiling or netting worn over the head or face or attached for protection or ornament to a hat or headdress **c :** HUMERAL VEIL **2 :** a concealing curtain or cover of cloth **3 :** something that hides or obscures like a veil **4 :** a covering body part or membrane: as **a :** VELUM **b :** CAUL

²**veil** *vt* **:** to cover, provide, obscure, or conceal with or as if with a veil **~** *vi* **:** to put on or wear a veil

veiled \'vā(ə)ld\ *adj* **1 a :** having or wearing a veil or concealing cover ⟨a ~ hat⟩ **b :** characterized by a softening tonal distortion **2 :** obscured as if by a veil **:** DISGUISED ⟨~ threats⟩

veil·ing \'vā-liŋ\ *n* **1 :** VEIL **2 :** any of various light sheer fabrics (as net or chiffon)

¹**vein** \'vān\ *n* [ME *veine*, fr. OF, fr. L *vena*] **1 a :** a narrow water channel in rock or earth, or ice **b** (1) **:** LODE 2, 3 (2) **:** a bed of useful mineral matter **2 a :** BLOOD VESSEL **b :** one of the tubular branching vessels that carry blood from the capillaries toward the heart **3 a :** one of the vascular bundles forming the framework of a leaf **b :** one of the thickened cuticular ribs that serve to stiffen the wings of an insect **4 :** something suggesting veins (as in reticulation); *specif* **:** a wavy variegation (as in marble) **5 a :** a distinctive mode of expression **:** STYLE **b :** a pervasive element or quality **:** STRAIN **c :** a line of thought or action **6 a :** a special aptitude **:** TALENT **b :** MOOD **c :** top form **:** FETTLE **syn** see MOOD — **vein·al** \-ᵊl\ *adj*

²**vein** *vt* **:** to pattern with or as if with veins

veined \'vānd\ *adj* **:** patterned with or as if with veins **:** STREAKED

vein·er \'vā-nər\ *n* **:** a small V gouge used in wood carving

vein·ing \'vā-niŋ\ *n* **:** a pattern of veins **:** VENATION

vein·let \'vān-lət\ *n* **:** a small vein esp. of a leaf

vein·stone \-,stōn\ *n* **:** GANGUE

veiny \'vā-nē\ *adj* **:** full of veins **:** VEINED

ve·la·men \və-'lā-mən\ *n, pl* **ve·lam·i·na** \-'lam-ə-nə\ [NL, fr. L, covering, fr. *velare* to cover, fr. *velum* veil] **1 :** MEMBRANE, VELUM **2 :** the thick corky epidermis of aerial roots of an epiphytic orchid that absorbs water from the atmosphere — **vel·a·men·tous** \,vel-ə-'ment-əs\ *adj*

ve·lar \'vē-lər\ *adj* [NL *velaris*, fr. *velum*] **1 :** of, forming, or relating to a velum and esp. the soft palate **2 :** formed with the back of the tongue touching or near the soft palate ⟨the ~ \k\ of \'kül\ *cool*⟩ — **velar** *n*

ve·lar·i·um \vi-'lar-ē-əm, -'ler-\ *n, pl* **ve·lar·ia** \-ē-ə\ [L, fr. *velum* veil] **:** an awning over an ancient Roman theater or amphitheater

ve·lar·iza·tion \,vē-lə-rə-'zā-shən\ *n* **1 :** the quality or state of being velarized **2 :** an act or instance of velarizing

ve·lar·ize \'vē-lə-,rīz\ *vt* **:** to modify (as the \l\ of \'pül\ *pool*) by a simultaneous velar articulation as a result of the assimilative influence of the vowel

ve·late \'vē-lət, -,lāt\ *adj* [partly fr. L *velatus* (pp. of *velare* to cover, veil) & partly fr. NL *velatus*, fr. *velum*] **:** having a veil or velum — **ve·la·tion** \vi-'lā-shən\ *n*

veld *or* **veldt** \'felt, 'velt\ *n* [Afrik *veld*, fr. MD, field; akin to OE *feld* field] **:** a grassland esp. of southern Africa usu. with scattered shrubs or trees

vel·i·ta·tion \,vel-ə-'tā-shən\ *n* [L *velitation-*, *velitatio*, fr. *velitatus*, pp. of *velitari* to skirmish, fr. *velit-*, *veles* light-armed foot soldier; akin to L *vehere* to carry] **1 :** SKIRMISH **2 :** DISPUTE

vel·le·ity \ve-'lē-ət-ē\ *n* [NL *velleitas*, fr. L *velle* to wish, will — more at WILL **1 :** the lowest degree of volition **2 :** a slight wish or tendency **:** INCLINATION

¹**vel·lum** \'vel-əm\ *n* [ME *velim*, fr. MF *veelin*, fr. *veelin*, adj., of a calf, fr. *veel* calf — more at VEAL] **1 :** a fine-grained unsplit lambskin, kidskin, or calfskin prepared esp. for writing on or for binding books **2 :** a strong cream-colored paper resembling vellum

²**vellum** *adj* **1 :** of, resembling, or bound in vellum **2 :** having a finish resembling eggshell but finer grained

ve·lo·ce \vā-'lō-(,)chā\ *adv* (*or adj*) [It, fr. L *veloc-*, *velox*] **:** RAPIDLY — used as a direction in music

ve·loc·i·pede \və-'läs-ə-,pēd\ *n* [F *vélocipède*, fr. L *veloc-*, *velox* + *ped-*, *pes* foot — more at FOOT] **:** a lightweight wheeled vehicle propelled by the rider: as **a** *archaic* **:** BICYCLE **b :** TRICYCLE **c :** a 3-wheeled railroad handcar

ve·loc·i·ty \və-'läs-ət-ē, -'läs-tē\ *n* [MF *velocité*, fr. L *velocitat-*, *velocitas*, fr. *veloc-*, *velox* quick; akin to L *vehere* to carry — more at WAY] **1 :** quickness of motion **:** SPEED ⟨the ~ of sound⟩ **2 :** time rate of linear motion in a given direction **3 a :** rate of occurrence or action **:** RAPIDITY **b :** rate of turnover ⟨~ of money⟩

ve·lour *or* **ve·lours** \və-'lù(ə)r\ *n, pl* **velours** \-'lù(ə)rz\ *often attrib* [F *velours* velvet, velour, fr. MF *velours*, *velour*, fr. OF *velous*, fr. L *villosus* shaggy, fr. *villus* shaggy hair] **1 :** any of various fabrics with a pile or napped surface resembling velvet used in heavy weights for upholstery and curtains and in light weights for coats and jackets **2 :** a fur felt usu. of rabbit, hare, beaver, or nutria finished with a long velvety nap and used esp. for hats

ve·lum \'vē-ləm\ *n, pl* **ve·la** \-lə\ [NL, fr. L, curtain, veil] **:** a membrane or membranous part likened to a veil or curtain; *esp* **:** SOFT PALATE

ve·lure \vel-ˈ(y)u̇(ə)r, ˈvel-yər\ *n* [modif. of MF *velour*] *obs* **:** velvet or a fabric resembling it

ve·lu·ti·nous \və-ˈlüt-ᵊn-əs\ *adj* [NL *velutinus*, fr. ML *velutum* velvet, prob. fr. OIt *velluto* shaggy, fr. (assumed) VL *villutus*] **:** covered with a silky pubescence **:** VELVETY

[1]**vel·vet** \ˈvel-vət\ *n* [ME *veluet, velvet*, fr. MF *velu* shaggy, fr. (assumed) VL *villutus*, fr. L *villus* shaggy hair; akin to L *vellus* fleece — more at WOOL] **1 :** a clothing and upholstery fabric in a wide range of constructions and weights made of silk, rayon, cotton, nylon, or wool and characterized by a short soft dense pile **2 a :** something suggesting velvet **b** (1) **:** SOFTNESS (2) **:** SMOOTHNESS **3 :** the soft vascular skin that envelops and nourishes the developing antlers of deer **4 a :** the cash or chips a player is ahead in a gambling game **:** WINNINGS **b :** a profit or gain beyond ordinary expectation

[2]**velvet** *adj* **1 :** made of or covered with velvet; *also* **:** clad in velvet **2 :** resembling or suggesting velvet **:** VELVETY

velvet ant *n* **:** any of various solitary usu. brightly colored and hairy fossorial wasps (family Mutillidae) with the female wingless

velvet bean *n* **:** an annual legume (*Stizolobium deeringianum*) grown esp. in the southern U. S. for green manure and grazing; *also* **:** its seed often used as stock feed

vel·ve·teen \ˌvel-və-ˈtēn\ *n, often attrib* **1 :** a clothing fabric usu. of cotton in twill or plain weaves made with a short close weft pile in imitation of velvet **2** *pl* **:** clothes made of velveteen

velvet sponge *n* **:** a fine soft usu. flat and rounded commercial sponge (*Hippiospongia equina meandriformis*) found in the Gulf of Mexico and off the West Indies

vel·vety \ˈvel-vət-ē\ *adj* **1 :** soft and smooth like velvet **2 :** smooth to the taste **:** MILD ⟨~ rum⟩

ven- *or* **veni-** *or* **veno-** *comb form* [L *vena*] **:** vein ⟨venation⟩ ⟨venipuncture⟩ ⟨venostasis⟩

ve·na \ˈvā-nə, ˈvē-\ *n, pl* **ve·nae** \ˈvā-ˌnī, ˈvē-ˌnē\ [ME, fr. L] **:** VEIN

ve·na ca·va \ˌvā-nə-ˈkäv-ə, ˌvē-nə-ˈkā-və\ *n, pl* **ve·nae ca·vae** \ˌvā-ˌnī-ˈkäv-ˌī, ˌvē-nē-ˈkā-(ˌ)vē\ [NL, lit., hollow vein] **:** one of the large veins by which in air-breathing vertebrates the blood is returned to the right atrium of the heart

ve·nal \ˈvēn-ᵊl\ *adj* [L *venalis*, fr. *venum* (acc.) sale; akin to Gk *ōneisthai* to buy, Skt *vasna* price] **:** capable of being bought or obtained for money or other valuable consideration **:** PURCHASABLE; *esp* **:** MERCENARY, CORRUPT — **ve·nal·ly** \-ᵊl-ē\ *adv*

ve·nal·i·ty \vi-ˈnal-ət-ē\ *n* **:** the quality or state of being venal esp. as open to improper influence or bribery

ve·nat·ic \vi-ˈnat-ik\ *adj* [L *venaticus*, fr. *venatus*, pp. of *venari* to hunt — more at VENISON] **1 :** of, relating to, or used in hunting ⟨~ equipment⟩ **2 :** fond of or living by hunting ⟨the ~ tribes of ancient Europe⟩

ve·na·tion \vā-ˈnā-shən, vē-\ *n* [L *vena* vein] **:** an arrangement or system of veins ⟨the ~ of the hand⟩: as **a :** that in the tissue of a leaf blade **b :** that in the wing of an insect — **ve·na·tion·al** \-shnəl, -shən-ᵊl\ *adj*

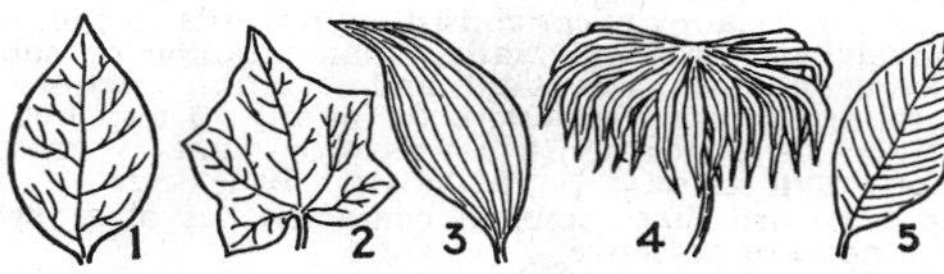

venation a: *1* pinnately veined, *2* palmately veined, *3* base to tip, *4* base to midrib, *5* midrib to margin

vend \ˈvend\ *vb* [L *vendere* to sell, v.t., contr. for *venum dare* to give for sale] *vi* **:** to change hands by sale **:** SELL; *also* **:** to engage in selling ~ *vt* **1 :** to sell esp. as a hawker or peddler **2 :** to utter publicly **:** PUBLISH

ven·dace \ˈven-dəs\ *n, pl* **vendace** *also* **ven·dac·es** [NL *vandesius*, fr. MF *vandoise*] **:** a whitefish (*Coregonus vandesius*) native to various lakes of Scotland and England

vend·ee \ven-ˈdē\ *n* **:** one to whom a thing is sold **:** BUYER

vend·er \ˈven-dər\ *n* **:** VENDOR

ven·det·ta \ven-ˈdet-ə\ *n* [It, lit., revenge, fr. L *vindicta* — more at VINDICTIVE] **:** BLOOD FEUD

vend·ibil·i·ty \ˌven-də-ˈbil-ət-ē\ *n* **:** the quality or state of being vendible

[1]**vend·ible** *or* **vend·able** \ˈven-də-bəl\ *adj* **1 :** capable of being vended **:** SALABLE **2** *obs* **:** VENAL — **vend·ibly** \-blē\ *adv*

[2]**vendible** *n* **:** a vendible article — usu. used in pl.

vending machine *n* **:** a slot machine for vending merchandise

ven·di·tion \ven-ˈdish-ən\ *n* [L *vendition-, venditio*, fr. *venditus*, pp. of *vendere* to vend] **:** the act of selling **:** SALE

ven·dor \ˈven-dər, *for 1 also* ven-ˈdȯ(ə)r\ *n* **1 :** one that vends **:** SELLER **2 :** VENDING MACHINE

ven·due \ven-ˈd(y)ü, van-, vän-\ *n* [obs. F, fr. MF, fr. *vendre* to sell, fr. L *vendere*] **:** a public sale at auction

[1]**ve·neer** \və-ˈni(ə)r\ *n* [G *furnier*, fr. *furnieren* to veneer, fr. F *fournir* to furnish — more at FURNISH] **1 :** a thin sheet of a material: as **a :** a layer of wood of superior value or excellent grain to be glued to an inferior wood **b :** any of the thin layers bonded together to form plywood **2 :** a protective or ornamental facing (as of brick or stone) **3 :** a superficial or meretricious show **:** GLOSS

[2]**veneer** *vt* **1 :** to overlay or plate (as a common wood) with a thin layer of finer wood for outer finish or decoration; *broadly* **:** to face with a material giving a superior surface **2 :** to cover over with a veneer; *esp* **:** to conceal (as a defect of character) under a superficial and specious attractiveness — **ve·neer·er** *n*

ve·neer·ing *n* **1 :** material for veneering **2 :** a veneered surface

ven·e·nate \ˈven-ə-ˌnāt\ *vb* [L *venenatus*, pp. of *venenare* to poison, fr *venenum* poison — more at VENOM] *vt* **:** POISON; *specif* **:** to inject a toxic substance into ~ *vi* **:** to use a toxic substance in preying or feeding — **ven·e·na·tion** \ˌven-ə-ˈnā-shən\ *n*

ven·er·a·bil·i·ty \ˌven-(ə-)rə-ˈbil-ət-ē\ *n* **:** the quality or state of being venerable

ven·er·a·ble \ˈven-ər-(ə-)bəl, ˈven-rə-bəl\ *adj* **1 :** deserving to be venerated—used as a title for an Anglican archdeacon or a Roman Catholic who has attained the lowest of three degrees of sanctity **2 :** made sacred by association (as religious or historic) **3 a :** calling forth respect through age, character, and attainments; *broadly* **:** conveying an impression of aged goodness and benevolence **b :** impressive by reason of age ⟨under ~ pines⟩ **syn** see OLD — **ven·er·a·ble·ness** *n* — **ven·er·a·bly** \-blē\ *adv*

ven·er·ate \ˈven-ə-ˌrāt\ *vt* [L *veneratus*, pp. of *venerari*, fr. *vener-, venus* love, charm — more at WIN] **:** to regard with reverential respect or with admiration and deference **syn** see REVERE

ven·er·a·tion \ˌven-ə-ˈrā-shən\ *n* **1 :** respect or awe excited by personal dignity or consecration **2 :** the act of venerating **3 :** the condition of one that is venerated

ven·er·a·tor \ˈven-ə-ˌrāt-ər\ *n* **:** one that venerates

ve·ne·re·al \və-ˈnir-ē-əl\ *adj* [ME *venereall*e, fr. L *venereus*, fr. *vener-, venus* love, sexual desire] **1 :** of or relating to sexual pleasure or indulgence **2 a :** resulting from or contracted during sexual intercourse **b :** of, relating to, or affected with venereal disease **c :** involving the genital organs

venereal disease *n* **:** a contagious disease that is typically acquired in sexual intercourse

ve·ne·re·ol·o·gist \və-ˌnir-ē-ˈäl-ə-jəst\ *n* [ISV *venereology*, fr. L *venereus* + ISV *-o-* + *-logy*] **:** a physician specializing in venereal diseases

ve·ne·re·ol·o·gy \-jē\ *or* **ven·er·ol·o·gy** \ˌven-ə-ˈräl-ə-jē\ *n* [*venereology* ISV *venereal* + *-o-* + *-logy; venerology* fr. G *venerologie*, fr. *venerisch* venereal (fr. L *vener-, venus*) + *-o-* + *-logie* -logy] **:** a branch of medical science concerned with venereal diseases

[1]**ven·ery** \ˈven-ə-rē\ *n* [ME *venerie*, fr. MF, fr. *vener* to hunt, fr. L *venari* — more at VENISON] **1 :** the art, act, or practice of hunting **2 :** animals that are hunted **:** GAME

[2]**venery** *n* [ME *venerie*, fr. ML *veneria*, fr. L *vener-, venus* sexual desire] **1 :** the pursuit of sexual indulgence or pleasure **2 :** SEXUAL INTERCOURSE

vene·sec·tion *or* **veni·sec·tion** \ˈven-ə-ˌsek-shən, ˌven-ə-ˈ\ *n* [NL *venae section-, venae sectio*, lit., cutting of a vein] **:** the operation of opening a vein for letting blood **:** PHLEBOTOMY

Ve·ne·ti \ˈven-ə-ˌtī, ˈwen-ə-ˌtē\ *also* **Ve·netes** \ˈven-ə-ˌtēz, vā-ˈnet\ *n pl* [L *Veneti*] **1 :** an ancient people in Gaul conquered by Caesar 56 B.C. **2 :** an ancient people in northeastern Italy allied politically to the Romans

ve·ne·tian blind \və-ˌnē-shən-\ *n* [*Venetian* of Venice, Italy] **:** a blind (as for a window) having numerous horizontal slats that may be set simultaneously at any of several angles so as to vary the amount of light admitted

venetian glass *n, often cap V* **:** a dainty delicate and artistic glassware made at Murano near Venice

Venetian red *n* **:** an earthy hematite used as a pigment; *also* **:** a synthetic iron oxide pigment

Ve·net·ic \və-ˈnet-ik\ *n* [L *veneticus* of the Veneti, fr. *Veneti* an ancient people of northeastern Italy] **:** the Italian language of the ancient Veneti of Italy — **Venetic** *adj*

venge \ˈvenj\ *vb* [ME *vengen*, fr. OF *vengier*] **:** AVENGE

ven·geance \ˈven-jən(t)s\ *n* [ME, fr. OF, fr. *vengier* to avenge, fr. L *vindicare* to lay claim to, avenge — more at VINDICATE] **:** punishment inflicted in retaliation for an injury or offense **:** RETRIBUTION — **with a vengeance 1 :** VIOLENTLY **2 :** EXTREMELY

venge·ful \ˈvenj-fəl\ *adj* [obs. E *venge* (revenge)] **:** REVENGEFUL: as **a :** seeking to avenge **:** VINDICTIVE **b :** serving to gain vengeance — **venge·ful·ly** \-fə-lē\ *adv* — **venge·ful·ness** *n*

V–en·gine \ˈvē-ˈ\ *n* **:** an internal-combustion engine the cylinders of which are arranged in two banks forming an acute angle

veni- *or* **veno-** — see VEN-

ve·nial \ˈvē-nē-əl, -nyəl\ *adj* [ME, fr. OF, fr. LL *venialis*, fr. L *venia* favor, indulgence, pardon; akin to L *venus* love, charm — more at WIN] **1 :** FORGIVABLE, PARDONABLE; *also* **:** EXCUSABLE **2 :** committed in a minor matter or without reflection or full consent and held in Roman Catholicism to merit only temporal punishment ⟨~ sin⟩ — compare MORTAL — **ve·nial·ly** \ˈvē-nē-ə-lē, -nyə-\ *adv* — **ve·nial·ness** *n*

ven·in \ˈven-ən\ *n* [*venom* + *-in*] **:** any of various toxic substances in snake venom

veni·punc·ture \ˈven-ə-ˌpəŋ(k)-chər\ *n* **:** surgical puncture of a vein esp. for the withdrawal of blood or for intravenous medication

ve·ni·re \və-ˈnī(ə)r-ē, -ˈni(ə)r-\ *n* [*venire facias*] **:** an entire panel from which a jury is drawn

ve·ni·re fa·ci·as \-ˌnī-rē-ˈfā-shē-əs, -ˌnir-ē-\ *n* [ME, fr. ML, you should cause to come] **:** a judicial writ directing the sheriff to summon a number of qualified persons to serve as jurors

ve·ni·re·man \və-ˈnī-rē-mən, -ˈnir-\ *n* **:** a member of a venire

ven·i·son \ˈven-ə-sən *also* -ə-zən\ *n, pl* **venisons** *also* **venison** *often attrib* [ME, fr. OF *veneison* hunting, game, fr. L *venation-, venatio*, fr. *venatus*, pp. of *venari* to hunt, pursue; akin to OE *winnan* to struggle — more at WIN] **1 :** the edible flesh of a wild animal taken by hunting **2 :** the flesh of a deer ⟨elk ~⟩

Ve·ni·te \və-ˈnīt-ē, -ˈnē-ˌtā\ *n* [L, O come, fr. *venire* to come; fr. the opening word of Ps 95:1 — more at COME] **:** a liturgical chant composed of parts of Psalms 95 and 96

[1]**ven·om** \ˈven-əm\ *n* [ME *venim, venom*, fr. OF *venim*, fr. (assumed) VL *venimen*, alter. of L *venenum* magic charm, drug, poison; akin to L *venus* love, charm — more at WIN] **1 :** poisonous matter normally secreted by some animals (as snakes, scorpions, or bees) and communicated chiefly by biting or stinging; *broadly* **:** material that is poisonous **2 :** something that embitters or blights the mind or spirit **:** MALIGNITY

[2]**venom** *vt* **:** ENVENOM

ven·om·ous \ˈven-ə-məs\ *adj* **1 :** full of venom: as **a :** POISONOUS, ENVENOMED **b :** VIRULENT, BANEFUL **c :** SPITEFUL, MALIGNANT **2 :** having a venom-producing gland and able to inflict a poisoned wound ⟨~ snakes⟩ — **ven·om·ous·ly** *adv* — **ven·om·ous·ness** *n*

ve·nose \ˈvē-ˌnōs\ *adj* [L *venosus*] **:** VENOUS; *esp* **:** having numerous or conspicuous veins ⟨insects with ~ wings⟩

ve·nos·i·ty \vi-ˈnäs-ət-ē\ *n* **:** the quality or state of being venous

ve·no·sta·sis \ˌvē-nə-ˈstā-səs, -ˈstas-is; vē-ˈnäs-tə-səs\ *n* [NL] **:** abnormal slowing or stoppage of the flow of blood in a vein

ve·nous \ˈvē-nəs\ *adj* [L *venosus*, fr. *vena* vein] **1 :** of, relating to or full of veins ⟨a ~ rock⟩ ⟨a ~ system⟩ **2** *of blood***:** having passed

through the capillaries and given up oxygen for the tissues and become charged with carbon dioxide : UNOXYGENATED — **ve·nous·ly** *adv*

1**vent** \'vent\ *vt* [ME *venten*, prob. fr. MF *esventer* to expose to the air, fr. *es-* ex- (fr. L *ex-*) + *vent* wind, fr. L *ventus* — more at WIND] **1** : to provide with a vent **2 a** : to serve as a vent for ⟨chimneys ~ smoke⟩ **b** : DISCHARGE, EXPEL **c** : to give expression to **3** : to relieve by venting **syn** see EXPRESS

2**vent** *n* **1** : an opportunity or way of escape or passage : OUTLET **2** : an opening for the escape of a gas or liquid or for the relief of pressure: as **a** : the external opening of the rectum or cloaca : ANUS **b** : PIPE 3c, FUMAROLE **c** : an opening at the breech of a gun through which fire is touched to the powder **d** *chiefly Scot* : CHIMNEY, FLUE

3**vent** *n* [ME *vente*, alter. of *fente*, fr. MF, slit, fissure, fr. *fendre* to split, fr. L *findere* — more at BITE] : a slit in a garment; *specif* : an opening in the lower part of a seam (as of a jacket or skirt)

vent·age \'vent-ij\ *n* : a small hole (as a flute stop) : VENT

ven·tail \'ven-,tāl\ *n* [ME, fr. MF *ventaille*, fr. *vent* wind] : the lower movable front of a medieval helmet

ven·ter \'vent-ər\ *n* [AF, fr. L, belly, womb; akin to OHG *wanast* paunch, L *vesica* bladder] **1** : a wife or mother that is a source of offspring **2** : a protuberant and often hollow anatomical structure: as **a** : ABDOMEN **b** : BELLY 4b **c** : a broad shallow concavity esp. of a bone

ven·ti·fact \'vent-ə-,fakt\ *n* [L *ventus* + E *-ifact* (as in *artifact*)] : a stone worn, polished, or faceted by windblown sand — called also *rillstone*

ven·ti·late \'vent-ᵊl-,āt\ *vt* [LL *ventilatus*, pp. of *ventilare*, fr. L, to fan, winnow, fr. *ventulus*, dim. of *ventus* wind — more at WIND] **1 a** : to examine, discuss, or investigate freely and openly : EXPOSE **b** : to make public : UTTER **2** *archaic* : to free from chaff by winnowing **3** : to expose to air and esp. to a current of fresh air for purifying, curing, or refreshing **4** *of a current of air* : to pass or circulate through so as to freshen — **ven·ti·la·tive** \'vent-ᵊl-,āt-iv\ *adj*

ven·ti·la·tion \,vent-ᵊl-'ā-shən\ *n* **1** : the act or process of ventilating **2** : circulation of air ⟨a room with good ~⟩ **3** : a system or means of providing fresh air

ven·ti·la·tor \'vent-ᵊl-,āt-ər\ *n* : one that ventilates; *esp* : a contrivance for introducing fresh air or expelling foul or stagnant air

ven·ti·la·to·ry \-ᵊl-ə-,tōr-ē, -,tȯr-\ *adj* : of, relating to, or provided with ventilation

ventr- *or* **ventro-** *comb form* [L *ventr-*, *venter* belly] : ventral and ⟨*ventro*lateral⟩

ven·tral \'ven-trəl\ *adj* [F, fr. L *ventralis*, fr. *ventr-*, *venter*] **1 a** : of or relating to the belly : ABDOMINAL **b** : being or located near or on the anterior or lower surface of an animal that is opposite the back **2 a** : AXIAL **b** : being or located on the lower surface of a dorsiventral plant structure — **ventral** *n* — **ven·tral·ly** \-trə-lē\ *adv*

ven·tri·cle \'ven-tri-kəl\ *n* [ME, fr. L *ventriculus*, fr. dim. of *ventr-*, *venter* belly] : a cavity of a bodily part or organ: as **a** : a chamber of the heart which receives blood from a corresponding atrium and from which blood is forced into the arteries **b** : one of the system of communicating cavities in the brain that are continuous with the central canal of the spinal cord

ven·tri·cose \'ven-tri-,kōs\ *adj* [NL *ventricosus*, fr. L *ventr-*, *venter* + *-icosus* (as in *varicosus* varicose)] : DISTENDED, INFLATED; *esp* : markedly swollen on one side — **ven·tri·cos·i·ty** \,ven-trə-'käs-ət-ē\ *n*

ven·tric·u·lar \ven-'trik-yə-lər\ *adj* : of, relating to, or being a ventricle or ventriculus

ven·tric·u·lus \-ləs\ *n, pl* **ven·tric·u·li** \-,lī, -,lē\ [NL, fr. L, dim. of *venter*] : a digestive cavity: as **a** : STOMACH **b** : GIZZARD 1 **c** : the digestive part of an insect's stomach

ven·tri·lo·qui·al \,ven-trə-'lō-kwē-əl\ *adj* : of or relating to ventriloquism — **ven·tri·lo·qui·al·ly** \-kwē-ə-lē\ *adv*

ven·tril·o·quism \ven-'tril-ə-,kwiz-əm\ *n* [LL *ventriloquus* ventriloquist, fr. L *ventr-*, *venter* + *loqui* to speak; fr. the belief that the voice is produced from the ventriloquist's stomach] : the production of the voice in such a manner that the sound appears to come from a source other than the vocal organs of the speaker

ven·tril·o·quist \-kwəst\ *n* : one who uses or is skilled in ventriloquism; *esp* : one who entertains by ventriloquism usu. through holding a dummy and apparently carrying on a conversation with it — **ven·tril·o·quis·tic** \(,)ven-,tril-ə-'kwis-tik\ *adj*

ven·tril·o·quize \ven-'tril-ə-,kwīz\ *vi* : to use ventriloquism ~ *vt* : to utter in the manner of a ventriloquist

ven·tril·o·quy \-kwē\ *n* : VENTRILOQUISM

ven·tro·lat·er·al \,ven-(,)trō-'lat-ə-rəl, -'la-trəl\ *adj* : ventral and lateral — **ven·tro·lat·er·al·ly** \-ē\ *adv*

ven·tro·me·di·al \-'mēd-ē-əl\ *adj* : ventral and medial — **ven·tro·me·di·al·ly** \-ē-ə-lē\ *adv*

1**ven·ture** \'ven-chər\ *vb* **ven·tur·ing** \'vench-(ə-)riŋ\ [ME *venteren*, by shortening & alter. fr. *aventuren*, fr. *aventure* adventure] *vt* **1** : to expose to hazard : RISK **2** : to undertake the risks and dangers of : BRAVE **3** : to offer at the risk of rebuff, rejection, or censure ~ *vi* : to proceed despite danger : DARE

2**venture** *n* **1** *obs* : FORTUNE, CHANCE **2 a** : an undertaking involving chance, risk, or danger; *esp* : a speculative business enterprise **b** : a venturesome act **3** : something at hazard in a speculative venture (as a trading ship or its cargo) — **at a venture** : at hazard or random

venture capital *n* : money invested or available for investment in stocks esp. of new or speculative enterprises

ven·tur·er \'vench-(ə-)rər\ *n* : one that ventures or puts to hazard; *specif* : a person who engages in business ventures

ven·ture·some \'ven-chər-səm\ *adj* **1** : disposed to court or incur risk or danger : DARING ⟨~ hunter⟩ **2** : involving risk : HAZARDOUS ⟨~ journey⟩ **syn** see ADVENTUROUS — **ven·ture·some·ly** *adv* — **ven·ture·some·ness** *n*

ven·tu·ri \ven-'tu̇(ə)r-ē\ *n* [G. B. *Venturi* †1822 It physicist] : a short tube that is inserted in a pipeline, that has flaring ends connected by a constricted middle, that depends for operation upon the fact that as the velocity of flow of a fluid increases in the constricted part the pressure decreases, and that is used for measuring the quantity of a fluid flowing, in connection with other devices for measuring airspeed, and for producing suction esp. for driving aircraft instruments

ven·tur·ous \'vench-(ə-)rəs\ *adj* **1** : VENTURESOME ⟨~ spirit⟩ **2** : HAZARDOUS ⟨~ enterprise⟩ — **ven·tur·ous·ly** *adv* — **ven·tur·ous·ness** *n*

ven·ue \'ven-(,)yü, -yə-w\ *n* [ME *venyw* action of coming, fr. MF *venue*, fr. *venir*, to come, fr. L *venire* — more at COME] **1 a** : the place or county in which alleged events from which a legal action arises take place **b** : the place from which the jury is drawn and in which trial is held in such an action **2** : a statement showing that a case is brought to the proper court or authority

ven·ule \'ven-(,)yü(ə)l\ *n* [L *venula*, dim. of *vena* vein] : a small vein; *esp* : one of the minute veins connecting the capillary bed with the larger systemic veins

Ve·nus \'vē-nəs\ *n* [ME, fr. L *Vener-*, *Venus*] **1** : the goddess of love and beauty in Roman mythology **2** : the planet second in order from the sun — see PLANET table

Ve·nus·berg \'vē-nəs-,bərg\ *n* : a mountain in central Germany containing a cavern in which according to medieval legend Venus held court

Ve·nus·hair \-,ha(ə)r, -,he(ə)r\ *n* : a delicate maidenhair fern (*Adiantum capillus-veneris*) with a slender black stipe and branches

Ve·nu·sian \vi-'n(y)ü-zhən\ *adj* : of or relating to the planet Venus — **Venusian** *n*

Ve·nus's-fly·trap \,vē-nə-səz-'flī-,trap\ *n* : an insectivorous plant (*Dionaea muscipula*) of the sundew family of the Carolina coast with the leaf apex modified into an insect trap

ve·ra·cious \və-'rā-shəs\ *adj* [L *verac-*, *verax* — more at VERY] **1** : TRUTHFUL, HONEST **2** : ACCURATE, TRUE — **ve·ra·cious·ly** *adv* — **ve·ra·cious·ness** *n*

ve·rac·i·ty \və-'ras-ət-ē\ *n* **1** : devotion to the truth : TRUTHFULNESS **2** : power of conveying or perceiving truth : CORRECTNESS **3** : conformity with truth or fact : ACCURACY **4** : something true **syn** see TRUTH

ve·ran·da *or* **ve·ran·dah** \və-'ran-də\ *n* [Hindi *varaṇḍā*] : a usu. roofed open gallery or portico attached to the exterior of a building : PORCH

ve·rat·ri·dine \və-'ra-trə-,dēn\ *n* [*veratr*ine + *-idine*] : a poisonous amorphous alkaloid $C_{36}H_{51}NO_{11}$ occurring esp. in sabadilla seed

ver·a·trine \'ver-ə-,trēn\ *n* [NL *veratrina*, fr. *Veratrum*, genus of herbs] : a poisonous irritant mixture of alkaloids from sabadilla seed that has been used as a counterirritant, insecticide, and c-mitotic agent

ve·ra·trum \və-'rā-trəm\ *n* [NL, genus name, fr. L, hellebore] **1** : HELLEBORE 1b **2** : the dried rhizome and roots of a hellebore (esp. *Veratrum viride* or *V. album*) used in the treatment of hypertension

verb \'vərb\ *n, often attrib* [ME *verbe*, fr. MF, fr. L *verbum* word, verb — more at WORD] : a word that characteristically is the grammatical center of a predicate and expresses an act, occurrence, or mode of being, that in various languages is inflected for agreement with the subject, for tense, for voice, for mood, or for aspect, and that typically has rather full descriptive meaning and characterizing quality but is sometimes nearly devoid of these esp. when used as an auxiliary or copula

1**ver·bal** \'vər-bəl\ *adj* [MF or LL; MF, fr. LL *verbalis*, fr. L *verbum* word] **1 a** : of, relating to, or consisting in words **b** : of, relating to, or involving words only rather than meaning or substance **c** : consisting of or using words only and not effective action **2** : of, relating to, or formed from a verb ⟨~ noun⟩ **3** : spoken rather than written ⟨~ contract⟩ **4** : WORD-FOR-WORD, VERBATIM ⟨~ translation⟩ **syn** see ORAL — **ver·bal·ly** \-bə-lē\ *adv*

2**verbal** *n* : a word that combines characteristics of a verb with those of a noun or adjective

verbal auxiliary *n* : an auxiliary verb

ver·bal·ism \'vər-bə-,liz-əm\ *n* **1 a** : a verbal expression : TERM **b** : PHRASING, WORDING **2** : words used as a substitute for more significant things **3 a** : an empty form of words **b** : VERBOSITY

ver·bal·ist \-ləst\ *n* **1** : one who stresses words above substance or reality **2** : a person skilled with words — **ver·bal·is·tic** \,vər-bə-'lis-tik\ *adj*

ver·bal·iza·tion \,vər-bə-lə-'zā-shən\ *n* : the act or an instance of verbalizing

ver·bal·ize \'vər-bə-,līz\ *vi* **1** : to speak or write in wordy or empty fashion **2** : to express something in words ~ *vt* **1** : to convert into a verb **2** : to name or describe in words **3** : to express in empty, verbose, or pretentious manner : INFLATE — **ver·bal·iz·er** *n*

verbal noun *n* : a noun derived directly from a verb or verb stem and in some uses having the sense and constructions of a verb

ver·ba·tim \(,)vər-'bāt-əm\ *adv* (*or adj*) [ME, fr. ML, fr. L *verbum* word] : word for word : in the same words

ver·be·na \(,)vər-'bē-nə\ *n* [NL, genus of subshrubs, fr. L, sing. of *verbenae* sacred boughs, certain medicinal plants — more at VERVAIN] : VERVAIN; *esp* : any of numerous garden plants of hybrid origin widely grown for their showy spikes of white, pink, red, or blue flowers which are borne in profusion over a long season

ver·biage \'vər-bē-ij *also* -bij\ *n* [F, fr. MF *verbier* to chatter, fr. *verbe* speech, fr. L *verbum* word] **1** : superfluity of words in proportion to sense or content : WORDINESS **2** : DICTION, WORDING ⟨concise military ~⟩

ver·bid \'vər-bəd\ *n* : VERBAL

verb·ify \'vər-bə-,fī\ *vt* : to make into a verb

ver·bile \'vər-,bīl\ *n* [L *verb*um word] : one whose mental imagery consists of words

ver·bose \(,)vər-'bōs\ *adj* : excessively wordy or prolix : DIFFUSE **syn** see WORDY — **ver·bose·ly** *adv* — **ver·bose·ness** *n* — **ver·bos·i·ty** \-'bäs-ət-ē\ *n*

ver·bo·ten \vər-'bōt-ᵊn\ *adj* [G] : FORBIDDEN; *esp* : prohibited unreasonably

ver·bum sap \,vərb-ᵊm-'sap, -əm-\ [short for NL *verbum sapienti (sat est)* a word to the wise (is sufficient)] : enough said

ver·dan·cy \'vərd-ᵊn-sē\ *n* : the quality or state of being verdant

ver·dant \-ᵊnt\ *adj* [modif. of MF *verdoyant*, fr. prp. of *verdoyer* to be green, fr. OF *verdoier*, fr. *verd*, *vert* green, fr. L *viridis*, fr. *virēre* to be green] **1 a** : green in tint or color ⟨~ grass⟩ **b** : green with growing plants ⟨~ fields⟩ **2** : unripe in experience or judgment : GREEN — **ver·dant·ly** *adv*

verd an·tique *or* **verde an·tique** \,vər-,dan-'tēk\ *n* [It *verde antico*, lit., ancient green] **1** : a green mottled or veined serpentine marble or calcareous serpentine much used for indoor decoration esp. by the ancient Romans **2** : an andesite porphyry showing crystals of feldspar in a dark green groundmass

ver·der·er *or* **ver·der·or** \'vərd-ər-ər\ *n* [AF, fr. OF *verdier*, fr.

verd green] : an English judicial officer having charge of the king's forest

ver·dict \'vər-(,)dikt\ *n* [alter. of ME *verdit*, fr. AF, fr. OF *ver* true (fr. L *verus*) + *dit* saying, dictum, fr. L *dictum* — more at VERY] **1 :** the finding or decision of a jury on the matter submitted to them in trial **2 :** OPINION, JUDGMENT

ver·di·gris \'vərd-ə-,grēs, -,gris, -grəs, -,grē\ *n* [ME *vertegrez*, fr. OF *vert de Grice*, lit., green of Greece] **1 a :** a green or greenish blue poisonous pigment resulting from the action of acetic acid on copper and consisting of one or more basic copper acetates **b :** normal copper acetate $Cu(C_2H_3O_2)_2H_2O$ **2 :** a green or bluish deposit esp. of copper carbonates formed on copper, brass, or bronze surfaces

ver·din \'vərd-ᵊn\ *n* [F, yellowhammer] : a very small yellow-headed titmouse (*Auriparus flaviceps*) found from Texas to California and southward

ver·di·ter \'vərd-ət-ər\ *n* [MF *verd de terre*, lit., earth green] : either of two basic carbonates of copper prepared respectively from azurite and malachite as well as artificially and yielding a blue and a green pigment

ver·dure \'vər-jər\ *n* [ME, fr. MF, fr. *verd* green] **1 :** the greenness of growing vegetation; *also* **:** such vegetation itself **2 :** a condition of health and vigor — **ver·dur·ous** \'vərj-(ə-)rəs\ *adj* — **ver·dur·ous·ness** *n*

ver·dured \'vər-jərd\ *adj* **:** covered with verdure

1verge \'vərj\ *n* [ME, fr. MF, fr. L *virga* rod, stripe — more at WHISK] **1 a** (1) **:** a rod or staff carried as an emblem of authority or symbol of office (2) *obs* **:** a stick or wand held by a person being admitted to tenancy while he swears fealty **b :** the spindle of a watch balance; *esp* **:** a spindle with pallets in an old vertical escapement **c :** the male intromittent organ of any of various invertebrates **2 a :** something that borders, limits, or bounds: as (1) **:** an outer margin of an object or structural part (2) *obs* **:** CIRCLET, RING; *also* **:** RIM, BRIM (3) **:** the edge of the tiling projecting over the gable of a roof **b :** BRINK, THRESHOLD **syn** see BORDER

2verge *vi* **1 :** to be contiguous **2 :** to be on the verge or border

3verge *vi* [L *vergere* to bend, incline — more at WRENCH] **1 a** *of the sun* **:** to incline toward the horizon **:** SINK **b :** to move or extend in some direction or toward some condition **2 :** to be in transition or change

verg·er \'vər-jər\ *n* **1** *Brit* **:** an attendant that carries a verge (as before a bishop or justice) **2 :** a church official who keeps order during services or serves as an usher or a sacristan

Ver·gil·ian \(,)vər-'jil-ē-ən, -'jil-yən\ *adj* **:** of, relating to, or characteristic of Vergil or his writings

ver·glas \ve(ə)r-'glä\ *n* [F, fr. OF *verre-glaz*, lit., glass ice] **:** a thin film of ice on rock

ve·rid·i·cal \və-'rid-i-kəl\ *adj* [L *veridicus*, fr. *verus* true + *dicere* to say — more at VERY, DICTION] **1 :** TRUTHFUL, VERACIOUS **2 :** not illusory **:** GENUINE — **ve·rid·i·cal·ly** \-k(ə-)lē\ *adv*

ver·i·fi·able \'ver-ə-,fī-ə-bəl\ *adj* **:** capable of being verified — **ver·i·fi·able·ness** *n*

ver·i·fi·ca·tion \,ver-ə-fə-'kā-shən\ *n* **:** the act or process of verifying **:** the state of being verified

ver·i·fi·er \'ver-ə-,fī(-ə)r\ *n* **:** one that verifies

ver·i·fy \-,fī\ *vt* [ME *verifien*, fr. MF *verifier*, fr. ML *verificare*, fr. L *verus* true — more at VERY] **1 :** to confirm or substantiate in law by oath **2 :** to establish the truth, accuracy, or reality of **syn** see CONFIRM

ver·i·ly \'ver-ə-lē\ *adv* [ME *verraily*, fr. *verray* very] **1 :** in very truth **:** CERTAINLY **2 :** TRULY, CONFIDENTLY

veri·sim·i·lar \,ver-ə-'sim-(ə-)lər\ *adj* [L *verisimilis*] **:** having the appearance of truth **:** PROBABLE — **veri·sim·i·lar·ly** *adv*

veri·si·mil·i·tude \-sə-'mil-ə-,t(y)üd\ *n* [L *verisimilitudo*, fr. *verisimilis* verisimilar, fr. *veri similis* like the truth] **1 :** the quality or state of being verisimilar **2 :** something verisimilar **syn** see TRUTH

ve·rism \'vi(ə)r-,iz-əm, 've(ə)r-\ *n* [It *verismo*, fr. *vero* true, fr. L *verus*] **:** artistic preference of the ordinary to the heroic or legendary esp. in grand opera — **ve·rist** \-əst\ *n or adj* — **ve·ris·tic** \vi(ə)r-'is-tik, ve(ə)r-\ *adj*

ver·i·ta·ble \'ver-ət-ə-bəl\ *adj* **:** ACTUAL, TRUE **syn** see AUTHENTIC — **ver·i·ta·ble·ness** *n* — **ver·i·ta·bly** \-blē\ *adv*

ver·i·ty \'ver-ət-ē\ *n* [ME *verite*, fr. MF *verité*, fr. L *veritat-, veritas*, fr. *verus* true] **1 :** the quality or state of being true or real **2 :** a true fact or statement; *esp* **:** a necessary truth **3 :** HONESTY, VERACITY **syn** see TRUTH

ver·juice \'vər-,jüs\ *n* [ME *verjus*, fr. MF, fr. *vert jus*, lit., green juice] **1 :** the sour juice of crab apples or of unripe fruit (as grapes or apples); *also* **:** an acid liquor made from verjuice **2 :** acidity of disposition or manner

ver·meil *n* [MF, fr. *vermeil*, adj. — more at VERMILION] **1** \'vər-məl, -,māl\ **:** VERMILION **2** \ve(ə)r-'mā\ **:** gilded silver, bronze, or copper — **vermeil** *adj*

vermi- *comb form* [NL, fr. LL, fr. L *vermis* — more at WORM] **:** worm ⟨*vermi*form⟩

ver·mi·an \'vər-mē-ən\ *adj* [ISV] **:** of, relating to, or resembling worms

ver·mi·cel·li \,vər-mə-'chel-ē, -'sel-\ *n* [It, fr. pl. of *vermicello*, dim. of *verme* worm, fr. L *vermis*] **:** a dough made in long solid strings smaller in diameter than spaghetti

ver·mi·cide \'vər-mə-,sīd\ *n* **:** an agent that destroys worms

ver·mic·u·lar \(,)vər-'mik-yə-lər\ *adj* [NL *vermicularis*, fr. L *vermiculus*, dim. of *vermis*] **1 a :** resembling a worm in form or motion **b :** VERMICULATE **2 :** of, relating to, or caused by worms

ver·mic·u·late \-lət\ *or* **ver·mic·u·lat·ed** \-,lāt-əd\ *adj* [L *vermiculatus*, fr. *vermiculus*] **1 a :** VERMIFORM **b :** marked with irregular fine lines or with wavy impressed lines ⟨a ~ nut⟩ **2 :** TORTUOUS, INVOLUTE **3 :** full of worms **:** WORM-EATEN — **ver·mic·u·la·tion** \-,mik-yə-'lā-shən\ *n*

ver·mic·u·lite \(,)vər-'mik-yə-,līt\ *n* [L *vermiculus* little worm] **:** any of a number of micaceous minerals that are hydrous silicates derived usu. from alteration of mica whose granules expand greatly at high temperatures to give a lightweight highly water-absorbent material

ver·mi·form \'vər-mə-,fórm\ *adj* [NL *vermiformis*, fr. *vermi-* + *-formis* form] **:** resembling a worm in shape

vermiform appendix *n* **:** a narrow blind tube usu. about three or four inches long that extends from the cecum in the lower right-hand part of the abdomen

ver·mi·fuge \'vər-mə-,fyüj\ *adj* [prob. fr. (assumed) NL *vermifugus*, fr. *vermi-* + L *fugare* to put to flight — more at -FUGE] **:** serving to destroy or expel parasitic worms **:** ANTHELMINTIC — **vermifuge** *n*

ver·mil·ion *or* **ver·mil·lion** \vər-'mil-yən\ *n* [ME *vermilioun*, fr. OF *vermeillon*, fr. *vermeil*, adj., bright red, vermilion, fr. LL *vermiculus* kermes, fr. L, little worm] **1 a :** a bright red pigment consisting of mercuric sulfide **b :** any of various other red pigments **2 :** a variable color averaging a vivid reddish orange

ver·min \'vər-mən\ *n, pl* **vermin** [ME, fr. MF, fr. L *vermis* worm — more at WORM] **1 :** noxious, mischievous, or disgusting animals of small size, of common occurrence, and difficult to control; *also* **:** birds and mammals that prey upon game **2 :** a noxious or offensive person

ver·min·o·sis \,vər-mə-'nō-səs\ *n* **:** infestation with or disease caused by parasitic worms

ver·min·ous \'vər-mə-nəs\ *adj* **1 :** consisting of or being vermin **:** NOXIOUS ⟨a ~ brood⟩ **2 :** forming a breeding place for or infested by vermin **:** FILTHY ⟨~ garbage⟩ **3 :** caused by vermin ⟨~ disease⟩ — **ver·min·ous·ly** *adv*

ver·miv·o·rous \(,)vər-'miv-ə-rəs\ *adj* [ISV] **:** feeding on worms

ver·mouth \vər-'müth\ *n* [F *vermout*, fr. G *wermut* wormwood, fr. OHG *wermuota* — more at WORMWOOD] **:** a white wine flavored with aromatic herbs and used as an aperitif or in mixed drinks

1ver·nac·u·lar \və(r)-'nak-yə-lər\ *adj* [L *vernaculus* native, fr. *verna* slave born in his master's house, native] **1 a :** using a language or dialect native to a region or country rather than a literary, cultured, or foreign language **b :** of, relating to, or being a nonstandard or substandard language or dialect of a place region, or country **c :** of, relating to, or being the normal spoken form of a language **2 :** applied to a plant or animal in the common native speech as distinguished from the Latin nomenclature of scientific classification — **ver·nac·u·lar·ly** *adv*

2vernacular *n* **1 :** a vernacular language **2 :** the mode of expression of a group or class **3 :** a vernacular name of a plant or animal **syn** see DIALECT

ver·nac·u·lar·ism \-lə-,riz-əm\ *n* **:** a vernacular word or idiom

ver·nal \'vərn-ᵊl\ *adj* [L *vernalis*, alter. of *vernus*, fr. *ver* spring; akin to Gk *ear* spring] **1 :** of, relating to, or occurring in the spring ⟨~ equinox⟩ ⟨~ sunshine⟩ **2 :** fresh or new like the spring; *also* **:** YOUTHFUL — **ver·nal·ly** \-ᵊl-ē\ *adv*

ver·nal·iza·tion \,vərn-ᵊl-ə-'zā-shən\ *n* **:** the act or process of vernalizing

ver·nal·ize \'vərn-ᵊl-,īz\ *vt* **:** to hasten the flowering and fruiting of (plants) by treating seeds, bulbs, or seedlings to induce a shortening of the vegetative period

ver·na·tion \(,)vər-'nā-shən\ *n* [NL *vernation-, vernatio*, fr. L *vernatus*, pp. of *vernare* to behave as in spring, fr. *vernus* vernal] **:** the arrangement of foliage leaves within the bud

Ver·ner's law \,ve(ə)r-nərz-\ *n* [Karl A. *Verner* †1896 Dan philologist] **:** a statement in historical linguistics: in medial or final position in voiced environments and when the immediately preceding vowel did not bear the principal accent in Proto-Indo-European, the Proto-Germanic voiceless fricatives *f*, *þ*, and *χ* derived from the Proto-Indo-European voiceless stops *p*, *t*, and *k* and the Proto-Germanic voiceless fricative *s* derived from Proto-Indo-European *s* became the voiced fricatives *ƀ*, *ð*, *g*, and *z* represented in various recorded Germanic languages by *b*, *d*, *g*, and *r*

1ver·ni·er \'vər-nē-ər\ *n* [Pierre *Vernier* †1637 F mathematician] **1 :** a short scale made to slide along the divisions of a graduated instrument for indicating parts of divisions **2 :** a small auxiliary device used with a main device to obtain fine adjustment

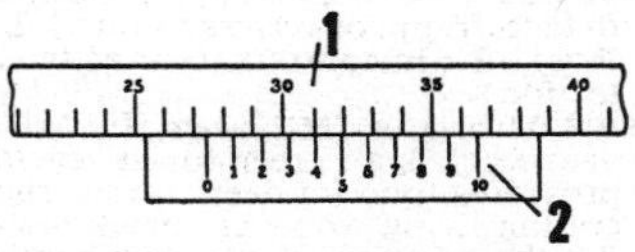

vernier 1: *1* regular scale, *2* vernier scale indicating measurement of 27.4

2vernier *adj* **:** having or comprising a vernier

vernier caliper *n* **:** a caliper gauge with a graduated beam and a sliding jaw having a vernier

vernier micrometer *n* **:** a micrometer caliper having on its barrel a vernier scale in order to subdivide the smallest readings of the micrometer

Ver·o·nal \'ver-ə-,nól, -ən-ᵊl\ *trademark* — used for barbital

1ve·ron·i·ca \və-'rän-i-kə\ *n* [NL, genus of herbs] **:** SPEEDWELL

2veronica *n* [ML, fr. *Veronica* St. Veronica] **:** an image of Christ's face said to have been impressed on the handkerchief that St. Veronica gave him to wipe his face with on the way to his crucifixion; *also* **:** a cloth resembling the legendary one of St. Veronica

ver·ru·ca \və-'rü-kə\ *n, pl* **ver·ru·cae** \-(,)kē, -,kī, -,sī\ [L — more at WART] **1 :** a wart or warty skin lesion **2 :** a warty elevation on a plant or animal surface

ver·ru·cose \və-'rü-,kōs\ *adj* **:** covered with warty elevations

ver·sal \'vər-səl, 'vär-\ *adj* [short for *universal*] *archaic* **:** ENTIRE, WHOLE ⟨as pale as any clout in the ~ world —Shak.⟩

1ver·sant \'vərs-ᵊnt\ *adj* [L *versant-, versans*, pres. part. of *versare, versari* to turn, occupy oneself, meditate] **1 :** mentally engaged or occupied **2 :** EXPERIENCED, PRACTICED **3 :** closely acquainted **:** CONVERSANT

2ver·sant \'vərs-ᵊnt, ve(ə)r-'säⁿ\ *n* [F, fr. MF, fr. prp. of *verser* to turn, pour, fr. L *versare* to turn; fr. its shedding of water] **1 :** the slope of a side of a mountain chain **2 :** the general slope of a country **:** INCLINATION

ver·sa·tile \'vər-sət-ᵊl\ *adj* [F or L; F, fr. L *versatilis* turning easily, fr. *versatus*, pp. of *versare* to turn, fr. *versus*, pp. of *vertere*] **1 :** changing or fluctuating readily **:** VARIABLE **2 :** embracing a variety of subjects, fields, or skills; *also* **:** turning with ease from one thing to another **3 a** (1) **:** capable of turning forward or backward **:** REVERSIBLE ⟨a ~ toe of a bird⟩ (2) **:** capable of moving laterally and up and down ⟨~ antennae⟩ **b** *of an anther* **:** having the filaments attached at or near the middle so as to swing freely **4 :** having many uses or applications — **ver·sa·tile·ly** \-ᵊl-(l)ē\ *adv* — **ver·sa·tile·ness** \-ᵊl-nəs\ *n*

syn VERSATILE, MANY-SIDED, ALL-AROUND mean having several skills or abilities. VERSATILE stresses aptitude and facility in several activities that require skill; MANY-SIDED implies breadth of interests as well as variety of talents; ALL-AROUND stresses completeness and symmetry of development as a person or within an activity that has many phases

ver·sa·til·i·ty \ˌvər-sə-ˈtil-ət-ē\ *n* **:** the quality or state of being versatile ⟨a writer of great ~⟩

vers de so·cié·té \ˌve(ə)r-də-ˌsȯs-ˌyā-ˈtā\ *n* [F, society verse] **:** witty and typically ironic light verse

1**verse** \ˈvərs\ *n* [ME *vers,* fr. OF, fr. L *versus,* lit., turning, fr. *versus,* pp. of *vertere* to turn — more at WORTH] **1 :** a line of metrical writing **2 a** (1) **:** metrical language (2) **:** metrical writing distinguished from poetry esp. by its lower level of intensity (3) **:** POETRY 2 **b :** POEM **c :** a body of metrical writing (as of a period) **3 :** STANZA **4 :** one of the short divisions into which a chapter of the Bible is traditionally divided

2**verse** *vi* **:** to make verse **:** VERSIFY ~ *vt* **1 :** to tell or celebrate in verse **2 :** to turn into verse

3**verse** *vt* [back-formation fr. *versed,* fr. L *versatus,* pp. of *versari* to be active, be occupied (in), pass. of *versare* to turn, fr. *versus,* pp.] **:** to familiarize by close association, study, or experience ⟨*versed* himself in the theater⟩

versed sine \ˈvərs(t)-\ *n* [NL *versus* turned, fr. L, pp. of *vertere*] **:** 1 minus the cosine of an angle

verse·man \ˈvərs-mən\ *n* **:** a maker of verses **:** VERSIFIER

vers·er \ˈvər-sər\ *n* **:** VERSIFIER

ver·si·cle \ˈvər-si-kəl\ *n* [ME, fr. L *versiculus,* dim. of *versus* verse] **1 :** a short verse or sentence said or sung in public worship by a priest or minister and followed by a response from the people **2 :** a little verse

ver·si·col·or \ˈvər-si-ˌkəl-ər\ *or* **ver·si·col·ored** \-ərd\ *adj* [L *versicolor,* fr. *versus,* pp. of *vertere* to turn, change + *color*] **1 :** having various colors **:** VARIEGATED **2 :** changeable in color **:** IRIDESCENT

ver·sic·u·lar \ˌvər-ˈsik-yə-lər\ *adj* [L *versiculus* little verse] **:** of or relating to verses or versicles

ver·si·fi·ca·tion \ˌvər-sə-fə-ˈkā-shən\ *n* **1 :** the making of verses **2 :** metrical structure **:** PROSODY

ver·si·fi·er \ˈvər-sə-ˌfī(-ə)r\ *n* **:** one that versifies

ver·si·fy \-ˌfī\ *vi* **:** to compose verses ~ *vt* **1 :** to relate or describe in verse **2 :** to turn into verse

ver·sine *or* **ver·sin** \ˈvər-ˌsīn\ *n* [by contr.] **:** VERSED SINE

ver·sion \ˈvər-zhən, -shən\ *n* [MF, fr. ML *version-, versio* act of turning, fr. L *versus,* pp. of *vertere*] **1 :** a translation from another language; *esp* **:** a translation of the Bible or a part of it **2 a :** an account or description from a particular point of view esp. as contrasted with another account **b :** an adaptation of a literary work ⟨a stage ~ of the novel⟩ **c :** an arrangement of a musical composition **3 :** a form or variant of a type or original ⟨an experimental ~ of the plane⟩ **4 a :** a condition in which an organ and esp. the uterus is turned from its normal position **b :** manual turning of a fetus in the uterus to aid delivery — **ver·sion·al** \ˈvərzh-nəl, ˈvərsh-, -ən-ᵊl\ *adj*

vers li·bre \ve(ə)r-ˈlēbrᵊ\ *n, pl* **vers li·bres** *same*\ [F] **:** FREE VERSE

vers–li·brist \-ˈlē-brəst\ *n* [F *vers-libriste*] **:** a writer of free verse

ver·so \ˈvər-(ˌ)sō\ *n* [NL *verso* (*folio*) the page being turned] **1 :** the side of a leaf (as of a manuscript) that is to be read second — compare RECTO **2 :** a left-hand page

verst \ˈvərst\ *n* [F *verste* & G *werst,* fr. Russ *versta;* akin to L *vertere* to turn] **:** a Russian unit of distance equal to 0.6629 miles

ver·sus \ˈvər-səs, -səz\ *prep* [ML, towards, against, fr. L, adv., so as to face, fr. pp. of *vertere* to turn] **1 :** AGAINST ⟨John Doe ~ Richard Roe⟩ **2 :** in contrast to or as the alternative of ⟨free trade ~ protection⟩

vert \ˈvərt\ *n* [ME *verte,* fr. MF *vert,* fr. *vert* green — more at VERDANT] **1 a :** green forest vegetation esp. when forming cover or providing food for deer **b :** the right or privilege (as in England) of cutting living wood or sometimes of pasturing animals in a forest **2 :** the color green esp. as a heraldic tincture

ver·te·bra \ˈvərt-ə-brə\ *n, pl* **ver·te·brae** \-(ˌ)brē, -ˌbrā\ *or* **vertebras** [L, joint, vertebra, fr. *vertere* to turn — more at WORTH] **:** one of the bony or cartilaginous segments composing the spinal column, consisting in some lower vertebrates of several distinct elements which never become united, and in higher vertebrates having a short more or less cylindrical body whose ends articulate by pads of elastic or cartilaginous tissue with those of adjacent vertebrae and a bony arch that encloses the spinal cord

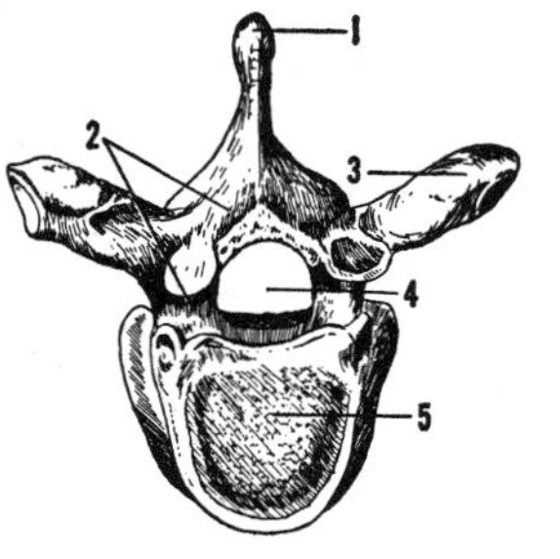

sixth thoracic vertebra, seen from above: *1* neural spine, *2* neural arch, *3* transverse process, *4* spinal foramen, *5* centrum

ver·te·bral \ˈvərt-ə-brəl, ˌvər-ˈtē-\ *adj* **1 :** of, relating to, or being vertebrae or the vertebral column **:** SPINAL **2 :** composed of or having vertebrae — **vertebral** *n* — **ver·te·bral·ly** \-ē\ *adv*

vertebral column *n* **:** SPINAL COLUMN

1**ver·te·brate** \ˈvərt-ə-brət, -ˌbrāt\ *adj* [NL *vertebratus,* fr. L, jointed, fr. *vertebra*] **1 a :** having a spinal column **b :** of or relating to the vertebrates **2 :** having a strong framework suggesting vertebrae **3 :** organized or constructed in orderly or developed form ⟨a ~ piece of composition⟩

2**vertebrate** *n* [deriv. of NL *vertebratus*] **:** any of a comprehensive division (Vertebrata) usu. held to be a subphylum of chordates comprising animals with a segmented spinal column together with a few primitive forms in which the backbone is represented by a notochord

ver·te·bra·tion \ˌvərt-ə-ˈbrā-shən\ *n* **:** highly developed organization **:** FIRMNESS ⟨the solid ~ of his logic⟩

ver·tex \ˈvər-ˌteks\ *n, pl* **ver·tex·es** *or* **ver·ti·ces** \ˈvərt-ə-ˌsēz\ [L *vertic-, vertex, vortic-, vortex* whirl, whirlpool, top of the head, summit, fr. *vertere* to turn] **1 a** (1) **:** the point opposite to and farthest from the base in a figure (2) **:** the termination or intersection of lines or curves **b :** ZENITH 1 **2 :** the top of the head **3 :** a principal or highest point **:** SUMMIT, APEX ⟨a monument on the ~ of the hill⟩

ver·ti·cal \ˈvərt-i-kəl\ *adj* [MF or LL; MF, fr. LL *verticalis,* fr. L *vertic-, vertex*] **1 a :** situated at the highest point **:** directly overhead or in the zenith **b :** being an aerial photograph taken with the camera pointing straight down or nearly so **2 a :** perpendicular to the plane of the horizon or to a primary axis **:** UPRIGHT **b** (1) **:** located at right angles to the plane of a supporting surface (2) **:** lying in the direction of an axis **:** LENGTHWISE **3 :** composed of economic units on different levels of production or distribution ⟨a ~ business organization⟩ — **vertical** *n* — **ver·ti·cal·ly** \-k(ə-)lē\ *adv* — **ver·ti·cal·ness** \-kəl-nəs\ *n*

syn VERTICAL, PERPENDICULAR, PLUMB mean being at a right angle with the plane of the horizon. VERTICAL suggests a line or direction rising upward toward or approximately toward a zenith; PERPENDICULAR may suggest a stiff straightness; it is more likely than VERTICAL to suggest a straight downward drop; PLUMB stresses an exact verticality as determined by the force of gravity

vertical circle *n* **:** a great circle of the celestial sphere whose plane is perpendicular to that of the horizon

vertical file *n* **:** a collection of pamphlets, clippings, and ephemera (as in a library) that is maintained to answer brief questions quickly or to provide points of information not easy to locate elsewhere

ver·ti·cal·i·ty \ˌvərt-ə-ˈkal-ət-ē\ *n* **:** the quality or state of being vertical

vertical union *n* **:** INDUSTRIAL UNION

ver·ti·cil \ˈvərt-ə-ˌsil\ *n* [NL *verticillus,* dim. of L *vertex* whirl] **:** a circle of similar parts (as leaves, flowers, or inflorescences) about the same point on the axis **:** WHORL

ver·ti·cil·las·ter \ˌvərt-ə-ˌsil-ˈas-tər\ *n* [NL, fr. *verticillus* + L *-aster,* suffix denoting partial resemblance] **:** a mixed inflorescence esp. of mints that consists of a pair of much-condensed nearly sessile cymes arranged around an axis like a true verticil — **ver·ti·cil·las·trate** \-ˈas-ˌtrāt\ *adj*

ver·ti·cil·late \ˌvərt-ə-ˈsil-ət\ *adj* **:** arranged in verticils **:** WHORLED; *esp* **:** arranged in a transverse whorl like the spokes of a wheel ⟨~ leaves⟩ ⟨a ~ shell⟩ — **ver·ti·cil·late·ly** *adv* — **ver·ti·cil·la·tion** \ˌvərt-ə-ˌsil-ˈā-shən\ *n*

ver·ti·cil·li·um \ˌvərt-ə-ˈsil-ē-əm\ *n* [NL, genus name, fr. *verticillus*] **:** any of a genus (*Verticillium*) of imperfect fungi including several that cause destructive wilts in plants

ver·tig·i·nous \(ˌ)vər-ˈtij-ə-nəs\ *adj* [L *vertiginosus,* fr. *vertigin-, vertigo*] **1 :** characterized by or suffering from vertigo **:** DIZZY **2 :** GIDDY, INCONSTANT **3 :** causing or tending to cause dizziness **4 :** marked by turning **:** ROTARY ⟨the ~ motion of the earth⟩ — **ver·tig·i·nous·ly** *adv*

ver·ti·go \ˈvərt-i-ˌgō\ *n, pl* **ver·ti·goes** *or* **ver·tig·i·nes** \(ˌ)vər-ˈtij-ə-ˌnēz\ [L *vertigin-, vertigo,* fr. *vertere* to turn] **1 a :** a disordered state in which the individual or his environs seem to whirl dizzily **:** GIDDINESS **b :** a dizzy confused state of mind **2 :** disordered vertiginous movement as a symptom of disease in lower animals; *also* **:** a disease (as gid) causing this

ver·tu \ˌvər-ˈtü, ve(ə)r-\ *var of* VIRTU

Ver·tum·nus \(ˌ)vər-ˈtəm-nəs\ *n* [L] **:** the god of the changing seasons and of developing vegetation in Roman mythology

ver·vain \ˈvər-ˌvān\ *n* [ME *verveine,* fr. MF, fr. L *verbena,* sing. of *verbenae* sacred boughs, certain medicinal plants; akin to L *verber* rod, Gk *rhabdos*] **:** any of a genus (*Verbena* of the family Verbenaceae, the vervain family) of plants; *esp* **:** one with small spicate flowers

verve \ˈvərv, ˈve(ə)rv\ *n* [F, fantasy, caprice, animation, fr. L *verba,* pl. of *verbum* word — more at WORD] **1** *archaic* **:** special ability or talent **2 a :** the spirit and enthusiasm animating artistic composition or performance **:** VIVACITY **b :** ENERGY, VITALITY

ver·vet \ˈvər-vət\ *n* [F] **:** a southern and eastern African guenon monkey (*Cercopithecus pygerythrus*) related to the grivet but having the face, chin, hands, and feet black

1**very** \ˈver-ē\ *adj* [ME *verray, verry,* fr. OF *verai,* fr. (assumed) VL *veracus,* alter. of L *verac-, verax* truthful, fr. *verus* true; akin to OE *wǣr* true, OHG *wāra* trust, care, Gk *ēra* (acc.) favor] **1 a :** properly entitled to the name or designation **:** TRUE **b :** ACTUAL, REAL **c :** SIMPLE, PLAIN ⟨in ~ truth⟩ **2 a :** EXACT, PRECISE ⟨~ heart of the city⟩ **b :** exactly suitable or necessary ⟨the ~ thing for the purpose⟩ **3 a :** ABSOLUTE, UTTER ⟨the *veriest* fool alive⟩ **b :** SHEER, UNQUALIFIED ⟨the ~ shame of it⟩ **4 :** MERE, BARE ⟨the ~ thought terrified him⟩ **5 :** SELFSAME, IDENTICAL ⟨the ~ man I saw⟩ **6 :** SPECIAL, PARTICULAR **syn** see SAME

2**very** *adv* **1 :** to a high degree **:** EXCEEDINGLY ⟨a ~ hot day⟩ ⟨~ much better⟩ **2 :** in actual fact **:** TRULY ⟨the ~ best store in town⟩ ⟨told the ~ same story⟩

very high frequency *n* **:** a radio frequency in the range of the radio spectrum above high frequency; *specif* **:** such a frequency in the part of the band between 100 and 156 megacycles — see RADIO FREQUENCY table

Very light \ˌver-ē-, ˌvi(ə)r-ē-\ *n* [Edward W. *Very* †1910 Am naval officer] **:** a pyrotechnic signal in a system of signaling using white or colored balls of fire projected from a special pistol

very low frequency *n* **:** a radio frequency in the lowest range of the radio spectrum — see RADIO FREQUENCY table

Very pistol *n* [Edward W. *Very*] **:** a pistol for firing Very lights

Very Reverend — used as a title for various ecclesiastical officials (as cathedral deans and canons, rectors of Roman Catholic colleges and seminaries, superiors of some religious houses, and some prelates having the title monsignor)

ve·si·ca \və-ˈsē-kə, -ˈsī-\ *n, pl* **ve·si·cae** \-ˈsē-ˌkī; -ˈsī-(ˌ)kē, -ˈsī-(ˌ)sē\ [L — more at VENTER] **:** BLADDER

ves·i·cal \ˈves-i-kəl\ *adj* **:** of or relating to a bladder and esp. to the urinary bladder

ves·i·cant \-kənt\ *n* [L *vesica* bladder, blister] **:** an agent (as a drug or a plant substance) that induces blistering — **vesicant** *adj*

ves·i·cate \ˈves-ə-ˌkāt\ *vb* [L *vesica* blister] **:** BLISTER — **ves·i·ca·tion** \ˌves-ə-ˈkā-shən\ *n*

ves·i·ca·to·ry \ˈves-i-kə-ˌtōr-ē, -ˌtȯr-\ *adj or n* **:** VESICANT

ves·i·cle \ˈves-i-kəl\ *n* [MF *vesicule,* fr. L *vesicula* small bladder, blister, fr. dim. of *vesica*] **:** a body felt to resemble a bladder esp. in constituting a small thin-walled cavity: as **a :** a plant or animal structure (as a cyst, vacuole, or cell) in the form of a membranous cavity; *esp* **:** one filled with fluid **b :** a small elevation of the cuticle

of the skin containing a clear watery fluid : BLISTER **c** : a small cavity in a mineral or rock

ve·sic·u·lar \və-ˈsik-yə-lər, ve-\ *adj* [NL *vesicula* vesicle, fr. L, small bladder] **1** : of or relating to vesicles and esp. to the alveoli of the lungs **2** : having the form of structure of a vesicle **3** : containing, composed of, or characterized by vesicles : VESICULATE — **ve·sic·u·lar·ly** *adv*

1**ve·sic·u·late** \-lət\ *adj* **1** : containing or covered with vesicles **2** : VESICULAR 2

2**ve·sic·u·late** \-ˌlāt\ *vt* : to make vesicular ~ *vi* : to become vesicular — **ve·sic·u·la·tion** \və-ˌsik-yə-ˈlā-shən, (ˌ)ve-\ *n*

ves·pal \ˈves-pəl\ *adj* [L *vespa* wasp — more at WASP] : of or relating to wasps

1**ves·per** \ˈves-pər\ *n* [ME, fr. L, evening, evening star — more at WEST] **1** *cap* : EVENING STAR **2** : a vesper bell **3** *archaic* : EVENING, EVENTIDE

2**vesper** *adj* : of or relating to vespers or the evening

1**ves·per·al** \ˈves-p(ə-)rəl\ *adj* : VESPER ⟨a ~ breeze⟩; *esp* : CREPUSCULAR 2 ⟨~ insects⟩

2**vesperal** *n* **1** : a book containing the office and music for vespers **2** : an altar cover used to protect the white altar cloths between ceremonies

ves·pers \ˈves-pərz\ *n pl but sing or pl in constr, often cap* [F *vespres*, fr. ML *vesperae*, fr. L, pl. of *vespera* evening; akin to L *vesper* evening] **1** : the 6th of the canonical hours **2** : EVENSONG 2 **3** : a late afternoon or evening worship service

ves·per·til·ian \ˌves-pər-ˈtil-ē-ən, -ˈtil-yən\ *adj* [L *vespertilio* bat, fr. *vesper*] : of or relating to bats

ves·per·ti·nal \-ˈtīn-ᵊl\ *adj* : VESPERTINE

ves·per·tine \ˈves-pər-ˌtīn\ *adj* [L *vespertinus*, fr. *vesper*] **1 a** : of, relating to, or occurring in the evening **b** : resembling that of evening ⟨~ shadows⟩ **2** : active or flourishing in the evening : CREPUSCULAR: as **a** : feeding or flying in early evening **b** : blossoming in the evening

ves·pi·ary \ˈves-pē-ˌer-ē\ *n* [L *vespa* + E *-iary* (as in *apiary*)] : a nest of a social wasp or the colony inhabiting it

ves·pid \ˈves-pəd\ *n* [deriv. of L *vespa* wasp — more at WASP] : any of a cosmopolitan family (Vespidae) of hymenopterous insects comprising the social wasps that live in colonies like bees — **vespid** *adj*

ves·pine \ˈves-ˌpīn\ *adj* [L *vespa* wasp] : of, relating to, or resembling wasps and esp. vespid wasps

ves·sel \ˈves-əl\ *n* [ME, fr. OF *vaissel*, fr. LL *vascellum*, dim. of L *vas* vase, vessel — more at VASE] **1 a** : a hollow or concave utensil (as a hogshead, bottle, kettle, cup, or bowl) for holding something **b** : a person into whom some quality (as grace) is infused **2 a** : a hollow structure designed for navigation on the water; *esp* : one bigger than a rowboat **b** : any of various aircraft **3 a** : a tube or canal (as an artery) in which a body fluid is contained and conveyed or circulated **b** : a conducting tube in a vascular plant formed by the fusion and loss of end walls of a series of cells

1**vest** \ˈvest\ *vb* [ME *vesten*, fr. MF *vestir* to clothe, invest, fr. L *vestire* to clothe, fr. *vestis* clothing, garment — more at WEAR] *vt* **1 a** : to place or give into the possession or discretion of some person or authority; *esp* : to give to a person a legally fixed immediate right of present or future enjoyment of (as an estate) **b** : to clothe with a particular authority, right, or property **2** : to clothe with or as if with a garment; *esp* : to garb in ecclesiastical vestments ~ *vi* **1** : to become legally vested **2** : to put on garments; *esp* : to robe in ecclesiastical vestments

2**vest** *n* [F *veste*, fr. It, fr. L *vestis* garment] **1** *archaic* **a** : a loose outer garment : ROBE **b** : CLOTHING, GARB **2 a** : a man's sleeveless garment worn under a suit coat : WAISTCOAT **b** : a similar garment for women **c** : a protective garment worn on active military duty or in or on the water **3 a** *chiefly Brit* : a man's undershirt **b** : a knitted undershirt for women **4** : a plain or decorative piece used to fill in the front neckline of a woman's outer garment (as a waist, coat, or gown) — **vest·like** \-ˌlīk\ *adj*

ves·ta \ˈves-tə\ *n* [L *Vesta*] **1** *cap* : the goddess of the hearth and hearth fire in Roman mythology **2** : a short match with a shank of wax; *also* : a short wooden match

1**ves·tal** \ˈvest-ᵊl\ *adj* **1** : of or relating to the Roman goddess Vesta **2 a** : of or relating to a vestal virgin **b** : CHASTE — **ves·tal·ly** \-ᵊl-ē\ *adv*

2**vestal** *n* **1** : a virgin consecrated to the Roman goddess Vesta and to the service of watching the sacred fire perpetually kept burning upon her altar **2** : a chaste woman

vested interest *n* **1 a** : an interest (as a title to an estate) carrying a legal right of present or future enjoyment and of present alienation **b** : an interest (as in an existing political, economic, or social arrangement) in which the holder has a strong personal commitment **2** : one having a vested interest in something and esp. an existing economic or political privilege

vest·ee \ve-ˈstē\ *n* **1** : DICKEY; *esp* : one made to resemble a vest and worn under a coat **2** : VEST 4

ves·ti·ary \ˈves-tē-ˌer-ē, ˈves(h)-chē-\ *n* [ME *vestiarie*, fr. OF, vestry — more at VESTRY] **1** : a room (as in a monastery) where clothing is kept **2** : CLOTHING, RAIMENT; *esp* : a set of clerical vestments

ves·tib·u·lar \ve-ˈstib-yə-lər\ *adj* : of, relating to, or functioning as a vestibule

ves·ti·bule \ˈves-tə-ˌbyü(ə)l\ *n* [L *vestibulum*] **1 a** : a passage, hall, or room between the outer door and the interior of a building : LOBBY **b** : an enclosed entrance at the end of a railway passenger car **2** : any of various bodily cavities esp. when serving as or resembling an entrance to some other cavity or space: as **a** : the central cavity of the bony labyrinth of the ear or the parts of the membranous labyrinth that it contains **b** : the part of the left ventricle below the aortic orifice

ves·ti·buled \-ˌbyü(ə)ld\ *adj* : having a vestibule

vestibule school *n* : a school organized in an industrial plant to train new workers in specific skills

ves·tige \ˈves-tij\ *n* [F, fr. L *vestigium* footstep, footprint, track, vestige] **1 a** (1) : a trace or visible sign left by something vanished or lost (2) : a minute remaining amount **b** : the mark of a foot on the earth : TRACK **2** : a small and degenerate or imperfectly developed bodily part or organ that remains from one more fully developed in an earlier stage of the individual, in a past generation, or in closely related forms **syn** see TRACE — **ves·ti·gial** \ve-ˈstij-(ē-)əl\ *adj* — **ves·ti·gial·ly** \-ē\ *adv*

vest·ment \ˈves(t)-mənt\ *n* [ME *vestement*, fr. OF, fr. L *vestimentum*, fr. *vestire* to clothe] **1 a** : an outer garment; *esp* : a robe of ceremony or office **b** *pl* : CLOTHING, GARB **2** : a covering resembling a garment ⟨the verdant ~ which spring spreads over the land⟩ **3** : one of the articles of the ceremonial attire and insignia worn by ecclesiastical officiants and assistants as indicative of their rank and appropriate to the rite being celebrated — **vest·men·tal** \ves(t)-ˈment-ᵊl\ *adj*

vestments 3 of 16th century archbishop: *1* alb, *2* apparel on alb, *3* stole, *4* tunicle, *5* dalmatic, *6* chasuble, *7* maniple, *8* pallium, *9* amice, *10* miter, *11* lappet, *12* crosier

vest–pock·et \ˌvest-ˌpäk-ət\ *adj* : adapted to fit into the vest pocket : of very small size or scope

ves·try \ˈves-trē\ *n* [ME *vestrie*, prob. modif. of MF *vestiarie*, fr. ML *vestiarium*, fr. L *vestire*] **1 a** : a room in a church building for the vestments of the clergy, the altar linen and hangings, and the sacred vessels — called also *sacristy* **b** : a storage place for clothing **c** : a room used for church meetings and classes **2 a** : the business meeting of an English parish; *also* : the parishioners assembled for it **b** : an elective body administering the temporal affairs and ministerial relations of an Episcopal parish

ves·try·man \-mən\ *n* : a member of a vestry

1**ves·ture** \ˈves(h)-chər\ *n* [ME, fr. MF, fr. *vestir* to clothe — more at VEST] **1 a** : a covering garment (as a robe or vestment) **b** : CLOTHING, APPAREL **2** : something that covers like a garment

2**vesture** *vt* : to cover with vesture : CLOTHE

ve·su·vi·an \və-ˈsü-vē-ən\ *n* **1** [G, fr. *Vesuv* Vesuvius, volcano in Italy] : IDOCRASE **2** [*Vesuvian*, adj. (of Vesuvius)] : a match or fusee used esp. formerly for lighting cigars

ve·su·vi·an·ite \-vē-ə-ˌnīt\ *n* : IDOCRASE

1**vet** \ˈvet\ *n* : VETERINARIAN, VETERINARY

2**vet** *vt* **vet·ted**; **vet·ting** **1 a** : to provide veterinary care for (an animal) or medical care for (a person) **b** : to subject (a person or animal) to a physical examination or checkup **2** : to subject to expert appraisal or correction

3**vet** *adj or n* : VETERAN

vetch \ˈvech\ *n* [ME *vecche*, fr. ONF *veche*, fr. L *vicia*; akin to OE *wicga* insect, L *vincire* to bind, OE *wīr* wire] : any of a genus (*Vicia*) of herbaceous twining leguminous plants including valuable fodder and soil-building plants

vetch·ling \-liŋ\ *n* : any of various small leguminous plants (genus *Lathyrus* and esp. *L. pratensis*)

vet·er·an \ˈvet-ə-rən, ˈve-trən\ *n* [L *veteranus*, fr. *veteranus* old, of long experience, fr. *veter-*, *vetus* old — more at WETHER] **1 a** (1) : an old soldier of long service (2) : a former member of the armed forces **b** : a person of long experience in politics, a profession, or some other occupation or skill **2** : an old tree usu. over two feet in diameter breast high — **veteran** *adj*

Veterans Day *n* : November 11 observed as a legal holiday in the U.S. in commemoration of the end of hostilities in 1918 and 1945

veterans' preference *n* : preferential treatment given qualified veterans of the U. S. armed forces under federal or state law; *specif* : special consideration (as by allowance of points) on a civil service examination

vet·er·i·nar·i·an \ˌvet-ə-rən-ˈer-ē-ən, ˌve-trən-, ˌvet-ᵊn-\ *n* : one qualified and authorized to treat diseases and injuries of animals

1**vet·er·i·nary** \ˈvet-ə-rən-ˌer-ē, ˈve-trən-, ˈvet-ᵊn-\ *adj* [L *veterinarius* of beasts of burden, fr. *veterinae* beasts of burden, fr. fem. pl. of *veterinus* of beasts of burden; akin to L *veter-*, *vetus* old] : of, relating to, or being the science and art of prevention, cure, or alleviation of disease and injury in animals and esp. domestic animals

2**veterinary** *n* : VETERINARIAN

veterinary surgeon *n, Brit* : VETERINARIAN

vet·i·ver \ˈvet-ə-vər\ *n* [F *vétiver*, fr. Tamil *veṭṭivēr*] : an East Indian grass (*Vetiveria zizanioides*) cultivated in warm regions esp. for its fragrant roots used for making mats and screens and in perfumes; *also* : its root

1**ve·to** \ˈvēt-(ˌ)ō\ *n, pl* **vetoes** [L, I forbid, fr. *vetare* to forbid] **1** : an authoritative prohibition : INTERDICTION **2 a** : a power of one department or branch of a government to forbid or prohibit finally or provisionally the carrying out of projects attempted by another department; *esp* : a power vested in a chief executive to prevent permanently or temporarily the enactment of measures passed by a legislature **b** (1) : the exercise of such authority (2) : a message communicating the reasons of an executive and esp. the president of the U. S. for vetoing a proposed law

2**veto** *vt* : to refuse to admit or approve : PROHIBIT; *also* : to refuse assent to (a legislative bill) so as to prevent enactment or cause reconsideration — **ve·to·er** \-ˌō(-ə)r\ *n*

vex \ˈveks\ *vt* **vexed** *also* **vext**; **vex·ing** [ME *vexen*, fr. MF *vexer*, fr. L *vexare* to agitate, trouble, vex] **1 a** : to bring trouble, distress, or agitation to **b** : to bring physical distress to **c** : to irritate or annoy by petty provocations : HARASS **d** : PUZZLE, BAFFLE **2** : to debate or discuss at length ⟨a *vexed* question⟩ **3** : to shake or toss about **syn** see ANNOY

vex·a·tion \vek-ˈsā-shən\ *n* **1** : the quality or state of being vexed : IRRITATION **2** : the act of harassing or vexing : TROUBLING **3** : a cause of trouble : AFFLICTION

vex·a·tious \-shəs\ *adj* **1 a** : causing vexation : DISTRESSING **b** : intended (as litigation) to harass **2** : full of disorder or stress : TROUBLED — **vex·a·tious·ly** *adv* — **vex·a·tious·ness** *n*

vexed·ly \ˈvek-səd-lē, ˈveks-tlē\ *adv* : in a vexed manner

1**vex·il·lary** \ˈvek-sə-ˌler-ē\ *n* [L *vexillarius*, fr. *vexillum*] **1** : a veteran under a special standard in an ancient Roman army **2** : STANDARD-BEARER

2**vexillary** *adj* **1 :** of or relating to an ensign or standard **2 :** of, relating to, or being a vexillum
vex·il·late \'vek-sə-,lāt, vek-'sil-ət\ *adj* **:** having a vexillum
vex·il·lum \vek-'sil-əm\ *n, pl* **vex·il·la** \-ə\ [L] **1 :** a square flag of the ancient Roman cavalry **2 :** STANDARD 8a **3 :** the web or vane of a feather **4 :** a company of ancient Roman troops serving under one standard
via \,vī-ə, ,vē-ə\ *prep* [L, abl. of *via* way; akin to Gk *hiesthai* to hurry — more at VIM] **1 :** by way of **2 :** through the medium of; *also* **:** by means of
vi·a·bil·i·ty \,vī-ə-'bil-ət-ē\ *n* **:** the quality or state of being viable
vi·a·ble \'vī-ə-bəl\ *adj* [F, fr. MF, fr. *vie* life, fr. L *vita* — more at VITAL] **1 :** capable of living; *esp* **:** born alive with such form and development of organs as to be normally capable of living **2 :** capable of growing or developing ⟨~ seeds⟩ ⟨~ eggs⟩ **3 :** WORKABLE — **vi·a·bly** \-blē\ *adv*
via·duct \'vī-ə-,dəkt\ *n* [L *via* way, road + E *-duct* (as in *aqueduct*)] **1 :** a bridge esp. when resting on a series of narrow reinforced concrete or masonry arches, having high supporting towers or piers, and carrying a road or railroad over an obstruction (as a valley or river) **2 :** a steel bridge made up of short spans carried on high steel towers

viaduct

vi·al \'vī(-ə)l\ *n* [ME *fiole, viole,* fr. MF *fiole,* fr. OProv *fiola,* fr. L *phiala* — more at PHIAL] **:** a small vessel for liquids
via me·dia \,vī-ə-'mēd-ē-ə; ,vē-ə-'mād-ē-ə, -'med-\ *n* [L] **:** a middle way
vi·and \'vī-ənd\ *n* [ME, fr. MF *viande,* fr. ML *vivanda* food, alter. of L *vivenda,* neut. pl. of *vivendus,* gerundive of *vivere* to live — more at QUICK] **1 :** an article of food **2** *pl* **:** PROVISIONS, FOOD
vi·at·i·cum \vī-'at-i-kəm, vē-\ *n, pl* **viaticums** *or* **vi·at·i·ca** \-kə\ [L — more at VOYAGE] **1 a :** an allowance (as of transportation or supplies and money) for traveling expenses **b :** provisions for a journey **2 :** the Christian Eucharist given to a person in danger of death
vi·a·tor \vī-'āt-ər, vē-'ä-,tȯ(ə)r\ *n* [L, fr. *via*] **:** TRAVELER, WAYFARER
vi·bran·cy \'vī-brən-sē\ *n* **:** the quality or state of being vibrant **:** VIBRATION
vi·brant \-brənt\ *adj* **1 a** (1) **:** VIBRATING, PULSING (2) **:** pulsating with life, vigor, or activity **b** (1) **:** readily set in vibration (2) **:** RESPONSIVE, SENSITIVE **2 :** sounding as a result of vibration **:** RESONANT — **vi·brant·ly** *adv*
vi·bra·phone \'vī-brə-,fōn\ *n* [L *vibrare* + ISV *-phone*] **:** a percussion musical instrument resembling the xylophone but having metal bars and motor-driven resonators for sustaining the tone and producing a vibrato — **vi·bra·phon·ist** \-,fō-nəst\ *n*
vi·brate \'vī-,brāt\ *vb* [L *vibratus,* pp. of *vibrare* to shake, vibrate — more at WIPE] *vt* **1 :** to swing or move to and fro **2 :** to emit with or as if with a vibratory motion **3 :** to mark or measure by oscillation ⟨a pendulum *vibrating* seconds⟩ **4 :** to set in vibration ~ *vi* **1 a :** to move to and fro or from side to side **:** OSCILLATE **b :** WAVER ⟨~ between opinions⟩ **2 :** to be in a state of vibration **:** QUIVER **3 :** to respond sympathetically **:** THRILL ⟨~ to the opportunity⟩ **syn** see SWING
vi·bra·tile \'vī-brət-ᵊl, -brə-,tīl\ *adj* **1 :** characterized by vibration **2 :** adapted to or used in vibratory motion ⟨the ~ organs of insects⟩ — **vi·bra·til·i·ty** \,vī-brə-'til-ət-ē\ *n*
vi·bra·tion \vī-'brā-shən\ *n* **1 a :** a periodic motion of the particles of an elastic body or medium in alternately opposite directions from the position of equilibrium when that equilibrium has been disturbed (as when a stretched cord produces musical tones or particles of air transmit sounds to the ear) **b :** the action of vibrating **:** the state of being vibrated or in vibratory motion: as (1) **:** OSCILLATION (2) **:** a quivering or trembling motion **:** QUIVER **2 :** an instance of vibration **3 :** vacillation in opinion or action **:** WAVERING — **vi·bra·tion·al** \-shnəl, -shən-ᵊl\ *adj* — **vi·bra·tion·less** \-shən-ləs\ *adj*
vi·bra·tive \'vī-,brāt-iv, -brət-\ *adj* **:** VIBRATORY
vi·bra·to \vē-'brät-(,)ō\ *n, pl* **vibratos** [It, pp. of *vibrare* to vibrate, fr. L] **1 :** a slightly tremulous effect imparted to vocal or instrumental tone for added warmth and expressiveness by slight and rapid variations in pitch **2 :** TREMOLO 1b
vi·bra·tor \'vī-,brāt-ər\ *n* **1 :** one that vibrates or causes vibration: as **a :** a vibrating electrical apparatus used in massage **b :** a vibrating device (as in an electric bell or buzzer) **2 :** an electromagnetic device that converts low direct current to pulsating direct current or alternating current
vi·bra·to·ry \'vī-brə-,tōr-ē, -,tȯr-\ *adj* **1 :** consisting in, capable of, or causing vibration or oscillation **2 :** VIBRANT, VIBRATING
vib·rio \'vib-rē-,ō\ *n* [NL, genus name, fr. L *vibrare* to vibrate] **:** any of a genus (*Vibrio*) of short rigid motile bacteria typically shaped like a comma or an S — **vib·ri·oid** \-rē-,ȯid\ *adj* — **vib·ri·on·ic** \,vib-rē-'än-ik\ *adj*
vib·ri·o·sis \,vib-rē-'ō-səs\ *n* [NL, fr. *Vibrio*] **:** infestation with or disease caused by vibrios
vi·bris·sa \vī-'bris-ə, və-\ *n, pl* **vi·bris·sae** \vī-'bris-(,)ē; və-'bris-(,)ē, -,ī\ [L; akin to L *vibrare*] **1 :** one of the stiff hairs esp. about the nostrils or on other parts of the face in many mammals that often serve as tactile organs **2 :** one of the bristly feathers near the mouth of many and esp. insectivorous birds that may help to prevent the escape of insects — **vi·bris·sal** \-'bris-əl\ *adj*
vi·bro·graph \'vī-brə-,graf\ *n* [L *vibrare* + ISV *-o-* + *-graph*] **:** an instrument to observe, measure, and record vibrations
vi·brom·e·ter \vī-'bräm-ət-ər\ *n* [L *vibrare* + *-o-* + *-meter*] **:** VIBROGRAPH
vi·bur·num \vī-'bər-nəm\ *n* [NL, genus name, fr. L, wayfaring tree] **:** any of a genus (*Viburnum*) of widely distributed shrubs or trees of the honeysuckle family with simple leaves and white or rarely pink cymose flowers
vic·ar \'vik-ər\ *n* [ME, fr. L *vicarius,* fr. *vicarius* vicarious] **1 :** one serving as a substitute or agent; *specif* **:** an administrative deputy **2 :** the priest of an Anglican parish of which the tithes are owned by a layman or formerly by an ecclesiastical corporation **3 :** an Anglican minister having charge of a mission or dependent parish — **vic·ar·ship** \-,ship\ *n*
Vi·cara \vī-'kar-ə\ *trademark* — used for a woolly protein textile fiber from corn zein used esp. in blends with other fibers
vic·ar·age \'vik-ə-rij\ *n* **1 :** the benefice of a vicar **2 :** the house of a vicar **3 :** VICARIATE 1
vicar apostolic *n, pl* **vicars apostolic :** a Roman Catholic titular bishop who governs a territory not yet organized as a diocese
vic·ar·ate \'vik-ə-rət, -,rāt\ *n* **:** VICARIATE
vicar fo·rane \-fō-'rān, -fə-; -'fȯr-ən, -'fär-\ *n, pl* **vicars forane** [LL *foranus* situated on the outside — more at FOREIGN] **:** DEAN 1b
vicar–general *n, pl* **vicars–general :** an administrative deputy of a Roman Catholic or Anglican bishop or of the head of a religious order
vi·car·i·al \vī-'kar-ē-əl, və-, -'ker-\ *adj* [L *vicarius*] **1 :** DELEGATED, DEPUTED **2 :** of or relating to a vicar
vi·car·i·ate \-ē-ət\ *n* [ML *vicariatus,* fr. L *vicarius* vicar] **1 :** the office, jurisdiction, or tenure of a vicar **2 :** the office or district of a governmental administrative deputy
vi·car·i·ous \vī-'kar-ē-əs, -'ker-\ *adj* [L *vicarius,* fr. *vicis* change, alternation, stead — more at WEEK] **1 :** serving instead of someone or something else **:** DELEGATED **2 :** performed or suffered by one person as a substitute for another or to the benefit or advantage of another **:** SUBSTITUTIONARY ⟨~ sacrifice⟩ **3 :** experienced or realized through imaginative or sympathetic participation in the experience of another **4 :** occurring in an unexpected or abnormal part of the body instead of the usual one ⟨bleeding from the gums sometimes replaces the discharge from the uterus in ~ menstruation⟩ — **vi·car·i·ous·ly** *adv* — **vi·car·i·ous·ness** *n*
Vicar of Christ : the Roman Catholic pope
1**vice** \'vīs\ *n* [ME, fr. OF, fr. L *vitium* fault, vice] **1 a :** moral depravity or corruption **:** WICKEDNESS **b :** a moral fault or failing **c :** FOIBLE **2 :** BLEMISH, DEFECT **3 :** a physical imperfection, deformity, or taint **4 a** *often cap* **:** a character representing one of the vices in an English morality play **b :** BUFFOON, JESTER **5 :** an abnormal behavior pattern in a domestic animal detrimental to its health or usefulness **6 :** sexual immorality; *esp* **:** PROSTITUTION **syn** see FAULT, OFFENSE
2**vice** *n* [ME *vis, vice* screw, fr. MF *vis, viz* something winding] *chiefly Brit* **:** VISE
3**vice** *vt, chiefly Brit* **:** VISE
4**vi·ce** \'vī-sē\ *prep* [L, abl. of *vicis* change, alternation, stead — more at WEEK] **:** in the place of **:** SUCCEEDING
vice- \(')vīs, ,vīs\ *prefix* [ME *vis-, vice-,* fr. MF, fr. LL *vice-,* fr. L *vice,* abl. of *vicis*] **:** one that takes the place of ⟨*vice*-consul⟩
vice ad·mi·ral \(')vī-'sad-m(ə-)rəl\ *n* [MF *visamiral,* fr. *vis-* vice- + *amiral* admiral] **:** a commissioned officer in the navy ranking below an admiral and above a rear admiral
vice–chan·cel·lor \(')vīs-'chan(t)-s(ə-)lər\ *n* [ME *vichauncellor,* fr. MF *vischancelier,* fr. *vis-* + *chancelier* chancellor] **:** an officer ranking next below a chancellor and serving as his deputy; *esp* **:** a judge appointed to act for or to assist a chancellor
vice–con·sul \-'kän(t)-səl\ *n* **:** a consular officer subordinate to a consul general or to a consul
vice·ge·ren·cy \-'jir-ən-sē\ *n* **:** the office or jurisdiction of a vicegerent
vice·ge·rent \-ənt\ *n* [ML *vicegerent-, vicegerens,* fr. LL *vice-* + L *gerent-, gerens,* prp. of *gerere* to carry, carry on — more at CAST] **:** an administrative deputy of a king or magistrate
vi·cen·ni·al \vī-'sen-ē-əl\ *adj* [LL *vicennium* period of 20 years, fr. L *vicies* 20 times + *annus* year; akin to L *viginti* twenty — more at VIGESIMAL, ANNUAL] **:** occurring once every 20 years
vice–pres·i·den·cy \(')vīs-'prez-əd-ən-sē, -'prez-dən- *also* -ə-,den(t)-sē\ *n* **:** the office of vice-president
vice–pres·i·dent \-'prez-əd-ənt, -'prez-dənt *also* -ə-,dent\ *n* **1 :** an officer next in rank to a president and usu. empowered to serve as president in that officer's absence or disability **2 :** a president's deputy in charge of a particular location or function
vice·re·gal \(')vīs-'rē-gəl\ *adj* **:** of or relating to a viceroy — **vice·re·gal·ly** \-gə-lē\ *adv*
vice–re·gent \-'rē-jənt\ *n* **:** a regent's deputy
vice·reine \'vīs-,rān\ *n* [F, fr. *vice-* + *reine* queen, fr. L *regina,* fem. of *reg-, rex* king — more at ROYAL] **1 :** the wife of a viceroy **2 :** a woman viceroy
vice·roy \'vīs-,rȯi\ *n* [MF *vice-roi,* fr. *vice-* + *roi* king, fr. L *reg-, rex* — more at ROYAL] **1 :** the governor of a country or province who rules as the representative of his king or sovereign **2 :** a showy American butterfly (*Limenitis archippus*) closely mimicking the monarch in coloration but smaller
vice·roy·al·ty \'vīs-,rȯi(-ə)l-tē, vīs-'\ *n* **:** the office, jurisdiction, or term of service of a viceroy
vice·roy·ship \'vīs-,rȯi-,ship\ *n* **:** VICEROYALTY
vice squad *n* **:** a police squad charged with enforcement of laws concerning vice
vice ver·sa \,vī-si-'vər-sə, (')vīs-'vər-\ *adv* [L] **:** with the alternation or order changed **:** CONVERSELY
vi·chys·soise \,vish-ē-'swäz, ,vē-shē-\ *n* [F, fr. fem. of *vichyssois* of Vichy, fr. *Vichy,* France] **:** a soup made of pureed leeks or onions and potatoes, cream, chicken stock, and seasoning and usu. served cold
Vi·chy water \'vish-ē-\ *n* **:** a natural sparkling mineral water from Vichy, France; *also* **:** an imitation of or substitute for this
vic·i·nage \'vis-ᵊn-ij, 'vis-nij\ *n* [ME *vesinage,* fr. MF, fr. *vesin* neighboring, fr. L *vicinus*] **:** a neighboring or surrounding district **:** VICINITY
vic·i·nal \'vis-ᵊn-əl, 'vis-nəl\ *adj* [L *vicinalis,* fr. *vicinus* neighbor, fr. *vicinus* neighboring] **1 :** of or relating to a limited district **:** LOCAL **2 :** of, relating to, or being subordinate forms or faces on a crystal which sometimes take the place of fundamental ones
vi·cin·i·ty \və-'sin-ət-ē\ *n* [MF *vicinité,* fr. L *vicinitat-, vicinitas,* fr. *vicinus* neighboring, fr. *vicus* row of houses, village; akin to Goth *weihs* village, Gk *oikos, oikia* house] **1 :** the quality or state of being near **:** PROXIMITY **2 :** a surrounding area or district **:** NEIGHBORHOOD
vi·cious \'vish-əs\ *adj* **1 :** having the nature or quality of vice or immorality **:** DEPRAVED **2 :** DEFECTIVE, FAULTY; *also* **:** INVALID **3 :** IMPURE, NOXIOUS **4 :** dangerously aggressive **:** SAVAGE **5 :** MALICIOUS, SPITEFUL **6 :** worsened by internal causes that reciprocally augment each other ⟨~ wage-price spiral⟩ — **vi·cious·ly** *adv* — **vi·cious·ness** *n*

syn VILLAINOUS, INIQUITOUS, NEFARIOUS, FLAGITIOUS, INFAMOUS, CORRUPT, DEGENERATE: VICIOUS may directly oppose *virtuous* in implying moral depravity, or may connote malignancy, cruelty, or destructive violence; VILLAINOUS applies to any evil, depraved, or vile conduct or characteristic; INIQUITOUS implies absence of all signs of justice or fairness; NEFARIOUS suggests flagrant breaching of time-honored laws and traditions of conduct; FLAGITIOUS and INFAMOUS suggest shameful and scandalous wickedness; CORRUPT stresses a loss of moral integrity or probity causing betrayal of principle or sworn obligations; DEGENERATE suggests having sunk to an esp. vicious or enervated condition

vicious circle *n* **1 :** a chain of events in which the solution of one difficulty creates a new problem involving increased difficulty **2 :** an argument or definition that assumes something that is to be proved or defined **3 :** a chain of abnormal processes in which a primary disorder leads to a second which in turn aggravates the first

vi·cis·si·tude \və-'sis-ə-,t(y)üd, vī-\ *n* [MF, fr. L *vicissitudo*, fr. *vicissim* in turn, fr. *vicis* change, alternation — more at WEEK] **1 a :** the quality or state of being changeable **:** MUTABILITY **b :** natural change or mutation visible in nature or in human affairs **2 a :** an accident of fortune (as of prosperity or happiness) **b :** alternating change **:** SUCCESSION **syn** see CHANGE, DIFFICULTY

vi·cis·si·tu·di·nous \və-,sis-ə-'t(y)üd-nəs, (,)vī-, -ᵊn-əs\ *adj* [L *vicissitudin-, vicissitudo*] **:** marked by or filled with vicissitudes

vic·tim \'vik-təm\ *n* [L *victima;* akin to OHG *wīh* holy, Skt *vinakti* he sets apart] **1 :** a living being sacrificed to a deity or in the performance of a religious rite **2 :** someone injured, destroyed, or sacrificed under any of various conditions **3 :** someone tricked or duped

vic·tim·iza·tion \,vik-tə-mə-'zā-shən\ *n* **:** the act of victimizing **:** the state of being victimized

vic·tim·ize \'vik-tə-,mīz\ *vt* **1 :** to make a victim of **:** SACRIFICE **2 :** to subject to deception or fraud **:** CHEAT — **vic·tim·iz·er** *n*

vic·tor \'vik-tər\ *n* [ME, fr. L, fr. *victus*, pp. of *vincere* to conquer, win; akin to OE *wīgan* to fight, OSlav *věkŭ* strength] **:** one that defeats an enemy or opponent **:** WINNER — **victor** *adj*

Victor — a communications code word for the letter *v*

vic·to·ria \vik-'tōr-ē-ə, -'tȯr-\ *n* [*Victoria* †1901 queen of England] **1 :** a low four-wheeled pleasure carriage for two with a calash top and a raised seat in front for the driver **2 :** an open passenger automobile with a calash top that usu. extends over the rear seat only **3** [NL, genus name, fr. Queen *Victoria*] **:** any of a genus (*Victoria*) of So. American aquatic plants of the water-lily family with large spreading leaves often over 5 feet in diameter and immense rose-white flowers

victoria 1

Victoria Cross *n* [Queen *Victoria*] **:** a bronze Maltese cross awarded to members of the British armed services for acts of remarkable valor

1**Vic·to·ri·an** \vik-'tōr-ē-ən, -'tȯr-\ *adj* **1 :** of or relating to the reign of Queen Victoria of England or the art, letters, or taste of her time **2 :** typical of the moral standards or conduct of the age of Victoria esp. when stuffy or hypocritical

2**Victorian** *n* **:** a person living during Queen Victoria's reign; *esp* **:** a representative author of that time

Vic·to·ri·an·ism \-ē-ə-,niz-əm\ *n* **1 :** the quality or state of being Victorian esp. in taste, habits of thought, or conduct **2 :** a typical instance or product of Victorian expression, taste, or conduct

vic·to·ri·an·ize \-,nīz\ *vt, often cap* **:** to make Victorian (as in style or taste)

vic·to·ri·ous \vik-'tōr-ē-əs, -'tȯr-\ *adj* **1 a :** having won a victory **b :** of, relating to, or characteristic of victory **2 :** evincing moral harmony or a sense of fulfillment — **vic·to·ri·ous·ly** *adv*

vic·to·ri·ous·ness \-ē-ə-snəs\ *n* **:** the quality or state of being victorious

vic·to·ry \'vik-t(ə-)rē\ *n* [ME, fr. MF *victorie*, fr. L *victoria*, fr. fem. of (assumed) L *victorius* of winning or conquest, fr. L *victus*, pp. of *vincere*] **1 :** the overcoming of an enemy or antagonist **2 :** achievement of mastery or success in a struggle or endeavor against odds or difficulties

syn VICTORY, CONQUEST, TRIUMPH mean a successful outcome in a contest or struggle. VICTORY stresses the fact of winning against an opponent or against odds. CONQUEST implies the subjugation of a defeated opponent or enemy; TRIUMPH suggests a brilliant or decisive victory or an overwhelming conquest

vic·tress \-trəs\ *n* **:** a female victor

1**vict·ual** \'vit-ᵊl\ *n* [alter. of ME *vitaille*, fr. MF, fr. LL *victualia*, pl., provisions, victuals, fr. neut. pl. of *victualis* of nourishment, fr. L *victus* nourishment, fr. *victus*, pp. of *vivere* to live — more at QUICK] **1 :** food usable by man **2** *pl* **:** supplies of food **:** PROVISIONS

2**victual** *vb* **vict·ualed** *or* **vict·ualled; vict·ual·ing** *or* **vict·ual·ling** *vt* **:** to supply with food ~ *vi* **1 :** EAT **2 :** to lay in provisions

vict·ual·ler *or* **vict·ual·er** \'vit-ᵊl-ər\ *n* **1 :** the keeper of a restaurant or tavern **2 :** one that provisions an army, a navy, or a ship with food **3 :** an army or navy provision ship

vi·cu·ña *or* **vi·cu·na** \vi-'kün-yə, vī-; vī-'k(y)ü-nə, və-\ *n* [Sp *vicuña*, fr. Quechua *wikúña*] **1 :** a wild ruminant (*Lama vicugna*) of the Andes from Ecuador to Bolivia that is related to the domesticated llama and alpaca **2 a :** the wool from the vicuña's fine lustrous undercoat **b :** a fabric made of vicuña wool; *also* **:** a sheep's wool imitation of this

vi·de \'vīd-ē, 'vē-,dā\ *v imper* [L, fr. *vidēre* to see — more at WIT] **:** SEE — used to direct a reader to another item

vi·de·li·cet \və-'del-ə-,set, vī-; vi-'dā-li-,ket\ *adv* [ME, fr. L, fr. *vidēre* to see + *licet* it is permitted, fr. *licēre* to be permitted — more at LICENSE] **:** that is to say **:** NAMELY

1**vid·eo** \'vid-ē-,ō\ *adj* [L *vidēre* to see + E *-o* (as in *audio*)] **:** relating to or used in the transmission or reception of the television image ⟨~ channel⟩ ⟨~ frequency⟩ — compare AUDIO

2**video** *n* **:** TELEVISION

vid·eo·ge·nic \,vid-ē-ō-'jen-ik, -'jē-nik\ *adj* **:** TELEGENIC

vid·eo·tape \'vid-ē-ō-,tāp\ *vt* [*video tape*] **:** to make a recording on magnetic tape of (a television production) — **videotape** *n*

vi·dette *var of* VEDETTE

vid·icon \'vid-i-,kän\ *n, often cap* [*video* + *iconoscope*] **:** a camera tube using the principle of photoconductivity

vi·du·ity \vid-'(y)ü-ət-ē\ *n* [ME (Sc) *viduite*, fr. MF *viduite*, fr. L *viduitat-, viduitas*, fr. *vidua* widow — more at WIDOW] **:** WIDOWHOOD

vie \'vī\ *vb* **vied; vy·ing** \'vī-iŋ\ [modif. of MF *envier* to invite, challenge, wager, fr. L *invitare* to invite] *vi* **:** to strive for superiority **:** CONTEND ~ *vt* **:** HAZARD, WAGER ⟨~ money on the turn of a card⟩; *also* **:** to exchange in rivalry **:** MATCH ⟨~ accusation against accusation⟩ — **vi·er** \'vī(-ə)r\ *n*

Vi·en·na sausage \vē-,en-ə-\ *n* [*Vienna*, Austria] **:** a short slender frankfurter in a thin casing usu. having the ends cut off

Viet·cong \vē-'et-'käŋ, vyet-, ,vē-ət-, vēt-, -'kȯŋ\ *n, pl* **Vietcong** [Vietnamese *Viet Nam cong san* Vietnam communists] **:** an adherent of the Vietnamese communist movement supported by North Vietnam and engaged esp. in guerrilla warfare in South Vietnam

Viet·minh \vē-'et-'min, vyet-, ,vē-ət-, vēt-\ *n, pl* **Vietminh** [Vietnamese *Viet Nam Doc Lap Dong Minh* League for the Independence of Vietnam] **:** an adherent of the Vietnamese communist movement

Viet·nam·ese \vē-,et-nä-'mēz, ,vyet-, ,vē-ət-, ,vēt-, -na-, -'mēs\ *n, pl* **Vietnamese 1 :** a native or inhabitant of Vietnam **2 :** the language of the largest group in Vietnam and the official language of the country — **Vietnamese** *adj*

1**view** \'vyü\ *n* [ME *vewe*, fr. MF *veue, vue*, fr. OF, fr. *veeir, voir* to see, fr. L *vidēre* — more at WIT] **1 :** the act of seeing or examining **:** INSPECTION; *also* **:** SURVEY **2 :** ESTIMATE, JUDGMENT **3 :** SCENE, PROSPECT **4:** extent or range of vision **:** SIGHT **5 a :** something that is looked toward or kept in sight **:** OBJECT **b :** something that is expected or anticipated **6 :** a pictorial representation **:** SKETCH **syn** see OPINION — **in view of :** in regard to **:** in consideration of

2**view** *vt* **1 :** SEE, BEHOLD **2 :** to look at attentively **:** SCRUTINIZE **3 :** to survey or examine mentally **:** CONSIDER

view·er \-ər\ *n* **:** one that views: as **a :** a person legally appointed to inspect and report on property **b :** an optical device used in viewing **c :** a person who watches television

view halloo *n* **:** a shout uttered by a hunter on seeing a fox break cover

view·less \'vyü-ləs\ *adj* **1 :** INVISIBLE, UNSEEN **2 :** affording no view **3 :** expressing no views or opinions — **view·less·ly** *adv*

view·point \'vyü-,pȯint\ *n* **:** POINT OF VIEW, STANDPOINT

viewy \'vyü-ē\ *adj* **1 :** possessing visionary, impractical, or fantastic views **2 :** spectacular or arresting in appearance **:** SHOWY

vi·ges·i·mal \vī-'jes-ə-məl\ *adj* [L *vicesimus, vigesimus* twentieth; akin to L *viginti* twenty] **:** based on the number 20

vig·il \'vij-əl\ *n* [ME *vigile*, fr. OF, fr. LL & L; LL *vigilia* watch on the eve of a feast, fr. L, wakefulness, watch, fr. *vigil* awake, watchful; akin to L *vigēre* to be vigorous, *vegēre* to be active, rouse — more at WAKE] **1 a :** a watch formerly kept on the night before a religious feast with prayer or other devotions **b :** the day before a religious feast observed as a day of spiritual preparation **c :** evening or nocturnal devotions or prayers — usu. used in pl. **2 :** the act of keeping awake at times when sleep is customary; *also* **:** a period of wakefulness **3 :** an act of surveillance (as for protection)

vig·i·lance \'vij-ə-lən(t)s\ *n* **:** the quality or state of being vigilant

vigilance committee *n* **:** a volunteer committee of citizens organized to suppress and punish crime summarily (as when the processes of law appear inadequate)

vig·i·lant \'vij-ə-lənt\ *adj* [ME, fr. MF, fr. L *vigilant-, vigilans*, fr prp. of *vigilare* to keep watch, stay awake, fr. *vigil* awake] **:** alertly watchful esp. to avoid danger **syn** see WATCHFUL — **vig·i·lant·ly** *adv*

vig·i·lan·te \,vij-ə-'lant-ē\ *n* [Sp, watchman, guard, fr. *vigilante* vigilant, fr. L *vigilant-, vigilans*] **:** a member of a vigilance committee

vig·i·lan·tism \-'lan-,tiz-əm\ *n* **:** the summary action resorted to by vigilantes when law fails

vigil light *n* **1 :** a candle lighted by a worshiper in a Roman Catholic church (as for the veneration of a saint) **2 :** a candle or small lamp burning before a shrine, memorial, or image

vi·gin·til·lion \,vī-,jin-'til-yən\ *n, often attrib* [L *viginti* twenty + E *-illion* (as in *million*) — more at VIGESIMAL] — see NUMBER table

1**vi·gnette** \vin-'yet, vēn-\ *n* [F, fr. MF *vignete*, fr. dim. of *vigne* vine — more at VINE] **1 :** a running ornament (as of vine leaves, tendrils, and grapes) put on or just before a title page or at the beginning or end of a chapter; *also* **:** a small decorative design or picture so placed **2 :** a picture (as an engraving or photograph) that shades off gradually into the surrounding ground or the unprinted paper **3 :** a brief word picture **:** SKETCH

2**vignette** *vt* **1 :** to finish (as a photograph) in the manner of a vignette **2 :** to describe or sketch briefly — **vi·gnett·er** *or* **vi·gnett·ist** \-'yet-əst\ *n*

vig·or *or chiefly Brit* **vig·our** \'vig-ər\ *n* [ME, fr. MF *vigor*, fr. L, fr. *vigēre* to be vigorous] **1 :** active strength or force of body or mind **2 :** strength or force in animal or vegetable nature or action **3 :** intensity of action or effect **:** FORCE **4 :** effective legal status

vi·go·ro·so \,vig-ə-'rō-(,)sō, ,vē-gə-, -(,)zō\ *adj* (*or adv*) [It, lit., vigorous, fr. MF *vigorous*] **:** energetic in style — used as a direction in music

vig·or·ous \'vig-(ə-)rəs\ *adj* [ME, fr. MF, fr. OF, fr. *vigor*] **1 :** possessing vigor **:** full of physical or mental strength or active force **:** STRONG ⟨a ~ youth⟩ ⟨a ~ plant⟩ **2 :** done with vigor **:** carried out forcefully and energetically ⟨~ enforcement of laws⟩ — **vig·or·ous·ly** *adv* — **vig·or·ous·ness** *n*

syn VIGOROUS, ENERGETIC, STRENUOUS, LUSTY, NERVOUS mean having great vitality and force. VIGOROUS further implies showing no signs of depletion or diminishing of freshness or robustness; ENERGETIC suggests a capacity for intense activity; STRENUOUS suggests a preference for coping with the arduous or the challenging; LUSTY implies exuberant energy and capacity for enjoyment; NERVOUS suggests esp. the forcibleness and sustained effectiveness resulting from mental vigor

Vi·king \'vī-kiŋ\ *n* [ON *vīkingr*] **1 a :** one of the pirate Northmen plundering the coasts of Europe in the 8th to 10th centuries **b** *not cap* **:** SEA ROVER **2 :** SCANDINAVIAN

1**vile** \'vī(ə)l\ *adj* [ME, fr. OF *vil*, fr. L *vilis*] **1 :** of small worth or account **:** COMMON; *also* **:** MEAN **2 a :** morally base **:** WICKED **b :** physically repulsive **:** FOUL **3 :** DEGRADED, LOW **4 :** DISGUST-

ING, CONTEMPTIBLE **syn** see BASE — **vile·ly** \'vī(ə)l-lē\ *adv* — **vile·ness** *n*
²**vile** *adv* : VILELY — used chiefly in combination ⟨*vile*-smelling⟩
vil·i·fi·ca·tion \,vil-ə-fə-'kā-shən\ *n* **1** : the act of vilifying : ABUSE **2** : a vilifying or defamatory utterance
vil·i·fi·er \'vil-ə-,fī(-ə)r\ *n* : one who vilifies
vil·i·fy \-,fī\ *vt* **1** : to lower in estimation or importance **2** : to utter slanderous and abusive statements against **syn** see MALIGN
vil·i·pend \'vil-ə-,pend\ *vt* [ME *vilipenden*, fr. MF *vilipender*, fr. ML *vilipendere*, fr. L *vilis* of small worth + *pendere* to weigh, estimate — more at PENDANT] **1** : to hold or treat as of small worth or account : CONTEMN **2** : to express a low opinion of : DISPARAGE
vill \'vil\ *n* [AF, fr. OF *ville* village] **1** : a division of a hundred : TOWNSHIP **2** : VILLAGE
vil·la \'vil-ə\ *n* [It, fr. L; akin to L *vicus* row of houses — more at VICINITY] **1** : a country estate **2** : the rural or suburban residence of a person of wealth
vil·la·dom \'vil-əd-əm\ *n, Brit* : the world constituted by villas and their occupants : SUBURBIA
vil·lage \'vil-ij\ *n, often attrib* [ME, fr. MF, fr. OF, fr. *ville* farm, village, fr. L *villa* country estate] **1 a** : a settlement usu. larger than a hamlet and smaller than a town **b** : an incorporated minor municipality **2** : the residents of a village **3** : something and esp. an aggregation of burrows or nests suggesting a village **4** : a territorial area having the status of a village esp. as a unit of local government
vil·lag·er \'vil-ij-ər\ *n* : an inhabitant of a village
vil·lage·ry \'vil-ij-rē\ *n* : VILLAGES
vil·lain \'vil-ən\ *n* [ME *vilain*, *vilein*, fr. MF, fr. ML *villanus*, fr. L *villa* country estate] **1** : VILLEIN **2** : a person of uncouth mind and manners : BOOR **3** : a deliberate scoundrel or criminal **4** : a scoundrel in a story or play — **vil·lain·ess** \'vil-ə-nəs\ *n*
vil·lain·ous \'vil-ə-nəs\ *adj* **1** : befitting a villain : DEPRAVED **2** : highly objectionable : WRETCHED **syn** see VICIOUS — **vil·lain·ous·ly** *adv* — **vil·lain·ous·ness** *n*
vil·lainy \'vil-ə-nē\ *n* **1** : villainous conduct; *also* : a villainous act **2** : the quality or state of being villainous : DEPRAVITY
vil·la·nel·la \,vil-ə-'nel-ə\ *n, pl* **vil·la·nel·le** \-'nel-ē\ [It, fr. *villano* villein, peasant, fr. ML *villanus*] **1** : a 16th century Italian rustic part-song unaccompanied and in free form **2** : an instrumental piece in the style of a rustic dance
vil·la·nelle \,vil-ə-'nel\ *n* [F, fr. It *villanella*] : a chiefly French verse form running on two rhymes and consisting typically of five tercets and a quatrain in which the first and third lines of the opening tercet recur alternately at the end of the other tercets and together as the last two lines of the quatrain
vil·lat·ic \vil-'at-ik\ *adj* [L *villaticus*, fr. *villa*] : of or relating to a villa or a village : RURAL
vil·lein \'vil-ən, 'vil-,ān, vil-'ān\ *n* [ME *vilain*, *vilein* — more at VILLAIN] **1** : a free common villager or village peasant of any of the feudal classes lower in rank than the thane **2** : a free peasant of a feudal class lower than a sokeman and higher than a cotter **3** : an unfree peasant standing as the slave of his feudal lord but free in his legal relations with respect to all others
vil·len·age \'vil-ə-nij\ *n* [ME *vilenage*, fr. MF, fr. OF, fr. *vilein*, *vilain*] **1** : tenure at the will of a feudal lord by villein services **2** : the status of a villein
vil·li·form \'vil-ə-,fȯrm\ *adj* [ISV] : having the form or appearance of villi; *also* : resembling bristles or the pile of velvet
vil·los·i·ty \vil-'äs-ət-ē\ *n* **1** : the state of being villous **2 a** : VILLUS **b** : a villous patch or area **3** : a coating of long slender hairs
vil·lous \'vil-əs\ *adj* **1** : covered or furnished with villi **2** : having soft long hairs ⟨leaves ~ underneath⟩ — compare PUBESCENT — **vil·lous·ly** *adv*
vil·lus \'vil-əs\ *n, pl* **vil·li** \'vil-,ī, -(,)ē\ [NL, fr. L, tuft of shaggy hair — more at VELVET] : a small slender vascular process: as **a** : one of the minute finger-shaped processes of the mucous membrane of the small intestine that serve in the absorption of nutriment **b** : one of the branching processes of the surface of the chorion of the developing egg of most mammals that help to form the placenta
vim \'vim\ *n* [L, accus. of *vis* strength; akin to Gk *is* strength, *hiesthai* to hurry, OE *wāth* pursuit] : robust energy and enthusiasm : VITALITY
vi·min·e·ous \vī-'min-ē-əs, və-\ *adj* [L *vimineus*, fr. *vimin-*, *vimen* pliant twig; akin to L *viēre* to plait — more at WITHY] : of or producing long slender twigs or shoots ⟨shrub of ~ habit⟩
vim·pa \'vim-pə\ *n* [ML] : a veil of silk worn over the shoulders and hands of acolytes carrying the crosier and the miter in Roman Catholic pontifical services
vi·na \'vē-nə\ *n* [Skt & Hindi; Hindi *bīnā*, fr. Skt *vīṇā*] : a musical instrument of India having usu. four strings and a long bamboo fingerboard with movable frets and a gourd resonator at each end
vi·na·ceous \vī-'nā-shəs\ *adj* [L *vinaceus* of wine, fr. *vinum* wine — more at WINE] : of the color wine
vin·ai·grette \,vin-i-'gret\ *n* [F, fr. *vinaigre* vinegar] : a small ornamental box or bottle with perforated top used for holding an aromatic preparation (as smelling salts)
vinaigrette sauce *n* : a sauce made typically of vinegar, oil, onions, parsley, and herbs and used esp. on cold meats or fish
¹**vi·nal** \'vīn-ᵊl\ *adj* [L *vinalis*, fr. *vinum* wine] : of or relating to wine : VINOUS
²**vi·nal** \'vī-,nal\ *n* [poly*vi*nyl *al*cohol] : a synthetic textile fiber that is a long-chain polymer consisting largely of vinyl alcohol units $-CH_2CHOH-$
vin·ca \'viŋ-kə\ *n* [NL, short for L *pervinca* periwinkle] : ¹PERIWINKLE
Vin·cen·tian \vin-'sen-chən\ *n* : a priest or brother of the Roman Catholic Congregation of the Mission founded in 1625 by St. Vincent de Paul and devoted to missions and clerical seminaries — **Vincentian** *adj*
Vin·cent's angina \,vin(t)-sən(t)s-, (,)vaⁿ-,säⁿz-\ *n* [Jean Hyacinthe *Vincent* †1950 F bacteriologist] : a contagious disease marked by ulceration of the mucous membrane of the mouth and adjacent parts and caused by a bacterium (*Fusobacterium fusiforme*) often in association with a spirochete (*Borrelia vincentii*) — called also *trench mouth*
Vincent's infection *n* : a bacterial infection of the respiratory tract and mouth marked by destructive ulceration esp. of the mucous membranes
vin·ci·ble \'vin(t)-sə-bəl\ *adj* [L *vincibilis*, fr. *vincere* to conquer — more at VICTOR] : capable of being overcome or subdued : SURMOUNTABLE
vin·cu·lum \'viŋ-kyə-ləm\ *n, pl* **vinculums** *or* **vin·cu·la** \-lə\ [L, fr. *vincire* to bind — more at VETCH] **1** : a unifying bond : LINK, TIE **2** : a straight horizontal mark placed over two or more members of a compound mathematical expression and equivalent to parentheses or brackets about them (as in $a-\overline{b-c}=a-[b-c]$)
vin·di·ca·ble \'vin-di-kə-bəl\ *adj* : capable of being vindicated : JUSTIFIABLE
vin·di·cate \'vin-də-,kāt\ *vt* [L *vindicatus*, pp. of *vindicare* to lay claim to, avenge, fr. *vindic-*, *vindex* claimant, avenger] **1** *obs* : to set free : DELIVER **2** : AVENGE **3 a** : EXONERATE, ABSOLVE **b** (1) : CONFIRM, SUBSTANTIATE (2) : to provide justification or defense for : JUSTIFY **c** : to protect from attack or encroachment : DEFEND **4** : to maintain a right to : ASSERT **syn** see EXCULPATE, MAINTAIN — **vin·di·ca·tor** \-,kāt-ər\ *n*
vin·di·ca·tion \,vin-də-'kā-shən\ *n* : the act of vindicating : the state of being vindicated; *specif* : justification against denial or censure : DEFENSE
vin·dic·a·tive \vin-'dik-ət-iv\ *adj* **1** *obs* : VINDICTIVE, VENGEFUL **2** *archaic* : PUNITIVE
vin·di·ca·to·ry *adj* **1** \'vin-di-kə-,tōr-ē, -,tȯr-\ : providing vindication : JUSTIFICATORY **2** \vin-'dik-ə-\ : PUNITIVE, RETRIBUTIVE
vin·dic·tive \vin-'dik-tiv\ *adj* [L *vindicta* revenge, vindication, fr. *vindicare*] **1 a** : disposed to seek revenge : VENGEFUL **b** : intended for or involving revenge **2** : VICIOUS, SPITEFUL — **vin·dic·tive·ly** *adv* — **vin·dic·tive·ness** *n*
¹**vine** \'vīn\ *n* [ME, fr. OF *vigne*, fr. L *vinea* vine, vineyard, fr. fem. of *vineus* of wine, fr. *vinum* wine — more at WINE] **1** : GRAPE 2 **2** : a plant whose stem requires support and which climbs by tendrils or twining or creeps along the ground; *also* : the stem of such a plant
²**vine** *vi* : to form or grow in the manner of a vine
vin·eal \'vin-ē-əl, 'vīn-\ *adj* [L *vinealis* of vines, fr. *vinea* vine] : of or relating to wine
vine·dress·er \'vīn-,dres-ər\ *n* : one that cultivates and prunes grapevines
vin·e·gar \'vin-i-gər\ *n* [ME *vinegre*, fr. OF *vinaigre*, fr. *vin* wine (fr. L *vinum*) + *aigre* keen, sour — more at EAGER] **1** : a sour liquid obtained by acetic fermentation of dilute alcoholic liquids and used as a condiment or preservative **2** : disagreeableness in speech, disposition, or attitude **3** : VIM
vinegar eel *n* : a minute nematode worm (*Turbatrix aceti*) often found in great numbers in vinegar or acid fermenting vegetable matter
vin·e·gar·ish \'vin-i-g(ə-)rish\ *adj* : VINEGARY 2
vin·e·gar·roon \,vin-i-gə-'rün\ *n* [MexSp *vinagrón*, aug. of Sp *vinagre* vinegar, fr. OF *vinaigre*] : a large whip scorpion (*Mastigoproctus giganteus*) of the southern U.S. and Mexico that emits a vinegary odor when disturbed and is popularly held to be venomous
vin·e·gary \'vin-i-g(ə-)rē\ *adj* **1** : resembling vinegar : SOUR **2** : disagreeable, bitter, or irascible in character or manner : CRABBED
vin·ery \'vīn-(ə-)rē\ *n* : an area or building in which vines are grown
vine·yard \'vin-yərd\ *n* **1** : a planting of grapevines **2** : an area or category of physical or mental occupation — **vine·yard·ist** \-yərd-əst\ *n*
vingt-et-un \,van-,tā-'ən\ *n* [F] : TWENTY-ONE 2
vi·nic \'vī-nik\ *adj* [ISV, fr. L *vinum* wine — more at WINE] : of, relating to, or derived from wine or alcohol ⟨~ ether⟩
vi·ni·cul·ture \'vin-ə-,kəl-chər, 'vī-nə-\ *n* [L *vinum* + ISV *-i-* + *culture*] : VITICULTURE
vi·nif·er·ous \vī-'nif-(ə-)rəs\ *adj* [L *vinifer*, fr. *vinum* + *-ifer* -iferous] : yielding or grown for the production of wine
vi·no \'vē-(,)nō\ *n* [It & Sp, fr. L *vinum*] : WINE
vi·nos·i·ty \vī-'näs-ət-ē\ *n* : the characteristic body, flavor, and color of a wine
vi·nous \'vī-nəs\ *adj* [L *vinosus*, fr. *vinum* wine] **1** : of, relating to, or made with wine ⟨~ medications⟩ **2** : showing the effects of the use of wine **3** : VINACEOUS — **vi·nous·ly** *adv*
¹**vin·tage** \'vint-ij\ *n* [ME, alter. of *vendage*, fr. MF *vendenge*, fr. L *vindemia*, fr. *vinum* wine, grapes + *demere* to take off, fr. *de-* + *emere* to take — more at WINE, REDEEM] **1 a** (1) : a season's yield of grapes or wine from a vineyard (2) : WINE; *specif* : a wine of a particular type, region, and year and usu. of superior quality that is dated and allowed to mature **b** : a collection of contemporaneous and similar persons or things : CROP **2** : the act or time of harvesting grapes or making wine **3 a** : a period of origin or manufacture **b** : length of existence : AGE
²**vintage** *adj* **1** : of old, recognized, and enduring interest, importance, or quality : CLASSIC **2** : OLD-FASHIONED, OUTMODED **3** : of the best and most characteristic — used with a proper noun ⟨~ Shaw: a wise and winning comedy —*Time*⟩
vin·tag·er \-ij-ər\ *n* : one that takes part in a vintage
vintage year *n* **1** : a year in which a vintage wine is produced **2** : a year of outstanding distinction or success
vint·ner \'vint-nər\ *n* [ME *vineter*, fr. OF *vinetier*, fr. ML *vinetarius*, fr. L *vinetum* vineyard, fr. *vinum* wine] : a wine merchant
viny \'vī-nē\ *adj* **1** : of, relating to, or resembling vines ⟨~ plants⟩ **2** : covered with or abounding in vines ⟨~ hillsides and forests⟩
vi·nyl \'vīn-ᵊl\ *n* [ISV, fr. L *vinum* wine] **1** : a univalent radical $CH_2=CH-$ derived from ethylene by removal of one hydrogen atom **2** : a polymer of a vinyl compound or product made from one
vinyl alcohol *n* : an unstable compound $CH_2=CHOH$ known only in the form of its polymers or derivatives
vi·nyl·i·dene \vī-'nil-ə-,dēn\ *n* [ISV *vinyl* + *-ide* + *-ene*] : a bivalent radical $CH_2=C<$ derived from ethylene by removal of two hydrogen atoms from one carbon atom
vinylidene resin *n* : any of a group of tough thermoplastic resins formed by polymerization of a vinylidene compound and used esp. for filaments, films, and molded articles
Vi·nyl·ite \'vīn-ᵊl-,īt\ *trademark* — used for any of a series of vinyl resins
vinyl plastic *n* : any of various tough durable plastics based on vinyl resins and used esp. in the form of films, coatings, foams, and molded and extruded products

vinyl resin *n* **:** any of various thermoplastic resinous materials consisting essentially of polymers of vinyl compounds

vi·ol \'vī-(ə)l, 'vī-(,)ōl\ *n* [MF *viole* viol, viola, fr. OProv *viola* viol] **:** a bowed stringed instrument chiefly of the 16th and 17th centuries with deep body, flat back, sloping shoulders, usu. six strings, fretted fingerboard, and low-arched bridge made in treble, alto, tenor, and bass sizes

¹**vi·o·la** \vē-'ō-lə\ *n* [It & Sp, viol, viola, fr. OProv, viol] **1 :** a musical instrument of the violin family that is intermediate in size and compass between the violin and violoncello and is tuned a fifth lower than the violin **2 :** VIOLIST

²**vi·o·la** \vī-'ō-lə, vē-; 'vī-ə-\ *n* [L] **:** VIOLET 1a; *esp* **:** any of various garden hybrids with solitary white, yellow, or purple often variegated flowers resembling but smaller than typical pansies

vi·o·la·bil·i·ty \,vī-ə-lə-'bil-ət-ē\ *n* **:** the quality or state of being violable

vi·o·la·ble \'vī-ə-lə-bəl\ *adj* **:** capable of being or likely to be violated — **vi·o·la·ble·ness** *n* — **vi·o·la·bly** \-blē\ *adv*

vi·o·la·ceous \,vī-ə-'lā-shəs\ *adj* [L *violaceus*, fr. *viola* violet] **:** of the color violet — **vi·o·la·ceous·ly** *adv*

vi·o·la da brac·cio \vē-,ō-ləd-ə-'bräch-(,)ō, -'bräch-ē-,ō\ *n* [It, arm viol] **:** a viol having roughly the range of the viola

viola da gam·ba \-'gäm-bə, -'gam-\ *n* [It, leg viol] **:** a bass member of the viol family having a range approximating the cello

viola d'a·mo·re \-ləd-ə-'mōr-ē, -'mȯr-\ *n* [It, viol of love] **:** a tenor viol having usu. seven gut and seven wire strings

¹**vi·o·late** \'vī-ə-,lāt\ *vt* [ME *violaten*, fr. L *violatus*, pp. of *violare;* akin to L *vis* strength — more at VIM] **1 :** BREAK, DISREGARD ⟨~ the law⟩ **2 :** to do harm to the person or esp. the chastity of; *specif* **:** RAPE **3 :** PROFANE, DESECRATE **4 :** INTERRUPT, DISTURB — **vi·o·la·tive** \-,lāt-iv\ *adj* — **vi·o·la·tor** \-,lāt-ər\ *n*

²**vi·o·late** \'vī-ə-lət\ *adj, archaic* **:** VIOLATED

vi·o·la·tion \,vī-ə-'lā-shən\ *n* **:** the act of violating **:** the state of being violated: as **a :** INFRINGEMENT, TRANSGRESSION; *specif* **:** an infringement of the rules in sports that is less serious than a foul and usu. involves technicalities of play **b :** an act of irreverence or desecration **:** PROFANATION **c :** INTERRUPTION, DISTURBANCE **d :** RAVISHMENT, RAPE

vi·o·lence \'vī-ə-lən(t)s\ *n* **1 a :** exertion of physical force so as to injure or abuse (as in effecting an entrance into a house) **b :** an instance of violent treatment or procedure **2 :** injury by or as if by distortion, infringement, or profanation **3 a :** intense, turbulent, or furious often destructive action or force **b :** vehement feeling or expression **:** FERVOR **c :** an instance of such action or feeling **:** a tendency to violent action **d :** jarring quality **:** DISCORDANCE **4 :** undue alteration of wording or sense (as in editing a text)

vi·o·lent \-lənt\ *adj* [ME, fr. MF, fr. L *violentus;* akin to L *violare* to violate] **1 :** marked by extreme force or sudden intense activity **2 :** furious or vehement to the point of being improper, unjust, or illegal **3 :** EXTREME, INTENSE **4 :** produced or effected by force ⟨a ~ death⟩ **5 :** tending to distort or misrepresent ⟨a ~ interpretation⟩ **6 :** extremely excited — **vi·o·lent·ly** *adv*

vi·o·let \'vī-ə-lət\ *n* [ME, fr. MF *violete*, dim. of *viole* violet, fr. L *viola*] **1 a :** any of a genus (*Viola* of the family Violaceae, the violet family) of herbs or subshrubs with alternate stipulate leaves and both aerial and cleistogamous flowers; *esp* **:** one with smaller usu. solid-colored flowers as distinguished from the usu. larger-flowered violas and pansies **b :** any of several plants of other genera — compare DOGTOOTH VIOLET **2 :** any of a group of colors of reddish blue hue, low lightness, and medium saturation **3 :** any of numerous small violet-colored butterflies (family Lycaenidae)

vi·o·let–ear \-,i(ə)r\ *n* **:** a tropical hummingbird of the genus *Colibri* having violet or bluish purple ear tufts

violet ray *n* **:** an ultraviolet ray

vi·o·lin \,vī-ə-'lin\ *n* [It *violino*, dim. of *viola*] **1 :** a bowed stringed instrument with four strings tuned at intervals of a fifth distinguished from the viol in having a shallower body, shoulders at right angles with the neck, and a more curved bridge **2 :** VIOLINIST

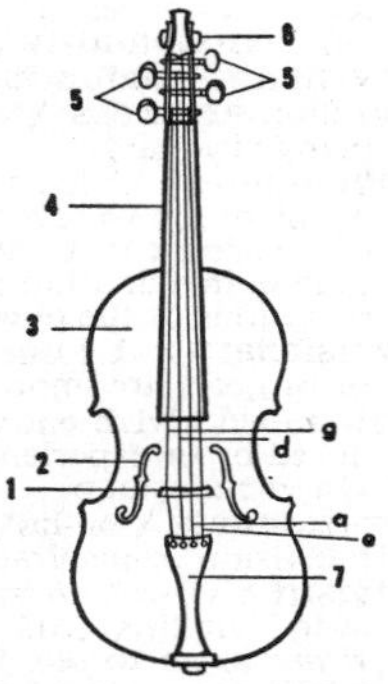

violin: *1* bridge, *2* sound hole, *3* soundboard, *4* fingerboard, *5* pegs, *6* scroll, *7* string holder, *g* G-string, *d* D-string, *a* A-string, *e* E-string

vi·o·lin·ist \-'lin-əst\ *n* **:** one who plays the violin

vi·o·list \vē-'ō-ləst\ *n* **:** one who plays the viola

vi·o·lon·cel·list \,vī-ə-lən-'chel-əst, ,vē-\ *n* **:** CELLIST

vi·o·lon·cel·lo \-'chel-(,)ō\ *n* [It, dim. of *violone*, aug. of *viola*] **:** CELLO

vi·os·ter·ol \vī-'äs-tə-,rȯl, -,rōl\ *n* [ultra*violet* + *sterol*] **:** vitamin D_2 esp. when dissolved in an edible vegetable oil

VIP \,vē-,ī-'pē\ *n* [*v*ery *i*mportant *p*erson] **:** a person of great influence or prestige; *esp* **:** a high official with special privileges

vi·per \'vī-pər\ *n* [MF *vipere*, fr. L *vipera*] **1 a :** a common European venomous snake (*Vipera berus*) that attains a length of two feet, varies in color from red, brown, or gray with dark markings to black, occurs across Eurasia from England to Sakhalin, and is rarely fatal to man; *broadly* **:** any of various Old World venomous snakes (family Viperidae) **b :** PIT VIPER **c :** a venomous or reputedly venomous snake **2 :** a malignant or treacherous person

vi·per·ine \'vī-pə-,rīn\ *adj* **:** of, relating to, or resembling a viper **:** VENOMOUS

vi·per·ish \'vī-p(ə-)rish\ *adj* **:** spitefully vituperative **:** VENOMOUS

vi·per·ous \'vī-p(ə-)rəs\ *adj* **1 :** VIPERINE **2 :** VENOMOUS — **vi·per·ous·ly** *adv*

viper's bugloss *n* **:** a coarse bristly Old World weed (*Echium vulgare*) of the borage family naturalized in No. America that has showy blue tubular flowers with exserted stamens

vi·rag·i·nous \və-'raj-ə-nəs\ *adj* [L *viragin-, virago* virago] **:** of, relating to, or characteristic of a virago

vi·ra·go \və-'räg-(,)ō, 'vir-ə-,gō\ *n, pl* **viragoes** *or* **viragos** [L *viragin-, virago*, fr. *vir* man — more at VIRILE] **1 :** a woman of great stature, strength, and courage **2 :** a loud overbearing woman **:** TERMAGANT

vi·ral \'vī-rəl\ *adj* **:** of, relating to, or caused by a virus

vir·e·lay \'vir-ə-,lā\ *n* [ME, fr. MF *virelai*] **:** a chiefly French verse form consisting of stanzas of indeterminate length and number with alternating long and short lines and interlaced rhyme (as *abab, bcbc, cdcd, dada*)

vir·eo \'vir-ē-,ō\ *n* [L, a small bird, fr. *virēre* to be green] **:** any of certain small insectivorous American passerine birds (family Vireonidae) chiefly olivaceous and grayish in color — **vir·eo·nine** \-ē-ō-,nīn\ *adj or n*

vires *pl of* VIS

vi·res·cence \və-'res-ᵊn(t)s, vī-\ *n* **:** the state or condition of becoming green; *esp* **:** such a condition due to the development of chloroplasts in plant organs (as petals) normally white or colored

vi·res·cent \-ᵊnt\ *adj* [L *virescent-, virescens*, prp. of *virescere* to become green, incho. of *virēre* to be green] **:** beginning to be green **:** GREENISH

vir·ga \'vər-gə\ *n* [NL, fr. L, branch, rod, streak in the sky suggesting rain — more at WHISK] **:** trailing wisps of precipitation evaporating before reaching the ground

¹**vir·gate** \'vər-,gāt\ *n* [ML *virgata*, fr. *virga*, a land measure, fr. L, rod] **:** an old English unit of land area equal to one quarter of a hide or one quarter of an acre

²**virgate** *adj* [NL *virgatus*, fr. L, made of twigs, fr. *virga*] **1 :** shaped like a rod or wand **2 :** bearing many small twigs

¹**vir·gin** \'vər-jən\ *n* [ME, fr. OF *virgine*, fr. L *virgin-, virgo* young woman, virgin] **1 a :** an unmarried woman devoted to religion **b** *cap* **:** VIRGIN MARY **2 a :** an absolutely chaste young woman **b :** an unmarried girl or woman **3 :** a person who has not had sexual intercourse **4 :** a female animal that has never copulated

²**virgin** *adj* **1 :** free of impurity or stain **:** UNSULLIED **2 :** CHASTE **3 :** relating to, characteristic of, or befitting a virgin **:** MODEST **4 :** FRESH, UNSPOILED; *specif* **:** not altered by human activity ⟨~ forest⟩ **5 a :** being used or worked for the first time **b :** INITIAL, FIRST **6 a :** NATIVE 8b ⟨~ sulfur⟩ **b** *of a vegetable oil* **:** obtained from the first light pressing and without heating **7 :** produced directly from ore or by primary smelting — used of metal

¹**vir·gin·al** \'vər-jən-ᵊl, 'vərj-nəl\ *adj* **1 :** of, relating to, or characteristic of a virgin or virginity; *esp* **:** PURE, CHASTE **2 :** PRISTINE, UNSULLIED — **vir·gin·al·ly** \-ē\ *adv*

²**virginal** *n* [prob. fr. L *virginalis* of a virgin, fr. *virgin-, virgo*] **:** a small rectangular spinet having no legs and only one wire to a note and popular in the 16th and 17th centuries — often used in pl.; called also *pair of virginals*

virgin birth *n* **1 :** birth from a virgin **:** PARTHENOGENESIS **2** *often cap V&B* **:** the theological doctrine that Jesus was miraculously begotten of God and born of a virgin mother

Vir·gin·ia cowslip \vər-,jin-yə-, -,jin-ē-ə-\ *n* [*Virginia*, state of the U.S.] **:** a smooth erect eastern No. American herb (*Mertensia virginica*) of the borage family with entire leaves and showy blue flowers pink in the bud — called also *Virginia bluebell*

Virginia creeper *n* **:** a common No. American tendril-climbing vine (*Parthenocissus quinquefolia*) of the grape family with palmately compound leaves and bluish black berries

Virginia fence *n* **:** WORM FENCE — called also *Virginia rail fence*

Virginia reel *n* **:** an American dance in which all couples in turn participate in a series of figures

vir·gin·i·ty \(,)vər-'jin-ət-ē\ *n* **1 :** the quality or state of being virgin; *esp* **:** MAIDENHOOD **2 :** the unmarried life **:** CELIBACY, SPINSTERHOOD

vir·gin·ium \vər-'jin-ē-əm, -'jin-yəm\ *n* [NL, fr. *Virginia*] **:** FRANCIUM

Virgin Mary *n* **:** the mother of Jesus

virgin's bower *n* **:** any of several usu. small-flowered and climbing clematises

virgin wool *n* **:** wool not used before in manufacture

Vir·go \'vər-(,)gō\ *n* [L (gen. *Virginis*), lit., virgin] **1 :** a zodiacal constellation on the celestial equator due south of the handle of the Dipper pictured as a woman holding a spike of grain **2 :** the 6th sign of the zodiac

vir·gu·late \'vər-gyə-lət, -,lāt\ *adj* **:** shaped like a rod

vir·gule \'vər-(,)gyü(ə)l\ *n* [F, fr. L *virgula* small stripe, obelus, fr. dim. of *virga* rod — more at WHISK] **:** DIAGONAL 3

vi·ri·ci·dal \,vī-rə-'sīd-ᵊl\ *adj* **:** of, relating to, or being a viricide

vi·ri·cide \'vī-rə-,sīd\ *n* [NL *virus* + E *-i-* + *-cide*] **:** an agent that destroys or inactivates viruses

vir·id \'vir-əd\ *adj* [L *viridis* green — more at VERDANT] **:** vividly green **:** VERDANT

vir·i·des·cent \,vir-ə-'des-ᵊnt\ *adj* [L *viridis* green — more at VERDANT] **:** slightly green **:** GREENISH

vi·rid·i·an \və-'rid-ē-ən\ *n* [L *viridis*] **:** a chrome green held to be chromic oxide Cr_2O_3

vi·rid·i·ty \və-'rid-ət-ē\ *n* [ME *viridite*, fr. MF *viridité*, fr. L *viriditat-, viriditas*, fr. *viridis*] **1 :** GREENNESS **2 :** FRESHNESS

vir·ile \'vir-əl *also* 'vi(ə)r-,īl\ *adj* [MF or L; MF *viril*, fr. L *virilis*, fr. *vir* man, male; akin to OE & OHG *wer* man, Skt *vīra*] **1 :** having the nature, properties, or qualities of a man; *specif* **:** capable of functioning as a male in copulation **2 :** ENERGETIC, VIGOROUS **3 :** characteristic of or associated with men **:** MASCULINE **4 :** MASTERFUL, FORCEFUL **syn** see MALE

vir·il·ism \'vir-ə-,liz-əm\ *n* **1 :** precocious development of secondary sex characters in the male **2 :** the appearance of secondary male characters in the female

vi·ril·i·ty \və-'ril-ət-ē\ *n* **:** the quality or state of being virile: **a :** MANHOOD **b :** manly vigor **:** MASCULINITY

virl \'vər(-ə)l\ *n* [ME *virole* — more at FERRULE] *Scot* **:** FERRULE 1

vi·ro·log·i·cal \,vī-rə-'läj-i-kəl\ *adj* **:** of or relating to virology

vi·rol·o·gist \vī-'räl-ə-jəst\ *n* **:** a specialist in virology

vi·rol·o·gy \-jē\ *n* [NL *virus* + ISV *-logy*] **:** a branch of science that deals with viruses

vi·ro·sis \vī-'rō-səs\ *n* **:** infection with or disease caused by a virus

vir·tu \,vər-'tü, vi(ə)r-\ *n* [It *virtù*, lit., virtue, fr. L *virtut-, virtus*] **1 :** a love of or taste for curios or objets d'art **2 :** productions of art esp. of a curious or antique nature **:** OBJETS D'ART

vir·tu·al \'vərch-(ə-)wəl, 'vər-chəl\ *adj* [ME, possessed of certain physical virtues, fr. ML *virtualis*, fr. L *virtus* strength, virtue] **:** being in essence or effect but not in fact — **vir·tu·al·i·ty** \,vər-chə-'wal-ət-ē\ *n* — **vir·tu·al·ly** \'vərch-(ə-)wə-lē, 'vərch-(ə-)lē\ *adv*

virtual focus *n* **:** a point from which divergent rays (as of light) seem to emanate but do not actually do so (as in the image of a point source seen in a plane mirror)

virtual image *n* **:** an image (as seen in a plane mirror) formed of virtual foci

vir·tu·al·ism \'vərch-(ə-)wə-,liz-əm, 'vər-chə-,liz-\ *n* **:** the theological doctrine attributed to John Calvin that though the eucharistic elements remain unchanged the spiritual body, blood, and benefits of Jesus Christ are conveyed through them

vir·tue \'vər-(,)chü, -chə-w\ *n* [ME *virtu*, fr. OF, fr. L *virtut-, virtus* strength, manliness, virtue, fr. *vir* man — more at VIRILE] **1 a :** conformity to a standard of right **:** MORALITY **b :** a particular moral excellence **2** *cap* **:** an angel of the fifth highest rank **3 :** a beneficial quality or power of a thing **4 :** manly strength or courage **:** VALOR **5 :** a commendable quality or trait **:** MERIT **6 :** a capacity to act **:** POTENCY **7 :** chastity esp. in a woman — **by virtue of** *or* **in virtue of :** through the force of **:** by authority of

vir·tue·less \-(,)chü-ləs\ *adj* **1 :** devoid of excellence or worth **2 :** lacking in moral goodness

vir·tu·o·sa \,vər-chə-'wō-sə, -zə\ *n* [It, fem. of *virtuoso*] **:** a female virtuoso

vir·tu·o·sic \,vər-chə-'wäs-ik; -'wō-sik, -zik\ *adj* **:** characteristic of a virtuoso

vir·tu·os·i·ty \-'wäs-ət-ē\ *n* **1 :** taste for or interest in virtu **2 :** great technical skill in the practice of the fine arts

vir·tu·o·so \-'wō-(,)sō, -(,)zō\ *n, pl* **virtuosos** *or* **vir·tu·o·si** \-(,)sē, -(,)zē\ [It, fr. *virtuoso*, adj., virtuous, skilled, fr. LL *virtuosus* virtuous, fr. L *virtus*] **1 :** an experimenter or investigator esp. in the arts and sciences **:** SAVANT **2 :** one skilled in or having a taste for the fine arts **3 :** one who excels in the technique of an art; *esp* **:** a musical performer (as on the violin) — **virtuoso** *adj*

vir·tu·ous \'vərch-(ə-)wəs\ *adj* **1 :** POTENT, EFFICACIOUS **2 a :** having or exhibiting virtue **b :** morally excellent **:** RIGHTEOUS **3 :** CHASTE **syn** see MORAL — **vir·tu·ous·ly** *adv* — **vir·tu·ous·ness** *n*

vi·ru·cide \'vī-rə-,sīd\ *n* [NL *virus* + E *-cide*] **:** an agent that kills viruses

vir·u·lence \'vir-(y)ə-lən(t)s\ *or* **vir·u·len·cy** \-lən-sē\ *n* **:** the quality or state of being virulent: as **a :** extreme bitterness or malignity of temper **b :** VENOMOUSNESS, MALIGNANCY **c :** the relative capacity of a pathogen to overcome body defenses

vir·u·lent \-lənt\ *adj* [ME, fr. L *virulentus*, fr. *virus* poison] **1 a :** marked by a rapid, severe, and malignant course ⟨a ~ infection⟩ **b :** able to overcome bodily defensive mechanisms ⟨a ~ pathogen⟩ **2 :** extremely poisonous or venomous **:** NOXIOUS **3 :** full of malice **:** MALIGNANT **4 :** objectionably harsh or strong — **vir·u·lent·ly** *adv*

vi·rus \'vī-rəs\ *n* [L, slimy liquid, poison, stench; akin to OE *wāse* marsh, Gk *ios* poison, Skt *viṣa*; in senses 2 & 4, fr. NL, fr. L] **1** *archaic* **:** VENOM 1 **2 a :** the causative agent of an infectious disease **b :** FILTERABLE VIRUS; *specif* **:** any of a large group of submicroscopic infective agents that are held by some to be living organisms and by others to be complex protein molecules containing nucleic acids and comparable to genes, that are capable of growth and multiplication only in living cells, and that cause various important diseases in man, lower animals, or plants **c :** a disease caused by a filterable virus **3 :** something that poisons the mind or soul **4 :** an antigenic but not infective material (as vaccine lymph) obtainable from a case of an infectious disease

vi·ru·stat·ic \,vī-rə-'stat-ik\ *adj* [*virus* + Gk *statikos* causing to stand — more at STATIC] **:** tending to check the growth of viruses

vis \'vis\ *n, pl* **vi·res** \'vī-,rēz\ [L — more at VIM] **:** FORCE, POWER

[1]**vi·sa** \'vē-zə\ *n* [F, fr. L, neut. pl. of *visus*, pp.] **1 :** an endorsement made on a passport by the proper authorities denoting that it has been examined and that the bearer may proceed **2 :** a signature of formal approval by a superior upon a document

[2]**visa** *vt* **vi·saed** \-zəd\ **vi·sa·ing** \-zə-iŋ\ **:** to give a visa to (a passport)

vis·age \'viz-ij\ *n* [ME, fr. OF, fr. *vis* face, fr. L *visus* sight, fr. *visus*, pp. of *vidēre* to see — more at WIT] **1 :** the face, countenance, or appearance of a person or sometimes an animal **2 :** ASPECT, APPEARANCE **syn** see FACE — **vis·aged** \-ijd\ *adj*

[1]**vis-à-vis** \,vē-zə-'vē, -zä-\ *n, pl* **vis-à-vis** \-zə-'vē(z), -zä-\ [F, lit., face to face] **1 :** one that is face to face with another **2 a :** ESCORT, DATE **b :** COUNTERPART, OPPOSITE NUMBER **3 :** TÊTE-À-TÊTE

[2]**vis-à-vis** \,vē-zə-,vē, -zä-\ *prep* **1 :** face to face with **:** OPPOSITE **2 :** in relation to **3 :** as compared with

[3]**vis-à-vis** \,vē-zə-'vē, -zä-\ *adv* **:** in company **:** TOGETHER

Vi·sa·yan \və-'sī-ən\ *var of* BISAYAN

vis·ca·cha *var of* VIZCACHA

viscera *pl of* VISCUS

vis·cer·al \'vis(-ə)-rəl\ *adj* **1 :** felt in or as if in the viscera **:** DEEP ⟨~ sensation⟩ **2 :** INSTINCTIVE, APPETITIVE **3 :** EARTHY **4 :** of, relating to, or located on or among the viscera **:** SPLANCHNIC — **vis·cer·al·ly** \-rə-lē\ *adv*

vis·cero·gen·ic \,vis-(ə-)rə-'jen-ik\ *adj* [L *viscera* + E *-genic*] **:** arising within the body

vis·cero·mo·tor \-'mōt-ər\ *adj* **:** causing or concerned in the functional activity of the viscera ⟨~ nerves⟩

vis·cid \'vis-əd\ *adj* [LL *viscidus*, fr. L *viscum* birdlime — more at VISCOUS] **1 a :** having an adhesive quality **:** STICKY **b :** having a glutinous consistency **:** VISCOUS **2 :** covered with a sticky layer — **vis·cid·i·ty** \vis-'id-ət-ē\ *n* — **vis·cid·ly** \'vis-əd-lē\ *adv*

vis·co·elas·tic \,vis-(,)kō-i-'las-tik\ *adj* [*viscous* + *elastic*] **:** having both viscous and elastic properties in appreciable degree

vis·com·e·ter \vis-'käm-ət-ər\ *n* [*viscosity* + *-meter*] **:** an instrument with which to measure viscosity — **vis·co·met·ric** \,vis-kə-'me-trik\ *adj*

[1]**vis·cose** \'vis-,kōs *also esp for 2* -,kōz\ *adj* **1 :** VISCOUS **2 :** of, relating to, or made from viscose

[2]**vis·cose** \-,kōs, -,kōz\ *n* **1 :** a viscous golden-brown solution made by treating cellulose with caustic alkali solution and carbon disulfide and used in making rayon and films of regenerated cellulose **2 :** viscose rayon

vis·co·sim·e·ter \,vis-kə-'sim-ət-ər\ *n* [ISV *viscosity* + *-meter*] **:** VISCOMETER — **vis·cosi·met·ric** \(,)vis-,käs-ə-'me-trik\ *adj*

vis·cos·i·ty \vis-'käs-ət-ē\ *n* **1 :** the quality or state of being viscous; *specif* **:** the property of a fluid that resists internal flow by releasing counteracting forces **2 :** the capability possessed by a solid of yielding continually under stress

vis·count \'vī-,kaùnt\ *n* [ME *viscounte*, fr. MF *viscomte*, fr. ML *vicecomit-, vicecomes*, fr. LL *vice-* + *comit-, comes* count — more at COUNT] **:** a member of the peerage in Great Britain ranking below an earl and above a baron — **vis·count·cy** \-,kaùn(t)-sē\ *n* — **vis·count·ess** \-,kaùnt-əs\ *n* — **vis·county** \-,kaùnt-ē\ *n*

vis·cous \'vis-kəs\ *adj* [ME *viscouse*, fr. LL *viscosus* full of birdlime, viscous, fr. L *viscum* mistletoe, birdlime; akin to OHG *wīhsila* cherry, Gk *ixos* mistletoe] **1 :** VISCID, GLUEY **2 :** having or characterized by viscosity — **vis·cous·ly** *adv* — **vis·cous·ness** *n*

vis·cus \'vis-kəs\ *n, pl* **vis·cera** \'vis-(ə-)rə\ [L (pl. *viscera*)] **:** an internal organ of the body; *esp* **:** one (as the heart, liver, or intestine) located in the great cavity of the trunk proper

[1]**vise** \'vīs\ *n* [MF *vis* something winding, fr. L *vitis* vine — more at WITHY] **:** any of various tools having two jaws for holding work that close usu. by a screw, lever, or cam

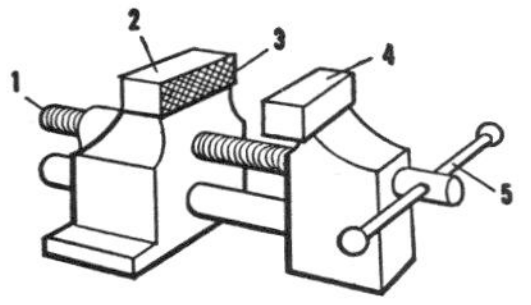

vise: *1* screw, *2* fixed jaw, *3* jaw plate, *4* movable jaw, *5* handle

[2]**vise** *vt* **:** to hold, force, or squeeze with or as if with a vise

[3]**vi·sé** \'vē-,zā, vē-'\ *vt* **vi·séd** *also* **vi·séed; vi·sé·ing** [F] **:** VISA

[4]**visé** *n* [F] **:** VISA

Vish·nu \'vish-(,)nü\ *n* [Skt *Viṣṇu*] **:** a Hindu god worshiped in the Trimurti as the Preserver and in a major cult in various incarnations (as Rama, Krishna) — **Vish·nu·ism** \-,iz-əm\ *n* — **Vish·nu·ite** \-,īt\ *n*

vis·i·bil·i·ty \,viz-ə-'bil-ət-ē\ *n* **1 :** the quality or state of being visible **2 a :** the degree of clearness of the atmosphere; *specif* **:** the greatest distance toward the horizon that prominent objects can be identified visually with the naked eye **b :** capability of affording an unobstructed view **3 :** a measure of the ability of radiant energy to evoke visual sensation

vis·i·ble \'viz-ə-bəl\ *adj* [ME, fr. MF or L; MF, fr. L *visibilis*, fr. *visus*, pp.] **1 :** capable of being seen ⟨~ stars⟩ **2 a :** exposed to view ⟨the ~ horizon⟩ **b :** MANIFEST, APPARENT **c :** CONSPICUOUS **3 :** DISCOVERABLE, RECOGNIZABLE ⟨no ~ means of support⟩ **4 :** AVAILABLE 4 **5 :** devised to keep a particular part or item always in full view or readily seen or referred to ⟨~ file⟩ — **vis·i·ble·ness** *n* — **vis·i·bly** \-blē\ *adv*

visible speech *n* **1 :** a set of phonetic symbols based on symbols for articulatory position **2 :** speech exhibited spectrographically

Visi·goth \'viz-ə-,gäth\ *n* [LL *Visigothi*, pl.] **:** a member of the western division of the Goths — called also *West Goth;* compare OSTROGOTH

Visi·goth·ic \,viz-ə-'gäth-ik\ *adj* **:** of or relating to the Visigoths

[1]**vi·sion** \'vizh-ən\ *n* [ME, fr. OF, fr. L *vision-, visio*, fr. *visus*, pp. of *vidēre* to see — more at WIT] **1 a :** something seen in a dream, trance, or ecstasy; *specif* **:** a supernatural appearance that conveys a revelation **b :** an object of imagination **c :** a manifestation to the senses of something immaterial **2 a :** the act or power of imagination **b** (1) **:** mode of seeing or conceiving (2) **:** unusual discernment or foresight **c :** direct mystical awareness of the supernatural usu. in visible form **3 a :** the act or power of seeing **:** SIGHT **b :** the special sense by which the qualities of an object (as color, luminosity, shape and size) constituting its appearance are perceived and which is mediated by the eye **4 a :** something seen **b :** a lovely or charming sight — **vi·sion·al** \'vizh-nəl, -ən-ᵊl\ *adj* — **vi·sion·al·ly** \-ē\ *adv*

[2]**vision** *vt* **vi·sion·ing** \'vizh-(ə-)niŋ\ **:** IMAGINE, ENVISION

vi·sion·ar·i·ness \'vizh-ə-,ner-ē-nəs\ *n* **:** the quality or state of being visionary

[1]**vi·sion·ary** \'vizh-ə-,ner-ē\ *adj* **1 a :** able or likely to see visions **b :** disposed to reverie or imagining **:** DREAMY **2 a :** of the nature of a vision **:** ILLUSORY **b :** IMPRACTICABLE, UTOPIAN **c :** existing only in imagination **:** UNREAL **3 :** of, relating to, or characterized by visions or the power of vision **syn** see IMAGINARY

[2]**visionary** *n* **1 :** one who sees visions **:** SEER **2 :** one whose ideas or projects are impractical **:** DREAMER

vi·sioned \'vizh-ənd\ *adj* **1 :** seen in a vision ⟨a ~ face⟩ **2 :** produced by or experienced in a vision ⟨~ agony⟩ **3 :** endowed with vision **:** INSPIRED

vi·sion·less \-ən-ləs\ *adj* **1 :** SIGHTLESS, BLIND ⟨~ eyes⟩ **2 :** lacking vision or inspiration ⟨a ~ leader⟩

[1]**vis·it** \'viz-ət\ *vb* **vis·it·ed** \'viz-ət-əd, 'viz-təd\ **vis·it·ing** \'viz-ət-iŋ, 'viz-tiŋ\ [ME *visiten*, fr. OF *visiter*, fr. L *visitare*, freq. of *visare* to go to see, fr. *visus*, pp.] *vt* **1 :** to go to see in order to comfort or help **2 a :** to pay a call upon as an act of friendship or courtesy **b :** to go or come to see in an official or professional capacity **:** INSPECT **c :** to dwell with temporarily as a guest **3 a :** to come to or upon as a reward, affliction, or punishment **b :** INFLICT ~ *vi* **1 :** to make a visit; *also* **:** to make frequent or regular visits **2 :** CHAT, CONVERSE

[2]**visit** *n* **1 a :** a short stay **:** CALL **b :** a brief residence as a guest **c :** an extended stay **:** SOJOURN **2 :** a journey to and stay or short sojourn at a place **3 :** an official call or tour **:** VISITATION **4 :** the act of a naval officer in boarding a merchant ship on the high seas in exercise of the right of search

vis·it·able \'viz-ət-ə-bəl, 'viz-tə-\ *adj* **1 :** subject to or allowing visitation or inspection **2 :** socially eligible to receive visits

Vis·i·tan·dine \,viz-ə-'tan-,dēn\ *n* [F, fr. L *visitandum*, gerund of *visitare* to visit] **:** a nun of the Roman Catholic Order of the Visitation of the Blessed Virgin Mary founded in France in 1610 and devoted to contemplation and education

vis·i·tant \'viz-ət-ənt, 'viz-tənt\ *n* **1 :** VISITOR; *esp* **:** one thought to come from a spirit world **2 :** a migratory bird that appears at intervals for a limited period — **visitant** *adj*

vis·i·ta·tion \,viz-ə-'tā-shən\ *n* **1 :** VISIT; *esp* **:** an official visit (as for inspection) **2 a :** a special dispensation of divine favor or wrath **b :** a severe trial **:** AFFLICTION **3** *cap* **:** a Christian feast on July 2 commemorating the visit of the Virgin Mary to Elisabeth before the birth of Elisabeth's son John the Baptist — **vis·i·ta·tion·al** \-shnəl, -shən-ᵊl\ *adj*

vis·i·ta·tor \'viz-ə-,tāt-ər\ *n* **:** an official visitor in the Roman Catholic Church
vis·i·ta·to·ri·al \,viz-ət-ə-'tōr-ē-əl, ,viz-tə-, -'tȯr-\ *adj* **:** of or relating to visitation or to a judicial visitor or superintendent
visiting card *n* **:** a small card bearing the name and sometimes the address of a person or married couple presented when calling — called also *calling card*
visiting fireman *n* **:** a usu. important or influential visitor whom it is desirable or expedient to show about or entertain impressively
visiting nurse *n* **:** a nurse employed by a hospital or social-service agency to visit sick persons or perform other public health services in a community
visiting professor *n* **:** a professor invited to join a college or university faculty for a limited time (as an academic year)
visiting teacher *n* **:** an educational officer employed by a public school system to enforce attendance regulations or to instruct sick or handicapped pupils unable to attend school
vis·i·tor \'viz-ət-ər, 'viz-tər\ *n* **:** one that visits; *specif* **:** one that makes formal visits of inspection
vi·sive \'viz-iv, 'vī-siv\ *adj* [ML *visivus*, fr. L *visus*, pp. of *vidēre* to see — more at WIT] **1** *archaic* **:** of, relating to, or serving for vision **2** *archaic* **:** capable of seeing or of being seen
vi·sor \'vī-zər\ *n* [ME *viser*, fr. AF, fr. OF *visiere*, fr. *vis* face — more at VISAGE] **1 :** the front piece of a helmet; *esp* **:** a movable upper piece **2 a :** a face mask **b :** DISGUISE **3 a :** a projecting front on a cap for shading the eyes **b :** a projecting piece on an automobile windshield to protect the eyes — **vi·sored** \-zərd\ *adj* — **vi·sor·less** \-zər-ləs\ *adj*
vis·ta \'vis-tə\ *n* [It, sight, fr. *visto*, pp. of *vedere* to see, fr. L *vidēre* — more at WIT] **1 :** a distant view through or along an avenue or opening **:** PROSPECT **2 :** an extensive mental view over a stretch of time or a series of events
vis·taed \-təd\ *adj* **1 :** affording or made to form a vista **2 :** seen in or as if in a vista
vi·su·al \'vizh-(ə-)wəl, 'vizh-əl\ *adj* [ME, fr. LL *visualis*, fr. L *visus* sight, fr. *visus*, pp. of *vidēre* to see] **1 :** of, relating to, or used in vision **2 :** attained or maintained by sight **3 :** OPTICAL ⟨~ focus of a lens⟩ **4 :** VISIBLE **5 :** producing mental images **:** VIVID **6 :** done or executed by sight only ⟨~ navigation⟩ **7 :** of, relating to, or constituting a means of instruction (as a map or film) by means of sight ⟨~ aid⟩ — **vi·su·al·ly** \'vizh-(ə-)wə-lē, 'vizh-(ə-)lē\ *adv*
visual acuity *n* **:** the relative ability of the visual organ to resolve detail that is usu. expressed as the reciprocal of the minimum angular separation in minutes of two lines just resolvable as separate and that forms in the average human eye an angle of one minute
visual–aural radio range *n* **:** a radio aid to air navigation by which a pilot determines if he is on course by an appropriate aural signal, a meter reading, or both — called also *visual-aural range*
vi·su·al·iza·tion \,vizh-(ə-)wə-lə-'zā-shən, ,vizh-(ə-)lə-\ *n* **:** the act of visualizing or state of being visualized
vi·su·al·ize \'vizh-(ə-)wə-,līz, 'vizh-ə-,līz\ *vt* **:** to make visible; *esp* **:** to see or form a mental image of **:** ENVISAGE ~ *vi* **:** to form a visual mental image
vi·su·al·iz·er \-,lī-zər\ *n* **:** one that visualizes; *esp* **:** one whose mental imagery is prevailingly visual — compare AUDILE, MOTILE
visual purple *n* **:** a photosensitive red or purple pigment in the retinal rods of various vertebrates; *esp* **:** RHODOPSIN
vi·ta \'vīt-ə, 'wē-,tä\ *n, pl* **vi·tae** \'vīt-ē, 'vī-,tē, 'wē-,tī\ [L, lit., life] **:** a brief autobiographical sketch (as in a doctoral thesis)
vi·tal \'vīt-ᵊl\ *adj* [ME, fr. MF, fr. L *vitalis* of life, fr. *vita* life; akin to L *vivere* to live — more at QUICK] **1 a :** existing as a manifestation of life **b :** concerned with or necessary to the maintenance of life ⟨~ organs⟩ **2 :** full of life and vigor **:** ANIMATED **3 :** characteristic of life or living beings **4 a :** fundamentally concerned with or affecting life or living beings: as (1) **:** INVIGORATING (2) **:** destructive to life **:** MORTAL **b :** of the utmost importance **:** ESSENTIAL **5 :** recording data relating to lives **syn** see ESSENTIAL, LIVING — **vi·tal·ly** \-ᵊl-ē\ *adv*
vital capacity *n* **:** the breathing capacity of the lungs expressed as the number of cubic inches or cubic centimeters of air that can be forcibly exhaled after a full inspiration
vi·tal·ism \'vīt-ᵊl-,iz-əm\ *n* **1 :** a doctrine that the functions of a living organism are due to a vital principle distinct from physicochemical forces **2 :** a doctrine that the processes of life are not explicable by the laws of physics and chemistry alone and that life is in some part self-determining — **vi·tal·ist** \-ᵊl-əst\ *n* — **vi·tal·is·tic** \,vīt-ᵊl-'is-tik\ *adj*
vi·tal·i·ty \vī-'tal-ət-ē\ *n* **1 a :** the peculiarity distinguishing the living from the nonliving **b :** capacity to live and develop; *also* **:** physical or mental vigor esp. when highly developed **2 a :** power of enduring or continuing **b :** lively and animated character **:** VIGOR
vi·tal·iza·tion \,vīt-ᵊl-ə-'zā-shən\ *n* **:** the quality or state of being vitalized
vi·tal·ize \'vīt-ᵊl-,īz\ *vt* **:** to endow with vitality **:** ANIMATE
vi·tals \'vīt-ᵊlz\ *n pl* **1 :** vital organs **2 :** essential parts
vital statistics *n pl but sing or pl in constr* **:** statistics relating to births, deaths, marriages, health, and disease
vi·ta·mer \'vīt-ə-mər\ *n* [*vitamin* + *isomer*] **:** any of two or more compounds that relieve a particular vitamin deficiency — **vi·ta·mer·ic** \,vīt-ə-'mer-ik\ *adj*
vi·ta·min \'vīt-ə-mən\ *n* [L *vita* life + ISV *amine*] **:** any of various organic substances that are essential in minute quantities to the nutrition of most animals and some plants, act in the regulation of metabolic processes but do not provide energy or serve as building units, and are present in natural foodstuffs or sometimes produced within the body
vitamin A *n* **:** any of several fat-soluble vitamins found esp. in animal products (as egg yolk, milk, or fish-liver oils) or a mixture of them whose lack in the animal body causes epithelial tissues to become keratinous (as in the eye with resulting visual defects)
vitamin B *n* **1 :** VITAMIN B COMPLEX **2** *or* **vitamin B_1 :** THIAMINE
vitamin B_c \-'bē-'sē\ *n* **:** FOLIC ACID
vitamin B complex *n* **:** a group of water-soluble vitamins found esp. in yeast, seed germs, eggs, liver and flesh, and vegetables that have varied metabolic functions and include coenzymes and growth factors — called also *B complex;* compare BIOTIN, CHOLINE, NICOTINIC ACID, PANTOTHENIC ACID
vitamin B_6 \-'bē-'siks\ *n* **:** pyridoxine or a closely related compound found widely in combined form and considered essential to vertebrate nutrition
vitamin B_{12} \-'bē-'twelv\ *n* **:** a complex cobalt-containing compound $C_{63}H_{90}CoN_{14}O_{14}P$ that occurs esp. in liver, is essential to normal blood formation, neural function, and growth, and is used esp. in treating pernicious and related anemias and in animal rations; *also* **:** any of several compounds of similar action but different chemistry
vitamin B_2 \-'bē-'tü\ *n* **:** RIBOFLAVIN
vitamin C *n* **:** a water-soluble vitamin $C_6H_8O_6$ found in plants and esp. in fruits and leafy vegetables or made synthetically and used in the prevention and treatment of scurvy and as an antioxidant for foods
vitamin D *n* **:** any or all of several fat-soluble vitamins chemically related to steroids, essential for normal bone and tooth structure, and found esp. in fish-liver oils, egg yolk, and milk or produced by activation (as by ultraviolet irradiation) of sterols: as **a** *or* **vitamin D_2 :** an alcohol $C_{28}H_{43}OH$ usu. prepared by irradiation of ergosterol and used as a dietary supplement in nutrition and medicinally in the control of rickets and related disorders — called also *calciferol* **b** *or* **vitamin D_3 :** an alcohol $C_{27}H_{43}OH$ that is the predominating form of vitamin D in most fish-liver oils and is formed in the skin on exposure to sunlight or ultraviolet rays **c** *or* **vitamin D_4 :** an alcohol $C_{28}H_{45}OH$ of doubtful biological activity obtained by irradiation of a derivative of ergosterol
vitamin E *n* **:** any of the tocopherols that are essential in the nutrition of various vertebrates in which their absence is associated with infertility, muscular dystrophy, or vascular abnormalities, are found esp. in leaves and in seed germ oils, and are used chiefly in animal feeds and as antioxidants
vitamin G *n* **:** RIBOFLAVIN
vitamin H *n* **:** BIOTIN
vi·ta·min·ize \'vīt-ə-mə-,nīz\ *vt* **1 :** to provide or supplement with vitamins **2 :** to make vigorous as if by the feeding of vitamins
vitamin K *n* [Dan *koagulation* coagulation] **1 :** either of two naturally occurring fat-soluble vitamins $C_{31}H_{46}O_2$ and $C_{41}H_{56}O_2$ essential for the clotting of blood because of their role in the production of prothrombin — called also respectively *vitamin K_1*, *vitamin K_2* **2 :** any of several synthetic compounds closely related chemically to natural vitamins K_1 and K_2 and of similar biological activity
vitamin P *n* [*p*aprika & *p*ermeability] **:** BIOFLAVONOID
vitamin PP \-'pē-'pē\ *n* [*p*ellagra-*p*reventive] **:** a pellagra-preventive vitamin (as nicotinamide or nicotinic acid)
vi·ta·scope \'vīt-ə-,skōp\ *n* [L *vita* life + E *-scope* — more at VITAL] **:** an early motion-picture projector — **vi·ta·scop·ic** \,vīt-ə-'skäp-ik\ *adj*
vi·tel·lin \vī-'tel-ən, və-\ *n* **:** a protein in egg yolk
vi·tel·line \-'tel-ən, -,ēn, -,īn\ *adj* **1 :** resembling the yolk of an egg esp. in yellow color **2 :** of, relating to, or producing yolk
vi·tel·lus \-'tel-əs\ *n* [L, lit., small calf — more at VEAL] **:** YOLK 1c
vi·ti·ate \'vish-ē-,āt\ *vt* [L *vitiatus*, pp. of *vitiare*, fr. *vitium* fault] **1 :** CONTAMINATE, POLLUTE **2 :** DEBASE, PERVERT **3 :** to make ineffective or weak **:** INVALIDATE **syn** see DEBASE — **vi·ti·a·tor** \'vish-ē-,āt-ər\ *n*
vi·ti·a·tion \,vish-ē-'ā-shən\ *n* **1 :** the quality or state of being vitiated ⟨the air in the room showed marked ~⟩ **2 :** the act of vitiating ⟨protesting his ~ of the agreement⟩
vi·ti·cul·tur·al \,vit-ə-'kəlch-(ə-)rəl, ,vīt-\ *adj* **:** of, relating to, or used in viticulture
vi·ti·cul·ture \'vit-ə-,kəl-chər, 'vīt-\ *n* [L *vitis* vine + E *culture* — more at WITHY] **:** the cultivation or culture of grapes — **vi·ti·cul·tur·ist** \,vit-ə-'kəlch-(ə-)rəst, ,vīt-\ *n*
vit·i·li·go \,vit-ᵊl-'ī-(,)gō\ *n* [NL, fr. L, tetter] **:** a skin disorder manifested by smooth white spots on various parts of the body
vi·ti·os·i·ty \,vish-ē-'äs-ət-ē\ *n, archaic* **:** VICIOUSNESS, DEPRAVITY
vit·re·ous \'vi-trē-əs\ *adj* [L *vitreus*, fr. *vitrum* glass — more at WOAD] **1 :** of, relating to, derived from, or consisting of glass **2 :** resembling glass (as in color, composition, brittleness, or luster) **:** GLASSY ⟨~ rocks⟩ **3 :** of, relating to, or constituting the vitreous humor — **vit·re·ous·ly** *adv* — **vit·re·ous·ness** *n*
vitreous enamel *n* **:** a fired-on opaque glassy coating on steel or other metals
vitreous humor *n* **:** the clear colorless transparent jelly that fills the eyeball posterior to the lens
vitreous silica *n* **:** a chemically stable and refractory glass made from silica alone — compare QUARTZ GLASS
vit·ri·fi·able \'vi-trə-,fī-ə-bəl\ *adj* **:** of a kind that can be vitrified
vit·ri·fi·ca·tion \,vi-trə-fə-'kā-shən\ *n* **:** the process of vitrifying or state of being vitrified
vit·ri·fy \'vi-trə-,fī\ *vb* [F *vitrifier*, fr. MF, fr. L *vitrum* glass] *vt* **:** to change into glass or a glassy substance by heat and fusion ~ *vi* **:** to undergo vitrification
¹**vit·ri·ol** \'vi-trē-əl\ *n* [ME, fr. MF, fr. ML *vitriolum*, alter. of LL *vitreolum*, neut. of *vitreolus* glassy, fr. L *vitreus* vitreous] **1 a :** a sulfate of any of various metals (as copper, iron, or zinc); *esp* **:** a glassy hydrate of such a sulfate **b :** OIL OF VITRIOL **2 :** something felt to resemble vitriol esp. in caustic quality; *esp* **:** virulence of feeling or of speech — **vit·ri·ol·ic** \,vi-trē-'äl-ik\ *adj*
²**vitriol** *vt* **:** to expose to the action of vitriol; *esp* **:** to dip in dilute sulfuric acid
vit·ta \'vit-ə\ *n, pl* **vit·tae** \'vit-ē, 'vi-,tē, 'vi-,tī\ [NL, fr. L, fillet; akin to L *viēre* to plait — more at WIRE] **1 :** one of the oil tubes in the fruits of plants of the carrot family **2 :** STRIPE, STREAK
vit·tate \'vi-,tāt\ *adj* **1 :** bearing or containing vittae **2 :** striped longitudinally
vit·tle *n* **:** VICTUAL
vi·tu·per·ate \vī-'t(y)ü-pə-,rāt, və-\ *vt* [L *vituperatus*, pp. of *vituperare*, fr. *vitium* fault + *parare* to make — more at PARE] **:** to abuse or censure severely or abusively **:** BERATE **syn** see SCOLD — **vi·tu·per·a·tive** \-'t(y)ü-p(ə-)rət-iv, -pə-,rāt-\ *adj* — **vi·tu·per·a·tive·ly** *adv* — **vi·tu·per·a·tor** \-pə-,rāt-ər\ *n*
vi·tu·per·a·tion \(,)vī-,t(y)ü-pə-'rā-shən, və-\ *n* **:** sustained and bitter railing and condemnation **syn** see ABUSE

vi·tu·per·a·to·ry \vī-'t(y)ü-p(ə-)rə-ˌtōr-ē, və-, -ˌtȯr-\ *adj* : VITUPERATIVE

vi·va \'vē-və, -ˌvä\ *interj* [It, long live, fr. 3d pers. sing. pres. subj. of *vivere* to live, fr. L — more at QUICK] — used to express goodwill or approval

vi·va·ce \vē-'väch-(ˌ)ā\ *adv* (*or adj*) [It, vivacious, fr. L *vivac-, vivax*] : in a brisk spirited manner — used as a direction in music

vi·va·cious \və-'vā-shəs *also* vī-\ *adj* [L *vivac-, vivax*, lit., long-lived, fr. *vivere* to live — more at QUICK] : lively in temper or conduct : SPRIGHTLY **syn** see LIVELY — **vi·va·cious·ly** *adv* — **vi·va·cious·ness** *n*

vi·vac·i·ty \-'vas-ət-ē\ *n* : the quality or state of being vivacious

vi·van·dière \ˌvē-ˌvä^{n}-'dye(ə)r\ *n* [F] : a woman formerly accompanying troops to sell provisions and liquor

vi·var·i·um \vī-'var-ē-əm, -'ver-\ *n, pl* **vi·var·ia** \-ē-ə\ *or* **vi·var·i·ums** [L, park, preserve, fr. *vivus* alive — more at QUICK] : an enclosure for keeping or raising and observing animals or plants indoors; *esp* : one for terrestrial animals — called also *terrarium*

1**vi·va vo·ce** \ˌvī-və-'vō-(ˌ)sē\ *adv* [ML, with the living voice] : by word of mouth : ORALLY

2**viva voce** *adj* : expressed or conducted by word of mouth : ORAL

3**viva voce** *n* : an examination conducted viva voce

vi·ver·rine \vī-'ver-ən, 'vī-və-ˌrīn\ *adj* [deriv. of L *viverra* ferret; akin to OE *ācweorna* squirrel, Czech *veverka*] : of or relating to a family (Viverridae) of small carnivores including the civets

vi·vers \'vē-vərz, 'vī-\ *n pl* [MF *vivres*, pl. of *vivre* food, fr. *vivre* to live, fr. L *vivere*] *chiefly Scot* : VICTUALS, FOOD

Viv·i·an *or* **Viv·i·en** \'viv-ē-ən\ *n* : the mistress of Merlin in Arthurian legend — called also *Lady of the Lake*

viv·id \'viv-əd\ *adj* [L *vividus*, fr. *vivere* to live — more at QUICK] **1** : having the appearance of vigorous life or freshness : LIVELY ⟨~ sketch⟩ **2** *of a color* : very strong : very high in chroma **3** : producing a strong or clear impression on the senses : SHARP, INTENSE; *specif* : producing distinct mental images ⟨a ~ description⟩ **4** : acting clearly and vigorously ⟨a ~ imagination⟩ **syn** see GRAPHIC — **viv·id·ly** *adv* — **viv·id·ness** *n*

vi·vif·ic \vī-'vif-ik\ *adj* : VIVIFYING, ENLIVENING

viv·i·fi·ca·tion \ˌviv-ə-fə-'kā-shən\ *n* : the act of vivifying : the state of being vivified

viv·i·fi·er \'viv-ə-ˌfī(-ə)r\ *n* : one that vivifies

viv·i·fy \'viv-ə-ˌfī\ *vt* [MF *vivifier*, fr. LL *vivificare*, fr. L *vivificus* enlivening, fr. *vivus* alive — more at QUICK] **1** : to endue with life : QUICKEN, ANIMATE **2** : to make vivid **syn** see QUICKEN

vi·vi·par·i·ty \ˌvī-və-'par-ət-ē\ *n* : the quality or state of being viviparous

vi·vip·a·rous \vī-'vip-(ə-)rəs\ *adj* [L *viviparus*, fr. *vivus* alive + *-parus* -parous] **1** : producing living young instead of eggs from within the body in the manner of nearly all mammals, many reptiles, and a few fishes **2** : germinating while still attached to the parent plant ⟨the ~ seed of the mangrove⟩ — **vi·vip·a·rous·ly** *adv* — **vi·vip·a·rous·ness** *n*

vivi·sect \'viv-ə-ˌsekt\ *vb* [back-formation fr. *vivisection*] *vt* : to perform vivisection on ~ *vi* : to practice vivisection — **vivi·sec·tor** \-ˌsek-tər\ *n*

vivi·sec·tion \ˌviv-ə-'sek-shən, 'viv-ə-ˌ\ *n* [L *vivus* + E *section*] : the cutting of or operation on a living animal usu. for physiological or pathological investigation; *broadly* : animal experimentation esp. if considered to cause distress to the subject — **vivi·sec·tion·al** \ˌviv-ə-'sek-shnəl, -shən-^{ə}l\ *adj* — **vivi·sec·tion·al·ly** \-ē\ *adv* — **vivi·sec·tion·ist** \-'sek-sh(ə-)nəst\ *n*

vix·en \'vik-sən\ *n* [(assumed) ME (southern dial.) *vixen*, alter. of ME *fixen*, fr. OE *fyxe*, fem. of *fox*] **1** : a female fox **2** : a shrewish ill-tempered woman — **vix·en·ish** \-s(ə-)nish\ *adj* — **vix·en·ish·ly** *adv* — **vix·en·ish·ness** *n*

viz·ard \'viz-ərd\ *n* [alter. of ME *viser* mask, visor] **1** : a mask for disguise or protection **2** : DISGUISE, GUISE

viz·ca·cha \vis-'käch-ə\ *n* [Sp *vizcacha*, fr. Quechua *wiskácha*] : any of several So. American burrowing rodents closely related to the chinchilla

vi·zier \və-'zi(ə)r\ *n* [Turk *vezir*, fr. Ar *wazīr*] : a high executive officer of various Muslim countries and esp. of the former Turkish Empire — **vi·zier·ate** \-'zir-ət, -'zi(ə)r-ˌāt\ *n* — **vi·zier·ial** \-'zir-ē-əl\ *adj* — **vi·zier·ship** \-'zi(ə)r-ˌship\ *n*

vi·zor *var of* VISOR

vizs·la \'vizh-ˌlō\ *n* [*Vizsla*, Hungary] : any of a Hungarian breed of hunting dog resembling the weimaraner but having a rich deep red coat and brown eyes

vo·ca·ble \'vō-kə-bəl\ *n* [MF, fr L *vocabulum*, fr. *vocare* to call — more at VOICE] : TERM, NAME; *specif* : a word composed of various sounds or letters without regard to its meaning

vo·cab·u·lar \vō-'kab-yə-lər, və-\ *adj* [back-formation fr. *vocabulary*] : of or relating to words or phraseology : VERBAL

vo·cab·u·lary \vō-'kab-yə-ˌler-ē, və-\ *n* [MF *vocabulaire*, prob. fr. ML *vocabularium*, fr. neut. of *vocabularius* verbal, fr. L *vocabulum*] **1** : a list or collection of words or of words and phrases usu. alphabetically arranged and explained or defined : LEXICON **2** : a sum or stock of words employed by a language, group, individual, or work or in a field of knowledge

vocabulary entry *n* : a word (as the noun *book*), hyphened or open compound (as the verb *book-match* or the noun *book review*), word element (as the affix *pro-*), abbreviation (as *agt*), verbalized symbol (as *Na*), or term (as *man in the street*) entered alphabetically in a dictionary for the purpose of definition or identification or expressly included as an inflectional form (as the noun *mice* or the verb *saw*) or as a derived form (as the noun *godlessness* or the adverb *globally*) or related phrase (as *one for the book*) run on at its base word and usu. set in a type (as boldface) readily distinguishable from that of the lightface running text which defines, explains, or identifies the entry

1**vo·cal** \'vō-kəl\ *adj* [ME, fr. L *vocalis*, fr. *voc-, vox* voice — more at VOICE] **1 a** : uttered by the voice : ORAL **b** : produced in the larynx : uttered with voice **2** : relating to, composed or arranged for, or sung by the human voice ⟨~ music⟩ **3** : VOCALIC **4 a** : having or exercising the power of producing voice, speech, or sound **b** : EXPRESSIVE **c** : full of voices : RESOUNDING **d** : given to expressing oneself freely or insistently : OUTSPOKEN **e** : expressed in words **5** : of, relating to, or resembling the voice — **vo·cal·i·ty** \vō-'kal-ət-ē\ *n* — **vo·cal·ly** \'vō-kə-lē\ *adv*

2**vocal** *n* **1** : a vocal sound **2** : the vocal solo in a dance or jazz number

vocal cords *n pl* : either of two pairs of folds of mucous membrane that project into the cavity of the larynx and have free edges extending dorsoventrally toward the middle line

1**vo·cal·ic** \vō-'kal-ik, və-\ *adj* [L *vocalis* vowel, fr. *vocalis* vocal] **1** : marked by or consisting of vowels **2 a** : being or functioning as a vowel **b** : of, relating to, or associated with a vowel — **vo·cal·i·cal·ly** \-i-k(ə-)lē\ *adv*

2**vocalic** *n* : a vowel sound or sequence in its function as the most sonorous part of a syllable

vo·cal·ism \'vō-kə-ˌliz-əm\ *n* **1** : VOCALIZATION **2** : vocal art or technique : SINGING **3** : the vowel system of a language or dialect

vo·cal·ist \-kə-ləst\ *n* : SINGER

vo·cal·iza·tion \ˌvō-kə-lə-'zā-shən\ *n* : an act, process, or instance of vocalizing

vo·cal·ize \'vō-kə-ˌlīz\ *vt* **1** : to give voice to : UTTER; *specif* : SING **2 a** : to make voiced rather than voiceless : VOICE **b** : to convert to a vowel **3** : to furnish (as a consonantal Hebrew or Arabic text) with vowels or vowel points ~ *vi* **1** : to utter vocal sounds **2** : SING; *specif* : to sing without words — **vo·cal·iz·er** *n*

vo·ca·tion \vō-'kā-shən\ *n* [ME *vocacioun*, fr. L *vocation-, vocatio* summons, fr. *vocatus*, pp. of *vocare* to call — more at VOICE] **1 a** : a summons or strong inclination to a particular state or course of action; *specif* : a divine call to the religious life **b** : the special function of an individual or group **2 a** : the work in which a person is regularly employed : OCCUPATION **b** : the persons engaged in a particular occupation

vo·ca·tion·al \-shnəl, -shən-^{ə}l\ *adj* **1** : of, relating to, or concerned with a vocation **2** : of, relating to, or being in training in a skill or trade to be pursued as a career — **vo·ca·tion·al·ly** \-ē\ *adv*

vo·ca·tion·al·ism \-shnə-ˌliz-əm, -shən-^{ə}l-ˌiz-\ *n* : emphasis on vocational training in education

1**voc·a·tive** \'väk-ət-iv\ *adj* [ME *vocatif*, fr. MF, fr. L *vocativus*, fr. *vocatus*, pp.] **1** : of, relating to, or being a grammatical case marking the one addressed ⟨Latin *Domine* in *miserere, Domine* "have mercy, O Lord" is in the ~ case⟩ **2** *of a word or word group* : marking the one addressed ⟨*mother* in "mother, come here" is a ~ expression⟩ — **voc·a·tive·ly** *adv*

2**vocative** *n* **1** : the vocative case of a language **2** : a form in the vocative case

vo·cif·er·ance \vō-'sif-ə-rən(t)s\ *n* : VOCIFERATION, CLAMOROUSNESS

vo·cif·er·ant \-rənt\ *adj* : CLAMOROUS, VOCIFEROUS

vo·cif·er·ate \-ˌrāt\ *vb* [L *vociferatus*, pp. of *vociferari*, fr. *voc-, vox* voice + *ferre* to bear — more at VOICE, BEAR] *vi* : to cry out loudly : CLAMOR ~ *vt* : to utter loudly : SHOUT — **vo·cif·er·a·tor** \-ˌrāt-ər\ *n*

vo·cif·er·a·tion \vō-ˌsif-ə-'rā-shən\ *n* : the act of vociferating : OUTCRY

vo·cif·er·ous \vō-'sif-(ə-)rəs\ *adj* : making or given to loud outcry : CLAMOROUS — **vo·cif·er·ous·ly** *adv* — **vo·cif·er·ous·ness** *n*

syn CLAMOROUS, BLATANT, STRIDENT, BOISTEROUS, OBSTREPEROUS: VOCIFEROUS implies vehement deafening shouting or calling out; CLAMOROUS suggests insistent vociferousness often in complaint or demand; BLATANT implies an offensive bellowing or insensitive loudness; STRIDENT suggests a harsh, unpleasant, inescapable quality of sound; BOISTEROUS suggests a noisiness and turbulence due to high spirits; OBSTREPEROUS implies resistance to or defiance of efforts to restrain noisy or excited behavior

vo·cod·er \'vō-ˌkōd-ər\ *n* [*vo*ice *coder*] : an electronic mechanism that reduces speech signals to slowly varying signals which can be transmitted over communication systems of limited frequency band width

vo·der \'vōd-ər\ *n* [*vo*ice operation *de*monstrato*r*] : an electronic device that is capable of producing a recognizable approximation of speech

vod·ka \'väd-kə\ *n* [Russ, fr. *voda* water; akin to OE *wæter* water] : a colorless and unaged liquor of neutral spirits distilled from a mash (as of rye or wheat)

vo·dun \vō-'dü^{n}\ *n* [Haitian Creole] : VOODOOISM 1

vo·gie \'vō-gē\ *adj* [origin unknown] *Scot* : PROUD, VAIN

vogue \'vōg\ *n* [MF, action of rowing, course, fashion, fr. OIt *voga*, fr. *vogare* to row; akin to OSp *bogar* to row] **1** : the leading place in popularity or acceptance **2 a** : popular acceptation or favor : POPULARITY **b** : a period of popularity **3** : one that is in fashion at a particular time **syn** see FASHION — **vogue** *adj*

vogu·ish \'vō-gish\ *adj* **1** : FASHIONABLE, SMART **2** : suddenly or temporarily popular

1**voice** \'vȯis\ *n* [ME, fr. OF *vois*, fr. L *voc-, vox*; akin to OHG *giwahanen* to mention, L *vocare* to call, Gk *epos* word, speech] **1 a** : sound produced by vertebrates by means of lungs, larynx, or syrinx; *esp* : sound so produced by human beings **b** (1) : musical sound produced by the vocal cords and resonated by the cavities of head and throat (2) : the power or ability to produce musical tones (3) : SINGER (4) : one of the melodic parts in a vocal or instrumental composition (5) : condition of the vocal organs with respect to production of musical tones **c** : expiration of air with the vocal cords drawn close so as to vibrate audibly (as in uttering vowels and consonant sounds as \v\ or \z\) **d** : the faculty of utterance : SPEECH **2** : a sound resembling or suggesting vocal utterance **3** : an instrument or medium of expression **4 a** : wish, choice, or opinion openly or formally expressed **b** : right of expression : SUFFRAGE **5** : distinction of form or a system of inflections of a verb to indicate the relation of the subject of the verb to the action which the verb expresses — **with one voice** : UNANIMOUSLY

2**voice** *vt* **1** : UTTER **2** : to regulate the tone of **3** : to pronounce (as a consonant) with voice **syn** see EXPRESS

voice box *n* : LARYNX

voiced \'vȯist\ *adj* **1 a** : furnished with a voice ⟨soft-*voiced*⟩ **b** : expressed by the voice ⟨a frequently ~ opinion⟩ **2** : uttered with vocal cord vibration ⟨~ consonant⟩ — **voiced·ness** \'vȯis(t)-nəs, 'vȯi-səd-nəs\ *n*

voice·ful \'vȯis-fəl\ *adj* : having a voice or vocal quality; *also* : having a loud voice or many voices — **voice·ful·ness** *n*

voice·less \'vȯi-sləs\ *adj* **1** : having no voice : MUTE **2** : not voiced : SURD ⟨~ glide⟩ — **voice·less·ly** *adv* — **voice·less·ness** *n*

voice part *n* : VOICE 1b(4)

voice·print \'vȯi-ˌsprint\ *n* : an individually distinctive pattern of certain voice characteristics that is spectrographically produced

1**void** \'vȯid\ *adj* [ME *voide*, fr. OF, fr. (assumed) VL *vocitus*, deriv. of L *vacuus* — more at VACUUM] **1** : containing nothing ⟨~ space⟩

2 : IDLE, LEISURE 3 a : UNOCCUPIED, VACANT ⟨~ bishopric⟩ b : DESERTED 4 a : WANTING, DEVOID b : having no members or examples ⟨bid a ~ suit as a slam signal⟩ 5 : VAIN, USELESS 6 a : of no legal force or effect : NULL b : VOIDABLE **syn** see EMPTY

[2]void *n* 1 a : empty space : EMPTINESS, VACUUM b : OPENING, GAP 2 : LACK, ABSENCE 3 : a feeling of want or hollowness 4 : absence of cards of a particular suit in a hand as dealt

[3]void *vt* [ME *voiden*, fr. MF *vuidier*, fr. (assumed) VL *vocitare*, fr. *vocitus*] 1 a : to make empty or vacant : CLEAR b : VACATE, LEAVE 2 : DISCHARGE, EMIT ⟨~ excrement⟩ 3 : NULLIFY, ANNUL ⟨~ a contract⟩ — **void·er** *n*

void·able \ˈvȯid-ə-bəl\ *adj* : capable of being voided; *specif* : capable of being adjudged void, invalid, and of no force — **void·able·ness** *n*

void·ance \ˈvȯid-ᵊn(t)s\ *n* 1 : the act of voiding 2 *of a benefice* : the state of being without an incumbent

void·ed \ˈvȯid-əd\ *adj* : having the inner part cut away or left vacant with a narrow border left at the sides

void·ness \-nəs\ *n* : the quality or state of being void : EMPTINESS

voile \ˈvȯi(ə)l\ *n* [F, veil, fr. L *vela*, neut. pl. of *velum*] : a fine soft sheer fabric from various fibers used for women's summer clothing or curtains

voir dire \ˈ(v)wä(r)-ˈdi(ə)r\ *n* [AF, fr. OF, to speak the truth] : a preliminary examination to determine the competency of a witness or juror

voix cé·leste \ˌvwäs-ā-ˈlest\ *n* [F, lit., heavenly voice] : a labial organ stop with soft tremulous tone

vo·lant \ˈvō-lənt\ *adj* [MF, fr. L *volant-*, *volans*, prp. of *volare* to fly] 1 : having the wings extended as if in flight — used of a heraldic bird 2 : FLYING : capable of flying 3 : QUICK, NIMBLE

vo·lan·te \vō-ˈlän-(ˌ)tā\ *adj* [It, lit., flying, fr. L *volant-*, *volans*, prp.] : moving with light rapidity — used as a direction in music

Vo·la·pük \ˈvō-lə-ˌpu̇k, ˈväl-ə-\ *n* [Volapük, lit., world's speech, fr. *vola* of the world (gen. of *vol* world, modif. of E *world*) + *pük* speech, modif. of E *speak*] : an artificial international language based largely on English but with some root words from German, French, and Latin

vo·lar \ˈvō-lər\ *adj* [L *vola* palm of the hand, sole of the foot] : relating to the palm of the hand or the sole of the foot

[1]vol·a·tile \ˈväl-ət-ᵊl, *esp Brit* -ə-ˌtīl\ *n* [ME *volatil*, fr. OF, fr. *volatilie* group of birds, fr. ML *volatilia*, fr. L, neut. pl. of *volatilis* winged, volatile] 1 : a winged creature (as a bird or insect) 2 : a volatile substance

[2]volatile *adj* [F, fr. L *volatilis*, fr. *volatus*, pp. of *volare* to fly] 1 : FLYING : having the power to fly 2 : readily vaporizable at a relatively low temperature 3 a : LIGHTHEARTED, LIVELY b : easily aroused c : tending to erupt into violent action : EXPLOSIVE 4 : CHANGEABLE, FICKLE 5 : EVANESCENT, TRANSITORY

vol·a·tile·ness \-nəs\ *n* : VOLATILITY

volatile oil *n* : an oil that vaporizes readily; *specif* : essential oil

vol·a·til·i·ty \ˌväl-ə-ˈtil-ət-ē\ *n* : the quality or state of being volatile **syn** see LIGHTNESS

vol·a·til·iza·tion \ˌväl-ət-ᵊl-ə-ˈzā-shən\ *n* : the act or process of volatilizing : the state of being volatilized

vol·a·til·ize \ˈväl-ət-ᵊl-ˌīz\ *vt* : to make volatile; *esp* : to cause to pass off in vapor ~ *vi* : to pass off in vapor

vol·a·tize \ˈväl-ə-ˌtīz\ *vb* : VOLATILIZE

vol–au–vent \ˌvȯ-lō-ˈvä^n\ *n* [F, lit., flight in the wind] : a large patty shell filled with a ragout of meat, fowl, game, or fish after baking

[1]vol·can·ic \väl-ˈkan-ik, vȯl- *also* -ˈkān-\ *adj* 1 a : of or relating to a volcano b : characterized by volcanoes c : made of materials from volcanoes 2 : explosively violent : VOLATILE — **vol·can·i·cal·ly** \-i-k(ə-)lē\ *adv*

[2]volcanic *n* : a volcanic rock

volcanic glass *n* : natural glass produced by the cooling of molten lava too rapidly to permit crystallization

vol·ca·nic·i·ty \ˌväl-kə-ˈnis-ət-ē, ˌvȯl-\ *n* : VOLCANISM

vol·ca·nism \ˈväl-kə-ˌniz-əm, ˈvȯl-\ *n* : volcanic power or action

vol·ca·nist \-nəst\ *n* : a specialist in the study of volcanic phenomena

vol·ca·nize \-ˌnīz\ *vt* : to subject to or affect by volcanic heat

vol·ca·no \väl-ˈkā-(ˌ)nō, vȯl-\ *n, pl* **volcanoes** *or* **volcanos** [It *vulcano*, fr. L *Volcanus*, *Vulcanus* Vulcan] : a vent in the earth's crust from which molten or hot rock and steam issue; *also* : a hill or mountain composed wholly or in part of the ejected material

vol·ca·no·log·ic \ˌväl-kən-ᵊl-ˈäj-ik, ˌvȯl-\ *adj* : of or relating to volcanology — **vol·ca·no·log·i·cal** \-i-kəl\ *adj*

vol·ca·nol·o·gist \ˌväl-kə-ˈnäl-ə-jəst, ˌvȯl-\ *n* : a geophysicist who specializes in volcanology

vol·ca·nol·o·gy \-jē\ *n* : a branch of science that deals with volcanic phenomena

[1]vole \ˈvōl\ *n* [F, prob. fr. *voler* to fly — more at VOLLEY] : GRAND SLAM 1 — **go the vole** : to risk all for great gains

[2]vole *n* [earlier *vole-mouse*, fr. *vole-* (of Scand origin; akin to ON *vǫllr* field) + *mouse*] : any of various small rodents (family Cricetidae and esp. genus *Microtus*) closely related to the lemmings and muskrats but in general resembling stocky mice or rats

vo·li·tion \vō-ˈlish-ən, və-\ *n* [F, fr. ML *volition-*, *volitio*, fr. L *vol-* (stem of *velle* to will, wish) + *-ition-*, *-itio* (as in L *position-*, *positio* position) — more at WILL] 1 : an act of making a choice or decision; *also* : a choice or decision made 2 : the power of choosing or determining : WILL — **vo·li·tion·al** \-ˈlish-nəl, -ən-ᵊl\ *adj*

vol·i·tive \ˈväl-ət-iv\ *adj* 1 : of or relating to the will 2 : expressing a wish or permission

volks·lied \ˈfōk-ˌslēt, ˈfȯlk-\ *n, pl* **volks·lie·der** \-ˌslēd-ər\ [G, fr. *volk* people + *lied* song] : a folk song

[1]vol·ley \ˈväl-ē\ *n* [MF *volee* flight, fr. *voler* to fly, fr. L *volare*] 1 a : a flight of missiles (as arrows) b : simultaneous discharge of a number of missile weapons c : one round per gun in a battery fired as soon as each gun is ready without regard to order d (1) : the flight of the ball in tennis or its course before striking the ground; *also* : a return of the ball before it touches the ground (2) : a kick of the ball in soccer before it rebounds (3) : the exchange of the shuttlecock in badminton following the serve 2 a : a burst or emission of many things at once b : a burst of simultaneous or immediately sequential nerve impulses passing to an end organ, synapse, or center

[2]volley *vb* **vol·leyed**; **vol·ley·ing** *vt* 1 : to discharge in or as if in a volley 2 : to propel (an object) while in the air and before touching the ground; *specif* : to hit (a tennis ball) on the volley ~ *vi* 1 : to become discharged in or as if in a volley 2 : to make a volley; *specif* : to volley an object of play (as in tennis) — **vol·ley·er** *n*

vol·ley·ball \ˈväl-ē-ˌbȯl\ *n* : a game played by volleying a large inflated ball over a net

[1]vol·plane \ˈväl-ˌplān\ *n* [F *vol plané*, fr. *vol* flight (fr. *voler*) + *plané*, pp. of *planer* to glide — more at PLANE] : a glide in an airplane

[2]volplane *vi* 1 : to glide in or as if in an airplane 2 : GLIDE 3

Vol·sci \ˈvȯl-ˌskē, ˈväl-ˌsī\ *n pl* [L] : a people of ancient Italy dwelling between the Latins and Samnites

Vol·scian \ˈväl-shən, -skē-ən\ *n* 1 : a member of the Volsci 2 : the Italic language of the Volsci — **Volscian** *adj*

[1]volt \ˈvōlt, ˈvȯlt\ *n* [F *volte*, fr. It *volta* turn, fr. *voltare* to turn, fr. (assumed) VL *volvitare*, freq. of L *volvere* to roll — more at VOLUBLE] 1 a : a tread or gait in which a horse going sideways makes a turn around a center b : a circle traced by a horse in this movement 2 : a leaping movement in fencing to avoid a thrust

[2]volt \ˈvōlt\ *n* [Alessandro *Volta* †1827 It physicist] 1 : the practical mks unit of electrical potential difference and electromotive force equal to the difference of potential between two points in a conducting wire carrying a constant current of one ampere when the power dissipated between these two points is equal to one watt and equivalent to the potential difference across a resistance of one ohm when one ampere is flowing through it 2 : a unit of electrical potential difference and electromotive force equal to 1.00034 volts and formerly taken as the standard in the U. S. — called also *international volt*

volt·age \ˈvōl-tij\ *n* : electric potential or potential difference expressed in volts

voltage divider *n* : a resistor or series of resistors provided with taps at certain points and used to provide various potential differences from a single power source

vol·ta·ic \väl-ˈtā-ik, vōl-\ *adj* [A. *Volta*] : of, relating to, or producing direct electric current by chemical action (as in a battery) : GALVANIC ⟨~ cell⟩

voltaic couple *n* : GALVANIC COUPLE

voltaic pile *n* : [3]PILE 4a

vol·ta·ism \ˈvōl-tə-ˌiz-əm, ˈväl-\ *n* : GALVANISM 1

vol·ta·me·ter \vōl-ˈtam-ət-ər, ˈvōl-tə-ˌmēt-\ *n* [ISV *voltaic* + *-meter*] : an apparatus for measuring the quantity of electricity passed through a conductor by the amount of electrolysis produced — **vol·ta·met·ric** \ˌvōl-tə-ˈme-trik\ *adj*

volt–am·me·ter \ˈvōl-ˈtam-ˌēt-ər\ *n* : an instrument for indicating one or more ranges of volts and amperes by changing terminal connections

volt–am·pere \-ˈtam-ˌpi(ə)r\ *n* : a unit of electric measurement equal to the product of a volt and an ampere that for direct current constitutes a measure of power equivalent to a watt and for alternating current a measure of apparent power

Vol·ta's pile \ˌvōl-təz-, ˌväl-, ˌvȯl-\ *n* [Alessandro *Volta*] : [3]PILE 4a

volte–face \ˌvȯlt-(ə-)ˈfäs\ *n* [F, fr. It *voltafaccia*, fr. *volta* turn + *faccia* face, fr. (assumed) VL *facia* — more at VOLT] : a facing about esp. in policy : ABOUT-FACE

volt·me·ter \ˈvōlt-ˌmēt-ər\ *n* [ISV] : an instrument (as a galvanometer) for measuring in volts the differences of potential between different points of an electrical circuit

vol·u·bil·i·ty \ˌväl-yə-ˈbil-ət-ē\ *n* : the quality or state of being voluble

vol·u·ble \ˈväl-yə-bəl\ *adj* [MF or L; MF, fr. L *volubilis*, fr. *volvere* to roll; akin to OE *wealwian* to roll, Gk *eilyein* to roll, wrap] 1 a : easily rolling or turning : ROTATING b : having the power or habit of twining ⟨~ plant stem⟩ 2 : characterized by ready or rapid speech : GLIB, FLUENT **syn** see TALKATIVE — **vol·u·bly** \-blē\ *adv*

vol·u·ble·ness \-bəl-nəs\ *n* : VOLUBILITY

[1]vol·ume \ˈväl-yəm, -(ˌ)yüm\ *n* [ME, fr. MF, fr. L *volumen* roll of writing, fr. *volvere* to roll] 1 : SCROLL 1a 2 a : a series of printed sheets bound typically in book form : BOOK b : an arbitrary number of issues of a periodical c : ALBUM 1c 3 : space occupied as measured in cubic units (as inches, quarts, or pecks) : CAPACITY — see MEASURE table, METRIC SYSTEM table 4 a (1) : AMOUNT; *also* : BULK, MASS (2) : a considerable quantity b : the amount of a substance occupying a particular volume c : mass or the representation of mass in art or architecture 5 : the degree of loudness or the intensity of a sound; *also* : LOUDNESS **syn** see BULK — **volume** *adj* — **vol·umed** \-yəmd, -(ˌ)yümd\ *adj*

VOLUME FORMULAS

FIGURE	FORMULA	MEANING OF LETTERS
cube	$V=a^3$	a=one of the dimensions
rectangular prism	$V=abc$	a=length; b=width; c=depth
pyramid	$V=\frac{Ah}{3}$	A=area of base; h=height
cylinder	$V=\pi r^2 h$	π=3.1416; r=radius of the base; h=height
cone	$V=\frac{\pi r^2 h}{3}$	π=3.1416; r=radius of the base; h=height
sphere	$V=\frac{4\pi r^3}{3}$	π=3.1416; r=radius

[2]volume *vi* : to roll or rise in volume ~ *vt* : to send or give out in volume

vol·u·meter \ˈväl-yu̇-ˌmēt-ər\ *n* [ISV, blend of *volume* and *-meter*] : an instrument for measuring volumes (as of gases or liquids) directly or (as of solids) by displacement of a liquid

vol·u·met·ric \ˌväl-yu̇-ˈme-trik\ *adj* : of or relating to the measurement of volume — **vol·u·met·ri·cal·ly** \-tri-k(ə-)lē\ *adv*

volumetric analysis *n* 1 : quantitative analysis by the use of

definite volumes of standard solutions of reagents **2 :** analysis of gases by volume

vo·lu·mi·nos·i·ty \və-ˌlü-mə-ˈnäs-ət-ē\ *n* **:** the quality or state of being voluminous

vo·lu·mi·nous \və-ˈlü-mə-nəs\ *adj* [LL *voluminosus*, fr. L *volumin-, volumen*] **1 :** consisting of many folds, coils, or convolutions **:** WINDING **2 a :** having or marked by great volume or bulk **:** LARGE; *specif* **:** FULL **b :** NUMEROUS **3 a :** filling or capable of filling a large volume or several volumes **b :** writing or speaking much or at great length — **vo·lu·mi·nous·ly** *adv* — **vo·lu·mi·nous·ness** *n*

vol·un·tar·i·ly \ˌväl-ən-ˈter-ə-lē\ *adv* **:** of one's own free will

vol·un·tar·i·ness \ˈväl-ən-ˌter-ē-nəs\ *n* **:** the quality or state of being voluntary

vol·un·ta·rism \ˈväl-ən-tə-ˌriz-əm, -ˌter-ˌiz-\ *n* **1 :** the principle or system of doing something by or relying on voluntary action **2 :** a theory that conceives will to be the dominant factor in experience or in the world — **vol·un·ta·rist** \-tə-rəst, -ˌter-əst\ *n* — **vol·un·ta·ris·tic** \ˌväl-ən-tə-ˈris-tik, -ˌter-ˈis-\ *adj*

1vol·un·tary \ˈväl-ən-ˌter-ē\ *adj* [ME, fr. L *voluntarius*, fr. *voluntas* will, fr. *velle* to will, wish — more at WILL] **1 :** proceeding from the will or from one's own choice or consent **2 :** unconstrained by interference **:** SELF-DETERMINING **3 :** done by design or intention **:** INTENTIONAL ⟨~ manslaughter⟩ **4 :** of, relating to, subject to, or regulated by the will ⟨~ behavior⟩ **5 :** having power of free choice ⟨man is a ~ agent⟩ **6 :** provided or supported by voluntary action **7 :** acting or done of one's own free will without valuable consideration or legal obligation

syn VOLUNTARY, INTENTIONAL, DELIBERATE, WILLFUL, WILLING mean done or brought about of one's own will. VOLUNTARY implies freedom and spontaneity of choice or action without external compulsion, or it may suggest control of the will over actions or movements in contrast with *involuntary;* INTENTIONAL stresses an awareness of an end to be achieved; DELIBERATE implies full consciousness of the nature of one's act and its consequences; WILLFUL stresses a refusal to be taught, advised, or commanded; WILLING implies a readiness and eagerness to accede to or anticipate the wishes of another

2voluntary *n* **1 a :** a prefatory often extemporized musical piece **b :** an improvisatory organ piece played before, during, or after a religious service **2 :** one who participates voluntarily **:** VOLUNTEER

vol·un·tary·ism \ˈväl-ən-ˌter-ē-ˌiz-əm\ *n* **:** VOLUNTARISM — **vol·un·tary·ist** \-ē-əst\ *n*

voluntary muscle *n* **:** muscle under voluntary control

1vol·un·teer \ˌväl-ən-ˈti(ə)r\ *n* [obs. F *voluntaire* (now *volontaire*), fr. *voluntaire*, adj., voluntary, fr. L *voluntarius*] **1 :** one who enters into or offers himself for any service of his own free will: as **a :** one who enters into military service voluntarily **b** (1) **:** one who renders a service or takes part in a transaction while having no legal concern or interest (2) **:** one who receives a conveyance or transfer of property without giving valuable consideration **2 :** a volunteer plant

2volunteer *adj* **1 :** of, relating to, or consisting of volunteers **:** VOLUNTARY **2 :** growing spontaneously without direct human control or supervision esp. from seeds lost from a previous crop

3volunteer *vt* **:** to offer or bestow voluntarily ⟨~ one's services⟩ ~ *vi* **:** to offer oneself as a volunteer

Volunteers of America *n* **:** a religious and philanthropic organization similar to the Salvation Army founded in 1896 by Commander and Mrs. Ballington Booth

vo·lup·tu·ary \və-ˈləp-chə-ˌwer-ē\ *n* **:** one whose chief interest is luxury and the gratification of sensual appetites — **voluptuary** *adj*

vo·lup·tu·ate \-chə-ˌwāt\ *vi* [*voluptuous* + *-ate*] **:** LUXURIATE

vo·lup·tuous \-chə(-wə)s\ *adj* [ME, fr. L *voluptuosus*, fr. *voluptas* pleasure; akin to Gk *elpis* hope, L *velle* to wish — more at WILL] **1 a :** full of delight or pleasure to the senses **b :** ministering or inclining to or arising from sensuous or sensual gratification **:** LUXURIOUS ⟨~ palace⟩ **c :** suggesting sensual pleasure by fullness and beauty of form **2 :** given to or spent in enjoyments of luxury, pleasure, or sensual gratifications **syn** see SENSUOUS — **vo·lup·tuous·ly** *adv* — **vo·lup·tuous·ness** *n*

vo·lute \və-ˈlüt\ *n* [L *voluta*, fr. fem. of *volutus*, pp. of *volvere* to roll] **1 :** a spiral or scroll-shaped form **2 a :** a spiral scroll-shaped ornament forming the chief feature of the Ionic capital **b :** a turn of a spiral shell **3 :** any of numerous marine gastropod mollusks (family Volutidae) with a thick short-spired shell — **volute** *or* **vo·lut·ed** \-ˈlüt-əd\ *adj*

vo·lu·tin \ˈväl-yə-ˌtin, və-ˈlüt-ᵊn\ *n* [G, fr. NL *volutans*, specific epithet of the bacterium *Spirillum volutans* in which it was first found] **:** a granular basophilic substance that is probably a nucleic acid compound and is common in microorganisms

vol·va \ˈväl-və, ˈvȯl-\ *n* [NL, fr. L *volva, vulva* integument — more at VULVA] **:** a membranous sac or cup about the base of the stipe in many gill fungi — **vol·vate** \-ˌvāt\ *adj*

vol·vox \-ˌväks\ *n* [NL, genus name, fr. L, *volvere* to roll — more at VOLUBLE] **:** any of a genus (*Volvox*) of green flagellates that form spherical colonies

vol·vu·lus \ˈväl-vyə-ləs, ˈvȯl-\ *n* [NL, fr. L *volvere*] **:** a twisting of the intestine upon itself that causes obstruction

vo·mer \ˈvō-mər\ *n* [NL, fr L. plowshare] **:** a bone of the skull of most vertebrates situated below the ethmoid region that in man forms part of the nasal septum — **vo·mer·ine** \ˈvō-mə-ˌrīn\ *adj*

1vom·it \ˈväm-ət\ *n* [ME, fr. MF, fr. L *vomitus*, fr. *vomitus*, pp. of *vomere* to vomit; akin to ON *vāma* nausea, Gk *emein* to vomit] **1 :** an act or instance of disgorging the contents of the stomach through the mouth; *also* **:** the disgorged matter **2 :** EMETIC

2vomit *vi* **1 :** to disgorge the stomach contents **2 :** to spew forth **:** BELCH, GUSH ~ *vt* **1 :** to disgorge (the contents of the stomach) through the mouth **2 :** to eject violently or abundantly **:** SPEW **3 :** to cause to vomit — **vom·it·er** *n*

vomiting gas *n* **:** CHLOROPICRIN

vom·i·to·ry \ˈväm-ə-ˌtōr-ē -ˌtȯr-\ *n* [LL *vomitorium*, fr. L *vomitus*, pp.; fr. its disgorging the spectators] **:** an entrance piercing the banks of seats of a theater or amphitheater

vom·i·tu·ri·tion \ˌväm-ə-chə-ˈrish-ən, -ə-tü-\ *n* [*vomit* + *-urition* (as in *micturition*)] **:** repeated ineffectual attempts at vomiting

vom·i·tus \ˈväm-ət-əs\ *n* [L] **:** matter vomited

V–1 \ˈvē-ˈwən\ *n* [G, abbr. for *vergeltungswaffe 1*, lit., reprisal weapon 1] **:** ROBOT BOMB

1voo·doo \ˈvüd-(ˌ)ü\ *n* [LaF *voudou*, of African origin; akin to Ewe *vo¹du³* tutelary deity, demon] **1 :** VOODOOISM **2 a :** one who deals in spells and necromancy **b** (1) **:** a sorcerer's spell (2) **:** a hexed object — **voodoo** *adj*

2voodoo *vt* **:** to bewitch by or as if by means of voodoo **:** HEX

voo·doo·ism \ˈvüd-(ˌ)ü-ˌiz-əm\ *n* **1 :** a religion derived from African ancestor worship, practiced chiefly by Negroes of Haiti, and characterized by propitiatory rites and communication by trance with animistic deities **2 :** the practice of witchcraft — **voo·doo·ist** \-ü-əst\ *n* — **voo·doo·is·tic** \ˌvüd-(ˌ)ü-ˈis-tik\ *adj*

vo·ra·cious \vȯ-ˈrā-shəs, və-\ *adj* [L *vorac-, vorax*, fr. *vorare* to devour; akin to OHG *querdar* bait, L *gurges* whirlpool] **1 :** having a huge appetite **:** RAVENOUS **2 :** excessively eager **:** INSATIABLE — **vo·ra·cious·ly** *adv* — **vo·ra·cious·ness** *n* — **vo·rac·i·ty** \-ˈras-ət-ē\ *n*

vor·la·ge \ˈfōr-ˌläg-ə, ˈfȯr-\ *n* [G, lit., forward position, fr. *vor* fore + *lage* position] **:** the position of a skier leaning forward from the ankles usu. without lifting the heels from the skis

-v·o·rous \v-(ə-)rəs\ *adj comb form* [L *-vorus*, fr. *vorare* to devour] **:** eating **:** feeding on ⟨frugi*vorous*⟩

vor·tex \ˈvȯr-ˌteks\ *n, pl* **vor·ti·ces** \ˈvȯrt-ə-ˌsēz\ *also* **vor·tex·es** [NL *vortic-, vortex*, fr. L *vertex* whirlpool — more at VERTEX] **:** a mass of fluid esp. of a liquid having a whirling or circular motion tending to form a cavity or vacuum in the center of the circle and to draw toward this cavity or vacuum bodies subject to its action; *specif* **:** WHIRLPOOL, EDDY

vor·ti·cal \ˈvȯrt-i-kəl\ *adj* **:** of, relating to, or resembling a vortex **:** SWIRLING — **vor·ti·cal·ly** \-k(ə-)lē\ *adv*

vor·ti·cel·la \ˌvȯrt-ə-ˈsel-ə\ *n, pl* **vor·ti·cel·lae** \-ˈsel-(ˌ)ē\ *or* **vorticellas** [NL, genus name, fr. L *vortic-, vortex*] **:** any of a genus (*Vorticella*) of stalked bell-shaped ciliates

vor·ti·cism \ˈvȯrt-ə-ˌsiz-əm\ *n* [L *vortic-, vortex*] **:** an English offshoot of futurism designed to relate all art forms directly to the machine and industrial civilization — **vor·ti·cist** \-səst\ *n*

vor·tic·i·ty \vȯr-ˈtis-ət-ē\ *n* **:** the state of a fluid in vortical motion

vor·ti·cose \ˈvȯrt-i-ˌkōs\ *adj* **:** VORTICAL

vor·tig·i·nous \vȯr-ˈtij-ə-nəs\ *adj* [L *vortigin-, vortigo, vertigin-, vertigo* action of whirling, vertigo] **1** *archaic* **:** VORTICAL **2** *archaic* **:** moving in a series of eddies **:** SWIRLING

vo·ta·ress \ˈvōt-ə-rəs\ *n* **:** a female votary

vo·ta·rist \-rəst\ *n* **:** VOTARY

vo·ta·ry \ˈvōt-ə-rē\ *n* [L *votum* vow] **1** *archaic* **:** a sworn adherent **2 a :** ENTHUSIAST, DEVOTEE **b :** a devoted admirer **3 a :** a devout or zealous worshiper **b :** a staunch believer or advocate

1vote \ˈvōt\ *n* [ME (Sc), fr. L *votum* vow, wish — more at VOW] **1 a :** a usu. formal expression of opinion or will in response to a proposed decision; *esp* **:** one given as an indication of approval or disapproval of a proposal, motion, or candidate for office **b :** the total number of such expressions of opinion made known at a single time (as at an election) **c :** an expression of opinion or preference held to resemble a vote **d :** BALLOT 1 **2 :** the collective opinion or verdict of a body of persons expressed by voting **3 :** the right to cast a vote; *specif* **:** the right of suffrage **:** FRANCHISE **4 a :** the act or process of voting **b :** a method of voting **5 :** a formal expression of a wish, will, or choice voted by a meeting **6 a :** VOTER **b :** a group of voters with some common and identifying characteristics **7** *chiefly Brit* **a :** a proposition to be voted upon; *esp* **:** a legislative money item **b :** APPROPRIATION **8** *often cap* **:** a daily record of proceedings in the House of Commons

2vote *vi* **1 :** to express one's views in response to a poll; *esp* **:** to exercise a political franchise **2 :** to express an opinion ~ *vt* **1 :** to choose, endorse, decide the disposition of, defeat, or authorize by vote **2 a :** to adjudge by general agreement **:** DECLARE **b :** to offer as a suggestion **:** PROPOSE **3 a :** to cause to vote in a given way **b :** to cause to be cast for or against a proposal

vote·less \ˈvōt-ləs\ *adj* **:** having no vote; *esp* **:** denied the political franchise

vot·er \ˈvōt-ər\ *n* **:** one that votes or has the legal right to vote

voting machine *n* **:** a mechanical device for recording and counting votes cast in an election

vo·tive \ˈvōt-iv\ *adj* [L *votivus*, fr. *votum* vow] **1 :** offered or performed in fulfillment of a vow or in gratitude or devotion **2 :** consisting of or expressing a vow, wish, or desire ⟨a ~ prayer⟩ — **vo·tive·ly** *adv* — **vo·tive·ness** *n*

votive mass *n* **:** a mass celebrated for a special intention in place of the mass of the day

vo·tress \ˈvō-trəs\ *n* [by alter.] *archaic* **:** VOTARESS

1vouch \ˈvau̇ch\ *vb* [ME *vochen, vouchen*, fr. MF *vocher*, fr. L *vocare* to call, summon, fr. *voc-, vox* voice — more at VOICE] *vt* **1 :** to summon into court to warrant or defend a title **2** *archaic* **a :** ASSERT, AFFIRM **b :** ATTEST **3** *archaic* **:** to cite or refer to as authority or supporting evidence **4 a :** PROVE, SUBSTANTIATE **b :** to verify (a business transaction) by examining documentary evidence ~ *vi* **1 :** to give a guarantee **:** become surety **2 a :** to supply supporting evidence or testimony **b :** to give personal assurance

2vouch *n, obs* **:** ALLEGATION, DECLARATION

vouch·ee \vau̇-ˈchē\ *n* **:** one for whom another vouches

1vouch·er \ˈvau̇-chər\ *n* **1 :** an act of vouching **2 a :** a piece of supporting evidence **:** PROOF **b :** a documentary record of a business transaction **c :** a written affidavit or authorization

2voucher *vt* **:** to establish the authenticity of; *esp* **:** to certify by a voucher

3voucher *n* **:** one that guarantees **:** SURETY

vouch·safe \vau̇ch-ˈsāf, ˈvau̇ch-ˌ\ *vt* **1 a :** to grant or furnish often in a condescending manner **b :** to choose to give by way of reply **2 a :** to grant as a privilege **:** PERMIT **b :** to grant as a special favor **syn** see GRANT — **vouch·safe·ment** \-mənt\ *n*

vous·soir \vü-ˈswär, ˈvü-ˌ\ *n* [F, fr. (assumed) VL *volsorium*, fr. *volsus*, pp. of L *volvere* to roll — more at VOLUBLE] **:** one of the wedge-shaped pieces forming an arch or vault

1vow \ˈvau̇\ *n* [ME *vowe*, fr. OF, fr. L *votum*, fr. neut. of *votus*, pp. of *vovēre* to vow; akin to Gk *euchesthai* to pray, vow] **:** a solemn promise or assertion; *specif* **:** one by which a person binds himself to an act, service, or condition

2vow *vt* **1 :** to make as a vow **2 :** to bind or consecrate by a vow ~ *vi* **:** to make a vow — **vow·er** \ˈvau̇(-ə)r\ *n*

3vow *vb* [ME *vowen*, short for *avowen*] **:** AVOW, DECLARE

vow·el \ˈvau̇(-ə)l\ *n* [ME, fr. MF *vouel*, fr. L *vocalis* — more at VOCALIC] **1 :** one of a class of speech sounds in the articulation of which the oral part of the breath channel is not blocked and is not

constricted enough to cause audible friction; *broadly* : the one most prominent sound in a syllable **2** : a letter or other symbol representing a vowel — usu. used in English of *a, e, i, o, u,* and sometimes *y*

vow·el·ize \'vaù-(ə-),līz\ *vt* : to furnish with vowel signs or points

vowel point *n* : a mark placed below or otherwise near a consonant in some languages (as Hebrew) and representing the vowel sound that precedes or follows the consonant sound

vowel rhyme *n* : ASSONANCE 2b

vox an·gel·i·ca \,väk-san-'jel-i-kə\ *n* [NL, lit., angelic voice] : VOIX CÉLESTE

vox hu·ma·na \,väks-h(y)ü-'män-ə, ,väks-yü-\ *n* [NL, lit., human voice] : a reed pipe-organ stop made to give a sound imitative of the human voice

vox po·pu·li \'väk-'späp-yə-,lī, -,lē\ *n* [L, voice of the people] : popular sentiment

¹voy·age \'vói-ij, 'vò(-)ij\ *n* [ME, fr. OF *voiage,* fr. LL *viaticum,* fr. L, traveling money, fr. neut. of *viaticus* of a journey, fr. *via* way — more at VIA] **1** : an act or instance of traveling : JOURNEY **2 a** : a journey by water : CRUISE **b** : a journey through air or space **3** : an account of a journey esp. by sea

²voyage *vi* : to take a trip : TRAVEL ~ *vt* : SAIL, TRAVERSE — **voy·ag·er** *n*

voya·geur \,vwä-,yä-'zhər, ,vói-ä-\ *n* [CanF, fr. F, traveler, fr. *voyager* to travel, fr. *voyage* voyage, fr. OF *voiage*] : a man employed by a fur company to transport goods and men to and from remote stations in the Northwest

voy·eur \vwä-'yər, vói-'(y)ər\ *n* [F, lit., one who sees, fr. MF, fr. *voir* to see, fr. L *videre* — more at WIT] : one obtaining sexual gratification from seeing sex organs and sexual acts — **voy·eur·ism** \-,iz-əm\ *n* — **voy·eur·is·tic** \,vwä-,yər-'is-tik, ,vói-,(y)ər\ *adj* — **voy·eur·is·ti·cal·ly** \-ti-k(ə-)lē\ *adv*

V–par·ti·cle \'vē-\ *n* : a charged or uncharged short-lived elementary particle produced by collisions of very high energy protons or neutrons with nuclei

vrouw *or* **vrow** \'vrō, 'frō, 'vròü, 'fròü\ *n* [D *vrouw* & Afrik *vrou*] : a Dutch or Afrikaner woman

V sign *n* : a sign made by raising the index and middle fingers in a V and used as a victory salute, a gesture of approval, or an okay

VT fuze \'vē-'tē-\ *n* [*variable time fuze*] : PROXIMITY FUZE

V–2 \'vē-'tü\ *n* [G, abbr. for *vergeltungswaffe* 2, lit., reprisal weapon 2] : a rocket-propelled bomb of German invention

vug *or* **vugg** *or* **vugh** \'vəg\ *n* [Corn dial. *vooga* underground chamber, fr. L *fovea* small pit] : a small unfilled cavity in a lode or in rock

Vul·can \'vəl-kən\ *n* [L *Volcanus, Vulcanus*] : the god of fire and of metalworking in Roman mythology

vul·ca·ni·an \,vəl-'kā-nē-ən\ *adj* **1** *cap* : of or relating to Vulcan or to working in iron or other metals **2 a** : VOLCANIC **b** : of or relating to a volcanic eruption in which highly viscous or solid lava is blown into fragments and dust

vul·can·ic·i·ty \,vəl-kə-'nis-ət-ē\ *n* : VOLCANICITY

vul·can·ism \'vəl-kə-,niz-əm\ *n* : VOLCANISM

vul·can·ite \-,nīt\ *n* [obs. E *vulcan* fire, fr. *Vulcan*] : a hard vulcanized rubber

vul·can·izate \'vəl-kə-nə-,zāt\ *n* [back-formation fr. *vulcanization*] : a vulcanized product

vul·can·iza·tion \,vəl-kə-nə-'zā-shən\ *n* : the process of treating crude or synthetic rubber or similar plastic material chemically to give it useful properties (as elasticity, strength, and stability)

vul·can·ize \'vəl-kə-,nīz\ *vb* [ISV, fr. L *Vulcanus* Vulcan, fire] *vt* : to subject to vulcanization ~ *vi* : to undergo vulcanization — **vul·can·iz·er** *n*

vulcanized fiber *n* [fr. *Vulcanized Fibre,* a trademark] : a tough substance made by treatment of cellulose (as paper from rags) and used for luggage and for electrical insulation

vul·can·ol·o·gist \,vəl-kə-'näl-ə-jəst\ *n* : VOLCANOLOGIST

vul·can·ol·o·gy \-jē\ *n* [ISV] : VOLCANOLOGY

vul·gar \'vəl-gər\ *adj* [ME, fr. L *vulgaris* of the mob, vulgar, fr. *volgus, vulgus* mob, common people; akin to Skt *varga* group] **1 a** : generally used, applied, or accepted **b** : having or under-

standing in the ordinary sense **2** : VERNACULAR **3 a** : of or relating to the common people : PLEBEIAN **b** : generally current : PUBLIC **c** : of the usual, typical, or ordinary kind **4 a** : lacking in cultivation, perception, or taste : COARSE **b** : morally crude, undeveloped, or unregenerate : GROSS **c** : ostentatious or excessive in expenditure or display : PRETENTIOUS **5 a** : offensive in language : EARTHY **b** : OBSCENE, PROFANE **syn** see COARSE, COMMON — **vul·gar·ly** *adv*

vulgar era *n* : CHRISTIAN ERA

vul·gar·i·an \,vəl-'gar-ē-ən, -'ger-\ *n* : a vulgar person

vul·gar·ism \'vəl-gə-,riz-əm\ *n* **1 a** : a word or expression originated or used chiefly by illiterate persons : a substandard use **b** : a coarse word or phrase **2** : VULGARITY

vul·gar·i·ty \,vəl-'gar-ət-ē\ *n* **1** : the quality or state of being vulgar **2** : something vulgar

vul·gar·iza·tion \,vəl-g(ə-)rə-'zā-shən\ *n* **1** : a making widely familiar : POPULARIZATION **2** : COARSENING, DEBASEMENT

vul·gar·ize \'vəl-gə-,rīz\ *vt* **1** : to diffuse generally : POPULARIZE **2** : to make vulgar : COARSEN — **vul·gar·iz·er** *n*

Vulgar Latin *n* : the nonclassical Latin of ancient Rome including the speech of plebeians and the informal speech of the educated established by comparative evidence as the chief source of the Romance languages

vul·gate \'vəl-,gāt, -gət\ *n* [ML *vulgata,* fr. LL *vulgata editio* edition in general circulation] **1** *cap* : a Latin version of the Bible authorized and used by the Roman Catholic Church **2** : any commonly accepted text or reading

vul·gus \'vəl-gəs\ *n* [prob. alter. of obs. *vulgars* (English sentences to be translated into Latin)] : a short composition in Latin verse formerly common as an exercise in some English public schools

vul·ner·a·bil·i·ty \,vəln-(ə-)rə-'bil-ət-ē\ *n* : the quality or state of being vulnerable

vul·ner·a·ble \'vəln-(ə-)rə-bəl, 'vəl-nər-bəl\ *adj* [LL *vulnerabilis,* fr. L *vulnerare* to wound, fr. *vulner-, vulnus* wound; akin to Goth *wilwan* to rob, L *vellere* to pluck, Gk *oulē* wound] **1** : capable of being wounded **2** : open to attack or damage : ASSAILABLE **3** : liable to increased penalties but entitled to increased bonuses after winning a game of contract bridge — **vul·ner·a·ble·ness** *n* — **vul·ner·a·bly** \-blē\ *adv*

¹vul·ner·ary \'vəl-nə-,rer-ē\ *adj* [L *vulnerarius,* fr. *vulner-, vulnus*] : used for or useful in healing wounds ⟨~ plants⟩

²vulnerary *n* : a vulnerary remedy

vul·pine \'vəl-,pīn\ *adj* [L *vulpinus,* fr. *vulpes* fox; akin to Gk *alōpēx* fox] **1** : of, relating to, or resembling a fox **2** : FOXY, CRAFTY

vul·ture \'vəl-chər\ *n* [ME, fr. L *vultur*] **1** : any of various large raptorial birds (families Aegypiidae and Cathartidae) that are related to the hawks, eagles, and falcons but have weaker claws and the head usu. naked and that subsist chiefly or entirely on carrion **2** : a rapacious or predatory person

vulture

vul·tur·ine \-chə-,rīn\ *adj* **1 a** : of or relating to the vultures **b** : characteristic of a vulture **2** : marked by a vile rapacity : PREDATORY

vul·tur·ous \'vəlch-(ə-)rəs\ *adj* : resembling a vulture esp. in rapacity or scavenging habits

vul·va \'vəl-və\ *n* [NL, fr. L *volva, vulva* integument, womb; akin to Skt *ulva* womb, L *volvere* to roll — more at VOLUBLE] : the external parts of the female genital organs; *also* : the opening between the projecting parts of the external organs — **vul·val** \-vəl\ *or* **vul·var** \-vər\ *adj* — **vul·vate** \-,vāt\ *adj*

vul·vi·form \'vəl-və-,fòrm\ *adj* [NL *vulva* + E *-iform*] **1** : having an oval shape with a middle cleft and projecting lips **2** : suggesting a cleft with projecting edges — used of plant forms

vul·vi·tis \,vəl-'vīt-əs\ *n* [NL] : inflammation of the vulva

vul·vo·vag·i·ni·tis \,vəl-(,)vō-,vaj-ə-'nīt-əs\ *n* [NL] : coincident inflammation of the vulva and vagina

vying *pres part of* VIE

w \'dəb-əl-(,)yü, -yə(-w), *rapid* 'dəb(-ə)-yə(-w), 'dəb-yē\ *n, often cap, often attrib* **1 a :** the 23d letter of the English alphabet **b :** a graphic representation of this letter **c :** a speech counterpart of orthographic *w* **2 :** a graphic device for reproducing the letter *w* **3 :** one designated *w* esp. as the 22d or when j is used for the 10th the 23d in order or class **4 :** something shaped like the letter W

wab·ble \'wäb-əl\ *var of* WOBBLE

Wac \'wak\ *n* [*W*omen's *A*rmy *C*orps] **:** a member of the Women's Army Corps established in the U.S. during World War II

wack·i·ly \'wak-ə-lē\ *adv* **:** in a wacky manner

wack·i·ness \'wak-ē-nəs\ *n* **:** the quality or state of being wacky **:** CRAZINESS

wacky \'wak-ē\ *adj* [perh. fr. E dial. *whacky* (fool)] **:** absurdly or amusingly eccentric or irrational **:** CRAZY

1**wad** \'wäd\ *n* [origin unknown] **1 a :** a small mass, bundle, or tuft **b :** a soft mass esp. of a loose fibrous material variously used (as to stop an aperture, pad a garment, or hold grease around an axle) **c** (1) **:** a soft plug used to retain a powder charge or to avoid windage esp. in a muzzle-loading cannon or gun (2) **:** a felt or paper disk to separate the components of a shotgun cartridge **2 :** a considerable amount **3 a :** a roll of paper money **b :** MONEY **c :** a large amount of money

2**wad** *vt* **wad·ded; wad·ding 1 :** to form into a wad or wadding; *esp* **:** to roll or crush into a tight wad **2 a :** to insert a wad into **b :** to hold in by a wad ⟨~ a bullet in a gun⟩ **3 :** to stuff or line with some soft substance (as cotton) **:** PAD — **wad·der** *n*

wad·able *or* **wade·able** \'wād-ə-bəl\ *adj* **:** capable of being waded ⟨a ~ stream⟩

wad·ding \'wäd-iŋ\ *n* **1 :** wads or material for making wads **2 :** a soft mass or sheet of short loose fibers used for stuffing or padding

1**wad·dle** \'wäd-ᵊl\ *vi* **wad·dling** \'wäd-liŋ, -ᵊl-iŋ\ [freq. of *wade*] **1 :** to walk with short steps swinging the forepart of the body from side to side **2 :** to move clumsily in a manner suggesting a waddle — **wad·dler** \-lər, -ᵊl-ər\ *n*

2**waddle** *n* **:** an awkward clumsy swaying gait

1**wad·dy** \'wäd-ē\ *n* [native name in Australia] *Austral* **:** CLUB — **waddy** *vt, Austral*

2**wad·dy** *or* **wad·die** \'wäd-ē\ *n* [origin unknown] *West* **:** COWBOY

1**wade** \'wād\ *vb* [ME *waden,* fr. OE *wadan;* akin to OHG *watan* to go, wade, L *vadere* to go] *vi* **1 :** to step in or through a medium (as water) offering more resistance than air **2 :** to move or proceed with difficulty or labor **3 :** to set to work or attack with determination or vigor — used with *in* or *into* ~ *vt* **:** to pass or cross by wading

2**wade** *n* **:** an act of wading ⟨a ~ in the brook⟩

wad·er \'wād-ər\ *n* **1 :** one that wades **2 :** WADING BIRD **3 :** high waterproof boots or trousers for wading

wa·di \'wäd-ē\ *n* [Ar *wādiy*] **1 :** the bed or valley of a stream in regions of southwestern Asia and northern Africa that is usu. dry except during the rainy season and that often forms an oasis **:** GULLY, WASH **2 :** a shallow usu. sharply defined depression in a desert region

wading bird *n* **:** any of many long-legged birds including the shorebirds (as sandpipers and snipe) and the inland water birds (as cranes and herons) that wade in water in search of food

wading pool *n* **:** a shallow pool of portable or permanent construction used by children for wading

wad·mal *or* **wad·mol** *or* **wad·mel** \'wäd-məl\ *n* [ME *wadmale,* fr. ON *vathmāl,* lit., standard cloth, fr. *vāth* cloth, clothing + *māl* measure; akin to L *metiri* to measure — more at WEED, MEASURE] **:** a coarse rough woolen fabric formerly used in the British Isles and Scandinavia for protective coverings and warm clothing

wae·sucks \'wā-,səks\ *interj* [Sc *wae* woe (fr. ME *wa*) + *sucks,* alter. of E *sakes* — more at WOE] *Scot* — used to express grief or pity

Waf \'waf\ *n* [*W*omen in the *A*ir *F*orce] **:** a member of the women's component of the air force formed after World War II

1**wa·fer** \'wā-fər\ *n* [ME, fr. ONF *waufre,* of Gmc origin; akin to MD *wafel, wafer* waffle] **1 a :** a thin crisp cake or cracker **b :** a round thin piece of unleavened bread in the Eucharist **2 :** an adhesive disk of dried paste with added coloring matter used as a seal **3 :** a thin disk or ring resembling a wafer and variously used (as for a valve or diaphragm)

2**wafer** *vt* **wa·fer·ing** \-f(ə-)riŋ\ **:** to seal, close, or fasten with a wafer

waff \'waf\ *n* [E dial. *waff* (to wave)] **1** *chiefly Scot* **:** a waving motion **2** *chiefly Scot* **:** PUFF, GUST

waf·fle \'wäf-əl, 'wȯf-\ *n* [D *wafel,* fr. MD *wafel, wafer;* akin to OE *wefan* to weave] **:** a crisp cake of pancake batter baked in a waffle iron

waffle iron *n* **:** a utensil for cooking waffles consisting of two hinged metal parts that shut upon each other and impress surface projections on the waffle

1**waft** \'wäft, 'waft\ *vb* [(assumed) ME *waughten* to guard, convoy, fr. MD or MLG *wachten* to watch, guard; akin to OE *wæccan* to watch — more at WAKE] *vt* **:** to cause to move or go lightly by or as if by the impulse of wind or waves ~ *vi* **:** to become wafted on or as if on a buoyant medium — **waft·er** *n*

2**waft** *n* **1 :** a faint odor **:** WHIFF **2 :** a slight breeze **:** PUFF **3 :** the act of waving **4 :** a pennant or flag used to signal or to show wind direction

waft·age \'wäf-tij, 'waf-\ *n* **:** the act of wafting or state of being wafted; *broadly* **:** CONVEYANCE

waf·ture \-chər\ *n* **:** the act of waving or a wavelike motion

1**wag** \'wag\ *vb* **wagged; wag·ging** [ME *waggen;* akin to MHG *wacken* to totter, OE *wegan* to move — more at WAY] *vi* **1 :** to be in motion **:** STIR **2 :** to move to and fro or up and down esp. with quick jerky motions **3 :** to move in chatter or gossip ⟨scandal caused tongues to ~⟩ **4** *archaic* **:** DEPART **5 :** WADDLE ~ *vt* **1 :** to swing to and fro or up and down esp. with quick jerky motions **:** SWITCH; *specif* **:** to nod (the head) or shake (a finger) at (as in assent or mild reproof) **2 :** to move (as the tongue) animatedly in conversation — **wag·ger** *n*

2**wag** *n* [prob. short for obs. E *waghalter* (gallows bird), fr. E 1*wag* + *halter*] **1** *obs* **:** a young man **:** CHAP **2 :** WIT, JOKER **3 :** an act of wagging **:** SHAKE

1**wage** \'wāj\ *vb* [ME *wagen* to pledge, give as security, fr. ONF *wagier,* fr. *wage*] *vt* **:** to engage in or carry on ⟨~ war⟩ ⟨~ a campaign⟩ ~ *vi* **:** to be in process of being waged

2**wage** *n* [ME, pledge, wage, fr. ONF, of Gmc origin; akin to Goth *wadi* pledge — more at WED] **1 a :** a payment usu. of money for labor or services usu. according to contract and on an hourly, daily, or piecework basis **b** *pl* **:** the share of the national product attributable to labor as a factor in production **2 :** RECOMPENSE, REWARD — usu. used in pl. but sing. or pl. in constr. ⟨the ~s of sin is death — Rom 6:23 (RSV)⟩

syn WAGE OR WAGES, SALARY, STIPEND, FEE, PAY, HIRE, EMOLUMENT mean the price paid for services or labor. WAGE OR WAGES applies to an amount paid daily or weekly esp. for chiefly physical labor; SALARY and STIPEND apply to a fixed amount paid for services requiring training or special ability; FEE applies to the price asked or paid for the services of a physician, lawyer, artist, or other professional; PAY may apply to wages or salaries but often specif. to those of the military services; HIRE is archaic for WAGE or PAY; EMOLUMENT may suggest rewards, other than pay, of one's work or office

wage earner *n* **:** one that works for wages or salary

wage·less \'wāj-ləs\ *adj* **:** having no wages **:** UNPAID

wage level *n* **:** the approximate position of wages at any given time in any occupation or trade or esp. in industry at large

1**wa·ger** \'wā-jər\ *n* [ME, pledge, bet, fr. AF *wageure,* fr. ONF *wagier* to pledge] **1 a :** something risked on an uncertain event **:** STAKE **b :** something on which bets are laid **:** GAMBLE **2** *archaic* **:** an act of giving a pledge to take and abide by the result of some action

2**wager** *vb* **wa·ger·ing** \'wāj-(ə-)riŋ\ *vt* **:** to hazard on an issue **:** RISK, VENTURE; *specif* **:** to lay as a gamble ~ *vi* **:** to make a bet — **wa·ger·er** \'wā-jər-ər\ *n*

wage scale *n* **1 :** a schedule of rates of wages paid for related tasks **2 :** the level of wages paid by an employer

wage·work·er \'wāj-,wər-kər\ *n* **:** WAGE EARNER

wag·gery \'wag-ə-rē\ *n* **1 :** mischievous merriment **:** PLEASANTRY **2 :** JEST; *esp* **:** PRACTICAL JOKE

wag·gish \'wag-ish\ *adj* **1 :** resembling or characteristic of a wag **:** FROLICSOME **2 :** done or made in waggery or for sport **:** HUMOROUS ⟨a ~ trick⟩ — **wag·gish·ly** *adv* — **wag·gish·ness** *n*

wag·gle \'wag-əl\ *vb* **wag·gling** \-(ə-)liŋ\ [freq. of 1*wag*] *vi* **:** to reel, sway, or move from side to side **:** WAG ~ *vt* **:** to move frequently one way and the other **:** WAG — **waggle** *n* — **wag·gly** \-(ə-)lē\ *adj*

1**Wag·ne·ri·an** \väg-'nir-ē-ən\ *adj* [Richard *Wagner* †1883 G composer and writer] **:** of, relating to, or characteristic of Wagner or his music or theories

2**Wagnerian** *n* **:** an admirer of the musical theories and style of Wagner — **Wag·ner·ite** \'väg-nə-,rīt\ *n*

1**wag·on** *or chiefly Brit* **wag·gon** \'wag-ən\ *n* [D *wagen,* fr. MD — more at WAIN] **1 a :** a four-wheel vehicle for transporting bulky commodities drawn orig. by animals **b :** a lighter typically horse-drawn vehicle for transporting goods or passengers **c :** PATROL WAGON **2** *Brit* **:** a railway freight car **3 :** a low four-wheel vehicle with an open rectangular body and a retroflex tongue made for the play or use (as for carrying newspapers) of a child **4 :** a small wheeled table used for the service of a dining room **5 :** a delivery truck ⟨milk ~⟩ **6 :** STATION WAGON — **off the wagon :** no longer abstaining from alcoholic beverages — **on the wagon :** abstaining from alcoholic beverages

2**wagon** *vi* **:** to travel or transport goods by wagon ~ *vt* **:** to trans port (goods) by wagon

wag·on·er \'wag-ə-nər\ *n* **1 :** the driver of a wagon **2** *cap* **a :** AURIGA **b :** CHARLES'S WAIN

wag·on·ette \,wag-ə-'net\ *n* **:** a light wagon with two facing seats along the sides back of a transverse front seat

wa·gon–lit \vȧ-gōⁿ-lē\ *n, pl* **wagons–lits** *or* **wagon–lits** \-gōⁿ-lē\ [F, fr. *wagon* railroad car + *lit* bed] **:** a railroad sleeping car

wagon master *n* **:** a person in charge of one or more wagons esp. for transporting freight

wagon train *n* **:** a group of wagons (as of supplies for a column of troops) traveling overland

wag·tail \'wag-,tāl\ *n* **1 :** any of numerous chiefly Old World birds (family Motacillidae) related to the pipits and having a trim slender body and a very long tail that they habitually jerk up and down **2 :** a bird resembling a wagtail (as an American water thrush)

Wah·ha·bi *or* **Wa·ha·bi** \wə-'häb-ē, wä-'häb-\ *n* [Ar *wahhābīy,* fr. Muḥammad b. ʽAbd al-*Wahhāb* (Abdul-Wahhab) †1787 Arab religious reformer] **:** a member of a puritanical Muslim sect founded in Arabia in the 18th century by Muhammad ibn-Abdul Wahhab and revived by ibn-Saud in the 20th century — **Wah·ha·bism** \-'häb-,iz-əm\ *n* — **Wah·ha·bite** \-,īt\ *adj or n*

wa·hi·ne \wä-'hē-(,)nā\ *n* [Maori & Hawaiian] **:** a Polynesian woman

1**wa·hoo** \'wä-,hü, 'wȯ-\ *n* [Creek *ûhawhu* wahoo (def. **a**)] **:** any of various American trees or shrubs: as **a :** either of two elms (*Ulmus racemosa* and *U. alata*) **b :** CASCARA BUCKTHORN **c :** BASSWOOD 1

2**wahoo** *n* [Dakota *wāhu,* lit., arrowwood] **:** either of two No. American spindle trees: **a :** a shrub or small shrubby tree (*Euonymus atropurpureus*) having purple capsules which in dehiscence expose the scarlet-ariled seeds — called also *burning bush* **b :** a strawberry bush (*Euonymus americanus*)

3**wa·hoo** \'wä-,hü\ *interj, chiefly West* — used to express exuberance or enthusiasm or to attract attention

1**waif** \'wāf\ *n* [ME, fr. ONF, adj., lost, unclaimed] **1 a :** a piece of property found (as washed up by the sea) but unclaimed **b** *pl* **:** stolen goods thrown away by a thief in flight **2 a :** something found without an owner and esp. by chance **b :** a stray person or animal; *esp* **:** a homeless child

2**waif** *n* **:** WAFT 4

1**wail** \'wā(ə)l\ *vb* [ME *wailen,* of Scand origin; akin to ON *væla, vāla* to wail; akin to ON *vei* woe — more at WOE] *vi* **1 :** to express sorrow audibly **:** LAMENT **2 :** to make a sound suggestive of a mournful cry **3 :** to express dissatisfaction plaintively **:** COMPLAIN ~ *vt, archaic* **:** BEWAIL — **wail·er** *n*

2**wail** *n* **1 :** the act or practice of wailing **:** loud lamentation **2 a :** a usu. prolonged cry or sound expressing grief or pain **b :** a sound suggestive of wailing ⟨the ~ of an air-raid siren⟩ **c :** a

querulous expression of grievance : COMPLAINT

wail·ful \'wā(ə)l-fəl\ *adj* **1** : SORROWFUL, MOURNFUL **2** : uttering a sound suggestive of wailing — **wail·ful·ly** \-fə-lē\ *adv*

wailing wall *n* **1** *cap* : an ancient wall in Jerusalem which is held to contain stones from Solomon's temple and at which Jews traditionally gather to lament and pray **2** : a source of comfort and consolation in misfortune ⟨a soldier making the chaplain's office his *wailing wall*⟩

wain \'wān\ *n* [ME, fr. OE *wægn;* akin to MD *wagen* wagon, OE *wegan* to move — more at WAY] **1** : a usu. large and heavy vehicle for farm use **2** *cap* : CHARLES'S WAIN

¹wain·scot \'wān-,skōt, -,skät, -skət\ *n* [ME, fr. MD *wagenschot*] **1** *Brit* : a fine grade of oak imported for woodwork **2 a** (1) : a usu. paneled wooden lining of an interior wall (2) : a lining of an interior wall irrespective of material **b** : the lower three or four feet of an interior wall when finished differently from the remainder of the wall

²wainscot *vt* **wain·scot·ed** *or* **wain·scot·ted; wain·scot·ing** *or* **wain·scot·ting** : to line with or as if with boards or paneling

wain·scot·ing *or* **wain·scot·ting** \-,skōt-iŋ, -,skät-, -skət-\ *n* **1** : the material used to wainscot a house **2** : WAINSCOT 2a, 2b

wain·wright \'wān-,rīt\ *n* : a maker and repairer of wagons

waist \'wāst\ *n* [ME *wast;* akin to OE *weaxan* to grow — more at WAX] **1 a** : the narrowed part of the body between the thorax and hips **b** : the greatly constricted basal part of the abdomen of some insects (as wasps and flies) **2** : the part of something corresponding to or resembling the human waist: as **a** (1) : the part of a ship's deck between the poop and forecastle (2) : the middle part of a sailing ship between foremast and mainmast **b** : the middle section of the fuselage of an airplane **3** : a garment or the part of a garment covering the body from the neck to the waistline or just below: **a** : the upper part of a woman's dress **b** : BLOUSE **c** : a child's undergarment to which other garments may be buttoned

waist·band \'wās(t)-,band\ *n* : a band or sash worn around the waist; *specif* : a fitted band forming the top edge of trousers, shorts, or skirt

waist·coat \'wes-kət, 'wās(t)-,kōt\ *n* **1** : an ornamental garment worn under a doublet **2 a** *chiefly Brit* : VEST **b** : a similar design worn by a woman — **waist·coat·ed** \-əd\ *adj*

waist·er \'wā-stər\ *n* : a usu. green or broken-down seaman stationed in the waist of a ship (as a whaling ship)

waist·line \'wāst-,līn\ *n* **1** : an arbitrary line encircling the narrowest part of the waist; *also* : the part of a garment that covers this line or may be above or below it as fashion dictates **2** : body circumference at the waist

¹wait \'wāt\ *vb* [ME *waiten,* fr. ONF *waitier* to watch, of Gmc origin; akin to OHG *wahta* watch, OE *wæccan* to watch — more at WAKE] *vt* **1 a** : to stay in place in expectation of : AWAIT **b** : to delay in hope of a favorable change in ⟨~ out a storm⟩ **2** : to delay serving (a meal) **3** : to serve as waiter for ⟨~ table⟩ ~ *vi* **1 a** : to remain stationary in readiness or expectation ⟨~ for a train⟩ **b** : to pause for another to catch up **2** : to look forward expectantly or hold back expectantly **3** : to serve at meals **4 a** : to be ready and available **b** : to remain temporarily neglected or unrealized **syn** see STAY — **wait on** *or* **wait upon 1 a** : to attend as a servant **b** : to supply the wants of : SERVE **2** : to make a formal call on **3** : to follow as a consequence — **wait up** : to delay going to bed

²wait *n* [ME *waite* watchman, public musician, wait, fr. ONF, watchman, watch, of Gmc origin; akin to OHG *wahta* watch] **1 a** : one of a band of public musicians in England employed to play for processions or public entertainments **b** (1) : one of a group who serenade for gratuities esp. at the Christmas season (2) : a piece of music by these **2 a** : a position of concealment usu. with intent to attack or surprise — used chiefly in the expression *lie in wait* **b** : a state or attitude of watchfulness and expectancy **3** : an act or period of waiting

wait–a–bit \'wāt-ə-,bit\ *n* [trans. of Afrik *wag-'n-bietjie*] : any of several plants bearing thorns or stiff hooked appendages

wait·er \'wāt-ər\ *n* **1** : one that waits upon another; *esp* : a man who waits on table (as in a restaurant) **2** : a tray on which something is carried : SALVER

waiting game *n* : a strategy in which one or more participants withhold action temporarily in the hope of having a favorable opportunity for more effective action later

waiting list *n* : a list or roster of those waiting (as for election to a club or appointment to a position)

waiting room *n* : a room (as at a railroad station) for the use of persons waiting

wait·ress \'wā-trəs\ *n* : a girl or woman who waits on table

waive \'wāv\ *vt* [ME *weiven,* fr. ONF *weyver,* fr. *waif* lost, unclaimed] **1** *archaic* : to give up : FORSAKE **2** : to throw away (stolen goods) : ABANDON **3** *archaic* : to shunt aside (as a danger or duty) : EVADE **4 a** : to relinquish voluntarily (as a legal right) ⟨~ a jury trial⟩ **b** : to refrain from pressing or enforcing (as a claim or rule) : FORGO **5** : to put off from immediate consideration : POSTPONE **6** : to dismiss with or as if with a wave of the hand

waiv·er \'wā-vər\ *n* [AF *weyver,* fr. ONF *weyver* to abandon, waive] : the act of intentionally relinquishing or abandoning a known right, claim, or privilege or an instrument evidencing such an act

¹wake \'wāk\ *vb* **waked** \'wākt\ *or* **woke** \'wōk\ **waked** *or* **wo·ken** \'wō-kən\ *or* **woke; wak·ing** [partly fr. ME *waken* (past *wook,* pp. *waken*), fr. OE *wacan* to awake (past *wōc,* pp. *wacen*) and partly fr. ME *wakien, waken* (past & pp. *waked*), fr. OE *wacian* to be awake (past *wacode,* pp. *wacod*); akin to OE *wæccan* to watch, L *vegēre* to rouse, excite] *vi* **1 a** : to be or remain awake **b** : to remain awake on watch esp. over a corpse **c** *obs* : to stay up late in revelry **2** : AWAKE — often used with *up* ~ *vt* **1** : to stand watch over (as a dead body); *esp* : to hold a wake over **2** : to rouse from or as if from sleep : AWAKE — often used with *up* — **wak·er** *n*

²wake *n* **1** : the state of being awake **2 a** (1) : an annual English parish festival formerly held in commemoration of the church's patron saint (2) : VIGIL 1a **b** : the festivities orig. connected with the wake of an English parish church — usu. used in pl. but sing. or pl. in constr. **c** *Brit* : an annual holiday or vacation — usu. used in pl. but sing. or pl. in constr. **3** : a watch held over the body of a dead person prior to burial and sometimes accompanied by festivity

³wake *n* [of Scand origin; akin to ON *vök* hole in ice; akin to ON *vökr* damp — more at HUMOR] : the track left by a moving body (as a ship) in the water; *broadly* : a track or path left

wake·ful \'wāk-fəl\ *adj* : not sleeping or able to sleep : SLEEPLESS — **wake·ful·ly** \-fə-lē\ *adv* — **wake·ful·ness** *n*

wake·less \'wā-kləs\ *adj, of sleep* : SOUND, UNBROKEN

wak·en \'wā-kən\ *vb* **wak·en·ing** \'wāk-(ə-)niŋ\ [ME *waknen,* fr. OE *wæcnian;* akin to ON *vakna* to awaken, OE *wæccan* to watch] : AWAKE — often used with *up*

wak·en·er \'wāk-(ə-)nər\ *n* : one that causes to waken

wake·rife \'wā-,krīf\ *adj* [ME (Sc) *walkryfe,* fr. *walk* awake (fr. *waken, walken* to wake) + *ryfe* rife] *Scot* : WAKEFUL, ALERT

wake–rob·in \'wā-,kräb-ən\ *n* **1** *Brit* **a** : any of various arums; *esp* : CUCKOOPINT **b** : a European orchid (*Orchis maculata*) **2** : TRILLIUM **3** : JACK-IN-THE-PULPIT

Wal·den·ses \wȯl-'den(t)-(,)sēz, wäl-\ *n pl* [ME *Waldensis,* fr. ML *Waldenses, Valdenses,* fr. Peter *Waldo* (or *Valdo*), 12th cent. F heretic] : a Christian sect arising in southern France in the 12th century, adopting Calvinist doctrines in the 16th century, and later living chiefly in Piedmont — **Wal·den·sian** \-'den-chən, -'den(t)-sē-ən\ *adj or n*

Wal·dorf salad \,wȯl-,dȯrf-\ *n* [*Waldorf*-Astoria Hotel, New York City] : a salad made typically of diced apples, celery, and nuts and dressed with mayonnaise

¹wale \'wā(ə)l\ *n* [ME, fr. OE *walu;* akin to ON *valr* round, L *volvere* to roll — more at VOLUBLE] **1 a** : a streak or ridge made on the skin esp. by the stroke of a whip : WEAL **b** : a narrow raised surface : RIDGE **2** : one of a number of strakes usu. of extra thick and strong planks in the sides of a wooden ship : — usu. used in pl. **3 a** : one of a series of even ribs in a fabric **b** : the texture esp. of a fabric

²wale *vt* : to mark (as the skin) with welts

³wale *n* [ME (Sc & northern dial.) *wal,* fr. ON *val;* akin to OHG *wala* choice, OE *wyllan* to wish — more at WILL] **1** *dial Brit* : CHOICE **2** *dial Brit* : the best part : PICK

⁴wale *vb, dial Brit* : CHOOSE

wal·er \'wā-lər\ *n, often cap* [New So. *Wales,* Australia] : a horse from New So. Wales; *esp* : a rather large rugged saddle horse of mixed ancestry formerly exported in quantity from Australia to British India for military use

Wal·hal·la \väl-'häl-ə\ *n* [G] : VALHALLA

¹walk \'wȯk\ *vb* [partly fr. ME *walken* (past *welk,* pp. *walken*), fr. OE *wealcan* to roll, toss (past *wēolc,* pp. *wealcen*) and partly fr. ME *walkien* (past *walked,* pp. *walked*), fr. OE *wealcian* to roll up, muffle up; akin to MD *walken* to knead, press, full, L *valgus* bowlegged] *vi* **1 a** *obs* : ROAM, WANDER **b** *of a spirit* : to move about in visible form : APPEAR **c** *of a ship* : to make headway **2 a** : to move along on foot : advance by steps **b** : to go on foot for exercise or pleasure **c** : to go at a walk **3 a** : to pursue a course of action or way of life : conduct oneself : BEHAVE ⟨~ in darkness —Jn 8:12 (AV)⟩ **b** : to be or act in association : continue in union **4** : to go to first base as the result of a base on balls **5** *of an inanimate object* **a** : to move in a manner that is suggestive of walking **b** : to stand with an appearance suggestive of strides ⟨pylons ~*ing* across the valley⟩ ~ *vt* **1 a** : to pass on foot or as if on foot through, along, over, or upon : TRAVERSE, PERAMBULATE ⟨~ the streets⟩ ⟨~ a tightrope⟩ **b** : to perform or accomplish by going on foot ⟨~ guard⟩ **2 a** : to cause (an animal) to go at a walk ⟨~*ing* a dog⟩ **b** : to cause to move by walking ⟨~*ed* his bicycle up the hill⟩; *specif* : to haul (as an anchor) by walking round the capstan **3** : to follow on foot for the purpose of measuring, surveying, or inspecting ⟨~ a boundary⟩ **4 a** : to accompany on foot : walk with **b** : to compel to walk **c** : to bring to a specified condition by walking ⟨~*ed* us off our feet⟩ **5** : to move (an object) in a manner suggestive of walking **6** : to perform (a dance) at a walking pace ⟨~ a quadrille⟩ **7** : to give a base on balls to — **walk away from 1** : to outrun or get the better of without difficulty **2** : to survive (an accident) with little or no injury — **walk into 1 a** : ATTACK **b** : to reprimand harshly : criticize severely **2 a** : to eat or drink greedily ⟨*walked* right *into* the beer and pretzels⟩ **b** : to use up rapidly — **walk off with 1 a** : to steal and take away **b** : to take over unexpectedly from someone else : STEAL 1d **2** : to win or gain esp. by outdoing one's competitors without difficulty — **walk over** : to disregard the wishes or feelings of : treat contemptuously — **walk the plank 1** : to walk under compulsion over the side of a ship into the sea **2** : to resign an office or position under compulsion — **walk through 1** : to go through (a play or acting part) perfunctorily as in an early stage of rehearsal **2** : to deal with or carry out perfunctorily

²walk *n* **1** : an act or instance of going on foot esp. for exercise or pleasure ⟨go for a ~⟩ **2** : accustomed place of walking : HAUNT **3** : a place designed for walking: **a** : a railed platform above the roof of a dwelling house **b** (1) : a path specially arranged or paved for walking (2) : SIDEWALK **c** : a public avenue for promenading : PROMENADE **d** : ROPEWALK **4** : a place or area of land in which animals feed and exercise with minimal restraint **5** : distance to be walked **6** *Brit* : a ceremonial procession **7** : manner of living : CONDUCT, BEHAVIOR **8 a** : the gait of a biped in which the feet are lifted alternately with one foot not clear of the ground before the other touches **b** : the gait of a quadruped in which there are always at least two feet on the ground; *specif* : a four-beat gait of a horse in which the feet strike the ground in the sequence near hind, near fore, off hind, off fore **c** : an extremely low rate of speed **9** : a route regularly traversed by a person in the performance of a particular activity (as patrolling, begging, vending) **10** : characteristic manner of walking ⟨his ~ is just like his father's⟩ **11 a** : social or economic status ⟨all ~*s* of life⟩ **b** (1) : range or sphere of action : FIELD, PROVINCE (2) : VOCATION **12** : a plantation of trees arranged in rows with wide spaces between them **13** : BASE ON BALLS

walk·away \'wȯ-kə-,wā\ *n* : an easily won contest

walk·er \'wȯ-kər\ *n* **1** : one that walks: as **a** : one that conducts himself in a specified way **b** : a competitor in a walking race **c** : a peddler going on foot **2** : something used in walking: as **a** : a framework with wheels designed to support one learning to walk **b** : a walking shoe

walk·ie–look·ie \,wȯ-kē-'lu̇k-ē\ *n* : a portable one-man television camera

walk·ie–talk·ie \-'tȯ-kē\ *n* : a compact battery-operated radio

transmitting and receiving set carried on a person's back to provide two-way communication

¹**walk–in** \'wȯ-ˌkin\ *adj* **1 :** large enough to be walked into **2 :** arranged so as to be entered directly rather than through a lobby ⟨~ apartment⟩

²**walk–in** *n* **1 :** a walk-in refrigerator or cold storage room **2 :** an easy election victory

¹**walk·ing** \'wȯ-kiŋ\ *n* **1 :** the action of one that walks ⟨~ is good exercise⟩ **2 :** the condition of a surface for one going on foot ⟨the ~ is slippery⟩

²**walking** *adj* **1 a :** LIVING, HUMAN ⟨a ~ encyclopedia⟩ **b :** able to walk **:** AMBULATORY **2 a :** used for or in walking ⟨~ shoes⟩ **b :** characterized by or consisting of the action of walking ⟨a ~ tour⟩ **3 :** of or appropriate to a person being dismissed **4 :** that moves or appears to move in a manner suggestive of walking; *esp* **:** that swings or rocks back and forth ⟨~ beam⟩ **5 :** not requiring bed rest **6 :** guided or operated by a man on foot ⟨~ plow⟩

walking delegate *n* **:** a labor union representative appointed to visit members and their places of employment, to secure enforcement of union rules and agreements, and at times to represent the union in dealing with employers

walking leaf *n* **1 :** any of a genus (*Camptosorus*) of ferns — called also *walking fern* **2 :** any of a family (Phasmatidae) of insects with wings and legs resembling leaves

walking papers *n pl* **:** DISMISSAL, DISCHARGE — called also *walking ticket*

walking stick *n* **1 :** a stick used in walking **2** *usu* **walk·ing·stick :** STICK INSECT; *esp* **:** an orthopterous insect (*Diapheromera femorata*) common in parts of the U.S.

walk–on \'wȯ-ˌkȯn, -ˌkän\ *n* **:** a small usu. nonspeaking part in a dramatic production

walk out *vi* **1 :** to go on strike **2 :** to leave suddenly often as an expression of disapproval — **walk out on :** to leave in the lurch **:** ABANDON, DESERT

walk·out \'wȯ-ˌkau̇t\ *n* **1 :** STRIKE 3a **2 :** the action of leaving a meeting or organization as an expression of disapproval

walk·over \'wȯ-ˌkō-vər\ *n* **1 :** a horse race with only one starter **2 :** a one-sided contest or an easy or uncontested victory

walk–up \'wȯ-ˌkəp\ *n* **:** a building or apartment house without an elevator; *also* **:** an apartment or office in such a building — **walk–up** *adj*

walk·way \'wȯ-ˌkwā\ *n* **:** a passage for walking **:** WALK

Wal·ky·rie \väl-'kir-ē, -'kī(ə)r-ē, 'väl-ˌ\ *n* [G *walküre* & ON *valkyrja*] **:** VALKYRIE

¹**wall** \'wȯl\ *n* [ME, fr. OE *weall;* akin to MHG *wall;* both fr. a prehistoric WGmc word borrowed fr. L *vallum* rampart, fr. *vallus* stake, palisade; akin to ON *völr* round stick, L *volvere* to roll — more at VOLUBLE] **1 a :** a high thick masonry structure forming a long rampart or an enclosure chiefly for defense — often used in pl. **b :** a masonry fence around a garden, park, or estate **c :** a structure that serves to hold back pressure (as of water or sliding earth) **2 :** one of the sides of a room or building connecting floor and ceiling or foundation and roof **3 :** the side of a footpath next to buildings **4 :** an extreme or desperate position or a state of defeat, failure, or ruin — usu. used in the phrase *to the wall* **5 :** a material layer enclosing space ⟨~ of a container⟩ ⟨heart ~*s*⟩ **6 :** something resembling a wall in appearance; *esp* **:** something that acts as a barrier or defense ⟨~ of reserve⟩ ⟨tariff ~⟩ — **walled** \'wȯld\ *adj* — **wall–like** \'wȯl-ˌlīk\ *adj*

²**wall** *vt* **1 a :** to provide, cover with, or surround with or as if with a wall ⟨~ in the garden⟩ **b :** to separate by or as if by a wall ⟨~*ed* off half the house⟩ **2 a :** IMMURE **b :** to close (an opening) with or as if with a wall

³**wall** *vb* [ME (Sc) *wawlen,* prob. fr. ME *wawil-* (in *wawil-eghed* walleyed)] *vt* **:** to roll (one's eyes) in a dramatic manner **~** *vi, of the eyes* **:** to roll in a dramatic manner

wal·la·by \'wäl-ə-bē\ *n, pl* **wallabies** *also* **wallaby** [*wolabā,* native name in New So. Wales, Australia] **:** any of various small or medium-sized usu. brightly colored kangaroos (esp. genus *Macropus*)

wal·lah \'wäl-ə, *in combination usu* ˌwäl-ə\ *n* [Hindi *-wālā* man, one in charge, fr. Skt *pāla* protector; akin to Skt *pāti* he protects — more at FUR] **:** a person who is associated with a particular work or who performs a specific duty or service — usu. used in combination

wal·la·roo \ˌwäl-ə-'rü\ *n* [*wolarū,* native name in New So. Wales, Australia] **:** EURO

wall·board \'wȯl-ˌbō(ə)rd, -ˌbȯ(ə)rd\ *n* **:** a structural boarding of any of various materials (as wood pulp, gypsum, or plastic) made in large rigid sheets and used esp. for sheathing interior walls and ceilings

wal·let \'wäl-ət\ *n* [ME *walet*] **1 :** a bag for carrying miscellaneous articles while traveling **2 a :** BILLFOLD **b :** a pocketbook with compartments for change, photographs, cards, and keys **c :** a large pocketbook usu. carried in a breast pocket

wall·eye \'wȯ-ˌlī\ *n* [back-formation fr. *walleyed*] **1 a :** an eye with a whitish iris **b :** an eye with an opaque white cornea **c :** an eye that turns outward showing more than a normal amount of white **2 a :** LEUCOMA **b :** strabismus in which the eye turns outward **3** *pl* **:** eyes affected with divergent strabismus **4** *or* **walleyed pike :** a large vigorous American freshwater food and sport fish (*Stizostedion vitreum*) that has prominent eyes and is related to the perches but resembles the true pike

wall·eyed \-'līd\ *adj* [by folk etymology fr. ME *wawil-eghed* part trans. of ON *vagl-eygr* walleyed, fr. *vagl* beam, roost + *eygr* eyed; akin to OE *wegan* to move, carry — more at WAY] **1 :** having walleyes or affected with walleye **2 :** marked by a wild irrational staring of the eyes

wall fern *n* **:** a low-growing mat-forming fern (*Polypodium vulgare*)

wall·flow·er \'wȯl-ˌflau̇(-ə)r\ *n* **1 a :** any of several Old World herbaceous or subshrubby perennial plants (genus *Cheiranthus*) of the mustard family; *esp* **:** a hardy erect herb (*C. cheiri*) widely cultivated for its showy fragrant flowers **b :** any of a related genus (*Erysimum*) **2 :** a person who from shyness or unpopularity remains on the sidelines of a social activity (as a dance)

wall hanging *n* **:** a drapery or tapestry hung against a wall for decoration

Wal·loon \wä-'lün\ *n* [MF *Wallon,* adj. & n., of Gmc origin; prob. akin to OHG *Walah* Celt, Roman, OE *Wealh* Celt, Welshman — more at WELSH] **1 :** a member of a chiefly Celtic people of southern and southeastern Belgium and adjacent parts of France **2 :** a French dialect of the Walloons — **Walloon** *adj*

¹**wal·lop** \'wäl-əp\ *n* [ME, gallop, fr. ONF *walop,* fr. *waloper* to gallop] **1 a :** a powerful blow **:** ²PUNCH 2 **b :** the ability (as of a boxer) to hit hard **2 a :** emotional or psychological force **:** IMPACT **b :** an exciting emotional response **:** THRILL

²**wallop** *vb* [ME *walopen* to gallop, fr. ONF *waloper*] *vi* **1 a :** to move with reckless or disorganized haste **:** advance in a headlong rush **b :** WALLOW, FLOUNDER **2 :** to boil noisily **~** *vt* **1 a :** to thrash soundly **:** BEAT **b :** to beat by a wide margin **:** TROUNCE **2 :** to hit with force **:** SOCK — **wal·lop·er** *n*

wal·lop·ing \'wäl-ə-piŋ\ *adj* **1 :** LARGE, WHOPPING **2 :** exceptionally fine or impressive

¹**wal·low** \'wäl-(ˌ)ō, -ə(-w)\ *vi* [ME *walwen,* fr. OE *wealwian* to roll — more at VOLUBLE] **1 :** to roll oneself about in an indolent or ungainly manner **2 :** to billow forth **:** SURGE **3 :** to devote oneself entirely; *esp* **:** to take unrestrained pleasure **:** DELIGHT **4 a :** to become abundantly supplied **b :** to indulge oneself immoderately ⟨~*ing* in luxury⟩ **5 :** to become helpless — **wal·low·er** \'wäl-ə-wər\ *n*

²**wallow** *n* **1 :** an act or instance of wallowing **2 a :** a muddy area or one filled with dust used by animals for wallowing **b :** a depression formed by or as if by the wallowing of animals **3 :** a state of degradation or degeneracy

wall painting *n* **:** FRESCO

¹**wall·pa·per** \'wȯl-ˌpā-pər\ *n* **:** decorative paper for the walls of a room

²**wallpaper** *vt* **:** to provide the walls of (as a room) with wallpaper **~** *vi* **:** to put wallpaper on a wall

wall pellitory *n* **:** a European herb (*Parietaria officinalis*) of the nettle family with diuretic properties that grows esp. on old walls

wall plate *n* **:** PLATE 5

wall plug *n* **:** an electric receptacle in a wall

wall rock *n* **:** a rock through which a fault or vein runs

wall rocket *n* **:** any of several plants (genus *Diplotaxis*) of the mustard family; *esp* **:** a yellow-flowered European weed (*D. tenuifolia*) adventive in No. America

wall rue *n* **:** a small delicate spleenwort (*Asplenium rutamuraria*) found esp. on walls or cliffs

Wall Street \'wȯl-\ *n* [*Wall Street,* near southern end of New York City] **:** the influential financial interests of the U.S. economy

wal·ly \'wā-lē\ *adj* [prob. fr. ³*wale*] *Scot* **:** FINE, STURDY

wal·ly·drai·gle \'wā-lē-ˌdrā-gəl, 'wäl-ē-\ *n* [origin unknown] *Scot* **:** a feeble, imperfectly developed, or slovenly creature

wal·nut \'wȯl-(ˌ)nət\ *n* [ME *walnot,* fr. OE *wealhhnutu,* lit., foreign nut, fr. *Wealh* Welshman, foreigner + *hnutu* nut — more at WELSH, NUT] **1 a :** an edible nut of any of a genus (*Juglans* of the family Juglandaceae, the walnut family) of trees; *also* **:** one of these trees or its wood often valued for cabinetmaking and veneers **b :** a hickory tree or its nut — called also *white walnut* **2 :** a moderate reddish brown that is the color of the heartwood of the black walnut

Wal·pur·gis Night \väl-'pu̇r-gəs-\ *n* [part trans. of G *walpurgisnacht,* fr. *Walpurgis* St. Walburga †A.D. 777 E saint whose feast day falls on May Day + G *nacht* night] **:** the eve of May Day on which witches are held to ride to an appointed rendezvous

wal·rus \'wȯl-rəs, 'wäl-\ *n, pl* **walrus** *or* **wal·rus·es** [D, of Scand origin; akin to Dan & Norw *hvalros* walrus, ON *rosmhvalr*] **:** either of two large marine mammals (*Odobenus rosmarus* and *O. divergens* of the family Odobenidae) of northern seas related to the seals and hunted for the tough heavy hide, the ivory tusks, the oil yielded by the blubber, and locally for the flesh

¹**waltz** \'wȯl(t)s\ *n* [G *walzer,* fr. *walzen* to roll, dance, fr. OHG *walzan* to turn, roll — more at WELTER] **1 :** a round dance in ¾ time with strong accent on the first beat **2 :** music for a waltz or a concert composition in ¾ time

²**waltz** *vi* **1 :** to dance a waltz **2 :** to move or advance in a lively or conspicuous manner **:** FLOUNCE **3 :** to advance easily and successfully **:** BREEZE — usu. used with *through* **~** *vt* **1 :** to dance a waltz with **2 :** to grab and lead unceremoniously **:** MARCH — **waltz·er** *n*

¹**wam·ble** \'wäm-bəl\ *vi* **wam·bling** \-b(ə-)liŋ\ [ME *wamlen;* akin to Dan *vamle* to become nauseated, L *vomere* to vomit — more at VOMIT] **1 a :** to feel nausea **b** *of a stomach* **:** RUMBLE 1 **2 :** to move unsteadily or with a weaving or rolling motion

²**wamble** *n* **1 :** a wambling esp. of the stomach **2 :** a reeling or staggering gait or movement

wame \'wām\ *n* [ME, alter. of *wamb* — more at WOMB] *chiefly Scot* **:** BELLY

wam·pum \'wäm-pəm\ *n* [short for *wampumpeag*] **1 :** beads of polished shells strung in strands, belts, or sashes and used by No. American Indians as money, ceremonial pledges, and ornaments **2** *slang* **:** MONEY

wam·pum·peag \-ˌpēg\ *n* [Narraganset *wampompeag,* fr. *wampan* white + *api* string + *-ag,* pl. suffix] **:** WAMPUM; *esp* **:** that made of the less valuable white shell beads

¹**wan** \'wän\ *adj* [ME, fr. OE, dark, livid] **1 a :** SICKLY, PALLID **b :** FEEBLE **2 :** DIM, FAINT **3 :** LANGUID ⟨a ~ smile⟩ — **wan·ly** *adv* — **wan·ness** \'wän-nəs\ *n*

²**wan** *vi* **wanned; wan·ning :** to grow or become pale or sickly

wand \'wänd\ *n* [ME, slender stick, fr. ON *vöndr;* akin to OE *windan* to wind, twist — more at WIND] **1 :** a slender staff carried in a procession **:** VERGE **2 :** a slender rod used by conjurers and magicians **3 :** a slat 6 feet by 2 inches used as a target in archery

wan·der \'wän-dər\ *vb* **wan·der·ing** \-d(ə-)riŋ\ [ME *wandren,* fr. OE *wandrian;* akin to MHG *wandern* to wander, OE *windan* to wind, twist] *vi* **1 a :** to move about without a fixed course, aim, or goal **b :** to go idly about **:** RAMBLE **2 :** to follow a winding course **:** MEANDER **3 a :** to deviate (as from a course) **:** STRAY **b :** to go astray morally **:** ERR **c :** to stray in thought **~** *vt* **:** to roam over — **wander** *n* — **wan·der·er** \-dər-ər\ *n*

¹**wan·der·ing** *n* **1 :** a going about from place to place — often used in pl. **2 :** movement away from the proper, normal, or usual course — often used in pl.

²**wandering** *adj* **:** characterized by aimless, slow, or pointless movement: as **a :** WINDING, MEANDERING ⟨a ~ course⟩ **b :** not keeping a rational or sensible course **:** VAGRANT **c :** NOMADIC ⟨~ tribes⟩ **d** *of a plant* **:** having long runners or tendrils

wandering jenny *n* **:** MONEYWORT

Wandering Jew *n* **1 :** a Jew held in medieval legend to be condemned to wander the earth until the second coming of Christ for having mocked at Him on the day of the crucifixion **2** *not cap W*

: any of several plants (genera *Zebrina* and *Tradescantia*) of the spiderwort family; *esp* : either of two trailing or creeping cultivated plants (*Z. pendula* and *T. fluminensis*)

wan·der·lust \'wän-dər-,ləst\ *n* [G, fr. *wandern* to wander + *lust* desire, pleasure] : strong or unconquerable longing for or impulse toward wandering

wan·de·roo \,wän-də-'rü\ *n* [Sinhalese *vanduru*, pl. of *vandurā*, fr. Skt *vānara* monkey, fr. *vanar-*, *vana* forest; akin to Av *vana* forest] **1** : a purple-faced langur (*Presbytis cephalopterus*) of Ceylon **2** : a macaque (*Macaca albibarbata*) of the Indian peninsula with a tufted tail

1wane \'wān\ *vi* [ME *wanen*, fr. OE *wanian;* akin to OHG *wanōn* to wane, OE *wan* wanting, deficient, L *vanus* empty, vain] **1** : to decrease in size or extent : DWINDLE: as **a** : to diminish in phase or intensity — used chiefly of the moon **b** : to become less brilliant or powerful : DIM **c** : to flow out : EBB **2** : to fall gradually from power, prosperity, or influence : DECLINE **syn** see ABATE

2wane *n* **1 a** : the act or process of waning **b** : a period or time of waning; *specif* : the period from full phase of the moon to the new moon **2** [ME, defect, fr. OE *wana;* akin to OE *wan* deficient] : a defect in lumber characterized by bark or a lack of wood at a corner or edge

wan·ey *or* **wany** \'wā-nē\ *adj* **wan·i·er; wan·i·est** **1** : waning or diminished in some parts **2** *of sawed timber* : marked by wane

wan·gle \'waŋ-gəl\ *vb* **wan·gling** \-g(ə-)liŋ\ [perh. alter. of *waggle*] *vi* **1** : to extricate oneself (as from difficulty) : WIGGLE **2** : to resort to trickery or devious methods ~ *vt* **1** : SHAKE, WIGGLE **2** : to adjust or manipulate for personal or fraudulent ends **3** : to make or get by devious means : FINAGLE ⟨~ an invitation⟩ — **wan·gler** \-g(ə-)lər\ *n*

wan·i·gan *or* **wan·ni·gan** \'wän-i-gən\ *n* [of Algonquian origin; akin to Abnaki *waniigan* trap, lit., that into which something strays] : a shelter often mounted on wheels or tracks and towed by tractor or mounted on a raft or boat

wan·ion \'wän-yən\ *n* [fr. the obs. phrase *in the waniand* unluckily, lit., in the waning (moon), fr. ME, fr. *waniand*, northern pres. part. of *wanien, wanen* to wane] *archaic* : PLAGUE, VENGEANCE — used in the phrase *with a wanion*

1want \'wȯnt, 'wänt, 'wənt\ *vb* [ME *wanten*, fr. ON *vanta;* akin to OE *wan* deficient] *vt* **1** : to fail to possess : LACK **2 a** (1) : to desire earnestly ⟨~*s* to be home⟩ (2) : CRAVE **b** : to be inclined to : LIKE **3** : NEED, REQUIRE **4** : to suffer from the lack of **5** : to wish or demand the presence of ~ *vi* **1** : to be deficient or short ⟨it ~*s* three minutes to twelve⟩ **2** : to be needy or destitute **3** : to have or feel need : LONG ⟨never ~*s* for friends⟩ **4** : to be necessary or needed **syn** see DESIRE

2want *n* **1 a** : the quality or state of lacking a required or usual amount **b** : dire need : DESTITUTION **2** : something wanted : NEED, DESIRE **3** : personal defect : FAULT **syn** see POVERTY

want ad *n* : a newspaper advertisement stating that something (as an employee, employment, or a specified item) is wanted

1want·ing *adj* **1** : not present or in evidence : ABSENT **2 a** : not being up to standards or expectations **b** : lacking in ability or capacity : DEFICIENT

2wanting *prep* **1** : WITHOUT ⟨a book ~ a cover⟩ **2** : LESS, MINUS ⟨a month ~ two days⟩

1wan·ton \'wȯnt-ᵊn, 'wänt-\ *adj* [ME, fr. *wan-* deficient, wrong, mis- (fr. OE, fr. *wan* deficient) + *towen*, pp. of *teen* to draw, train, discipline, fr. OE *tēon* — more at TOW] **1** *archaic* : UNDISCIPLINED, UNRULY **2** : FROLICSOME **3** : UNCHASTE, LEWD; *also* : SENSUAL **4** *obs* : VOLUPTUOUS **5 a** : MERCILESS, INHUMANE ⟨~ cruelty⟩ **b** : having no just foundation or provocation : MALICIOUS ⟨a ~ attack⟩ **6** : UNRESTRAINED, EXTRAVAGANT; *esp* : luxuriantly rank **syn** see SUPEREROGATORY — **wan·ton·ly** *adv* — **wan·ton·ness** \-ᵊn-(n)əs\ *n*

2wanton *n* **1** : a pampered person or animal : PET; *esp* : a spoiled child **2** : a frolicsome child or animal **3 a** : a person given to luxurious self-enjoyment **b** : a lascivious person

3wanton *vi* : to be wanton or act wantonly ~ *vt* : to pass or waste wantonly or in wantonness — **wan·ton·er** *n*

wa·pen·take \'wap-ən-,tāk, 'wäp-\ *n* [ME, fr. OE *wǣpentæc*, fr. ON *vāpnatak* act of grasping weapons, fr. *vāpn* weapon + *tak* act of grasping, fr. *taka* to take; prob. fr. the brandishing of weapons as an expression of approval when the chief of the wapentake entered upon his office — more at WEAPON, TAKE] : a subdivision of some English shires corresponding to a hundred

wa·pi·ti \'wäp-ət-ē, wə-'pēt-ē\ *n, pl* **wapiti** *or* **wapitis** [of Algonquian origin; akin to Cree *wapitew* white, whitish; fr. its white rump and tail] : an American elk (*Cervus canadensis* and related forms) similar to the European red deer but larger

wap·pen·schaw·ing \'wap-ən-,shȯ(-)iŋ\ *n* [ME (northern dial.) *wapynschawing*, fr. *wapen* weapon (fr. ON *vāpn*) + *schawing*, gerund of *schawen* to show, fr. OE *scēawian* to look, look at — more at WEAPON, SHOW] : an exhibition of arms formerly held at various seasons in each district of Scotland : MUSTER

wap·per–jawed \,wäp-ər-'jȯd, ,wäp-ē-'jȯd\ *adj* [origin unknown] : having a crooked, undershot, or wry jaw

1war \'wȯ(ə)r\ *n* [ME *werre*, fr. ONF, of Gmc origin; akin to OHG *werra* strife; akin to OHG *werran* to confuse, L *verrere* to sweep] **1 a** (1) : a state of usu. open and declared armed hostile conflict between states or nations (2) : a period of such armed conflict (3) : STATE OF WAR **b** : the art or science of warfare **c** (1) *obs* : weapons and equipment for war (2) *archaic* : soldiers armed and equipped for war **2 a** : a state of hostility, conflict, or antagonism **b** : a struggle between opposing forces or for a particular end

2war *vi* **warred; war·ring** **1** : to engage in warfare **2** : to be in active or vigorous conflict

3war \'wär\ *adv (or adj)* [ME *werre*, fr. ON *verri*, adj., *verr*, adv. — more at WORSE] *chiefly Scot* : WORSE

4war \'wär\ *vt* **warred; war·ring** *Scot* : WORST, OVERCOME

1war·ble \'wȯr-bəl\ *n* [ME *werble* tune, fr. ONF, of Gmc origin; akin to MHG *wirbel* whirl, tuning peg, OHG *wirbil* whirlwind — more at WHIRL] **1** : a melodious succession of low pleasing sounds **2** : a musical trill **3** : the action of warbling

2warble *vb* **war·bling** \-b(ə-)liŋ\ *vi* **1** : to sing in a trilling manner or with many turns and variations **2** : to become sounded with trills, quavers, and rapid modulations in pitch **3** : SING ~ *vt* : to render with turns, runs, or rapid modulations : TRILL

3warble *n* [perh. of Scand origin; akin to obs. Sw *varbulde* boil, fr. *var* pus + *bulde* swelling] **1** : a swelling under the hide esp. of the back of cattle, horses, and some other mammals caused by the maggot of a botfly or warble fly **2** : the maggot of a warble fly — **war·bled** \-bəld\ *adj*

warble fly *n* : any of various two-winged flies (family Oestridae) whose larvae live under the skin of various mammals and cause warbles

war·bler \'wȯr-blər\ *n* **1** : one that warbles : SONGSTER **2 a** : any of numerous small Old World singing birds (family Sylviidae) many of which are noted songsters and are closely related to the thrushes **b** : any of numerous small brightly colored American songbirds (family Parulidae) with a usu. weak and unmusical song — called also *wood warbler*

war·bon·net \'wȯr-,bän-ət\ *n* : a ceremonial headdress of some Plains Indians with a feathered extension

war chest *n* : a fund accumulated to finance a war; *broadly* : a fund earmarked for a specific purpose, action, or campaign

war club *n* : a club used by warriors; *esp* : a club-shaped implement used as a weapon by American Indians

war crime *n* : a crime (as genocide or maltreatment of prisoners) committed during or in connection with war — usu. used in pl.

war cry *n* **1** : a cry used by a body of fighters in war **2** : a slogan used esp. to rally people to a cause

1ward \'wȯ(ə)rd\ *n* [ME, fr. OE *weard;* akin to OHG *warta* act of watching, OE *warian* to beware of, guard — more at WARE] **1 a** : the action or process of guarding **b** : a group acting as guards **2** : the state of being under guard; *esp* : CUSTODY **3 a** : the inner court of a castle or fortress **b** : a division (as a cell or block) of a prison **c** : a division in a hospital **4 a** : a division of a city for representative, electoral, or administrative purposes **b** : a division of some English and Scottish counties corresponding to a hundred **c** : the Mormon local congregation having auxiliary organizations (as Sunday schools and relief societies) and one or more quorums of each office of the Aaronic priesthood **5** : a projecting ridge of metal in a lock casing or keyhole permitting only the insertion of a key with a corresponding notch; *also* : a corresponding notch in a bit of a key **6** : a person under guard, protection, or surveillance: as **a** : a minor subject to wardship **b** : a person who by reason of incapacity (as minority or lunacy) is under the protection of a court either directly or through a guardian appointed by the court **c** : a person or body of persons under the protection or tutelage of a government **7** : means of defense : PROTECTION — **ward·ed** \'wȯrd-əd\ *adj*

2ward *vt* [ME *warden*, fr. OE *weardian;* akin to OHG *wartēn* to watch, ON *vartha* to guard, OE *weard* ward] **1** : to keep watch over : GUARD **2** : DEFLECT — usu. used with *off*

1-ward \wərd\ *also* **-wards** \wərdz\ *adj suffix* [*-ward* fr. ME, fr. OE *-weard;* akin to OHG *-wart*, *-wert* -ward, L *vertere* to turn; *-wards* fr. *-wards*, adv. suffix — more at WORTH] **1** : that moves, tends, faces, or is directed toward ⟨door on the river*ward* side — D.C.Peattie⟩ ⟨by means of advances land*wards* from the . . . coast — W. G. East⟩ **2** : that occurs or is situated in the direction of ⟨sunrise to right, sunset left*ward* —George Meredith⟩

2-ward *or* **-wards** *adv suffix* [*-ward* fr. ME, fr. OE *-weard*, fr. *-weard*, adj. suffix; *-wards* fr. ME, fr. OE *-weardes*, gen. sing. neut. of *-weard*, adj. suffix] **1** : in a (specified) spatial or temporal direction ⟨aimed up*ward* from the ground⟩ ⟨after*ward* plague broke out⟩ ⟨plain . . . confined land*wards* by . . . mountains —W.G.East⟩ **2** : toward a (specified) point, position, or area ⟨bent earth*ward* by a thousand gales —Norman Douglas⟩

war dance *n* : a dance performed by primitive peoples as preparation for battle or in celebration of victory

ward·ed \'wȯrd-əd\ *adj* : provided with a ward ⟨~ lock⟩

war·den \'wȯrd-ᵊn\ *n* [ME *wardein*, fr. ONF, fr. *warder* to guard, of Gmc origin; akin to OHG *wartēn* to watch] **1** : one having care or charge of something : GUARDIAN, KEEPER **2 a** : REGENT 2 **b** : the governor of a town, district, or fortress **c** : a member of the governing body of a guild **3 a** : an official charged with special supervisory duties or with the enforcement of specified laws or regulations ⟨game ~⟩ ⟨air raid ~⟩ **b** : an official in charge of the operation of a prison **c** : any of various British officials having designated administrative functions ⟨~ of the mint⟩ **4 a** : one of two ranking lay officers of an Episcopal parish **b** : any of various British college officials whose duties range from the administration of academic matters to the supervision of student discipline

war·den·ship \-,ship\ *n* : the office, jurisdiction, or powers of a warden

1ward·er \'wȯrd-ər\ *n* [ME, fr. AF *wardere*, fr. *warde* act of guarding, of Gmc origin; akin to OHG *warta* act of watching] **1** : WATCHMAN, PORTER **2** *Brit* **a** : WARDEN; *esp* : CARETAKER, CUSTODIAN **b** : a prison guard

2warder *n* [ME, perh. fr. *warden* to ward] : a truncheon used by a king or commander in chief to signal orders

war·der·ship \-,ship\ *n* : the office, position, or function of a warder

ward heeler *n* : a political heeler working in a ward or other local area

ward off *vt* : to fend off : AVERT, PARRY **syn** see PREVENT

ward·ress \'wȯr-drəs\ *n* : a female warden in a prison

ward·robe \'wȯr-,drōb\ *n* [ME *warderobe*, fr. ONF, fr. *warder* to guard + *robe* robe] **1 a** : a room or closet where clothes are kept **b** : CLOTHESPRESS **c** : a large trunk in which clothes may be hung upright **2** : a collection of wearing apparel (as of one person or for one activity) **3** : the department of a royal or noble household entrusted with the care of wearing apparel, jewels, and personal articles

ward·room \'wȯr-,drüm, -,drům\ *n* **1** : the space in a warship allotted for living quarters to the commissioned officers excepting the captain; *specif* : the messroom assigned to these officers **2** : the officers dining in a wardroom

ward·ship \'wȯrd-,ship\ *n* **1 a** : GUARDIANSHIP **b** : the right to the custody of an infant heir of a feudal tenant and of his property **2** : the state of being under a guardian

1ware \'wa(ə)r, 'we(ə)r\ *adj* [ME *war, ware* careful, aware, fr. OE *wær* — more at WARY] **1** : AWARE, CONSCIOUS **2** *archaic* : WARY, VIGILANT

[2]ware *vt* [ME *waren*, fr. OE *warian;* akin to OHG *biwarōn* to protect, OE *wær* aware] **:** to beware of — used chiefly as a command to hunting animals ⟨~ chase⟩

[3]ware *n* [ME, fr. OE *waru;* akin to MHG *ware* ware and prob. to OE *wær* aware] **1 a :** manufactured articles, products of art or craft, or produce **:** GOODS — often used in combination ⟨tin*ware*⟩ **b :** an article of merchandise **2 :** pottery or dishes of fired clay ⟨earthen*ware*⟩ **3 :** an intangible item (as a service) that is a marketable commodity

[4]ware *vt* [ME *waren*, fr. ON *verja* to clothe, invest, spend — more at WEAR] *Scot* **:** SPEND, EXPEND

[1]ware·house \ˈwa(ə)r-ˌhau̇s, ˈwe(ə)r-\ *n* **:** a structure or room for the storage of merchandise or commodities — **ware·house·man** \-ˌhau̇s-mən, -ˌhau̇z-\ *n*

[2]ware·house \-ˌhau̇z, -ˌhau̇s\ *vt* **:** to deposit, store, or stock in or as if in a warehouse

ware·room \ˈwa(ə)r-ˌrüm, ˈwe(ə)r-, -ˌru̇m\ *n* **:** a room in which goods are exhibited for sale

war·fare \ˈwȯr-ˌfa(ə)r, -ˌfe(ə)r\ *n* [ME, fr. *werre, warre* war + *fare* journey, passage — more at FARE] **1 :** military operations between enemies **:** HOSTILITIES, WAR; *broadly* **:** activity undertaken by a political unit (as a nation) to weaken or destroy another ⟨economic ~⟩ **2 :** struggle between competing entities **:** CONFLICT

war·fa·rin \ˈwȯr-fə-rən\ *n* [*W*isconsin *A*lumni *R*esearch *F*oundation (its patentee) + coum*arin*] **:** a crystalline anticoagulant compound $C_{19}H_{16}O_4$ used as a rodent poison and in medicine

war footing *n* **:** the condition of being prepared to undertake or maintain war

war game *n* **1 :** a simulated battle or campaign to test military concepts and usu. conducted in conferences by officers acting as the opposing staffs **2 :** a two-sided umpired training maneuver with actual elements of the armed forces participating

war gas *n* **:** a gas for use in warfare

war hawk *n* **:** one who clamors for war; *esp* **:** an American jingo favoring war with Britain around 1812

war·head \ˈwȯ(ə)r-ˌhed\ *n* **:** the section of a missile (as a torpedo) containing the explosive, chemical, or incendiary charge

war–horse \-ˌhȯ(ə)rs\ *n* **1 :** a horse used in war **:** CHARGER **2 :** a veteran soldier or public person (as a politician) **3 :** a work of art (as a musical composition) that from much repetition as part of the standard repertory has become hackneyed

war·i·ly \ˈwar-ə-lē, ˈwer-\ *adv* **:** in a wary manner **:** CAUTIOUSLY

war·i·ness \ˈwar-ē-nəs, ˈwer-\ *n* **:** the quality or state of being wary

war·i·son \ˈwar-ə-sən\ *n* [prob. a misunderstanding by Sir Walter Scott in the *Lay of the Last Minstrel* (1805) of ME *waryson* reward, fr. ONF *warison* defense, possessions, fr. *warir* to protect, provide, of Gmc origin; akin to OHG *werien* to defend — more at WEIR] **:** a bugle call to attack

war·less \ˈwȯr-ləs\ *adj* **:** free from war

war·like \ˈwȯ(ə)r-ˌlīk\ *adj* **1** *obs* **:** ready for war **:** equipped to fight **2 :** fit for, disposed to, or fond of war **:** BELLICOSE **3 :** of, relating to, or useful in war **:** MARTIAL **4 :** befitting or characteristic of war or a soldier **syn** see MARTIAL

war·lock \-ˌläk\ *n* [ME *warloghe*, fr. OE *wǣrloga* one that breaks faith, the Devil, fr. *wǣr* faith, troth + *-loga* (fr. *lēogan* to lie); akin to OE *wǣr* true — more at VERY, LIE] **1 :** one given to black magic **:** SORCERER **2 :** CONJUROR

war·lord \-ˌlȯ(ə)rd\ *n* **1 :** a supreme military leader **2 :** a military commander exercising civil power by force usu. in a limited area

[1]warm \ˈwȯ(ə)rm\ *adj* [ME, fr. OE *wearm;* akin to OHG *warm* warm, L *formus*, Gk *thermos* warm, hot] **1 a :** having heat to a moderate degree **b :** having the heat appropriate to a living warm-blooded animal **c :** sending or giving out heat **:** WARMING **d :** tending to maintain or preserve heat esp. to a satisfactory degree ⟨a ~ sweater⟩ **e** (1) **:** feeling or causing sensations of heat brought about by strenuous exertion (2) **:** ready for action after preliminary exercise **2 :** comfortably established **:** SECURE **3 a :** ARDENT, ZEALOUS **b :** marked by excitement, disagreement, temper, or anger **4 a** 1) **:** readily showing or reacting to love, affection, or gratitude (2) **:** giving rise to a feeling of love, tenderness, or well-being **b :** AMOROUS, PASSIONATE **5 :** accompanied or marked by extreme danger, duress, or pain **6 a :** newly made **:** FRESH ⟨a ~ scent⟩ **b :** near to a goal **7 :** having the color or tone of something that imparts heat; *specif* **:** of a hue in the range yellow through orange to red — **warm·ly** *adv* — **warm·ness** *n*

[2]warm *vt* **1 :** to make warm **2 a :** to infuse with a feeling of love, friendship, well-being, or pleasure **b :** to fill with anger, zeal, or passion **c :** to impart life, color, or zest to **3 :** to reheat (cooked food) for eating — often used with *over* **4 :** to make ready for operation or performance by preliminary exercise or operation — often used with *up* ~ *vi* **1 :** to become warm **2 a :** to become ardent or interested **b :** to become filled with affection or love — used with *to* or *toward* **3 :** to experience feelings of pleasure **:** BASK **4 :** to become ready for operation or performance by preliminary activity

[3]warm *adv* **:** WARMLY — usu. used in combination ⟨*warm*-clad⟩ ⟨*warm*-tinted⟩

warm–blood·ed \-ˈbləd-əd\ *adj* **1 :** having warm blood; *specif* **:** having a relatively high and constant body temperature relatively independent of the surroundings **2 :** fervent or ardent in spirit — **warm–blood·ed·ness** *n*

warmed–over \ˈwȯrm-ˈdō-vər\ *adj* **:** REHEATED ⟨*warmed-over* cabbage⟩

warm·er \ˈwȯr-mər\ *n* **:** one that warms; *esp* **:** a device for keeping warm ⟨foot ~⟩

warm front *n* **:** an advancing edge of a warm air mass

warm·heart·ed \ˈwȯ(ə)rm-ˈhärt-əd\ *adj* **:** marked by warmth of feeling — **warm·heart·ed·ness** *n*

warming pan *n* **:** a long-handled covered pan filled with live coals used to warm a bed

warm·ish \ˈwȯr-mish\ *adj* **:** somewhat warm

war·mon·ger \ˈwȯ(ə)r-ˌməŋ-gər, -ˌmäŋ-\ *n* **:** one who stirs up war **:** JINGO — **war·mon·ger·ing** \-g(ə-)riŋ\ *n*

warm spot *n* **1 :** a cutaneous sensory end organ that is stimulated by an increase of temperature **2 :** a lasting affection for a particular person or object

warmth \ˈwȯ(ə)rm(p)th\ *n* **1 :** the quality or state of being warm in temperature **2 :** emotional intensity (as passion, anger, or love) **3 :** a glowing effect such as is produced by the use of warm colors

warm up *vi* **1 :** to engage in exercise or practice esp. before entering a game or contest **2 :** to approach a state of violence, conflict, or danger

warm–up \ˈwȯr-ˌməp\ *n* **:** the act or an instance of warming up; *also* **:** a procedure (as a set of exercises) used in warming up

warn \ˈwȯ(ə)rn\ *vb* [ME *warnen*, fr. OE *warnian;* akin to OHG *warnōn* to take heed, OE *wær* careful, aware — more at WARY] *vt* **1 a :** to give notice to beforehand esp. of danger or evil **b :** ADMONISH, COUNSEL **c :** to notify or apprise esp. in advance **:** INFORM **2 :** to bid to go or leave ~ *vi* **:** to give a warning — **warn·er** \ˈwȯr-nər\ *n*

syn FOREWARN, CAUTION: WARN may range in meaning from simple notification of something to be watched for or guarded against to admonition or threats of violence or reprisal; FOREWARN heightens the implication of notifying well in advance of impending danger or peril; CAUTION stresses giving advice that puts one on guard or suggests the need of precaution

[1]warn·ing \ˈwȯr-niŋ\ *n* **1 :** the act of warning **:** the state of being warned ⟨he had ~ of his illness⟩ **2 :** something that warns or serves to warn

[2]warning *adj* **:** serving as an alarm, signal, summons, or admonition ⟨~ bell⟩ ⟨~ shot⟩ — **warn·ing·ly** \-niŋ-lē\ *adv*

warning coloration *n* **:** a conspicuous coloration possessed by an animal otherwise defended

war of nerves : a conflict characterized by psychological tactics (as bluff, threats, and intimidation) designed primarily to create confusion, indecision, or breakdown of morale

[1]warp \ˈwȯ(ə)rp\ *n* [ME, fr. OE *wearp;* akin to OHG *warf* warp, ON *verpa* to throw] **1 a** (1) **:** a series of yarns extended lengthwise in a loom and crossed by the woof (2) **:** the cords forming the carcass of a pneumatic tire **b :** FOUNDATION, BASE **2 :** a rope for warping a ship or boat **3 :** a bed or layer of deposited sediment **4** [[2]*warp*] **a :** the state or fact of being out of true in plane or line; *also* **:** an instance of warping ⟨a ~ in a door panel⟩ **b :** a mental twist or aberration

[2]warp *vb* [ME *warpen*, fr. OE *weorpan* to throw; akin to ON *verpa* to throw, Gk *rhembein* to whirl] *vt* **1 a :** to turn or twist out of shape; *esp* **:** to twist or bend out of a plane **b :** to cause to judge, choose, or act wrongly **:** PERVERT **c :** FALSIFY, DISTORT **d :** to deflect from a course **2** [ME *warpen*, fr. [1]*warp*] **:** to arrange (yarns) so as to form a warp **3** [[1]*warp*] **:** to move (as a ship) by hauling on a line attached to a fixed object ~ *vi* **1 :** to become warped **2** *of a ship* **:** to become moved by warping **syn** see DEFORM — **warp·er** *n*

war paint *n* **1 :** paint put on parts of the body (as the face) by American Indians as a token of going to war **2 :** ceremonial or official dress **:** REGALIA **3 :** MAKEUP 3a

warp and woof *n* **:** WARP 1b ⟨the vigorous Anglo-Saxon base had become the *warp and woof* of English speech —H.R. Warfel⟩

war party *n* **1 :** a group of No. American Indians on the warpath **2 :** a usu. jingoist political party advocating or upholding a war

war·path \ˈwȯ(ə)r-ˌpath, -ˌpȧth\ *n* **1 :** the route taken by a party of American Indians going on a warlike expedition **2 :** a hostile course of action or frame of mind

warp beam *n* **:** a roll on which warp is wound for a loom

war·plane \ˈwȯ(ə)r-ˌplān\ *n* **:** a military airplane; *esp* **:** one for combat

war power *n* **:** the power to make war; *specif* **:** an extraordinary power exercised usu. by the executive branch of a government in the prosecution of a war

[1]war·rant \ˈwȯr-ənt, ˈwär-\ *n* [ME, protector, warrant, fr. ONF *warant*, modif. of a Gmc noun represented by OHG *werēnto* guarantor, fr. prp. of *werēn* to warrant; akin to OHG *wāra* trust, care — more at VERY] **1 a** (1) **:** SANCTION, AUTHORIZATION; *also* **:** evidence for or token of authorization (2) **:** GUARANTEE, SECURITY **b** (1) **:** GROUND, JUSTIFICATION (2) **:** CONFIRMATION, PROOF **2 a :** a commission or document giving authority to do something; *specif* **:** a writing that authorizes a person to pay or deliver to another and the other to receive money or other consideration **b :** a precept or writ issued by a competent magistrate authorizing an officer to make an arrest, a seizure, or a search or to do other acts incident to the administration of justice **c :** an official certificate of appointment issued to an officer of lower rank than a commissioned officer **d** (1) **:** a short-term obligation of a municipality or other governmental body issued in anticipation of revenue (2) **:** an instrument issued by a corporation giving to the holder the right to subscribe to the capital stock of the corporation at a fixed price either for a limited period or perpetually

[2]warrant *vt* [ME *warranten*, fr. ONF *warantir*, fr. *warant*] **1 a :** to declare or maintain with certainty **b :** to assure (a person) of the truth of what is said **2 a :** to guarantee to a person good title to and undisturbed possession of (as an estate) **b :** to provide a guarantee of the security of (as title to property sold) usu. by an express covenant in the deed of conveyance **c :** to guarantee to be as represented **d :** to guarantee (as goods sold) esp. in respect of the quality or quantity specified **3 :** to guarantee security or immunity to **:** SECURE **4 :** to give warrant or sanction to **:** AUTHORIZE ⟨the law ~*s* this procedure⟩ **5 a :** to give proof of **:** ATTEST **b :** to give assurance of the nature of or for the undertaking of **:** GUARANTEE **6 :** to serve as or give ground or reason for **:** JUSTIFY

war·rant·able \-ənt-ə-bəl\ *adj* **:** capable of being warranted **:** JUSTIFIABLE — **war·rant·able·ness** \-bəl-nəs\ *n* — **war·rant·ably** \-blē\ *adv*

war·ran·tee \ˌwȯr-ən-ˈtē, ˌwär-\ *n* **:** the person to whom a warranty is made

war·rant·er \ˈwȯr-ənt-ər, ˈwär-\ *n* **:** WARRANTOR

warrant officer *n* **:** an officer in the army, air force, navy, or marine corps ranking below a commissioned officer and above a noncommissioned officer and holding a warrant from the president

war·ran·tor \ˌwȯr-ən-ˈtȯ(ə)r, ˌwär-; ˈwȯr-ənt-ər, ˈwär-\ *n* **:** one that warrants or gives a warranty

war·ran·ty \ˈwȯr-ənt-ē, ˈwär-\ *n* [ME *warantie*, fr. ONF, fr. *warantir* to warrant] **1 a :** a real covenant binding the grantor of an estate and his heirs to warrant and defend the title **b :** a collateral undertaking that a fact regarding the subject of a contract is or will be as it is expressly or by implication declared or promised to be **2 :** something that authorizes, sanctions, supports, or justifies **:** WARRANT **3 :** a usu. written guarantee of the integrity of a product and of the maker's responsibility for the repair or replacement of defective parts

warranty deed *n* **:** a deed warranting that the grantor has a good title free and clear of all liens and encumbrances and will defend the grantee against all claims

war·ren \ˈwȯr-ən, ˈwär-\ *n* [ME *warenne*, fr. ONF] **1 a :** a place legally authorized for keeping small game (as hare or pheasant) **b :** the privilege of hunting game in such a warren **2 a :** an area esp. of uncultivated ground where rabbits breed **b :** the rabbits of a warren **3 :** a crowded tenement or district

war·ren·er \-ə-nər\ *n* **1 :** GAMEKEEPER **2 :** one that maintains a rabbit warren

war·rior \ˈwȯr-yər, ˈwȯr-ē-ər, ˈwär-ē- *also* ˈwär-yər\ *n, often attrib* [ME *werriour*, fr. ONF *werreieur*, fr. *werreier* to make war, fr. *werre* war] **:** a man engaged or experienced in warfare

war risk insurance *n* **:** term insurance written by the government for members of the military and naval forces

war·saw \ˈwȯr-(ˌ)sȯ\ *n* [modif. of AmerSp *guasa*] **:** a large grouper (esp. *Garrupa nigrita*)

war·ship \ˈwȯ(ə)r-ˌship\ *n* **:** a government ship employed for war purposes; *esp* **:** one armed for combat

war·sle *or* **wars·tle** \ˈwä(r)s-əl\ *vb* [ME *werstelen, warstelen*, alter. of *wrestlen, wrastlen*] *Scot* **:** WRESTLE, STRUGGLE — **warsle** *n, Scot*

wart \ˈwȯ(ə)rt\ *n* [ME, fr. OE *wearte*; akin to OHG *warza* wart, L *verruca*] **1 a :** a horny projection on the skin usu. of the extremities caused by a virus — called also *ver·ru·ca vul·ga·ris* \və-ˌrü-kə-ˌvəl-ˈgar-əs, -ˈger-\ **b :** any of numerous similar skin lesions **2 :** an excrescence or protuberance resembling a true wart; *specif* **:** a glandular excrescence or hardened protuberance on a plant — **wart·ed** \ˈwȯrt-əd\ *adj* — **warty** \ˈwȯrt-ē\ *adj*

wart·hog \ˈwȯ(ə)rt-ˌhȯg, -ˌhäg\ *n* **:** any of a genus (*Phacochoerus*) of African wild hogs with two pairs of rough warty excrescences on the face and large protruding tusks

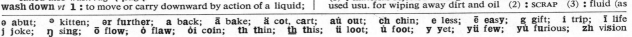

warthog

war·time \ˈwȯ(ə)r-ˌtīm\ *n, often attrib* **:** a period during which a war is in progress

war vessel *n* **:** WARSHIP

war whoop *n* **:** a war cry esp. of American Indians

wary \ˈwa(ə)r-ē, ˈwe(ə)r-\ *adj* [¹*ware*, fr. ME *war, ware*, fr. OE *wær* careful, aware, wary; akin to OHG *giwar* aware, attentive, L *vereri* to fear, Gk *horan* to see] **:** marked by keen caution, cunning, and watchful prudence in detecting and escaping danger **syn** see CAUTIOUS

war zone *n* **1 :** a zone in which belligerents are conducting hostile operations during a war **2 :** a designated area esp. on the high seas within which rights of neutrals are not respected by a belligerent nation in time of war

was [ME, fr. OE, 1st & 3d sing. past indic. of *wesan* to be; akin to ON *vera* to be, *var* was, Skt *vasati* he lives, dwells] *past 1st & 3d sing of* BE

¹wash \ˈwȯsh, ˈwäsh\ *vb* [ME *washen*, fr. OE *wascan*; akin to OHG *waskan* to wash, OE *wæter* water] *vt* **1 a :** to cleanse by or as if by the action of liquid (as water) **b :** to remove (as dirt) by rubbing or drenching with liquid **2 :** to cleanse (fur) by licking or by rubbing with a paw moistened with saliva **3 a :** to flush or moisten (a bodily part or injury) with a liquid **b** (1) **:** to wet thoroughly **:** SATURATE (2) **:** OVERSPREAD **:** SUFFUSE **c :** to pass water over or through esp. so as to carry off material from the surface or interior **4 :** to flow along or dash or overflow against **:** LAVE **5 :** to move, carry, or deposit by or as if by the force of water in motion **6 a :** to subject (as crushed ore) to the action of water to separate valuable material **b :** to separate (particles) from a substance (as ore) by agitation with or in water **c** (1) **:** to pass through a bath to carry off impurities or soluble components (2) **:** to pass (a gas or gaseous mixture) through or over a liquid to purify it esp. by removing soluble components **7 a :** to cover or daub lightly with or as if with an application of a thin liquid (as whitewash or varnish) **b :** to depict or paint by a broad sweep of thin color with a brush **8 :** to cause to swirl **~** *vi* **1 :** to wash oneself or a part of one's body **2 :** to become worn away by the action of water **3 :** to clean something by rubbing or dipping in water **4 a :** to become carried or floated along on water **:** DRIFT **b :** to pour, sweep, or flow in a stream or current **5 :** to serve as a cleansing agent **6 a :** to undergo laundering without damage **b :** to move with a lapping or splashing sound

²wash *n* **1 a :** the act or process or an instance of washing or being washed **b :** articles to be washed or being washed **2 :** the surging action of waves or its sound **3 a :** a piece of ground washed by the sea or river **b :** BOG, MARSH **c :** a shallow body of water or creek **d** *West* **:** the dry bed of a stream — called also *dry wash* **4 :** worthless esp. liquid waste **:** REFUSE **5 a :** an insipid beverage **b :** vapid writing or speech **6 a :** a sweep or splash esp. of color made by or as if by a long stroke of a brush **b :** a thin coat of paint (as watercolor) **c :** a thin liquid used for coating a surface (as a wall) **7 :** LOTION 2 **8 :** loose or eroded surface material of the earth (as rock debris) transported and deposited by running water **9 a :** BACKWASH 1 **b :** a disturbance in the air produced by the passage of an airfoil or propeller

³wash *adj* **:** WASHABLE

wash·able \ˈwȯsh-ə-bəl, ˈwäsh-\ *adj* **:** capable of being washed without damage

wash and wear *adj* **:** of, relating to, or constituting a fabric or garment not needing to be ironed after washing

wash·ba·sin \ˈwȯsh-ˌbās-ᵊn, ˈwäsh-\ *n* **:** WASHBOWL

wash·board \ˈwȯsh-ˌbō(ə)rd, ˈwäsh-, -ˌbȯ(ə)rd\ *n, often attrib* **1 :** a broad thin plank along a gunwale or on the sill of a lower deck port to keep out the sea **2 :** BASEBOARD **3 a :** a corrugated rectangular surface to scrub clothes on **b :** a road or pavement so worn by traffic as to be corrugated transversely

wash·bowl \-ˌbōl\ *n* **:** a large bowl for water to wash one's hands and face

wash·cloth \-ˌklȯth\ *n* **:** a cloth for washing one's face and body — called also *wash·rag* \-ˌrag\

wash down *vt* **1 :** to move or carry downward by action of a liquid; *specif* **:** to facilitate the passage of (food) down the gullet with accompanying swallows of liquid **2 :** to wash the whole length or extent of ⟨*washed down* and scrubbed the front porch⟩

wash drawing *n* **:** water-color painting in or chiefly in washes esp. in black, white, and gray tones only

washed–out \ˈwȯsh-ˈtau̇t, ˈwäsh-\ *adj* **1 :** faded in color **2 :** depleted in vigor or animation **:** EXHAUSTED

washed–up \-ˈtəp\ *adj* **1 :** left with no effective power and no capacity or opportunity for recovery **2** *usu* **washed up :** ready to quit esp. from disgust **:** THROUGH

wash·er \ˈwȯsh-ər, ˈwäsh-\ *n* **1 :** one that washes; *specif* **:** WASHING MACHINE **2 :** a flat thin ring or a perforated plate used in joints or assemblies to ensure tightness, prevent leakage, or relieve friction

wash·er·man \-mən\ *n* **:** LAUNDRYMAN — **wash·er·wom·an** \-ˌwu̇m-ən\ *n*

wash·house \ˈwȯsh-ˌhau̇s, ˈwäsh-\ *n* **:** a house or building used or equipped for washing; *esp* **:** one for washing clothes

wash·ing \ˈwȯsh-iŋ, ˈwäsh-\ *n* **1 :** material obtained by washing **2 :** a thin covering or coat ⟨a **~** of silver⟩ **3 :** articles washed or to be washed **:** WASH

washing machine *n* **:** a machine for washing; *specif* **:** one for washing clothes and household linen

washing soda *n* **:** hydrated sodium carbonate

Wash·ing·ton pie \ˌwȯsh-iŋ-tən-, ˌwäsh-\ *n* [George *Washington* †1799] **:** cake layers put together with a jam or jelly filling

Washington's Birthday *n* [George *Washington* †1799 first president of the U.S.] **:** February 22 observed as a legal holiday in most of the states of the U.S.

wash out *vt* **1 :** to wash free of an extraneous substance (as dirt) **2 a :** to drain the color from in laundering **b :** to deplete the strength or vitality of **c :** to eliminate as useless or unsatisfactory **3 a:** to destroy or make useless by the force or action of water ⟨the storm *washed out* the bridge⟩ **b :** to rain out ⟨the game was *washed out*⟩ **~** *vi* **1 :** to become depleted of color or vitality **:** FADE **2 :** to fail to meet requirements or measure up to a standard

wash·out \ˈwȯsh-ˌau̇t, ˈwäsh-\ *n* **1 :** the washing out or away of earth esp. in a roadbed by a freshet; *also* **:** a place where earth is washed away **2 :** one that fails to measure up **:** FAILURE; *specif* **:** one who fails in a course of training or study

wash·room \-ˌrüm, -ˌru̇m\ *n* **:** a room equipped with washing and toilet facilities **:** LAVATORY

wash·stand \ˈwȯsh-ˌ(s)tand, ˈwäsh-\ *n* **1 :** a stand holding articles needed for washing one's face and hands **2 :** a washbowl permanently set in place and attached to water and drainpipes

wash·tub \-ˌtəb\ *n* **:** a tub in which clothes are washed or soaked

wash up *vi* **1 :** to wash one's face and hands **2** *Brit* **:** to wash the dishes after a meal **~** *vt* **1 :** to get rid of by washing ⟨*wash up* the spilled milk⟩ **2 :** EXHAUST, FINISH

wash·wom·an \ˈwȯsh-ˌwu̇m-ən, ˈwäsh-\ *n* **:** WASHERWOMAN

washy \ˈwȯsh-ē, ˈwäsh-\ *adj* **1 a :** WEAK, WATERY **b :** deficient in color **:** PALLID **c :** lacking in vigor, individuality, or definiteness **2 :** lacking in condition and in firmness of flesh

wasn't \ˈwəz-ᵊnt, ˈwäz-\ **:** was not

¹wasp \ˈwäsp, ˈwȯsp\ *n* [ME *waspe*, fr. OE *wæps, wæsp*; akin to OHG *wafsa* wasp, L *vespa* wasp, OE *wefan* to weave — more at WEAVE] **1 :** any of numerous social or solitary winged hymenopterous insects that usu. have a slender smooth body with the abdomen attached by a narrow stalk, well-developed wings, biting mouthparts, and in the females and workers an often formidable sting, and that are largely carnivorous and often provision their nests with caterpillars, insects, or spiders killed or paralyzed by stinging for their larvae to feed on — compare BEE **2 :** any of various hymenopterous insects with larvae that are parasitic on other arthropods

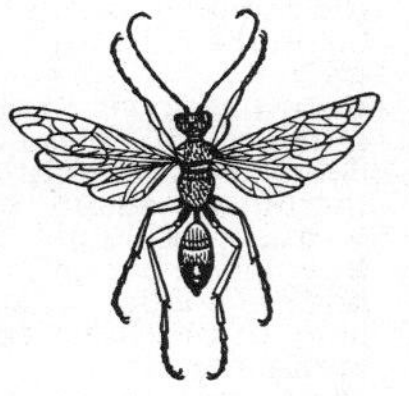
wasp

²wasp *n, often cap W or all cap* [white *A*nglo-*S*axon *P*rotestant] **:** an American of English Protestant ancestral background

wasp·ish \ˈwäs-pish, ˈwȯs-\ *adj* **1 :** resembling a wasp in behavior; *esp* **:** SNAPPISH, PETULANT **2 :** resembling a wasp in form; *esp* **:** slightly built — **wasp·ish·ly** *adv* — **wasp·ish·ness** *n*

wasp waist *n* **:** a very slender waist

¹was·sail \ˈwäs-əl, wä-ˈsā(ə)l\ *n* [ME *wæs hæil*, fr. ON *ves heill* be well, fr. *ves* (imper. sing. of *vera* to be) + *heill* healthy — more at WAS, WHOLE] **1 :** an early English toast to someone's health **2 :** a liquor formerly drunk in England on festive occasions (as at Christmas) and made of ale or wine with spices and other ingredients (as sugar, toast, or roasted apples) **3 :** riotous drinking **:** REVELRY

²wassail *vi* **1 :** to hold a wassail **:** CAROUSE **2** *dial Eng* **:** to sing carols from house to house at Christmas **~** *vt* **:** to drink to the health or thriving of

was·sail·er \ˈwäs-ə-lər, wä-ˈsā-lər\ *n* **1 :** one that carouses **:** REVELER **2** *archaic* **:** one who goes about singing carols

Was·ser·mann reaction \ˈwäs-ər-mən-; ˈväs-ər-ˌmän-, -ˌmän-\ *n* [August von *Wassermann* †1925 G bacteriologist] **:** a complement-fixing reaction occurring with the serum of syphilitic patients and used as a test for syphilis

Wassermann test *n* **:** a test for the detection of syphilitic infection using the Wassermann reaction

wast \wəst, (ˈ)wäst\ *archaic past 2d sing of* BE

wast·age \ˈwā-stij\ *n* **:** loss by use, decay, erosion, or leakage or through wastefulness

¹waste \ˈwāst\ *n* [ME *waste, wast*; in sense 1, fr. ONF *wast*, fr. *wast*, adj., desolate, waste, fr. L *vastus*; akin to OHG *wuosti* desolate, waste, L *vanus* empty; in other senses, fr. ME *wasten* to waste — more at WANE] **1 a :** a sparsely settled or barren region **:** DESERT **b :** uncultivated land **c :** a broad and empty expanse (as of water) **2 :** the act or an instance of wasting **:** the state of being wasted **3 a :** loss through breaking down of bodily tissue **b :** gradual loss or decrease by use, wear, or decay **4 a :** damaged, defective, or superfluous material produced by a manufacturing process: as (1) **:** material rejected during a textile manufacturing process and used usu. for wiping away dirt and oil (2) **:** SCRAP (3) **:** fluid (as

steam) allowed to escape without being utilized **b :** refuse from places of human or animal habitation: as (1) **:** GARBAGE, RUBBISH (2) *pl* **:** EXCREMENT (3) **:** SEWAGE **c :** material derived by mechanical and chemical weathering of the land and moved down sloping surfaces or carried by streams to the sea

2**waste** *vb* [ME *wasten*, fr. ONF *waster*, fr. L *vastare*, fr. *vastus* desolate, waste] *vt* **1 :** to lay waste **:** DEVASTATE **2 :** to cause to shrink in physical bulk or strength **:** EMACIATE, ENFEEBLE **3 :** to wear away or diminish gradually **:** CONSUME **4 a :** to spend or use carelessly **:** SQUANDER **b :** to allow to be used inefficiently or become dissipated ~ *vi* **1 :** to lose weight, strength, or vitality — often used with *away* **2 a :** to become diminished in bulk or substance **b :** to become consumed **3 :** to spend money or consume property extravagantly or improvidently **syn** see RAVAGE

3**waste** *adj* [ME *waste, wast*, fr. ONF *wast*] **1 a** (1) **:** being wild and uninhabited **:** DESOLATE (2) **:** ARID, EMPTY **b :** UNCULTIVATED, UNPRODUCTIVE **2 :** RUINED, DEVASTATED **3** [1*waste*] **:** discarded as worthless, defective, or of no use **:** REFUSE ⟨~ power⟩ **4** [1*waste*] **:** serving to conduct or hold refuse material; *specif* **:** carrying off superfluous water

waste·bas·ket \'wās(t)-,bas-kət\ *n* **:** a receptacle for unwanted odds and ends esp. of wastepaper

wast·ed *adj* **1 :** laid waste **:** RAVAGED **2 :** impaired in strength or health **:** EMACIATED **3** *obs* **:** ELAPSED ⟨the chronicle of ~ time —Shak.⟩ **4 :** unprofitably used, made, or expended ⟨~ effort⟩

waste·ful \'wāst-fəl\ *adj* **:** given to or marked by waste **:** LAVISH, PRODIGAL — **waste·ful·ly** \-fə-lē\ *adv* — **waste·ful·ness** *n*

waste·land \'wāst-,land\ *n* **:** barren or uncultivated land

waste·ness \'wās(t)-nəs\ *n* **:** DESOLATION, BARRENNESS

waste·pa·per \'wās(t)-'pā-pər\ *n* **:** paper discarded as used, superfluous, or not fit for use

waste pipe *n* **:** a pipe for carrying off waste fluid

waste product *n* **1 :** debris resulting from a process (as of manufacture) that is of no further use to the system producing it **2 :** material discharged from or stored in an inert form in a living body as a by-product of its vital activities

wast·er \'wā-stər\ *n* **1 a** (1) **:** one that spends or consumes extravagantly **:** SPENDTHRIFT (2) **:** a dissolute person **:** WASTREL **b :** one that uses wastefully or causes or permits waste ⟨a procedure that is a ~ of time⟩ **c :** one that lays waste **:** DESTROYER **2 :** an imperfect or inferior manufactured article or object

wast·ing \'wā-stiŋ\ *adj* **1 :** laying waste **:** DEVASTATING **2 :** causing decay or loss of strength — **wast·ing·ly** \-stiŋ-lē\ *adv*

wast·rel \'wā-strəl\ *n* [irreg. fr. 2*waste*] **1 a :** PROFLIGATE **b :** VAGABOND, WAIF **2 :** SPENDTHRIFT, WASTER

wast·ry \'wā-strē\ *n*, *Scot* **:** PRODIGALITY, WASTE

1**watch** \'wäch\ *vb* [ME *wacchen*, fr. OE *wæccan* — more at WAKE] *vi* **1 a :** to keep vigil as a devotional exercise **b :** to be awake during the night **2 a :** to be attentive or vigilant **b :** to keep guard **3 a :** to keep someone or something under close observation **b :** to observe as a spectator **4 :** to be expectant **:** WAIT ~ *vt* **1 :** to keep under guard **2 a :** to observe closely in order to check on action or change **b :** to look at **:** OBSERVE **c :** to look on at **3 a :** to take care of **:** TEND **b :** to be careful of ⟨~*es* his diet⟩ **4 :** to be on the alert for **:** BIDE **syn** see SEE

2**watch** *n* **1 a :** the act of keeping awake to guard, protect, or attend **b** *obs* **:** WAKEFULNESS **c :** WAKE **d :** a state of alert and continuous attention **e :** close observation **:** SURVEILLANCE **2 a :** any of the definite divisions of the night made by ancient peoples **b :** one of the indeterminate wakeful intervals marking the passage of night — usu. used in pl. **3 a :** one that watches **:** LOOKOUT, WATCHMAN **b** *archaic* **:** the office or function of a sentinel or guard **4 a :** a body of soldiers or sentinels making up a guard **b :** a watchman or body of watchmen formerly assigned to patrol the streets of a town at night, announce the hours, and act as police **5 a** (1) **:** a portion of time during which a part of a ship's company is on duty (2) **:** the part of a ship's company required to be on duty during a particular watch (3) **:** a sailor's assigned duty period **b :** a period of duty **:** SHIFT **6 a :** a portable timepiece that has a movement driven in any of several ways (as by a spring or a battery) and is designed to be worn (as on the wrist) or carried in the pocket — compare CLOCK **b :** a ship's chronometer

watch·band \-,band\ *n* **:** the bracelet or strap of a wristwatch

watch cap *n* **:** a knitted close-fitting navy-blue cap worn esp. by enlisted men in the U. S. navy in cold or stormy weather

watch·case \'wäch-,kās\ *n* **:** the outside metal covering of a watch

1**watch·dog** \-,dȯg\ *n* **1 :** a dog kept to guard property **2 :** one that guards against loss, waste, theft, or undesirable practices

2**watchdog** *vt* **:** to act as a watchdog for

watch·er \'wäch-ər\ *n* **:** one that watches: as **a :** one that sits up or continues awake at night **b :** WATCHMAN **c** (1) **:** one that keeps watch beside a dead person (2) **:** one that attends a sick person at night **d :** OBSERVER, VIEWER **e :** a representative of a party or candidate stationed at the polls on an election day to watch the conduct of officials and voters

watch·eye \'wäch-,ī\ *n* **:** WALLEYE 1; *esp* **:** a walleye of a dog

watch fire *n* **:** a fire lighted as a signal or for the use of a guard

watch·ful \'wäch-fəl\ *adj* **1** *archaic* **a :** WAKEFUL **b :** causing sleeplessness **c :** SLEEPLESS **2 :** marked by vigilance **:** VIGILANT, ATTENTIVE — **watch·ful·ly** \-fə-lē\ *adv* — **watch·ful·ness** *n*

syn WATCHFUL, VIGILANT, WIDE-AWAKE, ALERT mean being on the lookout esp. for danger or opportunity. WATCHFUL is the least explicit term; VIGILANT suggests keen, unremitting, wary watchfulness; WIDE-AWAKE applies to watchfulness for opportunities more often than dangers and suggests awareness of relevant developments and situations; ALERT stresses readiness or promptness in apprehending and meeting danger or emergency or in seizing opportunity

watch·mak·er \'wäch-,mā-kər\ *n* **:** one that makes or repairs watches or clocks — **watch·mak·ing** \-kiŋ\ *n*

watch·man \-mən\ *n* **:** one who keeps watch **:** GUARD

watch night *n* **:** a devotional service lasting until after midnight esp. on New Year's Eve

watch out *vi* **:** to be vigilant **:** look out — often used with *for* ⟨*watch out* for speeding cars⟩

watch·tow·er \'wäch-,tau̇(-ə)r\ *n* **:** a tower for a lookout

watch·word \-,wərd\ *n* **1 :** a word or phrase used as a sign of recognition among members of the same society, class, or group **2 :** a motto that embodies a principle or guide to action of an individual or group **:** SLOGAN

1**wa·ter** \'wȯt-ər, 'wät-\ *n*, *often attrib* [ME, fr. OE *wæter;* akin to OHG *wazzar* water, Gk *hydōr*, L *unda* wave] **1 a :** the liquid that descends from the clouds as rain, forms streams, lakes, and seas, and is a major constituent of all living matter and that is an odorless, tasteless, very slightly compressible liquid oxide of hydrogen H_2O which appears bluish in thick layers, freezes at 0° C and boils at 100° C, has a maximum density at 4° C and a high specific heat, is feebly ionized to hydrogen and hydroxyl ions, and is a poor conductor of electricity and a good solvent **b :** a natural mineral water — usu. used in pl. **2 a** (1) *pl* **:** the water occupying or flowing in a particular bed (2) *chiefly Brit* **:** LAKE, POND **b :** a quantity or depth of water adequate for some purpose (as navigation) **c** *pl* (1) **:** a band of seawater abutting on the land of a particular sovereignty and under the control of that sovereignty (2) **:** the sea of a particular part of the earth **3 :** travel or transportation on water **4 :** the level of water at a particular state of the tide **:** TIDE **5 :** liquid containing or resembling water: as **a** (1) **:** a pharmaceutical or cosmetic preparation made with water (2) **:** a watery solution of a gaseous or readily volatile substance — compare AMMONIA WATER **b** *archaic* **:** a distilled fluid (as an essence); *esp* **:** a distilled alcoholic liquor **c :** a watery fluid (as tears, urine, or sap) formed or circulating in a living body **6 a :** the limpidity and luster of a precious stone and esp. a diamond **b :** degree of excellence **c :** a wavy lustrous pattern (as of a textile) **7 :** WATERCOLOR **8 a :** capital stock not representing assets of the issuing company and not backed by earning power **b :** fictitious or exaggerated asset entries that give a stock an unrealistic book value — **above water :** out of difficulty — **in deep water :** in serious difficulties

2**water** *vt* **1 :** to moisten, sprinkle, or soak with water **2 :** to supply with water for drink **3 :** to supply water to **4 :** to treat with or as if with water; *specif* **:** to impart a lustrous appearance and wavy pattern to (cloth) by calendering **5 a :** to dilute by or as if by the addition of water **b :** to add to the aggregate par value of (securities) without a corresponding addition to the assets represented by the securities ~ *vi* **1 :** to form or secrete water or watery matter (as tears or saliva) **2 :** to get or take water: as **a :** to take on a supply of water **b :** to drink water

water back *n* **:** a water heater set in the firebox of a stove

water bag *n* **1 :** a bag for holding water; *esp* **:** one designed to keep water cool for drinking by evaporation through a slightly porous surface **2 a :** the reticulum of a camel or a closely related animal **b :** the fetal membranes enclosing the amniotic fluid

water ballet *n* **:** a synchronized sequence of evolutions performed by a group of swimmers

water beetle *n* **:** any of numerous oval flattened aquatic beetles (esp. family Dytiscidae) that swim by means of their fringed hind legs which act together as oars

water bird *n* **:** a swimming or wading bird — compare WATERFOWL

water biscuit *n* **:** a cracker of flour and water and sometimes fat

water blister *n* **:** a blister with a clear watery content that is not purulent or sanguineous

water bloom *n* **:** an accumulation of algae and esp. of blue-green algae at or near the surface of a body of water; *also* **:** an alga causing this

water boatman *n* **:** any of various aquatic bugs (family Corixidae) with one pair of legs modified into paddles

wa·ter·borne \'wȯt-ər-,bō(ə)rn, 'wät-, -,bȯ(ə)rn\ *adj* **:** supported or carried by water

water boy *n* **:** one who keeps a group (as of football players) supplied with drinking water

wa·ter·brain \-,brān\ *n* **:** GID

water brash \-,brash\ *n* [Sc *brash* an eruption of fluid] **:** combined salivation and acid regurgitation

wa·ter·buck \'wȯt-ər-,bək, 'wät-\ *n*, *pl* **waterbuck** *or* **waterbucks :** any of various Old World antelopes that commonly frequent streams or wet lands

water buffalo *n* **:** an often domesticated Asiatic buffalo (*Bubalus bubalis*)

water bug *n* **:** any of various small arthropods (as insects) that frequent water; *esp* **:** CROTON BUG

water chestnut *n* **1 :** any of a genus (*Trapa* and esp. *T. natans* and *T. bicornis*) of aquatic herbs of the evening-primrose family; *also* **:** its edible nutlike spiny-angled fruit — called also *water caltrop* **2 :** a Chinese sedge (*Eleocharis tuberosa*); *also* **:** its edible tuber

water chinquapin *n* **:** an American lotus (*Nelumbo lutea*); *also* **:** its edible seed that has the flavor of a chinquapin

water clock *n* **:** an instrument designed to measure time by the fall or flow of a quantity of water

water closet *n* **1 a :** a compartment or room for defecation and excretion into a hopper **:** BATHROOM **b :** the hopper and its accessories **2** *dial* **:** PRIVY

wa·ter·col·or \'wȯt-ər-,kəl-ər, 'wät-\ *n* **1 :** a paint of which the liquid is a water dispersion of the binding material (as glue, casein, or gum) **2 :** the art or method of painting with watercolors **3 :** a picture or design executed in watercolors — **watercolor** *adj* — **wa·ter·col·or·ist** \-,kəl-ə-rəst\ *n*

wa·ter–cool \,wȯt-ər-'kül, ,wät-\ *vt* **:** to cool by means of water and esp. circulating water (as in a water jacket)

wa·ter·course \'wȯt-ər-,kō(ə)rs, -,kȯ(ə)rs\ *n* **1 :** a natural or made channel through which water flows **2 :** a stream of water (as a river, brook, or underground stream)

wa·ter·craft \-,kraft\ *n* **1 :** skill in managing boats or in other aquatic activities **2 a :** SHIP, BOAT **b :** craft for water transport

water crake *n* **1 :** WATER OUZEL **2 :** any of several rails

wa·ter·cress \-,kres\ *n* **:** any of several water-loving cresses; *esp* **:** a perennial cress (*Nasturtium officinale*) found chiefly in springs or running water and used in salads or as a potherb

water cure *n* **:** HYDROPATHY, HYDROTHERAPY

water cycle *n* [*water* + *-cycle* (as in *bicycle*)] **:** any of various watercraft propelled by treadles

water dog *n* **1 :** a dog accustomed to the water and usu. trained to retrieve waterfowl **2 a :** OTTER **b :** a large salamander; *esp* **:** MUD PUPPY **3 :** a person (as a skilled sailor or seaman) who is quite at ease in or on water **4 :** a small cloud that is held to indicate the approach of rain

wa·ter·er \'wȯt-ər-ər, 'wät-\ *n* **:** one that waters: as **a :** a person who obtains or supplies drinking water **b :** a device used for supplying water to livestock and poultry

wa·ter·fall \'wȯt-ər-,fȯl, 'wät-\ *n* **:** a perpendicular or very steep descent of the water of a stream

wa·ter–fast \-,fast\ *adj* **1** *chiefly Scot* : WATERTIGHT **2** : not capable of being leached by water ⟨a ∼ dye⟩

water flea *n* : any of various small active dark or brightly colored aquatic entomostracan crustaceans (as of the genera *Cyclops* and *Daphnia*)

wa·ter·fowl \'wȯt-ər-,faùl, 'wät-\ *n* **1** : a bird that frequents water; *esp* : a swimming bird **2** *pl* : swimming game birds as distinguished from upland game birds and shorebirds

wa·ter·front \-,frənt\ *n, often attrib* : land, land with buildings, or a section of a town fronting or abutting on a body of water

water gap *n* : a pass in a mountain ridge through which a stream runs

water gas *n* : a poisonous flammable gaseous mixture that consists chiefly of carbon monoxide and hydrogen with small amounts of methane, carbon dioxide, and nitrogen, is usu. made by blowing air and then steam over red-hot coke or coal, and is used as a fuel and after carbureting as an illuminant

water gate *n* **1** : a gate (as of a building) giving access to a body of water **2** : FLOODGATE

water gauge *n* : an instrument to measure or find the depth or quantity of water or to indicate the height of its surface esp. in a steam boiler

water glass *n* **1** : WATER CLOCK **2** : a glass vessel (as a drinking glass) for holding water **3** : an instrument consisting of an open box or tube with a glass bottom used for examining objects in or under water **4** : a substance consisting usu. of sodium silicate but sometimes of potassium silicate or of both found in commerce as a glassy mass, a stony powder, or dissolved in water as a viscous syrupy liquid, and used esp. as a cement, as a protective coating and fireproofing agent, and in preserving eggs **5** : WATER GAUGE

water gum *n* : a gum tree (as a tupelo) that grows on wet land

water hammer *n* : a concussion or sound of concussion of moving water against the sides of a containing pipe or vessel (as a steam pipe)

water heater *n* : an apparatus for heating and usu. storing hot water (as for domestic use)

water hemlock *n* : any of several poisonous plants (genus *Cicuta*) of the carrot family; *esp* : a tall Eurasian perennial herb (*C. virosa*)

water hen *n* : any of various birds of the rail group (as a coot or gallinule)

water hole *n* **1** : a natural hole or hollow containing water **2** : a hole in a surface of ice

water hyacinth *n* : a floating aquatic plant (*Eichhornia crassipes* of the family Pontederiaceae) often clogging waterways in the southern U.S.

water ice *n* : a frozen dessert consisting of water, sugar, and flavoring

wa·ter–inch \,wȯt-ə-'rinch, ,wät-\ *n* : the discharge from a circular orifice one inch in diameter which is commonly estimated at 14 pints per minute and constitutes an old unit of hydraulic measure

wa·ter·i·ness \'wȯt-ə-rē-nəs, 'wät-\ *n* : the quality or state of being watery

watering place *n* **1** : a place where animals come to drink **2** : a place where water may be obtained **3** : a health or recreational resort featuring water activities

watering pot *n* : a vessel usu. with a spout used to sprinkle water esp. on plants — called also *watering can*

wa·ter·ish \'wȯt-ə-rish, 'wät-\ *adj* : somewhat watery — **wa·ter·ish·ness** *n*

water jacket *n* : an outer casing which holds water or through which water circulates to cool the interior; *specif* : the enclosed space surrounding the cylinder block of an internal-combustion engine and containing the cooling liquid

water jump *n* : an obstacle (as in a steeplechase) consisting of a pool, stream, or ditch of water

wa·ter·leaf \'wȯt-ər-,lēf, 'wät-\ *n, pl* **waterleafs** \-,lēfs\ : any of a genus (*Hydrophyllum* of the family Hydrophyllaceae, the waterleaf family) of perennial woodland herbs

wa·ter·less \-ləs\ *adj* **1** : destitute of water : DRY **2** : not requiring water (as for cooling or cooking) — **wa·ter·less·ly** *adv* — **wa·ter·less·ness** *n*

water level *n* **1** : an instrument to show the level by means of the surface of water in a trough or in a U-shaped tube **2** : the surface of still water: as **a** : the level assumed by the surface of a particular body or column of water **b** : the waterline of a vessel **c** : WATER TABLE 2

water lily *n* : any of a family (Nymphaeaceae, the water-lily family) of aquatic plants with floating leaves and usu. showy flowers; *broadly* : an aquatic plant (as a water hyacinth) with showy flowers

wa·ter·line \'wȯt-ər-,līn, 'wät-\ *n* : any of several lines that are marked upon the outside of a ship and correspond with the surface of the water when it is afloat on an even keel

wa·ter·log \-,lȯg, -,läg\ *vt* [back-formation fr. *waterlogged*] **1** : to make (as a boat) unmanageable by flooding **2** : to saturate with water to the point of sogginess or loss of buoyancy

water lily

wa·ter·logged \-,lȯgd, -,lägd\ *adj* ['*water* + *log* (to accumulate in the hold)] : so filled or soaked with water as to be heavy or hard to manage ⟨∼ boats⟩

wa·ter·loo \,wȯt-ər-'lü, ,wät-\ *n* [*Waterloo*, Belgium, scene of Napoleon's defeat in 1815] : a decisive defeat

water main *n* : a pipe or conduit for conveying water

wa·ter·man \'wȯt-ər-mən, 'wät-\ *n* : a man who lives and works mostly in or near water; *esp* : a boatman who plies for hire

wa·ter·man·ship \-,ship\ *n* : the business, skill, or art of a waterman: as **a** : expertness or technique in rowing **b** : expertness or technique in swimming

¹wa·ter·mark \'wȯt-ər-,märk, 'wät-\ *n* **1** : a mark indicating the height to which water has risen **2** : a marking in paper resulting from differences in thickness usu. produced by pressure of a projecting design in the mold or on a processing roll and visible when the paper is held up to the light; *also* : the design or the metal pattern producing the marking

²watermark *vt* **1** : to mark (paper) with a watermark **2** : to impress (a given design) as a watermark

wa·ter·mel·on \-,mel-ən\ *n* **1** : a large oblong or roundish fruit with a hard green or white rind often striped or variegated, a sweet watery pink, yellowish, or red pulp, and many seeds **2** : a widely grown African vine (*Citrullus vulgaris*) of the gourd family whose fruits are watermelons

water meter *n* : an instrument for recording the quantity of water passing through a particular outlet

water milfoil *n* : any of a genus (*Myriophyllum* of the family Haloragaceae) of aquatic plants with finely pinnate submersed leaves

water mill *n* : a mill whose machinery is moved by water

water moccasin *n* **1** : a venomous semiaquatic pit viper (*Agkistrodon piscivorus*) of the southern U.S. closely related to the copperhead **2** : a water snake (genus *Natrix*)

water nymph *n* : a goddess (as a naiad, Nereid, or Oceanid) associated with a body of water

water oak *n* : any of numerous American oaks that thrive in wet soils

water of crystallization : water of hydration present in many crystallized substances that is usu. essential for maintenance of a particular crystal structure

water of hydration : water chemically combined with a substance to form a hydrate that can be expelled (as by heating) without essentially altering the composition of the substance

water ouzel *n* : any of several birds (genus *Cinclus* and esp. *C. cinclus* and *C. mexicanus*) that are related to the thrushes and are not web-footed but dive into swift mountain streams and walk on the bottom in search of food — called also *dipper*

water ox *n* : WATER BUFFALO

water parting *n* : a summit or boundary line separating the drainage districts of two streams or coasts

water pepper *n* : an annual smartweed (*Polygonum hydropiper*) of moist soils with extremely acrid peppery juice

water pimpernel *n* : either of two small white-flowered herbs (*Samolus valerandí* of Europe and *S. floribundus* of the U.S.) of the primrose family that grow in wet places

water pipe *n* : a tobacco smoking device so arranged that the smoke is drawn through water

water pistol *n* : a toy pistol designed to throw a jet of liquid — called also *water gun*

water plantain *n* : any of a genus (*Alisma* of the family Alismaceae, the water-plantain family) of marsh or aquatic herbs with acrid sap and scapose 3-petaled flowers

water polo *n* : a goal game played in water by teams of swimmers with a ball resembling a soccer ball

wa·ter·pow·er \'wȯt-ər-,paù-(ə)r, 'wät-\ *n* **1 a** : the power of water employed to move machinery **b** : a fall of water suitable for such use **2** : a water privilege for a mill

¹wa·ter·proof \,wȯt-ər-'prüf, 'wät-\ *adj* : impervious to water; *esp* : covered or treated with a material (as a solution of rubber) to prevent permeation by water — **wa·ter·proof·ness** *n*

²waterproof \'wȯt-ər-,, 'wät-\ *n* **1** : a waterproof fabric **2** *chiefly Brit* : RAINCOAT

³waterproof \,wȯt-ər-', 'wät-\ *vt* : to make waterproof

wa·ter·proof·er \-'prü-fər\ *n* : one that waterproofs something (as roofs or fabrics)

wa·ter·proof·ing **1 a** : the act or process of making something waterproof **b** : the condition of being made waterproof **2** : something (as a coating) capable of imparting waterproofness

water rat *n* **1** : a rodent that frequents water **2** : a waterfront loafer or petty thief

wa·ter·re·pel·lent \,wȯt-ə(r)-ri-'pel-ənt, ,wät-\ *adj* : treated with a finish that is resistant but not impervious to penetration by water

wa·ter·re·sis·tant \-ri-'zis-tənt\ *adj* : resistant to but not wholly proof against the action or entry of water

water right *n* : a right to the use of water (as for irrigation); *esp* : RIPARIAN RIGHT

water sapphire *n* : a deep blue cordierite sometimes used as a gem

wa·ter·scape \'wȯt-ər-,skāp, 'wät-\ *n* : a water or sea view : SEASCAPE

water scorpion *n* : any of numerous aquatic bugs (family Nepidae) with the end of the abdomen prolonged by a long breathing tube

wa·ter·shed \'wȯt-ər-,shed, 'wät-\ *n* **1** : WATER PARTING **2** : a region or area bounded peripherally by a water parting and draining ultimately to a particular watercourse or body of water **3** : a crucial dividing point or line

water shield *n* : an aquatic plant (*Brasenia schreberi*) of the water-lily family having floating oval leaves with a gelatinous coating and small dull purple flowers; *also* : any of a related genus (*Cabomba*)

¹wa·ter·side \-,sīd\ *n* : the land bordering a body of water

²waterside *adj* **1** : of, relating to, or located on the waterside ⟨∼ trees⟩ **2** : employed along the waterside ⟨∼ workers⟩; *also* : of or relating to the workers along the waterside ⟨a ∼ strike⟩

water ski *n* : a ski used in planing over water towed by a speedboat — **wa·ter·ski** \'wȯt-ər-,skē, 'wät-\ *vi*

water snake *n* : any of numerous snakes (esp. genus *Natrix*) frequenting or inhabiting fresh waters and feeding largely on aquatic animals

wa·ter·soak \'wȯt-ər-,sōk, 'wät-\ *vt* : to soak in water

water spaniel *n* : a rather large spaniel with a heavy curly coat used esp. for retrieving waterfowl

water spot *n* : any of several diseases of fruits characterized by water-soaked lesions

wa·ter·spout \'wȯt-ər-,spaùt, 'wät-\ *n* **1** : a pipe, duct, or orifice from which water is spouted or through which it is carried **2** : a funnel-shaped or tubular column of rotating cloud-filled wind usu. extending from the underside of a cumulus or cumulonimbus cloud down to a cloud of spray torn up by the whirling winds from the surface of an ocean or lake

water sprite *n* : a sprite supposed to inhabit or haunt water : WATER NYMPH

water sprout *n* **:** an extremely vigorous but usu. unproductive shoot from an adventitious or latent bud on a tree

water strider *n* **:** any of various long-legged bugs (family Gerridae) that move about on the surface of the water

water supply *n* **:** source, means, or process of supplying water (as for a community) usu. including reservoirs, tunnels, and pipelines

water system *n* **1 :** a river with its tributaries **2 :** WATER SUPPLY

water table *n* **1 :** a stringcourse or similar member when projecting so as to throw off water **2 :** the upper limit of the portion of the ground wholly saturated with water

water thrush *n* **1 :** any of several No. American warblers (genus *Seiurus*) usu. living in the vicinity of streams **2 :** a European water ouzel (*Cinclus cinclus*)

wa·ter·tight \ˌwȯt-ər-ˈtīt, ˌwät-\ *adj* **1 :** of such tight construction or fit as to be impermeable to water **2 :** leaving no possibility of misconstruction or evasion — **wa·ter·tight·ness** *n*

water tower *n* **:** a tower or standpipe serving as a reservoir to deliver water at a required head; *specif* **:** a fire apparatus having a vertical pipe that can be extended to various heights and supplied with water under high pressure

water vapor *n* **:** water in a vaporous form esp. when below boiling temperature and diffused (as in the atmosphere)

water–vascular system *n* **:** a system of vessels in echinoderms that contains a circulating watery fluid used for the movement of tentacles and tube feet and that may also function in excretion and respiration

water wave *n* **:** a method or style of setting hair by dampening with water and forming into waves — **wa·ter–waved** \ˈwȯt-ər-ˌwāvd, ˈwät-\ *adj*

wa·ter·way \ˈwȯt-ər-ˌwā, ˈwät-\ *n* **1 :** a way or channel for water **2 :** a groove at the edge of a ship's deck for draining the deck **3 :** a navigable body of water

wa·ter·weed \-ˌwēd\ *n* **:** any of various aquatic plants (as a pondweed) with inconspicuous flowers — compare WATER LILY

wa·ter·wheel \-ˌhwēl, -ˌwēl\ *n* **1 :** a wheel made to rotate by direct action of water **2 :** a wheel for raising water

water wings *n pl* **:** a pneumatic device to give support to the body of a person swimming or learning to swim

water witch *n* **:** a dowser for water — called also *water witch·er* \-ˌwich-ər\ — **water witch·ing** \-iŋ\ *n*

wa·ter·works \ˈwȯt-ər-ˌwərks, ˈwät-\ *n pl* **1 :** an ornamental fountain or cascade **2 :** the system of reservoirs, channels, mains, and pumping and purifying equipment by which a water supply is obtained and distributed (as to a city) **3 :** TEARS **:** the shedding of tears

wa·ter·worn \-ˌwō(ə)rn, -ˌwȯ(ə)rn\ *adj* **:** worn, smoothed, or polished by the action of water

wa·tery \ˈwȯt-ə-rē, ˈwät-\ *adj* **1 a :** consisting of or filled with water **b :** containing, sodden with, or yielding water or a thin liquid ⟨a ~ solution⟩ ⟨~ vesicles⟩ **2 a :** felt to resemble water or watery matter esp. in thin fluidity, soggy texture, paleness, or lack of savor ⟨~ blood⟩ ⟨~ blues⟩ ⟨a ~ soup⟩ **b :** exhibiting weakness and vapidity **:** WISHY-WASHY

watt \ˈwät\ *n* [James *Watt* †1819 Sc engineer] **:** the absolute mks unit of power equal to the work done at the rate of one absolute joule per second or to the rate of work represented by a current of one ampere under a pressure of one volt and taken as the standard in the U.S. **:** 1/746 horsepower

watt·age \ˈwät-ij\ *n* **:** amount of power expressed in watts

Wat·teau \(ˌ)wä-ˌtō\ *adj* [Antoine *Watteau* †1721 F painter] **1** *of women's dress* **:** having back pleats falling loosely from neckline to hem **2** *of a hat* **:** shallow-crowned with wide brim turned up at the back to hold flower trimmings

watt·er \ˈwät-ər\ *n* **:** something having a specified wattage

watt–hour \ˈwät-ˈau̇(ə)r\ *n* **:** a unit of work or energy equivalent to the power of one watt operating for one hour

¹wat·tle \ˈwät-ᵊl\ *n* [ME *wattel*, fr. OE *watel*; akin to OHG *wadal* bandage] **1 a :** a fabrication of poles interwoven with slender branches, withes, or reeds and used esp. formerly in building **b :** material for such construction **c** *pl* **:** poles laid on a roof to support thatch **2 a :** a fleshy dependent process usu. about the head or neck (as of a bird) **b :** BARBEL 2 **3** *Austral* **:** ACACIA 1 — **wat·tled** \-ᵊld\ *adj*

²wattle *vt* **wat·tling** \ˈwät-liŋ, -ᵊl-iŋ\ **1 :** to form or build of or with wattle **2 a :** to form into wattle **:** interlace to form wattle **b :** to unite or make solid by interweaving light flexible material

wat·tle·bird \ˈwät-ᵊl-ˌbərd\ *n* **:** any of several Australasian honey eaters (genus *Anthochaera*) having fleshy pendulous ear wattles

watt·me·ter \ˈwät-ˌmēt-ər\ *n* [ISV] **:** an instrument for measuring electric power in watts

¹wave \ˈwāv\ *vb* [ME *waven*, fr. OE *wafian* to wave with the hands; akin to OE *wǣfre* restless — more at WAVER] *vi* **1 :** to float, play, or shake in an air current **:** move loosely to and fro **:** FLUTTER **2 :** to motion with the hands or with something held in them in signal or salute **3** *of water* **:** to move in waves **:** HEAVE **4 :** to become moved or brandished to and fro **5 :** to move before the wind with a wavelike motion ⟨field of *waving* grain⟩ **6 :** to follow a curving line or take a wavy form **:** UNDULATE ~ *vt* **1 :** to swing (something) back and forth or up and down **2 :** to impart a curving or undulating shape to **3 a :** to motion to (someone) to go in an indicated direction or to stop **:** FLAG, SIGNAL ⟨*waved* him aside⟩ **b :** to gesture with (the hand or an object) in greeting or farewell or in homage **c :** to convey by waving ⟨*waved* farewell⟩ **4 :** BRANDISH, FLOURISH ⟨*waved* a pistol menacingly⟩ **syn** see SWING — **wav·er** *n*

²wave *n, often attrib* **1 a :** a moving ridge or swell on the surface of a liquid (as of the sea) **b :** open water **2 a :** a shape or outline having successive curves **b :** a waviness of the hair **c :** an undulating line or streak or a pattern formed by such lines **3 :** something that swells and dies away: as **a :** a surge of sensation or emotion **b :** a movement sweeping large numbers in a common direction **:** CONTAGION **c :** a peak or climax of activity ⟨~ of buying⟩ **4 :** a sweep of hand or arm or of some object held in the hand used as a signal or greeting **5 :** a rolling or undulatory movement or one of a series of such movements passing along a surface or through the air **6 :** a movement like that of an ocean wave: as **a :** one of a succession of influxes of people migrating into a region **b** (1) **:** a moving group of animals of one kind (2) **:** a sudden rapid increase in a population **c :** a line of attacking or advancing troops or airplanes **7 :** a disturbance or variation that transfers energy progressively from point to point in a medium and that may take the form of an elastic deformation or of a variation of pressure, electric or magnetic intensity, electric potential, or temperature **8 :** a marked change in temperature **:** a period of hot or cold weather **9 :** an undulating or jagged line constituting a graphic representation of an action

Wave \ˈwāv\ *n* [*W*omen *A*ccepted for *V*olunteer *E*mergency Service] **:** a woman serving in the navy

wave band *n* **:** a band of radio-wave frequencies

waved \ˈwāvd\ *adj* **:** having a wavelike form or outline: as **a :** UNDULATING, CURVING ⟨the ~ cutting edge of a bread knife⟩ **b :** having wavy lines of color **:** WATERED ⟨~ cloth⟩

wave front *n* **:** a surface composed at any instant of all the points just reached by a vibrational disturbance in its propagation through a medium

wave guide *n* **:** a metal pipe of circular or rectangular cross section or a dielectric cylinder of such dimensions that it will propagate electromagnetic waves of a given frequency used for channeling ultrahigh-frequency waves

wave·length \ˈwāv-ˌleŋ(k)th\ *n* **:** the distance in the line of advance of a wave from any one point to the next point at which at the same instant there is the same phase

wave·less \-ləs\ *adj* **:** having no waves **:** CALM

wave·let \ˈwāv-lət\ *n* **:** a little wave **:** RIPPLE

wave·like \-ˌlīk\ *adj* **:** characteristic of a wave

wave mechanics *n pl but sing or pl in constr* **:** a theory of matter holding that elementary particles (as electrons, protons, or neutrons) have wave properties and seeking a mathematical interpretation of the structure of matter on the basis of these properties

¹wa·ver \ˈwā-vər\ *vi* **wa·ver·ing** \ˈwāv-(ə-)riŋ\ [ME *waveren*; akin to OE *wǣfre* restless, *wefan* to weave — more at WEAVE] **1 :** to vacillate irresolutely between choices **:** fluctuate in opinion, allegiance, or direction **2 a :** to weave or sway unsteadily to and fro **:** REEL, TOTTER **b :** QUIVER, FLICKER ⟨~*ing* flames⟩ **c :** FALTER **3 :** to give an unsteady sound **:** QUAVER **syn** see HESITATE, SWING — **wa·ver·er** \ˈwā-vər-ər\ *n* — **wa·ver·ing·ly** \ˈwāv-(ə-)riŋ-lē\ *adv*

²waver *n* **:** an act of wavering, quivering, or fluttering

wa·very \ˈwāv-(ə-)rē\ *adj* **:** WAVERING

wave theory *n* **:** UNDULATORY THEORY

wave train *n* **:** a succession of similar waves at equal intervals

wav·i·ly \ˈwā-və-lē\ *adv* **:** in a wavy manner

wav·i·ness \-vē-nəs\ *n* **:** the quality or state of being wavy

wavy \ˈwā-vē\ *adj* **1 :** rising or swelling in waves; *also* **:** abounding in waves **2 :** UNDULATING, FLUCTUATING; *also* **:** WAVERING **3 :** UNDULATORY, ROLLING

waw \ˈväv, ˈvȯv\ *n* [Heb *wāw*] **:** the 6th letter of the Hebrew alphabet — symbol ו

¹wax \ˈwaks\ *n* [ME, fr. OE *weax*; akin to OHG *wahs* wax, Lith *vaškas*] **1 :** a substance secreted by bees and used by them for constructing the honeycomb that is a dull yellow solid plastic when warm and composed of a mixture of esters, cerotic acid, and hydrocarbons — called also *beeswax* **2 :** any of various substances resembling beeswax: as **a :** any of numerous substances of plant or animal origin that differ from fats in being less greasy, harder, and more brittle and in containing principally esters of higher fatty acids and higher alcohols, free higher acids and alcohols, and saturated hydrocarbons **b :** a solid substance (as ozokerite or paraffin wax) of mineral origin consisting usu. of higher hydrocarbons **c :** a pliable or liquid composition used esp. in uniting surfaces, excluding air, making patterns or impressions, or producing a polished surface **d :** a resinous preparation used by shoemakers for rubbing thread **3 :** something likened to wax as soft, impressionable, or readily molded **4 :** a waxy secretion; *esp* **:** CERUMEN **5 :** a phonograph recording — **wax·like** \ˈwak-ˌslīk\ *adj*

²wax *vt* **1 :** to treat or rub with wax usu. for polishing or stiffening **2 :** to record on phonograph records

³wax *vi* [ME *waxen*, fr. OE *weaxan*; akin to OHG *wahsan* to increase, Gk *auxanein*, L *augēre* — more at EKE] **1 a :** to increase in size, numbers, strength, prosperity, or intensity **b :** to grow in volume or duration **c :** to grow toward full development **2 :** to increase in phase or intensity — used chiefly of the moon, other satellites, and inferior planets **3 :** to assume a (specified) characteristic, quality, or state **:** BECOME ⟨~ indignant⟩

⁴wax *n* [ME, fr. *waxen* to increase, grow] **1 :** INCREASE, GROWTH **2 :** the period from the new moon to the full phase of the moon

⁵wax *n* [perh. fr. ³*wax*] **:** a fit of temper **:** RAGE

wax bean *n* **:** a kidney bean with pods creamy yellow to bright yellow when fit for use as snap beans

wax·ber·ry \ˈwaks-ˌber-ē\ *n* **1 :** the wax-covered fruit of the wax myrtle; *also* **:** WAX MYRTLE **2 :** SNOWBERRY

wax·bill \-ˌbil\ *n* **:** any of numerous Old World birds (family Ploceidae and esp. genus *Estrilda*) having white, pink, or reddish bills of a waxy appearance

waxed paper *n* **:** paper coated or otherwise treated with wax to make it impervious to water and grease and used esp. as a wrapping

wax·en \ˈwak-sən\ *adj* **1 :** made of or covered with wax **2 :** resembling wax: as **a :** PLIABLE, IMPRESSIONABLE **b :** PALLID **c :** lustrously smooth

wax·er \-sər\ *n* **:** one whose work is applying or polishing with wax

wax·i·ness \ˈwak-sē-nəs\ *n* **:** the quality or state of being waxy

wax·ing *n* **1 :** the act of applying wax (as in polishing) **2 a :** the making of a phonograph record **b :** a phonograph record

wax insect *n* **:** a scale insect (family Coccidae) that secretes a wax from its body; *esp* **:** a Chinese insect (*Ericerus pe-la*) that yields much of the commercial Chinese wax

wax light *n* **:** a wax candle **:** TAPER

wax myrtle *n* **:** any of a genus (*Myrica* of the family Myricaceae, the wax-myrtle family) of trees or shrubs with aromatic foliage; *esp* **:** an American shrub (*M. cerifera*) having small hard berries with a thick coating of white wax used for candles

wax palm *n* **:** any of several palms that yield wax: as **a :** an Andean pinnate-leaved palm (*Ceroxylon andicolum*) whose stem yields a resinous wax used in candles **b :** CARNAUBA

wax·wing \ˈwak-ˌswiŋ\ *n* **:** any of several American and Eurasian passerine birds (genus *Bombycilla*) chiefly brown with a showy crest and velvety plumage

wax·work \ˈwak-ˌswərk\ *n* **1 :** an effigy in wax usu. of a person **2** *pl but sing or pl in constr* **:** an exhibition of wax effigies

waxy \ˈwak-sē\ *adj* **1 :** made of, abounding in, or covered with wax **:** WAXEN ⟨a ~ surface⟩ ⟨~ berries⟩ **2 :** felt to resemble wax:

as **a** : readily shaped or molded : PLASTIC, IMPRESSIONABLE **b** : marked by smooth or lustrous whiteness ⟨a ~ complexion⟩ **c** : containing white insoluble deposits or being degeneration marked by such deposits : AMYLOID

1way \'wā\ *n* [ME, fr. OE *weg;* akin to OHG *weg* way, OE *wegan* to move, L *vehere* to carry] **1 a** : a thoroughfare for travel or transportation from place to place **b** : an opening for passage **2** : the course traveled from one place to another : ROUTE **3 a** : a nonspatial course (as a series of actions or sequence of events) leading in a direction or toward an objective **b** (1) : a course of action (2) : opportunity, capability, or fact of doing as one pleases **c** : a possible course : POSSIBILITY **4 a** : manner or method of doing or happening; *also* : method of accomplishing : MEANS **b** : FEATURE, RESPECT **c** : the state of being or acting on a specified scale ⟨active in real estate in a small ~⟩ **d** : usual or characteristic state of affairs **e** : STATE, CONDITION — used with *the, this,* or *that* in phrases that stand in predicative or modifying relation esp. to the verb *be* **5 a** (1) : characteristic or habitual manner of acting (2) : a personal trait : IDIOSYNCRASY (3) : an ingratiating mode of behavior (4) : a recognized practice, tendency, or quality (5) : an endearing trick of behavior **b** : regular continued course or mode **6** : the length of a course : DISTANCE **7** : movement or progress along a course; *specif* : advancement in one's career **8 a** : DIRECTION ⟨is coming this ~⟩ **b** : LOCALITY, DISTRICT ⟨lives out our ~⟩ **c** : direction with reference to the lie of a natural growth (as hair) **d** : PARTICIPANT — usu. used in combination ⟨three-*way* discussion⟩ **9** : state of affairs : CONDITION **10 a** : room or opportunity to advance, pass, or progress **b** : freedom of action **c** : a place or position to be occupied by another — used as object of *make* **11** : scope or range of observation, experience, or possible acquisition **12 a** *pl but sometimes sing in constr* : an inclined structure upon which a ship is built or supported in launching **b** *pl* : the guiding surfaces on the bed of a machine along which a table or carriage moves **13** : CATEGORY, KIND — usu. used in a prepositional phrase introduced by *in* **14** : motion or speed of a ship or boat through the water **syn** see METHOD — **by way of 1** : for the purpose of ⟨*by way of* illustration⟩ **2** : by the route through : VIA — **out of the way 1** : WRONG, IMPROPER **2 a** : in or to a secluded place **b** : UNUSUAL, REMARKABLE **3** : COMPLETED, DONE — **under way 1** : in motion through the water **2** : in progress

2way *adj* : of, connected with, or constituting an intermediate point on a route ⟨~ station⟩

3way *adv* : 1AWAY 7

way·bill \'wā-,bil\ *n* : a document prepared by the carrier of a shipment of goods and containing details of the shipment, route, and charges

way car *n* **1** : CABOOSE 2 **2** : a freight car for less-than-carload shipments to way stations

way·far·er \'wā-,far-ər, -,fer-\ *n* : a traveler esp. on foot — **way·far·ing** \-,far-iŋ, -,fer-\ *adj*

way·go·ing \-,gō-ən, -iŋ\ *n, chiefly Scot* : DEPARTURE

Way·land \'wā-lənd\ *n* [OE *Wēland*] : a supernatural and invisible smith of Germanic legend — called also *Wayland the Smith*

way·lay \'wā-,lā\ *vt* **way·laid** \-,lād\ **way·lay·ing** : to lie in wait for

way·less \-ləs\ *adj* : having no road or path

Way of the Cross : STATIONS OF THE CROSS

way-out \'wā-'au̇t\ *adj* [*way out* (adverbial phrase), fr. 3*way* + *out*] : FAR-OUT

-ways \,wāz\ *adv suffix* [ME, fr. *ways*, gen. of *way*] : in (such) a way, course, direction, or manner ⟨side*ways*⟩ ⟨flat*ways*⟩

ways and means *n pl* **1** : methods and resources for accomplishing something and esp. for defraying expenses **2** *often cap W&M* **a** : methods and resources for raising the necessary revenues for the expenses of a nation or state **b** : a legislative committee concerned with this function

way·side \'wā-,sīd\ *n* : the side of or land adjacent to a road or path — **wayside** *adj*

way station *n* : an intermediate station between principal stations on a line of travel (as a railroad)

way·ward \'wā-wərd\ *adj* [ME, short for *awayward* turned away, fr. *away*, adv. + *-ward*] **1** : following one's own capricious, wanton, or depraved inclinations : DISOBEDIENT **2** : following no clear principle or law : UNPREDICTABLE **3** : opposite to what is desired or expected : UNTOWARD ⟨~ fate⟩ **syn** see CONTRARY — **way·ward·ly** *adv* — **way·ward·ness** *n*

way·worn \-,wō(ə)rn, -,wȯ(ə)rn\ *adj* : wearied by traveling

we \(')wē\ *pron, pl in constr* [ME, fr. OE *wē;* akin to OHG *wir* we, Skt *vayam*] **1** : I and the rest of a group that includes me : you and I : you and I and another or others : I and another or others not including you — used as pronoun of the first person plural; compare I, OUR, OURS, US **2** : 2I — used by sovereigns; used by writers to keep an impersonal character or to avoid the egotistical sound of a repeated *I*

weak \'wēk\ *adj* [ME *weike*, fr. ON *veikr;* akin to OE *wīcan* to yield, L *vicis* change — more at WEEK] **1** : lacking strength: as **a** : deficient in physical vigor : FEEBLE, DEBILITATED **b** : not able to sustain or exert much weight, pressure, or strain **c** : not able to resist external force or withstand attack **2 a** : mentally or intellectually deficient **b** : WAVERING, VACILLATING **c** : resulting from or indicating lack of judgment or discernment **d** : not able to withstand temptation or persuasion **3** : not factually grounded or logically presented ⟨a ~ argument⟩ **4 a** : not able to function properly **b** : lacking skill or proficiency : indicative of a lack of skill or aptitude **c** : wanting in vigor of expression or effect **5 a** : deficient in the usual or required ingredients : DILUTE ⟨~ coffee⟩ **b** : lacking normal intensity or potency ⟨~ strain of virus⟩ **6 a** : not having or exerting authority or political power ⟨~ government⟩ **b** : INEFFECTIVE, IMPOTENT **7** : of, relating to, or constituting a verb or verb conjugation that forms the past tense and past participle by adding the suffix *-ed* or *-d* or *-t* **8 a** : bearing the minimal degree of stress occurring in the language ⟨~ syllable⟩ **b** : having little or no stress and obscured vowel sound ⟨*'d* is the ~ form of *would*⟩ — **weak·ly** *adv*

syn WEAK, FEEBLE, FRAIL, FRAGILE, INFIRM, DECREPIT mean not strong enough to endure strain, pressure, or strenuous effort. WEAK is of wide application in implying deficiency or inferiority in strength or power of any sort; FEEBLE suggests extreme weakness inviting pity or contempt; FRAIL implies delicacy and slightness of constitution or structure; FRAGILE suggests frailty and brittleness unable to resist rough usage; INFIRM suggests instability, unsoundness, and insecurity due to old age or crippling illness; DECREPIT implies being worn out or broken down from long use or old age

weak·en \'wē-kən\ *vb* **weak·en·ing** \'wēk-(ə-)niŋ\ *vt* **1** : to make weak : lessen the strength of **2** : to reduce in intensity or effectiveness ~ *vi* : to become weak — **weak·en·er** \-(ə-)nər\ *n*

syn WEAKEN, ENFEEBLE, DEBILITATE, UNDERMINE, SAP, CRIPPLE, DISABLE mean to lose or cause to lose strength or vigor. WEAKEN may imply loss of physical strength, health, soundness, or stability or of quality, intensity, or effective power; ENFEEBLE implies an obvious and pitiable condition of weakness and helplessness; DEBILITATE suggests a less marked or more temporary impairment of strength or vitality; UNDERMINE and SAP suggest a weakening by something working surreptitiously and insidiously; CRIPPLE implies causing a serious loss of functioning power through damaging or removing an essential part or element; DISABLE suggests a usu. sudden crippling or enfeebling that makes one unable to carry on customary work or activity

weak·fish \'wēk-,fish\ *n* [obs. D *weekvis*, fr. D *week* soft + *vis* fish; fr. its tender flesh] : any of several marine percoid food fishes (genus *Cynoscion*); *esp* : a common sport and market fish (*C. regalis*) of the eastern coast of the U.S.

weak·heart·ed \-'härt-əd\ *adj* : lacking courage : FAINTHEARTED

weak·ish \'wē-kish\ *adj* : somewhat weak ⟨~ tea⟩

weak-kneed \'wēk-'nēd\ *adj* : lacking willpower or resolution

weak·li·ness \'wē-klē-nəs\ *n* : the quality or state of being weakly

weak·ling \'wē-kliŋ\ *n* : one that is weak in body, character, or mind — **weakling** *adj*

weak·ly \'wē-klē\ *adj* : FEEBLE, WEAK

weak-mind·ed \'wēk-'mīn-dəd\ *adj* : having or indicating a weak mind: **a** : lacking in judgment or good sense : FOOLISH **b** : FEEBLE-MINDED — **weak-mind·ed·ness** *n*

weak·ness \'wēk-nəs\ *n* **1** : the quality or state of being weak; *also* : an instance or period of being weak **2** : FAULT, DEFECT **3** : an object of special desire or fondness

1weal \'wē(ə)l\ *n* [ME *wele*, fr. OE *wela;* akin to OE *wel* well] **1** : a sound, healthy, or prosperous state : WELL-BEING **2** *obs* : BODY POLITIC, COMMONWEAL

2weal *n* [alter. of *wale*] : WELT

weald \'wē(ə)ld\ *n* [the *Weald*, wooded district in Kent, Surrey, & Sussex, England] **1** : a heavily wooded area : FOREST ⟨*Weald* of Kent⟩ **2** : a wild or uncultivated usu. upland region

wealth \'welth\ *n* [ME *welthe*, fr. *wele* weal] **1** *obs* : WEAL, WELFARE **2** : abundance of valuable material possessions or resources : AFFLUENCE **3** : abundant supply : PROFUSION **4 a** : all property that has a money value or an exchangeable value **b** : all material objects that have economic utility; *esp* : the stock of useful goods having economic value in existence at any one time ⟨national ~⟩

wealth·i·ly \'wel-thə-lē\ *adv* : in a wealthy manner

wealth·i·ness \-thē-nəs\ *n* : the quality or state of being wealthy

wealthy \'wel-thē\ *adj* **1** : having wealth : AFFLUENT **2** : characterized by abundance : AMPLE **syn** see RICH

wean \'wēn\ *vt* [ME *wenen*, fr. OE *wenian* to accustom, wean; akin to OE *wunian* to be used to — more at WONT] **1** : to accustom (as a child) to take food otherwise than by nursing **2** : to detach the affections of from something long followed or desired **syn** see ESTRANGE — **wean·er** *n*

wean·ling \'wēn-liŋ\ *n* : a child or animal newly weaned — **weanling** *adj*

1weap·on \'wep-ən\ *n* [ME *wepen*, fr. OE *wǣpen;* akin to ON *vāpn* weapon] **1** : an instrument of offensive or defensive combat : something to fight with **2** : a means of contending against another

2weapon *vt* : ARM

weap·on·less \'wep-ən-ləs\ *adj* : lacking weapons : UNARMED

weap·on·ry \-rē\ *n* **1** : the science of designing and making weapons **2** : WEAPONS

1wear \'wa(ə)r, 'we(ə)r\ *vb* **wore** \'wō(ə)r, 'wȯ(ə)r\ **worn** \'wō(ə)rn, 'wȯ(ə)rn\ **wear·ing** [ME *weren*, fr. OE *werian;* akin to ON *verja* to clothe, invest, spend, L *vestis* clothing, garment, Gk *hennynai* to clothe] *vt* **1** : to bear or have upon the person ⟨*wore* a coat⟩ **2 a** : to use habitually for clothing or adornment ⟨~*s* a toupee⟩ **b** : to carry on the person ⟨~ a sword⟩ **3 a** : to hold the rank or dignity or position signified by (an ornament) ⟨~ the royal crown⟩ **b** : to have or show an appearance of ⟨*wore* a happy smile⟩ **c** : to show or fly (a flag or colors) on a ship **4 a** : to cause to deteriorate by use **b** : to impair or diminish by use or attrition : consume or waste gradually ⟨letters on the stone *worn* away by weathering⟩ **5** : to produce gradually by friction or attrition ⟨~ a hole in the rug⟩ **6** : to exhaust or lessen the strength of : WEARY, FATIGUE **7** : to cause (a ship) to go about with the stern presented to the wind ~ *vi* **1 a** : to endure use : last under use or the passage of time **b** : to retain quality or vitality **2** : to diminish or decay through use ⟨it grew colder as the day *wore* on⟩ **3** : to grow or become by attrition or use **4** *of a ship* : to go about by turning the stern to the wind — compare TACK — **wear·able** \'war-ə-bəl, 'wer-\ *adj* — **wear·er** *n* — **wear on** : IRRITATE, FRAY — **wear stripes** : to serve in prison

2wear *n* **1** : the act of wearing : the state of being worn : USE ⟨clothes for everyday ~⟩ **2 a** : clothing or an article of clothing usu. of a particular kind; *esp* : clothing worn for a special occasion or popular during a specific period **b** : FASHION, VOGUE **3** : wearing quality : durability under use **4** : the result of wearing or use : diminution or impairment due to use ⟨*wear*-resistant surface⟩

wear and tear *n* : the loss or injury to which something is subjected by or in the course of use; *esp* : normal depreciation

wear down *vt* : to weary and overcome by persistent resistance or pressure

wea·ri·ful \'wir-ē-fəl\ *adj* **1** : causing weariness; *esp* : TEDIOUS **2** : WEARIED — **wea·ri·ful·ly** \-fə-lē\ *adv* — **wea·ri·ful·ness** *n*

wea·ri·less \'wir-ē-ləs\ *adj* : TIRELESS — **wea·ri·less·ly** *adv*

wea·ri·ly \'wir-ə-lē\ *adv* : in a weary manner

wea·ri·ness \'wir-ē-nəs\ *n* : the quality or state of being weary

1wear·ing \'wa(ə)r-iŋ, 'we(ə)r-\ *adj* : intended for wear ⟨~ apparel⟩

2wearing *adj* **:** subjecting to or inflicting wear; *esp* **:** FATIGUING ⟨a ~ journey⟩ — **wear·ing·ly** \-iŋ-lē\ *adv*

wea·ri·some \'wir-ē-səm\ *adj* **:** causing weariness **:** TIRESOME — **wea·ri·some·ly** *adv* — **wea·ri·some·ness** *n*

wear off *vi* **:** to diminish gradually in effect **:** pass away

wear out *vt* **1 :** to make useless esp. by long or hard usage **2 :** TIRE, EXHAUST **3 :** ERASE, EFFACE **4 :** to endure through **:** OUTLAST ⟨*wear out* a storm⟩ **5 :** to consume (as time) tediously ⟨*wear out* idle days⟩ ~ *vi* **:** to become useless from long or excessive wear or use

1wea·ry \'wi(ə)r-ē\ *adj* [ME *wery*, fr. OE *wērig;* akin to OHG *wuorag* intoxicated, Gk *hōrakian* to faint] **1 :** worn out in strength, endurance, vigor, or freshness **2 :** expressing or characteristic of weariness **3 :** having one's patience, tolerance, or pleasure exhausted — used with *of* **4 :** WEARISOME

2weary *vi* **:** to become weary ~ *vt* **:** to make weary **syn** see TIRE

wea·sand \'wēz-ᵊnd, 'wiz-ᵊn(d)\ *n* [ME *wesand*, fr. (assumed) OE *wǣsend* gullet; akin to OE *wāsend* gullet, OHG *weisunt* windpipe] **:** THROAT, GULLET; *also* **:** WINDPIPE

1wea·sel \'wē-zəl\ *n, pl* **weasels** [ME *wesele*, fr. OE *weosule;* akin to OHG *wisula* weasel, L *virus* slimy liquid, stench — more at VIRUS] **1** *or pl* **weasel :** any of various small slender active carnivorous mammals (genus *Mustela*) related to the minks that consume small birds and mammals and esp. great numbers of vermin (as mice or rats) and are mostly reddish brown with white or yellowish underparts and in northern forms turn white in winter **2 :** a light self-propelled tracked vehicle built either for traveling over snow or ice or sand or as an amphibious vehicle

2weasel *vi* **wea·sel·ing** \'wēz-(ə-)liŋ\ [*weasel word*] **1 :** to use weasel words **:** EQUIVOCATE **2 :** to escape from or evade a situation or obligation — often used with *out*

weasel word *n* [fr. the weasel's reputed habit of sucking the contents out of an egg while leaving the shell superficially intact] **:** a word used in order to evade or retreat from a direct or forthright statement or position

1weath·er \'weth-ər\ *n* [ME *weder*, fr. OE; akin to OHG *wetar* weather, OSlav *vetrŭ* wind] **1 :** state of the atmosphere with respect to heat or cold, wetness or dryness, calm or storm, clearness or cloudiness **2 :** state of life or fortune **3 :** disagreeable atmospheric conditions: as **a :** RAIN, STORM **b :** cold air with dampness **4 :** WEATHERING — **under the weather :** somewhat ill or drunk

2weather *adj* **:** WINDWARD — compare LEE

3weather *vb* **weath·er·ing** \'weth-(ə-)riŋ\ *vt* **1 :** to expose to the open air **:** subject to the action of the elements **2 :** to sail or pass to the windward of **3 :** to bear up against and come safely through ⟨~ a storm⟩ ~ *vi* **:** to undergo or endure the action of the elements

weath·er·abil·i·ty \,weth-(ə-)rə-'bil-ət-ē\ *n* **:** capability of withstanding weather ⟨~ of a plastic⟩

weath·er–beat·en \'weth-ər-,bēt-ᵊn\ *adj* **1 :** worn or damaged by exposure to weather **2 :** toughened, tanned, or bronzed by the weather ⟨~ face⟩

weath·er·board \-,bō(ə)rd, -,bȯ(ə)rd\ *n* **1 :** CLAPBOARD, SIDING **2 :** the weather side of a ship

weath·er·board·ing \-,bōrd-iŋ, -,bȯrd-\ *n* **:** CLAPBOARDS, SIDING

weath·er–bound \-,baủnd\ *adj* **:** kept in port or at anchor or from travel or sport by bad weather

weather bureau *n* **:** a bureau engaged in the collection of weather reports as a basis for weather predictions, storm warnings, and the compiling of statistical records

weath·er·cock \-,käk\ *n* **1 :** a vane often in the figure of a cock mounted so as to turn freely with the wind and show its direction **2 :** a person or thing that changes readily or often

weather deck *n* **:** a deck having no overhead protection from the weather

weath·ered \'weth-ərd\ *adj* **1 a :** seasoned by exposure to the weather **b :** altered in color, texture, composition, or form by such exposure or by artificial means producing a similar effect ⟨~ oak⟩ **2 :** made sloping so as to throw off water ⟨~ windowsill⟩

weather eye *n* **:** an eye quick to observe coming changes in the weather

weath·er·glass \'weth-ər-,glas\ *n* **:** a simple instrument for showing changes in atmospheric pressure by the changing level of liquid in a spout connected with a closed reservoir; *broadly* **:** BAROMETER

weath·er·ing *n* **:** the action of the elements in altering the color, texture, composition, or form of exposed objects; *specif* **:** the physical disintegration and chemical decomposition of earth materials at or near the earth's surface

weath·er·ly \'weth-ər-lē\ *adj* **:** able to sail close to the wind with little leeway

weath·er·man \-,man\ *n* **:** one who reports and forecasts the weather **:** METEOROLOGIST

weather map *n* **:** a map or chart showing the principal meteorological elements at a given hour and over an extended region

weath·er·proof \,weth-ər-'prüf\ *adj* **:** able to withstand exposure to weather without damage or loss of function — **weatherproof** *vt* — **weath·er·proof·ness** *n*

weather ship *n* **:** a ship that makes observations for use by meteorologists

weather station *n* **:** a station for taking, recording, and reporting meteorological observations

weather strip *n* **:** a strip of material to cover the joint of a door or window and the sill, casing, or threshold so as to exclude rain, snow, and cold air — called also *weather stripping* — **weath·er–strip** \'weth-ər-,strip\ *vt*

weath·er·tight \,weth-ər-'tīt\ *adj* **:** proof against wind and rain ⟨~ storage bin⟩

weather vane *n* **:** VANE 1a

weath·er–wise \'weth-ər-,wīz\ *adj* **:** skillful in forecasting changes in the weather or in opinion or feeling

weath·er·worn \-,wō(ə)rn, -,wȯ(ə)rn\ *adj* **:** worn by exposure to the weather

1weave \'wēv\ *vb* **wove** \'wōv\ **wo·ven** \'wō-vən\ **weav·ing** [ME *weven*, fr. OE *wefan;* akin to OHG *weban* to weave, Gk *hyphos* web] *vt* **1 a :** to form (cloth) by interlacing strands (as of yarn); *specif* **:** to make (cloth) on a loom by interlacing warp and filling threads **b :** to interlace (as threads) into cloth **c :** to make (as a basket) by intertwining **2 :** SPIN — used of spiders and insects **3 :** to interlace esp. to form a texture, fabric, or design **4 a :** to produce by elaborately combining elements **:** CONTRIVE **b :** to unite in a coherent whole **c :** to introduce as an appropriate element **:** work in — usu. used with *in* or *into* **5 :** to direct (as the body) in a winding or zigzag course esp. to avoid obstacles ~ *vi* **1 :** to work at weaving **:** make cloth **2 :** to move in a devious, winding, or zigzag course esp. to avoid obstacles

2weave *n* **:** any of the patterns or methods for interlacing the threads of woven fabrics

3weave *vi* [ME *weven* to move to and fro, wave; akin to ON *veifa* to wave, Skt *vepate* he trembles] **:** to move waveringly from side to side **:** SWAY

weav·er \'wē-vər\ *n* **1 :** one that weaves esp. as an occupation **2 :** WEAVERBIRD

weav·er·bird \-,bərd\ *n* **:** any of numerous Old World passerine birds (family Ploceidae) that resemble finches and mostly construct elaborate nests of interlaced vegetation

weaver's knot *n* **:** SHEET BEND — called also *weaver's hitch*

1web \'web\ *n, often attrib* [ME, fr. OE; akin to ON *vefr* web, OE *wefan* to weave] **1 :** a fabric on a loom or in process of being removed from a loom **2 a :** COBWEB 1, 2 **b :** SNARE, ENTANGLEMENT **3 :** a tissue or membrane of an animal or plant; *esp* **:** that uniting fingers or toes either at their bases (as in man) or for a greater part of their length (as in many water birds) **4 a :** a thin metal sheet, plate, or strip **b :** the plate connecting the upper and lower flanges of a girder or rail **c :** the arm of a crank **5 :** an intricate structure suggestive of something woven **:** NETWORK **6 :** the series of barbs implanted on each side of the shaft of a feather **:** VANE **7 a :** a continuous sheet of paper manufactured or undergoing manufacture on a paper machine **b :** a reel of such paper for use in a rotary printing press **8 :** the part of a ribbed vault between the ribs — **web·like** \-,līk\ *adj*

2web *vb* **webbed; web·bing** *vt* **1 :** to cover with a web or network **2 :** ENTANGLE, ENSNARE **3 :** to provide with a web ⟨*webbed* feet⟩ ~ *vi* **:** to construct or form a web

web·bing \'web-iŋ\ *n* **:** a strong narrow closely woven tape designed for bearing weight and used esp. for straps, harness, or upholstery

web·by \'web-ē\ *adj* **:** of, relating to, or consisting of a web

we·ber \'web-ər, 'vā-bər\ *n* [Wilhelm E. *Weber* †1891 G physicist] **:** the practical mks unit of magnetic flux equal to that flux which in linking a circuit of one turn produces in it an electromotive force of one volt as the flux is reduced to zero at a uniform rate of one ampere per second **:** 10^8 maxwells

web·foot *n* **1** \'web-'fủt\ **:** a foot having webbed toes **2** \-,fủt\ **:** an animal having web feet — **web–foot·ed** \-'fủt-əd\ *adj*

web member *n* **:** one of the several members joining the top and bottom chords of a truss or lattice girder

web press *n* **:** a press that prints a continuous roll of paper

web spinner *n* **:** an insect that spins a web; *esp* **:** any of an order (Embiodea) of small slender insects with biting mouthparts that live in silken tunnels which they spin

web·ster \'web-stər\ *n* [ME, fr. OE *webbestre* female weaver, fr. *webbian* to weave; akin to OE *wefan* to weave] *archaic* **:** WEAVER

Web·ste·ri·an \web-'stir-ē-ən\ *adj* **1 :** of, relating to, or characteristic of the statesman Daniel Webster **2 :** of, relating to, or characteristic of the lexicographer Noah Webster or his dictionary

web·worm \'web-,wərm\ *n* **:** any of various caterpillars that are more or less gregarious and spin large webs

wed \'wed\ *vb* **wed·ded** *also* **wed; wed·ding** [ME *wedden*, fr. OE *weddian;* akin to MHG *wetten* to pledge, OE *wedd* pledge, OHG *wetti*, Goth *wadi*, L *vad-, vas* bail, security] *vt* **1 :** to take for wife or husband by a formal ceremony **:** MARRY **2 :** to join in marriage **3 :** to unite as if by the bond of marriage ~ *vi* **:** to enter into matrimony — **wed·der** *n*

we'd \(,)wēd\ **:** we had **:** we would **:** we should

wed·ding \'wed-iŋ\ *n, often attrib* **1 :** a marriage ceremony usu. with its accompanying festivities **:** NUPTIALS **2 :** an act, process, or instance of joining in close association **3 :** a wedding anniversary or its celebration — usu. used in combination

wedding march *n* **:** a march of slow tempo and stately character composed or played to accompany the bridal procession

wedding ring *n* **:** a ring often of plain gold or platinum given by the groom to the bride during the wedding service; *also* **:** a similar ring given by the bride to the groom in a double-ring service

1wedge \'wej\ *n* [ME *wegge*, fr. OE *wecg;* akin to OHG *wecki* wedge, Lith *vagis*] **1 :** a piece of a substance (as wood or iron) that tapers to a thin edge and is used for splitting wood and rocks, raising heavy bodies, or for tightening by being driven into something **2 a :** something (as a policy) causing a breach or separation **b :** something used to initiate an action or development **3 :** something wedge-shaped: as **a :** an array of troops or tanks in the form of a wedge **b :** the wedge-shaped stroke in cuneiform characters **c :** a shoe having a heel extending from the back of the shoe to the front of the shank and a tread formed by an extension of the sole **d :** an iron golf club with a broad low-angled face for maximum loft

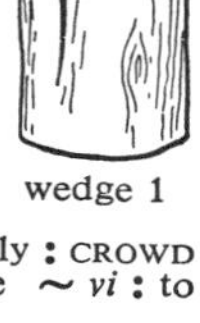

wedge 1

2wedge *vt* **1 :** to fasten or tighten by driving in a wedge **2 :** to force (an object) into something for holding tightly **:** CROWD **3 :** to separate or force apart with or as if with a wedge ~ *vi* **:** to become wedged

wedged \'wejd, 'wej-əd\ *adj* **:** shaped like a wedge ⟨the ~ formation of flying geese⟩

Wedg·ies \'wej-ēz\ *trademark* — used for shoes having a wedge-shaped piece serving as the heel and joining the half sole to form a continuous flat undersurface

Wedg·wood \'wej-,wủd\ *trademark* — used for a pottery (as bone china or jasper)

wedgy \'wej-ē\ *adj* **:** resembling a wedge in shape

wed·lock \'wed-,läk\ *n* [ME *wedlok*, fr. OE *wedlāc* marriage bond, fr. *wedd* pledge + *-lāc*, suffix denoting activity] **:** the state of being married **:** MARRIAGE, MATRIMONY — **out of wedlock :** with the natural parents not legally married to each other

Wednes·day \'wenz-dē\ *n* [ME, fr. OE *wōdnesdæg;* akin to ON *ōthinsdagr* Wednesday; both fr. a prehistoric WGmc-NGmc compound whose components are represented by OE *Wōden* Odin, the chief god in Germanic mythology, and by OE *dæg* day] **:** the fourth day of the week — **Wednes·days** \-dēz\ *adv*

wee \'wē\ *adj* [ME *we*, fr. *we*, n., little bit, fr. OE *wǣge* weight; akin to OE *wegan* to move, weigh — more at WAY] **1 :** very small

: LITTLE **2** : very early ⟨~ hours of the morning⟩ **syn** see SMALL

1weed \'wēd\ *n* [ME, fr. OE *wēod;* akin to OS *wiod* weed] **1 a** (1) : a plant of no value and usu. of rank growth; *esp* : one that tends to overgrow or choke out more desirable plants (2) : a weedy growth of plants **b** : an aquatic plant; *esp* : SEAWEED **c** (1) : TOBACCO (2) : MARIJUANA **2 a** : an obnoxious growth, thing, or person **b** : something like a weed in detrimental quality; *esp* : an animal unfit to breed from

2weed *vi* : to remove weeds or something harmful ~ *vt* **1 a** : to clear of weeds ⟨~ a garden⟩ **b** (1) : to free from something hurtful or offensive (2) : to remove the less desirable portions of : CULL **2** : to get rid of (something harmful or superfluous) — often used with *out*

3weed *n* [ME *wede*, fr. OE *wǣd, gewǣde;* akin to ON *vāth* cloth, clothing, Lith *austi* to weave] **1** : GARMENT — often used in pl. **2 a** : dress worn as a sign of mourning (as by a widow) — usu. used in pl. **b** : a band of crape worn on a man's hat as a sign of mourning — usu. used in pl.

weed·ed \'wēd-əd\ *adj* [in sense 1, fr. pp. of *2weed;* in sense 2, fr. *1weed* + *-ed*] **1** : cleared of weeds **2** : having many weeds : WEEDY

weed·er \-ər\ *n* : one that weeds; *specif* : any of various devices for freeing an area from weeds

weed·i·cide \'wēd-ə-,sīd\ *n* : HERBICIDE

weed·less \'wēd-ləs\ *adj* : free from weeds ⟨a ~ garden⟩

weedy \'wēd-ē\ *adj* **1** : abounding with or consisting of weeds **2** : resembling a weed esp. in rank growth or ready propagation **3** : noticeably lean and scrawny : LANKY ⟨light carriage with its pair of ~ young horses —Joseph Hergesheimer⟩

week \'wēk\ *n* [ME *weke*, fr. OE *wicu, wucu;* akin to OHG *wehha* week, L *vicis* change, alternation, OE *wīr* wire — more at WIRE] **1 a** : one of a series of seven-day cycles used in various calendars **b** (1) : a week beginning with a specified day or containing a specified holiday ⟨the ~ of the 18th⟩ ⟨Easter ~⟩ (2) : a week appointed for public recognition of some cause ⟨Fire Prevention *Week*⟩ **2 a** : any seven consecutive days **b** : a series of regular working, business, or school days during each seven-day period **3** : a time seven days before or after a specified day

week·day \'wēk-,dā\ *n* : a day of the week except Sunday or sometimes except Saturday and Sunday

week·days \-,dāz\ *adv* : on weekdays repeatedly : on any weekday ⟨takes a bus ~⟩

1week·end \'wē-,kend\ *n* : the end of the week; *specif* : the period between the close of one working or business or school week and the beginning of the next

2weekend *vi* : to spend the weekend

weekend bag *n* : a traveling bag of a size to carry clothing and personal articles for a weekend trip — called also *weekend case*

week·end·er \'wē-,ken-dər\ *n* **1** : one that vacations or visits for a weekend **2** : WEEKEND BAG

week·ends \'wē-,ken(d)z\ *adv* : on weekends repeatedly : on any weekend ⟨travels ~⟩

1week·ly \'wē-klē\ *adv* : every week : once a week : by the week

2weekly *adj* **1** : occurring, appearing, or done weekly **2** : reckoned by the week

3weekly *n* : a weekly newspaper or periodical

ween \'wēn\ *vt* [ME *wenen*, fr. OE *wēnan;* akin to ON *væna* to hope, L *venus* love, charm — more at WIN] *archaic* : IMAGINE, SUPPOSE

wee·ny \'wē-nē\ *also* **ween·sy** \'wēn(t)-sē\ *adj* [*wee* + *tiny*] : exceptionally small : TINY

1weep \'wēp\ *vb* **wept** \'wept\ **weep·ing** [ME *wepen*, fr. OE *wēpan;* akin to OHG *wuoffan* to weep, OSlav *vabiti* to call to] *vt* **1** : to express deep sorrow for usu. by shedding tears : BEWAIL **2** : to pour forth (tears) from the eyes **3** : to exude (a fluid) slowly : OOZE ~ *vi* **1** : to express passion (as grief) by shedding tears **2 a** : to give off or leak fluid slowly : OOZE **b** *of a fluid* : to flow sluggishly or in drops

2weep *n* [imit.] : LAPWING

weep·er \'wē-pər\ *n* **1 a** : one that weeps **b** : a professional mourner **2** : a small statue of a figure in mourning on a funeral monument **3** : a badge of mourning worn esp. in the 18th and 19th centuries **4** : CAPUCHIN 3

weep·ing \'wē-piŋ\ *adj* **1** : TEARFUL; *also* : RAINY **2** : having slender pendent branches

weeping willow *n* : an Asiatic willow (*Salix babylonica*) with weeping branches

weepy \'wē-pē\ *adj* : inclined to weep : TEARFUL

weet \'wēt\ *vb* [ME *weten*, alter. of *witen* — more at WIT] *archaic* : KNOW

wee·ver \'wē-vər\ *n* [ONF *wivre* viper — more at WYVERN] : any of several edible marine percoid fishes (family Trachinidae) with a broad spinose head and venomous spines on the dorsal fin

wee·vil \'wē-vəl\ *n* [ME *wevel*, fr. OE *wifel;* akin to OHG *wibil* beetle, OE *wefan* to weave] : any of numerous mostly small beetles (group Rhynchophora) having the head elongated and usu. curved downward to form a snout bearing the jaws at the tip and including many very injurious esp. as larvae to nuts, fruit, and grain or to living plants — **wee·vily** *or* **wee·vil·ly** \'wēv-(ə-)lē\ *adj*

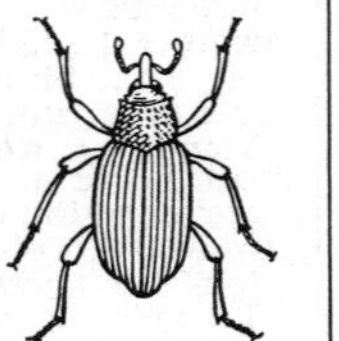
weevil

wee·viled *or* **wee·villed** \'wē-vəld\ *adj* : WEEVILY

weft \'weft\ *n* [ME, fr. OE; akin to ON *veptr* weft, OE *wefan* to weave — more at WEAVE] **1 a** : 1WOOF 1a **b** : yarn used for the woof **2** : WEB, FABRIC; *also* : an article of woven fabric

wei·ge·la \wī-'jē-lə\ *n* [NL, genus name, fr. Christian E. *Weigel* †1831 G physician] : any of a genus (*Weigela*) of showy shrubs of the honeysuckle family; *esp* : one (*W. florida*) of China widely grown for its pink or red flowers

1weigh \'wā\ *vb* [ME *weyen*, fr. OE *wegan* to move, carry, weigh — more at WAY] *vt* **1** : to ascertain the heaviness of by or as if by a balance **2 a** : OUTWEIGH **b** : COUNTERBALANCE **c** : to make heavy : WEIGHT **3** : to consider carefully : PONDER **4** : to heave up (an anchor) preparatory to sailing **5** : to measure or apportion (a definite quantity) on or as if on a scales ~ *vi* **1 a** : to have weight or a specified weight **b** : to register a weight (as on a scales) — used with *in* or *out* — compare WEIGH IN **2** : to merit consideration as important : COUNT ⟨evidence will ~ heavily against him⟩ **3 a** : to press down with or as if with a heavy weight **b** : to have a saddening or disheartening effect **4** : to weigh anchor **syn** see CONSIDER — **weigh·able** \'wā-ə-bəl\ *adj*

2weigh *n* [alter. of *way*] : WAY — used in the phrase *under weigh*

weigh down *vt* **1** : to cause to bend down : OVERBURDEN **2** : OPPRESS, DEPRESS

weigh·er \'wā-ər\ *n* : one that weighs

weigh in *vi* **1** : to have oneself or one's possessions (as baggage) weighed; *esp* : to have oneself weighed in connection with an athletic contest **2** : to enter as a participant

1weight \'wāt\ *n* [ME *wight, weght*, fr. OE *wiht;* akin to ON *vætt* weight, OE *wegan* to weigh] **1 a** : the amount that a thing weighs **b** (1) : the standard or established amount that a thing should weigh (2) : one of the classes into which contestants in a sports event are divided according to body weight (3) : poundage required to be carried by a horse in a handicap race **2 a** : a quantity or thing weighing a fixed and usu. specified amount **b** : a heavy object (as a metal ball) thrown, put, or lifted as an athletic exercise **3 a** : a unit of weight or mass — see MEASURE table, METRIC SYSTEM table **b** : a piece of material (as metal) of known specified weight for use in weighing articles **c** : a system of related units of weight **4 a** : something heavy : LOAD **b** : a heavy object to hold or press something down or to counterbalance **5 a** : BURDEN, PRESSURE **b** : PONDEROUSNESS **6 a** : relative heaviness **b** : the force with which a body is attracted toward the earth or a celestial body by gravitation and which is equal to the product of the mass by the local gravitational acceleration **7 a** : the relative importance or authority accorded something **b** : measurable influence esp. upon others **8** : overpowering force **9** : the quality (as lightness) that makes a fabric or garment suitable for a particular use or season — often used in combination ⟨dress-weight⟩ **10** : a numerical coefficient assigned to an item to express its relative importance in a frequency distribution **syn** see IMPORTANCE, INFLUENCE

2weight *vt* **1 a** : to load or make heavy with or as if with a weight **b** : to increase in heaviness by adding an ingredient **2** : to oppress with a burden ⟨~*ed* down with cares⟩ **3 a** : WEIGH 1 **b** : to feel the weight of : HEFT **4** : to assign a statistical weight to **5** : to cause to incline in a particular direction by manipulation **6** : to shift the burden of weight upon

weight·ed *adj* **1** : made heavy : LOADED ⟨~ silk⟩ **2 a** : having a statistical weight attached **b** : compiled from weighted data ⟨~ mean⟩

weight·i·ly \'wāt-ᵊl-ē\ *adv* : in a weighty manner

weight·i·ness \'wāt-ē-nəs\ *n* : the quality or state of being weighty

weight·less \'wāt-ləs\ *adj* : having little weight : lacking apparent gravitational pull — **weight·less·ly** *adv* — **weight·less·ness** *n*

weight lifter *n* : one that lifts barbells in competition or as an exercise — **weight lifting** *n*

weighty \'wāt-ē\ *adj* **1 a** : of much importance or consequence : MOMENTOUS **b** : SOLEMN **2 a** : weighing a considerable amount : CORPULENT **b** : heavy in proportion to its bulk ⟨~ metal⟩ **3** : POWERFUL, TELLING ⟨~ arguments⟩ **syn** see HEAVY

wei·ma·ra·ner \,vī-mə-'rän-ər; 'vī-mə-,, 'wī-\ *n* [G, fr. *Weimar*, Germany] : any of a German breed of large gray short-haired sporting dogs

weir \'wa(ə)r, 'we(ə)r, 'wi(ə)r\ *n* [ME *were*, fr. OE *wer;* akin to ON *ver* fishing place, OHG *werien, werren* to defend, L *aperire* to open, *operire* to close, cover] **1** : a fence or enclosure set in a waterway for taking fish **2** : a dam in a stream to raise the water level or divert its flow

1weird \'wi(ə)rd\ *n* [ME *wird, werd*, fr. OE *wyrd;* akin to ON *urthr* fate, OE *weorthan* to become — more at WORTH] **1 a** : FATE, DESTINY; *esp* : ill fortune **b** *cap* : 1FATE 4, NORN **2** : SOOTHSAYER

2weird *adj* **1** *archaic* : of, relating to, or dealing with fate or the Fates **2 a** : of, relating to, or caused by witchcraft or the supernatural : MAGICAL **b** : UNEARTHLY, MYSTERIOUS **3** : of strange or extraordinary character : ODD, FANTASTIC — **weird·ly** *adv* — **weird·ness** *n*

syn WEIRD, EERIE, UNCANNY mean mysteriously strange or fantastic. WEIRD may imply an unearthly or preternatural strangeness or it may stress queerness or oddness; EERIE suggests an uneasy or fearful consciousness that mysterious and malign powers are at work; UNCANNY may imply disquieting strangeness or mysteriousness, or it may apply to powers or perceptions so remarkable as to seem magical

Weird Sisters *n pl* : FATES

wei·sen·hei·mer *var of* WISENHEIMER

Weis·mann·ism \'vī-,smän-,iz-əm, 'wī-smən-\ *n* : the theories of heredity proposed by August Weismann; *esp* : the concepts of continuity of the germ plasm and dichotomy of germ and soma with the resulting impossibility of transmitting acquired characters

weka \'wek-ə\ *n* [Maori] : any of several flightless New Zealand rails (genus *Gallirallus*)

welch \'welch\, **welcher** *var of* WELSH, WELSHER

Welch \'welch\ *var of* WELSH

1wel·come \'wel-kəm\ *interj* [ME, alter. of *wilcume*, fr. OE, fr. *wilcuma* desirable guest; akin to OHG *willicomo* desirable guest; prob. both fr. a prehistoric WGmc compound whose constituents are represented by OE *willa, will* desire and by OE *cuma* guest; akin to OE *cuman* to come — more at WILL, COME] — used to express a greeting to a guest or newcomer upon his arrival

2welcome *vt* **1** : to greet hospitably and with courtesy or cordiality **2** : to accept with pleasure the occurrence of ⟨~*s* danger⟩ — **wel·com·er** *n*

3welcome *adj* **1** : received gladly into one's presence or companionship **2** : giving pleasure : received with gladness or delight esp. in response to a need **3** : willingly permitted or admitted **syn** see PLEASANT — **wel·come·ly** *adv* — **wel·come·ness** *n*

4welcome *n* : a cordial greeting or reception upon arrival

1weld \'weld\ *n* [ME *welde;* akin to MLG *wolde* weld] : a European mignonette (*Reseda luteola*) yielding a yellow dye; *also* : a yellow dye from this

2weld *vb* [alter. of obs. E *well* to weld, fr. ME *wellen* to boil, well, weld] *vi* : to become or be capable of being welded ~ *vt* **1 a** : to unite (metallic parts) by heating and allowing the metals to flow

ə abut; ᵊ kitten; ər further; a back; ā bake; ä cot, cart; au̇ out; ch chin; e less; ē easy; g gift; i trip; ī life
j joke; ŋ sing; ō flow; ȯ flaw; ȯi coin; th thin; t͟h this; ü loot; u̇ foot; y yet; yü few; yu̇ furious; zh vision

together or by hammering or compressing with or without previous heating **b** : to unite (plastics) in a similar manner by heating **c** : to repair (as an article) by this method **d** : to produce or create as if by such a process **2** : to unite closely or intimately — **weld·able** \'wel-də-bəl\ *adj*

³**weld** *n* **1** : a welded joint **2** : union by welding : the state or condition of being welded

weld·er \'wel-dər\ *n* : one that welds: as **a** : one whose work is welding **b** : a machine used in welding

weld·ment \'wel(d)-mənt\ *n* : a unit formed by welding together an assembly of pieces

wel·dor \'wel-dər\ *n* : one whose work is welding

wel·fare \'wel-,fa(ə)r, -,fe(ə)r\ *n* [ME, fr. the phrase *wel faren* to fare well] **1** : the state of doing well esp. in respect to good fortune, happiness, well-being, or prosperity **2** : WELFARE WORK **3** : RELIEF 2b — **welfare** *adj*

welfare state *n* **1** : a social system based upon the assumption by a political state of primary responsibility for the individual and social welfare of its citizens **2** : a nation or state characterized by the operation of the system of the welfare state

welfare work *n* : organized efforts by a community or organization for the social betterment of a group in society — **welfare worker** *n*

wel·far·ism \'wel-,fa(ə)r-,iz-əm, -,fe(ə)r-\ *n* : the complex of policies, attitudes, and beliefs associated with the welfare state

wel·kin \'wel-kən\ *n* [ME, lit., cloud, fr. OE *wolcen;* akin to OHG *wolkan* cloud, OSlav *vlaga* moisture] **1** : SKY **2** : AIR

¹**well** \'wel\ *n* [ME *welle,* fr. OE (northern & Midland dial.) *welle;* akin to OHG *wella* wave, OE *weallan* to bubble, boil] **1 a** : an issue of water from the earth : a pool fed by a spring **b** : FOUNTAIN, WELLSPRING **2** : a pit or hole sunk into the earth to reach a supply of water **3 a** : an enclosure in the middle of a ship's hold to protect from damage and facilitate the inspection of the pumps **b** : a compartment in the hold of a fishing boat in which fish are kept alive **4** : a shaft or hole sunk to obtain oil, brine, or gas **5** : an open space extending vertically through floors of a structure **6** : a space having a construction or shape suggesting a well for water **7 a** : something resembling a well in being damp, cool, deep, or dark **b** : a deep vertical hole **c** : a deep reservoir from which one may draw

²**well** *vb* [ME *wellen,* fr. OE (northern & Midland dial.) *wellan* to cause to well; akin to MHG *wellen* to cause to well, OE *weallan* to bubble, boil, L *volvere* to roll — more at VOLUBLE] *vi* **1** : to rise to the surface and usu. flow forth **2** : to rise to the surface like a flood of liquid ⟨longing ~*ed* up in his breast⟩ ~ *vt* : to pour forth from the depths

³**well** *adv* **bet·ter** \'bet-ər\ **best** \'best\ [ME *wel,* fr. OE; akin to OHG *wela* well, OE *wyllan* to wish — more at WILL] **1 a** : in a good or proper manner : JUSTLY, RIGHTLY **b** : satisfactorily with respect to conduct or action ⟨did ~ in math⟩ **2** : in a kindly or friendly manner **3 a** : with skill or aptitude : EXPERTLY ⟨paints ~⟩ **b** : SATISFACTORILY **c** : with good appearance or effect : ELEGANTLY ⟨carried himself ~⟩ **4** : ATTENTIVELY **5** : to a high degree ⟨~ deserved the honor⟩ ⟨*well*-equipped kitchen⟩ **6** : FULLY, QUITE ⟨~ worth the price⟩ **7 a** : FITTINGLY, RIGHTLY **b** : in a prudent manner : SENSIBLY — used with *do* **8** : in accordance with the occasion or circumstances : NATURALLY ⟨cannot ~ refuse⟩ **9 a** : as one could wish : FAVORABLY **b** : ADVANTAGEOUSLY, PROPERLY ⟨married ~⟩ **10 a** : EASILY, READILY **b** : in all likelihood : INDEED **11** : in a prosperous or affluent manner ⟨he lives ~⟩ **12** : THOROUGHLY, COMPLETELY ⟨after being ~ dried with a sponge⟩ **13** : without doubt or question : CLEARLY **14** : CONSIDERABLY, FAR ⟨~ over a million⟩ — **as well 1** : in addition : ALSO ⟨other features *as well*⟩ **2** : to the same extent or degree : as much ⟨open *as well* to the poor as to the rich⟩ **3** : with equivalent or comparable effect — **as well as** : and not only : and in addition ⟨skillful *as well as* strong⟩

⁴**well** *interj* **1** — used to express surprise or expostulation **2** — used to indicate resumption of a thread of discourse or to introduce a remark

⁵**well** *adj* **1** : being in good standing or favor **2** : SATISFACTORY, PLEASING ⟨all's ~ that ends well⟩ **3 a** : PROSPEROUS, WELL-OFF **b** : being in satisfactory condition or circumstances **4** : ADVISABLE, DESIRABLE ⟨not ~ to anger him⟩ **5 a** : free or recovered from infirmity or disease : HEALTHY ⟨a ~ man⟩ **b** : CURED, HEALED ⟨the wound is nearly ~⟩ **6** : pleasing or satisfactory in appearance **7** : being a cause for thankfulness : FORTUNATE ⟨it is ~ that this has happened⟩ **syn** see HEALTHY

we'll \(,)wē(ə)l, wil\ : we will : we shall

well-ad·vised \,wel-əd-'vīzd\ *adj* **1** : acting with wisdom, wise counsel, or proper deliberation : PRUDENT **2** : resulting from, based on, or showing careful deliberation or wise counsel ⟨~ plans⟩

wel·la·way \,wel-ə-'wā\ *interj* [ME *welaway,* fr. OE *weilāwei,* lit., woe! lo! woe!, alter. of *wālāwā,* fr. *wā* woe + *lā* lo + *wā* woe — more at WOE] — used to express sorrow or lamentation

well-be·ing \'wel-'bē-iŋ\ *n* : the state of being happy, healthy, or prosperous : WELFARE

well-be·loved \,wel-bi-'ləvd\ *adj* **1** : sincerely and deeply loved ⟨my ~ wife⟩ **2** : sincerely respected — used in various ceremonial forms of address

well·born \'wel-'bȯ(ə)rn\ *adj* : born of good stock either socially or genetically

well-bred \-'bred\ *adj* **1** : having or displaying good breeding : REFINED **2** : having a good pedigree ⟨*well-bred* swine⟩

well-con·di·tioned \,wel-kən-'dish-ənd\ *adj* **1** : characterized by proper disposition, morals, or behavior **2** : having a good physical condition : SOUND ⟨a ~ animal⟩

well-dis·posed \-dis-'pōzd\ *adj* : having a good disposition; *esp* : disposed to be friendly, favorable, or sympathetic

well-done \'wel-'dən\ *adj* **1** : rightly or properly performed **2** : cooked thoroughly

Wel·ler·ism \'wel-ə-,riz-əm\ *n* [Sam *Weller,* witty servant of Mr. Pickwick in the story *Pickwick Papers* (1836–37) by Charles Dickens] : an expression of comparison comprising a usu. well-known quotation followed by a facetious sequel (as "'every one to his own taste,' said the old woman as she kissed the cow")

well-fa·vored \'wel-'fā-vərd\ *adj* : good-looking : HANDSOME — **well-fa·vored·ness** *n*

well-fixed \-'fikst\ *adj* : having plenty of money or property : WELL-TO-DO

well-found \-'faund\ *adj* : fully furnished : properly equipped ⟨a *well-found* ship⟩

well-found·ed \-'faun-dəd\ *adj* : based on excellent reasoning, information, judgment, or grounds

well-groomed \-'grümd, -'grumd\ *adj* **1** : well dressed and scrupulously neat ⟨~ men⟩ **2** : made neat, tidy, and attractive down to the smallest details ⟨a ~ lawn⟩

well-ground·ed \-'graun-dəd\ *adj* : having a firm foundation

well-han·dled \-'han-dᵊld\ *adj* **1** : managed or administered efficiently **2** : having been handled a great deal ⟨~ goods on a store counter⟩

well·head \'wel-,hed\ *n* **1** : the source of a spring or a stream **2** : principal source : FOUNTAINHEAD **3** : the top of or a structure built over a well

well-heeled \-'hē(ə)ld\ *adj* : having plenty of money : WELL-FIXED

Wel·ling·ton \'wel-iŋ-tən\ *n* [Arthur Wellesley, 1st Duke of *Wellington* †1852 Brit general and statesman] : a leather boot having a loose top with the front usu. coming above the knee

well-knit \'wel-'nit\ *adj* : firmly knit; *esp* : firmly and strongly constructed, compacted, or framed

well-known \'wel-'nōn\ *adj* : fully or widely known

well-mean·ing \-'mē-niŋ\ *adj* : having good intentions

well·ness \'wel-nəs\ *n* : the quality or state of being in good health

well-nigh \-'nī\ *adv* : ALMOST, NEARLY

well-off \'wel-'ȯf\ *adj* **1** : being in good condition or circumstances **2** : well provided **3** : WELL-TO-DO

well-or·dered \-'ȯrd-ərd\ *adj* : being simply ordered and having every subset containing a first element

well-read \'wel-'red\ *adj* : well informed or deeply versed through reading ⟨~ in history⟩

well-set \-'set\ *adj* **1** : well or firmly established **2** : strongly built ⟨a ~ young man⟩

well-spo·ken \-'spō-kən\ *adj* **1** : speaking well, fitly, or courteously **2** : spoken with propriety ⟨~ words⟩

well·spring \'wel-,spriŋ\ *n* **1** : a source of continual supply **2** : FOUNTAINHEAD 1

well-thought-of \wel-'thȯt-,əv, -,äv\ *adj* : being of good repute

well-tim·bered \'wel-'tim-bərd\ *adj* **1 a** : well braced or strengthened by timbers ⟨a ~ house⟩ **b** : having a good structure or constitution ⟨a ~ horse⟩ **2** : having a good quantity of growing timber ⟨a ~ tract of land⟩

well-timed \'wel-'tīmd\ *adj* : happening at an opportune moment : TIMELY

well-to-do \,wel-tə-'dü\ *adj* : having more than adequate esp. financial resources : PROSPEROUS

well-turned \'wel-'tərnd\ *adj* **1** : symmetrically shaped or rounded : SHAPELY **2** : concisely and appropriately expressed ⟨a ~ phrase⟩ **3** : expertly rounded or turned ⟨a ~ column⟩

well-wish·er \'wel-,wish-ər, -'wish-\ *n* : one that wishes well to another — **well-wish·ing** \-iŋ\ *adj or n*

well-worn \-'wō(ə)rn, -'wȯ(ə)rn\ *adj* **1 a** : having been much used or worn ⟨~ shoes⟩ **b** : made stale or threadbare by use : TRITE ⟨a ~ quotation⟩ **2** : worn well or properly ⟨~ honors⟩

Wels·bach \,welz-,bak, -,bäk\ *trademark* — used for a burner for producing gaslight by the combustion of a mixture of air and gas or vapor to heat to incandescence a gas mantle or for the mantle used with such a burner

welsh \'welsh, 'welch\ *vi* [prob. fr. *Welsh,* adj.] : to cheat by avoiding payment of bets — **welsh·er** *n*

Welsh \'welsh\ *n* [ME *Walsche, Welsse,* fr. *walisch, welisch,* adj., Welsh, fr. OE (northern & Midland dial.) *wælisc, welisc* Celtic, Welsh, foreign, fr. OE *Wealh* Celt, Welshman, foreigner, of Celtic origin; akin to the source of L *Volcae,* a Celtic people of southeastern Gaul] **1** *pl in constr* : the natives or inhabitants of Wales **2** : the Celtic language of the Welsh people **3** : a breed of cattle or of swine developed in Wales — **Welsh** *adj*

Welsh cor·gi \-'kȯr-gē\ *n* [W *corgi,* fr. *cor* dwarf + *ci* dog] : a short-legged long-backed dog with foxy head belonging to either of two Welsh varieties

Welsh·man \'welsh-mən\ *n* : one of the Welsh — **Welsh·wom·an** \-,wum-ən\ *n*

Welsh rabbit *n* : melted often seasoned cheese poured over toast or crackers

Welsh rare·bit \-'ra(ə)r-bət, -'re(ə)r-\ *n* [by alter.] : WELSH RABBIT

Welsh springer spaniel *n* : any of a Welsh breed of red and white or orange and white small-eared springer spaniels

Welsh terrier *n* : any of a breed of wiry-coated terriers resembling airedales but smaller and developed in Wales for hunting

¹**welt** \'welt\ *n* [ME *welte*] **1** : a strip between a shoe sole and upper through which they are stitched or stapled together **2** : a doubled edge, strip, insert, or seam for ornament or reinforcement **3** : a ridge or lump raised on the body usu. by a blow; *also* : a heavy blow

²**welt** *vt* **1** : to furnish with a welt **2 a** : to raise a welt on the body of **b** : to hit hard

welt·an·schau·ung \'vel-,tän-,shau-əŋ\ *n, pl* **weltanschauungs** \-əŋz\ *or* **welt·an·schau·ung·en** \-əŋ-ən\ *often cap* [G, fr. *welt* world + *anschauung* view] : a comprehensive conception or apprehension of the world esp. from a specific standpoint

¹**wel·ter** \'wel-tər\ *vi* **wel·ter·ing** \-t(ə-)riŋ\ [ME *welteren;* akin to MD *welteren* to roll, OHG *walzan,* L *volvere* — more at VOLUBLE] **1 a** : WRITHE, TOSS; *also* : WALLOW **b** : to rise and fall or toss about in or with waves **2** : to become deeply sunk, soaked, or involved **3** : to be in turmoil

²**welter** *n* **1** : a state of wild disorder : TURMOIL **2** : a chaotic mass or jumble

³**welter** *n* [prob. fr. ¹*welt*] : WELTERWEIGHT

wel·ter·weight \'wel-tər-,wāt\ *n* [³*welter*] : a boxer weighing more than 135 but not over 147 pounds

welt·schmerz \'velt-,shme(ə)rts\ *n, often cap* [G, fr. *welt* world + *schmerz* pain] **1** : mental depression or apathy caused by comparison of the actual state of the world with an ideal state **2** : a mood of sentimental sadness

¹**wen** \'wen\ *n* [ME *wenn,* fr. OE; akin to MLG *wene* wen] : a cyst formed by obstruction of a sebaceous gland and filled with sebaceous material

²**wen** *n* [OE] : a rune adopted into the Old English alphabet with the value of Modern English *w*

¹wench \'wench\ n [ME wenche, short for wenchel child, fr. OE wencel; akin to OHG winchan to stagger — more at WINK] **1 a** : a young woman : GIRL **b** : a female servant **2** : a lewd woman : PROSTITUTE

²wench vi : to consort with lewd women; esp : to practice fornication — **wench·er** n

wend \'wend\ vb [ME wenden, fr. OE wendan; akin to OHG wenten to turn, OE windan to twist — more at WIND] vi : to direct one's course : TRAVEL ~ vt : to proceed on (one's way) : DIRECT

Wend \'wend\ n [G Wende, fr. OHG Winida; akin to OE Winedas, pl., Wends] : a member of a Slavic people of eastern Germany

¹Wend·ish \'wen-dish\ adj : of or relating to the Wends or their language

²Wendish n : the West Slavic language of the Wends

went [ME, past & pp. of wenden] past of GO

wen·tle·trap \'went-ᵊl-‚trap\ n [D wenteltrap winding stair, fr. MD wendeltrappe, fr. wendel turning + trappe stairs] : any of a family (Epitoniidae) of marine snails with usu. white shells; also : one of the shells

wept past of WEEP

were [ME were (suppletive sing. past subj. & 2d sing. past indic. of been to be), weren (suppletive past pl. of been), fr. OE wǣre (past subj. sing. & 2d sing. past indic. of wesan to be), wǣron (past pl. indic. of wesan), wǣren (past pl. subj. of wesan) — more at WAS] past 2d sing, past pl, or past subjunctive of BE

we're \(‚)wi(ə)r, (‚)wər, ‚wē-ər\ : we are

weren't \(')wərnt, 'wər-ənt\ : were not

were·wolf \'wi(ə)r-‚wu̇lf, 'wər-, 'we(ə)r-\ n, pl **were·wolves** \-‚wu̇lvz\ [ME, fr. OE werwulf; akin to OHG werwolf werewolf; both fr. a prehistoric WGmc compound whose constituents are represented by OE wer man and by OE wulf wolf — more at VIRILE, WOLF] : a person transformed into a wolf or capable of assuming a wolf's form : LYCANTHROPE

wer·gild \'wər-‚gild\ or **wer·geld** \-‚geld\ n [ME wergeld, fr. OE; akin to OHG wergelt wergild; both fr. a prehistoric WGmc compound whose constituents are represented by OE wer man and by OE gield, geld payment, tribute — more at GELD] : the value set in Anglo-Saxon and Germanic law upon the life of a man in accordance with his rank and paid as compensation to the kindred or lord of a slain person

wert \(')wərt\ archaic past 2d sing of BE

wes·kit \'wes-kət\ n [alter. of waistcoat] : VEST 2a, 2b

Wes·ley·an \'wes-lē-ən, 'wez-\ adj **1** : of or relating to John or Charles Wesley **2** : of or relating to the Arminian Methodism taught by John Wesley — **Wesleyan** n

Wes·ley·an·ism \-ə-‚niz-əm\ n : METHODISM 1; specif : the system of Arminian Methodism taught by John Wesley

¹west \'west\ adv [ME, fr. OE; akin to OHG westar to the west and prob. to L vesper evening, Gk hesperos] : to, toward, or in the west : WESTWARD

²west adj **1** : situated toward or at the west **2** : coming from the west

³west n **1 a** : the general direction of sunset : the direction to the left of one facing north **b** : the place on the horizon where the sun sets when it is near one of the equinoxes **c** : the cardinal point directly opposite to east **2** cap : regions or countries lying to the west of a specified or implied point of orientation **3** : the end of a church opposite the chancel

west·bound \'wes(t)-‚ba͟und\ adj : traveling or headed west

west by north n : a compass point one point north of due west : N 78° 45' W

west by south n : a compass point one point south of due west : S 78° 45' W

¹west·er \'wes-tər\ vi **west·er·ing** \-t(ə-)riŋ\ [ME westren, fr. ¹west] : to turn or move westward

²wester n [²west] : a westerly wind; esp : a storm from the west

¹west·er·ly \'wes-tər-lē\ adv (or adj) [obs. wester (western)] **1** : from the west **2** : toward the west

²westerly n : a wind blowing from the west

¹west·ern \'wes-tərn\ adj [ME westerne, fr. OE; akin to OHG westrōni western, OE west] **1** often cap : of, relating to, or characteristic of a region conventionally designated West **2 a** : lying toward the west **b** : coming from the west ⟨~ wind⟩ **3** cap : of or relating to the Roman Catholic or Protestant segment of Christianity ⟨Western liturgies⟩ — **west·ern·most** \-‚mōst\ adj

²western n **1** : one that is produced in or characteristic of a western region and esp. the western U.S. **2** often cap : a novel, story, motion picture, or broadcast dealing with life in the western U.S. during the latter half of the 19th century

West·ern·er \'wes-tə(r)-nər\ n **1** : a native or inhabitant of the West; esp : a native or resident of the western part of the U.S. **2** : one advocating the adoption of western European culture esp. in 19th century Russia

western hemisphere n : the half of the earth comprising No. and So. America and surrounding waters

west·ern·iza·tion \‚wes-tər-nə-'zā-shən\ n, often cap : conversion to or adoption of western traditions or techniques

west·ern·ize \'wes-tər-‚nīz\ vt : to imbue with qualities native to or associated with a western region; esp : OCCIDENTALIZE ~ vi : to become occidentalized

West Germanic n : a subdivision of the Germanic languages including English, Frisian, Dutch, and German

West Highland n [fr. West Highlands, western part of the High-lands of Scotland] : any of a breed of small very hardy beef cattle from the Highlands of Scotland

West Highland white terrier n : a small white long-coated dog of a breed developed in Scotland

west·ing \'wes-tiŋ\ n **1** : difference in longitude to the west from the last preceding point of reckoning **2** : westerly progress

west–northwest n — see COMPASS CARD

West·pha·lian ham \‚wes(t)-‚fāl-yən-, -‚fā-lē-ən-\ n [Westphalia, former province of Prussia] : a ham of distinctive flavor produced by smoking with juniper brush

West Saxon n **1** : a native or inhabitant of the West Saxon kingdom **2** : a dialect of Old English used as the chief literary dialect in pre-Conquest England

west–southwest n — see COMPASS CARD

¹west·ward \'wes-twərd\ adv (or adj) : toward the west

²westward n : westward direction or part ⟨sail to the ~⟩

west·wards \'wes-twərdz\ adv : WESTWARD

¹wet \'wet\ adj **wet·ter**; **wet·test** [ME, partly fr. pp. of weten to wet & partly fr. OE wǣt wet; akin to ON vātr wet, OE wæter water] **1 a** : consisting of, containing, covered with, or soaked with liquid (as water) **b** of natural gas : containing appreciable quantities of readily condensable hydrocarbons **2** : RAINY **3** : still moist enough to smudge or smear ⟨~ paint⟩ **4** of a fish : not processed, dried, or reduced **5 a** : permitting the manufacture and sale of alcoholic liquor **b** : advocating a policy of permitting such traffic ⟨a ~ candidate⟩ **6** : preserved in liquid **7** : employing or done by means of or in the presence of water or other liquid ⟨~ extraction of copper⟩ **8** : perversely wrong : MISGUIDED ⟨all ~⟩ — **wet·ly** adv — **wet·ness** n

syn DAMP, DANK, MOIST, HUMID: WET usu. implies saturation but may suggest a covering of a surface with water or something (as paint) not yet dry; DAMP implies a slight or moderate absorption and often connotes an unpleasant degree of moisture; DANK implies a more distinctly disagreeable or unwholesome dampness often connoting lack of fresh air and sunlight; MOIST applies to what is slightly damp or not felt as dry; HUMID implies the presence of much water vapor in the air

²wet n **1** : WATER; also : WETNESS, MOISTURE **2** : rainy weather : RAIN **3** : an advocate of a policy of permitting the sale of intoxicating liquors

³wet vb **wet** or **wet·ted**; **wet·ting** [ME weten, fr. OE wǣtan, fr. wǣt, adj.] vt **1** : to make wet **2** : to urinate in or on ~ vi : to become wet — **wet one's whistle** : to take a drink esp. of liquor

wet·back \'wet-‚bak\ n : a Mexican who enters (as by wading the Rio Grande) the U.S. illegally

wet blanket n : one who quenches or dampens enthusiasm or pleasure

wet–blan·ket \'wet-'blaŋ-kət\ vt : to quench or dampen with or as if with a wet blanket : DEPRESS

wet down vt : to dampen by sprinkling with water

weth·er \'weth-ər\ n [ME, ram, fr. OE; akin to OHG widar ram, L vitulus calf, vetus old, Gk etos year] : a male sheep castrated before sexual maturity

wet·land \'wet-‚land\ n : land containing much soil moisture

wet nurse n : one that cares for and suckles young not her own

wet–nurse \'wet-‚nərs\ vt **1** : to care for and suckle as a wet nurse **2** : to devote unremitting or excessive care to

wet·ta·bil·i·ty \‚wet-ə-'bil-ət-ē\ n : the quality or state of being wettable : the degree to which something can be wet

wet·ta·ble \'wet-ə-bəl\ adj : capable of being wetted

wet·ter \'wet-ər\ n : one that wets

wetting agent n : a substance that by becoming adsorbed prevents a surface from being repellent to a wetting liquid and is used in mixing solids with liquids or spreading liquids on surfaces

wet·tish \'wet-ish\ adj : somewhat wet : MOIST

wet wash n : laundry returned damp and not ironed

we've \(‚)wēv\ : we have

¹whack \'hwak, 'wak\ vb [prob. imit.] vt **1 a** : to strike with a smart or resounding blow **b** : to cut with or as if with a whack : CHOP **2** chiefly Brit : to get the better of : DEFEAT ~ vi : to strike a smart or resounding blow — **whack·er** n

²whack n **1** : a smart or resounding blow; also : the sound of or as if of such a blow **2** : PORTION, SHARE **3** : CONDITION; esp : proper working order **4 a** : an opportunity or attempt to do something **b** : a single action or occasion

whack·ing \'hwak-iŋ, 'wak-\ adj : very large : WHOPPING

whack up vt : to divide into shares

whacky \'hwak-ē, 'wak-\ var of WACKY

¹whale \'hwā(ə)l, 'wā(ə)l\ n, pl **whales** often attrib [ME, fr. OE hwæl; akin to OHG hwal whale] **1** or pl **whale** : an aquatic mammal (order Cetacea) that superficially resembles a large fish and is valued commercially for its oil, flesh, and sometimes whalebone; esp : one of the larger members of this group **2** : a person or thing impressive in size or qualities ⟨a ~ of a difference⟩ ⟨a ~ of a story⟩

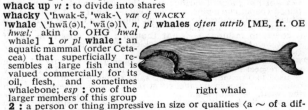

right whale

²whale vi : to engage in whale fishing

³whale vt [origin unknown] **1** : LASH, THRASH **2** : to strike or hit vigorously **3** : to defeat soundly

whale·back \-‚bak\ n : something shaped like the back of a whale; specif : a freight steamer with a convex upper deck

whale·boat \-‚bōt\ n **1** : a long narrow rowboat made with both ends sharp and raking, often steered with an oar, and formerly used by whalers for hunting whales **2** : a long narrow rowboat or motorboat that is sharp and rounded at both ends in the manner of the original whaleboats and is often carried by warships and merchant ships

whale·bone \-‚bōn\ n **1** : a horny substance found in two rows of plates from 2 to 12 feet long attached along the upper jaw of whalebone whales and used esp. to stiffen stays or fans **2** : an article made of whalebone

whalebone whale n : any of various usu. large whales (suborder Mysticeti) having whalebone instead of teeth

whal·er \'hwā-lər, 'wā-\ n **1** : a person or ship engaged in whale fishing **2** : WHALEBOAT 2

whal·ing \-liŋ\ n : the occupation of catching and rendering whales

¹wham \'hwam, 'wam\ n [imit.] **1** : the loud sound of a hard impact **2** : a solid blow

²wham vb **whammed**; **wham·ming** vt : to propel, strike, or beat so as to produce a loud impact ~ vi : to hit or explode with a loud impact

wham·my \'hwam-ē, 'wam-\ n [prob. fr. ¹wham] : a supernatural power bringing bad luck : JINX

1whang \'hwaŋ, 'waŋ\ *n* [alter. of ME *thong, thwang*] **1** *dial* **a :** THONG **b :** RAWHIDE **2** *Brit* **:** a large piece **:** CHUNK

2whang *vt* **1** *dial* **:** BEAT, THRASH **2 :** to propel or strike with force ~ *vi* **:** to beat or work with force or violence

3whang *n* [imit.] **:** a loud sharp vibrant or resonant sound ⟨the ~ of hammer on anvil⟩

4whang *vi* **:** to make a whang ~ *vt* **:** to strike with a whang

whan·gee \hwaŋ-'gē, waŋ-\ *n* [prob. fr. Chin (Pek) *huang² li²*, fr. *huang²* yellow + *li²* bamboo cane] **1 :** any of several Chinese bamboos (genus *Phyllostachys*) **2 :** a walking stick or riding crop of whangee

whap \'hwäp, 'wäp\ *var of* WHOP

1wharf \'hwȯrf, 'wȯrf\ *n, pl* **wharves** \'hwȯrvz, 'wȯrvz\ *also* **wharfs** [ME, fr. OE *hwearf* embankment, wharf; akin to OE *hweorfan* to turn, OHG *hwerban*, Gk *karpos* wrist] **1 :** a structure built along or at an angle from the shore of navigable waters so that ships may lie alongside to receive and discharge cargo and passengers **2** *obs* **:** the bank of a river or the shore of the sea

2wharf *vt* **wharfed; wharf·ing :** to place upon or bring to a wharf ~ *vi* **:** DOCK

wharf·age \'hwȯr-fij, 'wȯr-\ *n* **1 a :** the provision or the use of a wharf **b :** the handling or stowing of goods on a wharf **2 :** the charge for the use of a wharf **3 :** the wharf accommodations of a place **:** WHARVES

wharf·in·ger \-fən-jər\ *n* [irreg. fr. *wharfage*] **:** the operator or manager of a commercial wharf

wharf·mas·ter \'hwȯrf-,mas-tər, 'wȯrf-\ *n* **:** the manager of a wharf **:** WHARFINGER

wharve \'hwȯrv, 'wȯrv\ *n* [ME *wherve*, fr. OE *hweorfa;* akin to OE *hweorfan* to turn] **:** WHORL 1

1what \(')hwät, (')hwət, (')wät, (')wət\ *pron* [ME, fr. OE *hwæt*, neut of *hwā* who — more at WHO] **1 a** (1) — used as an interrogative expressing inquiry about the identity of an object or matter ⟨~ is this⟩ ⟨~ are those things on the table⟩; often used to ask for repetition of an utterance or part of an utterance not properly heard or understood ⟨found ~⟩ (2) **:** a person or thing of how much value or consequence ⟨~ is wealth without friends⟩ **b** (1) *archaic* **:** WHO 1 — used as an interrogative expressing inquiry about the identity of a person (2) — used as an interrogative expressing inquiry about the character, occupation, position, or role of a person ⟨~ do you think I am, a fool⟩ **c :** how much ⟨~ does breakfast cost⟩ **d** — used as an exclamation expressing surprise or excitement and frequently introducing a question ⟨~, no breakfast⟩ **e :** one or ones of what sort ⟨do not recognize him for ~ he is⟩ **f :** SOMETHING — used in expressions directing attention to a statement that the speaker is about to make ⟨I'll tell you ~⟩ **g** — used at the end of a question to express inquiry about additional possibilities ⟨is it raining, or snowing, or ~⟩ **h** *chiefly Brit* — used at the end of an utterance as a tag apparently inviting agreement or disagreement ⟨a clever play, ~⟩ **2** *chiefly substand* **:** 4THAT 1, WHICH 3, WHO 3 **3 a :** that which **:** the one or ones that ⟨no income but ~ he gets from his writings⟩ — sometimes used in reference to a clause or phrase that is yet to come or is not yet complete ⟨gave also, ~ is more valuable, understanding⟩ **b :** as much or as many as **c :** the kind that **:** the same as ⟨the speech was very much ~ everyone expected⟩ **4 a :** WHATEVER 1a ⟨say ~ you will⟩ **b** *obs* **:** WHOEVER — **what for 1** *chiefly dial* **:** what kind of — used either inseparably or with a verb and its subject between *what* and *for* ⟨*what* is he *for* a fool —Shak.⟩ ⟨*what for* tobacco are you smoking⟩ **2 :** for what purpose or reason **:** WHY — usu. used with the other words of a question between *what* and *for* ⟨*what* did you do that *for*⟩ except when used alone **3 :** punishment esp. by blows or by a sharp reprimand ⟨gave him *what for* in violent Spanish —*New Yorker*⟩ — **what have you :** what not — **what if 1 :** what will or would be the result if **2 :** what does it matter if — **what it takes :** the qualities or resources needed for success or for attainment of a goal — **what not :** any of various other things that might also be mentioned ⟨paper clips, pins, and *what not*⟩ — **what of 1 :** what is the situation with respect to **2 :** what importance can be assigned to — **what's what :** the true state of things ⟨knows *what's what* when it comes to fashion⟩ — **what though :** what does it matter if ⟨*what though* the rose have prickles, yet 'tis plucked —Shak.⟩ ⟨*what though* the sky is cloudy today⟩

2what *adv* [ME, fr. OE *hwæt*, fr. *hwæt*, pron.] **1** *obs* **:** WHY **2 a :** in what respect **:** HOW **b :** how much ⟨~ does he care⟩ **3 a :** PARTLY — used two or more times in the same sentence to introduce prepositional phrases in parallel construction ⟨~ with the war, ~ with the sweat, ~ with the gallows, and ~ with poverty, I am custom-shrunk —Shak.⟩ **b** — used to introduce a prepositional phrase that expresses cause and usu. has more than one object; used principally before phrases beginning with *with* ⟨~ with unemployment and high prices⟩

3what *adj* [1*what*] **1 a** (1) — used as an interrogative expressing inquiry about the identity or nature of a person, object, or matter ⟨~ minerals do we export⟩ (2) **:** how much **b :** how remarkable or surprising esp. for good or bad qualities or great or small size — used esp. in exclamatory utterances and dependent clauses ⟨~ mountains⟩ ⟨remember ~ fun we had⟩ ⟨~ a suggestion⟩ ⟨~ a charming girl⟩ **2 a** (1) **:** WHATEVER 1a (2) **:** ANY ⟨ornament of ~ description soever⟩ **b :** the . . . that **:** as much or as many . . . as ⟨~ survivors had been found⟩

1what·ev·er \hwät-'ev-ər, wät-, (,)(h)wət-\ *pron* **1 a :** anything or everything that ⟨take ~ you want⟩ **b :** no matter what **c :** what not ⟨buffalo or rhinoceros or ~ —Alan Moorehead⟩ **2 :** WHAT 1a (1) — used in questions expressing astonishment or perplexity ⟨~ do you mean by that⟩

2whatever *adj* **1 a :** any . . . that **:** all . . . that **b :** no matter what **2 :** of any kind at all — used for emphasis after the substantive it modifies ⟨no food ~⟩

what·man \'hwät-mən, 'wät-\ *n* [James *Whatman*, 18th cent. E paper manufacturer] **:** a drawing paper or board of high quality

what·not \'hwät-,nät, 'hwət-, 'wät-, 'wət-\ *n* [*what not?*] **1 :** a nondescript person or thing **2 :** a light open set of shelves for bric-a-brac

what·so·ev·er \,hwät-sə-'wev-ər, ,hwət-, ,wät-, ,wət-\ *pron or adj* **:** WHATEVER

whaup \'hwȯp, 'wȯp\ *n, pl* **whaup** *also* **whaups** [imit.] *Scot & dial Eng* **:** a European curlew (*Numenius arquata*)

wheal \'hwē(ə)l, 'wē(ə)l\ *n* [alter. of *wale*] **:** a suddenly formed elevation of the skin surface: as **a :** WELT **b :** a flat burning or itching eminence on the skin

wheat \'hwēt, 'wēt\ *n, often attrib* [ME *whete*, fr. OE *hwǣte;* akin to OHG *weizzi* wheat, *hwīz, wīz* white — more at WHITE] **1 :** a cereal grain that yields a fine white flour, is the chief breadstuff of temperate climates, is used also in pastes (as macaroni or spaghetti), and is important in animal feeds esp. as bran or middlings **2 :** any of various grasses (genus *Triticum*) of wide climatic adaptability that are cultivated in most temperate areas for the wheat they yield; *esp* **:** an annual cereal grass (*T. aestivum*) known only as a cultigen — called also *common wheat*

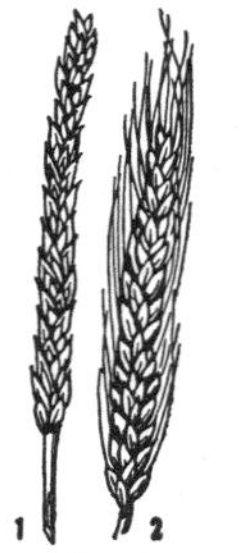

1 2

wheat: *1* beardless; *2* bearded

wheat bread *n* **:** a bread made of a combination of white and whole wheat flours as distinguished from bread made entirely of whole wheat flour or white flour

wheat cake *n* **:** a griddle cake made of wheat flour

wheat·ear \'hwēt-,i(ə)r, 'wēt-\ *n* [back-formation fr. earlier *wheatears* wheatear, prob. by folk etymology or euphemism fr. *white* + *arse* (rump)] **:** a small northern bird (*Oenanthe oenanthe*) related to the stonechat and whinchat

wheat·en \'hwēt-ᵊn, 'wēt-\ *adj* **:** of, relating to, or made of wheat

wheat germ *n* **:** the embryo of the wheat kernel separated in milling and used esp. as a source of vitamins

wheat rust *n* **:** a destructive disease of wheat caused by rust fungi; *also* **:** a fungus (as *Puccinia graminis*) causing a wheat rust

Wheat·stone bridge \,hwēt-,stōn-, ,wēt-, *chiefly Brit* -stən-\ *n* [Sir Charles *Wheatstone* †1875 E physicist] **:** a bridge for measuring electrical resistances consisting of a conductor joining two branches of a circuit

wheat·worm \'hwēt-,wərm, 'wēt-\ *n* **:** a small nematode worm (*Anguina tritici*) parasitic on wheat and other grasses — called also *wheat eel*

whee \'hwē, 'wē\ *interj* — used to express delight or general exuberance

whee·dle \'hwēd-ᵊl, 'wēd-\ *vb* **whee·dling** \'(h)wēd-liŋ, -ᵊl-iŋ\ [origin unknown] *vt* **1 :** to influence or entice by soft words or flattery **2 :** to gain or get by wheedling ⟨~ his way into favor⟩ ~ *vi* **:** to use soft words or flattery

1wheel \'hwē(ə)l, 'wē(ə)l\ *n, often attrib* [ME, fr. OE *hweogol, hwēol;* akin to ON *hvēl* wheel, Gk *kyklos* circle, wheel, Skt *cakra*, L *colere* to cultivate, inhabit, Gk *telos* end] **1 :** a circular frame of hard material that may be solid, partly solid, or spoked and that is capable of turning on an axle **2 :** a contrivance or apparatus having as its principal part a wheel: as **a :** a chiefly medieval instrument of torture designed for stretching, disjointing, or otherwise mutilating a victim **b :** BICYCLE **c :** any of many revolving disks or drums used as gambling paraphernalia **3 :** an imaginary turning wheel symbolizing the inconstancy of fortune **4 :** something resembling a wheel in shape or motion; *specif* **:** a firework that rotates while burning **5 a :** a curving or circular movement **b :** a rotation or turn usu. about an axis or center; *specif* **:** a turning movement of troops or ships in line in which the units preserve alignment and relative positions as they change direction **6 a :** a moving or essential part of something likened to a machine ⟨the ~*s* of government⟩ **b :** a directing or controlling force **c :** a person of importance esp. in an organization ⟨big ~⟩ **7 :** the refrain or burden of a song **8 a :** a circuit of theaters or places of entertainment **b :** a sports league

2wheel *vi* **1 :** to turn on or as if on an axis **:** REVOLVE **2 :** to change direction as if revolving on a pivot ⟨the battalion would have ~*ed* to the flank —Walter Bernstein⟩ ⟨~*ed* about and walked briskly aft —L.C.Douglas⟩ ⟨her mind will ~ around to the other extreme —Liam O'Flaherty⟩ **3 :** to move or extend in a circle or curve ⟨birds in ~*ing* flight⟩ ⟨valleys where young cotton ~*ed* slowly in fanlike rows —William Faulkner⟩ **4 :** to drive or go on or as if on wheels or in a wheeled vehicle ~ *vt* **1 :** to cause to turn on or as if on an axis **:** ROTATE **2 :** to convey or move on or as if on wheels or in a wheeled vehicle; *esp* **:** to drive (a vehicle) at high speed **3 :** to cause to change direction as if revolving on a pivot **4 :** to make or perform in a circle or curve

wheel and axle *n* **:** a mechanical device consisting of a grooved wheel turned by a cord or chain with a rigidly attached axle (as for winding up a weight) together with the supporting standards

wheel animal *n* **:** ROTIFER — called also *wheel animalcule*

1wheel·bar·row \'hwē(ə)l-,bar-(,)ō, 'wē(ə)l-, -,bar-ə(-w)\ *n* **:** a small vehicle with handles and one or more wheels for carrying small loads

2wheelbarrow *vt* **:** to convey in a wheelbarrow

wheel·base \-,bās\ *n* **:** the distance in inches between the front and rear axles of an automotive vehicle

wheel bug *n* **:** a large No. American bug (*Arilus cristatus*) having a high serrated crest on its prothorax and sucking the blood of other insects

wheel·chair \-,che(ə)r, -,cha(ə)r\ *n* **:** a chair mounted on wheels and usu. propelled by the occupant

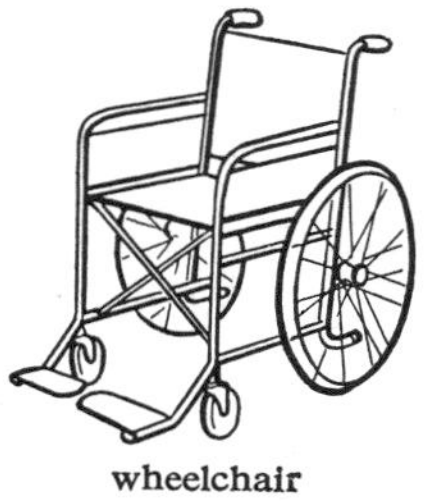

wheelchair

wheeled \'hwē(ə)ld, 'wē(ə)ld\ *adj* **1 :** equipped with wheels ⟨~ vehicles⟩ **2 :** moving or functioning by means of wheels ⟨~ traffic⟩

wheel·er \'hwē-lər, 'wē-\ *n* **1 :** one that wheels **2 :** a draft animal (as a horse) pulling in the position nearest the front wheels of a wagon **3 :** something (as a vehicle or ship) that has wheels — used esp. in combinations ⟨side-*wheeler*⟩

wheel·horse \'hwē(ə)l-,hȯ(ə)rs, 'wē(ə)l-\ *n* **1 :** a horse in a position nearest the wheels in a tandem or similar arrangement **2 :** a steady and effective worker esp. in a political body

wheel·house \-,hau̇s\ *n* **:** PILOTHOUSE

wheel·ing \'hwē-liŋ, 'wē-\ *n* **1 :** the act or process of one that wheels **2 :** the condition of a road relative to passage on wheels

wheel lock *n* **:** an obsolete gunlock in which sparks are struck from a flint or a piece of iron pyrites by a revolving wheel

wheel·man \'hwē(ə)l-mən, 'wē(ə)l-\ *n* **1 a :** HELMSMAN **b :** the driver of an automobile **2 :** CYCLIST

wheels·man \'hwē(ə)lz-mən, 'wē(ə)lz-\ *n* **:** one who steers with a wheel; *esp* **:** HELMSMAN

wheel·work \'hwē(ə)l-,wərk, 'wē(ə)l-\ *n* **:** wheels in gear and their connections in a machine or mechanism

wheel·wright \-,rīt\ *n* **:** a man whose occupation is to make or repair wheels and wheeled vehicles

1**ween** \'hwēn, 'wēn\ *adj* [ME (Sc) *quheyne*, fr. OE *hwǣne, hwēne*, adv., somewhat, fr. instr. of *hwōn* little, few] *dial Brit* **:** 2FEW 2

2**ween** *n, dial Brit* **:** a considerable number or amount

1**wheeze** \'hwēz, 'wēz\ *vi* [ME *whesen*, prob. of Scand origin; akin to ON *hvæsa* to hiss; akin to OE *hwǣst* action of blowing, L *queri* to complain] **1 :** to breathe with difficulty usu. with a whistling sound **2 :** to make a sound resembling that of wheezing

2**wheeze** *n* **1 :** a sound of wheezing **2 a :** a stage joke esp. when often repeated and widely known **b :** a trite saying or witticism

wheez·i·ly \'hwē-zə-lē, 'wē-\ *adv* **:** in a wheezy manner

wheez·i·ness \-zē-nəs\ *n* **:** the quality or state of being wheezy

wheezy \-zē\ *adj* **1 :** inclined to wheeze **2 :** having a wheezing sound

1**whelk** \'hwelk, 'welk, 'wilk\ *n* [ME *welke*, fr. OE *weoloc;* akin to L *volvere* to turn — more at VOLUBLE] **:** any of numerous large marine snails (as of the genus *Buccinum*); *esp* **:** one (*B. undatum*) much used as food in Europe

2**whelk** \'hwelk, 'welk\ *n* [ME *whelke*, fr. OE *hwylca*, fr. *hwelian* to suppurate] **1 :** PAPULE, PUSTULE **2 :** WELT, WHEAL

whelm \'hwelm, 'welm\ *vb* [ME *whelmen*] *vt* **1 :** to turn (as a dish or vessel) upside down usu. to cover something **:** cover or engulf completely with usu. disastrous effect **2 :** to overcome in thought or feeling **:** OVERWHELM ~ *vi* **:** to pass or go over something so as to bury or submerge it

1**whelp** \'hwelp, 'welp\ *n* [ME, fr. OE *hwelp;* akin to OHG *hwelf* whelp] **1 a :** one of the young of various carnivorous mammals and esp. of the dog **b :** a young boy or girl **2 :** an ill-considered or despised person or his offspring **3 a :** any of the longitudinal ribs or ridges on the barrel of a capstan or windlass — usu. used in pl. **b :** SPROCKET

2**whelp** *vt* **:** to give birth to — used of the dog and some other carnivores ~ *vi* **:** to bring forth young

1**when** \(')hwen, (')wen, (h)wən\ *adv* [ME, fr. OE *hwanne, hwenne;* akin to OHG *hwanne* when, OE *hwā* who — more at WHO] **1 :** at what time ⟨asked him ~ it happened⟩ ⟨~ will he return⟩ **2 a :** at or during which time **b :** and then **3 :** at a former and usu. less prosperous time ⟨brag fondly of having known him ~ —Vance Packard⟩

2**when** *conj* [ME, fr. OE *hwanne, hwenne*, fr. *hwanne, hwenne*, adv.] **1 a :** at or during the time that **:** WHILE ⟨went fishing ~ he was a boy⟩ **b :** just after the moment that ⟨stop writing ~ the bell rings⟩ **c :** at any or every time that ⟨~ he listens to music, he falls asleep⟩ **2 :** in the event that **:** IF ⟨the batter is out ~ he bunts foul with two strikes on him⟩ **3 a :** considering that ⟨why use water at all ~ you can drown in it —Stuart Chase⟩ **b :** in spite of the fact that **:** ALTHOUGH ⟨gave up politics ~ he might have made a great career in it⟩

3**when** \,hwen, ,wen\ *pron* **:** what or which time ⟨in 1934, since ~ he has been working at landscapes and portraits —*Horizon*⟩

4**when** \'hwen, 'wen\ *n* **:** the time in which something is done or comes about

when·as \hwe-'naz, we-, (h)wə-\ *conj* [ME (Sc) *when as*, fr. ME *when* + *as*] *archaic* **:** WHEN

1**whence** \(')hwen(t)s, (')wen(t)s\ *adv* [ME *whennes*, fr. *whenne* whence (fr. OE *hwanon*) + *-s*, adv. suffix, fr. *-s*, gen. sing. ending; akin to OHG *hwanān* whence, OE *hwā* who] **:** from what place, source, or cause ⟨~ do these questionings well up —A.C.Pepper⟩

2**whence** *conj* **1 :** from what place, source, or cause ⟨inquired ~ the water came —Maria Edgeworth⟩ **2 a :** from or out of which place, source, or cause ⟨the lawless society ~ the ballads sprang —De Lancey Ferguson⟩ **b :** by reason of which fact **:** WHEREFORE ⟨nothing broke — ~ I infer that my bones are not yet chalky —O. W. Holmes †1935⟩

whence·so·ev·er \'hwen(t)(s)-sə-,wev-ər, 'wen(t)(s)-\ *conj* **:** from whatever place or source

1**when·ev·er** \hwe-'nev-ər, we-, (h)wə-\ *conj* **:** at any or every time that

2**whenever** *adv* **:** at whatever time

1**when·so·ev·er** \'hwen(t)-sə-,wev-ər, 'wen(t)-\ *conj* **:** WHENEVER

2**whensoever** *adv, obs* **:** at any time whatever

1**where** \(')hwe(ə)r, (')hwa(ə)r, (')we(ə)r, (')wa(ə)r, (,)(h)wər\ *adv* [ME, fr. OE *hwǣr;* akin to OHG *hwār* where, OE *hwā* who — more at WHO] **1 a :** at, in, or to what place ⟨~ is the house⟩ ⟨~ are we going⟩ **b :** at, in, or to what situation, position, direction, circumstances, or respect ⟨~ does this plan lead⟩ ⟨~ is he wrong⟩ **2** *archaic* **:** HERE, THERE ⟨lo, ~ it comes again —Shak.⟩

2**where** *conj* **1 a :** at, in, or to what place ⟨knows ~ the house is⟩ **b :** at, in, or to what situation, position, direction, circumstances, or respect ⟨shows ~ the plan leads⟩ **2 :** WHEREVER ⟨goes ~ he likes⟩ **3 a :** at, in, or to which place ⟨the town ~ she lives⟩ **b :** at or in which ⟨has reached the size ~ traffic is a problem⟩ **4 a :** at, in, or to the place at, in, or to which ⟨stay ~ you are⟩ ⟨send him away ~ he'll forget⟩ **b :** in a case, situation, or respect in which ⟨outstanding ~ endurance is called for⟩

3**where** \'hwe(ə)r, 'hwa(ə)r, 'we(ə)r, 'wa(ə)r\ *n* **1 :** PLACE, LOCATION ⟨the ~ and the how of the accident⟩ **2 :** what place, source, or cause ⟨~ is he from⟩

1**where·abouts** \-ə-,bau̇ts\ *also* **where·about** \-,bau̇t\ *adv* [ME *wherabouts* (fr. *wher aboute* + *-s*, adv. suffix) & *wher aboute*, fr. *where, wher* where + *about, aboute* about — more at WHENCE] **:** about where **:** near what place ⟨~ is the house⟩

2**whereabouts** *also* **whereabout** *conj* **1** *obs* **:** on what business or errand **2 :** near what place **:** WHERE ⟨know ~ he lives⟩

3**whereabouts** *n pl but sing or pl in constr, also* **whereabout :** the place or general locality where a person or thing is

1**where·as** \hwer-'az, hwar-, wer-, war-, (,)(h)wər-\ *conj* [ME *where as*, fr. *where* + *as*] **1 :** in view of the fact that **:** SINCE — used esp. to introduce a preamble **2 :** while on the contrary

2**whereas** *n* **1 :** an introductory statement of a formal document **:** PREAMBLE **2 :** a conditional or qualifying statement

where·at \-'at\ *conj* **1 :** at or toward which **2 :** in consequence of which **:** WHEREUPON

1**where·by** \hwe(ə)r-'bī, hwa(ə)r-, we(ə)r-, wa(ə)r-, (,)(h)wər-\ *conj* **:** by, through, or in accordance with which

2**whereby** *adv, obs* **:** by what **:** HOW

1**where·fore** \'hwe(ə)r-,fō(ə)r, 'hwa(ə)r-, 'we(ə)r-, 'wa(ə)r-, -,fȯ(ə)r\ *adv* [ME *wherfor, wherfore*, fr. *where, wher* + *for, fore* for] **1 :** for what reason or purpose **:** WHY **2 :** THEREFORE

2**wherefore** *n* **:** an answer or statement giving an explanation **:** REASON

where·from \-,frəm, -,främ\ *conj* **:** from which

1**where·in** \hwer-'in, hwar-, wer-, war-, (,)(h)wər-\ *adv* **:** in what **:** in what particular or respect ⟨~ was he wrong⟩

2**wherein** *conj* **1 a :** in which **:** WHERE ⟨the city ~ he resides⟩ **b :** during which **2 :** in what way **:** HOW ⟨showed him ~ he was wrong⟩

where·in·to \-'in-(,)tü, -tə-(w)\ *conj* **:** into which

1**where·of** \-'əv, -'äv\ *conj* **1 :** of what ⟨knows ~ she speaks⟩ **2 a :** of which ⟨books ~ the best are lost⟩ **b :** of whom **3** *archaic* **:** with or by which

2**whereof** *adv, archaic* **:** of what ⟨~ are you made —Shak.⟩

1**where·on** \-'ȯn, -'än\ *conj* **1** *archaic* **:** on what ⟨tell me ~ the likelihood depends —Shak.⟩ **2 :** on which ⟨the base ~ it rests⟩

2**whereon** *adv, archaic* **:** on what ⟨~ do you look —Shak.⟩

where·so·ev·er \'hwer-sə-,wev-ər, 'hwar-, 'wer-, 'war-\ *conj, archaic* **:** WHEREVER

where·through \'hwe(ə)r-,thrü, 'hwa(ə)r-, 'we(ə)r-, 'wa(ə)r-\ *conj* **:** through which

1**where·to** \-,tü\ *adv* **:** to what place, purpose, or end ⟨~ tends all this —Shak.⟩

2**whereto** *conj* **:** to which

where·un·to \hwer-'ən-(,)tü, hwar-, wer-, war-, (,)(h)wər-, -'ən-tə-(w)\ *adv or conj* **:** WHERETO

where·up·on \'hwer-ə-,pȯn, 'hwar-, 'wer-, 'war-, -,pän\ *conj* **1 :** on which **2 :** closely following and in consequence of which

1**wher·ev·er** \hwer-'ev-ər, hwar-, wer-, war-, (,)(h)wər-\ *adv* **1 :** where in the world ⟨~ did she get that hat⟩ **2 :** anywhere at all ⟨explore northward or ~ —Bernard De Voto⟩

2**wherever** *conj* **1 :** at, in, or to any or all places that ⟨thrives ~ he goes⟩ **2 :** in any circumstance in which ⟨~ it is possible, he tries to help⟩

1**where·with** \'hwe(ə)r-,wit͟h, 'hwa(ə)r-, 'we(ə)r-, 'wa(ə)r-, -,with\ *conj* **:** with or by means of which ⟨metal tools ~ to break ground —Russell Lord⟩

2**wherewith** *pron* **:** that with or by which — used with an infinitive ⟨had not ~ to feed himself⟩

3**wherewith** *adv, obs* **:** with what ⟨~ shall it be salted —Mt 5:13 (AV)⟩

1**where·with·al** \'hwe(ə)r-wit͟h-,ȯl, 'hwa(ə)r-, 'we(ə)r-, 'wa(ə)r-, -with-\ *conj* [*where* + *withal*] **:** WHEREWITH

2**wherewithal** *pron* **:** WHEREWITH

3**wherewithal** *n* **:** MEANS, RESOURCES; *specif* **:** MONEY ⟨the ~ for a dinner⟩

wher·ry \'hwer-ē, 'wer-\ *n* [ME *whery*] **1 :** any of various light boats: as **a :** a long light rowboat made sharp at both ends and used to transport passengers on rivers and about harbors **b :** a racing scull for one person **2 :** a large light barge, lighter, or fishing boat varying in type in different parts of Great Britain

1**whet** \'hwet, 'wet\ *vt* **whet·ted; whet·ting** [ME *whetten*, fr. OE *hwettan;* akin to OHG *wezzen* to whet, *waz* sharp] **1 :** to sharpen by rubbing on or with something (as a stone) ⟨~ a knife⟩ **2 :** to make keen or more acute **:** EXCITE, STIMULATE ⟨~ the appetite⟩ — **whet·ter** *n*

2**whet** *n* **1** *dial* **a :** a spell of work between two whettings of the scythe **b :** TIME, WHILE **2 :** something that sharpens or makes keen: **a :** GOAD, INCITEMENT **b :** APPETIZER; *also* **:** a drink of liquor

1**wheth·er** \'hwet͟h-ər, 'wet͟h-, (,)(h)wət͟h-\ *pron* [ME, fr. OE *hwæther, hwether;* akin to OHG *hwedar* which of two, L *uter*, Gk *poteros*, OE *hwā* who — more at WHO] **1** *archaic* **:** which one of the two **2** *archaic* **:** whichever one of the two

2**whether** *conj* [ME, fr. OE *hwæther, hwether*, fr. *hwæther, hwether*, pron.] **1** — used as a function word followed usu. by correlative *or* or by *or whether* to indicate (1) until the early 19th century a direct question involving alternatives; (2) an indirect question involving alternatives ⟨decide ~ he should agree or raise objections⟩; (3) alternative conditions or possibilities ⟨see me no more, ~ he be dead or no —Shak.⟩ **2 :** EITHER ⟨seated him next to her ~ by accident or design⟩

whether or no *also* **whether or not** *adv* **:** in any case

whet·stone \'hwet-,stōn, 'wet-\ *n* **:** a stone for whetting edge tools

whew *often read as* 'hwü, 'wü, 'hyü\ *n* [imit.] **1 :** a whistling sound **2 :** a sound like a half-formed whistle uttered as an exclamation ⟨gave a long ~ when he realized the size of the job⟩ — used interjectionally chiefly to express amazement, discomfort, or relief

whey \'hwā, 'wā\ *n* [ME, fr. OE *hwæg;* akin to MD *wey* whey] **:** the serum or watery part of milk separated from the more thick or coagulable part or curd esp. in the process of making cheese — **whey·ey** \'hwā-ē, 'wā-\ *adj*

whey–face \-,fās\ *n* **:** a person having a pale face (as from fear) — **whey–faced** \-,fāst\ *adj*

1**which** \(')hwich, (')wich\ *adj* [ME, of what kind, which, fr. OE *hwilc;* akin to OHG *wilīh* of what kind, which; both fr. a prehistoric Gmc compound whose first constituent is akin to OE *hwā* who & whose second constituent is represented by OE *-līc* -ly — more at WHO, -LY] **1 :** being what one or ones out of a group — used as an interrogative ⟨~ tie should I wear⟩ ⟨kept a record of ~ employees took their vacations in July⟩ **2 :** 2WHICHEVER ⟨it will not fit, turn it ~ way you like⟩ **3** — used as a function word to introduce a nonrestrictive relative clause and to modify a noun in that clause and to refer together with that noun to a word or word group in a preceding clause or to an entire preceding clause or sentence or longer unit of discourse ⟨in German, ~ language might . . . have been the medium of transmission —Thomas Pyles⟩ ⟨that this city is a rebellious city . . . for ~ cause was this city destroyed —Ezra 4:15 (AV)⟩

2**which** *pron* **1 :** what one or ones out of a group — used as an interrogative ⟨~ of those houses do you live in⟩ ⟨~ of you want tea and ~ want lemonade⟩ ⟨he is swimming or canoeing, I don't know ~⟩ **2 :** 1WHICHEVER ⟨take ~ you like⟩ **3** — used as a function word to introduce a relative clause; used in any grammatical relation except that of a possessive; used esp. in reference to animals, inanimate objects, groups, or ideas ⟨the bonds ~ represent the debt

--G.B.Robinson⟩ ⟨the Samnite tribes, ~ settled south and southeast of Rome —Ernst Pulgram⟩; used freely in reference to persons as recently as the 17th century ⟨our Father ~ art in heaven —Mt 6:9 (AV)⟩, and still occas. so used but usu. with some implication of emphasis on the function or role of the person rather than on the person himself ⟨chiefly they wanted husbands, ~ they got easily —Lynn White⟩; used by speakers on all educational levels and by many reputable writers, though disapproved by some grammarians, in reference to an idea expressed by a word or group of words that is not necessarily a noun or noun phrase ⟨in August of that year he resigned that post, after ~ he engaged in ranching —*Current Biog.*⟩

[1]**which·ev·er** \hwich-'ev-ər, wich-\ *pron* **:** whatever one or ones out of a group ⟨take two of the four elective subjects, ~ you prefer⟩

[2]**whichever** *adj* **:** being whatever one or ones out of a group **:** no matter which ⟨walk . . . back to ~ chair he happened to be using at the time —Grace Metalious⟩ ⟨its soothing . . . effect will be the same ~ way you take it —*Punch*⟩

which·so·ev·er \ˌhwich-sə-'wev-ər, ˌwich-\ *pron or adj* **:** WHICHEVER

whick·er \'hwik-ər, 'wik-\ *vi* **whick·er·ing** \-(ə-)riŋ\ [imit.] **:** NEIGH, WHINNY — **whicker** *n*

whid \'hwid, 'wid\ *vi* [Sc *whid* silent rapid motion] *Scot* **:** to move nimbly and silently

whidah *var of* WHYDAH

[1]**whiff** \'hwif, 'wif\ *n* [imit.] **1 a :** a quick puff or slight gust esp. of air, odor, gas, smoke, or spray **b :** an inhalation of odor, gas, or smoke **c :** a slight puffing or whistling sound **2 :** a slight trace **:** HINT

[2]**whiff** *vi* **1 :** to move with or as if with a puff of air **2 :** to emit whiffs **:** PUFF **3 :** to inhale an odor **4 :** FAN 3 ~ *vt* **1 a :** to carry or convey by or as if by a whiff **:** BLOW **b :** to expel or puff out in a whiff **:** EXHALE **c :** SMOKE 3 **2 :** FAN 8

whif·fet \'hwif-ət, 'wif-\ *n* [prob. alter. of *whippet*] **:** a small, young, or unimportant person

whif·fle \'hwif-əl, 'wif-\ *vb* **whif·fling** \-(ə-)liŋ\ [prob. freq. of *whiff*] *vi* **1 a** *of the wind* **:** to blow unsteadily or in gusts **b :** VACILLATE **2 :** to emit or produce a light whistling or puffing sound ~ *vt* **:** to blow, disperse, emit, or expel with or as if with a whiff

[1]**whif·fler** \'hwif-lər, 'wif-\ *n* [alter. of earlier *wifler*, fr. obs. *wifle* (battle-ax)] *Brit* **:** one that clears the way for a procession

[2]**whif·fler** \'hwif-(ə-)lər, 'wif-\ *n* [*whiffle*] **1 :** one that frequently changes his opinion or course **2 :** one that uses shifts and evasions in argument

whif·fle·tree \'hwif-əl-(ˌ)trē, 'wif-\ *n* [alter. of *whippletree*, perh. irreg. fr. *whip* + *tree*] **:** the pivoted swinging bar to which the traces of a harness are fastened and by which a vehicle or implement is drawn

Whig \'hwig, 'wig\ *n* [short for *Whiggamore* (member of a Scottish group that marched to Edinburgh in 1648 to oppose the court party)] **1 :** a member or supporter of a major British political group of the 18th and early 19th centuries seeking to limit the royal authority and increase parliamentary power — compare TORY **2 :** an American favoring independence from Great Britain during the American Revolution **3 :** a member or supporter of an American political party formed about 1834 in opposition to the Jacksonian Democrats, associated chiefly with manufacturing, commercial, and financial interests, and succeeded about 1854 by the Republican party — **Whig** *adj* — **Whig·gish** \'hwig-ish, 'wig-\ *adj* — **Whig·gism** \-ˌiz-əm\ *n*

Whig·gery \'hwig-ə-rē, 'wig-\ *n* **:** the principles or practices of Whigs

whig·ma·lee·rie \ˌhwig-mə-'li(ə)r-ē, ˌwig-\ *n* [origin unknown] **1 :** WHIM **2 :** an odd or fanciful contrivance **:** GIMCRACK

[1]**while** \'hwī(ə)l, 'wī(ə)l\ *n* [ME, fr. OE *hwīl*; akin to OHG *hwīla* time, L *quies* rest, quiet] **1 :** a period of time esp. when short and marked by the occurrence of an action or a condition **:** TIME ⟨stay here for a ~⟩ **2 :** the time and effort used (as in the performance of an action) **:** TROUBLE ⟨worth your ~⟩

[2]**while** *conj* **1 a :** during the time that ⟨take a nap ~ I'm out⟩ **b :** as long as ⟨~ there's life there's hope⟩ **2 a :** at the same time that on the contrary ⟨easy for an expert, ~ it is dangerous for a novice⟩ **:** WHEREAS **b :** in spite of the fact that **:** ALTHOUGH ⟨~ respected, he is not liked⟩ **3 :** at the same time that in a similar manner ⟨~ the book will be welcomed by scholars, it will make an immediate appeal to the general reader —*Brit. Bk. News*⟩

[3]**while** *prep, archaic* **:** UNTIL

[4]**while** *vt* **:** to cause to pass esp. without boredom or in a pleasant manner — usu. used with *away* ⟨~ away the time⟩

syn WHILE, WILE, BEGUILE, FLEET mean to pass idle or leisure time without being bored. WHILE or WILE (with *away*) implies filling time with something pleasant or amusing but not useful; BEGUILE has less suggestion of wasting time; FLEET implies causing time to pass quickly or imperceptibly

[1]**whiles** \'hwī(ə)lz, 'wī(ə)lz\ *conj* [ME, fr. *while* + *-s*, adv. suffix — more at WHENCE] *archaic* **:** WHILE

[2]**whiles** *adv, chiefly Scot* **:** SOMETIMES

[1]**whi·lom** \'hwī-ləm, 'wī-\ *adv* [ME, lit., at times, fr. OE *hwīlum*, dat. pl. of *hwīl* time, while] *archaic* **:** FORMERLY

[2]**whilom** *adj* **:** FORMER ⟨grievous treatment at the hands of ~ friends —Agnes Repplier⟩

whilst \'hwī(ə)lst, 'wī(ə)lst\ *conj* [ME *whilest*, alter. of *whiles*] *chiefly Brit* **:** WHILE

whim \'hwim, 'wim\ *n* [short for *whim-wham*] **1 :** a sudden turn or start of the mind **:** NOTION, FANCY **2 :** a large capstan made with one or more radiating arms to which a horse may be yoked and used in mines for raising ore or water **syn** see CAPRICE

whim·brel \'hwim-brəl, 'wim-\ *n* [perh. imit.] **:** a small European curlew (*Phaeopus phaeopus*); *broadly* **:** a small curlew

[1]**whim·per** \'hwim-pər, 'wim-\ *vi* **whim·per·ing** \-p(ə-)riŋ\ [imit.] **1 :** to make a low whining plaintive or broken sound **2 :** to complain or protest with or as if with a whimper

[2]**whimper** *n* **1 :** a whimpering cry or sound **2 :** a petulant complaint or protest

whim·si·cal \'hwim-zi-kəl, 'wim-\ *adj* [*whimsy*] **1 :** full of, actuated by, or exhibiting whims **2 a :** resulting from or characterized by whim or caprice **b :** subject to erratic behavior or unpredictable change — **whim·si·cal·i·ty** \ˌhwim-zə-'kal-ət-ē, ˌwim-\ *n* — **whim·si·cal·ly** \'hwim-zi-k(ə-)lē, 'wim-\ *adv* — **whim·si·cal·ness** \-kəl-nəs\ *n*

whim·sied \'hwim-zēd, 'wim-\ *adj* **:** filled with whimsies **:** WHIMSICAL

whim·sy *or* **whim·sey** \'hwim-zē, 'wim-\ *n* [irreg. fr. *whim-wham*] **1 :** WHIM, CAPRICE **2 :** a fanciful or fantastic device, object, or creation esp. in writing or art

whim-wham \'hwim-ˌhwam, 'wim-ˌwam\ *n* [origin unknown] **1 :** a whimsical object or device esp. of ornament or dress **2 :** FANCY, WHIM **3** *pl* **:** JIMJAMS, JITTERS

[1]**whin** \'hwin, 'win\ *n* [ME (northern) *quin*] **:** a hard rock that on weathering cumbers the ground with large fragments **:** WHINSTONE

[2]**whin** *n* [ME *whynne*, of Scand origin; akin to Norw *kvein* bent grass] **:** FURZE

whin·chat \'hwin-ˌchat, 'win-\ *n* [[2]*whin*] **:** a small brown and buff European singing bird (*Saxicola rubetra*) of grassy meadows

[1]**whine** \'hwīn, 'wīn\ *vb* [ME *whinen*, fr. OE *hwīnan* to whiz; akin to ON *hvīna* to whiz] *vi* **1 a :** to utter a high-pitched plaintive or distressed cry **b :** to make a sound similar to such a cry **2 :** to utter a complaint with or as if with a whine ~ *vt* **:** to utter or express with or as if with a whine — **whin·er** *n* — **whin·ing·ly** \'hwī-niŋ-lē, 'wī-\ *adv*

[2]**whine** *n* **1 a :** a prolonged high-pitched cry usu. expressive of distress or pain **b :** a sound resembling such a cry **2 :** a complaint uttered with or as if with a whine — **whiny** *or* **whin·ey** \-nē\ *adj*

whing-ding \'wiŋ-ˌdiŋ, 'hwiŋ-\ *n* [by alter.] **:** WINGDING

[1]**whin·ny** \'hwin-ē, 'win-\ *vb* [prob. imit.] *vi* **:** to neigh esp. in a low or gentle fashion ~ *vt* **:** to utter with or as if with a whinny

[2]**whinny** *n* **1 :** NEIGH **2 :** a sound resembling a neigh

whin·stone \'hwin-ˌstōn, 'win-\ *n* **:** basaltic rock **:** TRAP; *also* **:** any of various other dark resistant rocks (as chert)

[1]**whip** \'hwip, 'wip\ *vb* **whipped; whip·ping** [ME *wippen, whippen;* akin to MD *wippen* to move up and down, sway, OE *wīpian* to wipe] *vt* **1 :** to take, pull, snatch, jerk or otherwise move very quickly and forcefully ⟨*whipped* out his gun —Green Peyton⟩ ⟨*whipped* a fast ball across⟩ **2 a :** to strike with a slender lithe implement (as a lash or rod) esp. as a punishment; *broadly* **:** SPANK **b :** to drive or urge on by or as if by using a whip **c :** to strike as a lash does ⟨rain *whipped* the pavement⟩ **3 a :** to bind or wrap (as a rope or fishing rod) with cord in order to protect and strengthen **b :** to wind or wrap around something **4 :** to belabor with stinging words **5 :** to seam or hem with shallow overcasting stitches **6 :** to thoroughly overcome **:** DEFEAT **7 :** to stir up **:** INCITE — usu. used with *up* ⟨trying to ~ up a new emotion —Ellen Glasgow⟩ **8 :** to produce in a hurry — usu. used with *up* ⟨a sketch . . . an artist might ~ up —*N.Y.Times*⟩ **9 :** to fish (water) with rod, line, and artificial lure **10 :** to beat (as eggs or cream) into a froth usu. with a whisk, fork, or other instrument **11 :** to gather together or hold together for united action in the manner of a party whip ~ *vi* **1 :** to move nimbly or quickly **:** WHISK **2 :** to thrash about flexibly in the manner of a whiplash ⟨a flag . . . *whipping* out from its staff — H. A. Calahan⟩

[2]**whip** *n* **1 :** an instrument consisting usu. of a handle and lash forming a flexible rod that is used for whipping **2 :** a stroke or cut with or as if with a whip **3 a :** a dessert made by whipping a portion of the ingredients **b :** a kitchen utensil made of braided or coiled wire or perforated metal with a handle and used in whipping **4 :** one of the arms of a windmill **5 :** a hoisting apparatus; *esp* **:** a purchase consisting of a single block and a small rope for lifting light articles **6 :** one that handles a whip: as **a :** a driver of horses **:** COACHMAN **b :** WHIPPER-IN 1 **7 a :** a member of a legislative body appointed by his political party to enforce party discipline and to secure the attendance of party members at important sessions **b** *often cap* **:** a notice of forthcoming business sent weekly to each member of a political party in the British House of Commons **8 :** a whipping or thrashing motion **9 :** the quality of resembling a whip esp. in being flexible **10 :** any of various pieces of machinery that operate with a quick vibratory motion (as a spring in an electrical device for making a circuit) **11 :** a flexible radio antenna — **whip·like** \-ˌlīk\ *adj*

whip·cord \-ˌkȯ(ə)rd\ *n, often attrib* **1 a :** a thin tough cord made of braided or twisted hemp or catgut **b :** a cloth that is made of hard-twisted yarns and has fine diagonal cords or ribs **2 :** either of two marine brown algae (*Chorda filum* and *Chordaria flagelliformis*) having very long slender flexible fronds

whip hand *n* **1 :** the hand holding the whip in driving **2 :** positive control **:** ADVANTAGE

whip in *vt* **1 :** to keep (hounds in a pack) from scattering by use of a whip **2 :** to collect or keep together (members of a political party) for legislative action

whip·lash \'hwip-ˌlash, 'wip-\ *n* **:** the lash of a whip

whip·per \'hwip-ər, 'wip-\ *n* **:** one that whips

whip·per-in \ˌhwip-ə-'rin, ˌwip-\ *n, pl* **whip·pers-in** \-ər-'zin\ **1 :** a huntsman's assistant who whips in the hounds **2 :** WHIP 7a

whip·per·snap·per \'hwip-ər-ˌsnap-ər, 'wip-\ *n* [alter. of *snipper-snapper*] **:** a diminutive, insignificant, or presumptuous person

whip·pet \'hwip-ət, 'wip-\ *n* [prob. fr. [1]*whip*] **1 :** a small swift slender dog of greyhound type developed from a cross between the Italian greyhound and a terrier **2 :** a small tank used in World War I by the Allied armies

whip·ping *n* **1 :** the act of one that whips: as **a :** a severe beating or chastisement **b :** a stitching with small overcasting stitches **2 :** material used to whip or bind

whipping boy *n* **1 :** a boy formerly educated with a prince and punished in his stead **2 :** SCAPEGOAT

whipping post *n* **:** a post to which offenders are tied to be legally whipped

whip·ple·tree \'hwip-əl-(ˌ)trē, 'wip-\ *var of* WHIFFLETREE

whip·poor·will \ˌhwip-ər-'wil, 'hwip-ər-ˌ, ˌwip-, 'wip-\ *n* [imit.] **:** a nocturnal goatsucker (*Caprimulgus vociferus*) of the eastern U.S. and Canada related to the European nightjar

whip·py \'hwip-ē, 'wip-\ *adj* **1 :** of, relating to, or resembling a whip **2 :** unusually resilient **:** SPRINGY ⟨a ~ fishing rod⟩

whip ray \'hwip-ˌrā, -rē, 'wip-\ *n* **:** STINGRAY

[1]**whip·saw** \'hwip-ˌsȯ, 'wip-\ *n* [[2]*whip*] **1 :** a narrow pit saw tapering from butt to point, having hook teeth, and averaging from 5 to 7½ feet in length **2 :** a two-man crosscut saw

[2]**whipsaw** *vt* **1 :** to saw with a whipsaw **2 :** to worst or victimize in gambling or negotiation

whip scorpion *n* **:** any of an order (Pedipalpida) of arachnids somewhat resembling true scorpions but having a long slender caudal process and no sting

whip stall *n* **:** a stall during a vertical climb in which the nose of the

airplane whips violently forward and then downward

1**whip·stitch** \'hwip-ˌstich, 'wip-\ *vt* : WHIP 5

2**whipstitch** *n* **1** : a shallow overcasting stitch **2** : a small interval of time

whip·stock \-ˌstäk\ *n* : the handle of a whip

whip·worm \-ˌwərm\ *n* : a parasitic nematode worm (family Trichuridae) with a body thickened posteriorly and very long and slender anteriorly; *esp* : one (*Trichuris trichiura*) of the human intestine

1**whir** *also* **whirr** \'hwər, 'wər\ *vb* **whirred; whir·ring** [ME (Sc) *quirren*, prob. of Scand origin; akin to Dan *hvirre* to whirl, whir; akin to OE *hweorfan* to turn — more at WHARF] *vi* : to fly, revolve, or move rapidly with a whir ~ *vt* : to move or carry rapidly with a whir

2**whir** *also* **whirr** *n* : a continuous fluttering or vibratory sound made by something in rapid motion

1**whirl** \'hwər(-ə)l, 'wər(-ə)l\ *vb* [ME *whirlen*, prob. of Scand origin; akin to ON *hvirfla* to whirl; akin to OHG *wirbil* whirlwind, OE *hweorfan* to turn — more at WHARF] *vi* **1** : to move in a circle or similar curve esp. with force or speed **2 a** : to turn on or around an axis like a wheel : ROTATE **b** : to turn abruptly around or aside : WHEEL **3** : to pass, move, or go quickly **4** : to become giddy or dizzy : REEL ⟨my head is ~*ing*⟩ ~ *vt* **1** : to drive, impel, or convey with or as if with a rotary motion **2 a** : to cause to turn usu. rapidly on or around an axis : ROTATE **b** : to cause to turn abruptly around or aside **3** *obs* : to throw or hurl violently with a revolving motion

2**whirl** *n* **1 a** : a rapid rotating or circling movement **b** : something undergoing such a movement : VORTEX **2 a** : a confused tumult : BUSTLE **b** : a confused or disturbed mental state **3** : an experimental or brief attempt : TRY

whirl·er \'hwər-lər, 'wər-\ *n* : one that whirls

whirl·i·gig \'hwər-li-ˌgig, 'wər-\ *n* [ME *whirlegigg*, fr. *whirlen* to whirl + *gigg* top — more at GIG] **1** : a child's toy having a whirling motion **2** : MERRY-GO-ROUND **3** : something or someone that continuously whirls, moves, or changes; *also* : a whirling or circling course

whirligig beetle *n* : any of numerous beetles (family Gyrinidae) that live mostly on the surface of water where they move swiftly about in curves

whirl·pool \'hwər(-ə)l-ˌpül, 'wər(-ə)l-\ *n* **1** : water moving rapidly in a circle so as to produce a depression in the center into which floating objects may be drawn : EDDY, VORTEX **2 a** : a confused tumult and bustle **b** : a magnetic or impelling force by which something may be engulfed

whirl·wind \-ˌwind\ *n, often attrib* **1** : a small rotating windstorm of limited extent marked by an inward and upward spiral motion of the lower air that is followed by an outward and upward spiral motion and usu. a progressive motion at all levels **2 a** : a confused rush : WHIRL **b** : a destructive force or agency

1**whirly** \'hwər-lē, 'wər-\ *adj* : marked by or exhibiting a whirling motion

2**whirly** *n* : a small whirlwind

whirly·bird \-ˌbərd\ *n* : HELICOPTER

whir·ry \'hwər-ē, 'wər-, '(h)wə-rē\ *vb* [perh. blend of *whir* and *hurry*] *Scot* : to move quickly : HURRY

1**whish** \'hwish, 'wish\ *vb* [imit.] *vt* : to urge on or cause to move with a whish ~ *vi* **1** : to make a sibilant sound **2** : to move with a whish esp. at high speed

2**whish** *n* : a rushing sound : SWISH

whisht \'hwisht, 'wisht\ *n or vb* [imit.] *chiefly Irish* : HUSH — often used interjectionally to enjoin silence

1**whisk** \'hwisk, 'wisk\ *n* [ME *wisk*, prob. of Scand origin; akin to ON *visk* wisp; akin to OE *wiscian* to plait, L *virga* branch, rod] **1** : a quick light brushing or whipping motion **2 a** : a small usu. wire kitchen implement used for hand beating of food **b** : a flexible bunch (as of twigs, feathers, or straw) attached to a handle for use as a brush

2**whisk** *vi* : to move nimbly and quickly ~ *vt* **1** : to move or convey briskly **2** : to mix or fluff up by or as if by beating with a whisk **3** : to brush or wipe off lightly

whisk broom *n* : a small broom with a short handle used esp. as a clothes brush

whisk·er \'hwis-kər, 'wis-\ *n* [2*whisk*] **1 a** : a hair of the beard **b** *pl* (1) *archaic* : MOUSTACHE (2) : the part of the beard growing on the sides of the face or on the chin **2** : one of the long projecting hairs or bristles growing near the mouth of an animal (as a cat or bird) **3** : an outrigger extending on each side of the bowsprit to spread the jib and flying jib guys — usu. used in pl. **4** : a shred or filament likened to a whisker — **whisk·ered** \-kərd\ *adj*

whisk·ery \-k(ə-)rē\ *adj* : having or resembling whiskers ⟨~ eyebrows⟩

whis·key *or* **whis·ky** \'hwis-kē, 'wis-\ *n, often attrib* [IrGael *uisce beathadh* & ScGael *uisge beatha*, lit., water of life] **1** : a distilled alcoholic liquor made from fermented mash of grain (as rye, corn, barley, or wheat) **2** : a drink of whiskey

Whiskey — a communications code word for the letter *w*

whiskey sour *n* : a cocktail usu. made of whiskey, bitters, sugar, and lemon juice shaken up in cracked ice and served with a fruit garnish (as orange or maraschino cherry)

1**whis·per** \'hwis-pər, 'wis-\ *vb* **whis·per·ing** \-p(ə-)riŋ\ [ME *whisperen*, fr. OE *hwisperian*; akin to OHG *hwispalōn* to whisper, ON *hvīsla* — more at WHISTLE] *vi* **1** : to speak softly with little or no vibration of the vocal cords esp. with the aim of preserving secrecy **2** : to make a sibilant sound that resembles whispering ~ *vt* **1** : to address in a whisper **2** : to utter or communicate in or as if in a whisper

2**whisper** *n* **1 a** : an act or instance of whispering; *specif* : speech without vibration of the vocal cords **b** : a sibilant sound that resembles whispered speech **2** : something communicated by or as if by whispering

whis·per·er \-pər-ər\ *n* : one that whispers; *specif* : RUMORMONGER

1**whis·per·ing** *n* **1 a** : whispered speech **b** : GOSSIP, RUMOR **2** : a sibilant sound : WHISPER

2**whispering** *adj* : spreading confidential and esp. derogatory reports ⟨~ tongues can poison truth —S.T.Coleridge⟩ — **whis·per·ing·ly** \-p(ə-)riŋ-lē\ *adv*

whispering campaign *n* : the systematic dissemination by word of mouth of derogatory rumors or charges esp. against a candidate for public office

whis·pery \'hwis-p(ə-)rē, 'wis-\ *adj* **1** : resembling a whisper **2** : full of whispers

1**whist** \'hwist, 'wist\ *vi* [imit.] *dial Brit* : to be silent : HUSH — often used interjectionally to enjoin silence

2**whist** *adj* : QUIET, SILENT

3**whist** *n* [alter. of earlier *whisk*, prob. fr. 2*whisk*; fr. whisking up the tricks] : a card game for four players in two partnerships that is played with a pack of 52 cards and that scores one point for each trick in excess of six

1**whis·tle** \'hwis-əl, 'wis-\ *n, often attrib* [ME, fr. OE *hwistle*; akin to ON *hvīsla* to whisper, *hvína* to whiz — more at WHINE] **1 a** : a small wind instrument in which sound is produced by the forcible passage of breath through a slit in a short tube ⟨police ~⟩ **b** : a device through which air or steam is forced into a cavity or against a thin edge to produce a loud sound ⟨factory ~⟩ **2 a** : a shrill clear sound produced by forcing breath out or air in through the puckered lips **b** : the sound produced by a whistle **c** : a signal given by or as if by whistling **3** : a sound that resembles a whistle; *specif* : the shrill clear note of a bird or other animal

2**whistle** *vb* **whis·tling** \-(ə-)liŋ\ *vi* **1 a** : to utter a shrill clear sound by blowing or drawing air through the puckered lips **b** : to utter a shrill note or call resembling a whistle **c** : to make a shrill clear sound esp. by rapid movement **d** : to blow or sound a whistle **2** : to give a signal or issue an order or summons by or as if by whistling ⟨~ to a dog⟩; *specif* : to make a demand without result ⟨did a sloppy job so he can ~ for his money⟩ ~ *vt* **1** : to send, bring, signal, or call by or as if by whistling **2** : to produce, utter, or express by whistling ⟨~ a tune⟩

whis·tle·able \'hwis-ə-lə-bəl, 'wis-\ *adj* : capable of being whistled ⟨a ~ tune⟩

whis·tler \'hwis-(ə-)lər, 'wis-\ *n* : one that whistles; as: **a** : any of various birds; *esp* : GOLDENEYE 1 **b** : a large mountain marmot (*Marmota caligata*) of northwestern No. America **c** : a broken-winded horse **d** : a rising and falling noise heard on radio that results from an electrical disturbance caused by lightning discharge

1**whis·tle–stop** \'hwis-əl-ˌstäp, 'wis-\ *n* **1 a** : a small station at which trains stop only on signal : FLAG STOP **b** : a small community **2** : a brief personal appearance esp. by a political candidate usu. on the rear platform of a train during the course of a tour

2**whistle–stop** *vi* : to make a tour esp. in a political campaign with many brief personal appearances in small communities

whis·tling *n* **1** : the act or sound of one that whistles : WHISTLE **2** : ROARING

whit \'hwit, 'wit\ *n* [alter. of ME *wiht*, *wight* creature, thing, bit — more at WIGHT] : the smallest part or particle imaginable : BIT ⟨cared not a ~⟩

1**white** \'hwīt, 'wīt\ *adj* [ME, fr. OE *hwīt*; akin to OHG *hwīz* white, Skt *śveta*] **1 a** : free from color **b** : of the color of new snow or milk; *specif* : of the color white **c** : light or pallid in color ⟨~ hair⟩ ⟨~ wine⟩ ⟨lips ~ with fear⟩ **d** : lustrous pale gray : SILVERY; *also* : made of silver **2 a** : being a member of a group or race characterized by reduced pigmentation **b** : of, relating to, or consisting of white people ⟨~ Australia⟩ ⟨~ schools⟩ **c** *slang* : marked by upright fairness ⟨a ~ man if ever there was one⟩ **3** : free from spot or blemish: as **a** : free from moral impurity : INNOCENT **b** : unmarked by writing or printing **c** : not intended to cause harm ⟨~ lie⟩ ⟨~ magic⟩ **d** : FAVORABLE, FORTUNATE **4 a** : wearing or habited in white ⟨~ friars⟩ **b** : marked by the presence of snow : SNOWY ⟨~ Christmas⟩ **5 a** : heated to the point of whiteness **b** : notably ardent : PASSIONATE ⟨~ fury⟩ **6** : conservative or reactionary in political outlook and action

2**white** *n* **1** : the achromatic object color of greatest lightness characteristically perceived to belong to objects that reflect diffusely nearly all incident energy throughout the visible spectrum **2 a** : a white or light-colored part of something: as (1) : a mass of albuminous material surrounding the yolk of an egg (2) : the white part of the ball of the eye (3) : the light-colored pieces in a two-handed board game; *also* : the player by whom these are played **b** (1) *archaic* : a white target (2) : the fifth or outermost circle of an archery target; *also* : a shot that hits it **3** : one that is or approaches the color white: as **a** : white clothing **b** : a white mammal (as a horse or a hog) **c** : a white-colored product (as flour, pins, or sugar) — usu. used in pl. **4** *pl* : LEUKORRHEA **5** : a person belonging to a light-skinned race **6** : a member of a conservative or reactionary political group

3**white** *vt* [ME *whiten*, fr. *white*, adj] *archaic* : WHITEN

white ant *n* : TERMITE

white·bait \'hwīt-ˌbāt, 'wīt-\ *n* **1** : the young of several European herrings and esp. of the common herring (*Clupea harengus*) or of the sprat (*C. sprattus*) **2** : any of various small fishes likened to the European whitebait and used as food

white bass *n* : a No. American freshwater food fish (*Lepibema chrysops*)

white·beard \'hwīt-ˌbi(ə)rd, 'wīt-\ *n* : an old man : GRAYBEARD

white beet *n* : CHARD

white blood cell *n* : a blood cell that does not contain hemoglobin : LEUKOCYTE

white book *n* : an official report of government affairs bound in white

white·cap \'hwīt-ˌkap, 'wīt-\ *n* **1** : a wave crest breaking into white foam **2** *cap* : a member of a self-appointed vigilance committee attempting by lynch-law methods to drive away or coerce persons obnoxious to it

white cedar *n* : any of various No. American timber trees including true cedars, junipers, and cypress

white chip *n* **1** : a white-colored poker chip usu. of minimum value **2** : a thing or quantity of little worth

white–col·lar \'hwīt-'käl-ər, 'wīt-\ *adj* : of, relating to, or constituting the class of salaried employees whose duties call for well-groomed appearance

white corpuscle *n* : WHITE BLOOD CELL — called also *white cell*

white crappie *n* : a silvery No. American sunfish (*Pomoxis annularis*) highly esteemed as a panfish and often used for stocking small ponds

whit·ed \'hwīt-əd, 'wīt-\ *adj* **1 :** covered with white; *esp* **:** WHITEWASHED **2 :** made white **:** WHITENED

whited sepulcher *n* [fr. the simile in Mt 23:27 (AV)] **:** a person inwardly corrupt or wicked but outwardly virtuous or holy **:** HYPOCRITE

white Dutch clover *n* **:** a Eurasian clover (*Trifolium repens*) with round heads of white flowers that is widely used in lawn and pasture grass-seed mixtures and is an important honey plant

white elephant *n* **1 :** an Indian elephant of a pale color that is sometimes venerated in India, Ceylon, Thailand, and Burma **2 a :** a property requiring much care and expense and yielding little profit **b :** an object no longer esteemed by its owner though not without value to others

white·face \'hwīt-ˌfās, 'wīt-\ *n* **1 :** a white-faced animal; *specif* **:** HEREFORD **2 :** dead-white facial makeup

white–faced \-'fāst\ *adj* **1 :** having a wan pale face **2 :** having the face white in whole or in part — used esp. of an animal otherwise dark in color

white feather *n* [fr. the superstition that a white feather in the plumage of a gamecock is a mark of a poor fighter] **:** a mark or symbol of cowardice — used chiefly in the phrase *show the white feather*

white·fish \'hwīt-ˌfish, 'wīt-\ *n* **1 a :** any of various freshwater food fishes (family Salmonidae and esp. genus *Coregonus*) related to the salmons and trouts **b :** any of various fishes felt to resemble the true whitefishes **c** *Brit* **:** any of various market fishes with white flesh that is not oily **2 :** the flesh of a whitefish esp. as an article of food **3 :** BELUGA

white flag *n* **1 :** a flag of plain white used as a flag of truce or as a token of surrender **2 :** a token of weakness or yielding

white·fly \'hwīt-ˌflī, 'wīt-\ *n* **:** any of numerous small injurious homopterous insects (family Aleyrodidae) related to the scale insects

white friar *n, often cap W&F* [fr. his white habit] **:** CARMELITE

white gasoline *n* **:** gasoline containing no tetraethyl lead — called also *white gas*

white gold *n* **:** a pale alloy of gold resembling platinum in appearance and usu. containing nickel with or without other metals (as tin, zinc, or copper)

white goods *n pl* **1 a :** white fabrics esp. of cotton or linen **b :** articles (as sheets or towels) orig. or typically made of white cloth **2 :** major household appliances (as stoves or refrigerators) that are typically finished in white enamel

white grease *n* **:** an inedible fat from hogs that resembles lard in appearance

White·hall \'hwīt-ˌhȯl, 'wīt-\ *n* [*Whitehall*, thoroughfare of London in which are located the chief offices of British government] **:** the British government

white·head \-ˌhed\ *n* **1 :** any of various birds with more or less white about the head **2 :** MILIUM 3

white–head·ed \-'hed-əd\ *adj* **1 :** having the hair, fur, or plumage of the head white or very light **2 :** highly favored **:** FORTUNATE

white heat *n* **1 :** a temperature (as for copper and iron from 1500° to 1600° C.) higher than red heat at which a body becomes brightly incandescent **2 :** a state of intense mental or physical strain, emotion, or activity

White Horde *n* **:** a Mongolian people powerful in Russia in the 14th century

white–hot \'hwīt-'hät, 'wīt-\ *adj* **:** being at or radiating white heat

White House \-ˌhau̇s\ *n* [the *White House*, mansion in Washington, D.C. assigned to the use of the president of the U.S.] **:** the executive department of the U.S. government

white hunter *n* **:** a white man serving as guide and professional hunter to an African safari

white lead *n* **:** any of several white-lead-containing pigments; *esp* **:** a heavy poisonous basic lead carbonate of variable composition that is marketed as a powder or as a paste in linseed oil, has good hiding power, and is used chiefly in exterior paints

white leather *n* **:** leather prepared with alum and salt

white line *n* **:** a band or edge of something white; *esp* **:** a stripe painted on a road and used to guide traffic

white–liv·ered \'hwīt-'liv-ərd, 'wīt-\ *adj* [fr. the former belief that the choleric temperament depends on the body's producing large quantities of yellow bile] **:** COWARDLY, PUSILLANIMOUS

white·ly \'hwīt-lē, 'wīt-\ *adv* **:** so as to show or appear white

white man's burden *n* ["The White Man's Burden" (1899), poem by Rudyard Kipling] **:** the alleged duty of the white peoples to manage the affairs of the less developed colored peoples

white matter *n* **:** neural tissue that consists largely of medullated nerve fibers, has a whitish color, and underlies the cortical gray matter or is gathered into central tracts and peripheral nerves

white metal *n* **1 :** any of several lead-base or tin-base bearing metals **2 :** any of several white alloys (as pewter or britannia metal)

white mustard *n* **:** a Eurasian mustard (*Brassica hirta*) grown for its seeds that yield mustard and mustard oil

whit·en \'hwīt-ᵊn, 'wīt-\ *vb* **whit·en·ing** \'hwīt-niŋ, 'wīt-, -ᵊn-iŋ\ *vt* **:** to make white or whiter ~ *vi* **:** to become white or whiter

syn BLANCH, BLEACH: WHITEN implies a making white usu. by the application or addition of something; BLANCH implies the removal or withdrawal of color esp. from living tissue; BLEACH implies the action of sunlight or chemicals in removing color

whit·en·er \'hwīt-nər, -ᵊn-ər, 'wīt-\ *n* **:** one that whitens; *specif* **:** an agent (as a bleach) used to impart whiteness to something

white·ness \'hwīt-nəs, 'wīt-\ *n* **1 :** the quality or state of being white: as **a :** white color **b :** PALENESS **c :** freedom from stain **:** CLEANNESS **2 :** white substance

whit·en·ing *n* **1 :** the act or process of making or becoming white **2 :** something that is used to make white **:** WHITING

white noise *n* [fr. the analogy of its composition with that of white light] **:** a heterogeneous mixture of sound waves extending over a wide frequency range

white oak *n* **:** any of various oaks (esp. *Quercus sessiliflora* of Europe and *Q. alba* of No. America) with acorns that mature in one year and leaf veins that never extend beyond the margin of the leaf; *also* **:** the hard, strong, durable, and moisture-resistant wood of a white oak

white oil *n* **:** any of various colorless odorless tasteless mineral oils used esp. in medicine and in pharmaceutical and cosmetic preparations

white·out \'hwīt-ˌau̇t, 'wīt-\ *n* [*white* + *-out* (as in *blackout*)] **:** a surface weather condition in an arctic area in which no object casts a shadow, the horizon cannot be seen, and only dark objects are discernible

white paper *n* **:** a government report on any subject; *esp* **:** an English publication that is usu. less extensive than a blue book

white perch *n* **1 :** a small silvery anadromous sea bass (*Morone americana*) of the coast and coastal streams of the eastern U.S. **2 :** a croaker (*Aplodinotus grunniens*) of the Great Lakes and Mississippi valley that sometimes attains a weight of 50 pounds or more **3 :** WHITE CRAPPIE

white pine *n* **1 a :** a tall-growing pine (*Pinus strobus*) of eastern No. America with leaves in clusters of five — called also *eastern white pine* **b :** any of several trees felt to resemble the white pine esp. in having leaves in bundles of five **2 :** the wood of a white pine and esp. of the eastern white pine which is much used in building construction

white plague *n* **:** tuberculosis of the lungs

white primary *n* **:** a party primary in a southern state open to white voters only

White Russian *n* **:** BELORUSSIAN

white sale *n* **:** a sale of white goods

white sauce *n* **:** a sauce consisting essentially of milk, cream, or stock with flour and seasoning

white sea bass *n* **:** a large croaker (*Cynoscion nobilis*) of the Pacific coast that is closely related to the Atlantic weakfishes and is an important sport and food fish

white slave *n* **:** a woman or girl held unwillingly for purposes of commercial prostitution

white slav·er \-'slā-vər\ *n* **:** one engaged in white-slave traffic

white slavery *n* **:** enforced prostitution

white·smith \'hwīt-ˌsmith, 'wīt-\ *n* **1 :** TINSMITH **2 :** a worker in iron who finishes or polishes the work

white su·prem·a·cist \-sü-'prem-ə-səst\ *n* **:** an advocate of or believer in white supremacy

white supremacy *n* **:** a doctrine based on a belief in the inherent superiority of the white race over the Negro race and the correlative necessity for the subordination of Negroes to whites in all relationships

white·tail \'hwīt-ˌtāl, 'wīt-\ *n* **:** a No. American deer (*Odocoileus virginianus*) with a rather long tail white on the undersurface and forward-arching antlers — called also *white-tailed deer* \ˌ(h)wīt-ˌtāl(d)-'di(ə)r\

white·throat \'hwīt-ˌthrōt, 'wīt-\ *n* **:** any of several birds with white on the throat; *esp* **:** an Old World warbler (*Sylvia communis*) with rusty upper surfaces and largely pale buff underparts

white tie *n* **:** formal evening dress for men

white·wall \'hwīt-ˌwȯl, 'wīt-\ *n* **:** an automobile tire having a white sidewall

white walnut *n* **1 a :** a butternut tree **b :** WALNUT 1b **2 :** the light-colored wood of a white walnut

¹white·wash \'hwīt-ˌwȯsh, 'wīt-, -ˌwäsh\ *vt* **1 :** to whiten with whitewash **2 a :** to gloss over or cover up (as vices or crimes) **b :** to exonerate by means of a perfunctory investigation or through biased presentation of data **3 :** to hold (an opponent) scoreless

²whitewash *n* **1 :** a liquid composition for whitening a surface: as **a :** a preparation for whitening the skin **b :** a composition (as of lime and water or whiting, size, and water) for whitening structural surfaces **2 a :** an act or instance of glossing over or of exonerating **b :** a defeat in a contest in which the loser fails to score

white·wash·er \-ər\ *n* **:** one that whitewashes; *esp* **:** one who puts on whitewash

white water *n* **:** frothy water (as in breakers, rapids, or waterfalls)

white way *n* [the *Great White Way*, nickname for the theatrical section of Broadway, New York City] **:** a brilliantly lighted street or avenue esp. in a city's business or theater district

white whale *n* **:** BELUGA 2

white·wing \'hwīt-ˌwiŋ, 'wīt-\ *n* **:** a person and esp. a street sweeper wearing a white uniform

white·wood \-ˌwu̇d\ *n* **1 :** any of various trees with pale or white wood: as **a :** BASSWOOD 1 **b :** COTTONWOOD **c :** the American tulip tree **2 :** the wood of a whitewood; *esp* **:** the pale soft wood of the tulip tree

¹whith·er \'hwith-ər, 'with-\ *adv* [ME, fr. OE *hwider;* akin to L *quis* who and to OE *hider* hither — more at WHO, HITHER] **1 :** to what place ⟨~ will they go⟩ **2 :** to what situation, position, degree, or end ⟨~ will this abuse drive him⟩

²whither *conj* **1 a :** to what place ⟨knew ~ to go —Daniel Defoe⟩ **b :** to what situation, position, degree, or end **2 a :** to the place at, in, or to which **b :** to which place **3 :** to whatever place

whith·er·so·ev·er \ˌhwith-ər-sə-'wev-ər, ˌwith-\ *conj* **:** to whatever place

whith·er·ward \'hwith-ər-wərd, 'with-\ *adv* **:** toward what or which place

¹whit·ing \'hwīt-iŋ, 'wīt-\ *n* [ME, fr. MD *witinc*, fr. *wit* white; akin to OE *hwīt* white] **:** any of various marine food fishes: as **a** (1) **:** a common European fish (*Merlangus merlangus*) of the cod family (2) **:** a hake (genus *Merluccius*) **b :** any of several No. American sciaenid fishes (genus *Menticirrhus*)

²whiting *n* [ME, fr. gerund of *whiten* to white] **:** calcium carbonate prepared as fine powder by grinding and washing and used esp. as a pigment and extender, in putty, and in rubber compounding and paper coating

whit·ish \'hwīt-ish, 'wīt-\ *adj* **:** somewhat white

whit·low \'hwit-(ˌ)lō, 'wit-\ *n* [ME *whitflawe, whitflowe, whitlowe*] **:** ³FELON

Whit·mon·day \'hwit-'mən-dē, 'wit-, -ˌmən-\ *n* [*Whit-* (as in *Whitsunday*) + *Monday*] **:** the day after Whitsunday observed as a legal holiday in England, Wales, and Ireland

Whit·sun \'hwit-sən, 'wit-\ *adj* [ME *Whitson*, fr. *Whitsonday*] **:** of, relating to, or observed on Whitsunday or at Whitsuntide

Whit·sun·day \-(ˌ)sən-dē, -'sən-dē, -sən-ˌdā\ *n* [ME *Whitsonday*, fr. OE *hwīta sunnandæg*, lit., white Sunday; prob. fr. the custom of wearing white robes by the newly baptized, who were numerous at this season] **:** PENTECOST 2

Whit·sun·tide \-sən-ˌtīd\ *n* **:** the week beginning with Whitsunday and esp. the first three days of this week

¹whit·tle \'hwit-ᵊl, 'wit-\ *n* [ME *whittel*, alter. of *thwitel*, fr. *thwiten* to whittle, fr. OE *thwītan;* akin to ON *thveita* to hew] **:** a large knife

2**whittle** *vb* **whit·tling** \'hwit-liŋ, -ᵊl-iŋ, 'wit-\ *vt* **1 a :** to pare or cut off chips from the surface of (wood) with a knife **b :** to shape or form by so paring or cutting **2 :** to reduce, remove, or destroy gradually as if by cutting off bits with a knife **:** PARE — usu. used with an adverb ⟨~ down expenses⟩ ~ *vi* **1 :** to cut or shape wood by slowly paring it with a knife **2 :** to wear oneself or another out with fretting — **whit·tler** \-lər, -ᵊl-ər\ *n*

whit·tling *n* **:** a piece cut away in whittling

whit·tret \'hwi-trət, 'wi-\ *n* [ME *whitrat*, fr. *white, whit* white + *rat*] *chiefly Scot* **:** WEASEL

whity *or* **whit·ey** \'hwīt-ē, 'wīt-\ *adj* **:** WHITISH — usu. used in combination

1**whiz** *or* **whizz** \'hwiz, 'wiz\ *vb* **whizzed; whiz·zing; whiz·zes** [imit.] *vi* **1 :** to hum, whir, or hiss like a speeding object (as an arrow or ball) passing through air **2 :** to fly or move swiftly with a whiz ~ *vt* **:** to cause to whiz; *esp* **:** to rotate very rapidly

2**whiz** *or* **whizz** *n, pl* **whiz·zes 1 :** a hissing, buzzing, or whirring sound **2 :** a movement or passage of something accompanied by a whizzing sound

3**whiz** *n, pl* **whiz·zes** [prob. by shortening & alter.] **:** WIZARD 3

whiz·bang *or* **whizz·bang** \'hwiz-,baŋ, 'wiz-, -'baŋ\ *n* **1 a :** a small shell of such high velocity that the sound it makes in passing through the air is almost simultaneous with its explosion **b :** a firecracker or similar firework resembling such a shell **c :** ROBOT BOMB **2 :** someone or something conspicuous for noise, speed, or startling effect

whiz–bang *adj* **:** EXCELLENT, NOTABLE

whiz·zer \'hwiz-ər, 'wiz-\ *n* **:** one that whizzes: as **a :** BULL-ROARER **b :** a centrifugal machine for drying something (as grain, sugar, or nitrated cotton)

who \(')hü, ü\ *pron* [ME, fr. OE *hwā;* akin to OHG *hwer*, interrog. pron., who, L *quis*, Gk *tis*, L *qui*, rel. pron., who] **1 :** what or which person or persons — used as an interrogative ⟨~ was elected president⟩ ⟨find out ~ they are⟩; used by speakers on all educational levels and by many reputable writers, though disapproved by some grammarians, as the object of a verb or a following preposition ⟨~ did I see but a Spanish lady —Padraic Colum⟩ ⟨do not know ~ the message is from —G.K.Chesterton⟩ **2 :** the person or persons that **:** WHOEVER **3** — used as a function word to introduce a relative clause; used esp. in reference to persons ⟨my father, ~ was a lawyer⟩ but also in reference to groups ⟨a generation ~ had known nothing but war —R.B.West⟩ or to animals ⟨dogs ~ . . . fawn all over tramps —Nigel Balchin⟩ or to inanimate objects esp. with the implication that the reference is really to a person ⟨earlier sources ~ maintain a Davidic ancestry —F.M.Cross⟩ — **as who** *archaic* **:** as one that **:** as if someone — **as who should say** *archaic* **:** so to speak — **who's who :** the identity of or the noteworthy facts about each of a number of persons

whoa \'wō, 'hō, 'hwō\ *v imper* [ME *whoo, who*] — a command to a draft animal to stand still

who·dun·it \hü-'dən-ət\ *n* [substandard *who done it?*] **:** a detective story or mystery story presented as a novel, play, or motion picture

who·ev·er \hü-'ev-ər\ *pron* **:** whatever person **:** no matter who — used in any grammatical relation except that of a possessive

1**whole** \'hōl\ *adj* [ME *hool* healthy, unhurt, entire, fr. OE *hāl;* akin to OHG *heil* healthy, unhurt, ON *heill*, OSlav *cělŭ*] **1 a** (1) **:** free of wound or injury **:** UNHURT (2) **:** recovered from a wound or injury **:** RESTORED (3) **:** HEALED **b :** free of defect or impairment **:** INTACT, UNBROKEN **c :** physically sound and healthy **:** free of disease or deformity **2 :** having all its proper parts or components **:** ENTIRE, UNMODIFIED ⟨~ milk⟩ **3 a :** constituting the total sum or undiminished entirety of **:** INTEGRAL **b :** each or all of the **4 a :** constituting an undivided unit **:** UNBROKEN, UNCUT ⟨a ~ roast suckling pig⟩ **b :** directed to one end **:** not scattered or dispersed **:** CONCENTRATED ⟨promised to give it his ~ attention⟩ **5 :** seemingly complete or total **6 :** having the same father and mother ⟨~ brother⟩

syn WHOLE, ENTIRE, TOTAL, ALL, GROSS mean including everything or everyone without exception. WHOLE implies that nothing has been omitted, ignored, abated, or taken away; ENTIRE may suggest a being completed or perfected; TOTAL implies that everything has been counted, weighed, measured, or considered; ALL may equal WHOLE, ENTIRE, or TOTAL; GROSS implies that customary or expected deductions have not been made **syn** see in addition PERFECT

2**whole** *n* **1 :** a complete amount or sum **:** a number, aggregate, or totality lacking no part, member, or element **2 :** something constituting a complex unity **:** a coherent system or organization of parts fitting or working together as one **syn** see SUM — **on the whole 1 :** in view of all the circumstances or conditions **:** all things considered **2 :** in general **:** in most instances **:** TYPICALLY

whole gale *n* **:** wind having a speed of 55 to 63 miles per hour

whole·heart·ed \'hōl-'härt-əd\ *adj* **:** undivided in purpose, enthusiasm, or will **:** HEARTY, ZESTFUL ⟨~ effort⟩ **syn** see SINCERE — **whole·heart·ed·ly** *adv* — **whole·heart·ed·ness** *n*

whole hog *n* **:** the whole way or farthest limit **:** ALL — used esp. in the phrase *go the whole hog*

whole·ness \'hōl-nəs\ *n* **:** the quality or state of being whole

whole note *n* **:** a musical note equal in value to four quarter notes or two half notes

whole number *n* **:** INTEGER

1**whole·sale** \'hōl-,sāl\ *n* **1 :** the sale of commodities in quantity usu. for resale (as by a retail merchant) **2 :** a large scale or indiscriminate proceeding — used esp. in the phrase *by wholesale*

2**wholesale** *adj* **1 :** of, relating to, or engaged in the sale of commodities in quantity for resale ⟨a ~ grocer⟩ **2 :** performed on a large scale esp. without discrimination ⟨~ slaughter⟩ **syn** see INDISCRIMINATE

3**wholesale** *adv* **:** in a wholesale manner

4**wholesale** *vb* **:** to sell at wholesale

whole·sal·er \-,sā-lər\ *n* **:** a merchant middleman who sells chiefly to retailers, other merchants, or industrial, institutional, and commercial users mainly for resale or business use

whole·some \'hōl-səm\ *adj* **1 :** promoting health or well-being of mind or spirit **2 :** promoting health of body **3 a :** sound in body, mind, or morals **b :** having the simple health or vigor of normal domesticity **4 a :** based on well-grounded fear **:** PRUDENT **b :** SAFE **syn** see HEALTHY — **whole·some·ly** *adv* — **whole·some·ness** *n*

whole–souled \'hōl-'sōld\ *adj* **:** moved by ardent enthusiasm or single-minded devotion **:** WHOLEHEARTED

whole step *n* **:** a musical interval comprising two half steps (as C–D or F♯–G♯) — called also *whole tone*

whole wheat *adj* **:** made of ground entire wheat kernels

whole wheat flour *n* **:** flour that is ground from the whole grain and contains all the constituents of the wheat kernels

whol·ly \'hō(l)-lē\ *adv* [ME *hoolly*, fr. *hool* whole] **1 :** to the full or entire extent **:** COMPLETELY **2 :** to the exclusion of other things **:** SOLELY

whom \(')hüm, üm\ *pron, objective case of* WHO — used as an interrogative or relative; used as object of a verb or a preceding preposition ⟨to know for ~ the bell tolls —John Donne⟩ or less frequently as the object of a following preposition ⟨the man ~ you wrote to⟩ though now often considered stilted esp. as an interrogative and esp. in oral use; occas. used as predicate nominative with a copulative verb or as subject of a verb esp. in the vicinity of a preposition or a verb of which it might mistakenly be considered the object ⟨~ say ye that I am —Mt 16:15 (AV)⟩ ⟨people . . . ~ you never thought would sympathize —Shea Murphy⟩

whom·ev·er \hü-'mev-ər\ *pron, objective case of* WHOEVER

1**whomp** \'hwämp, 'hwȯmp, 'wämp, 'wȯmp\ *n* [imit.] **:** a loud slap, crash, or crunch

2**whomp** *vb* **:** BANG, SLAP

whomp up *vt* **1 :** to stir up **:** AROUSE **2 :** to put together esp. hastily

whom·so \'hüm-(,)sō\ *objective case of* WHOSO

whom·so·ev·er \,hüm-sə-'wev-ər\ *objective case of* WHOSOEVER

1**whoop** \'h(w)üp, 'h(w)u̇p, *least frequently for vi 3* 'wüp *or* 'wu̇p\ *vb* [ME *whopen*, fr. MF *houpper*, of imit. origin] *vi* **1 :** to utter a whoop in expression of eagerness, enthusiasm, or enjoyment **:** SHOUT **2 :** to utter the cry of an owl **:** HOOT **3 :** to make the characteristic whoop of whooping cough **4 :** to go or pass with a loud noise ~ *vt* **1 a :** to utter or express with a whoop **b :** to urge, drive, or cheer on with a whoop **2 :** to agitate in behalf of **3 :** BOOST, RAISE — **whoop it up 1 :** to celebrate riotously **:** CAROUSE **2 :** to stir up enthusiasm

2**whoop** \'h(w)üp, 'h(w)u̇p, *least frequently for 3* 'wüp *or* 'wu̇p\ *n* **1 a :** a loud yell expressive of eagerness, exuberance, or jubilation — often used interjectionally **b :** a shout of hunters or of men in battle or pursuit **2 :** the cry of an owl **:** HOOT **3 :** the crowing intake of breath following a paroxysm in whooping cough **4 :** the smallest bit ⟨not worth a ~⟩

whoop–de–do *or* **whoop–de–doo** \,h(w)üp-dē-'dü, ,h(w)u̇p, ,wüp-, ,wu̇p-\ *n* [prob. irreg. fr. 2*whoop*] **1 :** noisy and conspicuous activity esp. in entertainment, politics, or commercial promotion **2 :** agitated public discussion

1**whoop·ee** \'(h)wu̇p-(,)ē, '(h)wü-(,)pē; (h)wu̇-'pē, (h)wü-\ *interj* [irreg. fr. 2*whoop*] — used to express exuberant delight

2**whoop·ee** \'(h)wu̇p-(,)ē, '(h)wü-(,)pē\ *n* **1 :** the feverish participation in alcohol-and-sex orgies first widely conspicuous during the U.S. prohibition era — often used in the phrase *make whoopee* **2 :** boisterous convivial fun

whooping cough *n* **:** an infectious disease esp. of children caused by a bacterium (*Bordetella pertussis*) and marked by a convulsive spasmodic cough sometimes followed by a crowing intake of breath — called also *pertussis*

whoop·la \'h(w)ü-,plä, 'h(w)üp-,lä\ *n* [alter. of *hoopla*] **1 :** a noisy commotion **2 :** boisterous merrymaking

1**whoosh** \'hwüsh, 'wüsh, '(h)wu̇sh\ *vb* [imit.] **:** to move with an explosive or sibilant rush

2**whoosh** *n* **:** a swift or explosive rush

1**whop** \'hwäp, 'wäp\ *vt* **whopped; whop·ping** [ME *whappen*, alter. of *wappen* to throw violently] **1 :** to pull or whip out **2 a :** BEAT, STRIKE **b :** to defeat totally

2**whop** *n* **:** a heavy blow **:** THUMP

whop·per \'hwäp-ər, 'wäp-\ *n* [1*whop*] **1 :** something unusually large or extreme of its kind **2 :** a monstrous lie

whop·ping \'hwäp-iŋ, 'wäp-\ *adj* **:** extremely large

1**whore** \'hō(ə)r, 'hȯ(ə)r\ *n* [ME *hore*, fr. OE *hōre;* akin to ON *hōra* whore, *hōrr* adulterer, L *carus* dear — more at CHARITY] **:** a woman who practices unlawful sexual intercourse esp. for hire **:** PROSTITUTE

2**whore** *vi* **1 :** to have unlawful sexual intercourse as or with a whore **2 :** to pursue a faithless, unworthy, or idolatrous desire ~ *vt, obs* **:** to corrupt by lewd intercourse

whore·dom \'hōrd-əm, 'hȯrd-\ *n* [ME *hordom* sexual immorality, idolatrous practices, fr. ON *hōrdōmr* adultery, fr. *hōrr*] **1 :** the practice of whoring **2 :** faithless, unworthy, or idolatrous practices or pursuits

whore·house \'hō(ə)r-,hau̇s, 'hȯ(ə)r-\ *n* **:** a building in which prostitutes are available

whore·mas·ter \-,mas-tər\ *n* **:** a man consorting with whores or given to lechery

whore·mon·ger \-,məŋ-gər, -,mäŋ-\ *n, archaic* **:** WHOREMASTER

whore·son \'hōrs-ᵊn, 'hȯrs-\ *n, often attrib* **1 :** BASTARD **2 :** a coarse fellow — used as a generalized term of abuse

whor·ish \'hōr-ish, 'hȯr-\ *adj* **:** of or resembling a whore **:** LEWD

whorl \'hwȯr(ə)l, 'wȯr(ə)l, '(h)wər(-ə)l\ *n* [ME *wharle, whorle*, prob. alter. of *whirle*, fr. *whirlen* to whirl] **1 :** a drum-shaped section on the lower part of a spindle in spinning or weaving machinery serving as a pulley for the tape drive that rotates the spindle **2 :** an arrangement of similar anatomical parts (as leaves) in a circle around a point on an axis **3 :** something that whirls, coils, or spirals or whose form suggests such movement **4 :** one of the turns of a univalve shell **5 :** a fingerprint in which the central papillary ridges turn through at least one complete circle

whorled \'hwȯr(ə)ld, 'wȯr(ə)ld, '(h)wər(-ə)ld\ *adj* **:** having or arranged in whorls; *esp* **:** VERTICILLATE ⟨~ leaves⟩

whort \'hwərt, 'wərt\ *or* **whor·tle** \'hwərt-ᵊl, 'wərt-\ *n* **:** WHORTLEBERRY 1

whor·tle·ber·ry \'hwərt-ᵊl-,ber-ē, 'wərt-\ *n* [alter. of earlier *hurtleberry*, fr. ME *hurtilberye*, irreg. fr. OE *horte* whortleberry + ME *berye* berry] **1 :** a European blueberry (*Vaccinium myrtillus*); *also* **:** its glaucous blackish edible berry **2 :** BLUEBERRY

1**whose** \(')hüz, üz\ *adj* [ME *whos*, gen. of *who, what*] **:** of or relat-

ing to whom or which esp. as possessor or possessors ⟨~ gorgeous vesture heaps the ground —Robert Browning⟩, agent or agents ⟨the law courts, ~ decisions were important —F.L.Mott⟩, or object or objects of an action ⟨the first poem ~ publication he ever sanctioned —J.W.Krutch⟩

2**whose** *pron, sing or pl in constr* **:** whose one or whose ones — used without a following noun as a pronoun equivalent in meaning to the adjective *whose* ⟨tell me ~ it was —Shak.⟩

whose·so·ev·er \ˌhüz-sə-'wev-ər\ *adj* **:** of or relating to whomsoever ⟨~ sins ye remit —Jn 20:23 (AV)⟩

who·so \'hü-(ˌ)sō\ *pron* **:** WHOEVER

who·so·ev·er \ˌhü-sə-'wev-ər\ *pron* **:** WHOEVER

1**why** \(')hwī, (')wī\ *adv* [ME, fr. OE *hwȳ*, instr. of *hwæt* what — more at WHAT] **:** for what cause, reason, or purpose ⟨~ did you do it⟩

2**why** *conj* **1 :** the cause, reason, or purpose for which ⟨know ~ you did it⟩ ⟨that is ~ you did it⟩ **2 :** for which **:** on account of which ⟨know the reason ~ you did it⟩

3**why** \'hwī, 'wī\ *n* **1 :** REASON, CAUSE **2 :** a baffling problem **:** ENIGMA

4**why** \(ˌ)wī, (ˌ)hwī\ *interj* [1*why*] — used to express surprise, hesitation, approval, disapproval, or impatience ⟨~, here's what I was looking for⟩

whyd·ah \'hwid-ə, 'wid-\ *n* [alter. of *widow* (*bird*)] **:** any of various mostly black and white African weaverbirds often kept as cage birds and distinguished in the male by long drooping tail feathers during the breeding season

wick \'wik\ *n* [ME *weke*, *wicke*, fr. OE *wēoce*; akin to OHG *wiohha* wick, OIr *figim* I weave] **:** a bundle of fibers or a loosely twisted cord, tape, or tube of soft spun cotton threads that by capillary attraction draws up to be burned a steady supply of the oil in lamps or the melted tallow or wax in candles

wick·ed \'wik-əd\ *adj* [ME, alter. of *wicke* wicked] **1 :** morally bad **:** EVIL **2 a :** FIERCE, VICIOUS **b :** causing or likely to cause harm or trouble **c :** disgustingly unpleasant **:** VILE ⟨~ odor⟩ **d :** disposed to mischief **:** ROGUISH **syn** see BAD — **wick·ed·ly** *adv* — **wick·ed·ness** *n*

wick·er \'wik-ər\ *n* [ME *wiker*, of Scand origin; akin to Sw dial. *vikker* willow, ON *veikr* weak — more at WEAK] **1 :** a small pliant twig or osier **:** WITHE **2 a :** WICKERWORK **b :** something made of wicker — **wicker** *adj*

wick·er·work \-ˌwərk\ *n* **:** work of osiers, twigs, or rods **:** BASKETRY

wick·et \'wik-ət\ *n* [ME *wiket*, fr. ONF, of Gmc origin; akin to MD *wiket* wicket, OE *wīcan* to yield — more at WEAK] **1 :** a small gate or door; *esp* **:** one forming part of or placed near a larger gate or door **2 :** an opening like a window; *esp* **:** a grilled or grated window through which business is transacted **3 :** a small gate for emptying the chamber of a canal lock or regulating the amount of water passing through a channel **4 a :** either of the 2 sets of 3 stumps topped by 2 crosspieces and set 22 yards apart at which the ball is bowled in cricket **b :** an area 10 feet wide bounded by these wickets **c :** one innings of a batsman; *specif* **:** one that is not completed or never begun ⟨win by 3 ~*s*⟩ **5 :** an arch or hoop in croquet

wick·et·keep·er \-ˌkē-pər\ *n* **:** the player who fields immediately behind the wicket in cricket

wick·ing \'wik-iŋ\ *n* **:** material for wicks

wick·i·up \'wik-ē-ˌəp\ *n* [Sac, Fox, & Kickapoo *wikiyap* dwelling] **1 :** a hut used by the nomadic Indians of the arid regions of the western and southwestern U.S. with a usu. oval base and a rough frame covered with reed mats, grass, or brushwood **2 :** any rude temporary shelter or hut

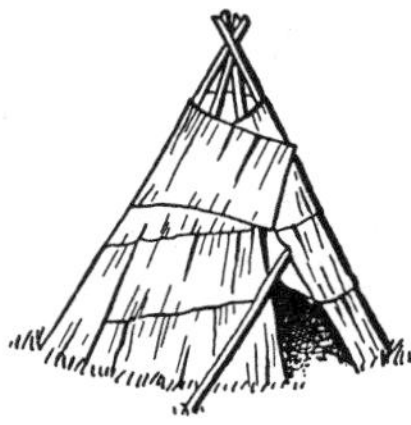
wickiup

wic·o·py *or* **wick·a·pe** \'wik-ə-pē\ *n* [Cree *wikupiy* inner bark of basswood] **1 :** LEATHERWOOD **2 :** a basswood (*Tilia glabra*) **3 :** WILLOW HERB 1

wid·der·shins \'wid-ər-shənz, 'with-ər-\ *adv* [MLG *weddersinnes*] **:** in a left-handed, wrong, or contrary direction **:** COUNTERCLOCKWISE — compare DEASIL

wid·dy \'wid-ē\ *n* [ME (Sc), fr. ME *withy*] **1** *Scot & dial Eng* **:** a rope of osiers **:** WITHY **2** *Scot & dial Eng* **:** a hangman's noose

1**wide** \'wīd\ *adj* [ME, fr. OE *wīd*; akin to OHG *wīt* wide] **1 a :** having great extent **:** VAST **b :** extending over a vast area **:** EXTENSIVE **c :** extending throughout a specified area or scope ⟨nation*wide*⟩ **d :** COMPREHENSIVE, INCLUSIVE **2 a :** having a specified extension from side to side ⟨3 feet ~⟩ **b :** having much extent between the sides **:** BROAD **c :** fully opened **d :** LAX 4 **3 a :** extending or fluctuating considerably between limits **b :** straying or deviating from something specified ⟨~ of the truth⟩ **4** *of an animal ration* **:** relatively rich in carbohydrate as compared with protein **syn** see BROAD — **wide·ly** *adv* — **wide·ness** *n*

2**wide** *adv* **1 a :** over a great distance or extent **:** WIDELY ⟨searched far and ~⟩ **b :** over a specified distance, area, or extent ⟨expanded the business country-*wide*⟩ **2 a :** so as to leave much space or distance between **b :** so as to pass at or clear by a considerable distance ⟨ran ~ around left end⟩ **3 :** COMPLETELY, FULLY ⟨opened her eyes ~⟩ **4 :** so as to diverge or miss **:** ASTRAY ⟨the bullet went ~⟩

wide-an·gle \ˌwī-ˌdaŋ-gəl\ *adj* **:** having or covering an angle of view wider than the ordinary — used esp. of lenses of shorter than normal focal length

wide-awake \ˌwīd-ə-'wāk\ *adj* **:** fully awake; *also* **:** KNOWING, ALERT **syn** see WATCHFUL

wide-awake·ness \-nəs\ *n* **:** the quality or state of being wide-awake

wide-eyed \'wī-'dīd\ *adj* **1 :** having the eyes wide open **2 :** struck with wonder or astonishment **:** AMAZED **3 :** marked by unsophisticated or uncritical acceptance or admiration **:** NAÏVE ⟨a ~ belief in the goodness of everybody⟩

wide·mouthed \'wīd-'mau̇thd, -'mau̇tht\ *adj* **1 :** having a wide mouth ⟨~ jars⟩ **2 :** having one's mouth opened wide (as in awe)

wid·en \'wīd-ᵊn\ *vb* **wid·en·ing** \'wīd-niŋ, -ᵊn-iŋ\ **:** to make or become wide or wider **:** BROADEN — **wid·en·er** \-nər, -ᵊn-ər\ *n*

wide·spread \'wīd-'spred\ *adj* **1 :** widely extended or spread out **2 :** widely diffused or prevalent

wide-spread·ing \-iŋ\ *adj* **1 :** stretching or extending far ⟨~ plains⟩ **2 :** spreading over or affecting a wide area

wid·geon *also* **wi·geon** \'wij-ən\ *n, pl* **widgeon** *or* **widgeons** [origin unknown] **:** any of several freshwater ducks (genus *Mareca*) between the teal and the mallard in size

wid·get \'wij-ət\ *n* [alter. of *gadget*] **1 :** GADGET **2 :** an unnamed article considered for purposes of hypothetical example

wid·ish \'wīd-ish\ *adj* **:** somewhat wide

1**wid·ow** \'wid-(ˌ)ō, 'wid-ə(-w)\ *n* [ME *widewe*, fr. OE *wuduwe*; akin to OHG *wituwa* widow, L *vidua* widow, *-videre* to separate, Gk *ēitheos* unmarried youth] **1 a :** a woman who has lost her husband by death; *esp* **:** one who has not remarried **b :** GRASS WIDOW 2 **2 :** an extra hand or part of a hand of cards dealt face down and usu. placed at the disposal of the highest bidder **3 :** a short line ending a paragraph and appearing at the top or bottom of a printed page or column

2**widow** *vt* **1 :** to cause to become a widow **2 :** to survive as the widow of **3 :** to deprive of something greatly loved or needed

widow bird *n* [fr. its dark plumage and long black tail feathers like a widow's veil] **:** WHYDAH

wid·ow·er \'wid-ə-wər\ *n* [ME *widewer*, alter. of *wedow* widow, widower, fr. OE *wuduwa* widower; akin to OE *wuduwe* widow] **:** a man who has lost his wife by death and has not married again

wid·ow·hood \'wid-ō-ˌhu̇d, 'wid-ə-ˌhu̇d\ *n* **:** the state or period of being a widow

widow lady *n, chiefly dial* **:** WIDOW

widow's mite *n* [fr. the widow who cast two mites into the Temple treasury (Mark 12:12)] **:** a small contribution that is willingly given and is all one can afford

widow's peak *n* **:** PEAK 7

widow's walk *n* **:** a railed observation platform atop a coastal house

width \'width, 'witth\ *n* [1*wide*] **1 :** the measurement taken at right angles to the length **:** BREADTH **2 a :** largeness of extent or scope **b :** GENEROSITY, LIBERALITY **3 :** a measured and cut piece of material ⟨a ~ of calico⟩ ⟨a ~ of lumber⟩

width·ways \-ˌwāz\ *adv* **:** WIDTHWISE

width·wise \-ˌwīz\ *adv* **:** in the direction of the width **:** CROSSWISE

wield \'wē(ə)ld\ *vt* [ME *welden* to control, fr. OE *wieldan*; akin to OHG *waltan* to rule, L *valēre* to be strong, be worth] **1** *chiefly dial* **:** to deal successfully with **:** MANAGE **2 :** to handle (as a tool) effectively ⟨~ a broom⟩ **3 :** to exert one's authority by means of ⟨~ influence⟩ **syn** see HANDLE — **wield·er** *n*

wieldy \'wē(ə)l-dē\ *adj* **:** capable of wielding or being wielded

wie·ner \'wē-nər, 'wē-nē, 'win-ē\ *n* [short for *wienerwurst*] **:** FRANKFURTER

Wie·ner schnit·zel \'vē-nər-ˌs(h)nit-səl, 'wē-nər-ˌsnit-\ *n* [G, lit., Vienna cutlet] **:** a thin breaded veal cutlet served with a garnish

wie·ner·wurst \'wē-nə(r)-ˌwərst, -ˌwu̇(ə)rst; 'wē-nər-ˌwu̇st\ *n* [G, fr. *Wiener* of Vienna + *wurst* sausage] **1 :** VIENNA SAUSAGE **2 :** FRANKFURTER

wife \'wīf\ *n, pl* **wives** \'wīvz\ [ME *wif*, fr. OE *wīf*; akin to OHG *wīb* wife] **1 a** *dial* **:** WOMAN **b :** a woman acting in a specified capacity — used in combination ⟨fish*wife*⟩ **2 :** a married woman

wife·hood \'wīf-ˌhu̇d\ *n* **:** the quality or state of being a wife

wife·less \'wī-fləs\ *adj* **:** having no wife

1**wife·like** \'wī-ˌflīk\ *adv* **:** in a wifely manner ⟨laid, ~, her hand in one of his —Alfred Tennyson⟩

2**wifelike** *adj* **:** WIFELY

wife·li·ness \'wī-flē-nəs\ *n* **:** the quality or state of being wifely

wife·ly \'wī-flē\ *adj* **:** of, relating to, or befitting a wife

1**wig** \'wig\ *n* [short for *periwig*] **1 a :** a manufactured covering of hair for the head usu. made of human hair and worn to conceal baldness or as part of a costume **b :** TOUPEE 2 **2 :** an act of wigging **:** REBUKE

2**wig** *vt* **wigged; wig·ging 1 :** to supply with a wig **2 :** to scold severely **:** REBUKE

wig·an \'wig-ən\ *n* [*Wigan*, England] **:** a stiff plain-weave cotton fabric used for interlining

wigged \'wigd\ *adj* **:** wearing a wig ⟨the judge, all ~ and robed⟩

1**wig·gle** \'wig-əl\ *vb* **wig·gling** \-(ə-)liŋ\ [ME *wiglen*, fr. or akin to MD or MLG *wiggelen* to totter; akin to OE *wegan* to move — more at WAY] *vi* **1 :** to move to and fro with quick jerky or shaking motions **:** JIGGLE **2 :** to proceed with twisting and turning movements **:** WRIGGLE **~** *vt* **:** to cause to wiggle

2**wiggle** *n* **1 :** the act of wiggling **2 :** shellfish or fish in cream sauce with peas — **wig·gly** \'wig-(ə-)lē\ *adj*

wig·gler \'wig-(ə-)lər\ *n* **1 :** one that wiggles **2 :** a larva or pupa of the mosquito — called also *wriggler*

1**wight** \'wīt\ *n* [ME, creature, thing, fr. OE *wiht*; akin to OHG *wiht* creature, thing, OSlav *veštĭ* thing] **:** a living being **:** CREATURE

2**wight** *adj* [ME, of Scand origin; akin to ON *vīgr* skilled in fighting (neut. *vīgt*); akin to OE *wīgan* to fight — more at VICTOR] *archaic* **:** VALIANT, STALWART

wig·mak·er \'wig-ˌmā-kər\ *n* **:** one that makes or deals in wigs

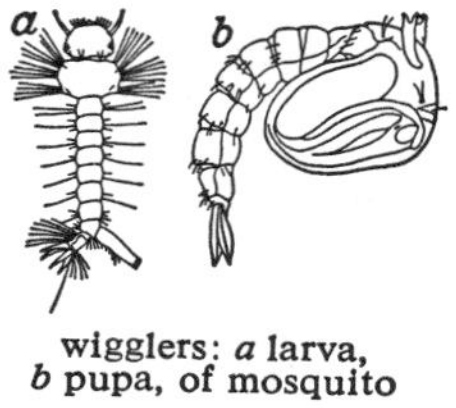

wigglers: *a* larva, *b* pupa, of mosquito

1**wig·wag** \'wig-ˌwag\ *vb* [E dial. *wig* to move + E *wag*] *vi* **1 :** to send a signal by or as if by a flag or light waved according to a code **2 :** to make a signal (as with the hand or arm) **~** *vt* **1 :** to signal by wigwagging **2 :** to cause to wigwag

2**wigwag** *n* **1 :** the art or practice of wigwagging **2 :** a wigwagged message

wig·wam \'wig-ˌwäm\ *n* [Abnaki & Massachuset *wīkwām*] **:** a hut of the Indians of the Great Lakes region and eastward having typically an arched framework of poles overlaid with bark, rush mats, or hides; *also* **:** a rough hut

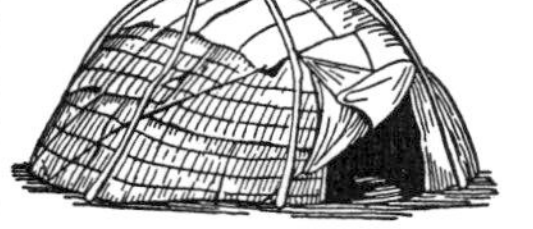
wigwam

wil·co \'wil-(ˌ)kō\ *interj* [*will comply*] — used esp. in radio and signaling to indicate that a message received will be complied with

1**wild** \'wī(ə)ld\ *adj* [ME *wilde*, fr. OE; akin to OHG *wildi* wild, W *gwyllt*] **1 a :** living in a state of nature and not ordinarily tame or domesticated ⟨~ duck⟩ **b** (1) **:** growing or produced without the aid and care of man ⟨~ honey⟩ (2) **:** related to or

resembling a corresponding cultivated or domesticated organism **c :** of or relating to wild organisms ⟨the ~ state⟩ **2 a :** not inhabited or cultivated ⟨~ land⟩ **b :** WASTE, DESOLATE **3 a** (1) **:** not subjected to restraint or regulation **:** UNCONTROLLED ⟨~ mobs⟩ (2) **:** overcome by emotion ⟨~ with grief⟩; *also* **:** passionately eager or enthusiastic (3) **:** not amenable to control or restraint **:** UNRULY ⟨the zebra is too ~ to be used as a draft animal⟩ **b :** marked by turbulent agitation **:** STORMY ⟨a ~ night⟩ **c :** EXTRAVAGANT, FANTASTIC **d :** escaped from normal restraints or control **e :** indicative of strong passion, desire, or emotion **4 :** UNCIVILIZED, BARBARIC **5 :** characteristic of, appropriate to, or expressive of wilderness, wildlife, or a simple or uncivilized society **6 :** deviating from the natural or expected course **7** *of a playing card* **:** having a denomination determined by the holder — **wild·ly** \ˈwī(ə)l-(d)lē\ *adv* — **wild·ness** \ˈwī(ə)l(d)-nəs\ *n*

2**wild** *n* **1 :** a sparsely inhabited or uncultivated region or tract **:** WILDERNESS **2 :** a wild, free, or natural state or existence

3**wild** *adv* **1 :** WILDLY **2 :** without regulation or control

wild allspice *n* **:** SPICEBUSH

wild and woolly *adj* **:** marked by a boisterous and untamed lack of polish and refinement ⟨a *wild and woolly* town⟩

wild boar *n* **:** an Old World wild hog (*Sus scrofa*) from which most domestic swine have been derived

wild carrot *n* **:** a widely naturalized Eurasian weed (*Daucus carota*) that is prob. the original of the cultivated carrot and has an acrid ill-flavored root — called also *Queen Anne's lace*

1**wild·cat** \ˈwī(ə)l(d)-ˌkat\ *n, pl* **wildcats 1 a :** either of two cats (*Felis sylvestris* of Europe and *F. ocreata* of Africa) that resemble but are heavier in build than the domestic tabby cat and are usu. held to be among the ancestors of the domestic cat **b** *or pl* **wildcat :** any of various small or medium-sized cats (as the lynx or ocelot) **c :** a feral domestic cat **2 :** a savage quick-tempered person

2**wildcat** *adj* **1 a** (1) **:** financially irresponsible or unreliable ⟨~ banks⟩ (2) **:** issued by a financially irresponsible banking establishment ⟨~ currency⟩ **b :** operating, produced, or carried on outside the bounds of standard or legitimate business practices **c :** of, relating to, or being an oil or gas well drilled in territory not known to be productive **d :** initiated by a group of workers without formal union approval or in violation of a contract ⟨~ strike⟩ ⟨~ work stoppage⟩ **2 a :** *of a cartridge* **:** having a bullet of standard caliber but using an expanded case or a case designed for a bullet of greater caliber necked down for the smaller bullet **b** *of a rifle* **:** using wildcat cartridges

3**wildcat** *vi* **wild·cat·ted; wild·cat·ting :** to prospect and drill an experimental oil or gas well or mine shaft in territory not known to be productive

wild·cat·ter \-ˌkat-ər\ *n* **1 :** one that drills wells in the hope of finding oil in territory not known to be an oil field **2 :** one that promotes unsafe and unreliable enterprises; *esp* **:** one that sells stocks in enterprises of this kind **3** [*wildcat* (*cartridge*) + *-er*] **:** one that designs, builds, or fires wildcat cartridges and rifles as a hobby

wild celery *n* **:** TAPE GRASS

wil·de·beest \ˈwil-də-ˌbēst, ˈvil-\ *n, pl* **wildebeests** *also* **wildebeest** [Afrik *wildebees*, fr. *wilde* wild + *bees* ox] **:** GNU

wil·der \ˈwil-dər\ *vb* [prob. irreg. fr. *wilderness*] *vt* **1** *archaic* **:** to lead astray **2** *archaic* **:** BEWILDER, PERPLEX ~ *vi, archaic* **:** STRAY, WANDER — **wil·der·ment** \-dər-mənt\ *n, archaic*

wil·der·ness \ˈwil-dər-nəs\ *n* [ME, fr. *wildern* wild, fr. OE *wilddēoren* of wild beasts; akin to OE *wilde* wild] **1 a :** a tract or region uncultivated and uninhabited by human beings **:** WASTE **b :** an empty or pathless area or region **c :** a part of a garden devoted to wild growth **2** *obs* **:** WILDNESS **3 :** a confusing multitude or mass **:** a great number or quantity ⟨I would not have given it for a ~ of monkeys —Shak.⟩

wilderness area *n* **:** an area (as of national forest land) set aside by government for preservation of natural conditions for scientific or recreational purposes

wild–eyed \ˈwī(ə)l-ˈdīd\ *adj* **1 :** appearing or being furious or raving ⟨haggard and ~ men⟩ **2 :** consisting of or favoring extreme political or social measures ⟨~ schemes designed to circumvent the law⟩

wild fig *n* **:** CAPRIFIG

wild·fire \ˈwī(ə)l(d)-ˌfī(ə)r\ *n* **1 :** a sweeping and destructive conflagration **2 a :** GREEK FIRE **b :** something of unquenchable intensity or all-inclusive action ⟨the news spread through the town like ~⟩ **3 :** the ignis fatuus or a similar phosphorescent appearance **4 :** HEAT LIGHTNING

wild flax *n* **1 :** GOLD OF PLEASURE **2 :** TOADFLAX

wild flower *n* **:** the flower of a wild or uncultivated plant or the plant bearing it

wild·fowl \ˈwī(ə)l(d)-ˌfau̇l\ *n* **:** a game bird; *esp* **:** a game waterfowl (as a wild duck or goose) — **wild·fowl·er** \-ˌfau̇-lər\ *n* — **wild·fowl·ing** \-liŋ\ *n*

wild ginger *n* **:** a No. American perennial herb (*Asarum canadense*) of the birthwort family with a pungent creeping rhizome

wild–goose chase *n* **:** the pursuit of something unattainable

wild hyacinth *n* **1 :** a camas (*Camassia scilloides*) with white racemose flowers **2 :** WOOD HYACINTH

wild indigo *n* **:** any of a genus (*Baptisia*) of American leguminous plants; *esp* **:** a tumbleweed (*B. tinctoria*) with bright yellow flowers and trifoliolate leaves

1**wild·ing** \ˈwīl-diŋ\ *n* **1 a :** a plant growing uncultivated in the wild either as a native or an escape; *esp* **:** a wild apple or crab apple **b :** the fruit of a wilding **2 :** a wild animal

2**wilding** *adj* **:** not domesticated or cultivated **:** WILD

wild·ish \ˈwīl-dish\ *adj* **:** somewhat wild

wild land *n* **:** land that is uncultivated or unfit for cultivation **:** WASTELAND, DESERT

wild·life \ˈwī(ə)l-ˌ(d)līf\ *n, often attrib* **:** living things that are neither human nor domesticated; *esp* **:** mammals, birds, and fishes hunted by man

wild·ling \ˈwī(ə)l-(d)liŋ\ *n* **:** a wild plant or animal

wild madder *n* **1 :** MADDER 1, 2a **2 :** either of two bedstraws (*Gallium mollugo* and *G. tinctorium*)

wild mustard *n* **:** CHARLOCK

wild oat *n* **1 a :** any of several wild grasses (genus *Avena*); *esp* **:** a European annual weed (*A. fatua*) common in meadows and pastures **b :** any of a genus (*Uvularia*) of small herbs of the lily family with drooping bell-shaped yellowish flowers **2** *pl* **:** offenses and indiscretions ascribed to youthful exuberance — usu. used in the phrase *sow one's wild oats*

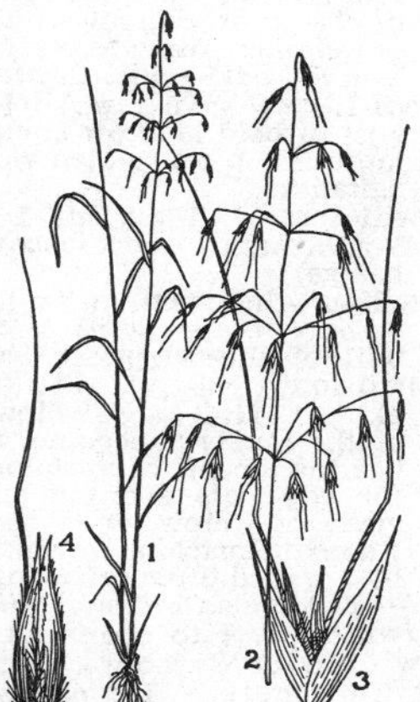

wild oat 1a: *1* whole plant, *2* panicle, *3* single spikelet, *4* lemma

wild olive *n* **:** any of various trees that resemble the olive or have fruits resembling its fruit

wild pansy *n* **:** a common and long-cultivated European viola (*Viola tricolor*) which has short-spurred flowers usu. blue or purple mixed with white and yellow and from which most of the garden pansies are derived — called also *heartsease, Johnny-jump-up*

wild parsley *n* **:** any of numerous wild plants of the carrot family with finely divided foliage

wild pink *n* **:** an American catchfly (genus *Silene*); *esp* **:** one (*S. caroliniana*) of the eastern U.S. with pink or whitish flowers

wild pitch *n* **:** a baseball pitch that cannot be caught by the catcher and that enables a base runner to advance

wild rice *n* **:** a tall aquatic No. American perennial grass (*Zizania aquatica*) yielding an edible grain

wild rye *n* **:** any of several grasses (genus *Elymus*)

wild type *n* **:** the typical form of an organism as ordinarily encountered in nature in contrast to atypical mutant individuals

wild vanilla *n* **:** a perennial composite herb (*Trilisa odoratissima*) of the southeastern U.S. with vanilla-scented leaves

wild West *n* **:** the western U.S. in its frontier period

wild·wood \ˈwī(ə)l-ˌ(d)wu̇d\ *n* **:** a wood unaltered or unfrequented by man

1**wile** \ˈwī(ə)l\ *n* [ME *wil*, fr. (assumed) ONF, prob. of Gmc origin; akin to OE *wigle* divination — more at WITCH] **1 :** a trick or stratagem intended to ensnare or deceive; *also* **:** a beguiling or playful trick **2 :** TRICKERY, GUILE **syn** see TRICK

2**wile** *vt* **1 :** to lure by or as if by a magic spell **:** ENTICE **2** [perh. alter. of *while*] **:** to pass or spend pleasurably **syn** see WHILE

wi·li·ly \ˈwī-lə-lē\ *adv* **:** in a wily manner

wi·li·ness \ˈwī-lē-nəs\ *n* **:** the quality or state of being wily

1**will** \wəl, (ə)l, (ˈ)wil\ *vb, past* **would** \wəd, (ə)d, (ˈ)wu̇d\ *pres sing & pl* **will** [ME (1st & 3d sing. pres. indic.), fr. OE *wille* (infin. *wyllan*); akin to OHG *wili* (3d sing. pres. indic.) wills, L *velle* to wish, will] *vt* **:** DESIRE, WISH ⟨call it what you ~⟩ ~ *verbal auxiliary* **1** — used to express desire, choice, willingness, consent, or in negative constructions refusal ⟨could find no one who *would* take the job⟩ ⟨if we ~ all do our best⟩ ⟨~ you please stop that racket⟩ **2** — used to express frequent, customary, or habitual action or natural tendency or disposition ⟨~ get angry over nothing⟩ ⟨~ work one day and loaf the next⟩ **3** — used to express simple futurity ⟨tomorrow morning I ~ wake up in this first-class hotel suite —Tennessee Williams⟩ **4** — used to express capability or sufficiency ⟨back seat ~ hold three passengers⟩ **5** — used to express probability or recognition and often equivalent to the simple verb ⟨that ~ be the milkman⟩ **6 a** — used to express determination, insistence, persistence, or willfulness ⟨I have made up my mind to go and go I ~⟩ **b** — used to express inevitability ⟨accidents ~ happen⟩ **7** — used to express a command, exhortation, or injunction ⟨you ~ do as I say, at once⟩ ~ *vi* **:** to have a wish or desire

2**will** \ˈwil\ *n* [ME, fr. OE *willa* will, desire; akin to OE *wille*] **1 :** DESIRE, WISH: as **a :** DISPOSITION, INCLINATION **b :** APPETITE, PASSION **c :** CHOICE, DETERMINATION **2 a :** something desired; *esp* **:** a choice or determination of one having authority or power **b** (1) *archaic* **:** REQUEST, COMMAND (2) [fr. the phrase *our will is* which introduces it] **:** the part of a summons or other signet letter that expresses its will or command **3 :** the act, process, or experience of willing **:** VOLITION **4 a :** mental powers manifested as wishing, choosing, desiring, intending **b :** a disposition to act according to principles or ends **c :** the collective desire of a group **5 :** SELF-CONTROL **6 :** a legal declaration of a person's mind as to the manner in which he would have his property or estate disposed of after his death; *esp* **:** a written instrument legally executed by which a man makes disposition of his estate to take effect after his death

3**will** \ˈwil\ *vt* **1 a :** to order or direct by a will **b :** to dispose of by or as if by a will **:** BEQUEATH **2 a :** to determine by an act of choice **b :** DECREE, ORDAIN ⟨Providence ~s it⟩ **c :** INTEND, PURPOSE ~ *vi* **1 :** to exercise the will **2 :** CHOOSE

will·able \ˈwil-ə-bəl\ *adj* **:** capable of being willed, wished, or determined by will

willed \ˈwild\ *adj* **:** having a will esp. of a specified kind — usu. used in combination ⟨strong-*willed*⟩

wil·lem·ite \ˈwil-ə-ˌmīt\ *n* [G *willemit*, fr. *Willem* (William) I †1843 king of the Netherlands] **:** a mineral Zn_2SiO_4 consisting of zinc silicate, occurring in hexagonal prisms and in massive or granular forms, and varying in color

wil·let \ˈwil-ət\ *n, pl* **willet** [imit.] **:** a large shorebird (*Catoptrophorus semipalmatus*) of the eastern and Gulf coasts and the central parts of No. America

will·ful *or* **wil·ful** \ˈwil-fəl\ *adj* **1 :** governed by will without regard to reason **:** OBSTINATE **2 :** done deliberately **:** INTENTIONAL **syn** see UNRULY, VOLUNTARY — **will·ful·ly** \-fə-lē\ *adv* — **will·ful·ness** *n*

Wil·liam Tell \ˌwil-yəm-ˈtel\ *n* **:** a legendary Swiss patriot sentenced to shoot an apple from his son's head

wil·lies \ˈwil-ēz\ *n pl* [origin unknown] **:** a fit of nervousness **:** JITTERS

wil·lie–waught \ˈwil-ē-ˌwäkt\ *n* [*guid willie-waught*, by incorrect division fr. Sc *guidwillie waught* cheering drink] **:** a deep draft (as of ale)

will·ing \'wil-iŋ\ *adj* **1 :** inclined or favorably disposed in mind **:** READY **2 :** prompt to act or respond **3 :** done, borne, or accepted of choice or without reluctance **4 :** of or relating to the will or power of choosing **:** VOLITIONAL **syn** see VOLUNTARY — **will·ing·ly** \-iŋ-lē\ *adv* — **will·ing·ness** *n*

wil·li·waw \'wil-ē-,wȯ\ *n* [origin unknown] **1 a :** a sudden violent gust of cold land air common along mountainous coasts of high latitudes **b :** a sudden violent wind **2 :** a violent commotion or agitation

will–less \'wil-ləs\ *adj* **1 :** involving no exercise of the will **:** INVOLUNTARY ⟨~ obedience⟩ **2 :** not exercising the will ⟨~ human beings⟩

will–o'–the–wisp \,wil-ə-thə-'wisp\ *n* [*Will* (nickname fr. *William*) + *of* + *the* + *wisp*] **1 :** IGNIS FATUUS **2 :** a delusive goal — **will–o'–the–wisp·ish** \-'wis-pish\ *adj*

1**wil·low** \'wil-(,)ō, 'wil-ə(-w)\ *n* [ME *wilghe, wilowe,* fr. OE *welig;* akin to MHG *wilge* willow, Gk *helikē*] **1 :** any of a genus (*Salix* of the family Salicaceae, the willow family) of trees and shrubs bearing aments of apetalous flowers and including forms of value for wood, osiers, or tanbark and a few ornamentals **2 :** an object made of willow wood; *esp* **:** a cricket bat **3** [alter. of 1*willy*] **:** a textile machine in which cotton or wool is opened and cleaned by a spiked drum revolving in a box studded internally with spikes — called also *willower, willy* — **wil·low·like** \-ō-,līk, -ə-,līk\ *adj*

2**willow** *vt* **:** to open and clean (textile fibers) with a willow

wil·low·er \'wil-ə-wər\ *n* **:** a textile worker who operates a willow

willow herb *n* **1 :** any of a genus (*Epilobium*) of herbs of the evening-primrose family; *esp* **:** a perennial (*E. angustifolium*) with tall spikes of pinkish purple flowers that is an important honey plant where abundant **2 :** LOOSESTRIFE; *esp* **:** a purplish-flowered form (*Lythrum salicaria*) common in marshes

willow oak *n* **:** an oak (as *Quercus phellos* of the eastern U.S.) with lanceolate leaves

willow pattern *n* **:** a design used in decorating willowware

wil·low·ware \'wil-ə-,wa(ə)r, 'wil-ō-, -,we(ə)r\ *n* **:** blue-and-white dinnerware decorated with a storytelling design featuring a large willow tree by a little bridge

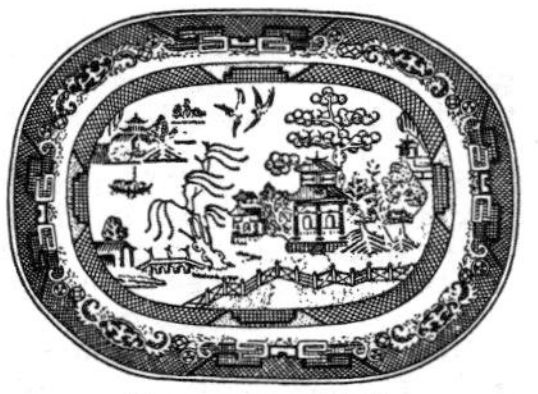
willowware platter

wil·lowy \'wil-ə-wē\ *adj* **1 :** abounding with willows **2 a :** resembling a willow **:** PLIANT **b :** gracefully tall and slender

will·pow·er \'wil-,pau̇(-ə)r\ *n* **:** energetic determination **:** RESOLUTENESS

will to power **1 :** the drive of the superman in the philosophy of Nietzsche to perfect and transcend the self through the possession and exercise of creative power **2 :** a conscious or unconscious desire to exercise authority over others

1**wil·ly** \'wil-ē\ *n* [(assumed) ME, basket, fr. OE *wiliga;* akin to OE *welig* willow] **:** WILLOW 3

2**willy** *vt* **:** WILLOW

wil·ly–nil·ly \,wil-ē-'nil-ē\ *adv* (*or adj*) [alter. of *will I nill I* or *will ye nill ye* or *will he nill he*] **:** by compulsion **:** HELPLESSLY

Wil·so·ni·an \wil-'sō-nē-ən\ *adj, usu cap* **:** of, relating to, or characteristic of Woodrow Wilson or his political principles or policies

1**wilt** \wəlt, (')wilt\ *archaic pres 2d sing of* WILL

2**wilt** \'wilt\ *vb* [alter. of earlier *welk,* fr. ME *welken,* prob. fr. MD; akin to OHG *erwelkēn* to wilt] *vi* **1 :** to lose freshness and become flaccid (as a plant on a dry day) **:** DROOP **2 :** to grow weak or faint **:** LANGUISH **~** *vt* **:** to cause to wilt

3**wilt** \'wilt\ *n* **1 :** an act or instance of wilting **:** the state of being wilted **2 a :** a disorder (as a fungus) of plants marked by loss of turgidity in soft tissues with subsequent drooping and often shriveling **b :** a destructive virus disease of various caterpillars marked by visceral liquefaction and shriveling of the body

Wil·ton \'wilt-ᵊn\ *n* [*Wilton,* borough in England] **:** a carpet woven with loops like the Brussels carpet but having a velvet cut pile and being generally of better materials

Wilt·shire \'wilt-,shi(ə)r, -shər\ *n* [*Wiltshire,* county of England] **:** any of an old English breed of pure-white sheep with long spirally curved horns and long arched head — called also *Wiltshire horn*

wily \'wī-lē\ *adj* **:** full of wiles **:** CRAFTY **syn** see SLY

1**wim·ble** \'wim-bəl\ *n* [ME, fr. AF, fr. MD *wimmel* auger; akin to MLG *wimmel* auger] **:** any of various instruments for boring holes

2**wimble** *vb* **wim·bling** \-b(ə-)liŋ\ *archaic* **:** to bore with or as if with a wimble

1**wim·ple** \'wim-pəl\ *n* [ME *wimpel,* fr. OE; akin to OE *wīpian* to wipe] **1 :** a cloth covering worn outdoors over the head and around the neck and chin by women esp. in the late medieval period and by some nuns **2** *Scot* **a :** a crafty turn **:** TWIST **b :** CURVE, BEND

2**wimple** *vb* **wim·pling** \-p(ə-)liŋ\ *vt* **1 :** to cover with or as if with a wimple **:** VEIL **2 :** to cause to ripple **~** *vi* **1 :** to fall or lie in folds **2** *chiefly Scot* **:** to follow a winding course (as of a stream) **:** MEANDER **3 :** RIPPLE

1**win** \'win\ *vb* **won** \'wən\ **win·ning** [ME *winnen,* fr. OE *winnan* to struggle; akin to OHG *winnan* to struggle, L *venus* love, charm] *vi* **1 :** to gain the victory in a contest **:** SUCCEED **2 :** to succeed in arriving at a place or a state **~** *vt* **1 :** to get possession of esp. by effort **:** GAIN **2 a :** to gain in or as if in battle or contest **b :** to be the victor in ⟨*won* the war⟩ **3 :** to obtain by work **:** EARN **4 :** to solicit and gain the favor of; *specif* **:** to induce to accept oneself in marriage **5 a :** to obtain (as ore, coal, or clay) by mining **b :** to prepare (as a vein or bed) for regular mining **c :** to recover (as metal) from ore **syn** see GET

2**win** *n* **:** VICTORY; *specif* **:** first place at the finish of a horse race — compare PLACE, SHOW

3**win** *vt* [prob. fr. E dial. *win* to take in, harvest, fr. ME *winnen* to win] *dial Brit* **:** to dry (as hay) by exposure to the air or heat

1**wince** \'win(t)s\ *vi* [ME *wenchen* to be impatient, dart about, fr. (assumed) ONF *wenchier,* of Gmc origin; akin to OHG *wankōn* to totter, OE *wincian* to wink] **:** to shrink back involuntarily (as from pain) **:** FLINCH **syn** see RECOIL

2**wince** *n* **:** an act or instance of wincing

1**winch** \'winch\ *n* [ME *winche* roller, reel, fr. OE *wince;* akin to OE *wincian* to wink] **1 :** any of various machines or instruments for hauling or pulling; *esp* **:** a powerful machine with one or more drums on which to coil a rope, cable, or chain for hauling or hoisting **:** WINDLASS **2 :** a crank with a handle for giving motion to a machine (as a grindstone)

2**winch** *vt* **:** to hoist or haul with or as if with a winch — **winch·er** *n*

1**wind** \'wind, *archaic or poetic* 'wīnd\ *n, often attrib* [ME, fr. OE; akin to OHG *wint* wind, L *ventus,* Gk *aēnai* to blow, Skt *vāti* it blows] **1 a :** a natural movement of air of any velocity; *esp* **:** air in natural motion horizontally **b :** an artificially produced movement of air **2 a :** a destructive force or influence **b :** a force or agency that carries along or influences **:** TENDENCY, TREND **3 a :** BREATH 4a **b :** BREATH 2a **c :** the pit of the stomach **:** SOLAR PLEXUS **4 :** gas generated in the stomach or the intestines **5 a :** compressed air or gas **b** *archaic* **:** AIR **6 :** something that is insubstantial: as **a :** mere talk **:** idle words **b :** NOTHING, NOTHINGNESS **c :** vain self-satisfaction **7 a :** air carrying a scent (as of a hunter or game) **b :** slight information esp. about something secret **:** INTIMATION **8 a :** musical wind instruments esp. as distinguished from strings and percussion **b** *pl* **:** players of wind instruments **9 a :** a direction from which the wind may blow **:** a point of the compass; *esp* **:** one of the cardinal points **b :** the direction from which the wind is blowing — **get the wind up :** to become excited or alarmed — **have in the wind :** to be on the scent of — **have the wind of 1 :** to be to windward of **2 :** to be on the scent of **3 :** to have a superior position to — **in the wind :** about to happen **:** ASTIR, AFOOT — **near the wind 1 :** CLOSE-HAULED **2 :** close to a point of danger **:** near the permissible limit — **off the wind :** away from the direction from which the wind is blowing — **under the wind 1 :** to leeward **2 :** in a place protected from the wind **:** under the lee

2**wind** \'wind\ *vt* **1 :** to detect or follow by scent **2 :** to expose to the air or wind **:** dry by exposing to air **3 :** to make short of breath **4 :** to regulate the wind supply of (an organ pipe) **5 :** to rest (as a horse) in order to allow the breath to be recovered **~** *vi* **1 :** to scent game **2** *dial* **:** to pause for breath

3**wind** \'wīnd, 'wind\ *vb* **wind·ed** \'wīn-dəd, 'win-\ *or* **wound** \'wau̇nd\ **wind·ing** *vt* [1*wind*] **1 :** to cause (as a horn) to sound by blowing **:** BLOW ⟨little fishing boats ~ their conchs —Mary H. Vorse⟩ **2 :** to sound (as a call or note) on a horn ⟨*wound* a rousing call —R.L.Stevenson⟩ **~** *vi* **:** to produce a sound on a horn

4**wind** \'wīnd\ *vb* **wound** \'wau̇nd\ *also* **wind·ed; wind·ing** [ME *winden,* fr. OE *windan* to twist, move with speed or force, brandish; akin to OHG *wintan* to wind, Umbrian *ohavendu* let him turn aside] *vi* **1 :** BEND, WARP **2 :** to have a curving course or shape **:** extend in curves **3 :** to move so as to encircle **4 :** to turn when lying at anchor **~** *vt* **1 a** *obs* **:** WEAVE **b :** ENTANGLE, INVOLVE **c :** to introduce sinuously or stealthily **:** INSINUATE **2 a :** to encircle or cover with something pliable **:** bind with loops or layers **b :** to turn completely or repeatedly about an object **:** COIL, TWINE **c** (1) **:** to hoist or haul by means of a rope or chain and a windlass (2) **:** to move (a ship) by hauling on a capstan **d** (1) **:** to tighten the spring of ⟨~ a clock⟩ ⟨~ up a toy train⟩ (2) *obs* **:** to make tighter **:** TIGHTEN, TUNE (3) **:** CRANK ⟨*wound* down the car window⟩ **e :** to raise to a high level (as of excitement or tension) **3 a :** to cause to move in a curving line or path **b** *archaic* **:** to turn the course of; *esp* **:** to lead (a person) as one wishes **c** (1) **:** to cause (as a ship) to change direction **:** TURN (2) **:** to turn (a ship) end for end **d :** to traverse on a curving course ⟨the river ~*s* the valley⟩ **e :** to effect by curving — **wind·er** *n*

5**wind** \'wīnd\ *n* **1 :** a mechanism (as a winch) for winding **2 :** an act of winding **:** the state of being wound **3 :** COIL, TURN **4 :** a particular method of winding

wind·age \'win-dij\ *n* **1 a :** the space between the projectile of a smoothbore gun and the surface of the bore **b :** the difference between the diameter of the bore of a muzzle-loading rifled cannon and that of the projectile cylinder **2 a :** the amount of sight deflection necessary to compensate for wind displacement in aiming a gun **b** (1) **:** the influence of the wind in deflecting the course of a projectile (2) **:** the amount of deflection due to the wind **3 :** the disturbance of the air caused by a passing object (as a projectile) **4 :** the surface exposed (as by a ship) to the wind

wind·bag \'win(d)-,bag\ *n* **:** an idly talkative person

wind·blown \-,blōn\ *adj* **1 :** blown by the wind; *esp* **:** having a permanent set or character of growth determined by the prevailing winds ⟨~ trees⟩ **2** *of hair* **:** cut so that the ends turn outward and to the front as if blown by a wind from behind

wind·bound \-,bau̇nd\ *adj* **:** prevented from sailing by a contrary or a high wind

wind·break \-,brāk\ *n* **:** a growth of trees or shrubs serving to break the force of wind; *broadly* **:** a shelter (as a fence) from the wind

Wind·break·er \-,brā-kər\ *trademark* — used for an outer jacket made of wind-resistant material

wind–bro·ken \-,brō-kən\ *adj, of a horse* **:** affected with pulmonary emphysema or with heaves

wind·burn \-,bərn\ *n* **:** irritation caused by wind — **wind·burned** \-,bərnd\ *adj*

wind cone *n* **:** WIND SOCK

wind·er \'wīn-dər\ *n* **:** one that winds: as **a :** a worker who winds yarn or thread **b :** any of various textile machines for winding thread and yarn **c :** a key for winding a mechanism (as a clock) **d :** a step that is wider at one end than at the other (as in a spiral staircase)

wind·fall \'win(d)-,fȯl\ *n, often attrib* **1 :** something (as a tree or fruit) blown down by the wind **2 :** an unexpected or sudden gain or advantage

wind·flaw \-,flȯ\ *n* **:** a gust of wind **:** FLAW

wind·flow·er \-,flau̇(-ə)r\ *n* **1 :** ANEMONE 1 **2 :** RUE ANEMONE

wind·gall \-,gȯl\ *n* **:** a soft tumor or synovial swelling on a horse's leg in the region of the fetlock joint — **wind·galled** \-,gȯld\ *adj*

wind gap *n* **:** a notch in the crest of a mountain ridge

wind harp *n* **:** AEOLIAN HARP

wind·hov·er \'wind-,həv-ər, -,häv-\ *n, Brit* **:** KESTREL

wind·i·ly \'win-də-lē\ *adv* **:** in a windy manner

wind·i·ness \-dē-nəs\ *n* **:** the quality or state of being windy

1**wind·ing** \'wīn-diŋ\ *n* **1 :** material (as wire) wound or coiled about an object (as an armature); *also* **:** a single turn of the wound material **2 a :** the act of one that winds **b :** manner of winding **3 :** a curved or sinuous course, line, or progress

2**winding** *adj* **:** marked by winding: as **a :** having a pronounced curve; *esp* **:** SPIRAL ⟨a ~ stairway⟩ **b :** having a course that winds ⟨a ~ road⟩

wind·ing–sheet \\-ˌshēt\\ *n* **:** a sheet in which a corpse is wrapped **:** SHROUD

wind instrument *n* **:** a musical instrument sounded by wind and esp. by the breath

wind·jam·mer \\ˈwin(d)-ˌjam-ər\\ *n* **:** a sailing ship or one of its crew

[1]**wind·lass** \\ˈwin-(d)ləs\\ *n* [ME *wyndlas,* alter. of *wyndas,* fr. ON *vindāss,* fr. *vinda* to wind + *āss* pole; akin to OHG *wintan* to wind] **:** any of various machines for hoisting or hauling: as **a :** a horizontal barrel supported on vertical posts and turned by a crank so that the hoisting rope is wound around the barrel **b :** a steam or electric winch with horizontal or vertical shaft and two drums used to raise a ship's anchor

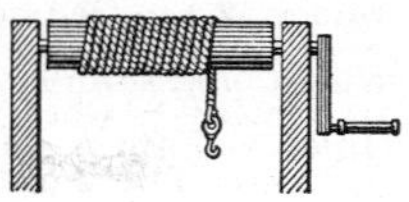

windlass

[2]**windlass** *vt* **:** to hoist or haul with a windlass

win·dle·straw \\ˈwin-(d)ᵊl-ˌstrȯ\\ *n* [(assumed) ME, fr. OE *windel-strēaw,* fr. *windel* basket (fr. *windan* to wind) + *strēaw* straw] *Brit* **:** a dry thin stalk of grass

[1]**wind·mill** \\ˈwin(d)-ˌmil\\ *n* **1 a :** a mill operated by the wind usu. acting on oblique vanes or sails which radiate from a horizontal shaft; *esp* **:** a wind-driven water pump **b :** the wind-driven wheel of a windmill **2 :** something that resembles or suggests a windmill: as **a :** PINWHEEL 1 **b** *slang* **:** HELICOPTER **3** [fr. the episode in *Don Quixote* by Cervantes in which the hero attacks windmills under the illusion that they are giants] **:** an imaginary wrong, evil, or opponent — used in the phrase *to tilt at windmills*

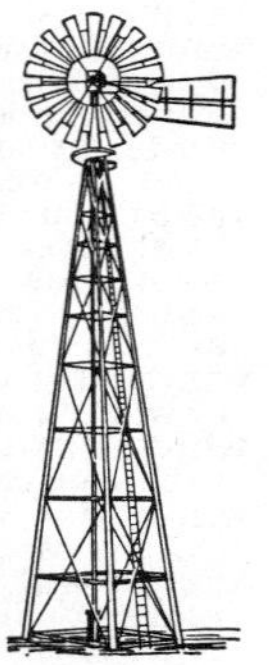

windmill

[2]**windmill** *vt* **:** to cause to move like a windmill ~ *vi* **:** to move like a windmill

win·dow \\ˈwin-(ˌ)dō, -də(-w)\\ *n, often attrib* [ME *windowe,* fr. ON *vindauga,* fr. *vindr* wind + *auga* eye; akin to OE *wind* and to OE *ēage* eye — more at EYE] **1 :** an opening esp. in the wall of a building for admission of light and air usu. closed by casements or sashes containing transparent material (as glass) and capable of being opened and shut **2 :** WINDOWPANE **3 :** an opening like or suggestive of a window (as a shutter, slot, valve) **4 :** the transparent panel of a window envelope **5 :** the framework (as a shutter or sash with its fittings) that closes a window opening **6 :** strips of foil dropped from airplanes to interfere with radar detection **7 :** a range of wavelengths in the electromagnetic spectrum to which the earth's atmosphere is transparent **8 :** an interval of time within which a rocket or spacecraft must be launched to accomplish a particular mission **9 :** an area at the limits of the earth's sensible atmosphere through which a spacecraft must pass for successful reentry

window box *n* **1 :** one of the hollows in the sides of a window frame for the weights that counterbalance a lifting sash **2 :** a box designed to hold soil for growing plants on a windowsill

win·dow–dress \\ˈwin-dō-ˌdres, -də-ˌdres\\ *vt* [back-formation fr. *window dresser*] **:** to make appear more attractive or favorable

window dresser *n* **1 :** one that arranges merchandise and decorations in a show window **2 :** one that distorts facts or puts up a front in order to make a favorable impression

window dressing *n* **1 :** the display of merchandise in a retail store window **2 :** a showing (as financial) made to create a good but sometimes false impression

window envelope *n* **:** an envelope having a transparent panel through which the address on the enclosure is visible

win·dow·pane \\ˈwin-də-ˌpān, -dō-\\ *n* **:** a pane in a window

window seat *n* **:** a seat built into a window recess

window shade *n* **:** a shade or curtain for a window

win·dow–shop \\ˈwin-də-ˌshäp, -dō-\\ *vi* **:** to look at the displays in store windows without going inside the stores to make purchases — **win·dow–shop·per** *n*

win·dow·sill \\-ˌsil\\ *n* **:** the horizontal member at the bottom of a window opening

wind·pipe \\ˈwin(d)-ˌpīp\\ *n* **:** the passage for the breath from the larynx to the lungs **:** TRACHEA

wind–pol·li·nat·ed \\-ˈpäl-ə-ˌnāt-əd\\ *adj* **:** pollinated by wind-borne pollen

wind·proof \\-ˈprüf\\ *adj* **:** proof against the wind ⟨a ~ jacket⟩

wind rose \\ˈwin-ˌdrōz\\ *n* [G *windrose* compass card] **:** a diagram showing for a given place the relative frequency or frequency and strength of winds from different directions

wind·row \\ˈwin-ˌ(d)rō\\ *n* **1 a :** a row of hay raked up to dry before being baled **b :** a similar row (as of grain) for drying **2 :** a row heaped up by or as if by the wind **3 a :** a long low ridge of road-making material scraped to the side of a road **b :** BANK, RIDGE, HEAP — **windrow** *vt*

wind scale *n* **:** a series of numbers or words corresponding to various ranges of wind speeds for indicating the force of the wind

wind·screen \\ˈwin(d)-ˌskrēn\\ *n, Brit* **:** an automobile windshield

wind shake *n* **:** shake in timber attributed to high winds — **wind-shak·en** \\ˈwin(d)-ˌshā-kən\\ *adj*

wind·shield \\ˈwin(d)-ˌshēld\\ *n* **:** a transparent screen (as of glass) in front of the occupants of a vehicle to protect them from the wind

wind sock *n* **:** a truncated cloth cone open at both ends and mounted in an elevated position to indicate the direction of the wind — called also *wind sleeve*

Wind·sor chair \\ˌwin-zər-\\ *n* [*Windsor,* borough in England and seat of Windsor Castle, residence of English sovereigns] **:** a wooden chair with spindle back and raking legs

Windsor knot *n* **:** a knot used for tying four-in-hand ties that is wider than the usual four-in-hand knot

Windsor tie *n* **:** a broad necktie usu. tied in a loose bow

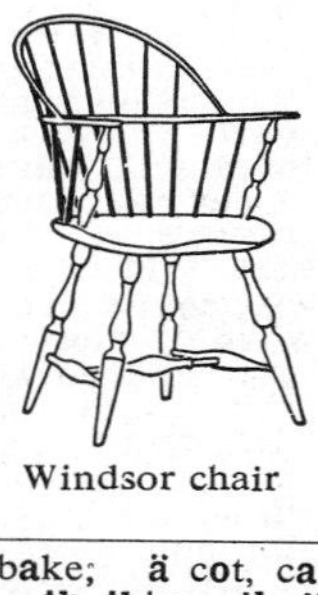

Windsor chair

wind sprint *n* **:** a sprint performed as a training exercise to develop the wind

wind·storm \\ˈwin(d)-ˌstȯ(ə)rm\\ *n* **:** a storm marked by high wind with little or no precipitation

wind·suck·er \\-ˌsək-ər\\ *n* **:** a wind-sucking horse

wind sucking *n* **:** a vice of horses in which the animal swallows or goes through the motions of swallowing quantities of air

wind·swept \\ˈwin(d)-ˌswept\\ *adj* **:** swept by or as if by wind

wind tee *n* **:** a large weather vane shaped like a horizontal letter T on or near a landing field

wind tunnel *n* **:** a tunnellike passage through which air is blown at a known velocity to determine the effects of wind pressure on an object (as an airplane part or model or a guided missile) placed in the passage

wind up *vt* **1 :** to bring to a conclusion **:** END **2 :** to put in order **:** SETTLE ~ *vi* **1 a :** to come to a conclusion **b :** to arrive in a place, situation, or condition at the end or as a result of a course of action ⟨*wound up* as millionaires⟩ **2 :** to give a preliminary swing to the arm (as before pitching a baseball)

[1]**wind·up** \\ˈwīn-ˌdəp\\ *n* **1 a :** the act of bringing to an end **b :** a concluding act or part **:** FINISH **2 :** a preliminary swing of the arm before pitching a baseball

[2]**windup** *adj* **:** having a spring wound up by hand for operation

[1]**wind·ward** \\ˈwin-(d)wərd\\ *adj* **:** moving or situated toward the direction from which the wind is blowing — compare LEEWARD

[2]**windward** *n* **:** the side or direction from which the wind is blowing — **to windward :** into or in an advantageous position

wind·way \\ˈwin-ˌ(d)wā\\ *n* **:** a passage for air

wind–wing \\-ˌ(d)wiŋ\\ *n* **:** a small panel in an automobile window that can be turned outward for ventilation

windy \\ˈwin-dē\\ *adj* **1 a** (1) **:** WINDSWEPT (2) **:** marked by strong wind or by more wind than usual **b :** VIOLENT, STORMY **2 :** FLATULENT 1 **3 a :** VERBOSE, BOMBASTIC **b :** lacking substance **:** EMPTY

[1]**wine** \\ˈwīn\\ *n* [ME *win,* fr. OE *wīn;* akin to OHG *wīn* wine; both fr. a prehistoric Gmc word borrowed fr. L *vinum* wine, of non-IE origin; akin to the source of Gk *oinos* wine] **1 a :** fermented grape juice containing varying percentages of alcohol together with ethers and esters that give it bouquet and flavor **b :** wine or a substitute used in Christian communion services **2 :** the usu. fermented juice of a plant product (as a fruit) used as a beverage **3 :** something that invigorates or intoxicates **4 :** a variable color averaging a dark red

[2]**wine** *vt* **:** to treat to wine ~ *vi* **:** to drink wine

wine cellar *n* **:** a room for storing wines; *also* **:** a stock of wines

wine cooler *n* **:** a vessel or container in which wine is cooled; *specif* **:** a metal-lined wooden container on legs with casters used esp. in the 18th and early 19th centuries for cooling wine

wine·glass \\ˈwīn-ˌglas\\ *n* **1 :** a stemware drinking glass for wine **2 :** a four-ounce unit of measure used in mixing drinks

wine·grow·er \\-ˌgrō(-ə)r\\ *n* **:** one that cultivates a vineyard and makes wine

wine palm *n* **:** any of several palms whose sap is used to make wine

wine·press \\-ˌpres\\ *n* **:** a vat in which juice is expressed from grapes by treading or by means of a plunger

win·ery \\ˈwīn-(ə-)rē\\ *n* **:** a wine-making establishment

wine·shop \\ˈwīn-ˌshäp\\ *n* **:** a tavern that specializes in serving wine

wine·skin \\-ˌskin\\ *n* **:** a bag made from the skin of an animal and used for holding wine

wine taster *n* **1 :** one that tests wine by tasting **2 :** a small flat bowl used to hold a sample of wine being tested

win·ey *var of* WINY

[1]**wing** \\ˈwiŋ\\ *n, often attrib* [ME *winge,* of Scand origin; akin to Dan & Sw *vinge* wing; akin to Skt *vāti* it blows — more at WIND] **1 a :** one of the movable feathered or membranous paired appendages by means of which a bird, bat, or insect is able to fly; *also* **:** such an appendage even though rudimentary if possessed by an animal belonging to a group characterized by the power of flight **b :** any of various organic structures esp. of a flying fish or flying lemur providing means of limited flight **2 :** an appendage or part likened to a wing in shape, appearance, or position: as **a :** a device (as for swimming) attached to the shoulders **b :** ALA **c :** a turned-back or extended edge on an article of clothing **d :** a sidepiece at the top of an armchair **e** (1) **:** a foliaceous, membranous, or woody expansion of a plant esp. along a stem or on a samara or capsule (2) **:** either of the two lateral petals of a papilionaceous flower **f :** a vane of a windmill or arrow **g :** SAIL **h :** one of the airfoils that develop a major part of the lift which supports a heavier-than-air aircraft **3 :** a means of flight or rapid progress **4 :** the act or manner of flying **:** FLIGHT **5 :** ARM; *esp* **:** a throwing or pitching arm **6 :** a side or outlying region or district **7 :** a part or feature usu. projecting from and subordinate to the main or central part **8 a :** one of the pieces of scenery at the side of a stage **b** *pl* **:** the area at the side of the stage out of sight **9 a :** a left or right section of an army or fleet **b :** one of the positions or players on either side of a center position or line of a field, court, or rink; *esp* **:** such a position or player on the forward line of a team **10 a :** either of two opposing groups within an organization or society **:** FACTION **b :** a section of an organized body (as a legislative chamber) representing a group or faction holding distinct opinions or policies — compare LEFT WING, RIGHT WING **11 a :** a unit of the U.S. Air Force higher than a group and lower than an air division **b :** two or more squadrons of naval airplanes not carrier based **12 :** a dance step marked by a quick outward and inward rolling glide of one foot — **on the wing :** in flight **:** FLYING — **under one's wing :** under one's protection **:** in one's care

[2]**wing** *vt* **1 a :** to fit with wings **b :** to enable to fly or move swiftly **2 a :** to wound in the wing **:** disable the wing of **b :** to wound (as with a bullet) without killing **3 a :** to traverse with or as if with wings **b :** to effect or achieve by flying **4 :** to let fly **:** DISPATCH ~ *vi* **:** to go with or as if with wings **:** FLY

wing and wing *adv* **:** with sails extended on both sides

wing·back \\ˈwiŋ-ˌbak\\ *n* **:** a football back whose position on offense is beyond the offensive end; *also* **:** the position of a player so stationed

wing bow *n* **:** the lesser coverts of the shoulder or bend of a bird's wing when distinctively colored

wing case *n* **:** ELYTRON

wing chair *n* **:** an upholstered armchair with high solid back and sides that provide a rest for the head and protection from drafts

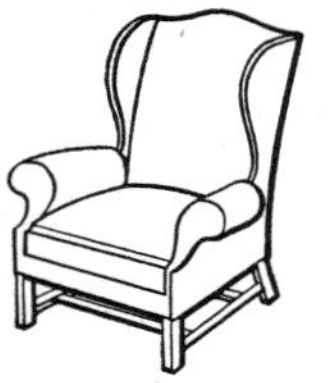

wing chair

wing covert *n* **:** one of the coverts of the wing quills

wing·ding \ˈwiŋ-ˌdiŋ\ *n* [origin unknown] **:** a wild or lively or lavish party

winged \ˈwiŋd *also except for 1a "esp." sense* ˈwiŋ-əd\ *adj* **1 a :** having wings esp. of a specified character **b :** using wings in flight **2 a :** soaring with or as if with wings **:** ELEVATED **b :** SWIFT, RAPID

wing–foot·ed \ˈwiŋ-ˈfu̇t-əd\ *adj* **:** having winged feet **:** SWIFT ⟨~ messenger⟩

wing·less \ˈwiŋ-ləs\ *adj* **:** having no wings or very rudimentary wings — **wing·less·ness** *n*

wing·let \ˈwiŋ-lət\ *n* **1 :** a very small wing **2 :** BASTARD WING

wing·like \-ˌlīk\ *adj* **:** resembling a wing in form or lateral position

wing loading *n* **:** the gross weight of an airplane fully loaded divided by the area of the supporting surface — called also *wing load*

wing·man \-mən\ *n* **:** a pilot that flies behind and outside the leader of a flying formation

wing nut *n* **:** a nut with wings affording a grip for the thumb and finger

wing·over \ˈwiŋ-ˌō-vər\ *n* **:** a flight maneuver in which a plane is put into a climbing turn until nearly stalled after which the nose is allowed to fall while the turn is continued until normal flight is attained in a direction opposite to that in which the maneuver was entered

wings \ˈwiŋz\ *n pl* **:** insignia consisting of an outspread pair of stylized bird's wings which are awarded on completion of prescribed training to a qualified pilot, bombardier, gunner, navigator, observer, flight surgeon, or other crew member or a balloon pilot in armed services

wing shooting *n* **:** the act or practice of shooting at game birds in flight or at flying targets

wing·span \ˈwiŋ-ˌspan\ *n* **:** the length of an airplane wing measured between outermost tips

wing·spread \-ˌspred\ *n* **:** the spread of the wings **:** WINGSPAN; *specif* **:** the extreme measurement between the tips or outer margins of the wings (as of a bird or insect)

wing tip *n* **1 :** a toe cap having a point extending back toward the throat of the shoe and curving sides extending toward the shank **2 :** a shoe having a wing tip

wingy \ˈwiŋ-ē\ *adj* **1 :** having wings **2 :** soaring with or as if with wings **3 :** resembling or suggesting a wing in shape or position ⟨~ sleeves⟩

1**wink** \ˈwiŋk\ *vb* [ME *winken*, fr. OE *wincian;* akin to OHG *winchan* to stagger, wink, L *vacillare* to sway — more at PREVARICATE] *vi* **1 :** to shut one eye briefly as a signal or in teasing **2 :** to close and open the eyelids quickly **3 :** to avoid seeing or noting something — usu. used with *at* **4 :** to gleam or flash intermittently **:** TWINKLE **5 a :** to come to an end — usu. used with *out* **b :** to stop shining — usu. used with *out* **6 :** to signal a message with a light **~** *vt* **1 :** to cause to open and shut **2 :** to affect or influence by or as if by blinking the eyes

syn WINK, BLINK mean to close and open one's eyelids. WINK implies rapid, light, and usu. involuntary motion; BLINK commonly implies a slower closing and opening that may suggest a dazzled or dazed state or a struggle against drowsiness; in figurative use WINK implies connivance or indulgence, BLINK suggests evasion or shirking

2**wink** *n* **1 :** a brief period of sleep **:** NAP **2 a :** a hint or sign given by winking **b :** an act of winking **3 :** the time of a wink **:** INSTANT **4 :** a flicker of the eyelids **:** BLINK

wink·er \ˈwiŋ-kər\ *n* **1 :** one that winks **2 a :** a horse's blinder **:** BLINKER **b :** EYE; *also* **:** EYELASH

1**win·kle** \ˈwiŋ-kəl\ *n* [short for *periwinkle*] **1 :** 2PERIWINKLE **2 :** any of various whelks (esp. genus *Busycon*) that destroy large numbers of oysters and clams by drilling their shells and rasping away their flesh

2**winkle** *vt* **win·kling** \-k(ə-)liŋ\ **:** to displace, extract, or evict from a position — usu. used with *out*

3**winkle** *vi* [freq. of *wink*] **:** TWINKLE

win·na·ble \ˈwin-ə-bəl\ *adj* **:** able to be won

win·ner \ˈwin-ər\ *n* **:** one that wins: as **a :** one that is successful esp. through praiseworthy ability and hard work **b :** a victor esp. in games and sports

winner's circle *n* **:** an enclosure near a racetrack where the winning horse and jockey are brought for photographs and awards

1**win·ning** \ˈwin-iŋ\ *n* **1 :** the act of one that wins **:** VICTORY **2 :** something won **:** CONQUEST **3 a :** a shaft or pit opening made to win coal **b :** a more or less isolated section of a mine

2**winning** *adj* **:** ATTRACTIVE, CHARMING — **win·ning·ly** \-iŋ-lē\ *adv*

winning gallery *n* **:** the netted opening which is farthest from the dedans and into which a ball counted as winning in court tennis is played

winning opening *n* **:** the dedans, grille, or winning gallery of a court-tennis court

win·nock \ˈwin-ək\ *n* [ME (Sc) *windok, windowe*] *Scot* **:** WINDOW

1**win·now** \ˈwin-(ˌ)ō, ˈwin-ə(-w)\ *vb* [ME *winewen*, fr. OE *windwian* to fan, winnow; akin to OHG *wintōn* to fan, L *vannus* winnowing fan, *ventus* wind — more at WIND] *vt* **1 a** (1) **:** to remove (as chaff) by a current of air (2) **:** to get rid of (something undesirable or unwanted) **b :** SEPARATE, SIFT **2 :** to treat (as grain) by exposure to a current of air so that waste matter is eliminated **3 :** FAN **~** *vi* **1 :** to separate chaff from grain by fanning **2 :** to separate desirable and undesirable elements

2**winnow** *n* **1 :** a device for winnowing **2 a :** the act of winnowing **b :** a motion resembling that of winnowing

win·now·er \ˈwin-ə-wər\ *n* **:** one that winnows; *esp* **:** a winnowing machine

wino \ˈwī-(ˌ)nō\ *n, pl* **winos :** one who is chronically addicted to drinking wine

win·some \ˈwin(t)-səm\ *adj* [ME *winsum*, fr. OE *wynsum*, fr. *wynn* joy; akin to OHG *wunna* joy, L *venus* love — more at WIN] **1 :** causing joy or pleasure **:** WINNING **2 :** CHEERFUL, GAY — **win·some·ly** *adv* — **win·some·ness** *n*

1**win·ter** \ˈwint-ər\ *n* [ME, fr. OE; akin to OHG *wintar* winter] **1 :** the season between autumn and spring comprising in the northern hemisphere usu. the months December, January, and February or as reckoned astronomically extending from the December solstice to the March equinox **2 :** the colder half of the year **3 :** YEAR **4 :** a period of inactivity or decay

2**winter** *vb* **win·ter·ing** \ˈwint-ə-riŋ, ˈwin-triŋ\ *vi* **1 :** to pass the winter **2 :** to feed or find food during the winter — used with *on* **~** *vt* **:** to keep, feed, or manage during the winter

3**winter** *adj* **:** sown in autumn for harvesting in the following spring or summer ⟨~ wheat⟩ ⟨~ rye⟩

winter aconite *n* **:** a small Old World perennial herb (*Eranthis hyemalis*) of the crowfoot family grown for its bright yellow flowers which often bloom through the snow

win·ter·ber·ry \ˈwint-ər-ˌber-ē\ *n* **:** any of various American hollies with bright red berries persistent through the winter

win·ter·bourne \-ˌbō(ə)rn, -ˌbȯ(ə)rn, -ˌbu̇(ə)rn\ *n* **:** a stream that flows only or chiefly in winter

winter crookneck *n* **:** any of several crooknecks that are winter squashes of the pumpkin group noted for their keeping qualities

win·ter·er \ˈwint-ər-ər\ *n* **:** one that winters; *specif* **:** a winter resident or visitor

winter flounder *n* **:** a rusty brown flounder (*Pseudopleuronectes americanus*) of the northwestern Atlantic important as a market fish esp. in winter

win·ter·green \ˈwint-ər-ˌgrēn\ *n* **1 :** any of a genus (*Pyrola* of the family Pyrolaceae, the wintergreen family) of evergreen perennial herbs related to the heaths; *esp* **:** one (*P. minor*) with small round basal leaves **2 a :** any of a genus (*Gaultheria*) of the heath family; *esp* **:** a low evergreen plant (*G. procumbens*) with white flowers and spicy red berries — called also *checkerberry* **b :** an essential oil from this plant or its flavor ⟨~ lozenges⟩

win·ter·ish \ˈwint-ə-rish, ˈwin-trish\ *adj* **:** suitable to or suggestive of winter **:** somewhat wintry

win·ter·iza·tion \ˌwint-ə-rə-ˈzā-shən\ *n* **:** the process of winterizing **:** the state of being winterized

win·ter·ize \ˈwint-ə-ˌrīz\ *vt* **:** to make ready for winter or winter use and esp. resistant or proof against winter weather

win·ter–kill \ˈwint-ər-ˌkil\ *vt* **:** to kill (as a plant) by exposure to winter conditions **~** *vi* **:** to die as a result of exposure to winter conditions — **winterkill** *n*

win·ter·ly \ˈwint-ər-lē\ *adj* **:** WINTRY, CHEERLESS

winter melon *n* **:** a muskmelon (*Cucumis melo inodorus*) with smooth rind and sweet white or greenish flesh that keeps well

winter quarters *n pl but sing or pl in constr* **:** a winter residence or station (as of a military unit or a circus)

winter squash *n* **:** any of various squashes derived from a natural species (*Cucurbita maxima*) or pumpkins from a species (*C. moschata*) that can be stored for several months

win·ter·tide \ˈwint-ər-ˌtīd\ *n* **:** the season of winter

win through *vi* **:** to survive difficulties and reach a desired or satisfactory end

win·tle \ˈwin(t)-ᵊl\ *vi* [perh. fr. Flem *windtelen* to reel] *Scot* **:** STAGGER, REEL; *also* **:** WRIGGLE

win·tri·ly \ˈwin-trə-lē\ *adv* **:** in a wintry manner

win·tri·ness \-trē-nəs\ *n* **:** the quality or state of being wintry

win·try \ˈwin-trē\ *or* **win·tery** \ˈwint-ə-rē, ˈwin-trē\ *adj* **1** *archaic* **:** of or relating to winter **2 :** characteristic of winter **:** COLD, STORMY **3 a :** AGED **b :** WHITE **c :** CHILLING, CHEERLESS

winy \ˈwī-nē\ *adj* **1 :** having the taste or qualities of wine **:** VINOUS **2** *of the air* **:** EXHILARATING

1**winze** \ˈwinz\ *n* [alter. of earlier *winds*, prob. fr. pl. of 5*wind*] **:** a steeply inclined passageway connecting a mine working place with a lower one

2**winze** *n* [Flem or D *wensch* wish] *Scot* **:** CURSE

1**wipe** \ˈwīp\ *vt* [ME *wipen*, fr. OE *wīpian;* akin to OHG *wīfan* to wind around, L *vibrare* to vibrate] **1 a :** to rub with or as if with something soft for cleaning **b :** to clean or dry by rubbing **c :** to draw, pass, or move for or as if for rubbing or cleaning **2 a :** to remove by or as if by rubbing **b** (1) **:** to expunge completely **:** OBLITERATE (2) **:** to cause to cease to exist **:** ANNIHILATE — usu. used with *out* **3 a :** to spread by or as if by wiping **b :** to form (a joint between lead pipes) by applying solder in repeated increments individually spread and shaped with greased cloth pads

2**wipe** *n* **1 a :** BLOW, STRIKE **b :** GIBE, JEER **2 :** an act or instance of wiping **3 :** something used for wiping

wip·er \ˈwī-pər\ *n* **1 :** one that wipes **2 a :** something (as a towel or sponge) used for wiping **b :** a projecting tooth, tumbler, eccentric, tappet, or cam on a rotating or oscillating piece used esp. for raising a stamper, the helve of a power hammer, or other part intended to fall by its own weight **c :** a moving contact for making connections with the terminals of an electrical device (as a rheostat)

wipe up *vt* **:** to make clean by or as if by wiping **:** mop up

wir·able \ˈwī-rə-bəl\ *adj* **:** capable of being wired

1**wire** \ˈwī(ə)r\ *n, often attrib* [ME, fr. OE *wīr;* akin to OHG *wiara* fine gold, L *viēre* to plait, Gk *iris* rainbow] **1 a :** metal in the form of a usu. very flexible thread or slender rod **b :** a thread or rod of such material **2 a :** WIREWORK **b :** the meshwork of parallel or woven wire on which the wet web of paper forms **3 :** something wirelike (as a thin plant stem) **4** *usu pl* **a :** a system of wires used to operate the puppets in a puppet show **b :** hidden influences controlling the action of a person or organization **5 a :** a line of wire for conducting electrical current — compare CORD 3b **b :** a telephone or telegraph wire or system **c :** TELEGRAM, CABLEGRAM **6 :** fencing or a fence of usu. barbed wire **7 :** the finish line of a race — **wire·like** \-ˌlīk\ *adj* — **under the wire 1 :** at the finish line **2 :** at the last moment

2**wire** *vt* **1 :** to provide with wire **:** use wire on for any purpose **2 :** to send or send word to by telegraph **~** *vi* **:** to send a telegraphic message

wire cloth *n* **:** a fabric of woven metallic wire (as for strainers)

wire coat *n* **:** a coat (as of a dog) of harsh and dense outer hair

wired \ˈwī(ə)rd\ *adj* **1 :** reinforced by wire (as for strength) **2 :** furnished with wires (as for electric connections) **3 :** bound with wire ⟨a ~ container⟩ **4 :** having a wirework netting or fence

wired radio *n* **:** a system for distributing radio programs over wire lines — called also *wired wireless, wire radio*

wire·draw \ˈwī(ə)r-ˌdrȯ\ *vt* **1 a :** to draw or stretch forcibly **b :** to draw or spin out to great length, tenuity, or overrefinement **:** ATTENUATE **2 :** to draw (metal) into wire — **wire·draw·er** \-ˌdrȯ(-ə)r\ *n*

wire·draw·ing *n* : the act, process, or occupation of drawing metal into wire
wire·drawn \-ˌdrȯn\ *adj* : excessively minute and subtle ⟨~ distinctions⟩
wire gauge *n* **1** : a gauge esp. for measuring the diameter of wire or thickness of sheet metal **2** : any of various systems consisting of a series of standard sizes used in describing the diameter of wire or the thickness of sheet metal
wire gauze *n* : a gauzelike texture of fine wires
wire glass *n* : a glass with wire netting embedded in it
wire grass *n* : any of various grasses having wiry culms or leaves; *esp* : a European slender-stemmed meadow grass (*Poa compressa*) widely naturalized in the U.S. and Canada
wire·hair \'wī(ə)r-ˌha(ə)r, -ˌhe(ə)r\ *n* : a wirehaired fox terrier
wire·haired \-'ha(ə)rd, -'he(ə)rd\ *adj* : having a stiff wiry outer coat of hair
wirehaired pointing griffon *n* : a large European bird dog with a harsh wiry coat
wirehaired terrier *n* : a wirehaired fox terrier
1**wire·less** \'wī(ə)r-ləs\ *adj* **1** : having no wire or wires **2** *chiefly Brit* : of or relating to radiotelegraphy, radiotelephony, or radio
2**wireless** *n* **1** : WIRELESS TELEGRAPHY **2** : RADIOTELEPHONY **3** *chiefly Brit* : RADIO — **wireless** *vb*
wireless telegraphy *n* : telegraphy carried on by radio waves and without connecting wires — called also *wireless telegraph*
wireless telephone *n* : RADIOTELEPHONE
wire·man \'wī(ə)r-mən\ *n* : a maker of or worker with wire; *esp* : LINEMAN
wire netting *n* : a texture of woven wire coarser than wire gauze
Wire·pho·to \'wī(ə)r-'fōt-(ˌ)ō\ *trademark* — used for a photograph transmitted by electrical signals over telephone wires
wire–pull·er \-ˌpu̇l-ər\ *n* : one who uses secret or underhand means to influence the acts of a person or organization — **wire–pull·ing** \ˌpu̇l-iŋ\ *n*
wir·er \'wīr-ər\ *n* : one that wires or uses wire : WIREMAN; *esp* : a trapper who uses a wire trap
wire–re·cord \ˌwī(ə)(r)-ri-'kȯ(ə)rd\ *vt* : to make a wire recording of
wire recorder *n* : a magnetic recorder using magnetic wire
wire recording *n* : magnetic recording on magnetic wire; *also* : the recording made by this process
wire rope *n* : a rope formed wholly or chiefly of wires
wire service *n* : a news agency that sends out syndicated news copy by wire to subscribers
1**wire·tap** \'wī(ə)r-ˌtap\ *vi* : to tap a telephone or telegraph wire to get information
2**wiretap** *n* **1** : the act or an instance of wiretapping **2** : an electrical connection for wiretapping
wire·tap·per \-ˌtap-ər\ *n* : one that taps telephone or telegraph wires
wire·way \'wī(ə)r-ˌwā\ *n* : a conduit for wires
wire·work \-ˌwərk\ *n* **1** : work of wires; *esp* : meshwork, netting, or grillwork of wire **2** : walking on wires esp. by acrobats
wire·worm \-ˌwərm\ *n* **1** : a worm that is the slender hard-coated larva of various click beetles and is esp. destructive to plant roots **2** : MILLIPEDE
wir·i·ness \'wī-rē-nəs\ *n* : the quality or state of being wiry
wir·ing \'wī(ə)r-iŋ\ *n* **1** : the act of providing or using wire **2** : a system of wires : WIREWORK; *esp* : an arrangement of wires used for electric distribution
wir·ra \'wir-ə\ *interj* [*oh wirra*, fr. IrGael *a Muire*, lit., O Mary] *Irish* — usu. used to express lament, grief, or concern
wiry \'wī(ə)r-ē\ *adj* **1 a** : made or consisting of wire **b** : resembling wire esp. in form and flexibility **c** *of sound* : produced by or suggestive of the vibration of wire **2** : being lean, supple, and vigorous : SINEWY
wis \'wis\ *vb* [by incorrect division fr. *iwis* (understood as *I wis*, with *wis* taken to be an archaic pres. indic. of 1*wit*)] *archaic* : KNOW
wis·dom \'wiz-dəm\ *n* [ME, fr. OE *wīsdōm*, fr. *wīs* wise] **1 a** : accumulated philosophic or scientific learning : KNOWLEDGE **b** : ability to discern inner qualities and relationships : INSIGHT **c** : good sense : JUDGMENT **2** : a wise attitude or course of action **3** : the teachings of the ancient wise men **syn** see SENSE
wisdom tooth *n* [fr. being cut usu. in the late teens] : the last tooth of the full set on each half of each jaw in man
1**wise** \'wīz\ *n* [ME, fr. OE *wīse*; akin to OHG *wīsa* manner, Gk *eidos* form, *idein* to see — more at WIT] : MANNER, WAY
2**wise** *adj* [ME *wis*, fr. OE *wīs*; akin to OHG *wīs* wise, OE *witan* to know — more at WIT] **1 a** : having wisdom : SAGE **b** : exercising sound judgment : PRUDENT **2** : evidencing or hinting at the possession of inside information : KNOWING; *also* : CRAFTY, SHREWD **3** *obs* : skilled in magic or divination — **wise·ly** *adv*
syn SAGE, SAPIENT, JUDICIOUS, PRUDENT, SENSIBLE, SANE: WISE suggests great understanding of people and of situations and unusual discernment and judgment in dealing with them; SAGE suggests wide experience, great learning, and wisdom; SAPIENT is chiefly ironical and implies chiefly an appearance of sageness; JUDICIOUS stresses a capacity for reaching wise decisions or just conclusions; PRUDENT suggests exercise of the restraint of sound practical wisdom and discretion; SENSIBLE applies to action guided and restrained by good sense and rationality; SANE stresses mental soundness, rationality, and levelheadedness
3**wise** *vt* : INFORM, INSTRUCT — usu. used with *up* ~ *vi* : to become informed or knowledgeable : LEARN — used with *up*
4**wise** *vt* [ME *wisen*, fr. OE *wīsian*; akin to ON *vīsa* to show the way, OE *wīs* wise] **1** *chiefly Scot* **a** : DIRECT, GUIDE **b** : ADVISE, PERSUADE **2** *chiefly Scot* : to divert or impel in a given direction : SEND
-wise \ˌwīz\ *adv comb form* [ME, fr. OE *-wīsan*, fr. *wīse* manner] **1 a** : in the manner of ⟨crab*wise*⟩ ⟨fan*wise*⟩ **b** : in the position or direction of ⟨slant*wise*⟩ ⟨clock*wise*⟩ **2** : with regard to : in respect of ⟨dollar*wise*⟩
wise·acre \'wī-ˌzā-kər\ *n* [MD *wijssegger* soothsayer, modif. of OHG *wīzzago*; akin to OE *wītega* soothsayer, *witan* to know] : one who pretends to knowledge or cleverness : SMART ALECK
1**wise·crack** \'wīz-ˌkrak\ *n* : a sophisticated or knowing witticism **syn** see JEST
2**wisecrack** *vi* : to make a wisecrack — **wise·crack·er** *n*
wise guy \'wīz-ˌgī\ *n* : a cocky conceited fellow : KNOW-IT-ALL
wise·ness \'wīz-nəs\ *n* : the quality or state of being wise : WISDOM
wi·sen·hei·mer \'wīz-ᵊn-ˌhī-mər\ *n* [2*wise* + G *-enheimer* (as in G family names such as *Guggenheimer, Oppenheimer*)] : one who has the air of knowing all about something or everything : WISEACRE
wi·sent \'vē-ˌzent\ *n* [G, fr. OHG *wisunt* — more at BISON] : a European bison (*Bison bonasus*) — called also *aurochs*
wise·wom·an \'wīz-ˌwu̇m-ən\ *n* **1** : a woman versed in charms, conjuring, or fortune-telling **2** : MIDWIFE
1**wish** \'wish\ *vb* [ME *wisshen*, fr. OE *wȳscan*; akin to OHG *wunsken* to wish, L *venus* love, charm — more at WIN] *vt* **1** : to have a desire for : CRAVE **2** : to invoke upon : BID ⟨~ him good night⟩ **3 a** : to give form to (a wish) **b** : to express a wish for **c** : to request in the form of a wish : ORDER **4** : to confer (something unwanted) upon : FOIST ~ *vi* **1** : to have a desire : WANT **2** : to make a wish **syn** see DESIRE — **wish·er** *n*
2**wish** *n* **1 a** : an act or instance of wishing or desire : WANT **b** : an object of desire : GOAL **2 a** : an expressed will or desire : MANDATE **b** : a request or command couched as a wish **3** : an invocation of good or evil fortune on someone
wisha \'wish-ə\ *interj* [IrGael *ō* oh + *muise* indeed] *chiefly Irish* — used as an intensive or to express surprise
wish·bone \'wish-ˌbōn\ *n* [fr. the superstition that when two persons pull it apart the one getting the longer fragment will have his wish granted] : a furcula in front of the breastbone in a bird consisting chiefly of the two clavicles fused at their median or lower end
wish·ful \'wish-fəl\ *adj* **1 a** : expressive of a wish : HOPEFUL **b** : having a wish : DESIROUS **2** : according with wishes rather than reality — **wish·ful·ly** \-fə-lē\ *adv* — **wish·ful·ness** *n*
wish fulfillment *n* : the gratification of a desire esp. as gained symbolically (as in dreams)
wishful thinking *n* **1** : illusory attribution of actuality to what one wishes to be or become true and discovery of justifications for what one wants to believe through unconscious motivation in order to avoid facing painful or unpleasant facts **2** : AUTISM
wish·ing *adj* **1** *archaic* : WISHFUL **2** : regarded as having the power to grant wishes ⟨~ well⟩
wish–wash \'wish-ˌwȯsh, -ˌwäsh\ *n* [redupl. of 2*wash*] : any weak thin drink
wishy–washy \'wish-ē-ˌwȯsh-ē, -ˌwäsh-\ *adj* [redupl. of *washy*] : WEAK, INSIPID; *also* : morally feeble
1**wisp** \'wisp\ *n* [ME] **1** : a small handful (as of hay or straw) **2 a** : a thin strip or fragment **b** : a thready streak ⟨a ~ of smoke⟩ **c** : something frail, slight, or fleeting ⟨a ~ of a girl⟩ ⟨a ~ of a smile⟩ **3** : WILL-O'-THE-WISP — **wispy** \'wis-pē\ *adj*
2**wisp** *vt* : to roll into a wisp
wisp·ish \'wis-pish\ *adj* : resembling a wisp : INSUBSTANTIAL
wist \'wist\ *vt* [alter. of *wis*] *archaic* : KNOW ⟨it . . . took at last a certain shape I ~ —S.T.Coleridge⟩
wis·tar·ia \wis-'tir-ē-ə *also* -'ter-\ *n* [NL, alter. of *Wisteria*] : WISTERIA
wis·te·ria \-'tir-ē-ə\ *n* [NL, genus name, fr. Caspar *Wistar* †1818 Am. physician] : any of a genus (*Wisteria*) of chiefly Asiatic mostly woody leguminous vines having pinnately-compound leaves and showy blue, white, purple, or rose pealike flowers in long racemes and including several grown as ornamentals
wist·ful \'wist-fəl\ *adj* [blend of *wishful* and obs. E *wistly* (intently)] : full of unfulfilled longing or desire : YEARNING — **wist·ful·ly** \-fə-lē\ *adv* — **wist·ful·ness** *n*
1**wit** \'wit\ *vb* **wist** \'wist\ **wit·ting**; *pres 1st & 3d sing* **wot** \'wät\ [ME *witen* (1st & 3d sing. pres. *wot*, past *wiste*), fr. OE *witan* (1st & 3d sing. pres. *wāt*, past *wisse, wiste*); akin to OHG *wizzan* to know, L *vidēre* to see, Gk *eidenai* to know, *idein* to see] *archaic* : KNOW, LEARN
2**wit** *n* [ME, fr. OE; akin to OHG *wizzi* knowledge, OE *witan* to know] **1 a** : MIND, MEMORY **b** : reasoning power : INTELLIGENCE **2 a** : SENSE 2a — usu. used in pl. **b** (1) : mental soundness : SANITY — usu. used in pl. (2) : RESOURCEFULNESS, INGENUITY **3 a** : ACUMEN, WISDOM **b** : the ability to relate seemingly disparate things so as to illuminate or amuse **c** (1) : a talent for banter or persiflage (2) : a facetious or satirical retort or comment **4 a** : a man of superior intellect : THINKER **b** : an imaginatively perceptive and articulate individual esp. skilled in banter or persiflage
syn HUMOR, IRONY, SARCASM, SATIRE, REPARTEE: WIT suggests the power to evoke laughter by remarks showing verbal felicity or ingenuity and swift perception esp. of the incongruous; HUMOR implies an ability to perceive the ludicrous, the comical, and the absurd in human life and to express these usu. without bitterness; IRONY applies to a manner of expression in which the intended meaning is the opposite of what is seemingly expressed; SARCASM applies to expression frequently in the form of irony that is intended to cut or wound; SATIRE applies to writing that exposes or ridicules conduct, doctrines, or institutions either by direct criticism or more often through irony, parody, or caricature; REPARTEE implies the power of answering quickly, pointedly, wittily, and often humorously
— **at wit's end** : at a loss
wi·tan \'wi-ˌtän\ *n pl* [OE, pl. of *wita* sage, adviser; akin to OHG *wizzo* sage, OE *witan* to know] **1** : members of the king's advisory council in Anglo-Saxon England **2** : WITENAGEMOT
1**witch** \'wich\ *n* [ME *wicche*, fr. OE *wicca*, masc., wizard & *wicce*, fem., witch; akin to MHG *wicken* to bewitch, OE *wigle* divination, OHG *wīh* holy — more at VICTIM] **1 a** *dial Brit* : WIZARD, SORCERER **b** (1) : a woman practicing the black arts : SORCERESS (2) : an ugly old woman : HAG **c** : one supposed to possess supernatural powers esp. by compact with the devil or a familiar **d** *or* **witch·er** \'wich-ər\ : DOWSER **2** : a charming or alluring woman
2**witch** *vb* **1** : BEWITCH **2** : DOWSE
witch·craft \'wich-ˌkraft\ *n* **1 a** : the use of sorcery or magic **b** : intercourse with the devil or with a familiar **2** : an irresistible influence or fascination : ENCHANTMENT
witch doctor *n* : a professional worker of magic in a primitive society resembling a shaman or medicine man
witch·ery \'wich-(ə-)rē\ *n* **1 a** : the practice of witchcraft : SORCERY **b** : an act of witchcraft **2** : an irresistible fascination : CHARM
witch·es'–broom \'wich-əz-ˌbrüm, -ˌbru̇m\ *n* : an abnormal tufted

growth of small branches on a tree or shrub caused esp. by fungi or viruses — called also *hex·en·be·sen* \'hek-sən-,bāz-ᵊn\

witches' Sabbath *n* **:** a midnight assembly of witches, devils, and sorcerers for the celebration of rites and orgies

witch·grass \'wich-,gras\ *n* **1 :** COUCH GRASS **2 :** a No. American grass (*Panicum capillare*) with slender brushy panicles that is often a weed on cultivated land

witch ha·zel \'wich-,hā-zəl\ *n* [*witch* (a tree with pliant branches)] **1 :** any of a genus (*Hamamelis* of the family Hamamelidaceae, the witch-hazel family) of shrubs with slender-petaled yellow flowers borne in late fall or early spring; *esp* **:** one (*H. virginiana*) of eastern No. America that blooms in the fall **2 :** an alcoholic solution of a distillate of the bark of a witch hazel (*H. virginiana*) used as a soothing and mildly astringent lotion

witch–hunt \'wich-,hənt\ *n* **1 :** a searching out and persecution of persons accused of witchcraft **2 :** an investigation of or campaign against dissenters — **witch–hunt·er** *n*

[1]**witch·ing** \'wich-iŋ\ *n* **:** the practice of witchcraft **:** SORCERY

[2]**witching** *adj* **1 :** of, relating to, or suitable for sorcery or supernatural occurrences ⟨the very ~ time of night —Shak.⟩ **2 :** BEWITCHING, FASCINATING

witch moth *n* **:** any of various noctuid moths (as of the genus *Erebus*)

witchy \'wich-ē\ *adj* **1 :** of, relating to, or characteristic of a witch **2 :** produced by or suggestive of witchcraft

[1]**wite** \'wīt\ *n* [ME, fr. OE *wīte* punishment; akin to OHG *wīzi* punishment, OE *witan* to know] *chiefly Scot* **:** BLAME, RESPONSIBILITY

[2]**wite** *vt, chiefly Scot* **:** BLAME, CENSURE

wi·te·na·ge·mot *or* **wi·te·na·ge·mote** \'wit-ᵊn-ə-gə-,mōt\ *n* [OE *witena gemōt*, fr. *witena* (gen. pl. of *wita* sage, adviser) + *gemōt* gemot] **:** an Anglo-Saxon council of perhaps 100 nobles, prelates, and influential officials convened from time to time to advise the king on administrative and judicial matters — called also *witan*

with \(')with, (')with, wəth, wəth\ *prep* [ME, against, from, with, fr. OE; akin to OE *wither* against, OHG *widar* against, back, Skt *vi* apart] **1 a :** in opposition to **:** AGAINST ⟨had a fight ~ his brother⟩ **b :** so as to be separated or detached from ⟨broke ~ his family⟩ **2** — used as a function word to indicate one to whom a usu. reciprocal communication is made ⟨talking ~ a friend⟩ **3 a** — used as a function word to indicate one that shares in an action, transaction, or arrangement ⟨works ~ his father⟩ **b** — used as a function word to indicate the object of attention, behavior, or feeling ⟨get tough ~ him⟩ ⟨angry ~ her⟩ **c :** in respect to **:** so far as concerns ⟨on friendly terms ~ all nations⟩ **d** — used to indicate the object of an adverbial expression of imperative force ⟨off ~ his head⟩ **e :** OVER, ON ⟨no longer has any influence ~ him⟩ **f :** in the performance, operation, or use of ⟨the trouble ~ this machine⟩ **4 a** — used as a function word to indicate the object of a statement of comparison or equality ⟨a dress identical ~ her hostess's⟩ **b** — used as a function word to express agreement or sympathy ⟨must conclude, ~ him, that the painting is a forgery⟩ **c :** on the side of **:** FOR ⟨if he's for lower taxes, I'm ~ him⟩ **d :** as well as ⟨can pitch ~ the best of them⟩ **5 a** — used as a function word to indicate combination, accompaniment, presence, or addition ⟨heat milk ~ honey⟩ ⟨went there ~ her⟩ ⟨his money, ~ his wife's, comes to a million⟩ **b :** inclusive of ⟨costs five dollars ~ the tax⟩ **6 a :** in the judgment or estimation of ⟨stood well ~ his classmates⟩ **b :** in or according to the experience or practice of ⟨~ many of us, our ideas seem to fall by the wayside —W.J.Reilly⟩ **7 a** — used as a function word to indicate the means, cause, or agent ⟨hit him ~ a rock⟩ ⟨pale ~ anger⟩ ⟨threatened ~ tuberculosis⟩ **b** *archaic* **:** by the direct act of **8 a** — used as a function word to indicate manner of action ⟨ran ~ effort⟩ ⟨acknowledge your contribution ~ thanks⟩ **b** — used as a function word to indicate an attendant fact or circumstance ⟨stood there ~ his hat on⟩ **c** — used as a function word to indicate a result attendant on a specified action ⟨got off ~ a light sentence⟩ **9 a** (1) **:** in possession of **:** HAVING ⟨came ~ good news⟩ (2) **:** in the possession or care of ⟨left the money ~ his mother⟩ **b :** characterized or distinguished by ⟨a man ~ a sharp nose⟩ **10 a** — used as a function word to indicate a close association in time ⟨~ the outbreak of war they went home⟩ ⟨mellows ~ time⟩ **b :** in proportion to ⟨the pressure varies ~ the depth⟩ **11 a :** in spite of **:** NOTWITHSTANDING ⟨a really tip-top man, ~ all his wrongheadedness —H.J.Laski⟩ **b :** except for ⟨finds that, ~ one group of omissions and one important addition, they reflect that curriculum —Gilbert Highet⟩ **12 :** in the direction of ⟨~ the wind⟩ ⟨~ the grain⟩

[1]**with·al** \with-'ȯl, with-\ *adv* [ME, fr. *with* + *all, al* all] **1 :** together with this **:** BESIDES **2** *archaic* **:** THEREWITH **3 :** on the other hand **:** NEVERTHELESS

[2]**withal** *prep, archaic* **:** WITH — used postpositively with a relative or interrogative pronoun as object

with·draw \with-'drȯ, with-\ *vb* [ME, fr. *with* from + *drawen* to draw] *vt* **1 a :** to take back or away **b :** to remove from use or cultivation **c :** to turn away (as the eyes) from an object of attention **d :** to draw back or aside **2 a :** to remove from consideration or set outside a group **b** (1) **:** to take back **:** RETRACT (2) **:** to recall or remove (a motion) under parliamentary procedure **~** *vi* **1 a :** to move back or away **:** RETIRE **b :** to draw back from a battlefield **:** RETREAT **2 a :** to remove oneself from participation **b :** to become socially or emotionally detached **3 :** to recall a motion under parliamentary procedure **syn** see GO

with·draw·al \-'drȯ(-ə-)l\ *n* **1 a :** retreat or retirement esp. into a more secluded or less exposed place or position **b :** an operation by which a military force disengages from the enemy **c :** DETACHMENT **2 :** RETRACTION, REVOCATION **3 :** the act of drawing someone or something back from or out of a place or position **4 a :** the act of taking back or away something that has been granted or possessed **b :** removal from a place of deposit or investment **c :** the discontinuance of administration or use of a drug

withdrawing room *n* **:** a room to retire to (as from a dining room); *esp* **:** DRAWING ROOM

with·drawn \-'drȯn\ *adj* **1 :** removed from immediate contact or easy approach **:** ISOLATED **2 :** socially detached and unresponsive **:** INTROVERTED — **with·drawn·ness** \-'drȯn-nəs\ *n*

withe \'with, 'with, 'wīth\ *n* [ME, fr. OE *withthe;* akin to OE *wīthig* withy] **:** a slender flexible branch or twig; *esp* **:** one used as a band or rope

with·er \'with-ər\ *vb* **with·er·ing** \-(ə-)riŋ\ [ME *widren;* prob. akin to ME *weder* weather] *vi* **1 :** to become dry and sapless; *esp* **:** to shrivel from or as if from loss of bodily moisture **2 :** to lose vitality, force, or freshness **~** *vt* **1 :** to cause to wither **2 :** to make speechless or incapable of action **:** STUN ⟨a ~*ing* glance⟩

with·ered *adj* **:** shriveled and shrunken from drying **:** WIZENED

with·er·ing *adj* **:** acting or serving to cut down or destroy **:** DEVASTATING ⟨a ~ fire from the enemy⟩

with·er·ite \'with-ə-,rīt\ *n* [G *witherit*, irreg. fr. William *Withering* †1799 E physician] **:** a mineral $BaCO_3$ consisting of barium carbonate occurring as white or gray twin crystals and in columnar or granular masses

withe rod *n* **:** either of two No. American viburnums (*Viburnum cassinoides* and *V. nudum*) with tough slender shoots

with·ers \'with-ərz\ *n pl* [prob. fr. obs. E *wither-* (against), fr. ME, fr. OE, fr. *wither* against; fr. the withers being the parts which resist the pull in drawing a load — more at WITH] **:** the ridge between the shoulder bones of a horse or the corresponding part in other quadrupeds

with·er·shins *var of* WIDDERSHINS

with·hold \with-'hōld, with-\ *vb* **with·held** \-'held\ **with·hold·ing** [ME *withholden*, fr. *with* from + *holden* to hold — more at WITH] *vt* **1 :** to hold back **:** RESTRAIN; *also* **:** RETAIN **2 :** to refrain from granting, giving, or allowing ⟨~ permission⟩ **~** *vi* **:** FORBEAR, REFRAIN **syn** see KEEP — **with·hold·er** *n*

withholding tax *n* **:** a deduction levied as a tax upon income (as salaries, wages, fees, or dividends) at the source

[1]**with·in** \with-'in, with-\ *adv* [ME *withinne*, fr. OE *withinnan*, fr. *with* + *innan* inwardly, within, fr. *in*] **1 :** in or into the interior **:** INSIDE **2 :** in one's inner thought, disposition, or character **:** INWARDLY

[2]**within** *prep* **1 :** in the inner part of **2 :** in or into the limits or compass of: as **a :** before the end of ⟨gone ~ a week⟩ **b** (1) **:** not beyond the quantity, degree, or limitations of ⟨lives ~ his income⟩ (2) **:** in or into the scope or sphere of ⟨~ the jurisdiction of the state⟩ (3) **:** in or into the range of ⟨~ reach⟩ ⟨~ sight⟩ (4) — used as a function word to indicate a specified difference or margin of error ⟨came ~ two points of a perfect mark⟩ **c :** not farther than **:** nearer than ⟨~ a mile of the town⟩ **3 :** to the inside of **:** INTO

[3]**within** *n* **:** an inner place or area ⟨revolt from ~⟩

[4]**within** *adj* **:** being inside **:** ENCLOSED

with·in·doors \with-,in-'dō(ə)rz, with-, -'dȯ(ə)rz\ *adv* **:** INDOORS

[1]**with·out** \with-'au̇t, with-\ *prep* [ME *withoute*, fr. OE *withūtan*, fr. *with* + *ūtan* outside, fr. *ūt* out] **1 :** OUTSIDE 1, 2, 3 **2** — used as a function word to indicate something or someone that is absent or lacking ⟨fight ~ fear⟩ ⟨left ~ him⟩ ⟨looks ~ seeing⟩

[2]**without** *adv* **1 :** on the outside **:** EXTERNALLY **2 :** with something lacking or absent ⟨has learned to do ~⟩

[3]**without** *conj, chiefly dial* **:** UNLESS

[4]**without** *n* **:** an outer place or area ⟨came from ~⟩

with·out·doors \with-,au̇t-'dō(ə)rz, with-\ *adv* **:** OUTDOORS

with·stand \with-'stand, with-\ *vt* [ME *withstanden*, fr. OE *withstandan*, fr. *with* against + *standan* to stand — more at WITH] **1 a :** to stand up against **:** oppose; *esp* **:** to resist successfully **b :** to be proof against **c :** to resist the attraction or influence of **:** FORBEAR ⟨~ temptation⟩ **2** *archaic* **:** to stop or obstruct the course of **syn** see OPPOSE

[1]**withy** \'with-ē\ *n* [ME, fr. OE *wīthig;* akin to OHG *wīda* willow, L *vitis* vine, *viēre* to plait — more at WIRE] **1 :** WILLOW; *esp* **:** OSIER 1 **2 :** a flexible slender twig or branch (as of osier) **:** WITHE

[2]**withy** \'with-ē, 'with-ē, 'wī-thē\ *adj* [*withe*] **:** flexible and tough like a withy; *specif* **:** AGILE, WIRY

wit·less \'wit-ləs\ *adj* **:** destitute of wit or understanding **:** FOOLISH, MAD — **wit·less·ly** *adv* — **wit·less·ness** *n*

wit·ling \'wit-liŋ\ *n* **:** a pretender to wit

wit·loof \'wit-,lōf\ *n* [D dial. *witloof* chicory, fr. D *wit* white + *loof* foliage] **:** CHICORY 1; *also* **:** its crown of foliage as a salad green **:** ENDIVE 2

[1]**wit·ness** \'wit-nəs\ *n* [ME *witnesse*, fr. OE *witnes* knowledge, testimony, witness, fr. [2]*wit*] **1 :** attestation of a fact or event **:** TESTIMONY **2 :** one that gives evidence; *specif* **:** one who testifies in a cause or before a judicial tribunal **3 :** one asked to be present at a transaction so as to be able to testify to its having taken place **4 :** one who has personal knowledge of something **5 :** something serving as evidence or proof **:** SIGN

[2]**witness** *vt* **1 :** to testify to **:** ATTEST **2 :** to act as legal witness of **3 :** to furnish proof of **:** BETOKEN **4 :** to see or know by personal presence or direct cognizance **5 :** to constitute the scene of **~** *vi* **1 :** to bear witness **:** TESTIFY **2 :** to bear witness to one's religious convictions

wit·ness–box \-,bäks\ *n, chiefly Brit* **:** an enclosure in which a witness sits or stands while testifying in court

witness stand *n* **:** a stand or an enclosure from which a witness gives evidence in a court

wit·ted \'wit-əd\ *adj* **:** having wit or understanding — usu. used in combination ⟨dull-*witted*⟩

wit·ti·cism \'wit-ə-,siz-əm\ *n* [*witty* + *-cism* (as in *criticism*)] **:** a witty saying **syn** see JEST

wit·ti·ly \'wit-ᵊl-ē\ *adv* **:** in a witty manner

wit·ti·ness \'wit-ē-nəs\ *n* **:** the quality or state of being witty

[1]**wit·ting** \'wit-ᵊn, -iŋ\ *n* **1** *chiefly dial* **:** knowledge or awareness of something **:** COGNIZANCE **2** *chiefly dial* **:** information obtained or communicated **:** NEWS

[2]**wit·ting** \-iŋ\ *adj* **1 :** cognizant or aware of something **:** CONSCIOUS **2 :** done deliberately **:** INTENTIONAL — **wit·ting·ly** \-iŋ-lē\ *adv*

wit·tol \'wit-ᵊl\ *n* [ME *wetewold*, fr. *weten, witen* to know + *-wold* (as in *cokewold* cuckold) — more at WIT] *archaic* **:** a man who knows of his wife's infidelity and submits to it

wit·ty \'wit-ē\ *adj* **1** *chiefly dial* **:** CLEVER, INTELLIGENT **2 :** marked by or full of wit **:** AMUSING **3 :** quick or ready to see or express illuminating or amusing relationships or insights

syn WITTY, HUMOROUS, FACETIOUS, JOCULAR, JOCOSE mean provoking or intended to provoke laughter. WITTY suggests cleverness and quickness of mind and often a caustic tongue; HUMOROUS applies broadly to anything that evokes usu. genial laughter and may contrast with WITTY in suggesting whimsicality or eccentricity; FACETIOUS stresses a desire to produce laughter and may be derogatory in implying dubious or ill-timed attempts at wit or humor; JOCULAR may suggest a studied avoidance of seriousness in speech or manner; JOCOSE is somewhat less derogatory than FACETIOUS in suggesting habitual waggishness or playfulness

wive \'wīv\ *vb* [ME *wiven*, fr. OE *wīfian*, fr. *wīf* woman, wife]

vi : to marry a woman ~ *vt* **1** : to marry to a wife **2** : to take for a wife

wi·vern *var of* WYVERN

wives *pl of* WIFE

wiz \'wiz\ *n* : WIZARD 3

1wiz·ard \'wiz-ərd\ *n* [ME *wysard,* fr. *wis, wys* wise] **1** *archaic* : a wise man : SAGE **2** : one skilled in magic : SORCERER **3** : a very clever or skillful person

2wizard *adj* **1** : having magical influence or power **2** : of or relating to wizardry : ENCHANTED **3** *chiefly Brit* : worthy of the highest praise : EXCELLENT — **wiz·ard·ly** \-lē\ *adj*

wiz·ard·ry \'wiz-ə(r)-drē\ *n* **1** : the art or practices of a wizard : SORCERY **2** : a seemingly magical transforming power or influence

wiz·en \'wiz-ᵊn\ *vb* [ME *wisenen,* fr. OE *wisnian;* akin to OHG *wesanēn* to wither, L *viēre* to twist together, plait — more at WIRE] : WITHER, SHRIVEL

wiz·ened \-ᵊnd\ *or* **wizen** *adj* : dried up : SHRIVELED

woad \'wōd\ *n* [ME *wod,* fr. OE *wād;* akin to OHG *weit* woad, L *vitrum* woad, glass] : a European herb (*Isatis tinctoria*) of the mustard family formerly grown for the blue dyestuff yielded by its leaves; *also* : this dyestuff

1wob·ble \'wäb-əl\ *vb* **wob·bling** \-(ə-)liŋ\ [prob. fr. LG *wabbeln;* akin to OE *wǣfre* restless — more at WAVER] *vi* **1 a** : to move or proceed with an irregular rocking or staggering motion or unsteadily and clumsily from side to side **b** : TREMBLE, QUAVER **2** : WAVER, VACILLATE ~ *vt* : to cause to wobble — **wob·bler** \-(ə-)lər\ *n* — **wob·bly** \-(ə-)lē\ *adj*

2wobble *n* **1 a** : a hobbling or rocking unequal motion (as of a wheel unevenly hung) **b** : an uncertainly directed movement : FLUCTUATION **2** : an intermittent variation (as in volume of sound) ⟨a vocal ~⟩

wobble pump *n* : an auxiliary hand pump used to supply fuel to the carburetor of an airplane engine when the power-driven pump fails or for forcing fuel from an extra tank

Wo·den \'wōd-ᵊn\ *n* [OE *Wōden*] : ODIN

1woe \'wō\ *interj* [ME *wa, wo,* fr. OE *wā;* akin to ON *vei,* interj., woe, L *vae*] — used to express grief, regret, or distress

2woe *n* [ME *wo,* fr. *wo,* interj.] **1** : a condition of deep suffering from misfortune, affliction, or grief **2** : CALAMITY, MISFORTUNE **syn** see SORROW

woe·be·gone \'wō-bi-,gȯn *also* -,gän\ *adj* [ME *wo begon,* fr. *wo,* n. + *begon,* pp. of *begon* to go about, beset, fr. OE *begān,* fr. *be-* + *gān* to go — more at GO] **1** *archaic* : overwhelmed with woe : WOEFUL **2 a** : exhibiting great woe, sorrow, or misery **b** : DISMAL, DESOLATE

woe·be·gone·ness \-,gȯn-nəs *also* -,gän-\ *n* : the quality or state of being woebegone

woe·ful *also* **wo·ful** \'wō-fəl\ *adj* **1** : full of woe : AFFLICTED **2** : involving, bringing, or relating to woe **3** : PALTRY, DEPLORABLE — **woe·ful·ly** \-f(ə-)lē\ *adv* — **woe·ful·ness** \-fəl-nəs\ *n*

woke *past of* WAKE

woken *past part of* WAKE

1wold \'wōld\ *n* [ME *wald, wold,* fr. OE *weald, wald* forest; akin to OHG *wald* forest] **1** : an upland plain : a region without woods **2** : an open hilly or rolling region

2wold *var of* WELD

1wolf \'wu̇lf\ *n, pl* **wolves** \'wu̇lvz\ *often attrib* [ME, fr. OE *wulf;* akin to OHG *wolf,* L *lupus,* Gk *lykos*] **1** *pl also* **wolf a** : any of various large mammals (genus *Canis* and esp. *C. lupus*) that resemble the related dogs, are crafty, rapacious, and very destructive to game, sheep, and cattle, and will sometimes attack man esp. in a pack — compare COYOTE, JACKAL **b** : the fur of a wolf **2 a** (1) : a fierce, rapacious, or destructive person (2) : a crafty person (3) : a man forward, direct, and zealous in amatory attentions to women **b** (1) : a corrupting or destructive agency (2) : dire poverty : STARVATION **c** (1) : a beetle grub or moth grub that infests granaries (2) : the maggot of a warble fly **3** [G; fr. the howling sound] **a** (1) : dissonance in some chords on organs, pianos, or other instruments with fixed tones tuned by unequal temperament (2) : an instance of such dissonance **b** : a harshness due to faulty vibration in various tones in a bowed instrument — **wolf·like** \'wu̇l-,flīk\ *adj* — **wolf in sheep's clothing** : one who cloaks a hostile intention with a friendly manner

2wolf *vt* : to eat greedily : DEVOUR

wolf·ber·ry \'wu̇lf-,ber-ē\ *n* : a white-berried western American shrub (*Symphoricarpos occidentalis*) of the honeysuckle family

wolf dog *n* **1** : any of various large dogs formerly kept for hunting wolves **2** : the offspring of a wolf and a domestic dog **3** : a dog felt to resemble a wolf

wolff·ian \'wu̇l-fē-ən, 'vȯl-\ *adj, often cap* : discovered or first described by Kaspar Friedrich Wolff

wolffian body *n, often cap W* : MESONEPHROS

wolf·fish \'wu̇lf-,fish\ *n* : any of several large marine blennies notable for their strong teeth and ferocity

wolf·hound \'wu̇lf-,hau̇nd\ *n* : any of several large dogs used in hunting large animals (as wolves)

wolf·ish \'wu̇l-fish\ *adj* : **1** : of or relating to wolves ⟨~ lore⟩ **2** : resembling a wolf; *esp* : FEROCIOUS — **wolf·ish·ly** *adv* — **wolf·ish·ness** *n*

wolf·ling \'wu̇l-fliŋ\ *n* : a young or little wolf

wolf pack *n* : a group of submarines that make a coordinated attack on shipping; *also* : a group of two or more fighter planes making a coordinated attack

wol·fram \'wu̇l-frəm\ *n* [G] **1** : TUNGSTEN — see ELEMENT table **2** : WOLFRAMITE

wol·fram·ic \wu̇l-'fram-ik\ *adj* : TUNGSTIC

wol·fram·ite \'wu̇l-frə-,mīt\ *n* [G *wolframit,* fr. *wolfram*] : a mineral $(Fe,Mn)WO_4$ that consists of an iron manganese tungstate of a usu. brownish or grayish black color and slightly metallic luster, occurs in monoclinic crystals and in granular or columnar masses, and is used as a source of tungsten

wolfs·bane \'wu̇lfs-,bān\ *n* : ACONITUM 1; *esp* : a highly variable yellow-flowered Eurasian herb (*Aconitum lycoctonum*)

wolf spider *n* : any of various active wandering ground spiders (family Lycosidae)

wol·las·ton·ite \'wu̇l-ə-stə-,nīt\ *n* [William H. *Wollaston* †1828 E chemist] : a triclinic mineral $CaSiO_3$ of a white to gray, red, yellow, or brown color consisting of a native calcium silicate occurring usu. in cleavable masses

wol·ver·ine \,wu̇l-və-'rēn\ *n, pl* **wolverines** [prob. irreg. fr. *wolv-* (as in *wolves*)] **1** *pl also* **wolverine a** : a northern No. American carnivorous mammal (*Gulo luscus*) that resembles and is often held conspecific with the glutton of Europe and is noted for its thievishness, strength, and cunning — called also *carcajou* **b** : the fur of the wolverine **2** *cap* : a native or resident of Michigan — used as a nickname

1wom·an \'wu̇m-ən\ *n, pl* **wom·en** \'wim-ən\ [ME, fr. OE *wīfman,* fr. *wīf* woman, wife + *man* human being, man] **1** : an adult female person **2** : WOMANKIND **3** : distinctively feminine nature : WOMANLINESS **4** : a female servant or personal attendant **5** : MISTRESS **syn** see FEMALE

2woman *adj* **1** : of, belonging to, or characteristic of a woman : WOMANLY **2** : FEMALE ⟨~ doctor⟩

wom·an·hood \'wu̇m-ən-,hu̇d\ *n* **1 a** : the state of being a woman **b** : the distinguishing character or qualities of a woman or of womankind **2** : WOMEN, WOMANKIND

wom·an·ish \'wu̇m-ə-nish\ *adj* **1** *archaic* : of or belonging to women ⟨~ work⟩ **2** : characteristic of a woman **3** : unsuitable to a man or to a strong character of either sex : EFFEMINATE ⟨~ fears⟩ **syn** see FEMININE — **wom·an·ish·ly** *adv* — **wom·an·ish·ness** *n*

wom·an·ize \-ə-,nīz\ *vt* : to make effeminate ~ *vi* : to pursue or associate illicitly with women

wom·an·iz·er \-,nī-zər\ *n* : a man who pursues or associates illicitly with women

wom·an·kind \'wu̇m-ən-,kīnd\ *n sing but sing or pl in constr* : the females of the human race : WOMEN

wom·an·like \-,līk\ *adj* : resembling or characteristic of a woman : WOMANLY **syn** see FEMININE

wom·an·li·ness \-lē-nəs\ *n* : the quality of being womanly

wom·an·ly \-lē\ *adj* : marked by qualities characteristic of a woman **syn** see FEMININE — **womanly** *adv*

woman's rights *n pl* **1** : legal, political, and social rights for women equal to those of men **2** : FEMINISM 2

woman suffrage *n* : possession and exercise of suffrage by women

womb \'wüm\ *n* [ME *wamb, womb,* fr. OE; akin to OHG *wamba* belly] **1** : UTERUS **2 a** : a cavity or space that resembles a womb in containing and enveloping **b** : a place where something is generated — **wombed** \'wümd\ *adj*

wom·bat \'wäm-,bat\ *n* [native name in New So. Wales] : any of several stocky Australian marsupials (family Vombatidae) resembling small bears

wom·en·folk \'wim-ən-,fōk\ *or* **wom·en·folks** \-,fōks\ *n pl* : WOMEN

womp \'wämp, 'wȯmp\ *n* [imit. of the sound of a small explosion] : an abrupt increase in the illumination of a television screen resulting from an abrupt increase in signal strength

1won \'wən, 'wōn\ *vi* **wonned; won·ning** [ME *wonen,* fr. OE *wunian*] *archaic* : DWELL, ABIDE

2won \'wən\ *past of* WIN

3won \'wȯn\ *n* [Korean *wŏn*] — see MONEY table

1won·der \'wən-dər\ *n* [ME, fr. OE *wundor;* akin to OHG *wuntar* wonder] **1 a** : a cause of astonishment or surprise : MARVEL **b** : MIRACLE **2** : the quality, sense, or a state of exciting amazed admiration **3** : a feeling of doubt or uncertainty

2wonder *adj* : WONDROUS, WONDERFUL: as **a** *archaic* : MAGICAL, MIRACULOUS **b** : effective or efficient far beyond anything previously known or anticipated ⟨~ drugs⟩

3wonder *vb* **won·der·ing** \-d(ə-)riŋ\ *vi* **1 a** : to be in a state of wonder : MARVEL **b** : to feel surprise **2** : to feel curiosity or doubt ~ *vt* : to be curious or in doubt about — **won·der·er** \-dər-ər\ *n*

won·der·ful \'wən-dər-fəl\ *adj* **1** : exciting wonder : MARVELOUS, ASTONISHING **2** : unusually good : ADMIRABLE — **won·der·ful·ly** \-f(ə-)lē\ *adv* — **won·der·ful·ness** \-fəl-nəs\ *n*

won·der·land \'wən-dər-,land, -lənd\ *n* **1** : a fairylike imaginary realm **2** : a place that excites admiration or wonder

won·der·ment \-mənt\ *n* **1** : ASTONISHMENT, SURPRISE **2** : a cause of or occasion for wonder **3** : curiosity about something

won·der·work \-,wərk\ *n* **1** : WONDER 1b **2** : something that arouses wonder

won·der–work·er \-,wər-kər\ *n* : one that performs wonders

won·drous \'wən-drəs\ *adj* [alter. of ME *wonders,* fr. gen. of *1wonder*] : WONDERFUL, MARVELOUS — **wondrous** *adv, archaic* — **won·drous·ly** *adv* — **won·drous·ness** *n*

won·ky \'wäŋ-kē\ *adj* [alter. of E dial. *wankle,* fr. ME *wankel,* fr. OE *wancol*] **1** *Brit* : UNSTEADY, SHAKY **2** *Brit* : AWRY, WRONG

1wont \'wȯnt, 'wōnt, 'wənt\ *adj* [ME *woned, wont,* fr. pp. of *wonen* to dwell, be used to, fr. OE *wunian;* akin to OHG *wonēn* to dwell, be used to, L *venus* love, charm — more at WIN] **1** : ACCUSTOMED, USED ⟨as he is ~ to do⟩ **2** : INCLINED, APT ⟨revealing as letters are ~ to be⟩

2wont *n* : CUSTOM, USAGE **syn** see HABIT

3wont *vb* **wont;** **wont** *or* **wont·ed; wont·ing** *vt* : ACCUSTOM, HABITUATE ~ *vi* : to have the habit of doing something

won't \(')wōnt, ,wənt, 'wənt\ : will not

wont·ed \'wȯnt-əd, 'wōnt-, 'wənt-\ *adj* : ACCUSTOMED, CUSTOMARY **syn** see USUAL — **wont·ed·ly** *adv* — **wont·ed·ness** *n*

woo \'wü\ *vb* [ME *wowen,* fr. OE *wōgian*] *vt* **1** : to sue for the affection of and usu. marriage with : COURT **2** : to solicit or entreat esp. with importunity **3** : to seek to gain or bring about ~ *vi* : to court a woman

1wood \'wüd, 'wōd, 'wu̇d\ *adj* [ME, fr. OE *wōd* insane; akin to OHG *wuot* madness — more at VATIC] *archaic* : MAD, VIOLENT

2wood \'wu̇d\ *n* [ME *wode,* fr. OE *widu, wudu;* akin to OHG *witu* wood, OIr *fid* tree] **1 a** : a dense growth of trees usu. greater in extent than a grove and smaller than a forest — often used in pl. but sing. or pl. in constr. **b** : WOODLAND **2 a** : the hard fibrous substance basically xylem that makes up the greater part of the stems and branches of trees or shrubs beneath the bark and is found to a limited extent in herbaceous plants **b** : this material suitable or prepared for some use (as burning); *esp* : TIMBER, LUMBER **3** : something made of wood; *esp* : a golf club having a wooden head — **out of the woods** : escaped from peril or difficulty

³**wood** \'wu̇d\ *adj* **1 :** WOODEN **2 :** suitable for cutting or working with wood **3** *or* **woods** \'wu̇dz\ **:** living or growing in woods
⁴**wood** \'wu̇d\ *vt* **1 :** to supply or load with wood esp. for fuel **2 :** to cover with a growth of trees or plant with trees ~ *vi* **:** to gather or take on wood
wood alcohol *n* **:** METHANOL
wood anemone *n* **:** any of several anemones (esp. *Anemone quinquefolia* of the U.S. and *A. memorosa* of Europe)
wood betony *n* **1 :** a common betony (*Stachys betonica*) **2 :** a lousewort (*Pedicularis canadensis*) of eastern No. America with pinnately parted leaves and red or yellowish flowers in bracted spikes
wood·bin \'wu̇d-,bin\ *n* **:** a bin for holding firewood
wood·bine \'wu̇d-,bīn\ *n* [ME *wodebinde*, fr. OE *wudubinde*, fr. *wudu* wood + *bindan* to tie, bind; fr. its winding around trees] **1 :** any of several honeysuckles; *esp* **:** a European twining shrub (*Lonicera periclymenum*) **2 :** VIRGINIA CREEPER
wood block *n* **:** WOODCUT
wood–block \,wu̇d-,bläk\ *adj* **:** made of, done with, or printed from wood blocks ⟨~ print⟩
wood–bor·ing \-,bōr-iŋ, -,bȯr-\ *adj* **:** excavating galleries in wood in feeding or in constructing a nest — used chiefly of an insect
wood–carv·er \-,kär-vər\ *n* **:** a person whose occupation is wood carving
wood carving *n* **:** the art of fashioning or ornamenting objects of wood by cutting with a sharp implement held in the hand; *also* **:** an object of wood so fashioned or ornamented
wood·chat \'wu̇d-,chat\ *n* **1 :** any of several Asiatic thrushes (genus *Erithacus*) having brightly colored males **2 :** a European shrike (*Lanius senator*)
wood·chop·per \-,chäp-ər\ *n* **:** one engaged esp. in chopping down trees
wood·chuck \-,chək\ *n* [by folk etymology fr. Ojibwa *otchig* fisher, marten, or Cree *otcheck*] **:** a grizzled thickset marmot (*Marmota monax*) of the northeastern U.S. and Canada; *also* **:** any of several marmots of mountainous western No. America
wood coal *n* **1 :** CHARCOAL **2 :** LIGNITE
wood·cock \'wu̇d-,käk\ *n, pl* **woodcocks 1** *or pl* **woodcock :** a widespread Old World limicoline bird (*Scolopax rusticola*); *also* **:** a smaller related American bird (*Philohela minor*) prized as a game bird **2** *archaic* **:** SIMPLETON
wood·craft \-,kraft\ *n* **1 :** skill and practice in anything relating to the woods and esp. in maintaining oneself and making one's way in the woods or in hunting or trapping **2 :** skill in shaping or constructing articles from wood
wood·cut \-,kət\ *n* **1 :** a letterpress printing surface consisting of a wooden block with a usu. pictorial design cut with the grain **2 :** a print from a woodcut
wood·cut·ter \-,kət-ər\ *n* **:** a person who cuts wood
wood·cut·ting \-,kət-iŋ\ *n* **1 :** WOODCUT **2 :** the action or occupation of cutting wood or timber
wood·ed \'wu̇d-əd\ *adj* **:** covered with growing trees
wood·en \'wu̇d-ᵊn\ *adj* **1 :** made or consisting of wood **2 a :** lacking resilience **:** STIFF **b :** AWKWARD, CLUMSY — **wood·en·ly** *adv* — **wood·en·ness** \-ᵊn-(n)əs\ *n*
wood engraver *n* **:** an engraver on wood; *esp* **:** one that makes wood engravings
wood engraving *n* **1 a :** the art or process of cutting a design upon wood for use as a letterpress printing surface **b :** a wooden letterpress printing surface bearing a usu. pictorial design produced by wood engraving **2 :** a design printed from a wood engraving
wood·en·head \'wu̇d-ᵊn-,hed\ *n* **:** BLOCKHEAD — **wood·en–head·ed** \,wu̇d-ᵊn-'hed-əd\ *adj*
wooden Indian *n* **:** a standing wooden image of an American Indian brave used esp. formerly for advertising before a cigar store
wood·en·ware \'wu̇d-ᵊn-,wa(ə)r, -,we(ə)r\ *n* **:** articles made of wood for domestic use
wood hyacinth *n* **:** a European squill (*Scilla nonscripta*) having scapose racemes of drooping bell-shaped flowers — called also *harebell*
wood ibis *n* **:** a large wading bird (*Mycteria americana* of the family Ciconiidae) that frequents wooded swamps of So. and Central America and the southern U.S.
wood·i·ness \'wu̇d-ē-nəs\ *n* **:** the quality or state of being woody
¹**wood·land** \'wu̇d-lənd, -,land\ *n* **:** land covered with woody vegetation **:** TIMBERLAND, FOREST — **wood·land·er** \-ər\ *n*
²**woodland** *adj* **1 :** of, relating to, or being woodland **2 :** growing or living in woodland
wood·lot \'wu̇d-,lät\ *n* **:** a restricted area devoted to the growing of forest trees
wood louse *n* **1 :** a terrestrial isopod crustacean (suborder Oniscoidea) with a flattened elliptical body often capable of being rolled into a ball **2 :** any of several small wingless insects (order Corrodentia) that live under bark, in the crevices of walls, and among old books and papers
wood·man \'wu̇d-mən\ *n* **:** WOODSMAN
wood·note \-,nōt\ *n* **:** a sound or call (as of a bird) natural in a wood
wood nymph *n* **1 :** a nymph living in woods — called also *dryad* **2 a :** any of several showy moths (genus *Euthisanotia*) with bright-colored larvae that feed on leaves **b :** SATYR 3
wood·peck·er \'wu̇d-,pek-ər\ *n* **:** any of numerous birds (family Picidae) with zygodactyl feet, stiff spiny tail feathers used in climbing or resting on tree trunks, a usu. extensile tongue, a very hard bill used to drill the bark or wood of trees for insect food or to excavate nesting cavities, and generally showy parti-colored plumage
wood·pile \-,pīl\ *n* **:** a pile of wood (as firewood)
wood·print \-,print\ *n* **:** WOODCUT
wood pulp *n* **:** pulp from wood used in making cellulose derivatives (as paper or rayon)
wood pussy *n* **:** SKUNK
wood rat *n* **:** any of numerous native voles (family Cricetidae and esp. genus *Neotoma*) of the southern U.S. and western No. America with soft fur light gray to ocherous above and white below, well-furred tails, and large ears
wood ray *n* **:** XYLEM RAY
wood·ruff \'wu̇d-(,)rəf\ *n* [ME *woderove*, fr. OE *wudurofe*, fr. *wudu* wood + *-rofe* (perh. akin to OHG *rāba* turnip) — more at RAPE] **:** any of a genus (*Asperula*) of herbs of the madder family; *esp* **:** a small European sweet-scented herb (*A. odorata*) used in perfumery and for flavoring wine
wood·shed \'wu̇d-,shed\ *n* **:** a shed for storing wood and esp. firewood
woods·man \'wu̇dz-mən\ *n* **:** one who frequents or works in the woods; *esp* **:** one skilled in woodcraft
wood sorrel *n* **1 :** any of a genus (*Oxalis* of the family Oxalidaceae, the wood-sorrel family) of herbs with acid sap, compound leaves, and regular flowers; *esp* **:** a stemless herb (*O. montana*) with trifoliolate leaves sometimes held to be the original shamrock **2 :** SHEEP SORREL
wood spirit *n* **:** METHANOL
wood sugar *n* **1 :** xylose from plant sources **2 :** a mixture of pentose and hexose sugars obtained by hydrolysis of pentosans and cellulose of wood
woodsy \'wu̇d-zē\ *adj* **:** relating to or characteristic or suggestive of woods
wood tar *n* **:** tar obtained by the destructive distillation of wood either as a deposit from pyroligneous acid or as a residue from the distillation of the acid or of wood turpentine
wood·turn·er \'wu̇d-,tər-nər\ *n* **:** one whose occupation is wood turning
wood turning *n* **:** the art or process of fashioning wooden pieces or blocks into various forms and shapes by means of a lathe
wood·wax·en \'wu̇d-,wak-sən\ *n* [ME *wodewexen*, alter. of OE *wuduweaxe*, fr. *wudu* wood + *-weaxe* (prob. fr. *weaxan* to grow) — more at WAX] **:** a low bushy yellow-flowered Eurasian leguminous shrub (*Genista tinctoria*) grown for ornament or formerly as the source of a yellow dye
wood·wind \'wu̇d-,wind\ *n* **1 :** one of a group of wind instruments comprised of flutes, clarinets, oboes, bassoons, and sometimes saxophones **2 :** the woodwind section of a band or orchestra — **woodwind** *adj*
wood·work \-,wərk\ *n* **:** work made of wood; *esp* **:** interior fittings (as moldings or stairways) of wood
wood·work·er \-,wər-kər\ *n* **:** one that works on wood
wood·work·ing \-,wər-kiŋ\ *n* **:** the act, process, or occupation of working with wood — **woodworking** *adj*
wood·worm \-,wərm\ *n* **:** a larva that bores in wood
woody \'wu̇d-ē\ *adj* **1 :** abounding or overgrown with woods **2 :** of or containing wood or wood fibers **:** LIGNEOUS **3 :** characteristic of or resembling wood ⟨a ~ taste⟩
wood·yard \'wu̇d-,yärd\ *n* **:** a yard for storing or sawing wood
woo·er \'wü-ər\ *n* **:** one that woos
¹**woof** \'wu̇f, 'wüf\ *n* [alter. of ME *oof*, fr. OE *ōwef*, fr. *ō-* (fr. *on*) + *wefan* to weave — more at WEAVE] **1 a :** a filling thread or yarn in weaving **b :** woven fabric; *also* **:** the texture of such a fabric **2 :** a basic or essential element or material
²**woof** \'wu̇f\ *n* [imit.] **1 :** a low gruff sound typically produced by a dog **2 :** a low note emitted by sound reproducing equipment
woof·er \'wu̇f-ər\ *n* **:** a loudspeaker usu. larger than a tweeter, responsive only to the lower acoustic frequencies, and used for reproducing sounds of low pitch
wool \'wu̇l\ *n, often attrib* [ME *wolle*, fr. OE *wull;* akin to OHG *wolla* wool, L *vellus* fleece, *lana* wool, *lanugo* down] **1 :** the soft wavy or curly hypertrophied undercoat of various hairy mammals and esp. the sheep made up of fibers of keratin molecules within a matrix and covered with minute scales **2 :** a product of wool; *esp* **:** a woven fabric or garment of such fabric **3 a :** a dense felted pubescence esp. on a plant **:** TOMENTUM **b :** a filamentous mass — usu. used in combination; compare MINERAL WOOL, STEEL WOOL **c :** short thick often crisp curly hair on a human head **4 :** something that conceals the truth or impedes understanding — **wooled** \'wu̇ld\ *adj*
wool clip *n* **:** the annual crop of wool
¹**wool·en** *or* **wool·len** \'wu̇l-ən\ *adj* **1 :** made of wool — compare WORSTED **2 :** of or relating to the manufacture or sale of woolen products
²**woolen** *or* **woollen** *n* **1 :** a fabric made of wool **2 :** garments of woolen fabric — usu. used in pl.
wool·er \'wu̇l-ər\ *n* **:** an animal (as an Angora rabbit) bred or kept for its wool
wool fat *n* **:** wool grease esp. after refining **:** LANOLIN
wool·fell \'wu̇l-,fel\ *n, Brit* **:** WOOLSKIN
wool–gath·er \'wu̇l-,gath-ər, -,geth-\ *vi* **:** to indulge in woolgathering — **wool·gath·er·er** \-ər-ər\ *n*
wool·gath·er·ing \-,gath-(ə-)riŋ, -,geth-\ *n* **:** the act of indulging in vagrant fancies
wool grease *n* **:** a fatty slightly sticky wax coating the surface of the fibers of sheep's wool — called also *wool fat;* compare LANOLIN
wool·li·ness \'wu̇l-ē-nəs\ *n* **:** the quality or state of being woolly
¹**wool·ly** *also* **wooly** \'wu̇l-ē\ *adj* **1 a :** of, relating to, or bearing wool **b :** resembling wool **2 :** CONFUSED, BLURRY **3 :** marked by a lack of order or restraint; *esp* **:** having the rough virility of the West in frontier times
²**wool·ly** *also* **wool·ie** *or* **wooly** \'wu̇l-ē\ *n* **1 :** a garment made from wool; *esp* **:** underclothing of knitted wool — usu. used in pl. **2** *West & Austral* **:** SHEEP
woolly aphid *n* **:** a plant louse (genus *Eriosoma*) covered with a dense coat of white filaments
woolly bear *n* **:** any of various rather large very hairy caterpillars; *esp* **:** one that is the larva of a moth (family Arctiidae)
wool·ly–head·ed \,wu̇l-ē-'hed-əd\ *adj* **1 :** having hair resembling wool **2 :** marked by vague or confused perception or thinking
wool·pack \'wu̇l-,pak\ *n* **1 a :** a wrapper of strong fabric into which fleeces are packed for shipment **b :** the complete package of wool and wrapper **2 :** a rounded cumulus cloud springing from a horizontal base
wool·sack \-,sak\ *n* **1 :** a sack for wool **2 :** the official seat of the Lord Chancellor or of one of the judges of the High Court of Justice in the House of Lords
wool·shed \-,shed\ *n* **:** a building or range of buildings (as on an Australian sheep station) in which sheep are sheared and wool is prepared for market
wool·skin \-,skin\ *n* **:** a sheepskin having the wool still on it
wool·sort·er's disease \'wu̇l-,sȯrt-ərz-\ *n* **:** pulmonary anthrax resulting esp. from inhalation of bacterial spores (*Bacillus anthracis*) from contaminated wool or other hair

wool sponge *n* **:** a soft-fibered durable commercial sponge; *esp* **:** one (*Hippiospongia lachne*) found in the Gulf of Mexico, the Caribbean sea, and off the southeastern coast of Florida

wool stapler *n* **:** a dealer in wool

woo·zi·ly \ˈwü-zə-lē, ˈwu̇z-ə-\ *adv* **:** in a woozy manner

woo·zi·ness \ˈwü-zē-nəs, ˈwu̇z-ē-\ *n* **:** the quality or state of being woozy

woo·zy \ˈwü-zē, ˈwu̇z-ē\ *adj* [prob. alter. of *oozy*] **1 :** BEFUDDLED **2 :** affected with dizziness, mild nausea, or weakness **:** SICK

Worces·ter china \ˌwu̇s-tər-\ *n* **:** china made at Worcester, England since 1751

Worcester porcelain *n* **:** porcelain made at Worcester, England, since 1751

Worces·ter·shire sauce \ˌwu̇s-tə(r)-ˌshi(ə)r-, -shər-\ *n* **:** a pungent sauce orig. made in Worcester, England, of soy, vinegar, and many other ingredients

1**word** \ˈwərd\ *n, often attrib* [ME, fr. OE; akin to OHG *wort* word, L *verbum*, Gk *eirein* to say, speak] **1 a :** something that is said **b** *pl* (1) **:** TALK, DISCOURSE (2) **:** the text of a vocal musical composition **c :** a brief remark or conversation **2 a** (1) **:** a speech sound or series of speech sounds that symbolizes and communicates a meaning without being divisible into smaller units capable of independent use (2) **:** the entire set of linguistic forms produced by combining a single base with various inflectional elements without change in the part of speech elements **b :** a written or printed character or combination of characters representing a spoken word **c :** a combination of electrical or magnetic impulses conveying a quantum of information in communication and computer work **3 :** ORDER, COMMAND **4** *often cap* **a :** LOGOS **b :** GOSPEL 1a **c :** the expressed or manifested mind and will of God **5 a :** NEWS, INFORMATION **b :** RUMOR **6 :** the act of speaking or of making verbal communication **7 :** SAYING, PROVERB **8 :** PROMISE, DECLARATION **9 :** a quarrelsome utterance or conversation — usu. used in pl. **10 :** a verbal signal **:** PASSWORD

2**word** *vi, archaic* **:** SPEAK ~ *vt* **:** to express in words **:** PHRASE

word·age \ˈwərd-ij\ *n* **1 a :** WORDS **b :** VERBIAGE 1 **2 :** the number or quantity of words **3 :** WORDING

word blindness *n* **:** ALEXIA

word·book \ˈwərd-ˌbu̇k\ *n* **:** VOCABULARY, DICTIONARY

word class *n* **:** a linguistic form class whose members are words; *esp* **:** PART OF SPEECH

word for word *adv* **:** in the exact words **:** VERBATIM — **word–for–word** \ˌwərd-fə(r)-ˈwərd\ *adj*

word–hoard \ˈwərd-ˌhō(ə)rd, -ˌhȯ(ə)rd\ *n* **:** a supply of words **:** VOCABULARY

word·i·ly \ˈwərd-ᵊl-ē\ *adv* **:** in a wordy manner

word·i·ness \ˈwərd-ē-nəs\ *n* **:** VERBOSITY

word·ing \ˈwərd-iŋ\ *n* **:** the act or manner of expressing in words **:** PHRASEOLOGY

word·less \ˈwərd-ləs\ *adj* **1 :** not expressed in or accompanied by words **2 :** SILENT, INARTICULATE — **word·less·ly** *adv* — **word·less·ness** *n*

word·mon·ger \-ˌməŋ-gər, -ˌmäŋ-\ *n* **:** a dealer in words; *esp* **:** one that uses words for show

word of mouth **:** oral communication

word–of–mouth \ˌwərd-ə(v)-ˈmau̇th\ *adj* **:** orally communicated

word order *n* **:** the order of arrangement of words in a phrase, clause, or sentence

word·play \ˈwərd-ˌplā\ *n* **:** verbal wit

word square *n* **:** ACROSTIC 3

word stress *n* **:** the manner in which stresses are distributed on the syllables of a word — called also *word accent*

Words·wor·thi·an \ˌwərdz-ˈwər-thē-ən, -t͟hē-\ *adj* **:** of, relating to or characteristic of the poet Wordsworth or his writings

wordy \ˈwərd-ē\ *adj* **1 :** using or containing many words **:** VERBOSE **2 :** of or relating to words **:** VERBAL

syn WORDY, VERBOSE, PROLIX, DIFFUSE, REDUNDANT mean using more words than necessary to express thought. WORDY may also imply loquaciousness or garrulity; VERBOSE suggests a resulting dullness, obscurity, or lack of effectiveness; PROLIX suggests unreasonable and tedious dwelling on details; DIFFUSE stresses lack of compactness and pointedness of style; REDUNDANT applies to what is repetitious or logically superfluous

wore *past of* WEAR

1**work** \ˈwərk\ *n* [ME *werk, work*, fr. OE *werc, weorc*; akin to OHG *werc*, Gk *ergon*] **1 :** activity in which one exerts strength or faculties to do or perform something: **a :** sustained physical or mental effort to overcome obstacles and achieve an objective or result **b :** the labor, task, or duty that affords one his accustomed means of livelihood **c :** a specific task, duty, function, or assignment often being a part or phase of some larger activity **2 a :** energy expended by natural phenomena **b :** the result of such energy ⟨sand dunes are the ~ of sea and wind⟩ **c :** the transference of energy that is produced by the motion of the point of application of a force and is measured by multiplying the force and the displacement of its point of application in the line of action **3 a :** something that results from a particular manner or method of working, operating, or devising ⟨careful police ~⟩ ⟨clever camera ~⟩ **b :** something that results from the use or fashioning of a particular material ⟨porcelain ~⟩ **4 a :** a fortified structure (as a fort, earthen barricade, or trench) **b** *pl* **:** structures in engineering (as docks, bridges, or embankments) or mining (as shafts or tunnels) **5** *pl but sing or pl in constr* **:** a place where industrial labor is carried on **:** PLANT, FACTORY **6** *pl* **:** the working or moving parts of a mechanism ⟨~*s* of a clock⟩ **7 :** froth or foam caused by fermentation **8 a :** something produced or accomplished by effort, exertion, or exercise of skill ⟨this book is the ~ of many hands⟩ **b :** something produced by the exercise of creative talent or expenditure of creative effort **:** artistic production **9** *pl* **:** performance of moral or religious acts ⟨salvation by ~*s*⟩ **10 a :** effective operation **:** EFFECT, RESULT ⟨wait for time to do its healing ~⟩ **b :** manner of working **:** WORKMANSHIP, EXECUTION **11 a :** the material or piece of material that is operated upon at any stage in the process of manufacture **b :** ore before it is dressed **12** *pl* **a :** everything possessed, available, or belonging ⟨the whole ~*s*, rod, reel, tackle box, went overboard⟩ **b :** subjection to drastic treatment **:** all possible abuse including murder — usu. used with *get* ⟨get the ~*s*⟩ or *give* ⟨gave him the ~*s*⟩

syn WORK, LABOR, TRAVAIL, TOIL, DRUDGERY, GRIND mean activity involving effort or exertion. WORK may imply activity of body, of mind, or of a machine or it may apply to the effort or to what is produced by the effort; LABOR applies to physical or intellectual work involving great and often strenuous exertion; TRAVAIL is bookish for labor involving pain or suffering; TOIL implies prolonged and fatiguing labor; DRUDGERY suggests dull and irksome labor; GRIND implies labor exhausting to mind or body

syn WORK, EMPLOYMENT, OCCUPATION, CALLING, PURSUIT, MÉTIER, BUSINESS mean a specific sustained activity engaged in esp. in earning one's living; WORK may apply to any purposeful activity whether remunerative or not; EMPLOYMENT stresses activity that fills one's time; OCCUPATION implies work in which one engages regularly esp. as a result of training; CALLING applies to an occupation viewed esp. in relation to the one engaged in it; PURSUIT suggests a trade, profession, or avocation followed with zeal or steady interest; MÉTIER implies a calling or pursuit for which one believes oneself to be especially fitted; BUSINESS suggests activity in commerce or the management of money and affairs rather than in directly productive or effective work

— **at work** **1 :** engaged in working **:** BUSY; *esp* **:** engaged in one's regular occupation **2 :** having effect **:** OPERATING, FUNCTIONING — **in work** **1 :** in process of being done **2** *of a horse* **:** in training — **out of work** **:** without regular employment **:** JOBLESS

2**work** *adj* **1 :** suitable or styled for wear while working ⟨~ clothes⟩ **2 :** used for work ⟨~ elephant⟩

3**work** *vb* **worked** \ˈwərkt\ *or* **wrought** \ˈrȯt\ **work·ing** [ME *werken, worken*, fr. OE *wyrcan*; akin to OE *weorc*] *vt* **1 :** to bring to pass **:** EFFECT **2 a :** to fashion or create by expending labor or exertion upon **:** FORGE, SHAPE ⟨~ flint into tools⟩ **b :** to make or decorate with needlework; *esp* **:** EMBROIDER **3 a :** to prepare for use by stirring or kneading **b :** to bring into a desired form by a gradual process of cutting, hammering, scraping, pressing, or stretching ⟨~ cold steel⟩ **4 :** to set or keep in motion, operation, or activity **:** cause to operate or produce ⟨a pump ~*ed* by hand⟩ ⟨~ farmland⟩ **5 :** to solve (a problem) by reasoning or calculation **6 a :** to cause to toil or labor **:** get work out of **b :** to make use of **:** EXPLOIT **c :** to control or guide the operation of ⟨switches are ~*ed* from a central tower⟩ **7 :** to carry on an operation through or in or along ⟨fisherman ~*ed* the stream from the bridge down to the pool⟩ **8 :** to pay for with labor or service ⟨~ off a debt⟩ **9 a :** to get (oneself or an object) into or out of a condition or position by gradual stages **b :** CONTRIVE, ARRANGE ⟨we can ~ it so that you can take your vacation⟩ **10 a :** to practice trickery or cajolery on for some end ⟨~*ed* the management for a free ticket⟩ **b :** EXCITE, PROVOKE ⟨~*ed* himself into a rage⟩ ~ *vi* **1 a :** to exert oneself physically or mentally esp. in sustained effort for a purpose or under compulsion or necessity **b :** to perform or carry through a task requiring sustained effort or continuous repeated operations **c :** to perform work or fulfill duties regularly for wages or salary **2 :** to function or operate according to plan or design ⟨hinges ~ better with oil⟩ **3 :** to exert an influence or tendency **4 :** to produce a desired effect or result **:** SUCCEED **5 a :** to make way slowly and with difficulty **:** move or progress laboriously **b :** to sail to windward **6 :** to permit of being worked **:** react in a specified way to being worked ⟨this wood ~*s* easily⟩ **7 a :** to be in agitation or restless motion **b :** FERMENT 1 **c :** to move slightly in relation to another part **d :** to get into a specified condition by slow or imperceptible movements ⟨the knot ~*ed* loose⟩ — **work on** **1 :** AFFECT ⟨*worked on* his sympathies⟩ **2 :** to strive to influence or persuade — **work upon** **:** to have effect upon **:** operate on **:** PERSUADE, INFLUENCE

work·abil·i·ty \ˌwər-kə-ˈbil-ət-ē\ *n* **:** the quality or state of being workable

work·able \ˈwər-kə-bəl\ *adj* **1 :** capable of being worked **2 :** PRACTICABLE, FEASIBLE — **work·able·ness** *n*

work·a·day \ˈwər-kə-ˌdā\ *adj* [alter. of earlier *workyday*, fr. obs. *workyday*, n., (workday)] **1 :** relating to or suited for working days **2 :** PROSAIC, ORDINARY

work·bag \ˈwərk-ˌbag\ *n* **:** a bag for implements or materials for work; *esp* **:** a bag for needlework

work·bank \-ˌbaŋk\ *n* **:** a stand on which type matter in galleys is corrected and prepared for makeup

work·bas·ket \-ˌbas-kət\ *n* **:** a basket for needlework

work·bench \-ˌbench\ *n* **:** a bench on which work esp. of mechanics, machinists, and carpenters is performed

work·book \-ˌbu̇k\ *n* **1 :** a booklet outlining a course of study **2 :** a workman's handbook or manual **3 :** a record book of work done **4 :** a student's individual exercise book of problems to be solved directly on the pages

work·box \-ˌbäks\ *n* **:** a box for work instruments and materials

work camp *n* **:** a camp for workers: as **a :** PRISON CAMP 1 **b :** a short-term group project in which individuals from one or more religious organizations volunteer their labor

work·day \-ˌdā\ *n* **1 :** a day on which work is performed as distinguished from Sunday or a holiday **2 :** the period of time in a day during which work is performed — **workday** *adj*

worked \ˈwərkt\ *adj* **:** that has been subjected to some process of development, treatment, or manufacture

worked up *adj* **:** emotionally aroused **:** EXCITED

work·er \ˈwər-kər\ *n* **1 a :** one that works esp. at manual or industrial labor or with a particular material — often used in combination **b :** a member of the working class **2 :** one of the sexually underdeveloped and usu. sterile members of a colony of social ants, bees, wasps, or termites that perform most of the labor and protective duties of the colony **3 :** a usu. electrotype plate from which printing is done

work farm *n* **:** a farm on which minor offenders are confined and put to work

work·folk \ˈwərk-ˌfōk\ *or* **work·folks** \-ˌfōks\ *n pl* **:** working people; *esp* **:** farm workers

work force *n* **1 :** the workers engaged in a specific activity ⟨the factory's *work force*⟩ **2 :** the number of workers potentially assignable for any purpose ⟨the nation's *work force*⟩

work·horse \-ˌhȯ(ə)rs\ *n* **1 :** a horse used chiefly for labor as distinguished from driving, riding, or racing **2 a :** a person who undertakes arduous labor **b :** a markedly useful or durable vehicle, craft, or machine

work·house \\-ˌhau̇s\\ *n* **1** *Brit* **:** POORHOUSE **2 :** a house of correction for minor offenders

work in *vt* **1 :** to insert or cause to penetrate by repeated or continued effort **2 :** to interpose or insinuate gradually or unobtrusively

¹work·ing *adj* **1 :** adequate to permit work to be done ⟨a ~ majority⟩ **2 :** assumed or adopted to permit or facilitate further work or activity ⟨~ draft⟩

²working *n* **:** an excavation or group of excavations made in mining, quarrying, or tunneling — used chiefly in pl.

working asset *n* **:** an asset other than a capital asset

working capital *n* **1 :** the excess of current assets over current liabilities **2 :** all capital of a business except that invested in capital assets

working class *n* **:** the class of people who are employed for wages usu. in manual labor

work·ing–class \\ˌwər-kiŋ-ˌklas\\ *adj* **:** relating to, deriving from, or suitable to the class of wageworkers ⟨~ virtues⟩

working day *n* **:** WORKDAY

working drawing *n* **:** a scale drawing of an object to be made or structure to be built for direct use by the workman

work·ing·man \\ˈwər-kiŋ-ˌman\\ *n* **:** one who works for wages usu. at manual labor

working papers *n pl* **:** official documents legalizing the employment of a minor

working substance *n* **:** a usu. fluid substance that through changes of temperature, volume, and pressure is the means of carrying out thermodynamic processes or cycles (as in a heat engine)

work·less \\ˈwər-kləs\\ *adj* **:** being without work **:** UNEMPLOYED — **work·less·ness** *n*

work load *n* **1 :** the amount of work or of working time expected from or assigned to an employee **2 :** the total amount of work to be performed by a group (as a department) of workers in a period of time

work·man \\ˈwərk-mən\\ *n* **1 :** WORKINGMAN **2 :** ARTISAN, CRAFTSMAN

work·man·like \\-ˌlīk\\ *or* **work·man·ly** \\-lē\\ *adj* **:** worthy of a good workman **:** SKILLFUL

work·man·ship \\-ˌship\\ *n* **1 :** the art or skill of a workman **:** CRAFTSMANSHIP; *also* **:** the quality imparted to a thing in the process of making ⟨a vase of exquisite ~⟩ **2 :** something effected, made, or produced **:** WORK

workmen's compensation insurance *n* **:** insurance against statutory damages arising from injury to employees while in the employ of the insured employer

work of art : a product of one of the fine arts; *esp* **:** a painting or sculpture of high artistic quality

work out *vt* **1 :** to effect by labor and exertion **2 a :** SOLVE **b :** to devise, arrange, or achieve esp. by resolving difficulties **c :** DEVELOP, ELABORATE **3 :** to discharge (as a debt) by labor **4 :** to exhaust (as a mine) by working **~** *vi* **1 a :** to prove effective, practicable, or suitable **b :** to amount to a total or calculated figure — used with *at* **2 :** to go through a training or practice session esp. in an athletic specialty ⟨*works out* daily with sparring partners⟩

work·out \\ˈwər-ˌkau̇t\\ *n* **:** a practice or exercise to test or improve one's fitness esp. for athletic competition, ability, or performance

work·peo·ple \\ˈwərk-ˌpē-pəl\\ *n pl, chiefly Brit* **:** WORKERS, EMPLOYEES

work·room \\ˈwər-ˌkrüm, -ˌkru̇m\\ *n* **:** a room used esp. for manual work

work·shop \\ˈwərk-ˌshäp\\ *n* **1 :** a small establishment where manufacturing or handicrafts are carried on **2 :** a seminar emphasizing free discussion, exchange of ideas, and practical methods, skills, and principles that is given mainly for adults already employed in the field

work stoppage *n* **:** concerted cessation of work by a group of employees usu. more spontaneous and less serious than a strike

work·ta·ble \\ˈwərk-ˌtā-bəl\\ *n* **:** a table for holding working materials and implements; *esp* **:** a small table with drawers and other conveniences for needlework

work–up \\ˈwər-ˌkəp\\ *n* **:** an unintended mark on a printed sheet caused by the rising of spacing material

work·week \\ˈwər-ˌkwēk\\ *n* **:** the hours or days of work in a calendar week ⟨40-hour ~⟩ ⟨a 5-day ~⟩

work·wom·an \\ˈwər-ˌkwu̇m-ən\\ *n* **:** a woman who works

world \\ˈwər(-ə)ld\\ *n, often attrib* [ME, fr. OE *woruld* human existence, this world, age; akin to OHG *weralt* age, world; both fr. a prehistoric WGmc-NGmc compound whose first constituent is represented by OE *wer* man and whose second constituent is akin to OE *eald* old — more at VIRILE, OLD] **1 a :** the earthly state of human existence **b :** life after death — used with a qualifier ⟨the next ~⟩ **2 :** the earth with its inhabitants and all things upon it **3 :** individual course of life **:** CAREER **4 :** the inhabitants of the earth **:** the human race **5 a :** the concerns of the earth and its affairs as distinguished from heaven and the life to come **b :** secular affairs **6 :** the system of created things **:** UNIVERSE **7 a :** a division, section, or generation of the inhabitants of the earth **b :** a distinctive class of persons or their sphere of interest ⟨academic ~⟩ ⟨sports ~⟩ **8 :** human society ⟨withdraw from the ~⟩ **9 :** a part or section of the earth that is a separate independent unit **10 :** the sphere or scene of one's life and action **11 :** an indefinite multitude or a great quantity or amount ⟨makes a ~ of difference⟩ **12 :** KINGDOM 5 ⟨animal ~⟩ **13 :** a celestial body (as a planet); *esp* **:** one that is inhabited **syn** see EARTH — **in the world :** among innumerable possibilities **:** EVER — used as an intensive ⟨what *in the world* is it⟩ — **out of this world :** of extraordinary excellence **:** SUPERB

world–beat·er \\ˈwərl(d)-ˌbēt-ər\\ *n* **:** one that excels all others of its kind **:** CHAMPION

World Communion Sunday *n* **:** the first Sunday in October observed with Communion in many churches as an expression of Christian unity

World Day of Prayer : the first Friday in Lent observed by many churches esp. as a day of prayer for missions

world federalism *n* **1 :** federalism on a worldwide basis **2** *cap W&F* **a :** the principles and policies of the World Federalists **b :** the body or movement composed of World Federalists

world federalist *n* **1 :** an adherent or advocate of world federalism **2** *cap W&F* **:** a member of a movement arising after World War II advocating the formation of a federal union of the nations of the world with limited but positive governmental powers

World Island *n* **:** the landmass consisting of Europe, Asia, and Africa

world·li·ness \\ˈwərl-(d)lē-nəs\\ *n* **:** the quality or state of being worldly

world·ling \\ˈwər(-ə)l-dliŋ, ˈwərl-liŋ\\ *n* **:** a person engrossed in the concerns of this present world

world·ly \\ˈwər(-ə)l-dlē, ˈwərl-lē\\ *adj* **1 :** of, relating to, or devoted to this world and its pursuits rather than to religion or spiritual affairs **2 :** WORLDLY-WISE **syn** see EARTHLY

world·ly–mind·ed \\ˌwərl-(d)lē-ˈmīn-dəd\\ *adj* **:** devoted to or engrossed in worldly interests — **world·ly–mind·ed·ness** *n*

world·ly–wise \\ˈwərl-(d)lē-ˌwīz\\ *adj* **:** wise as to things and ways of this world

world power *n* **:** a political unit (as a nation or state) powerful enough to affect the entire world by its influence or actions

world series *n* **:** a series of baseball games played each fall between the pennant winners of the major leagues to decide the professional championship of the U.S.

world–shak·ing \\ˈwərl(d)-ˌshā-kiŋ\\ *adj* **:** EARTHSHAKING

world soul *n* **:** a spiritual being related to the world as the soul is to the individual being

world war *n* **:** a war engaged in by the principal nations of the world

world–wea·ri·ness \\ˈwərl-ˌdwir-ē-nəs\\ *n* **:** fatigue from or boredom with the life of the world and esp. with material pleasures — **world–wea·ry** \\-ˌdwir-ē\\ *adj*

world·wide \\ˈwər(-ə)l-ˈdwīd\\ *adj* **:** extended throughout the entire world

¹worm \\ˈwərm\\ *n, often attrib* [ME, fr. OE *wyrm* serpent, worm; akin to OHG *wurm* serpent, worm, L *vermis* worm] **1 a :** EARTHWORM; *broadly* **:** an annelid worm **b :** any of numerous relatively small elongated usu. naked and soft-bodied animals: as (1) **:** an insect larva; *esp* **:** one that is a destructive grub, caterpillar, or maggot (2) **:** SHIPWORM (3) **:** BLINDWORM **2 a :** a human being who is an object of contempt, loathing, or pity **:** WRETCH **b :** something that inwardly torments or devours **3** *archaic* **:** SNAKE, SERPENT **4 :** HELMINTHIASIS — usu. used in pl. **5 :** something (as a mechanical device) spiral or vermiculate in form or appearance: as **a :** the thread of a screw **b :** a short revolving screw whose threads gear with the teeth of a worm wheel or a rack **c :** a spiral condensing tube used in distilling **d :** ARCHIMEDES' SCREW; *also* **:** a conveyor working on the principle of such a screw — **worm·like** \\-ˌlīk\\ *adj*

²worm *vi* **1 :** to move or proceed sinuously **2 a :** to proceed or make one's way insidiously or deviously — usu. used with *into* ⟨spies ~ into important positions⟩ **b :** to evade or escape in indirect or subtle fashion **:** WRIGGLE — usu. used with *out of* **~** *vt* **1 :** to free (as a dog) from worms **2 a :** to cause to move or proceed in or as if in the manner of a worm **b :** to insinuate or introduce (oneself) by devious or subtle means **3 :** to wind rope or yarn spirally round and between the strands of (a cable or rope) before serving **4 :** to obtain or extract by artful or insidious questioning or by pleading, asking, or persuading — usu. used with *out of* — **worm·er** *n*

worm–eat·en \\ˈwər-ˌmēt-ᵊn\\ *adj* **1 a :** eaten or burrowed by worms ⟨~ timber⟩ **b :** PITTED **2 :** WORN-OUT, ANTIQUATED

worm fence *n* **:** a zigzag fence consisting of interlocking rails supported by crossed poles — called also *snake fence, Virginia fence*

worm gear *n* **1 :** WORM WHEEL **2 :** a gear of a worm and a worm wheel working together

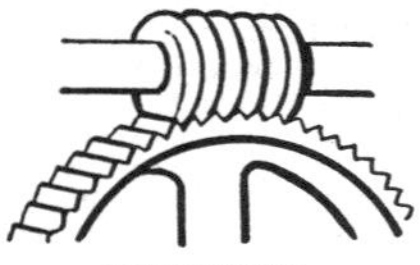

worm gear

worm·hole \\ˈwərm-ˌhōl\\ *n* **:** a hole or passage burrowed by a worm

worm·root \\-ˌrüt, -ˌru̇t\\ *n* **:** PINKROOT

worm·seed \\ˈwərm-ˌsēd\\ *n* **1 :** any of various plants whose seeds possess anthelmintic properties: as **a :** any of several ragweeds (as *Artemisia santonica* and *A. pauciflora*) **b :** a goosefoot (*Chenopodium ambrosioides*) **2 :** SANTONICA 2

worm snake *n* **:** any of various small harmless burrowing snakes suggesting earthworms

worm wheel *n* **:** a toothed wheel gearing with the thread of a worm

worm·wood \\ˈwərm-ˌwu̇d\\ *n* [ME *wormwode,* alter. of *wermode,* fr. OE *wermōd;* akin to OHG *wermuota* wormwood] **1 :** any of a genus (*Artemisia*) of composite woody herbs; *esp* **:** a European plant (*A. absinthium*) yielding a bitter slightly aromatic dark green oil used in absinthe **2 :** something bitter or grievous **:** BITTERNESS

wormy \\ˈwər-mē\\ *adj* **1 :** containing, abounding in, or infested with worms ⟨~ flour⟩ ⟨a ~ dog⟩; *also* **:** damaged by worms **:** WORM-EATEN ⟨~ timbers⟩ **2 :** resembling or suggestive of a worm

worn *past part of* WEAR

worn–out \\ˈwō(ə)r-ˈnau̇t, ˈwȯ(ə)r-\\ *adj* **:** exhausted or used up by or as if by wear

wor·ri·er \\ˈwər-ē-ər, ˈwə-rē-\\ *n* **:** one that worries

wor·ri·ment \\ˈwər-ē-mənt, ˈwə-rē-\\ *n* **:** an act or instance of worrying; *also* **:** TROUBLE, WORRY

wor·ri·some \\-səm\\ *adj* **1 :** causing distress or worry **2 :** inclined to worry or fret — **wor·ri·some·ly** *adv*

¹wor·ry \\ˈwər-ē, ˈwə-rē\\ *vb* [ME *worien,* fr. OE *wyrgan;* akin to OHG *wurgen* to strangle, Lith *veržti* to constrict] *vt* **1** *dial Brit* **:** CHOKE, STRANGLE **2 a :** to harass by tearing, biting, or snapping esp. at the throat **b :** to shake or pull at with the teeth ⟨terrier *~ing* a rat⟩ **c :** to touch or disturb something repeatedly **d :** to change the position of or adjust by repeated pushing or hauling **3 a :** to assail with rough or aggressive attack or treatment **:** TORMENT **b :** to subject to persistent or nagging attention or effort **4 :** to afflict with mental distress or agitation **:** make anxious **:** FRET **~** *vi* **1** *dial Brit* **:** STRANGLE, CHOKE **2 :** to move, proceed, or progress by unceasing or difficult effort **:** STRUGGLE **3 :** to feel or experience concern or anxiety **:** FRET

syn ANNOY, HARASS, HARRY, PLAGUE, PESTER, TEASE, TANTALIZE: WORRY implies an incessant goading or attacking that drives one to desperation; ANNOY suggests molesting, interfering or intruding causing anger or discomfort in the victim; HARASS implies persecution with small attacks or exactions that wear down or distract; HARRY may imply heavier oppression or maltreatment than HARASS; PLAGUE suggests the torment of a painful disease or anything comparable in effect; PESTER implies a continual annoyance as by

vermin or demanding children; TEASE suggests an attempt to break down one's resistance or rouse to wrath; TANTALIZE implies awakening expectation and then withholding or frustrating satisfaction

2**worry** *n* **1 a :** mental distress or agitation resulting from concern usu. for something impending or anticipated **:** ANXIETY **b :** an instance or occurrence of such distress or agitation **c :** a cause of worry **:** TROUBLE, DIFFICULTY **2 :** the act of seizing an animal with the teeth and shaking it so as to kill or injure it **syn** see CARE

wor·ry·wart \-ˌwȯ(ə)rt\ *n* **:** one who is inclined to worry unduly

1**worse** \ˈwərs\ *adj, comparative of* BAD *or of* ILL [ME *werse, worse,* fr. OE *wiersa, wyrsa;* akin to OHG *wirsiro* worse] **1 :** of more inferior quality, value, or condition **2 a :** more unfavorable, unpleasant, or painful **b :** more faulty, unsuitable, or incorrect **c :** less skillful or efficient **3 :** bad, evil, ill, or corrupt in a greater degree **:** more reprehensible

2**worse** *n* **1 :** one that is worse **2 :** a greater degree of ill or badness

3**worse** *adv, comparative of* BAD *or of* ILL **:** in a worse manner **:** to a worse extent or degree

wors·en \ˈwərs-ᵊn\ *vb* **wors·en·ing** \ˈwərs-niŋ, -ᵊn-iŋ\ *vt* **:** to make worse ~ *vi* **:** to become worse

wors·er \ˈwər-sər\ [*worse* + *-er*] *comparative of* BAD, *substand comparative of* ILL

1**wor·ship** \ˈwər-shəp\ *n* [ME *worshipe* worthiness, repute, respect, reverence paid to a divine being, fr. OE *weorthscipe* worthiness, repute, respect, fr. *weorth* worthy, worth + *-scipe* -ship] **1** *chiefly Brit* **:** a person of importance — used as a title for various officials (as magistrates and some mayors) ⟨sent a petition to his *Worship*⟩ **2 :** reverence tendered a divine being or supernatural power; *also* **:** an act of expressing such reverence **3 :** a form of religious practice with its creed and ritual **4 :** extravagant respect or admiration for or devotion to an object of esteem ⟨~ of the dollar⟩

2**worship** *vb* **wor·shiped** *or* **wor·shipped; wor·ship·ing** *or* **wor·ship·ping** *vt* **1 :** to honor or reverence as a divine being or supernatural power **2 :** to regard with extravagant respect, honor, or devotion **:** IDOLIZE ~ *vi* **:** to perform or take part in worship or an act of worship **syn** see REVERE — **wor·ship·er** *or* **wor·ship·per** *n*

wor·ship·ful \ˈwər-shəp-fəl\ *adj* **1 a** *archaic* **:** NOTABLE, DISTINGUISHED **b** *chiefly Brit* — used as a title for various persons or groups of rank or distinction **2 :** VENERATING, WORSHIPING — **wor·ship·ful·ly** \-fə-lē\ *adv* — **wor·ship·ful·ness** *n*

wor·ship·less \-shə-pləs\ *adj* **:** lacking worship or worshipers

1**worst** \ˈwərst\ *adj, superlative of* BAD *or of* ILL [ME *werste, worste,* fr. OE *wierresta, wyrsta,* superl. of the root of OE *wiersa* worse] **1 :** most bad, evil, ill, or corrupt **2 a :** most unfavorable, unpleasant, or painful **b :** most unsuitable, faulty, unattractive, or ill-conceived **c :** least skillful or efficient **3 :** most wanting in quality, value, or condition

2**worst** *n* **1 :** one that is worst **2 :** the greatest degree of ill or badness

3**worst** *adv, superlative of* ILL *or* ILLY *or of* BAD *or* BADLY **:** to the extreme degree of badness or inferiority **:** in the worst manner

4**worst** *vt* **:** to get the better of **:** DEFEAT

wor·sted \ˈwu̇s-təd, ˈwər-stəd\ *n* [ME, fr. *Worsted* (now *Worstead*), England] **1 :** a smooth compact yarn from long wool fibers used esp. for firm napless fabrics, carpeting, or knitting **2 :** a fabric made from worsted yarns — **worsted** *adj*

1**wort** \ˈwərt, ˈwȯ(ə)rt\ *n* [ME, fr. OE *wyrt* root, herb, plant — more at ROOT] **1 :** PLANT; *esp* **:** an herbaceous plant — usu. used in combination **2** *archaic* **:** POTHERB

2**wort** *n* [ME, fr. OE *wyrt;* akin to MHG *würze* brewer's wort, OE *wyrt* root, herb] **:** a dilute solution of sugars obtained by infusion from malt and fermented to form beer

1**worth** \ˈwərth\ *vi* [ME *worthen,* fr. OE *weorthan;* akin to OHG *werdan* to become, L *vertere* to turn] *archaic* **:** BECOME — usu. used in the phrase *woe worth*

2**worth** *adj* [ME, fr. OE *weorth* worthy, of (a specified) value; akin to OHG *werd* worthy, worth] **1** *archaic* **:** having monetary or material value **2** *archaic* **:** ESTIMABLE

3**worth** *prep* **1 a :** equal in value to **b :** having possessions or income equal to **2 :** deserving of ⟨well ~ the effort⟩ **3 :** capable of ⟨ran for all he was ~⟩

4**worth** *n* **1 a :** monetary value **b :** the equivalent of a specified amount or figure **2 :** the value of something measured by its qualities or by the esteem in which it is held **3 a :** moral or personal value **b :** MERIT, EXCELLENCE **4 :** WEALTH, RICHES

syn WORTH, VALUE mean the quality of being useful, important, or excellent. WORTH applies to what is intrinsically or enduringly excellent, meritorious, or desirable; VALUE may suggest the immediate estimation of the worth of something to an individual or in a particular situation

worth·ful \ˈwərth-fəl\ *adj* **1 :** full of merit **:** HONORABLE **2 :** having value **:** ESTEEMED

wor·thi·ly \ˈwər-t͟hə-lē\ *adv* **:** in a worthy manner

wor·thi·ness \-t͟hē-nəs\ *n* **:** the quality or state of being worthy

worth·less \ˈwərth-ləs\ *adj* **1 a :** lacking worth **:** VALUELESS **b :** USELESS **2 :** LOW, DESPICABLE — **worth·less·ly** *adv* — **worth·less·ness** *n*

worth·while \ˈwərth-ˈhwī(ə)l, -ˈwī(ə)l\ *adj* **:** being worth the time or effort spent — **worth·while·ness** *n*

1**wor·thy** \ˈwər-t͟hē\ *adj* **1 a :** having worth or value **:** ESTIMABLE **b :** HONORABLE, MERITORIOUS **2 :** having sufficient worth ⟨a man ~ of the honor⟩

2**worthy** *n* **:** a worthy person

1**wot** *pres 1st & 3d sing of* WIT

2**wot** \ˈwät\ *vb* **wot·ted; wot·ting** [ME *woten,* alter. of *witen* — more at WIT] *dial chiefly Brit* **:** KNOW

would \wəd, əd, d, (ˈ)wu̇d\ *past of* WILL [ME *wolde,* fr. OE; akin to OHG *wolta* wished, desired] **1 a** *archaic* **:** WISHED, DESIRED **b** *archaic* **:** wish for **:** WANT **c** (1) **:** strongly desire **:** WISH ⟨I ~ I were young again⟩ (2) — used in auxiliary function with *rather* or *sooner* to express preference ⟨he ~ sooner die than face them⟩ **2 a** — used in auxiliary function to express wish, desire, or intent ⟨those who ~ forbid gambling⟩ **b** — used in auxiliary function to express willingness or preference ⟨as ye ~ that men should do to you —Lk 6:31 (AV)⟩ **c** — used in auxiliary function to express plan or intention ⟨said he ~ come⟩ **3** — used in auxiliary function to express custom or habitual action ⟨we ~ meet often for lunch⟩ **4** — used in auxiliary function to express consent or choice ⟨~ put it off if he could⟩ **5 a** — used in auxiliary function in the conclusion of a conditional sentence to express a contingency or possibility ⟨if he were coming, he ~ be here now⟩ **b** — used in auxiliary function in a noun clause completing a statement of desire, request, or advice ⟨we wish that he ~ go⟩ **6** — used in auxiliary function to express probability or presumption in past or present time ⟨~ have won if he had not tripped⟩ **7 :** COULD ⟨the barrel ~ hold 20 gallons⟩ **8** — used in auxiliary function to express a request with which voluntary compliance is expected ⟨~ you please help us⟩ **9** — used in auxiliary function to express doubt or uncertainty ⟨the explanation . . . ~ seem satisfactory⟩ **10 :** SHOULD ⟨knew I ~ enjoy the trip⟩ ⟨~ be glad to know the answer⟩

would-be \ˈwu̇d-ˌbē\ *adj* **:** desiring or professing to be

wouldn't \ˈwu̇d-ᵊnt\ **:** would not

wouldst \wədst, (ˈ)wu̇dst, wətst, (ˈ)wu̇tst\ *or* **would·est** \ˈwu̇d-əst\ *archaic past 2d sing of* WILL

1**wound** \ˈwünd\ *n* [ME, fr. OE *wund;* akin to OHG *wunta* wound] **1 a :** an injury to the body consisting of a laceration or breaking of a membrane (as the skin) usu. by a hard or sharp instrument forcefully driven or applied **b :** a cut or breach in a plant due to external violence **2 :** a mental or emotional hurt or blow

2**wound** *vt* **:** to cause a wound to or in ~ *vi* **:** to inflict a wound

3**wound** *past of* WIND

wound·ed \ˈwün-dəd\ *n pl* **:** wounded persons

wound·less \ˈwün-(d)ləs\ *adj* **1** *obs* **:** INVULNERABLE ⟨the ~ air —Shak.⟩ **2 :** free from wounds **:** UNWOUNDED

wound·wort \ˈwün-ˌdwərt, -ˌdwȯ(ə)rt\ *n* **:** any of various plants whose soft downy leaves have been used in the dressing of wounds; *esp* **:** any of several mints (genus *Stachys*)

wove *past of* WEAVE

woven *past part of* WEAVE

wove paper \ˈwōv-\ *n* [*wove* (archaic pp. of *weave*)] **:** paper made by means of a revolving roller covered with wires so woven as to produce no fine lines running across the grain — compare LAID PAPER

1**wow** \ˈwau̇\ *interj* — used to express pleasure, surprise, or strong feeling

2**wow** *n* [1*wow*] **:** a striking success **:** HIT

3**wow** *vt* **:** to excite to enthusiastic admiration

4**wow** *n* [imit.] **:** a distortion in reproduced sound consisting of a slow rise and fall of pitch caused by speed variation in the reproducing system

wow·ser \ˈwau̇-zər\ *n* [origin unknown] *chiefly Austral* **:** an obtrusively puritanical person

1**wrack** \ˈrak\ *n* [ME, fr. OE *wræc* misery, punishment, something driven by the sea; akin to OE *wrecan* to drive, punish — more at WREAK] **1 :** RUIN, DESTRUCTION **2 :** a remnant of something destroyed

2**wrack** *n* [ME *wrak,* fr. MD or MLG; akin to OE *wræc* something driven by the sea] **1 a :** a wrecked ship **b :** WRECKAGE **c :** WRECK **d** *dial* **:** the violent destruction of a structure, machine, or vehicle **2 a :** marine vegetation; *esp* **:** KELP **b :** dried seaweeds

3**wrack** *vt* **:** to utterly ruin **:** WRECK

4**wrack** *vb* [by alter.] **:** 4RACK

5**wrack** *n* **:** 3RACK 2

6**wrack** *n* **:** 1RACK

wrack·ful \ˈrak-fəl\ *adj* **:** DESTRUCTIVE

wraith \ˈrāth\ *n* [origin unknown] **1 a :** an apparition of a living person in his exact likeness seen usu. just before his death **b :** GHOST, SPECTER **2 :** an insubstantial appearance **:** SHADOW **3 :** a barely visible gaseous or vaporous column

1**wran·gle** \ˈraŋ-gəl\ *vb* **wran·gling** \-g(ə-)liŋ\ [ME *wranglen;* akin to OHG *ringan* to struggle — more at WRING] *vi* **1 :** to dispute angrily or peevishly **:** BICKER **2 :** to engage in argument or controversy ~ *vt* **1 :** to obtain by persistent arguing **:** WANGLE **2 :** to herd and care for (livestock and esp. horses) on the range

2**wrangle** *n* **1 :** an angry, noisy, or prolonged dispute or quarrel **2 :** the action or process of wrangling **syn** see QUARREL

wran·gler \-g(ə-)lər\ *n* **1 :** a bickering disputant **2 :** a ranch hand who takes care of the saddle horses; *broadly* **:** COWBOY

1**wrap** \ˈrap\ *vb* **wrapped; wrap·ping** [ME *wrappen*] *vt* **1 a :** to cover esp. by winding or folding **b :** to envelop and secure for transportation or storage **:** BUNDLE **c :** ENFOLD, EMBRACE **d :** to coil, fold, draw, or twine about something **2 a :** SURROUND, ENVELOP **b :** SUFFUSE **c :** to involve completely **:** ENGROSS **3 a :** to conceal or obscure as if by enveloping or enfolding **b :** VEIL **4 :** to enclose as if with a protective covering ~ *vi* **1 :** to wind, coil, or twine so as to encircle or cover something **2 :** to put on clothing **:** DRESS — usu. used with *up* **3 :** to be subject to covering, enclosing, or packaging — usu. used with *up*

2**wrap** *n* **1 a :** WRAPPER, WRAPPING **b :** an article of clothing that may be wrapped round a person; *esp* **:** an outer garment (as a coat or shawl) **c :** BLANKET **d :** a 4-page insert folded around text leaves of a book and sewed in — called also *wraparound* **2 :** a single turn or convolution of something wound round an object **3** *pl* **a :** RESTRAINT **b :** SECRECY, CENSORSHIP

wrap·around \ˈrap-ə-ˌrau̇nd\ *n* **1 :** a garment (as a dress or coat) made with a full-length opening and adjusted to the figure by wrapping around **2 :** WRAP 1d **3 :** an object that encircles or esp. curves and laps over another

wrap·per \ˈrap-ər\ *n* **1 :** that in which something is wrapped: as **a :** a tobacco leaf used for the outside covering esp. of cigars **b** (1) **:** JACKET 3c(1) (2) **:** the paper cover of a book not bound in boards **c :** a paper wrapped around a newspaper or magazine in the mail **2 :** one that wraps **3 :** an article of clothing worn wrapped around the body

wrap·ping \ˈrap-iŋ\ *n* **:** something used to wrap an object **:** WRAPPER

wrap up *vt* **1 :** END, CONCLUDE **2 :** to make a single comprehensive report of

wrap-up \ˈrap-ˌəp\ *n* **:** a summarizing news report

wrasse \ˈras\ *n* [Corn *gwragh, wragh*] **:** any of numerous elongate compressed usu. brilliantly colored marine spiny-finned fishes

ə abut; ᵊ kitten; ər further; a back; ā bake; ä cot, cart; au̇ out; ch chin; e less; ē easy; g gift; i trip; ī life
j joke; ŋ sing; ō flow; ȯ flaw; ȯi coin; th thin; t͟h this; ü loot; u̇ foot; y yet; yü few; yu̇ furious; zh vision

(family Labridae) that include important food fishes esp. of warm seas as well as some believed to be poisonous

1**wrath** \'rath, *chiefly Brit* 'rȯth\ *n* [ME, fr. OE *wrǣththo*, fr. *wrāth* wroth — more at WROTH] **1** : violent anger : RAGE **2** : retributory punishment for an offense or a crime : divine chastisement **syn** see ANGER

2**wrath** *adj* [alter. of WROTH] *archaic* : WRATHFUL

wrath·ful \-fəl\ *adj* **1** : filled with wrath : IRATE **2** : arising from, marked by, or indicative of wrath — **wrath·ful·ly** \-fə-lē\ *adv* — **wrath·ful·ness** *n*

wrathy \-ē\ *adj* : WRATHFUL

wreak \'rēk\ *vt* [ME *wreken*, fr. OE *wrecan* to drive, punish, avenge; akin to OHG *rehhan* to avenge, L *urgēre* to drive on, urge] **1 a** *archaic* : AVENGE **b** : to cause the infliction of (vengeance or punishment) : EXACT **2** : to give free play or course to (malevolent feeling) ⟨~ one's wrath⟩ **3** : CAUSE, INFLICT

wreak·ful \-fəl\ *adj* : REVENGEFUL

wreath \'rēth\ *n, pl* **wreaths** \'rēthz, 'rēths\ [ME *wrethe*, fr. OE *writha;* akin to OE *wrīthan* to twist — more at WRITHE] : something intertwined into a circular shape; *esp* : GARLAND, CHAPLET

wreathe \'rēth\ *vb* [*wreath*] *vt* **1** : to twist or contort so as to show folds or creases ⟨*wreathed* with smiles⟩ **2 a** : to shape into a wreath **b** : INTERWEAVE **c** : to cause to coil about something **3** : to encircle or adorn with or as if with a wreath ~ *vi* **1** : to twist in coils : WRITHE **2 a** : to take on the shape of a wreath **b** : to move or extend in circles or spirals

wreathy \'rē-thē, -thē\ *adj* **1** : having the form of a wreath **2** : constituting a wreath

1**wreck** \'rek\ *n* [ME *wrek*, fr. AF, of Scand origin; akin to ON *rek* wreck; akin to OE *wrecan* to drive] **1** : something cast up on the land by the sea esp. after a shipwreck **2 a** : SHIPWRECK **b** : the action of wrecking or fact or state of being wrecked : DESTRUCTION **3 a** : a hulk or the ruins of a wrecked ship **b** : the broken remains of something wrecked or otherwise ruined **c** : something disabled or in a state of ruin or dilapidation; *also* : a person or animal of broken constitution, health, or spirits

2**wreck** *vt* **1** : to cast ashore **2 a** : to reduce to a ruinous state by or as if by violence **b** : SHIPWRECK **c** : to ruin, damage, or imperil by wreck **d** : to involve in disaster or ruin **3** : WREAK 3 ~ *vi* **1** : to become wrecked **2** : to rob, salvage, or repair wreckage or a wreck

wreck·age \'rek-ij\ *n* **1** : the act of wrecking : the state of being wrecked; *also* : the remains of a wreck **2** : broken, disrupted, and disordered parts or material from a wrecked structure **3** : wretched or degraded beings cast off by society

wreck·er \'rek-ər\ *n* **1** : one that wrecks; *specif* : one whose work is the demolition of buildings **2 a** : one that searches for or works upon the wrecks of ships (as for rescue or for plunder) **b** : an automotive vehicle with hoisting apparatus and equipment for towing wrecked or disabled automobiles or freeing automobiles stalled in snow or mud — called also *tow car* **c** : one that salvages junked automobile parts and material

wrecking bar *n* : a small crowbar with a claw for pulling nails at one end and a slight bend for prying at the other end

wren \'ren\ *n* [ME *wrenne*, fr. OE *wrenna;* akin to OHG *rentilo* wren] **1** : any of numerous small more or less brown singing birds (family Troglodytidae); *esp* : a very small European bird (*Troglodytes troglodytes*) that has a short erect tail and is a good singer **2** : any of numerous small singing birds resembling the true wrens in size and habits

1**wrench** \'rench\ *vb* [ME *wrenchen*, fr. OE *wrencan;* akin to OHG *renken*, L *vergere* to bend, incline] *vi* **1** : to move with a violent twist; *also* : to undergo twisting **2** : to pull or strain at something with violent twisting ~ *vt* **1** : to twist violently **2** : to injure or disable by a violent twisting or straining **3** : CHANGE; *esp* : DISTORT, PERVERT **4 a** : to pull or tighten by violent twisting or with violence **b** : to snatch forcibly : WREST **5** : to cause to suffer anguish : RACK

2**wrench** *n* **1 a** : a violent twisting or a pull with or as if with twisting **b** : a sharp twist or sudden jerk straining muscles or ligaments; *also* : the resultant injury (as of a joint) **c** : ALTERATION; *esp* : DISTORTION **d** : acute emotional distress : sudden violent mental change **2** : a hand or power tool for holding, twisting, or turning an object (as a bolt or nut)

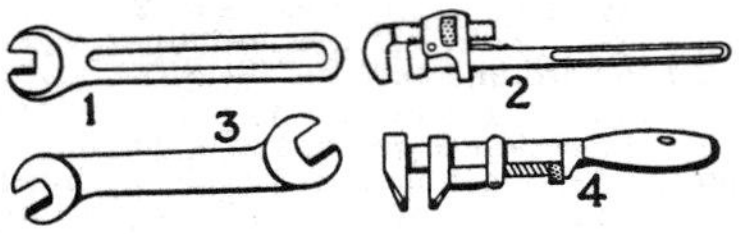

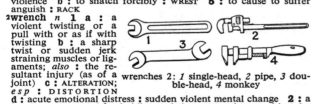

wrenches 2: *1* single-head, *2* pipe, *3* double-head, *4* monkey

1**wrest** \'rest\ *vt* [ME *wrasten, wresten*, fr. OE *wrǣstan;* akin to OE *wrīthan* to twist — more at WRITHE] **1** : to pull, force, or move by violent wringing or twisting movements **2** : to gain with difficulty by or as if by force or violence **3 a** : to divert to an unnatural or improper use **b** : to deflect or change from a true or normal bearing, significance, or interpretation : DISTORT — **wrest·er** *n*

2**wrest** *n* **1** : the action of wresting : WRENCH **2** : a key or wrench formerly used for turning wrest pins

1**wres·tle** \'res-əl, 'ras-\ *vb* **wres·tling** \-(ə-)liŋ\ [ME *wrastlen, wrestlen*, fr. OE *wrǣstlian*, freq. of *wrǣstan*] *vi* **1** : to contend by grappling with and striving to trip or throw down an opponent **2** : to combat or overcome an opposing tendency or force **3** : to engage in deep thought, consideration, or debate **4** : to strive earnestly in or as if in a violent or determined struggle ~ *vt* **1 a** : to engage in (a match, bout, or fall) in wrestling **b** : to wrestle with ⟨~ an alligator⟩ **2** : to move by or as if by force — **wres·tler** \'res-lər, 'ras-\ *n*

2**wrestle** *n* : the action or an instance of wrestling : STRUGGLE; *specif* : a wrestling bout

wres·tling \'res-liŋ, 'ras-\ *n* : the sport of hand-to-hand combat between two unarmed contestants who seek to throw each other

wrest pin *n* [2*wrest*] : a pin in a stringed instrument (as a harp or piano) around which the ends of the strings are coiled and by which the instrument is tuned

wretch \'rech\ *n* [ME *wrecche*, fr. OE *wrecca*, outcast, exile; akin to OE *wrecan* to drive, drive out — more at WREAK] **1** : a miserable person : one who is profoundly unhappy or in great misfortune **2** : a base, despicable, or vile person

wretch·ed \'rech-əd\ *adj* [irreg. fr. *wretch*] **1** : deeply afflicted, dejected, or distressed : MISERABLE **2** : WOEFUL, GRIEVOUS ⟨a ~ accident⟩ **3** : hatefully contemptible : DESPICABLE **4** : very poor in quality or ability : INFERIOR — **wretch·ed·ly** *adv* — **wretch·ed·ness** *n*

1**wrig·gle** \'rig-əl\ *vb* **wrig·gling** \-(ə-)liŋ\ [ME *wrigglen*, fr. or akin to MLG *wriggeln* to wriggle; akin to OE *wrigian* to turn — more at WRY] *vi* **1** : to move the body or a bodily part to and fro with short writhing motions like a worm : SQUIRM **2** : to move or advance by twisting and turning **3** : to extricate or insinuate oneself or reach a goal by maneuvering, equivocation, or ingratiation ~ *vt* **1** : to cause to move in short quick contortions **2** : to introduce, insinuate, or bring into a state or place by or as if by wriggling — **wrig·gly** \-(ə-)lē\ *adj*

2**wriggle** *n* **1** : a short or quick writhing motion or contortion **2** : a formation or marking of sinuous design

wrig·gler \'rig-(ə-)lər\ *n* : one that wriggles; *specif* : WIGGLER 2

wright \'rīt\ *n* [ME, fr. OE *wyrhta, wryhta* worker, maker; akin to OE *weorc* work] : a workman in wood : CARPENTER — usu. used in combination ⟨ship*wright*⟩

wring \'riŋ\ *vb* **wrung** \'rəŋ\ **wring·ing** \'riŋ-iŋ\ [ME *wringen*, fr. OE *wringan;* akin to OHG *ringan* to struggle, OE *wyrgan* to strangle — more at WORRY] *vt* **1** : to squeeze or twist esp. so as to make dry or to extract moisture or liquid **2 a** : to extract or obtain by or as if by twisting and compressing **b** : to exact or acquire by violence or coercion **3 a** : to twist so as to strain or sprain into a distorted shape : CONTORT **b** : to twist together (clasped hands) as a sign of anguish **4** : to place or insert by a twisting movement **5** : to affect painfully as if by wringing : TORMENT **6** : to shake (a hand) vigorously in greeting ~ *vi* : SQUIRM, WRITHE — **wring** *n*

wring·er \'riŋ-ər\ *n* : one that wrings; *specif* : a machine or device for pressing out liquid or moisture ⟨clothes ~⟩

1**wrin·kle** \'riŋ-kəl\ *n* [ME, back-formation fr. *wrinkled* twisted, winding, prob. fr. OE *gewrinclod*, pp. of *gewrinclian* to wind, fr. *ge-*, perfective prefix + *-wrinclian* (akin to *wrencan* to wrench) — more at CO-] **1** : a small ridge or furrow esp. when formed on a surface by the shrinking or contraction of a smooth substance : CREASE; *specif* : one in the skin esp. when due to age, care, or fatigue **2 a** : METHOD, TECHNIQUE; *also* : information about a method : HINT **b** : an innovation in method, technique, or equipment — **wrin·kly** \-k(ə-)lē\ *adj*

2**wrinkle** *vb* **wrin·kling** \-k(ə-)liŋ\ *vi* : to become marked with or contracted into wrinkles ~ *vt* : to contract into wrinkles : PUCKER

wrist \'rist\ *n* [ME, fr. OE; akin to OE *wrǣstan* to twist, wrest — more at WREST] **1** : the joint or the region of the joint between the human hand and the arm or a corresponding part on a lower animal **2** : the part of a garment or glove covering the wrist

wrist·band \'ris(t)-,band\ *n* **1** : the part of a sleeve covering the wrist **2** : a band encircling the wrist

wrist·let \'ris(t)-lət\ *n* : a band encircling the wrist; *specif* : a close-fitting knitted band worn for warmth

wrist·lock \'rist-,läk\ *n* : a wrestling hold in which one contestant is thrown or made helpless by a twisting grip on the wrist

wrist pin *n* : a stud or pin that forms a journal (as in a crosshead) for a connecting rod

wrist shot *n* : a short golf stroke played chiefly from the wrists and usu. with an iron

wrist·watch \'ris-,twäch\ *n* : a small watch attached to a bracelet or strap to fasten about the wrist

writ \'rit\ *n* [ME, fr. OE; akin to OE *wrītan* to write] **1** : something written : WRITING ⟨Holy *Writ*⟩ **2 a** : a formal written document; *specif* : a legal instrument in epistolary form issued under seal in the name of the English monarch **b** : an order or mandatory process in writing issued under seal in the name of the sovereign or of a court or judicial officer commanding the person to whom it is directed to perform or refrain from performing an act specified therein ⟨~ of detinue⟩ ⟨~ of entry⟩ ⟨~ of execution⟩ **c** : such a written order constituting a symbol of the power and authority of the issuer — usu. used with *run* ⟨outside the United States where . . . our ~ does not run —Dean Acheson⟩

writ·able \'rīt-ə-bəl\ *adj* : capable of being put in writing

write \'rīt\ *vb* **wrote** \'rōt\ **writ·ten** \'rit-ᵊn\ *also* **writ** \'rit\ **writ·ing** \'rīt-iŋ\ [ME *writen*, fr. OE *wrītan* to scratch, draw, inscribe; akin to OHG *rīzan* to tear, Gk *rhinē* file, rasp] *vt* **1 a** (1) : to draw or form by or as if by scoring or incising a surface (2) : to trace (a symbol or combination of symbols) by carving or scoring : INSCRIBE **b** (1) : to form or trace (a character or series of characters) on paper or other suitable material ⟨~ *7* instead of *9*⟩ (2) : to form or record (a meaningful sign) by a series of written characters ⟨~ the word *dog*⟩ (3) : to spell in writing **c** : to write characters upon ⟨~ a check⟩ **2 a** : to set down in writing **b** : to draw up : DRAFT **c** (1) : to be the author of : COMPOSE (2) : to compose in musical form ⟨~ a string quartet⟩ **d** : to express by means of words **e** : to communicate by letter ⟨~*s* that he is coming⟩ **f** : to use or exhibit (a specific script, language, or literary form or style) in writing ⟨~ Braille⟩ ⟨~*s* French with ease⟩ **g** : to write contracts or orders for; *esp* : UNDERWRITE **3** : to make a permanent impression of **4** : to communicate with in writing **5** : ORDAIN, FATE ⟨so be it, it is *written* —D.C.Peattie⟩ **6** : to make evident or obvious ⟨guilt *written* on his face⟩ **7** : to force, effect, introduce, or remove by writing **8** : to take part in or bring about (something worth recording) ~ *vi* **1 a** : to make significant characters or inscriptions; *also* : to permit or be adapted to writing **b** : to form or produce written letters, words, or sentences **2** : to compose, communicate by, or send a letter **3 a** : to produce a written work **b** : to compose music

write down *vt* **1** : to record in written form **2** : to record, regard, or reveal (as oneself) as being **3 a** : to depreciate, disparage, or injure by writing **b** : to reduce in status, rank, or value **c** : to play down in writing ~ *vi* : to write so as to appeal to a lower level of taste, comprehension, or intelligence

write-down \'rīt-,daůn\ *n* : a deliberate reduction in the book value of an asset

write in *vt* **1 a** : to insert in a document or text **b** (1) : to insert (a name not listed on a ballot or voting machine) in an appropriate space by writing or use of a printed sticker (2) : to cast (a vote) in this manner **2** : to write to a center of activity or source of supply

write-in campaign \'rīt-,in-\ *n* : a political campaign carried on to encourage writing in a candidate's name

write-in vote *n* : a vote cast by writing in the name of a candidate

write off *vt* **1** : to reduce the estimated value of : DEPRECIATE

2 : to take off the books : CANCEL

write-off \'rīt-,óf\ *n* **1** : an elimination from the books : CANCELLATION **2** : a reduction in book value : DEPRECIATION

write out *vt* **1** : to put in writing; *esp* : to put into a full and complete written form **2** : to exhaust the literary ability or resources of (oneself) by writing too much

writ·er \'rīt-ər\ *n* : one who practices writing as an occupation; *esp* : AUTHOR

writer's cramp *n* : a painful spasmodic cramp of muscles of the hand or fingers brought on by excessive writing

write up *vt* **1 a** : to write an account of : DESCRIBE **b** : to put into finished written form **2** : to bring up to date the writing of **3** : to set down an unduly high value for **4** : to write a summons for

write-up \'rīt-,əp\ *n* **1** : a written account; *esp* : a flattering article **2** : an increase in the book value or alleged assets of a corporation

writhe \'rīth\ *vb* [ME *writhen*, fr. OE *wrīthan;* akin to ON *rītha* to twist, OE *wrigian* to turn — more at WRY] *vt* **1 a** : to twist into coils or folds **b** : to twist so as to distort : WRENCH **c** : to twist (the body or a bodily part) in pain **2** : INTERTWINE ~ *vi* **1** : to move or proceed with twists and turns **2** : to become twisted in or as if in pain or struggling **3** : to suffer keenly from torment — **writhe** *n*

writh·en \'rīth-ən\ *adj* [ME, fr. OE, fr. pp. of *wrīthan*] *archaic* : WRITHED, CONTORTED

writ·ing \'rīt-iŋ\ *n* **1** : the act or process of one who writes: as **a** : the act or art of forming visible letters or characters; *specif* : HANDWRITING 1 **b** : the act or practice of literary, journalistic, or other composition **2** : something written: as **a** : letters or characters that serve as visible signs of ideas, words, or symbols **b** : a letter, note, or notice used to communicate or record **c** : a written composition **d** : INSCRIPTION **e** (1) : a written or printed paper or document (2) : an impression of characters on a substance (as paper) **3** : a style or form of composition **4** : the occupation of a writer; *esp* : the profession of authorship

writing desk *n* : a desk often with a sloping top for writing upon; *also* : a portable case containing writing materials and having a surface for writing

writing paper *n* : paper intended for writing upon with ink and usu. finished with a smooth surface and sized

Writ·ings \'rīt-iŋz\ *n pl* [trans. of LHeb *kĕthūbhīm*] : HAGIOGRAPHA

writ of assistance **1** : a writ issued to a law officer (as a sheriff or marshal) for the enforcement of a court order or decree **2** : a writ issued to a sheriff or other officer to aid in the search for smuggled or illegal goods

writ of certiorari : CERTIORARI

writ of election : a writ to order the holding of an election; *specif* : one used to call a special election to fill a vacancy in an elective office

writ of error : a writ directing a court usu. to remit the record of a legal action to an appellate court in order that some alleged error in the proceedings or in the judgment may be corrected if it exists

writ of extent : a writ formerly used to recover debts of record to the British crown and under which the lands, goods, and person of the debtor might all be seized to secure payment

writ of privilege : a writ to deliver a privileged person from custody when arrested in a civil suit

writ of prohibition : a writ issued by a superior tribunal and commanding an inferior court to cease from the prosecution of a suit depending before it

writ of protection : a judicial writ issued to a person required to attend court as party or juror and intended to secure him from arrest in coming, staying, and returning

writ of summons : a writ issued on behalf of the British monarch summoning a lord spiritual or a lord temporal to attend parliament

¹wrong \'róŋ\ *n* [ME, fr. OE *wrang*, fr. (assumed) *wrang*, adj., wrong] **1** : an injurious, unfair, or unjust act **2** : something wrong, immoral, or unethical; *esp* : principles, practices, or conduct contrary to justice, goodness, equity, or law **3** : action or conduct inflicting harm without due provocation or just cause **4** : the state, position, or fact of being or doing wrong: as **a** : the state of being mistaken or incorrect **b** : the state of being guilty **5** : a violation or invasion of the legal rights of another; *esp* : TORT **syn** see INJUSTICE

²wrong *adj* [ME, fr. (assumed) OE *wrang*, of Scand origin; akin to ON *rangr* awry, wrong; akin to OE *wringan* to wring] **1** : not according to the moral standard : SINFUL, IMMORAL **2** : not right

or proper according to a code, standard, or convention : IMPROPER **3** : not suitable or appropriate **4** : not according to truth or facts : INCORRECT **5** : not satisfactory (as in condition, results, health, or temper) **6** : of, relating to, or constituting the side of something that is usu. held to be opposite to the principal one, that is the one naturally or by design turned down, inward, or away, or that is the least finished or polished **syn** see FALSE — **wrong** *adv* — **wrong·ly** \'róŋ-lē\ *adv* — **wrong·ness** *n*

³wrong *vt* **wrong·ing** \'róŋ-iŋ\ **1 a** : to do wrong to : INJURE, HARM **b** : to treat disrespectfully or dishonorably : VIOLATE **2** : DEFRAUD **3** : DISHONOR, MALIGN — **wrong·er** \'róŋ-ər\ *n* **syn** WRONG, OPPRESS, PERSECUTE, AGGRIEVE mean to injure unjustly or outrageously. WRONG implies inflicting injury either unmerited or out of proportion to what one deserves; OPPRESS suggests inhumane imposing of burdens one cannot endure or exacting more than one can perform; PERSECUTE implies a relentless and unremitting subjection to annoyance or suffering; AGGRIEVE suggests a giving cause for protest by wronging, oppressing, or persecuting

wrong·do·er \'róŋ-'dü-ər\ *n* : one that does wrong; *esp* : a transgressor of moral laws

wrong·do·ing \-dü-iŋ\ *n* **1** : evil behavior or action **2** : an instance of doing wrong

wronged \'róŋd\ *adj* : suffering a wrong : HARMED

wrong font *n* : a character not of the right font

wrong·ful \'róŋ-fəl\ *adj* **1** : WRONG, UNJUST **2** : not rightful esp. in law **3** : ILLEGITIMATE — **wrong·ful·ly** \-fə-lē\ *adv* — **wrong·ful·ness** *n*

wrong·head·ed \'róŋ-'hed-əd\ *adj* : stubborn in adherence to wrong opinion or principles : PERVERSE — **wrong·head·ed·ly** *adv* — **wrong·head·ed·ness** *n*

wroth \'róth *also* 'rōth\ *adj* [ME, fr. OE *wrāth;* akin to OHG *reid* twisted, OE *wrīthan* to writhe] : highly incensed : WRATHFUL

wrought \'rót\ *adj* [ME, fr. pp. of *worken* to work] **1** : FASHIONED, FORMED **2** : elaborately embellished : ORNAMENTED **3** : MANUFACTURED **4** : beaten into shape by tools : HAMMERED — used of metals **5** : deeply stirred : EXCITED — often used with *up* ⟨gets easily ~ up over nothing⟩

wrought iron *n* : a commercial form of iron that is tough, malleable, and relatively soft, contains less than 0.3 percent and usu. less than 0.1 percent carbon, and carries 1 or 2 percent of slag mechanically mixed with it

wrung *past of* WRING

¹wry \'rī\ *vb* **wried; wry·ing** [ME *wrien*, fr. OE *wrigian* to turn; akin to MHG *rigel* kerchief wound around the head, Gk *rhoikos* crooked] : TWIST, WRITHE

²wry *adj* **wri·er** \'rī(-ə)r\ *or* **wri·est** \'rī-əst\ **1 a** : turned abnormally to one side ⟨~ neck⟩ **b** : TWISTED, CONTORTED **2** : made by distortion of the facial muscles ⟨a ~ smile⟩ **3** : marked by perversity : WRONGHEADED **4** : cleverly and often ironically or grimly humorous — **wry·ly** *adv* — **wry·ness** *n*

wry·neck \'rī-,nek\ *n* **1** : any of various woodpeckers (genus *Jynx*) that differ from the typical woodpeckers in having soft tail feathers and a peculiar manner of writhing the neck **2 a** : one that has a wry neck **b** : TORTICOLLIS

wud \'wüd\ *adj* [alter. of ¹*wood*] *chiefly Scot* : INSANE, MAD

wul·fen·ite \'wúl-fə-,nīt\ *n* [G *wulfenit*, fr. F. X. von *Wulfen* †1805 Austrian mineralogist] : a tetragonal mineral PbMoO₄ consisting of a compound of lead, molybdenum, and oxygen that is bright orange-yellow to red, gray, green, or brown usu. in tabular crystals

wun·der·kind \'vún-dər-,kint\ *n, pl* **wun·der·kin·der** \-,kin-dər\ [G, fr. *wunder* wonder + *kind* child] : a child prodigy

wurst \'wərst, 'wú(ə)rst\ *n* [G; akin to OHG *werran* to confuse — more at WAR] : SAUSAGE 1

wurzel *n* : MANGEL-WURZEL

Wy·an·dot \'wī-ən-,dät\ *n* : a member of a subgroup of the Hurons

wy·an·dotte \-,dät\ *n* [prob. fr. *Wyandotte* (Wyandot)] : any of an American breed of medium-sized domestic fowls derived largely from dark brahmas and spangled Hamburgs

Wyc·liff·ite \'wik-lə-,fīt\ *n* [John *Wycliffe* †1384 E religious reformer] : LOLLARD — **Wycliffite** *adj*

wye \'wī\ *n* : the letter *y*

wy·lie·coat \'wī-lē-,kōt, 'wil-ē-\ *n* [ME (Sc) *wyle cot*] **1** *chiefly Scot* : a warm undergarment **2** *chiefly Scot* : PETTICOAT

wy·vern \'wī-vərn\ *n* [alter. of ME *wyvere* viper, fr. ONF *wivre*, modif. of L *vipera*] : a fabulous animal usu. represented as a 2-legged winged creature resembling a dragon

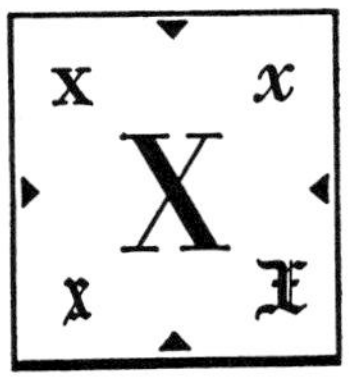

[1]**x** \'eks\ *n, often cap, often attrib* **1 a :** the 24th letter of the English alphabet **b :** a graphic representation of this letter **c :** a speech counterpart of orthographic *x* **2 :** TEN **3 :** a graphic device for reproducing the letter *x* **4 :** one designated *x* esp. as the 24th in order or class, the 23d in order or class when j is not used, the 21st in order or class when j, v, and w are not used, or the first in an order or class that includes x, y, and sometimes z **5 a :** an unknown quantity **b :** an arbitrarily chosen value from the domain of a variable **6 :** something shaped like or marked with the letter X

[2]**x** *vt* **x-ed** *also* **x'd** *or* **xed** \'ekst\ **x-ing** *or* **x'ing** \'ek-siŋ\ **1 :** to mark with an *x* **2 :** to cancel or obliterate with a series of *x's* — usu. used with *out*

xanth- *or* **xantho-** *comb form* [NL, fr. Gk, fr. *xanthos*] **1 :** yellow ⟨*xanth*ene⟩ **2 :** xanthic acid ⟨*xanth*ate⟩

xan·thate \'zan-ˌthāt\ *n* **:** a salt or ester of xanthic acid

xan·thene \-ˌthēn\ *n* **1 :** a white crystalline heterocyclic compound $C_{13}H_{10}O$; *also* **:** an isomer of this that is the parent of the colored forms of the xanthene dyes **2 :** any of various derivatives of xanthene

xanthene dye *n* **:** any of various brilliant fluorescent yellow to pink to bluish red dyes characterized by the presence of the xanthene nucleus

xan·thic \'zan(t)-thik\ *adj* [F *xanthique*, fr. Gk *xanthos*] **1 a :** of, relating to, or tending toward a yellow color **b** *of a flower* **:** colored with some tint of yellow **2 a :** of or relating to xanthin or xanthine **b :** of, relating to, or being any of various unstable thio acids and esp. a colorless oily acid $C_3H_6OS_2$

xan·thin \-thən\ *n* [ISV] **:** a carotenoid pigment soluble in alcohol **:** XANTHOPHYLL

xan·thine \'zan-ˌthēn\ *n* [ISV] **:** a feebly basic compound $C_5H_4N_4O_2$ that is found esp. in animal or plant tissue, is formed by hydrolysis of guanine, and yields uric acid on oxidation; *also* **:** any of various derivatives

Xan·thip·pe \zan-'t(h)ip-ē\ *or* **Xan·tip·pe** \-'tip-ē\ *n* [Gk *Xanthippē*, shrewish wife of Socrates] **:** an ill-tempered woman

xan·thoch·roi \zan-'thäk-rə-ˌwī, -'thäk-ˌrȯi\ *n pl* [NL, fr. *xanth-* + Gk *ōchroi*, nom. pl. masc. of *ōchros* pale] **:** white persons having light hair and fair skin — **xan·tho·chro·ic** \ˌzan(t)-thə-'krō-ik\ *adj* — **xan·tho·chroid** \'zan(t)-thə-ˌkrȯid, zan-'thäk-ˌrȯid\ *adj or n*

xan·tho·ma \zan-'thō-mə\ *n, pl* **xanthomas** *or* **xan·tho·ma·ta** \-mət-ə\ [NL] **:** a condition marked by irregular yellow patches or nodules on the skin — **xan·tho·ma·tous** \-'thäm-ət-əs, -'thōm-\ *adj*

xan·thone \'zan-ˌthōn\ *n* [ISV] **:** a ketone $C_{13}H_8O_2$ that is the parent of several natural yellow pigments

xan·tho·phyll \'zan(t)-thə-ˌfil\ *n* [F *xanthophylle*, fr. *xanth-* + *-phylle* -phyll] **:** any of several neutral yellow carotenoid pigments esp. that are oxygen derivatives of carotenes; *esp* **:** LUTEIN 1 — **xan·tho·phyl·lic** \ˌzan(t)-thə-'fil-ik\ *adj* — **xan·tho·phyl·lous** \-'fil-əs\ *adj*

Xa·ve·ri·an Brother \zā-ˌvir-ē-ən-, za-\ *n* **:** a member of a teaching congregation of lay brothers in the Roman Catholic Church founded in 1839 in Bruges

x-ax·is \'ek-ˌsak-səs\ *n* **1 :** the axis of abscissas in a plane Cartesian coordinate system **2 :** one of the three axes in a three-dimensional rectangular coordinate system

X chromosome *n* **:** a sex chromosome that carries factors for femaleness and usu. occurs paired in each female zygote and cell and single in each male zygote and cell — compare Y CHROMOSOME

X-dis·ease \'eks-diz-ˌēz\ *n* **:** any of various usu. virus diseases of obscure etiology and relationships; *esp* **:** a viral encephalitis of man first detected in Australia

xe·bec \'zē-ˌbek, zi-'\ *n* [prob. modif. of F *chebec*, fr. Ar *shabbāk*] **:** a usu. 3-masted Mediterranean sailing ship with long overhanging bow and stern

xen- *or* **xeno-** *comb form* [LL, fr. Gk, fr. *xenos* stranger, guest, host] **1 :** guest **:** foreigner ⟨*xeno*phobia⟩ **2 :** strange **:** foreign ⟨*xeno*lith⟩

xe·nia \'zē-nē-ə, -nyə\ *n* [NL, fr. Gk, hospitality, fr. *xenos* host] **:** the effect of genes introduced by a male nucleus on structures (as endosperm or the fruit of a seed plant) other than the embryo

xeno·di·ag·no·sis \ˌzen-ō-ˌdī-ig-'nō-səs\ *n* [NL] **:** the detection of a parasite (as of man) by feeding a suitable intermediate host (as an insect) on supposedly infected material (as blood) and later examining it for the parasite — **xeno·di·ag·nos·tic** \-'näs-tik\ *adj*

xeno·gen·e·sis \-'jen-ə-səs\ *n* [NL] **:** the fancied production of an organism altogether and permanently unlike the parent

xeno·lith \'zen-ᵊl-ˌith\ *n* **:** a fragment of a rock included in another rock — **xeno·lith·ic** \ˌzen-ᵊl-'ith-ik\ *adj*

xe·non \'zē-ˌnän, 'zen-ˌän\ *n* [Gk, neut. of *xenos* strange] **:** a heavy colorless inert gaseous element occurring in air as about one part in 20 million by volume and used in thyratrons and specialized electric lamps — see ELEMENT table

xeno·phobe \'zen-ə-ˌfōb\ *n* [ISV] **:** one unduly fearful of what is foreign and esp. of people of foreign origin — **xeno·pho·bic** \ˌzen-ə-'fō-bik, -'fäb-ik\ *adj*

xeno·pho·bia \ˌzen-ə-'fō-bē-ə\ *n* [NL] **:** fear and hatred of strangers or foreigners or of anything that is strange or foreign

xeno·plas·tic \ˌzen-ə-'plas-tik\ *adj* **:** involving or occurring between distantly related individuals — **xeno·plas·ti·cal·ly** \-ti-k(ə-)lē\ *adv*

xer- *or* **xero-** *comb form* [LL, fr. Gk *xēr-*, *xēro-*, fr. *xēros* — more at SERENE] **:** dry ⟨*xer*ic⟩ ⟨*xero*phyte⟩

xe·rarch \'zi(ə)r-ˌärk\ *adj, of an ecological succession* **:** developing in a dry place

xe·ric \'zi(ə)r-ik\ *adj* **1 :** low or deficient in available moisture for the support of life **2 :** XEROPHYTIC — **xe·ri·cal·ly** \'zir-i-k(ə-)lē\ *adv*

xe·ro·graph·ic \ˌzir-ə-'graf-ik\ *adj* **:** relating to, used in, or prepared by xerography

xe·rog·ra·phy \zə-'räg-rə-fē, zi(ə)r-'äg-\ *n* [ISV] **:** the formation of pictures or copies of graphic matter by the action of light on an electrically charged photoconductive insulating surface in which the latent image usu. is developed with powders

xe·roph·i·lous \zə-'räf-ə-ləs, zi(ə)r-'äf-\ *or* **xe·ro·phile** \'zir-ə-ˌfīl\ *adj* **:** thriving in or tolerant or characteristic of xeric environment — **xe·roph·i·ly** \zə-'räf-ə-lē, zi(ə)r-'äf-\ *n*

xe·roph·thal·mia \ˌzir-ˌäf-'thal-mē-ə, -ˌäp-'thal-\ *n* [LL, fr. Gk *xērophthalmia*, fr. *xēr-* xer- + *ophthalmia*] **:** a dry thickened lusterless condition of the eyeball resulting from a severe systemic deficiency of vitamin A — **xe·roph·thal·mic** \-mik\ *adj*

xe·ro·phyte \'zir-ə-ˌfīt\ *n* **:** a plant structurally adapted for life and growth with a limited water supply esp. by means of mechanisms that limit transpiration or that provide for the storage of water — **xe·ro·phyt·ic** \ˌzir-ə-'fit-ik\ *adj* — **xe·ro·phyt·i·cal·ly** \-i-k(ə-)lē\ *adv* — **xe·ro·phyt·ism** \'zir-ə-ˌfīt-ˌiz-əm\ *n*

xe·ro·ther·mic \ˌzir-ə-'thər-mik\ *adj* **1 :** characterized by heat and dryness **2 :** adapted to or thriving in a hot dry environment

x height *n* **:** the distance between the top and bottom of a printed letter (as *x*, a, r, w) without an ascender or descender

xi \'zī, 'ksī\ *n* [Gk *xei*] **:** the fourteenth letter of the Greek alphabet — symbol Ξ or ξ

xiphi·ster·num \ˌzif-i-'stər-nəm\ *n, pl* **xiphi·ster·na** \-nə\ [NL, fr. Gk *xiphos* sword + NL *sternum*] **:** the posterior segment of the sternum — called also *xiphoid process*

[1]**xiph·oid** \'zif-ˌȯid\ *adj* [NL *xiphoides*, fr. Gk *xiphoeidēs*, fr. *xiphos*] **1 :** shaped like a sword **:** ENSIFORM **2 :** of, relating to, or being the xiphisternum

[2]**xiphoid** *n* **:** XIPHISTERNUM

xiph·os·uran \ˌzif-ə-'su̇r-ən\ *n* [deriv. of Gk *xiphos* + *oura* tail — more at SQUIRREL] **:** any of an order (Xiphosura) of arthropods comprising the king crabs and extinct related forms — **xiphosuran** *adj* — **xiph·os·ure** \'zif-ə-ˌsu̇(ə)r\ *n* — **xiph·os·urous** \ˌzif-ə-'su̇r-əs\ *adj*

Xmas \'kris-məs *also* 'ek-sməs\ *n* [*x* (symbol for *Christ*) + *-mas* (in *Christmas*)] **:** CHRISTMAS

X-radiation *n* **1 :** exposure to X rays — called also *X-irradiation* **2 :** radiation composed of X rays

X ray \'eks-ˌrā\ *n* **1 :** any of the electromagnetic radiations of the same nature as visible radiation but of an extremely short wavelength less than 100 angstroms that is produced by bombarding a metallic target with fast electrons in vacuum or by transition of atoms to lower energy states and that has the properties of ionizing a gas upon passage through it, of penetrating various thicknesses of all solids, of producing secondary radiations by impinging on material bodies, of acting on photographic films and plates as light does, and of causing fluorescent screens to emit light **2 :** a photograph obtained by use of X rays

X-ray *vt, often cap X* **:** to examine, treat, or photograph with X rays

Xray — a communications code word for the letter *x*

X-ray photograph *n* **:** a shadow picture made with X rays

X-ray therapy *n* **:** medical treatment (as of a cancer) by controlled application of X rays

X-ray tube *n* **:** a vacuum tube in which a concentrated stream of electrons strikes a metal target and produces X rays

xyl- *or* **xylo-** *comb form* [L, fr. Gk, fr. *xylon*] **1 :** wood ⟨*xylo*phone⟩ **2 :** xylene ⟨*xyl*ic⟩

xy·lan \'zī-ˌlan\ *n* [ISV] **:** a yellow gummy pentosan present in plant cell walls and woody tissue

xy·lem \'zī-ləm, -ˌlem\ *n* [G, fr. Gk *xylon*] **:** a complex tissue in the vascular system of higher plants consisting of vessels, tracheids, or both usu. together with wood fibers and parenchyma cells, functioning chiefly in conduction but also in support and storage, and typically constituting the woody element (as of a plant stem) — compare PHLOEM

xylem ray *or* **xy·la·ry ray** \ˌzī-lə-rē-\ *n* **:** a vascular ray or portion of a vascular ray located in xylem — called also *wood ray;* compare PHLOEM RAY

xy·lene \'zī-ˌlēn\ *n* [ISV] **:** any of three toxic flammable oily isomeric aromatic hydrocarbons C_8H_{10} that are di-methyl homologues of benzene and are obtained from wood tar, coal tar, coke-oven gas, or petroleum distillates; *also* **:** a mixture of xylenes and ethyl-benzene used chiefly as a solvent

xy·lic acid \ˌzī-lik-, ˌzil-ik-\ *n* [ISV] **:** any of six isomeric crystalline carboxylic acids $C_9H_{10}O_2$ derived from xylene

xy·li·dine \'zī-lə-ˌdēn, 'zil-ə-\ *n* [ISV] **:** any or a mixture of six toxic liquid or low-melting crystalline isomeric amino derivatives $C_8H_{11}N$ of the xylenes used chiefly as intermediates for azo dyes and in organic synthesis

xy·lo·graph \'zī-lə-ˌgraf\ *n* **:** a product of xylography — **xy·log·ra·pher** \zī-'läg-rə-fər\ *n* — **xy·lo·graph·ic** \ˌzī-lə-'graf-ik\ *adj* — **xy·lo·graph·i·cal** \-i-kəl\ *adj*

xy·log·ra·phy \zī-'läg-rə-fē\ *n* [F *xylographie*, fr. *xyl-* + *-graphie* -graphy] **:** the art of engraving on wood or of taking impressions from engravings so made

xy·lol \'zī-ˌlȯl, -ˌlōl\ *n* [ISV] **:** XYLENE

xy·loph·a·gous \zī-'läf-ə-gəs\ *adj* [Gk *xylophagos*, fr. *xyl-* + *-phagos* -phagous] **:** feeding on or in wood

xy·loph·i·lous \-'läf-ə-ləs\ *adj* **:** growing or living in or on wood

xy·lo·phone \'zī-lə-ˌfōn, 'zil-ə-\ *n* **:** a percussion instrument consisting of a series of wooden bars graduated in length to sound the musical scale, supported on belts of straw or felt, and sounded by striking with two small wooden hammers — **xy·lo·phon·ist** \-ˌfō-nəst\ *n*

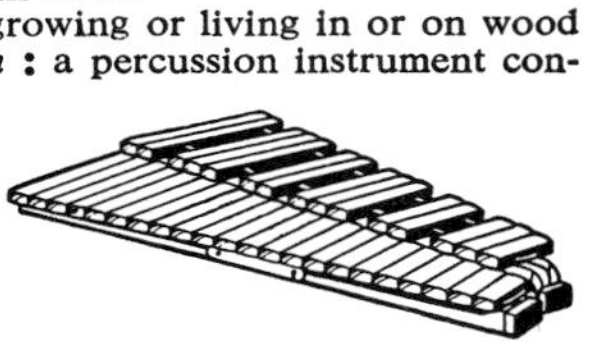

xylophone

xy·lose \'zī-ˌlōs, -ˌlōz\ *n* [ISV] **:** a crystalline aldose sugar $C_5H_{10}O_5$ not fermentable with ordinary yeasts that is found esp. as a constituent of xylans from which it is obtained by hydrolysis

xy·lo·tom·ic \ˌzī-lə-'täm-ik\ *adj* **:** of or relating to xylotomy — **xy·lo·tom·i·cal** \-i-kəl\ *adj*

xy·lot·o·mous \zī-'lät-ə-məs\ *adj* **:** capable of boring or cutting wood — used of an insect

xy·lot·o·my \-mē\ *n* **:** the art of preparing sections of wood for microscopic examination

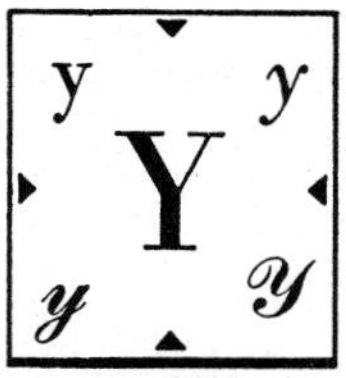

y \'wī\ *n, often cap, often attrib* **1 a :** the 25th letter of the English alphabet **b :** a graphic representation of this letter **c :** a speech counterpart of orthographic *y* **2 :** a graphic device for reproducing the letter *y* **3 :** one designated *y* esp. as the 25th in order or class, the 24th in order or class when j is not used, the 22nd in order or class when j, v, and w are not used, or the second in order or class when x is made the first **4 :** an arbitrarily chosen value from the domain of a variable **5 :** something shaped like the letter Y

y- *prefix* [ME *y-, i-*, fr. OE *ge-*, perfective prefix — more at CO-] — used in a few esp. archaic past participles and occas. in other verb forms coined by analogy with such past participles ⟨*y*pointing⟩

[1]**-y** *also* **-ey** \ē\ *adj suffix* [ME, fr. OE *-ig*; akin to OHG *-īg* -y, L *-icus*, Gk *-ikos*, Skt *-ika*] **1 a :** characterized by **:** full of ⟨blossom*y*⟩ ⟨dirt*y*⟩ ⟨mudd*y*⟩ ⟨clay*ey*⟩ **b :** having the character of **:** composed of ⟨ic*y*⟩ ⟨wax*y*⟩ **c :** like **:** like that of ⟨hom*ey*⟩ ⟨wintr*y*⟩ — often with a disparaging connotation ⟨stag*y*⟩ **d :** devoted to **:** addicted to **:** enthusiastic over ⟨hors*y*⟩ **2 a :** tending or inclined to ⟨sleep*y*⟩ ⟨chatt*y*⟩ **b :** giving occasion for (specified) action ⟨tear*y*⟩ **c :** performing (specified) action ⟨curl*y*⟩ **3 a :** somewhat **:** rather **:** -ISH ⟨chill*y*⟩ **b :** having (such) characteristics to a marked degree or in an affected or superficial way ⟨French*y*⟩

[2]**-y** \ē\ *n suffix, pl* **-ies** [ME *-ie*, fr. OF, fr. L *-ia*, fr. Gk *-ia, -eia*] **1 :** state **:** condition **:** quality ⟨beggar*y*⟩ **2 :** activity, place of business, or goods dealt with ⟨chandler*y*⟩ ⟨laundr*y*⟩ **3 :** whole body or group ⟨soldier*y*⟩

[3]**-y** *n suffix, pl* **-ies** [ME *-ie*, fr. AF, fr. L *-ium*] **:** instance of a (specified) action ⟨entreat*y*⟩ ⟨inquir*y*⟩

[4]**-y** — see -IE

[1]**yacht** \'yät\ *n* [obs. D *yaght*, fr. MLG *jacht*, short for *jachtschiff*, lit., hunting ship] **:** any of various relatively small sailing or mechanically driven ships that characteristically have a sharp prow and graceful lines and are ordinarily used for pleasure cruising or racing

[2]**yacht** *vi* **:** to race or cruise in a yacht

yacht·ing *n* **:** the action, fact, or pastime of racing or cruising in a yacht

yacht rope *n* **:** rope of the best quality usu. made from fine soft white Manila hemp

yachts·man \'yät-smən\ *n* **:** a person who owns or sails a yacht

yack *slang var of* [2]YAK, [3]YAK

ya·gi \'yäg-ē, 'yag-\ *n* [Hidetsugu *Yagi b* 1886 Jap engineer] **:** a highly directional and selective shortwave antenna consisting of a horizontal conductor of one or two dipoles connected with the receiver or transmitter and of a set of nearly equal insulated dipoles parallel to and on a level with the horizontal conductor

ya·hoo \'yā-(,)hü, 'yä-\ *n* **1** *cap* **:** a member of a race of brutes in Swift's *Gulliver's Travels* who have the form and all the vices of man **2 :** an uncouth or rowdy person

Yah·weh \'yä-(,)wā, -(,)vā\ *also* **Yah·veh** *or* **Yah·vè** \-(,)vā\ *n* [Heb *Yahweh*] **:** the God of the Hebrews — compare TETRAGRAMMATON

Yah·wism \-,wiz-əm, -,viz-\ *n* **:** the worship of Yahweh among the ancient Hebrews

Yah·wis·tic \yä-'wis-tik, -'vis-\ *adj* **1 :** characterized by the use of *Yahweh* as the name of God **2 :** of or relating to Yahwism

[1]**yak** \'yak\ *n, pl* **yaks** *also* **yak** [Tibetan *gyak*] **:** a large long-haired wild or domesticated ox (*Bos grunniens*) of Tibet and adjacent elevated parts of Central Asia

[2]**yak** *n* [prob. imit.] **:** persistent or voluble talk

[3]**yak** *vi* **yakked; yakking :** to talk persistently **:** CHATTER

[4]**yak** \'yäk, 'yak\ *n* [imit.] **1** *slang* **:** LAUGH **2** *slang* **:** JOKE, GAG

Yak·i·ma \'yak-ə-,mȯ\ *n, pl* **Yakima** *or* **Yakimas 1 a :** a Shahaptian people or group of peoples of the lower Yakima river valley, south central Washington **b :** a member of this people **2 :** the language of the Yakima people

yam \'yam\ *n* [earlier *iname*, fr. Pg *inhame* & Sp *ñame*] **1 :** the edible starchy tuberous root of various plants (genus *Dioscorea* of the family Dioscoreaceae) used as a staple food in tropical areas; *also* **:** a plant producing these **2 :** a moist-fleshed and usu. orange-fleshed sweet potato

ya·men \'yäm-ən\ *n* [Chin (Pek) *ya*[2]*-men*[2]] **:** the headquarters or residence of a Chinese government official or department

yam·mer \'yam-ər\ *vi* **yam·mer·ing** \-(ə-)riŋ\ [alter. of ME *yomeren* to murmur, be sad, fr. OE *gēomrian;* akin to OHG *jāmarōn* to be sad] **1 :** WHIMPER **2 :** CHATTER — **yammer** *n*

yang \'yäŋ\ *n* [Chin (Pek) *yang*[2]] **:** the masculine active principle (as of light, heat, or dryness) in nature that in Chinese cosmology combines with yin to produce all that comes to be

[1]**yank** \'yaŋk\ *n* [origin unknown] **:** a strong sudden pull **:** JERK

[2]**yank** *vt* **:** to pull or extract with a quick vigorous movement ~ *vi* **:** to pull on something with a quick vigorous movement

Yank \'yaŋk\ *n* **:** YANKEE

[1]**Yan·kee** \'yaŋ-kē\ *n, often attrib* [origin unknown] **1 a :** a native or inhabitant of New England **b :** a native or inhabitant of the northern U. S. **2 :** a native or inhabitant of the U. S. — **Yan·kee·dom** \-kēd-əm\ *n* — **Yan·kee·ism** \-kē-,iz-əm\ *n*

[2]**Yankee** — a communications code word for the letter *y*

Yan·kee-Doo·dle \,yaŋ-kē-'düd-ᵊl\ *n* [*Yankee Doodle*, popular song during the American Revolution] **:** YANKEE

yan·qui \'yäŋ-kē\ *n, often cap* [Sp, fr. E [1]*Yankee*] **:** a citizen of the U.S. as distinguished from a Latin American

[1]**yap** \'yap\ *vi* **yapped; yap·ping** [imit.] **1 :** to bark snappishly **:** YELP **2 :** CHATTER, SCOLD

[2]**yap** *n* **1 a :** a snappish bark **:** YELP **b :** CHATTER **2 :** BUMPKIN **3** *slang* **:** MOUTH

ya·pock *or* **ya·pok** \yə-'päk\ *n* [*Oyapock, Oyapok*, river in So. America] **:** a gray and white So. American aquatic opossum (*Chironectes minimus*) with webbed hind feet

Yar·bor·ough \'yär-,bər-ə, -,bə-rə, -b(ə-)rə\ *n* [2d Earl of *Yarborough* †1897 E nobleman said to have bet a thousand to one against the dealing of such a hand] **:** a hand in bridge or whist containing no card higher than a nine

[1]**yard** \'yärd\ *n* [ME *yarde*, fr. OE *gierd* twig, measure, yard; akin to OHG *gart* stick, L *hasta* spear] **1 :** any of various units of measure: as **a :** a unit of length equal in the U.S. to 0.9144 meter — see MEASURE table **b :** a unit of volume equal to a cubic yard **2 :** a long spar tapered toward the ends to support and spread the head of a square sail, lateen, or lugsail

[2]**yard** *n, often attrib* [ME, fr. OE *geard* enclosure, yard; akin to OHG *gart* enclosure, L *hortus* garden] **1 a :** a small usu. walled area open to the sky and adjacent to a building **:** COURT **b :** the grounds of a building or group of buildings **2 a :** an enclosure for livestock (as poultry) **b** (1) **:** an area set aside for a particular business or activity (2) **:** an assembly or storage area **c :** a system of tracks for storage and maintenance of cars and making up trains **3 :** a locality in a forest where deer herd in winter

[3]**yard** *vt* **1 :** to drive into or confine in a restricted area **:** HERD, PEN **2 :** to deliver to or store in a yard ~ *vi* **:** to congregate in or as if in a yard

[1]**yard·age** \'yärd-ij\ *n* **1 :** the use of a livestock enclosure for animals in transit provided by a railroad at a station **2 :** a charge made by a railroad for the use of a livestock enclosure

[2]**yardage** *n* **:** an aggregate number of yards; *also* **:** the length, extent, or volume of something as measured in yards

yard·arm \'yär-,därm\ *n* **:** either end of the yard of a square-rigged ship

yard·bird \'yärd-,bərd\ *n* **1 :** a soldier assigned to a menial task **2 :** an untrained or inept enlisted man

yard goods *n pl* **:** fabrics sold by the yard **:** PIECE GOODS

yard grass *n* **:** a coarse annual grass (*Eleusine indica*) with digitate spikes that is widely distributed as a weed

yard·man \'yärd-mən, -,man\ *n* **:** a man employed in or about a yard; *specif* **:** a railroad man employed in yard service

yard·mas·ter \-,mas-tər\ *n* **:** the man in charge of operations in a railroad yard

yard·stick \'yärd-,stik\ *n* **1 a :** a graduated measuring stick three feet long **b :** a standard basis of calculation **2 :** a standard for making a critical judgment **:** CRITERION **syn** see STANDARD

yare \'ya(ə)r, 'ye(ə)r, 'yär\ *adj* [ME, fr. OE *gearu;* akin to OHG *garo* ready] **1** *archaic* **:** set for action **:** READY **2** *or* **yar** \'yär\ **a :** NIMBLE, LIVELY **b** *of a ship* **:** easily handled **:** MANEUVERABLE — **yare** *adv* — **yare·ly** *adv, archaic*

yar·mul·ke *or* **yar·mel·ke** \'yär-məl-kə, 'yäm-əl-\ *n* [Yiddish, fr. Ukrainian & Pol *yarmulka* skullcap] **:** a skullcap worn esp. by Orthodox and Conservative Jewish males in the synagogue and the home

[1]**yarn** \'yärn\ *n* [ME, fr. OE *gearn;* akin to OHG *garn* yarn, Gk *chordē* string, L *hernia* rupture] **1 a :** a continuous often plied strand composed of fibers or filaments, and used in weaving and knitting to form cloth **b :** a similar strand of metal, glass, asbestos, paper, or plastic **c :** THREAD **d :** ROPE YARN **2 :** a narrative of adventures **:** STORY; *esp* **:** a tall tale

[2]**yarn** *vi* **:** to tell a yarn

yarn-dye \-,dī\ *vt* **:** to dye before weaving or knitting

yar·row \'yar-(,)ō, -ə(-w)\ *n* [ME *yarowe*, fr. OE *gearwe;* akin to OHG *garwa* yarrow] **:** a widely naturalized strong-scented Eurasian composite herb (*Achillea millefolium*) with finely dissected leaves and small usu. white corymbose flowers; *also* **:** any of several congeneric plants

yat·a·ghan \'yat-ə-,gan, 'yat-i-gən\ *n* [Turk *yatağan*] **:** a long knife or short saber common among Muslims that is made without a cross guard and usu. with a double curve to the edge and a nearly straight back

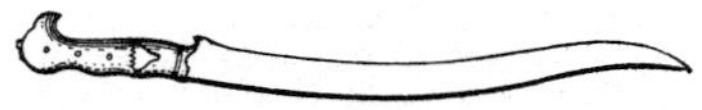

yataghan

yauld \'yȯl(d)\ *adj* [origin unknown] *chiefly Scot* **:** VIGOROUS, ENERGETIC

yau·pon \'yü-,pän *also* 'yō-, 'yȯ-\ *n* [Catawba *yopún*, dim. of *yop* tree] **:** a holly (*Ilex vomitoria*) of the southern U.S. with smooth elliptical leaves used as a substitute for tea

[1]**yaw** \'yȯ\ *n* [origin unknown] **:** the action of yawing; *also* **:** the extent of the movement in yawing

[2]**yaw** *vi* **1 a** *of a ship* **:** to deviate erratically from a course (as when struck by a heavy sea) **b** *of an airplane or projectile* **:** to turn by angular motion about the vertical axis **2 :** to become deflected **:** SWERVE

yawl \'yȯl\ *n* [LG *jolle*] **1 :** a ship's small boat **:** JOLLY BOAT **2 :** a fore-and-aft rigged sailboat carrying a mainsail and one or more jibs with a mizzenmast far aft

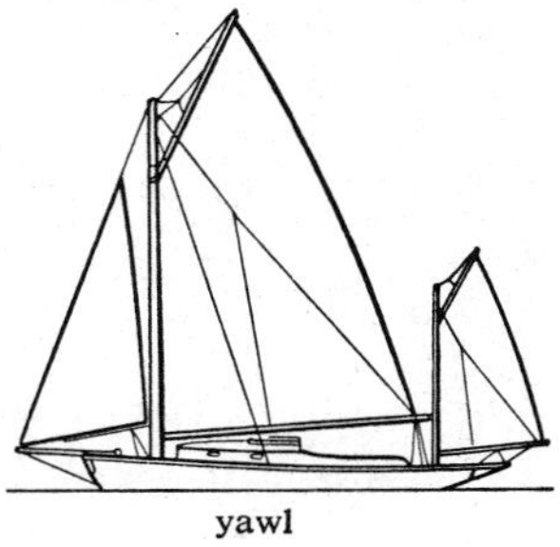

yawl

[1]**yawn** \'yȯn, 'yän\ *vb* [ME *yenen, yanen*, fr. OE *ginian;* akin to OHG *ginēn* to yawn, L *hiare*, Gk *chainein*] *vi* **1 :** to open wide **:** GAPE **2 :** to open the mouth wide usu. as an involuntary reaction to fatigue or boredom ~ *vt* **:** to utter with a yawn — **yawn·er** *n*

[2]**yawn** *n* **1 :** GAP, CAVITY **2 :** a deep usu. involuntary intake of breath through the wide open mouth

yawn·ing *adj* **1 :** wide open **:** CAVERNOUS ⟨a ~ hole⟩ **2 :** showing fatigue or boredom by yawns ⟨a ~ congregation⟩

[1]**yawp** *or* **yaup** \'yȯp\ *vi* [ME *yolpen*] **1 :** to make a raucous noise **:** SQUAWK **2 :** CLAMOR, COMPLAIN — **yawp·er** *n*

[2]**yawp** *also* **yaup** *n* **1 :** a raucous noise **:** SQUAWK **2 :** something suggestive of a raucous noise; *specif.* **:** rough vigorous language ⟨sound my barbaric ~ over the roofs of the world —Walt Whitman⟩

yawp·ing *n* **:** a strident utterance

yaws \'yȯz\ *n pl but sing or pl in constr* [of Cariban origin; akin to Calinago *yáya* yaws] **:** an infectious contagious tropical disease caused by a spirochete (*Treponema pertenue*) and marked by ulcerating lesions with later bone involvement — called also *fram·be·sia* \fram-'bē-zh(ē-)ə\

y-ax·is \'wī-,ak-səs\ *n* **1 :** the axis of ordinates in a plane Cartesian

coordinate system **2 :** one of the three axes in a three-dimensional rectangular coordinate system

Y chromosome *n* **:** a sex chromosome occurring in male zygotes and cells and formerly held to carry factors for maleness that are prob. actually in autosomes — compare X CHROMOSOME

ycleped *or* **yclept** [ME, fr. OE *geclipod,* pp. of *clipian* to cry out, name] *past part of* CLEPE

1**ye** \(')yē\ *pron* [ME, fr. OE *gē;* akin to OHG *ir* you — more at YOU] **:** YOU 1 — used orig. only as a plural pronoun of the second person in the nominative case

2**ye** \yē, yə, *or like* 1THE\ *definite article* [alter. of OE *þē* the; fr. the use by early printers of the letter *y* to represent *þ* (*th*) of manuscripts] *archaic* **:** THE ⟨*Ye* olde Gifte Shoppe⟩

1**yea** \'yā\ *adv* [ME *ye, ya,* fr. OE *gēa;* akin to OHG *jā* yes] **1 :** YES — used in oral voting **2** — used as a function word to introduce a more explicit or emphatic phrase

2**yea** *n* **1 :** AFFIRMATION, ASSENT **2 a :** an affirmative vote **b :** a person casting a yea vote

yean \'(y)ēn\ *vi* [ME *yenen,* fr. (assumed) OE *geēanian,* fr. OE *ge-,* perfective prefix + *ēanian* to yean; akin to L *agnus* lamb, Gk *amnos*] **:** to bring forth young — used of a sheep or goat

yean·ling \-liŋ, -lən\ *n* **:** LAMB, KID 1a

year \'yi(ə)r\ *n* [ME *yere,* fr. OE *gēar;* akin to OHG *jār* year, Gk *hōros* year, *hōra* season, hour, L *ire* to go — more at ISSUE] **1 a :** the period of about 365¼ solar days required for one revolution of the earth around the sun **b :** the time required for the apparent sun to return to an arbitrary fixed or moving reference point in the sky **2 a :** a cycle in the Gregorian calendar of 365 or 366 days divided into 12 months beginning with January and ending with December **b :** a period of time equal to one year of the Gregorian calendar but beginning at a different time **3 :** a calendar year specified usu. by a number **4** *pl* **:** a time or era having a special significance **5** *pl* **:** AGE; *also* **:** the final stage of the normal life span **6 :** a period of time (as the usu. nine-month period in which a school is in session) other than a calendar year

year·book \-,bu̇k\ *n* **:** a book published yearly as a report or summary of the statistics or facts **:** ANNUAL

year·ling \'yi(ə)r-liŋ, 'yər-lən\ *n* **:** one that is a year old; as **a :** an animal one year old or in the second year of its age **b :** a racehorse between January 1st of the year after the year in which it was foaled and the next January 1st — **yearling** *adj*

year·long \'yi(ə)r-'lȯŋ\ *adj* **:** lasting through a year

1**year·ly** \'yi(ə)r-lē\ *adj* **1 :** reckoned by the year **2 :** occurring, appearing, made, done, or acted upon every year or once a year **:** ANNUAL

2**yearly** *adv* **:** every year **:** ANNUALLY

Yearly Meeting *n* **:** an organization uniting several Quarterly Meetings of the Society of Friends

yearn \'yərn\ *vi* [ME *yernen,* fr. OE *giernan;* akin to OHG *gerōn* to desire, L *hortari* to urge, encourage, Gk *chairein* to rejoice] **1 :** to feel a longing or craving **2 :** to feel tenderness or compassion **syn** see LONG — **yearn·er** *n*

year of grace : a year of the Christian era ⟨the *year of grace* 1962⟩

year-round \'yi(ə)r-'rau̇nd, 'yiə-'rau̇nd\ *adj* **:** effective, employed, or operating for the full year **:** not seasonal ⟨a ~ resort⟩

1**yeast** \'yēst\ *n* [ME *yest,* fr. OE *gist;* akin to MHG *jest* foam, Gk *zein* to boil] **1 a :** a yellowish surface froth or sediment that occurs esp. in saccharine liquids (as fruit juices) in which it promotes alcoholic fermentation, consists largely of cells of a fungus (family Saccharomycetaceae) and is used esp. in the making of alcoholic liquors and as a leaven in baking **b :** a commercial product containing yeast plants in a moist or dry medium **c** (1) **:** a minute fungus (esp. *Saccharomyces cerevisiae*) that is present and functionally active in yeast, usu. has little or no mycelium, and reproduces by budding (2) **:** any of various similar fungi (esp. orders Endomycetales and Moniliales) **2 :** the foam or spume of waves **3 :** something that causes ferment or activity

2**yeast** *vi* **:** FERMENT, FROTH

yeasty \'yē-stē\ *adj* **1 :** of, relating to, or resembling yeast **2 a :** IMMATURE, UNSETTLED **b :** marked by change **c :** EXUBERANT **d :** FRIVOLOUS

yegg \'yeg\ *n* [origin unknown] **:** SAFECRACKER, ROBBER

1**yell** \'yel\ *vb* [ME *yellen,* fr. OE *giellan;* akin to OHG *gellan* to yell, OE *galan* to sing] *vi* **1 :** to utter a loud cry, scream, or shout **2 :** to give a cheer usu. in unison ~ *vt* **:** to utter or declare with or as if with a yell **:** SHOUT — **yell·er** *n*

2**yell** *n* **1 :** SCREAM, SHOUT **2 :** a usu. rhythmic cheer used esp. in schools or colleges to encourage athletic teams

1**yel·low** \'yel-(,)ō, -ə(-w)\ *adj* [ME *yelwe, yelow,* fr. OE *geolu;* akin to OHG *gelo* yellow, L *helvus* light bay, Gk *chlōros* greenish yellow, Skt *hari* yellowish] **1 a :** of the color yellow **b :** become yellowish through age, disease, or discoloration **:** SALLOW **c :** having a yellow complexion or skin **2 a :** featuring sensational or scandalous items or ordinary news sensationally distorted ⟨~ journalism⟩ **b :** MEAN, COWARDLY

2**yellow** *vt* **:** to make or turn yellow ~ *vi* **:** to become or turn yellow

3**yellow** *n* **1 a :** a color whose hue resembles that of ripe lemons or sunflowers or is that of the portion of the spectrum lying between green and orange **b :** a pigment or dye that colors yellow **2 :** something yellow or marked by a yellow color: as **a :** a person having yellow skin **b :** the yolk of an egg **3** *pl* **:** JAUNDICE **4** *pl* **:** any of several plant diseases caused esp. by viruses and marked by yellowing of the foliage and stunting

yellow bile *n* **:** a humor of medieval physiology believed to be secreted by the liver and to cause irascibility

yel·low·bird \'yel-ō-,bərd, -ə-,bərd\ *n* **1 :** any of various American goldfinches **2 :** a small mostly yellow American warbler (*Dendroica petechia*)

yellow daisy *n* **:** BLACK-EYED SUSAN

yellow-dog \,yel-ō-'dȯg, -ə-'dȯg\ *adj* **1 :** MEAN, CONTEMPTIBLE **2 :** of or relating to opposition to trade unionism or a labor union

yellow-dog contract *n* **:** an employment contract in which a worker disavows membership in and agrees not to join a labor union during the period of his employment

yellow enzyme *n* **:** any of several yellow flavoprotein respiratory enzymes widely distributed in nature

yellow fever *n* **:** an acute destructive infectious disease of warm regions marked by sudden onset, prostration, fever, albuminuria, jaundice, and often hemorrhage and caused by a virus transmitted by a mosquito — called also *yellow jack*

yellow-fever mosquito *n* **:** a small dark-colored mosquito (*Aëdes aegypti*) that is the usual vector of yellow fever

yellow grease *n* **:** fat from hogs considered unfit for food and used as a lubricant

yellow-green alga *n* **:** any of a division (Chrysophyta) of algae with the chlorophyll masked by brown or yellow pigment

yel·low·ham·mer \'yel-ō-,ham-ər, -ə-,ham-\ *n* [alter. of earlier *yelambre,* fr. (assumed) ME *yelwambre,* fr. ME *yelwe* yellow + (assumed) ME *ambre* yellowhammer, fr. OE *amore;* akin to OHG *amaro* yellowhammer, *amari* emmer] **1 :** a common European finch (*Emberiza citrinella*) having the male largely bright yellow — called also *yellow bunting* **2 :** YELLOW-SHAFTED FLICKER

yel·low·ish \'yel-ə-wish\ *adj* **:** somewhat yellow

yellow jack *n* **1 :** YELLOW FEVER **2 :** a flag raised on ships in quarantine **3 :** a silvery and golden food fish (*Caranx bartholomaei*) of Florida and the West Indies

yellow jacket *n* **:** any of various small yellow-marked social wasps (family Vespidae) that commonly nest in the ground

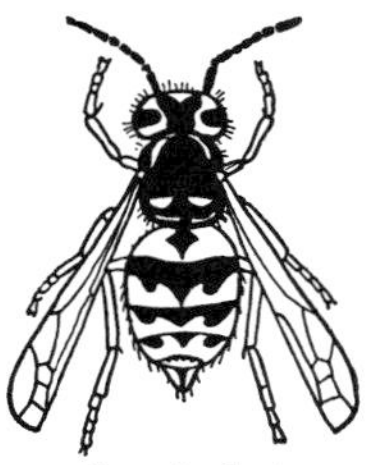
yellow jacket

yellow jessamine *also* **yellow jasmine** *n* **1 :** JASMINE 1a(2) **2 :** a twining evergreen shrub (*Gelsemium sempervirens*) of the family Loganiaceae with fragrant yellow flowers

yel·low·legs \'yel-ō-,legz, -ə-,legz, -,lāgz\ *n pl but sing or pl in constr* **:** either of two American shorebirds (*Tringa melanoleuca* and *Totarus flavipes*) that are related to the greenshank and have long yellow legs — called also respectively *greater yellowlegs, lesser yellowlegs*

yellow ocher *n* **1 :** a mixture of limonite usu. with clay and silica used as a pigment **2 :** a moderate orange yellow

yellow peril *n, often cap Y&P* **1 :** a danger to Western civilization held to arise from expansion of the power and influence of Oriental peoples **2 :** a threat to Western living standards from the incursion into Western countries of Oriental laborers willing to work for very low wages

yellow pine *n* **:** the yellowish wood of any of several No. American pines; *also* **:** a tree yielding this

yellow poplar *n* **1 a :** the American tulip tree **b :** TULIPWOOD 1 **2 :** the soft and light but durable wood of the common cucumber tree (*Magnolia acuminata*) of the southeastern U.S.

yel·low-shaft·ed flicker \,yel-ō-,shaf-təd-, -ə-,shaf-\ *n* **:** a common large woodpecker (*Colaptes auratus*) of eastern No. America with bright symmetrical markings among which are a black crescent on the breast, red nape, white rump, and yellow shafts to the tail and wing feathers — called also *yellowhammer*

yellow spot *n* **:** the most sensitive area on the human retina — called also *mac·u·la lu·tea* \,mak-yə-lə-'lüt-ē-ə\

yel·low·tail \'yel-ō-,tāl, -ə-,tāl\ *n, pl* **yellowtail** *or* **yellowtails :** any of various fishes having a yellow or yellowish tail: as **a :** any of several carangid fishes (genus *Seriola*) **b :** a croaker (*Bairdiella chrysura*) **c :** RAINBOW RUNNER **d :** a pinfish (*Lagodon rhomboides*) **e :** a common snapper (*Ocyurus chrysurus*) of the tropical western Atlantic and West Indies that is olive above and broadly striped with yellow along the sides and on the tail and highly esteemed for sport and food **f :** SPOT 6

yel·low·throat \-,thrōt\ *n* **:** any of several largely olive American warblers (genus *Geothlypis*); *esp* **:** one with yellow breast and throat

yel·low·weed \-,wēd\ *n* **:** any of various yellow-flowered weedy plants: as **a :** SNEEZEWEED 1 **b :** any of several goldenrods **c :** 1RAPE

yel·low·wood \-,wu̇d\ *n* **1 :** any of various trees having yellowish wood or yielding a yellow extract: as **a :** a leguminous tree (*Cladrastis lutea*) of the southern U.S. having showy white fragrant flowers and yielding a yellow dye — called also *gopherwood* **b :** OSAGE ORANGE **c :** BUCKTHORN **d :** SMOKE TREE **2 :** the wood of a yellowwood tree

1**yelp** \'yelp\ *vb* [ME *yelpen* to boast, cry out, fr. OE *gielpan* to boast, exult; akin to OHG *gelph* outcry, Lith *gulbinti* to praise] *vi* **:** to utter a sharp quick shrill cry ⟨dogs ~⟩ ~ *vt* **:** to utter with a yelp

2**yelp** *n* **:** the sharp shrill bark or cry (as of a dog)

yelp·er \'yel-pər\ *n* **1 :** one that yelps; *specif* **:** a yelping dog **2 :** an instrument used by hunters to produce a call or whistle imitating the yelp of the wild turkey hen

1**yen** \'yen\ *n, pl* **yen** [Jap *en*] — see MONEY table

2**yen** *n* [Chin (Cant) *yăn* craving] **:** a strong desire or propensity **:** LONGING; *also* **:** URGE — **yen** *vi* **yenned; yen·ning**

yeo·man \'yō-mən\ *n* [ME *yoman*] **1 a :** an attendant or officer in a royal or noble household **b :** a person attending or assisting another **:** RETAINER **c :** YEOMAN OF THE GUARD **d :** a naval petty officer who performs clerical duties **2 a :** a small farmer who cultivates his own land; *specif* **:** one belonging to a class of English freeholders below the gentry **b :** a person of the social rank of yeoman **3 :** one that performs great and laborious services

1**yeo·man·ly** \-lē\ *adj* **1 :** of, relating to, or having the rank of a yeoman **2 :** becoming or suitable to a yeoman

2**yeomanly** *adv* **:** in a manner befitting a yeoman **:** BRAVELY

yeoman of the guard : a member of a military corps attached to the British royal household and serving as ceremonial attendants of the sovereign and as warders of the Tower of London

yeo·man·ry \'yō-mən-rē\ *n* **1 :** the body of yeomen; *specif* **:** the body of small landed proprietors of the middle class **2 :** a British volunteer cavalry force created from yeomen in 1761 as a home defense force and reorganized in 1907 as part of the territorial force

yeoman's service *or* **yeoman service** *n* **:** great and loyal service, assistance, or support

-yer — see -ER

yer·ba ma·té \,yer-bə-'mä-,tā, ,yər-\ *n* [AmerSp *yerba mate,* fr. *yerba* herb + *mate* maté] **:** MATÉ

1**yerk** \'yərk\ *vt* [ME *yerken* to bind tightly] **1 :** to beat vigorously **:** THRASH **2 :** to attack or excite vigorously **:** GOAD

2**yerk** *n* **1** *Scot* **:** a lashing out **:** KICK **2** *dial* **:** JERK 1

1**yes** \'yes, 'yeu̇, 'e-(y)ə *are three of many variants*\ *adv* [ME, fr. OE *gēse*] **1** — used as a function word to express assent or agreement ⟨are you ready? *Yes,* I am⟩ **2** — used as a function word usu. to introduce correction or contradiction of a negative assertion, direction, or request ⟨don't say that! *Yes,* I will⟩ **3** — used as a function word to introduce a more emphatic or explicit phrase

4 — used as a function word to indicate uncertainty or polite interest or attentiveness

2**yes** \'yes\ *n* **:** an affirmative reply **:** YEA

ye·shi·va *or* **ye·shi·vah** \yə-'shē-və\ *n, pl* **yeshivas** *or* **yeshivahs** *or* **ye·shi·voth** \-,shē-'vōt(h)\ [LHeb *yĕshībhāh*] **1 :** a school for Talmudic study **2 :** an orthodox Jewish rabbinical seminary **3 :** a Jewish day school providing secular and religious instruction

yes–man \'yes-,man\ *n* **:** a person who agrees with everything that is said to him; *esp* **:** one who endorses or supports without criticism every opinion or proposal of an associate or superior

yes·ter \'yes-tər\ *adj, archaic* **:** of or relating to yesterday

1**yes·ter·day** \'yes-tərd-ē\ *adv* [ME *yisterday*, fr. OE *giestran dæg*, fr. *giestran* yesterday + *dæg* day; akin to OHG *gestaron* yesterday, L *heri*, Gk *chthes*] **1 :** on the day last past **:** on the day preceding today **2 :** at a time not long past **:** only a short time ago — **yesterday** *adj*

2**yesterday** *n* **1 :** the day last past **:** the day next before the present **2 :** recent time **:** time not long past **3 :** past time — usu. used in pl. ⟨all our ~s have lighted fools the way to dusty death —Shak.⟩

yes·ter·year \'yes-tər-,yi(ə)r\ *n* [*yesterday* + *year*] **1 :** last year **2 :** the recent past — **yesteryear** *adv*

1**yes·treen** \ye-'strēn\ *adv* [ME (Sc) *yistrevin*, fr. *yisterday* yesterday + *evin* evening, alter. of ME *even*] *chiefly Scot* **:** on yesterday evening

2**yestreen** *n, chiefly Scot* **:** last evening or night

1**yet** \(')yet\ *adv* [ME, fr. OE *giet;* akin to OFris *ieta* yet] **1 a :** in addition **:** BESIDES ⟨gives ~ another reason⟩ **b :** EVEN 2c ⟨a ~ higher speed⟩ **2 a** (1) **:** up to now **:** so far ⟨hasn't done much ~⟩ (2) **:** at this or that time **:** so soon as now ⟨not time to go ~⟩ **b :** continuously up to the present or a specified time **:** STILL ⟨is ~ a new country⟩ **c :** at a future time **:** EVENTUALLY ⟨may ~ see the light⟩ **3 :** NEVERTHELESS, HOWEVER

2**yet** *conj* **:** but nevertheless **:** BUT

yeti \'yet-ē\ *n* [Tibetan] **:** ABOMINABLE SNOWMAN

yeuk \'yük\ *vi* [ME (northern) *yukyn*, fr. OE *giccan*] *chiefly Scot* **:** ITCH — **yeuk** *n, chiefly Scot* — **yeuky** \'yü-kē\ *adj, chiefly Scot*

yew \'yü\ *n* [ME *ew*, fr. OE *īw;* akin to OHG *īwa* yew, OIr *ēo*] **1 a :** any of a genus (*Taxus* of the family Taxaceae, the yew family) of evergreen trees and shrubs with stiff linear leaves and fruits with a fleshy aril; *esp* **:** a long-lived Eurasian tree (*T. baccata*) — called also *English yew* **b :** the wood of a yew; *esp* **:** the heavy fine-grained wood of English yew **2** *archaic* **:** an archery bow made of yew

Ygerne \ē-'ge(ə)rn\ *n* **:** IGRAINE

Ygg·dra·sil \'ig-drə-,sil\ *n* [ON] **:** a huge ash tree in Norse mythology that overspreads the world and binds earth, hell, and heaven together

YHWH *n* **:** YAHWEH — compare TETRAGRAMMATON

Yid·dish \'yid-ish\ *n* [Yiddish *yidish*, short for *yidish daytsh*, lit., Jewish German] **:** a High German language spoken by Jews chiefly in eastern Europe and areas to which Jews from eastern Europe have migrated and commonly written in Hebrew characters — **Yiddish** *adj*

1**yield** \'yē(ə)ld\ *vb* [ME *yielden*, fr. OE *gieldan;* akin to OHG *geltan* to pay] *vt* **1** *archaic* **:** RECOMPENSE, REWARD **2 :** to give or render as fitting, rightfully owed, or required **3 :** to give up possession of upon claim or demand: as **a :** to give up (as one's breath) and so die **b :** to surrender or relinquish to the physical control of another **:** hand over possession of **c :** to surrender or submit (oneself) to another **d :** to give (oneself) up to an inclination, temptation, or habit **e :** to relinquish one's possession of (as a position of advantage or point of superiority) ⟨~ precedence⟩ **4 a :** to bear or bring forth as a natural product esp. as a result of cultivation **b :** to furnish as return or result of expended effort **c** (1) **:** to produce as return from an expenditure or investment **:** furnish as profit or interest (2) **:** to produce as revenue **:** bring in ~ *vi* **1 :** to be fruitful or productive **:** BEAR, PRODUCE **2 :** to give up and cease resistance or contention **:** SUBMIT, SUCCUMB **3 :** to give way to pressure or influence **:** submit to urging, persuasion, or entreaty **4 :** to give way under physical force so as to bend, stretch, or break **5 a :** to give place or precedence **:** acknowledge the superiority of someone else **b :** to give way to or become succeeded by someone or something else **6 :** to relinquish the floor of a legislative assembly

syn SUBMIT, CAPITULATE, SUCCUMB, RELENT, DEFER: YIELD may apply to any sort of giving way or giving in before force, argument, or entreaty; SUBMIT suggests surrendering after resistance or conflict to the will or control of another; CAPITULATE stresses the act of giving up to a stronger force or power; SUCCUMB suggests a giving way in weakness or helplessness; RELENT applies to a yielding through mercy or pity by one who has the upper hand; DEFER suggests yielding or submitting voluntarily through respect or reference **syn** see in addition RELINQUISH

2**yield** *n* **1 :** something yielded **:** PRODUCT; *esp* **:** the amount or quantity resulting often expressed as the percentage of what is theoretically possible **2 :** the capacity of yielding produce

yield·er \'yē(ə)l-dər\ *n* **:** one that yields: as **a :** a person who surrenders, concedes, or gives in **b :** something that yields produce or products

yield·ing *adj* **1 :** PRODUCTIVE ⟨a high-*yielding* wheat⟩ **2 :** lacking rigidity or stiffness **:** FLEXIBLE ⟨a ~ mass⟩ **3 :** disposed to submit or comply

yill \'yil\ *chiefly Scot var of* ALE

yin \'yin\ *n* [Chin (Pek) *yin*[1]] **:** the feminine passive principle (as of darkness, cold, or wetness) in nature that in Chinese cosmology combines with yang to produce all that comes to be

yip \'yip\ *vi* **yipped; yip·ping** [imit.] **:** YELP — used chiefly of a dog — **yip** *n*

yip·pee \'yip-ē\ *interj* — used to express exuberant delight or triumph

yird \'yird\ *chiefly Scot var of* EARTH

-yl \əl, ᵊl, (,)il, ,ēl, *chiefly Brit* ,īl\ *n comb form* [Gk *hylē* matter, material, lit., wood] **:** chemical and usu. univalent radical ⟨eth*yl*⟩ ⟨hydrox*yl*⟩

ylang–ylang *var of* ILANG-ILANG

Ymir \'ē-,mi(ə)r\ *n* [ON] **:** a giant from whose body the Norse gods are held to have created the world

yod \'yȯd, 'yu̇d\ *n* [Heb *yōdh*] **:** the 10th letter of the Hebrew alphabet — symbol '

1**yo·del** \'yōd-ᵊl\ *vb* **yo·deled** *or* **yo·delled; yo·del·ing** *or* **yo·del·ling** \'yōd-liŋ, -ᵊl-iŋ\ [G *jodeln*] *vi* **:** to sing by suddenly changing from chest voice to head voice or falsetto and the reverse; *also* **:** to shout or call in a similar manner ~ *vt* **:** to sing (a tune) by yodeling — **yo·del·er** \-lər, -ᵊl-ər\ *n*

2**yodel** *n* **:** a song or refrain sung by yodeling; *also* **:** a yodeled shout or cry

yo·ga \'yō-gə\ *n* [Skt, lit., yoking, fr. *yunakti* he yokes; akin to L *jungere* to join — more at YOKE] **1** *cap* **:** a Hindu theistic philosophy teaching the suppression of all activity of body, mind, and will in order that the self may realize its distinction from them and attain liberation **2 :** a system of exercises for attaining bodily or mental control and well-being — **yo·gic** \-gik\ *adj, often cap*

yogh \'yōk, 'yōg\ *n* [ME *yogh, ȝogh*] **:** a letter ȝ used in Middle English to represent a voiced velar fricative or palatal fricative or sometimes a voiceless velar or palatal fricative

yo·gi \'yō-gē\ *or* **yo·gin** \-gən\ *n* [Skt *yogin*, fr. *yoga*] **1 :** a person who practices yoga **2** *cap* **:** an adherent of Yoga philosophy

yo·gurt *or* **yo·ghurt** \'yō-gərt\ *n* [Turk *yoğurt*] **:** a fermented slightly acid semifluid milk food made of skimmed cow's milk and milk solids to which cultures of two bacteria (*Lactobacillus acidophilus* and *Streptococcus thermophilus*) have been added

yo·him·bine \yō-'him-,bēn\ *n* [ISV, fr. *yohimbé* (an African tree)] **:** an alkaloid $C_{21}H_{26}N_2O_3$ with sympathomimetic and hypotensive effects that has been used as an aphrodisiac

yoicks \'yȯiks\ *interj, archaic* — used as a cry of encouragement to foxhounds

1**yoke** \'yōk\ *n, pl* **yokes** [ME *yok*, fr. OE *geoc;* akin to OHG *joh* yoke, L *jugum*, Gk *zygon*, L *jungere* to join] **1 a :** a wooden bar or frame by which two draft animals (as oxen) are joined at the heads or necks for working together **b :** an arched device formerly laid upon the neck of a defeated person **c :** a frame fitted to a person's shoulders to carry a load in two equal portions **d :** a bar by which the end of the tongue of a wagon or carriage is suspended from the collars of the harness **e** (1) **:** a crosspiece on the head of a boat's rudder (2) **:** an airplane lever operating the elevators and the ailerons **f :** a frame from which a bell is hung **g :** a clamp or similar piece that embraces two parts to hold or unite them in position **2** *pl usu* **yoke :** two animals yoked or worked together **3 a** (1) **:** an oppressive agency (2) **:** SERVITUDE, BONDAGE **b :** TIE, LINK; *esp* **:** MARRIAGE **4 :** a fitted or shaped piece at the top of a skirt or at the shoulder of various garments

2**yoke** *vt* **1 a** (1) **:** to put a yoke on (2) **:** to join in or with a yoke **b :** to attach a draft animal to; *also* **:** to attach (a draft animal) to something **2 :** to join as if by a yoke **3 :** to put to work ~ *vi* **:** to become joined or linked

yoke·fel·low \-,fel-(,)ō, -ə(-w)\ *n* **:** a close companion **:** MATE

yo·kel \'yō-kəl\ *n* [perh. fr. E dial. *yokel* green woodpecker, of imit. origin] **:** a rude, naïve, or gullible inhabitant of a rural area or small town

yolk \'yōk, 'yōlk\ *or* **yoke** *n* [ME *yolke*, fr. OE *geoloca*, fr. *geolu* yellow — more at YELLOW] **1 a :** the yellow spheroidal mass of stored food that forms the inner portion of the egg of a bird or reptile and is surrounded by the white **b** *archaic* **:** the whole contents of an ovum consisting of a protoplasmic formative portion and an inert nutritive portion **c :** the material stored in an ovum that supplies food material to the developing embryo and consists chiefly of proteins, lecithin, and cholesterol **2** [akin to MD *ieke* yolk (of wool), OE *ēowu* ewe] **:** oily material in unprocessed sheep wool consisting of wool fat, suint, and debris — **yolked** \'yō(l)kt\ *adj* — **yolky** \'yō(l)-kē\ *adj*

yolk sac *n* **:** a membranous sac that is attached to an embryo and encloses food yolk, that is continuous through the vitelline duct with the intestinal cavity of the embryo, that being abundantly supplied with blood vessels is throughout embryonic life and in some forms later the chief organ of nutrition, and that in placental mammals is nearly vestigial and functions chiefly prior to the elaboration of the placenta

yolk stalk *n* **:** the narrow tubular stalk connecting the yolk sac with the embryo

Yom Kip·pur \,yȯm-'kip-ər, ,yəm-, ,yōm-, ,yäm-, -ki-'pu̇(ə)r\ *n* [Heb *yōm kippūr*, fr. *yōm* day + *kippūr* atonement] **:** a Jewish holiday observed with fasting on the 10th day of Tishri in accordance with the rites described in Leviticus 16

1**yon** \'yän\ *adj* [ME, fr. OE *geon;* akin to OHG *ienēr*, adj., that, Gk *enē* day after tomorrow] **:** YONDER

2**yon** *pron, dial* **:** that or those yonder

3**yon** *adv* **1 :** YONDER **2 :** THITHER ⟨ran hither and ~⟩

1**yond** \'yänd\ *adv* [ME, fr. OE *geond;* akin to OE *geon*] *archaic* **:** YONDER

2**yond** *adj, dial* **:** YONDER

1**yon·der** \'yän-dər\ *adv* [ME, fr. *yond* + *-er* (as in *hither*)] **:** at or in that indicated more or less distant place usu. within sight

2**yonder** *adj* **1 :** farther removed **:** more distant **2 :** being at a distance within view or at a place or in a direction known or indicated

3**yonder** *pron* **:** something that is or is in an indicated more or less distant place

yo·ni \'yō-nē\ *n* [Skt, vulva] **:** the formal symbol under which Shakti is worshiped — compare LINGAM

yoo–hoo \'yü-hü\ *interj* — used to attract attention or as a call to persons

yore \'yō(ə)r, 'yȯ(ə)r\ *n* [ME, fr. *yore*, adv., long ago, fr. OE *geāra*, fr. *gēar* year] **:** time past and esp. long past — usu. used in the phrase *of yore*

York·ist \'yȯr-kəst\ *n* **:** a member or supporter of the English royal house of York founded by Richard, Duke of York, in the time of Henry VI and continued by Edward IV, Edward V, and Richard III — compare LANCASTRIAN — **Yorkist** *adj*

York rite \'yȯ(ə)rk-\ *n* [*York*, England] **1 :** a ceremonial observed by one of the Masonic systems **2 :** a system or organization that observes the York rite and confers in the U.S. 13 degrees of which the last three are in commanderies of Knights Templar — compare SCOTTISH RITE

York·shire \'yȯ(ə)rk-,shi(ə)r, -shər\ *n* **:** a white swine of any of

several breeds or strains originated in Yorkshire, England
Yorkshire pudding *n* [*Yorkshire*, England] **:** a batter of eggs, flour, and milk baked in meat drippings
Yorkshire terrier *n* **:** a compact toy terrier with long straight silky hair mostly bluish gray but tan on the head and chest
Yor•u•ba \'yȯr-ə-bə\ *n, pl* **Yoruba** *or* **Yorubas** **1 :** a member of a Negro people of the eastern Guinea coast mainly between Dahomey and the lower Niger **2 :** the language of the Yorubas
you \(')yü, yə, yē\ *pron* [ME, fr. OE *ēow*, dat. & accus. of *gē* you; akin to OHG *iu*, dat. of *ir* you, Skt *yūyam* you] **1 :** the one or ones being addressed — used as the pronoun of the second person singular or plural in any grammatical relation except that of a possessive ⟨~ may sit in that chair⟩ ⟨~ are my friends⟩ ⟨can I pour ~ a cup of tea⟩; used formerly only as a plural pronoun of the second person in the dative or accusative case as direct or indirect object of a verb or as object of a preposition; compare THEE, THOU, YE, YOUR, YOURS **2 :** 2ONE 2
you–all \(')yü-'ȯl, 'yȯl\ *pron* **:** YOU — usu. used in addressing two or more persons or sometimes one person as representing also another or others ⟨down here we can always spot Yankees by the way they use ~ in the singular —Arthur Gordon⟩
you'd \(,)yüd, (,)yu̇d, yəd\ **:** you had **:** you would
you'll \(,)yü(ə)l, (,)yu̇l, yəl\ **:** you will **:** you shall
1young \'yəŋ\ *adj* **youn•ger** \'yəŋ-gər\ **youn•gest** \'yəŋ-gəst\ [ME *yong*, fr. OE *geong;* akin to OHG *jung* young, L *juvenis*] **1 a :** being in the first or an early stage of life, growth, or development **b :** JUNIOR 1a **2 :** having little experience **3 a :** recently come into being **:** NEW **b :** YOUTHFUL 5 **4 :** of, relating to, or having the characteristics of youth or a young person **5** *cap* **:** representing a new or rejuvenated esp. political group or movement
2young *n, pl* **young** **1** *pl* **a :** young persons **:** YOUTH **b :** immature offspring esp. of lower animals **2 :** a single recently born or hatched animal — **with young :** PREGNANT — used of a female animal
young•ber•ry \'yəŋ-,ber-ē\ *n* [B. M. *Young fl* 1900 Am fruit grower] **:** the large sweet reddish black fruit of a hybrid between a trailing blackberry and a southern dewberry grown in western and southern U.S.; *also* **:** the trailing hybrid bramble
youn•ger \'yəŋ-gər\ *n* **:** an inferior in age **:** JUNIOR — usu. used with a possessive pronoun ⟨is several years his ~⟩
youn•gest \'yəŋ-gəst\ *n* **:** one that is the least old esp. of a family
young•ish \'yəŋ-ish\ *adj* **:** somewhat young
young•ling \'yəŋ-liŋ\ *n* **:** one that is young; *esp* **:** a young person or animal — **youngling** *adj*
young•ster \'yəŋ(k)-stər\ *n* **1 a :** a young person **:** YOUTH **b :** CHILD **2 :** a sophomore at the U.S. Naval Academy **3 :** a young mammal, bird, or plant esp. of a domesticated or cultivated breed or type
Young Turk *n* [*Young Turk*, member of a 20th cent. revolutionary party in Turkey] **:** an insurgent or a member of an insurgent group in a political party **:** RADICAL
youn•ker \'yəŋ-kər\ *n* [D *jonker* young nobleman] **1 :** a young man **2 :** CHILD, YOUNGSTER
your \yər, (')yu̇(ə)r, (')yō(ə)r, (')yȯ(ə)r\ *adj* [ME, fr. OE *ēower;* akin to OE *ēow* you — more at YOU] **1 :** of or relating to you or yourself or yourselves esp. as possessor or possessors ⟨~ bodies⟩, agent or agents ⟨~ contributions⟩, or object or objects of an action ⟨~ discharge⟩ **2 :** of or relating to one or oneself ⟨when you face the north, east is at ~ right⟩
you're \yər, (,)yu̇(ə)r, (,)yō(ə)r, (,)yȯ(ə)r, ,yü-ər\ **:** you are
yours \'yu̇(ə)rz, 'yō(ə)rz, 'yȯ(ə)rz\ *pron, sing, or pl in constr* [ME fr. *your* + *-s* -'s] **:** your one **:** your ones — often used esp. with an adverbial modifier in the complimentary close of a letter ⟨~ truly⟩ — **yours truly :** I, ME, MYSELF ⟨I can take care of *yours truly*⟩
your•self \yər-'self\ *pron* **1 a :** that identical one that is you — used reflexively ⟨you might hurt ~⟩, for emphasis ⟨carry them ~⟩, or in absolute constructions **b :** your normal, healthy, or sane condition or self **2 :** ONESELF ⟨it is more restful to ride in a car that someone else is driving than to drive a car ~⟩
your•selves \-'selvz\ *pron pl* **1 :** those identical ones that are you — used reflexively ⟨get ~ a treat⟩, for emphasis, or in absolute constructions **2 :** the normal, healthy, or sane condition or selves of you persons
youth \'yüth\ *n, pl* **youths** \'yüt͟hz, 'yüths\ [ME *youthe*, fr. OE *geoguth;* akin to OE *geong* young — more at YOUNG] **1 :** the time of life marked by growth and development; *esp* **:** the period between childhood and maturity **2 a :** a young person; *esp* **:** a young male between adolescence and maturity **b :** young persons or creatures — usu. pl. in constr. **3 :** YOUTHFULNESS
youth•ful \'yüth-fəl\ *adj* **1 :** of, relating to, or appropriate to youth **2 :** being young and not yet mature **3 :** marked by or possessing youth **4 :** FRESH, VIGOROUS **5 :** having accomplished or undergone little erosion — **youth•ful•ly** \-fə-lē\ *adv* — **youth•ful•ness** *n*
youth hostel *n* **:** HOSTEL 2
you've \(,)yüv, yəv\ **:** you have
1yowl \'yau̇(ə)l\ *vb* [ME *yowlen*] *vi* **:** to utter a loud long often mournful cry **:** WAIL ~ *vt* **:** to express with yowling
2yowl *n* **:** a loud long mournful wail or howl (as of a cat)
yo–yo \'yō-(,)yō\ *n* [native name in Philippines] **:** a thick grooved double disk with a string attached to its center which is made to fall and rise to the hand by unwinding and rewinding on the string
yt•ter•bic \i-'tər-bik, ə-\ *adj* **:** of, relating to, or containing ytterbium esp. when trivalent
yt•ter•bi•um \-bē-əm\ *n* [NL, fr. *Ytterby*, Sweden] **:** a bivalent or trivalent metallic element of the rare-earth group that resembles yttrium and occurs with it and related elements in several minerals (as gadolinite) — see ELEMENT table
yt•ter•bous \-bəs\ *adj* **:** of, relating to, or containing ytterbium when bivalent
yt•tri•um \'i-trē-əm\ *n* [NL, fr. *yttria* (yttrium oxide)] **:** a trivalent metallic element usu. included among the rare-earth metals which it resembles chemically and with which it occurs in minerals — see ELEMENT table
yttrium metal *n* **:** any of several metals separable as a group from other metals occurring with them and including yttrium, holmium, erbium, thulium, ytterbium, and lutetium and sometimes gadolinium, terbium, and dysprosium
yu•an \'yü-ən, yu̇-'än\ *n, pl* **yuan** [Chin (Pek) *yüan²*] — see MONEY table
Yu•ca•tec \'yü-kə-,tek\ *n* [Sp *yucateco*, fr. *Yucatán* peninsula, Mexico] **1 :** a member of an Indian people of the Yucatán peninsula, Mexico **2 :** a Mayan language of the Yucatecs — **Yu•ca•tec•an** \,yü-kə-'tek-ən\ *adj*
yuc•ca \'yək-ə\ *n* [NL, genus name, fr. Sp *yuca*] **:** any of a genus (*Yucca*) of sometimes arborescent plants of the lily family having long often rigid fibrous-margined leaves on a woody base and bearing a large panicle of white blossoms
yu•ga \'yu̇g-ə\ *n* [Skt, yoke, age; akin to L *jugum* yoke — more at YOKE] **:** one of the four ages of a Hindu world cycle
Yu•kon time \'yü-,kän-\ *n* **:** the time of the 9th time zone west of Greenwich that includes the Yukon Territory and part of southern Alaska
yule \'yü(ə)l\ *n, often cap, often attrib* [ME *yol*, fr. OE *geōl;* akin to ON *jōl* yule] **:** the feast of the nativity of Jesus Christ **:** CHRISTMAS, CHRISTMASTIDE
Yule log *n* **:** a large log formerly put on the hearth on Christmas Eve as the foundation of the fire
yule•tide \'yü(ə)l-,tīd\ *n, often cap* **:** the Christmas season; *esp* **:** CHRISTMASTIDE
Yu•man \'yü-mən\ *n* **:** an Amerindian language family of southwestern U.S. and northern Mexico — **Yuman** *adj*
yum•my \'yəm-ē\ *adj* [*yum-yum* (interj. expressing pleasure in the taste of food)] **:** highly attractive or pleasing **:** DELECTABLE, DELICIOUS
yurt \'yu̇(ə)rt\ *n* [Russ *yurta*, of Turkic origin; akin to Turk *yurt* dwelling] **:** a circular domed tent of skins or felt stretched over a collapsible lattice framework and used by the Kirghiz and other Mongol nomads of Siberia

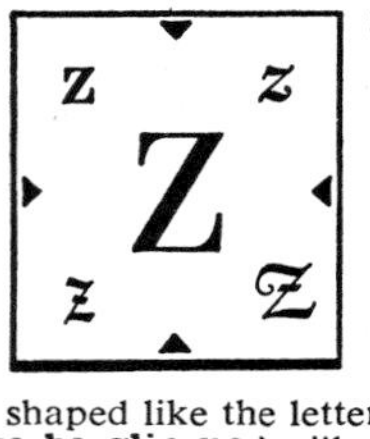

z \'zē, *chiefly Brit* 'zed\ *n, often cap, often attrib* **1 a :** the 26th and last letter of the English alphabet **b :** a graphic representation of this letter **c :** a speech counterpart of orthographic *z* **2 :** a graphic device for reproducing the letter *z* **3 :** one designated *z* esp. as the 26th in order or class, the 25th in order or class when j is not used, the 23d in order or class when j, v, and w are not used, or the third in order or class when x is made the first **4 :** an arbitrarily chosen value from the domain of a variable **5 :** something shaped like the letter Z
za•ba•glio•ne \,zäb-əl-'yō-nē\ *n* [It] **:** a mixture of eggs, sugar, and wine or fruit juice beaten over hot water until thick and light and served warm or cold in a glass
zaf•fer *or* **zaf•fre** \'zaf-ər\ *n* [It *zaffera*] **:** an impure oxide of cobalt used in the manufacture of smalt and as a blue ceramic coloring
zaire \'zī(ə)r\ *n* [F *zaïre*, fr. *Zaïre*, former name of Congo river] — see MONEY table
za•mia \'zā-mē-ə\ *n* [NL, genus name, fr. L *zamiae nuces* false MS reading for *azaniae nuces* pine nuts] **:** any of a genus (*Zamia*) of American cycads with a short thick woody base, a crown of palmlike leaves, and oblong cones
za•min•dar *or* **ze•min•dar** \zə-,mēn-'där\ *n* [Hindi *zamīndār*, fr. Per, fr. *zamīn* land + *-dār* holder] **1 :** a collector of the land revenue of a district for the government during the period of Muslim rule in India **2 :** a feudatory in British India and the early period of Indian independence paying the government a fixed revenue
za•min•dari *or* **ze•min•dary** \-'där-ē\ *n* [Hindi *zamīndārī*, fr. Per, fr. *zamīndār*] **1 :** the system of landholding and revenue collection by zamindars **2 :** the land held or administered by a zamindar
zan•der \'zan-dər, 'tsän-\ *n, pl* **zander** *or* **zanders** [G] **:** a pike perch (*Lucioperca sandra*) of central Europe related to the walleyed pike
za•ni•ly \'zān-ᵊl-ē\ *adv* **:** in a zany manner
za•ni•ness \'zā-nē-nəs\ *n* **:** the quality or state of being zany
1za•ny \'zā-nē\ *n* [It *zanni*, a traditional masked clown, fr. It (dial.) *Zanni*, nickname for *Giovanni* John] **1 :** a subordinate clown or acrobat in old comedies who mimics ludicrously the tricks of his principal **:** MERRY-ANDREW **2 :** a slavish follower **:** TOADY **3 :** one who acts the buffoon to amuse others **4 :** SIMPLETON
2zany *adj* **1 :** being or having the characteristics of a zany **2 :** fantastically or irrationally ludicrous — **za•ny•ism** \-nē-,iz-əm\ *n*
za•re•ba *or* **za•ri•ba** \zə-'rē-bə\ *n* [Ar *zarībah* enclosure] **:** an improvised stockade constructed esp. of thorny bushes in parts of Africa
zar•zue•la \,zärz-(ə-)'wā-lə\ *n* [Sp] **:** a usu. comic Spanish opera with spoken dialogue
z–ax•is \'zē-,ak-səs\ *n* **:** one of the axes in a three-dimensional rectangular coordinate system
za•yin \'zä-yən, 'zī(-ə)n\ *n* [Heb] **:** the 7th letter of the Hebrew alphabet — symbol ז
zeal \'zē(ə)l\ *n* [ME *zele*, fr. LL *zelus*, fr. Gk *zēlos*] **:** eagerness and ardent interest in pursuit of something **:** FERVOR **syn** see PASSION
zeal•ot \'zel-ət\ *n* [LL *zelotes*, fr. Gk *zēlōtēs*, fr. *zēlos*] **1** *cap* **:** one of a fanatical sect of ancient Judea bitterly opposing the Roman domination of Palestine **2 :** a zealous person; *esp* **:** a fanatical partisan — **zealot** *adj*
zeal•ot•ry \'zel-ə-trē\ *n* **:** excess of zeal **:** fanatical devotion
zeal•ous \'zel-əs\ *adj* **:** filled with, characterized by, or due to zeal — **zeal•ous•ly** *adv* — **zeal•ous•ness** *n*

Zeb·e·dee \'zeb-əd-ē, -ə-ˌdē\ *n* [Gk *Zebedaios*, fr. Aram *Zabhdai*] **:** the father of the disciples James and John

ze·bra \'zē-brə, *Brit also* 'zeb-rə\ *n, pl* **zebras** *also* **zebra** [It, fr. Sp *cebra*] **:** any of several fleet African mammals (genus *Equus*) related to the horse but distinctively and conspicuously patterned in stripes of black or dark brown and white or buff — **ze·brine** \-ˌbrīn\ *adj* — **ze·broid** \-ˌbrȯid\ *adj*

zebra finch *n* **:** a small largely gray-and-white Australian weaverbird (*Poephila castanotis*) that has black bars on the tail coverts and is often kept as a cage bird

zebra fish *n* **:** any of various barred fishes; *esp* **:** a very small blue-and-silver-striped Indian danio (*Brachydanio rerio*) often kept in the tropical aquarium — called also *zebra danio*

ze·bra·wood \'zē-brə-ˌwu̇d\ *n* **1 :** any of several trees or shrubs having mottled or striped wood; *esp* **:** a tropical tree (*Connarus guianensis* of the family Connaraceae) with strikingly marked hard wood used in cabinetwork **2 :** the wood of a zebrawood

ze·bu \'zē-(ˌ)b(y)ü\ *n* [F *zébu*] **:** an Asiatic ox (*Bos indicus*) domesticated and differentiated into many breeds, used chiefly for draft or for milk or flesh, and distinguished from European cattle with which it crosses freely by the presence of a large fleshy hump over the shoulders, a loose skin prolonged into dewlap and folds under the belly, large pendulous ears, and marked resistance to the injurious effects of heat and insect attack

Zeb·u·lun \'zeb-yə-lən\ *n* [Heb *Zĕbhūlūn*] **:** a son of Jacob and ancestor of one of the tribes of Israel

zec·chi·no \ze-'kē-(ˌ)nō, tse-\ *n, pl* **zec·chi·ni** \-(ˌ)nē\ *or* **zec·chinos** [It] **:** SEQUIN 1

Zech·a·ri·ah \ˌzek-ə-'rī-ə\ *n* [Heb *Zĕcharyāh*] **:** a Hebrew prophet of the 6th century B.C.

zech·in \'zek-ən\ *n* [It *zecchino*] **:** SEQUIN 1

zed \'zed\ *n* [ME, fr. MF *zede*, fr. LL *zeta* zeta, fr. Gk *zēta*] *chiefly Brit* **:** the letter *z*

zee \'zē\ *n* **:** the letter *z*

ze·in \'zē-ən\ *n* [NL *Zea*, genus including Indian corn, fr. Gk, wheat; akin to Skt *yava* barley] **:** a protein from Indian corn used in making textile fibers, plastics, printing inks, coatings (as varnish), and adhesives and sizes

zeit·geist \'tsīt-ˌgīst, 'zīt-\ *n* [G, fr. *zeit* time + *geist* spirit] **:** the general intellectual, moral, and cultural state of an era

Zen \'zen\ *n* [Jap, religious meditation, fr. Chin (Pek) *ch'an*², fr. Pali *jhāna*, fr. Skt *dhyāna*, fr. *dhyāti* he thinks — more at SEMANTIC] **:** a Japanese sect of Mahayana Buddhism that teaches self-discipline, meditation, and attainment of enlightenment by direct intuition by means of paradoxical and nonlogical statements

ze·nai·da \zə-'nā-əd-ə, -'nīd-ə\ *n* [NL, genus name, fr. *Zénaïde* †1854 wife of Prince Charles Lucien Bonaparte] **:** either of two wild pigeons (*Zenaida aurita* of tropical America and *Z. asiatica* of the southwestern U.S.) — called also *zenaida dove*

ze·na·na \zə-'nän-ə\ *n* [Hindi *zanāna*] **:** HAREM, SERAGLIO

Zend-Aves·ta \ˌzen-də-'ves-tə\ *n* [F, fr. MPer *Avastāk va Zand* Avesta and commentary] **:** AVESTA

ze·nith \'zē-nəth, *esp Brit* 'zen-ith\ *n* [ME *senith*, fr. MF *cenith*, fr. ML, fr. OSp *zenit*, modif. of Ar *samt* (*ar-ra's*) way (of the head)] **1 :** the point of the celestial sphere that is directly opposite the nadir and vertically above the observer **2 :** the highest point reached in the heavens by a celestial body **3 :** culminating point **:** ACME **syn** see SUMMIT

ze·nith·al \-əl\ *adj* **1 :** of, relating to, or located at or near the zenith **2 :** drawn to show correct directions from the center ⟨a ~ map⟩

ze·o·lite \'zē-ə-ˌlīt\ *n* [Sw *zeolit*, fr. Gk *zein* to boil + *-o-* + Sw *-lit* -lite, fr. F *-lite* — more at YEAST] **:** any of various hydrous silicates that are analogous in composition to the feldspars, occur as secondary minerals in cavities of lavas, and can act as ion-exchangers; *also* **:** any of various natural or synthesized silicates of similar structure used in water softening and as adsorbents — **ze·o·lit·ic** \ˌzē-ə-'lit-ik\ *adj*

Zeph·a·ni·ah \ˌzef-ə-'nī-ə\ *n* [Heb *Ṣĕphanyāh*] **:** a Hebrew prophet of the 7th century B.C.

Zeph·i·ran \'zef-ə-ˌran\ *trademark* — used for a cationic surface-active mixture of ammonium chloride derivatives used esp. as a skin disinfectant

zeph·yr \'zef-ər\ *n* [ME *Zephirus*, west wind (personified), fr. L *Zephyrus*, god of the west wind, & *zephyrus* west wind, zephyr, fr. Gk *Zephyros*, god of the west wind, & *zephyros* west wind, zephyr] **1 a :** a breeze from the west **b :** a gentle breeze **2 :** any of various lightweight fabrics and articles of clothing (as a shawl, duster, or hat)

Zeph·y·rus \'zef-ə-rəs\ *n* [L] **:** the west wind personified

zep·pe·lin \'zep-(ə-)lən\ *n* [Count Ferdinand von *Zeppelin* †1917 G airship manufacturer] **:** a rigid airship consisting of a cylindrical trussed and covered frame supported by internal gas cells; *broadly* **:** AIRSHIP

[1]**ze·ro** \'zē-(ˌ)rō, 'zi(ə)r-(ˌ)ō\ *n, pl* **zeros** *also* **zeroes** [F or It; F *zéro*, fr. It *zero*, fr. ML *zephirum*, fr. Ar *ṣifr*] **1 a :** the numerical symbol 0 **:** CIPHER **b :** the number represented by the symbol 0 that leaves unchanged any number to which it is added — see NUMBER table **c :** the number between the set of all positive numbers and the set of all negative numbers **2 a** (1) **:** the point of departure in reckoning; *specif* **:** the point from which the graduation of a scale (as of a thermometer) commences (2) **:** the temperature represented by the zero mark on a thermometer **b :** the setting or adjustment of the rear sight of a firearm that causes it to hit where aimed **3 :** a person or thing with no importance or independent existence **:** NONENTITY **4 a :** a state of total absence or neutrality **b :** the lowest point **:** NADIR **5 :** something arbitrarily or conveniently designated zero

[2]**zero** *adj* **1 a :** of, relating to, or being a zero **b** (1) **:** ABSENT, LACKING ⟨the ~ modification in the past of *cut*⟩ (2) **:** having no modified inflectional form ⟨~ plural⟩ **2 a** *of a cloud ceiling* **:** limiting vision to 50 feet or less **b** *of horizontal visibility* **:** limited to 165 feet or less

[3]**zero** *vt* **1 :** to determine or adjust the zero of (as a rifle) **2 a :** to concentrate firepower on the exact range of — usu. used with *in* **b :** to bring to bear on the exact range of a target — usu. used with *in* ~ *vi* **1 :** to adjust fire (as of artillery) on a specific target — usu. used with *in* **2 :** to move near to or focus attention as if on a target **:** CLOSE — usu. used with *in*

zero hour *n* **1 :** the hour at which a previously planned military operation is started **2 :** the scheduled time for an action or operation (as the firing of a rocket) to begin

zero-zero *adj* **1 :** characterized by or being atmospheric conditions that reduce ceiling and visibility to zero **2 :** limited to zero by atmospheric conditions

zest \'zest\ *n* [obs. F (now *zeste*), orange or lemon peel (used as flavoring)] **1 :** a quality of enhancing enjoyment **:** PIQUANCY **2 :** keen enjoyment **:** RELISH, GUSTO **syn** see TASTE — **zest·ful** \-fəl\ *adj* — **zest·ful·ly** \-fə-lē\ *adv* — **zest·ful·ness** *n*

zesty \'zes-tē\ *adj* **:** having or characterized by zest **:** PIQUANT

ze·ta \'zāt-ə, 'zēt-\ *n* [Gk *zēta*] **:** the 6th letter of the Greek alphabet — symbol Z or ζ

zeug·ma \'züg-mə\ *n* [L, fr. Gk, lit., joining, fr. *zeugnynai* to join; akin to L *jungere* to join — more at YOKE] **:** the use of a word to modify or govern two or more words usu. in such a manner that it applies to each in a different sense or makes sense with only one

Zeus \'züs\ *n* [Gk] **:** the chief of the Olympian gods and husband of Hera

zib·e·line *or* **zib·el·line** \'zib-ə-ˌlēn, -ˌlīn\ *n* [MF, sable, fr. OIt *zibellino*, of Slav origin; akin to Russ *sobol'* sable] **:** a soft lustrous wool fabric with mohair, alpaca, or camel's hair

zib·et *or* **zib·eth** \'zib-ət\ *n* [It *zibetto* & ML *zibethum*, fr. Ar *zabād* civet perfume] **:** a common Asiatic civet cat (*Viverra zibetha*)

[1]**zig** \'zig\ *n* [*zigzag*] **:** one of the sharp turns or changes or a straight section of a zigzag course

[2]**zig** *vi* **zigged; zig·ging :** to execute a turn or follow a section of a zigzag course

zig·gu·rat \'zig-ə-ˌrat\ *n* [Akkadian *ziqqurratu* pinnacle] **:** an ancient Babylonian temple tower consisting of a lofty pyramidal structure built in successive stages with outside staircases and a shrine at the top

[1]**zig·zag** \'zig-ˌzag\ *n* [F] **:** one of a series of short sharp turns, angles, or alterations in a course; *also* **:** something marked by such a series

[2]**zigzag** *adv* **:** in or by a zigzag path or course

[3]**zigzag** *adj* **:** having short sharp turns or angles

[4]**zigzag** *vb* **zig·zagged; zig·zag·ging** *vt* **:** to form into a zigzag ~ *vi* **:** to lie in, proceed along, or consist of a zigzag course

zil·lion \'zil-yən\ *n* [*z* + *-illion* (as in *million*)] **:** a large indeterminate number

Zil·pah \'zil-pə\ *n* [Heb *Zilpāh*] **:** the mother of Gad and Asher

[1]**zinc** \'ziŋk\ *n, often attrib* [G *zink*] **:** a bluish white crystalline bivalent metallic element of low to intermediate hardness that is ductile when pure but in the commercial form is brittle at ordinary temperatures and becomes ductile on slight heating, occurs abundantly in minerals, and is used esp. as a protective coating for iron and steel — see ELEMENT table — **zinc·ic** \'ziŋ-kik\ *adj* — **zin·cous** \-kəs\ *adj*

[2]**zinc** *vt* **zinced** *or* **zincked** \'ziŋ(k)t\ **zinc·ing** *or* **zinck·ing** \'ziŋ-kiŋ\ **:** to treat or coat with zinc **:** GALVANIZE

zinc·ate \'ziŋ-ˌkāt\ *n* **:** a compound formed by reaction of zinc oxide or zinc with solutions of alkalies

zinc blende *n* **:** SPHALERITE

zinc·ite \'ziŋ-ˌkīt\ *n* [G *zinkit*, fr. *zink*] **:** a brittle deep-red to orange-yellow hexagonal mineral ZnO consisting of zinc oxide that occurs in massive or granular form — called also *red oxide of zinc, red zinc ore*

zincky *or* **zinky** *or* **zincy** \'ziŋ-kē\ *adj* **:** containing or having the appearance of zinc

zin·cog·ra·phy \ziŋ-'käg-rə-fē\ *n* [ISV] **1 :** the art or process of engraving or photoengraving letterpress printing surfaces on zinc **2 :** the art or process of preparing planographic printing surfaces on zinc

zinc·oid \'ziŋ-ˌkȯid\ *adj* **:** of, relating to, or resembling zinc

zinc ointment *n* **:** an ointment containing about 20 percent of zinc oxide and used in treating skin diseases

zinc oxide *n* **:** an infusible white solid ZnO used esp. as a pigment, in compounding rubber, and in pharmaceutical and cosmetic preparations

zinc white *n* **:** a white pigment used esp. in house paints and glazes that consists of zinc oxide

zin·fan·del \'zin-fən-ˌdel\ *n* [origin unknown] **:** a red table wine of the claret type made from a small black grape that is grown chiefly in California

zing \'ziŋ\ *n* [imit.] **1 :** a shrill humming noise **2 :** VITALITY, VIM — **zing** *vi*

zinj·an·thro·pus \zin-'jan(t)-thrə-pəs, ˌzin-ˌjan-'thrō-\ *n, pl* **zinj·an·thro·pi** \-ˌpī, -ˌpē\ *or* **zinj·an·thro·pus·es** [NL, genus name, fr. Ar *Zinj* eastern Africa + Gk *anthrōpos* human being] **:** any of a genus (*Zinjanthropus*) of fossil hominids based on a skull found in eastern Africa, characterized by very low brow and large molars, and tentatively assigned to the Lower Pleistocene

zin·ken·ite \'ziŋ-kə-ˌnīt\ *n* [G *zinkenit*, fr. J. K. L. *Zinken* †1862 G mineralogist] **:** a steel-gray mineral $Pb_6Sb_{14}S_{27}$ of metallic luster consisting of a lead antimony sulfide

zin·nia \'zin-ē-ə, 'zin-yə, 'zēn-\ *n* [NL, genus name, fr. Johann G. *Zinn* †1759 G botanist] **:** any of a small genus (*Zinnia*) of tropical American composite herbs with showy flower heads and long-lasting ray flowers

Zi·on \'zī-ən\ *n* [*Zion*, citadel in Palestine which was the nucleus of Jerusalem, fr. ME *Sion*, fr. OE, fr. LL, fr. Heb *Ṣīyōn*] **1 a :** the Jewish people **:** ISRAEL **b :** the Jewish homeland that is symbolic of Judaism or of Jewish national aspiration **c :** the ideal nation or society envisaged by Judaism **2 :** HEAVEN **3 :** UTOPIA

Zi·on·ism \'zī-ə-ˌniz-əm\ *n* **:** a theory, plan, or movement for setting up a Jewish national or religious community in Palestine — **Zi·on·ist** \-nəst\ *adj or n* — **Zi·on·is·tic** \ˌzī-ə-'nis-tik\ *adj*

[1]**zip** \'zip\ *vb* **zipped; zip·ping** [imit. of the sound of a speeding object] *vi* **1 :** to move or act with speed and vigor **2 :** to travel with a sharp hissing or humming sound ~ *vt* **1 :** to impart speed or force to **2 :** to add zest, interest, or life to — often used with *up*

[2]**zip** *n* **1 :** a sudden sharp hissing or sibilant sound **2 :** ENERGY, VIM

[3]**zip** *vb* **zipped; zip·ping** [back-formation fr. *zipper*] *vt* **1 :** to close or open with a zipper **2 :** to cause (a zipper) to open or shut

~ *vi* **:** to become open, closed, or attached by means of a zipper
zip code *n, often cap Z&I&P* [zone *i*mprovement *p*lan] **:** a five-digit number that identifies each postal delivery area in the U.S.
zip gun *n* **:** a gun that is made from a toy pistol or length of pipe, has a firing pin usu. powered by a rubber band, and fires a .22 caliber bullet
zip·per \'zip-ər\ *n* [fr. *Zipper*, a trademark] **:** a fastener consisting of two rows of metal or plastic teeth on strips of tape and a sliding piece that closes an opening by drawing the teeth together
zip·pered \-ərd\ *adj* **:** equipped with a zipper
zip·py \'zip-ē\ *adj* **:** full of zip **:** BRISK, SNAPPY
zi·ram \'zī(ə)r-,am\ *n* [*zinc* + *-ram* (as in *thiram*)] **:** a zinc salt $[(CH_3)_2NCSS]_2Zn$ used as a rubber accelerator and agricultural fungicide
zir·con \'zər-,kän\ *n* [G, modif. of F *jargon* jargoon, zircon, fr. It *giargone*] **:** a tetragonal mineral $ZrSiO_4$ consisting of a zirconium silicate and occurring usu. in square prisms of adamantine luster and brown or grayish color with transparent kinds esp. of reddish or brownish color being used as gems
zir·con·ate \'zər-kə-,nāt\ *n* **:** any of various compounds obtained usu. by heating zirconium oxide and a metal oxide or carbonate
zir·co·nia \,zər-'kō-nē-ə\ *n* [NL, fr. ISV *zircon*] **:** ZIRCONIUM OXIDE
zir·con·ic \,zər-'kän-ik\ *adj* **:** of, relating to, or containing zirconium
zir·co·ni·um \,zər-'kō-nē-əm\ *n* [NL, fr. ISV *zircon*] **:** a steel-gray strong ductile chiefly tetravalent metallic element with a high melting point that occurs widely in combined form esp. in zircon, is highly resistant to corrosion, and is used in alloys and in refractories and ceramics — see ELEMENT table
zirconium oxide *n* **:** a white crystalline compound ZrO_2 used esp. in refractories, in thermal and electric insulation, in abrasives, and in enamels and glazes — called also *zirconia*
zith·er \'zith-ər, 'zith-\ *n* [G, fr. L *cithara* lyre, fr. Gk *kithara*] **:** a musical instrument having 30 to 40 strings over a shallow horizontal soundboard and played with plectrum and fingers — **zith·er·ist** \-ə-rəst\ *n*

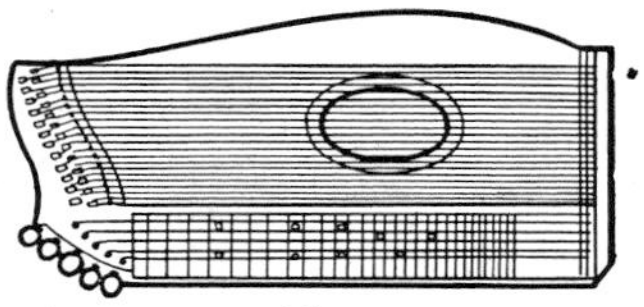
zither

zi·zith \'tsit-səs, tsēt-'sēt\ *n pl* [Heb *ṣīṣīth*] **:** the tassels of entwined threads worn by Jewish males at the 4 corners of the outer garment on the tallith
zlo·ty \'zlȯt-ē, zə-'lȯt-\ *n, pl* **zlo·tys** \-ēz\ *also* **zloty** [Pol *złoty*] — see MONEY table
zo- *or* **zoo-** *comb form* [Gk *zōi, zōio-*, fr. *zōion;* akin to Gk *zōē* life] **1 :** animal **:** animal kingdom or kind ⟨zooid⟩ ⟨*zoo*logy⟩ **2** [Gk *zō-* alive, fr. *zōos;* akin to Gk *zōē*] **:** motile ⟨*zoo*spore⟩
zoa *pl of* ZOON
-zoa \'zō-ə\ *n pl comb form* [NL, fr. Gk *zōia*, pl. of *zōion*] **:** animals — in taxa ⟨Meta*zoa*⟩
zo·an·thar·i·an \,zō-,an-'thar-ē-ən, -'ther-\ *n* [deriv. of *zo-* + Gk *anthos* flower — more at ANTHOLOGY] **:** any of a subclass (Zoantharia) of anthozoans having a hexamerous arrangement of tentacles or septa or both and including most of the recent corals and sea anemones — **zoantharian** *adj*
zo·ar·i·al \zō-'ar-ē-əl, zə-'war-, -'er-, -'wer-\ *adj* **:** of or relating to a zoarium
zo·ar·i·um \-ē-əm\ *n, pl* **zo·ar·ia** \-ē-ə\ [NL] **:** a colony of colonial bryozoans
zo·di·ac \'zōd-ē-,ak\ *n* [ME, fr. MF *zodiaque*, fr. L *zodiacus*, fr. Gk *zōidiakos*, fr. *zōidiakos*, adj., of carved figures, of the zodiac, fr. *zōidion* carved figure, sign of the zodiac, fr. dim. of *zōion* living being, figure; akin to Gk *zōē* life — more at QUICK] **1 a :** an imaginary belt in the heavens usu. 18 degrees wide that encompasses the apparent paths of all the principal planets except Pluto, that has the ecliptic as its central line, and that is divided into 12 constellations or signs each taken for astrological purposes to extend 30 degrees of longitude **b :** a figure representing the signs of the zodiac and their symbols **2 :** a cyclic course (as of time) — **zo·di·a·cal** \zō-'dī-ə-kəl, zə-\ *adj*

THE SIGNS OF THE ZODIAC

NUMBER	NAME	SYMBOL	SUN ENTERS
1	Aries the Ram	♈	March 21
2	Taurus the Bull	♉	April 20
3	Gemini the Twins	♊	May 21
4	Cancer the Crab	♋	June 22
5	Leo the Lion	♌	July 23
6	Virgo the Virgin	♍	August 23
7	Libra the Balance	♎	September 23
8	Scorpio the Scorpion	♏	October 24
9	Sagittarius the Archer	♐	November 22
10	Capricorn the Goat	♑	December 22
11	Aquarius the Water Bearer	♒	January 20
12	Pisces the Fishes	♓	February 19

zodiacal light *n* **:** a diffuse glow seen in the west after twilight and in the east before dawn
zo·ea \zō-'ē-ə\ *n, pl* **zo·eae** \-'ē-,ē\ *or* **zo·eas** \-'ē-əz\ [NL, fr. Gk *zōē* life] **:** an early larval form of many decapod crustaceans and esp. crabs with a relatively large cephalothorax, conspicuous eyes, and large fringed antennae and mouthparts used for swimming — **zo·e·al** \zō-'ē-əl\ *adj*
¹-zo·ic \'zō-ik\ *adj comb form* [Gk *zōikos* of animals, fr. *zōion* animal — more at ZO-] **:** having a (specified) animal mode of existence ⟨holo*zoic*⟩ ⟨endo*zoic*⟩ ⟨sapro*zoic*⟩
²-zoic *adj comb form* [Gk *zōē* life] **:** of, relating to, or being a (specified) geological era ⟨Archeo*zoic*⟩ ⟨Meso*zoic*⟩
zois·ite \'zȯi-,sīt\ *n* [G *zoisit*, fr. Baron Sigismund *Zois* von Edelstein †1819 Slovenian nobleman] **:** a mineral $Ca_2Al_3Si_3O_{12}OH$ consisting of a basic calcium aluminum silicate related to epidote
Zo·la·esque \,zō-lə-'esk, -,lä-\ *adj* **:** of, relating to, or characteristic of Zola or his writings
zom·bi *or* **zom·bie** \'zäm-bē\ *n* [of Niger-Congo origin; akin to Kongo *nzambi* god] **1 a :** the voodoo snake deity **b :** the supernatural power that according to voodoo belief may enter into and reanimate a dead body **c :** a will-less and speechless human in the West Indies capable only of automatic movement who is held to have died and been reanimated but often believed to have been drugged into a catalepsy for the hours of interment **2 :** a tall mixed drink made of several kinds of rum, liqueur, and fruit juice — **zom·bi·ism** \-bē-,iz-əm\ *n*
zon·al \'zōn-ᵊl\ *adj* **1 :** of, relating to, or having the form of a zone **2 :** of, relating to, or being a soil or major soil group marked by well-developed characteristics that are determined primarily by the action of climate and organisms esp. vegetation — compare AZONAL, INTRAZONAL — **zon·al·ly** \-ᵊl-ē\ *adv*
zon·ary \'zō-nə-rē\ *adj* **:** ZONAL 1
zon·ate \'zō-,nāt\ *also* **zon·at·ed** \-,nāt-əd\ *adj* **:** marked with or arranged in zones
zo·na·tion \zō-'nā-shən\ *n* **1 :** zonate structure **2 :** distribution of kinds of organisms in biogeographic zones
¹zone \'zōn\ *n* [L *zona* belt, zone, fr. Gk *zōnē;* akin to Lith *juosti* to gird] **1 :** any of five great divisions of the earth's surface with respect to latitude and temperature — compare FRIGID ZONE, TEMPERATE ZONE, TORRID ZONE **2** *archaic* **:** GIRDLE, BELT **3 a :** an encircling anatomical structure **b** (1) **:** a subdivision of a biogeographic region that supports a similar fauna and flora throughout its extent (2) **:** such a zone dominated by a particular life form **c :** a distinctive belt, layer, or series of layers of earth materials (as rock) **4 :** a region or area set off as distinct from surrounding or adjoining parts **5 :** one of the sections of an area or territory created for a particular purpose: as **a :** a zoned section of a city **b :** any of the eight concentric bands of territory centered on a given postal shipment point designated as a distance bracket for U.S. parcel post to which mail is charged at a single rate — called also *parcel post zone* **c :** one of the numbered sections into which a metropolitan area is divided in the U.S. postal system **d :** a distance within which the same fare is charged by a common carrier **e :** an area on a field of play **f :** a stretch of roadway or a space in which certain traffic regulations are in force

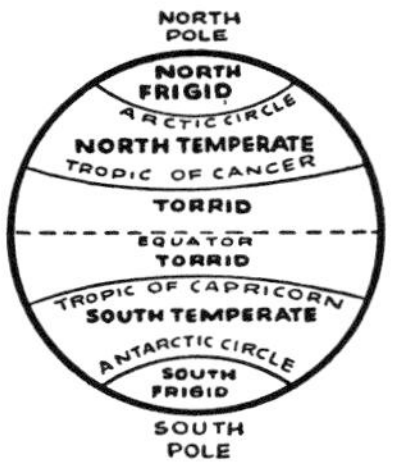

zones 1

²zone *vt* **1 :** to surround with a zone **:** ENCIRCLE **2 :** to arrange in or mark off into zones; *specif* **:** to partition (a city, borough, or township) by ordinance into sections reserved for different purposes (as residence, business, manufacturing)
Zon·ta \'zänt-ə\ *n* [Sioux *zon'-ta* honest] **:** one of an organization of service clubs made up of executive women each of whom is a sole representative of one business or profession in a community
zo·nu·lar \'zō-nyə-lər\ *adj* **:** of or relating to a zonule
zo·nule \'zō-(,)nyü(ə)l\ *n* **:** a little zone, belt, or girdle
zoo \'zü\ *n* [short for *zoological garden*] **:** a zoological garden or collection of living animals usu. for public display
zoo- — see ZO-
zoo–ecol·o·gy \,zō-ə-wē-'käl-ə-jē\ *n* **:** a branch of ecology dealing with the relation of animals to their environment and to other animals
zoo·fla·gel·late \,zō-ə-'flaj-ə-lət, -,lāt; -flə-'jel-ət\ *n* **:** a flagellate protozoan lacking photosynthesis and other plantlike characteristics — compare PLANTLIKE FLAGELLATE
zoo·ga·mete \,zō-ə-gə-'mēt, -'gam-,ēt\ *n* [ISV] **:** a motile gamete esp. of a plant (as an alga)
zoo·gen·ic \,zō-ə-'jen-ik\ *or* **zo·og·e·nous** \zō-'äj-ə-nəs\ *adj* [ISV] **:** caused by or associated with animals or their activities ⟨~ humus⟩
zoo·ge·og·ra·pher \,zō-ə-jē-'äg-rə-fər\ *n* **:** a student of animal distribution
zoo·geo·graph·ic \-,jē-ə-'graf-ik\ *adj* **:** of or relating to zoogeography — **zoo·geo·graph·i·cal** \-i-kəl\ *adj* — **zoo·geo·graph·i·cal·ly** \-i-k(ə-)lē\ *adv*
zoo·ge·og·ra·phy \-jē-'äg-rə-fē\ *n* [ISV] **:** a branch of biogeography concerned with the geographical distribution of animals and esp. with the determination of the areas characterized by special groups of animals and the study of the causes and significance of such groups
zoo·glea \zō-'äg-lē-ə, ,zō-ə-'glē-ə\ *n, pl* **zoo·gle·as** *or* **zoo·gle·ae** \-lē-,ē, -'glē-,ē\ [NL, fr. *zo-* + MGk *glia, gloea* glue — more at CLAY] **:** a gelatinous or mucilaginous mass formed by bacteria growing in fluid media rich in organic material and made up of bacterial bodies embedded in a matrix of swollen confluent capsule substance — **zoo·gle·al** \-lē-əl, -'glē-əl\ *adj*
zoo·graph·ic \,zō-ə-'graf-ik\ *adj* **:** of or relating to zoography — **zoo·graph·i·cal** \-i-kəl\ *adj*
zo·og·ra·phy \zō-'äg-rə-fē, zə-'wäg-\ *n* **1 :** descriptive zoology **2 :** ZOOGEOGRAPHY
zo·oid \'zō-,ȯid\ *n* **:** an entity that resembles but is not wholly the same as a separate individual organism: as **a :** an organized body (as a phagocyte or a sperm cell) having locomotion **b :** a more or less independent animal produced (as by fission, proliferation, or strobilation) by other than direct sexual methods and so having an equivocal individuality — **zo·oi·dal** \zō-'ȯid-ᵊl, zə-'wȯid-\ *adj*
zooks \'zu̇ks\ *interj* — used as a mild oath
zo·ol·a·try \zō-'äl-ə-trē, zə-'wäl-\ *n* [NL *zoolatria*, fr. *zo-* + LL *-latria* -latry] **:** animal worship
zoo·log·i·cal \,zō-ə-'läj-i-kəl\ *adj* **1 :** of, relating to, or occupied with zoology **2 :** of, relating to, or affecting lower animals often as distinguished from man — **zoo·log·i·cal·ly** \-i-k(ə-)lē\ *adv*
zoological garden *n* **:** a garden or park where wild animals are kept for exhibition
zo·ol·o·gist \zō-'äl-ə-jəst, zə-'wäl-\ *n* **:** a specialist in zoology
zo·ol·o·gy \-jē\ *n* [NL *zoologia*, fr. *zo-* + *-logia* -logy] **1 :** a science that deals with animals and is the branch of biology concerned with the animal kingdom and its members as individuals and classes and with animal life **2 :** a treatise on zoology **3 a :** animal life (as of a region) **:** FAUNA **b :** the properties and vital phenomena exhibited by an animal, animal type, or group
¹zoom \'züm\ *vb* [imit.] *vi* **1 :** to move with a loud low hum or buzz **2** *of an airplane* **:** to climb for a short time at an angle greater than that which can be maintained in steady flight so that the machine is carried upward at the expense of stored kinetic energy **3** *of a motion-picture or television camera* **:** to move toward or away

from an object rapidly so that the image appears to come closer to or to move away from the observer ~ *vt* : to cause to zoom

²**zoom** *n* **1** : an act or process of zooming; *specif* : a sharp upward movement **2** : a zooming sound

zoo·met·ric \ˌzō-ə-'me-trik\ *adj* : designed for the measurement of animals and esp. for the estimation of a measure of bulk through determination of some linear measurement ⟨a ~ tape⟩ — **zoo·met·ri·cal** \-tri-kəl\ *adj*

zoom lens *n* : a camera lens in which the image size can be varied continuously so that the image remains in focus at all times

zoo·mor·phic \ˌzō-ə-'mȯr-fik\ *adj* [ISV] **1** : having the form of an animal **2** : of or relating to a deity conceived of in animal form or with the attributes of an animal

zoo·mor·phism \-ˌfiz-əm\ *n* [ISV] **1** : the representation of deity in the form or with the attributes of the lower animals **2** : the use of animal forms in art or symbolism

zo·on \'zō-ˌän\ *n, pl* **zoa** \'zō-ə\ [NL, fr. Gk *zōion* animal — more at ZO-] **1** : the whole product of one fertilized egg whether a single individual, a colony of associated zooids, or an asexual progeny of a sexually produced individual **2** : ZOOID — **zo·on·al** \'zō-ən-ᵊl, -ˌän-\ *adj*

-zo·on \'zō-ˌän *also* zə-\ *n comb form, pl* **-zoa** \'zō-ə\ [NL, fr. Gk *zōion*] : animal : zooid ⟨hematozoon⟩ ⟨spermatozoon⟩

zoo·no·sis \ˌzō-'än-ə-səs, zə-'wän-; ˌzō-ə-'nō-səs\ *n* [NL, fr. zo- + Gk *nosos* disease] : a disease communicable from lower animals to man under natural conditions — **zoo·not·ic** \ˌzō-ə-'nät-ik\ *adj*

zoo·par·a·site \ˌzō-ə-'par-ə-ˌsīt\ *n* : a parasitic animal — **zoo·par·a·sit·ic** \-ˌpar-ə-'sit-ik\ *adj*

zo·oph·a·gous \zō-'äf-ə-gəs, zə-'wäf-\ *adj* [ISV] : feeding on animals : CARNIVOROUS

zo·oph·i·lous \zō-'äf-ə-ləs, zə-'wäf-\ *or* **zoo·phil·ic** \ˌzō-ə-'fil-ik\ *adj* : having an attraction to or preference for animals; *esp* : adapted to pollination by animals other than insects — compare ENTOMOPHILOUS

zoo·phyte \'zō-ə-ˌfīt\ *n* [Gk *zōophyton*, fr. *zōi-, zō-* zo- + *phyton* plant — more at PHYT-] : any of numerous invertebrate animals (as a coral, sea anemone, or sponge) more or less resembling plants in appearance or mode of growth; *esp* : one that forms a branching arborescent colony attached to a substrate — **zoo·phyt·ic** \ˌzō-ə-'fit-ik\ *adj*

zoo·plank·ton \ˌzō-ə-'plaŋ(k)-tən, -ˌtän\ *n* : animal life of the plankton — **zoo·plank·ton·ic** \-ˌplaŋ(k)-'tän-ik\ *adj*

zoo·sperm \'zō-ə-ˌspərm\ *n* [ISV] **1** : SPERMATOZOID, SPERMATOZOON **2** : ZOOSPORE

zoo·spo·ran·gi·um \ˌzō-ə-spə-'ran-jē-əm\ *n* [NL] : a spore case or sporangium bearing zoospores

zoo·spore \'zō-ə-ˌspō(ə)r, -ˌspȯ(ə)r\ *n* [ISV] : an independently motile spore: as **a** : a motile usu. naked and flagellated asexual spore esp. of an alga or lower fungus **b** : a minute amoeboid or flagellated product of protozoan sporocyst division whether sexual or asexual

zo·os·ter·ol \zō-'äs-tə-ˌrȯl, zə-'wäs-, -ˌrōl\ *n* : any of a group of sterols (as cholesterol) of animal origin — compare PHYTOSTEROL

zoo·tech·ni·cal \ˌzō-ə-'tek-ni-kəl\ *adj* : of or relating to zootechny

zoo·tech·ni·cian \-(ˌ)tek-'nish-ən\ *n* : a specialist in zootechny

zoo·tech·nics \-'tek-niks\ *n pl but sing or pl in constr* : ZOOTECHNY

zoo·tech·ny \'zō-ə-ˌtek-nē\ *n* [ISV zo- + Gk *technē* art — more at TECHNICAL] : the system of maintaining and improving animals under domestication that constitutes the technology of animal husbandry

zo·ot·o·my \zō-'ät-ə-mē, zə-'wät-\ *n* : animal anatomy esp. as studied on a comparative basis

zoot suit \'züt-\ *n* [origin unknown] : a flashy suit of extreme cut typically consisting of a thigh-length jacket with wide padded shoulders and peg-top trousers tapering to narrow cuffs — **zoot-suit·er** \-ˌsüt-ər\ *n*

Zo·ro·as·tri·an \ˌzōr-ə-'was-trē-ən, ˌzȯr-\ *adj* : of or relating to the Persian prophet Zoroaster or the religion founded by him and marked by belief in a cosmic war between good and evil — **Zoroastrian** *n* — **Zo·ro·as·tri·an·ism** \-trē-ə-ˌniz-əm\ *n*

zos·ter \'zōs-tər, 'zäs-\ *n* [L, fr. Gk *zōstēr* girdle; akin to Gk *zōnē* zone] : HERPES ZOSTER

Zou·ave \zü-'äv\ *n* [F, fr. *Zwāwa*, Algerian tribe] **1** : a member of a French infantry unit orig. composed of Algerians wearing a brilliant uniform and conducting a quick spirited drill **2** : a member of a military unit modeled on the Algerian Zouaves

zounds \'zaún(d)z\ *interj* [euphemism for *God's wounds*] — used as a mild oath

zoy·sia \'zȯi-sē-ə\ *n* [NL, alter. of *Zoisia*, genus name, fr. Karl von Zois †1800 G botanist] : any of a genus (*Zoisia*) of creeping perennial grasses having fine wiry leaves and including some suitable for lawn grasses in warm regions

zuc·chet·to \zü-'ket-(ˌ)ō, tsü-\ *n* [It, fr. *zucca* gourd, head, fr. LL *cucutia* gourd] : a small round skullcap worn by Roman Catholic ecclesiastics in colors that vary according to the rank of the wearer

zuc·chi·ni \zü-'kē-nē, tsü-\ *n, pl* **zucchini** *or* **zucchinis** [It, pl. of *zucchino*, dim. of *zucca* gourd] : a summer squash of bushy growth with smooth slender cylindrical dark green fruits

¹**Zu·lu** \'zü-(ˌ)lü\ *n* **1** : a member of a Bantu-speaking people of Natal **2** : the Bantu language of the Zulus — **Zulu** *adj*

²**Zulu** — a communications code word for the letter *z*

Zu·ñi \'zü-n(y)ē\ *n, pl* **Zuñi** *or* **Zuñis** [Sp, fr. Keresan *sīni* middle] **1 a** : a people occupying a pueblo in western New Mexico **b** : a member of this people **2** : the language of the Zuñi people — **Zu·ñi·an** \-n(y)ē-ən\ *adj*

Zu·ñi·an \-n(y)ē-ən\ *n* : a language family consisting of Zuñi only

zwie·back \'swē-ˌbak, -ˌbäk, 'swī-, 'zwē-, zə-'wē-, 'zwī-, zə-'wī-\ *n* [G, lit., twice baked, fr. *zwie-* twice (fr. OHG *zwi-*) + *backen* to bake, fr. OHG *bahhan* — more at TWI-, BAKE] : a usu. sweetened bread enriched with eggs that is baked and then sliced and toasted until dry and crisp

Zwing·li·an \'zwiŋ-(g)lē-ən, 'swiŋ-; 'tsfiŋ-lē-\ *adj* : of or relating to Ulrich Zwingli or his doctrine that in the Lord's Supper there is an influence of Christ upon the soul but that the true body of Christ is present by the contemplation of faith and not in essence or reality — **Zwinglian** *n* — **Zwing·li·an·ism** \-ə-ˌniz-əm\ *n* — **Zwing·li·an·ist** \-nəst\ *n or adj*

zwit·ter·ion \'tsfit-ə-ˌrī-ən, -ˌrī-ˌän\ *n* [G, fr. *zwitter* hybrid + *ion*] : a dipolar ion — **zwit·ter·ion·ic** \ˌtsfit-ə-(ˌ)rī-'än-ik\ *adj*

zyg- *or* **zygo-** *comb form* [NL, fr. Gk *zygon* — more at YOKE] **1** : yoke ⟨zygomorphic⟩ **2** : pair ⟨zygodactyl⟩ **3** : union : zygosis ⟨zygospore⟩

zyg·apoph·y·sis \ˌzī-gə-'päf-ə-səs\ *n* [NL] : one of the articular processes of the neural arch of a vertebra of which there are usu. two anterior and two posterior

zy·go·dac·tyl \ˌzī-gə-'dak-tᵊl\ *or* **zy·go·dac·ty·lous** \-tə-ləs\ *adj* [ISV *zyg-* + Gk *daktylos* toe] : having the toes arranged two in front and two behind — used of a bird — **zygodactyl** *n*

zy·go·gen·e·sis \-'jen-ə-səs\ *n* [NL] : reproduction by means of specialized germ cells or gametes

zy·goid \'zī-ˌgȯid\ *adj* : of or relating to a zygote : ZYGOTIC

zy·go·ma \zī-'gō-mə\ *n, pl* **zy·go·ma·ta** \-mət-ə\ *also* **zygomas** [NL *zygomat-, zygoma*, fr. Gk *zygōma*, fr. *zygoun* to join, fr. *zygon* yoke] **1 a** : ZYGOMATIC ARCH **b** : a slender bony process of the zygomatic arch **2** : ZYGOMATIC BONE

zy·go·mat·ic \ˌzī-gə-'mat-ik\ *adj* : of, relating to, constituting, or situated in the region of the zygoma and esp. the zygomatic arch as a whole

zygomatic arch *n* : the arch of bone that extends along the front or side of the skull beneath the orbit

zygomatic bone *n* : a bone of the side of the face below the eye that in mammals forms part of the zygomatic arch and part of the orbit — called also *cheekbone*

zygomatic process *n* : any of several bony processes that enter into or strengthen the zygomatic arch

zy·go·mor·phic \ˌzī-gə-'mȯr-fik\ *adj* : bilaterally symmetrical and capable of division into essentially symmetrical halves by only one longitudinal plane passing through the axis — compare ACTINOMORPHIC — **zy·go·mor·phism** \-ˌfiz-əm\ *n or* **zy·go·mor·phy** \'zī-gə-ˌmȯr-fē\ *n*

zy·gose \'zī-ˌgōs\ *adj* : of or relating to zygosis

zy·go·sis \zī-'gō-səs\ *n, pl* **zy·go·ses** \-'gō-ˌsēz\ [NL] : zygote formation by union of gametes : CONJUGATION — compare HETEROZYGOSIS

zy·gos·i·ty \zī-'gäs-ət-ē\ *n* : zygotic quality or characteristics

zy·go·sphere \'zī-gə-ˌsfi(ə)r\ *n* : a plant gamete capable of uniting with a similar one to form a zygospore

zy·go·spore \'zī-gə-ˌspō(ə)r, -ˌspȯ(ə)r\ *n* [ISV] : a plant spore that is formed by conjugation of two similar sexual cells, usu. serves as a resting spore, and ultimately produces the sporophytic phase of the plant — compare OOSPORE — **zy·go·spor·ic** \ˌzī-gə-'spōr-ik, -'spȯr-\ *adj*

zy·gote \'zī-ˌgōt\ *n* [Gk *zygōtos* yoked, fr. *zygoun* to join together — more at ZYGOMA] : a cell formed by the union of two gametes; *broadly* : the developing individual produced from such a cell — **zy·got·ic** \zī-'gät-ik\ *adj* — **zy·got·i·cal·ly** \-i-k(ə-)lē\ *adv*

zy·go·tene \'zī-gə-ˌtēn\ *n* [ISV *zyg-* + *-tene* filament, fr. Gk *tainia* band, fillet] : the synaptic stage in meiosis in which homologous chromosomes pair intimately

-zy·gous \'zī-gəs, z-i-gəs\ *adj comb form* [Gk *-zygos* yoked, fr. *zygon* yoke — more at YOKE] : having (such) a zygotic constitution ⟨heterozygous⟩

zym- *or* **zymo-** *comb form* [NL, fr. Gk leaven, fr. *zymē*] **1** : fermentation ⟨zymogen⟩ **2** : enzyme ⟨zymase⟩

zy·mase \'zī-ˌmās, -ˌmāz\ *n* [ISV] : an enzyme or enzyme complex that promotes glycolysis

-zyme \ˌzīm\ *n comb form* [Gk *zymē* leaven] : enzyme ⟨lysozyme⟩

zy·mo·gen \'zī-mə-jən\ *n* [ISV] : an inactive protein precursor of an enzyme secreted by living cells and activated by catalysis (as by a kinase or an acid) — called also *proenzyme*

zy·mo·gen·ic \ˌzī-mə-'jen-ik\ *adj* **1** : producing fermentation **2** : of or relating to a zymogen

zy·mol·o·gy \zī-'mäl-ə-jē\ *n* [NL *zymologia*, fr. *zym-* + *-logia* -logy] : a science that deals with fermentation

zy·mo·plas·tic \ˌzī-mə-'plas-tik\ *adj* : participating in the formation of enzymes — compare THROMBOPLASTIC

zy·mo·scope \'zī-mə-ˌskōp\ *n* [ISV] : an apparatus for determining the fermenting power of yeast by measuring the carbon dioxide evolved from a known quantity of sugar

zy·mo·sis \zī-'mō-səs\ *n* [NL, fr. Gk *zymōsis*, fr. *zymoun* to ferment, fr. *zymē* leaven] : FERMENTATION

zy·mo·sthen·ic \ˌzī-məs-'then-ik\ *adj* : strengthening the activity of an enzyme

zy·mot·ic \zī-'mät-ik\ *adj* **1** : of, relating to, causing, or caused by fermentation **2** : relating to, constituting, or causing an infectious or contagious disease — **zy·mot·i·cal·ly** \-i-k(ə-)lē\ *adv*

zy·mur·gy \'zī-(ˌ)mər-jē\ *n* : a branch of applied chemistry that deals with fermentation processes

ABBREVIATIONS

AND SYMBOLS FOR CHEMICAL ELEMENTS

For a list of special abbreviations used in this dictionary see page 22a preceding the vocabulary.
Most of these abbreviations have been normalized to one form. Variation in use of periods, in typeface,
and in capitalization is frequent and widespread (as *mph, MPH, m.p.h., Mph*)

---

a acre, ampere, anode, answer, ante, anterior, are
A ace, angstrom unit, argon
aa ana
AA Alcoholics Anonymous, antiaircraft, associate in arts, author's alterations
AAA Agricultural Adjustment Administration, American Automobile Association
AAAL American Academy of Arts and Letters
AAAS American Association for the Advancement of Science
AACS Airways and Air Communications Service
A and M agricultural and mechanical
A and R artists and repertory
AAR against all risks
AAS associate in applied science
AAU Amateur Athletic Union
AAUN American Association for the United Nations
AAUP American Association of University Professors
AAUW American Association of University Women
AB able-bodied seaman, airborne, bachelor of arts
ABA American Bar Association
abbr abbreviation
ABC American Bowling Congress, American Broadcasting Company, Australian Broadcasting Company
abd, abdom abdomen, abdominal
AB in Th bachelor of arts in theology
abl ablative
abn airborne
abp archbishop
abr abridged, abridgment
abs absolute
ABS American Bible Society
abstr abstract
ac account
Ac actinium, altocumulus
AC alternating current, ante Christum (L, before Christ), ante cibum (L, before meals), athletic club
acad academic, academy
acc, accus accusative
ACC Air Coordinating Committee
acct account
ACE American Council on Education
ack acknowledge, acknowledgment
ACLS American Council of Learned Societies
ACP American College of Physicians
acpt acceptance
ACS American Chemical Society, American College of Surgeons, antireticular cytotoxic serum
act active, actual
A.C.T. Australian Capital Territory
actg acting
ACTH adrenocorticotropic hormone
AD active duty, after date, air-dried, anno Domini, assembly district
ADC aide-de-camp
addn addition
addnl additional
ADF automatic direction finder
ADH antidiuretic hormone
ad int ad interim (L, in the meantime)
ADIZ air defense identification zone
adj adjective, adjunct, adjustment, adjutant
ad loc ad locum (L, to or at the place)

adm administration, administrative, admiral
admin administration
adv adverb, adversus (L, against), advertisement, advertising, advisory
ad val ad valorem
advt advertisement
AEC Atomic Energy Commission
AEF American Expeditionary Force
aeq aequales (L, equal)
aet, aetat aetatis (L, of age, aged)
AF air force, audio frequency
AFAM Ancient Free and Accepted Masons
AFB air force base
AFC automatic frequency control
aff affirmative
afft affidavit
AFL–CIO American Federation of Labor and Congress of Industrial Organizations
Afr Africa, African
aft afternoon
Ag argentum (L, silver)
AG adjutant general, attorney general
agcy agency
agr, agric agricultural, agriculture
agt agent
ah ampere-hour
AH anno hegirae
AHA American Historical Association
a.i. ad interim (L, in the meantime)
AI airborne intercept, air interception
AIA American Institute of Architects
AIChE American Institute of Chemical Engineers
AID Agency for International Development
AIEE American Institute of Electrical Engineers
AK Alaska
AKC American Kennel Club
Al aluminum
AL Alabama, American Legion
Ala Alabama
ALA American Library Association, Automobile Legal Association
Alb Albanian
alc alcohol
ald alderman
alg algebra
alk alkaline
alky alkalinity
ALS autograph letter signed
alt alternate, altitude
Alta Alberta
alw allowance
a.m. ante meridiem
Am America, American, americium
AM air medal, Albert medal, amplitude modulation, master of arts
AMA American Medical Association
amb ambassador
amdt amendment
Amer America, American
AMF airmail field
AMG allied military government
amp ampere
amp hr ampere-hour
AMS Agricultural Marketing Service
amt amount
AMU atomic mass unit
AMVETS American Veterans (of World War II)
an anno, annum
ANA American Nurses Association

anal analogy, analysis, analytic
anat anatomical, anatomy
anc ancient
Ang Anglesey
anhyd anhydrous
ann annals, annual
anon anonymous
ans answer
ant antenna, antonym
Ant Antrim
anthrop anthropological, anthropology
antilog antilogarithm
antiq antiquarian, antiquary
a/o account of
AOH Ancient Order of Hibernians
aor aorist
ap apostle
AP additional premium, airplane, antipersonnel, arithmetic progression, armor-piercing, Associated Press, author's proof
APA American Philological Association
APB all points bulletin
API air position indicator, American Petroleum Institute
APO army post office
app apparatus, appendix
appl applied
approx approximate, approximately
apps appendixes
appt appoint, appointed
apptd appointed
Apr April
apt apartment
aq aqua, aqueous
AQ accomplishment quotient, achievement quotient
ar arrival, arrive
Ar argon
AR acknowledgment of receipt, all rail, all risks, annual return, Arkansas, army regulation, autonomous republic
Arab Arabian, Arabic
ARC American Red Cross
arch, archit architecture
archeol archeology
arg argent
Arg Argyle
ARIBA Associate of the Royal Institute of British Architects
arith arithmetic
Ariz Arizona
Ark Arkansas
Arm Armagh, Armenian
ARP air-raid precautions
arr arranged, arrival, arrive
ARS Agricultural Research Service
art article, artificial, artillery
arty artillery
As altostratus, arsenic
AS after sight, airspeed, Anglo-Saxon, antisubmarine
ASA American Standards Association
asb asbestos
ASCAP American Society of Composers, Authors and Publishers
ASCE American Society of Civil Engineers
asg assigned, assignment
asgd assigned
asgmt assignment
ASI airspeed indicator
ASLA American Society of Landscape Architects
ASME American Society of Mechanical Engineers
ASR airport surveillance radar, air-sea rescue
assn association
asso, assoc associate, association
ASSR Autonomous Soviet Socialist Republic
asst assistant
asstd assented, assorted

assy assembly
Assyr Assyrian
ASTM American Society for Testing and Materials
ASTP army specialized training program
astrol astrology
astron astronomer, astronomy
ASV American Standard Version
at airtight, atomic
At astatine
AT antitank
Atl Atlantic
atm atmosphere, atmospheric
at. no. atomic number
ATP adenosine triphosphate
att attached, attention, attorney
attn attention
attrib attributive, attributively
atty attorney
atty gen attorney general
at. wt. atomic weight
Au aurum (L, gold)
AU angstrom unit
aud audit, auditor
aug augmentative
Aug August
AUS Army of the United States
Austral Australian
auth authentic, author, authorized
aux auxiliary
av avenue, average, avoirdupois
AV ad valorem, audiovisual, Authorized Version
AVC American Veterans Committee, automatic volume control
avdp avoirdupois
ave avenue
avg average
avn aviation
AW actual weight, aircraft warning, all water, articles of war, automatic weapon
AWOL absent without leave
ax axiom
Ayr Ayrshire
az azimuth, azure
AZ Arizona

b bacillus, black, blue, book, born
B bachelor, Baumé, bishop, bolivar, boliviano, boron, brightness, bulb
Ba barium
BA bachelor of arts, Buenos Aires
bact bacterial, bacteriology, bacterium
bal balance
b & w black and white
bar barometer, barometric
BAR Browning automatic rifle
BArch bachelor of architecture
Bart, Bt baronet
Bav Bavarian
BB ball bearing, best of breed
BBB Better Business Bureau
BBC British Broadcasting Corporation
bbl barrel, barrels
B.C. before Christ, British Columbia
BCG bacillus Calmette-Guérin
BChE bachelor of chemical engineering
BCL bachelor of canon law, bachelor of civil law
bcn beacon
BCS bachelor of commercial science
bd board, bound
BD bachelor of divinity, bank draft, barrels per day, bills discounted, bomb disposal, brought down
bd ft board foot
bdl bundle
bds boards, bound in boards
Be beryllium
Bé Baumé
BE bachelor of education, bachelor of engineering, bill of exchange

BEC Bureau of Employees' Compensation
BEd bachelor of education
Beds Bedfordshire
bef before
BEF British Expeditionary Force, British Expeditionary Forces
Belg Belgian, Belgium
BEM British Empire Medal
Berks Berkshire
Berw Berwick
bet between
BEV billion electron volts
bf boldface
BF brought forward
BFA bachelor of fine arts
bg bag
BHC benzene hexachloride
bhd bulkhead
BHN Brinell hardness number
BHP brake horsepower
Bi bismuth
bib Bible, biblical
bibliog bibliographer, bibliography
BID bis in die (L, twice a day)
biochem biochemistry
biog biographical, biography
biol biologic, biological, biology
BJ bachelor of journalism
bk bank, book
Bk berkelium
bkg banking
bkgd background
bks barracks, books
bkt basket, bracket
bl bale
B/L bill of lading
bldg building
BldgE building engineer
bldr builder
BLitt, BLit bachelor of letters, bachelor of literature
blk black, block
bls bales
BLS Bureau of Labor Statistics
blvd boulevard
bm beam
BM basal metabolism, bench mark, board measure, bowel movement
B/M bill of material
BMEP brake mean effective pressure
BMOC big man on campus
BMR basal metabolic rate
bn battalion
BNA Basle Nomina Anatomica
BO bad order, body odor, box office, branch office, buyer's option
BOD biochemical oxygen demand
BOQ bachelor officers' quarters
bor borough
bot botanical, botany
botan botanical
bp bishop, boiling point
BP bills payable, blood pressure, British Pharmacopoeia
BPD barrels per day
bpl birthplace
BPOE Benevolent and Protective Order of Elks
BPW Board of Public Works, Business and Professional Women's Clubs
br branch, brass, brown
Br British, bromine
BR bedroom, bills receivable
Braz Brazilian
Breck, Brecon Brecknockshire
brig brigade, brigadier
brig gen brigadier general
Brit Britain, British
brl barrel
bro brother, brothers
bros brothers
BS bachelor of science, balance sheet, bill of sale
BSA bachelor of science in agriculture, Boy Scouts of America
BSc bachelor of science
BSEd, BSE bachelor of science in education
BSFS bachelor of science in foreign service
BSI British Standards Institution
BS in CE bachelor of science in chemical engineering, bachelor of science in civil engineering
BS in ChE bachelor of science in chemical engineering
BS in Ed bachelor of science in education
BS in LS bachelor of science in library science, bachelor of science in library service

bskt basket
BT berth terms
btry battery
Btu British thermal unit, British thermal units
bu bureau, bushel, bushels
Bucks Buckinghamshire
Bulg Bulgarian
bull bulletin
bur bureau
bus business
BV Blessed Virgin
bvt brevet
B.W.I. British West Indies
bx box

c candle, capacitance, carat, cathode, cent, centime, century, chapter, circa, copyright, cup, cycle
C carbon, cedi, Celsius, centigrade, centum
ca centare, circa
Ca calcium
CA California, capital account, chartered accountant, chief accountant, chronological age, commercial agent, controller of accounts, crown agent, current account
CAB Civil Aeronautics Board
CADO Central Air Documents Office
CAF cost and freight
Caith Caithness
cal calendar, caliber, calorie, calories
Cal large calorie
calc calculate, calculated
Calif, Cal California
Cambs Cambridgeshire
Can, Canad Canada, Canadian
canc, can canceled
C and F cost and freight
C and LC capitals and lower case
Cantab Cantabrigiensis (L, of Cambridge)
cap capacity, capital, capitalize, capitalized
CAP Civil Air Patrol
caps capitals, capsule
capt captain
Car Carlow
CAR civil air regulations
card cardinal
Card Cardiganshire
CARE Cooperative for American Relief Everywhere
Carm Carmarthenshire
Carn Caernarvonshire
cat catalog
cath cathedral
caus causative
cav cavalry
CAVU ceiling and visibility unlimited
Cb columbium, cumulonimbus
CB confined to barracks, county borough
CBC Canadian Broadcasting Corporation
CBD cash before delivery
CBS Columbia Broadcasting System
cc cubic centimeter, cubic centimeters
Cc cirrocumulus
CC carbon copy, chief clerk, common carrier
CCC Civilian Conservation Corps, Commodity Credit Corporation
CCF Chinese communist forces, Cooperative Commonwealth Federation (of Canada)
ccw counterclockwise
cd cord
Cd cadmium
CD carried down, certificate of deposit, civil defense, corps diplomatique (F, diplomatic corps), current density
CDD certificate of disability for discharge
cdr commander
Ce cerium
CE chemical engineer, civil engineer, International Society of Christian Endeavor
CEA Council of Economic Advisors
CED Committee for Economic Development
cem cement
CEMF counter electromotive force
cen central
cent centigrade, central, centum, century
cert certificate, certification, certified, certify

cf calf, confer (L, compare)
Cf californium
CF carried forward, centrifugal force, cost and freight
CFI cost, freight and insurance
CFM cubic feet per minute
CFS cubic feet per second
cg, cgm centigram
CG center of gravity, coast guard, commanding general
cgs centimeter-gram-second
CGT Confédération Générale du Travail (Fr, General Confederation of Labor)
ch chain, chains, champion, chaplain, chapter, chief, child, children, church
CH clearinghouse, courthouse, customhouse
chan channel
chap chapter
chem chemical, chemist, chemistry
Ches Cheshire
chg charge
Chin Chinese
chm chairman
chron chronicle, chronological, chronology
Ci cirrus
CI cast iron, certificate of insurance, cost and insurance
cía compañía (Sp, company)
CIA Central Intelligence Agency
CID Criminal Investigation Department (Scotland Yard)
cie compagnie (F, company)
CIF cost, insurance and freight
C in C commander in chief
cir, circ circular
cit citation, cited, citizen
civ civil, civilian
CJ chief justice
ck cask, check
cl centiliter, class, clause, close, closet, cloth
Cl chlorine
CL carload, center line
Cla Clackmannan
cld called, cleared
clin clinical
clk clerk
clo clothing
clr clear
CLU chartered life underwriter
cm centimeter, centimeters
Cm curium
CM center matched, circular mil, Congregation of the Mission, countermarked
cmd, comd command
cmdg, comdg commanding
CMG Companion of (the Order of) St. Michael and St. George
cml commercial
CN credit note
CNO chief of naval operations
CNS central nervous system
co company, county
c/o care of
Co cobalt
CO cash order, Colorado, commanding officer, conscientious objector
cod codex
COD cash on delivery, collect on delivery
coeff, coef coefficient
C of C Chamber of Commerce
C of S chief of staff
cog cognate
col college, colonel, colonial, colony, color, colored, column
coll collection, collector, college
collat, coll collateral
colloq colloquial
Colo Colorado
colog cologarithm
com comedy, command, commandant, commander, commissioner, committee, common
comb combination, combining
comdr, cmdr commander
comdt commandant
coml commercial
comm commission, commonwealth
commo commodore
comp comparative, compiled, compiler, composition, compound
compd compound
comr commissioner
con conjunx (L, wife), consolidated, consul, continued, contra (L, against)
conc concentrate, concentrated, concentration, concrete
conch, conchol conchology
concn concentration

cond conductivity
conf conference
Confed Confederate
cong congress
conj conjunction
Conn Connecticut
cons consonant
consol consolidated
const constant, constitution, constitutional
constr construction
cont containing, contents, continent, continental, continued, control
contd continued
contg containing
contr contract, contraction
contrib contribution, contributor
conv convention, convertible
Cop, Copt Coptic
cor corner, corrected, correction
Corn Cornwall
corp corporal, corporation
corr corrected, correction, correspondence, corresponding, corrugated
cos companies, cosine, counties
COS cash on shipment, chief of staff
cosec cosecant
cot cotangent
cp compare, coupon
CP candlepower, Cape Province, center of pressure, charter party, chemically pure, command post, communist party, Congregation of the Passion, custom of port
CPA certified public accountant
cpd compound
CPFF cost plus fixed fee
cpl corporal
CPM cycles per minute
CPO chief petty officer
CPS Civilian Public Service, cycles per second
CQ call to quarters (general call preceding transmission of radio signals), charge of quarters
cr cathode ray, credit, creditor, creek, crown, cruzeiro
Cr chromium
CR carrier's risk, company's risk, conditioned reflex, conditioned response, critical ratio
cresc crescendo
crim con criminal conversation
crit critical, criticism
CRT cathode-ray tube
cryst crystalline, crystallized
cs case, cases
c/s cycles per second
Cs cesium, cirrostratus
CS chief of staff, civil service, conditioned stimulus
CSA Confederate States of America
csc cosecant
CSC Civil Service Commission, Congregation of the Holy Cross (L, Congregatio Sanctae Crucis)
CSF cerebrospinal fluid
CSsR Congregation of the Most Holy Redeemer (L, Congregatio Sanctissimi Redemptoris)
CST central standard time
ct carat, cent, count, court
CT central time, combat team, Connecticut
CTC centralized traffic control
ctge cartage
ctn carton, cotangent
c to c center to center
ctr center
cts cents
cu cubic
Cu cumulus, cuprum (L, copper)
CU closeup
cum cumulative
Cumb Cumberland
cur currency, current
cv, cvt convertible
CV cardiovascular, chief value
CVA Columbia Valley Authority
cw clockwise
CW chemical warfare, continuous wave
CWO cash with order, chief warrant officer
CWS Chemical Warfare Service
cwt hundredweight
cyc, cycl cyclopedia
cyl cylinder
CYO Catholic Youth Organization
cytol cytological, cytology
CZ Canal Zone

d date, daughter, day, days, degree, denarius, denarii, density,

died, drizzling, pence, penny
D Democrat, Democratic, deuterium, diameter, dimensional, doctor, dollar, dose, drachma
DA days after acceptance, delayed action, deposit account, district attorney, documents against acceptance, documents for acceptance, don't answer
DAB Dictionary of American Biography
Dan Danish
DAR Daughters of the American Revolution
dat dative
DAV Disabled American Veterans
db debenture, decibel, decibels
DB day book
DBA doing business as
DBE Dame Commander (of the Order of the) British Empire
DBH diameter at breast height
dbl double
DC da capo (It, from the beginning), decimal classification, direct current, District of Columbia, doctor of chiropractic, double crochet
dd delivered
DD days after date, demand draft, dishonorable discharge, doctor of divinity
DDS doctor of dental science, doctor of dental surgery
DE Delaware
deb debenture
dec deceased, declaration, declared, declination, decorated, decorative, decrease
Dec December
decd deceased
def defendant, defense, deferred, defined, definite, definition
deg degree, degrees
del delegate, delegation
Del Delaware
dely delivery
dem demurrage
Dem Democrat, Democratic
Den Denmark
Den, Denb Denbighshire
dent dental, dentistry
dep depart, department, departure, deponent, deposed, deposit, depot, deputy
depr depreciation
dept department
der, deriv derivation, derivative
Derby Derbyshire
det detached, detachment, detail, determiner
detd determined
detn determination
dev deviation
Devon Devonshire
DEW distant early warning
DF damage free, direction finder, direction finding
DFA doctor of fine arts
DFC distinguished flying cross
DFM distinguished flying medal
dft defendant, draft
dg decigram, decigrams
DG Dei gratia (LL, by the grace of God), director general
DI drill instructor
dia, diam diameter
diag diagonal, diagram
dial dialect, dialectical
dict dictionary
dif, diff difference
dig digest
dil dilute
dim dimension, diminished, diminuendo, diminutive
din dinar
dir director
dis discharge, discount
disc discount
disp dispensary
diss dissertation
dist distance, district
distn distillation
distr distribute, distribution
div divided, dividend, division, divorced
dj dust jacket
DJ disk jockey
dk dark, deck, dock
dkg decagram
dkl decaliter
dkm decameter
dks decastere
dl deciliter
DLitt, DLit doctor of letters, doctor of literature
DLO dead letter office, dispatch loading only
dm decimeter
DM deutsche mark

DMD doctor of dental medicine
dn down
DNA deoxyribonucleic acid
DNB Dictionary of National Biography
do ditto
DO defense order
DOA dead on arrival
doc document
dol dollar
dom domestic, dominant, dominion
DOM Deo optimo maximo (ML, to God, the best and greatest)
Don Donegal
Dors Dorset
doz dozen
DP degree of polymerization, diametrical pitch, direct port, documents against payment, documents for payment, domestic prelate
DPH, DPhil doctor of philosophy
dpt department, deponent
dr debit, debtor, drachma, drachmas, dram, drams, drive, drum
Dr doctor
DR dead reckoning, dining room
dram dramatic, dramatist
DS dal segno (It, from the sign), days after sight, detached service, document signed, drop siding
DSc doctor of science
DSC distinguished service cross, doctor of surgical chiropody
DSM distinguished service medal
DSO distinguished service order
dsp decessit sine prole (L, died without issue)
DST daylight saving time
DT double time
Du Dutch
Dub Dublin
Dumb Dumbarton
Dumf Dumfries
dup duplicate
Dur Durham
DV Deo volente (L, God willing), Douay Version
DVM doctor of veterinary medicine
dw deadweight, dust wrapper
DW dock warrant
dwt deadweight ton, pennyweight
DX distance
dy delivery, deputy, duty
Dy dysprosium
dynam dynamics
dz dozen

e erg
E east, eastern, edge, einsteinium, engineer, English, excellent
ea each
EA enemy aircraft
E and OE errors and omissions excepted
EB eastbound
eccl ecclesiastic, ecclesiastical
ECG electrocardiogram
ech echelon
ecol ecological, ecology
econ economics, economist, economy
Ecua Ecuador
ed edited, edition, editor, education
ED extra duty
EdM master of education
EDP electronic data processing
eds editions, editors
EDT eastern daylight time
educ education, educational
EE electrical engineer
EEG electroencephalogram
EENT eye, ear, nose and throat
eff efficiency
e.g. exempli gratia (L, for example)
Eg Egypt, Egyptian
Egypt Egyptian
ehf extremely high frequency
EHP effective horsepower, electric horsepower
EKG electrocardiogram
el, elev elevation
elec electric, electrical, electricity
elem elementary
EM electromagnetic, end matched, engineer of mines, enlisted man, mining engineer
embryol embryology
emer emeritus
EMF electromotive force
emp emperor, empress
emu electromagnetic unit, electromagnetic units

enc, encl enclosure
ency, encyc encyclopedia
eng engine, engineer, engineering
Eng England, English
engr engineer, engraved, engraving
engrs engineers
enl enlarged, enlisted
ens ensign
entom, entomol entomological, entomology
env envelope
EO executive order
EOM end of month
EP estimated position, extended play
eq equation
EQ educational quotient
equip equipment
equiv equivalent
Er erbium
Es einsteinium
Esk Eskimo
esp especially
ESP extrasensory perception
esq, esqr esquire
est established, estimate, estimated
EST eastern standard time
esu electrostatic unit, electrostatic units
Et ethyl
ET eastern time
ETA estimated time of arrival
et al et alii (L, and others)
etc et cetera
ETD estimated time of departure
ethnol ethnology
ETO European theater of operations
et seq et sequens (L, and the following one), et sequentes or et sequentia (L, and those that follow)
Eu europium
Eur Europe, European
EV electron volt
evap evaporate
eve, evg evening
EW enlisted woman
ex example, exchange, executive, express, extra
exc excellent, except
exch exchange, exchanged
ex div without dividend
exec executive
exhbn exhibition
exor executor
exp expense, experiment, experimental, export, express
expt experiment
exptl experimental
exrx executrix
exs examples
ext extension, exterior, external, externally, extra, extract
extg extracting
exx examples

f farad, farthing, female, feminine, fine, focal length, following, force, forte, franc, frequency
F Fahrenheit, false, fellow, filial generation, fluorine, French
FA field artillery
FAA Federal Aviation Agency, free of all average
fac facsimile, faculty
FACP Fellow of the American College of Physicians
FACS Fellow of the American College of Surgeons
FAdm fleet admiral
FAGS Fellow of the American Geographical Society
Fahr Fahrenheit
FAIA Fellow of the American Institute of Architects
fam familiar, family
FAO Food and Agriculture Organization of the United Nations
FAQ fair average quality
far farthing
FAS firsts and seconds, Foreign Agricultural Service, free alongside
fasc fascicle
FB freight bill
FBA Fellow of the British Academy
FBI Federal Bureau of Investigation
FBM foot board measure
FBOA Fellow of the British Optical Association
FC fire control, fire controlman, follow copy

FCA Farm Credit Administration, Fellow of the Chartered Accountants
FCC Federal Communications Commission
FCIS Fellow of the Chartered Institute of Secretaries
fcp foolscap
FCS Fellow of the Chemical Society
fcy fancy
FD fire department, free dock
FDA Food and Drug Administration
FDIC Federal Deposit Insurance Corporation
Fe ferrum (L, iron)
Feb February
fec fecit (L, he [she] made)
fed federal, federation
fedn federation
fem feminine
FEPC Fair Employment Practices Commission
Ferm Fermanagh
ff folios, following, fortissimo
FFA Future Farmers of America
FFR Fellow of the Faculty of Radiologists
FFV first families of Virginia
FG fine grain, flat grain
FGA free of general average
FGS Fellow of the Geographical Society
FHA Federal Housing Administration
FIC Fellow of the Institute of Chemistry
FICA Federal Insurance Contributions Act
fict fiction
fi fa fieri facias (L, cause to be done)
FIFO first in, first out
fig figurative, figuratively, figure
figs figures
fin finance, financial, finish
Finn Finnish
fin sec financial secretary
FIO free in and out
fir firkin
FJP Federation of Jewish Philanthropies of New York
fl floor, florin, flourished, fluid
Fla, FL Florida
fl dr fluidram
Flem Flemish
Flint, Flints Flintshire
fl oz fluidounce
FLS Fellow of the Linnean Society
fm fathom
Fm fermium
FM frequency modulation
FMB Federal Maritime Board
FMCS Federal Mediation and Conciliation Service
fn footnote
FNMA Federal National Mortgage Association
fo, fol folio
FO field officer, field order, finance officer, flight officer, forward observer
FOB free on board
FOC free of charge
FOE Fraternal Order of Eagles
for foreign, forestry
FOR free on rail
FOS free on steamer
FOT free on truck
fow first open water
fp freezing point
FPA free of particular average
FPC Federal Power Commission
fpm feet per minute
FPO fleet post office
fps feet per second, foot-pound-second
fr father, franc, friar, from
Fr francium, French
FRCM Fellow of the Royal College of Music
FRCO Fellow of the Royal College of Organists
FRCP Fellow of the Royal College of Physicians, London
FRCS Fellow of the Royal College of Surgeons
freq frequent, frequentative, frequently
FRGS Fellow of the Royal Geographical Society
Fri Friday
FRIBA Fellow of the Royal Institute of British Architects
front frontispiece
FRS Federal Reserve System, Fellow of the Royal Society
frt freight
frwy freeway

FS filmstrip
FSA Fellow of the Society of Actuaries, Fellow of the Society of Antiquaries
FSH follicle-stimulating hormone
ft feet, foot, fort
FTC Federal Trade Commission
fth, fath fathom
ft lb foot-pound
fund fundamental
fur furlong
fut future
FV folio verso (L, on the back of the page)
fwd forward
FYI for your information
FZS Fellow of the Zoological Society

g acceleration of gravity, gauge, gram, grams, gravity, guinea
G German, giga-, good, guilder, gulf
ga gauge
Ga gallium, Georgia
GA general agent, general assembly, general average, Georgia
gal gallon, gallons
galv galvanized
GAO General Accounting Office
GAPA ground-to-air pilotless aircraft
gar garage
GAR Grand Army of the Republic
GATT General Agreement on Tariffs and Trade
GAW guaranteed annual wage
gaz gazette
GB Great Britain
GCA ground-controlled approach
GCB Knight Grand Cross of the Bath
GCD greatest common divisor
GCF greatest common factor
GCT Greenwich civil time
gd good
Gd gadolinium
ge gilt edges
Ge germanium
gen general, genitive, genus
genl general
geog geographic, geographical, geography
geol geologic, geological, geology
geom geometrical, geometry
geophys geophysical, geophysics
ger gerund
Ger German
GFE government-furnished equipment
GFWC General Federation of Women's Clubs
GHA Greenwich hour angle
GHQ general headquarters
GI galvanized iron, gastrointestinal, general issue, government issue
Gib Gibraltar
Gk Greek
GL gunlaying
Glam Glamorganshire
Glos Gloucestershire
gloss glossary
gm gram, grams
GM general manager, George medal, grand master, guided missile
GMT Greenwich mean time
GMV gram-molecular volume
GNP gross national product
GO general order
GOP Grand Old Party (Republican)
Goth Gothic
gov government, governor
govt government
gp group
GP general practitioner, geometric progression
GPA grade-point average
gpd gallons per day
GPI ground position indicator
gpm gallons per minute
GPO general post office, Government Printing Office
gps gallons per second
GQ general quarters
gr grade, grain, grains, gram, grams, gravity, gross
Gr Greece, Greek
grad graduate
gram grammar
gro gross
gr wt gross weight
GS general staff, ground speed
GSA General Services Administration, Girl Scouts of America
GSC general staff corps
GSO general staff officer
GST Greenwich sidereal time
gt gilt top, great, gutta (L, drop)
GT gross ton
Gt Brit Great Britain
GTC good till canceled
gtd guaranteed
gtt guttae (L, drops)
GU genitourinary
gyn, gynecol gynecology

h harbor, hard, hardness, height, henry, heroin, high, hit, hour, hours, house, hundred, husband
H hydrogen
ha hectare, hoc anno (L, this year)
HA hour angle
hab corp habeas corpus (ML, you should have the body)
handbk handbook
Hants Hampshire
hav haversine
Hb hemoglobin
HBM Her Britannic Majesty, His Britannic Majesty
h.c. honoris causa (L, for the sake of honor)
HC Holy Communion, House of Commons
HCF highest common factor
HCL high cost of living
hd head
HD heavy-duty
hdbk handbook
hdkf handkerchief
hdqrs headquarters
hdwe hardware
He helium
HE high explosive, his eminence, his excellency
Heb Hebrew, Hebrews
her heraldry
Heref Herefordshire
Herts Hertfordshire
hex hexagon, hexagonal
hf half, high-frequency
Hf hafnium
hg hectogram, hectograms, hemoglobin
Hg hydrargyrum (L, mercury)
HG High German
hgt height
HH Her Highness, His Highness, His Holiness
hhd hogshead, hogsheads
HHFA Housing and Home Finance Agency
HI Hawaii
hist historian, historical, history
hl hectoliter
HL House of Lords
hm hectometer
HM Her Majesty, His Majesty
HMS Her Majesty's Ship, His Majesty's Ship
Ho holmium
hon honor, honorable, honorary
hor horizontal
hort horticultural, horticulture
hosp hospital
hp horsepower
HP half pay, high pressure, hire purchase
HQ headquarters
hr hour, hours
HR House of Representatives
HRH Her Royal Highness, His Royal Highness
HS high school, house surgeon
ht height
HT high-tension
Hung Hungarian, Hungary
Hunts Huntingdonshire
HV high-voltage
hvy heavy
HW high water
HWM high-water mark
hwy highway
hy henry
hyd hydraulics, hydrostatics
hydraul hydraulics
hyp, hypoth hypothesis, hypothetical
Hz hertz

I inclination, intensity, iodine, island, isle, moment of inertia
Ia, IA Iowa
IADB Inter-American Defense Board
IAS indicated airspeed
ib, ibid ibidem (L, in the same place)
IB in bond, incendiary bomb
ICA International Cooperation Administration, International Cooperative Alliance
ICAAAA, IC4A Intercollegiate Association of Amateur Athletes of America
ICAO International Civil Aviation Organization
ICBM intercontinental ballistic missile
ICC Indian Claims Commission, International Chamber of Commerce, Interstate Commerce Commission
ICFTU International Confederation of Free Trade Unions
ichth, ich ichthyology
ICI international commission on illumination
ICJ International Court of Justice
ICSH interstitial cell-stimulating hormone
id idem (L, same)
ID Idaho, identification, inside diameter, inside dimensions, intelligence department
i.e. id est (L, that is)
IF intermediate frequency
IFC International Finance Corporation
IFF identification, friend or foe
IFR instrument flight rules
IG inspector general
IGY International Geophysical Year
IHM Servants of the Immaculate Heart of Mary
ihp indicated horsepower
IL Illinois
ILA International Longshoremen's Association
ILGWU International Ladies' Garment Workers' Union
ill, illus illustrated, illustration
Ill Illinois
ILO International Labor Organization
ILS instrument landing system
IMCO Inter-Governmental Maritime Consultative Organization
IMF International Monetary Fund
imit imitative
imp imperative, imperfect, imperial, import, imported, imprimatur (NL, let it be printed)
imperf imperfect
in inch, inches
In indium
IN Indiana
inc incorporated, increase
incl including, inclusive
incog incognito
incr increase, increased
ind independent, index, industrial, industry
Ind Indiana
indef indefinite
indic indicative
indus industrial, industry
inf infantry, infinitive
infl influenced
inorg inorganic
INP International News Photo
INRI Iesus Nazarenus Rex Iudaeorum (L, Jesus of Nazareth, King of the Jews)
ins inches, insurance
insol insoluble
insp inspector
inst instant, institute, institution, institutional
instr instructor, instrument, instrumental
int interest, interior, internal, international
interj interjection
interrog interrogative
intl international
intrans intransitive
in trans in transitu (L, in transit)
introd introduction
inv inventor, invoice
Inv Inverness
IOOF Independent Order of Odd Fellows
IORM Improved Order of Red Men
IP initial point, intermediate pressure
IPA International Phonetic Alphabet
ipm inches per minute
ips inches per second
i.q. idem quod (L, the same as)
IQ intelligence quotient
Ir iridium, Irish
IR infrared, inland revenue
IRBM intermediate range ballistic missile
Ire Ireland
irreg irregular

IRS Internal Revenue Service
is island
Isr Israel, Israeli
ISV International Scientific Vocabulary
It, Ital Italian
ital italic, italicized
ITO International Trade Organization
ITU International Telecommunication Union
IU international unit, international units
IUCD intrauterine contraceptive device
IUD intrauterine device
IV intravenous, intravenously
IW Isle of Wight
IWW Industrial Workers of the World

J jack, joule, journal, judge, justice
JA joint account, judge advocate
JAG judge advocate general
Jam Jamaica
Jan January
Jap Japan, Japanese
Jav Javanese
JCB bachelor of canon law
JCC Junior Chamber of Commerce
JCD doctor of canon law
JCL licentiate in canon law
JCS joint chiefs of staff
jct junction
JD doctor of law
jg junior grade
JND just noticeable difference
jour journal, journeyman
JP jet propulsion, justice of the peace
JPS Jewish Publication Society
jr junior
JRC Junior Red Cross
JSD doctor of juristic science
jt, jnt joint
jun junior
junc junction
juv juvenile
JV junior varsity
JWB Jewish Welfare Board

k karat, kitchen, kilo, knit, knot, koruna
K kalium (L, potassium), Kelvin (scale), king, kip, kopeck, krone, kroner
ka cathode
Kans Kansas
kc kilocycle, kilocycles
KC Kansas City, king's counsel
kcal kilocalorie
KCB knight commander of the Bath
kc/s kilocycles per second
KD kiln-dried, knocked down
Ker Kerry
kg keg, kilogram
KG knight of the Garter
kgps kilogram per second
KIA killed in action
Kild Kildare
Kilk Kilkenny
Kin Kinross
Kinc Kincardine
Kirk Kirkudbright
KKK Ku Klux Klan
kl kiloliter
km kilometer, kilometers
kmps kilometers per second
kn knot
K of C Knights of Columbus
K of P Knights of Pythias
kop kopeck
KP kitchen police
kr krona, krone
Kr krypton
KS Kansas
kt karat, knight
kv kilovolt
kva kilovolt-ampere
kvar kilovar
kw kilowatt
kwhr, kwh kilowatt hour
Ky, KY Kentucky

l left, length, line, liter, lumen
L lake, lambert, large, Latin, libra (L, pound), lira, lire
La lanthanum, Louisiana
LA law agent, Los Angeles, Louisiana
Lab Labrador
lam laminated
Lancs Lancashire
lang language, languages
lat latitude
Lat Latin
LAT local apparent time

lav lavatory
lb pound, pounds
lbs pounds
lc lowercase
LC landing craft, left center, letter of credit, Library of Congress
LCD lowest common denominator
LCL less-than-carload lot
LCM least common multiple
LCT local civil time
ld load, lord
LD lethal dose, line of departure
ldg landing, loading
ldr leader
LDS Latter-day Saints
LE leading edge
lea leather
LEA local education authority (Brit)
lect lecture
leg legal, legato, legislative, legislature
legis legislative, legislature
Leics, Leic Leicester
Leit Leitrim
lf lightface, low frequency
LF ledger folio
lg large
LG Low German
LH left hand, lower half, luteinizing hormone
LHD doctor of humanities
li link, links
Li lithium
LI Long Island
lib liberal, librarian, library
lieut lieutenant
LIFO last in, first out
Lim Limerick
lin lineal, linear
Lincs Lincolnshire
ling linguistics
liq liquid, liquor
lit liter, literal, literally, literary, literature
lith, litho lithographic, lithography
LittB, LitB bachelor of letters, bachelor of literature
LittD, LitD doctor of letters, doctor of literature
LJ lord justice
ll lines
LL Late Latin
LLB bachelor of laws
LLD doctor of laws
LLM master of laws
LM legion of merit, long meter
LMG light machine gun
LMT local mean time
ln natural logarithm
loc cit loco citato (L, in the place cited)
log logarithm
Lond London, Londonderry
long longitude
Long Longford
LOOM Loyal Order of Moose
loq loquitur (L, he speaks, she speaks)
Lou Louth
LP low pressure
LPG liquefied petroleum gas
LR living room, log run
LS left side, letter signed, locus sigilli (L, place of the seal), long shot
LSS lifesaving service, lifesaving station
lt lieutenant, light
LT long ton, low-tension
lt col lieutenant colonel
lt comdr lieutenant commander
ltd limited
lt gen lieutenant general
lt gov lieutenant governor
LTL less than truckload
ltr letter, lighter
Lu lutetium
lub lubricant, lubricating
lv leave
LW low water
LWM low-water mark
LWV League of Women Voters
LZ landing zone

m male, mark, married, masculine, meridian, meridies (L, noon), meter, meters, mile, miles, mill, minim, minute, minutes, month, moon
m- meta-
M mach, master, metal, mille (L, thousand), molecular weight, moment, monsieur
ma milliampere
MA Massachusetts, master of arts, mental age

mach machine, machinery, machinist
mag magazine, magnetism, magneto, magnitude
maj major
maj gen major general
man manual
Man Manitoba
manuf manufacture, manufacturing
mar maritime
Mar March
masc masculine
Mass Massachusetts
MAT master of arts in teaching
math mathematical, mathematician, mathematics
MATS Military Air Transport Service
max maximum
mb millibar
MBA master of business administration
MBS Mutual Broadcasting System
mc megacycle, millicurie
MC master of ceremonies, member of Congress
MCL Marine Corps League
MCO mill culls out
m.d. mano destra (It, with the right hand)
Md Maryland, mendelevium
MD doctor of medicine, Maryland, medical department, months after date
mdnt midnight
MDS master of dental surgery
mdse merchandise
me marbled edges
Me Maine, methyl
ME Maine, mechanical engineer, medical examiner, Middle English
Mea, Mth Meath
meas measure
mech mechanical, mechanics
med medical, medicine, medieval, medium
MEd master of education
meg megohm
mem member, memoir, memorial
mep mean effective pressure
meq milliequivalent
mer meridian
Merion Merionethshire
Messrs messieurs
met meteorological, meteorology, metropolitan
metal, metall metallurgy
metaph metaphysics
meteorol meteorology
METO Middle East Treaty Organization
MEV million electron volts
Mex Mexican, Mexico
mf medium frequency, mezzo forte, microfarad, millifarad
MF machine finish, master of forestry
MFA master of fine arts
mfd manufactured, microfarad
mfg manufacturing
MFH master of foxhounds
MFN most favored nation
mfr manufacture, manufacturer
MFS master of foreign study
mg milligram, milligrams
Mg magnesium
MG machine gun, military government
MGB Ministerstvo Gosudarstvennoi Bezopasnosti (Russ, Ministry of State Security)
mgr manager, monseigneur, monsignor
mgt management
mh millihenry
MH medal of honor
MHW mean high water
mi mile, miles, mill
MI Michigan, military intelligence
MIA missing in action
Mich Michigan
mid middle
Middx Middlesex
MidL Midlothian
midn midshipman
mil military
min minim, minimum, mining, minister, minor, minute, minutes
mineral mineralogy
Minn Minnesota
MIO minimum identifiable odor
misc miscellaneous
Miss Mississippi
mixt mixture
mk mark, markka
mks meter-kilogram-second
ml milliliter, milliliters

mL millilambert
MLA Modern Language Association
MLD minimum lethal dose
Mlle mademoiselle
Mlles mesdemoiselles
MLW mean low water
mm millimeter, millimeters
MM Maryknoll Missioners, messieurs, mutatis mutandis (L, with the necessary changes having been made)
Mme madame
Mmes mesdames
MMF magnetomotive force
mmfd micromicrofarad
MMus master of music
Mn manganese
MN magnetic north, Minnesota
mo month
Mo Missouri, molybdenum
MO mail order, medical officer, Missouri, money order
mod moderate, modern, modification, modified
modif modification
mol molecular, molecule
mol wt molecular weight
MOM middle of month
mon monastery, monetary
Mon Monaghan, Monday, Monmouthshire
Mont Montana
Montg Montgomeryshire
mor morocco
morph, morphol morphology
MOS military occupational specialty
mp melting point
MP member of parliament, metropolitan police, military police, military policeman
MPA master of public administration
mpg miles per gallon
mph miles per hour
MPH master of public health
mphps miles per hour per second
mps meters per second
mr milliroentgen
Mr mister
MR mill run
Mrs mistress
m.s. mano sinistra (It, with the left hand)
MS manuscript, master of science, Mississippi, motor ship, multiple sclerosis
MSc master of science
msec millisecond
msg message
msgr monseigneur, monsignor
MSgt master sergeant
MS in LS master of science in library science
msl mean sea level
MSS manuscripts
MST mountain standard time
MSTS Military Sea Transportation Service
MSW master of social work
mt mount, mountain
MT metric ton, Montana, mountain time
mtg, mtge mortgage
MTO Mediterranean theater of operations
mts mountains
mun, munic municipal
mus museum, music, musical, musician
MusM master of music
mv millivolt
Mv mendelevium
MV mean variation, motor vessel
MVA Missouri Valley Authority
MVD Ministerstvo Vnutrennikh Del (Russ, Ministry of Internal Affairs)
MVP most valuable player
mw milliwatt
MWA Modern Woodmen of America
mxd mixed
myc, mycol mycology
myg myriagram
myl myrialiter
mym myriameter
mythol mythology

n name, net, neuter, noon, note, noun, number
N navy, nitrogen, normal, north, northern
Na natrium (L, sodium)
NA national academician, no account
NAACP National Association for the Advancement of Colored People

NAD National Academy of Design, no appreciable disease
NAM National Association of Manufacturers
NAS National Academy of Sciences, naval air station
NASA National Aeronautics and Space Administration
NASD National Association of Security Dealers
nat national, native, natural
natl national
NATO North Atlantic Treaty Organization
naut nautical
nav naval, navigable, navigation
Nb niobium
NB Nebraska, northbound, nota bene (L, mark well)
N.B. New Brunswick
NBA National Basketball Association, National Boxing Association
NBC National Broadcasting Company
NBS National Bureau of Standards
NC nitrocellulose, no charge, nurse corps
N.C., NC North Carolina
NCAA National Collegiate Athletic Association
NCCJ National Conference of Christians and Jews
NCCM National Council of Catholic Men
NCCW National Council of Catholic Women
NCE New Catholic Edition
NCO noncommissioned officer
NCTE National Council of Teachers of English
ncv no commercial value
Nd neodymium
ND no date
N. Dak, N.D., ND North Dakota
Ne neon
NE New England, no effects, northeast
NEA National Education Association of the United States
NEB New English Bible
Nebr, Neb Nebraska
NED New English Dictionary
neg negative
NEI not elsewhere included
nem con nemine contradicente (NL, no one contradicting)
nem diss nemine dissentiente (NL, no one dissenting)
NES not elsewhere specified
Neth Netherlands
neurol neurological, neurology
neut neuter
Nev Nevada
New Eng New England
NF national fine, national formulary, no funds
NFL National Football League
Nfld Newfoundland
NG national guard, no good
NGk New Greek
N.H., NH New Hampshire
NHG New High German
NHI national health insurance (Brit)
NHL National Hockey League
nhp nominal horsepower
Ni nickel
ni pri nisi prius (L, unless before)
N.J., NJ New Jersey
nl non licet (L, it is not permitted)
NL New Latin, night letter, north latitude
NLRB National Labor Relations Board
NLT night letter
NM nautical mile, night message, no mark, not marked
N. Mex, N.M., NM New Mexico
nn notes
no north, number
No nobelium
nol pros nolle prosequi (L, to be unwilling to prosecute)
nom nominative
non obst, non obs non obstante (L, notwithstanding)
non pros non prosequitur (L, he does not prosecute)
non seq non sequitur (L, it does not follow)
NOP not otherwise provided for
Norf Norfolk
norm normal
Northants, Nthptn Northamptonshire

Norw Norway, Norwegian
nos numbers
NOS not otherwise specified
Notts Nottinghamshire
nov novelist
Nov November
Np neptunium
NP neuropsychiatric, neuropsychiatry, no place, no protest, notary public, noun phrase
NPF not provided for
NPH neutral protamine Hagedorn (new insulin)
n pl noun plural
NPN nonprotein nitrogen
nr near, number
NRA National Recovery Administration
NRC National Research Council
Ns nimbostratus
NS national special, new series, new style, not specified, not sufficient, nuclear ship
N.S. Nova Scotia
NSA National Shipping Authority
NSC National Security Council
NSF National Science Foundation, not sufficient funds
N.S.W. New South Wales
NT New Testament
Nthmb Northumberland
ntp normal temperature and pressure
nt wt, n wt net weight
NU name unknown
num numeral
numb numbered
numis numismatic, numismatical, numismatics
NV Nevada, nonvoting
NW northwest
NWT Northwest Territories
N.Y., NY New York
NYA National Youth Administration
NYC New York City
NYSE New York Stock Exchange
N.Z. New Zealand

o ohm
o- ortho-
O ocean, Ohio, old, order, oxygen
o/a on account
OAS Organization of American States
ob obiit (L, he died, she died), obstetrical, obstetrics
OBE Officer (of the Order) of the British Empire
obj object, objective
obl oblique, oblong
obs observation, observatory, obsolete, obstetrical, obstetrics
obstet obstetrical, obstetrics
obv obverse
oc ocean
OC officer commanding, Order of Cistercians, overcharge
OCarm Order of Carmelites
OCart Order of Carthusians
OCC Order of Calced Carmelites
occas occasionally
OCD Office of Civil Defense, Order of Discalced Carmelites
OCDM Office of Civil and Defense Mobilization
oceanog oceanography
OCS officer candidate school
OCSO Order of Cistercians of the Strict Observance
oct octavo
Oct October
o/d on demand
OD doctor of optometry, oculus dexter (L, right eye), officer of the day, olive drab, outside diameter, outside dimension, overdraft, overdrawn
ODC Order of Discalced Carmelites
OE Old English
OED Oxford English Dictionary
OEEC Organization for European Economic Cooperation
OES Order of the Eastern Star
off office, officer, official
offic official
OFM Order of Friars Minor
O.F.S. Orange Free State
OG officer of the guard, original gum
OH Ohio
OHMS on her majesty's service, on his majesty's service
OIT Office of International Trade
Okla, OK Oklahoma

OM order of merit
OMI Oblates of Mary Immaculate
ONI Office of Naval Intelligence
ONR Office of Naval Research
Ont Ontario
op opus, out of print
OP observation post, Order of Preachers
OPA Office of Price Administration
op cit opere citato (L, in the work cited)
opp opposite
opt optical, optician, optics, optional
OR Oregon, owner's risk
ORC Organized Reserve Corps
orch orchestra
ord order, ordnance
Oreg, Ore Oregon
org organic, organization, organized
orig original, originally
Ork Orkney
ornith ornithology
o/s out of stock
Os osmium
OS oculus sinister (L, left eye), old series, old style, ordinary seaman
OSA Order of St. Augustine
OSB Order of St. Benedict
OSF Order of St. Francis
OSM Order of the Servants of Mary
OSU Order of St. Ursula
OT occupational therapy, Old Testament, overtime
OTS officers' training school
Oxon Oxonia (L, Oxford, Oxfordshire), Oxoniensis (L, of Oxford)
oz ounce, ounces

p page, part, participle, past, penny, per, piano, pint, pipe, pitch, pole, post, port, power, pro, purl
p- para-
P parental generation, pater, pawn, peseta, peso, phosphorus, pressure
pa per annum (L, annually)
Pa Pennsylvania, protactinium
PA particular average, passenger agent, Pennsylvania, power amplifier, power of attorney, press agent, private account, prothonotary apostolic, public address, purchasing agent
Pac Pacific
PAC Political Action Committee
PAL Police Athletic League
paleon, pal paleontology
pam pamphlet
Pan Panama
P and L profit and loss
par paragraph, parallel, parish
part participial, participle, particular
pass passenger, passive
pat patent
path, pathol pathological, pathology
PAU Pan American Union
PAYE pay as you earn, pay as you enter
payt payment
Pb plumbum (L, lead)
PBX private branch exchange
pc percent, piece, postcard, post cibum (L, after meals)
PC petty cash, police constable, privy council, privy councillor
pcs pieces
pct percent
pd paid
Pd palladium
PD per diem, police department, postal district, potential difference
PE probable error, professional engineer
Peeb Peebles
P.E.I. Prince Edward Island
Pemb Pembrokeshire
pen peninsula
PEN International Association of Poets, Playwrights, Editors, Essayists and Novelists
Penn, Penna Pennsylvania
per period, person
perf perfect, perforated
perh perhaps
perm permanent
perp perpendicular
pers person, personal
Pers Persia, Persian
pert pertaining

pet petroleum
petrol petrology
pf pfennig, preferred
PF power factor
pfc private first class
pfd preferred
pg page
PG paying guest, postgraduate, preacher general
PGA Professional Golfers' Association
ph phase
Ph phenyl
PH purple heart
PHA Public Housing Administration
phar pharmacopoeia, pharmacy
pharm pharmaceutical, pharmacist, pharmacy
PhB bachelor of philosophy
PhC pharmaceutical chemist
PhD doctor of philosophy
phil, philol philological, philology
Phila Philadelphia
philos philosopher, philosophy
phon phonetics
photog photographic, photography
phr phrase
PHS Public Health Service
phys physical, physician, physics
physiol physiologist, physiology
pi, pias piaster
pibal pilot balloon
pizz pizzicato
pj pajama
pk park, peak, peck
PK psychokinesis
pkg, pkge package
pkt packet
pkwy parkway
pl place, plate, plural
PL partial loss, private line
PL and R postal laws and regulations
plat platoon
plf plaintiff
plu plural
pm phase modulation, premium
p.m. post meridiem
Pm promethium
PM paymaster, permanent magnet, police magistrate, postmaster, postmortem, prime minister, provost marshal
pmh production man-hour
pmk postmark
pmt payment
PN promissory note
pnxt, pinx pinxit (L, he painted, she painted)
Po polonium
PO petty officer, postal order, post office
POC port of call
POD pay on delivery, post office department
POE port of embarkation, port of entry
pol political
Pol Poland, Polish
polit political, politician
poly, polytech polytechnic
pon pontoon
POO post office order
pop popular, population
POP printing-out paper
por portrait
POR pay on return
Port Portugal, Portuguese
pos position, positive
poss possessive
pot potential
POW prisoner of war
pp pages, per procurationem (L, by proxy), pianissimo
PP parcel post, past participle, postpaid, prepaid
ppa per power of attorney
PPC pour prendre congé (Fr, to take leave)
ppd postpaid, prepaid
PPI policy proof of interest, plan position indicator
ppm parts per million
PPS post postscriptum (L, an additional postscript)
ppt precipitate
pptn precipitation
PQ previous question, Province of Quebec
pr pair, price, printed
Pr praseodymium, propyl
PR payroll, proportional representation, public relations, Puerto Rico
prec preceding
pred predicate
pref preface, preference, pre-

ferred, prefix
prelim preliminary
prem premium
prep preparatory, prepare, preposition
prepd prepared
prepg preparing
prepn preparation
pres present, president
prev previous
prf proof
PRF pulse recurrence frequency, pulse repetition frequency
prim primary, primitive
prin principal
priv privative
prn pro re nata (L, for the emergency, as needed)
PRO public relations officer
prob probable, probably, problem
proc proceedings
prod production
prof professor
prom promontory
pron pronoun, pronounced, pronunciation
prop propeller, property, proposition, proprietor
pros prosody
Prot Protestant
prov province, provincial, provisional
prox proximo
prs pairs
ps pieces
PS postscriptum (L, postscript), public school
pseud pseudonym, pseudonymous
psf pounds per square foot
psi pounds per square inch
PST Pacific standard time
psych psychology
psychol psychologist, psychology
pt part, payment, pint, point, port
Pt platinum
PT Pacific time, patrol torpedo boat, physical therapy, physical training
pta peseta
PTA Parent-Teacher Association
pte private (British)
ptg printing
PTO please turn over
pts parts, pints, points
pty proprietary
Pu plutonium
PU pickup
pub public, publication, published, publisher, publishing
publ publication, published
PUD pickup and delivery
pvt private
PW prisoner of war
PWA Public Works Administration
pwr power
pwt pennyweight
PX please exchange, post exchange

q quart, quarto, query, question, quetzal, quintal, quire
Q quartile, queen
QB queen's bench
QC queen's counsel
qd quaque die (L, daily)
qda quantity discount agreement
QED quod erat demonstrandum (L, which was to be demonstrated)
QEF quod erat faciendum (L, which was to be done)
QEI quod erat inveniendum (L, which was to be found out)
QF quick-firing
QID quater in die (L, four times a day)
Qld, Q'land Queensland
QM quartermaster
QMC quartermaster corps
QMG quartermaster general
qp, q pl quantum placet (L, as much as you please)
qq questions
qq v quae vide (L pl, which see)
qr quarter, quire
qs quantum sufficit (L, as much as suffices)
qt quantity, quart
q.t. quiet
qtd quartered
qto quarto
qts quarts
qty quantity

qu, ques question
quad quadrant
qual qualitative
quant quantitative
quar quarterly
Que Quebec
quot quotation
q.v. quod vide (L, which see)
qy query

r rain, range, rare, red, right, river, roentgen, run
R rabbi, radius, real, reales, Reaumur, regina, Republican, resistance, rex, rook, rough, ruble, rupee
Ra radium
RA regular army, right ascension, royal academy
RAAF Royal Australian Air Force
rad radical, radio, radius, radix
Rad Radnorshire
RAdm rear admiral
RAF Royal Air Force
RAM Royal Academy of Music
R and D research and development
rap rapid
Rb rubidium
RBA Royal Society of British Artists
RBC red blood cells, red blood count
RBI runs batted in
RBS Royal Society of British Sculptors
rc resistance capacitance
RC Red Cross, Roman Catholic
RCAF Royal Canadian Air Force
RCMP Royal Canadian Mounted Police
RCP Royal College of Physicians
RCS Royal College of Surgeons
rct recruit
rd road, rod, round
RD refer to drawer, rural delivery
RDF radio direction finder, radio direction finding
re reference, regarding
Re rhenium, rupee
REA Rural Electrification Administration
Reaum Reaumur
rec receipt, record, recording, recreation
recd received
recip reciprocal, reciprocity
rec sec recording secretary
rect rectangle, rectangular, receipt, rectified
red reduce, reduction
ref referee, reference, referred, refining, reformed, refunding
refl reflex, reflexive
refr refraction
refrig refrigerating, refrigeration
reg region, register, registered, regular, regulation
regd registered
regt regiment
rel relating, relative, released, religion, religious
relig religion
Renf Renfrew
rep repair, report, reporter, representative, republic
Rep Republican
repl replace, replacement
rept report
req require, required, requisition
reqd required
res research, reserve, residence, resolution
RES reticuloendothelial system
resp respective, respectively
ret retain, retired, return
retd retained, retired, returned
rev revenue, reverend, reverse, review, reviewed, revised, revision, revolution
RF radio frequency, refunding
RFD rural free delivery
RGS Royal Geographical Society
Rh rhodium
RH relative humidity, right hand
rhet rhetoric
RI refractive index
R.I., RI Rhode Island
RIBA Royal Institute of British Architects
RIP requiescat in pace (L, may he [she] rest in peace)
rit ritardando
riv river
RJ road junction

rm ream, room
RM Reichsmark
RMA Royal Military Academy (Sandhurst)
rms root mean square
RMS Royal Mail Service, royal mail steamer, royal mail steamship
Rn radon
RN registered nurse, Royal Navy
RNA ribonucleic acid
rnd round
RNR Royal Naval Reserve
RNVR Royal Naval Volunteer Reserve
RNZAF Royal New Zealand Air Force
ROG receipt of goods
Rom Roman, Romance, Romania, Romanian
ROP record of production, run of paper
Ros, Rosc Roscommon
Ross Ross and Cromarty
rot rotating, rotation
ROTC Reserve Officers' Training Corps
Rox Roxburgh
RP reply paid, reprint, reprinting
Rpf Reichspfennig
rpm revolutions per minute
RPO railway post office
rps revolutions per second
rpt repeat, report
RQ respiratory quotient
RR railroad, rural route
RRB Railroad Retirement Board
Rs reis, rupees
RS recording secretary, revised statutes, right side, Royal Society
RSA Royal Scottish Academy
RSCJ Religious of the Sacred Heart of Jesus
RSE Royal Society of Edinburgh
RSFSR Russian Socialist Federated Soviet Republic
RSV Revised Standard Version
RSVP répondez s'il vous plait (Fr, please reply)
RSWC right side up with care
rt right
RT radiotelephone
rte route
Ru ruthenium
RU rat unit
Rum Rumania, Rumanian
Russ Russia, Russian
Rutland Rutlandshire
RW radiological warfare, right worshipful, right worthy
rwy, ry railway

s second, section, semi, series, shilling, sine, singular, snow, son, sou, stere
S sabbath, saint, schilling, senate, signor, small, smooth, society, south, southern, subject, sulfur
SA Salvation Army, sex appeal, sine anno (L, without date), sociedad anonima (Sp, corporation), société anonyme (Fr, corporation), South Africa, subject to approval
SAC Strategic Air Command
SAE Society of Automotive Engineers
Salop Shropshire
S and SC sized and supercalendered
sanit sanitary, sanitation
s.ap. scruple, apothecaries'
Sask Saskatchewan
sat saturate, saturated, saturation
Sat Saturday
satd saturated
S. Aust, S.A. South Australia
sb substantive
Sb stibium (L, antimony)
SB bachelor of science, simultaneous broadcast, southbound
SBA Small Business Administration
sc scale, scene, science, scilicet, sculpsit (L, he or she carved or engraved it), small capitals
Sc scandium, Scots, stratocumulus
SC Sisters of Charity, supercalendered
S.C., SC South Carolina
Scand Scandinavia, Scandinavian
SCAP supreme commander, allied powers

ScD doctor of science
sch school
sci science, scientific
scil scilicet
Scot Scotland, Scottish
scp spherical candlepower
scr scruple
script scripture
sctd scattered
sd sewed
SD sea-damaged, sight draft, sine die (L, without day), special delivery, standard deviation
SDA specific dynamic action
S. Dak, S.D., SD South Dakota
Se selenium
SE southeast
SEATO Southeast Asia Treaty Organization
sec secant, second, secondary, seconds, secretary, section, secundum (L, according to)
SEC Securities and Exchange Commission
Sec Nav Secretary of the Navy
secs seconds, sections
sect section
secy secretary
sed sediment, sedimentation
sel select, selected, selection
Selk Selkirk
sem seminary
sen senate, senator, senior
sep separate, separated
sepd separated
sepg separating
sepn separation
Sept, Sep September
seq sequens (L, the following)
seqq sequentia (L pl, the following)
ser serial, series
Serb Serbian
serg, sergt sergeant
serv service
sf science fiction, sforzando, surface foot
SF sinking fund
sfc sergeant first class
sfz sforzando
sg senior grade, singular, specific gravity
SG solicitor general, surgeon general
sgd signed
sgt sergeant
sh share
SH semester hour, semester hours
SHA sidereal hour angle
Shak Shakespeare
shf superhigh frequency
shp shaft horsepower
shpt, shipt shipment
sht sheet
shtg shortage
Si silicon
SIC specific inductive capacity
sig signal, signature, signor
sigill sigillum (L, seal)
sin sine
sing singular
SJ Society of Jesus
SJD doctor of juridical science
sk sack
Skt Sanskrit
sl slightly
SL salvage loss, sea level, south latitude
s.l.a.n. sine loco, anno, vel nomine (L, without place, year, or name)
sld sailed, sealed
Slo Sligo
sm small
Sm samarium
SM master of science, Society of Mary, soldier's medal
SMaj sergeant major
Sn stannum (LL, tin)
so south
SO seller's option
soc social, societies, society
sociol sociologist, sociology
SOD seller's option to double
SOF sound on film
sol solicitor, soluble, solution
soln solution
Soms Somersetshire
SOP standing operating procedure
soph sophomore
sp special, specialist, species, specific, specimen, spelling, spirit
Sp Spain, Spanish
SP self-propelled, shore patrol, shore patrolman, shore police, sine prole (L, without issue), single pole
Span Spanish

SPCA Society for the Prevention of Cruelty to Animals
SPCC Society for the Prevention of Cruelty to Children
spec special, specifically
specif specific, specifically
sp. gr. specific gravity
sp. ht. specific heat
spp species (pl)
SPQR senatus populusque Romanus (L, the senate and the people of Rome), small profits, quick returns
SPR Society for Psychical Research
sps sine prole supersite (L, without surviving issue)
sp vol specific volume
sq squadron, square
sr senior
Sr senor, sister, strontium
SR sedimentation rate, shipping receipt
S-R stimulus-response
Sra senora
Sres senores
SRO standing room only
Srta senorita
ss scilicet (L, namely), semis (L, one half)
SS saints, same size, steamship, Sunday school, sworn statement
SSA Social Security Administration
SSgt staff sergeant
ssp subspecies
SSR Soviet Socialist Republic
SSRC Social Science Research Council
SSS Selective Service System
st saint, stanza, state, stitch, stone, street
St stratus
ST short ton, single throw
sta stationary
Staffs Staffordshire
stat statim (L, immediately), statute
STB bachelor of sacred theology, bachelor of theology
stbd starboard
std standard
STD doctor of sacred theology
ste sainte
stg, ster sterling
stge storage
Sthptn Southampton
Stir Stirling
stk stock
STL licentiate of sacred theology
STM master of sacred theology, master of theology
STOL short takeoff and landing
stor storage
STP standard temperature and pressure
str steamer, strophe
STR submarine thermal reactor
stud student
sub subaltern, suburb
subg subgenus
subj subject, subjunctive
subpar subparagraph
subsec subsection
suff sufficient, suffix
suffr suffragan
Sun Sunday
sup superior, supplement, supplementary, supply, supra (L, above)
super superfine
superl superlative
supp, suppl supplement, supplementary
supr supreme
supt superintendent
supvr supervisor
sur surface
surg surgeon, surgery, surgical
surv survey, surveying, surveyor
Suss Sussex
Suth Sutherland
SV sailing vessel, sub verbo or sub voce (L, under the word)
svc, svce service
svgs savings
sw switch
Sw, Swed Sweden, Swedish
SW seawater, shipper's weight, shortwave, southwest
S.W.A. South-West Africa
swbd switchboard
SWG standard wire gauge
Switz Switzerland
syll syllable
sym symbol, symmetrical
syn synonym, synonymous, synonymy
syst system

t teaspoon, temperature, tempore (L, in the time of), time, ton, transitive, troy

T tablespoon, tension, township, true
Ta tantalum
TAG the adjutant general
tal qual talis qualis (L, such as it is)
tan tangent
Tas, Tasm Tasmania
TAS true airspeed
taxon taxonomic, taxonomy
Tb terbium
TB trial balance, tubercle bacillus, tuberculosis
tbs, tbsp tablespoon, tablespoonful
TBS talk between ships (short range radio)
tc tierce
Tc technetium
TC teachers college, terra-cotta, till countermanded
tchr teacher
TD tank destroyer, touchdown
TDN total digestible nutrients
TDY temporary duty
Te tellurium
TE table of equipment, trailing edge
tec technical
tech technical, technically, technician, technological, technology
technol technological, technology
tel telegram, telegraph, telephone
TEL tetraethyl lead
teleg telegraphy
temp temperature, temporary, tempore (L, in the time of)
Tenn Tennessee
ter terrace, territory
terr territory
Tex Texas
TF task force, territorial force, till forbidden
tfr transfer
tg type genus
tgt target
Th thorium, Thursday
TH true heading
ThD doctor of theology
theat theatrical
theol theological, theology
theor theorem
theoret theoretical, theoretically
therap therapeutics
therm thermometer
thou thousand
thp thrust horsepower
Thurs, Thu Thursday
Ti titanium
TID ter in die (L, three times a day)
tinct tincture
Tip Tipperary
tit title
tk tank, truck
TKO technical knockout
tkt ticket
Tl thallium
TL total loss, truckload
TLC tender, loving care
TLO total loss only
tlr tailor, trailer
Tm thulium
TM technical manual, trademark, true mean
TMO telegraph money order
tn ton, town, train
TN Tennessee, true north
tng training
tnpk turnpike
TO table of organization, telegraph office, turn over
tonn tonnage
topog, topo topography
tot total
TOT time on target
tp title page, township
tpk turnpike
tps townships
tr translated, translation, translator, transpose, troop, trustee
TR tons registered, transmit-receive
trag tragedy, tragic
trans transactions, transitive, translated, translation, translator, transportation, transverse
transf transferred
transl translated, translation
transp transportation
trav travels
treas treasurer, treasury
trf tuned radio frequency
trib tributary
trig trigonometry

trit triturate
trop tropic, tropical
ts tensile strength
TSgt technical sergeant
TSH thyroid-stimulating hormone
tsp teaspoon, teaspoonful
TT telegraphic transfer, teletypewriter, tuberculin tested
TU trade union, transmission unit
TUC Trades Union Congress (British)
Tues, Tue Tuesday
Turk Turkey, Turkish
TV television, terminal velocity
TVA Tennessee Valley Authority
Tvl Transvaal
twp township
TWX teletypewriter exchange
TX Texas
typo, typ typographical
Tyr Tyrone

u uncle, und (G, and), unit, upper
U university, uranium
UAR United Arab Republic
UAW United Auto, Aircraft and Agricultural Implements Workers of America
uc upper case
UC under charge
UDC universal decimal classification
UFO unidentified flying object
UGT urgent
UH upper half
uhf ultrahigh frequency
UK United Kingdom
ult ultimate, ultimo
UMT Universal Military Training
UMW United Mine Workers of America
UN United Nations
unan unanimous
unasgd unassigned
UNESCO United Nations Educational, Scientific, and Cultural Organization
UNICEF United Nations Children's Fund
univ universal, university
unp unpaged
UNRWA United Nations Relief and Works Agency
uns unsymmetrical
up upper
UP underproof
UPI United Press International
UPU Universal Postal Union
urol urological, urology
u.s. ubi supra (L, where above [mentioned]), ut supra (L, as above)
US United States, unserviceable
USA United States Army, United States of America
USAF United States Air Force
USAFI United States Armed Forces Institute
USC United States Code
USCG United States Coast Guard
USDA United States Department of Agriculture
USES United States Employment Service
USIA United States Information Agency
USLTA United States Lawn Tennis Association
USM United States mail
USMA United States Military Academy
USMC United States Marine Corps
USN United States Navy
USNA United States Naval Academy
USNR United States Naval Reserve
USO United Service Organizations
USP United States Pharmacopeia
USS United States Ship
USSR Union of Soviet Socialist Republics
usu usual, usually
usw und so weiter (G, et cetera)
UT Utah
ut dict ut dictum (L, as directed)

UV ultraviolet
UW underwriter
ux uxor (L, wife)
UXB unexploded bomb

v vector, velocity, verb, verse, versus, very, vice, vide (L, see), voice, volume, vowel
V vanadium, victory, volt, voltage
va verb active
Va, VA Virginia
VA Veterans Administration, vicar apostolic, vice admiral, volt-ampere
vac vacuum
VAdm vice admiral
val value
var variable, variant, variation, variety, various
VAR visual-aural range, volt-ampere reactive
vb verb
VC valuation clause, veterinary corps, vice-chancellor, vice-consul, Victoria Cross, Vietcong
VD vapor density, various dates, venereal disease
veg vegetable
vel vellum, velocity
ven venerable
ver verse
vers versed sine
vert vertebrate, vertical
Vert Vertebrata
ves vessel
vet veterinarian, veterinary
VF very fair, very fine, vicar forane, video frequency, visual field
VFD volunteer fire department
VFW Veterans of Foreign Wars
VG very good, vicar general
vhf very high frequency
vi verb intransitive, vide infra (L, see below)
VI Virgin·Islands, viscosity index, volume indicator
vic vicinity
Vic Victoria
vil village
vis visibility, visual
viz videlicet
vlf very low frequency
VLR very long range
vn verb neuter
VNA Visiting Nurse Association
VO verbal order
VOA Voice of America
voc vocative
vocab vocabulary
vol volume, volunteer
vols volumes
VOP valued as in original policy
VOR very-high-frequency omnirange
vou voucher
VP variable pitch, various places, verb phrase, vice-president
vs verse, versus, vide supra (L, see above)
VS veterinary surgeon
vss verses, versions
vt verb transitive
Vt, VT Vermont
VT vacuum tube, variable time, voice tube
VTOL vertical takeoff and landing
VU volume unit
Vulg Vulgate
vv verses, vice versa

w warden, water, watt, week, weight, white, wicket, wide, width, wife, with, work
W Welsh, west, western, wolfram
WA Washington, with average
WAC Women's Army Corps
WAE when actually employed
WAF Women in the United States Air Force
war warrant
War Warwickshire
Wash Washington
Wat Waterford
W. Aust, W.A. Western Australia
WB water ballast, waybill, weather bureau, westbound
WBC white blood cells, white blood count
WBS without benefit of salvage
WC water closet, without charge
WCTU Women's Christian Tem-

perance Union
wd wood, word, would
WD War Department
Wed Wednesday
Westm Westmeath, Westmorland
Wex Wexford
wf wrong font
WFTU World Federation of Trade Unions
wg wing, wire gauge
wh watt-hour, which, white
whf wharf
WHO World Health Organization
WHP water horsepower
whr watt-hour
whs, whse warehouse
whsle wholesale
WI when issued, Wisconsin, wrought iron
W.I. West Indies
WIA wounded in action
WIBC Women's International Bowling Congress
Wick Wicklow
wid widow, widower
Wig Wigtown
Wilts Wiltshire
Wis, Wisc Wisconsin
wk week, work
WL waterline, wavelength
wm wattmeter
W/M weight or measurement
wmk watermark
WMO World Meteorological Organization
w/o water-in-oil, without
WO warrant officer
WOC without compensation
Worcs Worcestershire
WP weather permitting, white phosphorus
WPA with particular average, Works Progress Administration
WPB wastepaper basket
wpc watts per candle
wpm words per minute
wpn weapon
WR warehouse receipt, Wasserman reaction, with rights
WRAC Women's Royal Army Corps
WRAF Women's Royal Air Force
WRNS Women's Royal Naval Service
wrnt warrant
wt weight
WT watertight, wireless telegraphy
W. Va., WV West Virginia
WVS Women's Voluntary Services (British)
WW warehouse warrant, with warrants, world war
Wyo, WY Wyoming

X experimental
xc, x cp without coupon
xd, x div without dividend
Xe xenon
x in, x int without interest
XL extra large
Xn Christian
Xnty Christianity
xr without rights
xw without warrants

y yard, year
Y yen, yeoman, YMCA, yttrium
Yb ytterbium
YB yearbook
yd yard
yeo yeomanry
YMCA Young Men's Christian Association
YMHA Young Men's Hebrew Association
Yorks Yorkshire
yr year, younger, your
yrbk yearbook
yrs years, yours
YT Yukon Territory
YWCA, YW Young Women's Christian Association
YWHA Young Women's Hebrew Association

z zero, zone
ZI zone of interior
Zl zloty
Zn azimuth, zinc
zoochem zoochemistry
zoogeog zoogeography
zool zoological, zoology
Zr zirconium

ASTRONOMY

SUN, GREATER PLANETS, ETC.

⊙ or ☉   the sun; Sunday
◍, ☾, or ☽   the moon; Monday
●   new moon
☽, ◍, ☽,)   first quarter
○ or ☉   full moon
☾, ◍, ☾, ☾   last quarter
☿   Mercury; Wednesday
♀   Venus; Friday
⊕, ⊖, or ♁   the earth
♂   Mars; Tuesday
♃   Jupiter; Thursday
♄ or ♄   Saturn; Saturday
♅, ♅, or ♅   Uranus
♆, ♆, or ♃   Neptune
♇   Pluto
☄   comet
✳ or ✷   fixed Star

SIGNS OF THE ZODIAC

spring signs {
1 ♈ Aries, *the Ram*
2 ♉ Taurus, *the Bull*
3 ♊, □, or ♊ Gemini, *the Twins*

summer signs {
4 ♋ or ♋ Cancer, *the Crab*
5 ♌ Leo, *the Lion*
6 ♍ or ♍ Virgo, *the Virgin*

autumn signs {
7 ♎ Libra, *the Balance*
8 ♏ Scorpio, *the Scorpion*
9 ♐ or ♐ Sagittarius, *the Archer*

winter signs {
10 ♑ or ♑ Capricorn, *the Goat*
11 ♒ or ♒ Aquarius, *the Water Bearer*
12 ♓ or ♓ Pisces, *the Fishes*

ASPECTS AND NODES

☌   conjunction—indicating that the bodies have the same longitude, or right ascension
✶   sextile—indicating a difference of 60° in longitude, or right ascension
□   quadrature—indicating a difference of 90° in longitude, or right ascension
△   trine—indicating a difference of 120° in longitude, or right ascension
☍   opposition—indicating a difference of 180° in longitude, or right ascension; as, ☍ ♆ ⊙, opposition of Neptune to the sun
☊   ascending node
☋   descending node

BIOLOGY

○, ⊙, or ①   annual plant
②, ♂, or ○   biennial plant
♃   perennial herb
♄   tree or shrub
♀   female   ♂ or ♂   male
♀   neuter
☿ or ☿   hermaphrodite
×   crossed with; hybrid
⁎   northern hemisphere
⁎   southern hemisphere
✳   Old World
✳| New World
∞   indefinitely numerous
·|·   bilaterally symmetrical
⊕   radially symmetrical
§   section of a species or genus
!   seen by the author

BOOKS

f°   folio
4° or 4to   quarto
8° or 8vo   octavo
12° or 12mo   duodecimo; twelvemo
16° or 16mo   sextodecimo; sixteenmo
18° or 18mo   octodecimo; eighteenmo
24° or 24mo   twenty-fourmo
32° or 32mo   thirty-twomo
48° or 48mo   forty-eightmo
sizes above 48° are rare

BUSINESS

@   at; each ⟨4 apples @ 5¢=20¢⟩
℔   per ⟨sheep $4 ℔ head⟩
number if it precedes a numeral ⟨track #3⟩; pounds if it follows ⟨a 5# sack of sugar⟩
℔   pound; pounds
%   percent   ‰   per thousand
$ dollars   ¢   cents
£   pounds   /   shillings
(for other currency symbols see MONEY table)
©   copyrighted   ®   registered trademark

CHEMISTRY

+   signifies "plus", "and", "together with", and is used between the symbols of substances brought together for, or produced by, a reaction; placed above a symbol or to its right above the line, it signifies a unit charge of positive electricity: Ca^{++} denotes the ion of calcium, which carries two positive charges; the plus sign is used also to indicate dextrorotation (as +143°); it is sometimes used to indicate a base or alkaloid when placed above the initial letter of the name of the substance; (as $\overset{+}{M}$, morphine or $\overset{+}{Q}$, quinine)

−   signifies a single "bond", or unit of attractive force or affinity, and is used between the symbols of elements or groups which unite to form a compound: H−Cl for HCl, H−O−H for H_2O; placed above a symbol or to its right above the line, it signifies a unit charge of negative electricity: Cl^- denotes a chlorine ion carrying a negative charge; the dash indicates levorotation (as −92°); it also indicates an acid, when placed above the initial letter of the name of the acid (as $\overline{C}$, citric acid); it is used also to indicate the removal of a part from a compound

/   often indicates valence (as $Fe^{//}$ denotes bivalent iron, $Fe^{///}$, trivalent iron); sometimes its use is restricted to negative ions so that it is equivalent to −

.   is often used: (1) to indicate a bond (as H.Cl for H−Cl) or (2) to denote a unit positive charge of electricity (as Ca.. denotes two positive charges) or (3) to separate parts of a compound regarded as loosely joined (as $CuSO_4.5H_2O$)

◯   denotes the benzene ring

=   indicates a double bond; placed above a symbol or to its right above the line, it signifies two unit charges of negative electricity (as $SO_4=$, the negative ion of sulfuric acid, carrying two negative charges)

≡   signifies a triple bond or negative charge
⋮   indicates a double bond
⋮   indicates a triple bond
( )   mark groups or radicals within a compound [as in $C_6H_4(CH_3)_2$, the formula for xylene which contains two methyl radicals (CH_3)]

— or —   join separated atoms or groups in structural formulas, as in that for glucose:

$$CH_2OHCH(CHOH)_3CHOH$$

=   give or form
→   give, pass over to, or lead to
⇄   forms and is formed from
↓   indicates precipitation of the substance
↑   indicates that the substance passes off as a gas
≕ or ⇌   is equivalent—used in statements to show how much of one substance will react with a given quantity of another so as to leave no excess of either

1-, 2-, etc.   used initially in names, referring to the positions of substituting groups, attached to the first, etc., of the numbered atoms of the parent compound

H^2 or ^2H deuterium H^3 or ^3H tritium (for element symbols see ELEMENT table)
pH   hydrogen-ion concentration
R   denotes a hydrocarbon radical
Z_2 atomic number

MATHEMATICS

+   plus; positive ⟨a+b=c⟩—used also to indicate omitted figures or an approximation
−   minus; negative
±   plus or minus ⟨the square root of $4a^2$ is ± 2a⟩
×   multiplied by; times ⟨6×4=24⟩—also indicated by placing a dot between the factors ⟨6·4=24⟩ or by writing factors other than numerals without signs
÷ or :   divided by ⟨24÷6=4⟩—also indicated by writing the divisor under the dividend with a line between ⟨$\frac{24}{6}$=4⟩ or by writing the divisor after the dividend with an oblique line between ⟨3/8⟩
=   equals ⟨6+2=8⟩
≠ or ≠   is not equal to
>   is greater than ⟨6>5⟩
<   is less than ⟨3<4⟩
≧ or ≥   is greater than or equal to
≦ or ≤   is less than or equal to
≯   is not greater than
≮   is not less than
≈   is approximately equal to
≡   is identical to
∼   equivalent; similar
≅   is congruent to
∝   varies directly as ⟨a∝b⟩
:   is to; the ratio of
∴   therefore
∞   infinity   0   zero
∠   angle; the angle ⟨∠ABC⟩
∟   right angle ⟨∟ABC⟩
⊥   the perpendicular; is perpendicular to ⟨AB ⊥ CD⟩
∥   parallel; is parallel to ⟨AB ∥ CD⟩
⊙ or ○   circle
△   triangle   □   square   ▭   rectangle
√ or √   root—used without a figure to indicate a square root ⟨as in √4=2⟩ or with an index above the sign to indicate another degree

⟨as in $\sqrt[3]{3}$, $\sqrt[5]{7}$⟩; also denoted by a fractional index at the right of a number whose denominator expresses the degree of the root ⟨$3^{1/2}=\sqrt[2]{3}$⟩

( )   parentheses ⎫
[ ]   brackets   ⎬ indicate that the quantities enclosed by them are to be taken together
{ }   braces ⎭

f or F function; function ⟨$y=f(x)$⟩ indicates that y is a function of x⟩—also indicated by other signs (as ϕ, Φ, ψ, Ψ, π, Π)
d differential ⟨dx; the differential of x⟩
δ variation ⟨δx; the variation of x⟩
Δ increment
D differential coefficient; derivative
$\int$ integral; integral of ⟨$\int 2x\,dx=x^2$⟩
$\int_b^a$ the integral taken between the value b of the variable and its value a
s standard deviation of a sample
σ standard deviation of a population
Σ sum; summation
$\bar{x}$ arithmetic mean of a sample of a variable x
μ arithmetic mean of a population
π pi; the number 3.14159265+; the ratio of the circumference of a circle to its diameter
Π product
!   —used to indicate the product of all the whole numbers up to and including a given preceding number
e or ϵ (1) the number 2.7182818+; the base of the natural system of logarithms (2) the eccentricity of a conic section
°   degree ⟨60°⟩
′   minute; foot ⟨30′⟩—used also to distinguish between different values of the same variable or between different variables (as a', a'', a''', usu. read a prime, a double prime, a triple prime)
″   second, inch ⟨30″⟩
2, 3, etc.   —used as exponents placed above and at the right of an expression to indicate that it is raised to a power whose degree is indicated by the figure ⟨a^2, the square of a⟩
n —used as a constant denoting an unspecified degree, order, class, or power
i imaginary unit; $+\sqrt{-1}$
∪   union of two sets
∩   intersection of two sets
⊂   is included in, is a subset of
⊃   contains as a subset
∈ or ϵ is an element of
∉   is not an element of
Λ or 0 or ϕ or { }   empty set, null set

MEDICINE

ĀĀ, Ā, or āā   ana; of each
℞   take—used on prescriptions
S or Sig   write—used in a prescription to indicate directions to be put on the medicine package
☠   poison

APOTHECARIES' MEASURES

C   congius; gallon
O or 0   octarius; pint
℥   ounce
ƒ℥   fluidounce   ƒ℈   fluidram
℔, ℔, ℔, or min   minim

APOTHECARIES' WEIGHTS

℔   pound
℥   ounce (as ℥ i or ℥ j, one ounce; ℥ ss, half an ounce; ℥ iss or ℥ jss, one ounce and a half; ℥ ij, two ounces)
℈   dram
℈   scruple

MISCELLANEOUS

&   and
&c   et cetera; and so forth
<   derived from
>   whence derived ⎫
+   and   ⎬ used in etymologies
*   assumed ⎭
†   died—used esp. in genealogies
✝   cross (for variations see CROSS illustration)
☧   monogram from Greek XP signifying Jesus
卐 or 卍   gammadion (the first is called also swastika)
✡   Magen David
♀   ankh
℣   versicle   ℟   response
✳   —used in Roman Catholic and Anglican service books to divide each verse of a psalm, indicating where the response begins
✠ or +   —used in some service books to indicate where the sign of the cross is to be made; also used by certain Roman Catholic and Anglican prelates as a sign of the cross preceding their signatures
LXX   Septuagint
f/ or f: relative aperture of a photographic lens
🛡   civil defense

for Roman numerals see NUMBER table
for Greek alphabet see ALPHABET table

MUSIC

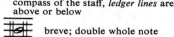

staff with notes—whole note, half note, quarter, eighth, sixteenth, thirty-second; a dot after a note adds to it half the length of the note without the dot; to extend the compass of the staff, *ledger lines* are added above or below

breve; double whole note

rests—whole, half, quarter, eighth, etc.

brace—used to connect two or more staffs indicating that the parts on these staffs are to be performed simultaneously

bar—a vertical line across the staff, dividing it into equal measures of time; a double bar marks the end of a division, movement, or composition, while a single heavy bar is used (as in a hymn tune) to mark the end of a verse or period

G clef; treble clef—used to indicate that the second line represents the first G above middle C

F clef; bass clef—used to indicate that the fourth line represents the first F below middle C

C clefs—used to indicate that any line or space on which they are placed represents middle C

♯ sharp

♭ flat

♮ natural—used to annul the effect of a previous ♯ or ♭; the *sharps* or *flats* placed at the beginning of a composition or section are called collectively the *key signature*

╳ *or* ※ double sharp—used to raise a note two half steps

♭♭ double flat—used to lower a note two half steps

♮♯ single sharp—used after a double sharp

♮♭ single flat—used after a double flat

repeat—used to indicate the beginning and end respectively of a passage to be played or sung twice

𝄋 *or* :𝄇: segno; sign—used to mark the beginning or end of a passage to be repeated

:𝄇:, +, ※ presa—used to indicate where successive voice parts take up the theme

𝄴 common time $\frac{4}{4}$

𝄵 alla breve—used to indicate $\frac{4}{2}$ or $\frac{2}{2}$ time

♪ *or* ♩ long appoggiatura—used as an embellishing note a degree above or below the principal note

♪ acciaccatura; short appoggiatura—used to indicate that the note is to be performed very quickly

~ ∾ turn—a grace consisting of four tones: 1) the one above the principal tone; 2) the principal tone; 3) the one below the principal tone; 4) the principal tone

ↄ ↄ inverted turn—a grace of four tones like the turn but beginning with the *tone below* instead of the *tone above*

∿∿ mordent

tr ∿∿∿ trill; shake

arpeggio

8va all' ottava; at the octave—used above the staff to indicate that the tone or tones are to be sounded an octave higher than written; used below the staff to indicate that they are to be an octave lower

⌢ *or* ⌣ fermata; hold—used over or under a note; when placed over a double bar denotes the conclusion of the piece

< crescendo

> decrescendo; diminuendo

<> swell

> ♪ ∧ accent marks—used to indicate that a tone or chord is to be given additional stress

▔ tenuto mark—used to indicate that a note is to be held to its full value

' *or* . staccato—placed over or under a note

⌢ *or* ⌣ slur; tie

⊔ ⊓ ∧ down-bow ⎱ used in music for
     ∨ up-bow   ⎰ stringed instru-
                      ments

PHYSICS

Å	angstrom unit
A	mass number
α	alpha particle
β	beta ray
C	capacitance
c	velocity of light
e	electronic charge
g	acceleration due to gravity
k	susceptibility to magnetism
L	inductance
λ	wavelength
μ	micron or microns; permeability; modulus (used with a specifying subscript); index of refraction
mμ	millimicron
μμ	micromicron
m₀	rest mass of a particle
n	neutron
ν	frequency
p	proton
R	resistance
ρ	density
T	kinetic energy
V	potential energy
X	reactance
Z	impedance

PUNCTUATION
see page 1193

PROOFREADERS' MARKS

𝒮 *or* ⸜ *or* ⸝ (L *dele*) dele *or* delete; take out or expunge

𝒮 take out a letter and close up

⌢ print as a ligature; thus, a͡e (i. e., print æ); also, close up

∨ *or* ⌣ less space

⌒ close up entirely; no space

℈ turn a reversed letter

∧ *or* > caret; insert at this point the marginal addition

♯ *or* # space or more space

Eq ♯ space evenly—used in the margin

⌐ *or* ⌐ *or* [carry farther to the left

⌐ *or* ⌐ *or*] carry farther to the right

⊓ elevate a letter or word

⊔ sink or depress a letter or word

☐ em quad space; or indent one em

$\frac{1}{m}$, ⊢⊣, $\frac{1}{em}$ *or* $\frac{1}{em}$ *or* ᵉᵐ one-em dash

‖ straighten ends of lines

≡ *or* /// *or* \\\ straighten a crooked line or lines

⊥ *or* ⊥ push down a space which prints as a mark

╳ *or* + *or* ⊗ broken or imperfect type—used in the margin

¶ make a new paragraph

○ (a ring drawn around an abbreviation, figure, etc.) spell out—used in the text

(sp) spell out—used in the margin

⊙ period

↱ *or* ,/ comma

:/ *or* ⊙ colon

;/ semicolon

ꞌ apostrophe or single closing quotation mark

ꞌꞌ double closing quotation mark

ꞌ inverted comma or single opening quotation mark

ꞌꞌ double opening quotation mark

=/ *or* -/ hyphen

[/] brackets

(/) parentheses

wf wrong font—used when a character is of a wrong size or style

ital put in italic type—used in the margin with ____ under text matter

rom put in roman type—used in the margin with _____ under text matter

bf put in boldface type—used in the margin with _____ under text matter

⌐___⌐ transpose

tr transpose—used in the margin

lc lowercase—used in the margin with a slanting line drawn through the letter in the text

= *or* sc *or* sm *caps* put in small capitals—the double lines drawn under the letters or word

≡ *or* *caps* put in capitals—the triple lines drawn under the letters or word

ld insert a lead between lines

stet restore words crossed out—usually written in the margin (with dots under the words to be kept)

∨ set as a superscript; thus, ³∨ (i. e., print ³)—used in the margin

∧ set as a subscript; thus, ₃∧ (i. e., print ₃)—used in the margin

? is this correct as set?—used in the margin

see following page for illustration of the application of these marks

PROOFS OF LINCOLN'S GETTYSBURG ADDRESS WITH CORRECTIONS
MARKED (above) AND MADE (below)

"Four score and 7 years ago our fathers brought forth on this continent a new nation, conceived in in liberty, and dedicated to the proposition, that all men are created equal. Now we're engaged in a great Civil War, testing whether that nation, or any nation conceived so and dedicated so, can long endure.

We are met on a great battle field of that war] we have come to dedicate a portion of this field, as a final resting place for those who here have given their lives that this nation might live/it is altogether proper and fitting that we should do this. But, in a larger sense, we can not dedicate—we cannot consecrate—we cannot Hallow—this ground. The brave men, living and dead, who struggled here, have have consecrated it, far above our power to de-tract or add. The world will little note, nor long remember, what we say here, but it can never forget what we did here. It is for us, the living, rather, to be dedicated here to the great Task remaining before us,—that from these honored dead we take increased devotion to that cause for which they gave the last full measure of devotion—that we now highly resolve that these dead shall not have died in vain—that this nation, under God, shall have a new birth of freedom—and, Government of the people, by the people, for the people, shall never perish from the earth.

"Fourscore and seven years ago our fathers brought forth on this continent a new nation, conceived in liberty, and dedicated to the proposition that all men are created equal. Now we are engaged in a great civil war, testing whether that nation, or any nation so conceived and so dedicated, can long endure. We are met on a great battle-field of that war. We have come to dedicate a portion of that field, as a final resting place for those who here gave their lives that that nation might live. It is altogether fitting and proper that we should do this. But, in a larger sense, we cannot dedicate—we cannot consecrate—we cannot hallow—this ground. The brave men, living and dead, who struggled here, have consecrated it, far above our poor power to add or detract. The world will little note, nor long remember, what we say here, but it can never forget what they did here. It is for us the living, rather, to be dedicated here to the unfinished work which they who fought here have thus far so nobly advanced. It is rather for us to be here dedicated to the great task remaining before us,—that from these honored dead we take increased devotion to that cause for which they gave the last full measure of devotion—that we here highly resolve that these dead shall not have died in vain—that this nation, under God, shall have a new birth of freedom—and that government of the people, by the people, for the people, shall not perish from the earth."

BIOGRAPHICAL NAMES

OVER FIVE THOUSAND NAMES WITH PRONUNCIATIONS

The aim of this section is to give dates, nationality, and status or occupation of the persons included and to indicate the syllabification and pronunciation of such part of their names as they are most often known by. Such boldface items as roman numerals, connectives (as *von* and *de*), and place names (as in *Alexander of Tunis*) are usually not pronounced. Other name elements (as prenames and titles) are pronounced sparingly. A large proportion of the pronunciations shown for names in languages other than English are anglicized to some extent (see the section on foreign names in "Guide to Pronunciation").

Names containing connectives like *d'*, *de*, *di*, *van*, or *von* are alphabetized usually under the part of the name following the connective; exceptions are chiefly American or British names.

Dates of birth and death follow the name. A doubtful or approximate date is indicated by a question mark; in some instances only the years of principal activity are given, preceded by the abbreviation *fl* (flourished). The dates of a reign or other term of office are also given in parentheses.

Most of the abbreviations used will be found in the list on page 22a; for others consult the longer list of Abbreviations on pages 1042 ff.

Ab·bey \'ab-ē\ Edwin Austin 1852–1911 Am. painter & illustrator
Ab·bott \'ab-ət\ Jacob 1803–1879 Am. clergyman & author
Abbott Lyman 1835–1922 Am. clergyman & author
Abd-el-Ka·der \,ab-,del-'käd-ər\ *or* **Abd-al-Ka·dir** \-,dal-\ 1807?–1883 Arab leader in Algeria
Abd-er-Rah·man Khan \,ab-,der-ə-'män-,kän\ 1830?–1901 amir of Afghanistan (1880–1901)
Abd-ul-Aziz \,ab-,dül-ə-'zēz\ 1830–1876 sultan of Turkey (1861–76); deposed
Abd·ul Ba·ha \,ab-,dül-bə-'hä\ 1844–1921 *Ab·bas Ef·fen·di* \a-,bäs-ə-'fen-dē\ Pers. Bahai leader
Abd·ul-Ha·mid II \,ab-,dül-hä-'mēd\ 1842–1918 sultan of Turkey (1876–1909); deposed
Abd·ul·lah ibn-Hu·sein \,ab-də-'lä-,ib-ən-hü-'sān\ 1882–1951 ruler of Transjordan; amir (1921–46); king (1946–51)
Abd·ul-Me·djid I *or* **Abd·ul Me·jid** \,ab-,dül-mə-'jēd\ 1823–1861 sultan of Turkey (1839–61)
Abel \'ā-bəl\ Sir Frederick Augustus 1827–1902 Eng. chem.
Ab·e·lard \'ab-ə-,lärd\ Peter *Fr.* Pierre **Abé·lard** *or* **Abai·lard** \-,ab-ā-'lär\ 1079–1142 Fr. philos. & theol.
Ab·er·crom·bie *or* **Ab·er·crom·by** \'ab-ər-,kräm-bē, -,krəm-\ James 1706–1781 Brit. gen. in Am.
Abercromby Sir Ralph 1734–1801 Brit. gen.
Ab·ing·ton \'ab-iŋ-tən\ Frances *or* Fanny 1737–1815 née *Barton* Eng. actress
Abruz·zi \ä-'brüt-sē\ Duke of the 1873–1933 Prince *Luigi of Savoy-Aosta* naval officer & explorer
abu-Bakr \,äb-ü-'bak-ər\ *also* **Abu Bekr** \-'bek-ər\ 573–634 1st caliph of Mecca
Abul Ka·sim \,äb-,ül-'käs-əm\ *Lat.* **Al·bu·ca·sis** \,al-byə-'kā-səs\ *d* ?1013 Arab surgeon & medical writer
Ach·e·son \'ach-ə-sən\ Dean Gooderham 1893– Am. diplomat
Ac·ton \'ak-tən\ 1st Baron 1834–1902 *John Emerich Edward Dal·berg-Acton* \,dȯl-,bərg-\ Eng. hist.
Ad·am \'ad-əm\ Robert 1728–1792 & his bro. James 1730–1794 Eng. architects & furniture designers
Ad·ams \'ad-əmz\ Charles Francis 1807–1886 *son of J.Q.* Am. lawyer & diplomat
— Franklin Pierce 1881–1960 *F.P.A.* Am. journalist
— Henry Brooks 1838–1918 *son of C.F.* Am. hist.
— James Truslow 1878–1949 Am. hist.
— John 1735–1826 Am. lawyer & 2d pres. of the U.S. (1797–1801)
— John Quin·cy \'kwin-zē, 'kwin(t)-sē\ 1767–1848 *son of John* 6th pres. of the U.S. (1825–29)
— Maude 1872–1953 *Maude Kiskadden* Am. actress
— Samuel 1722–1803 Am. Revolutionary patriot
— Samuel Hopkins 1871–1958 Am. author
Ad·dams \'ad-əmz\ Jane 1860–1935 Am. social worker
Ad·di·son \'ad-ə-sən\ Joseph 1672–1719 Eng. essayist & poet
Ade \'ād\ George 1866–1944 Am. humorist
Ade·nau·er \'ad-ᵊn-,au̇(-ə)r, 'äd-\ Konrad 1876–1967 chancellor of West Germany (1949–63)
Ad·ler \'äd-lər, 'ad-\ Alfred 1870–1937 Austrian psychiatrist
— \'ad-\ Cyrus 1863–1940 Am. educ. & author
— \'ad-\ Felix 1851–1933 Am. educ. & reformer
— \'ad-\ Mortimer Jerome 1902– Am. philos. & educ.
Adri·an \'ā-drē-ən\ name of 6 popes: esp. **IV** (*Nicholas Break·spear* \'brāk-,spi(ə)r\) 1100?–1159 the only Eng. pope (1154–59)
— Rom. emp. *see* HADRIAN
— Edgar Douglas 1889– 1st Baron of *Cambridge* Eng. physiol.
Æ *or* **A.E.** *see* George William RUSSELL
Æl·fric \'al-frik\ *ab* 955–*ab* 1020 *Gram·mat·i·cus* \grə-'mat-i-kəs\ Eng. abbot & writer
Aeneas Silvius *or* **Sylvius** *see* PIUS II
Aes·chi·nes \'es-kə-,nēz\ 389–314 B.C. Athenian orator
Aes·chy·lus \'es-kə-ləs, 'ēs-\ 525–456 B.C. Greek dram.
Ae·sop \'ē-,säp, -səp\ *ab* 620–*ab* 560 B.C. Greek fabulist
Aga Khan III \,äg-ə-'kän, ,ag-\ 1877–1957 *Aga Sultan Sir Mahomed Shah* head of Ismailian Muslims (1885–1957)
— **IV** 1936– *grandson, Shah Karim* head of Ismailian Muslims (1957–)

Ag·as·siz \'ag-ə-(,)sē\ Alexander 1835–1910 *son of J.L.R.* Am. zool.
—(Jean) Louis (Rodolphe) 1807–1873 Am. (Swiss-born) naturalist
Agath·o·cles \ə-'gath-ə-,klēz\ 361–289 B.C. tyrant of Syracuse
Agee \'ā-(,)jē\ James 1909–1955 Am. author
Ages·i·la·us II \ə-,jes-ə-'lā-əs\ *d ab* 360 B.C. king of Sparta (*ab* 400–360)
Ag·nes \'ag-nəs\ Saint *d* A.D. 304 R.C. virgin martyr
Ag·new \'ag-,n(y)ü\ Spiro \'spi(ə)r-(,)ō\ Theodore 1918– Am. polit.; vice-pres. of the U.S. (1969–)
Agric·o·la \ə-'grik-ə-lə\ Gnae·us Julius 37–93 Rom. gen.
Agrip·pa \ə-'grip-ə\ Marcus Vipsanius 63–12 B.C. Rom. statesman
Ag·rip·pi·na \,ag-rə-'pī-nə, -'pē-\ the elder 13 B.C.?–A.D. 33 *dau. of Agrippa, wife of Germanicus Caesar, mother of Caligula*
— the younger A.D. 15?–59 & *dau. of prec. mother of Emp. Nero*
Agui·nal·do \,äg-ē-'näl-(,)dō\ Emilio 1869–1964 Filipino leader
Ah·med III \ä-'met, -'med\ 1673–1736 sultan of Turkey (1703–30)
Ai·ken \'ā-kən\ Conrad Potter 1889– Am. poet
Ains·worth \'ānz-(,)wərth\ William Harrison 1805–1882 Eng. nov.
Ai·sha *or* **Aye·sha** \'ī-shə, 'ä-ē-shə\ 611–678 *favorite wife of Muhammad*
Ait·ken \'āt-kən\ Robert Ingersoll 1878–1949 Am. sculptor
Ak·bar \'ak-bər, -,bär\ 1542–1605 *the Great* emp. of Hindustan (1556–1605)
a Kempis *see* THOMAS A KEMPIS
Aken·side \'ā-kən-,sīd\ Mark 1721–1770 Eng. poet & physician
Akhe·na·ten *or* **Akhe·na·ton** *or* **Akh·na·ton** \,äk-(ə-)'nät-ᵊn\ *var of* IKHNATON
Alanbrooke Viscount *see* Alan Francis BROOKE
Alar·cón \,ä-,lär-'kōn, -'kȯn\ Pedro Antonio 1833–1891 Span. writer & statesman
Al·a·ric \'al-ə-rik\ 370?–410 Visigoth king; conqueror of Rome
— **II** *d* 507 Visigoth king; issued legal code
Al·bee \'ȯl-(,)bē, 'al-\ Edward Franklin 1928– Am. dram.
Albemarle Duke of *see* George MONCK
Al·bé·niz \äl-'bā-(,)nēs, -(,)nēth\ Isaac 1860–1909 Span. pianist & composer
Al·bert I \'al-bərt\ 1875–1934 king of the Belgians (1909–34)
Albert of Saxe–Co·burg-Go·tha \-,saks-,kō-,bərg-'gō-thə, -'gȯt-ə\ Prince 1819–1861 *consort of Queen Victoria of Gr. Brit.*
Al·ber·tus Mag·nus \al-'bərt-ə-'smag-nəs\ Saint 1193? (or 1206?)–1280 *Albert Count von Boll·städt* \-'bȯl-,shtet\ Ger. philos. & theol.
Al·boin \'al-,bȯin, -bə-wən\ *d* 573 Lombard king (*ab* 565–573)
Albucasis *see* ABUL KASIM
Al·bu·quer·que, de \'al-bə-,kər-kē, ,al-bə-'\ Alfonso 1453–1515 Port. viceroy & conqueror in India
Al·cae·us \al-'sē-əs\ *fl ab* 600 B.C. Greek poet
Al·ci·bi·a·des \,al-sə-'bī-ə-,dēz\ *ab* 450–404 B.C. Athenian gen. & polit.
Al·cott \'ȯl-kət\ Amos Bronson 1799–1888 Am. teacher & philos.
— Louisa May 1832–1888 *dau. of A.B.* Am. author
Al·cuin \'al-kwən\ 735–804 Eng. theol. & scholar
Al·da \'äl-də, 'ȯl-, 'al-\ Frances 1883–1952 N.Z.-born soprano
Al·den \'ȯl-dən\ John 1599?–1687 *Mayflower* pilgrim
Al·der \'äl-dər\ Kurt 1902–1958 Ger. chem.
Al·drich \'ȯl-drich\ Thomas Bailey 1836–1907 Am. author
Al·drin \'ȯl-drən\ Edwin Eugene Jr. 1930– Am. astronaut; 2d man on the moon
Aldus Manutius *see* MANUTIUS
Ale·mán \,äl-ā-'män\ Mateo 1547?–1610 Span. nov.
Ale·mán Val·dés \-väl-'däs\ Miguel 1902– Mex. lawyer; pres. of Mexico (1946–52)
Alem·bert, d' \,dal-əm-'ba(ə)r, -'be(ə)r\ Jean Le Rond 1717?–1783 Fr. math. & philos.
Al·ex·an·der \,al-ig-'zan-dər, ,el-\ name of 8 popes: esp. **VI** (*Rodrigo Lanzol y Borja*) 1431?–1503 (pope 1492–1503)
— **III of Macedon** 356–323 B.C. *the Great* king (336–323)
— *Russ.* **Alek·sandr** name of 3 emps. of Russia: **I** 1777–1825

ə abut; ᵊ kitten; ər further; a back; ā bake; ä cot, cart; au̇ out; ch chin; e less; ē easy; g gift; i trip; ī life
j joke; ŋ sing; ō flow; ȯ flaw; ȯi coin; th thin; th̲ this; ü loot; u̇ foot; y yet; yü few; yu̇ furious; zh vision
ᵊ F table; ᴬ F bac; ḵ G ich, Buch; ⁿ F vin; œ F bœuf; œ̄ F feu; ᵫ G füllen; ᵫ̄ F rue; ʸ F digne \dēnʸ\, nuit \nwʸē\

1053

(reigned 1801–25); **II** 1818–1881 (reigned 1855–81); **III** 1845–1894 (reigned 1881–94)
— **I** Obre·no·vich \-ə-'bren-ə-,vich\ 1876–1903 king of Serbia (1889–1903)
— **I** 1888–1934 king of Yugoslavia (1921–34)
— **of Hillsborough** 1st Earl 1885–1965 *Albert Victor Alexander* Brit. polit.
— **Nev·ski** \-'nev-skē, -'nef-\ 1220?–1263 Russ. saint & mil. hero
— **Se·ve·rus** \-sə-'vir-əs\ 208?–235 Rom. emp. (222–235)
— **of Tunis** 1st Earl 1891–1969 *Harold Rupert Leofric George Alexander* Brit. field marshal; gov. gen. of Canada (1946–52)
Alex·is I Mi·khai·lo·vich \ə-,lek-sə-smə-'kī-lə-,vich\ 1629–1676 *father of Peter the Great* czar of Russia (1645–76)
Alexis Pe·tro·vich \pə-'trō-vich\ 1690–1718 *son of Peter the Great* czarevitch of Russia
Alex·i·us I Com·ne·nus \ə-'lek-sē-ə-,skäm-'nē-nəs\ 1048–1118 Eastern Rom. emp. (1081–1118)
Al·fie·ri \,al-fē-'e(ə)r-ē\ Count Vittorio 1749–1803 Ital. dram.
Al·fon·so \al-'fän(t)-,sō, -'fän-(,)zō\ *Port.* **Afon·so** *older* **Af·fon·so** \ə-'fōⁿ-(,)sü\ name of 6 kings of Portugal: esp. **I** 1112–1185 (1st king; 1139–85); **V** 1432–1481 (reigned 1438–81)
Alfonso *or* **Al·phon·so XIII** 1886–1941 king of Spain (1886–1931); deposed
Al·fred \'al-frəd, -fərd\ 849–899 *the Great* king of the West Saxons (871–899)
Al·ger \'al-jər\ Horatio 1832–1899 Am. author
Al·gren \'ȯl-grən\ Nelson 1909– Am. author
Ali \a-'lē, 'al-ē, äl-ē\ *Arab.* **Ali ibn·abi·Tālib** 600?–661 *cousin & son-in-law of Muhammad* 4th orthodox caliph (656–661)
Ali *or* **Ali Pa·sha** \,äl-ē-pə-'shä\ 1741–1822 *the Lion of Janaina* Turk. pasha
Al·len \'al-ən\ Charles Grant Blairfindie 1848–1899 Brit. author
— **Ethan** 1738–1789 Am. Revolutionary soldier
— **Frederick Lewis** 1890–1954 Am. editor & hist.
— **William** 1532–1594 Eng. cardinal
Al·len·by \'al-ən-bē\ 1st Viscount 1861–1936 *Edmund Henry Hynman Allenby* Brit. field marshal
Al·leyn \'al-ən, 'al-,ān, ə-'lēn\ Edward 1566–1626 Eng. actor
All·ston \'ȯl-stən\ Washington 1779–1843 Am. painter
Al·ma-Tad·e·ma \,al-mə-'tad-i-mə\ Sir Lawrence 1836–1912 Eng. (Du.-born) painter
Al·va \'al-və\ *or* **Al·ba** \'al-bə\ Fernando Ál·va·rez \'al-və-,rez; 'äl-və-,räs, -,räth\ de Toledo Duke of 1508–1582 Span. gen.
Al·va·ra·do, de \,äl-və-'räd-(,)ō\ Alonso 1490?–1554 Span. soldier in Mexico (under Cortes) & Peru
— **Pedro** 1495?–1541 Span. soldier; companion of Cortes in Mexico
Al·ve·ar, de \,äl-vā-'är\ Carlos María 1789–1853 Argentine revolutionist
A·ma·ti \ä-'mät-ē, ə-\ family of Ital. violin makers of Cremona: esp. Nicolò or Nicola 1596–1684
Am·brose \'am-,brōz\ Saint 340?–397 bishop of Milan
Amen·ho·tep \,äm-ən-'hō-,tep, ,am-\ *or* **Am·e·no·phis** \,am-ə-'nō-fəs\ name of 4 kings of Egypt: esp. **III** (reigned *ab* 1411–1375 B.C.); **IV** see IKHNATON
Amerigo Vespucci see VESPUCCI
Am·herst \'am-(,)ərst\ Baron 1717–1797 *Jeffrey or Jeffery Amherst* Brit. gen.; gov. gen. of Brit. N. Am. (1760–63)
Amis \'ā-məs\ Kingsley 1922– Eng. author
Am·père \äⁿ-'pe(ə)r\ André Marie¯1775–1836 Fr. physicist
Amund·sen \'äm-ən-sən, 'am-\ Roald 1872–1928 Norw. polar explorer; disc. South Pole (1911)
Anac·re·on \ə-'nak-rē-ən\ 572?–?488 B.C. Greek poet
An·ax·ag·o·ras \,an-,ak-'sag-ə-rəs\ 500?–428 B.C. Greek philos.
Anax·i·man·der \ə-'nak-sə-,man-dər\ 611–547 B.C. Greek philos. & astron.
An·ders \'än-dərs, -dərz\ Wladyslaw 1892–1970 Pol. gen.
An·der·sen \'an-dər-sən\ Hans Christian 1805–1875 Danish writer of fairy tales
An·der·son \'an-dər-sən\ Carl David 1905– Am. physicist
— **John** 1882–1958 1st Viscount *Wa·ver·ley* \'wā-vər-lē\ Brit. polit.
— **Dame Judith** 1898– *orig. Frances Margaret Anderson* Australian actress
— **Sir Kenneth Arthur Noel** 1891–1959 Brit. gen.
— **Marian** 1902– Am. contralto
— **Maxwell** 1888–1959 Am. dram.
— **Sherwood** 1876–1941 Am. poet & storywriter
An·drás·sy \'än-(,)dräsh-ē\ Gyu·la \'jü-lə\ Count, father 1823–1890 & son 1860–1929 Hung. statesmen
An·dré \'an-drē, 'än-(,)drā\ John 1751–1780 Brit. major; spy in Am. Rev.; hanged
An·drea del Sar·to \än-,drā-ə-,del-'särt-(,)ō\ 1486–1531 *Andrea Domenico d' Agnolo di Francesco* Florentine painter
An·dre·ev \än-'drā-(y)əf\ Andrei Andreevich 1895– Russ. polit.
Andreev *or* **An·dre·yev** \än-'drā-(y)əf\ Leonid Nikolaevich 1871–1919 Russ. nov., storywriter, & dram.
An·drews \'an-,drüz\ Roy Chapman 1884–1960 Am. naturalist
An·dros \'an-,dräs, -drəs\ Sir Edmund 1637–1714 Brit. colonial gov. in Am.
An·ge·la Me·ri·ci \,an-jə-lə-mə-'rē-chē\ Saint 1474?–1540 Ital. religious; founder of Ursuline order (1535)
Angelico Fra see FIESOLE
An·gell \'än-jəl\ Sir Norman 1872–1967 *Ralph Norman Angell Lane* Eng. author & lecturer
Ång·ström \'aŋ-strəm, 'ȯŋ-\ Anders Jonas 1814–1874 Swed. physicist
An·na Iva·nov·na \'an-ə-ē-'vän-əv-nə\ 1693–1740 empress of Russia (1730–40)
Anne \'an\ 1665–1714 *dau. of James II* queen of Gr. Brit. (1702–14)
— **of Austria** 1601–1666 *consort of Louis XIII of France* regent (1643–61) for her son Louis XIV
— **of Cleves** \,an-əv-'klēvz\ 1515–1557 *4th wife of Henry VIII of Eng.*
Annunzio, D' Gabriele see D'ANNUNZIO
Anouilh \a-'nü-(y)ə, -'nü-ē\ Jean 1910– Fr. dram.
An·selm \'an-,selm\ Saint 1033–1109 archbishop of Canterbury
An·tho·ny \'an(t)-thə-nē, *chiefly Brit* 'an-tə-\ Saint *ab* 250–350 Egyptian monk; regarded as founder of Christian monachism
— **Mark** see Marcus ANTONIUS
— **Susan Brownell** 1820–1906 Am. suffragist

— **of Padua** Saint 1195–1231 Franciscan monk
An·tig·o·nus I \an-'tig-ə-nəs\ 382–301 B.C. *Cyclops* gen. of Alexander the Great & king of Macedonia (306–301)
An·ti·o·chus \an-'tī-ə-kəs\ name of 13 Seleucid kings of Syria: esp. **III** *the Great* 242–187 B.C. (reigned 223–187); **IV** (*Epiph·a·nes* \-i-'pif-ə-,nēz\) *d* 163 B.C. (reigned 175–163)
An·tip·a·ter \an-'tip-ət-ər\ 398?–319 B.C. Macedonian gen. & statesman
An·tis·the·nes \an-'tis-thə-,nēz\ 444?–after 371 B.C. Athenian philos.; founder of Cynic school
An·toine Père \pe(ə)r-'an-,twän\ 1748–1829 *Antonio de Se·di·lla* \sə-'dē-(y)ə\ Span. Capuchin priest in New Orleans
An·to·ne·scu \,an-tə-'nes-(,)kü\ Ion \'yön\ 1882–1946 Romanian gen.; dictator (1940–44); executed
An·to·ni·nus \,an-tə-'nī-nəs\ Marcus Au·re·lius \ȯ-'rēl-yəs, -'rē-lē-əs\ 121–180 *nephew, son-in-law, and adopted son of Antoninus Pius* Rom. emp. (161–180) & Stoic philos.
— **Pi·us** \'pī-əs\ 86–161 Rom. emp. (138–161)
An·to·ni·us \an-'tō-nē-əs\ Marcus *Eng.* Mark or Marc An·to·ny or An·tho·ny \'an(t)-thə-nē, *chiefly Brit* 'an-tə-\ 83?–30 B.C. Rom. orator, triumvir, & gen.
Ao·ki \ä-'ō-kē\ Shuzo Viscount 1844–1914 Jap. diplomat; 1st Jap. ambassador to U.S. (1905–09)
Apel·les \ə-'pel-ēz\ 4th cent. B.C. Greek painter
Apol·li·naire \ə-,päl-ə-'na(ə)r, -'ne(ə)r\ Guillaume 1880–1918 *Guillaume Apollinaire de Kostrowitsky* Fr. poet
Ap·ol·lo·ni·us \,ap-ə-'lō-nē-əs\ **of Rhodes** 3d–2d cent. B.C. Greek poet
Appius Claudius see CLAUDIUS
Appleseed Johnny see John CHAPMAN
Ap·ple·ton \'ap-əl-tən, -əlt-ᵊn\ Sir Edward (Victor) 1892–1965 Eng. physicist
Aprak·sin *or* **Aprax·in** \ə-'prak-sən\ Fëdor Matveevich 1671–1728 Russ. admiral
Ap·u·le·ius \,ap-yə-'lē-(y)əs\ Lucius 2d cent. A.D. Rom. philos. & satirist
Aqui·nas \ə-'kwī-nəs\ Saint Thomas 1225–1274 Ital. theol.
Ar·am \'ar-əm, 'er-\ Eugene 1704–1759 Eng. philologist & murderer
Ara·nha \ə-'ran-yə\ Oswaldo 1894–1960 Brazil. lawyer & polit.
Ar·ber \'är-bər\ Edward 1836–1912 Eng. editor
Arblay, d' Madame see Fanny BURNEY
Ar·buth·not \är-'bəth-nət, 'är-bəth-,nät\ John 1667–1735 Scot. physician & author
Ar·cher \'är-chər\ William 1856–1924 Scot. critic & dram.
Ar·chi·me·des \,är-kə-'mēd-ēz\ 287?–212 B.C. Greek math. & inventor
Ar·chi·pen·ko \,är-kə-'peŋ-(,)kō\ Alexander 1887–1964 Am. (Russ.-born) sculptor
Are·ti·no \,ar-ə-'tē-(,)nō\ Pietro 1492–1556 Ital. satirist
Ar·gall \'är-gȯl, -gəl\ Sir Samuel *fl* 1609–1625 Eng. mariner
Ar·gyll \är-'gī(ə)l, 'är-,gīl\ 9th Duke of 1845–1914 *John Douglas Sutherland Campbell* gov. gen. of Canada (1878–83)
Ari·o·sto \,ar-ē-'ō-(,)stō\ Lodovico 1474–1533 Ital. poet
Ar·is·tar·chus \,ar-ə-'stär-kəs\ 220?–150 B.C. Greek grammarian
— **of Samos** 3d cent. B.C. Greek astron.
Ar·is·ti·des *or* **Ar·is·tei·des** \,ar-ə-'stīd-ēz\ 530?–?468 B.C. *the Just* Athenian statesman
Ar·is·tip·pus \,ar-ə-'stip-əs\ 435?–?356 B.C. Greek philos.
Ar·is·toph·a·nes \,ar-ə-'stäf-ə-,nēz\ 448?–?380 B.C. Athenian dram.
— **of Byzantium** 257?–?180 B.C. Greek scholar
Ar·is·tot·le \'ar-ə-,stät-ᵊl\ 384–322 B.C. Greek philos.
Ari·us \ə-'rī-əs; 'ar-ē-əs, 'er-\ *d* 336 A.D. Greek theol.
Ark·wright \'är-,krīt\ Sir Richard 1732–1792 Eng. inventor
Ar·len \'är-lən\ Michael 1895–1956 *Di·kran* \dik-'rän\ *Kou·youm·djian* \-kü-'yüm-jē-,än\ Brit. (Armenian-born) nov.
Ar·min·i·us \är-'min-ē-əs\ *or* **Ar·min** \är-'mēn\ 17 B.C.?–A.D. 21 sometimes *Her·mann* \'he(ə)r-,män\ Ger. hero
— **Jacobus** 1560–1609 *Jacob Har·men·sen* \'här-mən-sən\ or *Her·mansz* \'he(ə)r-,män(t)s\ Du. theol.
Arm·strong \'ärm-,strȯŋ\ Hamilton Fish 1893– Am. editor
— **Louis** 1900– *Satch·mo* \'sach-,mō\ Am. jazz musician
— **Neil Alden** 1930– Am. astronaut; 1st man on the moon
— **William George** 1810–1900 Baron *Armstrong of Cragside* Eng. inventor & industrialist
— **-Jones** Antony Charles Robert 1930– Earl of *Snowdon; husband of Princess Margaret Rose of Gt. Brit.*
Arne \'ärn\ Thomas Augustine 1710–1778 Eng. composer
Ar·nim, von \fə-'när-nəm, və-\ Jürgen 1889– Ger. gen.
Ar·nold \'ärn-ᵊld\ Benedict 1741–1801 Am. Revolutionary gen. & traitor
— **Sir Edwin** 1832–1904 Eng. poet
— **Henry Harley** 1886–1950 Am. gen. of the army
— **Matthew** 1822–1888 *son of Thomas* Eng. poet & critic
— **Thomas** 1795–1842 Eng. educ.
Ar·nold·son \'ärn-ᵊl-sən\ Klas Pontus 1844–1916 Swed. pacifist
Arouet François Marie see VOLTAIRE
Arp \'ärp\ Jean (or Hans) 1887–1966 Fr. artist & poet
Ar·pád \'är-,päd\ *d* 907 Hung. national hero
Ar·rhe·ni·us \ə-'rē-nē-əs, -'rā-\ Svanté August 1859–1927 Swed. physicist & chem.
Ar·son·val, d' \'därs-ᵊn-,väl, -,val\ Jacques Arsène 1851–1940 Fr. physicist
Ar·ta·xer·xes \,ärt-ə(g)-'zərk-,sēz\ name of 3 Pers. kings: **I** *d* 424 B.C. (reigned 464–24); **II** *d* 359 B.C. (reigned 404–359); **III** *d* 338 B.C. (reigned 359–338)
Ar·te·vel·de, van \vä-'närt-ə-,vel-də, və-'närt-\ Jacob 1290?–1345 & his son Philip 1340?–1382 Flem. leaders
Ar·thur \'är-thər\ 6th cent. A.D. Brit. real or legendary king
— **Chester Alan** 1830–1886 21st pres. of the U.S. (1881–85)
Ar·tzy·ba·sheff \,ärt-si-'bäsh-əf\ Boris 1899–1965 Am. (Russ.-born) illustrator
As·bury \'az-,ber-ē, -b(ə-)rē\ Francis 1745–1816 1st Methodist bishop in Am.
Asch \'ash\ Sho·lem \'shō-ləm\ *or* Sha·lom \shə-'lōm\ *or* Sho·lom \'shö-ləm\ 1880–1957 Am. (Pol.-born) Yiddish nov. & dram.
As·cham \'as-kəm\ Roger 1515–1568 Eng. scholar & author
Ashburton Baron see Alexander BARING
Ashur·ba·ni·pal *also* **A(s·)sur·ba·ni·pal** \,äs(h)-ər-'bän-ə-,päl

,as(h)-ər-'ban-ə-,pal\ king of Assyria (669–626 B.C.)

Aso·ka or **Aço·ka** \ə-'s(h)ōkə\ *d* 232 B.C. king of Magadha, India (273–232)

As·pa·sia \as-'pā-zh(ē-)ə, əs-\ 470?–410 B.C. *consort of Pericles*

As·quith \'as-,kwith, -kwəth\ Herbert Henry 1852–1928 *1st earl of Oxford and Asquith* Brit. statesman

As·ser \'äs-ər\ Tobias Michael Carel 1838–1913 Du. jurist

Astaire \ə-'sta(ə)r, -'ste(ə)r\ Fred 1899–   Am. dancer & actor

As·ton \'as-tən\ Francis William 1877–1945 Eng. physicist

As·tor \'as-tər\ John Jacob 1763–1848 Am. (Ger.-born) fur trader & capitalist

— Viscountess 1879–1964 *Nancy Langhorne Astor* 1st woman member of Brit. Parliament (1919–45)

At·a·hual·pa \,at-ə-'wäl-pə\ 1500?–1533 last Inca king of Peru

Ath·a·na·sius \,ath-ə-'nā-zh(ē-)əs, -'nā-sh(ē-)əs\ Saint 293?–373 Greek church father

Ath·el·stan \'ath-əl-,stan\ 895–940 king of Eng. *(ab 924–940)*

Ath·er·ton \'ath-ərt-ᵊn\ Gertrude Franklin 1857–1948 née *Horn* Am. nov.

At·tar \'ät-ər, 'a-,tär\ 1119–?1229 Pers. poet

At·ti·la \'at-ᵊl-ə\ 406?–453 *the Scourge of God* king of the Huns

Att·lee \'at-lē\ 1st Earl 1883–1967 *Clement Richard Attlee* Brit. polit.

At·tucks \'at-əks\ Crispus 1723?–1770 Am. Negro; one of 3 men killed in Boston Massacre

Au·ber \ō-'be(ə)r\ Daniel François Esprit 1782–1871 Fr. composer

Au·brey \'ȯ-brē\ John 1626–1697 Eng. antiquary

Au·chin·closs \'ȯ-kən-,kläs\ Louis Stanton 1917–   Am. writer

Au·chin·leck \,ȯ-kən-'lek\ Sir Claude John Eyre 1884–   Brit. field marshal

Au·den \'ȯd-ᵊn\ Wystan Hugh 1907–   Am. (Eng.-born) poet

Au·du·bon \'ȯd-ə-bən, -,bän\ John James 1785–1851 Am. artist & naturalist

Au·er·bach \'au̇(-ə)r-,bäk, -,bȧk\ Berthold 1812–1882 Ger. nov.

Au·gier \ō-'zh(y)ā, ō-zhē-'ā\ Émile 1820–1889 Fr. poet & dram.

Au·gus·tine \'ȯ-gə-,stēn; ȯ-'gəs-tən, ə-\ Saint 354–430 church father; bishop of Hippo (396–430)

— also **Austin** Saint *d* 604 *Apostle of the English* 1st archbishop of Canterbury

Au·gus·tus \ȯ-'gəs-təs, ə-\ 63 B.C.–A.D. 14 *Gaius Julius Caesar Octavianus* 1st Rom. emp. (27 B.C.–A.D. 14)

Au·rang·zeb or **Au·rung·zeb** or **Au·rung·zebe** \'ȯr-ən-,zeb, 'au̇-rən-\ 1618–1707 emp. of Hindustan (1658–1707)

Au·re·lian \ȯ-'rēl-yən\ 212?–275 *Lucius Domitius Aurelianus* Rom. emp. (270–275)

Au·ri·ol \,ȯr-ē-'ȯl, -'ōl\ Vincent 1884–1966 Fr. lawyer; 1st pres. of 4th Republic (1947–54)

Aus·ten \'ȯs-tən, 'äs-\ Jane 1775–1817 Eng. nov.

Aus·tin \'ȯs-tən, 'äs-\ Alfred 1835–1913 Eng. poet; poet laureate (1896–1913)

— John 1790–1859 Eng. jurist

— Mary 1868–1934 née *Hunter* Am. nov.

— Stephen Fuller 1793–1836 Am. colonizer in Texas

Avebury 1st Baron see LUBBOCK

Av·en·zo·ar \,av-ən-'zō-ər, -zə-'wär\ 1091?–1162 Arab physician in Spain

Aver·ro·ës or **Aver·rho·ës** \ə-'ver-ə-,wēz, ,av-ə-'rō-(,)ēz\ 1126–1198 also *ibn-Rushd* Span.-Arab philos. & physician

Av·i·cen·na \,av-ə-'sen-ə\ 980–1037 also *ibn-Sina* Arab (Persian-born) philos. & physician

Ávila Camacho Manuel see CAMACHO

Avo·ga·dro \,av-ə-'gäd-(,)rō, ,äv-\ Amedeo Count 1776–1856 Ital. chemist & physicist

Avon Earl of see Anthony EDEN

Ay·de·lotte \'ād-ᵊl-,ät\ Frank 1880–1956 Amer. educ.

Aza·ña \ə-'thän-yə, -'sän-\ Manuel 1880–1940 Span. lawyer; pres. of Spain (1936–39)

Azu·ma \ə-'zü-mə, 'ä-zə-,mä\ Tokuho 1909–   Jap. dancer

Bab·bitt \'bab-ət\ Irving 1865–1933 Am. scholar & educ.

Ba·ber or **Ba·bur** or **Ba·bar** \'bäb-ər\ 1483–1530 *Zahir ud-Din Muhammad* founder of the Mogul dynasty of India; emp. (1526–30)

Ba·beuf or **Ba·bœuf** \bä-'bəf, bȧ-'bœf\ François Émile 1760–1797 Fr. communist

Bab·ing·ton \'bab-iŋ-tən\ Anthony 1561–1586 Eng. R.C. conspirator against Queen Elizabeth I

Bab·son \'bab-sən\ Roger Ward 1875–1967 Am. statistician

Bach \'bäk̇, 'bäk\ Johann Sebastian 1685–1750 Ger. organist & composer

Ba·con \'bā-kən\ Francis 1561–1626 1st Baron *Ver·u·lam* \'ver-(y)ə-ləm\ Viscount *St. Al·bans* \sȧnt-'ȯl-bənz, sənt-\ Eng. philos. & author

— Roger, Friar 1214?–1294 Eng. philos.

Ba·den-Pow·ell \,bād-ᵊn-'pō-əl\ Robert Stephenson Smyth 1857–1941 1st Baron of *Gilwell* Brit. gen.; founder of Boy Scout movement

Ba·do·glio \bə-'dōl-(,)yō\ Pietro 1871–1956 Ital. gen.; premier (1943–44)

Bae·yer, von \fən-'bā-(y)ər, vən-\ Adolf 1835–1917 Ger. chem.

Baez \'bä-,ez, 'bīz\ Joan 1941–   Am. folk singer

Baf·fin \'baf-ən\ William 1584–1622 Eng. navigator

Bage·hot \'baj-ət\ Walter 1826–1877 Eng. econ. & journalist

Ba·gra·tion \bə-,grät-ē-'ȯn, ,bäg-rə-'tyȯn\ Prince Pëtr Iva·no·vich 1765–1812 Russ. gen.

Ba·ha·ul·lah \bä-,hä-ü-'lä\ Mirza Husayn Ali 1817–1892 Pers. founder of Bahaism

Bai·ley \'bā-lē\ Liberty Hyde 1858–1954 Am. botanist

— Nathan or Nathaniel *d* 1742 Eng. lexicographer

Bail·lie \'bā-lē\ Joanna 1762–1851 Scot. dram. & poet

Bain \'bān\ Alexander 1818–1903 Scot. psychol.

Baird \'ba(ə)rd, 'be(ə)rd\ John Lo·gie \'lō-gē\ 1888–1946 *father of television* Scot. inventor

Bairns·fa·ther \'ba(ə)rnz-,fȧth-ər, 'be(ə)rnz-\ Bruce 1888–1959 Eng. soldier & cartoonist

Ba·jer \'bī(-ə)r\ Fredrik 1837–1922 Dan. statesman & writer

Ba·ker \'bā-kər\ Newton Diehl 1871–1937 Am. lawyer & statesman

— Ray Stannard 1870–1946 Am. author

— Sir Samuel White 1821–1893 Eng. explorer in Africa

Bakst \'bäkst\ Léon Nikolaevich 1866?–1924 Russ. painter

Ba·ku·nin \bə-'kün-(y)ən, bä-\ Mikhail Aleksandrovich 1814–1876 Russ. anarchist

Bal·an·chine \,bal-ən-'shēn\ George 1904–   *George Meletonovitch Balanchinvadze* Am. (Russ.-born) choreographer

Bal·bo \'bäl-(,)bō\ Italo 1896–1940 Ital. aviator & polit.

Bal·boa, de \bal-'bō-ə\ Vasco Núñez 1475–1519 Span. explorer; disc. Pacific Ocean

Balch \'bȯlch\ Emily Greene 1867–1961 Am. econ. & sociol.

Bal·dwin I \'bȯl-dwən-\ 1058–1118 *bro. of Godfrey of Bouillon* king of Jerusalem (1100–18)

— James 1924–   Am. writer

— James Mark 1861–1934 Am. psychol.

— Stanley 1867–1947 1st Earl *Baldwin of Bewdley* \-'byüd-lē\ Brit. statesman

Balfe \'balf\ Michael William 1808–1870 Irish composer & singer

Bal·four \'bal-,fu̇(ə)r\ 1st Earl of 1848–1930 *Arthur James Balfour* Brit. philos. & statesman

Ba·liol, de \'bāl-yəl\ John 1249–1315 king of Scotland (1292–96)

Ball \'bȯl\ John *d* 1381 Eng. priest & social agitator

Bal·lan·tyne \'bal-ən-,tīn\ James 1772–1833 Scot. printer

Baltimore Lord see George CALVERT

Bal·zac, de \'bȯl-,zak, 'bal-, *F* bȧl-zȧk\ Honoré 1799–1850 Fr. nov.

Ban·croft \'ban-,krȯft, 'baŋ-\ George 1800–1891 Am. hist.

— Richard 1544–1610 Eng. prelate

Ban·del·lo \ban-'del-(,)ō, bän-\ Matteo 1480?–1562 Ital. writer

Bangs \'baŋz\ John Kendrick 1862–1922 Am. humorist

Banks \'baŋ(k)s\ Sir Joseph 1743–1820 Eng. naturalist

Ban·ting \'bant-iŋ\ Sir Frederick Grant 1891–1941 Canad. physician; discovered (with others) insulin treatment of diabetes

Ba·ra·nov \bə-'rän-əf\ Aleksandr Andreevich 1747–1819 Russ. fur trader; 1st gov. of Russ. America

Bá·rány \'bär-,än-yə\ Robert 1876–1936 Austrian physician

Bar·ba·ros·sa \,bär-bə-'rȯs-ə, -'rȯs-\ see FREDERICK I

— name of 2 Algerian corsairs, brothers: **I** 1473?–1518; **II** 1466?–1546

Bar·ber \'bär-bər\ Samuel 1910–   Am. composer

Bar·busse \bär-büs, bär-'b(y)üs\ Henri 1873–1935 Fr. author

Bar·clay \'bär-klē\ Robert 1648–1690 Scot. Quaker author

Bar·clay de Tol·ly \(,)bär-,klī-də-'tȯ-lē\ Prince Mikhail 1761–1818 Russ. field marshal

Bar·deen \bär-'dēn\ John 1908–   Am. physicist

Ba·rents \'bar-ən(t)s, 'bär-\ Willem *d* 1597 Du. navigator

Bar·ing \'ba(ə)r-iŋ, 'be(ə)r-\ Alexander 1774–1848 1st Baron *Ash·bur·ton* \'ash-,bərt-ᵊn\ Brit. financier & diplomat

— Eve·lyn \'ēv-lən, 'ev-\ 1841–1917 1st Earl of *Cro·mer* \'krō-mər\ Brit. diplomat

Bark·la \'bär-klə\ Charles Glover 1877–1944 Eng. physicist

Bark·ley \'bär-klē\ Al·ben \'al-bən\ William 1877–1956 Am. lawyer & polit.; vice-pres. of U.S. (1949–53)

Bar·low \'bär-,lō\ Joel 1754–1812 Am. poet & diplomat

Bar·nard \'bär-nərd\ George Grey 1863–1938 Am. sculptor

Barnes \'bärnz\ Harry Elmer 1889–1968 Am. sociol. & educ.

Bar·ne·veldt or **Bar·ne·veld** \'bär-nə-,velt\ Jan van Olden 1547–1619 Du. statesman

Bar·num \'bär-nəm\ Phineas Taylor 1810–1891 Am. showman

Barocchio or **Barozzi** Giacomo see VIGNOLA

Ba·ro·ja \bə-'rȯ-(,)hä\ Pío 1872–1956 Span. nov. & essayist

Bar·rès \ba-'res, bə-\ Auguste Maurice 1862–1923 Fr. nov. & polit.

Bar·rie \'bar-ē\ Sir James Matthew 1860–1937 Scot. nov. & dram.

Bar·ros, de \'bär-,üsh\ João 1496–1570 Port. hist.

Bar·row \'bar-(,)ō, 'bar-ō-(w)\ Isaac 1630–1677 Eng. math. & theol.

Bar·ry \'bar-ē\ Philip 1896–1949 Am. dram.

Bar·ry·more \'bar-i-,mō(ə)r, -,mȯ(ə)r\ family of Amer. actors: Maurice 1847–1905 real name *Herbert Blythe;* his wife Georgiana Emma 1856–1893 dau. of John Drew; their children Lionel 1878–1954, Ethel 1879–1959, & John Blythe 1882–1942

Bart \'bär\ or **Barth** \'bärt\ Jean 1651?–1702 Fr. naval hero

Barth \'bärt\ Karl 1886–1968 Swiss theol.

Bar·thol·di \bär-'t(h)äl-dē, -'t(h)ȯl-\ Frédéric Auguste 1834–1904 Fr. sculptor

Bart·lett \'bärt-lət\ John 1820–1905 Am. publisher

— Vernon 1894–   Eng. author

Bar·tók \'bär-,täk, -,tȯk\ Béla 1881–1945 Hung. composer

Bar·to·lom·meo \,bär-,tȯl-ə-'mā-(,)ō\ Fra 1475–1517 *Baccio della Porta* Florentine painter

Bar·ton \'bärt-ᵊn\ Clara *in full* Clarissa Harlowe 1821–1912 founder of Am. Red Cross Society

Bar·tram \'bär-trəm\ John 1699–1777 Am. botanist

Ba·ruch \bə-'rük\ Bernard Man·nes \-'man-əs\ 1870–1965 Am. businessman & statesman

Bar·zun \'bärz-ᵊn\ Jacques 1907–   Am. (Fr.-born) hist.

Ba·sil \'baz-əl, 'bas-, 'bȧz-, 'bäs-\ or **Ba·sil·i·us** \bə-'sil-ē-əs, -'zil-\ Saint 330?–?379 *the Great* church father; bishop of Caesarea

Bas·ker·ville \'bas-kər-,vil\ John 1706–1775 Eng. typographer

Bates \'bāts\ Katharine Lee 1859–1929 Am. poet & educator

Ba·tis·ta y Zal·dí·var \bə-'tēs-tə-,ē-,säl-'dē-,vär\ Fulgencio 1901–   Cuban soldier; pres. of Cuba (1940–44; 1952–59)

Bat·ta·ni, al- \,al-bə-'tän-ē\ *ab* 850–929 *Al·ba·teg·ni·us* \,al-bə-'teg-nē-əs\ or *Al·ba·te·ni·us* \-'tē-nē-\ Arab astron.

Bau·de·laire \,bōd-'la(ə)r, -'le(ə)r\ Charles Pierre 1821–1867 Fr. poet

Bau·douin \bō-'dwaⁿ\ 1930–   king of Belgium (1951–   )

Baum \'bäm\ Lyman Frank 1856–1919 Am. journalist & story-

ə abut; ᵊ kitten; ər further; a back; ā bake; ä cot, cart; au̇ out; ch chin; e less; ē easy; g gift; i trip; I life
j joke; ŋ sing; ō flow; ȯ flaw; ȯi coin; th thin; th̤ this; ü loot; u̇ foot; y yet; yü few; yu̇ furious; zh vision
• F table; ȧ F bac; ⸯ G ich, Buch; ⁿ F vin; œ F bœuf; ō̤ F feu; ɯ G füllen; œ̄ F rue; ʸ F digne \dēnʸ\, nuit \nwᵉʸ\

writer
— \'baùm\ Vicki 1888–1960 Am. (Austrian-born) nov.
Bau·mé \bō-'mā\ Antoine 1728–1804 Fr. chem.
Bax·ter \'bak-stər\ Richard 1615–1691 Eng. Puritan scholar & writer
Ba·yard, de \'bī-ərd, 'bā-ərd, F. bà-yàr\ Seigneur Pierre Ter·rail \tə-'rī\ 1473?–1524 Fr. mil. hero
Bayle \'bā(ə)l\ Pierre 1647–1706 Fr. philos. & critic
Bay·lor \'bā-lər\ Robert Emmet Bledsoe 1793?–1873 Am. jurist
Beaconsfield Earl of see Benjamin DISRAELI
Bea·dle \'bēd-ᵊl\ George Wells 1903– Am. biologist
Beard \'bi(ə)rd\ Charles Austin 1874–1948 & his wife Mary née *Ritter* 1876–1958 Am. historians
— Daniel Carter 1850–1941 Am. painter & illustrator; organizer of Boy Scouts in U.S. (1910)
Beards·ley \'bi(ə)rdz-lē\ Aubrey Vincent 1872–1898 Eng. illustrator
Beat·tie \'bēt-ē\ James 1735–1803 Scot. poet
Beat·ty \'bēt-ē\ David 1871–1936 1st Earl of *the North Sea & of Brooks·by* \'brùks-bē\ Brit. admiral
Beau·fort \'bō-fərt\ Sir Francis 1774–1857 Brit. admiral
— Henry 1377?–1447 Eng. cardinal & statesman
Beau·har·nais, de \,bō-,är-'nā\ Fr. family including: Vicomte Alexandre 1760–1794 gen.; his wife Joséphine 1763–1814 later the 1st wife of Napoleon I; their son Eugène 1781–1824 prince of Eich·stätt \'īk-,shtet\ their daughter Hortense 1783–1837 wife of Louis Bonaparte & mother of Napoleon III
Beau·mar·chais, de \,bō-,mär-'shā\ Pierre Augustin Caron 1732–1799 Fr. dram. & man of affairs
Beau·mont \'bō-,mänt, -mənt\ Francis 1584–1616 Eng. dram.
— William 1785–1853 Am. surgeon
Beau·re·gard, de \'bōr-ə-,gärd, 'bòr-\ Pierre Gustave Toutant 1818–1893 Am. Confed. gen.
Beau·voir, de \bōv-'wär\ Simone 1908– Fr. author
Bea·ver·brook \'bē-vər-,brùk\ 1st Baron 1879–1964 *William Maxwell Aitken* Brit. (Canad.-born) newspaper publisher
Be·bel \'bā-bəl\ August 1840–1913 Ger. Social Democrat leader & writer
Beck·et, à \ə-'bek-ət, ä-\ Saint Thomas 1118?–1170 archbishop of Canterbury
Beck·ett \'bek-ət\ Samuel 1906– Irish author in France
Beck·ford \'bek-fərd\ William 1760–1844 Eng. author
Bec·que·rel \be-'krel, bek-ə-'rel\ family of Fr. physicists including: Antoine César 1788–1878; his son Alexandre Edmond 1820–1891; the latter's son Antoine Henri 1852–1908
Bed·does \'bed-(,)ōz\ Thomas Lovell 1803–1849 Eng. poet & dram.
Bede \'bēd\ *or* **Bae·da** *or* **Be·da** \'bēd-ə\ Saint 673–735 *the Venerable Bede* Eng. scholar, hist., & theol.
Bed·ford \'bed-fərd\ Duke of 1389–1435 *John of Lancaster; son of Henry IV of England* regent for Henry V
Bee·be \'bē-bē\ (Charles) William 1877–1962 Am. naturalist & explorer
Bee·cham \'bē-chəm\ Sir Thomas 1879–1961 Eng. conductor
Bee·cher \'bē-chər\ Henry Ward 1813–1887 Am. clergyman
— Lyman 1775–1863 *father of H.W. & of Harriet Beecher Stowe* Am. Presbyterian clergyman
Beer·bohm \'bi(ə)r-,bōm, -bəm\ Sir Max 1872–1956 Eng. critic & caricaturist
Beer·naert \'be(ə)r-,närt\ Auguste Marie François 1829–1912 Belg. statesman
Bee·tho·ven, van \vän-'bā-,tō-vən\ Ludwig 1770–1827 Ger. composer
Be·han \'bē-ən, 'bā-ən\ Brendan Francis 1923–1964 Irish dram.
Beh·ring, von \fän-'be(ə)r-iŋ, vän-\ Emil 1854–1917 Ger. bacteriol.
Behr·man \'be(ə)r-mən\ Samuel Nathaniel 1893– Am. dram.
Bel·a·fon·te \,bel-ə-'fänt-ē\ Harry 1927– Am. singer
Be·las·co \bə-'las-(,)kō\ David 1854–1931 Am. dram. & producer
Bel·i·sar·i·us \,bel-ə-'sar-ē-əs, -'ser-\ 505?–565 gen. of the Eastern Rom. Empire
Bell \'bel\ Alexander Graham 1847–1922 Am. (Scot.-born) inventor of the telephone
Bel·la·my \'bel-ə-mē\ Edward 1850–1898 Am. author
Bel·lay, du \,d(y)ü-bə-'lā\ Joachim 1522–1560 Fr. poet
Bel·li·ni \bə-'lē-nē\ family of Venetian painters including: Iacopo *ab* 1400–*ab* 1470 and his sons Gentile 1429?–1507 and Giovanni 1430?–1516
— Vincenzo 1801–1835 Ital. composer
Bel·loc \'bel-,äk, -ək\ Hil·a·ry \'hil-ərē \hil-'a(ə)r, -'e(ə)r\ 1870–1953 Eng. author *pen name Hi·laire*
Bel·low \'bel-(,)ō, -ə(-w)\ Saul 1915– Am. (Canad.-born) writer
Bel·lows \'bel-(,)ōz\ Albert Fitch 1829–1883 Am. painter
— George Wesley 1882–1925 Am. painter & lithographer
Be·mis \'bē-məs\ Samuel Flagg 1891– Am. hist.
Be·na·ven·te y Mar·tí·nez \,ben-ə-,vent-ē-,ē-,mär-'tē-nəs\ Jacinto 1866–1954 Span. dram.
Ben·bow \'ben-,bō\ John 1653–1702 Eng. admiral
Bench·ley \'bench-lē\ Robert Charles 1889–1945 Am. humorist
Ben·e·dict \'ben-ə-,dikt\ name of 15 popes: esp. **XIV** (*Prospero Lambertini*) 1675–1758 (pope 1740–58); **XV** (*Giacomo della Chiesa*) 1854–1922 (pope 1914–22)
— **of Nur·sia** \'nər-sh(ē-)ə\ Saint 480?–?543 Ital. founder of Benedictine order
Benedict Ruth 1887–1948 née *Fulton* Am. anthropologist
Be·nes \'ben-,esh\ Eduard 1884–1948 Czech statesman; pres. (1935–38; 1939–48)
Be·nét \bə-'nā\ Stephen Vincent 1898–1943 Am. poet & story-writer
— William Rose 1886–1950 Am. poet, nov., & editor
Ben-Gu·rion \,ben-gùr-'yón\ David 1886– Israeli (Pol.-born) laborite; prime minister of Israel (1949–53; 1955–63)
Ben·ja·min \'benj-(ə-)mən\ Judah Philip 1811–1884 Am. Confed. statesman & lawyer
Ben·nett \'ben-ət\ (Enoch) Arnold 1867–1931 Eng. nov.
— James Gordon 1795–1872 Am. (Scot.-born) journalist; founder of New York *Herald* (1835)
— Viscount 1870–1947 *Richard Bedford Bennett* Canad. prime min. (1930–35)
Be·noît de Sainte-Maure \(,)ben-'wäd-ə-(,)sänt-'mò(ə)r\ 12th cent. Fr. trouvère

Ben·son \'ben(t)-sən\ Arthur Christopher 1862–1925 Eng. educ. & author
Ben·tham \'ben(t)-thəm\ Jeremy 1748–1832 Eng. jurist & philos.
Ben·tinck \'bent-iŋk\ Lord William Cavendish 1774–1839 *son of W.H.C.* 1st gov. gen. of India (1833)
— William Henry Cavendish 1738–1809 3d Duke of *Portland* Brit. prime min. (1783; 1807–09)
Bent·ley \'bent-lē\ Richard 1662–1742 Eng. clergyman, scholar, & critic
Ben·ton \'bent-ᵊn\ Thomas Hart 1889– Am. painter
Bé·ran·ger, de \bā-rä⁸-zhā\ Pierre Jean 1780–1857 Fr. poet
Ber·dya·ev \bərd-'yä-yəf, bər-'jä-\ Nikolai Aleksandrovich 1874–1948 Russ. philos.
Ber·en·son \'ber-ən-sən\ Bernard 1865–1959 Am. art critic
Berg \'be(ə)rg\ Alban 1885–1935 Austrian composer
Bergerac, de Cyrano see CYRANO DE BERGERAC
Ber·gi·us \'ber-gē-əs\ Friedrich 1884–1949 Ger. chem.
Berg·son \'be(ə)rg-sən, berg-'sō⁸\ Henri 1859–1941 Fr. philos.
Be·ria *or* **Be·ri·ya** \bə-'rē-ə, 'ber-ē-ə\ Lavrenti Pavlovich 1899–1953 Russ. polit.
Be·ring \'bi(ə)r-iŋ, 'be(ə)r-\ Vitus 1680–1741 Dan. navigator; disc. Bering Strait and Bering Sea
Berke·ley \'bär-klē, 'bər-\ George 1685–1753 Irish bishop & philos.
— \'bər-\ Sir William 1606–1677 colonial gov. of Virginia
Ber·le \'bər-lē\ Adolf Augustus 1895– Am. diplomat
Ber·lich·ing·en, von \fän-'ber-lik-,iŋ-ən, vän-\ Götz *or* Gottfried 1480–1562 Ger. knight
Ber·lin \(,)bər-'lin\ Irving 1888– Am. (Russ.-born) composer
Ber·li·ner \'bər-lə-nər\ Emile 1851–1929 Am. (Ger.-born) inventor
Ber·li·oz \'ber-lē-,ōz\ (Louis) Hector 1803–1869 Fr. composer
Ber·na·dette of Lourdes \,bər-nə-'det\ 1844–1879 *Bernadette Sou·bi·rous* \,sü-bē-'rü\ Fr. religious
Ber·na·dotte \,bər-nə-,dät\ Jean Baptiste Jules 1763?–1844 Fr. gen.; king (1818–44) of Sweden as *Charles XIV John* founding present Swed. dynasty
Ber·nard \ber-'när\ Claude 1813–1878 Fr. physiol.
Ber·nard of Clair·vaux \bər-'närd-əv-,kla(ə)r-'vō, ber-'när-, -,kle(ə)r-\ Saint 1091–1153 Fr. ecclesiastic
Ber·nar·din de Saint-Pierre \,ber-nər-'da⁸-də-,sänt-pē-'e(ə)r\ Jacques Henri 1737–1814 Fr. author
Berners Baron see TYRWHITT-WILSON
Bern·hardt \'bərn-,härt, 'be(ə)rn-\ Sarah 1844–1923 orig. *Rosine Ber·nard* ber-när\ Fr. actress
Ber·ni·ni \bər-'nē-nē\ Giovanni Lorenzo 1598–1680 Ital. sculptor, architect, & painter
Bern·stein \'bərn-,stīn, -,stēn\ Leonard 1918– Am. conductor & composer
Bern·storff \'be(ə)rn-,shtórf\ Count Johann-Heinrich 1862–1939 Ger. diplomat
Ber·ry·man \'ber-ē-mən\ John 1914– Am. writer
Ber·til·lon \,ber-tē-'(y)ō⁸, 'bərt-ᵊl-,än\ Alphonse 1853–1914 Fr. anthropol. & criminol.
Ber·ze·li·us \(,)bər-'zē-lē-əs, -'zā-\ Baron Jöns Jakob 1779–1848 Swed. chem.
Bes·ant \'bes-ᵊnt, 'bez-\ Annie née *Wood* 1847–1933 Eng. theosophist
Bes·se·mer \'bes-ə-mər\ Sir Henry 1813–1898 Eng. engineer
Be·tan·court \,be-,tän-'kù(ə)r(t), -'täŋ\ Rómulo 1908– Venezuelan pres. (1959–63)
Beth·mann–Holl·weg, von \fän-,bet-mən-'hòl-,väg, vän-, -,män-\ Theobald 1856–1921 Ger. statesman; chancellor (1909–17)
Bet·je·man \'bech-ə-mən\ John 1906– Eng. poet
Bet·ter·ton \'bet-ərt-ᵊn\ Thomas 1635?–1710 Eng. actor
Bev·an \'bev-ən\ Aneurin \ə-'nī-rən\ 1897–1960 Brit. socialist leader
Bev·er·idge \'bev-(ə-)rij\ Albert Jeremiah 1862–1927 Am. polit. & hist.
— 1st Baron 1879–1963 *William Henry Beveridge* Eng. econ.
Bev·in \'bev-ən\ Ernest 1884–1951 Brit. labor leader & polit.
Beyle Marie Henri see STENDHAL
Bi·dault \bē-'dō\ Georges 1899– Fr. statesman
Bid·dle \'bid-ᵊl\ John 1615–1662 founder of Eng. Unitarianism
Bien·ville, de \bē-'en-,vil, -vəl; bya⁸-'vē(ə)l\ Sieur Jean Baptiste Lemoyne 1680–1767 Fr. colonial gov. of Louisiana
Bierce \'bi(ə)rs\ Ambrose (Gwinnett) 1842–?1914 Am. author
Big·gers \'big-ərz\ Earl Derr 1884–1933 Am. author
Bi·on \'bī-,än, -ən\ 2d cent. B.C. Greek poet
Birk·beck \'bər(k)-,bek\ George 1776–1841 Eng. physician; founder of mechanics' institutions
Bir·ken·head \'bər-kən-,hed\ 1st Earl of 1872–1930 *Frederick Edwin Smith* Eng. jurist & statesman
Bi·ron \'bē-,rón\ Ernst Johann 1690–1772 orig. *Büh·ren* \'bǖ-rən\ Duke of *Kurland* Russ. statesman
Bir·rell \'bir-əl\ Augustine 1850–1933 Eng. author
Bis·marck, von \'biz-,märk, 'bis-\ Prince Otto Eduard Leopold 1815–1898 in full *Bismarck-Schön·hau·sen* \-,shēn-'haùz-ᵊn\ 1st chancellor of Ger. Empire
Bi·zet \bē-'zā\ Alexandre César Léopold 1838–1875 Fr. composer
Björn·son \'byörn-sən\ Björnstjerne 1832–1910 Norw. poet, dram., & nov.
Black \'blak\ Hugo LaFayette 1886– Am. jurist & polit.
Black·ett \'blak-ət\ Patrick Maynard Stuart 1897– Brit. physicist
Black Hawk \'blak-,hòk\ 1767–1838 *Ma-ka-tae-mish-kia-kiak* Am. Indian (Sac) chief
Black·more \'blak-,mō(ə)r, -,mò(ə)r\ Richard Doddridge 1825–1900 Eng. nov.
Black·mun \'blak-mən\ Harry Andrew 1908– Am. jurist
Black·stone \'blak-,stōn, *chiefly Brit* -stən\ Sir William 1723–1780 Eng. jurist
Black·wood \'blak-,wùd\ William 1776–1834 Scot. publisher
Blaine \'blān\ James Gillespie 1830–1893 Am. statesman
Blake \'blāk\ Robert 1599–1657 Eng. admiral
— William 1757–1827 Eng. artist, poet, & mystic
Blas·co-Ibá·ñez \'bläs-(,)kō-ē-'bän-(,)yäth, -'vän-, -(,)yäs\ Vicente 1867–1928 Span. nov.
Bla·vat·sky \blə-'vat-skē, -'vät-\ Elena Petrovna 1831–1891 née (*Helena*) *Hahn* \'hän\ Russ. traveler & theosophist
Blé·ri·ot \'bler-ē-,ō, 'blä-rē-\ Louis 1872–1936 Fr. engineer & pioneer aviator

Bligh \'blī\ William 1754–1817 Eng. naval officer
Bliss \'blis\ Tasker Howard 1853–1930 Am. gen.
Bloc \'blòk, -'bläk\ André 1896–1966 Fr. sculptor
Bloch \'bläk, 'blòk, 'blòk\ Ernest 1880–1959 Am. (Swiss-born) composer
—\'bläk\ Felix 1905–   Am. physicist
Block \'bläk\ Herbert Lawrence 1909–   *Her·block* \'hər-ˌbläk\ Am. editorial cartoonist
Bloom·field \'blüm-ˌfēld\ Leonard 1887–1949 Am. linguist
Blü·cher, von \'blü-kər, 'blʉk-ər\ Gebhard Leberecht 1742–1819 Pruss. field marshal
Blum \'blüm\ Léon 1872–1950 Fr. polit.; provisional pres. (1946)
Bluntsch·li \'blunch-lē\ Johann Kaspar 1808–1881 Swiss legal scholar
Bo·ab·dil \ˌbō-əb-'dē(ə)l\ d 1533 or 1534 last Moorish king of Granada
Bo·ad·i·cea \(ˌ)bō-ˌad-ə-'sē-ə\ d 62 queen of the Iceni
Bo·as \'bō-ˌas, -ˌaz\ Franz 1858–1942 Am. (Ger.-born) anthropol. & ethnol.
Bo·ba·dil·la, de \ˌbō-bə-'dē-(y)ə, -'thē-(y)ə, -'thēl-yə\ Francisco d 1502 Span. viceroy of Indies
Boc·cac·cio \bō-'käch-ē-ˌō, -'käch-(ˌ)ō\ Giovanni 1313–1375 Ital. author
Bock, von \'bäk, 'bòk\ Fedor 1880–1945 Ger. gen.
Bod·ley \'bäd-lē\ Sir Thomas 1545–1613 Eng. diplomat & founder of Bodleian library
Bo·do·ni \bə-'dō-nē\ Giambattista 1740–1813 Ital. printer & type designer
Bo·ethi·us \bō-'ē-thē-əs\ Anicius Manlius Severinus 480?–?524 Rom. philos.
Böh·len \'bō-lən\ Charles Eustis 1904–   Am. diplomat
Böh·me \'bə(r)m-ə, 'bœ̄-mə\ or **Böhm** \'bə(r)m, 'bœ̄m\ Jakob \'yä-ˌkóp\ 1575–1624 Ger. mystic & theosophist
Bohr \'bō(ə)r, 'bò(ə)r\ Niels 1885–1962 Dan. physicist
Bo·iar·do \bòi-'ärd-(ˌ)ō, bō-'yärd-\ Matteo Maria 1434–1494 Ital. poet
Boi·leau-Des·pré·aux \'bwäl-ō-ˌdā-prē-'ō\ Nicolas 1636–1711 Fr. critic & poet
Bo·jer \'bòi-(ə)r\ Johan \yō-'hän\ 1872–1959 Norw. nov. & dram.
Bok \'bäk\ Edward William 1863–1930 Am. (Du.-born) editor
Bol·eyn \'bul-ən, bə-'lin\ Anne 1507–1536 2d wife of Henry VIII of England & mother of Queen Elizabeth I
Bo·ling·broke \'bäl-iŋ-ˌbruk (usu Brit pronunc), 'bō-liŋ-, -ˌbrok\ 1st Viscount 1678–1751 Henry St. John \'sin-jən (usu Brit pronunc); (ˌ)sänt-'jän, sənt-\ Eng. statesman
Bo·lí·var Si·món \si-ˌmōn-bə-'lē-ˌvär, ˌsī-mən-'bäl-ə-vər\ 1783–1830 So. Am. liberator
Bo·na·parte \'bō-nə-ˌpärt\ *Ital.* **Buo·na·par·te** \ˌbwòn-ə-'pärt-ē\ Corsican family including Na·po·leon I \nə-'pōl-yən, -'pō-lē-ən\ (q.v.) & his bros.: Joseph 1768–1844 king of Naples & Spain; Lucien 1775–1840 prince of Ca·ni·no \kə-'nē-(ˌ)nō\; Louis 1778–1846 king of Holland & father of Napoleon III; Jérôme 1784–1860 king of Westphalia
Bonar Law see LAW
Bon·a·ven·tu·ra \ˌbän-ə-ˌven-'t(y)ur-ə\ or **Bon·a·ven·ture** \ˌbän-ə-'ven-chər, 'bän-ə-ˌ\ Saint 1221–1274 the Seraphic Doctor Ital. philos.
Bone \'bōn\ Sir Muirhead 1876–1953 Scot. etcher & painter
Bon·heur \bä-'nər\ Rosa 1822–1899 Marie Rosalie Fr. painter
Bon·i·face \'bän-ə-fəs, -ˌfās\ Saint 680?–755 Winfrid or Wynfrith Eng. missionary in Germany
— name of 9 popes: esp. **VIII** (Benedetto Caetani) 1235?–1303 (pope 1294–1303)
Bon·ner or **Bon·er** \'bän-ər\ Edmund 1500?–1569 Eng. prelate
Bon·net \bò-'nā\ Georges 1889–   Fr. polit. & diplomat
— Henri 1888–   Fr. hist. & diplomat
Boone \'bün\ Daniel 1734–1820 Am. pioneer
Booth \'büth, chiefly Brit 'büth\ family of Am. actors: Junius Brutus 1796–1852 b in England & his sons Edwin Thomas 1833–1893 & John Wilkes 1838–1865 assassin of Lincoln
— William 1829–1912 Eng. founder of Salvation Army & father of: William Bramwell 1856–1929 Salvation Army gen.; Ballington 1859–1940 founder of Volunteers of America; Evangeline Cory 1865–1950 Salvation Army gen.
Boothe Clare see Clare Boothe LUCE
Bo·rah \'bōr-ə, 'bòr-\ William Edgar 1865–1940 Am. lawyer & polit.
Bor·den \ˌbòrd-ᵊn\ Sir Robert (Laird) 1854–1937 Canad. lawyer & statesman; prime min. (1911–20)
Bor·det \bòr-'dā\ Jules 1870–1961 Belg. bacteriol.
Bor·gia \'bòr-(ˌ)jä, -jə\ Cesare 1475(or 1476)–1507 son of Rodrigo Ital. cardinal & mil. leader
— Lucrezia 1480–1519 dau. of Rodrigo duchess of Ferrara
— Rodrigo 1431?–1503 see Pope ALEXANDER VI
Bor·glum \'bòr-gləm\ (John) Gut·zon \'gət-sən\ (de la Mothe) 1871–1941 Am. sculptor
Bo·ri \'bòr-ē, 'bòr-\ Lucrezia 1887–1960 Span. soprano in U.S.
Bo·ris III \'bōr-əs, 'bòr-, 'bär-\ 1894–1943 tsar of Bulgaria (1918–43)
Born \'bò(ə)rn\ Max 1882–1970 Ger. physicist
Bo·ro·din \ˌbòr-ə-'dēn, ˌbär-\ Aleksandr Porfirevich 1834–1887 Russ. composer & chem.
Bor·row \'bär-(ˌ)ō\ George 1803–1881 Eng. author & linguist
Bosch \'bäs, 'bòs\ Hieronymus ab 1450–1516 Du. painter
— \'bäsh, 'bòsh\ Karl 1874–1940 Ger. industrial chem.
Bose \'bōs, 'bòs(h)\ Sir Ja·ga·dis \ˌjəg-ə-'dēs\ Chan·dra \'chən-drə\ 1858–1937 Indian physicist & plant physiol.
Bos·suet \bò-'swā\ Jacques Bénigne 1627–1704 Fr. bishop
Bos·well \'bäz-ˌwel, -wəl\ James 1740–1795 Boz·zy \'bäz-ē\ Scot. lawyer & author; biographer of Samuel Johnson
Bo·tha \'bō-tä, 'bòt-ə\ Louis 1862–1919 Boer gen.; 1st prime min. of Transvaal (1907) & of Union of S. Africa (1910–19)
Bo·the \'bòt-ə\ Walter 1891–1957 Ger. physicist
Bot·ti·cel·li \ˌbät-ə-'chel-ē\ Sandro 1444?–1510 Alessandro di Mariano dei Filipepi Ital. painter
Bou·cher \bü-'shā\ François 1703–1770 Fr. painter
Bou·ci·cault \'bü-si-ˌkō\ or **Bour·ci·cault** \'bùr-\ Dion 1820?–

1890 Dionysius Lardner Boursiquot Irish actor & dram.
Bou·gain·ville, de \'bü-gən-ˌvil\ Louis Antoine 1729–1811 Fr. navigator
Bou·lan·ger \ˌbü-län-'zhā\ Georges Ernest Jean Marie 1837–1891 Fr. gen.
Bour·bon, de \'bù(ə)r-bən, bùr-'bōⁿ\ Duc Charles 1490–1527 Fr. gen.; constable of France
Bour·geois \bùrzh-'wä, 'bù(ə)rzh-,\ Léon Vic·tor Auguste 1851–1925 Fr. statesman
Bour·get \bùr-'zhā\ (Charles Joseph) Paul 1852–1935 Fr. poet, critic, & nov.
Bour·gui·ba \bùr-'gē-bə\ Habib ben Ali 1904–   Tunisian pres. (1957–   )
Bo·vet \bō-'vā\ Daniel 1907–   Ital. (Swiss-born) chem.
Bow·ditch \'baùd-ich\ Nathaniel 1773–1838 Am. math. & astron.
Bow·en \'bō-ən\ Elizabeth 1899–   Eng. author
Bow·ers \'baù-ərz\ Claude Ger·nade \zhər-'näd\ 1878–1958 Am. hist. & diplomat
Bowles \'bōlz\ Chester 1901–   Am. econ. & diplomat
— Samuel: father 1797–1851 & son 1826–1878 Am. newspaper editors & publishers
Boyd \'bòid\ Alan Stephenson 1922–   Am. secy. of transportation (1967–69)
Boy·den \'bòid-ᵊn\ Seth 1788–1870 Am. inventor
Boyd Orr \'bòid-'ò(ə)r, -'ō(ə)r\ 1st Baron 1880–   *John Boyd Orr* Scot. agriculturist
Boyle \'bòi(ə)l\ Kay 1903–   Am. author
— Robert 1627–1691 Brit. physicist & chem.
Brabazon of Tara Baron see MOORE-BRABAZON
Brad·bury \'brad-ˌber-ē, -b(ə-)rē\ Ray Douglas 1920–   Am. writer
Brad·dock \'brad-ək\ Edward 1695–1755 Brit. gen. in Am.
Brad·ford \'brad-fərd\ Gamaliel 1863–1932 Am. biographer
— Roark 1896–1948 Am. writer
— William 1590–1657 Pilgrim father; 2d gov. of Plymouth colony
— William 1663–1752 Am. printer
Brad·ley \'brad-lē\ Francis Herbert 1846–1924 Eng. philos.
— Henry 1845–1923 Eng. philologist & lexicographer
— Omar Nelson 1893–   Am. gen. of the army
Brad·street \'brad-ˌstrēt\ Anne 1612?–1672 née Dudley; wife of Simon Am. poet
— Simon 1603–1697 colonial gov. of Mass.
Bragg \'brag\ Braxton 1817–1876 Am. Confed. gen.
— Sir William (Henry) 1862–1942 Eng. physicist
— Sir (William) Lawrence 1890–   son of prec. Eng. physicist
Brahe \'brä; 'brä-hē, -hə\ Ty·cho \'tē-(ˌ)kō\ 1546–1601 Dan. astron.
Brahms \'brämz\ Johannes 1833–1897 Ger. composer & pianist
Braille \'brā(ə)l, 'brī\ Louis 1809–1852 Fr. blind teacher of the blind
Bra·man·te \brə-'mänt-ē, -'män-(ˌ)tä\ 1444–1514 Donato d'Agnolo or d'Angelo Ital. architect
Bran·cu·si \brän-'kü-sē\ Constantin 1876–1957 Fr. (Romanian-born) sculptor
Bran·deis \'bran-ˌdīs, -ˌdīz\ Louis Dembitz 1856–1941 Am. jurist
Bran·des \'brän-dəs\ Georg Morris 1842–1927 Dan. lit. critic
Brandt \'bränt, 'brant\ Wil·ly \'vil-ē, 'wil-ē\ 1913–   W. Ger. polit.; chancellor of West Germany (from 1969)
Bran·ting \'brant-iŋ\ Karl Hjal·mar \'yäl-ˌmär\ 1860–1925 Swed. statesman & socialist leader
Braque \'brak\ Georges 1882–1963 Fr. cubist painter
Brat·tain \'brat-ᵊn\ Walter Houser 1902–   Am. physicist
Brau·chitsch, von \'braùk-ich, 'braùk-\ Heinrich Alfred Hermann Walther 1881–1948 Ger. gen.
Braun \'braùn\ Karl Ferdinand 1850–1918 Ger. physicist
Breas·ted \'bres-təd\ James Henry 1865–1935 Am. Orientalist
Brecht \'brekt, 'brekt\ Bertolt 1898–1956 Ger. dram.
Breck·in·ridge \'brek-ən-(ˌ)rij\ John Cabell 1821–1875 Am. lawyer; vice-pres. of the U.S. (1857–61)
Bren·nan \'bren-ən\ Francis 1894–1968 Am. cardinal
— William Joseph, Jr. 1906–   Am. jurist
Bresh·kov·sky \bresh-'kòf-skē, -'kòv-\ Catherine 1844–1934 Russ. revolutionist
Bre·ton \brə-'tōⁿ\ André 1896–1966 Fr. surrealist poet
Brew·ster \'brü-stər\ William 1567–1644 Pilgrim father
Brezh·nev \'brezh-nef\ Leonid I. 1906–   Russ. polit.; pres. U.S.S.R. (1960–64); 1st secy. of communist party (from 1964)
Bri·an Bo·ru \ˌbrī-ən-bə-'rü\ Irish **Brian Bo·ram·ha** or **Bo·raim·he** \ˌbrēn-bə-'rò, -'rü\ 926–1014 king of Ireland (1002–14)
Bri·and \brē-'äⁿ\ Aristide 1862–1932 Fr. statesman
Brid·ges \'brij-əz\ Robert Seymour 1844–1930 Eng. poet; poet laureate (1913–30)
Bridg·man \'brij-mən\ Percy Williams 1882–1961 Am. physicist
Briggs \'brigz\ Lyman James 1874–1963 Am. physicist
Bright \'brīt\ John 1811–1889 Eng. orator & statesman
Brig·id \'brij-əd, 'brē-əd\ also **Brid·get** \'brij-ət\ or **Brig·it** \'brij-ət, 'brē-ət\ or **Brighid** \'brēd\ or **Bride** \'brīd\ of Kildare Saint 453–523 a patron saint of Ireland
Bril·lat-Sa·va·rin \brē-(ˌ)yä-ˌsav-ə-'raⁿ, -ˌsäv-; -'sav-ə-rən\ Anthelme 1755–1826 Fr. gastronomist
Brit·ten \'brit-ᵊn\ (Edward) Benjamin 1913–   Eng. composer
Bro·gan \'brō-gən\ Sir Denis William 1900–   Brit. hist.
Broglie, de \'brói\ Louis Victor 1892–   Fr. physicist
Brom·field \'bräm-ˌfēld\ Louis 1896–1956 Am. nov.
Bron·të \'bränt-ē\ a family of Eng. writers: Charlotte 1816–1855 & her sisters Emily 1818–1848 & Anne 1820–1849
Brooke \'brük\ Alan Francis 1883–1963 1st Viscount Al·an·brooke \'al-ən-ˌbrük\ Brit. field marshal
— Edward William 1919–   Am. polit.
— Rupert 1887–1915 Eng. poet
Brooks \'brüks\ Phillips 1835–1893 Am. bishop
— Van Wyck \van-'wik, vən-\ 1886–1963 Am. essayist & critic
Bro·sio \'brō-zē-ˌō\ Manlio 1897–   Ital. lawyer & diplomat; secy.-gen. of N.A.T.O. (from 1964)
Brown \'braùn\ Charles Brockden 1771–1810 Am. nov.
— Ford Mad·ox \'mad-əks\ 1821–1893 Eng. painter
— John Mason 1900–1969 Am. literary critic

ə abut; ᵊ kitten; ər further; a back; ā bake; ä cot, cart; aù out; ch chin; e less; ē easy; g gift; i trip; ī life
j joke; ŋ sing; ō flow; ò flaw; òi coin; th thin; t̷h this; ü loot; u̇ foot; y yet; yü few; yu̇ furious; zh vision
ə F table; à F bac; ᵏ G ich, Buch; ⁿ F vin; œ F bœuf; œ̄ F feu; ʉ G füllen; œ̄ F rue; ʸ F digne \dēnʸ\, nuit \nwʸē\

— John, of Osa·wat·o·mie \,ō-sə-'wät-ə-mē, ,äs-ə-\ 1800–1859 Am. abolitionist

Browne \'braún\ Charles Farrar 1834–1867 pseud. *Ar·te·mus* \'ärt-ə-məs\ *Ward* Am. humorist

— Sir Thomas 1605–1682 Eng. physician & author

Brow·ning \'braú-niŋ\ Elizabeth Bar·rett \'bar-ət\ 1806–1861 *wife of Robert* Eng. poet

— Robert 1812–1889 Eng. poet

Broz \'brōz, 'bróz\ *or* **Bro·zo·vitch** \'brō-zə-,vich, 'brô-\ Josip 1892– *Ti·to* \'tēt-(,)ō\ Yugoslav marshal; prime minister (1945–53); pres. (1953–)

Bruce \'brüs\ Sir David 1855–1931 Brit. physician & bacteriol.

— David K. E. 1898– Am. diplomat

— Robert 1274–1329 liberator & king (1306–29) of Scotland

— Viscount 1883–1967 *Stanley Melbourne Bruce* Austral. statesman; prime min. (1923–29)

Bruck·ner \'brúk-nər\ Anton 1824–1896 Austrian composer

Brue·ghel *or* **Breu·ghel** \'brü-gəl, 'brói-, 'brə(r)-\ family of Flem. painters including: Pieter 1520?–1569 & his sons Pieter 1564?–?1638 & Jan 1568–1625

Brum·mell \'brəm-əl\ George Bryan 1778–1840 *Beau Brummell* Eng. dandy

Bru·nel·le·schi \,brün-ᵊl-'es-kē\ *or* **Bru·nel·le·sco** \-(,)kō\ Filippo 1377?–1446 Ital. architect

Bru·ne·tière \,brü-nə-'tye(ə)r, ,brūᵉ-\ Vincent de Paul Marie Ferdinand 1849–1906 Fr. critic

Brü·ning *or* **Brue·ning** \'brü-niŋ, 'brūᵉ-\ Heinrich 1885–1970 chancellor of Germany (1930–32)

Bru·no \'brü-(,)nō\ Giordano 1548?–1600 Ital. philos.

Bru·tus \'brüt-əs\ Marcus Junius 85?–42 B.C. Rom. polit.; one of Caesar's assassins

Bry·an \'brī-ən\ William Jennings 1860–1925 Am. lawyer & polit.

Bry·ant \'brī-ant\ William Cul·len \'kəl-ən\ 1794–1878 Am. poet & editor

Bryce \'brīs\ Viscount 1838–1922 *James Bryce* Brit. jurist, hist., & diplomat

Bu·ber \'bü-bər\ Martin 1878–1965 Israeli (Austrian-born) philos.

Buch·an \'bək-ən, 'bək-\ John 1875–1940 1st Baron *Tweeds·muir* \'twēdz-,myù(ə)r\ Scot. author; gov. gen. of Canada (1935–40)

Bu·chan·an \byü-'kan-ən, bə-\ James 1791–1868 Am. polit. & diplomat; 15th pres. of the U.S. (1857–61)

Buch·man \'bùk-mən, 'bək-\ Frank Nathan Daniel 1878–1961 Am. evangelist

Buch·ner \'bùk-nər\ Eduard 1860–1917 Ger. chem.

Buck \'bək\ Pearl 1892– *née Sy·den·strick·er* \'sīd-ᵊn-,strik-ər\ Am. nov.

Buckingham 1st & 2d Dukes of see George VILLIERS

Buck·le \'bək-əl\ Henry Thomas 1821–1862 Eng. hist.

Buck·ner \'bək-nər\ Simon Bolivar 1823–1914 Am. Confed. gen. & polit.

— Simon Bolivar 1886–1945 *son of S.B.* Am. gen.

Buddha see GAUTAMA BUDDHA

Bu·dën·ny \büd-'yòn-ē, bü-'den-\ Semën Mikhailovich 1883– Russ. gen.

Buffalo Bill see William Frederick CODY

Buf·fon, de \,bə-'fōⁿ, byü-, bȳⁱ-\ Comte Georges Louis Leclerc 1707–1788 Fr. naturalist

Buis·son \bwē-'sōⁿ\ Ferdinand 1841–1932 Fr. educ.

Bul·finch \'bùl-,finch\ Charles 1763–1844 Am. architect

Bul·ga·nin \bùl-'gan-ən\ Nikolai Aleksandrovich 1895– Russ. polit. & marshal

Bull \'bùl\ Ole \'ō-lə\ Bor·ne·mann 1810–1880 Norw. violinist

Bul·litt \'bùl-ət\ William Christian 1891–1967 Am. diplomat

Bü·low, von \'byü-(,)lō, 'bū̇-\ Prince Bernhard 1849–1929 Ger. diplomat & statesman; chancellor of Germany (1900–09)

Bulwer–Lytton see LYTTON

Bunche \'bənch\ Ralph Johnson 1904– Am. diplomat

Bu·nin \'bün-(y)ən, -,(y)ēn\ Ivan Alekseevich 1870–1953 Russ. poet & nov.

Bun·ker \'bəŋ-kər\ Ellsworth 1894– Am. diplomat

Bun·sen \'bùn-zən, 'bən(t)-sən\ Robert Wilhelm 1811–1899 Ger. chem.

Bun·yan \'bən-yən\ John 1628–1688 Eng. preacher & author

Buonaparte Ital. spelling of BONAPARTE

Bur·bage \'bər-bij\ Richard 1567?–1619 Eng. actor

Bur·bank \'bər-,baŋk\ Luther 1849–1926 Am. horticulturist

Bur·ger \'bər-gər\ Warren Earl 1907– Am. jurist; chief justice U.S. Supreme Court (1969–)

Bür·ger \'bùr-gər, 'bir-, 'būᵉr-\ Gottfried August 1747–1794 Ger. poet

Bur·gess \'bər-jəs\ Frank Ge·lett \jə-'let\ 1866–1951 Am. humorist & illustrator

— Thornton Waldo 1874–1965 Am. writer

Burghley *or* **Burleigh** 1st Baron see CECIL

Bur·goyne \(,)bər-'gòin, 'bər-,\ John 1722–1792 Brit. gen. in Am. & dram.

Burke \'bərk\ Edmund 1729–1797 Brit. statesman & orator

Bur·lin·game \'bər-lən-,gām\ An·son \'an(t)-sən\ 1820–1870 Am. lawyer & diplomat

Burne–Jones \'bərn-'jōnz\ Sir Edward Co·ley \'kō-lē\ 1833–1898 orig. *Jones* Eng. painter & designer

Bur·net \(,)bər-'net, 'bər-nət\ Sir (Frank) Macfarlane 1899– Austral. physician

Bur·nett \(,)bər-'net, 'bər-nət\ Frances Eliza 1849–1924 *née Hodg·son* \'häj-sən\ Am. (Eng.-born) writer

Bur·ney \'bər-nē\ Fanny 1752–1840 orig. *Frances; Madame d'Ar·blay* \'där-(,)blā\ Eng. nov. & diarist

Burns \'bərnz\ Robert 1759–1796 Scot. poet

Burn·side \'bərn-,sīd\ Ambrose Everett 1824–1881 Am. gen.

Burr \'bər\ Aaron 1756–1836 3d vice-pres. of the U.S. (1801–05)

Bur·roughs \'bər-(,)ōz 'bə-(,)rōz\ Edgar Rice 1875–1950 Am. writer

— John 1837–1921 Am. naturalist

— William Seward 1914– Am. writer

Bur·ton \'bərt-ᵊn\ Harold Hitz 1888–1964 Am. jurist

— Sir Richard Francis 1821–1890 Brit. explorer & orientalist

— Robert 1577–1640 Eng. clergyman & author

Bush \'bùsh\ Van·ne·var \və-'nē-vər\ 1890– Am. electrical engineer

Bu·te·nandt \'büt-ᵊn-,änt\ Adolph 1903– Ger. chem.

But·ler \'bət-lər\ Benjamin Franklin 1818–1893 Am. gen. & polit.

— Joseph 1692–1752 Eng. theol.

— Nicholas Murray 1862–1947 Am. educ.

— Samuel 1612–1680 Eng. satirical poet

— Samuel 1835–1902 Eng. nov. & satirist

Bux·te·hu·de \,bùk-stə-'hüd-ə\ Dietrich 1637?–1707 Dan. organist & composer

Buys Bal·lot \,bīs-bə-'lät, ,bòis-\ Christoph Hendrik Didericus 1817–1890 Du. meteorol.

Byng \'biŋ\ George 1663–1733 Brit. admiral

— Julian Hed·worth George 1862–1935 1st Baron *Byng of Vimy* Brit. gen.; gov. gen. of Canada (1921–26)

Byrd \'bərd\ Richard Eve·lyn \'ēv-(ə-)lən\ 1888–1957 Am. admiral & polar explorer

Byrnes \'bərnz\ James Francis 1879– Am. polit. & jurist

By·ron \'bī-rən\ 6th Baron 1788–1824 *George Gordon Byron* Eng. poet

Caballero Francisco Largo see LARGO CABALLERO

Cab·ell \'kab-əl\ James Branch 1879–1958 Am. nov. & essayist

Ca·be·za de Va·ca \kə-,bā-thə-də-'väk-ə, -,bā-sə-\ Álvar Núñez 1490?–?1577 Span. explorer

Ca·ble \'kā-bəl\ George Washington 1844–1925 Am. nov.

Cab·ot \'kab-ət\ John 1450–1498 *Giovanni Ca·bo·to* \kä-'bō-(,)tō\ Venetian navigator; disc. continent of No. America for England

— Sebastian 1476?–1557 *son of John* Eng. navigator

Ca·bral \kə-'bräl, kəv-'räl\ Pedro \'pā-,thrü\ Álvares \'äl-vä-,rēsh\ 1460?–?1526 Port. navigator; claimed Brazil for Portugal

Ca·bri·ni \kə-'brē-nē\ Saint Frances Xavier 1850–1917 1st Am. citizen canonized (1946)

Cade \'kād\ Jack *d* 1450 Eng. rebel

Cad·il·lac \'kad-ᵊl-,ak, *F* kȧ-dē-yȧk\ Sieur Antoine de la Mothe \də-,lä-'mót\ 1658–1730 Fr. founder of Detroit

Ca·dor·na \kə-'dòr-nə\ Count Luigi 1850–1928 Ital. gen.

Caed·mon \'kad-mən\ *fl* 670 Anglo-Saxon poet

Cae·sar \'sē-zər\ Gaius Julius 100–44 B.C. Rom. gen., statesman, & writer

Caf·fery \'kaf-(ə-)rē\ Jefferson 1886– Am. diplomat

Cage \'kāj\ John 1912– Am. composer

Ca·glio·stro, di \kal-'yò-(,)strō, käl-\ Count Alessandro 1743–1795 real name *Giuseppe Bal·sa·mo* \'bäl-sə-,mō\ Ital. imposter

Caine \'kān\ Sir (Thomas Henry) Hall 1853–1931 Eng. nov.

Calamity Jane 1852?–1903 *Martha Jane Burke née Canary* Am. frontier markswoman

Cal·der \'kòl-dər\ Alexander 1898– Am. sculptor

Cal·de·rón de la Bar·ca \,käl-də-'rōn-də-(,)lä-'bär-kə, -'rón-\ Pedro 1600–1681 Span. dram. & poet

Cald·well \'kòl-,dwel, -dwəl, 'käl-\ Erskine 1903– Am. nov.

— (Janet) Taylor 1900– Am. author

Cal·houn \kal-'hün\ John Caldwell 1782–1850 Am. lawyer; vice-pres. of the U.S. (1825–32)

Ca·lig·u·la \kə-'lig-yə-lə\ 12–41 *Gaius Caesar* Rom. emp. (37–41)

Cal·las \'kal-əs, 'käl-,äs\ Maria 1924– Am. soprano

Cal·les \'kī-,äs, 'kä-,yäs\ Plutarco Elías 1877–1945 Mex. gen.; pres. of Mexico (1924–28)

Cal·lim·a·chus \kə-'lim-ə-kəs\ 5th cent. B.C. Greek sculptor

— *b ab* 310 B.C. Greek scholar & Alexandrian librarian

Cal·lis·the·nes \kə-'lis-thə-,nēz\ 360?–?328 B.C. Greek philos. & hist.

Cal·lis·tra·tus \kə-'lis-trət-əs\ *d* 355 B.C. Athenian orator & gen.

Cal·vert \'kal-vərt\ George 1580?–1632 1st Baron *Baltimore* Eng. proprietor in Am.

— Leonard 1606–1647 *son of George* gov. of Maryland province (1634–47)

Cal·vin \'kal-vən\ John 1509–1564 orig. *Jean Chau·vin* \shō-vaⁿ\ *or Caul·vin* \kōl-vaⁿ\ Fr. theol. & reformer

Ca·ma·cho \kə-'mäch-(,)ō\ Manuel Ávila 1897–1955 Mex. gen.; pres. of Mex. (1940–46)

Cam·ba·cé·rès, de \,käⁿ-bas-ə-'res, -,bäs-\ Duc 1753–1824 *Jean Jacques Ré·gis* \rā-'zhēs\ Fr. jurist; counsellor of Napoleon I

Cam·by·ses \kam-'bī-(,)sēz\ *d* 522 B.C. *son of Cyrus the Great* king of Persia (529–22)

Cam·den \'kam-dən\ William 1551–1623 Eng. antiquary & hist.

Cam·er·on of Loch·iel \'kam-(ə-)rə-nəv-lä-'kēl\ 1629–1719 Sir *Ewen Cameron* Scot. chieftain

— 1695?–1748 *Donald Cameron; the gentle Lochiel* Scot. chieftain

Ca·mões, Vaz de \,väzh-də-kə-'mōiⁿsh\ *Eng.* **Ca·mo·ens** \kə-'mō-ənz, 'kam-ə-wənz\ Luiz 1524–1580 Port. poet

Camp \'kamp\ Walter Chauncey 1859–1925 Am. football coach

Camp·bell \'kam-(b)əl\ Alexander 1788–1866 Am. (Irish-born) founder of Disciples of Christ

— Colin 1792–1863 orig. *Mac·li·ver* \mə-'klē-vər\; Baron *Clyde* Brit. field marshal

— John 1705–1782 4th Earl of *Lou·doun* \-'laúd-ᵊn\ Brit. gen. in Am.

— Thomas 1777–1844 Brit. poet

— -Ban·ner·man \-'ban-ər-mən\ Sir Henry 1836–1908 Brit. statesman; prime min. (1905–08)

Cam·pi \'käm-(,)pē\ Ital. family of painters in Cremona including: Galeazzo 1477–1536 & his three sons Giulio *ab* 1502–1572, Antonio *d* 1591?, & Vincenzo 1536–1591

Cam·pi·on \'kam-pē-ən\ Thomas 1567–1620 Eng. poet & musician

Ca·mus \kȧ-mᵫ\ Albert 1913–1960 Fr. nov., essayist, & dram.

Can·by \'kan-bē\ Henry Sei·del \-'sīd-ᵊl\ 1878–1961 Am. editor & educ.

Can·dolle, de \käⁿ-dòl\ Augustin Pyrame 1778–1841 Swiss botanist

Can·ning \'kan-iŋ\ Earl Charles John 1812–1862 Brit. gov. gen. of India (1856–62)

— George 1770–1827 *father of C.J.* Brit. statesman; prime min. (1827)

— Stratford 1786–1880 1st Viscount *Stratford de Red·cliffe* \'red-,klif\ Brit. diplomat

Can·non \'kan-ən\ Joseph Gur·ney \'gər-nē\ 1836–1926 *Uncle Joe* Am. lawyer & polit.

Ca·no·va \kə-'nō-və, -'nò-\ Antonio 1757–1822 Ital. sculptor

Can·ro·bert \ˌkän-rō-'be(ə)r\ François Cer·tain \ser-taⁿ\ 1809–1895 Fr. marshal

Can·til·lon \ˌkän-tē-'(y)ōⁿ\ Richard 1680?–1734 Irish econ.

Ca·nute \kə-'n(y)üt\ 994?–1035 *the Great* king of England (1016–35); of Denmark (1018–35); of Norway (1028–35)

Ča·pek \'chäp-ˌek\ Karel \'kär-əl\ 1890–1938 Czech nov. & dram.

Capet Hugh see HUGH CAPET

Ca·po·te \kə-'pōt-ē\ Truman 1924– Am. author

Car·a·cal·la \ˌkar-ə-'kal-ə\ 188–217 *Marcus Aurelius Antoninus* orig. *Bas·si·a·nus* \ˌbas-ē-'an-əs\ Rom. emp. (211–217)

Ca·rac·ta·cus \kə-'rak-ti-kəs\ *or* **Ca·rat·a·cus** \kə-'rat-i-\ *Eng.*

Ca·rad·oc \kə-'rad-ək\ *fl* 43–50 Brit. chieftain

Cár·de·nas \'kärd-ᵊn-ˌäs, 'kär-thä-ˌnäs\ Lázaro 1895– Mex. gen. & polit.; pres. of Mex. (1934–40)

Car·do·zo \kär-'dō-(ˌ)zō\ Benjamin Nathan 1870–1938 Am. jurist

Car·duc·ci \kär-'dü-(ˌ)chē\ Giosuè 1835–1907 Ital. poet

Ca·rew \kə-'rü; 'ka(ə)r-ē, 'ke(ə)r-\ Thomas 1595?–?1645 Eng. poet

Carle·ton \'kär(-ə)l-tən, 'kärlt-ᵊn\ Guy 1724–1808 1st Baron *Dorchester* Brit. gen. & administrator in Am.

Car·los \'kär-ləs, -ˌlōs\ Don 1788–1855 infante & pretender to Span. throne

— **de Austria** 1545–1568 prince of Asturias & heir to Span. throne

Car·lo·ta \kär-'lōt-ə, -'lät-\ *Eng.* **Charlotte** 1840–1927 empress of Mexico (1864–67)

Car·lyle \kär-'lī(ə)l, 'kär-ˌ\ Thomas 1795–1881 Scot. essayist & hist.

Car·man \'kär-mən\ (William) Bliss 1861–1929 Canad. poet

Car·mo·na \kär-'mō-nə\ Antonio Oscar de Fra·go·so \frə-'gō(ˌ)zü\ 1869–1951 Port. gen.; pres. of Portugal (1926–51)

Car·ne·gie \kär-nə-gē, kär-'neg-ē\ Andrew 1835–1919 Am. (Scot.-born) industrialist & philanthropist

Car·not \kär-'nō\ Lazare \lä-zär\ Nicolas \nē-kò-lä\ Marguerite 1753–1823 Fr. statesman & gen.

— **Marie François Sadi** 1837–1894 pres. of France (1887–94)

Car·ol II \'kar-əl\ 1893–1953 king of Romania (1930–40)

Car·ran·za \kə-'ran-zə, -'rän-\ Venustiano 1859–1920 pres. of Mexico (1915–20)

Car·rel \kə-'rel, 'kar-əl\ Alexis 1873–1944 Fr. surgeon & biologist

Car·rère \kə-'re(ə)r\ John Merven 1858–1911 Am. architect

Car·roll \'kar-əl\ Charles 1737–1832 *Carroll of Car·roll·ton* \'kar-əl-tən\ Am. patriot

Carroll Lewis see Charles Lutwidge DODGSON

Car·son \'kärs-ᵊn\ Christopher 1809–1868 *Kit* \'kit\ Am. trapper & frontiersman

— **Rachel** 1907–1964 Am. scientist & writer

Carte, D'Oy·ly \'dòi-lē-'kärt\ Richard 1844–1901 Eng. opera impresario

Car·ter \'kärt-ər\ Howard 1873–1939 Eng. archaeologist

Car·ter·et \ˌkärt-ə-'ret\ John 1690–1763 Earl *Gran·ville* \'gran-ˌvil\ Eng. statesman

Car·tier \kär-'tyā, ˌkärt-ē-'ā\ Jacques 1491–1557 Fr. navigator & explorer; disc. St. Lawrence River

Cart·wright \'kärt-ˌrīt\ Edmund 1743–1823 Eng. inventor

Ca·ru·so \kə-'rü-(ˌ)sō, -(ˌ)zō\ En·ri·co \en-'rē-(ˌ)kō\ 1873–1921 orig. *Errico* Ital. tenor

Car·ver \'kär-vər\ George Washington 1864–1943 Am. botanist

— **John** 1576?–1621 Eng. *Mayflower* pilgrim; 1st gov. of Plymouth colony

Cary \'ka(ə)r-ē, 'ke(ə)r-ē\ (Arthur) Joyce (Lunel) 1888–1957 Brit. nov.

— **Henry Francis** 1772–1844 Eng. clergyman; translator of Dante

Ca·sa·bian·ca, de \ˌkäz-ə-'byäŋ-kə, ˌkäs-\ Louis 1755?–1798 Fr. naval officer

Ca·sals \kə-'sälz, -'zälz\ Pablo 1876– Span. violoncellist, conductor, & composer

Cas·a·no·va \ˌkas-ə-'nō-və, ˌkas-\ *or* **Casanova de Sein·galt** \saⁿ-gäl\ Giacomo Girolamo 1725–1798 *also Giovanni Jacopo* Ital. adventurer

Ca·sau·bon \kə-'sò-bən, ˌkaz-(ˌ)ō-'bōⁿ\ Isaac 1559–1614 Fr. theol. & scholar

Case·ment \'kā-smənt\ Sir Roger David 1864–1916 Irish rebel; hanged by British

Ca·si·mir-Pé·rier \ˌkaz-ə-ˌmi(ə)r-ˌper-ē-'ā\ Jean Paul Pierre 1847–1907 Fr. statesman; pres. of France (1894–95)

Cas·lon \'kaz-lən\ William 1692–1766 Eng. type founder

Cass \'kas\ Lewis 1782–1866 Am. statesman

Cas·satt \kə-'sat\ Mary 1845–1926 Am. painter

Cas·si·o·do·rus \ˌkas-ē-ə-'dōr-əs, -'dòr-\ Flavius Magnus Aurelius *d* A.D. 575 Rom. statesman & author

Cas·si·us Lon·gi·nus \'kash-(ē)-ə-,slän-'jī-nəs, 'kas-ē-ə-\ Gaius *d* 42 B.C. Rom. gen. & conspirator

Cas·te·lar y Ri·poll \ˌkas-tə-'lär-ē-rē-'pòlʸ\ Emilio 1832–1899 Span. statesman & writer

Ca·stel·ve·tro \ˌkas-tᵊl-'ve-(ˌ)trō\ Lodovico 1505–1571 Ital. critic & philologist

Ca·sti·glio·ne \ˌkäs-tēl-'yō-(ˌ)nā\ Con·te \ˌkōn-tā-\ Bal·das·sa·re \ˌbäl-də-'sär-(ˌ)ā\ 1478–1529 Ital. statesman & author

Cas·ti·lho, de \ˌvēs-con-de \ˌvēs(h)-'kōⁿ-dē\ Antônio Feliciano 1800–1875 Port. poet

Castlereagh Viscount see Robert STEWART

Castriota George see SCANDERBEG

Cas·tro \'kas-(ˌ)trō, 'käs-\ Cipriano 1858?–1924 Venezuelan gen.; pres. of Venezuela (1902–08)

—, **de Inés** *Eng.* Agnes 1320?–1355 Span. noblewoman

— **(Ruz)** \'rüs\ Fi·del \fē-'del\ 1927– Cuban premier (1959–)

Cates·by \'kāts-bē\ Mark 1679?–1749 Eng. naturalist

— **Robert** 1573–1605 Eng. rebel

Cath·er \'kath-ər\ Wil·la \'wil-ə\ Si·bert \'sī-bərt\ 1873–1947 Am. nov.

Cath·er·ine \'kath-(ə-)rən\ name of 1st, 5th, & 6th wives of Henry VIII of England: Catherine of Aragon 1485–1536; Catherine Howard 1520?–1542; Catherine Parr \-'pär\ 1512–1548

— **I** 1684?–1727 *wife of Peter the Great* empress of Russia (1725–27)

— **II** 1729–1796 *the Great* empress of Russia (1762–96)

— **of Braganza** 1638–1705 *queen of Charles II of England*

Cath·er·ine de Mé·di·cis \'kath-(ə-)rən-də-med-ə-(ˌ)chē, -ˌmäd-ə-'sēs\ *Ital* **Caterina de' Me·di·ci** \'med-ə-(ˌ)chē\ 1519–1589 *queen of Henry II of France*

Cat·i·line \'kat-ᵊl-ˌīn\ 108?–62 B.C. *Lucius Sergius Cat·i·li·na* \ˌkat-ᵊl-'ī-nə, -ē-nə\ Rom. polit. & conspirator

Ca·to \'kät-(ˌ)ō\ Marcus Porcius 234–149 B.C. *the Elder; the Censor* Rom. statesman

— **Marcus Porcius** 95–46 B.C. *the Younger; great-grandson of prec.* Rom. Stoic philos.

Catt \'kat\ Carrie Chapman 1859–1947 née *Lane* Am. suffragist

Cat·tell \kə-'tel\ James McKeen 1860–1944 Am. psychol. & editor

Cat·ton \'kat-ᵊn\ (Charles) Bruce 1899– Am. journalist & hist.

Ca·tul·lus \kə-'təl-əs\ Gaius Valerius 84?–54 B.C. Rom. poet

Cau·lain·court, de \ˌkō-ˌlaⁿ-'kù(ə)r\ Marquis Armand Augustin Louis 1772–1827 Fr. gen. & diplomat

Ca·vell \'kav-əl, kə-'vel\ Edith Louisa 1865–1915 Eng. nurse; executed by Germans

Cav·en·dish \'kav-ən-(ˌ)dish\ Henry 1731–1810 Eng. scientist

— **Spencer Compton** 1833–1908 8th Duke of *Devonshire* Eng. statesman

— **Sir William** 1505?–1557 Eng. statesman

— **William** 1640–1707 1st Duke of *Devonshire* Eng. statesman

Ca·vour, di \kə-'vù(ə)r, kä-\ Con·te \ˌkōn-(ˌ)tā-\ Camillo Benso 1810–1861 Ital. statesman

Ca·xi·as, de \kə-'shē-əs\ Du·que \'dü-kə\ 1803–1880 *Luiz Alves de Lima e Silva* Brazil. gen. & statesman

Cax·ton \'kak-stən\ William 1422?–1491 1st Eng. printer

Ce·cil \'ses-əl, 'sis-\ (Edgar Algernon) Robert 1864–1958 1st Viscount *Cecil of Chel·wood* \'chel-ˌwůd\ Eng. statesman

— **Lord** (Edward Christian) David 1902– Eng. biographer

— **Robert** 1563?–1612 1st Earl of *Salisbury* & 1st Viscount *Cran·borne* \'kran-ˌbò(ə)rn\ Eng. statesman

— **Gas·coyne-** \'gas-ˌkòin-\ Robert Arthur Talbot 1830–1903 3d Marquis of *Salisbury* Eng. statesman

— **William** 1520–1598 1st Baron *Burgh·ley* or *Bur·leigh* \'bər-lē\ Eng. statesman

Cel·li·ni \chə-'lē-nē\ Ben·ve·nu·to \ˌben-və-'nü-(ˌ)tō\ 1500–1571 Ital. goldsmith & sculptor

Cel·sius \'sel-sē-əs, -shəs\ Anders 1701–1744 Swed. astron.

Cen·ci \'chen-(ˌ)chē\ Be·a·tri·ce \ˌbā-ä-'trē-(ˌ)chā\ 1577–1599 Ital. woman executed for parricide

Cer·van·tes Saa·ve·dra, de \sər-'van-ˌtēz-,sä-(ə-)'vä-drə\ Miguel 1547–1616 Span. writer

Cer·ve·ra y To·pe·te \sər-'ver-ə-,ē-tō-'pāt-ē\ Pascual 1839–1909 Con·de \'kòn-(ˌ)dā\ *de Jerez*; Mar·qués \mär-'käs\ *de San·ta Ana* \ˌsant-ə-'an-ə\ Span. admiral

Cé·zanne \sā-'zan\ Paul 1839–1906 Fr. painter

Chad·wick \'chad-ˌwik\ Sir James 1891– Eng. physicist

Cha·gall \shə-'gäl\ Marc 1887– Russ. painter in France

Chain \'chān\ Ernst Boris 1906– Brit. (Ger.-born) biochem.

Cha·lia·pin \shəl-'yäp-(ˌ)ēn, -ən\ Feodor Ivanovitch 1873–1938 Russ. basso

Chal·mers \'chäm-ərz, 'chal-mərz\ Alexander 1759–1834 Scot. biographer & editor

Cham·ber·lain \'chām-bər-lən\ Joseph 1836–1914 & his sons Sir (Joseph) Austen 1863–1937 & (Arthur) Neville 1869–1940 Brit. statesmen

— **Owen** 1920– Am. physicist

Cham·ber·lin \'chām-bər-lən\ Thomas Chrow·der \'kraůd-ər\ 1843–1928 Am. geologist

Cham·bers \'chām-bərz\ Robert 1802–1871 Scot. publisher & editor

Cham·bord, de \shäⁿ-'bò(ə)r\ Comte 1820–1883 Duc *de Bordeaux* Bourbon claimant to Fr. throne

Cham·plain, de \sham-'plān\ Samuel 1567?–1635 Fr. explorer in Am.; founder of Quebec

Cham·pol·lion \shäⁿ-pól-yōⁿ\ Jean François 1790–1832 Fr. Egyptologist

— **-Fi·geac** \-fē-zhàk\ Jean Jacques 1778–1867 *bro. of prec.* Fr. archaeologist

Chan·dra·gup·ta \ˌchən-drə-'gùp-tə\ 4th cent. B.C. *also San·dro·cot·tus* or *San·dra·cot·tus* \ˌsan-drə-'kät-əs\ Indian ruler of Maurya dynasty

— **II** Indian ruler of Gupta dynasty (383?–413)

Cha·nel \shə-'nel, sha-\ Gabrielle 1882?– Fr. fashion designer & perfumer

Chang Hsüeh-liang \'jäŋ-shü-'ā-lē-'äŋ\ *son of Chang Tso-lin* 1898– Chin. gen.

— **Tso-lin** \-'(t)sō-'lin\ 1873–1928 Chin. gen.

Chan·ning \'chan-iŋ\ William Ellery 1780–1842 Am. clergyman

Chao K'uang-yin \'jaů-'kwäŋ-'yin\ *or* **T'ai-tsu** \'tīd-'zü\ Chin. emp. (960–976); founder of Sung dynasty

Chap·man \'chap-mən\ Frank Mich·ler \'mik-lər\ 1864–1945 Am. ornithologist

— **George** 1559?–1634 Eng. dram. & translator

— **John** 1774–1845 *Johnny Ap·ple·seed* \'ap-əl-ˌsēd\ Am. pioneer

Char·cot \shär-'kō\ Jean Mar·tin \mär-'taⁿ\ 1825–1893 Fr. neurologist

Char·le·magne \'shär-lə-ˌmān\ 742–814 *Charles the Great* or *Charles I* Frankish king (768–814) & emp. of the West (800–814)

Charles I \'chär(-ə)lz\ 1600–1649 *Charles Stuart* king of Gt. Brit. (1625–49); executed

— **II** 1630–1685 *son of Charles I* king of Gt. Brit. (1660–85)

— **1948–** *son of Elizabeth II* prince of Wales

— **I** 1887–1922 *Charles Francis Joseph; nephew of Francis Ferdinand* emp. of Austria & (as *Charles IV*) king of Hungary (1916–18)

— **I** or **II** 823–877 *the Bald* king of France as *Charles I* (840–877); emp. as *Charles II* (875–877)

— **IV** 1294–1328 *the Fair* king of France (1322–28)

— **V** 1337–1380 *the Wise* king of France (1364–80)

— **VI** 1368–1422 *the Mad* or *the Beloved* king of France (1380–1422)

— **VII** 1403–1461 *the Victorious* king of France (1422–61)

— **IX** 1550–1574 king of France (1560–74)

— **X** 1757–1836 king of France (1824–30)

— **V** 1500–1558 Holy Rom. emp. (1519–56); king of Spain as *Charles I* (1516–56)

— **XII** 1682–1718 king of Sweden (1697–1718)

— **Prince** 1903– *bro. of King Leopold* regent of Belgium (1944–50)

— **XIV John** see BERNADOTTE

— **Edward Stuart** 1720–1788 *the Young Pretender; (Bonnie) Prince Charlie* Eng. prince

— *or* **Karl Ludwig** 1771–1847 archduke of Austria

— **Mar·tel** \mär-'tel\ 689?–741 *grandfather of Charlemagne* Frankish ruler (715–741)

Charlotte Empress of Mexico see CARLOTA

Chase \'chās\ Mary Ellen 1887– Am. educ. & author

— **Sal·mon** \'sam-ən, 'sal-mən\ Portland 1808–1873 Am. statesman; chief justice U.S. Supreme Court (1864–73)

Cha·teau·bri·and, de \,sha-,tō-brē-'äⁿ\ Vi·comte \vē-kōⁿt\ François René 1768–1848 Fr. author

Chatham 1st Earl of see William PITT

Chatrian Alexandre see ERCKMANN-CHATRIAN

Chat·ter·ji \'chät-ər-jē\ Ban·kim \'bóŋ-kim\ Chan·dra \-'chòn-(,)dró\ 1838–1894 Indian nov.

Chat·ter·ton \'chat-ərt-ᵊn\ Thomas 1752–1770 Eng. poet

Chau·cer \'chò-sər\ Geoffrey 1340?–1400 Eng. poet

Chau·temps \shō-täⁿ\ Camille 1885–1963 Fr. lawyer & polit.; premier (1930; 1933–34; 1937–38)

Chavannes, de see PUVIS DE CHAVANNES

Chá·vez \'chäv-(,)ās\ Carlos 1899– Mex. conductor & composer

Chee·ver \'chē-vər\ John 1912– Am. writer

Che·khov \'chek-,óf\ Anton Pavlovich 1860–1904 *also Che·kov* Russ. dram. & storywriter

Ché·nier, de \shän'yā\ André Marie 1762–1794 Fr. poet

Chen·nault \shə-'nólt\ Claire Lee 1890–1958 Am. gen.

Cheops see KHUFU

Che·ren·kov \chə-'reŋ-kəf\ Pavel Alekseevich 1904– Russ. physicist

Cher·ny·shev·ski \,cher-ni-'shef-skē, -'shev-\ Nikolai Gavrilovich 1829–1889 Russ. revolutionist & author

Che·ru·bi·ni \,ker-ə-'bē-nē, ,kā-rü-\ Lu·i·gi \lü-'ē-(,)jē\ Carlo Zenobio Salvatore 1760–1842 Ital. composer

Ches·ter·field \'ches-tər-,fēld\ 4th Earl of 1694–1773 *Philip Dor·mer Stan·hope* \'stan-əp\ Eng. statesman & author

Ches·ter·ton \'ches-tərt-ᵊn\ Gilbert Keith 1874–1936 Eng. journalist & author

Che·va·lier \shə-'val-(,)yā\ Mau·rice \mó-'rēs\ 1888– Fr. entertainer

Chiang Kai-shek \jē-'äŋ-'kī-'shek, 'chaŋ-\ 1887– Chin. gen. & statesman; pres. of China (1948–49, 1950–54; 1954–)

Ch'ien-lung \chē-'en-'luŋ\ 1711–1799 Chin. emp. (1736–96)

Chi·ka·ma·tsu Mon·za·e·mon \,chē-kə-'mät-(,)sü-mən-'zī-,mòn\ 1653–?1724 *the Shakespeare of Japan* Jap. dram.

Child \'chī(ə)ld\ Francis James 1825–1896 Am. philologist & ballad editor

Childe \'chī(ə)ld\ Vere Gordon 1892–1957 Brit. anthropol. & archaeol.

Chip·pen·dale \'chip-ən-,dāl\ Thomas 1718?–1779 Eng. cabinetmaker

Chi·ri·co, de \'kir-i-,kō, 'kē-ri-\ Gior·gio \'jōr-(,)jō\ 1888– Ital. painter

Chit·ty \'chit-ē\ Joseph 1776–1841 Eng. lawyer & legal writer

Choate \'chōt\ Joseph Hod·ges \'häj-əz\ 1832–1917 Am. lawyer & diplomat

— **Rufus** 1799–1859 Am. jurist

Choi·seul, de \shwä-'zəl, -'zər(-ə)l\ Duc Étienne 1719–1785 Fr. statesman

Cho·pin \'shō-,pan, -,paⁿ\ Frédéric François 1810–1849 Pol. pianist & composer

Chou En-lai \'jō-'en-'lī\ 1898– Chin. Communist polit.

Chré·tien de Troyes \krā-tyaⁿ-də-trwä\ *also Chres·tien* \krā-tyaⁿ\ 12th cent. Fr. trouvère

Christ Jesus see JESUS

Chris·tian X \'kris(h)-chən\ 1870–1947 king of Denmark (1912–47)

Chris·tie \'kris-tē\ Agatha 1891– *née Miller* Eng. writer

Chris·ti·na \kris-'tē-nə\ 1626–1689 *dau. of Gustavus Adolphus* queen of Sweden (1632–54)

Chris·tophe \krē-stóf\ Henri 1767–1820 king of Haiti (1811–20)

Chris·ty \'kris-tē\ Howard Chandler 1873–1952 Am. painter & illustrator

Chry·sos·tom \'kris-əs-təm, kris-'äs-təm\ Saint John 345?–407 church father & patriarch of Constantinople

Chu \'jü\ Hsi \'shē\ 1130–1200 Chin. philos.

— **Teh** \'də\ 1886– Chin. Communist gen.

Chur·chill \'chər-,chil, 'chərch-,hil\ John 1650–1722 1st Duke of *Marl·bor·ough* \'märl-,bər-ə, 'mól-, -,bə-rə, -b(ə-)rə\ Eng. gen.

— **Randolph Henry Spencer** 1849–1895 Lord *Randolph Churchill* Brit. statesman

— **Winston** 1871–1947 Amer. nov.

— **Sir Winston Leonard Spencer** 1874–1965 *son of Lord Randolph* Brit. statesman; prime min. (1940–45; 1951–55)

Cia·no \'chän-(,)ō\ Con·te \'kōn-(,)tā\ Galeazzo 1903–1944 *son-in-law of Mussolini* Ital. statesman

Ciar·di \'chärd-ē\ John 1916– Am. poet

Cib·ber \'sib-ər\ Col·ley \'käl-ē\ 1671–1757 Eng. dram. & actor; poet laureate (1730–57)

Cic·ero \'sis-ə-,rō\ Marcus Tullius 106–43 B.C. Rom. statesman, orator, & author

Cid, the \'sid\ 1040?–1099 *Rodrigo* (or *Ruy*) *Díaz de Bi·var* \bē-'vär\ Span. soldier & hero

Ci·ma·bue \,chē-mə-'bü-(,)ā\ Giovanni *ab* 1240–*ab* 1302 *properly Cen·ni de Pe·po* \,chen-ē-dā-'pā-(,)pō\ Florentine painter

Ci·mon \'sī-mən\ 507?–449 B.C. Athenian gen. & statesman

Cin·cin·na·tus \,sin(t)-sə-'nat-əs, -'nät-\ Lucius Quinctius 5th cent. B.C. Rom. gen. & statesman

Clarendon Earl of see Edward HYDE

Clark \'klärk\ Champ \'champ\ 1850–1921 *James Beau·champ* \'bē-chəm\ *Clark* Am. polit.

— **George Rogers** 1752–1818 Am. soldier & frontiersman

— **Kenneth Bancroft** 1914– Am. psychologist

— **Mark Wayne** 1896– Am. gen.

— **Thomas Campbell** 1899– Am. jurist

— **William** 1770–1838 Am. explorer (with Meriwether Lewis)

— **William Ramsey** 1927– Am. lawyer; U.S. attorney general (1967–69)

Clarke \'klärk\ Charles Cow·den \'kaùd-ᵊn\ 1787–1877 & his wife Mary Victoria Cowden-Clarke 1809–1898 Eng. Shakespearean scholars

Clau·di·us \'klód-ē-əs\ Rom. gens including. **Ap·pi·us** \'ap-ē-əs\ **Claudius Cras·sus** \'kras-əs\ consul (471 & 451 B.C.) & decemvir (451–450 B.C.); **Appius Claudius Cae·cus** \'sē-kəs\ censor (312–307 B.C.), consul (307 & 296 B.C.), & dictator who began building of Appian Way (312 B.C.)

— **I** 10 B.C.–A.D. 54 *Tiberius Claudius Drusus Ne·ro* \'nē-(,)rō, 'nir-(,)ō\ *Germanicus* Rom. emp. (41–54)

— **II** 214–270 *Marcus Aurelius Claudius Gothicus* Rom. emp. (268–270)

Clau·se·witz, von \'klaù-zə-,vits\ Karl 1780–1831 Pruss. gen. & military strategist

Clay \'klā\ Henry 1777–1852 Am. statesman & orator

— **Lucius Du Bi·gnon** \dü-'bin-yən\ 1897– Am. gen.

Cle·an·thes \klē-'ar-,thēz\ 3d cent. B.C. Greek Stoic philos.

Cle·ar·chus \klē-'är-kəs\ *fl* 408–401 B.C. Greek soldier; gov. of Byzantium

Cleis·the·nes \'klīs-thə-,nēz\ *or* **Clis·the·nes** \'klis-\ *fl ab* 507 B.C. Athenian statesman

Cle·men·ceau \,klem-ən-'sō, klā-mäⁿ-sō\ Georges 1841–1929 *the Tiger* Fr. statesman

Clem·ens \'klem-ənz\ Samuel Langhorne 1835–1910 pseud. *Mark Twain* \'twān\ Am. humorist

Clem·ent \'klem-ənt\ name of 14 popes: esp. **VII** (*Giulio de' Me·di·ci* \'med-ə-(,)chē\) 1478–1534 (pope 1523–34)

— **of Alexandria** 150?–?220 *Titus Flavius Cle·mens* \'klem-,enz\ Greek Christian theologian & church father

Cle·om·e·nes \klē-'äm-ə-,nēz\ name of 3 kings of Sparta: esp. **III** (reigned 235–219 B.C.)

Cle·o·pa·tra \,klē-ə-'pa-trə, -'pā-, -'pä-\ 69–30 B.C. queen of Egypt (51–49; 48–30)

Clerk-Maxwell James see James Clerk MAXWELL

Cleve·land \'klēv-lənd\ (Stephen) Grover 1837–1908 22d & 24th pres. of the U.S. (1885–89; 1893–97)

Cli·burn \'klī-bərn\ Van \'van\ 1934– Am. pianist

Clif·ford \'klif-ərd\ Clark McAdams 1906– Am. lawyer; secy. of defense (1968–69)

Clin·ton \'klint-ᵊn\ De Witt \di-'wit\ 1769–1828 Am. statesman

— **George** 1739–1812 vice-pres. of the U.S. (1805–12)

— **Sir Henry** 1738?–1795 Eng. gen. in Am.

Clive \'klīv\ Robert 1725–1774 Baron *Clive of Plassey* Brit. gen.; founder of the empire of Brit. India

Cloots, de \'klōts\ Baron 1755–1794 *Jean Baptiste du Val-de Grâce; An·a·char·sis* \,an-ə-'kär-səs\ *Cloots* Prussian-Fr. revolutionist

Clough \'kləf\ Arthur Hugh 1819–1861 Eng. poet

Clo·vis I \'klō-vəs\ Ger. **Chlod·wig** \'klōt-(,)vik\ 466?–511 Frankish king of Merovingian dynasty (481–511)

Clyde Baron see Colin CAMPBELL

Cnut \'kə-'n(y)üt\ *var of* CANUTE

Coates \'kōts\ Joseph Gordon 1878–1943 N. Z. statesman

Cobb \'käb\ Irvin Shrewsbury 1876–1944 Am. journalist & humorist

Cob·bett \'käb-ət\ William 1763–1835 *Peter Porcupine* Eng. polit. writer

Cob·den \'käb-dən\ Richard 1804–1865 Eng. statesman & econ.

Cobham Lord see Sir John OLDCASTLE

Cock·croft \'käk-,róft, 'kō-,króft\ Sir John Douglas 1897–1967 Brit. physicist

Coc·teau \käk-'tō, kók-\ Jean 1889–1963 Fr. author

Co·dy \'kōd-ē\ John Patrick 1907– Am. cardinal

— **William Frederick** 1846–1917 *Buf·fa·lo Bill* Am. scout, Indian fighter, & showman

Coen \'kün\ Jan Pie·ters·zoon \'pēt-ər-sən\ 1587–1629 Du. colonial gov.; founder of Du. East Indian empire

Coeur de Lion see RICHARD I of England

Cof·fin \'kóf-ən, 'käf-\ Robert Peter Tristram 1892–1955 Am. author

Co·han \'kō-,han\ George Michael 1878–1942 Am. actor, dram., & producer

Co·hen \'kō-ən\ Octavus Roy 1891–1959 Am. author

Cohn \'kōn\ Ferdinand Julius 1828–1898 Ger. botanist; called founder of bacteriology

Coke \'kük, 'kōk\ Sir Edward 1552–1634 *Lord Coke* Eng. jurist

Col·bert \kól-'be(ə)r\ Jean Baptiste 1619–1683 Fr. statesman & financier

Cole \'kōl\ Thomas 1801–1848 Am. (Eng.-born) painter

Cole·pep·er \'kəl-,pep-ər\ Thomas 1635–1689 2d Baron *Colepeper of Thores·way* \'thō(ə)rz-,wā, 'thó(ə)rz-\ Eng. colonial administrator; gov. of Virginia

Cole·ridge \'kōl-rij, 'kō-lə-rij\ Samuel Taylor 1772–1834 Eng. poet

Col·et \'käl-ət\ John 1466?–1519 Eng. theol. & scholar

Co·lette \kò-'let\ Sidonie Gabrielle Claudine 1873–1954 Fr. author

Col·fax \'kōl-,faks\ Schuy·ler \'skī-lər\ 1823–1885 vice-pres. of the U. S. (1869–73)

Co·li·gny *or* **Co·li·gni, de** \,kò-,lēn-'yē, ,kō-\ Gaspard (II) 1519–1572 Fr. admiral & Huguenot leader

Col·lier \'käl-yər, 'käl-ē-ər\ Jeremy 1650–1726 Eng. clergyman

— **John Payne** 1789–1883 Eng. editor

— **Peter Fen·e·lon** \'fen-ᵊl-ən\ 1849–1909 Am. publisher

Col·lins \'käl-ənz\ Michael 1890–1922 Irish revolutionist

— **Michael** 1930– Am. astronaut

— **William** 1721–1759 Eng. poet

— (**William**) **Wilkie** 1824–1889 Eng. nov.

Col·man \'kōl-mən\ George 1732–1794 Eng. dram.

Col·um \'käl-əm\ Mary Gun·ning \-gən-iŋ\ 1887?–1957 *née Ma·guire* \mə-'gwī(ə)r\ *wife of Padraic* Am. (Irish-born) writer

— **Pad·raic** \'pothʲ-rig\ 1881– Am. (Irish-born) poet & dram.

Co·lum·ba \kə-'ləm-bə\ Saint **Col·um** \'käl-əm\ *or* **Col·um·cille** \'käl-əm-,kil\ Saint 521–597 *apostle of Caledonia* Irish missionary in Scot.

Co·lum·bus \kə-'ləm-bəs\ Christopher *Ital.* Cristoforo **Co·lom·bo** \kə-'läm-(,)bō\ *Span.* Cristóbal **Co·lón** \kə-'lōn\ 1451–1506 Ital. navigator; disc. Am.

Col·vin \'käl-vən\ Sir Sidney 1845–1927 Eng. author & critic

Co·me·ni·us \kə'mē-nē-əs\ *Czech* **Ko·men·ský** \'kȯ-mən-skē\ John Amos 1592–1670 Czech theol. & educ.

Co·mines *or* Com·mines *or* Com·mynes *or* Co·mynes, de \kə-'mēn\ Philippe 1447?–?1511 Sire *d'Ar·gen·ton* \'siər-ˌdär-zhäⁿ-töⁿ\ Fr. chronicler

Com·ma·ger \'käm-i-jər\ Henry Steele 1902– Am. hist.

Com·mo·dus \'käm-ə-dəs\ Lucius Aelius Aurelius 161–192 Rom. emp. (180–192)

Comp·ton \'käm(p)-tən\ Arthur Holly 1892–1962 Am. physicist
— Karl Taylor 1887–1954 *bro. of A.H.* Am. physicist

Com·stock \'kəm-ˌstäk\ Anthony 1844–1915 Am. reformer

Comte \kôⁿt\ Auguste 1798–1857 *Isidore Auguste Marie François Comte* Fr. math. & philos.

Co·nant \'kō-nənt\ James Bryant 1893– Am. chem. & educ.

Con·dé, de \kôⁿ-'dā\ Prince 1621–1687 *Louis II de Bour·bon* \'bu̇(ə)r-bən, bu̇r-'bôⁿ; *Duc d'En·ghien* \dän-gaⁿ\ Fr. gen.

Con·don \'kän-dən\ Edward Uhler 1902– Am. physicist

Con·dor·cet, de \kôⁿ-dȯr-sā\ Marquis 1743–1794 *Marie Jean Antoine Nicholas de Ca·ri·tat* \ˌkar-ə-'tä\ Fr. philos. & polit.

Con·fu·cius \kən-'fyü-shəs\ *Chin.* **K'ung Fu-tzu** *or* **Kung Fu-tse** *ab* 551–479 B.C. Chin. philos.

Con·greve \'kän-ˌgrēv, 'käŋ-\ William 1670–1729 Eng. dram.

Con·ing·ham \'kən-iŋ-ˌham, *chiefly Brit* -iŋ-əm\ Sir Arthur 1895–1948 Brit. air marshal

Con·nor \'kän-ər\ John Thomas 1914– Am. lawyer; U.S. secretary of commerce (1965–67)

Con·rad \'kän-ˌrad\ Joseph 1857–1924 *orig. Teodor Józef Konrad Kor·ze·niow·ski* \ˌkȯr-zən-'yȯf-skē\ Brit. (Ukrainian-born of Pol. parents) nov.

Con·sta·ble \'kən(t)-stə-bəl, 'kän(t)-\ John 1776–1837 Eng. painter

Cons·tant \kôⁿ-stäⁿ\ Benjamin 1845–1902 Fr. painter
— de Re·becque \rə-'bek\ 1767–1830 Fr. writer & polit.

Con·stan·tine \'kän(t)-stən-ˌtēn, -ˌtīn\ 1940– king of Greece (from 1964)
— I 280?–337 *the Great* Rom. emp. (306–337)
— I 1868–1923 king of Greece 1913–17; 1920–22)

Con·ta·ri·ni \ˌkänt-ə-'rē-nē\ Venetian family including esp. Gasparo 1483–1542 cardinal (1535) & diplomat

Con·ti, de' \'kônt-ē\ Niccolò 15th cent. Venetian traveler

Cook \'ku̇k\ Capt. James 1728–1779 Eng. navigator & explorer

Cooke \'ku̇k\ (Alfred) Al·is·tair \'al-ə-stər\ 1908– Am. (Brit.-born) essayist & journalist
— Jay 1821–1905 Am. financier
— Terence James 1921– Am. cardinal

Coo·lidge \'kü-lij\ (John) Calvin 1872–1933 30th pres. of the U. S. (1923–29)
— Julian Lowell 1873–1954 Am. math.

Coo·per \'kü-pər, 'ku̇p-ər\ Anthony Ashley see SHAFTESBURY
— Hugh Lincoln 1865–1937 Am. engineer
— James Fen·i·more \'fen-ə-ˌmō(ə)r, -ˌmȯ(ə)r\ 1789–1851 Am. nov.
— Peter 1791–1883 Am. manufacturer & philanthropist

Co·per·ni·cus \kō-'pər-ni-kəs\ Nicolaus *Pol.* **Mikolaj Ko·per·nik** \kȯ-'per-nēk\ *or* **Niklas Kop·per·nigk** \'käp-ər-ˌnik\ 1473–1543 Pol. (or Prussian) astron.; founder of modern astronomy

Cop·land \'kō-plənd\ Aaron 1900– Am. composer

Cop·ley \'käp-lē\ John Sin·gle·ton \'siŋ-gəl-tən\ 1738–1815 Am. portrait painter

Co·que·lin \kȯ-klaⁿ\ Benoît Constant 1841–1909 Fr. actor

Cor·co·ran \'kȯr-k(ə-)rən\ Thomas Gardiner 1900– Am. lawyer & polit.

Cor·day \kȯr-'dā\ Charlotte 1768–1793 *Marie Anne Charlotte Corday d'Ar·mont* \där-'môⁿ\ Fr. patriot; assassinated Marat

Co·ri \'kȯr-ē, 'kȯr-\ Carl Ferdinand 1896– & his wife Ger·ty \'gert-ē\ Theresa 1896–1957 *née Rad·nitz* \'räd-ˌnits\ Am. (Czech-born) biochemists

Corneille \kȯr-'nā\ Pierre 1606–1684 Fr. dram.

Cor·ne·lia \kȯr-'nēl-yə, -'nē-lē-ə\ 2d cent. B.C. *Mother of the Gracchi* Rom. matron
— d ?67 B.C. *wife of Julius Caesar*

Cor·ne·lius, von \kȯr-'nāl-yəs, -'nā-lē-əs\ Peter \'pāt-ər\ 1783–1867 Ger. painter

Cor·nell \kȯr-'nel\ Ezra 1807–1874 Am. financier & philanthropist
— Katharine 1898– Am. actress

Corn·wal·lis \kȯrn-'wäl-əs\ 1st Marquis 1738–1805 *Charles Cornwallis* Brit. gen. & statesman

Co·ro·na·do \ˌkȯr-ə-'näd-(ˌ)ō, ˌkär-, -'näth-\ Francisco Vásquez de 1510–1554 Span. explorer of southwestern U.S.

Co·rot \kə-'rō\ Jean Baptiste Camille 1796–1875 Fr. painter

Cor·reg·gio \kə-'rej-(ē-ˌ)ō\ 1494–1534 *Antonio Allegri da Correggio* Ital. painter

Cor·tes *or* Cor·tez \ˌkȯr-tez, 'kȯr-\ Hernando 1485–1547 Span. conqueror of Mexico

Cos·grave \'käz-ˌgrāv\ William Thomas 1880–1965 Irish statesman

Cos·ta Ca·bral, da \ˌkäs(h)-tə-kə-'bräl\ Antonio Bernardo 1803–1889 *Con·de* \'kôn-dē\ *de Tho·mar* \tü-'mär\ Port. statesman

Cot·ton \'kät-ᵊn\ Charles 1630–1687 Eng. author & translator
— John 1584–1652 Eng. Puritan clergyman in Am.

Co·ty \kȯ-'tē, kō-\ René 1882–1962 Fr. lawyer; 2d pres. of 4th Republic (1954–59)

Cou·lomb, de \kü-lôⁿ; 'kü-ˌläm, -ˌlōm, kü-'\ Charles Augustin 1736–1806 Fr. physicist

Cou·pe·rin \kü-praⁿ\ François 1668–1733 Fr. composer

Cour·bet \ku̇r-'bā\ Gustave 1819–1877 Fr. painter

Cour·nand \ku̇r-'näⁿ\ André Frédéric 1895– Am. (Fr.-born) physiologist

Cou·sin \kü-zaⁿ\ Victor 1792–1867 Fr. philos.

Cous·ins \'kəz-ᵊnz\ Norman 1912– Am. editor & essayist

Co·var·ru·bias \ˌkō-və-'rü-bē-əs\ Miguel 1904–1957 Mex. illustrator

Cov·er·dale \'kəv-ər-ˌdāl\ Miles 1488–1568 Eng. Bible translator

Cow·ard \'kau̇-(ə)rd\ Noel Pierce 1899– Eng. actor & dram.

Cow·ell \'kau̇-(ə)l\ Henry Dixon 1897–1965 Am. composer

Cowl \'kau̇(ə)l\ Jane 1884–1950 *orig. Cowles* Am. actress

Cow·ley \'kau̇-lē\ Abraham 1618–1667 Eng. poet
— Malcolm 1898– Am. literary critic

Cow·per \'kü-pər, 'ku̇p-ər, 'kau̇-pər\ William 1731–1800 Eng. poet

Cox·ey \'käk-sē\ Jacob Sechler 1854–1951 Am. polit. reformer

Coz·zens \'kəz-ᵊnz\ James Gould 1903– Am. author

Crabbe \'krab\ George 1754–1832 Eng. poet

Craig·av·on \krā-'gav-ən\ 1st Viscount 1871–1940 *James Craig Craigavon* Brit. statesman; 1st prime min. of Northern Ireland (1921–40)

Crai·gie \'krā-gē\ Sir William Alexander 1867–1957 Brit. philologist & lexicographer

Craik \'krāk\ Dinah Maria 1826–1887 *née Mu·lock* \'myü-ˌläk\ Eng. nov.

Cram \'kram\ Ralph Adams 1863–1942 Am. architect & author

Cra·nach \'krän-ˌäk\ Lucas 1472–1553 Ger. painter & engraver

Cranborne Viscount see CECIL

Crane \'krān\ Stephen 1871–1900 Am. writer
— Walter 1845–1915 Eng. painter & illustrator

Cran·mer \'kran-mər\ Thomas 1489–1556 Eng. reformer; archbishop of Canterbury

Cras·sus \'kras-əs\ Marcus Licinius 115?–53 B.C. *Di·ves* \'dī-(ˌ)vēz\ Rom. polit.

Cré·bil·lon \krā-bē-'(y)ôⁿ\ 1674–1762 pseud. of *Prosper Jolyot* Fr. dram.

Cre·mer \'krē-mər\ Sir William Randal 1838–1908 Eng. pacifist

Cres·ton \'kres-tən\ Paul 1906– real name *Joseph Guttoveggio* Am. composer

Crève·coeur, de \krev-'kər, -'ku̇(ə)r\ Michel Guillaume St. Jean 1735–1813 Am. (Fr.-born) essayist

Crich·ton \'krīt-ᵊn\ James 1560?–1582 *the Admirable Crichton* Scot. prodigy

Crile \'krī(ə)l\ George Washington 1864–1943 Am. surgeon

Cripps \'krips\ Sir (Richard) Stafford 1889–1952 Brit. lawyer & socialist statesman

Cri·spi \'kris-pē, 'krēs-\ Francesco 1819–1901 Ital. statesman; premier (1887–91; 1893–96)

Cro·ce \'krō-(ˌ)chā\ Benedetto 1866–1952 Ital. philos. & statesman

Crock·ett \'kräk-ət\ David 1786–1836 *Davy* Am. frontiersman & polit.

Croe·sus \'krē-səs\ d 546 B.C. king of Lydia (560–546); amassed vast wealth

Cro·ker \'krō-kər\ John Wilson 1780–1857 Brit. essayist & editor

Cromp·ton \'kräm(p)-tən\ Samuel 1753–1827 Eng. inventor of the spinning mule

Crom·well \'kräm-ˌwel, 'krəm-, -wəl\ Oliver 1599–1658 Eng. gen. & statesman; lord protector of England (1653–58)
— Richard 1626–1712 *son of Oliver* lord protector (1658–59)
— Thomas 1485?–1540 Earl of *Essex* Eng. statesman

Cro·nin \'krō-nən\ Archibald Joseph 1896– Eng. physician & nov.

Cron·jé \krôn-'yā\ Piet Arnoldus 1840?–1911 Boer leader & gen.

Crookes \'kru̇ks\ Sir William 1832–1919 Eng. physicist & chem.

Cross \'krȯs\ Wilbur Lucius 1862–1948 Am. educ. & polit.

Crouse \'krau̇s\ Russel 1893–1966 Am. journalist & dram.

Cru·den \'krüd-ᵊn\ Alexander 1701–1770 Scot. compiler of a biblical concordance

Cruik·shank \'kru̇k-ˌshaŋk\ George 1792–1878 Eng. caricaturist & illustrator

Cud·worth \'kəd-(ˌ)wərth\ Ralph 1617–1688 Eng. philos.

Cul·pep·er \'kəl-ˌpep-ər\ var of COLEPEPER

Cum·mings \'kəm-iŋz\ Edward Estlin 1894–1962 Am. poet

Cu·nha, da Tris·tão \ tris-tən-də-'kü-nə, trēs(h)-ˌtau̇ⁿ-də-'kün-yə\ 1460?–?1540 Port. navigator & explorer

Cun·ning·ham \'kən-iŋ-ˌham, *chiefly Brit* -iŋ-əm\ Allan 1784–1842 Scot. author
— Andrew Browne 1883–1963 1st Viscount *Cunningham of Hynd·hope* Brit. admiral
— Merce 1922?– Am. choreographer

Cu·rie \kyu̇-'rē, 'kyu̇(ə)r-(ˌ)ē\ Eve 1904– *dau. of Marie & Pierre* Fr. author
— Marie 1867–1934 *née Marja Skło·dow·ska* \sklə-'dȯf-skə\ Fr. (Pol.-born) chem.
— Pierre 1859–1906 *husband of Marie* Fr. chem.
— Joliot see JOLIOT-CURIE

Cur·ley \'kər-lē\ James Michael 1874–1958 Am. polit.

Cur·ri·er \'kər-ē-ər, ˌkə-rē-\ Nathaniel 1813–1888 Am. lithographer

Cur·ry \'kər-ē, ˌkə-rē\ John Steuart 1897–1946 Am. painter

Cur·tin \'kərt-ᵊn\ John 1885–1945 Austral. polit.; prime min. (1941–45)

Cur·tis \'kərt-əs\ Charles 1860–1936 vice-pres. of the U. S. (1929–33)
— Cyrus Hermann Kotzsch·mar \'käch-ˌmär\ 1850–1933 Am. publisher
— George Ticknor 1812–1894 Am. lawyer & writer
— George William 1824–1892 Am. author

Cur·tiss \'kərt-əs\ Glenn Hammond 1878–1930 Am. aviator & inventor

Cur·ti·us \'ku̇rt-sē-əs\ Ernst 1814–1896 Ger. philologist & archaeologist

Cur·wen \'kər-wən\ John 1816–1880 Eng. music teacher

Cur·zon \'kərz-ᵊn\ George Nathaniel 1859–1925 1st Baron & 1st Marquis *Curzon of Ked·le·ston* \'ked-ᵊl-stən\ Eng. statesman; viceroy of India (1899–1905)

Cush·ing \'ku̇sh-iŋ\ Caleb 1800–1879 Am. lawyer & diplomat
— Harvey 1869–1939 Am. surgeon
— Richard James 1895– Am. cardinal

Cus·ter \'kəs-tər\ George Armstrong 1839–1876 Am. gen.

Cuth·bert \'kəth-bərt\ Saint 635?–687 Eng. monk

Cu·vier \'k(y)ü-vē-ˌā\ Baron Georges Léopold Chrétien Frédéric Dagobert 1769–1832 Fr. naturalist

Cyne·wulf \'kin-ə-ˌwu̇lf\ *or* Cyn·wulf \'kin-ˌwu̇lf\ *fl* 750 Anglo-Saxon poet

Cyp·ri·an \'sip-rē-ən\ Saint d 258 *Thascius Caecilius Cyprianus* Christian martyr; bishop of Carthage (248–258)

Cy·ran·kie·wicz \ˌ(t)sir-ən-'kyā-vich\ Jozef 1911?– Pol. polit.; prime min. (1947; 1954; 1961)

Cy·ra·no de Ber·ge·rac, de \sir-ə-ˌnō-də-'ber-zhə-ˌrak\ Savinien

1619–1655 Fr. poet & soldier

Cyr·il \\'sir-əl\\ Saint 827–869 *Constantine* Slavic apostle

Cy·rus \\'sī-rəs\\ 600?–529 B.C. *the Great* or *the Elder* king of Persia (550–529)

— 424?–401 B.C. *the Younger* Persian prince & satrap

D', De, Du, etc. for many names beginning with these elements see the specific family names

Da·guerre \\də-'ge(ə)r\\ Louis Jacques Mandé 1789–1851 Fr. painter; inventor of the daguerrotype

Da·kin \\'dā-kən\\ Henry Drys·dale \\'drīz-,dāl\\ 1880–1952 Eng. chem.

Da·la·dier \\də-'läd-ē-,ā, ,dal-əd-'yā\\ Édouard 1884– Fr. statesman

D' Al·bert \\'dal-bərt\\ Eugen 1864–1932 Scot. pianist & composer

Dalcroze Émile Jaques see Émile JAQUES-DALCROZE

Dale \\'dā(ə)l\\ Sir Henry Hallett 1875–1968 Eng. physiol.

— Sir Thomas *d* 1619 Eng. colonial administrator in Virginia (1611–16)

Da·lén \\də-'lān\\ Nils Gustaf 1869–1937 Swed. inventor

Dalhousie Earl & Marquis of see RAMSAY

Da·li \\'däl-ē, dä-'lē; *the second is his own accentuation*\\ Salvador 1904– Span. painter; leader of surrealist school

Dal·las \\'dal-əs\\ George Mifflin 1792–1864 vice-pres. of the U.S. (1845–49)

Dal·rym·ple \\dal-'rim-pəl, 'dal-,\\ Sir James 1619–1695 1st Viscount *Stair* Scot. jurist

— Sir John 1673–1747 2d Earl of *Stair* Brit. gen. & diplomat

Dal·ton \\'dôlt-ᵊn\\ Baron 1887–1962 *Hugh Dalton* Brit. polit.

— John 1766–1844 Eng. chem. & physicist

Da·ly \\'dā-lē\\ (John) Augustin 1838–1899 Am. dram. & theater manager

Dam \\'dam, 'däm\\ (Carl Peter) Henrik 1895– Dan. biochem.

Da·mien de Veus·ter \\,dä-mē-ən-də-'vyüs-tər, ,dam-ē-,aⁿ-də-,vȯ(r)s-'te(ə)r\\ Joseph 1840–1889 *Father Da·mien* \\'dā-mē-ən\\ Belg. R.C. missionary to lepers on Molokai

Dam·pi·er \\'dam-pē-ər\\ William 1652–1715 Eng. buccaneer & navigator

Dam·rosch \\'dam-,räsh\\ Walter Johannes 1862–1950 Am. (Ger.-born) musician & conductor

Da·na \\'dā-nə\\ Charles Anderson 1819–1897 Am. newspaper editor

— Edward Salisbury 1849–1935 Am. mineralogist

— James Dwight 1813–1895 Am. geologist

— Richard Henry 1815–1882 Am. lawyer & author

Dane \\'dān\\ Clemence 1888–1965 pseud. of *Winifred Ash·ton* \\'ash-tən\\ Eng. nov.

Dan·iel \\'dan-yəl\\ Samuel 1563?–1619 Eng. poet

Dan·iels \\'dan-yəlz\\ Josephus 1862–1948 Am. journalist & statesman

Da·ni·lo·va \\də-'nē-lə-və\\ Alexandra 1906– Russ. ballet dancer in U.S.

D'An·nun·zio \\dä-'nünt-sē-,ō\\ Gabriele 1863–1938 Ital. author & soldier

Dan·te \\'dant-ē, 'dän-(,)tā\\ 1265–1321 *Dante Ali·ghie·ri* \\,al-əg-'ye(ə)r-ē\\ Ital. poet

Dan·ton \\däⁿ-tōⁿ\\ Georges Jacques 1759–1794 Fr. revolutionist

Dare \\'da(ə)r, 'de(ə)r\\ Virginia 1587–? 1st child born in Am. of Eng. parents

Da·ri·us \\də-'rī-əs\\ name of 3 kings of Persia: esp. **I** 558?–486 B.C. (reigned 521–486) *Darius Hys·tas·pis* \\his-'tas-pəs\\; *the Great*

Dar·lan \\där-'läⁿ\\ Jean Louis Xavier 1881–1942 Fr. admiral

Darn·ley \\'därn-lē\\ Lord 1545–1567 *Henry Stewart* or *Stuart; husband of Mary, Queen of Scots*

Dar·row \\'dar-(,)ō\\ Clarence Seward 1857–1938 Am. lawyer & author

Dar·win \\'där-wən\\ Charles Robert 1809–1882 Eng. naturalist

— Erasmus 1731–1802 *grandfather of C. R.* Eng. physiol. & poet

Dau·bi·gny \\,dō-bēn-'yē\\ Charles François 1817–1878 Fr. painter

Dau·det \\dō-'dā\\ Alphonse 1840–1897 Fr. nov.

— Léon 1867–1942 *son of Alphonse* Fr. journalist & writer

Dau·mier \\dō-myā\\ Honoré 1808–1879 Fr. caricaturist & painter

Dav·e·nant or **D'Av·e·nant** \\'dav-(ə-)nənt\\ Sir William 1606–1668 Eng. poet & dram.; poet laureate (1638–68)

Dav·en·port \\dav-ən-,pō(ə)rt, 'dav-ᵊm-, -,pȯ(ə)rt\\ John 1597–1670 Eng. clergyman; founder of New Haven colony

Da·vid \\'dā-vəd\\ **I** 1084–1153 king of Scotland (1124–53)

— \\'däv-ət\\ Gerard 1450? or 1460?–1523 Du. painter

Da·vid \\dä-'vēd\\ Jacques Louis 1748–1825 Fr. painter

— **d'An·gers** \\däⁿ-zhä\\ Pierre Jean 1788–1856 Fr. sculptor

Da·vid·son \\'dā-vəd-sən\\ Jo 1883–1952 Am. sculptor

Dá·vi·la y Pa·dil·la \\'dä-vē-lə-,ē-pə-'the̱-(y)ə\\ Agustín 1562–1604 Mex. monk & hist.

Da·vis \\'dā-vəs\\ Elmer Holmes 1890–1958 Am. radio broadcaster & news commentator

— Harold Le·noir \\lə-'nȯ(ə)r, -'nȯ(ə)r\\ 1896–1960 Am. author & poet

— Jefferson 1808–1889 Am. statesman; pres. of Confed. states (1861–65)

— Richard Harding 1864–1916 Am. author

Da·vis·son \\'dā-və-sən\\ Clinton Joseph 1881–1958 Am. physicist

Da·vout \\də-'vü\\ Louis Nicolas 1770–1823 Duc *d'Au·er·staedt* \\'daú(ə)r-,stat\\ & Prince *d'Eck·mühl* \\'dek-,myül\\ marshal of France

Da·vy \\'dā-vē\\ Sir Humphry 1778–1829 Eng. chem.

Dawes \\'dȯz\\ Charles Gates 1865–1951 Am. lawyer & financier; vice-pres. of U.S. (1925–29)

Daw·son \\'dȯs-ᵊn\\ Sir John William 1820–1899 Canad. geologist

Day \\'dā\\ Clarence Shepard 1874–1935 Am. author

— Thomas 1748–1789 Eng. author

— William Rufus 1849–1923 Am. statesman & jurist

Da·yan \\dī-'än, dä-'yän\\ Moshe 1915– Israeli soldier and statesman

Day–Lewis Cecil 1904– Eng. writer; poet laureate (from 1968)

De·ák \\'de-,äk\\ Ferencz \\'fer-,ents\\ 1803–1876 Hung. statesman

Dean \\'dēn\\ Sir Patrick 1909– Brit. diplomat

Deane \\'dēn\\ Silas 1737–1789 Am. lawyer & diplomat

De·bierne \\də-'bye(ə)rn\\ André Louis 1874–1949 Fr. chem.

Debs \\'debz\\ Eugene Victor 1855–1926 Am. socialist

De·bus·sy \\,deb-yü-'sē, ,däb-yü-, də-,byü-; də-'byü-sē\\ Claude

Achille 1862–1918 Fr. composer

De·bye \\də-'bī\\ Peter Joseph Wilhelm 1884–1966 Du.-born physicist in Am.

De Cas·ser·es \\də-'kas-ə-rəs\\ Benjamin 1873–1945 Am. journalist & poet

De·ca·tur \\di-'kāt-ər\\ Stephen 1779–1820 Am. naval officer

De·cazes \\də-'käz\\ Duc Élie 1780–1860 Fr. jurist & statesman

De·ci·us \\'dē-sh(ē-)əs\\ 201–251 *Gaius Messius Quintus Trajanus Decius* Rom. emp. (249–51)

Dee·ping \\'dē-piŋ\\ George Warwick 1877–1950 Eng. nov.

Def·fand, du \\de-fäⁿ\\ Marquise 1697–1780 née *Marie de Vichy-Cham·rond* \\-shäⁿ-rōⁿ\\ Fr. noblewoman

De·foe \\di-'fō\\ Daniel *ab* 1660–1731 Eng. journalist & nov.

De For·est \\di-'fȯr-əst, -'fär-\\ Lee 1873–1961 Am. inventor

De·gas \\də-'gä\\ Hilaire Germain Edgar 1834–1917 Fr. artist

de Gaulle \\də-'gōl\\ Charles André Joseph Marie 1890– Fr. gen.; interim pres. of France (1945–46); pres. of Fifth Republic (1959–69)

De·grelle \\də-'grel\\ Léon 1906– Belg. polit.

Dek·ker or **Deck·er** \\'dek-ər\\ Thomas 1572?–?1632 Eng. dram.

de Koo·ning \\də-'kō-niŋ\\ Willem 1904– Du.-born painter in Am.

De Ko·ven \\də-'kō-vən\\ (Henry Louis) Reginald 1859–1920 Am. composer

De Kruif \\də-'krīf\\ Paul 1890– Am. bacteriol. & author

De·la·croix \\,del-ə-'krwä\\ Ferdinand Victor Eugène 1798–1863 Fr. painter

de la Mare \\,del-ə-'ma(ə)r, -'me(ə)r\\ Walter John 1873–1956 Eng. poet & nov.

De·land \\də-'land\\ Margaret 1857–1945 née (*Margaretta Wade*) *Campbell* Am. nov.

De La Rey \\,del-ə-'rī\\ Jacobus Hercules 1847–1914 Boer gen. & statesman

De·la·roche \\,del-ə-'rōsh, -'rȯsh\\ Hippolyte Paul 1797–1856 Fr. painter

De·la·vigne \\,del-ə-'vēnʸ\\ Casimir 1793–1843 Fr. poet & dram.

De La Warr \\'del-ə-,wa(ə)r, -,we(ə)r\\ Baron 1577–1618 *Thomas West; Lord Delaware* Eng. colonial administrator in Am.

De·led·da \\də-'led-ə\\ Grazia 1875–1936 Ital. nov.

De·li·us \\'dē-lē-əs, 'dēl-yəs\\ Frederick 1862–1934 Eng. composer

Del·lin·ger \\'del-ən-jər\\ John Howard 1886–1962 Am. radio engineer

De Long \\də-'lȯŋ\\ George Washington 1844–1881 Am. naval officer & explorer

De·lorme or **de l'Orme** \\de-'lȯ(ə)rm\\ Philibert 1515?–1570 Fr. architect

De Mille \\də-'mil\\ Agnes George 1909– Am. dancer & choreographer

— Cec·il \\'ses-əl\\ Blount \\'blənt\\ 1881–1959 Am. motion-picture producer

De·moc·ri·tus \\di-'mäk-rət-əs\\ *b ab* 460 B.C. *the Laughing Philosopher* Greek philos.

De Mor·gan \\di-'mȯr-gən\\ William Frend 1839–1917 Eng. artist & nov.

De·mos·the·nes \\di-'mäs-thə-,nēz\\ 385?–322 B.C. Athenian orator & statesman

De·ni·ker \\,dā-nē-'ke(ə)r\\ Joseph 1852–1918 Fr. anthropol.

De·nis or **De·nys** \\'den-əs, də-'nē\\ Saint 3d cent. A.D. 1st bishop of Paris; patron saint of France

Dent \\'dent\\ Joseph Mal·a·by \\'mal-ə-bē\\ 1849–1926 Eng. publisher

De·pew \\di-'pyü\\ Chauncey Mitchell 1834–1928 Am. lawyer & polit.

De Quin·cey \\di-'kwin(t)-sē, -'kwin-zē\\ Thomas 1785–1859 Eng. author

De·rain \\də-'raⁿ\\ André 1880–1954 Fr. painter

Der·vish Pa·sha \\,dər-vish-pə-'shä\\ Ibrahim 1817–1896 Turk. gen.

Der·zha·vin \\dər-'zhäv-ən\\ Gavriil Romanovich 1743–1816 Russ. poet

De·saix de Vey·goux \\də-,sād-ə-(,)vā-'gü\\ Louis Charles Antoine 1768–1800 Fr. gen.

De·sar·gues \\dā-'zärg\\ Gérard 1593–1662 Fr. math.

Des·cartes \\dā-'kärt\\ René 1596–1650 Lat. *Renatus Car·te·sius* \\kär-'tē-zh(ē-)əs\\ Fr. math. & philos.

Des·cha·nel \\,dā-shä-'nel\\ Paul Eugène Louis 1856–1922 Fr. statesman; pres. of France (1920)

de Se·ver·sky \\də-sə-'ver-skē\\ Alexander Procofieff 1894– Am. (Russ.-born) aeronautical engineer

Des·mond \\'dez-mənd\\ Shaw 1877–1960 Irish author

Des·mou·lins \\,dā-mü-laⁿ\\ Camille 1760–1794 *Lucie Simplice Camille Benoît Desmoulins* Fr. revolutionist

de So·to \\di-'sōt-(,)ō\\ Hernando or Fernando 1500?–1542 Span. explorer in Am.

Des Prez \\dā-'prā\\ Jos·quin \\zhȯs-kwᵊaⁿ\\ 1450?–1521 Du. contrapuntist

Des·saix \\də-'sā\\ Comte Joseph Marie 1764–1834 Fr. gen. under Napoleon

Des·sa·lines \\,dā-sə-'lēn\\ Jean Jacques 1758–1806 emp. as Jacques I of Haiti

De·taille \\də-'tī\\ (Jean Baptiste) Édouard 1848–1912 Fr. painter

De·us Ra·mos, de \\dā-əsh-'ram-(,)üsh\\ João \\zhwaúⁿ\\ 1830–1896 Port. poet

De Va·le·ra \\,dev-ə-'ler-ə, -'lir-ə\\ Ea·mon \\'ā-mən\\ 1882– Irish polit.; prime min. of Ireland (1937–48; 1951–54; 1957–59); pres. of Ireland (1959–)

de Vere \\də-'vi(ə)r\\ Aubrey Thomas 1814–1902 Irish poet

Dev·er·eux \\'dev-ə-,rü(ks)\\ Robert 1566–1601 2d Earl of *Essex* Eng. soldier & courtier

De Vin·ne \\də-'vin-ē\\ Theodore Low 1828–1914 Am. printer

Devonshire dukes of see CAVENDISH

De Vo·to \\di-'vōt-(,)ō\\ Bernard Augustine 1897–1955 Am. author

De Vries \\də-'vrēs\\ Hugo 1848–1935 Du. botanist

Dew·ar \\'d(y)ü-ər\\ Sir James 1842–1923 Scot. chem. & physicist

De Wet \\də-'vet\\ Christiaan Rudolph 1854–1922 Boer soldier & polit.

Dew·ey \\'d(y)ü-ē\\ George 1837–1917 Am. admiral

— John 1859–1952 Am. philos. & educ.

— Melvil 1851–1931 Am. librarian

— Thomas Edmund 1902– Am. lawyer & polit.

De Witt \də-'vit\ Jan 1625–1672 Du. statesman

Dia·ghi·lev \dē-'äg-ə-ˌlef, 'dyäg-\ Sergei Pavlovich 1872–1929 Russ. ballet producer & art critic

Di·as *or* **Di·az** \'dē-ˌäsh\ Bartholomeu 1450?–1500 Port. navigator; discovered Cape of Good Hope

Dí·az \'dē-ˌäts\ Armando 1861–1928 *Duca della Vittoria* Ital. gen.; marshal of Italy (1920)

Dí·az \'dē-ˌäs\ Porfirio 1830–1915 *José de la Cruz Porfirio* Mex. gen.; pres. of Mexico (1877–80; 1884–1911)

Díaz de Bivar *see* CID

Dick \'dik\ George Frederick 1881–1967 Am. physician

Dick·ens \'dik-ənz\ Charles John Huf·fam \'həf-əm\ 1812–1870 *Boz* \'bäz, 'bōz\ Eng. nov.

Dick·in·son \'dik-ən-sən\ Emily Elizabeth 1830–1886 Am. poet

— John 1732–1808 Am. statesman

Di·de·rot \dē-'drō, 'dēd-ə-ˌrō\ Denis 1713–1784 Fr. encyclopedist

Die·fen·ba·ker \'dē-fən-ˌbā-kər\ John George 1895– prime min. of Canada (1957–63)

Diels \'dē(ə)lz, 'dē(ə)ls\ Otto 1876–1954 Ger. chem.

Die·sel \'dē-zəl, -səl\ Rudolf 1858–1913 Ger. mechanical engineer

Diez \'dēts\ Friedrich Christian 1794–1876 Ger. philologist

Dig·by \'dig-bē\ Sir Ken·elm \'ken-ˌelm\ 1603–1665 Eng. naval commander, diplomat, & author

Dill \'dil\ Sir John Greer 1881–1944 Brit. gen.

Dil·lon \'dil-ən\ (Clarence) Douglas 1909– Am. secy. of the treasury (1961–65)

— John 1851–1927 Irish nationalist polit.

Dim·net \dim-'nā\ Ernest 1866–1954 Fr. abbé & writer

Di·ne·sen \'dē-nə-sən\ Isak \'ē-ˌsäk\ 1885–1962 pen name of *Baroness Karen Blix·en* \'blik-sən\ née *Dinesen* Dan. author

Din·wid·die \din-'wid-ē, 'din-ˌ\ Robert 1693–1770 Eng. colonial administrator in Am.

Di·o·cle·tian \ˌdī-ə-'klē-shən\ 245–313 *Gaius Aurelius Valerius Diocletianus* Rom. emp. (284–305)

Di·og·e·nes \dī-'äj-ə-ˌnēz\ 412?–323 B.C. Greek Cynic philos.

Di·o·ny·sius \ˌdī-ə-'nis(h)-ē-əs, -'nish-əs, -'nī-sē-əs\ 430?–?367 B.C. *the Elder* Greek tyrant of Syracuse (405–367)

— *the Younger* tyrant of Syracuse (367–356; 347–344 B.C.)

— **Ex·ig·u·us** \eg-'zig-yə-wəs\ 6th cent. Christian monk; introduced method of reckoning the Christian era

— **of Alexandria** Saint 3d cent. theol. & bishop of Alexandria (247)

— **of Halicarnassus** *d ab* 7 B.C. Greek scholar

Di·rac \di-'rak\ Paul Adrien Maurice 1902– Eng. physicist

Dirk·sen \'dərk-sən\ Everett McKinley 1896–1969 Am. polit.

Dis·ney \'diz-nē\ Walter Elias 1901–1966 Am. producer of animated motion-picture cartoons

Dis·rae·li \diz-'rā-lē\ Benjamin 1804–1881 1st Earl of *Bea·cons·field* \'bē-kənz-ˌfēld, 'bek-ənz-\; *Diz·zy* \'diz-ē\ Brit. polit. & author; prime min. (1868; 1874–80)

Dit·mars \'dit-ˌmärz\ Raymond Lee 1876–1942 Am. naturalist

Dix Dorothy *see* Elizabeth Meriwether GILMER

Dix·on \'dik-sən\ Jeremiah *fl* 1763–1767 Eng. surveyor in Am.

Dmow·ski \də-'mȯf-skē\ Roman 1864–1939 Pol. statesman

Dö·be·rei·ner \'də(r)b-ə-ˌrī-nər\ Johann Wolfgang 1780–1849 Ger. chem.

Do·bie \'dō-bē\ James Frank 1888–1964 Am. folklorist

Do·brée \'dō-ˌbrā\ Bon·a·my \'bän-ə-mē\ 1891– Eng. scholar

Dob·son \'däb-sən\ (Henry) Austin 1840–1921 Eng. poet & essayist

Dodge \'däj\ Mary Elizabeth 1831–1905 née *Mapes* \'māps\ Am. author

Dodg·son \'däj-sən\ Charles Lut·widge \'lət-wij\ 1832–1898 pseud. *Lewis Car·roll* \'kar-əl\ Eng. math. & storywriter

Dods·ley \'dädz-lē\ Robert 1703–1764 Eng. author & bookseller

Doe·nitz \'də(r)n-əts\ Karl 1891– Ger. grand admiral

Doi·sy \'dȯi-zē\ Edward Adelbert 1893– Am. biochem.

Dole \'dōl\ Sanford Ballard 1844–1926 Am. jurist; pres. (1894–98) & gov. (1900–03) of Hawaii

Doll·fuss \'dȯl-ˌfüs\ Engelbert 1892–1934 Austrian statesman

Do·magk \'dō-ˌmäk\ Gerhard 1895–1964 Ger. chem.

Do·me·ni·chi·no, Il \ˌ(ˌ)dō-mä-nə-'kē-(ˌ)nō\ 1581–1641 *Domenico Zam·pie·ri* \ˌtsäm-pē-'e(ə)r-ē, ˌzäm-\ Ital. painter ·

Dom·i·nic \'däm-ə-(ˌ)nik\ Saint 1170–1221 *Domingo de Guz·mán* \güz-'män\ Span.-born founder of the Dominican order of friars

Do·mi·tian \də-'mish-ən\ 51–96 *Titus Flavius Domitianus Augustus* Rom. emp. (81–96)

Don·a·tel·lo \ˌdän-ə-'tel-(ˌ)ō\ 1386?–1466 *Donato di Niccolò di Betto Bardi* Ital. sculptor

Don·i·zet·ti \ˌdän-ə(d)-'zet-ē\ Gaetano 1797–1848 Ital. composer

Donne \'dən, 'dän\ John *ab* 1572–1631 Eng. divine & poet

Don·o·van \'dän-ə-vən, 'dən-\ William Joseph 1883–1959 *Wild Bill* Am. lawyer & gen.

Doo·lit·tle \'dü-ˌlit-ᵊl\ James Harold 1896– Am. aviator & gen.

Dopp·ler \'däp-lər\ Christian Johann 1803–1853 Austrian physicist & math.

Do·ra·ti \də-'rät-ē\ An·tal \'än-ˌtäl\ 1906– Am. (Hung.-born) conductor

Do·ré \dȯ-'rā, də-\ Paul Gustave 1833–1883 Fr. illustrator & painter

Dor·nier \'dȯrn-ˌyā\ Claude 1884–1969 Ger. airplane builder

Dorr \'dȯ(ə)r\ Thomas Wilson 1805–1854 Am. lawyer & polit.

Dorset 1st Earl of *see* Thomas SACKVILLE

Dos Pas·sos \də-'spas-əs\ John Roderigo 1896– Am. writer

Dos·to·ev·ski \ˌdäs-tə-'yef-skē, -'yev-\ Fëdor Mikhailovich 1821–1881 Russ. nov.

Dou *or* **Dow** *or* **Douw** \'daů\ Gerard 1613–1675 Du. painter

Dou·gher·ty \'dȯ-(h)ərt-ē\ Denis Joseph 1865–1951 Am. cardinal

Dough·ty \'daůt-ē\ Charles Montagu 1843–1926 Eng. poet & traveler

Doug·las \'dəg-ləs\ John Shol·to \'shȯl-(ˌ)tō\ 1844–1900 8th Marquis & Earl of *Queens·ber·ry* \'kwēnz-ˌber-ē, -b(ə-)rē\ Scot. boxing patron

— Norman 1868–1952 Eng. author

— Stephen Arnold 1813–1861 Am. polit.

— William Orville 1898– Am. jurist

— **Home** Sir Alec *see* HOME

— **of Kir·tle·side** \'kərt-ᵊl-ˌsīd\ 1st Baron 1893–1969 *William Sholto Douglas* Brit. air marshal

Doug·lass \'dəg-ləs\ Frederick 1817?–1895 orig. *Frederick Augustus Washington Bailey* Am. abolitionist

Dou·mer \dü-'me(ə)r\ Paul 1857–1932 pres. of France (1931–32)

Dou·mergue \dü-'me(ə)rg\ Gaston 1863–1937 Fr. statesman; pres. of France (1924–31)

Dow·den \'daůd-ᵊn\ Edward 1843–1913 Irish literary critic

Dow·ie \'daů-ē\ John Alexander 1847–1907 Scot.-born religious leader in Am.

Downes \'daůnz\ (Edwin) Olin \'ō-lən\ 1886–1955 Am. music critic

Dow·son \'daůs-ᵊn\ Ernest Christopher 1867–1900 Eng. lyric poet

Dox·ia·dis \dȯk-'syä-thēs\ Constantinos Apostolos 1913– Gk. architect

Doyle \'dȯi(ə)l\ Sir Arthur Co·nan \'kō-nən\ 1859–1930 Brit. physician, nov., & detective-story writer

D'Oyly Carte *see* CARTE

Drach·mann \'dräk-mən\ Holger Henrik Herholdt 1846–1908 Dan. author

Dra·co \'drā-(ˌ)kō\ late 7th cent. B.C. Athenian lawgiver

Drake \'drāk\ Sir Francis 1540?–1596 Eng. navigator & admiral

Dra·per \'drā-pər\ Henry 1837–1882 Am. astron.

— John William 1811–1882 Am. (Eng.-born) scientist & writer

Dray·ton \'drāt-ᵊn\ Michael 1563–1631 Eng. poet

— William Henry 1742–1779 Am. Revolutionary polit.

Drei·ser \'drī-sər, -zər\ Theodore 1871–1945 Am. editor & nov.

Drew \'drü\ John 1826–1862 Am. (Irish-born) actor

— John 1853–1927 *son of prec.* Am. actor

Drey·fus \'drī-fəs, 'drā-; drā-'füs\ Alfred 1859–1935 Fr. army officer

Driesch \'drēsh\ Hans Adolf Eduard 1867–1941 Ger. biologist & philos.

Drink·wa·ter \'driŋ-ˌkwȯt-ər, -ˌkwät-\ John 1882–1937 Eng. poet & dram.

Drou·et d' Er·lon \drü-ˌā-(ˌ)der-'lōⁿ\ Comte Jean Baptiste 1765–1844 Fr. gen.; marshal of France

Drum·mond \'drəm-ənd\ Henry 1851–1897 Scot. clergyman & writer

— William 1585–1649 1st Laird of *Haw·thorn·den* \'hȯ-ˌthȯrn-dən\ Scot. poet

— William Henry 1854–1907 Canad. (Irish-born) poet

Dru·sus \'drü-səs\ 38–9 B.C. *Ne·ro* \'nē-(ˌ)rō, 'nir-(ˌ)ō\ *Claudius Drusus Ger·man·i·cus* \(ˌ)jər-'man-i-kəs\ Rom. gen.

Dry·den \'drīd-ᵊn\ John 1631–1700 Eng. poet & dram.; poet laureate (1670–89)

Du Bar·ry \d(y)ü-'bar-ē\ Comtesse 1746 (or 1743?)–1793 *Marie Jeanne Bécu; mistress of Louis XV of France*

Du·bois \d(y)üb-'wä\ Paul 1829–1905 Fr. sculptor

— Théodore 1837–1924 Fr. composer

Du Bois \d(y)ü-'bȯis\ William Edward Burghardt 1868–1963 Am. educ. & writer

Du·buf·fet \ˌd(y)ü-bə-'fā\ Jean 1901– Fr. artist

Du Cange \d(y)ü-'käⁿzh\ Sieur Charles du Fresne 1610–1688 Fr. scholar & glossarist

Du Chail·lu \də-'shal-(ˌ)yü, -'shī-(ˌ)ü\ Paul Belloni 1831–1903 Am. (Fr.-born) explorer in Africa

Du·champ \d(y)ü-'shäⁿ\ Marcel 1887–1968 Fr. painter

Du·com·mun \ˌd(y)ü-kə-'mœⁿ\ Élie 1833–1906 Swiss journalist

Dudevant Aurore *see* George SAND

Dud·ley \'dəd-lē\ Robert 1532?–1588 1st Earl of *Leicester* Eng. courtier

— Thomas 1576–1653 colonial administrator in Massachusetts Bay Colony

Duf·fer·in and Ava \ˌdəf-(ə-)rə-nə-'näv-ə\ 1st Marquis of 1826–1902 *Frederick Temple Hamilton-Temple-Blackwood* Brit. diplomat & administrator

Duff-Gor·don \'dəf-'gȯrd-ᵊn\ Lady Lucie *or* Lucy 1821–1869 Eng. author

Duf·fy \'dəf-ē\ Sir Charles Gavan 1816–1903 Irish nationalist & Austral. polit.

Du·fy \d(y)ü-'fē\ Raoul 1877–1953 Fr. painter

Du Gard Roger Martin *see* MARTIN DU GARD

Du Gues·clin \ˌd(y)ü-ge-'kläⁿ\ Bertrand 1320?–1380 constable of France

Du·ha·mel \ˌdü-à-mel\ Georges 1884–1966 pseud. *Denis Thévenin* Fr. writer

Duke \d(y)ük\ Benjamin Newton 1855–1929 & his bro. James Buchanan 1856–1925 Am. tobacco industrialists

Dul·les \'dəl-əs\ John Foster 1888–1959 Am. lawyer; secy. of state (1953–59)

Du·mas \d(y)ü-'mä, 'd(y)ü-ˌ\ Alexandre 1802–1870 *Dumas père* \'pe(ə)r\ Fr. nov. & dram.

— Alexandre 1824–1895 *Dumas fils* \'fēs\ Fr. nov. & dram.

du Mau·rier \d(y)ů-'mȯr-ē-ˌā\ George Louis Palmella Busson 1834–1896 Brit. artist & nov.

Du·mou·riez \d(y)ů-ˌmür-ē-ˌā\ Charles François 1739–1823 Fr. gen.

Du·nant \d(y)ü-'näⁿ\ Jean Henri 1828–1910 Swiss philanthropist; founder of the Red Cross

Dun·bar \'dən-ˌbär\ Paul Laurence 1872–1906 Am. poet

— William 1460?–?1520 Scot. poet

Dun·can \'dəŋ-kən\ Isadora 1878–1927 Am. dancer

Dun·das \ˌdən-'das, 'dən-\ Henry 1742–1811 1st Viscount *Melville* & Baron *Dun·ira* \ˌdə-'nir-ə\ Brit. statesman

Dun·lop \ˌdən-'läp, 'dən-\ John Boyd 1840–1921 Scot. inventor

Dun·more \ˌdən-'mō(ə)r, -'mȯ(ə)r\ 4th Earl of 1732–1809 *John Murray* Scot. colonial administrator in Am.

Dunne \'dən\ Finley Peter 1867–1936 Am. humorist

Du·nois, de \d(y)ün-'wä\ Comte Jean 1403?–1468 *the bastard of Orléans* Fr. gen.

Dun·sa·ny \ˌdən-'sā-nē\ 18th Baron 1878–1957 *Edward John Moreton Drax Plunkett; Lord Dunsany* Irish poet & dram.

Duns Sco·tus \ˌdən(z)-'skōt-əs\ John 1265?–?1308 Scot. scholastic

theol.

Dun·stan \\'dən(t)-stən\\ Saint 925?–988 Archbishop of Canterbury (961)

Du·pleix \\d(y)ü-'plāks, -'pleks\\ Marquis Joseph François 1697–1763 Fr. colonial administrator in India

Duplessis–Mornay see Philippe de MORNAY

Du Pont \\d(y)ü-'pänt, 'd(y)ü-,\\ Éleuthère Irénée 1771–1834 *son of P.S. Du Pont de Nemours* Am. (Fr.-born) industrialist

Du Pont de Ne·mours \\-də-nə-'mü(ə)r\\ Pierre Samuel 1739–1817 Fr. econ. & statesman

Du·pré \\d(y)ü-'prā\\ Jules \\zhül\\ 1811–1889 Fr. painter

Du·quesne \\d(y)ü-'kān\\ Marquis Abraham 1610–1688 Fr. naval officer

Du·rant \\d(y)ù-'rant\\ William James 1885–   Am. educ. & writer

Dü·rer \\'d(y)ùr-ər, 'dūer-\\ Albrecht 1471–1528 Ger. painter & engraver

D'Ur·fey \\'dər-fē\\ Thomas 1653–1723 Eng. songwriter & dram.

Du·roc \\d(y)ù-'räk\\ Géraud Christophe Michel 1772–1813 Duc de Friuli Fr. gen. under Napoleon

Dur·rell \\'dər-əl, 'də-rəl, də-'rel\\ Lawrence 1912–   Eng. author & poet

Du·ruy \\,dùr-(ə-)'wē\\ Victor 1811–1894 Fr. hist.

Du·se \\'dü-(,)zā\\ Eleanora 1859–1924 Ital. actress

Du·tra \\'dü-trə\\ Eurico Gaspar 1885–   Brazilian gen.; pres. of Brazil (1946–51)

Du·val \\d(y)ü-'väl\\ Paul 1850?–1906 pseud. *Jean Lorrain* Fr. author

Du·ve·neck \\'d(y)ù-və-,nek\\ Frank 1848–1919 orig. *Frank Decker* Am. artist

du Vi·gneaud \\d(y)ù-'vēn-(,)yō\\ Vincent 1901–   Am. biochem.

Dvo·řák \\(də-)'vòr-,zhäk\\ Anton 1841–1904 Czech composer

Dwig·gins \\'dwig-ənz\\ William Addison 1880–1956 Am. type designer

Dwight \\'dwīt\\ Timothy 1758–1817 Am. clergyman; pres. Yale U. (1795–1817)

— Timothy 1826–1916 *grandson of prec.* Am. clergyman; pres. Yale U. (1886–98)

Dwy·for Earl of see LLOYD GEORGE

Dyce \\'dīs\\ Alexander 1798–1869 Scot. editor

Dy·er \\'dī(ə)r\\ John 1700?–1758 Brit. poet

Eads \\'ēdz\\ James Buchanan 1820–1887 Am. engineer & inventor

Ea·ker \\'ā-kər\\ Ira Clarence 1896–   Am. aviator & gen.

Ea·kins \\'ā-kənz\\ Thomas 1844–1916 Am. artist

Ear·hart \\'e(ə)r-,härt, 'i(ə)r-\\ Amelia 1898–1937 Am. aviator

Ear·ly \\'ər-lē\\ Ju·bal \\'jü-bəl\\ Anderson 1816–1894 Am. Confed. gen.

Earp \\'ərp\\ Wyatt 1848–1929 Am. lawman

East·man \\'ēs(t)-mən\\ George 1854–1932 Am. inventor & industrialist

— Max Forrester 1883–1969 Am. editor & writer

Ea·ton \\'ēt-ᵊn\\ Theophilus 1590–1658 Eng. colonial administrator in Am.; gov. of New Haven colony (1638–58)

Ebert \\'ā-bərt\\ Friedrich 1871–1925 Ger. polit.; pres. of the Reich (1919–25)

Ec·cles \\'ek-əlz\\ Marriner Stoddard 1890–   Am. banker & econ.

Eche·ga·ray y Ei·za·guir·re \\,ā-chə-gə-'rī-,ē-,ā-thə-'gwi(ə)r-(,)ā, -,ē-,ā-sə-\\ José 1832–1916 Span. dram.

Eck \\'ek\\ Johann 1486–1543 orig. *Mayer* Ger. R.C. theol.

Eck·er·mann \\'ek-ər-,män, -mən\\ Johann Peter 1792–1854 Ger. writer

Eck·hart *or* **Eck·art** *or* **Eck·ardt** \\'ek-,(h)ärt\\ Johannes 1260?–?1327 Ger. Dominican theol.; founder of Ger. mysticism

Ed·ding·ton \\'ed-iŋ-tən\\ Sir Arthur Stanley 1882–1944 Eng. astron.

Ed·dy \\'ed-ē\\ Mary Morse 1821–1910 née *Baker* Am. founder of the Christian Science Church

Eden \\'ēd-ᵊn\\ (Robert) Anthony 1897–   Earl of *Avon* Eng. statesman; prime min. (1955–57)

Edge·worth \\'ej-(,)wərth\\ Maria 1767–1849 Brit. nov.

Edinburgh Duke of see PHILIP

Ed·i·son \\'ed-ə-sən\\ Thomas Alva 1847–1931 Am. inventor

Ed·mund *or* **Ead·mund II** \\'ed-mənd\\ 980?–1016 *Ironside* king of the English (1016)

Ed·ward \\'ed-wərd\\ name of 8 post-Norman Eng. (Brit.) kings: **I** 1239–1307 (reigned 1272–1307) *Longshanks*

— **II** 1284–1327 (reigned 1307–27)

— **III** 1312–1377 (reigned 1327–77)

— **IV** 1442–1483 (reigned 1461–70; 1471–83)

— **V** 1470–1483 (reigned 1483)

— **VI** 1537–1553 (reigned 1547–53) *son of Henry VIII & Jane Seymour*

— **VII** 1841–1910 (reigned 1901–10) *Albert Edward, son of Victoria*

— **VIII** 1894–   (reigned 1936; abdicated) Duke of *Windsor, son of George V*

— 1330–1376 *the Black Prince; son of Edward III* prince of Wales

— *or* **Ead·ward** \\'ed-\\ 1002?–1066 *the Confessor* king of the English (1042–66)

Ed·wards \\'ed-wərdz\\ Jonathan 1703–1758 Am. theol.

Ed·win *or* **Ead·wine** \\'ed-wən\\ 585?–633 king of Northumbria (617–633)

Eg·bert \\'eg-bərt\\ 775?–839 king of the West Saxons (802–839) & 1st king of the English (828–839)

Eg·gle·ston \\'eg-əl-stən\\ Edward 1837–1902 Am. writer

— George Cary 1839–1911 *bro. of Edward* Am. writer

Eg·mont, d' \\'deg-,mänt\\ Comte Lamoral 1522–1568 Flem. gen. & statesman

Eh·ren·burg \\'er-ən-,bù(ə)rg\\ Ilya Grigorievich 1891–1967 Russ. writer

Ehr·lich \\'e(ə)r-lik, 'ār-lik\\ Paul 1854–1915 Ger. bacteriol.

Eich·mann \\'īk-,män, 'īsh-\\ Adolf 1906–1962 Ger. Nazi leader

Eif·fel \\'ī-fəl, ā-fel\\ Alexandre Gustave 1832–1923 Fr. engineer

Eijk·man \\'īk-,män, 'āk-\\ Christiaan 1858–1930 Du. hygienist

Ein·stein \\'īn-,stīn\\ Albert 1879–1955 Am. (Ger.-born) physicist

Eint·ho·ven \\'īnt-,hō-vən, 'änt-\\ Willem 1860–1927 Du. physiol.

Ei·sen·how·er \\'īz-ᵊn-,hau̇(-ə)r\\ Dwight David 1890–1969 Am.

gen. of the army; 34th pres. of the U.S. (1953–61)

El·a·gab·a·lus \\,el-ə-'gab-ə-ləs\\ *var of* HELIOGABALUS

El·don \\'el-dən\\ 1st Earl of 1751–1838 *John Scott* Eng. jurist

El·ea·nor \\'el-ə-nər, -,nó(ə)r\\ *of Aquitaine* 1122?–1204 *queen of Louis VII of France (divorced 1152) & of Henry II of England*

— *of Castile* d 1290 *queen of Edward I of England*

— *of Provence* d 1291 *queen of Henry III of England*

El·gar \\'el-gär, -gər\\ Sir Edward 1857–1934 Eng. composer

El·iot \\'el-ē-ət, 'el-yət\\ Charles William 1834–1926 Am. educ.; pres. Harvard U. (1869–1909)

— George 1819–1880 pseud. of *Mary Ann (or Marian) Evans* Eng. nov.

— Sir John 1592–1632 Eng. statesman

— John 1604–1690 *apostle to the Indians* Am. clergyman

— Thomas Stearns 1888–1965 Brit. (Am.-born) poet & critic

Eliz·a·beth \\i-'liz-ə-bəth\\ name of 2 Eng. (Brit.) queens: **I** 1533–1603 *dau. of Henry VIII & Anne Boleyn* queen of England (1558–1603)

— **II** 1926–   *Elizabeth Alexandra Mary; dau. of George VI, wife of Prince Philip; mother of Prince Charles* queen of Gt. Brit. (1952–)

— 1596–1662 *Queen of Hearts; queen of Frederick V of Bohemia*

— 1900–   *Elizabeth Angela Marguerite Bowes-Ly·on* \\'bōz-'lī-ən\\; *queen of George VI of Gt. Brit.*

— 1843–1916 pseud. *Carmen Syl·va* \\,kär-mən-'sil-və\\ queen of Romania & writer

— pseud. of Countess RUSSELL

— **Pe·trov·na** \\pə-'tróv-nə\\ 1709–1762 empress of Russia (1741–62)

Ellenborough 1st Baron see LAW

El·ling·ton \\'el-iŋ-tən\\ Edward Kennedy 1899–   *Duke Ellington* Am. band leader & composer

El·liott \\'el-ē-ət, 'el-yət\\ Maxine 1871–1940 pseud. of *Jessie Dermot* Am. actress

El·lis \\'el-əs\\ Alexander John 1814–1890 orig. surname *Sharpe* Eng. philologist

— (Henry) Have·lock \\'hav-,läk, -lək\\ 1859–1939 Eng. psychol. & writer

El·li·son \\'el-ə-sən\\ Ralph (Waldo) 1914–   Am. writer

Ells·berg \\'elz-,bərg\\ Edward 1891–   Am. engineer & naval officer

Ells·worth \\'elz-(,)wərth\\ Lincoln 1880–1951 Am. explorer

El·man \\'el-mən\\ Mi·scha \\'mē-shə\\ 1891–1967 Am. (Russ.-born) violinist

El·phin·stone \\'el-fən-,stōn, *chiefly* Brit -stən\\ Mount·stu·art \\mau̇nt-'st(y)ü-ərt\\ 1779–1859 Brit. statesman in India

— William 1431–1514 Scot. bishop & statesman

El·yot \\'el-ē-ət, 'el-yət\\ Sir Thomas 1490?–1546 Eng. scholar & diplomat

El·ze·vir *or* **El·ze·vier** \\'el-zə-,vi(ə)r\\ family of Du. printers including esp. Louis 1540?–1617, his son Bonaventure 1583–1652, & his grandson Abraham 1592?–1652

Em·er·son \\'em-ər-sən\\ Ralph Waldo 1803–1882 Am. essayist & poet

Em·met \\'em-ət\\ Robert 1778–1803 Irish nationalist & rebel

Em·ped·o·cles \\em-'ped-ə-,klēz\\ 5th cent. B.C. Greek philos. & statesman

En·de·cott *or* **En·di·cott** \\'en-di-kət, -də-,kät\\ John 1589?–1665 colonial gov. of Massachusetts

En·ders \\'en-dərz\\ John Franklin 1897–   Am. bacteriol.

Eng·els \\'eŋ-(g)əlz, *G* 'eŋ-əls\\ Friedrich 1820–1895 Ger. socialist; collaborator with Karl Marx

En·ver Pa·sha \\'en-,ve(ə)r-pə-'shä\\ 1881?–1922 *Enver Bey* Turk. soldier & polit.

Epam·i·non·das \\i-,pam-ə-'nän-dəs\\ 418?–362 B.C. Theban gen. & statesman

Ep·ic·te·tus \\,ep-ik-'tēt-əs\\ 1st–2d cent. A.D. Greek Stoic philos. in Rome

Ep·i·cu·rus \\,ep-i-'kyùr-əs\\ 342?–270 B.C. Greek philos.

Ep·stein \\'ep-,stīn\\ Sir Jacob 1880–1959 Brit. sculptor *b* in U.S.

Eras·mus \\i-'raz-məs\\ Desiderius 1466?–1536 *Gerhard Gerhards or Geert Geerts* Du. scholar

Er·a·tos·the·nes \\,er-ə-'täs-thə-,nēz\\ 3d cent. B.C. Greek astron.

Erck·mann–Cha·tri·an \\'erk-,män-,shä-trē-'äⁿ\\ joint pseud. of Émile Erckmann 1822–1899 & Alexandre Chatrian 1826–1890 Fr. authors

Er·hard \\'e(ə)r-,härt\\ Ludwig 1897–   chancellor of West Germany (1963–66)

Er·ic \\'er-ik\\ 10th cent. *the Red* Norw. navigator; explored Greenland coast

Er·ic·son \\'er-ik-sən\\ Leif \\'lāv, 'lēf\\ *Old Norse* Leifr Eiriksson *fl* 1000 *son of Eric the Red* Norw. mariner; discovered "Vinland"

Er·ics·son \\'er-ik-sən\\ John 1803–1889 Am. (Swed.-born) engineer & inventor

Erig·e·na \\i-'rij-ə-nə\\ Johannes Scotus 815?–?877 Scot.-Irish (?) philos. & theol.

Er·lan·der \\er-'län-dər\\ Tage Frithiof 1901–   Swed. polit.

Er·lang·er \\'ər-,laŋ-ər\\ Joseph 1874–1965 Am. physiol.

Er·len·mey·er \\'ər-lən-,mī-(ə)r, 'er-\\ Emil 1825–1909 Ger. chem.

Ernst \\'e(ə)rn(t)st, 'ərn(t)st\\ Max 1891–   Ger. painter

Er·skine \\'ər-skən\\ John 1695–1768 Scot. jurist

— John 1879–1951 Am. educ. & writer

Er·vine \\'ər-vən\\ St. John \\sänt-'jän, sant-; 'sin-jən\\ Greer 1883– Irish dram. & nov.

Erz·ber·ger \\'erts-,ber-gər\\ Matthias 1875–1921 Ger. statesman

Ese·nin \\(y)is-'än-yən\\ Sergei Aleksandrovich 1895–1925 Russ. poet

Esh·kol \\esh-'kól\\ Levi 1895–1969 premier of Israel (1963–69)

Es·par·te·ro \\,es-pər-'te(ə)r-(,)ō\\ Baldomero 1792–1879 Con·de \\'kón-(,)dā\\ *de Lu·cha·na* \\lü-'chän-ə\\ Span. gen. & statesman

Esquemeling see EXQUEMELIN

Es·sen, von \\'es-ᵊn\\ Count Hans Henrik 1755–1824 Swed. field marshal & statesman

Essex 2d Earl of see DEVEREUX

Es·taing, d' \\'des-taⁿ\\ Comte Jean Baptiste Charles Henri Hector 1729–1794 Fr. admiral

Este \\'es-(,)tā\\ Ital. princely family beginning with *Alberto Az·zo II* \\'äd-(,)zō\\ 996–1097 & ending with *Er·co·le III* \\'er-kə,lā\\ *Rinaldo* 1727–1803

Es·ter·ha·zy \\'es-tər-,häz-ē, ,es-tə-(,)rä-'zē\\ Marie Charles Ferdinand Walsin 1847–1923 Fr. army officer

Es·tienne \es-'tyen\ or Étienne \ā-'tyen\ Fr. family of printers & bookdealers including esp.: Henri I d 1520; his son Robert 1503–1559; & Robert's son Henri II 1528?–1598

Es·ti·mé \,es-ti-'mā\ Dumarsais 1900–1953 pres. of Haiti (1946–50)

Es·tour·nelles de Cons·tant, d' \,des-,tür-'nel-də-kōⁿ-'stäⁿ\ Baron Constant de Re·becque \rə-'bek\ 1852–1924 Paul Henri Benjamin Bal·luat \bà-lwᵃ\ Fr. diplomat & polit.

Eth·el·bert \'eth-əl-(,)bərt\ 552?–616 King of Kent

Eth·el·red II \'eth-əl-,red\ 968?–1016 the Unready king of England (978–1016)

Eth·er·ege \'eth-(ə-)rij\ Sir George 1635?–1691 Eng. dram.

Euck·en \'oi-kən\ Rudolf Christoph 1846–1926 Ger. philos.

Eu·clid \'yü-kləd\ fl ab 300 B.C. Greek geometer

Eu·gene or Eu·gène \yü-'jēn, 'yü-,, F œ-zhen, ū-zhen\ 1663–1736 François Eugène de Sa·voie-Ca·ri·gnan \sᵊv-'wä-,kär-ēn-'yäⁿ\ prince of Savoy & Austrian gen.

Eu·gé·nie \'yü-jə-,nē; yü-'jā-nē, -'jē-; F œ-zhā-nē, ē-\ 1826–1920 Eugénie Marie de Montijo de Guzmán; wife of Napoleon III empress of the French (1853–71)

Eu·ler \'oi-lər\ Leonhard 1707–1783 Swiss math. & physicist

Eu·ler-Chel·pin, von \,oi-lər-'kel-pən\ Hans August Simon 1873–1964 Swed. (Ger.-born) chem.

Eu·rip·i·des \yü-'rip-ə-,dēz\ 480?–?406 B.C. Greek dram.

Eus·den \'yüz-dən\ Laurence 1688–1730 Eng. poet; poet laureate (1718–30)

Eu·se·bi·us of Caesarea \yü-'sē-bē-əs\ 260?–?340 theol. & church hist.

Eu·sta·chio \eú-'stäk-ē-,ō\ Bartolommeo 1524?–1574 Lat. Eu·sta·chius \yü-'stā-kē-əs, -'stā-sh(ē-)əs\ Ital. anatomist

Ev·ans \'ev-ənz\ Sir Arthur John 1851–1941 Eng. archaeologist
— Herbert McLean 1882– Am. anatomist & embryologist
— Maurice 1901– Eng. actor
— Robley Dun·gli·son \'dəŋ-glə-sən\ 1846–1912 Am. admiral
— Rudulph 1878–1960 Am. sculptor

Ev·arts \'ev-ərts\ William Maxwell 1818–1901 Am. lawyer & statesman

Ev·att \'ev-ət\ Herbert Vere 1894–1965 Austral. lawyer & statesman

Eve·lyn \'ēv-lən, 'ev-\ John 1620–1706 Eng. diarist

Ev·er·ett \'ev-(ə-)rət\ Edward 1794–1865 Am. clergyman, orator, & statesman

Ewald or Evald \'iv-,äl\ Johannes 1743–1781 Dan. poet & dram.

Ew·ell \'yü-əl\ Richard Stoddert 1817–1872 Am. Confed. gen.

Ex·que·me·lin \ik-'skä-mə-lən\ Alexandre Olivier 1645?–1707 Fr. pirate, surgeon, & author

Eyck, van \'īk\ Hubert or Huybrecht 1366?–1426 & his bro. Jan 1370?–1440 Flem. painters

Eze·kiel \i-'zēk-yəl\ Moses Jacob 1844–1917 Am. sculptor

Fa·bi·o·la \,fab-ē-'ō-lə, fəb-'yō-\ 1928– queen of King Baudouin I of Belgium

Fa·bi·us \'fā-bē-əs\ d 203 B.C. Quintus Fabius Maximus Verrucosus Cunc·ta·tor \,kəŋk-'tāt-ər\ Rom. gen. against Hannibal

Fa·bre \'fäbrᵊ\ Jean Henri 1823–1915 Fr. entomologist

Fad·i·man \'fad-ə-mən\ Clifton 1904– Am. writer & editor

Fah·ren·heit \'far-ən-,hīt, 'fär-\ Gabriel Daniel 1686–1736 Ger. physicist

Fair·banks \'fa(ə)r-,baŋks, 'fe(ə)r-\ Charles Warren 1852–1918 Am. lawyer & polit.; vice-pres. of U.S. (1905–09)
— Douglas 1883–1939 Am. actor

Fair·fax \'fa(ə)r-,faks, 'fe(ə)r-\ Baron Thomas 1612–1671 Eng. gen.
— Baron Thomas 1692–1782 proprietor in Va.

Fai·sal \'fī-səl, 'fā-\ 1904– king of Saudi Arabia (from 1964)

Fai·sal or Fei·sal or Fei·sul I \'fī-səl, 'fā-\ 1885–1933 king of Syria (1920), of Iraq (1921–1933)
— II 1935–1958 king of Iraq (1939–58)

Fa·lie·ri \fəl-'ye(ə)r-ē\ or Fa·lie·ro \-(,)ō\ Marino 1278?–1355 doge of Venice (1354–55)

Fal·ken·hau·sen, von \'fäl-kən-,haúz-ⁿn\ Baron Ludwig 1844–1936 Ger. gen.

Fal·ken·hayn, von \'fäl-kən-,hīn\ Erich 1861–1922 Ger. gen.

Falkner William see FAULKNER

Fal·la, de \'fä-yə, 'fī-ə\ Manuel 1876–1946 Span. composer

Fal·lières \fal-'ye(ə)r\ Clément Armand 1841–1931 Fr. statesman; pres. of France (1906–13)

Fan·euil \'fan-yəl, 'fan-ᵊl, 'fan-yə-wəl\ Peter 1700–1743 Am. merchant

Far·a·day \'far-ə-,dā, -əd-ē\ Michael 1791–1867 Eng. chem. & physicist

Fa·ri·na \fə-'rē-nə\ Salvatore 1846–1918 Ital. nov.

Far·ley \'fär-lē\ James Aloysius 1888– Am. polit.

Far·man \'fär-'mäⁿ\ Henri 1874–1958 & his brother Maurice 1877–1964 Fr. pioneer aviators and airplane manufacturers

Far·mer \'fär-mər\ Fannie Merritt 1857–1915 Am. cookery expert

Far·ne·se \fär-'nā-zē, -sē\ Alessandro 1545–1592 Duke of Parma Ital. gen. in Span. service

Far·quhar \'fär-k(w)ər\ George 1678–1707 Brit. dram.

Far·ra·gut \'far-ə-gət\ David Glasgow 1801–1870 Am. admiral

Far·rar \'far-ər\ Frederic William 1831–1903 Eng. clergyman & writer

Far·rell \'far-əl\ James Thomas 1904– Am. nov.

Fa·ruk or Fa·rouk \fə-'rük\ I 1920–1965 king of Egypt (1936–52; abdicated); citizen of Monaco (1959–65)

Fat·i·ma \'fat-ə-mə\ 606–632 dau. of Muhammad

Faulk·ner \'fók-nər\ William 1897–1962 sometimes Falkner Am. nov.

Faure \'fó(ə)r\ François Félix 1841–1899 Fr. statesman; pres. of France (1895–99)

Fau·ré \fó-'rā\ Gabriel Urbain 1845–1924 Fr. composer

Faus·ta \'fó-stə, 'faù-\ 289–326 Flavia Maximiana Fausta; wife of Constantine the Great Rom. empress

Fawkes \'fóks\ Guy 1570–1606 Eng. R.C. conspirator

Fäy \'fā, 'fī\ Bernard 1893– Fr. hist.

Fech·ner \'fek-nər, 'feḵ\ Gustav Theodor 1801–1887 Ger. physicist & psychol.

Fei·ning·er \'fī-niŋ-ər\ Lyonel Charles Adrian 1871–1956 Am. painter

Fell·tham or Fel·tham \'fel-thəm\ Owen 1602?–1668 Eng. writer

Fé·ne·lon \,fān-ᵊl-'ōⁿ\ François de Salignac de La Mothe- 1651–1715 Fr. prelate & writer

Feng Yü-hsiang \'fəŋ-'yü-shē-'äŋ\ 1880–1948 Chin. gen.

Fer·ber \'fər-bər\ Edna 1887–1968 Am. writer

Fer·di·nand I \'fərd-ⁿn-,and\ 1503–1564 Holy Rom. emp. (1556–64)
— II 1578–1637 king of Bohemia (1617–19; 1620–37) & of Hungary (1621–37); Holy Rom. emp. (1619–37)
— III 1608–1657 king of Hungary (1625–57); Holy Rom. emp. (1637–57)
— I 1861–1948 Maximilian Karl Leopold Maria king of Bulgaria (1908–18)
— I 1065 the Great king of Castile (1033–65); of Navarre and León (1037–65); emp. of Spain (1056–65)
— V of Castile or II of Aragon 1452–1516 the Catholic king of Castile (1474–1504); of Aragon (1479–1516); of Naples (1504–16); founder of the Span. monarchy
— VII 1784–1833 king of Spain (1808; 1814–33)

Fe·rish·tah \,fer-ish-'tä\ Mohammed Kasim 1550?–?1626 Pers. hist.

Fer·mat, de \fer-'mä\ Pierre 1601–1665 Fr. math.

Fer·mi \'fe(ə)r-,mē\ Enrico 1901–1954 Ital. physicist

Fer·nan·dez \fər-'nan-,dez\ Juan 1536–?1602 Span. navigator

Fer·re·ro \fə-'re(ə)r-,(,)ō\ Guglielmo 1871–1942 Ital. hist. & author

Fes·sen·den \'fes-ⁿn-dən\ William Pitt 1806–1869 Am. polit.; secy. of the treas. (1864–65)

Fes·tus \'fes-təs\ Porcius d ab A.D. 62 Rom. procurator of Judea (58 or 60–62)

Feucht·wang·er \'fóikt-,väŋ-ər, 'fóiḵt-\ Li·on \'lē-,ón\ 1884–1958 Ger. nov. & dram.

Feuil·let \,fə-'yā\ Octave 1821–1890 Fr. nov. & dram.

Fey \'fī\ Emil 1888–1938 Austrian soldier & polit.

Fi·bi·ger \'fē-bē-gər\ Johannes 1867–1928 Dan. pathologist

Fich·te \'fik-tə, 'fiḵ\ Johann Gottlieb 1762–1814 Ger. philos.

Field \'fē(ə)ld\ Cyrus West 1819–1892 Am. financier
— Eugene 1850–1895 Am. poet & journalist
— Marshall 1834–1906 Am. merchant

Field·ing \'fē(ə)l-diŋ\ Henry 1707–1754 Eng. nov.
— Sarah 1710–1768 sister of prec. Eng. writer

Fie·so·le, da \fē-'ā-zə-,lā, 'fyā-zə-\ Giovanni 1387–1455 Fra An·ge·li·co \an-'jel-i-,kō\ orig. Guido di Pietro Ital. painter

Figl \'fē-gəl\ Leopold 1902–1965 Austrian agrarian & polit.

Fi·gue·roa, de \,fē-gə-'rō-ə\ Francisco 1536?–1620 Span. poet

Fill·more \'fil-,mō(ə)r, -,mò)r\ Millard 1800–1874 13th pres. of the U.S. (1850–53)

Fin·lay \fin-'lī\ Carlos Juan 1833–1915 Cuban physician & biologist

Fin·sen \'fin(t)-sən\ Niels Ryberg 1860–1904 Dan. physician

Fir·dau·si \fər-'daú-sē, -'dō-\ or Fir·du·si \-'dü-\ 940?–?1020 Abul Qasim Mansur or Hasan Pers. epic poet

Fi·scher \'fish-ər\ Emil 1852–1919 Ger. chem.
— Hans 1881–1945 Ger. chem.

Fish \'fish\ Hamilton 1808–1893 Am. statesman

Fish·bein \'fish-,bīn\ Morris 1889– Am. physician & editor

Fish·er \'fish-ər\ Dorothy 1879–1958 Dorothea Frances née Can·field \'kan-,fēld\ Am. nov.
— Herbert Albert Laurens 1865–1940 Eng. hist.
— Irving 1867–1947 Am. econ.
— John Arbuthnot 1841–1920 1st Baron Fisher of Kil·ver·stone \'kil-vər-stən\ Brit. admiral

Fiske \'fisk\ John 1842–1901 orig. Edmund Fisk Green Am. philos. & hist.

Fitch \'fich\ John 1743–1798 Am. inventor
— (William) Clyde 1865–1909 Am. dram.

Fitz·ger·ald \'fits-'jer-əld\ Francis Scott Key 1896–1940 Am. author

FitzGerald Edward 1809–1883 Eng. poet & translator

Fitz·her·bert \'fits-'hər-bərt\ Maria Anne 1756–1837 née Smythe; wife of George IV of England

Flagg \'flag\ James Montgomery 1877–1960 Am. painter, illustrator, & writer

Flag·stad \'fläg-,stä, 'flag-,stad\ Kir·sten \'kish-tən, 'ki(ə)r-stən\ 1895–1962 Norw. soprano

Fla·min·i·us \flə-'min-ē-əs\ Gaius d 217 B.C. Rom. gen. & statesman

Flam·ma·rion \flə-'mar-ē-,ōⁿ\ (Nicolas) Camille 1842–1925 Fr. astron. & writer

Flan·a·gan \'flan-i-gən\ Edward Joseph 1886–1948 Am. (Irish-born) R.C. priest & founder of Boys Town

Flan·din \'fläⁿ-daⁿ\ Pierre Étienne 1889–1958 Fr. lawyer; premier (1934–35)

Flau·bert \flō-'be(ə)r\ Gustave 1821–1880 Fr. nov.

Flax·man \'flak-smən\ John 1755–1826 Eng. sculptor

Fleet·wood \'flēt-,wùd\ Charles d 1692 Eng. gen.

Flem·ing \'flem-iŋ\ Sir Alexander 1881–1955 Brit. bacteriol.
— Sir John Ambrose 1849–1945 Eng. electrical engineer

Fletch·er \'flech-ər\ John 1579–1625 Eng. dram.

Fleu·ry, de \,flər-'ē, ,flə-'rē\ André Hercule 1653–1743 Fr. cardinal & statesman
— Claude 1640–1723 Fr. ecclesiastical hist.

Flint \'flint\ Austin: father 1812–1886 & son 1836–1915 Am. physicians

Flo·res \'flór-,ās, 'flór-\ Juan José 1800–1864 Ecuadorian soldier; pres. of Ecuador (1830–35; 1839–45)

Flo·rey \'flór-ē, 'flór-\ Sir Howard Walter 1898–1968 Brit. pathologist

Flo·rio \'flōr-ē-,ō, 'flòr-\ John 1553?–1625 Eng. lexicographer & translator

Flo·tow, von \'flō-(,)tō\ Baron Friedrich 1812–1883 Ger. composer

Foch \'fòsh, 'fäsh\ Ferdinand 1851–1929 Fr. gen.; marshal of France (1918)

Fo·kine \'fò-,kēn, fò-'\ Michel 1880–1942 Am. (Russ.-born) choreographer

ə abut; ᵊ kitten; ər further; a back; ā bake; ä cot, cart; aú out; ch chin; e less; ē easy; g gift; i trip; ī life
j joke; ŋ sing; ō flow; ò flaw; òi coin; th thin; th this; ü loot; ù foot; y yet; yü few; yù furious; zh vision
ᵊ F table; â F bac; ḵ G ich, Buch; ⁿ F vin; œ F bœuf; œ̄ F feu; ᵫ G füllen; ū̄ F rue; ʸ F digne \dēnʸ\, nuit \nwᵉē\

Fok·ker \\'fäk-ər, 'fôk-\\ Anthony Herman Gerard 1890–1939 Am. (Du.-born) aircraft designer & builder

Fo·ley \\'fō-lē\\ John Henry 1818–1874 Irish sculptor

Fol·ger \\'fōl-jər\\ Henry Clay 1857–1930 Am. bibliophile

Fon·tanne \\fän-'tan, 'fän-\\ Lynn 1887?– *wife of Alfred Lunt* Am. (Eng.-born) actress

Fon·teyn \\fän-'tān, 'fän-\\ Dame Margot 1919– *Margot Hook·ham* \\'hùk-əm\\ Eng. dancer

Foote \\'fùt\\ Andrew Hull 1806–1863 Am. admiral

Forbes–Rob·ert·son \\'fòrbz-'räb-ərt-sən\\ Sir Johnston 1853–1937 Eng. scholar

Ford \\'fō(ə)rd, 'fò(ə)rd\\ Ford Mad·ox \\'mad-əks\\ 1873–1939 orig. *Huef·fer* \\'hyü-fər\\ Eng. author
— Henry 1863–1947 Am. automobile manuf.
— John 1586?–after 1638 Eng. dram.
— Paul Leicester 1865–1902 Am. hist. & nov.

For·es·ter \\'fòr-əs-tər, 'fär-\\ Cecil Scott 1899–1966 Eng. nov.

For·rest \\'fòr-əst, 'fär-\\ Edwin 1806–1872 Am. actor
— Nathan Bedford 1821–1877 Am. Confed. gen.

For·res·tal \\'fòr-əs-t³l, 'fär-, -,tòl\\ James Vincent 1892–1949 Am. banker; 1st U.S. secy. of defense (1947–49)

Forss·mann \\'fòr-,smän\\ Werner Theodor Otto 1904– Ger. surgeon

For·ster \\'fòr-stər\\ Edward Morgan 1879–1970 Brit. nov.

For·syth \\'fòr-,sīth, fər-\\ John 1780–1841 Am. statesman

For·tas \\'fòrt-əs\\ Abe 1910– Am. jurist

Fos·dick \\'fäz-,dik\\ Harry Emerson 1878–1969 Am. clergyman

Fos·ter \\'fòs-tər, 'fäs-\\ Stephen Collins 1826–1864 Am. songwriter
— William Zebulon 1881–1961 Am. Communist

Fou·cault \\fü-'kō\\ Jean Bernard Léon 1819–1868 Fr. physicist

Fouqué see LA MOTTE-FOUQUÉ

Fou·quet *or* **Fouc·quet** \\fü-'kā\\ Nicolas 1615–1680 Fr. superintendent of finance

Fou·quier–Tin·ville \\fü-kyā-ta^n-vēl\\ Antoine Quentin 1746–1795 Fr. polit.

Four·dri·nier \\,fòr-drə-'ni(ə)r, ,fòr-; fùr-'drin-ē-ər, fōr-, fòr-\\ Henry 1766–1854 & his bro. Sealy *d* 1847 Eng. papermakers & inventors

Fou·rier \\'fùr-ē-,ā\\ François Marie Charles 1772–1837 Fr. sociol. & reformer

Fow·ler \\'faù-lər\\ Henry H. 1908– Am. secy. of the treasury (1965–68)
— Henry Watson 1858–1933 Eng. lexicographer

Fox \\'fäks\\ Charles James 1749–1806 Eng. statesman & orator
— Dixon Ryan 1887–1945 Am. educ. & hist.
— George 1624–1691 Eng. preacher; founder of Society of Friends (Quakers)
— Henry 1705–1774 1st Baron *Hol·land* \\'häl-ənd\\ Brit. statesman
— John William 1863–1919 *John Fox, Jr.* Am. nov.

Foxe \\'fäks\\ John 1517–1587 Eng. martyrologist
— *or* **Fox** Richard 1448?–1528 Eng. prelate & statesman

Fra·go·nard \\,frag-ə-'när\\ Jean Honoré 1732–1806 Fr. painter & engraver

France \\'fran(t)s, fräⁿs\\ Anatole 1844–1924 pseud. of *Jacques Anatole François Thibault* Fr. nov. & satirist

Fran·ce·sca, della \\fran-'ches-kə, frän-\\ Piero 1420?–1492 *Piero dei Fran·ce·schi* \\-'ches-kē\\ Ital. painter

Fran·ce·sca da Ri·mi·ni \\fran-,ches-kəd-ə-'rim-ə-(,)nē, frän-, -'rē-mə-\\ *d* 1285? Ital. lady immortalized by Dante

Fran·cis I \\'fran(t)-səs\\ 1494–1547 king of France (1515–47)
— II 1768–1835 last Holy Rom. emp. (1792–1806); emp. of Austria (as *Francis I*) 1804–35
— **Ferdinand** 1863–1914 archduke of Austria; assassinated
— **Joseph I** 1830–1916 emp. of Austria (1848–1916)
— **of Assisi** Saint 1182–1226 *Giovanni Francesco Bernardone* Ital. friar; founder of Franciscan order
— **of Sales** \\'sä(ə)lz\\ Saint 1567–1622 Fr. R.C. bishop of Geneva

Franck \\'fräŋk\\ César Auguste 1822–1890 Belg.-Fr. organist & composer
— James 1882–1964 Am. (Ger.-born) physicist

Francke \\'fräŋ-kə\\ Kuno 1855–1930 Am. (Ger.-born) hist. & educ.

Fran·co \\'fräŋ-(,)kō, 'fraŋ-\\ Francisco 1892– *Francisco Paulino Hermenegildo Teódulo Franco-Bahamonde* Span. gen. & head of Span. state

Frank \\'fraŋk, 'fräŋk\\ Ilya Mikhailovich 1908– Russ. physicist

Frank·furt·er \\'fraŋk-fə(r)t-ər, -,fərt-\\ Felix 1882–1965 Am. (Austrian-born) jurist

Frank·lin \\'fraŋ-klən\\ Benjamin 1706–1790 Am. statesman & philos.
— Sir John 1786–1847 Eng. arctic explorer

Franks \\'fraŋ(k)s\\ Baron 1905– *Oliver Shewell Franks* Eng. philos. & diplomat

Fra·ser \\'frā-zər, -zhər\\ James Earle 1876–1953 Am. sculptor
— Peter 1884–1950 N.Z. statesman; prime min. (1940–49)
— Simon 1667?–1747 12th Baron *Lov·at* \\'ləv-ət\\ Scot. Jacobite

Fraun·ho·fer, von \\'fraùn-,hō-fər\\ Joseph 1787–1826 Bavarian optician & physicist

Fra·zer \\'frā-zər, -zhər\\ Sir James (George) 1854–1941 Scot. anthropologist

Fré·chette \\frā-'shet\\ Louis Honoré 1839–1908 Canad. journalist & poet

Fred·er·ick I \\'fred-(ə-)rik\\ 1123?–1190 *Frederick Bar·ba·ros·sa* \\,bär-bə-'räs-ə, -'rós-\\ Holy Rom. emp. (1152–90)
— II 1194–1250 Holy Rom. emp. (1215–50); king of Sicily (1198–1250)
— I 1657–1713 king of Prussia (1701–13)
— II 1712–1786 *Frederick the Great* king of Prussia (1740–86)
— IX 1899– king of Denmark (1947–)

Frederick William 1620–1688 *the great Elector* elector of Brandenburg (1640–88)
— name of 4 kings of Prussia: I 1688–1740 (reigned 1713–40); II 1744–1797 (reigned 1786–97); III 1770–1840 (reigned 1797–1840); IV 1795–1861 (reigned 1840–61)

Free·man \\'frē-mən\\ Douglas Sou·thall \\'saù-,thól, -,thòl\\ 1886–1953 Am. editor & hist.
— Mary Eleanor 1852–1930 née *Wilkins* Am. writer
— Orville L. 1918– U.S. secy. of agric. (1961–69)

Fre·ling·huy·sen \\'frē-liŋ-,hīz-³n\\ Frederick Theodore 1817–1885 Am. statesman

Fré·mont \\'frē-,mänt\\ John Charles 1813–1890 Am. gen. & explorer

Frem·stad \\'frem-,städ, -,stad\\ Anna Olivia 1872–1951 *Olive* Am. (Swed.-born) soprano

French \\'french\\ Alice 1850–1934 pseud. *Octave Than·et* \\'than-ət\\ Am. nov.
— Daniel Chester 1850–1931 Am. sculptor
— John Denton Pinkstone 1st Earl of *Ypres* 1852–1925 Brit. field marshal

Fre·neau \\frə-'nō, 'frē-\\ Philip Morin 1752–1832 Am. poet

Fres·nel \\frā-'nel\\ Augustin Jean 1788–1827 Fr. physicist

Freud \\'fròid\\ Sigmund 1856–1939 Austrian neurologist; founder of psychoanalysis

Frey·berg \\'frī-,bərg\\ 1st Baron 1889–1963 *Bernard Cyril Freyberg* N.Z. gen.

Frey·tag \\'frī-,täk, -,täg\\ Gustav 1816–1895 Ger. author

Frick \\'frik\\ Henry Clay 1849–1919 Am. industrialist

Fried \\'frēt\\ Alfred Hermann 1864–1921 Austrian pacifist

Fro·bish·er \\'frō-bi-shər\\ Sir Martin 1535?–1594 Eng. navigator

Froe·bel *or* **Frö·bel** \\'frā-bəl, 'frä(r)-bəl\\ Friedrich 1782–1852 Ger. educ.

Froh·man \\'frō-mən\\ Charles 1860–1915 Am. theater manager

Frois·sart \\frwä-'sär, 'fròi-,särt\\ Jean 1333?–?1400 Fr. chronicler

Fromm \\'främ\\ Erich 1900– Am. (Ger.-born) psychoanalyst

Fron·di·zi \\frän-'dē-zē, -sē\\ Arturo 1908– Argentinian pres. (1958–62)

Fron·te·nac, de \\'fränt-³n-,ak\\ Comte *de Pal·lu·au* \\,pal-ə-'wō\\ *et* 1620–1698 *Louis de Buade* \\'bw^yäd\\ Fr. gen. & colonial administrator

Frost \\'fròst\\ Robert Lee 1874–1963 Am. poet

Froude \\'früd\\ James Anthony 1818–1894 Eng. hist.

Fry \\'frī\\ Christopher 1907– Eng. dram.

Fu·ad I \\fù-'äd\\ 1868–1936 orig. *Ahmed Fuad Pasha* sultan (1917–22) & king (1922–36) of Egypt

Fu·en·tes \\fü-'en-tās\\ Carlos 1928– Mex. author

Fuer·tes \\'fyù(ə)rt-ēz\\ Louis Agassiz 1874–1927 Am. illustrator

Ful·bright \\'fùl-,brīt\\ James William 1905– Am. polit.

Ful·da \\'fùl-də\\ Ludwig 1862–1939 Ger. writer

Ful·ler \\'fùl-ər\\ Melville Weston 1833–1910 Am. jurist; chief justice U.S. Supreme Court (1888–1910)
— Richard Buckminster 1895– Am. engineer
— (Sarah) Margaret 1810–1850 Marchioness *Os·so·li* \\'ò-sə-(,)lē\\ Am. critic & reformer
— Thomas 1608–1661 Eng. divine & author

Ful·ton \\'fùlt-³n\\ Robert 1765–1815 Am. engineer & inventor

Funk \\'fùŋk, 'faŋk\\ Casimir 1884–1967 Am. (Pol.-born) biochem.
— \\'faŋk\\ Isaac Kauffman 1839–1912 Am. editor & publisher
— \\'fùŋk\\ Walther 1890–1960 Ger. journalist & econ.

Fun·ston \\'fən(t)-stən\\ Frederick 1865–1917 Am. gen.

Fur·ness \\'fər-nəs\\ Horace Howard: father 1833–1912 & son 1865–1930 Am. Shakespeare scholars

Fur·ni·vall \\'fər-nə-vəl\\ Frederick James 1825–1910 Eng. philologist

Ga·bo \\'gäb-(,)ō\\ Naum 1890– orig. *Naum Pevs·ner* \\'pevz-nər\\ Am. (Russ.-born) sculptor

Ga·bo·riau \\,gä-,bòr-'yō, gə-'bòr-ē-,ō\\ Emile 1835–1873 Fr. writer

Gads·den \\'gadz-dən\\ James 1788–1858 Am. army officer & diplomat

Gad·ski \\'gät-skē\\ Johanna 1872–1932 Ger. soprano

Ga·ga·rin \\gə-'gär-ən\\ Yu·ri \\'yù(ə)r-ē\\ Alekseyevich 1934–1968 Russ. astronaut; first man in space (1961)

Gage \\'gāj\\ Thomas 1721–1787 Brit. gen. & colonial gov. in Am.

Gail·lard \\gil-'yärd\\ David DuBose \\-d(y)ü-'bōz\\ 1859–1913 Am. army officer & engineer

Gaines \\'gānz\\ Edmund Pendleton 1777–1849 Am. gen.

Gains·bor·ough \\'gānz-,bər-ə, -,bə-rə, -b(ə-)rə\\ Thomas 1727–1788 Eng. painter

Gait·skell \\'gāt-skəl\\ Hugh Todd Naylor 1906–1963 Brit. socialist leader

Ga·ius \\'gā-(y)əs, 'gī-əs\\ *or* **Ca·ius** \\'kā-, 'kī-\\ 2d cent. A.D. Rom. jurist

Gal·ba \\'gal-bə, 'gòl-\\ Servius Sulpicius 5 B.C.?–A.D. 69 Rom. emp. (68–69)

Gal·braith \\'gal-,brāth\\ John Kenneth 1908– Am. (Canad.-born) econ.

Gale \\'gā(ə)l\\ Zona 1874–1938 Am. nov.

Ga·len \\'gā-lən\\ *ab* 130– *ab* 200 Greek physician & writer

Ga·le·ri·us \\gə-'lir-ē-əs\\ *d* 311 *Gaius Galerius Valerius Maximianus* Rom. emp. (305–311)

Gal·i·lei \\,gal-ə-'lā-,ē\\ Ga·li·leo \\,gal-ə-'lē-(,)ō, -'lā-\\ 1564–1642 *Galileo* Ital. astron. & physicist

Gal·land \\gə-'läⁿ\\ Antoine 1646–1715 Fr. orientalist & translator

Gal·la·tin \\'gal-ət-³n\\ (Abraham Alfonse) Albert 1761–1849 Am. (Swiss-born) financier & statesman

Gal·lau·det \\,gal-ə-'det\\ Thomas Hopkins 1787–1851 Am. teacher for the deaf & dumb

Gal·le·gos \\gä-'yā-(,)gōs\\ Freire Rómulo 1884–1969 Venezuelan nov.; pres. of Venezuela (1948)

Gal·li–Cur·ci \\,gal-ē-'kùr-chē, ,gal-ē-, ,gäl-, -'kər-\\ Amelita 1889–1963 née *Galli* Am. (Ital.-born) soprano

Gal·lie·ni \\,gal-yā-'nē\\ Joseph Simon 1849–1916 Fr. gen. & colonial administrator

Gal·lie·nus \\,gal-ē-'ē-nəs, -'ā-nəs\\ Publius Licinius Valerianus Egnatius *d* 268 Rom. emp. (253–268)

Gal·lup \\'gal-əp\\ George Horace 1901– Am. statistician

Gal·ois \\gal-'wä\\ Évariste 1811–1832 Fr. math.

Gals·wor·thy \\'gòlz-,wər-thē\\ John 1867–1933 Eng. nov. & dram.

Galt \\'gòlt\\ John 1779–1839 Scot. nov.

Gal·ton \\'gòlt-³n\\ Sir Francis 1822–1911 Eng. scientist

Gal·va·ni \\gal-'vän-ē, gäl-\\ Luigi *or* Aloisio 1737–1798 Ital. physician & physicist

Gál·vez \\'gäl-,vāth, -,väs\\ José 1729–1787 Marqués *de la Sonora* Span. jurist & colonial administrator

Ga·ma, da \\'gam-ə, 'gäm-\\ Vasco 1469?–1524 Port. navigator

Ga·mar·ra \gə-'mär-ə\ Agustín 1785–1841 Peruvian gen.; pres. of Peru (1829–33; 1839–41)

Gam·bet·ta \gam-'bet-ə, ˌgam-bə-'tä\ Léon 1838–1882 Fr. lawyer & statesman

Ga·me·lin \ˌgam-(ə-)'laⁿ\ Maurice Gustave 1872–1958 Fr. gen.

Gan·dhi \'gän-dē, 'gan-\ Indira Nehru *see* NEHRU

— Mohandas Karamchand 1869–1948 *Ma·hat·ma* \mə-'hät-mə, -'hat-\ *Gandhi* Hindu nationalist leader

Gar·a·mond \'gar-ə-ˌmänd, ˌgar-ə-'mōⁿ\ Claude *d* 1561 Fr. typefounder

Ga·rand \gə-'rand, 'gar-ənd\ John Cantius 1888– Am. (Canad.-born) inventor

Gar·cía Gu·tiér·rez \gär-'sē-ə-gü-'tyer-ˌās, -'thē-ə-, -'tyer-ˌāth\ Antonio *c*1813–1884 Span. dram.

Gar·cía Iñi·guez \gär-'sē-ə-'ēn-yē-gäs\ Calixto 1836?–1898 Cuban lawyer & revolutionist

Gar·cía Lor·ca \gär-'sē-ə-'lȯr-kə\ Frederico 1899–1936 Span. poet & dram.

Gar·cía Mo·re·no \gär-'sē-ə-mə-'rā-(ˌ)nō\ Gabriel 1821–1875 Ecuadorian journalist; pres. of Ecuador (1861–65; 1869–75)

Gar·ci·la·so de la Ve·ga \ˌgär-sə-'läs-(ˌ)ō, -ˌdā-lə-'vā-gə\ 1539?–1616 *El Inca* Peruvian hist.

Gar·den \'gärd-ᵊn\ Mary 1874–1967 Am. (Scot.-born) soprano

Gar·di·ner \'gärd-nər, -ᵊn-ər\ Samuel Rawson 1829–1902 Eng. hist.

— Stephen 1483?–1555 Eng. prelate & statesman

Gard·ner \'gärd-nər\ Erle Stanley 1889–1970 Am. writer

— John W. 1912– U.S. secy. health, ed. & welfare (1965–68)

Gar·field \'gär-ˌfēld\ James Abram 1831–1881 20th pres. of the U.S. (1881)

Gar·i·bal·di \ˌgar-ə-'bȯl-dē\ Giuseppe 1807–1882 Ital. patriot

Gar·land \'gär-lənd\ Hamlin 1860–1940 Am. nov.

Gar·ner \'gär-nər\ John Nance 1868–1967 Am. polit.; vice-pres. of the U.S. (1933–41)

Gar·nett \'gär-nət\ Constance 1862–1946 née *Black* Eng. translator

Gar·rick \'gar-ik\ David 1717–1779 Eng. actor

Gar·ri·son \'gar-ə-sən\ Mabel 1886–1963 Am. soprano

— William Lloyd 1805–1879 Am. abolitionist

Gar·shin \'gär-shən\ Vsevolod Mikhailovich 1855–1888 Russ. writer

Gar·vey \'gär-vē\ Marcus 1887–1940 Jamaican Black Nationalist

Gary \'ga(ə)r-ē, 'ge(ə)r-\ Elbert Henry 1846–1927 Am. lawyer & industrialist

Gas·coigne \'gas-ˌkȯin\ George 1535?–1577 Eng. poet

Gas·kell \'gas-kəl\ Elizabeth Cleghorn 1810–1865 née *Stevenson* Eng. nov.

Gas·ser \'gas-ər\ Herbert Spencer 1888–1963 Am. physiol.

Gasset *see* José ORTEGA Y GASSET

Gates \'gāts\ Horatio 1728?–1806 Am. gen. in Revolution

Gau·guin \gō-'gaⁿ\ Eugène Henri Paul 1848–1903 Fr. painter

Gauss \'gaús\ Karl Friedrich 1777–1855 Ger. math. & astron.

Gau·ta·ma Bud·dha \ˌgaút-ə-mə-'büd-ə, -'büd-\ 563?–?483 B.C. orig. Prince *Siddhartha* Indian philos.; founder of Buddhism

Gau·tier \gō-'tyā\ Théophile 1811–1872 Fr. author

Gay \'gā\ John 1685–1732 Eng. poet & dram.

Gay–Lus·sac \ˌgā-lə-'sak\ Joseph Louis 1778–1850 Fr. chem. & physicist

Ge·ber \'jē-bər\ *fl* 721–766 Arab scholar

Ged·des \'ged-əs\ Sir Eric (Campbell) 1875–1937 & his bro. 1st Baron 1879–1954 *Auckland Campbell Geddes* Eng. statesmen

— \'ged-ēz\ Norman Bel \'bel\ 1893–1958 Am. designer

Gei·kie \'gē-kē\ Sir Archibald 1835–1924 Scot. geologist

Gellée Claude *see* Claude LORRAIN

Ge·nêt \zhə-'nā\ Edmond Charles Édouard 1763–1834 Fr. diplomat in U.S.

— Jean 1909– Fr. dram.

Gen·ghis Khan \ˌjeŋ-gə-'skän, ˌgeŋ-\ 1162–1227 Mongol conqueror

Gen·ser·ic \'gen(t)-sə-rik, 'jen(t)-\ *d* 477 king of the Vandals (428–477)

Gen·ti·le da Fa·bri·a·no \jen-'tē-lē-də-ˌfäb-rē-'än-(ˌ)ō\ 1370?–?1427 *Gentile Massi* Ital. painter

Geof·frey of Monmouth \'jef-rē\ 1100?–1154 Eng. ecclesiastic & chronicler

George \'jȯ(ə)rj\ Saint *d ab* 303 Christian martyr & patron saint of Eng.

— name of 6 kings of Gt. Britain: **I** 1660–1727 (reigned 1714–27); **II** 1683–1760 (reigned 1727–60); **III** 1738–1820 (reigned 1760–1820); **IV** 1762–1830 (reigned 1820–30); **V** 1865–1936 (reigned 1910–36); **VI** 1895–1952 (reigned 1936–52)

— **I** 1845–1913 king of Greece (1863–1913)

— **II** 1890–1947 king of Greece (1922–23; 1935–47)

— David Lloyd *see* David LLOYD GEORGE

— Henry 1839–1897 Am. econ.

Ge·rard \jə-'rärd, 'jer-ˌärd\ Charles 1618?–1694 1st Baron *Gerard of Bran·don* \'bran-dən\; Viscount *Brandon* Eng. royalist commander

— James Watson 1867–1951 Am. lawyer & diplomat

Gé·rard \zhā-'rär\ Comte Étienne Maurice 1773–1852 Fr. Napoleonic gen.; marshal of France

Gé·rôme \zhā-'rōm\ Jean Léon 1824–1904 Fr. painter

Ge·ron·i·mo \jə-'rän-ə-ˌmō\ 1829–1909 Apache chieftain

Ger·ry \'ger-ē\ Elbridge 1744–1814 Am. statesman; vice-pres. of the U.S. (1813–14)

Gersh·win \'gərsh-wən\ George 1898–1937 Am. composer

Ge·sell \gə-'zel\ Arnold Lucius 1880–1961 Am. psychol. & pediatrician

Ges·ner, von \'ges-nər\ Konrad 1516–1565 Swiss naturalist

Get·ty \'get-ē\ George Washington 1819–1901 Am. gen.

— Jean Paul 1892– Am. business executive

Ghaz·za·li *or* Gha·za·li, al- \ˌal-gə-'zäl-ē\ 1058–1111 Arab (Persian-born) philos.

Ghi·ber·ti \gē-'bert-ē\ Lorenzo 1378–1455 Florentine goldsmith, painter, & sculptor

Ghir·lan·da·jo \ˌgir-lən-'dä-(ˌ)yō, -'dī-(ˌ)ō\ Domenico 1449–1494 Florentine painter & mosaicist

Ghorm·ley \'gȯrm-lē\ Robert Lee 1883–1958 Am. admiral

Ghose \'gōs\ Sri Aurobindo 1872–1950 Indian philos. & nationalist statesman

Giar·di·no \jär-'dē-(ˌ)nō\ Gaetano 1864–1935 Ital. gen.

Gi·auque \jē-'ōk\ William Francis 1895– Am. chem.

Gib·bon \'gib-ən\ Edward 1737–1794 Eng. hist.

Gib·bons \'gib-ənz\ James 1834–1921 Am. cardinal

Gibbs \'gibz\ Josiah Willard 1839–1903 Am. math. & physicist

— Sir Philip 1877–1962 Eng. journalist & nov.

Gib·ran \jə-'brän\ Gibran Khalil 1883–1931 Lebanese novelist, poet, & artist in U.S.

Gib·son \'gib-sən\ Charles Dana 1867–1944 Am. illustrator

Gide \'zhēd\ André 1869–1951 Fr. nov., critic, & essayist

Giel·gud \'gil-ˌgúd, 'gēl-\ Sir (Arthur) John 1904– Eng. actor

Gie·se·king \'gē-zə-kiŋ\ Walter Wilhelm 1895–1956 Ger. (Fr.-born) pianist

Gil·bert \'gil-bərt\ Cass 1859–1934 Am. architect

— Sir Humphrey 1539?–1583 Eng. navigator

— William 1540–1603 Eng. physician & physicist

— Sir William Schwenck 1836–1911 Eng. librettist & poet; collaborator with Sir Arthur Sullivan

Gil·der \'gil-dər\ Richard Watson 1844–1909 Am. poet & editor

Gil·lette \jə-'let\ King Camp 1855–1932 Am. inventor & manuf.

— William 1855–1937 Am. actor

Gil·man \'gil-mən\ Arthur 1837–1909 Am. educ.; developed Radcliffe College

— Daniel Coit \'kȯit\ 1831–1908 Am. educ.; pres. Johns Hopkins U. (1875–1901)

Gil·mer \'gil-mər\ Elizabeth 1870–1951 née *Mer·i·weth·er* \'mer-ə-weth-ər\; pseud. *Dorothy Dix* \'diks\ Am. journalist

Gil·pin \'gil-pən\ Charles Sidney 1878–1930 Am. actor

Gior·gio·ne, Il \ˌēl-(ˌ)jȯr-'jō-nē\ *ab* 1478–1511 *Giorgione da Castelfranco*, orig. *Giorgio Barbarelli* Venetian painter

Giot·to \'jȯ(t)-(ˌ)tō, jē-'ät-(ˌ)ō\ 1266?–1337 *Giotto di Bondone* Florentine painter, architect, & sculptor

Gipps \'gips\ Sir George 1791–1847 Brit. gov. of New So. Wales (1836–46)

Gi·rard \zhē-'rär\ Jean Baptiste 1765–1850 Swiss Franciscan & educ.

Gi·rard \jə-'rärd\ Stephen 1750–1831 Am. (Fr.-born) financier & philanthropist

Gi·raud \zhē-'rō\ Henri Honoré 1879–1949 Fr. gen.

Gi·rau·doux \ˌzhir-ō-'dü\ Jean 1882–1944 Fr. writer

Gir·tin \'gərt-ᵊn\ Thomas 1775–1802 Eng. founder of art of modern watercolor painting

Gis·sing \'gis-iŋ\ George Robert 1857–1903 Eng. nov.

Gjel·le·rup \'gel-ə-ˌrúp\ Karl 1857–1919 Dan. writer

Glad·stone \'glad-ˌstōn, *chiefly Brit* -stən\ William Ewart 1809–1898 Brit. statesman; prime min. (1868–74; 1880–85; 1886; 1892–94)

Gla·ser \'glā-zər\ Donald Arthur 1926– Am. physicist

Glas·gow \'glas-(ˌ)kō, -(ˌ)gō, 'glaz-(ˌ)gō\ Ellen Anderson Gholson 1874–1945 Am. nov.

Glas·pell \'glas-ˌpel\ Susan 1882–1948 Am. nov. & dram.

Glass \'glas\ Carter 1858–1946 Am. statesman

Glen·dow·er \glen-'daú-(ə)r\ Owen 1359?–?1416 Welsh chieftain & rebel against Henry IV of Eng.

Glenn \'glen\ John Herschel 1921– Am. astronaut; first Am. man to orbit the earth (1962)

Glen·nan \'glen-ən\ Thomas Keith 1905– Am. engineer

Glin·ka \'gliŋ-kə\ Mikhail Ivanovich 1803–1857 Russ. composer

Gloucester Duke of *see* HUMPHREY

Glov·er \'gləv-ər\ John 1732–1797 Am. Revolutionary gen.

— Sarah Ann 1785–1867 Eng. music teacher; invented tonic sol-fa system of notation

Gluck \'glúk\ Alma 1884–1938 née (*Reba*) *Fiersohn* Am. (Romanian-born) soprano

— Christoph Willibald 1714–1787 Ger. composer

Glyn \'glin\ Elinor 1864–1943 née *Sutherland* Brit. nov.

Go·bat \gō-'bä\ Charles Albert 1843–1914 Swiss statesman

God·dard \'gäd-ərd\ Robert Hutchings 1882–1945 Am. physicist

God·frey of Bouil·lon \ˌgäd-frē-əv-(ˌ)bü-'yōⁿ\ *Fr.* Godefroy de Bouillon 1061?–1100 Fr. crusader

Go·dol·phin \gə-'däl-fən\ Sidney 1645–1712 1st Earl of *Godolphin* Eng. statesman

Go·doy, de \gə-'thȯi\ Manuel 1767–1851 Span. statesman

Go·du·nov \'gȯd-ᵊn-ˌȯf, 'gȯd-, 'gäd-\ Boris Fëdorovich 1551?–1605 czar of Russia (1598–1605)

God·win \'gäd-wən\ *d* 1053 earl of the West Saxons

— William 1756–1836 Eng. philos. & nov.

Godwin–Aus·ten \-'ȯs-tən, -'äs-\ Henry Haversham 1834–1923 Eng. explorer & geologist

Goeb·bels \'gə(r)b-əlz, 'gœb-\ Joseph Paul 1897–1945 Ger. Nazi propagandist

Goering *see* GÖRING

Goes \'güs\ Hugo van der 1440?–1482 Du. painter

Goe·thals \gō-thəlz\ George Washington 1858–1928 Am. gen. & engineer

Goe·the, von \'gə(r)t-ə, 'gœ-tə\ Johann Wolfgang 1749–1832 Ger. poet & dram.

Gogh, van \van-'gō, vän-'kȯk\ Vincent 1853–1890 Du. painter

Go·gol \'gȯ-gəl, -ˌgȯl\ Nikolai Vasilievich 1809–1852 Russ. writer

Gold·berg \'gōl(d)-ˌbərg\ Arthur Joseph 1908– Am. lawyer; U.S. ambassador to U.N. (1965–68)

Gol·den \'gōl-dən\ Harry Lewis 1902– Am. journalist

Gol·den·wei·ser \'gōl-dən-ˌwī-zər\ Alexander A. 1880–1940 Am. (Russ.-born) anthropologist & sociologist

Gol·ding \'gōl-diŋ\ William (Gerald) 1911– Eng. author

Gol·do·ni \gäl-'dō-nē, gōl-\ Carlo 1707–1793 Ital. dram.

Gold·smith \'gōl(d)-ˌsmith\ Oliver 1728–1774 Brit. author

Gold·wa·ter \'gōl-ˌdwȯt-ər, -ˌdwät-\ Barry Morris 1909– Am. polit.

Gol·gi \'gȯl-(ˌ)jē\ Camillo \kä-'mēl-(ˌ)lō\ 1844–1926 Ital. physi-

ə abut; ᵊ kitten; ər further; a back; ā bake; ä cot, cart; aú out; ch chin; e less; ē easy; g gift; i trip; ī life
j joke; ŋ sing; ō flow; ȯ flaw; ȯi coin; th thin; th this; ü loot; ú foot; y yet; yü few; yú furious; zh vision
ə F table; à F bac; ᵏ G ich, Buch; ⁿ F vin; œ F bœuf; œ̄ F feu; ᵫ G füllen; ᵫ̄ F rue; ʸ F digne \dēnʸ\, nuit \nwʸē\

cian

Gol·lancz \gə-'lan(t)s, 'gäl-ən(t)s\ Sir Hermann 1852-1930 Eng. Semitic scholar

Goltz, von der \'gólts, 'gölts\ Baron Kol·mar \-'kól-,mär\ 1843-1916 Ger. gen.

Gó·mez \'gō-,mās, -,mez\ Juan Vicente 1857?-1935 Venezuelan gen. & polit.; dictator (1908-35)

Gom·pers \'gäm-pərz\ Samuel 1850-1924 Am. (Brit.-born) labor leader

Go·mul·ka \gō-'múl-kə, -'məl-\ Wladyslaw 1905- Pol. polit. official

Gon·çal·ves Di·as \gən-,säl-vəs-'dē-əs\ Antônio 1823-1864 Brazilian poet

Gon·cha·ro·va \gən-'chär-ə-və\ Nathalie 1883-1962 Russ. artist

Gon·court, de \gōⁿ-'kü(ə)r\ Edmond Louis Antoine 1822-1896 & his bro. Jules Alfred Huot 1830-1870 Fr. nov. & collaborators

Gon·do·mar \,gän-də-'mär\ Count of 1567-1626 *Diego Sarmiento de Acuña* Span. diplomat

Gon·za·ga \gən-'zäg-ə, -'zag-\ Saint Aloysius 1568-1591 Ital. Jesuit cleric

Gon·zá·lez \gən-'zäl-əs, -əz\ Manuel 1833-1893 Mex. gen.; pres. of Mexico (1880-84)

— **Vi·de·la** \və-'thā-lə, -'dā-\ Gabriel 1898- Chilean lawyer; pres. of Chile (1946-52)

Gon·za·lo de Cór·do·ba \gən-,zäl-ō-də-'kórd-ə-bə, -'kórd-ə-və\ Hernández 1453-1515 *el Gran Capitán* Span. soldier

Good·hue \'gúd-(,)(h)yü\ Bertram Grosvenor 1869-1924 Am. architect

Good·rich \'gúd-(,)rich\ Samuel Griswold 1793-1860 pseud. *Peter Par·ley* \'pär-lē\ Am. writer

Good·year \'gúd-,yi(ə)r, 'gúj-,i(ə)r\ Charles 1800-1860 Am. inventor

Gor·cha·kov \,gór-chə-'kóf, -'kóv\ Prince Aleksandr Ivanovich 1764-1825 Russ. gen. & statesman

— Prince Aleksandr Mikhailovich 1798-1883 Russ. statesman & diplomat

Gor·din \'górd-ən\ Jacob 1853-1909 Am. (Russ.-born) Yiddish dram.

Gor·don \'górd-ən\ Charles George 1833-1885 *Chinese Gordon, Gordon Pasha* Brit. soldier

— Charles William 1860-1937 pseud. *Ralph Connor* Canad. clergyman & nov.

— Lord George 1751-1793 Eng. polit. agitator

Go·re·my·kin \,gór-ə-'mē-kən\ Ivan Longinovich 1839-1917 Russ. statesman; prime min. (1906; 1914-16)

Gor·gas \'gór-gəs\ William Crawford 1854-1920 Am. army surgeon & sanitation expert

Gö·ring \'gər-iŋ, 'ger-\ Hermann Wilhelm 1893-1946 Ger. Nazi polit.

Gor·ki \'gór-kē\ Maksim *also* Maxim **Gorky** 1868-1936 pseud. of *Aleksei Maksimovich Pesh·kov* \'pesh-,kóf, -,kóv\ Russ. writer

Gort \'gó(ə)rt\ 6th Viscount 1886-1946 *John Standish Surtees Prendergast Ver·e·ker* \'ver-i-kər\ Brit. field marshal

Gor·ton \'górt-ən\ John Grey 1911- Austral. polit.; prime minister (from 1968)

Go·schen \'gō-shən\ George Joachim 1st Viscount 1831-1907 Brit. statesman

Gosse \'gäs\ Sir Edmund William 1849-1928 Eng. poet & critic

Go·ta·ma Buddha \'gōt-ə-mə-\ *var of* GAUTAMA BUDDHA

Gou·dy \'gaúd-ē\ Frederic William 1865-1947 Am. type designer

Gough \'gäf\ Sir Hugh 1st Viscount 1779-1869 Eng. field marshal

Gould \'güld\ Jay *orig.* Jason 1836-1892 Am. financier

Gou·nod \'gü-(,)nō\ Charles François 1818-1893 Fr. composer

Gou·raud \gü-'rō\ Henri Joseph Eugène 1867-1946 Fr. gen.

Gour·mont, de \gúr-'mōⁿ\ Remy 1858-1915 Fr. writer

Gow·er \'gaú(-ə)r, 'gō-(ə)r, 'gó(-ə)r\ John 1325?-1408 Eng. poet

Go·ya y Lu·cien·tes, de \'gói-(y)ə-,ē-,lü-sē-'en-,täs\ Francisco José 1746-1828 Span. painter

Grac·chus \'grak-əs\ Gaius Sempronius 153-121 B.C. & his bro. Tiberius Sempronius 163-133 *the Grac·chi* \'grak-,ī\ Rom. statesmen

Gra·ham \'grā-əm, 'gra-(ə)m\ John 1649?-1689 *Graham of Cla·ver·house* \'kla-vər-,haús\; *Bonny Dundee*; 1st Viscount of *Dundee* Scot. Jacobite

— Martha 1894?- Am. dancer

— Thomas 1805-1869 Scot. chem.

— William Franklin 1918- *Billy* Am. evangelist

Gra·hame \'grā-əm, 'gra-(ə)m\ Kenneth 1859-1932 Brit. writer

Gramme \gram\ Zénobe Théophile 1826-1901 Belg. electrician

Gra·mont, de \gra-'mōⁿ\ Comte Philibert 1621?-1707 Fr. soldier & courtier

Gran·di \'grän-(,)dē\ Count (di Mordano) Dino 1895- Ital. Fascist polit.

Grant \'grant, 'gránt\ Heber Jedediah 1856-1945 Am. Mormon; pres. of the church (1918-45)

— Ulysses Simpson 1822-1885 *Ulysses Hiram* (baptized *Hiram Ulysses*) *Grant* Am. gen.; 18th pres. of the U.S. (1869-77)

Gran·ville-Bar·ker \,gran-vil-'bär-kər\ Harley Granville 1877-1946 Eng. actor-manager & dram.

Grass \'gräs\ Günter (Wilhelm) 1927- Ger. writer

Grasse, de \'gras, 'gräs\ Comte François Joseph Paul 1722-1788 Marquis *de Grasse-Tilly* \-tē-'yē\ Fr. naval officer

Gra·tian \'grā-sh(ē-)ən\ *Lat.* **Flavius Gratianus** 359-383 Rom. emp. (375-383)

Grat·tan \'grat-ən\ Henry 1746-1820 Irish orator & statesman

Grau San Mar·tín \'graú-,san-(,)mär-'tēn, -,sän-\ Ramón 1887-1969 Cuban physician & polit.; pres. of Cuba (1944-48)

Graves \'grāvz\ Robert Ranke 1895- Brit. author

Gray \'grā\ Asa 1810-1888 Am. botanist

— Thomas 1716-1771 Eng. poet

Grayson David *see* Ray Stannard BAKER

Gra·zia·ni \,grät-sē-'ä-nē, ,gräd-zē-\ Rodolfo 1882-1955 Marchese *di Neghelli* Ital. marshal & colonial administrator

Gre·co, El \'grek-(,)ō, 'gräk-, -(,)ō\ 1548?-?1614 or ?1625 *Domenico Theotocopuli* Span. (Cretan-born) painter

Gree·ley \'grē-lē\ Horace 1811-1872 Am. journalist & polit.

Gree·ly \'grē-lē\ Adolphus Washington 1844-1935 Am. gen. & arctic explorer

Green \'grēn\ Anna Katharine 1846-1935 Am. writer

— John Richard 1837-1883 Eng. hist.

— Julian 1900- Am. nov. in France

— William 1873-1952 Am. labor leader

Green·a·way \'grē-nə-,wā\ Catherine 1846-1901 *Kate* Eng. painter & illustrator

Greene \'grēn\ Graham 1904- Brit. nov.

— Nathanael 1742-1786 Am. Revolutionary gen.

— Robert 1558-1592 Eng. poet & dram.

Gree·nough \'grē-(,)nō\ Horatio 1805-1852 Am. sculptor

Greg·o·ry \'greg-(ə-)rē\ name of 16 popes: esp. **I** Saint 540?-604 *the Great* (pope 590-604); **VII** Saint (*Hil·de·brand* \'hil-də-,brand\) 1020?-1085 (pope 1073-85); **XIII** (*Ugo Buoncompagni*) 1502-1585 (pope 1572-85)

— Lady Augusta 1859?-1932 née *Persse* Irish dram.

— of Nys·sa \-'nis-ə\ Saint 331?-?396 Eastern church father

— of Tours Saint 538?-593 Frankish ecclesiastic & hist.

Gren·fell \'gren-,fel\ Sir Wilfred Thomason 1865-1940 Eng. medical missionary to Labrador

Gren·ville \'gren-,vil\ George 1712-1770 Eng. statesman

— *or* Greynville Sir Richard 1541?-1591 Brit. admiral

Gresh·am \'gresh-əm\ Sir Thomas 1519?-1579 Eng. financier

Greuze \'grə(r)z, 'grœz\ Jean Baptiste 1725-1805 Fr. painter

Gré·vy \grā-'vē\ François Paul Jules 1807-1891 Fr. lawyer; 3d pres. of the Republic (1879-87)

Grey \'grā\ 2d Earl 1764-1845 *Charles Grey* Eng. statesman; prime min. (1830-34)

— Edward 1862-1933 Viscount *Grey of Fal·lo·don* \'fal-əd-ən\ Eng. statesman

— Lady Jane 1537-1554 Eng. noblewoman beheaded as a possible rival for the throne

— Zane 1875-1939 Am. nov.

Grieg \'grēg, 'grig\ Edvard Hagerup 1843-1907 Norw. composer

Grier·son \'gri(ə)rs-ən\ Sir Herbert John Clifford 1866-1960 Brit. scholar

Grif·fin \'grif-ən\ Walter Burley 1876-1937 Am. architect

Grif·fith \'grif-əth\ Arthur 1872-1922 Irish polit.

— David Lewelyn Wark 1875-1948 Am. motion-picture producer

Gri·gnard \grēn-'yär(d)\ Victor 1871-1934 Fr. chem.

Grill·par·zer \'gril-,pärt-sər\ Franz 1791-1872 Austrian dram. & poet

Grimm \'grim\ Jacob 1785-1863 & his bro. Wilhelm 1786-1859 Ger. philologists & fairy-tale collaborators

Gris \'grēs\ Juan 1887-1927 Span. painter in France

Gro·fé \'grō-,fā\ Fer·de \'fərd-ē\ 1892- Am. conductor & composer

Gro·lier de Ser·vières \'grōl-,yā-də-,ser-vē-'e(ə)r\ Jean 1479-1565 Fr. bibliophile

Gro·my·ko \grə-'mē-(,)kō\ Andrei Andreevich 1909- Russ. econ. & diplomat

Gro·nou·ski \grə-'naú-skē\ John Austin 1919- U.S. postmaster general (1963-65)

Groo·te \'grōt-ə\ Gerhard 1340-1384 *Ge·rar·dus Mag·nus* \jə-,rärd-ə-'smag-nəs\ Du. religious reformer

Gro·pi·us \'grō-pē-əs\ Walter 1883-1969 Ger.-born architect in Am.

Grop·per \'gräp-ər\ William 1897- Am. painter

Gros·ve·nor \'grōv-nər\ Gilbert Hovey 1875-1966 Am. geographer

Grote \'grōt\ George 1794-1871 Eng. hist.

Gro·tius \'grō-sh(ē-)əs\ Hugo 1583-1645 *Huig de Groot* \'grōt\ Du. jurist & statesman

Grou·chy, de \grü-'shē\ Marquis Emmanuel 1766-1847 Fr. gen.

Grove \'grōv\ Sir George 1820-1900 Eng. writer on music

Groves \'grōvz\ Leslie Richard 1896- Am. gen.

Grü·ne·wald \'grü-nə-,wóld\ Matthias *fl* 1500-1530 Ger. painter

Gryph·i·us \'grif-ē-əs\ Andreas 1616-1664 Ger. **Greif** \'grīf\ Ger. poet & dram.

Guar·ne·ri \gwär-'ne(ə)r-ē\ Lat. **Guar·ne·ri·us** \gwär-'nir-ē-əs, -'ner-\ family of Italian violinmakers: esp. Giuseppe Antonio 1638-1745

Gu·de·ri·an \gü-'der-ē-ən\ Heinz 1886-1954 Ger. gen.

Gue·dal·la \gwə-'dal-ə\ Philip 1889-1944 Eng. writer

Gué·rard \gā-'rär(d)\ Albert Léon 1880-1959 Am. (Fr.-born) educ. & writer

Gue·rin \'ger-ən\ Jules 1866-1946 Am. painter

Guesde \ged\ Jules 1845-1922 *Mathieu Basile* Fr. socialist

Guest \'gest\ Edgar Albert 1881-1959 Am. journalist & poet

Gui·do d' Arez·zo \'gwēd-(,)ō-də-'ret-(,)sō\ *or* **Guido Are·ti·no** \,ar-ə-'tē-(,)nō\ 995?-?1050 Benedictine monk & music reformer

Guil·laume \gē-'yōm\ Charles Édouard 1861-1938 Fr. physicist

Guis·card \gē-'skär\ Robert 1015?-1085 Norman conqueror in Italy

Guise, de \'gēz, 'gwēz\ 1st Duc 1519-1563 *François de Lorraine; le Balafré* Fr. soldier & polit.

— 3d Duc 1550-1588 *Henri I de Lorraine;* also *le Balafré* Fr. soldier & polit.

Gui·te·ras \gē-'ter-əs\ Juan 1852-1925 Cuban physician

Gui·zot \gē-'zō\ François Pierre Guillaume 1787-1874 Fr. hist. & statesman

Gull·strand \'gəl-,stran(d)\ Allvar 1862-1930 Swed. ophthalmologist

Gun·nars·son \'gən-ər-sən\ Gunnar 1889- Icelandic poet & nov.

Gun·ter \'gənt-ər\ Edmund 1581-1626 Eng. math.

Gus·ta·vus \(,)gə-'stä-vəs, -'stäv-əs\ name of 6 kings of Sweden: **I** (*Gustavus Va·sa* \-'väs-ə\) 1496-1560 (reigned 1523-60); **II** (*Gustavus Adolphus*) 1594-1632 (reigned 1611-32); **III** 1746-1792 (reigned 1771-92); **IV** (*Gustavus Adolphus*) 1778-1837 (reigned 1792-1809); **V** (*Gus·taf* \'gəs-,täv, 'güs-, -,täf\) 1858-1950 (reigned 1907-50); **VI** 1882- (reigned 1950-)

Gu·ten·berg \'güt-ən-,bərg\ Johann 1400?-?1468 *Johann Gensfleisch* Ger. inventor of printing from movable type

Gutz·kow \'güts-(,)kō\ Karl 1811-1878 Ger. journalist, nov., & dram.

Guz·mán Blan·co \gü-'smän-'blän-(,)kō\ Antonio 1829-1899 Venezuelan soldier & statesman; pres. of Venezuela (alternate terms of two years 1870-89)

Gwin·nett \gwin-'et\ Button 1735-1777 Am. Revolutionary leader

Gwyn *or* **Gwynne** \'gwin\ Eleanor 1650-1687 *Nell* Eng. actress; *mistress of Charles II*

Haa·kon VII \'hó-kən, -,kän\ 1872-1957 king of Norway (1905- -57)

Ha·ber \'häb-ər\ Fritz 1868–1934 Ger. chem.
Há·cha \'hä-(‚)kä\ Emil 1872–1945 Czech jurist & statesman
Had·field \'had-‚fēld\ Sir Robert Abbott 1858–1940 Eng. metallurgist
Had·ley \'had-lē\ Henry Kimball 1871–1937 Am. composer
Had·ow \'had-(‚)ō\ Sir (William) Henry 1859–1937 Eng. educ. & writer on music
Ha·dri·an \'hā-drē-ən\ var of ADRIAN
Hadrian 76–138 Rom. emp. (117–138)
Haeck·el \'hek-əl\ Ernst Heinrich 1834–1919 Ger. biologist & philos.
Ha·fiz \hä-'fiz\ 14th cent. Shams ud-din Mohammed Pers. poet
Hag·e·dorn \'hag-ə-‚dò(ə)rn\ Hermann 1882–1964 Am. poet, nov., & critic
Hag·gard \'hag-ərd\ Sir (Henry) Ri·der \-'rīd-ər\ 1856–1925 Eng. nov.
Hahn \'hän\ Otto 1879–1968 Ger. physical chem.
Hah·ne·mann \'hän-ə-mən\ (Christian Friedrich) Samuel 1755–1843 Ger. physician; founder of homeopathy
Hai·dar (or **Hy·der**) **Ali** \‚hīd-ə-rə-'lē\ 1722–1782 Muslim ruler of Mysore, India
Haig \'hāg\ 1st Earl 1861–1928 Douglas Haig Brit. field marshal
Hai·le Se·las·sie \‚hī-lē-sə-'las-ē, -'läs-\ 1891– Ras Taffari or Tafari emp. of Ethiopia (1930–36; 1941–)
Hak·luyt \'hak-‚lüt, -lət\ Richard 1552–1616 Eng. geographer & hist.
Hal·dane \'hòl-‚dān\ John Burdon Sanderson 1892–1964 Brit. scientist
— John Scott 1860–1936 Brit. physiologist
— Richard Burdon 1856–1928 Viscount Haldane of Cloan \'klōn\; bro. of J.S. Brit. lawyer, philos., & statesman
Hal·der \'häl-dər\ Franz 1884– Ger. gen.
Hale \'hā(ə)l\ Edward Everett 1822–1909 Am. Unitarian clergyman & writer
— George Ellery 1868–1938 Am. astron.
— Sir Matthew 1609–1676 Eng. jurist
— Nathan 1755–1776 Am. Revolutionary officer; executed as a spy by the British
Ha·lé·vy \‚(h)al-ā-'vē, ‚(h)äl-\ 1799–1862 pseud. of Jacques Fromental Élie Lé·vy \lā-'vē\ Fr. composer
— Ludovic 1834–1908 nephew of prec. Fr. dram. & nov.
Hal·i·fax \'hal-ə-‚faks\ Earl of 1881–1959 Edward Frederick Lindley Wood Eng. statesman & diplomat
Hall \'hòl\ Charles Francis 1821–1871 Am. arctic explorer
— Charles Martin 1863–1914 Am. chem. & manuf.
— Granville Stanley 1846–1924 Am. psychol. & educ.
— James Norman 1887–1951 Am. nov.
Hal·lam \'hal-əm\ Henry 1777–1859 Eng. hist.
Hal·leck \'hal-ək, -ik\ Fitz-Greene 1790–1867 Am. poet
— Henry Wager 1815–1872 Am. gen.
Hal·ler \'häl-ər\ Józef 1873–1960 Pol. soldier
Hal·ley \'hal-ē, 'hā-lē\ Edmund 1656–1742 Eng. astron.
Hals \'hälz, 'häls\ Frans 1580?–1666 Du. painter
Hal·sey \'hòl-sē, -zē\ William Frederick 1882–1959 Am. admiral of the fleet
Hal·sted \'hòl-stəd, -‚sted\ William Stewart 1852–1922 Am. surgeon
Ham·bro \'häm-‚brō\ Carl Joachim 1885–1964 Norw. statesman
Ha·mil·car Bar·ca \hə-'mil-‚kär-'bär-kə, 'ham-əl-\ 270?–228 B.C. father of Hannibal Carthaginian gen.
Ham·il·ton \'ham-əl-tən, -əlt-ᵊn\ Alexander 1755–1804 Am. statesman
— Edith 1867–1963 Am. classicist
— Lady Emma 1761?–1815 née Lyon, mistress of Lord Nelson
— Sir Ian (Standish Mon·teith \män-'tēth\) 1853–1947 Brit. gen.
Ham·lin \'ham-lən\ Hannibal 1809–1891 Am. polit.; vice-pres. of the U.S. (1861–65)
Ham·mar·skjöld \'häm-ər-‚shəld, 'häm-, -‚shùld, -‚shēld\ Dag \'däg\ Hjalmar Agné Carl 1905–1961 Swed. U.N. official; secy.-gen. (1953–61)
Ham·mer·stein \'ham-ər-‚stīn, -‚stēn\ Oscar 1847?–1919 Ger.-born theater manager in Am.
— Oscar 1895–1960 grandson of prec. Am. dram.
Ham·mond \'ham-ənd\ John Hays 1855–1936 Am. mining engineer
— John Hays 1888–1965 son of prec. Am. electrical engineer & inventor
Ham·mu·ra·bi \‚ham-ə-'räb-ē\ king of Babylon (ab 1955–1913 B.C. or earlier)
Hamp·den \'ham(p)-dən\ John 1594–1643 Eng. statesman
— Walter 1879–1955 stage name of W. H. Dougherty Am. actor
Hamp·ton \'ham(p)-tən\ Wade 1752?–1835 Am. gen.
— Wade 1818–1902 grandson of prec. Am. polit. & Confed. gen.
Ham·sun \'häm-sən\ Knut 1859–1952 pseud. of Knut Pedersen Norw. writer
Han·cock \'han-‚käk\ John 1737–1793 Am. Revolutionary statesman
— Winfield Scott 1824–1886 Am. gen.
Hand \'hand\ Learned 1872–1961 Am. jurist
Han·del \'han-dəl\ George Frederick 1685–1759 Brit. (Ger.-born) composer
Han·na \'han-ə\ Marcus Alonzo 1837–1904 Mark Am. businessman & polit.
Han·nay \'han-‚ā, 'han-ē\ James Owen 1865–1950 Irish clergyman & nov.
Han·ni·bal \'han-ə-bəl\ 247–183 B.C. son of Hamilcar Barca Carthaginian gen.
Han·no \'han-(‚)ō\ 3d cent. B.C. Carthaginian statesman
Ha·no·taux \‚an-ə-'tō, ‚än-\ (Albert Auguste) Gabriel 1853–1944 Fr. hist. & statesman
Han·sard \'han(t)-sərd, 'han-‚särd\ Luke 1752–1828 Eng. printer
Han·son \'han(t)-sən\ Howard 1896– Am. composer
Hans·son \'han(t)-sən\ Per Albin 1885–1946 Swed. statesman
Han Yü \'hän-'yü\ 768–824 Han Wen-kung Chin. poet, essayist, & philos.
Har·bach \'här-‚bäk\ Otto Abels 1873–1963 Am. dram. & musical-comedy librettist

Har·court \'här-kərt, -‚kō(ə)rt, -‚kò(ə)rt\ Sir Cecil Halliday Jepson 1892–1959 Brit. admiral
Har·de·ca·nute \‚här-di-kə-'n(y)üt\ 1019?–1042 king of Denmark (1035–42) and of Eng. (1040–42)
Har·den \'härd-ᵊn\ Sir Arthur 1865–1940 Eng. chem.
— Maximilian 1861–1927 orig. Witkowski Ger. journalist & writer
Har·den·berg, von \'härd-ᵊn-‚bərg\ Prince Karl August 1750–1822 Pruss. statesman
Har·ding \'härd-iŋ\ Warren Gamaliel 1865–1923 29th pres. of the U.S. (1921–23)
Hard·wicke \'här-‚dwik\ Sir Ce·dric \'sē-drik\ Webster 1893–1964 Eng. actor
Har·dy \'härd-ē\ Thomas 1840–1928 Eng. nov. & poet
Har·greaves \'här-‚grēvz\ James d 1778 Eng. inventor of the spinning jenny
Har·ing·ton or **Har·ring·ton** \'har-iŋ-tən\ Sir John 1561–1612 Eng. writer & translator
Ha·ri·ri, al- \‚al-hə-'ri(ə)r-ē\ 1054–1122 Arab scholar & poet
Har·lan \'här-lən\ John Marshall 1899– Am. jurist
Har·ley \'här-lē\ Robert 1661–1724 1st Earl of Oxford Eng. statesman
Harms·worth \'härmz-(‚)wərth\ Alfred Charles William 1865–1922 Viscount North·cliffe \'nòrth-‚klif\ Eng. publisher & polit.
— Harold Sidney 1868–1940 1st Viscount Roth·er·mere \'räth-ər-‚mi(ə)r\ bro. of A.C.W. Eng. publisher & poet
Har·old \'har-əld\ I d 1040 Harold Hare·foot \'ha(ə)r-‚fùt, 'he(ə)r-\ king of Eng. (1035–40)
— II 1022?–1066 king of Eng. (1066)
— name of 3 kings of Norway: esp. III Haard·raa·de \'hòr-‚ròd-ə\ 1015–1066 (reigned 1047–66)
Har·ri·man \'har-ə-mən\ (William) Aver·ell \'āv-(ə-)rəl\ 1891– Am. businessman, diplomat, & polit.
Har·ris \'har-əs\ Sir Arthur Travers 1892– Brit. air marshal
— Frank 1854–1931 Am. (Irish-born) writer
— Joel Chandler 1848–1908 Am. writer
— Roy 1898– Am. composer
— William Torrey 1835–1909 Am. philos. & educ.
Har·ri·son \'har-ə-sən\ Benjamin 1833–1901 23d pres. of the U.S. (1889–93)
— Frederic 1831–1923 Eng. writer & philos.
— William Henry 1773–1841 9th pres. of the U.S. (1841)
Hart \'härt\ Albert Bushnell 1854–1943 Am. hist. & editor
— Lorenz 1895–1943 Am. librettist
— Moss 1904–1961 Am. librettist & dram.
— Sir Robert 1835–1911 Brit. diplomat
— William Shakespeare 1872–1946 Am. actor
Harte \'härt\ Francis Brett 1836–1902 Bret \'bret\ Am. writer
Ha·run al-Ra·shid \hə-‚rü-‚nal-rə-'shēd, -‚när-rə-\ 764?–809 caliph of Baghdad (786–809)
Har·vard \'här-vərd\ John 1607–1638 Eng. clergyman in Am.
Har·vey \'här-vē\ George Brinton McClellan 1864–1928 Am. journalist & diplomat
— Sir John Martin 1863–1944 Eng. actor & producer
— William 1578–1657 Eng. physician & anatomist
Has·dru·bal \'haz-‚drü-bəl, haz-'\ d 207 B.C. bro. of Hannibal Carthaginian gen.
Has·sam \'has-əm\ Childe 1859–1935 Am. painter & etcher
Hass·ler \'häs-lər\ Hans Leo 1564–1612 Ger. composer
Has·tings \'hā-stiŋz\ 1st Marquis of 1754–1826 Francis Raw·don Hastings \‚ròd-ᵊn-\ Brit. gen. & colonial administrator
— Thomas 1860–1929 Am. architect
— Warren 1732–1818 Eng. statesman & administrator in India
Ha·ta \'hä-(‚)tä\ Shun·ro·ku \'shùn-rō-‚kü\ 1879–1962 Jap. gen.
Haupt·mann \'haùp(t)-‚män\ Gerhart 1862–1946 Ger. writer
Haus·ho·fer \'haùs-‚hō-fər\ Karl 1860–1946 Ger. gen. & geographer
Hauss·mann \'ō-‚smän\ Baron Georges Eugène 1809–1891 Fr. administrator; improver of Paris
Have·lock \'hav-‚läk, -lək\ Sir Henry 1795–1857 Brit. gen.
Hawke \'hòk\ 1st Baron 1705–1781 Edward Hawke Eng. admiral
Haw·kins \'hò-kənz\ Sir Anthony Hope 1863–1933 pseud. Anthony Hope Eng. nov. & dram.
— or **Hawkyns** Sir John 1532–1595 Eng. admiral
Ha·worth \'härth, 'hò₀-rth\ Sir (Walter) Norman 1883–1950 Eng. chem.
Haw·thorne \'hò-‚thò(ə)rn\ Nathaniel 1804–1864 Am. author
Hay \'hā\ John Milton 1838–1905 Am. statesman
Hay·dn \'hīd-ᵊn\ (Franz) Joseph 1732–1809 Austrian composer
Hayes \'hāz\ Carlton Joseph Huntley 1882–1964 Am. hist. & diplomat
— Helen 1900– Helen Hayes Brown, wife of Charles MacArthur Am. actress
— Isaac Israel 1832–1881 Am. arctic explorer
— Patrick Joseph 1867–1938 Am. cardinal
— Roland 1887– Am. tenor
— Rutherford Birchard 1822–1893 19th pres. of the U.S. (1877–81)
Haynes \'hānz\ Elwood 1857–1925 Am. inventor
Hays \'hāz\ Will Harrison 1879–1954 Am. lawyer & polit.
Haz·ard \'haz-ərd\ Caroline 1856–1945 Am. educ.; pres. Wellesley College (1899–1910)
Ha·zard \ä-'zär\ Paul Gustave Marie Camille 1878–1944 Fr. literary hist.
Haz·litt \'haz-lət\ William 1778–1830 Eng. essayist
Hea·ly \'hē-lē\ Timothy Michael 1855–1931 Irish nationalist statesman
Hearn \'hərn\ Laf·ca·dio \laf-'kad-ē-‚ō, -'käd-\ 1850–1904 Yakumo Koizumi Jap. (Greek-born) writer of Irish-Greek descent
Hearst \'hərst\ William Randolph 1863–1951 Am. newspaper publisher
Heav·i·side \'hev-ē-‚sīd\ Oliver 1850–1925 Eng. physicist & electrician
Heb·bel \'heb-əl\ Friedrich 1813–1863 Ger. dram.
He·ber \'hē-bər\ Reginald 1783–1826 Eng. prelate & hymn writer
Hé·bert \ā-'be(ə)r\ Jacques René 1755–1794 Fr. revolutionary journalist
He·din \hā-'dēn\ Sven Anders 1865–1952 Swed. explorer

ə abut; ᵊ kitten; ər further; a back; ā bake; ä cot, cart; aù out; ch chin; e less; ē easy; g gift; i trip; ī life
j joke; ŋ sing; ō flow; ò flaw; òi coin; th thin; t̲h̲ this; ü loot; ù foot; y yet; yü few; yù furious; zh vision
ᵊ F table; á F bac; ḱ G ich, Buch; ⁿ F vin; œ F bœuf; œ̄ F feu; ս G füllen; ᴈ F rue; ʸ F digne \dēnʸ\, nuit \nwʸē\

He·gel \'hā-gəl\ Georg Wilhelm Friedrich 1770–1831 Ger. philos.
Hei·deg·ger \'hīd-i-gər, 'hī-,deg-ər\ Martin 1889– Ger. philos.
Hei·den·stam, von \'hād-ᵊn-,stam, -,stäm\ Verner 1859–1940 Swed. writer
Hei·fetz \'hī-fəts\ Ja·scha \'yäsh-ə\ 1901– Am. (Russ.-born) violinist
Hei·ne \'hī-nə\ Heinrich 1797–1856 Ger. poet & critic
Hei·sen·berg \'hīz-ᵊn-,bərg, -,be(ə)rk\ Werner 1901– Ger. physicist
Hei·ser \'hī-zər\ Victor George 1873– Am. public-health physician & writer
He·li·o·gab·a·lus \,hē-lē-ō-'gab-ə-ləs\ 204–222 Varius Avitus Bassianus Rom. emp. (218–222)
Hell·man \'hel-mən\ Lillian 1905– Am. dram.
Helm·holtz, von \'helm-,hōlts\ Hermann Ludwig Ferdinand 1821–1894 Ger. physicist, anatomist, & physiol.
Hé·lo·ïse \'ā-lō-,wēz\ 1101?–1164 wife of Abelard Fr. abbess
Hel·vé·tius \hel-'vā-sh(ē-)əs, -'vē-; ,(h)el-,vās-'yüs\ Claude Adrien 1715–1771 Fr. philos.
He·mans \'hem-ənz, 'hē-mənz\ Felicia Dorothea 1793–1835 née Browne Eng. poet
Hem·ing or Hem·minge \'hem-iŋ\ John 1556?–1630 Eng. actor
Hem·ing·way \'hem-iŋ-,wā\ Ernest Miller 1899–1961 Am. story-writer & journalist
Hé·mon \'ā-mōⁿ\ Louis 1880–1913 Fr. nov.
Hench \'hench\ Philip Showalter 1896–1965 Am. physician
Hen·der·son \'hen-dər-sən\ Arthur 1863–1935 Brit. labor leader & statesman
— Leon 1895– Am. econ. & administrator
— Sir Nev·ile \-'nev-əl\ Meyrick 1882–1942 Brit. diplomat
Hen·dricks \'hen-driks\ Thomas Andrews 1819–1885 Am. polit.; vice-pres. of the U.S. (1885)
Hen·gist \'heŋ-gəst, -,gist\ and Hor·sa \'hȯr-sə\ d 488 and 455 A.D. resp. bros. Jute invaders of Britain (ab 449)
Hen·ley \'hen-lē\ William Ernest 1849–1903 Eng. editor & author
Hen·ne·pin \'hen-ə-pən, en-'pan\ Louis 1640?–1701 Belg. friar & explorer in Am.
Hen·ry \'hen-rē\ name of 8 kings of Eng.: I 1068–1135 (reigned 1100–35); II 1133–1189 (reigned 1154–89); III 1207–1272 (reigned 1216–72); IV 1367–1413 (reigned 1399–1413); V 1387–1422 (reigned 1413–22); VI 1421–1471 (reigned 1422–61 & 1470–71); VII 1457–1509 (reigned 1485–1509); VIII 1491–1547 (reigned 1509–47)
— name of 4 kings of France: I 1008–1060 (reigned 1031–60); II 1519–1559 (reigned 1547–59); III 1551–1589 (reigned 1574–89); IV of Navarre 1553–1610 (reigned 1589–1610)
— 1394–1460 the Navigator Port. prince; promoter of navigation
— Joseph 1797–1878 Am. physicist
— O. see PORTER
— Patrick 1736–1799 Am. statesman & orator
Hens·lowe \'henz-(,)lō\ Philip d 1616 Eng. theater manager & diarist
Hep·burn \'hep-(,)bərn\ Katharine 1909– Am. actress
Hep·ple·white \'hep-əl-,(h)wīt\ George d 1786 Eng. cabinetmaker
Her·a·cli·tus \,her-ə-'klīt-əs\ 6th–5th cent. B.C. Greek philos.
He·ra·cli·us \,her-ə-'klī-əs, hi-'rak-lē-\ 575?–641 Byzantine emp. (610–641)
Her·bart \'he(ə)r-,bärt\ Johann Friedrich 1776–1841 Ger. philos. & educ.
Her·bert \'hər-bərt\ George 1593–1633 Eng. divine & poet
— Victor 1859–1924 Am. (Irish-born) composer & conductor
— William 1580–1630 3d Earl of Pembroke Eng. statesman & poet
Herblock see Herbert Lawrence BLOCK
Her·der, von \'herd-ər\ Johann Gottfried 1744–1803 Ger. philos. & writer
He·re·dia, de \,er-ā-'dyä, (h)ā-'rād-ē-ə\ José María 1842–1905 Fr. (Cuban-born) poet
Her·ford \'hər-fərd\ Oliver 1863–1935 Eng. writer & illustrator
Her·ges·hei·mer \'hər-gəs-,hī-mər, -gə-,shī-\ Joseph 1880–1954 Am. nov.
He·ring \'her-iŋ, 'hā-riŋ\ Ewald 1834–1918 Ger. physiol. & psychol.
Her·ki·mer \'hər-kə-mər\ Nicholas 1728–1777 Am. Revolutionary gen.
Hern·don \'hərn-dən\ William Henry 1818–1891 Am. lawyer
He·ro \'hē-(,)rō, 'hi(ə)r-(,)ō\ or He·ron \'hē-,rän\ 3d cent. A.D. Greek scientist
Her·od \'her-əd\ 73?–4 B.C. the Great Rom. king of Judea (37–4)
— An·ti·pas \'ant-ə-,pas, -pəs\ d after A.D. 40 son of prec. Rom. tetrarch of Galilee (4 B.C.–A.D. 40)
He·rod·o·tus \hi-'räd-ə-təs\ 5th cent. B.C. Greek hist.
Her·re·ra, de \(h)ə-'rer-ə\ Francisco 1576–1656 el Viejo Span painter
Her·rick \'her-ik\ Myron Timothy 1854–1929 Am. diplomat
— Robert 1591–1674 Eng. poet
— Robert 1868–1938 Am. nov.
Her·riot \,er-ē-'ō\ Édouard 1872–1957 Fr. statesman
Her·schel \'hər-shəl\ Sir John Frederick William 1792–1871 & his father Sir William 1738–1822 Eng. astronomers
Her·sey \'hər-sē, -zē\ John Richard 1914– Am. nov. & journalist
Her·ter \'hərt-ər\ Christian Archibald 1895–1966 Am. diplomat; secy. of state (1959–61)
Her·ty \'hərt-ē\ Charles Holmes 1867–1938 Am. chem.
Hertz \'he(ə)rts, 'hərts\ Gustav 1887– Ger. physicist
— Heinrich Rudolf 1857–1894 Ger. physicist
Her·tzog \'hərt-,sȯg, -,säg\ Enrique 1897?– pres. of Bolivia (1947–49)
— James Barry Munnik 1866–1942 S. African gen. & statesman
Herzl \'hert-səl\ Theodor 1860–1904 Austrian (Hung.-born) Zionist
He·si·od \'hē-sē-əd, 'hes-ē-\ 8th cent. B.C. Greek poet
Hess \'hes\ Dame Myra 1890–1965 Eng. pianist
— Victor Franz 1883–1964 Austrian physicist
— (Walther Richard) Rudolf 1894– Ger. Nazi polit.
— Walter Rudolf 1881– Swiss physiol.
Hes·se \'hes-ə\ Hermann 1877–1962 Ger. author
He·ve·sy, de \'hev-ə-shē\ George 1885–1966 Hung. chem.
Hey·drich \'hī-drik, -driḵ\ Reinhard 1904–1942 the Hangman

Ger. Nazi administrator
Hey·mans \'hā-,mänz, ā-'mäⁿs\ Corneille 1892–1968 Belg. physiol.
Hey·rov·sky \'hā-raf-skē, -rav-\Jaroslav\'yär-ȯ-,släf\1890–1967 Czech chem.
Hey·se, von \'hī-zə\ Paul 1830–1914 Ger. nov., dram., & poet
Hey·ward \'hā-wərd\Du·Bose\d(y)ü-'bōz\1885–1940 Am. author
Hey·wood \'hā-,wu̇d\ John 1497?–?1580 Eng. author
— Thomas 1574?–1641 Eng. dram.
Hich·ens \'hich-ənz\ Robert Smythe 1864–1950 Eng. nov.
Hick·ok \'hik-,äk\ James Butler 1837–1876 Wild Bill Am. scout & U.S. marshal
Hi·ero I \'hī-ə-,rō\ or Hi·er·on \-,rän\ d 466 B.C. tyrant of Syracuse (478–466)
Hieronymus Saint Eusebius see JEROME
Hig·gin·son \'hig-ən-sən\ Thomas Wentworth Storrow 1823–1911 Am. clergyman & writer
High·et \'hī-ət\ Gilbert 1906– Am. (Scot.-born) author, critic, & educ.
Hildebrand see Pope GREGORY VII
Hill \'hil\ Ambrose Powell 1825–1865 Am. Confed. gen.
— Archibald Vivian 1886– Eng. physiol.
— James Jerome 1838–1916 Am. financier & railway promoter
— Sir Rowland 1795–1879 Eng. postal reformer
Hil·la·ry \'hil-ə-rē\ Sir Edmund 1919– N.Z. apiarist & mountaineer
Hil·lel \'hil-əl, -,el\ fl 30 B.C.–A.D. 9 Jewish teacher; first to formulate definite hermeneutic principles
Hill·man \'hil-mən\ Sidney 1887–1946 Am. labor leader
Hil·precht \'hil-,prekt\ Hermann Volrath 1859–1925 Am. (Ger.-born) Assyriologist
Hil·ton \'hilt-ᵊn\ James 1900–1954 Eng. nov.
Himm·ler \'him-lər\ Heinrich 1900–1945 Ger. Nazi polit.
Hin·de·mith \'hin-də-,mit(h), -mət(h)\ Paul 1895–1963 Am. (Ger.-born) violist & composer
Hin·den·burg, von \'hin-dən-,bərg, -,bu̇(ə)rg\ Paul 1847–1934 Paul Ludwig Hans Anton von Beneckendorff und von Hindenburg Ger. field marshal; pres. of Germany (1925–34)
Hin·shel·wood \'hin-chəl-,wu̇d\ Sir Cyril Norman 1897–1967 Brit. chem.
Hip·par·chus \hip-'är-kəs\ 6th cent. B.C. tyrant of Athens (527–514 B.C.)
— fl 130 B.C. Greek astron.
Hip·pi·as \'hip-ē-əs\ 6th cent. B.C. bro. of Hipparchus ruled Athens with his brother
Hip·poc·ra·tes \hip-'äk-rə-,tēz\ 460?–?377 B.C. father of medicine Greek physician
Hi·ra·nu·ma \,hir-ə-'nü-mə\ Baron Kiichiro 1867–1952 Jap. statesman
Hi·ro·hi·to \,hir-ō-'hē-(,)tō\ 1901– emp. of Japan (1926–)
Hi·ro·shi·ge \,hir-ə-'shē-gē\ Ando 1797–1858 Jap. painter
Hitch·cock \'hich-,käk\ Edward 1793–1864 Am. geologist
— Ethan Allen 1835–1909 Am. diplomat & administrator
Hit·ler \'hit-lər\ Adolf 1889–1945 Ger. chancellor & führer
Hit·ti \'hit-ē\ Philip Khuri 1886– Am. (Lebanese-born) orientalist
Hit·torf \'hi-,tȯrf\ Johann Wilhelm 1824–1914 Ger. physicist
Hoare \'hō(ə)r, 'hȯ(ə)r\ Samuel John Gurney 1880–1959 Viscount Templewood Eng. statesman
Ho·bart \'hō-,bärt, -bərt\ Garret Augustus 1844–1899 Am. lawyer; vice-pres. of the U.S. (1897–99)
Hob·be·ma \'häb-i-mə\ Meindert 1638–1709 Du. painter
Hobbes \'häbz\ Thomas 1588–1679 Eng. philos.
Hob·son \'häb-sən\ Richmond Pearson 1870–1937 Am. naval officer
Hoc·cleve \'häk-,lēv\ Thomas 1370?–?1450 Eng. poet
Ho Chi Minh \,hō-,chē-'min, ,hō-,shē-\ 1890–1969 pres. of North Vietnam (from 1954)
Hock·ing \'häk-iŋ\ William Ernest 1873–1966 Am. philos.
Hoe \'hō\ Richard March 1812–1886 son of Robert Am. inventor
— Robert 1784–1833 Am. (Eng.-born) printing-press manuf.
Ho·fer \'hō-fər\ Andreas 1767–1810 Tyrolese patriot
Hof·fa \'häf-ə\ James Riddle 1913– Am. labor leader
Hoff·man \'häf-mən, 'hȯf-\ Mal·vi·na \mal-'vē-nə\ 1887–1966 Am. sculptor
Hoff·mann \'häf-mən, 'hȯf-, -,män\ August Heinrich 1798–1874 Ger. poet, philologist, & hist.
— Ernst Theodor Wilhelm 1776–1822 Ernst Theodor Amadeus Ger. composer, writer, & illustrator
Hof·mann \'häf-mən, 'hȯf-\ Hans 1880–1966 Am. (Ger.-born) painter
— Josef Casimir 1876–1957 Pol. pianist
Hof·mann, von \'häf-mən, 'hȯf-, -,män\ August Wilhelm 1818–1892 Ger. chem.
Hof·manns·thal, von \'häf-mənz-,täl, 'hȯf-\ Hugo 1874–1929 Austrian poet & dram.
Ho·garth \'hō-,gärth\ William 1697–1764 Eng. painter & engraver
Hog·ben \'hȯg-bən, 'häg-\ Lancelot Thomas 1895– Eng. scientist & writer
Hogg \'hȯg, 'häg\ James 1770–1835 Scot. poet
Hohenzollern Michael see MICHAEL
Ho·ku·sai \'hō-kə-,sī\ Katsushika 1760–1849 Jap. artist
Hol·bein \'hōl-,bīn, 'hȯl-\ Hans father 1465?–1524 & son 1497?–1543 Ger. painters
Hol·comb \'häl-kəm\ Thomas 1879–1965 Am. marine-corps gen.
Hol·in·shed \'häl-ənz-,hed, -ən-,shed\ or Hol·lings·head \-iŋz-,hed\ Raphael d ab 1580 Eng. chronicler
Hol·land \'häl-ənd\ John Philip 1840–1914 Irish-born inventor in Am.
Holman-Hunt William see Holman HUNT
Holmes \'hōmz, 'hōlmz\ John Haynes 1879–1964 Am. clergyman
— Oliver Wendell 1809–1894 Am. physician & author
— Oliver Wendell 1841–1935 son of prec. Am. jurist
Holt \'hōlt\ Harold Edward 1908–1967 Austral. polit.; prime min. (1966–67)
— Luther Emmett 1855–1924 Am. pediatrician
Hol·yoake \'hȯl-,yōk, 'hō-lē-,ōk\ Keith J. 1904– prime min. of N.Z. (from 1960)
Home \'hyüm\ Sir Alec Douglas- 1903– Brit. prime min. (1963–64)
— William Douglas- 1912– Brit. dram.
Ho·mer \'hō-mər\ fl 850? B.C.; traditional Greek epic poet

— Winslow 1836–1910 Am. painter

Ho·neg·ger \\,än-ē-'ge(ə)r, ,ȯn-; 'hän-ē-gər\ Arthur 1892–1955 Fr. composer

Ho·no·ri·us \hə-'nȯr-ē-əs, -'nȯr-\ Flavius 384–423 Rom. emp. of the West (395–423)

Hood \'hu̇d\ John Bell 1831–1879 Am. Confed. gen.

— Samuel 1st Viscount 1724–1816 Brit. admiral

— Thomas 1799–1845 Eng. poet

Hooke \'hu̇k\ Robert 1635–1703 Eng. experimental philos.

Hook·er \'hu̇k-ər\ Joseph 1814–1879 Am. army officer

— Sir Joseph Dalton 1817–1911 Eng. botanist

— Richard 1554–1600 Eng. theol.

— Thomas 1586?–1647 Eng. Puritan clergyman; a founder of Connecticut

Hoo·ton \'hu̇t-ᵊn\ Earnest Albert 1887–1954 Am. anthropol.

Hoo·ver \'hü-vər\ Herbert Clark 1874–1964 31st pres. of the U.S. (1929–33)

— John Edgar 1895– Am. criminologist; F.B.I. director

Hope \'hōp\ Anthony see Sir Anthony Hope HAWKINS

— Victor Alexander John 1887–1951 son of prec. 8th Earl of *Hope·toun* \'hōp-tən, -,tau̇n\ & 2d Marquis of *Lin·lith·gow* \lin-'lith-(,)gō\ Brit. soldier; viceroy of India (1936–43)

Hop·kins \'häp-kənz\ Sir Frederick Gow·land \'gau̇-lənd\ 1861–1947 Eng. biochem.

— Gerard Manley 1844–1889 Eng. poet

— Harry Lloyd 1890–1946 Am. polit. & administrator

— Johns \'jänz\ 1795–1873 Am. financier

— Mark 1802–1887 Am. educ.

Hop·kin·son \'häp-kən-sən\ Francis 1737–1791 Am. lawyer & satirist

Hop·pe \'häp-ē\ William Frederick 1887–1959 Am. billiard player

Hop·per \'häp-ər\ Edward 1882–1967 Am. artist

— (William) DeWolf 1858–1935 Am. actor

Hop·wood \'häp-,wu̇d\ (James) Avery 1882–1928 Am. dram.

Hor·ace \'hȯr-əs, 'här-\ 65–8 B.C. *Quintus Horatius Flaccus* Rom. poet & satirist

Hore-Be·li·sha \,hō(ə)r-bə-'lē-shə, ,hȯ(ə)r-, -'lish-ə\ Leslie 1893–1957 Eng. polit.

Hor·na·day \'hȯr-nə-,dā\ William Temple 1854–1937 Am. zool.

Hor·ney \'hȯr-,nī\ Karen 1885–1952 née *Danielson* Am. (Ger.-born) psychoanalyst & author

Ho·ro·witz \'hȯr-ə-,wits, 'här-\ Vla·di·mir \'vlad-ə-,mi(ə)r, vlə-'dē-,mi(ə)r\ 1904– Am. (Russ.-born) pianist

Horsa see HENGIST

Hortense de Beauharnais see BEAUHARNAIS

Hor·thy \'hȯrt-ē\ Miklós von Nagybánya 1868–1957 Hung. admiral; regent of Hungary (1920–44)

Hos·kins \'häs-kənz\ Roy Graham 1880–1964 Am. physiol.

Hou·di·ni \hü-'dē-nē\ Harry 1874–1926 *Ehrich Weiss* Am. magician

Hou·don \'hü-,dän, ü-dōⁿ\ Jean Antoine 1741–1828 Fr. sculptor

Hou·dry \'hü-drē\ Eugene Jules 1892–1962 Am. (Fr.-born) engineer

House \'hau̇s\ Edward Mandell 1858–1938 *Colonel House* Am. diplomat

Hous·man \'hau̇-smən\ Alfred Edward 1859–1936 Eng. classical scholar & poet

— Laurence 1865–1959 *bro. of prec.* Eng. writer & illustrator

Hous·say \ü-'sī\ Bernardo Alberto 1887– Argentine physiol

Hous·ton \'(h)yü-stən\ Samuel 1793–1863 *Sam* Am. gen.; pres. of the Republic of Texas (1836–38; 1841–44)

Hov·ey \'həv-ē\ Richard 1864–1900 Am. poet

How·ard \'hau̇(-ə)rd\ Catherine see CATHERINE

— Henry 1517?–1547 Earl of *Surrey* Eng. soldier & poet

— Sidney Coe 1891–1939 Am. dram.

Howe \'hau̇\ Ed 1853–1937 *Edgar Watson* Am. journalist

— Elias 1819–1867 Am. inventor

— Julia 1819–1910 née *Ward* Am. suffragist & reformer

— Mark Antony De Wolfe 1864–1960 Am. writer

— Earl 1726–1799 *Richard Howe* Eng. admiral of the fleet

— 5th Viscount 1729–1814 *William Howe* Eng. gen. in Am.

How·ells \'hau̇-əlz\ William Dean 1837–1920 Am. author

Hoyt \'hȯit\ Charles Hale 1860–1900 Am. dram.

Hr·dlič·ka \'hərd-lich-,kä\ Aleš \'äl-,esh\ 1869–1943 Am. (Bohemian-born) anthropol.

Hsü Shih-ch'ang \'shü-'shi(ə)r-'chäŋ\ 1858–1939 Chin. gen.; pres. of China (1918–22)

Hsüan-t'ung \shü-'än-'tùŋ\ 1906–1967 *Henry P'u-yi* \'pü-'(y)ē\ Chin. emp. (1908–12); last of Manchu dynasty; puppet emp. of Manchukuo (1934–45)

Hu Shih \'hü-'shi(ə)r, -'shē\ 1891–1962 Chin. philos., diplomat, & writer

Huás·car \'wäs-,kär\ 1495?–1533 Inca prince

Hub·bard \'həb-ərd\ Elbert Green 1856–1915 Am. writer, editor, & printer

Hud·son \'həd-sən\ Henry *d* 1611 erroneously *Hen·drick* \'hen-drik\ Eng. navigator & explorer

— Manley Ottmer 1886–1960 Am. jurist

— William Henry 1841–1922 Eng. naturalist & writer

Huer·ta \'wert-ə, ü-'ert-\ Victoriano 1854–1916 Mex. gen.; provisional pres. of Mexico (1913–14)

Hug·gins \'həg-ənz\ Sir William 1824–1910 Eng. astron.

Hugh Ca·pet \'kā-pət, 'kap-ət, kə-'pā\ *Fr.* **Hugues Capet** 940?–996 king of France (987–996)

Hughes \'hyüz\ Charles Evans 1862–1948 Am. jurist; chief justice of the U.S. (1930–41)

— (James) Langston 1902–1967 Am. writer

— Rupert 1872–1956 Am. writer

— Thomas 1822–1896 Eng. jurist, reformer, & writer

— William Morris 1864–1952 Austral. statesman

Hu·go \'(h)yü-(,)gō\ Victor Marie 1802–1885 Fr. poet, nov., & dram.

Hui·zinga \'hī-ziŋ-ə\ Johan 1872–1945 Du. historian

Hu·la·gu \hü-'lä-(,)gü\ 1217–1265 *grandson of Genghis Khan* Mongol ruler

Hull \'həl\ Cordell 1871–1955 Am. statesman; U.S. secy. of state (1933–44)

— Isaac 1773–1843 Am. naval officer

— William 1753–1825 Am. gen.

Hu·ma·yun \hü-'mä-,yün\ 1508–1556 emp. of Hindustan (1530–56)

Hum·bert I \'həm-bərt\ *Ital.* **Um·ber·to** \üm-'be(ə)r-(,)tō\ 1844–1900 king of Italy (1878–1900)

— II 1904– Prince of *Piedmont;* Count of *Sarre;* king of Italy (1946)

Hum·boldt, von \'həm-,bōlt, 'hùm-\ Baron (Friedrich Heinrich) Alexander 1769–1859 Ger. naturalist, traveler, & statesman

— Baron Wilhelm 1767–1835 *bro. of prec.* Ger. philologist & diplomat

Hume \'hyüm\ David 1711–1776 Scot. philos. & hist.

Hum·per·dinck \'hùm-pər-,diŋk, 'həm-\ Engelbert 1854–1921 Ger. composer

Hum·phrey \'həm(p)-frē\ 1391–1447 *son of Henry IV* Duke of *Gloucester (the Good Duke)* & Earl of *Pembroke* Eng. statesman & book collector

— Hubert Horatio 1911– Am. polit.; vice-pres. of the U.S. (1965–69)

Hun·e·ker \'hən-i-kər\ James Gibbons 1860–1921 Am. musician & critic

Hung-wu \'hùŋ-'wü\ 1328–1398 *Chu Yüan-chang* \'jü-yü-'än-'jäŋ\ Chin. emp. (1368–98); founder of Ming dynasty

Hunt \'hənt\ (James Henry) Leigh 1784–1859 Eng. writer

— (William) Holman 1827–1910 Eng. painter

Hun·ter \'hənt-ər\ John 1728–1793 Brit. anatomist & surgeon

Hun·ting·ton \'hənt-iŋ-tən\ Collis Potter 1821–1900 Am. pioneer railroad builder

— Ellsworth 1876–1947 Am. geographer & explorer

— Henry E. 1850–1927 Am. bibliophile

— Samuel 1731–1796 Am. Revolutionary polit.

Hun·tzi·ger \,(h)ənt-sē-'zhe(ə)r\ Charles Léon Clément 1880–1941 Fr. gen.

Hu·nya·di *or* **Hu·nya·dy** \'hùn-,yäd-ē, -,yȯd-\ Já·nos \'yän-(,)ōsh\ 1387?–1456 Hung. soldier & hero

Hur·ley \'hər-lē\ Patrick Jay 1883–1963 Am. lawyer & diplomat

Hurst \'hərst\ Sir Cecil James Barrington 1870–1963 Eng. jurist

— Fannie 1889–1968 Am. writer

Hu·sein ibn-Ali \hü-'sā-,nib-ən-ə-'lē\ 1856–1931 first king of the Hejaz (1916–24)

Huss *or* **Hus** \'həs, 'hùs\ John *or* Jan *ab* 1374–1415 *Johannes Hus von Husinetz* Bohemian religious reformer

Hus·sein I \hü-'sān\ 1935– king of Jordan (1953–)

Hu·szár \'hùs-,är\ Károly 1882– Hung. journalist & polit.

Hutch·ins \'həch-ənz\ Robert Maynard 1899– Am. educ.

Hutch·in·son \'həch-ə(n)-sən\ Anne 1591–1643 née *Marbury* religious liberal in Am.

— Thomas 1711–1780 Am. colonial administrator

Hut·ten, von \'hùt-ᵊn\ Ulrich 1488–1523 Ger. humanist & supporter of Luther

Hux·ley \'hək-slē\ Al·dous \'ȯl-dəs\ Leonard 1894–1963 *bro. of J.S.* Eng. nov. & critic

— Andrew Fielding 1917– Am. educator

— Sir Julian Sorell 1887– *grandson of T.H.* Eng. biologist

— Thomas Henry 1825–1895 Eng. biologist

Huy·gens *or* **Huy·ghens** \'hī-gənz, 'hȯi-\ Christian 1629–1695 Du. math., physicist, & astron.

Huys·mans \wē-'smä's\ Camille 1871–1968 Belg. polit.

— Joris Karl 1848–1907 *orig. Charles Marie Georges* Fr. nov.

Hy·att \'hī-ət\ Alpheus 1838–1902 Am. naturalist

Hyde \'hīd\ Douglas 1860–1949 Irish author; pres. of Republic of Ireland (1938–45)

— Edward 1609–1674 1st Earl of *Clarendon* Eng. statesman & hist.

Hyder Ali see HAIDAR ALI

Hy·mans \'hī-mənz\ Paul 1865–1941 Belg. statesman

Hy·pse·lan·tes \,ēp-sə-'län-dēs\ *var of* YPSILANTI

Ibáñez Vicente Blasco- see BLASCO-IBÁÑEZ

Iber·ville, d' \'dē-bər-,vil, -,vēl; 'dī-bər-,vil\ Sieur 1661–1706 *Pierre Lemoyne* Fr.-Canad. explorer; founder of Louisiana

ibn-Khal·dun \,ib-ən-,kal-'dün\ 1332–1406 Arab hist.

ibn-Rushd see AVERROËS

ibn-Saud \,ib-ən-sä-'üd, -'saùd\ Abdul-Aziz 1880–1953 king of Saudi Arabia (1932–53)

ibn-Zuhr \,ib-ən-'zü(ə)r\ *or* **ibn-Zohr** \-'zō(ə)r, -'zȯ(ə)r\ *var of* AVENZOAR

Ibra·him Pa·sha \i-,brä-'him-pə-'shä\ 1789–1848 Egyptian gen. & viceroy

Ib·sen \'ib-sən, 'ip-\ Henrik 1828–1906 Norw. poet & dram.

Ick·es \'ik-əs\ Harold LeClair 1874–1952 Am. lawyer & administrator

Ic·ti·nus \ik-'tī-nəs\ 5th cent. B.C. Greek architect

Ig·na·tius \ig-'nā-sh(ē-)əs\ Saint 1st–2d cent. A.D. *Theophorus* bishop of Antioch & church father

— of **Loyola** Saint see LOYOLA

Ike·da \ē-'käd-ə, -'ked-\ Hayato 1899–1965 Jap. polit.; premier (1960–64)

Ikh·na·ton \ik-'nät-ᵊn\ *Amen·ho·tep IV* \,äm-ən-'hō-,tep, ,am-\ king of Egypt (*ab* 1375–1358 B.C.); religious reformer

Im·mel·mann \'im-əl-,män, -mən\ Max 1890–1916 Ger. aviator

In·dy, d' \'dan-dē; dan-'dē, daⁿ-\ Vincent 1851–1931 Fr. composer

Inés de Castro see CASTRO

Inge \'iŋ\ William Ralph 1860–1954 Eng. prelate & author; dean of St. Paul's (1911–34)

In·ger·soll \'iŋ-gər-,sȯl, -səl\ Robert Green 1833–1899 Am. lawyer & agnostic

In·gram \'iŋ-grəm\ Arthur Foley Winnington 1858–1946 Eng. prelate; bishop of London (1901–39)

In·gres \'aⁿgrᵊ\ Jean Auguste Dominique 1780–1867 Fr. painter

In·ness \'in-əs\ George, father 1825–1894 & son 1854–1926 Am. painters

In·no·cent \'in-ə-sənt\ name of 13 popes: esp. **II** *d* 1143 (pope 1130–43); **III** 1161–1216 (pope 1198–1216); **IV** *d* 1254 (pope 1243–54); **XI** 1611–1689 (pope 1676–89)

Inö·nü \,in-ə-'n(y)ü\ Ismet \is-'met\ 1884– Turk. states-

ə abut; ᵊ kitten; ər further; a back; ā bake; ä cot, cart; aù out; ch chin; e less; ē easy; g gift; i trip; ī life
j joke; ŋ sing; ō flow; ȯ flaw; ȯi coin; th thin; t͟h this; ü loot; ù foot; y yet; yü few; yù furious; zh vision
ᵊ F table; á F bac; ķ G ich, Buch; ⁿ F vin; œ F bœuf; ō̄ F feu; ɶ G füllen; ɶ̄ F rue; ᵞ F digne \dēnᵞ\, nuit \nwᵞē\

man; pres. of Turkey (1938–50); premier (1961–65)

In·sull \'in(t)-səl\ Samuel 1859–1938 Am. (Eng.-born) utilities executive

Io·nes·co \,ē-ə-'nes-(,)kō\ Eugene 1912–   Fr. dram.

Ipa·tieff or **Ipa·tiev** \i-'pät-ē-,ef\ Vladimir Nikolaevich 1867–1952 Russ.-born chem. in Am.

Ire·dell \'ī(ə)r-,del\ James 1751–1799 Am. jurist

Ire·ton \'ī(ə)rt-ºn\ Henry 1611–1651 Eng. Parliamentary commander & regicide

Iri·go·yen \,ir-i-'gō-,yen\ Hi·pó·li·to \ē-'pō-lē-,tō\ 1850–1933 pres. of Argentina (1916–22; 1928–30)

Iron·side \'ī-(ə)rn-,sīd\ William Edmund 1880–1959 1st Baron of *Archangel and Ironside* Brit. field marshal

Ir·ving \'ər-viŋ\ Sir Henry 1838–1905 orig. *John Henry Brodribb* Eng. actor

— Washington 1783–1859 Am. essayist, nov., & hist.

Ir·win \'ər-wən\ Wallace 1875–1959 Am. journalist & humorist

— William Henry 1873–1948 *Will* Am. journalist & writer

Isaacs \'ī-ziks, -zəks\ Sir Isaac Alfred 1855–1948 Austral. jurist & statesman; gov. of Australia (1931–36)

— Rufus Daniel see Marquis of READING

Is·a·bel·la I \,iz-ə-'bel-ə\ 1451–1504 *wife of Ferdinand II of Aragon* queen of Castile (1474–1504); aided Columbus

Ish·er·wood \'ish-ər-,wùd\ Christopher William Bradshaw-1904–   Am. (Brit.-born) writer

Ishii \'ē-shē-,ē, 'ish-ē-\ Viscount Kikujiro 1866–1945 Jap. diplomat

Is·i·dore of Seville \'iz-ə-,dō(ə)r, -,dò(ə)r\ Saint *ab* 570–636 *Isidorus Hispalensis* Span. prelate & scholar

Iskender Bey see SCANDERBEG

Is·ma·il Pa·sha \is-'mä-,ēl-pə-'shä\ 1830–1895 *Ismail I* khedive of Egypt (1863–79)

Isoc·ra·tes \ī-'säk-rə-,tēz\ 436–338 B.C. Athenian orator

Ito \'ē-(,)tō\ Marquis Hirobumi 1841–1909 Jap. statesman

— Yuko or Sukenori 1843–1914 Jap. admiral

Itur·bi \i-'tùr-bē\ José 1895–   Span.-born pianist & conductor in Am.

Itur·bi·de, de \,ē-,tùr-'bē-(,)thā, -'vē-\ Agustín 1783–1824 Mex. soldier; emp. of Mex. (1822–23)

Ivan III \ē-'vän, 'ī-vən\ **Vasilievich** 1440–1505 *Ivan the Great* grand duke of Russia (1462–1505)

— **IV Vasilievich** 1530–1584 *Ivan the Terrible* ruler of Russia (1533–84)

Ives \'īvz\ Charles Edward 1874–1954 Am. composer

— James Merritt 1824–1895 Am. lithographer

Iye·ya·su or **Ie·ya·su** \,ē-ə-'yäs-(,)ü, ,ē-yä-'yäs-\ 1542–1616 Jap. gen.; founder (1603) of Tokugawa shogunate

Iz·ard \'iz-ərd\ Ralph 1742–1804 Am. Revolutionary leader

Jabir var of GEBER

Jack·son \'jak-sən\ Andrew 1767–1845 Am. gen.; 7th pres. of the U. S. (1829–37)

— Helen Maria Hunt 1830–1885 née *Fiske* Am. nov.

— Robert Hough·wout \'haù-ət\ 1892–1954 Am. jurist

— Thomas Jonathan 1824–1863 *Stone·wall* \'stōn-,wòl\ *Jackson* Am. Confed. gen.

Jac·quard \zha-'kär, 'jak-,ärd\ Joseph Marie 1752–1834 Fr. inventor

Jacques I see Jean Jacques DESSALINES

Jag·a·tai \'jag-ə-,tī\ d 1242 *2d son of Genghis Khan* Mongol ruler

Ja·han·gir \jə-'hän-,gi(ə)r\ 1569–1627 emp. of Hindustan (1605–27)

Ja·lal-ud-din Ru·mi \jə-,läl-ə-,dēn-'rü-mē\ 1207–1273 Pers. poet

James \'jāmz\ name of 6 kings of Scot. & 2 kings of Gt. Britain: **I** 1566–1625 (reigned 1603–25); **II** 1633–1701 (reigned 1685–88)

— Henry 1811–1882 Am. philos.

— Henry 1843–1916 *son of prec.* Brit. writer

— Jesse 1847–1882 Am. outlaw

— William 1842–1910 *bro. of Henry.* Am. psychol. & philos.

— **Edward Stuart** 1688–1766 *the Old Pretender* Eng. prince

Jame·son \'jām(p)-sən, 'jā-mə-sən\ Sir Leander Starr 1853–1917 *Doctor Jameson* Scot. physician & administrator in So. Africa

Ja·mi \'jäm-ē\ 1414–1492 Pers. poet & mystic

Ja·ná·ček \'yän-ə-,chek\ Leoš 1854–1928 Czech. composer

Jan·sen \'jan(t)-sən, 'yän(t)-\ Cor·ne·lis \kòr-'nā-ləs\ 1585–1638 *Cornelius Jansenius* Du. R.C. theol.

Jaques–Dal·croze \'zhäk-,dal-'krōz\ Émile 1865–1950 Swiss composer & creator of eurythmics

Ja·rir \jə-'ri(ə)r\ d 729? Arab poet

Jas·pers \ yäs-pərs\ Karl 1883–1969 Ger. philos.

Jauregg Julius Wagner von see WAGNER VON JAUREGG

Jau·rès \zhō-'res\ Jean Léon 1859–1914 Fr. socialist

Jay \'jā\ John 1745–1829 Am. jurist & statesman; 1st chief justice of the U. S. (1789–95)

Jeanne d'Arc see JOAN OF ARC

Jeans \'jēnz\ Sir James Hopwood 1877–1946 Eng. physicist, astron., & author

Jebb \'jeb\ Sir Richard Claverhouse 1841–1905 Scot. Greek scholar

Jef·fers \'jef-ərz\ (John) Robinson 1887–1962 Am. poet

Jef·fer·son \'jef-ər-sən\ Joseph 1829–1905 Am. actor

— Thomas 1743–1826 Am. statesman; 3d pres. of the U. S. (1801–09)

Jef·frey \'jef-rē\ Lord Francis 1773–1850 Scot. critic & jurist

Jef·freys \'jef-rēz\ George 1648–1689 1st Baron *Jeffreys of Wem* Eng. jurist

Jel·li·coe \'jel-i-,kō\ 1st Earl 1859–1935 *John Rushworth Jellicoe* Brit. admiral of the fleet

Jenghiz Khan var of GENGHIS KHAN

Jen·ner \'jen-ər\ Edward 1749–1823 Eng. physician

— Sir William 1815–1898 Eng. physician

Jen·sen \'yen(t)-sən, 'jen(t)-\ Johannes Vilhelm 1873–1950 Dan. poet & nov.

Jep·son \'jep-sən\ Helen 1907–   Am. singer

Je·ri·tza \'yer-ət-sə\ Maria 1887–   Am. (Austrian-born) soprano

Je·rome \jə-'rōm, *chiefly Brit* 'jer-əm\ Saint 340?–420 *Eusebius Hieronymus* Latin church father

Jer·vis \'jär-vəs, 'jər-\ John 1735–1823 Earl of *St. Vincent* Brit. admiral

Jes·per·sen \'yes-pər-sən\ (Jens) Otto (Harry) 1860–1943 Dan. philologist

Je·sus \'jē-zəs, -zəz\ or **Jesus Christ** \'krīst\ or **Christ Jesus** 4–8? B.C.–A.D.? 29 *Jesus of Nazareth; the Son of Mary* source of the Christian religion & Savior in the Christian faith

Jev·ons \'jev-ənz\ William Stanley 1835–1882 Eng. econ. & logician

Jew·ett \'jü-ət\ Sarah Orne 1849–1909 Am. writer

Ji·mé·nez \hē-'mā-(,)nāth, -(,)nās\ Juan Ramón 1881–1958 Span. poet

— **de Cis·ne·ros** \the-'snā-(,)rōs, sē-'snā-\ Francisco 1436–1517 Span. prelate & statesman

Jin·nah \'jin-(,)ä, 'jin-ə\ Mohammed Ali 1876–1948 Muslim lawyer; 1st gov. gen. of dominion of Pakistan (1947–48)

Jo·achim \'yō-ə-,kim, yō-'äk-(,)im\ Joseph 1831–1907 Hung. violinist

Joan of Arc \,jō-nə-'värk, ,jō-ə-nə-, jō,-an-ə-\ Fr. **Jeanne d'Arc** \zhän-'därk\ Saint 1412–1431 *the Maid of Orleans* Fr. national heroine

Jodl \'yōd-ºl\ Alfred 1892?–1946 Ger. gen.

Jof·fre \zhòfrª\ Joseph Jacques Césaire 1852–1931 Fr. field marshal; marshal of France (1917)

John \'jän\ name of 21 popes: esp. **XXIII** (*Angelo Giuseppe Roncalli*) 1881–1963 (pope 1958–63)

John 1167?–1216 *John Lack·land* \'lak-,land\ king of England (1199–1216)

— **I** 1357–1433 *the Great* king of Portugal (1385–1433)

— Augustus Edwin 1878–1961 Brit. painter & etcher

— **of Austria** 1547–1578 Don *John* Span. soldier

— **of Gaunt** \'gónt, 'gänt\ 1340–1399 Duke of *Lancaster; son of Edward III of Eng.*

— **of Lancaster** see Duke of BEDFORD

— **of Leiden** 1509–1536 Du. Anabaptist fanatic

— **of Salisbury** d 1180 Eng. ecclesiastic

— **III So·bies·ki** \sō-'byes-kē, ,sō-bē-'es-\ 1624–1697 king of Poland (1674–96)

John·son \'jän(t)-sən\ Andrew 1808–1875 17th pres. of the U. S. (1865–69)

— Gerald White 1890–   Am. author

— James Weldon 1871–1938 Am. author

— Lyn·don \'lin-dən\ Baines \'bānz\ 1908–   Am. polit.; 36th pres. of the U. S. (1963–69)

— Richard Mentor 1780–1850 Am. vice-pres. of the U. S. (1837–41)

— Samuel 1709–1784 *Dr. Johnson* Eng. lexicographer & author

— Sir William 1715–1774 Brit. administrator in Am.

John·ston \'jän(t)-stən, -sən\ Albert Sidney 1803–1862 Am. Confed. gen.

— Joseph Eggleston 1807–1891 Am. Confed. gen.

— Mary 1870–1936 Am. nov.

Join·ville, de \zhwanⁿ-'vē(ə)l\ Jean 1224?–1317 Fr. chronicler

Jó·kai \'yō-,kòi\ Mau·rus \'mòr-əs\ or Mó·ricz \'mōr-əts, 'mór-\ 1825–1904 Hung. nov. & dram.

Jo·li·ot-Cu·rie \'zhō-lē-,ō-kyù-'rē, -'kyù(ə)r-(,)ē\ Frédéric 1900–1958 orig. *Joliot* Fr. physicist

— Irène 1897–1956 formerly *Irène Curie-Joliot, dau. of Marie & Pierre Curie & wife of prec.* Fr. physicist

Jo·mi·ni \,zhō-mə-'nē\ Baron Henri 1779–1869 Swiss-born soldier & military strategist

Jones \'jōnz\ Anson 1798–1858 pres. of the Republic of Texas (1844–46)

— Daniel 1881–1968 Eng. phonetician

— Henry Arthur 1851–1929 Eng. dram.

— Howard Mumford 1892–   Am. educ. & critic

— In·i·go \'in-i-,gō\ 1573–1652 Eng. architect

— Jesse Holman 1874–1956 Am. financier & administrator

— John Paul 1747–1792 orig. in full *John Paul* Am. (Scot.-born) naval officer

— Thomas Hudson 1892–1969 Am. sculptor

Jon·son \'jän(t)-sən\ Ben 1573?–1637 orig. *Benjamin* Eng. dram.; poet laureate (1619–37)

Jor·dan \'jòrd-ºn\ David Starr 1851–1931 Am. biologist & educ.

Jo·seph II \'jō-zəf *also* -səf\ 1741–1790 king of Germany (1764–90); Holy Rom. emp. (1765–90)

Josephine Empress see BEAUHARNAIS

Jo·se·phus \jō-'sē-fəs\ Flavius 37–?100 Jewish hist.

Jou·bert \zhü-'be(ə)r\ Joseph 1754–1824 Fr. essayist & moralist

— \yü-'\ Petrus Jacobus 1834–1900 *Piet* Boer gen. & statesman

Jou·haux \zhü-ō\ Léon 1879–1954 Fr. trade-union leader

Joule \'jül, 'jaù(ə)l\ James Prescott 1818–1889 Eng. physicist

Jour·dan \zhùr-'dänⁿ\ Comte Jean Baptiste 1762–1833 Fr. soldier; marshal of France (1804)

Jo·vi·an \'jō-vē-ən\ 331?–364 *Flavius Claudius Jovianus* Rom. emp. (363–364)

Jow·ett \'jaù-ət, 'jō-\ Benjamin 1817–1893 Eng. Greek scholar

Joyce \'jòis\ James 1882–1941 Irish writer

Juan Car·los \'wän-'kär-ləs, -,lōs\ 1938–   Span. king-designate

Juan Ma·nuel \'wän-man-'wel\ Don 1282–1349 Span. writer

Juá·rez \'wär-(,)äs\ Benito Pablo 1806–1872 Mex. lawyer; pres. of Mexico (1857–72)

Ju·das Mac·ca·bae·us \'jüd-ə-,smak-ə-'bē-əs\ d 160 B.C. Jewish patriot; with 4 bros. (the Mac·ca·bees \'mak-ə-(,)bēz\) revolted against Antiochus Epiphanes

Ju·gur·tha \jù-'gər-thə\ d 104 B.C. king of Numidia (113–104 B.C.)

Ju·lian \'jül-yən\ 331–363 *Flavius Claudius Julianus, the Apostate* Rom. emp. (361–363)

Ju·li·ana \,jü-lē-'an-ə\ 1909–   *dau. of Wilhelmina* queen of the Netherlands (1948–   )

Jung \'yùŋ\ Carl Gustav 1875–1961 Swiss psychol.

Junius \'jü-nyəs, -nē-əs\ Franciscus 1589–1677 Eng. (Ger.-born) philologist

Jun·kers \'yùŋ-kərz, -kərs\ Hugo 1859–1935 Ger. airplane designer & builder

Ju·not \zhü-'nō\ Andoche 1771–1813 Duc d'*Abran·tès* \,dab-,ränⁿ-'tes\ Fr. gen. under Napoleon

Jus·se·rand \zhüs-rä"\ Jean Jules 1855–1932 *Jean Adrien Antoine Jules Jusserand* Fr. scholar & diplomat

Jus·tin \'jəs-tən\ Saint 100?–?165 *Justin (the) Martyr* church father

Jus·tin·i·an I \,jə-'stin-ē-ən\ 483–565 *the Great* Byzantine emp. (527–565)

Ju·ve·nal \'jü-vən-ºl\ 60?–?140 *Decimus Junius Juvenalis* Rom. poet & satirist

Kaf·ka \'käf-kə, 'kaf-\ Franz 1883–1924 Austrian poet & nov.
Ka·ga·no·vich \ˌkäg-ə-'nō-vich, ˌkag-, -'nò-\ Lazar Moiseevich 1893– Russ. polit.
Ka·ga·wa \kä-'gä-wə\ Toyohiko 1888–1960 Jap. social reformer
Kai·ser \'kī-zər\ Henry John 1882–1967 Am. industrialist
Kalb \'kälp, 'kalb\ Johann 1721–1780 Baron de Kalb \di-'kalb\ Ger. gen. in Am.
Ka·li·da·sa \ˌkäl-i-'däs-ə\ 5th cent. A.D. Hindu dram. & poet
Ka·li·nin \kə-'lē-nən, -'lēn-ˌyēn\ Mikhail Ivanovich 1875–1946 Russ. polit.; pres. U. S. S. R. (1923–46)
Ka·me·ha·me·ha I \kə-ˌmä-ə-'mä-(ˌ)hä\ 1758?–1819 the Great king of Hawaii (1795–1819)
Ka·mer·lingh On·nes \ˌkäm-ər-ˌliŋ-'òn-əs\ Heike 1853–1926 Du. physicist
Kan·din·ski \kan-'din(t)-skē\ Vasili 1866–1944 Russ. painter
Kane \'kān\ Elisha Kent 1820–1857 Am. arctic explorer
K'ang–hsi \'käŋ-'shē\ 1654–1722 Chin. emp. (1662–1722)
Kant \'kant, 'känt\ Immanuel 1724–1804 Ger. philos.
Kar·a·george \ˌkar-ə-'jò(ə)rj\ 1766?–1817 orig. George Petrović Serbian nationalist; founder of Kar·a·geor·ge·vich \-'jòr-jə-vich\ dynasty
Ka·ra·jan \'kär-ə-ˌyän\ Herbert von 1908– Austrian conductor
Karl·feldt \'kär(ə)l-ˌfelt\ Erik Axel 1864–1931 Swed. poet
Ka·ro·lyi \'kar-əl-yē, 'kär-\ Count Mihály 1875–1955 Hung. polit.
Kar·rer \'kär-ər\ Paul 1889– Swed. chemist
Kar·sa·vi·na \kär-'sav-ə-nə, -'säv-\ Tamara 1885– Russ. dancer
Kauf·man \'kòf-mən\ George Simon 1889–1961 Am. dram.
Kau·nitz, von \'kaù-ˌnits, -nəts\ Count Wenzel Anton 1711–1794 Prince von Kaunitz-Riet·berg \-'rēt-ˌberk\ Austrian statesman
Kaut·sky \'kaùt-skē\ Karl Johann 1854–1938 Ger. socialist writer
Kaye–Smith \'kā-'smith\ Sheila 1887–1956 Eng. nov.
Ka·zan·tza·kis \ˌkäz-ˌän-'tsäk-ēs\ Nikos 1885–1957 Greek poet, nov., & translator
Kean \'kēn\ Edmund 1787–1833 Eng. actor
Kear·ny \'kär-nē\ Philip 1814–1862 Am. gen.
Keats \'kēts\ John 1795–1821 Eng. poet
Ke·ble \'kē-bəl\ John 1792–1866 Eng. clergyman & poet
Kee·ley \'kē-lē\ Leslie Enraught 1834–1900 Am. physician & founder of a sanitarium for alcoholics
Kei·tel \'kīt-ᵊl\ Wilhelm 1882–1946 Ger. field marshal
Kel·land \'kel-ənd\ Clarence Bud·ing·ton \-'bəd-iŋ-tən\ 1881–1964 Am. nov.
Kel·ler \'kel-ər\ Helen Adams 1880–1968 Am. deaf & blind lecturer
Kel·logg \'kel-ˌòg, -ˌäg\ Frank Billings 1856–1937 Am. statesman
Kel·ly \'kel-ē\ James Edward 1855–1933 Am. sculptor
Kel·vin \'kel-vən\ 1st Baron 1824–1907 William Thomson Brit. math. & physicist
Ke·mal Ata·türk \kə-ˌmal-'at-ə-ˌtərk, -'ät-\ 1881–1938 Mustafa or Mustapha Kemal Turk. gen.; pres. of Turkey (1923–38)
Kem·ble \'kem-bəl\ Frances Anne 1809–1893 Fanny Eng. actress
— John Philip 1757–1823 Eng. actor
Kempis Thomas a see THOMAS A KEMPIS
Ken or Kenn \'ken\ Thomas 1637–1711 Eng. prelate & hymn writer
Ken·dall \'ken-dᵊl\ Edward Calvin 1886– Am. chemist
— (William) Sergeant 1869–1938 Am. painter & sculptor
Ken·nan \'ken-ən\ George Frost 1904– Am. hist. & diplomat
Ken·ne·dy \'ken-əd-ē\ David Matthew 1905– Am. banker; U.S. secy. of the treasury (from 1969)
— John Fitzgerald 1917–1963 Am. polit.; 35th pres. of the U.S. (1961–63)
— Joseph Patrick 1888–1969 father of J. F. & R. F. Am. businessman & diplomat
— Robert Francis 1925–1968 Am. lawyer; atty. gen. of the U.S. (1961–64)
Ken·nel·ly \'ken-ᵊl-ē\ Arthur Edwin 1861–1939 Am. electrical engineer
Ken·ny \'ken-ē\ Elizabeth 1886–1952 Austral. nurse & physiotherapist
Kent \'kent\ James 1763–1847 Am. jurist
— Rockwell 1882– Am. painter
Ken·wor·thy \'ken-ˌwər-thē\ Joseph Montague 1886–1953 10th Baron Stra·bol·gi \strə-'bō-gē\ Brit. naval officer
Ken·yon \'ken-yən\ John Samuel 1874–1959 Am. phonetician
Kep·ler \'kep-lər\ Johannes 1571–1630 Ger. astronomer
Kep·pel \'kep-əl\ 1st Viscount 1725–1786 Augustus Keppel Brit. admiral
Ker \'ke(ə)r\ William Paton 1855–1923 Brit. scholar
Ke·ren·ski \kə-'ren(t)-skē\ Aleksandr Feodorovich 1881–1970 Russ. revolutionist
Kern \'kərn\ Jerome David 1885–1945 Am. composer
Kes·sel·ring \'kes-əl-riŋ\ Albert 1887–1960 Ger. field marshal
Ket·ter·ing \'ket-ə-riŋ\ Charles Franklin 1876–1958 Am. electrical engineer & inventor
Key \'kē\ Francis Scott 1779–1843 Am. lawyer; author of "The Star-Spangled Banner"
Keyes \'kēz\ 1st Baron 1872–1945 Roger John Brownlow Keyes Brit. admiral
Keynes \'kānz\ John Maynard 1883–1946 Eng. econ.
Key·ser·ling \'kī-zər-liŋ\ Count Hermann Alexander 1880–1946 Ger. philos. & writer
Kha·cha·tu·ri·an \ˌkäch-ə-'tùr-ē-ən, ˌkach-\ Aram 1903– Russ.-Armenian composer
Khe·ra·skov \kə-'räs-kəf, -'ras-\ Mikhail Matveevich 1733–1807 Russ. poet
Khru·shchev \krüsh-'(ch)òf, -'(ch)óv, -'(ch)ef, -'(ch)ev, 'krüsh-, Ni·ki·ta \nə-'kēt-ə\ Sergeevich 1894– Russ. polit.; premier of Soviet Union (1958–64)
Khu·fu \'kü-(ˌ)fü\ Greek Che·ops \'kē-ˌäps\ king of Egypt (ab 2900–2877 B.C.) & pyramid builder
Khwa·riz·mi, al- \al-'kwär-əz-mē\ 780–?850 Arab math.
Kidd \'kid\ William 1645?–1701 Captain Kidd Scot. pirate

Kie·ran \'kir-ən\ John Francis 1892– Am. journalist
Kier·ke·gaard \'kir-kə-ˌgär(d), -ˌgò(ə)r\ Sören Aabye 1813–1855 Dan. philos. & theol.
Kie·sing·er \'kē-ziŋ-ər, -siŋ-\ Kurt Georg 1904– chancellor of West Germany (1966–69)
Kil·learn \kil-'ərn\ 1st Baron 1880–1964 Miles Wedderburn Lampson Brit. diplomat
Kil·lian \'kil-ē-ən, 'kil-yən\ James Rhyne 1904– Am. educator
Kil·mer \'kil-mər\ (Alfred) Joyce 1886–1918 Am. poet
Kil·patrick \kil-'pa-trik\ Hugh Judson 1836–1881 Am. gen.
Kim·mel \'kim-əl\ Husband Edward 1882–1968 Am. admiral
Kin·di, al- \al-'kin-dē\ 9th cent. A.D. Arab philos.
King \'kiŋ\ Ernest Joseph 1878–1956 Am. admiral of the fleet
— Martin Luther 1929–1968 Am. clergyman
— Rufus 1755–1827 Am. polit. & diplomat
— William Lyon Mackenzie 1874–1950 Canad. statesman; prime min. (1921–26; 1926–30; 1935–48)
— William Rufus DeVane 1786–1853 Am. polit.; vice-pres. of the U.S. (1853)
King·lake \'kiŋ-ˌlāk\ Alexander William 1809–1891 Eng. hist.
Kings·ley \'kiŋz-lē\ Charles 1819–1875 Eng. clergyman & nov.
— Sidney 1906– Am. dram.
Kin·kaid \kin-'kād\ Thomas Cassin 1888– Am. admiral
Kin·sey \'kin-zē\ Alfred Charles 1894–1956 Am. zoologist
Kip·ling \'kip-liŋ\ Rud·yard \'rəd-yərd, 'rəj-ərd\ 1865–1936 Eng. author
Kir·by–Smith \ˌkər-bē-'smith\ Edmund 1824–1893 Am. Confed. gen.
Kirch·hoff \'ki(ə)r-ˌkóf\ Gustav Robert 1824–1887 Ger. physicist
Ki·rov \'kē-ˌróf, -ˌròv, 'kir-əf\ Sergei Mironovich 1888–1934 Russ. revolutionist
Kir·sten \'ki(ə)r-stən\ Dorothy 1917– Am. soprano
Kir·wan \'kər-wən\ Richard 1733–1812 Irish chem.
Kitch·e·ner \'kich-(ə-)nər\ Horatio Herbert 1850–1916 1st Earl Kitchener of Khartoum and of Broome Brit. field marshal
Kit·tredge \'ki-trij\ George Lyman 1860–1941 Am. educ.
Klee \'klā\ Paul 1879–1940 Swiss painter
Kleist, von \'klīst\ Heinrich 1777–1811 Ger. dram.
— Paul Ludwig Ewald 1881–1954 Ger. gen.
Klop·stock \'kläp-ˌstäk, 'klòp-ˌshtòk\ Friedrich Gottlieb 1724–1803 Ger. poet
Knel·ler \'nel-ər\ Sir Godfrey 1646–1723 orig. Gottfried Kniller Ger.-born portrait painter in Eng.
Knob·lock \'näb-ˌläk\ Edward 1874–1945 Brit. dram. & nov.
Knox \'näks\ Frank 1874–1944 William Franklin Am. publisher
— Henry 1750–1806 Am. Revolutionary gen.
— John 1505–1572 Scot. reformer & statesman
— Philander Chase 1853–1921 Am. statesman
Knud·sen \(kə-)'nüd-sən\ William Signius 1879–1948 Am. (Dan.-born) industrialist & administrator
Knut \kə-'n(y)üt\ var of CANUTE
Koch \'kòk, 'kók, or ō, ä\ Robert 1843–1910 Ger. bacteriologist
Ko·cher \'kók-ər, 'kòk\ Emil Theodor 1841–1917 Swiss surgeon
Kock, de \'kòk\ Paul 1794–1871 Fr. nov. & dram.
Ko·dály \'kō-ˌdī\ Zol·tán \'zól-ˌtän\ 1882–1967 Hung. composer
Koest·ler \'kes(t)-lər\ Arthur 1905– Brit. (Hung.-born) writer
Koh·ler \'kō-lər\ Foy David 1908– Am. diplomat
Koi·so \'kòi-(ˌ)sō, 'kò-ē-(ˌ)sō\ Kuniaki 1880–1950 Jap. gen.
Ko·kosch·ka \kə-'kòsh-kə, 'kò-kəsh-\ Oskar 1886– Brit. (Austrian-born) painter
Kol·chak \'kòl-'chäk\ Aleksandr Vasilievich 1874–1920 Russ. admiral & counterrevolutionist
Kol·lon·tai \ˌkäl-ən-'tī\ Aleksandra Mikhailovna 1872–1952 Russ. diplomat
Kol·tsov \kòlt-'sóf, -'sòv\ Aleksei Vasilievich 1808–1842 Russ. poet
Ko·mu·ra \kō-'mür-ä, 'kò-mə-ˌrä\ Marquis Jutaro 1855–1911 Jap. diplomat
Kon·dy·les \kòn-'dē-ləs, -lēs\ Georgios 1879–1936 Greek gen. & statesman
Ko·nev \'kòn-ˌyef, -ˌyev, -yəf\ Ivan Stepanovich 1897– Russ. gen. & marshal of Soviet Union
Ko·no·ye \kə-'nòi-(ˌ)ā\ Prince Fumimaro 1891–1945 Jap. statesman
Koo \'kü\ Vi Kyuin Wel·ling·ton \'wel-iŋ-tən\ 1887– orig. Ku Wei-chün Chin. statesman & diplomat
Kopernik or Koppernigk see COPERNICUS
Korn·berg \'kó(ə)rn-ˌbərg\ Arthur 1918– Am. biochemist
Korn·gold \'kó(ə)rn-ˌgōld, -ˌgòlt\ Eric Wolfgang 1897–1957 Austrian composer, conductor, & pianist
Kor·ni·lov \kòr-'nē-ləf\ Lavr Georgievich 1870–1918 Russ. gen.
Ko·ro·len·ko \ˌkòr-ə-'leŋ-(ˌ)kō, ˌkär-\ Vladimir Galaktionovich 1853–1921 Russ. nov.
Kor·zyb·ski \kòr-'zip-skē\ Alfred Habdank Skarbek 1879–1950 Am. (Pol.-born) scientist & writer
Kos·cius·ko \ˌkäs-ē-'əs-ˌkō, ˌkòsh-'chùsh-(ˌ)kō\ Thaddeus 1746–1817 Pol. patriot
Kos·sel \'kòs-əl\ Albrecht 1853–1927 Ger. physiological chem.
Kos·suth \'kä-ˌsüth, kä-'; 'kò-ˌshùt\ Fe·renc \'fer-ˌen(t)s\ 1841–1914 son of Lajos Hung. polit.
— La·jos \'lòi-ˌōsh\ 1802–1894 Hung. patriot & statesman
Ko·sy·gin \kò-'sē-gən, -'sig-ən\ Aleksei Nikolaevich 1904– Russ. polit.; premier of Soviet Union (from 1964)
Kot·ze·bue, von \'kät-sə-ˌbü, 'kòt-\ August Friedrich Ferdinand 1761–1819 Ger. dram.
Koun·dou·rio·tes \(ˌ)kün-ˌdùr-ē-'òt-ēs\ Pavlos 1855–1935 Greek admiral & statesman
Kous·se·vitz·ky \ˌkü-sə-'vit-skē\ Serge \'sərj, 'se(ə)rzh\ 1874–1951 Sergei Alexandrovitch Russ.-born conductor
Krafft–Ebing, von \'kräf-'tā-biŋ, 'kraf-\ Baron Richard 1840–1902 Ger. neurologist
Krebs \'krebz\ Sir Hans (Adolf) 1900– Brit. (Ger.-born) biochemist
Kreis·ler \'krī-slər\ Fritz 1875–1962 Am. (Austrian-born) violinist
Kreym·borg \'krām-ˌbò(ə)rg\ Alfred 1883–1966 Am. poet
Krock \'kräk\ Arthur 1886– Am. journalist
Krogh \'króg\ August 1874–1949 Dan. physiol.

ə abut; ᵊ kitten; ər further; a back; ā bake; ä cot, cart; aù out; ch chin; e less; ē easy; g gift; i trip; ī life
j joke; ŋ sing; ō flow; ò flaw; òi coin; th thin; t̲h̲ this; ü loot; ù foot; y yet; yü few; yù furious; zh vision
ᵊ F table; ȧ F bac; ᴋ G ich, Buch; ⁿ F vin; œ F bœuf; œ̄ F feu; ᵫ F rue; ʸ F digne \dēnʸ\, nuit \nʸwē\

Krol \'krōl\ John Joseph 1910– Am. cardinal
Kroll \'krōl\ Leon 1884– Am. painter
Kro·pot·kin \krə-'pät-kən\ Prince Pëtr Alekseevich 1842–1921 Russ. geographer & revolutionist
Kru·ger \'krü-gər\ Stephanus Johannes Paulus 1825–1904 *Oom Paul* \'ōm-'pòl, 'üm-\ So. African statesman
Krupp \'krùp, 'krəp\ family of Ger. munition makers including: Friedrich 1787–1826; his son Alfred 1812–1887; Alfred's son Friedrich Alfred 1854–1902; Friedrich Alfred's daughter Bertha 1886–1957; & Bertha's son Alfred Felix 1907–1967
Krup·ska·ya \'krùp-skə-yə\ Na·dezh·da \nə-'dezh-də\ Konstantinovna 1869–1939 *wife of Nikolai Lenin* Russ. social worker
Krutch \'krüch\ Joseph Wood 1893–1970 Am. author & critic
Ku·blai Khan \,kü-,blī-'kän, -blə-\ 1216–1294 founder of Mongol dynasty in China
Kuhn \'kün\ Richard 1900–1967 Austrian chem.
Kui·by·shev \'kwē-bə-,shef, 'kü-ē-bə-, -,shev\ Valerian Vladimirovich 1888–1935 Russ. Bolshevik
Kun \'kün\ Bé·la \'bā-lə\ 1885–1937 Hung. Communist
Kung \'gùŋ\ Prince 1833–1898 Manchu statesman
— \'kùŋ\ H. H. 1881–1967 orig. *K'ung Hsiang-hsi* Chin. statesman
Ku·ro·pat·kin \,kùr-ə-'pat-kən, -'pät-\ Aleksei Nikolaevich 1848–1925 Russ. gen.
Ku·ru·su \kù-'rü-(,)sü, ,kùr-ə-'sü\ Saburo 1888–1954 Jap. diplomat
Kusch \'kùsh\ Polykarp 1911– Am. (Ger.-born) physicist
Ku·tu·zov \kə-'tü-,zòf, -,zòv\ Mikhail Ilarionovich 1745–1813 Prince of *Smolensk* Russ. field marshal
Kyd *or* **Kid** \'kid\ Thomas 1558–1594 Eng. dram.
Kynewulf *var of* CYNEWULF

La Bru·yère, de \də-,lä-brü-'ye(ə)r, -brē-'e(ə)r\ Jean 1645–1696 Fr. moralist
La Chaise, de \də-lə-'shāz\ François d'Aix 1624–1709 Fr. Jesuit
La Farge \lə-'färzh\ John 1835–1910 Am. artist
La·fa·yette, de \,läf-ē-'et, ,laf-\ Marquis 1757–1834 *Marie Joseph Paul Yves Roch Gilbert du Mo·tier* Fr. gen. & statesman; served in Am.
Laf·fite *or* **La·fitte** \lə-'fēt\ Jean *ab* 1780–*ab* 1826 Fr. pirate
La Fol·lette \lə-'fäl-ət\ Robert Marion 1855–1925 Am. polit.
La·fon·taine \lə-,fän-'tān, -'fän-,\ Henri 1854–1943 Belg. lawyer & statesman
La Fon·taine, de \lə-(,)lä-,fän-'tān, -'fän-,\ Jean 1621–1695 Fr. fabulist
La·ger·kvist \'läg-ər-,kvist, -,kwist\ Pär Fabian 1891– Swed. dram., poet, & nov.
La·ger·löf \'läg-ər-,lə(r)v\ Sel·ma \'sel-mə\ Ottiliana Lovisa 1858–1940 Swed. nov. & poet
La·grange \lə-'gränj, -'gränzh\ Comte Joseph Louis 1736–1813 Fr. geometer & astron.
La Guar·dia \lə-'g(w)ärd-ē-ə\ Fio·rel·lo \,fē-ə-'rel-(,)ō\ Henry 1882–1947 Am. lawyer & polit.
Lahm \'läm\ Frank Purdy 1877–1963 Am. aeronaut
Laird \'la(ə)rd, le(ə)rd\ Melvin Robert 1922– U.S. polit.; U.S. secy. of defense (from 1969)
Lake \'lāk\ Simon 1866–1945 Am. naval architect
La·marck, de \də-lə-'märk, -(,)lä-\ Chevalier 1744–1829 *Jean Baptiste Pierre Antoine de Monet* Fr. naturalist
La·mar·tine, de \də-,lä-,mär-'tēn, -,lam-ər-'tēn\ Alphonse Marie Louis de Prat 1790–1869 Fr. poet
Lamas Carlos Saavedra *see* Carlos SAAVEDRA LAMAS
Lamb \'lam\ Charles 1775–1834 Eng. essayist & critic
— William 1779–1848 2d Viscount *Melbourne* Eng. statesman
— Willis Eugene 1913– Am. physicist
Lam·bert \'lam-bərt\ John 1619–1683 Eng. Parliamentary gen.
Lam·masch \'läm-,äsh\ Heinrich 1853–1920 Austrian jurist
La Motte–Fou·qué \lə-,mät-,fü-'kā\ Baron Friedrich Heinrich Karl 1777–1843 Ger. nov.
Lan·dis \'lan-dəs\ Ken·e·saw \'ken-ə-,sò\ Mountain 1866–1944 Am. jurist & baseball commissioner
Lan·don \'lan-dən\ Alfred Mossman 1887– Am. polit.
Lan·dor \'lan-,dó(ə)r, -dər\ Walter Savage 1775–1864 Eng. author
Lan·dow·ska \lan-'dóf-skə, län-\ Wanda 1877–1959 Pol. pianist
Land·seer \'lan(d)-,si(ə)r\ Sir Edwin Henry 1802–1873 Eng. painter
Land·stei·ner \'lan(d)-,stī-nər, 'länt-,shtī-\ Karl 1868–1943 Austrian-born pathologist in Am.
Lane \'lān\ Edward William 1801–1876 Eng. orientalist
Lan·franc \'lan-,fraŋk\ 1005?–1089 Ital.-born prelate & scholar in Eng.
Lang \'laŋ\ Andrew 1844–1912 Scot. scholar & author
— Cosmo Gordon 1864–1945 Brit. prelate; archbishop of Canterbury
Lange \'läŋ-ə\ Christian Louis 1869–1938 Norw. pacifist & hist.
Lang·er \'laŋ-ər\ Susanne Knauth 1895– Am. educator
Lang·land \'laŋ-lənd\ *or* **Lang·ley** \'laŋ-lē\ William 1332?–?1400 Eng. poet
Lang·ley \'laŋ-lē\ Samuel Pierpont 1834–1906 Am. astron. & airplane pioneer
Lang·muir \'laŋ-,myù(ə)r\ Irving 1881–1957 Am. chem.
Lang·ton \'laŋ(k)-tən\ Stephen *d* 1228 Eng. theol., hist., & poet
Lang·try \'laŋ-trē\ Lillie 1852–1929 née (*Emily Charlotte*) *Le Breton;* the *Jersey Lily* Eng. actress
La·nier \lə-'ni(ə)r\ Sidney 1842–1881 Am. poet
Lan·kes·ter \'laŋ-kəs-tər; 'lan-,kes-, 'laŋ-\ Sir Edwin Ray 1847–1929 Eng. zool.
Lannes \'län, 'lan\ Jean 1769–1809 Duc *de Montebello* Fr. soldier under Napoleon; marshal of France (1804)
Lan·sing \'lan(t)-siŋ\ Robert 1864–1928 Am. lawyer & statesman
Lao-tzu *or* **Lao-tse** *or* **Lao-tze** \'laùd-'zə\ 604?–?531 B.C. Chin. philos.
La Pé·rouse, de \də-,lä-pā-'rüz\ Comte 1741–1788 *Jean François de Galoup* Fr. navigator & explorer
La·place, de \də-(,)lä-'pläs\ Marquis Pierre Simon 1749–1827 Fr. astron. & math.
Lard·ner \'lärd-nər\ Ring 1885–1933 *Ringgold Wilmer* Am. writer
La·re·do Brú \lə-,räd-ō-'brü, -,rä͟th-\ Federico 1875–1946 Cuban soldier; pres. of Cuba (1936–40)

Lar·go Ca·ba·lle·ro \'lär-(,)gō-,kab-ə(l)-'ye(ə)-(,)rō, -,käb-, -ə-'le(ə)r-\ Francisco 1869–1946 Span. labor leader; prime min. (1936–37)
La Roche·fou·cauld, de \də-(,)lä-,rōsh-fü-'kō, də-lə-, -,rōsh-\ Duc François 1613–1680 Fr. writer & moralist
La·rousse \lə-'rüs\ Pierre Athanase 1817–1875 Fr. grammarian & lexicographer
Lar·tet \lär-'tā\ Édouard Armand Isidore Hippolyte 1801–1871 Fr. archaeologist
La Salle, de \də-lə-'sal\ Sieur 1643–1687 *Robert Cavelier* Fr. explorer in Am.
Las Ca·sas, de \də-lə-(,)lä-'käs-əs\ Bartolomé 1474–1566 Span. Dominican missionary & hist.
Las·ki \'las-kē\ Harold Joseph 1893–1950 Eng. polit. scientist
Las·salle \lə-'säl, -'sal\ Ferdinand 1825–1864 Ger. socialist
Lat·i·mer \'lat-ə-mər\ Hugh 1485?–1555 Eng. Protestant martyr
La·tou·rette \,lät-ə-'ret\ Kenneth Scott 1884–1968 Am. religious hist. & sinologue
La·trobe \lə-'trōb\ Benjamin Henry 1764–1820 Am. (Eng.-born) architect & engineer
Lat·ti·more \'lat-ə-,mō(ə)r, -,mó(ə)r\ Owen 1900– Am. orientalist
Latz·ko \'lät-(,)skō\ Andreas \än-'drā-,äs\ 1876– Hung.-born writer in Austria
Laud \'lòd\ William 1573–1645 Eng. prelate; archbishop of Canterbury; executed
Lau·der \'lòd-ər\ Sir Harry 1870–1950 orig. *MacLennan* Scot. singer
Laue, von \'laù-ə\ Max 1879–1960 Ger. physicist
Laugh·ton \'lòt-ᵊn\ Charles 1899–1962 Am. (Eng.-born) actor
Lau·rens \lò-'räⁿs\ Henri 1885–1954 Fr. sculptor
Lau·ri·er \'lòr-ē-,ā, 'lär-\ Sir Wilfrid 1841–1919 Canad. statesman
La·val \lə-'val, -'väl\ Pierre 1883–1945 Fr. lawyer & polit.
La Val·liè·re, de \də-,lä-val-'ye(ə)r\ Duchesse 1644–1710 *mistress of Louis XIV of France*
La·ve·ran \lav-'räⁿ\ Charles Louis Alphonse 1845–1922 Fr. physiol. & bacteriol.
La Vé·ren·drye, de \də-(,)lä-,ver-ən-'drē, -'ver-ən-,drī\ Sieur 1685–1749 *Pierre Gaultier de Varennes* Canad. explorer in Am.
La·very \'lāv-(ə-)rē, 'lav-\ Sir John 1856–1941 Brit. painter
La·voi·sier \ləv-'wäz-ē-,ā\ Antoine Laurent 1743–1794 Fr. chem.
Law \'lò\ (Andrew) Bon·ar \'bän-ər\ 1858–1923 Brit. statesman
— Edward 1750–1818 1st Baron *El·len·bor·ough* \'el-ən-,bər-ō, -,bə-rō, -b(ə-)rə\ Eng. jurist
— John 1671–1729 Scot. financier & speculator
— William 1686–1761 Eng. devotional writer
Lawes \'lòz\ Henry 1596–1662 Eng. composer
— Lewis Edward 1883–1947 Am. penologist
Law·rence \'lòr-ən(t)s, 'lär-\ David 1888– Am. journalist
— David Herbert 1885–1930 Eng. nov.
— Ernest Orlando 1901–1958 Am. physicist
— Gertrude 1901–1952 orig. *Gertrud Alexandra Dagmar Lawrence Klasen* Eng. actress
— James 1781–1813 Am. naval officer
— Sir Thomas 1769–1830 Eng. painter
— Thomas Edward 1888–1935 *Lawrence of Arabia* later surname *Shaw* Brit. archaeologist, soldier, & writer
Law·rie \'lòr-ē, 'lär-ē\ Lee 1877–1963 Am. sculptor
Lax·ness \'läk-,snes\ Hall·dór \'häl-,dō(ə)r, -,dò(ə)r\ Kiljan 1902– Icelandic writer
Lay·a·mon \'lī-ə-mən, 'lä-ə-\ *fl* 1200 Eng. poet
Lay·ard \'la(ə)rd, 'le(ə)rd\ Sir Austen Henry 1817–1894 Eng. archaeologist & diplomat
Lea·cock \'lē-,käk\ Stephen Butler 1869–1944 Canad. econ. & humorist
Leaf \'lēf\ Walter 1852–1927 Eng. banker & scholar
Lea·hy \'lā-(,)hē\ William Daniel 1875–1959 Am. admiral of the fleet
Lea·key \'lē-kē\ Louis Seymour Bazett 1903– Brit. paleontologist
Lear \'li(ə)r\ Edward 1812–1888 Eng. painter & nonsense poet
Lea·ry \'li(ə)r-ē\ Herbert Fairfax 1885–1957 Am. admiral
Le·brun \lə-'brœⁿ, -'bran, -'brœn\ Albert 1871–1950 Fr. statesman; pres. of France (1932–40)
— Mme. Vigée– *see* VIGÉE-LEBRUN
Le Brun *or* **Le·brun** \lə-'brœⁿ, -'braⁿ, -'brœn\ Charles 1619–1690 Fr. painter
Lecky \'lek-ē\ William Edward Hartpole 1838–1903 Irish hist. & essayist
Le·conte de Lisle \lə-,kōⁿt-də-'lē(ə)l\ Charles Marie 1818–1894 orig. *Leconte* Fr. poet
Le Cor·bu·sier \lə-,kòr-'b(y)ü-zē-,ā\ 1887–1965 pseud. of *Charles Édouard Jeanneret-Gris* Fr. (Swiss-born) architect, painter, & writer
Le·der·berg \'lād-ər-,bərg\ Joshua 1925– Am. geneticist
Lee \'lē\ Ann 1736–1784 Eng. mystic; founder of Shaker society in U. S.
— Charles 1731–1782 Am. (Eng.-born) gen.
— Fitzhugh 1835–1905 *nephew of R. E. Lee* Am. gen.
— Francis Lightfoot 1734–1797 Am. Revolutionary statesman
— Henry 1756–1818 *Light-Horse Harry* Am. gen.
— Richard Henry 1732–1794 Am. Revolutionary statesman
— Robert Edward 1807–1870 Am. Confed. gen.
— Sir Sidney 1859–1926 Eng. editor & scholar
— Tsung-Dao \'lē-'dzùŋ-'daù\ 1926– Chin. physicist
Leeu·wen·hoek *or* **Leu·wen·hoek, van** \'lā-vən-,hùk\ Anton 1632–1723 Du. naturalist
Le·fe·bvre \lə-'fevrᵊ\ François Joseph 1755–1820 Duc *de Dantzig* Fr. gen.; marshal of France (1807)
Le Gal·lienne \lə-'gal-yən, -,yen\ Eva 1899– *dau. of Richard* Eng. actress in Am.
— Richard 1866–1947 Eng. writer
Le·gen·dre \lə-'zhändrᵊ, -'zhäⁿdrᵊ\ Adrien Marie 1752–?1833 Fr. math.
Lé·ger \lā-'zhā\ Alexis Saint-Léger 1887– pseud. *St. John Perse* Fr. diplomat & poet
— Fernand 1881–1955 Fr. painter
Le·guía y Sal·ce·do \lə-,gē-ə-,ē-(,)säl-'sā-(,)thō, -'sād-(,)ō\ Augusto Bernardino 1863–1932 Peruvian banker; pres. of Peru (1908–12; 1919–30)
Le·hár \'lā-,här\ Franz 1870–1948 Hung. composer
Leh·man \'lē-mən\ Herbert Henry 1878–1963 Am. banker & polit.

Leh·mann \'lā-ˌmän\ Lot·te \'lȯt-ə, 'lät-ə\ 1888– Ger. soprano

Leib·niz or **Leib·nitz, von** \'līp-ˌnits\ Baron Gottfried Wilhelm 1646–1716 Ger. philos. & math.

Leicester 1st Earl of see Robert DUDLEY see also de MONTFORT

Leif Ericson see ERICSON

Leigh–Mal·lo·ry \'lē-'mal-(ə-)rē\ Sir Trafford Leigh 1892–1944 Brit. air marshal

Leigh·ton \'lāt-ᵊn\ Frederick 1830–1896 Baron *Leighton of Stretton* Eng. painter

Leins·dorf \'līnz-ˌdȯrf, 'līn(t)s-\ Erich 1912– Am. (Austrian-born) conductor

Leith–Ross \'lē-'thrȯs\ Sir Frederick (William) 1887–1968 Brit. econ. & financier

Le·jeune \lə-'zhə(r)n, -'jün\ John Archer 1867–1942 Am. marine-corps gen.

Le·land or **Ley·land** \'lē-lənd\ John 1506?–1552 Eng. antiquary

Le·ly \'lē-lē, 'lā-lē\ Sir Peter 1618–1680 orig. *Pieter Van der Faes* Du. painter in Eng.

Le·maî·tre \lə-'mātrᵊ\ (Fran·çois Élie) Jules 1853–1914 Fr. writer & literary critic

— Abbé Georges Édouard 1894– Belg. astrophysicist & math.

Lemoyne Pierre see IBERVILLE

Le·nard \'lā-ˌnärt\ Philipp 1862–1947 Ger. physicist

Len·clos \läⁿ-klō\ Anne 1620–1705 *Ninon de Lenclos* Fr. wit & lady of fashion

L'En·fant \'län-ˌfänt, läⁿ-fäⁿ\ Pierre Charles 1754–1825 Fr. engineer in Am.

Le·nin \'len-ən, 'län-, -ˌēn\ Nikolai 1870–1924 *Vladimir Ilich Ul·ya·nov* \ül-'yän-əf, -ˌȯf\ Russ. Communist

Leo \'lē-(ˌ)ō\ name of 13 popes: esp. **I** Saint 390?–461 (pope 440?–61); **III** Saint 750?–816 (pope 795–816); **XIII** 1810–1903 (pope 1878–1903)

Leon·ard \'len-ərd\ William Ellery 1876–1944 Am. educ. & poet

Leonardo da Vinci see Leonardo da VINCI

Le·on·ca·val·lo \ˌlā-ˌōn-kə-'väl-(ˌ)ō\ Ruggiero 1858–1919 Ital. composer & librettist

Le·on·i·das \lē-'än-əd-əs\ 5th cent. B.C. Greek hero; king of Sparta (490?–480)

Le·o·par·di \ˌlā-ə-'pärd-ē\ Conte Giacomo 1798–1837 Ital. poet

Le·o·pold I \'lē-ə-ˌpōld\ 1640–1705 king of Hungary (1655–1705) & Holy Rom. emp. (1658–1705)

— **II** 1747–1792 Holy Rom. emp. (1790–92)

— **I** 1790–1865 king of Belgium (1831–65)

— **II** 1835–1909 king of Belgium (1865–1909)

— **III** 1901– king of Belgium (1934–51)

Lep·i·dus \'lep-əd-əs\ Marcus Aemilius *d* 13 B.C. Rom. triumvir

Ler·mon·tov \'ler-mən-ˌtȯf, -ˌtəf\ Mikhail Yurievich 1814–1841 Russ. poet & nov.

Ler·ner \'lər-nər\ Alan Jay 1918– Am. dram.

Le·sage \lə-'säzh\ Alain René 1668–1747 Fr. nov. & dram.

Le·sche·tiz·ky \ˌlesh-ə-'tit-skē\ Theodor 1830–1915 Pol. pianist & composer

Les·seps, de \le-'seps, 'les-əps\ Vicomte Ferdinand Marie 1805–1894 Fr. diplomat; promoter of Suez Canal

Les·sing \'les-iŋ\ Gotthold Ephraim 1729–1781 Ger. critic & dram.

Les·ter \'les-tər\ Seán \'shȯn\ 1889–1959 Irish journalist & diplomat; last secy.-gen. of League of Nations (1940–46)

L'Es·trange \lə-'stränj\ Sir Roger 1616–1704 Eng. journalist & translator

Leu·tze \'lȯit-sə\ Emanuel 1816–1868 Ger.-born painter

Le·vas·seur \lə-ˌväs-'ər\ Pierre Émile 1828–1911 Fr. econ.

Le·ver \'lē-vər\ Charles James 1806–1872 Brit. nov.

Lewes \'lü-əs\ George Henry 1817–1878 Eng. philos. & critic

Lew·is \'lü-əs\ Cecil Day see DAY-LEWIS

— Clive Staples 1898–1963 Eng. nov. & essayist

— (Harry) Sinclair 1885–1951 Am. nov.

— Isaac Newton 1858–1931 Am. army officer & inventor

— John Llewellyn 1880–1969 Am. labor leader

— Matthew Gregory 1775–1818 *Monk Lewis* Eng. author

— Mer·i·weth·er \'mer-ə-ˌweth-ər\ 1774–1809 Am. explorer

— (Percy) Wyndham 1884–1957 Brit. painter & author

Lew·i·sohn \'lü-ə-sən, -ˌzən\ Ludwig 1883–1955 Ger.-born nov. & critic

Ley \'lī\ Robert 1890–1945 Ger. Nazi leader

Li Hung-chang \'lē-'hùŋ-'jäŋ\ 1823–1901 Chin. statesman

— Po \-'bō, -'pō\ or Tai-po \-'tī-\ *d* 762 A.D. Chin. poet

— Shih-min \-'shē-'min\ 597–649 *T'ai-tsung* \'tīd-'zùŋ\ Chin. emp. (627–649)

Lib·by \'lib-ē\ Willard Frank 1908– Am. chem.

Li·cin·i·us \lə-'sin-ē-əs\ 270?–325 *Valerius Licinianus Licinius* Rom. emp. (308–324)

Lid·dell Hart \ˌlid-ᵊl-'härt\ Basil Henry 1895–1970 Eng. military scientist

Lie \'lē\ Jonas 1833–1909 Norw. nov. & dram.

— Jonas 1880–1940 *nephew of prec.* Norw.-born painter in Am.

— Tryg·ve \'trig-vē, -və\ 1896–1968 Norw. lawyer & statesman; secy.-gen. of U.N. (1946–53)

Lie·big, von \'lē-big\ Baron Justus 1803–1873 Ger. chem.

Li·far \'lē-ˌfär, lē-'\ Serge 1905– Russ. dancer

Lil·ien·thal \'lil-yən-ˌthȯl\ David Eli 1899– Am. lawyer & administrator

Lil·ien·thal \'lil-yən-ˌtäl, -ˌthȯl\ Otto 1848–1896 Ger. aeronautical engineer

Li·li·u·o·ka·la·ni \lə-ˌlē-ə-(ˌ)wō-kə-'län-ē\ Lydia Kamekeha 1838–1917 queen of the Hawaiian Islands (1891–93)

Lil·lo \'lil-(ˌ)ō\ George 1693?–1739 Eng. dram.

Li·món \lē-'mōn\ José 1908– Mex. dancer & choreographer in the U. S.

Lin Sen \'lin-'sen\ or **Shen** \-'shen\ 1876?–1943 Chin. statesman; pres. of the National government (1932–43)

— Yutang \-'yü-ˌtäŋ, -ˈtaŋ\ 1895– Chin. author & philologist

Lin·a·cre \'lin-i-kər\ Thomas 1460?–1524 Eng. humanist & physician

Lin·coln \'liŋ-kən\ Abraham 1809–1865 16th pres. of the U. S. (1861–65)

— Benjamin 1733–1810 Am. Revolutionary gen.

— Joseph Crosby 1870–1944 Am. nov.

Lind \'lind\ Jenny 1820–1887 *Johanna Maria; the Swedish Nightingale* Swed. soprano

Lind·bergh \'lin(d)-ˌbərg\ Anne Spencer 1907– *née Morrow; wife of C. A.* Am. aviator & author

— Charles Augustus 1902– Am. aviator

Lind·ley \'lin-(d)lē\ John 1799–1865 Eng. botanist

Lind·say \'lin-zē\ Howard 1889–1968 Am. dram. & actor

— (Nicholas) Va·chel \'vā-chəl\ 1879–1931 Am. poet

Link·la·ter \'liŋ-ˌklāt-ər\ Eric 1899– Brit. writer

Linlithgow Marquis of see HOPE

Lin·nae·us \lə-'nē-əs\ Carolus 1707–1778 *Carl von Lin·né* \lə-'nā\ Swed. botanist

Lip·mann \'lip-mən\ Fritz Albert 1899– Am. (Ger.-born) biochem.

Lip·pi \'lip-ē\ Fra Filippo or Lip·po \'lip-(ˌ)ō\ 1406?–1469 Florentine painter

— Filippo or Filippino 1457?–1504 *son of prec.* Florentine painter

Lipp·mann \'lep-ˌmän, 'lip-mən\ Gabriel 1845–1921 Fr. physicist

Lipp·mann \'lip-mən\ Walter 1889– Am. journalist & author

Lip·ton \'lip-tən\ Sir Thomas Johnstone 1850–1931 Eng. merchant & yachtsman

Lisle, de see LECONTE DE LISLE, ROUGET DE LISLE

Lis·ter \'lis-tər\ Joseph 1827–1912 1st Baron *Lister of Lyme Regis* Eng. surgeon

Liszt \'list\ Franz 1811–1886 Hung. pianist & composer

Lit·tle \'lit-ᵊl\ Sir Charles James Colebrooke 1882– Brit. admiral

Lit·tle·ton \'lit-ᵊl-tən\ Sir Thomas 1407?–1481 Eng. jurist

Lit·tré \li-'trā\ Maximilien Paul Émile 1801–1881 Fr. lexicographer

Lit·vi·nov \lit-'vē-ˌnȯf, -nəf\ Maksim Maksimovich 1876–1951 Russ. Communist

Liu Shao-ch'i \'lē-ü-' shaù-'chē\ 1905– Chin. Communist

Liv·ing·ston \'liv-iŋ-stən\ Robert R. 1746–1813 Am. statesman

Liv·ing·stone \'liv-iŋ-stən\ David 1813–1873 Scot. explorer in Africa

Livy \'liv-ē\ 59 B.C.–A.D. 17 *Titus Livius* Rom. hist.

Lloyd George \'lȯid-'jȯ(ə)rj\ David 1863–1945 1st Earl of *Dwy·for* \'dü-ē-ˌvȯ(ə)r\ Brit. statesman; prime min. (1916–22)

Lo·ba·chev·ski \ˌlō-bə-'chef-skē, ˌläb-ə-, -'chev-\ Nikolai Lyanovich 1793–1856 Russ. math.

Lo·ben·gu·la \ˌlō-bən-'g(y)ü-lə\ 1833–1894 Zulu king of the Matabele

Locke \'läk\ John 1632–1704 Eng. philos.

Lock·er–Lamp·son \ˌläk-ər-'lam(p)-sən\ Frederick 1821–1895 Eng. poet

Lock·hart \'läk-ərt, 'läk-, -(ˌ)härt\ John Gibson 1794–1854 Scot. nov. & biographer

Lock·yer \'läk-yər\ Sir Joseph Norman 1836–1920 Eng. astron.

Lodge \'läj\ Henry Cabot 1850–1924 Am. statesman & author

— Henry Cabot 1902– *grandson of prec.* Am. polit. & diplomat

— Sir Oliver Joseph 1851–1940 Eng. physicist

— Thomas 1558–1625 Eng. poet & dram.

Loeb \'lōb\ Jacques 1859–1924 Ger.-born physiol. in Am.

Loewe \'lō\ Frederick 1904– Austrian composer in the U. S.

Loewi \'lō-ē\ Otto 1873–1961 Am. (Ger.-born) pharmacologist

Löff·ler \'lef-lər\ Friedrich August Johannes 1852–1915 Ger. bacteriol.

Lo·max \'lō-ˌmaks\ John Avery 1872–1948 Am. folklorist

Lom·bard \'läm-ˌbärd, -bərd\ Peter 1100?–1160 or 1164 *Petrus Lombardus* Ital. theol.

Lom·bro·so \lȯm-'brō-(ˌ)sō\ Ce·sa·re \'chā-zä-ˌrā\ 1836–1909 Ital. physician & psychiatrist

Lon·don \'lən-dən\ Jack 1876–1916 Am. writer

— Stephen Harriman 1784–1864 Am. army officer & explorer

Long \'lȯŋ\ Hu·ey \'hyü-ē\ Pierce 1893–1935 Am. lawyer & polit.

Long·fel·low \'lȯŋ-ˌfel-ə, -ˌfel-ə-(w)\ Henry Wads·worth \'wädz-(ˌ)wərth\ 1807–1882 Am. poet

Lon·gi·nus \län-'jī-nəs\ Dionysius Cassius *d* A.D. 273 Greek philos.

Long·street \'lȯŋ-ˌstrēt\ James 1821–1904 Am. Confed. gen.

Lönn·rot \'len-ˌrüt, 'lə(r)n-, -ˌrüt\ Elias 1802–1884 Finnish scholar

Lons·dale \'länz-ˌdāl\ Frederick 1881–1954 Brit. dram.

Ló·pez \'lō-ˌpez, -ˌpäs\ Carlos Antonio 1790–1862 pres. of Paraguay (1844–62)

— Francisco Solano 1827–1870 *son of prec.* pres. of Paraguay (1862–70)

Lo·rentz \'lōr-ˌen(t)s, 'lȯr-\ Hendrik Antoon 1853–1928 Du. physicist

Lo·renz \'lōr-ˌen(t)s, 'lȯr-\ Adolf 1854–1946 Austrian orthopedic surgeon

Lor·rain \lə-'rān, lȯ-, -'raⁿ\ Claude 1600–1682 pseud. of *Claude Gellée* Fr. painter

Lo·thair I \lō-'t(h)a(ə)r, -'t(h)e(ə)r, 'lō-\ 795?–855 king of Germany (840–43) & Holy Rom. emp. (840–855)

— **II** (*or* **III**) 1070?–1137 *the Saxon* king of Germany & Holy Rom. emp. (1125–37)

Lo·ti \lō-'tē, lȯ-\ Pierre 1850–1923 pseud. of *Louis Marie Julien Viaud* Fr. naval officer & nov.

Lou·bet \lü-'bā\ Émile 1838–1929 Fr. statesman; pres. of France (1899–1906)

Loudoun 4th Earl of see John CAMPBELL

Lou·is \'lü-ē, lü-'ē, 'lü-əs\ name of 18 kings of France: esp. **I** (*le Débonnaire*) 778–840 (reigned 814–840); **V** (*le Fainéant*) 966?–987 (reigned — last Carolingian — 986–987); **IX** (*Saint*) 1214–1270 (reigned 1226–70); **XI** 1423–1483 (reigned 1461–83); **XII** 1462–1515 (reigned 1498–1515); **XIII** 1601–1643 (reigned 1610–43); **XIV** 1638–1715 (reigned 1643–1715); **XV** 1710–1774 (reigned 1715–74); **XVI** 1754–1793 (reigned 1774–92; guillotined); **XVII** 1785–1795 (nominally reigned 1793–95); **XVIII** 1755–1824 (reigned 1814–15; 1815–24)

— **IV** 1287?–1347 *Duke of Bavaria* king of Germany & Holy Rom. emp. (1314–47)

ə abut; ᵊ kitten; ər further; a back; ā bake; ä cot, cart; aù out; ch chin; e less; ē easy; g gift; i trip; ī life
j joke; ŋ sing; ō flow; ȯ flaw; ȯi coin; th thin; th̲ this; ü loot; ù foot; y yet; yü few; yù furious; zh vision
ᵊ F table; ȧ F bac; ḳ G ich, Buch; ⁿ F vin; œ F bœuf; œ̄ F feu; ᵫ G füllen; ᵫ̄ F rue; ʸ F digne \dēnʸ\, nuit \nwʸē\

— **II de Bourbon** see CONDÉ

— **Napoleon** see NAPOLEON III

— **Phi·lippe** \fə-'lēp\ 1773–1850 *the Citizen King* king of the French (1830–48)

Louns·bury \'laúnz‚ber-ē, -b(ə-)rē\ Thomas Raynesford 1838–1915 Am. scholar & educ.

Louÿs \lü-'ē\ Pierre 1870–1925 Fr. writer

Lovat 12th Baron see FRASER

Love·lace \'lǝv-‚lās, -ləs\ Richard 1618–1658 Eng. Cavalier poet

Lov·ell \'lǝv-əl\ Sir (Alfred Charles) Bernard 1913– Brit. radio astron.

Lov·er \'lǝv-ər\ Samuel 1797–1868 Irish nov.

Low \'lō\ Sir David 1891–1963 Brit. cartoonist

Low·ell \'lō-əl\ Amy 1874–1925 Am. poet & critic

— James Russell 1819–1891 Am. poet, essayist, & dram.

— Percival 1855–1916 *bro. of Amy* Am. astron.

— Robert (Traill Spence) 1917– Am. poet

Lowes \'lōz\ John Livingston 1867–1945 Am. educ.

Lowndes \'laún(d)z\ William Thomas 1798–1843 Eng. bibliographer

Loy·o·la \lói-'ō-lə\ Saint Ignatius of 1491–1556 *Íñigo de Oñez y Loyola* Span. soldier & ecclesiastic; founder of the Society of Jesus

Lu Hsun \'lü-'shün\ 1881–1936 Chin. writer

Lub·bock \'lǝb-ək\ Sir John 1834–1913 1st Baron *Avebury; son of Sir J. W.* Eng. financier & author

— Sir John William 1803–1865 Eng. astron. & math.

Lu·can \'lü-kən\ 39–65 *Marcus Annaeus Lucanus* Rom. poet

Luce \'lüs\ Clare 1903– née *Boothe* \'büth\ *wife of H. R.* Am. dram., polit., & diplomat

— Henry Robinson 1898–1967 Am. editor & publisher

Lu·cre·ti·us \lü-'krē-sh(ē-)əs\ 96?–55 B.C. *Titus Lucretius Carus* Rom. poet & philos.

Lu·cul·lus \lü-'kəl-əs\ Lucius Licinius *fl* 79?–?57 B.C. Rom. gen. & epicure

Lu·den·dorff \'lüd-ᵊn-‚dórf\ Erich Friedrich Wilhelm 1865–1937 Ger. gen.

Lul·ly \lü-'lē\ Jean Baptiste 1632–1687 Fr. (Ital.-born) composer

Lul·ly \'lǝl-ē\ Raymond 1235?–1315 Span. ecclesiastic & philos.

Lunt \'lənt\ Alfred 1893– Am. actor

Lu·ther \'lü-thər\ Martin 1483–1546 Ger. Reformation leader

Lyau·tey \lē-‚ō-'tā\ Louis Hubert Gonzalve 1854–1934 Fr. soldier; marshal of France (1921)

Ly·cur·gus \lī-'kər-gəs\ 9th cent. B.C. Spartan lawgiver

Lyd·gate \'lid-‚gāt, -gət\ John 1370?–?1451 Eng. poet

Ly·ell \'lī-əl\ Sir Charles 1797–1875 Brit. geologist

Lyly \'lil-ē\ John 1554?–1606 Eng. author

Lynd \'lind\ Robert Staugh·ton \'stót-ᵊn\ 1892– & his wife Helen née *Merrell* 1897– Am. sociologists

Ly·on \'lī-ən\ Mary 1797–1849 Am. educ.

Ly·ons \'lī-ənz\ Joseph Aloysius 1879–1939 Austral. statesman; prime min. (1932–39)

Ly·san·der \lī-'san-dər\ *d* 395 B.C. Spartan commander

Ly·sen·ko \lə-'seŋ-(‚)kō\ Trofim Denisovich 1898– Russ. scientist

Lys·i·as \'lis-ē-əs\ 450?–?380 B.C. Athenian orator

Ly·sim·a·chus \lī-'sim-ə-kəs\ 361?–281 B.C. Macedonian gen. under Alexander the Great; king of Thrace (306)

Ly·sip·pus \lī-'sip-əs\ 4th cent. B.C. Greek sculptor

Lyt·ton \'lit-ᵊn\ 1st Baron 1803–1873 *Edward George Earle Lytton Bul·wer-Lytton* \‚búl-wər-\; *bro. of Sir Henry Bulwer* Eng. nov. & dram.

— 1st Earl of 1831–1891 *Edward Robert Bulwer-Lytton; pseud. Owen Meredith; son of prec.* Brit. statesman & poet

— 2d Earl of 1876–1947 *Victor Alexander George Robert Lytton; son of 1st Earl* Brit. administrator & author

M'-, Mc- names beginning with these prefixes are alphabetized as if spelled MAC-

Mc·Adoo \'mak-ə-‚dü\ William Gibbs 1863–1941 Am. lawyer & administrator

Mac·Ar·thur \mə-'kär-thər\ Arthur 1845–1912 Am. gen.

— Charles 1895–1956 Am. dram.

— Douglas 1880–1964 *son of Arthur* Am. gen. of the army

Ma·cau·lay \mə-'kó-lē\ Dame Rose 1881–1958 Eng. nov.

— 1st Baron 1800–1859 *Thomas Babington Macaulay* Eng. hist., author, & statesman

Mac·beth \mək-'beth\ *d* 1057 king of Scotland (1040–57)

Mc·Bur·ney \mək-'bər-nē\ Charles 1845–1913 Am. surgeon

Mc·Car·thy \mə-'kär-thē *also* -'kärt-ē\ Eugene Joseph 1916– Am. polit.

— Joseph Raymond 1908–1957 Am. polit.

M'·Car·thy \mə-'kär-thē *also* -'kärt-ē\ Justin 1830–1912 Irish writer & polit.

— Justin Huntly 1861–1936 *son of Justin* Irish dram., nov., & hist.

Mc·Clel·lan \mə-'klel-ən\ George Brinton 1826–1885 Am. gen.

Mc·Clos·key \mə-'kläs-kē\ John 1810–1885 1st Am. cardinal

Mc·Cloy \mə-'klói\ John Jay 1895– Am. banker & govt. official

Mc·Clure \mə-'klú(ə)r\ Samuel Sidney 1857–1949 Am. (Irish-born) editor & publisher

Mc·Cor·mack \mə-'kór-mək, -mik\ John 1884–1945 Am. (Irish-born) tenor

Mc·Cor·mick \mə-'kór-mik\ Cyrus Hall 1809–1884 Am. inventor

— Joseph Me·dill \mə-'dil\ 1877–1925 & his bro. Robert Rutherford 1880–1955 Am. newspaper publishers

Mac·Crack·en \mə-'krak-ən\ Henry Noble 1880–1970 Am. educ.

Mc·Crae \mə-'krā\ John 1872–1918 Canad. physician & poet

Mac·don·ald \mək-'dän-ᵊld\ George 1824–1905 Scot. nov. & poet

— Sir John Alexander 1815–1891 Canad. statesman; 1st prime min. of Dominion of Canada (1867–73) and again (1878–91)

Mac·don·ough \mək-'dän-ə\ Thomas 1783–1825 Am. naval officer

Mac·Dow·ell \mək-'daú(-ə)l\ Edward Alexander 1861–1908 Am. composer

Mc·Dow·ell \mək-'daú(-ə)l\ Ir·vin \'ər-vən\ 1818–1885 Am. gen.

Mc·Fee \mək-'fē\ William 1881–1966 Eng. writer

Mc·Gill \mə-'gil\ James 1744–1813 Canad. (Scot.-born) businessman & philanthropist

— Ralph Emerson 1898–1969 Am. journalist

Mc·Guf·fey \mə-'gəf-ē\ William Holmes 1800–1873 Am. educ.

Ma·cha·do y Mo·ra·les \mä-'chä-(‚)thō-ē-mō-'rä-(‚)läs\ Gerardo \hā-'rär-(‚)thō\ 1871–1939 pres. of Cuba (1925–33)

Ma·chi·a·vel·li \‚mak-ē-ə-'vel-ē\ Niccolò 1469–1527 Ital. statesman & polit. philos.

Mc·In·tyre \'mak-ən-‚tī(ə)r\ James Francis Aloysius 1886– Am. cardinal

Mac·Kaye \mə-'kī\ Percy 1875–1956 Am. poet & dram.

Mc·Ken·na \mə-'ken-ə\ Sio·bhan \shə-'vón\ 1923– Irish actress

Mack·en·sen, von \'mäk-ən-zən\ August 1849–1945 Ger. field marshal

Mac·Ken·zie \mə-'ken-zē\ Alexander 1822–1892 Canad. (Scot.-born) statesman; prime min. (1873–78)

— Sir Alexander Campbell 1847–1935 Brit. composer & conductor

— William Lyon 1795–1861 Canad. (Scot.-born) insurgent leader

Mackenzie Sir Compton 1883– Eng. nov.

Mc·Kim \mə-'kim\ Charles Follen 1847–1909 Am. architect

Mac·kin·der \mə-'kin-dər\ Sir Halford John 1861–1947 Eng. geographer

Mc·Kin·ley \mə-'kin-lē\ William 1843–1901 25th pres. of the U. S. (1897–1901)

Mack·in·tosh \'mak-ən-‚täsh\ Sir James 1765–1832 Scot. philos. & hist.

Maclaren Ian see John WATSON

Mac·Leish \mə-'klēsh\ Archibald 1892– Am. poet & administrator

Mac·Len·nan \mə-'klen-ən\ Hugh 1907– Canad. nov.

Mac·leod \mə-'klaúd\ Iain \'ē-ən\ Norman 1913– Brit. polit.

— John James Rickard 1876–1935 Scot. physiol.

Mc·Lu·han \mə-'klü-ən\ Marshall 1911– Canad. educator

Mac·Ma·hon, de \‚mak-‚mä-'ōⁿ; mək-'ma(-ə)n, -'mäⁿ\ Comte Marie Edme Patrice Maurice 1808–1893 marshal (1859) & pres. (1873–79) of France

Mac·mil·lan \mək-'mil-ən\ Harold 1894– Brit. prime min. (1957–63)

Mac·Mil·lan \mək-'mil-ən\ Donald Baxter 1874– Am. arctic explorer

Mc·Mil·lan \mək-'mil-ən\ Edwin Mattison 1907– Am. chem.

Mac·Mon·nies \mək-'mil-ən\ Frederick William 1863–1937 Am. sculptor

Mc·Na·mara \‚mak-nə-'mar-ə, 'mak-nə-‚mar-ə\ Robert Strange 1916– Am. secy. of defense (1961–68)

Mc·Naugh·ton \mək-'nót-ᵊn\ Andrew George Latta 1887–1966 Canad. gen. & diplomat

Mac·Neice \mək-'nēs\ Louis 1907–1963 Brit. poet & classical scholar

Mac·Neil \mək-'nē(ə)l\ Hermon Atkins 1866–1947 Am. sculptor

Mc·Nutt \mək-'nət\ Paul Vo·ries \'vōr-ēz, 'vór-\ 1891–1955 Am. lawyer & administrator

Mac·pher·son \mək-'fərs-ᵊn\ James 1736–1796 Scot. writer

Mac·rea·dy \mə-'krēd-ē\ William Charles 1793–1873 Eng. actor

Ma·da·ri·a·ga y Ro·jo, de \‚mäth-ə-rē-'äg-ə-(‚)ē-'rò-(‚)hō\ Salvador 1886– Span. writer & diplomat

Ma·de·ro \mä-'de(ə)r-(‚)ō, -'thā(ə)r-\ Francisco Indalecio 1873–1913 pres. of Mexico (1911–13)

Mad·i·son \'mad-ə-sən\ Dolley 1768–1849 née (*Dorothea*) *Payne; wife of James* Am. hostess

— James 1751–1836 4th pres. of the U. S. (1809–17)

Mae·ce·nas \mi-'sē-nəs\ Gaius 70?–8 B.C. Rom. statesman & patron of literature

Maes *or* **Maas** \'mäs\ Nicolaes 1632–1693 Du. painter

Mae·ter·linck \'mat-ər-‚liŋk, 'mät-\ Count Maurice 1862–1949 Belg. poet, dram., & essayist

Ma·gel·lan \mə-'jel-ən, *chiefly Brit* -'gel-\ Ferdinand 1480?–1521 *Fernão de Magalhães* Port. navigator

Ma·gi·not \‚mazh-ə-'nō, -maj-\ André 1877–1932 Fr. polit.; min. of war (1922–24; 1926–29; 1929–30; 1931)

Ma·han \mə-'han\ Alfred Thayer 1840–1914 Am. admiral & hist.

Mah·ler \'mäl-ər\ Gustav 1860–1911 Austrian composer

Mah·mud II \mä-'müd\ 1785–1839 sultan of Turkey (1803–39)

Ma·hom·et \mə-'häm-ət\ *or* **Ma·hom·ed** \-əd\ *var of* MUHAMMAD

Mai·ler \'mā-lər\ Norman 1923– Am. author

Mai·mon·i·des \mī-'män-ə-‚dēz\ 1135–1204 Rabbi *Moses ben Maimon* Span.-born philos.

Maine \'mān\ Sir Henry James Sumner 1822–1888 Eng. jurist

Main·te·non, de \‚maⁿt-ᵊn-‚óⁿ, mant-\ Marquise 1635–1719 *Françoise d' Aubigné; consort of Louis XIV*

Mait·land \'māt-lənd\ Frederic William 1850–1906 Eng. hist.

Ma·ki·no \mä-'kē-(‚)nō\ Count Nobuaki 1861–1949 Jap. statesman

Ma·lan \mə-'lan, -'län, 'läⁿ\ Daniel François 1874–1959 So. African editor; prime min. (1948–54)

Mal·colm X \‚mal-kə-'meks\ 1925–1965 *Malcolm Little* Am. civil rights leader

Male·branche, de \‚mal-(ə-)'bräⁿsh, ‚mäl-\ Nicolas 1638–1715 Fr. philos.

Ma·len·kov \‚mal-(y)ən-'kóf, ‚mäl-\ Georgi Maximilianovich 1901– Russ. polit.

Mal·herbe, de \ma-'le(ə)rb, mä-\ François 1555–1628 Fr. poet

Ma·li·nov·sky \‚mal-ə-'nóf-skē, ‚mäl-, -'nóv-\ Rodion Yakovlevich 1899–1967 Russ. gen.

Ma·li·now·ski \‚mal-ə-'nóf-skē, ‚mäl-, -'nóv-\ Bronislaw Kasper 1884–1942 Pol.-born anthropologist

Mal·lar·mé \‚mal-‚är-'mā\ Stéphane 1842–1898 Fr. poet

Ma·lone \mə-'lōn\ Edmund *or* Edmond 1741–1812 Irish Shakespearean scholar

Mal·o·ry \'mal-(ə-)rē\ Sir Thomas *fl* 1470 Eng. author

Mal·pi·ghi \mal-'pē-gē, -'pig-ē\ Marcello 1628–1694 Ital. anatomist

Mal·raux \mal-'rō\ André 1901– Fr. writer & polit.

Mal·thus \'mal-thəs\ Thomas Robert 1766–1834 Eng. econ.

Man·del \man-'del, män-, mäⁿ\ Georges 1885–1943 orig. *Jéroboam Rothschild* Fr. polit.

Man·de·ville \'man-də-‚vil\ Bernard 1670?–1733 Du.-born physician & satirist in Eng.

— Sir John *d* 1372 pseud. of an unidentified author of travel books

Ma·net \ma-'nā, mä-\ Édouard 1832–1883 Fr. painter

Ma·nil·i·us \mə-'nil-ē-əs\ Gaius 1st cent. B.C. Rom. polit.

Mann \'man\ Horace 1796–1859 Am. educ.

— \'män, 'man\ Thomas 1875–1955 Am. (Ger.-born) author

Man·ner·heim, von \'män-ər-ˌhām, 'man-, -ˌhīm\ Baron Carl Gustaf Emil 1867–1951 Fin. gen. & statesman

Man·ning \'man-iŋ\ Henry Edward 1808–1892 Eng. cardinal

Mans·field \'manz-ˌfēld, 'man(t)s-\ Katherine 1888–1923 pseud. of *Kathleen* née *Beau·champ* \'bē-chəm\ *Murry* Brit. writer

— Richard 1854–1907 Eng. actor in Am.

Man·son \'man(t)-sən\ Sir Patrick 1844–1922 Brit. parasitologist

Man·sur, al- \ˌal-ˌman-'sù(ə)r\ 712?–775 Arab caliph (754–775); founder of Baghdad

Man·te·gna \män-'tān-yə\ Andrea 1431–1506 Ital. painter & engraver

Man·tle \'mant-ᵊl\ (Robert) Burns 1873–1948 Am. journalist

Manuel *Don Juan* see JUAN MANUEL

Ma·nu·tius \mə-'n(y)ü-sh(ē-)əs\ Al·dus \'òl-dəs, 'al-\ 1450–1515 *Teobaldo Mannucci* or *Manuzio* Ital. painter & classical scholar

Man·zo·ni \män(d)-'zō-nē\ Alessandro Francesco Tommaso Antonio 1785–1873 Ital. nov. & poet

Mao Tse-tung \'maù-(')dzə-'dùŋ\ 1893–   Chin. Communist

Map \'map\ Walter 1140?–?1209 Welsh writer

Ma·rat \mə-'rä\ Jean Paul 1743–1793 Fr. (Swiss-born) revolutionist

Mar·cel·lus \mär-'sel-əs\ Marcus Claudius 268?–208 B.C. Rom. gen.

March 1st Earl of see Roger de MORTIMER

Mar·co·ni \mär-'kō-nē\ Marchese Guglielmo 1874–1937 Ital. electrical engineer & inventor

Marco Polo see POLO

Mar·cos \'mär-kəs, -(ˌ)kōs\ Ferdinand E. 1917–   pres. of the Philippine Republic (from 1965)

Marcus Aurelius see Marcus Aurelius ANTONINUS

Mar·ga·ret \'mär-g(ə-)rət\ **of Anjou** 1430–1482 *queen of Henry VI of England*

— **of Navarre** 1492–1549 queen of Navarre (1544–49) & writer

— **of Valois** 1553–1615 queen of Navarre

— **Rose** 1930–   *wife of Earl of Snowdon* princess of Gt. Britain

Ma·ria The·re·sa \mə-ˌrē-ə-tə-'rē-sə, -'rä-sə, -'rā-zə\ 1717–1780 *wife of Emp. Francis I* queen of Hungary & Bohemia

Ma·rie \mə-'rē\ 1875–1938 queen of Romania (1914–27); queen dowager (1927–38)

— **An·toi·nette** \ˌan-t(w)ə-'net\ 1755–1793 *dau. of Maria Theresa & wife of Louis XVI of France;* guillotined

— **Louise** 1791–1847 *dau. of Francis I of Austria & 2d wife of Napoleon I*

Marie de Mé·di·cis \-də-'med-ə-(ˌ)chē, ˌmäd-ə-'sēs\ 1573–1642 *2d wife of Henry IV of France*

Mar·in \'mar-ən\ John 1870–1953 Am. painter

Ma·ri·net·ti \ˌmar-ə-'net-ē, ˌmär-\ Emilio Filippo Tommaso 1876–1944 Ital. poet

Ma·ri·ni \mə-'rē-nē\ or **Ma·ri·no** \-(ˌ)nō\ Giambattista 1569–1625 Ital. poet

Mar·i·on \'mer-ē-ən, 'mar-ē-, 'mā-rē-\ Francis 1732?–1795 *the Swamp Fox* Am. Revolutionary commander

Ma·ri·tain \ˌmar-ə-'taⁿ\ Jacques 1882–   Fr. philos. & diplomat

Mar·i·us \'mer-ē-əs, 'mar-\ Gaius 155?–86 B.C. Rom. gen.

Ma·ri·vaux, de \ˌmar-ə-'vō\ Pierre Carlet de Chamblain 1688–1763 Fr. dram. & nov.

Mark Antony or **Anthony** see Marcus ANTONIUS

Mark·ham \'mär-kəm\ (Charles) Edwin 1852–1940 Am. poet

Mar·ko·va \mär-'kō-və\ Ali·cia \ə-'lē-sē-ə\ 1910–   *Alice Marks* Eng. dancer

Marlborough 1st Duke of see John CHURCHILL

Mar·lowe \'mär-(ˌ)lō\ Christopher 1564–1593 Eng. dram.

— **Julia** 1866–1950 pseud. of *Sarah Frances Frost* Am. (Eng.-born) actress

Mar·mont, de \ˌmär-'mōⁿ\ Auguste Frédéric Louis Viesse 1774–1852 Duc *de Raguse* Fr. gen.; marshal of France (1809)

Mar·mon·tel \ˌmär-(ˌ)mōⁿ-'tel\ Jean François 1723–1799 Fr. author

Ma·rot \ma-'rō, mə-\ Clément 1495?–1544 Fr. poet

Mar·quand \'mär-ˌkwänd\ John Phillips 1893–1960 Am. writer

Mar·quette \mär-'ket\ Jacques 1637–1675 *Père* \ˌpi(ə)r, ˌpe(ə)r\ *Marquette* Jesuit missionary & explorer in Am.

Mar·quis \'mär-kwəs\ Donald Robert Perry 1878–1937 *Don* Am. humorist

Mar·ry·at \'mar-ē-ət\ Frederick 1792–1848 Eng. naval commander & nov.

Marsh \'märsh\ Dame Ngaio \'nī-(ˌ)ō\ 1899–   N.Z. writer

Mar·shall \'mär-shəl\ George Catlett 1880–1959 Am. gen. of the army & diplomat

— **John** 1755–1835 Am. jurist; chief justice U.S. Supreme Court (1801–35)

— **Thomas Riley** 1854–1925 vice-pres. of the U.S. (1913–21)

— **Thurgood** 1908–   Am. jurist

Mar·sil·i·us of Padua \mär-'sil-ē-əs\ 1290?–?1343 Ital. scholar

Mar·ston \'mär-stən\ John 1575?–1634 Eng. dram.

Martel Charles see CHARLES MARTEL

Mar·tens \'märt-ᵊnz\ Fëdor Fëdorovich 1845–1909 Russ. jurist

Mar·tial \'mär-shəl\ ab 40–ab 102 *Marcus Valerius Martialis* Rom. epigrammatist

Mar·tin \'märt-ᵊn, mär-taⁿ\ Saint 315?–?399 *Martin of Tours* \-'tù(ə)r\ patron saint of France

Mar·tin \'märt-ᵊn\ Archer John Porter 1910–   Brit. chem.

— **Glenn Luther** 1886–1955 Am. airplane manuf.

— **Homer Dodge** 1836–1897 Am. painter

— **Joseph William** 1884–1968 Am. publisher & polit.

— **Sir Theodore** 1816–1909 Brit. author

Mar·tin du Gard \ˌmär-taⁿ-dü-'gär\ Roger 1881–1958 Fr. nov.

Mar·ti·neau \'märt-ᵊn-ˌō\ Harriet 1802–1876 Eng. nov. & econ.

— **James** 1805–1900 *bro. of Harriet* Eng. theol. & philos.

Mar·ti·ni \mär-'tē-nē\ Simone 1283?–1344 Ital. painter

Mar·vell \'mär-vəl\ Andrew 1621–1678 Eng. poet & satirist

Marx \'märks\ Karl 1818–1883 Ger. polit. philos. & socialist

Mary \'me(ə)r-ē, 'ma(ə)r-ē, 'mā-rē\ 1867–1953 Princess *Victoria Mary of Teck; queen of George V of Eng.*

— **I** 1516–1558 *Mary Tudor; Bloody Mary* queen of Eng. (1553–58)

— **II** 1662–1694 joint Brit. sovereign with William III

— **Stuart** 1542–1587 *Mary, Queen of Scots* queen of Scot. (1542–67); beheaded

Ma·sac·cio \mə-'zäch-(ˌ)ō, -ē-ˌō\ 1401–1428 orig. *Tommaso Guidi* Ital. painter

Ma·sa·ryk \'mas-ə-(ˌ)rik\ Jan \'yän, 'yan\ Gar·rigue \gə-'rēg\ 1886–1948 *son of T. G.* Czech diplomat & polit.

— **To·máš** \'tò-ˌmäsh, 'täm-əs\ Garrigue 1850–1937 Czech philos.; 1st pres. of Czechoslovakia (1918–35)

Ma·sca·gni \mä-'skän-yē, ma-\ Pietro 1863–1945 Ital. composer

Mase·field \'mās-ˌfēld\ John 1878–1967 Eng. author; poet laureate (1930–67)

Mas·i·nis·sa or **Mas·si·nis·sa** \ˌmas-ᵊn-'is-ə\ 238?–149 B.C. king of Numidia

Ma·son \'mās-ᵊn\ Charles 1730–1787 Eng. astron. & surveyor

Mas·sa·soit \ˌmas-ə-'sòit\ d 1661 sachem of Wampanoag Indians in eastern Massachusetts

Mas·sé·na \ˌmas-ā-'nä, mə-'sä-nə\ André 1758–1817 Duc *de Rivoli;* Prince *d'Ess·ling* \'des-liŋ\ Fr. soldier under Napoleon; marshal of France (1804)

Mas·se·net \ˌmas-ᵊn-'ā, ma-'snā\ Jules Émile Frédéric 1842–1912 Fr. composer

Mas·sey \'mas-ē\ Raymond 1896–   Am. (Canad.-born) actor & producer

— **William Ferguson** 1856–1925 N. Z. statesman

Mas·sine \ma-'sēn, mə-\ Léonide 1894–   Am. (Russ.-born) dancer & choreographer

Mas·sing·er \'mas-ᵊn-jər\ Philip 1583–1640 Eng. dram.

Mas·son \'mas-ᵊn\ David 1822–1907 Scot. editor & author

Mas·ters \'mas-tərz\ Edgar Lee 1869–1950 Am. author

Math·er \'math-ər, 'math-\ Cotton 1663–1728 Am. clergyman & author

— **Increase** 1639–1723 *father of Cotton* Am. clergyman & author; pres. Harvard College (1685–1701)

Ma·tisse \ma-'tēs, mə-\ Henri 1869–1954 Fr. painter

Ma·tsu·o·ka \ˌmat-sə-'wō-kə, ˌmät-, -(ˌ)kä\ Yosuke \'yō-sùk-e\ 1880–1946 Jap. statesman

Mat·te·ot·ti \ˌmat-ē-'ōt-ē, ˌmät-, -'òt-\ Giacomo 1885–1924 Ital. socialist

Mat·thews \'math-ˌyüz\ (James) Brander 1852–1929 Am. educ. & author

Mat·ting·ly \'mat-iŋ-lē\ Garrett 1900–1962 Am. hist.

Maugham \'mò(-ə)m\ William Somerset 1874–1965 Eng. nov. & dram.

Mau·nou·ry \ˌmō-nù-'rē\ Michel Joseph 1847–1923 Fr. gen.

Maupassant, de \ˌmō-pə-'säⁿ\ (Hen·ri René Albert) Guy 1850–1893 Fr. short-story writer

Mau·riac \mòr-'yäk, ˌmòr-ē-'äk\ François 1885–   Fr. author

Mau·rice \'mòr-əs, 'mär-əs; mò-'rēs, mə-\ Ger. **Mo·ritz** \'mōr-əts, 'mòr-\ 1521–1553 elector of Saxony (1547–53) & gen.

— **of Nassau** 1567–1625 Prince of *Orange* Du. gen. & statesman

Mau·rois \mòr-'wä\ André 1885–1967 pseud. of *Émile Salomon Wilhelm Her·zog* \-er-zòg\ Fr. writer

Mau·ry \'mòr-ē, 'mär-\ Matthew Fontaine 1806–1873 Am. naval officer & oceanographer

Mau·ser \'maù-zər\ Peter Paul 1838–1914 & his bro. Wilhelm 1834–1882 Ger. inventors

Maw·son \'mòs-ᵊn\ Sir Douglas 1882–1958 Brit. antarctic explorer & geologist

Max·im \'mak-səm\ Sir Hiram Stevens 1840–1916 Brit. (Am.-born) inventor

— **Hudson** 1853–1927 *bro. of Sir Hiram* Am. inventor & explosives expert

Max·i·mil·ian \ˌmak-sə-'mil-yən\ 1832–1867 *bro. of Francis Joseph I of Austria* emp. of Mexico (1864–67); executed

— **I** 1459–1519 Holy Rom. emp. (1493–1519)

— **II** 1527–1576 Holy Rom. emp. (1564–76)

Max·well \'mak-ˌswel, -swəl\ James Clerk \'klärk\ 1831–1879 Scot. physicist

May \'mā\ Sir Thomas Erskine 1815–1886 1st Baron *Farn·bor·ough* \'färn-ˌbər-ə, -ˌbə-ˌrō, -b(ə-)rə\ Eng. constitutional jurist

Mayo \'mā-(ˌ)ō\ Charles Horace 1865–1939 & his bro. William James 1861–1939 Am. surgeons

— **Henry Thomas** 1856–1937 Am. admiral

Ma·za·rin \ˌmaz-ə-'raⁿ, 'maz-ə-rən, ˌmaz-ə-'rēn\ Jules 1602–1661 Fr. cardinal & statesman

Maz·zi·ni \mät-'sē-nē, mat-; mäd-'zē-, mad-\ Giuseppe 1805–1872 Ital. patriot

Mc- see MAC-

Mead \'mēd\ Margaret 1901–   Am. anthropol.

Meade \'mēd\ George Gordon 1815–1872 Am. gen.

Mea·ny \'mē-nē\ George 1894–   Am. labor leader

Med·a·war \'med-ə-wər\ Peter Brian 1915–   Eng. anatomist

Me·di·ci, de' \'med-ə-(ˌ)chē\ Catherine see CATHERINE DE MÉDICIS

— **Cosimo** or **Cosmo** 1389–1464 Florentine financier & polit.

— **Cosimo I** 1519–1574 *Cosimo the Great;* Duke of *Florence;* Grand Duke of *Tuscany*

— **Giulio** see CLEMENT VII

— **Lorenzo** 1449–1492 *Lorenzo the Magnificent* Florentine statesman, ruler, & patron

Me·di·na-Si·do·nia \mə-'dē-nə-sə-'dōn-yə, mä-'thē-nə-sə-'thōn-\ 7th Duke of 1550–1615 *Alonso Pérez de Guzmán* Span. admiral

Meer van Delft, van der see Jan VERMEER

Me·he·met Ali \mä-ˌmet-(ˌ)ä-'lē\ or **Mohammed Ali** 1769–1849 viceroy of Egypt (1805–48)

Meigh·en \'mē-ən\ Arthur 1874–1960 Canad. statesman; prime min. (1920–21; 1926)

Meis·so·nier \ˌmās-ᵊn-'yā\ Jean Louis Ernest 1815–1891 Fr. painter

Meit·ner \'mīt-nər\ Li·se \'lē-zə\ 1878–1968 Ger. physicist

Me·lanch·thon \mə-'laŋ(k)-t(h)ən\ 1497–1560 *Philipp Schwarzert* Ger. scholar & religious reformer

Mel·ba \'mel-bə\ Dame Nellie 1861–1931 orig. *Helen Porter Mitchell* Austral. soprano

Mel·chers \'mel-chərz\ Gari 1860–1932 Am. painter

Mel·chi·or \'mel-kē-ˌó(ə)r\ Lau·ritz \'laù-rəts\ Lebrecht Hommel 1890–   Am. (Dan.-born) tenor

Mel·lon \'mel-ən\ Andrew William 1855–1937 Am. financier

Mel·ville \'mel-ˌvil\ Herman 1819–1891 Am. nov.

ə abut; ᵊ kitten; ər further; a back; ā bake; ä cot, cart; aù out; ch chin; e less; ē easy; g gift; i trip; ī life
j joke; ŋ sing; ō flow; ò flaw; òi coin; th thin; th this; ü loot; ù foot; y yet; yü few; yù furious; zh vision
ᵊ F table; à F bac; ķ G ich, Buch; ⁿ F vin; œ F bœuf; œ̄ F feu; ᵫ F rue; ᵞ F digne \dēnᵞ\, nuit \nwᵞē\

Mem·ling \'mem-liŋ\ *or* **Mem·linc** \-liŋk\ Hans 1430?–1495 Flem. painter

Me·nan·der \mə-'nan-dər\ 343?–?291 B.C. Greek dram.

Men·cius \'men-ch(ē-)əs\ 372?–?289 B.C. *Mêng-tzŭ or Meng-tse* Chin. philos.

Menc·ken \'meŋ-kən, 'men-\ Henry Louis 1880–1956 Am. editor

Men·del \'men-dᵊl\ Gregor Johann 1822–1884 Austrian botanist

Men·de·le·ev \,men-dᵊl-'ā-əf\ Dmitri Ivanovich 1834–1907 Russ. chem.

Men·dels·sohn \'men-dᵊl-sən\ Moses 1729–1786 Ger. philos.

Mendelssohn-Bar·thol·dy \-,bär-'t(h)ȯl-dē\ Ludwig Felix 1809–1847 *grandson of Moses Mendelssohn* Ger. composer, pianist, & conductor

Men·do·za, de \men-'dō-zə\ Antonio 1485?–1552 Span. colonial administrator

Men·e·lik II \'men-ᵊl-(,)ik\ 1844–1913 emp. of Ethiopia (1889–1913)

Me·nén·dez de Av·i·lés \mə-'nen-dəs-dā-,äv-ə-'lās\ Pedro 1519–1574 Span. admiral; colonizer of Florida

Me·nes \'mē-(,)nēz\ *fl* 3400 (3500?) B.C. Egyptian king; uniter of north & south kingdoms

Men·ning·er \'men-iŋ-ər\ Karl Augustus 1893– Am. psychiatrist

Me·not·ti \mə-'nät-ē, -'nȯt-\ Gian-Carlo 1911– Am. (Ital.-born) composer

Me·nu·hin \'men-yə-wən, mə-'n(y)ü-ən\ Ye·hu·di \yə-'hüd-ē\ 1916– Am. violinist

Men·zies \'men-(,)zēz\ Sir Robert Gordon 1894– Austral. statesman; prime min. (1949–66)

Mer·ca·tor \(,)mər-'kāt-ər\ Gerhardus 1512–1594 *Gerhard Kremer* Flem. geographer

Mer·cier \mer-'syā, 'mer-sē-,ā\ Désiré Joseph 1851–1926 Belg. cardinal; primate of Belgium

Mer·e·dith \'mer-əd-əth\ George 1828–1909 Eng. nov. & poet
— Owen see E. R. Bulwer LYTTON

Mer·gen·tha·ler \'mər-gən-,thäl-ər, 'mer-gən-,täl-\ Ottmar 1854–1899 Am. (Ger.-born) inventor

Mé·ri·mée \'mer-ə-,mā, ,mā-rə-'\ Prosper 1803–1870 Fr. nov. & hist.

Mer·ritt \'mer-ət\ Wesley 1834–1910 Am. gen.

Mer·ton \'mərt-ᵊn\ Thomas 1915–1968 Am. clergyman & author

Mes·mer \'mez-mər, 'mes-\ Franz *or* Friedrich Anton 1734–1815 Austrian physician

Mes·sa·la Cor·vi·nus \mə-'säl-ə-,kȯr-'vī-nəs\ Marcus Valerius 1st cent. B.C. Rom. gen. & statesman

Mes·sa·li·na \,mes-ə-'lī-nə, -'lē-\ Valeria *d* A.D. 48 *3d wife of Emp. Claudius*

Mes·ser·schmitt \'mes-ər-,shmit\ Willy 1898– Ger. aircraft designer & manuf.

Mes·sier \mes-'yā, 'mes-ē-,ā\ Charles 1730–1817 Fr. astron.

Mes·tro·vic \'mesh-trə-,vich\ Ivan 1883–1962 Am. (Yugoslavian-born) sculptor

Me·tax·as \,met-ək-'säs\ Joannes 1871–1941 Greek gen. & dictator

Metch·ni·koff \'mech-nə-,kȯf\ Élie 1845–1916 Russ. zool. & bacteriol.

Met·ter·nich, von \'met-ər-(,)nik\ Prince Klemens Wenzel Nepomuk Lothar 1773–1859 Austrian statesman

Mey·er \'mī-(-ə)r\ Albert Gregory 1903–1965 Am. cardinal
— Annie 1867–1951 née *Nathan* Am. educ. & writer

Mey·er·beer \'mī-ər-,bi(ə)r, -,be(ə)r\ Giacomo 1791–1864 *Jakob Liebmann Beer* Ger. composer

Mey·er·hof \'mī-ər-,hȯf\ Otto 1884–1951 Ger. physiol.

Mi·chael \'mī-kəl\ *Romanian* **Mi·hai** \mē-'hī\ 1921– *Michael Hohenzollern* king of Romania (1927–30; 1940–47); abdicated

Mi·chel·an·ge·lo Buo·nar·ro·ti \,mī-kə-'lan-jə-,lō-,bwȯn-ə-'rȯt-ē, ,mik-ə-'lan-, - jə-\ 1475–1564 Ital. sculptor, painter, architect, & poet

Mi·che·let \mēsh-'lā\ Jules 1798–1874 Fr. hist.

Mi·chel·son \'mī-kəl-sən\ Albert Abraham 1852–1931 Am. (Ger.-born) physicist

Mich·e·ner \'mich-ə-nər\ James Albert 1907– Am. author
— Roland 1900– Canad. polit.; gov. gen. of Canada (from 1967)

Mic·kie·wicz \mits-'kyā-vich\ Adam 1798–1855 Pol. poet

Mid·dle·ton \'mid-ᵊl-tən\ Thomas 1570?–1627 Eng. dram.

Mies van der Ro·he \'mēs-,vän-də-'rō(-ə), ,mēz-\ Ludwig 1886–1969 Am. (Ger.-born) architect

Miff·lin \'mif-lən\ Thomas 1744–1800 Am. Revolutionary gen.

Mi·haj·lo·vić *or* **Mi·khai·lo·vitch** \mi-'hī-lə-,vich\ Draža *or* Dra·ja \'dräzh-ə\ 1893?–1946 Yugoslav gen.

Mi·ko·yan \,mik-ə-'yän, ,mē-kə-\ Anas·tas \'än-ə-'stäs\ Ivanovich 1895– Russ. polit.; pres. U.S.S.R. (1964–65)

Miles \'mī(ə)lz\ Nelson Appleton 1839–1925 Am. gen.

Mi·lhaud \mē-'(y)ō\ Darius 1892– Fr. composer

Mill \'mil\ James 1773–1836 Scot. philos., hist., & econ.
— John Stuart 1806–1873 *son of James* Eng. philos. & econ.

Mil·lais \mil-'ā\ Sir John Everett 1829–1896 Eng. painter

Mil·lay \mil-'ā\ Edna St. Vincent 1892–1950 Am. poet

Mil·ler \'mil-ər\ Arthur 1915– Am. dram. & nov.
— Cincinnatus Hiner 1839–1913 pseud. *Joa·quin* \wä-'kēn\ *Miller* Am. poet
— Henry 1891– Am. writer
— Perry Gilbert Eddy 1905–1963 Am. literary critic & scholar
— William 1782–1849 Am. Adventist

Mil·le·rand \mēl-rä°\ Alexandre 1859–1943 Fr. statesman; pres. of France (1920–24)

Mil·let \mil-'ā\ Jean François 1814–1875 Fr. painter

Mil·li·kan \'mil-i-kən\ Robert Andrew 1868–1953 Am. physicist

Mil·man \'mil-mən\ Henry Hart 1791–1868 Eng. poet & hist.

Milne \'mil(n)\ Alan Alexander 1882–1956 Eng. poet & dram.

Mil·ner \'mil-nər\ 1st Viscount 1854–1925 *Alfred Milner* Brit. administrator in So. Africa

Mil·ti·a·des \,mil-'tī-ə-,dēz\ 540?–?489 B.C. Athenian gen.

Mil·ton \'milt-ᵊn\ John 1608–1674 Eng. poet

Mil·yu·kov \,mil-yə-'kȯf\ Pavel Nikolaevich 1859–1943 Russ. polit. & hist.

Mi·nié \'min-ē-,ā, men-'yā\ Claude Étienne 1814–1879 Fr. army officer & inventor

Mi·not \'mī-nət\ George Richards 1885–1950 Am. physician

Min·ton \'mint-ᵊn\ Sherman 1890–1965 Am. jurist

Min·u·it \'min-yə-wət\ *or* **Min·ne·wit** \'min-ə-,wit\ Peter 1580–1638 Du. colonial administrator in Am.

Mi·ra·beau, de \'mir-ə-,bō\ Comte 1749–1791 *Honoré Gabriel Victor Riqueti* Fr. orator & revolutionist

Mi·ró \mē-'rō\ Joan \zhü-'än\ 1893– Span. painter

Mis·tral \mi-'stral\ Frédéric 1830–1914 Provençal poet

Mis·tral \mi-'sträl\ Gabriela 1889–1957 *Lucila Godoy de Alcayaga* Chilean poet & educ.

Mitch·ell \'mich-əl\ John 1870–1919 Am. labor leader
— John Newton 1913– Am. lawyer; U.S. attorney general (from 1969)
— Maria 1818–1889 Am. astron.
— William 1879–1936 *Billy Mitchell* Am. gen.

Mit·ford \'mit-fərd\ Mary Russell 1787–1855 Eng. nov. & dram.
— William 1744–1827 Eng. hist.

Mith·ri·da·tes VI \,mith-rə-'dāt-ēz\ *ab* 132–63 B.C. *the Great* king of Pontus (120–63)

Mi·tro·pou·los \mə-'träp-ə-ləs\ Di·mi·tri \də-'mē-trē\ 1896–1960 Am. (Greek-born) conductor

Mo·di·glia·ni \,mō-(,)dēl-'yän-ē, mō-,dēl-ē-'än-ē\ Amedeo 1884–1920 Ital. painter in France

Mo·djes·ka \mə-'jes-kə\ Helena 1840–1909 orig. *Modrzejewska* née *Opid* Pol.-born actress in Am.

Mohammed *var of* MUHAMMAD

Mo·ham·med Ri·za Pah·la·vi *or* **Pah·le·vi** \mō-'ham-əd-ri-'zä-'pal-ə-(,)vē, -'häm-\ 1919– shah of Iran (1941–)

Mois·san \mwä-'sä°\ Henri 1852–1907 Fr. chem.

Mo·ley \'mō-lē\ Raymond 1886– Am. journalist

Mo·lière \mōl-'ye(ə)r, 'mȯl-,\ 1622–1673 pseud. of *Jean Baptiste Poquelin* Fr. actor & dram.

Molina, de Tirso see TIRSO DE MOLINA

Mol·nár \'mōl-,när, 'mȯl-\ Fe·renc \'fer-ən(t)s\ 1878–1952 Hung. author

Mo·lo·tov \'mäl-ə-,tȯf, 'mȯl-, 'mōl-, -,tȯv\ Vyacheslav Mikhailovich 1890– orig. *Skryabin* Russ. statesman

Molt·ke, von \'mōlt-kə\ Count Helmuth 1800–1891 Pruss. field marshal

Momm·sen \'mōm-zən\ Theodor \'tä-ō-,dȯr\ 1817–1903 Ger. classical scholar & hist.

Monck *or* **Monk** \'məŋk\ George 1608–1670 1st Duke of *Albemarle* Eng. gen.

Mon·dri·an \'mȯn-drē-,än\ Piet 1872–1944 *Pieter Cor·ne·lis* \kȯr-'nā-ləs\ *Mondriaan* Du. painter

Mo·net \mō-'nā\ Claude 1840–1926 Fr. painter

Mo·ne·ta \mō-'nät-ə\ Ernesto Teodoro 1833–1918 Ital. journalist & pacifist

Mon·i·er-Wil·liams \'mən-ē-ər-'wil-yəmz, 'män-\ Sir Monier 1819–1899 Eng. Sanskrit scholar

Mo·niz \mū-'nēsh\ Antonio Caetano de Abrere Freire Egas 1874–1955 Port. medical scientist

Mon·mouth \'mən-məth, 'män-\ Duke of 1649–1685 *James Scott, son of Charles II of Eng.* Eng. rebel & claimant to the throne

Mon·roe \mən-'rō\ James 1758–1831 5th pres. of U.S. (1817–25)

Mon·ta·gna \mən-'tän-yə\ Bartolommeo 1450?–1523 Ital. painter

Mon·ta·gu \'mänt-ə-,gyü, 'mənt-\ Lady Mary Wortley 1689–1762 Eng. letter writer

Mon·taigne, de \män-'tän\ Michel Eyquem 1533–1592 Fr. essayist

Mont·calm de Saint-Vé·ran, de \,mänt-'kä(l)m-də-,saⁿ-və-'räⁿ\ Marquis Louis Joseph 1712–1759 Fr. field marshal in Canada

Mon·tes·pan, de \,mō°-tes-pä°, ,mänt-ə-'span\ Marquise 1641–1707 née (*Françoise Athénaïs*) *Rochechouart; Mistress of Louis XIV*

Mon·tes·quieu, de \,mänt-əs-'kyü, ,män-,tes-, -'kyə(r)\ Baron *de La Brède et* 1689–1755 *Charles de Secondat* Fr. lawyer & polit. philos.

Mon·tes·so·ri \,mänt-ə-'sȯr-ē, -'sȯr-\ Maria 1870–1952 Ital. physician & educator

Mon·teux \mōⁿ-'tə(r)\ Pierre 1875–1964 Am. (Fr.-born) conductor

Mon·te·ver·di \,mänt-ə-'ve(ə)rd-ē, -'vərd-\ Claudio Giovanni Antonio 1567–1643 Ital. composer

Mon·te·zu·ma II \,mänt-ə-'zü-mə\ 1480?–1520 last Aztec emp. of Mexico (1502–20)

Mont·fort, de \'mänt-fərt\ Simon 1208?–1265 Earl of *Leicester* Eng. soldier & statesman
— l'Amau·ry \,lam-ə-'rē\ Simon IV 1160?–1218 Earl of *Leicester* & Comte de *Toulouse; father of prec.* Fr. crusader

Mont·gol·fier \mänt-'gäl-fē-ər, -fē-,ā\ Joseph Michel 1740–1810 & his bro. Jacques Étienne 1745–1799 Fr. inventors & aeronauts

Mont·gom·ery \(,)mən(t)-'gəm-(ə-)rē, män(t)-, -'gäm-\ Bernard Law 1887– 1st Viscount Brit. field marshal

Mont·mo·ren·cy, de \,mänt-mə-'ren(t)-sē\ Duc Anne 1493–1567 Fr. soldier; constable (1537)

Mont·rose \män-'trōz\ James Graham 1st Marquis of 1612–1650 Scot. Royalist

Moo·dy \'müd-ē\ Dwight Lyman 1837–1899 Am. evangelist
— William Vaughn 1869–1910 Am. poet & dram.

Moo·ney \'mü-nē\ Edward 1882–1958 Am. cardinal

Moore \'mō(ə)r, 'mȯ(ə)r, 'mu(ə)r\ George 1852–1933 Irish author
— George Edward 1873–1958 Eng. philos.
— Henry 1898– Brit. sculptor
— John Bassett 1860–1947 Am. jurist
— Marianne Craig 1887– Am. poet
— Thomas 1779–1852 Irish poet
— -Brab·a·zon \-'brab-ə-zən\ John Theodore Cuthbert 1884–1964 1st Baron *Brabazon of Tara* Brit. aviator & administrator

Mo·ra·via \mō-'räv-ē-ə\ Alberto 1907– real name *Pincherle* Ital. writer

More \'mō(ə)r, 'mȯ(ə)r\ Hannah 1745–1833 Eng. religious writer
— Henry 1614–1687 Eng. philos.
— Paul Elmer 1864–1937 Am. essayist & critic
— Sir Thomas 1478–1535 *Saint* Eng. statesman & author

Mo·reau \mȯ-rō\ Jean Victor 1763–1813 Fr. soldier

Mor·gan \'mȯr-gən\ Conway Lloyd 1852–1936 Eng. zool. & psychol.
— Daniel 1736–1802 Am. Revolutionary gen.
— Sir Henry 1635?–1688 Eng. buccaneer
— John Hunt 1825–1864 Am. Confed. cavalry officer
— John Pier·pont \'pi(ə)r-,pänt\ 1837–1913 Am. financier
— John Pierpont 1867–1943 *son of J. P.* Am. financier
— Thomas Hunt 1866–1945 Am. zool.

Mor·gen·thau \\'mȯr-gən-ˌthȯ\ Henry 1891–1967 U.S. secy. of the treas. (1934–45)

Mor·i·son \\'mȯr-ə-sən, 'mär-\ Samuel Eliot 1887–   Am. hist.

— Stanley 1889–1968 Eng. type designer

Mor·land \\'mȯ(ə)r-lənd\ Sir Thomas Lethbridge Napier 1865–1925 Brit. (Canad.-born) gen.

Mor·ley \\'mȯr-lē\ Christopher Darlington 1890–1957 Am. writer

— John 1838–1923 Viscount *Morley of Blackburn* Eng. statesman & writer

Mor·nay, de \\'mȯr-nā\ Philippe 1549–1623 Seigneur du *Plessis= Marly; Duplessis-Mornay* Fr. Huguenot

Mor·ris \\'mȯr-əs, 'mär-\ Gou·ver·neur \ˌgəv-ə(r)-'ni(ə)r\ 1752–1816 Am. statesman & diplomat

— Robert 1734–1806 Am. financier & statesman

— William 1834–1896 Eng. poet, artist, & socialist

Mor·ri·son \\'mȯr-ə-sən, 'mär-\ **of Lambeth** Baron 1888–1965 *Herbert Stanley Morrison* Eng. labor leader & polit.

— Robert 1782–1834 Scot. missionary in China

Morse \\'mȯ(ə)rs\ Samuel Finley Breese 1791–1872 Am. artist & inventor

Mor·ti·mer, de \\'mȯrt-ə-mər\ Roger (IV) 1287–1330 1st Earl of *March* Welsh rebel & paramour of Isabella, Queen of Edward II of Eng.

Mor·ton \\'mȯrt-ⁿn\ Levi Parsons 1824–1920 Am. banker; vice= pres. of the U.S. (1889–93)

— William Thomas Green 1819–1868 Am. dentist

Mos·by \\'mȯz-bē\ John Singleton 1833–1916 Am. lawyer & Confed. cavalry officer

Moś·cic·ki \mȯsh-'tsit-skē\ Ignacy 1867–1946 Pol. chem.; pres. of Poland (1926–39)

Mo·ses \\'mō-zəz *also* -zəs\ Anna Mary Robertson 1860–1961 *Grandma Moses* Am. painter

Mos·ley \\'mōz-lē\ Sir Oswald Er·nald \\'ərn-ⁿld\ 1896–   Eng. polit.

Moth·er·well \\'məth-ər-ˌwel, -wəl\ Robert 1915–   Am. artist

Mo Ti \\'mō-'dē\ *or* **Mo-tzu** \\'mōd-'zə\ 5th-4th cent. B.C. Chin. philos.

Mot·ley \\'mät-lē\ John Lothrop 1814–1877 Am. hist.

Mo·ton \\'mōt-ⁿn\ Robert Russa 1867–1940 Am. educ.

Mott \\'mät\ John Raleigh 1865–1955 Am. Y.M.C.A. leader

— Lucretia 1798–1880 *nee Coffin* Am. social reformer

Mot·teux \mä-'tə(r)\ Peter Anthony 1660 *or* 1663–1718 Eng. (Fr.-born) dram. & translator

Moul·ton \\'mōlt-ⁿn\ Forest Ray 1872–1952 Am. astron.

Moul·trie \\'mül-trē\ William 1730–1805 Am. Revolutionary gen.

Mount·bat·ten \maunt-'bat-ⁿn\ Louis, Earl 1900–   Prince *Louis of Bat·ten·berg* \\'bat-ⁿn-ˌbərg\ Brit. admiral; 1st gov. gen. of India (1947–48); chief of defense staff (1959–65)

— Philip, Duke of Edinburgh *see* PHILIP

Mo·zart \\'mōt-ˌsärt\ Wolfgang Amadeus 1756–1791 Austrian composer

Muench \\'minch\ Aloisius Joseph 1889–1962 Am. cardinal

Mu·ham·mad \mō-'ham-əd, -'häm- *also* mü-\ 570–632 Arab prophet & founder of Islam

Müh·len·berg \\'myü-lən-ˌbərg\ Henry Melchior 1711–1787 Ger.= born Lutheran clergyman in Am.

Muir \\'myù(ə)r\ John 1838–1914 Am. (Scot.-born) naturalist

Mul·ler \\'məl-ər\ Hermann Joseph 1890–1967 Am. geneticist

Mül·ler \\'myül-ər, 'mil-, 'məl-\ Friedrich Max 1823–1900 Brit. (Ger.-born) philologist

— Johann 1436–1476 *Regiomontanus* Ger. astron.

— Paul 1899–1965 Swiss chem.

Mulock Dinah Maria *see* CRAIK

Mum·ford \\'məm(p)-fərd\ Lewis 1895–   Am. writer

Munch \\'munch, 'mənch\ Charles 1891–   Fr.-born conductor

Münch·hau·sen, von \\'muŋk-ˌhauz-ⁿn\ Baron Karl Friedrich Hieronymus 1720–1797 Baron *Mun·chau·sen* \\'mən-ˌchauz-ⁿn, 'mùn-, -ˌchȯz-\ Ger. hunter, soldier, & supposed teller of absurdly exaggerated stories

Mun·de·lein \\'mən-də-ˌlīn\ George William 1872–1939 Am. cardinal

Mu·ñoz Ma·rín \ˌ(ˌ)mün-ˌyōs-mə-'rēn, -ˌyōz-\ Luis 1898–   Puerto Rican polit.

Munro H.H. *see* SAKI

Mun·sey \\'mən(t)-sē, 'mən-zē\ Frank Andrew 1854–1925 Am. publisher

Mün·ster·berg \\'mùn(t)-stər-ˌbərg, 'myün(t)-, 'mən(t)-\ Hugo 1863–1916 Ger.-born psychol. in Am.

Mu·ra·sa·ki \ˌmùr-ə-'säk-ē\ Baroness 11th cent. *Murasaki Shikibu* Jap. poet

Mu·rat \myù-'rä\ Joachim 1767?–1815 Fr. gen.; marshal of France (1804); king of Naples (1808–15)

Mu·ril·lo \myù-'ril-ˌō, m(y)ù-'rē-(ˌ)ō, -'rēl-(ˌ)yō\ Bartolomé Esteban 1617–1682 Span. painter

Mur·phy \\'mər-fē\ Frank 1890–1949 Am. jurist

— Robert Daniel 1894–   Am. diplomat

— William Parry 1892–   Am. physician

Mur·ray \\'mər-ē, 'mə-rē\ (George) Gilbert (Aimé) 1866–1957 Brit. classical scholar

— Sir James Augustus Henry 1837–1915 Brit. lexicographer

— Lindley 1745–1826 Am. grammarian

— Philip 1886–1952 Am. labor leader

Mur·row \\'mər-(ˌ)ō, 'mə-(ˌ)rō\ Edward Roscoe 1908–1965 Am. news commentator

Mus·kie \\'məs-kē\ Edmund Sixtus 1914–   Am. polit.

Mu·sorg·ski *or* **Mous·sorg·sky** \mù-'sȯrg-skē, -'zȯrg-\ Mo·dest \mō-'dest\ Petrovich 1835–1881 Russ. composer

Mus·set, de \myü-'sā\ (Louis Charles) Alfred 1810–1857 Fr. poet

Mus·so·li·ni \ˌmü-sə-'lē-nē, ˌmùs-ə-\ Be·ni·to \bə-'nēt-(ˌ)ō\ 1883–1945 *Il Du·ce* \ēl-'dü-(ˌ)chā\ Ital. Fascist premier (1922–45)

Mustafa (*or* **Mustapha**) **Kemal Pasha** *see* KEMAL ATATÜRK

Mu·tsu·hi·to \ˌmüt-sə-'hē-(ˌ)tō\ 1852–1912 *Mei·ji* \\'mā-(ˌ)jē\ emp. of Japan (1867–1912)

Muz·zey \\'məz-ē\ David Sav·ille \\'sav-əl\ 1870–1965 Am. hist.

My·ron \\'mī(ə)-rən\ 5th cent. B.C. Greek sculptor

Na·bo·kov \nə-'bȯ-kəf\ Vladimir Vladimirovich 1899–   Am. (Russ.-born) nov. & poet

Na·ga·no \nə-'gän-(ˌ)ō\ Osami 1888–1947 Jap. admiral

Nai·du \\'nīd-(ˌ)ü\ Sa·ro·ji·ni \sə-'rō-jə-(ˌ)nē\ 1879–1949 Hindu poet & reformer

Na·mi·er \\'nā-mē-ər\ Sir Lewis Bernstein 1888–1960 Brit. hist.

Na·nak \\'nän-ək\ 1469–1538 founder of the Sikh faith in India

Nan·sen \\'nän(t)-sən, 'nan(t)-\ Frid·tjof \\'frich-ˌȯf\ 1861–1930 Norw. arctic explorer, zool., & statesman

Na·pier \\'nā-pē-ər, nə-'pi(ə)r\ Sir Charles James 1782–1853 Brit. gen.

— John 1550–1617 Laird of *Mer·chis·ton* \\'mər-kə-stən\ Scot. math.

— Robert Cornelis 1810–1880 1st Baron *Napier of Mag·da·la* \\'mag-də-lə\ Brit. field marshal

Na·po·leon I \nə-'pōl-yən, -'pō-lē-ən\ *or* **Napoleon Bo·na·parte** \\'bō-nə-ˌpärt\ 1769–1821 emp. of the French (1804–15)

— **II** 1811–1832 *L'Ai·glon* \lā-'glōⁿ\; Duc de Reichstadt; son of *Napoleon I & Marie Louise*

— **III** 1808–1873 *Louis Napoleon; son of Louis Bonaparte & Hortense de Beauharnais* emp. of the French (1852–70)

Nar·vá·ez, de \när-'vä-ˌās, -ˌäth\ Pánfilo 1480?–1528 Span. soldier in Am.

Nash \\'nash\ Ogden 1902–   Am. poet

Nash *or* **Nashe** \\'nash\ Thomas 1567–1601 Eng. satirist & dram.

Nas·myth \\'nāz-məth, 'naz-\ Alexander 1758–1840 Scot. painter

Nas·ser \\'näs-ər, 'nas-\ Ga·mal \gə-'mäl\ Ab·del \\'äb-d'l\ 1918–   Egyptian polit.; pres. of Egypt (1956–   ) & of U. A. R. (1958–   )

Nast \\'nast\ Thomas 1840–1902 Am. (Ger.-born) cartoonist

Na·than \\'nā-thən\ George Jean 1882–1958 Am. editor & dramatic critic

— Robert 1894–   Am. nov.

Na·tion \\'nā-shən\ Car·ry \\'kar-ē\ Amelia 1846–1911 *née Moore* Am. temperance agitator

Neb·u·chad·nez·zar \ˌneb-(y)ə-kəd-'nez-ər\ *or* **Neb·u·cha·drez·zar** \-kə-'drez-\ d 562 B.C. Chaldean king of Babylon (605–562)

Nec·ker \ne-'ke(ə)r, 'nek-ər\ Jacques 1732–1804 *father of Mme. de Staël* Fr. (Swiss-born) financier & statesman

Neh·ru \\'ne(ə)r-(ˌ)ü, 'nā-(ˌ)rü\ Ja·wa·har·lal \jə-'wä-hər-ˌläl\ 1889–1964 *son of Motilal* Indian nationalist; prime min. (1947–64); his daughter In·di·ra \\'in-də-rə\ Nehru Gandhi 1918–   prime min. (from 1966)

— Pun·dit \\'pən-dət\ Mo·ti·lal \\'mōt-ⁿl-ˌäl\ 1861–1931 Indian nationalist

Neil·son \\'nē(ə)l-sən\ William Allan 1869–1946 Am. (Scot.-born) educ.; pres. Smith Coll. (1917–39)

Nel·son \\'nel-sən\ Viscount 1758–1805 *Horatio Nelson* Brit. admiral

Ne·pos \\'nē-ˌpäs, 'nep-ˌäs\ Cornelius 1st cent. B.C. Rom. hist.

Ne·ri, de' \\'ne(ə)r-ē, 'nā-rē\ San Filippo 1515–1595 Saint *Philip Neri* Ital. founder (1564) of "Fathers of the Oratory"

Nernst \\'ne(ə)rn(t)st\ Walther Hermann 1864–1941 Ger. physicist & chem.

Ne·ro \\'nē-(ˌ)rō, 'ni(ə)r-(ˌ)ō\ 37–68 *Nero Claudius Caesar Drusus Germanicus* orig. *Lucius Domitius Ahenobarbus* Rom. emp. 54–68

Ner·va \\'nər-və\ Marcus Cocceius 35?–98 Rom. emp. (96–98)

Ner·vi \\'ne(ə)r-vē\ Pier Luigi 1891–   Ital. structural engineer

Nes·to·ri·us \ne-'stȯr-ē-əs, -'stȯr-\ d ab 451 patriarch of Constantinople (428–431)

Neu·rath, von \\'nȯi-ˌrät\ Baron Konstantin 1873–1956 Ger. diplomat

Neville Richard *see* Earl of WARWICK

Nev·in \\'nev-ən\ Ethelbert Woodbridge 1862–1901 Am. composer

Nev·ins \\'nev-ənz\ Allan 1890–   Am. hist.

New·bolt \\'n(y)ü-ˌbōlt\ Sir Henry John 1862–1938 Eng. author

New·man \\'n(y)ü-mən\ John Henry 1801–1890 Eng. cardinal & writer

New·ton \\'n(y)üt-ⁿn\ Sir Isaac 1642–1727 Eng. math. & natural philos.

Ney \nā\ Michel 1769–1815 Duc *d'Elchingen; Prince de la Moskova* Fr. soldier; marshal of France (1804); executed

Nich·o·las \\'nik-(ə-)ləs\ Saint 4th cent. Christian prelate; patron saint of children

— **I** 1796–1855 czar of Russia (1825–55)

— **II** 1868–1918 czar of Russia (1894–1917)

— Grand Duke 1856–1929 Russ. gen. & monarchist

— of Cu·sa \\'kyü-sə\ 1401–1464 R.C. prelate, math., & philos.

Nich·ols \\'nik-əlz\ Anne 1891–1966 Am. dram.

Nich·ol·son \\'nik-əl-sən\ Sir Francis 1655–1728 Eng. administrator in Am.

— Francis 1753–1844 Eng. watercolorist

Ni·ci·as \\'nis-(h)-ē-əs\ d 413 B.C. Athenian gen. & statesman

Nic·o·lay \\'nik-ə-ˌlā\ John George 1832–1901 Am. biographer

Ni·colle \nē-kȯl\ Charles Jean Henri 1866–1936 Fr. physician & bacteriol.

Nic·ol·son \\'nik-əl-sən\ Harold 1886–1968 Eng. biographer & diplomat

Nie·buhr \\'nē-ˌbù(ə)r\ Barthold Georg 1776–1831 Ger. hist., statesman, & philologist

— Rein·hold \\'rīn-ˌhōld\ 1892–   Am. theol.

Niel·sen \\'nēl-sən\ Carl August 1865–1931 Dan. composer

Niem·ce·wicz \nē-ˌem-'sā-vich\ Julian Ursyn 1758–1841 Pol. patriot & writer

Nie·mey·er \\'nē-ˌmī-(ə)r\ Oscar 1907–   Brazilian architect

Nie·möl·ler \\'nē-ˌmə(r)l-ər\ Martin 1892–   Ger. anti-Nazi Protestant theol.

Nietz·sche \\'nē-chə, -chē\ Friedrich Wilhelm 1844–1900 Ger. philos.

Night·in·gale \\'nīt-ⁿn-ˌgāl, -iŋ-\ Florence 1820–1910 Eng. nurse & philanthropist

Ni·jin·ska \nə-'jin-skə, -'zhin-\ Bro·ni·sla·va \ˌbrän-ə-'släv-ə\ 1891–   Russ. dancer & choreographer

Ni·jin·sky \nə-'jin-skē, -'zhin-\ Was·law \vät-'släf\ 1890–1950 Russ. ballet dancer; bro. of prec.

Nim·itz \\'nim-əts\ Chester William 1885–1966 Am. admiral of the fleet

Nin \\'nēn\ Anaïs 1903–   Am. (Fr.-born) author

Nit·ti \\'nit-ē, 'nēt-\ Francesco Saverio 1868–1953 Ital. econ. & statesman

Nix·on \'nik-sən\ Richard Mil·hous \'mil-ˌhaůs\ 1913– Am. lawyer; 37th pres. of the U.S. (1969–)

Nkru·mah \en-'krü-mə, eŋ-\ Kwa·me \'kwäm-i\ 1909– Ghanaian prime min. (1957–60); first president (1960–66)

No·bel \nō-'bel\ Alfred Bernhard 1833–1896 Swed. manuf., inventor, & philanthropist

No·bi·le \'nō-bə-ˌlā\ Umberto 1885– Ital. arctic explorer & aeronautical engineer

No·ble \'nō-bəl\ Sir Percy Lockhart Harnam 1880–1955 Brit. admiral

No·el–Ba·ker \ˌnō-əl-'bā-kər\ Philip John 1889– Brit. polit.

No·gu·chi \nō-'gü-chē\ Hideyo 1876–1928 Jap.-born bacteriol. in Am.

— Isamu 1904– Am. sculptor

No·guès \nō-'ges\ Auguste 1876– Fr. gen.

No·mu·ra \nō-'mùr-ə\ Kichisaburo 1877–1964 Jap. admiral & diplomat

Nor·dau \'nȯ(ə)r-ˌdaů\ Max Simon 1849–1923 orig. *Süd·feld* \'zūēt-ˌfelt\ Ger. physician, author, & Zionist

Nor·den·skjöld \'nùrd-ᵊn-ˌshəld, -ˌshēld\ Baron Nils Adolf Erik 1832–1901 Swed. arctic explorer

Nor·di·ca \'nȯrd-i-kə\ Lillian 1857–1914 pseud. *of Lillian Norton* Am. soprano

Nor·ris \'nȯr-əs, 'när-\ Charles Gilman 1881–1945 Am. nov.

— Frank 1870–1902 *bro. of C.G.* Am. nov.

— George William 1861–1944 Am. statesman

— Kathleen 1880–1966 *wife of C.G.* Am. nov.

North \'nȯ(ə)rth\ Christopher see WILSON

— Frederick 1732–1792 *Lord North* Eng. statesman; prime min. (1770–82)

— Sir Thomas 1535–?1601 Eng. translator

Northcliffe Viscount see HARMSWORTH

Nor·throp \'nȯr-thrəp\ John Howard 1891– Am. scientist

Nor·ton \'nȯrt-ᵊn\ Charles Eliot 1827–1908 Am. author & educ.

— Thomas 1532–1584 Eng. lawyer & poet

Nos·tra·da·mus \ˌnäs-trə-'dā-məs, ˌnȯs-trə-'däm-əs\ 1503–1566 Fr. physician & astrologer

No·vi·kov \'nō-və-ˌkȯf, -ˌkȯv\ Nikolai Vasilievich 1903– Russ. diplomat

Noyes \'nȯiz\ Alfred 1880–1958 Eng. poet

Nu·re·yev \nů-'rā-yəf\ Rudolph 1939– Russ. dancer

Nut·ting \'nət-iŋ\ Wallace 1861–1941 Am. antiquarian

Nye \'nī\ Edgar Wilson 1850–1896 *Bill* Am. humorist

Oates \'ōts\ Titus 1649–1705 Eng. fabricator of the Popish Plot

O'·Boyle \ō-'bȯil\ Patrick Aloysius 1896– Am. cardinal

Obrenović Alexander I see ALEXANDER

O'·Bri·en \ō-'brī-ən\ Lawrence Francis 1917– U.S. postmaster general (1965–68)

O'·Ca·sey \ō-'kā-sē\ Sean \'shȯn\ 1880–1964 Irish dram.

Oc·cleve \'äk-ˌlēv\ *var of* HOCCLEVE

Ochoa \ō-'chō-ə\ Severo 1905– Am. (Span.-born) biochem.

Ochs \'äks\ Adolph Simon 1858–1935 Am. newspaper publisher

Ock·ham *or* **Oc·cam** \'äk-əm\ William of 1300?–?1349 Eng. philos.

O'·Con·nell \ō-'kän-ᵊl\ Daniel 1775–1847 Irish polit. agitator

— William Henry 1859–1944 Am. cardinal

O'·Con·nor \ō-'kän-ər\ Frank 1903–1966 pseud. *of Michael John O'Donovan* Irish author

— Thomas Power 1848–1929 *Tay Pay* \'tā-'pā\ Irish journalist

Octavian *or* **Octavianus** see AUGUSTUS

Odets \ō-'dets\ Clifford 1906–1963 Am. playwright

Odo·a·cer \ˌōd-ə-ˌwā-sər\ 434?–493 1st barbarian ruler of Italy (476–493)

Oeh·len·schlä·ger \'ə(r)l-ən-ˌshlā-gər\ Adam Gottlob 1779–1850 Dan. poet & dram.

O'·Fao·láin \ˌō-fə-'lȯn, -'līn\ Seán \'shȯn\ 1900– Irish author

Of·fen·bach \'ȯf-ən-ˌbäk, -ˌbäk\ Jacques 1819–1880 Fr. composer

O'·Fla·her·ty \ō-'fla-hər-tē\ Li·am \'lē-əm\ 1896– Irish nov.

Og·a·dai \ˌäg-ə-'dī\ 1185–1241 Mongol khan (1229–41)

Og·den \'ȯg-dən, 'äg-\ Charles Kay 1889–1957 Brit. psychol.

Ogle·thorpe \'ō-gəl-ˌthȯrp\ James Edward 1696–1785 Eng. philanthropist & gen.; founder of Georgia

O'·Hara \ō-'har-ə\ John (Henry) 1905–1970 Am. author

O'·Hig·gins \ō-'hig-ənz, ō-'ē-gēn(t)s\ Bernardo 1778–1842 *Liberator of Chile* Chilean soldier & statesman

Ohm \'ōm\ Georg Simon 1787–1854 Ger. physicist

O'·Keeffe \ō-'kēf\ Georgia 1887– Am. muralist & painter

O'·Kel·ly \ō-'kel-ē\ Seán \'shȯn\ Thomas 1883–1966 Irish journalist; pres. of Republic of Ireland (1945–59)

— Seu·mas \'shā-məs\ 1881–1918 Irish writer

Olaf I \'ō-ləf\ 969–1000 *Olaf Trygg·ves·son* \'trig-və-sən\ king of Norway (995–1000)

— **II** 995?–1030 Saint *Olaf* king of Norway (1016–28)

Olav V \'ō-ləf, -ləv\ 1903– king of Norway (from 1957)

Old·cas·tle \'ōl(d)-ˌkas-əl\ Sir John 1377?–1417 Baron *Cob·ham* \-'käb-əm\ Eng. Lollard; executed

Oliv·i·er \ō-'liv-ē-ˌā\ Sir Laurence Kerr 1907– Eng. actor

Omar Khay·yám \ˌō-ˌmär-ˌkī-'(y)äm, ˌō-mər-, -'(y)am\ *d ab* 1123 Pers. poet & astron.

O'·Neill \ō-'nē(ə)l\ Eugene Gladstone 1888–1953 Am. dram.

On·ions \'ən-yənz\ Charles Talbut 1873–1965 Eng. lexicographer

Op·pen·heim \'äp-ən-ˌhīm\ Edward Phillips 1866–1946 Eng. nov.

Op·pen·hei·mer \-ˌhī-mər\ Julius Robert 1904–1967 Am. physicist

Or·ca·gna \ȯr-'kän-yə\ 1308?–?1368 *Andrea di Cione* Florentine painter, sculptor, & architect

Or·czy \'ȯrt-sē\ Baroness Em·mus·ka \'em-əsh-kə\ 1865–1947 Eng. (Hung.-born) nov. & dram.

Orff \'ȯ(ə)rf\ Carl 1895– Ger. composer

Or·i·gen \'ȯr-ə-jən, 'är-\ 185?–?254 Greek writer, teacher, & church father

Or·lan·do \ȯr-'lan-(ˌ)dō, -'län-\ Vittorio Emanuele 1860–1952 Ital. statesman

Or·man·dy \'ȯr-mən-dē\ Eugene 1899– Hung.-born conductor in U.S.

Orms·by–Gore \ˌȯrmz-bē-'gō(ə)r, -'gȯ(ə)r\ (William) David 1918– 5th Baron *Harlech* Brit. diplomat

Oroz·co \ə-'rō-(ˌ)skō, -'rō-\ José Clemente 1883–1949 Mex. painter

— **Romero** \rō-'me(ə)-(ˌ)ō\ Carlos 1898– Am. caricaturist & painter

Or·te·ga y Gas·set \ȯr-'tā-gə-ˌē-gä-'set\ José 1883–1955 Span. philos., writer, & statesman

Or·tiz Ru·bio \ˌȯr-ˌtēz-'rü-bē-ˌō\ Pascual 1877–1963 pres. of Mexico (1930–32)

Or·well \'ȯr-ˌwel, -wəl\ George 1903–1950 pseud. *of Eric Blair* Eng. author

Os·born \'äz-bərn, -ˌbȯrn\ Henry Fairfield 1857–1935 Am. paleontologist

Os·borne \'äz-bərn, -ˌbȯrn\ John James 1929– Brit. dram.

— Thomas Mott 1859–1926 Am. penologist

Os·car II \'äs-kər, 'ȯs-\ 1829–1907 king of Sweden (1872–1907) & of Norway (1872–1905)

Osce·o·la \ˌäs-ē-'ō-lə, ˌō-sē-\ 1800?–1838 chief of the Seminole Indians

Os·ler \'ō-slər, 'ōz-lər\ Sir William 1849–1919 Canad. physician

Os·man \'ȯs-ˌmän\ *or* **Oth·man** \'ȯth-\ 1259–1326 founder of the Ottoman Empire

Os·me·ña \ˌōz-'mān-yə, ōs-\ Sergio 1878–1961 pres. of Philippine Commonwealth (1944–46)

Os·si·etz·ky, von \ˌäs-ē-'et-skē\ Carl 1889–1938 Ger. writer & pacifist

Ossoli Marchioness see Margaret FULLER

Os·ten·so \'äs-tən-ˌsō\ Martha 1900–1963 Norw.-born nov. in U.S.

Ost·wald \'ōs-ˌtwȯld\ Wilhelm 1853–1932 Ger. physical chem. & philos.

Otis \'ōt-əs\ Elwell Stephen 1838–1909 Am. gen.

— Harrison Gray 1837–1917 Am. gen. & journalist

— James 1725–1783 Am. Revolutionary statesman

Ot·ter·bein \'ät-ər-ˌbīn\ Philip William 1726–1813 Ger.-born clergyman in Am.

Ot·to I \'ät-(ˌ)ō\ 912–973 *the Great* Holy Rom. emp. (936–973)

Ot·way \'ät-ˌwā\ Thomas 1652–1685 Eng. dram.

Ouida see Marie Louise de la RAMÉE

Ov·id \'äv-əd\ 43 B.C.–?A.D. 17 *Publius Ovidius Naso* Rom. poet

Ow·en \'ō-ən\ Robert 1771–1858 Welsh social reformer

Ox·en·stier·na \'ük-sən-ˌsher-nə, 'äk-\ *or* **Ox·en·stiern** \'äk-sən-ˌsti(ə)rn\ Count Axel Gustafsson 1583–1654 Swed. statesman

Oxford Earl of see Robert HARLEY

Oya·ma \ō-'yäm-ə\ Prince Iwao 1842–1916 Jap. field marshal

Paa·si·ki·vi \'päs-ə-ˌkiv-ē, -ˌkē-vē, ˌpäs-ə-'\ Ju·ho \'yü-(ˌ)hō\ K. 1870–1956 Finnish businessman; pres. of Finland (1946–56)

Pa·de·rew·ski \ˌpad-ə-'ref-skē, -'rev-\ Ignace \ēn-'yäs\ Jan \'yän\ 1860–1941 Pol. pianist & statesman

Pa·ga·ni·ni \ˌpag-ə-'nē-nē, ˌpäg-\ Nicolò 1782–1840 Ital. violinist

Page \'pāj\ Thomas Nelson 1853–1922 Am. nov. & diplomat

— Walter Hines 1855–1918 Am. journalist & diplomat

Pag·et \'paj-ət\ Sir James 1814–1899 Eng. surgeon & pathologist

Paine \'pān\ Albert Bigelow 1861–1937 Am. author

— Thomas 1737–1809 Am. (Eng.-born) polit. philos. & author

Pain·le·vé \ˌpaⁿ-lə-vā\ Paul 1863–1933 Fr. math. & statesman

Pa·le·stri·na, da \ˌpal-ə-'strē-nə\ Giovanni Pierluigi 1526?–1594 Ital. composer

Pa·ley \'pā-lē\ William 1743–1805 Eng. theol. & philos.

Pal·grave \'pȯl-ˌgrāv, 'pal-\ Francis Turner 1824–1897 Eng. poet & anthologist

Pal·la·dio \pə-'läd-ē-ˌō\ Andrea 1518–1580 Ital. architect

Pal·ma \'päl-mə\ Tomás Estrada 1835–1908 1st pres. of Cuba (1902–06)

Palm·er \'päm-ər, 'päl-mər\ Alice Elvira 1855–1902 née *Freeman;* wife of G.H. Am. educ.

— Daniel David 1845–1913 Canad.-born father of chiropractic

— George Herbert 1842–1933 Am. scholar & educ.

Palm·er·ston \'päm-ər-stən, 'päl-mər-\ 3d Viscount 1784–1865 *Henry John Temple* Eng. statesman; prime min. (1855–58; 1859–65)

Palm·gren \'päm-grən, 'pälm-\ Se·lim \'sā-ləm, 'sel-əm\ 1878–1951 Finnish pianist & composer

Pa·ni·ni \'pän-(y)ə-(ˌ)nē\ *fl* 350 B.C. Sanskrit grammarian

Pank·hurst \'paŋk-ˌhərst\ Emmeline 1858–1928 née *Goulden* Eng. suffragist

Pa·o·li, di \'paů-lē, 'pä-ō-ˌlē\ Pasquale 1725–1807 Corsican patriot

Pa·pen, von \'päp-ən\ Franz 1879–1969 Ger. diplomat

Pap·pen·heim, zu \'päp-ən-ˌhīm, 'pap-\ Count Gottfried Heinrich 1594–1632 Ger. gen.

Par·a·cel·sus \ˌpar-ə-'sel-səs\ Philippus Aureolus 1493–1541 *Theophrastus Bombastus von Hohenheim* Swiss-born alchemist & physician

Pares \'pa(ə)rz, 'pe(ə)rz\ Sir Bernard 1876–1949 Eng. hist.

Pa·re·to \pə-'rāt-(ˌ)ō\ Vilfredo 1848–1923 Ital. econ. & sociol.

Pa·ris \'par-əs\ Gaston 1839–1903 Fr. philologist

Par·is \'par-əs\ Matthew 1200?–1259 Eng. monk & hist.

Park \'pärk\ Mungo 1771–1806 Scot. explorer in Africa

Par·ker \'pär-kər\ Dorothy 1893–1967 née *Rothschild* Am. writer

— Sir Gilbert 1862–1932 Canad. author

— Matthew 1504–1575 Eng. theol.

— Theodore 1810–1860 Am. Unitarian clergyman

Parkes \'pärks\ Sir Henry 1815–1896 Austral. statesman

Park·man \'pärk-mən\ Francis 1823–1893 Am. hist.

Parley Peter see Samuel Griswold GOODRICH

Par·men·i·des \pär-'men-ə-ˌdēz\ 5th cent. B.C. Greek philos.

Par·nell \pär-'nel, 'pärn-ᵊl\ Charles Stewart 1846–1891 Irish nationalist

Parr Catherine see CATHERINE

Par·ring·ton \'par-iŋ-tən\ Vernon Louis 1871–1929 Am. literary hist.

Par·rish \'par-ish\ Maxfield 1870–1966 Am. painter

Par·ry \'par-ē\ Sir William Edward 1790–1855 Eng. arctic explorer

Par·sons \'pärs-ᵊnz\ William 1800–1867 3d Earl of *Rosse* Eng. astron.

Pas·cal \pa-'skal\ Blaise 1623–1662 Fr. math. & philos.

Pa·šić \'päsh-(ˌ)ich\ Nikola \'nē-kō-lä\ 1845?–1926 Serbian & Yugoslav statesman

Passfield 1st Baron see WEBB

Pas·sy \pa-'sē\ Frédéric 1822–1912 Fr. econ. & statesman

— Paul Édouard 1859–1940 *son of prec.* Fr. phonetician

Pas·ter·nak \\'pas-tər-ˌnak\\ Boris Leonidovich 1890–1960 Russ. poet, nov., & translator

Pas·teur \\pa-'stər\\ Louis 1822–1895 Fr. chem.

Pa·ter \\'pāt-ər\\ Walter Horatio 1839–1894 Eng. essayist & critic

Pat·more \\'pat-ˌmō(ə)r, -ˌmò(ə)r\\ Coventry Kersey Dighton 1823–1896 Eng. poet

Pa·ton \\'pāt-ᵊn\\ Alan Stewart 1903– S. African writer

Pa·tri \\'pä-trē\\ Angelo 1877–1965 Am. (Ital.-born) educ. & author

Pat·rick \\'pa-trik\\ Saint 389?–?461 apostle & patron saint of Ireland

Pat·ti \\'pat-ē, 'pät-ē\\ Adelina 1843–1919 Ital. (Span.-born) operatic coloratura soprano

Pat·ti·son \\'pat-ə-sən\\ Mark 1813–1884 Eng. scholar & author

Pat·ton \\'pat-ᵊn\\ George Smith 1885–1945 Am. gen.

Pau·ker \\'pau̇-kər\\ Ana 1889?–1960 née *Ra·bin·sohn* Romanian Communist

Paul \\'pòl\\ name of 6 popes: esp. **III** 1468–1549 (pope 1534–49); **V** 1552–1621 (pope 1605–21); **VI** 1897– (pope 1963–)
— **I** 1754–1801 emp. of Russia (1796–1801); assassinated
— **I** 1901–1964 king of Greece (1947–64)
— Jean see RICHTER

Paul-Bon·cour \\'pòl-(ˌ)bōⁿ-'kù(ə)r\\ Joseph 1873– Fr. lawyer & statesman

Paul·ding \\'pòl-diŋ\\ James Kirke 1778–1860 Am. author

Pau·li \\'pau̇-lē\\ Wolfgang 1900–1958 Austrian-born physicist in Am.

Pau·ling \\'pò-liŋ\\ Li·nus \\'lī-nəs\\ Carl 1901– Am. chem.

Pau·lus \\'pau̇-ləs\\ Friedrich 1890–1957 Ger. field marshal (1943)
— \\'pò-ləs\\ Julius 2d–3d cent. A.D. Rom. jurist

Pau·sa·ni·as \\pò-'sā-nē-əs\\ 2d cent. A.D. Greek traveler & geographer

Pav·lov \\'päv-ˌlòf, 'pav-, -ˌlòv\\ Ivan Petrovich 1849–1936 Russ. physiol.

Pa·vlo·va \\'pav-lə-və, pav-'lò-\\ Anna 1885–1931 Russ. ballerina

Payne \\'pān\\ John Howard 1791–1852 Am. actor & dram.

Pea·body \\'pē-ˌbäd-ē, -bəd-ē\\ Endicott 1857–1944 Am. educ.
— George 1795–1869 Am. merchant & philanthropist

Pea·cock \\'pē-ˌkäk\\ Thomas Love 1785–1866 Eng. nov. & poet

Peale \\'pē(ə)l\\ Charles Willson 1741–1827 & his bro. James 1749–1831 & Charles's son Rembrandt 1778–1860 Am. painters

Pear·son \\'pi(ə)rs-ᵊn\\ Karl 1857–1936 Eng. scientist
— Lester Bowles 1897– prime min. of Canada (1963–68)

Pea·ry \\'pi(ə)r-ē\\ Robert Edwin 1856–1920 Am. arctic explorer

Pe·co·ra \\pi-'kòr-ə, -'kòr-\\ Ferdinand 1882– Am. jurist

Peel \\'pē(ə)l\\ Sir Robert 1788–1850 Eng. statesman

Peele \\'pē(ə)l\\ George 1556–1596 Eng. dram. & poet

Pe·gram \\'pē-grəm\\ George Braxton 1876–1958 Am. physicist

Peirce \\'pərs, 'pi(ə)rs\\ Charles Sanders 1839–1914 Am. math. & logician

Pei·xot·to \\pā-'shòt-(ˌ)ō\\ Ernest Clifford 1869–1940 Am. painter & illustrator

Pe·la·gius \\pə-'lā-j(ē-)əs\\ 360?–?420 Brit. monk & theol.

Pe·lop·i·das \\pə-'läp-əd-əs\\ d 364 B.C. Theban gen.

Penn \\'pen\\ Sir William 1621–1670 Eng. admiral
— William 1644–1718 *son of prec.* Eng. Quaker; founder of Pennsylvania

Pen·nell \\'pen-ᵊl, pə-'nel\\ Joseph 1857–1926 Am. etcher

Pep·in the Short \\ˌpep-ən-\\ 714?–768 king of the Franks (751–768)

Pepys \\'pēps\\ Samuel 1633–1703 Eng. diarist

Per·cy \\'pər-sē\\ Sir Henry 1364–1403 *Hotspur* Eng. soldier
— Thomas 1729–1811 Eng. antiquary & poet

Pé·rez Gal·dós \\ˌper-əs-(ˌ)gäl-'dòs\\ Benito 1843–1920 Span. nov. & dram.

Per·i·cles \\'per-ə-ˌklēz\\ d 429 B.C. Athenian statesman

Per·kins \\'pər-kənz\\ Frances 1882–1965 Am. social worker & administrator

Pe·rón \\pā-'rōn, pə-\\ Juan Domingo 1895– Argentine polit.; pres. of Argentina (1946–55)

Per·rault \\pə-'rō, pe-\\ Charles 1628–1703 Fr. fairy-tale writer

Per·rin \\pə-'ran, pe-, -'raⁿ\\ Jean Baptiste 1870–1942 Fr. physicist

Per·ry \\'per-ē\\ Bliss 1860–1954 Am. educ. & critic
— Matthew Cal·braith 1794–1858 Am. commodore
— Oliver Hazard 1785–1819 *bro. of prec.* Am. naval officer
— Ralph Barton 1876–1957 Am. philos. & educ.

Perse \\'pe(ə)rs\\ St. John see Alexis Saint-Léger LÉGER

Per·shing \\'pər-shiŋ, -zhiŋ\\ John Joseph 1860–1948 Am. gen. of the armies

Per·sius \\'pər-shəs, -shē-əs\\ 34–62 *Aulus Persius Flaccus* Rom. satirist

Pe·ru·gi·no, Il \\ˌper-ə-'jē-(ˌ)nō\\ 1446–1523 *Pietro Vannucci* Ital. painter

Pe·ruz·zi \\pə-'rüt-sē, pā-\\ Baldassare 1481–1536 Ital. architect & painter

Pes·ta·loz·zi \\ˌpes-tə-'lät-sē\\ Johann Heinrich 1746–1827 Swiss educ.

Pé·tain \\pā-taⁿ\\ Henri Philippe 1856–1951 Fr. gen.; marshal of France (1918); premier of Vichy France (1940–44)

Pe·ter \\'pēt-ər\\ Saint *d* A.D. ?67 disciple of Jesus; regarded, esp. by Roman Catholics, as vicar of Christ on earth [Mt. 16:16–19]
— **I** 1672–1725 *the Great* czar of Russia (1682–1725)
— **I** Ka·ra·geor·ge·vich \\ˌkar-ə-'jòr-jə-ˌvich\\ 1844–1921 king of Serbia (1903–21)
— **II** 1923– king of Yugoslavia (1934–45)
— the Hermit 1050?–?1115 Fr. preacher of the 1st Crusade

Pe·ters \\'pāt-ərz, -ərs\\ Carl 1856–1918 Ger. explorer in Africa

Pe·tö·fi \\'pet-ə-fē\\ Sán·dor \\'shän-ˌdò(ə)r\\ 1823–1849 Hung. poet

Pe·trarch \\'pē-ˌträrk, 'pe-\\ *or* Pe·trar·ca \\pā-'trär-kə\\ Francesco 1304–1374 Ital. poet

Pe·trie \\'pē-trē\\ Sir (William Matthew) Flin·ders \\'flin-dərz\\ 1853–1942 Eng. Egyptologist

Pe·tro·ni·us \\pə-'trō-nē-əs\\ Gaius 1st cent. A.D. *Ar·bi·ter Ele·gan·ti·ae* \\'är-bət-ər-,el-ə-'gan-chē-ˌē\\ Rom. satirist

Pet·ty \\'pet-ē\\ Sir William 1623–1687 Eng. polit. econ.

Pevs·ner \\'pefs-nər, 'pevz-\\ Antoine 1886–1962 Fr. (Russ.-born) sculptor & painter

Phae·drus \\'fē-drəs\\ 5th cent. B.C. Greek philos.
— 1st cent. A.D. Rom. fabulist

Phid·i·as \\'fid-ē-əs\\ 5th cent. B.C. Greek sculptor

Phil·ip \\'fil-əp\\ *d* 1676 *Met·a·com·et* \\ˌmet-ə-'käm-ət\\ sachem of the Wampanoag Indians
— name of 6 kings of France: esp. **II** *or* Philip Augustus 1165–1223 (reigned 1180–1223); **IV** (*the Fair*) 1268–1314 (reigned 1285–1314); **VI** 1293–1350 (reigned 1328–50)
— name of 5 kings of Spain esp.: **II** 1527–1598 (reigned 1556–98); **V** 1683–1746 (reigned 1700–46)
— **II** 382–336 B.C. king of Macedon (359–336)
— Prince 1921– *consort of Queen Elizabeth II of Gr. Britain* 3d Duke of Edinburgh (from 1947)
— the Good 1396–1467 Duke of Burgundy (1419–67)

Phil·ips \\'fil-əps\\ Ambrose 1675?–1749 *Nam·by-Pam·by* \\ˌnam-bē-'pam-bē\\ Eng. poet & dram.

Phil·lips \\'fil-əps\\ Stephen 1868–1915 Eng. poet & dram.
— Wendell 1811–1884 Am. orator & reformer

Phill·potts \\'fil-ˌpäts\\ Eden 1862–1960 Eng. nov. & dram.

Phi·lo Ju·dae·us \\'fī-(ˌ)lō-jü-'dē-əs\\ 1st cent. B.C.–1st cent. A.D. Hellenistic Jewish philos. of Alexandria

Pho·ci·on \\'fō-sē-ˌän, -sē-ən\\ 402?–317 B.C. Athenian gen. & statesman

Phu·mi·phon Adul·det \\'pü-mē-ˌpōn-ä-'dùn-lə-ˌdāt—*sic*\\ 1927– *Ra·ma IX* \\'räm-ə\\ king of Thailand (1946–)

Phyfe \\'fīf\\ Duncan 1768–1854 Am. (Scot.-born) cabinetmaker

Pi·card \\pē-'kär\\ Jean 1620–1682 Fr. astron.

Pi·cas·so \\pi-'käs-(ˌ)ō, -'kas-\\ Pablo 1881– Span. painter & sculptor

Pic·card \\pē-'kär\\ Auguste 1884–1962 Swiss physicist & aeronaut
— Jacques Ernst *son of Auguste* 1922– Swiss (Belg.-born) oceanographer; developer of bathyscaphe

Pick·er·ing \\'pik-(ə-)riŋ\\ Edward Charles 1846–1919 & his bro. William Henry 1858–1938 Am. astronomers

Pick·ett \\'pik-ət\\ George Edward 1825–1875 Am. Confed. gen.

Pi·co del·la Mi·ran·do·la \\'pē-(ˌ)kō-,del-ə-mə-'ran-də-lə, -'rän-\\ Count Giovanni 1463–1494 Ital. humanist

Pieck \\'pēk\\ Wilhelm 1876–1960 Ger. Communist

Pierce \\'pi(ə)rs\\ Franklin 1804–1869 14th pres. of the U.S. (1853–57)

Pike \\'pīk\\ Zebulon Montgomery 1779–1813 Am. gen. & explorer

Pi·late \\'pī-lət\\ Pon·tius \\'pän-chəs, 'pən-chəs\\ 1st cent. A.D. Rom. procurator of Judea; tried & condemned Jesus Christ

Pil·sud·ski \\pil-'süt-skē, -'züt-\\ Józef 1867–1935 Pol. gen. & statesman

Pin·chot \\'pin-(ˌ)shō\\ Gifford 1865–1946 Am. forester & polit.

Pinck·ney \\'piŋk-nē\\ Charles Cotesworth 1746–1825 Am. statesman

Pin·dar \\'pin-dər\\ 522?–443 B.C. Greek poet

Pi·ne·ro \\pə-'ni(ə)r-(ˌ)ō, -'ne(ə)r-\\ Sir Arthur Wing 1855–1934 Eng. dram.

Pin·ker·ton \\'piŋ-kərt-ᵊn\\ Allan 1819–1884 Scot.-born detective in Am.

Pin·ter \\'pint-ər\\ Harold 1930– Eng. dram.

Pin·tu·ric·chio \\ˌpint-ə-'rē-kē-ˌō, ˌpēnt-\\ 1454–1513 *Bernardino Betti* Ital. painter

Pin·zón \\pin-'zōn, pēn-'thòn\\ Martín Alonso 1440?–1493 & his bro. Vicente Yáñez 1460?–?1524 Span. navigators with Columbus

Pioz·zi \\pē-'òt-sē\\ Hester Lynch 1741–1821 *Mrs. Thrale* \\'thrā(ə)l\\ Eng. writer

Pi·ran·del·lo \\ˌpir-ən-'del-(ˌ)ō\\ Luigi 1867–1936 Ital. author

Pire \\'pi(ə)r\\ Dominique-Georges 1910–1969 Belg. priest; founder of charitable organizations

Pi·sa·no \\pi-'sän-(ˌ)ō\\ Giovanni 1245–1314 & his father Nicola 1220–1284 Ital. sculptors

Pi·sis·tra·tus *or* **Pei·sis·tra·tus** \\pī-'sis-trət-əs, pə-\\ *d* 527 B.C. tyrant of Athens

Pis·sar·ro \\pə-'sär-(ˌ)ō\\ Camille 1830–1903 Fr. painter

Pis·ton \\'pis-tən\\ Walter 1894– Am. composer

Pit·man \\'pit-mən\\ Sir Isaac 1813–1897 Eng. phonographer

Pitt \\'pit\\ William 1708–1778 Earl of *Chatham; the Elder Pitt* Eng. statesman
— William 1759–1806 *the Younger Pitt; son of prec.* Eng. statesman

Pitt-Riv·ers \\'pit-'riv-ərz\\ Augustus Henry 1827–1900 Eng. archaeologist

Pi·us \\'pī-əs\\ name of 12 popes: esp. **II** (*Enea Silvio de Piccolomini or Aeneas Silvius or Sylvius*) 1405–1464 (pope 1458–64); **VII** 1742–1823 (pope 1800–23); **IX** 1792–1878 (pope 1846–78); **X** 1835–1914 (pope 1903–14); **XI** (*Achille Ratti*) 1857–1939 (pope 1922–39); **XII** (*Eugenio Pacelli*) 1876–1958 (pope 1939–58)

Pi·zar·ro \\pə-'zär-(ˌ)ō\\ Francisco 1470?–1541 Span. conqueror of Peru

Planck \\'pläŋk\\ Max Karl Ernst Ludwig 1858–1947 Ger. physicist

Pla·to \\'plāt-(ˌ)ō\\ 427?–347 B.C. Greek philos.

Plau·tus \\'plòt-əs\\ Titus Maccius 254?–184 B.C. Rom. dram.

Ple·kha·nov \\plə-'kän-ˌòf, -ˌòv\\ Georgi Valentinovich 1857–1918 Russ. Marxist philos.

Ple·ven \\'plā-ven\\ René 1901– Fr. polit.

Plim·soll \\'plim(p)-səl, 'plim-ˌsäl\\ Samuel 1824–1898 *the Sailor's Friend* Eng. shipping reformer

Pliny \\'plin-ē\\ 23–79 *Gaius Plinius Secundus; the Elder* Rom. scholar
— 62–113 *Gaius Plinius Caecilius Secundus; the Younger; nephew of prec.* Rom. author

Plo·ti·nus \\plō-'tī-nəs\\ 205?–270 Rom. (Egyptian-born) philos.

Plu·tarch \\'plü-ˌtärk\\ 46?–?120 Greek biographer & moralist

Po·ca·hon·tas \\ˌpō-kə-'hänt-əs\\ 1595?–1617 *dau. of Powhatan* Am. Indian

Pod·gor·ny \\pòd-'gòr-nē\\ Nikolai Viktorovich 1903– Soviet polit.; pres. U.S.S.R. (from 1965)

Poe \\'pō\\ Edgar Allan 1809–1849 Am. poet & storywriter

Poin·ca·ré \\ˌpwaⁿ-kə-'rā, ˌpwaŋ-kə-\\ Jules Henri 1854–1912 Fr. math.
— Raymond 1860–1934 *cousin of J.H.* Fr. statesman; pres. of France (1913–20)

Poi·tier \\'pwä-ˌtyā\\ Sidney 1924– Am. actor

Pole \'pōl, 'púl\ Reginald 1500-1558 Eng. cardinal; archbishop of Canterbury

Po·li·tian \pə-'lish-ən\ 1454-1494 *Angelo Poliziano* Ital. classical scholar & poet

Polk \'pōk\ James Knox 1795-1849 11th pres. of the U.S. (1845-49)

Pol·lio \'päl-ē-,ō\ Gaius Asinius 75 B.C.-A.D. 5 Rom. soldier, orator, & polit.

Pol·lock \'päl-ək\ Channing 1880-1946 Am. nov. & dram.
— Sir Frederick 1845-1937 Eng. jurist
— Jackson 1912-1956 Am. painter

Po·lo \'pō-(,)lō\ Mar·co \'mär-(,)kō\ 1254?-?1324 Ital. traveler

Po·lyb·i·us \pə-'lib-ē-əs\ 205?-?125 B.C. Greek hist.

Pol·y·carp \'päl-i-,kärp\ Saint 69?-?155 Christian martyr & Apostolic Father; bishop of Smyrna

Pol·y·cli·tus *or* Pol·y·clei·tus \,päl-i-'klīt-əs\ 5th cent. B.C. Greek sculptor & architect

Po·lyc·ra·tes \pə-'lik-rə-,tēz\ *d ab* 522 B.C. tyrant of Samos

Pol·y·do·rus \,päl-i-'dōr-əs, -'dör-\ 1st cent. B.C. Rhodian scholar

Pol·yg·no·tus \,päl-ig-'nōt-əs\ 5th cent. B.C. Greek painter

Pom·pa·dour, de \'päm-pə-,dō(ə)r, -,dö(ə)r, -,dü(ə)r\ Marquise 1721-1764 *Jeanne Antoinette Poisson; mistress of Louis XV*

Pom·pey \'päm-pē\ 106-48 B.C. *Gnaeus Pompeius Magnus; the Great* Rom. gen. & statesman

Pom·pi·dou \'päm-pi-,dü\ Georges Jean Raymond 1911-   Fr. polit.; premier of France (1962-68); pres. of France (1969-   )

Ponce de Le·ón \,pän(t)s-də-'lē-ən, ,pän(t)-sə-,dā-lē-'ōn\ Juan 1460?-1521 Span. explorer; disc. Florida

Pons \'pōⁿs\ Lily 1904-   Am. (Fr.-born) soprano

Pon·selle \pän-'sel\ Rosa Melba 1897-   Am. soprano

Pon·ti·ac \'pänt-ē-,ak\ *d* 1769 Ottawa Indian chief

Pon·top·pi·dan \pän-'täp-ə-,dan\ Henrik 1857-1943 Dan. nov.

Pope \'pōp\ Alexander 1688-1744 Eng. poet
— John 1822-1892 Am. gen.

Por·son \'pòrs-ən\ Richard 1759-1808 Eng. scholar

Por·tal \'pōrt-əl, 'pört-\ Sir Charles Frederick Algernon 1893-   1st Viscount *Portal of Hungerford* Brit. air marshal

Por·ter \'pōrt-ər, 'pört-\ Cole 1893-1964 Am. composer & songwriter
— David 1780-1843 & his son David Dixon 1813-1891 Am. naval officers
— Gene 1868-1924 née *Stratton* Am. nov.
— Katherine Anne 1890-   Am. writer
— Noah 1811-1892 Am. philos. & lexicographer; pres. Yale U. (1871-86)
— William Sydney 1862-1910 pseud. *O. Hen·ry* \(')ō-'hen-rē\ Am. short-story writer

Portland Duke of *see* BENTINCK

Post \'pōst\ Emily 1873?-1960 née *Price* Am. columnist & writer; authority on etiquette

Po·tem·kin \pə-'tyòm(p)-kən, pō-'tem(p)-\ Grigori Aleksandrovich 1739-1791 Russ. field marshal & statesman

Pot·ter \'pät-ər\ Paul 1625-1654 Du. painter

Pou·lenc \'pü-,laŋk\ Francis 1899-1963 Fr. composer

Pound \'paúnd\ Sir (Alfred) Dudley (Pickman Rogers) 1877-1943 Brit. admiral of the fleet
— Ezra Loomis 1885-   Am. poet
— Roscoe 1870-1964 Am. jurist

Pous·sin \pü-'saⁿ\ Nicolas 1594-1665 Fr. painter

Pow·ell \'paú(ə)l\ Adam Clayton 1908-   Am. clergyman & polit.
— Anthony 1905-   Eng. writer
— Cecil Frank 1903-1969 Brit. physicist
— Maud 1868-1920 Am. violinist

Pow·ha·tan \,paú-ə-'tan, paú-'hat-ⁿn\ 1550?-1618 *father of Pocahontas* Am. Indian chief

Pow·nall \'paú-nəl\ Sir Henry Royds 1887-1961 Brit. gen.

Pow·ys \'pō-əs\ John Cow·per \'kü-pər, 'kúp-ər\ 1872-1963 & his bros. Theodore Francis 1875-1953 & Llewelyn 1884-1939 Eng. authors

Pra·do Ugar·te·che \'präth-(,)ō-,ü-(,)gär-'tech-ē\ Manuel 1889-1967 Peruvian banker; pres. of Peru (1939-45; 1956-62)

Pra·ja·dhi·pok \prə-'chät-i-,päk\ 1893-1941 king of Siam (1925-35)

Pratt \'prat\ Bela Lyon 1867-1917 Am. sculptor
— Edwin John 1883-1964 Canad. poet

Prax·it·e·les \prak-'sit-ⁿl-,ēz\ 4th cent. B.C. Athenian sculptor

Pre·ble \'preb-əl\ Edward 1761-1807 Am. naval officer

Pregl \'prā-gəl\ Fritz 1869-1930 Austrian chem.

Pres·cott \'pres-kət\ William Hickling 1796-1859 Am. hist.

Pre·to·ri·us \pri-'tōr-ē-əs, -'tör-\ Andries Wilhelmus Jacobus 1799-1853 & his son Marthinus Wessels 1819-1901 S. African Du. colonizers & soldiers

Pré·vost d'Ex·iles \prā-'vō-(,)deg-'zē(ə)l\ Antoine François 1697-1763 Fr. abbé & writer

Price \'prīs\ Byron 1891-   Am. journalist
— (Mary) Leontyne 1927-   Am. singer

Pride \'prīd\ Thomas *d* 1658 Eng. Parliamentary commander

Priest·ley \'prēst-lē\ John Boynton 1894-   Eng. author
— Joseph 1733-1804 Eng. clergyman & chem.

Primo de Rivera y Orbaneja *see* RIVERA Y ORBANEJA

Prior \'prī-(ə)r\ Matthew 1664-1721 Eng. poet

Pris·cian \'prish-ən, -ē-ən\ *fl* 500 *Priscianus Caesariensis* Latin grammarian at Constantinople

Pro·clus \'prō-kləs, 'präk-ləs\ 410?-485 Greek philos.

Pro·cc·pi·us \prə-'kō-pē-əs\ 6th cent. A.D. Byzantine hist.

Pro·kof·iev \prə-'kóf-yəf, -,yef\ Sergei Sergeevich 1891-1953 Russ. composer

Pro·per·tius \prō-'pər-sh(ē-)əs\ Sextus 50?-?15 B.C. Rom. poet

Pro·tag·o·ras \prō-'tag-ə-rəs\ 5th cent. B.C. Greek philos.

Prou·dhon \prü-'dōⁿ\ Pierre Joseph 1809-1865 Fr. journalist

Proust \'prüst\ Marcel 1871-1922 Fr. nov.

Prynne \'prin\ William 1600-1669 Eng. Puritan pamphleteer

Prze·val·ski \,pər-və-'väl-skē, ,prezh-ə-\ Nikolai Mikhailovich 1839-1888 Russ. explorer

Ptol·e·my \'täl-ə-mē\ name of 14 kings of Egypt
— 2d cent. A.D. *Claudius Ptolemaeus*, Alexandrian astron.

Puc·ci·ni \pü-'chē-nē\ Giacomo 1858-1924 Ital. composer

Pu·las·ki \pə-'las-kē, pyü-\ Casimir 1748?-1779 Pol. soldier in Am. Rev.

Pu·lit·zer \'púl-ət-sər (*family's pronunciation*), 'pyü-lət-\ Joseph 1847-1911 Am. (Hung.-born) journalist

Pull·man \'púl-mən\ George Mortimer 1831-1897 Am. inventor

Pu·pin \p(y)ü-'pēn\ Michael Idvorsky 1858-1935 Am. (Yugoslavian-born) physicist & inventor

Pur·cell \'pər-səl, (,)pər-'sel\ Edward Mills 1912-   Am. physicist
— Henry 1658?-1695 Eng. composer

Pur·chas \'pər-chəs\ Samuel 1575?-1626 Eng. compiler

Pur·kin·je \'púr-kən-,yā, (,)pər-'kin-jē\ Johannes Evangelista 1787-1869 Czech physiol.

Pu·sey \'pyü-zē, -sē\ Edward Bou·ver·ie \'bü-və-rē\ 1800-1882 Eng. theol.

Push·kin \'púsh-kən\ Aleksander Sergeevich 1799-1837 Russ. poet

Put·nam \'pət-nəm\ Israel 1718-1790 Am. Revolutionary gen.
— Rufus 1738-1824 *cousin of Israel* Am. Revolutionary gen. & pioneer in Ohio region

Pu·vis de Cha·vannes \pīē-,vēs-də-shà-vàn, pīē-,vēd-shà-\ Pierre 1824-1898 Fr. painter & muralist

P'u-yi Henry *see* HSÜAN-T'UNG

Pye \'pī\ Henry James 1745-1813 Eng. poet laureate (1790-1813)

Pyle \'pī(ə)l\ Ernest 1900-1945 *Ernie* Am. journalist

Pym \'pim\ John 1584-1643 Eng. parliamentary statesman

Pyn·chon \'pin-chən\ William 1590?-1662 Eng. pioneer in Am.

Pyr·rhus \'pir-əs\ 318?-272 B.C. king of Epirus (306-272 B.C.)

Py·thag·o·ras \pə-'thag-ə-rəs, pī-\ *d ab* 497 B.C. Greek philos. & math.

Qua·dros \'kwäd-rōs\ Jânio \'zhän-ē-,ō\ da Silva 1917-   Brazilian pres. (1961)

Quarles \'kwòr(ə)lz, 'kwär(ə)lz\ Francis 1592-1644 Eng. poet

Qua·si·mo·do \,kwäs-ə-'mōd-(,)ō\ Salvatore \,säl-vä-'tō-(,)rā\ 1901-1968 Ital. poet & critic

Queensberry Marquis of *see* DOUGLAS

Quer·cia, del·la \'kwer-chə\ Jacopo 1378?-1438 Sienese sculptor

Ques·nay \kā-'nā\ François 1694-1774 Fr. physician & econ.

Que·zon y Mo·li·na \'kā-,sò-,nē-mə-'lē-nə\ Manuel \män-'wel\ Luis 1878-1944 pres. of the Philippine Commonwealth (1935-44)

Quid·de \'kfid-ə, 'kwid-\ Ludwig 1858-1941 Ger. hist. & pacifist

Quil·ler-Couch \'kwil-ər-,küch\ Sir Arthur Thomas 1863-1944 Eng. author

Quin·cy \'kwin-zē, 'kwin(t)-sē\ Josiah 1744-1775 Am. lawyer

Quin·te·ro, Ál·va·rez \'äl-və-,räth-kēn-'te(ə)r-(,)ō, -,räs-\ Se·ra·fín \,ser-ə-'fēn\ 1871-1938 & his bro. Joa·quín \wä-'kēn\ 1873-1944 Span. dramatists

Quin·til·ian \kwin-'til-yən\ 1st cent. A.D. *Marcus Fabius Quintilianus* Rom. rhetorician

Qui·ri·no \kē-'rē-(,)nō\ Elpidio 1891?-1956 pres. of the Philippine Republic (1948-53)

Quo Tai-chi \'gwò-'tī-'chē\ 1889-1952 Chin. diplomat

Ra·be·lais \'rab-(ə-),lā, ,rab-(ə-)'lā\ François 1494?-1553 Fr. humorist & satirist

Ra·bi \'räb-ē\ Isidor Isaac 1898-   Am. (Austrian-born) physicist

Ra·chel \ra-'shel\ Mlle. 1820-1858 pseud. of *Élisa Félix* Fr. actress

Rach·ma·ni·noff \rak-'man-ə-,nóf, räk-'män-, -,nòv\ Sergei Wassilievitch 1873-1943 Russ. composer, pianist, & conductor

Ra·cine \rə-'sēn\ Jean Baptiste 1639-1699 Fr. dram.

Rack·ham \'rak-əm\ Arthur 1867-1939 Brit. illustrator

Rad·cliffe \'rad-,klif\ Ann 1764-1823 née *Ward* Eng. nov.

Ra·dek \'räd-,ek, 'räd-(y)ik\ Karl Bernadovich 1885-   Russ. Communist

Ra·detz·ky \rə-'det-skē\ Joseph Wenzel 1766-1858 Count *Radetzky von Radetz* Austrian field marshal

Rae \'rā\ John 1813-1893 Scot. arctic explorer

Rae·burn \'rā-(,)bərn\ Sir Henry 1756-1823 Scot. painter

Rae·der \'rād-ər\ Erich 1876-1960 Ger. admiral

Rae·mae·kers \'räm-,äk-ərz, -,ers\ Louis 1869-1956 Du. cartoonist

Rag·lan \'rag-lən\ 1st Baron 1788-1855 *Fitzroy James Henry Somerset* Brit. field marshal

Rai·mon·di \rī-'män-dē, -'mòn-\ Marcantonio 1475?-?1534 Ital. engraver

Ra·ja·go·pa·la·cha·ria \'räj-ə-(,)gō-,päl-ə-'chär-yə\ Chakravarti 1879-   Indian lawyer; gov. gen. of India (1948-50)

Ra·leigh *or* Ra·legh \'ròl-ē, 'räl-\ Sir Walter 1552?-1618 Eng. courtier, navigator, & hist.

Ra·ma·krish·na \,räm-ə-'krish-nə\ 1836-1886 Hindu saint

Ra·man \'räm-ən\ Sir Chan·dra·se·kha·ra \,chən-drə-'shā-kə-rə\ Venkata 1888-   Indian physicist

Ra·mée, de la \,del-ə-rə-'mā\ Marie Louise 1839-1908 pseud. *Oui·da* \'wēd-ə\ Eng. nov.

Ra·món y Ca·jal \rə-,mōn-(,)ē-kə-'häl\ Santiago 1852-1934 Span. histologist

Ram·say \'ram-zē\ Allan 1686-1758 Scot. poet
— James Andrew Broun 1812-1860 10th Earl & 1st Marquis of *Dalhousie* Brit. colonial administrator
— Sir William 1852-1916 Brit. chem.

Ram·ses \'ram-,sēz\ *or* Ram·e·ses \'ram-ə-,sēz\ name of 12 kings of Egypt esp.: II (reigned 1292-1225 B.C.); III (reigned 1198-1167 B.C.)

Rand \'rand\ Ayn \'īn\ 1905-   Am. (Russ.-born) writer

Ran·dolph \'ran-,dälf\ Asa Philip 1889-   Am. labor leader
— Edmund Jennings 1753-1813 Am. statesman
— John 1773-1833 Am. statesman

Ran·jit Singh \,rən-jət-'siŋ\ Maharaja 1780-1839 founder of Sikh kingdom

Ran·ke \'räŋ-kə\ Leopold 1795-1886 Ger. hist.

Ran·som \'ran(t)-səm\ John Crowe 1888-   Am. educator & poet

Ra·pha·el \'raf-ē-əl, 'rā-fē-, 'räf-ē-\ 1483-1520 *Raffaello Santi* or *Sanzio* Ital. painter

Rask \'räsk, 'rask\ Rasmus Christian 1787-1832 Dan. philologist & orientalist

Ras·mus·sen \'räs-,mús-ⁿn, 'ras-mə-sən\ Knud Johan Victor 1879-1933 Dan. arctic explorer & ethnologist

Ras·pu·tin \ra-'sp(y)üt-ⁿn\ Grigori Efimovich 1871?-1916 Russ. holy man & polit.

Ra·the·nau \'rät-ⁿn-,aú\ Emil 1838-1915 Ger. industrialist

Rausch·ning \'raù-shniŋ\ Hermann 1887– Am. (Ger.-born) polit. & writer

Ra·vel \rə-'vel, ra-\ Mau·rice \mò-'rēs\ Joseph 1875–1937 Fr. composer

Raw·lin·son \'rò-lən-sən\ George 1812–1902 Eng. orientalist & hist.
— Sir Henry Cres·wicke \'krez-ik\ 1810–1895 *bro. of prec.* Eng. Assyriologist

Ray \'rā\ John 1627?–1705 Eng. naturalist

Ray·burn \'rā-(,)bərn\ Sam 1882–1961 Am. lawyer & polit.

Ray·leigh \'rā-lē\ 3d Baron 1842–1919 *John William Strutt* Eng. math & physicist

Read \'rēd\ George 1733–1798 Am. lawyer & revolutionist
— Sir Herbert 1893–1968 Eng. writer
— Thomas Buchanan 1822–1872 Am. poet & painter

Reade \'rēd\ Charles 1814–1884 Eng. nov. & dram.

Read·ing \'red-iŋ\ 1st Marquis of 1860–1935 *Rufus Daniel Isaacs* Brit. statesman; viceroy of India (1921–26)

Ré·au·mur, de \,rā-ō-'myú(ə)r\ René Antoine Ferchault 1683–1757 Fr. naturalist & physicist

Ré·ca·mi·er \rā-'kam-ē-,ā\ Jeanne Françoise Julie Adélaïde 1777–1849 Fr. society wit

Red·mond \'red-mənd\ John Edward 1856–1918 Irish polit.

Reed \'rēd\ John 1887–1920 Am. journalist, poet, & Communist
— Stanley Forman 1884– Am. jurist
— Thomas Brackett 1839–1902 Am. polit.
— Walter 1851–1902 Am. army surgeon

Reg·u·lus \'reg-yə-ləs\ Marcus Atilius *d ab* 250 B.C. Rom. gen.

Rei·che·nau, von \'rī-kə-,naù\ Walther 1884–1942 Ger. field marshal

Reich·stein \'rīk-,s(h)tīn\ Tadeus 1897– Swiss (Pol.-born) chem.

Reid \'rēd\ Thomas 1710–1796 Scot. philos.
— Whitelaw 1837–1912 Am. journalist & diplomat

Rei·nach \rā-'näk\ Salomon 1858–1932 Fr. archaeologist

Rein·hardt \'rīn-,härt\ Max 1873–1943 orig. *Goldmann* Austrian theater director

Re·marque \rə-'märk\ Erich Maria 1898– Am. (Ger.-born) nov.

Rem·brandt van Rijn *or* **Ryn** \'rem-,brant-vän-'rīn, -,bränt-, -vən-, -(,)vän-\ 1606–1669 Du. painter

Rem·ing·ton \'rem-iŋ-tən\ Frederic 1861–1909 Am. artist

Rem·sen \'rem(p)-sən, 'rem-zən\ Ira 1846–1927 Am. chem.

Re·nan \rə-'näⁿ, -'nän\ Joseph Ernest 1823–1892 Fr. philologist & hist.

Re·nault \rə-'nō\ Louis 1843–1918 Fr. jurist & pacifist

Re·ni \'rā-nē\ Guido 1575–1642 Ital. painter

Ren·ner \'ren-ər\ Karl 1870–1950 Austrian statesman; pres. of Austria (1945–50)

Re·noir \'ren-,wär, rən-'\ Pierre Auguste 1841–1919 Fr. painter

Rep·plier \'rep-,li(ə)r, -lē-ər\ Agnes 1855–1950 Am. essayist

Re·spi·ghi \rə-'spē-gē, re-\ Ottorino 1879–1936 Ital. composer

Res·ton \'res-tən\ James Barrett 1909– Am. journalist

Resz·ke, de \'resh-kē\ Jean \'zhäⁿ\ 1850–1925 *Jan Mieczisław* Pol. tenor

Retz, de \'rets\ Cardinal 1614–1679 *Jean François Paul de Gondi* Fr. ecclesiastic & polit.

Reuch·lin \'ròik-lən; 'ròi-,klēn, ròi-'\ Johann 1455–1522 *Cap·nio* \'kap-nē-,ō\ Ger. humanist

Reu·ter, von \'ròit-ər\ Ludwig 1869–1943 Ger. admiral
— Baron Paul Julius 1816–1899 orig. *Israel Beer Josaphat* Brit. (Ger.-born) news agent

Reu·ter·dahl \'ròit-ər-,däl\ Henry 1871–1925 Swed.-born painter in U.S.

Reu·ther \'rü-thər\ Walter Philip 1907–1970 Am. labor leader

Re·vere \ri-'vi(ə)r\ Paul 1735–1818 Am. patriot & silversmith

Rey·mont \'rā-,mänt\ Władysław \vlä-'dis-,läf\ Sta·ni·slaw \stä-'ne-,släf\ 1867–1925 Pol. nov.

Rey·naud \rā-'nō\ Paul 1878–1966 premier of France (1940)

Reyn·olds \'ren-ᵊl(d)z\ Sir Joshua 1723–1792 Eng. painter

Rhee \'rē\ Syng·man \'siŋ-mən, 'sig-\ 1875–1965 So. Korean polit.

Rhodes \'rōdz\ Cecil John 1853–1902 Brit. administrator & financier in So. Africa

Rhond·da \'rän-də\ Viscount 1856–1918 *David Alfred Thomas* Brit. industrialist & administrator

Rib·ben·trop, von \'rib-ən-,träp, -,tròp\ Joachim 1893–1946 Ger. diplomat

Ri·be·ra, de \rē-'ber-ə\ Jusepe 1588–1652 *Lo Spa·gno·let·to* \,lō-,spän-yə-'let-(,)ō\ Span. painter & etcher

Ri·car·do \rik-'ärd-(,)ō\ David 1772–1823 Eng. econ.

Rice \'rīs\ Elmer L. 1892–1967 orig. *Elmer Reizenstein* Am. dram.

Rich·ard \'rich-ərd\ name of 3 kings of England: **I** (*Coeur de Li·on* \,kərd-ᵊl-'ī-ən, -'ē-ən, -ē-'ōⁿ\) 1157–1199 (reigned 1189–99); **II** 1367–1400 (reigned 1377–99); **III** 1452–1485 (reigned 1483–85)

Rich·ards \'rich-ərdz\ Dickinson Woodruff 1895– Am. physician
— Theodore William 1868–1928 Am. chem.

Rich·ard·son \'rich-ərd-sən\ Henry Handel 1870–1946 pseud. of *Ethel Florence Lindesay Richardson* Austral. nov.
— Henry Hobson 1838–1886 Am. architect
— Sir Owen Williams 1879–1959 Eng. physicist
— Samuel 1689–1761 Eng. nov.

Ri·che·lieu, de \'rish-ə-,lü, -ə-,lyü, ,rē-shə-lyœ\ Duc 1585–1642 *Armand Jean du Plessis* Fr. cardinal & statesman

Ri·chet \rē-'shā\ Charles Robert 1850–1935 Fr. physiol.

Rich·ter \'rik-tər, 'riḵ-\ Jean Paul Friedrich 1763–1825 pseud. *Jean Paul* \'zhäⁿ-'paù(ə)l, 'jēn-'pòl\ Ger. writer

Ric·i·mer \'ris-ə-mər\ *d* 472 Rom. gen.

Rick·en·back·er \'rik-ən-,bak-ər\ Edward Vernon 1890– Am. aviator

Rick·o·ver \'rik-,ō-vər\ Hy·man \'hī-mən\ George 1900– Am. admiral

Rid·ley \'rid-lē\ Nicholas 1500?–1555 Eng. reformer & martyr

Rid·path \'rid-,path\ John Clark 1840–1900 Am. hist.

Ri·el \rē-'el\ Louis 1844–1885 Canad. insurgent

Rie·mann \'rē-,män\ Georg Friedrich Bernhard 1826–1866 Ger. math.

Ri·en·zi \rē-'en-zē\ *or* **Ri·en·zo** \-(,)zō\, di Cola 1313–1354 *Niccolo Gabrini; Last of the Romans* Ital. patriot; tribune of Rome

Ries·man \'rēs-mən, 'rēz-\ David 1909– Am. social scientist

Riis \'rēs\ Jacob August 1849–1914 Am. (Dan.-born) social worker & writer

Ri·ley \'rī-lē\ James Whit·comb \'hwit-kəm, 'wit-\ 1849–1916 Am. poet

Ril·ke \'ril-kə\ Rai·ner \'rī-nər\ Maria 1875–1926 Ger. poet

Rim·baud \raⁿ(m)-bō\ (Jean Nicholas) Arthur 1854–1891 Fr. poet

Rimini Francesca da see FRANCESCA DA RIMINI

Rim·ski-Kor·sa·kov \,rim(p)-skē-'kòr-sə-,kòf\ Nikolai Andree·vich 1844–1908 Russ. composer

Rin·cón, del \riŋ-'kòn, rin-\ Antonio 1446–1500 Span. painter

Rine·hart \'rīn-,härt\ Mary 1876–1958 née *Roberts* Am. writer

Rí·os \'rē-,ōs\ Juan Antonio 1888–1946 Chilean lawyer; pres. of Chile (1942–46)

Rip·ley \'rip-lē\ George 1802–1880 Am. literary critic & socialist

Ri·sto·ri \ri-'stòr-ē, -'stòr-\ Adelaide 1822–1906 Ital. actress

Rit·ten·house \'rit-ᵊn-,haùs\ Jessie Belle 1869–1948 Am. critic & poet

Rit·ter \'rit-ər\ Joseph Elmer 1891–1967 Am. cardinal

Ri·ve·ra \ri-'ver-ə\ Diego 1886–1957 Mex. painter & muralist

Ri·ve·ra y Or·ba·ne·ja, de \-,ē-,òr-bə-'nā-(,)hä\ Miguel Primo 1870–1930 *Marqués de Estella* Span. gen.; dictator (1925–30)

Ri·zal \ri-'zäl, -'säl\ José 1861–1896 Filipino patriot

Ri·za Shah Pah·la·vi *or* **Pah·le·vi** \ri-'zä-,shä-'päl-ə-(,)vē, -,shò-\ 1877–1944 shah of Iran (1925–41)

Riz·zio \'rit-sē-,ō\ *or* **Ric·cio** \'rich-ē-,ō\ David 1533?–1566 Ital. musician & favorite of Mary, Queen of Scots

Rob·bia, del·la \,del-ə-'räb-ē-ə, -'ròb-\ Luca 1400?–1482 Florentine sculptor

Rob·bins \'räb-ənz\ Frederick C. 1916– Am. physician
— Jerome 1918– Am. dancer & choreographer

Rob·ert \'räb-ərt\ see Robert BRUCE
— **I** *d* 1035 *Robert the Devil* Duke of Normandy (1028–35) *father of William the Conqueror*

Rob·erts \'räb-ərts\ Sir Charles George Douglas 1860–1943 Canad. poet
— Frederick Sleigh 1832–1914 1st Earl *Roberts of Kandahar, Pretoria, and Waterford* Brit. field marshal
— Kenneth 1885–1957 Am. nov.
— Owen Josephus 1875–1955 Am. jurist

Rob·ert·son \'räb-ərt-sən\ William 1721–1793 Scot. hist.
— Sir William Robert 1860–1933 Brit. field marshal

Robe·son \'rōb-sən\ Paul 1898– Am. actor & singer

Robes·pierre, de \'rōbz-,pi(ə)r, -,pye(ə)r; ,rō-,bes-'pye(ə)r\ Maximilien François Marie Isidore 1758–1794 Fr. revolutionist

Rob·in·son \'räb-ən-sən\ Edwin Arlington 1869–1935 Am. poet
— George Frederick Samuel 1827–1909 1st Marquis of *Ripon* Brit. statesman
— James Harvey 1863–1936, Am. hist.
— Sir Robert 1886– Eng. chem.

Ro·cham·beau, de \,rō-shäm-'bō, rä-, -,sham-\ Comte 1725–1807 *Jean Baptiste Donatien de Vimeur* Fr. gen.

Rocke·fel·ler \'räk-i-,fel-ər, 'räk-,fel-\ John Davison father 1839–1937 & son 1874–1960 Am. oil magnates & philanthropists
— Nelson Aldrich 1908– *grandson & son of prec.* Am. polit.

Rock·ing·ham \'räk-iŋ-əm, *US also* -iŋ-,ham\ 2d Marquis of 1730–1782 *Charles Watson-Wentworth* Eng. statesman

Rock·ne \'räk-nē\ Knute \'nüt\ Kenneth 1888–1931 Norw.-born football coach in U.S.

Rock·well \'räk-,wel, -wəl\ Norman 1894– Am. illustrator

Ro·de \'rō-thə\ Hel·ge \'hel-gə\ 1870–1937 Dan. poet

Rod·gers \'räj-ərz\ Richard 1902– Am. composer

Ro·din \rō-'daⁿ, -'dan\ François Auguste René 1840–1917 Fr. sculptor

Rod·ney \'räd-nē\ George Bryd·ges \'brij-əz\ 1719–1792 1st Baron *Rodney* Eng. admiral

Ro·dzin·ski \rō-'jin(t)-skē\ Ar·tur \'är-,tù(ə)r\ 1894–1958 Am. conductor

Roeb·ling \'rō-bliŋ\ John Augustus 1806–1869 Am. (Ger.-born) civil engineer

Roent·gen *or* **Rönt·gen** \'rent-gən, 'rənt-, -jən; 'ren-chən, 'rən-\ Wilhelm Conrad 1845–1923 Ger. physicist

Roe·rich \'rər-ik, 're(ə)r-\ Nicholas Konstantin 1874–1947 Russ. painter

Rog·ers \'räj-ərz\ Bruce 1870–1957 Am. printer & book designer
— Henry Hut·tle·ston \'hət-ᵊl-stən\ *or* Hud·dle·ston \'həd-ᵊl-\ 1840–1909 Am. financier
— James Gamble 1867–1947 Am. architect
— Samuel 1763–1855 Eng. poet
— William Penn Adair 1879–1935 *Will* Am. actor & humorist
— William Pierce 1913– Am. lawyer; U.S. secy. of state (from 1969)

Ro·get \rō-'zhā, 'rō-,\ Peter Mark 1779–1869 Eng. physician & scholar

Ro·kos·sov·ski \,räk-ə-'sòf-skē, -'sòv-\ Konstantin 1896–1968 Russ. marshal

Rolfe \'rälf\ John 1585–1622 *husband of Pocahontas* Eng. colonist

Rol·land \rò-läⁿ\ Romain 1866–1944 Fr. author

Rol·lo \'räl-(,)ō\ *or* **Hrolf** \'(h)rälf\ 860?–?931 Norse chieftain

Röl·vaag \'rōl-,väg\ Ole \'ō-lə\ Ed·vart \'ed-,värt\ 1876–1931 Norw.-born educ. & nov. in Am.

Ro·mains \rò-maⁿ, rō-'mänz\ Jules 1885– pseud. of *Louis Farigoule* Fr. author

Ro·ma·no \rō-'män-(,)ō, rə-\ Giulio 1499–1546 *Giulio Pippi de' Gianuzzi* Ital. painter & architect

Ro·ma·nov *or* **Ro·ma·noff** \rō-'män-əf, 'rō-mə-,näf\ Mikhail Feodorovich 1596–1645 1st czar (1613–45) of Russ. Romanov dynasty (1613–1917)

Rom·berg \'räm-,bərg\ Sig·mund \'sig-mənd\ 1887–1951 Hung.-born composer in Am.

Rom·mel \'räm-əl\ Erwin 1891–1944 Ger. field marshal

Rom·ney \\'räm-nē\ George 1734–1802 Eng. painter
Ron·sard, de \rōⁿ-'sär\ Pierre 1524–1585 Fr. poet
Roo·se·velt \\'rō-zə-vəlt (*Roosevelts' usual pronunciation*), -,velt *also* \\'rü-\ (Anna) Eleanor 1884–1962 née Roosevelt, wife of F.D. Am. lecturer & writer
— Franklin Del·a·no \\'del-ə-,nō\ 1882–1945 32d pres. of the U.S. (1933–45)
— Theodore 1858–1919 26th pres. of the U.S. (1901–09)
— Theodore 1887–1944 *son of prec.* Am. gen., explorer, & polit.
Root \\'rüt, 'rüt\ Elihu 1845–1937 Am. lawyer & statesman
Ro·sa \\'rō-zə\ Salvator 1615–1673 Ital. painter & poet
Rose·bery \\'rōz-,ber-ē, -b(ə-)rē\ 5th Earl of 1847–1929 *Archibald Philip Primrose* Eng. statesman
Rose·crans \\'rōz-,kran(t)s, 'rō-zə-,kranz\ William Starke \\'stärk\ 1819–1898 Am. gen.
Ro·sen·berg \\'rōz-ⁿn-,bərg, -,be(ə)rk\ Alfred 1893–1946 Ger. Nazi & writer
Ro·sen·wald \\'rōz-ⁿn-,wóld\ Julius 1862–1932 Am. merchant & philanthropist
Ross \\'rós\ Betsy 1752–1836 née *Griscom* maker of first Am. flag
— Sir James Clark 1800–1862 Scot. polar explorer
— Sir John 1777–1856 *uncle of prec.* Scot. arctic explorer
— Sir Ronald 1857–1932 Brit. physician
Ros·set·ti \rō-'zet-ē, -'set-\ Christina Georgina 1830–1894 *sister of D.G.* Eng. poet
— Dante Gabriel 1828–1882 Eng. painter & poet
Ros·si \\'rós-ē\ Bruno 1905– Ital.-born physicist in Am.
Ros·si·ni \rò-'sē-nē, rō-\ Gio·ac·chi·no \jō-ə-'kē-(,)nō\ Antonio 1792–1868 Ital. composer
Ros·tand \rò-stäⁿ, 'räs-,tand\ Edmond 1868–1918 Fr. poet & dram.
Roth·ko \\'räth-(,)kō\ Mark 1903–1970 Am. (Russ.-born) painter
Roth·schild \\'rôth(s)-,chīld, 'räth(s)-, -'räs-, 'rós-, *Ger* 'rōt-,shilt\ Meyer Amschel 1743–1812 Ger. financier
— Nathan Meyer 1777–1836 *son of prec.* financier in London
Rou·ault \rü-'ō\ Georges 1871–1958 Fr. painter
Rou·get de Lisle \(,)rü-,zhā-də-'lē(ə)l\ Claude Joseph 1760–1836 Fr. army officer & composer
Rous·seau \rü-'sō\ Henri 1844–1910 *the Douanier* Fr. painter
— Jean Jacques 1712–1778 Fr. (Swiss-born) philos. & writer
— Théodore 1812–1867 Fr. painter
Rowe \\'rō\ Nicholas 1674–1718 Eng. poet & dram.; poet laureate (1715–18)
Row·ley \\'rō-lē, 'raü-\ William 1585?–?1642 Eng. actor & dram.
Ro·xas y Acu·ña \'rō-,häs-,ē-ə-'kün-yə\ Manuel 1892–1948 Philippine statesman; pres. of the Philippine Republic (1946–48)
Roy·all \\'rói(-ə)l\ Kenneth Claiborne 1894– Am. lawyer & statesman
Royce \\'róis\ Josiah 1855–1916 Am. philos.
Rozh·dest·ven·ski \räzh-'dest-vən-skē\ Zinovi Petrovich 1848–1909 Russ. admiral
Ru·bens \\'rü-bənz\ Peter Paul 1577–1640 Flem. painter
Ru·bin·stein \\'rü-bən-,stīn\ An·ton \än-'tón\ 1829–1894 Russ. pianist & composer
— Artur 1889– Pol.-born pianist in Am.
Ru·dolf I of Haps·burg \,rü-,dälf-thə-'(')fər-stəv-'haps-,bərg, -'häps-,bù(ə)rg\ 1218–1291 Holy Rom. emp. (1273–91); 1st of the Hapsburgs
Rudolf *or* **Rudolph of Haps·burg** 1858–1889 archduke & crown prince of Austria
Ru·ger \\'rü-gər\ Thomas Howard 1833–1907 Am. gen.
Ruis·dael *or* **Ruys·dael, van** \\'rīz-,däl, 'rīs-\ Jacob 1628?–1682 & his uncle Salomon 1600?–1670 Du. painters
Rumford Count *see* Benjamin THOMPSON
Rund·stedt, von \\'rùn(t)-,s(h)tet\ Karl Rudolf Gerd 1875–1953 Ger. field marshal
Ru·ne·berg \\'rü-nə-,bərg, -,be(ə)r\ Johan Ludvig 1804–1877 Finnish poet
Runjit Singh *see* RANJIT SINGH
Run·yon \\'rən-yən\ (Alfred) Da·mon \\'dā-mən\ 1880–1946 Am. author
Ru·pert \\'rü-pərt\ Prince 1619–1682 *nephew of Charles I of Eng.* Ger.-Eng. gen. & admiral
— *or* **Rup·precht** \\'rùp-,rekt, -,reĸt\ 1869–1955 crown prince of Bavaria & Ger. field marshal
Rush \\'rəsh\ Benjamin 1745?–1813 Am. physician & Revolutionary patriot
— Richard 1780–1859 *son of prec.* Am. lawyer & statesman
Rusk \\'rəsk\ Dean 1909– Am. secy. of state (1961–69)
Rus·kin \\'rəs-kən\ John 1819–1900 Eng. essayist, critic, & reformer
Rus·sell \\'rəs-əl\ 3d Earl 1872–1970 *Bertrand Arthur Russell* Eng. math. & philos.
— Charles Taze 1852–1916 Am. pastor
— Countess 1866–1941 *Elizabeth Mary Beauchamp Russell* pseud. *Elizabeth* Austral.-born nov.
— George William 1867–1935 pseud. *Æ* Irish author
— Lord John 1792–1878 1st Earl *Russell of Kingston Russell* Brit. statesman
— Lillian 1861–1922 *Helen Louise Leonard* Am. soprano
Rus·tin \\'rəs-tən\ Bayard 1910– Am. civil rights leader
Ruth·er·ford \\'rəth-ə(r)-fərd\ Ernest 1871–1937 1st Baron *Rutherford of Nelson* Brit. physicist
— Joseph Franklin 1869–1942 *Judge* Am. leader of Jehovah's Witnesses
Rut·ledge \\'rət-lij\ Ann 1816–1835 fiancée of Abraham Lincoln
— John 1739–1800 Am. statesman & jurist
— Wiley Blount \\'blənt\ 1894–1949 Am. jurist
Ruy·ter *or* **Rui·ter, de** \\'rīt-ər\ Michel Adriaanszoon 1607–1676 Du. admiral
Ru·žič·ka \\'rü-,z(h)ich-kə, rü-\ Leopold 1887– Yugoslav chem.
Ry·der \\'rīd-ər\ Albert Pinkham 1847–1917 Am. painter
Rys·kind \\'ris-kənd\ Morris 1895– Am. dram.

Saa·ri·nen \\'sär-ə-,nen, -nən\ Ee·ro \\'ā-(,)rō\ 1910–1961 Am. architect
— Gottlieb Eliel 1873–1950 *father of prec.* Finnish architect
Saa·ve·dra La·mas \sä-,väd-rə-'läm-əs, -,väth-\ Carlos 1880–1959 Argentine lawyer & diplomat
Sa·ba·tier \,sab-ə-'tyā\ Paul 1854–1941 Fr. chem.

Sa·ba·ti·ni \,sab-ə-'tē-nē\ Rafael 1875–1950 Ital. author
Sachs \\'zäks, 'saks\ Hans 1494–1576 Ger. cobbler & Meistersinger
Sack·ville \\'sak-,vil\ Thomas 1536–1608 1st Earl of *Dorset* Eng. poet & diplomat
Sack·ville–West \,sak-,vil-'west\ Victoria Mary 1892–1962 Eng. writer
Sade, de \\'säd, 'sad\ Comte Donatien Alphonse François 1740–1814 *Marquis de Sade* Fr. soldier & pervert
Sage \\'sāj\ Russell 1816–1906 Am. financier
Saint-Cyr \saⁿ-'si(ə)r\ Marquis Laurent de Gouvion 1764–1830 Fr. gen. under Napoleon; marshal of France (1812)
St. Den·is \,sānt-'den-əs, sənt-\ Ruth 1878–1968 Am. dancer
Sainte-Beuve \saⁿt-bœv, sənt-, ,sant-(ə)-\ Charles Augustin 1804–1869 Fr. critic & author
Saint-Gau·dens \,sānt-'gód-ⁿnz, sənt-\ Augustus 1848–1907 Irish-born sculptor in Am.
St. John Henry *see* BOLINGBROKE
Saint-Just, de \saⁿ-zhüst, -'zhüst; ,sānt-'jəst, sənt-\ Louis Antoine Léon 1767–1794 Fr. Revolutionist
St. Lau·rent \saⁿ-lò-räⁿ\ Louis Stephen 1882– Canad. lawyer; prime min. (1948–57)
Saint-Pierre *see* BERNARDIN DE SAINT-PIERRE
Saint-Saëns \saⁿ-säⁿs\ (Charles) Camille 1835–1921 Fr. composer
Saints·bury \\'sānts-,ber-ē, -b(ə-)rē\ George Edward Bateman 1845–1933 Eng. critic
Saint-Si·mon, de \saⁿ-sē-mōⁿ\ Comte 1760–1825 *Claude Henri de Rouvroy* Fr. philos. & social scientist
— Duc 1675–1755 *Louis de Rouvroy* Fr. soldier, statesman, & writer
Sai·on·ji \sī-'än-jē, -'ón-\ Marquis Kimmochi 1849–1940 Jap. statesman
Sa·ki \\'säk-ē\ 1870–1916 pseud. of *Hector Hugh Mun·ro* \(,)mən-'rō\ Brit. humorist
Sal·a·din \\'sal-əd-ⁿn\ 1138–1193 sultan of Egypt & Syria
Sa·la·zar \,sal-ə-'zär, ,säl-\ Antonio de Oliveira 1889– Port. chief of state
Sal·in·ger \\'sal-ən-jər\ Jerome David 1919– Am. nov.
Salisbury 1st Earl of & 3d Marquis of *see* CECIL
Sal·lust \\'sal-əst\ 86–34 B.C. *Gaius Sallustius Crispus* Rom. hist. & polit.
Sal·ve·mi·ni \,sal-'vā-mə-nē, ,säl-\ Gaetano 1873–1957 Ital. hist.
Sal·vi·ni \,sal-'vē-nē, ,säl-\ Tommaso 1829–1916 Ital. actor
Samp·son \\'sam(p)-sən\ William Thomas 1840–1902 Am. admiral
Sán·chez de Bus·ta·man·te y Sir·vén \'sän-chəz-də-,büs-tə-'mänt-ē-,ē-sər-'ven\ Antonio 1865–1951 Cuban jurist
Sand \\'sand, säⁿd\ George 1804–1876 pseud. of *Amandine Aurore Lucie* née *Dupin; Baronne Dudevant* Fr. writer
Sand·burg \\'san(d)-,bərg\ Carl 1878–1967 Am. author
Sandracottus *or* **Sandrocottus** *see* CHANDRAGUPTA
San·gal·lo, da \sän-'gäl-(,)ō, säŋ-\ Giuliano 1445–1516 Florentine architect & sculptor
Sang·er \\'saŋ-ər\ Frederick 1918– Brit. chem.
— Margaret 1883–1966 née *Higgins* Am. birth-control leader
San Mar·tín, de \,san-(,)mär-'tēn, ,sän-\ José 1778–1850 So. Am. soldier & statesman
San·ta An·na *or* **San·ta Ana, de** \,sant-ə-'an-ə, ,sänt-ə-'än-ə\ Antonio López 1795?–1876 Mex. gen. & pres.
San·tan·der \,sän-,tän-'de(ə)r, ,san-,tan-\ Francisco de Paula 1792–1840 gen. & polit. of New Granada
San·ta·ya·na \,sant-ə-'yän-ə, ,sant-ē-'än-, ,sänt-\ George 1863–1952 Am. (Span.-born) poet & philos.
San·tos-Du·mont \,sant-əs-dü-'mänt, -'mōⁿ\ Alberto 1873–1932 Brazilian aeronaut in France
Sa·pir \sə-'pi(ə)r\ Edward 1884–1939 Am. (Pomerania-born) anthropol. & linguist
Sap·pho \\'saf-(,)ō\ *fl ab* 600 B.C. Greek poet
Sar·da·na·pa·lus \,särd-ⁿn-'ap-ə-ləs, -ⁿn-ə-'pā-ləs\ king of Assyria (*ab* 822 B.C.); sometimes identified with Ashurbanipal
Sar·dou \sär-'dü\ Victorien 1831–1908 Fr. dram.
Sar·gent \\'sär-jənt\ John Singer 1856–1925 Am. painter
Sar·gon II \\'sär-,gän, -gən\ *d* 705 B.C. king of Assyria (722–705)
Sa·roy·an \sə-'rói-ən\ William 1908– Am. writer
Sar·tre \\'särtr²\ Jean-Paul 1905– Fr. philos., dram., & nov.
Sas·soon \sa-'sün, sə-\ Siegfried 1886–1967 Eng. writer
Sa·to \\'sä-(,)tō\ Eisaku 1901– Jap. premier (from 1964)
— Naotake 1882– Jap. diplomat
Sa'ud Ibn Abd·ul \sä-'üd-,ib-ə-nəb-'dül, 'saùd-\ 1902–1969 king of Saudi Arabia (1953–64)
Sav·age \\'sav-ij\ Richard 1697?–1743 Eng. poet
Sa·vo·na·ro·la \,sav-ə-nə-'rō-lə, ,säv-; sə-,vän-ə-'rō-\ Gi·ro·la·mo \ji-'rō-lə-,mō\ 1452–1498 Ital. reformer
Saw·yer \\'só-yər, 'sói-ər\ Charles 1887– Am. lawyer & administrator
Saxe, de \\'saks\ Comte Hermann Maurice 1696–1750 Fr. soldier; marshal of France (1744)
Saxo Gram·mat·i·cus \,sak-(,)sō-grə-'mat-i-kəs\ 1150?–?1220 Dan. hist.
Say·ers \\'sā-ərz, 'sa(ə)rz, 'se(ə)rz\ Dorothy Leigh 1893–1957 Eng. writer
Scal·i·ger \\'skal-ə-jər\ Joseph Justus 1540–1609 Ital.-born physician & scholar
— Julius Caesar 1484–1558 *father of prec.* Ital. physician
Scan·der·beg \\'skan-dər-,beg\ *Turk.* Iskender Bey 1403?–1468 *George Castriota* Albanian chieftain
Scar·lat·ti \skär-'lät-ē\ Alessandro 1659–1725 Ital. composer
Scar·ron \ska-'rōⁿ\ Paul 1610–1660 Fr. author
Schacht \\'shäkt, 'shäĸt\ (Horace Greeley) Hjal·mar \\'yäl-,mär\ 1877–1970 Ger. financier
Scharn·horst, von \\'shärn-,hórst\ Gerhard Johann David 1755–1813 Prussian gen.
Schar·wen·ka \shär-'veŋ-kə\ Philipp 1847–1917 & his bro. Xaver 1850–1924 Ger. pianists & composers
Schei·de·mann \\'shīd-ə-,män\ Philipp 1865–1939 Ger. polit.
Schel·ling, von \\'shel-iŋ\ Friedrich Wilhelm Joseph 1775–1854 Ger. philos.
Schia·pa·rel·li \,skyäp-ə-'rel-ē, ,skap-\ Giovanni Virginio 1835–1910 Ital. astron.
Schick \\'shik\ Bé·la \\'bā-lə\ 1877–1967 Am. (Hung.-born) pediatrician

Schil·ler, von \'shil-ər\ Johann Christoph Friedrich 1759–1805 Ger. poet & dram.

Schi·rach, von \'shē-ˌräk, -ˌräk\ Baldur 1907– Ger. Nazi polit.

Schle·gel, von \'shlā-gəl\ August Wilhelm 1767–1845 Ger. author

— Friedrich 1772–1829 *bro. of prec.* Ger. philos. & writer

Schlei·cher, von \'shlī-kər, -ˌkər\ Kurt 1882–1934 Ger. soldier & statesman

Schlei·er·ma·cher \'shlī-(-ə)r-ˌmäk-ər, -ˌmäk-\ Friedrich Ernst Daniel 1768–1834 Ger. theol. & philos.

Schle·sing·er \'s(h)les-ʼn-jər, 'shlāz-, 's(h)lez-, -iŋ-ər\ Arthur Meier father 1888–1965 & son 1917– Am. historians

Schley \'slī\ Winfield Scott 1839–1911 Am. admiral

Schlie·mann \'shlē-ˌmän\ Heinrich 1822–1890 Ger. archaeologist

Schna·bel \'shnäb-əl\ Ar·tur \'är-ˌtu̇(ə)r\ 1882–1951 Am. (Austrian-born) pianist & composer

Schnitz·ler \'shnit-slər\ Arthur 1862–1931 Austrian physician, dram., & nov.

Scho·field \'skō-ˌfēld\ John McAllister 1831–1906 Am. gen.

Schön·berg \'shə(r)n-ˌbərg, -ˌbe(ə)rk\ Arnold 1874–1951 Am. (Austrian-born) composer

Scho·pen·hau·er \'shō-pən-ˌhau̇(-ə)r\ Arthur 1788–1860 Ger. pessimist philos.

Schrö·ding·er \'shrād-iŋ-ər\ Erwin 1887–1961 Austrian physicist

Schu·bert \'shü-bərt\ Franz Peter 1797–1828 Austrian composer

Schu·man \'shü-ˌmän, -mən\ Robert 1886–1963 Fr. statesman

Schu·man \'shü-mən\ William Howard 1910– Am. composer

Schu·mann \'shü-ˌmän, -mən\ Robert 1810–1856 Ger. composer

Schu·mann–Heink \ˌshü-mən-'hiŋk\ Ernestine 1861–1936 née *Roessler* Austrian-born contralto

Schur·man \'shu̇(ə)r-mən, 'shər-\ Jacob Gould 1854–1942 Am. philos. & diplomat

Schurz \'shu̇(ə)rts, 'shərts\ Carl 1829–1906 Am. (Ger.-born) lawyer, gen., & polit.

Schusch·nigg, von \'shu̇sh-(ˌ)nik\ Kurt 1897– Austrian statesman

Schuy·ler \'skī-lər\ Philip John 1733–1804 Am. gen. & statesman

Schweit·zer \'shvīt-sər, 's(h)wīt-\ Albert 1875–1965 Fr. Protestant clergyman, philos., physician, & music scholar

Scip·io \'sip-ē-ˌō, 'skip-\ **Aemilianus Af·ri·ca·nus** \ˌaf-rə-'kän-əs, -'kän-, -'kan-\ **Numantinus** Publius Cornelius 185–129 B.C. *Scipio the Younger* Rom. gen.

Scipio Africanus Publius Cornelius 237–183 B.C. *Scipio the Elder* Rom. gen.

Scopes \'skōps\ John Thomas 1900– Am. teacher

Scott \'skät\ Dred \'dred\ 1795?–1858 Am. Negro slave; central figure in U.S. lawsuit

— Sir George Gilbert 1811–1878 Eng. architect

— Robert Falcon 1868–1912 Eng. antarctic explorer

— Sir Walter 1771–1832 Scot. poet & nov.

— Winfield 1786–1866 Am. gen.

Scotus Duns see DUNS SCOTUS

— Johannes see ERIGENA

Scria·bin *or* **Scria·bine** \skrē-'äb-ən\ Alexander 1872–1915 Russ. composer

Scribe \skrēb\ Augustin Eugène 1791–1861 Fr. dram.

Scud·der \'skəd-ər\ Horace Elisha 1838–1902 Am. author

Scu·dé·ry, de \ˌsküd-ə-'rē, skü-dā-rē\ Magdeleine 1607–1701 *Sa·pho* \sà-fō\ Fr. poet, nov., & lady of fashion

Sea·borg \'sē-ˌbȯ(ə)rg\ Glenn Theodore 1912– Am. chem.

See \'sē\ Thomas Jefferson Jackson 1866–1962 Am. astronomer & math.

Seeckt, von \'zākt\ Hans 1866–1936 Ger. army officer

See·ger \'sē-gər\ Alan 1888–1916 Am. poet

Se·fe·ri·a·des \ˌsef-ə-'yäth-ēs\ Giorgos Stylianou 1900– pseud. *George Se·fe·ris* \se-'fer-ēs\ Greek diplomat & poet

Se·go·via \sā-'gō-vyə, -vē-ə\ Andrés 1894– Span. guitarist & composer

Se·grè \sə-'grā\ Emilio 1905– Am. (Ital.-born) physicist

Se·ja·nus \si-'jā-nəs\ Lucius Aelius *d* A.D. 31 Rom. conspirator

Sel·den \'sel-dən\ George Baldwin 1846–1922 Am. lawyer & inventor

— John 1584–1654 Eng. jurist & antiquary

Se·leu·cus I \sə-'lü-kəs\ 358?–280 B.C. ruler (306–280) of a Greek dynasty in Syria

Sel·in·court, de \'sel-ən-ˌkō(ə)rt, -ˌkȯ(ə)rt\ Hugh 1878–1951 Eng. nov. & dram.

Sel·kirk \'sel-ˌkərk\ Alexander 1676–1721 Scot. sailor marooned on one of Juan Fernández islets; original of Defoe's Robinson Crusoe

Sem·brich \'sem-brik\ Marcella 1858–1935 *Praxede Marcelline Kochańska* Austrian-born soprano

Se·më·nov \sə-'myȯn-əf\ Nikolai Nikolaevitch 1896– Russ. chem.

Semmes \'semz\ Raphael 1809–1877 Am. Confed. admiral

Sen·e·ca \'sen-i-kə\ Lucius Annaeus 4 B.C.?–A.D. 65 Rom. statesman & philos.

Sen·nach·er·ib \sə-'nak-ə-rəb\ *d* 681 B.C. king of Assyria (705–681)

Se·quoya \si-'kwȯi-ə\ 1770?–1843 Cherokee Indian scholar

Ser·ra, no Su·ñer \'ser-ə\ Ju·ní·pe·ro \hü-'nē-pə-ˌrō\ 1713–1784 orig. *Miguel José* Span. missionary in Mexico & California

Ser·ra·no Su·ñer \sə-ˌrän-ō-sün-'ye(ə)r\ Ramón 1901– *bro.◦ in-law of Franco* Span. lawyer & polit.

Ser·to·ri·us \(ˌ)sər-'tōr-ē-əs, -'tȯr-\ Quintus *d* 72 B.C. Rom. gen. & statesman

Ser·ve·tus \(ˌ)sər-'vēt-əs\ Michael 1511–1553 Span. theol. & martyr

Ser·vice \'sər-vəs\ Robert William 1874–1958 Canad. writer

Ses·sions \'sesh-ənz\ Roger 1896– Am. composer

Se·ton \'sēt-ʼn\ Ernest Thompson 1860–1946 orig. surname *Thompson* Eng.-born writer & illustrator in Am.

Seu·rat \sə-'rä\ Georges 1859–1891 Fr. painter

Se·ve·rus \sə-'vir-əs\ Lucius Septimius 146–211 Rom. emp. (193–211)

Sé·vi·gné, de \ˌsā-(ˌ)vēn-'yä, sā-'vēn-(ˌ)yä\ Marquise 1626–1696 née *Marie de Rabutin-Chantal* Fr. writer & lady of fashion

Sew·ard \'sü-ərd\ William Henry 1801–1872 Am. statesman; secy. of state (1861–69)

Sey·mour \'sē-ˌmō(ə)r, -ˌmȯ(ə)r\ Jane 1509?–1537 *3d wife of Henry VIII of Eng. & mother of Edward VI*

Seyss-In·quart, von \'zī-ˌsiŋ(k)-ˌfärt\ Ar·tur \'är-ˌtu̇(ə)r\ 1892–1946 Ger. Nazi polit.

Sfor·za \'sfȯrt-sə\ Count Carlo 1873–1952 Ital. anti-Fascist statesman

Shack·le·ton \'shak-əl-tən, -əlt-ʼn\ Sir Ernest Henry 1874–1922 Brit. antarctic explorer

Shad·well \'shad-ˌwel, -wəl\ Thomas 1642?–1692 Eng. dram.; poet laureate (1689–92)

Shaf·ter \'shaf-tər\ William Rufus 1835–1906 Am. gen.

Shaftes·bury \'shaf(t)s-ˌber-ē, -b(ə-)rē\ 1st Earl of 1621–1683 *Anthony Ashley Cooper* Eng. statesman

Shah Ja·han \ˌshäj-ə-'hän\ 1592–1666 Mogul emp. of Hindustan (1628–58)

Shake·speare *or* **Shak·spere** \'shāk-ˌspi(ə)r\ William 1564–1616 Eng. dram. & poet

Sha·piro \shə-'pir-(ˌ)ō\ Karl Jay 1913– Am. poet & critic

Sha·posh·ni·kov \'shäp-əsh-ni-ˌkȯf, 'shap-, -ˌkȯv\ Boris Mikhailovich 1882–1945 Russ. field marshal

Shas·tri \'shäs-trē\ Shri Lal \'läl\ Bahadur 1904–1966 Indian polit.; prime min. of India (1964–66)

Shaw \'shȯ\ George Bernard 1856–1950 Brit. author & socialist

— Thomas Edward see T. E. LAWRENCE

Shawn \'shȯn\ Ted 1891– Am. dancer & choreographer

Shays \'shāz\ Daniel 1747?–1825 Am. Revolutionist & rebel

She·han \'shē-ən\ Lawrence Joseph 1898– Am. cardinal

Shel·ley \'shel-ē\ Mary Woll·stone·craft \'wu̇l-stən-ˌkraft\ 1797–1851 née *Godwin; wife of P.B.* Eng. nov.

— Percy Bysshe \'bish\ 1792–1822 Eng. poet

Shen·stone \'shen-ˌstōn, 'shen(t)-stən\ William 1714–1763 Eng. poet

Shep·ard \'shep-ərd\ Alan Bartlett 1923– Am. astronaut; 1st Am. man in space (1961)

Sher·a·ton \'sher-ət-ʼn\ Thomas 1751–1806 Eng. furniture maker & designer

Sher·i·dan \'sher-əd-ʼn\ Philip Henry 1831–1888 Am. gen.

— Richard Brins·ley \'brinz-lē\ 1751–1816 Irish dram. & orator

Sher·man \'shər-mən\ James Schoolcraft 1855–1912 vice-pres. of the U.S. (1909–12)

— John 1823–1900 *bro. of W. T.* Am. statesman

— Roger 1721–1793 Am. jurist & statesman

— Stuart Pratt 1881–1926 Am. critic

— William Tecumseh 1820–1891 Am. gen.

Sher·riff \'sher-əf\ Robert Cedric 1896– Eng. writer

Sher·ring·ton \'sher-iŋ-tən\ Sir Charles Scott 1861–1952 Eng. physiol.

Sher·wood \'shər-ˌwu̇d *also* 'she(ə)r-\ Robert Emmet 1896–1955 Am. dram.

Shi·de·ha·ra \ˌshēd-ə-'här-ə\ Baron Kijuro 1872–1951 Jap. diplomat & statesman

Shi·ge·mit·su \ˌshē-gə-'mit-(ˌ)sü\ Mamoru 1887–1957 Jap. diplomat

Shih Huang-ti \'shi(ə)r-'hwäŋ-'tē, 'shē-\ 259–210 B.C. Chin. emp. Ch'in dynasty

Shin·well \'shin-ˌwel, -wəl\ Emanuel 1884– Brit. Labourite polit.

Shi·rer \'shīr-ər\ William Lawrence 1904– Am. journalist

Shir·ley \'shər-lē\ James 1596–1666 Eng. dram.

Shock·ley \'shäk-lē\ William Bradford 1910– Am. physicist

Sho·lo·khov \'shȯl-ə-ˌkȯf, -ˌkȯv\ Mikhail Aleksandrovich 1905– Russ. nov.

Short \'shȯ(ə)rt\ Walter Campbell 1880–1949 Am. gen.

Sho·sta·ko·vich \ˌshäs-tə-'kō-vich, ˌshȯs-, -'kȯ-\ Di·mi·tri \də-'mē-trē\ Dimitrievich 1906– Russ. composer

Shute \'shüt\ Nev·il \'nev-əl\ 1899–1960 *Nevil Shute Norway* Eng. aeronautical engineer & writer

Shver·nik \'shfer-nik\ Nikolai M. 1888– Russ. polit.; pres. U.S.S.R. (1946–53)

Si·be·lius \sə-'bāi-yəs, -'bā-lē-əs\ Jean \'zhän, 'yän\ 1865–1957 Finnish composer

Sick·les \'sik-əlz\ Daniel Edgar 1825–1914 Am. gen. & polit.

Sid·dons \'sid-ʼnz\ Sarah 1755–1831 née *Kemble* Eng. actress

Sid·ney \'sid-nē\ Sir Philip 1554–1586 Eng. poet, statesman, & soldier

Sieg·bahn \'sēg-ˌbän\ Karl Manne Georg 1886– Swed. physicist

Sie·mens \'sē-mənz, 'zē-\ Sir William 1823–1883 Brit. (Ger.-born) inventor

Sien·kie·wicz \shen-'kyā-vich\ Henryk 1846–1916 Pol. nov.

Sie·vers \'sē-vərz; 'zē-fərs, -vərs\ Eduard 1850–1932 Ger. philologist

Sie·yès \sē-ˌā-'yes, sā-'yes\ Emmanuel Joseph 1748–1836 *Abbé Sieyès* Fr. Revolutionist

Sig·is·mund \'sig-ə-smənd\ 1368–1437 Holy Rom. emp. (1411–37)

Sigs·bee \'sigz-bē\ Charles Dwight 1845–1923 Am. admiral

Si·gurds·son \'sig-ərd-ˌsən, -ˌerth-\ Jón \'yōn\ 1811–1879 Icelandic statesman & author

Si·kor·sky \sə-'kȯr-skē\ Igor Ivan 1889– Am. (Russ.-born) aeronautical engineer

Sil·lan·pää \'sil-an-ˌpa\ Frans Ee·mil 1888–1964 Finnish nov.

Si·lo·ne \si-'lō-nē\ Ignazio real name *Secondo Tranquilli* 1900– Ital. author

Sim·e·on Sty·li·tes \ˌsim-ē-ən-stə-'līt-ēz, -ˌstī-\ Saint 390?–459 Syrian ascetic & stylite

Si·mon \'sī-mən\ 1st Viscount 1873–1954 *John Allsebrook Simon* Brit. jurist & statesman

Si·mon·i·des \sī-'män-ə-ˌdēz\ **of Ceos** 6th–5th cent. B.C. Greek poet

Simp·son \'sim(p)-sən\ William Hood 1888– Am. gen.

Sims \'simz\ William Sow·den \'sau̇d-ʼn\ 1858–1936 Am. admiral

Sin·clair \'sin-ˌkla(ə)r, 'siŋ-, -ˌkle(ə)r, sin-', siŋ-'\ May 1865?–1946 Eng. nov.

— Upton Beall \'bel\ 1878–1968 Am. writer & polit.

Sing·er \'siŋ-ər\ Isaac Merrit 1811–1875 Am. inventor

ə abut; ᵊ kitten; ər further; a back; ā bake; ä cot, cart; au̇ out; ch chin; e less; ē easy; g gift; i trip; ī life
j joke; ŋ sing; ō flow; ȯ flaw; ȯi coin; th thin; th̷ this; ü loot; u̇ foot; y yet; yü few; yu̇ furious; zh vision
ᵊ F table; à F bac; ḵ G ich, Buch; ⁿ F vin; œ F bœuf; ᴔ F feu; ᵁᴇ G füllen; ᵁᴇ F rue; ʸ F digne \dēnʸ\, nuit \nwᵊyᵉ\

Si·quei·ros \si-'kā-(,)rōs\ David Al·fa·ro \äl-'fär-(,)ō\ 1898– Mex. muralist

Si·raj-ud-dau·la \sə-,räj-ə-'daù-lə\ 1728?–1757 nawab of Bengal (1756–57)

Sis·ley \'sis-lē, sē-'slā\ Alfred 1839–1899 Eng.-born painter in France

Sis·mon·di, de \sis-'män-dē\ Jean Charles Léonard Simonde 1773–1842 Swiss hist. & econ.

Sit·ter, de \'sit-ər\ Willem 1872–1934 Du. astron.

Sit·ting Bull \,sit-iŋ-'bùl\ 1834–1890 Sioux leader & medicine man

Sit·well \'sit-,wel, -wəl\ Sir George Reres·by \'ri(ə)rz-bē\ 1860–1943 & his 3 children: Dame Edith 1887–1964; Sir Osbert 1892–1969; & Sa·chev·er·ell \sə-'shev-(ə-)rəl\ 1897– Eng. authors

Skeat \'skēt\ Walter William 1835–1912 Eng. philologist

Skel·ton \'skelt-ᵊn\ John 1460?–1529 Eng. poet

Skin·ner \'skin-ər\ Cornelia Otis 1901–   *dau. of Otis* Am. actress

— Otis 1858–1942 Am. actor

Sko·da, von \'skōd-ə, 'shkód-(,)ä\ Emil 1839–1900 Czech engineer & industrialist

Sla·ter \'slāt-ər\ Samuel 1768–1835 Eng.-born industrialist in Am.

Slich·ter \'slik-tər\ Sumner Huber 1892–1959 Am. economist

Sli·dell \slī-'del, *by collateral descendants* 'slīd-ᵊl\ John 1793–1871 Am. Confed. diplomat

Sloan \'slōn\ John 1871–1951 Am. painter

Slo·cum \'slō-kəm\ Henry Warner 1827–1894 Am. gen.

Slo·nim·sky \slō-'nim(p)-skē\ Nicolas 1894–   Russ.-born composer in U.S.

Sme·ta·na \'smet-ə-nə\ Be·dřich \'bed-ər-,zhik\ 1824–1884 Czech pianist, composer, & conductor

Smig·ly-Rydz \,s(h)mig-lē-'rits, -'ridz\ Edward 1886–   Pol. gen.

Smith \'smith\ Adam 1723–1790 Scot. econ.

— Alfred Emanuel 1873–1944 Am. polit.

— Edmund Kirby see KIRBY-SMITH

— Goldwin 1823–1910 Brit. hist.

— John 1580–1631 Eng. colonist in Am.

— Joseph 1805–1844 Am. founder of Mormon Church

— Sydney 1771–1845 Eng. essayist

— Walter Be·dell \bə-'del\ 1895–1961 Am. gen. & diplomat

— William 1769–1839 Eng. geologist

— Winchell 1871–1933 Am. author

Smith-Dor·ri·en \'smith-'dòr-ē-ən, -'där-\ Sir Horace Lockwood 1858–1930 Brit. gen.

Smith·son \'smith-sən\ James 1765–1829 Brit. chem. & mineralogist

Smol·lett \'smäl-ət\ Tobias George 1721–1771 Brit. author

Smuts \'sməts, 'smœts\ Jan \'yän\ Christiaan 1870–1950 So. African field marshal; prime min. (1919–24; 1939–48)

Smyth \'smīth\ Henry DeWolf 1898–   Am. physicist

Snor·ri Stur·lu·son \,snòr-ē-'stər-lə-sən, ,snär-\ 1178–1241 Icelandic statesman & hist.

Snow \'snō\ Baron 1905–   *Charles Percy Snow* Eng. nov. & physicist

Snow·den \'snōd-ᵊn\ Philip 1864–1937 1st Viscount *Snowden of Ick·orn·shaw* \'ik-,òrn,shò\ Eng. econ. & polit.

Snow·don \'snōd-ᵊn\ Earl of — see ARMSTRONG-JONES

Sny·der \'snīd-ər\ John Wesley 1895–   Am. banker & administrator

Sobieski John see JOHN III SOBIESKI

So·ci·nus \sō-'sī-nəs\ Faustus 1539–1604 *Fausto Soz·zi·ni* \-sōt-'sē-nē\ Ital. religious reformer

Soc·ra·tes \'säk-rə-,tēz\ 470?–399 B.C. Greek philos.

Sod·dy \'säd-ē\ Frederick 1877–1956 Eng. chem.

Sö·der·blom \'sə(r)d-ər-,blùm\ Nathan 1866–1931 Swed. theol.

So·do·ma, Il \'sòd-ə-mə\ 1477?–1549 *Giovanni Antonio de' Bazzi* Ital. painter

So·kol·ni·kov \sə-'kòl-ni-,kóf, -,kòv\ Grigori Yakovlevich 1888–   Russ. polit.

So·lon \'sō-lən, -,län\ 638?–?559 B.C. Athenian lawgiver

Sol·y·man \'säl-i-mən\ *var of* SULEIMAN

Som·er·ville \'səm-ər-,vil\ Sir James Fownes \'fōnz\ 1882–1949 Brit. admiral of the fleet

Soong \'sùŋ\ Ai-ling \'ī-'liŋ\ 1888–   *wife of H.H.Kung*

— Ch'ing-ling \'chiŋ-'liŋ\ 1890–   *wife of Sun Yat-Sen*

— Mei-ling \'mā-'liŋ\ 1898–   *wife of Chiang Kai-shek*

— Tse-ven *or* Tsŭ-wên \'tsù-'wən\ 1891–   *T.V.Soong, bro. of the 3 prec.* Chin. financier & statesman

Soph·o·cles \'säf-ə-,klēz\ 496?–406 B.C. Greek dram.

Sor·del·lo \sòr-'del-(,)ō\ 13th cent. Ital. troubadour

So·rol·la y Bas·ti·da \sə-'ról-yə-,ē-(,)bä-'stē-də, -'rói-ə-, -'stē-thə\ Joaquín 1863–1923 Span. painter

Soult \sült\ Nicolas Jean de Dieu 1769–1851 *Duc de Dal·ma·tie* \dàl-mà-sē\ Fr. soldier; marshal of France (1804)

Sou·sa \'sü-zə, 'sü-sə\ John Philip 1854–1932 *the March King* Am. bandmaster & composer

South \'saùth\ Robert 1634–1716 Eng. clergyman

Sou·they \'saù-the, 'səth-ē\ Robert 1774–1843 Eng. author; poet laureate (1813–43)

Sou·tine \sü-'tēn\ Chaim 1894–1943 Lith.-born painter in France

Spaak \späk\ Paul Henri 1899–   Belg. lawyer & polit.; premier (1938–39; 1947–49); secy.-gen. of N.A.T.O. (1957–61)

Spaatz \'späts\ Carl 1891–   *orig. Spatz* Am. gen.

Spal·ding \'spòl-diŋ\ Albert 1888–1953 Am. violinist & composer

Sparks \'spärks\ Jar·ed \'jar-əd, 'jer-\ 1789–1866 Am. hist.

Spar·ta·cus \'spärt-ə-kəs\ *d* 71 B.C. Rom. slave & insurrectionist

Spee \'shpā\ Count Maximilian 1861–1914 Ger. admiral

Spell·man \'spel-mən\ Francis Joseph 1889–1967 Am. cardinal

Spe·mann \'shpā-,män\ Hans 1869–1941 Ger. zool.

Spen·cer \'spen(t)-sər\ Herbert 1820–1903 Eng. philos.

Spen·der \'spen-dər\ Stephen Harold 1909–   Eng. poet & critic

Speng·ler \'shpeŋ-lər\ Oswald 1880–1936 Ger. philos.

Spen·ser \'spen(t)-sər\ Edmund 1552–1599 Eng. poet

Sper·ry \'sper-ē\ Elmer Ambrose 1860–1930 Am. inventor

Spin·garn \'spin-,gärn\ Joel Elias 1875–1939 Am. author

Spi·no·za \spin-'ō-zə\ Baruch *or* Benedict 1632–1677 Du. philos.

Spit·te·ler \'shpit-ᵊl-ər, 'shpit-,lər\ Carl 1845–1924 pseud. *Felix Tan·dem* \'tän-,dem\ Swiss writer

Spock \'späk\ Benjamin McLane 1903–   Am. physician

Spode \'spōd\ Josiah 1754–1827 Eng. potter

Spru·ance \'sprü-ən(t)s\ Raymond Ames 1886–1969 Am. admiral

Spy·ri \'s(h)pi(ə)r-ē\ Johanna 1827–1901 née *Heusser* Swiss author

Staël, de \'stäl\ Mme. Anne Louise Germaine 1766–1817 Baronne *de Staël Holstein* née *Necker* Fr. writer

Ståhl·berg \'stöl-,be(ə)r(-yə), -,bərg\ Kaarlo Ju·ho \'yü-(,)hó\ 1865–1952 Finnish statesman

Stair Viscount & Earl of see DALRYMPLE

Sta·lin \'stäl-ən, 'stal-, -,ēn\ Joseph 1879–1953 *Iosif Vissarionovich Dzhu·gash·vi·li* \,jü-gəsh-'vē-lē\ Russ. polit. leader

Stan·dish \'stan-dish\ Myles *or* Miles 1584?–1656 Eng. colonist in Am.

Stan·is·las \'stan-ə-,slòs\ I Lesz·czyń·ski \lesh-'chin-skē\ 1677–1766 king of Poland (1704–09; 1733–35)

Stan·i·slav·ski \,stan-ə-'slaf-skē, -'släv-\ Konstantin 1863–1938 Russ. actor

Stan·ley \'stan-lē\ Sir Henry Morton 1841–1904 orig. *John Rowlands* Brit. explorer in Africa

— Wendell Meredith 1904–   Am. biochem.

Stan·ton \'stant-ᵊn\ Edwin McMasters 1814–1869 Am. lawyer & secy. of war (1862–68)

— Elizabeth 1815–1902 nee *Cady* Am. suffragist

Star·hem·berg, von \'stär-əm-,bərg, 'shtär-əm-,be(ə)rk\ Prince Ernst Rüdiger 1899–1956 Austrian anti-Nazi statesman

Stark \'stärk\ Harold Raynsford 1880–   Am. admiral

— \'s(h)tärk\ Johannes 1874–1957 Ger. physicist

— \'stärk\ John 1728–1822 Am. Revolutionary gen.

Star·zyń·ski \stär-'zin(t)-skē\ Stefan 1893–?1940 Pol. polit. & hero

Stas·sen \'stas-ᵊn\ Harold Edward 1907–   Am. lawyer & polit.

Sta·ti·us \'stā-sh(ē-)əs\ Publius Papinius 45?–?96 Rom. poet

Stau·ding·er \'s(h)taùd-iŋ-ər\ Hermann 1881–1965 Ger. chem.

Steed \'stēd\ Henry Wick·ham \'wik-əm\ 1871–1956 Eng. journalist

Steele \'stē(ə)l\ Sir Richard 1672–1729 Brit. essayist & dram.

Steen \'stān\ Jan 1626–1679 Du. painter

Ste·fans·son \'stef-ən-sən\ Vil·hjal·mur \'vil-,yaùl-mər\ 1879–1962 Canad. arctic explorer

Stef·fens \'stef-ənz\ (Joseph) Lincoln 1866–1936 Am. journalist & editor

Stein \'stīn\ Gertrude 1874–1946 Am. writer

Stein, vom und zum \,fòm-ənt-,sùm-'s(h)tīn, -,süm-\ Baron Heinrich Friedrich Karl 1757–1831 Prussian statesman

Stein·beck \'stīn-,bek\ John Ernst 1902–1968 Am. nov.

Stein·metz \'s(h)tīn-,mets\ Charles Proteus 1865–1923 Am. (Ger.-born) electrical engineer

Sten·dhal \sten-'däl, stan-, *F* staⁿ-dâl\ 1783–1842 pseud. of *Marie Henri Beyle* Fr. writer

Ste·phen \'stē-vən\ 1097?–1154 king of England (1135–54)

— Sir Leslie 1832–1904 Eng. philos., critic, & biographer

Ste·phens \'stē-vənz\ Alexander Hamilton 1812–1883 Am. polit.; vice-pres. of the Confed. states

— James 1882–1950 Irish poet & nov.

Ste·phen·son \'stē-vən-sən\ George 1781–1848 Eng. inventor & founder of railroads

— Robert 1803–1859 *son of George* Eng. engineer

Stern \'stərn\ Isaac 1920–   Russ.-born violinist in Am.

— Otto 1888–1969 Am. physicist

Stern·berg \'stərn-,bərg\ George Miller 1838–1915 Am. physician & bacteriol.

Sterne \'stərn\ Laurence 1713–1768 Brit. nov.

Stet·tin·i·us \stə-'tin-ē-əs\ Edward Riel·ley \'rī-lē\ 1900–1949 Am. financier & statesman

Steu·ben, von \'st(y)ü-bən, 'shtói-; st(y)ü-'ben\ Baron Friedrich Wilhelm Ludolf Gerhard Augustin 1730–1794 Prussian-born gen. in Am.

Ste·vens \'stē-vənz\ John 1749–1838 Am. inventor

— Thad·de·us \'thad-ē-əs, tha-'dē-\ 1792–1868 Am. lawyer & legislator

— Wallace 1879–1955 Am. poet

Ste·ven·son \'stē-vən-sən\ Ad·lai \'ad-lē\ Ewing 1835–1914 Am. polit.; vice-pres. of U.S. (1893–97)

— Adlai Ewing 1900–1965 *grandson of prec.* Am. lawyer & diplomat

— Robert Louis Balfour 1850–1894 *R.L.S.* Scot. author

Stew·art \'st(y)ü-ərt, 'st(y)ù-(-ə)rt\ Du·gald \'dü-gəld\ 1753–1828 Scot. philos.

— Potter 1915–   Am. jurist

— Robert 1769–1822 Viscount *Cas·tle·reagh* \'kas-əl-,rā\ Eng. statesman

Steyn \'stān, 'stīn\ Martinus Theunis 1857–1916 So. African lawyer & statesman

Stieg·litz \'stē-,glits\ Alfred 1864–1946 Am. photographer & editor

Stik·ker \'stik-ər\ Dirk 1897–   Dutch diplomat & statesman; secy.-gen. of N.A.T.O. (1961–64)

Stil·i·cho \'stil-i-,kō\ Flavius 359?–408 Rom. gen. & statesman

Still \'stil\ Andrew Taylor 1828–1917 Am. physician; founder of osteopathy

Stil·well \'stil-,wel, -wəl\ Joseph Warren 1883–1946 Am. gen.

Stim·son \'stim(p)-sən\ Henry Lewis 1867–1950 Am. statesman

Stin·nes \'s(h)tin-əs\ Hugo 1870–1924 Ger. industrialist

Stock·mar, von \'stäk-,mär\ Baron Christian Friedrich 1787–1863 Anglo-Belg. statesman

Stock·ton \'stäk-tən\ Francis Richard 1834–1902 *Frank R.* Am. writer

Stod·dard \'städ-ərd\ Richard Henry 1825–1903 Am. poet & critic

Stokes \'stōks\ Sir Frederick Wilfrid Scott 1860–1927 Eng. engineer & inventor

Sto·kow·ski \stə-'kòf-skē, -'kòv-\ Leopold Antoni Stanisław 1887–   Eng.-born conductor in Am.

Stone \'stōn\ Edward Durell 1902–   Am. architect

— Harlan Fiske 1872–1946 Am. jurist; chief justice U.S. Supreme Court (1941–46)

— Lucy 1818–1893 Mrs. *Henry Brown Blackwell* Am. suffragist

Sto·ry \'stōr-ē, 'stòr-ē\ Joseph 1779–1845 Am. jurist

— William Wetmore 1819–1895 *son of Joseph* Am. sculptor

Stow \'stō\ John 1525?–1605 Eng. hist. & antiquary

Stowe \'stō\ Harriet Elizabeth 1811–1896 née *Beecher* Am. author

Stra·bo \'strā-(,)bō\ 63 B.C.?–?A.D. 24 Greek geographer

Stra·chey \'strā-chē\ Evelyn John St. Loe 1901–1963 Eng. socialist

— (Giles) Lytton 1880–1932 Eng. biographer

— John St. Loe 1860–1927 *father of Evelyn* Eng. journalist

Stra·di·va·ri \strad-ə-'vär-ē, -'var-, -'ver-\ Antonio 1644–1737 *Antonius Strad·i·var·i·us* \,strad-ə-'var-ē-əs, -'ver-\ Ital. violin maker

Straf·ford \'straf-ərd\ 1st Earl of 1593–1641 *Thomas Wentworth* Eng. statesman

Stratford de Redcliffe Viscount see CANNING

Strath·co·na \strath-'kō-nə\ **and Mount Royal** 1st Baron 1820–1914 *Donald Alexander Smith* Canad. (Scot.-born) railroad builder & administrator

Straus \'s(h)traús\ Oskar 1870–1954 Fr. (Austrian-born) composer

Strauss \'s(h)traús\ David Friedrich 1808–1874 Ger. theol. & philos.

— Johann father 1804–1849 & son 1825–1899 Austrian composers

— Ri·chard \'rik-,ärt, 'rik-\ 1864–1949 Ger. composer

Stra·vin·sky \strə-'vin(t)-skē\ Igor \'ē-,gó(ə)r\ Fëdorovich 1882– Am. (Russ.-born) composer

Strei·cher \'s(h)trī-kər, -kər\ Julius 1885–1946 Ger. Nazi administrator

Stre·se·mann \'s(h)trā-zə-,män\ Gustav 1878–1929 Ger. statesman

Strind·berg \'strin(d)-,bərg, 'strin-,be(ə)r(-yə)\ August 1849–1912 Swed. dram. & nov.

Stritch \'strich\ Samuel Alphonsus 1887–1958 Am. cardinal

Strong \'stróŋ\ George Veazey 1880–1946 Am. gen.

Stru·en·see, von \'s(h)trü-ən-,zā\ Count Johann Friedrich 1737–1772 Ger.-Dan. statesman & philos.

Struth·er \'strəth-ər\ Jan \'jan\ 1901–1953 pseud. of *Joyce Maxtone Graham* née *Anstruther* Eng. writer

Strutt \'strət\ Joseph 1749–1802 Eng. antiquary

Stu·art \'st(y)ü-ərt, 'st(y)ù-(,ə)rt\ see CHARLES I & MARY STUART

— *Charles the Young Pretender* see CHARLES

— Gilbert Charles 1755–1828 Am. painter

— James Ewell Brown 1833–1864 *Jeb* Am. Confed. gen.

— *James Francis Edward the Old Pretender* see JAMES

Stubbs \'stəbz\ William 1825–1901 Eng. hist. & prelate

Stülp·na·gel, von \'s(h)túlp-,näg-əl\ Otto 1880–1948 Ger. gen.

Stur·dee \'stərd-ē\ Sir Frederick Charles Doveton 1859–1925 Brit. admiral

Stur·gis \'stər-jəs\ Russell 1836–1909 Am. architect & writer

Sturluson see SNORRI STURLUSON

Štur·sa \'shtü(ə)r-sə\ Jan \'yän\ 1880–1925 Czech sculptor

Stuy·ve·sant \'stī-və-sənt\ Peter 1592–1672 Du. administrator in Am.

Suck·ling \'sək-liŋ\ Sir John 1609–1642 Eng. Cavalier poet

Su·cre, de \'sü-(,)krā\ Antonio José 1795–1830 So. Am. liberator & gen.

Sue \'sü, sǖ\ Eugène 1804–1857 *Marie Joseph* Fr. nov.

Sue·to·ni·us \swē-'tō-nē-əs\ 2d cent. A.D. *Gaius Suetonius Tranquillus* Rom. biographer & hist.

Su·gi·ya·ma \,sü-gē-'yäm-ə\ Hajime 1880–1945 Jap. field marshal

Su·kar·no \sü-'kär-(,)nō\ 1901– pres. of Indonesian Republic (1945–1967)

Su·lei·man I \'sü-lā-,män\ 1496?–1566 *the Magnificent* Ottoman sultan (1520–66)

Sul·la \'səl-ə\ 138–78 B.C. *Lucius Cornelius Sulla Felix* Rom. gen. & polit.

Sul·li·van \'səl-ə-vən\ Sir Arthur Seymour 1842–1900 Eng. composer

— John 1740–1795 Am. Revolutionary gen.

— John Lawrence 1899– Am. lawyer & administrator

— Louis 1856–1924 Am. architect

Sul·ly \'səl-ē\ Thomas 1783–1872 Eng.-born painter in Am.

Sul·ly, de \'səl-ē, sə-'lē\ Duc 1560–1641 *Maximilien de Béthune Baron de Ros·ny* \-rō-'nē\ Fr. statesman

Sul·ly Pru·dhomme \-(,)prü-'dóm, -'dəm\ René François Armand 1839–1907 Fr. poet & critic

Sum·ner \'səm-nər\ Charles 1811–1874 Am. statesman & orator

— James Batchelier 1887–1955 Am. biochem.

— William Graham 1840–1910 Am. sociol. & educ.

Sun Yat-sen \'sün-'yät-'sen\ 1866–1925 Chin. statesman

Sun·day \'sən-dē\ William Ashley 1862–1935 *Billy* Am. evangelist

Su·raj·ah Dow·lah var of SIRAJ-UD-DAULA

Surrey Earl of see Henry HOWARD

Sur·tees \'sərt-(,)ēz\ Robert Smith 1805–1864 Eng. nov. & editor

Sut·ter \'sət-ər, 'süt-\ John Augustus 1803–1880 Ger.-born pioneer in California

Sutt·ner, von \'zút-nər, 'sút-\ Bertha 1843–1914 née Countess *Kinsky* Austrian writer & pacifist

Su·vo·rov \sü-'vór-əf, -'vär-\ Count Aleksandr Vasilievich 1730–1800 Russ. field marshal

Sved·berg \'sfed-,bərg, sfäd-,be(ə)r(-yə)\ The or Theodor 1884– Swed. chem.

Sver·drup \'sve(ə)r-drəp\ Otto Neumann 1855–1930 Norw. arctic explorer

Sver·re \'sver-ə\ 1152?–1202 *Sverre Si·gurds·son* \'sig-ərd-sən\ king of Norway (1184–1202)

Swe·den·borg \'swēd-ᵊn-,bórg\ Emanuel 1688–1772 orig. *Svedberg* Swed. philos. & religious writer

Sweet \'swēt\ Henry 1845–1912 Eng. phonetician & philologist

Swift \'swift\ Jonathan 1667–1745 Eng. (Irish-born) satirist

Swin·burne \'swin-(,)bərn\ Algernon Charles 1837–1909 Eng. poet

Swin·ner·ton \'swin-ərt-ᵊn\ Frank Arthur 1884– Eng. nov. & critic

Swin·ton \'swint-ᵊn\ 1st Earl of 1884– *Philip Cunliffe-Lister* Eng. statesman

Sykes \'sīks\ George 1822–1880 Am. gen.

Sylva Carmen see ELIZABETH Queen of Romania

Sy·ming·ton \'sī-miŋ-tən\ (William) Stuart 1901– Am. industrialist & polit.

Sy·monds \'sīm-ən(d)z, 'sim-\ John Addington 1840–1893 Eng. scholar

Sy·mons \'sīm-ənz, 'sim-\ Arthur 1865–1945 Brit. poet & critic

Synge \'siŋ\ John Millington 1871–1909 Irish poet & dram.

— Richard Laurence Millington 1914– Brit. biochem.

Szent-Györ·gyi \sent-'jər-jē\ **von Nagy·ra·polt** \'näj-'räp-,ōlt\ Albert 1893– Hung. chem.

Szi·lard \'zil-,ärd, zə-'lärd\ Leo 1898–1964 Am. (Hung.-born) physicist

Szold \'zōld\ Henrietta 1860–1945 Am. Zionist; founder of Hadassah

---

Tac·i·tus \'tas-ət-əs\ Cornelius 55?–after 117 Rom. hist.

Taft \'taft\ Lo·ra·do \lə-'räd-(,)ō\ 1860–1936 Am. sculptor

— Robert Alphonso 1889–1953 son of W.H. Am. lawyer & polit.

— William Howard 1857–1930 27th pres. of the U.S. (1909–13); chief justice U.S. Supreme Court (1921–30)

Ta·gore \tə-'gō(ə)r, -'gò(ə)r\ Sir Ra·bin·dra·nath \rə-'bin-drə-,nät\ 1861–1941 Hindu poet

Taine \'tān\ Hippolyte Adolphe 1828–1893 Fr. philos. & critic

Tall·chief \'tól-,chēf\ Maria 1925– Am. dancer

Tal·ley·rand-Pé·ri·gord, de \'tal-ē-,ran(d)-'per-ə-,gó(ə)r\ Charles Maurice 1754–1838 Prince *de Bénévent* Fr. statesman

Ta·ma·yo \tə-'mä-(,)yō, -'mī-(,)ō\ Rufino 1899– Mex. painter

Tam·er·lane \'tam-ər-,lān\ or **Tam·bur·laine** \'tam-bər-,lān\ 1336?–1405 *Timur Lenk* also *Timour* Eastern conqueror

Tamm \'täm, 'tam\ Igor Eugenievich 1895– Russ. physicist

Tan·cred \'taŋ-krəd\ 1078?–1112 Norman leader in 1st crusade

Ta·ney \'tó-nē\ Roger Brooke 1777–1864 Am. jurist; chief justice U.S. Supreme Court (1836–64)

Tar·bell \'tär-,bel\ Ida Minerva 1857–1944 Am. author

Tar·dieu \tär-'dyə(r)\ André Pierre Gabriel Amédée 1876–1945 Fr. statesman

Tar·king·ton \'tär-kiŋ-tən\ (Newton) Booth 1869–1946 Am. nov.

Tas·man \'taz-mən, 'täs-,män\ Abel Janszoon 1603–1659 Du. mariner

Tas·so \'tas-(,)ō, 'täs-\ Tor·qua·to \tòr-'kwät-(,)ō\ 1544–1595 Ital. poet

Tate \'tāt\ Nahum 1652–1715 Brit. dram.; poet laureate (1692–1715)

Ta·tum \'tāt-əm\ Edward Lawrie 1909– Am. biochem.

Taus·sig \'taú-sig\ Frank William 1859–1940 Am. econ.

Taw·ney \'tó-nē\ Richard Henry 1880–1962 Eng. economic hist.

Tay·lor \'tā-lər\ Bay·ard \'bī-ərd, 'bā-\ 1825–1878 Am. writer

— Deems \'dēmz\ 1885–1966 Am. composer & music critic

— Edward 1645?–1729 Am. clergyman & poet

— Jeremy 1613–1667 Eng. prelate & author

— Maxwell Davenport 1901– Am. gen.

— Myron Charles 1874–1959 Am. lawyer, businessman, & diplomat

— Tom 1817–1880 Eng. dram.

— Zachary 1784–1850 12th pres. of the U.S. (1849–50)

Tchai·kov·sky \chī-'kóf-skē, chə-, -'kóv-\ Pëtr Ilich 1840–1893 Russ. composer

Tchekhov var of CHEKHOV

Teas·dale \'tēz-,dāl\ Sara 1884–1933 Am. poet

Te·cum·seh \tə-'kəm(p)-sə, -sē\ or **Te·cum·tha** \-'kəm(p)-thə\ 1768?–1813 Shawnee Indian chief

Ted·der \'ted-ər\ 1st Baron 1890–1967 *Arthur William Tedder* Brit. air marshal

Teil·hard de Char·din \tā-yàr-də-shàr-daⁿ\ Pierre 1881–1955 Fr. priest & author

Tek·a·kwitha \,tek-ə-'kwith-ə\ Ka·teri \'kät-ə-rē\ 1656–1680 *Lily of the Mohawks* Am. Indian ascetic

Tel·ler \'tel-ər\ Edward 1908– Am. (Hung.-born) physicist

Téllez Gabriel see TIRSO DE MOLINA

Tem·ple \'tem-pəl\ Sir William 1628–1699 Eng. statesman

Te·niers \tə-'ni(ə)rz, 'ten-yərz\ David father 1582–1649 & son 1610–1690 Flemish painters

Ten·niel \'ten-yəl\ Sir John 1820–1914 Eng. cartoonist & illustrator

Ten·ny·son \'ten-ə-sən\ 1st Baron 1809–1892 *Alfred Tennyson* Eng. poet; poet laureate (1850–92)

Ter·borch or **Ter Borch** \tər-'bórk, -'bórk\ Gerard 1617–1681 Du. painter

Ter·ence \'ter-ən(t)s\ 190?–159 B.C. *Publius Terentius Afer* Rom. dram.

Ter·hune \(,)tər-'hyün\ Albert Payson 1872–1942 Am. author

Ter·ry \'ter-ē\ Ellen Alicia or Alice 1847–1928 Eng. actress

Ter·tul·lian \tər-'təl-yən\ 160?–?230 *Quintus Septimius Florens Tertullianus* Latin church father

Tes·la \'tes-lə\ Nikola 1856–1943 Am. (Austrian-born) electrician & inventor

Tet·zel or **Te·zel** \'tet-səl\ Johann 1465?–1519 Ger. Dominican monk

Thack·er·ay \'thak-(ə-)rē\ William Makepeace 1811–1863 Eng. author

Tha·les \'thā-(,)lēz\ 640?–546 B.C. Greek philos.

Thanet Octave see Alice FRENCH

Thant \'thänt\ U \'ü\ 1909– Burmese U.N. official; secy.-gen. (1961–)

Thay·er \'tha(ə)r, 'the(ə)r\ Sylvanus 1785–1872 *father of West Point* Am. army officer & educ.

— William Roscoe 1859–1923 Am. hist. & biographer

Thei·ler \'tī-lər\ Max 1899– So. African-born specialist in tropical medicine in U.S.

The·mis·to·cles \thə-'mis-tə-,klēz\ 527?–?460 B.C. Athenian gen. & statesman

The·oc·ri·tus \thē-'äk-rət-əs\ 3d cent. B.C. Greek poet

The·od·o·ric \thē-'äd-ə-rik\ 454?–526 *the Great* king of the Ostrogoths (474–526)

The·o·do·si·us I \,thē-ə-'dō-sh(ē-)əs\ 346?–395 *the Great* Rom. gen. & emp. (379–395)

The·o·phras·tus \,thē-ə-'fras-təs\ ab 371–287 B.C. Greek philos. & naturalist

The·o·rell \'tā-ə-,rel\ Axel Hugo Theodor 1903– Swed. biochem.

The·re·sa or **Te·re·sa** \tə-'rē-sə, -'rā-sə, -'rā-zə\ Saint 1515–1582 Span. Carmelite nun

---

ə abut; ᵊ kitten; ər further; a back; ā bake; ä cot, cart; aú out; ch chin; e less; ē easy; g gift; i trip; ī life
j joke; ŋ sing; ō flow; ó flaw; ói coin; th thin; t̶h this; ü loot; ú foot; y yet; yü few; yú furious; zh vision
ᵊ F table; á F bac; ӄ G ich, Buch; ⁿ F vin; œ F bœuf; ȫ F feu; ᴜᴇ G füllen; ᴜᴇ̄ F rue; ʸ F digne \dēnʸ\, nuit \nwᵊē\

Thes·pis \\'thes-pəs\\ 6th cent. B.C. Greek poet
Thiers \\tē-'e(ə)r\\ Louis Adolphe 1797–1877 Fr. statesman & hist.; pres. of France (1871–73)
Thom·as \\'täm-əs\\ Augustus 1857–1934 Am. dram.
— Dyl·an \\'dil·ən\\ 1914–1953 Brit. poet
— George Henry 1816–1870 Am. gen.
— Norman Mat·toon \\ma-'tün, mə-\\ 1884–1969 Am. socialist polit.
— Seth 1785–1859 Am. clock manufacturer
— Theodore 1835–1905 Ger.-born conductor in Am.
— à Becket see BECKET
— a Kem·pis \\ə-'kem-pəs, (ˌ)ä-'kem-\\ 1380–1471 Ger. ecclesiastic & writer
— of Er·cel·doune \\'ər-səl-ˌdün\\ fl 1220–1297 Thomas the Rhymer Scot. seer & poet
Thomp·son \\'täm(p)-sən\\ Benjamin 1753–1814 Count Rum·ford \\'rəm(p)-fərd\\ Brit. (Am.-born) physicist & statesman
— Francis 1859–1907 Eng. poet
— Llewellyn E. 1904– Am. diplomat
Thom·son \\'täm(p)-sən\\ George Pag·et \\'paj-ət\\ 1892– son of Sir Joseph John Eng. physicist
— James 1700–1748 Scot. poet
— James 1834–1882 B. V. Scot. poet
— John Arthur 1861–1933 Scot. biologist
— Sir Joseph John 1856–1940 Eng. physicist
— Virgil 1896– Am. composer
— William see Baron KELVIN
Tho·reau \\'thȯr-(ˌ)ō, thə-'rō\\ Henry David 1817–1862 Am. writer
Tho·rez \\tȯ-'rez\\ Maurice 1900–1964 Fr. Communist
Thorn·dike \\'thȯ(ə)rn-ˌdīk\\ Ashley Horace 1871–1933 & his brother Lynn 1882–1965 Am. educators
Thorn·ton \\'thȯrnt-ən\\ William 1759–1828 Am. architect
Thor·vald·sen or **Thor·wald·sen** \\'tür-ˌväl-sən\\ Ber·tel \\'bert-ᵊl\\ 1768–1844 Dan. sculptor
Thras·y·bu·lus \\ˌthras-ə-'byü-ləs\\ d 389 B.C. Athenian gen.
Thu·cyd·i·des \\th(y)ü-'sid-ə-ˌdēz\\ 471?–?400 B.C. Greek hist.
Thur·ber \\'thər-bər\\ James 1894–1961 Am. writer
Thys·sen \\'tis-ᵊn\\ Fritz 1873–1951 Ger. industrialist
Tib·bett \\'tib-ət\\ Lawrence Mervil 1896–1960 Am. baritone
Ti·be·ri·us \\tī-'bir-ē-əs\\ 42 B.C.–A.D. 37 Tiberius Claudius Nero Caesar Rom. emp. (14–37)
Ti·bul·lus \\tə-'bəl-əs\\ Albius 54?–?18 B.C. Rom. poet
Tieck \\'tēk\\ Ludwig 1773–1853 Ger. author
Tie·po·lo \\tē-'ā-pə-ˌlō\\ Giovanni Battista 1696–1770 Ital. painter
Tig·lath-pi·le·ser III \\'tig-ˌlath-(ˌ)pī-'lē-zər-, -pə-\\ d 727 B.C. king of Assyria (745–727)
Til·den \\'til-dən\\ Samuel Jones 1814–1886 Am. lawyer & polit.
Til·dy \\'til-dē\\ Zol·tán \\'zōl-ˌtän\\ 1889–1961 Hung. polit.; pres. of Hungary (1946–48)
Til·lich \\'til-ik\\ Paul Johannes 1886–1965 Am. (Ger.-born) theol.
Til·lot·son \\'til-ət-sən\\ John 1630–1694 Eng. divine
Til·ly \\'til-ē\\ Count of 1559–1632 Johan Tser·claes \\tsər-'kläs\\ Flem. field marshal
Ti·mo·shen·ko \\ˌtim-ə-'shen-(ˌ)kō\\ Se·mën \\səm-'yȯn\\ Konstantinovich 1895–1970 Russ. marshal
Timour, Timur, Timur Lenk see TAMERLANE
Ting·ley \\'tiŋ-lē\\ Katherine Augusta 1847–1929 née Westcott Am. theosophist
Tin·to·ret·to, Il \\ˌtin-tə-'ret-(ˌ)ō\\ 1518–1594 Jacopo Robusti Ital. painter
Ti·pu Sa·hib or **Tip·poo Sa·hib** \\ˌtip-(ˌ)ü-'sä-,(h)ib\\ 1751–1799 sultan of Mysore (1782–99)
Tir·pitz, von \\'ti(ə)r-pəts, 'tər-\\ Alfred 1849–1930 Ger. admiral
Tir·so de Mo·li·na \\ˌtir-(ˌ)sō-(ˌ)dā-mə-'lē-nə, -(ˌ)sō-(ˌ)thä-\\ 1571?–1648 pseud. of Gabriel Téllez Span. dram.
Ti·se·li·us \\tə-'sā-lē-əs, -'zā-\\ Arne Wilhelm Kaurin 1902– Swed. biochem.
Ti·so \\'tē-(ˌ)sō\\ Josef 1887–1947 Slovakian pres.
Ti·tian \\'tish-ən\\ 1477–1576 Tiziano Vecellio Ital. painter
Tito see BROZ
Ti·tus \\'tīt-əs\\ 40?–81 Titus Flavius Sabinus Vespasianus Rom. emp. (79–81)
Tocque·ville, de \\'tōk-ˌvil, 'tȯk-, 'täk-, -ˌvēl, -vəl\\ Alexis Charles Henri Maurice Clérel 1805–1859 Fr. statesman & author
Todd \\'täd\\ Sir Alexander Robertus 1907– Brit. chem.
— David 1855–1939 Am. astron.
Todt \\'tōt\\ Fritz 1891–1942 Ger. mil. engineer
To·gliat·ti \\tōl-'yät-ē\\ Pal·mi·ro \\päl-'mē-(ˌ)rō\\ 1893?–1964 Ital. Communist
To·go \\'tō-(ˌ)gō\\ Marquis Heihachiro 1847–1934 Jap. admiral
— Shigenori 1882–1950 Jap. diplomat & polit.
To·jo \\'tō-(ˌ)jō\\ Hideki 1885–1948 Jap. gen. & polit.
Tol·kien \\'täl-ˌkēn, 'tȯl-\\ John Ronald Reuel 1892– Eng. author
Tol·ler \\'tȯl-ər, 'täl-\\ Ernst 1893–1939 Ger. dram. & polit.
Tol·stoi \\tȯl-'stȯi, tōl-', täl-', 'tȯl-, 'tōl-, 'täl-\\ Count Lev Nikolaevich 1828–1910 Russ. nov., philos., & mystic
Tom·ma·si·ni \\ˌtäm-ə-'zē-nē\\ Vicenzo 1880–1950 Ital. composer
Tomp·kins \\'täm(p)-kənz\\ Daniel D. 1774–1825 Am. polit.; vice-pres. of the U. S. (1817–25)
Tone \\'tōn\\ (Theobald) Wolfe 1763–1798 Irish revolutionist
Tooke \\'tùk\\ (John) Horne 1736–1812 Eng. polit. radical & philologist
Toombs \\'tümz\\ Robert Augustus 1810–1885 Am. lawyer & Confed. statesman
Tor·que·ma·da, de \\ˌtȯr-kə-'mäd-ə, -'math-ə\\ Tomás 1420?–1498 Span. grand inquisitor
Tor·ri·cel·li \\ˌtȯr-ə-'chel-ē, ˌtär-\\ Evangelista 1608–1647 Ital. math. & physicist
Tos·ca·ni·ni \\ˌtäs-kə-'nē-nē, ˌtȯs-\\ Ar·tu·ro \\är-'tù(ə)r-(ˌ)ō\\ 1867–1957 Ital. conductor
Tot·le·ben or **Tod·le·ben** \\'tȯt-lə-bən\\ Count Frants Eduard Ivanovich 1818–1884 Russ. gen.
Tou·louse-Lau·trec, de \\tü-ˌlüz-lō-'trek\\ Henri 1864–1901 Fr. painter
Tour·neur \\'tər-nər\\ Cyril 1575?–1626 Eng. dram.
Tous·saint L'Ou·ver·ture \\'tü-ˌsaⁿ-'lü-vər-,t(y)ù(ə)r\\ Pierre Dominique 1743–1803 Haitian gen. & liberator
Tov·ey \\'təv-ē\\ 1st Baron 1885– John Cronyn Tovey Brit. admiral of the fleet

Toyn·bee \\'tȯin-bē\\ Arnold Joseph 1889– Eng. hist.
Tra·jan \\'trā-jən\\ 52 or 53–117 Marcus Ulpius Trajanus Rom. emp. (98–117)
Tree \\'trē\\ Sir Herbert Beerbohm 1853–1917 Eng. actor-manager
Treitsch·ke, von \\'trīch-kə\\ Heinrich 1834–1896 Ger. hist.
Trench \\'trench\\ Richard Chen·e·vix \\'shen-ə-ˌvē\\ 1807–1886 Eng. poet & prelate
Tren·chard \\'tren-chärd, -chərd\\ 1st Viscount 1873–1956 Hugh Montague Trenchard Brit. air marshal
Tre·vel·yan \\tri-'vel-yən, -'vil-\\ George Macaulay 1876–1962 Eng. hist.
— Sir George Otto 1838–1928 father of prec. Eng. polit., biographer, & hist.
Trol·lope \\'träl-əp\\ Anthony 1815–1882 Eng. nov.
Tromp \\'trȯmp, 'trämp\\ Maarten Harpertszoon 1597–1653 Du. admiral
Trots·ky or **Trots·ki** \\'trät-skē, 'trȯt-\\ Leon 1879–1940 Leib or Lev Davydovich Bronstein Russ. Communist
Troy·on \\tr(ə)-wä-'yōⁿ\\ Constant 1813–1865 Fr. painter
Tru·deau \\'trü-(ˌ)dō\\ Pierre Elliott 1921– Canad. polit.; prime minister (from 1968)
Tru·ji·llo Mo·li·na \\trü-'hē-(ˌ)(y)ō-mə-'lē-nə\\ Rafael Leonidas 1891–1961 Dominican gen. & polit.; pres. of Dominican Republic (1930–38; 1942–52)
Tru·man \\'trü-mən\\ Harry S 1884– 33d pres. of the U.S. (1945–53)
Trum·bull \\'trəm-bəl\\ John 1756–1843 Am. painter
— Jonathan 1710–1785 father of prec. Am. patriot & statesman
Tsai Ting-kai \\'(ˌ)tsī-'tiŋ-'gī\\ 1890– Chin. gen.
Tsal·da·res or **Tsal·da·ris** \\(ˌ)säl-'där-əs, -ēs\\ Pa·na·ges or Pa·na·gis \\ˌpän-ə-'yēs\\ 1868–1936 Greek statesman
Tsao Hsueh-chin \\'tsaù-'shü-'chin\\ d. 1764 Chin. author
Tschaikovsky var of TCHAIKOVSKY
Tu Fu \\'tü-'fü\\ 712–770 Chin. poet
Tub·man \\'təb-mən\\ William Vacanarat Shadrach 1895– Liberian lawyer; pres. of Liberia (1944–)
Tul·si Das \\ˌtùl-sē-'däs\\ 1532–1623 Hindu poet
Tu·renne, de \\tù-'ren\\ Vicomte 1611–1675 Henri de la Tour d'Auvergne Fr. marshal
Tur·ge·nev \\'tùr-ˌgän-yəf, -'gen-\\ Ivan Sergeevich 1818–1883 Russ. nov.
Tur·got \\tùr-'gō\\ Anne Robert Jacques 1727–1781 Baron de l'Aulne \\'lōn\\ Fr. statesman & econ.
Tur·ner \\'tər-nər\\ Frederick Jackson 1861–1932 Am. hist.
— Joseph Mallord William 1775–1851 Eng. painter
— Nat 1800–1831 Am. slave leader
Tut·ankh·a·men \\ˌtü-ˌtaŋ-'käm-ən, -ˌtäŋ-\\ or **Tut·enkh·a·mon** \\-ˌteŋ-\\ fl ab 1358 B.C. king of Egypt
Twacht·man \\'twäk(t)-mən\\ John Henry 1853–1902 Am. painter
Twain Mark see CLEMENS
Tweed \\'twēd\\ William Marcy 1823–1878 Am. polit.
Tweedsmuir see BUCHAN
Ty·ler \\'tī-lər\\ John 1790–1862 10th pres. of the U. S. (1841–45)
— Wat \\'wät\\ or Walter d 1381 Eng. leader of Peasants' Revolt (1381)
Tyn·dale \\'tin-dᵊl\\ William 1492?–1536 Eng. reformer & martyr
Tyn·dall \\'tin-dᵊl\\ John 1820–1893 Brit. physicist
Tyr·whitt-Wil·son \\ˌtir-ət-'wil-sən\\ Gerald Hugh 1883–1950 14th Baron Ber·ners \\'bər-nərz\\ Eng. composer & painter
Tz'u-hsi \\'tsü-'shē\\ 1835–1908 Chin. empress dowager

Udall \\'yü-ˌdȯl, 'yüd-ᵊl\\ or **Uve·dale** \\'yüv-ˌdāl\\ Nicholas 1505–1556 Eng. schoolmaster & dram.
Udall \\'yü-ˌdȯl\\ Stewart Lee 1920– U.S. secretary of interior (1961–69)
Ugar·te \\ü-'gärt-ē\\ Manuel 1874–1951 Argentine writer
Uh·land \\'ü-ˌlänt\\ Johann Ludwig 1787–1862 Ger. poet & hist.
Ul·fi·las \\'ùl-fə-ˌläs, 'əl-, -ləs, -ˌlas\\ or **Ul·fi·la** \\-lə\\ or **Wul·fi·la** \\'wùl-fə-lə\\ 311?–381 bishop of the Goths
Ul·pi·an \\'əl-pē-ən\\ 170?–228 Domitius Ulpianus Rom. jurist
Una·mu·no y Ju·go, de \\ˌü-nə-'mü-(ˌ)nō-(ˌ)ē-'hü-(ˌ)gō\\ Miguel 1864–1936 Span. philos. & writer
Un·cas \\'əŋ-kəs\\ 1588?–?1683 Pequot Indian chief
Und·set \\'ùn-ˌset\\ Si·grid \\'sig-rē, -ˌrid\\ 1882–1949 Norw. nov.
Un·ter·mey·er \\'ənt-ər-ˌmī(-ə)r\\ Louis 1885– Am. poet
Up·dike \\'əp-ˌdīk\\ John 1932– Am. writer
Up·ton \\'əp-tən\\ Emory 1839–1881 Am. gen. & author
Ur·ban \\'ər-bən\\ name of 8 popes: esp. II (Odo \\'ōd-(ˌ)ō\\ or Udo \\'üd-\\) 1042?–1099 (pope 1088–99)
Urey \\'yù(ə)r-ē\\ Harold Clayton 1893– Am. chem.
Ur·quhart \\'ər-kərt, -ˌkärt\\ Sir Thomas 1611–1660 Scot. author & translator
Ussher \\'əsh-ər\\ James 1581–1656 Irish archbishop
Utril·lo \\ü-'trē-(ˌ)lō, -'trēl-(ˌ)yō, -'trē-(ˌ)(y)ō\\ Maurice 1883–1955 Fr. painter

Vail·lant \\vä-'yäⁿ, vī-'äⁿ\\ Jean Baptiste Philibert 1790–1872 Fr. army officer; marshal of France (1851)
Valdemar see WALDEMAR
Val·di·via, de \\val-'dē-vē-ə\\ Pedro 1500?–1553 Span. conqueror of Chile
Va·lens \\'vā-lənz, -ˌlenz\\ 328?–378 Rom. emp. of the East (364–378)
Val·en·tin·ian \\ˌval-ən-'tin-ē-ən, -'tin-yən\\ Lat. Valentinianus name of 3 Rom. emperors: I 321–375 (reigned 364–375); II 372–392 (reigned 375–392); III 419–455 (reigned 425–455)
Valera Eamon de see DE VALERA
Va·le·ra y Al·ca·lá Ga·lia·no \\və-'ler-ə-ˌē-ˌal-kə-'lä-ˌgal-ē-'än-(ˌ)ō, -ˌä-ˌgäl-\\ Juan 1824–1905 Span. writer & statesman
Va·le·ri·an \\və-'lir-ē-ən\\ d ?269 Publius Licinius Valerianus Rom. emp. (253–260)
Va·lé·ry \\və-lā-'rē, val-ə-'rē, val-ˌā-\\ Paul Ambroise 1871–1945 Fr. poet & philos.
Va·lin \\va-'laⁿ\\ Martial Henri 1898– Fr. gen. & diplomat
Va·llar·ta \\vä-'yärt-ə, vī-'ärt-\\ Manuel Sandoval 1899– Mex. physicist
Val·le·jo \\və-'lā-(ˌ)ō, -'yā-(ˌ)(h)ō\\ Mariano Guadalupe 1808–1890 soldier & pioneer in Calif.

Van Al·len \va-'nal-ən, və-\ James Alfred 1914– Am. physicist

Van·brugh \van-'brü, vən-, -'bruk; 'van-brə\ Sir John 1664–1726 Eng. dram. & architect

Van Bu·ren \van-'byur-ən, vən-\ Martin 1782–1862 8th pres. of the U.S. (1837–41)

Van·cou·ver \van-'kü-vər\ George 1757–1798 Eng. navigator & explorer

Van·de·grift \'van-də-,grift\ Alexander Archer 1887– Am. marine-corps gen.

Van·den·berg \'van-dən-,bərg\ Arthur Hendrick 1884–1951 Am. journalist & polit.

Van·der·bilt \'van-dər-,bilt\ Cornelius 1794–1877 Am. capitalist

Van Dine see WRIGHT

van Don·gen \van-'däŋ-ən, vän-, vən-, 'doŋ-\ Cornelius 1877–1968 Kees van Dongen Du. painter

Van Do·ren \van-'dōr-ən, vən-, -'dor-\ Carl 1885–1950 & his bro. Mark 1894– Am. writers & editors

Van·dyke or **Van Dyck** \van-'dīk, vən-\ Sir Anthony 1599–1641 Flem.-born painter in Eng.

Vane \'vān\ Sir Henry or Harry 1613–1662 Eng. statesman

Van Rens·se·laer \,van-'ren(t)-sə-'li(ə)r, -,ren-'sli(ə)r, vən-; -'ren-t-s(ə)-)lər\ Stephen 1764–1839 Am. gen. & polit.

Van·sit·tart \van-'sit-ərt, vən-\ Robert Gilbert 1881–1957 1st Baron Vansittart of Den·ham \'den-əm\ Brit. diplomat

van't Hoff \vänt-'hof, vant-\ Jacobus Hen·dri·cus \hen-'drē-kəs\ 1852–1911 Du. physical chem.

Van Zyl \fän-'zī(ə)l, vän-, vən-, -'zā(ə)l\ Gideon Brand 1873–1956 So. African lawyer

Va·rèse \və-'räz, -'rez\ Edgard 1883–1965 Am. (Fr.-born) composer

Var·gas \'vär-gəs\ Getulio Dornelles 1883–1954 Brazilian lawyer; pres. of Brazil (1930–45; 1951–54)

Var·ro \'var-(,)ō\ Marcus Terentius 116–27 B.C. Rom. author

Va·sa·ri \və-'zär-ē\ Giorgio 1511–1574 Ital. painter

Vasco da Gama see GAMA

Va·tu·tin \və-'tüt-ən, -'tü-,tēn\ Nikolai 1900?–1944 Russ. gen.

Vau·ban, de \vō-'bän\ Marquis 1633–1707 Sébastien Le Pres·tre \lə-'pretrᵊ\ Fr. mil. engineer; marshal of France (1703)

Vaughan \'vón, 'vän\ Henry 1622–1695 the Sil·u·rist \'sil-yə-rəst\ Brit. poet
— **Wil·liams** \'wil-yəmz\ Ralph 1872–1958 Eng. composer

Veb·len \'veb-lən\ Thor·stein \'thó(ə)r-,stīn\ Bunde 1857–1929 Am. sociol. & econ.

Ved·der \'ved-ər\ Elihu 1836–1923 Am. painter & illustrator

Ve·ga, de \'vā-gə\ Lo·pe \'lō-(,)pā\ 1562–1635 Lope Félix de Vega Carpio Span. dram.

Ve·láz·quez or **Ve·lás·quez** \və-'läs-kəs, -'las-, -(,)kās; -'läth-(,)kāth\ Diego Rodríguez de Silva y 1599–1660 Span. painter

Ven·dôme, de \vän-'dōm, vä^n-\ Duc Louis Joseph 1654–1712 Fr. soldier; marshal of France

Ve·ni·ze·los \,ven-ə-'zā-ləs, -'zel-əs\ Eleutherios 1864–1936 Greek statesman

Ver·di \'ve(ə)rd-ē\ Giuseppe 1813–1901 Ital. composer

Vereker see GORT

Ve·re·shcha·gin \,ver-əsh-'chäg-ən, ,ver-ə-'shäg-\ Vasili Vasilievich 1842–1904 Russ. painter

Ver·gil or **Vir·gil** \'vər-jəl\ 70–19 B.C. Publius Vergilius Maro Rom. poet

Ver·laine \ve(ə)r-'lān, vər-\ Paul 1844–1896 Fr. poet

Ver·meer \vər-'me(ə)r, ver-, -'mi(ə)r\ Jan 1632–1675 Jan van der Meer van Delft Du. painter

Verne \'vərn, 've(ə)rn\ Jules 1828–1905 Fr. writer

Ver·ner \'ve(ə)r-nər\ Karl Adolph 1846–1896 Dan. philologist

Ver·nier \'ve(ə)rn-,yā, 'vər-nē-ər\ Pierre 1580–1637 Fr. math.

Ver·non \'vər-nən\ Edward 1684–1757 Eng. admiral

Ve·ro·ne·se \,ver-ə-'nā-sē, -'nā-zē\ Paolo 1528–1588 Paolo Cagliari Ital. painter

Ver·ra·za·no, da or **Ver·raz·za·no** \,ver-ə-'zän-(,)ō, ,ver-,ät-'sän-\ Giovanni 1485?–?1528 Florentine navigator

Ver·roc·chio, del \və-'rók-ē-,ō, -'rōk-, -'räk-\ Andrea 1435–1488 Andrea di Michele Cione Florentine sculptor & painter

Verulam see Francis BACON

Ve·rus \'vir-əs\ Lucius Aurelius 130–169 Lucius Ceionius Commodus Rom. emp. (161–169)

Ver·woerd \fər-'vu(ə)rt\ Hendrik Frensch 1901–1966 South African polit.; prime min. (1958–66)

Ves·pa·sian \ve-'spā-zh(ē-)ən\ 9–79 Titus Flavius Sabinus Vespasianus Rom. emp. (69–79)

Ves·puc·ci \ve-'spü-chē\ Ame·ri·go \,äm-ə-'rē-(,)gō\ 1454–1512 Amer·i·cus Ves·pu·cius \ə-'mer-ə-kəs,-ves-'pyü-sh(ē-)əs\ Ital. navigator; eponym of America

Victor Emmanuel I 1759–1824 king of Sardinia (1802–21)
— **II** 1820–1878 king of Sardinia (1849–61) & 1st king of Italy (1861–78)
— **III** 1869–1947 king of Italy (1900–46)

Vic·to·ria \vik-'tōr-ē-ə, -'tor-\ Alexandrina 1819–1901 queen of Gr. Brit. (1837–1901)

Vi·da \'vēd-ə\ Marco Girolamo 1480?–1566 Ital. polit.

Videla see GONZÁLEZ VIDELA

Vi·e·tor \'fē-ə-,tó(ə)r\ Wilhelm 1850–1918 Ger. philologist

Vi·gée–Le·brun \vē-'zhā-lə-'brən, -'brə^n, -'brœ^n\ Marie Ann Élisabeth 1755–1842 Fr. painter

Vi·gno·la, da \vēn-'yē\ Giacomo 1507–1573 Giacomo Barocchio or Barozzi Ital. architect

Vi·gny, de \vēn-'yē\ Comte Alfred Victor 1797–1863 Fr. author

Vil·la \'vē-(y)ə\ Francisco 1877–1923 Pan·cho \'pän-(,)chō, 'pan-\ Doroteo Arango Mex. bandit & revolutionist

Vil·la-Lo·bos \,vil-ə-'lō-bəs\ Heitor 1881–1959 Braz. composer

Vil·lard \və-'lär(d)\ Oswald Garrison 1872–1949 Am. journalist

Vil·lars, de \və-'lär\ Duc Claude Louis Hector 1653–1734 Fr. soldier; marshal of France (1702)

Ville·neuve, de \vēl-'nə(r)v\ Pierre Charles Jean Baptiste Silvestre 1763–1806 Fr. admiral

Vil·liers \'vil-(y)ərz\ George 1592–1628 1st Duke of Buck·ing·ham \'bək-iŋ-əm, US also -,ham\ Eng. statesman & admiral
— **George** 1628–1687 2d Duke of Buckingham, son of prec. Eng. courtier & dram.

Vil·lon \vē-'(y)ō^n\ François 1431–after 1462 François de Montcorbier Fr. poet
— **Jacques** 1875–1963 real name Gaston Duchamp Fr. painter

Vin·cent de Paul \,vin(t)-sənt-də-'pól\ Saint 1581?–1660 Fr. priest

Vin·ci, da \'vin-chē, 'vēn-\ Leonardo 1452–1519 Florentine painter, sculptor, architect, & engineer

Vi·no·gra·doff \,vin-ə-'grad-,óf, -,óv\ Sir Paul Gavrilovich 1854–1925 Russ. jurist & hist. in Eng.

Vin·son \'vin(t)-sən\ Carl 1883– Am. lawyer & administrator
— **Frederick Moore** 1890–1953 Am. chief justice U.S. Supreme Court (1946–53)

Viol·let-le-Duc \,vē-ə-'lā-lə-'d(y)ük, vyō-,lā-lə-'dük\ Eugène Emmanuel 1814–1879 Fr. architect

Vir·chow \'fi(ə)r-,(,)kō, 'vi(ə)r-, -(,)kō\ Rudolf 1821–1902 Ger. pathologist

Vir·ta·nen \'vi(ə)r-tə-,nen\ Art·tu·ri \'ärt-ə-rē\ Ilmari 1895– Finnish biochem.

Vi·tru·vi·us Pol·lio \və-'trü-vē-ə-'späl-ē-,ō\ Marcus 1st cent. B.C. Rom. architect & engineer

Vi·val·di \vi-'väl-dē, -'vol-\ Antonio 1675?–1741 Ital. violinist and composer

Vla·di·mir \'vlad-ə-,mi(ə)r, vlə-'dē-,mi(ə)r\ 956?–1015 the Great ruler of Russia (980–1015)

Vla·minck, de \vlə-'maŋk, -'ma^n\ Maurice 1876–1958 Fr. painter

Vo·gler \'fō-glər\ Georg Joseph 1749–1814 Abt \äpt, apt\ or Abbé Vogler Ger. musician

Vol·stead \'väl-,sted, 'vól-, 'vōl-, -stəd\ Andrew John 1860–1947 Am. legislator

Vol·ta \'vōl-tə, 'väl-, 'vól-\ Count Alessandro 1745–1827 Ital. physicist

Vol·taire \vōl-'ta(ə)r, väl-, vól-, -'te(ə)r\ 1694–1778 François Marie Arouet Fr. writer

Von Braun \vän-'braun, fən-, vən-\ Wern·her \'ver-nər\ 1912– Am. (Ger.-born) engineer

Vo·ro·shi·lov \,vór-ə-'shē-,lóf, vär-, -,lóv\ Kliment Efremovich 1881–1969 Russ. marshal; pres. U.S.S.R. (1953–60)

Vor·ster \'fór-stər\ Balthazar Johannes 1915– prime min. of Union of South Africa (from 1966)

Voz·ne·sen·ski \,väz-nə-'sen(t)-skē\ Nikolai Alekseevich 1904– Russ. econ. & polit.

Voz·ne·sen·sky \,väz-nə-'sen(t)-skē\ Andrei 1933– Russ. poet

Vy·shin·sky \və-'shin(t)-skē\ Andrei Yanuarievich 1883–1954 Russ. lawyer & statesman

Waals, van der \'van-dər-,wólz\ Johannes Diderik 1837–1923 Du. physicist

Wace \'wäs, 'wās\ 12th cent. Anglo-Norman poet

Wag·ner \'väg-nər\ (Wilhelm) Richard 1813–1883 Ger. poet & composer
— **von Jau·regg** \'yau-,rek\ Julius 1857–1940 Austrian neurologist & psychiatrist

Wag·ner \'wag-nər\ Robert Ferdinand 1910– Am. polit.

Wain·wright \'wān-,rīt\ Jonathan Mayhew 1883–1953 Am. gen.
— **Richard** father 1817–1862 & son 1849–1926 Am. naval officers

Waite \'wāt\ Morrison R. 1816–1888 Am. jurist; chief justice U.S. Supreme Court (1874–88)

Waks·man \'wäk-smən, 'wak-\ Sel·man \'sel-mən\ Abraham 1888– Am. (Ukrainian-born) microbiologist

Wal·de·mar \'wól-də-,mär, Dan. Val·de·mar \'väl-, 'val-\ name of 4 kings of Denmark: esp. **I** (the Great) 1131–1182 (reigned 1157–82)

Wal·der·see, von \'väl-dər-,zā, 'wól-\ Count Alfred 1832–1904 Ger. field marshal

Wal·do \'wól-(,)dō, 'wäl-\ or **Val·do** \'val-(,)dō, 'väl-\ Peter fl 1173–1179 Fr. heretic

Walk·er \'wó-kər\ Francis Am·a·sa \'am-ə-sə\ 1840–1897 Am. econ.
— **William** 1824–1860 Am. filibuster in Lower California & in Nicaragua

Wal·lace \'wäl-əs\ Alfred Russel 1823–1913 Eng. naturalist
— **Henry Agard** \'ā-,gärd\ 1888–1965 Am. agriculturist, editor, & polit.; vice-pres. of U.S. (1941–45)
— **Lewis** 1827–1905 Lew Am. lawyer, gen., & nov.
— **Sir William** 1272?–1305 Scot. patriot

Wal·lach \'wäl-ək, 'väl-\ Otto 1847–1931 Ger. chem.

Wal·len·stein, von \'wäl-ən-,stīn\ Albrecht Eusebius Wenzel 1583–1634 Duke of Friedland and Mecklenburg; Prince of Sagan Austrian gen.

Wal·ler \'wäl-ər\ Edmund 1606–1687 Eng. poet

Wal·pole \'wól-,pōl, 'wäl-\ Horace or Horatio 1717–1797 4th Earl of Orford Eng. author
— **Sir Hugh Seymour** 1884–1941 Eng. nov.
— **Sir Robert** 1676–1745 1st Earl of Orford; father of Horace Eng. statesman

Wal·ter \'väl-tər, 'wól-\ Bruno 1876–1962 orig. Bruno Schle·sing·er \'s(h)lā-ziŋ-ər\ Am. (Ger.-born) conductor
— \'wól-tər\ John 1739–1812 Eng. founder of The (London) Times

Wal·ther von der Vo·gel·wei·de \'väl-tər-,fón-dər-'fō-gəl-,vīd-ə\ 1170?–?1230 Ger. minnesinger

Wal·ton \'wólt-ən\ Ernest Thomas Sinton 1903– Irish physicist
— **Izaak** \'ī-zik, -zək\ 1593–1683 Eng. writer
— **Sir William** (Turner) 1902– Eng. composer

Wan·a·ma·ker \'wän-ə-,mā-kər\ John 1838–1922 Am. merchant

Wang Ching-wei \'wäŋ-'jiŋ-'wā\ 1884–1944 Chin. polit.

War·beck \'wór-,bek\ Perkin 1474–1499 Walloon impostor; pretender to the Eng. throne

War·burg \'wór-,bərg, 'vär-,bu̇(ə)rk\ Otto Heinrich 1883– Ger. physiol.

Ward \'wó(ə)rd\ Sir Adolphus William 1837–1924 Eng. hist.
— **Ar·te·mas** \'ärt-ə-məs\ 1727–1800 Am. Revolutionary gen.
— **Artemus** see Charles Farrar BROWNE
— **Barbara** 1914– Lady Jackson Eng. econ. & writer

ə abut; ᵊ kitten; ər further; a back; ā bake; ä cot, cart; au̇ out; ch chin; e less; ē easy; g gift; i trip; ī life
j joke; ŋ sing; ō flow; ó flaw; ói coin; th thin; t̷h this; ü loot; u̇ foot; y yet; yü few; yu̇ furious; zh vision
ᵊ F table; à F bac; ḵ G ich, Buch; ^n F vin; œ F bœuf; œ̄ F feu; ᴜᴇ G füllen; ᴜᴇ F rue; ʸ F digne \dēnʸ\, nuit \nwᵊ^e\

— Sir Joseph George 1856–1930 N.Z. statesman

— Mary Augusta 1851–1920 Mrs. *Humphry Ward; née Arnold* Eng. nov.

War·field \\'wȯr-ˌfēld\\ William Caesar 1920–   Am. baritone

War·ner \\'wȯr-nər\\ Charles Dudley 1829–1900 Am. editor & essayist

War·ren \\'wȯr-ən, 'wär-\\ Earl 1891–   Am. lawyer & polit.; chief justice U.S. Supreme Court (1953–69)

— Gou·ver·neur \\ˌgəv-ə(r)-'ni(ə)r\\ Kemble 1830–1882 Am. gen.

— Joseph 1741–1775 Am. physician & gen.

— Robert Penn 1905–   Am. author & educ.

— Whitney 1864–1943 Am. architect

War·ton \\'wȯrt-ᵊn\\ Thomas 1728–1790 Eng. literary hist. & critic; poet laureate (1785–90)

War·wick \\'wär-ik, *US also* 'wȯr-ik, 'wȯ(ə)r-ˌ(ˌ)wik, 'wär-ˌ(ˌ)wik\\ Earl of 1428–1471 *Richard Nev·ille* \\'nev-əl\\; *the Kingmaker* Eng. soldier & statesman

Wash·ing·ton \\'wȯsh-iŋ-tən, 'wäsh-\\ Book·er \\'bu̇k-ər\\ Tal·ia·ferro \\'täl-ə-vər\\ 1856–1915 Am. educ.

— George 1732–1799 Am. gen.; 1st pres. of the U.S. (1789–97)

Was·ser·mann, von \\'väs-ər-mən, -ˌmän; 'wäs-ər-mən\\ August 1866–1925 Ger. bacteriol.

Wa·ters \\'wȯt-ərz, 'wät-\\ Ethel 1900–   Am. actress & singer

Wat·son \\'wät-sən\\ John 1850–1907 *pseud. Ian Mac·lar·en* \\mə-'klar-ən\\ Scot. clergyman & author

— John Broadus 1878–1958 Am. psychol.

— Sir William 1858–1935 Eng. poet

Watt \\'wät\\ James 1736–1819 Scot. inventor

— Sir Robert Alexander Watson 1892–   Scot. physicist

Wat·teau \\wä-'tō, vä-\\ Jean Antoine 1684–1721 Fr. painter

Wat·ter·son \\'wät-ər-sən, 'wȯt-\\ Henry 1840–1921 Am. journalist & polit.

Watts \\'wäts\\ George Frederic 1817–1904 Eng. painter & sculptor

— Isaac 1674–1748 Eng. theol. & hymn writer

— **-Dunton** Walter Theodore 1832–1914 Eng. critic & poet

Waugh \\'wȯ\\ Arthur Evelyn St. John \\ˌsānt-'jän, sənt-; 'sin-jən\\ 1903–1966 Eng. writer

Wa·vell \\'wā-vəl\\ 1st Earl 1883–1950 *Archibald Percival Wavell* Brit. field marshal; viceroy of India (1943–47)

Wayne \\'wān\\ Anthony 1745–1796 *Mad Anthony* Am. Revolutionary gen.

Wea·ver \\'wē-vər\\ Robert Clifton 1907–   Am. economist; U.S. secy. of housing and urban development (1966–69)

Webb \\'web\\ Beatrice 1858–1943 née *Potter; wife of S.J.* Eng. socialist

— Sidney James 1859–1947 1st Baron *Passfield* Eng. socialist

We·ber \\'vā-bər\\ Ernst Heinrich 1795–1878 Ger. physiol.

Web·er \\'web-ər\\ Max 1881–1961 Am. (Russ.-born) artist

—, **von** Baron Karl Maria Friedrich Ernst 1786–1826 Ger. composer & conductor

We·bern \\'vā-bərn\\ Anton von 1883–1945 Austrian composer

Web·ster \\'web-stər\\ Daniel 1782–1852 Am. statesman & orator

— John 1580?–?1625 Eng. dram.

— Noah 1758–1843 Am. lexicographer

Wedg·wood \\'wej-ˌwu̇d\\ Josiah 1730–1795 Eng. potter

Weems \\'wēmz\\ Mason Locke 1759–1825 *Parson Weems* Am. clergyman & biographer

Weill \\'wī(ə)l, 'vī(ə)l\\ Kurt \\'ku̇(ə)rt\\ 1900–1950 Ger.-born composer in the U.S.

Weir \\'wi(ə)r\\ Robert Walter 1803–1889 & his 2 sons John Ferguson 1841–1926 & Julian Alden 1852–1919 Am. painters

Weis·mann \\'vī-ˌsmän, 'wī-smən\\ August 1834–1914 Ger. biologist

Weiz·mann \\'vīt-ˌsmän; 'vīt-smən, 'wīt-\\ Cha·im \\'kī-im\\ 1874–1952 Israeli (Russ.-born) chem.; 1st pres. of Israel (1948–52)

Welch \\'welch, 'welsh\\ William Henry 1850–1934 Am. pathologist

Wel·ler \\'wel-ər\\ Thomas Huckle 1915–   Am. public health specialist

Welles \\'welz\\ (George) Or·son \\'ȯrs-ᵊn\\ 1915–   Am. actor & producer

— Gideon 1802–1878 Am. polit. & writer

— Sumner 1892–1961 Am. diplomat

Welles·ley \\'welz-lē\\ 1st Marquis 1760–1842 *Richard Colley Wellesley* Brit. statesman; gov. gen. of India (1797–1805)

Wel·ling·ton \\'wel-iŋ-tən\\ 1st Duke of 1769–1852 *Arthur Wellesley; the Iron Duke* Brit. gen. & statesman

Wells \\'welz\\ Herbert George 1866–1946 Eng. nov. & hist.

Wemyss \\'wēmz\\ Sir Henry Colville Barclay 1891–1959 Brit. gen.

Wen·ces·laus \\'wen(t)-sə-ˌslȯs, -sləs\\ *Ger.* **Wen·zel** \\'ven(t)-səl\\ 1361–1419 king of Germany & Holy Rom. Emp. (1378–1400) & (as Wenceslaus IV) king of Bohemia (1378–1419)

Wen·dell \\'wen-dᵊl\\ Bar·rett \\'bar-ət\\ 1855–1921 Am. scholar

Went·worth \\'went-ˌ(ˌ)wərth\\ William Charles 1793–1872 Austral. statesman

Wer·fel \\'ver-fəl\\ Franz 1890–1945 Ger. author

Wer·ner \\'ver-nər\\ Alfred 1866–1919 Swiss chem.

Wes·ley \\'wes-lē, 'wez-\\ Charles 1707–1788 *bro. of John* Eng. Methodist preacher & hymn writer

— John 1703–1791 Eng. theol., evangelist, & founder of Methodism

West \\'west\\ Benjamin 1738–1820 Am. painter in Eng.

— Nathanael 1902–1940 *Nathan Wallenstein Wein·stein* \\'wīn-ˌstīn\\ Am. nov.

— Dame Rebecca 1892–   *pseud. of Cicily Isabel Fairfield* Eng. critic & nov.

West·cott \\'wes(t)-kət\\ Edward Noyes 1846–1898 Am. banker & nov.

Wes·ter·marck \\'wes-tər-ˌmärk, 'ves-\\ Edward Alexander 1862–1939 Finnish philos. & anthropol.

Wes·ting·house \\'wes-tiŋ-ˌhau̇s\\ George 1846–1914 Am. inventor

Wey·gand \\vā-gäⁿ\\ Maxime 1867–1965 Fr. gen.

Whar·ton \\'hwȯrt-ᵊn, 'wȯrt-\\ Edith Newbold 1862–1937 née *Jones* Am. nov.

Whate·ly \\'hwāt-lē, 'wāt-\\ Richard 1787–1863 Eng. theol. & logician

Wheat·stone \\'hwēt-ˌstōn, 'wēt-, *chiefly Brit.* -stən\\ Sir Charles 1802–1875 Eng. physicist & inventor

Whee·ler \\'hwē-lər, 'wē-\\ Joseph 1836–1906 Am. Confed. gen.

— William Almon 1819–1887 Am. lawyer & polit.; vice-pres. of the U.S. (1877–81)

Whee·lock \\'hwē-ˌläk, 'wē-\\ Eleazar 1711–1779 Am. clergyman & educ.

Whip·ple \\'hwip-əl, 'wip-\\ George Hoyt 1878–   Am. pathol.

Whis·tler \\'hwis-lər, 'wis-\\ James Abbott McNeill 1834–1903 Am. painter & etcher

White \\'hwīt, 'wīt\\ Andrew Dickson 1832–1918 Am. educ. & diplomat

— Byron Raymond 1917–   Am. jurist and polit.

— Edward Douglass 1845–1921 Am. jurist; chief justice U.S. Supreme Court (1910–21)

— Elwyn Brooks 1899–   Am. journalist & writer

— Gilbert 1720–1793 Eng. clergyman & naturalist

— Stanford 1853–1906 Am. architect

— Stewart Edward 1873–1946 Am. nov.

— William Allen 1868–1944 Am. journalist & writer

White·field \\'hwit-ˌfēld, 'hwīt-, 'wit-, 'wīt-\\ George 1714–1770 Eng. Methodist revivalist

White·head \\'hwīt-ˌhed, 'wīt-\\ Alfred North 1861–1947 Eng. math. & philos.

— William 1715–1785 Eng. dram.; poet laureate (1757–85)

Whit·man \\'hwit-mən, 'wit-\\ Marcus 1802–1847 Am. missionary & pioneer in the Oregon region

— Walt \\'wȯlt\\ 1819–1892 orig. *Walter* Am. poet

Whit·ney \\'hwit-nē, 'wit-\\ Eli 1765–1825 Am. inventor

— Josiah Dwight 1819–1896 Am. scientist

— William Dwight 1827–1894 *bro. of J.D.* Am. philologist

Whit·ta·ker \\'hwit-i-kər, 'wit-\\ Charles Evans 1901–   Am. jurist

Whit·ti·er \\'hwit-ē-ər, 'wit-\\ John Greenleaf 1807–1892 *the Quaker Poet* Am. poet

Wic·lif *or* **Wick·liffe** *var of* WYCLIFFE

Wi·dor \\vē-'dȯ(ə)r\\ Charles Marie 1845–1937 Fr. organist & composer

Wie·land \\'vē-ˌlänt\\ Christoph Martin 1733–1813 Ger. author

— Heinrich 1877–1957 Ger. chem.

Wien \\'vēn\\ Wilhelm 1864–1928 Ger. physicist

Wies·ner \\'wēs-nər, 'wēz-\\ Jerome Bert 1915–   Am. engineer

Wig·gin \\'wig-ən\\ Kate Douglas 1856–1923 née *Smith* Am. writer & educ.

Wig·gins \\'wig-ənz\\ Carleton 1848–1932 & his son Guy Carleton 1883–1962 Am. painters

Wig·ner \\'wig-nər\\ Eugene Paul 1902–   Am. (Hung.-born) physicist

Wil·ber·force \\'wil-bər-ˌfō(ə)rs, -ˌfȯ(ə)rs\\ William 1759–1833 Eng. philanthropist & abolitionist

Wil·bur \\'wil-bər\\ Richard Purdy 1921–   Am. writer

Wilde \\'wī(ə)ld\\ Oscar Fingal O'Flahertie Wills 1854–1900 Irish author

Wil·der \\'wīl-dər\\ Thornton Niven 1897–   Am. author

Wi·ley \\'wī-lē\\ Harvey Washington 1844–1930 Am. chem. & food expert

Wil·hel·mi·na \\ˌwil-(ˌ)hel-'mē-nə, ˌwil-ə-'mē-\\ 1880–1962 queen of the Netherlands (1890–1948)

Wilkes \\'wilks\\ Charles 1798–1877 Am. naval officer & explorer

— John 1727–1797 Eng. polit. reformer

Wil·kins \\'wil-kənz\\ Sir George Hubert 1888–1958 Austral. polar explorer

— Mary Eleanor   *see* Mary E. FREEMAN

— Roy 1901–   Am. civil rights leader

Wil·kin·son \\'wil-kən-sən\\ Ellen Cicely 1891–1947 Eng. feminist & polit.

— James 1757–1825 Am. gen. & adventurer

Wil·lard \\'wil-ərd\\ Emma 1787–1870 née *Hart* Am. educ.

— Frances Elizabeth Caroline 1839–1898 Am. educ. & reformer

Will·cocks \\'wil-ˌkäks, -ˌkäks\\ Sir William 1852–1932 Brit. engineer

Wil·liam \\'wil-yəm\\ name of 4 kings of Eng.: **I** (*the Conqueror*) 1027–1087 (reigned 1066–87); **II** (*Ru·fus* \\'rü-fəs\\) 1056?–1100 (reigned 1087–1100); **III** 1650–1702 (reigned 1689–1702; *see* MARY); **IV** 1765–1837 (reigned 1830–37)

— **I** 1533–1584 *the Silent* prince of Orange & founder of the Du. Republic

— **I** 1797–1888 king of Prussia (1861–88) Ger. emp. (1871–88)

— **II** 1859–1941 Ger. emp. & king of Prussia (1888–1918)

— 1882 *or* 1951 *Friedrich Wilhelm Victor August Ernst* crown prince of Germany (1888–1918)

— **of Malmes·bury** \\'mämz-ˌber-ē, 'mälmz-, -b(ə-)rē\\ between 1090 and 1096–?1143 Eng. hist.

Wil·liams \\'wil-yəmz\\ Roger 1603?–1683 Eng.-born clergyman; founder of Rhode Island colony

— Tennessee 1914–   *Thomas Lanier Williams* Am. dram.

— William Carlos 1883–1963 Am. writer

Wil·lis \\'wil-əs\\ Sir Algernon Usborne 1889–   Brit. admiral of the fleet

— Nathaniel Parker 1806–1867 Am. editor & writer

Will·kie \\'wil-kē\\ Wendell Lewis 1892–1944 Am. lawyer, businessman, & polit.

Will·stät·ter \\'vil-ˌshtet-ər, 'wil-ˌstet-\\ Ri·chard \\'rik-ˌärt\\ 1872–1942 Ger. chem.

Wil·son \\'wil-sən\\ Charles Thomson Rees 1869–1959 Scot. physicist

— Edmund 1895–   Am. writer

— Harold 1916–   Brit. socialist leader; prime min. (1964–   )

— Henry orig. name *Jeremiah Jones Colbath* 1812–1875 Am. polit.; vice-pres. of the U.S. (1873–75)

— Sir Henry Hughes 1864–1922 Brit. field marshal

— 1st Baron 1881–1964 *Henry Maitland Wilson* Brit. field marshal

— John 1785–1854 pseud. *Christopher North* Scot. author

— (Thomas) Wood·row \\'wu̇d-(ˌ)rō\\ 1856–1924 28th pres. of the U.S. (1913–21)

Winck·el·mann \\'viŋ-kəl-ˌmän, -mən; 'wiŋ-kəl-mən\\ Johann Joachim 1717–1768 Ger. archaeologist & art hist.

Win·daus \\'vin-ˌdau̇s\\ Adolf 1876–1959 Ger. chem.

Win·disch-Graetz, zu \\ˌvin-dish-'grāts\\ Prince Alfred Candidus Ferdinand 1787–1862 Austrian field marshal

Windsor Duke of   *see* EDWARD VIII

Win·gate \\'win-ˌgāt, -gət\\ Sir Francis Reginald 1861–1953 Brit. gen.

— Orde \\'ȯ(ə)rd\\ Charles 1903–1944 Brit. gen.

Win·kel·ried, von \\'viŋ-kəl-ˌrēt\\ Arnold 14th cent. Swiss patriot

Wins·low \\'winz-(ˌ)lō\\ Edward 1595–1655 gov. of Plymouth colony (1633, 1636, 1644)

Win·sor \\'win-zər\\ Justin 1831–1897 Am. librarian & hist.

Win·throp \\'win-(ˌ)thrəp\\ John 1588–1649 1st gov. of Massachusetts Bay colony

— John 1606–1676 *son of prec.* gov. of Connecticut colony

— John 1638–1707 *son of prec.* gov. of Connecticut colony

Wirtanen Arturi see Artturi VIRTANEN

Wirtz \'wərts\ William Willard 1912–   U.S. secretary of labor (1962–69)

Wise \'wīz\ Stephen Samuel 1874–1949 Am. (Hung.-born) rabbi
— Thomas James 1859–1937 Eng. bibliophile & forger

Wise·man \'wīz-jən\ Nicholas Patrick Stephen 1802–1865 Eng. cardinal & author

Wiss·ler \'wis-lər\ Clark 1870–1947 Am. anthropol.

Wis·ter \'wis-tər\ Owen 1860–1938 Am. nov.

With·er \'with-ər\ or **With·ers** \-ərz\ George 1588–1667 Eng. poet & pamphleteer

Wit·te \'vit-ə\ Count Sergei Yulievich 1849–1915 Russ. statesman

Wit·te·kind \'vit-ə-ˌkint\ or **Wi·du·kind** \'vēd-ə-\ d ab 807 Saxon warrior

Witt·gen·stein \'vit-gən-ˌs(h)tīn\ Ludwig 1889–1951 Ger. philosopher

Wode·house \'wùd-ˌhaùs, 'wōd-\ Pel·ham \'pel-əm\ Grenville 1881–   Eng. nov.

Wof·fing·ton \'wäf-iŋ-tən\ Margaret 1714?–1760 *Peg* Irish-born actress

Wol·cott \'wùl-kət\ Oliver 1726–1797 *son of Roger* gov. of Connecticut (1796–97)
— Oliver 1760–1833 *son of prec.* gov. of Connecticut (1817–27)
— Roger 1679–1767 gov. of Connecticut (1751–58)

Wolf \'vòlf\ Friedrich August 1759–1824 Ger. philologist

Wolfe \'wùlf\ Charles 1791–1823 Irish poet
— James 1727–1759 Brit. gen.
— Thomas Clayton 1900–1938 Am. nov.

Wolff \'vòlf\ Kaspar Friedrich 1733–1794 Ger. anatomist
— or **Wolf, von** \'vòlf\ Baron Christian 1679–1754 Ger. philos. & math.

Wol·fram \'wùl-frəm, 'vòl-ˌfräm\ **von Esch·en·bach** \'esh-ən-ˌbäk, -ˌbäk\ 1170?–?1220 Ger. poet

Wol·las·ton \'wùl-ə-stən\ William Hyde 1766–1828 Eng. chem. & physicist

Wolse·ley \'wùlz-lē\ 1st Viscount 1833–1913 *Garnet Joseph Wolseley* Brit. field marshal

Wol·sey \'wùl-zē\ Thomas 1475?–1530 Eng. cardinal & statesman

Wood \'wùd\ Grant 1892–1942 Am. painter
— Leonard 1860–1927 Am. physician, gen., & colonial administrator

Woolf \'wùlf\ Virginia 1882–1941 *née Stephen* Eng. author

Wooll·cott \'wùl-kət\ Alexander 1887–1943 Am. journalist & writer

Wool·ley \'wùl-ē\ Sir Charles Leonard 1880–1960 Eng. archaeologist

Wool·ton \'wùlt-ᵊn\ 1st Earl of 1883–1964 *Frederick James Marquis* Eng. businessman & administrator

Wool·worth \'wùl-(ˌ)wərth\ Frank Winfield 1852–1919 Am. merchant

Worces·ter \'wùs-tər\ Dean \'dēn\ Co·nant \'kō-nənt\ 1866–1924 Am. administrator in the Philippines
— Joseph Emerson 1784–1865 Am. lexicographer

Worde \'wò(ə)rd\ Wynkyn de d. 1534? Eng. printer

Words·worth \'wərdz-(ˌ)wərth\ William 1770–1850 Eng. poet; poet laureate (1843–50)

Wot·ton \'wät-ᵊn\ Sir Henry 1568–1639 Eng. diplomat & poet

Wran·gel \'(v)räŋ-gəl\ Baron Pëtr Nikolaevich 1878–1928 Russ. gen.

Wren \'ren\ Sir Christopher 1632–1723 Eng. architect

Wright \'rīt\ Frank Lloyd 1869–1959 Am. architect
— John Joseph 1909–   Am. cardinal
— Joseph 1855–1930 Eng. philologist
— Louis Booker 1899–   Am. educ. & librarian
— Or·ville \'òr-vəl\ 1871–1948 & his bro. Wilbur 1867–1912 Am. pioneers in aviation
— Richard 1908–1960 Am. author
— Willard Huntington 1888–1939 pseud. *S. S. Van Dine* \van-'dīn, vən-\ Am. writer

Wundt \'vùnt\ Wilhelm 1832–1920 Ger. physiol. & psychol.

Wu-ti \'wü-'dē\ 157–87 B.C. Chin. emp. (140–87)

Wy·att or **Wy·at** \'wī-ət\ Sir Thomas 1503–1543 Eng. poet & diplomat

Wych·er·ley \'wich-ər-lē\ William 1640?–1716 Eng. dram.

Wyc·liffe \'wik-ˌlif, -ləf\ John 1320?–1384 Eng. religious reformer & Bible translator

Wy·eth \'wī-əth\ Andrew 1917–   Am. artist

Wyld \'wī(ə)ld\ Henry Cecil Kennedy 1870–1945 Eng. lexicographer

Wy·lie \'wī-lē\ Elinor Morton 1885–1928 Mrs. *William Rose Benét*, née *Hoyt* Am. poet & nov.
— Philip 1902–   Am. writer

Wynd·ham \'win-dəm\ Sir Charles 1837–1919 Charles *Culverwell* Eng. actor-manager
— George 1863–1913 Eng. polit. & writer

Xan·thip·pe \zan-'t(h)ip-ē\ or **Xan·tip·pe** \-'tip-ē\ 5th cent. B.C. *wife of Socrates*

Xa·vi·er \'zā-vē-ər, ig-'zā-\ Saint Francis 1506–1552 *Francisco Ja·vier* \häv-'ye(ə)r\; *Apostle of the Indies* Span. Jesuit missionary

Xe·noc·ra·tes \zi-'näk-rə-ˌtēz\ 396–314 B.C. Greek philos.

Xe·noph·a·nes \zi-'näf-ə-ˌnēz\ 6th cent. B.C. Greek philos.

Xen·o·phon \'zen-ə-fən\ 434?–?355 B.C. Greek hist., essayist, & soldier

Xer·xes I \'zərk-ˌsēz\ 519?–465 B.C. *the Great* king of Persia (486–465)

Yale \'yā(ə)l\ Elihu 1649–1721 Eng. merchant in Am.

Ya·ma·ga·ta \ˌyäm-ə-'gät-ə\ Prince Aritomo 1838–1922 Jap. gen. & statesman

Ya·ma·mo·to \ˌyäm-ə-'mōt-(ˌ)ō\ Isoroku 1884–1943 Jap. admiral

Ya·ma·shi·ta \ˌyäm-ə-'shēt-ə\ Tomoyuki 1885–1946 Jap. gen.

Yang Chen Ning \'yäŋ-'jən-'niŋ\ 1922–   Chin. physicist

Ya·su·da \yä-'süd-ə, 'yäs-ə-ˌdä\ Takeo 1889–   Jap. gen.

Yeats \'yāts\ William Butler 1865–1939 Irish poet & dram.

Yen \'yen\ W. W. 1877–1950 orig. *Yen Hui-ch'ing* \'yen-'hwä-'chiŋ\ Chin. statesman
— Hsi-shan \-'shē-'shän\ 1882–1960 Chin. gen.

Ye·re·men·ko \ˌyer-ə-'meŋ-(ˌ)kō\ Andrei Ivanovich 1892–   Russ. gen.

Yer·kes \'yər-kēz, -kəs\ Charles Ty·son \'tīs-ᵊn\ 1837–1905 Am. financier

Yev·tu·shen·ko \ˌyef-tə-'shen-(ˌ)kō\ Yevgeny 1932–   Russ. writer

Yo·nai \'yō-ˌnī\ Mitsumasa 1880–1948 Jap. admiral & statesman

York \'yò(ə)rk\ Alvin Cullum 1887–1964 Am. soldier

Yo·shi·hi·to \ˌyō-shi-'hē-(ˌ)tō\ 1879–1926 emp. of Japan (1912–26)

Yost \'yōst\ Charles Woodruff 1907–   Am. diplomat; U.S. ambassador to U.N. (from 1969)

You·mans \'yü-mənz\ Vincent 1898–1946 Am. composer

Young \'yəŋ\ Brig·ham \'brig-əm\ 1801–1877 Am. Mormon leader
— Edward 1683–1765 Eng. poet
— Francis Brett 1884–1954 Eng. nov.
— Owen D. 1874–1962 Am. lawyer
— Whitney Moore 1921–   Am. civil rights leader

Young·hus·band \'yəŋ-ˌhəz-bənd\ Sir Francis (Edward) 1863–1942 Brit. explorer & author

Yp·si·lan·ti \ˌip-sə-'lant-ē\ Alexander 1792–1828 & his bro. Demetrius 1793–1832 Greek revolutionists

Yüan Shih-k'ai \yü-'än-'shi(ə)r-'kī, -'shē-\ 1859–1916 Chin. statesman; pres. of China (1913–16)

Yu·ka·wa \yü-'kä-wə\ Hideki 1907–   Jap. physicist

Yung-lo \'yùŋ-'lə\ 1359–1424 Chin. emp. (1403–24)

Zagh·lul Pa·sha \zag-ˌlül-'päsh-ə\ Saad \'sad\ 1860?–1927 Egyptian lawyer & statesman

Za·ha·roff \zə-'här-əf, -'här-ˌòf\ Sir Basil 1850–1936 Brit. (Russ.-born) banker & armament contractor

Za·i·mes or **Za·i·mis** \zä-'ē-məs, -mēs\ Alexandros 1855–1936 Greek statesman

Za·les·ki \zə-'les-kē\ August 1883–   Pol. statesman

Za·mo·ra y Tor·res \zə-'mōr-ə-ē-'tòr-(ˌ)äs, thə-'mōr-, -'mòr-\ Niceto Alcalá 1877–1949 Span. polit.; pres. of Spain (1931–36)

Zan·gwill \'zaŋ-ˌ(g)wil\ Israel 1864–1926 Eng. dram. & nov.

Zee·man \'zā-ˌmän, -mən\ Pieter 1865–1943 Du. physicist

Zeitz·ler \'tsīt-slər, 'zīt-\ Kurt 1895–   Ger. gen.

Ze·lin·ski \zə-'lin(t)-skē\ Nikolai Dimitrievich 1861–1953 Russ. chem.

Zeng·er \'zeŋ-(g)ər\ John Peter 1697–1746 Am. journalist & printer

Ze·no \'zē-(ˌ)nō\ 4th–3d cent. B.C. Greek philos.; founder of Stoic school
— of Elea \'ē-lē-ə\ 5th cent. B.C. Greek philos.

Ze·no·bia \zə-'nō-bē-ə\ d after 272 queen of Palmyra (267–272)

Zep·pe·lin, von \ˌtsep-ə-'lēn, 'zep-ə-lən\ Count Ferdinand 1838–1917 Ger. gen. & aeronaut

Zer·ni·ke \'zer-ni-kə, 'zər-\ Frits 1888–1966 Du. physicist

Zeux·is \'zük-səs\ 5th cent. B.C. Greek painter

Zhda·nov \'zhdän-əf, 'shtän-, -ˌòf, -ˌòv\ Andrei Aleksandrovich 1896–1948 Russ. polit. & gen.

Zhu·kov \'zhü-ˌkòf, -ˌkòv\ Georgi Konstantinovich 1894–   Russ. marshal

Zim·ba·list \'zim-bə-ləst\ Ef·rem \'ef-rəm\ 1889–   Russ.-born violinist

Zim·mer·mann \'zim-ər-mən, 'tsim-ər-ˌmän\ Arthur 1864–1940 Ger. statesman; author of "Zimmermann telegram"

Zim·mern \'zim-ərn\ Sir Alfred 1879–1957 Eng. polit. scientist

Zi·nov·iev \zə-'nòv-yəf, -ˌyef, -ˌyev\ Grigori Evseevich 1883–1936 orig. *Hirsch Apfelbaum* Russ. Communist

Zins·ser \'zin(t)-sər\ Hans 1878–1940 Am. bacteriol.

Zin·zen·dorf, von \'zin(t)-sən-ˌdòrf, 'tsin(t)-\ Count Nikolaus Ludwig 1700–1760 Ger. leader of the Bohemian Brethren

Žiž·ka \'zhish-kə\ Ger. **Zis·ka** \'tsis-kə, 'zis-\ Jan Ger. Johann 1360?–1424 Bohemian gen. & Hussite

Zog I \'zòg\ or **Zogu I** \'zòg-wə\ 1895–1961 *Scanderbeg III*; orig. *Ahmed Bey Zogu* king of the Albanians (1928–46)

Zo·la \'zō-lə, 'zō-ˌlä, zō-'lä\ Émile 1840–1902 Fr. nov.

Zorn \'sò(ə)rn, 'zò(ə)rn\ Anders Leonhard 1860–1920 Swed. painter, etcher, & sculptor

Zo·ro·as·ter \'zōr-ə-ˌwas-tər, 'zòr-\ or **Zar·a·thu·stra** \ˌzar-ə-'thü-strə\ 6th cent. B.C. founder of ancient Pers. religion

Zor·ri·lla y Mo·ral \zə-'rēl-yə-ˌē-mə-'räl, thə-, -'rē-(y)ə-\ José 1817–1893 Span. poet & dram.

Zsig·mon·dy \'zhig-ˌmón-dē\ Richard 1865–1929 Ger. chem.

Zu·lo·a·ga \ˌthü-lə-'wäg-ə, ˌzü-\ Ignacio 1870–1945 Span. painter

Zweig \'zwīg, 'swīg, 'tsfīk\ Arnold 1887–1968 Ger. author
— Stefan 1881–1942 Brit. (Austrian-born) writer

Zwing·li \'zwiŋ-(g)lē, 'swiŋ-(g)lē, 'tsfiŋ-lē\ Huldreich or Ulrich 1484–1531 Swiss Reformation leader

---

ə abut; ᵊ kitten; ər further; a back; ā bake; ä cot, cart; aù out; ch chin; e less; ē easy; g gift; i trip; ī life
j joke; ŋ sing; ō flow; ò flaw; òi coin; th thin; th this; ü loot; ù foot; y yet; yü few; yù furious; zh vision
ꞓ F table; à F bac; ᵏ G ich Buch; ⁿ F vin; œ F bœuf; ̄œ F feu; ᴜᴇ G füllen; ̄ᴜᴇ F rue; ʸ F digne \dēnʸ\, nuit \nwᵉⁱ\

A PRONOUNCING GAZETTEER

CONTAINING MORE THAN TEN THOUSAND
NAMES OF PLACES

The purpose of this section is to give basic information about the countries of the world and their most important regions, cities, and natural features. The information includes the spelling, syllabication, and pronunciation of the names, the location of the place or natural feature, and for the more important entries the legal or political status (for example, town, city, urban district, commune, state) and statistical data. All urban centers in the United States having 15,000 or more inhabitants at the 1960 census and all incorporated places in Canada having 15,000 or more inhabitants at the 1956 census have been included.

This section complements the general Vocabulary by entering many derivative forms, such as *Abyssinian* at ABYSSINIA, *Costa Rican* at COSTA RICA, and *Monacan* and *Monegasque* at MONACO.

The abbreviations used are listed in the abbreviations section in the front matter of this book. The letters N, E, S, and W when not followed by a period indicate direction and are not part of a place name; thus, northern North Dakota appears as N N. Dak. The symbol ✳ denotes a capital or seat of administration. Areas are given in square miles except where acres are specified.

Aa·chen \'äk-ən\ *or* F **Aix-la-Cha·pelle** \,āk-,slä-shə-'pel\ city W Germany near Belgian & Dutch borders *pop* 168,200
Aaland — see AHVENANMAA
Aal·borg \'ȯl-,bȯ(ə)rg\ city & port Denmark in N E Jutland *pop* 83,210
Aalst \'älst\ *or* **Alost** \ä-'lȯst\ commune cen Belgium W N W of Brussels *pop* 45,196
Aa·rau \'är-,au̇\ commune N Switzerland ✳ of Aargau canton *pop* 14,700
Aa·re \'är-ə\ *or* **Aar** \'är\ river 175 *m*, cen & N Switzerland flowing E & N E into the Rhine
Aar·gau \'är-,gau̇\ *or* F **Ar·go·vie** \,är-gə-'vē\ canton N Switzerland ✳ Aarau *area* 542, *pop* 300,782
Aar·hus \'ȯ(ə)r-,hüs\ city & port Denmark in E Jutland on the Kattegat *pop* 118,943
Ab·a·co \'ab-ə-,kō\ two islands of the Bahamas (**Great Abaco** [80 *m* long] & **Little Abaco**) N of New Providence I. *area* 776, *pop* 3407
Aba·dan \,äb-ə-'dän, ,ab-; ,ab-ə-'dan\ 1 island W Iran in Shatt-al-Arab delta 2 city & port on Abadan I. *pop* 302,189
Ab·bai \ä-'bī\ the upper course of the Blue Nile
Ab·be·ville \ab-'vēl\ commune N France on the Somme N W of Amiens *pop* 19,500
Ab·er·dare \,ab-ə(r)-'da(ə)r, -'de(ə)r\ urban district S Wales in Glamorganshire *pop* 40,916
Ab·er·deen, 1 \'ab-ər-,dēn\ city N E S. Dak. *pop* 23,073 **2** city & port W Wash. on Grays Harbor *pop* 18,741 **3** \,ab-ər-'dēn\ *or* **Ab·er·deen·shire** \-,shi(ə)r, -shər\ county N E Scotland *area* 1971, *pop* 308,008 **4** burgh & port ✳ of Aberdeenshire *pop* 182,200 — **Ab·er·do·ni·an** \,ab-ər-'dō-nē-ən\ *adj or n*
Ab·er·yst·wyth \,ab-ə-'ris-,twith\ municipal borough W Wales on Cardigan Bay ✳ of Cardiganshire
Ab-i-Diz — see DIZ
Ab·i·djan \,ab-i-'jän\ city & port ✳ of Ivory Coast *pop* 127,500
Abila — see MUSA (Jebel)
Ab·i·lene \'ab-ə-,lēn\ city N W cen Tex. *pop* 90,368
Ab·in·ger \'ab-ən-jər\ village S England in Surrey, at 51°12'N, 0°24'W
Ab·ing·ton \'ab-iŋ-tən\ urban township S E Pa. N of Philadelphia *pop* 55,831
Ab·i·ti·bi \,ab-ə-'tib-ē\ 1 lake Canada on E boundary of Ont. *area* 356 2 river 230 *m* Canada flowing N into Moose river
Ab·kha·sia *or* **Ab·kha·zia** \ab-'kā-zh(ē)-ə, -'käz-ē-ə\ *or* **Ab·kha·sian Republic** \-'kā-zhən, -'käz-ē-ən\ autonomous republic U.S.S.R. in N W Georgia on Black sea ✳ Sukhumi *area* 3358, *pop* 400,000 — **Ab·khas** \-'käs\ *or* **Ab·kha·sian** *or* **Ab·kha·zian** \-'kā-zhən, -'käz-ē-ən\ *n*
Abo — see TURKU
Abo·mey \,ab-ə-'mā, ə-'bō-mē\ city S Dahomey *pop* 16,906
Abruz·zi \ä-'brüt-sē, ə-\ area cen Italy bordering on the Adriatic & including highest of the Apennines; with Molise (to S), forms **Abruzzi e Mo·li·se** \-,ä-'mō-lə-,zā\ region (✳ Aquila)
Ab·sa·ro·ka \ab-'sär-ə-kə, -'sȯ(ə)r-kē\ mountain range S Mont. & N W Wyo. E of Yellowstone National Park — see FRANKS PEAK
Ab·se·con \ab-'sē-kən\ inlet (strait) S E N. J. through barrier reef N of Atlantic City
Ab·u·kir \,ab-(,)ü-'ki(ə)r, ,äb-\ 1 bay N Egypt between Alexandria & Rosetta mouth of the Nile 2 village on the bay — see CANOPUS
Abu Sim·bel \,äb-ü-'sim-bəl\ *or* **Ip·sam·bul** \,ip-səm-,bül\ locality S Egypt on left bank of the Nile 140 *m* S W of Aswân; site of two rock temples
Aby·dos \ə-'bīd-əs\ 1 ancient town Asia Minor on the Hellespont 2 ancient town S Egypt on left bank of the Nile
Abyla — see MUSA (Jebel)
Ab·ys·sin·ia \,ab-ə-'sin-ē-ə, -'sin-yə\ — see ETHIOPIA — **Ab·ys·sin·ian** \-ē-ən, -yən\ *adj or n*
Aca·dia \ə-'kād-ē-ə\ *or* F **Aca·die** \à-kà-dē\ NOVA SCOTIA — an early name — **Aca·di·an** \ə-'kād-ē-ən\ *adj or n*
Acadia National Park section of coast of Me. including chiefly mountainous areas on Mount Desert I. & Isle au Haut *area* 42
Aca·pul·co \,äk-ə-'pül-(,)kō, ,ak-\ *or* **Acapulco de Juá·rez** \-thä-'hwär-,es, -'wär-əz\ city & port S Mexico in Guerrero on the Pacific S of Mexico City *pop* 27,913
Ac·ar·na·nia \,ak-ər-'nā-nē-ə, -'nā-nyə\ *or* NGk **Akar·na·nía** \,äk-,är-nə-'nē-ə\ region W Greece on Ionian sea — **Ac·ar·na·nian** \,ak-ər-'nā-nē-ən, -'nā-nyən\ *adj or n*
Ac·cad \'ak-,ad, 'äk-,äd\ — see AKKAD — **Ac·ca·di·an** \ə-'kād-ē-ən, -'käd-\ *adj or n*
Ac·cra *or* **Ak·kra** \ə-'krä\ city & port ✳ of Ghana on Gulf of Guinea *pop* 532,600
Ac·cring·ton \'ak-riŋ-tən\ municipal borough N W England in S E Lancashire N of Manchester *pop* 40,671
Achaea \ə-'kē-ə\ *or* **Acha·ia** \ə-'kī-ə, -'kā-(y)ə\ region S Greece in N Peloponnesus bordering on gulfs of Corinth & Patras — **Achae·an** \ə-'kē-ən\ *or* **Acha·ian** \ə-'kī-ən, -'kā-(y)ən\ *adj or n*
Ach·e·lo·us *or* NGk **Akhe·ló·os** *or* **Ach·e·lo·os** \,ak-ə-'lō-əs\ river 100 *m* W Greece flowing S to Ionian sea
Ach·ill \'ak-əl\ island 15 *m* long N W Ireland in County Mayo
Achray, Loch \ə-'krä\ lake cen Scotland in S W Perthshire
Acon·ca·gua \,ak-ən-'käg-wə, ,äk-\ mountain 22,835 *ft* W Argentina W N W of Mendoza near Chilean border; highest in Andes & western hemisphere
Açores — see AZORES
Acragas — see AGRIGENTO
Acre \'äk-rə, 'ä-(,)krä\ territory W Brazil bordering on Peru & Bolivia ✳ Rio Branco *area* 57,153, *pop* 114,755
Acre \'äk-ər, 'ā-kər, 'äk-rə\ *or* Heb **Ak·ko** *or* **Ac·cho** \ä-'kō\ *or anc* **Ptol·e·ma·is** \,täl-ə-'mā-əs\ city & port N W Israel at N end of Bay of Acre N of Mt. Carmel *pop* 25,128
Acroceraunia — see LINGUETTA (Cape)
Ac·te *or* **Ak·te** \'ak-(,)tē\ peninsula N E Greece, the most easterly of the three peninsulas of Chalcidice — see ATHOS
Ac·ti·um \'ak-stē-əm, 'ak-tē-\ promontory & ancient town W Greece in N W Acarnania
Ac·ton \'ak-tən\ municipal borough S E England in Middlesex, W suburb of London *pop* 67,424
Adak \'ā-,dak\ island S W Alaska in Andreanof group of the Aleutians
Adalia — see ANTALYA
Ad·ams, Mount \'ad-əmz\ 1 mountain 5798 *ft* N N.H. in White mountains N of Mt. Washington 2 mountain 12,307 *ft* S W Wash. in Cascade range S S E of Mt. Rainier
Ad·am's Bridge \,ad-əmz-\ chain of shoals 30 *m* long between Ceylon & S E India
Adam's Peak mountain 7365 *ft.* S cen Ceylon
Ada·na \'äd-ə-nə, -,nä, ə-'dän-ə\ *or* **Sey·han** \sā-'hän\ city S Turkey on Seyhan river *pop* 309,024
Ada·pa·za·ri \,äd-ə-,päz-ə-'rē\ city N W Turkey in Asia E of Istanbul *pop* 80,160
Ad·dis Ab·a·ba \,ad-ə-'sab-ə-bə\ city ✳ of Ethiopia *pop* 400,000
Ad·e·laide \'ad-ºl-,ād\ city Australia ✳ of So. Australia *pop* (with suburbs) 562,500
Aden \'äd-ºn, 'ād-, 'ad-\ 1 former Brit. protectorate S Arabia comprising coast area between Yemen on W & Oman on E; since 1967 part of So. Yemen *area* 112,000, *pop* 660,000 2 former Brit. colony on coast of & surrounded by Aden protectorate comprising Aden & Little Aden peninsulas, a small area of hinterland, & Perim I.; since 1967 part of So. Yemen *area* 75, *pop* 138,441 3 seaport, former ✳ of Aden colony & protectorate; now a township comprising a number of settlements (largest Crater) *pop* 99,285
Aden, Gulf of arm of Indian ocean between Aden & Somalia
Adi·ge \'äd-ə-,jā\ river 220 *m* N Italy flowing S E into the Adriatic
Adi·gey *or* **Ady·gei** \,äd-ə-'gā\ autonomous region U.S.S.R. in S Soviet Russia, Europe ✳ Maikop *area* 1505, *pop* 254,100
Ad·i·ron·dack \,ad-ə-'rän-,dak\ mountains N E N.Y. — see MARCY (Mount)
Ad·mi·ral·ty \'ad-m(ə-)rəl-tē\ 1 island 90 *m* long S E Alaska in N Alexander archipelago 2 islands W Pacific N of New Guinea in Bismarck archipelago *area* 800, *pop* 18,400
Adour \à-'dü(ə)r\ river 200 *m* S W France flowing from the Pyrenees N W & W into Bay of Biscay
Adri·an \'ā-drē-ən\ city S E Mich. *pop* 20,347
Adrianople — see EDIRNE
Adri·at·ic \,ā-drē-'at-ik, ,ad-rē-\ sea arm of the Mediterranean between Italy & Balkan peninsula
Adu·wa *or* **Ado·wa** \'äd-ə-wə, 'ad-\ town N Ethiopia
Ad·vent Bay \,ad-,vent, -vənt-\ inlet of Arctic ocean West Spitsbergen on W coast

Adzha·ria \ə-'jär-ē-ə\ *or* **Adzhar Republic** \,aj-,är-\ autonomous republic U.S.S.R. in SW Georgia on Black sea ✳ Batum *area* 1080, *pop* 242,000 — **Adzhar** \'äj,är\ *n* — **Adzhar·i·an** \ə-'jär-ē-ən\ *adj or n*

Aegadian, Aegates — *see* EGADI

Ae·ge·an \i-'jē-ən\ **1** sea arm of the Mediterranean between Asia Minor & Greece **2** islands Aegean sea including the Cyclades & the Northern & Southern Sporades

Ae·gi·na \i-'jī-nə\ *or* NGk **Ai·gi·na** \'ä-yē-,nä\ island & ancient state SE Greece in Saronic gulf — **Ae·gi·ne·tan** \,ē-jə-'nēt-ᵊn\ *adj or n*

Ae·gos·pot·a·mi \,ē-gə-'spät-ə-,mī\ *or* **Ae·gos·pot·a·mos** \-məs\ river & town of ancient Thrace in the Chersonese

Aemilia — *see* EMILIA-ROMAGNA

Aeolian islands — *see* LIPARI

Ae·o·lis \'ē-ə-ləs\ *or* **Ae·o·lia** \ē-'ō-lē-ə, -'ōl-yə\ ancient country of NW Asia Minor

Aetna — *see* ETNA

Ae·to·lia \ē-'tō-lē-ə, -'tōl-yə\ region W *cen* Greece N of Gulf of Patras & E of Acarnania — **Ae·to·lian** \-lē-ən, -yən\ *adj or n*

Afars and the Issas, French Territory of the — *see* FRENCH SOMALILAND

Af·ghan·i·stan \af-'gan-ə-,stan\ country W Asia E of Iran; a kingdom ✳ Kabul *area* 250,000, *pop* 12,000,000

Afog·nak \ə-'fóg-,nak, -'fäg-\ island S Alaska N of Kodiak I.

Af·ri·ca \'af-ri-kə\ continent of the eastern hemisphere S of the Mediterranean & adjoining Asia on NE *area* 11,596,000

Afyon *or* **Afyon Ka·ra·hi·sar** \äf-'yōn-,kär-ə-his-'är\ city W *cen* Turkey *pop* 38,392

Aga·dir \,äg-ə-'di(ə)r, ,ag-\ city & port SW Morocco *pop* 30,111

Aga·na \ə-'gän-yə\ town ✳ of Guam on W coast *pop* 1642

Agar·ta·la \,əg-ər-tə-'lä\ city E India ✳ of Tripura *pop* 42,600

Ag·as·siz, Lake \'ag-ə-(,)sē\ prehistoric lake 700 *m* long in S Man., E Sask., E N.Dak., & NW Minn.

Age·nais \,äzh-ə-'nä\ *or* **Age·nois** \,äzh-ən-'wä\ ancient region SW France S of Périgord ✳ Agen

Aghrim — *see* AUGHRIM

Ag·in·court — *see* AZINCOURT

Ag·no \'äg-(,)nō\ river 128 *m* Philippines in NW Luzon

Agra \'äg-rə\ **1** region N India roughly equivalent to present Uttar Pradesh excluding Oudh region **2** city N India in W Uttar Pradesh SSE of Delhi *pop* 375,665

Agram — *see* ZAGREB

Agri Dagi — *see* ARARAT

Agri·gen·to \,äg-ri-'jen-(,)tō\ *or formerly* **Gir·gen·ti** \jər-'jent-ē\ *or anc* **Ag·ri·gen·tum** \,ag-rə-'jent-əm\ *or* **Ac·ra·gas** \'ak-rə-gəs\ commune Italy in SW Sicily near coast *pop* 35,100

Agua·di·lla \,äg-wə-'thē-(y)ə\ city & port NW Puerto Rico *pop* 15,943

Aguas·ca·lien·tes \,äg-wə-,skäl-'yen-,tās\ **1** state *cen* Mexico *area* 2499, *pop* 208,719 **2** its ✳ *pop* 122,809

Agul·has, Cape \ə-'gəl-əs\ headland Republic of So. Africa in S Cape Province; southernmost point of Africa, at 34°50′S, 20°E

Ahag·gar \ə-'häg-ər, ,ä-hə-'gär\ *or* **Hog·gar** \'häg-ər, hə-'gär\ mountains S Algeria in W *cen* Sahara; highest Tahat 9573 *ft*

Ah·mad·abad *or* **Ah·med·abad** \'äm-əd-ə-,bäd\ city W India N of Bombay ✳ of Gujarat *pop* 788,300

Ah·ven·an·maa \'ä(k)-və-,nän-,mä\ *or* Sw **Åland** *or* **Aa·land** \'ō-,länd\ **1** archipelago SW Finland in Baltic sea ✳ Maarianhamina (Sw Mariehamn) **2** island, chief of the group

Ah·waz \ä-'wäz\ city SW Iran on Karun river *pop* 119,828

Ail·sa Craig \'āl-sə-,krāg, -,krag\ small rocky island Scotland S of Arran at mouth of Firth of Clyde

Ain \aⁿ\ river 118 *m* E France rising in Jura mountains & flowing SSW into the Rhone

Aintab — *see* GAZIANTEP

Air·drie \'a(ə)r-,drē, 'e(ə)r-\ burgh S *cen* Scotland in Lanark E of Glasgow *pop* 30,308

Aire \'a(ə)r, 'e(ə)r\ river 70 *m* N England in W Yorkshire flowing to the Ouse; its valley is **Aire·dale** \-,dāl\

Aisne \'ān\ river *ab* 175 *m* N France flowing NW & W from Argonne Forest into the Oise near Compiègne

Aix \'āks\ *or* **Aix-en-Pro·vence** \,āk-,säⁿ-prō-'väⁿs\ city SE France N of Marseilles *pop* 54,217

Aix-la-Chapelle — *see* AACHEN

Ajac·cio \ä-'yäch-(,)ō\ city & port France ✳ of Corsica *pop* 32,997

Ajan·ta \ə-'jənt-ə\ village W *cen* India in N *cen* Maharashtra in Ajanta range NNE of Aurangabad; caves

Aj·mer \,əj-'mi(ə)r, -'me(ə)r\ **1** *or* **Ajmer-Mer·wa·ra** \-,me(ə)r-'wär-ə\ former state NW India, now part of Rajasthan *area* 2425 **2** city, its ✳, SW of Delhi *pop* 196,633

Ajodh·ya *or* **Ayodh·ya** \ə-'yōd-yə\ former city N India, now part of city of Faizabad

Akaba — *see* 'AQABA

Akarnania — *see* ACARNANIA

Aka·shi \ä-'käsh-ē\ city Japan in W Honshu on Akashi strait W of Kobe *pop* 120,000

Akheloós — *see* ACHELOUS

Ak·hi·sar \,äk-(h)is-'är\ *or anc* **Thy·a·ti·ra** \,thī-ə-'tī-rə\ city W Turkey in Asia NE of Izmir *pop* 40,013

Aki·ta \ä-'kēt-ə\ city & port Japan in N Honshu on Sea of Japan *pop* 190,202

Ak·kad *or* **Ac·cad** \'ak-,ad, 'äk-,äd\ **1** the N division of ancient Babylonia **2** *or* **Aga·de** \ə-'gäd-ə\ ancient city, its ✳

Akkerman — *see* BELGOROD-DNESTROVSKI

Akko — *see* ACRE

Akkra — *see* ACCRA

Ak·ron \'ak-rən\ city NE Ohio *pop* 290,351

Ak·sum *or* **Ax·um** \'äk-,süm\ town N Ethiopia ✳ of an ancient kingdom (the Axumite Empire)

Akte — *see* ACTE

Ak·yab \ak-'yab\ city & port W Burma; chief town of Arakan coast *pop* 42,329

Al·a·bama \,al-ə-'bam-ə\ **1** river 315 *m* S Ala. flowing SW into Tensaw & Mobile rivers **2** state SE U.S. ✳ Montgomery *area* 51,609, *pop* 3,266,740 — **Al·a·bam·i·an** \-'bam-ē-ən\ *or* **Al·a·bam·an** \-'bam-ən\ *adj or n*

Ala·go·as \,al-ə-'gō-əs\ state NE Brazil ✳ Maceió *area* 11,031, *pop* 1,093,137

Alai \'ä-,lī\ mountain range U.S.S.R. in Soviet Central Asia in SW Kirgiz Republic; highest peak 19,554 *ft*

Al·a·me·da \,al-ə-'mēd-ə\ city & port W Calif. on island in San Francisco Bay near Oakland *pop* 63,855

Ala·mein *or* **El Alamein** \,el-,al-ə-'mān\ village NW Egypt on the Mediterranean N of NE corner of Qattara Depression

Ala·mo·gor·do \,al-ə-mə-'górd-(,)ō\ city S N. Mex. *pop* 21,723

Ala·se·hir \,al-ə-shə-'hi(ə)r, ,äl-\ *or anc* **Philadelphia** town W Turkey 75 *m* E of Izmir

Alas·ka \ə-'las-kə\ **1** state (territory 1912–59) of the U.S. NW No. America ✳ Juneau *area* 586,400, *pop* 226,167 **2** peninsula SW Alaska SW of Cook inlet **3** mountain range S Alaska extending from Alaska peninsula to Yukon boundary — *see* MCKINLEY (Mount) — **Alas·kan** \-kən\ *adj or n*

Alaska, Gulf of inlet of the Pacific off S Alaska between Alaska peninsula on W & Alexander archipelago on E

Ala Tau \,al-ə-'taù, ,äl-\ several ranges of the Tien Shan mountain system Soviet Central Asia in E Kazakh & Kirgiz republics around & NE of Issyk Kul; 10,000 to 18,000 *ft* high

Ala·va \'äl-ə-və\ province N Spain S of Vizcaya; one of the Basque Provinces ✳ Vitoria *area* 1175, *pop* 135,029

Al·a·va, Cape \'al-ə-və\ cape NW Wash. 17 *m* S of Cape Flattery; westernmost point of conterminous U.S., at 124°44′W

Al·ba·ce·te \,al-bə-'sāt-ē\ **1** province SE Spain N of Murcia province *area* 5737, *pop* 387,752 **2** commune, its ✳ *pop* 77,807

Al·ba Lon·ga \,al-bə-'lóŋ-gə\ ancient city *cen* Italy SE of Rome

Al·ban hills \,ól-bən-, ,al-\ *or anc* **Al·ba·nus Mons** \äl-,bän-ə-'smón(t)s\ mountain group Italy SE of Rome

Al·ba·nia \al-'bā-nē-ə, -nyə *also* äl-\ **1** ancient country Europe in E Caucasus region on W side of Caspian sea **2** country S Europe in Balkan peninsula on the Adriatic; a republic ✳ Tirane *area* 10,630, *pop* 1,560,000

Al·ba·no, Lake \al-'bän-(,)ō, äl-\ *or anc* **La·cus Al·ba·nus** \,lā-kə-(,)sal-'bā-nəs\ lake Italy SE of Rome

Al·ba·ny \'ól-bə-nē\ **1** city SW Ga. *pop* 55,890 **2** city ✳ of N.Y. *pop* 129,726 **3** river 610 *m* N Canada in Ont. flowing E into James Bay — **Al·ba·ni·an** \ól-'bā-nē-ən, -'bän-yən\ *adj or n*

Al·be·marle \'al-bə-,märl\ **1** sound inlet of Atlantic ocean NE N.C. **2** — *see* ISABELA

Al·bert, Lake \'al-bərt\ lake 100 *m* long E Africa between Uganda & Congo in course of the Victoria Nile

Al·ber·ta \al-'bərt-ə\ province W Canada ✳ Edmonton *area* 248,800, *pop* 1,123,116 — **Al·ber·tan** \-'bərt-ᵊn\ *adj or n*

Albert Lea \,al-bərt-'lē\ city S Minn. *pop* 17,108

Albert Nile — *see* NILE

Al·bert·ville \,al-,bər-'vē(ə)l, 'al-bərt-,vil\ city & port E Republic of the Congo on Lake Tanganyika *pop* 27,931

Al·bi \'al-'bē\ commune S France N of Toulouse *pop* 34,693

Al·bu·quer·que \'al-b(y)ə-,kər-kē\ city *cen* N. Mex. *pop* 201,189 — **Al·bu·quer·que·an** \,al-b(y)ə-'kər-kē-ən\ *n*

Al·ca·mo \'äl-kə-,mō\ commune NW Sicily *pop* 42,000

Al·ca·traz \'al-kə-,traz\ rocky island Calif. in San Francisco Bay

Al·coy \äl-'kói\ commune E Spain N of Alicante *pop* 50,239

Al·dab·ra \al-'dab-rə\ island (atoll) NW Indian ocean N of Madagascar, chief of Aldabra group; in Brit. Indian Ocean Territory

Al·dan \äl-'dän\ river 1500 *m* U.S.S.R. in E Soviet Russia, Asia, in SE Yakutsk Republic flowing into the Lena

Al·der·ney \'ól-dər-nē\ island in English channel, northernmost of the Channel islands ✳ St. Anne *area* 3, *pop* 1500

Al·der·shot \'ól-dər-,shät\ municipal borough S England in Hampshire *pop* 37,646

Aleksandrovsk — *see* ZAPOROZHE

Aleksandrovsk Grushevski — *see* SHAKHTY

Alen·çon \,al-,äⁿ-'sōⁿ\ city NW France N of Le Mans *pop* 21,893

Alep·po \ə-'lep-(,)ō\ *or* **Alep** \ä-'lep\ *or* Ar **Ha·leb** \hə-'leb\ *or* **Ha·lab** \-'läb\ *or anc* **Be·roea** *or* **Be·rea** \bə-'rē-ə\ city N Syria *pop* 451,435 — **Alep·pine** \ə-'lep-,ən, -,īn, -,ēn\ *adj or n*

Ales·san·dria \,al-ə-'san-drē-ə\ commune NW Italy *pop* 79,327

Aleu·tian \ə-'lü-shən\ **1** islands SW Alaska extending in an arc 1200 *m* SW & W from Alaska peninsula — *see* ANDREANOF, FOX, NEAR, RAT **2** mountain range SW Alaska, the SW extension of Alaska range, running along NW shore of Cook inlet to SW tip of Alaska peninsula with mountains of the Aleutian chain forming its SW extension — *see* SHISHALDIN

Al·ex·an·der \,al-ig-'zan-dər, ,el-\ archipelago of *ab* 1100 islands SE Alaska — *see* ADMIRALTY, BARANOF, CHICHAGOF, KUPREANOF, PRINCE OF WALES, REVILLAGIGEDO

Alexander I island Antarctica W of base of Antarctic peninsula

Alexandretta — *see* ISKENDERUN

Al·ex·an·dria \,al-ig-'zan-drē-ə, ,el-\ **1** city *cen* La. *pop* 40,279 **2** city N Va. on the Potomac S of Washington, D.C. *pop* 91,023 **3** city & port N Egypt between Lake Mareotis & the Mediterranean *pop* 1,416,000 — **Al·ex·an·dri·an** \-drē-ən\ *adj or n*

Al·föld \'ól-,fə(r)ld\ the central plain of Hungary

Al·gar·ve \äl-'gär-və, al-\ medieval Moorish kingdom now a province of Portugal on S coast

Al·ge·ci·ras \,al-jə-'sir-əs\ city & port SW Spain W of Gibraltar on Bay of Algeciras *pop* 62,592

Al·ge·ria \al-'jir-ē-ə\ *or* F **Al·gé·rie** \àl-zhā-rē\ country NW Africa bordering on the Mediterranean ✳ Algiers *area* 919,352, *pop* 9,529,726 — **Al·ge·ri·an** \-ē-ən\ *adj or n*

Al·giers \al-'ji(ə)rz\ **1** section of New Orleans, La., on right bank of the Mississippi **2** former Barbary state N Africa now Algeria **3** *or* F **Al·ger** \àl-zhā\ *or* Ar **Al·je·zair** \,al-jə-'zaєr\ city & port ✳ of Algeria on Bay of Algiers *pop* 361,285 — **Al·ge·rine** \,al-jə-'rēn\ *adj or n*

Al·goa Bay \al-,gō-ə-\ inlet of Indian ocean S Republic of So. Africa on SE coast of Cape Province

Al·ham·bra \al-'ham-brə\ **1** city SW Calif. E of Los Angeles *pop* 54,807 **2** hill in Granada, Spain; site of remains of Moorish palace & fortifications

Ali·can·te \,al-ə-'kant-ē, ,äl-ə-'känt-ē\ **1** province E Spain on the Mediterranean S of Valencia province *area* 2185, *pop* 708,425 **2** city & port, its ✳ *pop* 119,908

ə abut; ᵊ kitten; ər further; a back; ā bake; ä cot, cart; aù out; ch chin; e less; ē easy; g gift; i trip; ī life
j joke; ŋ sing; ō flow; ó flaw; ói coin; th thin; t̲h̲ this; ü loot; ù foot; y yet; yü few; yù furious; zh vision
ᵊ F table; ȧ F bac; ᵏ G ich, Buch; ⁿ F vin; œ F bœuf; œ̄ F feu; ᵫ G füllen; ᵫ̄ F rue; ʸ F digne \dēnʸ\, nuit \nwʸē\

GAZ.

Al·ice \'al-əs\ city S Tex. W of Corpus Christi *pop* 20,861
Ali·garh \,al-i-'gär\ city N India in NW Uttar Pradesh N of Agra *pop* (including old town of **Ko·il** \'kō-əl\) 141,618
Al·i·quip·pa \,al-ə-'kwip-ə\ borough W Pa. *pop* 26,369
Al·i·sal \,al-ə-'sal\ urban area W Calif. NE of Monterey *pop* 16,473
Al Ittihad — see MEDINA AS-SHAAB
Alk·maar \'alk-,mär\ commune NW Netherlands *pop* 42,507
Al Kuwait — see KUWAIT
Al·lah·abad \'al-ə-hə-,bad, -,bäd\ city N India in S Uttar Pradesh on the Ganges W of Banaras *pop* 332,300
Al·le·ghe·ny \,al-ə-'gā-nē\ **1** river 325 *m* W Pa. uniting with the Monongahela at Pittsburgh to form the Ohio **2** mountains of Appalachian system E U.S. in Pa., Md., Va., & W. Va.; 2000 to over 4800 *ft* high — **Al·le·ghe·ni·an** \-'gā-nē-ən\ *adj*
Al·len Park \,al-ən-\ city SE Mich. WSW of Detroit *pop* 37,052
Allenstein — see OLSZTYN
Al·len·town \'al-ən-,taun\ city E Pa. on the Lehigh *pop* 108,347
Al·lep·pey \ə-'lep-ē\ city & port S India in Kerala NW of Trivandrum *pop* 116,300
Al·li·ance \ə-'lī-ən(t)s\ city NE Ohio NE of Canton *pop* 28,362
Al·lier \al-'yā\ river *ab* 250 *m* S *cen* France flowing to the Loire
Al·ma \'al-mə\ river 50 *m* U.S.S.R. in S Soviet Russia, Europe, in SW Crimea
Al·ma–Ata \,al-mə-ə-'tä\ *or formerly* **Ver·nyi** \'ve(ə)rn-yē\ city U.S.S.R. in Soviet Central Asia ✳ of Kazakh Republic *pop* 650,000
Al·ma·dén \,al-mə-'dān, ,äl-, -'thān\ town S *cen* Spain in the Sierra Morena
Al·me·lo \'äl-mə-,lō\ commune E Netherlands *pop* 49,603
Al·me·ría \,al-mə-'rē-ə\ **1** province S Spain SE of Granada province *area* 3360, *pop* 375,296 **2** city & port, its ✳ *pop* 87,044
Alor \'al-,ȯ(ə)r, 'äl-\ *or* **Om·bai** \'ȯm-,bī\ island Indonesia in Lesser Sundas N of Timor; with **Pan·tar** \'pan-,tär\, forms **Alor islands** group
Alor Star \-'stär\ city NW Malaya ✳ of Kedah *pop* 52,772
Alost — see AALST
Al·phe·us \al-'fē-əs\ *or* NGk **Al·fiós** \al-'fyȯs, äl-\ river *ab* 75 *m* S Greece in W Peloponnesus flowing NW into Ionian sea
Alps \'alps\ mountain system S *cen* Europe extending from Mediterranean coast at border between France & Italy into NW & W Yugoslavia — see MONT BLANC
Al·sace \al-'sas, -'sās, 'al-,\ *or* G **El·sass** \'el-,zäs\ *or anc* **Al·sa·tia** \al-'sā-sh(ē-)ə\ region & former province NE France between Rhine river & Vosges mountains — **Al·sa·tian** \al-'sā-shən\ *adj or n*
Alsace–Lor·raine \-lə-'rān, -lȯ-\ *or* G **El·sass–Lo·thring·en** \,el-,zäs-'lō-triŋ-ən\ region NE France including Alsace & part of Lorraine
Al·sek \'al-,sek\ river 260 *m* NW Canada & SE Alaska flowing S into the Pacific
Al·ta California \'äl-tə-\ upper California — the former Spanish name for the S & *cen* part of present state of Calif., used to differentiate it from Baja (Lower) California
Al·ta·de·na \,al-tə-'dē-nə\ urban area SW Calif. N of Pasadena *pop* 40,568
Al·tai \'al-,tī\ **1** mountain system *cen* Asia between Outer Mongolia & Sinkiang region of W China & between Kazakh & Russian republics — see TABUN BOGDO **2** territory U.S.S.R. in SW Soviet Russia, Asia ✳ Barnaul *area* 71,885, *pop* 2,358,700
Al·ta·ma·ha \'ȯl-tə-mə-,hȯ\ river 137 *m* SE Ga. formed by junction of Ocmulgee & Oconee rivers & flowing SE into **Altamaha Sound** (estuary)
Al·ta·mi·ra \,al-tə-'mir-ə\ caverns N Spain WSW of Santander
Alt·dorf \'alt-,dȯrf, 'ält-\ *or* **Al·torf** \'al-,tȯrf, 'äl-\ town *cen* Switzerland ✳ of Uri canton
Al·ten·burg \'ält-^{ə}n-,bu̇(ə)rg\ city E Germany E of Weimar *pop* 51,800
Altin Tagh *or* **Altyn Tagh** — see ASTIN TAGH
Al·to Adi·ge \,äl-(,)tō-'äd-i-,jā\ *or* **Upper Adige** *or* **South Tirol** district N Italy in S Tirol in N Trentino-Alto Adige region
Al·ton \'ȯlt-^{ə}n\ city SW Ill. on the Mississippi *pop* 43,047
Al·too·na \al-'tü-nə\ city S *cen* Pa. *pop* 69,407
Alto Paraná — see PARANÁ
Al·trin·cham \'ȯl-triŋ-əm\ urban district NW England in Cheshire SSW of Manchester *pop* 39,787
Al·tus \'al-təs\ city SW Okla. *pop* 21,225
Al·um Rock \'al-əm-\ urban area W Calif. NE of San Jose *pop* 18,942
Aluta — see OLT
Ama·ga·sa·ki \,am-ə-gə-'säk-ē\ city Japan in W *cen* Honshu on Osaka Bay *pop* 405,955
Amal·fi \ə-'mäl-fē\ commune & port S Italy in Campania on Gulf of Salerno — **Amal·fi·an** \-fē-ən\ *adj or n*
Ama·mi \ə-'mäm-ē\ island group W Pacific in *cen* Ryukyus belonging to Japan *area* 498
Ama·pá \,am-ə-'pä\ territory N Brazil NW of Amazon delta ✳ Macapá *area* 55,489, *pop* 37,477
'Ama·ra \ə-'mär-ə, -'mär-(,)ä\ city SE Iraq on the Tigris *pop* 44,064
Am·a·ril·lo \,am-ə-'ril-(,)ō, -'ril-ə\ city NW Tex. *pop* 137,969
Am·a·zon \'am-ə-,zän, -zən\ river *ab* 3900 *m* N So. America flowing from Peruvian Andes into the Atlantic in N Brazil — see UCAYALI, SOLIMÕES
Ama·zo·nas \,am-ə-'zō-nəs\ state NW Brazil ✳ Manaus *area* 595,474, *pop* 514,099
Am·ba·to \äm-'bät-(,)ō\ city *cen* Ecuador S of Quito *pop* 33,908
Am·bon \'am-,bän\ *or* **Am·boi·na** \am-'bȯi-nə\ **1** island E Indonesia in the Moluccas S of Ceram *area* 314, *pop* 66,800 **2** city & port on Ambon I. ✳ of Maluku province *pop* 31,600 — **Am·bo·nese** \,am-bə-'nēz, -'nēs\ *or* **Am·boi·nese** \,am-,bȯi-\ *adj or n*
Am·bra·cian Gulf \am-,brā-shən-\ *or* **Gulf of Ar·ta** \'ärt-ə\ *or* NGk **Am·vra·ki·kós Kól·pos** \,äm-,vräk-i-,kȯ-'skȯl-,pȯs\ inlet of Ionian sea 25 *m* long W Greece in S Epirus
Am·brose \'am-,brōz\ channel SE N. Y. at entrance to N. Y. harbor N of Sandy Hook; 40 *ft* deep, 2000 *ft* wide
Am·chit·ka \am-'chit-kə\ island SW Alaska in the Aleutians at E end of Rat group
Amer·i·ca \ə-'mer-ə-kə\ **1** either continent (No. America or So. America) of the western hemisphere **2** *or* **the Amer·i·cas** \-kəz\ the lands of the western hemisphere including No., Central, & So. America & the West Indies **3** UNITED STATES OF AMERICA
American Samoa *or* **Eastern Samoa** island group of E Samoa SW *cen* Pacific ✳ Pago Pago (on Tutuila I.) *area* 76, *pop* 20,051
Amers·foort \'äm-ərz-,fō(ə)rt, -ərs-, -,fȯ(ə)rt\ commune *cen* Netherlands NE of Utrecht *pop* 68,906
Ames \'āmz\ city *cen* Iowa N of Des Moines *pop* 27,003
Am·ga \äm-'gä\ river 800 *m* U.S.S.R. in E Soviet Russia, Asia, flowing NE to the Aldan
Am·hara \am-'har-ə, -'här-ə\ former kingdom now province of NW Ethiopia ✳ Gondar
Amiens \am-'ya^{n}\ city N France on the Somme *pop* 92,506
Amin·di·vi \,əm-ən-'dē-vē\ island group India in the N Laccadives
Am·i·rante \'am-ə-,rant\ islands W Indian ocean SW of Seychelles; a dependency of Seychelles
Am·man \a-'man\ *or anc* **Philadelphia** *or Bib* **Rab·bah** \'rab-ə\ *or* **Rab·bath** \'rab-əth\ city ✳ of Jordan *pop* 245,000
Am·mon \'am-ən\ ancient country NW Arabia E of Gilead ✳ Rabbah
Ammonium — see SIWA
Am·ne Ma·chin \,am-nē-mə-'jin\ **1** range of the Kunlun mountains W China in E *cen* Tsinghai **2** its highest peak *ab* 25,000 *ft*
Amnok — see YALU
Amor·gos \ə-'mȯr-gəs\ *or* NGk **Amor·gós** \,äm-(,)ȯr-'gȯs\ island Greece in the Aegean in SE Cyclades SE of Naxos *area* 52
Amoy \ä-'mȯi, a-, ə-\ *or* **Sze·ming** \'sü-'miŋ\ city & port SE China in S Fukien on Amoy & Kulangsu islands *pop* 224,300
Am·rao·ti \,əm-'rau̇t-ē\ city *cen* India in NE Maharashtra WSW of Nagpur; chief city of Berar region *pop* 87,100
Am·rit·sar \,əm-'rit-sər\ city N India in NW Punjab *pop* 325,747
Am·ster·dam \'am(p)-stər-,dam\ **1** city E N.Y. on the Mohawk *pop* 28,772 **2** city & port, official ✳ of Netherlands *pop* 872,428
Amu Dar·ya \,äm-ü-'där-yə\ *or* **Ox·us** \'äk-səs\ river over 1400 *m*, *cen* & W Asia flowing from Pamir plateau into Lake Aral
Amund·sen \'äm-ən-sən, 'am-\ **1** sea arm of the S Pacific Antarctica off Marie Byrd Land **2** gulf arm of Beaufort sea N Canada W of Victoria I.
Amur \ä-'mu̇(ə)r\ *or* **Hei·lung·kiang** \'hā-'lu̇ŋ-jē-'äŋ\ river 1780 *m* E Asia formed by junction of Shilka & Argun rivers, flowing into the Pacific at N end of Tatar strait, & forming part of boundary between Manchuria & Soviet Russia, Asia
Ana·dyr *or* **Ana·dir** \,än-ə-'di(ə)r, ,an-\ river 450 *m* U. S. S. R. in Soviet Russia, Asia, flowing S & E to Gulf of Anadyr
Anadyr, Gulf of inlet of N Bering sea U.S.S.R. in Soviet Russia, Asia, S of Chukotski peninsula
An·a·heim \'an-ə-,hīm\ city SW Calif. *pop* 104,184
Aná·huac \ə-'nä-,wäk\ the central plateau of Mexico
Anarajapura — see ANURADHAPURA
An·a·to·lia \,an-ə-'tō-lē-ə, -'tōl-yə\ the part of Turkey comprising the peninsula of Asia Minor
An·chor·age \'aŋ-k(ə-)rij\ city & port S *cen* Alaska at head of Cook inlet *pop* 44,237
An·co·hu·ma \,aŋ-kə-'h(y)ü-mə\ mountain peak 20,873 *ft* W Bolivia; highest in the Illampu massif
An·co·na \aŋ-'kō-nə\ city & port *cen* Italy ✳ of the Marches on the Adriatic *pop* 64,501
An·da·lu·sia \,an-də-'lü-zh(ē-)ə\ *or* Sp **An·da·lu·cía** \,än-də-(,)lü-'sē-ə, -(,)lü-'thē-\ region S Spain including Sierra Nevada & valley of the Guadalquivir — **An·da·lu·sian** \,an-də-'lü-zhən\ *adj or n*
An·da·man \'an-də-mən, -,man\ **1** islands India in Bay of Bengal S of Burma & N of Nicobar islands *area* 2508 **2** sea SE Asia, the E section of Bay of Bengal — **An·da·man·ese** \,an-də-mə-'nēz\ *adj or n*
Andaman and Nic·o·bar \'nik-ə-,bär\ territory India comprising Andaman & Nicobar groups ✳ Port Blair *area* 3143, *pop* 31,000
An·der·lecht \'än-dər-,lekt\ commune *cen* Belgium, WSW suburb of Brussels *pop* 92,642
An·der·matt \'än-dər-,mät\ commune *cen* Switzerland S of Altdorf
An·der·son \'an-dər-sən\ **1** city *cen* Ind. *pop* 49,061 **2** city NW S. C. *pop* 41,316 **3** river 430 *m* Canada in NW Mackenzie District flowing W & N into Beaufort sea
An·des \'an-(,)dēz\ mountain system of So. America extending along W coast from Panama to Tierra del Fuego — see ACONCAGUA
An·dhra Pra·desh \,än-drə-prə-'dāsh, -'desh\ state SE India N of Madras state bordering on Bay of Bengal ✳ Hyderabad *area* 105,677, *pop* 31,260,133
An·di·zhan \,an-di-'zhan, ,än-di-'zhän\ city U.S.S.R. in Uzbekistan ESE of Tashkent *pop* 129,000
An·dor·ra \an-'dȯr-ə, -'där-ə\ country SW Europe in E Pyrenees between France & Spain; a republic ✳ Andorra la Vella *area* 179, *pop* 5200 — **An·dor·ran** \-ən\ *adj or n*
An·dre·a·nof \,an-drē-'an-əf, -,ȯf\ islands SW Alaska in *cen* Aleutian chain — see ADAK, ATKA
An·dria \'än-drē-ə\ commune SE Italy in Apulia *pop* 67,900
An·dros, 1 \'an-drəs\ island, largest of the Bahamas *area* 1600 **2** \'an-drəs, -,dräs\ island 25 *m* long Greece in N Cyclades
An·dros·cog·gin \,an-drə-'skäg-ən\ river 157 *m* NE N. H. & SW Me. flowing into the Kennebec
Ane·to, Pi·co de \,pē-(,)kō-,thā-ə-'nāt-(,)ō, -(,)kō-,dā-\ *or* F **Pic de Né·thou** \,pēk-də-(,)nā-'tü\ mountain 11,174 *ft* NE Spain; highest in the Pyrenees
An·gara \an-'gar-ə\ river 1100 *m* U. S. S. R. in Soviet Russia, Asia, flowing from Lake Baikal into the Yenisei — see TUNGUSKA
An·garsk \an-'gärsk\ city U.S.S.R. in E *cen* Soviet Russia, Asia, on the Angara NW of Irkutsk *pop* 160,000
An·gel Falls \,ān-jəl-\ waterfall 3212 *ft* SE Venezuela on Auyán-tepuí Mountain in a headstream of the Caroní
An·gers \ä^{n}-zhā\ city W France ENE of Nantes *pop* 102,142
Ang·kor \'aŋ-,kȯ(ə)r\ ruins of ancient city NW Cambodia N of Tonle Sap; ✳ of the Khmers
An·gle·sey *or* **An·gle·sea** \'aŋ-gəl-sē\ **1** *or anc* **Mo·na** \'mō-nə\ island NW Wales **2** county comprising Anglesey I. & Holyhead I. ✳✳ Beaumaris & Llangefni *area* 276, *pop* 50,637
Anglia, 1 — see ENGLAND **2** — see EAST ANGLIA — **An·gli·an** \'aŋ-glē-ən\ *adj or n*
Anglo–Egyptian Sudan — see SUDAN
An·go·la \aŋ-'gō-lə, an-\ *or* **Portuguese West Africa** country SW Africa S of mouth of the Congo river ✳ Luanda *area* 481,351, *pop* 8,441,312 — **An·go·lan** \-lən\ *adj or n*
An·gou·lême \,ä^{n}-gü-'lām\ city W France NE of Bordeaux *pop* 38,060

An·gou·mois \ˌäⁿ-güm-ˈwä\ region & former duchy & province W France S of Poitou ✻ Angoulême

An·guil·la \aŋ-ˈgwil-ə, an-\ island Brit. West Indies NW of St. Kitts *area* 34

An·gus \ˈaŋ-gəs\ *or formerly* For·far \ˈfȯr-fər\ *or* For·far·shire \-ˌshi(ə)r, -shər\ county E Scotland ✻ Forfar *area* 874, *pop* 274,876

An·halt \ˈän-ˌhält\ former state *cen* Germany ✻ Dessau

An·hwei *or* An·hui \ˈän-ˈ(h)wā\ province E China W of Kiangsu ✻ Hofei *area* 54,015, *pop* 30,633,000

An·i·ak·chak Crater \ˌan-ē-ˈak-ˌchak\ active volcano 4420 *ft* SW Alaska on Alaska peninsula 140 *m* SW of Mt. Katmai; crater 6 *m* in diameter

An·jou \ˈan-ˌjü, äⁿ-zhü\ region & former province NW France in Loire valley SE of Brittany ✻ Angers

An·ka·ra \ˈaŋ-kə-rə, ˈäŋ-\ *or formerly* An·go·ra \aŋ-ˈgōr-ə, an-, -ˈgȯr-\ *or anc* An·cy·ra \an-ˈsī-rə\ city ✻ of Turkey in N *cen* Anatolia *pop* 646,151

An·king \ˈän-ˈkiŋ\ *or* Hwai·ning \ˈhwī-ˈniŋ, ˈwī-\ city E China in Anhwei on the Yangtze *pop* 105,300

Ann, Cape \kā-ˈpan\ peninsula NE Mass.

An Najaf — *see* NAJAF

An·nam \a-ˈnam, ə-, ˈan-ˌam\ region & former kingdom E Indochina in *cen* Vietnam ✻ Hue *area* 57,000

An·nap·o·lis \ə-ˈnap-(ə-)ləs\ city & port ✻ of Md. *pop* 23,385

Annapolis Basin inlet of Bay of Fundy Canada in W N.S.

An·na·pur·na *or* An·a·pur·na \ˌan-ə-ˈpu̇r-nə, -ˈpər-\ massif N Nepal in the Himalayas; highest peak Annapurna I 26,503 *ft*

Ann Ar·bor \ˈan-ˈär-bər\ city SE Mich. *pop* 67,340

An·ne·cy \an-(ə-)ˈsē\ city E France ENE of Lyons *pop* 33,114

An·nis·ton \ˈan-ə-stən\ city NE Ala. *pop* 33,657

An·shan \ˈän-ˈshän\ city NE China in *cen* Liaoning SSW of Mukden *pop* 548,900

An·so·nia \an-ˈsō-nē-ə, -ˈsōn-yə\ city SW Conn. *pop* 19,819

An·ta·kya \ˌant-ə-ˈkyä\ *or* An·ta·ki·yah \-ˈkē-(y)ə\ *or anc* An·ti·och \ˈant-ē-ˌäk\ city S Turkey on Orontes river *pop* 30,400

An·tal·ya \ant-ˈl-ˌyä\ *or formerly* Ada·lia \ˌäd-ˈl-ē-(y)ə\ city & port SW Turkey on Gulf of Antalya *pop* 50,963

Antananarivo — *see* TANANARIVE

Ant·arc·tic \(ˈ)ant-ˈärk-tik, -ˈärt-ik\ 1 ocean surrounding Antarctica including the southern regions of the So. Atlantic, So. Pacific, & Indian oceans esp. S of ab 60° S 2 the Antarctic regions 3 *or formerly* Palm·er peninsula \ˈpäm-ər-, ˈpäl-mər-\ *or* Gra·ham Land \ˈgrä-əm, ˈgra-\ peninsula 1200 *m* long W Antarctica S of S end of So. America 4 *or* Palmer archipelago islands W of N end of Antarctic peninsula in Falkland Islands Dependencies

Ant·arc·ti·ca \-ˈärk-ti-kə, -ˈärt-i-\ *or* Antarctic continent body of land around the So. Pole; a plateau 6000 to 10,000 *ft* covered by a great ice cap & having mountain peaks 10,000 to 15,000 *ft* high *area ab* 6,000,000

An·tibes \äⁿ-ˈtēb\ city & port SE France SW of Nice *pop* 25,000

Antibes, Cap d' — *see* CAP D'ANTIBES

An·ti·cos·ti \ˌant-ə-ˈkȯ-stē\ island E Canada in E Que. at mouth of the St. Lawrence *area* 3043

An·tie·tam \an-ˈtēt-əm\ creek S Pa. & N Md. flowing S into the Potomac N of Harpers Ferry, W.Va.

An·ti·gua \an-ˈtē-g(w)ə, -ˈtig-(w)ə\ 1 island Brit. West Indies in the Leewards ✻ St. Johns *area* 108, *pop* (with Barbuda & Redonda) 56,800 2 *or* Antigua Guatemala city S *cen* Guatemala WSW of Guatemala City; former ✻ of Guatemala *pop* 22,942 — An·ti·guan \an-ˈtē-g(w)ən, -ˈtig-(w)ən\ *adj or n*

An·ti-Leb·a·non \ˈant-i-ˈleb-ə-nən, -ˌnän\ mountains SW Asia E of Bika valley on Syria-Lebanon border — *see* HERMON (Mount)

Antilles the West Indies excluding the Bahamas — *see* GREATER ANTILLES, LESSER ANTILLES — An·til·le·an \an-ˈtil-ē-ən\ *adj*

An·ti·och \ˈant-ē-ˌäk\ 1 city W Calif. NE of Oakland *pop* 17,305 2 — *see* ANTAKYA 3 ancient city Asia Minor in Pisidia, at certain periods within boundaries of Phrygia; its ruins are near Yalvac in W *cen* Turkey

An·ti·sa·na \ˌant-i-ˈsän-ə\ volcano 18,714 *ft* N *cen* Ecuador

An·to·fa·gas·ta \ˌant-ə-fə-ˈgäs-tə\ city & port N Chile *pop* 89,114

An·trim \ˈan-trəm\ county E Northern Ireland ✻ Belfast *area* 1098, *pop* 231,149 (with Belfast, 674,769)

An·tung \ˈän-ˈdu̇ŋ, -ˈtu̇ŋ\ city & port NE China in SE Liaoning at mouth of the Yalu *pop* 360,000

Ant·werp \ˈant-(ˌ)wərp\ *or* F An·vers \äⁿ-ve(ə)r\ *or* Flem Ant·wer·pen \ˈänt-ver-pə(n)\ 1 province N Belgium *area* 1104, *pop* 1,429,761 2 city & port, its ✻, on the Scheldt *pop* 302,569

Anu·ra·dha·pu·ra \ˌən-ə-ˌräd-ə-ˈpu̇r-ə\ *or* Ana·ra·ja·pu·ra \-ˌräj-ə-\ town *cen* Ceylon; an ancient ✻ of Ceylon *pop* 124,900

An·yang \ˈän-ˈyäŋ\ city E China in N Honan N of Kaifeng *pop* 124,900

An·zio \ˈan-zē-ˌō, ˈän-\ town & port Italy SSE of Rome

Ao·mo·ri \ˈau̇-mə-(ˌ)rē\ city & port N Japan in NE Honshu on Mutsu Bay *pop* 183,744

Aorangi — *see* COOK (Mount)

Aos·ta \ä-ˈȯ-stə\ 1 commune NW Italy in Piedmont at junction of Great & Little St. Bernard passes *pop* 26,500 2 — *see* VAL D'AOSTA

Ap·a·lach·i·co·la \ˌap-ə-ˌlach-i-ˈkō-lə\ river 90 *m* NW Fla. flowing from Lake Seminole S into Apalachicola Bay (inlet of Gulf of Mexico)

Apa·po·ris \ˌäp-ə-ˈpōr-(ˌ)ēs, -ˈpȯr-\ river *ab* 500 *m* S Colombia flowing SE into the Japurá on Colombia-Brazil boundary

Apel·doorn \ˈap-əl-ˌdȯ(ə)rn, -ˌdō(ə)rn\ commune E *cen* Netherlands N *or* Arnhem *pop* 101,492

Ap·en·nines \ˈap-ə-ˌnīnz\ mountain chain Italy extending the length of the peninsula — *see* CORNO (Monte) — Ap·en·nine \-ˌnīn\ *adj*

Apia \ä-ˈpē-ə\ town & port Samoa ✻ of Western Samoa on Upolu I.

Apo, Mount \ˈäp-(ˌ)ō\ volcano 9689 *ft* S Philippines in SE Mindanao; highest peak in the Philippines

Ap·pa·la·chia \ˌap-ə-ˈlā-ch(ē-)ə, -ˈlach-(ē-)ə\ region SE U.S. comprising Appalachian mountains from SW Pa. southward

Ap·pa·la·chian \ˌap-ə-ˈlā-chən, -ˈlach-ən\ mountain system E No. America extending from S Que. to N Ala.; highest peak Mt. Mitchell (N.C.; in Blue Ridge) 6684 *ft*

Ap·pen·zell \ˈap-ən-ˌzel, ˈäp-ən(t)-ˌsel\ canton NE Switzerland; subdivided into half cantons: Appenzell In·ner Rhodes \-ˈin-ər-ˌrōdz\ *or* G Appenzell Inner Rho·den \-ˌrōd-ˈn\ (✻ Appen-

---

zell, *area* 61, *pop* 13,427) & Appenzell Out·er Rhodes \-ˈau̇t-ə(r)-\ *or* G Appenzell Aus·ser Rhoden \-ˈau̇-sə(r)-\ (✻ Herisau, *area* 101, *pop* 47,938)

Ap·ple·ton \ˈap-əl-tən\ city E Wis. *pop* 48,411

Ap·po·mat·tox Court House National Historical Park \ˌap-ə-ˈmat-əks\ reservation *cen* Va. E of Lynchburg & ENE of town of Appomattox

Apra Harbor \ˌäp-rə-\ seaport Guam on W coast

Ap·she·ron \ˌäp-shə-ˈrȯn\ peninsula U. S. S. R. projecting into the Caspian sea on coast of E Azerbaidzhan Republic

Apu·lia \ə-ˈpyü-lē-ə\ *or* It Pu·glia \ˈpül-(ˌ)yä\ *or* Le Pu·glie \lā-ˈpül-(ˌ)yä\ region SE Italy bordering on the Adriatic & Gulf of Taranto ✻ Bari — Apu·lian \ə-ˈpyül-yən, -ˈpyü-lē-ən\ *adj or n*

Apu·re \ə-ˈpu̇(ə)r-(ˌ)ā\ river 420 *m* W Venezuela flowing E into the Orinoco

Apu·rí·mac \ˌäp-ə-ˈrē-ˌmäk\ river 550 *m* S & *cen* Peru flowing N to unite with the Urubamba forming the Ucayali

Aqa·ba *or* Aka·ba \ˈäk-ə-bə, ˈak-\ *or anc* Elath \ˈē-ˌlath\ town & port SW Jordan on border of Israel at head of NE arm (Gulf of 'Aqaba) of Red sea

Aquid·neck \ə-ˈkwid-ˌnek\ *or* Rhode island SE R. I. in Narragansett Bay; site of city of Newport

Aqui·la \ˈäk-wi-lə, ˈak-\ *or* L'A·qui·la \ˈläk-, -ˈlak-\ *or* Aquila de·gli Abruz·zi \ˌdāl-yē-ä-ˈbrüt-sē, -yē-ə-\ commune *cen* Italy NE of Rome ✻ of Abruzzi e Molise *pop* 25,600

Aq·ui·taine \ˈak-wə-ˌtān\ old region of SW France comprising area later known as Guienne ✻ Toulouse

Aq·ui·ta·nia \ˌak-wə-ˈtā-nyə, -nē-ə\ a Roman division of SW Gaul under Caesar consisting of country between Pyrenees mountains & Garonne river & under Augustus expanded to Loire & Allier rivers — Aq·ui·ta·nian \-nyən, -nē-ən\ *adj or n*

Ara·ba, Wa·di el \ˌwäd-ē-el-ˈar-ə-bə\ valley extending S from Dead sea to Gulf of 'Aqaba

Ara·bia \ə-ˈrā-bē-ə\ peninsula of SW Asia *ab* 1400 *m* long & 1250 *m* wide including Saudi Arabia, Yemen, Oman, Trucial Oman, & Aden; in earlier times divided into Arabia Petraea, "Rocky Arabia", the NW part; Arabia Deserta, "Desert Arabia", the N part; & Arabia Felix, "Fertile Arabia" (on assumption that the interior was as fertile as the coastal strip), the main part of the peninsula but by some geographers restricted to Yemen — Ara·bi·an \ə-ˈrā-bē-ən\ *adj or n*

Arabian, 1 desert E Egypt between the Nile & the Red sea 2 sea, NW section of the Indian ocean between India & Arabia

Ara·ca·ju \ˌar-ə-kə-ˈzhü\ city & port NE Brazil ✻ of Sergipe *pop* 67,539

Arad \ä-ˈräd\ city W Romania on Mures river *pop* 112,139

Ara·fu·ra \ˌar-ə-ˈfu̇r-ə\ sea between N Australia & West New Guinea

Ar·a·gon \ˈar-ə-ˌgän, -gən\ region NE Spain bordering on France; once an independent kingdom ✻ Zaragoza — Ar·a·go·nese \ˌar-ə-gə-ˈnēz, -ˈnēs\ *adj or n*

Ara·guaia *or* Ara·guaya \ˌar-ə-ˈgwī-ə\ river *ab* 1100 *m*, *cen* Brazil flowing N into the Tocantins

Arak \ä-ˈräk, ə-ˈrak\ *or* Iraq \i-ˈräk, i-ˈrak\ *or* Sul·tan·abad \ˌsu̇l-ˈtän-ə-ˌbäd\ city W Iran SW of Tehran *pop* 58,929

Ara·kan \ə-ˈräks, ə-ˈkän, -ˈkan\ coast region SW Burma on Bay of Bengal; chief town Akyab

Araks \ə-ˈräks\ *or* Aras \ə-ˈräs\ *or anc* Arax·es \ə-ˈrak-(ˌ)sēz\ river 635 *m* W Asia rising in mountains of Turkish Armenia & flowing E to join the Kura in E Azerbaidzhan, U. S. S. R.

Ar·al sea \ˈar-əl-\ *or* Lake Aral brackish lake U.S.S.R. in SW Soviet Central Asia between Kazakhstan & Uzbekistan *area* 26,000

Ar·am \ˈar-əm, ˈer-\ ancient Syria — its Hebrew name

Ar·an \ˈar-ən\ islands W Ireland off coast of Galway; largest island Inishmore

Aran·sas \ə-ˈran(t)-səs\ 1 bay (inlet) of Gulf of Mexico S Tex. NE of Corpus Christi Bay between mainland & St. Joseph I. 2 pass (channel) S Tex. between Mustang & St. Joseph islands leading to Corpus Christi & Aransas bays

Ar·a·rat \ˈar-ə-ˌrat\ *or* Ag·ri Da·gi \ˈä(g)-rē-(ˌ)dä(g)-ˈē\ mountain 16,946 *ft* E Turkey near border of Iran

Arau·ca·nia \ə-ˌrau̇-ˈkän-ē-ə, ˌär-ˌau̇-\ region *cen* Chile S of Bío-Bío river — Arau·ca·ni·an \ə-ˌrau̇-ˈkän-ē-ən, ˌar-(ˌ)ȯ-ˈkā-nē-\ *adj or n*

Ara·val·li \ə-ˈräv-ə-(ˌ)lē\ mountain range NW India E of Thar desert 300 *m* long; highest peak Mt. Abu 5650 *ft*

Arbela, Arbil — *see* ERBIL

Ar·bon \är-ˈbōⁿ\ commune NE Switzerland in Thurgau canton on Lake Constance

Ar·buck·le mountains \ˈär-ˌbək-əl\ hilly region S *cen* Okla.

Ar·bu·tus \är-ˈbyüt-əs\ urban area N *cen* Md. SW of Baltimore *pop* (with Halethorpe & Relay) 22,402

Ar·cade \är-ˈkād\ *or* Town and Country Village urban area N *cen* Calif. NE of Sacramento *pop* (with Arden) 73,352

Ar·ca·dia \är-ˈkād-ē-ə\ 1 city SW Calif. ENE of Los Angeles *pop* 41,005 2 mountainous region S Greece in *cen* Peloponnesus

Archangel, Gulf of — *see* DVINA GULF

Arch·es National Monument \ˈär-chəz\ reservation E Utah including wind-eroded natural arch formations *area* 125

Ar·cos de la Fron·te·ra \ˈär-ˌkȯz-də-ˌlä-ˌfrȯn-ˈter-ə\ commune SW Spain NE of Cádiz

Ar·cot \är-ˈkät\ city SE India in N Madras state WSW of Madras; once ✻ of the nawabs of Carnatic *pop* 16,583

Arc·tic \ˈärk-tik, ˈärt-ik\ 1 ocean N of the Arctic circle 2 the Arctic regions 3 archipelago N Canada in Arctic ocean constituting larger part of Franklin District, Northwest Territories

Arctic Red river 310 *m* Canada in NW Mackenzie District, Northwest Territories, flowing N into the Mackenzie

Ar·cueil \är-ˈkə(r), -ˈkəi\ commune N France S of Paris *pop* 18,067

Ar·de·bil *or* Ar·da·bil \ˌärd-ə-ˈbē(ə)l\ city NW Iran in E Azerbaijan province *pop* 65,720

Ar·den \ˈärd-ˈn\ 1 urban area N *cen* Calif. NE of Sacramento *pop* (with Arcade) 73,352 2 district *cen* England in N Warwickshire W of Stratford on Avon; site of former Forest of Arden

Ar·dennes \är-ˈden\ wooded plateau region in NE France, W

ə abut; ᵊ kitten; ər further; a back; ā bake; ä cot, cart; au̇ out; ch chin; e less; ē easy; g gift; i trip; ī life
j joke; ŋ sing; ō flow; ȯ flaw; ȯi coin; th thin; t̲h̲ this; ü loot; u̇ foot; y yet; yü few; yu̇ furious; zh vision
ᵊ F table; á F bac; ᴋ G ich, Buch; ⁿ F vin; œ F bœuf; œ̄ F feu; ᵫ G füllen; ᵫ̄ F rue; ʸ F digne \dēnʸ\, nuit \nwᵉʸ\

Luxembourg, & SE Belgium E of the Meuse; average height under 1600 ft

Ard·more \'ärd-‚mō(ə)r, -‚mȯ(ə)r\ city S Okla. *pop* 20,184

Are·ci·bo \‚ar-ə-'sē-(‚)bō\ city & port N Puerto Rico *pop* 28,828

Are·na, Point \ə-'rē-nə\ promontory N Calif. in the Pacific *ab* midway between Cape Mendocino & San Francisco Bay

Are·qui·pa \‚ar-ə-'kē-pə\ city S Peru *pop* 121,896

Arez·zo \ə-'ret-(‚)sō\ commune *cen* Italy in Tuscany SE of Florence *pop* 66,700

Ar·gen·tan \‚är-zhän-'tän\ town NW France in Normandy NNW of Alençon

Ar·gen·teuil \‚är-zhən-'tə(r), -'tœi\ commune N France on the Seine NNW of Paris *pop* 59,314

Ar·gen·ti·na \‚är-jən-'tē-nə\ *or* **Ar·gen·tine Republic** \‚är-jən-‚tēn-\ *or* the **Ar·gen·tine** \'är-jən-‚tēn\ country S So. America between the Andes & the Atlantic S of Pilcomayo river; a federal republic ✳ Buenos Aires *area* 1,079,965, *pop* 20,435,000 — **Ar·gen·tine** *adj or n* — **Ar·gen·tin·ean** *or* **Ar·gen·tin·i·an** \‚är-jən-'tin-ē-ən\ *adj or n*

Ar·gi·nu·sae \‚är-jə-'n(y)ü-‚sē\ group of small islands in the Aegean SE of Lesbos

Ar·go·lis \'är-gə-ləs\ district & ancient country S Greece in E Peloponnesus comprising a plain around Argos & area between Gulf of Argolis & Saronic gulf — **Ar·gol·ic** \är-'gäl-ik\ *adj*

Argolis, Gulf of *or* **Gulf of Nau·plia** \'nȯ-plē-ə\ inlet of the Aegean S Greece on E coast of Peloponnesus

Ar·gonne \är-'gän, 'är-‚\ wooded plateau NE France S of the Ardennes near Belgian border between Meuse & Aisne rivers

Ar·gos \'är-‚gäs, -gəs\ town Greece in E Peloponnesus on Argive plain at head of Gulf of Argolis; once a Greek city-state

Argovie — see AARGAU

Ar·guel·lo, Point \är-'gwel-(‚)ō\ cape SW Calif. WNW of Santa Barbara

Ar·gun \är-'gün\ river 450 m NE Asia forming boundary between Inner Mongolia (China) & U. S. S. R. & uniting with the Shilka to form the Amur

Ar·gyll \är-'gī(ə)l, 'är-‚gīl\ *or* **Ar·gyll·shire** \-‚shi(ə)r, -shər\ county W Scotland ✳ Lochgilphead *area* 3110, *pop* 63,300

Aria \'ar-ē-ə, 'er-; ə-'rī-ə\ **1** an E province of ancient Persian Empire; district now in NW Afghanistan & E Iran **2** — see HERAT

Ari·ca \ə-'rē-kə\ city & port N Chile near Peruvian border *pop* 46,542 — see TACNA

Ar·i·ma·thea *or* **Ar·i·ma·thaea** \‚ar-ə-mə-'thē-ə\ town in ancient Palestine; location not certainly identified

Ariminum — see RIMINI

Ari·pua·nã \‚är-əp-wə-'naⁿ\ river 600 m W *cen* Brazil rising in Mato Grosso state & flowing N into the Madeira

Arius — see HARI RUD

Ar·i·zo·na \‚ar-ə-'zō-nə\ state SW U. S. ✳ Phoenix *area* 113,909, *pop* 1,302,161 — **Ar·i·zo·nan** \-nən\ *or* **Ar·i·zo·nian** \-nē-ən, -nyən\ *adj or n*

Ar·kan·sas \'är-kən-‚sȯ; 1 *is also* är-'kan-zəs\ **1** river 1450 m SW *cen* U.S. rising in *cen* Colo. & flowing E & SE through S Kans., NE Okla., & Ark. into the Mississippi **2** state S *cen* U. S. ✳ Little Rock *area* 53,104, *pop* 1,786,272 — **Ar·kan·san** \är-'kan-zən\ *adj or n*

Ar·khan·gelsk \är-'kän-‚gelsk\ *or* **Arch·an·gel** \'är-‚kān-jəl\ city & port U. S. S. R. in N Soviet Russia, Europe, on the Northern Dvina *pop* 256,000

Arl·berg \'är(ə)l-‚bərg, -‚be(ə)rg\ Alpine valley, pass, & tunnel W Austria in the Tirol

Arles \'ärl(z)\ **1** medieval kingdom E & SE France; also called Kingdom of Burgundy **2** *or* **Ar·e·las** \'ar-ə-‚las\ *or* **Ar·e·la·te** \‚ar-ə-'lāt-ē\ city SE France on the Rhone *pop* 23,776 — **Ar·le·sian** \är-'lē-zhən\ *n*

Ar·ling·ton \'är-liŋ-tən\ **1** county N Va. on the Potomac; an urban area, suburb of Washington, D. C. *pop* 163,401 **2** town E Mass. NW of Boston *pop* 49,953 **3** city N Texas E of Fort Worth *pop* 44,775

Arlington Heights village NE Ill. NW of Chicago *pop* 27,878

Ar·lon \är-'lōⁿ\ commune SE Belgium ✳ of Luxembourg province *pop* 23,509

Ar·magh \är-'mä, 'är-‚\ **1** county S Northern Ireland *area* 489, *pop* 108,800 **2** urban district, its ✳

Ar·ma·gnac \‚är-mən-'yak\ district SW France in old province of Gascony; chief town Auch

Ar·me·nia \är-'mē-nē-ə, -nyə\ **1** *or* Bib **Min·ni** \'min-‚ī\ former kingdom W Asia in mountainous region SE of Black sea & SW of Caspian sea; area now divided between U.S.S.R., Turkey, & Iran **2** *or* **Ar·me·nian Republic** \är-‚mē-nē-ən-, -nyən-\ constituent republic of U. S. S. R. in S Transcaucasia ✳ Yerevan *area* 11,580, *pop* 1,800,000 — see LESSER ARMENIA

Ar·men·tières \‚är-mən-tye(ə)r, -'ti(ə)rz\ commune N France W of Lille *pop* 24,940

Ar Misr — see EGYPT

Ar·mor·i·ca \är-'mȯr-ə-kə, -'mär-\ **1** *or* **Ar·e·mor·i·ca** \‚ar-ə-\ ancient region NW France between Seine & Loire rivers **2** BRITTANY — **Ar·mor·ic** \-ik\ *or* **Ar·mor·i·can** \-ə-kən\ *adj or n*

Arn·hem \'ärn-‚hem, 'är-nəm\ commune E Netherlands ✳ of Gelderland *pop* 123,238

Arnhem Land \'är-nəm\ region N Australia on N coast of Northern Territory

Ar·no \'är-(‚)nō\ *or anc* **Ar·nus** \-nəs\ river 140 m, *cen* Italy flowing W from the Apennines through Florence into Ligurian sea

Aroos·took \ə-'rüs-tək, -'rüs-\ river 140 m N Me. flowing NE across N. B. border & into St. John river

Aro·sa \ä-'rō-zä\ village E Switzerland in Graubünden SE of Chur

Ar·ran \'ar-ən\ island SW Scotland in Firth of Clyde *area* 165

Ar·ras \'a-‚räs, 'ar-əs\ city N France SSW of Lille *pop* 36,242

Ar Rimal — see RUB' AL KHALI

Arsanias — see MURAT

Arta, Gulf of — see AMBRACIAN GULF

Ar·te·movsk \är-'tem-əfsk\ *or formerly* **Bakh·mut** \'bäk-‚müt\ city U.S.S.R. in E Ukraine in the Donets basin N of Donetsk *pop* 61,000

Ar·tois \är-'twä\ former province N France between Flanders & Picardy ✳ Arras

Aru *or* **Aroe** *or* **Ar·roe** \'är-(‚)ü\ islands E Indonesia S of W New Guinea *area* 3305, *pop* 18,200

Aru·ba \ə-'rü-bə\ island Netherlands Antilles off coast of NW Venezuela; chief town Oranjestad *area* 69, *pop* 53,600

Aru·wi·mi \‚är-ə-'wē-mē, ‚ar-\ river 800 m N Congo flowing SW & W into Congo river

Ar·vada \är-'vad-ə, -'väd-\ town *cen* Colo., NW suburb of Denver *pop* 19,242

Ar·wad \'är-‚wad, -‚wäd\ *or* **Ru·ad** \rü-'ad\ *or* Bib **Ar·vad** \'är-‚vad\ island Syria off coast of S Latakia

Asa·hi·ka·wa \‚äs-ə-'hē-'kä-wə\ *or* **Asa·hi·ga·wa** \-'gä-wə\ city Japan in *cen* Hokkaido *pop* 164,971

Asa·ma \ə-'säm-ə\ *or* **Asa·ma·ya·ma** \ə-‚säm-ə-'yäm-ə\ volcano 8340 ft Japan in *cen* Honshu

Asan·sol \'äs-ᵊn-‚sȯl\ city NE India in West Bengal *pop* 76,277

As·bury Park \‚az-‚ber-ē-, -b(ə-)rē-\ city E N.J. on the Atlantic *pop* 17,366

As·cen·sion \ə-'sen-chən\ island in S Atlantic at 7°55′S, 14°25′W belonging to Brit. colony of St. Helena *area* 34, *pop* 326

As·co·li Pi·ce·no \‚äs-kə-(‚)lē-pi-'chā-(‚)nō\ *or anc* **As·cu·lum Pi·ce·num** \‚as-kyə-ləm-(‚)pī-'sē-nəm\ commune *cen* Italy in the Marches 87 m NE of Rome *pop* 47,000

Ascoli Sa·tria·no \-‚sä-trē-'än-(‚)ō\ *or anc* **As·cu·lum Ap·u·lum** \‚as-kyə-lə-'map-yə-ləm\ *or* **As·cu·lum Apulum** \‚ȯs-\ commune SE Italy in Apulia S of Foggia

As·cot \'as-kət, -‚kät\ village S England in Berkshire SW of London

As·cut·ney, Mount \ə-'skət-nē\ mountain 3320 ft SE Vermont

Ashan·ti \ə-'shant-ē, -'shänt-\ region *cen* Ghana; formerly a native kingdom & later a Brit. colony ✳ Kumasi *area* 24,379, *pop* 578,100

Ash·bur·ton \'ash-‚bərt-ᵊn\ river 500 m Australia in NW Western Australia flowing NW into Indian ocean

Ash·dod \'ash-‚däd\ town & port Israel W of Jerusalem

Ashe·ville \'ash-‚vil, -vil\ city W N.C. *pop* 60,192

Ashi·ka·ga \‚äsh-i-'käg-ə\ city Japan in *cen* Honshu *pop* 52,810

Ash·ke·lon \'as-kə-‚län\ *or* **As·ca·lon** \'as-kə-‚län\ ancient city & port SW Palestine, site in Israel WSW of Jerusalem

Ashkh·a·bad \'ash-kə-‚bad, -‚bäd\ *or formerly* **Pol·to·ratsk** \‚päl-tə-'rätsk\ city U.S.S.R. in Soviet Central Asia ✳ of Turkmen Republic *pop* 170,000

Ash·land \'ash-lənd\ **1** city NE Ky. on the Ohio *pop* 31,283 **2** city N *cen* Ohio *pop* 17,419

Ash·ley \'ash-lē\ river 40 m S S.C. flowing SE into Charleston harbor

Ash·ta·bu·la \‚ash-tə-'byü-lə\ city NE Ohio on Lake Erie *pop* 24,559

Asia \'ā-zhə, -shə\ continent of the eastern hemisphere N of equator forming a single landmass with Europe (the conventional dividing line between Asia & Europe being the Ural mountains & main range of the Caucasus mountains); has numerous large offshore islands including Cyprus, Ceylon, Malay archipelago, Formosa, the Japanese chain, & Sakhalin *area* 16,988,000

Asia Mi·nor \-'mī-nər\ peninsula forming W extremity of Asia between Black sea on N, Mediterranean sea on S, & Aegean sea on W — see ANATOLIA

Asir \ə-'si(ə)r\ principality SW Arabia on Red sea; dependency of the Nejd, Saudi Arabia ✳ As Sabya *area* 13,857, *pop* 750,000

As·ma·ra \az-'mär-ə, -'mar-ə\ city N Ethiopia ✳ of Eritrea *pop* 120,000

As·nières \än-'ye(ə)r\ commune N France NW of Paris *pop* 77,838

Aso \'äs-(‚)ō\ *or* **Aso·san** \‚äs-ō-'sän\ volcanic mountain Japan in *cen* Kyushu; has five volcanic cones (highest 5225 ft) grouped around crater 15 m long with walls 2000 ft high

Aso·lo \'äz-ə-‚lō\ commune NE Italy NW of Treviso

As·pern \'as-pərn, 'äs-\ former village Austria ENE of Vienna; since 1905 part of Vienna

Asphaltites, Lacus — see DEAD SEA

Aspinwall — see COLÓN

As·sam \ə-'sam, a-; 'as-‚am\ state NE India on edge of Himalayas ✳ Shillong *area* 85,012, *pop* 9,043,700

As·sin·i·boine \ə-'sin-ə-‚bȯin\ river 450 m Canada rising in SE Sask. & flowing S & E across S Man. into Red river

Assiniboine, Mount mountain 11,870 ft Canada in SW Alta. on B.C. border

As·si·si \ə-'sis-ē, -'sē-zē, -'sē-sē, -'siz-ē\ commune *cen* Italy ESE of Perugia *pop* 24,206

As·syr·ia \ə-'sir-ē-ə\ *or* Bibl **As·sur** \ä-'su̇(ə)r, 'ä-‚\ *or* **Ash·ur** \'ash-ər\ ancient empire W Asia extending along middle Tigris & over foothills to the E; early ✳ Calah, later ✳ Nineveh

Astacus — see IZMIT

Asterabad — see GURGAN

Asti \'äs-tē\ commune NW Italy W of Alessandria *pop* 52,000

As·tin Tagh \‚as-tən-'tä(g)\ *or* **Al·tin Tagh** *or* **Al·tyn Tagh** \‚al-tən-\ mountain range W China in S Sinkiang; highest peak *ab* 17,000 ft

As·tra·khan \'as-trə-‚kan, -kən\ city U.S.S.R. in Soviet Russia, Europe, on the Volga at head of its delta; 50 ft below sea level *pop* 294,000

As·tu·ri·as \a-'st(y)u̇r-ē-əs\ **1** region & old kingdom NW Spain on Bay of Biscay **2** OVIEDO (province) — **As·tu·ri·an** \a-'st(y)u̇r-ē-ən\ *adj or n*

Asun·ción \ə-‚sün(t)-sē-'ōn, (‚)ä-\ city ✳ of Paraguay on Paraguay river at confluence with the Pilcomayo *pop* 205,605

As·wân *or* **As·souan** *or* **As·suan** \ä-'swän, ä-\ *or anc* **Sy·e·ne** \sī-'ē-nē\ city S Egypt on right bank of the Nile near site of dam built 1898–1902 & of **Aswân High Dam** (under construction to form **Lake Nas·ser** \'näs-ər, 'nas-\) *pop* 48,000

As·yût *or* **As·siout** *or* **As·siut** \as-'yüt\ city *cen* Egypt on left bank of the Nile *pop* 121,000

Ata·ca·ma \‚at-ə-'käm-ə\ **1** region N Chile between Copiapó & Peru border **2** — see PUNA DE ATACAMA

At·ba·ra \'at-bə-rə\ river *ab* 500 m NE Africa rising in N Ethiopia & flowing through E Sudan into the Nile

Atchaf·a·laya \(ə-)‚chaf-ə-'lī-ə\ river 225 m S La. flowing S into **Atchafalaya Bay** (inlet of Gulf of Mexico)

Ath·a·bas·ca *or* **Ath·a·bas·ka** \‚ath-ə-'bas-kə\ **1** river 765 m Canada in Alta. flowing NE & N into Lake Athabasca **2** lake Canada on Alta.-Sask. boundary *area* 3058

Ath·ens \'ath-ənz\ **1** city NE Ga. *pop* 31,355 **2** city SE Ohio on Hocking river *pop* 16,470 **3** *or* NGk **Athí·nai** \'ä-‚thē-(‚)nē\ *or anc* **Athe·nae** \ə-'thē-(‚)nē\ city ✳ of Greece near Saronic Gulf *pop* (with suburbs) 1,850,000 — **Athe·nian** \ə-'thē-nē-ən, -nyən\ *adj or n*

Athos \'ath-‚äs, 'ā-‚thäs\ mountain NE Greece at E end of Acte

peninsula; site of a number of monasteries comprising **Mount Athos** (autonomous area)

Ati·tlán \ˌät-ē-ˈtlän\ lake 24 *m* long SW Guatemala at 4700 *ft* altitude occupying a crater 1000 *ft* deep N of Atitlán Volcano

At·ka \ˈat-kə, ˈät-\ island SW Alaska in Andreanof group of the Aleutians

At·lan·ta \ət-ˈlant-ə, at-\ city ✳ of Ga. *pop* 487,455

At·lan·tic \ət-ˈlant-ik, at-\ ocean separating No. & So. America from Europe & Africa *area* 41,105,000

Atlantic City city SE N.J. on Atlantic coast *pop* 59,544

At·las \ˈat-ləs\ mountains NW Africa extending from SW Morocco to NE Tunisia; its highest peaks (over 13,000 *ft*) are in the **Grand,** or **High, Atlas** in SW cen Morocco

Atrek \ə-ˈtrek\ or **Atrak** \-ˈtrak\ river 300 *m* NE Iran flowing into the Caspian on U.S.S.R. border

Atropatene — see AZERBAIJAN

At·ta·wa·pis·kat \ˌat-ə-wə-ˈpis-kət\ river 465 *m* Canada in N Ont. flowing E into James Bay

At·ti·ca \ˈat-i-kə\ region E Greece, chief city Athens; a state of ancient Greece

At·tle·boro \ˈat-ᵊl-ˌbər-ə, -ˌbə-rə\ city SE Mass. *pop* 27,118

At·tu \ˈat-(ˌ)ü\ island SW Alaska, most westerly of the Aleutians, in Near group

Aube \ˈōb\ river 125 *m* N cen France flowing into the Seine

Au·ber·vil·liers \ˌō-bər-ˌvēl-ˈyā\ commune N France NNE of Paris *pop* 58,740

Au·burn \ˈȯ-bərn\ **1** city E Ala. *pop* 16,261 **2** city SW Me. *pop* 24,449 **3** city cen N.Y. *pop* 35,249

Auch \ˈōsh, ˈȯsh\ city SW France W of Toulouse *pop* 15,253

Auck·land \ˈȯ-klənd\ **1** provincial district N New Zealand on North I. *area* 25,420, *pop* 950,609 **2** city & port, its ✳ *pop* 547,900

Audenarde — see OUDENAARDE

Au·ghra·bies Falls \ō-ˌgräb-ēz-\ or **King George's Falls** waterfall 480 *ft* Republic of So. Africa in Orange river in NW Cape Province

Au·ghrim or **Aghrim** \ˈȯ-grəm\ town W Ireland in E Galway

Augs·burg \ˈȯgz-ˌbərg, ˈauks-ˌbu̇(ə)rk\ city W Germany in Bavaria on Lech river *pop* 205,000

Au·gus·ta \ȯ-ˈgəs-tə, ə-\ **1** city E Ga. on Savannah river *pop* 70,626 **2** city ✳ of Me. on the Kennebec *pop* 21,680

Au·lis \ˈȯ-ləs\ harbor E Greece in Boeotia on Evripos strait

Au·nis \ō-ˈnēs\ former province W France on Gironde estuary & Bay of Biscay ✳ La Rochelle

Au·rang·a·bad \au̇-ˈrəŋ-gə-ˌbäd\ city W India in cen Maharashtra ENE of Bombay *pop* 66,600

Au·rès \ȯ-ˈres\ massif ab 7600 *ft* NE Algeria in Saharan Atlas

Au·ri·gnac \ˌȯ-rēn-ˈyak\ village SW France SW of Toulouse

Au·ril·lac \ˌȯ-rē-ˈ(y)ak, -ˈ(y)ak\ city S cen France NW of Cahors *pop* 22,224

Au·ro·ra \ə-ˈrōr-ə, ȯ-, -ˈrȯr-\ **1** city NE cen Colo. *pop* 48,548 **2** city NE Ill. *pop* 63,715

Au·sa·ble \ȯ-ˈsā-bəl\ river 20 *m* NE N.Y. flowing E into Lake Champlain through **Ausable Chasm** (gorge 2 *m* long)

Auschwitz — see OSWIECIM

Aus·ter·litz \ˈȯ-stər-ˌlits, ˈau̇-\ or Czech **Slav·kov** \ˈsläf-ˌkȯf, ˈsläv-ˌkȯv\ town Czechoslovakia ESE of Brno

Aus·tin \ˈȯs-tən, ˈäs-\ **1** city S Minn. *pop* 27,908 **2** city ✳ of Tex. on the Colorado *pop* 186,545

Austral — see TUBUAÏ

Aus·tral·asia \ˌȯs-trə-ˈlā-zhə, ˌäs-, -ˈlā-shə\ **1** Australia, Tasmania, New Zealand, & Melanesia **2** the Brit. Commonwealth nations of the SW Pacific: Australia, New Zealand, Fiji, & Western Samoa — **Aus·tral·asian** \-zhən, -shən\ *adj or n*

Aus·tra·lia \ȯ-ˈstrāl-yə, ä-\ **1** continent of the eastern hemisphere SE of Asia & S of the equator *area* 2,948,366 **2** or **Commonwealth of Australia** dominion of the British Commonwealth of Nations including the continent of Australia & the island of Tasmania ✳ Canberra *area* 2,967,909, *pop* (1965 est.) 11,359,510 — **Aus·tra·lian** \-yən\ *adj or n*

Australian Alps mountain range SE Australia in E Victoria & SE New So. Wales forming S end of Great Dividing range

Australian Capital Territory or formerly **Federal Capital Territory** district SE Australia including two areas, one around Canberra & the other on Jervis Bay, surrounded by New So. Wales *area* 939, *pop* 44,780

Aus·tra·sia or **Os·tra·sia** \ȯ-ˈstrā-zhə, ä-, -shə\ the E dominions of the Merovingian Franks extending from Meuse river to Bohemian Forest — **Aus·tra·sian** \-zhən, -shən\ *adj or n*

Aus·tria \ˈȯs-trē-ə, ˈäs-\ or G **Ös·ter·reich** \ˈœ̄-stə(r)-ˌrīk\ country cen Europe in E & N of E Alps with the Danube crossing it in N; a republic *area* 32,375, *pop* 7,073,807 — **Aus·tri·an** \-ən\ *adj or n*

Austria–Hun·ga·ry \-ˈhəŋ-gə-rē\ dual monarchy 1867–1918 cen Europe including Austria, Hungary, Czechoslovakia, Bukovina & Transylvania in Romania, NW half of Yugoslavia, Galicia in Poland, & NE Italy — **Aus·tro-Hun·gar·i·an** *adj or n* \ˈȯs-(ˌ)trō-ˌhəŋ-ˈgar-ē-ən, ä-\

Aus·tro·ne·sia \ˌȯs-trə-ˈnē-zhə, ˌäs-, -ˈnē-shə\ **1** the islands of the S Pacific **2** area extending from Madagascar through the Malay peninsula & archipelago to Hawaii & Easter I.

Au·teuil \ō-ˈtə(r), -ˈtœi\ district in W Paris, France

Au·vergne \ō-ˈve(ə)rn, -ˈvərn\ **1** region & former province S cen France ✳ Clermont (now Clermont-Ferrand) **2** mountains S cen France; highest in the Massif Central — see SANCY (Puy de)

Aux Cayes — see CAYES

Aux Sources, Mont \ˌmōⁿ-ˌtō-ˈsu̇(ə)rs\ mountain 10,822 *ft* N Basutoland in Drakensberg mountains on Natal border

Au·yán-te·puí \ˌau̇-ˌyän-təp-ˈwē\ or **Devil Mountain** plateau ab 20 *m* long SE Venezuela E of Caroní river — see ANGEL FALLS

Av·a·lon \ˈav-ə-ˌlän\ **1** peninsula Canada in SE Nfld. **2** or **Isle of Avalon** district, orig. an island, SW England in Somerset including Glastonbury; considered by some to be the Avalon of Arthurian legend

Ave·bury \ˈāv-b(ə-)rē, US also -ˌber-ē\ village S England in

Wiltshire E of Bristol

Ave·lla·ne·da \ˌä-və-zhə-ˈnā-thə\ city E Argentina on Río de la Plata, E suburb of Buenos Aires *pop* 278,621

Avenches \a-ˈvä°sh\ or anc **Aven·ti·cum** \ə-ˈvent-i-kəm\ town W Switzerland in Vaud canton ✳ of ancient Helvetia

Av·en·tine \ˈav-ən-ˌtīn, -ˌtēn\ hill in Rome, Italy, one of seven (including also the Caelian, Capitoline, Esquiline, Palatine, Quirinal, & Viminal) on which the ancient city was built

Aver·nus \ə-ˈvər-nəs\ or It **Aver·no** \ä-ˈve(ə)r-(ˌ)nō\ lake S Italy in crater of extinct volcano W of Naples

Avi·gnon \ˌa-(ˌ)vēn-ˈyōⁿ\ city SE France near confluence of Rhone & Durance rivers *pop* 62,768

Ávi·la \ˈäv-i-lə\ **1** province cen Spain *area* 3042, *pop* 256,422 **2** city, its ✳, WNW of Madrid *pop* 26,533

Avlona — see VLONE

Avon \ˈā-vən, ˈav-ən, US also ˈā-ˌvän\ **1** river 96 *m*, cen England rising in Northamptonshire & flowing WSW past Stratford on Avon into the Severn at Tewkesbury **2** river 65 *m* S England rising near Devizes in Wiltshire & flowing S into English channel **3** river 62 *m* SW England rising in Gloucestershire & flowing S & W through city of Bristol into Bristol channel at Avonmouth **4** \ˈav-ən\ — see SWAN

Avranches \av-ˈrä°sh\ town NW France in SW Normandy on inlet of Gulf of St-Malo

Awa·ji \ə-ˈwäj-ē\ island Japan S of Honshu & NE of Shikoku I.

Awash — see HAWASH

Ax·el Hei·berg \ˌak-səl-ˈhī-ˌbərg\ island N Canada in the Sverdrup islands W of Ellesmere I. *area* 15,779

Axum — see AKSUM — **Ax·um·ite** \ˈak-sə-ˌmīt\ *adj or n*

Aya·cu·cho \ˌī-ə-ˈkü-(ˌ)chō\ city S Peru SE of Lima *pop* 21,531

Ay·din \ˈī-ˌdin\ city SW Turkey SE of Izmir *pop* 35,671

Ayers Rock \ˈa(ə)rz-, ˈe(ə)rz-\ monolith cen Australia in SW Northern Territory; 1½ *m* long, 1143 *ft* high

Ayles·bury \ˈā(ə)lz-b(ə-)rē, US also -ˌber-ē\ municipal borough SE cen England ✳ of Buckinghamshire *pop* 21,054

Ayodhya — see AJODHYA

Ayr \ˈa(ə)r, ˈe(ə)r\ **1** or **Ayr·shire** \-ˌshər\ county SW Scotland *area* 1132, *pop* 321,184 **2** burgh & port, its ✳ *pop* 43,011

Ayut·tha·ya or **Ayu·dhya** \ä-ˈyùt-ə-yə\ city S Thailand N of Bangkok on an island in the lower Chao Phraya *pop* 25,000

Azer·bai·dzhan or **Azer·bai·jan** or **Azer·bai·dzhan Republic** \ˌaz-ər-ˌbī-ˈjän-, ˌäz-\ constituent republic of the U.S.S.R. in E Transcaucasia bordering on Caspian sea ✳ Baku *area* 33,200, *pop* 3,800,000

Azerbaijan or anc **At·ro·pa·te·ne** or **Me·dia Atropatene** \ˈmēd-ē-ə-ˌa-trō-pə-ˈtē-nē\ region NW Iran; chief city Tabriz

Azin·court \ˌa-za°-ˈkür\ or earlier **Agin·court** \ˈaj-ən-ˌkō(ə)rt, -kō(ə)rt; ˈäzh-ən-ˌkü,(ə)r\ village N France WNW of Arras

Azores \ˈā-ˌzō(ə)rz, -ˌzȯ(ə)rz, ə-\ or Port **Aço·res** \ə-ˈsōr-ēsh\ islands N Atlantic belonging to Portugal & lying ab 800 *m* off coast of Portugal; chief town Ponta Delgada *area* 888, *pop* 327,480 — **Azor·e·an** or **Azor·i·an** \ā-ˈzōr-ē-ən, -ˈzȯr-, ə-\ *adj or n*

Azov, Sea of \ˈaz-ȯf, ˈäz-, -ȯv\ gulf of the Black sea E of Crimea connected with the Black sea by the Kerch strait *area* 14,520

Az·tec Ruins National Monument \ˌaz-ˌtek-\ reservation NW N. Mex. NE of Farmington; site of a prehistoric pueblo

Azu·sa \ə-ˈzü-sə\ city SW Calif. ENE of Los Angeles *pop* 20,497

Baal·bek \ˈbā-əl-ˌbek, ˈbäl-ˌbek\ town E Lebanon N of Damascus on site of ancient city of **He·li·op·o·lis** \ˌhē-lē-ˈäp-(ə-)ləs\

Ba·bar \ˈbäb-ˌär\ islands Indonesia ENE of Timor

Bab el Man·deb \ˌbab-ˌel-ˈman-ˌdeb\ strait between SW Arabia & Africa connecting Red sea & Gulf of Aden

Ba·bel·thu·ap \ˌbäb-əl-ˈtü-ˌäp\ or **Pa·lau** \pə-ˈlau̇\ or **Pe·lew** \pə-ˈlü\ island W Pacific, chief of the Palau islands *area* 143

Ba·bu·yan \ˌbäb-(ˌ)yän\ **1** islands N Philippines N of Luzon *area* 225 **2** chief island of the group

Bab·y·lon \ˈbab-ə-lən, -ˌlän\ ancient city ✳ of Babylonia; its site ab 50 *m* S of Baghdad near the Euphrates

Bab·y·lo·nia \ˌbab-ə-ˈlō-nyə, -nē-ə\ ancient country in valley of lower Euphrates & Tigris rivers ✳ Babylon

Back \ˈbak\ river 605 *m* Canada in NE Northwest Territories flowing ENE into Arctic ocean

Ba·co·lod \ba-ˈkō-ˌlȯd\ city Philippines on Negros I. *pop* 101,432

Bactra — see BALKH

Bac·tria \ˈbak-trē-ə\ or **Bac·tri·a·na** \ˌbak-trē-ˈan-ə, -ˈän-ə, -ˈā-nə\ ancient country SW Asia between Hindu Kush & Oxus river ✳ Bactra — see BALKH — **Bac·tri·an** \ˈbak-trē-ən\ *adj or n*

Ba·da·joz \ˌbäth-ə-ˈhōs, -ˈhōz\ **1** province SW Spain in valley of Guadiana river *area* 8451, *pop* 875,735 **2** city, its ✳ *pop* 102,464

Ba·da·lo·na \ˌbäth-ə-ˈlō-nə\ city & port NE Spain on the Mediterranean NE of Barcelona *pop* 82,845

Bad Ems — see EMS

Ba·den \ˈbäd-ᵊn\ **1** region SW Germany bordering on Switzerland & France; formerly a grand duchy (1805–1918), a state of the Weimar republic (1918–33), an administrative division of the Third Reich (1933–49), & a state of the Bonn Republic (1949–51) ✳ Karlsruhe — see BADEN-WÜRTTEMBERG **2** BADEN-BADEN

Ba·den–Ba·den \ˌbäd-ᵊn-ˈbäd-ᵊn\ city & spa SW Germany in Baden-Württemberg SSW of Karlsruhe *pop* 40,200

Ba·den–Würt·tem·berg \ˌbäd-ᵊn-ˈwərt-əm-ˌbərg, -ˈwùrt-; -ˈvirt-əm-ˌbe(ə)rk\ state W Germany W of Bavaria; formed 1951 from former Baden, Württemberg-Baden, & Württemberg-Hohenzollern states ✳ Stuttgart *area* 13,800, *pop* 7,726,900

Bad Gastein — see GASTEIN

Bad Godesberg — see GODESBERG

Badlands National Monument reservation SW S. Dak. E of Black hills comprising an area of badlands topography *area* 156

Bad Mergentheim — see MERGENTHEIM

Baf·fin \ˈbaf-ən\ island NE Canada N of Hudson strait; largest in Arctic archipelago *area* 183,810

Baffin Bay inlet of the Atlantic between W Greenland & E Baffin I.

Baffin Land Baffin I. — a former name

Ba·fing \bə-'faŋ\ river 350 *m* W Africa in W Mali & Guinea; the upper course of the Senegal

Bagh·dad *or* **Bag·dad** \'bag-,dad\ city ✻ of Iraq on the middle Tigris *pop* 730,549 — **Bagh·dadi** \bag-'dad-ē\ *n*

Ba·guio \'bäg-ē-,ō\ city, summer ✻ of the Philippines, in NW *cen* Luzon *pop* 50,331

Ba·ha·ma \bə-'häm-ə, *by outsiders also* -'hā-mə\ islands in the Atlantic SE of Florida; a British self-governing colony ✻ Nassau *area* 4404, *pop* 136,229 — see TURKS AND CAICOS — **Ba·ha·mi·an** \bə-'hā-mē-ən, -'häm-ē-\ *adj or n*

Ba·ha·wal·pur \bə-'hä-wəl-,pù(ə)r\ region W Pakistan in SW Punjab in Thar desert; until 1947 a princely state of India

Bahia, 1 — see BAÍA   **2** — see SALVADOR

Ba·hía Blan·ca \bä-,hē-ə-'bläŋ-kə, -'bläŋ-\ city & port E Argentina 350 *m* SW of Buenos Aires *pop* 112,597

Bahnasa, El — see OXYRHYNCHUS

Bah·rein *or* **Bah·rain** \bä-'rān\ **1** islands in Persian gulf off coast of Arabia; a nominally independent sultanate ✻ Manama (on Bahrein I.) *area* 213, *pop* 120,000   **2** island, largest of the group, 27 *m* long

Bahr el Gha·zal \,bär,el-gä-'zal\ river *ab* 500 *m* SW Sudan flowing E to unite at Lake No with the **Bahr el Je·bel** \'jeb-əl\ forming the White Nile

Ba·ía *or* **Ba·hía** \bä-'ē-ə\ **1** state E Brazil ✻ Salvador *area* 215,329, *pop* 4,834,575   **2** — see SALVADOR

Bai·kal *or* **Bay·kal** \bī-'kól, -'kal\ lake U.S.S.R. in S Soviet Russia, Asia, in mountains N of Mongolia; 5712 *ft* deep, *ab* 375 *m* long *area* 13,200

Baile Atha Cliath — see DUBLIN

Baja California — see LOWER CALIFORNIA

Bakan — see SHIMONOSEKI

Ba·ker \'bā-kər\ island (atoll) *cen* Pacific near equator at 176°31′W; belongs to U.S.

Baker, Mount mountain 10,750 *ft* NW Wash. in Cascade range E of Bellingham

Baker Lake — see DUBAWNT

Ba·kers·field \'bā-kərz-,fēld\ city S Calif. at SE end of San Joaquin valley *pop* 56,848

Bakhmut — see ARTEMOVSK

Ba·ku \bä-'kü\ city U.S.S.R. ✻ of Azerbaidzhan Republic on W shore of Caspian sea *pop* 968,000

Ba·kwan·ga \bə-'kwäŋ-gə\ city S Congo in S Kasai E of Luluabourg in diamond field *pop* 18,900

Ba·la·kla·va *or* **Ba·la·cla·va** \,bal-ə-'klav-ə, -'kläv-; ,bäl-ə-'kläv-ə\ town & port U.S.S.R. in S Soviet Russia, Europe, in Crimea on Black sea SE of Sevastopol

Bal·a·ton \'bal-ə-,tän, 'ból-ə-,tōn\ *or* G **Plat·ten·see** \'plät-ᵊn-,zā\ lake W Hungary; largest in *cen* Europe *area* 266

Bal·boa Heights \(,)bal-,bō-ə-\ town Panama Canal Zone, suburb of Balboa, at Pacific entrance to the canal adjacent to Panama City; administrative center of Canal Zone

Bal·dwin \'ból-dwən\ **1** urban area SE N.Y. on S shore of Long I. *pop* 30,204   **2** borough SW Pa. S of Pittsburgh *pop* 24,489

Baldwin Park city SW Calif. W of Los Angeles *pop* 33,951

Bâle — see BASEL

Bal·e·ar·es \,bal-ē-'ar-ēz\ **1** the Balearic islands   **2** province E Spain comprising the Balearic islands ✻ Palma *area* 1936, *pop* 445,994

Bal·e·ar·ic \,bal-ē-'ar-ik\ islands E Spain in the W Mediterranean — see BALEARES, IVIZA, MAJORCA, MINORCA

Ba·li \'bäl-ē, 'bal-\ island Indonesia off E end of Java; chief town Singaradja *area* 2147, *pop* 1,101,400 — **Ba·li·nese** \,bäl-i-'nēz, -bal-, -'nes\ *adj or n*

Ba·li·ke·sir \,bäl-ē-ke-'si(ə)r\ city NW Turkey in Asia SW of Bursa *pop* 61,012

Ba·lik·pa·pan \,bäl-ik-'päp-,än\ city & port Indonesia on SE Borneo on inlet of Makassar strait *pop* 29,843

Bal·kan \'ból-kən\ **1** mountain range *cen* Bulgaria extending from Yugoslavia border to Black sea; highest point Botev Peak 7795 *ft*   **2** peninsula SE Europe between Adriatic & Ionian seas on W & Aegean & Black seas on E

Balkan States *or* **Bal·kans** \'ból-kənz\ the countries occupying the Balkan peninsula: Yugoslavia, Romania, Bulgaria, Albania, Greece, & Turkey in Europe

Bal·kar·ia \ból-'kar-ē-ə, bal-, -'ker-\ mountain region U.S.S.R. in S Soviet Russia, Europe, in S Kabardinian Republic

Balkh \'bälk\ **1** district N Afghanistan corresponding closely to ancient Bactria   **2** *or anc* **Bac·tra** \'bak-trə\ town N Afghanistan ✻ of ancient Bactria

Bal·khash *or* **Bal·kash** \bal-'kash, bäl-'käsh\ lake 440 *m* long U.S.S.R. in Soviet Central Asia in SE Kazakh Republic *area* 6700

Bal·la·rat \'bal-ə-,rat\ city SE Australia in *cen* Victoria WNW of Melbourne *pop* (with suburbs) 49,500

Bal·sas \'ból-səs, 'bäl-\ river 426 *m*, *cen* Mexico flowing from Tlaxcala to the Pacific on border between Michoacán & Guerrero

Bal·tic \'ból-tik\ sea arm of the Atlantic N Europe enclosed by Denmark & the Scandinavian peninsula *area ab* 160,000

Bal·ti·more \'ból-tə-,mō(ə)r, -,mó(ə)r, -mər\ city & port N *cen* Md. on Patapsco river estuary near Chesapeake Bay *pop* 939,024 — **Bal·ti·mor·ean** \,ból-tə-'mōr-ē-ən, -'mór-\ *n*

Bal·ti·stan \,ból-tə-'stan\ region N Kashmir; the W section of Ladakh district

Ba·lu·chi·stan \bə-,lü-chə-'stan\ arid region S Asia bordering on Arabian sea in West Pakistan & SE Iran & SW of Afghanistan

Ba·ma·ko \'bam-ə-,kō\ city ✻ of Mali on the Niger *pop* 32,800

Bam·berg \'bam-bərg, 'bäm-,be(ə)rk\ city W Germany in N Bavaria NNW of Nuremberg *pop* 73,600

Ba·na·hao \bə-'nä-,haù\ extinct volcano 7141 *ft* Philippines on S Luzon *ab* 50 *m* W of Manila

Ba·nana river \bə-,nan-ə-\ lagoon E Fla. between Canaveral peninsula & Merritt I.

Ba·na·ras *or* **Be·na·res** \bə-'när-əs, -ēz\ *or* **Va·ra·na·si** \və-'rän-ə-(,)sē\ city N India in SE Uttar Pradesh *pop* 355,800

Ba·nat \bə-'nät, 'bän-,ät\ region SE *cen* Europe in Danube basin between Tisza & Mures rivers & the Transylvanian Alps; once entirely in Hungary, divided 1919 between Yugoslavia & Romania

Ban·da \'ban-də\ **1** islands Indonesia in Moluccas S of Ceram *area* 16   **2** sea E Malay archipelago SE of Celebes, S of the Moluccas, W of Aru islands, & NE of Timor

Ban·da Ori·en·tal \,bän-də-,ör-ē-,en-'täl, -,ór-\ URUGUAY — a former name, used with reference to its position on E shore of

Uruguay river

Bandar — see MASULIPATNAM

Ban·dar Shah·pur \ban-,där-shə-'pù(ə)r\ town & port SW Iran at head of Persian gulf ENE of Abadan

Ban·de·lier National Monument \,ban-də-,li(ə)r\ reservation N *cen* N. Mex. W of Santa Fe containing cliff-dweller ruins *area* 42

Ban·djar·ma·sin *or* **Ban·jer·ma·sin** \,ban-jər-'mäs-ᵊn, ,bän-\ city Indonesia in S Borneo on Martapura river *pop* 176,800

Ban·dol \bäⁿ-dól\ town SE France W of Toulon

Ban·dung *or* D **Ban·doeng** \,bän-,dùŋ, 'ban-, -,dəŋ\ city Indonesia in W Java SE of Djakarta *pop* 839,200

Banff \'bam(p)f\ **1** *or* **Banff·shire** \-,shi(ə)r, -shər\ county NE Scotland *area* 630, *pop* 50,148   **2** burgh, its ✻

Banff National Park reservation W Canada in E Alta. on E slopes of Rocky mountains *area* 2585

Ban·ga·lore \'baŋ-gə-,lō(ə)r, -,ló(ə)r\ city S India W of Madras ✻ of Mysore *pop* 778,000

Bang·ka *or* **Ban·ka** \'baŋ-kə\ island, Indonesia off SE Sumatra; chief town Pangkalpinang *area* 4609, *pop* 205,400

Bang·kok \'baŋ-,käk, baŋ-'\ city & port ✻ of Thailand on the Chao Phraya *ab* 20 *m* above its mouth *pop* 1,328,228

Ban·gor \'ban-,gò(ə)r & 'baŋ-,gò(ə)r (*these usual for* 1), 'baŋ-gər\ **1** city E *cen* Me. on Penobscot river *pop* 38,912   **2** municipal borough SE Northern Ireland in County Down *pop* 20,615   **3** municipal borough & city NW Wales in Caernarvonshire

Ban·gui \bäŋ-'gē\ city ✻ of Central African Republic *pop* 82,500

Bang·we·u·lu \,baŋ-wē-ü-(,)lü\ lake *ab* 50 *m* long N Northern Rhodesia in swamp region; its area fluctuates seasonally; drains into the Luapula, a headstream of the Congo

Banks \'baŋ(k)s\ **1** island N Canada at W end of Canadian Arctic archipelago *area* 23,230   **2** islands SW Pacific N of New Hebrides

Ban·nock·burn \'ban-ək-,bərn, ,ban-ək-'\ town *cen* Scotland in Stirlingshire SSE of Stirling

Ban·tam \'bant-əm\ village Indonesia in NW corner of Java; once ✻ of Sultanate of Bantam

Ban·try Bay \,ban-trē-\ bay SW Ireland in SW County Cork

Ba·paume \bä-'pōm\ town N France S of Arras

Ba·ra·cal·do \,bar-ə-'käl-(,)dō, ,bär-\ commune N Spain W of Bilbao *pop* 73,308

Ba·ra·coa \,bar-ə-'kō-ə, ,bär-\ town & port E Cuba on N coast near E tip of island

Bar·a·nof \'bar-ə-,nòf, bə-'rän-əf\ island SE Alaska in Alexander archipelago S of Chicagof I. *area ab* 1600

Bar·a·tar·ia Bay \,bar-ə-,tar-ē-ə, -,ter-\ lagoon SE La. on coast NW of delta of the Mississippi

Bar·ba·dos *or* **Bar·ba·does** \bär-'bād-(,)ōz, -əz\ island Brit. West Indies in Lesser Antilles E of the Windward group; a dominion of the Brit. Commonwealth since 1966 ✻ Bridgetown *area* 166, *pop* 246,452 — **Bar·ba·di·an** \-'bād-ē-ən\ *adj or n*

Bar·ba·ry \'bär-b(ə-)rē\ region N Africa on coast extending from Egyptian border to the Atlantic & including the former **Barbary States** (Morocco, Algiers, Tunis, & Tripoli) — a former name

Bar·bers Point \,bär-bərz-\ *or* **Ka·la·eloa Point** \kə-,lä-(,)ā-,lō-ə-\ cape Hawaii at SW corner of Oahu W of Pearl Harbor

Bar·ber·ton \'bär-bərt-ᵊn\ city NE Ohio SW of Akron *pop* 33,805

Bar·bi·zon \,bär-bə-'zōⁿ\ village N France SSE of Paris near Forest of Fontainebleau

Bar·bu·da \bär-'büd-ə\ island Brit. West Indies in the Leewards N of Antigua, to which it is a dependency *area* 62

Bar·ca \'bär-kə\ *or It* **Bar·ce** \-,chä\ town Libya in NW Cyrenaica

Bar·ce·lo·na \,bär-sə-'lō-nə\ **1** province NE Spain in Catalonia on the Mediterranean *area* 2968, *pop* 2,817,857   **2** city & port, its ✻ *pop* 1,538,710   **3** city NE Venezuela near coast *pop* 38,000

Bar·dia \'bärd-ē-ə\ town & port Libya in NE Cyrenaica

Ba·reil·ly *or* **Ba·re·li** \bə-'rā-lē\ **1** city N India in NW *cen* Uttar Pradesh ESE of Delhi *pop* 208,100   **2** — see ROHILKHAND

Ba·rents \'bar-ən(t)s, 'bär-\ sea comprising the part of the Arctic ocean between Spitsbergen & Novaya Zemlya

Ba·ri \'bär-ē\ *or anc* **Bar·i·um** \'bar-ē-əm, 'ber-\ commune & port SE Italy ✻ of Apulia on the Adriatic *pop* 273,801

Ba·ri·lo·che *or* **San Car·los de Bariloche** \san-,kär-ləs-də-,bar-ə-'lō-ə\ town SW Argentina on Lake Nahuel Huapí

Bar·i·sal \,bär-ə-,sól\ city E Pakistan in East Bengal in Ganges delta *pop* 61,300

Bar·king \'bär-kiŋ\ *or* **Barking Town** urban district SE England in Essex; E suburb of London *pop* 78,197

Bar·let·ta \bär-'let-ə\ commune & port SE Italy in Apulia on the Adriatic *pop* 57,386

Bar·na·ul \,bär-nə-'ül\ city U.S.S.R. in Soviet Russia, Asia, on the Ob ✻ of Altai Territory *pop* 320,000

Bar·ne·gat Bay \,bär-ni-,gat, -gət\ inlet of the Atlantic E N. J.

Bar·net \'bär-nət\ urban district SE England in Hertfordshire N of London *pop* 25,017

Barns·ley \'bärnz-lē\ county borough N England in West Riding, Yorkshire *pop* 75,625

Ba·ro·da \bə-'rōd-ə\ **1** former state W India near head of Gulf of Cambay ✻ Baroda *area* 8176   **2** city W India in SE Gujarat SE of Ahmadabad *pop* 211,400

Ba·rot·se·land \bə-'rät-sē-,land\ province W Zambia ✻ Mongu Lealui; a protectorate

Bar·qui·si·me·to \,bär-kə-sə-'māt-(,)ō\ city NW Venezuela *pop* 105,108

Bar·ran·qui·lla \,bär-ən-'kē-(y)ə\ city & port N Colombia on the Magdalena *pop* 411,330

Barren Grounds treeless plains N Canada W of Hudson Bay

Bar·rie \'bar-ē\ town Canada in S Ont. *pop* 16,851

Bar·row \'bar-(,)ō\ *or* **Barrow-in-Fur·ness** \,bar-ə-wən-'fər-nəs\ county borough NW England in NW Lancashire *pop* 67,473

Barrow, Point most northerly point of Alaska & of the U.S., at *ab* 71°25′N, 156°30′W

Bar·tles·ville \'bärt-ᵊlz-,vil\ city NE Okla. *pop* 27,893

Ba·sel \'bäz-əl\ *or F* **Bâle** *or older* **Basle** \'bäl\ **1** canton NW Switzerland *area* 179, *pop* 304,000   **2** city, its ✻ & ✻ of **Ba·sel·Stadt** \'bäz-əl-,shtät\ (half canton) *pop* 203,300

Ba·shan \'bā-shən\ region in ancient Palestine E & NE of Sea of Galilee

Ba·shi Channel \,bäsh-ē-\ strait between Philippines & Formosa

Bash·kir·ia \bash-'kir-ē-ə\ *or* **Bash·kir Republic** \,bash-,ki(ə)r-\ autonomous republic U.S.S.R. in E Soviet Russia, Europe, in S Ural mountains ✻ Ufa *area* 54,233, *pop* 3,342,000

Ba·si·lan \bə-'sē-,län\ island Philippines, chief of Basilan islands, SW of Mindanao; chief town Isabela *area* 495, *pop* 57,561

Ba·si·li·ca·ta \bə-,sil-ə-'kät-ə\ *or formerly* **Lu·ca·nia** \lü-'kān-yə, -'kän-\ region S Italy on Gulf of Taranto

Basin ranges — see GREAT BASIN

Basque Provinces \'bask\ region N Spain on Bay of Biscay including provinces of Álava, Guipúzcoa, & Vizcaya

Bas·ra \'bäs-rə, 'bəs-, 'bäz-, 'bəz-, 'baz-\ *or* **Bus·ra** \'bäs-rə, 'bəs-\ city & port S Iraq on Shatt-al-Arab *pop* 159,355

Bass \'bas\ strait separating Tasmania & continent of Australia

Bas·sein \bə-'sān\ **1** city S Burma W of Rangoon *pop* 77,905 **2** town & port W India in Maharashtra N of Bombay

Basse·terre \bas-'te(ə)r, bäs-\ town & port Brit. West Indies ✳ of St. Kitts I. & of St. Kitts-Nevis-Anguilla State

Basse-Terre \bas-'te(ə)r, bäs-\ **1** island French West Indies constituting the W part of Guadeloupe *area* 364, *pop* 99,736 **2** town & port ✳ of Guadeloupe

Bas·tia \'bas-tē-ə, 'bäs-\ city & port France on NE coast of Corsica *pop* 52,208

Bas·togne \ba-'stōn\ town SE Belgium in the Ardennes

Bas·trop \'bas-trəp\ city NE La. *pop* 15,193

Ba·su·to·land \bə-'süt-ō-,land\ former Brit. territory S Africa NE of Drakensberg mountains surrounded by Republic of o. Africa; since 1966 the independent constitutional monarchy of **Le·so·tho** \lə-'sō-(,)tō ✳ Maseru *area* 11,716, *pop* 975,000

Ba·taan \bə-'tan, -'tän\ peninsula Philippines in W Luzon on W side of Manila Bay

Ba·ta·via \bə-'tā-vē-ə\ **1** city W N.Y. SW of Rochester *pop* 18,210 **2** *or* **Batavian Republic** Netherlands under the French (1795–1806) **3** — see DJAKARTA — **Ba·ta·vi·an** \-vē-ən\ *adj & n*

Bath \'bath, 'bäth\ city & county borough SW England in Somerset ESE of Bristol *pop* 79,294

Bath·urst \'bath-(,)ərst\ **1** city & port ✳ of Gambia on Island of St. Mary in Gambia river *pop* 19,602 **2** island N Canada in Parry group *area* 6041

Bat·on Rouge \,bat-ᵊn-'rüzh\ city ✳ of La. on the Mississippi *pop* 152,419

Bat·ter·sea \'bat-ər-sē\ metropolitan borough SW London, England, on S bank of the Thames *pop* 117,130

Bat·tle Creek \'bat-ᵊl-,krēk\ city S Mich. *pop* 44,169

Ba·tum \bə-'tüm\ *or* **Ba·tu·mi** \-'tü-mē\ city & port U.S.S.R. in SW Georgia on Black sea ✳ of Adzhar Republic *pop* 82,000

Baut·zen \'baùt-sən\ city E Germany on Spree river ENE of Dresden *pop* 42,000

Ba·var·ia \bə-'ver-ē-ə, -'var-\ *or G* **Bay·ern** \'bī-(ə)rn\ state S Germany bordering on Austria & Czechoslovakia ✳ Munich *area* 27,232, *pop* 9,494,900

Ba·ya·món \,bī-ə-'mōn\ city NE *cen* Puerto Rico *pop* 15,109

Bay City city E Mich. at head of Saginaw Bay *pop* 53,604

Ba·yeux \bī-'ü, bä-'(y)ü, bä-'yə(r)\ town NW France WNW of Caen

Baykal — see BAIKAL

Bay·onne \bā-'ōn\ city & port NE N.J. *pop* 74,215

Ba·yonne \,bā-'ōn, bä-'yón\ city SW France on the Adour near Bay of Biscay *pop* 32,575

Bay·reuth \bī-'ròit, 'bī-,\ city W Germany in Bavaria NE of Nuremberg *pop* 60,600

Bay·town \'bā-,taùn\ city SE Tex. on Galveston Bay *pop* 28,159

Beachy Head headland SE England on coast of East Sussex

Bear \ba(ə)r, 'be(ə)r\ **1** river 75 *m* N Calif. flowing SW to Feather river **2** river 350 *m* N Utah, SW Wyo., & SE Idaho flowing to Great Salt Lake

Beard·more \'bi(ə)rd-,mō(ə)r, -,mò(ə)r\ glacier Antarctica descending to Ross Shelf Ice at *ab* 170° E

Bear Mountain mountain 1305 *ft* SE N.Y. on the Hudson

Bé·arn \bā-'är(n)\ region & former province SW France in Pyrenees SW of Gascony ✳ Pau

Be·as *or* **Bi·as** \'bē-,äs\ river 300 *m* N India in the Punjab flowing to the Sutlej

Beau·fort \'bō-fərt\ sea comprising the part of the Arctic ocean NE of Alaska & NW of Canada

Beau·mar·is \bō-'mar-əs, byü-\ municipal borough NW Wales, a ✳ of Anglesey, on E Anglesey I. on Beaumaris Bay

Beau·mont \'bō-,mänt, bō-'\ city & port SE Tex. on Neches river *pop* 119,175

Beaune \'bōn\ commune E France SSW of Dijon

Beau·so·leil \,bō-sə-'lā\ commune SE France N of Monaco

Beau·vais \bō-'vā\ commune N France NNW of Paris *pop* 18,869

Bea·ver \'bē-vər\ river 305 *m* Canada in Alta. & Sask. flowing E into the Churchill

Beaver Falls city W Pa. S of New Castle *pop* 16,240

Bea·ver·head \'bē-vər-,hed\ mountain range on Idaho-Mont. boundary; SE part of Bitterroot range of the Rockies — see GARFIELD

Bech·u·a·na·land \,bech-(ə-)'wän-ə-,land\ **1** region S Africa N of Orange river & W of Transvaal & including Kalahari desert & Okovanggo Basin **2** former Brit. protectorate in the region N of Molopo river; since 1966 the independent republic of **Bo·tswa·na** \bät-'swän-ə\ ✳ Gaberones *area ab* 222,000, *pop* 540,401 **3** *or* **British Bechuanaland** former Brit. colony in the region S of Molopo river; became part of Union of So. Africa 1895 — **Bech·u·a·na** \,bech-(ə-)'wän-ə\ *adj or n*

Beck·en·ham \'bek-(ə-)nəm\ urban district SE England in Kent, S suburb of London *pop* 74,834

Beck·ley \'bek-lē\ city S W. Va. *pop* 18,642

Bed·ford \'bed-fərd\ **1** city NE Ohio SE of Cleveland *pop* 15,223 **2** *or* **Bed·ford·shire** \-,shi(ə)r, -shər\ county SE *cen* England *area* 473, *pop* 311,844 **3** municipal borough, its ✳ *pop* 53,065

Bed·loe's \'bed-,lōz\ — see LIBERTY

Be·dzin \'ben-,jēn\ *or* **Ben·din** \'ben-,dēn\ commune S Poland in Silesia *pop* 50,721

Beer·she·ba \bi(ə)r-'shē-bə, be(ə)r-, bər-\ city S Israel in N Negeb, in Bible times marking extreme S limit of Palestine *pop* 43,158

Behar — see BIHAR

Be·his·tun \,bā-his-'tün\ *or* **Bi·su·tun** \,bē-sə-'tün\ village W Iran 22 *m* E of Kermanshah

Bei·da \'bād-ə\ town NE Libya in Cyrenaica NE of Benghazi

Bei·ra \'bā-rə\ town & port SE Mozambique *pop* 81,000

Bei·rut *or* **Bay·rut** *or* **Bey·routh** \bā-'rüt\ *or anc* **Be·ry·tus** \bə-'rīt-əs\ city & port ✳ of Lebanon *pop* 500,000

Bekaa — see BIKA

Be·kes·csa·ba \'bā-,kāsh-,chò-,bò\ city SE Hungary *pop* 50,000

Be·la·wan \bə-'lä-,wän\ town Indonesia in NE Sumatra; port for Medan

Be·la·ya \'bel-ə-yə\ river 700 *m* U.S.S.R. in Soviet Russia, Europe, rising in the S Urals & flowing S, W, & NW to the Kama

Be·lém \bə-'lem\ *or* **Pa·rá** \pə-'rä\ city N Brazil ✳ of Pará state on Pará river *pop* 225,218

Bel·fast \'bel-,fast, bel-'\ county borough & port ✳ of Northern Ireland & of County Antrim at head of **Belfast Lough** (inlet) *pop* 443,670

Bel·fort \bel-'fò(ə)r, 'bel-,\ commune E France commanding **Belfort Gap** (wide pass between Vosges & Jura mountains) *pop* 45,625

Belgian Congo *or earlier* **Congo Free State** former Belgian colony W *cen* Africa — see CONGO

Belgian East Africa — see RUANDA-URUNDI

Bel·gium \'bel-jəm\ *or F* **Bel·gique** \bel-zhēk\ *or Flem* **Bel·gië** \'bel-gē-ə\ country W Europe bordering on North sea; a constitutional monarchy ✳ Brussels *area* 11,774, *pop* 8,512,195

Bel·go·rod–Dnes·trov·ski *or* **Byel·go·rod–Dnes·trov·ski** \'b(y)el-gə-,räd-(,)nə-'stróf-skē, -'stróv-\ *or Rom* **Ce·ta·tea Al·ba** \chə-,tät-ē-ə-'äl-bə\ *or formerly* Turk & Russ **Ak·ker·man** \,äk-ər-'män\ city U.S.S.R. in SW Ukraine on the Dniester estuary *pop* 33,500

Bel·grade \'bel-,grād, -,gräd, -,grad, bel-'\ *or* **Be·o·grad** \'bā-ə-,gräd\ city ✳ of Yugoslavia & of Serbia *pop* 470,172

Bel·gra·via \bel-'grā-vē-ə\ district of W *cen* London, England

Be·li·tung \bə-'lē-təŋ\ *or* **Bil·li·ton** \'bil-ə-,tän\ island Indonesia between Bangka & Borneo *area* 1866, *pop* 73,400

Be·lize \bə-'lēz\ **1** city & port ✳ of Brit. Honduras *pop* 21,886 **2** BRITISH HONDURAS

Bell \'bel\ city SW Calif. SE of Los Angeles *pop* 19,450

Bel·la Coo·la \,bel-ə-'kü-lə\ river *ab* 60 *m* Canada in B.C. flowing W to Burke channel E of Queen Charlotte Sound

Bel·laire \be-'la(ə)r, -'le(ə)r\ city SE Tex. entirely within city of Houston *pop* 19,872

Bel·leau \be-'lō, 'be-,\ village N France NW of Château-Thierry & N of **Belleau Wood**, F **Bois de Belleau** \,bwäd-ə-be-'lō\

Belle Fourche \bel-'füsh\ river *ab* 350 *m* NE Wyo. & W S. Dak. flowing SE & E into the Cheyenne

Belle Isle, Strait of \be-'lī(ə)l\ channel between N tip of Newfoundland I. & SE Labrador

Belle·ville \'bel-,vil\ **1** city SW Ill. *pop* 37,264 **2** town NE N.J. N of Newark *pop* 35,005 **3** city Canada in SE Ont. *pop* 20,605

Bell·flow·er \'bel-,flaù(-ə)r\ city SW Calif. *pop* 45,909

Bell Gardens urban area SW Calif. *pop* 26,467

Bel·ling·ham \'bel-iŋ-,ham\ city & port NW Wash. on **Bellingham Bay** (inlet at N end of Puget Sound) *pop* 34,688

Bel·lings·hau·sen \'bel-iŋz-,haùz-ᵊn\ sea comprising a large bay of the S Pacific W of base of Antarctic peninsula

Bel·lin·zo·na \,bel-ən-'zō-nə\ commune S Switzerland E of Locarno ✳ of Ticino

Bel·lu·no \bə-'lü-(,)nō\ commune N Italy on Piave river

Bell·wood \'bel-,wùd\ village NE Ill. W of Chicago *pop* 20,729

Bel·mont \'bel-,mänt\ **1** city W Calif. SE of San Francisco *pop* 15,996 **2** town E Mass. W of Boston *pop* 28,715

Beloe More — see WHITE

Be·lo Ho·ri·zon·te \'bā-(,)lō-,hór-ə-'zänt-ē, 'bel-(,)ō-, -,här-\ city E Brazil ✳ of Minas Gerais *pop* 338,585

Be·loit \bə-'lòit\ city S Wis. on Ill. border *pop* 32,846

Be·lo·rus·sia \,bel-ō-'rəsh-ə\ *or* **Bye·lo·rus·sia** \bē-,el-ō-, ,byel-ō-\ *or* **White Russia, 1** former region E Europe N of & including the Pripet Marshes inhabited by the White Russians **2** *or* **Be·lo·rus·sian Republic** \-'rəsh-ən-\ constituent republic of the U.S.S.R. bordering on Poland, Lithuania, & Latvia ✳ Minsk *area* 88,044, *pop* 10,154,287

Belostok — see BIALYSTOK

Bel·sen *or* **Ber·gen–Belsen** \,ber-gən-'bel-zən, ,bər-\ locality NW Germany on Lüneburg Heath NW of Celle

Be·lu·kha \bə-'lü-kə\ mountain 15,157 *ft* U.S.S.R. in S Soviet Russia, Asia; highest in Altai mountain region

Benares — see BANARAS

Ben·di·go \'ben-di-,gō\ city SE Australia in N Victoria NNW of Melbourne *pop* (with suburbs) 38,100

Bene·lux \'ben-ᵊl-,əks\ customs union comprising Belgium, the Netherlands, & Luxembourg; formed 1947

Be·ne·ven·to \,ben-ə-'ven-(,)tō\ commune S Italy in Campania NE of Naples *pop* 36,800

Ben·gal \ben-'gól, beŋ-\ region E India (subcontinent) including delta of Ganges & Brahmaputra rivers; formerly a presidency & (1937–47) a province of Brit. India; divided 1947 between Pakistan & Republic of India — see EAST BENGAL, EAST PAKISTAN, WEST BENGAL — **Ben·gal·ese** \,ben-gə-'ēz, beŋ-, -'lēs\ *adj or n*

Bengal, Bay of arm of the Indian ocean between India & Ceylon on the W & Burma & Malay peninsula on the E

Ben·gha·zi *or* **Ben·ga·zi** *or* **Ben·ga·si** \ben-'gäz-ē, -'gaz-\ *or anc* **Ber·e·ni·ce** \,ber-ə-'nī-sē\ city & port NE Libya ✳ of Cyrenaica & a ✳ of Libya *pop* 70,533

Ben·guela \ben-'gel-ə\ town & port W Angola S of Luanda

Be·ni \'bā-nē\ river 1000 *m*, *cen* & N Bolivia flowing N to unite with Mamoré river forming the Madeira

Be·nin \bə-'nin, -'nēn; 'ben-ən\ **1** river *ab* 100 *m* S Nigeria W of the Niger flowing into Bight of Benin **2** *or* **Benin City** city SW Nigeria in W delta of the Niger *pop* 54,000

Benin, Bight of the N section of Gulf of Guinea W Africa off coast of SW Nigeria & Dahomey

Be·ni Su·ef \,ben-ē-sù-'äf\ city N *cen* Egypt SSW of Cairo *pop* 78,800

Ben Lomond — see LOMOND (Ben)

Ben Nevis — see NEVIS (Ben)

Be·no·ni \bə-'nō-,nī, -nē\ city NE Republic of So. Africa in S Transvaal on the Witwatersrand E of Johannesburg *pop* 139,300

Ben·ton Harbor \'bent-ᵊn-\ city SW Mich. *pop* 19,136

Be·nue \'bān-(,)wā\ *or* **Bin·ue** \'bin-(,)wā\ river 870 *m* W Africa flowing W into the Niger

Bep·pu \'bep-(,)ü\ city Japan in NE Kyushu on **Beppu Bay** (arm of Inland sea) *pop* 102,330
Be·rar \bā-'rär, bə-\ region W *cen* India; in Central Provinces & Berar 1903–47, in Madhya Pradesh 1947–56, in Bombay 1956–60, in Maharashtra since 1960; chief city Amraoti
Ber·be·ra \'bər-b(ə-)rə\ city & port N Somalia *pop* 20,000
Berch·tes·ga·den \'berk-təs-,gäd-ᵊn\ town W Germany in E Bavarian Alps S of Salzburg, Austria
Be·rea \bə-'rē-ə\ **1** city NE Ohio SW of Cleveland *pop* 16,592 **2** — see ALEPPO **3** — see VÉROIA
Be·re·zi·na \bə-'rāz-ᵊn-ə\ river 350 *m* U.S.S.R. in Belorussia flowing SE into the Dnieper
Bergama — see PERGAMUM
Ber·ga·mo \'be(ə)r-gə-,mō, 'bər-\ commune N Italy in Lombardy NE of Milan *pop* 104,968
Ber·gen, 1 \'bər-gən, 'be(ə)r-\ city & port SW Norway *pop* 114,711 **2** — see MONS
Ber·gen·field \'bər-gən-,fēld\ borough NE N.J. *pop* 27,203
Be·ring \'bi(ə)r-iŋ, 'be(ə)r-\ **1** sea arm of the N Pacific between Alaska & NE Siberia & between the Aleutians & Bering strait *area* 878,000 **2** strait *ab* 56 *m* wide separating Asia (U.S.S.R.) from No. America (Alaska)
Berke·ley \'bər-klē\ **1** city & port W Calif. on San Francisco Bay N of Oakland *pop* 111,268 **2** city E Mo. NW of St. Louis *pop* 18,676
Berk·ley \'bər-klē\ city SE Mich. NW of Detroit *pop* 23,275
Berk·shire \'bərk-,shi(ə)r, -shər\ **1** hills W Mass. W of the Connecticut — see GREYLOCK (Mount) **2** *Brit usu* 'bärk-\ county S England in Thames river basin ✻ Reading *area* 725, *pop* 402,939
Ber·lin, 1 \'bər-lən, -,lin\ city N *cen* N.H. *pop* 17,821 **2** \(,)bər-'lin\ city E *cen* Germany on Spree river, before 1945 ✻ of Germany & of Prussia; divided under postwar occupation between East & West Germany, East Berlin being made ✻ of East Germany (1949) & West Berlin a state (not yet formally incorporated) of West Germany *pop* (1950) 3,187,500 — **Ber·lin·er** \(,)bər-'lin-ər\ *n*
Ber·me·jo \bər-'mā-(,)hō\ river 1000 *m* N Argentina rising on Bolivian frontier & flowing SE into Paraguay river
Ber·mond·sey \'bər-mən(d)-zē\ metropolitan borough E *cen* London, England, on S bank of the Thames *pop* 60,661
Ber·mu·da \bər-'myüd-ə\ islands W Atlantic ESE of Cape Hatteras; a British colony ✻ Hamilton *area* 21, *pop* 43,480 — **Ber·mu·di·an** \-'myüd-ē-ən\ *or* **Ber·mu·dan** \-'myüd-ᵊn\ *adj or n*
Bern *or* **Berne** \'bərn, 'be(ə)rn\ **1** canton NW & W *cen* Switzerland *area* 2658, *pop* 801,943 **2** city, its ✻ & ✻ of Switzerland on the Aare *pop* 163,000 — **Ber·nese** \(,)bər-'nēz, -'nēs\ *adj or n*
Bern·burg \'bərn-,bərg, 'be(ə)rn-,bu̇(ə)rk\ city E Germany W of Dessau *pop* 53,367
Bernese Alps *or* **Bernese Oberland** — see OBERLAND
Ber·ni·cia \(,)bər-'nish-(ē-)ə\ Anglian kingdom of 6th century A.D. located between Tyne & Forth rivers ✻ Bamborough
Ber·ni·na \(,)bər-'nē-nə\ the S extension of Rhaetian Alps on border between Italy & Switzerland; highest peak **Piz Bernina** \,pēts-\ (highest in the Rhaetian Alps) 13,295 *ft*
Beroea, 1 — see ALEPPO **2** — see VÉROIA
Ber·ry *or* **Ber·ri** \be-'rē\ former province *cen* France S of Orléanais ✻ Bourges
Ber·thoud \'bər-thəd\ mountain pass 11,315 *ft* N Colo. in Front range WNW of Denver
Ber·wick \'ber-ik\ *or* **Ber·wick·shire** \-,shi(ə)r, -shər\ county SE Scotland ✻ Duns *area* 457, *pop* 25,060
Ber·wyn \'bər-wən\ city NE Ill. W of Chicago *pop* 54,224
Berytus — see BEIRUT
Be·san·çon \bə-'zan(t)-sən, bə-zäⁿ-sōⁿ\ city E France *pop* 65,022
Bes·kids \'bes-,kidz, be-'skēdz\ mountain ranges *cen* Europe in W Carpathians; include **West Beskids** (in Poland & Czechoslovakia W of Tatra mountains) & **East Beskids** (in NE Czechoslovakia)
Bes·sa·ra·bia \,bes-ə-'rā-bē-ə\ region SE Europe between Dniester & Prut rivers; now mostly in Moldavian Republic of the U.S.S.R. — **Bes·sa·ra·bi·an** \-bē-ən\ *adj or n*
Bes·se·mer \'bes-ə-mər\ city N *cen* Ala. *pop* 33,054
Beth·a·ny \'beth-ə-nē\ village Palestine E of Jerusalem on Mount of Olives; now in W Jordan
Beth·el \'beth-əl\ **1** borough SW Pa. S of Pittsburgh *pop* 23,650 **2** \'beth-əl, be-'thel\ ruined town Palestine in W Jordan *ab* 11 *m* N of Jerusalem
Be·thes·da \bə-'thez-də\ urban area *cen* Md. *pop* 56,527
Beth·le·hem \'beth-li-,hem, -lē-(h)əm\ **1** city E Pa. on the Lehigh *pop* 75,408 **2** town Palestine in Judea SW of Jerusalem; now in W Jordan
Beth·nal Green \,beth-nəl-\ metropolitan borough E London, England *pop* 58,374
Beth·page \beth-'pāj\ urban area SE N.Y. in *cen* Long I. *pop* (with Old Bethpage) 20,515
Beth·sa·i·da \beth-'sā-əd-ə\ ruined town Palestine on NE side of Sea of Galilee E of the Jordan; its site in SE Syria
Be·tio \'bā-chē-,ō\ islet & village W Pacific in N Gilbert islands at S end of Tarawa
Beuthen — see BYTOM
Bev·er·ley \'bev-ər-lē\ municipal borough N England ✻ of East Riding, Yorkshire *pop* 15,499
Bev·er·ly \'bev-ər-lē\ city NE Mass. *pop* 36,108
Beverly Hills city SW Calif. W of Los Angeles *pop* 30,817
Bex·ley \'bek-slē\ urban district SE England in Kent SE of London *pop* 88,767
Bey·o·glu \,bā-ə-'(g)lü\ *or formerly* **Pera** \'per-ə\ section of Istanbul, Turkey, comprising area N of the Golden Horn
Beyrouth — see BEIRUT
Bé·ziers \bāz-'yā\ city S France SW of Montpellier *pop* 64,929
Bezwada — see VIJAYAWADA
Bha·gal·pur \'bäg-əl-,pu̇(ə)r\ city E India in E Bihar on the Ganges *pop* 114,500
Bhak·ra Dam \,bäk-rə-\ hydroelectric & irrigation dam 680 *ft* high N India in Punjab NW of Bilaspur in gorge of the Sutlej
Bha·mo \bə-'mȯ, -'mō\ town N Burma on the upper Irrawaddy
Bharat — see INDIA
Bhat·pa·ra \bät-'pär-ə\ city E India in West Bengal N of Calcutta *pop* 134,900
Bhav·na·gar *or* **Bhau·na·gar** \bau̇-'nəg-ər\ city & port W India in S Gujarat on Gulf of Cambay *pop* 138,000
Bho·pal \bō-'päl\ **1** former state N *cen* India in & N of Vindhya mountains ✻ Bhopal; now part of Madhya Pradesh **2** city N *cen* India NW of Nagpur ✻ of Madhya Pradesh *pop* 102,300
Bhu·ba·nes·war *or* **Bhu·va·nesh·war** \,bu̇v-ə-'nāsh-wər\ town E India S of Cuttack ✻ of Orissa
Bhu·tan \bü-'tan, -'tän\ country Asia in Himalayas on NE border of India; a protectorate of India ✻ Thimbu *area* 18,000, *pop* 700,000 — **Bhu·ta·nese** \,büt-ᵊn-'ēz, -'ēs\ *adj or n*
Bi·a·fra, Bight of \bē-'äf-rə, -'af-\ the E section of Gulf of Guinea, W Africa
Bi·ak \bē-'(y)äk\ island off West New Guinea; largest of the Schouten islands
Bia·ly·stok \bē-'äl-i-,stȯk\ *or Russ* **Be·lo·stok** \,bel-ə-'stȯk\ city NE Poland *pop* 111,400
Biar·ritz \byä-'rits, ,bē-ə-'\ commune SW France on Bay of Biscay *pop* 20,691
Bias — see BEAS
Bid·de·ford \'bid-ə-fərd\ city SW Me. SW of Portland *pop* 19,255
Biel \'bē(ə)l\ *or F* **Bienne** \bē-'en\ commune NW Switzerland in Bern canton NE of NE end of **Lake of Biel** (10 *m* long) *pop* 56,600
Bie·le·feld \'bē-lə-,felt\ city W Germany E of Münster *pop* 174,500
Big Bend section of Columbia river E *cen* Wash. where river turns in its course S to make a wide bend W, S, & E
Big Bend National Park reservation SW Tex. comprising mountain & desert area in bend of Rio Grande *area* 1094
Big Black river 330 *m* W *cen* Miss. flowing to the Mississippi
Big Diomede — see DIOMEDE
Big Hole Battlefield National Monument reservation SW Mont. in mountain valley SW of Anaconda near Idaho border
Big·horn \'big-,hȯ(ə)rn\ *or* **Big Horn, 1** river 336 *m* N Wyo. & SE Mont. flowing N into Yellowstone river — see WIND **2** mountains N Wyo. extending S from Mont. border E of Bighorn river — see CLOUD PEAK
Big Sandy river 22 *m* between W. Va. & Ky. formed by confluence of Levisa Fork & Tug Fork & flowing N into the Ohio
Big Sioux \'sü\ river 300 *m* S.Dak. & Iowa flowing S to the Missouri & forming Iowa-S.Dak. boundary
Big Spring city W Tex. NE of Odessa *pop* 31,230
Big Stone lake *ab* 30 *m* long between W Minn. & NE S. Dak. — see MINNESOTA (river)
Big Sur \'sü(ə)r\ region W Calif. centering on Big Sur river & extending *ab* 80 *m* along coast SE of Point Sur
Bi·har *or* **Be·har** \bi-'här\ **1** state NE India bordering on Nepal; winter ✻ Patna, summer ✻ Ranchi *area* 67,164, *pop* 38,779,600 **2** city *cen* Bihar state SE of Patna *pop* 63,124
Bijanagar — see VIJAYANAGAR
Bi·ka *or* **Be·kaa** \bi-'kä\ *or* **El Bika** *or* **El Bekaa** \,el-\ *or anc* **Coe·le-Syria** \,sē-lē-\ valley Lebanon & Syria between Lebanon & Anti-Lebanon mountain ranges
Bi·ka·ner \,bik-ə-'ne(ə)r, ,bē-kə-, -'ni(ə)r\ city NW India in N Rajasthan in Thar desert *pop* 117,100
Bi·ki·ni \bə-'kē-nē\ island (atoll) W Pacific in Marshall islands at NW end of Ratak chain
Bi·las·pur \bə-'läs-,pu̇(ə)r\ city E *cen* India in SE Madhya Pradesh SE of Jabalpur *pop* 39,099
Bil·bao \bil-'bä-,ō, -'bä-(,)ō\ city N Spain ✻ of Vizcaya *pop* 292,059
Bil·lings \'bil-iŋz\ city S *cen* Mont. *pop* 52,851
Billiton — see BELITUNG
Bi·loxi \bə-'lək-sē, -'läk-\ city & port SE Miss. *pop* 44,053
Bim·i·ni \'bim-ə-nē\ two islands of the Bahamas NW of Andros
Bing·en \'biŋ-ən\ city W Germany at confluence of the Rhine & the Nahe *pop* 18,700
Bing·ham·ton \'biŋ-əm(p)-tən\ city S *cen* N.Y. *pop* 75,941
Binh Dinh \'bin-'din\ city S Vietnam in S Annam *pop* 75,000
Binue — see BENUE
Bío-Bío \,bē-ō-'bē-(,)ō\ river 238 *m* S *cen* Chile flowing into the Pacific at Concepción
Bir·ken·head \'bər-kən-,hed, ,bər-kən-'\ county borough NW England in Cheshire on the Mersey estuary opposite Liverpool *pop* 142,392
Bir·ming·ham \'bər-miŋ-,ham, *Brit usu* -miŋ-əm\ **1** city N *cen* Ala. *pop* 340,887 **2** city SE Mich. N of Detroit *pop* 25,525 **3** city & county borough W *cen* England in Warwickshire, Staffordshire, & Worcestershire *pop* 1,112,340
Bi·ro·bi·dzhan \,bir-ō-bi-'jän, -'jan\ **1** — see JEWISH AUTONOMOUS REGION **2** city U.S.S.R. ✻ of Jewish Autonomous Region *pop* 41,000
Bisayas — see VISAYAN
Biscay *or* **Biscaya** — see VIZCAYA
Bis·cay, Bay of \'bis-(,)kā, -kē\ inlet of the Atlantic between W coast of France & N coast of Spain
Bis·cayne \bis-'kān, 'bis-,\ bay SE Fla. on which Miami is situated
Bisk \'bisk, 'bēsk\ *or* **Biysk** *or* **Biisk** \'bē(-ə)sk\ city U.S.S.R. in Soviet Russia, Asia, in E Altai Territory *pop* 146,000
Bis·kra \'bis-krə, -(,)krä\ city NE Algeria at an oasis on S edge of Atlas mountains *pop* 52,511
Bis·marck \'biz-,märk\ **1** sea comprising the part of the W Pacific enclosed by the islands of the Bismarck archipelago **2** archipelago W Pacific N of E end of New Guinea *area* 22,290, *pop* 156,700 **3** mountain range North-East New Guinea NW of Owen Stanley range; highest point Mt. Wilhelm, over 14,000 *ft* **4** city ✻ of N. Dak. on the Missouri *pop* 27,670
Bis·sau *or* **Bis·são** \bis-'au̇(ⁿ)\ town & port ✻ of Portuguese Guinea *pop* 18,309
Bisutun — see BEHISTUN
Bit·burg \'bit-,bərg, -,bu̇(ə)rg\ town W Germany in Eifel region SSW of Bonn
Bi·thyn·ia \bə-'thin-ē-ə\ ancient country NW Asia Minor bordering on the Propontis & Euxine — **Bi·thyn·i·an** \-ē-ən\ *adj or n*
Bitola *or* **Bitolj** — see MONASTIR
Bitter Lakes two lakes (Great Bitter Lake & Little Bitter Lake) in NE Egypt N of Suez; connected & traversed by the Suez canal
Bit·ter·root \'bit-ə(r)-,rüt, -,ru̇t\ range of the Rocky mountains on Idaho-Mont. boundary — see BEAVERHEAD, GARFIELD
Bi·wa \'bē-(,)wä\ lake 40 *m* long Japan on Honshu NE of Kyoto; largest lake in Japan
Bi·zerte \bə-'zərt-ē, bi-'ze(ə)rt\ *or* **Bi·zer·ta** \bə-'zərt-ə\ city & port N Tunisia on **Lake Bizerte** (a deep lagoon) *pop* 39,327
Björneborg — see PORI
Black \'blak\ **1** *or* **Eux·ine** \'yük-sən, -,sīn\ *or anc* **Pon·tus** *or*

Pontus Eux·i·nus \'pänt-əs-,yük-'sī-nəs\ sea between Europe & Asia connected with Aegean sea through the Bosporus, Sea of Marmara, & Dardanelles *area* 168,500 **2** mountains W N.C.; a range of the Blue Ridge mountains — see MITCHELL (Mount) **3** hills W S. Dak. & NE Wyo. — see HARNEY PEAK **4** canyon of the Colorado between Ariz. & Nev. S of Hoover Dam **5** canyon of the Gunnison SW *cen* Colo. partly in **Black Canyon of the Gunnison National Monument** (*area* 21) **6** — see BO
Black·burn \'blak-(,)bərn\ county borough NW England in Lancashire *pop* 111,217
Blackburn, Mount mountain 16,523 *ft* S Alaska; highest in the Wrangell mountains
Black Forest *or* G **Schwarz·wald** \'shfärts-,vält, 'shwȯrt-,swȯld\ forested mountain region SW Germany along the upper Rhine between the Neckar & Swiss border
Black·pool \'blak-,pül\ county borough NW England in Lancashire on Irish sea *pop* 147,131
Black Volta — see VOLTA
Black Warrior river 178 *m*, *cen* Ala. flowing into the Tombigbee
Bla·go·vesh·chensk \,bläg-ə-'vesh-,(ch)en(t)sk\ city U.S.S.R. in E Soviet Russia, Asia, on the Amur *pop* 94,000
Blanc, Cape \'blaŋk, 'blä^n\ **1** cape N Tunisia; northernmost point of Africa, at 37°14′N **2** promontory NW Africa on the Atlantic at tip of peninsula divided by Mauritania — Spanish Sahara boundary
Blanc, Mont — see MONT BLANC
Blan·ca Peak \,blaŋ-kə-\ mountain 14,317 *ft* S Colo.; highest in Sangre de Cristo mountains
Blan·co, Cape \'blaŋ-(,)kō\ cape SW Oreg.
Blan·tyre–Lim·be \blan-'tī(ə)r-'lim-bā\ city S Malawi *pop* 62,600
Blar·ney \'blär-nē\ town SW Ireland in *cen* County Cork
Blas·ket \'blas-kət\ islands SW Ireland N of entrance to Dingle Bay
Bled \'bled\ resort village NW Yugoslavia in Slovenia NW of Ljubljana
Blen·heim \'blen-əm\ *or* G **Blind·heim** \'blint-,hīm\ village W Germany in Bavaria NNW of Augsburg
Bli·da \'blēd-ə\ city N Algeria SW of Algiers *pop* 93,000
Block \'bläk\ island R.I. SSW of Point Judith
Bloem·fon·tein \'blüm-,fän-,tān\ city Republic of So. Africa ✻ of Orange Free State & judicial ✻ of the Republic *pop* 112,406
Blois \blə-'wä\ city N *cen* France SW of Orléans *pop* 28,190
Bloom·field \blüm-,fēld\ town NE N.J. *pop* 51,867
Bloo·ming·ton \'blü-miŋ-tən\ **1** city *cen* Ill. *pop* 36,271 **2** city SW *cen* Ind. *pop* 31,357 **3** village SE Minn. SW of Minneapolis *pop* 50,498
Blooms·bury \'blümz-b(ə-)rē, *US also* -,ber-ē\ district of *cen* London, England
Blue, 1 mountains NE Oreg. & SE Wash. W of Wallowa mountains; highest Rock Creek Butte 9097 *ft* **2** mountains SE Australia in Great Dividing range in E New So. Wales; highest 4460 *ft* **3** mountains E Jamaica; highest Blue Mountain Peak 7402
Blue·field \'blü-,fēld\ city S W. Va. on Va. border *pop* 19,256
Blue Island city NE Ill. S of Chicago *pop* 19,618
Blue Nile river 850 *m* Ethiopia & Sudan flowing from Lake Tana NNW into the Nile at Khartoum — see ABBAI
Blue Ridge \-,rij\ *or* **Blue Ridge Mountains** the E range of the Appalachian mountains E U.S. extending from South Mountain, S Pa., into N Ga. — see MITCHELL (Mount)
Bluff \'bləf\ town S New Zealand; port for Invercargill
Blythe·ville \'blī(th)-,vil, 'blīth-, -vəl\ city NE Ark. *pop* 20,797
Bo \'bō\ *or* **Black** \'blak\ river 500 *m* SE Asia rising in *cen* Yunnan, China, & flowing SE to Red river
Bo·bruisk \bä-'brü-isk\ city U.S.S.R. in White Russia on the Berezina *pop* 84,100
Bo·chum \'bō-kəm\ city W Germany in Ruhr valley *pop* 362,000
Bodensee — see CONSTANCE (Lake)
Boe·o·tia \bē-'ō-sh(ē-)ə\ *or* NGk **Voi·o·tía** \vyȯ-'tē-ə\ district E *cen* Greece NW of Attica — **Boe·o·tian** \bē-'ō-shən\ *adj or n*
Boetoeng — see BUTUNG
Bo·ga·lu·sa \,bō-gə-'lü-sə\ city E La. *pop* 21,423
Bo·gor \'bō-,gȯ(ə)r\ *or formerly* **Bui·ten·zorg** \'bīt-^{ə}n-,zȯ(ə)rg\ city Indonesia in W Java S of Djakarta *pop* 123,800
Bo·go·tá \,bō-gə-'tȯ, -'tä\ city ✻ of Colombia on plateau of the Andes at altitude of 8563 *ft*, *pop* 1,123,600
Bo·he·mia \bō-'hē-mē-ə\ region W Czechoslovakia; once a kingdom, later a province ✻ Prague
Bohemian Forest *or* G **Böh·mer Wald** \'bə(r)m-ər-,vält\ forested mountain region Czechoslovakia & Germany along boundary between E Bavaria & SW Bohemia
Bo·hol \bō-'hȯl\ island S *cen* Philippines, one of the Visayan islands, N of Mindanao *area* 1492
Bois de Belleau *or* **Bois de la Brigade Marine** — see BELLEAU
Bois de Bou·logne \,bwäd-ə-bü-'lōn, -'lȯin\ park France just W of Paris *area* 2155 acres
Boi·se \'bȯi-sē, -zē\ *or* **Boise City** city ✻ of Idaho on Boise river (60 *m* long) *pop* 34,481
Bo·ja·dor, Cape \'bäj-ə-,dȯ(ə)r\ headland NW Africa in the Atlantic on W coast of Spanish Sahara, at 26°15′N
Bokhara — see BUKHARA — **Bo·kha·ran** \-ən\ *adj or n*
Boks·burg \'bäks-,bərg\ city NE Republic of So. Africa in S Transvaal E of Johannesburg *pop* 64,264
Bo·lan \bō-'län\ mountain pass 5900 *ft* Pakistan in N Baluchistan
Bolbitine — see ROSETTA
Bo·lí·var, Cer·ro \,ser-(,)ō-bə-'lē-,vär\ *or* **La Pa·ri·da** \,läp-ə-'rē-thə\ iron mountain 2018 *ft* E Venezuela S of Ciudad Bolívar
Bo·lí·var, Pi·co \,pē-(,)kō-bə-'lē-,vär\ *or* **La Co·lum·na** \,läk-ə-'lüm-nə\ mountain 16,411 *ft* W Venezuela in Cordillera Mérida; highest in Venezuela
Bo·liv·ia \bə-'liv-ē-ə\ country W *cen* So. America; a republic; administrative ✻ La Paz, constitutional ✻ Sucre *area* 424,200, *pop* 3,019,031 — **Bo·liv·i·an** \-ē-ən\ *adj or n*
Bo·lo·gna \bə-'lōn-(y)ə\ *or anc* **Bo·no·nia** \bə-'nō-nē-ə\ commune N Italy ✻ of Emilia-Romagna at foot of the Apennines *pop* 350,676 — **Bo·lo·gnan** \-yən\ *or* **Bo·lo·gnese** \,bō-lən-'(y)ēz, -'(y)ēs, bə-'lōn-,yēz, -,yēs\ *adj or n*
Bol·se·na, Lake \bōl-'sā-nə\ lake *cen* Italy in NW Latium NW of Viterbo
Bol·ton *or* **Bolton-le-Moors** \,bōlt-^{ə}n-lə-'mu̇(ə)rz\ county borough NW England in Lancashire NW of Manchester *pop* 167,162
Bol·za·no \bōlt-'sän-(,)ō, bōl-'zän-\ **1** former province N Italy in S Tirol, now part of Trentino-Alto Adige region **2** commune in Trentino-Alto Adige region *pop* 76,900
Bo·ma \'bō-mə\ city & port W Congo on Congo river *pop* 20,531
Bom·bay \bäm-'bā\ **1** former state W India ✻ Bombay; divided 1960 into Gujarat & Maharashtra states; once a presidency & (1937–47) a province of Brit. India **2** island W India on which city of Bombay is situated *area* 24 **3** city & port W India ✻ of Maharashtra & of former Bombay state *pop* 2,839,270
Bo·mu \'bō-(,)mü\ *or* **Mbo·mu** \əm-'bō-\ river 500 *m* W *cen* Africa forming boundary between Republic of Congo (✻ Léopoldville) & Central African Republic & uniting with Uele river to form the Ubangi
Bon, Cape \'bō^n\ *or* **Ras el Tib** \,räs-,el-'tib\ *or* **Ras Ad·dar** \,räs-ə-'där\ headland NE Tunisia on **Cape Bon Peninsula**
Bo·na, Mount \'bō-nə\ mountain 16,421 *ft* S Alaska at W end of Wrangell mountains
Bon·aire \bə-'na(ə)r, -'ne(ə)r\ island Netherlands Antilles E of Curaçao *area* 95, *pop* 5775
Bon·di \'bän-'dī\ town SE Australia, SE suburb of Sydney, S of entrance to Port Jackson on **Bondi Beach**
Bône \'bōn\ commune & port NE Algeria *pop* 114,068
Bo·nin \'bō-nən\ *or* **Oga·sa·wa·ra** \(,)ō-,gäs-ə-'wär-ə\ islands W Pacific *ab* 600 *m* SSE of Tokyo; belong to Japan; administered by U.S. 1945–68 *area* 40, *pop* 7361
Bonn \'bän, 'bȯn\ city W Germany on the Rhine SSE of Cologne ✻ of West German Federal Republic (often called **Bonn Republic**) *pop* 146,500
Bon·ne·ville, Lake \'bän-ə-,vil\ prehistoric lake 350 *m* long in Utah, E Nev., & S Idaho; its remnant is Great Salt Lake
Bonneville Dam dam in Columbia river *ab* 35 *m* above Vancouver, Wash.
Bonneville Salt Flats *or* **Bonneville Flats** broad level area of Great Salt Lake desert E of Wendover, Utah
Boo·thia \'bü-thē-ə\ peninsula N Canada W of Baffin I.; its N tip (at *ab* 72°N, 94°W) is the northernmost point on No. American mainland
Boothia, Gulf of gulf N Canada between Baffin I. & Melville peninsula on E & Boothia peninsula on W
Boo·tle \'büt-^{ə}l\ county borough NW England in Lancashire, N suburb of Liverpool *pop* 74,302
Bo·ra Bo·ra \,bōr-ə-'bōr-ə, ,bȯr-ə-'bȯr-ə\ island S Pacific in Leeward group of the Society islands NW of Tahiti *area* 14.6
Bo·rah Peak \,bōr-ə-, ,bȯr-\ mountain 12,662 *ft* E *cen* Idaho in Lost River range; highest point in state
Bo·rås \bü-'rōs\ city SW Sweden E of Göteborg *pop* 67,647
Bor·deaux \bȯr-'dō\ city & port SW France on the Garonne *pop* 257,900
Bor·di·ghe·ra \,bȯrd-i-'ger-ə\ commune & port NW Italy in Liguria SW of San Remo
Bor·ger \'bȯr-gər\ city NW Tex. NE of Amarillo *pop* 20,911
Bor·ger·hout \'bȯr-gər-,hau̇t\ commune N Belgium, E suburb of Antwerp *pop* 50,645
Borgne, Lake \'bȯ(ə)rn\ inlet of the Mississippi Sound E of New Orleans, La.
Bo·ri·sov \bə-'rē-səf\ city U.S.S.R. in N *cen* White Russia on the Berezina *pop* 59,000
Bor·neo \'bȯr-nē-,ō\ island Malay archipelago SW of Philippines *area* 290,012 — see BRUNEI, NORTH BORNEO, KALIMANTAN, SARAWAK — **Bor·ne·an** \-nē-ən\ *adj or n*
Born·holm \'bȯrn-,hō(l)m\ island Denmark in Baltic sea ✻ Rönne *area* 228, *pop* 48,632
Bos·nia \'bäz-nē-ə\ region W *cen* Yugoslavia; formerly a kingdom, now part of **Bosnia and Her·ze·go·vi·na** \,hert-sə-gō-'vē-nə, ,hərt-\ federated republic (✻ Sarajevo *area* 19,904, *pop* 2,847,790) — **Bos·ni·an** *adj or n*
Bos·po·rus \'bäs-p(ə-)rəs\ *or* **Bos·pho·rus** \-f(ə-)rəs\ strait *ab* 18 *m* long between Turkey in Europe & Turkey in Asia connecting Sea of Marmara & Black sea — **Bos·po·ran** \-pə-rən\ *adj*
Bos·sier City \,bō-zhər-\ city NW La. *pop* 32,776
Bos·ton \'bȯ-stən\ **1** mountains NW Ark. & E Okla. in Ozark plateau; highest over 2000 *ft* **2** city & port ✻ of Mass. on Massachusetts Bay *pop* 697,197 **3** municipal borough & port E England in Lincolnshire ✻ of Parts of Holland *pop* 24,453 — **Bos·ton·ese** \,bȯ-stə-'nēz, -'nēs\ *adj* — **Bos·to·nian** \bȯ-'stō-nē-ən, -nyən\ *adj or n*
Bo·ta·fo·go Bay \,bōt-ə-,fō-(,)gō-\ inlet of Guanabara Bay in Rio de Janeiro, Brazil
Bot·a·ny Bay \,bät-^{ə}n-ē-, ,bät-nē-\ inlet of the S Pacific SE Australia in New So. Wales on S border of city of Sydney
Both·nia, Gulf of \'bäth-nē-ə\ arm of Baltic sea between Sweden & Finland
Botswana — see BECHUANALAND (protectorate)
Bot·trop \'bä-,träp\ city W Germany NNW of Essen *pop* 110,800
Bou·gain·ville \'bü-gən-,vil, 'bō-\ island S Pacific, largest of the Solomons; chief town Kieta *area* 3500, *pop* 46,300
Bou·gie \bü-'zhē\ city & port NE Algeria *pop* 43,934
Bouil·lon \bü'-yō^n\ town SE Belgium in the Ardennes
Boul·der \'bōl-dər\ **1** canyon of the Colorado between Ariz. & Nev. now covered by Lake Mead **2** city N *cen* Colo. *pop* 37,718
Boulder Dam — see HOOVER DAM
Bou·logne \bü-'lōn, -'lȯin\ *or* **Bou·logne–sur–Mer** \-,su̇(ə)r-'me(ə)r\ city & port N France on English channel *pop* 41,870
Boulogne–Bil·lan·court \,bē-,(y)ä^n-'kü(ə)r\ commune N France SW of Paris on the Seine *pop* 93,998
Boundary Peak mountain 13,145 *ft* SW Nev. in White mountains; highest point in state
Boun·ti·ful \'bau̇nt-i-fəl\ city N Utah *pop* 17,039
Bour·bon·nais \,bu̇r-bə-'nā\ former province *cen* France W of Burgundy ✻ Moulins
Bourges \'bu̇(ə)rzh\ commune *cen* France SSE of Orléans *pop* 53,879
Bourgogne — see BURGUNDY
Bourne·mouth \'bō(ə)rn-məth, 'bȯ(ə)rn-, 'bu̇(ə)rn-\ county borough S England in Hampshire on English channel SW of Southampton *pop* 144,726

ə abut; ^{ə} kitten; ər further; a back; ā bake; ä cot, cart; au̇ out; ch chin; e less; ē easy; g gift; i trip; ī life
j joke; ŋ sing; ō flow; ȯ flaw; ȯi coin; th thin; th this; ü loot; u̇ foot; y yet; yü few; yu̇ furious; zh vision
^{ə} F table; ȧ F bac; k G ich, Buch; ^{n} F vin; œ F bœuf; œ̄ F feu; ue G füllen; ue̅ F rue; ^{y} F digne \dēn^y\, nuit \nw^{y}ē\

Bou·vet \'bü-(,)vā\ island S Atlantic SSW of Cape of Good Hope at *ab* 54°S, 5°E; belongs to Norway

Bow \'bō\ river 315 *m* Canada in SW Alta. rising in Banff National Park & joining the Oldman to form the So. Saskatchewan

Bowl·ing Green \,bō-liŋ-'grēn\ city S Ky. *pop* 28,338

Boyne \'bȯin\ river 70 *m* E Ireland in Leinster flowing to Irish sea S of Drogheda

Boz·caa·da \,bōz-jä-'dä\ *or anc* **Ten·e·dos** \'ten-ə-,däs\ island Turkey in NE Aegean sea S of the Dardanelles

Bra·bant \brə-'bant, -'bänt\ **1** old duchy of W Europe including region now forming No. Brabant province of the Netherlands & Brabant & Antwerp provinces of Belgium **2** *or* **South Brabant** province *cen* Belgium ✻ Brussels *pop* 1,973,729

Bra·den·ton \'brād-ᵊn-tən\ city & port W Fla. *pop* 19,380

Brad·ford \'brad-fərd\ **1** city NW Pa. near N.Y. border *pop* 15,061 **2** city & county borough N England in Yorkshire *pop* 292,394

Bra·ga \'bräg-ə\ city NW Portugal *pop* 32,600

Bra·gan·ça \brə-'gan(t)-sə\ *or* **Bra·gan·za** \-'gan-zə\ town NE Portugal near Spanish border

Brah·ma·pu·tra \,bräm-ə-'p(y)ü-trə\ river 1680 *m* S Asia flowing from the Himalayas in Tibet to the Ganges delta in NE India (subcontinent) — see JAMUNA, TSANGPO

Bra·i·la \brə-'ē-lə\ city E Romania on the Danube *pop* 109,394

Brain·tree \'brān-(,)trē\ town E Mass. S of Boston *pop* 31,069

Brak·pan \'brak-,pan\ city NE Republic of So. Africa in S Transvaal on the Witwatersrand S of Johannesburg *pop* 54,811

Bran·co \'braŋ-(,)kō, 'braŋ-(,)kü\ river 350 *m* N Brazil flowing S into the Negro

Bran·den·burg \'bran-dən-,bərg, 'brän-dən-,bu̇(ə)rk\ **1** region & former province NE *cen* Germany **2** city E Germany on the Havel WSW of Berlin *pop* 87,700

Bran·don \'bran-dən\ city Canada in SW Man. *pop* 24,796

Bran·dy·wine \'bran-dē-,wīn\ creek *ab* 20 *m* SE Pa. & N Del. flowing SE to join Christina river at Wilmington, Del.

Brant·ford \'brant-fərd\ city Canada in SE Ont. *pop* 51,869

Bras d'Or Lake \,brä-,dȯ(ə)r-\ tidal lake *ab* 50 *m* long Canada in N.S. on Cape Breton I.

Bra·sí·lia \brə-'zil-yə, -'zēl-\ city ✻ (since 1960) of Brazil in Federal District in E Goiás *pop* 185,000

Bra·sov \brä-'shȯv\ *or formerly* **Sta·lin** \'stäl-ən, 'stal-, -,ēn\ *or* **Ora·sul Stalin** \,ōr-ə-,shül-, ,ȯr-\ city *cen* Romania *pop* 127,829

Bra·ti·sla·va \,brat-ə-'släv-ə, ,brät-\ *or* G **Press·burg** \'pres-,bərg, -,bu̇(ə)rk\ city Czechoslovakia, chief city of Slovakia, on the Danube *pop* 246,695

Bratsk \'brätsk\ town U.S.S.R. in E *cen* Soviet Russia, Asia, NNE of Irkutsk near site of **Bratsk Dam** (in Angara river)

Braunschweig — see BRUNSWICK

Bravo, Río — see RIO GRANDE

Bra·zil \brə-'zil\ *or* Port **Bra·sil** *or* **Es·ta·dos Uni·dos do Bra·sil** \ish-'täth-ə-zü-'nē-thəz-,dü-brə-'zil\ country E & *cen* So. America; a federal republic ✻ Brasília *area* 3,286,169, *pop* 70,967,185 — **Bra·zil·ian** \brə-'zil-yən\ *adj or n*

Braz·os \'braz-əs\ river 870 *m*, *cen* Tex. flowing SE into Gulf of Mexico

Braz·za·ville \'braz-ə-,vil, 'bräz-ə-,vēl\ city & port ✻ of Congo Republic on W bank of Stanley Pool in Congo river *pop* 100,000

Breck·nock \'brek-,näk, -nək\ *or* **Brec·on** \'brek-ən\ **1** *or* **Breck·nock·shire** \-,shi(ə)r, -shər\ *or* **Brec·on·shire** county SE Wales *area* 733, *pop* 56,484 **2** municipal borough, its ✻

Brecknock Beacons *or* **Brecon Beacons** two mountain peaks SE Wales in Brecknockshire; highest Pen y Fan 2907 *ft*

Bre·da \brā-'dä\ commune S Netherlands *pop* 105,531

Bre·genz \'brā-,gen(t)s\ commune W Austria on Lake Constance ✻ of the Vorarlberg *pop* 20,277

Brei·ten·feld \'brīt-ᵊn-,felt\ village E Germany NNW of Leipzig

Bre·men \'brem-ən, 'brā-mən\ **1** former duchy N Germany between the lower Weser & the lower Elbe **2** state NW Germany including cities of Bremen & Bremerhaven *area* 156, *pop* 704,300 **3** city & port, its ✻ *pop* 557,100

Bre·mer·ha·ven \'brem-ər-,häv-ən, ,brā-mər-'häf-ən\ city & port NW Germany in Bremen state at mouth of the Weser; includes former city of Wesermünde *pop* 140,000

Brem·er·ton \'brem-ərt-ᵊn\ city & port W Wash. *pop* 28,922

Bren·ner \'bren-ər\ mountain pass 4494 *ft* in the Alps between Austria & Italy

Bren·ta \'brent-ə\ river 100 *m* N Italy flowing SE into the Adriatic S of Chioggia

Brent·ford and Chis·wick \,brent-fərd-ᵊn-'chiz-ik\ municipal borough SE England in Middlesex on the Thames *pop* 59,354

Brent·wood \'brent-,wu̇d\ urban area SE N.Y. in *cen* Long I. *pop* 15,387

Bre·scia \'bresh-ə, 'brā-shə\ *or anc* **Brix·ia** \'brik-sē-ə\ commune N Italy in E Lombardy ENE of Milan *pop* 147,288

Breslau — see WROCLAW

Brest \'brest\ **1** commune & port NW France in Brittany *pop* 110,713 **2** *or* **Brest Li·tovsk** \,brest-lə-'tȯfsk, -'tȯvsk\ city U.S.S.R. in SW Belorussia on the Bug *pop* 55,374

Bret·on, Cape \'bret-ᵊn, 'brit-\ headland Canada, easternmost point of Cape Breton I. & of N.S., at 59°48′ W

Bri·an·çon \brē-äⁿ-sōⁿ\ town SE France SE of Grenoble

Bridge·port \'brij-,pō(ə)rt, -,pȯ(ə)rt\ city SW Conn. on Long Island Sound *pop* 156,748

Bridge·ton \'brij-tən\ city SW N.J. *pop* 20,966

Bridge·town \'brij-,tau̇n\ city & port Brit. West Indies ✻ of Barbados *pop* 18,850

Brie \'brē\ district & medieval county NE France E of Paris; chief town Meaux

Bri·enne \brē-'en\ **1** former county NE France in the Champagne NNE of Troyes **2** town, its ✻

Bri·enz \brē-'en(t)s\ town Switzerland in SE Bern canton at NE end of **Lake of Brienz** (9 *m* long, in course of the Aare)

Brigh·ton \'brīt-ᵊn\ county borough S England in East Sussex on English channel *pop* 156,440

Brin·di·si \'brin-də-(,)zē, 'brēn-\ *or anc* **Brun·di·si·um** \,brən-'diz(h)-ē-əm\ city & port SE Italy in Apulia *pop* 41,699

Bris·bane \'briz-bən, -,bān\ city & port E Australia ✻ of Queensland on Brisbane river near its mouth *pop* (with suburbs) 527,500

Bris·tol \'brist-ᵊl\ **1** city W *cen* Conn. WSW of Hartford *pop* 45,499 **2** urban township SE Pa. NE of Philadelphia *pop* 59,298 **3** city NE Tenn. adjacent to Bristol, Va. *pop* 17,582 **4** city SW Va. *pop* 17,144 **5** channel between S Wales & SW England **6** city & county borough & port SW England in Gloucestershire on Avon river near Severn estuary *pop* 442,281 — **Bris·to·li·an** \bris-'tō-lē-ən, -'tōl-yən\ *n*

Bristol Bay arm of Bering sea SW Alaska W of Alaska peninsula

Brit·ain \'brit-ᵊn\ **1** *or* L **Bri·tan·nia** \bri-'tan-yə, -'tan-ē-ə\ the island of Great Britain **2** UNITED KINGDOM **3** BRITISH COMMONWEALTH OF NATIONS

British America, 1 *or* **British North America** CANADA **2** all Brit. possessions in & adjacent to No. & So. America

British Bechuanaland — see BECHUANALAND

British Cameroons former Brit. trust territory W equatorial Africa comprising two areas in the Cameroons between Nigeria & Republic of Cameroon ✻ Buea *area* 34,081; divided 1961 between Nigeria (N section) & Cameroon (S section)

British Columbia province W Canada on Pacific coast ✻ Victoria *area* 359,279, *pop* 1,398,464

British Commonwealth of Nations *or* **British Commonwealth** Great Britain & Northern Ireland, the Brit. dominions & republics, & the Brit. dependencies

British East Africa, 1 KENYA — a former name **2** the former Brit. dependencies in E Africa: Kenya, Uganda, Zanzibar, & Tanganyika

British Empire Great Britain & the Brit. dominions & dependencies — a chiefly former usage

British Guiana — see GUYANA

British Honduras country Central America bordering on the Caribbean; a Brit. colony ✻ Belize *area* 8688, *pop* 88,156

British India the part of India formerly under direct Brit. administration — see INDIAN STATES

British Indian Ocean Territory Brit. colony in Indian ocean comprising Chagos archipelago & Aldabra, Farquhar, & Desroches islands

British Isles island group W Europe comprising Great Britain, Ireland, & adjacent islands

British Malaya former dependencies of Great Britain on Malay peninsula & in Malay archipelago including Federation of Malaya, Singapore, No. Borneo, Sarawak, & Brunei

British Solomon Islands Brit. protectorate comprising the Solomons (except Bougainville, Buka, & adjacent small islands) & the Santa Cruz islands ✻ Honiara *area* 11,500, *pop* 114,350

British Somaliland former Brit. protectorate E Africa bordering on Gulf of Aden ✻ Hargeisa; since 1960 part of Somalia

British Virgin Islands the E islands of the Virgin islands group; a Brit. possession ✻ Road Town (on Tortola I.) *area* 58, *pop* 7600

British West Indies islands of the West Indies including Jamaica, the Bahamas, Caymans, Brit. Virgin islands, Leeward & Windward islands, Trinidad, & Tobago

Brit·ta·ny \'brit-ᵊn-ē\ *or* F **Bre·tagne** \brə-tänʸ\ region & former province NW France SW of Normandy

Br·no \'bər-(,)nō\ *or* G **Brünn** \'brʊen, 'bru̇n\ city *cen* Czechoslovakia, chief city of Moravia *pop* 306,371

Broads \'brȯdz\ low-lying district E England in Norfolk (the **Norfolk Broads**) & Suffolk (the **Suffolk Broads**)

Brock·en \'bräk-ən\ mountain 3747 *ft* E Germany; highest in Harz mountains

Brock·ton \'bräk-tən\ city SE Mass. *pop* 72,813

Bro·ken Hill \,brō-kən-\ **1** city SE Australia in W New So. Wales *pop* 32,200 **2** city *cen* Zambia *pop* 26,700

Bromberg — see BYDGOSZCZ

Brom·ley \'bräm-lē\ municipal borough SE England in Kent, SE suburb of London *pop* 64,178

Bronx \'bräŋ(k)s\ *or* **The Bronx** borough of New York City on the mainland NE of Manhattan I. *pop* 1,424,815

Brook·field \'bru̇k-,fēld\ **1** village NE Ill. W of Chicago *pop* 20,429 **2** city SE Wis. W of Milwaukee *pop* 19,812

Brook·line \'bru̇k-,līn\ town E Mass. W of Boston *pop* 54,044

Brook·lyn \'bru̇k-lən\ borough of New York City at SW end of Long I. *pop* 2,627,319 — **Brook·lyn·ite** \-lə-,nīt\ *n*

Brooklyn Center village SE Minn. NW of Minneapolis *pop* 24,356

Brooks \'bru̇ks\ mountain range N Alaska extending from Kotzebue Sound to Canada border; highest peak Mt. Michelson 9239 *ft*

Browns·ville \'brau̇nz-,vil, -vəl\ **1** urban area NW Fla. W of Pensacola *pop* 38,417 **2** city & port S Tex. on Rio Grande *pop* 48,040

Brown·wood \'brau̇n-,wu̇d\ city *cen* Tex. *pop* 16,974

Bruges \'brüzh\ *or* Flem **Brug·ge** \'brʊeg-ə\ commune NW Belgium ✻ of West Flanders *pop* 52,167

Bru·nei \'brü-,nī, -(,)nā\ **1** sultanate & Brit. protectorate NW Borneo *area* 2226, *pop* 80,277 **2** town & port, its ✻

Bruns·wick \'brənz-(,)wik\ **1** city & port SE Ga. on Atlantic coast *pop* 21,703 **2** *or* G **Braun·schweig** \'brau̇n-,shwīg, -,shfīk\ former state *cen* Germany ✻ Brunswick **3** *or* G **Braunschweig** city W *cen* Germany W of Berlin *pop* 244,100

Brus·sels \'brəs-əlz\ *or* F **Bru·xelles** \brʊe(k)-sel\ *or* Flem **Brus·sel** \'brʊes-əl\ city ✻ of Belgium & of Brabant *pop* (with suburbs) 1,000,744

Bruttium — see CALABRIA

Bry·an \'brī-ən\ city E *cen* Tex. *pop* 27,542

Bryansk *or* **Briansk** \brē-'än(t)sk\ city U.S.S.R. in SW Soviet Russia, Europe, SW of Moscow *pop* 206,000

Bryce Canyon National Park \'brīs\ reservation S Utah NE of Zion National Park *area* 56

Bu·bas·tis \byü-'bas-təs\ ancient city N Egypt; ruins near modern city of Zagazig

Bu·ca·ra·man·ga \,bü-kə-rə-'mäŋ-gə\ city N Colombia NNE of Bogotá *pop* 184,670

Bu·cha·rest \'b(y)ü-kə-,rest\ *or* Rom **Bu·cu·res·ti** \,bü-kə-'resht(-ē)\ city ✻ of Romania *pop* 1,291,351

Bu·chen·wald \'bü-kən-,wȯld, -,vält\ village E Germany NW of Weimar

Buck·ing·ham \'bək-iŋ-əm, *U. S. also* -iŋ-,ham\ *or* **Buck·ing·ham·shire** \-,shi(ə)r, -shər\ *or* **Bucks** \'bəks\ county SE *cen* England ✻ Aylesbury *area* 749, *pop* 386,164

Bu·da·pest \'büd-ə-,pest *also* 'byüd-, 'bu̇d-, -,pesht\ city ✻ of Hungary on the Danube *pop* 1,850,000

Buddh Ga·ya \,bu̇d-gə-'yä\ village NE India in *cen* Bihar

Budweis — see CESKE BUDEJOVICE

Bue·na Park \,byü-nə-\ city Calif. near Los Angeles *pop* 46,401

Bue·na·ven·tu·ra \,bwen-ə-,ven-'t(y)u̇r-ə, ,bwā-nə-\ city & port W Colombia on the Pacific *pop* 102,887

Bue·nos Ai·res \,bwā-nə-'sa(ə)r-ēz, ,bō-nə-, -'se(ə)r-, -'sī(ə)r-\ city & port ✱ of Argentina on Rio de la Plata *pop* 3,767,887

Buenos Aires, Lake lake 80 *m* long S Argentina & S Chile in the Andes; drains to the Pacific

Buf·fa·lo \'bəf-ə-,lō\ city & port W N.Y. on Lake Erie & Niagara river *pop* 532,759

Bug \'büg\ **1** river 450 *m*, *cen* Poland rising in W Ukraine, U.S.S.R., & flowing into the Vistula **2** river 500 *m* U.S.S.R. in SW Ukraine flowing SE to the Dnieper estuary

Bu·gan·da \b(y)ü-'gan-də\ province & former native kingdom E Africa in SE Uganda ✱ Kampala

Buitenzorg — see BOGOR

Bujumbura — see USUMBURA

Bu·ka \'bü-kə\ island W Pacific in the Solomons N of Bougainville

Bu·ka·vu \bü-'käv-(,)ü\ *or formerly* Cos·ter·mans·ville \'käs-tər-mənz-,vil\ city E Congo at S end of Lake Kivu *pop* 26,800

Bu·kha·ra \bü-'kär-ə, -'kar-, -'här-, -'har-\ *or* Bo·kha·ra \bō-\ **1** former emirate W Asia occupying region around city of Bukhara **2** city U.S.S.R. in Soviet Central Asia in W Uzbek Republic E of the Amu Darya *pop* 69,000 — **Bu·kha·ran** \-ən\ *adj or n*

Bu·kit·ting·gi \,bü-kə-'tin-gē\ *or formerly* Fort de Kock \-də-'kók, -'käk\ town Indonesia in W *cen* Sumatra

Bu·ko·vi·na *or* **Bu·co·vi·na** \,bü-kə-'vē-nə\ region E *cen* Europe in foothills of E Carpathians; now in N E Romania & W Ukraine

Bu·la·wayo *or* **Bu·lu·wayo** \,bùl-ə-'wä-(,)ō, -'wī-\ city SW Southern Rhodesia, chief town of Matabeleland *pop* 210,900

Bul·gar·ia \,bəl-'gar-ē-ə, bùl-, -'ger-\ country SE Europe on Black sea; a republic ✱ Sofia *area* 42,858, *pop* 7,629,254

Bull Run \'bùl-'rən\ stream 20 *m* N Va. W of Washington, D.C., flowing into Occoquan creek (small tributary of the Potomac)

Bun·del·khand \'bùn-d'l-,kənd\ region N *cen* India containing headwaters of the Jumna; now chiefly in N Madhya Pradesh

Bun·ker Hill \,bəŋ-kər-\ height in Charlestown section of Boston, Mass.

Bur·bank \'bər-,baŋk\ city SW Calif. *pop* 90,155

Bur·gas \bùr-'gäs\ city & port SE Bulgaria *pop* 72,795

Bur·gen·land \'bər-gən-,land, 'bùr-gən-,länt\ province E Austria SE of Vienna on Hungarian border ✱ Eisenstadt

Bur·gos \'bù(ə)r-,gōs\ **1** province N Spain *area* 5480, *pop* 405,543 **2** city, its ✱ & once of Old Castile *pop* 89,367

Bur·gun·dy \'bər-gən-dē\ *or* F Bour·gogne \bür-gón'\ **1** region & former kingdom, duchy, & province E France S of Champagne **2** county France E of Burgundy province; later called Franche-Com·té \frän‿sh-kō͞n-'tā\ — **Bur·gun·di·an** \(,)bər-'gən-dē-ən\ *adj or n*

Bur·lin·game \'bər-lən-,gām, -,liŋ-\ city W Calif. SSE of San Francisco on San Francisco Bay *pop* 24,036

Bur·ling·ton \'bər-liŋ-tən\ **1** city SE Iowa *pop* 32,430 **2** city N *cen* N.C. *pop* 33,199 **3** city NW Vt. *pop* 35,531

Bur·ma \'bər-mə\ *or* Union of Burma country SE Asia on Bay of Bengal; a federal republic ✱ Rangoon *area* 261,789, *pop* 19,242,000 — **Bur·man** \'bər-mən\ *adj or n*

Burn·ley \'bərn-lē\ county borough NW England in Lancashire N of Manchester *pop* 84,950

Bur·rard \bə-'rärd\ inlet of Strait of Georgia, W Canada, in B.C.; city of Vancouver is situated on it

Bur·sa \'bùr-'sä, 'bər-sə\ *or formerly* Bru·sa \brü-'sä, 'brü-sə\ city NW Turkey in Asia near Sea of Marmara *pop* 153,574

Bu·run·di \bù-'rün-dē\ *or formerly* Urun·di \ù-'rün-\ country E *cen* Africa; a kingdom ✱ Usumbura *area* 10,744, *pop* 2,500,000 — see RUANDA-URUNDI — **Bu·run·di·an** *adj or n*

Bury \'ber-ē\ county borough NW England in Lancashire NNW of Manchester *pop* 58,829

Bur·yat, *or* **Bur·iat, Republic** \bùr-,yät-, ,bùr-ē-,ät-\ autonomous republic U.S.S.R. in S Soviet Russia, Asia, adjacent to Outer Mongolia & E of Lake Baikal ✱ Ulan-Ude *area* 127,020, *pop* 673,000 — **Buryat** *or* **Buriat** *n*

Bury Saint Ed·munds \,ber-ē-(,)sānt-'ed-mən(d)z, -sənt-\ municipal borough ✱ of West Suffolk *pop* 20,045

Bu·shire \bü-'shi(ə)r\ city & port SW Iran *pop* 27,317

Busra — see BASRA

Butaritari — see MAKIN

Bute \'byüt\ **1** island SW Scotland W of Firth of Clyde **2** *or* **Bute·shire** \-,shi(ə)r, -shər\ county SW Scotland comprising Bute, Arran, the Cumbraes, & several smaller islands in the Firth of Clyde ✱ Rothesay (on Bute) *area* 218, *pop* 19,285

But·ler \'bət-lər\ city W Pa. N of Pittsburgh *pop* 20,975

Butte \'byüt\ city SW Mont. *pop* 27,877

Bu·tung \'bü-,tùŋ\ *or* **Bu·ton** \'bü-,tón\ *or* D **Boe·toeng** \'bü-,tùŋ\ island Indonesia off SE Celebes *area ab* 2000

Bu·zau \bə-'zaù, -'zō\ city E Romania *pop* 50,320

Buz·zards Bay \,bəz-ərdz-\ inlet of the Atlantic SE Mass. W of Cape Cod

Byd·goszcz \'bid-,gósh(ch)\ *or* G **Brom·berg** \'bräm-,bərg, 'bróm-,be(ə)rk\ city NW *cen* Poland NE of Poznan *pop* 219,700

Byelgorod–Dnestrovski — see BELGOROD-DNESTROVSKI

Byelorussia — see BELORUSSIA — **Byelorussian** *adj or n*

By·tom \'bē-,tóm, 'bi-\ *or* G **Beu·then** \'bóit-ᵊn\ city SW Poland in Silesia *pop* 175,100

Byzantium — see ISTANBUL

Ca·ba·na·tuan \,käb-ə-nə-'twän\ city Philippines in S *cen* Luzon *pop* 70,398

Ca·bin·da \kə-'bin-də\ territory W equatorial Africa on the Atlantic between Congo Republic (✱ Brazzaville) & Republic of Congo (✱ Léopoldville); belongs to Angola ✱ Cabinda *area* 3000, *pop* 50,503

Cab·ot \'kab-ət\ strait *ab* 70 *m* wide E Canada between SW Nfld. & Cape Breton I. connecting Gulf of St. Lawrence with the Atlantic

Ca·bo Yu·bi \,käb-(,)ō-'yü-bē\ *or* **Cabo Ju·by** \-'hü-bē\ *or* **Vil·la Bens** \,vil-ə-'benz\ town on SW coast of Morocco SW of Ifni; former seat of administration for Spanish Sahara & Ifni

Ca·ca·hua·mil·pa \,käk-ə-wə-'mil-pə\ caverns S Mexico in Guerrero NNE of Taxco

Cá·ce·res \'käs-ə-,rās, 'käth-\ **1** province W Spain in N Estremadura *area* 7667, *pop* 571,370 **2** city, its ✱ *pop* 48,881

Cache la Pou·dre \,kash-lə-'pü-drə\ river 125 *m* N Colo. flowing into the So. Platte

Cad·do \'kad-(,)ō\ lake 20 *m* long NW La. & N E Tex. draining to Red river

Cá·diz \kə-'diz; 'kād-əz, 'käd-, kad-; *Sp* 'kä-,thēth, -,thēs\ **1** province SW Spain in Andalusia *area* 2834, *pop* 829,016 **2** *or anc* **Ga·dir** \'gäd-ər\ *or* **Ga·des** \'gäd-(,)ēz\ city & port, its ✱, on Bay of Cádiz NW of Gibraltar *pop* 116,333

Cae·li·an \'sē-lē-ən\ hill in Rome, Italy, one of seven on which the ancient city was built — see AVENTINE

Caen \kän\ city NW France in Normandy *pop* 67,851

Caer·nar·von *or* **Car·nar·von** \kär-'när-vən, kər-\ **1** *or* **Caernar·von·shire** *or* **Car·nar·von·shire** \-,shi(ə)r, -shər\ county NW Wales *area* 569, *pop* 124,074 **2** municipal borough, its ✱

Cae·sa·rea \,sē-zə-'rē-ə; ,ses-ə-, ,sez-\ **1** ancient seaport Palestine 22 *m* S of Haifa **2** *or* **Caesarea Mazaca** — see KAYSERI

Caesarea Phi·lip·pi \-'fil-ə-,pī, -fə-'lip-,ī\ ancient city N Palestine SW of Mt. Hermon; site at modern village of Baniyas \,ban-ē-'yas\ in SW Syria

Caesena — see CESENA

Ca·ga·yan \,käg-ə-'yän\ *or* **Rio Gran·de de Cagayan** \,rē-ō-'grän-dē-,dā-\ river 220 *m* Philippines in N E Luzon flowing N

Ca·glia·ri \'käl-yə-(,)rē\ commune & port Italy ✱ of Sardinia *pop* 142,744

Ca·guas \'käg-,wäs\ town E *cen* Puerto Rico *pop* 32,015

Ca·ho·kia \kə-'hō-kē-ə\ village SW Ill. S of East St. Louis *pop* 15,829

Cahokia Mounds group of prehistoric Indian mounds Ill. E N E of East St. Louis

Ca·hors \kə-'(h)ó(ə)r\ town S *cen* France on the Lot N of Toulouse

Caicos — see TURKS AND CAICOS

Cairn·gorm \'ka(ə)rn-,gó(ə)rm, 'ke(ə)rn-\ **1** mountain range of the Grampians N E *cen* Scotland; highest point Ben Macdhui 4296 *ft* **2** mountain 4084 *ft* in Cairngorm mountains in N Banffshire

Cai·ro \'kī-(,)rō\ city N Egypt ✱ of United Arab Republic *pop* 3,035,000 — **Cai·rene** \kī-'rēn\ *adj or n*

Caith·ness \'käth-,nes, käth-'\ *or* **Caith·ness–shire** \'käth-nəs(h)-,shi(ə)r, -shər, käth-'nes(h)-\ county N Scotland ✱ Wick *area* 684, *pop* 22,704

Ca·ja·mar·ca \,kä-hə-'mär-kə\ city NW Peru *pop* 18,324

Ca·jon \kə-'hōn\ pass 4301 *ft* S Calif. NW of San Bernardino between San Bernardino & San Gabriel mountains

Cal·a·bar \'kal-ə-,bär\ city & port SE Nigeria *pop* 46,000

Ca·la·bria \kə-'lā-brē-ə, -'läb-rē-\ **1** district of ancient Italy comprising area forming heel of the Italian peninsula; now the S part of Apulia **2** *or* It **Le Ca·la·brie** \,lā-kə-'läb-rē-,ā\ *or anc* **Brut·ti·um** \'brüt-ē-əm, 'brət-\ region S Italy occupying toe of the Italian peninsula ✱ Reggio *area* 5823, *pop* 2,044,287 — **Ca·la·bri·an** \kə-'lā-brē-ən, -'läb-rē-\ *adj or n*

Calah — see KALAKH

Ca·lais \ka-'lā, 'kal-(,)ā\ city & port N France on Strait of Dover *pop* 60,340

Calais, Pas de — see DOVER (Strait of)

Ca·la·ma \kə-'läm-ə\ city N Chile N E of Antofagasta *pop* 56,330

Ca·la·mian \,käl-ə-mē-'än\ islands W Philippines N E of Palawan I.

Cal·ca·sieu \'kal-kə-,shü\ river 200 *m* SW La. flowing through **Calcasieu Lake** (*ab* 15 *m* long) & **Calcasieu Pass** (channel 5 *m* long) into Gulf of Mexico

Cal·cut·ta \kal-'kət-ə\ city & port E India on Hooghly river ✱ of West Bengal *pop* 2,548,700 — **Cal·cut·tan** \-'kət-ᵊn\ *n*

Cal·e·do·nia \,kal-ə-'dō-nyə, -nē-ə\ — see SCOTLAND — **Cal·e·do·nian** \-nyən, -nē-ən\ *adj or n*

Caledonian Canal ship canal N Scotland in the Great Glen connecting Loch Linnhe & Moray firth & uniting lochs Ness, Oich, Lochy, & Eil

Cal·ga·ry \'kal-gə-rē\ city Canada in SW Alta. *pop* 181,780

Ca·li \'käl-ē\ city W Colombia on the Cauca *pop* 545,410

Calicut — see KOZHIKODE

Cal·i·for·nia \,kal-ə-'fór-nyə, -nē-ə\ state SW U.S. ✱ Sacramento *area* 158,693, *pop* 15,717,204 — **Cal·i·for·nian** *adj or n*

California, Gulf of arm of the Pacific NW Mexico between Lower California & states of Sonora & Sinaloa

Cal·lao \kə-'yä-(,)ō, -'yaù\ city & port W Peru on Callao Bay W of Lima *pop* 129,365

Ca·loo·sa·hatch·ee \kə-,lü-sə-'hach-ē\ river 75 *m* S Fla. flowing W into Gulf of Mexico

Calpe — see GIBRALTAR (Rock of)

Cal·ta·nis·set·ta \,käl-tə-ni-'set-ə, ,kal-\ commune Italy in *cen* Sicily *pop* 46,800

Cal·u·met \'kal-yə-,met, -mət\ industrial region NW Ind. & N E Ill. SE of & adjacent to Chicago; includes chiefly cities of East Chicago, Gary, & Hammond, Ind., & Calumet City & Lansing, Ill.

Calumet City city N E Ill. S of Chicago *pop* 25,000

Calumet Harbor harbor district SE Chicago, Ill., on Lake Michigan at mouth of Calumet river draining Lake Calumet in S Chicago

Cal·va·dos reef \'kal-və-,dōs, -'dōs, -'däs\ *or* F **Ro·chers du Calvados** \rō-shä-dü‿\ long reef of rocks NW France in English channel at mouth of Orne river

Cal·va·ry \'kalv-(ə-)rē\ *or Heb* **Gol·go·tha** \'gäl-gə-thə, gäl-'gäth-ə\ place outside ancient Jerusalem where Christ was crucified

Cal·y·don \'kal-ə-,dän, -əd-ᵊn\ ancient city *cen* Greece in S Aetolia near Gulf of Patras — **Cal·y·do·nian** \,kal-ə-'dō-nyən, -nē-ə\ *adj*

Calydon, Gulf of — see PATRAS (Gulf of)

Cam \'kam\ river 40 *m* E *cen* England in Cambridgeshire flowing into the Ouse

Ca·ma·güey \,kam-ə-'gwä\ city E *cen* Cuba *pop* 110,388

Ca·margue \kə-'märg\ *or* **La Ca·margue** \,läk-ə-\ marshy island S France in delta of the Rhone

Cam·ba·luc \,kam-bə-,lək\ — see KHANBALIK

Cam·bay \kam-'bā\ city & former port W India in Gujarat W of Baroda *pop* 39,038

Cambay, Gulf of inlet of Arabian sea in India N of Bombay

Cam·ber·well \'kam-bər-,wel, -wəl\ **1** city SE Australia in S Victoria E of Melbourne *pop* 76,125 **2** metropolitan borough S London, England *pop* 179,729

Cam·bo·dia \kam-'bōd-ē-ə\ country SE Asia bordering on Gulf of Siam; a kingdom ✱ Phnom Penh *area* 69,866, *pop* 5,040,000

Cam·brai *or formerly* **Cam·bray** \kam-'brā, kä^n-\ city N France on the Scheldt *pop* 29,567
Cam·bria \'kam-brē-ə\ — see WALES
Cam·bri·an \'kam-brē-ən\ mountains *cen* Wales
Cam·bridge \'kām-brij\ **1** city E Mass. W of Boston *pop* 107,716 **2** *or* **Cam·bridge·shire** \-,shi(ə)r, -shər\ formerly, & still as a postal & geographical name, a county in E England comprising the present administrative counties of Cambridge & Isle of Ely **3** *or* **Cambridgeshire** administrative county E England ✻ Cambridge *area* 492, *pop* 166,863 **4** *or* ML **Can·ta·brig·ia** \,kant-ə-'brij-(ē-)ə\ municipal borough E England on the Cam ✻ of Cambridgeshire *pop* 66,789
Cam·den \'kam-dən\ **1** city S Ark. *pop* 15,823 **2** city & port SW N.J. on the Delaware opposite Philadelphia, Pa. *pop* 117,159
Cam·er·oon \,kam-ə-'rün\ **1** *or* **Fa·ko** \'fäk-(,)ō\ massif 13,353 *ft* Republic of Cameroon NW of Buea near coast **2** *or* **Cam·er·oun** country W equatorial Africa in Cameroons region; a republic, formerly a trust territory under France ✻ Yaoundé *area* 183,080, *pop* 4,907,000 — **Ca·me·roo·nian** \-'rü-nē-ən, -nyən\ *adj or n*
Cam·er·oons \,kam-ə-'rünz\ region W Africa bordering on NE Gulf of Guinea formerly comprising Brit. & French Cameroons but now divided between Nigeria & Republic of Cameroon— **Cam·er·oo·nian** \-'rü-nē-ən, -nyən\ *adj or n*
Ca·mi·guin \,kam-ə-'gēn\ **1** island N Philippines N of Luzon; site of Camiguin Volcano 2750 *ft* **2** island S Philippines off N coast of Mindanao — see HIBOKHIBOK
Ca·mo·ni·ca \kə-'mō-ni-kə\ valley N Italy in the Alps N of Brescia
Ca·mo·tes \kə-'mō-,tās\ sea S *cen* Philippines W of Leyte
Cam·pa·gna di Ro·ma \kam-,pän-yə-dē-'rō-mə, -'pan-\ *or* **Ro·man Campagna** region *cen* Italy around Rome *area ab* 800
Cam·pa·nia \kam-'pā-nyə, -nē-ə\ region S Italy bordering on Tyrrhenian sea ✻ Naples *area* 5214, *pop* 4,346,264 — **Cam·pa·nian** \-nyən, -nē-ən\ *adj or n*
Cam·pe·che \kam-'pē-chē\ **1** state SE Mexico in W Yucatán peninsula *area* 19,670, *pop* 122,098 **2** city & port, its ✻, on Bay of Campeche *pop* 31,279
Campeche, Bay of the SW section of Gulf of Mexico
Cam·pi·na Gran·de \kam-,pē-nə-'gran-də, -dē\ city E Brazil in E Paraíba *pop* 72,464
Cam·pi·nas \kam-'pē-nəs\ city SE Brazil in E São Paulo state *pop* 99,156
Cam·po·bel·lo \,kam-pə-'bel-(,)ō\ island Canada in SW N.B.
Cam·po·for·mi·do \,kam-(,)pō-'fȯr-mə-,dō\ *or formerly* **Cam·po For·mio** \-mē,ō\ village NE Italy SW of Udine
Cam·pos \'kam-pəs\ city SE Brazil in Rio de Janeiro state on the Paraíba *pop* 61,633
Cam Ranh Bay \,kam-,ran-\ inlet of So. China sea SE Vietnam *ab* 180 *m* NE of Saigon
Ca·na \'kā-nə\ village N Palestine in Galilee 4 *m* NE of Nazareth; now in Israel
Ca·naan \'kā-nən\ ancient region corresponding vaguely to later Palestine
Can·a·da \'kan-əd-ə\ country N No. America including Nfld. & Arctic islands N of mainland; a dominion of the British Commonwealth ✻ Ottawa *area* 3,560,238, *pop* 16,080,791 — **Ca·na·di·an** \kə-'nād-ē-ən\ *adj or n*
Canadian *or, above its junction with the No. Canadian,* **South Canadian** river 906 *m* S *cen* U.S. flowing E from NE N. Mex. to Arkansas river in E Okla.
Canadian Shield — see LAURENTIAN HIGHLANDS
Ca·nal Zone *or* **Panama Canal Zone** strip of territory Panama under perpetual lease to the U.S. for Panama canal; administrative center Balboa Heights; *area* (including 191 *sq m* of inland waters) 553, *pop* 42,122
Can·an·dai·gua \,kan-ən-'dā-gwə\ lake 15 *m* long W *cen* N.Y.; one of the Finger Lakes
Ca·nary \kə-'ne(ə)r-ē\ islands in the Atlantic off NW coast of Africa S of Madeira belonging to Spain *area* 2807 *pop* 890,381 — see LAS PALMAS, SANTA CRUZ DE TENERIFE — **Ca·nar·i·an** \kə-'ner-ē-ən\ *adj or n*
Ca·nav·er·al \kə-'nav-(ə-)rəl\ **1** peninsula 100 *m* long E Fla. enclosing Mosquito lagoon & Indian river (lagoon) **2** — see KENNEDY (Cape)
Can·ber·ra \'kan-,ber-ə, -b(ə-)rə\ city ✻ of Australia in Australian Capital Territory on a headstream of the Murrumbidgee SW of Sydney *pop* 70,775
Can·dia \'kan-dē-ə\ **1** CRETE **2** *or* **He·rak·li·on** \hi-'rak-lē-ən\ *or* NGk **Irá·kli·on** \i-'rak-\ city & port Greece on N coast of Crete *pop* 54,541
Candia, Sea of — see CRETE (Sea of)
Ca·nea \kə-'nē-ə\ *or* NGk **Kha·niá** \kän-'yä\ *or anc* **Cy·do·nia** \sī-'dō-nē-ə, -nyə\ city & port Greece ✻ of Crete *pop* 35,237
Ca·ney *or* **El Caney** \,el-kə-'nā\ town E Cuba NE of Santiago de Cuba
Can·nae \'kan-(,)ē\ ancient town SE Italy in Apulia WSW of modern Barletta
Can·na·nore \'kan-ə-,nō(ə)r, -,nȯ(ə)r\ *or* **Ka·na·nur** \,kən-ə-'nu̇(ə)r\ city SW India in Kerala on Malabar coast NNW of Calicut *pop* 34,600
Cannes \'kan\ commune & port SE France *pop* 50,192
Cann·stadt \'kän-,s(h)tät\ a N section of Stuttgart, Germany
Ca·no·pus \kə-'nō-pəs\ ancient city N Egypt E of Alexandria at modern Abukir — **Ca·no·pic** \kə-'nō-pik, -'näp-ik\ *adj*
Can·so, Cape \'kan(t)-(,)sō\ cape Canada at NE end of N.S. mainland
Canso, Strait of narrow channel Canada separating Cape Breton I. from mainland of Nova Scotia
Can·ta·bri·an \kan-'tā-brē-ən\ mountains N & NW Spain running E–W near coast of Bay of Biscay — see CERREDO
Cantabrigia — see CAMBRIDGE
Can·ter·bury \'kant-ə(r)-,ber-ē\ **1** provincial district New Zealand on E coast of South I. ✻ Christchurch *area* 13,940, *pop* 329,920 **2** city SE Australia in E New So. Wales, SW suburb of Sydney *pop* 79,058 **3** city & county borough SE England in Kent *pop* 27,778 — **Can·ter·bu·ri·an** \,kant-ə(r)-'byu̇r-ē-ən\ *adj*
Can·ti·gny \,kä^n-,tēn-'yē\ village N France S of Amiens
Can·ton \'kant-^{ə}n\ **1** city NE Ohio *pop* 113,631 **2** island (atoll) *cen* Pacific in Phoenix islands; controlled jointly by U.S. & Great Britain
Can·ton \'kan-,tän, kan-'\ **1** — see PEARL **2** *or* **Kwang·chow** *or* **Kuang-chou** \'gwäŋ-'jō\ city & port SE China ✻ of Kwangtung on Pearl river *pop* 1,598,900 — **Can·ton·ese** \-,kant-^{ə}n-'ēz, -'ēs\ *adj or n*
Cantyre — see KINTYRE
Canyon de Chel·ly National Monument \də-'shā\ reservation NE Ariz. containing cliff-dweller ruins *area* 131
Can·yon·lands National Park reservation SE Utah surrounding junction of Colorado & Green rivers *area* 403
Cap d'An·tibes \,kap-(,)dä^n-'tēb\ point of land SE France in the Mediterranean SSW of city of Antibes
Cap-de-la-Ma·de·leine \,kap-də-,lä-,mad-^{ə}l-'ān\ city Canada in S Que. on the St. Lawrence ENE of Trois-Rivières *pop* 22,943
Cape Bret·on \kāp-'bret-^{ə}n, kə-'bret-, -'brit-\ **1** island Canada in NE N.S. *area* 3970 **2** — see BRETON (Cape)
Cape Breton Highlands National Park reservation Canada in NE N.S. near N end of Cape Breton I. *area* 390
Cape Cod Bay the S end of Massachusetts Bay W of Cape Cod
Cape Cod National Seashore — see COD (Cape)
Cape Fear \'fi(ə)r\ **1** river 202 *m*, *cen* & SE N.C. flowing SE into the Atlantic **2** — see FEAR (Cape)
Cape Gi·rar·deau \jə-'rä(r)d-(,)ō\ city SE Mo. *pop* 24,947
Cape Hai·tien \kāp-'hā-shən\ *or* F **Cap-Ha·ï·tien** \kȧ-pȧ-ē-syä^n, -ē-tyä^n\ city & port N Haiti *pop* 24,957
Cape Hatteras National Seashore Recreational Area — see HATTERAS
Cape of Good Hope, 1 — see GOOD HOPE (Cape of) **2** *or* **Cape Province** *or* **Kaap·land** \'käp-,länt\ *or formerly* **Cape Colony** province S Republic of So. Africa ✻ Cape Town *area* 278,465, *pop* 4,426,726
Ca·per·na·um \kə-'pər-nē-əm\ city of ancient Palestine on NW shore of Sea of Galilee
Cape Sa·ble \'sā-bəl\ **1** island 7 *m* long Canada off S coast of N.S. **2** — see SABLE (Cape)
Cape Town *or* **Cape·town** \'kāp-,tau̇n\ *or* **Kaap·stad** \'käp-,stät\ city & port, legislative ✻ of Republic of So. Africa & ✻ of Cape of Good Hope, on Table Bay *pop* 577,648 — **Cape·to·ni·an** \kāp-'tō-nē-ən\ *n*
Cape Verde \'vərd\ **1** islands in the Atlantic off W Africa belonging to Portugal ✻ Praia (on São Tiago) *area* 1557, *pop* 148,331 **2** — see VERT (Cape) — **Cape Verd·ian** \'vərd-ē-ən\ *n*
Cape York peninsula peninsula NE Australia in N Queensland having at its N tip **Cape York** (on Torres strait)
Cap Fer·rat \,kap-fə-'rä\ cape SE France E of Nice
Cap·i·to·line \'kap-ət-^{ə}l-,īn, *Brit often* kə-'pit-^{ə}l-\ hill in Rome, Italy, one of seven on which the ancient city was built — see AVENTINE
Capitol Reef National Monument reservation S *cen* Utah containing archaeological remains, petrified forests, & unusual erosion forms *area* 397
Capodistria — see KOPER
Caporetto — see KOBARID
Cap·pa·do·cia \,kap-ə-'dō-sh(ē-)ə\ ancient district E Asia Minor chiefly in valley of the upper Kizil Irmak in modern Turkey ✻ Caesarea Mazaca — **Cap·pa·do·cian** \-sh(ē-)ən\ *adj or n*
Ca·pri \ka-'prē, kə-; 'käp-(,)rē, 'kap-\ *or anc* **Cap·re·ae** \'kap-rē-,ē\ island Italy S of Bay of Naples *area* 5 — **Cap·ri·ote** \'kap-rē-,ōt, -rē-ət\ *n*
Capsa — see GAFSA
Cap·ua \'kap-yə-wə\ town S Italy on the Volturno N of Naples near site of original ancient city of Capua — **Cap·u·an** \-wən\ *adj or n*
Ca·pu·lin, Mount \'kap-(y)ə-lən\ **1** cinder cone 8215 *ft* NE N. Mex. ESE of Raton; main feature of **Capulin Mountain National Monument** (*area* 1) **2** *or* **Capulin Peak** mountain 9198 *ft* N N. Mex. NW of Los Alamos
Ca·ra·cas \kə-'rak-əs, -'räk-\ city ✻ of Venezuela near Caribbean coast *pop* 695,100
Car·cas·sonne \,kär-kə-'sȯn, -'sän\ city S France on the Aude SE of Toulouse *pop* 37,035
Car·che·mish \'kär-kə-,mish, kär-'kē-mish\ ruined city S Turkey on Euphrates river at Syrian border N of modern Jerablus, Syria
Cár·de·nas \'kärd-^{ə}n-,äs, 'kär-t͟hā-,näs\ city & port N Cuba E of Matanzas *pop* 43,750
Car·diff \'kärd-əf\ county borough & port ✻ of Wales & of Glamorganshire on Bristol channel *pop* 243,627
Car·di·gan \'kärd-i-gən\ *or* **Car·di·gan·shire** \-,shi(ə)r, -shər\ county W Wales ✻ Aberystwyth *area* 692, *pop* 53,267
Cardigan Bay inlet of St. George's channel on W coast of Wales
Carelia — see KARELIA — **Ca·re·lian** \kə-'rēl-yən, -'rē-lē-ən\ *adj or n*
Ca·ren·tan \,kar-ən-'tä^n\ town NW France at base of Cotentin peninsula
Car·ia \'kar-ē-ə, 'ker-\ ancient region SW Asia Minor bordering on Aegean sea ✻ Halicarnassus — **Car·i·an** \-ē-ən\ *adj or n*
Ca·rib·be·an \,kar-ə-'bē-ən, kə-'rib-ē-\ sea arm of Atlantic ocean bounded on N & E by West Indies, on S by So. America, & on W by Central America
Car·ib·bees \'kar-ə-,bēz\ LESSER ANTILLES
Car·i·boo \'kar-ə-,bü\ mountains W Canada in E *cen* B.C. W of the Rocky mountains; highest point *ab* 11,750 *ft*
Ca·rin·thia \kə-'rin(t)-thē-ə\ region *cen* Europe in E Alps; once a duchy, Austrian crownland 1849–1918, divided between Austria & Yugoslavia 1918 — **Ca·rin·thi·an** \-thē-ən\ *adj or n*
Car·lisle \kär-'lī(ə)l, kər-\ **1** borough S *cen* Pa. *pop* 16,623 **2** city & county borough NW England ✻ of Cumberland *pop* 57,304
Car·low \'kär-(,)lō\ **1** county SE Ireland in Leinster *area* 346, *pop* 33,345 **2** urban district, its ✻
Carls·bad \'kär(ə)lz-,bad\ **1** caverns SE N. Mex. in **Carlsbad Caverns National Park** (*area* 72) **2** city SE N. Mex. on the Pecos *pop* 25,541 **3** — see KARLOVY VARY
Carmana, Carmania — see KERMAN
Car·mar·then \kər-'mär-t͟hən, kär-\ **1** *or* **Car·mar·then·shire** \-,shi(ə)r, -shər\ county S Wales *area* 919, *pop* 171,742 **2** municipal borough & port, its ✻, on Towy river
Car·mel, Mount \'kär-məl\ mountain ridge NW Palestine; highest point 1791 *ft*
Car·mi·chael \'kär-,mī-kəl\ urban area N *cen* Calif. ENE of Sacramento *pop* 20,455
Carnarvon, Carnarvonshire — see CAERNARVON
Car·nat·ic \kär-'nat-ik\ region SE India between Eastern Ghats & Coromandel coast
Car·ney \'kär-nē\ urban area N *cen* Md. NE of Baltimore *pop* (with Parkville) 27,236

Car·nic Alps \,kär-nik-\ mountain range E Alps between Austria & Italy — see KELLERWAND

Car·nio·la \,kär-nē-'ō-lə, kärn-'yō-\ region NW Yugoslavia NE of Istrian peninsula — **Car·nio·lan** \-lən\ *adj*

Car·ol City \,kar-əl-\ urban area SE Fla. N of Miami *pop* 21,749

Car·o·li·na \,kar-ə-'lī-nə\ English colony 1663–1729 on E coast of No. America divided 1729 into No. Carolina & So. Carolina (the **Car·o·li·nas** \-nəz\)

Car·o·line \'kar-ə-,līn, -lən\ islands W Pacific E of S Philippines; part of Trust Territory of the Pacific Islands *area* 550 — see PALAU

Ca·ro·ní \,kär-ə-'nē, ,kar-\ river 373 *m* E Venezuela flowing N into the Orinoco

Car·pa·thi·an \kär-'pā-thē-ən\ mountain system E *cen* Europe along boundary between Czechoslovakia & Poland & in N & *cen* Romania — see GERLACHOVKA, TATRA, TRANSYLVANIAN ALPS

Carpathian Ruthenia — see RUTHENIA

Carpathos — see KARPATHOS

Car·pen·tar·ia, Gulf of \,kär-pən-'ter-ē-ə, ,kärp-°m-, -'tar-\ inlet of Arafura sea on N coast of Australia

Car·pen·ters·ville \'kär-pən-tərz-,vil, 'kärp-°m-\ village NE Ill. NW of Chicago *pop* 17,424

Car·qui·nez \kär-'kē-nəs\ strait 8 *m* long Calif. joining San Pablo & Suisun bays

Car·ran·tuo·hill \,kar-ən-'tü-əl\ mountain 3414 *ft* SW Ireland in County Kerry; highest in Macgillicuddy's Reeks & in Ireland

Car·ra·ra \kə-'rär-ə\ commune N Italy ESE of La Spezia *pop* 62,287

Carrhae — see HARAN

Car·rick on Shan·non \,kar-i-,kȯn-'shan-ən, -,kän-\ town N *cen* Ireland ✳ of County Leitrim

Car·shal·ton \kər-'shȯlt-°n\ urban district S England in Surrey S of London *pop* 62,804

Carso — see KRAS

Car·son \'kärs-°n\ **1** river 125 *m* W Nev. flowing NE into **Carson Lake 2** urban area SW Calif. SE of Los Angeles *pop* 38,059

Carson City city ✳ of Nev. E of Lake Tahoe *pop* 5163

Carson Sink intermittent lake W Nev. S of Humboldt Lake; has no outlet to ocean

Car·stensz, Mount \'kär-stənz\ mountain 16,404 *ft* W New Guinea in Nassau range of Snow mountains; highest in New Guinea

Car·ta·ge·na \,kärt-ə-'gā-nə, -'hā-\ **1** city & port NW Colombia on Caribbean sea *pop* 167,980 **2** city & port SE Spain SSE of Murcia *pop* 121,122

Car·ta·go \kär-'täg-(,)ō\ city *cen* Costa Rica *pop* 23,498

Car·ter·et \,kärt-ə-'ret\ borough NE N.J. S of Elizabeth *pop* 20,502

Car·thage \'kär-thij\ *or anc* **Car·tha·go** \kär-'täg-(,)ō\ ancient city & state N Africa on coast NE of modern Tunis — **Car·tha·gin·ian** \,kär-thə-'jin-yən, -'jin-ē-ən\ *adj or n*

Ca·sa·blan·ca \,käs-ə-'blaŋ-kə, ,kaz-; ,käs-ə-'bläŋ-, ,käz-\ *or* **Ar Dar el Bei·da** \,dä-,rel-bī-'dä, -bā-'dä\ city & port W Morocco on the Atlantic *pop* 1,177,000

Casa Gran·de National Monument \,kas-ə-'gran-dē\ reservation S *cen* Ariz. SE of Phoenix containing prehistoric ruins *area* 473 acres

Cas·cade \ka-'skād\ mountain range W U.S., N continuation of the Sierra Nevada extending N from Lassen Peak, N Calif., across Oreg. & Wash. — see RAINIER (Mount), COAST

Cas·co Bay \,kas-(,)kō-\ inlet of the Atlantic S Me. on which Portland is situated

Ca·ser·ta \kə-'zert-ə, -'zərt-\ commune S Italy NNE of Naples *pop* 31,200

Cash·el \'kash-əl\ urban district S Ireland in *cen* Tipperary at base of **Rock of Cashel** (hill 300 *ft* high with ruins of cathedral & castle)

Cashmere — see KASHMIR

Ca·si·quia·re \,käs-i-'kyär-ē\ river 125 *m* S Venezuela connecting the upper course of the Negro with the Orinoco

Cas·per \'kas-pər\ city *cen* Wyo. on No. Platte river *pop* 38,930

Cas·pi·an \'kas-pē-ən\ sea (salt lake) between Europe & Asia; *ab* 85 *ft* below sea level *area* 169,381

Caspian Gates pass on W shore of Caspian sea near Derbent

Cassel — see KASSEL

Cas·si·no \kə-'sē-(,)nō\ commune *cen* Italy ESE of Frosinone; site of Monte Cassino monastery

Cas·tel Gan·dol·fo \(,)käs-,tel-(,)gän-'dȯl-(,)fō\ commune *cen* Italy on Lake Albano SE of Rome

Cas·te·llón *or* **Castellón de la Pla·na** \,kas-təl-'yōn-də-,lä-'plän-ə\ **1** province E Spain *area* 2495, *pop* 339,290 **2** city & port, its ✳, on the Mediterranean NE of Valencia *pop* 61,007

Castellorizo *or* **Castelrosso** — see KASTELLORIZON

Cas·tile \ka-'stē(ə)l\ *or Sp* **Cas·ti·lla** \kä-'stē-l'ä, -'stē-yä\ region & ancient kingdom *cen* & N Spain divided by the Sierra de Guadarrama into regions & old provinces of **Old Castile** (to the N, ✳ Burgos) & **New Castile** (to the S, ✳ Toledo)

Castilla la Nue·va \-lä-'nwä-vä\ NEW CASTILE — see CASTILE

Castilla la Vie·ja \-lä-'vye-ká\ OLD CASTILE — see CASTILE

Cas·tle·bar \,kas-əl-'bär\ urban district NW Ireland ✳ of County Mayo

Castres \'kästr°\ city S France E of Toulouse *pop* 28,982

Cas·tries \-kä-'strē, kä-,trēs\ *or* **Port Castries** city & port Brit. West Indies in the Windward islands ✳ of St. Lucia *pop* 22,356

Ca·strop–Raux·el *or* **Ka·strop–Rauxel** \,käs-,trȯp-'rauk-səl\ city W Germany SSW of Münster *pop* 87,300

Cas·tro Valley \,kas-(,)trō-\ urban area W Calif. ESE of Oakland *pop* 37,120

Ca·tal·ca *or* **Cha·tal·ja** \chät-°l-'jä\ city Turkey in Europe W of Istanbul *pop* 22,000

Cat·a·li·na *or* **San·ta Catalina** \,sant-ə-,kat-°l-'ē-nə\ island SW Calif. in Santa Barbara islands *area* 70

Cat·a·lo·nia \,kat-°l-'ō-nē-ə, -nyə\ *or Sp* **Ca·ta·lu·ña** \,kät-°l-'ü-nyə\ region NE Spain bordering on France & the Mediterranean; chief city Barcelona *area* 12,431 — **Cat·a·lo·nian** \-'ō-nyən, -nē-ən\ *adj or n*

Ca·ta·mar·ca \,kät-ə-'mär-kə\ city NW Argentina SSW of Tucumán *pop* 31,067

Ca·ta·nia \kə-'tän-yə, -'tän-\ *or anc* **Cat·a·na** \'kat-ə-nə\ com-

mune Italy in E Sicily on E coast on Gulf of Catania at foot of Mt. Etna *pop* 301,682

Ca·tan·za·ro \,kä-,tän-'zär-(,)ō\ city S Italy in Calabria *pop* 40,300

Ca·taw·ba \kə-'tȯ-bə\ river 250 *m* flowing S from W N.C. into S.C. — see WATEREE

Ca·thay \kə-'thā, ka-\ CHINA — an old name

Catherine, Mount — see KATHERINA (Gebel)

Ca·toc·tin Mountain \kə-,täk-tən-\ mountain ridge NW Md. & N Va. in Blue Ridge mountains

Ca·tons·ville \'kāt-°nz-,vil, -vəl\ urban area N *cen* Md. SW of Baltimore *pop* 37,372

Cats·kill \'kat-,skil\ mountains SE N.Y. in the Appalachian system W of the Hudson — see SLIDE MOUNTAIN

Cattaro — see KOTOR

Cau·ca \'kau̇-kə\ river 600 *m* W Colombia flowing N into the Magdalena

Cau·ca·sia \kȯ-'kā-zhə, -shə\ *or* **Cau·ca·sus** \'kȯ-kə-səs\ region U.S.S.R. between the Black & Caspian seas; divided by Caucasus mountains into **Cis·cau·ca·sia** \,sis-\ (to the N) & **Trans·cau·ca·sia** \,tran(t)s-\ (to the S)

Caucasus mountain system U.S.S.R. in Caucasia — see ELBORUS

Caucasus Indicus — see HINDU KUSH

Cau·dine Forks \,kȯ-,dīn-, -,dēn-\ two mountain passes S Italy in the Apennines between Benevento & Capua

Caul·field \'kȯl-,fēld\ city SE Australia in S Victoria SE of Melbourne; part of Greater Melbourne *pop* 75,217

Causses \'kōs\ limestone region S *cen* France on S border of Massif Central

Cau·ve·ry \'kȯ-və-rē\ *or* **Ka·ve·ri** \'kä-və-rē\ river 475 *m* S India flowing E & entering Bay of Bengal in a wide delta

Cauvery Falls waterfall 300 *ft* India in Cauvery river on Madras-Mysore boundary

Cav·an \'kav-ən\ **1** county NE Republic of Ireland in Ulster *area* 730, *pop* 56,597 **2** urban district, its ✳

Ca·vi·te \kə-'vēt-ē\ city Philippines in Luzon on Cavite peninsula in Manila Bay SW of Manila *pop* 35,052

Cawnpore — see KANPUR

Ca·xi·as \kə-'shē-əs\ **1** town NE Brazil in Maranhão WNW of Teresina **2** *or* **Du·que de Caxias** \,dü-kəd-ə-'shē-əs\ city SE Brazil in Rio de Janeiro state N of city of Rio de Janeiro *pop* 74,557 **3** *or* **Caxias do Sul** \də-'sül\ city S Brazil in Rio Grande do Sul N of Pôrto Alegre *pop* 31,561

Ca·yenne \kī-'en, kā-\ town & port ✳ of French Guiana on island in Cayenne river near the coast

Cayes *or* **Aux Cayes** \ō-'kā\ town & port SW Haiti on Tiburon peninsula

Ca·yey \kä-'yā\ city SE *cen* Puerto Rico *pop* 19,738

Cay·man \kā-'man, *attributively* 'kā-mən\ islands West Indies NW of Jamaica; a Brit. colony ✳ Georgetown (on **Grand Cayman,** chief island) *area* 93, *pop* 9374

Ca·yu·ga \kē-'ü-gə, 'kyü-, kā-(y)ü-\ lake 40 *m* long W *cen* N.Y.; one of the Finger Lakes

Ce·a·rá \,sā-ə-'rä\ **1** state NE Brazil bordering on the Atlantic ✳ Fortaleza *area* 57,371, *pop* 2,695,450 **2** — see FORTALEZA

Ce·bu \sā-'bü\ **1** island E *cen* Philippines, one of the Visayan islands *area* 1707 **2** city on E coast of Cebu I. *pop* 167,503

Ce·dar \'sēd-ər\ river 329 *m* SE Minn. & E Iowa flowing SE into the Iowa

Cedar Breaks National Monument reservation SW Utah NE of Zion National Park containing unusual erosion forms *area* 8

Cedar Falls city NE *cen* Iowa NW of Waterloo *pop* 21,195

Cedar Rapids city E *cen* Iowa on Cedar river *pop* 92,035

Cel·e·bes \'sel-ə-,bēz, sə-'lē-bēz\ **1** *or* **Su·la·we·si** \,sü-lə-'wā-sē\ island Indonesia E of Borneo ✳ Makassar *area* 69,255, *pop* 4,231,900 **2** sea arm of SW Pacific enclosed on N by Mindanao & Sulu archipelago, on S by Celebes, & on W by Borneo — **Cel·e·be·sian** \,sel-ə-'bē-zhən\ *adj*

Celestial Empire the former Chinese Empire

Cel·le \'tsel-ə\ city W Germany NE of Hannover *pop* 56,500

Ce·nis, Mont \,mȯⁿ-sə-'nē, mȯⁿ-'snē\ *or It* **Mon·te Ce·ni·sio** \,mȯnt-ē-chə-'nēz-,(,)yō\ **1** mountain pass 6831 *ft* between France & Italy over Mont Cenis massif (11,792 *ft*) in Graian Alps **2** tunnel piercing the Fréjus massif SW of Mont Cenis

Central African Republic country N *cen* Africa, formerly Ubangi-Shari; a republic ✳ Bangui *area* 238,224, *pop* 1,227,000

Central America, 1 the narrow S portion of No. America connecting that continent with So. America & extending from the Isthmus of Tehuantepec to the Isthmus of Panama **2** the republics of Guatemala, El Salvador, Honduras, Nicaragua, & Costa Rica & often also Panama & Brit. Honduras — **Central American** *adj or n*

Central Falls city N R.I. N of Providence *pop* 19,858

Central India former group of 89 Indian states N *cen* India ✳ Indore; area now chiefly in W & N Madhya Pradesh

Central Karroo — see KARROO

Central Provinces and Be·rar \bā-'rär, bə-\ former province of India reorganized 1950 & renamed Madhya Pradesh

Central Valley valley *cen* Calif. comprising the valleys of the Sacramento & San Joaquin rivers

Ceos — see KEOS

Ceph·a·lo·nia \,sef-ə-'lō-nyə, -nē-ə\ *or NGk* **Ke·fal·li·nía** \,kef-ə-lə-'nē-ə\ island W Greece in the Ionian islands *area* 277

Ce·phi·sus \sə-'fī-səs\ *or* **Ce·phis·sus** \-'fis-əs\ any of three small rivers *cen* Greece in Attica & Boeotia

Ce·ram *or* **Se·ram** \'sā-,räm\ island E Indonesia in *cen* Moluccas *area* 6621

Cerigo — see KÍTHIRA

Cernauti — see CHERNOVTSY

Cer·re·do *or* **Tor·re de Cerredo** \'tȯr-ē-də-sə-'räd-(,)ō\ mountain 8687 *ft* N Spain SW of Santander; highest in the Cantabrians

Cerro Bolívar — see BOLÍVAR (Cerro)

Cer·ro de Pas·co \,ser-(,)ō-də-'pas-(,)kō\ **1** mountain 15,100 *ft*, *cen* Peru NE of Lima **2** town near the mountain *pop* 22,688

Cerro de Pun·ta \'pün-tə\ mountain 4389 *ft*, *cen* Puerto Rico in Cordillera Central; highest on the island

Cer·ro Gor·do \\,ser-ō-'gȯrd-(,)ō\\ mountain pass E Mexico between Veracruz & Jalapa
Cervin, Mont — see MATTERHORN
Ce·se·na \\chə-'zā-nə\\ *or anc* **Cae·se·na** \\sə-'zē-nə\\ commune N Italy in Emilia-Romagna SE of Forlì *pop* 70,390
Ces·ke Bu·de·jo·vi·ce \\,ches-kə-'büd-ə-,yō-vət-sə\\ *or* G **Bud·weis** \\'büt-,vīs\\ city W Czechoslovakia in S Bohemia on the Vltava *pop* 38,194
Cetatea Alba — see BELGOROD-DNESTROVSKI
Ce·ti·nje \\'tset-^{ə}n-,yä\\ town S Yugoslavia SE of Kotor near coast; formerly ✻ of Montenegro
Cette — see SÈTE
Ceu·ta \\'sā-,üt-ə\\ city & port N Morocco opposite Gibraltar; a Spanish presidio *pop* 65,680
Cé·vennes \\sā-'ven\\ mountain range S France W of the Rhone at E edge of Massif Central — see MÉZENC
Cey·lon \\sə-'län, sē-, sā-\\ *or* **Lan·ka** \\'läŋ-kə\\ **1** *or* Ar **Ser·en·dib** \\'ser-ən-,dib, -,dip\\ *or* L & Gk **Ta·prob·a·ne** \\tə-'präb-ə-(,)nē\\ island 270 *m* long & 140 *m* wide in Indian ocean off S India **2** country coextensive with island; a dominion of the Brit. Commonwealth ✻ Colombo *area* 25,332, *pop* 9,172,042 — **Cey·lon·ese** \\,sā-lə-'nēz, ,sē-lə-, ,sel-ə-, -'nēs\\ *adj or n*
Cha·co *or* **Gran Chaco** \\'grän-'chäk-(,)ō\\ region S *cen* So. America drained by the Paraguay & its chief W tributaries the Pilcomayo & Bermejo; divided between Argentina, Bolivia, & Paraguay
Chaco Canyon National Monument \\,chäk-(,)ō-\\ reservation NW N. Mex. containing cliff-dweller ruins *area* 28
Chad *or* F **Tchad** \\'chad\\ **1** shallow lake N *cen* Africa at junction of boundaries of Chad, Niger, & Nigeria *maximum area ab* 8000 **2** country N *cen* Africa ✻ Fort-Lamy; a republic within French Community; before 1959 a territory of French Equatorial Africa *area* 495,752, *pop* 2,675,000 — **Chad·ian** \\'chad-ē-ən\\ *adj or n*
Chae·ro·nea \\,ker-ə-'nē-ə, ,kir-\\ *or* **Chae·ro·neia** \\-'nī-ə\\ ancient city E *cen* Greece in W Boeotia SE of Mt. Parnassus
Cha·gres \\'chäg-rəs, 'chag-\\ river Panama flowing through Gatun Lake to the Caribbean
Cha·gua·ra·mas \\,chäg-wə-'räm-əs\\ district NW Trinidad W of Port of Spain on **Chaguaramas Bay** (inlet of Gulf of Paria)
Cha·har \\'chä-'här\\ former province NE China in E Inner Mongolia ✻ Kalgan
Chalcedon — see KADIKOY
Chal·cid·i·ce \\kal-'sid-ə-(,)sē\\ *or* NGk **Khal·ki·di·kí** \\,käl-kə-thi-'kē\\ peninsula NE Greece in E Macedonia projecting SE into N Aegean sea; terminates in three peninsulas: Kassandra (*anc* Pallene), Sithonia, & Acte — see ACTE
Chal·cis \\'kal-səs\\ *or* **Chal·kis** \\-kəs\\ *or* NGk **Khal·kís** \\käl-'kēs\\ city *cen* Greece ✻ of Euboea on Evripos strait *pop* 23,786 — **Chal·cid·i·an** \\kal-'sid-ē-ən\\ *adj or n*
Chal·dea *or* **Chal·daea** \\kal-'dē-ə\\ ancient region SW Asia on Euphrates river & Persian gulf
Cha·leur Bay \\shə-'lü(ə)r-, -'lər-\\ inlet of Gulf of St. Lawrence SE Canada between N N.B. & Gaspé peninsula, Que.
Chal·na \\'chəl-nə\\ town & port E Pakistan in SW East Bengal
Cha·lon *or* **Cha·lon-sur-Saône** \\shä-'lō^{n}-,sü(ə)r-'sōn\\ city E *cen* France N of Mâcon *pop* 37,399
Châ·lons *or* **Châ·lons-sur-Marne** \\shä-'lō^{n}-,sü(ə)r-'märn\\ commune NE France on the Marne *pop* 36,834
Cha·mar·tín de la Ro·sa \\,chäm-,är-'tēn-də-,lä-'rō-zə\\ commune *cen* Spain, NNE suburb of Madrid *pop* 64,874
Cham·bal \\'chəm-bəl\\ river 650 *m*, *cen* India flowing from Vindhya mountains E into the Jumna
Cham·bers·burg \\'chām-bərz-,bərg\\ borough S *cen* Pa. *pop* 17,670
Cham·bé·ry \\,shä^{n}-(,)bā-'rē\\ city E France E of Lyons *pop* 32,139
Cham·bord \\shä^{n}-'bō(ə)r\\ village N *cen* France NE of Blois
Cham·do \\'chäm-'dō\\ **1** region E Tibet; chief town Changtu **2** — see CHANGTU
Cha·mo·nix *or* **Cha·mou·ni** \\,sham-ə-'nē\\ town & valley SE France NW of Mont Blanc
Cham·pagne \\sham-'pān\\ region & former province NE France W of Lorraine & N of Burgundy ✻ Troyes
Cham·paign \\sham-'pān\\ city E *cen* Ill. *pop* 49,583
Cham·pi·gny-sur-Marne \\,shä^{n}-(,)pēn-'yē-,sü(ə)r-'märn\\ commune N France, SSE suburb of Paris *pop* 36,903
Cham·plain, Lake \\sham-'plān\\ lake 125 *m* long between N.Y. & Vt. extending N into Quebec *area* 600
Chan·der·na·gor *or* **Chan·der·na·gor** \\,chən-dər-nə-'gō(ə)r, -'gȯ(ə)r\\ *or* **Chan·der·na·gar** \\'nəg-ər\\ city E India in West Bengal N of Calcutta; before 1950 part of French India *pop* 49,900
Chan·di·garh \\'chən-dē-gər\\ city N India N of Delhi; a union territory administered by the national government; joint ✻ of Punjabi Suba & Hariana; founded 1953, *pop* 90,000
Changan — see SIAN
Chang·chow \\'jäŋ-'jō, 'chaŋ-'chaü\\ **1** *or* **Lung·ki** \\'lüŋ-'kē\\ city SE China in S Fukien W of Amoy *pop* 81,200 **2** *or formerly* **Wu·tsin** \\'wü-'jin\\ city E China in S Kiangsu *pop* 296,500
Chang·chun \\'chäŋ-'chün\\ city NE China ✻ of Kirin *pop* 855,200
Chang·hua \\'chäŋ-'hwä\\ city China in W Formosa *pop* 62,452
Chang·jin \\'chäŋ-'jin\\ *or* Jap **Cho·shin** \\'chō-'shin\\ **1** river 160 *m* N Korea flowing NE into the Yalu **2** reservoir in Changjin river
Changkiakow — see KALGAN
Chang·sha \\'chäŋ-'shä\\ city SE *cen* China ✻ of Hunan on Siang river *pop* 650,600
Chang·shu \\'chäŋ-'shü\\ city E China in S Kiangsu *pop* 101,400
Chang·teh \\'chäŋ-'də\\ city SE *cen* China in N Hunan on Yuan river *pop* 94,800
Chang·tu \\'chäŋ-'tü\\ *or* **Cham·do** \\'chäm-'dō\\ town E Tibet on the Mekong
Chan·kiang \\'chän-jē-'äŋ\\ *or* **Tsam·kong** \\'jäm-'gȯŋ\\ *or formerly* **Fort Bay·ard** \\'bā-ərd, 'bī-\\ city SE China in SE Kwangtung on Luichow peninsula *pop* 166,000
Channel, 1 — see SANTA BARBARA (islands) **2** islands in English channel belonging to Great Britain *area* 75, *pop* 158,059 — see ALDERNEY, GUERNSEY, JERSEY, SARK
Channel Islands National Monument reserve SW Calif. in Santa Barbara islands including areas on Anacapa islands (E of Santa Cruz I.) & Santa Barbara I. (W of Santa Catalina I.)
Chan·til·ly \\shä^{n}-tē-yē\\ town N France NNE of Paris
Chao·chow \\'chaü-'jō\\ *or* **Chao·an** \\'chaü-'än\\ city E China in NE Kwangtung on Han river above Swatow *pop* 101,300
Chao Phra·ya \\chaü-'prī-ə\\ *or* **Me Nam** \\mā-'näm\\ river 160 *m* W *cen* Thailand formed by confluence of Nan & Ping rivers & flowing S into Gulf of Siam
Cha·pa·la \\chə-'päl-ə\\ lake 50 *m* long W *cen* Mexico in Jalisco & Michoacán SE of Guadalajara
Cha·pul·te·pec \\chə-'pül-tə-,pek\\ fortress *cen* Mexico on a hill 3 *m* SW of Mexico City
Cha·rente \\shə-'ränt\\ river 225 *m* W France flowing W into Bay of Biscay
Chari — see SHARI
Char·i·ton \\'shar-ət-^{ə}n\\ river 280 *m* S Iowa & N Mo. flowing S into the Missouri
Charle·roi \\'shär-lə-,rȯi, ,shärl-rə-'wä\\ city SW Belgium in Hainaut *pop* 26,433
Charles \\'chär(ə)lz\\ river 47 *m* Mass. flowing into Boston harbor
Charles, Cape cape E Va. N of entrance to Chesapeake Bay
Charles·ton \\'chärl-stən\\ **1** city & port SE S.C. *pop* 65,925 **2** city ✻ of W. Va. on the Kanawha *pop* 85,796
Charleston Peak mountain 10,874 *ft* SE Nev. WNW of Las Vegas
Charles·town \\'chärl-,staün\\ section of Boston, Mass., on Boston harbor between mouths of Charles & Mystic rivers
Char·lotte \\'shär-lət\\ city S N.C. *pop* 201,564
Charlotte Ama·lie \\ə-'mäl-yə\\ *or formerly* **Saint Thomas** city & port ✻ of Virgin Islands of the U.S., on St. Thomas I. *pop* 12,880
Charlotte Harbor inlet of Gulf of Mexico SW Fla.
Char·lot·ten·burg \\shär-'lät-^{ə}n-,bərg, -,bü(ə)rg\\ a W section of Berlin, Germany
Char·lottes·ville \\'shär-ləts-,vil, -vəl\\ city *cen* Va. *pop* 29,427
Char·lotte·town \\'shär-lət-,taün\\ city & port Canada ✻ of P.E.I. on Northumberland Strait *pop* 16,707
Chartres \\'shärt, 'shärtr^{ə}\\ city N *cen* France SW of Paris *pop* 28,750
Chatalja — see CATALCA
Châ·teau·roux \\,shä-,tō-'rü\\ commune *cen* France S of Orléans *pop* 36,420
Châ·teau-Thier·ry \\,sha-,tō-,tye-'rē, ,shä-\\ town N France on the Marne SW of Reims
Chat·ham \\'chat-əm\\ **1** — see SAN CRISTÓBAL **2** islands S Pacific belonging to New Zealand & comprising two islands (Chatham & Pitt) *area* 372 **3** strait SE Alaska between Admiralty I. & Kuiu I. on E & Baranof I. & Chichagof I. on W **4** city Canada in SE Ont. E of Lake St. Clair *pop* 22,262 **5** municipal borough SE England in Kent *pop* 46,940
Chat·ta·hoo·chee \\,chat-ə-'hü-chē\\ river 410 *m* SE U.S. rising in N Ga., flowing SW & S along Ala.-Ga. boundary into Lake Seminole
Chat·ta·noo·ga \\,chat-ə-'nü-gə, ,chat-^{ə}n-'ü-\\ city SE Tenn. on the Tennessee *pop* 130,009
Chau·tau·qua \\shə-'tȯ-kwə\\ lake 18 *m* long SW N.Y.
Che·bok·sa·ry \\,cheb-,äk-'sär-ē\\ city U.S.S.R. in Soviet Russia, Europe ✻ of Chuvash Republic WNW of Kazan *pop* 83,000
Che·cheno-In·gush Republic \\chə-,chen-ō-in-,güsh-\\ autonomous republic of the U.S.S.R. in SE Soviet Russia, Europe, on N slopes of Caucasus mountains *area* 6064, *pop* 710,000
Che·du·ba \\chə-'dü-bə\\ island W Bengal *area* 220
Cheek·to·waga \\,chēk-tə-'wäg-ə\\ urban area W N.Y. N of Buffalo *pop* 52,362
Che·foo \\'jə-'fü\\ *or* **Yen·tai** \\'yen-'tī\\ city & port E China in NE Shantung on Shantung peninsula on Po Hai *pop* 116,000
Che·ju \\'chē-,jü\\ *or* **Quel·part** \\'kwel-,pärt\\ *or* Jap **Sai·shu** \\'sī-(,)shü\\ **1** island S Korea in N East China sea *area* 710 **2** city & port on N coast of the island *pop* 57,905
Che·kiang \\'jəj-ē-'äŋ\\ province E China bordering on East China sea ✻ Hangchow *area* 39,305, *pop* 22,866,000
Che·lan \\shə-'lan\\ lake *ab* 55 *m* long N *cen* Wash.
Chelms·ford \\'chelm(p)s-fərd\\ municipal borough SE England ✻ of Essex *pop* 37,888
Chel·sea \\'chel-sē\\ **1** city E Mass. NE of Boston *pop* 33,749 **2** metropolitan borough SW London, England, on N bank of the Thames *pop* 50,912
Chel·ten·ham \\'chelt-^{ə}n-,ham, *Brit usu* 'chelt-nəm *or* -^{ə}n-əm\\ **1** urban township SE Pa. *pop* 35,990 **2** municipal borough SW *cen* England in Gloucestershire *pop* 62,823
Che·lya·binsk \\chel-'yä-bən(t)sk\\ city U.S.S.R. in W Soviet Russia, Asia, S of Sverdlovsk *pop* 688,000
Che·lyus·kin \\chel-'yüs-kən\\ cape U.S.S.R. in NW Soviet Russia, Asia, on Taimyr peninsula; northernmost point of Asian mainland, at 77°35′N, 105°E
Chem·nitz \\'kem-,nits, -nəts\\ *or* **Karl-Marx-Stadt** \\kärl-'märk-,s(h)tät\\ city E Germany SE of Leipzig *pop* 250,188
Chemulpo — see INCHON
Che·nab \\chə-'näb\\ river 590 *m* NW India (subcontinent) in Kashmir & the Punjab flowing SW to unite with the Sutlej forming the Panjnad
Cheng·chow \\'jəŋ-'jō\\ city NE *cen* China ✻ of Honan on Yellow river *pop* 594,700
Cheng·teh \\'chəŋ-'də\\ *or formerly* **Je·hol** \\jə-'hōl, 'rō-'hō\\ city NE China in NE Hopei NE of Peking *pop* 92,900
Cheng·tu \\'chəŋ-'dü\\ city SW *cen* China ✻ of Szechwan on Min river *pop* 856,700
Chenstokhov — see CZESTOCHOWA
Cher \\'she(ə)r\\ river 220 *m*, *cen* France flowing into the Loire
Cher·bourg \\'she(ə)r-,bü(ə)r(g), 'shər-; sher-'bü(ə)r\\ city & port NW France on Cotentin peninsula on English channel *pop* 35,246
Che·rem·kho·vo \\chə-'rem-kə-,vō\\ city U.S.S.R. in E *cen* Soviet Russia, Asia, NW of Irkutsk *pop* 123,000
Cheribon — see TJIREBON
Cher·kessk \\cher-'kesk\\ city U.S.S.R. in SE Soviet Russia, Europe, in N Caucasia SE of Stavropol *pop* 41,000
Cher·ni·gov \\cher-'nē-gəf\\ city U.S.S.R. in Ukraine *pop* 89,000
Cher·nov·tsy \\cher-'nȯft-sē\\ *or* Rom **Cer·na·u·ti** \\,cher-nə-'üts(-ē)\\ city U.S.S.R. in W Ukraine on the Prut *pop* 145,000
Cher·o·kee Outlet *or* **Cherokee Strip** \\,cher-ə-,kē-\\ strip of land N Okla. along S border of Kans. E of 100° W opened to settlement 1893; 50 *m* wide, *ab* 220 *m* long
Cherry Hill \\,cher-ē-\\ *or formerly* **Del·a·ware** \\'del-ə-,wa(ə)r, -,we(ə)r\\ urban township W N.J. *pop* 31,522
Cher·so·nese \\'kər-sə-,nēz, -,nēs\\ *or anc* **Cher·so·ne·sus** \\,kər-sə-'nē-səs\\ any of several peninsulas: as (1) Jutland (the **Cim·bri·an** \\'sim-brē-ən\\, *or* **Cim·bric** \\-brik\\, **Chersonese**); (2) the Malay peninsula (the **Golden Chersonese**); (3) the Crimea (the

Tau·ric Chersonese \'tȯr-ik\); (4) the Gallipoli peninsula (the **Thra·cian Chersonese** \'thrā-shən\)

Cher·well \'chär-wəl\ river 30 m, cen England in Northampton-shire & Oxfordshire flowing S into the Thames at Oxford

Ches·a·peake \'ches-(ə-)ˌpēk\ city SE Va. pop 73,647

Chesapeake Bay inlet of the Atlantic 200 m long in Va. & Md.

Chesh·ire \'chesh-ər, 'chesh-ˌi(ə)r\ or **Ches·ter** \'ches-tər\ county NW England ✻ Chester area 973, pop 1,258,050

Ches·ter \'ches-tər\ 1 city SE Pa. pop 63,658 2 city & county borough NW England ✻ of Cheshire on the Dee pop 48,229

Ches·ter·field \'ches-tər-ˌfēld\ 1 inlet ab 250 m long N Canada on NW coast of Hudson Bay in Keewatin District 2 municipal borough N cen England in Derbyshire S of Sheffield pop 68,540

Chev·i·ot \'chev-ē-ət\ 1 hills extending NE to SW along English-Scottish border 2 peak 2676 ft, highest in the Cheviots

Chey·enne \shī-'an, -'en\ 1 river 290 m S. Dak. flowing NE into the Missouri 2 city ✻ of Wyo. pop 43,505

Chi·ai \jē-'ī\ city China in W cen Formosa pop 123,819

Chiang Mai \jē-'äŋ-'mī\ or **Chieng·mai** \jē-'eŋ-'mī\ city NW Thailand on Ping river pop 60,942

Chia·pas \chē-'äp-əs\ state SE Mexico bordering on the Pacific ✻ Tuxtla Gutiérrez area 28,729, pop 1,106,329

Chi·ba \'chē-bə\ city E Japan in Honshu on Tokyo Bay E of Tokyo pop 133,844

Chi·ca·go \shə-'käg-(ˌ)ō, -'kȯg-\ 1 river Chicago, Ill., having two branches (No. Branch & So. Branch) & orig. flowing E into Lake Michigan but now flowing S through So. Branch & Chicago Sanitary & Ship canal into Des Plaines river 2 city ✻ port NE Ill. on Lake Michigan pop 3,550,404 — **Chi·ca·go·an** \-'käg-ə-wən, -'kȯg-\ n

Chicago Heights city NE Ill. S of Chicago pop 34,331

Chich·a·gof \'chich-ə-ˌgȯf, -ˌgäf\ island SE Alaska in Alexander archipelago N of Baranof I. area 2100

Chi·chén It·zá \chə-ˌchen-ət-'sä\ village SE Mexico in Yucatán 75 m ESE of Mérida at site of ruins of important Mayan city

Chich·es·ter \'chich-ə-stər\ municipal borough S England ENE of Portsmouth ✻ of West Sussex pop 19,110

Chick·a·hom·i·ny \ˌchik-ə-'häm-ə-nē\ river 90 m E Va. flowing SE into the James

Chi·cla·yo \shə-'klī-(ˌ)ō\ city NW Peru near coast pop 54,400

Chic·o·pee \'chik-ə-(ˌ)pē\ city SW Mass. pop 61,553

Chi·cou·ti·mi \shə-'küt-ə-mē\ 1 river 100 m Canada in S Que. flowing N into the Saguenay 2 city Canada in S cen Que. on the Saguenay pop 24,878

Chihli — see HOPEI

Chihli, Gulf of — see PO HAI

Chi·hua·hua \chə-'wä-wə, shə-\ 1 state N Mexico bordering on the U.S. area 94,822, pop 1,044,350 2 city, its ✻ pop 144,653

Chilachap — see TJILATJAP

Chile \'chil-ē\ country S So. America between the Andes & Pacific ocean; a republic ✻ Santiago area 286,396, pop 7,364,498 — **Chil·ean** \'chil-ē-ən\ adj or n

Chil·koot \'chil-ˌküt\ pass 3502 ft between SE Alaska & SW Yukon Territory, Canada, in N Coast mountains

Chil·lán \chē-'(y)än\ city cen Chile NE of Concepción pop 82,947

Chil·li·cothe \ˌchil-ə-'käth-ē, -'kȯ-thē\ city S Ohio pop 24,957

Chi·loé \ˌchil-ə-'wā\ island S cen Chile area 4700

Chil·pan·cin·go \ˌchil-pən-'siŋ-(ˌ)gō\ town S Mexico ✻ of Guerrero

Chil·tern \'chil-tərn\ hills S cen England in Oxfordshire, Buck-inghamshire, Hertfordshire, & Bedfordshire

Chim·bo·ra·zo \ˌchim-bə-'räz-(ˌ)ō, ˌshim-\ mountain 20,702 ft W cen Ecuador

Chim·kent \chim-'kent\ city U.S.S.R. in S Kazakh Republic N of Tashkent pop 153,000

Chin \'chin\ hills W Burma; highest Mt. Victoria 10,018 ft

Chi·na \'chī-nə\ country E Asia; a republic, until 1912 an empire ✻ Peking; area 3,691,502, pop 604,666,212 — see FORMOSA

China sea the East & So. China seas

Chin·chow \'jin-'jō\ city NE China in SW Liaoning on Gulf of Liaotung pop 352,200

Chin·co·teague \ˌshiŋ-kə-'tēg\ bay Md. & Va. on Atlantic coast

Chin·dwin \'chin-ˌdwin\ river 550 m NW Burma flowing S into the Irrawaddy

Chinese Turkestan or **Kash·gar·ia** \kash-'gar-ē-ə, -'ger-\ region W China in W & cen Sinkiang

Chinghai — see TSINGHAI

Chin·ju \'jin-'jü\ or Jap **Shin·shu** \'shin-'shü\ city S Korea W of Pusan pop 77,473

Chin·kiang \'jin-jē-'äŋ\ city & port E China in NW cen Kiangsu on the Yangtze at its junction with the Grand canal pop 201,400

Chinmen — see QUEMOY

Chinnampo — see NAMPO

Chinnereth, Sea of — see GALILEE (Sea of)

Chin·wang·tao \'chin-'(h)wäŋ-'daù\ city & port NE China in NE Hopei on Po Hai pop 186,800

Chiog·gia \kē-'ȯ-jə\ commune & port NE Italy on island in Lagoon of Venice pop 39,915

Chi·os \'kī-ˌäs, or NGk **Khí·os** \'kē-ˌȯs\ 1 island E Greece in the Aegean off W coast of Turkey area 355 2 or NGk **Ká·stron** \'käs-ˌtrȯn\ city & port Greece on E coast of Chios pop 24,361 — **Chi·an** \'kī-ən\ adj or n

Chip·pe·wa \'chip-ə-ˌwȯ, -ˌwä\ river 183 m NW Wis. flowing S into the Mississippi

Chire — see SHIRE

Chir·i·ca·hua National Monument \ˌchir-i-'kä-wə\ reservation SE Ariz. containing curious natural rock formations area 16.5

Chi·ri·quí \ˌchir-i-'kē\ volcano 11,070 ft Panama near Costa Rican border

Chis·holm Trail \ˌchiz-əm-\ pioneer cattle trail between San Antonio, Tex., & Abilene, Kans., used esp. 1866–85

Chisimaio — see KISMAYU

Chisinau — see KISHINEV

Chis·le·hurst and Sid·cup \ˌchiz-əl-ˌhər-stən-'sid-kəp\ urban district SE England in Kent, SE suburb of London pop 83,837

Chi·ta \chi-'tä\ city U.S.S.R. in SE Soviet Russia, Asia, E of Lake

Baikal pop 171,000

Chi·tral \chi-'träl\ 1 river 300 m West Pakistan & Afghanistan flowing SW into the Kabul 2 district N West Pakistan ✻ Chitral

Chit·ta·gong \'chit-ə-ˌgäŋ, -ˌgȯŋ\ city & port Pakistan in SE East Pakistan on Bay of Bengal pop 294,000

Chiu·si \kē-'ü-sē\ or anc **Clu·si·um** \'klü-z(h)ē-əm\ town cen Italy in Tuscany SE of Siena

Chka·lov \chə-'käl-əf\ or **Oren·burg** \'ȯr-ən-ˌbərg, 'ȯr-\ city U.S.S.R. in E Soviet Russia, Europe, on Ural river pop 267,000

Choaspes — see KARKHEH

Choi·seul \shwä-'zə(r)l\ island W Pacific in the Solomons SE of Bougainville I. area 1500

Choi·sy or **Choisy-le-Roi** \shwä-ˌzē-lər-'wä, -lə-rə-'wä\ commune N France on Seine river SSE of Paris pop 27,213

Cho·lon \shə-'lȯn, chə-'lȯn\ city & port S Vietnam on Saigon river adjoining Saigon pop 481,000

Cho·lu·la \chə-'lü-lə\ town SE cen Mexico in Puebla state

Cho·mo Lha·ri \ˌchō-mō-'lär-ē\ mountain 23,997 ft in the Himalayas between Tibet & NW Bhutan; sacred to Buddhists

Chomolungma — see EVEREST

Chong·jin \'chȯŋ-ˌjin\ or Jap **Sei·shin** \'sā-ˌshen\ city & port NE Korea on Sea of Japan pop 184,301

Chong·ju \'chȯŋ-ˌjü\ or Jap **Sei·shu** \'sā-(ˌ)shü\ city S cen Korea N of Taejon pop 64,571

Chon·ju \'jən-ˌjü\ or Jap **Zen·shu** \'zen-(ˌ)shü\ city SW Korea SW of Taejon pop 100,624

Cho Oyu \ˌchō-ō-'yü\ mountain 26,967 ft Nepal & Tibet in the Himalayas; 6th highest in the world

Cho·ras·mia \kə-'raz-mē-ə\ province of ancient Persia on the Oxus extending W to Caspian sea; equiv. to Khwarazm — see KHIVA

Cho·rzow \'kȯ-ˌzhüf\ city SW Poland in Silesia pop 143,800

Chosen — see KOREA

Choshin — see CHANGJIN

Cho·ta Nag·pur \ˌchȯt-ə-'näg-ˌpù(ə)r\ plateau region E India N of Mahanadi basin in N Orissa & S Bihar

Cho·wan \chə-'wän\ river 50 m NE N.C. formed by confluence of Blackwater & Nottoway rivers & flowing into Albemarle sound

Christ·church \'krīs(t)-ˌchərch\ city New Zealand on E coast of South I. pop 220,322

Christiania — see OSLO

Chris·tians·haab \kris(h)-chənz-ˌhȯb\ town W Greenland on Disko Bay SE of Godhavn

Chris·tian·sted \'kris(h)-chən-ˌsted\ town Virgin Islands of the U.S. on N coast of St. Croix I.

Christ·mas \'kris-məs\ 1 island E Indian ocean 225 m S of W end of Java; administered by Australia area 64, pop 2619 2 island (atoll) in the Line islands belonging to Great Britain; largest atoll in the Pacific area (including lagoon) 234

Chu \'chü\ 1 — see PEARL 2 river 600 m U.S.S.R. in Soviet Central Asia in SE Kazakh Republic flowing E into Issyk Kul

Chü·an·chow \chə-'wän-jō\ city & port SE China in SE Fukien on Formosa strait pop 107,700

Chubb Crater \'chəb\ lake-filled meteoric crater Canada in N Que. in N Ungava peninsula; 3 m in diameter

Chu·but \chə-'büt, -'vüt\ river 500 m S Argentina flowing E across Patagonia into the Atlantic

Chu·chow \'chü-'jō\ city SE China in E Hunan pop 127,300

Chuck·chee or **Chuk·chi** \'chək-chē, 'chúk-\ sea of the Arctic ocean N of Bering strait

Chudskoe — see PEIPUS (Lake)

Chu·gach \'chü-ˌgach also -ˌgash\ mountains S Alaska extending along coast from Cook inlet to St. Elias range; highest Mt. Marcus Baker 13,250 ft

Chu·kot·ski \chə-'kät-skē\ or **Chu·kot** \'-ˌkät\ peninsula U.S.S.R. in NE Soviet Russia, Asia, between Bering & Chuckchee seas — see EAST CAPE

Chu·la Vis·ta \ˌchü-lə-'vis-tə\ urban area SW Calif. S of San Diego pop 42,034

Chu·lym or **Chu·lim** \chə-'lim\ river 700 m U.S.S.R. in E cen Soviet Russia, Asia, flowing W into the Ob

Chun·chon \'chün-ˌchon\ or Jap **Shun·sen** \'shün-ˌsen\ city S cen Korea NE of Seoul pop 54,539

Chung·king \'chùŋ-'kiŋ\ or **Pa·hsien** \'bä-shē-'en\ city ✻ of China 1937–46 in SE Szechwan on the Yangtze pop 1,772,500

Chur \'kù(ə)r\ or F **Coire** \'kwär\ commune E Switzerland ✻ of Graubünden canton pop 19,382

Chur·chill \'chər-ˌchil, 'chərch-ˌhil\ 1 river ab 1000 m Canada flowing E across N Sask. & N Man. into Hudson Bay 2 — see HAMILTON

Churchill Falls — see GRAND FALLS

Chu Shan \'chü-'shän\ archipelago E China in East China sea at entrance to Hangchow Bay

Chu·vash Republic \chü-'väsh-\ or **Chu·vash·ia** \-'väsh-ē-ə\ autonomous republic U.S.S.R. in E cen Soviet Russia, Europe, S of the Volga ✻ Cheboksary area 6909, pop 1,098,000

Chu·zen·ji \chü-'zen-jē\ lake Japan in cen Honshu W of Nikko

Cí·bo·la \'sē-bə-lə\ historical region in present N N.Mex. including seven pueblos (the **Seven Cities of Cíbola**) believed by early Spanish explorers to contain vast treasures

Cic·ero \'sis-ə-ˌrō\ town NE Ill. W of Chicago pop 69,130

Cien·fue·gos \sē-ˌen-'fwā-ˌgōs\ city & port W cen Cuba on S coast on Cienfuegos Bay pop 52,910

Cieszyn — see TESCHEN

Ci·li·cia \sə-'lish-(ē-)ə\ ancient country & region SE Asia Minor extending along Mediterranean coast S of Taurus mountains — see LESSER ARMENIA — **Ci·li·cian** \-'lish-ən\ adj or n

Cilician Gates mountain pass S Turkey in Taurus mountains

Cim·ar·ron \'sim-ə-ˌrōn, -ˌrän, -rən\ river 600 m flowing E from NE N. Mex. through SW Kans. into the Arkansas in NE Okla.

Cimbrian, or **Cimbric, Chersonese** — see CHERSONESE

Cim·me·ri·an Bosporus \sə-ˌmir-ē-ən-\ the Kerch strait

Cin·cin·nati \ˌsin(t)-sə-'nat-ē, -'nat-ə\ city SW Ohio pop 502,550

Cinque Ports \'siŋk\ group of seaport towns SE England on coast of Kent & Sussex, orig. five (Dover, Sandwich, Romney, Hastings, & Hythe) to which were later added Winchelsea, Rye, & other minor places, granted special privileges (abolished in 19th century) in return for services in coast defense

Cintra — see SINTRA

ə abut; ᵊ kitten; ər further; a back; ā bake; ä cot, cart; aù out; ch chin; e less; ē easy; g gift; i trip; ī life
j joke; ŋ sing; ō flow; ȯ flaw; ȯi coin; th thin; th̲ this; ü loot; ù foot; y yet; yü few; yù furious; zh vision
ᵊ F table; á F bac; ḵ G ich, Buch; ⁿ F vin; œ F bœuf; œ̄ F feu; ᵫ G füllen; œ̄̄ F rue; ʸ F digne \dēnʸ\, nuit \nwᵉy\

Circars — see NORTHERN CIRCARS

Cir·cas·sia \(,)sər-'kash-(ē-)ə\ region U.S.S.R. in S Soviet Russia, Europe, on NE coast of Black sea N of W end of Caucasus mountains

Cirenaica — see CYRENAICA

Cis·al·pine Gaul \sis-,al-,pīn-\ the part of Gaul lying S & E of the Alps

Ciscaucasia — see CAUCASIA

Ci·thae·ron \sə-'thē-,rän\ or NGk **Ki·thai·ron** \,kē-the-'rón\ or formerly **El·a·tea** \,el-ə-'tē-ə\ mountain 4629 ft Greece on NW border of ancient Attica

Ci·tlal·te·petl \sē-,tläl-'tā-,pet-ᵊl\ or **Ori·za·ba** \,ōr-ə-'zäb-ə, ,ór-\ inactive volcano 18,700 ft SE Mexico on Puebla-Veracruz boundary; highest point in Mexico

Città del Vaticano — see VATICAN CITY

Ci·u·dad Bo·lí·var \,sē-ü-,thä-bə-'lē-,vär, -ü-,dad-\ city & port E cen Venezuela on the Orinoco pop 31,009

Ciudad Guayana — SANTO TOMÉ DE GUAYANA

Ciudad Juá·rez \-'hwär-,es, -'wär-əz\ or **Juárez** city Mexico in Chihuahua on Rio Grande opposite El Paso, Tex. pop 294,373

Ciudad Re·al \-rā-'äl\ **1** province S cen Spain area 7620, pop 591,577 **2** commune, its ✳, S of Toledo pop 35,509

Ciudad Trujillo — see SANTO DOMINGO

Ciudad Vic·to·ria \-,vik-'tōr-ē-ə, -'tór-\ city E cen Mexico ✳ of Tamaulipas pop 31,815

Ci·vi·ta·vec·chia \,chē-vē-tä-'vek-(,)yä\ commune & port cen Italy in Latium on Tyrrhenian sea WNW of Rome pop 35,100

Clack·man·nan \klak-'man-ən\ or **Clack·man·nan·shire** \-,shi(ə)r, -,shər\ **1** county cen Scotland bordering on Forth river where it widens into Firth of Forth area 55, pop 37,528 **2** town, its ✳

Clac·ton \'klak-tən\ urban district SE England in Essex on North sea pop 24,065

Clair·ton \'kla(ə)rt-ᵊn, 'kle(ə)rt-\ city SW Pa. SE of Pittsburgh on the Monongahela pop 18,389

Clare \'kla(ə)r, 'kle(ə)r\ county W Ireland in Munster ✳ Ennis area 1231, pop 73,710

Clark Fork \'klärk\ river 300 m W Mont. & N Idaho flowing NW into Pend Oreille Lake

Clarks·burg \'klärks-,bərg\ city N W. Va. pop 28,112

Clarks·dale \'klärks-,dāl\ city NW Miss. pop 21,105

Clarks Fork \'klärks\ river 120 m NW Wyo. & S Mont. flowing into Yellowstone river in Mont.

Clarks·ville \'klärks-,vil, -vəl\ city N Tenn. NW of Nashville pop 22,021

Clay·ton \'klāt-ᵊn\ city E Mo. W of St. Louis pop 15,245

Clear, Cape \'kli(ə)r\ cape SW Ireland at S end of Clear I.

Clear·wa·ter \'kli(ə)r-,wòt-ər, -,wät-\ **1** mountains N cen Idaho; highest ab 8000 ft **2** city W Fla. NW of St. Petersburg on Gulf of Mexico pop 34,653

Cle·burne \'klē-bərn\ city NE cen Tex. pop 15,381

Clee \'klē\ hills W England in Shropshire; highest 1790 ft

Cler·mont–Fer·rand \,kler-,mōⁿ-fə-'räⁿ\ city S cen France in Allier valley on edge of Auvergne mountains pop 113,391

Cleve·land \'klēv-lənd\ **1** city & port NE Ohio on Lake Erie pop 876,050 **2** city SE Tenn. ENE of Chattanooga pop 16,196 **3** district N England in N Yorkshire between Tees estuary & the Cleveland hills — **Cleve·land·er** \-lən-dər\ n

Cleveland Heights city NE Ohio E of Cleveland pop 61,813

Cleves \'klēvz\ or G **Kle·ve** \'klā-və\ city NW Germany WSW of Münster near the Rhine pop 21,500

Cli·chy or **Clichy-la-Ga·renne** \kli-,shē-,läg-ə-'ren\ commune N France NW of Paris pop 55,591

Cliff·side Park \klif-,sīd-\ borough NE N.J. pop 17,642

Clif·ton \'klif-tən\ city NE N.J. N of Newark pop 82,084

Clinch \'klinch\ river 200 m SW Va. & E Tenn. flowing SW into the Tennessee

Cling·mans Dome \,kliŋ-mənz-\ mountain 6642 ft on N.C.-Tenn. boundary; highest in Great Smoky mountains

Clin·ton \'klint-ᵊn\ city E Iowa on the Mississippi pop 33,589

Clip·per·ton \'klip-ərt-ᵊn\ island E Pacific at 10°N, 109°W belonging to France

Clon·mel \klän-'mel\ municipal borough S Ireland ✳ of County Tipperary

Cloud Peak mountain 13,165 ft N Wyo.; highest in Bighorn mountains

Clo·vel·ly \klō-'vel-ē\ village SW England in NW Devon

Clo·vis \'klō-vəs\ city E N. Mex. pop 23,713

Cluj \'klüzh\ city NW cen Romania in Transylvania pop 162,419

Clu·ny \'klü-nē, klü-'nē\ town E cen France NNW of Lyons

Clusium — see CHIUSI

Clu·tha \'klü-thə\ river 210 m New Zealand in SE South I. flowing SE into the Pacific

Clyde \'klīd\ river 106 m SW Scotland flowing NW into **Firth of Clyde** (estuary)

Clyde·bank \'klīd-,baŋk\ burgh W cen Scotland in Dunbartonshire on the Clyde pop 44,625

Clydes·dale \'klīdz-,dāl\ valley of the upper Clyde, Scotland

Cni·dus \'nīd-əs\ ancient town SW Asia Minor in Caria at end of a long promontory

Cnossus — see KNOSSOS

Coa·chel·la \kō-'chel-ə\ valley SE Calif. between Salton sea & San Bernardino mountains

Coa·hui·la \,kō-ə-'wē-lə, kwä-'wē-\ state N Mexico bordering on the U.S. ✳ Saltillo area 58,062, pop 867,365

Coast, 1 mountains Canada in W B.C.; N continuation of Cascade range **2** mountain ranges W No. America extending along Pacific coast W of Sierra Nevada & Cascade range & N through Vancouver I., B.C., to Kenai peninsula & Kodiak I., Alaska — see LOGAN (Mount)

Coat·bridge \'kōt-(,)brij\ burgh S cen Scotland in Lanark E of Glasgow pop 47,538

Coats Land \'kōts\ section of Antarctica SE of Weddell sea

Cobh \'kōv\ or formerly **Queens·town** \'kwēn-,staún\ urban district & port SW Ireland on island in Cork Harbor

Coblenz — see KOBLENZ

Co·burg, 1 \'kō-,bərg\ city SE Australia in S Victoria, N suburb of Melbourne pop 62,077 **2** \-,bərg, -,bù(ə)rg\ city W Germany in N Bavaria NW of Bayreuth pop 44,000

Cocanada — see KAKINADA

Co·cha·bam·ba \,kō-chə-'bäm-bə\ city W cen Bolivia pop 80,795

Co·chin \'kō-chən, 'käch-ən\ region SW India in Kerala on Malabar coast — see TRAVANCORE AND COCHIN

Cochin China region S Vietnam bordering on So. China sea & Gulf of Siam area 29,974

Cochinos Bay — see PIGS (Bay of)

Coco — see SEGOVIA

Co·co·ni·no \,kō-kə-'nē-(,)nō, -'nē-nə\ plateau NW Ariz. S of Grand Canyon

Co·cos \'kō-kəs\ or **Kee·ling** \'kē-liŋ\ islands E Indian ocean belonging to Australia area 1

Cod, Cape \'käd\ peninsula 65 m long SE Mass.; part of area is included in **Cape Cod National Seashore** (created 1961; area 42)

Coele–Syria — see BIKA

Coeur d'A·lene \,kòrd-ᵊl-'ān\ lake ab 25 m long N Idaho E of Spokane, Wash.; drained by Spokane river

Cof·fey·ville \'kò-fē-,vil, 'käf-ē-\ city SE Kans. pop 17,382

Coglians, Monte — see KELLERWAND

Co·hoes \kə-'hōz\ city E N.Y. NW of Troy pop 20,129

Coi — see RED

Coim·ba·tore \,kòim-bə-'tō(ə)r, -'tò(ə)r\ city S India in W Madras on S slope of Nilgiri hills pop 197,800

Co·im·bra \kù-'im-brə\ city W cen Portugal pop 41,977

Coire — see CHUR

Col·ches·ter \'kōl-,ches-tər, -chəs-\ municipal borough SE England in Essex pop 57,436

Col·chis \'käl-kəs\ ancient country bordering on Black sea S of Caucasus mountains; area now constitutes W part of Georgian Republic, U.S.S.R. — **Col·chi·an** \'käl-kē-ən\ adj or n

Co·li·ma \kə-'lē-mə\ **1** volcano 12,792 ft SW Mexico in S Jalisco **2** state SW Mexico bordering on the Pacific area 2009, pop 122,325 **3** city, its ✳, SSW of Guadalajara pop 28,658

College Park, 1 city NW Ga. S of Atlanta pop 23,469 **2** city SW Md. NE of Washington, D.C. pop 18,482

Col·lings·wood \'käl-iŋz-,wúd\ borough SW N.J. pop 17,370

Col·mar or **Kol·mar** \'kōl-,mär, kōl-\ commune NE France at E edge of Vosges mountains pop 47,305

Co·logne \kə-'lōn\ or G **Köln** \'kœln\ city W Germany in No. Rhine-Westphalia on the Rhine pop 789,300

Co·lomb-Bé·char \kə-,lōⁿ-bā-'shär\ commune NW Algeria SSE of Oran pop 26,960

Co·lombes \kə-'lōm, -'lōⁿb\ commune N France, NW suburb of Paris pop 67,909

Co·lom·bia \kə-'ləm-bē-ə, -'lōm-\ country NW So. America bordering on Caribbean sea & Pacific ocean ✳ Bogotá area 439,825, pop 13,823,600 — **Co·lom·bi·an** \-bē-ən\ adj or n

Co·lom·bo \kə-'ləm-(,)bō\ city & port ✳ of Ceylon pop 426,127

Co·lón \kə-'lōn\ or formerly **As·pin·wall** \'as-pən-,wòl\ city & port N Panama on the Caribbean at entrance to Panama canal pop 52,035

Colón archipelago — see GALÁPAGOS ISLANDS

Col·o·phon \'käl-ə-fən, -,fän\ ancient city W Asia Minor in Lydia

Col·o·ra·do \,käl-ə-'rad-(,)ō, -'räd-\ **1** river 1450 m SW U.S. & NW Mexico rising in N Colo. & flowing SW into Gulf of California **2** river 840 m S Tex. flowing SE into Gulf of Mexico **3** desert SE Calif. W of Colorado river **4** plateau SW U.S. W of Rocky mountains in Colorado river basin N in Ariz., S & E Utah, W Colo., & NW N. Mex. **5** state W U.S. ✳ Denver area 104,247, pop 1,753,947 **6** river 530 m, cen Argentina flowing SE to the Atlantic — **Col·o·ra·dan** \-'rad-ᵊn, -'räd-\ adj or n — **Col·o·ra·do·an** \-'rad-ə-wən, -'räd-\ adj or n

Colorado National Monument reservation W Colo. W of Grand Junction containing many unusual erosion formations area 28

Colorado Springs city cen Colo. E of Pikes Peak pop 70,194

Co·los·sae \kə-'läs-(,)ē\ ancient city SW cen Asia Minor in SW Phrygia — **Co·los·sian** \kə-'läsh-ən\ adj or n

Col·ton \'kōlt-ᵊn\ city SW Calif. S of San Bernardino pop 18,666

Co·lum·bia \kə-'ləm-bē-ə\ **1** river 1270 m SW Canada & NW U.S. rising in S B.C. & flowing S & W into the Pacific **2** city E Wash., E Oreg., & SW Idaho in Columbia river basin **3** city cen Mo. pop 36,650 **4** city ✳ of S.C. pop 97,433 **5** city cen Tenn. pop 17,624 — **Co·lum·bi·an** \-bē-ən\ adj or n

Columbia, Cape cape N Canada on Ellesmere I.; northernmost point of Canada, at 83°07′N

Columbia, District of — see DISTRICT OF COLUMBIA

Columbia Heights city SE Minn. N of Minneapolis pop 17,533

Co·lum·bus \kə-'ləm-bəs\ **1** city W Ga. on the Chattahoochee pop 116,779 **2** city S cen Ind. pop 20,778 **3** city E Miss. pop 24,771 **4** city ✳ of Ohio on the Scioto pop 471,316

Col·ville \'kōl-,vil, 'käl-\ river 320 m N Alaska flowing NE into Beaufort sea

Col·wyn Bay \,käl-wən-\ urban district N Wales in Denbighshire pop 22,276

Co·mil·la \kə-'mil-ə\ city East Pakistan pop 47,526

Commander — see KOMANDORSKIE

Communism Peak — see GARMO PEAK

Co·mo \'kō-(,)mō\ commune N Italy in Lombardy at SW end of **Lake Como** (37 m long) pop 72,100

Comodoro Rivadavia — see RIVADAVIA

Com·o·rin, Cape \'käm-ə-rən\ cape S India in Madras; southernmost point of India, at 8°5′N

Com·o·ro \'käm-ə-,rō\ islands off SE Africa between Mozambique & Madagascar belonging to France area 790, pop 156,150

Com·piègne \kōmp-'yän\ town N France E of Beauvais on the Oise pop 22,325

Compostela SANTIAGO DE COMPOSTELA

Comp·ton \'käm(p)-tən\ city SW Calif. SSE of Los Angeles pop 71,812

Com·stock lode \'käm-,stäk-\ gold & silver lode at Virginia City, Nev., discovered 1859

Con·a·kry or **Kon·a·kry** \'kän-ə-krē\ city & port ✳ of Guinea on the Atlantic pop 52,521

Co·nan·i·cut \kə-'nan-i-kət\ island R.I. in Narragansett Bay W of Aquidneck I.

Con·cep·ción \kən-,sep-sē-'ōn, -'sep-shən\ city S cen Chile pop 167,468

Con·chos \'kän-chəs\ river 300 m N Mexico flowing NE into Rio Grande

Con·cord, 1 \'kän-,kò(ə)rd, 'käŋ-\ city W Calif. NE of Oakland pop 36,208 **2** \'käŋ-,kə(ə)rd\ city ✳ of N.H. on the Merrimack pop 28,991 **3** \'käŋ-,kò(ə)rd, 'käŋ-\ city S cen N.C. pop 17,799

Co·ney Island \,kō-nē-\ resort section of New York City in S Brooklyn; formerly an island

Con·ga·ree \'käŋ-gə-(,)rē\ river 60 *m*, *cen* S.C. flowing SE to unite with the Wateree forming the Santee

Con·go \'käŋ-(,)gō\ **1** river *ab* 3000 *m*, *cen* Africa flowing N, W, & SW into the Atlantic — see LUALABA **2** or **Republic of (the) Congo** or formerly **Belgian Congo** country *cen* Africa comprising most of Congo river basin E of lower Congo river ❋ Kinshasa *area* 893,000, *pop* 14,150,000 **3** or **Congo Republic** or formerly **Middle Congo** country W *cen* Africa W of the lower Congo ❋ Brazzaville *area* 132,046, *pop* 795,000 — see FRENCH EQUATORIAL AFRICA — **Con·go·lese** \,käŋ-gə-'lēz, -'lēs\ *adj or n*

Congo Free State — see BELGIAN CONGO

Conjeeveram — see KANCHIPURAM

Con·nacht \'kän-,ȯt\ or formerly **Con·naught** province W Ireland *area* 6611, *pop* 419,221

Con·nect·i·cut \kə-'net-i-kət\ **1** river 407 *m* NE U.S. rising in N N.H. & flowing S into Long Island Sound **2** state NE U.S. ❋ Hartford *area* 5009, *pop* 2,535,234

Con·ne·ma·ra \,kän-ə-'mär-ə, -'mar-\ district W Ireland in W Galway on Atlantic coast

Con·ners·ville \'kän-ərz-,vil\ city E Ind. *pop* 17,698

Con·stance \'kän(t)-stən(t)s\ or G **Kon·stanz** \'kȯn-,stän(t)s\ commune W Germany on Lake Constance *pop* 52,900

Constance, Lake or G **Bo·den·see** \'bōd-ᵊn-,zā\ lake 46 *m* long W Europe on border between Germany, Austria, & Switzerland

Con·stan·ta or **Con·stan·tsa** \kən-'stän(t)-sə\ city & port SE Romania on Black sea *pop* 110,485

Con·stan·tine \'kän(t)-stən-,tēn\ city NE Algeria S of Philippeville *pop* 116,706

Constantinople — see ISTANBUL

Cooch Be·har \,küch-bə-'här\ former state NE India W of Assam, since 1947 attached to West Bengal *area* 1321

Cook \'kuk\ **1** islands S Pacific SW of Society islands; belong to New Zealand ❋ Avarua (on Rarotonga) *area* 89, *pop* 17,654 **2** strait New Zealand between North I. & South I. **3** inlet of the Pacific S Alaska W of Kenai peninsula

Cook, Mount or **Ao·rangi** \au̇-'räŋ-ē\ mountain 12,349 *ft* New Zealand in W *cen* South I.; highest peak in Southern Alps & New Zealand

Coomassie — see KUMASI

Coorg or **Kurg** \'ku(ə)rg\ former state S India ❋ Mercara; merged with Mysore state 1956

Coo·sa \'kü-sə\ river 286 *m* NW Ga. & N Ala. flowing SW to join the Tallapoosa forming the Alabama

Coos Bay \'küs\ inlet of the Pacific SW Oreg.

Co·pán \kō-'pän\ ruined Mayan city W Honduras

Co·pen·ha·gen \,kō-pən-'hā-gən, -'häg-ən, 'kō-pən-,\ or Dan **Kø·ben·havn** \,kœb-ən-'haun\ city & port ❋ of Denmark on E Sjælland I. & N Amager I. *pop* 960,319 — **Co·pen·ha·gen·er** \,kō-pən-'hā-gə-nər, -'häg-ə-\ *n*

Co·pia·pó \,kō-pē-ə-'pō\ **1** volcano 19,947 *ft* N *cen* Chile **2** city W of the volcano *pop* 38,004

Cop·per·mine \'käp-ər-,mīn\ river 525 *m* N Canada in Northwest Territories flowing NW into Arctic ocean

Co·quil·hat·ville \kō-'kē-ə-,vil, ,kō-kē-'at-,vil\ or since 1966 **Mban·da·ka** \,em-bän-'däk-ə\ city W Congo on Congo river *pop* 25,457

Co·quim·bo \kō-'kim-(,)bō, -'kēm-\ city & port N *cen* Chile *pop* 41,304

Coral sea arm of the SW Pacific bounded on W by Queensland, Australia, on N by the Solomons, & on E by New Hebrides & New Caledonia

Coral Gables city SE Fla. SW of Miami *pop* 34,793

Cor·co·va·do \,kȯr-kə-'väd-(,)ō\ **1** mountain 2310 *ft* SE Brazil on S side of city of Rio de Janeiro

Cor·di·lle·ra Cen·tral \,kȯrd-ᵊl-'(y)er-ə,-,sen-'träl, ,kȯrd-ē-'er-\ **1** range of the Andes in Colombia **2** chief range of the Dominican Republic **3** range of the Andes in Peru E of the Marañón **4** range Philippines in N Luzon — see PULOG **5** range S *cen* Puerto Rico — see CERRO DE PUNTA

Cordillera Mé·ri·da \-'mer-əd-ə\ or **Sier·ra Ne·va·da de Mérida** \sē-,er-ə-nə-'väd-əd-ə, -'vad-\ mountain range W Venezuela — see BOLÍVAR (Pico)

Cór·do·ba \'kȯrd-ə-bə, -ə-və\ **1** province S Spain *area* 5299, *pop* 811,562 **2** or **Cor·do·va** city, its ❋, on the Guadalquivir *pop* 189,969 **3** city N *cen* Argentina *pop* 369,886 — **Cor·do·ban** \-bən\ *adj or n*

Cor·fu \kȯr-'fü, 'kȯr-,\ f(y)ü\ or NGk **Kér·ky·ra** or **Kér·ki·ra** \'ker-ki-rə\ or anc **Cor·cy·ra** \kȯr-'sī-rə\ **1** island NW Greece, one of the Ionian islands *area* 227 **2** city & port on E Corfu *pop* 30,739 — **Cor·fi·ote** \'kȯr-fē-,ōt, -ət\ *n*

Cor·inth \'kȯr-ən(t)th, 'kär-\ or NGk **Kó·rin·thos** \'kȯr-ən-,thȯs\ **1** or **Co·rin·thia** \kə-'rin(t)-thē-ə\ region of ancient Greece occupying most of Isthmus of Corinth & part of NE Peloponnesus **2** city & port Greece on Isthmus of Corinth at head of Gulf of Corinth NE of site of ancient city of Corinth *pop* 17,699

Corinth, Gulf of or **Gulf of Le·pan·to** \'lep-ən-,tō, li-'pan-(,)tō\ inlet of Ionian sea *cen* Greece W of Isthmus of Corinth (neck of land connecting Peloponnesus with rest of Greece)

Cork \'kȯ(ə)rk\ **1** county SW Ireland in Munster *area* 2881, *pop* 252,246 **2** city & county borough & port, its ❋, at head of Cork Harbor *pop* 77,860

Corn \'kȯ(ə)rn\ two small islands in the Caribbean 40 *m* off E coast of Nicaragua leased by Nicaragua to U.S.

Cor·ner Brook \'kȯr-nər-,bruk\ city Canada in W Nfld. on Gulf of St. Lawrence *pop* 23,225

Corneto — see TARQUINIA

Cor·ning \'kȯr-niŋ\ city S N.Y. WNW of Elmira *pop* 17,085

Cor·no, Mon·te \,mänt-ē-'kȯr-(,)nō\ mountain 9585 *ft*, *cen* Italy NE of Rome; highest in the Apennines

Corn·wall \'kȯrn-,wȯl, -wəl\ **1** city Canada in SE Ont. on the St. Lawrence *pop* 18,158 **2** county SW England on peninsula projecting into the Atlantic ❋ Truro *area* 1357, *pop* 345,612

Co·ro \'kȯr-(,)ō, 'kōr-\ city NW Venezuela near coast at base of Paraguaná peninsula *pop* 39,000

Cor·o·man·del \,kȯr-ə-'man-dᵊl, ,kär-\ coast region SE India on Bay of Bengal S of the Kistna

Cor·o·na·do \,kȯr-ə-'näd-(,)ō, ,kär-\ city SW Calif. on San Diego Bay opposite San Diego *pop* 18,039

Co·ro·nel \,kȯr-ə-'nel, ,kär-\ city & port S *cen* Chile S of Concepción *pop* 17,372

Cor·pus Chris·ti \,kȯr-pə-'skris-tē\ city & port S Tex. on Corpus Christi Bay at mouth of Nueces river *pop* 167,690

Cor·reg·i·dor \kə-'reg-ə-,dȯ(ə)r\ island N Philippines at entrance to Manila Bay *area ab* 2

Cor·rien·tes \,kȯr-ē-'en-,tās, ,kär-\ city NE Argentina on the Paraná *pop* 56,544

Cor·si·ca \'kȯr-si-kə\ or F **Corse** \'kȯrs\ island France in the Mediterranean N of Sardinia ❋ Ajaccio *area* 3367, *pop* 246,995 — **Cor·si·can** \'kȯr-si-kən\ *adj or n*

Cor·si·ca·na \,kȯr-si-'kan-ə\ city NE *cen* Tex. *pop* 20,344

Cor·ti·na or **Cortina d'Am·pez·zo** \kȯr-'tē-nə-,däm-'pet-(,)sō\ resort village N Italy in the Dolomites N of Belluno

Cort·land \'kȯrt-lənd\ city S *cen* N.Y. *pop* 19,181

Coruña, La; Corunna — see LA CORUÑA

Cor·val·lis \kȯr-'val-əs\ city W Oreg. SW of Salem *pop* 20,669

Cos — see KOS

Co·sen·za \kō-'zen(t)-sə\ commune S Italy in Calabria *pop* 49,500

Cos·ta Bra·va \,käs-tə-'bräv-ə, ,kȯs-, ,kōs-\ coast region NE Spain in Catalonia on the Mediterranean extending NE from Barcelona

Cos·ta del Sol \-thel-'sȯl, -'sōl\ coast region S Spain on the Mediterranean extending E from Gibraltar

Cos·ta Me·sa \,kōs-tə-'mā-sə\ city SW Calif. SE of Long Beach on Pacific coast *pop* 37,550

Cos·ta Ri·ca \,käs-tə-'rē-kə, ,kȯs-, ,kōs-\ country Central America between Nicaragua & Panama; a republic ❋ San José *area* 19,238, *pop* 1,134,62 — **Cos·ta Ri·can** \-kən\ *adj or n*

Costermansville — see BUKAVU

Côte d'A·zur \,kōt-də-'zù(ə)r\ coastal region SE France on the Mediterranean; part of the Riviera

Côte d'Ivoire — see IVORY COAST

Côte d'Or \kōt-'dȯ(ə)r\ range of hills E France SW of Dijon

Co·ten·tin \kō-täⁿ-taⁿ\ peninsula NW France projecting into English channel W of mouth of the Seine

Co·to·nou \,kōt-ᵊn-'ü\ city & port S Dahomey *pop* 56,200

Co·to·pax·i \,kōt-ə-'pak-sē, -'pä-(,)hē\ volcano 19,347 *ft* N *cen* Ecuador

Cots·wold \'kät-,swōld, -swəld\ hills SW *cen* England in Gloucestershire; highest point Cleeve Cloud 1031 *ft*

Cott·bus or **Kott·bus** \'kät-bəs, -,bùs\ city E Germany on Spree river SE of Berlin *pop* 64,500

Cot·ti·an Alps \,kät-ē-ən\ range of W Alps France & Italy — see VISO

Couls·don and Pur·ley \'kōlz-də-nən-'pər-lē\ urban district S England in Surrey S of London *pop* 63,770

Coun·cil Bluffs \,kauṅ(t)-səl-'bləfs\ city SW Iowa *pop* 55,641

Cou·ran·tyne or **Co·ren·tyne** \'kȯr-ən-,tīn, 'kȯr-\ or D **Co·ran·tijn** \-,tīn\ river 300 *m* N So. America flowing N into the Atlantic & forming boundary between Brit. Guiana & Surinam

Cour·be·voie \,kùr-bəv-'wä\ commune N France on the Seine NW of Paris *pop* 59,730

Courland — see KURLAND

Cour·ma·yeur \,kùr-mə-'yər\ resort village NW Italy in Val d'Aosta SE of Mont Blanc

Courtrai — see KORTRIJK

Cov·en·try \usu Brit 'käv-ən-trē; 'kəv-\ city & county borough *cen* England in Warwickshire *pop* 258,211

Co·vi·na \kō-'vē-nə\ city SW Calif. E of Los Angeles *pop* 20,124

Cov·ing·ton \'kəv-iŋ-tən\ city N Ky. *pop* 60,376

Cowes \'kauz\ urban district S England in N Isle of Wight *pop* 17,154

Cow·litz \'kaù-ləts\ river 150 *m* SW Wash. flowing into the Columbia

Co·zu·mel \,kō-zə-'mel\ island SE Mexico off NE coast of Quintana Roo

Crab — see VIEQUES

Cracow — see KRAKOW

Cra·io·va \krə-'yō-və\ city S Romania *pop* 106,276

Cran·ford \'kran-fərd\ urban township NE N.J. *pop* 26,424

Cran·ston \'kran(t)-stən\ city E R.I. S of Providence *pop* 66,766

Cra·ter \'krāt-ər\ lake 1932 *ft* deep SW Oreg. in Cascade range at altitude of 6164 *ft*; main feature of **Crater Lake National Park** (*area* 250) — see MAZAMA (Mount)

Craters of the Moon National Monument reservation SE *cen* Idaho including lava flows & other volcanic formations *area* 74

Cré·cy \krā-'sē, 'kres-ē\ or **Cres·sy** \'kres-ē\ or **Cré·cy-en-Pon·thieu** \krā-,sē-,äⁿ-pōⁿ-'tyə(r)\ commune N France NW of Amiens

Cre·mo·na \krə-'mō-nə\ commune N Italy in Lombardy on the Po ESE of Milan *pop* 56,200

Crete \'krēt\ or NGk **Krí·ti** \'krēt-ē\ island Greece in the E Mediterranean ❋ Canea *area* 3199, *pop* 460,844 — **Cre·tan** \'krēt-ᵊn\ *adj or n*

Crete, Sea of or **Sea of Can·dia** \'kan-dē-ə\ the S section of Aegean sea between Crete & the Cyclades

Crewe \'krü\ municipal borough NW England in Cheshire *pop* 52,415

Cri·mea \krī-'mē-ə, krə-\ or Russ **Krim** \'krim\ peninsula U.S.S.R. in S Soviet Russia, Europe, extending into Black sea SW of Sea of Azov — **Cri·me·an** \-'mē-ən\ *adj*

Cris·to·bal \kris-'tō-bəl\ or Sp **Cris·tó·bal** town NW Panama Canal Zone adjoining Colón, in Canal Zone

Cro·atan \krō-ə-'tan\ or **Cro·ato·an** \-'tō-ən\ island of uncertain identity, probably Okracoke I., off coast of N.C. between Pamlico Sound & the Atlantic thought to be place to which Raleigh's Roanoke I. colony moved 1587

Cro·atia \krō-'ā-sh(ē-)ə\ **1** region S Europe in NW Yugoslavia SE of Slovenia **2** constituent republic Yugoslavia comprising Croatia, Slavonia, & most of Istria & the Dalmatian coast ❋ Zagreb *area* 21,726, *pop* 3,918,817

Crocodile — see LIMPOPO

Cros·by \'krȯz-bē\ or **Great Crosby** municipal borough NW England in Lancashire on Irish sea NNW of Liverpool *pop* 58,362

ə abut; ᵊ kitten; ər further; a back; ā bake; ä cot, cart; au̇ out; ch chin; e less; ē easy; g gift; i trip; ī life
j joke; ŋ sing; ō flow; ȯ flaw; ȯi coin; th thin; th this; ü loot; ù foot; y yet; yü few; yù furious; zh vision
ᵊ F table; a F bac; ᵏ G ich, Buch; ⁿ F vin; œ F bœuf; ō̄ F feu; ᵫ G füllen; ᵫ̄ F rue; ʸ F digne \dēnʸ\, nuit \nwᵉē\

Cross \'kròs\ river 300 *m* W Africa in W Cameroun & SE Nigeria flowing W & S into Gulf of Guinea
Cro·to·ne \krə-'tō-nē\ *or anc* **Cro·to·na** \-nə\ *or* **Cro·ton** \'krō-,tän, 'krōt-ᵊn\ commune S Italy in Calabria on Gulf of Taranto *pop* 31,200
Crow·ley \'kraù-lē\ city S La. W of Lafayette *pop* 15,617
Croy·don \'kròid-ᵊn\ county borough S England in Surrey S of London *pop* 249,592
Cro·zet \krō-'zā\ islands S Indian ocean WNW of Kerguelen
Crys·tal \'krist-ᵊl\ village SE Minn. N of Minneapolis *pop* 24,283
Ctes·i·phon \'tes-ə-,fän, 'tē-sə-\ ancient city *cen* Iraq on the Tigris opposite Seleucia ✻ of Parthia & of later Sassanid empire
Cuan·za \'kwän-zə\ river 500 *m* SW Africa in *cen* Angola flowing NW into the Atlantic
Cu·ba \'kyü-bə\ **1** island in the West Indies N of Caribbean sea *area* 41,634 **2** country largely coextensive with island; a republic ✻ Havana *area* 46,736, *pop* 7,800,000 — **Cu·ban** \-bən\ *adj or n*
Cubango — see OKOVANGGO
Cú·cu·ta \'kü-kət-ə\ city N Colombia *pop* 131,410
Cud·a·hy \'kəd-ə-(,)hē\ city SE Wis. *pop* 17,975
Cuen·ca \'kweŋ-kə\ **1** city S Ecuador *pop* 46,428 **2** province E *cen* Spain *area* 6636, *pop* 328,983 **3** commune, its ✻, ESE of Madrid *pop* 26,826
Cuer·na·va·ca \,kwer-nə-'väk-ə, -vak-\ city S *cen* Mexico S of Mexico City ✻ of Morelos *pop* 30,597
Cufra — see KUFRA
Cu·lia·cán \,kül-yə-'kän\ **1** river 175 *m* NW Mexico flowing SW into the Pacific at mouth of Gulf of California **2** city NW Mexico on the Culiacán ✻ of Sinaloa *pop* 48,963
Cul·lo·den Moor \kə-,läd-ᵊn-, -,lōd-\ moorland N Scotland in N Inverness-shire E of Inverness
Cul·ver City \,kəl-vər-\ city SW Calif. *pop* 32,163
Cu·mae \'kyü-(,)mē\ ancient town S Italy on Tyrrhenian coast W of modern Naples — **Cu·mae·an** \kyü-'mē-ən\ *adj*
Cu·ma·ná \,kü-mə-'nä\ city & port NE Venezuela on the Caribbean NE of Barcelona *pop* 64,000
Cum·ber·land \'kəm-bər-lənd\ **1** river 687 *m* S Ky. & N Tenn. flowing W into the Ohio **2** falls SE Ky. in upper course of the Cumberland **3** caverns *cen* Tenn. SE of McMinnville **4** city NW Md. on the Potomac *pop* 33,415 **5** county NW England ✻ Carlisle *area* 1511, *pop* 285,347 — **Cum·bri·an** \'kəm-brē-ən\ *adj or n*
Cumberland Gap mountain pass 1304 *ft* NE Tenn. through a ridge of the Cumberlands SE of Middlesboro, Ky.
Cumberland plateau *or* **Cumberland mountains** mountain region E U.S., part of the S Appalachian mountains W of Tennessee river extending from S W. Va. to NE Ala.
Cumbre, La — see USPALLATA
Cumbria — see STRATHCLYDE
Cum·bri·an \'kəm-brē-ən\ mountains NW England in Cumberland, Westmorland, & Lancashire — see SCAFELL PIKE
Cu·naxa \kyü-'nak-sə\ town in ancient Babylonia E of the Euphrates *ab* 87 *m* NW of Babylon
Cu·ne·ne *or* **Ku·ne·ne** \kü-'nā-nə\ river 700 *m* SW Africa in SW Angola flowing S & W into the Atlantic
Cu·par \'kü-pər\ burgh E Scotland ✻ of Fifeshire
Cuquenán — see KUKENAAM
Cu·ra·çao \,k(y)ùr-ə-'saù, -'sō\ island Netherlands Antilles in the S Caribbean; chief town Willemstad *area* 210, *pop* 115,929
Cu·ri·ti·ba \,kùr-ə-'tē-bə\ city S Brazil SW of São Paulo ✻ of Paraná *pop* 361,309
Cush or **Kush** \'kəsh, 'kùsh\ ancient country NE Africa in Nile valley S of Egypt — **Cush·ite** \-,īt\ *adj or n* — **Cush·it·ic** \,kəsh-'it-, kùsh-\ *adj*
Cus·ter Battlefield National Monument \,kəs-tər-\ site SE Mont. on Little Bighorn river of battle 1876
Cutch — see KUTCH
Cut·tack \'kət-ək\ city E India in Orissa *pop* 102,500
Cux·ha·ven \kùks-'häf-ən\ city & port W Germany on North sea at mouth of the Elbe *pop* 43,300
Cuy·a·hoga \,kī-(ə-)'hō-gə, kə-'hō-, -'hä-, -'hō-\ river 100 *m* NE Ohio flowing into Lake Erie at Cleveland
Cuyahoga Falls city NE Ohio N of Akron *pop* 47,922
Cu·yu·ni \kù-'yü-nē\ river 300 *m* N So. America rising in E Venezuela & flowing E into the Essequibo in N Guyana
Cuz·co *or* **Cus·co** \'kü-(,)skō\ city S Peru *pop* 68,500
Cyc·la·des \'sik-lə-,dēz\ *or* NGk **Ki·klá·dhes** \kē-'kläth-(,)es\ islands Greece in the S Aegean *area* 996 — **Cy·clad·ic** \sik-'lad-ik, sī-'klad-\ *adj*
Cydonia — see CANEA — **Cy·do·nian** \sī-'dō-nē-ən, -'dō-nyən\ *adj or n*
Cymru — see WALES
Cy·prus \'sī-prəs\ **1** island E Mediterranean S of Turkey **2** country coextensive with the island; a republic of the Brit. Commonwealth ✻ Nicosia *area* 3572, *pop* 614,000 — **Cyp·ri·ot** \'sip-rē-ət -rē-,ät\ *or* **Cyp·ri·ote** \-,ōt, -ət\ *adj or n*
Cy·re·na·ica \,sir-ə-'nā-ə-kə, ,sī-rə-\ *or It* **Ci·re·na·ica** \,chē-rā-'nä-ē-kä\ **1** *or* **Cy·re·ne** \sī-'rē-(,)nē\ ancient coastal region N Africa dominated by city of Cyrene **2** province E Libya ✻ Benghazi *area* 330,173, *pop* 291,328 — **Cy·re·na·ican** \,sir-ə-'nā-ə-kən, ,sī-rə-\ *adj or n* — **Cy·re·ni·an** \sī-'rē-nē-ən\ *adj or n*
Cy·re·ne \sī-'rē-(,)nē\ ancient city N Africa on the Mediterranean in NE Libya; site at modern village of Shahat — **Cy·re·na·ic** \,sir-ə-'nā-ik, ,sī-rə-\ *adj or n* — **Cy·re·ni·an** \sī-'rē-nē-ən\ *n*
Cythera — see KÍTHIRA
Cyz·i·cus \'siz-i-kəs\ **1** — see KAPIDAGI **2** ancient city in Mysia on isthmus leading to Kapidagi peninsula
Czecho·slo·va·kia \,chek-ə-slō-'väk-ē-ə, -'vak-\ country *cen* Europe; a republic ✻ Prague *area* 49,373, *pop* 13,745,577 — **Czecho·slo·vak** \-'slō-,väk, -,vak\ *adj or n* — **Czecho·slo·va·ki·an** \-slō-'väk-ē-ən, -'vak-\ *adj or n*
Cze·sto·cho·wa \,chen(t)-stə-'kō-və\ *or* Russ **Chen·sto·khov** \,chen(t)-stə-'kòf, -'kòv\ city S Poland on the Warta *pop* 148,000

Dac·ca \'dak-ə, 'däk-ə\ city Pakistan ✻ of East Pakistan & legislative ✻ of Pakistan *pop* 411,000
Da·chau \'däk-,aù\ city W Germany in S Bavaria *pop* 27,800
Da·cia \'dā-sh(ē-)ə\ ancient country SE Europe roughly equivalent to Romania & Bessarabia — **Da·cian** \-shən\ *adj or n*
Dag·en·ham \'dag-(ə-)nəm\ municipal borough SE England in Essex, NE suburb of London *pop* 114,588
Da·ge·stan *or* **Da·ghe·stan** \,dag-ə-'stan, ,däg-ə-'stän\ autonomous republic U.S.S.R. in SE Soviet Russia, Europe, on W shore of the Caspian ✻ Makhachkala *area* 13,124, *pop* 1,063,000
Da·ho·mey \də-'hō-mē\ country W Africa on Gulf of Guinea; a republic within the French Community; formerly a territory of French West Africa ✻ Porto-Novo *area* 44,749, *pop* 2,370,000 — **Da·ho·man** \-mən\ *adj or n* — **Da·ho·me·an** \-mē-ən\ *adj or n* — **Da·ho·mey·an** \-mē-ən\ *adj or n*
Daido — see TAEDONG
Dai·ren \'dī-'ren\ city & port NE China in S Liaoning on Liaotung peninsula *pop* 766,400 — see LÜTA
Da·kar \də-'kär, 'dak,-är\ city & port ✻ of Senegal *pop* 230,887
Da·ko·ta \də-'kōt-ə\ **1** — see JAMES **2** territory (1861–89) NW U.S. divided 1889 into states of N. Dak. & S. Dak. (the **Da·ko·tas** \-əz\) — **Da·ko·tan** \-'kōt-ᵊn\ *adj or n*
Dal·e·car·lia \,dal-ə-'kär-lē-ə\ region W *cen* Sweden — **Dal·e·car·li·an** \-lē-ən\ *adj*
Dal·las \'dal-əs, -is\ city NE Tex. E of Fort Worth *pop* 679,684
Dal·ma·tia \dal-'mā-sh(ē-)ə\ region W Yugoslavia on the Adriatic — **Dal·ma·tian** \-shən\ *adj or n*
Dal·ton \'dòlt-ᵊn\ city NW Ga. *pop* 17,868
Da·ly City \,dā-lē-\ city W Calif. S of San Francisco *pop* 44,791
Da·man \də-'man\ *or* **Da·mão** \də-'maù^{n}\ **1** district W India, formerly part of Portuguese India, on Gulf of Cambay *area* 148, *pop* 57,000 **2** its chief town & port
Da·man·hûr \,dam-ən-'hù(ə)r\ city N Egypt E of Alexandria *pop* 126,000
Da·mas·cus \də-'mas-kəs\ *or* Ar **Esh Sham** \(')esh-'sham\ city ✻ of Syria *pop* 529,963
Damavand — see DEMAVEND
Dam·i·et·ta \,dam-ē-'et-ə\ city & port N Egypt *pop* 63,100
Dam·mam \də-'mam\ town & port Saudi Arabia on Persian gulf
Da·mo·dar \'däm-ə-,där\ river 350 *m* NE India in *cen* Bihar & West Bengal flowing ESE into the Hooghly
Dan \'dan\ **1** river 180 *m* S Va. & N N. C. flowing E into the Roanoke **2** ancient village at N extremity of Palestine N of Waters of Merom
Da Nang \'dän-'äŋ\ *or* **Tou·rane** \tü-'rän\ city & port S Vietnam in Annam SE of Hue *pop* 108,800
Dan·bury \'dan-,ber-ē, -b(ə-)rē\ city SW Conn. *pop* 22,928
Danger islands — see PUKAPUKA
Dangerous archipelago — see TUAMOTU
Danish West Indies the W islands of the Virgin islands group that were until 1917 a Danish possession & now constitute the Virgin Islands of the U. S.
Danmark — see DENMARK
Dan·ube \'dan-(,)yüb\ *or anc* **Da·nu·bi·us** \də-'n(y)ü-bē-əs, da-\ *or* **Is·ter** \'is-tər\ river 1725 *m*, *cen* & SE Europe flowing SE from S Germany into Black sea — **Da·nu·bi·an** \da-'nyü-bē-ən\ *adj*
Dan·vers \'dan-vərz\ town NE Mass. N of Lynn *pop* 21,926
Dan·ville, **1** \'dan-,vil\ city E Ill. *pop* 41,856 **2** \-,vil, -vəl\ city S Va. on the Dan *pop* 46,577
Dan·zig \'dan(t)-sig, 'dän(t)-\ **1** — see GDANSK **2** territory surrounding & including Danzig that (1920–39) constituted a free city under the League of Nations *area* 754
Danzig, Gulf of inlet of S Baltic sea in N Poland & W U.S.S.R.
Dapsang — see GODWIN AUSTEN
Dar·da·nelles \,därd-ᵊn-'elz\ *or* **Hel·les·pont** \'hel-ə-,spänt\ *or anc* **Hel·les·pon·tus** \,hel-ə-'spänt-əs\ strait NW Turkey connecting Sea of Marmara with the Aegean
Dar el Beida — see CASABLANCA
Dar es Sa·laam \,där-,es-sə-'läm\ city & port ✻ of Tanganyika & of Tanzania on Indian ocean *pop* 128,742
Dar·fur \där-'fù(ə)r\ region W Sudan; chief city El Fasher
Dar·i·en \,dar-ē-'en, ,der-\ Spanish colonial settlement Central America W of Gulf of Darien
Darien, Gulf of inlet of the Caribbean between E Panama & NW Colombia
Darien, Isthmus of — see PANAMA (Isthmus of)
Dar·jee·ling *or* **Dar·ji·ling** \där-'jē-liŋ\ city NE India in West Bengal on Sikkim border *pop* 33,600
Dar·ling \'där-liŋ\ **1** river 1160 *m* SE Australia in Queensland & New So. Wales flowing SW into the Murray **2** mountain range SW Western Australia extending *ab* 250 *m* N–S along coast; highest point Mt. Cooke 1910 *ft*
Dar·ling·ton \'där-liŋ-tən\ county borough N England in Durham *pop* 84,861
Darm·stadt \'därm-,stat, -,s(h)tät\ city W Germany in Hesse SSW of Frankfurt *pop* 136,600
Dart·moor \'därt-,mù(ə)r, -,mō(ə)r, -,mò(ə)r\ tableland SW England in S Devonshire *area* 215
Dart·mouth \'därt-məth\ **1** city Canada in S N. S. on Halifax harbor opposite Halifax *pop* 21,093 **2** municipal borough & port SW England in S Devon on Dart river
Dar·win \'där-wən\ *or formerly* **Port Darwin** town & port N Australia ✻ of Northern Territory on **Port Darwin** (inlet of Timor sea)
Dar·yal Gorge *or* **Dar·ial Gorge** \där-,yal-\ mountain pass U.S.S.R. in S Soviet Russia, Europe, through Caucasus mountains; a gorge cut by Terek river
Dau·gav·pils \'daù-gəf-,pilz\ *or* Russ **Dvinsk** \də-'vin(t)sk\ city U. S. S. R. in E Latvia on the Dvina *pop* 65,000
Dau·phi·né \,dō-fi-'nā\ region & former province SE France N of Provence ✻ Grenoble
Da·vao \'däv-,aù, də-'vaù\ **1** gulf of the Pacific Philippines in SE Mindanao **2** city Philippines on Davao gulf *pop* 47,846
Dav·en·port \'dav-ən-,pō(ə)rt, -,pò(ə)rt\ city E Iowa *pop* 88,981
Da·vis \'dā-vəs\ **1** mountains W Texas N of the Big Bend of the Rio Grande **2** strait between SW Greenland & E Baffin I. connecting Baffin Bay with the Atlantic
Da·vos \dä-'vōs\ commune E Switzerland in Graubünden ESE of Chur
Dax \'daks\ commune SW France in the Landes on the Adour NE of Biarritz
Day·ton \'dāt-ᵊn\ city SW Ohio on the Miami *pop* 262,332
Day·to·na Beach \dā-,tō-nə-\ city NE Fla. *pop* 37,395
Dead sea \'ded\ *or Bib* **Salt sea** \'sòlt\ *or L* **La·cus As·phal·ti·tes** \'lā-kə-,sas-,fòl-tīt-ēz\ salt lake *ab* 50 *m* long on boundary between Israel & Jordan *area* 370, surface 1286 *ft* below sea level
Dean, Forest of \'dēn\ forested district SW England in W Gloucestershire between Severn & Wye rivers; an ancient royal forest

Dear·born \'di(ə)r-ˌbȯ(ə)rn, -bȯrn\ city SE Mich. *pop* 112,007

Death Valley arid valley E Calif. & S Nev. containing lowest point in the U.S. (280 *ft* below sea level); most of area included in **Death Valley National Monument** (*area* 2891)

Deau·ville \'dō-ˌvil, dō-'vē(ə)l\ town NW France on Bay of the Seine SSW of Le Havre

De·bre·cen \'deb-rət-ˌsen\ city E Hungary *pop* 130,000

De·cap·o·lis \di-'kap-ə-ləs\ confederation of 10 ancient cities N Palestine in region chiefly SE of Sea of Galilee

De·ca·tur \di-'kāt-ər\ **1** city N Ala. *pop* 29,217 **2** city NW *cen* Ga. E of Atlanta *pop* 22,026 **3** city *cen* Ill. *pop* 78,004

Dec·can \'dek-ən, -ˌan\ plateau region S *cen* India lying between Eastern & Western Ghats

Ded·ham \'ded-əm\ town E Mass. SW of Boston *pop* 23,869

Dee \'dē\ **1** river 90 *m* NE Scotland flowing E into North sea **2** river 50 *m* S Scotland flowing S into Solway firth **3** river 70 *m* N Wales & W England flowing E & N into Irish sea

Deer Park urban area SE N. Y. in S *cen* Long I. *pop* 16,726

Deh·ra Dun \ˌder-ə-'dün\ city N India in NW Uttar Pradesh *pop* 144,202

De Kalb \di-'kalb\ city N Ill. *pop* 18,486

Del·a·goa Bay \ˌdel-ə-ˌgō-ə\ inlet of Indian ocean S Mozambique

Del·a·ware \'del-ə-ˌwa(ə)r, -ˌwe(ə)r, -wər\ **1** river 296 *m* E U.S. flowing S from S N.Y. into Delaware Bay **2** state E U.S. ✳ Dover *area* 2057, *pop* 446,292 **3** — see CHERRY HILL — **Del·a·war·ean** or **Del·a·war·ian** \ˌdel-ə-'war-ē-ən, -'wer-\ *adj or n*

Delaware Bay inlet of the Atlantic between SW N.J. & E Del.

Delft \'delft\ commune SW Netherlands *pop* 72,261

Del·ga·do, Cape \del-'gäd-(ˌ)ō\ cape NE Mozambique

Del·hi \'del-ē\ **1** territory N India W of Uttar Pradesh ✳ Delhi *area* 578, *pop* 1,744,100 **2** city, its ✳ *pop* 2,061,758 — see NEW DELHI

Dells of the Wisconsin or **Wisconsin Dells** gorge of Wisconsin river in S *cen* Wis. N of Baraboo

Del·mar·va \del-'mär-və\ or **Del·mar·via** \-vē-ə\ peninsula E U.S. between Chesapeake & Delaware bays comprising Del. & parts of Md. & Va. — see EASTERN SHORE

Del·men·horst \'del-mən-ˌhȯrst\ city NW Germany in Lower Saxony WSW of Bremen *pop* 55,700

De·los or NGk **Dhí·los** \'dē-ˌläs\ island Greece in *cen* Cyclades *area* 2 — **De·lian** \'dē-lē-ən, 'dēl-yən\ *adj or n*

Del·phi \'del-ˌfī\ ancient town *cen* Greece in Phocis on S slope of Mt. Parnassus near present village of **Dhel·foí** \thel-'fē\

Del Rio \del-'rē-(ˌ)ō\ city S Tex. on Rio Grande *pop* 18,612

Dem·a·vend \'dem-ə-ˌvend\ or **Dam·a·vand** \'dam-ə-ˌvand\ mountain 18,934 *ft* N Iran NE of Tehran; highest in Elburz mountains

Dem·e·rara \ˌdem-ə-'rar-ə, -'rär-\ river 200 *m* Guyana flowing N into the Atlantic

Denali — see MCKINLEY (Mount)

Den·bigh \'den-bē\ or **Den·bigh·shire** \-ˌshi(ə)r, -shər\ county N Wales ✳ Ruthin *area* 669, *pop* 170,699

Den·der·mon·de \ˌden-dər-'män-də\ or **Ter·monde** \te(ə)r-'mōⁿd\ commune NW *cen* Belgium *pop* 62,502

Den Hel·der \də(n)-'hel-dər\ commune W Netherlands in No. Holland on an outlet from Wadden Zee to North sea *pop* 47,451

Den·i·son \'den-ə-sən\ city NE Tex. on Red river *pop* 22,748

De·niz·li \ˌden-əz-'lē\ city SW Turkey SE of Izmir *pop* 49,042

Den·mark \'dan-ˌmärk\ or Dan **Dan·mark** \'dän-ˌmärk\ **1** country N Europe occupying most of Jutland peninsula & adjacent islands in Baltic & North seas; a kingdom ✳ Copenhagen *area* 16,576, *pop* 4,448,401 **2** strait 130 *m* wide between SE Greenland & Iceland connecting Arctic ocean with the Atlantic

Dent Blanche \däⁿ-blänsh\ mountain 14,304 *ft* S Switzerland in Pennine Alps

Dent du Mi·di \däⁿ-dū-mē-dē\ mountain 10,686 *ft* SW Switzerland in W Alps

Den·ton \'dent-ᵊn\ city N Tex. NW of Dallas *pop* 26,844

D'En·tre·cas·teaux \ˌdäⁿ-trə-'kas-(ˌ)tō\ islands SW Pacific N of E tip of New Guinea belonging to Territory of Papua *area* 1200, *pop* 40,000

Den·ver \'den-vər\ city ✳ of Colo. *pop* 493,887

Dept·ford \'det-fərd\ metropolitan borough SE London, England, on S bank of the Thames *pop* 75,694

Der·be \'dər-(ˌ)bē\ ancient town S Asia Minor in S Lycaonia on border of Cilicia; exact site unknown

Der·bent or **Der·bend** \dər-'bent\ city U.S.S.R. in SE Soviet Russia, Europe, in Dagestan on Caspian sea *pop* 35,000

Der·by \'där-bē, *U.S. also* 'dər-\ **1** or **Der·by·shire** \-ˌshi(ə)r, -shər\ county N *cen* England *area* 1012, *pop* 826,336 **2** county borough, its ✳ *pop* 141,264

Der·na \'de(ə)r-nə\ city & port NE Libya *pop* 20,782

Derry — see LONDONDERRY

Der·went \'dər-wənt\ river 130 *m* Australia in Tasmania flowing SE into Tasman sea

Der·went·wa·ter \'dər-wənt-ˌwȯt-ər, -ˌwät-\ lake NW England in Lake District in Cumberland

Desaguadero — see SALADO

Des·chutes \dā-'shüt\ river 250 *m*, *cen* & N Oreg. E of Cascade range flowing N into the Columbia

Des·er·et \ˌdez-ə-'ret\ provisional state of the U.S. S of 42d parallel & W of the Rockies organized 1849 by Mormons; part of it became Utah territory 1850

Des Moines \di-'mȯin\ **1** river 327 *m* Iowa flowing SE into the Mississippi **2** city ✳ of Iowa on Des Moines river *pop* 208,982

Des·na \də-'snä\ river 550 *m* U.S.S.R. in SW Soviet Russia, Europe, & N Ukraine flowing S into the Dnieper

Des Plaines \de-'splānz\ **1** river 150 *m* NE Ill. flowing S to unite with the Kankakee forming the Illinois **2** city NE Ill. NW of Chicago *pop* 34,886

Des·sau \'des-ˌaú\ city E Germany N of Halle *pop* 94,300

Destêrro — see FLORIANÓPOLIS

De·troit \di-'trȯit\ **1** river 31 *m* Ont. & SE Mich. connecting Lakes Erie & St. Clair **2** city SE Mich. *pop* 1,670,144 — **De·troit·er** \-ər\ *n*

Detskoe Selo — see PUSHKIN

Deur·ne \'dər-nə\ commune N Belgium, E suburb of Antwerp *pop* 64,406

Deutschland — see GERMANY

De·ven·ter \'dā-vən-tər\ commune E Netherlands *pop* 54,389

Devil Mountain — see AUYÁN-TEPUÍ

Devil's Island or F **Île du Dia·ble** \ēl-dü-dyàblᵊ\ island French Guiana in the Safety islands group; former penal colony

Devils Lake salt lake NE *cen* N. Dak.

Devils Post·pile \'pōst-ˌpīl\ lava formation E *cen* Calif. SE of Yosemite National Park; feature of **Devils Postpile National Monument** (*area* 1.3)

Devils Tower or **Ma·to Tepee** \ˌmät-(ˌ)ō-\ columnar rock formation NE Wyo. rising 865 *ft* above base, in **Devils Tower National Monument** (*area* 2)

Dev·on \'dev-ən\ **1** island N Canada in Northwest Territories N of Baffin I. *area* 20,861 **2** or **Dev·on·shire** \-ˌshi(ə)r, -shər\ county SW England between Bristol & English channels ✳ Exeter *area* 2612, *pop* 798,283

Dews·bury \'d(y)üz-ˌber-ē, -b(ə-)rē\ county borough N England in Yorkshire S of Leeds *pop* 53,476

Dezhnev, Cape — see EAST CAPE

Dhah·ran \dä-'rän, dä-hə-'rän\ town SE Saudi Arabia on Persian gulf near Bahrein islands

Dhau·la·gi·ri \ˌdaú-lə-'gi(ə)r-ē\ mountain 26,810 *ft* W *cen* Nepal in the Himalayas

Di·a·blo, Mount \dē-'äb-(ˌ)lō, dī-'ab-\ mountain 3849 *ft*, *cen* Calif. E of Oakland

Di·a·man·ti·na, 1 \ˌdī-ə-ˌman-'tē-nə\ river 470 *m* E *cen* Australia in SW Queensland flowing SW into the Warburton **2** \ˌdē-ə-\ town E Brazil in *cen* Minas Gerais

Diamond — see KUMGANG

Di·a·mond, Cape \dī-(ə)mənd\ promontory Canada at E end of city of Quebec

Diamond Head promontory Hawaii on Oahu I. SE of Honolulu

Dié·go–Sua·rez \dē-ˌā-gō-'swär-əs\ city & port Malagasy Republic near N tip of Madagascar *pop* 23,900

Dien Bien Phu \ˌdyen-ˌbyen-'fü\ village NW Vietnam

Di·eppe \dē-'ep\ city & port N France N of Rouen *pop* 26,427

Di·jon \dē-'jōⁿ\ city E France *pop* 112,844

Diks·mui·de or **Dix·mui·de** \dik-'smīd-ə\ or **Dix·mude** \dē(k)-ˌsmüd\ town N Belgium in West Flanders N of Ieper

Di·mi·trov·grad \də-'mē-trəf-ˌgrad\ city S Bulgaria on Maritsa river ESE of Plovdiv *pop* 45,000

Di·mi·tro·vo \də-'mē-trə-vō\ or **Per·nik** \'pe(ə)r-nik\ city W Bulgaria SW of Sofia *pop* 59,721

Di·nar·ic Alps \də-ˌnar-ik-\ range of E Alps W Yugoslavia; highest point Djeravica (SW of Pec) 8714 *ft*

Din·gle Bay \ˌdiŋ-gəl-\ inlet of the Atlantic SW Ireland

Ding·wall \'diŋ-ˌwȯl, -wəl\ burgh N Scotland of Ross and Cromarty

Dinosaur National Monument reservation NW Colo. & NE Utah at junction of Green & Yampa rivers; rich fossil deposits *area* 328

Di·o·mede \'dī-ə-ˌmēd\ islands in Bering strait comprising **Big Diomede** (U.S.S.R.) & **Little Diomede** (U.S.)

Diospolis — see THEBES

Di·re·da·wa \ˌdir-id-ə-'wä\ city E Ethiopia *pop* 30,000

Dis·ko \'dis-(ˌ)kō\ island W Greenland in Davis strait

Dismal swamp SE Va. & NE N.C. between Chesapeake Bay & Albemarle Sound *ab* 40 *m* long, 10 *m* wide

District of Co·lum·bia \kə-'ləm-bē-ə\ federal district E U.S. coextensive with city of Washington *area* 69, *pop* 763,956

Distrito Federal — see FEDERAL DISTRICT

Diu \'dē-(ˌ)ü\ district W India, formerly part of Portuguese India, at S end of Kathiawar peninsula *area* 20, *pop* 4856

Dix·on \'dik-sən\ city NW Ill. on Rock river *pop* 19,565

Dixon Entrance strait between N Queen Charlotte islands, B.C., & Prince of Wales I., Alaska

Di·yar·ba·kir \di-ˌ(y)är-bä-'ki(ə)r\ or **Di·ar·bekr** \-'bek-ər\ city SE Turkey on the Tigris *pop* 80,645

Diz or **Ab-i-Diz** \ˌäb-ə-'dēz, ˌab-ə-'diz\ river 250 *m* W Iran flowing S to the Karun

Diz·ful \diz-'fül\ city SW Iran on the Karun *pop* 52,153

Djailolo — see HALMAHERA

Dja·kar·ta or **Ja·kar·ta** \jə-'kärt-ə\ or *formerly* **Ba·ta·via** \bə-'tā-vē-ə\ city & port ✳ of Indonesia on NW coast of Java *pop* 1,492,100

Djam·bi or **Jam·bi** \'jäm-bē\ city & port Indonesia in SE *cen* Sumatra on Hari river *pop* 63,200

Djawa — see JAVA

Djer·ba or **Jer·ba** \'jər-bə, 'je(ə)r-\ island SE Tunisia in the Mediterranean at entrance to Gulf of Gabes *area* 16, *pop* 35,000

Dji·bou·ti or **Ji·bu·ti** \jə-'büt-ē\ city ✳ of French Somaliland on Gulf of Tadjoura *pop* 31,300

Djok·ja·kar·ta \ˌjäk-yə-'kärt-ə\ or **Jog·ja·kar·ta** \ˌjäg-\ city Indonesia in S Java *pop* 268,300

Dne·pro·dzer·zhinsk \nep-ˌrōd-ər-'zhin(t)sk\ city U.S.S.R. in E *cen* Ukraine on the Dnieper W of Dnepropetrovsk *pop* 194,000

Dne·pro·pe·trovsk \ˌnep-rō-pə-'trȯfsk\ or *formerly* **Eka·te·ri·no·slav** \i-ˌkat-ə-'rē-nə-ˌslät, -ˌslav\ city U.S.S.R. in E *cen* Ukraine on the Dnieper *pop* 658,000

Dnie·per \'nē-pər\ river 1400 *m* U.S.S.R. rising in S Valdai hills & flowing S through Ukraine into Black sea

Dnies·ter \'nēs-tər\ river 850 *m* U.S.S.R. rising on N slope of Carpathian mountains & flowing SE into Black sea

Do·bru·ja or **Do·bru·dja** \'dō-brə-ˌjä\ region S Europe in Romania & Bulgaria on Black sea S of the Danube

Do·dec·a·nese \dō-'dek-ə-ˌnēz, -ˌnēs\ islands Greece in the SE Aegean comprising the Southern Sporades S of Icaria & Samos; belonged to Italy 1923–47 *area* 486 — see RHODES — **Do·dec·a·ne·sian** \(ˌ)dō-ˌdek-ə-'nē-zhən, -shən\ *adj or n*

Do·do·na \də-'dō-nə\ ancient city NW Greece in Epirus on Mt. Tomarus

Dog·ger Bank \ˌdȯg-ər-, ˌdäg-\ submerged sandbank *ab* 150 *m* long in North sea *ab* 60 *m* E of N England

Dol·gel·ley or **Dol·gel·ly** \däl-'gel-ē\ urban district W Wales ✳ of Merionethshire

---

ə abut; ᵊ kitten; ər further; a back; ā bake; ä cot, cart; aú out; ch chin; e less; ē easy; g gift; i trip; ī life
j joke; ŋ sing; ō flow; ȯ flaw; ȯi coin; th thin; th this; ü loot; ü foot; ȳ yet; yü few; yú furious; zh vision
ᵊ F table; à F bac; ₖ G ich, Buch; ⁿ F vin; œ F bœuf; œ̄ F feu; ü G füllen; ₵ F rue; ʸ F digne \dēnʸ\, nuit \nwᵊē\

Do·lo·mites \'dō-lə-ˌmīts, 'däl-ə-\ *or* **Dolomite Alps** range of E Alps NE Italy between Adige & Piave rivers — see MARMOLADA
Dol·ton \'dōlt-ᵊn\ village NE Ill. S of Chicago *pop* 18,746
Dôme, Puy de \ˌpwē-ə-'dōm\ mountain 4805 *ft* S *cen* France in Auvergne mountains
Dom·i·ni·ca \ˌdäm-ə-'nē-kə, -'nik-ə, də-'min-i-kə\ island Brit. West Indies in the Leeward islands ✻ Roseau *area* 305, *pop* 66,645
Do·min·i·can Republic \də-ˌmin-i-kən-\ *or formerly* **San·to Do·min·go** \ˌsant-əd-ə-'min-(ˌ)gō\ *or* **San Domingo** \ˌsan-də-\ country West Indies on E Hispaniola; a republic ✻ Santo Domingo *area* 18,700, *pop* 4,070,108 — **Dominican** *adj or n*
Dom·ré·my-la-Pu·celle \ˌdō-(ˌ)rā-ˌmē-(ˌ)läp-(y)ü-'sel\ village NE France on the Meuse SW of Nancy
Don \'dän\ river 1200 *m* U.S.S.R. in SW Soviet Russia, Europe, flowing SE & then SW into Sea of Azov
Don·cas·ter \'däŋ-kə-stər\ county borough N England in West Riding, Yorkshire *pop* 81,896
Don·e·gal \ˌdän-i-'gól, -'gol\ county NW Republic of Ireland in Ulster ✻ Lifford *area* 1865, *pop* 113,815
Donegal Bay inlet of the Atlantic NW Ireland
Don·el·son \'dän-ᵊl-sən\ urban area N *cen* Tenn. *pop* 17,195
Do·nets \də-'nets\ river 670 *m* U.S.S.R. in SE Ukraine & SW Soviet Russia, Europe, flowing SE into the Don
Donets basin *or* **Don·bass** *or* **Don·bas** \'dän-ˌbas\ region U.S.S.R. in E Ukraine SW of Donets river
Do·netsk \də-'netsk\ *or formerly* **Sta·li·no** \'stäl-i-ˌnō, 'stal-\ *or* **Sta·lin** \'stäl-in, 'stal-, -ᵊn\ *or* **Yu·zov·ka** \'yü-zəf-kə\ city U.S.S.R. in E Ukraine in Donets basin *pop* 701,000
Don·ner \'dän-ər\ mountain pass 7135 *ft* E Calif. in Sierra Nevada NW of Lake Tahoe
Don·ny·brook \'dän-ē-ˌbruk\ city E Ireland in Leinster, SE suburb of Dublin *pop* 37,228
Doon \'dün\ river 25 *m* SW Scotland in Ayrshire flowing through **Loch Doon** (5 *m* long) into Firth of Clyde
Door \'dōr\ peninsula E Wis. between Green Bay & Lake Michigan
Doornik — see TOURNAI
Dor·ches·ter \'dór-chə-stər, -ˌches-tər\ municipal borough S England ✻ of Dorset
Dor·dogne \dór-'dōn\ river 300 *m* SW France flowing SW & W to unite with the Garonne forming the Gironde estuary
Dor·drecht \'dór-ˌdrekt\ *or* **Dort** \'dó(ə)rt\ commune SW Netherlands in So. Holland on the Maas *pop* 80,503
Dore, Monts \mōⁿ-'dó(ə)r, -'dó(ə)r\ mountain group S *cen* France in Auvergne mountains — see SANCY (Puy de)
Do·ris \'dōr-əs, 'dór-, -'där-\ 1 ancient country *cen* Greece between Mounts Oeta & Parnassus 2 ancient district SW Asia Minor on coast of Caria
Dor·noch \'dór-ˌnäk, -nək\ burgh N Scotland ✻ of Sutherland
Dorpat — see TARTU
Dor·set \'dór-sət\ *or* **Dor·set·shire** \-ˌshi(ə)r, -shər\ county S England ✻ Dorchester *area* 973, *pop* 291,157
Dort·mund \'dó(ə)rt-ˌmunt, -mənd\ city W Germany in the Ruhr *pop* 637,600
Do·than \'dō-thən\ city SE Ala. *pop* 31,440
Dou·ai *or formerly* **Dou·ay** \dü-'ā\ city N France S of Lille *pop* 43,380
Dou·a·la *or* **Du·a·la** \dü-'äl-ə\ city & port SW Cameroon on Bight of Biafra *pop* 118,857
Doug·las \'dəg-ləs\ city & port ✻ of Isle of Man *pop* 20,288
Dou·ro \'dōr-(ˌ)ü, 'dór-\ *or Sp* **Due·ro** \'dwe(ə)r-(ˌ)ō\ river 485 *m* N Spain & N Portugal flowing W into the Atlantic
Do·ver \'dō-vər\ 1 city ✻ of Del. *pop* 7250 2 city SE N.H. *pop* 19,131 3 municipal borough SE England in Kent on Strait of Dover *pop* 35,217
Dover, Strait of *or F* **Pas de Ca·lais** \ˌpäd-kə-'lā\ channel between SE England & N France, easternmost section of English channel; 20 *m* wide at narrowest point
Down \'daun\ county SE Northern Ireland ✻ Downpatrick *area* 952, *pop* 241,105
Dow·ners Grove \ˌdau-nərz-\ village NE Ill. W of Chicago *pop* 21,154
Dow·ney \'dau-nē\ city SW Calif. SE of Los Angeles *pop* 82,505
Down·pat·rick \ˌdaun-'pa-trik\ urban district SE Northern Ireland ✻ of County Down
Downs \'daunz\ 1 two ranges of hills SE England — see NORTH DOWNS, SOUTH DOWNS 2 roadstead in English channel along SE coast of Kent protected by the Goodwin Sands
Dra·chen·fels \'dräk-ən-ˌfelz\ hill 1053 *ft* W Germany in the Siebengebirge on the Rhine S of Bonn
Dra·kens·berg \'dräk-ənz-ˌbərg\ *or* **Quath·lam·ba** \kwät-'läm-bə\ mountains E Republic of So. Africa in Cape of Good Hope & Natal; highest Thabantshonyana 11,425 *ft*
Drake Passage *or* **Drake Strait** \'dräk\ strait S of So. America between Cape Horn & So. Shetlands
Dram·men \'dräm-ən\ city & port SE Norway on a branch of Oslo Fjord *pop* 30,704
Dran·cy \dräⁿ-'sē\ commune N France, NE suburb of Paris *pop* 50,654
Dra·va *or* **Dra·ve** \'dräv-ə\ river 450 *m* S Austria & N Yugoslavia flowing SE into the Danube
Dren·the *or* **Dren·te** \'drent-ə\ province NE Netherlands ✻ Assen *area* 1030, *pop* 308,028
Dres·den \'drez-dən\ city E Germany in Saxony *pop* 496,500
Dri·na \'drē-nə\ river 160 *m*, *cen* Yugoslavia flowing N along the border between Bosnia & Serbia into the Sava
Dro·ghe·da \'dró(i)-əd-ə, 'dróid-ə\ municipal borough E Ireland in County Louth on the Boyne *pop* 17,071
Drug \'drüg\ city E *cen* India in SE Madhya Pradesh E of Nagpur *pop* 133,371
Drum·mond·ville \'drəm-ən-,(d)vil\ city Canada in S Que. NE of Montreal *pop* 26,284
Druz, Jebel (ed) — see JEBEL ED DRUZ
Dry Tor·tu·gas \ˌtór-'tü-gəz\ small island group S Fla. WNW of Key West; site of **Fort Jef·fer·son National Monument** \'jef-ər-sən\
Du·bawnt \dü-'bónt\ 1 lake N Canada in SE Northwest Territories E of Great Slave Lake *area* 1654 2 river 580 *m* N Canada flowing NE through Dubawnt Lake to **Ba·ker Lake** \ˌbā-kər-\ (W expansion of Chesterfield inlet)
Dub·lin \'dəb-lən\ *or Gael* **Bai·le Atha Cli·ath** \ˌblä-'klē-ə\ 1 county E Ireland in Leinster *area* 356, *pop* 726,116 2 city

& county borough & port ✻ of Republic of Ireland & of County Dublin at mouth of the Liffey on **Dublin Bay** (inlet of Irish sea) *pop* 593,251 — **Dub·lin·er** \'dəb-lə-nər\ *n*
Du·brov·nik \'dü-ˌbróv-nik\ *or It* **Ra·gu·sa** \rə-'gü-zə\ city & port SW Yugoslavia in Montenegro *pop* 19,063
Du·buque \də-'byük\ city E Iowa on the Mississippi *pop* 56,606
Dud·ley \'dəd-lē\ county W *cen* England in Worcestershire WNW of Birmingham *pop* 62,536
Dui·no \dü-'ē-(ˌ)nō, 'dwē-\ village NE Italy on the Adriatic NW of Trieste
Duis·burg *or formerly* **Duisburg–Ham·born** \'d(y)üs-ˌbù(ə)rg-ˌhäm-ˌbórn, -ˌbòr(ə)n\ city W Germany at junction of Rhine & Ruhr rivers *pop* 501,800
Du·luth \də-'lüth\ city & port N E Minn. at W end of Lake Superior *pop* 106,884 — **Du·luth·ian** \-'lü-thē-ən\ *adj or n*
Dul·wich \'dəl-ij, -ich\ a SW district of London, England, in Camberwell metropolitan borough
Dum·bar·ton \ˌdəm-'bärt-ᵊn\ 1 burgh W *cen* Scotland ✻ of Dunbartonshire *pop* 23,703 2 *or* **Dum·bar·ton·shire** \-ˌshi(ə)r, -shər\ DUNBARTON
Dum·fries \ˌdəm-'frēs\ 1 *or* **Dum·fries·shire** \-'frēs(h)-ˌshi(ə)r, -shər\ county S Scotland *area* 1073, *pop* 85,656 2 burgh, its ✻ *pop* 26,320
Du·mont \'d(y)ü-ˌmänt\ borough NE N.J. E of Paterson *pop* 18,882
Dun·bar·ton \ˌdən-'bärt-ᵊn\ *or* **Dun·bar·ton·shire** \-ˌshi(ə)r, -shər\ county W *cen* Scotland ✻ Dumbarton *area* 244, *pop* 164,263
Dun·can \'dəŋ-kən\ city S Okla. *pop* 20,009
Dun·dalk, 1 \ˌdən-'dók\ urban area N *cen* Md. SE of Baltimore *pop* 82,428 2 \ˌdən-'dó(l)k\ urban district & port NE Republic of Ireland on Dundalk Bay ✻ of County Louth *pop* 21,142
Dun·dee \ˌdən-'dē\ burgh & port E Scotland in Angus on Firth of Tay *pop* 177,333
Dun·edin \ˌdə-'nēd-ᵊn\ 1 — see EDINBURGH 2 city New Zealand on SE coast of South I. at head of Otago Harbor *pop* (with suburbs) 102,500
Dun·ferm·line \ˌdən-'fərm-lən, ˌdəm-\ burgh E Scotland in Fife *pop* 44,710
Dun·kerque *or* **Dun·kirk** \'dən-ˌkərk, dən-'\ city & port N France on Strait of Dover *pop* 21,136
Dun·kirk \'dən-ˌkərk\ city SW N.Y. on Lake Erie *pop* 18,205
Dun Laoghai·re \ˌdən-'le(ə)r-ə\ *or* **Dun·lea·ry** \-'li(ə)r-ē\ *or formerly* **Kings·town** \'kiŋ-ˌstaun\ city borough & port E Ireland in Leinster on Dublin Bay *pop* 68,048
Dun·more \'dən-ˌmō(ə)r, -ˌmó(ə)r\ borough NE Pa. *pop* 18,917
Dun·net Head \ˌdən-ət-\ headland N Scotland on N coast in Caithness W of John o' Groat's; northernmost point of mainland of Scotland, at 58°50′N
Duns \'dənz\ burgh SE Scotland ✻ of Berwick
Duque de Caxias — see CAXIAS
Du·quesne \dü-'kān\ city SW Pa. *pop* 15,019
Du·rance \d(y)ù-'räns\ river 160 *m* SE France flowing SW into the Rhone
Du·ran·go \d(y)ù-'raŋ-(ˌ)gō\ 1 state NW *cen* Mexico *area* 42,272, *pop* 629,874 2 city, its ✻ *pop* 59,496
Dur·ban \'dər-bən\ city & port E Republic of So. Africa in E Natal on Natal Bay *pop* (with suburbs) 527,400
Dur·ham \'dər-əm, 'də-rəm, 'dur-əm\ 1 city NE *cen* N.C. NW of Raleigh *pop* 78,302 2 county N England bordering on North sea *area* 1015, *pop* 1,463,416 3 municipal borough, its ✻, S of Newcastle *pop* 19,283
Dur·res \'dur-əs\ *or It* **Du·raz·zo** \dù-'rät-(ˌ)sō\ *or anc* **Ep·i·dam·nus** \ˌep-ə-'dam-nəs\ *or* **Dyr·ra·chi·um** \də-'rā-kē-əm\ town & port Albania on Adriatic sea W of Tirane
Du·sham·be \d(y)ü-'sham-bə, -'shäm-\ *or formerly* **Sta·lin·abad** \ˌstäl-i-nə-'bäd, ˌstal-i-nə-'bad\ city U.S.S.R. in Soviet Central Asia ✻ of Tadzhik Republic *pop* 224,000
Düs·sel·dorf \'d(y)üs-əl-ˌdórf\ city W Germany on the Rhine N of Cologne ✻ of No. Rhine-Westphalia *pop* 694,700
Dutch Borneo — see KALIMANTAN
Dutch East Indies NETHERLANDS EAST INDIES
Dutch Guiana — see SURINAM
Dutch New Guinea NETHERLANDS NEW GUINEA
Dutch West Indies — see NETHERLANDS ANTILLES
Dvi·na \də-ˌvē-'nä\ 1 river 630 *m* U.S.S.R. rising in Valdai hills & flowing W into Gulf of Riga 2 — see NORTHERN DVINA
Dvíña Gulf *or* **Dvina Bay** *or formerly* **Gulf of Arch·an·gel** \'är-ˌkān-jəl\ arm of White sea U.S.S.R. in N Soviet Russia, Europe
Dvinsk — see DAUGAVPILS
Dzau·dzhi·kau \ˌdzaü-'jē-ˌkau\ *or* **Or·dzho·ni·kid·ze** \ˌór-jän-ə-'kid-zə\ city U.S.S.R. in SE Soviet Russia, Europe, on Terek river ✻ of No. Ossetia *pop* 164,000
Dzer·zhinsk \dər-'zhin(t)sk\ city U.S.S.R. in *cen* Soviet Russia, Europe, on Oka river W of Gorki *pop* 163,000
Dzun·gar·ia *or* **Zun·gar·ia** \(d)zəŋ-'gar-ē-ə, (d)zùŋ-, -'ger-\ region W China in N Sinkiang N of the Tien Shan

Ea·gle \'ē-gəl\ lake 13 *m* long N Calif. ENE of Lassen Peak
Ea·ling \'ē-liŋ\ municipal borough SE England in Middlesex, W suburb of London *pop* 187,306
East Anglia region E England including Norfolk & Suffolk; one of kingdoms in Anglo-Saxon heptarchy — **East Anglian** *adj or n*
East Bengal the part of Bengal now in East Pakistan
East Beskids — see BESKIDS
East·bourne \'ēs(t)-ˌbō(ə)rn, -ˌbó(ə)rn\ county borough S England in East Sussex on English channel *pop* 57,801
East Cape *or* **Cape Dezh·nev** \'dezh-nəf\ cape U.S.S.R. in NE Soviet Russia, Asia, at E end of Chukotski peninsula
East Chicago city NW Ind. SE of Chicago, Ill. *pop* 57,669
East China sea W Pacific between China (on W), Korea (on N), Japan & Ryukyu islands (on E), & Formosa (on S)
East Cleveland city NE Ohio NE of Cleveland *pop* 37,991
East Detroit city SE Mich. NE of Detroit *pop* 45,756
Eas·ter \'ē-stər\ *or* **Ra·pa Nui** \ˌräp-ə-'nü-ē\ *or Sp* **Is·la de Pas·cua** \ˌēz-klä-thā-'päs-kwä\ island SE Pacific 2000 *m* W of Chilean coast belonging to Chile *area* 50
Eastern Ghats chain of mountains SE India extending SW & S from near delta of Mahanadi river in Orissa to W Madras &

S Kerala; highest point Mt. Dodabetta (in Nilgiri hills) 8647 *ft* — see WESTERN GHATS

Eastern Rumelia *or* **Eastern Roumelia** region S Bulgaria including Rhodope mountains & Maritsa river valley *area* 12,585

Eastern Samoa — see AMERICAN SAMOA

Eastern Shore region E Md. & E Va. of Chesapeake Bay; sometimes considered as including Del. — see DELMARVA

Eastern Thrace — see THRACE

East Flanders province NW *cen* Belgium ✳ Ghent *area* 1147, *pop* 1,272,161

East Frisian — see FRISIAN

East Ham \'ēst-'ham\ county borough SE England in Essex, E suburb of London *pop* 120,873

East Hartford town *cen* Conn. *pop* 43,977

East Haven \'est-,hā-vən\ town S Conn. SE of New Haven *pop* 21,388

East Indies, 1 *or* **East India** southeastern Asia including India, Indochina, Malaya, & Malay archipelago — a chiefly former name **2** the Malay archipelago — **East Indian** *adj or n*

East Lansing city S Mich. *pop* 30,198

East-lawn \'ēst-,lón\ urban area SE Mich. S of Ann Arbor *pop* 17,652

East Liverpool city E Ohio on the Ohio *pop* 22,306

East London city & port S Republic of So. Africa in SE Cape of Good Hope on Indian ocean *pop* 91,264

East Los Angeles urban area SW Calif. *pop* 104,270

East Lothian *or* **Had-ding-ton** \'had-iŋ-tən\ *or* **Had-ding-ton-shire** \-,shi(ə)r, -shər\ county SE Scotland ✳ Haddington *area* 267, *pop* 52,240

East-main \'ēst-,mān\ river 375 *m* Canada in W Que. flowing W into James Bay

East Meadow urban area SE N.Y. on Long I. *pop* 46,036

East Moline city NW Ill. on the Mississippi *pop* 16,732

Eas-ton \'ē-stən\ city E Pa. NE of Bethlehem at junction of Lehigh & Delaware rivers *pop* 31,955

East Orange city NE N.J. NW of Newark *pop* 77,259

East Pakistan the E division of Pakistan comprising the E portion of Bengal; a province ✳ Dacca *area* 54,501, *pop* 42,063,000

East Paterson borough NE N.J. *pop* 19,344

East Point city NW *cen* Ga. SW of Atlanta *pop* 35,633

East Providence city E R.I. *pop* 41,955

East Prussia region N Europe bordering on the Baltic E of Pomerania; formerly a province of Prussia, for a time (1919–39) forming an exclave separated from rest of Prussia by Polish Corridor; since 1945 in Poland & U.S.S.R.

East Punjab — see PUNJAB

East Ridge town SE Tenn. SE of Chattanooga *pop* 19,570

East Ri-ding \'rīd-iŋ\ administrative county N England comprising SE part of Yorkshire ✳ Beverley *area* 1172, *pop* 510,800

East river strait SE N.Y. connecting Upper New York Bay with Long Island Sound & separating Manhattan I. from Long I.

East Saint Louis city SW Ill. *pop* 81,712

East Siberian sea arm of Arctic ocean N of Yakutsk Republic, U.S.S.R., extending from New Siberian islands to Wrangel I.

East Suffolk — see SUFFOLK

East Sussex — see SUSSEX

East-view \'ēst-,vyü\ town Canada in SE Ont. NE of Ottawa on Ottawa river *pop* 19,283

East Whittier urban area SW Calif. *pop* 19,884

Eau Claire \ō-'kla(ə)r, -'kle(ə)r\ city W Wis. *pop* 37,987

Eb-bw Vale \'eb-ü-,vāl\ urban district W England in Monmouthshire N of Cardiff, Wales *pop* 29,205

Eboracum — see YORK

Ebro \'ā-(,)brō\ river 480 *m* NE Spain flowing from Cantabrian mountains ESE into the Mediterranean

Ecbatana — see HAMADAN

Ecorse \'ē-,kórs\ city SE Mich. SSW of Detroit *pop* 17,328

Ec-ua-dor \'ek-wə-,dó(ə)r\ country W So. America bordering on the Pacific; a republic ✳ Quito *area* 104,510, *pop* 3,906,907 — **Ec-ua-dor-an** \,ek-wə-'dór-ən, -'dór-\ *adj or n* — **Ec-ua-dor-ian** \-ē-ən\ *adj or n*

Edam \'ēd-əm, 'ē-,dam\ commune NW Netherlands on the IJsselmeer NNE of Amsterdam

Ede, 1 \'ād-ə\ commune E Netherlands NW of Arnhem *pop* 58,132 **2** \'ā-,dā\ city SW Nigeria NE of Ibadan *pop* 52,000

Edes-sa \i-'des-ə, ē-\ **1** *or* **Vo-de-na** \vó-the-'nä\ town N Greece in W Macedonia; ancient ✳ of Macedonian kings *pop* 15,000 **2** — see URFA

Edfu — see IDFU

Edi-na \i-'dī-nə\ village SE Minn. SW of Minneapolis *pop* 28,501

Ed-in-burg \'ed-°n-,bərg\ city S Tex. W of Harlingen *pop* 18,706

Ed-in-burgh \'ed-°n-,bər-ə, -,bə-rə, -b(ə-)rə\ **1** *or* Gael **Dun-edin** \,də-'nēd-°n\ city & burgh of Scotland & of Midlothian on Firth of Forth *pop* 466,770 **2** *or* **Edinburghshire** \-,shi(ə)r, -shər\ — see MIDLOTHIAN

Edir-ne \ā-'dir-nə\ **1** *or formerly* **Adri-a-no-ple** \,ā-drē-ə-'nō-pəl\ city Turkey in Europe on Maritsa river *pop* 31,865

Ed-i-son \'ed-ə-sən\ urban township NE *cen* N.J. *pop* 44,799

Ed-is-to \'ed-ə-,stō\ river 150 *m* S S.C. flowing SE into the Atlantic

Edith Ca-vell, Mount \-'kav-əl, -kə-'vell\ mountain 11,033 *ft* Canada in SW Alta. in Jasper National Park

Ed-mon-ton \'ed-mən-tən\ **1** city Canada ✳ of Alta. on the No. Saskatchewan *pop* 226,002 **2** municipal borough SE England in Middlesex, N suburb of London *pop* 104,244

Edo — see TOKYO

Edom \'ēd-əm\ *or* **Id-u-maea** *or* **Id-u-mea** \,ij-ə-'mē-ə\ ancient country SW Asia S of Judea & the Dead sea

Edward, Lake \'ed-wərd\ lake E Africa SW of Lake Albert on boundary between NE Congo & SW Uganda *area* 830

Ed-wards \'ed-wərdz\ plateau 2000–5000 *ft* SW Tex.

Efa-te \ā-'fät-ē\ *or* **Va-té** \vä-'tā\ island SW Pacific in *cen* New Hebrides; chief town Vila ✳ of New Hebrides *area* 200

Effigy Mounds National Monument site NE Iowa on the Mississippi including prehistoric mounds *area* 2

Ega-di \'eg-ə-dē\ *or* **Ae-ga-di-an** \ē-'gād-ē-ən\ *or anc* **Ae-ga-tes** \ē-'gāt-ēz\ islands Italy off W coast of Sicily *area* 15

Eger \'ā-gər\ *or* Czech **Ohre** \'ór-zhə\ river 193 *m* S Germany & W Czechoslovakia flowing NE into the Elbe

Eg-gerts-ville \'eg-ərts-,vil\ urban area W N.Y. E of Buffalo *pop* 44,807

Eg-mont, Mount \'eg-,mänt\ *or* **Ta-ra-na-ki** \,tar-ə-'näk-ē\ mountain 8260 *ft* New Zealand in W *cen* North I.

Egorevsk — see YEGOREVSK

Egypt \'ē-jəpt\ *or* **Ar Misr** \'misr°\ country NE Africa & Sinai peninsula bordering on Mediterranean & Red seas ✳ Cairo — see UNITED ARAB REPUBLIC

Ei-fel \'ī-fəl\ plateau region W Germany NW of the Moselle & NE of Luxembourg

Ei-ger \'ī-gər\ mountain 13,036 *ft* W *cen* Switzerland NE of the Jungfrau

Eind-ho-ven \'īnt-,hō-vən, 'änt-\ commune S Netherlands in No. Brabant *pop* 157,621

Eire — see IRELAND

Ei-se-nach \'īz-°n-,äk, -,äk\ city E Germany in Thuringia W of Erfurt *pop* 51,800

Ekaterinburg — see SVERDLOVSK

Ekaterinodar — see KRASNODAR

Ekaterinoslav — see DNEPROPETROVSK

El Alamein — see ALAMEIN

Elam \'ē-ləm\ *or* **Su-si-ana** \,sü-zē-'an-ə, -'än-ə, -'ā-nə\ ancient kingdom SW Asia at head of Persian gulf E of Babylonia ✳ Susa — **Elam-ite** \'ē-lə-,mīt\ *adj or n*

Elatea — see CITHAERON

Elath \'ē-,lath\ **1** — see 'AQABA **2** *or* **Ei-lat** \ā-'lät\ town & port S Israel at head of Gulf of 'Aqaba

Ela-zig \,el-ə-'zig\ city E *cen* Turkey in valley of the upper Murat *pop* 60,438

El-ba \'el-bə\ island Italy in the Mediterranean between Corsica & mainland; chief town Portoferraio *area* 86, *pop* 27,000

El Bahnasa — see OXYRHYNCHUS

El-be \'el-bə, 'elb\ *or* Czech **La-be** \'lä-be\ river 720 *m* NW Czechoslovakia & N Germany flowing NW into North sea

El-bert, Mount \'el-bərt\ mountain 14,431 *ft*, *cen* Colo. in Sawatch mountains; highest in Colo. & Rocky mountains

El Bika *or* **El Bekaa** — see BIKA

El-blag \'el-,blóŋ\ *or* G **El-bing** \'el-biŋ\ city & port N Poland near the Frisches Haff *pop* 65,000

El-brus \el-'brüz\ *or* **El-bo-rus** \,el-bə-'rüz\ mountain 18,481 *ft* U.S.S.R. in Georgia; highest in the Caucasus & in Europe

El-burz \el-'bù(ə)rz\ mountains N Iran parallel with S shore of Caspian sea — see DEMAVEND

El Ca-jon \,el-kə-'hón\ city SW Calif. E of San Diego *pop* 37,618

El Caney — see CANEY

El Cen-tro \el-'sen-(,)trō\ city S Calif. in Imperial valley *pop* 16,811

El Cer-ri-to \,el-sə-'rēt-(,)ō\ city W Calif. on San Francisco Bay N of Berkeley *pop* 25,437

El-che \'el-(,)chā\ city SE Spain SW of Alicante *pop* 67,088

El Do-ra-do \,el-də-'räd-(,)ō\ city S Ark. *pop* 25,292

Electric Peak mountain 11,155 *ft* S Mont. in Yellowstone National Park; highest in Gallatin range

El-e-phan-ta \,el-ə-'fant-ə\ *or* **Gha-ra-pu-ri** \,gär-ə-'pù(ə)r-ē\ island W India in Bombay harbor

El-e-phan-ti-ne \,el-ə-,fan-'tī-nē, -'tē-\ island S Egypt in the Nile opposite Aswān

Eleu-sis \i-'lü-səs\ *or* NGk **Elev-sís** \,el-əf-'sēs\ ancient ruined city E Greece in Attica NW of Athens on inlet of Saronic gulf opposite Salamis I. — **El-eu-sin-i-an** \,el-yü-'sin-ē-ən\ *adj or n*

Eleu-thera \i-'lü-thə-rə\ island Bahamas E of New Providence I. *area* 164

El Faiyûm *or* **El Fayum** — see FAIYŪM

El Fa-sher \el-'fash-ər\ city W Sudan in Darfur *pop* 26,161

El Fer-rol *or* **El Ferrol del Cau-di-llo** \,el-fə-'ról,del-,kaù-'dē-(,)(y)ō, -'dēl-(,)(y)ō\ city & port NW Spain on the Atlantic NE of La Coruña *pop* 81,376

El-gin, 1 \'el-jən\ city NE Ill. *pop* 49,447 **2** \'el-gən\ *or* **El-gin-shire** \-,shi(ə)r, -shər\ — see MORAY **3** \'el-gən\ borough NE Scotland ✳ of Moray

El Giza *or* **El Gizeh** — see GIZA

El-gon, Mount \'el-,gän\ extinct volcano 14,178 *ft* E Africa on boundary between Uganda & Kenya NE of Lake Victoria

El Hamad — see HAMAD

El Hasa — see HASA

Elis \'ē-ləs\ *or* NGk **Ilía** \ē-'lē-ə\ region S Greece in NW Peloponnesus S of Achaea bordering on Ionian sea

Elisabethville — see LUBUMBASHI

Elisavetgrad — see KIROVOGRAD

Elisavetpol — see KIROVABAD

Eliz-a-beth \i-'liz-ə-bəth\ **1** short river SE Va. flowing between cities of Norfolk & Portsmouth into Hampton Roads **2** islands SE Mass. between Buzzards Bay & Vineyard Sound **3** city & port NE N.J. SW of Newark on Newark Bay *pop* 107,698

El Jezira — see GEZIRA

Elk-hart \'el-,kärt\ city N Ind. E of So. Bend *pop* 40,274

Elk Island National Park reservation Canada in E *cen* Alta. *area* 51

Éllas — see GREECE

Elles-mere \'elz-,mi(ə)r\ island Canada in Franklin District of Northwest Territories W of NW Greenland — see COLUMBIA (Cape)

El-lice \'el-əs\ islands W Pacific N of Fiji & SSE of Gilbert islands *area* 10, *pop* 4938 — see GILBERT

El-lis \'el-əs\ island SE N.Y. in Upper New York Bay

El-lo-ra \e-'lōr-ə, -'lór-\ *or* **Elu-ra** \-'lür-ə\ village W India in *cen* Maharashtra NW of Aurangabad; caves

El-lore \e-'lō(ə)r, -'ló(ə)r\ *or* **Elu-ru** \e-'lù(ə)r-(,)ü\ city SE India in E Andhra Pradesh N of Masulipatnam *pop* 108,367

El Maghreb al Aqsa — see MAGHREB

El Mansûra — see MANSŪRA

Elm-hurst \'elm-,hərst\ city NE Ill. W of Chicago *pop* 36,991

El Minya — see MINYA

El-mi-ra \el-'mī-rə\ city S N.Y. *pop* 46,517

El Misti — see MISTI

El·mont \'el-ˌmänt\ urban area SE N.Y. on Long I. *pop* 30,138

El Mor·ro National Monument \el-'mär-(ˌ)ō, -'mȯr-\ reservation W N. Mex. SE of Gallup; rock carvings, pueblo *area* 1.4

Elm·wood Park \ˌelm-ˈwu̇d-\ village NE Ill. NW of Chicago *pop* 23,866

El Obeid \ˌel-ō-ˈbād\ city *cen* Sudan in Kordofan *pop* 52,372

El Paso \el-ˈpas-(ˌ)ō\ city Tex. at W tip on Rio Grande *pop* 276,687 — **El Paso·an** \-ˈpas-ə-wən\ *n*

El Sal·va·dor \el-ˈsal-və-ˌdȯ(ə)r, ˌsal-və-ˈ\ country Central America bordering on the Pacific; a republic ✱ San Salvador *area* 8236 *pop* 2,510,984

Elsass, Elsass–Lothringen — see ALSACE, ALSACE-LORRAINE

Elsene — see IXELLES

Elsinore — see HELSINGÖR

El Uqsor — see LUXOR

Ely \'ē-lē\ urban district E England in Isle of Ely on the Ouse

Ely, Isle of administrative county E England ✱ March *area* 372, *pop* 89,038 — see CAMBRIDGE

Elyr·ia \i-ˈlir-ē-ə\ city NE Ohio SW of Cleveland *pop* 43,782

Em·bar·ras *or* **Em·bar·rass** \'am-ˌbrȯ\ river 150 *m* E Ill. flowing SE into the Wabash

Em·den \'em-dən\ city & port W Germany at the mouth of the Ems *pop* 44,500

Emesa — see HOMS

Emi·lia \ā-ˈmēl-yə\ **1** district N Italy comprising the W part of Emilia-Romagna region   **2** — see EMILIA-ROMAGNA

Emi·lia-Ro·ma·gna \ā-ˌmēl-yə-rō-ˈmän-yə\ *or formerly* **Emilia** *or anc* **Ae·mil·ia** \ē-ˈmil-yə, -ˈmēl-\ region N Italy bounded by the Po, the Adriatic, & the Apennines ✱ Bologna *area* 8546, *pop* 3,338,858

Em·men \'em-ən\ commune NE Netherlands *pop* 64,869

Em·men·thal *or* **Em·men·tal** \'em-ən-ˌtäl\ valley of the upper **Em·me** \'em-ə\ *or* **Em·men** \'em-ən\ (river 45 *m*) *cen* Switzerland in E Bern canton

Em·po·ria \em-ˈpȯr-ē-ə, -ˈpȯr-\ city E *cen* Kans. *pop* 18,190

Empty Quarter RUBʻ AL KHALI

Ems \'emz, 'em(p)s\ **1** river 200 *m* W Germany flowing N into North sea   **2** *or* **Bad Ems** \bät-\ town W Germany SE of Koblenz

Enchanted Mesa sandstone butte W N. Mex. NE of Acoma

En·der·bury \'en-dər-ˌber-ē\ island (atoll) *cen* Pacific in the Phoenix islands controlled jointly by U. S. & Great Britain

En·di·cott \'en-di-kət, -də-ˌkät\ **1** village S N. Y. W of Binghamton *pop* 18,775   **2** mountains N Alaska, the central range of Brooks range

En·field \'en-ˌfēld\ **1** town N Conn. *pop* 31,464   **2** urban district SE England in Middlesex, N suburb of London *pop* 110,458

En·ga·dine \'eŋ-gə-ˌdēn\ valley of Inn river 60 *m* long E Switzerland in Graubünden

Eng·land \'iŋ-glənd *also* 'iŋ-lənd\ **1** *or* LL **An·glia** \'aŋ-glē-ə\ country S Great Britain; a division of the United Kingdom of Great Britain & Northern Ireland ✱ London *area* 50,331, *pop* 43,460,525   **2** England & Wales   **3** UNITED KINGDOM

En·gle·wood \'eŋ-gəl-ˌwu̇d\ **1** city N *cen* Colo. S of Denver *pop* 33,398   **2** city NE N. J. on the Hudson opposite New York City *pop* 26,057

English channel *or* F **La Manche** \lä-ˈmäⁿsh\ channel between S England & N France connecting North sea & Atlantic ocean

Enid \'ē-nəd\ city N Okla. *pop* 38,859

Enisei — see YENISEI

Eni·we·tok \ˌen-i-ˈwē-ˌtäk\ island (atoll) W Pacific in the NW Marshalls

En·na \'en-ə\ commune Italy in *cen* Sicily *pop* 28,200

En·nis \'en-əs\ urban district W Ireland ✱ of County Clare

En·nis·kil·len \ˌen-ə-ˈskil-ən\ *or* **In·nis·kil·ling** \ˌin-ə-ˈskil-iŋ\ municipal borough SW Northern Ireland ✱ of County Fermanagh

Enns \'enz, 'en(t)s\ river 160 *m*, *cen* Austria flowing E & N from Styria into the Danube

En·sche·de \ˌen(t)-skə-ˈdā\ commune E Netherlands in Overijssel near German frontier *pop* 121,981

En·se·ña·da \ˌen(t)-sən-ˈ(y)äd-ə\ city & port NW Mexico in Baja California state on the Pacific SE of Tijuana *pop* 18,140

En·teb·be \en-ˈteb-ə\ town S Uganda on N shore of Lake Victoria; former ✱ of Uganda

Eolie, Isole — see LIPARI

Eph·e·sus \'ef-ə-səs\ ancient city W Asia Minor in Ionia near Aegean coast; its site SW of present town of Selsuk — **Ephe·sian** \i-ˈfē-zhən\ *adj or n*

Ephra·im \'ē-frē-əm\ **1** *or* **Mount Ephraim** hilly region Palestine N of Judaea   **2** — see ISRAEL

Epidamnus — see DURRES

Ep·i·dau·rus \ˌep-ə-ˈdȯr-əs\ ancient town S Greece in Argolis on Saronic gulf

Épi·nal \ˌā-pi-ˈnäl\ commune NE France on the Moselle SW of Strasbourg *pop* 28,688

Epi·rus *or* **Epei·rus** \i-ˈpī-rəs\ *or* NGk **Ípi·ros** \'ē-pē-ˌrós\ region NW Greece bordering on Ionian sea; once an independent kingdom & later (*ab* 200 B.C.) a republic — **Epi·rote** \i-ˈpī-ˌrōt, -rət\ *adj or n*

Ep·ping Forest \'ep-iŋ\ forested region SE England in Essex NE of London & S of **Epping** urban district

Ep·som and Ew·ell \ˌep-sə-mən-ˈ(d)yü-əl\ municipal borough SE England in Surrey SW of London *pop* 68,049

Equatorial Guinea country W Africa on Bight of Biafra comprising former Spanish Guinea; an independent republic since 1968 ✱ Santa Isabei *area* 10,831, *pop* 244,574 — see SPANISH GUINEA

Er·bil \'e(ə)r-ˌbil\ *or* **Ar·bil** \'är-\ *or anc* **Ar·be·la** \är-ˈbē-lə\ city N Iraq E of Mosul *pop* 34,313

Er·ci·yas Da·gi \ˌer-jē-ˌyäs-dä-ˈ(g)ē\ mountain 12,848 *ft*, *cen* Turkey; highest in Asia Minor

Er·e·bus, Mount \'er-ə-bəs\ volcano 12,450 *ft* E Antarctica on Ross I. in SW Ross sea

Ere·gli \ˌer-ˌī-ˈlē, ˌer-ə-ˈglē\ **1** city S Turkey SSE of Ankara *pop* 32,057   **2** town & port NW Turkey in Asia on Black sea NW of Ankara

Erevan — see YEREVAN

Er·furt \'e(ə)r-fərt, -ˌfu̇(ə)rt\ city E Germany WSW of Leipzig *pop* 188,100

Erie \'i(ə)r-ē\ **1** city & port NW Pa. on Lake Erie *pop* 138,440   **2** canal 363 *m* long N N.Y. from Hudson river at Albany to Lake

Erie at Buffalo; built 1817–25; superseded by **New York State Barge Canal** (*ab* 525 *m* long)

Erie, Lake lake 241 *m* long E *cen* No. America on boundary between the U.S. & Canada; one of the Great Lakes *area* 9940

Eriha — see JERICHO

Er·i·trea \ˌer-ə-ˈtrē-ə, -ˈtrā-\ country NE Africa bordering on Red sea ✱ Asmara; incorporated (1962) into Ethiopia *area* 46,000, *pop* 1,100,000 — **Er·i·tre·an** \-ˈtrē-ən, -ˈtrā-\ *adj*

Erivan — see YEREVAN

Er·lang·en \'e(ə)r-ˌläŋ-ən\ city W Germany in Bavaria NNW of Nuremberg *pop* 67,300

Er·moú·po·lis *or* **Her·moú·po·lis** \er-ˈmü-pə-ləs\ *or* **Her·mop·o·lis** \(ˌ)hər-ˈmäp-ə-ləs\ *or* **Sy·ros** \'sī-ˌräs\ city & port Greece on Syros; chief town of the Cyclades *pop* 21,156

Er Rif *or* **Er Riff** — see RIF

Erz·ge·bir·ge \'erts-gə-ˌbir-gə\ *or* **Ore mountains** mountain range E *cen* Germany & NW Czechoslovakia on boundary between Saxony & Bohemia; highest Klinovec (in Czechoslovakia) 4000 *ft*

Er·zin·can \ˌer-zin-ˈjän\ city E *cen* Turkey on the Euphrates W of Erzurum *pop* 36,465

Er·zu·rum \ˌerz-ə-ˈrüm, ˌȯrz-\ city NE Turkey in mountains of W Turkish Armenia *pop* 91,196

Es·bjerg \'es-ˌbē-ˌe)rg, -ˌȯrg\ city & port SW Denmark in SW Jutland peninsula on North sea *pop* 50,921

Es·ca·na·ba \ˌes-kə-ˈnäb-ə\ city NW Mich. on Green Bay *pop* 15,391

Escaut — see SCHELDT

Es·con·di·do \ˌes-kən-ˈdēd-(ˌ)ō\ city SW Calif. N of San Diego *pop* 16,377

Es·dra·e·lon, Plain of \ˌez-drə-ˈē-lən\ *or* **Plain of Jez·re·el** \'jez-rē-ˌel, -ˌrē(ə)l\ plain N Palestine NE of Mt. Carmel in valley of the upper Qishon

Esfahan — see ISFAHAN

Esher \'ē-shər\ urban district S England in Surrey SW of London *pop* 51,217

Esh Sham — see DAMASCUS

Es·kils·tu·na \'es-kəl-ˌstü-nə\ city SE Sweden S of Malar Lake *pop* 59,882

Es·ki·se·hir \ˌes-ki-shə-ˈhi(ə)r\ *or* **Es·ki·shehr** \-ˈshe(ə)r\ city W *cen* Turkey on tributary of the Sakarya *pop* 153,190

España — see SPAIN

Española — see HISPANIOLA

Es·pí·ri·to San·to \ə-ˌspir-ə-tü-ˈsan-(ˌ)tü\ state E Brazil bordering on the Atlantic ✱ Vitória *area* 16,543, *pop* 861,562

Es·pí·ri·tu San·to \ə-ˌspir-ə-tü-ˈsan-(ˌ)tü\ island SW Pacific in the NW New Hebrides; largest in the group *area* 1875

Es·qui·line \'es-kwə-ˌlīn, -lən\ hill in Rome, Italy, one of seven on which the ancient city was built — see AVENTINE

Es·sa·oui·ra \ˌes-ə-ˈwir-ə\ *or* **Mog·a·dor** \'mäg-ə-ˌdȯ(ə)r\ city & port W Morocco on the Atlantic W of Marrakesh *pop* 22,291

Es·sen \'es-ən\ city W Germany in the Ruhr *pop* 727,300

Es·se·qui·bo \ˌes-ə-ˈkē-(ˌ)bō\ river 600 *m* Guyana flowing N into the Atlantic through a wide estuary

Es·sex \'es-iks\ **1** urban area N *cen* Md. E of Baltimore *pop* 35,205   **2** county SE England bordering on North sea & N shore of the Thames; one of kingdoms in Anglo-Saxon heptarchy ✱ Chelmsford *area* 1528, *pop* 2,043,574

Ess·ling·en \'es-liŋ-ən\ city W Germany on the Neckar ESE of Stuttgart *pop* 83,300

Es Sur — see TYRE

Es·te·rel \ˌes-tə-ˈrel\ forested mountain region SE France on coast between Fréjus & Cannes; highest point 2020 *ft*

Es·tes Park \ˌes-tēz-\ valley N Colo. in Front range of the Rocky mountains at E border of Rocky Mountain National Park

Es·to·nia \e-ˈstō-nē-ə, -nyə\ *or* **Es·tho·nia** \e-ˈstō-, es-ˈthō-\ country N Europe bordering on Baltic sea; one of the Baltic Provinces of Russia 1721–1917, an independent republic 1918–40, since 1940 a constituent republic (**Estonian Republic**) of the U.S.S.R. ✱ Tallin *area* 18,361, *pop* 1,196,000

Es·to·ril \ˌēsh-tə-ˈril\ resort town Portugal on coast W of Lisbon

Es·tre·ma·du·ra \ˌes-trə-mə-ˈdu̇r-ə\ **1** region & old province W *cen* Portugal ✱ Lisbon; SW part included in present Estremadura province   **2** *or* **Ex·tre·ma·du·ra** \ˌek-strə-\ region & old province W Spain bordering on Portugal; area included in present Cáceres & Badajoz provinces

Ethi·o·pia \ˌē-thē-ˈō-pē-ə\ **1** ancient country NE Africa S of Egypt bordering on Red sea   **2** *or* **Ab·ys·sin·ia** \ˌab-ə-ˈsin-yə, -ˈsin-ē-ə\ country E Africa; an empire ✱ Addis Ababa *area* 400,000, *pop ab* 22,000,000

Et·na *or* **Aet·na** \'et-nə\ volcano 10,741 *ft* Italy in NE Sicily near the coast

Eton \'ēt-ᵊn\ urban district SE *cen* England in Buckinghamshire on the Thames

Étre·tat \ˌā-trə-ˈtä\ commune N France on coast NNE of Le Havre

Etru·ria \i-ˈtru̇r-ē-ə\ ancient country *cen* Italy coextensive with modern Tuscany & part of Umbria

Et·trick Forest \'e-trik-\ region, formerly a forest & hunting ground, in SE Scotland in Selkirkshire

Eu·boea \yu̇-ˈbē-ə\ *or* **Neg·ro·pont** \'neg-rə-ˌpänt\ *or* NGk **Év·voia** \'ev-(ˌ)yä\ island 90 *m* long E Greece in the Aegean NE of Attica & Boeotia ✱ Chalcis *area* 1457 — **Euboean** *adj or n*

Eu·clid \'yü-kləd\ city NE Ohio NE of Cleveland *pop* 62,998

Eu·ga·ne·an \yü-ˈgā-nē-ən, ˌyü-gə-ˈnē-\ hills NE Italy in SW Veneto between Padua & the Adige

Eu·gene \yü-ˈjēn\ city W Oreg. on the Willamette *pop* 50,977

Eu·pen \'ȯi-pən\ commune E Belgium E of Liège; formerly in Germany, transferred (with Malmédy) to Belgium 1919

Eu·phra·tes \yu̇-ˈfrāt-(ˌ)ēz\ river 1700 *m* SW Asia flowing from E Turkey SW & SE to unite with the Tigris forming the Shatt-al-Arab — see KARA SU

Eure \'ər\ river 140 *m* NW France flowing N into the Seine above Rouen

Eu·re·ka \yu̇-ˈrē-kə\ city & port NW Calif. *pop* 28,137

Eu·rope \'yu̇r-əp\ **1** continent of the eastern hemisphere between Asia & the Atlantic *area ab* 3,800,000; forms with Asia the landmass called **Eur·asia** \yu̇-ˈrā-zhə, -shə\   **2** the European continent as distinguished from the British Isles

Euxine — see BLACK (sea)

Ev·ans, Mount \'ev-ənz\ mountain 14,260 *ft* N *cen* Colo. WSW of Denver
Ev·ans·ton \'ev-ən(t)-stən\ city NE Ill. N of Chicago *pop* 79,283
Ev·ans·ville \'ev-ənz-,vil\ city SW Ind. on the Ohio *pop* 141,543
Ev·er·est, Mount \'ev-(ə-)rəst\ *or* Tibetan **Cho·mo·lung·ma** \,chō-mə-'lüŋ-mə\ mountain 29,028 *ft* S Asia on border between Nepal & Tibet in the Himalayas; highest in the world
Ev·er·ett \'ev-(ə-)rət\ **1** city E Mass. N of Boston *pop* 43,544 **2** city NW *cen* Wash. on Puget Sound N of Seattle *pop* 40,304
Ev·er·glades \'ev-ər-,glādz\ swamp region S Fla. S of Lake Okeechobee; now partly drained; S part forms **Everglades National Park** (*area* 423)
Evergreen Park village NE Ill. S of Chicago *pop* 24,178
Eve·sham \'ēv-shəm\ municipal borough W *cen* England in Worcestershire S of Birmingham in **Vale of Evesham**
Évian *or* **Évian–les–Bains** \ā-vyä^{n}-le-ba^{n}\ commune E France on Lake Geneva; health resort
Évo·ra \'ev-ə-rə\ city S *cen* Portugal *pop* 25,400
Évreux \āv-'rə(r)\ commune N France WNW of Paris *pop* 23,647
Évros — see MARITSA
Ew·ing \'yü-iŋ\ urban township W N.J. NW of Trenton *pop* 26,628
Ex·e·ter \'ek-sət-ər\ city & county borough SW England ✻ of Devonshire *pop* 75,479
Ex·moor \'ek-,smu̇(ə)r, -,smō(ə)r, -,smȯ(ə)r\ moorland SW England in Somerset *area* 32
Ex·u·ma \ik-'sü-mə, ig-'zü-\ islands in *cen* Bahamas S of **Exuma Sound** (SE of New Providence I.); chief island **Great Exuma**
Eyre \'a(ə)r, 'e(ə)r\ peninsula Australia in S So. Australia W of Spencer gulf
Eyre, Lake intermittent lake *cen* Australia in NE So. Australia
Eyzies, Les — see LES EYZIES

Fa·en·za \fä-'en-zə, -'en(t)-sə\ commune N Italy SW of Ravenna *pop* 47,199
Faer·oe *or* **Far·oe** \'fa(ə)r-(,)ō, 'fe(ə)r-\ islands Denmark in the NE Atlantic NW of the Shetlands ✻ Thorshavn *area* 540, *pop* 32,465
Fair·born \'fa(ə)r-,bȯ(ə)rn, 'fe(ə)r-\ city SW *cen* Ohio NE of Dayton *pop* 19,453
Fair·field \'fa(ə)r-,fēld, 'fe(ə)r-\ **1** city N *cen* Ala. *pop* 15,816 **2** town SW Conn. SW of Bridgeport *pop* 46,183
Fair Lawn borough NE N.J. NE of Paterson *pop* 36,421
Fair·mont \'fa(ə)r-,mänt, 'fe(ə)r-\ city N W. Va. *pop* 27,477
Fair·weath·er, Mount \'fa(ə)r-,weth-ər, 'fe(ə)r-\ mountain 15,300 *ft* on boundary between Alaska & B.C.; highest in **Fairweather range** of the Coast ranges
Fai·yûm *or* **Fa·yum** *or* **El Faiyûm** *or* **El Fayum** \,el-fā-'(y)üm, -(,)fī-\ city N Egypt SSW of Cairo *pop* 101,100
Faiz·abad \'fī-zə-,bad\ **1** city NE Afghanistan *pop* 25,700 **2** *or* **Fyz·abad** \'fī-\ city N India in Uttar Pradesh *pop* 76,582
Fa·ka·ra·va \,fäk-ə-'räv-ə\ island (atoll) S Pacific, principal island of the Tuamotu archipelago
Fako — see CAMEROON
Fa·laise \fə-'lāz, fa-\ town NW France SSE of Caen
Fal·kirk \'fȯl-,kərk\ burgh *cen* Scotland in Stirlingshire ENE of Glasgow *pop* 37,528
Falk·land \'fȯ(l)-klənd\ *or* Sp **Is·las Mal·vi·nas** \,ēz-läz-mäl-'vē-näs\ islands SW Atlantic E of S end of Argentina; a British crown colony ✻ Stanley *area* 4618, *pop* 2230
Falkland Islands Dependencies islands & territories in the S Atlantic & in Antarctica administered by the British from Falkland islands, including So. Orkney, So. Sandwich, & So. Shetland islands, So. Georgia I., Antarctic (Palmer) peninsula, & Antarctic (Palmer) archipelago
Fall River \'fȯl\ city & port SE Mass. *pop* 99,942
Falls \'fȯlz\ urban township SE Pa. N of Philadelphia *pop* 29,082
False Bay \'fȯls\ inlet Republic of So. Africa in SW Cape Province E of Cape of Good Hope
Fal·ster \'fäl-stər, 'fȯl-\ island Denmark in Baltic sea S of Sjælland *area* 198
Fa·ma·gus·ta \,fäm-ə-'güs-tə, ,fam-\ city & port E Cyprus on **Famagusta Bay** (inlet of the Mediterranean) *pop* 18,693
Fan·ning \'fan-iŋ\ island *cen* Pacific in the Line islands belonging to Great Britain *area* 15
Far·al·lon \'far-ə-,län\ islands Calif. 27 *m* W of San Francisco
Far East the countries of E Asia & the Malay archipelago — usu. considered as comprising the Asian countries bordering on the Pacific but sometimes as including also India, Ceylon, East Pakistan, Tibet, & Burma — **Far Eastern** *adj*
Fare·well, Cape \'fa(ə)r-,wel, 'fe(ə)r-\ cape Greenland at S tip
Far·go \'fär-(,)gō\ city E N. Dak. on Red river *pop* 46,662
Far·i·bault \'far-ə-,bō\ city SE Minn. *pop* 16,926
Far·ming·ton \'fär-miŋ-tən\ town NW N. Mex. *pop* 23,786
Far·rukh·abad \fə-'rü-kə-,bad, -,bäd\ city N India in Uttar Pradesh on the Ganges WNW of Lucknow *pop* 74,205
Fars \'färz, 'färs\ *or* **Far·si·stan** \,fär-si-'stan\ region SW Iran, chief city Shiraz, corresponding closely with ancient region of **Per·sis** \'pər-səs\
Fársala — see PHARSALUS
Farther India — see INDOCHINA
Fashoda — see KODOK
Fá·ti·ma \'fat-ə-mə\ village *cen* Portugal NNE of Lisbon
Fat·shan \'fät-'shän\ *or* **Nam·hoi** \'näm-'hȯi\ city SE China in *cen* Kwangtung SW of Canton *pop* 122,500
Fa·yal \fə-'yäl, fī-'äl\ island *cen* Azores *area* 64
Fay·ette·ville \'fā-ət-,vil, -vəl\ **1** city NW Ark. *pop* 20,274 **2** city SE *cen* N.C. on Cape Fear river *pop* 47,106
Fear, Cape \'fi(ə)r\ cape SE N.C. at mouth of Cape Fear river
Feath·er \'feth-ər\ river 100 *m* N *cen* Calif. flowing S into the Sacramento
Federal Capital Territory — see AUSTRALIAN CAPITAL TERRITORY
Federal District *or* Sp & Port **Dis·tri·to Fe·de·ral** \di-'strē-tō-,feth-ə-'räl, dish-'trē-tü-\ **1** *or* **Federal Capital** *or* Sp **Ca·pi·tal Fe·de·ral** \,käp-ə-'täl-\ district E Argentina largely comprising ✻ city of Buenos Aires *area* 74, *pop* 3,799,200 **2** district E *cen* Brazil including ✻ city of Brasília *area* 2260, *pop ab* 150,000 **3** — see GUANABARA **4** district *cen* Mexico including ✻, Mexico City *area* 573, *pop* 4,460,413 **5** district N Venezuela including ✻ city of Caracas *area* 745, *pop* 709,602
Federated Malay States former Brit. protectorate (1895–1945) comprising the Malay states of Negri Sembilan, Pahang, Perak, & Selangor ✻ Kuala Lumpur
Federated Shan States — see SHAN STATE
Fen \'fen, 'fən\ river 300 *m* N China in *cen* Shansi flowing SSE into Yellow river
Fengtien, 1 — see LIAONING **2** — see MUKDEN
Fer·ga·na *or* **Fer·gha·na** \fər-'gän-ə\ valley U.S.S.R. in the Tien Shan in Kirgiz, Tadzhik & Uzbek republics SE of Tashkent
Fer·gu·son \'fər-gə-sən\ city E Mo. N of St. Louis *pop* 22,149
Fer·man·agh \fər-'man-ə\ county SW Northern Ireland ✻ Enniskillen *area* 653, *pop* 53,040
Fer·nan·do de No·ro·nha \fər-'nan-(,)dō-də-nə-'rōn-yə\ island Brazil in the Atlantic 300 *m* NE of city of Natal *area* 7
Fer·nan·do Po *or* **Fer·nan·do Poo** \fər-,nan-(,)dō-'pō\ island Equatorial Guinea in Bight of Biafra *area* 778, *pop* 61,197
Fern·dale \'fərn-,dāl\ city SE Mich. N of Detroit *pop* 31,347
Fer·ra·ra \fə-'rär-ə\ commune N Italy in Emilia-Romagna NE of Bologna near the Po *pop* 134,467
Ferro — see HIERRO
Ferrol, El — see EL FERROL
Ferryville — see MENZEL-BOURGUIBA
Fez \'fez\ *or* **Fès** \'fes\ city N *cen* Morocco *pop* 202,000
Fez·zan \fe-'zan\ province SW Libya, chiefly desert ✻ Sabha *area ab* 150,000, *pop* 54,438
Fich·tel·ge·bir·ge \'fik-t^{ə}l-gə-,bir-gə\ mountains S *cen* Germany in NE Bavaria; highest Schneeberg 3447 *ft*
Fie·so·le \fē-'ā-zə-,lā\ *or anc* **Fae·su·lae** \'fē-zə-,lē\ commune *cen* Italy in Tuscany NE of Florence
Fife \'fīf\ *or* **Fife·shire** \-,shi(ə)r, -shər\ county E Scotland between firths of Tay & Forth ✻ Cupar *area* 505, *pop* 306,855
Fi·ji \'fē-(,)jē\ islands SW Pacific E of New Hebrides constituting (with Rotuma I.) a Brit. crown colony ✻ Suva (on Viti Levu) *area* 7083, *pop* 374,284
Filch·ner Ice Shelf \'filk-nər\ ice sheet Antarctica in Weddell sea *area ab* 127,400
Filipinas, República de — see PHILIPPINES
Finch·ley \'finch-lē\ municipal borough SE England in Middlesex, NW suburb of London *pop* 69,990
Find·lay \'fin-(d)lē\ city NW Ohio *pop* 30,344
Fin·gal's Cave \,fiŋ-gəlz-\ sea cave W Scotland on Staffa I.
Fin·ger Lakes \'fiŋ-gər\ group of long narrow lakes W *cen* N.Y. comprised of Cayuga, Seneca, Keuka, Canandaigua, Skaneateles, Owasco, & several smaller lakes
Fin·is·terre, Cape \,fin-ə-'ste(ə)r, -'ster-ē\ cape NW Spain on coast of La Coruña province; westernmost point of Spanish mainland, at 9°18′W
Fin·land \'fin-lənd\ *or* Finn **Suo·mi** \'swȯ-mē\ country N Europe bordering on Gulf of Bothnia & Gulf of Finland; a republic ✻ Helsinki *area* 130,165, *pop* 4,394,700 — **Fin·land·er** *n*
Finland, Gulf of arm of Baltic sea between Finland & Estonia
Fin·lay \'fin-lē\ river 250 *m* Canada in N *cen* B.C. flowing SE to unite with **Pars·nip** \,pär-snəp-\ river (145 *m*) forming the Peace
Fins·bury \'finz-,ber-ē, -b(ə-)rē\ metropolitan borough E *cen* London, England *pop* 35,347
Fin·ster·aar·horn \,fin(t)-stə-'rär-,hȯ(ə)rn\ mountain 14,022 *ft* S Switzerland; highest of the Bernese Alps
Fiord·land \fē-'ȯ(ə)rd-,land, 'fyȯ(ə)rd-\ mountain region S New Zealand in SW South I.
Fitch·burg \'fich-,bərg\ city N *cen* Mass. *pop* 43,021
Fiume — see RIJEKA
Fiu·mi·ci·no \,fyü-mə-'chē-(,)nō\ **1** *or* **Ru·bi·con** \'rü-bi-,kän\ river 15 *m* N *cen* Italy flowing E into the Adriatic **2** town *cen* Italy on Tyrrhenian sea SW of Rome & WNW of Ostia
Flag·staff \'flag-,staf\ city N *cen* Ariz. *pop* 18,214
Flam·bor·ough Head \,flam-,bər-ə-, -,bə-rə-, -b(ə-)rə-\ promontory NE England on Yorkshire coast
Flan·ders \'flan-dərz\ *or* F **Flan·dre** \flä^{n}dr^{ə}\ *or* Flem **Vlaan·de·ren** \'vlän-də-rə(n)\ region W Belgium & N France bordering on North sea; a medieval county ✻ Lille — see EAST FLANDERS, WEST FLANDERS
Flat·head \'flat-,hed\ river 250 *m* SE B.C. & NW Mont. flowing S through **Flathead Lake** (30 *m* long, in Mont.) into Clark Fork
Flat·tery, Cape \'flat-ə-rē\ cape NW Wash. at entrance to Juan de Fuca strait
Flens·burg \'flenz-,bərg, 'flen(t)s-,bu̇(ə)rk\ city & port W Germany on inlet of the Baltic near Danish border *pop* 97,200
Fletsch·horn \'flech-,hȯ(ə)rn\ *or* **Ross·bo·den·horn** \'rȯs-'bōd-^{ə}n-,hȯ(ə)rn\ mountain 13,127 *ft* S Switzerland in Pennine Alps S of Simplon Pass
Flin·ders \'flin-dərz\ **1** river 500 *m* Australia in *cen* Queensland flowing NW into Gulf of Carpentaria **2** mountain ranges Australia in E So. Australia E of Lake Torrens
Flint \'flint\ **1** river 265 *m* W Ga. flowing S & SW into Lake Seminole **2** city SE *cen* Mich. *pop* 196,940 **3** *or* **Flint·shire** \-,shi(ə)r, -shər\ county NE Wales ✻ Mold *area* 256, *pop* 145,108
Flod·den \'fläd-^{ə}n\ hill N England in N Northumberland near Scottish border
Floral Park village SE N.Y. on E Long I. *pop* 17,499
Flor·ence \'flȯr-ən(t)s, 'flär-\ **1** city NW Ala. on the Tennessee *pop* 31,649 **2** urban area SW Calif. E of Los Angeles *pop* (with Graham) 38,164 **3** city E S.C. *pop* 24,722 **4** *or* It **Fi·ren·ze** \fē-'rent-sā\ commune *cen* Italy on the Arno ✻ of Tuscany *pop* 390,769 — **Flor·en·tine** \'flȯr-ən-,tēn, 'flär-, -,tīn\ *adj or n*
Flo·res \'flōr-əs, 'flȯr-\ **1** island NW Azores *area* 57 **2** island Indonesia in Lesser Sunda islands *area* 5509
Flo·ri·a·nó·po·lis \,flōr-ē-ə-'näp-ə-ləs, ,flȯr-\ *or formerly* **Des·têr·ro** \dēsh-'ter-ü\ city S Brazil ✻ of Santa Catarina state on island off coast *pop* 48,264
Flor·i·da \'flȯr-əd-ə, 'flär-\ **1** state SE U.S. ✻ Tallahassee *area* 58,560, *pop* 4,951,560 **2** \'flȯr-əd-ə, 'flär-; flə-'rēd-ə\ *or* **N'Ge·la**

ə abut; ^{ə} kitten; ər further; a back; ā bake; ä cot, cart; au̇ out; ch chin; e less; ē easy; g gift; i trip; ī life
j joke; ŋ sing; ō flow; ȯ flaw; ȯi coin; th thin; th this; ü loot; u̇ foot; y yet; yü few; yu̇ furious; zh vision
^{ə} F table; à F bac; k G ich, Buch; ^{n} F vin; œ F bœuf; œ̄ F feu; ue G füllen; ue̅ F rue; ^{y} F digne \dēn^{y}\, nuit \nw^{y}ē\

\en-'gā-lə\ *or* **Ge·la** \'gā-lə\ island W Pacific in SE Solomons N of Guadalcanal — **Flo·rid·i·an** \flə-'rid-ē-ən\ *adj or n* — **Flor·i·dan** \'flȯr-əd-ᵊn, 'flär-\ *adj or n*

Florida, Straits of *or* **Florida Strait** channel between Florida Keys (on NW) & Cuba & Bahamas (on S & E) connecting Gulf of Mexico with the Atlantic

Florida Keys chain of islands off the S tip of Florida peninsula

Flo·ris·sant \'flōr-ə-sənt, 'flȯr-\ city E Mo. NNW of St. Louis *pop* 38,166

Flowerpot Island National Park — see GEORGIAN BAY ISLANDS NATIONAL PARK

Flush·ing \'fləsh-iŋ\ **1** section of New York City on Long I. in Queens **2** — see VLISSINGEN

Fly \'flī\ river 650 *m* S New Guinea flowing SE into Gulf of Papua

Foc·sa·ni \fȯk-'shän(-ē)\ city E *cen* Romania in S Moldavia *pop* 29,390

Fog·gia \'fȯ-jə\ commune SE Italy in Apulia *pop* 109,100

Foggy Bottom section of Washington, D.C., along the Potomac

Foix \'fwä\ region & former province S France in the Pyrenees SE of Gascony

Folke·stone \'fōk-stən, *US also* -,stōn\ municipal borough SE England in Kent on Strait of Dover *pop* 45,200

Fond du Lac \'fän-dᵊl-,ak, 'fän-jə-,lak\ city E Wis. on Lake Winnebago *pop* 32,719

Fon·se·ca, Gulf of \fän-'sā-kə\ *or* **Fonseca Bay** inlet of the Pacific in Central America in Salvador, Honduras, & Nicaragua

Fon·taine·bleau \'fänt-ᵊn-,blō\ commune N France SSE of Paris *pop* 19,915

Fon·taine–de–Vau·cluse \'fän-,tān-də-vō-'klüz, 'fōⁿ-\ *or formerly* **Vaucluse** village S France E of Avignon near Monts de Vaucluse

Foo·chow \'fü-'jō, -'chaù\ *or* **Min·how** \'min-'hō\ city & port SE China ✻ of Fukien on Min river *pop* 553,000

For·a·ker, Mount \'fȯr-i-kər, 'fär-\ mountain 17,395 *ft* S Alaska in Alaska range SW of Mt. McKinley

Forest Hill village Canada in SE Ont. near Toronto *pop* 19,480

For·far \'fȯr-fər\ **1** *or* **For·far·shire** \-,shi(ə)r, -shər\ — see ANGUS **2** burgh E Scotland ✻ of Angus

For·lì \fȯr-'lē\ commune N Italy in Emilia-Romagna *pop* 48,100

For·mo·sa \fȯr-'mō-sə, fər-, -zə\ *or* **Tai·wan** \'tī-'wän\ **1** island China off SE coast E of Fukien; belonged to Japan 1895–1945; since 1949 seat of (Nationalist) Republic of China (✻ Taipei); provincial ✻ Taichung *area* 13,900, *pop* 9,077,643 **2** strait between Formosa & China mainland connecting East China & So. China seas — **For·mo·san** \-'mōs-ᵊn, -'mōz-\ *adj or n*

For·ta·le·za \,fȯrt-ᵊl-'ā-zə\ *or* **Ce·a·rá** \,sā-ə-'rä\ city & port NE Brazil on the Atlantic ✻ of Ceará *pop* 205,052

Fort Bayard — see CHANKIANG

Fort Col·lins \'käl-ənz\ city N Colo. *pop* 25,027

Fort–de–France \,fȯrd-ə-'fräⁿs\ city French West Indies ✻ of Martinique on W coast *pop* 60,648

Fort de Kock — see BUKITTINGGI

Fort Dodge \'däj\ city NW *cen* Iowa *pop* 28,399

Fort Fred·e·ri·ca National Monument \,fred-ə-'rē-kə, fre-'drē-\ reservation SE Ga. on W shore of St. Simon I. containing site of fort built by Oglethorpe 1736

Fort George \'jȯ(ə)rj\ river 480 *m* Canada in *cen* Que. flowing W into James Bay

Forth \'fō(ə)rth, 'fȯ(ə)rth\ river 114 *m* S *cen* Scotland flowing E into **Firth of Forth** (estuary 48 *m* long, inlet of North sea)

Fort Jefferson National Monument — see DRY TORTUGAS

Fort Knox \'näks\ military reservation N *cen* Ky. SSW of Louisville; location of U.S. Gold Bullion Depository

Fort–La·my \,fȯr-lə-'mē\ town ✻ of Chad on Chari river

Fort Lar·a·mie National Monument \'lar-ə-mē\ site SE Wyo. on the No. Platte NW of Torrington of a trading post & fort (1834–90) on Oregon Trail

Fort Lau·der·dale \'lȯd-ər-,dāl\ city SE Fla. N of Miami Beach on the Atlantic *pop* 83,648

Fort Lee \'lē\ borough NE N.J. on the Hudson *pop* 21,815

Fort Mc·Hen·ry National Monument \mə-'ken-rē\ site in Baltimore, Md., of a fort bombarded 1814 by the British

Fort Mad·i·son \'mad-ə-sən\ city SE Iowa on the Mississippi *pop* 15,247

Fort Ma·tan·zas National Monument \mə-'tan-zəs\ reservation *ab* 15 *m* SSE of St. Augustine, Fla., containing Fort Matanzas, built *ab* 1736 by the Spanish

Fort My·ers \'mī(-ə)rz\ city SW Fla. on estuary of the Caloosahatchee *pop* 22,523

Fort Nel·son \'nel-sən\ river 260 *m* Canada in NE B.C. flowing NW into Liard river

Fort Peck Reservoir \'pek\ reservoir *ab* 130 *m* long NE Mont. formed in Missouri river by **Fort Peck Dam**

Fort Pierce \'pi(ə)rs\ city E Fla. on the Atlantic *pop* 25,256

Fort Pu·las·ki National Monument \p(y)ə-'las-kē\ reservation E Ga. comprising island in mouth of Savannah river, site of a fort built 1829–47 to replace Revolutionary Fort Greene

Fort Ran·dall Dam — see FRANCIS CASE (Lake)

Fort Smith \'smith\ city NW Ark. on Arkansas river *pop* 52,991

Fort Sum·ter National Monument \'səm(p)-tər\ reservation S.C. at entrance to Charleston harbor containing site of Fort Sumter

Fort Union National Monument reservation NE N. Mex. 50 *m* ENE of Santa Fe containing site (1851–91) of military post

Fort Vancouver National Monument site SW Wash. in city of Vancouver of a trading & military post (founded 1825) that was W terminus of the Oregon Trail

Fort Wayne \'wān\ city NE Ind. *pop* 161,776

Fort Wil·liam \'wil-yəm\ city & port Canada in SW Ont. on Lake Superior *pop* 39,464

Fort Worth \'wərth\ city N Tex. W of Dallas *pop* 356,268

Fos·to·ria \fò-'stōr-ē-ə, -'stȯr-\ city NW *cen* Ohio *pop* 15,732

Four Forest Cantons the cantons of Uri, Schwyz, Unterwalden, & Lucerne in *cen* Switzerland surrounding the Lake of Lucerne

Four Forest Cantons, Lake of the — see LUCERNE (Lake of)

Fou·ta Djal·lon *or* **Fu·ta Jal·lon** \,füt-ə-jə-'lōn\ mountain region W Guinea; highest point *ab* 4200 *ft*

Fox \'fäks\ **1** islands SW Alaska in the E Aleutians — see UMNAK, UNALASKA, UNIMAK **2** river 220 *m* SE Wis. & NE Ill. flowing S into the Illinois **3** river 175 *m* E Wis. flowing NE & N through Lake Winnebago into Green Bay

Foxe Basin \'fäks\ inlet of the Atlantic N Canada in E Northwest Territories W of Baffin I.; connected with Hudson Bay by **Foxe channel**

Foyle \'fȯi(ə)l\ river *ab* 20 *m* N Ireland flowing NE past city of Londonderry to **Lough Foyle** (inlet of the Atlantic 18 *m* long)

Fra·ming·ham \'frā-miŋ-,ham\ town E Mass. *pop* 44,526

France \'fran(t)s\ country W Europe between English channel & the Mediterranean; a republic ✻ Paris *area* 212,659, *pop* 46,150,000

Franche–Com·té \fräⁿsh-kōⁿ-tā\ region & former county & province E France E of the Saône ✻ Besançon — see BURGUNDY

Francis Case, Lake \'kās\ reservoir *ab* 100 *m* long S S. Dak. formed in the Missouri by **Fort Randall Dam** \,ran-dᵊl\

Fran·co·nia \fraŋ-'kō-nē-ə, -nyə\ **1** former duchy in Austrasia **2** region W Germany in Bavaria — **Fran·co·ni·an** \-nē-ən, -nyən\ *adj or n*

Frank·fort \'fraŋk-fərt\ **1** city W *cen* Ind. *pop* 15,302 **2** city ✻ of Ky. *pop* 18,365

Frank·furt \'fraŋk-fərt, 'fräŋk-,fü(ə)rt\ *or* E **Frank·fort** \'fraŋk-fərt\ **1** *or* **Frankfurt am Main** \-(,)äm-'mīn\ *or* E **Frankfort on the Main** city W Germany on Main river *pop* 666,500 **2** *or* **Frankfurt an der Oder** \-,än-də-'rōd-ər\ *or* E **Frankfort on the Oder** city E Germany on Oder river *pop* 57,200

Frank·lin \'fraŋ-klən\ district Canada in N Northwest Territories including Arctic islands & Boothia & Melville peninsulas *area* 541,753

Franklin D. Roosevelt Lake reservoir 151 *m* long NE Wash. formed in Columbia river by Grand Coulee Dam

Franklin Park village NE Ill. W of Chicago *pop* 18,322

Franklin Square urban area SE N.Y. on Long I. *pop* 32,483

Franks Peak *or* **Francs Peak** \'fraŋ(k)s\ mountain 13,140 *ft* NW Wyo.; highest in Absaroka range

Franz Jo·sef Land \fran(t)s-'jō-zəf-,land *also* -səf-; frän(t)s-'yō-zəf-,länt\ archipelago U.S.S.R. in Soviet Russia, Europe, in Arctic ocean N of Novaya Zemlya

Fras·ca·ti \fra-'skät-ē, frä-\ commune *cen* Italy in Latium 11 *m* SE of Rome

Fra·ser \'frā-zər, -zhər\ river 850 *m* Canada in S *cen* B.C. flowing into Strait of Georgia

Frau·en·feld \'fraù(-ə)n-,felt\ commune NE Switzerland ✻ of Thurgau canton

Fred·er·ick \'fred-(ə-)rik\ city N Md. *pop* 21,744

Fred·er·ic·ton \'fred-(ə-)rik-tən\ city Canada ✻ of N.B. on St. John river *pop* 18,303

Fred·er·iks·berg \'fred-(ə-)riks-,bərg\ city Denmark on Sjælland I., W suburb of Copenhagen *pop* 113,584

Free·port \'frē-,pō(ə)rt, -,pȯ(ə)rt\ **1** city N Ill. W of Rockford *pop* 26,628 **2** village SE N.Y. on Long I. *pop* 34,419 **3** town NW Bahamas on *cen* Grand Bahama I.

Free·town \'frē-,taùn\ city & port ✻ of Sierra Leone on the Atlantic *pop* 100,000

Frei·burg \'frī-,bù(ə)rg, -,bərg, -,bù(ə)rk\ *or* **Freiburg im Breisgau** \-im-'brīs-,gaù\ **1** city W Germany at W foot of Black Forest *pop* 141,200 **2** — see FRIBOURG

Fré·jus, Mas·sif du \ma-,sēf-də-frā-'zhüs\ mountain mass on border between France & Italy at SW end of Graian Alps

Fre·man·tle \frē-'mant-ᵊl\ city Australia in SW Western Australia at mouth of Swan river; port for Perth *pop* 22,787

Fre·mont \'frē-,mänt\ **1** city W Calif. SE of Oakland *pop* 43,790 **2** city E Nebr. *pop* 19,698 **3** city N Ohio *pop* 17,573

French Community *or* F **Com·mu·nau·té fran·çaise** \kȯ-mūē-nō-tā-fräⁿ-sez, -säz\ federation (formed 1958) comprising metropolitan France, its overseas departments & territories, & the former French territories in Africa that on becoming republics chose to maintain their ties with France

French Equatorial Africa *or* **French Congo** former country W *cen* Africa N of Congo river comprising a federation of Chad, Gabon, Middle Congo, & Ubangi-Shari territories ✻ Brazzaville

French Guiana country N So. America bordering on the Atlantic & belonging to France ✻ Cayenne *area* 34,740, *pop* 32,000

French Guinea — see GUINEA

French India former French possessions in India including Chandernagore (ceded to India 1950) & Pondicherry, Karikal, Yanaon, & Mahé (ceded to India 1954) ✻ Pondicherry

French Indochina — see INDOCHINA

French Morocco — see MOROCCO

French Polynesia *or formerly* **French Oceania** islands in S Pacific belonging to France & including Society, Marquesas, Tuamotu, Gambier, & Tubuai groups ✻ Papeete (on Tahiti)

French Somaliland *or since 1967* **French Territory of the Afars and the Is·sas** \'ä-,färz . . . ē-'säz\ country E Africa on Gulf of Aden belonging to France ✻ Djibouti *area* 8492, *pop* 79,300

French Sudan — see MALI

French Togo — see TOGO

French Union former federation (1946–58) comprising metropolitan France & its overseas departments, territories, & associated states — see FRENCH COMMUNITY

French West Africa former country W Africa comprising the French territories of Dahomey, French Guinea, French Sudan, Ivory Coast, Mauritania, Niger, Senegal, & Upper Volta ✻ Dakar *area* 1,815,768

French West Indies islands of the West Indies belonging to France including Guadeloupe, Martinique, Désirade, Les Saintes, Marie Galante, St. Barthélemy, & part of St. Martin

Fres·no \'frez-(,)nō\ city S *cen* Calif. *pop* 133,929

Fri·bourg \frē-'bù(ə)r\ *or* G **Frei·burg** \'frī-,bù(ə)rg, -,bərg, -,bù(ə)rk\ **1** canton W *cen* Switzerland *area* 647, *pop* 158,695 **2** commune, its ✻, SW of Bern *pop* 30,300

Frid·ley \'frid-lē\ city SE Minn. N of St. Paul *pop* 15,173

Friendly — see TONGA

Fries·land \'frēz-lənd, 'frēs-, -,land\ **1** old region N Europe bordering on North sea **2** province N Netherlands ✻ Leeuwarden *area* 1431, *pop* 474,744

Frio, Cape \'frē-(,)ō\ **1** cape SE Brazil E of Rio de Janeiro **2** cape NW South-West Africa in the Atlantic

Fri·sches Haff \'frish-əs-,häf\ lagoon N Poland & E Soviet Russia, Europe; inlet of Gulf of Danzig

Fri·sian \'frizh-ən, 'frē-zhən\ islands NW Europe in North sea including **West Frisian** islands (off N coast of Netherlands), **East Frisian** islands (off NW coast of Germany), & **North Frisian** islands (off coast of Germany & Denmark, including Helgoland & Sylt)

Fri·u·li \'frē-ə-,lē, frē-'ü-lē\ district N Italy in Friuli-Venezia Giulia on Yugoslav border — **Fri·u·li·an** \frē-'ü-lē-ən\ *adj or n*
Friuli-Ve·ne·zia Giu·lia \-və-,net-sē-ə-'jül-yə\ region N Italy E of Veneto ✻ Udine *area* 6223, *pop* 1,226,121
Fro·bi·sher Bay \,frō-bi-shər-\ inlet of the Atlantic N Canada in Franklin District on SE coast of Baffin I.
Front \'frənt\ range of the Rockies extending from *cen* Colo. N into SE Wyo. — see GRAYS PEAK
Fro·ward, Cape \'frō-(w)ərd\ headland S Chile on N side of Strait of Magellan; southernmost point of mainland of So. America, at *ab* 53°54′S lat.
Frun·ze \'frün-zə\ *or formerly* **Pish·pek** \pish-'pek\ city U.S.S.R. on Chu river ✻ of Kirgiz Republic *pop* 217,000
Fu·ji \'f(y)ü-(,)jē\ *or* **Fu·ji·ya·ma** \,f(y)ü-jē-'(y)äm-ə\ *or* **Fu·ji·no-ya·ma** \-(,)nō-'yäm-ə\ *or* **Fu·ji-san** \,f(y)ü-(,)jē-'sän\ mountain 12,388 *ft* Japan in S *cen* Honshu; highest in Japan
Fu·kien \'fü-'kyen, -kē-'en\ province SE China bordering on Formosa strait ✻ Foochow *area* 47,529, *pop* 13,143,000
Fu·ku·o·ka \,fü-kə-'wō-kə\ city & port Japan on N Kyushu on inlet of Tsushima strait *pop* 647,122
Ful·da \'fül-də\ city W Germany NE of Frankfurt *pop* 44,700
Ful·ham \'fül-əm\ metropolitan borough SW London, England, N of the Thames *pop* 122,047
Ful·ler·ton \'fül-ərt-ᵊn\ city SW Calif. *pop* 56,180
Fu·na·fu·ti \,f(y)ü-nə-'f(y)üt-ē\ island (atoll) S Pacific in *cen* Ellice islands
Fun·chal \fün-'shäl, ,fən-\ city & port Portugal ✻ of Madeira I. *pop* 37,200
Fun·dy, Bay of \'fən-dē\ inlet of the Atlantic SE Canada between N.B. & N.S.
Fundy National Park reservation SE Canada in N.B. on upper Bay of Fundy *area* 80
Fur·neaux \'fər-(,)nō\ islands Australia off NE Tasmania
Fur·ness \'fər-nəs\ district N England comprising peninsula in Irish sea in NW Lancashire
Fürth \'fü(ə)rt, 'fi(ə)rt\ city W Germany NW of Nuremberg *pop* 98,200
Fusan — see PUSAN
Fu·se \'fü-(,)sā\ city Japan in S Honshu E of Osaka *pop* 272,000
Fusen — see PUJON
Fu·shun \'fü-'shün\ city NE China in NE Liaoning E of Mukden *pop* 678,600
Fu·sin \'fü-'shin\ city NE China in NE Liaoning WNW of Mukden *pop* 188,600
Futa Jallon — see FOUTA DJALLON
Fu·tu·na \fə-'tü-nə\ **1** *or* **Hoorn** \'hō(ə)rn, 'hȯ(ə)rn\ islands SW Pacific NE of Fiji; formerly a French protectorate, since 1959 part of Wallis & Futuna islands territory **2** island SW Pacific in Futuna group **3** island SW Pacific in SE New Hebrides
Fyn \'fin\ *or* G **Fü·nen** \'f(y)ü-nən\ island Denmark in the Baltic between Sjælland & Jutland; chief city Odense *area* 1149
Fyzabad — see FAIZABAD

Ga·be·ro·nes \,gäb-ə-'rō-nəs\ town ✻ of Botswana on SE border *pop ab* 6000
Ga·bes \'gäb-əs, -,es\ city & port SE Tunisia on **Gulf of Gabes** (*anc* **Syr·tis Mi·nor** \,sərt-ə-'smī-nər\, arm of the Mediterranean) *pop* 24,420
Ga·bon \ga-'bōⁿ\ **1** *or* **Ga·boon** *or* **Ga·bun** \gə-'bün, ga-\ river NW Gabon flowing into the Atlantic through long wide estuary **2** country W Africa bordering on the Atlantic; formerly a territory of French Equatorial Africa, since 1958 a republic within the French Community ✻ Libreville *area* 103,089, *pop* 440,000 — **Gab·o·nese** \,gab-ə-'nēz, -'nēs\ *adj or n*
Gad·a·ra \'gad-ə-rə\ ancient town Palestine SE of Sea of Galilee — **Gad·a·rene** \'gad-ə-,rēn, ,gad-ə-'\ *adj or n*
Gades *or* **Gadir** — see CÁDIZ — **Gad·i·tan** \'gad-ət-ᵊn\ *adj or n*
Gads·den \'gadz-dən\ city NE Ala. on Coosa river *pop* 58,088
Gadsden Purchase tract of land S of Gila river in present Ariz. & N. Mex. purchased 1853 by the U.S. from Mexico *area* 29,640
Ga·e·ta \gä-'āt-ə\ city & port *cen* Italy in Latium on **Gulf of Gaeta** (inlet of Tyrrhenian sea N of Bay of Naples) *pop* 18,900
Gaf·sa \'gaf-sə\ *or anc* **Cap·sa** \'kap-sə\ oasis W *cen* Tunisia
Gaines·ville \'gānz-,vil, -vəl\ **1** city N *cen* Fla. *pop* 29,701 **2** city N Ga. *pop* 16,523
Gaird·ner, Lake \'ga(ə)rd-nər, 'ge(ə)rd-\ salt lake Australia in So. Australia W of Lake Torrens *area* 1840
Ga·lá·pa·gos islands \gə-,läp-ə-gəs-, -,lap-\ *or* **Co·lón archi·pelago** \kə-,lōn-\ island group Ecuador in the Pacific 600 *m* W of mainland ✻ San Cristóbal *area* 3029 — see ISABELA
Gal·a·ta \'gal-ət-ə\ port & commercial section of Istanbul, Turkey
Ga·la·ti \gə-'läts(-ē)\ *or* **Ga·latz** \'gäl-,äts\ city E Romania on the Danube *pop* 101,878
Ga·la·tia \gə-'lā-sh(ē-)ə\ ancient country & Roman province *cen* Asia Minor in region centering around modern Ankara, Turkey — **Ga·la·tian** \-shən\ *adj or n*
Gald·hö·pig·gen \'gäl-,hə(r)-,pig-ən\ mountain 8097 *ft* S *cen* Norway in Jotenheim mountains; highest in Scandinavia
Gales·burg \'gā(ə)lz-,bərg\ city NW Ill. *pop* 37,243
Ga·li·cia \gə-'lish-(ē-)ə\ **1** region E *cen* Europe including N slopes of the Carpathians & valleys of the upper Vistula, Dniester, Bug, & Seret; former Austrian crown land; belonged to Poland between the two world wars; now divided between Poland & Ukraine **2** region & ancient kingdom NW Spain bordering on the Atlantic — **Ga·li·cian** \-'lish-ən\ *adj or n*
Gal·i·lee \'gal-ə-,lē, ,gal-ə-'\ hill region N Palestine N of Esdraelon plain — **Gal·i·le·an** \,gal-ə-'lē-ən\ *adj or n*
Galilee, Sea of *or Bib* **Lake of Gen·nes·a·ret** \gə-'nes-ə-,ret, -rət\ *or* **Sea of Ti·be·ri·as** \tī-'bir-ē-əs\ *or* **Sea of Chin·ne·reth** \'kin-ə-,reth\ *or* Heb **Yam Kin·ne·ret** \'yäm-'kin-ə-,ret\ lake 14 *m* long & 8 *m* wide N Israel on Syrian border traversed by the Jordan; 686 *ft* below sea level
Gal·la·tin \'gal-ət-ᵊn\ **1** mountain range S Mont. — see ELECTRIC PEAK **2** river 125 *m* SW Mont. — see THREE FORKS
Ga·lli·nas, Point \gə-'yē-nəs\ cape N Colombia; northernmost point of So. America, at 12°15′ N
Gal·lip·o·li \gə-'lip-ə-lē\ *or* **Ge·li·bo·lu** \,gel-ə-bə-'lü\ **1** peninsula Turkey in Europe between the Dardanelles & Saros gulf — see CHERSONESE **2** city & port Turkey on Gallipoli peninsula at entrance to Sea of Marmara *pop* 16,496
Gal·lo·way \'gal-ə-,wā\ district SW Scotland comprising Wigtown & Kirkcudbright — **Gal·we·gian** \gal-'wē-j(ē-)ən\ *adj or n*
Galt \'gȯlt\ city Canada in SE Ont. NW of Hamilton *pop* 23,738
Gal·ves·ton \'gal-və-stən\ city SE Tex. on **Galveston Island** (30 *m* long) at entrance to **Galveston Bay** (inlet of Gulf of Mexico) *pop* 67,175
Gal·way \'gȯl-,wā\ **1** county W Ireland in Connacht bordering on the Atlantic *area* 2293, *pop* 149,800 **2** municipal borough & port, its ✻, on **Galway Bay** (inlet) *pop* 23,661
Gam·bia \'gam-bē-ə\ **1** river 460 *m* W Africa flowing from Fouta Djallon in W Guinea W through Senegal into the Atlantic in Gambia **2** country W Africa; a British colony & protectorate ✻ Bathurst *area* 3977, *pop* 268,500 — **Gam·bi·an** \-bē-ən\ *adj or n*
Gam·bier \'gam-,bi(ə)r\ islands S Pacific SE of Tuamotu archipelago belonging to France — see MANGAREVA
Gana — see GHANA
Gand — see GHENT
Gan·dak \'gən-(,)dək\ river 400 *m* Nepal & N India flowing SW & SE into the Ganges
Gandzha — see KIROVABAD
Gan·ges \'gan-,jēz\ river 1550 *m* N India flowing from the Himalayas SE & E to unite with the Brahmaputra & empty into Bay of Bengal through the vast **Ganges delta** — see HOOGHLY — **Gan·get·ic** \gan-'jet-ik\ *adj or n*
Gang·tok \'gəŋ-,täk\ town ✻ of Sikkim
Gan·nett Peak \,gan-ət-\ mountain 13,785 *ft*, *cen* Wyo.; highest in Wind River range & in the state
Gar·da, Lake \'gärd-ə\ lake 35 *m* long N Italy between Lombardy & Veneto draining through the Mincio into the Po
Gar·de·na \gär-'dē-nə\ city SW Calif. S of Los Angeles *pop* 35,943
Garden City, **1** city SE Mich. SW of Detroit *pop* 38,017 **2** village SE N.Y. on Long I. *pop* 23,948
Garden City Park urban area SE N.Y. on Long I. *pop* (with Herricks) 15,364
Garden Grove city SW Calif. SW of Los Angeles *pop* 84,238
Gard·ner \'gärd-nər\ city N *cen* Mass. *pop* 19,038
Gar·field \'gär-,fēld\ **1** mountain 10,961 *ft* SW Mont. near Idaho border; highest in Beaverhead & Bitterroot ranges **2** city NE N.J. N of Newark *pop* 29,253
Garfield Heights city NE Ohio SSE of Cleveland *pop* 38,455
Ga·ri·glia·no \,gär-ēl-'yän-(,)ō\ river 100 *m*, *cen* Italy in Latium flowing SE & SW into Gulf of Gaeta
Gar·land \'gär-lənd\ city NE Tex. NNE of Dallas *pop* 38,501
Gar·misch-Par·ten·kir·chen \,gär-mish-,pärt-ᵊn-'ki(ə)r-kən, -'pärt-ᵊn-,\ city W Germany in Bavaria SW of Munich in foothills of the Alps *pop* 25,300
Gar·mo Peak \,gär-(,)mō\ *or* **Sta·lin Peak** \,stäl-ən, ,stal-, -,ēn\ *or since 1961* **Communism Peak** mountain 24,590 *ft* Soviet Central Asia in SE Tadzhik Republic in the Pamirs; highest in the U.S.S.R.
Ga·ronne \gə-'rän, -'rōn\ river 355 *m* SW France flowing NW to unite with the Dordogne forming Gironde estuary
Gar·ri·son Reservoir \,gar-ə-sən-\ reservoir 140 *m* long W N. Dak. formed in the Missouri by the **Garrison Dam**
Gar·tok \'gär-,täk\ town SW Tibet on the upper Indus
Gary \'ga(ə)r-ē, 'ge(ə)r-\ city NW Ind. *pop* 178,320
Gas·co·nade \,gas-kə-'nād\ river 250 *m* S *cen* Mo. flowing NE into the Missouri
Gas·co·ny \'gas-kə-nē\ *or* F **Gas·cogne** \gȧ-skȯnʸ\ region & former province SW France ✻ Auch
Ga·sher·brum \'gəsh-ər-,brüm, -,brüm\ mountain 26,470 *ft* N Kashmir in Karakoram range SE of Mt. Godwin Austen
Gas·pé \ga-'spā\ peninsula Canada in SE Que. between mouth of St. Lawrence river & Chaleur Bay — **Gas·pe·sian** \-'spē-zhən\ *adj*
Ga·stein *or* **Bad Ga·stein** \,bät-gä-'stīn\ town W *cen* Austria S of Salzburg
Gas·ti·neau \'gas-tə-,nō\ channel SE Alaska between Douglas I. & mainland; Juneau is situated on it
Gas·to·nia \ga-'stō-nē-ə, -nyə\ city S N.C. *pop* 37,276
Gates·head \'gāts-,hed\ county borough N England in Durham on the Tyne opposite Newcastle *pop* 115,017
Gat·i·neau \,gat-ᵊn-'ō\ river 240 *m* Canada in SW Que. flowing S into the Ottawa at Hull
Ga·tun \gə-'tün\ lake Panama Canal Zone formed by the **Gatun Dam** in Chagres river
Gaul \'gȯl\ *or* L **Gal·lia** \'gal-ē-ə\ ancient country W Europe comprising chiefly the region occupied by modern France & Belgium & at one time including also the Po valley in N Italy — see CISALPINE GAUL, TRANSALPINE GAUL
Ga·var·nie \,gav-ər-'nē\ waterfall 1385 *ft* SW France S of Lourdes in the **Cirque de Gavarnie** \,si(ə)rk-də-\ (natural amphitheater at head of Gave de Pau) — see PAU (Gave de)
Gave de Pau — see PAU
Gav·ins Point Dam \,gav-ənz-\ dam SE S. Dak. & NE Nebr. in the Missouri — see LEWIS AND CLARK
Gäv·le \'yev-lə\ city & port E Sweden on Gulf of Bothnia NNW of Stockholm *pop* 55,942
Ga·ya \gə-'yä\ city NE India in *cen* Bihar *pop* 133,700
Ga·za \'gäz-ə, 'gaz-, 'gāz-\ *or* Ar **Ghaz·ze** \'gaz-ē\ city S Palestine near the Mediterranean; with surrounding coastal district (**Gaza Strip**, adjoining Sinai peninsula), administered since 1949 by Egypt *pop* 38,000
Ga·zi·an·tep \,gäz-ē-(,)än-'tep\ *or formerly* **Ain·tab** \īn-'tab\ city S Turkey N of Alep, Syria *pop* 125,498
Gdansk \gə-'dän(t)sk, -'dan(t)sk\ *or* G **Dan·zig** \'dan(t)-sig, 'dän(t)-\ city & port N Poland on Gulf of Danzig *pop* 240,000
Gdyn·ia \gə-'din-ē-ə\ city & port N Poland on Gulf of Danzig NNW of Gdansk *pop* 140,200
Gebel Katherina — see KATHERINA (Gebel)
Gebel Musa — see MUSA (Gebel)
Ge·diz \gə-'dēz\ *or* **Sa·ra·bat** \,sär-ə-'bät\ river 200 *m* W Turkey in Asia flowing W into Gulf of Izmir

ə abut; ᵊ kitten; ər further; a back; ā bake; ä cot, cart; au̇ out; ch chin; e less; ē easy; g gift; i trip; ī life
j joke; ŋ sing; ō flow; ȯ flaw; ȯi coin; th thin; t͟h this; ü loot; u̇ foot; y yet; yü few; yu̇ furious; zh vision
ᵊ F table; ȧ F bac; k̲ G ich, Buch; ⁿ F vin; œ F bœuf; œ̄ F feu; ue G füllen; ue̅ F rue; ʸ F digne \dēnʸ\, nuit \nwʸē\

Gee·long \jə-ˈlȯŋ\ city & port SE Australia in S Victoria on Port Phillip Bay SW of Melbourne *pop* (with suburbs) 78,500
Geel·vink Bay \ˌgā(ə)l-ˌviŋk-\ inlet of W Pacific N West New Guinea
Gela — see FLORIDA
Gel·der·land \ˈgel-dər-ˌland\ province E Netherlands bordering on IJsselmeer ✱ Arnhem *area* 1965, *pop* 1,250,317
Gel·sen·kir·chen \ˌgel-zən-ˈki(ə)r-kən\ city W Germany in the Ruhr W of Dortmund *pop* 388,800
General San Martín — see SAN MARTÍN
Gen·e·see \ˌjen-ə-ˈsē\ river 144 *m* W N.Y. flowing N into Lake Ontario
Ge·ne·va \jə-ˈnē-və\ **1** city W *cen* N.Y. on Seneca Lake *pop* 17,286 **2** *or* F **Ge·nève** \zhə-nev\ *or* G **Genf** \ˈgenf\ canton SW Switzerland *area* 107, *pop* 202,918 **3** *or* F **Genève** *or* G **Genf** city, its ✱, at SW tip of Lake Geneva on the Rhone *pop* 172,000 — **Gen·e·vese** \ˌjen-ə-ˈvēz, -ˈvēs\ *adj or n*
Geneva, Lake *or* **Lake Le·man** \ˈlē-mən, ˈlem-ən, lə-ˈman\ lake 45 *m* long on border between SW Switzerland & E France; traversed by the Rhone
Gennesaret, Lake of — see GALILEE (Sea of)
Gen·oa \ˈjen-ə-wə\ *or* It **Ge·no·va** \ˈje-nō-vä\ *or anc* **Gen·ua** \ˈjen-yə-wə\ commune & port NW Italy ✱ of Liguria at foot of the Apennines & at head of **Gulf of Genoa** (arm of Ligurian sea) *pop* 768,520 — **Gen·o·ese** \ˌjen-ə-ˈwēz, -ˈwēs\ *adj or n* — **Gen·o·vese** \-ə-ˈvēz, -ˈvēs\ *adj or n*
Gensan *or* **Genzan** — see WONSAN
Gen·tof·te \ˈgen-ˌtəf-tə\ city Denmark on Sjælland I., N suburb of Copenhagen *pop* 68,718
George \ˈjȯ(ə)rj\ river 345 *m* Canada in NE Que. flowing N into Ungava Bay
George, Lake, 1 lake 14 *m* long NE Fla. in course of St. Johns river WNW of Daytona Beach **2** lake 33 *m* long E N.Y. S of Lake Champlain
George·town \ˈjȯ(ə)rj-ˌtau̇n\ **1** section of Washington, D.C., in W part of the city **2** city & port ✱ of Guyana on the Atlantic at mouth of the Demerara *pop* 162,000
George Town \ˈjȯ(ə)rj-ˌtau̇n\ *or* **Pe·nang** \pə-ˈnaŋ\ city & port Federation of Malaysia ✱ of Penang on Penang I. *pop* 234,855
Geor·gia \ˈjȯr-jə\ **1** state SE U.S. ✱ Atlanta *area* 58,876, *pop* 3,943,116 **2** *or* **Geor·gian Republic** \ˌjȯr-jən-\ constituent republic of the U.S.S.R. S of Caucasus mountains bordering on Black sea; an ancient & medieval kingdom ✱ Tiflis *area* 26,875, *pop* 4,049,000
Georgia, Strait of channel 150 *m* long NW Wash. & SW B.C. between S Vancouver I. & mainland
Georgian Bay inlet of Lake Huron, Canada, in SE Ont.
Georgian Bay Islands National Park reservation SE Canada including Flowerpot I. (formerly comprising a separate park, **Flowerpot Island National Park**) SE of Manitoulin I. & a group of small islands N of Midland, Ont. *area* 5.4
Ge·ra \ˈger-ə\ city E Germany ESE of Erfurt *pop* 99,241
Ger·la·chov·ka \ˈge(ə)r-lə-ˌkȯf-kə, -ˌkȯv-\ mountain 8737 *ft* E Czechoslovakia in N Slovakia in Tatra mountains; highest in Carpathian mountains
German East Africa former country E Africa comprising Tanganyika & Ruanda-Urundi (now Rwanda & Burundi); a German protectorate 1885–1920
Ger·ma·nia \(ˌ)jər-ˈmā-nē-ə, -nyə\ **1** region of ancient Europe E of the Rhine & N of the Danube including modern Germany **2** region of Roman Empire just W of the Rhine in what is now NE France & part of Belgium & the Netherlands
German ocean — see NORTH SEA
German Southwest Africa — see SOUTH-WEST AFRICA
Ger·man·town \ˈjər-mən-ˌtau̇n\ a NW section of Philadelphia, Pa.
Ger·ma·ny \ˈjərm-(ə-)nē\ *or* G **Deutsch·land** \ˈdȯich-ˌlänt\ country *cen* Europe bordering on North & Baltic seas, since 1949 constituting two republics: the West German Federal Republic (✱ Bonn, *area* 94,634, *pop* 55,958,300) & the East German Democratic Republic (✱ East Berlin, *area* 41,700, *pop* 17,313,700)
Ger·mis·ton \ˈjər-mə-stən\ city NE Republic of So. Africa in S Transvaal E of Johannesburg *pop* 168,139
Ge·ro·na \jə-ˈrō-nə\ **1** province NE Spain in Catalonia bordering on the Mediterranean *area* 2264, *pop* 349,163 **2** commune, its ✱ *pop* 33,037
Get·tys·burg National Military Park \ˈget-ēz-ˌbərg\ reservation S Pa. near borough of Gettysburg including site of battle 1863
Ge·zi·ra *or* **Je·zi·ra** *or* **El Jezira** \ˌel-jə-ˈzir-ə\ district E *cen* Sudan between the Blue Nile & White Nile
Gha·da·mes \gə-ˈdam-əs, -ˈdäm-\ oasis & town NW Libya in Tripolitania near Algerian border
Gha·na \ˈgän-ə, ˈgan-ə\ **1** *or* **Ga·na** ancient empire W Africa in what is now W Mali; flourished 4th–13th centuries **2** *or formerly* **Gold Coast** country W Africa bordering on Gulf of Guinea; a republic within Brit. Commonwealth; formerly (as Gold Coast) a Brit. territory comprising Gold Coast colony, Ashanti, Northern Territories, & Togoland trust territory ✱ Accra *area* 91,843, *pop* 6,691,000 — **Gha·na·ian** \gä-ˈnā-(y)ən, gə-, ga-; ˈgän-ə-yən, ˈgan-\ *adj or n* — **Gha·nian** \ˈgän-ē-ən, ˈgän-yən, ˈgan-\ *adj or n* — **Gha·nese** \gä-ˈnēz, ga-, -ˈnēs\ *adj*
Gharapuri — see ELEPHANTA
Ghar·da·ïa \gär-ˈdī-ə\ town & oasis N *cen* Algeria 300 *m* S of Algiers
Ghats \ˈgȯts\ mountains S India — see EASTERN GHATS, WESTERN GHATS
Ghazal, Bahr el — see BAHR EL GHAZAL
Ghaz·ni \ˈgäz-nē\ city E *cen* Afghanistan; once ✱ of a Muslim kingdom extending from the Tigris to the Ganges *pop* 27,084
Ghazze — see GAZA
Ghent \ˈgent\ *or* Flem **Gent** \ˈgent\ *or* F **Gand** \gäⁿ\ city NW *cen* Belgium ✱ of East Flanders at confluence of Scheldt & Lys rivers *pop* 179,613
Giant's Causeway formation of prismatic basaltic columns Northern Ireland on N coast of Antrim
Gib·e·on \ˈgib-ē-ən\ city of ancient Palestine NW of Jerusalem — **Gib·e·on·ite** \-ə-ˌnīt\ *n*
Gi·bral·tar \jə-ˈbrȯl-tər\ town & port on Rock of Gibraltar; a Brit. colony *area* 2.5, *pop* 23,232 — **Gi·bral·tar·i·an** \jə-ˌbrȯl-ˈter-ē-ən, ˌjib-ˌrȯl-, -ˈtar-\ *n*
Gibraltar, Rock of *or anc* **Cal·pe** \ˈkal-(ˌ)pē\ headland on S coast of Spain at E end of Strait of Gibraltar; highest point 1396 *ft* — see PILLARS OF HERCULES
Gibraltar, Strait of passage between Spain & Africa connecting the Atlantic & Mediterranean *ab* 8 *m* wide at narrowest point
Gies·sen \ˈgēs-ᵊn\ city W Germany N of Frankfort *pop* 64,800
Gi·fu \ˈgē-(ˌ)fü\ city Japan in *cen* Honshu *pop* 304,492
Gi·jón \hē-ˈhōn\ city & port NW Spain in Oviedo province on Bay of Biscay *pop* 119,008
Gi·la \ˈhē-lə\ river 630 *m* N. Mex. & Ariz. flowing W into the Colorado
Gila Cliff Dwellings National Monument reservation SW N. Mex. including cliff-dweller ruins
Gil·bert \ˈgil-bərt\ islands (*area* 166) W Pacific SSE of the Marshalls forming with other islands the Brit. colony of **Gilbert and El·lice Islands** (✱ Tarawa *area* 316, *pop* 36,000) — **Gil·bert·ese** \ˌgil-bər-ˈtēz, -ˈtēs\ *n*
Gil·boa, Mount \gil-ˈbō-ə\ mountain 1696 *ft* N Palestine W of the Jordan & S of Valley of Jezreel
Gil·e·ad \ˈgil-ē-əd\ mountainous region of Palestine E of Jordan river; now in Jordan — **Gil·e·ad·ite** \-ē-ə-ˌdīt\ *n*
Gil·ling·ham \ˈjil-iŋ-əm\ municipal borough SE England in Kent *pop* 68,099
Gin·za \ˈgin-zə, -ˌzä\ shopping street & entertainment district in downtown Tokyo, Japan
Gi·re·sun \ˌgir-ə-ˈsün\ *or* **Ke·ra·sun** \ˌker-ə-\ town & port NE Turkey on Black sea 70 *m* W of Trabzon
Girgenti — see AGRIGENTO
Gi·ronde \jə-ˈränd, zhē-rōⁿd\ estuary 45 *m* W France formed by junction of the Garonne & the Dordogne & flowing NW into Bay of Biscay
Gis·borne \ˈgiz-bərn\ borough & port New Zealand on E North I. *pop* 23,800
Gî·za *or* **Gi·zeh** \ˈgē-zə\ *or* **El Gîza** *or* **El Gizeh** \el-\ city N Egypt on W bank of the Nile near Cairo *pop* 250,000
Glace Bay \ˈglās\ town Canada in NE N.S. on Cape Breton I. *pop* 24,416
Gla·cier Bay \ˌglā-shər-\ inlet SE Alaska at S end of St. Elias range in **Glacier Bay National Monument** (*area* 3.5)
Glacier National Park, 1 reservation NW Mont. adjoining Waterton Lakes National Park, Canada, and with it forming **Wa·ter·ton–Glacier International Peace Park** \ˌwȯt-ərt-ᵊn-, ˌwät-\ **2** reservation W Canada in SE B.C. in Selkirk mountains W of Yoho National Park
Glad·beck \ˈglät-ˌbek, ˈglad-\ city W Germany in the Ruhr *pop* 83,200
Gla·mor·gan \glə-ˈmȯr-gən\ *or* **Gla·mor·gan·shire** \-ˌshi(ə)r, -shər\ county SE Wales ✱ Cardiff *area* 813, *pop* 1,201,989
Gla·rus \ˈglär-əs\ *or* F **Gla·ris** \gla-ˈrēs\ **1** canton E *cen* Switzerland *area* 267, *pop* 37,663 **2** commune, its ✱
Glas·gow \ˈglas-(ˌ)kō, ˈglas-(ˌ)gō, ˈglaz-(ˌ)gō\ burgh & port S *cen* Scotland on the Clyde *pop* 1,089,555 — **Glas·we·gian** \gla-ˈswē-jən\ *n*
Glas·ton·bury \ˈglas-tən-ˌber-ē, -b(ə-)rē *also* ˈglas-ᵊn-\ municipal borough SW England in Somerset SSW of Bristol
Glatzer Neisse — see NEISSE
Glen Canyon Dam \ˌglen-\ dam N Ariz. in Glen Canyon of Colorado river forming **Lake Pow·ell** \ˈpau̇(-ə)l\ (chiefly in SE Utah)
Glen·coe \glen-ˈkō\ valley W Scotland in Argyll
Glen Cove \ˈglen-ˈkōv\ city SE N.Y. on NW Long I. *pop* 23,817
Glen·dale \ˈglen-ˌdāl\ **1** city *cen* Ariz. NW of Phoenix *pop* 15,596 **2** city SW Calif. NE of Los Angeles *pop* 119,442
Glen·do·ra \glen-ˈdōr-ə, -ˈdȯr-\ city SW Calif. ENE of Los Angeles *pop* 20,752
Glen El·lyn \gle-ˈnel-ən\ village NE Ill. W of Chicago *pop* 15,972
Glen More — see GREAT GLEN
Glens Falls \ˈglenz\ city E N.Y. S of Lake George *pop* 18,580
Glen·view \ˈglen-ˌvyü\ village NE Ill. *pop* 18,132
Gli·wi·ce \gli-ˈvēt-sə\ *or* G **Glei·witz** \ˈglī-ˌvits\ city SW Poland in Silesia W of Katowice *pop* 124,700
Glom·ma \ˈglō-mə, ˈgläm-ə\ river 375 *m* E Norway flowing S into the Skagerrak
Glossa, Cape — see LINGUETTA (Cape)
Glouces·ter \ˈgläs-tər, ˈglȯs-\ **1** city NE Mass. on Cape Ann *pop* 25,789 **2** *or* **Glouces·ter·shire** \-ˌshi(ə)r, -shər\ county SW *cen* England *area* 1257, *pop* 938,618 **3** city & county borough, its ✱, on the Severn *pop* 67,268
Gloucester City city SW N.J. S of Camden *pop* 15,511
Glov·ers·ville \ˈgləv-ərz-ˌvil\ city E N.Y. *pop* 21,741
Gnossus — see KNOSSOS
Goa \ˈgō-ə\ *or* Port **Gôa** district W India; before 1962 belonged to Portugal ✱ Pangim *area* 1301, *pop* 672,000 — see PORTUGUESE INDIA — **Go·an** \ˈgō-ən\ *adj or n* — **Go·a·nese** \ˌgō-ə-ˈnēz, -ˈnēs\ *adj*
Go·bi \ˈgō-(ˌ)bē\ desert E *cen* Asia in Mongolia *area ab* 500,000
Go·da·va·ri \gə-ˈdäv-ə-rē\ river 900 *m*, *cen* India flowing SE across the Deccan into Bay of Bengal
Go·des·berg \ˈgōd-əs-ˌbərg, -ˌbe(ə)rk\ *or* **Bad Godesberg** \ˈbät-\ commune W Germany on the Rhine S of Bonn *pop* 65,500
Godt·haab \ˈgȯt-ˌhȯb, ˈgät-\ town ✱ of Greenland on SW coast
God·win Aus·ten \ˌgäd-wə-ˈnȯ-stən, -ˈnäs-tən\ *or* **K²** \ˈkā-ˈtü\ *or* **Dap·sang** \ˈdap-ˌsaŋ, ˈdəp-ˌsəŋ\ mountain 28,250 *ft* N Kashmir in Karakoram range; 2d highest mountain in the world
Go·ge·bic \gō-ˈgē-bik\ iron range N Wis. & W upper peninsula of Mich.
Gog·ra \ˈgäg-rə\ river 570 *m* S *cen* Asia flowing S from SW Tibet through Nepal into the Ganges in N India
Goi·â·nia *or formerly* **Goy·a·nia** \gȯi-ˈan-ē-ə\ city SE *cen* Brazil ✱ of Goiás *pop* 39,871
Goi·ás *or* **Goi·az** *or* **Goy·az** \gȯi-ˈäs\ state SE *cen* Brazil ✱ Goiânia *area* 244,330, *pop* 1,234,740
Gokcha — see SEVAN
Gol·con·da \gäl-ˈkän-də\ ruined city *cen* India in W Andhra Pradesh W of Hyderabad ✱ (1512–1687) of Golconda kingdom
Gold Coast, 1 region W Africa on N shore of Gulf of Guinea between the Ivory Coast (on W) & the Slave Coast (on E) **2** — see GHANA **3** former Brit. colony in S Gold Coast region ✱ Accra; now part of Ghana
Golden Chersonese — see CHERSONESE
Golden Gate strait 2 *m* wide W Calif. connecting San Francisco Bay with Pacific ocean
Golden Horn inlet of the Bosporus, Turkey in Europe; harbor of Istanbul

Golds·boro \'gōl(d)z-ˌbər-ə, -ˌbə-rə\ city E cen N.C. pop 28,873

Golgotha — see CALVARY

Go·mel \'gō-məl, 'gó-\ city U.S.S.R. in SE Belorussia pop 166,000

Go·mor·rah \gə-'mór-ə, -'mär-\ city of ancient Palestine in the plain of the Jordan

Go·na·ives, Gulf of \ˌgō-nə-'ēv\ arm of Caribbean sea on W coast of Haiti

Gon·dar \'gän-dər, -ˌdär\ town NW Ethiopia N of Lake Tana ✱ of Amhara & former ✱ of Ethiopia

Good Hope, Cape of \ˌgùd-'hōp\ cape S Republic of So. Africa in SW Cape Province W of False Bay, at 34°21′S — see CAPE OF GOOD HOPE

Good·win Sands \ˌgùd-wən-\ shoals SE England in Strait of Dover off E coast of Kent — see DOWNS

Goos·port \'gäs-ˌpō(ə)rt, -ˌpó(ə)rt\ urban area SW La. NE of Lake Charles pop 16,778

Go·rakh·pur \'gōr-ək-ˌpù(ə)r, 'gór-\ city NE India in E Uttar Pradesh N of Banaras pop 132,400

Go·ri·zia \gə-'rēt-sē-ə\ commune NE Italy in Venetia on Isonzo river pop 42,100

Gor·ki or **Gor·ky** or **Gor·kiy** \'gór-kē\ or formerly **Nizh·ni Nov·go·rod** \ˌnizh-nē-'näv-gə-ˌräd\ city in cen Soviet Russia, Europe, at confluence of Oka & Volga rivers pop 942,000

Gör·litz \'gər-ˌlits, -ˌlēts\ city E Germany on the Neisse pop 96,100

Gor·lov·ka \'gór-ˌlóf-kə, -'lóv-\ city U.S.S.R. in E Ukraine in the Donets basin N of Donetsk pop 293,000

Gor·no-Al·tai \ˌgór-(ˌ)nō-ˌal-'tī\ or formerly **Oi·rot** \'ói-rət\ autonomous region U.S.S.R. in S Soviet Russia, Asia, in SE Altai Territory in Altai mountains ✱ Gorno-Altaisk (formerly Oirot-Tura) area 35,800, pop 150,000

Gor·no-Ba·dakh·shan \ˌgór-(ˌ)nō-ˌbäd-ˌäk-'shän\ autonomous region U.S.S.R. in Soviet Central Asia in SE Tadzhik Republic in the Pamirs ✱ Khorog area 25,784, pop 41,800

Go·shen \'gō-shən\ district of ancient Egypt E of Nile delta

Gos·port \'gäs-ˌpō(ə)rt, -ˌpó(ə)rt\ municipal borough S England in Hampshire on Portsmouth harbor pop 58,246

Gö·te·borg \ˌyə(r)t-ə-'bór(-yə), ˌyät-\ or **Goth·en·burg** \'gäth-ən-ˌbərg, 'gät-ᵊn-\ city & port SW Sweden pop 408,436

Go·tha \'gōt(h)-ə\ city W Germany W of Erfurt pop 57,800

Got·land or **Gott·land** \'gät-ˌland, -lənd\ island Sweden in the Baltic off SE coast; chief town Visby area 1167, pop 55,000

Göt·ting·en \'gə(r)t-iŋ-ən, 'get-\ city W Germany SSW of Brunswick pop 77,800

Gott·wal·dov \'gät-vəl-ˌdóf, -ˌdóv\ or formerly **Zlin** \zə-'lēn\ city cen Czechoslovakia in SE Moravia pop 57,974

Gou·da \'gaùd-ə, 'güd-, 'haùd-\ commune SW Netherlands in So. Holland pop 33,300

Gra·ham \'grā-əm, 'gra(-ə)m\ urban area SW Calif. E of Los Angeles pop (with Florence) 38,164

Graham Land, 1 — see ANTARCTIC **2** the N section of the Antarctic peninsula

Gra·hams·town \'grā-əmz-ˌtaùn, 'gra(-ə)mz-\ city S Republic of So. Africa in SE Cape Province ENE of Port Elizabeth pop 23,741

Gra·ian Alps \ˌgrā-(y)ən-, ˌgrī-ən-\ section of W Alps S of Mont Blanc on border between France & Italy — see GRAN PARADISO

Grain coast \'grān-\ region W Africa in Liberia bordering on Gulf of Guinea

Gram·pi·an \'gram-pē-ən\ hills cen Scotland between the Lowlands & the Great Glen — see NEVIS (Ben)

Gra·na·da \grə-'näd-ə\ **1** city SW Nicaragua on NW shore of Lake Nicaragua pop 21,743 **2** medieval Moorish kingdom S Spain **3** province S Spain in Andalusia bordering on the Mediterranean area 4928, pop 787,116 **4** city, its ✱, in the Sierra Nevada pop 146,169

Gran·by \'gran-bē, 'gram-bē\ city Canada in S Que. pop 27,095

Gran Chaco — see CHACO

Grand, 1 river 260 m SW Mich. flowing N & W into Lake Michigan **2** river 300 m NW Mo. flowing SE into the Missouri **3** river 140 m W Mo. flowing SE into the Osage **4** river 200 m N S. Dak. flowing E into the Missouri **5** the Colorado river from its source to junction with Green river in SE Utah—a former name **6** — see NEOSHO **7** — see HAMILTON **8** canal ab 1000 m long E China from Hangchow to Tientsin

Grand Atlas — see ATLAS

Grand Bahama island Bahamas, NW island of group area 430

Grand Bank or **Grand Banks** shoals in W Atlantic SE of Nfld.

Grand Canary or Sp **Gran Ca·na·ria** \ˌgräŋ-kä-'när-yä\ island Spain in the Canaries; chief city Las Palmas area 523

Grand Canyon gorge of the Colorado NW Ariz. extending from mouth of the Little Colorado W to the Grand Wash Cliffs; over 1 m deep; area largely comprised in **Grand Canyon National Park** (at E end area 1008) & **Grand Canyon National Monument** (to the W area 306) — see MARBLE CANYON

Grand Canyon of the Snake — see HELLS CANYON

Grand Cayman — see CAYMAN

Grand Cou·lee \'kü-lē\ valley E Wash. extending SSW from S wall of canyon of the Columbia where it turns W in forming the Big Bend

Grand Coulee Dam dam NE cen Wash. in the Columbia — see FRANKLIN D. ROOSEVELT LAKE

Grande, Rio, 1 \ˌrē-ō-'grand(-ē), ˌrē-ə- also ˌrī-ō-'grand or ˌrī-ə-\ river U.S. & Mexico — see RIO GRANDE **2** \ˌrē-ō-'gran-də, ˌrē-ə-, -dē\ river 680 m E Brazil in Minas Gerais flowing W to unite with the Paranaíba forming the Paraná

Grande Soufrière — see SOUFRIÈRE

Grande-Terre \gran-'te(ə)r\ island French West Indies constituting the E portion of Guadeloupe area 220, pop 103,718

Grand Falls or now **Churchill Falls** waterfall 245 ft high Canada in W Labrador in Churchill river

Grand Forks city E N. Dak. on Red river pop 34,451

Grand Island city SE cen Nebr. on the Platte pop 25,742

Grand Junction city W Colo. on the Colorado pop 18,694

Grand Lac — see TONLE SAP

Grand Ma·nan \mə-'nan\ island 20 m long Canada in N.B. at entrance to Bay of Fundy

Grand Prairie city NE cen Tex. W of Dallas pop 30,386

Grand Rapids city SW Mich. pop 177,313

Grand Te·ton \'tē-ˌtän\ mountain 13,766 ft W Wyo.; highest in Teton range

Grand Teton National Park reservation NW Wyo. including Jackson Lake & main part of Teton range

Grand Trav·erse Bay \-ˌtrav-ərs-\ inlet of Lake Michigan in Mich. on NW coast of lower peninsula

Grand Turk — see TURKS AND CAICOS

Grange·mouth \'grānj-məth, -ˌmaùth\ burgh & port cen Scotland in Stirling county on Firth of Forth pop 15,305

Granicus — see KOCABAS

Granite City city SW Ill. on the Mississippi pop 40,073

Granite Peak mountain 12,799 ft S Mont. NE of Yellowstone National Park in Beartooth range (spur of Absaroka range); highest point in state

Gran Pa·ra·dis·o \ˌgran-ˌpar-ə-'dē-(ˌ)zō\ mountain 13,324 ft NW Italy in NW Piedmont; highest in Graian Alps

Gran Qui·vi·ra National Monument \ˌgran-kə-ˌvir-ə-\ reservation cen N. Mex. containing ruins of a pueblo & Spanish mission

Gras·mere \'gras-ˌmi(ə)r\ lake 1 m long NW England in Westmorland in Lake District

Grasse \'gras, 'gräs\ commune SE France W of Nice

Grau·bün·den \graù-'bün-dən, -'bùn-\ or F **Gri·sons** \grē-zōⁿ\ canton E Switzerland ✱ Chur area 2744, pop 137,100

Graudenz — see GRUDZIADZ

Gravenhage, 's — see HAGUE (The)

Graves·end \'grāv-ˌzend\ municipal borough SE England in Kent on Thames estuary pop 45,043

Grays Harbor \'grāz\ inlet of the Pacific W Wash.

Grays Peak \'grāz\ mountain 14,274 ft, cen Colo.; highest in Front range

Graz \'gräts\ city S Austria ✱ of Styria on the Mur pop 226,453

Great Abaco — see ABACO

Great Australian Bight wide bay on S coast of Australia

Great Barrier Reef coral reef 1250 m long Australia off NE coast of Queensland

Great Basin arid region W U.S. between Sierra Nevada & Wasatch mountains including most of Nev. & parts of Calif., Idaho, Utah, Wyo., & Oreg. & having no drainage to ocean; contains many isolated mountain ranges (the **Basin ranges**)

Great Bear lake Canada in N Mackenzie District, Northwest Territories area 12,000

Great Bend city cen Kans. on Arkansas river pop 16,670

Great Brit·ain \'brit-ᵊn\ or **Britain, 1** island W Europe comprising England, Scotland, & Wales area 88,745, pop 48,840,893 **2** UNITED KINGDOM

Great Crosby — see CROSBY

Great Dividing mountain range E Australia extending from Cape York peninsula to S Victoria &, interrupted by Bass strait, into Tasmania — see KOSCIUSKO (Mount)

Greater An·til·les \an-'til-ēz\ group of islands in the West Indies including Cuba, Hispaniola, Jamaica, & Puerto Rico

Greater Sunda — see SUNDA

Greater Walachia — see MUNTENIA

Great Exuma — see EXUMA

Great Falls, 1 or **Great Falls of the Potomac** waterfall 35 ft in the Potomac ab 15 m above Washington **2** city W cen Mont. on Missouri river N of the **Great Falls of the Missouri** (92 ft) pop 55,357

Great Glen \'glen\ or **Glen More** \glen-'mō(ə)r, -'mó(ə)r\ valley ab 50 m long N Scotland cutting through the Highlands from SW to NE & connecting Loch Linnhe & Moray firth — see CALEDONIAN CANAL

Great Inagua — see INAGUA

Great Kabylia — see KABYLIA

Great Karroo — see KARROO

Great Khingan — see KHINGAN

Great Lakes, 1 chain of five lakes (Superior, Michigan, Huron, Erie, & Ontario) cen No. America in the U. S. & Canada **2** group of lakes E cen Africa including Lakes Rudolf, Albert, Victoria, Tanganyika, & Nyasa

Great Namaqualand — see NAMAQUALAND

Great Ouse — see OUSE

Great Plains elevated plains region W cen U.S. & W Canada E of Rocky mountains & chiefly W of 100th meridian extending from NE B.C. & NW Alta. SE & S to include the Llano Estacado of N. Mex. & Tex.

Great Rift valley \-ˌrift-\ depression SW Asia & E Africa extending with several breaks from valley of the Jordan S to Mozambique

Great Saint Ber·nard \ˌsānt-bər-'närd\ mountain pass 8111 ft through Pennine Alps between Switzerland & Italy

Great Salt lake ab 70 m long & 35 m wide N Utah having strongly saline waters & no outlet

Great Salt Lake desert flat barren region NW Utah

Great Sand Dunes National Monument reservation S Colo. on W slope of Sangre de Cristo mountains area 56

Great Slave, 1 lake NW Canada in S Mackenzie District receiving Slave river on S & draining into the Mackenzie on W area 11,170 **2** — see SLAVE

Great Smoky mountains on N.C.-Tenn. boundary partly in **Great Smoky Mountains National Park** (area 720) — see CLINGMANS DOME

Great Yarmouth — see YARMOUTH

Greece \'grēs\ or Gk **Hel·las** \'hel-əs\ or NGk **El·lás** \e-'läs\ country S Europe at S end of Balkan peninsula; a kingdom ✱ Athens area 50,147, pop 7,632,801

Gree·ley \'grē-lē\ city N Colo. pop 26,314

Green \'grēn\ **1** river 730 m W U.S. flowing from Wind River range in W Wyo. S into the Colorado in SE Utah **2** mountains E No. America in the Appalachian system extending from S Que. S through Vt. into W Mass. — see MANSFIELD (Mount)

Green Bay, 1 inlet of NW Lake Michigan 120 m long in NW Mich. & NE Wis. **2** city NE Wis. on Green Bay pop 62,888

Green·field \'grēn-ˌfēld\ city SE Wis. near Milwaukee pop 17,636

Green·land \'grēn-lənd, -ˌland\ **1** island in N Atlantic off NE No. America belonging to Denmark ✱ Godthaab area 839,800, pop

ə abut; ᵊ kitten; ər further; a back; ā bake; ä cot, cart; aù out; ch chin; e less; ē easy; g gift; i trip; ī life
j joke; ŋ sing; ō flow; ó flaw; ói coin; th thin; t͡h this; ü loot; ù foot; y yet; yü few; yù furious; zh vision
ᵊ F table; à F bac; ᴋ G ich, Buch; ⁿ F vin; œ F bœuf; œ̄ F feu; ᵫ G füllen; ᵫ̄ F rue; ᵞ F digne \dēnᵞ\, nuit \nwᵞē\

33,140 **2** sea arm of Arctic ocean between Greenland and Spitsbergen — **Green·land·er** \-lən-dər, -,lan-\ *n*

Gree·nock \'grēn-ək, 'grin-, 'gren-\ burgh & port SW Scotland in Renfrewshire on Firth of Clyde *pop* 76,299

Greens·boro \'grēnz-,bər-ə, -,bə-rə\ city N *cen* N.C. *pop* 119,574

Greens·burg \'grēnz-,bərg\ city SW Pa. *pop* 17,383

Green·ville \'grēn-,vil, -vəl\ **1** city W Miss. on the Mississippi *pop* 41,502 **2** city E N.C. *pop* 22,860 **3** city NW S.C. *pop* 66,188 **4** city NE Tex. NE of Dallas on the Sabine *pop* 19,087

Green·wich, 1 \'grin-ich, 'grēn-,wich, 'grin-,wich\ town SW Conn. on Long Island Sound *pop* 53,793 **2** \'grin-ij, 'gren-, -ich\ metropolitan borough SE London, England, on S bank of the Thames *pop* 91,492

Green·wich Village \,gren-ich-, ,grin-, -ij-\ section of New York City in Manhattan on lower W side

Green·wood \'grēn-,wùd\ **1** city W Miss. *pop* 20,436 **2** city W S.C. *pop* 16,644

Gre·na·da \grə-'nād-ə\ island Brit. West Indies in S Windward islands; with S Grenadines, constitutes an Associated State of Brit. Commonwealth ✻ St. George's *area* 133, *pop* 91,700

Gren·a·dines \,gren-ə-'dēnz\ islands Brit. West Indies in *cen* Windwards between Grenada & St. Vincent; divided administratively between Grenada & St. Vincent

Gre·no·ble \grə-'nō-bəl, -'nóbl'\ city SE France *pop* 116,440

Gret·na \'gret-nə\ city SE La. S of New Orleans *pop* 21,967

Grey·lock, Mount \'grā-,läk\ mountain 3505 *ft* NW Mass.; highest in Berkshire hills & in state

Grif·fin \'grif-ən\ city W *cen* Ga. *pop* 21,735

Grims·by \'grimz-bē\ county borough E England in Lincolnshire in Parts of Lindsey near mouth of the Humber *pop* 94,527

Grin·del·wald \'grin-d'l-,wóld, -,vält\ valley & village *cen* Switzerland in Bern canton in the Bernese Alps E of Interlaken

Gri·qua·land East \,grik-wə-,land, 'grik-wə-\ district S Republic of So. Africa in E Cape of Good Hope S of Basutoland; one of the Transkeian Territories; chief town Kokstad

Griqualand West district NW Republic of So. Africa in N Cape of Good Hope N of Orange river; chief town Kimberley

Gris-Nez, Cape \grē-'nā\ headland N France projecting into Strait of Dover

Grisons — see GRAUBÜNDEN

Grod·no \'gräd-(,)nō, 'gród-\ city U.S.S.R. in W Belorussia on Neman river *pop* 72,000

Gro·ning·en \'grō-niŋ-ən\ **1** province NE Netherlands *area* 866, *pop* 471,745 **2** city, its ✻ *pop* 143,996

Grosse Pointe Park \,grō-,spóint-\ city SE Mich. NE of Detroit *pop* 15,457

Grosse Pointe Woods city SE Mich. NE of Detroit *pop* 18,580

Gross·glock·ner \'grōs-,gläk-nər\ mountain 12,457 *ft* SW Austria, highest in the Hohe Tauern & in Austria

Gros Ventre \'grō-,vänt\ river 100 *m* W Wyo. flowing W into the Snake

Groves \'grōvz\ city SE Tex. NE of Port Arthur *pop* 17,304

Groz·ny or **Groz·nyy** \'gróz-nē, 'gräz-\ city U.S.S.R. in S Soviet Russia, Europe, N of Caucasus mountains *pop* 240,000

Gru·dziadz \'grü-,jónts, -,jòn(t)s\ or G **Grau·denz** \'graù-,den(t)s\ city N Poland on the Vistula NE of Bydgoszcz *pop* 56,000

Gua·da·la·ja·ra \,gwäd-ə-lə-'här-ə, ,gwäth-\ **1** city W Mexico ✻ of Jalisco *pop* 734,346 **2** province E *cen* Spain in NE New Castile *area* 4676, *pop* 195,633 **3** commune, its ✻ *pop* 21,928

Gua·dal·ca·nal \,gwäd-'l-kə-'nal, ,gwäd-ə-kə-\ island W Pacific in the SE Solomons *area* 2500, *pop* 14,500

Gua·dal·qui·vir \,gwäd-'l-'kwiv-ər, -ki-'vi(ə)r\ river 374 *m* S Spain flowing W & SW into Gulf of Cádiz

Gua·da·lupe \'gwäd-'l-,üp\ **1** mountains S N. Mex. & W Tex., the S extension of Sacramento mountains; highest point Guadalupe Peak 8751 *ft* (highest in Tex.) **2** river 300 *m* SE Tex. flowing SE into San Antonio river

Gua·da·lupe Hi·dal·go \,gwäd-'l-,üp(-ē)-hi-'dal-(,)gō, -,üp-ē-ē-'thäl-\ former city *cen* Mexico N of Mexico City now part of city of Gustavo A. Madero

Gua·de·loupe \'gwäd-'l-,üp, ,gwäd-'l-'\ two islands, Basse-Terre (or Guadeloupe proper) & Grande-Terre, separated by a narrow channel, in French West Indies in *cen* Leeward islands; an overseas department of France ✻ Basse-Terre (on Basse-Terre I.) *area* 583, *pop* 203,454

Gua·di·a·na \,gwäd-ē-'än-ə, -'an-\ river 515 *m* Spain & Portugal flowing W & S into Gulf of Cádiz

Guai·rá Falls \gwī-'rä-\ or **Se·te Que·das** \,sā-tə-'kā-thəsh\ cataract in gorge of the Alto Paraná on Brazil-Paraguay boundary; total descent 374 *ft*

Guam \'gwäm\ island W Pacific in S Marianas belonging to U.S. ✻ Agana *area* 209, *pop* 67,044 — **Gua·ma·ni·an** \gwä-'mä-nē-ən\ *adj or n*

Gua·na·ba·coa \,gwän-ə-bə-'kō-ə\ city W Cuba E of Havana *pop* 32,490

Gua·na·ba·ra \,gwän-ə-'bar-ə\ state SE Brazil bordering on the Atlantic; created 1960 from former Federal District ✻ Rio de Janeiro *area* 451

Guanabara Bay or **Rio de Janeiro Bay** inlet of Atlantic ocean SE Brazil

Gua·na·jua·to \,gwän-ə-'(h)wät-(,)ō\ **1** state *cen* Mexico *area* 11,804, *pop* 1,566,333 **2** city, its ✻ *pop* 23,389

Guan·tá·na·mo \gwän-'tän-ə,mō\ city SE Cuba NW of **Guantánamo Bay** (inlet of the Caribbean; site of U.S. naval station) *pop* 64,671

Gua·po·ré \,gwäp-ə-'rā\ **1** or **Ité·nez** \ē-'tā-nəs\ river 950 *m* W Brazil & NE Bolivia flowing NW to the Mamoré **2** — see RONDÔNIA

Guar·da·fui, Cape \,g(w)ärd-əf-'wē, -ə-'fü-ē\ cape NE Somalia at entrance to Gulf of Aden

Guá·ri·co \'gwär-i-,kō\ river 225 *m* W Venezuela flowing SW & S into the Apure

Gua·te·ma·la \,gwät-ə-'mäl-ə\ **1** country Central America S of Mexico bordering on the Pacific & the Caribbean; a republic *area* 42,042, *pop* 4,575,000 **2** or **Guatemala City** city, its ✻ *pop* 404,940 — **Gua·te·ma·lan** \-'mäl-ən\ *adj or n*

Gua·via·re \gwäv-ē-'är-ē, ,gwäv-ē-'är-\ river 650 *m* Colombia flowing E into the Orinoco

Gua·ya·ma \gwə-'yäm-ə\ town SE Puerto Rico *pop* 19,183

Gua·ya·quil \,gwī-ə-'kē(ə)l, -'kil\ city & port W Ecuador on

Guayas river 40 *m* from **Gulf of Guayaquil** (inlet of the Pacific) *pop* 295,791

Gua·yas \'gwī-əs\ river *ab* 100 *m* W Ecuador forming delta in Gulf of Guayaquil

Guay·mas \'gwī-məs\ city & port NW Mexico in Sonora on Gulf of California *pop* 18,800

Gub·bio \'gü-bē-,ō\ commune *cen* Italy NE of Perugia

Guelph \'gwelf\ city Canada in SE Ont. *pop* 33,860

Guer·ni·ca \ger-'nē-kə\ town N Spain ENE of Bilbao

Guern·sey \'gərn-zē\ island English channel in the Channel islands ✻ St. Peter Port *area* 25, *pop* 40,588

Guer·re·ro \gə-'re(ə)r-(,)ō\ state S Mexico bordering on the Pacific ✻ Chilpancingo *area* 24,885, *pop* 1,074,826

Gui·ana \gē-'an-ə, -'än-ə, gī-'an-ə\ region N So. America bordering on the Atlantic & bounded on W & S by the Orinoco, the Negro, & the Amazon; includes Guyana, French Guiana, Surinam, & adjoining parts of Brazil & Venezuela — **Gui·an·an** \-ən\ *adj or n* — **Gui·a·nese** \,gī-ə-'nēz, ,gē-ə-, -'nēs\ *adj or n*

Gui·enne or **Guy·enne** \gē-'en\ region & former province SW France bordering on Bay of Biscay ✻ Bordeaux — see AQUITAINE

Guin·ea \'gin-ē\ or F **Gui·née** \gē-nā\ **1** region W Africa bordering on the Atlantic from Gambia (on N) to Angola (on S) **2** or *formerly* **French Guinea** country W Africa bordering on the Atlantic; a republic, formerly a territory of French West Africa ✻ Conakry *area* 108,455, *pop* 3,000,000 — **Guin·ean** \'gin-ē-ən\ *adj or n*

Guinea, Gulf of arm of the Atlantic W *cen* Africa; includes bights of Benin & Biafra

Gui·púz·coa \gē-'püth-kə-wə, -'püs-\ province N Spain; one of the Basque provinces ✻ San Sebastián *area* 728, *pop* 468,363

Gu·ja·rat or **Gu·je·rat** \,güj-ə-'rät, ,güj-ə-\ **1** region W India where Gujarati is spoken **2** state W India N & E of Gulf of Cambay; formed 1960 from NW portion of former Bombay state ✻ Ahmadabad *area* 72,245 *pop* 20,633,350

Guj·ran·wala \,güj-rən-'wäl-ə, ,güj-\ city Pakistan in NE West Pakistan N of Lahore *pop* 120,900

Gulf·port \'gəlf-,pō(ə)rt, -,pó(ə)rt\ city & port SE Miss. *pop* 30,204

Gulf Stream warm ocean current in N Atlantic flowing from Gulf of Mexico N along coast of U.S. to Nantucket I. & thence E

Gum·ti \'gùm(p)-tē\ river 500 *m* N India flowing SE into the Ganges

Gun·ni·son \'gən-ə-sən\ river 150 *m* W *cen* Colo. flowing W & NW into the Colorado

Gun·tur \gùn-'tù(ə)r\ city E India in *cen* Andhra Pradesh W of Masulipatnam *pop* 125,300

Gunzan — see KUNSAN

Gur·gan \gùr-'gän\ or **As·ter·abad** \'as-t(ə-)rə-,bad, -,bäd\ city N Iran near SE coast of Caspian sea *pop* 28,525

Gus·ta·vo A. Ma·de·ro \gə-'stäv-(,)ō-,äm-ə-'the(ə)r-(,)ō\ city *cen* Mexico in Federal District N of Mexico City *pop* 60,239

Guy·ana \gī-'an-ə\ or *formerly* **British Guiana** country N So. America on Atlantic coast; a dominion of the Brit. Commonwealth since 1966 ✻ Georgetown *area* 83,000 *pop* 638,030 — **Guy·a·nese** \,gī-ə-'nēz, -'nēs\ *adj or n*

Gwa·dar or **Gwa·dur** \'gwäd-ər\ town & port SW West Pakistan on Arabian sea; until 1958 belonged to Sultan of Oman

Gwa·li·or \'gwäl-ē-,ò(ə)r\ **1** former state *cen* India ✻ Lashkar; part of Madhya Pradesh since 1956 **2** city N *cen* India in NW Madhya Pradesh SSE of Agra *pop* (including adjacent city of **Lash·kar** \'ləsh-kər\) 241,400

Gyang·tse \gē-'äŋ(k)t-'sā\ town W China in SE Tibet

Gyor \'jər\ or G **Raab** \'räp\ city NW Hungary *pop* 68,000

Haar·lem \'här-ləm\ city W Netherlands ✻ of No. Holland *pop* 168,863

Haar·lem·mer·meer \'här-lə-mər-,me(ə)r\ commune W Netherlands *pop* 42,702

Habana — see HAVANA

Hab·ba·ni·ya \hə-'ban-ē-(y)ə\ lake *cen* Iraq along S bank of the Euphrates W of Baghdad

Hack·en·sack \'hak-ən-,sak\ city NE N.J. *pop* 30,521

Hack·ney \'hak-nē\ metropolitan borough NE London, England *pop* 171,337

Had·ding·ton \'had-iŋ-tən\ **1** or **Had·ding·ton·shire** \-,shi(ə)r, -shər\ — see EAST LOTHIAN **2** burgh Scotland ✻ of East Lothian

Had·don \'had-ən\ urban township SW N.J. *pop* 17,099

Ha·dhra·maut or **Ha·dra·maut** \,häd-rə-'müt, -'maùt\ region S Arabia bordering on Arabian sea E of Aden in South Yemen; chief city Mukalla *area* 58,500

Hadrumetum — see SOUSSE

Hae·ju \'hī-(,)jü\ or Jap **Kai·shu** \'kī-(,)shü\ city N Korea on inlet of Yellow sea S of Pyongyang *pop* 82,135

Ha·gen or **Hagen in West·fa·len** \'häg-ə-(,)nin-,vest-'fäl-ən\ city W Germany ENE of Düsseldorf *pop* 193,800

Ha·gers·town \'hā-gərz-,taùn\ city N Md. *pop* 36,660

Hague, The \thə-'hāg\ or D **'s Gra·ven·ha·ge** \,s(k)rävᵊn-ᵊ'häg-ə\ city SW Netherlands in So. Holland near coast of North sea; de facto ✻ of the Netherlands *pop* 606,825

Haichow — see SINHAILIEN

Haidarabad — see HYDERABAD

Hai·fa \'hī-fə\ city & port NW Israel *pop* 170,000

Haikow — see HOIHOW

Hai·nan \'hī-'nän\ **1** island SE China in Kwangtung in So. China sea *area* 13,000 **2** strait between Hainan I. & Luichow peninsula connecting Gulf of Tonkin with So. China sea

Hai·naut \(h)ā-'nō\ **1** medieval county in Low Countries SE of Flanders in modern SW Belgium & N France **2** province SW Belgium ✻ Mons *area* 1436, *pop* 1,276,552

Hai·phong \'hī-'fóŋ\ city & port N Vietnam in Tonkin in delta of Red river *pop* 188,600

Hai·ti or *formerly* **Hay·ti** \'hāt-ē\ **1** — see HISPANIOLA **2** country West Indies on W Hispaniola; a republic ✻ Port-au-Prince *area* 10,714, *pop ab* 4,500,000 — **Hai·tian** \'hā-shən, 'hāt-ē-ən\ *adj or n*

Ha·ko·da·te \,häk-ə-'dät-ē\ city & port Japan in SW Hokkaido on Tsugaru strait *pop* 242,582

Halab or **Haleb** — see ALEPPO

Ha·le·a·ka·la \,häl-ē-,äk-ə-'lä\ dormant volcano 10,023 *ft* Hawaii on E Maui I.; crater 2720 *ft* deep, 20 *m* in circumference; in

Haleakala National Park (*area* 33) — see HAWAII NATIONAL PARK

Hal·fa·ya Pass \hal-ˌfī-ə-\ pass NW Egypt through hills near Mediterranean coast

Hal·i·car·nas·sus \ˌhal-ə-(ˌ)kär-'nas-əs\ ancient city SW Asia Minor in SW Caria on Aegean sea; its site at modern town of **Bo·drum** \bō-'drüm\

Hal·i·fax \'hal-ə-ˌfaks\ **1** city & port Canada ✳ of N.S. pop 93,301 **2** county borough N England in Yorkshire pop 98,376

Hal·le \'häl-ə\ city E Germany on Saale river pop 278,828

Hall·statt \'hȯl-ˌstat, 'häl-ˌs(h)tät\ village W cen Austria on shore of **Hall·stät·ter Lake** \'hȯl-ˌstet-ər, ˌhäl-ˌs(h)tet-\

Hal·ma·he·ra \ˌhal-mə-'her-ə, ˌhäl-\ or **Djai·lo·lo** \jī-'lō-(ˌ)lō\ island E Indonesia in Moluccas; largest in group area 6928

Halm·stad \'hälm-ˌstä(d)\ city & port SW Sweden pop 39,724

Häl·sing·borg \'hel-siŋ-ˌbȯ(ə)r\ city & port SW Sweden on Öresund opposite Helsingör, Denmark pop 77,006

Hal·tom City \ˌhȯl-təm-\ village N Tex. NE of Fort Worth pop 23,133

Halys — see KIZIL IRMAK

Ha·ma \'ham-ə\ or Bib **Ha·math** \'hā-ˌmath\ city W Syria on the Orontes pop 104,016

Ha·mad or **El Hamad** \ˌel-hə-'mad\ the SW portion of Syrian desert

Ha·ma·dan \ˌham-ə-'dan, -'dän\ or anc **Ec·bat·a·na** \ek-'bat-ᵊn-ə\ city W Iran WSW of Tehran pop 100,029

Ha·ma·ma·tsu \ˌhäm-ə-'mät-(ˌ)sü\ city Japan in S Honshu SE of Nagoya near Pacific coast pop 333,009

Ham·burg \'ham-ˌbərg, 'häm-ˌbu̇(ə)rg, -ˌbu̇(ə)rk\ city & port W Germany on the Elbe 90 m from its mouth; since 1948 a state of the Bonn Republic area 288, pop 1,837,000 — **Ham·burg·er** n

Ham·den \'ham-dən\ town S Conn. N of New Haven pop 41,056

Ha·meln \'häm-əln\ city W Germany in Lower Saxony SW of Hannover pop 50,300

Ham·hung \'häm-ˌhu̇ŋ\ or Jap **Kan·ko** \'kän-(ˌ)kō\ city N Korea NW of Hungnam near coast pop 112,184

Ha·mi \'hä-ˌmē\ or **Qo·mul** \'kō-ˌmül\ oasis W China in E Sinkiang NE of Takla Makan desert

Ham·il·ton \'ham-əl-tən, -əlt-ᵊn\ **1** city SW Ohio N of Cincinnati pop 72,354 **2** or **Hamilton Square** urban township W N.J. E of Trenton pop 65,035 **3** town & port ✳ of Bermuda **4** or **Grand** or now **Churchill** river 208 m Canada in Nfld. in S cen Labrador flowing E to **Hamilton Inlet** (inlet of the Atlantic 150 m long) **5** city & port Canada in SE Ont. on Lake Ontario pop 239,625 **6** borough New Zealand on cen North I. pop 45,200

Hamilton, Mount mountain 4209 ft W Calif. E of San Jose

Hamm \'häm, 'ham\ city W Germany on the Lippe SSE of Münster pop 68,400

Ham·mer·fest \'ham-ər-ˌfest, 'häm-\ town & port N Norway on island in Arctic ocean; northernmost town in Europe, at 70°38′N

Ham·mer·smith \'ham-ər-ˌsmith\ metropolitan borough W London, England, N of the Thames pop 119,317

Ham·mond \'ham-ənd\ city NW Ind. SE of Chicago pop 111,698

Hamp·shire \'ham(p)-ˌshi(ə)r, -shər\ **1** or **Hants** \'han(t)s\ formerly, and still as a postal and geographical name, a county of S England comprising the mainland administrative counties of Hampshire & Isle of Wight **2** or officially **South·amp·ton** \sau̇-'tham(p)-tən, sau̇th-'ham(p)-\ administrative county S England on English channel ✳ Winchester area 1503, pop 1,196,617

Hamp·stead \'ham(p)-stəd, -ˌsted\ metropolitan borough NW London, England pop 95,073

Hamp·ton \'ham(p)-tən\ city & port SE Va. E of Newport News on Hampton Roads pop 89,258

Hampton Roads channel SE Va. through which the James & Elizabeth rivers flow into Chesapeake Bay

Ham·tramck \ham-'tram-ik\ city SE Mich. entirely within city of Detroit pop 34,137

Han \'hän\ **1** river 900 m E cen China in Shensi & Hupei flowing SE into the Yangtze **2** or Jap **Kan** \'kän\ river 220 m S Korea flowing W & NW into Yellow sea

Han Cities WUHAN

Hang·chow \'haŋ-'chau̇, 'häŋ-'jō\ city E China ✳ of Chekiang at head of **Hangchow Bay** (inlet of East China sea) pop 696,600

Hanka — see KHANKA

Han·ko \'haŋ-ˌkȯ\ or Sw **Hangö** \'häŋ-ə(r)\ town & port SW Finland on Hanko (Hangö) peninsula in the Baltic SE of Turku

Han·kow \'haŋ-ˌkau̇, -ˌkō; 'hän-ˌkō\ former city E cen China — see WUHAN

Han·ni·bal \'han-ə-bəl\ city NE Mo. on the Mississippi pop 20,028

Han·no·ver or **Han·o·ver** \'han-ˌō-vər, 'han-ə-vər, G hä-'nō-vər, -'nō-fər\ city W Germany WNW of Brunswick pop 572,300

Ha·noi \ha-'nȯi, hə-\ city ✳ of No. Vietnam in Tonkin on Red river; formerly ✳ of French Indochina pop ab 500,000

Han·o·ver \'han-ə-vər\ borough S Pa. SW of York pop 15,538

Han·yang \'hän-'yäŋ\ former city E cen China — see WUHAN

Ha·ran \hə-'rän\ or **Car·rhae** \'kar-(ˌ)ē\ town SE Turkey an ancient city of N Mesopotamia

Ha·rap·pa \hə-'rap-ə\ locality W Pakistan in Indus valley NE of Multan; site of a prehistoric civilization

Ha·rar \'här-ər\ city E Ethiopia E of Addis Ababa pop 40,000

Har·bin \'här-bən, här-'bin\ or **Pin·kiang** \'bin-jē-'äŋ\ city NE China ✳ of Heilungkiang on Sungari river pop 1,163,000

Har·gei·sa \här-'gā-sə\ city NW Somalia

Hariana — see PUNJAB

Ha·ri Rud \ˌhar-ē-'rüd\ or **He·ri Rud** \ˌher-\ or anc **Ari·us** \'ar-ē-əs, 'er-; ə-'rī-əs\ river 700 m NW Afghanistan, NE Iran, & S Turkmen Republic flowing W & N into Kara Kum desert

Har·lech \'här-ˌlek\ village NW Wales on Cardigan Bay

Har·lem \'här-ləm\ **1** river channel SE N.Y. NE of Manhattan I.; with Spuyten Duyvil Creek, connects Hudson & East rivers **2** section of New York City in NE Manhattan bordering on Harlem & East rivers **3** HAARLEM — **Har·lem·ite** \-lə-ˌmīt\ n

Har·ling·en \'här-liŋ-ən\ **1** city S Tex. NNW of Brownsville pop 41,207 **2** town & port N Netherlands in Friesland

Har·ney Lake \ˌhär-nē-\ salt lake SE Oreg. in **Harney basin** (depression, area 2500)

Harney Peak mountain 7242 ft SW S. Dak.; highest in Black hills & in state

Har·pers Fer·ry National Monument \ˌhär-pərz-'fer-ē\ historical site Md.-W. Va. at town of Harpers Ferry, W. Va., at junction of Shenandoah & Potomac rivers

Har·per Woods \ˌhär-pər-\ city SE Mich. NE of Detroit pop 19,995

Harris — see LEWIS WITH HARRIS

Har·ris·burg \'har-əs-ˌbərg\ city ✳ of Pa. pop 79,697

Har·ri·son \'har-ə-sən\ urban township SW Pa. pop 15,710

Har·ro·gate \'har-ə-gət, -ˌgāt\ municipal borough N England in Yorkshire N of Leeds pop 50,454

Har·row \'har-(ˌ)ō\ urban district SE England in Middlesex NW of London pop 219,463

Hart·ford \'härt-fərd\ city ✳ of Conn. pop 162,178

Har·vard, Mount \'här-vərd\ mountain 14,420 ft, cen Colo. in Collegiate range of Sawatch mountains SE of Mt. Elbert

Har·vey \'här-vē\ city NE Ill. S of Chicago pop 29,071

Har·wich \'har-ij, -ich, US also 'här-(ˌ)wich\ municipal borough SE England in Essex on North sea

Harz \'härts\ mountains cen Germany between Elbe & Leine rivers — see BROCKEN

Ha·sa or **El Hasa** \el-'has-ə\ region NE Saudi Arabia in E Nejd bordering on Persian gulf

Has·selt \'häs-əlt\ commune NE Belgium ✳ of Limburg pop 36,630

Has·tings \'hā-stiŋz\ **1** city S Nebr. pop 21,412 **2** county borough SE England in East Sussex on Strait of Dover pop 65,506

Ha·tay \hä-'tī\ district S Turkey E of Gulf of Iskenderun; chief city Iskenderun

Hat·ter·as \'hat-ə-rəs, 'ha-trəs\ island N. C. between Pamlico sound & Atlantic ocean; a long barrier island, mostly in **Cape Hatteras National Seashore Recreational Area** (area 39)

Hatteras, Cape cape N. C. on SE Hatteras I.

Hat·ties·burg \'hat-ēz-ˌbərg\ city SE Miss. pop 34,989

Hau·ra·ki Gulf \hau̇-ˌrak-ē-, -ˌräk-\ inlet of the Pacific N New Zealand on N coast of North I.

Haute–Volta — see UPPER VOLTA

Ha·vana or **Ha·ba·na** \hə-'van-ə\ or Sp **La Ha·ba·na** \ˌlä-(ä-)-'vän-ə\ city & port ✳ of Cuba on Gulf of Mexico pop 785,455 — **Ha·van·an** \hə-'van-ən\ adj or n

Ha·vel \'häf-əl\ river 225 m E Germany flowing SW through Berlin into the Elbe

Hav·er·ford \'hav-ə(r)-fərd\ urban township SE Pa. NW of Philadelphia pop 54,019

Hav·er·ford·west \ˌhav-ə(r)-fər-'dwest\ municipal borough & port SW Wales ✳ of Pembrokeshire

Ha·ver·hill \'hāv-(ə-)rəl\ city NE Mass. pop 46,346

Havre — see LE HAVRE

Ha·waii \hə-'wä-(ˌ)(y)ē, -'wī-(ˌ)(y)ē, -'wȯ-(ˌ)(y)ē, -'wä-yə, -'wȯ-yə, -'wī-(y)ə\ **1** or **Ha·wai·ian islands** \hə-ˌwä-yən-, -ˌwī-(y)ən-, -ˌwȯ-yən-\ or formerly **Sand·wich islands** \ˌsan-(d)wich-\ group of islands cen Pacific **2** state of the U. S. coextensive with Hawaiian islands; annexed 1898, a territory 1900–59 ✳ Honolulu area 6423, pop 632,772 **3** island SE Hawaii, largest of the group; chief city Hilo area 4021, pop 61,332

Hawaii National Park reservation Hawaii including Mauna Loa & Kilauea volcanoes on Hawaii I. area 244; formerly included also Haleakala crater (now in Haleakala National Park) on Maui I.

Ha·wash \'hä-ˌwäsh\ or **Awash** \'ä-\ river 500 m E Ethiopia flowing NE into the desert

Hawke Bay \'hȯk\ inlet of the S Pacific N New Zealand on SE coast of North I.

Hawke's Bay \'hȯks\ provincial district N New Zealand on SE coast of North I. ✳ Napier area 4260, pop 108,800

Haw·thorne \'hȯ-ˌthȯ(ə)rn\ **1** city SW Calif. SW of Los Angeles pop 33,035 **2** borough NE N. J. N of Paterson pop 17,735

Hay \'hā\ river 530 m Canada in N Alta. & SW Mackenzie District flowing NE into Great Slave Lake

Hayes \'hāz\ **1** river 300 m Canada in E Man. flowing NE into Hudson Bay **2** or **Hayes and Har·ling·ton** \'här-liŋ-tən\ urban district SE England in Middlesex W of London pop 65,608

Hayti — see HAITI

Hay·ward \'hā-wərd\ city W Calif. SE of Oakland pop 72,700

Ha·zel Park \ˌhā-zəl-\ city SE Mich. N of Detroit pop 25,631

Ha·zle·ton \'hā-zəl-tən\ city E Pa. S of Wilkes-Barre pop 32,056

Heard \'hərd\ island S Indian ocean SE of Kerguelen, at 53°10′S, 74°10′E; claimed by Australia

Heb·ri·des \'heb-rə-ˌdēz\ or **Western** islands W Scotland in the Atlantic divided by Little Minch into **Inner Hebrides** (near the mainland) & **Outer Hebrides** (to NW) area 2900, pop 61,795 — see LEWIS WITH HARRIS — **Heb·ri·de·an** \ˌheb-rə-'dē-ən\ adj or n

He·bron \'hē-brən\ or anc **Kir·jath-ar·ba** \ˌkər-jath-'är-bə, ˌki(ə)r-\ city cen Palestine SSW of Jerusalem in modern Jordan pop 35,983

Hec·ate \'hek-ət\ strait Canada in W B.C., inlet of the Pacific between Queen Charlotte islands & the coast

Heer·len \'he(ə)r-lə(n)\ commune SE Netherlands in Limburg NE of Maastricht pop 56,600

Hei·del·berg \'hīd-ᵊl-ˌbərg, -ˌbe(ə)rg\ city W Germany on the Neckar ESE of Mannheim pop 127,400

Heijo — see PYONGYANG

Heil·bronn \'hī(ə)l-ˌbrän, hīl-'brȯn\ city W Germany on the Neckar N of Stuttgart pop 86,100

Hei·lung·kiang \'hā-'lu̇ŋ-jē-'äŋ\ **1** — see AMUR **2** province NE China in N Manchuria bordering on the Amur ✳ Harbin area 178,996, pop 11,897,000

He·jaz \he-'jaz, hij-'az\ region W Saudi Arabia on Red sea; a viceroyalty ✳ Mecca area 150,000, pop 2,000,000 — **He·jazi** \-ē\ adj or n

Hek·la or **Hec·la** \'hek-lə\ volcano 4747 ft SW Iceland

Hel·e·na \'hel-ə-nə\ city ✳ of Mont. pop 20,227

Hel·go·land \'hel-gō-ˌländ\ or **Hel·i·go·land** \'hel-ə-gō-ˌland, -ˌlänt\ island NW Germany in North sea, in No. Frisian islands

Hel·i·con \'hel-ə-ˌkän, -i-kən\ mountain 5738 ft E cen Greece in SW Boeotia near Gulf of Corinth

He·li·op·o·lis \ˌhē-lē-'äp-ə-ləs\ **1** — see BAALBEK **2** ancient ruined city N Egypt S of modern Cairo **3** ancient ruined city 6 m N of modern Cairo **4** or Ar **Masr-el-Ge·di·da** \ˌmis-ə-ˌrel-jə-'dēd-ə\ a NE suburb of Cairo

Hellas — see GREECE

Hel·les, Cape \'hel-(,)ēz\ headland Turkey in Europe at S tip of Gallipoli peninsula

Hellespont, Hellespontus — see DARDANELLES

Hell Gate a narrow part of East river in New York City between Long I. & Manhattan I.

Hells Canyon \'helz\ or **Grand Canyon of the Snake** canyon of Snake river on Idaho-Oreg. border 40 m long; deepest point over 7000 ft

Hel·mand or **Hel·mund** \'hel-mənd\ river 650 m SW Afghanistan flowing SW & W into a morass on Iranian border

Hel·mond \'hel-,mónt\ commune S Netherlands pop 42,442

Helm·stedt \'helm-,s(h)tet\ city cen Germany E of Brunswick on border between East and West Germany pop 29,100

Hel·sing·ör \,hel-siŋ-'ər\ or **El·si·nore** \'el-sə-,nō(ə)r, -,nó(ə)r\ city & port Denmark on N Sjælland I. pop 21,828

Hel·sin·ki \'hel-,siŋ-kē, hel-'\ or Sw **Hel·sing·fors** \'hel-siŋ-,fó(ə)rz\ city & port ✳ of Finland on Gulf of Finland pop 445,200

Hel·vel·lyn \hel-'vel-ən\ mountain 3118 ft NW England on Cumberland-Westmorland border in Lake District

Helvetia — see SWITZERLAND

Hemp·field \'hem(p)-,fēld\ urban township SW Pa. pop 29,704

Hemp·stead \'hem(p)-,sted, -stəd\ village SE N. Y. on Long I. pop 34,641

Hen·der·son \'hen-dər-sən\ city NW Ky. pop 16,892

Hen·don \'hen-dən\ urban district SE England in Middlesex, NW suburb of London pop 155,835

Heng·e·lo \'heŋ-ə-,lō\ commune E Netherlands in Overijssel pop 59,350

Heng·yang \'həŋ-'yäŋ\ city SE cen China in SE Hunan on the Siang pop 235,000

Hen·ley \'hen-lē\ or **Henley on Thames** municipal borough SE cen England in Oxfordshire W of London

Hen·lo·pen, Cape \hen-'lō-pən\ headland SE Del. at entrance to Delaware Bay

Hen·ry, Cape \'hen-rē\ headland SE Va. S of entrance to Chesapeake Bay

Her·a·clea \,her-ə-'klē-ə\ ancient city S Italy in Lucania near Gulf of Taranto

Heraklion — see CANDIA

He·rat \he-'rät, hə-\ or anc **Ar·ia** \'ar-ē-ə, 'er-; ə-'rī-ə\ city NW Afghanistan on the Hari Rud pop 75,632

Her·cu·la·ne·um \,hər-kyə-'lā-nē-əm\ ancient city S Italy in Campania on Tyrrhenian sea; destroyed A.D. 79 by eruption of Mt. Vesuvius

Her·e·ford \'her-ə-fərd, ,US also 'hər-fərd-\ 1 or **Her·e·ford·shire** \-,shi(ə)r, -shər\ county W England on Welsh border area 842, pop 127,092 2 municipal borough, its ✳, on the Wye

Her·ford \'he(ə)r-,fó(ə)rt\ city W Germany in North Rhine-Westphalia NE of Bielefeld pop 55,100

Heri Rud — see HARI RUD

Her·i·sau \'her-ə-,zaú\ commune NE Switzerland ✳ of Appenzell Outer Rhodes half canton

Her·mon, Mount \'hər-mən\ mountain 9232 ft on border between Syria & Lebanon; highest in Anti-Lebanon mountains

Hermopolis or **Hermoúpolis** — see ERMOÚPOLIS

Her·mo·sa Beach \(,)hər-,mō-sə-\ city SW Calif. pop 16,115

Her·mo·si·llo \,er-mə-'sē-(,)(y)ō\ city NW Mexico ✳ of Sonora on Sonora river pop 43,516

Her·ne \'he(ə)r-nə\ city W Germany in the Ruhr pop 113,700

Herst·mon·ceux or **Hurst·mon·ceux** \,hərs(t)-mən-'sü\ village S England in East Sussex NE of Eastbourne

Her·ten \'he(ə)rt-ᵊn\ city W Germany in North Rhine-Westphalia N of Essen pop 51,600

Hert·ford \'härf-ərd also 'härt-, US also 'hərt-\ 1 or **Hert·ford·shire** \-,shi(ə)r, -shər\ county SE England area 632, pop 609,735 2 municipal borough, its ✳, N of London

Hertogenbosch, 's — see 's HERTOGENBOSCH

Her·ze·go·vi·na \,hert-sə-gō-'vē-nə, ,hərt-\ or Serb **Her·ce·go·vi·na** \'kərt-sə-gō-vē-nə\ region W cen Yugoslavia S of Bosnia & NW of Montenegro; now part of Bosnia & Herzegovina federated republic — see BOSNIA — **Her·ze·go·vi·nian** \,hert-sə-gō-'vēn-ē-ən, ,hərt-, -'vēn-yən, -ē-\ adj

Hesse \'hes, 'hes-ē\ or G **Hes·sen** \'hes-ᵊn\ 1 region SW Germany N of Baden-Württemberg including district **Hesse-Darmstadt** (in the S) & **Hes·se–Cas·sel** \'kas-əl, 'käs-\ (in the N), the latter being united with Prussia in 1866 as part of the province of **Hesse-Nassau** along with the duchy of Nassau & the city of Frankfurt 2 state of the Weimar Republic, equivalent to Hesse-Darmstadt 3 state of the Bonn Republic, including larger part of Hesse-Darmstadt & part of Hesse-Nassau ✳ Wiesbaden area 8148, pop 4,783,400

Hes·ton and Isle·worth \,hes-tə-nə-'nī-zəl-(,)wərth, ,hes-ᵊn-ə-'nī-\ municipal borough SE England in Middlesex, W suburb of London pop 106,636

Hi·a·le·ah \,hī-ə-'lē-ə\ city SE Fla. N of Miami pop 66,972

Hib·bing \'hib-iŋ\ village NE Minn. pop 17,731

Hi·ber·nia — see IRELAND

Hi·bok·hi·bok \,hē-,bók-'hē-,bók\ volcano 5620 ft S Philippines on Camiguin I.

Hick·o·ry \'hik-(ə-)rē\ city W cen N.C. pop 19,328

Hicks·ville \'hiks-,vil\ urban area SE N. Y. on Long I. pop 50,405

Hi·dal·go \hid-'al-(,)gō, ē-'thäl-\ state cen Mexico ✳ Pachuca area 8057, pop 909,119

Hierosolyma — see JERUSALEM

Hier·ro \'ye(ə)r-(,)ō\ or formerly **Fer·ro** \'fe(ə)r-(,)ō\ island Spain, westernmost of the Canary islands area 107

High Atlas — see ATLAS

High·land \'hī-lənd\ town NW Ind. S of Hammond pop 16,284

Highland Park, 1 city NE Ill. N of Chicago pop 25,532 **2** city SE Mich. entirely within city of Detroit pop 38,063

High·lands \'hī-lən(d)z\ the chiefly mountainous N part of Scotland N of a line connecting Firth of Clyde & Firth of Tay

Highlands of Na·ve·sink \'nav-ə-,siŋk, 'näv-, 'nev-\ or **Navesink Highlands** or **Navesink Hills** range of hills E N. J. extending from near Sandy Hook to Raritan Bay

Highlands of the Hudson hilly region SE N. Y. on both sides of the Hudson; includes Storm King 1340 ft

High Plains the Great Plains esp. from Nebr. southward

High Point city N cen N.C. SW of Greensboro pop 62,063

High Sierra the Sierra Nevada (in Calif.)

High Tatra — see TATRA

High Wyc·ombe \'wik-əm\ municipal borough SE cen England in Buckinghamshire WNW of London pop 39,352

Hiiumaa — see KHIUMA

Hil·des·heim \'hil-dəs-,hīm\ city W Germany SSE of Hannover pop 92,500

Hill·crest Heights \,hil-,krest-\ urban area S Md. pop 15,295

Hill·side \'hil-,sīd\ urban township NE N. J. N of Elizabeth pop 22,304

Hi·lo \'hē-(,)lō\ city & port Hawaii in E Hawaii I. pop 25,966

Hil·ver·sum \'hil-vər-səm\ city cen Netherlands in No. Holland SE of Amsterdam pop 100,369

Hi·ma·chal Pra·desh \hə-,mäch-əl-prə-'desh\ territory NW India comprising two areas NW of Uttar Pradesh area 10,904, pop 1,109,500 — see SIMLA

Hi·ma·la·ya \,him-ə-'lā-ə, hə-'mäl-(ə-)yə\ mountains S Asia on border between India & Tibet & in Kashmir, Nepal, Sikkim, & Bhutan — see EVEREST — **Hi·ma·la·yan** \,him-ə-'lā-ən, hə-'mäl-(ə-)yən\ adj

Hi·me·ji \hi-'mej-ē\ city Japan in W Honshu pop 328,689

Hindenburg — see ZABRZE

Hin·du Kush \,hin-(,)dü-'kúsh, -'kəsh\ or anc **Cau·ca·sus In·di·cus** \,kó-kə-sə-'sin-di-kəs\ mountain range cen Asia SW of the Pamirs on border of Kashmir & in Afghanistan — see TIRICH MIR

Hin·du·stan or **Hin·do·stan** \,hin-(,)dü-'stan, -də-, -'stän\ 1 region N India N of the Deccan including the plain drained by the Indus, the Ganges, & the Brahmaputra 2 the subcontinent of India 3 the Republic of India

Hip·po \'hip-(,)ō\ or **Hippo Re·gi·us** \-'rē-j(ē-)əs\ ancient city N Africa S of modern Bône, Algeria; chief town of Numidia

Hi·ro·sa·ki \hi-'rō-sə-kē, hir-ə-'säk-ē\ city Japan in N Honshu SW of Aomori pop 138,953

Hi·ro·shi·ma \,hir-ə-'shē-mə, hə-'rō-shə-mə\ city & port Japan in SW Honshu on Inland sea pop 431,336

His·pa·nia \his-'pān-ē-ə, -'pān-yə, -'pan-\ the Iberian peninsula

His·pan·io·la \,his-pən-'yō-lə\ or Sp **Es·pa·ño·la** \,es-,pän-'yō-lə\ or formerly **Hai·ti** \'hāt-ē\ or **San·to Do·min·go** \,sant-əd-ə-'miŋ-(,)gō\ or **San Domingo** \,san-də-\ island West Indies in the Greater Antilles; divided between Haiti (on W) & Dominican Republic (on E) area 29,979

His·sar·lik \,his-ər-'lik\ site of ancient Troy NW Turkey in Asia 4 m SE of mouth of the Dardanelles

Hi·va Oa \,hē-və-'ō-ə\ island S Pacific in SE Marquesas area 154

Hi·was·see \hī-'wäs-ē\ river 150 m E U.S. flowing from N E Ga. WNW through W N.C. into the Tennessee in Tenn.

Ho·bart, 1 \'hō-bərt\ city NW Ind. pop 18,680 **2** \-,bärt\ city & port Australia ✳ of Tasmania pop (with suburbs) 99,500

Hobbs \'häbz\ city SE N. Mex. pop 26,275

Ho·bo·ken \'hō-,bō-kən\ 1 city NE N.J. N of Jersey City pop 48,441 **2** commune N Belgium, suburb of Antwerp pop 30,552

Höch·städt \'hœ(r)k-,s(h)tet\ town W Germany in Bavaria on the Danube NE of Ulm

Ho·dei·da \hō-'dād-ə\ city & port W Yemen pop 30,000

Hod·me·zo·va·sar·hely \'hód-mə-,zə(r)-'väsh-ər-,hā\ city SE Hungary NE of Szeged near Tisza river pop 38,000

Hof \'hōf, 'hóf\ city W Germany in Bavaria on the Saale NE of Bayreuth pop 56,100

Ho·fei \'hə-'fā\ or **Lu·chow** \'lü-'jō\ city E China ✳ of Anhwei W of Nanking pop 183,600

Ho·fuf \hü-'füf\ city NE Saudi Arabia in E Nejd; chief town of Hasa region pop 100,000

Hoggar — see AHAGGAR

Ho·hen·lin·den \,hō-ən-,lin-dən, ,hō-ən-'\ village W Germany in Bavaria E of Munich

Ho·hen·zol·lern \'hō-ən-,zäl-ərn, ,hō-ən-'\ region SW Germany, formerly a province of Prussia — see WÜRTTEMBERG

Ho·he Tau·ern \,hō-ə-'taú-(ə)rn\ range of the E Alps W Austria between Carinthia & Tirol — see GROSSGLOCKNER

Hoi·how \'hói-'haú, 'hī-'hō\ or **Hai·kow** \'hī-'kaú, -'kō\ city & port SE China in Kwangtung on NE Hainan I. pop 135,300

Hok·kai·do \hä-'kīd-(,)ō\ or **Ye·zo** \'yez-(,)ō\ island N Japan N of Honshu area 30,077

Hol·born \'hō(l)-bərn\ metropolitan borough W cen London, England pop 24,806

Hol·guin \(h)ól-'gēn\ city E Cuba NW of Santiago de Cuba pop 57,573

Hol·land \'häl-ənd\ 1 city W Mich. on Lake Michigan pop 24,777 **2** medieval county of Holy Roman Empire bordering on North sea, now forming No. & So. Holland provinces of the Netherlands **3** — see NETHERLANDS — **Hol·land·er** \-ən-dər\ n

Holland, Parts of administrative county E England in SE Lincolnshire ✳ Boston area 420, pop 101,500

Hol·lan·dia \hä-'lan-dē-ə\ or **Ko·ta·ba·ru** \,kōt-ə-'bär-(,)ü\ or now **Su·kar·na·pu·ra** \sü-,kär-nə-'púr-ə\ city & port ✳ of West New Guinea pop 16,300

Hol·ly·wood \'häl-ē-,wúd\ 1 section of Los Angeles, Calif. NW of the downtown district **2** city SE Fla. N of Miami pop 35,237

Hol·stein \'hōl-,stīn, -,stēn\ region NW Germany S of Jutland peninsula adjoining Schleswig; once a duchy of Denmark, became a part of Prussia 1866 — see SCHLESWIG-HOLSTEIN

Hol·ston \'hōl-stən\ river 140 m E Tenn. flowing SW to unite with the French Broad forming the Tennessee

Ho·ly \'hō-lē\ 1 or **Lin·dis·farne** \'lin-dəs-,färn\ island N England cliff NE coast of Northumberland **2** or **Holy·head** \'häl-ē-,hed\ island NW Wales in St. George's channel off W coast of Anglesey

Holy Cross, Mount of the mountain 13,996 ft NW cen Colo. in Sawatch range

Holy·head \'häl-ē-,hed\ urban district & port NW Wales in Anglesey on Holy I.

Holy Land PALESTINE

Holy Loch inlet of Firth of Clyde W Scotland on NW shore of the firth opposite mouth of Clyde river

Hol·yoke \'hōl-,yōk\ city SW Mass. pop 52,689

Homestead National Monument site SE Nebraska W of Beatrice of first homestead entered under General Homestead Act of 1862

Home·wood \'hōm-,wúd\ city cen Ala. pop 20,289

Homs \'hōmz, 'hóm(p)s\ 1 or formerly **Leb·da** \'leb-də\ or anc **Lep·tis Mag·na** \,lep-tə-'smag-nə\ town & port Libya ESE of Tripoli **2** or anc **Em·e·sa** \'em-ə-sə\ city W Syria pop 132,637

Ho·nan \'hō-'nän\ province E *cen* China ✻ Chengchow *area* 64,479, *pop* 44,215,000

Hon·du·ras \hän-'d(y)ùr-əs\ country Central America bordering on the Caribbean & the Pacific; a republic ✻ Tegucigalpa *area* 59,160, *pop* 1,953,094 — **Hon·du·ran** \-ən\ *adj or n* — **Hon·du·ra·ne·an** *or* **Hon·du·ra·ni·an** \,hän-d(y)ə-'rā-nē-ən\ *adj or n*

Honduras, Gulf of inlet of the Caribbean between S Brit. Honduras, E Guatemala, & N Honduras

Hon·fleur \ōⁿ-'flœr\ town & port N France on Seine estuary

Hong Kong *or* **Hong·kong** \'häŋ-,käŋ, -'käŋ; 'hòŋ-,kòŋ, -'kòŋ\ **1** Brit. crown colony on SE coast of China E of mouth of Pearl river including Hong Kong I., Kowloon peninsula & adjacent area (New Territories) on mainland, & nearby islands ✻ Victoria *area* 391, *pop* 3,642,500 **2** — see VICTORIA

Ho·ni·a·ra \,hō-nē-'är-ə\ town W Pacific ✻ of the Brit. Solomons on Guadalcanal I.

Ho·no·lu·lu \,hän-ə-'lü-(,)lü, ,hōn-ə-l\ city & port ✻ of Hawaii on Oahu I. *pop* 294,194

Hon·shu \'hän-(,)shü\ *or* **Hon·do** \-(,)dō\ island Japan, chief island of the group *area* 88,000

Hood, Mount \'hùd\ mountain 11,245 *ft* NW Oreg. in Cascade range; highest point in state

Hood Canal inlet of Puget Sound 80 *m* long W Wash. along E shore of Olympic peninsula

Hoo·ghly *or* **Hu·gli** \'hü-glē\ river 120 *m* E India flowing S into Bay of Bengal; most westerly channel of the Ganges in its delta

Hook of Holland \,hùk-\ headland SW Netherlands in So. Holland on coast SW of The Hague

Hoorn — see FUTUNA

Hoo·sac \'hü-sək, -sik\ mountain range W Mass. in Green mountains; highest peak Spruce Hill 2588 *ft*

Hoo·ver Dam \,hü-vər-\ *or* **Boul·der Dam** \,bōl-dər-\ dam 726 *ft* high in Colorado river between Nev. & Ariz. — see MEAD (Lake)

Ho·pat·cong, Lake \hə-'pat-,kän, ,kän\ lake 8 *m* long N N.J.

Ho·pei *or* **Ho·peh** \'hō-'pā\ *or formerly* **Chih·li** \'chē-'lē\ province NE China bordering on Po Hai ✻ Tientsin *area* 84,865, *pop* 43,348,000

Hope·well \'hōp-,wel, -wəl\ city SE Va. *pop* 17,895

Hop·kins·ville \'häp-kənz-,vil\ city SW Ky. *pop* 19,465

Hor \'hò(ə)r\ mountain 4430 *ft* SW Jordan

Ho·reb \'hōr-,eb, 'hòr-\ *or* **Si·nai** \'sī-,nī *also* -nē-,ī\ mountain where according to the Bible the Law was given to Moses; thought to be in the Gebel Musa on Sinai peninsula

Hor·muz *or* **Or·muz** \'(h)òr-,muz, (h)òr-'müz\ **1** ancient town S Iran on Strait of Hormuz (strait between Iran & N Trucial Oman connecting Persian gulf & Gulf of Oman) **2** island SE Iran in Strait of Hormuz

Horn, Cape \'hò(ə)rn\ headland S Chile on Horn I. in Tierra del Fuego; southernmost point of So. America, at 55°59'S

Horn·church \'hòrn-,chərch\ urban district SE England in Essex ENE of London *pop* 104,128

Horn of Africa the easternmost projection of Africa S of Gulf of Aden including Somalia & SE Ethiopia; its E tip is Cape Guardafui

Horn·sey \'hòrn-zē\ municipal borough SE England in Middlesex, N suburb of London *pop* 98,134

Hor·sens \'hòr-sənz, -sən(t)s\ city & port Denmark in E Jutland *pop* 36,138

Hos·pi·ta·let \,(h)äs-,pit-ᵊl-'et\ city NE Spain in Barcelona province, SW suburb of Barcelona *pop* 69,748

Hot Springs city W *cen* Ark. in **Hot Springs National Park** (reservation containing numerous hot mineral springs) *pop* 28,337

Hou·ma \'hō-mə, 'hü-\ city SE La. *pop* 22,561

Hou·sa·ton·ic \,hü-sə-'tän-ik, ,hü-zə-\ river 148 *m* W Mass. & W Conn. flowing from Berkshire hills S into Long Island Sound

Hous·ton \'(h)yü-stən\ city & port SE Tex. NW of Galveston Bay; connected with Gulf of Mexico by ship canal *pop* 938,219

Hove \'hōv\ municipal borough S England in East Sussex on English channel, W suburb of Brighton *pop* 69,435

Ho·ven·weep National Monument \,hō-vən-,wēp-\ site SE Utah & SW Colo. of prehistoric pueblos & cliff dwellings

How·rah \'haù-rə\ city E India in West Bengal on the Hooghly opposite Calcutta *pop* 433,600

Hra·dec Kra·lo·ve \,(h)räd-,ets-'kräl-ə-,vā\ *or* G **Kö·nig·grätz** \'kā-nig-,grāts, 'kə(r)n-ig-\ city W Czechoslovakia *pop* 51,480

Hsiang — see SIANG

Hsin·chu \'shin-'chü\ city & port China in NW Formosa on coast SW of Taipei *pop* 124,596

Hua·lla·ga \wä-'yäg-ə\ river 700 *m* N *cen* Peru flowing N into the Marañón

Huam·bo \'wäm-(,)bō\ *or* **No·va Lis·boa** \,nò-və-lēzh-'vō-ə\ city Angola in the W *cen* highlands *pop* 28,000

Huang — see YELLOW

Huas·ca·rán \,wäs-kə-'rän\ *or* **Huas·cán** \wä-'skän\ mountain 22,205 *ft* W Peru; highest in the country

Hud·ders·field \'həd-ərz-,fēld\ county borough N England in West Riding, Yorkshire, NE of Manchester *pop* 129,021

Hud·son \'həd-sən\ **1** river 306 *m* E N.Y. flowing from Adirondack mountains S into New York Bay **2** bay inlet of the Atlantic in N Canada; an inland sea 850 *m* long **3** strait 450 *m* long NE Canada between S Baffin I. & N Que. connecting Hudson Bay with the Atlantic — **Hud·so·ni·an** \,həd-'sō-nē-ən\ *adj*

Hue *or* F **Hué** \h(y)ü-'ā, 'wā\ city & port S *cen* Vietnam in Annam; formerly ✻ of Annam *pop* 113,000

Huel·va \'wel-və\ **1** province SW Spain in Andalusia on Gulf of Cádiz *area* 3913, *pop* 408,287 **2** city, its ✻ *pop* 78,878

Hues·ca \'wes-kə\ **1** province NE Spain in Aragon *area* 5848, *pop* 241,812 **2** commune, its ✻ *pop* 24,973

Hu·he·hot \'hü-(,)hā-'hòt\ *or* **Kwei·sui** \'gwā-'swä\ *or* **Ku·ku·Kho·to** \,kü-(,)kü-'kōt-(,)ō, -'hōt-\ city N China ✻ of Inner Mongolia E of Paotow *pop* 148,400

Hui·la \'wē-(,)lä\ volcano 18,700 *ft* SW *cen* Colombia

Hule, Lake — see MEROM (Waters of)

Hull \'həl\ **1** city Canada in SW Que. on Ottawa river opposite Ottawa, Ont. *pop* 49,243 **2** *or* **Kings·ton upon Hull** \,kiŋ(k)-stən-\ county borough & port N England in East Riding, Yorkshire, on the Humber *pop* 299,068

Hum·ber \'həm-bər\ estuary 40 *m* E England formed by the Ouse & the Trent & flowing E & SE into North sea

Hum·boldt \'həm-,bōlt\ **1** river 290 *m* N Nev. flowing W & SW into Rye Patch reservoir & formerly into Humboldt Lake **2** glacier NW Greenland; largest known glacier **3** bay NW Calif. on which Eureka is situated

Humboldt Lake *or* **Humboldt Sink** intermittent lake 20 *m* long W Nev. formerly receiving Humboldt river; has no outlet to ocean

Hum·phreys, Mount \'həm(p)-frēz\ mountain peak 12,670 *ft* N *cen* Ariz. — see SAN FRANCISCO PEAKS

Hu·nan \'hü-'nän\ province SE *cen* China ✻ Changsha *area* 81,274, *pop* 33,227,000 — **Hu·na·nese** \,hü-nə-'nēz, -'nēs\ *adj or n*

Hun·ga·ry \'həŋ-g(ə-)rē\ *or* Hung **Ma·gyar·or·szag** \'mäj-,är-,òr-,säg\ country *cen* Europe; formerly a kingdom, since 1946 a republic ✻ Budapest *area* 35,912, *pop* 9,977,870

Hung·nam \'hùŋ-,näm\ *or* Jap **Ko·nan** \'kō-,nän\ city & port N Korea on Sea of Japan *pop* 143,600

Hung·shui \'hùŋ-'shwā\ river 800 *m* S China flowing from E Yunnan E to unite with the Yü in E Kwangsi forming West river

Hung·tze \'hùŋ-'(d)zə\ lake 65 *m* long E China in W Kiangsu; traversed by Yellow river

Hun·ter \'hənt-ər\ river 287 *m* SE Australia in E New So. Wales flowing E into the Pacific

Hun·ting·don \'hənt-iŋ-dən\ **1** *or* **Hun·ting·don·shire** \-,shi(ə)r, -shər\ *or* **Hunts** \'hən(t)s\ county E *cen* England *area* 366, *pop* 69,273 **2** municipal borough, its ✻, on the Great Ouse

Hun·ting·ton \'hənt-iŋ-tən\ **1** city NE Ind. SW of Fort Wayne *pop* 16,185 **2** city W Va. on the Ohio *pop* 83,627

Huntington Park city SW Calif. S of Los Angeles *pop* 29,920

Huntington Station urban area SE N.Y. on Long I. *pop* 23,438

Hunts·ville \'hən(t)s-,vil, -vil\ city N Ala. *pop* 72,365

Hun·za \'hùn-zə\ district NW Jammu & Kashmir N of Hunza river ✻ Baltit *area* 8000, *pop* 32,000

Hu·on \'hyü-,än\ gulf inlet of Solomon sea on SE coast of North-East New Guinea S of Huon peninsula

Hu·pei *or* **Hu·peh** \'hü-'pā\ province E *cen* China ✻ Wuhan *area* 72,394, *pop* 27,790,000

Hu·ron, Lake \'(h)yùr-ən, '(h)yù(ə)r-,än\ lake E *cen* No. America between the U.S. & Canada; one of the Great Lakes *area* 23,010

Hürt·gen \'hi(ə)rt-gən, 'hùrt-\ town W Germany E of Aachen near **Hürtgen Forest**

Hurstmonceux — see HERSTMONCEUX

Hutch·in·son \'həch-ə(n)-sən\ city *cen* Kans. *pop* 37,574

Hutt \'hət\ city New Zealand on S North I. *pop* 93,000

Huy \'wē\ commune E Belgium SW of Liège *pop* 60,398

Huy·ton with Ro·by \,hīt-ᵊn-with-'rō-bē, -with-\ urban district NW England in Lancashire E of Liverpool *pop* 55,783

Hwai \'(h)wī\ river 600 *m* E China flowing from S Honan E into Hungtze Lake

Hwai·nan \'(h)wī-'nän\ *or formerly* **Show·hsien** \'shō-shē-'en\ city E China in N *cen* Anhwei SW of Pengpu *pop* 286,900

Hwaining — see ANKING

Hwang Ho — see YELLOW

Hwang Pu *or* **Whang·poo** \'(h)wäŋ-'pü\ river 70 *m* E China flowing E & N past Shanghai into the Yangtze

Hwang·shih \'(h)wäŋ-'shē\ city E China in E Hupei on the Yangtze SE of Wuhan *pop* 110,500

Hy·atts·ville \'hī-əts-,vil, -vəl\ city SW Md. *pop* 15,168

Hy·bla \'hī-blə\ ancient town in Sicily on S slope of Mt. Etna

Hydaspes — see JHELUM

Hy·der·abad \'hīd-(ə-)rə-,bad, -,bäd\ **1** former state S *cen* India in the Deccan ✻ Hyderabad **2** *or* **Hai·dar·abad** city S *cen* India ✻ of Andhra Pradesh *pop* 1,085,700 **3** city Pakistan in S West Pakistan in Sind on the Indus *pop* 241,800

Hy·dra \'hī-drə\ *or* NGk **Ídhra** \'ēth-rə\ island Greece in S Aegean sea off E coast of Peloponnesus *area* 20 — **Hy·dri·ot** \'hī-drē-ət, -drē-,ät\ *or* **Hy·dri·ote** \-,ōt, -ət\ *n*

Hydraotes — see RAVI

Hy·ères \ē-'e(ə)r, 'ye(ə)r\ **1** islands (F **Îles d'Hyères** \,ēl-dē-'ē(ə)r, ēl-'dye(ə)r\) in the Mediterranean off SE coast of France **2** commune SE France on Côte d'Azur E of Toulon *pop* 26,400

Hy·met·tus \hī-'met-əs\ mountain ridge 3370 *ft*, *cen* Greece E & SE of Athens — **Hy·met·ti·an** \-'met-ē-ən\ *adj*

Hyr·ca·nia \,hər-'kā-nē-ə\ province of ancient Persia on SE coast of Caspian sea NE of Media & NW of Parthia — **Hyr·ca·ni·an** \-nē-ən\ *adj*

Ia·si \'yäsh(-ē)\ *or* **Jas·sy** \'yäs-ē\ city NE Romania *pop* 122,780

Iba·dan \ē-'bäd-ᵊn\ city SW Nigeria *pop* 459,000

Ibe·ria \ī-'bir-ē-ə\ **1** ancient Spain **2** the Iberian peninsula **3** ancient region S of the Caucasus W of Colchis in modern Georgia

Ibe·ri·an \-ē-ən\ peninsula SW Europe between the Mediterranean & the Atlantic occupied by Spain & Portugal

Ibi·cuí \,ē-bi-'kwē\ river 400 *m* S Brazil in Rio Grande do Sul flowing W into the Uruguay

Ibiza — see IVIZA

Içá — see PUTUMAYO

Icar·ia \ī-'ker-ē-ə, -'kar-; ik-'er-, -'ar-\ *or* NGk **Ika·ría** \,ē-kə-'rē-ə\ *or* **Ni·ka·ría** \,nē-kə-\ island Greece WSW of Samos *area* 99

Icel — see MERSIN

Ice·land \'ī-slənd, 'ī-,sland\ *or* Dan **Is·land** \'ē-,slän\ *or* Icelandic **Ís·land** \'ē-,slänt\ island between the Arctic & the Atlantic SE of Greenland; a republic formerly (1380–1944) belonging to Denmark, latterly (1918–44) as an independent kingdom in personal union with Denmark ✻ Reykjavík *area* 39,709, *pop* 143,973 — **Ice·land·er** \'ī-,slan-dər, 'ī-slən-\ *n*

Ichang \'ē-'chäŋ\ city *cen* China in W Hupei *pop* 81,000

Iconium — see KONYA

Ida \'īd-ə\ **1** *or* NGk **Ídhi** \'ē-thē\ mountain 8195 *ft* Greece in *cen* Crete; highest on island **2** *or* Turk **Kaz Da·gi** \,käz-dä-'(g)ē\ mountain 5810 *ft* NW Turkey in Asia SE of ancient Troy

Ida·ho \'īd-ə-,hō\ state NW U.S. ✻ Boise *area* 83,557, *pop* 667,-191 — **Ida·ho·an** \,īd-ə-'hō-ən\ *adj or n*

Idaho Falls city SE Idaho on the Snake *pop* 33,161

Id·fu \'id-(,)fü\ *or* **Ed·fu** \'ed-\ city S Egypt on Nile *pop* 20,700

Idumaea *or* **Idumea** — see EDOM — **Id·u·mae·an** *or* **Id·u·me·an** \ˌij-ə-ˈmē-ən\ *adj or n*
Ie·per \ˈyā-pər\ *or* F **Ypres** \ˈēprᵊ\ commune NW Belgium in West Flanders *pop* 17,682
Ife \ˈē-(ˌ)fā\ city SW Nigeria NE of Ibadan *pop* 111,000
If·ni \ˈif-nē\ **1** territory SW Morocco; administered by Spain 1934–69 *area* 741, *pop* 38,295 **2** *or* **Si·di Ifni** \ˌsēd-ē-\ town, its ✻
Igua·çu *or* **Iguas·su** *or* Sp **Igua·zú** \ˌē-gwə-ˈsü\ river 380 *m* S Brazil in Paraná state flowing W into the Alto Paraná; contains **Iguaçu Falls** (waterfall over 2 *m* wide composed of numerous cataracts averaging 200 *ft* in height)
IJs·sel *or* **Ijs·sel** *or* **Ys·sel** \ˈī-səl\ river 70 *m* E Netherlands flowing out of Rhine river N into IJsselmeer
IJs·sel·meer \ˈī-səl-ˌme(ə)r\ *or* **Lake Ijs·sel** \ˈī-səl\ *or formerly* **Zui·der,** *or* **Zuy·der, Zee** \ˌzīd-ər-ˈzā, -ˈzē\ lake N Netherlands separated from North sea by a dike & bordered by reclaimed lands
Île-de-France \ˌēl-də-ˈfräⁿs\ region & former province N *cen* France bounded on N by Picardy, on E by Champagne, on S by Orléanais, & on W by Normandy ✻ Paris
Île du Diable — see DEVIL'S ISLAND
Îles de la Société — see SOCIETY
Îles du Vent — see WINDWARD
Îles sous le Vent — see LEEWARD
Il·ford \ˈil-fərd\ municipal borough SE England in Essex, NE suburb of London *pop* 184,707
Il·fra·combe \ˈil-frə-ˌküm\ urban district SW England in Devon on Bristol channel
Ili \ˈē-ˈlē\ river 800 *m, cen* Asia flowing from W Sinkiang, China, W & NW into Lake Balkhash in Kazakhstan
Ilía — see ELIS
Il·i·am·na \ˌil-ē-ˈam-nə\ **1** lake 80 *m* long SW Alaska NE of Bristol Bay **2** volcano 10,085 *ft* NE of Iliamna Lake
Ilion *or* **Ilium** — see TROY — **Il·i·an** \ˈil-ē-ən\ *adj or n*
Illam·pu \ē-ˈ(y)äm-(ˌ)pü\ **1** *or* **So·ra·ta** \sə-ˈrät-ə\ massif in the Andes W Bolivia E of Lake Titicaca — see ANCOHUMA **2** peak 21,276 *ft* in the Illampu massif
Illi·ma·ni \ˌē-(y)ə-ˈmän-ē\ mountain 22,579 *ft* Bolivia E of La Paz
Il·li·nois \ˌil-ə-ˈnȯi *also* -ˈnȯiz\ **1** river 273 *m* Ill. flowing SW into the Mississippi **2** state *cen* U.S. ✻ Springfield *area* 56,400, *pop* 10,081,158 — **Il·li·nois·an** \ˌil-ə-ˈnȯi-ən, -ˈnȯiz-ᵊn\ *adj or n*
Il·lyr·ia \ə-ˈlir-ē-ə\ ancient region S Europe in Balkan peninsula bordering on the Adriatic — **Il·lyr·ic** \-ˈlir-ik\ *adj*
Il·lyr·i·cum \ə-ˈlir-i-kəm\ province of Roman Empire in Illyria
Il·men \ˈil-mən\ lake U.S.S.R. in NW Soviet Russia, Europe, S of Lake Ladoga
Ilo·ilo \ˌē-lə-ˈwē-(ˌ)lō\ city Philippines on S coast of Panay I. *pop* 46,416
Im·pe·ria \im-ˈpir-ē-ə, -ˈper-\ commune & port NW Italy in Liguria SW of Genoa *pop* 28,295
Im·pe·ri·al \im-ˈpir-ē-əl\ valley U.S. & Mexico in SE Calif. & NE Baja California state in Colorado desert; most of area below sea level — see SALTON SEA
Imperial Beach city SW Calif. S of San Diego *pop* 17,773
Imp·hal \ˈimp-ˌhəl\ city NE India ✻ of Manipur *pop* 132,000
Im·roz \im-ˈrȯz\ *or* Gk **Im·bros** \ˈim-brəs, ˈēm-ˌvrȯs\ island Turkey in the NE Aegean W of Gallipoli peninsula *area* 110
Ina·gua \in-ˈäg-wə\ two islands in the SE Bahamas: **Great Inagua** (50 *m* long) & **Little Inagua** (8 *m* long)
In·chon \ˈin-ˌchän\ *or* **Che·mul·po** \jə-ˈmu̇l-(ˌ)pō\ *or* Jap **Jin·sen** \ˈjin-ˌsen\ city & port S Korea W of Seoul *pop* 318,683
In·de·pen·dence \ˌin-də-ˈpen-dən(t)s\ city W Mo. *pop* 62,328
In·dia \ˈin-dē-ə\ **1** peninsula region (often called a subcontinent) S Asia S of the Himalayas between Bay of Bengal & Arabian sea occupied by India & Pakistan & formerly often considered as also including Burma (but not Ceylon) **2** those parts of India until 1947 under Brit. rule or protection together with Baluchistan & the Andaman & Nicobar islands &, prior to 1937, Burma **3** *or* **Indian Union** *or* **Bha·rat** \ˈbər-ət, ˈbə-rət\ country comprising major portion of peninsula; a republic within the Brit. Commonwealth; until 1947 a part of the Brit. Empire ✻ New Delhi *area* 1,262,275, *pop* 439,235,082
In·di·an \ˈin-dē-ən\ **1** ocean E of Africa, S of Asia, W of Australia & Tasmania, & N of Antarctica *area* 28,925,000 **2** — see THAR
In·di·ana \ˌin-dē-ˈan-ə\ state E *cen* U.S. ✻ Indianapolis *area* 36,291, *pop* 4,662,498 — **In·di·an·an** \-ˈan-ən\ *adj or n* — **In·di·an·i·an** \-ˈan-ē-ən\ *adj or n*
Indiana Harbor harbor district in East Chicago, Ind., on Lake Michigan
In·di·a·nap·o·lis \ˌin-dē-ə-ˈnap-(ə-)ləs\ city ✻ of Ind. *pop* 476,258
Indian river lagoon 165 *m* long E Fla. between mainland & coastal islands
Indian States *or* **Native States** former semi-independent states of the Indian Empire ruled by native princes subject to varying degrees of Brit. authority — see BRITISH INDIA
Indian Territory former territory S U.S. in present state of Okla.
In·dies \ˈin-(ˌ)dēz\ **1** EAST INDIES **2** WEST INDIES
In·di·gir·ka \ˌin-də-ˈgi(ə)r-kə\ river 850 *m* U.S.S.R. in NE Yakutsk Republic flowing N into East Siberian sea
In·do·chi·na \ˈin-(ˌ)dō-ˈchī-nə\ **1** *or* **Farther India** peninsula SE Asia; includes Burma, Cambodia, Laos, Malaya, Thailand, & Vietnam **2** *or* **French Indochina** former country SE Asia bordering on So. China sea & Gulf of Siam & comprising Annam, Cambodia, Cochin China, Laos, & Tonkin ✻ Hanoi
In·do·ne·sia \ˌin-də-ˈnē-zhə, -shə\ **1** country SE Asia in Malay archipelago comprising Sumatra, Java, S & E Borneo, Celebes, W Timor, W New Guinea, the Moluccas, & many adjacent smaller islands; a republic since 1949; formerly (as **Netherlands East Indies**) an overseas territory of the Netherlands ✻ Djakarta (formerly Batavia) *area* 575,450, *pop* 97,085,348 **2** the Malay archipelago
In·dore \in-ˈdō(ə)r, -ˈdȯ(ə)r\ **1** former state *cen* India in Narbada valley ✻ Indore; area now in Madhya Pradesh **2** city NW *cen* India in W Madhya Pradesh *pop* 310,900
In·dus \ˈin-dəs\ river 1800 *m* S Asia flowing from Tibet NW & SSW through W Pakistan into Arabian sea
In·gle·wood \ˈiŋ-gəl-ˌwu̇d\ **1** city SW Calif. SW of Los Angeles *pop* 63,390 **2** urban area N *cen* Tenn. near Nashville *pop* 26,527
In·gol·stadt \ˈiŋ-gəl-ˌs(h)tät\ city W Germany in Bavaria N of Munich *pop* 51,500
Ink·ster \ˈiŋ(k)-stər\ village SE Mich. W of Detroit *pop* 39,097
In·land \ˈin-ˌland, -lənd\ sea inlet of the Pacific 240 *m* long SW Japan between Honshu on E & N, Kyushu on W, & Shikoku on S
Inland Empire region NW U.S. between Cascade range & Rocky mountains in E Wash., N Idaho, W Mont., & NE Oreg.; chief city Spokane, Wash.
Inn \ˈin\ river 320 *m* flowing from SE Switzerland NE through Austria into the Danube in Germany — see ENGADINE
Inner Hebrides — see HEBRIDES
Inner Mongolia region N China in SE Mongolia & W Manchuria ✻ Huhehot *area* 454,633, *pop* 7,338,000
Inniskilling — see ENNISKILLEN
Inns·bruck \ˈinz-ˌbru̇k, ˈin(t)s-\ city W Austria *pop* 95,055
Inside Passage *or* **Inland Passage** protected shipping route from Puget Sound, Wash., to Skagway, Alaska, following channels between mainland & coastal islands
In·ter·la·ken \ˌint-ər-ˈläk-ən\ commune W *cen* Switzerland in Bern canton on the Aare between Lake of Thun & Lake of Brienz
International Zone — see MOROCCO
Inu·vik \in-ˈü-vik\ town NW Canada in NW Mackenzie District in Mackenzie delta
In·ver·car·gill \ˌin-vər-ˈkär-gəl\ borough & port New Zealand on S coast of South I. *pop* 42,400
In·ver·ness \ˌin-vər-ˈnes\ **1** *or* **In·ver·ness-shire** \-ˈnes(h)-ˌshi(ə)r, -shər\ county NW Scotland *area* 4211, *pop* 84,924 **2** burgh, its ✻ *pop* 28,115
Io·an·ni·na \yō-ˈän-ē-(ˌ)nä\ *or* **Yan·ni·na** \ˈyän-ē-(ˌ)nä\ city NW Greece in N Epirus *pop* 32,268
Io·na \ī-ˈō-nə\ island Scotland in S Inner Hebrides off SW tip of Mull I. *area* 6
Io·nia \ī-ˈō-nē-ə\ ancient region W Asia Minor bordering on the Aegean W of Lydia & Caria — **Io·ni·an** \-nē-ən\ *adj or n*
Ionian, 1 sea arm of the Mediterranean between SE Italy & W Greece **2** islands W Greece in Ionian sea
Io·wa \ˈī-ə-wə\ **1** river 291 *m* Iowa flowing SE into the Mississippi **2** state *cen* U.S. ✻ Des Moines *area* 56,290, *pop* 2,757,537 — **Io·wan** \-wən\ *adj or n*
Iowa City city E Iowa *pop* 33,443
Ipin \ˈē-ˈpin, -ˈpēn\ *or formerly* **Sü·chow** \ˈs(h)ü-ˈjō, ˈsü-ˈchau̇\ *or* **Sui·fu** \ˈswā-ˈfü\ city *cen* China in S Szechwan *pop* 177,500
Ípiros — see EPIRUS
Ipoh \ˈē-(ˌ)pō\ city Federation of Malaysia in Perak *pop* 125,855
Ipsambul — see ABU SIMBEL
Ip·sus \ˈip-səs\ ancient village W *cen* Asia Minor in S Phrygia
Ips·wich \ˈip-(ˌ)swich\ **1** city E Australia in SE Queensland SW of Brisbane *pop* 40,900 **2** county borough SE England ✻ of East Suffolk *pop* 104,788
Iqui·que \i-ˈkē-kē\ city & port N Chile on the Pacific *pop* 39,576
Iqui·tos \i-ˈkēt-(ˌ)ōs\ city NE Peru on the Amazon *pop* 54,300
Iráklion — see CANDIA
Iran \i-ˈran, -ˈrän; ī-ˈran\ *or esp formerly* **Per·sia** \ˈpər-zhə, *esp Brit* -shə\ country SW Asia bordering in N on Caspian sea & in S on Persian gulf & Gulf of Oman; a kingdom ✻ Tehran *area* 628,000, *pop* 18,944,821 — **Irani** \-ˈran-ē, -ˈrän-\ *adj or n*
Iraq \i-ˈräk, -ˈrak\ **1** *or* **Irak** country SW Asia in Mesopotamia; a republic since 1958, formerly a kingdom ✻ Baghdad *area* 171,555, *pop* 6,538,109 **2** — see ARAK — **Iraqi** \-ˈräk-ē, -ˈrak-\ *adj or n*
Ire·land \ˈī(ə)r-lənd\ **1** *or* L **Hi·ber·nia** \hī-ˈbər-nē-ə\ island W Europe in the Atlantic, one of the Brit. Isles *area* 32,375; divided between Republic of Ireland & Northern Ireland **2** *or* **Republic of Ireland** *or* **Eire** \ˈar-ə, ˈar-ē, ˈer-, ˈār-, ˈīr-\ country occupying major portion of island; a republic since 1949; a division of the United Kingdom of Great Britain & Ireland 1801–1921 & (as **Irish Free State**) a dominion of the Brit. Commonwealth 1922–37 ✻ Dublin *area* 26,602, *pop* 2,814,703 **3** — see NORTHERN IRELAND
Irian — see NEW GUINEA
Irish sea arm of the Atlantic between Great Britain & Ireland
Ir·kutsk \i(ə)r-ˈkütsk, ˌər-\ city U.S.S.R. in E *cen* Soviet Russia, Asia, on the Angara near Lake Baikal *pop* 365,000
Iron Gate \ˌī(-ə)rn-\ river gorge 2 *m* long of the Danube at place where it cuts around end of Transylvanian Alps on border between Romania & Yugoslavia
Iron·ton \ˈī(-ə)rn-tən\ city S Ohio on the Ohio *pop* 15,745
Ir·ra·wad·dy \ˌir-ə-ˈwäd-ē\ river 1350 *m* Burma flowing S into Bay of Bengal through several mouths
Ir·tysh *or* **Ir·tish** \i(ə)r-ˈtish, ˌər-\ river 2200 *m, cen* Asia flowing from Altai mountains in Sinkiang, China, NW & N into the Ob in U.S.S.R.
Irún \ē-ˈrün\ commune N Spain in Guipúzcoa E of San Sebastián near French border *pop* 19,452
Ir·ving \ˈər-viŋ\ city NE Tex. W of Dallas *pop* 45,985
Ir·ving·ton \-tən\ town NE N.J. WSW of Newark *pop* 59,379
Is·a·bela \ˌiz-ə-ˈbel-ə\ *or* **Al·be·marle** \ˈal-bə-ˌmärl\ island Ecuador; largest of the Galápagos *area* 1650
Isar \ˈē-ˌzär\ river 219 *m* W Europe flowing from Tirol, Austria, NW through Bavaria, Germany, into the Danube
Isau·ria \ī-ˈsȯr-ē-ə\ ancient district in E Pisidia S Asia Minor on N slope of W Taurus mountains — **Isau·ri·an** \-ē-ən\ *adj or n*
Is·chia \ˈis-kē-ə\ island Italy WSW of Naples *area* 18
Ise Bay \ˌē-ˌsā-\ inlet of the Pacific S Japan on S coast of Honshu
Iseo, Lake \ē-ˈzā-(ˌ)ō\ lake 14 *m* long N Italy in Lombardy NW of Bergamo
Isère \ē-ˈze(ə)r\ river 150 *m* SE France flowing from Graian Alps WSW into the Rhone
Iser·lohn \ˌē-zər-ˈlōn, ˈē-zər-ˌ\ city W Germany in Ruhr valley SE of Dortmund *pop* 55,100
Is·fa·han \ˌis-fə-ˈhän, -ˈhan\ *or* **Es·fa·han** \ˌes-\ *or* **Is·pa·han** \ˌis-pə-\ city W *cen* Iran; former ✻ of Persia *pop* 254,876
Ishim \i-ˈshim\ river 1330 *m* U.S.S.R. flowing from N Kazakh Republic N into the Irtysh
Isis \ˈī-səs\ the Thames river, England, at & above Oxford
Is·ken·de·run \(ˌ)is-ˌken-də-ˈrün\ *or* **Is·ken·de·ron** \-ˈrän\ *or formerly* **Al·ex·an·dret·ta** \ˌal-ig-(ˌ)zan-ˈdret-ə, ˌel-\ city & port S Turkey on **Gulf of Iskenderun** (inlet of the Mediterranean) *pop* 63,736
Is·lam·abad \is-ˈläm-ə-ˌbäd, iz-ˈlam-ə-ˌbad\ projected ✻ of Pakistan in NE West Pakistan in Murree hills NE of Rawalpindi
Island *or* **Ísland** — see ICELAND
Is·lay \ˈī-(ˌ)lā, -lə\ island Scotland in S Inner Hebrides *area* 234

Isle au Haut \ˌī-lə-'hō, ˌē-\ island Me. at entrance to Penobscot Bay — see ACADIA NATIONAL PARK

Isle of Ely — see ELY (Isle of)

Isle of Man — see MAN (Isle of)

Isle of Pines, 1 or Sp **Is·la de Pi·nos** \ˌēz-lä-thä-'pē-nōs\ island W Cuba in the Caribbean area 1180 **2** — see KUNIE

Isle of Wight — see WIGHT (Isle of)

Isle Roy·ale \ˌī(ə)l-'roi(-ə)l\ island Mich. in NW Lake Superior in **Isle Royale National Park** (area 209)

Is·ling·ton \'iz-liŋ-tən\ metropolitan borough N cen London, England pop 235,645

Is·ma·ilia \ˌiz-mā-ə-'lē-ə\ city NE Egypt on the Suez canal pop 115,200

Ison·zo \ē-'zón(t)-(ˌ)sō\ river 75 m NW Yugoslavia & NE Italy flowing S into Gulf of Trieste

Is·par·ta \is-(ˌ)pär-'tä\ city SW Turkey N of Antalya pop 36,201

Is·ra·el \'iz-rē-əl\ **1** ancient kingdom Palestine comprising the lands occupied by the Hebrew people; established ab 1025 B.C.; divided ab 933 B.C. into a S kingdom (Judah) & a N kingdom (Israel) **2** or **Northern Kingdom** or **Ephra·im** \'ē-frē-əm\ the N portion of the Hebrew kingdom after the division **3** country Palestine bordering on the Mediterranean; a republic since 1948 ✻ Jerusalem area 7993, pop 2,170,082 — see PALESTINE

Is·sus \'is-əs\ ancient town S Asia Minor N of modern Iskenderun, Turkey

Is·syk Kul \ˌis-ik-'kəl\ lake 115 m long U.S.S.R. in Soviet Central Asia in NE Kirgiz Republic area 2250

Is·tan·bul \ˌis-təm-'bül, -ˌtäm-, -ˌtam-, -ˌtän-\ or formerly **Con·stan·ti·no·ple** \ˌkän-ˌstant-ᵊn-'ō-pəl\ or anc **By·zan·ti·um** \bə-'zan-sh(ē-)əm, -'zant-ē-əm\ city NW Turkey on the Bosporus & Sea of Marmara; former ✻ of Turkey & of Ottoman Empire pop 1,459,528

Ister — see DANUBE

Is·tok·po·ga \ˌis-ˌtäk-'pō-gə\ lake S Fla. NW of Lake Okeechobee

Is·tria \'is-trē-ə\ peninsula NW Yugoslavia in Croatia & Slovenia projecting into the N Adriatic — **Is·tri·an** \-trē-ən\ adj or n

Italian East Africa former territory E Africa comprising Eritrea, Ethiopia, & Italian Somaliland

Italian Somaliland former country E Africa bordering on Indian ocean; an Italian colony before World War II, a U.N. trust territory under Italian administration 1950–60 ✻ Mogadishu (Mogadiscio) area 194,000 — see SOMALIA

It·a·ly \'it-ᵊl-ē\ or It **Ita·lia** \ē-'täl-yə\ or L **Ita·lia** \ə-'tal-yə, i-\ **1** peninsula 760 m long S Europe projecting into the Mediterranean between Adriatic & Tyrrhenian seas **2** country comprising the peninsula of Italy, Sicily, Sardinia, & numerous other islands; a republic since 1946, formerly a kingdom ✻ Rome area 119,764, pop 49,230,000

Itas·ca, Lake \ī-'tas-kə\ lake NW cen Minn.; source of the Mississippi

Iténez — see GUAPORÉ

Ith·a·ca \'ith-i-kə\ **1** city S cen N.Y. on Cayuga Lake pop 28,799 **2** or NGk **Ithá·ki** \ē-'thäk-ē\ island W Greece in the Ionian islands NE of Cephalonia area 36 — **Ith·a·can** \'ith-i-kən\ adj or n

Itsukushima — see MIYAJIMA

It·u·raea or **It·u·rea** \ˌich-ə-'rē-ə\ ancient country NE Palestine S of Damascus — **It·u·rae·an** or **It·u·re·an** \-'rē-ən\ adj or n

Iva·no·vo or formerly **Ivanovo Voz·ne·sensk** \i-'vän-ə-və-ˌväz-nə-'sen(t)sk\ city U.S.S.R. in cen Soviet Russia, Europe, WNW of Gorki pop 483,000

Ivi·za or Sp **Ibi·za** \ē-'vē-zə\ island Spain in the Balearics SW of Majorca area 230

Ivory Coast or **Côte d'Ivoire** \ˌkōt-dēv-'wär\ **1** region W Africa bordering on the Atlantic W of the Gold Coast **2** country W Africa including the Ivory Coast & its hinterland; a republic of the French Community since 1959, formerly a territory of French West Africa ✻ Abidjan area 127,520, pop 3,300,000 — **Ivo·ry Coast·er** \ˌīv-(ə-)'kō-stər\ n

Iwo \'ē-(ˌ)wō\ city SW Nigeria NE of Ibadan pop 100,000

Iwo Ji·ma \ˌē-(ˌ)wō-'jē-mə\ island W Pacific in the Volcano islands 660 nautical m S of Tokyo

Ix·elles \ēk-'sel\ or Flem **El·se·ne** \'el-sə-nə\ commune cen Belgium in Brabant; suburb of Brussels pop 92,657

Iza·bal \ˌē-sə-'bäl, -zə-\ lake 25 m long E Guatemala

Izal·co \i-'zal-(ˌ)kō, ē-'säl-\ volcano 6200 ft W El Salvador

Izhevsk \'ē-ˌzhefsk\ city U.S.S.R. in E Soviet Russia, Europe ✻ of Udmurt Republic pop 283,000

Iz·ma·il or Rom **Is·ma·il** \ˌiz-mā-'ē(ə)l\ city U.S.S.R. in SW Ukraine on the Danube delta pop 40,000

Iz·mir \iz-'mi(ə)r\ or **Smyr·na** \'smər-nə\ city & port W Turkey in Asia on an inlet of the Aegean pop 370,923

Iz·mit or **Iz·mid** \iz-'mit\ or anc **As·ta·cus** \'as-tə-kəs\ or **Nic·o·me·dia** \ˌnik-ə-'mēd-ē-ə\ city & port NW Turkey in Asia on **Gulf of Izmit** (E arm of Sea of Marmara) pop 73,705

Iz·nik \iz-'nik\ lake 14 m long NW Turkey in Asia S of E arm of Sea of Marmara

Iz·tac·ci·huatl or **Ix·ta·ci·huatl** \ˌēs-tä(k)-'sē-ˌwät-ᵊl\ extinct volcano 17,343 ft S Mexico N of Popocatepetl

Ja·bal·pur \'jəb-əl-ˌpù(ə)r\ or **Jub·bul·pore** \ˌjəb-əl-ˌpō(ə)r, -ˌpò(ə)r\ city cen India in cen Madhya Pradesh pop 257,000

Jack·son \'jak-sən\ **1** city S Mich. pop 50,720 **2** city ✻ of Miss. on Pearl river pop 144,422 **3** city W Tenn. pop 33,849

Jackson Hole valley NW Wyo. S of Teton range & partly in Grand Teton National Park; contains **Jackson Lake** (reservoir)

Jack·son·ville \'jak-sən-ˌvil\ **1** city NE Fla. near mouth of the St. Johns pop 201,030 **2** city W cen Ill. pop 21,690

Jacques–Car·tier \ˌzhak-(ˌ)kär-'tyā, ˌkärt-ē-'ā\ city Canada in S Que. on the St. Lawrence opposite Montreal pop 33,132

Ja·dot·ville \zha-'dō-ˌvil\ city SE Congo in SE Katanga pop 76,877

Ja·en \hä-'ān\ **1** province S Spain in N Andalusia area 5203, pop 781,285 **2** commune, its ✻ pop 66,518

Jaf·fa \'jaf-ə, 'yaf-ə\ or **Jop·pa** \'jäp-ə\ or **Ya·fo** \yä-'fō\ former city & port W Israel, since 1950 a S section of Tel Aviv

Jaff·na \'jäf-nə\ city N Ceylon on Palk strait pop 76,664

Jagannath — see PURI

Jain·tia \'jīnt-ē-ə\ hills E India in N cen Assam E of Khasi hills

Jai·pur \'jī-ˌpù(ə)r\ **1** former state NW India; now part of Rajasthan **2** city, its ✻, now ✻ of Rajasthan pop 291,000

Jakarta — see DJAKARTA

Ja·la·pa \hə-'läp-ə\ city E Mexico ✻ of Veracruz pop 51,166

Ja·lis·co \hə-'lis-(ˌ)kō\ state W cen Mexico ✻ Guadalajara area 31,149, pop 2,016,403

Jal·u·it \'jal-(y)ə-ˌwət\ island (atoll) 38 m long & 21 m wide W Pacific, largest of the Marshalls, in Ralik chain

Ja·mai·ca \jə-'mā-kə\ island West Indies in the Greater Antilles; a dominion of Brit. Commonwealth since 1962; formerly a Brit. colony & (1958–61) a territory of the West Indies Federation ✻ Kingston area 4411, pop 1,613,148 — **Ja·mai·can** \-kən\ adj or n

Jamaica Bay inlet SE N.Y. in SW Long I.

Jambi — see DJAMBI

James \'jāmz\ **1** or **Da·ko·ta** \də-'kōt-ə\ river 710 m N. & S. Dak. flowing S to the Missouri **2** river 340 m Va. flowing E into Chesapeake Bay at Hampton Roads

James Bay the S extension of Hudson Bay 280 m long & 150 m wide Canada between NE Ont. & W Que.

James·town \'jām-ˌstaùn\ **1** city SW N.Y. pop 41,818 **2** city SE cen N. Dak. on the James pop 15,163

Jam·mu \'jəm-ə-ˌü\ **1** district N India (subcontinent) S of Kashmir in valley of the upper Chenab **2** city S of Srinagar, winter ✻ of Jammu & Kashmir pop 50,400

Jammu and Kashmir — see KASHMIR

Jam·na·gar \ˌjäm-'nəg-ər\ or **Na·va·na·gar** \ˌnäv-ə-'nəg-ər\ city W India in W Gujarat on Gulf of Kutch pop 104,400

Jam·shed·pur \ˌjäm-ˌshed-ˌpù(ə)r\ city E India in S Bihar SE of Ranchi pop 218,200

Ja·mu·na \'jəm-ə-nə\ the lower Brahmaputra

Janes·ville \'jānz-ˌvil\ city S Wis. SE of Madison pop 35,164

Ja·nic·u·lum \jə-'nik-yə-ləm\ hill in Rome, Italy, on right bank of the Tiber opposite the Seven Hills — see AVENTINE

Jan Ma·yen \yän-'mī-ən\ island in Arctic ocean E of Greenland & NNE of Iceland belonging to Norway area 147

Ja·pan \jə-'pan, ji-, ja-\ or Jap **Nip·pon** \nip-'än\ or **Ni·hon** \'nē-'hòn\ country E Asia comprising Honshu, Hokkaido, Kyushu, Shikoku, & other islands in the W Pacific; an empire ✻ Tokyo area 146,690, pop 93,418,501

Japan, Sea of arm of the Pacific between Japan on E & Asian mainland on W

Ja·pu·rá \ˌzhäp-ə-'rä\ river 1750 m S Colombia & NW Brazil flowing SE into the Amazon

Jar·vis \'jär-vəs\ island cen Pacific in the Line islands; occupied by the U.S.

Jas·per National Park \'jas-pər\ reservation W Canada in W Alta. on E slopes of the Rockies NE of & adjoining Banff National Park area 4200

Jasper Place town Canada in cen Alta., W suburb of Edmonton pop 15,957

Jassy — see IASI

Ja·va \'jäv-ə, 'jav-ə\ or Indonesian **Dja·wa, 1** island Indonesia SE of Sumatra; chief city Djakarta area 48,830, pop (including Madura) 56,800,000 **2** sea arm of the Pacific bounded on S by Java, on W by Sumatra, on N by Borneo, & on E by Celebes

Java Head cape Indonesia at W end of Java on Sunda strait

Ja·va·rí \ˌzhäv-ə-'rē\ or **Ya·ca·ra·na** \ˌyäk-ə-'rän-ə\ river 650 m Peru & Brazil flowing NE on the boundary & into the Amazon

Jaxartes — see SYR DARYA

Jean·nette \jə-'net\ city SW Pa. ESE of Pittsburgh pop 16,565

Jebel, Bahr el — see BAHR EL GHAZAL

Je·bel ed Druz \ˌjeb-ə-led-'drüz\ or **Jebel Druz** region S Syria E of Sea of Galilee on border of Jordan; formerly (1921–42) an autonomous state of Syria ✻ Es Suweida area 2700

Jebel Musa — see MUSA (Jebel)

Jed·burgh \'jed-b(ə-)rə\ burgh SE Scotland ✻ of Roxburgh

Jef·fer·son \'jef-ər-sən\ river 250 m SW Mont. — see THREE FORKS

Jefferson, Mount mountain 10,495 ft NW Oreg. in Cascades

Jefferson City city ✻ of Mo. on the Missouri pop 28,228

Jefferson Heights urban area SE La. pop 19,353

Jef·fer·son·ville \'jef-ər-sən-ˌvil\ city S Ind. pop 19,522

Je·hol \'rə-'hōl, 'rō-'hò\ **1** former province NE China ✻ Chengteh; divided 1955 among Hopei, Liaoning, & Inner Mongolia **2** — see CHENGTEH

Je·mappes \zhə-'map\ commune SW Belgium W of Mons

Je·na \'yā-nə\ city E Germany on the Saale E of Erfurt pop 83,100

Jen·nings \'jen-iŋz\ city E Mo., N suburb of St. Louis pop 19,965

Je·qui·ti·nho·nha \ˌzhə-ˌkēt-ən-'yōn-yə\ river 500 m E Brazil flowing NE into the Atlantic

Jerba — see DJERBA

Je·rez \hə-'rās\ or **Je·rez de la Fron·te·ra** \hə-'rez-də-lə-ˌfrən-'ter-ə\ or formerly **Xe·res** \'sher-ēz\ city SW Spain NE of Cádiz pop 124,600

Jer·i·cho \'jer-i-ˌkō\ **1** or Ar **Eri·ha** \ə-'rē-ə\ city W Jordan 5 m N of Dead sea pop 41,593 **2** ancient Palestinian city near site of modern Jericho

Jer·sey \'jər-zē\ **1** island English channel in the Channel islands ✻ St. Helier area 45 **2** NEW JERSEY — **Jer·sey·an** \-ən\ n — **Jer·sey·ite** \-ˌīt\ n

Jersey City city & port NE N.J. pop 276,101

Je·ru·sa·lem \jə-'rü-s(ə-)ləm, -'rüz-(ə-)ləm\ or anc **Hi·er·o·sol·y·ma** \ˌhī-ə-rō-'säl-ə-mə\ city cen Palestine NW of Dead sea; divided since 1948 between Jordan (old city) & Israel (new city) ✻ of Israel since 1950 & formerly ✻ of ancient kingdoms of Israel & Judah pop 183,000

Jer·vis Bay \ˌjär-vəs\ inlet of the Pacific SE Australia on SE coast of New So. Wales on which is situated district (area 28) that is part of Australian Capital Territory

Jes·sel·ton \'jes-əl-tən\ or now **Ko·ta Kin·a·ba·lu** \'kōt-ə-ˌkin-ə-bə-'lü\ town & port Malaysia ✻ of Sabah (No. Borneo)

Jewel Cave National Monument limestone cave SW S. Dak.

Jewish Autonomous Region or **Bi·ro·bi·dzhan** \ˌbir-ō-bi-'jän\

---

autonomous region U.S.S.R. in E Soviet Russia, Asia, bordering on the Amur ✱ Birobidzhan *area* 14,085, *pop* 198,400

Jezira — see GEZIRA

Jez·re·el \'jez-rē-,el, -,rē(ə)l\ ancient town *cen* Palestine in Samaria NW of Mt. Gilboa in Valley of Jezreel

Jezreel, Plain of the Plain of Esdraelon

Jezreel, Valley of the E end of the Plain of Esdraelon

Jhan·si \'jän(t)-sē\ city N India in S Uttar Pradesh SW of Kanpur *pop* 127,400

Jhe·lum \'jā-ləm\ *or anc* **Hy·das·pes** \hī-'das-(,)pēz\ river 450 *m* NW India (subcontinent) flowing from Kashmir S & SW into the Chenab

Jibuti — see DJIBOUTI

Jid·da \'jid-ə\ *or* **Jed·da** \'jed-ə\ city & port W Saudi Arabia in Hejaz on Red sea; port for Mecca *pop* 100,000

Jin·ja \'jin-jə\ city & port SE Uganda on Lake Victoria *pop* 30,000

Jinsen — see INCHON

João Pes·soa \,zhwaů^n(m)-pə-'sō-ə\ *or formerly* **Pa·ra·í·ba** \,par-ə-'ē-bə\ city NE Brazil ✱ of Paraíba *pop* 141,057

Jodh·pur \'jäd-pər, -,pů(ə)r\ **1** *or* **Mar·war** \'mär-,wär\ former state NW India bordering on Thar desert & Rann of Kutch; since 1949 part of Rajasthan state **2** city, its *pop* 180,700

Jod·rell Bank \,jäd-rəl-\ locality W England in NE Cheshire near Macclesfield

Jogjakarta — see DJOKJAKARTA

Jo·han·nes·burg \jō-'han-əs-,bərg, -'hän-\ city NE Republic of So. Africa in S Transvaal in *cen* Witwatersrand *pop* 884,007 — **Jo·han·nes·burg·er** \-,bər-gər\ *n*

John Day \'jän-'dā\ river 281 *m* N Oreg. flowing W & N into the Columbia

John o' Groat's \,jän-ə-'grōts\ *or* **John o' Groat's House** locality N Scotland on N coast in Caithness; popularly considered the northernmost point of mainland of Scotland & Great Britain — see DUNNET HEAD

John·son City \,jän(t)-sən-\ **1** village N N.Y. NW of Binghamton *pop* 19,118 **2** city NE Tenn. *pop* 29,892

John·ston \'jän(t)-stən, -sən\ island (atoll) *cen* Pacific 700 *m* SW of Honolulu, Hawaii; belongs to the U.S.

Johns·town \'jän-,staůn\ city SW *cen* Pa. *pop* 53,949

Jo·hore \jə-'hō(ə)r, -'hö(ə)r\ state S Federation of Malaysia at S end of Malay peninsula ✱ Johore Bahru *area* 7321, *pop* 927,565

Johore Bah·ru \-'bär-(,)ü\ city S Federation of Malaysia ✱ of Johore on an inlet opposite Singapore I. *pop* 74,495

Join·vi·le *or formerly* **Join·vil·le** \zhoin-'vē-lē\ city S Brazil N NW of Florianópolis *pop* 20,951

Jo·li·et \,jō-lē-'et, *chiefly by outsiders* ,jäl-ē-\ city NE Ill. SW of Chicago *pop* 66,780

Jo·liette \,zhô-lē-'et\ city Canada in S Que. N of Montreal *pop* 16,940

Jo·lo \'hō-(,)lō\ *or* **Su·lu** \'sü-(,)lü\ island S Philippines, chief island of Sulu archipelago *area* 345

Jones·boro \'jōnz-,bər-ə, -,bə-rə\ city N E Ark. *pop* 21,418

Jön·kö·ping \'yə(r)n-,chə(r)p-iŋ\ city S Sweden at S end of Lake Vatter *pop* 50,941

Jon·quière \,zhō^n-kē-'e(ə)r\ city Canada in S *cen* Que. *pop* 25,550

Joplin \'jäp-lən\ city SW Mo. *pop* 38,958

Joppa — see JAFFA

Jor·dan \'jord-ən\ **1** river 45 *m*, *cen* Utah flowing from Utah Lake N into Great Salt Lake **2** river 200 *m* NE Palestine flowing from Anti-Lebanon mountains S through Sea of Galilee into Dead sea **3** *or* **Trans·jor·dan** \(')tran(t)s-, (')tranz-\ *or officially* **Hash·im·ite Kingdom of Jordan** \'hash-ə-,mīt\ country SW Asia in NW Arabia ✱ Amman *area* 39,460, *pop* 1,600,000 — **Jor·da·ni·an** \jòr-'dā-nē-ən, -'dan-ē-\ *adj or n*

Josh·ua Tree National Monument \'jäsh-(ə-)wə\ reservation S Calif. N of Salton sea containing unusual desert flora *area* 1025

Jo·tun·heim \'yōt-ůn-,hām\ *or* **Jo·tun·hei·men** \-,hā-mən\ mountains S *cen* Norway — see GALDHÖPIGGEN

Juan de Fu·ca \,(h)wän-də-'fyü-kə\ strait 100 *m* long between Vancouver I., B.C., & Olympic peninsula, Wash.

Juan Fer·nán·dez \,(h)wän-fər-'nan-dəs\ group of three islands SE Pacific 400 *m* W of Chile; belongs to Chile *area* 70

Juan-les-Pins \zhwä^n-lā-'pa^n\ town SE France on Cap d'Antibes

Juárez — see CIUDAD JUÁREZ

Ju·ba \'jü-bə\ river 1000 *m* E Africa flowing from S Ethiopia S through Somalia into Indian ocean

Jubbulpore — see JABALPUR

Juby, Cape — see YUBI (Cape)

Jú·car \'hü-,kär\ river 300 *m* E Spain flowing S & E into the Mediterranean S of Valencia

Ju·dah \'jüd-ə\ ancient kingdom S Palestine ✱ Jerusalem — see ISRAEL

Ju·dea *or* **Ju·daea** \jù-'dē-ə\ ancient region Palestine constituting the S division (Judah) of the country under Persian, Greek, & Roman rule — **Ju·de·an** *or* **Ju·dae·an** \-'dē-ən\ *adj or n*

Juggernaut — see PURI

Jugoslavia — see YUGOSLAVIA — **Jugoslav** *or* **Jugoslavian** *adj or n*

Juiz de Fo·ra \zha-,wēzh-də-'fòr-ə, -'fòr-\ city E Brazil in S Minas Gerais *pop* 84,995

Ju·juy \hü-'hwē\ city NW Argentina N of Tucumán *pop* 31,091

Ju·lian Alps \,jül-yən\ section of E Alps NW Yugoslavia N of Istrian peninsula; highest peak Triglav 9393 *ft*

Julian Venetia — see VENEZIA GIULIA

Jul·lun·dur \'jəl-ən-dər\ city NW India in Punjab *pop* 168,800

Jum·na \'jəm-nə\ river 860 *m* N India in Uttar Pradesh flowing from the Himalayas S & SE into the Ganges

Junc·tion City \,jəŋ(k)-shən-\ city N E *cen* Kans. *pop* 18,700

Ju·neau \'jü-(,)nō\ city & port ✱ of Alaska in SE coastal strip *pop* 6,797

Jung·frau \'yůŋ-,fraů\ mountain 13,642 *ft* SW *cen* Switzerland in Bernese Alps between Bern & Valais cantons

Ju·ni·ata \,jü-nē-'at-ə\ river 150 *m* S *cen* Pa. flowing E into the Susquehanna

Ju·nín \hü-'nēn\ **1** city N Argentina 150 *m* W of Buenos Aires *pop* 36,149 **2** town *cen* Peru at S end of Lake Junín (25 *m* long)

Ju·ra \'jůr-ə\ **1** mountains France & Switzerland extending 200 *m* along the boundary; highest Crêt de la Neige 5652 *ft* **2** island 24 *m* long W Scotland in the Inner Hebrides W of Mull

Juramento — see SALADO

Ju·ruá \,zhůr-(ə-)'wä\ river 1200 *m* NW cen So. America flowing

from E *cen* Peru NE into the Solimões in NW Brazil

Ju·rue·na \,zhůr-(ə-)'wä-nə\ river 600 *m* W *cen* Brazil flowing N to unite with the São Manuel forming the Tapajoz

Jut·land \'jət-lənd\ *or* Dan **Jyl·land** \'yüe-,län\ **1** peninsula N Europe projecting into North sea & comprising mainland of Denmark & N portion of Schleswig-Holstein, Germany **2** the mainland of Denmark

Kaapland — see CAPE OF GOOD HOPE

Kaapstad — see CAPE TOWN

Kab·ar·din·i·an \,kab-ər-,din-ē-ən-\ *or* **Kab·ar·di·no-Bal·kar·i·an Republic** \,kab-ər-'dē-(,)nō-,bòl-'kar-ē-ən-, -,bal-, -'ker-\ *or* **Kabardino-Bal·kar Republic** \-'bòl-,kär, -'bal-\ autonomous republic U.S.S.R. in S Soviet Russia, Europe, on N slopes of the Caucasus ✱ Nalchik *area* 4600, *pop* 420,000 — **Kab·ardinian** *adj or n*

Ka·bul \'käb-əl, kə-'bül\ **1** river 360 *m* Afghanistan & W Pakistan flowing E into the Indus **2** city ✱ of Afghanistan on Kabul river *pop* 206,200 — **Ka·bu·li** \kä-'bü-,lē, kə-'bü-lē\ *adj or n*

Ka·by·lia \kə-'bī-lē-ə, -'bil-ē-\ mountainous region N Algeria on coast E of Algiers; comprises two areas: **Great Kabylia** (to W) & **Little Kabylia** (to E)

Ka·chin \kə-'chin\ state N Burma between China & India

Ka·desh-bar·nea \,kā-,desh-'bär-nē-ə\ ancient town S Palestine SW of Dead sea; exact location uncertain

Kadiak — see KODIAK

Ka·di·koy \,käd-i-'kòi\ *or anc* **Chal·ce·don** \'kal-sə-,dän, kal-'sēd-ən\ former city NW Turkey in Asia on the Bosporus; now a district of Istanbul

Ka·di·yev·ka *or* **Ka·di·ev·ka** \kə-'dē-(y)əf-kə\ city U.S.S.R. in E Ukraine in Donets basin *pop* 180,000

Kae·song \'kā-,sòŋ\ *or* Jap **Kai·jo** \'kī-(,)jō\ city S Korea NW of Seoul *pop* 88,708

Kaf·frar·ia \kə-'frar-ē-ə, ka-, -'frer-\ region Republic of So. Africa in E Cape Province S of Natal & bordering on Indian ocean

Kafiristan — see NURISTAN

Ka·fue \kə-'fü-ē\ river 500 *m* Zambia flowing into the Zambezi

Ka·ge·ra \kə-'ger-ə\ river 430 *m* Burundi, Rwanda, & NW Tanganyika flowing N & E into Lake Victoria on Uganda border

Ka·go·shi·ma \,käg-ə-'shē-mə, kä-'gō-shə-\ city & port S Japan in S Kyushu on **Kagoshima Bay** (inlet of the Pacific) *pop* 274,340

Ka·hoo·la·we \kä-hō-'lä-vē, -wē\ island Hawaii SW of Maui *area* 45

Kai·bab \'kī-,bab\ plateau N Ariz. N of Grand Canyon

Kai·e·teur Falls \,kī-ə-'tù(ə)r-\ waterfall 741 *ft* high & 350 *ft* wide *cen* Guyana in Potaro river

Kai·feng \'kī-'fəŋ\ city E *cen* China in NE Honan *pop* 299,100

Kai·lua \kī-'lü-ə\ urban area Hawaii on Oahu NE of Honolulu *pop* (with Lanikai) 25,622

Kair·ouan \ker-'wän\ *or* **Kair·wan** \kī(ə)r-'wän\ city NE Tunisia *pop* 32,299

Kai·sers·lau·tern \,kī-zerz-'laůt-ərn\ city W Germany W of Ludwigshafen *pop* 88,200

Kaishu — see HAEJU

Ka·ki·na·da *or* **Coc·a·na·da** \,käk-ə-'näd-ə\ city & port E India in NE Andhra Pradesh on Bay of Bengal *pop* 100,000

Ka Lae \kä-'lä-ā\ *or* **South Cape** *or* **South Point** headland Hawaii, southernmost point of Hawaii I.

Kalaeloa Point — see BARBERS POINT

Kal·a·ha·ri \,kal-ə-'här-ē\ desert region S Africa N of Orange river & S of Lake Ngami in Bechuanaland Protectorate & NW Republic of So. Africa

Ka·lakh \'käl-,äk\ *or* Bib **Ca·lah** \'kā-lə\ ancient city ✱ of Assyria on the Tigris 20 *m* SW of modern Mosul; its site now called **Nim·rud** \nim-'rüd\

Ka·la·ma·ta \,kal-ə-'mät-ə\ *or* NGk **Ka·lá·mai** \kə-'läm-ē\ city & port S Greece in SW Peloponnesus *pop* 38,663

Kal·a·ma·zoo \,kal-ə-mə-'zü\ city SW Mich. *pop* 82,089

Ka·lat *or* **Khe·lat** \kə-'lät\ region NW West Pakistan including S & *cen* Baluchistan; a former princely state ✱ Kalat

Kal·gan \'kal-'gan\ *or* **Chang·kia·kow** \'jäŋ-jē-'ä-'kō\ city NE China in NW Hopei NW of Peking *pop* 229,300

Kal·goor·lie \kal-'gů(ə)r-lē\ city Australia in S *cen* Western Australia *pop* (with suburbs) 23,000

Ka·li·man·tan \,kal-ə-'man-,tan, ,käl-ə-'män-,tän\ **1** BORNEO — its Indonesian name **2** the S & E part of Borneo belonging to Indonesia; formerly (as **Dutch Borneo**) part of Netherlands Indies

Ka·li·nin \kə-'lē-nən\ *or formerly* **Tver** \tə-'ve(ə)r\ city U.S.S.R. in W *cen* Soviet Russia, Europe, on the Volga *pop* 261,000

Ka·li·nin·grad \kə-'lē-nən-,grad\ *or* G **Kö·nigs·berg** \'kā-nigz-,bərg, 'kö(r)n-igz-, -,be(ə)rg, -,be(ə)rk\ city & port U.S.S.R. in W Soviet Russia, Europe, near the Frisches Haff; formerly ✱ of East Prussia *pop* 202,000

Ka·lisz \'käl-ēsh\ commune *cen* Poland W of Lodz *pop* 66,100

Kal·mar \'käl-,mär, 'kal-\ city & port SE Sweden *pop* 31,425

Kal·myk Republic \(,)kal-,mik-\ autonomous republic of the U.S.S.R. in S Soviet Russia, Europe, on NW shore of Caspian sea W of the Volga ✱ Elista *area* 29,417 *pop* 185,000

Ka·lu·ga \kə-'lü-gə\ city U.S.S.R. in W *cen* Soviet Russia, Europe, on the Oka WNW of Tula *pop* 133,000

Ka·ma \'käm-ə\ river 1200 *m* U.S.S.R. in E Soviet Russia, Europe, flowing SW into the Volga S of Kazan

Ka·ma·ku·ra \,käm-ə-'kůr-ə, ,kam-\ city Japan in SE Honshu on Sagami sea S of Yokohama *pop* 91,328

Kam·chat·ka \kam-'chat-kə\ peninsula 750 *m* long U.S.S.R. in NE Soviet Russia, Asia, projecting into the Pacific between Sea of Okhotsk & Bering sea

Ka·met \'kəm-,āt\ mountain 25,447 *ft* N India in Uttar Pradesh in the NW Himalayas

Kam·pa·la \käm-'päl-ə\ city ✱ of Uganda in Buganda N of Entebbe *pop* 22,094

Kan, 1 \'kän\ river 350 *m* SE China in Kiangsi flowing N through Poyang Lake into the Yangtze **2** \'kän\ — see HAN

Kananur — see CANNANORE

Ka·na·wha \kə-'nó-(ə), -'nòi\ river 97 *m* W W. Va. flowing NW into the Ohio

Ka·na·za·wa \kə-'näz-ə-wə, ,kan-ə-'zä-wə\ city & port Japan in W *cen* Honshu near Sea of Japan *pop* 277,283

Kan·chen·jun·ga \ˌkan-chən-ˈjən-gə, -ˈjùn-\ or **Kang·chen·jun·ga** \ˌkaŋ-chen-\ or **Kin·chin·jun·ga** \ˌkin-chən-\ mountain 28,146 ft Nepal & Sikkim in the Himalayas; 3d highest in world

Kan·chi·pu·ram \ˈkän-ˈchē-pə-rəm\ or **Con·jee·ve·ram** \-ˈjē-və-rəm\ city SE India in N Madras state SW of Madras pop 84,800

Kan·da·har \ˈkan-də-ˌhär\ city SE Afghanistan pop 77,186

Kand·la \ˈkən-dlə\ town & port W India in Gujarat near E end of Gulf of Kutch

Kan·dy \ˈkan-dē\ city W cen Ceylon ENE of Colombo pop 57,000

Kane Basin \ˈkān\ section of the channel between NW Greenland & Ellesmere I. N of Baffin Bay

Ka·ne·o·he Bay \ˌkän-ē-ˌō-ē-\ inlet of the Pacific Hawaii on E coast of Oahu I.

Kan·i·a·pis·kau \ˌkan-ē-ə-ˈpis-(ˌ)kō\ river 575 m Canada in N Que. flowing N to unite with the Larch forming the **Kok·so·ak** \ˈkäk-sə-ˌwak\ river (85 m flowing into Ungava Bay)

Kan·ka·kee \ˌkaŋ-kə-ˈkē\ 1 river 225 m Ind. & Ill. flowing SW & W to unite with the Des Plaines forming the Illinois 2 city NE Ill. on the Kankakee pop 27,666

Kanko — see HAMHUNG

Kan·nap·o·lis \kə-ˈnap-(ə-)ləs\ urban area S cen N.C. NE of Charlotte pop 34,647

Ka·no \ˈkän-(ˌ)ō\ city N cen Nigeria pop 130,000

Ka·noya \kə-ˈnòi-ə\ city Japan in S Kyushu pop 75,488

Kan·pur \ˈkän-ˌpu̇(ə)r\ or **Cawn·pore** \ˈkȯn-ˌpō(ə)r, -ˌpȯ(ə)r\ city N India in S Uttar Pradesh on the Ganges pop 705,400

Kan·sas \ˈkan-zəs also ˈkan(t)-səs\ 1 or **Kaw** \ˈkȯ\ river 169 m E Kans. flowing E into the Missouri 2 state cen U.S. ✻ Topeka area 82,276, pop 2,178,611 — **Kan·san** \ˈkan-zən also ˈkan(t)-sən\ adj or n

Kansas City \ˌkan-zə(s)-ˈsit-ē\ 1 city NE Kans. adjacent to Kansas City, Mo. pop 121,901 2 city W Mo. pop 475,539

Kan·su \ˈkan-ˈsü, ˈgän-\ province N cen China ✻ Lanchow area 137,104, pop 11,106,000

Kanto Plain — see KWANTO PLAIN

Kaoh·siung \ˈkaủ-shē-ˈủŋ, ˈgaủ-\ city & port China in SW Formosa pop 275,000

Kaolan — see LANCHOW

Ka·pi·da·gi \ˌkäp-ē-dä-ˈ(g)ē\ or anc **Cyz·i·cus** \ˈsiz-i-kəs\ peninsula NW Turkey in Asia projecting into Sea of Marmara

Ka·ra, 1 \ˈkär-ə\ sea arm of Arctic ocean off coast of N U.S.S.R. E of Novaya Zemlya 2 — see MESTA

Ka·ra·chi \kə-ˈräch-ē\ city & port Pakistan in S West Pakistan on an arm of Arabian sea NW of mouths of the Indus pop 1,409,138

Karafuto — see SAKHALIN

Ka·ra·gan·da \ˌkar-ə-gən-ˈdä\ city U.S.S.R. in cen Kazakh Republic pop 398,000

Ka·ra-Kal·pak Republic \ˌkar-ə-ˌkal-ˈpak\ autonomous republic U.S.S.R. in NW Uzbek Republic SE of Lake Aral ✻ Nukus area 61,600, pop 510,000

Kar·a·ko·ram or **Kar·a·ko·rum** \ˌkar-ə-ˈkōr-əm, -ˈkȯr-\ mountain system S cen Asia in N Kashmir & NW Tibet on Sinkiang border; westernmost system of the Himalaya complex, connecting the Himalayas with the Pamirs — see GODWIN AUSTEN

Karakoram Pass or **Karakorum Pass** mountain pass 18,290 ft NE Kashmir through Karakoram range

Kar·a·ko·rum \-əm\ ruined city Outer Mongolia on the upper Orkhon ✻ of Mongol Empire

Ka·ra Kum \ˌkar-ə-ˈküm\ desert U.S.S.R. in Soviet Central Asia in Turkmen Republic S of Lake Aral extending from Caspian sea to the Amu Darya area 110,000

Karashahr — see QARA SHAHR

Ka·ra Su \ˌkar-ə-ˈsü\ the Euphrates above its junction with the Murat in E cen Turkey

Kar·ba·la \ˈkär-bə-lə\ or **Ker·be·la** \ˈkər-bə-lə\ city cen Iraq SSW of Baghdad pop 44,600

Ka·re·lia or **Ca·re·lia** \kə-ˈrē-lē-ə, -ˈrēl-yə\ 1 region NE Europe between Gulf of Finland & White sea in the U.S.S.R. & Finland 2 or **Ka·re·lian Republic** \-ˌrē-lē-ən, -ˌrēl-yən-\ autonomous republic U.S.S.R. in NW Soviet Russia, Europe, in Karelia region; formerly (1940–56), as the **Ka·re·lo-Finnish Republic** \kə-ˌrē-(ˌ)lō-\, a constituent republic of the U.S.S.R. ✻ Petrozavodsk area 68,900, pop 651,000

Ka·re·lian \-ˌrē-lē-ən-, -ˌrēl-yən-\ isthmus NW U.S.S.R. in Karelia between Gulf of Finland & Lake Ladoga

Ka·ren \kə-ˈren\ state S Burma bordering on Andaman sea

Karenni — see KAYAH

Ka·ri·ba \kə-ˈrē-bə\ lake 165 m long SE Zambia & N Southern Rhodesia formed in the Zambezi by **Kariba Dam**

Ka·ri·kal \ˌkar-ə-ˈkäl\ 1 territory of former French India S of Pondicherry; incorporated 1954 in India area 52 2 city & port, its ✻, on Bay of Bengal pop 24,600

Kar·kheh or **Ker·kheh** \kär-ˈkā\ or anc **Cho·as·pes** \kō-ˈas-(ˌ)pēz\ river 340 m flowing from W Iran S & W into marshlands E of the Tigris in SE Iraq

Karl-Marx-Stadt — see CHEMNITZ

Kar·lov·ci Srem·ski \ˈkär-lȯv-tsē-ˈsrem(p)-skē\ or G **Kar·lo·witz** \ˈkär-lə-ˌvits\ town NE Yugoslavia in N Serbia

Kar·lo·vy Va·ry \ˌkär-lə-vē-ˈvär-ē\ or G **Karls·bad** or E **Carls·bad** \ˈkär(ə)lz-ˌbad, -ˌbät\ city NW Czechoslovakia in NW Bohemia NNW of Plzen pop 30,915

Karls·kro·na \kärl-ˈskrü-nə\ city & port SE Sweden on Baltic sea pop 33,227

Karls·ru·he \ˈkärlz-ˌrü-ə\ city W Germany in Baden-Württemberg on the Rhine pop 237,100 — **Karls·ru·her** \-ˌrü-ər\ n

Karl·stad \ˈkär(ə)l-ˌstä(d)\ city SW Sweden pop 43,618

Kar·nak \ˈkär-ˌnak\ town E Egypt on the Nile N of Luxor on N part of site of ancient Thebes

Kár·pa·thos or **Car·pa·thos** \ˈkär-pə-ˌthäs\ or It **Scar·pan·to** \ˈskär-pən-ˌtō\ island Greece in the S Dodecanese area 118

Kar·roo or **Ka·roo** \kə-ˈrü\ plateau region W Republic of So. Africa W of Drakensberg mountains divided into **Little,** or **Southern, Karroo** (in S Cape Province); **Great,** or **Central, Karroo** (in S Cape Province); and **Northern,** or **Upper, Karroo** (in N Cape Province, Orange Free State, & W Transvaal)

Kars \ˈkärz, ˈkärs\ city NE Turkey pop 20,524

Karst — see KRAS

Ka·run \kə-ˈrün\ river 450 m W Iran flowing into Shatt-al-Arab

Ka·sai \kə-ˈsī\ 1 river 1200 m N Angola & W Congo flowing N & W into the Congo 2 region S cen Congo

Ka·shan \kə-ˈshän\ city cen Iran N of Isfahan pop 44,994

Kash·gar \ˈkash-ˌgär\ city W China in SW Sinkiang at oasis on Kashgar river pop 91,000

Kashgaria — see CHINESE TURKESTAN

Kash·mir \ˈkash-ˌmi(ə)r, ˈkazh-, kash-ˈ, kazh-ˈ\ or formerly **Cashmere,** 1 mountain region N India (subcontinent) W of Tibet & SW of Sinkiang; includes valley (**Vale of Kashmir**) watered by Jhelum & Kishenganga rivers 2 or **Jam·mu and Kashmir** \ˈjəm-(ˌ)ü\ state including Kashmir region & Jammu (to the S); claimed by India & Pakistan; summer ✻ Srinagar, winter ✻ Jammu area 92,780, pop 4,410,000 — **Kash·mir·i·an** \kash-ˈmir-ē-ən, kazh-\ adj or n

Kas·kas·kia \kə-ˈskas-kē-ə\ river 300 m SW Ill. flowing SW into the Mississippi

Kas·sa·la \ˈkas-ə-lə\ city NE Sudan pop 35,621

Kas·sel or **Cas·sel** \ˈkas-əl, ˈkäs-\ city W Germany WNW of Erfurt pop 204,400

Kas·ser·ine Pass \ˌkas-ə-ˌrēn\ mountain pass cen Tunisia

Ka·stel·lór·i·zon \ˌkäs-tə-ˈlȯr-ə-ˌzän\ or It **Ca·stel·lo·ri·zo** \ˌkäs-tə-ˈlȯr-ə-ˌzō\ or **Cas·tel·ros·so** \ˌkäs-tel-ˈrȯs-(ˌ)ō\ island Greece in the E Dodecanese off SW coast of Turkey area 4

Kastro — see MYTILENE

Ká·stron \ˈkäs-ˌtrȯn\ 1 town Greece on Lemnos 2 — see CHIOS

Kastrop-Rauxel — see CASTROP-RAUXEL

Ka·tah·din, Mount \kə-ˈtäd-ᵊn\ mountain 5268 ft N cen Me.; highest point in state

Ka·tan·ga \kə-ˈtäŋ-gə, -ˈtaŋ-\ region SE Congo; chief city Lubumbashi — **Ka·tan·gan** \-gən\ or **Ka·tan·gese** \kə-ˌtäŋ-ˈgēz, -ˌtaŋ-, -ˈgēs\ adj or n

Katar — see QATAR

Kath·er·i·na, Ge·bel \ˌjeb-əl-ˌkath-ə-ˈrē-nə\ or **Mount Kath·er·ine** \ˈkath-(ə-)rən\ mountain 8652 ft NE Egypt on Sinai peninsula; highest in the Gebel Musa

Ka·thi·a·war \ˌkät-ē-ə-ˈwär\ peninsula W India in Gujarat between Gulf of Kutch & Gulf of Cambay

Kat·mai, Mount \ˈkat-ˌmī\ volcano 6715 ft S Alaska in Aleutian range at NE end of Alaska peninsula

Katmai National Monument reservation S Alaska including Mt. Katmai & Valley of Ten Thousand Smokes area 4215

Kat·man·du or **Kath·man·du** or **Khat·man·du** \ˌkat-man-ˈdü, -mən-\ city ✻ of Nepal pop 195,300

Ka·to·wi·ce \ˌkät-ə-ˈvēt-sə\ city S Poland in Silesia WNW of Krakow pop 206,500

Kat·rine, Loch \ˈka-trən\ lake 9 m long cen Scotland in SW Perthshire E of Loch Lomond

Kat·te·gat \ˈkat-i-ˌgat\ arm of North sea between Sweden & Jutland peninsula of Denmark

Kau·ai \ˈkaủ-ˌī\ island Hawaii WNW of Oahu area 551, pop 27,922

Kau·nas \ˈkaủ-nəs, -ˌnäs\ or Russ **Kov·no** \ˈkȯv-(ˌ)nō\ city U.S.S.R. in cen Lithuania on Neman river; a former (1918–40) ✻ of Lithuania pop 214,000

Ka·vál·la \kə-ˈval-ə\ city & port NE Greece in Macedonia on coast pop 42,250

Kaveri — see CAUVERY

Kaw — see KANSAS

Ka·wa·gu·chi \ˌkä-wə-ˈgü-chē\ city Japan in E Honshu N of Tokyo pop 130,599

Ka·war·tha Lakes \kə-ˌwȯr-thə-\ group of lakes Canada in SE Ont. E of Lake Simcoe; traversed by Trent canal system

Ka·wa·sa·ki \ˌkä-wə-ˈsäk-ē\ city Japan in E Honshu on Tokyo Bay, S suburb of Tokyo pop 632,975

Ka·yah \ˈkī-ə\ or formerly **Ka·ren·ni** \kə-ˈren-ē\ state S Burma

Kay·se·ri \ˌkī-zə-ˈrē\ or anc **Cae·sa·rea** \ˌsē-zə-ˈrē-ə, ˌsez-ə-, ˌses-ə-\ or **Maz·a·ca** \ˈmaz-ə-kə\ or **Caesarea Mazaca** city cen Turkey in Asia at foot of Erciyas Dagi; chief city of ancient Cappadocia pop 102,795

Ka·zakh·stan or **Ka·zak·stan** \kə-ˌzak-ˈstan; kə-ˌzäk-ˈstän, kä-\ or **Ka·zakh Republic** \kə-ˌzak-, -ˌzäk-\ constituent republic of the U.S.S.R. in Soviet Central Asia extending from Caspian sea to Altai mountains ✻ Alma-Ata area 1,047,930, pop 9,800,000

Ka·zan, 1 \kə-ˈzan\ river 455 m Canada flowing through a series of lakes into Baker Lake 2 \kə-ˈzan, -ˈzän-(yə)\ city U.S.S.R. in E Soviet Russia, Europe ✻ of Tatar Republic pop 643,000

Kazan Retto — see VOLCANO ISLANDS

Kaz·bek or **Kas·bek** \käz-ˈbek\ mountain 16,541 ft U.S.S.R. in S Soviet Russia, Europe, in cen Caucasus mountains

Kaz Dagi — see IDA

Kaz·vin or **Qaz·vin** \kaz-ˈvēn\ city NW Iran S of Elburz mountains & NW of Tehran pop 66,386

Ke·a·la·ke·kua Bay \ˌkā-ˌäl-ə-kə-ˌkü-ə-\ inlet of the Pacific Hawaii in W Hawaii I. on Kona coast W of Mauna Loa

Kearns \ˈkərnz\ urban area N Utah pop 17,172

Kear·ny \ˈkär-nē\ town NE N.J. N of Newark pop 37,472

Kear·sarge, Mount \ˈki(ə)r-ˌsärj\ mountain 2937 ft S cen N.H.

Kecs·ke·met \ˈkech-kə-ˌmāt\ city cen Hungary pop 39,000

Ked·ah \ˈked-ə\ state Federation of Malaysia in N Malaya bordering on Strait of Malacca ✻ Alor Star area 3660, pop 701,643

Kedron — see KIDRON

Keeling — see COCOS

Kee·lung \ˈkē-ˈlùŋ\ city & port China in N Formosa pop 145,405

Keene \ˈkēn\ city SW N.H. pop 17,562

Kee·wa·tin \kē-ˈwāt-ᵊn\ district Canada in E Northwest Territories N of Manitoba & Ontario & including Hudson Bay area 218,460

Kefallinía — see CEPHALONIA

Kef·la·vík \ˈkyep-lə-ˌvēk\ town SW Iceland WSW of Reykjavík

Keigh·ley \ˈkēth-lē\ municipal borough N England in West Riding, Yorkshire, NW of Leeds pop 56,938

Keijo — see SEOUL

Ke·lan·tan \kə-ˈlan-ˌtan\ state Federation of Malaysia in N Malaya on So. China sea ✻ Kota Bharu area 5746, pop 505,585

Kel·er·wand \ˈkel-ər-ˌvänt\ or **Mon·te Co·glians** \ˌmȯnt-ē-kōl-ˈyän(t)s\ mountain 9217 ft on Austria-Italy border; highest in the Carnic Alps

Keltsy — see KIELCE

Ke·me·ro·vo \'kem-ə-rə-və, -ˌrō-və, -rə-ˌvō\ city U.S.S.R. in S Soviet Russia, Asia, in Kuznetsk basin on the Tom *pop* 277,000
Ke·nai \'kē-ˌnī\ peninsula S Alaska E of Cook inlet
Ken·dal \'ken-dᵊl\ municipal borough NW England ✻ of Westmorland *pop* 18,543
Ken·il·worth \'ken-ᵊl-ˌwərth\ urban district *cen* England in Warwickshire
Ke·ni·tra \kə-'nē-trə\ *or formerly* **Port Lyau·tey** \ˌpȯr-lē-ˌō-'tā\ city N Morocco NE of Rabat *pop* 55,905
Ken·more \'ken-ˌmō(ə)r, -ˌmȯ(ə)r\ village W N.Y. N of Buffalo *pop* 21,261
Ken·ne·bec \ˌken-ə-'bek\ river 164 *m* S Me. flowing S from Moosehead Lake into the Atlantic
Ken·ne·dy, Cape \'ken-əd-ē\ cape E Fla. in the Atlantic on E shore of Canaveral peninsula; site of Air Force Missile Test Center; formerly **Cape Canaveral**
Kennedy, Mount mountain 13,095 *ft* NW Canada in Yukon Territory in St. Elias range SE of Mt. Logan near Alaska border
Ken·ner \'ken-ər\ city SE La. W of New Orleans *pop* 17,037
Ken·ne·saw Mountain \ˌken-ə-ˌsȯ-\ mountain 1809 *ft* NW Ga. NW of Atlanta
Ke·no·sha \kə-'nō-shə\ city SE Wis. S of Racine *pop* 67,899
Ken·sing·ton \'ken-ziŋ-tən, 'ken(t)-siŋ-\ metropolitan borough W London, England, N of the Thames *pop* 168,054
Kent \'kent\ **1** city NE Ohio SE of Cleveland *pop* 17,836 **2** county SE England bordering on Strait of Dover; one of kingdoms in Anglo-Saxon heptarchy ✻ Maidstone *area* 1525, *pop* 1,563,286 — **Kent·ish** \'kent-ish\ *adj*
Ken·tucky \kən-'tək-ē\ **1** river 259 *m* N *cen* Ky. flowing NW into the Ohio **2** state E *cen* U.S. ✻ Frankfort *area* 40,395, *pop* 3,038,156 — **Ken·tuck·i·an** \-ē-ən\ *adj or n*
Ken·ya \'ken-yə, 'kēn-\ **1** extinct volcano 17,040 *ft*, *cen* Kenya near equator **2** republic E Africa S of Ethiopia bordering on Indian ocean; former Brit. crown colony & protectorate ✻ Nairobi *area* 224,960, *pop* 6,351,000 — **Ken·yan** \'ken-yən, 'kēn-\ *adj or n*
Ke·o·kuk \'kē-ə-ˌkək\ city SE Iowa on the Mississippi *pop* 16,316
Ke·os \'kē-ˌäs\ *or* **Kea** \'kē-ə\ *or anc* **Ce·os** \'sē-ˌäs\ island Greece in NW Cyclades; chief town Kea *area* 67
Ker·a·la \'ker-ə-lə\ state SW India bordering on Arabian sea; formed 1956 from former Travancore and Cochin state & part of Madras state ✻ Trivandrum *area* 15,035, *pop* 13,550,600
Kerasun — see GIRESUN
Kerbela — see KARBALA
Kerch \'ke(ə)rch\ **1** peninsula U.S.S.R. in S Soviet Russia, Europe, projecting E from the Crimea **2** strait between Kerch peninsula & Taman peninsula connecting Sea of Azov & Black sea **3** city & port in Crimea on Kerch strait *pop* 99,000
Ker·gue·len \'kər-gə-lən, ˌker-gə-'len\ **1** archipelago S Indian ocean belonging to France *area* 7000 **2** island in the archipelago
Ke·rin·tji \kə-'rin-chē\ volcano 12,484 *ft* Indonesia in W *cen* Sumatra; highest on the island
Kerkheh — see KARKHEH
Kérkira *or* **Kérkyra** — see CORFU
Kerk·ra·de \'ke(ə)r-ˌkräd-ə\ commune SE Netherlands *pop* 48,167
Ker·mad·ec \(ˌ)kər-'mad-ək\ islands SW Pacific *ab* 500 *m* NE of New Zealand; belong to New Zealand *area* 13
Ker·man \kər-'män, ke(ə)r-\ **1** *or anc* **Car·ma·nia** \kär-'mā-nē-ə, -nyə\ region SE Iran bordering on Gulf of Oman & Persian gulf S of ancient Parthia **2** *or anc* **Car·ma·na** \kär-'mān-ə, -'man-, -'män-\ city SE *cen* Iran in NW Kerman region *pop* 62,175
Ker·man·shah \ˌker-ˌmän-'shä, -'shȯ\ city W Iran *pop* 125,181
Kern \'kərn\ river 150 *m* S *cen* Calif. flowing SW into Buena Vista reservoir
Ker·ry \'ker-ē\ county SW Ireland in Munster ✻ Tralee *area* 1815, *pop* 116,405
Ker·u·len \'ker-ə-ˌlen\ river 650 *m* E Mongolia flowing S & E into the Argun in Manchuria
Kes·te·ven, Parts of \ke-'stē-vən\ administrative county E England in SW Lincolnshire ✻ Sleaford *area* 724, *pop* 131,600
Kes·wick \'kez-ik\ urban district NW England in Cumberland near Derwentwater
Ket·ter·ing \'ket-ə-riŋ\ city SW Ohio S of Dayton *pop* 54,462
Keu·ka \'kyü-kə, kā-'yü-\ lake 18 *m* long W *cen* N.Y.; one of the Finger Lakes
Kew \'kyü\ **1** city SE Australia in S Victoria, NE suburb of Melbourne *pop* 31,518 **2** parish S England in Surrey on the Thames, W suburb of London
Ke·wa·nee \ki-'wän-ē\ city NW Ill. *pop* 16,324
Ke·wee·naw \'kē-wə-ˌnȯ\ peninsula NW Mich. projecting from upper Mich. peninsula into Lake Superior W of **Keweenaw Bay**
Key Lar·go \'lär-(ˌ)gō\ island S Fla. in the Florida Keys
Key West \'west\ city SW Fla. on Key West I. at W end of Florida Keys *pop* 33,956
Kha·ba·rovsk \kə-'bär-əfsk\ **1** territory U.S.S.R. in E Soviet Russia, Asia, bordering on Sea of Okhotsk & Bering sea *area* 965,400, *pop* 1,250,000 **2** city, its ✻, on the Amur *pop* 322,000
Kha·kass \kə-'kas\ autonomous region U.S.S.R. in S Soviet Russia, Asia, in SW Krasnoyarsk Territory N of the Sayan mountains ✻ Abakan *area* 24,000, *pop* 300,000
Khalkidikí — see CHALCIDICE
Khalkís — see CHALCIS
Khan·ba·lik \ˌkän-bə-'lēk\ ancient city ✻ of China under the Mongols, corresponding to modern Peking
Khaniá — see CANEA
Khan·ka \'kaŋ-kə\ *or* **Han·ka** \'haŋ-kə\ lake E Asia on border between Maritime Territory, U.S.S.R., & Heilungkiang, China *area* 1700
Khan Tengri — see TENGRI KHAN
Kha·rag·pur \'kər-əg-ˌpu̇(ə)r\ city E India in SW West Bengal WSW of Calcutta *pop* 129,600
Khar·kov \'kär-ˌkȯf, -ˌkȯv, -kəf\ city U.S.S.R. in NE Ukraine on edge of Donets Basin *pop* 930,000
Khar·toum *or* **Khar·tum** \kär-'tüm\ city ✻ of Sudan at junction of the White Nile & Blue Nile *pop* 93,103
Khartoum North city *cen* Sudan *pop* 39,082
Kha·si \'käs-ē\ hills E India in NW *cen* Assam; region constitutes an autonomous district of India
Kha·tan·ga \kə-'täŋ-gə, -'taŋ-\ river 800 *m* N Soviet Russia, Asia, in NE Krasnoyarsk Territory flowing N into Laptev sea
Khatmandu — see KATMANDU
Khelat — see KALAT
Kher·son \ke(ə)r-'sȯn\ city & port U.S.S.R. in S Ukraine on the Dnieper 19 *m* from its mouth *pop* 157,000
Khing·an \'shiŋ-'än\ mountains NE China divided into the **Great Khingan** (running N–S in NE Inner Mongolia) & the **Lesser Khingan** (extending NW–SE in Heilungkiang)
Khíos — see CHIOS
Khirbat Qumran — see QUMRAN
Khi·u·ma \'kē-ə-ˌmä\ *or* Estonian **Hii·u·maa** \'hē-ə-ˌmä\ island U.S.S.R. in Estonia in Baltic sea N of Sarema I. *area* 371
Khi·va \'kē-və\ **1** *or* **Kho·rezm** \kə-'rez-əm\ oasis U.S.S.R. in Uzbekistan on the lower Amu Darya **2** *or* **Khwa·razm** \kwə-'raz-əm\ former khanate *cen* Asia including Khiva oasis **3** city in the oasis, ✻ of the khanate *pop* 15,000
Khor·ram·shahr \ˌkȯr-əm-'shär, ˌkär-\ city & port W Iran on Shatt-al-Arab NNW of Abadan *pop* 30,000
Kho·tan \'kō-'tän\ oasis W China in SW Sinkiang on S edge of the Takla Makan at foot of Kunlun mountains
Khu·ra·san \ˌkür-ə-'sän\ *or* **Khor·a·san** \ˌkȯr-ə-'sän, ˌkär-\ region NE Iran; chief city Meshed
Khu·zi·stan \ˌkü-zi-'stän, -'stan\ region SW Iran bordering on Persian gulf; chief city Khorramshahr
Khy·ber \'kī-bər\ mountain pass 33 *m* long on border between Afghanistan & Pakistan in Safed Koh range WNW of Peshawar
Kia·mu·sze \jē-'ä-'mü-'sü\ city NE China in NE Heilungkiang on the Sungari *pop* 146,000
Kiang·si \jē-'äŋ-'sē\ province SE China ✻ Nanchang *area* 63,629, *pop* 16,773,000
Kiang·su \jē-'äŋ-'sü\ province E China bordering on Yellow sea ✻ Nanking *area* 41,699, *pop* 47,167,000
Kiangtu — see YANGCHOW
Kiao·chow Bay \jē-ˌau̇-ˌjō-\ inlet of Yellow sea E China in E Shantung *area* 200
Ki·bo \'kē-(ˌ)bō\ mountain peak 19,317 *ft* NE Tanganyika; highest peak of Kilimanjaro & highest point in Africa
Kid·der·min·ster \'kid-ər-ˌmin(t)-stər\ municipal borough W *cen* England in Worcestershire SW of Birmingham *pop* 37,423
Kid·ron \'kid-rən, 'kī-drən\ *or* **Ked·ron** \'ked-rən, 'kē-drən\ valley *cen* Palestine between Jerusalem & Mount of Olives; source of stream (Kidron) flowing E to Dead sea
Kiel \'kē(ə)l\ **1** city & port N Germany ✻ of Schleswig-Holstein on SE coast of Jutland peninsula *pop* 270,700 **2** ship canal 61 *m* N Germany across base of Jutland peninsula connecting Baltic sea & North sea
Kiel·ce \kē-'elt-(ˌ)sā\ *or* Russ **Kelt·sy** \'kelt-sē\ city S Poland S of Warsaw *pop* 77,500
Ki·ev *or* **Ki·yev** \'kē-ˌ(y)ef, -ˌ(y)ev, -(y)əf\ city U.S.S.R. ✻ of Ukraine on the Dnieper *pop* 1,102,000
Ki·ga·li \ki-'gäl-ē\ town E *cen* Africa ✻ of Rwanda
Kikládhes — see CYCLADES
Ki·lau·ea \ˌkē-ˌlau̇-'ā-ə\ volcanic crater 2 *m* wide Hawaii on Hawaii I. on E slope of Mauna Loa
Kil·dare \kil-'da(ə)r, -'de(ə)r\ county E Ireland in Leinster ✻ Naas *area* 654, *pop* 64,346
Kil·i·man·ja·ro \ˌkil-ə-mən-'jär-(ˌ)ō, -'jar-\ mountain NE Tanganyika near Kenya border — see KIBO
Kil·ken·ny \kil-'ken-ē\ **1** county SE Ireland in Leinster *area* 796, *pop* 61,670 **2** municipal borough, its ✻
Kil·lar·ney, Lakes of \kil-'är-nē\ three lakes SW Ireland in County Kerry
Kill Dev·il \'kil-ˌdev-əl\ hill E N.C. near village of **Kit·ty Hawk** \'kit-ē-ˌhȯk\ on sand barrier opposite Albemarle Sound; included in Wright Brothers National Memorial
Kil·leen \kil-'ēn\ city *cen* Tex. N of Austin *pop* 23,377
Kil·lie·cran·kie \ˌkil-ē-'kraŋ-kē\ mountain pass *cen* Scotland in Perth in the SE Grampians
Kill Van Kull \ˌkil-(ˌ)van-'kəl, -vən-\ channel between N.J. & Staten I., N.Y., connecting Newark Bay & Upper New York Bay
Kil·mar·nock \kil-'mär-nək\ burgh SW Scotland in Ayrshire *pop* 42,120
Kim·ber·ley \'kim-bər-lē\ city Republic of So. Africa in N Cape of Good Hope WNW of Bloemfontein *pop* 58,777
Kim·ber·leys \-lēz\ plateau region N Western Australia N of 19°30'S lat.
Kin·a·ba·lu *or* **Kin·a·bu·lu** \ˌkin-ə-bə-'lü\ mountain 13,455 *ft* N *cen* No. Borneo in Crocker range; highest in Borneo I.
Kin·car·dine \kin-'kärd-ᵊn\ *or* **Kin·car·dine·shire** \-ˌshi(ə)r, -shər\ *or formerly* **The Mearns** \'mərnz\ county E Scotland bordering on North sea ✻ Stonehaven *area* 382, *pop* 47,341
Kinchinjunga — see KANCHENJUNGA
Ki·nesh·ma \'kē-nish-mə\ city U.S.S.R. in *cen* Soviet Russia, Europe, NE of Moscow *pop* 84,000
King George's Falls — see AUGHRABIES FALLS
King·man \'kiŋ-mən\ reef *cen* Pacific at N end of Line islands
King's — see OFFALY
Kings Canyon National Park \'kiŋz-\ reservation SE *cen* Calif. in the Sierra Nevada N of Sequoia National Park *area* 708
King's Lynn \'kiŋz-'lin\ *or* **Lynn** *or* **Lynn Re·gis** \-'rē-jəs\ municipal borough E England in Norfolk near the Wash *pop* 26,173
Kings Mountain ridge N.C. & S.C. SW of Gastonia, N.C.
Kings Peak mountain 13,498 *ft* NE Utah in Uinta mountains; highest point in state
Kings·port \'kiŋz-ˌpō(ə)rt, -ˌpȯ(ə)rt\ city NE Tenn. *pop* 26,314
Kings·ton \'kiŋ(k)-stən\ **1** city SE N.Y. on the Hudson *pop* 29,260 **2** borough E Pa. SW of Scranton *pop* 20,261 **3** city Canada in SE Ont. on Lake Ontario *pop* 48,618 **4** *or* **Kingston on** (*or* **upon**) **Thames** municipal borough SE England WSW of London ✻ of Surrey *pop* 40,168 **5** city & port ✻ of Jamaica on **Kingston Harbor** (inlet of the Caribbean) *pop* 137,700
Kingston upon Hull — see HULL
Kings·town \'kiŋ-ˌstau̇n\ **1** town & port Brit. West Indies on St. Vincent I. ✻ of St. Vincent territory **2** — see DUN LAOGHAIRE
Kings·ville \'kiŋz-ˌvil, -vəl\ city S Tex. *pop* 25,297
Kinmen — see QUEMOY
Kinneret, Yam — see GALILEE (Sea of)
Kin·ross \kin-'rȯs\ **1** *or* **Kin·ross-shire** \-'rȯs(h)-ˌshi(ə)r, -shər\ county E *cen* Scotland *area* 82, *pop* 7418 **2** burgh, its ✻
Kinsen — see KUMCHON
Kin·sha·sa \kin-'shäs-ə\ *or formerly* **Lé·o·pold·ville** \'lē-ə-ˌpōld-ˌvil, 'lā-\ city ✻ of Republic of the Congo on Congo river at outlet of Stanley Pool *pop* 402,492
Kin·ston \'kin(t)-stən\ city E N.C. *pop* 24,819
Kin·tyre \kin-'tī(ə)r\ *or* **Can·tyre** \kan-\ peninsula 40 *m* long

SW Scotland between the Atlantic & Firth of Clyde; terminates in **Mull of Kintyre** \,mәl-\ (cape in No. channel)

Kioga — see KYOGA

Kir·giz Republic or **Kir·ghiz Republic** \,ki(ә)r-ˈgēz-\ or **Kir·gi·zia** or **Kir·ghi·zia** \-ˈgē-z(h)ē-ә, -zhә\ constituent republic of the U.S.S.R. in Soviet Central Asia on China border NE of Tadzhikistan ✱ Frunze *area* 76,100 *pop* 2,100,000

Ki·rik·ka·le \kә-ˈrik-ә-,lä\ city *cen* Turkey E of Ankara *pop* 42,838

Ki·rin \ˈkē-ˈrin\ **1** province NE China in E Manchuria ✱ Changchun *area* 72,201, *pop* 11,290,000 **2** or *formerly* **Yung·ki** \ˈyùŋ-ˈjē\ city NE China in Kirin E of Changchun *pop* 435,400

Kirjath–arba — see HEBRON

Kirk·caldy \(,)kәr-ˈkȯ(l)d-ē, -ˈkad-, -ˈkäd-\ burgh & port E Scotland in Fife on Firth of Forth N of Edinburgh *pop* 45,037

Kirk·cud·bright \(,)kәr-ˈkü-brē\ **1** or **Kirk·cud·bright·shire** \-,shi(ә)r, -shәr\ county S Scotland on Solway firth *area* 899, *pop* 30,472 **2** burgh. its ✱, SW of Dumfries

Kirk·pat·rick, Mount \,kәrk-ˈpa-trik\ mountain 14,800 *ft* E Antarctica in Queen Alexandra Range S of Ross sea

Kir·kuk \ki(ә)r-ˈkük\ city NE Iraq SE of Mosul *pop* 89,917

Kirk·wall \ˈkәr-,kwȯl\ burgh & port N Scotland ✱ of Orkney, on Mainland I.

Kirk·wood \ˈkәr-,kwùd\ city E Mo. W of St. Louis *pop* 29,421

Ki·rov \ˈkē-,rȯf, -,rȯv, -rәf\ or *formerly* **Vyat·ka** \vē-ˈat-kә, -ˈät-\ city U.S.S.R. in E Soviet Russia, Europe, on Vyatka river *pop* 252,000

Ki·ro·va·bad \ki-ˈrō-vә-,bad\ or *formerly* **Gan·dzha** \ˈgän-jә\ or **Eli·sa·vet·pol** \i-,liz-ә-ˈvet-,pȯl\ city U.S.S.R. in W Azerbaidzhan *pop* 116,000

Ki·ro·vo·grad \ki-ˈrō-vә-,grad\ or *formerly* **Zi·nov·ievsk** \zә-ˈnȯv-,yefsk, -,yevsk\ or **Eli·sa·vet·grad** \i-,liz-ә-ˈvet-,grad\ city U.S.S.R. in S *cen* Ukraine *pop* 30,000

Ki·ru·na \ˈkē-rә-,nä\ city N Sweden in Lapland *pop* 27,063

Ki·san·ga·ni \,kē-sәn-ˈgän-ē\ or *formerly* **Stan·ley·ville** \ˈstan-lē-,vil\ city NE Congo on Congo river *pop* 53,400

Kish \ˈkish\ ancient city of Sumer & Akkad E of site of Babylon

Ki·shi·nev \ˈkish-ә-,nef, -,nev\ or *Rom* **Chi·si·nau** \,kē-shi-ˈnaù\ city U.S.S.R. ✱ of Moldavia *pop* 214,000

Kishm — see QISHM

Kishon — see QISHON

Kis·ka \ˈkis-kә\ island SW Alaska in Rat group of the Aleutians

Kis·ma·yu \kis-ˈmī-(,)ü\ or *It* **Chi·si·ma·io** \,kē-zē-ˈmä-(,)yō\ town & port S Somalia on Indian ocean

Kis·sim·mee \kis-ˈim-ē\ river 150 *m* S *cen* Fla. flowing SSE from Lake Tohopekaliga through **Lake Kissimmee** (12 *m* long) into Lake Okeechobee

Kist·na \ˈkis(t)-nә\ or **Krish·na** \ˈkrish-nә\ river 800 *m* S India flowing from Western Ghats E across the Deccan into Bay of Bengal

Ki·su·mu \ki-ˈsü-(,)mü\ town & port E Kenya on Lake Victoria

Ki·ta-Kyu·shu \kē-ˈtä-ˈkyü-(,)shü\ city & port Japan in N Kyushu formed by amalgamation of former cities of Kokura, Moji, Tobata, Wakamatsu, & Yawata *pop* 1,056,381

Kitch·e·ner \ˈkich-(ә-)nәr\ city Canada in SE Ont. *pop* 59,562

Kithairon — see CITHAERON

Ki·thi·ra or **Ky·the·ra** \ˈkē-thә-(,)rä\ or **Cy·the·ra** \sә-ˈthir-ә, sī-\ or *It* **Ce·ri·go** \ˈcher-i-,gō\ island W Greece, southernmost of the Ionian islands ✱ Kíthira *area* 110

Kit·i·mat \ˈkit-ә-,mat\ river *ab* 50 *m* W Canada in NW B. C. flowing to Douglas channel (inlet of the Pacific)

Kit·ta·tin·ny Mountain \,kit-ә-,tin-ē-\ ridge E U.S. in the Appalachians extending from SE N. Y. through NW N. J. into E Pa.

Kit·tery Point \,kit-ә-rē-\ cape Me. at S tip

Kitz·bü·hel \ˈkits-,byü-(ә)l\ resort town W Austria in the Tirol

Kiushu — see KYUSHU

Kivu, Lake \ˈkē-(,)vü\ lake 60 *m* long & 30 *m* wide E Congo in Great Rift valley N of Lake Tanganyika *area* 1025

Ki·zil Ir·mak \kә-,zil-,i(ә)r-ˈmäk\ or *anc* **Ha·lys** \ˈhā-lәs\ river 600 *m* N *cen* Turkey flowing W & NE into Black sea

Kjö·len \ˈchȯ(r)l-әn\ mountains on border between NE Norway & NW Sweden; highest peak Kebnekaise (in Sweden) 6963 *ft*

Kla·gen·furt \ˈkläg-әn-,fù(ә)rt\ city S Austria ✱ of Carinthia WSW of Graz *pop* 62,782

Klaipeda — see MEMEL

Klam·ath \ˈklam-әth\ **1** river 250 *m* S Oreg. & NW Calif. flowing from Upper Klamath Lake SW into the Pacific **2** mountains S Oreg. & NW Calif. in the Coast ranges; highest point Mt. Eddy (in Calif.) 9038 *ft*

Klamath Falls city S Oreg. on Upper Klamath Lake at head of Klamath river *pop* 16,949

Kleve — see CLEVES

Klon·dike \ˈklän-,dīk\ **1** river 90 *m* Canada in *cen* Yukon Territory flowing W into the Yukon **2** the Klondike river valley

Kly·az·ma \klē-ˈaz-mә\ river 425 *m* U.S.S.R. in W *cen* Soviet Russia, Europe, flowing E to join the Oka W of Gorki

Knok·ke \kә-ˈnäk-ә\ town N Belgium NNE of Bruges

Knos·sos or **Cnos·sus** \(kә-)ˈnäs-әs\ or **Gnos·sus** \(gә-)ˈnäs-әs\ ruined city ✱ of ancient Crete near N coast SE of modern Candia

Knox·ville \ˈnäks-,vil, -vәl\ city E Tenn. *pop* 111,827

Knud Ras·mus·sen Land \ˈnüd-ˈräs-,műs-ᵊn, -mә-sәn\ region N & NW Greenland NE of Baffin Bay

Ko·ba·rid \ˈkō-bә-,rēd\ or *It* **Ca·po·ret·to** \,kap-ә-ˈret-(,)ō ,käp-\ village NW Yugoslavia on the Isonzo NE of Udine, Italy

Ko·be \ˈkō-bē, -,bā\ city & port Japan in S Honshu on Osaka Bay *pop* 1,113,977

København — see COPENHAGEN

Ko·blenz or **Co·blenz** \ˈkō-,blen(t)s\ city W Germany SSE of Cologne at confluence of the Rhine & the Moselle *pop* 97,500

Koca — see XANTHUS

Ko·ca·bas \,kȯ-jә-ˈbäsh\ or *anc* **Gra·ni·cus** \grә-ˈnī-kәs\ river *ab* 30 *m* NW Turkey in Asia flowing NE to Sea of Marmara

Ko·chi \ˈkō-chē\ city & port Japan in S Shikoku *pop* 180,146

Ko·di·ak \ˈkōd-ē-,ak\ or **Ka·diak** \kәd-ˈyak, -ˈyäk\ island S Alaska in Gulf of Alaska E of Alaska peninsula *area* 3465

Ko·dok \ˈkōd-,äk\ or *formerly* **Fa·sho·da** \fә-ˈshōd-ә\ town SE Sudan on the White Nile

Koedoes — see KUDUS

Ko·fu \ˈkō-(,)fü\ city Japan in S *cen* Honshu *pop* 154,494

Ko·ha·la \kō-ˈhäl-ә\ mountains Hawaii in N Hawaii I.; highest point *ab* 5500 *ft*

Koi — see RED

Koil — see ALIGARH

Ko·kand \kō-ˈkand\ **1** region & former khanate U.S.S.R. in Soviet Central Asia in E Uzbekistan **2** city in Kokand region SE of Tashkent *pop* 105,000

Ko·kiu or **Ko·chiu** \ˈgō-jē-ˈō\ city S China in SE Yunnan S of Kunming *pop* 159,700

Ko·ko·mo \ˈkō-kә-,mō\ city N *cen* Ind. *pop* 47,197

Koko Nor — see TSINGHAI

Ko·ku·ra \ˈkō-kә-,rä, kō-ˈkùr-ә\ former city Japan in N Kyushu — see KITA-KYUSHU

Ko·la \ˈkō-lә\ peninsula 250 *m* long & 150 *m* wide U.S.S.R. in NW Soviet Russia, Europe, between Barents & White seas

Kolar Gold Fields city S India in SE Mysore *pop* 159,100

Kol·ha·pur \ˈkōl-ә-,pù(ә)r\ city W India in SW Maharashtra SSE of Bombay *pop* 136,800

Kolmar — see COLMAR

Köln — see COLOGNE

Ko·ly·ma or **Ko·li·ma** \kә-ˈlē-mә\ **1** river 1110 *m* U.S.S.R. in NE Soviet Russia, Asia, flowing from Kolyma range NE into East Siberian sea **2** mountain range Soviet Russia, Asia, in NE Khabarovsk Territory parallel to coast of Penzhinskaya Bay

Ko·man·dor·skie \,käm-әn-ˈdȯr-skē\ or **Com·mand·er** \kә-ˈman-dәr\ islands U.S.S.R. in E Soviet Russia, Asia, in Bering sea E of Kamchatka peninsula *area* 850

Ko·ma·ti \kә-ˈmät-ē\ river 500 *m* S Africa flowing from N Drakensberg mountains in NE Republic of So. Africa E & N into Delagoa Bay in S Mozambique

Ko·mi Republic \,kō-mē-\ autonomous republic U.S.S.R. in NE Soviet Russia, Europe, W of N Ural mountains ✱ Syktyvkar *area* 145,221, *pop* 806,000

Ko·mo·do \kә-ˈmōd-(,)ō\ island Indonesia in the Lesser Sundas E of Sumbawa I. & W of Flores I. *area* 185

Kom·so·molsk \,käm-(,)sә-ˈmȯlsk\ city U.S.S.R. in E Soviet Russia, Asia, in S Khabarovsk Territory on the Amur *pop* 177,000

Ko·na \ˈkō-nә\ coast region Hawaii in W Hawaii I.

Konakry — see CONAKRY

Konan — see HUNGNAM

Kongo — see KUMGANG

Königgrätz — see HRADEC KRALOVE

Königsberg — see KALININGRAD

Kon·kan \ˈkäŋ-kәn\ region W India in W Maharashtra bordering on Arabian sea & extending from Bombay S to Goa

Konstanz — see CONSTANCE

Kon·ya or **Kon·ia** \ˈkōn-ˈyä\ or *anc* **Ico·ni·um** \ī-ˈkō-nē-әm\ city SW *cen* Turkey *pop* 122,704

Ko·o·lau \,kō-(,)ō-ˈlä-(,)ü\ mountains Hawaii in E Oahu; highest peak Konahuanui 3105 *ft*

Koo·te·nai or (*in Canada*) **Koo·te·nay** \ˈküt-ᵊn-,ā, -ᵊn-ē\ river 407 *m* SW Canada & NW U. S. in B. C., Mont., & Idaho flowing through Kootenay Lake (65 *m* long, in B. C.) into the Columbia

Kootenay National Park reservation Canada in SE B. C. including section of the upper Kootenay *area* 587

Ko·per \ˈkō-,pe(ә)r\ or *It* **Ca·po·dis·tria** \,kap-ә-ˈdis-trē-ә, ,käp-ә-ˈdēs-\ town & port Yugoslavia N end of Istrian peninsula SSW of Trieste

Ko·peysk or **Ko·peisk** \kō-ˈpāsk\ city U.S.S.R. in W Soviet Russia, Asia, SE of Chelyabinsk *pop* 160,000

Kor·do·fan \,kȯrd-ә-ˈfan\ region *cen* Sudan W & N of the White Nile; chief city El Obeid

Ko·rea \kә-ˈrē-ә, *esp South* (ˈ)kō-\ **1** peninsula 600 *m* long & 135 *m* wide E Asia between Yellow sea & Sea of Japan **2** strait 120 *m* wide between S Korea & SW Japan connecting Sea of Japan & Yellow sea **3** or **Cho·sen** \ˈchō-ˈsen\ country coextensive with Korea peninsula; once a kingdom & (1910–1945) a Japanese dependency ✱ Seoul; divided after World War II at 38th parallel into republics of No. Korea (✱ Pyongyang *area* 47,839, *pop* 19,996,000) & So. Korea (✱ Seoul *area* 37,427, *pop* 22,974,000)

Korea Bay arm of Yellow sea between Liaotung peninsula & NW Korea

Kórinthos — see CORINTH

Kort·rijk \ˈkȯrt-,rīk\ or **Cour·trai** \kùr-ˈtrā\ commune NW Belgium in West Flanders on the Lys NNE of Lille *pop* 44,331

Kos or **Cos** \ˈkäs\ **1** island Greece in the Dodecanese *area* 111 **2** chief town & port on the island

Kos·ci·us·ko, Mount \,käz-ē-ˈәs-(,)kō\ mountain 7305 *ft* SE Australia in SE New So. Wales; highest in Great Dividing range & Australia

Koshu — see KWANGJU

Ko·si·ce \ˈkȯ-shәt-,sā\ city E Czechoslovakia *pop* 60,658

Ko·stro·ma \,käs-trә-ˈmä\ city U.S.S.R. in N *cen* Soviet Russia, Europe, on the Volga *pop* 171,000

Kotabaru — see HOLLANDIA

Ko·ta Bha·ru \,kōt-ә-ˈbär-(,)ü\ city Federation of Malaysia in Malaya ✱ of Kelantan *pop* 22,765

Kota Kinabalu — see JESSELTON

Ko·tor \ˈkō-,tȯ(ә)r\ or *It* **Cat·ta·ro** \ˈkät-ә-,rō\ town & port SE Yugoslavia in Montenegro on an inlet of the Adriatic

Kottbus — see COTTBUS

Kot·ze·bue Sound \,kät-sә-,byü-\ arm of Chuckchee sea NW Alaska NE of Bering strait

Kovno — see KAUNAS

Kowait — see KUWAIT

Kow·loon \ˈkaù-ˈlün\ **1** peninsula SE China in Hong Kong colony opposite Hong Kong I. **2** city on Kowloon peninsula *pop* 500,000

Koy·u·kuk \ˈkī-ә-,kәk\ river 425 *m* N *cen* Alaska flowing from Brooks range SW into the Yukon

Ko·zhi·kode \ˈkō-zhә-,kōd\ or **Cal·i·cut** \ˈkal-i-kәt\ city & port SW India on Malabar coast in Kerala *pop* 158,700

Kozlov — see MICHURINSK

ә abut; ᵊ kitten; әr further; a back; ā bake; ä cot, cart; aù out; ch chin; e less; ē easy; g gift; i trip; ī life
j joke; ŋ sing; ō flow; ȯ flaw; ȯi coin; th thin; t̲h̲ this; ü loot; ù foot; y yet; yü few; yù furious; zh vision
ᵊ F table; å F bac; ḵ G ich, Buch; ⁿ F vin; œ F bœuf; œ̄ F feu; ᵫ G füllen; ᵫ̄ F rue; ʸ F digne \dēnʸ\, nuit \nwᵉʸ\

Kra, Isthmus of \'krä\ isthmus S Thailand in N *cen* Malay peninsula; 40 *m* wide at narrowest part

Krak·a·toa \,krak-ə-'tō-ə\ *or* **Krak·a·tau** *or* **Krak·a·tao** \-'tau̇\ island & volcano Indonesia between Sumatra & Java

Kra·kow *or* **Cra·cow** \'kräk-,au̇, 'krak-, 'kräk-, -(,)ō, *Pol* 'krä-,küf\ city S Poland on the Vistula *pop* 463,000

Kras \'kräs\ *or G* **Karst** \'kärst\ *or It* **Car·so** \'kär-(,)sō\ limestone plateau NW Yugoslavia N E of Istrian peninsula

Kras·no·dar \'kras-nə-,där\ **1** territory U.S.S.R. in S Soviet Russia, Europe, in N Caucasus region *area* 32,800, *pop* 3,000,000 **2** *or formerly* **Eka·te·ri·no·dar** \i-,kat-ə-'rē-nə-,där\ city, its ✻, on Kuban river *pop* 312,000

Kras·no·yarsk \,kras-nə-'yärsk\ **1** territory U.S.S.R. in W *cen* Soviet Russia, Asia, extending along valley of the Yenisei from Arctic ocean to Sayan mountains *area* 928,000, *pop* 2,100,000 **2** city, its ✻, on the upper Yenisei *pop* 409,000

Kre·feld \'krā-,felt\ *or formerly* **Krefeld-Uer·ding·en** \'ürd-iŋ-ən\ city W Germany on the Rhine WSW of Essen *pop* 209,300

Krim — see CRIMEA

Krishna — see KISTNA

Kristiania — see OSLO

Kris·tian·sand \'kris(h)-chən-,san(d)\ city & port SW Norway on the Skagerrak SW of Oslo *pop* 27,610

Kris·tian·sund \'kris(h)-chən-,sun(d)\ city & port W Norway WSW of Trondheim *pop* 16,805

Krīti — see CRETE

Kri·voy Rog *or* **Kri·voi Rog** \,kriv-,ȯi-'rȯg, -'rȯk\ city U.S.S.R. in SE *cen* Ukraine NE of Odessa *pop* 448,000

Kron·shtadt *or* **Kron·stadt** \'krōn-,stat, krän-'s(h)tät\ city U.S.S.R. in Soviet Russia, Europe, on island in E Gulf of Finland W of Leningrad *pop* 45,000

Kru·ger National Park \'krü-gər\ game reserve N E Republic of So. Africa in E Transvaal on Mozambique border *area* 8652

Kru·gers·dorp \'krü-gərz-,dȯrp\ city N E Republic of So. Africa in S Transvaal W of Johannesburg *pop* 75,647

K² — see GODWIN AUSTEN

Kua·la Lum·pur \,kwäl-ə-'lùm-,pù(ə)r, kù-,äl-, -'ləm-\ city ✻ of Federation of Malaysia & of Selangor in W Malaya *pop* 315,040

Kuang-chou — see CANTON

Ku·ban \kü-'ban, -'bän\ river 512 *m* U.S.S.R. flowing from the Caucasus N & W into Sea of Azov

Ku·ching \'kü-chiŋ\ city & port ✻ of Sarawak *pop* 37,949

Ku·dus *or D* **Koe·does** \'küd-,üs\ city Indonesia in *cen* Java NE of Semarang *pop* 54,524

Ku·fra *or* **Cu·fra** \'kü-frə\ group of five oases SE Libya

Kui·by·shev *or* **Kuy·by·shev** \'kwē-bə-,shef, 'kü-ē-bə-, -,shev\ *or formerly* **Sa·ma·ra** \sə-'mär-ə\ city U.S.S.R. in SE Soviet Russia, Europe, in valley of the Volga *pop* 806,000

Ku·ke·naam \,kü-kə-'nän\ *or* **Cu·que·nán** \,kü-kə-'nän\ **1** mountain 8620 *ft* on border between Brit. Guiana & Venezuela near Roraima **2** waterfall 2000 *ft* on this mountain

Kuku–Khoto — see HUHEHOT

Ku·la Gulf \,kü-lə-\ body of water 17 *m* long in the Solomons between New Georgia & adjacent islands

Kul·dja \'kùl-(,)jä\ city W China in NW Sinkiang *pop* 108,200

Kum \'küm\ river 247 *m* S Korea flowing into Yellow sea

Ku·ma·mo·to \,küm-ə-'mōt-(,)ō\ city Japan in W Kyushu *pop* 373,922

Ku·ma·si *or* **Coo·mas·sie** \kü-'mäs-ē, -'mas-\ city S *cen* Ghana in Ashanti *pop* 78,483

Kum·chon \'küm-,chän\ *or Jap* **Kin·sen** \'kin-,sen\ city S Korea NW of Taegu *pop* 51,300

Kum·gang \'küm-,gän\ *or Jap* **Kon·go** \'kän-(,)gō\ *or E* **Di·a·mond** \'dī-(ə-)mənd\ mountains N E *cen* Korea; highest 5374 *ft*

Kunene — see CUNENE

Ku·nie \'kün-(,)yā\ *or* **Isle of Pines** island SW Pacific in New Caledonia territory SE of New Caledonia I. *area* 58

Kun·lun *or* **Kuen·lun** \'kün-'lün\ mountains W China extending from the Pamirs & Karakoram range E along N edge of Tibetan plateau to SE Tsinghai — see ULUGH MUZTAGH

Kun·ming \'kün-'miŋ\ *or formerly* **Yun·nan** \yü-'nän\ *or* **Yun·nan-fu** \-'fü\ city S China ✻ of Yunnan *pop* 698,900

Kun·san \'gùn-,sän\ *or Jap* **Gun·zan** \'gùn-,zän\ city & port S Korea on Yellow sea at mouth of Kum river *pop* 75,000

Kun·tse·vo \'künt-sə-,vō\ city U.S.S.R. in Soviet Russia, Europe, SW suburb of Moscow *pop* 128,000

Ku·pre·a·nof \,kü-prē-'an-,ȯf\ island SE Alaska in E Alexander archipelago

Ku·ra \kə-'rä, 'kùr-ə\ river 825 *m* W Asia in Transcaucasia flowing from NE Turkey ESE through Georgia & Azerbaidzhan, U.S.S.R., into Caspian sea

Kur·di·stan \,kùrd-ə-'stan, ,kərd-\ region SW Asia chiefly in E Turkey, NW Iran, & N Iraq

Ku·re \'k(y)ù(ə)r-ē, 'kü-(,)rā\ **1** *or* **Ocean** island *cen* Pacific in Hawaii, westernmost of the Leewards **2** city & port Japan in SW Honshu on Inland sea SSE of Hiroshima *pop* 199,304

Kurg — see COORG

Kur·gan \kù(ə)r-'gan, -'gän\ city U.S.S.R. in W Soviet Russia, Asia, E of Chelyabinsk *pop* 145,000

Ku·ria Mu·ria \,k(y)ùr-ē-ə-'m(y)ùr-ē-ə\ islands in Arabian sea off SW coast of Oman belonging to Aden colony *area* 28

Ku·ril *or* **Ku·rile** \'kyù(ə)r-,ēl, kyü-'rē(ə)l\ islands U.S.S.R. in the Pacific between S Kamchatka & NE Hokkaido, Japan; belonged 1875–1945 to Japan *area* 3960

Kur·land *or* **Cour·land** \'kù(ə)r-lənd\ region U.S.S.R. in W Latvia bordering on the Baltic & Gulf of Riga

Kurland Gulf inlet of the Baltic W U.S.S.R. on border between Lithuania & Soviet Russia *area* 625

Kur·nool \kər-'nül\ city S India in W Andhra Pradesh SSW of Hyderabad *pop* 100,849

Kursk \'kù(ə)rsk\ city U.S.S.R. in SW Soviet Russia, Europe, on Seim river *pop* 203,000

Kush — see CUSH

Kus·ko·kwim \'kəs-kə-,kwim\ river 550 *m* SW Alaska flowing SW into **Kuskokwim Bay** (inlet of Bering sea)

Ku·tah·ya \kü-'tä-yə\ city W *cen* Turkey *pop* 39,851

Kut-al-Ima·ra *or* **Kut-el-Ama·ra** \,küt-,al-ə-'mär-ə, -,el-\ city SE Iraq on the Tigris SE of Baghdad *pop* 16,237

Kutch *or* **Cutch** \'kəch\ former principality & state W India N of Gulf of Kutch ✻ Bhuj; now part of Gujarat

Kutch, Gulf of inlet of Arabian sea W India N of Kathiawar

Kutch, Rann of \,ran-\ salt marsh in S West Pakistan & W India stretching in an arc from the mouths of the Indus to the head of Gulf of Kutch

Ku·wait *or* **Ku·weit** *or* **Ko·wait** \kə-'wāt\ *or* **Al Kuwait** \,al-\ **1** country SW Asia in Arabia at head of Persian gulf; a sheikhdom, before 1961 under Brit. protection *area* 6178, *pop* 468,389 **2** city & port, its ✻ *pop* 99,438 — **Ku·wai·ti** \kə-'wāt-ē\ *adj or n*

Kuz·netsk \küz-'netsk\ city U.S.S.R. in SE Soviet Russia, Europe, E of Penza *pop* 57,000

Kuznetsk Basin *or* **Kuz·bass** *or* **Kuz·bas** \'küz-,bas\ basin of Tom river U.S.S.R. in W *cen* Soviet Russia, Asia, extending from Novokuznetsk to Tomsk

Kwa·ja·lein \'kwäj-ə-lən, -,lān\ island (atoll) 78 *m* long W Pacific in Ralik chain of the Marshalls; encloses lagoon (*area* 650)

Kwan·do \'kwän-(,)dō\ river 600 *m* S Africa flowing from *cen* Angola SE & E into the Zambezi just above Victoria Falls

Kwangchow — see CANTON

Kwang·cho·wan \,gwäŋ-'jō-'wän, 'kwän-\ former territory SE China in Kwangtung on Luichow peninsula; leased 1898–1946 to France ✻ Fort Bayard *area* 325

Kwang·ju \'gwäŋ-(,)jü, 'kwän-\ *or Jap* **Ko·shu** \'kō-(,)shü\ city SW Korea NE of Mokpo *pop* 138,883

Kwang·si \'gwäŋ-'sē, 'kwän-\ *or* **Kwangsi-Chu·ang Region** \-chü-'äŋ\ region & former province S China W of Kwangtung ✻ Nanning *area* 85,096, *pop* 17,591,000

Kwang·tung \'gwäŋ-'dùŋ, 'kwän-, -'tùŋ\ province SE China bordering on So. China sea & Gulf of Tonkin ✻ Canton *area* 89,344, *pop* 36,740,000

Kwan·to Plain \,kwän-(,)tō-\ *or* **Kan·to Plain** \,kän-\ *or* **Tokyo Plain** region Japan in E *cen* Honshu; Tokyo is situated on it

Kwan·tung \'gwän-'dùŋ, 'kwän-, -'tùŋ\ former territory NE China in S Manchuria at tip of Liaotung peninsula; leased to Russia 1898–1905, to Japan 1905–45, & to Russia again 1945–55; included cities of Port Arthur & Dairen *area* 1444

Kwei \'gwā, 'kwā\ river 200 *m* SE China in E Kwangsi flowing S into West river

Kwei·chow \'gwā-'jō, 'kwā-\ province S China S of Szechwan ✻ Kweiyang *area* 67,181, *pop* 15,037,000

Kwei·lin \'gwā-'lin, 'kwā-\ city S China in NE Kwangsi on the Kwei *pop* 145,100

Kweisui — see HUHEHOT

Kwei·yang \,gwā-'yäŋ, 'kwā-\ *or* **Kwei·chu** \'gwā-'jü, 'kwā-\ city S China ✻ of Kweichow *pop* 270,900

Kyo·ga *or* **Kio·ga** \kē-'ō-gə\ lake *cen* Uganda N of Lake Victoria traversed by the Victoria Nile *area* 1000

Kyongsong — see SEOUL

Kyo·to \kē-'ōt-(,)ō\ city Japan in W *cen* Honshu NNE of Osaka; formerly (794–1869) ✻ of Japan *pop* 1,284,818

Kythera — see KÍTHIRA

Kyu·shu *or* **Kiu·shu** \kē-'ü-(,)shü\ island S Japan S of W end of Honshu *area* 16,240

Laaland — see LOLLAND

Labe — see ELBE

Lab·ra·dor \'lab-rə-,dȯ(ə)r\ **1** peninsula E Canada between Hudson Bay & the Atlantic; divided between Que. & Nfld. **2** the section of the peninsula belonging to Nfld. *area* 101,881, *pop* 10,814 **3** sea arm of the Atlantic between Labrador & Greenland — **Lab·ra·dor·ean** *or* **Lab·ra·dor·ian** \,lab-rə-'dȯr-ē-ən, -'dōr-\ *adj or n*

La·bu·an \lə-'bü-ən\ island Sabah off W coast

La Ca·na·da \,läk-ən-'yad-ə\ urban area SW Calif. NE of Glendale *pop* (with Flintridge) 18,338

Lac·ca·dive \'lak-ə-,dīv\ islands India in Arabian sea N of Maldive islands

Laccadive, Min·i·coy, and Amin·di·vi Islands \'min-i-,kȯi, ,əm-ən-'dē-vē\ territory India comprising the Laccadive group ✻ Kozhikode (in Kerala) *area* 11, *pop* 21,195

Lacedaemon — see SPARTA — **Lac·e·dae·mo·nian** \,las-əd-ə-'mō-nē-ən, -nyən\ *adj or n*

La Chaux-de-Fonds \lä-,shōd-ə-'fōⁿ\ commune W Switzerland in Neuchâtel canton in Jura mountains WNW of Bern *pop* 38,200

La·chine \lə-'shēn\ city Canada in S Que. above the **Lachine rapids** on the St. Lawrence SW of Montreal *pop* 34,494

La·chish \'lā-kish\ ancient city S Palestine W of Hebron

Lach·lan \'läk-lən\ river 800 *m* SE Australia in *cen* New So. Wales flowing W into the Murrumbidgee

La Cis·ter·na \,läs-is-'te(ə)r-nə, -'tər-\ city *cen* Chile, S suburb of Santiago *pop* 155,332

Lack·a·wan·na \,lak-ə-'wän-ə\ city W N.Y. on Lake Erie S of Buffalo *pop* 29,564

La·co·nia \lə-'kō-nē-ə, -nyə\ **1** city *cen* N.H. *pop* 15,288 **2** *or* **La·con·i·ca** \lə-'kän-i-kə\ ancient country S Greece in SE Peloponnesus bordering on the Aegean & the Mediterranean ✻ Sparta — **La·co·nian** \lə-'kō-nē-ən, -nyən\ *adj or n*

Laconia, Gulf of inlet of the Mediterranean on S coast of Greece in Peloponnesus between capes Matapan & Malea

La Co·ru·ña \,läk-ə-'rün-yə\ **1** province NW Spain in Galicia bordering on the Atlantic *area* 3051, *pop* 1,022,707 **2** *or* **Co·run·na** \kə-'rən-ə\ commune & port, its ✻ *pop* 164,770

La Crosse \lə-'krȯs\ city W Wis. *pop* 47,575

La·dakh \lə-'däk\ district N India in E Kashmir on border of Tibet ✻ Leh *area* 45,762 — **La·da·khi** \lə-'däk-ē\ *adj or n*

Lad·o·ga \'lad-ə-gə, 'läd-\ lake 130 *m* long & 75 *m* wide U.S.S.R. in NW Soviet Russia, Europe, NE of Gulf of Finland *area* 7000; largest in Europe

Ladrone — see MARIANA

La·dy·smith \'lād-ē-,smith\ city E Republic of So. Africa in W Natal *pop* 16,317

Lae \'lä-,ā\ town & port Territory of New Guinea on SE coast on Huon Gulf

La·fay·ette 1 \,läf-ē-'et *also* ,lä-fē-\ city W *cen* Ind. *pop* 42,330 **2** \,laf-ē-\ city S La. WSW of Baton Rouge *pop* 40,400

La·gash \'lā-,gash\ ancient city of Sumer between the Euphrates & the Tigris at modern village of Telloh \'te-,lō\ in S Iraq

Lagoa dos Patos — see PATOS (Lagoa dos)

La·gos \'lā-,gäs\ city & port ✻ of Nigeria on an offshore island in Bight of Benin & on mainland opposite *pop* 350,000

La Gou·lette \,lä-gü-'let\ city N Tunisia on Bay of Tunis; port for Tunis *pop* 26,323

La Grange \lə-'grānj\ **1** city W Ga. *pop* 23,632 **2** village NE Ill. W of Chicago *pop* 15,285

La Granja — see SAN ILDEFONSO

La Guai·ra \lə-'gwī-rə\ city N Venezuela on the Caribbean; port for Caracas *pop* 16,279

Laguna Madre — see MADRE (Laguna)

La Habana — see HAVANA

La Ha·bra \lə-'häb-rə\ city SW Calif. SE of Los Angeles *pop* 25,136

La Hague, Cape \lə-'häg\ *or* F **Cap de la Hague** \käp-də-là-àg\ headland NW France at tip of Cotentin peninsula projecting into English channel

La Hogue \lə-'hōg\ roadstead NW France in English channel off E coast of Cotentin peninsula

La·hon·tan, Lake \lə-'hänt-ᵊn\ prehistoric lake NW Nev. & NE Calif.

La·hore \lə-'hō(ə)r, -'hò(ə)r\ city Pakistan ✳ of West Pakistan near the Ravi *pop* 849,500

Lah·ti \'lät-ē\ city S Finland NNE of Helsinki *pop* 62,600

La Jol·la \lə-'hòi-ə\ a NW section of San Diego, Calif.

Lake Charles \'chär(ə)lz\ city SW La. *pop* 63,392

Lake District region NW England in Cumberland, Westmorland, & NW Lancashire containing many lakes & peaks

Lake·land \'lā-klənd\ city *cen* Fla. E of Tampa *pop* 41,350

Lake of the Four Forest Cantons — see LUCERNE (Lake of)

Lake·wood \'lā-,kwùd\ **1** city SW Calif. NE of Long Beach *pop* 67,126 **2** urban area *cen* Colo. W of Denver *pop* 19,338 **3** city NE Ohio on Lake Erie W of Cleveland *pop* 66,154

Lake Worth \'wərth\ city SE Fla. on Lake Worth (lagoon) S of West Palm Beach *pop* 20,758

La Lí·nea \lä-'lē-nē-ə\ commune SW Spain on Bay of Algeciras N of Gibraltar *pop* 63,376

La Man·cha \lə-'män-chə\ region S *cen* Spain in S New Castile

La Mar·sa \lə-'mär-sə\ town N Tunisia NE of Tunis

Lam·ba·ré·né \läm-bə-'rā-nē, -nə\ town W Gabon, Africa

Lam·beth \'lam-bəth, -,beth\ metropolitan borough SW *cen* London, England, on S bank of the Thames *pop* 230,105

La Me·sa \lə-'mā-sə\ city SW Calif. NE of San Diego *pop* 30,441

La·mia \lə-'mē-ə\ city E *cen* Greece NW of Thermopylae *pop* 25,843

Lam·mer·muir \'lam-ər-,myu(ə)r\ *or* **Lam·mer·moor** \-,mu(ə)r\ hills SE Scotland in East Lothian & Berwick — see SAYS LAW

Lam·pe·du·sa \,lam-pə-'dü-sə, -zə\ island Italy in the Pelagian islands

La·nai \lə-'nī\ island Hawaii W of Maui *area* 141, *pop* 2115

Lan·ark \'lan-ərk\ **1** *or* **Lan·ark·shire** \-,shi(ə)r, -shər\ county S *cen* Scotland; chief city Glasgow *area* 892, *pop* 1,614,125 **2** burgh, its ✳, on the Clyde SE of Glasgow

Lan·ca·shire \'laŋ-kə-,shi(ə)r, -shər\ *or* **Lan·cas·ter** \'laŋ-kə-stər\ county NW England bordering on Irish Sea ✳✳ Lancaster & Preston *area* 1875, *pop* 5,116,013

Lan·cas·ter \'laŋ-kə-stər, 'lan-,kas-tər, 'laŋ-\ **1** urban area SW Calif. NE of Los Angeles *pop* 26,012 **2** city S *cen* Ohio SE of Columbus *pop* 29,916 **3** city SE Pa. *pop* 61,055 **4** municipal borough NW England, a ✳ of Lancashire *pop* 51,650 — **Lan·cas·tri·an** \laŋ-'kas-trē-ən, lan-\ *adj or n*

Lan·chow \'län-'jō\ *or* **Kao·lan** \'kau-'län\ city N *cen* China ✳ of Kansu *pop* 700,000

Landes \lä[n](d)\ coastal region SW France on Bay of Biscay between Gironde estuary & the Adour

Lands End *or* **Land's End** \'lan(d)-'zend\ cape SW England at SW tip of Cornwall; extreme W point of England, at 5°41′ W

Lang·dale Pikes \,laŋ-,dāl-\ two mountain peaks NW England in Westmorland in Lake District

Lan·gue·doc \,laŋ-gə-'däk, lä[n]-'dòk, lä[n]g-dòk\ region & former province S France extending from Auvergne to the Mediterranean ✳✳ Toulouse & Montpellier

La·ni·kai \,län-i-'kī\ urban area Hawaii on Oahu *pop* (with Kailua) 25,622

Lanka — see CEYLON

Lan·sing \'lan(t)-siŋ\ **1** village NE Ill. SSE of Chicago *pop* 18,098 **2** city ✳ of Mich. *pop* 107,807

La·nús \lə-'nüs\ city E Argentina, S suburb of Buenos Aires *pop* 286,400

La·od·i·cea \,(,)lā-,äd-ə-'sē-ə\ **1** ancient city W *cen* Asia Minor in Phrygia **2** — see LATAKIA — **La·od·i·ce·an** \-'sē-ən\ *adj or n*

Laoighis \'lāsh, 'lēsh\ *or* **Leix** \'lāsh, 'lēsh\ *or formerly* **Queen's** county *cen* Ireland in Leinster ✳ Maryborough *area* 664, *pop* 45,086

Laon \'lä[n]\ commune N France NE of Paris *pop* 21,931

Laos \'laùs, 'läōs, 'lä-,ōs, 'lä-əs, 'laùz\ country SE Asia bordering on the Mekong; a kingdom, formerly a state of French Indochina; administrative ✳ Vientiane, royal ✳ Luang Prabang *area* 91,482, *pop ab* 2,500,000

La Pal·ma \lə-'päl-mə\ island Spain in Canary islands; chief town Santa Cruz de la Palma *area* 280

La Paz \lə-'paz, -'päz, -'päs\ **1** city, administrative ✳ of Bolivia E of Lake Titicaca at altitude of 11,910 *ft*, *pop* 339,279 **2** town W Mexico ✳ of Baja California Sur on La Paz Bay (inlet of Gulf of California)

Lap·land \'lap-,land, -lənd\ region N Europe above the arctic circle in N Norway, N Sweden, N Finland, & Kola peninsula of the U.S.S.R. — **Lap·land·er** \-,lan-dər, -lən-\ *n*

La Pla·ta \lə-'plät-ə\ city E Argentina SE of Buenos Aires *pop* 357,356

La Porte \lə-'pō(ə)rt, -'pò(ə)rt\ city N Ind. *pop* 21,157

Lap·tev \'lap-,tef, -,tev\ *or formerly* **Nor·den·skjöld** \'nòrd-ᵊn-,sheld, -,shùld, -,sheld\ sea arm of Arctic ocean U.S.S.R. between Taimyr peninsula & New Siberian islands

La Pu·en·te \,läp-ù-'ent-ē\ city SW Calif. ESE of Los Angeles *pop* 24,723

L'Aquila — see AQUILA

Lar·a·mie \'lar-ə-mē\ **1** river 200 *m* N Colo. & SE Wyo. flowing N & NE into the No. Platte **2** city SE Wyo. *pop* 17,520

Larch \'lärch\ river 270 *m* Canada in W Que. flowing NE to unite with the Kaniapiskau forming the Koksoak

La·re·do \lə-'rād-(,)ō\ city S Tex. on Rio Grande *pop* 60,678

La·ris·sa \lə-'ris-ə\ city N *cen* Greece in E Thessaly on the Peneus *pop* 41,016

Lar·i·stan \,lar-ə-'stan\ region S Iran bordering on Persian gulf

La Ro·chelle \,lär-ə-'shel\ city & port W France *pop* 58,799

Lar·vik \'lär-vik, -,vēk\ town & port SE Norway

La Salle \lə-'sal\ town Canada in S Que. on the St. Lawrence SSW of Montreal *pop* 18,973

Las·caux \la-'skō\ cave SW *cen* France SE of Périgueux near town of Montignac

Las Cru·ces \lä-'skrü-səs\ city S N. Mex. *pop* 29,367

La·shio \lə-'shō\ town E *cen* Burma ✳ of Shan state

Lashkar — see GWALIOR

Las Pal·mas \lä-'späl-məs\ **1** province NW Spain comprising the E Canary islands *area* 1279, *pop* 450,329 **2** city & port, its ✳, in NE Grand Canary I. *pop* 182,217

La Se·re·na \,läs-ə-'rā-nə\ city N *cen* Chile *pop* 55,708

La Spezia — see SPEZIA

Lassa — see LHASA

Las·sen Peak \,las-ᵊn-\ *or* **Mount Lassen** volcano 10,453 *ft* N Calif. at S end of Cascade range; central feature of **Lassen Volcanic National Park** (area 161)

Las Ve·gas \läs-'vā-gəs\ city SE Nev. *pop* 64,405

Lat·a·kia \,lat-ə-'kē-ə\ **1** region NW Syria bordering on the Mediterranean **2** *or anc* **La·od·i·cea** \(,)lā-,äd-ə-'sē-ə\ city & port, its chief town, on the Mediterranean *pop* 109,216

Latin America, **1** Spanish America & Brazil **2** all of the Americas S of the U.S. — **Latin-American** *adj* — **Latin American** *n*

La·tium \'lā-sh(ē-)əm\ *or* It **La·zio** \'lät-sē-,ō\ region *cen* Italy bordering on Tyrrhenian sea & traversed by the Tiber ✳ Rome

Lat·via \'lat-vē-ə\ country N *cen* Europe bordering on the Baltic; an independent republic 1918–40, since 1940 a constituent republic (**Lat·vi·an Republic** \,lat-vē-ən-\) of the U.S.S.R. ✳ Riga *area* 25,200, *pop* 2,100,000

Laun·ces·ton \'lòn(t)-sə-stən, 'län(t)-\ city & port Australia in N Tasmania *pop* (with suburbs) 55,950

Lau·rel \'lòr-əl, 'lär-\ city SE Miss. *pop* 27,889

Lau·ren·tian \lò-'ren-chən\ *or* **Lau·ren·tide** \'lòr-ən-,tīd, 'lär-, -,tēd\ hills Canada in S Que. N of the St. Lawrence on S edge of Laurentian Highlands

Laurentian Highlands *or* **Laurentian Upland** *or* **Canadian Shield** plateau region E Canada & NE U.S. extending from Mackenzie basin E to Davis strait & S to S Que., S Ont., NE Minn., N Wis., NW Mich., & NE N.Y. including the Adirondacks

Lau·ri·um \'lòr-ē-əm, 'lär-\ mountain SE Greece at SE tip of Attica

Lau·sanne \lō-'zän, -'zan\ commune W Switzerland ✳ of Vaud canton on Lake Geneva *pop* 118,900

Lausitz — see LUSATIA

Lausitzer Neisse — see NEISSE

Lava Beds National Monument reservation N Calif. SE of Lower Klamath Lake *area* 72

La Vendée — see VENDÉE

Lavongai — see NEW HANOVER

Lawn·dale \'lòn-,dāl, 'län-\ city SW Calif. SSW of Los Angeles *pop* 21,740

Law·rence \'lòr-ən(t)s, 'lär-\ **1** city NE Kans. W of Kansas City *pop* 32,858 **2** city NE Mass. *pop* 70,933

Law·ton \'lòt-ᵊn\ city SW Okla. *pop* 61,697

Lay·san \'lī-,sän\ island Hawaii in the Leewards *ab* 750 *m* NW of Niihau I.

Leam·ing·ton \'lem-iŋ-tən\ municipal borough S *cen* England in Warwickshire *pop* 36,345

Lea·side \'lē-,sīd\ town Canada in SE Ont., N suburb of Toronto *pop* 16,538

Leav·en·worth \'lev-ən-,wərth\ city NE Kans. on the Missouri NW of Kansas City *pop* 22,052

Leb·a·non, 1 \'leb-(ə-)nən\ city SE *cen* Pa. E of Harrisburg *pop* 30,045 **2** \'leb-,non, 'leb-ə-,nän\ *or anc* **Lib·a·nus** \'lib-ə-nəs\ mountains Lebanon running parallel to coast W of Bika valley; highest point Dahr el Qadib 10,131 *ft* **3** country SW Asia bordering on the Mediterranean; a republic since 1944, formerly (1920–44) a French mandate ✳ Beirut *area* 4105, *pop* 2,400,000 — **Leb·a·nese** \,leb-ə-'nēz, -'nēs\ *adj or n*

Lebda — see HOMS

Le Bour·get \lə-(,)bùr-'zhā\ commune N France, NE suburb of Paris

Lec·ce \'lā-chē, 'lech-ē\ commune SE Italy in Apulia SE of Brindisi *pop* 58,400

Lec·co \'lā-(,)kō, 'lek-(,)ō\ commune N Italy in Lombardy on branch (**Lake Lecco**) of Lake Como *area* 43,800

Lech \'lek, 'lek\ river 177 *m* Austria & Germany flowing from the Vorarlberg N into the Danube

Le·do \'lēd-(,)ō, 'lād-\ town NE India in NE Assam

Leeds \'lēdz\ city & county borough N England in West Riding, Yorkshire, on the Aire *pop* 504,954

Leeu·war·den \'lā-,värd-ᵊn\ commune N Netherlands ✳ of Friesland *pop* 81,985

Lee·ward \'lē-wərd, 'lü-ərd\ **1** island chain *cen* Pacific extending 1250 *m* WNW from main islands of the Hawaiian group; includes Nihoa, Necker, Laysan, Midway, & Kure islands **2** *or* F **Îles sous le Vent** \ēl-sü-lə-vä[n]\ islands S Pacific, W group of the Society islands **3** islands West Indies in the N Lesser Antilles extending from Virgin islands (on N) to Dominica (on S) **4** former colony Brit. West Indies in the Leewards including territories of Antigua, St. Kitts-Nevis, & Montserrat

Leg·horn \'leg-,(h)ò(ə)rn\ *or* It **Li·vor·no** \lē-'vòr-(,)nō\ commune & port *cen* Italy in Tuscany on Tyrrhenian sea *pop* 146,162

Leh \'lā\ town E Kashmir on the Indus ✳ of Ladakh

Le Ha·vre \lə-'hävrᵊ\ *or* **Havre** *or formerly* **Le Ha·vre-de-Grâce** \lə-,häv-rəd-ə-'gräs, -,häv-də-\ city & port N France on English channel on N side of Seine estuary *pop* 139,810

Le·high \'lē-,hī\ river 100 *m* E Pa. flowing SW & SE into the Delaware

Leh·man Caves \,lē-mən-\ limestone caverns E Nev. on E slope of Wheeler Peak in **Lehman Caves National Monument**

Leices·ter \'les-tər\ **1** *or* **Leices·ter·shire** \-,shi(ə)r, -shər\

ə abut; ᵊ kitten; ər further; a back; ā bake; ä cot, cart; aù out; ch chin; e less; ē easy; g gift; i trip; ī life
j joke; ŋ sing; ō flow; ò flaw; òi coin; th thin; th this; ü loot; ù foot; y yet; yü few; yù furious; zh vision
ᵊ F table; á F bac; ḵ G ich, Buch; ⁿ F vin; œ F bœuf; œ̄ F feu; ᵫ G füllen; ᵫ̄ F rue; ʸ F digne \dēnʸ\, nuit \nwʸē\

county cen England area 832, pop 630,893 **2** city & county borough, its ✳, ENE of Birmingham pop 285,061

Lei·den or **Ley·den** \'līd-ᵊn, Du usu 'lā-yə\ city W Netherlands in So. Holland on a branch of the lower Rhine pop 95,882

Leie — see LYS

Lein·ster \'len(t)-stər\ province E Ireland area 7580, pop 1,329,-625

Leip·zig \'līp-sig, -sik\ or **Leip·sic** \-sik\ city E Germany in Saxony SSW of Berlin pop 613,700

Lei·ria \lā-'rē-ə\ town W cen Portugal SSW of Coimbra

Leith \'lēth\ port section of Edinburgh, Scotland, on Firth of Forth; formerly a burgh

Lei·tha \'lī-(ˌ)tä\ river 112 m E Austria & NW Hungary flowing SE into the Raba

Lei·trim \'lē-trəm\ county NW Ireland in Connacht ✳ Carrick on Shannon area 589, pop 33,468

Leix — see LAOIGHIS

Lei·xões \lā-'shōish\ town NW Portugal on the Atlantic; port for Oporto

Lek \'lek\ river 40 m Netherlands flowing W into the Atlantic; the N branch of the lower Rhine

Le Maine — see MAINE

Leman, Lake — see GENEVA (Lake of)

Le Mans \lə-'mäⁿ\ city NW France pop 111,891

Le Marche — see MARCHES

Lemberg — see LVOV

Lem·nos \'lem-ˌnäs, -nəs\ or NGk **Lím·nos** \'lēm-ˌnòs\ island Greece in the Aegean ESE of Chalcidice peninsula; chief town Kástron area 175

Lemon Grove urban area SW Calif. E of San Diego pop 19,348

Le·na \'lē-nə, 'lā-\ river 3000 m U.S.S.R. in W Soviet Russia, Asia, flowing from mountains W of Lake Baikal NE & N into Laptev sea through wide delta

Len·in·grad \'len-ən-ˌgrad\ or formerly (1703–1914) **Saint Pe·ters·burg** \ˌsānt-'pēt-ərz-ˌbərg, sənt-\ or (1914–24) **Pet·ro·grad** \'pe-trə-ˌgrad\ city U.S.S.R. in NW Soviet Russia, Europe, at E end of Gulf of Finland ✳ of Russian Empire 1712–1917, pop 3,300,000 — **Len·in·grad·er** \'len-ən-ˌgrad-ər\ n

Le·nin Peak \ˌlen-ən-, ˌlān-, -ˌēn-\ mountain 23,386 ft on border between Kirgiz & Tadzhik republics; highest in Trans Alai range

Len·nox \'len-əks, -iks\ urban area SW Calif. SSW of Los Angeles pop 31,224

Leom·in·ster \'lem-ən-stər\ city cen Mass. N of Worcester pop 27,929

Le·ón \lā-'ōn\ **1** or **León de los Al·da·mas** \-də-ˌlò-ˌsal-'däm-əs\ city cen Mexico in Guanajuato pop 226,245 **2** city W Nicaragua pop 46,321 **3** region & ancient kingdom NW Spain W of Old Castile **4** province NW Spain in N León region area 5936, pop 600,384 **5** city, its ✳ pop 75,871

Le·o·ne, Mon·te \ˌmänt-ē-lā-'ō-nē\ mountain 11,684 ft on border between Switzerland & Italy SW of Simplon Pass; highest in Lepontine Alps

Le·o·pold II, Lake \'lē-ə-ˌpōld\ lake 90 m long W Congo

Léopoldville — see KINSHASA

Lepanto — see NÁVPAKTOS

Lepanto, Gulf of — see CORINTH (Gulf of)

Le·pa·ya \'lep-ə-yə\ or G **Li·bau** \'lē-ˌbaů\ city & port U.S.S.R. in W Latvia on the Baltic pop 68,800

Le·pon·tine Alps \li-ˌpän-ˌtīn-, ˌlep-ən-\ range of cen Alps on border between Switzerland & Italy — see LEONE (Monte)

Leptis Magna — see HOMS

Lé·ri·da \'lā-rəd-ə, 'ler-əd-\ **1** province NE Spain in NW Catalonia area 4690, pop 336,743 **2** commune, its ✳ pop 61,449

Ler·wick \'lər-(ˌ)wik, 'le(ə)r-\ burgh & port N Scotland ✳ of Shetland on Mainland I.

Les·bos \'lez-ˌbäs, -bəs\ or **Myt·i·le·ne** \ˌmit-ᵊl-'ē-nē\ or NGk **Lés·vos** \'lez-ˌvós\ or **Mi·ti·li·ni** \ˌmit-ᵊl-'ē-nē\ island Greece in the Aegean off NW coast of Turkey area 623

Les Ey·zies \lā-zā-'zē\ commune SW cen France SE of Périgueux

Lesotho — see BASUTOLAND

Lesser An·til·les \an-'til-ēz\ islands in the West Indies including Virgin, Leeward & Windward islands, Trinidad, Tobago, & islands in the S Caribbean N of Venezuela

Lesser Armenia region S Turkey corresponding to ancient Cilicia

Lesser Khingan — see KHINGAN

Lesser Slave \'slāv\ lake Canada in cen Alta. draining through the Lesser Slave river to the Athabasca area 461

Lesser Sunda — see SUNDA

Leth·bridge \'leth-(ˌ)brij\ city Canada in S Alta. pop 29,462

Le·ti·cia \lə-'tē-sē-ə\ town SE Colombia on the Amazon on Colombia-Peru border

Letzeburg — see LUXEMBOURG

Leu·cas \'lü-kəs\ or **Leu·ca·dia** \lü-'kād-ē-ə\ or NGk **Lev·kás** \lef-'käs\ island Greece in Ionian islands at entrance to Ambracian Gulf area 111

Leuc·tra \'lük-trə\ ancient village Greece in Boeotia SW of Thebes

Leuven — see LOUVAIN

Le·val·lois-Per·ret \lə-ˌval-(ˌ)wä-pə-'rā\ commune N France on the Seine, NW suburb of Paris pop 62,871

Le·vant \lə-'vant\ the countries bordering on the E Mediterranean — **Lev·an·tine** \'lev-ən-ˌtīn, -ˌtēn, lə-'van-\ adj or n

Levant States — see SYRIA

Le·ven, Loch \'lē-vən\ **1** inlet of Loch Linnhe W Scotland between Argyll & Inverness counties **2** lake 4 m long E Scotland in Kinross SSE of Perth

Le·ver·ku·sen \ˌlā-vər-'küz-ᵊn\ city W Germany on the Rhine SE of Düsseldorf pop 91,200

Lev·it·town \'lev-ət-ˌtaůn\ urban area SE N.Y. on Long I. pop 65,276

Lew·es \'lü-əs\ **1** the upper Yukon river S of its junction with the Pelly **2** municipal borough S England ✳ of East Sussex on the Ouse S of London

Lew·is and Clark \ˌlü-ə-sən-'klärk\ **1** lake 30 m long SE S. Dak. & NE Nebr. formed by Gavins Point Dam **2** or **Mor·ri·son Cave** \ˌmòr-ə-sən-, ˌmär-\ cavern cen Mont. WNW of Bozeman

Lew·i·sham \'lü-ə-shəm\ metropolitan borough SE London, England pop 227,551

Lew·is·ton \'lü-ə-stən\ city SW Me. on the Androscoggin opposite Auburn pop 40,804

Lew·is with Har·ris \ˌlü-ə-swəth-'har-əs, -swəth-\ island NW Scotland in the Outer Hebrides divided administratively into

Lewis (in the N, in Ross and Cromarty county, chief town & port Stornoway) & **Harris** (in the S, in Inverness county); largest of the Hebrides area 770

Lex·ing·ton \'lek-siŋ-tən\ **1** city N cen Ky. pop 62,810 **2** town NE Mass. NW of Boston pop 27,691 **3** city cen N.C. S of Winston-Salem pop 16,093

Leyden — see LEIDEN

Ley·te \'lāt-ē\ island Philippines in the Visayans SSW of Samar; chief town Tacloban area 2785

Leyte Gulf inlet of the Pacific in Philippines E of Leyte & S of Samar

Ley·ton \'lāt-ᵊn\ municipal borough SE England in Essex, NE suburb of London pop 105,183

Lha·sa or **Las·sa** \'läs-ə, 'las-\ city SE Tibet ✳ of Tibet pop 50,000

Lho·tse \'(h)lōt-'sā\ or **E¹** \'ē-'wən\ mountain 27,923 ft in Mt. Everest massif S of Mt. Everest

Liao \lē-'aů\ river 700 m NE China flowing into Gulf of Liaotung

Liao·ning \lē-'aů-niŋ\ or formerly **Feng·tien** \'fəŋ-tē-'en\ province NE China in S Manchuria ✳ Mukden area 58,301, pop 20,566,000

Liao·si \lē-'aů-'shē\ former province (1948–54) NE China in S Manchuria bordering on Gulf of Liaotung ✳ Chinchow area 2500

Liao·tung \lē-'aů-'dùŋ\ peninsula NE China in S Liaoning between Korea Bay & **Gulf of Liaotung** (arm of Po Hai)

Liao·yang \lē-'aů-'yäŋ\ city NE China in cen Liaoning NE of Anshan pop 100,000

Liao·yüan \lē-'aů-yü-'än\ city NE China in W Kirin S of Changchun on the Liao pop 120,100

Li·ard \'lē-ˌärd\ river 755 m W Canada flowing from Stikine mountains in Yukon Territory E & N into the Mackenzie

Libanus — see LEBANON

Li·be·rec \'lib-ə-ˌrets\ city W Czechoslovakia in N Bohemia pop 52,798

Li·be·ria \lī-'bir-ē-ə\ country W Africa; a republic ✳ Monrovia area 43,000, pop 2,750,000 — **Li·be·ri·an** \-ē-ən\ adj or n

Lib·er·ty \'lib-ərt-ē\ or **Bed·loe's** \'bed-ˌlōz\ island SE N.Y. in Upper New York Bay; comprises **Statue of Liberty National Monument**

Li·bre·ville \'lē-brə-ˌvil\ city & port ✳ of Gabon at mouth of Gabon river pop 21,565

Lib·ya \'lib-ē-ə\ **1** the part of Africa N of the Sahara between Egypt & Syrtis Major (Gulf of Sidra) — an ancient name **2** northern Africa W of Egypt — an ancient name **3** or It **Li·bia** \'lē-byə\ country N Africa bordering on the Mediterranean; a colony of Italy 1912–43 & independent kingdom since 1952 ✳✳ Tripoli & Benghazi area 679,358, pop 1,195,000

Lib·y·an \'lib-ē-ən\ desert N Africa W of the Nile in Libya, Egypt, & Sudan

Lich·field \'lich-ˌfēld\ municipal borough W cen England in Staffordshire

Lick·ing \'lik-iŋ\ river 350 m NE Ky. flowing NW into the Ohio

Li·di·ce \'lid-ə(t)-sē, -ˌsā\ village W Czechoslovakia in W cen Bohemia WNW of Prague

Li·do \'lēd-(ˌ)ō\ island Italy in the Adriatic separating Lagoon of Venice & Gulf of Venice

Liech·ten·stein \'lik-tən-ˌs(h)tīn\ country W Europe between Switzerland & Austria bordering on the Rhine; a principality ✳ Vaduz area 62, pop 14,757 — **Liech·ten·stein·er** \-ˌs(h)tī-nər\ n

Li·ège \lē-'āzh, -'ezh\ or Flem **Luik** \'līk\ **1** province E Belgium area 1525, pop 1,010,534 **2** city, its ✳ pop 155,042

Lif·fey \'lif-ē\ river 50 m E Ireland flowing into Dublin Bay

Lif·ford \'lif-ərd\ town NW Republic of Ireland in Ulster ✳ of County Donegal

Li·gu·ria \lə-'gyùr-ē-ə\ region NW Italy bordering on Ligurian sea ✳ Genoa — **Li·gu·ri·an** \-ē-ən\ adj or n

Ligurian sea arm of the Mediterranean N of Corsica

Lille \'lē(ə)l\ or formerly **Lisle** \lē(ə)l, 'lī(ə)l\ city N France; medieval ✳ of Flanders pop 194,616

Li·ma, \'lī-mə\ city NW Ohio pop 51,037 **2** \'lē-mə\ city ✳ of Peru E of Callao pop 1,186,212

Li·may \lē-'mī\ river 250 m W Argentina flowing out of Lake Nahuel Huapí & joining the Neuquén to form the Negro

Lim·burg \'lim-ˌbərg\ **1** region W Europe E of the Meuse including parts of present Limburg province, Netherlands, & Limburg province, Belgium **2** province NE Belgium ✳ Hasselt area 929, pop 571,655 **3** province SE Netherlands ✳ Maastricht area 851, pop 1,425,732

Lime·house \'līm-ˌhaůs\ district E London, England, on N bank of the Thames

Lim·er·ick \'lim-(ə)-rik\ **1** county SW Ireland in Munster area 1037, pop 82,528 **2** city & county borough & port, its ✳, on the Shannon pop 51,445

Límnos — see LEMNOS

Li·moges \lē-'mōzh\ city SW cen France pop 105,990

Li·món or **Puer·to Limón** \ˌpwert-ō-li-'mōn\ city & port E Costa Rica on the Caribbean pop 20,764

Li·mou·sin \ˌlē-mə-'zaⁿ, -'zēn\ region & former province S cen France W of Auvergne ✳ Limoges

Lim·po·po \lim-'pō-(ˌ)pō\ or **Croc·o·dile** \'kräk-ə-ˌdīl\ river 1000 m S Africa flowing from Transvaal, Republic of So. Africa, into Indian ocean in Mozambique

Li·na·res \li-'när-əs\ commune S Spain N of Jaén pop 56,154

Lin·coln \'liŋ-kən\ **1** city cen Ill. pop 16,890 **2** city ✳ of Nebr. pop 128,521 **3** or **Lin·coln·shire** \-ˌshi(ə)r, -shər\ county E England bordering on North sea between Humber river & the Wash area 2664, pop 706,574 — see HOLLAND (Parts of), KESTEVEN (Parts of), LINDSEY (Parts of) **4** city & county borough E England in Lincolnshire ✳ of Parts of Lindsey pop 69,412

Lincoln Park city SE Mich. SW of Detroit pop 53,933

Lin·den \'lin-dən\ city NE N.J. SSW of Elizabeth pop 39,931

Lin·den·hurst \'lin-dən-ˌhərst\ village SE N.Y. in cen Long I. pop 20,905

Lin·des·nes \'lin-də-ˌsnäs\ or **the Naze** \'nāz\ cape Norway at S tip projecting into North sea

Lindisfarne — see HOLY

Lind·sey, Parts of \'lin-zē\ administrative county E England in N Lincolnshire ✳ Lincoln area 1520, pop 473,500

Line \'līn\ islands cen Pacific S of Hawaii divided between the U.S. (Kingman Reef & Palmyra), & Great Britain (Washington, Fanning, & Christmas) with some in dispute

Lin·ga·yen Gulf \ˌliŋ-gə-ˌyen-\ inlet of So. China sea Philippines in NW Luzon

Lin·guet·ta, Cape \liŋ-'gwet-ə\ *or* **Cape Glos·sa** \'gläs-ə\ *or anc* **Ac·ro·ce·rau·nia** \ˌak-rō-sə-'rō-nē-ə\ cape SW Albania projecting into Strait of Otranto

Lin·kö·ping \'lin-ˌchə(r)p-iŋ\ city SE Sweden *pop* 66,016

Lin·lith·gow \lin-'lith-(ˌ)gō\ **1** *or* **Lin·lith·gow·shire** \-ˌshi(ə)r, -shər\ — see WEST LOTHIAN **2** burgh SE Scotland ✳ of West Lothian

Linn·he, Loch \'lin-ē\ inlet of the Atlantic on W coast of Scotland in Argyll extending NE from head of Firth of Lorne

Linz \'lin(t)s, 'linz\ city N Austria on the Danube *pop* 184,685

Li·ons, Gulf of \'lī-ənz\ *or* F **Golfe du Lion** \ˌgȯlf-dᵫ-lyōⁿ\ arm of the Mediterranean on S coast of France

Lip·a·ri \'lip-ə-rē\ **1** *or* **Ae·o·lian islands** \ē-'ō-lē-ən, -'ōl-yən\ *or It* **Iso·le Eo·lie** \'ē-zə-ˌlā-ā-'ō-lē-ˌā\ islands Italy in SE Tyrrhenian sea off NE Sicily *area* 45 — see STROMBOLI **2** *or anc* **Lip·a·ra** \'lip-ə-rə\ island in the Lipari group

Li·petsk \'lē-ˌpetsk\ city U.S.S.R. in S cen Soviet Russia, Europe, N of Voronezh *pop* 157,000

Lip·pe \'lip-ə\ **1** river 150 *m* W Germany flowing from Teutoberger Wald W into the Rhine **2** former principality & state Germany between Teutoberger Wald & the Weser ✳ Detmold

Li·ri \'lir-ē\ river 100 *m*, cen Italy flowing into Gulf of Gaeta

Lis·bon \'liz-bən\ *or* **Port Lis·boa** \lēzh-'vō-ə\ city & port ✳ of Portugal on estuary of the Tagus *pop* 794,434 — **Lis·bo·an** \liz-'bō-ən\ *n*

Lis·burne, Cape \'liz-bərn\ cape NW Alaska projecting into Arctic ocean near W end of Brooks range

Li·sieux \lēz-'yə(r)\ city NW France E of Caen *pop* 15,342

Lith·u·a·nia \ˌlith-(y)ə-'wā-nē-ə, -nyə\ *or* Lith **Lie·tu·va** \ˌlē-e-tü-'vä\ country N cen Europe bordering on the Baltic; remnant of a medieval principality extending from Baltic sea to Black sea; a republic 1918–40, since 1940 a constituent republic (**Lithuanian Republic**) of the U.S.S.R. ✳ Vilnius *area* 31,200, *pop* 2,800,000

Little Abaco — see ABACO

Little America base for American exploration of Antarctica located in different years at various spots on Ross Ice Shelf E of Bay of Whales

Little Bighorn river 80 *m* N Wyo. & S Mont. flowing N into the Bighorn

Little Colorado river 300 *m* NE Ariz. flowing NW into the Colorado

Little Diomede — see DIOMEDE

Little Inagua — see INAGUA

Little Kabylia — see KABYLIA

Little Karroo — see KARROO

Little Minch — see MINCH

Little Missouri river 560 *m* W U.S. flowing from NE Wyo. N into the Missouri in W N. Dak.

Little Namaqualand — see NAMAQUALAND

Lit·tle Rock \'lit-ᵊl-ˌräk\ city ✳ of Ark. on Arkansas River *pop* 107,813

Little Saint Bernard mountain pass 7177 *ft* over Savoy Alps between France & Italy S of Mont Blanc

Little Walachia — see OLTENIA

Liuchiu — see RYUKYU

Liu·chow \lē-'ü-'jō\ city S China in cen Kwangsi *pop* 158,800

Liv·er·more \'liv-ər-ˌmō(ə)r, -ˌmȯ(ə)r\ city W Calif. SE of Oakland *pop* 16,058

Liv·er·pool \'liv-ər-ˌpül\ city & county borough & port NW England in Lancashire on Mersey estuary *pop* 789,532 — **Liv·er·pud·li·an** \ˌliv-ər-'pəd-lē-ən\ *adj or n*

Liv·ing·ston \'liv-iŋ-stən\ urban township NE N.J. *pop* 23,124

Liv·ing·stone \'liv-iŋ-stən\ city S Zambia on the Zambezi near Victoria Falls *pop* 20,100

Livingstone Falls rapids in lower Congo river W equatorial Africa below Stanley Pool; a series of cascades dropping *ab* 900 *ft* in 220 *m*

Li·vo·nia \lə-'vō-nē-ə, -nyə\ **1** region cen Europe bordering on the Baltic in Latvia & Estonia **2** city SE Mich. W of Detroit *pop* 66,702 — **Li·vo·nian** \-nē-ən, -nyən\ *adj or n*

Livorno — see LEGHORN

Lizard Head *or* **Lizard Point** headland SW England in S Cornwall at S tip of the **Lizard** (peninsula projecting into English channel); extreme S point of Great Britain at 49°57′30″N, 5°12′W

Lju·blja·na \lē-ˌü-blē-'än-ə\ city NW Yugoslavia ✳ of Slovenia on the Sava *pop* 138,981

Llan·ber·is \(h)lan-'ber-əs\ village NW Wales in Caernarvonshire near Mt. Snowdon at entrance to **Pass of Llanberis** (1169 *ft*)

Llan·drin·dod Wells \(h)lan-ˌdrin-ˌdäd-\ urban district E Wales ✳ of Radnorshire

Llan·dud·no \(h)lan-'did-(ˌ)nō, -'dəd-\ urban district NW Wales on coast of Caernarvonshire *pop* 16,712

Lla·nel·ly \(h)la-'neth-lē\ municipal borough & port S Wales in Carmarthenshire *pop* 34,329

Llan·gef·ni \(h)lan-'gef-nē\ urban district NW Wales, a ✳ of Anglesey, on Anglesey I.

Lla·no Es·ta·ca·do \ˌlan-(ˌ)ō-ˌes-tə-'käd-(ˌ)ō, 'län-\ *or* **Staked Plain** \'stāk(t)-\ plateau region SE N. Mex. & NW Tex.

Llu·llai·lla·co \ˌyü-yī-'yäk-(ˌ)ō\ volcano 22,057 *ft* N Chile in Andes mountains on Argentina border SE of Antofagasta

Loanda — see LUANDA

Lo·an·ge \lō-'äŋ-gə\ *or* **Port Lu·an·gue** \lü-'äŋ-gə\ river 425 *m* NE Angola & SW Congo flowing N into the Kasai

Lo·bi·to \lō-'bēt-(ˌ)ō\ town & port W Angola

Lo·bos, Point \'lō-bəs\ **1** promontory Calif. in San Francisco on S side of entrance to the Golden Gate **2** promontory Calif. on the Pacific SW of Monterey

Lo·car·no \lō-'kär-(ˌ)nō\ commune SE cen Switzerland in Ticino canton on N shore of Lake Maggiore

Loch·gilp·head \ˌläk-'gilp-ˌhed\ burgh W Scotland ✳ of Argyll

Loch Ra·ven \lä-'krā-vən\ urban area N cen Md. *pop* 23,278

Lock·port \'läk-ˌpō(ə)rt, -ˌpȯ(ə)rt\ city W N.Y. NE of Buffalo *pop* 26,443

Lo·cris \'lō-krəs, 'läk-rəs\ region of ancient Greece N of Gulf of Corinth — **Lo·cri·an** \'lō-krē-ən, 'läk-rē-\ *adj or n*

Lod — see LYDDA

Lo·di, 1 \'lōd-ˌī\ city cen Calif. SSE of Sacramento *pop* 22,229 **2** \'lōd-ˌī\ borough NE N.J. SE of Paterson *pop* 23,502 **3** \'lōd-(ˌ)ē\ commune N Italy in Lombardy SE of Milan *pop* 36,500

Lodz \'lüj, 'lädz\ city cen Poland WSW of Warsaw *pop* 698,000

Lo·fo·ten \'lō-ˌfōt-ᵊn\ island group Norway off NW coast SW of Vesterålen *area* 475

Lo·gan \'lō-gən\ city N Utah *pop* 18,731

Logan, Mount mountain 19,850 *ft* Canada in SW Yukon Territory; highest in St. Elias & Coast ranges & in Canada

Lo·gans·port \'lō-gənz-ˌpō(ə)rt, -ˌpȯ(ə)rt\ city N cen Ind. NNW of Kokomo *pop* 21,106

Lo·gro·ño \lə-'grōn-(ˌ)yō\ **1** province N Spain in NE Old Castile *area* 1946, *pop* 234,099 **2** commune, its ✳, on the Ebro *pop* 59,368

Loire \lə-'wär\ river 625 *m*, cen France flowing from the Massif Central NW & W into Bay of Biscay

Lol·land \'läl-ənd\ *or* **Laa·land** \'lȯ-ˌlän\ island Denmark in the Baltic S of Sjælland *area* 477

Lo·ma·mi \lō-'mäm-ē\ river 900 *m*, cen Congo flowing N into Congo river

Lo·mas \'lō-ˌmäs\ *or* **Lo·mas de Za·mo·ra** \ˌlō-ˌmäz-də-zə-'mōr-ə, -'mȯr-\ city E Argentina SW of Buenos Aires *pop* 125,943

Lom·bard \'läm-ˌbärd\ village NE Ill. W of Chicago *pop* 22,561

Lom·bar·dy \-ˌbärd-ē, -bərd-\ *or It* **Lom·bar·dia** \ˌläm-bər-'dē-ə\ region N Italy chiefly N of Po river ✳ Milan

Lom·blen \läm-'blen\ island Indonesia in the Lesser Sundas E of Flores *area* 468

Lom·bok \läm-'bäk\ island Indonesia in the Lesser Sundas E of Bali; chief town Mataram *area* 1825

Lo·mé \lō-'mā\ city & port ✳ of Togo *pop* 65,000

Lo·mond, Ben \ben-'lō-mənd\ mountain 3192 *ft* S cen Scotland on E side of Loch Lomond

Lomond, Loch lake 24 *m* long S cen Scotland *area* 27

Lon·don \'lən-dən\ **1** city Canada in SE Ont. on the Thames *pop* 101,693 **2** city & port SE England constituting an administrative county ✳ of United Kingdom; comprises City of London & 28 metropolitan boroughs *area* 117, *pop* 3,348,336 **3** *or* **City of London** *or anc* **Lon·din·i·um** \län-'din-ē-əm, ˌlun-\ city within county of London, England, on the Thames *area* 675 acres, *pop* 5268 **4** *or* **Greater London** urban area SE England comprising county of London & the Outer Ring (Middlesex & parts of Essex, Kent, Surrey, & Hertfordshire) *area* 693, *pop* 8,346,137 — **Lon·don·er** \-də-nər\ *n*

Lon·don·der·ry \ˌlən-dən-'der-ē, 'lən-dən-\ *or* **Der·ry** \'der-ē\ **1** county NW Northern Ireland *area* 804, *pop* 155,520 **2** county borough & port, its ✳, on the Foyle *pop* 50,099

Long \'lȯŋ\ island 118 *m* long SE N.Y. S of Conn. *area* 1401

Long Beach, 1 city & port SW Calif. S of Los Angeles on San Pedro Bay *pop* 344,168 **2** city SE N.Y. on island S of Long I. *pop* 26,473

Long Branch city E cen N.J. on the Atlantic *pop* 26,228

Long·fel·low mountains \'lȯŋ-fel-(ˌ)ō, -ˌfel-ə(-w)\ the Appalachian mountains in Me.; so named 1959

Long·ford \'lȯŋ-fərd\ **1** county E cen Ireland in Leinster *area* 403, *pop* 30,642 **2** urban district, its ✳

Long Island City section of New York City on East river in NW Queens

Long Island Sound inlet of the Atlantic between Conn. & Long I.

Longs Peak \'lȯŋz-\ mountain 14,255 *ft* N cen Colo. in Front range in Rocky Mountain National Park

Long·view \'lȯŋ-ˌvyü\ **1** city NE Tex. *pop* 40,050 **2** city SW Wash. on the Columbia *pop* 23,349

Long·xuyên \ˌlaùŋ-'swē-ən\ town S Vietnam in SW Cochin China on S side of Mekong delta

Lookout, Cape cape E N.C. on the Atlantic SW of Cape Hatteras

Lookout Mountain ridge 2126 *ft* SE Tenn., NW Ga., & NE Ala. near Chattanooga, Tenn.

Lo·rain \lō-'rān\ city N Ohio on Lake Erie *pop* 68,932

Lor·ca \'lȯr-kə\ commune SE Spain SW of Murcia *pop* 68,481

Lord Howe \lȯ(ə)rd-'haù\ island Australia in Tasman sea 436 *m* ENE of Sydney belonging to New So. Wales *area* 5

Lo·re·to \lə-'rāt-(ˌ)ō, -'ret-\ commune cen Italy S of Ancona

Lo·ri·ent \ˌlȯr-ē-'äⁿ\ commune & port NW France in Brittany on Bay of Biscay *pop* 47,095

Lorne, Firth of \'lȯ(ə)rn\ strait W Scotland between E Mull I. & mainland

Lor·raine \lə-'rān, lȯ-\ *or* G **Lo·thring·en** \'lō-triŋ-ən\ region & former duchy NE France around upper Moselle & Meuse rivers; remnant (Upper Lorraine) of medieval kingdom of **Lo·tha·rin·gia** \ˌlō-thə-'rin-j(ē-)ə\ including also territory to N (Lower Lorraine) between the Rhine & the Scheldt — see ALSACE-LORRAINE

Los Al·tos \lȯ-'sal-təs\ city W Calif. SSE of Palo Alto *pop* 19,696

Los An·ge·les, 1 \lȯ-'san-jə-ləs *also* -'saŋ-g(ə-)ləs\ city & port SW Calif. on the Pacific *pop* 2,479,015 **2** \lȯ-'säŋ-hā-ˌläs\ city S cen Chile *pop* 75,639

Lot \'lȯt\ river 300 *m* S France flowing W into the Garonne

Lo·thi·an \'lō-thē-ən\ region S Scotland bordering on Firth of Forth; now divided into three counties (the **Lothians**): East Lothian, Midlothian, & West Lothian

Lough·bor·ough \'ləf-ˌbər-ə, -ˌbə-rə, -b(ə-)rə\ municipal borough cen England in Leicestershire S of Nottingham *pop* 34,731

Lou·ise, Lake \lü-'ēz\ lake W Canada in SW Alta. in Banff National Park at altitude of 5670 *ft*

Lou·i·si·ade \lü-ˌē-zē-'äd, -ˌād\ archipelago in Solomon sea SE of New Guinea; belongs to Territory of Papua

Lou·i·si·ana \lü-ˌē-zē-'an-ə, ˌlü-ə-zē-, lü-ˌzē-\ state S U.S. ✳ Baton Rouge *area* 48,523, *pop* 3,257,022 — **Lou·i·si·an·an** \-'an-ən\ *adj or n* — **Lou·i·si·an·ian** \-'an-ē-ən, -'an-yən\ *adj or n*

Louisiana Purchase region W cen U.S. between the Mississippi & the Rockies purchased (1803) from France *area* 885,000

Lou·is·ville \'lü-i-ˌvil, -vəl\ city N Ky. on the Ohio *pop* 390,639

Loup \'lüp\ river 70 (290 *m* with longest headstream, the Middle Loup) E cen Nebr. flowing E into the Platte

ə abut; ᵊ kitten; ər further; a back; ā bake; ä cot, cart; aù out; ch chin; e less; ē easy; g gift; i trip; ī life
j joke; ŋ sing; ō flow; ȯ flaw; ȯi coin; th thin; t͟h this; ü loot; u̇ foot; y yet; yü few; yu̇ furious; zh vision
œ F table; ȧ F bac; ᴋ G ich, Buch; ⁿ F vin; œ F bœuf; œ̄ F feu; ᵫ G füllen; ᵫ F rue; ᵞ F digne \dēnᵞ\, nuit \nwᵞē\

Lourdes \ˈlu̇(ə)rd(z)\ commune SW France on the Gave de Pau SSW of Tarbes *pop* 15,829

Lou·ren·ço Mar·ques \lə-ˌren(t)-(ˌ)sō-ˌmär-ˈkes\ city & port ✱ of Mozambique on Delagoa Bay *pop* 184,000

Louth \ˈlau̇th\ county E Ireland in Leinster bordering on Irish sea ✱ Dundalk *area* 317, *pop* 67,284

Lou·vain \lü-ˈvaⁿ\ *or* Flem **Leu·ven** \ˈlə(r)v-ə(n)\ city *cen* Belgium in Brabant E of Brussels *pop* 32,474

Low — see TUAMOTU

Low Countries region W Europe bordering on North sea & comprising modern Belgium, Luxembourg, & the Netherlands

Low·ell \ˈlō-əl\ city NE Mass. NW of Boston *pop* 92,107

Lower California *or* Sp **Ba·ja Ca·li·for·nia** \ˌbä-(ˌ)hä-\ peninsula 760 *m* long NW Mexico between the Pacific & Gulf of California; divided into the state of **Baja California** (to the N ✱ Mexicali *area* 27,653, *pop* 470,089) & the territory of **Baja California Sur** \ˈsü(ə)r\ (to the S ✱ La Paz *area* 27,976, *pop* 68,315)

Lower Canada the chiefly French province of Canada 1791–1841 corresponding to modern Que. — see UPPER CANADA

Lower Klamath lake N Calif. on Oreg. border SSE of Upper Klamath Lake (in Oreg.); now usu. dry

Lower Mer·i·on \ˈmer-ē-ən\ urban township SE Pa. NW of Philadelphia *pop* 59,420

Lower Saxony *or* G **Nie·der·sach·sen** \ˌnēd-ər-ˈzäk-sən\ state of the Bonn Republic W Germany bordering on North sea ✱ Hannover *area* 18,289, *pop* 6,576,100 — see SAXONY

Lowes·toft \ˈlō-stəf(t), -ˌstȯft\ municipal borough & port E England in East Suffolk on North sea *pop* 42,837

Low·lands \ˈlō-lən(d)z, -ˌlan(d)z\ the *cen* & E part of Scotland lying between the Highlands & the Southern Uplands

Loyalty islands SW Pacific E of New Caledonia; a dependency of New Caledonia *area* 800, *pop* 16,000

Lo·yang \ˈlō-ˈyäŋ\ city E China in N Honan in Yellow river basin *pop* 500,000

Lu·a·la·ba \ˌlü-ə-ˈläb-ə\ river 400 *m* SE Congo flowing N to join the **Lu·a·pu·la** \-ˈpü-lə\ (350 *m*, outlet of Lake Bangweulu) forming the Congo

Lu·an·da \lü-ˈan-də\ *or* **Lo·an·da** \lō-\ city & port ✱ of Angola *pop* 137,139

Luang Pra·bang \lü-ˌäŋ-prə-ˈbäŋ\ city, royal ✱ of Laos, on the Mekong NNW of Vientiane *pop* 25,000

Luangue — see LOANGE

Lub·bock \ˈləb-ək\ city NW Tex. *pop* 128,691

Lü·beck \ˈlü-bek\ city & port N Germany NE of Hamburg *pop* 231,800

Lu·blin \ˈlü-blən, -ˌblēn\ city E Poland SE of Warsaw *pop* 148,200

Lu·bum·ba·shi \ˌlü-büm-ˈbä-shē\ *or formerly* **Elis·a·beth·ville** \i-ˈliz-ə-bəth-ˌvil\ city SE Congo in SE Katanga *pop* 117,879

Lucania — see BASILICATA

Lu·ca·nia, Mount \lü-ˈkā-nē-ə, -nyə\ mountain 17,150 *ft* Canada in SW Yukon Territory in St. Elias range N of Mt. Logan

Luc·ca \ˈlü-kə\ commune *cen* Italy in Tuscany NW of Florence *pop* 42,300

Lu·cerne \lü-ˈsərn\ *or* G **Lu·zern** \lüt-ˈse(ə)rn\ **1** canton *cen* Switzerland *area* 579, *pop* 223,249 **2** commune, its ✱, on Lake of Lucerne *pop* 67,100

Lucerne, Lake of *or* **Lake of the Four Forest Cantons** lake 24 *m* long *cen* Switzerland *area* 44

Lu·chow \ˈlü-ˈjō\ **1** city S *cen* China in SE Szechwan on the Yangtze SW of Chungking *pop* 289,000 **2** — see HOFEI

Luck·now \ˈlək-ˌnau̇\ city N India ✱ of Uttar Pradesh *pop* 496,900

Lü·de·ritz \ˈlüd-ə-rəts\ town & port SW South-West Africa

Lu·dhi·a·na \ˌlüd-ē-ˈän-ə\ city NW India in Punjab SE of Amritsar *pop* 153,800

Lud·wigs·burg \ˈlüd-(ˌ)vigz-ˌbu̇(ə)rg\ city SW Germany in Baden-Württemberg N of Stuttgart *pop* 73,200

Lud·wigs·ha·fen \ˌlüd-(ˌ)vigz-ˈhäf-ən\ city W Germany on the Rhine opposite Mannheim *pop* 161,900

Luf·kin \ˈləf-kən\ city E Tex. NNE of Houston *pop* 17,641

Lu·ga·no \lü-ˈgän-(ˌ)ō\ commune S Switzerland in Ticino canton on Lake Lugano *pop* 18,300

Lugano, Lake lake on border between Switzerland & Italy E of Lake Maggiore *area* 19

Lu·gansk \lü-ˈgän(t)sk\ *or formerly* **Vo·ro·shi·lov·grad** \ˌvȯr-ə-ˈshē-ləf-ˌgrad\ city U.S.S.R. in E Ukraine in Donets basin *pop* 274,000

Lu·go \ˈlü-(ˌ)gō\ **1** province NW Spain in NE Galicia on Bay of Biscay *area* 3814, *pop* 502,652 **2** commune, its ✱ *pop* 53,833

Lui·chow \ˈlā-ˈjō\ peninsula SE China in Kwangtung between So. China sea & Gulf of Tonkin

Luik — see LIÈGE

Lu·leå \ˈlü-lə-ˌō, -lē-ˌō\ city & port N Sweden near head of Gulf of Bothnia *pop* 31,588

Lu·le·bur·gaz \ˌlül-ə-(ˌ)bu̇r-ˈgäz\ town *cen* Turkey in Europe

Lu·lua·bourg \lü-ˈlü-ə-ˌbu̇(ə)r\ city S *cen* Congo 27,252

Lum·ber·ton \ˈləm-bərt-ᵊn\ city SE N.C. *pop* 15,305

Lund \ˈlənd\ city SW Sweden NE of Malmö *pop* 40,985

Lun·dy \ˈlən-dē\ island SW England at mouth of Bristol channel off coast of Devonshire *area* 2

Lü·ne·burg \ˈlü-nə-ˌbu̇(ə)rg\ city W Germany SE of Hamburg & NE of **Lüneburg Heath** *or* G **Lü·ne·bur·ger Hei·de** \ˌlü-nə-ˌbu̇r-gər-ˈhīd-ə\ (50 *m* long) *pop* 58,600

Lü·nen \ˈlü-nən\ city W Germany S of Münster *pop* 72,200

Lu·né·ville \ˈlü-nə-ˌvil\ city NE France on the Meurthe SE of Nancy *pop* 22,690

Lungki — see CHANGCHOW

Lungkiang — see TSITSIHAR

Lu·ray \ˈlü-(ˌ)rā\ caverns N Va. in Blue Ridge mountains

Lu·ri·stan \ˈlu̇r-ə-ˌstan, -ˌstän\ region W Iran; chief town Burujird

Lu·sa·ka \lü-ˈsäk-ə\ city ✱ of Zambia *pop* 30,700

Lu·sa·tia \lü-ˈsā-sh(ē-)ə\ *or* G **Lau·sitz** \ˈlau̇-ˌzits\ region E Germany NW of Silesia between Elbe & Oder rivers

Lüshun — see PORT ARTHUR

Lusitania — see PORTUGAL — **Lu·si·ta·ni·an** \ˌlü-sə-ˈtā-nē-ən, -nyən\ *adj or n*

Lü·ta *or* **Lü·dä** \ˈlü-ˈdä\ *or* **Port Arthur–Dairen** municipality NE China in Liaoning including cities of Dairen & Port Arthur & adjacent area *pop* 1,200,000

Lutetia — see PARIS

Lu·ton \ˈlüt-ᵊn\ municipal borough SE *cen* England in Bedfordshire *pop* 110,370

Lüt·zen \ˈlüt-sən\ town E Germany in Saxony SW of Leipzig

Lux·em·bourg *or* **Lux·em·burg** \ˈlu̇k-səm-ˌbu̇(ə)rg, ˈlək-səm-ˌbərg\ *or* **Let·ze·burg** \ˈlet-sə-ˌbu̇(ə)rg\ **1** province SE Belgium ✱ Arlon *area* 1705, *pop* 218,784 **2** country W Europe between Belgium & Germany; a grand duchy *area* 999, *pop* 317,853 **3** city, its ✱ *pop* 70,158 — **Lux·em·bourg·er** *or* **Lux·em·burg·er** \-ˌbu̇r-gər, -ˌbər-\ *n* — **Lux·em·bourg·ian** *or* **Lux·em·burg·ian** \ˌlu̇k-səm-ˈbu̇r-gē-ən, ˌlək-səm-ˈbər-\ *adj*

Lux·or \ˈlək-ˌsȯ(ə)r, ˈlük-\ *or* **Ar El Uq·sor** \e-ˈlük-ˌsu̇(ə)r\ city S Egypt on the Nile on S part of site of ancient Thebes *pop* 30,100

Lu·zon \lü-ˈzän\ island N Philippines, chief island of the group *area* 40,420, *pop* 3,800,000

Lvov \lə-ˈvȯf, -ˈvȯv\ *or* Pol **Lwow** \lə-ˈvüf, -ˈvüv\ *or* G **Lem·berg** \ˈlem-ˌbərg\ city U.S.S.R. in W Ukraine *pop* 410,000

Lya·khov \lē-ˈäk-əf\ islands U.S.S.R. in Arctic ocean S of New Siberian islands *area* 2660

Ly·all·pur \ˈlī-əl-ˌpu̇(ə)r\ city Pakistan in NE West Pakistan W of Lahore *pop* 179,100

Ly·ca·bet·tus *or* Gk **Ly·ka·bet·tos** \ˌlik-ə-ˈbet-əs, ˌlī-kə-\ mountain 909 *ft* in NE part of Athens, Greece

Lyc·a·o·nia \ˌlik-ə-ˈō-nē-ə, ˌlī-kə-, -nyə\ ancient region & Roman province SE *cen* Asia Minor N of Cilicia

Ly·cia \ˈlish-(ē-)ə\ ancient region & Roman province SW Asia Minor on coast SE of Caria — **Ly·cian** \-(ē-)ən\ *adj or n*

Lyd·da \ˈlid-ə\ *or* **Lod** \ˈlȯd\ city *cen* Israel *pop* 18,600

Lyd·ia \ˈlid-ē-ə\ ancient country W Asia Minor bordering on the Aegean ✱ Sardis — **Lyd·i·an** \-ən\ *adj or n*

Lyn·brook \ˈlin-ˌbru̇k\ village SE N.Y. on Long I. *pop* 19,881

Lynch·burg \ˈlinch-ˌbərg\ city S *cen* Va. on the James *pop* 54,790

Lynd·hurst \ˈlind-ˌhərst\ **1** urban township NE N.J. N of Newark *pop* 21,867 **2** city NE Ohio E of Cleveland *pop* 16,805

Lynn \ˈlin\ **1** city NE Mass. NE of Boston *pop* 94,478 **2** *or* **Lynn Re·gis** — see KING'S LYNN

Lynn Canal narrow inlet of the Pacific 80 *m* long SE Alaska extending N from Juneau

Lyn·wood \ˈlin-ˌwu̇d\ city SW Calif. S of Los Angeles *pop* 31,614

Ly·on·nais *or* **Ly·o·nais** \ˌlē-ə-ˈnā\ former province SE *cen* France NE of Auvergne & W of the Saône & the Rhone ✱ Lyons

Ly·ons \lē-ˈōⁿ, ˈlī-ənz\ *or* F **Lyon** \lyōⁿ\ *or anc* **Lug·du·num** \ˌlu̇g-ˈdü-nəm, ˌləg-\ city SE *cen* France *pop* 471,300

Lys \ˈlēs\ *or* **Leie** \ˈlā-ə, ˈlī-\ river 120 *m* France & Belgium flowing NE into the Scheldt

Lyt·tel·ton \ˈlit-ᵊl-tən\ borough New Zealand on South I.; port for Christchurch, on Port Lyttelton (inlet)

Maas — see MEUSE

Maas·tricht *or* **Maes·tricht** \ˈmäs-ˌtrikt\ commune SE Netherlands on the Meuse ✱ of Limburg *pop* 89,354

Mc·Al·es·ter \mə-ˈkal-ə-stər\ city E *cen* Okla. *pop* 17,419

Mc·Al·len \mə-ˈkal-ən\ city S Tex. WNW of Brownsville *pop* 32,728

Ma·cao \mə-ˈkau̇\ *or* Port **Ma·cau** \mə-ˈkau̇\ **1** island SE China in Kwangtung in Si delta W of Hong Kong **2** Portuguese colony comprising peninsula on SE Macao I. & adjacent islands *area* 6, *pop* 187,772 **3** city & port, its ✱ — **Mac·a·nese** \ˌmak-ə-ˈnēz, -ˈnēs\ *n*

Ma·ca·pá \ˌmak-ə-ˈpä\ town & port N Brazil ✱ of Amapá

Macassar — see MAKASSAR

Mac·cles·field \ˈmak-əlz-ˌfēld\ municipal borough W England in E Cheshire SSE of Manchester *pop* 35,999

Mac·don·nell ranges \mək-ˈdän-ᵊl\ series of mountain ridges *cen* Australia in S Northern Territory; highest point Mt. Ziel 4955 *ft*

Mac·e·do·nia \ˌmas-ə-ˈdō-nyə, -nē-ə\ **1** region S Europe in Balkan peninsula in NE Greece, S Yugoslavia, & SW Bulgaria including territory of ancient kingdom of Macedonia (**Mac·e·don** \ˈmas-əd-ən, -ə-ˌdän\ ✱ Pella) **2** the Yugoslav section of Macedonia; a federated republic ✱ Skoplje *area* 10,229, *pop* 1,153,000

Ma·ceió \ˌmas-ā-ˈō\ city NE Brazil ✱ of Alagoas *pop* 99,088

Mac·gil·li·cud·dy's Reeks \mə-ˌgil-ə-ˌkəd-ēz-\ mountains SW Ireland in County Kerry — see CARRANTUOHILL

Ma·chu Pic·chu \ˌmä-(ˌ)chü-ˈpēk-(ˌ)chü\ site SE Peru of ancient Inca city on a mountain NW of Cuzco

Mc·Kees·port \mə-ˈkēz-ˌpō(ə)rt, -ˌpȯ(ə)rt\ city SW Pa. S of Pittsburgh *pop* 45,489

Mac·ken·zie \mə-ˈken-zē\ **1** river 1120 *m* NW Canada flowing from Great Slave Lake NW into Beaufort sea; sometimes considered to include the Finlay, Peace, & Slave rivers (total length 2635 *m*) **2** mountain range NW Canada in the Rockies in Yukon Territory & Mackenzie District **3** district Canada in W Northwest Territories in basin of Mackenzie river *area* 493,225, *pop* 12,492

Mack·i·nac \ˈmak-ə-ˌnak, -ˌnȯ\ *or formerly* **Mich·i·li·mack·i·nac** \ˌmish-ə-lē-\ island N Mich. in Straits of Mackinac

Mack·i·nac, Straits of \ˈmak-ə-ˌnȯ\ channel N Mich. connecting Lakes Huron & Michigan; 4 *m* wide at narrowest point; site of Mackinac bridge connecting upper & lower peninsulas of Mich.

Mc·Kin·ley, Mount \mə-ˈkin-lē\ *or native* **De·na·li** \də-ˈnäl-ē\ mountain 20,320 *ft cen* Alaska in Alaska range; highest in U.S. & No. America; in **Mount McKinley National Park** (*area* 3030)

Mc·Mur·do Sound \mək-ˌmərd-ō-\ inlet of W Ross sea Antarctica between Ross I. & coast of Victoria Land

Ma·con \ˈmā-kən\ city *cen* Ga. *pop* 69,764

Mâ·con \mä-ˈkōⁿ\ city E *cen* France *pop* 22,393

Mac·quar·ie \mə-ˈkwär-ē\ river 750 *m* E *cen* New So. Wales flowing NNW to Darling river

Mac·tan \mäk-ˈtän\ island S *cen* Philippines off E coast of Cebu

Mad·a·gas·car \ˌmad-ə-ˈgas-kər\ island W Indian ocean off SE coast of Africa; formerly a French territory; became (1958), as the **Mal·a·gasy Republic** \ˌmal-ə-ˌgas-ē-\ *or* F **Ré·pu·blique Mal·gache** \rā-pū-ˌblēk-mal-ˈgäsh\, a republic of the French Community ✱ Tananarive *area* 227,678, *pop* 5,487,000 — **Mad·a·gas·can** \ˌmad-ə-ˈgas-kən\ *adj or n*

Ma·dei·ra \mə-ˈdir-ə, -ˈder-ə\ **1** river 2100 *m* W Brazil formed at Bolivian border by confluence of Mamoré & Beni rivers & flowing NE to the Amazon **2** islands in N Atlantic N of the Canaries belonging to Portugal ✱ Funchal *area* 302, *pop* 250,124 **3** island, chief of group *area* 285 — **Ma·dei·ran** \-ˈdir-ən, -ˈder-\ *adj or n*

Ma·dhya Bha·rat \ˌmäd-yə-ˈbär-ət\ former state *cen* India; a

union of 20 states including Gwalior, Indore, & Malwa formed 1948; became part of Madhya Pradesh 1956

Madhya Pra·desh \-prə-'däsh, -'desh\ state *cen* India ✻ Bhopal *area* 171,201, *pop* 26,072,300 — see CENTRAL PROVINCES AND BERAR, MADHYA BHARAT

Mad·i·son \'mad-ə-sən\ **1** river 180 *m* SW Mont. — see THREE FORKS **2** borough NE N.J. W of Newark *pop* 15,122 **3** city ✻ of Wis. *pop* 126,706

Madison Heights city SE Mich. N of Detroit *pop* 33,343

Ma·dras \mə-'dras, -'dräs\ **1** *or since 1967* **Ta·mizh·gam** \'täm-izh-,gäm\ state SE India bordering on Bay of Bengal ✻ Madras *area* 50,110, *pop* 29,974,200 **2** city & port, its ✻ *pop* 1,416,100

Ma·dre, La·gu·na \lə-,gü-nə-'mäd-rē\ inlet of Gulf of Mexico S Tex. between Padre I. & mainland

Ma·dre de Dios \,mäd-rē-,dād-ē-'ōs\ river 900 *m* rising in SE Peru & flowing E into the Beni in Brazil

Ma·drid \mə-'drid\ **1** province *cen* Spain in NW New Castile *area* 3084, *pop* 2,360,934 **2** city, its ✻ & ✻ of Spain *pop* 2,028,091 — **Mad·ri·le·nian** \,mad-rə-'lē-nē-ən, -nyən\ *adj or n*

Ma·du·ra *or* D **Ma·doe·ra** \mə-'dùr-ə\ island Indonesia off coast of NE Java *area* (with adjacent islands) 2113 — **Mad·u·rese** \,mad-ə-'rēz, ,maj-, -'rēs\ *adj or n*

Ma·du·rai \mäd-ə-'rī\ *or* **Mad·u·ra** \'maj-ə-rə\ city S India in S Madras state *pop* 361,800

Maeander — see MENDERES

Maf·e·king \'maf-ə-kiŋ\ town S Republic of So. Africa in N Cape Province near W Transvaal border

Ma·fia \'mäf-ē-ə, 'maf-\ island Tanganyika in Indian ocean S of Zanzibar *area* 170

Ma·ga·dan \,mäg-ə-'dan, -'dän\ city & port U.S.S.R. in E Soviet Russia, Asia, on N shore of Sea of Okhotsk *pop* 62,000

Magallanes — see PUNTA ARENAS

Mag·da·la \'mag-də-lə\ **1** ancient city N Palestine on W shore of Sea of Galilee N of Tiberias **2** town N *cen* Ethiopia

Mag·da·len \'mag-də-lən\ *or* F **Îles de la Ma·de·leine** \ēl-də-là-mà-dlen\ islands Canada in Que. in Gulf of St. Lawrence between Nfld. & P. E. I. *area* 102, *pop* 11,556

Mag·da·le·na \,mag-də-'lā-nə, -'lē-\ river 1000 *m* Colombia flowing N into the Caribbean

Mag·de·burg \'mäg-də-,bù(ə)rg, 'mag-də-,bərg\ city E Germany on the Elbe WSW of Berlin *pop* 258,712

Ma·ge·lang \,mäg-ə-'läŋ\ city Indonesia in *cen* Java *pop* 78,800

Ma·gel·lan, Strait of \mə-'jel-ən, *chiefly Brit* -'gel-\ strait 370 *m* long at S end of So. America between mainland & Tierra del Fuego archipelago

Mageröy — see NORTH CAPE

Mag·gio·re, Lake \mə-'jōr-ē, -'jòr-\ lake 40 *m* long N Italy & S Switzerland traversed by the Ticino

Ma·ghreb *or* **Ma·ghrib** \'məg-rəb\ **1** northwestern Africa &, at time of the Moorish occupation, Spain; now considered as including Morocco, Algeria, Tunisia, & sometimes Libya **2** *or* **El Ma·ghreb al Aq·sa** \el-,məg-rə-ba-'lək-sə\ MOROCCO — **Ma·ghre·bi** *or* **Ma·ghri·bi** \'məg-rə-bē\ *adj or n* — **Ma·ghreb·i·an** \mə-'greb-ē-ən\ *or* **Ma·ghrib·i·an** \-'grib-\ *adj or n*

Mag·na Grae·cia \,mag-nə-'grē-shə\ the ancient Greek colonies in S Italian peninsula including Tarentum, Sybaris, Crotona, Heraclea, & Neapolis

Magnesia — see MANISA

Mag·ni·to·gorsk \mag-'nēt-ə-,gòrsk\ city U.S.S.R. in W Soviet Russia, Asia, on Ural river *pop* 311,000

Magyarorszag — see HUNGARY

Ma·hal·la el Ku·bra \mə-,hal-ə-,el-'kü-brə\ city N Egypt in Nile delta NE of Tanta *pop* 162,900

Ma·ha·na·di \mə-'hän-əd-ē\ river 512 *m* E India flowing into Bay of Bengal in Orissa through several mouths

Ma·ha·rash·tra \,mä-hə-'räsh-trə\ **1** region W *cen* India S of the Narbada; the original home of the Marathas **2** state W India bordering on Arabian sea formed 1960 from SE part of former Bombay state ✻ Bombay

Ma·hé \ma-'hā\ **1** island in Indian ocean, chief of the Seychelles group **2** *or formerly* **May·ya·li** \mī-'yäl-ē\ town SW India in N Kerala NW of Kozhikode; a settlement of French India until 1954

Ma·hón \mə-'hōn\ *or* **Port Ma·hon** \mə-'hōn\ city & port Spain on Minorca I. *pop* 15,732

Ma·hone Bay \mə-,hōn-\ inlet of the Atlantic E Canada in S N.S. SW of Halifax

Maid·en·head \'mād-ᵊn-,hed\ municipal borough S England in Berkshire on the Thames W of London *pop* 27,125

Maid·stone \'mād-stən, -,stōn\ municipal borough SE England ✻ of Kent on the Medway ESE of London *pop* 54,026

Mai·kop \mī-'kòp\ city U.S.S.R. in S Soviet Russia, Europe ✻ of Adygei autonomous region *pop* 67,000

Main \'mīn, 'mān\ river 305 *m* W Germany rising in N Bavaria in the Fichtel Gebirge & flowing W into the Rhine

Maine \'mān\ **1** state NE U.S. ✻ Augusta *area* 33,215, *pop* 969,265 **2** *or* **Le Maine** \lə-\ region & former province NW France S of Normandy ✻ Le Mans **3** — see MAYENNE

Main·land \'mān-,land, -lənd\ **1** Honshu, the chief island of Japan **2** *or* **Po·mo·na** \pə-'mō-nə\ island N Scotland, largest of the Orkneys **3** island N Scotland, largest of the Shetlands

Mainz \'mīn(t)s\ *or* F **Ma·yence** \mà-yäⁿs\ city W Germany on the Rhine ✻ of Rhineland-Palatinate *pop* 130,900

Ma·jor·ca \mə-'jòr-kə\ *or* Sp **Ma·llor·ca** \mə(l)-'yòr-kə\ island Spain, largest of the Balearic islands; chief city Palma *area* 1405 — **Ma·jor·can** \mə-'jòr-kən\ *adj or n*

Ma·jun·ga \mə-'jəŋ-gə\ city & port NW Madagascar *pop* 51,687

Ma·ka·lu \'mək-ə-,lü\ mountain 27,824 *ft* in the Himalayas in NE Nepal SE of Mt. Everest; 5th highest in world

Ma·kas·sar *or* **Ma·kas·ar** *or* **Ma·cas·sar** \mə-'kas-ər\ **1** city & port Indonesia ✻ of Celebes on SW coast of the island *pop* 360,000 **2** strait Indonesia between E Borneo & W Celebes — **Ma·kas·sa·rese** *or* **Ma·cas·sa·rese** \mə-,kas-ə-'rēz, -'rēs\ *n*

Ma·ka·téa \,mäk-ə-'tā-ə\ island S Pacific in NW Tuamotu archipelago *area* 8

Ma·ke·ev·ka *or* **Ma·ke·yev·ka** \mə-'kā-əf-kə\ city U.S.S.R. in E Ukraine in Donets basin NE of Donetsk *pop* 358,000

Ma·khach·ka·la \mə-,käch-kə-'lä\ *or formerly* **Pe·trovsk** \pə-'tròfsk\ city U.S.S.R. in SE Soviet Russia, Europe, on the Caspian ✻ of Dagestan *pop* 119,000

Ma·kin \'mäk-ən, 'mā-kən\ *or* **Bu·ta·ri·ta·ri** \bù-,tär-ē-'tär-ē\ island (atoll) W Pacific at N end of the Gilberts *area* 4

Makira — see SAN CRISTOBAL

Makka — see MECCA

Mal·a·bar \'mal-ə-,bär\ coast region SW India on Arabian sea in Mysore & Kerala states

Ma·lac·ca *or* **Ma·lak·ka** \mə-'lak-ə\ **1** state Federation of Malaysia on W coast of Malaya; formerly in Straits Settlements *area* 633, *pop* 239,400 **2** city & port, its ✻, on Strait of Malacca *pop* 69,865 — **Ma·lac·can** \-'lak-ən\ *adj*

Malacca, Strait of channel 500 *m* long between S Malay peninsula & island of Sumatra

Má·la·ga \'mal-ə-gə\ **1** province S Spain in Andalusia *area* 2812, *pop* 779,613 **2** city & port, its ✻, on the Mediterranean *pop* 285,699

Malagasy Republic — see MADAGASCAR

Ma·lai·ta \mə-'lāt-ə\ island SW Pacific in the SE Solomons NE of Guadalcanal *area* 2500, *pop* 46,000

Ma·la·moc·co \,mal-ə-'mäk-(,)ō\ village N Italy on Lido I.

Ma·lang \mə-'läŋ\ city Indonesia in E Java *pop* 281,700

Ma·lar \'mā-,lär\ *or* **Mä·lar·en** \'mā-,lär-ən\ lake SE Sweden extending from Baltic sea 70 *m* inland

Mal·a·spi·na \,mal-ə-'spē-nə\ glacier S Alaska SE of Mt. St. Elias

Ma·la·tya \,mäl-ə-'tyä\ *or anc* **Mel·i·te·ne** \,mel-ə-'tē-nē\ city E Turkey NE of Gaziantep *pop* 84,162

Malawi — see NYASALAND — **Ma·la·wi·an** \mə-'lä-wē-ən\ *adj or n*

Ma·lay \mə-'lā, 'mā-(,)lā\ **1** archipelago SE Asia including Sumatra, Java, Borneo, Celebes, Moluccas, & Timor; usu. considered as including also the Philippines & sometimes New Guinea **2** peninsula 700 *m* long SE Asia divided between Thailand & Federation of Malaysia **3** sea SE Asia surrounding the Malay archipelago

Ma·laya \mə-'lā-ə, mā-\ **1** the Malay peninsula **2** BRITISH MALAYA **3** *or* **Federation of Malaya** former country SE Asia; a Brit. dominion 1957–63, since 1963 a territory of Federation of Malaysia ✻ Kuala Lumpur *area* 50,690, *pop* 7,136,804

Ma·lay·sia \mə-'lā-zh(ē-)ə, -sh(ē-)ə\ **1** the Malay archipelago **2** *or* **Federation of Malaysia** country SE Asia, a union of Malaya, Sabah (No. Borneo), Sarawak, & (until 1965) Singapore; a limited constitutional monarchy ✻ Kuala Lumpur *area* 128,319 *pop* 8,491,259 — **Ma·lay·sian** \mə-'lā-zhən\ *adj or n*

Mal·den \'mòl-dən\ **1** city E Mass. N of Boston *pop* 57,676 **2** island *cen* Pacific, one of the Line islands; claimed by U.S. & Great Britain

Mal·dive \'mal-,dīv, 'mòl-\ islands in Indian ocean S of the Laccadives; a sultanate; under Brit. protection until 1965 ✻ Male *area* 115, *pop* 81,900 — **Mal·div·i·an** \-'div-ē-ən\ *adj or n*

Ma·le \'mäl-ē\ island (atoll), chief of the Maldives

Ma·lea, Cape \mə-'lē-ə\ cape S Greece at extremity of E peninsula of the Peloponnesus

Malgache, République — see MADAGASCAR

Mal·heur \mal-'hù(ə)r\ lake SE Oreg. in Harney basin

Ma·li \'mäl-ē\ **1** federation 1959–60 of Senegal and Sudanese Republic **2** *or formerly* **Sudanese Republic** country W Africa in W Sahara & Sudan regions; a republic; before 1958 constituted **French Sudan** (a territory of France) ✻ Bamako *area* 461,389, *pop* 4,100,000 — **Ma·li·an** \-ē-ən\ *adj or n*

Malines — see MECHELEN

Mal·in Head \,mal-ən-\ cape Republic of Ireland in County Donegal; northernmost tip of Ireland

Mal·mé·dy \,mal-mā-'dē\ commune E Belgium SE of Liège; formerly in Germany, transferred (with Eupen) to Belgium 1919

Malmö \'mal-,mə(r)\ city & port SW Sweden on Öresund opposite Copenhagen, Denmark *pop* 233,370

Mal·ta \'mòl-tə\ *or anc* **Mel·i·ta** \'mel-ət-ə\ **1** *or* **Mal·tese islands** \,mòl-,tēz-, -,tēs-\ group of islands in the Mediterranean S of Sicily; a former British colony; independent since 1964 ✻ Valletta *area* 122, *pop* 241,600 **2** island, chief of the group *area* 95

Maluku — see MOLUCCAS

Mal·vern \'mò(l)-vərn\ hills W England between Worcestershire & Herefordshire; highest point 1395 *ft*

Malvinas, Islas — see FALKLAND

Ma·mar·o·neck \mə-'mar-ə-,nek, -nik\ village SE N.Y. NE of New Rochelle *pop* 17,673

Mam·be·ra·mo \,mam-bə-'räm-(,)ō\ river 500 *m* West New Guinea flowing NW into the Pacific

Mam·moth Cave \,mam-əth-\ limestone caverns SW *cen* Ky. in **Mammoth Cave National Park** (*area* 79)

Ma·mo·ré \,mäm-ə-'rā\ river 1200 *m* Bolivia flowing N to unite with the Beni on Brazilian border forming the Madeira

Man, Isle of \'man\ *or anc* **Mo·na·pia** \mə-'nā-pē-ə\ *or* **Mo·na** \'mō-nə\ island Brit. Isles in Irish sea; has own legislature & laws ✻ Douglas *area* 221, *pop* 49,308 — **Manx·man** \'maŋ(k)-smən\ *n*

Ma·na·do *or* **Me·na·do** \mə-'näd-(,)ō\ city & port Indonesia in NE Celebes I. on Celebes sea *pop* 62,000

Ma·na·gua \mə-'näg-wə\ **1** lake 38 *m* long W Nicaragua draining S through Tipitipa river to Lake Nicaragua **2** city ✻ of Nicaragua on Lake Managua *pop* 107,444

Ma·naus \mə-'naùs\ *or* **Ma·ná·os** \mə-'naùs\ city W Brazil ✻ of Amazonas on the Negro 12 *m* from its junction with the Amazon *pop* 89,612

Mancha, La — see LA MANCHA

Manche, La — see ENGLISH CHANNEL

Man·ches·ter \'man-,ches-tər, -chə-stər\ **1** town *cen* Conn. E of Hartford *pop* 42,102 **2** city S N.H. on the Merrimack *pop* 88,282 **3** city & county borough NW England in Lancashire *pop* 703,175 — **Man·cun·ian** \man-'kyü-nē-ən, -nyən\ *adj or n*

Man·chu·kuo \'man-'chü-'kwō, man-'chü-(,)\ former country (1931–45) E Asia in Manchuria & E Inner Mongolia ✻ Changchun

Man·chu·ria \man-'chùr-ē-ə\ region NE China E of the Great Khingan mountains & S of the Amur including Heilungkiang, Kirin, & Liaoning provinces & part of Inner Mongolia — **Man·chu·ri·an** \-ē-ən\ *adj or n*

Man·da·lay \,man-də-'lā\ city *cen* Burma *pop* 182,367

Man·ga·ia \mäŋ-'(g)ī-ə\ island S Pacific in SE Cook islands; completely encircled by reef *area* 25

Man·ga·lore \'maŋ-gə-,lō(ə)r, -,lȯ(ə)r\ city S India in Mysore on Malabar coast W of Bangalore *pop* 117,100
Man·ga·r·eva \,mäŋ-(g)ə-'rā-və\ island S Pacific, chief of the Gambier islands *area* 7
Man·hat·tan \man-'hat-ᵊn, mən-\ **1** city NE *cen* Kans. on Kansas river *pop* 22,993 **2** island 13 *m* long SE N.Y. on New York Bay **3** borough of New York City comprising Manhattan I., several small adjacent islands, & a small area (Marble Hill) on mainland *pop* 1,698,281 — **Man·hat·tan·ese** \-,hat-ᵊn-'ēz, -'ēs\ *adj or n* — **Man·hat·tan·ite** \-'hat-ᵊn-,īt\ *n*
Manhattan Beach city SW Calif. SW of Los Angeles *pop* 33,934
Ma·ni·hi·ki \,män-ə-'hē-kē\ *or* **Northern Cook** \'ku̇k\ islands S *cen* Pacific N of Cook islands; belong to New Zealand; chief island Manihiki (atoll)
Ma·nila \mə-'nil-ə\ city & port Philippines on W coast of Luzon on **Manila Bay** (inlet of So. China sea) ✻ of the Philippines until 1948 & present seat of government *pop* 983,906 — see QUEZON CITY
Man·i·pur \,man-ə-'pu̇(ə)r, ,mən-\ **1** river 210 *m* NE India & W Burma flowing into the Chindwin **2** territory NE India between Assam & Burma ✻ Imphal *area* 8628, *pop* 983,900
Ma·ni·sa *or* **Ma·nis·sa** \,män-ə-'sä\ *or anc* **Mag·ne·sia** \mag-'nē-shə, -zhə\ city W Turkey NE of Izmir *pop* 59,223
Man·i·to·ba \,man-ə-'tō-bə\ province S *cen* Canada ✻ Winnipeg *area* 251,000, *pop* 850,040 — **Man·i·to·ban** \-bən\ *adj or n*
Manitoba, Lake lake 120 *m* long Canada in S Man. *area* 1817
Man·i·tou·lin \,man-ə-'tü-lən\ island 80 *m* long Canada in Ont. in Lake Huron NW of Georgian Bay; largest freshwater island in the world *area* 1068
Man·i·to·woc \'man-ət-ə-,wäk\ city E Wis. *pop* 32,275
Ma·ni·za·les \,man-ə-'zäl-əs, -'zal-\ city W *cen* Colombia in Cauca valley *pop* 161,000
Man·ka·to \man-'kāt-(,)ō\ city S Minn. on Minnesota river SW of Minneapolis *pop* 23,797
Man·nar, Gulf of \mə-'när\ inlet of Indian ocean between Ceylon & S tip of India SW of Palk strait
Mann·heim \'man-,hīm, 'män-\ city W Germany at confluence of the Rhine & the Neckar *pop* 308,700
Mans·field \'manz-,fēld, 'man(t)s-\ **1** city N *cen* Ohio *pop* 47,325 **2** municipal borough N *cen* England in Nottinghamshire N of Nottingham *pop* 51,343
Mansfield, Mount mountain 4393 *ft* N Vt.; highest in Green mountains & in state
Man·sû·ra *or* **El Mansûra** \,el-(,)man-'su̇r-ə\ city N Egypt in Nile delta *pop* 146,700
Man·tua \'manch-(ə-)wə, 'mant-ə-wə\ *or* **Man·to·va** \'män-tə-və\ commune N Italy in Lombardy WSW of Venice *pop* 55,400 — **Man·tu·an** \'manch-(ə-)wən, 'mant-ə-wən\ *adj or n*
Ma·nua \mə-'nü-ə\ islands SW Pacific in American Samoa E of Tutuila *area* 22
Ma·nus \'män-(,)üs\ island SW Pacific in Admiralty islands; largest of group *area* 600
Man·za·la, Lake \man-'zäl-ə\ *or anc* **Ta·nis** \'tā-nəs\ lagoon N Egypt in Nile delta W of N entrance of Suez canal
Man·za·ni·llo \,man-zə-'nē-(,)(y)ō\ **1** city & port E Cuba on the Caribbean *pop* 42,252 **2** town & port SW Mexico in Colima
Ma·ple Heights \,mā-pəl-\ city NE Ohio SE of Cleveland *pop* 31,667
Ma·ple·wood \'mā-pəl-,wu̇d\ **1** village SE Minn. E of St. Paul *pop* 18,519 **2** urban township NE N.J. W of Newark *pop* 23,977
Ma·quo·ke·ta \mə-'kō-kət-ə\ river 150 *m* E Iowa flowing SE into the Mississippi
Mar·a·cai·bo \,mar-ə-'kī-(,)bō\ city NW Venezuela on channel between Lake Maracaibo & Gulf of Venezuela *pop* 235,750
Maracaibo, Gulf of — see VENEZUELA (Gulf of)
Maracaibo, Lake the S extension of Gulf of Venezuela in NW Venezuela *area* 6300
Maracanda — see SAMARKAND
Ma·ra·cay \,mär-ə-'kī\ city N Venezuela WSW of Caracas *pop* 64,535
Marais des Cygnes \'merd-ə-,zēn\ river 150 *m* E Kans. & W Mo. flowing into the Osage
Ma·ra·nhão \,mar-ən-'yau̇ⁿ\ state NE Brazil bordering on the Atlantic ✻ São Luís *area* 133,674, *pop* 1,600,400
Ma·ra·ñón \,mär-ən-'yōn\ river 800 *m* N Peru flowing from the Andes NNW & E to join the Ucayali forming the Amazon
Ma·ras *or* **Ma·rash** \mə-'räsh\ city S *cen* Turkey *pop* 54,646
Mar·a·thon \'mar-ə-,thän, -thən\ **1** plain E Greece in Attica NE of Athens on the Aegean **2** ancient town on the plain
Marble Canyon canyon of Colorado river N Ariz. just above the Grand Canyon, sometimes considered its upper portion
Mar·ble·head \'mär-bəl-,hed, ,mär-bəl-'\ town E Mass. NE of Lynn on Massachusetts Bay *pop* 18,521
Mar·burg \'mär-,bu̇(ə)rg, -,bərg\ city W Germany in Hesse N of Frankfurt *pop* 43,500
March \'märch\ **1** *or* **Mo·ra·va** \'mȯr-ə-və\ river 180 *m*, *cen* Czechoslovakia in Moravia flowing S into the Danube **2** urban district E England ✻ of Isle of Ely E of Leicester
Marche \'märsh\ region & former province *cen* France NW of Auvergne ✻ Guéret
March·es \'mär-chəz\ *or* **Le Mar·che** \lā-'mär-(,)kā\ region *cen* Italy on the Adriatic NW of Abruzzi e Molise ✻ Ancona
Mar·cus \'mär-kəs\ island W Pacific E of the Bonins; occupied by the U.S. *area* 1
Mar·cy, Mount \'mär-sē\ mountain 5344 *ft* NE N.Y.; highest in Adirondack mountains & in state
Mar del Pla·ta \,mär-,del-'plät-ə\ city & port E Argentina SSE of Buenos Aires *pop* 114,729
Mare \'ma(ə)r, 'me(ə)r\ island W Calif. in San Pablo Bay
Ma·rem·ma \mə-'rem-ə\ low-lying district W Italy on Tyrrhenian coast in SW Tuscany
Ma·ren·go \mə-'reŋ-(,)gō\ village NW Italy in SE Piedmont SE of Alessandria
Mar·eo·tis, Lake \,mar-ē-'ōt-əs\ *or* Ar **Mar·yût** \mər-'yüt\ lake N Egypt in Nile delta; Alexandria is situated between it & the Mediterranean
Ma·reth \'mär-əth, 'mar-\ town SE Tunisia SSE of Gabes
Mar·ga·ri·ta \,mär-gə-'rēt-ə\ island N Venezuela in the Caribbean, chief of the **Nue·va Es·par·ta** \nù-,ā-və-es-'pärt-ə\ group; chief town & port Porlamar *area* 444
Mar·gate \'mär-,gāt, -gət\ municipal borough SE England in Kent on coast of Isle of Thanet *pop* 42,487
Mar·i·ana \,mar-ē-'an-ə, ,mer-\ *or formerly* **La·drone** \lə-'drōn\ islands W Pacific S of Bonin islands; except Guam, a Japanese mandate 1919–45 & since 1947 in Trust Territory of the Pacific Islands administered by the U.S. *area* 246
Ma·ri·a·nao \,mär-ē-ə-'nau̇\ city W Cuba, W suburb of Havana *pop* 219,278
Ma·ri·an·ske Laz·ne \,mär-ē-,än(t)-skə-'läz-nə\ *or* G **Ma·ri·en·bad** \mə-'rē-ən-,bad, -,bät\ town W Czechoslovakia in NW Bohemia NE of Plzen
Ma·ri·as \mə-'rī-əs\ **1** river 250 *m* NW Mont. flowing SE to the Missouri **2** mountain pass 5213 *ft* NW Mont. in Lewis range at SE corner of Glacier National Park
Ma·ri·bor \'mär-i-,bȯ(ə)r\ city NW Yugoslavia *pop* 80,700
Ma·rie Byrd Land \mə-,rē-'bərd-\ *or* **Byrd Land** region W Antarctica E of Ross Ice Shelf & Ross sea
Ma·rie Ga·lante \mə-,rē-gə-'länt\ island E West Indies in the Leewards; a dependency of Guadeloupe *area* 60, *pop* 16,037
Mar·i·et·ta \,mar-ē-'et-ə, ,mer-\ **1** city NW Ga. NW of Atlanta *pop* 25,565 **2** city SE Ohio on the Ohio *pop* 16,847
Ma·rin·du·que \,mar-ən-'dü-(,)kā, ,mär-\ island Philippines in Sibuyan sea S of Luzon; chief town Boac *area* 355
Mar·i·on \'mer-ē-ən, 'mar-\ **1** city N *cen* Ind. *pop* 37,854 **2** city *cen* Ohio *pop* 37,079
Ma·ri Republic \,mär-ē-\ autonomous republic U.S.S.R. in E *cen* Soviet Russia, Europe ✻ Ioshkar Ola *area* 8900, *pop* 648,000
Maritime Alps section of the W Alps SE France & NW Italy extending to the Mediterranean; highest point Punta Argentera 10,814 *ft*
Maritime Provinces *or* **Maritimes** the Canadian provinces of N.B., N.S., & P.E.I.
Maritime Territory *or* **Pri·mor·ski Krai** \prə-,mȯr-skē-'krī\ territory U.S.S.R. in E Soviet Russia, Asia, bordering on Sea of Japan ✻ Vladivostok *area* 64,900, *pop* 1,475,000
Ma·ri·tsa \mə-'rēt-sə\ *or* NGk **Év·ros** \'ev-,rȯs\ *or* Turk **Me·ric** \mə-'rēch\ river 320 *m* S Europe flowing from W Rhodope mountains in S Bulgaria E & S through Thrace into the Aegean
Mariupol — see ZHDANOV
Mar·ken \'mär-kə(n)\ island W Netherlands in SW Lake IJssel
Mark·ham \'mär-kəm\ river 200 *m* E New Guinea flowing S & SE into Solomon sea
Markham, Mount mountain 14,270 *ft* Antarctica in Queen Elizabeth Range W of Ross Ice Shelf
Marl \'mär(ə)l\ city W Germany in the Ruhr *pop* 72,200
Marl·bor·ough \'märl-,bər-ə, -,bə-rə\ **1** *or* **Marl·boro** city E Mass. E of Worcester *pop* 18,819 **2** provincial district New Zealand on NE coast of South I. ✻ Blenheim *area* 4220, *pop* 27,800
Mar·ly–le–Roi \(,)mär-,lē-lə-rə-'wä, -lər-'wä\ village N France, NW suburb of Versailles, on edge of Marly Forest
Mar·ma·ra, Sea of *or* **Sea of Mar·mo·ra** \'mär-mə-rə\ *or anc* **Pro·pon·tis** \prə-'pänt-əs\ sea NW Turkey connected with Black sea by the Bosporus & with Aegean sea by the Dardanelles *area* 4250
Mar·mo·la·da \,mär-mə-'läd-ə\ mountain 10,965 *ft* NE Italy; highest in the Dolomites
Marne \'märn\ river 325 *m* NE France flowing W into the Seine
Ma·ro·ni \mə-'rō-nē\ *or* D **Ma·ro·wij·ne** \,mär-ə-'vī-nə\ river 420 *m* on border between Surinam & French Guiana flowing N into the Atlantic
Maros — see MURES
Mar·ple \'mär-pəl\ urban township SE Pa. W of Philadelphia *pop* 19,722
Mar·que·sas \mär-'kā-zəz, -'kā-səz\ *or* F **Îles Mar·quises** \,ē(ə)l-(,)mär-'kēz\ islands S Pacific N of Tuamotu archipelago in French Polynesia *area* 480, *pop* 3936
Mar·quette \mär-'ket\ city NW Mich. in upper peninsula on Lake Superior *pop* 19,824
Mar·ra·kesh *or* **Mar·ra·kech** \mə-'räk-ish, ,mar-ə-'kesh\ *or formerly* **Mo·roc·co** \mə-'räk-(,)ō\ city *cen* Morocco in foothills of the Grand Atlas *pop* 220,000
Mar·sa·la \mär-'säl-ə\ city & port Italy on W coast of Sicily S of Trapani *pop* 42,488
Mar·seilles \mär-'sā, -'sā(ə)lz\ *or* F **Mar·seille** \mär-'sā\ *or anc* **Mas·sil·ia** \mə-'sil-ē-ə\ city & port SE France on Gulf of Lions *pop* 661,500
Mar·shall \'mär-shəl\ **1** city NE Tex. *pop* 23,846 **2** islands W Pacific E of the Carolines comprising the Ratak & Ralik chains; a Japanese mandate 1920–45; now part of Trust Territory of the Pacific Islands administered by the U.S. *area* 66, *pop* 14,290
Mar·shall·town \'mär-shəl-,tau̇n\ city *cen* Iowa *pop* 22,521
Mar·ston Moor \,mär-stən-\ locality N England in West Riding, Yorkshire, W of York
Mar·ta·ban, Gulf of \,märt-ə-'bän, -'ban\ arm of Andaman sea S Burma
Mar·tha's Vineyard \,mär-thəz-\ island 20 *m* long SE Mass. in the Atlantic off SW coast of Cape Cod WNW of Nantucket
Mar·ti·nique \,märt-ᵊn-'ēk\ island West Indies in the Windwards; an overseas department of France ✻ Fort-de-France *area* 385, *pop* 239,130
Mar·tins·burg \'märt-ᵊnz-,bərg\ city NE W. Va. *pop* 15,179
Mar·tins·ville \'märt-ᵊnz-,vil, -vəl\ city S Va. *pop* 18,798
Marwar — see JODHPUR
Mary·bor·ough \'mer-ē-,bər-ə, 'mar-, -,bə-rə, -b(ə)rə\ *or* **Port Laoigh·i·se** \'lā-ə-shə\ town *cen* Ireland ✻ of County Laoighis
Mary·land \'mer-ə-lənd\ state E U.S. ✻ Annapolis *area* 10,577, *pop* 3,100,689 — **Mary·land·er** \-lən-dər, -,lan-\ *n*
Mary·le·bone \'mar-(ə-)lə-bən, 'mar-i-bən\ *or* **Saint Marylebone** \'mar-ē-lə-'bōn, 'mer-\ metropolitan borough W *cen* London, England *pop* 75,764
Ma·sa·da \mə-'säd-ə\ fortress town of ancient Palestine in SE Israel W of Dead Sea
Ma·san \'mäs-,än\ *or formerly* **Ma·sam·po** \'mäs-,äm-,pō\ city & port S Korea on an inlet of Korea strait E of Pusan *pop* 91,291
Mas·ba·te \mäs-'bät-ē\ island *cen* Philippines in the Visayans NE of Panay *area* 1571
Mas·ca·rene \,mas-kə-'rēn\ islands W Indian ocean E of Madagascar including Mauritius & Réunion
Mashhad — see MESHED
Mas·e·ru \'maz-ə-,rü\ town ✻ of Lesotho on NW border on Caledon river
Ma·son City \,mās-ᵊn-\ city N Iowa *pop* 30,642
Masqat — see MUSCAT
Masr–el–Gedida — see HELIOPOLIS

Mas·sa·chu·setts \,mas-(ə-)'chü-səts, -zəts\ state NE U.S. ✳ Boston *area* 8257, *pop* 5,148,578
Massachusetts Bay inlet of the Atlantic E Mass.
Mas·sa·nut·ten Mountain \,mas-ə-'nət-ᵊn\ ridge N Va. in Blue Ridge mountains
Mas·sa·pe·qua \,mas-ə-'pē-kwə\ urban area SE N.Y. on Long I. *pop* 32,900
Massapequa Park village SE N.Y. on Long I. *pop* 19,904
Mas·sa·wa *or* **Mas·saua** \mə-'sä-wə, -'saú-ə\ city & port N Ethiopia in Eritrea on an inlet of Red sea *pop* 17,000
Mas·se·na \mə-'sē-nə\ village N N.Y. *pop* 15,478
Mas·sif Cen·tral \ma-,sēf-,sen·träl, -,säⁿ-\ plateau *cen* France rising sharply just W of the Rhone-Saône valley & sloping N to the Paris basin & W to the basin of Aquitaine
Mas·sil·lon \'mas-ə-lən, -,län\ city NE Ohio *pop* 31,236
Mas·sive, Mount \'mas-iv\ mountain 14,418 *ft*, *cen* Colo. in Sawatch mountains N of Mt. Elbert
Ma·su·li·pat·nam \,mə-,sü-li-ə-'pat-nəm\ *or* **Ma·su·li·pa·tam** \-'pət-əm\ *or* **Ban·dar** \'bən-dər\ city & port SE India in E Andhra Pradesh SW of Kakinada *pop* 78,000
Ma·su·ria \mə-'zür-ē-ə, -'sür-\ *or* **G Ma·su·ren** \mə-'zúr-ən\ region N Poland S of Gulf of Danzig; formerly in East Prussia, Germany — **Ma·su·ri·an** \mə-'zúr-ē-ən, -'sür-\ *adj*
Mat·a·be·le·land \,mat-ə-'bē-lē-,land\ region SW Southern Rhodesia between the Limpopo & the Zambezi; chief town Bulawayo
Ma·ta·di \mə-'täd-ē\ town & port W Congo on Congo river *pop* 48,000
Mat·a·gor·da Bay \,mat-ə-,górd-ə-\ inlet of Gulf of Mexico 30 *m* long SE Tex.
Mat·a·mo·ros \,mat-ə-'mōr-əs, -'mór-\ city NE Mexico in Tamaulipas on Rio Grande opposite Brownsville, Tex. *pop* 120,277
Mat·a·nus·ka \,mat-ə-'nü-skə\ river 90 *m* S Alaska flowing SW to head of Cook inlet
Ma·tan·zas \mə-'tan-zəs\ city & port W Cuba on Straits of Florida E of Havana *pop* 63,900
Mat·a·pan \,mat-ə-'pan\ *or* **Ma·ta·pás** \,mät-ə-'päs\ *or* **Taí·na·ron** \'tä-nə,rón\ cape S Greece at S tip of Peloponnesus between gulfs of Laconia & Messenia
Ma·ta·ra·ni \,mät-ə-'rän-ē\ town & port S Peru NW of Mollendo
Ma·thu·ra \'mət-ə-rə\ *or* **Mut·tra** \'mə-trə\ city N India in W Uttar Pradesh NW of Agra *pop* 105,800
Ma·to Gros·so \,mat-ə-'grō-(,)sō\ **1** state SW Brazil ✳ Cuiabá *area* 485,405, *pop* 522,044 **2** plateau region in E Mato Grosso state
Mato Tepee — see DEVILS TOWER
Ma·trûh *or* **Mer·sa Matrûh** \mər-,säm-ə-'trü\ town NW Egypt
Mat·su \'mät-,sü, 'mat-, -(,)sü\ island SE China in Formosa strait E of Foochow
Ma·tsue \'mät-sə-,wä, -sù-,yä\ city of Japan in W Honshu NW of Hiroshima *pop* 97,857
Ma·tsu·mo·to \,mät-sə-'mōt-(,)ō\ city Japan in *cen* Honshu NE of Nagoya *pop* 145,228
Ma·tsu·shi·ma \,mät-sü-'shē-mə, mät-'sü-shi-mə\ group of over 800 islets Japan off N Honshu in Ishinomaki Bay NE of Sendai
Mat·su·ya·ma \mät-sə-'yäm-ə/ city & port Japan in W Shikoku *pop* 213,457
Mat·tag·a·mi \mə-'tag-ə-mē\ river 275 *m* Canada in E Ont. flowing into Moose river
Mat·ta·po·ni \,mat-ə-pə-'nī\ river 125 *m* E Va. uniting with the Pamunkey to form York river
Mat·ter·horn \'mat-ər-,hó(ə)rn, 'mät-\ *or* **F Mont Cer·vin** \,mōⁿ-sər-'vaⁿ\ mountain 14,690 *ft* in Pennine Alps on border between Switzerland & Italy
Mat·toon \mə-'tün, ma-\ city SE *cen* Ill. *pop* 19,088
Ma·tu·rín \,mät-ə-'rēn\ city NE Venezuela *pop* 42,000
Maui \'maù-ē\ island Hawaii NW of Hawaii I. *area* 728
Mau·mee \mò-'mē\ river 175 *m* NE Ind. & NW Ohio flowing NE into Lake Erie at Toledo
Mau·na Kea \,maù-nə-'kā-ə\ extinct volcano 13,796 *ft* Hawaii in N *cen* Hawaii I.
Mauna Loa \-'lō-ə\ volcano 13,680 *ft* Hawaii in S *cen* Hawaii I. in Hawaii National Park — see KILAUEA
Maures, Monts des \,mōⁿd-ā-'mō(ə)r, -'mó(ə)r\ mountains SE France along French Riviera
Mau·re·ta·nia *or* **Mau·ri·ta·nia** \,mór-ə-'tā-nē-ə, ,mär-, -nyə\ ancient country N Africa W of Numidia in modern Morocco & W Algeria — **Mau·re·ta·nian** *or* **Mau·ri·ta·nian** \-nē-ə, -nyə\ *adj or n*
Mauritania *or* **F Mau·ri·ta·nie** \mò-rē-tà-nē\ country NW Africa bordering on the Atlantic N of Senegal river; a republic (**Islamic Republic of Mauritania**) within the French Community, formerly a territory ✳ Nouakchott *area* 419,229, *pop* 727,000 — **Mau·ri·ta·nian** \-nē-ən, -nyən\ *adj or n*
Mau·ri·ti·us \mò-'rish-(ē-)əs\ island in Indian ocean in *cen* Mascarenes; constitutes with Rodrigues & other dependencies a Brit. colony ✳ Port Louis *area* 720, *pop* 749,069 — **Mau·ri·tian** \-'rish-ən\ *adj or n*
May, Cape \'mā\ cape S N.J. at entrance to Delaware Bay
Ma·a·gua·na \,mä-ə-'gwän-ə\ island in the SE Bahamas NNE of Great Inagua I. *area* 96
Ma·ya·güez \,mī-ə-'gwäs\ city & port W Puerto Rico *pop* 50,147
Ma·ya·pán \,mī-ə-'pän\ ruined city ✳ of the Mayas SE Mexico in Yucatán SSE of Mérida
Mayence — see MAINZ
Ma·yenne \mä-'yen\ river 125 *m* NW France uniting with the Sarthe to form the **Maine** \'mān\ (8 *m* long, flowing into the Loire)
May·fair \'mā-,fa(ə)r, -,fe(ə)r\ district of W London, England, in Westminster borough
May·nooth \mā-'nüth\ town E Ireland in County Kildare
Mayo, 1 \'mī-(,)ō\ river 250 *m* NW Mexico in Sonora flowing SW into Gulf of California **2** \'mā-(,)ō\ county NW Ireland in Connacht *area* 2084, *pop* 123,180
Ma·yon \mä-'yōn\ volcano 7943 *ft* Philippines in SE Luzon
May·wood \'mā-,wùd\ village NE Ill. W of Chicago *pop* 27,330
Mayyali — see MAHÉ
Mazaca — see KAYSERI

Ma·za·ma, Mount \mə-'zäm-ə\ prehistoric volcano SW Oreg. the collapse of whose summit formed Crater Lake
Ma·za·tlán \,mäs-ə-'tlän\ city & port W Mexico in Sinaloa on the Pacific *pop* 41,459
Mba·bane \,em-bə-'bän\ town ✳ of Swaziland *pop* 14,000
Mbandaka — see COQUILHATVILLE
Mbomu — see BOMU
M'·Clure Strait \mə-,klù(ə)r-\ channel N Canada between Banks I. & Melville I. opening on the W into Arctic ocean
Mead, Lake \'mēd\ reservoir NW Ariz. & SE Nev. formed by Hoover Dam in Colorado river — see BOULDER
Mead·ville \'mēd-,vil\ city NW Pa. *pop* 16,671
Mearns, The — see KINCARDINE
Meath \'mēth, 'mēth\ county E Ireland in NE Leinster ✳ Trim *area* 903, *pop* 65,106
Meaux \'mō\ commune N France ENE of Paris *pop* 16,767
Mec·ca \'mek-ə\ *or* **Mak·ka** \'mak-ə\ city ✳ of Hejaz & a ✳ of Saudi Arabia *pop ab* 250,000 — **Mec·can** \'mek-ən\ *adj or n*
Mech·lin \'mek-lən\ *or* Flem **Me·che·len** \'mek-ə-lə(n)\ *or* **F Ma·lines** \mə-'lēn\ commune N Belgium *pop* 63,298
Meck·len·burg \'mek-lən-,bərg\ region E Germany SE of Jutland peninsula & E of the Elbe; in 18th & 19th centuries divided into duchies of **Mecklenburg–Schwe·rin** \-shfā-'rēn\ & **Mecklen·burg–Stre·litz** \-'s(h)trā-ləts\ which became grand duchies 1815 & states of Weimar Republic 1919
Me·dan \mā-'dän\ city Indonesia in NE Sumatra *pop* 310,000
Me·de·llín \,med-ᵊl-'ēn, ,mā-thə-'yēn\ city NW Colombia NW of Bogotá *pop* 578,940
Med·ford \'med-fərd\ **1** city E Mass. N of Boston *pop* 64,971 **2** city SW Oreg. *pop* 24,425
Me·dia \'mēd-ē-ə\ ancient country & province of Persian Empire SW Asia in NW modern Iran — **Me·di·an** \-ē-ən\ *adj or n*
Media Atropatene — see AZERBAIJAN
Medicine Bow \-,bō\ **1** river 120 *m* S Wyo. flowing into the No. Platte **2** mountains N Colo. & S Wyo. in the Rockies; highest **Medicine Bow Peak** (in Wyo.) 12,005 *ft*
Medicine Hat city Canada in SE Alta. *pop* 20,826
Me·di·na \me-'dē-nə\ city W Saudi Arabia *pop ab* 30,000
Medina as–Shaab \-,ash-'shäb\ city ✳ of So. Yemen & formerly (as **Al It·ti·had** \,al-,it-i-'had, -'häd\) ✳ of Federation of So. Arabia
Mediolanum — see MILAN
Med·i·ter·ra·nean \,med-ə-tə-'rā-nē-ən, -nyən\ sea 2330 *m* long between Europe & Africa connecting with the Atlantic through Strait of Gibraltar & with Red sea through Suez canal
Mé·doc \mā-'däk\ district SW France N of Bordeaux
Med·way \'med-,wā\ river 60 *m* SE England in Kent flowing NE into the Thames
Mee·rut \'mā-rət, 'mir-ət\ city N India in NW Uttar Pradesh NE of Delhi *pop* 233,200
Meg·a·ra *or* NGk **Mé·ga·ra** \'meg-ə-rə\ town & port Greece on Saronic gulf W of Athens; chief town of ancient **Meg·a·ris** \'meg-ə-rəs\ (district between Saronic gulf & Gulf of Corinth) — **Me·gar·i·an** \mi-'gar-ē-ən, -'ger-\ *or* **Me·gar·ic** \-'gar-ik\ *adj or n*
Megh·na \'mäg-nə\ the lower course of the Surma river, India
Me·gid·do \mi-'gid-(,)ō\ ancient city N Palestine N of Samaria
Meis·sen \'mīs-ᵊn\ city E Germany NW of Dresden *pop* 49,900
Méjico — see MEXICO
Mek·nes \mek-'nes\ city N Morocco WSW of Fez; former ✳ of Morocco *pop* 150,000
Me·kong \'mā-,koŋ, -'käŋ\ river 2600 *m* SE Asia flowing from S Tsinghai, China, S & SE into So. China sea in S Vietnam
Mel·a·ne·sia \,mel-ə-'nē-zhə, -shə\ the islands in the Pacific NE of Australia & S of Micronesia including Bismarck archipelago, the Solomons, New Hebrides, New Caledonia, & the Fijis
Mel·bourne \'mel-bərn\ city & port SE Australia ✳ of Victoria on Port Phillip Bay *pop* (with suburbs) 1,595,300 — **Mel·bur·ni·an** \mel-'bər-nē-ən\ *n*
Me·li·lla \mə-'lē-(y)ə\ city & port NE Morocco on coast NE of Fez; a Spanish presidio *pop* 88,809
Melita — see MALTA
Melitene — see MALATYA
Me·li·to·pol \,mel-ə-'tó-pəl\ city U.S.S.R. in S Ukraine near Sea of Azov *pop* 95,000
Me·los *or* NGk **Mí·los** \'mē-,läs\ *or* It **Mi·lo** \'mē-(,)lō\ island Greece in SW Cyclades *area* 57 — **Me·li·an** \'mē-lē-ən\ *adj or n*
Mel·rose \'mel-,rōz\ city E Mass. N of Boston *pop* 29,619
Melrose Park village NE Ill. W of Chicago *pop* 22,291
Mel·ville \'mel-,vil\ **1** island Canada in N Northwest Territories in Parry islands *area* 16,141 **2** peninsula Canada in E Northwest Territories between Foxe Basin & an arm of Gulf of Boothia
Melville, Lake lake Canada in Nfld. in Labrador; the inner basin of Hamilton inlet *area* 1133
Me·mel \'mā-məl\ **1** — see NEMAN **2** *or* **Klai·pe·da** \'klī-pəd-ə\ city & port U.S.S.R. in W Lithuania on the Baltic *pop* 89,000
Mem·phis \'mem(p)-fəs\ **1** city N Tenn. *pop* 497,524 **2** ancient city N Egypt on the Nile S of modern Cairo; once ✳ of Egypt — **Mem·phi·an** \-fē-ən\ *adj or n* — **Mem·phite** \-,fīt\ *adj or n*
Mem·phre·ma·gog, Lake \,mem(p)-fri-'mā-,gäg\ lake 30 *m* long on border between Canada & the U.S. in Que. & Vt.
Menado — see MANADO
Men·ai \'men-,ī\ strait 14 *m* long N Wales between Anglesey I. & mainland
Me Nam — see CHAO PHRAYA
Men·den·hall \'men-dən-,hól\ glacier SE Alaska N of Juneau
Men·de·res \,men-də-'res\ **1** *or anc* **Mae·an·der** \mē-'an-dər\ river 240 *m* W Turkey in Asia flowing SW & W into the Aegean **2** *or anc* **Sca·man·der** \skə-'man-dər\ river 60 *m* NW Turkey in Asia flowing from Mt. Ida W & NW across the plain of ancient Troy into the Dardanelles
Men·dip \'men-,dip\ hills SW England in NE Somerset; highest point Blackdown 1068 *ft*
Men·do·ci·no, Cape \,men-də-'sē-(,)nō\ headland NW Calif. SSW of Eureka; extreme W point of Calif., at 124°8' W
Men·do·ta \men-'dōt-ə\ lake 6 *m* long S Wis. NW of Madison
Men·do·za \men-'dō-zə\ city W Argentina *pop* 115,161

ə abut; ᵊ kitten; ər further; a back; ā bake; ä cot, cart; aú out; ch chin; e less; ē easy; g gift; i trip; ī life
j joke; ŋ sing; ō flow; ó flaw; ói coin; th thin; th this; ü loot; ù foot; y yet; yü few; yù furious; zh vision
ᵊ F table; à F bac; ḵ G ich, Buch; ⁿ F vin; œ F bœuf; œ̄ F feu; ᵫ G füllen; ᵫ̄ F rue; ʸ F digne \dēnʸ\, nuit \nwʸē\

Men·lo Park \ˌmen-(ˌ)lō-\ city W Calif. SE of San Francisco *pop* 26,957
Me·nom·i·nee \mə-'näm-ə-nē\ **1** river 125 *m* NE Wis. flowing SE on Mich.–Wis. border into Green Bay **2** iron range NE Wis. & NW Mich. in upper peninsula
Me·nom·o·nee Falls \mə-ˌnäm-ə-nē-\ village SE Wis. NW of Milwaukee *pop* 18,276
Menorca — see MINORCA
Men·ton \mäⁿ-tōⁿ\ *or* It **Men·to·ne** \men-'tō-nē\ city SE France on the Mediterranean ENE of Nice *pop* 17,109
Men·zel–Bour·gui·ba \men-ˌzel-bür-'gē-bə\ *or formerly* **Fer·ry·ville** \'fer-ē-ˌvil\ city N Tunisia on S shore of Lake Bizerte *pop* 34,732
Me·ra·no \mə-'rän-(ˌ)ō\ commune N Italy in Trentino-Alto Adige NW of Bolzano *pop* 29,400
Mer·ced \(ˌ)mər-'sed\ **1** river 150 *m, cen* Calif. flowing W through Yosemite valley into San Joaquin river **2** city *cen* Calif. in San Joaquin valley *pop* 20,068
Mer·ce·da·rio \ˌmer-sə-'där-ē-ˌō\ mountain 22,210 *ft* W Argentina in the Andes N of Aconcagua
Mer·cia \'mər-sh(ē-)ə\ ancient Anglian kingdom *cen* England; one of kingdoms in the Anglo-Saxon heptarchy
Mer·gent·heim *or* **Bad Mergentheim** \bät-'mer-gənt-ˌhīm\ town W Germany in Baden-Württemberg NNE of Stuttgart
Meric — see MARITSA
Mé·ri·da \'mer-əd-ə\ **1** city SE Mexico ✻ of Yucatán *pop* 198,970 **2** city W Venezuela S of Lake Maracaibo *pop* 44,404
Mer·i·den \'mer-əd-ᵊn\ city S *cen* Conn. S of Hartford *pop* 51,850
Me·rid·i·an \mə-'rid-ē-ən\ city E *cen* Miss. *pop* 49,374
Merín — see MIRIM
Mer·i·on·eth \ˌmer-ē-'än-əth\ *or* **Mer·i·on·eth·shire** \-ˌshi(ə)r, -shər\ county W Wales ✻ Dolgelley *area* 660, *pop* 41,456
Mer·o·ë \'mer-ə-ˌwē\ ancient city, site in N *cen* Sudan on the Nile — **Mero·ite** \'mer-ə-ˌwīt\ *n* — **Mero·itic** \ˌmer-ə-'wit-ik\ *adj*
Meroë, Isle of ancient region E Sudan between the Nile & Blue Nile & the Atbara
Me·rom, Waters of \'mir-əm\ or **Lake Hu·le** \'hü-lə\ lake 4 *m* long N Israel in the course of the Jordan N of Sea of Galilee
Mer·rick \'mer-ik\ urban area SE N. Y. on Long I. *pop* 18,789
Mer·ri·mack \'mer-ə-ˌmak\ river 110 *m* S N. H. & NE Mass. flowing S & NE into the Atlantic
Mer·ritt \'mer-ət\ island 40 *m* long E Fla. W of Canaveral peninsula between Indian & Banana rivers
Mersa Matrûh — see MATRÛH
Mers–el–Ke·bir \ˌme(ə)r-ˌsel-kə-'bi(ə)r\ town NW Algeria on the Mediterranean W of Oran
Mer·sey \'mər-zē\ river 70 *m* NW England flowing NW & W into Irish sea through a large estuary
Mer·sin \me(ə)r-'sēn\ *or* **Icel** \ē-'chel\ city & port S Turkey on the Mediterranean WSW of Adana *pop* 68,574
Mer·thyr Tyd·fil \ˌmər-thər-'tid-ˌvil\ county borough SE Wales in Glamorganshire *pop* 61,093
Mer·ton and Mor·den \ˌmərt-ᵊn-ən-'mȯrd-ᵊn\ urban district S England in Surrey, SW suburb of London *pop* 74,602
Me·ru \'mā-(ˌ)rü\ mountain 14,954 *ft* N Tanganyika W of Kilimanjaro
Me·sa \'mā-sə\ city SW *cen* Ariz. E of Phoenix *pop* 33,772
Me·sa·bi \mə-'säb-ē\ iron range NE Minn. NW of Duluth
Me·sa Verde National Park \ˌmā-sə-'vərd, -'ve(ə)rd-ē\ reservation SW Colo. containing prehistoric cliff dwellings *area* 80
Me·se·ta \mə-'sāt-ə\ the central plateau of Spain
Me·shed \mə-'shed\ *or* **Mash·had** \mə-'shad\ city NE Iran *pop* 242,165
Me·so·lón·gi·on \ˌmes-ə-'lȯŋ-gē(-ˌȯn)\ *or* **Mis·so·lon·ghi** \ˌmis-ə-'lȯŋ-gē\ town *cen* Greece on Gulf of Patras
Mes·o·po·ta·mia \ˌmes-(ə-)pə-'tā-mē-ə, -myə\ region SW Asia between Tigris & Euphrates rivers extending from the mountains of Asia Minor to the Persian gulf — **Mes·o·po·ta·mian** \-mē-ən, -myən\ *adj or n*
Mes·quite \mə-'skēt, me-\ city NE Tex. E of Dallas *pop* 27,526
Mes·se·ne *or* NGk **Mes·sí·ni** \mə-'sē-nē\ town S Greece in SW Peloponnesus, ancient ✻ of Messenia
Mes·se·nia \mə-'sē-nē-ə, -nyə\ region S Greece in SW Peloponnesus bordering on Ionian sea
Messenia, Gulf of inlet of the Mediterranean S Greece on S coast of Peloponnesus
Mes·si·na \mə-'sē-nə\ *or anc* **Mes·sa·na** \mə-'sän-ə\ *or* **Zancle** \'zaŋ-(ˌ)klē\ city & port Italy in NE Sicily on Strait of Messina *pop* 222,899 — **Mes·si·nese** \ˌmes-ᵊn-'ēs\ *n*
Messina, Strait of channel between S Italy & NE Sicily
Mes·ta \me-'stä\ *or* Turk **Ka·ra** \'kär-ə\ *or* Gk **Nes·tos** \'nes-ˌtäs\ river 130 *m* SW Bulgaria & NE Greece flowing from W end of Rhodope mountains SE into the Aegean
Me·ta \'māt-ə\ river 685 *m* NE Colombia flowing into the Orinoco on Venezuela-Colombia boundary
Me·tau·ro \mə-'tau̇(ə)r-(ˌ)ō\ *or anc* **Me·tau·rus** \-'tȯr-əs\ river 70 *m* E *cen* Italy flowing E into the Adriatic
Me·thu·en \mə-'th(y)ü-ən\ town NE Mass. *pop* 28,114
Metz \'mets, *F* mes\ city NE France on the Moselle *pop* 85,701
Meurthe \'mərt\ river 100 *m* NE France flowing NW from Vosges mountains to the Moselle
Meuse \'myüz, 'mə(r)z\ *or* D **Maas** \'mäs\ river 575 *m* W Europe flowing from NE France through S Belgium into North sea in the Netherlands
Mewar — see UDAIPUR
Mex·i·cali \ˌmek-si-'kal-ē\ city NW Mexico ✻ of Baja California state on Mexico–Calif. border *pop* 196,600
Mex·i·co \'mek-si-ˌkō\ *or* Sp **Mé·ji·co** \'me-hē-(ˌ)kō\ *or* MexSp **Mé·xi·co** \'me-hē-(ˌ)kō\ **1** *or* **Es·ta·dos Uni·dos Me·xi·ca·nos** \ā-ˌstäth-(ˌ)ō-sü-ˌnē-(ˌ)thōz-ˌme-hē-'kän-(ˌ)ōs\ country S No. America S of the U. S.; a republic ✻ Mexico *area* 761,830, *pop* 33,304,253 **2** state S *cen* Mexico ✻ Toluca *area* 8267, *pop* 1,592,886 **3** *or* **Mexico City** city ✻ of Republic of Mexico in Federal District (area surrounded on three sides by state of Mexico) *pop* 3,301,757 — see TENOCHTITLÁN
Mexico, Gulf of inlet of the Atlantic on SE coast of No. America
Mé·zenc \mā-'zaŋk\ mountain 5753 *ft* S France; highest in the Cévennes
Mez·zo·gior·no \ˌmet-sō-'jȯr-(ˌ)nō, ˌmed-zō-\ the Italian peninsula S of *ab* the latitude of Rome
Mfumbiro — see VIRUNGA
Mi·ami \mī-'am-ē, -'am-ə\ city & port SE Fla. on Biscayne Bay *pop* 291,688 — **Mi·ami·an** \-'am-ē-ən\ *n*
Miami Beach city SE Fla. *pop* 63,145
Mich·i·gan \'mish-i-gən\ state N U. S. in Great Lakes region including an upper (NW) & a lower (SE) peninsula ✻ Lansing *area* 58,216, *pop* 7,823,194 — **Mich·i·gan·der** \ˌmish-i-'gan-dər\ *n* — **Mich·i·gan·ite** \'mish-i-gə-ˌnīt\ *n*
Michigan, Lake lake N *cen* U. S.; one of the Great Lakes *area* 22,400
Michigan City city N Ind. on Lake Michigan *pop* 36,653
Michilimackinac — see MACKINAC
Mi·cho·a·cán \ˌmē-chə-wä-'kän\ state SW Mexico bordering on the Pacific ✻ Morelia *area* 23,200, *pop* 1,616,556
Mi·chu·rinsk \mə-'chu̇r-ən(t)sk\ *or formerly* **Koz·lov** \käz-'lȯf, -'lȯv\ city U. S. S. R. in S *cen* Soviet Russia, Europe *pop* 80,000
Mi·cro·ne·sia \ˌmī-krə-'nē-zhə, -shə\ the islands of the W Pacific E of the Philippines & N of Melanesia including the Caroline, Gilbert, Mariana, & Marshall groups
Mid·del·burg \'mid-ᵊl-ˌbərg\ city SW Netherlands on Walcheren I. ✻ of Zeeland *pop* 21,805
Middle America region of western hemisphere including Mexico, Central America, often the West Indies, & sometimes Colombia & Venezuela — **Middle American** *adj*
Middle Congo former French territory W *cen* Africa — see CONGO, FRENCH EQUATORIAL AFRICA
Middle East *or* **Mid·east** \'mid-'ēst\ the countries of SW Asia & N Africa — usu. considered as including the countries extending from Libya on the W to Afghanistan on the E — **Middle Eastern** *or* **Mid·east·ern** \'mid-'ē-stərn\ *adj*
Mid·dles·brough \'mid-ᵊlz-brə\ county borough N England in No. Riding, Yorkshire, on the Tees *pop* 147,336
Mid·dle·sex \'mid-ᵊl-ˌseks\ county SE England including NW part of Greater London *area* 232, *pop* 2,268,776
Mid·dle·town \'mid-ᵊl-ˌtau̇n\ **1** city *cen* Conn. S of Hartford *pop* 33,250 **2** urban township E N. J. *pop* 39,675 **3** city SE N. Y. *pop* 23,475 **4** city SW Ohio SW of Dayton *pop* 42,115 **5** urban township SE *cen* Pa. SE of Harrisburg *pop* 26,894
Middle West *or* **Mid·west** \'mid-'west\ region N *cen* U. S. including area around Great Lakes & in upper Mississippi valley from Ohio & sometimes Ky. on the E to N. & S. Dak., Nebr., & Kans. on the W — **Middle Western** *or* **Mid·west·ern** \'mid-'wes-tərn\ *adj* — **Middle Westerner** *or* **Mid·west·ern·er** \-tə(r)-nər\ *n*
Mi·di \mē-'dē\ the south of France
Mid·i·an \'mid-ē-ən\ ancient region NW Arabia E of Gulf of 'Aqaba
Mid·land \'mid-lənd\ **1** city *cen* Mich. NW of Saginaw *pop* 27,779 **2** city W Tex. NE of Odessa *pop* 62,625
Mid·lands \'mid-lən(d)z\ the central counties of England usu. considered as comprising Derby, Nottingham, Lincoln, Stafford, Leicester, Rutland, Worcester, Warwick, Northampton, Huntingdon, Cambridge, Oxford, Buckingham, & Bedford
Mid·lo·thi·an \mid-'lō-th̲ē-ən\ *or formerly* **Ed·in·burgh** \'ed-ᵊn-ˌbər-ə, -ˌbə-rə, -b(ə-)rə\ *or* **Ed·in·burgh·shire** \-ˌshi(ə)r, -shər\ county SE Scotland ✻ Edinburgh *area* 366, *pop* 565,746
Mid·way \'mid-ˌwā\ **1** urban area N *cen* Ga. NE of Macon *pop* (with Hardwick) 16,909 **2** atoll *cen* Pacific 1300 *m* WNW of Honolulu belonging to the U. S.; includes two islets: Sand I. & Eastern I. *area* 2
Midwest City city *cen* Okla. E of Oklahoma City *pop* 36,058
Mie·res \mē-'er-əs\ commune NW Spain in Oviedo province SSE of Oviedo *pop* 68,031
Míkonos — see MYKONOS
Mi·lan \mə-'lan, -'län\ *or* It **Mi·la·no** \mē-'län-(ˌ)ō\ *or anc* **Me·dio·la·num** \ˌmed-ē-ō-'lā-nəm\ commune N Italy ✻ of Lombardy *pop* 1,276,521 — **Mil·a·nese** \ˌmil-ə-'nēz, -'nēs\ *adj or n*
Mi·laz·zo \mi-'lät-(ˌ)sō\ *or anc* **My·lae** \'mī-(ˌ)lē\ town & port Italy in NE Sicily W of Messina
Mi·le·tus \mī-'lēt-əs, mə-\ ancient city on W coast of Asia Minor in Caria near mouth of the Maeander
Mil·ford \'mil-fərd\ city S Conn. on Long Island Sound *pop* 41,662
Milford Haven urban district & port SW Wales in Pembrokeshire on Milford Haven (inlet of St. George's channel)
Milk \'milk\ river 625 *m* Canada & U. S. in Alta. & Mont. flowing into the Missouri
Mill·brae \'mil-(ˌ)brā\ city W Calif. on San Francisco Bay S of San Francisco *pop* 15,873
Mill·burn \'mil-bərn\ urban township NE N. J. *pop* 18,799
Mill·creek \'mil-ˌkrēk\ urban township S *cen* Pa. *pop* 28,441
Mille Lacs \mil-'(l)ak(s)\ lake 20 *m* long E *cen* Minn.
Mill·ville \'mil-ˌvil\ city S N. J. *pop* 19,096
Milo *or* **Mílos** — see MELOS
Mil·ton \'milt-ᵊn\ town E Mass. S of Boston *pop* 26,375
Mil·wau·kee \mil-'wȯ-kē\ city & port SE Wis. *pop* 741,324
Min \'min\ **1** river 350 *m, cen* China in Szechwan flowing SE into the Yangtze **2** river 250 *m* SE China in Fukien flowing SE into East China sea
Mi·nas Basin \ˌmī-nəs-\ landlocked bay E Canada in *cen* N.S.; the NE extension of Bay of Fundy
Mi·nas de Rí·o·tin·to \'mē-nəs-(ˌ)dā-ˌrē-ə-'tin-(ˌ)tō\ commune SW Spain in Huelva province NE of Huelva
Mi·nas Ge·rais \ˌmē-nə-zhə-'rīs\ state E Brazil ✻ Belo Horizonte *area* 226,179, *pop* 7,717,792
Minch \'minch\ channel NW Scotland comprising **North Minch** & **Little Minch** between Outer Hebrides & NW coast of Scotland
Min·cio \'mēn-(ˌ)chō, 'min-chē-ˌō\ *or anc* **Min·cius** \'min-sh(ē-)əs, 'min(t)-sē-əs\ river 115 *m* N Italy issuing from Lake Garda & emptying into the Po
Min·da·nao \ˌmin-də-'nä-ˌō, -'nau̇\ **1** island S Philippines *area* (including adjacent islands) 36,537, *pop* 1,997,300 **2** sea S Philippines bordered on N by islands of Negros, Cebu, Bohol, & Leyte & on S by Mindanao
Min·do·ro \min-'dōr-(ˌ)ō, -'dȯr-\ island *cen* Philippines SW of Luzon *area* 3759, *pop* 131,600
Min·e·o·la \ˌmin-ē-'ō-lə\ village SE N.Y. on Long I. *pop* 20,519
Minhow — see FOOCHOW
Min·i·coy \'min-i-ˌkȯi\ island India, southernmost of the Laccadive group
Min·ne·ap·o·lis \ˌmin-ē-'ap-(ə-)ləs\ city SE Minn. *pop* 482,872 — **Min·ne·apol·i·tan** \-ē-ə-'päl-ət-ᵊn\ *n*
Min·ne·so·ta \ˌmin-ə-'sōt-ə\ **1** river 332 *m* S Minn. flowing from

Big Stone Lake to the Mississippi **2** state N U.S. ✽ St. Paul *area* 84,068, *pop* 3,413,864 — **Min•ne•so•tan** \-'sōt- n\ *adj or n*

Min•ne•ton•ka \,min-ə-'täŋ-kə\ village SE Minn. E of **Lake Minnetonka** (12 *m* long) *pop* 25,037

Minni — see ARMENIA

Mi•nor•ca \mə-'nȯr-kə\ *or* Sp **Me•nor•ca** \mā-\ island Spain in the Balearic islands ENE of Majorca; chief city Mahón *area* 264 — **Mi•nor•can** \mə-'nȯr-kən\ *adj or n*

Mi•not \'mī-,nät\ city NW *cen* N. Dak. on Souris river *pop* 30,604

Minsk \'min(t)sk\ city U.S.S.R. ✽ of Belorussia *pop* 509,000

Min•ya *or* **El Minya** \el-'min-yə\ city *cen* Egypt *pop* 93,300

Min•ya Kon•ka \,min-yə-'käŋ-kə\ mountain 24,900 *ft* W China in SW *cen* Szechwan; highest in China

Miq•ue•lon \'mik-ə-,län\ island off S coast of Nfld., Canada, belonging to France — see SAINT PIERRE

Mi•ra•da Hills \mə-,räd-ə-\ city SW Calif. SE of Los Angeles *pop* 22,444

Mi•rim \mə-'rim\ *or* Sp **Me•rín** \mā-'rēn\ lake 108 *m* long on boundary between Brazil & Uruguay near Atlantic coast

Mir•za•pur \'mi(ə)r-zə-,pu̇(ə)r\ city N India in SE Uttar Pradesh on the Ganges SW of Banaras *pop* 86,500

Mish•a•wa•ka \,mish-ə-'wȯ-kə, -'wäk-ə\ city N Ind. *pop* 33,361

Mis•kolc \'mish-,kōlts\ city NE Hungary *pop* 150,000

Misr — see EGYPT

Missionary Ridge mountain SE Tenn. & NW Ga. SE of Chattanooga & E of Lookout Mountain

Mis•sis•sip•pi \,mis-(ə-)'sip-ē\ **1** river 2470 *m*, *cen* U.S. flowing from N *cen* Minn. to Gulf of Mexico — see ITASCA (Lake) **2** river 105 *m* Canada in SE Ont. flowing NE & N into the Ottawa **3** sound inlet of Gulf of Mexico E of Lake Pontchartrain **4** state S U.S. ✽ Jackson *area* 47,716, *pop* 2,178,141

Missolonghi — see MESOLÓNGION

Mis•sou•la \mə-'zü-lə\ city W Mont. *pop* 27,090

Mis•sou•ri \mə-'zu̇(ə)r-ē, -'zu̇r-ə\ **1** river 2700 *m* W U.S. flowing from SW Mont. into the Mississippi in E Mo. — see THREE FORKS **2** state *cen* U.S. ✽ Jefferson City *area* 69,674, *pop* 4,319,813 — **Mis•sou•ri•an** \-'zu̇r-ē-ən\ *adj or n*

Mis•tas•si•ni \,mis-tə-'sē-nē\ **1** lake Canada in S *cen* Que. draining W to James Bay *area* 840 **2** river 185 *m* Canada in S Que. flowing S into Lake St. John

Mis•ti *or* **El Misti** \el-'mēs-tē, -'mis-\ volcano 19,110 *ft* S Peru NE of Arequipa

Mitch•am \'mich-əm\ municipal borough S England in Surrey, SSW suburb of London *pop* 67,273

Mitch•ell, Mount \'mich-əl\ mountain 6684 *ft* W N.C. in Black mountains of the Blue Ridge mountains; highest point in U.S. E of Mississippi river

Mitilíni — see MYTILENE

Mi•ya•ji•ma \,mē-(y)ə-'jē-mə\ *or* **Itsu•ku•shi•ma** \it-,sü-kə-'shē-mə\ island *ab* 5 *m* long Japan in Inland sea SW of Hiroshima

Mi•ya•za•ki \mē-,(y)äz-'äk-ē\ city & port Japan in Kyushu on SE coast *pop* 140,782

Mo•ab \'mō-,ab\ region Jordan E of Dead sea; in biblical times a kingdom between Edom & the country of the Amorites

Mo•bile \mō-'bē(ə)l, 'mō-,bēl\ **1** river 38 *m* long SW Ala. formed by Alabama & Tombigbee rivers & flowing S into **Mobile Bay** (inlet of Gulf of Mexico) **2** city & port SW Ala. *pop* 202,779

Moçambique — see MOZAMBIQUE

Moçâmedes — see MOSSÂMEDES

Mo•cha \'mō-kə\ *or* Ar **Mu•kha** \mu̇-'kä\ town & port SW Arabia in SW Yemen on the Red sea

Mod•der \'mäd-ər\ river 180 *m* Republic of So. Africa in Orange Free State; a tributary of the Vaal

Mo•de•na \'mȯd-ᵊn-ə, -ᵊn-,ä\ *or anc* **Mu•ti•na** \'myüt-ᵊn-ə\ commune N Italy in Emilia SW of Venice *pop* 114,450 — **Mod•e•nese** \,mȯd-ᵊn-'ēz, -'ēs\ *n*

Mo•des•to \mə-'des-(,)tō\ city *cen* Calif. *pop* 36,585

Moe•sia \'mē-sh(ē-)ə\ ancient country & Roman province SE Europe in modern Serbia & Bulgaria S of the Danube from the Drina to Black sea

Mog•a•di•shu \,mäg-ə-'dish-(,)ü, -'dēsh-\ *or* **Mog•a•di•scio** \-'dish-(,)ō, -'dēsh-, -ē-,ō\ city & port ✽ of Somalia & formerly of Italian Somaliland on Indian ocean *pop* 86,600

Mogador — see ESSAOUIRA

Mo•gi•lev \mäg-ə-,lef, -,lev\ city U.S.S.R. in E Belorussia on the Dnieper *pop* 121,000

Mo•go•llon \,məg-ē-'ōn, ,mōg-\ **1** mountains SW N.Mex.; highest point Whitewater Baldy 10,892 *ft* **2** plateau *ab* 8000 *ft*, *cen* Ariz.

Mo•hacs \'mō-,hach, -,häch\ town S Hungary on the Danube

Mo•hawk \'mō-,hȯk\ river 148 *m* E *cen* N.Y. flowing E into the Hudson

Mo•hen•jo-Da•ro \mō-,hen-(,)jō-'där-(,)ō\ prehistoric city W Pakistan in Indus valley 140 *m* NE of modern Karachi

Mo•ja•ve *or* **Mo•ha•ve** \mə-'häv-ē\ desert S Calif. SE of S end of the Sierra Nevada

Mo•ji \'mō-(,)jē\ former city Japan in N Kyushu on Shimonoseki strait — see KITA-KYUSHU

Mok•po \'mäk-(,)pō\ *or* Jap **Mop•po** \'mȯ-(,)pō\ city & port SW Korea on Yellow sea SW of Kwangju *pop* 111,128

Mold \'mōld\ urban district NE Wales ✽ of Flintshire

Moldau — see VLTAVA

Mol•da•via \mäl-'dā-vē-ə, -vyə\ **1** region Europe in NE Romania & SE U.S.S.R. between the Carpathians & Transylvanian Alps on the W & the Dniester on the E **2** *or* **Mol•da•vian Republic** \-,dā-vē-ən-, -vyən-\ constituent republic of the U.S.S.R. in E Moldavia region ✽ Kishinev *area* 13,100, *pop* 3,000,000 — **Mol•da•vian** \-'dā-vē-ən, -vyən\ *adj or n*

Mo•len•beek *or* **Sint-Jans-Molenbeek** \sint-'yän(t)s-'mō-lən-,bāk\ *or* **Molenbeek-Saint-Jean** \-saⁿ-'zhäⁿ\ commune *cen* Belgium in Brabant W of Brussels *pop* 63,900

Mo•line \mō-'lēn\ city NW Ill. on the Mississippi *pop* 42,705

Mo•li•se \'mȯ-li-,zā\ area *cen* Italy between the Apennines & the Adriatic S of Abruzzi — see ABRUZZI

Mo•llen•do \mō-'yen-(,)dō\ city & port S Peru *pop* 25,700

Mo•lo•kai \,mäl-ə-'kī, ,mō-lə-\ island *cen* Hawaii ESE of Oahu *area* 259

Mo•lo•po \mə-'lō-(,)pō\ river 600 *m* S Africa flowing W along border between Botswana & Republic of So. Africa & thence S into the Orange; now usu. dry

Molotov — see PERM

Mo•luc•cas \mə-'lək-əz\ *or* **Spice** \'spīs\ *or* Indonesian **Ma•lu•ku** \mə-'lü-(,)kü\ islands Indonesia in Malay archipelago between Celebes & New Guinea *area* 32,300, *pop* 600,000 — see HALMAHERA — **Mo•luc•ca** \mə-'lək-ə\ *or* **Mo•luc•can** \-ən\ *adj*

Mom•ba•sa \mäm-'bäs-ə\ **1** island Kenya on coast N of Pemba **2** city & port on Mombasa I. & adjacent mainland *pop* 178,400

Mona, 1 — see ANGLESEY **2** *or* **Monapia** — see MAN (Isle of)

Mo•na•co \'män-ə-,kō, mə-'näk-(,)ō\ **1** country S Europe on the Mediterranean coast of France; a principality *area* 368 acres, *pop* 20,422 **2** commune, its ✽ — **Mo•na•can** \'män-ə-kən, mə-'näk-ən\ *adj or n* — **Mon•e•gasque** \,män-i-'gask\ *adj or n*

Mo•nad•nock, Mount \mə-'nad-,näk\ mountain 3186 *ft* SW N.H.

Mon•a•ghan \'män-i-gən, -ə-,han\ **1** county NE Republic of Ireland in Ulster *area* 498, *pop* 47,077 **2** urban district, its ✽

Mo•na Passage \,mō-nə-\ strait West Indies between Hispaniola & Puerto Rico connecting the Caribbean & the Atlantic

Mon•a•stir \,män-ə-'sti(ə)r\ *or* **Bi•tolj** \'bē-,tōl(-yə), -,tȯi\ *or* **Bi•to•la** \'bēt-ᵊl-,yä\ city S Yugoslavia in S Macedonia *pop* 31,131

Mönchen-Gladbach — see MÜNCHEN-GLADBACH

Monc•ton \'məŋ(k)-tən\ city Canada in E N.B. *pop* 36,003

Mo•nes•sen \mə-'nes-ᵊn\ city SW Pa. *pop* 18,424

Mon•go•lia \män-'gōl-yə, mäŋ-, -'gō-lē-ə\ **1** region E Asia W of Khingan mountains & E of Altai mountains; includes Gobi desert **2** *or* **Mongolian Republic** *or* **Outer Mongolia** country E Asia comprising major portion of Mongolia region; a republic ✽ Ulan Bator *area* 580,158, *pop* 1,000,000 **3** INNER MONGOLIA

Mon•he•gan \män-'hē-gən\ island Me. ESE of Boothbay Harbor

Mon•mouth \'mən-məth, 'män-\ *or* **Mon•mouth•shire** \-,shi(ə)r, -shər\ county W England bordering on SE Wales; often regarded as part of Wales ✽ Newport *area* 546, *pop* 424,647

Mo•no \'mō-(,)nō\ saline lake 14 *m* long E Calif.

Mo•noc•a•cy \mə-'näk-ə-sē\ river 60 *m* S Pa. & N Md. flowing S into the Potomac

Mo•non•ga•he•la \mə-,nän-gə-'hē-lə, -,näŋ-gə-, -'hā-lə\ river 128 *m* N W. Va. & SW Pa. flowing N to unite with the Allegheny at Pittsburgh forming the Ohio

Mon•roe \mən-'rō\ **1** city N La. *pop* 52,219 **2** city SE Mich. SSW of Detroit on Lake Erie *pop* 22,968

Mon•roe•ville \mən-'rō-,vil\ borough SW Pa. E of Pittsburgh *pop* 22,446

Mon•ro•via \mən-'rō-vē-ə\ **1** city SW Calif. E of Pasadena *pop* 27,079 **2** city & port ✽ of Liberia on the Atlantic *pop* 60,000

Mons \mōⁿs\ *or* Flem **Ber•gen** \'be(ə)r-k̲ə(n)\ commune SW Belgium ✽ of Hainaut *pop* 27,144

Mon•tana \män-'tan-ə\ state NW U.S. ✽ Helena *area* 147,138, *pop* 674,767 — **Mon•tan•an** \-ən\ *adj or n*

Mont•au•ban \,mänt-ō-'bäⁿ\ city SW France on the Tarn N of Toulouse *pop* 32,000

Mon•tauk Point \,män-,tȯk-\ headland SE N.Y. at E tip of Long I.

Mont Blanc \mōⁿ-bläⁿ\ **1** mountain 15,771 *ft* SE France on Italian border in Savoy Alps; highest of the Alps **2** tunnel 7½ *m* long France & Italy under Mont Blanc

Mont•clair \mänt-'kla(ə)r, -'kle(ə)r\ town NE N.J. SSW of Paterson *pop* 43,129

Mon•te Al•bán \,mänt-ē-äl-'bän\ ruined city of the Zapotecs S Mexico in Oaxaca state SW of Oaxaca

Mon•te•bel•lo \,mänt-ə-'bel-(,)ō\ city SW Calif. ESE of Los Angeles *pop* 32,097

Mon•te Car•lo \,mänt-i-'kär-(,)lō\ commune Monaco

Mon•te•go Bay \män-,tē-(,)gō-\ town & port NW Jamaica on Montego Bay (inlet of the Caribbean)

Mon•te•ne•gro \,mänt-ə-'nē-(,)grō\ federated republic S Yugoslavia on the Adriatic; formerly a kingdom (✽ Cetinje) ✽ Titograd *area* 5343, *pop* 377,200 — **Mon•te•ne•grin** \-grən\ *adj or n*

Mon•te•rey \,mänt-ə-'rā\ city W Calif. on Monterey peninsula at S end of **Monterey Bay** (inlet of the Pacific) *pop* 22,618

Monterey Park city SW Calif. E of Los Angeles *pop* 37,821

Mon•ter•rey \,mänt-ə-'rā\ city NE Mexico ✽ of Nuevo León *pop* 600,609

Mon•te•vi•deo \,mänt-ə-və-'dā-(,)ō, -'vid-ē-,ō\ city & port ✽ of Uruguay on N shore of Río de la Plata *pop* 922,885

Mon•te•zu•ma Castle National Monument \,mänt-ə-,zü-mə-\ reservation *cen* Ariz. containing prehistoric cliff dwellings

Mont•gom•ery \(,)mən(t)-'gəm-(ə-)rē, män(t)-, -'gäm-\ **1** city ✽ of Ala. on the Alabama *pop* 134,393 **2** *or* **Mont•gom•ery•shire** \-,shi(ə)r, -shər\ county E Wales ✽ Welshpool *area* 797, *pop* 45,989

Mont•mar•tre \mōⁿ-'märtrᵊ\ section of Paris, France, on a hill in N *cen* part of the city

Mont•mo•ren•cy \,mänt-mə-'ren(t)-sē\ commune N France, N suburb of Paris

Mont•mo•ren•cy Falls \,mänt-mə-,ren(t)-sē-\ waterfall 270 *ft* Canada in S Que. NE of Quebec city in **Montmorency** river (60 *m* flowing S into the St. Lawrence)

Mont•par•nasse \mōⁿ-(,)pär-'näs, -'nas\ section of Paris, France, in S *cen* part of the city — **Mont•par•nas•sian** \-'nash-ən, -'nas-ē-ən\ *adj*

Mont•pe•lier \mänt-'pēl-yər\ city ✽ of Vt. *pop* 8782

Mont•pel•lier \mōⁿ-pe-lyā\ city S France WNW of Marseilles *pop* 97,501

Mon•tre•al \,män-trē-'ȯl, ,mən-\ *or* **Mont•ré•al** \mōⁿ-rā-äl\ city & port Canada in S Que. on **Montreal Island** (32 *m* long, in the St. Lawrence) *pop* 1,109,439 — **Mon•tre•al•er** \,män-trē-'ȯ-lər, ,mən-\ *n*

Montreal North *or* **Montréal-Nord** \-nȯr\ town Canada in S Que. on Montreal I. *pop* 25,407

Mon•treuil *or* **Montreuil-sous-Bois** \mōⁿ-'trə(r)-(,)süb-'wä, -'trəi-\ commune N France, E suburb of Paris *pop* 76,252

Mon•treux \mōⁿ-'trə(r)\ group of villages W Switzerland in Vaud canton at E end of Lake Geneva

Mont-Roy•al \mōⁿ-rwä-yäl\ *or* **Mount Roy•al** \mau̇nt-'rȯi(-ə)l\ town Canada in S Que. on Montreal I. *pop* 16,990

Mont-Saint-Mi•chel \mōⁿ-saⁿ-mē-shel\ small island NW France in Gulf of St-Malo

ə abut; ᵊ kitten; ər further; a back; ā bake; ä cot, cart; au̇ out; ch chin; e less; ē easy; g gift; i trip; ī life
j joke; ŋ sing; ō flow; ȯ flaw; ȯi coin; th thin; t̲h̲ this; ü loot; u̇ foot; y yet; yü few; yu̇ furious; zh vision
ᵊ F table; ȧ F bac; k̲ G ich, Buch; ⁿ F vin; œ F bœuf; œ̄ F feu; ue G füllen; ue̅ F rue; ʸ F digne \dēnʸ\, nuit \nwʸē\

Mont·ser·rat \ˌmän(t)-sə-'rat\ island Brit. West Indies in the Leewards SW of Antigua; chief town Plymouth area 33, pop 14,500
Monument Valley region NE Ariz. & SE Utah containing red sandstone buttes, mesas, & arches
Mon·za \'mȯn(t)-sə\ commune N Italy in Lombardy SE of Milan pop 73,800
Mo·oréa \ˌmō-ə-'rā-ə\ island S Pacific in Society islands NW of Tahiti area 51
Moor·head \'mō(ə)r-ˌhed, 'mȯ(ə)r-, 'mu̇(ə)r-\ city W Minn. on Red river opposite Fargo, N. Dak. pop 22,934
Moose \'müs\ river 50 m Canada in NE Ont. flowing NE into James Bay; estuary of Abitibi, Mattagami, & other rivers
Moose·head \'müs-ˌhed\ lake 35 m long NW cen Me.
Moose Jaw city Canada in S Sask. W of Regina pop 29,603
Moppo — see MOKPO
Mo·rad·abad \mə-'räd-ə-ˌbäd, -'rad-ə-ˌbad\ city N India in NW Uttar Pradesh ENE of Delhi pop 161,900
Mo·ra·tu·wa \mə-'rät-ə-wə\ city W Ceylon on Indian ocean S of Colombo pop 50,700
Mo·ra·va \'mȯr-ə-və\ **1** — see MARCH **2** river 134 m E Yugoslavia in Serbia flowing N into the Danube
Mo·ra·via \mə-'rā-vē-ə\ region cen Czechoslovakia S of Silesia traversed by Morava river; chief city Brno
Mo·ra·vi·an Gate or **Moravian Gap** \mə-'rā-vē-ən-\ mountain pass cen Europe between Sudeten & Carpathian mountains
Moravska Ostrava — see OSTRAVA
Mor·ay \'mər-ē, 'mə-rē\ or **Mor·ay·shire** \-ˌshi(ə)r, -shər\ or **El·gin** \'el-gən\ or **El·gin·shire** \-ˌshi(ə)r, -shər\ county NE Scotland bordering on North sea ✳ Elgin area 476, pop 48,211
Moray firth inlet of North sea N Scotland
Mord·vin·i·an Republic \ˌmȯrd-ˌvin-ē-ən-\ or **Mor·do·vi·an Republic** \ˌmȯr-ˌdō-vē-ən-\ autonomous republic U.S.S.R. in cen Soviet Russia, Europe, S & W of middle Volga ✳ Saransk area 10,100, pop 1,000,000
Morea — see PELOPONNESUS
Mo·reau \'mȯr-ˌō, 'mȯr-\ river 250 m NW S. Dak. flowing E into the Missouri
More·cambe and Hey·sham \ˌmȯr-kəm-ən(d)-'hā-shəm, ˌmȯr-\ municipal borough NW England in N Lancashire on **Morecambe Bay** (inlet of Irish sea) pop 37,000
Mo·re·lia \mə-'rāl-yə\ city SW Mexico ✳ of Michoacán pop 63,245
Mo·re·los \mə-'rā-ləs\ state S cen Mexico ✳ Cuernavaca area 1916, pop 359,679
More·ton Bay \ˌmō(ə)rt-ᵊn-, ˌmȯrt-\ inlet of the Pacific Australia in SE Queensland at mouth of Brisbane river
Mor·gan·town \'mȯr-gən-ˌtau̇n\ city N W. Va. pop 22,487
Mo·ri·ah \mə-'rī-ə\ hill cen Palestine in E part of Jerusalem
Mo·ri·o·ka \ˌmȯr-ē-'ō-kə, ˌmȯr-\ city Japan in N Honshu E of Akita pop 142,875
Mo·roc·co \mə-'räk-ˌō\ **1** country NW Africa bordering on the Atlantic & the Mediterranean; a kingdom; formerly (1911–56) divided into **French Morocco** (protectorate ✳ Rabat area 153,870), **Spanish Morocco** (protectorate ✳ Tetuán area 18,009), **Southern Morocco** (Spanish protectorate, chief town Cabo Yubi area 10,039), & the **International Zone** of Tangier (area 225) ✳ Rabat, summer ✳ Tangier area ab 175,000, pop 11,626,000 **2** — see MARRAKESH — **Mo·roc·can** \-'räk-ən\ adj or n
Mo·ro Gulf \ˌmōr-ˌō, -ˌmȯr-\ arm of Celebes sea S Philippines off SW coast of Mindanao
Mor·ris Jes·up, Cape \ˌmȯr-əs-'jes-əp, ˌmär-\ headland N Greenland in Peary Land on Arctic ocean
Mor·ri·son, Mount \'mȯr-ə-sən, ˌmär-\ or **Yü Shan** \'yü-ˌshän\ mountain 13,599 ft China in cen Formosa; highest on island
Morrison Cave — see LEWIS AND CLARK
Mor·ris·town \'mȯr-ə-ˌstau̇n, ˌmär-\ **1** town NE cen N.J. pop 17,712 **2** city E Tenn. ENE of Knoxville pop 21,267
Mor·ton Grove \'mȯrt-ᵊn-\ village NE Ill. W of Evanston pop 20,533
Mos·cow \'mäs-ˌkō, -(ˌ)kō\ or Russ **Mos·kva** \mäsk-'vä\ **1** river 315 m U.S.S.R. in W cen Soviet Russia, Europe, flowing E into the Oka **2** city ✳ of U.S.S.R. & of the Russian Republic on Moscow river pop 6,464,000 — see MUSCOVY
Mo·selle \mō-'zel\ or G **Mo·sel** \'mō-zəl\ river 320 m E France & W Germany flowing from the Vosges into the Rhine at Koblenz
Mosquito Coast or **Mos·qui·tia** \mə-'skēt-ē-ə\ region Central America bordering on the Caribbean in E Honduras & E Nicaragua
Mos·sâ·me·des or **Mos·çâ·me·des** \mə-'sam-ə-ˌdēz\ town & port SW Angola
Mos·sel Bay \ˌmȯ-səl-\ town & port S Republic of So. Africa in S Cape of Good Hope on Mossel Bay (inlet of Indian ocean)
Mos·tag·a·nem \mə-ˌstag-ə-ˌnem\ city & port NW Algeria ENE of Oran pop 60,186
Mo·sul \mō-'sül, 'mō-səl\ city N Iraq on the Tigris pop 140,245
Moth·er·well and Wish·aw \ˌmə̱th-ər-, ˌwel-ən-'wish-ˌȯ, -mȯ-lən-\ burgh cen Scotland in Lanark SE of Glasgow pop 68,137
Moul·mein \mül-'mān, mōl-, -'mīn\ city S Burma on Gulf of Martaban at mouth of the Salween pop 101,720
Moul·trie \'mōl-trē\ city S Ga. pop 15,764
Mound City Group National Monument \'mau̇n(d)-'sit-ē\ reservation S Ohio N of Chillicothe containing prehistoric mounds
Mounds·ville \'mau̇n(d)z-ˌvil, -vəl\ city N W. Va. on the Ohio S of Wheeling pop 15,163
Mountain View city W Calif. NW of San Jose pop 30,889
Mount Clem·ens \'klem-ənz\ city SE Mich. pop 21,016
Mount De·sert \də-'zərt, 'dez-ərt\ island S Me. in the Atlantic E of Penobscot Bay area 100 — see ACADIA NATIONAL PARK
Mount Leb·a·non \'leb-(ə-)nən\ urban township SW Pa. S of Pittsburgh pop 35,361
Mount McKinley National Park — see MCKINLEY (Mount)
Mount Pros·pect \'präs-ˌpekt\ village NE Ill. pop 18,906
Mount Rainier National Park — see RAINIER (Mount)
Mount Rev·el·stoke National Park \'rev-əl-ˌstōk\ reservation Canada in SE B. C. on a plateau including Mt. Revelstoke (over 7000 ft) W of Selkirk mountains area 100
Mount Royal — see MONT-ROYAL
Mount Ver·non \'vər-nən\ **1** city S Ill. pop 15,566 **2** city SE N.Y. N of New York City pop 76,010
Mourne \'mō(ə)rn, 'mȯ(ə)rn\ mountains SE Northern Ireland
Mouse — see SOURIS
Mo·zam·bique \ˌmō-zəm-'bēk\ or Port **Mo·çam·bi·que** \ˌmü-səm-'bē-kə\ **1** channel 950 m long SE Africa between Madagascar

& Mozambique **2** or **Portuguese East Africa** country SE Africa bordering on Mozambique channel ✳ Lourenço Marques area 297,654, pop 5,738,911 — **Mo·zam·bi·can** \ˌmō-zəm-'bē-kən\ adj
Mtwa·ra \em-'twär-ə\ town & port SE Tanganyika
Mu·gu, Point \mə-'gü\ cape SW Calif. W of Los Angeles & SE of Oxnard
Muir Woods National Monument \ˌmyu̇(ə)r-\ reservation N Calif. NW of San Francisco containing a redwood grove
Mui·zen·berg \'māz-ᵊn-ˌbərg\ town Republic of So. Africa on False Bay, SSE suburb of Cape Town
Mu·kal·la \mu̇-'kal-ə\ city & port South Yemen on Gulf of Aden; chief town of the Hadhramaut pop 20,000
Muk·den \'mu̇k-dən, 'mək-\ or **Shen·yang** \'shən-'yäŋ\ or formerly **Feng·tien** \'fəŋ-tē-'en\ city NE China ✳ of Liaoning on Hun river; chief city of Manchuria pop 2,299,900
Mukha — see MOCHA
Mül·heim or **Mülheim an der Ruhr** \'m(y)ül-ˌhī-ˌmän-də(r)-'ru̇(ə)r, 'mül-\ city W Germany on Ruhr river near its junction with the Rhine pop 182,300
Mul·house \mə-'lüz\ commune NE France in Alsace pop 99,079
Mull \'məl\ island W Scotland in the Inner Hebrides area 351
Mul·lin·gar \ˌməl-ən-'gär\ town N cen Ireland ✳ of Westmeath
Mul·tan \mu̇l-'tän\ city Pakistan in NE West Pakistan SW of Lahore pop 190,100
Mult·no·mah Falls \ˌməlt-ˌnō-mə-\ waterfall 620 ft NW Oreg. E of Portland in a tributary of the Columbia
Mün·chen–Glad·bach \ˌm(y)ün-kən-'glät-ˌbäk, ˌmin-\ or **Mön·chen–Glad·bach** \ˌmen-\ city W Germany W of Düsseldorf pop 152,400
Mun·cie \'mən(t)-sē\ city E Ind. pop 68,603
Mun·hall \'mən-ˌhȯl\ borough SW Pa. E of Pittsburgh on the Monongahela pop 17,312
Mu·nich \'myü-nik\ or G **Mün·chen** \'mu̇en-kən\ city S Germany ✳ of Bavaria on the Isar pop 1,079,400
Mun·ster \'mən(t)-stər\ province S Ireland area 9317, pop 848,368
Mün·ster \'min(t)-stər, 'm(y)ün(t)-, 'mün(t)-, 'mən(t)-\ city W Germany; formerly ✳ of Westphalia pop 180,300
Mun·te·nia \ˌmən-'tē-nē-ə\ or **Greater Walachia** region SE Romania in E part of Walachia
Mur \'mu̇(ə)r\ or **Mu·ra** \'mu̇r-ə\ river 230 m Austria & N Yugoslavia flowing into the Drava
Mu·ra·no \mü-'rän-(ˌ)ō\ town NE Italy in Venetia on islands in Lagoon of Venice N of Venice
Mu·rat \mü-'rät\ or anc **Ar·sa·ni·as** \är-'sā-nē-əs\ river 380 m E Turkey flowing WSW into the Euphrates
Mur·chi·son \'mər-chə-sən\ river 400 m Australia in W Western Australia flowing W into Indian ocean
Murchison Falls waterfall 120 ft W Uganda in the Victoria Nile above Lake Albert
Mur·cia \'mər-sh(ē-)ə\ **1** region & ancient kingdom SE Spain bordering on the Mediterranean **2** province SE Spain bordering on the Mediterranean area 4453, pop 817,498 **3** commune, its ✳ & ✳ of ancient kingdom of Murcia, on Segura river pop 246,208
Mu·res or **Mu·resh** \'mü-ˌresh\ or **Ma·ros** \'mȯr-ˌōsh\ river 400 m, cen Romania & E Hungary flowing W into the Tisza
Mur·frees·boro \'mər-f(r)ēz-ˌbər-ə, -ˌbə-rə\ city cen Tenn. SE of Nashville pop 18,991
Mur·mansk \'mu̇r-ˌman(t)sk, -'män(t)sk\ city & port U.S.S.R. in NW Soviet Russia, Europe, on Kola peninsula on an inlet of Barents sea pop 226,000
Mu·ro·ran \ˌmu̇r-ə-'rän\ city & port Japan in SW Hokkaido on an inlet of the Pacific pop 123,533
Mur·ray \'mər-ē, 'mə-rē\ **1** city N Utah pop 16,806 **2** river 1200 m SE Australia flowing from near Mt. Kosciusko in E Victoria W into Indian ocean in SE So. Australia
Mur·ree \'mər-ē, 'mə-rē\ **1** hills NE West Pakistan **2** town in the Murree hills N of Rawalpindi
Mur·rum·bidg·ee \ˌmər-əm-'bij-ē, ˌmə-rəm-\ river 1000 m SE Australia in New So. Wales flowing W into the Murray
Murua — see WOODLARK
Murviedro — see SAGUNTO
Mu·sa, Ge·bel \ˌjeb-əl-'mü-sə\ mountain group NE Egypt in S Sinai peninsula — see HOREB, KATHERINA (Gebel)
Mu·sa, Je·bel \ˌjeb-əl-'mü-sə\ or anc **Ab·i·la** or **Ab·y·la** \'ab-ə-lə\ mountain 2775 ft N Morocco opposite Rock of Gibraltar — see PILLARS OF HERCULES
Mus·cat or **Mas·qat** \'məs-ˌkat, -kət\ town & port ✳ of Oman on Gulf of Oman
Muscat and Oman — see OMAN
Mus·ca·tine \ˌməs-kə-'tēn\ city E Iowa pop 20,997
Mus·co·vy \(ˌ)mə-'skō-vē; 'məs-kə-, -ˌkō-\ **1** the principality of Moscow (founded 1295) which in 15th century came to dominate Russia **2** RUSSIA
Mus·ke·gon \ˌməs-'skē-gən\ **1** river 200 m W cen Mich. flowing SW into Lake Michigan **2** city & port SW Mich. pop 46,485
Muskegon Heights city SW Mich. S of Muskegon pop 19,552
Mus·kin·gum \mə-'skiŋ-(g)əm\ river 120 m E Ohio flowing SSE into the Ohio
Mus·ko·gee \mə-'skō-gē\ city E Okla. pop 38,059
Mus·ko·ka, Lake \mə-'skō-kə\ lake Canada in SE Ont. E of Georgian Bay & N of Lake Simcoe area 54
Mus·sel·shell \'məs-əl-ˌshel\ river 300 m, cen Mont. flowing E & N into the Missouri
Mu·tan·kiang \'mü-ˌdän-jē-'äŋ\ city NE China in S Heilungkiang on the **Mu·tan** \'mü-ˌdän\ river (310 m flowing NE into the Sungari) SE of Harbin pop 151,400
Mutina — see MODENA
Mu·tsu Bay \ˌmüt-(ˌ)sü\ inlet N Japan on NE Honshu on Tsugaru strait
Muttra — see MATHURA
Mwe·ru \mə-'we(ə)r-(ˌ)ü\ lake 80 m long on border between Congo & Northern Rhodesia SW of Lake Tanganyika
Myc·a·le \'mik-ə-(ˌ)lē\ promontory W Turkey opposite Samos I.
My·ce·nae \mī-'sē-(ˌ)nē\ ancient city S Greece in NE Peloponnesus N of Argos
Myit·ky·i·na \ˌmē-chi-'nȯ\ town N Burma on the upper Irrawaddy in Kachin state
Myk·o·nos \'mik-ə-ˌnäs, -nəs\ or NGk **Mí·ko·nos** \'mē-kə-ˌnȯs\ island Greece in the Aegean in NE Cyclades SE of Tenos area 35
Mylae — see MILAZZO
My·men·singh \ˌmī-mən-'siŋ\ city E Pakistan pop 45,000

My·ra \'mī-rə\ ancient city S Asia Minor on coast of Lycia
My·sia \'mish-ē-ə\ ancient country NW Asia Minor bordering on the Propontis — **My·si·an** \-ē-ən\ *adj or n*
My·sore \mī-'sō(ə)r, -'sò(ə)r\ **1** state SW India ✳ Bangalore *area* 74,326, *pop* 19,399,300 **2** city in S Mysore state *pop* 244,300
Mys·tic \'mis-tik\ river E Mass. flowing SE into Boston harbor
Myt·i·le·ne *or* NGk **Mi·ti·li·ni** \,mit-ᵊl-'ē-nē\ **1** — see LESBOS **2** *or formerly* **Ka·stro** \'käs-(,)trō\ city & port Greece on E coast of Lesbos I. *pop* 27,125

Naas \'nās\ urban district E Ireland in Leinster ✳ of Kildare
Nab·a·taea *or* **Nab·a·tea** \,nab-ə-'tē-ə\ ancient Arab kingdom SE of Palestine — **Nab·a·taean** *or* **Nab·a·tean** \-'tē-ən\ *adj or n*
Nab·lus \'nab-ləs, 'näb-\ *or anc* **She·chem** \'shē-kəm, -,kem\ *or* **Ne·ap·o·lis** \nē-'ap-ə-ləs\ city *cen* Palestine in Samaria; now in W Jordan *pop* 19,700
Na·fud *or* **Ne·fud** \nə-'füd\ desert N Saudi Arabia in N Nejd
Na·ga \'näg-ə\ hills E India & N Burma SE of the Brahmaputra; highest Saramati 12,553 *ft*
Na·ga·land \'näg-ə-,land\ state E India N of Manipur in Naga hills ✳ Kohima *area* 6336, *pop* 369,200
Na·ga·o·ka \,näg-ə-'ō-kə, nä-gä-ō-(,)kä\ city Japan in N *cen* Honshu SSW of Niigata *pop* 130,785
Na·ga·sa·ki \,näg-ə-'säk-ē, ,nag-; ,nag-ə-'sak-ē\ city & port Japan in W Kyushu on East China sea *pop* 344,153
Na·gor·no–Ka·ra·bakh Region \nə-,gór-(,)nō-'kär-ə-,bäk-\ autonomous region U.S.S.R. in SW Azerbaidzhan ✳ Stepanakert *area* 1700, *pop* 130,000
Na·goya \nə-'gói-ə\ city Japan in S *cen* Honshu *pop* 1,591,935
Nag·pur \'näg-,pu(ə)r\ city E *cen* India in NE Maharashtra *pop* 449,100
Nagyvarad — see ORADEA
Na·ha \'nä-(,)hä\ *or* **Na·wa** \'nä-(,)wä\ city & port Ryukyu islands in SW Okinawa I. ✳ of Okinawa *pop* 223,000
Nairn \'na(ə)rn, 'ne(ə)rn\ **1** *or* **Nairn·shire** \-,shi(ə)r, -shər\ county NE Scotland bordering Moray firth *area* 163, *pop* 8719 **2** burgh, its ✳, on Moray firth
Nai·ro·bi \nī-'rō-bē\ city ✳ of Kenya *pop* 288,500
Na·jaf *or* **An Najaf** \an-'naj-,əf\ city S *cen* Iraq *pop* 74,089
Najd — see NEJD — **Najdi** \'naj-dē\ *adj or n*
Na·jin \'näj-,ēn\ *or* Jap **Ra·shin** \'räsh-,ēn\ city & port N Korea on Sea of Japan NE of Chongjin *pop* 34,338
Na·khi·che·van \,näk-i-chə-'vän\ **1** *or* **Nakhichevan Republic** autonomous republic U.S.S.R.; part of Azerbaidzhan *area* 2100, *pop* 160,000 **2** city, its ✳, on the Araks *pop* 25,000
Nak·tong \'näk-,tón\ *or* Jap **Ra·ku·to** \'räk-ə-,tō\ river 260 *m* S Korea flowing S & E into Korea strait near Pusan
Na·ma·qua·land \nə-'mäk-wə-,land\ *or* **Na·ma·land** \'näm-ə-\ region SW Africa bordering on the Atlantic; divided by Orange river into **Great Namaqualand** (in South-West Africa) & **Little Namaqualand** (in Cape Province, Republic of So. Africa, chief town Springbok)
Namhoi — see FATSHAN
Namibia — see SOUTHWEST AFRICA
Nam·pa \'nam-pə\ city SW Idaho W of Boise *pop* 18,013
Nam·po \'nam-(,)pō\ *or* **Chin·nam·po** \'chē(n)-,näm-(,)pō\ city & port N Korea SW of Pyongyang *pop* 82,162
Na·mur \nə-'m(y)ù(ə)r\ **1** province S Belgium *area* 1413, *pop* 32,345 **2** commune, its ✳ *pop* 105,836
Nan \'nän\ river 350 *m* N Thailand flowing S to join the Ping forming the Chao Phraya
Nan·chang \'nän-'chäŋ\ city SE China ✳ of Kiangsi on the Kan SW of Poyang Lake *pop* 398,200
Nan·chung \'nän-'chùŋ\ city *cen* China in E *cen* Szechwan on Kialing river *pop* 164,700
Nan·cy \'nan(t)-sē, näⁿ-'sē\ city NE France *pop* 124,797
Nan·da De·vi \,nən-də-'dā-vē\ mountain 25,645 *ft* N India in the Himalayas in Uttar Pradesh
Nan·di *or* **Na·di** \'nän-(,)dē\ village Fiji on W Viti Levu I.
Nan·ga Par·bat \,nəŋ-gə-'pər-bət\ mountain 26,660 *ft* NW Kashmir in the W Himalayas
Nan·king \'nan-'kiŋ, 'nän-\ city E China on the Yangtze ✳ of Kiangsu & (1928–37 & 1946–49) ✳ of China *pop* 1,091,600
Nan Ling \'nän-'liŋ\ *or* **Nan Shan** \'nän-'shän\ mountain system SE China roughly separating Kwangtung & Kwangsi from Hunan & Kweichow
Nan·ning \'nän-'niŋ\ *or formerly* **Yung·ning** \'yùŋ-'niŋ\ city S China ✳ of Kwangsi on Yü river *pop* 194,600
Nansei — see RYUKYU
Nan Shan \'nän-'shän\ mountain range W China extending from Kunlun mountains along NE edge of Tibetan plateau to NE Tsinghai
Nan·terre \näⁿ-'te(ə)r\ commune N France W of Paris *pop* 53,037
Nantes \'nan(t)s\ city NW France on the Loire *pop* 222,800
Nan·ti·coke \'nant-i-,kōk\ city NE *cen* Pa. *pop* 15,601
Nan·tuck·et \nan-'tək-ət\ island Mass. in the Atlantic S of Cape Cod on **Nantucket Sound** (inlet of the Atlantic)
Nan·tung \'nän-'tùŋ\ city & port E China in SE Kiangsu on Yangtze estuary NW of Shanghai *pop* 260,400
Na·pa \'nap-ə\ city W Calif. N of Vallejo *pop* 22,170
Na·pi·er \'nā-pē-ər\ borough & port New Zealand in E North I. on Hawke Bay *pop* 29,600
Na·ples \'nā-pəlz\ *or* It **Na·po·li** \'näp-ə-lē\ *or anc* **Ne·ap·o·lis** \nē-'ap-ə-ləs\ city & port S Italy on **Bay of Naples** (inlet of Tyrrhenian sea) ✳ of Campania *pop* 1,024,543 — **Ne·a·pol·i·tan** \,nē-ə-'päl-ət-ᵊn\ *adj or n*
Na·po \'näp-(,)ō\ river 550 *m* NW So. America rising near Mt. Cotopaxi in *cen* Ecuador & flowing E & SE into the Amazon
Na·ra \'när-ə\ city Japan in W *cen* Honshu E of Osaka; an early ✳ of Japan *pop* 115,700
Nar·ba·da \nər-'bəd-ə\ river 800 *m*, *cen* India flowing W between Vindhya mountains & Satpura range into Gulf of Cambay
Nar·bonne \när-'bän, -'bòn\ city S France near the Mediterranean sea E of Carcassonne *pop* 32,060
Na·rew \'när-,ef, -,ev\ *or* Russ **Na·rev** \när-'yòf, -'yòv\ river 285 *m* NE Poland flowing W & SW into the Bug

Nar·ra·gan·sett Bay \,nar-ə-,gan(t)-sət-\ inlet of the Atlantic SE R.I.
Nar·vik \'när-vik, -,vēk\ town & port N Norway
Nash·ua \'nash-ə-wə, -ə-,wä\ city S N.H. *pop* 39,096
Nash·ville \'nash-,vil, -vəl\ city ✳ of Tenn. *pop* 170,874
Nas·sau \'nas-,ò\ **1** town & port ✳ of the Bahamas on NE coast of New Providence I. **2** region W Germany N & E of the Rhine; chief city Wiesbaden **3** mountain range *cen* West New Guinea
Nasser, Lake — see ASWÂN
Na·tal \nə-'tal, -'täl\ **1** city & port NE Brazil ✳ of Rio Grande do Norte *pop* 161,917 **2** province E Republic of So. Africa between Drakensberg mountains & Indian ocean ✳ Pietermaritzburg *area* 35,284, *pop* 2,202,400
Natal Bay *or formerly* **Port Natal** inlet of Indian ocean Republic of So. Africa in Natal — see DURBAN
Natch·ez \'nach-əz\ city SW Miss. on the Mississippi *pop* 23,791
Natchez Trace pioneer road between Natchez, Miss., & Nashville, Tenn., used in the early 19th century
Na·tick \'nāt-ik\ town E Mass. W of Boston *pop* 28,831
National City city SW Calif. S of San Diego *pop* 32,771
Native States — see INDIAN STATES
Natural Bridges National Monument reservation SE Utah containing three large natural bridges
Nau·cra·tis \'nò-krət-əs\ ancient Greek city N Egypt in Nile delta W of Rosetta branch
Nau·ga·tuck \'nò-gə-,tək\ borough SW *cen* Conn. *pop* 19,511
Nau·plia \'nò-plē-ə\ *or* NGk **Náv·pli·on** \'näf-plē-on\ town & port S Greece in E Peloponnesus near head of Gulf of Argolis
Nauplia, Gulf of — see ARGOLIS (Gulf of)
Na·u·ru \nä-'ü-(,)rü\ *or formerly* **Pleas·ant** \'plez-ᵊnt\ island (atoll) W Pacific 26 *m* S of the equator; formerly a joint Brit., New Zealand, & Australian trust territory; since 1968 an independent republic *area* 8, *pop* 3100
Nav·a·jo National Monument \'nav-ə-,hō, 'näv-\ reservation N Ariz. SW of Monument Valley near Utah line
Navanagar — see JAMNAGAR
Navarino — see PYLOS
Na·varre \nə-'vär\ *or* Sp **Na·var·ra** \nə-'vär-ə\ **1** region & former kingdom N Spain & SW France in W Pyrenees **2** province N Spain ✳ Pamplona *area* 4055, *pop* 403,896
Navesink Highlands *or* **Navesink Hills** — see HIGHLANDS OF NAVESINK
Navigators — see SAMOA
Náv·pak·tos \'näf-,päk-təs\ *or* It **Le·pan·to** \'lep-ən-,tō, li-'pan-(,)tō\ *or anc* **Nau·pac·tus** \nò-'pak-təs\ town & port Greece on N shore of strait connecting gulfs of Corinth & Patras
Nawa — see NAHA
Nax·os \'nak-səs, -,säs\ **1** *or* NGk **Ná·xos** \'näk-,sòs\ island Greece, largest of the Cyclades *area* 171 **2** oldest Greek colony in Sicily; ruins SW of Taormina
Na·ya·rit \,nī-ə-'rēt\ state W Mexico bordering on the Pacific ✳ Tepic *area* 10,444, *pop* 354,741
Naz·a·reth \'naz-(ə)-rəth\ city N Israel in Galilee SE of Haifa *pop* 25,066
Naze \'näz\ **1** headland SE England on E coast of Essex **2** — see LINDESNES
Na·zil·li \,näz-ə-'lē\ city SW Turkey SE of Izmir *pop* 36,601
Neagh, Lough \'nā\ lake *cen* Northern Ireland *area* 153; largest in British Isles
Neapolis, 1 — see NABLUS **2** — see NAPLES
Near \'ni(ə)r\ islands SW Alaska at W end of the Aleutians — see ATTU
Near East, 1 the Balkan states **2** the region included in the former Ottoman Empire **3** the countries of SE Europe, N Africa, & SW Asia — often considered as including the area extending from Morocco, the Republic of Sudan, & Somalia N & E to the Balkans, Turkey, Iran, & Afghanistan — **Near Eastern** *adj*
Nebo — see PISGAH
Ne·bras·ka \nə-'bras-kə\ state *cen* U.S. ✳ Lincoln *area* 77,227, *pop* 1,411,330 — **Ne·bras·kan** *adj or n*
Ne·chako \ni-'chak-(,)ō\ river 287 *m* Canada in *cen* B.C. flowing N & E into the Fraser
Nech·es \'nech-əz\ river 280 *m* E Tex. flowing S & SE into Sabine Lake
Neck·ar \'nek-ər, -,är\ river 246 *m* SW Germany rising in the Black Forest & flowing N & W into the Rhine
Neck·er \'nek-ər\ island Hawaii in Leewards 300 *m* NW of Niihau I.
Need·ham \'nēd-əm\ town E Mass. WSW of Boston *pop* 25,793
Nee·nah \'nē-nə\ city E Wis. on Lake Winnebago *pop* 18,057
Nefud — see NAFUD
Neg·ev \'neg-,ev\ *or* **Neg·eb** \-,eb\ region S Israel, a triangular wedge of desert touching Gulf of 'Aqaba in S
Ne·gri Sem·bi·lan \nə-,grē-səm-'bē-lən\ state Federation of Malaysia on Strait of Malacca ✳ Seremban *area* 2550, *pop* 267,700
Ne·gro \'nā-(,)grō\ **1** river 630 *m* S *cen* Argentina flowing E into the Atlantic **2** river 1400 *m* E Colombia & N Brazil flowing into the Amazon **3** river 290 *m*, *cen* Uruguay flowing SW into Uruguay river
Negropont — see EUBOEA
Ne·gros \'nā-(,)grōs\ island Philippines, one of the Visayan islands *area* 4905
Nei·kiang \'nā-jē-'äŋ\ city *cen* China in S *cen* Szechwan SE of Chengtu *pop* 190,200
Neis·se \'nī-sə\ *or* Pol **Ny·sa** \'nis-ə\ **1** *or* **Lau·sitz·er Neisse** \'laù-zət-sər-,\ river 140 *m* N Europe flowing from N Czechoslovakia N into the Oder **2** *or* **Glatz·er Neisse** \'glät-sər-,\ river 120 *m* SW Poland rising on Czechoslovak border & flowing NE into the Oder
Nejd \'nejd\ *or* **Najd** \'najd\ region *cen* & E Saudi Arabia; a viceroyalty ✳ Riyadh *area* 447,000, *pop* 4,000,000 — **Nejdi** \'nej-dē\ *adj or n*
Nel·son \'nel-sən\ **1** river 400 *m* Canada in Man. flowing from N end of Lake Winnipeg to Hudson Bay **2** provincial district New Zealand in N South I. *area* 10,870, *pop* 58,100 **3** city & port, its ✳ *pop* 26,700

ə abut; ᵊ kitten; ər further; a back; ā bake; ä cot, cart; aù out; ch chin; e less; ē easy; g gift; i trip; ī life
j joke; ŋ sing; ō flow; ò flaw; òi coin; th thin; t̲h̲ this; ü loot; ù foot; y yet; yü few; yù furious; zh vision
ᵊ F table; â F bac; ᵏ G ich, Buch; ⁿ F vin; œ F bœuf; ȫ F feu; ue G füllen; t̄e F rue; ʸ F digne \dēnʸ\, nuit \nwʸē\

Ne·man \'nem-ən\ *or* **Nie·men** \nē-'em-ən, 'nē-mən\ *or* **Me·mel** \'mā-məl\ river 500 *m* W U.S.S.R. flowing from *cen* Belorussia N & W into Kurland gulf

Ne·mea \'nē-mē-ə\ valley & town Greece in NE Peloponnesus W of Corinth — **Ne·me·an** \'nē-mē-ən, ni-'mē-\ *adj*

Ne·o·sho \nē-'ō-(,)shō, -shə\ *or* **Grand** river 460 *m* SE Kans. & NE Okla. flowing SE & S into Arkansas river

Ne·pal \nə-'pȯl, -'päl, -'pal\ country Asia on NE border of India in the Himalayas; a kingdom ✻ Katmandu *area* 54,000, *pop* 9,500,000 — **Nep·a·lese** \,nep-ə-'lēz, -'lēs\ *adj or n*

Nep·tune \'nep-,t(y)ün\ urban township E N.J. on the Atlantic *pop* 21,487

Ness, Loch \'nes\ lake 23 *m* long NW Scotland in Inverness

Nestos — see MESTA

Neth·er·lands \'neth-ər-lən(d)z\ **1** LOW COUNTRIES — an historical usage **2** *or* **Hol·land** \'häl-ənd\ *or* D **Ne·der·land** \'nād-ər-,länt\ country NW Europe on North sea; a kingdom, official ✻ Amsterdam, de facto ✻ The Hague *area* 15,785, *pop* 12,535,307 — **Neth·er·land** \'neth-ər-lənd\ *adj* — **Neth·er·land·er** \-,lan-dər, -lən-\ *n* — **Neth·er·land·ish** \-dish\ *adj*

Netherlands Antilles *or* **Dutch West Indies** the islands of the West Indies belonging to the Netherlands: Aruba, Bonaire, Curaçao, Saba, St. Eustatius, & S part of St. Martin; an overseas territory ✻ Willemstad (on Curaçao) *area* 403, *pop* 194,056

Netherlands Guiana — see SURINAM

Netherlands East Indies — see INDONESIA

Netherlands India *or* **Netherlands Indies** NETHERLANDS EAST INDIES

Netherlands New Guinea — see WEST NEW GUINEA

Netherlands Timor — see TIMOR

Néthou, Pic de — see ANETO (Pico de)

Net·tu·no \nā-'tü-(,)nō\ commune Italy on Tyrrhenian sea SSE of Rome adjoining Anzio

Neu·châ·tel \,n(y)ü-shə-'tel, ,nə(r)sh-ə-\ *or* G **Neu·en·burg** \'nȯi-ən-,bərg\ **1** canton W Switzerland in Jura mountains *area* 312, *pop* 128,152 **2** commune, its ✻, on **Lake of Neuchâtel** (*area* 84) *pop* 29,500

Neuil·ly-sur-Seine \,nə(r)-,yē-,sü(ə)r-'sän\ commune N France NW of Paris near the Bois de Boulogne *pop* 66,095

Neu·mün·ster \nȯi-; *see* MÜNSTER\ city W Germany SSW of Kiel *pop* 73,100

Neu·quén \nyü-'kān\ river 375 *m* W Argentina flowing from the Andes E to join the Limay forming the Negro

Neuse \'n(y)üs\ river 260 *m* E *cen* N.C. flowing SE into Pamlico Sound

Neuss \'nȯis\ city W Germany W of Düsseldorf *pop* 91,600

Neus·tria \'n(y)ü-strē-ə\ **1** the western part of the dominions of the Franks after the conquest by Clovis in 511, comprising the NW part of modern France between the Meuse, the Loire, & the Atlantic **2** NORMANDY — **Neus·tri·an** \-ən\ *adj or n*

Ne·va \'nē-və, 'nā-\ river 40 *m* U.S.S.R. in NW Soviet Russia, Europe, flowing from Lake Ladoga to Gulf of Finland at Leningrad

Ne·vada \nə-'vad-ə, -'väd-ə\ state W U.S. ✻ Carson City *area* 110,540, *pop* 285,278 — **Ne·vad·an** \-'vad-ᵊn, -'väd-ᵊn\ *or* **Ne·vad·i·an** \-'vad-ē-ən, -'väd-\ *adj or n*

Ne·vers \nə-'ve(ə)r\ city *cen* France on the Loire SE of Orléans *pop* 33,700

Ne·ves \'nā-vəs\ city SE Brazil on Guanabara Bay *pop* 53,052

Ne·vis \'nē-vəs, 'nev-əs\ island Brit. West Indies, part of St. Kitts-Nevis Associated State in the Leewards; chief town Charlestown *area* 50

Ne·vis, Ben \ben-\ mountain 4406 *ft* W Scotland in SW Inverness in the Grampians; highest peak in Great Britain

New Al·ba·ny \'ȯl-bə-nē\ city S Ind. *pop* 37,812

New Am·ster·dam \'am(p)-stər-,dam\ town founded 1625 on Manhattan I. by the Dutch; renamed New York 1664 by the British

New·ark \'n(y)ü-ərk, 'n(y)ü(-ə)rk\ **1** city & port NE N.J. on **Newark Bay** (W extension of Upper New York Bay) *pop* 405,220 **2** city *cen* Ohio *pop* 41,790

New Bed·ford \'bed-fərd\ city & port SE Mass. *pop* 102,477

New Ber·lin \'bər-lən\ city SE Wis. W of Milwaukee *pop* 15,788

New Bern \'n(y)ü-(,)bərn, n(y)ü-'\ city & port E N.C. at mouth of Neuse river *pop* 15,717

New Braun·fels \'braün-fəlz\ city SE *cen* Tex. *pop* 15,631

New Brit·ain \'brit-ᵊn\ **1** city *cen* Conn. *pop* 82,201 **2** island Bismarck archipelago; largest of group *area* 14,000, *pop* 100,373

New Bruns·wick \'brənz-(,)wik\ **1** city N *cen* N.J. *pop* 40,139 **2** province SE Canada bordering on Gulf of St. Lawrence & Bay of Fundy ✻ Fredericton *area* 27,985, *pop* 554,616

New·burgh \'n(y)ü-,bərg\ city SE N.Y. on the Hudson S of Poughkeepsie *pop* 30,979

New Cal·e·do·nia \,kal-ə-'dō-nyə, -nē-ə\ island SW Pacific SW of the New Hebrides; with nearby islands, constitutes an overseas department of France ✻ Nouméa *area* 8548, *pop* 72,478

New Castile — see CASTILE

New·cas·tle \'n(y)ü-,kas-əl, -,kȧs-, n(y)ü-'\ **1** city & port SE Australia in E New So. Wales NE of Sydney at mouth of Hunter river *pop* (with suburbs) 185,200 **2** *or* **Newcastle upon Tyne** \'tīn\ city & county borough & port N England ✻ of Northumberland *pop* 291,723 **3** *or* **Newcastle under Lyme** \'līm\ municipal borough W *cen* England in Staffordshire *pop* 70,028

New Cas·tle \'n(y)ü-,kas-əl\ **1** city E Ind. S of Muncie *pop* 20,349 **2** city W Pa. ESE of Youngstown, Ohio *pop* 44,790

Newchwang — see YINGKOW

New Delhi \'del-ē\ city ✻ of India in Delhi Territory S of city of (Old) Delhi

New England, 1 the NE section of the U.S. comprising the states of Me., N.H., Vt., Mass., R.I., & Conn. **2** mountain range & plateau SE Australia in NE New So. Wales; part of Great Dividing range — **New En·gland·er** \-'iŋ-glən-dər *also* -'iŋ-lən-\ *n*

New Forest forested area S England in Hampshire between the Avon & Southampton Water; once a royal hunting ground

New·found·land \'n(y)ü-fən-(d)lənd, -,(d)land; n(y)ü-'faün-(d)lənd\ **1** island Canada in the Atlantic E of Gulf of St. Lawrence *area* 42,734, *pop* 404,260 **2** province E Canada comprising Newfoundland I. & Labrador ✻ St. John's *area* 154,734, *pop* 415,074 — **New·found·land·er** *n*

New France the possessions of France in No. America before 1763

New Geor·gia \'jȯr-jə\ **1** island group W Pacific in *cen* Solomons **2** island 50 *m* long, chief island of the group

New Goa — see PANGIM

New Gra·na·da \grə-'näd-ə\ Spanish viceroyalty in NW So. America 1717–1819 comprising area included in modern Panama, Colombia, Venezuela, & Ecuador

New Guin·ea \'gin-ē\ **1** *or* **Pap·ua** \'pap-yə-wə\ *or* Indonesian **Iri·an** \,ir-ē-'än\ island in Malay archipelago N of E Australia divided among West New Guinea on W, Territory of New Guinea on NE, & Territory of Papua on SE *area* 306,600 **2** the Territory of New Guinea — **New Guin·e·an** \'gin-ē-ən\ *adj or n*

New Guinea, Territory of territory comprising NE New Guinea, Bismarck archipelago, & Bougainville, Buka, & adjacent islands in the NW Solomons; a UN trust territory administered jointly with Territory of Papua by Australia *area* 93,000, *pop* 1,311,610

New Hamp·shire \'ham(p)-shər, -,shi(ə)r\ state NE U.S. ✻ Concord *area* 9304, *pop* 606,921 — **New Hamp·shire·man** \-mən\ *n* — **New Hamp·shir·ite** \-,īt\ *n*

New Han·o·ver \'han-ə-vər, 'han-,ō-\ **1** urban township S N.J. *pop* 28,528 **2** *or* **La·von·gai** \lə-'vȯŋ-,gī\ island W Pacific in Bismarck archipelago NW of New Ireland *area* 460

New Ha·ven \'hā-vən\ city & port S Conn. *pop* 152,048

New Heb·ri·des \'heb-rə-,dēz\ islands SW Pacific NE of New Caledonia & W of Fiji; under joint Brit. & French administration ✻ Vila (on Efate) *area* 5700 *pop* 53,888

New Ibe·ria \ī-'bir-ē-ə\ city S La. SE of Lafayette *pop* 29,062

New Ire·land \'ī(ə)r-lənd\ island W Pacific in Bismarck archipelago N of New Britain ✻ Kavieng *area* 3340, *pop* 37,225

New Jer·sey \'jər-zē\ state E U.S. ✻ Trenton *area* 7836, *pop* 6,066,782 — **New Jer·sey·ite** \-,īt\ *n*

New Ken·sing·ton \'ken-ziŋ-tən, 'ken(t)-siŋ-\ city SW Pa. NE of Pittsburgh on the Allegheny *pop* 23,485

New Lon·don \'lən-dən\ city & port SE Conn. on Long Island Sound at mouth of Thames river *pop* 34,182

New·mar·ket \'n(y)ü-,mär-kət\ urban district E England in West Suffolk

New Mex·i·co \'mek-si-,kō\ state SW U.S. ✻ Santa Fe *area* 121,666, *pop* 951,023 — **New Mex·i·can** \-si-kən\ *adj or n*

New Mil·ford \'mil-fərd\ borough NE N.J. *pop* 18,810

New Neth·er·land \'neth-ər-lənd\ Dutch colony in No. America 1613–64 occupying lands bordering on the Hudson & later also on the lower Delaware ✻ New Amsterdam

New Or·leans \'ȯr-lē-ənz, 'ȯrl-(y)ənz, (,)ȯr-'lēnz\ city & port SE La. between Lake Pontchartrain & the Mississippi *pop* 627,525 — **New Or·lea·nian** \(,)ȯr-'lē-nyən, -nē-ən\ *n*

New·port \'n(y)ü-,pō(ə)rt, -,pȯ(ə)rt\ **1** city N Ky. on the Ohio opposite Cincinnati, Ohio *pop* 30,070 **2** city & port SE R.I. on Narragansett Bay *pop* 47,049 **3** municipal borough S England ✻ of Isle of Wight *pop* 20,426 **4** county borough W England ✻ of Monmouthshire WNW of Bristol *pop* 105,285

Newport Beach city SW Calif. SE of Long Beach *pop* 26,564

Newport News \,n(y)ü-,pōrt-'n(y)üz, -,pȯrt-, -pərt-\ city & port SE Va. on the James & Hampton Roads *pop* 113,662

New Prov·i·dence \'präv-əd-ən(t)s, -ə-,den(t)s\ island in NW *cen* Bahamas E of Andros; chief town Nassau *area* 58, *pop* 46,125

New Quebec region Canada in N Que. N of Eastmain river between Hudson Bay & Labrador — see UNGAVA

New Ro·chelle \,n(y)ü-rə-'shel\ city SE N.Y. on Long Island Sound E of Mount Vernon *pop* 76,812

New Sarum — see SALISBURY

New Siberian islands U.S.S.R. in N Soviet Russia, Asia, N of Yakutsk Republic in Arctic ocean between Laptev & East Siberian seas *area* 11,000

New South Wales state SE Australia bordering on the Pacific ✻ Sydney *area* 309,432, *pop* 3,745,201

New Spain former Spanish viceroyalty 1521–1821 including territory now in SW U.S., Mexico, Central America N of Panama, the West Indies, & the Philippines ✻ Mexico City

New Sweden Swedish colony in No. America 1638–55 bordering on W bank of the Delaware from modern Trenton, N.J., to its mouth

New·ton \'n(y)üt-ᵊn\ **1** city S *cen* Iowa E of Des Moines *pop* 15,381 **2** city E Mass. W of Boston *pop* 92,384

New West·min·ster city Canada in SW B.C. *pop* 31,665

New Windsor — see WINDSOR

New York \'yȯ(ə)rk\ **1** state NE U.S. ✻ Albany *area* 49,576, *pop* 16,782,304 **2** *or* **New York City** city & port SE N.Y. at mouth of the Hudson; includes boroughs of Bronx, Brooklyn, Manhattan, Queens, & Richmond *pop* 7,781,984 — **New York·er** \'yȯr-kər\ *n*

New York Bay inlet of the Atlantic SE N.Y. & NE N.J. at mouth of the Hudson forming harbor of metropolitan New York & consisting of **Upper New York Bay** & **Lower New York Bay** connected by the **Narrows** (strait separating Staten I. & Long I.)

New York State Barge Canal — see ERIE

New Zea·land \'zē-lənd\ country SW Pacific ESE of Australia comprising chiefly North I. & South I.; a dominion of the Brit. Commonwealth ✻ Wellington *area* 103,736, *pop* 2,414,064 — **New Zea·land·er** \-lən-dər\ *n*

Nga·mi, Lake \eŋ-'gäm-ē\ marshy depression NW Botswana N of Kalahari desert; formerly a large lake

Ngau·ru·hoe \eŋ-,gaü-rə-'hō-ē\ volcano 7515 *ft* New Zealand in *cen* North I. in Tongariro National Park

N'Gela — see FLORIDA

Ni·ag·a·ra Falls \(,)nī-,ag-(ə-)rə-\ **1** waterfall on border between N.Y. & Ont. in the **Niagara** river (36 *m* flowing from Lake Erie N into Lake Ontario); divided by Goat I. into Horseshoe, or Canadian, Falls (158 *ft* high, 3010 *ft* wide at crest) & American Falls (167 *ft* high, 1060 *ft* wide) **2** city W N.Y. at the falls *pop* 102,394 **3** city Canada in SE Ont. *pop* 23,563

Nia·mey \nē-'äm-(,)ā\ city ✻ of Niger on Niger river *pop* 18,600

Ni·as \'nē-,äs\ island Indonesia in Indian ocean off W coast of Sumatra *area* 1569 — **Ni·as·san** \'nē-ə-sən\ *n*

Ni·caea \nī-'sē-ə\ *or* **Nice** \'nīs\ ancient city of Byzantine Empire, site at modern village of Iznik in NW Turkey in Asia at E end of Iznik Lake — **Ni·cae·an** \nī-'sē-ən\ *adj* — **Ni·cene** \nī-'sēn\ *adj*

Nic·a·ra·gua \,nik-ə-'räg-wə\ **1** lake 100 *m* long S Nicaragua *area* 3000 **2** country Central America bordering on the Pacific & the Caribbean; a republic ✻ Managua *area* 57,143, *pop* 1,331,000 — **Nic·a·ra·guan** \-'räg-wən\ *adj or n*

Nice \'nēs\ *or anc* **Ni·caea** \nī-'sē-ə\ city & port SE France on the Mediterranean *pop* 244,400

Nic·o·bar \'nik-ə-ˌbär\ islands India in Indian ocean S of Andaman islands *area* 635 — see ANDAMAN AND NICOBAR

Nicomedia — see IZMIT

Ni·cop·o·lis \nə-'käp-ə-ləs, nī-\ ancient city NW Greece in Epirus near entrance to Ambracian gulf

Nic·o·sia \ˌnik-ə-'sē-ə\ city ✳ of Cyprus *pop* 37,728

Nidwald *or* **Nidwalden** — see UNTERWALDEN

Niedersachsen — see LOWER SAXONY

Niemen — see NEMAN

Nieuw·poort *or* **Nieu·port** \'n(y)ü-ˌpō(ə)rt, -ˌpȯ(ə)rt\ commune NW Belgium in West Flanders on the Yser SW of Ostend

Ni·ger \'nī-jər\ **1** river 2600 *m* W Africa flowing from Fouta Djallon NE, SE, & S into Gulf of Guinea **2** country W Africa; a republic of the French Community since 1958, formerly a territory of French West Africa ✳ Niamey *area* 458,874, *pop* 3,100,000

Ni·ge·ria \nī-'jir-ē-ə\ country W Africa bordering on Gulf of Guinea; a dominion of the Brit. Commonwealth, formerly a colony & protectorate ✳ Lagos *area* 356,669, *pop* 55,653,821 — **Ni·ge·ri·an** \-ē-ən\ *adj or n*

Nihon — see JAPAN

Nii·ga·ta \nē-'gät-ə\ city & port Japan in N Honshu on Sea of Japan *pop* 314,528

Nii·hau \'nē-ˌhaů\ island Hawaii WSW of Kauai *area* 72

Nij·me·gen \'nī-ˌmā-gə(n)\ *or* **Nim·we·gen** \'nim-ˌvā-gən\ *or* **Ni·me·guen** \'nī-ˌmā-gə(n)\ commune E Netherlands in Gelderland on the Waal S of Arnhem *pop* 127,110

Nik·ko \'nik-(ˌ)ō\ city Japan in E *cen* Honshu *pop* 33,490

Ni·ko·la·yev *or* **Ni·ko·la·yev** \ˌnik-ə-'lī-əf\ *or* **Ver·no·len·insk** \ˌver-nə-'len-ˌin(t)sk\ city & port U.S.S.R. in S Ukraine at confluence of Bug & Ingul rivers *pop* 224,000

Ni·ko·pol \ni-'kȯ-pəl\ city U.S.S.R. in E *cen* Ukraine on the Dnieper *pop* 81,000

Nile \'nī(ə)l\ river 4037 *m* E Africa flowing from Lake Victoria in Uganda N into the Mediterranean in Egypt; in various sections called specifically: **Vic·to·ria** \vik-'tōr-ē-ə, -'tȯr-\, *or* **Som·er·set** \'səm-ər-sət, -ˌset\ **Nile**, between Lake Victoria & Lake Albert; **Al·bert** \'al-bərt\ **Nile**, between Lake Albert & Lake No; & **White Nile**, from Lake No to Khartoum — see BLUE NILE

Niles \'nī(ə)lz\ **1** village NE Ill. NW of Chicago *pop* 20,393 **2** city N Ohio SE of Warren *pop* 19,545

Nil·gi·ri \'nil-gə-rē\ hills S India in W Madras state; highest point Mt. Dodabetta 8647 *ft*

Nîmes \'nēm\ city S France NE of Montpellier *pop* 89,130

Nimrud — see KALAKH

Nin·e·veh \'nin-ə-və\ *or* L **Ni·nus** \'nī-nəs\ ancient city ✳ of Assyria; ruins in Iraq on the Tigris opposite Mosul

Ning·po \'niŋ-'pō\ *or formerly* **Ning·hsien** \'niŋ-shē-'en\ city E China in N Chekiang ESE of Hangchow *pop* 237,500

Ning·sia *or* **Ning·hsia** \'niŋ-shē-'ä\ **1** region N China; formerly a province ✳ Yinchwan *area* 30,039 **2** — see YINCHWAN

Ni·o·brara \ˌnī-ə-'brar-ə, -'brer-\ river 431 *m* E Wyo. & N Nebr. flowing E into the Missouri

Niort \nē-'ȯ(ə)r\ city W France ENE of La Rochelle *pop* 33,167

Nip·i·gon, Lake \'nip-i-ˌgän\ lake Canada in W Ont. N of Lake Superior *area* 1870

Nip·is·sing, Lake \'nip-ə-siŋ\ lake Canada in SE Ont. NE of Georgian Bay *area* 330

Nippon — see JAPAN

Nip·pur \nip-'ů(ə)r\ ancient city of Sumer 100 *m* SSE of Babylon

Nis *or* **Nish** \'nish\ city E Yugoslavia in E Serbia *pop* 62,100

Ni·shi·no·mi·ya \nish-ə-'nō-mē-,(y)ä\ city Japan in *cen* Honshu on Osaka Bay E of Kobe *pop* 210,179

Ni·te·rói *or formerly* **Nic·the·roy** \ˌnēt-ə-'rȯi\ city SE Brazil ✳ of Rio de Janeiro state on Guanabara Bay opposite Rio de Janeiro *pop* 255,585

Ni·u·a·foo \nē-'ü-ə-ˌfō\ island SW *cen* Pacific in the N Tongas

Ni·ue \nē-'ü-(ˌ)(w)ä\ *or* **Sav·age** \'sav-ij\ island S *cen* Pacific W of Cook islands; a dependency of New Zealand *area* 100

Ni·velles \nē-'vel\ commune *cen* Belgium *pop* 75,863

Ni·ver·nais \ˌniv-ər-'nā\ region & former province *cen* France E of the upper Loire ✳ Nevers

Nizhni Novgorod — see GORKI

Nizh·ni Ta·gil \ˌnizh-nē-tə-'gil\ city U.S.S.R. in W Soviet Russia, Asia, on E slope of the Urals *pop* 338,000

No \'nō\ lake S *cen* Sudan where Bahr el Jebel & Bahr el Ghazal join to form the White Nile *area* 40

Noem·foor *or* **Num·for** \'nüm-ˌfō(ə)r, -ˌfȯ(ə)r\ island West New Guinea in W Schouten islands *area* 28

No·gal·es \nō-'gal-əs, -'gäl-\ city NW Mexico in Sonora adjacent to Nogales, Ariz. *pop* 24,478

No·ga·ta \nō-'gät-ə\ city Japan in N Kyushu *pop* 62,520

Nome, Cape \'nōm\ cape W Alaska on S side of Seward peninsula

Non·ni \'nän-'nē\ river 660 *m* NE China in N Manchuria flowing from the Great Khingan mountains S into the Sungari

Noot·ka Sound \ˌnůt-kə-, ˌnüt-\ inlet of the Pacific Canada in SW B.C. on W coast of Vancouver I.

Nordenskjöld — see LAPTEV

Nord·kyn, Cape \'nȯ(ə)r-kən, 'nȯ(ə)r-\ cape NE Norway on Barents sea E of North Cape; northernmost point of European mainland, at 71°8′N

Nor·folk \'nȯr-fək, *US also* -ˌfȯk\ **1** city & port SE Va. on Elizabeth river S of Hampton Roads *pop* 304,869 **2** island S Pacific between New Caledonia & New Zealand; administered by Australia *area* 13 **3** county E England bordering on North sea ✳ Norwich *area* 2055, *pop* 546,550

Norfolk Broads — see BROADS

Norge — see NORWAY

Nor·i·cum \'nȯr-i-kəm\ ancient country & Roman province S *cen* Europe S of the Danube in modern Austria & S Germany

No·rilsk \nə-'rēlsk\ city U.S.S.R. in NW Soviet Russia, Asia, N of Arctic circle near mouth of the Yenisei *pop* 124,000

Nor·man \'nȯr-mən\ city *cen* Okla. on the Canadian *pop* 33,412

Nor·man·dy \'nȯr-mən-dē\ *or* F **Nor·man·die** \ˌnȯr-män-'dē\ region & former province NW France NE of Brittany ✳ Rouen

Nor·ris·town \'nȯr-ə-ˌstaůn, 'när-\ borough SE Pa. NW of Philadelphia on the Schuylkill *pop* 38,925

Norr·kö·ping \'nȯ(ə)r-, chə(r)p-iŋ\ city & port SE Sweden SW of Stockholm at head of an inlet of the Baltic *pop* 91,671

North island N New Zealand *area* 44,280, *pop* 1,610,000

North Ad·ams \'ad-əmz\ city NW Mass. *pop* 19,905

North·al·ler·ton \nȯr-'thal-ərt-ᵊn\ urban district N England ✳ of No. Riding, Yorkshire

North America continent of the western hemisphere NW of So. America bounded by Atlantic, Arctic, & Pacific oceans *area* 9,385,000 — **North American** *adj or n*

North·amp·ton \nȯr-'tham(p)-tən, nȯrth-'ham(p)-\ **1** city W *cen* Mass. on the Connecticut N of Holyoke *pop* 30,058 **2** *or* **North·amp·ton·shire** \-ˌshi(ə)r, -shər\ county *cen* England *area* 914, *pop* 359,550 **3** county borough, its ✳ *pop* 104,429

North Arlington borough NE N.J. NE of Newark *pop* 17,477

North Bay \'nȯrth-ˌbā\ city Canada in SE Ont. on Lake Nipissing *pop* 21,020

North Bell·more \'bel-ˌmō(ə)r, -ˌmȯ(ə)r\ urban area SE N.Y. on Long I. *pop* 19,639

North Ber·gen \'bər-gən\ urban township NE N.J. NNE of Jersey City *pop* 42,387

North Borneo *or* **British North Borneo** *or since 1963* **Sa·bah** \'säb-ˌä\ country NE Borneo, since 1963 a territory of Federation of Malaysia; formerly a Brit. colony & earlier a protected state ✳ Jesselton *area* 29,388, *pop* 400,836

North Brabant *or* D **Noord·bra·bant** \ˌnōrt-brä-'bänt\ province S Netherlands ✳ 's Hertogenbosch *area* 1965, *pop* 2,038,196

North Canadian river 760 *m* S *cen* U.S. flowing ESE from NE N. Mex. into the Canadian in E Okla.

North Cape, 1 cape New Zealand at N tip of North I. **2** cape NE Norway on **Ma·ger·öy** \ˌmäg-ə-'rȯi\ island (*area* 111), at 71°10′20″N

North Car·o·li·na \ˌkar-ə-'lī-nə\ state E U.S. ✳ Raleigh *area* 52,712, *pop* 4,556,155 — **North Car·o·lin·ian** \-'lin-ē-ən, -'lin-yən\ *adj or n*

North channel strait between NE Ireland & SW Scotland connecting Irish sea & the Atlantic

North Chicago city NE Ill. S of Waukegan *pop* 20,517

North Da·ko·ta \də-'kōt-ə\ state NW *cen* U.S. ✳ Bismarck *area* 70,665, *pop* 632,446 — **North Da·ko·tan** \-'kōt-ᵊn\ *adj or n*

North Downs hills S England chiefly in Kent & Surrey

North-East Frontier Agency autonomous district NE India in N Assam bordering on China

North-East New Guinea the section of the Territory of New Guinea on the island of New Guinea

Northern Cir·cars \(ˌ)sər-'kärz\ coast region E India now in E Andhra Pradesh but historically constituting the four N districts of Madras province

Northern Cook — see MANIHIKI

Northern Dvi·na \də-ˌvē-'nä\ *or* Russ **Se·ver·na·ya Dvina** \'sā-vər-nə-yə\ river 1100 *m* U.S.S.R. in N Soviet Russia, Europe, flowing NW into White sea

Northern Ireland region NE Ireland; a division of the United Kingdom of Great Britain & Northern Ireland ✳ Belfast *area* 5242, *pop* 1,370,709 — see ULSTER

Northern Karroo — see KARROO

Northern Kingdom — see ISRAEL

Northern Region *or formerly* **Northern Territories** region N Ghana N of Ashanti; formerly a Brit. protectorate administered as part of Gold Coast ✳ Tamale *area* 37,600, *pop* 1,036,603

Northern Rhodesia *or since 1964* **Zam·bia** \'zam-bē-ə\ country S Africa; formerly a Brit. protectorate; independent republic within Brit. Commonwealth since 1964 ✳ Lusaka *area* 290,410, *pop* 2,270,000

Northern Sporades — see SPORADES

Northern Territory territory *cen* & N Australia bordering on Arafura sea ✳ Darwin *area* 523,620, *pop* 35,744

North Frisian — see FRISIAN

North Highlands urban area N *cen* Calif. NNE of Sacramento *pop* 21,271

North Holland *or* D **Noord·hol·land** \ˌnōrt-'hȯ-ˌlänt\ province NW Netherlands ✳ Haarlem *area* 1163, *pop* 2,038,196

North Las Vegas city SE Nev. *pop* 18,422

North Little Rock city *cen* Ark. *pop* 58,032

North Miami city SE Fla. *pop* 28,708

North Miami Beach city SE Fla. *pop* 21,405

North Minch — see MINCH

North New Hyde Park urban area SE N.Y. in W Long I. W of Garden City *pop* 17,929

North Olm·sted \'əm-ˌsted\ city NE Ohio *pop* 16,290

North Ossetia *or* **North Ossetian Republic** autonomous republic U.S.S.R. in SE Soviet Russia, Europe, on the N slopes of Caucasus mountains ✳ Dzaudzhikau *area* 3500, *pop* 450,000

North Plainfield borough NE N.J. SW of Elizabeth *pop* 16,993

North Platte, 1 river 618 *m* W U.S. flowing from N Colo. N & E through Wyo. into Nebr. to unite with the So. Platte forming the Platte **2** city SW *cen* Nebr. *pop* 17,184

North Providence urban township NE R.I. *pop* 18,220

North Rhine–Westphalia *or* G **Nord·rhein–West·fa·len** \'nȯrt-ˌrīn-vest-'fä-lən\ state W Germany formed 1946 by union of former Westphalia province, Lippe state, & N Rhine Province ✳ Düsseldorf *area* 13,107, *pop* 15,852,500

North Riding \'rīd-iŋ\ administrative county N England comprising N part of Yorkshire ✳ Northallerton *area* 2128, *pop* 525,496

North river estuary of the Hudson between SE N.Y. & NE N.J.

North Saskatchewan — see SASKATCHEWAN

North sea *or* **German ocean** arm of the Atlantic 600 *m* long & 350 *m* wide E of Great Britain

North Tonawanda city W N.Y. N of Buffalo *pop* 34,757

North Truchas Peak — see TRUCHAS PEAK

North·um·ber·land \nȯr-'thəm-bər-lənd\ **1** strait 180 *m* long Canada in Gulf of St. Lawrence between P.E.I. & the mainland **2** county N England ✳ Newcastle upon Tyne *area* 2019, *pop* 798,175

North·um·bria \nȯr-'thəm-brē-ə\ ancient country Great Britain between the Humber & Firth of Forth; one of kingdoms in Anglo‑Saxon heptarchy

North Valley Stream urban area SE N.Y. on Long I. *pop* 17,239

North Vancouver city Canada in SW B.C. *pop* 19,951

North-West Frontier Province former province of British India & later of Pakistan on Afghanistan border ✻ Peshawar; merged 1955 in new province of West Pakistan

Northwest Territories territory N Canada comprising the arctic islands, the mainland N of 60° between Yukon Territory & Hudson Bay, & the islands in Hudson Bay; divided into Mackenzie, Keewatin, & Franklin districts ✻ Yellowknife *area* 1,253,438, *pop* 19,313

Nor·ton Sound \ˌnȯrt-ᵊn-\ arm of Bering sea W Alaska between Seward peninsula & the mouths of the Yukon

Nor·walk \ˈnȯ(ə)r-ˌwȯk\ **1** city SW Calif. SE of Los Angeles *pop* 88,739 **2** city SW Conn. on Long Island Sound *pop* 67,775

Nor·way \ˈnȯ(ə)r-ˌwā\ *or* Norw **Nor·ge** \ˈnȯr-gə\ country N Europe in Scandinavia bordering on Atlantic & Arctic oceans; a kingdom ✻ Oslo *area* 119,085, *pop* 3,510,199

Nor·we·gian \nȯr-ˈwē-jən\ sea arm of the N Atlantic W of Norway

Nor·wich \ˈnȯ(ə)r-(ˌ)wich; ˈnȯr-ich, ˈnär-\ **1** city SE Conn. N of New London *pop* 38,506 **2** \ˈnär-ij, -ich\ city & county borough E England ✻ of Norfolk *pop* 121,226

Nor·wood \ˈnȯ(ə)r-ˌwu̇d\ **1** town E Mass. SW of Boston *pop* 24,898 **2** city SW Ohio NE of Cincinnati *pop* 34,580

Not·ta·way \ˈnät-ə-ˌwā\ river 400 *m* Canada in SW Que. flowing NW into James Bay

Not·ting·ham \ˈnät-iŋ-əm, *US also* -ˌham\ **1** *or* **Not·ting·ham·shire** \-ˌshi(ə)r, -shər\ *or* **Notts** \ˈnäts\ county N *cen* England *area* 844, *pop* 841,083 **2** city & county borough, its ✻, on the Trent *pop* 306,008

Nouak·chott \nü-ˈäk-ˌshät\ town ✻ of Mauritania, in SW part on the Atlantic *pop ab* 12,000

Nou·méa \nü-ˈmā-ə\ city & port ✻ of New Caledonia *pop* 35,000

No·va Igua·çu \ˌnȯ-və-ˌē-gwə-ˈsü\ city SE Brazil in Rio de Janeiro state NW of Rio de Janeiro *pop* 58,533

Nova Lisboa — see HUAMBO

No·va·ra \nō-ˈvär-ə\ commune NW Italy in Piedmont *pop* 65,682

No·va Sco·tia \ˌnō-və-ˈskō-shə\ province SE Canada comprising a peninsula (375 *m* long) & Cape Breton I. ✻ Halifax *area* 21,103, *pop* 694,717 — see ACADIA — **No·va Sco·tian** \-shən\ *adj or n*

No·va·to \nō-ˈvät-(ˌ)ō\ city W Calif. N of San Francisco *pop* 17,881

No·va·ya Zem·lya \ˌnō-və-yə-ˌzem-lē-ˈä\ two islands U.S.S.R. in NE Soviet Russia, Europe, in Arctic ocean between Barents sea & Kara sea *area* 36,000

Nov·go·rod \ˈnäv-gə-ˌräd\ **1** medieval principality E Europe extending from Lake Peipus & Lithuania to the Urals **2** city U.S.S.R. in NW Soviet Russia, Europe, N of Lake Ilmen *pop* 61,000

No·vi Sad \ˌnō-vē-ˈsäd\ city NE Yugoslavia on the Danube; chief city of Voivodina *pop* 84,500

No·vo·kuz·netsk \ˌnō-(ˌ)vō-ku̇z-ˈnetsk\ *or formerly* **Sta·linsk** \ˈstäl-ˌ(y)in(t)sk, ˈstal-\ city U.S.S.R. in SW Soviet Russia, Asia, at S end of Kuznetsk basin *pop* 377,000

No·vo·si·birsk \ˌnō-(ˌ)vō-sə-ˈbi(ə)rsk\ *or formerly* **No·vo·ni·ko·la·evsk** \-ˌnik-ə-ˈlī-ˌefsk, -ˌevsk\ city U.S.S.R. in SW Soviet Russia, Asia, on the Ob *pop* 1,013,000

Nu·bia \ˈn(y)ü-bē-ə\ region & ancient kingdom NE Africa along the Nile in S Egypt & N Sudan

Nu·bi·an \ˈn(y)ü-bē-ən\ desert NE Sudan E of the Nile

Nu·e·ces \n(y)ü-ˈā-səs\ river 338 *m* S Tex. flowing S & SE into Nueces Bay at head of Corpus Christi Bay

Nueva Esparta — see MARGARITA

Nue·vo La·re·do \nü-ˌā-(ˌ)vō-lə-ˈrād-(ˌ)ō\ city N Mexico in Tamaulipas on Rio Grande opposite Laredo, Tex. *pop* 107,473

Nue·vo Le·ón \lā-ˈōn\ state N Mexico in the Sierra Madre Oriental ✻ Monterrey *area* 25,134, *pop* 918,506

Nu·ku Hi·va *or* **Nu·ku·hi·va** \ˌnü-kə-ˈhē-və\ island S Pacific in the Marquesas; largest in group *area* 186

Null·ar·bor Plain \ˌnəl-ə-ˌbȯ(ə)r-, ˌnəl-ˌär-bər-\ treeless plain SW Australia in Western Australia & So. Australia bordering on Great Australian Bight

Numfor — see NOEMFOOR

Nu·mid·ia \n(y)ü-ˈmid-ē-ə\ ancient country N Africa E of Mauretania in modern Algeria; chief city Hippo — **Nu·mid·i·an** \-ē-ən\ *adj or n*

Nun·ea·ton \ˌnə-ˈnēt-ᵊn\ municipal borough *cen* England in Warwickshire E of Birmingham *pop* 54,408

Nu·ni·vak \ˈnü-nə-ˌvak\ island 50 *m* long W Alaska in Bering sea

Nu·rem·berg \ˈn(y)u̇r-əm-ˌbərg\ *or* G **Nürn·berg** \ˈnuērn-ˌberk\ city W Germany in N *cen* Bavaria on Pegnitz river *pop* 452,400

Nu·ri·stan \ˌnu̇r-i-ˈstan\ *or formerly* **Kaf·i·ri·stan** \ˌkaf-ə-ri-ˈstan\ district E Afghanistan S of the Hindu Kush ✻ Puchal

Nut·ley \ˈnət-lē\ town NE N.J. N of Newark *pop* 29,513

Ny·asa, Lake \nī-ˈas-ə, nē-\ *or* **Lake Malawi** lake SE Africa in Great Rift valley in Malawi, Mozambique, & Tanganyika *area* 11,000

Ny·asa·land \-ˌland\ *or since* 1964 **Ma·la·wi** \mə-ˈlä-wē\ country SE Africa bordering on Lake Nyasa; formerly a Brit. protectorate; independent within Brit. Commonwealth since 1964; a republic 1966 ✻ Zomba *area* 37,374, *pop* 2,680,000

Nyir·a·gon·go \nē-ˌir-ə-ˈgȯŋ-(ˌ)gō, -ˈgäŋ-\ volcano over 11,000 *ft* E Congo in Virunga mountains NE of Lake Kivu

Nysa — see NEISSE

Oa·he Reservoir \ə-ˌwä-ˌē-ˈrez-, -ˌwī-ˈrez-\ reservoir *ab* 225 *m* long N S. Dak. & S N. Dak. formed in Missouri river by **Oahe Dam**

Oa·hu \ə-ˈwä-(ˌ)hü\ island Hawaii, site of Honolulu *area* 589

Oak·ham \ˈō-kəm\ urban district E *cen* England ✻ of Rutland

Oak·land \ˈō-klənd\ city & port W Calif. on San Francisco Bay opposite San Francisco *pop* 367,548

Oak Lawn village NE Ill. SW of Chicago *pop* 27,471

Oak Park, 1 village NE Ill. W of Chicago *pop* 61,093 **2** city SE Mich. N of Detroit *pop* 36,632

Oak Ridge city E Tenn. W of Knoxville *pop* 27,169

Oa·xa·ca \wə-ˈhäk-ə\ **1** state SE Mexico bordering on the Pacific *area* 36,371, *pop* 1,603,783 **2** city, its ✻ *pop* 46,741

Ob \ˈäb, ˈōb\ river 2500 *m* U.S.S.R. in W Soviet Russia, Asia, flowing NW & N into **Gulf of Ob** (inlet of Arctic ocean 500 *m* long); with the Irtysh, 3200 *m* long

Ober·am·mer·gau \ˌō-bə-ˈräm-ər-ˌgau̇\ town SW Germany in Bavaria SSW of Munich

Ober·hau·sen \ˈō-bər-ˌhau̇z-ᵊn\ city W Germany in the Ruhr WNW of Essen *pop* 256,700

Ober·land \ˈō-bər-ˌland, -ˌlänt\ *or* **Bernese Oberland** *or* **Bernese Alps** section of the Alps S Switzerland in Bern & Valais cantons between the Lakes of Thun & Brienz on the N & the valley of the upper Rhone on the S — see FINSTERAARHORN

Oberpfalz — see PALATINATE

Obwald *or* **Obwalden** — see UNTERWALDEN

Ocean, 1 island W Pacific between Nauru I. & Gilbert islands; belongs to Gilbert & Ellice Islands colony *area* 2 **2** — see KURE

Oce·a·nia \ˌō-shē-ˈan-ē-ə, -ˈā-nē-ə\ *or* **Oce·an·i·ca** \-ˈan-i-kə\ the lands of the *cen* & S Pacific including Micronesia, Melanesia, Polynesia (including New Zealand), often Australia, & sometimes the Malay archipelago — **Oce·a·ni·an** \-ˈan-ē-ən, -ˈā-nē-\ *adj or n*

Ocean·side \ˈō-shən-ˌsīd\ **1** city SW Calif. NNW of San Diego *pop* 24,971 **2** urban area SE N.Y. on Long I. *pop* 30,448

Oc·mul·gee \ōk-ˈməl-gē\ river 255 *m*, *cen* Ga. flowing SE to join the **Oco·nee** \ō-ˈkō-nē\ (250 *m*) forming the Altamaha

Ocmulgee National Monument reservation *cen* Ga. at Macon containing Indian mounds & other remains

Ocra·coke \ˈō-krə-ˌkōk\ island off *cen* N.C. coast between Pamlico Sound & the Atlantic — see CROATAN

Oden·se \ˈō-t͟hən-sə, ˈōd-ᵊn-\ city Denmark in N Fyn I. *pop* 105,915

Oder \ˈōd-ər\ *or* **Odra** \ˈō-drə\ river 563 *m*, *cen* Europe rising in the mountains of Silesia, Czechoslovakia, & flowing N to join the Neisse & thence N into the Baltic sea

Odes·sa \ō-ˈdes-ə\ **1** city W Tex. *pop* 80,338 **2** city & port U.S.S.R. in S Ukraine on Black sea *pop* 667,000

Oea — see TRIPOLI

Oe·ta \ˈēt-ə\ mountains *cen* Greece, E spur of Pindus mountains

Of·fa·ly \ˈȯf-ə-lē, ˈäf-\ *or formerly* **King's** county *cen* Ireland in Leinster ✻ Tullamore *area* 771, *pop* 51,532

Of·fen·bach \ˈȯf-ən-ˌbäk\ city W Germany on the Main E of Frankfurt *pop* 113,000

Oga·den \ō-ˈgäd-ˌän\ plateau region SE Ethiopia

Ogasawara — see BONIN

Og·bo·mo·sho \ˌäg-bə-ˈmō-(ˌ)shō\ city W Nigeria *pop* 139,000

Og·den \ˈȯg-dən, ˈäg-\ city N Utah *pop* 70,197

Og·dens·burg \-dənz-ˌbərg\ city N N.Y. *pop* 16,122

Ogee·chee \ō-ˈgē-chē\ river 250 *m* E Ga. flowing SE into the Atlantic

Ohio \ō-ˈhī-(ˌ)ō\ **1** river 981 *m* E U.S. flowing from junction of Allegheny & Monongahela rivers in W Pa. into the Mississippi **2** state E *cen* U.S. ✻ Columbus *area* 41,222, *pop* 9,706,397 — **Ohio·an** \-ˈhī-ə-wən\ *n*

Ohre — see EGER

Oil City city NW Pa. on Allegheny river *pop* 17,692

Oirot — see GORNO-ALTAI

Oise \ˈwäz\ river 186 *m* N France flowing SW into the Seine

Oi·ta \ˈoi-ˌtä\ city & port Japan in NE Kyushu *pop* 112,429

Oji·na·ga \ˌō-hē-ˈnäg-ə\ town N Mexico on Rio Grande opposite Presidio, Tex.

Ojos del Sa·la·do \ˌō-(ˌ)hōz-ˌdel-sə-ˈläd-(ˌ)ō\ mountain 22,539 *ft* NW Argentina in the Andes W of Tucumán

Oka \ō-ˈkä\ **1** river 530 *m* U.S.S.R. in S *cen* Soviet Russia, Asia, flowing N from the Sayan mountains into the Angara **2** river 950 *m* U.S.S.R. in *cen* Soviet Russia, Europe, flowing into the Volga

Oka·nog·an *or (in Canada)* **Oka·na·gan** \ˌō-kə-ˈnäg-ən\ river 300 *m* U.S. & Canada flowing from **Okanagan Lake** (70 *m* long, in SE B.C.) into the Columbia in NE Wash.

Oka·ya·ma \ˌō-kə-ˈyäm-ə\ city & port Japan in W Honshu on Inland sea *pop* 235,754

Oka·za·ki \ō-ˌkäz-ˈäk-ē, ˌō-kə-ˈzäk-\ city Japan in S *cen* Honshu SE of Nagoya *pop* 155,902

Okee·cho·bee, Lake \ˌō-kə-ˈchō-bē\ lake 37 *m* long S *cen* Fla.

Oke·fe·no·kee *or* **Oke·fi·no·kee** \ˌō-kə-fə-ˈnō-kē\ swamp 40 *m* long SE Ga. & NE Fla.

Okhotsk, Sea of \ō-ˈkätsk\ inlet of the Pacific U.S.S.R. in E Soviet Russia, Asia, W of Kamchatka peninsula & Kuril islands

Oki \ˈō-(ˌ)kē\ archipelago Japan in Sea of Japan off SW Honshu

Oki·na·wa \ˌō-kə-ˈnä-wə, -ˈnau̇-ə\ **1** island group in *cen* Ryukyu islands ✻ Naha; occupied by the U.S. **2** island in the group; largest in the Ryukyus *area* 579, *pop* 665,315 — **Oki·na·wan** \-ˈnä-wən, -ˈnau̇-ən\ *adj or n*

Okla·ho·ma \ˌō-klə-ˈhō-mə\ state S *cen* U.S. ✻ Oklahoma City *area* 69,919, *pop* 2,328,284 — **Okla·ho·man** \-mən\ *adj or n*

Oklahoma City city ✻ of Okla. on the No. Canadian *pop* 324,253

Ok·mul·gee \ōk-ˈməl-gē\ city E *cen* Okla. *pop* 15,951

Oko·vang·go *or* **Oka·van·go** \ˌō-kə-ˈvaŋ-(ˌ)gō\ *or* Port **Cu·ban·go** \kü-ˈvaⁿ(ŋ)-(ˌ)gü\ river 1000 *m* SW *cen* Africa rising in *cen* Angola & flowing S & E to empty into **Okovanggo basin** (great marsh N of Lake Ngami in N Bechuanaland Protectorate)

Öland \ˈə(r)l-ˌänd\ island Sweden in Baltic sea off SE coast; chief town Borgholm *area* 519

Old·bury \ˈōl(d)-b(ə-)rē, *US also* -ˌber-ē\ municipal borough W *cen* England in Worcestershire W of Birmingham *pop* 53,895

Old Castile — see CASTILE

Ol·den·burg \ˈōl-dən-ˌbərg\ **1** former state NW Germany bordering on North sea **2** city NW Germany W of Bremen *pop* 121,800

Old·ham \ˈōl-dəm\ county borough NW England in Lancashire NE of Manchester *pop* 121,212

Old Point Comfort cape SE Va. on N shore of Hampton Roads

Old Sar·um \ˈsar-əm, ˈser-\ *or anc* **Sor·bi·o·du·num** \ˌsȯr-bē-ə-ˈd(y)ü-nəm\ ancient city S England in Wiltshire N of Salisbury

Ol·du·vai Gorge \ˈōl-də-ˌwā, -ˌvā\ canyon Tanzania in N Tanganyika SE of Serengeti Plain; fossil beds

Ole·an \ˈō-lē-ˌan, ˌō-lē-ˈ\ city SW N.Y. *pop* 21,868

Olek·ma \ō-ˈlek-mə\ river 700 *m* U.S.S.R. in E Soviet Russia, Asia, rising in Yablonoi mountains & flowing N into the Lena

Ole·nek \ˌäl-ən-ˈyȯk\ river 1325 *m* U.S.S.R. in N *cen* Soviet Russia, Asia, flowing NE into Laptev sea W of the Lena

Ol·i·fants \ˈäl-ə-fən(t)s\ river 350 *m* S Africa in Republic of So. Africa & Mozambique flowing from Transvaal into the Limpopo

Olives, Mount of *or* **Ol·i·vet** \ˈäl-ə-ˌvet, ˌäl-ə-ˈ\ mountain ridge 2680 *ft* W Jordan running N & S on E side of Jerusalem

Olo·mouc \ˈō-lə-ˌmōts\ *or* G **Ol·mütz** \ˈōl-ˌm(y)üts\ city Czechoslovakia in *cen* Moravia on March river *pop* 73,899

Olsz·tyn \ˈōlsh-tən\ *or* G **Al·len·stein** \ˈal-ən-ˌs(t)īn, ˈäl-\ city N Poland NNW of Warsaw *pop* 54,000

Olt \'ôlt\ *or* **Alu·ta** \ə-'lüt-ə\ river 308 *m* S Romania flowing S through the Transylvanian Alps into the Danube

Ol·te·nia \ôl-'tē-nē-ə\ *or* **Little Walachia** region S Romania W of the Olt; the W division of Walachia

Olym·pia \ə-'lim-pē-ə, ō-\ **1** city ✳ of Wash. on Puget Sound *pop* 18,273 **2** plain S Greece in NW Peloponnesus along Alpheus river — **Olym·pi·an** \-pē-ən\ *adj or n* — **Olym·pic** \-pik\ *adj*

Olym·pic \-'lim-pik\ **1** mountains NW Wash. in *cen* Olympic peninsula — see OLYMPUS (Mount) **2** peninsula NW Wash. W of Puget Sound

Olympic National Park scenic area NW Wash. including part of Olympic mountains & strip of land along coast to W *area* 1388

Olym·pus \-'lim-pəs\ **1** mountains NE Greece in Thessaly near coast of Gulf of Salonika; highest peak 9550 *ft* **2** — see ULU DAG

Olympus, Mount mountain 7954 *ft* NW Wash.; highest in Olympic mountains

Olyn·thus \ō-'lin(t)-thəs\ ancient city NE Greece in Macedonia on Chalcidice peninsula

Om \'ôm\ river 450 *m* U.S.S.R. in SW Soviet Russia, Asia, flowing into the Irtysh

Omagh \'ō-,(,)mä, -mə\ town W Northern Ireland ✳ of Tyrone

Oma·ha \'ō-mə-,hô, -,hä\ city E Nebr. *pop* 301,598

Oman \ō-'män\ *or* **Muscat and Oman** country SW Asia in SE Arabia bordering on Arabian sea; a sultanate ✳ Muscat *area* 82,000, *pop* 550,000 — **Omani** \ō-'män-ē\ *adj or n* — see TRUCIAL OMAN

Oman, Gulf of arm of Arabian sea between Oman & SE Iran

Ombai — see ALOR

Om·dur·man \,äm-dər-'man\ city *cen* Sudan on the Nile opposite Khartoum & Khartoum North *pop* 113,551

Omo·lon \,äm-ə-'lôn\ river 600 *m* U.S.S.R. in NE Soviet Russia, Asia, flowing from the Kolyma range N into Kolyma river

Omsk \'ôm(p)sk, 'äm(p)sk\ city U.S.S.R. in SW Soviet Russia, Asia, at confluence of Irtysh & Om rivers *pop* 579,000

Omu·ra \'ō-mə-,rä\ city & port Japan in NW Kyushu on Omura Bay NNE of Nagasaki *pop* 61,230

Omu·ta \'ō-mə-,tä, ō-'müt-ə\ city & port Japan in NW Kyushu *pop* 201,737

One·ga \ō-'neg-ə\ lake U.S.S.R. in NW Soviet Russia, Europe, in S Karelo-Finnish Republic *area* 3764

Onei·da \ō-'nīd-ə\ lake *ab* 22 *m* long *cen* N.Y. NE of Syracuse

On·tar·io \än-'ter-ē-,ō, -'tar-\ **1** city SW Calif. NW of Riverside *pop* 46,617 **2** lake U.S. & Canada in N.Y. & Ont.; easternmost of the Great Lakes *area* 7540 **3** province E Canada between Great Lakes & Hudson Bay ✳ Toronto *area* 363,282, *pop* 5,404,933 — **On·tar·i·an** \-ē-ən\ *adj or n* — **On·tar·io·an** \-ē-,ō-ən\ *n*

Ope·li·ka \,ō-pə-'lī-kə\ city E Ala. *pop* 15,678

Op·e·lou·sas \,äp-ə-'lü-səs\ city S La. N of Lafayette *pop* 17,417

Opo·le \ō-'pô-lə\ *or* G **Op·peln** \'ô-pəln\ city SW Poland on the Odra *pop* 55,000

Opor·to \ō-'pôrt-(,)ō, ə-'pôrt-\ city & port NW Portugal on the Douro *pop* 284,842 — see LEIXÕES

Oquirrh \'ō-kər\ mountain range N *cen* Utah S of Great Salt Lake; highest point *ab* 11,000 *ft*

Ora·dea *or* **Oradea Ma·re** \ō-,räd-ē-ə-'mär-(,)ā\ *or* Hung **Nagy·va·rad** \'näj-,vär-,ôd\ city NW Romania in Transylvania near Hungarian border *pop* 105,008

Oran \ō-'rän\ city & port NW Algeria *pop* 299,000

Or·ange \'ôr-inj, 'är-,-ənj\ **1** city SW Calif. N of Santa Ana *pop* 26,444 **2** city NE N.J. NW of Newark *pop* 35,789 **3** city E Tex. E of Beaumont on the Sabine *pop* 25,605 **4** river 1300 *m* S Africa flowing from the Drakensbergs in Basutoland W into the Atlantic

Orange \ō-räⁿzh\ town SE France N of Avignon

Orange Free State \'ôr-inj, 'är-, -ənj\ *or* **Oran·je Vry·staat** \ō-,rän-yə-'frü-,stät\ province E *cen* Republic of So. Africa between Orange & Vaal rivers ✳ Bloemfontein *area* 49,647, *pop* 519,166

Orasul Stalin — see BRASOV

Or·dos \'ôrd-,əs\ desert N China in SW Inner Mongolia N of Great Wall in N bend of Yellow river

Ordzhonikidze — see DZAUDZHIKAU

Öre·bro \,ər-ə-'brü\ city S *cen* Sweden *pop* 76,057

Or·e·gon \'ôr-i-gən, 'är-, *chiefly by outsiders* -,gän\ **1** the Columbia river — an old name used esp. prior to discovery of mouth & renaming of river (1791) by Capt. Robert Gray **2** state NW U.S. ✳ Salem *area* 96,981, *pop* 1,768,687 — **Or·e·go·nian** \,ôr-i-'gō-nē-ən, ,är-, -nyən\ *adj or n*

Oregon Caves limestone caverns SW Ore. SW of Medford in **Oregon Caves National Monument**

Oregon Country region W No. America between Pacific coast & the Rockies extending from N border of Calif. to Alaska — often so called *ab* 1818–46

Oregon Trail pioneer route to the Pacific Northwest *ab* 2000 *m* long from vicinity of Independence, Mo., to Fort Vancouver, Wash.; used esp. 1842–60

Orel \ō-'rel, ôr-'yôl\ city U.S.S.R. in SW Soviet Russia, Europe, on the Oka S of Moscow *pop* 152,000

Orem \'ôr-əm, 'ôr-\ city W Utah N of Provo *pop* 18,394

Ore mountains — see ERZGEBIRGE

Orenburg — see CHKALOV

Oren·se \ō-'ren(t)-(,)sā\ **1** province NW Spain *area* 2694, *pop* 472,676 **2** city, its ✳ *pop* 63,450

Öre·sund \'ər-ə,sən\ *or* **The Sound** strait between Sjælland I., Denmark, & S Sweden connecting Kattegat with Baltic sea

Orfani, Gulf of — see STRYMONIC GULF

Organ Pipe Cactus National Monument reservation S Ariz. on Mexican border S of Ajo *area* 513

Ori·no·co \,ōr-ə-'nō-(,)kō, ,ôr-\ river 1600 *m* Venezuela flowing from Brazilian border to Colombia border & thence into the Atlantic through wide delta

Oris·sa \ō-'ris-ə\ state E India bordering on Bay of Bengal ✳ Bhubaneswar *area* 60,136, *pop* 14,645,900

Ori·za·ba \,ōr-ə-'zäb-ə, ,ôr-\ **1** — see CITLALTEPETL **2** city E Mexico in Veracruz state *pop* 55,531

Or·khon \'ôr-,kän\ river 450 *m* N Outer Mongolia flowing NE from N edge of the Gobi into the Selenga

Ork·ney \'ôrk-nē\ islands N Scotland constituting a county ✳ Kirkwall (on Mainland I.) *area* 376, *pop* 21,258 — **Ork·ney·an** \'ôrk-nē-ən, ôrk-'\ *adj or n*

Or·lan·do \ôr-'lan-(,)dō\ city E *cen* Fla. *pop* 88,135

Or·lé·a·nais \,ôr-lē-ə-'nā\ region & former province N *cen* France ✳ Orléans

Or·lé·ans \ôr-lā-äⁿ\ commune N *cen* France *pop* 76,439

Or·ly \ôr-'lē\ commune France, SSE suburb of Paris

Or·moc Bay \,ôr-'mäk-\ inlet of Camotes sea Philippines in NW Leyte I.

Ormuz — see HORMUZ

Orne \'ô(ə)rn\ river 95 *m* NW France flowing N into Bay of the Seine

Oron·tes \ō-'ränt-ēz, -'rän-,tēz\ river 246 *m* Syria & Turkey rising in Lebanon in the Bika & flowing into the Mediterranean

Or·ping·ton \'ôr-piŋ-tən\ urban district SE England in Kent SE of London *pop* 63,344

Ore·fors \ō-rə-'fôrz, -'fôsh\ town SE Sweden NW of Kalmar

Orsk \'ô(ə)rsk\ city U.S.S.R. in SE Soviet Russia, Europe, on Ural river S of Magnitogorsk *pop* 176,000

Or·te·gal, Cape \,ôrt-i-'gäl\ cape NW Spain

Ort·les \'ôrt-,läs\ *or* G **Ort·ler** \-lər\ mountain range of E Alps N Italy between Venezia Tridentina & Lombardy; highest peak Ortles (or **Ort·ler·spit·ze** \-lər-,s(h)pit-sə\) 12,793 *ft*

Oru·ro \ō-'rü(ə)r-(,)ō\ city W Bolivia *pop* 62,975

Or·vie·to \,ôr-vē-'āt-(,)ō\ *or anc* **Vel·su·na** \vel-'sü-nə\ *or* **Vol·sin·ii** \,väl-'sin-ē-,ī\ town *cen* Italy WNW of Terni

Osage \ō-'sāj\ river 360 *m* E Kans. & Mo. flowing E into the Missouri

Osa·ka \ō-'säk-ə\ city & port Japan in S Honshu *pop* 3,011,563

Osh·a·wa \'äsh-ə-wə, -,wä, -,wô\ city Canada in SE Ont. on Lake Ontario ENE of Toronto *pop* 50,412

Osh·kosh \'äsh-,käsh\ city E Wis. on Lake Winnebago *pop* 45,110

Osi·jek \'ô-sē-,(y)ek\ city N Yugoslavia in Slavonia *pop* 58,600

Os·lo \'äz-(,)lō, 'äs-\ *or formerly* **Chris·ti·a·nia** *or* **Kris·ti·a·nia** \,kris(h)-chē-'an-ē-ə, ,kris-tē-, -'än-\ city ✳ of Norway at N end of **Oslo Fjord** (inlet of the Skagerrak) *pop* 461,591

Os·na·brück \'äz-nə-,brùk\ city NW Germany *pop* 135,100

Osor·no \ō-'sôr-(,)nō\ **1** volcano 8727 *ft* S *cen* Chile in lake district **2** city S *cen* Chile S of Valdivia *pop* 93,686

Os·sa \'äs-ə\ mountain 6490 *ft* NE Greece in E Thessaly

Os·se·tia \ä-'sē-sh(ē)-ə\ region U.S.S.R. in SE Soviet Russia, Europe, in *cen* Caucasus — see NORTH OSSETIA, SOUTH OSSETIA

Os·si·ning \'äs-ᵊn-iŋ, 'äs-niŋ\ village SE N.Y. *pop* 18,662

Ost·end \ä-'stend, 'äs-,tend\ *or* Flem **Oost·en·de** \ō-'sten-də\ *or* F **Os·tende** \ô-stäⁿd\ city & port NW Belgium *pop* 71,937

Österreich — see AUSTRIA

Os·tia \'äs-tē-ə\ town *cen* Italy at mouth of the Tiber E of site of ancient town of the same name which was the port for Rome

Ostrasia — see AUSTRASIA

Ostra·va *or* **Mo·rav·ska Ostrava** \,môr-əf-skə-'ô-strə-və\ city *cen* Czechoslovakia in Moravia *pop* 199,206

Osu·mi \'ō-sə-,mē, ō-'sü-mē\ island group Japan in N Ryukyus

Os·we·go \ä-'swē-(,)gō\ city N N.Y. on Lake Ontario *pop* 22,155

Os·wie·cim \ôsh-'vyeⁿ(n)-tsēm\ *or* **Ausch·witz** \'aùsh-,vits\ town S Poland W of Krakow

Ota·go \ō-'täg-(,)ō\ provincial district S New Zealand *area* 25,220, *pop* 266,300

Otago Harbor inlet of the Pacific S New Zealand on E coast of South I.; Dunedin is situated on it

Ota·ru \ō-'tär-(,)ü\ city & port Japan on Otaru Bay on W coast of Hokkaido I. *pop* 188,448

Otran·to \ō-'tran-(,)tō, 'ô-trən-,tō\ commune & port S Italy on coast at SE tip of Apulia

Otranto, Strait of strait between SE Italy & W Albania

Otsu \'ôt-(,)sü\ city Japan in W *cen* Honshu NE of Kyoto *pop* 107,498

Ot·ta·wa \'ät-ə-wə, -,wä, -,wô\ **1** city N *cen* Ill. *pop* 19,408 **2** river 696 *m* Canada in SE Ont. & S Que. flowing E into the St. Lawrence **3** city ✳ of Canada in SE Ont. *pop* 222,129

Ot·to·man Empire \'ät-ə-mən-\ former Turkish sultanate in SE Europe, W Asia, & N Africa including at greatest extent Turkey, Syria, Iraq, Palestine, Egypt, Barbary States, Balkan States, & parts of Russia & Hungary ✳ Constantinople

Ot·tum·wa \ä-'təm-wə, ə-'təm-\ city SE Iowa *pop* 33,871

Oua·chi·ta \'wäsh-ə-,tô\ **1** mountains W Ark. & E Okla. S of the Arkansas **2** *or* **Wash·i·ta** \'wäsh-ə-,tô\ river 605 *m* SW Ark. & E La. flowing into Black river

Oua·ga·dou·gou \,wäg-ə-'dü-(,)gü\ city ✳ of Upper Volta *pop* 37,678

Ouar·gla *or* **War·gla** \'wôr-glə, 'wär-\ town & oasis Algeria in the Sahara SW of Touggourt

Oubangui — see UBANGI

Oubangui–Chari — see UBANGI-SHARI

Ou·de·naar·de \,aùd-ᵊn-'ärd-ə\ *or* F **Au·de·narde** \ōd-'närd\ town Belgium in E Flanders on the Scheldt

Oudh \'aùd\ region N India in E *cen* Uttar Pradesh ✳ Lucknow

Oudts·hoorn \'ōts-,hô(ə)rn\ city S Republic of So. Africa in S Cape Province 220 *m* E of Cape Town *pop* 18,702

Ouessant, Île d' — see USHANT

Ouj·da \ùzh-'dä\ city NE Morocco *pop* 85,000

Ou·lu \'aù-(,)lü\ *or* Sw **Uleå·borg** \'ü-le-ō-,bô(ə)r\ city N *cen* Finland on Gulf of Bothnia *pop* 52,800

Ou·ro Prê·to \,ō-(,)rü-'prāt-(,)ü\ town E Brazil in Minas Gerais

Ouse \'üz\ **1** *or* **Great Ouse** river 160 *m*, *cen* & E England flowing into the Wash **2** river 57 *m* NE England flowing SE to unite with the Trent forming the Humber

Outer Banks chain of sand islands & peninsulas along N.C. coast

Outer Hebrides — see HEBRIDES

Outer Mongolia — see MONGOLIA — **Outer Mongolian** *adj or n*

Out islands islands of the Bahamas group excepting New Providence

Ou·tre·mont \'ü-trə-,mänt, F ü-trə-môⁿ\ city Canada in S Que. on Montreal I. *pop* 29,990

Ova·lle \ō-'vī-,ā, -'vä-,yā\ city N *cen* Chile *pop* 46,553

Over·ijs·sel \,ō-və-'rī-səl\ province E Netherlands ✳ Zwolle *area* 1318, *pop* 760,020

Over·land \'ō-vər-lənd\ city E Mo. NW of St. Louis *pop* 22,763
Overland Park urban area NE Kans. *pop* 21,110
Ovie·do \,ō-vē-'ā-(,)thō\ **1** province NW Spain on Bay of Biscay *area* 4025, *pop* 1,011,350 — see ASTURIAS **2** city * of Oviedo province *pop* 130,969
Owas·co \ō-'wäs-(,)kō\ lake 11 *m* long *cen* N.Y.; one of the Finger lakes
Ow·en Falls \,ō-ən-\ former waterfall 65 *ft* E Africa in Uganda in the Nile N of Lake Victoria; submerged when Owen Falls Dam was built
Ow·ens \'ō-ənz\ river E Calif. formerly flowing into **Owens Lake** (now dry), now supplying water to city of Los Angeles by way of Los Angeles Aqueduct
Ow·ens·boro \'ō-ənz-,bər-ə, -,bə-rə\ city NW Ky. *pop* 42,471
Owen Sound city Canada in SE Ont. on Georgian Bay *pop* 16,976
Owen Stan·ley \'stan-lē\ mountain range E New Guinea; highest peak Mt. Victoria 13,240 *ft*
Owos·so \ō-'wäs-(,)ō\ city S *cen* Mich. W of Flint *pop* 17,006
Owy·hee \ō-'wī-(,)(h)ē\ river 250 *m* SE Oreg. flowing NW into Snake river
Ox·ford \'äks-fərd\ **1** *or* **Ox·ford·shire** \-,shi(ə)r, -shər\ county *cen* England *area* 749, *pop* 275,765 **2** *or* ML **Ox·o·nia** \äk-'sō-nē-ə\ city & county borough, its *, on the Thames WNW of London *pop* 98,675 — **Ox·for·di·an** \äks-'förd-ē-ən, -'förd-\ *adj or n*
Ox·nard \'äk-,snärd\ city S Calif. SE of Santa Barbara *pop* 40,265
Oxus — see AMU DARYA
Oxy·rhyn·chus \,äk-si-'riŋ-kəs\ *or* Ar **El Bah·na·sa** \el-'ban-ə-sə\ archaeological site Egypt N of Minya & S of Faiyûm
Ozark plateau \,ō-,zärk-\ *or* **Ozark mountains** eroded tableland 1500–2500 *ft* high *cen* U.S. N of Arkansas river in N Ark., S Mo., & NE Okla. with E extension in S Ill. — **Ozark·er** \'ō-,zär-kər\ *n* — **Ozark·i·an** \ō-'zär-kē-ən\ *adj or n*
Ozarks, Lake of the reservoir 130 *m* long *cen* Mo. formed in Osage river by Bagnell Dam

Pa·bia·ni·ce \,päb-yə-'nēt-sə\ commune *cen* Poland SSW of Lodz *pop* 53,100
Pa·chu·ca \pə-'chü-kə\ city *cen* Mexico NE of Mexico City * of Hidalgo *pop* 53,400
Pa·cif·ic \pə-'sif-ik\ ocean extending from the arctic circle to the antarctic regions & from W No. America & W So. America to E Asia & Australia *area* 69,375,000
Pa·cif·i·ca \pə-'sif-i-kə\ city W Calif. S of San Francisco on the Pacific *pop* 20,995
Pacific Islands, Trust Territory of the islands in W Pacific under U.S. administration: the Marianas (except Guam), the Carolines (including the Palaus), & the Marshalls * on Saipan I.; a Japanese mandate 1919–45, *land area* 687, *pop* 77,913
Pac·to·lus \pak-'tō-ləs\ river Asia Minor in ancient Lydia flowing into the Hermus (modern Gediz) near Sardis
Pa·dang \'päd-,äŋ\ city & port Indonesia in W Sumatra *pop* 116,300
Pad·ding·ton \'pad-iŋ-tən\ metropolitan borough NW London, England *pop* 125,281
Pa·dre \'päd-rē\ island 100 *m* long S Tex. between Laguna Madre & Gulf of Mexico
Pad·ua \'paj-ə-wə\ *or* It **Pa·do·va** \'päd-ə-və\ commune NE Italy W of Venice *pop* 173,354
Pa·du·cah \pə-'d(y)ü-kə\ city W Ky. on the Ohio *pop* 34,479
Padus — see PO
Paes·tum \'pes-təm, 'pē-stəm\ *or earlier* **Pos·ei·do·nia** \,päs-,ī-'dō-nē-ə, ,pō-,sī-\ ancient city S Italy in W Lucania on Gulf of Salerno (ancient **Bay of Paestum**)
Pa·go Pa·go \,päŋ-(,)(g)ō-'päŋ-(,)(g)ō, ,päg-(,)ō-'päg-(,)ō\ *or* **Pan·go Pan·go** \,päŋ-(,)(g)ō-'päŋ-(,)(g)ō\ town & port * of American Samoa on Tutuila I. *pop* 1251
Pa·hang \pə-'haŋ\ state E Federation of Malaysia bordering on So. China sea * Kuala Lipis *area* 13,873, *pop* 6,278,763
Pahsien — see CHUNGKING
Paines·ville \'pānz-,vil\ city NE Ohio *pop* 16,116
Painted desert region NE Ariz. E of the Little Colorado
Pais·ley \'pāz-lē\ burgh SW Scotland * of Renfrew WSW of Glasgow *pop* 93,704
Pak·i·stan \,pak-i-'stan, ,päk-i-'stän\ country S Asia comprising an eastern division & a western division; a dominion 1947–56 & since 1956 a republic of the Brit. Commonwealth, formed from parts of former Brit. India; administrative * Rawalpindi, legislative * Dacca *area* 364,737, *pop* 93,720,613 — see EAST PAKISTAN, WEST PAKISTAN — **Pak·i·stani** \-'stan-ē, -'stän-ē\ *adj or n*
Pa·lat·i·nate \pə-'lat-ᵊn-ət\ *or* G **Pfalz** \'(p)fälts\ either of two districts SW Germany once ruled by counts palatine of the Holy Roman Empire: **Rhenish,** *or* **Rhine, Palatinate** *or* G **Rhein·pfalz** \'rīn-,(p)fälts\ (on the Rhine E of Saarland) & **Upper Palatinate** *or* G **Ober·pfalz** \'ō-bər-,(p)fälts\ (on the Danube around Regensburg) — see RHINELAND-PALATINATE
Pal·a·tine \'pal-ə-,tīn\ hill in Rome, Italy, one of seven on which the ancient city was built — see AVENTINE
Pa·lau \pə-'laủ\ *or* **Pe·lew** \pə-'lü\ **1** island group W Pacific SW of Yap; generally considered as part of the Carolines *area* 184 **2** — see BABELTHUAP
Pa·la·wan \pə-'lä-wən\ island 278 *m* long W Philippines W of the Visayans *area* 4550, *pop* (with adjacent islands) 93,700
Pa·lem·bang \,päl-əm-'bäŋ\ city & port Indonesia in SE Sumatra on Musi river *pop* 282,900
Pa·len·cia \pə-'len-ch(ē-)ə\ **1** province N Spain *area* 3256, *pop* 240,707 **2** city, its *, NNE of Valladolid *pop* 47,413
Pa·len·que \pə-'leŋ-(,)kā\ ruined Mayan city S Mexico in N Chiapas SW of present town of Palenque
Pa·ler·mo \pə-'lər-(,)mō, -'le(ə)r-\ *or anc* **Pan·or·mus** \pa-'nör-məs\ *or* **Pan·hor·mus** \pan-'hör-\ city & port Italy * of Sicily *pop* 503,137 — **Pa·ler·mi·tan** \pə-'lər-mət-ᵊn, -'ler-\ *adj or n*
Pal·es·tine \'pal-ə-,stīn, -,stēn\ *or* L **Pal·aes·ti·na** \,pal-ə-'stē-nə, -'stī-\ **1** ancient region SW Asia bordering on E coast of the Mediterranean & extending E of the Jordan **2** former country bordering on the Mediterranean on W & Dead sea on E; a part of the Ottoman Empire 1516–1917, a Brit. mandate 1923–48; now divided between Israel & Jordan, with Gaza Strip administered by Egypt — **Pal·es·tin·ian** \,pal-ə-'stin-ē-ən, -'stin-yən\ *adj or n*
Pal·i·sades \,pal-ə-'sādz\ line of cliffs 15 *m* long SE N.Y. & NE N.J. on W bank of the Hudson
Palk \'pö(l)k\ strait 40 *m* wide between N Ceylon & SE India connecting Gulf of Mannar & Bay of Bengal
Pal·ma *or* **Palma de Ma·llor·ca** \,päl-mə-(,)thā-mə(l)-'yór-kə\ commune & port Spain * of Baleares province on Majorca *pop* 152,040
Pal·mas, Cape \'päl-məs\ cape Liberia on extreme S coast
Palmer archipelago, Palmer peninsula — see ANTARCTIC
Palm·er Land \'päm-ər, 'päl-mər\ the S section of Antarctic peninsula
Palm·er·ston \'päm-ər-stən, 'päl-mər-\ island (atoll) *cen* Pacific NW of Rarotonga I.; belongs to New Zealand *area* 1
Palmerston North city New Zealand on S North I. NE of Wellington *pop* 40,800
Pal·my·ra \pal-'mī-rə\ **1** island *cen* Pacific in Line islands *area* 1 **2** *or Bib* **Tad·mor** \'tad-,mó(ə)r\ *or* **Ta·mar** \'tā-,mär, -mər\ ancient city Syria on N edge of Syrian desert NE of Damascus
Palo Al·to \,pal-ə-'wal-(,)tō\ city W Calif. SE of San Francisco on San Francisco Bay *pop* 52,287
Pal·o·mar, Mount \'pal-ə-,mär\ mountain 6126 *ft* S Calif. NNE of San Diego
Pa·los \'pä-(,)lōs\ *or* **Palos de la Fron·te·ra** \-(,)lōz-,dā-lə-,frən-'ter-ə\ town & former port SW Spain on Tinto river SE of Huelva
Pa·louse \pə-'lüs\ **1** river 150 *m* NW Idaho & SE Wash. flowing W & S into the Snake **2** fertile hilly region E Wash. & NW Idaho N of Snake & Clearwater rivers
Pa·mirs \pə-'mi(ə)rz\ *or* **Pa·mir** \-'mi(ə)r\ mountain region *cen* Asia in Tadzhik Republic & on borders of Sinkiang, Kashmir, & Afghanistan from which radiate Tien Shan to N, Kunlun & Karakoram to E, & Hindu Kush to W; has many peaks over 20,000 *ft*, highest Kungur 25,146 *ft*
Pam·li·co \'pam-li-,kō\ river E N.C., estuary of Tar river, flowing E into **Pamlico Sound** (inlet of the Atlantic between the mainland & offshore islands)
Pam·pa \'pam-pə\ city NW Tex. ENE of Amarillo *pop* 24,664
Pam·phyl·ia \pam-'fil-ē-ə\ ancient district & Roman province S Asia Minor on coast S of Pisidia — **Pam·phyl·i·an** \-ē-ən\ *adj or n*
Pam·plo·na \pam-'plō-nə\ *or formerly* **Pam·pe·lu·na** \,pam-pə-'lü-nə\ city N Spain * of Navarra province & once * of Navarre kingdom *pop* 91,434
Pan·a·ma *or* Sp **Pa·na·má** \'pan-ə-,mä, -,mó, ,pan-ə-'\ **1** country S Central America; a republic; before 1903 part of Colombia *area* (including Canal Zone) 29,129, *pop* 805,285 **2** *or* **Panama City** city & port, its *, on Gulf of Panama *pop* 200,000 **3** ship canal 51 *m* S Central America in the Canal Zone connecting the Atlantic (Caribbean sea) & the Pacific (Gulf of Panama) — **Pan·a·ma·ni·an** \,pan-ə-'mā-nē-ən\ *adj or n*
Panama, Gulf of inlet of the Pacific on S coast of Panama
Panama, Isthmus of *or formerly* **Isthmus of Dar·i·en** \-,dar-ē-'en, -,der-\ isthmus Central America connecting No. America & So. America & comprised in Republic of Panama
Panama Canal Zone — see CANAL ZONE
Panama City, 1 city & port NW Fla. on Gulf of Mexico *pop* 33,275 **2** — see PANAMA
Pan·a·mint \'pan-ə-,mint, -mənt\ mountains E Calif. W of Death valley — see TELESCOPE PEAK
Pa·nay \pə-'nī\ island Philippines in the Visayans; chief town Iloilo *area* 4446
Pan·gim *or* **Pan·jim** \pan-'jim\ *or* **New Goa** \'gō-ə\ town & port W India in Goa; former * of Portuguese India
Pa·ni·pat \'pän-i-,pət\ city NW India in SE Punjab state NNW of Delhi *pop* 55,000
Panjab — see PUNJAB
Panj·nad \,pənj-'näd\ river 50 *m* W Pakistan, the combined stream of the Chenab & the Sutlej, flowing SW into the Indus
Pan·mun·jom \,pän-,mün-'jəm\ village S Korea SE of Kaesong
Pan·no·nia \pə-'nō-nē-ə\ Roman province SE Europe including territory W of the Danube in Hungary & Yugoslavia
Pantar — see ALOR
Pan·tel·le·ria \,pan-,tel-ə-'rē-ə\ island Italy in the Mediterranean between Sicily & Tunisia
Pá·nu·co \'pän-ə-,kō\ river 240 *m*, *cen* Mexico flowing from Hidalgo state NE into Gulf of Mexico
Pão de Açú·car \,paů^{n}(n)-dē-ə-'sü-kər\ *or* E **Sugarloaf Mountain** peak 1280 *ft* SE Brazil in city of Rio de Janeiro on W side of entrance to Guanabara Bay
Pao·ki \'paủ-'kē\ city N *cen* China in SW Shensi on Wei river W of Sian *pop* 130,100
Paoking — see SHAOYANG
Pao·ting \'baů-'diŋ\ *or formerly* **Tsing·yuan** \'chiŋ-yü-'än\ city NE China SW of Peking *pop* 197,000
Pao·tow \'baů-'dō\ city N China in SW Inner Mongolia on Yellow river W of Huhehot *pop* 650,000
Papal States — see STATES OF THE CHURCH
Pa·pe·e·te \,päp-ē-'āt-ē, pə-'pēt-ē\ commune & port Society islands on Tahiti * of French Polynesia *pop* 17,247
Paph·la·go·nia \,paf-lə-'gō-nē-ə, -nyə\ ancient country & Roman province N Asia Minor bordering on Black sea — **Paph·la·go·nian** \-nē-ən, -nyən\ *adj or n*
Pa·phos \'pā-,fäs\ town SW Cyprus on coast 10 *m* WNW of site of ancient city of Paphos
Pap·ua \'pap-yə-wə\ **1** — see NEW GUINEA **2** the Territory of Papua
Papua, Gulf of arm of Coral sea SE New Guinea
Papua, Territory of territory comprising SE New Guinea & offshore islands; a UN trust territory administered jointly with the Territory of New Guinea by Australia * Port Moresby *area* 90,600, *pop* 467,518
Pa·rá \pə-'rä\ **1** river 200 *m* N Brazil, the E mouth of the Amazon **2** state N Brazil S of the Amazon * Belém *area* 470,752, *pop* 1,123,273 **3** — see BELÉM
Par·a·guay \'par-ə-,gwī, -,gwā\ **1** river 1500 *m*, *cen* So. America flowing from Mato Grosso plateau in Brazil S into the Paraná in Paraguay **2** country *cen* So. America traversed by Paraguay river; a republic * Asunción *area* 157,006, *pop* 1,341,333 — **Par·a·guay·an** \,par-ə-'gwī-ən, -'gwā-\ *adj or n*
Par·a·í·ba \,par-ə-'ē-bə\ **1** *or* **Paraíba do Nor·te** \-də-'nórt-ē\ river 240 *m* NE Brazil flowing E into the Atlantic **2** *or* **Paraíba do Sul** \-'sül\ river 660 *m* SE Brazil flowing NE into the Atlantic **3** state NE Brazil bordering on the Atlantic * João Pessoa *area* 21,591, *pop* 1,713,259 **4** — see JOÃO PESSOA
Par·a·mar·i·bo \,par-ə-'mar-ə-,bō\ city & port * of Surinam on Suriname river *pop* 107,000
Par·a·mount \'par-ə-,maůnt\ city SW Calif. N of Long Beach *pop* 27,249

Pa·ram·us \pə-ˈram-əs\ borough NE N. J. *pop* 23,238

Pa·ra·ná \ˌpar-ə-ˈnä\ **1** *or in upper course* **Al·to Paraná** \ˌal-(ˌ)tō-\ river 2040 *m*, *cen* So. America flowing from junction of Rio Grande & the Paraíba in Brazil SSW into the Río de la Plata in Argentina **2** state S Brazil E of the Paraná ✻ Curitiba *area* 82,741, *pop* 2,115,547 **3** city NE Argentina *pop* 84,153

Pa·ra·na·í·ba *or formerly* **Pa·ra·na·hi·ba** \ˌpar-ə-nə-ˈē-bə\ river 530 *m* S Brazil flowing SW to unite with the Rio Grande forming the Paraná

Par·du·bi·ce \ˈpärd-ə-ˌbit-sə\ city Czechoslovakia in Bohemia on the Elbe E of Prague *pop* 54,077

Pa·ria \ˈpär-ē-ə\ peninsula NE Venezuela

Paria, Gulf of inlet of the Atlantic between Trinidad & Venezuela

Pa·rí·cu·tin \pə-ˈrē-kə-ˌtēn\ volcano 7451 *ft* SW Mexico in NW Michoacán; first eruption 1943

Parida, La — see BOLÍVAR (Cerro)

Par·is \ˈpar-əs\ **1** city NE Tex. *pop* 20,977 **2** *or anc* **Lu·te·tia** \lü-ˈtē-sh(ē-)ə\ city ✻ of France *pop* 2,850,189 — **Pa·ri·sian** \pə-ˈrizh-ən, -ˈrēsh-\ *adj or n* — **Pa·ri·si·enne** \pə-ˌrē-zē-ˈen\ *n*

Par·kers·burg \ˈpär-kərz-ˌbərg\ city NW W. Va. *pop* 44,797

Park Forest village NE Ill. S of Chicago *pop* 29,993

Park Ridge city NE Ill. NW of Chicago *pop* 32,659

Park·ville \ˈpärk-ˌvil, -vəl\ urban area N *cen* Md. N of Baltimore *pop* (with Carney) 27,236

Par·ma \ˈpär-mə\ **1** city NE Ohio S of Cleveland *pop* 82,845 **2** commune N Italy in Emilia-Romagna *pop* 89,300

Parma Heights city NE Ohio S of Cleveland *pop* 18,100

Par·na·í·ba *or formerly* **Par·na·hy·ba** \ˌpär-nə-ˈē-bə\ river 900 *m* NE Brazil flowing NE into the Atlantic

Par·nas·sus \pär-ˈnas-əs\ *or* NGk **Par·nas·sós** \ˌpär-nə-ˈsȯs\ mountain 8060 *ft*, *cen* Greece N of Gulf of Corinth

Par·os \ˈpar-ˌäs, ˈper-\ *or* NGk **Pá·ros** \ˈpär-ˌȯs\ island Greece in *cen* Cyclades W of Naxos *area* 81

Par·ra·mat·ta \ˌpar-ə-ˈmat-ə\ town SE Australia, W suburb of Sydney, on Parramatta river (estuary, W arm of Port Jackson)

Par·ris \ˈpar-əs\ island S S.C. in Port Royal sound

Par·ry \ˈpar-ē\ islands Canada in N Northwest Territories in Arctic ocean N of Victoria I.

Parsnip — see FINLAY

Par·thia \ˈpär-thē-ə\ ancient country SW Asia in NE modern Iran

Pas·a·de·na \ˌpas-ə-ˈdē-nə\ **1** city SW Calif. E of Glendale *pop* 116,407 **2** city SE Tex. E of Houston *pop* 58,737

Pa·sar·ga·dae \pə-ˈsär-gə-ˌdē\ city of ancient Persia built by Cyrus the Great; ruins NE of site of later Persepolis

Pasay — see RIZAL

Pas·ca·gou·la \ˌpas-kə-ˈgü-lə\ city & port SE Miss. *pop* 17,155

Pasco, Cerro de — see CERRO DE PASCO

Pascua, Isla de — see EASTER

Pas de Calais — see DOVER (Strait of)

Pa·sig \ˈpäs-ig\ river 12 *m* Philippines on Luzon flowing from the Laguna de Bay through Manila into Manila Bay

Pas·sa·ic \pə-ˈsā-ik\ **1** river 100 *m* NE N.J. flowing into Newark Bay **2** city NE N.J. SSE of Paterson *pop* 53,963

Pas·sa·ma·quod·dy Bay \ˌpas-ə-mə-ˌkwäd-ē-\ inlet of Bay of Fundy between E Me. & SW N.B. at mouth of St. Croix river

Pas·se·ro, Cape \ˈpäs-ə-ˌrō\ headland Italy at SE point of Sicily

Pas·sy \pa-ˈsē\ section of Paris, France, on right bank of the Seine near Bois de Boulogne

Pas·ta·za \pə-ˈstäz-ə, -ˈstäs-\ river 400 *m* Ecuador & Peru flowing S into the Marañón

Pat·a·go·nia \ˌpat-ə-ˈgō-nyə, -nē-ə\ barren region So. America in S Argentina & S Chile between the Andes & the Atlantic S of *ab* 40° S lat.; sometimes considered as including Tierra del Fuego — **Pat·a·go·nian** \-nyən, -nē-ən\ *adj or n*

Pa·tan \ˈpä-ˌtən\ city E *cen* Nepal adjoining Katmandu *pop* 105,000

Pa·tap·sco \pə-ˈtap-(ˌ)skō\ river 80 *m* N *cen* Md. flowing SE into Chesapeake Bay

Pat·er·son \ˈpat-ər-sən\ city NE N.J. N of Newark *pop* 143,663

Pa·ti·a·la \ˌpət-ē-ˈäl-ə\ **1** former state NW India, now part of Punjab state **2** city, its ✻, 70 *m* SW of Simla *pop* 97,867

Pat·mos \ˈpat-məs\ island Greece in the NW Dodecanese

Pat·na \ˈpət-nə\ city NE India on the Ganges, winter ✻ of Bihar *pop* 283,500

Pa·tos, La·goa dos \lə-ˌgō-əd-ə-ˈspat-əs\ lagoon 124 *m* long S Brazil in Rio Grande do Sul

Pa·tras \pə-ˈtras, ˈpa-trəs\ *or* NGk **Pa·trai** \ˈpä-trā\ *or anc* **Pa·trae** \ˈpā-(ˌ)trē\ city & port W Greece in N Peloponnesus on Gulf of Patras *pop* 79,000

Patras, Gulf of *or* **Gulf of Cal·y·don** \ˈkal-əd-ᵊn, -ə-ˌdän\ inlet of Ionian sea W Greece W of Gulf of Corinth

Patrimony of St. Peter — see ROME (Duchy of)

Pa·tux·ent \pə-ˈtək-sənt\ river 100 *m*, *cen* Md. flowing S & SE into Chesapeake Bay

Pau \ˈpō\ **1** *or* F **Gave de Pau** \ˈgȧv-də-pō\ river 100 *m* SW France rising in the Pyrenees SE of Pau & flowing to the Adour — see GAVARNIE **2** commune SW France on the Pau *pop* 48,320

Paumotu — see TUAMOTU

Pa·via \pə-ˈvē-ə\ commune N Italy S of Milan *pop* 67,100

Pav·lof, Mount \ˈpav-ˌlȯf\ volcano 8215 *ft* SW Alaska on SW Alaska peninsula in Aleutian range

Paw·tuck·et \pə-ˈtək-ət, pȯ-\ city NE R.I. *pop* 81,001

Pay·san·dú \ˌpī-ˌsän-ˈdü\ city & port W Uruguay on Uruguay river NW of Montevideo *pop* 60,000

Pea·body \ˈpē-ˌbäd-ē, -bəd-ē\ city NE Mass. N of Lynn *pop* 32,202

Peace \ˈpēs\ river 945 *m* W Canada flowing E & NE in N B.C. & N Alta. into the Slave — see FINLAY

Pearl \ˈpər(-ə)l\ **1** river estuary 490 *m* S Miss. flowing S into Gulf of Mexico **2** *or* **Chu** \ˈjü\ *or* **Canton** river SE China SE of Canton at E side of West river delta

Pearl Harbor inlet Hawaii on S coast of Oahu W of Honolulu

Pea·ry Land \ˈpi(ə)r-ē\ region N Greenland — see MORRIS JESUP

Pe·chen·ga \pə-ˈcheŋ-gə\ *or* Finn **Pet·sa·mo** \ˈpet-sə-ˌmō\ town & port U.S.S.R. in NW Soviet Russia, Europe, on inlet of Barents sea in district that belonged to Finland 1920–44

Pe·cho·ra \pə-ˈchōr-ə, -ˈchȯr-\ river 1125 *m* U.S.S.R. in NE Soviet Russia, Europe, flowing N into Barents sea

Pe·cos \ˈpā-kəs\ river 735 *m* E N. Mex. & W Tex. flowing SE into the Rio Grande

Pecs \ˈpāch\ city S Hungary W of the Danube *pop* 110,000

Ped·er·nal·es \ˌpərd-ᵊn-ˈal-əs\ river 150 *m* *cen* Tex. flowing E into the Colorado

Pee·bles \ˈpē-bəlz\ **1** *or* **Pee·bles·shire** \ˈpē-bəl-ˌshi(ə)r, -shər\ *or* **Tweed·dale** \ˈtwēd-ˌdāl\ county SE Scotland including upper course of the Tweed *area* 347, *pop* 15,226 **2** burgh, its ✻

Pee Dee \ˈpē-ˌdē\ river 233 *m* N.C. & S.C. flowing SE into Winyah Bay — see YADKIN

Peeks·kill \ˈpēk-ˌskil\ city SE N.Y. N of Yonkers *pop* 18,737

Peel \ˈpē(ə)l\ river 425 *m* NW Canada rising in W Yukon Territory & flowing E & N into the Mackenzie

Pee·ne \ˈpā-nə\ river 70 *m* N Germany flowing E through Pomerania into Stettiner Haff

Pee·ne·mün·de \ˌpā-nə-ˈmu̇n-də\ village NE Germany on island at mouth of Peene river

Pei·pus \ˈpī-pəs\ *or* Estonian **Peip·si** \ˈpāp-sē\ *or* Russ **Chud·skoe** \ˈchüt-skə-yə\ lake U.S.S.R. in E Estonia & NW Soviet Russia, Europe *area* 1357

Peiraeus — see PIRAEUS

Pe·ka·long·an \pə-ˌkä-ˈlȯŋ-ˌän\ city Indonesia in *cen* Java on N coast *pop* 91,900

Pe·kin \ˈpē-kən, -ˌkin\ city N *cen* Ill. SSW of Peoria *pop* 28,146

Pe·king \ˈpē-ˈkiŋ\ *or* **Pei·ping** \ˈpā-ˈpiŋ, ˈbā-\ municipality N China; before 1928 & since 1949 ✻ of China *pop* 5,420,000

Pe·la·gian \pə-ˈlā-j(ē-)ən\ islands Italy in the Mediterranean S of Sicily between Malta & Tunisia

Pe·lee \ˈpē-lē\ island SE Canada in W Lake Erie SW of Point Pelee, Ont. *area* 18

Pe·lée, Mount \pə-ˈlā\ volcano French West Indies in N Martinique

Pelee, Point — see POINT PELEE NATIONAL PARK

Pel·e·liu \ˌpel-ə-ˈlē-(ˌ)ü, ˈpel-ə-lē-ˌü\ island W Pacific at S end of Palau islands

Pelew — see PALAU

Pe·li·on \ˈpē-lē-ən\ *or* NGk **Pí·lion** \ˈpēl-ˌyȯn\ mountain 5417 *ft* NE Greece in E Thessaly SE of Mt. Ossa

Pel·la \ˈpel-ə\ ancient city NE Greece, ancient ✻ of Macedonia

Pel·ly \ˈpel-ē\ river 330 *m* NW Canada in Yukon Territory flowing W into the Yukon

Pel·o·pon·ne·sus \ˌpel-ə-pə-ˈnē-səs\ *or* **Pel·o·pon·ne·sos** \-səs\ *or* **Pel·o·pon·nese** \ˈpel-ə-pə-ˌnēz, -ˌnēs\ *or* **Mo·rea** \mə-ˈrē-ə\ peninsula forming S part of mainland of Greece — **Pel·o·pon·ne·sian** \ˌpəl-ə-pə-ˈnē-zhən, -shən\ *adj or n*

Pe·lo·tas \pə-ˈlōt-əs\ city S Brazil in SE Rio Grande do Sul at S end of Lagoa dos Patos *pop* 78,014

Pem·ba \ˈpem-bə\ island Tanzania in Indian ocean N of island of Zanzibar

Pem·broke \ˈpem-ˌbru̇k, -ˌbrōk\ **1** town Canada in SE Ont. on Ottawa river *pop* 15,434 **2** *or* **Pem·broke·shire** \-ˌshi(ə)r, -shər\ county SW Wales ✻ Haverfordwest *area* 614, *pop* 90,896

Pe·nang \pə-ˈnaŋ\ **1** island SE Asia at N end of Strait of Malacca *area* 108 **2** state Federation of Malaysia comprising Penang I. & mainland opposite; until 1948 one of the Straits Settlements ✻ George Town *area* 400, *pop* 572,132 **3** — see GEORGE TOWN

Pend Oreille \ˌpän-də-ˈrā\ river 100 *m* N Idaho & NE Wash. flowing from **Pend Oreille Lake** (35 *m* long, in Idaho) W & N into the Columbia in B.C.

Pe·ne·us \pə-ˈnē-əs\ *or* NGk **Pi·niós** \pēn-ˈyȯs\ *or formerly* **Sa·lam·bria** \sə-ˈlam-brē-ə\ river 125 *m* N Greece in Thessaly flowing E into Gulf of Salonika

Peng·pu \ˈpəŋ-ˈpü\ city E China in N Anhwei *pop* 253,000

Pen·ki \ˈbən-ˈchē\ city NE China in E *cen* Liaoning *pop* 449,000

Penn Hills \ˈpen\ urban township SW Pa. *pop* 51,512

Pen·nine Alps \ˌpen-ˌīn-\ section of Alps on border between Switzerland & Italy NE of Graian Alps — see ROSA (Monte)

Pennine Chain mountains N England extending S from Scottish border to Derbyshire & Staffordshire; highest Cross Fell 2930 *ft*

Penn·sau·ken \pen-ˈsȯ-kən\ urban township SW N.J. E of Camden on Delaware river *pop* 33,771

Penn·syl·va·nia \ˌpen(t)-səl-ˈvā-nyə, -nē-ə, *rapid* -sə-ˈvā-\ state NE U.S. ✻ Harrisburg *area* 45,333, *pop* 11,319,366

Pe·nob·scot \pə-ˈnäb-skət, -ˌskät\ river 101 *m*, *cen* Me. flowing S into **Penobscot Bay** (inlet of the Atlantic)

Penrhyn — see TONGAREVA

Pen·sa·co·la \ˌpen(t)-sə-ˈkō-lə\ city & port NW Fla. on **Pensacola Bay** (inlet of Gulf of Mexico) *pop* 56,752

Pen·tap·o·lis \pen-ˈtap-ə-ləs\ any one of several groups of five ancient cities in Italy, Asia Minor, & Cyrenaica

Pen·tel·i·cus \pen-ˈtel-i-kəs\ *or* **Pen·tel·i·kon** \-kən, -ˌkän\ *or* NGk **Pen·de·li·kón** \ˌpen-ˌdel-ē-ˈkȯn\ mountain 3639 *ft* E Greece in Attica NE of Athens

Pent·land \ˈpent-lən(d)-\ **1** firth channel between Orkneys & mainland of Scotland **2** hills S Scotland in Midlothian, Lanark, & Peebles; highest peak Scald Law 1898 *ft*

Pen·za \ˈpen-zə\ city U.S.S.R. in S Soviet Russia, Europe, on Sura river 225 *m* W of Kuibyshev *pop* 254,000

Pen·zance \pen-ˈzan(t)s, pən-\ municipal borough & port SW England in Cornwall on English channel *pop* 20,648

Pen·zhin·ska·ya Bay \ˌpen-ˌzhin(t)-skə-yə-\ *or* **Pen·zhi·na Bay** \ˌpen-zhə-nə-\ arm of Sea of Okhotsk, U.S.S.R., between Kamchatka peninsula & mainland

Pe·o·ria \pē-ˈōr-ē-ə, -ˈȯr-\ city N *cen* Ill. *pop* 103,162

Pep·in, Lake \ˈpip-ən, ˈpep-\ expansion of the upper Mississippi 34 *m* long between SE Minn. & W Wis.

Pera — see BEYOGLU

Pe·raea *or* **Pe·rea** \pə-ˈrē-ə\ region of Palestine in New Testament times E of the Jordan

Pe·rak \ˈper-ə, ˈpir-ə\ state W Federation of Malaysia on Strait of Malacca ✻ Kuala Kangsar *area* 7980, *pop* 953,900

Perche \ˈpe(ə)rsh\ region NW France in old province of Maine

Per·di·do \pər-ˈdēd-(ˌ)ō\ river 60 *m* rising in SE Ala. & flowing S into Gulf of Mexico forming part of Ala.-Fla. boundary

Per·ga \ˈpər-gə\ ancient city S Asia Minor in Pamphylia

Per·ga·mum \ˈpər-gə-məm\ *or* **Per·ga·mus** \-məs\ *or* **Per·ga·mos** \-məs, -ˌmäs\ **1** ancient Greek kingdom covering most of Asia Minor; at its height 263–133 B.C. **2** *or modern* **Ber·ga·ma**

ə abut; ᵊ kitten; ər further; a back; ā bake; ä cot, cart; au̇ out; ch chin; e less; ē easy; g gift; i trip; ī life
j joke; ŋ sing; ō flow; ȯ flaw; ȯi coin; th thin; t͟h this; ü loot; u̇ foot; y yet; yü few; yu̇ furious; zh vision
ᵊ F table; ȧ F bac; k̟ G ich, Buch; ⁿ F vin; œ F bœuf; œ̄ F feu; ue G füllen; ue̅ F rue; ʸ F digne \dēnʸ\, nuit \nwʸē\

\,ber-gə-'mä\ city W Turkey N N E of Izmir * of ancient Pergamum *pop* 16,351

Pé·ri·gord \,per-ə-'gȯ(ə)r\ old division of N Guienne in SW France * Périgueux

Pé·ri·gueux \-'gə(r)\ commune SW *cen* France *pop* 40,785

Pe·rim \pə-'rim\ island in Bab el Mandeb strait at entrance to Red sea; belongs to Aden colony

Per·lis \'per-ləs\ state N Federation of Malaysia bordering on Thailand & Andaman sea * Kangar *area* 310, *pop* 70,500

Perm \'pərm, 'pe(ə)rm\ *or formerly* **Mo·lo·tov** \'mäl-ə-,tȯf, 'mȯ-lə-, 'mō-lə-, -,tȯv\ city U.S.S.R. in E Soviet Russia, Europe, on the Kama *pop* 628,000

Per·nam·bu·co \,pər-nəm-'b(y)ü-(,)kō, ,per-nəm-'bü-\ **1** state N E Brazil * Recife *area* 38,315, *pop* 3,395,185 **2** — see RECIFE

Pernik — see DIMITROVO

Per·pi·gnan \per-pē-nyäⁿ\ city S France S E of Toulouse near Mediterranean coast *pop* 70,051

Per·sep·o·lis \pər-'sep-ə-ləs\ city of ancient Persia, site in SW Iran N E of Shiraz

Persia — see IRAN

Persian Gulf arm of Arabian sea between SW Iran & Arabia

Persian Gulf States Kuwait, Bahrein, Qatar, & Trucial Oman

Persis — see FARS

Perth \'pərth\ **1** city * of Western Australia on Swan river *pop* (with suburbs) 369,000 — see FREMANTLE **2** *or* **Perth·shire** \-,shi(ə)r, -shər\ county *cen* Scotland *area* 249, *pop* 128,072 **3** burgh, its * *pop* 41,200

Perth Am·boy \,pər-'tham-,bȯi\ city & port N E N.J. on Raritan Bay at mouth of Raritan river *pop* 38,007

Pe·ru \pə-'rü\ country W So. America; a republic * Lima *area* 482,257, *pop* 6,207,967 — **Pe·ru·vi·an** \-'rü-vē-ən\ *adj or n*

Pe·ru·gia \pā-'rü-j(ē-)ə\ commune *cen* Italy between Lake Trasimeno & the Tiber * of Umbria *pop* 41,500

Perugia, Lake of — see TRASIMENO

Pe·sa·ro \'pā-zə-,rō\ commune & port *cen* Italy on the Adriatic NW of Ancona *pop* 35,900

Pes·ca·do·res \,pes-kə-'dōr-ēz, -'dȯr-, -əs\ *or* **Peng·hu** \'pəŋ-'hü\ islands E China in Formosa strait, attached to Formosa; chief town Makung (on Penghu, chief island) *area* 49, *pop* 80,000

Pes·ca·ra \pe-'skär-ə\ commune & port *cen* Italy on the Adriatic *pop* 71,500

Pe·sha·war \pə-'shä-wər, -'shau̇(-ə)r\ city Pakistan in N West Pakistan E S E of Khyber pass *pop* 151,800

Pe·tah Tiq·va *or* **Pe·tah Tik·va** \,pe-,tä-'tik-(,)vä\ city W Israel E of Tel Aviv *pop* 52,771

Pe·ter·bor·ough \'pēt-ər-,bər-ə, -,bə-rə, -b(ə-)rə\ **1** city Canada in S E Ont. N E of Oshawa *pop* 42,698 **2** municipal borough E *cen* England, * of Soke of Peterborough *pop* 53,412

Peterborough, Soke of \,sōk-\ administrative county E *cen* England in Northamptonshire * Peterborough *area* 84, *pop* 63,784

Pe·ters·burg \'pēt-ərz-,bərg\ **1** city S E Va. *pop* 36,750 **2** SAINT PETERSBURG — see LENINGRAD

Pet·it·co·di·ac \,pet-ə-'kōd-ē-,ak\ river 60 *m* S E Canada in S E N.B. flowing to head of Bay of Fundy

Pe·ti·tot \'pet-ē-,tō\ river 295 *m* W *cen* Canada flowing W into Liard river

Pe·tra \'pē-trə, 'pe-trə\ ancient city of NW Arabia on slope of Mt. Hor, site now in SW Jordan; ancient * of the Edomites & Nabataeans

Petrified Forest National Park reservation E Ariz. in Painted desert containing natural exhibit of petrified wood *area* 147

Pe·tro·dvo·rets \,pe-trə-və-'rets\ *or formerly* **Pe·ter·hof** \'pēt-ər-,hȯf-, -,häf\ town U.S.S.R. in NW Soviet Russia, Europe, W of Leningrad

Petrograd — see LENINGRAD

Pet·ro·pav·lovsk \,pe-trə-'pav-,lȯfsk\ city U.S.S.R. in Soviet Central Asia in N Kazakhstan *pop* 131,000

Pe·tró·po·lis \pə-'träp-ə-ləs\ city S E Brazil in Rio de Janeiro state *pop* 61,011

Petrovsk — see MAKHACHKALA

Pet·ro·za·vodsk \,pe-trə-zə-'vätsk\ city U.S.S.R. in NW Soviet Russia, Europe of Karelian Republic on Lake Onega *pop* 135,000

Petsamo — see PECHENGA

Pfalz — see PALATINATE

Pforz·heim \'(p)fȯrts-,hīm\ city W Germany S E of Karlsruhe *pop* 80,200

Pha·ros \'far-,äs, 'fer-\ peninsula N Egypt in city of Alexandria; formerly an island

Phar·sa·lus \fär-'sā-ləs\ *or modern* **Phar·sa·la** \'fär-sə-lə\ *or* N Gk **Fár·sa·la** \'fär-\ town N E Greece in E Thessaly in ancient district of **Phar·sa·lia** \fär-'sāl-yə, -'sā-lē-ə\

Phe·nix City \,fē-niks-\ city E Ala. *pop* 27,630

Phil·a·del·phia \,fil-ə-'del-fyə, -fē-ə\ **1** city & port S E Pa. on the Delaware *pop* 2,002,512 **2** — see ALASEHIR **3** — see AMMAN — **Phil·a·del·phian** \-fyən, -fē-ən\ *adj or n*

Phi·lae \'fī-(,)lē\ island S Egypt in the Nile above Aswân

Phi·lippe·ville \'fil-əp-,vil, fə-'lēp-\ city & port N E Algeria N of Constantine *pop* 70,406

Phi·lip·pi \'fil-ə-,pī, fə-'lip-,ī\ ancient town N E Greece in N *cen* Macedonia 10 *m* from the coast — **Phi·lip·pian** *adj or n*

Phil·ip·pine \'fil-ə-,pēn\ **1** islands of the Malay archipelago N E of Borneo — see PHILIPPINES **2** sea comprising the waters of the W Pacific E of & adjacent to the Philippines

Phil·ip·pines \'fil-ə-,pēnz, ,fil-ə-'\ *or* **Republic of the Philippines** *or* Sp **Re·pú·bli·ca de Fi·li·pi·nas** \re-'pü-li-kä-thä-,fē-lē-'pē-(,)näs\ country E Asia comprising the Philippine islands; a republic, once a Spanish possession & (1898-1945) a U.S. possession * Manila, official * Quezon City *land area* 114,830, *pop* 27,087,685 — **Phil·ip·pine** \'fil-ə-,pēn\ *adj*

Philippopolis — see PLOVDIV

Phi·lis·tia \fə-'lis-tē-ə\ ancient country SW Palestine on the coast; the land of the Philistines

Phil·lips·burg \'fil-əps-,bərg\ town W N.J. *pop* 18,502

Phnom Penh *or* **Pnom·penh** \(pə-)'nȯm-'pen\ city * of Cambodia on the Mekong *pop* 375,000

Pho·caea \fō-'sē-ə\ ancient city of Asia Minor on Aegean sea in N Ionia — **Pho·cae·an** \-ən\ *adj or n*

Pho·cis \'fō-səs\ region *cen* Greece N of Gulf of Corinth

Phoe·ni·cia *or* **Phe·ni·cia** \fi-'nish-(ē-)ə, -'nēsh-\ *or* **Phe·ni·ce**

\-'nī-sē\ ancient country SW Asia at E end of the Mediterranean in modern Syria & Lebanon

Phoe·nix \'fē-niks\ **1** city * of Ariz. on Salt river *pop* 439,170 **2** islands *cen* Pacific E S E of the Gilberts belonging (except for Canton & Enderbury) to Gilbert & Ellice Islands colony

Phryg·ia \'frij-(ē-)ə\ ancient country W *cen* Asia Minor divided *ab* 400 B.C. into **Greater Phrygia** (the inland region) & **Lesser Phrygia** (region along the Hellespont)

Pia·cen·za \pyä-'chen(t)-sə, ,pē-ə-'\ *or anc* **Pla·cen·tia** \plə-'sen-ch(ē-)ə\ commune N Italy on the Po S E of Milan *pop* 62,400

Pi·auí *or formerly* **Pi·au·hy** \pyau̇-'ē, pē-,au̇-\ state N E Brazil bordering on the Atlantic E of Parnaíba river * Teresina *area* 94,819, *pop* 1,045,696

Pia·ve \'pyäv-ē, -(,)ā, pē-'äv-\ river 137 *m* N E Italy flowing S & S E into the Adriatic

Pic·ar·dy \'pik-ərd-ē\ *or* F **Pi·car·die** \pē-kàr-dē\ region & former province N France bordering on English channel N of Normandy * Amiens — **Pic·ard** \'pik-ərd, -,ärd; pik-'ärd\ *adj or n*

Pi·co Ri·ve·ra \,pē-(,)kō-rə-'vir-ə\ city SW Calif. S E of Los Angeles *pop* 49,150

Pied·mont \'pēd-,mänt\ **1** plateau E U.S. lying E of the Appalachian & Blue Ridge mountains between S E N.Y. & *cen* Ala. **2** *or* It **Pie·mon·te** \pyā-'mȯn-(,)tā\ region NW Italy bordering on France & Switzerland W of Lombardy * Turin — **Pied·mon·tese** \,pēd-mən-'tēz, -'tēs\ *adj or n*

Pie·dras Ne·gras \pē-,ā-drə-'snä-grəs\ city N Mexico in Coahuila on Rio Grande opposite Eagle Pass, Tex. *pop* 27,578

Pi·e·ria \pī-'ir-ē-ə, -'er-\ ancient region N E Greece in Macedonia N of Thessaly

Pierre \'pi(ə)r\ city * of S. Dak. on the Missouri *pop* 10,088

Pie·ter·mar·itz·burg \,pēt-ər-'mar-əts-,bərg\ city E Republic of So. Africa * of Natal *pop* 73,189

Pigs, Bay of \'pigz\ *or* **Co·chi·nos Bay** \kə-,chē-nəs-\ bay W Cuba on S coast

Pikes Peak \'pīks\ mountain 14,110 *ft* E *cen* Colo. at S end of Front range

Pikes·ville \'pīks-,vil, -vəl\ urban area N *cen* Md. NW of Baltimore *pop* 18,737

Pi·la·tus \pi-'lät-əs\ mountain 6995 *ft*, *cen* Switzerland in Unterwalden SW of Lucerne

Pil·co·ma·yo \,pil-kə-'mī-(,)ō\ river 1000 *m* S *cen* So. America rising in Bolivia & flowing S E on Argentina-Paraguay boundary into Paraguay river

Pílion — see PELION

Pillars of Her·cu·les \'hər-kyə-,lēz\ the two promontories at E end of Strait of Gibraltar: Rock of Gibraltar (in Europe) & Jebel Musa (in Africa)

Pílos — see PYLOS

Pi·nar del Río \pi-,när-,del-'rē-(,)ō\ city & port W Cuba SW of Havana *pop* 38,885

Pin·dus \'pin-dəs\ mountains N Greece between Epirus & Thessaly; highest point over 7500 *ft*

Pine Bluff \'pīn-'bləf\ city S E *cen* Ark. *pop* 44,037

Pi·nel·las \pī-'nel-əs\ peninsula W Fla. between Tampa Bay & Gulf of Mexico

Pines, Isle of, 1 — see ISLE OF PINES **2** — see KUNIE

Ping \'piŋ\ river 360 *m* W Thailand flowing S S E to join the Nan forming the Chao Phraya

Piniós — see PENEUS

Pinkiang — see HARBIN

Pinnacles National Monument reservation W *cen* Calif. in Coast range S S E of Hollister *area* 20

Pinsk \'pin(t)sk\ city U.S.S.R. in SW Belorussia *pop* 30,000

Pinsk Marshes — see PRIPET

Piotr·kow \'pyȯt-ər-,küf, pē-'ȯt-, -,küv\ *or* Russ **Pe·tro·kov** \'pe-trə-,kȯf, -,kȯv\ commune *cen* Poland S S E of Lodz *pop* 52,900

Pipe Spring National Monument reservation NW Ariz. containing old stone fort

Pipe·stone National Monument \'pīp-,stōn\ reservation SW Minn. containing quarry once used by Indians

Piq·ua \'pik-(,)wä, -wə\ city W Ohio N of Dayton *pop* 19,219

Pi·rae·us *or* **Pei·rae·us** \pī-'rē-əs\ *or* N Gk **Pi·rai·évs** \,pē-re-'efs\ city E Greece on Saronic gulf; port for Athens *pop* 184,802

Pirineos — see PYRENEES

Pir·ma·sens \,pi(ə)r-mə-'zen(t)s\ city W Germany near French border E of the Saar *pop* 53,400

Pir·na \'pi(ə)r-nə\ city E Germany S E of Dresden *pop* 40,000

Pi·sa \'pē-zə, It -sä\ commune W *cen* Italy in Tuscany on the Arno *pop* 81,100 — **Pi·san** \'pēz-ᵊn\ *adj or n*

Pis·cat·a·qua \pis-'kat-ə-,kwȯ\ river 12 *m* Me. & N.H. formed by junction of Cocheco & Salmon Falls rivers & flowing S E on Me.-N.H. boundary into the Atlantic

Pis·gah \'piz-gə\ *or* **Ne·bo** \'nē-(,)bō\ mountain 2644 *ft* Palestine in Jordan E of N end of Dead sea

Pishpek — see FRUNZE

Pi·sid·ia \pə-'sid-ē-ə, pī-\ ancient country S Asia Minor N of Pamphylia — **Pi·sid·i·an** \-ē-ən\ *adj*

Pi·sto·ia \pi-'stȯi-ə, -'stō-yə\ commune *cen* Italy NW of Florence *pop* 34,100

Pit \'pit\ river 280 *m* N Calif. flowing SW into the Sacramento

Pit·cairn \'pit-,ka(ə)rn, -,ke(ə)rn\ island S Pacific S of tropic of Capricorn; a British colony, including several smaller islands

Pitts·burg \'pits-,bərg\ **1** city W Calif. N E of Oakland on San Joaquin river *pop* 19,062 **2** city S E Kans. *pop* 18,678

Pitts·burgh \'pits-,bərg\ city SW Pa. *pop* 604,332

Pitts·field \'pits-,fēld\ city W Mass. *pop* 57,879

Piz Bernina — see BERNINA

Pla·cen·tia Bay \plə-'sen-ch(ē-)ə-\ inlet of the Atlantic E Canada in S E Nfld.

Plac·id, Lake \'plas-əd\ lake 5 *m* long N E N.Y. in the Adirondacks

Plain·edge \'plā-,nej\ urban area S E N.Y. on Long I. *pop* 21,973

Plain·field \'plān-,fēld\ city N E N.J. *pop* 45,330

Plains of Abra·ham \'ā-brə-,ham\ plateau Canada in W part of city of Quebec

Plain·view \'plān-,vyü\ **1** urban area S E N.Y. on Long I. *pop* 27,710 **2** city NW Tex. N of Lubbock *pop* 18,735

Plant City city SW *cen* Fla. E of Tampa *pop* 15,711

Plas·sey \'plas-ē\ village N E India in West Bengal N of Calcutta

Pla·ta, Río de la \,rē-(,)ō-də-lə-'plät-ə\ *or* E **River Plate** \'plāt\ estuary of Paraná & Uruguay rivers So. America between Uruguay & Argentina; 225 *m* long

Pla·taea \plə-'tē-ə\ or **Pla·tae·ae** \-'tē-ˌē\ ancient city Greece in SE Boeotia S of Thebes — **Pla·tae·an** \-'tē-ən\ adj or n

Platte \'plat\ river 310 m (with No. Platte, 900 m) cen Nebr. formed by junction of the No. Platte & So. Platte & flowing E into the Missouri

Plattensee — see BALATON

Platt National Park \'plat\ reservation S Okla. containing numerous sulfur & other mineral springs area 912 acres

Platts·burgh or **Platts·burg** \'plats-ˌbərg\ city NE N.Y. on Lake Champlain pop 20,172

Plau·en \'plaú-ən\ or **Plauen im Vogt·land** \ˌplaú-(ə-),nim-'fōk-ˌtlänt\ city E Germany on the Weisse Elster SW of Zwickau pop 82,000

Pleasant — see NAURU

Pleasant Hill urban area W Calif. ENE of Oakland pop 23,844

Pleas·ant·ville \'plez-ᵊnt-ˌvil\ city SE N.J. W of Atlantic City pop 15,172

Plenty, Bay of inlet of the So. Pacific N New Zealand on NE coast of North I.

Ple·ven \'plev-ən\ or **Plev·na** \'plev-nə\ city NW Bulgaria pop 57,758

Plo·eş·ti \plô-'yesht(-ē)\ city SE cen Romania in E foothills of Transylvanian Alps pop 123,937

Plov·div \'plóv-ˌdif, -ˌdiv\ or Gk **Phil·ip·pop·o·lis** \ˌfil-ə-'päp-ə-ləs\ city S Bulgaria on the Maritsa N of the Rhodope mountains pop 162,512

Plym·outh \'plim-əth\ city & county borough & port SW England in Devonshire pop 208,985

Plzen \'pəl-ˌzen(-yə)\ or G **Pil·sen** \'pil-zən, -sən\ city Czechoslovakia in Bohemia WSW of Prague pop 134,273

Pnompenh — see PHNOM PENH

Po \'pō\ or anc **Pa·dus** \'pād-əs\ river 418 m N Italy flowing from slopes of Mt. Viso E into the Adriatic through several mouths

Po·ca·tel·lo \ˌpō-kə-'tel-(ˌ)ō, -'tel-ə\ city SE Idaho pop 28,534

Po·co·no \'pō-kə-ˌnō\ mountain ridge E Pa. NW of Kittatinny Mountain

Podgorica or **Podgoritsa** — see TITOGRAD

Po·do·lia \pə-'dō-lē-ə, -'dōl-yə\ or Russ **Po·dolsk** \pə-'dólsk\ region U.S.S.R. in W Ukraine N of middle Dniester river

Po·dolsk \pə-'dólsk\ town Soviet Russia, Europe, S of Moscow pop 124,000

Po Hai \'bō-'hī\ or **Gulf of Chih·li** \'chē-'lē, 'ji(ə)r-\ arm of Yellow sea NE China bounded on NE by Liaotung peninsula & on SE by Shantung peninsula

Po·hang \'pō-ˌhäŋ\ or **Pohang-dong** \-'dóŋ\ or Jap **Ho·ko** \'hō-(ˌ)kō\ city S Korea on an inlet of the Sea of Japan pop 52,473

Pointe-à-Pi·tre \ˌpwant-ə-'pētrᵊ\ city & port French West Indies in Guadeloupe on Grande-Terre pop 26,160

Pointe-Claire \ˌpóint-'kla(ə)r, -'kle(ə)r\ town Canada in S Que. on St. Lawrence river SW of Montreal pop 15,208

Pointe-Noire \ˌpwant-nə-'wär\ city & port SW Congo Republic on the Atlantic; formerly ✳ of Middle Congo pop 56,865

Point Pe·lee National Park \'pē-lē\ reservation Canada in SE Ont. on **Point Pelee** (cape projecting into Lake Erie)

Poi·tiers or formerly **Poic·tiers** \pwä-'tyā, 'pwät-ē-ˌā\ city W cen France SW of Tours pop 52,635

Poi·tou \pwä-'tü\ region & former province W France SE of Brittany ✳ Poitiers

Pola — see PULA

Po·land \'pō-lənd\ or Pol **Pol·ska** \'pól-skä\ country E Europe bordering on Baltic sea; in medieval period a kingdom, at one time extending to the lower Dnieper; partitioned 1772, 1793, 1795 among Russia, Prussia, & Austria; again a kingdom 1815–30; lost autonomy 1830–1918; since 1918 a republic ✳ Warsaw area 120,355, pop 29,527,000

Polish Corridor strip of land N Europe in Poland that between World War I & World War II separated East Prussia from main part of Germany; area was before 1919 part of Germany

Pol·ta·va \pəl-'tävə\ city U.S.S.R. in Ukraine on Vorskla river pop 141,000

Poltoratsk — see ASHKHABAD

Pol·y·ne·sia \ˌpäl-ə-'nē-zhə, -shə\ the islands of the cen & S Pacific including Hawaii, the Line, Ellice, Phoenix, Tonga, Cook, & Samoa islands, Easter I., French Polynesia, & often New Zealand

Pom·er·a·nia \ˌpäm-ə-'rē-lē-ə, -nyə\ or G **Pom·mern** \'päm-ərn\ or Pol **Po·mo·rze** \pó-'mó-zhe\ 1 region N Europe on Baltic sea; formerly in Germany, now mostly in Poland 2 former province of Prussia

Pom·er·elia \ˌpäm-ə-'rē-lē-ə, -'rēl-yə\ or G **Pom·me·rel·len** \ˌpò-mə-'rel-ən\ region E Europe on the Baltic W of the Vistula & E of Pomerania; originally part of Pomerania

Po·mo·na \pə-'mō-nə\ 1 city SW Calif. E of Los Angeles pop 67,157 2 — see MAINLAND

Pom·pa·no Beach \ˌpäm-pə-ˌnō-, ˌpäm-\ city SE Fla. on the Atlantic N of Fort Lauderdale pop 15,992

Pom·pe·ii \päm-'pā, -'pā-ˌē\ ancient city S Italy SE of Naples destroyed A.D. 79 by eruption of Mt. Vesuvius — **Pom·pe·ian** \-'pā-ən\ adj or n

Po·na·pe \'pō-nə-ˌpā\ island W Pacific in the E Carolines area 134, pop 14,644

Ponca City \ˌpäŋ-kə-\ city N Okla. on Arkansas river pop 24,411

Pon·ce \'pón(t)-(ˌ)sā\ city & port S Puerto Rico pop 114,286

Pon·di·cher·ry \ˌpän-də-'cher-ē, -'sher-\ or F **Pon·di·ché·ry** \pōⁿ-dē-shā-rē\ 1 territory SE India SSW of Madras surrounded by Madras state; a settlement of French India before 1954 area 112, pop 130,000 2 city & port, its ✳ pop 53,100

Pon·do·land \'pän-(ˌ)dō-ˌland\ territory Republic of So. Africa, one of the Transkeian Territories, between Umtata river & Natal

Pon·ta Del·ga·da \ˌpän-tə-del-'gäd-ə, -'gad-\ city & port Portugal in the Azores on São Miguel I. pop 22,700

Pont-Aven \ˌpōⁿt-ə-'ven\ village NW France WNW of Lorient

Pont·char·train, Lake \ˌpän-chər-ˌtrān, ˌpän-chər-'\ lake SE La. E of the Mississippi & N of New Orleans area 600

Pon·te·fract \'pänt-i-ˌfrakt\ municipal borough N England in West Riding, Yorkshire, SE of Leeds pop 23,173

Pon·te·ve·dra \ˌpänt-ə-'vā-drə\ 1 province NW Spain in SW Galicia on the Atlantic area 1695, pop 748,693 2 commune & port, its ✳, NW of Vigo pop 54,867

Pon·ti·ac \'pänt-ē-ˌak\ city SE Mich. NW of Detroit pop 82,233

Pon·ti·a·nak \ˌpänt-ē-'än-ək\ city Indonesia on SW coast of Borneo ✳ of West Kalimantan pop 121,100

Pon·tine \'pän-ˌtīn, -ˌtēn\ islands Italy in Tyrrhenian sea W of Naples; chief islands **Pon·za** \'pōn(t)-sə\ & **Pon·ti·ne** \pōn-'tē-nē\

Pontine marshes district cen Italy in SW Latium, separated from sea by low sand hills that prevent natural drainage; now reclaimed

Pon·tus \'pänt-əs\ 1 ancient country NE Asia Minor; a kingdom 4th century B.C. to 66 B.C., later a Roman province 2 or **Pontus Euxinus** — see BLACK SEA — **Pon·tic** \'pänt-ik\ adj

Pon·ty·pool \ˌpänt-i-'pül\ urban district W England in Monmouthshire pop 42,683

Pon·ty·pridd \ˌpänt-i-'prēth\ urban district SE Wales in Glamorganshire pop 38,622

Poole \'pül\ municipal borough S England in Dorset on English channel pop 82,958

Poo·na \'pü-nə\ city W India in Maharashtra ESE of Bombay pop 481,000

Po·o·pó \ˌpō-ə-'pō\ lake 60 m long W cen Bolivia S of Lake Titicaca at altitude of 12,000 ft

Pop·lar \'päp-lər\ metropolitan borough E London, England, on N bank of the Thames pop 73,544

Poplar Bluff city SE Mo. pop 15,926

Po·po·ca·te·petl \ˌpō-pə-'kat-ə-ˌpet-ᵊl, ˌkat-ə-'; -kə-'tā-ˌpet-\ volcano 17,887 ft SE cen Mexico in Puebla

Porcupine river 590 m in N Yukon Territory & NE Alaska flowing N & W into the Yukon

Po·ri \'pór-ē\ or Sw **Björ·ne·borg** \'byər-nə-ˌbó(ə)r(-yə)\ city & port SW Finland pop 51,000

Pork·ka·la \'pór-kə-lə, -ˌlä\ peninsula S Finland projecting into Gulf of Finland W of Helsinki

Por·la·mar \ˌpór-lə-'mär\ city & port NE Venezuela on Margarita I. pop 25,000

Port Ad·e·laide \'ad-ᵊl-ˌād\ city SE So. Australia on Gulf of St. Vincent at mouth of Torrens river; port for Adelaide pop 38,377

Port Ar·thur \'är-thər\ 1 city & port SE Tex. on Sabine Lake SE of Beaumont pop 66,676 2 city & port Canada in SW Ont. on Lake Superior pop 38,136 3 or **Lü·shun** \'lü-'shùn\ city & port NE China in S Liaoning at tip of Liaotung peninsula SW of Dairen pop 126,000 — see LÜTA

Port-au-Prince \ˌpōrt-ō-'prin(t)s, ˌpórt-, -'pran(t)s\ city & port ✳ of Republic of Haiti pop 135,687

Port Blair \'bla(ə)r, 'ble(ə)r\ town & port India on So. Andaman I. ✳ of Andaman & Nicobar Islands Territory

Port Castries — see CASTRIES

Port Ches·ter \'pórt-,ches-tər, 'pórt-\ village SE N.Y. NE of New Rochelle on Long Island Sound pop 24,960

Port Darwin — see DARWIN

Port Eliz·a·beth \ᵊl-'iz-ə-bəth, i-'liz-\ city & port S Republic of So. Africa in SE Cape Province on Algoa Bay pop 78,670

Port Ev·er·glades \'ev-ər-ˌglādz\ port SE Fla. on the Atlantic S of Fort Lauderdale

Port Hu·ron \'hyùr-ən\ city E Mich. on Lake Huron & St. Clair river pop 36,084

Port Jack·son \'jak-sən\ inlet of S Pacific SE Australia in New So. Wales; the harbor of Sydney

Port Jin·nah \'jin-ə\ seaport E Pakistan; port for Chalna

Port·land \'pōrt-lənd, 'pórt-\ 1 city & port S Me. on Casco Bay pop 72,566 2 city & port NW Oreg. at confluence of Columbia & Willamette rivers pop 372,676

Portland Canal inlet of the Pacific ab 80 m long Canada & U.S. between B.C. & SE tip of Alaska

Port Louis — see MARYBOROUGH

Port Lou·is \'lü-əs, 'lü-ē, lù-'ē\ city & port ✳ of Mauritius pop (with suburbs) 101,145

Port Lyautey — see KENITRA

Port Mahon — see MAHÓN

Port Mores·by \'mō(ə)rz-bē, 'mò(ə)rz-\ town & port SE New Guinea ✳ of joint territories of Papua & New Guinea

Port Natal — see NATAL BAY

Pôrto — see OPORTO

Pôr·to Ale·gre \ˌpórt-(ˌ)ō-ə-'leg-rə, ˌpórt-\ city & port S Brazil ✳ of Rio Grande do Sul state at N end of Lagoa dos Patos pop 375,049

Por·to·be·lo or **Por·to Bel·lo** \ˌpōrt-ə-'bel-(ˌ)ō, ˌpórt-\ or **Puer·to Bello** \ˌpwert-ə-\ town & port Panama on Caribbean coast; the great emporium of So. American trade in 16th & 17th centuries

Por·to·fi·no \ˌpōrt-ə-'fē-(ˌ)nō, ˌpórt-\ village N Italy in Liguria on the coast SE of Genoa

Port of Spain city & port ✳ of Trinidad & Tobago, on NW Trinidad I. pop 114,150

Por·to-No·vo \ˌpōrt-ə-'nō-(ˌ)vō\ city & port ✳ of Dahomey pop 27,500

Porto Rico — see PUERTO RICO

Port Phil·lip Bay \'fil-əp-\ inlet of Bass strait SE Australia in Victoria; the harbor of Melbourne

Port Roy·al \'rói(-ə)l\ town Jamaica at entrance to Kingston Harbor; early ✳ of Jamaica, destroyed by earthquakes 1692 & 1907 & partly engulfed by the sea

Port Royal sound inlet of the Atlantic S S.C.

Port Said \'sīd, sä-'ēd\ city & port NE Egypt on the Mediterranean at N end of Suez canal pop 226,600

Ports·mouth \'pōrt-sməth, 'pórt-\ 1 city & port SE N.H. on the Atlantic pop 25,833 2 city S Ohio at junction of Ohio & Scioto rivers pop 33,637 3 city & port SE Va. on Elizabeth river opposite Norfolk pop 114,773 4 city & county borough S England in Hampshire on **Port·sea** \'pōrt-sē, 'pórt-\ (island in English channel) pop 233,464

Port Stanley — see STANLEY

Port Sudan city & port NE Sudan on Red sea pop 47,562

Por·tu·gal \'pōr-chi-gəl, 'pór-\ or anc **Lu·si·ta·nia** \ˌlü-sə-'tā-nē-ə, -nyə\ country SW Europe in W Iberian peninsula bordering on the Atlantic; a republic, before 1910 a kingdom ✳ Lisbon (not including Azores & Madeira) 34,240, pop 7,856,913

Portuguese East Africa — see MOZAMBIQUE

Por·tu·guese Guinea \ˌpōr-chə-ˌgēz-, ˌpȯr-, -ˌgēs-\ country W Africa S of Senegal; a Portuguese colony ✻ Bissau *area* 13,948, *pop* 510,777

Portuguese India former Portuguese possessions on W coast of India peninsula, annexed 1962 by India; comprised territory of Goa & districts of Damão & Diu ✻ Pangim *area* 1537, *pop* 637,591

Portuguese Timor — see TIMOR

Portuguese West Africa — see ANGOLA

Port Wash·ing·ton \ˈwȯsh-iŋ-tən, ˈwäsh-\ urban area SE N.Y. in NW Long I. *pop* 15,657

Porz am Rhein \ˌpȯrt-säm-ˈrīn\ city W Germany E of Cologne *pop* 50,500

Poseidonia — see PAESTUM

Po·si·ta·no \ˌpō-zə-ˈtän-(ˌ)ō\ commune S Italy on Gulf of Salerno

Potch·ef·stroom \ˈpäch-əf-ˌstrüm\ city NE Republic of So. Africa in S Transvaal SW of Johannesburg *pop* 32,031

Po·to·mac \pə-ˈtō-mək, -mik\ river 287 *m* E U.S. flowing from W. Va. to Chesapeake Bay & forming S boundary of Md.

Po·to·sí \ˌpōt-ə-ˈsē\ city S Bolivia *pop* 51,065

Pots·dam \ˈpäts-ˌdam\ city E Germany SW of Berlin *pop* 117,600

Potts·town \ˈpät-ˌstau̇n\ borough SE Pa. *pop* 26,144

Potts·ville \ˈpäts-ˌvil\ city E *cen* Pa. NNW of Reading *pop* 21,659

Pough·keep·sie \pə-ˈkip-sē, pō-\ city SE N.Y. *pop* 38,330

Pow·der \ˈpau̇d-ər\ **1** river 150 *m* E Oreg. flowing into the Snake **2** river 375 *m* N Wyo. & SE Mont. flowing N into the Yellowstone

Powell, Lake — see GLEN CANYON DAM

Po·yang \ˈpō-ˈyäŋ\ lake 90 *m* long E China in N Kiangsi

Poz·nan \ˈpōz-ˌnan(-yə), ˈpȯz-, -ˌnän(-yə)\ *or* G **Po·sen** \ˈpōz-ᵊn\ city W *cen* Poland on the Warta *pop* 395,000

Poz·zuo·li \pȯt-ˈswȯ-lē\ *or anc* **Pu·te·o·li** \pyu̇-ˈtē-ə-ˌlī, pə-ˈtē-\ commune & port S Italy in Campania W of Naples *pop* 36,800

Prades \ˈpräd\ village S France in the Pyrenees 25 *m* SW of Perpignan

Prague \ˈpräg\ *or* Czech **Pra·ha** \ˈprä-(ˌ)hä\ city ✻ of Czechoslovakia in Bohemia on Vltava river *pop* 1,030,330

Prairie Provinces the Canadian provinces of Man., Sask., & Alta.

Prairie Village city NE Kans. S of Kansas City *pop* 25,356

Pra·to \ˈprät-ō\ commune *cen* Italy in Tuscany *pop* 48,100

Presque Isle \pre-ˈskī(ə)l\ peninsula NW Pa. in Lake Erie forming **Presque Isle Bay** (harbor of Erie, Pa.)

Pressburg — see BRATISLAVA

Pres·ton \ˈpres-tən\ county borough NW England, a ✻ of Lancashire on the Ribble *pop* 119,243

Prest·wich \ˈpres-(ˌ)twich\ urban district NW England in Lancashire NNW of Manchester *pop* 34,387

Prest·wick \ˈpres-(ˌ)twik\ burgh SW Scotland in Ayrshire

Pre·to·ria \pri-ˈtōr-ē-ə, -ˈtȯr-\ city, administrative ✻ of Republic of So. Africa & ✻ of Transvaal *pop* 151,100

Prib·i·lof \ˈprib-ə-ˌlȯf\ islands Alaska in Bering sea

Prich·ard \ˈprich-ərd\ city SW Ala. N of Mobile *pop* 47,371

Primorski Krai — see MARITIME TERRITORY

Prince Al·bert \ˈal-bərt\ city Canada in *cen* Sask. *pop* 20,366

Prince Albert National Park reservation Canada in *cen* Sask. on No. Saskatchewan river *area* 7

Prince Ed·ward Island \ˌed-wərd-\ island SE Canada in Gulf of St. Lawrence off E N.B. & N N.S.; a province ✻ Charlottetown *area* 2184, *pop* 99,285

Prince Edward Island National Park reservation Canada in P.E.I. *area* 7

Prince of Wales \ˈwā(ə)lz\ **1** island SE Alaska, largest in Alexander archipelago *area* 1500 **2** island N Canada between Victoria I. & Somerset I. *area* 12,830

Prince of Wales, Cape cape Alaska at W tip of Seward peninsula; most westerly point of No. America, at 168°W

Prince Wil·liam Sound \ˌwil-yəm-\ inlet of Gulf of Alaska S Alaska E of Kenai peninsula

Prin·ci·pe \ˈprin(t)-sə-ˌpā\ *or* **Prince** \ˈprin(t)s\ island W Africa in Gulf of Guinea N of São Tomé; belongs to Portugal *area* 58 — see SÃO TOMÉ

Prip·et \ˈprip-ˌet, -ət\ *or* Russ **Pri·pyat** \ˈprip-yət\ river 500 *m* E *cen* Europe in the U.S.S.R. in NW Ukraine & S White Russia flowing E through the **Pripet,** *or* **Pinsk, marshes** (marshlands *ab* 300 *m* long & 140 *m* wide) to the Dnieper

Pro·gre·so \prə-ˈgres-(ˌ)ō\ town & port SE Mexico on Yucatán peninsula; port for Mérida

Pro·ko·pevsk *or* **Pro·ko·pyevsk** \prə-ˈkȯp-yəfsk\ city U.S.S.R. in SW Soviet Russia, Asia, at S end of Kuznetsk basin NW of Novokuznetsk *pop* 282,000

Propontis — see MARMARA (Sea of)

Pro·vence \prə-ˈväⁿs\ region & former province SE France bordering on the Mediterranean ✻ Aix

Prov·i·dence \ˈpräv-əd-ən(t)s, -ə-ˌden(t)s\ city & port ✻ of R.I. *pop* 207,498

Pro·vo \ˈprō-(ˌ)vō\ city N *cen* Utah on Utah Lake *pop* 36,047

Prus·sia \ˈprəsh-ə\ *or* G **Preus·sen** \ˈprȯis-ᵊn\ **1** region N Germany bordering on Baltic sea **2** former kingdom & state of Germany ✻ Berlin — see EAST PRUSSIA, WEST PRUSSIA — **Prus·sian** \ˈprəsh-ən\ *adj or n*

Prut \ˈprüt\ river 500 *m* E Europe flowing from the Carpathians SSE into the Danube & since World War II forming the boundary between Romania & the U.S.S.R.

Pskov \pə-ˈskȯf, -ˈskȯv\ city U.S.S.R. in Soviet Russia, Europe, near **Lake Pskov** (S arm of Lake Peipus) *pop* 81,000

Ptol·e·ma·is \ˌtäl-ə-ˈmā-əs\ **1** ancient town in upper Egypt on left bank of the Nile NW of Thebes **2** ancient town in Cyrenaica NW of Barca; site at modern village of Tolmeta **3** — see ACRE

Pueb·la \pü-ˈeb-lə, ˈpweb-, pyü-ˈeb-\ **1** state SE *cen* Mexico *area* 13,124, *pop* 1,902,172 **2** city, its ✻ *pop* 285,284

Pueb·lo \pü-ˈeb-(ˌ)lō, ˈpweb-, pyü-ˈeb-, ˈpyeb-\ city SE *cen* Colo. *pop* 91,181

Puer·to Bar·rios \ˌpwert-ō-ˈbär-ē-ˌōs\ city & port E Guatemala on Gulf of Honduras *pop* 29,899

Puerto Bello — see PORTOBELO

Puerto Ca·be·llo \-kə-ˈbā-(ˌ)(y)ō\ city & port N Venezuela 70 *m* W of Caracas *pop* 45,000

Puerto La Cruz \-lə-ˈkrüz, -ˈkrüs\ city NE Venezuela NE of Barcelona *pop* 28,385

Puerto Limón — see LIMÓN

Puerto Montt \ˌpwert-ō-ˈmȯnt\ city & port S *cen* Chile *pop* 64,775

Puer·to Ri·co \ˌpwert-ə-ˈrē-(ˌ)kō, ˌpȯrt-, ˌpȯrt-\ *or formerly* **Por·to Ri·co** island West Indies E of Hispaniola; a self-governing commonwealth in union with the U.S. ✻ San Juan *area* 3435, *pop* 2,349,544 — **Puerto Ri·can** \-ˈrē-kən\ *adj or n*

Pu·get Sound \ˌpyü-jət-\ arm of the Pacific extending 80 *m* S into W Wash. from E end of Juan de Fuca strait

Puglia *or* **Le Puglie** — see APULIA

Pu·jon \ˈpüj-ˌȯn\ *or* Jap **Fu·sen** \ˈfü-ˌsen\ reservoir 11 *m* long N Korea E of Changjin reservoir; formed by dam in **Pujon river** (60 *m* flowing N into Changjin river)

Pu·ka·pu·ka \ˌpü-kə-ˈpü-kə\ *or* **Dan·ger islands** \ˌdān-jər-\ atoll *cen* Pacific N of Cook islands; chief island Pukapuka; administered with Cook islands by New Zealand

Puk·han \ˈpük-ˌhän\ river 110 *m*, *cen* Korea flowing into the Han

Pu·la \ˈpü-lə\ *or* **Pulj** \ˈpül-yə\ *or* It **Po·la** \ˈpō-lə\ city & port NW Yugoslavia at tip of Istrian peninsula *pop* 29,300

Pul·ko·vo \ˈpül-kə-və, -ˌvō\ village U.S.S.R. in Soviet Russia, Europe, 10 *m* S of Leningrad

Pu·log \ˈpü-ˌlȯg\ mountain 9606 *ft* Philippines in N Luzon at S end of Cordillera Central; highest in Luzon

Pu·na de Ata·ca·ma \ˌpü-nə-ˌdā-ˌat-ə-ˈkäm-ə, -ˌät-\ high plateau region NW Argentina NW of Tucumán

Pun·jab *or* **Pan·jab** \ˌpən-ˈjäb, -ˈjab, ˈpən-ˌ\ **1** region NW Indian subcontinent in West Pakistan & NW India occupying valleys of the Indus & its five tributaries; formerly a province of Brit. India ✻ Lahore **2** *or formerly* **East Punjab** state NW India in E Punjab divided 1966 into two states of **Pun·jabi Su·ba** \ˌpən-ˌjäb-ē-ˈsü-bə, -ˌjab-\ (in north) & **Ha·ri·a·na** \ˌhar-ē-ˈän-ə\ (in south); joint ✻ Chandigarh *area* 47,456, *pop* 16,134,890 **3** WEST PUNJAB

Punt \ˈpu̇nt\ — ancient Egyptian name for a part of Africa not certainly identified, probably Somaliland

Pun·ta Are·nas \ˌpünt-ə-ə-ˈrā-nəs\ *or* **Ma·ga·lla·nes** \ˌmäg-ə-ˈyän-əs\ city & port S Chile on Strait of Magellan *pop* 52,595

Punta del Es·te \-ˌdel-ˈes-tē\ town S Uruguay E of Montevideo

Pu·ra·cé \ˌpu̇r-ə-ˈsā\ volcano 15,420 *ft* SW *cen* Colombia

Pur·beck, Isle of \ˈpər-ˌbek\ peninsula region S England in Dorset extending E into English channel

Pur·ga·toire \ˈpər-gə-ˌtwär, ˈpik-ət-ˌwī(ə)r\ river 190 *m* SE Colo. flowing into the Arkansas

Pu·ri \ˈpu̇r-ē\ *or* **Ja·gan·nath** \ˈjəg-ə-ˌnät\ *or* **Jug·ger·naut** \ˈjəg-ər-ˌnȯt, -ˌnät\ city & port E India in SE Orissa on Bay of Bengal *pop* 49,057

Pu·rus \pə-ˈrüs\ river 2000 *m* NW *cen* So. America rising in the Andes in SE Peru & flowing NE into the Amazon in Brazil

Pu·san \ˈpü-ˌsän\ *or* Jap **Fu·san** \ˈfü-\ city & port SE Korea on Korea strait *pop* 1,044,581

Push·kin \ˈpu̇sh-kən\ *or formerly* **Tsar·skoe Se·lo** \ˌtsär-skə-yə-sə-ˈlō\ *or* **Det·skoe Selo** \ˌdet-skə-yə-\ city U.S.S.R. in NW Soviet Russia, Europe, S of Leningrad *pop* 50,000

Puteoli — see POZZUOLI

Put-in-Bay \ˌpu̇t-ˌin-\ inlet of Lake Erie in Ohio on So. Bass I. N of Sandusky Bay; site of Perry's Victory and International Peace Memorial National Monument

Pu·tu·ma·yo \ˌpüt-ə-ˈmī-(ˌ)ō\ *or* (*in Brazil*) **Içá** \ē-ˈsä\ river 980 *m* NW So. America flowing from SW Colombia into the Amazon in NW Brazil

Puy de Dôme — see DÔME (Puy de)

Puy de Sancy — see SANCY (Puy de)

Pya·ti·gorsk \pē-ˌat-i-ˈgȯ(ə)rsk\ city U.S.S.R. in S Soviet Russia, Europe, in N Caucasus SE of Stavropol *pop* 69,000

Py·los \ˈpī-ˌläs\ *or* **Na·va·ri·no** \ˌnav-ə-ˈrē-(ˌ)nō\ *or* NGk **Pi·los** \ˈpē-ˌlȯs\ town & port SW Greece in SW Peloponnesus

Pyong·yang \pē-ˈȯŋ-ˌyäŋ, -ˈəŋ-, -ˌyaŋ\ *or* Jap **Hei·jo** \ˈhā-(ˌ)jō\ city ✻ of No. Korea on the Taedong *pop* 285,000

Pyramid lake 30 *m* NW Nev. NE of Reno

Pyr·e·nees \ˈpir-ə-ˌnēz\ *or* F **Py·ré·nées** \pē-rā-nā\ *or* Sp **Pi·ri·ne·os** \ˌpē-rē-ˈnā-(ˌ)ōs\ mountains along French-Spanish border from Bay of Biscay to Gulf of Lions — see ANETO (Pico de) — **Pyr·e·ne·an** \ˌpir-ə-ˈnē-ən\ *adj or n*

Qa·ra Shahr *or* **Ka·ra·shahr** \ˌkär-ə-ˈshär\ town W China in *cen* Sinkiang on N edge of Takla Makan desert

Qa·tar *or* **Ka·tar** \ˈkät-ər\ peninsula E Arabia projecting into Persian gulf; a sheikdom ✻ Doha *area* 4000, *pop* 60,000

Qat·ta·ra Depression \kə-ˌtär-ə-\ region NW Egypt, a low area 40 *m* from coast; lowest point 440 *ft* below sea level

Qazvin — see KAZVIN

Qe·na \ˈkē-nə, ˈkā-\ city S Egypt N of Luxor *pop* 47,700

Qishm *or* **Kishm** \ˈkish-əm\ island S Iran in Strait of Hormuz

Qi·shon *or* **Ki·shon** \ˈkī-ˌshän, ˈkish-ˌän\ river 50 *m* N Palestine flowing NW through Plain of Esdraelon to the Mediterranean

Qomul — see HAMI

Quathlamba — see DRAKENSBERG

Que·bec \kwi-ˈbek\ *or* **Qué·bec** \kā-bek\ **1** province E Canada extending from Hudson Bay to Gaspé peninsula *area* 523,860, *pop* 4,628,378 **2** city & port, its ✻, on the St. Lawrence *pop* 170,703

Queen Char·lotte \ˈshär-lət\ **1** islands Canada in W B.C. in Pacific ocean *area* 3970 **2** sound S of Queen Charlotte islands

Queen Eliz·a·beth \ə-ˈliz-ə-bəth, i-ˈliz-\ islands N Canada N of water passage extending from M'Clure strait to Lancaster Sound; include Parry, Sverdrup, Devon, & Ellesmere islands

Queen Maud Land \ˈmȯd\ section of Antarctica on the Atlantic

Queens \ˈkwēnz\ borough of New York City on Long I. E of Brooklyn *pop* 1,809,578

Queen's — see LAOIGHIS

Queens·land \ˈkwēnz-ˌland, -lənd\ state NE Australia ✻ Brisbane *area* 670,500, *pop* 1,428,656 — **Queens·land·er** \-ər\ *n*

Queenstown — see COBH

Quelpart — see CHEJU

Que·moy \k(w)i-ˈmȯi\ *or* **Kin·men** *or* **Chin·men** \ˈjin-ˈmən\ island SE China in Formosa strait 15 *m* E of Amoy

Que·ré·ta·ro \kə-ˈret-ə-ˌrō\ **1** state *cen* Mexico *area* 4432, *pop* 318,866 **2** city, its ✻ *pop* 49,209

Quet·ta \ˈkwet-ə\ city Pakistan in N Baluchistan *pop* 84,300

Que·zal·te·nan·go *or* **Quet·zal·te·nan·go** \ke(t)-ˌsäl-tə-ˈnäŋ-(ˌ)gō\ city SW Guatemala *pop* 49,057

Que·zon City \ˌkā-ˌsȯn-\ city Philippines in Luzon adjoining Manila; official ✻ of the Philippines *pop* 107,977

Quil·mes \ˈkē(ə)l-ˌmās\ city E Argentina SE of Buenos Aires *pop* 115,113

Quim·per \kaⁿ(m)-'pe(ə)r\ commune NW France W of Rennes near Bay of Biscay *pop* 19,352

Qui·nault \kwi-'nȯlt\ river 65 *m* W Wash. flowing to the Pacific

Quin·cy, 1 \'kwin(t)-sē\ city W Ill. on the Mississippi *pop* 43,793 **2** \'kwin-zē\ city E Mass. SE of Boston *pop* 87,409

Quin·ta·na Roo \kēn-,tän-ə-'rō\ territory SE Mexico in E Yucatán ✳ Chetumal *area* 19,438, *pop* 34,639

Quin·ta Nor·mal \,kēn-tə-(,)nȯr-'mäl\ city *cen* Chile, W suburb of Santiago *pop* 150,810

Quin·te, Bay of \'kwint\ inlet of Lake Ontario in Canada in SE Ont.; connected with Georgian Bay by Trent canal

Quir·i·nal \'kwir-ən-°l\ hill in Rome, Italy, one of seven on which the ancient city was built — see AVENTINE

Qui·to \'kē-(,)tō\ city ✳ of Ecuador *pop* 237,103

Qui·vi·ra \ki-'vir-ə\ region, probably the area around present city of Great Bend, Kans., believed by first Spanish explorers of the Southwest to be a populous land of great wealth; reached by Coronado 1541 & found to be a settlement of Wichita Indians

Qum \'kùm\ city NW *cen* Iran *pop* 96,463

Qum·ran *or* **Khir·bat Qumran** \kir-,bät-kùm-'rän\ site Palestine in NW Jordan on Wadi Qumran near NW shore of Dead sea of an Essene community (*ab* 100 B.C.–A.D. 68) near a series of caves in which the Dead Sea Scrolls were found

Raab — see GYOR

Ra·ba \'räb-ə\ river 160 *m* SE Austria & W Hungary flowing E & NE into the Danube

Ra·bat \rə-'bät\ city ✳ of Morocco on Atlantic coast *pop* 160,000

Ra·baul \rə-'bau(ə)l\ town Bismarck archipelago at E end of New Britain; formerly ✳ of Territory of New Guinea

Rab·bah, Rabbath — see AMMAN

Race, Cape \'rās\ headland, SE point of Nfld., Canada

Ra·ci·borz \rät-'sē-,bùsh\ *or* G **Ra·ti·bor** \'rät-ə-,bȯ(ə)r\ city SW Poland in Silesia on the Odra *pop* 32,500

Ra·cine \rə-'sēn, rā-\ city SE Wis. S of Milwaukee *pop* 89,144

Rad·nor \'rad-nər\ **1** urban township SE Pa. WNW of Philadelphia *pop* 21,697 **2** *or* **Rad·nor·shire** \-,shi(ə)r, -shər\ county E Wales ✳ Llandrindod Wells *area* 471, *pop* 19,998

Ra·dom \'räd-,òm\ commune Poland NE of Kielce *pop* 121,200

Raetia — see RHAETIA

Rae·tian adj *or* n

Rages — see RHAGES

Ra·gu·sa \rə-'gü-zə\ **1** commune Italy in SE Sicily *pop* 42,429 **2** — see DUBROVNIK

Rah·way \'rȯ-,wā\ city NE N.J. SW of Elizabeth *pop* 27,699

Ra·ia·téa \,rī-ə-'tā-ə\ island S Pacific in Leeward group of the Society islands 130 *m* WNW of Tahiti *area* 75, *pop* 4000

Rainbow Bridge National Monument reservation S Utah near Ariz. line containing **Rainbow Bridge** (large natural bridge)

Rai·nier, Mount \rə-'ni(ə)r, rā-\ *or formerly* **Mount Ta·co·ma** \tə-'kō-mə\ mountain 14,410 *ft* W *cen* Wash., highest in the Cascade range & in Wash.; situated in **Mount Rainier National Park** (*area* 377)

Rainy \'rā-nē\ **1** river 80 *m* on Canada-U.S. boundary between Ont. & Minn. flowing from Rainy Lake into Lake of the Woods **2** lake Canada & U.S. between Ont. & Minn. *area* 366

Rai·pur \'rī-,pù(ə)r\ city E India in SE Madhya Pradesh E of Nagpur *pop* 139,983

Rai·sin \'rāz-°n\ river 150 *m* SE Mich. flowing into Lake Erie

Ra·ja·mun·dry \,räj-ə-'mùn-drē\ city E India in E Andhra Pradesh on Godavari river E of Kakinada *pop* 105,300

Ra·ja·sthan \'räj-ə-,stän\ **1** RAJPUTANA **2** state NW India bordering on W Pakistan ✳ Jaipur *area* 132,077, *pop* 15,972,000

Raj·kot \'räj-,kōt\ **1** former state W India in N *cen* Kathiawar peninsula **2** city, its ✳, now in Gujarat *pop* 132,069

Raj·pu·ta·na \,räj-pə-'tän-ə\ region NW India bordering on West Pakistan & including part of Thar desert

Rakuto — see NAKTONG

Ra·leigh \'rȯ-lē, 'räl-ē\ city ✳ of N.C. *pop* 93,931

Ra·lik \'räl-ik\ the W chain of the Marshall islands

Ram·a·po \'ram-ə-,pō\ mountains of the Appalachians N N.J. & S N.Y.

Ra·mat Gan \rə-'mät-,gän\ city W Israel E of Tel Aviv *pop* 90,234

Ram·bouil·let \räⁿ-bü-yā\ town N France 28 *m* SW of Paris

Ram·gan·ga \räm-'gəŋ-gə\ river 370 *m* N India in Uttar Pradesh flowing S into the Ganges

Ram·pur \'rəm-,pù(ə)r\ **1** former state N India NW of Bareilly ✳ Rampur *area* 894; district now in Uttar Pradesh **2** city N India in NW Uttar Pradesh ENE of Delhi *pop* 134,300

Rams·gate \'ramz-,gāt, -gət\ municipal borough SE England in Kent on North sea N of Dover *pop* 35,748

Ran·chi \'rän-chē\ city E India, summer ✳ of Bihar, NW of Calcutta *pop* 106,849

Rand \'rand, 'ränd\ WITWATERSRAND

Ran·ders \'rän-ərs\ city & port NE Denmark *pop* 41,720

Ran·dolph \'ran-,dälf\ town E Mass. S of Boston *pop* 18,900

Range·ley Lakes \'rānj-lē\ chain of lakes W Me. & N N.H. including Rangeley, Mooselookmeguntic, Upper Richardson, Lower Richardson, & Umbagog

Ran·goon \ran-'gün, ,raŋ-\ **1** river 185 *m* S Burma, the E outlet of the Irrawaddy **2** city & port ✳ of Burma on Rangoon river 21 *m* from its mouth *pop* 737,079

Ran·noch, Loch \'ran-ək, -ək\ lake 9 *m* long *cen* Scotland

Rann of Kutch — see KUTCH

Ran·toul \ran-'tül\ village E Ill. NNE of Champaign *pop* 22,116

Ra·pa \'räp-ə\ island S Pacific in SE Tubuaï group *area* 15

Ra·pal·lo \rə-'päl-(,)ō\ commune NW Italy in Liguria ESE of Genoa on Gulf of Rapallo (inlet of Ligurian sea)

Rapa Nui — see EASTER

Rap·i·dan \,rap-ə-'dan\ river 70 *m* N Va. rising in Blue Ridge mountains & flowing E into the Rappahannock

Rap·id City \,rap-əd-\ city W S. Dak. in Black hills *pop* 42,399

Rap·pa·han·nock \,rap-ə-'han-ək\ river 185 *m* NE Va. flowing into Chesapeake Bay

Rap·ti \'räp-tē\ river 400 *m* Nepal & N India flowing SE into the Gogra

Rar·i·tan \'rar-ət-°n\ **1** river 75 *m* N *cen* N.J. flowing E into **Raritan Bay** (inlet of the Atlantic S of Staten I., N.Y.) **2** urban township E *cen* N.J. S of Raritan Bay *pop* 15,334 **3** borough N *cen* N.J. on Raritan river *pop* 6137

Rar·o·ton·ga \,rar-ə-'tän-gə\ island S Pacific in SW part of Cook islands; site of Avarua, ✳ of the group

Ras Addar — see BON (Cape)

Ras Da·shan \,räs-də-'shän\ mountain 15,160 *ft* N Ethiopia NE of Lake Tana; highest in Ethiopia

Ras el Tib — see BON (Cape)

Rashid — see ROSETTA

Rashin — see NAJIN

Rasht \'rasht\ *or* **Resht** \'resht\ city NW Iran *pop* 109,493

Rat \'rat\ islands SW Alaska in W Aleutians — see AMCHITKA, KISKA

Ra·tak \'rä-,täk\ *or* **Ra·dak** \'räd-,äk\ the E chain of the Marshall islands

Rath·mines and Rath·gar \rath-'mīn-zən-(,)rath-'gär\ town E Ireland, S suburb of Dublin *pop* 45,629

Ra·ton \rə-'tōn, -,tün\ pass 7834 *ft* SE Colo. on Colo.-N. Mex. border in **Raton range** (E spur of Sangre de Cristo mountains)

Ra·ven·na \rə-'ven-ə\ commune N Italy NE of Florence near Adriatic coast; formerly a seaport *pop* 115,205

Ra·vi \'räv-ē\ *or anc* **Hy·dra·o·tes** \,hī-drə-'ōt-(,)ēz\ river 450 *m* N India flowing SW to the Chenab & forming part of boundary between East Punjab (Republic of India) & West Punjab (Pakistan)

Ra·wal·pin·di \,rä-wəl-'pin-dē, raùl-'\ city ✳ of Pakistan in NE West Pakistan NNW of Lahore *pop* 237,300

Ray·town \'rā-,taùn\ city W Mo. SE of Kansas City *pop* 17,083

Read·ing \'red-iŋ\ **1** town E Mass. N of Boston *pop* 19,259 **2** city SE Pa. on the Schuylkill *pop* 98,177 **3** county borough S England ✳ of Berkshire *pop* 114,176

Reb·ild \'reb-,il(d)\ village N Denmark in N Jutland S of Aalborg in **Rebild hills** (site of Rebild National Park)

Re·ci·fe \rə-'sē-fə\ *or formerly* **Per·nam·bu·co** \,pər-nəm-'b(y)ü-(,)kō\ city & port NE Brazil ✳ of Pernambuco state *pop* 512,370

Reck·ling·hau·sen \,rek-liŋ-'haùz-°n\ city W Germany SW of Münster *pop* 130,200

Red \'red\ **1** sea 1450 *m* long between Arabia & NE Africa **2** river 1018 *m* flowing E on Okla.-Tex. boundary & into the Mississippi in La. **3** river 310 *m* N *cen* U.S. & S *cen* Canada flowing N on Minn.-N. Dak. boundary & into Lake Winnipeg in Man. **4** — see ARCTIC RED **5** *or* **Coi** *or* **Koi** \'kȯi\ river 500 *m* SE Asia rising in *cen* Yunnan, China, & flowing SE across N Vietnam into Gulf of Tonkin

Red Deer river 385 *m* Canada in S Alta. flowing E & SE into the So. Saskatchewan

Red Lake lake 38 *m* long N Minn. divided into **Upper Red Lake** & **Lower Red Lake**; drained by **Red Lake river** (135 *m* flowing W into Red river)

Red·lands \'red-lən(d)z\ city S Calif. SE of San Bernardino *pop* 26,829

Re·don·do Beach \ri-,dän-dō-\ city SW Calif. *pop* 46,986

Red Volta river 200 *m* S Upper Volta & N Ghana flowing into the White Volta

Red·wood City \,red-,wùd-\ city W Calif. SE of San Francisco *pop* 46,290

Reel·foot \'rē(ə)l-,fùt\ lake NW Tenn. near the Mississippi

Re·gens·burg \'rā-gənz-,bərg, -,bù(ə)rg\ *or* **Rat·is·bon** \'rat-əs-,bän, -əz-\ city W Germany in Bavaria on the Danube 65 *m* NNE of Munich *pop* 123,400

Reg·gan \'reg-ən\ oasis *cen* Algeria in Tanezrouft SSE of Colomb-Béchar

Reg·gio, 1 *or* **Reggio di Ca·la·bria** *or* **Reggio Calabria** \,rej-(ē-)(,)ō-,dē-kə-'läb-rē-ə\ *or anc* **Rhe·gi·um** \'rē-jē-əm\ commune & port S Italy on Strait of Messina ✳ of Calabria *pop* 139,459 **2** *or* **Reggio nel·l'Emi·lia** \-,nel-ə-'mēl-yə\ *or* **Reggio Emilia** commune N Italy in Emilia-Romagna NW of Bologna *pop* 106,847

Re·gi·na \ri-'jī-nə\ city Canada ✳ of Sask. *pop* 89,755

Reims *or* **Rheims** \'rēmz, F raⁿs\ city NE France ENE of Paris *pop* 121,145

Reindeer lake Canada on Man.-Sask. border *area* 2444

Reisui — see YOSU

Re·ma·gen \'rā-,mäg-ən\ town W Germany on W bank of the Rhine NW of Koblenz

Rem·scheid \'rem-,shīt\ city W Germany in No. Rhine-Westphalia ESE of Düsseldorf *pop* 124,200

Ren·do·va \ren-'dō-və\ island W Pacific in *cen* Solomons off SW *cen* coast of New Georgia I.

Ren·frew \'ren-(,)frü\ *or* **Ren·frew·shire** \-,shi(ə)r, -shər\ county SW Scotland ✳ Paisley *area* 227, *pop* 324,652

Rennes \'ren\ city NW France N of Nantes *pop* 124,122

Re·no \'rē-(,)nō\ city W Nev. NNE of Lake Tahoe *pop* 51,470

Ren·ton \'rent-°n\ city W Wash. SE of Seattle *pop* 18,453

Republican river 445 *m* Nebr. & Kans. rising in E Colo. & flowing E to unite with the Smoky Hill forming Kansas river

Re·si·ta \'resh-ət-,sä\ *or* **Re·ci·ta** \'rech-\ commune SW Romania 65 *m* SE of Arad *pop* 45,583

Re·thondes \rə-'tōⁿd\ village N France E of Compiègne

Ré·u·nion \rē-'yün-yən\ island W Indian ocean in the W Mascarenes ✳ St-Denis; an overseas department of France *area* 970, *pop* 274,370

Reut·ling·en \'rȯit-liŋ-ən\ city W Germany in Baden-Württemberg S of Stuttgart *pop* 61,400

Reval *or* **Revel** — see TALLIN

Re·vere \ri-'vi(ə)r\ city E Mass. NE of Boston *pop* 40,080

Re·vil·la·gi·ge·do \ri-,vil-ə-gə-'gēd-(,)ō\ island SE Alaska in SE Alexander archipelago E of Prince of Wales I.

Re·vil·la Gi·ge·do \ri-,vē-(y)ə-hi-'hā-(,)thō\ islands Mexico in the Pacific *ab* 300 *m* SW of S end of Lower California

Reyes, Point \'rāz\ cape W Calif. at S extremity of peninsula extending into the Pacific 30 *m* NW of Golden Gate, in **Point Reyes National Seashore** (established 1962)

Rey·kja·vík \'rāk-yə-,vēk, -,vik\ city & port ✳ of Iceland *pop* 69,268

Rey·no·sa \rā-'nō-sə\ city NE Mexico in Tamaulipas on Rio Grande *pop* 108,540

Rezaieh *or* **Rezayeh** — see RIZAIYEH
Rhae·tia *or* **Rae·tia** \'rē-sh(ē-)ə\ ancient Roman province *cen* Europe S of the Danube including most of modern Tirol & Vorarlberg region of Austria & Graubünden canton of E Switzerland —**Rhae·tian** \-sh(ē-)ən\ *adj or n*
Rhaetian Alps section of Alps E Switzerland in E Graubünden — see BERNINA
Rha·ges \'rā-jəz\ *or* **Rha·gae** \-(,)jē\ *or Bib* **Ra·ges** \'rā-jəz\ city of ancient Media; ruins at modern village of Rai \'rī\ S of Tehran, Iran
Rheinfall — see SCHAFFHAUSEN
Rheinpfalz — see PALATINATE
Rhenish Palatinate *or* **Rhine Palatinate** — see PALATINATE
Rheydt \'rīt\ city W Germany S of München-Gladbach *pop* 94,900
Rhine \'rīn\ *or* G **Rhein** \'rīn\ *or* F **Rhin** \raⁿ\ *or* D **Rijn** \'rīn\ river 820 *m* W Europe flowing from SE Switzerland to North sea in the Netherlands — **Rhe·nish** \'ren-ish, 'rē-nish\ *adj*
Rhine, Falls of the — see SCHAFFHAUSEN
Rhine·land \'rīn-,land, -lənd\ *or* G **Rhein·land** \'rīn-,länt\ **1** the part of W Germany W of the Rhine **2** RHINE PROVINCE — **Rhine·land·er** \'rīn-,lan-dər, -lən-\ *n*
Rhineland-Palatinate *or* G **Rheinland-Pfalz** \-'(p)fälts\ state of Federal Republic of Germany chiefly W of the Rhine ✻ Mainz *area* 7654, *pop* 3,411,200
Rhine Province *or* **Rhenish Prussia** former province of Prussia, Germany, bordering on Belgium ✻ Koblenz
Rhode Is·land \rō-'dī-lənd\ **1** *or officially* **Rhode Island and Providence Plantations** state NE U.S. ✻ Providence *area* 1214, *pop* 859,488 **2** — see AQUIDNECK — **Rhode Is·land·er** \-lən-dər\ *n*
Rhodes \'rōdz\ *or* NGk **Ró·dhos** \'rò-,t͟hòs\ **1** island Greece in the SE Aegean, chief island of the Dodecanese *area* 545 **2** city, its ✻ *pop* 24,186 — **Rho·di·an** \'rōd-ē-ən\ *adj or n*
Rho·de·sia \rō-'dē-zh(ē-)ə\ region *cen* S Africa S of Congo — see NORTHERN RHODESIA, SOUTHERN RHODESIA — **Rho·de·sian** \-zh(ē-)ən\ *adj or n*
Rhodesia and Nyasaland, Federation of former country S Africa comprising Southern Rhodesia, Northern Rhodesia, & Nyasaland; a federal state within the Brit. Commonwealth; dissolved 1963
Rhod·o·pe \'räd-ə-(,)pē\ mountains S Bulgaria & NE Greece; highest point Slav Peak 7576 *ft*
Rhon·dda \'rän-də, '(h)rän-t͟hə\ urban district SE Wales in Glamorganshire *pop* 111,357
Rhone *or* F **Rhône** \'rōn\ river 500 *m* Switzerland & France flowing through Lake of Geneva into the Mediterranean
Rhyl \'ril\ urban district & port NE Wales in Flintshire at mouth of the Clwyd *pop* 18,745
Ri·al·to \rē-'al-(,)tō\ **1** city SW Calif. W of San Bernardino *pop* 18,567 **2** island & district of Venice, Italy
Riazan — see RYAZAN
Ri·bei·rão Prê·to \,rē-və-'raùⁿ-'prā-(,)tü\ city SE Brazil in N *cen* São Paulo state *pop* 63,312
Rich·ard·son \'rich-ərd-sən\ city NE Tex. N of Dallas *pop* 16,810
Rich·e·lieu \'rish-ə-,lü\ river 210 *m* Canada in S Que. flowing N from Lake Champlain to head of Lake St. Peter in the St. Lawrence
Rich·field \'rich-,fēld\ village SE Minn. *pop* 42,523
Rich·land \'rich-lənd\ city SE Wash. at confluence of Yakima & Columbia rivers *pop* 23,548
Rich·mond \'rich-mənd\ **1** city W Calif. NNW of Oakland on San Francisco Bay *pop* 71,854 **2** city E Ind. *pop* 44,149 **3** borough of New York City coextensive with Staten I. *pop* 221,991 **4** city ✻ of Va. on James river *pop* 219,958 **5** municipal borough S England in Surrey on the Thames *pop* 41,945
Richmond Heights city E Mo. W of St. Louis *pop* 15,622
Ri·deau \ri-'dō\ canal system Canada 126 *m* long in SE Ont. connecting Lake Ontario & Ottawa river & including **Rideau Lake** (20 *m* long) & **Rideau river** (flowing into the Ottawa)
Ridge·wood \'rij-,wùd\ township NE N.J. NNE of Paterson *pop* 25,391
Rid·ing Mountain National Park \,rīd-iŋ-\ reservation Canada in SW Man. *area* 1148
Rid·ley \'rid-lē\ urban township SE Pa. SW of Philadelphia *pop* 35,738
Rif *or* **Riff** *or* **Er Rif** *or* **Er Riff** \er-'rif\ mountain range N Morocco on the Mediterranean; highest Tidiguin 8058 *ft*
Rift valley GREAT RIFT VALLEY
Ri·ga \'rē-gə\ city & port U.S.S.R. ✻ of Latvia *pop* 605,000
Riga, Gulf of inlet of Baltic sea between Estonia & Latvia
Ri·je·ka *or* **Ri·e·ka** \rē-'(y)ek-ə\ *or* It **Fiu·me** \'fyü-(,)mā, fē-'ü-\ city & port NW Yugoslavia in Croatia *pop* 76,700
Rijs·wijk \'rīs-,vīk\ *or* E **Rys·wick** \'riz-(,)wik\ commune SW Netherlands near The Hague *pop* 35,372
Ri·mac \rē-'mäk\ river 80 *m* W Peru flowing SW through Lima into the Pacific
Ri·mi·ni \'rim-ə-(,)nē, 'rē-mə-\ *or anc* **Arim·i·num** \ə-'rim-ə-nəm\ commune & port N Italy on the Adriatic ESE of Ravenna *pop* 53,400
Rin·e·an·na \,rin-ē-'an-ə\ village SW Ireland in County Clare
Rio RIO DE JANEIRO
Rio Bran·co \,rē-(,)ō-'braŋ-(,)kō\ **1** — see BRANCO **2** territory NW Brazil bordering on Venezuela & Brit. Guiana ✻ Boa Vista *area* 97,438, *pop* 18,116
Rio de Ja·nei·ro \'rē-(,)ō-,dā-zhə-'ne(ə)r-(,)ō, -,dē-, -də-, -jə-, -'ni(ə)r-\ **1** city & port SE Brazil ✻ of Guanabara state on Guanabara Bay; former ✻ of Brazil *pop* 3,307,163 **2** state SE Brazil ✻ Niterói *area* 16,372, *pop* 2,297,194
Rio de Janeiro Bay — see GUANABARA BAY
Río de la Plata — see PLATA (Río de la)
Río de Oro \,rē-(,)ōd-ē-'ōr-(,)ō, -'ór-\ **1** territory NW Africa comprising the S zone of Spanish Sahara **2** SPANISH SAHARA
Rio Grande \,rē-(,)ō-'grand(-ē) *also* ,rī-(,)ō-'grand\ **1** *or* Mex **Río Bra·vo** \,rē-(,)ō-'bräv-(,)ō\ river 1885 *m* SW U.S. forming part of Mexico-U.S. boundary & flowing from San Juan mountains in SW Colo. to Gulf of Mexico **2** *or* **Rio Gran·de do Sul** \,rē-(,)ō-,grand-ē-də-'sül\ city S Brazil in Rio Grande do Sul state W of entrance to Lagoa dos Patos *pop* 63,235 **3** — see GRANDE (Rio)
Rio Grande de Cagayan — see CAGAYAN
Rio Gran·de do Nor·te \,rē-(,)ō-,grand-ē-də-'nórt-ə\ state NE Brazil ✻ Natal *area* 20,236, *pop* 967,921
Rio Grande do Sul \-'sül\ state SE Brazil bordering on Uruguay ✻ Pôrto Alegre *area* 100,150, *pop* 4,164,821
Río Mu·ni \,rē-(,)ō-'mü-nē\ mainland portion of Spanish Guinea bordering on Gulf of Guinea ✻ Bata *area* 10,040, *pop* 183,377
Río Pie·dras \,rē-(,)ō-pē-'ā-drəs\ former city, since 1951 part of San Juan, Puerto Rico
Ri·ouw \'rē-,aù\ *or* **Rhio** \'rē-(,)ō\ archipelago Indonesia S of Singapore; chief island Bintan *area* 2279, *pop* 77,000
Rip·on Falls \,rip-ən-\ former waterfall in the Victoria Nile N of Lake Victoria; submerged by Owen Falls Dam
Ri·va·da·via *or* **Co·mo·do·ro Rivadavia** \,käm-ə-'dōr-(,)ō-,rē-və-'däv-ē-ə, -'dór-\ city & port S Argentina *pop* 37,000
River Rouge \'rüzh, 'rüj\ city SE Mich. *pop* 18,147
Riv·er·side \'riv-ər-,sīd\ city S Calif. *pop* 84,332
Riv·i·era \,riv-ē-'er-ə\ coast region SE France & NW Italy bordering on the Mediterranean — see CÔTE D'AZUR
Ri·yadh \rē-'(y)äd\ city ✻ of the Nejd & a ✻ of Saudi Arabia *pop* 150,000
Ri·zai·yeh *or* **Re·zai·eh** *or* **Re·za·yeh** \ri-'zī-(y)ə\ *or* **Ur·mia** \'ùr-mē-ə\ **1** shallow saline lake NW Iran **2** city NW Iran W of Lake Rizaiyeh *pop* 67,580
Ri·zal \ri-'zäl, -'säl\ *or* **Pa·say** \'päs-,ī\ city Philippines in Luzon on Manila Bay *pop* 132,178
Rju·kan \rē-'ü-,kän\ town S Norway 75 *m* W of Oslo near **Rjukan Falls** (waterfall 780 *ft*)
Ro·a·noke \'rō-(ə-),nōk\ **1** river 380 *m* S Va. & NE N.C. flowing E & SE into Albemarle Sound **2** island N.C. S of entrance to Albemarle Sound **3** city W *cen* Va. *pop* 97,110
Rob·bins·dale \'räb-ənz-,dāl\ city SE Minn. NW of Minneapolis *pop* 16,381
Rob·erts, Point \'räb-ərts\ cape NW Wash., tip of a peninsula extending S into Strait of Georgia from B.C. & separated from U.S. mainland by Boundary Bay
Rob·son, Mount \'räb-sən\ mountain 12,972 *ft* W Canada in E B.C.; highest in Canadian Rockies
Ro·ca, Cape \'rō-kə\ *or* Port **Ca·bo da Ro·ca** \,kà-vü-t͟hə-'rò-kə\ cape Portugal; westernmost point of continental Europe, at 9°30′W
Roch·dale \'räch-,dāl\ county borough NW England in Lancashire NNE of Manchester *pop* 87,734
Roche·fort \ròsh-'fò(ə)r\ *or* **Rochefort-sur-Mer** \-,sùr-'me(ə)r\ city W France SSE of La Rochelle *pop* 30,858
Ro·cher Noir \,rò-,shän-(ə-)'wär, ,rō-\ town N Algeria 20 *m* E of Algiers
Roch·es·ter \'räch-ə-stər, -,es-tər\ **1** city SE Minn. *pop* 40,663 **2** city SE N.H. *pop* 15,927 **3** city W N.Y. on Genesee river *pop* 318,611 **4** municipal borough SE England in Kent *pop* 43,899
Rock \'räk\ river 300 *m* S Wis. & N Ill. flowing S & SW into the Mississippi at Rock Island
Rock·all \'räk-,òl\ islet N Atlantic NW of Ireland, at 57°36′ N, 13°41′ W
Rock·ford \'räk-fərd\ city N Ill. *pop* 126,706
Rock·hamp·ton \räk-'(h)am(p)-tən\ city & port E Australia in E Queensland on Fitzroy river *pop* 42,200
Rock Hill city N S.C. SSW of Charlotte, N.C. *pop* 29,404
Rock Island city NW Ill. on the Mississippi *pop* 51,863
Rock·ville \'räk-,vil, -vəl\ city SW Md. *pop* 26,090
Rockville Centre village SE N.Y. in W *cen* Long I. *pop* 26,355
Rocky \'räk-ē\ mountains W No. America extending from N Alaska SE to *cen* N. Mex. — see ELBERT (Mount), ROBSON (Mount)
Rocky Mount city NE *cen* N.C. *pop* 32,147
Rocky Mountain National Park reservation N Colo. NW of Denver *area* 400
Rocky River city NE Ohio on Lake Erie W of Cleveland *pop* 18,097
Ródhos — see RHODES
Ro·dri·gues *or* **Ro·dri·guez** \rō-'drē-gəs\ island Indian ocean in the Mascarenes; a dependency of Mauritius; chief town Port Mathurin *area* 40, *pop* 17,018
Rogue \'rōg\ river 220 *m* SW Oreg. rising in Crater Lake National Park & flowing W & SW into the Pacific
Ro·hil·khand \'rō-,hil-,kənd\ *or* **Ba·reil·ly** \bə-'rā-lē\ region N India in Uttar Pradesh; chief city Bareilly
Ro·ma·gna \rō-'män-yə\ district N Italy on the Adriatic comprising the E part of Emilia-Romagna region
Roman Campagna — see CAMPAGNA DI ROMA
Ro·ma·nia *or* **Ru·ma·nia** *or* **Rou·ma·nia** \rù-'mā-nē-ə, rō-, -nyə\ country SE Europe bordering on Black sea ✻ Bucharest *area* 91,934, *pop* 18,255,504
Rom·blon \räm-'blän\ **1** islands Philippines in N Visayan islands in Sibuyan sea *area* 512 **2** island, largest of the group
Rome \'rōm\ **1** city NW Ga. NW of Atlanta *pop* 32,226 **2** city E *cen* N.Y. NW of Utica *pop* 51,646 **3** *or* It **Ro·ma** \'rō-mä\ *or anc* **Ro·ma** \'rō-mə\ city ✻ of Italy on the Tiber *pop* 2,160,773 **4** the Roman Empire
Rome, Duchy of division of Byzantine Empire 6th to 8th century *cen* Italy comprising most of modern Latium; later a province of the States of the Church called **Patrimony of Saint Pe·ter** \'pēt-ər\
Rom·ford \'rəm(p)-fərd, 'räm(p)-\ municipal borough SE England in Essex ENE of London *pop* 87,991
Ron·ces·va·lles \,rón(t)-səs-'vä(l)-,yäs\ *or* F **Ron·ce·vaux** \,rōⁿs-(ə-)'vō\ commune N Spain 5 *m* from French boundary in the Pyrenees near **Pass of Roncesvalles** (3648 *ft*)
Ron·dô·nia \rōⁿ(n)-'dōn-yə\ *or formerly* **Gua·po·ré** \,gwäp-ə-'rā\ territory W Brazil ✻ Porto Velho *area* 96,986, *pop* 1,844,655
Rong·er·ik \'ròŋ-ə-(,)rik\ island W *cen* Pacific in the Marshalls in Ratak chain E of Bikini
Roo·de·poort-Ma·rais·burg \'rüd-ə-,pù(ə)rt-mə-'rāz-,bərg\ city Republic of So. Africa in Transvaal W of Johannesburg *pop* 78,296
Roo·se·velt \'rō-zə-,velt, -vəlt *also* 'rü-\ river 200 *m* W *cen* Brazil flowing from W Mato Grosso state N into the Aripuanã
Ro·rai·ma \rō-'rī-mə\ mountain 8620 *ft* N So. America in Serra Pacaraima on boundary between Venezuela, Brit. Guiana, & Brazil; has flat top 9 *m* long & 3 *m* wide
Ror·schach \'rò(ə)r-,shäk, -,shäk\ commune NE Switzerland on S shore of Lake Constance
Ro·sa, Mon·te \,mänt-ē-'rō-zə\ mountain 15,217 *ft* on Swiss-Italian border; highest point in Pennine Alps
Ro·sa·rio \rō-'zär-ē-,ō, -'sär-\ city E *cen* Argentina on the Paraná *pop* 551,276
Ros·com·mon \rä-'skäm-ən\ **1** county *cen* Ireland *area* 951, *pop* 59,215 **2** town, its ✻
Rose, Mount \'rōz\ mountain 10,800 *ft* W Nev. in Carson range SW of Reno

Ro·selle \rō-'zel\ borough NE N.J. W of Elizabeth *pop* 21,032

Rose·mead \'rōz-ˌmēd\ city SW Calif. E of Los Angeles *pop* 15,476

Ro·set·ta \rō-'zet-ə\ *or* **Ra·shid** \rä-'shēd\ *or anc* **Bol·bi·ti·ne** \ˌbäl-bə-'tī-nē\ **1** river 146 *m* N Egypt forming W branch of the Nile in its delta **2** city N Egypt on the Rosetta *pop* 32,800

Rose·ville \'rōz-ˌvil\ **1** city SE Mich. NE of Detroit *pop* 50,195 **2** village SE Minn. N of St. Paul *pop* 23,997

Ross \'ros\ **1** urban township SW Pa. near Pittsburgh *pop* 25,952 **2** sea arm of S Pacific extending into Antarctica E of Victoria Land

Ross and Crom·ar·ty \'kräm-ərt-ē\ county N Scotland ✶ Ding-wall *area* 3089, *pop* 60,503

Rossbodenhorn — see FLETSCHHORN

Ross Dependency section of Antarctica lying S of 60°S lat. & between 160°E & 150°W long.; administered by New Zealand

Ross Ice Shelf ice sheet Antarctica in S Ross sea *area ab* 208,400

Ros·tock \'räs-ˌtäk, 'rô-ˌstôk\ city & port E Germany on Warnow river near the Baltic coast *pop* 151,811

Ros·tov \rə-'stôf, -'stôv\ *or* **Rostov-on-Don** \-ˌon-'dän, -ˌän-\ city E S in Soviet Russia, Europe, on the Don *pop* 597,000

Ro·ta \'rōt-ə\ **1** island W Pacific at S end of the Marianas *area* 35 **2** town & port SW Spain on the Atlantic NW of Cádiz

Roth·er·ham \'räth-ə-rəm\ county borough N England in West Riding, Yorkshire, N of Sheffield *pop* 82,334

Rothe·say \'räth-sē\ burgh SW Scotland on island of Bute ✶ of Buteshire

Ro·to·rua \ˌrōt-ə-'rü-ə\ borough New Zealand in N *cen* North I.

Rot·ter·dam \'rät-ər-ˌdam\ **1** urban area E N.Y. NW of Schenectady *pop* 16,871 **2** city & port SW Netherlands on the Nieuwe Maas *pop* 731,047

Ro·tu·ma \rō-'tü-mə\ island SW Pacific N of Fiji islands *area* 14; belongs to Fiji

Rou·baix \rü-'bā\ city N France NE of Lille *pop* 110,067

Rou·en \rü-'än, -'än\ city & port N France on the Seine *pop* 116,540

Roumania — see ROMANIA

Rous·sil·lon \ˌrü-sē-'(y)ōⁿ\ region & former province S France bordering on the Pyrenees & the Mediterranean ✶ Perpignan

Rou·yn \'rü-ən\ urban area Canada in SW Que. *pop* 17,076

Rox·burgh \'räks-bər-ə, -ˌbə-rə, -b(ə-)rə\ *or* **Rox·burgh·shire** \-ˌshi(ə)r, -shər\ county SE Scotland ✶ Jedburgh *area* 666, *pop* 45,562

Royal Gorge section of the canyon of Arkansas river S *cen* Colo. W of Canon City

Royal Oak city SE Mich. N of Detroit *pop* 80,612

Ruad — see ARWAD

Ru·an·da–Urun·di \rü-ˌän-də-ü-'rün-dē\ *or* **Belgian East Africa** former country E *cen* Africa bordering on Lake Tanganyika & comprising two districts, **Ruanda** (✶ Kigali) & **Urundi** (✶ Usumbura), administered by Belgium under League of Nations mandate 1919–45 & under UN trusteeship 1946–62 ✶ Usumbura — see BURUNDI, RWANDA

Ru·a·pe·hu \ˌrü-ə-'pā-(ˌ)hü\ volcano 9175 *ft* New Zealand, highest peak in North I., in Tongariro National Park

Rub' al Kha·li \ˌrüb-ˌal-'käl-ē\ *or* **Ar Ri·mal** \ˌär-rə-'mal\ desert region S Arabia extending from Nejd S to Hadhramaut *area* 300,000

Rubicon — see FIUMICINO

Ru·dolf, Lake \'rü-ˌdälf\ lake N Kenya in Great Rift valley *area* 3500

Ru·fisque \rü-'fēsk\ city & port W Senegal *pop* 49,800

Rug·by \'rəg-bē\ municipal borough *cen* England in Warwickshire on the Avon *pop* 45,418

Rü·gen \'rü-gən, 'rē-\ island E Germany in Baltic sea off coast of Pomerania *area* 374

Ruhr \'ru̇(ə)r\ **1** river 144 *m* W Germany flowing NW & W to the Rhine **2** industrial district, valley of the Ruhr river

Ruis·lip North·wood \ˌrī-sləp-'nȯrth-ˌwu̇d\ urban district S England in Middlesex W of London *pop* 68,274

Rumania — see ROMANIA

Ru·me·lia *or* **Rou·me·lia** \rü-'mēl-yə, -'mē-lē-ə\ a division of the old Ottoman Empire including Albania, Macedonia, & Thrace

Run·ny·mede \'rən-i-ˌmēd\ meadow S England in Surrey on S bank of the Thames in Egham urban district

Ru·pert \'rü-pərt\ river 380 *m* Canada in W Que. flowing W into James Bay

Ru·pert's Land \'rü-pərts-\ territory of the Hudson's Bay Company 1670–1869 N Canada; the drainage basin of Hudson Bay

Ru·se \'rü-(ˌ)sā\ *or* Turk **Rus·chuk** \'rüs-ˌchük\ city NE Bulgaria on the Danube S of Bucharest *pop* 53,420

Rush·more, Mount \'rəsh-ˌmō(ə)r, -ˌmȯ(ə)r\ mountain 6200 *ft* W S. Dak. in Black hills on which are carved gigantic faces of Washington, Jefferson, Lincoln, Theodore Roosevelt; a national memorial

Rus·sell Cave National Monument \ˌrəs-əl-\ reservation NE Ala. including cavern where remains of early pre-Columbian man have been found

Rus·sia \'rəsh-ə\ *or* Russ **Ros·si·ya** \rä-'sē-yə\ **1** former empire E Europe & N Asia coextensive (except for Finland & Kars region) with the present U.S.S.R. ✶ Petrograd **2** RUSSIAN REPUBLIC **3** the U.S.S.R.

Russian Republic *or* **Soviet Russia** constituent republic of the U.S.S.R. in E Europe (**Soviet Russia, Europe**) & N Asia (**Soviet Russia, Asia**) bordering on Arctic & Pacific oceans & on Baltic & Black seas ✶ Moscow *area* 6,501,500, *pop* 118,900,000

Russian Turkestan region comprising the republics of Soviet Central Asia

Ru·the·nia \rü-'thē-nyə, -nē-ə\ *or* **Carpathian Ruthenia** *or* **Za·kar·pat·ska·ya** \ˌzäk-ər-'pät-skə-yə\ region U.S.S.R. in W Ukraine S of the Carpathian mountains; part of Hungary before 1918 & 1939–45; a province of Czechoslovakia 1918–38 ✶ Uzhgorod — **Ru·thene** \-'thēn\ *n* — **Ru·the·nian** \-'thē-nyən, -nē-ən\ *adj or n*

Ruth·er·ford \'rəth-ə(r)-fərd, 'rəth-\ borough NE N.J. SSE of Paterson on Passaic river *pop* 20,473

Ruth·in \'rith-ən\ municipal borough N Wales ✶ of Denbighshire

Rut·land \'rət-lənd\ **1** city W *cen* Vt. *pop* 18,325 **2** *or* **Rut·land·shire** \-lən(d)-ˌshi(ə)r, -shər\ county E *cen* England ✶ Oakham *area* 152, *pop* 63,784

Ru·vu·ma *or* **Port Ro·vu·ma** \rü-'vü-mə\ river 400 *m* SE Africa rising in S Tanganyika & flowing E into Indian ocean on Mozambique border

Ru·wen·zo·ri \ˌrü-(w)ən-'zōr-ē, -'zȯr-\ mountain group E *cen* Africa between Uganda & Congo — see STANLEY

Rwan·da \rü-'än-də\ *or formerly* **Ru·an·da** country E *cen* Africa; a republic ✶ Kigali *area* 10,166, *pop* 3,000,000 — see RUANDA-URUNDI — **Rwan·dan** *adj or n*

Rya·zan *or* **Ria·zan** \ˌrē-ə-'zän(-yə)\ city in *cen* Soviet Russia, Europe, on Oka river SE of Moscow *pop* 213,000

Ry·binsk \'rib-ən(t)sk\ *or* **Shcher·ba·kov** \ˌsh(ch)er-bə-'kȯf, -'kov\ city U.S.S.R. in *cen* Soviet Russia, Europe, NNE of Moscow on the Volga at SE end of Rybinsk reservoir *pop* 181,000

Rye \'rī\ municipal borough SE England in East Sussex

Ryswick — see RIJSWIJK

Ryu·kyu \rē-'(y)ü-(ˌ)k(y)ü\ *or* **Liu·chiu** \'lü-'chü\ *or* **Nan·sei** \'nän-ˌsā\ islands W Pacific extending from Kyushu, Japan, to Formosa, China; belonged to Japan 1895–1945; now divided between Japan & U.S. *area* 1803 — see AMAMI, OKINAWA, OSUMI, SAKISHIMA, TOKARA — **Ryu·kyu·an** \rē-ˌ(y)ü'k(y)ü-ən\ *adj or n*

Saa·le \'zäl-ə, 'sä-\ river 226 *m* Germany rising in NE Bavaria in the Fichtel Gebirge & flowing N into the Elbe

Saar \'sär, 'zär\ **1** *or* F **Sarre** \sàr\ river 84 *m* Europe flowing from Vosges mountains in France N to the Moselle in Germany **2** *or* **Saar·land** \'sär-ˌland, 'zär-\ region W Europe in basin of Saar river between France & Germany; once part of Lorraine, became part of Germany in 19th century; administered by League of Nations 1919–35; became a state of Germany 1935; came under control of France after World War II; to West Germany by a plebiscite Jan. 1, 1957, as a state (**Saarland**) ✶ Saarbrücken *area* 898, *pop* 1,060,500

Saar·brück·en \ˌzär-'brük-ən, sär-, -'brik-\ *or* F **Sar·re·bruck** \sà-rə-brük\ city W Germany ✶ of Saarland *pop* 128,700

Saaremaa — see SAREMA

Sa·ba, 1 \'säb-ə\ island SE West Indies in Netherlands Antilles ✶ The Bottom (situated in a crater 800 *ft* above sea level) *area* 5, *pop* 1085 **2** — see SHEBA

Sa·ba·dell \ˌsab-ə-'del(-ə)\ commune NE Spain N of Barcelona *pop* 82,970

Sabah — see NORTH BORNEO

Sa·bar·ma·ti \ˌsäb-ər-'mət-ē\ river 200 *m* W India flowing S into head of Gulf of Cambay

Sab·ha \'sab-ə\ *or* **Seb·ha** \'seb-\ town W Libya ✶ of Fezzan

Sa·bi \'säb-ē\ *or* **Sa·ve** \'säv-ə\ river 400 *m* SE Africa rising in *cen* Southern Rhodesia & flowing E across S Mozambique to Mozambique channel

Sa·bine \sə-'bēn\ river 380 *m* E Tex. & W La. flowing SE & emptying through **Sabine Lake** (15 *m* long) & **Sabine Pass** (channel) into Gulf of Mexico

Sa·ble, Cape \'sā-bəl\ **1** cape at SW tip of Fla., southernmost point of U.S. mainland, at *ab* 25°7'N **2** headland E Canada on an islet S of Cape Sable I. (20 *m* long, at S end of N.S.)

Sab·ra·tha \'sab-rə-thə\ *or anc* **Sab·ra·ta** \-rət-ə\ town Libya on the coast WNW of Tripoli

Sachsen — see SAXONY

Sa·co \'sȯ-(ˌ)kō\ river 104 *m* E N.H. & SW Me. flowing SE to the Atlantic

Sac·ra·men·to \ˌsak-rə-'ment-(ˌ)ō\ **1** mountains S N. Mex. — see GUADALUPE, SIERRA BLANCA **2** river 382 *m* N Calif. flowing S into Suisun Bay **3** city ✶ of Calif. on Sacramento river *pop* 191,667

Sa·do·wa \ˌsä-'dō-və, sä-\ village Czechoslovakia in NE Bohemia

Sa·fed Koh \sə-ˌfed-'kō\ mountain range E Afghanistan on Pakistan border; a S extension of the Hindu Kush

Sa·fi \'saf-ē\ city & port W Morocco *pop* 56,751

Sa·ga·mi \sə-'gäm-ē\ sea inlet of the Pacific Japan in *cen* Honshu SW of Tokyo Bay

Saghalien — see SAKHALIN

Sag·i·naw \'sag-ə-ˌnȯ\ city E *cen* Mich. *pop* 98,265

Saginaw Bay inlet of Lake Huron in E Mich.

Sa·gres \'sag-rēsh\ village SW Portugal E of Cape St. Vincent

Saguache — see SAWATCH

Sa·gua·ro National Monument \sə-'(g)wär-(ˌ)ō\ reservation SE Ariz. E of Tucson *area* 84

Sag·ue·nay \ˌsag-ə-'nā\ river 125 *m* Canada in S Que. flowing from Lake St. John E into the St. Lawrence

Sa·guia el Ham·ra \sə-ˌgē-ə-ˌel-'häm-rə\ *or* **Se·kia el Hamra** \-ˌkē-ə\ territory NW Africa, the N zone of Spanish Sahara

Sa·gun·to \sə-'gün-(ˌ)tō\ *or formerly* **Mur·vie·dro** \ˌmür-vē-'ā-(ˌ)thrō\ commune E Spain NNE of Valencia *pop* 26,987

Sahama — see SAJAMA

Sa·ha·ra \sə-'har-ə, -'her-, -'här-\ desert region N Africa N of the Sudan region extending from the Atlantic coast to Red sea or, as sometimes considered, to the Nile — **Sa·ha·ran** \-ən\ *adj*

Sa·ha·ran·pur \sə-'här-ən-ˌpu̇(ə)r\ city N India in NW Uttar Pradesh NNE of Delhi *pop* 148,400

Saida — see SIDON

Sai·gon \sī-'gän, 'sī-ˌ\ city & port ✶ of So. Vietnam in Cochin China on Saigon river *pop* 1,614,200

Sai·maa \'sī-ˌmä\ lake SE Finland, largest of the **Saimaa Lakes**

Saint Al·bans \'ȯl-bənz\ **1** city W W. Va. *pop* 15,103 **2** city & municipal borough SE England in Hertfordshire *pop* 44,106

Saint Ber·nard \ˌsānt-bə(r)-'närd\ two Alpine passes — see GREAT SAINT BERNARD, LITTLE SAINT BERNARD

Saint Bon·i·face \-'bän-ə-ˌfäs\ city Canada in SE Man. on Red river opposite Winnipeg *pop* 28,851

Saint Cath·a·rines \'kath-(ə-)rənz\ city Canada in SE Ont. NW of Niagara Falls on the Welland ship canal *pop* 39,708

Saint Charles \'chär(ə)lz\ city E Mo. on the Missouri *pop* 21,189

Saint Clair, Lake \'kla(ə)r, 'kle(ə)r\ lake SE Mich. & SE Ont. *area* 460, connected by **Saint Clair river** (40 *m*) with Lake Huron & draining through Detroit river into Lake Erie

Saint Clair Shores city SE Mich. NE of Detroit *pop* 76,657

ə abut; ᵊ kitten; ər further; a back; ā bake; ä cot, cart; au̇ out; ch chin; e less; ē easy; g gift; i trip; ī life
j joke; ŋ sing; ō flow; ȯ flaw; ȯi coin; th thin; t͟h this; ü loot; u̇ foot; y yet; yü few; yu̇ furious; zh vision
ᵊ F table; à F bac; ḵ G ich, Buch; ⁿ F vin; œ F bœuf; œ̄ F feu; ᴜe G füllen; ᵫ F rue; ʸ F digne \dēnʸ\, nuit \nwēʸ\

Saint Cloud \'klau̇d\ city *cen* Minn. on the Mississippi *pop* 33,815
Saint-Cloud \sant-'klau̇d, sənt-; sa^{n}-klü\ commune France, WSW suburb of Paris *pop* 16,600
Saint Croix \sānt-'krȯi, sənt-\ **1** river 75 *m* Canada & U.S. on border between N.B. & Me. **2** river 164 *m* NW Wis. & E Minn. flowing into the Mississippi
Saint Croix *or* **San·ta Cruz** \,sant-ə-'krüz\ island West Indies, largest of the Virgin Islands of the U.S. *area* 80, *pop* 14,973
Saint-Cyr-l'École \sa^{n}-si(ə)r-lā-kȯl\ town N France W of Versailles
Saint-De·nis \,sa^{n}(t)-də-'nē\ **1** commune N France NNE of Paris *pop* 80,705 **2** commune ✻ of Réunion I. *pop* 41,863
Saint Eli·as \,sānt-i-'lī-əs\ mountain range of the Coast ranges SW Yukon Territory & E Alaska — see LOGAN (Mount)
Saint Elias, Mount mountain 18,008 *ft* on Alaska-Canada boundary in St. Elias range
Saint-Étienne \sa^{n}-tā-tyen\ city SE *cen* France *pop* 181,730
Saint Eu·sta·ti·us \,sānt-yü-'stā-sh(ē-)əs\ island West Indies in Netherlands Antilles NW of St. Kitts *area* 7
Saint Fran·cis \sānt-'fran(t)-səs, sənt-\ **1** river 425 *m* SE Mo. & E Ark. flowing S into the Mississippi **2** *or* **Saint Fran·çois** \sa^{n}-frä^{n}-swä\ river 165 *m* Canada in S Que. flowing NW into the St. Lawrence
Saint Fran·cis, Lake \'fran(t)-səs\ expansion of St. Lawrence river Canada above Valleyfield, Que.
Saint Gall \sānt-'gȯl, sənt-, -'gal\ *or* G **Sankt Gal·len** \zäŋ(k)t-'gäl-ən\ **1** canton NE Switzerland *area* 800, *pop* 318,200 **2** commune, its ✻ *pop* 70,700
Saint George's channel \,jȯr-jəz-\ strait British Isles between SW Wales & Ireland
Saint-Ger·main \,sa^{n}-zhər-'ma^{n}\ *or* **Saint-Ger·main-en-Laye** \-,ma^{n}-,nä^{n}-'lā\ commune N France WNW of Paris *pop* 29,429
Saint-Gilles \sa^{n}-'zhē(ə)l\ *or* Flem **Sint-Gil·lis** \sənt-'gil-əs\ commune *cen* Belgium near Brussels *pop* 56,532
Saint Gott·hard *or* **Saint Got·hard** \sānt-'gät-ərd, sənt-; ,sa^{n}-gə-'tär\ *or* G **Sankt Gott·hard** \zäŋ(k)t-'gȯt-,härt\ **1** mountains Switzerland in Lepontine Alps between Uri & Ticino cantons **2** mountain pass 6935 *ft* in St. Gotthard range
Saint He·le·na \,sānt-^{ə}l-'ē-nə, ,sānt-hə-'lē-\ island S Atlantic; a Brit. colony ✻ Jamestown *area* 47, *pop* 4802
Saint Hel·ens \sānt-'hel-ənz, sənt-\ county borough NW England in Lancashire ENE of Liverpool *pop* 110,276
Saint Helens, Mount mountain 9671 *ft* SW Wash. in Cascades
Saint Hel·ier \'hel-yər\ town Channel islands ✻ of Jersey *pop* 25,824
Saint-Hy·a·cinthe \sānt-'hī-ə-(,)sin(t)th, sənt-; ,sant-yə-'sant\ city Canada in S Que. E of Montreal *pop* 20,439
Saint James \'jāmz\ city Canada in SE Man. *pop* 26,502
Saint-Jean-Cap-Fer·rat \sa^{n}-'zhä^{n}-,kap-fə-'rä\ commune SE France on coast E of Nice
Saint-Jean-de-Luz \sa^{n}-,zhä^{n}-də-'lüz\ town SW France on Bay of Biscay SW of Biarritz
Saint-Jé·rôme \,sa^{n}-zhā-'rōm\ city Canada in S Que. NW of Montreal *pop* 20,645
Saint John \sānt-'jän, sənt-\ **1** river 450 *m* NE U.S. & SE Canada flowing from N Me. into Bay of Fundy in N.B. **2** city & port Canada in S N.B. on Bay of Fundy at mouth of the St. John *pop* 52,491 **3** island West Indies, one of the Virgin Islands of the U.S. *area* 20, *pop* 925
Saint John, Lake *or* **Lac Saint-Jean** \läk-sa^{n}-zhä^{n}\ lake Canada in S Que. draining through the Saguenay to the St. Lawrence *area* 350
Saint Johns \sānt-'jänz, sənt-\ **1** river 276 *m* NE Fla. flowing N & E into the Atlantic **2** town Brit. West Indies ✻ of Antigua on Antigua I. **3** *or* **Saint-Jean** \sa^{n}-zhä^{n}\ city Canada in S Que. SE of Montreal on Richelieu river *pop* 24,367
Saint John's \sānt-'jänz, sənt-\ city & port Canada ✻ of Nfld. *pop* 57,078
Saint Jo·seph \'jō-zəf *also* -səf\ city NW Mo. *pop* 79,673
Saint Kitts \'kits\ *or* **Saint Chris·to·pher** \'kris-tə-fər\ island Brit. West Indies in the Leewards; chief town Basseterre *area* 68; with Nevis forms **Saint Kitts-Nevis** Associated State (✻ Basseterre *area* 152, *pop* 58,578)
Saint-Lau·rent \,sa^{n}-lə-'rä^{n}\ city Canada in S Que. on Montreal I. *pop* 38,291
Saint Law·rence \sānt-'lȯr-ən(t)s, sənt-, -'lär-\ **1** island 95 *m* long W Alaska in N Bering sea **2** river 760 *m* E Canada in Ont. & Que. bordering on the U.S. in N.Y. & flowing from Lake Ontario NE into the Atlantic forming at its mouth a wide bay (the **Gulf of Saint Lawrence**) **3** seaway Canada & U.S. in & along the St. Lawrence from Lake Ontario to Montreal affording (with Welland ship canal) deep-draft navigation between Great Lakes & the Atlantic
Saint Lawrence, Lake expansion of St. Lawrence river Canada & U.S. above Cornwall, Ont.
Saint Lawrence Islands National Park reservation E Canada in Ont. comprising a number of islands in the Thousand islands group & an area on the shore of the St. Lawrence *area* 166 acres
Saint-Lô \sānt-'lō, sənt-; sa^{n}-lō\ commune NW France W of Caen
Saint Lou·is \sānt-'lü-əs, sənt-\ **1** river 220 *m* NE Minn. flowing to W tip of Lake Superior **2** city E Mo. *pop* 750,026
Saint-Louis \,sa^{n}-lü-'ē\ **1** city & port Senegal on island at mouth of Senegal river; formerly ✻ of Senegal *pop* 63,000 **2** city & port Réunion I. *pop* 25,220
Saint Louis, Lake \sānt-'lü-ē, sənt-\ expansion of St. Lawrence river Canada above Lachine rapids
Saint Louis Park \,lü-əs-\ city SE Minn. *pop* 43,310
Saint Lu·cia \sānt-'lü-shə, sənt-; ,sānt-lü-'sē-ə\ island Brit. West Indies in the Windwards S of Martinique; an Associated State ✻ Castries *area* 233, *pop* 92,089
Saint-Ma·lo \,sa^{n}-mə-'lō\ town & port NW France in Brittany on island in Gulf of St-Malo
Saint-Malo, Gulf of arm of English channel NW France between Cotentin peninsula & Brittany
Saint Mar·tin \sānt-'märt-^{ə}n, sənt-\ island West Indies in the N Leewards; divided between France & Netherlands *area* 38
Saint Marylebone — see MARYLEBONE
Saint Mar·ys \'me(ə)r-ēz, 'ma(ə)r-ēz, 'mā-rēz\ **1** river 175 *m* on Fla.-Ga. border flowing from Okefenokee swamp to the Atlantic **2** river 63 *m* between Canada & U.S. in Ont. & upper peninsula of Mich. flowing from Lake Superior into Lake Huron; descends 20 *ft* in a mile at **Saint Marys Falls** — see SAULT SAINTE MARIE CANALS
Saint-Maur-des-Fos·sés \sa^{n}-mȯr-dā-fō-sā\ commune N France SE of Paris on the Marne *pop* 64,387
Saint Mau·rice \sānt-'mȯr-əs, sənt-, -'mär-; ,sa^{n}-mə-'rēs, ,sānt-\ river 325 *m* Canada in S Que. flowing S into the St. Lawrence
Saint-Mi·chel \sa^{n}-mē-shel\ city Canada in S Que. on Montreal I. *pop* 24,706
Saint-Mi·hiel \sa^{n}-mē-yel\ town NE France on the Meuse NW of Nancy
Saint Mo·ritz \,sānt-mə-'rits\ *or* G **Sankt Mo·ritz** \,zäŋ(k)t-mə-'rits\ town E Switzerland in Graubünden canton SSE of Chur
Saint-Na·zaire \,sa^{n}-nə-'za(ə)r, -'ze(ə)r\ commune & port NW France at mouth of the Loire *pop* 39,350
Sain·tonge \sa^{n}-tō^{n}zh\ region & former province of France on Bay of Biscay N of the Gironde ✻ Saintes
Saint-Ouen \sa^{n}-twa^{n}\ commune France, N suburb of Paris *pop* 48,112
Saint Pan·cras \sānt-'paŋ-krəs, sənt-\ metropolitan borough NW London, England *pop* 138,364
Saint Paul \'pȯl\ city ✻ of Minn. *pop* 313,411
Saint Paul Rocks *or* **Saint Paul's Rocks** *or* **Saint Peter and Saint Paul Rocks** *or* Port **Ro·che·dos São Pau·lo** \rə-,shā-thəs-,sau̇n(m)-'pau̇-(,)lü\ rocky islets in the Atlantic 600 *m* NE of Natal, Brazil, at 1°N, 29°15'W; belong to Brazil
Saint Pe·ter, Lake \sānt-'pēt-ər, sənt-\ expansion of St. Lawrence river Canada between Sorel & Three Rivers, Que.
Saint Pe·ters·burg \'pēt-ərz-,bərg\ **1** city W Fla. on Pinellas peninsula SW of Tampa *pop* 181,298 **2** — see LENINGRAD
Saint Pierre \sānt-'pi(ə)r, sənt-; *F* sa^{n}-pyer\ island in the Atlantic off S Nfld.; with nearby island of Miquelon, constitutes French territory of **Saint Pierre and Miq·ue·lon** \'mik-ə-,län. *F* mē-klō^{n}\ (✻ St. Pierre, *area* 93, *pop* 4929)
Saint-Quen·tin \sānt-'kwent-^{ə}n, sənt-, *F* sa^{n}-kä^{n}-ta^{n}\ commune N France on the Somme NW of Laon *pop* 53,866
Saint Si·mon \sānt-'sī-mən, sənt-\ island SE Ga. in the Atlantic
Saint Thom·as \'täm-əs\ **1** island West Indies, one of Virgin Islands of the U.S. *area* 32, *pop* 16,201 **2** — see CHARLOTTE AMALIE **3** city Canada in SE Ont. S of London *pop* 19,129
Saint-Tro·pez \sa^{n}-trō-pā\ commune SE France on the Mediterranean SW of Cannes
Saint Vin·cent \sānt-'vin(t)-sənt, sənt-\ island Brit. West Indies in *cen* Windwards; with N Grenadines, constitutes an Associated State ✻ Kingstown *area* 150, *pop* 81,782
Saint Vincent, Cape *or* Port **Ca·bo de São Vi·cen·te** \'kä-vü-thə-,sau̇n-vē-'sa^{n}(n)-tə\ cape SW Portugal
Saint Vincent, Gulf of inlet of Indian ocean Australia in So. Australia E of Yorke peninsula
Sai·pan \sī-'pän, -'pan, 'sī-,\ island W Pacific in S *cen* Marianas *area* 70, *pop* 7424 — **Sai·pa·nese** \,sī-pə-'nēz, -'nēs\ *adj or n*
Sa·ïs \'sā-əs\ ancient city Egypt in Nile delta on Canopic branch
Saishu — see CHEJU
Sa·ja·ma *or* **Sa·ha·ma** \sə-'häm-ə\ mountain 21,390 *ft* W Bolivia near Chilean boundary
Sa·kai \'säk-,ī\ city Japan in S Honshu on Osaka Bay *pop* 339,863
Sa·kar·ya \sə-'kär-yə\ river 300 *m* NW Turkey in Asia flowing into the Black sea 80 *m* E of the Bosporus
Sa·kha·lin \'sak-ə-,lēn, -lən\ *or formerly* **Sa·ghal·ien** \,säg-əl-'yen\ *or* Jap **Ka·ra·fu·to** \,kär-ə-'füt-(,)ō\ island U.S.S.R. in Sea of Okhotsk N of Hokkaido; formerly (1905–45) divided between Russia & Japan *area* 24,560
Sakhar — see SUKKUR
Sa·ki·shi·ma \,säk-i-'shē-mə\ island group in S Ryukyus off E coast of N Formosa; occupied by the U.S. *area* 343
Sakkara — see SAQQARA
Sa·kon·net river \sə-,kän-ət- -,kən-\ tidal inlet of the Atlantic SE R.I. E of Aquidneck I.
Salaberry-de-Valleyfield — see VALLEYFIELD
Sa·la·do \sə-'läth-(,)ō\ **1** *or in upper course* **Ju·ra·men·to** \,hu̇r-ə-'men-(,)tō\ river 1120 *m* N Argentina flowing from the Andes SE into the Paraná **2** *or* **Des·agua·de·ro** \,dā-,säg-wə-'the(ə)r-(,)ō\ river 850 *m* W *cen* Argentina flowing S into the Colorado
Sa·la·jar *or* **Sa·la·yar** \sə-'lä-,yär\ island Indonesia off SW Celebes I. *area* 256
Sal·a·man·ca \,sal-ə-'maŋ-kə, ,säl-ə-'mäŋ-\ **1** province W Spain *area* 4829, *pop* 424,992 **2** commune, its ✻, WNW of Madrid *pop* 89,949
Sal·a·maua \,sal-ə-'mau̇-ə\ town E North-East New Guinea
Salambria — see PENEUS
Sal·a·mis \'sal-ə-məs\ **1** ancient city Cyprus on E coast **2** island Greece in Saronic gulf off Attica
Sa·lé \sa-'lā\ *or* **Sla** \'slä\ *or* **Sal·li** *or formerly* **Sal·lee** \'sal-ē\ city & port NW Morocco, N suburb of Rabat *pop* 46,582
Sa·lem \'sā-ləm\ **1** city & port NE Mass. NE of Lynn *pop* 39,211 **2** city ✻ of Oreg. on Willamette river *pop* 49,142 **3** town W *cen* Va. WNW of Roanoke *pop* 16,058 **4** city S India in N Madras state SW of Madras *pop* 202,300 **5** JERUSALEM — an ancient name
Sa·ler·no \sə-'lər-(,)nō, -'le(ə)r-\ commune & port S Italy on **Gulf of Salerno** (inlet of Tyrrhenian sea) ESE of Naples *pop* 125,654 — **Sa·ler·ni·tan** \-'lər-nə-tən\ *adj or n*
Sal·ford \'sȯl-fərd\ city & county borough NW England in Lancashire, W suburb of Manchester *pop* 178,036
Sa·li·na \sə-'lī-nə\ city *cen* Kans. on Smoky Hill river *pop* 43,202
Sa·li·nas \sə-'lē-nəs\ **1** river 150 *m* W Calif. flowing NW into Monterey Bay **2** city W Calif. near Monterey Bay *pop* 28,957
Salis·bury \'sȯlz-,ber-ē, 'salz-, -b(ə-)rē\ **1** city SE Md. *pop* 16,302 **2** city W *cen* N.C. SSW of Winston-Salem *pop* 21,297 **3** city ✻ of Southern Rhodesia *pop* 314,200 **4** *or* **New Sar·um** \'sar-əm, 'ser-\ municipal borough S England in Wiltshire on the Avon *pop* 32,910
Salisbury Plain plateau S England in Wiltshire NW of Salisbury
Salm·on \'sam-ən\ river 420 *m*, *cen* Idaho flowing into the Snake
Salmon River mountains *cen* Idaho; many peaks over 9000 *ft*
Sa·lo·ni·ka *or* **Sa·lo·ni·ca** \sə-'län-i-kə, ,sal-ə-'nē-kə\ *or* **Thes·sa·lo·ni·ca** \,thes-ə-lə-'nī-kə, -'län-i-\ *or* NGk **Thes·sa·lo·ní·ki** \,thes-ə-lə-'nē-kē\ *or* **Sa·lo·ní·ki** \,sal-ə-'nē-kē\ city & port N Greece in Macedonia *pop* 216,838
Salonika, Gulf of *or* **Ther·ma·ic Gulf** \,thər-,mā-ik-\ arm of Aegean sea N Greece W of Chalcidice
Salop, 1 — see SHROPSHIRE **2** — see SHREWSBURY — **Sa·lo·pi·an** \sə-'lō-pē-ən\ *adj or n*
Salt \'sȯlt\ **1** river 200 *m* Ariz. flowing W into the Gila **2** river 100 *m* N *cen* Ky. flowing into the Ohio **3** river 200 *m* NE Mo. flowing SE into the Mississippi

Sal·ta \'säl-tə\ city NW Argentina N of Tucumán *pop* 120,000

Sal·ti·llo \säl-'tē-(‚)(y)ō\ city NE Mexico ✳ of Coahuila *pop* 69,869

Salt Lake City *or* **Salt Lake** city ✳ of Utah *pop* 189,454

Sal·to \'säl-(‚)tō\ city & port NW Uruguay on Uruguay river *pop* 60,000

Sal·ton sea \‚sȯlt-ᵊn-\ saline lake *ab* 235 *ft* below sea level SE Calif. at N end of Imperial valley formed by diversion of water from Colorado river into depression formerly called **Salton sink**

Salt sea — see DEAD SEA

Sa·lu·da \sə-'lüd-ə\ river 200 *m* W cen S.C. flowing SE to unite with the Broad forming the Congaree

Sal·va·dor \'sal-və-‚dȯ(ə)r, ‚sal-və-'\ 1 EL SALVADOR 2 *or formerly* **São Salvador** \saůⁿ-\ *or* **Ba·ia** *or* **Ba·hia** \bä-'ē-ə\ city & port NE Brazil ✳ of Baía *pop* 389,422 — **Sal·va·do·ran** \‚sal-va-'dȯr-ən, -'dōr-\ *adj or n* — **Sal·va·do·re·an** *or* **Sal·va·do·ri·an** \-ē-ən\ *adj or n*

Sal·ween \'sal-‚wēn\ river 1750 *m* SE Asia flowing from Tibet S into Gulf of Martaban in Burma

Salz·burg \'sȯlz-‚bərg, 'sälz-, 'salz-, -‚bu̇(ə)rg, *G* 'zälts-‚bu̇rk\ city W Austria *pop* 102,927

Salz·git·ter *or formerly* **Wa·ten·stedt–Salzgitter** \'vät-ᵊn-‚s(h)tet-'zälts-‚git-ər\ city N cen Germany SW of Brunswick *pop* 107,600

Salz·kam·mer·gut \'zälts-‚käm-ər-‚gu̇t\ district N Austria E of Salzburg; chief town Bad Ischl

Sa·mar \'säm-‚är\ island cen Philippines in the Visayans NE of Leyte *area* 5050

Samara — see KUIBYSHEV

Samarang — see SEMARANG

Sa·mar·ia \sə-'mer-ē-ə, -'mar-\ 1 district of ancient Palestine W of the Jordan between Galilee & Judaea; city, its ✳ & ✳ of the Northern Kingdom (Israel); rebuilt by Herod the Great & renamed **Se·bas·te** \sə-'bas-tē\; site in Jordan at modern village of Sebastye

Sam·ar·kand \'sam-ər-‚kand\ *or anc* **Mar·a·can·da** \‚mar-ə-'kan-də\ city in E Uzbekistan U.S.S.R. *pop* 195,000

Sam·ni·um \'sam-nē-əm\ ancient country cen Italy E & SE of Latium — **Sam·nite** \-‚nīt\ *adj or n*

Sa·moa \sə-'mō-ə\ *or formerly* **Navigators** islands SW cen Pacific N of Tonga islands; divided at long. 171°W into American, or Eastern, Samoa & Western Samoa *area* 1209

Sa·mos \'sā-‚mäs\ island Greece in the Aegean off coast of Turkey N of the Dodecanese *area* 171 — **Sa·mi·an** \'sā-mē-ən\ *adj or n*

Sam·o·thrace \'sam-ə-‚thrās\ *or NGk* **Sa·mo·thrá·ke** \‚säm-ə-'thräk-ē\ island Greece in the NE Aegean — **Sam·o·thra·cian** \‚sam-ə-'thrā-shən\ *adj or n*

Sam·sun \'säm-‚sün\ city & port N Turkey on Black sea NW of Ankara *pop* 87,311

San·ʻa *or* **San·aa** \sä-'nä\ city S Arabia ✳ of Yemen *pop* 80,000

San An·ge·lo \sa-'nan-jə-‚lō\ city W cen Tex. *pop* 58,815

San An·to·nio \‚san-ən-'tō-nē-‚ō, -'tōn-yə\ 1 river 200 *m* S Tex. flowing SE into Gulf of Mexico 2 city S Tex. *pop* 587,718 — **San An·to·ni·an** \-nē-ən\ *n*

San Be·ni·to \‚san-bə-'nēt-(‚)ō\ city S Tex. SE of Harlingen *pop* 16,422

San Ber·nar·di·no \‚san-‚bər-nə(r)-'dē-(‚)nō\ 1 mountains S Calif. S of Mojave desert; highest Mt. San Gorgonio 11,485 *ft* 2 city SW Calif. E of Los Angeles *pop* 91,922

San Blas, Isthmus of \san-'bläs\ narrowest section of Isthmus of Panama

San Bru·no \san-'brü-(‚)nō\ city W Calif. S of San Francisco *pop* 29,063

San Buenaventura — see VENTURA

San Car·los \san-'kär-ləs\ city W Calif. SE of San Francisco *pop* 21,370

San Carlos de Bariloche — see BARILOCHE

San Cle·men·te \‚san-klə-'ment-ē\ island S Calif., southernmost of the Santa Barbara islands

San Cris·to·bal \‚san-kris-'tō-bəl\ *or* **San Cris·to·val** \-vəl\ *or* **Ma·ki·ra** \mə-'kir-ə\ island W Pacific in SE Solomons SE of Guadalcanal

San Cris·tó·bal \‚san-kris-'tō-bäl\ 1 *or* **Chat·ham** \'chat-əm\ island Ecuador in the Galápagos 2 city W Venezuela 100 *m* SSW of Lake Maracaibo *pop* 73,000

Sanc·ti Spí·ri·tus \‚säⁿ(k)-tē-'spir-ə-‚tüs\ city W cen Cuba *pop* 37,741

San·cy, Puy de \‚pwēd-ə-‚säⁿ-'sē\ mountain 6185 *ft* S cen France; highest in the Monts Dore & Auvergne mountains

San·da·kan \san-'däk-ən\ town & port Brit. No. Borneo on Sulu sea; former ✳ of colony

Sandalwood — see SUMBA

Sand·hurst \'sand-‚hərst\ town S England in E Berkshire SE of Reading

San·dia \san-'dē-ə\ mountains N cen N. Mex. E of Albuquerque; highest **Sandia Peak** 10,609 *ft*

San Di·e·go \‚san-dē-'ā-(‚)gō\ city & port SW Calif. on **San Diego Bay** (inlet of the Pacific) *pop* 573,224 — **San Di·e·gan** \-gən\ *n*

San Domingo, 1 — see HISPANIOLA 2 — see DOMINICAN REPUBLIC 3 — see SANTO DOMINGO

San·dring·ham \'san-driŋ-əm\ village E England in NW Norfolk

San·dus·ky \sən-'dəs-kē, san-\ 1 river 150 *m* N Ohio flowing N into Lake Erie 2 city N Ohio at entrance to **Sandusky Bay** (inlet of Lake Erie) *pop* 31,989

Sand·wich \'san-(‚)(d)wich\ 1 islands — see HAWAII 2 municipal borough SE England in Kent on the Stour

Sandy Hook peninsula E N.J. extending N toward New York Bay

San Fer·nan·do \‚san-fər-'nan-(‚)dō\ 1 valley S Calif. NW of Los Angeles; partly within Los Angeles city limits 2 city SW Calif. NW of Los Angeles *pop* 16,093

San·ford \'san-fərd\ city E Fla. NNE of Orlando *pop* 19,175

Sanford, Mount mountain 16,208 *ft* S Alaska at W end of Wrangell mountains

San Fran·cis·co \‚san-frən-'sis-(‚)kō\ city & port W Calif. on **San Francisco Bay** & the Pacific *pop* 740,316 — **San Fran·cis·can** \-kən\ *n*

San Francisco Peaks mountain N cen Ariz. N of Flagstaff; includes three peaks: Mt. Humphreys 12,670 *ft* (highest point in the state), Mt. Agassiz 12,340 *ft*, & Mt. Fremont 11,940 *ft*

San Ga·bri·el \san-'gā-brē-əl\ 1 mountains S Calif. SW of Mojave desert & NE of Los Angeles, highest point San Antonio Peak 10,080 *ft* 2 city SW Calif. S of Pasadena *pop* 22,561

San·ga·mon \'saŋ-gə-mən\ river 225 *m*, cen Ill. flowing SW & W into the Illinois

San·gay \säŋ-'gī\ volcano 17,159 *ft* SE cen Ecuador

San·gi·he \säŋ-'gē-ə\ *or* **Sangi** \'säŋ-ē\ 1 islands Indonesia NE of Celebes *area* 314 2 island, chief of the group

San Gi·mi·gna·no \‚sän-jē-mēn-'yän-(‚)ō\ commune cen Italy NW of Siena

San·gre de Cris·to \‚saŋ-grēd-ə-'kris-(‚)tō\ mountains S Colo. & N N. Mex. in Rocky mountains — see BLANCA PEAK

San·i·bel \'san-ə-bəl\ island SW Fla. SW of Fort Myers

San Il·de·fon·so \‚san-‚il-də-'fän(t)-(‚)sō\ *or* **La Gran·ja** \lə-'gränj-ə\ commune cen Spain NW of Segovia

San Isi·dro \‚san-ə-'sē-(‚)drō\ city E Argentina *pop* 90,086

San Ja·cin·to \‚san-jə-'sint-ə\ river 100 *m* SE Tex. flowing S into Galveston Bay

San Joa·quin \‚san-wä-'kēn\ river 350 *m*, cen Calif. flowing from the Sierra Nevada SW & then NW into the Sacramento

San Jo·se \‚san-ə-'zā\ city W Calif. SSE of San Francisco *pop* 204,196

San Jo·sé \‚san-ə-'zā\ city ✳ of Costa Rica *pop* 133,734

San Juan \san-'(h)wän\ 1 river 360 *m* SW Colo., NW N. Mex., & SE Utah flowing W into the Colorado 2 mountains SW Colo. in the Rocky mountains — see UNCOMPAHGRE PEAK 3 islands NW Wash. between Vancouver I. & the mainland 4 city & port ✳ of Puerto Rico *pop* 432,377 5 city W Argentina N of Mendoza *pop* 82,410 6 hill E Cuba near Santiago de Cuba — **San Jua·ne·ro** \‚san-(h)wä-'ne(ə)r-(‚)ō\ *n*

Sankt An·ton am Arl·berg \‚zän(k)-'tän-‚tōn-‚äm-'är(ə)l-‚bərg, ‚säŋ(k)-‚ -‚be(ə)rg\ village W Austria in Tirol W of Innsbruck

Sankt Gallen — see SAINT GALL

Sankt Gotthard — see SAINT GOTTHARD

Sankt Moritz — see SAINT MORITZ

San Le·an·dro \‚san-lē-'an-(‚)drō\ city W Calif. SE of Oakland *pop* 65,962

San Lo·ren·zo \‚san-lə-'ren-(‚)zō\ urban area W Calif. SSE of Oakland *pop* 23,773

San Lu·cas, Cape \‚san-'lü-kəs\ headland NW Mexico, the S extremity of Lower California

San Luis \san-'lü-əs\ valley S Colo. & N N. Mex. along the upper Rio Grande between San Juan & Sangre de Cristo mountains

San Luis Obis·po \san-‚lü-ə-sə-'bis-(‚)pō\ city W Calif. near the Pacific *pop* 20,437

San Lu·is Po·to·sí \‚sän-lü-‚ē-‚spōt-ə-'sē\ 1 state cen Mexico *area* 24,415, *pop* 1,004,560 2 city, its ✳ *pop* 173,886

San Ma·ri·no \‚san-mə-'rē-(‚)nō\ 1 country S Europe on Italian peninsula SSW of Rimini; a republic *area* 24, *pop* 13,500 2 town, its ✳

San Mar·tín *or* **Ge·ne·ral San Martín** \‚hä-nä-‚räl-sän-mär-'tēn\ city E Argentina, NW suburb of Buenos Aires *pop* 269,512

San Ma·teo \‚san-mə-'tā-(‚)ō\ city W Calif. SSE of San Francisco *pop* 69,870

San Pab·lo \san-'pab-(‚)lō\ city W Calif. N of Oakland on **San Pablo Bay** (N extension of San Francisco Bay) *pop* 19,687

San Pe·dro \san-'pē-(‚)drō, -'pā-\ 1 channel SW Calif. between Santa Catalina I. & the mainland 2 former city SW Calif. on San Pedro Bay, now a S section of Los Angeles; port

San Ra·fael \‚san-rə-'fel\ city W Calif. N of San Francisco on San Pablo Bay *pop* 20,460

San Re·mo \san-'rā-(‚)mō, -'rē-\ city & port NW Italy in Liguria near French border *pop* 30,705

San Sal·va·dor \san-'sal-və-‚dȯ(ə)r\ 1 *or* **Wat·ling** \'wät-liŋ\ *or* **Wat·lings** \-liŋz\ island cen Bahama islands *area* 60 — see GUANAHANI 2 city ✳ of Salvador *pop* 221,708

San Se·bas·tián \‚san-si-'bas-chən\ city & port N Spain ✳ of Guipúzcoa on Bay of Biscay *pop* 132,087

San Stefano — see YESILKOY

San·ta Ana \‚sant-ə-'an-ə\ 1 city SW Calif. ESE of Long Beach *pop* 100,350 2 city NW El Salvador *pop* 121,095

Santa Bar·ba·ra \-'bär-b(ə-)rə\ 1 channel SW Calif. between the N Santa Barbara islands & mainland 2 *or* **Chan·nel** \'chan-ᵊl\ islands Calif. in the Pacific off SW coast — see CATALINA, SAN CLEMENTE, SANTA CRUZ, SANTA ROSA 3 city S Calif. *pop* 58,768

Santa Catalina — see CATALINA

San·ta Cat·a·ri·na \‚sant-ə-‚kat-ə-'rē-nə\ state S Brazil bordering on the Atlantic *area* 31,118, *pop* 1,560,502

Santa Clara \-'klar-ə, -'kler-\ 1 city W Calif. NW of San Jóse *pop* 58,880 2 city W cen Cuba *pop* 77,398

Santa Cruz \-'krüz\ 1 island SW Calif. in NW Santa Barbara islands 2 city W Calif. S of San Jose on Monterey Bay *pop* 25,596 3 — see SAINT CROIX 4 river 250 *m* S Argentina flowing E into the Atlantic 5 city E Bolivia *pop* 58,272 6 islands SW Pacific N of the New Hebrides, chief island Ndeni; administratively attached to Brit. Solomon islands *area* 380

San·ta Cruz de Te·ne·ri·fè \‚sant-ə-‚krüz-də-‚ten-ə-'rē-fē\ 1 province Spain comprising W Canary islands *area* 1528, *pop* 477,688 2 city & port, its ✳, on NE Tenerife I. *pop* 126,651

San·ta Fe \‚sant-ə-'fā\ 1 city ✳ of N. Mex. *pop* 34,676 2 city cen Argentina *pop* 219,620 — **San·ta Fe·an** \-'fā-ən\ *n*

Santa Fe Springs \‚sant-ə-‚fā-\ city SW Calif. SE of Los Angeles *pop* 16,342

Santa Fe Trail pioneer route to the Southwest used esp. 1821–80 from vicinity of Kansas City, Mo., to Santa Fe, N. Mex.

San·ta Is·a·bel *or* **Santa Ys·a·bel** \‚sant-ə-'iz-ə-‚bel\ island W Pacific in the E cen Solomons NE of Guadalcanal *area* 1500 2 city N Fernando Po, ✳ of Equatorial Guinea *pop* 19,869

Santa Ma·ria \-mə-'rē-ə\ city W Calif. NW of Santa Barbara *pop* 20,027

Santa Ma·ría \-mə-'rē-ə\ volcano 12,300 *ft* W Guatemala

Santa Mar·ta \-'märt-ə\ city & port N Colombia on the Caribbean E of Barranquilla *pop* 59,290

Santa Mon·i·ca \-'män-i-kə\ city SW Calif. adjacent to Los Angeles on **Santa Monica Bay** (inlet of the Pacific) *pop* 83,249

San·tan·der \ˌsän-ˌtän-ˈde(ə)r, ˌsan-ˌtan-\ **1** province N Spain in N Old Castile bordering on Bay of Biscay *area* 2108, *pop* 434,499 **2** city & port, its ✱, on Bay of Biscay *pop* 116,525

San·ta·rém \ˌsant-ə-ˈrem\ town N Brazil in W Pará at confluence of the Tapajoz & Amazon rivers

San·ta Ro·sa \ˌsant-ə-ˈrō-zə\ **1** island SW Calif. in NW Santa Barbara islands **2** city W Calif. N of San Francisco *pop* 31,027

San·tee \san-ˈtē, ˈsan-ˌ\ river 143 *m* S. C. flowing SE into the Atlantic

San·ti·a·go \ˌsant-ē-ˈäg-(ˌ)ō, ˌsänt-\ **1** city ✱ of Chile *pop* 1,350,-409 **2** *or* **Santiago de los Ca·ba·lle·ros** \-də-ˌlōs-ˌkäb-ə-ˈye(ə)r-(ˌ)ōs\ city N *cen* Dominican Republic *pop* 113,630 **3** *or* **San·tia·go de Com·pos·te·la** \-də-ˌkäm-pə-ˈstel-ə\ commune NW Spain S of La Coruña *pop* 31,140 — **San·ti·a·gan** \ˌsant-ē-ˈäg-ən, ˌsänt-\ *n*

Santiago de Cu·ba \-ˌäg-(ˌ)ōd-ə-ˈkyü-bə\ city & port SE Cuba *pop* 163,237

Santiago del Es·te·ro \-ˈäg-ō-ˌdel-ə-ˈste(ə)r-(ˌ)ō\ city N Argentina SE of Tucumán *pop* 60,039

San·to Do·min·go \ˌsant-əd-ə-ˈmiŋ-(ˌ)gō\ *or* **San Domingo** \ˌsan-də-\ **1** *or* **Santo Domingo de Guz·mán** \-də-gü-ˈsmän\ *or formerly* **Tru·ji·llo** *or* **Ci·u·dad Trujillo** \ˌsē-ü-ˌthä-trü-ˈhē-(ˌ)(y)ō, ˌsē-ü-ˌdad-\ city & port ✱ of Dominican Republic on Caribbean sea *pop* 477,782 **2** — see HISPANIOLA **3** — see DOMINICAN REPUBLIC — **San·to Do·min·gan** \ˌsant-əd-ə-ˈmiŋ-gən\ *adj or n*

San·to·rin \ˌsant-ə-ˈrēn\ *or* NGk **San·to·ri·ni** \-ˈrē-nē\ *or* **Thí·ra** \ˈthir-ə\ *or anc* **The·ra** \ˈthir-ə\ island Greece in S Cyclades *area* 30

San·tos \ˈsant-əs\ city & port SE Brazil in SE São Paulo state SSE of São Paulo on an island in a tidal inlet *pop* 206,920

San·to To·mé de Gua·ya·na \ˌsänt-ō-tə-ˈmād-ə-gwə-ˈyän-ə\ *or* **San To·mé de Guayana** \ˌsän-tō-ˈmād-\ town E Venezuela near junction of the Caroní & Orinoco

San·tur·ce \sän-ˈtü(ə)r-(ˌ)sā\ a N section of San Juan, Puerto Rico

São Fran·cis·co \ˌsau̇^{n}(m)-frən-ˈsis-(ˌ)kō\ river 1800 *m* E Brazil flowing from S *cen* Minas Gerais NE & E into the Atlantic

São Luís \ˌsau̇^{n}-lü-ˈēs\ city & port NE Brazil ✱ of Maranhão state on Maranhão I. *pop* 152,176

São Ma·nuel \ˌsau̇^{n}-mən-ˈwel\ river 600 *m*, *cen* Brazil flowing NW to join the Juruena forming the Tapajoz

São Mi·guel \ˌsau̇^{n}-mi-ˈgel\ island Portugal in E Azores; chief town Ponta Delgada *area* 297

Saône \ˈsōn\ river 275 *m* E France flowing SSW into the Rhone

São Pau·lo \sau̇^{n}(m)-ˈpau̇-(ˌ)lü, -(ˌ)lō\ **1** state SE Brazil *area* 95,459, *pop* 9,134,423 **2** city, its ✱, on Tietê river *pop* 3,825,351

São Ro·que, Cape \sau̇^{n}-ˈrō-kə\ headland NE Brazil N of Natal

São Salvador — see SALVADOR

São Tia·go \ˌsau̇^{n}(n)t-ē-ˈäg-(ˌ)ü, -(ˌ)ō\ *or* **San·ti·a·go** \ˌsant-ə-ˈäg-(ˌ)ō\ island Cape Verde islands, largest of the group; chief town Praia *area* 359

São To·mé *or* **São Tho·mé** \ˌsau̇^{n}(n)t-ə-ˈmā\ island W Africa in Gulf of Guinea; with Principe I., forms Portuguese overseas territory of **São Tomé and Principe** (*area* 377, *pop* 60,159)

São Vicente, Cabo de — see SAINT VINCENT (Cape)

Sap·po·ro \sə-ˈpōr-(ˌ)ō, -ˈpȯr-\ city Japan on W Hokkaido *pop* 523,839

Saq·qa·ra *or* **Sak·ka·ra** \sə-ˈkär-ə\ village N Egypt SW of ruins of Memphis

Sarabat — see GEDIZ

Saragossa — see ZARAGOZA

Sa·ra·je·vo \ˈsär-ə-ye-ˌvȯ\ *or* **Se·ra·je·vo** \ˈser-\ city *cen* Yugoslavia ✱ of Bosnia & Herzegovina *pop* 136,283

Sar·a·nac \ˈsar-ə-ˌnak\ river 100 *m* NE N. Y. flowing NE from **Saranac Lakes** (three lakes in the Adirondacks: Upper Saranac, Middle Saranac, & Lower Saranac) into Lake Champlain

Sa·ransk \sə-ˈrän(t)sk, -ˈran(t)sk\ city U. S. S. R. in *cen* Soviet Russia, Europe ✱ of Mordvinian Republic *pop* 90,000

Sar·a·so·ta \ˌsar-ə-ˈsōt-ə\ city W Fla. S of Tampa *pop* 34,083

Sar·a·to·ga \ˌsar-ə-ˈtō-gə\ lake 7 *m* long E N. Y. S of Lake George

Saratoga Springs *or* **Saratoga** city NE N.Y. *pop* 16,630

Sa·ra·tov \sə-ˈrät-əf\ city U. S. S. R. in SE Soviet Russia, Europe, on a reservoir of Volga river *pop* 581,000

Sa·ra·wak \sə-ˈrä-(ˌ)wä(k), -ˌwak\ country N Borneo bordering on So. China sea; formerly a Brit. colony, since 1963 a territory of Federation of Malaysia ✱ Kuching *area* 47,000, *pop* 631,431

Sardica — see SOFIA

Sar·din·ia \sär-ˈdin-ē-ə, -ˈdin-yə\ *or* It **Sar·de·gna** \sär-ˈdān-yə\ island Italy S of Corsica ✱ Cagliari *area* 9283, *pop* 1,276,023

Sar·dis \ˈsärd-əs\ *or* **Sar·des** \ˈsärd-(ˌ)ēz\ ancient city W Asia Minor ✱ of ancient kingdom of Lydia; site *ab* 50 *m* E of Izmir — **Sar·di·an** \ˈsärd-ē-ən\ *adj or n*

Sa·re·ma *or* Estonian **Saa·re·maa** \ˈsär-ə-ˌmä\ island U. S. S. R. in Estonia at mouth of Gulf of Riga *area* 1010

Sar·gas·so sea \sär-ˌgas-(ˌ)ō-\ tract of comparatively still water N Atlantic lying chiefly between 25° & 35° N & 40° & 70° W

Sark \ˈsärk\ island in the English channel, one of the Channel islands *area* 2

Sar·ma·tia \sär-ˈmā-sh(ē-)ə\ ancient region E Europe in modern Poland & Russia between the Vistula & the Volga — **Sar·ma·tian** \-shən\ *adj or n*

Sar·nia \ˈsär-nē-ə\ city Canada in SE Ont. on St. Clair river opposite Port Huron, Mich. *pop* 43,447

Sa·ron·ic Gulf \sə-ˈrän-ik\ inlet of the Aegean SE Greece between Attica & the Peloponnesus

Sa·ros \ˈsar-ˌäs, ˈser-\ gulf inlet of the Aegean SW Turkey in Europe at base of Gallipoli peninsula

Sarre — see SAAR

Sarrebruck — see SAARBRÜCKEN

Sarthe \ˈsärt\ river 175 *m* NW France flowing S to unite with the Mayenne forming the Maine

Sarum, 1 New Sarum — see SALISBURY **2** OLD SARUM

Sa·se·bo \ˈsäs-ə-ˌbō\ city & port Japan in NW Kyushu on an inlet of East China sea *pop* 258,221

Sas·katch·e·wan \sə-ˈskach-ə-wən, sa-, -ˌwän\ **1** river 1205 *m* SW Canada flowing from the Rockies in W Alta. E into Lake Winnipeg in *cen* Man.; formed by confluence in *cen* Sask. of the **North Saskatchewan** (760 *m*) & the **South Saskatchewan** (865 *m*) **2** province SW Canada ✱ Regina *area* 237,975, *pop* 880,665 — **Sas·katch·e·wan·ian** \-ˌskach-ə-ˈwän-ē-ən\ *adj or n*

Sas·ka·toon \ˌsas-kə-ˈtün\ city Canada in *cen* Sask. *pop* 72,858

Sas·sa·ri \ˈsäs-ə-(ˌ)rē\ commune Italy in NW Sardinia *pop* 62,400

Sa·til·la \sə-ˈtil-ə\ river 220 *m* SE Ga. flowing E into the Atlantic

Sat·pu·ra \ˈsät-pə-rə\ range of hills W *cen* India between Narbada & Tapti rivers

Sa·tu-Ma·re \ˌsä-(ˌ)tü-ˈmär-(ˌ)ā\ city NW Romania in Transylvania on the Somes *pop* 56,463

Sau·di Arabia \ˌsau̇d-ē-, sä-ˌüd-ē-\ country SW Asia occupying most of Arabian peninsula; a kingdom, comprising former kingdoms of Nejd & Hejaz & principality of Asir ✱ ✱ Riyadh & Mecca *area* 870,000, *pop* 6,630,000 — **Saudi** *adj or n* — **Saudi Arabian** *adj or n*

Sau·gus \ˈsȯ-gəs\ town NE Mass. W of Lynn *pop* 20,666

Sault Sainte Ma·rie \ˌsü-ˌsānt-mə-ˈrē\ **1** city NE Mich. in upper peninsula *pop* 18,722 **2** city Canada in S Ont. *pop* 32,329

Sault Sainte Marie canals *or* **Soo canals** \ˈsü-\ *or* **Soo locks** three ship canals, two in the U. S. (four parallel locks) & one in Canada (one lock), at rapids in St. Marys river connecting Lakes Superior & Huron

Sau·mur \sō-ˈm(y)u̇(ə)r\ commune NW France on the Loire SE of Angers *pop* 18,169

Sau·rash·tra \sau̇-ˈräsh-trə\ former state (1948–56) W India on Kathiawar peninsula; in Bombay state 1956–60 & since 1960 in Gujarat

Sa·va \ˈsäv-ə\ river 450 *m* N Yugoslavia flowing from Italian border E into the Danube at Belgrade

Savage — see NIUE

Sa·vaii \sə-ˈvī-(ˌ)ē\ island SW *cen* Pacific, largest in Samoa, in Western Samoa

Sa·van·nah \sə-ˈvan-ə\ **1** river 314 *m* E Ga. flowing SE to the Atlantic & forming Ga.-S. C. boundary **2** city & port E Ga. at mouth of Savannah river *pop* 149,245

Save — see SABI

Sa·vo \ˈsäv-(ˌ)ō\ island W Pacific in SE Solomon islands N of W end of Guadalcanal

Sa·vo·na \sə-ˈvō-nə\ commune & port NW Italy SW of Genoa *pop* 68,300

Sa·voy \sə-ˈvȯi\ *or* F **Sa·voie** \så-vwå\ *or* It **Sa·vo·ia** \sä-ˈvȯ-yä\ region SE France in Savoy Alps SW of Switzerland & bordering on Italy; duchy 1416–1720, part of kingdom of Sardinia 1720–1860; became part of France 1860 — **Sa·voy·ard** \sə-ˈvȯi-ˌärd, ˌsav-ˌȯi-ˈärd, ˌsav-ˌwä-ˈyär(d)\ *adj or n*

Savoy Alps section of W Alps SE France — see BLANC (Mont)

Sa·watch *or* **Sa·guache** \sə-ˈwäch, ˈsə-wəch\ mountain range *cen* Colo. in Rocky mountains — see ELBERT (Mount)

Saxe \ˈsaks\ SAXONY — its French form, used in English chiefly in names of former duchies in Thuringia: **Saxe-Al·ten·burg** \ˈält-^{ə}n-ˌbu̇(ə)rg\, **Saxe-Co·burg** \ˈkō-ˌbərg\, **Saxe-Go·tha** \ˈgōt-ə, ˈgō-thə\, **Saxe-Mei·ning·en** \ˈmī-niŋ-ən\, & **Saxe-Wei·mar-Ei·se·nach** \-ˈvī-ˌmär-ˈīz-^{ə}n-ˌäk, -ˌäk\

Sax·o·ny \ˈsak-s(ə-)nē\ *or* G **Sach·sen** \ˈzäk-sən\ **1** region & former duchy NW Germany S of Jutland peninsula between the Elbe & the Rhine **2** region & former state E Germany N of the Erzgebirge — see LOWER SAXONY, SAXE

Sa·yan \sə-ˈyän\ mountains U. S. S. R. in S Soviet Russia, Asia, on border of Tuva N of Altai mountains

Sayre·ville \ˈsa(ə)r-ˌvil, ˈse(ə)r-\ borough E *cen* N. J. *pop* 22,553

Says Law \ˈsāz-ˌlȯ\ mountain 1749 *ft* SE Scotland; highest in Lammermuir hills

Sa·zan \ˈsäz-ˌän\ *or* It **Sa·se·no** \sə-ˈzā-(ˌ)nō\ island Albania at entrance to Bay of Vlone

Sca·fell \ˈskȯ-ˌfel\ mountain 3162 *ft* NW England in Cumbrians SW of Keswick; second highest peak in England

Scafell Pike mountain 3210 *ft* NW England in Cumberland 1 *m* NE of Scafell; highest in the Cumbrians & in England

Scamander — see MENDERES

Scan·di·na·via \ˌskan-də-ˈnā-vē-ə, -vyə\ **1** peninsula N Europe occupied by Norway & Sweden **2** Denmark, Norway, Sweden, & sometimes also Iceland, the Faeroe islands, & Finland

Scapa Flow \ˌskap-ə-ˈflō\ sea basin N Scotland in the Orkneys

Scarpanto — see KARPATHOS

Scars·dale \ˈskärz-ˌdāl\ town SE N. Y. NE of Yonkers *pop* 17,968

Schaer·beek *or* **Schaar·beek** \ˈskär-ˌbāk\ commune *cen* Belgium, NE suburb of Brussels *pop* 119,080

Schaff·hau·sen \shäf-ˈhau̇z-^{ə}n\ *or* F **Schaff·house** \shå-füz\ **1** *or* **Falls of the Rhine** *or* G **Rhein·fall** \ˈrīn-ˌfäl\ waterfall in the Rhine N Switzerland 370 *ft* wide, with two principal falls 50 *ft* & 60 *ft* high **2** canton N Switzerland bordering on Germany *area* 114, *pop* 57,515 **3** commune, its ✱ *pop* 26,400

Schaum·burg-Lip·pe \ˌshau̇m-ˌbu̇(ə)rg-ˈlip-ə\ state of Germany 1918–33 in NW between Westphalia & Hannover

Schei·degg \ˈshī-ˌdek\ village *cen* Switzerland in Bern canton on Little Scheidegg Pass

Scheldt \ˈskelt\ *or* **Schel·de** \ˈskel-də\ *or* F **Es·caut** \es-kō\ river 270 *m* W Europe flowing from N France through Belgium into North sea in Netherlands

Sche·nec·ta·dy \skə-ˈnek-təd-ē\ city E N. Y. *pop* 81,682

Sche·ve·ning·en \ˈskā-və-ˌniŋ-ə(n)\ town SW Netherlands on North sea W of The Hague

Schie·dam \skē-ˈdäm\ commune SW Netherlands *pop* 79,028

Schles·wig \ˈs(h)les-(ˌ)wig, -(ˌ)wik\ **1** *or* Dan **Sles·vig** \ˈslis-vē\ region N Germany & S Denmark in S Jutland peninsula **2** city N Germany *pop ab* 35,000

Schleswig-Hol·stein \-ˈhōl-ˌstīn\ state N Germany consisting of Holstein & part of Schleswig ✱ Kiel *area* 6052, *pop* 2,309,400

Schou·ten \ˈskau̇t-^{ə}n, ˈskau̇t-ə\ islands W New Guinea at mouth of Geelvink Bay *area* 1230

Schuyl·kill \ˈskül-ˌkil, ˈskü-kəl\ river 131 *m* SE Pa. flowing SE into the Delaware at Philadelphia

Schwaben — see SWABIA

Schwarzwald — see BLACK FOREST

Schwein·furt \ˈshfīn-ˌfu̇(ə)rt\ city W Germany on the Main *pop* 56,000

Schweiz — see SWITZERLAND

Schwe·rin \shfā-ˈrēn\ city E Germany in Mecklenburg E of Hamburg *pop* 94,200

Schwyz \ˈshfēts\ **1** canton E *cen* Switzerland *area* 351, *pop* 71,082 **2** town, its ✱, E of Lucerne

Scil·ly \ˈsil-ē\ island group SW England off Lands End comprised of 140 islands ✱ Hugh Town *area* 6

Sci·o·to \sī-ˈōt-ə\ river 237 *m* Ohio flowing S into the Ohio

Scone \ˈskün\ locality E Scotland NE of Perth

Sco·pus, Mount \ˈskō-pəs\ mountain Palestine in W Jordan in small area belonging to Israel

Scores·by Sound \,skō(ə)rz-bē-, ,skó(ə)rz-\ inlet of Norwegian sea E Greenland N of 70° N

Scotch Plains \'skäch\ urban township NE N. J. *pop* 18,491

Sco·tia \'skō-shə\ sea part of the S Atlantic SE of Falkland islands, W of So. Sandwich islands, & N of So. Orkney islands

Scot·land \'skät-lənd\ *or* L **Cal·e·do·nia** \,kal-ə-'dō-nyə, -nē-ə\ *or* ML **Scotia** country N Great Britain; a division of United Kingdom of Great Britain & Northern Ireland ✳ Edinburgh *area* 29,794, *pop* 5,095,969

Scott \'skät\ urban township SW Pa. SW of Pittsburgh *pop* 19,094

Scotts Bluff National Monument \,skäts-\ reservation W Nebr. on the No. Platte including **Scotts Bluff** (high butte that was a landmark on the Oregon Trail)

Scran·ton \'skrant-ᵊn\ city NE Pa. *pop* 111,443

Scun·thorpe \'skən-,thȯ(ə)rp\ municipal borough E England in Parts of Lindsey, Lincolnshire, WSW of Hull *pop* 54,245

Scu·ta·ri *or* **Sku·ta·ri** \'skü-tə-rē\ **1** *or* *Albanian* **Shko·der** \'shkȯd-ər\ city NW Albania *pop* 33,900 **2** lake NW Albania & S Yugoslavia *area* 130 **3** — see USKUDAR

Scyros — see SKYROS

Scyth·ia \'sith-ē-ə, 'sith-\ the country of the ancient Scythians comprising parts of Europe & Asia now in U. S. S. R. in regions N & NE of Black sea & E of Aral sea

Sea \'sē\ islands SE U. S. in the Atlantic off coast of S. C., Ga., & Fla. between mouths of Santee & St. Johns rivers

Sea·side \'sē-,sīd\ city W Calif. on Monterey Bay *pop* 19,353

Se·at·tle \sē-'at-ᵊl\ city & port W Wash. between Puget Sound & Lake Washington *pop* 557,087 — **Se·at·tle·ite** \-,īt\ *n*

Se·ba·go \sə-'bā-(,)gō\ lake 13 *m* long SW Me.

Sebaste, 1 *or* **Sebastia** — see SIVAS **2** — see SAMARIA

Sebha — see SABHA

Se·cun·der·abad *or* **Si·kan·dar·abad** \si-'kən-də-rə-,bad, -,bäd\ city S *cen* India in Andhra Pradesh, NE suburb of Hyderabad *pop* 225,400

Se·da·lia \si-'dāl-yə\ city W *cen* Mo. *pop* 23,874

Se·dan \si-'dan, F sə-däⁿ\ city NE France on the Meuse NE of Reims *pop* 17,637

Sedge·moor \'sej-,mú(ə)r, -,mō(ə)r, -,mȯ(ə)r\ tract of moorland SW England in *cen* Somerset

Sedom — see SODOM

Se·go·via \si-'gō-vē-ə\ **1** *or* **Co·co** \'kō-(,)kō\ *or* **Wanks** \'waŋ(k)s\ river 450 *m* N Nicaragua flowing NE into the Caribbean & forming part of Honduras-Nicaragua boundary **2** province N *cen* Spain in Old Castile *area* 2635, *pop* 205,793 **3** commune, its ✳, NW of Madrid *pop* 34,250

Seim *or* **Seym** \'sām\ river 435 *m* U.S.S.R. in SW *cen* Soviet Russia, Europe, flowing W into the Desna

Seine \'sān, 'sen\ river 480 *m* N France flowing NW into **Bay of the Seine** (inlet of English channel)

Seishin — see CHONGJIN

Seishu — see CHONGJU

Sekia el Hamra — see SAGUIA EL HAMRA

Sek·on·di \sek-ən-'dē\ city & port SW Ghana *pop* 26,757

Se·lang·or \sə-'laŋ-ər\ state *cen* Federation of Malaysia on Strait of Malacca ✳ Kuala Lumpur *area* 3166, *pop* 1,012,891

Sel·en·ga \,sel-ən-'gä\ river 750 *m* N *cen* Asia rising in W Outer Mongolia & flowing to Lake Baikal

Se·leu·cia \sə-'lü-sh(ē-)ə\ **1** *or* **Seleucia Tra·che·o·tis** \,trā-kē-'ōt-əs\ ancient city SE Asia Minor in Cilicia SW of Tarsus **2** ancient city, chief city of the Seleucid Empire; ruins now in Iraq on the Tigris SSE of Baghdad **3** *or* **Seleucia Pi·e·ria** \,pī-'ir-ē-ə, -'er-\ ancient city Asia Minor N of mouth of the Orontes; port for Antioch

Sel·kirk \'sel-,kərk\ **1** mountains SW Canada in SE B.C. W of the Rockies; highest Mt. Sir Sandford 11,590 *ft* **2** *or* **Sel·kirk·shire** \-,shi(ə)r, -shər\ county SE Scotland *area* 267, *pop* 21,724 **3** burgh, its ✳, SE of Edinburgh

Sel·ma \'sel-mə\ city W Ala. W of Montgomery *pop* 28,385

Se·ma·rang *or* **Sa·ma·rang** \sə-'mär-,äŋ\ city & port Indonesia in *cen* Java on N coast *pop* 373,900

Sem·i·nole, Lake \-'sem-ə-,nōl\ reservoir SW Ga. & NW Fla. formed by confluence of Chattahoochee & Flint rivers & emptying by the Apalachicola

Sem·i·pa·la·tinsk \,sem-i-pə-'lä-,tin(t)sk\ city U.S.S.R. in Soviet Central Asia in NE Kazakhstan on Irtysh river *pop* 155,000

Sen·dai \sen-'dī\ city Japan in NE Honshu *pop* 425,272

Sen·e·ca \'sen-i-kə\ lake 35 *m* long W *cen* N.Y.; one of the Finger lakes

Sen·e·gal \,sen-i-'gȯl\ **1** river 1050 *m* W Africa flowing from Fouta Djallon NW & W into the Atlantic **2** country W Africa on the Atlantic; a republic of the French Community, formerly a territory of French West Africa ✳ Dakar *area* 81,081, *pop* 2,973,000 — **Sen·e·ga·lese** \,sen-i-gə-'lēz, -'lēs\ *adj or n*

Sen·e·gam·bia \,sen-i-'gam-bē-ə\ region W Africa around Senegal & Gambia rivers — **Sen·e·gam·bi·an** \-ən\ *adj or n*

Sen·lac \'sen-,lak\ hill SE England in Sussex NW of Hastings

Sen·lis \säⁿ-lēs\ commune N France NNE of Paris

Sen·nar *or* **Sen·naar** \se-'när\ region E Sudan chiefly between the White Nile & the Blue Nile; an ancient kingdom

Sens \'säⁿs\ city NE *cen* France WSW of Troyes *pop* 18,612

Seoul \'sōl, 'sül, se-'ül\ *or* **Kyong·song** \kē-'ȯŋ-'sȯŋ\ *or* *Jap* **Kei·jo** \'kā-(,)jō\ city S Korea on Han river; formerly ✳ of Korea, since 1948 ✳ of So. Korea *pop* 1,642,599

Se·pik \'sā-pik\ river 600 *m* N New Guinea

Se·quoia National Park \si-,kwȯi-ə-\ reservation SE *cen* Calif. *area* 602; includes Mt. Whitney

Serajevo — see SARAJEVO

Seram — see CERAM

Ser·bia \'sər-bē-ə\ *or formerly* **Ser·via** \-vē-ə\ federated republic SE Yugoslavia traversed by the Morava; once a kingdom ✳ Belgrade *area* 34,080, *pop* 6,979,154

Serdica — see SOFIA

Serendib — see CEYLON

Ser·en·ge·ti Plain \,ser-ən-,get-ē-\ area N Tanzania comprising **Serengeti National Park,** a wild game reserve *area ab* 5,000

Ser·gi·pe \sər-'zhē-pə\ state NE Brazil ✳ Aracajú *area* 8321, *pop* 644,361

Se·rin·ga·pa·tam \sə-,riŋ-gə-pə-'tam\ *or* **Sri·ran·ga·pat·nam** \srē-,raŋ-gə-pət-'nam\ town S India N of city of Mysore

Se·rowe \sə-'rō-ē\ city S Africa in E Bechuanaland Protectorate *pop* 15,935

Ser·ra da Es·tre·la \,ser-ə-,dä-e-'strel-ə\ mountain range Portugal; highest point Malhão da Estrela (highest in Portugal) 6532 *ft*

Serra do Mar \-də-'mär\ mountain range S Brazil along coast chiefly in Santa Catarina, Paraná, & São Paulo states; highest point 7323 *ft*

Serra Pa·ca·rai·ma \-,pak-ə-'rī-mə\ *or* **Si·er·ra Pacaraima** \sē-,er-ə-\ mountain range N So. America in SE Venezuela, N Brazil, & W Brit. Guiana — see RORAIMA

Ser·ra Pa·ri·ma \,ser-ə-pə-'rē-mə\ *or* **Si·er·ra Parima** \sē-,er-ə-\ mountain range N So. America on Venezuela-Brazil border SW of Serra Pacaraima; source of the Orinoco; highest peak *ab* 8000 *ft*

Ses·tos \'ses-təs\ ruined town Turkey in Europe on the Dardanelles (Hellespont) at narrowest point

Sète \'set\ *or formerly* **Cette** \'set\ commune & port S France SSW of Montpellier *pop* 33,454

Sete Quedas — see GUAIRÁ FALLS

Sé·tif \sā-'tēf\ commune NE Algeria *pop* 53,057

Se·tú·bal \sə-'tü-bəl\ city & port SW Portugal *pop* 44,000

Se·van \sə-'vän\ *or* **Se·vang** \-'väŋ\ *or Turk* **Gok·cha** \'gə(r)k-chə\ lake U.S.S.R. in N Armenian Republic *area* 540

Se·vas·to·pol *or formerly* **Se·bas·to·pol** \sə-'vas-tə-,pōl, -,pȯl; ,sev-ə-'stȯ-pəl, -'stō-\ city & port U.S.S.R. in Soviet Russia, Europe, in SW Crimea *pop* 148,000

Sev·ern \'sev-ərn\ **1** inlet (**Severn river**) of Chesapeake Bay, Md., on which Annapolis is situated **2** river 610 *m* Canada in NW Ont. flowing NE into Hudson Bay **3** river 210 *m* Great Britain flowing from E *cen* Wales into Bristol channel

Severnaya Dvina — see NORTHERN DVINA

Se·ver·na·ya Zem·lya \'sev-ər-nə-,yä-,zem-lē-'ä\ islands U.S.S.R. in N Soviet Russia, Asia, in N Taimyr peninsula in Arctic ocean between Kara & Laptev seas *area* 14,300

Se·vier \sə-'vi(ə)r\ river 280 *m* SW *cen* Utah flowing into **Sevier Lake** (25 *m* long; saline)

Se·ville \sə-'vil\ *or Sp* **Se·vi·lla** \sā-'vē(l)-yä\ **1** province SW Spain *area* 5428, *pop* 1,241,844 **2** city, its ✳ *pop* 428,660

Sè·vres \'sevrᵊ\ commune N France SW of Paris *pop* 17,109

Sew·ard \'sü-ərd\ peninsula 180 *m* long & 130 *m* wide W Alaska projecting into Bering sea between Kotzebue & Norton sounds — see PRINCE OF WALES (Cape)

Sey·chelles \sā-'shel(z)\ island group W Indian ocean NE of Madagascar; a Brit. colony ✳ Victoria (on Mahé I.) *area* 100, *pop* 47,424

Sey·han \sā-'hän\ **1** *or* **Sei·hun** \-'hün\ river 300 *m* Turkey flowing SSW into the Mediterranean **2** — see ADANA

Seym — see SEIM

Sfax \'sfaks\ city & port Tunisia on Gulf of Gabes *pop* 65,635

's Gravenhage — see HAGUE (The)

Shah·ja·han·pur \,shäj-ə-'hän-,pú(ə)r, ,shȯ-jə-\ city N India in *cen* Uttar Pradesh NNW of Kanpur *pop* 104,800

Shah·pur \'shä-'pú(ə)r, shȯ-\ ancient city SW Iran W of Shiraz

Sha·ker Heights \,shā-kər-\ city NE Ohio E of Cleveland *pop* 36,460

Shakh·ty \'shäk-tē\ *or* **Ale·ksan·drovsk Gru·shev·ski** \,al-ik-'san-drəfsk-grü-'shef-skē, -ig-'zan, -'shev-\ city U.S.S.R. in SE Soviet Russia, Europe, N of Rostov *pop* 196,000

Sha·ler \'shā-lər\ urban township SW Pa. NE of Pittsburgh *pop* 24,939

Shang·hai \shaŋ-'hī\ municipality & port E China in SE Kiangsu on the Hwang Pu near the Yangtze estuary *pop* 7,100,000

Shang·kiu \'shäŋ-kē-'ü\ city E China in E Honan *pop* 134,400

Shan·non \'shan-ən\ river 240 *m* W Ireland flowing S & W into the Atlantic

Shan·si \'shän-'sē\ province N China bordering on Yellow river ✳ Taiyuan *area* 60,656, *pop* 14,314,000

Shan State \'shän, 'shan\ *or formerly* **Federated Shan States** province E Burma comprising a mountainous region (the **Shan hills**) ✳ Taunggyi

Shan·tung \'shan-'təŋ\ **1** peninsula E China projecting ENE between Yellow sea & Po Hai **2** province E China including Shantung peninsula ✳ Tsinan *area* 59,189, *pop* 48,877,000

Shao·hing *or* **Shao·hsing** \'shaú-'shiŋ\ city E China in N Chekiang SE of Hangchow *pop* 130,600

Shao·yang \'shaú-'yäŋ\ *or formerly* **Pao·king** \'baú-'chiŋ\ city SE China in *cen* Hunan W of Hengyang *pop* 117,700

Sha·ri *or* **Cha·ri** \'shär-ē\ river 1400 *m* N *cen* Africa in Chad flowing NW into Lake Chad

Shark Bay inlet of Indian ocean 150 *m* long W Western Australia, at *ab* 25°S

Shar·on \'shar-ən, 'sher-\ city NW Pa. *pop* 25,267

Sharon, Plain of region Israel on coast between Mt. Carmel & Jaffa

Sha·si \'shä-'sē\ city E *cen* China in S Hupei on the Yangtze *pop* 85,000

Shas·ta, Mount \'shas-tə\ mountain 14,162 *ft* N Calif. in Cascade range; an isolated volcanic cone

Shatt-al-Ar·ab \,shat,-al-'ar-əb\ river 120 *m* SE Iraq formed by Tigris & Euphrates rivers & flowing SE into Persian Gulf

Shaw·an·gunk Mountain \,shäŋ-gəm-\ mountain ridge SE N.Y.; part of Kittatinny Mountain

Sha·win·i·gan Falls \shə-,win-i-gən-\ city Canada in S Que. on St. Maurice river NW of Trois-Rivières *pop* 28,597

Shaw·nee \shȯ-'nē, shä-\ city *cen* Okla. *pop* 24,326

Shcherbakov — see RYBINSK

She·ba \'shē-bə\ *or* **Sa·ba** \'sā-bə\ ancient country S Arabia

She·boy·gan \shi-'bȯi-gən\ city & port E Wis. *pop* 45,747

Shechem — see NABLUS

Sheer·ness \shi(ə)r-'nes\ urban district & port SE England in Kent at mouth of the Thames *pop* 15,727

Shef·field \'shef-,ēld\ city & county borough N England in West Riding, Yorkshire *pop* 512,834

Shel·by \'shel-bē\ city S N.C. W of Charlotte *pop* 17,698

Shel·i·kof \'shel-i-ˌkóf\ strait S Alaska between Alaska peninsula & islands of Kodiak & Afognak

Shel·ton \'shelt-ᵊn\ city SW Conn. *pop* 18,190

Shen·an·do·ah \ˌshen-ən-'dō-ə, ˌshan-ə-'dō-ə\ river 55 *m* N Va. flowing NE between Allegheny & Blue Ridge mountains across NE tip of W. Va. & into the Potomac

Shenandoah National Park reservation N Va. in Blue Ridge mountains *area* 302

Shen·si \'shen-'sē\ province N *cen* China bordering on Yellow river ✳ Sian *area* 75,598, *pop* 15,881,000

Shenyang — see MUKDEN

Sher·brooke \'shər-ˌbrük\ city E Canada in S Que. *pop* 58,668

Sher·man \'shər-mən\ city NE Tex. N of Dallas *pop* 24,988

's Her·to·gen·bosch \'ser-ˌtō-gə(n)-ˌbós\ city S Netherlands ✳ of No. Brabant *pop* 70,194

Sher·wood Forest \ˌshər-ˌwůd- *also* ˌshe(ə)r-\ ancient royal forest *cen* England chiefly in Nottinghamshire

Shet·land \'shet-lənd\ 1 islands N Scotland NE of the Orkneys 2 *or* **Zet·land** \'zet-\ county comprising the Shetlands ✳ Lerwick (on Mainland I.) *area* 550, *pop* 19,352 — **Shet·land·er** \-lən-dər\ *n*

Shey·enne \shī-'an, -'en\ river 325 *m* SE *cen* N. Dak. flowing SE into Red river

Shi·beli *or* **She·beli** *or* **Web·be Shibeli** \ˌweb-ē-shə-'bel-ē\ river 700 *m* E Africa rising in *cen* Ethiopia & flowing SE to a swamp near Juba river in Somalia

Shi·bîn el Kôm \shib-ˌē-ˌnel-'kōm\ city N Egypt in Nile delta NNW of Cairo *pop* 56,900

Shi·ga·tse \shi-'gät-sə\ town W China in SE Tibet on Tsangpo river W of Lhasa

Shih·kia·chwang \'shi(ə)r-jē-'äj-'wän\ city NE China in SW Hopei NW of Paoting *pop* 373,400

Shi·kar·pur \shi-'kär-ˌpů(ə)r\ city Pakistan in S *cen* West Pakistan in Sind *pop* 45,400

Shi·ko·ku \shi-'kō-(ˌ)kü\ island S Japan E of Kyushu *area* 7246

Shil·ka \'shil-kə\ river 300 *m* U.S.S.R. in SE Soviet Russia, Asia, flowing NE to unite with the Argun forming the Amur

Shil·long \shil-'òn\ city NE India ✳ of Assam *pop* 53,800

Shi·loh \'shī-(ˌ)lō\ ancient village Palestine W of the Jordan on slope of Mt. Ephraim; site in modern Jordan at village of Seilun

Shi·mi·zu \shi-'mē-(ˌ)zü\ city & port Japan in *cen* Honshu on Suruga Bay; port for Shizuoka *pop* 88,472

Shi·mo·da \shi-'mōd-ə, -'mō-ˌdá\ city & port Japan in S Honshu SW of Yokohama on Sagami sea *pop* 27,369

Shi·mo·no·se·ki \ˌshim-ə-nō-'sek-ē\ 1 strait Japan between Honshu & Kyushu connecting Inland sea & Korea strait 2 *or* **Ba·kan** \'bäk-ən\ city & port Japan in SW Honshu on Shimonoseki strait *pop* 230,503

Shi·nar \'shī-ˌnär\ a country known to the early Hebrews as a plain in Babylonia; probably Sumer

Shingishu — see SINUIJU

Shin·kol·o·bwe \ˌshin-'käl-əb-ˌwā\ town SE Congo in Katanga

Shinshu — see CHINJU

Ship Rock isolated mountain 7178 *ft* N. Mex. in NW corner

Shi·raz \shi-'räz\ city SW Iran in Fars *pop* 169,088

Shi·re *or* **Chi·re** \'shē-(ˌ)rä\ river 370 *m* S Malawi & *cen* Mozambique flowing from Lake Nyasa S into the Zambezi

Shi·shal·din \shish-'al-dən\ volcano 9387 *ft* SW Alaska on Unimak I.; highest in Aleutian range

Shive·ly \'shīv-lē\ city N Ky. SW of Louisville *pop* 15,155

Shi·zu·o·ka \shi-'zü-ə-ˌkä\ city Japan in *cen* Honshu near Suruga Bay SW of Shimizu *pop* 328,819

Shkoder — see SCUTARI

Sho·la·pur \'shō-lə-ˌpů(ə)r\ city W India in SE Maharashtra SE of Bombay *pop* 266,000

Shore·ditch \'shō(ə)r-ˌdich, 'shò(ə)r-\ metropolitan borough N *cen* London, England *pop* 44,885

Shore·wood \-ˌwůd\ village SE Wis. *pop* 15,990

Short·land \'shórt-lənd\ islands W Pacific in the Solomons off S end of Bougainville; in Brit. Solomon Islands Protectorate

Sho·sho·ne \shə-'shō-nē\ river 120 *m* NW Wyo. flowing NE into the Bighorn

Shoshone Falls waterfall 210 *ft* S Idaho in Snake river

Showhsien — see HWAINAN

Shreve·port \'shrēv-ˌpō(ə)rt, -ˌpó)rt, *esp South* 'srēv-\ city NW La. *pop* 164,372

Shrews·bury \'shrüz-ˌber-ē, 'shróz-, -b(ə-)rē, *esp South* 'srüz-, 'sróz-\ *or* **Sal·op** \'sal-əp\ municipal borough W England ✳ of Shropshire on the Severn *pop* 44,926

Shrop·shire \'shräp-ˌshi(ə)r, -shər, *esp South* 'sräp-\ *or* **Sal·op** \'sal-əp\ county W England on border of Wales ✳ Shrewsbury *area* 1347, *pop* 289,844

Shunsen — see CHUNCHON

Shushan — see SUSA

Si — see WEST

Si·al·kot \sē-'äl-ˌkōt\ city Pakistan in NE West Pakistan NNE of Lahore *pop* 167,500

Siam — see THAILAND

Siam, Gulf of *or* **Gulf of Thailand** arm of So. China sea between Indochina & Malay peninsula

Si·an \'shē-'än\ *or formerly* **Chang·an** \'chän-'än\ city E *cen* China ✳ of Shensi on Wei river *pop* 787,300

Siang *or* **Hsiang** \'shē-'än\ 1 river 350 *m* SE *cen* China flowing from N Kwangsi N into Tungting Lake in Hunan 2 — see YÜ

Siang·tan \'shē-'än-'tän\ city SE China in E Hunan on the Siang S of Changsha *pop* 183,600

Si·be·ria \sī-'bir-ē-ə\ region U.S.S.R. E of the Urals, roughly coextensive with Soviet Russia, Asia — **Si·be·ri·an** \-ən\ *adj or n*

Si·biu \sē-'byü\ city W *cen* Romania in Transylvania *pop* 95,878

Si·bu·yan \ˌsē-bü-'yän\ sea *cen* Philippines bounded by Mindoro, S Luzon, & the Visayas

Sic·i·ly \'sis-(ə-)lē\ *or It* **Si·ci·lia** \sē-'chēl-yä\ *or anc* **Si·cil·ia** \sə-'sil-yə\ *or* **Tri·na·cria** \trə-'nak-rē-ə, trī-\ island S Italy in the Mediterranean; a region ✳ Palermo *area* 9926, *pop* 4,486,749 — **Si·cil·ian** \sə-'sil-yən\ *adj or n*

Si·cy·on \'sis(h)-ē-ˌän\ *or Gk* **Sik·y·on** \'sik-ē-\ ancient city S Greece in NE Peloponnesus NW of Corinth

Si·di Bar·râ·ni \ˌsēd-ē-bə-'rän-ē\ village NW Egypt on coast W of Mersa Matruh

Si·di-bel-Ab·bès \-ˌbel-ə-'bes\ commune NW Algeria S of Oran *pop* 105,000

Sidi Ifni — see IFNI

Si·don \'sīd-ᵊn\ *or Ar* **Sai·da** \'sīd-ə\ city & port SW Lebanon; a chief city of ancient Phoenicia *pop* 17,739 — **Si·do·ni·an** \sī-'dō-nē-ən\ *adj or n*

Sid·ra, Gulf of \'sid-rə\ *or anc* **Syr·tis Ma·jor** \ˌsərt-ə-'smā-jər\ inlet of the Mediterranean on coast of Libya

Sie·ben·ge·bir·ge \'zē-bən-gə-ˌbi)r-gə\ hills W Germany on right bank of the Rhine SSE of Bonn — see DRACHENFELS

Si·ena \sē-'en-ə\ commune *cen* Italy in Tuscany *pop* 40,722 — **Si·enese** *or* **Si·en·nese** \ˌsē-ə-'nēz, -'nēs\ *adj or n*

Si·er·ra Blan·ca \sē-ˌer-ə-'blaṇ-kə\ *or* **Sierra Blanca Peak** mountain 12,003 *ft* S *cen* N. Mex. in Sierra Blanca range of the Sacramento mountains

Sierra de Cór·do·ba \-də-'kórd-ə-bə\ mountain range *cen* Argentina chiefly in Córdoba province; highest Cerro Champaquí 9462 *ft*

Sierra de Gre·dos \-də-'grād-(ˌ)ōs\ mountain range W *cen* Spain, SW extension of the Sierra de Guadarrama; highest peak Plaza de Almanzor 8692 *ft*

Sierra de Gua·dar·ra·ma \-də-ˌgwäd-ə-'räm-ə\ mountain range *cen* Spain; highest peak Pico de Peñalara 7890 *ft*

Sier·ra Le·one \sē-ˌer-ə-lē-'ōn, ˌsir-ə\ country W Africa bordering on the Atlantic; a Brit. dominion ✳ Freetown *area* 27,925, *pop* 2,500,000 — **Sier·ra Le·o·ne·an** \-'ō-nē-ən\ *adj or n*

Si·er·ra Ma·dre del Sur \sē-ˌer-ə-ˌmäd-rē-ˌdel-'sü(ə)r\ mountain range S Mexico along Pacific coast in Guerrero & Oaxaca

Sierra Madre Oc·ci·den·tal \-ˌäk-sə-ˌden-'täl\ mountain range NW Mexico parallel to the Pacific coast

Sierra Madre Ori·en·tal \-ˌōr-ē-ˌen-'täl, -ˌór-\ mountain range E Mexico parallel to coast of Gulf of Mexico

Sier·ra Mo·re·na \-ˌmo-'rā-nə\ mountain range SW Spain between Guadiana & Guadalquivir rivers; highest peak Estrella 4274 *ft*

Sier·ra Ne·va·da \-nə-'vad-ə, -'väd-\ 1 mountain range E Calif. — see WHITNEY (Mount) 2 mountain range S Spain; highest peak Mulhacén 11,420 *ft*

Sierra Nevada de Mé·ri·da — see CORDILLERA MÉRIDA

Sierra Nevada de San·ta Mar·ta \-ˌsant-ə-'märt-ə\ mountain range N Colombia on Caribbean coast; highest 19,030 *ft*

Sierra Pacaraimc. — see SERRA PACARAIMA

Sierra Parima — see SERRA PARIMA

Sikandarabad — see SECUNDERABAD

Si·kang \'shē-'käṇ\ former province S China ✳ Yaan; incorporated 1955 in Szechwan & Chamdo

Si·kho·te Alin \ˌsē-kə-ˌtä-ə-'lēn\ mountain range U.S.S.R. in Soviet Russia, Asia, in Maritime Territory; highest point 6575 *ft*

Sik·kim \'sik-əm\ territory SE Asia on S slopes of the Himalayas between India & Tibet; a protectorate of Republic of India ✳ Gangtok *area* 2,818, *pop* 137,158 — **Sikkimese** *adj or n*

Si·le·sia \sī-'lē-zh(ē-)ə, sə-, -sh(ē-)ə\ region E *cen* Europe in valley of the upper Oder bordering on the Sudeten mountains; formerly chiefly in Germany, now chiefly in N Czechoslovakia & SW Poland — **Si·le·sian** \-zh(ē-)ən, -sh(ē-)ən\ *adj*

Silver Spring urban area SW Md. *pop* 66,348

Simbirsk — see ULYANOVSK

Sim·coe, Lake \'sim-(ˌ)kō\ lake E Canada in SE Ont. SE of Georgian Bay *area* 280

Sim·fe·ro·pol \ˌsim(p)-fə-'rò-pəl, -'rō\ city U.S.S.R. in S Soviet Russia, Europe, in the Crimea *pop* 189,000

Sim·la \'sim-lə\ city N India N of Delhi ✳ of Himachal Pradesh & former summer ✳ of India *pop* 46,100

Si·mons·town \'sī-mənz-ˌtaùn\ town & port SW Republic of So. Africa on False Bay S of Cape Town

Sim·plon \'sim-ˌplän\ 1 mountain pass 6589 *ft* in Lepontine Alps between Switzerland & Italy in Valais & Piedmont 2 tunnel 12.3 *m* long through Monte Leone near the pass

Si·nai \'sī-ˌnī *also* -nē-ˌī\ 1 peninsula extension of continent of Asia NE Egypt between Red sea & the Mediterranean 2 — see HOREB — **Si·na·it·ic** \ˌsī-nē-'it-ik\ *adj*

Si·na·loa \ˌsē-nə-'lō-ə, ˌsin-ə-\ state W Mexico bordering on Gulf of California ✳ Culiacán *area* 22,580, *pop* 757,563

Sind \'sind\ region Pakistan in S West Pakistan in lower Indus river valley; chief city Karachi

Sin·ga·pore \'siṇ-(g)ə-ˌpō(ə)r, -ˌpó(ə)r\ 1 island Malay archipelago in So. China sea off S end of Malay peninsula; formerly a Brit. crown colony, from 1963 to 1965 a state of Federation of Malaysia, an independent republic since 1965, *area* 224, *pop* 1,913,500 2 city & port, its ✳ on Singapore Strait *pop* 1,000,000 — **Sin·ga·por·ean** \ˌsiṇ-(g)ə-'pōr-ē-ən, -'pór-\ *adj or n*

Singapore Strait channel SE Asia between Singapore I. & Riouw archipelago connecting Strait of Malacca & So. China sea

Sin·hai·lien \'shiṇ-ˌhī-lē-'en\ *or formerly* **Tung·hai** \'tùṇ-'hī\ *or* **Hai·chow** \'hī-'jō\ city E China in N Kiangsu near coast *pop* 207,600

Si·ning \'shē-'niṇ\ city NW China WNW of Lanchow ✳ of Tsinghai *pop* 93,700

Sin·kiang \'shin-jē-'äṇ\ *or* **Sinkiang–Ui·ghur Region** \'wē-gər\ region W China between Kunlun & Altai mountains; formerly a province ✳ Urumchi *area* 635,829, *pop* 4,874,000

Si·nop \sə-'nóp\ *or anc* **Si·no·pe** \-'nō-pē\ town & port N Turkey on peninsula in Black sea NW of Ankara

Sin·siang \'shin-shē-'äṇ\ city E China in N Honan N of Chengchow *pop* 170,500

Sint-Gillis — see SAINT-GILLES

Sint-Jans-Molenbeek — see MOLENBEEK

Sin·tra *or* **Cin·tra** \'sēn-trə, 'sin-\ town W Portugal NW of Lisbon

Sin·ui·ju \'shin-ē-jü\ *or Jap* **Shin·gi·shu** \'shiṇ-gi-ˌshü\ city N Korea on the Yalu opposite Antung, China *pop* 118,414

Sion, 1 \sē-ˈōⁿ\ *or G* **Sit·ten** \'zit-ᵊn, 'sit-\ commune SW *cen* Switzerland ✳ of Valais 2 — see ZION

Sioux City \'sü\ city NW Iowa on Missouri river *pop* 89,159

Sioux Falls city SE S. Dak. on Big Sioux river *pop* 65,466

Sip·par \sip-'är\ ancient city of Babylonia on the Euphrates SSW of modern Baghdad; Sargon's capital

Sira *or* **Síros** — see SYROS

Siracusa — see SYRACUSE

Si·ret \sē-'ret\ river 270 *m* E Romania flowing from the Carpathians SE into the Danube

Sis·ki·you \'sis-ki-ˌyü\ mountains N Calif. & SW Oreg., a range of Klamath mountains; highest Mt. Ashland (in Oreg.) 7530 *ft*

Sit·ka National Monument \'sit-kə\ reservation SE Alaska on Baranof I. near town of Sitka; Indian & Russian relics

Sit·tang \'si-ˌtäŋ\ river 350 *m* E *cen* Burma flowing S into Gulf of Martaban

Si·vas \si-'väs\ *or anc* **Se·bas·te** \sə-'bas-tē\ *or* **Se·bas·tia** \sə-'bas-ch(ē-)ə, -tē-ə\ city E *cen* Turkey *pop* 93,849

Si·wa \'sē-wə\ *or anc* **Am·mo·ni·um** \ə-'mō-nē-əm\ oasis & town NW Egypt W of Qattara Depression

Si·wa·lik \si-'wäl-ik\ range of foothills of the Himalayas N India extending SE from N Punjab into Uttar Pradesh

Sjæl·land \'shel-ˌän\ *or* E **Zea·land** \'zē-lənd\ island, largest of islands of Denmark; site of Copenhagen *area* 2709

Skag·er·rak \'skag-ə-ˌrak\ arm of the North sea between Norway & Denmark

Skag·it \'skaj-ət\ river 200 *m* SW B.C. & NW Wash. flowing S & W into Puget sound

Skan·e·at·e·les \ˌskan-ē-'at-ləs, ˌskin-\ lake 16 *m* long *cen* N.Y. SW of Syracuse; one of the Finger Lakes

Skaw \'skȯ\ *or* **Cape Ska·gen** \'skäg-ən\ cape Denmark at N extremity of Jutland

Skee·na \'skē-nə\ river 360 *m* Canada in W B.C. flowing S & W into Hecate strait

Skid·daw \'skid-ˌȯ\ mountain 3054 *ft* NW England in *cen* Cumberland

Sko·kie \'skō-kē\ village NE Ill. N of Chicago *pop* 59,364

Skop·lje \'skäp-əl-ˌyä, 'skōp-\ *or* **Skop·je** \'skäp-(ˌ)yä, 'skōp-\ *or* Turk **Us·kub** \ù-'sküb\ city S Yugoslavia ✳ of Macedonia on Vardar river *pop* 170,000

Skunk river 264 *m* SE Iowa flowing SE into the Mississippi

Skutari — see SCUTARI, USKUDAR

Skye \'skī\ island Scotland, one of the Inner Hebrides *area* 670

Sky·ros \'skī-rəs, -ˌräs\ *or* **Scy·ros** \'sī-\ *or* NGk **Ský·ros** \'skē-ˌrós\ island Greece in the Northern Sporades E of Euboea

Sla — see SALÉ

Slave \'slāv\ *or* **Great Slave** river 258 *m* Canada flowing from W end of Lake Athabasca N into Great Slave Lake

Slave coast region W Africa bordering on Bight of Benin between Benin & Volta rivers

Slavkov — see AUSTERLITZ

Sla·vo·nia \slə-'vō-nē-ə, -nyə\ region N Yugoslavia in E Croatia between the Sava, the Drava, & the Danube

Slea·ford \'slē-fərd\ urban district E England ✳ of Parts of Kesteven, Lincolnshire

Slesvig — see SCHLESWIG

Slide Mountain \'slīd-\ mountain 4204 *ft* SE N.Y. W of Kingston; highest in the Catskills

Sli·go \'slī-(ˌ)gō\ **1** county N Republic of Ireland in N Connacht *area* 694, *pop* 53,588 **2** municipal borough & port, its ✳, on Sligo Bay

Slough \'slau\ urban district SE *cen* England in Buckinghamshire W of London *pop* 66,439

Slo·va·kia \slō-'väk-ē-ə, -'vak-\ region E Czechoslovakia ‑E of Moravia; chief city Bratislava

Slo·ve·nia \slō-'vē-nē-ə, -nyə\ federated republic NW Yugoslavia N & W of Croatia ✳ Ljubljana *area* 7708, *pop* 1,466,425

Smeth·wick \'smeth-ik\ county borough W *cen* England W of Birmingham *pop* 76,397

Smoky Hill river 540 *m*, *cen* Kans. flowing E to unite with Republican river forming the Kansas

Smo·lensk \smō-'len(t)sk\ city U.S.S.R. in W Soviet Russia, Europe, on upper Dnieper river WSW of Moscow *pop* 146,000

Smyrna — see IZMIR

Snake \'snāk\ river 1038 *m* NW U. S. flowing from NW Wyo. across S Idaho & into the Columbia in Wash.

Sno·qual·mie \snō-'kwäl-mē\ **1** mountain pass 3004 *ft* W *cen* Wash. in Cascade range SE of Seattle **2** waterfall 268 *ft* W *cen* Wash. in Snoqualmie river

Snow \'snō\ mountains West New Guinea; include Nassau & Orange ranges — see CARSTENSZ (Mount)

Snow·don \'snōd-ᵊn\ massif 3560 *ft* N Wales; highest point in Wales

Snow·do·nia \snō-'dō-nē-ə, -nyə\ mountain region NW Wales centering around Mt. Snowdon

Snowy, 1 mountains SE Australia in SE New So. Wales **2** river 240 *m* SE Australia flowing from Snowy mountains to the Pacific

So·bat \'sō-ˌbat\ river 460 *m* W Ethiopia & SE Sudan flowing W into the White Nile

Soche — see YARKAND

So·chi \'sō-chē\ city & port U.S.S.R. in S Soviet Russia, Europe, on NE coast of Black sea *pop* 95,000

So·ci·e·ty \sə-'sī-ət-ē\ *or* F **Îles de la So·cié·té** \ēl-də-là-sȯ-syā-tā\ islands S Pacific belonging to France ✳ Papeete (on Tahiti) *area* 650, *pop* 65,574

So·co·tra *or* **So·ko·tra** \sə-'kō-trə\ island Indian ocean E of Gulf of Aden in So. Yemen ✳ Tamrida (Hadibu) *area* 1400, *pop* 12,000

Sod·om \'säd-əm\ **1** city of ancient Palestine in plain of the Jordan **2** *or* **Se·dom** \sə-'dōm\ town Israel near S end of Dead sea

Soemba — see SUMBA

Soembawa — see SUMBAWA

Soenda — see SUNDA

Soerabaja — see SURABAJA

Soerakarta — see SURAKARTA

So·fia \'sō-fē-ə, 'sȯ-, sō-'\ *or* Bulg **So·fi·ya** \'sȯ-fē-(y)ə\ *or anc* **Ser·di·ca** \'sərd-i-kə\ *or* **Sar·di·ca** \'särd-\ city ✳ of Bulgaria *pop* 800,953

Sog·di·a·na \ˌsäg-dē-'an-ə, -'än-ə, -'ā-nə\ province of ancient Persian Empire between the Jaxartes (Syr Darya) & Oxus (Amu Darya) ✳ Maracanda (Samarkand)

Sog·ne Fjord \ˌsȯŋ-nə-\ inlet of Norwegian sea SW Norway

So·hâg \sō-'haj\ city *cen* Egypt on the Nile SE of Asyût *pop* 59,300

So·ho \'sō-ˌhō\ district of *cen* London, England, in Westminster

Sois·sons \swä-'sōⁿ\ commune N France NW of Paris

So·lent \'sō-lənt\ channel S England between Isle of Wight & the mainland

So·li·mões \ˌsü-lē-'mȯiⁿsh\ the upper Amazon, Brazil, from Peruvian border to the Negro

So·ling·en \'zō-liŋ-ən, 'sō-\ city W Germany in the Ruhr ESE of Düsseldorf *pop* 169,060

Sol·na \'sȯl-nə\ city E Sweden, N suburb of Stockholm *pop* 52,140

Solo — see SURAKARTA

Sol·o·mon \'säl-ə-mən\ **1** islands W Pacific E of New Guinea divided between the Australian trust territory of New Guinea & the Brit. Solomon islands *area* 16,120 **2** sea arm of Coral sea W of Solomon islands

So·lo·thurn \'zō-lə-ˌtú(ə)rn, 'sō-\ *or* F **So·leure** \sō-'lər\ **1** canton NW Switzerland *area* 306, *pop* 170,508 **2** commune, its ✳, on the Aare *pop* 16,743

Sol·way firth \ˌsäl-ˌwā-\ inlet of Irish sea in Great Britain on boundary between England & Scotland

So·ma·lia \sō-'mäl-ē-ə, -'mäl-yə\ *or* **So·ma·li Republic** \-ˌmäl-ē-\ country E Africa bordering on Gulf of Aden & Indian ocean; formed 1960 by union of Brit. Somaliland & Italian Somaliland ✳ Mogadishu *area* 262,000, *pop* 1,990,000 — **So·ma·lian** \-'mäl-ē-ən, -'mäl-yən\ *adj or n*

So·ma·li·land \sō-'mäl-ē-ˌland\ region E Africa comprising Somalia, French Somaliland, & Ogaden region of E Ethiopia

Som·er·set \'səm-ər-ˌset, -sət\ **1** island N Canada in Franklin District N of Boothia peninsula *area* 9370 **2** *or* **Som·er·set·shire** \-ˌshi(ə)r, -shər\ county SW England ✳ Taunton *area* 1620, *pop* 551,188

Somerset Nile — see NILE

Som·er·ville \'səm-ər-ˌvil, -vil\ city E Mass. N of Cambridge *pop* 94,697

So·mes \sō-'mesh\ *or* Hung **Sza·mos** \'sȯm-ˌōsh\ river 200 *m* NE Hungary & NW Romania flowing NW into the Tisza

Somme \'säm, 'səm\ river 147 *m* N France flowing NW into the English channel

So·no·ra \sə-'nōr-ə, -'nȯr-\ **1** river 300 *m* NW Mexico flowing SW into upper Gulf of California **2** state NW Mexico bordering on U. S. & Gulf of California ✳ Hermosillo *area* 70,477, *pop* 644,511 — **So·no·ran** \-ən\ *adj or n*

Soo locks *or* **Soo locks** — see SAULT SAINTE MARIE CANALS

Soo·chow *or* **Su·chou** \'sü-'jō, -'chau\ *or* **Wu·hsien** \'wü-shē-'en\ city E China in SE Kiangsu W of Shanghai *pop* 474,000

So·pot \'sȯ-ˌpȯt\ city N Poland NNW of Gdansk *pop* 40,000

Sop·ron \'shō-ˌprōn\ city W Hungary *pop* 37,000

Sorata — see ILLAMPU

Sorbiodunum — see OLD SARUM

So·rel \sə-'rel\ city Canada in S Que. on the St. Lawrence SW of Trois-Rivières *pop* 16,476

So·ria \'sōr-ē-ə, 'sȯr-\ **1** province N *cen* Spain *area* 3983, *pop* 154,789 **2** commune, its ✳, W of Zaragoza *pop* 18,544

So·ro·ca·ba \ˌsōr-ə-'kav-ə, ˌsȯr-\ city SE Brazil in SE São Paulo state *pop* 68,811

Sor·ren·to \sə-'ren-(ˌ)tō\ *or anc* **Sur·ren·tum** \sə-'rent-əm\ commune & port S Italy on S side of Bay of Naples

Sos·no·wiec \sə-'snȯv-ˌyets\ *or* **Sos·no·wi·ce** \ˌsȯs-nə-'vēt-sə\ city SW Poland NE of Katowice *pop* 125,000

Soudan — see SUDAN

Sou·fri·ère \ˌsü-frē-'e(ə)r\ **1** *or* **Grande Soufrière** \ˌgrän(n)d-\ volcano 4869 *ft* French West Indies in S Basse-Terre, Guadeloupe **2** volcano 4048 *ft* Brit. West Indies on St. Vincent I.

Sound, The — see ÖRESUND

Sou·ris \'sùr-əs\ *or* **Mouse** \'maús\ river 450 *m* Canada & U.S. flowing from SE Sask. SE into N N. Dak. & N into the Assiniboine in SW Man.

Sousse \'süs\ *or* **Su·sa** \'sü-sə, -zə\ *or anc* **Had·ru·me·tum** \ˌhad-rə-'mēt-əm\ city & port NE Tunisia *pop* 48,172

South island S New Zealand *area* 58,092, *pop* 716,000

South Africa, Republic of country S Africa S of the Limpopo, Molopo, & Orange rivers bordering on Atlantic & Indian oceans; a republic, until 1961 (as **Union of South Africa**) a Brit. dominion; administrative ✳ Pretoria, legislative ✳ Cape Town, judicial ✳ Bloemfontein *area* 472,359, *pop* 15,780,000

Sou·thall \'sau-ˌthȯl\ *or formerly* **Southall Nor·wood** \'nȯ(ə)r-ˌwùd\ municipal borough S England in Middlesex *pop* 55,900

South America continent of the western hemisphere lying between the Atlantic & Pacific oceans SE of No. America & chiefly S of the equator *area* 7,035,357 — **South American** *adj or n*

South·amp·ton \sauth-'(h)am(p)-tən\ **1** island N Canada in Keewatin District, Northwest Territories, between Hudson Bay & Foxe channel *area* 15,700 **2** — see HAMPSHIRE **3** county borough & port S England in Hampshire on **Southampton Water** (estuary of Test river) *pop* 178,326

South Arabia, Federation of — see SOUTH YEMEN

South Australia state S Australia ✳ Adelaide *area* 380,070, *pop* 914,763

South Bend \'bend\ city N Ind. *pop* 132,445

South Brabant — see BRABANT

South·bridge \'sauth-(ˌ)brij\ urban area S Mass. *pop* 15,889

South Canadian — see CANADIAN

South Cape — see KA LAE

South Car·o·li·na \ˌkar-ə-'lī-nə\ state SE U. S. ✳ Columbia *area* 31,055, *pop* 2,382,594 — **South Car·o·lin·ian** \-'lin-ē-ən, -'lin-yən\ *adj or n*

South Charleston city W W. Va. W of Charleston *pop* 19,180

South China sea W Pacific bounded by SE China, Formosa, Philippines, Indochina, Malaya, & Borneo

South Da·ko·ta \də-'kōt-ə\ state NW *cen* U. S. ✳ Pierre *area* 77,047, *pop* 680,514 — **South Da·ko·tan** \-'kōt-ᵊn\ *adj or n*

South Downs \'daunz\ hills S England chiefly in Sussex

South·end on Sea \ˌsau-ˌthend-\ county borough SE England in Essex at mouth of Thames estuary *pop* 151,830

Southern Alps mountain range New Zealand in W South I. extending almost the length of the island — see COOK (Mount)

Southern Morocco *or* **Southern Protectorate of Morocco** former Spanish protectorate W Africa S of former French Morocco

Southern ocean the Antarctic ocean

Southern Rhodesia country S Africa S of the Zambezi; a self‑governing territory within the Brit. Commonwealth ✳ Salisbury *area* 150,333, *pop* 2,590,000

Southern Uplands elevated moorland region S Scotland extending from English border to a line joining Girvan & Dunbar

South Euclid city NE Ohio E of Cleveland *pop* 27,569

South Far·ming·dale \'fär-miŋ-ˌdāl\ urban area SE N.Y. on Long I. *pop* 16,318

South·field \'sauth-ˌfēld\ city SE Mich. NW of Detroit *pop* 31,501

ə abut; ᵊ kitten; ər further; a back; ā bake; ä cot, cart; au̇ out; ch chin; e less; ē easy; g gift; i trip; ī life
j joke; ŋ sing; ō flow; ȯ flaw; ȯi coin; th thin; t͟h this; ü loot; ù foot; y yet; yü few; yù furious; zh vision
ᵊ F table; ȧ F bac; ḵ G ich, Buch; ⁿ F vin; œ F bœuf; œ̄ F feu; ᵫ G füllen; ᵫ̄ F rue; ʸ F digne \dēnʸ\, nuit \nwʸē\

South·gate, 1 \'sau̇th-,gāt\ city SE Mich. S of Detroit *pop* 29,404 **2** \-gət, -,gāt\ municipal borough SE England in Middlesex N of London *pop* 73,376
South Gate \,gāt\ city SW Calif. SE of Los Angeles *pop* 53,831
South Georgia island S Atlantic E of Tierra del Fuego in Falkland Islands Dependencies *area* 1450
South Holland *or* D **Zuid·hol·land** \zīt-'hȯ-,länt\ province SW Netherlands ✻ Rotterdam *area* 1212, *pop* 2,668,158
South Milwaukee city SE Wis. on Lake Michigan *pop* 20,307
South Mountain mountain ridge S Pa. & W Md. at N end of Blue Ridge mountains
South Na·han·ni \nə-'han-ē\ river 350 *m* Canada in SW Mackenzie District flowing SE into the Liard
South Norfolk former city SE Va.; now part of Chesapeake
South Orange village NE N. J. W of Newark *pop* 16,175
South Orkney islands S Atlantic SE of the Falklands in Falkland Islands Dependencies
South Ossetia *or* **South Ossetian Region** autonomous region U.S.S.R. in N Georgia on S slopes of the Caucasus ✻ Tskhinvali *area* 1500, *pop* 120,000
South Pasadena city SW Calif. *pop* 19,706
South Pass broad level valley SW *cen* Wyo. crossing continental divide near SE end of Wind River range
South Plainfield borough NE N. J. SW of Elizabeth *pop* 17,879
South Platte river 424 *m* Colo. & Nebr. flowing E to join the No. Platte forming the Platte
South Point — see KA LAE
South·port \'sau̇th-,pō(ə)rt, -,pȯ(ə)rt\ county borough NW England in Lancashire on coast N of Liverpool *pop* 84,057
South Portland city SW Me. *pop* 22,788
South Sacramento urban area N *cen* Calif. *pop* 16,443
South Saint Paul city SE Minn. on the Mississippi *pop* 22,032
South Sandwich islands S Atlantic SE of So. Georgia I. in Falkland Islands Dependencies
South San Francisco city W Calif. *pop* 39,418
South San Gabriel urban area SW Calif. *pop* 26,213
South Saskatchewan — see SASKATCHEWAN
South sea or **South seas** the areas of the Atlantic, Indian, & Pacific oceans in the southern hemisphere, esp. the S Pacific
South Shetland islands S Atlantic SE of Cape Horn off tip of Antarctic peninsula in Falkland Islands Dependencies
South Shields \'shē(ə)l(d)z\ county borough N England in Durham at mouth of the Tyne E of Newcastle *pop* 106,605
South Tirol — see ALTO ADIGE
South·wark \'səth-ərk, 'sau̇th-wərk\ metropolitan borough London, England, on S bank of the Thames *pop* 97,191
South-West Africa *or* **Suid·wes-Afri·ka** \,sīt-,ves-'äf-rē-kə\ *or* **Na·mib·ia** \nə-'mib-ē-ə\ *or formerly* **German Southwest Africa** territory SW Africa on the Atlantic; belonged to Germany before 1919, assigned as mandate by League of Nations to Union of So. Africa 1919 ✻ Windhoek *area* 318,099, *pop* 418,104
South Yemen republic S Arabian peninsula on Gulf of Aden formed 1967 from former **Federation of South Arabia** (Brit. protectorate comprising crown colony of Aden & numerous semi-independent Arab sultanates & amirates) ✻ Medina as-Shaab *area* 61,900, *pop* 900,000
So·vetsk \səv-'yetsk\ *or* G **Til·sit** \'til-sət, -zət\ city U. S. S. R. in W Soviet Russia, Europe, on Neman river *pop* 50,000
So·vet·ska·ya Ga·van \səv-,yet-skə-yə-'gäv-ən(-yə)\ city & port U. S. S. R. in SE Soviet Russia, Asia, in Khabarovsk Territory on Tatar strait
Soviet Central Asia the portion of *cen* Asia belonging to the U. S. S. R. & comprising the Kirgiz, Tadzhik, Turkmen, & Uzbek republics & sometimes the Kazakh Republic
Soviet Russia, 1 — see RUSSIAN REPUBLIC **2** the U.S.S.R.
Soviet Union — see UNION OF SOVIET SOCIALIST REPUBLICS
Spa \'spä, 'spȯ\ town E Belgium SE of Liège
Spain \'spān\ *or* Sp **Es·pa·ña** \ā-'spän-yä\ country SW Europe in the Iberian peninsula; nominally a kingdom ✻ Madrid *area* 193,144, *pop* 30,237,242
Span·dau \'s(h)pän-,dau̇\ a W section of Berlin, Germany
Spanish Africa the possessions of Spain in Africa: Spanish Sahara, Spanish Guinea, Ifni, & other areas *area* 117,123, *pop* 407,495
Spanish America, 1 the Spanish-speaking countries of Central & So. America **2** the parts of America settled & formerly governed by the Spanish — **Spanish–American** *adj* — **Spanish American** *n*
Spanish Guinea former Spanish colony W Africa bordering on Gulf of Guinea including Río Muni & Fernando Po & other islands — see EQUATORIAL GUINEA
Spanish Main, 1 the mainland of Spanish America esp. along N coast of So. America **2** the Caribbean sea & adjacent waters esp. at the time when region was infested by pirates
Spanish Morocco — see MOROCCO
Spanish Peaks two mountains (East Spanish Peak & West Spanish Peak) S Colo. E of Sangre de Cristo mountains; W peak 13,623 *ft*
Spanish Sahara region NW Africa SW of Morocco comprising the Spanish possessions Río de Oro & Saguia el Hamra ✻ Villa Cisneros *area* 105,448, *pop* 13,627
Spanish Town town SE *cen* Jamaica; former ✻ of Jamaica
Sparks \'spärks\ city W Nev. E of Reno *pop* 16,618
Spar·ta \'spärt-ə\ *or* **Lac·e·dae·mon** \,las-ə-'dē-mən\ ancient city S Greece in Peloponnesus ✻ of Laconia
Spar·tan·burg \'spärt-^{ə}n-,bərg\ city NW S. C. *pop* 44,352
Spen·cer Gulf \,spen(t)-sər-\ inlet of Indian ocean SE So. Australia
Spey \'spā\ river 110 *m* NE Scotland flowing into Moray firth
Spey·er \'s(h)pī(-ə)r\ *or* **Spires** \'spī(ə)rz\ city W Germany on W bank of the Rhine SW of Heidelberg *pop* 37,200
Spe·zia *or* **La Spezia** \lä-'spet-sē-ə\ city & port NW Italy in Liguria *pop* 112,245
Spice — see MOLUCCAS
Spits·ber·gen \'spits-,bər-gən\ group of islands in Arctic ocean N of Norway; belongs to Norway *area* 24,280 — see SVALBARD
Split \'split\ *or* **Spljet** \splē-'et\ *or* It **Spa·la·to** \'späl-ə-,tō\ city & port W Yugoslavia in Croatia on Dalmatian coast *pop* 77,100
Spo·kane \spō-'kan\ **1** river 120 *m* N Idaho & E Wash. flowing from Coeur d'Alene Lake W into the Columbia **2** city E Wash. at Spokane Falls in Spokane river *pop* 181,608
Spo·le·to \spə-'lāt-(,)ō\ commune *cen* Italy SE of Perugia
Spor·a·des \'spȯr-ə-,dēz, 'spär-\ two island groups Greece in the Aegean: the **Northern Sporades** (chief island Skyros, N of Euboea & E of Thessaly) & the **Southern Sporades** (chiefly Samos, Icaria, & the Dodecanese, off SW Turkey)
Spree \'s(h)prā\ river 220 *m* E Germany flowing N into the Havel
Spree·wald \-,vält\ marshy district E Germany in Spree valley
Spring·field \'spriŋ-,fēld\ **1** city ✻ of Ill. on the Sangamon *pop* 83,271 **2** city SW Mass. on the Connecticut *pop* 174,463 **3** city SW Mo. *pop* 95,865 **4** city W *cen* Ohio NE of Dayton *pop* 82,723 **5** city W Oreg. on the Willamette E of Eugene *pop* 19,616 **6** urban township SE Pa. in Delaware county *pop* 26,733 **7** urban township SE Pa. in Montgomery county *pop* 20,652
Springs \'spriŋz\ city NE Republic of So. Africa in S Transvaal *pop* 119,382
Spuy·ten Duy·vil Creek \,spīt-^{ə}n-,dī-vəl-\ channel New York City N of Manhattan I. connecting Hudson & Harlem rivers
Squaw \'skwȯ\ valley E Calif. on E slope of **Squaw Peak** 8960 *ft* in the Sierra Nevada W of Lake Tahoe
Sri·na·gar \sri-'nəg-ər\ city, summer ✻ of Jammu & Kashmir, in W Kashmir on Jhelum river NNE of Lahore *pop* 207,800
Srirangapatnam — see SERINGAPATAM
Staf·fa \'staf-ə\ islet W Scotland in the Inner Hebrides W of Mull — see FINGAL'S CAVE
Staf·ford \'staf-ərd\ **1** *or* **Staf·ford·shire** \-,shi(ə)r, -shər\ county W *cen* England *area* 1153, *pop* 1,621,013 **2** municipal borough, its ✻, NNW of Birmingham *pop* 40,275
Staked Plain — see LLANO ESTACADO
Stalin, 1 — see BRASOV **2** — see DONETSK **3** — see VARNA
Stalinabad — see DYUSHAMBE
Stalingrad — see VOLGOGRAD
Stalino — see DONETSK
Stalin Peak — see GARMO PEAK
Stalinsk — see NOVOKUZNETSK
Stam·boul *or* **Stam·bul** \stam-'bül\ **1** the older part of Istanbul S of the Golden Horn **2** ISTANBUL
Stam·ford \'stam(p)-fərd\ city SW Conn. *pop* 92,713
Stan·i·slav \,stan-ə-'slaf, -'slav\ city U. S. S. R. in SW Ukraine *pop* 66,000
Stan·ley \'stan-lē\ *or* **Port Stanley** town ✻ of the Falklands
Stanley, Mount mountain with two peaks (higher Margherita Peak 16,763 *ft*) E *cen* Africa; highest of Ruwenzori
Stanley Falls series of seven cataracts NE Congo in Lualaba river near head of Congo river with total fall of *ab* 200 *ft* in 60 *m*
Stanley Pool expansion of Congo river *ab* 20 *m* long 300 *m* above its mouth between Congo Republic & Republic of Congo; Brazzaville & Kinshasa are situated on its banks
Stanleyville — see KISANGANI
Stan·o·voi \,stan-ə-'vȯi\ mountain range U.S.S.R. in E Soviet Russia, Asia, N of Amur river; highest point 8143 *ft*
Sta·ra Za·go·ra \,stär-ə-zə-'gȯr-ə, -'gȯr-\ city *cen* Bulgaria *pop* 55,322
State College borough *cen* Pa. NE of Altoona *pop* 22,409
Stat·en \'stat-^{ə}n\ island SE N. Y. SW of mouth of the Hudson; part of New York City, constituting borough of Richmond
States of the Church *or* **Papal States** temporal domain of the popes in *cen* Italy 755–1870
States·ville \'stāts-,vil, -vəl\ city W *cen* N. C. *pop* 19,844
Statue of Liberty National Monument — see LIBERTY
Staun·ton \'stant-^{ə}n\ city NW *cen* Va. *pop* 22,232
Sta·vang·er \stə-'väŋ-ər\ city & port SW Norway *pop* 52,848
Stav·ro·pol \stav-'rō-pəl, -'rō-\ **1** territory U. S. S. R. in S Soviet Russia, Europe, N of the Caucasus *area* 29,600, *pop* 1,500,000 **2** city, its ✻ *pop* 140,000
Ste·bark \'ste(^{n})m-,bärk\ *or* G **Tan·nen·berg** \'tan-ən-,bərg, 'tän-ən-,berk\ village NE Poland SW of Olsztyn
Steens \'stēnz\ mountains SE Oreg.; highest point **Steens Mountain** (massif) 9354 *ft*
Stel·len·bosch \'stel-ən-,bu̇sh, ,stel-əm-'bȯs\ town SW Republic of So. Africa in SW Cape Province E of Cape Town
Step·ney \'step-nē\ metropolitan borough E London, England, on N bank of the Thames *pop* 98,581
Ster·ling \'stər-liŋ\ city NW Ill. on Rock river *pop* 15,688
Stet·tin \s(h)te-'tēn\ *or* Pol **Szcze·cin** \'shchet-,sēn\ city & port NW Poland on the Oder near its mouth *pop* 249,400
Stet·ti·ner Haff \s(h)te-'tē-nər-,häf\ lagoon on Baltic coast between NE Germany & NW Poland at mouth of the Oder
Steu·ben·ville \'st(y)ü-bən-,vil\ city E Ohio on the Ohio N of Wheeling, W. Va. *pop* 32,495
Ste·vens Point \,stē-vənz-\ city *cen* Wis. *pop* 17,837
Stew·art \'st(y)ü-ərt, 'st(y)u̇(-ə)rt\ **1** river 320 *m* Canada in *cen* Yukon Territory flowing W into the Yukon **2** island New Zealand S of South I. *area* 670
Sti·kine \stik-'ēn\ river 335 *m* Canada & Alaska flowing from **Stikine mountains** (in B. C. & Yukon Territory; highest point 8670 *ft*) into the Pacific
Still·wa·ter \'stil-,wȯt-ər, -,wät-\ city N *cen* Okla. *pop* 23,965
Stir·ling \'stər-liŋ\ **1** *or* **Stir·ling·shire** \-,shi(ə)r, -shər\ county *cen* Scotland *area* 451, *pop* 187,432 **2** burgh, its ✻ *pop* 26,960
Stock·holm \'stäk-,hō(l)m\ city & port ✻ of Sweden on Lake Malar *pop* 806,900 — **Stock·holm·er** \-,hō(l)-mər\ *n*
Stock·port \'stäk-,pō(ə)rt, -,pȯ(ə)rt\ county borough NW England in Cheshire S of Manchester *pop* 141,660
Stock·ton \'stäk-tən\ **1** city *cen* Calif. on San Joaquin river E of Oakland *pop* 86,321 **2** *or* **Stockton on Tees** \'tēz\ municipal borough N England in Durham *pop* 74,024
Stoke New·ing·ton \stōk-'n(y)ü-iŋ-tən\ metropolitan borough N London, England *pop* 49,137
Stoke on Trent \,stō-,kȯn-'trent, -,kän-\ city & county borough W *cen* England in Staffordshire *pop* 275,095
Stone·ham \'stō-nəm, 'stōn-,(h)am\ town E Mass. N of Boston *pop* 17,821
Stone·ha·ven \stōn-'hā-vən\ burgh & port E Scotland ✻ of Kincardine
Stone·henge \'stōn-'henj\ assemblage of megaliths S England in Wiltshire on Salisbury Plain erected by a prehistoric people
Stone·leigh \'stōn-lē\ urban area N *cen* Md. near Baltimore *pop* (with Rodgers Forge) 15,645
Stone Mountain mountain 1686 *ft* NW *cen* Georgia E of Atlanta
Stones \'stōnz\ river 60 *m*, *cen* Tenn. flowing NW into the Cumberland
Stour \'stau̇(ə)r, 'stu̇(ə)r, 'stō(ə)r\ **1** river 60 *m* SE England flow-

ing E between Essex & Suffolk into the North sea **2** river 55 *m* S England in Dorset & Hampshire flowing SE into the Avon **3** river 40 *m* SE England in Kent flowing NE into the North sea **4** river 20 *m*, *cen* England in Oxfordshire & Warwickshire flowing NW into the Avon **5** river 20 *m* W *cen* England in Staffordshire & Worcestershire flowing S into the Severn

Stour·bridge \'stau̇(ə)r-(,)brij\ municipal borough W *cen* England in Worcestershire W of Birmingham *pop* 37,247

Straits Settlements former country SE Asia bordering on Strait of Malacca & comprising Singapore I., Penang, & Malacca; now in Federation of Malaysia *area* 1242

Stral·sund \'s(h)träl-,zu̇nt, -,su̇nt\ city & port E Germany on the Baltic opposite Rügen I. *pop* 65,300

Stras·bourg \'sträs-,bu̇(ə)rg, 'sträz-\ *or* G **Strass·burg** \'s(h)träs-bu̇rk\ city NE France on Ill river W of its junction with the Rhine *pop* 200,900

Strat·ford \'strat-fərd\ **1** town SW Conn. *pop* 45,012 **2** city Canada in SE Ont. W of Kitchener *pop* 19,972

Stratford on Avon municipal borough *cen* England in Warwick

Strath·clyde \strath-'klīd\ Celtic kingdom of 7th to 9th centuries S Scotland & NW England ✻ Dumbarton; its S part called **Cum·bria** \'kəm-brē-ə\

Strath·more \strath-'mō(ə)r, -'mȯ(ə)r\ great valley of E *cen* Scotland S of the Grampians

Strea·tor \'strēt-ər\ city N *cen* Ill. *pop* 16,868

Stre·sa \'strā-zə\ town NW Italy in Piedmont on Lake Maggiore

Stret·ford \'stret-fərd\ municipal borough NW England in Lancashire SW of Manchester *pop* 61,532

Strom·bo·li \'sträm-bə-(,)lē\ *or anc* **Stron·gy·le** \'strän-jə-,lē\ **1** island Italy in Lipari islands **2** volcano 3040 *ft* on the island

Strom·lo, Mount \'sträm-(,)lō\ hill 2500 *ft* SE Australia in New So. Wales W of Canberra

Struth·ers \'strəth-ərz\ city E Ohio SE of Youngstown on Mahoning river *pop* 15,631

Stry·mon \'strī-,män\ *or* NGk **Stri·món** \strē-'mȯn\ *or* Bulg **Stru·ma** \'strü-mə\ river 225 *m* W Bulgaria & NE Greece flowing SE into Strymonic gulf

Stry·mon·ic Gulf \(,)strī-,män-ik-\ *or* **Gulf of Stri·món** \strē-'mȯn\ *or* **Gulf of Or·fa·ni** \ȯr-'fän-ē\ inlet of the Aegean NE Greece NE of Chalcidice peninsula

Stutt·gart \'s(h)tu̇t-,gärt, 'stət-\ city W Germany ✻ of Baden-Württemberg on the Neckar *pop* 634,000

Styr \'sti(ə)r\ river 300 *m* U.S.S.R. in NW Ukraine flowing N into Pripet river in the Pripet marshes

Styr·ia \'stir-ē-ə\ *or* G **Stei·er·mark** \'s(h)tī(-ə)r-,märk\ region *cen* & SE Austria; chief city Graz — **Styr·i·an** *adj or n*

Sua·kin \'swäk-ən\ town & port NE Sudan on Red sea

Süan·hwa \sü-'än-'(h)wä\ city NE China in NW Hopei near Kalgan *pop* 114,100

Su·bic \'sü-bik\ town Philippines in W Luzon at head of **Subic Bay** (inlet of So. China sea NW of Bataan peninsula)

Su·bo·ti·ca \'sü-bə-,tēt-sə\ city NE Yugoslavia in N Voivodina near Hungarian border *pop* 115,352

Suchon — see SOOCHOW

Sü·chow \'s(h)ü-'jō, 'sü-'chau̇\ **1** *or formerly* **Tung·shan** \'tu̇ŋ-'shän\ city E China in NW Kiangsu N of Pengpu *pop* 373,200 **2** — see IPIN

Su·cre \'sü-(,)krā\ city, constitutional ✻ of Bolivia, 265 *m* SE of La Paz *pop* 54,270

Su·da Bay \,süd-ə-\ inlet of Aegean sea Greece on N coast of Crete E of Canea

Su·dan \sü-'dan, -'dän\ *or* F **Sou·dan** \sü-däⁿ\ **1** region N Africa between the Atlantic & the upper Nile S of the Sahara including basins of Lake Chad & the Niger & upper Nile **2** country NE Africa S of Egypt; a republic, until 1956 a territory (**Anglo-Egyptian Sudan**) under joint Brit. & Egyptian rule ✻ Khartoum *area* 967,500, *pop* 12,109,000 — **Su·da·nese** \,süd-ᵊn-'ēz, -'ēs\ *adj or n*

Sud·bury \'səd-,ber-ē, -b(ə-)rē\ city Canada in SE Ont. N of Georgian Bay *pop* 46,482

Sudd \'səd\ swamp region S Sudan drained by the White Nile

Su·de·ten \sü-'dāt-ᵊn\ **1** *or* **Su·de·tes** \-'dēt-(,)ēz\ *or* **Su·det·ic** \-'det-ik\ mountains *cen* Europe W of the Carpathians between Czechoslovakia & Poland **2** *or* **Su·de·ten·land** \sü-'dāt-ᵊn-,land\ region N Czechoslovakia in Sudeten mountains — **Sudeten** *adj or n*

Su·ez \sü-'ez, *chiefly Brit* 'sü-iz\ **1** city & port NE Egypt at S end of Suez canal on **Gulf of Suez** (arm of Red sea) *pop* 156,300 **2** ship canal 92 *m* long NE Egypt traversing Isthmus of Suez

Suez, Isthmus of isthmus NE Egypt between Mediterranean & Red seas connecting Africa & Asia

Suf·folk \'səf-ək, *US also* -,ōk\ county E England bordering on North sea; divided into administrative counties of **East Suffolk** (✻ Ipswich *area* 871, *pop* 321,849) & **West Suffolk** (✻ Bury St. Edmunds *area* 611, *pop* 120,590)

Suffolk Broads — see BROADS

Sugarloaf Mountain — see PÃO DE AÇÚCAR

Suidwes-Afrika — see SOUTH-WEST AFRICA

Suifu — see IPIN

Suisse — see SWITZERLAND

Sui·sun Bay \sə-,sün-\ arm of San Francisco Bay *cen* Calif.

Sukarnapura — see HOLLANDIA

Su·khu·mi \'su̇k-ə-mē\ city & port U.S.S.R. in NW Georgia ✻ of Abkhazian Republic on Black sea *pop* 64,000

Suk·kur \'su̇k-ər\ *or* **Sa·khar** \'sək-ər\ city W Pakistan in N Sind on the Indus *pop* 77,057

Sulawesi — see CELEBES

Sul·grave \'səl-,grāv\ village England in S Northamptonshire

Sultanabad — see ARAK

Su·lu \'sü-(,)lü\ **1** archipelago SW Philippines SW of Mindanao **2** — see JOLO **3** sea W Philippines N of Celebes sea

Su·ma·tra \su̇-'mä-trə\ island W Indonesia S of Malay peninsula *area* 166,789 — **Su·ma·tran** \-trən\ *adj or n*

Sum·ba *or* D **Soem·ba** \'süm-bə\ *or* **San·dal·wood** \'san-dᵊl-,wu̇d\ island Indonesia in the Lesser Sundas S of Flores

Sum·ba·wa *or* D **Soem·ba·wa** \süm-'bä-wə\ island Indonesia in the Lesser Sundas E of Lombok

Su·mer \'sü-mər\ the S division of ancient Babylonia — see AKKAD, SHINAR

Sum·ga·it \,su̇m-gä-'ēt\ city & port U.S.S.R. in Azerbaidzhan on the Caspian NW of Baku *pop* 20,000

Sum·mit \'səm-ət\ city NE N.J. W of Newark *pop* 23,677

Sum·ter \'səm(p)-tər\ city E *cen* S.C. E of Columbia *pop* 23,062

Sun·da \'sən-də\ *or* D **Soen·da** \'sün-\ **1** islands Malay archipelago comprising the **Greater Sunda** islands (Sumatra, Java, Borneo, Celebes, & adjacent islands) & the **Lesser Sunda** islands (extending E from Bali to Timor); with exception of Brit. Borneo & Portuguese Timor, belong to Indonesia **2** strait between Java & Sumatra

Sun·der·land \'sən-dər-lənd\ county borough N England in Durham on North sea at mouth of the Wear *pop* 181,515

Sunds·vall \'sən(t)s-,väl\ city & port E Sweden on Gulf of Bothnia *pop* 29,783

Sun·ga·ri \'su̇ŋ-gə-rē\ **1** river 800 *m* NE China in E Manchuria flowing from Chang Pai Shan on Korean border NW & NE into the Amur **2** reservoir formed by dam in the upper Sungari

Sun·ny·vale \'sən-ē-,vāl\ city W Calif. WNW of San Jose *pop* 52,898

Sunset Crater volcanic crater N *cen* Ariz. in **Sunset Crater National Monument** (*area* 5)

Suomi — see FINLAND

Su·pe·ri·or \su̇-'pir-ē-ər\ city & port NW Wis. *pop* 33,563

Superior, Lake lake U.S. & Canada; largest, northernmost, & westernmost of the Great Lakes *area* 31,820

Superstition mountain range S *cen* Ariz. E of Phoenix; highest point **Superstition Mountain** 5060 *ft*

Sur, Point \'su̇(ə)r\ promontory Calif. on the Pacific 20 *m* S of Monterey

Su·ra·ba·ja *or* **Su·ra·ba·ya** *or* D **Soe·ra·ba·ja** \,su̇r-ə-'bī-ə\ city & port Indonesia in NE Java on **Surabaja strait** (between Java & W end of Madura) *pop* 935,700

Su·ra·kar·ta \,su̇r-ə-'kärt-ə\ *or* **So·lo** \'sō-(,)lō\ *or* D **Soe·ra·kar·ta** \,su̇r-ə-'kärt-ə\ city Indonesia in *cen* Java *pop* 369,800

Su·rat \'su̇r-ət, sə-'rat\ city W India in SE Gujarat *pop* 223,200

Sur·bi·ton \'sər-bət-ᵊn\ municipal borough S England in Surrey WSW of London *pop* 60,675

Su·ri·ba·chi, Mount \,su̇r-ə-'bäch-ē\ volcano 548 *ft* in the Volcano islands at S end of Iwo Jima

Su·ri·nam \'su̇r-ə-,nam\ *or* **Su·ri·na·me** \,su̇r-ə-'näm-ə\ *or* **Dutch Guiana** *or* **Netherlands Guiana** country N So. America between Guyana & French Guiana; a territory of the Netherlands ✻ Paramaribo *area* 55,142, *pop* 271,700 — **Su·ri·nam·ese** \,su̇r-ə-,nam-'ēz, -'ēs\ *adj or n*

Suriname *or* **Surinam** river 400 *m* N Surinam flowing N into the Atlantic

Sur·ma \'su̇r-mə\ river 560 *m* NE India (subcontinent) in Manipur & East Bengal — see MEGHNA

Surrentum — see SORRENTO

Sur·rey \'sər-ē, 'sə-rē\ county SE England S of London ✻ Kingston on Thames *area* 722, *pop* 1,601,555

Su·ru·ga Bay \,su̇r-ə-gə-\ inlet of the Pacific Japan on coast of SE Honshu W of Sagami sea

Su·sa \'sü-sə, -zə\ **1** \'sü-zə, -sə\ *or Bib* **Shu·shan** \'shü-shən, -,shan\ ancient city ✻ of Elam; ruins in SW Iran **2** — see SOUSSE

Su·sak \'sü-,shäk\ former city NW Yugoslavia, now an E section of Rijeka; seaport

Susiana — see ELAM

Sus·que·han·na \,səs-kwə-'han-ə\ river 444 *m* E U.S. flowing from *cen* N.Y. S through Pa. & into Chesapeake Bay in N Md.

Sus·sex \'səs-iks\ county SE England bordering on English channel; one of kingdoms in Anglo-Saxon heptarchy; divided into administrative counties of **East Sussex** (✻ Lewes *area* 829, *pop* 618,083) & **West Sussex** (✻ Chichester *area* 628, *pop* 318,661)

Suth·er·land \'səth-ər-lənd\ *or* **Suth·er·land·shire** \-lən(d)-,shi(ə)r, -shər\ county N Scotland ✻ Dornoch *area* 2028, *pop* 13,664

Sutherland Falls waterfall 1904 *ft* New Zealand in SW South I.

Sut·lej \'sət-,lej\ river 900 *m* N India (subcontinent) flowing from Tibet W & SW through the Punjab to join the Chenab

Sut·ton and Cheam \,sət-ᵊn-ən-'chēm\ municipal borough S England in Surrey S of London *pop* 80,664

Sut·ton Cold·field \,sət-ᵊn-'kōl(d)-,fēld\ municipal borough *cen* England in Warwickshire NE of Birmingham *pop* 29,928

Sutton in Ash·field \'ash-,fēld\ urban district N *cen* England in Nottinghamshire N of Nottingham *pop* 40,521

Su·va \'sü-və\ city & port ✻ of Fiji, on Viti Levu I. *pop* 37,371

Su·wal·ki *or* Russ **Su·val·ki** \sü-'väl-kē\ *or* Lithuanian **Su·val·kai** \-,kī\ **1** district NE Poland E of Masurian Lakes **2** city in the district *pop* 18,600

Su·wan·nee \sə-'wän-ē\ river 240 *m* SE Ga. & N Fla. flowing SW into Gulf of Mexico

Su·won \'sü-,wän\ *or* Jap **Sui·gen** \'sü-ē-,gen\ city S Korea S of Seoul *pop* 42,173

Sval·bard \'sfäl-,bär\ the Norwegian islands in the Arctic ocean including Spitsbergen, Bear I., & other small islands *area* 25,000

Sverd·lovsk \sferd-'lȯfsk\ *or formerly* **Eka·te·rin·burg** \i-'kat-ə-rən-,bərg\ city U.S.S.R. in W Soviet Russia, Asia, in *cen* Ural mountains *pop* 777,000

Sver·drup \'sfer-drəp\ islands N Canada W of Ellesmere I. including Axel Heiberg I. & the Ringnes islands

Swa·bia \'swā-bē-ə\ *or* G **Schwa·ben** \'shfäb-ən\ region SW Germany; the territory inhabited by the ancient Suevi — **Swa·bi·an** \'swā-bē-ən\ *adj or n*

Swan \'swän\ **1** two islands in the Caribbean NE of Honduras **2** *or in its upper course* **Av·on** \'av-ən\ river 150 *m* SW Western Australia flowing W into Indian ocean

Swan·sea \'swän-zē, 'swän(t)-sē\ county borough & port SE Wales in Glamorganshire *pop* 160,832

Swat \'swät\ river 400 *m* West Pakistan flowing into the Kabul

Swa·tow \'swä-'tau̇\ city & port SE China in E Kwangtung on So. China sea *pop* 280,400

Swa·zi·land \'swäz-ē-,land\ country SE Africa N of Natal between Transvaal & Mozambique; a former Brit. protectorate, independent since 1968 ✻ Mbabane *area* 6705, *pop* 237,041

Swe·den \'swēd-ᵊn\ *or* Swed **Sve·ri·ge** \'sfar-yə\ country N

ə abut; ᵊ kitten; ər further; a back; ā bake; ä cot, cart; au̇ out; ch chin; e less; ē easy; g gift; i trip; ī life
j joke; ŋ sing; ō flow; ȯ flaw; ȯi coin; th thin; th this; ü loot; u̇ foot; y yet; yü few; yu̇ furious; zh vision
ᵊ F table; à F bac; k G ich, Buch; ⁿ F vin; œ F bœuf; œ̄ F feu; ue G füllen; ue̅ F rue; ʸ F digne \dēnʸ\, nuit \nwʸē\

Europe on Scandinavian peninsula W of Baltic sea; a kingdom ✻ Stockholm *area* 173,349, *pop* 7,543,000
Swin·don \'swin-dən\ municipal borough S England in Wiltshire *pop* 68,932
Świ·no·ujs·cie \,shfē-nō-'üish-(,)chā\ *or* G **Swi·ne·mün·de** \,sfē-nə-'mün-də\ town & port NW Poland on N coast of Uznam I. at mouth of Swine river NNW of Szczecin
Swin·ton and Pen·dle·bury \,swint-ᵊn-ən-'pen-dᵊl-,ber-ē\ urban district NW England in Lancashire NW of Manchester *pop* 41,294
Swiss·vale \'swis-,vāl\ borough SW Pa. *pop* 15,089
Swit·zer·land \'swit-sər-lənd\ *or* F **Suisse** \swʸēs\ *or* G **Schweiz** \'shfīts\ *or* It **Sviz·ze·ra** \'zvēt-tsā-rä\ *or* L **Hel·ve·tia** \hel-'vē-sh(ē-)ə\ country W Europe in the Alps; a federal republic ✻ Bern *area* 15,940, *pop* 4,714,992
Syb·a·ris \'sib-ə-rəs\ ancient Greek city S Italy on Gulf of Tarentum; destroyed 510 B.C.
Syd·ney \'sid-nē\ **1** city & port SE Australia on Port Jackson ✻ of New So. Wales *pop* (with suburbs) 1,935,900 **2** city Canada in NE N.S. on Cape Breton I. *pop* 32,162 — **Syd·ney·ite** \-,īt\ *n*
Syene — see ASWÂN
Sylt \'zilt, 'silt\ island N Germany, chief of the No. Frisian islands
Syr·a·cuse \'sir-ə-,kyüs, -,kyüz\ **1** city *cen* N.Y. *pop* 216,038 **2** *or* It **Si·ra·cu·sa** \sē-rə-'kü-zə\ *or anc* **Syr·a·cu·sae** \,sir-ə-'kyü-(,)sē, -(,)zē\ city & port Italy in SE Sicily *pop* 63,300 — **Syr·a·cu·san** \,sir-ə-'kyüs-ᵊn, -'kyüz-\ *adj or n*
Syr Dar·ya \si(ə)r-'där-yə\ *or anc* **Jax·ar·tes** \jak-'särt-(,)ēz\ river 1500 *m* U.S.S.R. in Soviet Central Asia flowing from Tien Shan W & NW into Lake Aral
Syr·ia \'sir-ē-ə\ **1** ancient region SW Asia bordering on the Mediterranean & covering modern Syria, Lebanon, Israel, & Jordan **2** former French mandate (1920–44) comprising the **Le·vant States** \li-'vant\ (Syria, Lebanon, Latakia, & Jebel ed Druz), administrative ✻ Beirut, legislative ✻ Damascus *area* 76,030 **3** *or* **Syrian Arab Republic** country SW Asia bordering on the Mediterranean; a republic 1944–58 & since 1961; a province of United Arab Republic 1958–61 ✻ Damascus *area* 72,234, *pop* 4,420,587 — **Syr·i·an** \'sir-ē-ən\ *adj or n*
Syrian desert W Asia between Mediterranean coast & the Euphrates covering N Saudi Arabia, NE Jordan, SE Syria, & W Iraq
Sy·ros \'sī-,räs\ *or* **Sy·ra** \'sī-rə\ *or* NGk **Sí·ros** \'sē-,rȯs\ *or* **Sí·ra** \'sē-rə\ **1** island Greece in the Cyclades S of Andros **2** — see ERMOÚPOLIS
Syrtis Major — see SIDRA (Gulf of)
Syrtis Minor — see GABES (Gulf of)
Szamos — see SOMES
Szczecin — see STETTIN
Sze·chwan \'sech-'wän\ province SW China ✻ Chengtu *area* 219,691, *pop* 65,685,000
Sze·ged \'seg-,ed\ city S Hungary on Yugoslav border *pop* 100,000
Sze·kes·fe·her·var \'sā-,kesh-,fe-ər-,vär\ city W *cen* Hungary *pop* 52,000
Szeming — see AMOY
Sze·ping \'sü-'piŋ\ *or formerly* **Sze·ping·kai** \-'gī\ city NE China in W Kirin SW of Changchun *pop* 125,900
Szom·bat·hely \'sōm-,bȯt-,hā\ city W Hungary *pop* 53,000

Ta·bas·co \tə-'bas-(,)kō\ state SE Mexico on the Caribbean SW of Yucatán peninsula ✻ Villahermosa *area* 9782, *pop* 427,631
Ta·blas \'täb-ləs\ island *cen* Philippines in Romblon group
Table Bay harbor of Cape Town, Republic of So. Africa
Table Mountain mountain 3550 *ft* Republic of So. Africa S of Cape Town
Ta·bor, Mount \'tā-bər\ mountain 1929 *ft* N Palestine E of Nazareth
Ta·bo·ra \tə-'bōr-ə, -'bȯr-\ town Tanzania in W *cen* Tanganyika
Ta·briz \tə-'brēz\ *or anc* **Tau·ris** \'tȯr-əs\ city NW Iran in Azerbaijan *pop* 290,195
Ta·bun Bog·do \,täb-,ün-'bȯg-(,)dō\ mountain 15,266 *ft* W Outer Mongolia; highest in Altai mountains
Tac·na \'tak-nə\ town S Peru near Chilean border in region (**Tacna–Ari·ca** \,tak-nə-ə-'rē-kə\) occupied 1884–1930 by Chile & now divided between Chile & Peru
Ta·co·ma \tə-'kō-mə\ **1** city & port W Wash. on Puget Sound S of Seattle *pop* 147,979 **2** — see RAINIER (Mount)
Ta·con·ic \tə-'kän-ik\ mountains along Mass.-N.Y. boundary & in SW Vt.; highest peak Mt. Equinox (in Vt.) 3816 *ft*
Ta·cu·ba·ya \,täk-ə-'bī-ə\ a SW suburb of Mexico City
Ta·djou·ra, Gulf of *or* **Gulf of Ta·ju·ra** \tə-'jůr-ə\ inlet of Gulf of Aden in E French Somaliland
Tadmor — see PALMYRA
Ta·dzhik·i·stan *or* **Ta·jik·i·stan** \tä-,jik-i-'stan, tə-, -,jēk-, -'stän\ *or* **Ta·dzhik Republic** \tä-,jik-, -,jēk-\ constituent republic of the U.S.S.R. in Soviet Central Asia bordering on China (Sinkiang) & Afghanistan ✻ Dyushambe *area* 54,900, *pop* 2,000,000
Tae·dong \ta-'důŋ, tī-\ *or* Jap **Dai·do** \'dīd-(,)ō\ river 200 *m* N Korea flowing SW into Korea Bay
Tae·gu \ta-'gü, tī-\ *or* Jap **Tai·kyu** \'tī-(,)kyü\ city SE Korea NNW of Pusan *pop* 488,690
Tae·jon \ta-'jȯn, tī-\ *or* Jap **Tai·den** \'tī-,den\ city S Korea NW of Taegu *pop* 173,143
Ta·fi·la·let \,taf-i-lə-'let\ oasis SE Morocco; chief town Erfoud
Ta·gan·rog \'tag-ən-,räg\ city U.S.S.R. in Soviet Russia, Europe, on **Gulf of Taganrog** (NE arm of Sea of Azov) *pop* 201,000
Ta·gus \'tā-gəs\ *or* Sp **Ta·jo** \'tä-(,)hō\ *or* Port **Te·jo** \'tā-(,)zhü\ river 566 *m* Spain & Portugal flowing W into the Atlantic
Ta·hi·ti \tə-'hēt-ē\ island S Pacific in Windward group of the Society islands; chief town Papeete *area* 402, *pop* 44,247
Ta·hoe, Lake \'tä-(,)hō\ lake 22 *m* long on Calif.-Nev. boundary
Tai \'tī\ **1** mountain 5069 *ft* E China in W Shantung S of Tsinan **2** lake 40 *m* long & 35 *m* wide E China in Kiangsu W of Shanghai
Tai·chow \'tī-'jō, -'chaů\ city E China in *cen* Kiangsu NW of Shanghai *pop* 159,800
Tai·chung \'tī-'chůŋ\ city China, provincial ✻ of Formosa *pop* 199,519
Tai·myr *or* **Tai·mir** \tī-'mi(ə)r\ peninsula U.S.S.R. in NW Soviet Russia, Asia, between Yenisei & Khatanga rivers — see CHELYUSKIN
Tai·nan \'tī-'nän\ city China in SW Formosa *pop* 221,088
Taínaron — see MATAPAN
Tai·pei *or* **Tai·peh** \'tī-'pā, -'bā\ city ✻ of (Nationalist) China, on Formosa *pop* 759,800
Taiwan — see FORMOSA — **Tai·wan·ese** \,tī-,wäŋ-'ēz, -'ēs\ *n*
Tai·yu·an \'tī-yü-'än\ *or formerly* **Yang·ku** \'yäŋ-'kü\ city N China ✻ of Shansi *pop* 720,700
Ta·ju·mul·co \,tä-hü-'mül-(,)kō\ mountain 13,816 *ft* W Guatemala; highest in Central America
Ta·ka·mat·su \,täk-ə-'mät-(,)sü\ city & port Japan in NE Shikoku on Inland sea *pop* 144,812
Ta·ka·o·ka \tə-'kaů-kə\ city Japan in *cen* Honshu *pop* 131,531
Ta·kla Ma·kan \,täk-lə-mə-'kän\ desert W China in *cen* Sinkiang between Tien Shan & Kunlun mountains
Ta·ko·ma Park \tə-,kō-mə-\ city SW Md. *pop* 16,799
Ta·ko·ra·di \,täk-ə-'räd-ē\ city & port SW Ghana *pop* 17,800
Ta·laud \'täl-,aůt\ *or* **Ta·laur** \'täl-,aů(ə)r\ islands Indonesia NE of Celebes *area* 494
Tal·ca \'täl-kə\ city *cen* Chile 155 *m* S of Santiago *pop* 80,277
Tal·ca·hua·no \,täl-kə-'(h)wän-(,)ō\ city & port S *cen* Chile NW of Concepción *pop* 99,231
Tal·la·de·ga \,tal-ə-'dē-gə, -'dig-ə\ city E *cen* Ala. *pop* 17,742
Tal·la·has·see \,tal-ə-'has-ē\ city ✻ of Fla. *pop* 48,174
Tal·la·hatch·ie \,tal-ə-'hach-ē\ river 301 *m* N Miss. flowing SW to unite with the Yalobusha forming the Yazoo
Tal·la·poo·sa \,tal-ə-'pü-sə\ river 268 *m* NW Ga. & E Ala. flowing SW to join Coosa river forming the Alabama
Tal·linn *or* **Tal·lin** \'tal-ən, 'täl-\ *or* **Re·vel** \'rā-vəl\ *or* **Re·val** \-,väl\ city & port U. S. S. R. ✻ of Estonia *pop* 280,000
Tam·al·pais, Mount \,tam-əl-'pī-əs\ mountain 2606 *ft* W Calif. NW of San Francisco
Ta·man \tə-'män\ peninsula U.S.S.R. in S Soviet Russia, Europe, in Ciscaucasia between Sea of Azov & Black sea
Tam·an·ras·set \,tam-ən-'ras-ət\ wadi & oasis SE Algeria
Ta·mar, 1 \'tā-mər\ river 40 *m* Australia in N Tasmania flowing N to Bass strait **2** \'tā-mər\ river 60 *m* SW England flowing SE from NW Devon into English channel **3** — see PALMYRA
Ta·ma·tave \,tam-ə-'täv, ,täm-\ city & port NE Madagascar *pop* 28,700
Ta·mau·li·pas \,täm-,aů-'lē-pəs\ state NE Mexico bordering on Gulf of Mexico ✻ Ciudad Victoria *area* 30,731, *pop* 977,924
Tam·bo·ra \'täm-bə-rə\ volcano 9354 *ft* Indonesia on Sumbawa I.
Tam·bov \täm-'bȯf, -'bȯv\ city U.S.S.R. in *cen* Soviet Russia, Europe, SE of Moscow *pop* 170,000
Tamizhgam — see MADRAS
Tam·pa \'tam-pə\ city W Fla. on **Tampa Bay** (inlet of Gulf of Mexico) *pop* 274,970 — **Tam·pan** *adj or n*
Tam·pe·re \'tam-pə-,rā, 'täm-\ *or* Sw **Tam·mer·fors** \,täm-ər-'fō(ə)rz, -'fȯsh\ city SW Finland *pop* 95,753
Tam·pi·co \tam-'pē-(,)kō\ city & port E Mexico in S Tamaulipas on the Pánuco 7 *m* from its mouth *pop* 119,427
Ta·na \'tän-ə\ *or* **Tsa·na** \'(t)sän-ə\ **1** lake NW Ethiopia; source of the Blue Nile *area* 1100 **2** river 500 *m* E Africa in Kenya flowing into Indian ocean
Ta·na·gra \'tan-ə-grə, tə-'nag-rə\ village E *cen* Greece E of Thebes; an important town of ancient Boeotia
Tan·a·na \'tan-ə-,nȯ\ river 475 *m* E & *cen* Alaska flowing NW into the Yukon
Ta·nan·a·rive \tə-'nan-ə-,rēv\ *or* **An·ta·nan·a·ri·vo** \,an-tə-,nan-ə-'rē-(,)vō\ city Madagascar ✻ of Malagasy Republic *pop* 325,000
Tan·ez·rouft \,tan-əz-'rüft\ extremely arid region of W Sahara in SW Algeria & N Mali
Tan·ga \'taŋ-gə\ city & port NE Tanganyika *pop* 22,136
Tan·gan·yi·ka \,tan-gən-'yē-kə, ,taŋ-gən-, -gə-'nē-\ country E Africa between Lake Tanganyika & Indian ocean; administered by Britain 1920–61; became an independent member of Brit. Commonwealth 1961; since 1964 united with Zanzibar as United Republic of Tanzania ✻ Dar es Salaam *area* 361,800, *pop* 9,404,000 — see GERMAN EAST AFRICA — **Tan·gan·yi·kan** *adj or n*
Tanganyika, Lake lake E Africa in Great Rift valley between Congo & Tanganyika *area* 12,700
Tan·gier \tan-'ji(ə)r\ *or* **Tan·giers** \-'ji(ə)rz\ *or* Sp **Tán·ger** \'täŋ-,her\ **1** city & port N Morocco on Strait of Gibraltar; summer ✻ of Morocco *pop* 180,000 **2** the International Zone of Tangier — see MOROCCO — **Tan·ger·ine** \,tan-jə-'rēn\ *adj or n*
Tang·shan \'täŋ-'shän\ city NE China in E Hopei *pop* 693,300
Ta·nim·bar \tə-'nim-,bär, 'tan-əm-\ *or* **Ti·mor·laut** \'tē-,mȯr-,laůt\ islands Indonesia in SE Moluccas ENE of Timor
Ta·nis \'tā-nəs\ *or Bib* **Zo·an** \'zō-,an\ ancient city N Egypt in E Nile delta near Lake Tanis
Tanis, Lake — see MANZALA (Lake)
Tan·jung·pri·ok \(,)tän-,jůŋ-prē-'ȯk\ port of Djakarta, Indonesia
Tannenberg — see STEBARK
Tan·ta \'tänt-ə\ city N Egypt in *cen* Nile delta *pop* 175,400
Tan·za·nia \,tan-zə-'nē-ə\ republic E Africa formed 1964 by union of Tanganyika & Zanzibar ✻ Dar es Salaam *area* 362,844 *pop* 12,200,000 — **Tan·za·nian** *adj or n*
Ta·pa·joz \,tap-ə-'zhȯs\ river 500 *m* N Brazil flowing NE into the Amazon — see JURUENA
Tap·pan Zee \,tap-ən-'zē\ expansion of the Hudson SE New York
Taprobane — see CEYLON
Tap·ti \'täp-tē\ river 436 *m* W India S of Satpura range flowing W into Gulf of Cambay
Ta·qua·ri \,tak-wə-'rē\ river 450 *m* S *cen* Brazil rising in S *cen* Mato Grosso & flowing WSW into the Paraguay
Tar \'tär\ river 215 *m* NE N.C. flowing SE into Pamlico river
Tara \'tar-ə\ village Ireland in County Meath NW of Dublin near **Hill of Tara** (seat of ancient Irish kings)
Tarabulus — see TRIPOLI
Tar·a·na·ki \,tar-ə-'näk-ē\ **1** provincial district New Zealand in W North I. ✻ New Plymouth *area* 3750, *pop* 98,700 **2** — see EGMONT
Ta·ran·to \'tär-ən-,tō, tə-'rant-(,)ō\ *or anc* **Ta·ren·tum** \tə-'rent-əm\ city & port SE Italy on **Gulf of Taranto** (inlet of Ionian sea) *pop* 174,871
Ta·ra·wa \tə-'rä-wə, 'tar-ə-,wä\ island *cen* Pacific in N Gilbert islands ✻ of Gilbert & Ellice Islands colony *area* 8
Tarbes \'tärb\ city SW France ESE of Pau *pop* 40,242
Ta·rim \'dä-'rēm\ river 1250 *m* W China in Sinkiang in the Takla Makan flowing E & SE into Lop Nor (marshy depression)
Tar·lac \'tär-,läk\ city Philippines in *cen* Luzon *pop* 20,818
Tarn \'tärn\ river 233 *m* S France flowing W into the Garonne
Tar·now \'tär-,nüf\ city S Poland E of Krakow *pop* 58,000

Tar·qui·nia \tär-'kwēn-yə, -'kwen-ē-ə, -'kwin-\ *or formerly* **Cor·ne·to** \kór-'nāt-(,)ō\ *or anc* **Tar·quin·ii** \tär-'kwin-ē-,ī\ town *cen* Italy in N Latium NW of Viterbo

Tar·ra·go·na \,tar-ə-'gō-nə\ **1** province N E Spain on the Mediterranean *area* 2505, *pop* 369,997 **2** commune & port, its ✳, SW of Barcelona *pop* 45,509

Tar·ra·sa \tə-'räs-ə\ commune N E Spain N NW of Barcelona *pop* 81,702

Tar·shish \'tär-(,)shish\ an ancient maritime country referred to in the Bible, by some located in S Spain & identified with Tartessus

Tar·sus \'tär-səs\ city S Turkey near the Cilician Gates ✳ of ancient Cilicia *pop* 51,310

Tar·tes·sus *or* **Tar·tes·sos** \tär-'tes-əs\ ancient kingdom on SW coast of Spanish peninsula — see TARSHISH

Tar·tu \'tär-(,)tü\ *or G* **Dor·pat** \'dó(ə)r-,pät\ city E Estonia W of Lake Peipus *pop* 74,000

Tash·kent \tash-'kent\ *or* **Tash·kend** \-'kent, -'kend\ city U.S.S.R. in Soviet Central Asia E of the Syr Darya ✳ of Uzbekistan *pop* 911,000

Tas·man \'taz-mən\ sea comprising the part of the S Pacific between SE Australia & W New Zealand

Tas·ma·nia \taz-'mā-nē-ə, -nyə\ *or formerly* **Van Die·men's Land** \van-'dē-mənz\ island SE Australia S of Victoria; a state ✳ Hobart *area* 26,215, *pop* 342,315 — **Tas·ma·nian** \taz-'mā-nē-ən, -nyən\ *adj or n*

Ta·tar \'tät-ər\ strait between Sakhalin I. & mainland of Asia

Tatar Republic autonomous republic U.S.S.R. in E Soviet Russia, Europe, at bend of the middle Volga ✳ Kazan *area* 26,100, *pop* 2,850,000

Ta·ta·ry \'tät-ə-rē\ *or* **Tar·ta·ry** \'tärt-ə-\ an indefinite historical region in Asia & Europe extending from Sea of Japan to the Dnieper

Ta·tra \'tä-trə\ *or* **High Tatra** mountains E Czechoslovakia in *cen* Carpathian mountains — see GERLACHOVKA

Ta·tung \'dä-'tùŋ\ city N E China in N Shansi *pop* 228,500

Tau·ghan·nock Falls \tə-,gan-ək-\ waterfall 215 *ft* S *cen* N.Y. NW of Ithaca

Taung·gyi \'tàuŋ-'jē\ town E Burma ✳ of Shan State

Taun·ton \'tónt-ən, 'tänt-, 'tant-\ city SE Mass. *pop* 41,132

Tau·nus \'taù-nəs\ mountain range W Germany E of the Rhine & N of the lower Main; highest peak Grosser Feldberg 2886 *ft*

Tauric Chersonese — see CHERSONESE

Tauris — see TABRIZ

Tau·rus \'tór-əs\ *or* Turk **To·ros** \tò-'rós\ mountains S Turkey running parallel to Mediterranean coast; highest peak Ala Dag 12,251 *ft*

Tax·co \'täs-(,)kō\ *or* **Taxco de Alar·cón** \-(,)thä-,äl-,är-'kón\ town S Mexico in Guerrero SSW of Mexico City

Tay \'tā\ river 120 *m* E *cen* Scotland flowing into North sea through **Firth of Tay** (estuary 25 *m* long)

Tbilisi — see TIFLIS

Tchad — see CHAD

Tea·neck \'tē-,nek\ urban township N E N.J. E of Paterson *pop* 42,085

Teche, Bayou \'tesh\ stream 175 *m* S La. flowing SE into the Atchafalaya

Tees \'tēz\ river 70 *m* N England flowing E along boundary between Yorkshire & Durham & into North sea

Te·gu·ci·gal·pa \tə-,gü-sə-'gal-pə\ city ✳ of Honduras *pop* 106,949

Te·hach·a·pi \ti-'hach-ə-pē\ **1** mountains SE Calif. N of Mojave desert running E–W between S end of Sierra Nevada & the Coast ranges; highest point Double Mountain 7988 *ft* **2** pass 3793 *ft* at E end of the mountains

Teh·ran *or* **Te·he·ran** \te-'rän, tā-ə-,-'rän\ city ✳ of Iran at foot of S slope of Elburz mountains *pop* 1,513,164

Teh·ri *or* **Tehri Garh·wal** \,tā-rē-,gər-'wäl\ former state N India on Tibet border ✳ Tehri; merged with Uttar Pradesh 1949

Te·huan·te·pec, Isthmus of \tə-'wänt-ə-,pek\ the narrowest section of Mexico, between **Gulf of Tehuantepec** (on Pacific side) & Bay of Campeche; 130 *m* wide

Tejo — see TAGUS

Te·jon \tē-'hōn\ pass 4183 *ft* SW Calif. in Tehachapi mountains NW of Los Angeles

Tel Aviv \,tel-ə-'vēv\ city & port Israel *pop* 386,612 — see JAFFA

Tel·e·mark \'tel-ə-,märk\ mountain region SW Norway

Telescope Peak mountain 11,045 *ft* E Calif., highest in Panamint mountains

Tell \'tel\ hilly maritime region N Africa in N E Algeria & N Tunisia

Tell el 'Amar·na *or* **Tel el 'Amar·na** \,tel-,el-ə-'mär-nə\ *or* **Tell Amar·na** \,tel-ə-\ locality *cen* Egypt on E bank of the Nile NW of Asyût; site of Egyptian ruins

Te·ma \'tē-mə\ city & port Ghana E of Accra *pop* 40,000

Tem·bu·land \'tem-(,)bü-,land\ region Republic of So. Africa in E Cape Province; one of the Transkeian Territories ✳ Umtata *area* 3339

Temes — see TIMIS

Temesvar — see TIMISOARA

Tem·pe, 1 \'tem-'pē\ city S *cen* Ariz. SE of Phoenix *pop* 24,897 **2** \'tem-pē\ *or NGk* **Tém·bi** \'tem-bē\ valley (**Vale of Tempe**) in N E Thessaly between Mounts Olympus & Ossa

Tem·pel·hof \'tem-pəl-,hóf\ residential district of S Berlin, Germany

Tem·ple \'tem-pəl\ city N E *cen* Tex. SSW of Waco *pop* 30,419

Temple City urban area SW Calif. SE of Pasadena *pop* 31,838

Te·mu·co \tā-'mü-(,)kō\ city S *cen* Chile *pop* 111,641

Tenedos — see BOZCAADA

Ten·er·ife \,ten-ə-'rē-fē, -'rif, -'rēf\ *or formerly* **Ten·er·iffe** \,ten-ə-'rif, -'rēf\ island Spain, largest of the Canary islands; chief town Santa Cruz de Tenerife *area* 782

Ten·gri Khan \,teŋ-(g)rē-'kän\ *or* **Khan Tengri** mountain 23,620 *ft* on border between Kirgiz Republic (U.S.S.R.) & Sinkiang (China) in Tien Shan

Ten·nes·see \,ten-ə-'sē, 'ten-ə-\ **1** river 652 *m* E U.S., in Tenn., Ala., & Ky. flowing into the Ohio **2** state SE *cen* U.S. ✳ Nashville *area* 42,244, *pop* 3,567,089 — **Ten·nes·se·an** *or* **Ten·nes·see·an** \,ten-ə-'sē-ən\ *adj or n*

Te·noch·ti·tlán \tā-,näch-tē-'tlän\ MEXICO CITY — its name when capital of the Aztec Empire

Te·nos \'tē-,näs\ *or NGk* **Ti·nos** \'tē-,nòs\ *or* **Té·nos** \'tē-,nòs\ island Greece in N Cyclades SE of Andros

Ten·sas \'ten-,sò\ river 250 *m* N E La. uniting with the Ouachita to form the Black

Ten·saw \'ten-,sò\ river 40 *m* SW Ala. formed by Tombigbee & Alabama rivers & flowing S into Mobile Bay

Te·o·ti·hua·cán \,tā-ō-,tē-wə-'kän\ town S *cen* Mexico in Mexico state N E of Mexico City; once ✳ of the Toltecs

Te·pic \tā-'pēk\ city W Mexico ✳ of Nayarit *pop* 24,600

Te·quen·da·ma Falls \,tā-kən-,däm-ə-\ waterfall 475 *ft*, *cen* Colombia SW of Bogotá

Ter·cei·ra \tər-'sir-ə, -'ser-\ island *cen* Azores *area* 233

Ter·ek \'ter-ək\ river 380 *m* U.S.S.R. in S Soviet Russia, Europe, N of Caucasus mountains flowing into the Caspian

Te·re·si·na \,ter-ə-'zē-nə\ city N E Brazil ✳ of Piauí *pop* 111,811

Termonde — see DENDERMONDE

Ter·na·te \tər-'nät-ē\ **1** island Indonesia in N Moluccas off W Halmahera **2** city & port, chief city of Ternate I. *pop* 21,200

Ter·ni \'te(ə)r-nē\ commune *cen* Italy N NE of Rome *pop* 55,900

Ter·ra·ci·na \,ter-ə-'chē-nə\ city & port *cen* Italy in Latium SE of Pontine marshes *pop* 17,300

Ter·re Haute \,ter-ə-'hōt, ,ter-ē-, -'hət, -'hòt\ city W Ind. on Wabash river *pop* 72,500

Te·ruel \,ter-ə-'wel\ **1** province E Spain in S Aragon *area* 5720, *pop* 224,876 **2** commune, its ✳, S of Zaragoza *pop* 19,796

Te·schen \'tesh-ən\ *or* Czech **Te·sin** \tē-'esh-,ēn\ *or* Pol **Cie·szyn** \'chesh-ən\ region *cen* Europe in Silesia; once an Austrian duchy; divided 1920 between Poland & Czechoslovakia

Tessin — see TICINO

Te·ton \'tē-,tän\ mountain range NW Wyo. — see GRAND TETON

Te·tuán \tā-'twän\ city & port N Morocco on the Mediterranean SE of Tangier; formerly ✳ of Spanish Morocco

Teu·to·burg Forest \,t(y)üt-ə-,bərg-\ *or G* **Teu·to·bur·ger Wald** \'tóit-ə-,bùr-gər-,vält\ range of forested hills W Germany in region between the Ems & the Weser; highest point 1530 *ft*

Tewkes·bury \'t(y)üks-,ber-ē, -b(ə-)rē\ municipal borough SW *cen* England in Gloucestershire on Avon & Severn rivers

Tex·ar·ka·na \,tek-,sär-'kan-ə, ,tek-sər-\ **1** city SW Ark. adjacent to Texarkana, Tex. *pop* 19,788 **2** city N E Tex. *pop* 30,218

Tex·as \'tek-səs, -siz\ state S U.S. ✳ Austin *area* 267,339, *pop* 9,579,677 — **Tex·an** \-sən\ *adj or n*

Texas City city & port SE Tex. on Galveston Bay *pop* 32,065

Tex·co·co \tā-'skō-(,)kō\ *or* **Tez·cu·co** \tā-'skü-(,)kō\ town *cen* Mexico in Mexico state E of Mexico City

Thai·land \'tī-,land, -lənd\ *or* **Si·am** \sī-'am\ country SE Asia bordering on Gulf of Siam; a kingdom ✳ Bangkok *area* 198,247, *pop* 22,811,700 — **Thai·land·er** \-,lan-dər, -lən-\ *n*

Thailand, Gulf of — see SIAM (Gulf of)

Thames, 1 \'temz 'thämz, 'tāmz\ river 15 *m* SE Conn., an estuary flowing S into Long Island Sound **2** \'temz\ river 135 *m* Canada in SE Ont. flowing S & SW into Lake St. Clair **3** \'temz\ river 209 *m* S England flowing from the Cotswolds in Gloucestershire E into the North sea — see ISIS

Thamugadi *or* **Thamugadis** — see TIMGAD

Than·et, Isle of \'than-ət\ tract of land SE England in N E Kent cut off from mainland by arms of Stour river *area* 42

Thar \'tär\ *or* **Indian** desert NW India (subcontinent) in West Pakistan & Republic of India between Aravalli range & the Indus *area ab* 100,000

Tha·sos \'thā-,säs\ *or NGk* **Thá·sos** \'thäs-,òs\ island Greece in the N Aegean E of Chalcidice peninsula *area* 152

The·ba·id \thi-'bā-əd, 'thē-bā-,id\ district about Thebes, Egypt

Thebes \'thēbz\ **1** *or anc* **The·bae** \'thē-(,)bē\ *or* **Di·os·po·lis** \dī-'äs-pə-ləs\ ancient city S Egypt on the Nile S of modern Qena — see KARNAK, LUXOR **2** ancient city E Greece on site of modern village of Thívai 33 *m* N NW of Athens — **The·ban** \'thē-bən\ *adj or n*

The Hague — see HAGUE (The)

The·lon \'thē-,län\ river *ab* 550 *m* N Canada in E Northwest Territories flowing N E to Baker Lake

Thera — see SANTORIN

Thermaic Gulf — see SALONIKA (Gulf of)

Ther·mop·y·lae \(,)thər-'mäp-ə-(,)lē\ locality E Greece between Mt. Oeta & Gulf of Lamia; once a narrow pass along the coast, now a rocky plain 6 *m* from the sea

Thessalonica *or* **Thessaloníki** — see SALONIKA

Thes·sa·ly \'thes-ə-lē\ *or G* **Thes·sa·lia** \the-'sā-lē-ə, -'säl-yə\ region E Greece between Pindus mountains & the Aegean — **Thes·sa·lian** \the-'sā-lē-ən, -'säl-yən\ *adj or n*

Thet·ford Mines \,thet-fərd-\ city Canada in S Que. *pop* 19,511

Thim·bu \'thim-(,)bü\ town NW Bhutan ✳ of Bhutan

Thíra — see SANTORIN

Thom·as·ville \'täm-əs-,vil, -vəl\ **1** city S Ga. *pop* 18,246 **2** city *cen* N.C. SE of Winston-Salem *pop* 15,190

Thomp·son \'täm(p)-sən\ river 304 *m* Canada in S B.C. flowing S (as the **North Thompson** 210 *m*) & thence W & SW into the Fraser; joined by a branch (206 *m*) usu. known as the **South Thompson**

Thorn — see TORUN

Thors·havn \'tórs-'haùn\ town & port ✳ of the Faeroe islands, on Strömö I.

Thousand islands Canada & U.S. in the St. Lawrence in Ont. & N.Y.

Thrace \'thrās\ region SE Europe in Balkan peninsula N of the Aegean; as ancient country (**Thra·ce** \'thrā-,sē\ *or* **Thra·cia** \'thrā-sh(ē-)ə\), extended to the Danube; modern remnant divided between Greece (**Western Thrace**) & Turkey (**Eastern Thrace**, constituting Turkey in Europe) — **Thra·cian** \'thrā-shən\ *adj or n*

Thracian Chersonese — see CHERSONESE

Three Forks locality SW Mont. where Missouri river is formed by confluence of the Gallatin, Jefferson, & Madison

Three Rivers — see TROIS RIVIÈRES

Thu·le \'tü-lē\ settlement & district NW Greenland N of Cape York

---

ə abut; ᵊ kitten; ər further; a back; ā bake; ä cot, cart; aù out; ch chin; e less; ē easy; g gift; i trip; ī life j joke; ŋ sing; ō flow; ò flaw; òi coin; th thin; th̲ this; ü loot; ù foot; y yet; yü few; yù furious; zh vision ᵊ F table; à F bac; ᵏ G ich, Buch; ⁿ F vin; œ F bœuf; œ̄ F feu; ᵍ G füllen; ᵫ F rue; ʸ F digne \dēnʸ\, nuit \nwʸē\

Thun, Lake of \'tün\ *or* G **Thu·ner·see** \'tü-nər-,zā\ lake 10 *m* long *cen* Switzerland; an expansion of Aare river

Thur·gau \'tù(ə)r-,gaù\ *or* F **Thur·go·vie** \,tür-gə-'vē\ canton NE Switzerland ✳ Frauenfeld *area* 397, *pop* 149,738

Thu·rin·gia \th(y)ù-'rin-j(ē-)ə\ *or* G **Thü·ring·en** \'tüĔ-riŋ-ən\ region E Germany including the **Thu·rin·gian Forest** \th(y)ù-,rin-j(ē-)ən\ *or* G **Thü·ring·er Wald** \'tüĔ-riŋ-ər-,vält\ (wooded mountain range between the upper Werra & Czech border)

Thur·rock \'thər-ək, 'thə-rək\ urban district SE England in Essex *pop* 82,108

Thursday island NE Australia off N Queensland in Torres strait

Thyatira — see AKHISAR

Ti·a·hua·na·co \,tē-ə-wə-'näk-(,)ō\ locality W Bolivia near SE end of Lake Titicaca; site of prehistoric ruins

Ti·ber \'tī-bər\ *or* It **Te·ve·re** \'tā-vā-rā\ river 224 *m*, *cen* Italy flowing through Rome into Tyrrhenian sea

Ti·be·ri·as \tī-'bir-ē-əs\ city N Palestine in Galilee on W shore of Sea of Galilee; now in NE Israel *pop* 18,000

Tiberias, Sea of — see GALILEE (Sea of)

Ti·bes·ti \tə-'bes-tē\ mountains N *cen* Africa in the Sahara in NW Chad; highest peak Emi Koussi 11,204 *ft*

Ti·bet *or* **Thi·bet** \tə-'bet\ region SW China on high plateau (average altitude 16,000 *ft*) N of the Himalayas ✳ Lhasa *area* 471,660, *pop* 1,321,000

Ti·bu·rón \,tē-bə-'rōn\ island 34 *m* long NW Mexico in Gulf of California off coast of Sonora

Ti·ci·no \ti-'chē-(,)nō\ 1 river 154 *m* Switzerland & Italy flowing from slopes of St. Gotthard range SE & SW through Lake Maggiore into the Po 2 *or* F **Tes·sin** \te-saⁿ\ canton S Switzerland bordering on Italy ✳ Bellinzona

Tien Shan \tē-'en-'shän\ *or* **Tian Shan** \tē-'än-\ mountain system *cen* Asia extending from the Pamirs NE into Sinkiang; highest point Peak Pobeda (Pik Pobedy) 24,406 *ft*

Tien·tsin \tē-'en(t)-'sin, 'tin(t)-\ city & port NE China ✳ of Hopei SE of Peking *pop* 2,693,800

Tier·gar·ten \'ti(ə)r-,gärt-ᵊn\ section of W Berlin, Germany

Tier·ra del Fue·go \tē-,er-ə-,del-f(y)ù-'ā-(,)gō\ 1 archipelago off S So. America S of Strait of Magellan; divided between Chile & Argentina *area* 27,600 2 chief island of the archipelago; divided between Chile and Argentina *area* 18,530

Tif·fin \'tif-ən\ city N Ohio on Sandusky river *pop* 21,478

Ti·flis \'tif-ləs, tə-'flēs\ *or* **Tbi·li·si** *or* **Tpi·li·si** \tə-'bil-ə-sē, -'pil-\ city U.S.S.R. ✳ of Georgia on Kura river *pop* 694,000

Ti·gre \'tē-(,)grā\ 1 city E Argentina, NW suburb of Buenos Aires, on islands in Paraná delta *pop* 30,000 2 \tə-'grā\ region N Ethiopia bordering on Eritrea

Ti·gris \'tī-grəs\ river 1150 *m* Iraq & SE Turkey flowing SSE & uniting with the Euphrates to form the Shatt-al-Arab

Tihwa — see URUMCHI

Ti·jua·na \tē-'wän-ə\ city NW Mexico on U.S. border in Baja California state *pop* 191,609

Ti·kal \ti-'käl\ ancient Mayan city N Guatemala

Til·burg \'til-,bərg\ commune S Netherlands *pop* 134,974

Til·bury \'til-,ber-ē, -b(ə-)rē\ seaport SE England on the Thames in Essex E of London in Thurrock urban district

Til·la·mook Bay \'til-ə-,mùk-\ inlet of the Pacific NW Oreg.

Tilsit — see SOVETSK

Ti·ma·ga·mi, Lake \tə-'mäg-ə-mē\ lake Canada in Ont. N of Lake Nipissing

Tim·buk·tu *or* **Tim·buc·too** \,tim-,bək-'tü, tim-'bək-(,)tü\ *or* F **Tom·bouc·tou** \tōⁿ-bük-tü\ town W Africa in Mali (formerly French Sudan) near the Niger

Tim·gad \'tim-gad\ *or anc* **Tham·u·ga·di** \,tham-yə-'gäd-ē\ *or* **Tham·u·ga·dis** \-'gäd-əs\ ancient Roman city NE Algeria

Ti·mis \'tē-,mēsh\ *or* **Te·mes** \'tem-,esh\ river 270 *m* Romania & Yugoslavia flowing W & S into the Danube below Belgrade

Ti·mi·soa·ra \,tē-mish-(ə-)'wär-ə\ *or* Hung **Te·mes·var** \'tem-,esh-vär\ city SW Romania near Yugoslav border *pop* 148,176

Tim·mins \'tim-ənz\ town Canada in E Ont. N of Sudbury *pop* 27,551

Ti·mor \'tē-,mò(ə)r, tē-'\ 1 island SE Malay archipelago; W half (formerly **Netherlands Timor**) belonged to the Dutch until 1946; now part of Indonesia; E half (**Portuguese Timor**) an overseas territory of Portugal ✳ Dili *area* 5762, *pop* 517,079 2 sea between Timor I. & Australia — **Ti·mor·ese** \,(,)tē-,mò-'rēz, -'rēs\ *n*

Timorlaut — see TANIMBAR

Tim·pa·no·gos, Mount \,tim-pə-'nō-gəs\ mountain 12,008 *ft* N *cen* Utah N of Provo; highest in Wasatch mountains

Timpanogos Cave limestone cavern N *cen* Utah on N slope of Mt. Timpanogos in **Timpanogos Cave National Monument**

Ti·ni·an \,tin-ē-'an\ island W Pacific in the S Marianas

Tinos — see TENOS

Tin·tag·el Head \tin-,taj-əl-\ headland SW England in NW Cornwall

Tip·pe·ca·noe \,tip-ē-kə-'nü\ river 200 *m* N Indiana flowing SW into the Wabash

Tip·per·ary \,tip-ə-'re(ə)r-ē\ 1 county S Ireland in Munster ✳ Clonmel *area* 1643, *pop* 123,779 2 urban district in SW County Tipperary

Ti·ra·ne *or* **Ti·ra·na** \ti-'rän-ə\ city ✳ of Albania *pop* 57,000

Tir·gu-Mu·res \,ti(ə)r-(,)gü-'mü-,resh\ city NE *cen* Romania ESE of Cluj *pop* 69,962

Ti·rich Mir \,tir-ich-'mi(ə)r\ mountain 25,263 *ft* Pakistan on Afghan border; highest peak in the Hindu Kush

Ti·rol *or* **Ty·rol** \tə-'rōl, 'tī-,rōl, 'tir-əl, 'tir-al\ *or* It **Ti·ro·lo** \tē-'rò-(,)lō\ region Europe in E Alps chiefly in Austria; the section S of Brenner pass has belonged since 1919 to Italy — **Ti·ro·le·an** \tə-'rō-lē-ən, tī-; ,tir-ə-'lē-\ *adj or n* — **Ti·ro·lese** \,tir-ə-'lēz, ,tī-rə-, -'lēs\ *adj or n*

Ti·ru·chi·ra·pal·li \,tir-ə-chə-'räp-ə-lē\ *or* **Trich·i·nop·o·ly** \,trich-ə-'näp-ə-lē\ city S India in *cen* Madras state *pop* 218,900

Ti·ru·pa·thi *or* **Ti·ru·pa·ti** \,tir-ə-'pət-ē\ city SE India in Andhra Pradesh NW of Madras *pop* 20,000

Ti·ryns \'tir-ənz, 'tī-rənz\ city of pre-Homeric Greece; ruins in E Peloponnesus W of Argos

Ti·sza \'tis-,ò\ *or* **Ti·sa** \'tē-sə\ river 800 *m* E Europe flowing from the Carpathians in W Ukraine W & SW into the Danube

Ti·ti·ca·ca \,tit-i-'käk-ə\ lake on Peru-Bolivia boundary at altitude of 12,500 *ft*, *area* 3200

Ti·to·grad \'tēt-(,)ō-,grad\ *or* **Pod·go·ri·ca** *or* **Pod·go·ri·tsa** \'päd-gə-,rēt-sə\ city S Yugoslavia ✳ of Montenegro *pop* 17,000

Ti·vo·li \'tiv-ə-lē\ *or anc* **Ti·bur** \'tī-bər\ commune *cen* Italy in Latium ENE of Rome *pop* 23,000

Tji·la·tjap *or* **Chi·la·chap** \chi-'läch-əp\ city & port Indonesia in S Java ESE of Bandung *pop* 28,309

Tjir·e·bon \,chir-ə-'bon\ *or* **Cher·i·bon** \,cher-ə-\ city Indonesia in W Java on N coast E of Djakarta *pop* 106,700

Tlax·ca·la \tlä-'skäl-ə\ 1 state *cen* Mexico *area* 1555, *pop* 355,491 2 town, its ✳ E of Mexico City

Tlem·cen *or* **Tlem·sen** \tlem-'sen\ city NW Algeria SW of Oran *pop* 73,445

To·ba·go \tə-'bā-(,)gō\ island SE West Indies, a territory of Trinidad & Tobago; chief town Scarborough *area* 116, *pop* 27,161

To·bol \tə-'bòl\ river 800 *m* U.S.S.R. flowing from SE foothills of the Urals NNE into the Irtysh

To·bruk \tō-'brük\ town & port NE Libya in NE Cyrenaica

To·can·tins \,tō-kən-'tēⁿs\ river 1700 *m* E *cen* & NE Brazil rising in *cen* Goiás & flowing N into the Pará

To·go \'tō-(,)gō\ *or* **To·go·land** \-,land\ 1 region W Africa on Gulf of Guinea between Dahomey & Ghana; until 1919 a German protectorate, then divided into two trust territories: **British Togoland** (in W, *area* 13,041; since 1957 part of Ghana) & **French Togo** (in E, since 1958 the Republic of Togo) 2 republic W Africa ✳ Lomé *area* 21,893, *pop* 1,440,000 — **To·go·lese** \,tō-(,)gō-'lēz, -'lēs\ *adj or n* — **To·go·land·er** *n*

To·ho·pe·kal·i·ga \tə-,hō-pi-'kal-i-gə\ lake *cen* Fla. S of Orlando

To·ka·ra \tō-'kär-ə\ island group Japan in N Ryukyus

To·ke·lau \tō-kə-,laù\ *or* **Union** islands *cen* Pacific N of Samoa belonging to New Zealand

To·ku·shi·ma \,tō-kə-'shē-mə, tō-'kü-shi-mə\ city & port Japan on E coast of Shikoku I. *pop* 179,419

To·kyo \'tō-kē-,ō\ *or formerly* **Edo** \'ed-(,)ō\ *or* **Ye·do** \'yed-(,)ō\ city ✳ of Japan in SE Honshu on **Tokyo Bay** (inlet of the Pacific) *pop* 8,310,027 — **To·kyo·ite** \'tō-kē-(,)ō-,īt\ *n*

Tokyo Plain — see KWANTO PLAIN

To·le·do \tə-'lēd-(,)ō, -'lēd-ə\ 1 city & port NW Ohio *pop* 318,003 2 province *cen* Spain in W New Castile *area* 5919, *pop* 536,843 3 commune, its ✳ *pop* 40,700 — **To·le·dan** \-'lēd-ᵊn\ *adj or n*

Tol·i·ganj *or* **Tol·ly·ganj** *or* **Tol·ly·gunge** \'täl-ē-,gənj\ city E India in S West Bengal, SSE suburb of Calcutta *pop* 150,527

To·li·ma \tə-'lē-mə\ dormant volcano W *cen* Colombia 17,717 *ft*

To·lu·ca *or* **Toluca de Ler·do** \tə-,lü-kəd-ə-'le(ə)r-(,)dō\ city *cen* Mexico ✳ of Mexico state *pop* 52,968

To·lu·ca, Ne·va·do de \nə-,väth-(,)ō-,thät-ᵊl-'ü-kə\ extinct volcano 15,016 *ft* S *cen* Mexico in Mexico state; has two lakes in crater

Tom \'täm, 'tòm\ river 450 *m* U.S.S.R. in W Soviet Russia, Asia, rising in NW Altai mountains & flowing into the Ob

Tom·big·bee \täm-'big-bē\ river 300 *m* NE Miss. & W Ala. flowing S to the Mobile & Tensaw

Tomsk \'täm(p)sk, 'tòm(p)sk\ city U.S.S.R. in W *cen* Soviet Russia, Asia, on the Tom near its junction with the Ob *pop* 249,000

Ton·a·wan·da \,tän-ə-'wän-də\ 1 city W N.Y. N of Buffalo *pop* 21,561 2 urban area W N.Y. near Buffalo *pop* 83,771

Ton·ga \'täŋ-(g)ə\ *or* **Friendly** islands SW Pacific E of Fiji islands; a kingdom & Brit. protectorate ✳ Nukualofa (in Tongatabu group) *area* 270, *pop* 56,838 — **Ton·gan** \-(g)ən\ *adj or n*

Ton·ga·re·va \,täŋ-(g)ə-'rev-ə\ *or* **Pen·rhyn** \'pen-,rin\ island S Pacific in the Manihiki islands

Ton·ga·ri·ro \,täŋ-(g)ə-'ri(ə)r-(,)ō\ volcano 6458 *ft* New Zealand in *cen* North I. in **Tongariro National Park**

Tongue \'təŋ\ river 240 *m* N Wyo. & S Mont. flowing N into the Yellowstone

Ton·kin \'tän-'kin, 'täŋ-\ *or* **Tong·king** \'täŋ-'kiŋ\ region N Indochina bordering on China, since 1946 forming N part of Vietnam; chief city Hanoi *pop* 44,660 — **Ton·kin·ese** \,täŋ-kə-'nēz, -'nēs\ *or* **Tong·king·ese** \-kiŋ-'ēz, -'ēs\ *adj or n*

Tonkin, Gulf of arm of So. China sea between Indochina & Hainan I.

Ton·le Sap \,tän-,lā-'sap\ *or* F **Grand Lac** \gräⁿ-làk\ lake 87 *m* long SW Indochina in W Cambodia

Ton·to National Monument \'tän-(,)tō\ reservation S *cen* Ariz. E of Phoenix containing cliff-dweller ruins

Too·woom·ba \tə-'wùm-bə\ city E Australia in SE Queensland W of Brisbane *pop* 46,600

To·pe·ka \tə-'pē-kə\ city ✳ of Kans. on Kansas river *pop* 119,484

To·po·lo·bam·po \tə-,pō-lə-'bäm-(,)pō\ town & port NW Mexico in Sinaloa on Gulf of California

Tor·cel·lo \tòr-'chel-(,)ō\ island Italy in Lagoon of Venice

Tor·de·si·llas \,tòrd-ə-'sē-(y)əs, -'sēl-yəs\ village NW Spain on the Duero SW of Valladolid

Torino — see TURIN

Tor·ne \'tòr-nə\ *or* Finn **Tor·nio** \'tòr-nē-,ō\ river 250 *m* NE Sweden flowing S, forming part of Finnish-Swedish border, to head of Gulf of Bothnia

To·ron·to \tə-'ränt-(,)ō, -'ränt-ə\ city & port Canada ✳ of Ont. on Lake Ontario *pop* 667,706 — **To·ron·to·ni·an** \tə-,rän-'tō-nē-ən; ,tòr-ən-, ,tär-ən-\ *adj or n*

Toros — see TAURUS

Tor·quay \(')tòr-'kē\ municipal borough SW England in Devonshire on **Tor·bay** \-'bā\ (inlet of English channel) *pop* 53,216

Tor·rance \'tòr-ən(t)s, 'tär-\ city SW Calif. NW of Long Beach *pop* 100,991

Tor·re An·nun·zi·a·ta \'tòr-ē-ə-,nün(t)-sē-'ät-ə\ commune S Italy on Bay of Naples SE of Naples *pop* 54,800

Torre de Cerredo — see CERREDO

Tor·re del Gre·co \'tòr-ē-,del-'grek-(,)ō\ commune S Italy on Bay of Naples *pop* 53,500

Tor·rens, Lake \'tòr-ənz\ salt lake Australia in E So. Australia N of Spencer gulf; 25 *ft* below sea level

Tor·re·ón \,tòr-ē-'ōn\ city N Mexico in Coahuila *pop* 181,274

Tor·res \'tòr-əs\ strait 80 *m* wide between island of New Guinea & N tip of Cape York peninsula, Australia

Tor·res Ve·dras \,tòr-əs-'vā-drəs\ town W Portugal N of Lisbon

Tor·ring·ton \'tòr-iŋ-tən, 'tär-\ city NW Conn. *pop* 30,045

Tor·to·la \tòr-'tō-lə\ island Brit. West Indies, chief of the British Virgins; site of Road Town *area* 24, *pop* 6500

Tor·tu·ga \tòr-'tü-gə\ island Haiti off N coast; a resort of pirates in 17th century

To·run \'tòr-,ün-(yə)\ *or* G **Thorn** \'tò(ə)rn\ city N Poland on the Vistula *pop* 92,000

Toscana — see TUSCANY

Tot·ten·ham \'tät-^{ə}n-əm, 'tät-nəm\ municipal borough SE England in Middlesex N of London *pop* 126,921
Toug·gourt *or* **Tug·gurt** \tə-'gü(ə)rt\ oasis NE Algeria S of Biskra *pop* 17,380
Tou·lon \tü-'lō^{n}\ commune & port SE France *pop* 141,117
Tou·louse \tü-'lüz\ city SW France on the Garonne *pop* 268,900
Tou·raine \tə-'rān\ region & former province NW *cen* France ✻ Tours
Tourane — see DA NANG
Tour·coing \tü(ə)r-'kwa^{n}\ city N France NE of Lille *pop* 83,416
Tour·nai *or* **Tour·nay** \tü(ə)r-'nā\ *or* Flem **Door·nik** \'dōr-nik, 'dȯr-\ commune SW Belgium on the Scheldt *pop* 33,314
Tours \'tü(ə)r\ city NW *cen* France *pop* 83,618
Town and Country Village — see ARCADE
Towns·ville \'taůnz-,vil\ city & port NE Australia in NE Queensland *pop* 42,200
Tow·son \'taůs-^{ə}n\ urban area Md. N of Baltimore *pop* 19,090
To·ya·ma \tō-'yäm-ə\ city Japan in *cen* Honshu near **Toyama Bay** (inlet of Sea of Japan) *pop* 170,495
To·yo·ha·shi \,tō-yə-'häsh-ē\ city Japan in S Honshu SE of Nagoya *pop* 202,985
Tpilisi — see TIFLIS
Trab·zon \trab-'zän\ *or* **Treb·i·zond** \'treb-ə-,zänd\ *or anc* **Tra·pe·zus** \'trap-i-zəs\ city & port NE Turkey on Black sea *pop* 52,680
Tra·fal·gar, Cape \trə-'fal-gər, *Sp* ,trä-fäl-'gär\ cape SW Spain SE of Cádiz at W end of Strait of Gibraltar
Tra·lee \trə-'lē\ urban district & port SW Ireland ✻ of County Kerry
Trans Alai \,tran(t)s-ə-'lī, ,tranz-\ mountain range U.S.S.R. in NW Pamirs in Kirgiz & Tadzhik republics — see LENIN PEAK
Trans·al·pine Gaul \tran(t)s-'al-,pīn, tranz-\ the part of Gaul included chiefly in modern France & Belgium
Transcaucasia — see CAUCASIA — **Trans·cau·ca·sian** \,tran(t)s-(,)kȯ-'kā-zhən, -'kazh-ən\ *adj or n*
Transjordan — see JORDAN — **Trans·jor·da·ni·an** \,tran(t)s-, ,tranz-\ *adj or n*
Trans·kei \(')tran(t)s-'kā, -'kī\ territory E Republic of So. Africa; one of the Transkeian Territories ✻ Butterworth
Trans·kei·an Territories \(,)tran(t)s-,kā-ən-, -,kī-\ region Republic of So. Africa in E Cape Province comprising the part of Kaffraria N of the Great Kei & including the territories of Transkei, Tembuland, Griqualand East, & Pondoland ✻ Umtata
Trans·vaal \tran(t)s-'väl, tranz-\ province NE Republic of So. Africa between Vaal & Limpopo rivers; in 19th century a Boer republic (**South African Republic**) ✻ Pretoria *area* 110,450, *pop* 4,812,838
Tran·syl·va·nia *or* Rom **Tran·sil·va·nia** \,tran(t)s-əl-'vā-nyə, -nē-ə\ region W Romania bounded on the N, E, & S by the Carpathians & the Transylvanian Alps; part of Hungary 1867–1918 — **Tran·syl·va·nian** \-nyən, -nē-ən\ *adj or n*
Transylvanian Alps a S extension of the Carpathian mountains in *cen* Romania
Tra·pa·ni \'träp-ə-nē\ commune & port Italy at NW tip of Sicily *pop* 64,945
Tra·si·me·no, Lake \,traz-ə-'men-(,)ō\ *or* **Lake of Pe·ru·gia** \pə-'rü-jə\ *or anc* **La·cus Tras·i·me·nus** \,lā-kə-,straz-ə-'mē-nəs\ lake 10 *m* wide *cen* Italy W of Perugia
Trav·an·core \'trav-ən-,kō(ə)r, -,kȯ(ə)r\ region & former state SW India on Malabar coast extending N from Cape Comorin; included (1949–56) in former **Travancore and Co·chin** \'kō-chən, 'käch-ən\ state (✻ Trivandrum) — see KERALA
Trav·erse, Lake \'trav-ərs\ lake NE S. Dak. & W Minn.; drained by the Bois de Sioux (headstream of Red river)
Trav·erse City \,trav-ər(s)-'sit-ē\ city NW Mich. on Grand Traverse Bay *pop* 18,432
Treb·bia \'treb-ē-ə\ *or anc* **Tre·bia** \'trē-bē-ə\ river 71 *m* NW Italy flowing N into the Po
Treb·i·zond \'treb-ə-,zänd\ **1** — see TRABZON **2** Greek empire 1204–1461, an offshoot of Byzantine Empire; at greatest extent included Georgia, Crimea, & S coast of Black sea E of Sakarya river
Trem·blant, Mont \mō^{n}-trä^{n}-blä^{n}\ mountain 3150 *ft* Canada in S Que. in Laurentian hills NW of Montreal
Treng·ga·nu \treŋ-'gän-(,)ü\ state Federation of Malaysia bordering on So. China sea ✻ Kuala Trengganu *area* 5050
Trent \'trent\ **1** river 150 *m* Canada in SE Ont. flowing from Kawartha Lakes through Rice Lake into Lake Ontario (Bay of Quinte) **2** *or* **Trent–Sev·ern** \-'sev-ərn\ canal system Canada in SE Ont. connecting Lake Huron (Georgian Bay) with Lake Ontario (Bay of Quinte) **3** river 170 *m*, *cen* England flowing NNE & uniting with the Ouse to form the Humber **4** *or* **Tren·to** \'trān-(,)tō\ *or* G **Tri·ent** \trē-'ent\ *or anc* **Tri·den·tum** \trī-'dent-əm\ commune N Italy ✻ of Trentino-Alto Adige on Adige river *pop* 40,800
Tren·ti·no \tren-'tē-(,)nō\ district NE Italy in S Tirol; with Alto Adige, forms **Trentino–Alto Adige** region (✻ Trent *area* 6327, *pop* 728,604)
Tren·ton \'trent-^{ə}n\ **1** city SE Mich. on Detroit river *pop* 18,439 **2** city ✻ of N.J. on Delaware river *pop* 114,167
Tre·vi·so \trə-'vē-(,)zō\ commune NE Italy NW of Venice *pop* 56,300
Trichinopoly — see TIRUCHIRAPALLI
Trier \'tri(ə)r\ *or* **Treves** \'trēvz\ *or* F **Trèves** \'trev\ city W Germany on the Moselle near Luxembourg border *pop* 86,700
Tri·este \trē-'est, -'es-tē\ *or* G **Tri·est** \trē-'est\ *or* Yugoslav **Trst** \'tərst\ city & port NE Italy on **Gulf of Trieste** (inlet at head of the Adriatic NW of the Istrian peninsula) *pop* 270,164; once belonged to Austria; part of Italy 1919–47; in 1947 made with surrounding territory the **Free Territory of Trieste** (*area* 293, *pop* 345,000) under administration of the United Nations; city with N part of Free Territory returned to Italy 1953, S part of territory having previously been absorbed into Yugoslavia — **Tri·es·tine** \trē-'es-,tēn\ *adj*
Trim \'trim\ urban district E Ireland ✻ of County Meath
Trinacria — see SICILY — **Tri·nac·ri·an** \trə-'nak-rē-ən, trī-\ *adj*
Trin·co·ma·lee *or* **Trin·co·ma·li** \,triŋ-kō-mə-'lē\ city & port NE Ceylon on inlet of Koddiyar Bay *pop* 32,500
Trin·i·dad \'trin-ə-,dad\ island SE West Indies off coast of NE Venezuela; with Tobago, a dominion (**Trinidad and Tobago**) of Brit. Commonwealth since 1962; formerly a Brit. colony ✻ Port of Spain *area* 1864, *pop* 530,276 — **Trin·i·da·di·an** \,trin-ə-'dād-ē-ən, -'dad-\ *adj or n*
Trin·i·ty \'trin-ət-ē\ river 360 *m* E Tex. flowing SE into Galveston Bay
Trip·o·li \'trip-ə-lē\ **1** *or* Ar **Ta·ra·bu·lus** \tə-'räb-ə-ləs\ *or anc* **Oea** \'ē-ə\ city & port NW Libya ✻ of Tripolitania & a ✻ of Libya *pop* 172,202 **2** *or* Ar **Tarabulus** *or anc* **Trip·o·lis** \'trip-ə-ləs\ city & port NW Lebanon *pop* 70,842 **3** Tripolitania when it was one of the Barbary States — **Tri·pol·i·tan** \trip-'äl-ət-^{ə}n\ *adj or n*
Tri·po·li·ta·nia \trip-,äl-ə-'tān-yə, ,trip-ə-lə-\ *or anc* **Trip·o·lis** \'trip-ə-ləs\ region NW Libya bordering on the Mediterranean; now a province of Libya ✻ Tripoli *area* 353,000, *pop* 746,064 — see TRIPOLI — **Tri·po·li·ta·nian** \-yən\ *adj or n*
Tri·pu·ra \'trip-ə-rə\ territory E India between East Pakistan & Assam ✻ Agartala *area* 4032, *pop* 639,000
Tris·tan da Cu·nha \,tris-tən-də-'kü-nə\ island S Atlantic, chief of the Tristan da Cunha islands attached to Brit. colony of St. Helena *area* 42; volcanic eruptions 1961
Tri·van·drum \trə-'van-drəm\ city & port S India NW of Cape Comorin ✻ of Kerala *pop* 186,900
Tro·as \'trō-,as\ **1** *or* **the Tro·ad** \-,ad\ territory surrounding the ancient city of Troy in NW Mysia, Asia Minor **2** ancient city of Mysia S of site of Troy — **Tro·ad·ic** \trō-'ad-ik\ *adj*
Tro·bri·and \'trō-brē-,änd\ islands SW Pacific in Solomon sea; attached to Territory of Papua *area* 170 — **Tro·bri·and·er** \,trō-brē-'än-dər\ *n*
Trois–Ri·vières \trə-,wär-ēv-'ye(ə)r, *F* trwä-rē-vyer\ *or* **Three Rivers** city Canada in S Que. NE of Montreal on N bank of the St. Lawrence *pop* 50,483
Trom·sö \'träm-,sō, -,sə(r)\ town & port N Norway
Trond·heim \'trän-,hām\ city & port *cen* Norway on **Trondheim Fjord** (80 *m* long) *pop* 58,915
Tros·sachs \'träs-əks, -,aks\ valley *cen* Scotland in Perth between Lochs Katrine & Achray
Trou·ville *or* **Trouville–sur–Mer** \(,)trü-,vē(ə)l-(,)sür-'me(ə)r, -,vil-\ town & port N France on English channel S of Le Havre
Trow·bridge \'trō-(,)brij\ urban district S England ✻ of Wiltshire
Troy \'trȯi\ **1** city SE Mich. N of Detroit *pop* 19,058 **2** city E N.Y. on the Hudson NNE of Albany *pop* 67,492 **3** *or* **Il·i·um** \'il-ē-əm\ *or* **Il·i·on** \'il-ē-,än, -ē-ən\ *or* **Troia** \'trȯi-ə, 'trō-yə\ *or* **Tro·ja** \'trō-jə, -yə\ ancient city NW Asia Minor in Troas SW of the Dardanelles — see HISSARLIK
Troyes \trə-'wä\ city NE France SE of Paris *pop* 58,819
Tru·chas Peak \,trü-chəs-\ *or* **North Truchas Peak** mountain 13,110 *ft* N N. Mex. in Sangre de Cristo mountains NE of Sante Fe; highest of three peaks forming **Truchas Peaks**
Tru·cial Oman \,trü-shə-lō-'man, -'män\ *or* **Trucial States** region E Arabia on **Trucial coast** of Persian gulf between Qatar peninsula & Cape Musandam including seven (originally five) Arab sheikdoms (Abu Dhabi, Ajman, Dubai, Fujaira, Ras al Khaima, Sharja and Kalba, & Umm al Qaiwan) in treaty with Great Britain *area* 32,300, *pop* 86,000
Truck·ee \'trək-ē\ river 120 *m* E Calif. & W Nev. flowing from Lake Tahoe into Pyramid Lake
Tru·ji·llo \trü-'hē-(,)(y)ō\ **1** city NW Peru NW of Lima *pop* 60,400 **2** — see SANTO DOMINGO
Truk \'trək, 'trůk\ islands W Pacific in *cen* Carolines *pop* 21,010
Tru·ro \'trů(ə)r-(,)ō\ municipal borough SW England ✻ of Cornwall
Tsamkong — see CHANKIANG
Tsana — see TANA
Tsang·po \'(t)säŋ-'pō\ the upper Brahmaputra in Tibet
Tsaritsyn — see VOLGOGRAD
Tsarskoe Selo — see PUSHKIN
Tsi·nan \'jē-'nän\ city E China ✻ of Shantung *pop* 680,100
Tsing·hai *or* **Ching·hai** \'chiŋ-'hī\ **1** *or* **Ko·ko Nor** \,kō-(,)kō-'nō(ə)r\ shallow saline lake W *cen* China in NE Tsinghai province S of Nan Shan mountains at altitude of *ab* 10,000 *ft*, *area* 2300 **2** province W China ✻ Sining *area* 278,378, *pop* 1,676,000
Tsing·tao \'chiŋ-'daů, '(t)siŋ-'taů\ city & port E China in E Shantung on Kiaochow Bay *pop* 916,800
Tsingyuan — see PAOTING
Tsi·tsi·har \'(t)sēt-sē-,här, 'chē-chē-\ *or formerly* **Lung·kiang** \'lůŋ-jē-'äŋ\ city NE China in W Heilungkiang *pop* 344,700
Tskhin·va·li \'(t)skin-və-lē\ town N Georgia, U.S.S.R. NW of Tiflis ✻ of South Ossetia *pop* 27,000
Tsu·ga·ru \'(t)sü-gə-,rü\ strait Japan between Honshu & Hokkaido connecting Pacific ocean & Sea of Japan
Tsu·shi·ma \(t)sü-'shē-mə, '(t)sü-shi-,mä\ island Japan in Korea strait separated from Kyushu by **Tsushima strait** (the SE part of Korea strait) *area* 271
Tu·a·mo·tu \,tü-ə-'mō-(,)tü\ *or* **Pau·mo·tu** \paů-'mō-\ *or* **Dan·ger·ous** \'dānj-(ə-)rəs\ *or* **Low** \'lō\ archipelago S Pacific E of Society islands; belongs to France *area* 330
Tü·bing·en \'t(y)ü-biŋ-ən\ city W Germany on the Neckar S of Stuttgart *pop* 50,600
Tu·bu·aï \,tü-bə-'wī\ *or* **Aus·tral** \'ȯs-trəl, 'äs-\ islands S Pacific S of Tahiti belonging to France *area* 115, *pop* 3600
Tuc·son \'tü-,sän\ city SE Ariz. *pop* 212,892
Tu·cu·mán \,tü-kə-'män\ city NW Argentina *pop* 244,628
Tu·ge·la \tü-'gā-lə\ river 300 *m* E Republic of So. Africa in *cen* Natal flowing E to Indian ocean; near its source on Mt. Aux Sources are the **Tugela Falls** (3110 *ft*)
Tuggurt — see TOUGGOURT
Tu·la \'tü-lə\ **1** town *cen* Mexico in SW Hidalgo N of Mexico City; ancient ✻ of the Toltecs **2** city U.S.S.R. in *cen* Soviet Russia, Europe, S of Moscow on a tributary of the Oka *pop* 345,000
Tu·la·gi \tü-'läg-ē\ island S Pacific in S *cen* Solomons off S coast of Florida I. & N of Guadalcanal; formerly ✻ of the Brit. Solomons
Tu·lare \tü-'la(ə)r(-ē), -'le(ə)r(-ē)\ former lake S *cen* Calif. S of Fresno; now drained for farmland
Tul·la·more \,təl-ə-'mō(ə)r, -'mȯ(ə)r\ urban district *cen* Ireland ✻ of County Offaly
Tul·sa \'təl-sə\ city NE Okla. on Arkansas river *pop* 261,685

ə abut; ^{ə} kitten; ər further; a back; ā bake; ä cot, cart; aů out; ch chin; e less; ē easy; g gift; i trip; ī life
j joke; ŋ sing; ō flow; ȯ flaw; ȯi coin; th thin; th this; ü loot; ů foot; y yet; yü few; yů furious; zh vision
^{ə} F table; à F bac; k G ich, Buch; ^{n} F vin; œ F bœuf; œ̄ F feu; ue G füllen; ue̅ F rue; ^{y} F digne \dēn^{y}\, nuit \nw^{y}ē\

Tu·men \'tü-'mən\ river 220 m E Asia on border between Korea, China, & the U.S.S.R. flowing NE & SE into Sea of Japan

Tu·muc–Hu·mac or Brazilian **Tu·mu·cu·maque** \tə-,mü-kə-'mäk\ mountain [range NE Brazil on Surinam-French Guiana boundary

Tunghai — see SINHAILIEN

Tung·hwa \'tùŋ-'(h)wä\ city NE China in SW Kirin pop 129,100

Tungshan — see SÜCHOW

Tung·ting \'dùŋ-'tiŋ\ lake SE cen China in NE Hunan W of Poyang lake area 1450

Tun·gu·ska \tùŋ-'gü-skə, tən-\ any of three rivers in Soviet Russia, Asia, tributaries of the Yenisei: **Lower Tunguska** (2000 m), **Stony Tunguska** (1000 m), & **Upper Tunguska** (lower course of the Angara)

Tu·nis \'t(y)ü-nəs\ **1** city ✳ of Tunisia near site of ancient Carthage pop 410,000 **2** TUNISIA — used esp. of the former Barbary state — **Tu·ni·sian** \t(y)ü-'nē-zh(ē-)ən, -'nizh-(ē-)ən\ adj or n

Tu·ni·sia \t(y)ü-'nē-zh(ē-)ə, -'nizh-(ē-)ə\ country N Africa bordering on the Mediterranean; formerly one of the Barbary states; a French protectorate 1881–1956, a monarchy 1956–57, & a republic since 1957 ✳ Tunis area 48,300, pop 4,168,000

Tu·ol·um·ne \tü-'äl-ə-mē\ river 155 m, cen Calif. flowing W from Yosemite National Park into the San Joaquin

Tu·pe·lo \'t(y)ü-pə-,lō\ city NE Miss. pop 17,221

Tu·pun·ga·to \,tü-pəŋ-'gät-(,)ō\ mountain 22,310 ft in the Andes on Argentina-Chile boundary ENE of Santiago, Chile

Tur·fan \'tù(ə)r-'fän\ depression W China in E Sinkiang in NE part of Tarim basin; over 900 ft below sea level

Tu·rin \'t(y)ùr-ən, t(y)ü-'rin\ or It **To·ri·no** \tō-'rē-(,)nō\ commune NW Italy on the Po ✳ of Piedmont pop 994,089 — **Tu·ri·nese** \,t(y)ùr-ə-'nēz, -'nēs\ adj or n

Tur·ke·stan or **Tur·ki·stan** \,tər-kə-'stan, -'stän\ region cen Asia between Iran & Siberia; now divided between U.S.S.R., China, & Afghanistan — see CHINESE TURKESTAN, RUSSIAN TURKESTAN

Tur·key \'tər-kē\ country W Asia (**Turkey in Asia**) & SE Europe (**Turkey in Europe**) between Mediterranean & Black seas; formerly center of an empire (✳ Constantinople), since 1923 a republic ✳ Ankara area 296,185, pop 27,809,831 — see OTTOMAN EMPIRE

Turk·men Republic \,tərk-mən-\ or **Turk·me·nia** \,tərk-'mē-nē-ə\ or **Turk·men·i·stan** \,tərk-'men-ə-,stan\ constituent republic U.S.S.R. in cen Asia bordering on Afghanistan, Iran, & the Caspian ✳ Ashkhabad area 187,200, pop 1,626,000 — **Turk·man** \'tərk-mən\, — **Turk·men** \-mən\ adj — **Turk·me·ni·an** \,tərk-'mē-nē-ən\ adj

Turks and Cai·cos \,tərk-sən-'kā-kəs\ two groups of islands (Turks islands & Caicos islands) Brit. West Indies at SE end of the Bahamas; a Brit. colony; administered from Jamaica until 1962; chief island & seat of government **Grand Turk** (7 m long) area 166, pop 7000

Tur·ku \'tù(ə)r-(,)kü\ or Sw **Åbo** \'ō-(,)bü\ city & port SW Finland pop 119,900

Turn·hout \'tərn-,haùt\ commune N Belgium pop 36,334

Tus·ca·loo·sa \,təs-kə-'lü-sə\ city W cen Ala. on Black Warrior river SW of Birmingham pop 63,370

Tus·ca·ny \'təs-kə-nē\ or It **To·sca·na** \tō-'skän-ə\ region NW cen Italy bordering on Ligurian & Tyrrhenian seas ✳ Florence area 8861, pop 3,158,811

Tus·cu·lum \'təs-k(y)ə-ləm\ ancient town Italy in Latium SE of Rome & N of Alban hills near modern Frascati

Tu·tu·ila \,tüt-ə-'wē-lə\ island, chief of American Samoa group area 52, pop 16,814 — **Tu·tu·ilan** \-lən\ adj or n

Tux·tla or **Tuxtla Gu·tiér·rez** \tüst-lə-(,)gü-'tyer-əs\ city SE Mexico ✳ of Chiapas pop 28,260

Tu·zi·goot National Monument \'tü-zi-,güt\ reservation cen Ariz. SW of Flagstaff containing ruins of prehistoric pueblo

Tver — see KALININ

Tweed \'twēd\ river 96 m SE Scotland & NE England flowing E into North sea

Tweeddale — see PEEBLES

Twick·en·ham \'twik-(ə-)nəm\ municipal borough SE England in Middlesex on the Thames SW of London pop 105,645

Twin Cities the cities of Minneapolis & St. Paul, Minn.

Twin Falls city S Idaho SW of Twin Falls (125 ft) in Snake river pop 20,126

Ty·ler \'tī-lər\ city E Tex. ESE of Dallas pop 51,230

Tyn·dall, Mount \'tin-dᵊl\ **1** mountain 14,025 ft S cen Calif. in Sierra Nevada NW of Mt. Whitney **2** mountain 8280 ft New Zealand in cen South I. in Southern Alps

Tyne \'tīn\ river 35 m N England in Northumberland flowing E into North sea

Tyne·mouth \'tīn-,maùth\ county borough N England in Northumberland on North sea at mouth of the Tyne pop 66,544

Tyre \'tī(ə)r\ or Ar **Es Sur** \es-'sù(ə)r\ or Heb **Zor** \'tsò(ə)r, 'zò(ə)r\ town S Lebanon on the coast; ancient ✳ of Phoenicia — **Tyr·i·an** \'tir-ē-ən\ adj or n

Ty·ree, Mount \tī-'rē\ mountain 16,290 ft W Antarctica in Sentinel Range of Ellsworth mountains NW of Vinson Massif

Tyrol — see TIROL — **Ty·ro·le·an** \tə-'rō-lē-ən, tī-; ,tir-ə-'lē-\ adj or n — **Ty·ro·lese** \,tir-ə-'lēz, ,tī-rə-, -'lēs\ adj or n

Ty·rone \tir-'ōn\ county W cen Northern Ireland ✳ Omagh area 1218, pop 132,049

Tyr·rhe·ni·an \tə-'rē-nē-ən\ sea, the part of the Mediterranean W of Italy, N of Sicily, & E of Sardinia & Corsica

Tyu·men \tyü-'men\ city U.S.S.R. in W Soviet Russia, Asia, on the Tura (a tributary of the Tobol) pop 150,000

Tze·kung \'dzə-'gùŋ\ city S China in S Szechwan W of Chungking pop 291,300

Tze·po \'dzə-'pō\ city E China in cen Shantung E of Tsinan pop 184,200

Uap — see YAP

Uau·pés \waù-'pes\ or Sp **Vau·pés** \vaù-\ river 700 m Colombia & Brazil flowing ESE into the Negro

Uban·gi \(y)ü-'baŋ-(g)ē\ or F **Ou·ban·gui** \ü-bäⁿ-gē\ river 700 m W cen Africa on NW border of Republic of the Congo flowing W & S into Congo river

Ubangi–Sha·ri \-'shär-ē\ or F **Oubangui–Cha·ri** \-shä-rē\ former French territory N cen Africa — see CENTRAL AFRICAN REPUBLIC

Ube \'ü-bē, -(,)bä\ city & port Japan in SW Honshu on Inland sea pop 160,020

Uca·ya·li \,ü-kə-'yäl-ē\ river 1200 m, cen & N Peru flowing N to unite with the Marañón forming the Amazon

Uc·cle \'ükl³\ or Flem **Uk·kel** \'ək-əl\ commune cen Belgium pop 68,256

Udai·pur \ü-'dī-,pù(ə)r, ,ü-,dī-'\ **1** or **Me·war** \mā-'wär\ former state NW India, now part of Rajasthan state **2** city, its ✳, NE of Ahmadabad pop 89,600

Udi·ne \'üd-i,nä\ commune NE Italy NE of Venice ✳ of Friuli-Venezia Giulia region pop 76,400

Ud·murt Republic \'ùd-,mù(ə)rt\ autonomous republic U.S.S.R. in E Soviet Russia, Europe, in W foothills of the Urals ✳ Izhevsk area 16,200, pop 1,337,000

Ue·le or **Wel·le** \'wel-ē\ river 700 m, cen Africa flowing W in Republic of Congo to unite with the Bomu forming the Ubangi

Ufa \ü-'fä\ **1** river 430 m E Soviet Russia, Europe, in S Urals flowing NW & SW into the Belaya **2** city U.S.S.R. in E Soviet Russia, Europe ✳ of Bashkir Republic on the Belaya pop 546,000

Ugan·da \(y)ü-'gan-də\ country E Africa N of Lake Victoria; a Brit. protectorate until 1962; member of Brit. Commonwealth ✳ Kampala area 93,981, pop 6,523,628 — **Ugan·dan** \-dən\ n

Uin·ta \yù-'int-ə\ mountain range NE Utah — see KINGS PEAK

Uj·jain \'ü-,jīn\ city NW cen India in W Madhya Pradesh NNW of Indore pop 129,800

Uj·pest \'üē-,pes(h)t\ city cen Hungary on the Danube, N suburb of Budapest pop 68,530

Ukraine \yü-'krān, -'krīn, 'yü-,\ or **Ukrai·ni·an Republic** \yü-,krā-nē-ən-\ or Russ **Ukrai·na** \ü-'krī-nə\ constituent republic of the U.S.S.R. in E Europe on N coast of Black sea ✳ Kiev (✳ Kharkov 1921–34) area 222,600, pop 42,500,000

Ulan Ba·tor \,ü-,län-'bä-,to(ə)r\ or **Ur·ga** \'ù(ə)r-gə\ city ✳ of Outer Mongolia pop 100,000

Ulan–Ude \ü-,län-ü-'dä\ or formerly **Verkh·ne·udinsk** \,verk-nə-'ü-,din(t)sk\ city U.S.S.R. in E Soviet Russia, Asia ✳ of Buryat Republic on Selenga river pop 174,000

Uleåborg — see OULU

Ulm \'ùlm\ city W Germany on the Danube WNW of Munich pop 90,200

Ul·ster \'əl-stər\ **1** region N Ireland comprising Northern Ireland & N Republic of Ireland; ancient kingdom, later a province comprising nine counties three of which in 1921 joined Irish Free State (now Republic of Ireland) while the rest remained with United Kingdom **2** province N Republic of Ireland comprising counties Donegal, Cavan, & Monaghan area 3093, pop 217,489 **3** Northern Ireland comprising counties Antrim, Armagh, Down, Fermanagh, Londonderry, & Tyrone ✳ Belfast — **Ul·ster·ite** \-,īt\ n — **Ul·ster·man** \-mən\ n

Ulu Dag \,ü-lə-'dä(g)\ or anc **Olym·pus** \ō-'lim-pəs\ mountain 8224 ft NW Turkey in Asia SE of Bursa

Ulugh Muz·tagh \ü-lə-məz-'tä(g)\ mountain 25,340 ft W China in S Sinkiang; highest in Kunlun mountains

Ul·ya·novsk or **Ul·ia·novsk** \ül-'yä-nəfsk\ or formerly **Sim·birsk** \sim-'bi(ə)rsk\ city U.S.S.R. in E cen Soviet Russia, Europe, on the Volga pop 205,000

Uma·til·la \,yü-mə-'til-ə\ river 80 m NE Oreg. flowing W & N into the Columbia

Um·bria \'əm-brē-ə\ region cen Italy in the Apennines; ✳ Perugia

Um·nak \'üm-,nak\ island SW Alaska in Fox group of Aleutians

Ump·qua \'əm(p)-,kwò\ river 200 m SW Oreg. flowing into the Pacific

Un·alas·ka \,ən-ə-'las-kə\ island SW Alaska in Fox group of the Aleutians

Unalaska Bay bay SW Alaska on N coast of Unalaska I.

Un·com·pah·gre Peak \,ən-kəm-,päg-rē-\ mountain 14,309 ft SW Colo.; highest in San Juan mountains

Uncompahgre Plateau tableland W Colo. SW of Gunnison river

Un·ga·va \,ən-'gä-və, -'gäv-ə\ **1** peninsula Canada in N Que. between Hudson Bay & Ungava Bay **2** region Canada N of Eastmain river & W of Labrador including Ungava peninsula, divided 1927 between Que. & Nfld. — see NEW QUEBEC

Ungava Bay inlet of Hudson strait Canada in N Que.

Uni·mak \'yü-nə-,mak\ island SW Alaska in Fox group of the Aleutians

Union \'yün-yən\ **1** urban township NE N.J. WSW of Newark pop 51,499 **2** — see TOKELAU

Union City city NE N.J. N of Jersey City pop 52,180

Union·dale \'yün-yən-,dāl\ urban area SE N.Y. on Long I. pop 20,041

Union of South Africa — see SOUTH AFRICA (Republic of)

Union of Soviet Socialist Republics or **Soviet Union** country E Europe & N Asia bordering on the Arctic & Pacific oceans & Baltic & Black seas; a union of 15 constituent republics ✳ Moscow area 8,662,400, pop 216,200,000 — see RUSSIA

Union·town \'yün-yən-,taùn\ city SW Pa. pop 17,942

United Arab Republic country NE Africa & SW Asia, equivalent to Egypt; formerly (1958–61) a union of Egypt & Syria ✳ Cairo area 386,198, pop 4,734,000

United Kingdom, 1 or **United Kingdom of Great Britain and Northern Ireland** country W Europe comprising Great Britain & Northern Ireland ✳ London area 89,034, pop 50,354,115 **2** or **United Kingdom of Great Britain and Ireland** country 1801–1921 comprising Great Britain & all of Ireland

United Nations international territory, a small area in New York City in E cen Manhattan overlooking East river; seat since 1951 of permanent headquarters of the United Nations

United Provinces or **United Provinces of Agra and Oudh** former province N India formed 1902 ✳ Allahabad; as Uttar Pradesh, became a state of Republic of India 1950

United States of America or **United States** \yù-,nīt-əd-'stāts, esp South 'yü-\ **1** country No. America bordering on Atlantic, Pacific, & Arctic oceans; a federal republic ✳ Washington area 3,615,222, pop 179,323,175 **2** the United States of America with dependencies & possessions

University City city E Mo. WNW of St. Louis pop 51,249

University Heights city NE Ohio E of Cleveland pop 16,641

University Park city NE Tex. within city of Dallas pop 23,202

Un·ter·wal·den \'ùnt-ər-,väl-dən\ or F **Un·ter·wald** \ün-tər-väld\ canton S Switzerland subdivided into half cantons **Nid·wal·den** \'nēt-,väl-dən\ or F **Nid·wald** \nēd-väld\ (✳ Stans area 112, pop 19,389) & **Ob·wal·den** \'òp-,väl-dən\ or F **Ob·wald** \òb-väld\ (✳ Sarnen area 183, pop 22,125)

Up·land \'əp-lənd\ city SW Calif. W of San Bernardino *pop* 15,918
Upo·lu \ü-'pō-(,)lü\ island S Pacific in Western Samoa
Upper Adige — see ALTO ADIGE
Upper Arlington city *cen* Ohio W of Columbus *pop* 28,486
Upper Canada the Canadian province 1791–1841 corresponding to modern Ont. — see LOWER CANADA
Upper Dar·by \'där-bē\ urban township SE Pa. *pop* 93,158
Upper Karroo — see KARROO
Upper Klamath lake 30 *m* long S Oreg. SSE of Crater Lake National Park drained by Klamath river — see LOWER KLAMATH
Upper More·land \'mō(ə)r-lənd, 'mȯ(ə)r-\ urban township SE Pa. NW of Philadelphia *pop* 21,032
Upper Palatinate — see PALATINATE
Upper Vol·ta \'väl-tə\ or F **Haute-Vol·ta** \ōt-vȯl-tä\ country W Africa N of Ivory Coast, Ghana, & Togo; a republic; until 1958 a French territory * Ouagadougou *area* 121,892, *pop* 3,635,000 — **Upper Vol·tan** \'vält-ᵊn\ *n or adj*
Upp·sa·la *or* **Up·sa·la** \'əp-sə-,lä, -,säl-ə; ,əp-'säl-ə\ city E Sweden NW of Stockholm *pop* 74,802
Ur \'ər, 'ú(ə)r\ city of ancient Sumer in S Babylonia; site in S Iraq near the Euphrates 105 *m* NW of Basra
Ural \'yúr-əl\ **1** river 1400 *m* U. S. S. R. rising at S end of Ural mountains & flowing S into the Caspian **2** mountains U. S. S. R. extending from Kara sea to steppes N of Lake Aral; usu. considered the dividing line between Asia & Europe; highest point *ab* 6000 *ft*
Uralsk \yù-'ralsk\ city U.S.S.R. in Soviet Central Asia in W Kazakh Republic on Ural river *pop* 105,000
Ura·ri·coe·ra \ù-,rär-i-'kwer-ə\ river 360 *m* N Brazil, a headstream of the Branco
Ura·wa \u-'rä-wə\ city Japan in Honshu N of Tokyo *pop* 143,044
Ur·bana \ər-'ban-ə\ city E Ill. adjoining Champaign *pop* 27,294
Ur·bi·no \ù(ə)r-'bē-(,)nō\ commune *cen* Italy WNW of Ancona
Ur·fa \ùr-'fä\ *or anc* **Edes·sa** \i-'des-ə\ city SE Turkey E of Gaziantep *pop* 59,910
Urga — see ULAN BATOR
Uri \'ù(ə)r-ē\ canton *cen* Switzerland S of Lake of Lucerne * Altdorf *area* 415, *pop* 28,556
Urmia — see RIZAIYEH
Uru·bam·ba \,ùr-ə-'bäm-bə\ river 450 *m*, *cen* Peru flowing NNW to unite with the Apurímac forming the Ucayali
Uru·guay \'(y)ùr-ə-,gwī, -,gwä\ **1** river 980 *m* SE So. America rising in Brazil & flowing into the Río de la Plata **2** *or* **Re·pú·bli·ca Ori·en·tal del Uru·guay** \rä-'pü-bli-(,)kä-,ōr-ē-,en-'täl-,del-,ùr-ə-'gwī, -,ȯr-\ country SE So. America between the lower Uruguay & the Atlantic; a republic * Montevideo *area* 72,172, *pop* 2,800,000 — see BANDA ORIENTAL — **Uru·guay·an** \,(y)ùr-ə-'gwī-ən, -,gwä-\ *adj or n*
Urum·chi \ù-'rùm-chē\ *or* **Ti·hwa** \'dē-'(h)wä\ city NW China * of Sinkiang on N side of Tien Shan *pop* 140,700
Urundi — see BURUNDI
Ush·ant \'əsh-ənt\ *or* F **Île d'Oues·sant** \ēl-dwe-sän\ island NW France off tip of Brittany
Us·hua·ia \ü-'swī-ə\ town S Argentina on S coast of Tierra del Fuego I., at 54°50'S
Usk \'əsk\ river 60 *m* S Wales & W England flowing E & S into Severn estuary
Uskub — see SKOPLJE
Us·ku·dar \,üs-kə-'där\ *or* **Scu·ta·ri** *or* **Sku·ta·ri** \'sküt-ə-rē\ section of Istanbul, Turkey, on Asian side of the Bosporus
Us·pa·lla·ta \,ü-spə-'yät-ə, -'zhät-\ *or* **La Cum·bre** \lə-'kúm-brē\ mountain pass 12,600 *ft* S So. America in the Andes between Mendoza, Argentina, & Santiago, Chile
Us·su·ri \ù-'sú(ə)r-ē\ river 450 *m* E Asia on border between U.S.S.R. & China flowing N into the Amur
Usti nad La·bem \,ü-stē-'näd-lə-,bem\ city W Czechoslovakia in N Bohemia on the Elbe *pop* 56,328
Usum·bu·ra \,ü-səm-'bùr-ə\ *or* **Bu·jum·bu·ra** \,bü-jəm-'bùr-ə\ city * of Burundi on Lake Tanganyika *pop* 42,961
Utah \'yü-,tȯ, -,tä\ **1** lake 30 *m* long N *cen* Utah drained by Jordan river **2** state W U.S. * Salt Lake City *area* 84,916, *pop* 890,627 — **Utah·an** \-,tȯ(-ə)n, -,tä(-ə)n\ *adj or n* — **Utahn** \-,tȯ(-ə)n, -,tä(-ə)n\ *n*
Uti·ca \'yüt-i-kə\ **1** city E *cen* N.Y. on the Mohawk *pop* 100,410 **2** ancient city N Africa on coast NW of Carthage
Utrecht \'yü-,trekt\ **1** province *cen* Netherlands S of the IJsselmeer *area* 535, *pop* 662,847 **2** city, its * *pop* 252,104
Utsu·no·mi·ya \,üt-sə-'nō-mē-(y)ə\ city Japan in *cen* Honshu N of Tokyo *pop* 227,153
Ut·tar Pra·desh \,üt-ər-prə-'däsh, -'desh\ state N India bordering on Tibet & Nepal * Lucknow *area* 113,409, *pop* 63,215,700 — see UNITED PROVINCES
Ux·bridge \'əks-(,)brij\ urban area SE England in Middlesex WNW of London *pop* 55,944
Ux·mal \üz-'mäl\ ancient city SE Mexico in Yucatán S of modern Mérida * of the later Mayan Empire
Uz·bek Republic \'úz-,bek-, ,əz-\ *or* **Uz·bek·i·stan** \úz-,bek-i-'stan, ,əz-, -'stän\ constituent republic U.S.S.R. in W *cen* Asia E of the Amu Darya * Tashkent *area* 171,070, *pop* 8,400,000

Vaal \'väl\ river 700 *m* Republic of So. Africa rising in SE Transvaal & flowing W into the Orange in N Cape Province
Vaa·sa *or* Sw **Va·sa** \'väs-ə\ city & port W Finland *pop* 43,200
Va·duz \fä-'düts\ commune * of Liechtenstein on the upper Rhine
Vah \'vä(k)\ *or* Hung **Vag** \'väg\ river 210 *m* Czechoslovakia rising in Tatra mountains & flowing W & S into the Danube
Va·lais \va-'lā\ *or* G **Wal·lis** \'väl-əs\ canton SW *cen* Switzerland bordering on France & Italy * Sion *area* 2026, *pop* 159,178
Val·dai \väl-'dī\ hills U.S.S.R. in N Soviet Russia, Europe, SE of Lake Ilmen; highest point 1053 *ft*
Val d'Aos·ta \,väl-dä-'ós-tə\ *or* **Val·le d'Aos·ta** \,väl-ā-\ region NW Italy bordering on France & Switzerland NW of Piedmont * Aosta
Val·di·via \val-'dēv-ē-ə\ city & port S *cen* Chile *pop* 69,904
Val·dos·ta \val-'däs-tə\ city S Ga. *pop* 30,652
Va·lence \va-'läⁿs\ commune SE France S of Lyons *pop* 41,470
Va·len·cia \və-'len-ch(ē-)ə, -'len(t)-sē-ə\ **1** region & ancient kingdom E Spain between Andalusia & Catalonia **2** province

E Spain *area* 4150, *pop* 1,481,567 **3** commune & port, its * *pop* 558,728 **4** city N Venezuela WSW of Caracas *pop* 161,413
Va·len·ci·ennes \və-,len(t)-sē-'en(z)\ city N France SE of Lille *pop* 43,434
Va·len·tia *or* **Va·len·cia** \və-'len-ch(ē-)ə\ island SW Ireland in the Atlantic S of entrance to Dingle Bay
Val·la·do·lid \,val-əd-ə-'lid, -'lē\ **1** province NW *cen* Spain *area* 2922, *pop* 373,367 **2** commune, its * *pop* 149,195
Val·lau·ris \,val-ə-'rēs\ village SE France NE of Cannes
Val·le·cas \və(l)-'yä-kəs\ commune *cen* Spain, SE suburb of Madrid *pop* 60,604
Val·le·jo \və-'lā-(,)ō\ city W Calif. on San Pablo Bay *pop* 60,877
Val·let·ta *or* **Va·let·ta** \və-'let-ə\ city & port * of Malta *pop* 18,666
Val·ley·field \'val-ē-,fēld\ *or formerly* **Sal·a·ber·ry-de-Valley·field** \,sal-ə-,ber-ēd-ə-\ city Canada in S Que. on the St. Lawrence SW of Montreal *pop* 23,584
Valley of Ten Thousand Smokes volcanic region SW Alaska in Katmai National Monument
Valley Stream village SE N.Y. on Long I. *pop* 38,629
Val·lom·bro·sa \,val-əm-'brō-sə, -zə\ village *cen* Italy in Tuscany ESE of Florence
Va·lois \'val-,wä\ medieval county & duchy N France in NE Île-de-France * Crépy-en-Valois
Valona — see VLONE
Val·pa·rai·so, 1 \,val-pə-'rā-(,)zō\ city NW Ind. SE of Gary *pop* 15,227 **2** \-'rī-(,)zō, -'rā-\ *or* Sp **Val·pa·ra·í·so** \,väl-pä-rä-'ē-sō\ city & port *cen* Chile 75 *m* WNW of Santiago *pop* 259,241
Van \'van\ lake E Turkey in mountains of Armenia *area* 1425
Van·cou·ver \van-'kü-vər\ **1** island W Canada in B.C. off SW coast; chief city Victoria *area* 12,408 **2** city SW Wash. on the Columbia opposite Portland, Oreg. *pop* 32,464 **3** city & port Canada in SW B.C. on Burrard Inlet *pop* 365,844
Vancouver, Mount mountain 15,700 *ft* on Alaska-Canada boundary in St. Elias range
Van Die·men \van-'dē-mən\ gulf inlet of Arafura sea N Australia in N Northern Territory
Van Diemen's Land — see TASMANIA
Va·ner *or* **Vä·ner** *or* **Ve·ner** \'vä-nər\ *or* **Vä·nern** \-nərn\ lake SW Sweden *area* 2141
Va·nua Le·vu \,vä-,nü-ə-'lev-(,)ü\ island S Pacific in the Fijis NE of Viti Levu *area* 2128
Va·ra·de·ro \,vär-ə-'de(ə)r-(,)ō\ town Cuba on Straits of Florida
Varanasi — see BANARAS
Var·dar \'värd-ər\ *or* NGk **Var·dá·ris** \vär-'där-əs\ river 200 *m* SE Yugoslavia & N Greece flowing S into Gulf of Salonika
Va·re·se \və-'rā-sē\ commune N Italy NW of Milan *pop* 56,500
Var·na \'vär-nə\ *or formerly* **Sta·lin** \'stäl-ən, 'stal-, -,ēn\ city & port E Bulgaria on Black sea *pop* 119,769
Väs·ter·ås \,ves-tə-'rȯs\ city E Sweden on Lake Malar NW of Stockholm *pop* 79,210
Vaté — see EFATE
Vat·i·can City *or* **Vatican City State** \,vat-i-kən-\ *or* It **Cit·tà del Va·ti·ca·no** \chēt-'tä-del-,vä-ti-'kä-nō\ independent papal state within commune of Rome, Italy; created Feb. 11, 1929 *area* 108.7 acres, *pop* 1000
Vat·ter *or* **Vät·ter** *or* **Vet·ter** \'vet-ər\ *or* **Vät·tern** \-ərn\ lake S Sweden *area* 733
Vaucluse — see FONTAINE-DE-VAUCLUSE
Vaud \'vō\ *or* G **Waadt** \'vät\ canton W Switzerland N of Lake of Geneva * Lausanne *area* 1256, *pop* 377,585
Vaupés — see UAUPÉS
Ve·ii \'vē-,(y)ī\ ancient city of Etruria in *cen* Italy NNW of Rome
Vel·bert \'fel-bərt\ city W Germany in North Rhine-Westphalia in Ruhr valley NE of Düsseldorf *pop* 51,100
Vel·la La·vel·la \,vel-ə-lə-'vel-ə\ island SW Pacific in *cen* Solomons SW of Choiseul
Vel·lore \və-'lō(ə)r, -'lȯ(ə)r\ city SE India in N Madras state WSW of Madras *pop* 106,000
Vel·sen \'vel-sə(n)\ commune W Netherlands; outer port for Amsterdam *pop* 59,948
Velsuna — see ORVIETO
Vence \'väⁿs\ commune SE France W of Nice
Ven·dée *or* **La Ven·dée** \(,)lä-,vän(n)-'dā\ region W France bordering on Bay of Biscay S of Brittany
Ven·dôme \vän-'dōm\ town N *cen* France WSW of Orléans
Ve·ne·tia \vi-'nē-sh(ē-)ə\ *or* It **Ve·ne·zia** \və-'net-sē-ə\ **1** area NE Italy & NW Yugoslavia including territory between lower Po river & the Alps **2** VENEZIA EUGANEA
Ve·ne·to \'ven-ə-,tō, 'vä-nə-\ region N Italy comprising most of Venezia Euganea * Venice *area* 7092, *pop* 3,918,059
Ve·ne·zia Eu·ga·nea \və-,net-sē-ə,éü-'gän-ē-ə\ the S portion of Venetia
Venezia Tri·den·ti·na \,trē-,den-'tē-nə\ the NW portion of Venetia N of Lake Garda; included in Trentino–Alto Adige region
Ven·e·zu·e·la \,ven-əz-(ə-)'wā-lə, -(ə-)'wē-\ country N So. America; a republic * Caracas *area* 352,141, *pop* 7,361,703 — **Ven·e·zu·e·lan** \-lən\ *adj or n*
Venezuela, Gulf of *or* **Gulf of Maracaibo** inlet of the Caribbean NW Venezuela N of Lake Maracaibo
Ven·iam·i·nof Crater \ven-,yam-ə-,nȯf-\ volcano 8225 *ft* SW Alaska on *cen* Alaska peninsula in Aleutian range
Ven·ice \'ven-əs\ *or* It **Ve·ne·zia** \və-'net-sē-ə\ *or* L **Ve·ne·tia** \vi-'nē-sh(ē-)ə\ city & port N Italy * of Veneto, on islands in **Lagoon of Venice** (inlet of Gulf of Venice) *pop* 322,457 — **Ve·ne·tian** \və-'nē-shən\ *adj or n*
Venice, Gulf of arm of the Adriatic between Po delta & Istria
Ven·lo *or formerly* **Ven·loo** \'ven-(,)lō\ commune SE Netherlands on the Maas near German border *pop* 53,680
Ven·ta \'vent-ə\ *or* G **Win·dau** \'vin-,daù\ river 200 *m* U.S.S.R. in Lithuania & Latvia flowing into the Baltic
Ven·ti·mi·glia \,vent-i-'mēl-yə\ commune NW Italy on Ligurian sea W of San Remo near Menton, France

---

ə abut; ᵊ kitten; ər further; a back; ā bake; ä cot, cart; aú out; ch chin; e less; ē easy; g gift; i trip; ī life
j joke; ŋ sing; ō flow; ȯ flaw; ȯi coin; th thin; ṯẖ this; ü loot; ù foot; y yet; yü few; yù furious; zh vision
' F table; á F bac; k̬ G ich, Buch; ⁿ F vin; œ F bœuf; œ̄ F feu; ue G füllen; ue̅ F rue; ʸ F digne \dēnʸ\, nuit \nwʸē\

Vents·pils \'ven(t)-,spils\ *or* G **Win·dau** \'vin-,daů\ city & port Latvia at mouth of the Venta *pop* 20,000
Ven·tu·ra \ven-'t(y)ůr-ə\ *or officially* **San Buen·a·ven·tu·ra** \(,)san-,bwen-ə-,ven-'tůr-ə\ city & port SW Calif. on Santa Barbara channel ESE of Santa Barbara *pop* 29,114
Ve·nue, Ben \,ben-və-'n(y)ü\ mountain 2393 *ft*, *cen* Scotland in SW Perth S of Loch Katrine
Ve·ra·cruz *or* **Ve·ra Cruz** \,ver-ə-'krüz, -'krüs\ **1** state E Mexico ✻ Jalapa *area* 27,736, *pop* 2,392,606 **2** city & port E Mexico in Veracruz state on Gulf of Mexico *pop* 138,012
Ver·cel·li \ver-'chel-ē\ commune NW Italy *pop* 44,700
Ver·di·gris \'vərd-ə-grəs\ river 280 *m* SE Kans. & NE Okla. flowing into Arkansas river
Ver·dun \(,)vər-'dən, ver-\ **1** city Canada in S Que. on Montreal I. *pop* 78,262 **2** *or* **Verdun–sur–Meuse** \-,sů(ə)r-\ city NE France on the Meuse ESE of Reims *pop* 18,831
Ver·ee·ni·ging \fə-'rē-ni-giŋ, -ni-kiŋ\ city NE Republic of So. Africa in S Transvaal on the Vaal S of Johannesburg *pop* 109,200
Verkhneudinsk — see ULAN-UDE
Ver·mont \vər-'mänt\ state NE U.S. ✻ Montpelier *area* 9609, *pop* 389,881 — **Ver·mont·er** \-ər\ *n*
Vernoleninsk — see NIKOLAEV
Vernyi — see ALMA-ATA
Vé·roia \'ve(ə)r-yə\ *or anc* **Be·rea** *or* **Be·roea** \bə-'rē-ə\ town NE Greece in Macedonia W of Salonika
Ve·ro·na \və-'rō-nə\ commune NE Italy on the Adige *pop* 186,043 — **Ver·o·nese** \,ver-ə-'nēz, -'nēs\ *adj or n*
Ver·sailles \(,)vər-'sī, ver-\ city N France, WSW suburb of Paris *pop* 84,445
Vert, Cape \'vərt\ *or* **Cape Verde** \'vərd\ promontory W Africa on Cape Vert peninsula in Senegal; westernmost point of Africa, at 17°30′W
Ver·viers \verv-'yā\ commune E Belgium E of Liège *pop* 35,350
Ves·ter·å·len \'ves-tə-,rō-lən\ island group Norway off NW coast NE of Lofoten islands
Ve·su·vi·us \və-'sü-vē-əs\ *or* It **Ve·su·vio** \vā-'züv-yō\ volcano 4190 *ft* Italy on Bay of Naples — **Ve·su·vi·an** \və-'sü-vē-ən\ *adj*
Vet·lu·ga \vet-'lü-gə\ river 500 *m* U.S.S.R. in *cen* Soviet Russia, Europe, flowing S into the Volga
Ve·vey \və-'vā\ commune W Switzerland in Vaud on NE shore of Lake Geneva
Viatka — see VYATKA
Vi·cen·te Ló·pez \və-,sent-ē-'lō-,pez\ city E Argentina, N suburb of Buenos Aires, on Río de la Plata *pop* 149,958
Vi·cen·za \vi-'chen(t)-sə\ commune NE Italy W of Venice *pop* 63,700
Vi·cha·da \vi-'chäd-ə, -'chät͟h-ə\ river 335 *m*, *cen* & E Colombia flowing ENE into the Orinoco
Vichegda — see VYCHEGDA
Vi·chu·ga \və-'chü-gə\ city U.S.S.R. in *cen* Soviet Russia, Europe, NE of Moscow *pop* 51,000
Vi·chy \'vish-ē, 'vē-shē\ commune *cen* France on the Allier NE of Clermont-Ferrand *pop* 30,403
Vicks·burg \'viks-,bərg\ city W Miss. *pop* 29,143
Vic·to·ria \vik-'tōr-ē-ə, -'tȯr-\ **1** city SE Tex. on Guadalupe river *pop* 33,047 **2** city Canada ✻ of B.C. on SE Vancouver I. *pop* 54,584 **3** island N Canada SE of Banks I. *area* 81,930 **4** river 350 *m* Australia in NW Northern Territory flowing N & NW to Timor sea **5** state SE Australia ✻ Melbourne *area* 87,884, *pop* 2,796,959 **6** lake E Africa in Tanganyika, Kenya, & Uganda *area* 26,200 **7** *or* **Hong Kong** \'häŋ-,käŋ, 'hȯŋ-,kȯŋ, -'käŋ, -'kȯŋ\ city & port ✻ of Hong Kong colony on NW Hong Kong I. *pop* 3,113,131 — **Vic·to·ri·an** \vik-'tōr-ē-ən, -'tȯr-\ *adj or n*
Victoria Falls waterfall 200 to 350 *ft* high & 5580 *ft* wide S Africa in the Zambezi on border between Zambia & Southern Rhodesia
Victoria Land region E Antarctica S of New Zealand on W shore of Ross sea & Ross Ice Shelf
Victoria Nile — see NILE
Vic·to·ria·ville \vik-'tōr-ē-ə-,vil, -'tȯr-\ town Canada in S Que. NE of Drummondville *pop* 16,031
Vi·en·na \vē-'en-ə\ *or* G **Wien** \'vēn\ city ✻ of Austria on the Danube *pop* 1,627,566 — **Vi·en·nese** \,vē-ə-'nēz, -'nēs\ *adj or n*
Vi·enne \vē-'en\ **1** river 217 *m* SW *cen* France flowing NW into the Loire **2** city SE France on the Rhone *pop* 25,669
Vien·tiane \vyen-'tyän\ city, administrative ✻ of Laos, on the Mekong *pop* 80,000
Vie·ques \vē-'ā-kəs\ *or* **Crab** \'krab\ island West Indies off E Puerto Rico, belonging to Puerto Rico; chief town Isabela Secunda
Viet·nam *or* **Viet-Nam** or **Viet Nam** \vē-'et-'näm, vyet-, ,vē-ət-, vēt-, -'nam\ country SE Asia in Indochina; state, including Tonkin & N Annam, set up 1945–46; with S Annam & Cochin China, an associated state of French Union 1950–54; after civil war, divided 1954 at 17th parallel into republics of No. Vietnam (✻ Hanoi *area* 63,344, *pop* 17,000,000) & So. Vietnam (✻ Saigon *area* 66,262, *pop* 15,000,000)
Vi·go \'vē-(,)gō\ city & port NW Spain on **Vigo Bay** (inlet of the Atlantic) *pop* 162,114
Viipuri — see VYBORG
Vi·ja·ya·na·gar \,vij-ə-yə-'nəg-ər\ *or* **Bi·ja·na·gar** \,bij-ə-'nəg-\ Hindu kingdom (1336–1565) S India S of the Kistna
Vi·ja·ya·wa·da \,vij-ə-yə-'wäd-ə\ *or* **Vi·ja·ya·va·da** \-'väd-ə\ *or formerly* **Bez·wa·da** \bez-'wäd-ə\ city SE India in E Andhra Pradesh on Kistna river at head of its delta *pop* 161,198
Vi·la \'vē-lə\ town & port ✻ of New Hebrides in SW Efate I.
Villa Bens — see CABO YUBI
Vi·lla Cis·ne·ros \,vēl-yə-(,)sis-'ner-əs, ,vē-(y)ə-\ town & port NW Africa in Río de Oro ✻ of Spanish Sahara
Vi·lla·her·mo·sa \,vē-(y)ə-,er-'mō-sə\ city SE Mexico ✻ of Tabasco state *pop* 33,587
Vil·la Park \,vil-ə-\ village NE Ill. W of Chicago *pop* 20,391
Ville–d'Avray \,vēl-dəv-'rā\ commune N France W of Sèvres
Ville·franche \vēl-'frä^{n}sh\ **1** *or* **Villefranche–sur–Mer** \-sůr-'me(ə)r\ commune & port SE France E of Nice **2** *or* **Ville-franche–sur–Saône** \-'sōn\ commune E *cen* France NNW of Lyons *pop* 21,703
Ville·ur·banne \,vē-,lər-'ban, -,lů(ə)r-\ commune E France, E suburb of Lyons *pop* 81,769
Vil·ni·us *or* **Vil·ny·us** \'vil-nē-əs\ *or* Pol **Wil·no** \'vil-(,)nō\ *or* Russ **Vil·na** \'vil-nə\ *or* **Vil·no** \-(,)nō\ city U.S.S.R. ✻ of Lithuania *pop* 235,000
Vi·lyui \vil-'yü-ē\ river 1500 *m* U.S.S.R. in *cen* Soviet Russia, Asia, flowing E into the Lena
Vim·i·nal \'vim-ən-ᵊl\ hill in Rome, Italy, one of seven upon which the ancient city was built — see AVENTINE
Vi·my Ridge \,vē-mē-, ,vim-ē-\ ridge near Vimy commune N France N of Arras
Vi·ña del Mar \,vēn-yə-(,)del-'mär\ city & port *cen* Chile E of Valparaiso *pop* 126,441
Vin·cennes, 1 \vin-'senz\ city SW Ind. *pop* 18,046 **2** \vin-'senz, *F* va^{n}-sen\ commune N France, E suburb of Paris *pop* 50,434
Vin·dhya \'vin-dyə, -dē-ə\ mountain range N *cen* India N of & parallel to Narbada river
Vin·dhya Pra·desh \prə-'däsh, -'desh\ former state NE *cen* India ✻ Rewa; became (1956) part of Madhya Pradesh
Vine·land \'vīn-lənd\ city S N.J. *pop* 37,685
Vin·land \'vin-lənd\ a portion of the coast of No. America visited & so called by Norse voyagers *ab* A.D. 1000; perhaps N tip of Newfoundland
Vin·ni·tsa \'vin-ət-sə\ city U.S.S.R. in W *cen* Ukraine *pop* 121,000
Vin·son Massif \,vin(t)-sən-\ mountain 16,860 *ft* W Antarctica S of Ellsworth Land in Sentinel range of Ellsworth mountains; highest in Antarctica
Vir·gin \'vər-jən\ **1** river 200 *m* SW Utah & SE Nev. flowing to Lake Mead **2** islands West Indies E of Puerto Rico — see BRITISH VIRGIN ISLANDS, VIRGIN ISLANDS OF THE UNITED STATES
Vir·gin·ia \vər-'jin-yə, -'jin-ē-ə\ state E U.S. ✻ Richmond *area* 39,838, *pop* 3,966,949 — **Vir·gin·ian** \-yən, -ē-ən\ *adj or n*
Virginia Beach city SE Va. *pop* 85,218
Virginia Capes Cape Charles & Cape Henry in Va. forming entrance to Chesapeake Bay
Virgin Islands National Park reservation West Indies in Virgin islands of the U.S. on St. John I. *area* 8
Virgin Islands of the United States the W islands of the Virgin islands group including St. Croix, St. John, & St. Thomas; a territory ✻ Charlotte Amalie (on St. Thomas I.) *area* 132, *pop* 32,099 — see DANISH WEST INDIES
Vi·run·ga \və-'růŋ-gə\ *or* **Mfum·bi·ro** \em-'füm-bə-,rō\ volcanic mountain range E *cen* Africa in E Congo & SW Uganda N of Lake Kivu; highest peak Karisimbi 14,786 *ft*
Vi·sa·kha·pat·nam \vi-,säk-ə-'pət-nəm\ *or* **Vi·za·ga·pa·tam** \-,zäg-ə-'pət-əm\ city & port E India in NE Andhra Pradesh *pop* 108,000
Vi·sa·lia \və-'sāl-yə\ city S *cen* Calif. SE of Fresno *pop* 15,791
Vi·sa·yan \və-'sī-ən\ *or* **Bi·sa·yas** \bə-'sī-əz\ islands *cen* Philippines including Bohol, Cebu, Leyte, Masbate, Negros, Panay, Samar, & the Romblon group
Vis·by \'viz-bē\ town & port Sweden on Gotland I. in the Baltic
Vi·so \'vē-(,)zō\ mountain 12,605 *ft* NW Italy in Piedmont SW of Turin near French border; highest in Cottian Alps
Vis·tu·la \'vis(h)-chə-lə, 'vis-tə-\ *or* Pol **Wis·la** \'vē-(,)slä\ *or* Russ **Vis·la** \'vē-slə\ *or* G **Weich·sel** \'vīk-səl\ river 630 *m* Poland flowing from the Carpathians N into Gulf of Danzig
Vistula Lagoon FRISCHES HAFF
Vi·tebsk \'vē-,tepsk, -,tebzk, və-'\ city U.S.S.R. in NE Belorussia on the Dvina *pop* 148,000
Vi·ter·bo \vi-'te(ə)r-(,)bō\ commune *cen* Italy in Latium NNW of Rome *pop* 27,100
Vi·ti Le·vu \,vēt-ē-'lev-(,)ü\ island SW Pacific, largest of the Fiji group *area* 4053
Vi·tim \və-'tēm\ river 1100 *m* U.S.S.R. in S Soviet Russia, Asia, flowing NE & N into the Lena
Vi·to·ria \vi-'tōr-ē-ə, -'tȯr-\ city N Spain ✻ of Álava province SSE of Bilbao *pop* 68,443
Vi·tó·ria \vi-'tōr-ē-ə, -'tȯr-\ city & port E Brazil ✻ of Espírito Santo state on Espírito Santo I. *pop* 49,735
Vi·try–sur–Seine \vi-,trē-,sů(ə)r-'sān, -'sen\ commune N France, SSE suburb of Paris *pop* 52,540
Viz·ca·ya \vis-'kī-ə, vith-\ *or* **Bis·ca·ya** \bis-\ *or* **Bis·cay** \'bis-(,)kā, -kē\ province N Spain on Bay of Biscay; one of the Basque provinces ✻ Bilbao *area* 836, *pop* 746,232
Vlaanderen — see FLANDERS
Vlaar·ding·en \'vlär-diŋ-ə(n)\ commune & port SW Netherlands W of Rotterdam *pop* 66,740
Vla·di·mir \'vlad-ə-,mi(ə)r, vlə-'dē-,\ city U.S.S.R. in *cen* Soviet Russia, Europe, on Klyazma river E of Moscow *pop* 154,000
Vlad·i·vos·tok \,vlad-ə-və-'stäk, -'väs-,täk\ city & port U.S.S.R. in SE Soviet Russia, Asia ✻ of Maritime Territory *pop* 283,000
Vlis·sing·en \'vlis-iŋ-ə(n)\ *or* **Flush·ing** \'fləsh-iŋ\ city & port SW Netherlands on Walcheren I. *pop* 29,603
Vlo·ne *or* **Vlo·na** \'vlō-nə\ *or* **Vlo·re** *or* **Vlo·ra** \'vlōr-ə, 'vlȯr-\ *or* **Va·lo·na** \və-'lō-nə\ *or formerly* **Avlo·na** \av-'lō-nə\ town & port S Albania
Vlotslavsk — see WLOCLAWEK
Vlta·va \'vəl-tə-və\ *or* **Mol·dau** \'mōl-,daů, 'mȯl-\ river 270 *m* W Czechoslovakia in Bohemia flowing N into the Elbe
Vodena — see EDESSA
Vo·gel·kop \'vō-gəl-,käp\ peninsula NW New Guinea
Voiotía — see BOEOTIA
Voi·vo·di·na *or* **Voj·vo·di·na** \'vȯi-və-,dē-nə, -dē-,nä\ autonomous region NE Yugoslavia N of the Danube; chief city Novi Sad *area* 8683, *pop* 1,712,619
Volcano *or* Jap **Ka·zan Ret·to** \,käz-,än-'ret-(,)ō\ islands W Pacific S of Bonin islands; belong to Japan; under U.S. control 1945–68 *area* 11 — see IWO JIMA
Vo·len·dam \'vō-lən-,dam, -,däm\ village NW Netherlands on IJsselmeer SE of Edam
Vol·ga \'väl-gə, 'vȯl-, 'vōl-\ river 2325 *m* U.S.S.R. in Soviet Russia, Europe, rising in Valdai hills & flowing into the Caspian
Vol·go·grad \'väl-gə-,grad, 'vȯl-, 'vōl-\ *or formerly* **Sta·lin·grad** \'stäl-ən-,grad, 'stal-\ *or* **Tsa·ri·tsyn** \tsə-'rēt-sən\ city U.S.S.R. in S Soviet Russia, Europe, on the Volga *pop* 591,000
Vo·log·da \'vȯ-ləg-də\ city U.S.S.R. in N *cen* Soviet Russia, Europe, NNE of Moscow *pop* 138,000
Vo·los \'vō-,läs\ *or* NGk **Vó·los** \'vȯ-,lȯs\ city & port E Greece on **Gulf of Volos** (inlet of the Aegean) *pop* 51,134
Volsinii — see ORVIETO
Vol·ta \'väl-tə, 'vōl-, 'vȯl-\ river 250 *m* W Africa formed by confluence of **Black Volta** (540 *m*) & **White Volta** (450 *m*) in N *cen* Ghana & flowing S into Bight of Benin — see RED VOLTA
Vol·ta Re·don·da \,väl-tə-ri-'dän-də, ,vōl-, ,vȯl-\ city E Brazil on the Paraíba NW of city of Rio de Janeiro *pop* 32,143

Vol·ter·ra \väl-'ter-ə, vōl-, vȯl-\ *or anc* **Vo·la·ter·rae** \,vō-lə-'te(ə)r-,ī, -,(,)ē\ commune *cen* Italy in Tuscany SE of Pisa

Vol·tur·no \väl-'tü(ə)r-(,)nō, vōl-, vȯl-\ river 110 *m* S *cen* Italy flowing from the Apennines SE & SW into Gulf of Gaeta

Voor·burg \'vō(ə)r-,bȯrg, 'vō(ə)r-\ commune SW Netherlands, E suburb of The Hague *pop* 43,221

Vor·arl·berg \'fō(ə)r-,ärl-,berg, 'fȯ(ə)r-\ province W Austria W of Tirol bordering on Switzerland ✳ Bregenz

Vo·ro·nezh \və-'rō-nish\ city U.S.S.R. in S *cen* Soviet Russia, Europe, near the Don *pop* 454,000

Voroshilovgrad — see LUGANSK

Vosges \'vōzh\ mountains NE France on W side of Rhine valley; highest point Ballon de Guebwiller 4672 *ft*

Vrangelya — see WRANGEL

Vyat·ka *or* **Viat·ka** \vē-'ät-kə\ 1 river 800 *m* U.S.S.R. in E Soviet Russia, Europe, flowing into the Kama   2 — see KIROV

Vy·borg \'vē-,bȯ(ə)rg\ *or* Finn **Vii·pu·ri** \'vē-pə-rē\ city & port U.S.S.R. in NW Soviet Russia, Europe, on arm of Gulf of Finland; belonged to Finland 1917–40 *pop* 51,000

Vy·cheg·da *or* **Vi·cheg·da** \'vich-ig-də\ river 700 *m* U.S.S.R. in N Soviet Russia, Europe, flowing W to the Northern Dvina

Waadt — see VAUD

Waal \'väl\ river Netherlands, the S branch of the Lower Rhine

Wa·bash \'wȯ-,bash\ river 475 *m* Ind. & Ill. flowing into the Ohio

Wa·co \'wā-(,)kō\ city NE *cen* Tex. on Brazos river *pop* 97,808

Wad·den Zee \'väd-'n-zā, 'väd-ə-,zā\ inlet of North sea N Netherlands between West Frisian islands & IJsselmeer

Wad·ding·ton, Mount \'wäd-iŋ-tən\ mountain 13,260 *ft* W Canada in SW B.C. in Coast mountains; highest in province

Wa·gram \'väg-,räm\ village Austria NE of Vienna

Wa·hi·a·wa \,wä-hē-ə-'wä\ urban area Hawaii in *cen* Oahu *pop* 15,512

Wai·a·le·ale \wī-,äl-ē-'äl-ē\ mountain 5080 *ft* Hawaii in *cen* Kauai

Wai·ka·to \wī-'kät-(,)ō\ river 220 *m* New Zealand in NW North I. flowing NW into Tasman sea

Wai·ki·ki \,wī-kə-'kē\ resort section of; Honolulu, Hawaii, on Waikiki Beach

Wai·mea Canyon \wī-,mā-ə-\ gorge Hawaii on SW coast of Kauai I.

Wai·ta·ki \wī-'täk-ē\ river 135 *m* New Zealand in SE *cen* South I. flowing ESE into the Pacific

Wa·ka·ya·ma \,wäk-ə-'yäm-ə\ city & port Japan in SW Honshu on Inland sea *pop* 220,021

Wake \'wāk\ island N Pacific N of Marshall islands belonging to the U.S.

Wake·field \'wāk-,fēld\ 1 town E Mass. N of Boston *pop* 24,295   2 city & county borough N England W of West Riding, Yorkshire *pop* 60,380

Wa·la·chia *or* **Wal·la·chia** \wä-'lā-kē-ə\ region S Romania between the Transylvanian Alps & the Danube; includes Muntenia & Oltenia; chief city Bucharest — **Wa·la·chi·an** *or* **Wal·la·chi·an** \-ən\ *adj or n*

Wal·deck \'väl-,dek\ former county, principality, & state of Germany between Westphalia & Hesse-Nassau ✳ Arolsen

Wal·den Pond \,wȯl-dən-\ pond NE Mass. S of Concord

Wales \'wā(ə)lz\ *or* Welsh **Cym·ru** \'kəm-,rē\ *or* ML **Cam·bria** \'kam-brē-ə\ principality SW Great Britain; a division of the United Kingdom ✳ Cardiff *area* 7469, *pop* 2,172,339

Wal·la·sey \'wäl-ə-sē\ county borough NW England in Cheshire on coast W of Liverpool *pop* 101,331

Wal·la Wal·la \,wäl-ə-'wäl-ə, 'wäl-ə-,\ city SE Wash. *pop* 24,536

Wal·ling·ford \'wäl-iŋ-fərd, -,fō(ə)rd, -,fȯ(ə)rd\ town S Conn. NNE of New Haven *pop* 29,920

Wal·lis, 1 \'wäl-əs\ islands SW Pacific NE of Fiji islands; with Futuna islands, constitute a French overseas territory (**Wallis and Futuna Islands** \'wäl-əps\ island E Va. on the Atlantic SW of Chincoteague Bay

Wal·lops \'wäl-əps\ island E Va. on the Atlantic SW of Chincoteague Bay

Wal·lowa \wä-'laú-ə\ mountains NE Oreg. E of Blue mountains; highest point Sacajawea Peak 10,033 *ft*

Walnut Canyon National Monument reservation N *cen* Ariz. ESE of Flagstaff containing cliff dwellings

Wal·sall \'wȯl-,sȯl\ county borough W *cen* England in Staffordshire NNW of Birmingham *pop* 114,514

Wal·tham \'wȯl-,tham, *chiefly by outsiders* -thəm\ city E Mass. W of Boston *pop* 55,413

Wal·tham·stow \'wȯl-thəm-,stō\ municipal borough SE England in Essex NE of London *pop* 121,069

Wal·vis Bay \,wȯl-vəs-\ town, port, & district SW Africa on Walvis Bay (inlet) W of Windhoek; part of Republic of So. Africa but administered by South-West Africa *area* (of district) 374

Wands·worth \'wän(d)z-(,)wərth\ metropolitan borough SW London, England, S of the Thames *pop* 330,328

Wang·a·nui \,wäŋ-(g)ə-'nü-ē\ 1 river 150 *m* New Zealand in SW *cen* North I., flowing into Cook strait   2 city & port New Zealand in North I. on Cook strait *pop* 33,600

Wanks — see SEGOVIA

Wan·ne-Eick·el \,vän-ə-'ī-kəl\ city W Germany in the Ruhr N of Bochum *pop* 107,200

Wan·stead and Wood·ford \,wän-stəd-ən-'wúd-fərd\ municipal borough S England in Essex, NE suburb of London *pop* 61,620

Wan·tagh \'wän-,tȯ\ urban area SE N.Y. on Long I. *pop* 34,172

Wap·si·pin·i·con \,wäp-si-'pin-i-kən\ river 255 *m* SE Minn. & E Iowa flowing SE into the Mississippi

Wa·ran·gal \'wər-əŋ-gəl\ city S *cen* India in N Andhra Pradesh NE of Hyderabad *pop* 133,100

War·bur·ton \'wȯr-(,)bərt-°n\ river 275 *m* Australia in NE So. Australia flowing SW into Lake Eyre

Wargla — see OUARGLA

War·min·ster \'wȯr-,min(t)-stər\ urban township SE Pa. near Philadelphia *pop* 15,994

War·ner Rob·ins \,wȯr-nər-'räb-ənz\ city *cen* Ga. *pop* 18,633

War·ren \'wȯr-ən, 'wär-\ 1 city SE Mich. N of Detroit *pop* 89,246   2 city NE Ohio NW of Youngstown *pop* 59,648

War·ring·ton \'wȯr-iŋ-tən, 'wär-\ 1 urban area NW Fla. SW of Pensacola *pop* 16,752   2 county borough NW England in Lancashire on the Mersey E of Liverpool *pop* 80,681

War·saw \'wȯr-,sȯ\ *or* Pol **War·sza·wa** \vär-'shäv-ə\ city ✳ of Poland on the Vistula *pop* 1,095,000

War·ta \'värt-ə\ *or* G **War·the** \'värt-ə\ river 445 *m* Poland flowing NW & W into the Oder

War·wick \'wär-ik, *US also* 'wȯr-ik, 'wȯ(ə)r-(,)wik, 'wär-(,)wik\ 1 city *cen* R.I. S of Providence on Narragansett Bay *pop* 68,504   2 *or* **War·wick·shire** \-,shi(ə)r, -shər\ county *cen* England *area* 976, *pop* 1,860,874   3 municipal borough, its ✳ *pop* 15,350

Wa·satch \'wȯ-,sach\ mountain range SE Idaho & N & *cen* Utah — see TIMPANOGOS (Mount)

Wash \'wȯsh, 'wäsh\ inlet of North sea E England between Norfolk & Lincoln

Wash·ing·ton \'wȯsh-iŋ-tən, 'wäsh-\ 1 state NW U.S. ✳ Olympia *area* 68,192, *pop* 2,853,214   2 city ✳ of the U.S., coextensive with District of Columbia *pop* 763,956   3 city SW Pa. *pop* 23,545 — **Wash·ing·to·nian** \,wȯsh-iŋ-'tō-nē-ən, ,wäsh-, -nyən\ *adj or n*

Washington, Lake lake 20 *m* long W Wash. E of Seattle

Washington, Mount mountain 6288 *ft* N N.H.; highest in White mountains

Wash·i·ta \'wäsh-ə-,tȯ\ 1 river 500 *m* NW Tex. & SW Okla. flowing SE into Red river   2 — see OUACHITA

Wa·tau·ga \wä-'tȯ-gə\ river 60 *m* NW N.C. & NE Tenn. flowing into S fork of the Holston

Watenstedt–Salzgitter — see SALZGITTER

Wa·ter·bury \'wȯt-ə-(r)-,ber-ē, 'wät-\ city W *cen* Conn. on Naugatuck river *pop* 107,130

Wa·ter·ee \'wȯt-ə-,rē, 'wät-\ river S.C., lower course of the Catawba — see CONGAREE

Wa·ter·ford \'wȯt-ər-fərd, 'wät-\ 1 county S Ireland in Munster *area* 710, *pop* 43,205   2 city & port, its ✳, on Suir river *pop* 28,138

Wa·ter·loo \,wȯt-ər-'lü, ,wät-\ 1 city NE *cen* Iowa *pop* 71,755   2 city Canada in SE Ont. W of Kitchener *pop* 16,373   3 town *cen* Belgium S of Brussels

Waterton–Glacier International Peace Park — see GLACIER NATIONAL PARK

Wa·ter·ton Lakes National Park \'wȯt-ərt-°n, 'wät-\ reservation Canada in Rocky mountains in S Alta. on Mont. border *area* 521

Wa·ter·town \'wȯt-ər-,taún, 'wät-\ 1 town E Mass. W of Boston *pop* 39,092   2 city N *cen* N.Y. SE of Kingston, Ont. *pop* 33,306

Wa·ter·ville \'wȯt-ər-,vil, 'wät-\ city S *cen* Me. *pop* 18,695

Wat·ford \'wät-fərd\ municipal borough SE England in Hertfordshire NW of London *pop* 73,072

Watling *or* **Watlings** — see SAN SALVADOR

Wat·ten·scheid \'vät-°n-,shīt\ city W Germany E of Essen *pop* 78,300

Wau·ke·gan \wȯ-'kē-gən\ city NE Ill. N of Chicago *pop* 55,719

Wau·ke·sha \'wȯ-ki-,shȯ\ city SE Wis. *pop* 30,004

Wau·sau \'wȯ-,sȯ\ city N *cen* Wis. on Wisconsin river *pop* 31,943

Wau·wa·to·sa \,wȯ-wə-'tō-sə\ city SE Wis. *pop* 56,923

Way·cross \'wā-,krȯs\ city SE Ga. *pop* 20,944

Wayne \'wān\ 1 village SE Mich. SW of Detroit *pop* 16,034   2 urban township NE N.J. W of Paterson *pop* 29,353

Waynes·boro \'wānz-,bər-ə, -,bə-rə\ city W *cen* Va. *pop* 15,694

Wa·zir·i·stan \wə-,zir-i-'stan, -'stän\ region W Pakistan on border of Afghanistan NE of Baluchistan

Weald \'wē(ə)ld\ region SE England in Kent, Surrey, & Sussex, between North Downs & South Downs; once heavily forested

Webbe Shibeli — see SHIBELI

Web·ster Groves \,web-stər-\ city E Mo. *pop* 28,990

Wed·dell \wə-'del, 'wed-°l\ sea arm of the S Atlantic E of Antarctic peninsula

Wei \'wā\ river 400 *m* N *cen* China flowing E to join Yellow river

Weichsel — see VISTULA

Wei·fang \'wā-'fäŋ\ city E China in E *cen* Shantung NW of Tsingtao *pop* 148,900

Wei·hai \'wā-'hī\ *or formerly* **Wei·hai·wei** \,wā-,hī-'wā\ city & port E China in NE Shantung on Yellow sea *pop* 175,000

Wei·mar \'vī-,mär, 'wī-\ city E Germany W of Erfurt *pop* 66,700

Weimar Republic the German republic 1919–33

Weir·ton \'wi(ə)rt-°n\ city N W. Va. on the Ohio *pop* 28,201

Weiss·horn \'vīs-,hȯ(ə)rn\ mountain 14,804 *ft* SW *cen* Switzerland in Pennine Alps

Wel·land \'wel-ənd\ 1 city Canada in SE Ont. SW of Niagara Falls *pop* 16,405   2 ship canal 28 *m* Canada in SE Ont. connecting Lake Erie & Lake Ontario

Welle — see UELE

Welles·ley \'welz-lē\ town E Mass. WSW of Boston *pop* 26,071

Wel·ling·ton \'wel-iŋ-tən\ 1 provincial district New Zealand in S North I. *area* 10,870, *pop* 451,900   2 city & port, its ✳ & ✳ of New Zealand, on Port Nicholson (Wellington Harbor) on Cook strait *pop* 143,200

Wells \'welz\ municipal borough SW England in Somerset

Welsh·pool \'welsh-,pül\ municipal borough E Wales ✳ of Montgomeryshire

Wel·wyn Garden City \'wel-ən\ urban district SE England in Hertfordshire N of London *pop* 18,296

Wem·bley \'wem-blē\ municipal borough SE England in Middlesex W of London *pop* 131,369

We·natch·ee \wə-'nach-ē\ city *cen* Wash. *pop* 16,726

Wen·chow \'wən-'jō\ *or formerly* **Yung·kia** \'yúŋ-jē-'ä\ city & port E China in Chekiang on East China sea *pop* 201,600

Wer·ra \'ver-ə\ river 180 *m*, *cen* Germany flowing N to join the Fulda forming the Weser

We·ser \'vā-zər, 'wē-\ river 280 *m* W Germany formed by confluence of the Fulda & Werra & flowing into North sea

Wesermünde former city NW Germany — see BREMERHAVEN

Wes·la·co \'wes-lə-,kō\ city S Tex. NW of Brownsville *pop* 15,649

Wes·sex \'wes-iks\ ancient Anglian kingdom S England ✳ Winchester; one of kingdoms in Anglo-Saxon heptarchy

West \'west\ *or* Si \'shē\ river 300 *m* SE China in Kwangsi & Kwangtung formed by confluence of the Hungshui & the Yü & flowing E into So. China sea

West Al·lis \'al-əs\ city SE Wis. *pop* 68,157
West Bengal state E India comprising the W third of former Bengal province ✻ Calcutta *area* 33,945, *pop* 26,306,600
West Beskids — see BESKIDS
West Brom·wich \'brəm-ij, 'bräm-, -ich\ county borough W *cen* England in Staffordshire NW of Birmingham *pop* 87,985
West·ches·ter \'wes(t)-,ches-tər\ **1** county SE N.Y. N of New York City & E of the Hudson *pop* 808,891 **2** village NE Ill. W of Chicago *pop* 18,092
West Ches·ter \'wes(t)-,ches-tər\ borough SE Pa. *pop* 15,705
West Co·vi·na \kō-'vē-nə\ city SW Calif. *pop* 50,645
Western — see HEBRIDES
Western Australia state W Australia on Indian ocean ✻ Perth *area* 975,920, *pop* 639,771
Western Ghats \'gȯts\ chain of mountains SW India extending SSE parallel to coast from mouth of Tapti river to Cape Comorin; highest Anai Mudi 8841 *ft* — see EASTERN GHATS
Western Reserve tract of land NE Ohio on S shore of Lake Erie; part of western lands of Conn., ceded 1800 to Ohio *area ab* 5470
Western Samoa group of islands of Samoa W of 171° W; an independent state; until 1962 a territory administered by New Zealand ✻ Apia (on Upolu I.) *area* 1133, *pop* 102,860
Western Thrace — see THRACE
West·field \'wes(t)-,fēld\ **1** city SW Mass. WNW of Springfield *pop* 26,302 **2** town NE N.J. WSW of Elizabeth *pop* 31,447
West Flanders province NW Belgium bordering on North sea ✻ Bruges *area* 1248, *pop* 1,065,627
West Frisian — see FRISIAN
West Ham \'ham\ county borough SE England in Essex, E suburb of London *pop* 170,987
West Hartford town *cen* Conn. *pop* 62,382
West Har·tle·pool \'härt-lē-,pül, 'härt-ᵊl-,\ county borough N England in Durham on North sea *pop* 72,597
West Ha·ven \'west-,hā-vən\ town S Conn. *pop* 43,002
West Hempstead urban area SE N.Y. on Long I. *pop* (with Lakeview) 24,783
West Hollywood urban area SW Calif. *pop* 28,870
West Indies, 1 the islands lying between SE No. America & N So. America bordering the Caribbean & comprising the Greater Antilles, Lesser Antilles, & Bahamas **2** *or* **West Indies Federation** former country including all of the Brit. West Indies except the Bahamas & the Brit. Virgin islands; established 1958, dissolved 1961 — **West Indian** *adj or n*
West Indies Associated States the self-governing states of Antigua, Dominica, Grenada, St. Kitts-Nevis-Anguilla, & St. Lucia, associated with Great Britain in foreign relations & defense
West·land \'wes(t)-lənd\ provincial district New Zealand W South I. ✻ Hokitika *area* 4880, *pop* 18,700
West Lo·thi·an \'lō-t͟hē-ən\ *or* **Lin·lith·gow** \lin-'lith-(,)gō\ *or* **Lin·lith·gow·shire** \-,shi(ə)r, -shər\ county SE Scotland bordering on Firth of Forth ✻ Linlithgow *area* 120, *pop* 88,576
West·meath \(')wes(t)-'mēt͟h\ county E *cen* Ireland in Leinster ✻ Mullingar *area* 681, *pop* 52,774
West Memphis city E Ark. on the Mississippi *pop* 19,374
West Miff·lin \'mif-lən\ borough SW Pa. SE of Pittsburgh on the Monongahela *pop* 27,289
West·min·ster \'wes(t)-,min(t)-stər\ **1** city SW Calif. E of Long Beach *pop* 25,750 **2** metropolitan borough W *cen* London, England *pop* 98,895
West Monroe city N La. *pop* 15,215
West·mor·land \'wes(t)-mər-lənd, *US also* wes(t)-'mō(ə)r-, -'mȯ(ə)r-\ county NW England ✻ Kendal *area* 789, *pop* 67,383
West·mount \'wes(t)-,maunt\ city Canada in S Que. entirely within city of Montreal *pop* 24,800
West New Guinea *or* **West Iri·an** \,ir-ē-'än\ *or formerly* **Netherlands New Guinea** territory of Indonesia, the W half of New Guinea & adjacent islands; belonged to the Netherlands until 1962 ✻ Sukarnapura (Hollandia) *area* 159,334, *pop* 700,000
West New York town NE N.J. on the Hudson *pop* 35,547
Wes·ton su·per Mare \'wes-tən-,sü-pər-'ma(ə)r, -'me(ə)r\ municipal borough SW England in Somerset on Bristol channel *pop* 40,165
West Orange town NE N.J. NW of Newark *pop* 39,895
West Pakistan the W division of Pakistan in NW India (subcontinent); a province ✻ Lahore *area* 310,236, *pop* 33,779,000
West Palm Beach city SE Fla. on Lake Worth inlet *pop* 56,208
West·pha·lia \wes(t)-'fāl-yə, -'fā-lē-ə\ *or* G **West·fa·len** \vest-'fäl-ən\ region W Germany bordering on the Netherlands E of the Rhine; includes Ruhr valley; a province of Prussia 1816–1945 ✻ Münster — see NORTH RHINE-WESTPHALIA — **West·pha·lian** \wes(t)-'fāl-yən, -'fā-lē-ən\ *adj or n*
West·port \'wes(t)-,pō(ə)rt, -,pȯ(ə)rt\ town SW Conn. on Long Island Sound *pop* 20,955
West Prussia *or* G **West·preus·sen** \'vest-,prȯis-ᵊn\ region N Europe, now in Poland; the W part of original region of Prussia
West Punjab region W Pakistan — see PUNJAB
West Quod·dy Head \,kwäd-ē-\ cape NE Maine at entrance to Passamaquoddy Bay; easternmost point of the U.S., at 66°57′W
Wes·tra·lia \we-'strāl-yə, -'strā-lē-ə\ WESTERN AUSTRALIA
West Ri·ding \-'rīd-iŋ\ administrative county N England comprising W & SW part of Yorkshire ✻ Wakefield *area* 2781, *pop* 3,480,066
West Seneca urban area NW N.Y. SE of Buffalo *pop* 23,138
West Spitsbergen island in Arctic ocean, largest of the Spitsbergen group *area* 14,600
West Springfield town SW Mass. on the Connecticut *pop* 24,924
West Suffolk — see SUFFOLK
West Sussex — see SUSSEX
West Vir·gin·ia \vər-'jin-yə, -'jin-ē-ə\ state E U.S. ✻ Charleston *area* 24,181, *pop* 1,860,421 — **West Virginian** *adj or n*
West Warwick *see* WARWICK\ town *cen* R.I. *pop* 21,414
West·wood Lakes \,wes-,twu̇d-\ urban area SE Fla. near Miami *pop* 22,517
Weth·ers·field \'wet͟h-ərz-,fēld\ town *cen* Conn. *pop* 20,561
Wet·ter·horn \'vet-ər-,hȯ(ə)rn\ mountain 12,153 *ft* Switzerland in Bernese Alps N of the Finsteraarhorn
Wex·ford \'weks-fərd\ **1** county SE Ireland in Leinster *area* 908, *pop* 83,259 **2** municipal borough & port, its ✻
Wey·mouth \'wā-məth\ town E Mass. SE of Boston *pop* 48,177
Whales, Bay of inlet of Ross sea Antarctica in Ross Ice Shelf
Wham·poa \'hwäm-'pō-'ä, 'wäm-\ town & port SE China in Kwangtung on Pearl river below Canton
Whangpoo — see HWANG PU
Whea·ton \'hwēt-ᵊn, 'wēt-\ **1** city NE Ill. W of Chicago *pop* 24,312 **2** urban area SW Md. N of Washington, D.C. *pop* 54,635
Wheat Ridge urban area *cen* Colo. NW of Denver *pop* 21,619
Whee·ler Peak \,hwē-lər-, ,wē-\ **1** mountain 13,063 *ft* E Nev. in Snake range **2** mountain 13,160 *ft* N N. Mex. in Sangre de Cristo mountains; highest in the state
Whee·ling \'hwē-liŋ, 'wē-\ city N W. Va. on the Ohio *pop* 53,400
Whid·bey \'hwid-bē, 'wid-\ island 40 *m* long NW Wash. in upper Puget Sound E of Admiralty inlet
White, 1 river 690 *m* N Ark. & SW Mo. flowing SE into the Mississippi **2** river 160 *m* NW Colo. & E Utah flowing W into the Green **3** river 50 *m* SW Ind. formed by confluence of West Fork (300 *m*) & East Fork (250 *m*) & flowing W into the Wabash **4** river 325 *m* S S. Dak. flowing E into the Missouri **5** river 75 *m* NW Tex. flowing SE into the Salt Fork **6** mountains N N.H. in the Appalachians — see WASHINGTON (Mount) **7** mountain pass 2885 *ft* SE Alaska N of Skagway **8** *or* Russ **Be·loe Mo·re** \,bel-ə-yə-'mȯr-yə\ sea inlet of Barents sea U.S.S.R. on N coast of Soviet Russia, Europe, enclosed on the N by Kola peninsula
White·chap·el \'hwīt-,chap-əl, 'wīt-\ district of E London, England, N of the Thames in Stepney
Whitefish Bay village SE Wis. N of Milwaukee *pop* 18,390
White·friars \'hwīt-,frī(-ə)rz, 'wīt-\ district of *cen* London, England
White·hall \-,hȯl\ **1** city *cen* Ohio, E suburb of Columbus *pop* 20,818 **2** borough SW Pa., S suburb of Pittsburgh *pop* 16,075
White·horse \'hwīt-,hȯ(ə)rs, 'wīt-\ town NW Canada ✻ of Yukon Territory on the upper Yukon *pop* 5031
White Nile — see NILE
White Plains city SE N.Y. NE of Yonkers *pop* 50,485
White Russia — see BELORUSSIA
White Sands National Monument reservation S N. Mex. SW of Alamogordo comprising an area of gypsum sand dunes *area* 219
White Volta — see VOLTA
Whit·man National Monument \'hwit-mən, 'wit-\ reservation SE Wash. NW of Walla Walla, site of Marcus Whitman mission
Whit·ney, Mount \'hwit-nē, 'wit-\ mountain 14,494 *ft* SE *cen* Calif. in Sierra Nevada in Sequoia National Park; highest point in the U.S. outside of Alaska
Whit·ti·er \'hwit-ē-ər, 'wit-\ city SW Calif. SE of Los Angeles *pop* 33,663
Wich·i·ta \'wich-ə-,tȯ\ **1** city S *cen* Kans. on Arkansas river *pop* 254,698 **2** river 230 *m* N Tex. flowing ENE into Red river **3** mountains SW Okla.; highest Mt. Scott 2464 *ft*
Wichita Falls city N Tex. on Wichita river *pop* 101,724
Wick \'wik\ burgh N Scotland ✻ of Caithness
Wick·liffe \'wik-ləf, -(,)lif\ city NE Ohio NE of Cleveland *pop* 15,760
Wick·low \'wik-(,)lō\ **1** county E Ireland in Leinster *area* 782, *pop* 58,569 **2** urban district & port, its ✻, SSE of Dublin **3** mountains Ireland along E coast; highest peak Lugnaquilla 3039 *ft*
Wien — see VIENNA
Wies·ba·den \'vēs-,bäd-ᵊn, 'vis-\ city W Germany on the Rhine W of Frankfurt ✻ of Hesse *pop* 255,600
Wig·an \'wig-ən\ county borough NW England in Lancashire W of Manchester *pop* 84,546
Wight, Isle of \'wīt\ island S England in English channel constituting **Isle of Wight** administrative county (✻ Newport *area* 147, *pop* 95,594) — see HAMPSHIRE
Wig·town \'wig-tən, -,taun\ **1** *or* **Wig·town·shire** \-,shi(ə)r, -shər\ county SW Scotland *area* 487, *pop* 31,625 **2** burgh, its ✻
Wilderness Road trail from SW Va. to *cen* Ky. through Cumberland Gap blazed to site of Boonesborough by Daniel Boone 1775 & later extended to Falls of the Ohio at Louisville
Wil·helms·ha·ven \,vil-,helmz-'häf-ən, 'vil-əmz-,\ city & port W Germany NW of Bremen *pop* 100,300
Wilkes–Barre \'wilks-,bar-ə, -,bar-ē, -,ba(ə)r\ city NE Pa. on the Susquehanna SW of Scranton *pop* 63,551
Wilkes Land \'wilks\ coast region E Antarctica extending along Indian ocean S of Australia
Wil·kins·burg \'wil-kənz-,bərg\ borough SW Pa. *pop* 30,066
Wil·lam·ette \wə-'lam-ət\ river 190 *m* NW Oreg. flowing N into the Columbia
Wil·la·pa Bay \,wil-ə-,pȯ-, -,pä-\ inlet of the Pacific SW Wash.
Wil·lem·stad \'vil-əm-,stät\ city ✻ of Netherlands Antilles on Curaçao I. *pop* 44,062
Willes·den \'wilz-dən\ municipal borough SE England in Middlesex W of London *pop* 179,647
Wil·liam·son, Mount \'wil-yəm-sən\ mountain 14,384 *ft* SE *cen* Calif. in Sierra Nevada NNW of Mt. Whitney
Wil·liams·port \'wil-yəmz-,pō(ə)rt, -,pȯ(ə)rt\ city N *cen* Pa. on West Branch of the Susquehanna *pop* 41,967
Wil·lough·by \'wil-ə-bē\ city NE Ohio *pop* 15,058
Wil·lo·wick \'wil-ə-,wik\ city NE Ohio, E suburb of Cleveland *pop* 18,749
Wil·mette \wil-'met\ village NE Ill. N of Chicago on Lake Michigan *pop* 28,268
Wil·ming·ton \'wil-miŋ-tən\ **1** former city S Calif., now a port section of Los Angeles, NE of San Pedro section **2** city & port N Del. *pop* 95,827 **3** city & port SE N.C. *pop* 44,013
Wilno — see VILNYUS
Wil·son \'wil-sən\ city E *cen* N.C. E of Raleigh *pop* 28,753
Wilson, Mount mountain 5704 *ft* SW Calif. NE of Pasadena
Wilt·shire \'wilt-,shi(ə)r, -shər\ county S England ✻ Trowbridge *area* 1345, *pop* 387,379
Wim·ble·don \'wim-bəl-dən\ municipal borough SE England in Surrey SW of London *pop* 58,158
Win·ches·ter \'win-,ches-tər, -chə-stər\ **1** town E Mass. NW of Boston *pop* 19,376 **2** city N Va. in Shenandoah valley *pop* 15,110 **3** municipal borough S England ✻ of Hampshire *pop* 25,710
Wind \'wind\ river W *cen* Wyo., the upper course of the Bighorn
Windau — see VENTA, VENTSPILS
Wind Cave limestone cavern SW S. Dak. in Black hills in **Wind Cave National Park** (*area* 42)
Win·der·mere \'win-də(r)-,mi(ə)r\ lake 10 *m* long NW England on Westmorland-Lancashire border; largest in England
Wind·hoek \'vint-,hu̇k\ city ✻ of South-West Africa *pop* 33,000
Wind River, 1 mountain range W *cen* Wyo. — see GANNETT PEAK **2** — see WIND

Wind River Canyon gorge of the Bighorn river W cen Wyo.

Wind·sor \'win-zər\ **1** city Canada in SE Ont. opposite Detroit, Mich. pop 121,980 **2** or **New Windsor** municipal borough S England in Berkshire on the Thames W of London pop 23,181

Wind·ward \'win-dwərd\ **1** islands West Indies in the S Lesser Antilles extending S from Martinique but not including the Barbados, Tobago, or Trinidad **2** former colony Brit. West Indies comprising territories of St. Lucia, St. Vincent, & Grenada in the Windward group & Dominica in the Leewards **3** or F **Îles du Vent** \ēl-dœ-väⁿ\ islands S Pacific, E group of the Society islands, including Tahiti

Windward Passage channel between Cuba & Hispaniola

Win·ne·ba·go, Lake \,win-ə-'bā-(,)gō\ lake 30 m long E Wis.

Win·ni·peg \'win-ə-,peg\ **1** river 200 m Canada in W Ont. & SE Man. flowing from Lake of the Woods to Lake Winnipeg **2** city Canada ✳ of Man. pop 255,093 — **Win·ni·peg·ger** \-ər\ n

Winnipeg, Lake lake 275 m long Canada in S cen Man. drained by Nelson river area 9460

Win·ni·pe·go·sis, Lake \,win-ə-pə-'gō-səs\ lake Canada in W Man. W of Lake Winnipeg area 2086

Win·ni·pe·sau·kee, or **Win·ne·pe·sau·kee, Lake** \,win-ə-pə-'sȯ-kē\ lake cen N.H. area 71

Wi·no·na \wə-'nō-nə\ city SE Minn. pop 24,895

Wi·noo·ski \wə-'nü-skē\ river 100 m N cen Vt. flowing into Lake Champlain

Win·ston–Sa·lem \,win(t)-stən-'sā-ləm\ city N cen N.C. pop 111,135

Winter Haven city cen Fla. E of Lakeland pop 16,277

Winter Park city E Fla. N of Orlando pop 17,162

Win·ter·thur \'vint-ər-,tù(ə)r\ commune N Switzerland in Zurich canton NE of Zurich pop 77,400

Win·throp \'win(t)-thrəp\ town E Mass. ENE of Boston on Massachusetts Bay pop 20,303

Win·yah Bay \,win-,yȯ-\ inlet of the Atlantic E S.C.

Wis·con·sin \wis-'kän(t)-sən\ **1** river 430 m, cen Wis. flowing S & W into the Mississippi **2** state N cen U.S. ✳ Madison area 56,154, pop 3,951,777 — **Wis·con·sin·ite** \-sə-,nīt\ n

Wisconsin Dells — see DELLS OF THE WISCONSIN

Wisconsin Rapids city cen Wis. pop 15,042

Wisla — see VISTULA

Wis·mar \'vis-,mär\ city & port NE Germany SW of Rostock pop 54,800

Wis·sa·hick·on \,wis-ə-'hik-ən\ creek SE Pa. flowing into the Schuylkill at Philadelphia

With·la·coo·chee \,with-lə-'kü-chē\ **1** river 110 m S Ga. & NW Fla. flowing SE into the Suwannee **2** river 120 m NW cen Fla. flowing NW into Gulf of Mexico

Wit·ten \'vit-ⁿn\ city W Germany SW of Dortmund pop 96,200

Wit·ten·berg \'wit-ⁿn-,bərg\ city E Germany E of Dessau pop 48,100

Wit·wa·ters·rand \'wit-,wȯt-ərz-,ränd, -,wät-, -,rand\ ridge of auriferous rock 62 m long & 23 m wide NE Republic of So. Africa in S Transvaal

Wlo·cla·wek \vlȯt-'släv-,ek\ or Russ **Vlo·tslavsk** \vlät-'släfsk, -'slävzk\ commune N cen Poland on the Vistula pop 59,000

Wo·burn \'wü-bərn, 'wō-\ city E Mass. NW of Boston pop 31,214

Wolds \'wōl(d)z\ chalk hills N England in E Yorkshire & NE Lincolnshire on both sides of the Humber

Wolfs·burg \'wùlfs-,bərg\ city W Germany NE of Brunswick pop 60,600

Wol·lon·gong \'wùl-ən-,gäŋ, -,gȯŋ\ city & port SE Australia in E New So. Wales S of Sydney pop (with suburbs) 101,400

Wol·ver·hamp·ton \'wùl-vər-,ham(p)-tən\ county borough W cen England in Staffordshire NW of Birmingham pop 162,669

Won·san \'wən-,sän\ or Jap **Gen·san** \'gen-,sän\ or **Gen·zan** \'gen-,zän\ city & port N Korea on E coast pop 112,952

Wood·bridge \'wùd-,(,)brij\ city NE N.J. SW of Elizabeth pop 78,846

Wood Green municipal borough SE England in Middlesex N of London pop 52,224

Wood·lark \'wùd-,lärk\ or **Mu·rua** \'mùr-ə-wə\ island W Pacific in Solomon sea off SE end of New Guinea; attached to Territory of Papua area 400

Wood·lawn \'wùd-,lȯn, -,län\ urban area N cen Md. W of Baltimore pop (with Rockdale & Millford Mills) 19,254

Wood·mont \'wùd-,mänt\ urban area N cen Tenn. S of Nashville pop (with Green Hills & Glendale) 23,161

Woods, Lake of the lake S Canada & N U.S. in Ont., Man., & Minn. SE of Lake Winnipeg area 1485

Wood·stock \'wùd-,stäk\ town Canada in SE Ont. ENE of London on Thames river pop 18,347

Wool·wich \'wùl-ij, -ich\ metropolitan borough E London, England, on S bank of the Thames pop 147,824

Woom·era \'wùm-ə-rə\ town So. Australia W of Lake Torrens

Woon·sock·et \wün-'säk-ət, 'wün-,\ city N R.I. pop 47,080

Woos·ter \'wùs-tər\ city N Ohio SW of Akron pop 17,046

Worces·ter \'wùs-tər\ **1** city E cen Mass. pop 186,587 **2** or **Worces·ter·shire** \-tə(r)-,shi(ə)r, -shər\ county W cen England area 699, pop 522,974 **3** city & county borough, its ✳ pop 59,700

Worms \'wərmz, 'vȯrm(p)s\ city W Germany on the Rhine NNW of Mannheim pop 59,600

Worth, Lake lagoon inlet of the Atlantic SE Fla.

Wor·thing \'wər-thiŋ\ municipal borough S England in West Sussex on English channel pop 69,375

Wran·gel \'raŋ-gəl\ or Russ **Vran·ge·lya** \'vrän-gəl-yə\ island U.S.S.R. off NE Soviet Russia, Asia, in Arctic ocean

Wran·gell \'raŋ-gəl\ **1** island SE Alaska NE of Prince of Wales I. **2** mountain range S Alaska NW of St. Elias range — see BLACKBURN (Mount)

Wrangell, Cape cape on Attu I. in Aleutians, Alaska; westernmost point of U.S. at 172°27′ E

Wrangell, Mount active volcano 14,006 ft S Alaska in Wrangell mountains NW of Mt. Blackburn

Wrath, Cape \'rath\ extreme NW point of Scotland, at 58°35′ N

Wrex·ham \'rek-səm\ municipal borough N Wales in Denbighshire pop 30,962

Wro·claw \'vrȯt-,släf\ or G **Bres·lau** \'bres-,laù\ city SW Poland, chief city of Silesia pop 374,000

Wu \'wü\ river 500 m, cen China rising in W Kweichow & flowing through Szechwan into the Yangtze

Wu·chang \'wü-'chäŋ\ former city & ✳ of Hupei E cen China — see WUHAN

Wu·chow \'wü-'jō\ city S China in E Kwangsi at junction of Kwei & West rivers pop 110,800

Wu·han \'wü-'hän\ city E cen China ✳ of Hupei at junction of Han & Yangtze rivers; formed from the former separate cities of Hankow, Hanyang, & Wuchang pop 1,427,300

Wuhsien — see SOOCHOW

Wu·hu \'wü-'hü\ city E China in E Anhwei pop 242,100

Wu·pat·ki National Monument \wü-'pat-kē\ reservation N Ariz. NNE of Flagstaff containing prehistoric Indian dwellings

Wup·per·tal \'vùp-ər-,täl\ city W Germany in Ruhr valley ENE of Düsseldorf pop 420,500

Würt·tem·berg \'wərt-əm-,bərg, 'wùrt-; 'virt-əm-,be(ə)rk\ region SW Germany between Baden & Bavaria; chief city Stuttgart; once a kingdom 1813–1918, state 1918–45; divided 1945–51, S part being joined to Hohenzollern forming **Württemberg–Hohenzollern** state & N part to N Baden forming **Württemberg–Baden** state; since 1951 part of Baden-Württemberg state

Würz·burg \'wərts-,bərg, 'wùrts-; 'virts-,bù(ə)rk\ city W Germany on the Main in N Bavaria NW of Nuremberg pop 114,000

Wu·sih \'wü-'shē\ city E China in S Kiangsu NW of Soochow pop 581,500

Wutsin — see CHANGCHOW

Wu·tung·kiao \,wü-'tùŋ-chē-'aù\ city SW cen China in S Szechwan S of Chengtu pop 199,100

Wy·an·dotte \'wī-ən-,dät\ city SE Mich. pop 43,519

Wye \'wī\ river 130 m E Wales & W England flowing into the Severn

Wy·o·ming \wī-'ō-miŋ\ **1** state NW U.S. ✳ Cheyenne area 97,914, pop 330,066 **2** valley NE Pa. along the Susquehanna **3** city SW Mich. SW of Grand Rapids pop 45,829 — **Wy·o·ming·ite** \-miŋ-,īt\ n

Xan·thus \'zan(t)-thəs\ **1** or Turk **Ko·ca** \kō-'jä\ river 75 m S Turkey flowing SW & S into the Mediterranean **2** city of ancient Lycia near mouth of the Xanthus

Xe·nia \'zē-nyə, -nē-ə\ city SW cen Ohio pop 20,445

Xeres — see JEREZ

Xin·gu \shēŋ-'gü\ river 1300 m, cen & N Brazil rising on Mato Grosso plateau & flowing N into the Amazon near its mouth

Xo·chi·mil·co \,sō-chi-'mēl(,)-kō ,sō-shi- -'mil-\ city S cen Mexico, SE suburb of Mexico City pop 20,687

Ya·blo·noi \,yäb-lə-'nȯi\ or **Ya·blo·no·voi** \-lə-nə-'vȯi\ mountain range U.S.S.R. in S Soviet Russia, Asia, on E border of Buryat Republic; highest peak Sokhondo 8228 ft

Yacarana — see JAVARÍ

Yad·kin \'yad-kən\ river 202 m, cen N.C., the upper course of the Pee Dee

Yafo — see JAFFA

Yak·i·ma \'yak-ə-,mȯ\ **1** river 200 m S Wash. flowing SE into the Columbia **2** city S cen Wash. pop 43,284

Yak·u·tat Bay \,yak-ə-,tat-\ inlet of the Pacific SE Alaska

Ya·kutsk \yə-'kütsk\ city U.S.S.R. in E cen Soviet Russia, Asia ✳ of Yakutsk Republic pop 74,000

Yakutsk Republic or **Ya·kut Republic** \yə-'küt-\ or **Ya·ku·tia** \-'k(y)ü-sh(ē-)ə\ autonomous republic U.S.S.R. in E cen Soviet Russia, Asia ✳ Yakutsk area 1,182,300, pop 489,000

Yal·ta \'yȯl-tə\ city & port in S Soviet Russia, Europe, on S coast of Crimea pop 40,000

Ya·lu \'yäl-(,)ü\ or **Am·nok** \'am-,näk\ river 300 m SE Manchuria & NW Korea flowing N, W, & SW into Korea Bay

Ya·lung \'yä-'lùŋ\ river 725 m SW China in W Szechwan flowing S into the Yangtze

Ya·mal \yə-'mäl\ peninsula U.S.S.R. in NW Soviet Russia, Asia, at N end of Ural mountains between Gulf of Ob & Kara sea

Yam·pa \'yam-pə\ river 200 m NW Colo. flowing W into the Green

Ya·na \'yän-ə\ river 750 m U.S.S.R. in N Soviet Russia, Asia, flowing N into Laptev sea

Ya·naon \yə-'naùn\ or **Ya·nam** \yə-'näm\ town SE India in E Andhra Pradesh on N mouth of the Godavari; a territory of French India before 1954

Yang·chow \'yäŋ-'jō\ or formerly **Kiang·tu** \jē-'äŋ-'dü\ city E China in SW Kiangsu NW of Nanking pop 180,200

Yang·chuan \'yäŋ-chù-'än\ city N China in E Shansi E of Taiyuan pop 177,400

Yangku — see TAIYUAN

Yang·tze or **Yang·tse** \'yaŋ-'sē, 'yaŋ(k)t-'sē\ or **Yangtze Kiang** \kē-'aŋ\ river 3100 m, cen China flowing from Kunlun Shan in SW Tsinghai E into East China sea

Yannina — see IOANNINA

Yaoun·dé or **Yaun·de** \yaùn-'dā\ city W Africa ✳ of Cameroon pop 40,000

Yap \'yap, 'yäp\ or **Uap** \'wäp\ island group W Pacific in W Carolines including Yap, Map, Romung, & Tomil pop 6021

Ya·qui \yä-'kē\ river 420 m NW Mexico in Sonora flowing SW into Gulf of California

Yar·kand \'yär-,kand\ **1** river 500 m Kashmir & China flowing from Karakoram range N & W to join the Khotan in Sinkiang forming the Tarim **2** or **So·che** \'swä-'chə\ city W China in SW Sinkiang at oasis on Yarkand river pop 80,000

Yar·mouth \'yär-məth\ or **Great Yarmouth** county borough & port E England in Norfolk on North sea pop 51,105

Ya·ro·slavl \,yär-ə-'släv-əl\ city U.S.S.R. in W cen Soviet Russia, Europe, on the Volga NE of Moscow pop 406,000

Ya·wa·ta \yə-'wät-ə\ or **Ya·ha·ta** \-'hät-ə\ former city Japan in N Kyushu — see KITA-KYUSHU

Ya·zoo \ya-'zü\ river 188 m Miss. flowing SW into the Mississippi

Yedo — see TOKYO

Ye·gor·evsk or **Egor·evsk** \yə-'gȯr-(y)əfsk\ city W cen Soviet Russia, Europe, SE of Moscow pop 59,000

Yellow, 1 or **Hwang Ho** \'hwäŋ-'hō\ or **Huang** \'hwäŋ\ river 3000 m N China flowing from Kunlun mountains in Tsinghai E into Po Hai **2** sea inlet of East China sea between N China & Korea

Yel·low·knife \'yel-ə-ˌnīf\ town Canada ✳ of Northwest Territories in Mackenzie District on Great Slave Lake pop 3500

Yel·low·stone \'yel-ə-ˌstōn\ river 671 m NW Wyo. & S & E Mont. flowing N through **Yellowstone Lake** (area 140) & **Grand Canyon of the Yellowstone** in Yellowstone National Park & NE into the Missouri in NW N. Dak. near Mont. border

Yellowstone Falls two waterfalls NW Wyo. in Yellowstone river at head of Grand Canyon of the Yellowstone; upper fall 109 ft, lower fall 308 ft

Yellowstone National Park reservation NW Wyo., E Idaho, & S Mont. including plateau region notable for numerous geysers & hot springs area 3458

Ye·men \'yem-ən, 'yā-mən\ country SW Arabia bordering on Red sea; republic since 1962 ✳ San'a area 75,000, pop 4,500,000 — **Ye·me·ni** \'yem-ə-nē, 'yā-mə-\ adj or n — **Ye·men·ite** \-ˌnīt\ n

Yen·an \'yen-'än\ town N cen China in cen Shensi

Yen·i·sey or **Yen·i·sei** or **En·i·sei** \ˌyen-ə-'sā\ river ab 2300 m U.S.S.R. in Soviet Russia, Asia, flowing N into Arctic ocean

Yentai — see CHEFOO

Ye·re·van \ˌyer-ə-'vän\ or **Ere·van** or **Eri·van** \ˌ(y)er-ə-\ city U.S.S.R. ✳ of Armenian Republic pop 509,000

Ye·ru·pa·ja \ˌyer-ə-'pä-(ˌ)hä\ mountain 21,758 ft W cen Peru

Ye·sil Ir·mak \yə-ˌshē(ə)-lir-'mäk\ river ab 250 m N Turkey in Asia flowing N into Black sea

Ye·sil·koy \ˌyesh-(ˌ)ēl-'kȯi\ or formerly **San Ste·fa·no** \san-'stef-ə-ˌnō\ town Turkey in Europe on Sea of Marmara W of Istanbul

Yezd \'yezd\ or **Yazd** \'yazd\ city cen Iran pop 66,484

Yezo — see HOKKAIDO

Yin·chwan \'yin-chů-'än\ or formerly **Ning·sia** or **Ning·hsia** \'niŋ-shē-'ä\ city N China ✳ of Ningsia on Yellow river pop 84,000

Ying·kow \'yiŋ-'kaů, -'kō\ or **New·chwang** \'n(y)ü-chů-'äŋ\ city & port NE China in cen Liaoning on Gulf of Liaotung at mouth of Liao river pop 131,400

Yo·ho National Park \'yō-(ˌ)hō\ reservation W Canada in SE B.C. on Alta. border area 507

Yok·kai·chi \yō-'kī-chē\ city & port Japan in S Honshu SW of Nagoya pop 170,612

Yo·ko·ha·ma \ˌyō-kə-'häm-ə\ city & port Japan in SE Honshu on Tokyo Bay S of Tokyo pop 1,375,710

Yo·ko·su·ka \yō-'kȯ-s(ə-)kə\ city & port Japan in Honshu W of entrance to Tokyo Bay pop 279,132

Yo·ne·za·wa \yō-'näz-ə-wä, ˌyō-nä-'zä-wə\ city Japan in N Honshu E of Niigata pop 94,714

Yon·kers \'yäŋ-kərz\ city SE N.Y. N of New York City on the Hudson pop 190,634

Yonne \'yän\ river 120 m NE cen France flowing NNW into the Seine

York \'yȯ(ə)rk\ **1** city SE Pa. SE of Harrisburg pop 54,504 **2** or **York·shire** \-ˌshi(ə)r, -shər\ county N England bordering on North sea; comprises city of York & administrative counties of East, No., & West Riding area 6089, pop 4,621,698 **3** or anc **Ebo·ra·cum** \i-'bȯr-ə-kəm, -'bär-\ city & county borough in Yorkshire on the Ouse pop 105,336

York, Cape — see CAPE YORK PENINSULA

Yorke \'yȯ(ə)rk\ peninsula Australia in SE So. Australia between Spencer gulf and Gulf of St. Vincent

York river estuary 40 m E Va. formed by confluence of Pamunkey & Mattaponi rivers & flowing SE into Chesapeake Bay

Yo·sem·i·te \yō-'sem-ət-ē\ **1** waterfall E cen Calif. descending from rim of Yosemite valley in two falls (upper fall 1430 ft, lower fall 320 ft) **2** glaciated valley of the Merced river E cen Calif. on W slope of Sierra Nevada in **Yosemite National Park** (area 1182)

Yo·su \'yō-(ˌ)sü\ or **Jap Rei·sui** \'räs-,yē\ city & port S Korea on Korea strait pop 73,084

Yough·io·ghe·ny \ˌyäk-ə-'gā-nē\ river 150 m NW Md. & SW Pa. flowing N & NW into the Monongahela

Youngs·town \'yəŋ(k)-ˌstaůn\ city NE Ohio pop 166,689

Ypres — see IEPER

Yp·si·lan·ti \ˌip-sə-'lant-ē\ city SE Mich. pop 20,957

Yser \ē-'ze(ə)r\ river 55 m France & Belgium flowing into North sea

Yssel — see IJSSEL

Yü \'yü\ or **Siang** \shē-'äŋ\ river 400 m SE China in Yunnan & Kwangsi flowing E to unite with the Hungshui forming West river

Yu·an \yů-'än\ or **Yu·en** \-'än, -'en\ river 500 m SE cen China flowing from Kweichow NE to Tungting Lake

Yu·bi \'yü-bē\ or **Ju·by** \'jü-\, **Cape** cape NW Africa on NW coast of Spanish Sahara

Yu·ca·tán \ˌyü-kə-'tan, -'tän\ **1** peninsula SE Mexico & N Central America including Brit. Honduras & part of Guatemala **2** channel between Yucatán & W end of Cuba **3** state SE Mexico at N end of the peninsula ✳ Mérida area 23,926, pop 598,161

Yu·go·sla·via or **Ju·go·sla·via** \ˌyü-gō-'släv-ē-ə\ country S Europe bordering on the Adriatic; established 1918 as a kingdom (**Kingdom of the Serbs, Croats, and Slo·venes** \'sərbz-'krōt-sən-'slō-ˌvēnz\ also \-ˌkrō-ˌat-sən-\), became a federal republic 1945 ✳ Belgrade area 99,044, pop 16,936,573 — **Yu·go·slav** \ˌyü-gō-'släv, -'slav\ or **Yu·go·sla·vi·an** \-'släv-ē-ən\ adj or n

Yu·kon \'yü-ˌkän\ **1** river 1979 m Yukon Territory & Alaska flowing NW & SW into Bering sea — see LEWES **2** or **Yukon Territory** territory NW Canada between Alaska & B.C. bordering on Arctic ocean ✳ Whitehorse area 205,346, pop 12,190

Yu·ma \'yü-mə\ city SW Ariz. on Colorado river pop 23,974

Yungki — see KIRIN

Yungkia — see WENCHOW

Yungning — see NANNING

Yun·nan or **Yün·nan** \yü-'nän\ **1** province SW China bordering on Indochina & Burma ✳ Kunming area 168,417, pop 17,473,000 **2** or **Yunnanfu** — see KUNMING — **Yun·nan·ese** \ˌyü-nə-'nēz, 'nēs\ adj or n

Yun·que or **El Yunque** \el-'yüŋ-(ˌ)kā\ mountain 3496 ft E Puerto Rico

Yü Shan — see MORRISON (Mount)

Yuzovka — see DONETSK

Yver·don \ē-ver-dōⁿ\ commune W Switzerland N of Lausanne

Zaan·dam \zän-'dam, -'däm\ commune W Netherlands NW of Amsterdam pop 48,513

Zab·rze \'zäb-(ˌ)zhā\ or G **Hin·den·burg** \'hin-dən-ˌbȯrg, -ˌbů(ə)rg\ city SW Poland in Silesia pop 182,000

Za·ca·te·cas \ˌzak-ə-'tā-kəs, -'tek-əs\ **1** state N cen Mexico area 28,122, pop 744,626 **2** city, its ✳ pop 24,254

Za·dar \'zäd-ˌär\ or It **Za·ra** \'zär-ə\ town & port W Yugoslavia in Croatia; held by Italy 1920–47

Zag·a·zig \'zag-ə-ˌzig\ or **Za·qa·zîq** \zə-ˌkä-'zēk\ city N Egypt NNE of Cairo pop 123,200

Za·greb \'zäg-ˌreb\ or G **Agram** \'äg-ˌräm\ city NW Yugoslavia ✳ of Croatia pop 350,829

Zag·ros \'zag-rəs\ mountains W & S Iran bordering on Turkey, Iraq, & Persian gulf; highest over 14,000 ft

Zakarpatskaya — see RUTHENIA

Zá·kin·thos \'zäk-ən-ˌthȯs\ or **Zan·te** \'zant-ē\ or **Za·kyn·thos** or **Za·kyn·thus** \zə-'kin(t)-thəs\ **1** island W Greece, one of the Ionian islands, SSE of Cephalonia area 156 **2** its chief town

Za·ko·pa·ne \ˌzäk-ə-'pän-ē\ city S Poland in Tatra mountains S of Krakow pop 23,100

Za·ma \'zä-mə, 'zäm-ə\ ancient town N Africa SW of Carthage

Zam·be·zi or **Zam·be·si** \zam-'bē-zē\ river 1650 m SE Africa flowing from NW Zambia into Mozambique channel

Zambia — see NORTHERN RHODESIA

Zam·bo·an·ga \ˌzam-bə-'wäŋ-gə\ city & port Philippines on SW coast of Mindanao pop 17,000

Za·mo·ra \zə-'mȯr-ə, -'mȯr-\ **1** province NW Spain in cen León area 4097, pop 322,354 **2** city, its ✳ pop 46,834

Zancle — see MESSINA

Zanes·ville \'zānz-ˌvil\ city E cen Ohio pop 39,077

Zan·zi·bar \'zan-zə-ˌbär\ **1** island E Africa off NE Tanganyika area 640, pop 264,200; formerly a sultanate, with Pemba & adjacent islands forming a Brit. protectorate; became independent 1963; united 1964 with Tanganyika in United Republic of Tanzania **2** city & port ✳ of the island & protectorate pop 45,284 — **Zan·zi·ba·ri** \ˌzan-zə-'bär-ē\ n

Za·po·ro·zhe or **Za·po·ro·zhye** \ˌzäp-ə-'rȯ-zhə\ or formerly **Ale·ksan·drovsk** \ˌal-ik-'san-drəfsk\ city U.S.S.R. in SE Ukraine pop 434,000

Za·ra·go·za \ˌzar-ə-'gō-zə\ or **Sar·a·gos·sa** \ˌsar-ə-'gäs-ə\ **1** province NE Spain in W Aragon area 6726, pop 650,818 **2** city, its ✳, on the Ebro pop 309,702

Zealand — see SJÆLLAND

Zee·brug·ge \'zā-ˌbrəg-ə\ town NW Belgium; port for Bruges

Zee·land \'zē-lənd, 'zā-; 'zā-ˌlänt\ province SW Netherlands ✳ Middelburg area 1040, pop 283,356

Zeist \'zīst\ commune cen Netherlands E of Utrecht pop 50,865

Zem·po·al·te·pec \ˌzem-pə-'wäl-tə-ˌpek\ or **Zem·po·al·te·petl** \-ˌwäl-'tā-ˌpet-ᵊl\ mountain 11,138 ft SE Mexico in Oaxaca

Zenshu — see CHONJU

Zer·matt \(t)ser-'mät\ village SW cen Switzerland in Valais in Pennine Alps NE of the Matterhorn

Zetland — see SHETLAND

Zhda·nov \'zhdän-əf, zhə-'dän-\ or formerly **Ma·ri·u·pol** \ˌmar-ē-'ü-ˌpȯl\ city U.S.S.R. in E Ukraine on Sea of Azov pop 284,000

Zhi·to·mir \zhi-'tȯ-ˌmi(ə)r\ city U.S.S.R. in W Ukraine pop 105,000

Zim·ba·bwe \zim-'bäb-wē\ archaeological site NE Southern Rhodesia

Zinovievsk — see KIROVOGRAD

Zi·on \'zī-ən\ or **Si·on** \'sī-\ **1** the stronghold of Jerusalem conquered by David **2** a hill in Jerusalem occupied in ancient times by the Jewish Temple **3** JERUSALEM **4** ISRAEL

Zion National Park \'zī-ən\ reservation SW Utah (area 204) centering around **Zion Canyon** of Virgin river & including area to NW that until 1956 was separately maintained as **Zion National Monument**

Zi·pan·gu \zə-'paŋ-(ˌ)gü\ JAPAN — the name used by Marco Polo

Zi·pa·qui·rá \ˌsē-pə-kē-'rä\ town cen Colombia N of Bogotá

Zla·to·ust \ˌzlät-ə-'üst\ city U.S.S.R. in W Soviet Russia, Asia, in the S Urals pop 161,000

Zlin — see GOTTWALDOV

Zoan — see TANIS

Zom·ba \'zäm-bə\ town ✳ of Malawi 70 m S of Lake Nyasa

Zon·gul·dak \ˌzȯŋ-gəl-'däk\ city & port NW Turkey pop 54,026

Zor — see TYRE

Zug \'(t)sük\ or F **Zoug** \'züg\ **1** canton N cen Switzerland area 92, pop 42,239 **2** commune, its ✳, on Lake of Zug pop 15,700

Zug, Lake of lake N cen Switzerland in Zug & Schwyz cantons N of Lake of Lucerne area 15

Zug·spit·ze \'(t)sük-ˌs(h)pit-sə\ mountain 9719 ft SW Germany; highest in Bavarian Alps & in Germany

Zuider Zee or **Zuyder Zee** — see IJSSELMEER

Zuidholland — see SOUTH HOLLAND

Zu·lu·land \'zü-(ˌ)lü-ˌland\ territory E Republic of So. Africa in NE Natal bordering on Indian ocean N of Tugela river area 10,427, pop 362,400

Zungaria — see DZUNGARIA

Zu·rich \'zů(ə)r-ik\ or G **Zü·rich** \'tsüⸯ-rik\ **1** canton N Switzerland area 665, pop 777,002 **2** city, its ✳, at NW end of Lake of Zurich pop 433,400

Zurich, Lake of lake 25 m long N cen Switzerland

Zut·phen \'zət-fə(n)\ commune E Netherlands on IJssel river pop 23,793

Zwick·au \'tsfik-ˌaů, 'zwik-\ city E Germany S of Leipzig pop 135,800

Zwol·le \'zvȯl-ə, zə-'vȯl-\ city E Netherlands ✳ of Overijssel pop 55,145

FORMS OF ADDRESS

An exhaustive list of all alternative forms of address permissible in polite correspondence would extend far beyond the scope of this dictionary; especially in informal correspondence there is a great variety of possible salutations. In the table below we have usually put the most formal address and salutation first. Differences of local usage, however, inevitably introduce many exceptions. In the United States "My dear Mrs. Smith" is more formal than "Dear Mrs. Smith"; in Great Britain the reverse is true. In business correspondence the addressee's address is placed before the salutation; in most official and some social correspondence, it is placed at the foot of the letter, below and to the left of the signature. Social invitations to a married man are customarily addressed to the man and his wife; as, Senator and Mrs. ——; The President and Mrs. ——; Lord and Lady ——; Their Excellencies, the German Ambassador and Madame ——; etc.

Traditional masculine forms are used throughout for offices that are now sometimes held by women. Substitution of *Madam* for *Sir*, *Mrs.* for *Mr.*, *Her* for *His*, etc., (as at *ambassador, cabinet officer, professor, senator*) is always appropriate.

It will be noted that some of the addresses given below begin with the word "To", whereas most do not. There is no hard-and-fast rule. We have tried to suggest merely the more customary usage. Insertion or omission of the word "To" is optional. It will also be noted that the same word may be spelled differently according to the residence of the persons addressed. For example, in the United States the spellings *honor* and *honorable* are preferred; but in Great Britain, *honour* and *honourable*. In the address abbreviations are commonly used but they should never be used in the salutation or beginning of a letter.

*Such salutations as My Lord, Your Lordship, etc., are not ordinarily used in the United States of America, but should be used by an American writing to dignitaries of foreign countries entitled to such a title or mark of respect.

†When the person addressed holds several titles, as one from birth, another by marriage, and another by profession, the highest title should be preferred.

‡Clerical, naval, and military prefixes are written before other titles; initials indicative of distinction are written after the title and name; an officer is addressed by his official title when the communication refers to official business.

---

abbot
address: The Right Reverend —— ——, O.S.B. (or other initials of order), Abbot of ——; *or* The Right Rev. Abbot ——
begin: Right Reverend and dear Father
administrator same as governor
air force officer like army officer
alderman (in Canada and U.S.)
address: Honorable —— ——
begin: Dear Sir
ambassador†
address: His Excellency, The American Ambassador; *or* The Honorable ——, American Ambassador; *or* His Excellency, —— ——, Ambassador of Brazil at ——; *or* His Excellency, Her Majesty's Ambassador for the United Kingdom (the personal name or hereditary or professional title may be added after the words *His Excellency*; *His Excellency* is usually abbreviated to *H.E.*)
begin: Sir (*or* with the personal title, as Your Grace, etc.); *or* Excellency
ambassador and his wife
address: His Excellency, The —— Ambassador and Mrs. ——; *or* The Honorable —— ——, —— Ambassador and Madame ——
begin: Your Excellencies
apostolic delegate see papal nuncio
archbishop (Anglican)
address: The Most Reverend His Grace the Lord Archbishop of ——
begin: My Lord Archbishop; *or* Your Grace
In formal documents the archbishops of Canterbury and York are addressed as The Most Reverend Father in God ——, by Divine Providence Lord Archbishop of ——
archbishop (Roman Catholic)
address: The Most Reverend —— ——, D.D., Archbishop of ——
begin: Your Excellency
archdeacon
address: The Venerable The Archdeacon of ——; *or* The Venerable —— ——, Archdeacon of ——
begin: Venerable Sir
army officer
In the United States in letters from civilians:
address: The Commander in Chief, Army of the United States; *or* Lieutenant General ——, Commanding Officer, Army of the United States; Colonel (highest rank and full title) ——, U.S.A.; Lieutenant ——, U.S.A. (in case of retired officers U.S.A. is omitted)
begin: Sir; *or* (informal) My dear General —— (not My dear Lieutenant General ——); *or* Dear Commander —— (not Dear Pay-master Commander ——); and for all officers below the rank of captain, My dear (*Rank*) ——
In the British army and navy when an officer has a hereditary title or rank, his military or naval rank will ordinarily be prefixed to this; as, Admiral the Right Honourable the Earl of ——; General the Right Honourable Lord ——; but lieutenants in the army and sublieutenants in the navy are not addressed by their military or naval rank; thus, ——, Esq., 10th Hussars (not Lieutenant ——)
begin: Sir; *or* Dear General ——; *or* Dear Lord —— (but not Dear General Lord ——)
assemblyman
address: The Honorable —— ——, Member of Assembly; *or* Assemblyman ——
begin: Sir; *or* Dear Sir; *or* My dear Mr. ——
assistant secretary (assistant to a cabinet officer)
address: Honorable —— ——, Assistant Secretary of ——; *or* The Assistant Secretary of the —— Department
begin: Sir; *or* Dear Sir; *or* My dear Mr. ——; *or* Dear Mr. —— (never Mr. Secretary)
associate justice
address: The Honorable —— ——, United States Supreme Court; *or* Mr. Justice ——, The Supreme Court
begin: My dear Mr. Justice; *or* Dear Justice ——
attorney general see cabinet officers
auditor of the treasury
address: The Honorable —— ——, Auditor of the Treasury; *or* The Auditor of the Treasury
begin: Sir; *or* Dear Sir

baron
address: The Right Honourable Lord ——; *or* The Lord ——
begin: My Lord
baroness
address: The Right Honourable the Baroness ——; *or* The Right Honourable Lady ——; *or* The Lady ——
begin: Madam
baronet
address: Sir John ——, Bt. *or* Bart.
begin: Sir
baronet's wife see lady
baron's daughter
address: (if unmarried) The Honourable Helen ——; *or* (if married to a commoner or to the son of a baron or viscount or the younger son of an earl) The Honourable Mrs. ——; *or* (if her husband has a married brother) The Honourable Mrs. John ——; *or* (if married to a knight or baronet) The Honourable Lady ——. If she is married to a man of higher title, use feminine of husband's title
begin: Madam (or use higher title if one exists)
baron's son
address: The Honourable —— ——
begin: Sir
(no distinction for eldest son, except that in Scotland he is sometimes addressed as Master of ——)
baron's son's wife† like baron's married daughter
baron's wife = baroness
Benedictine see priest
bishop (Anglican)
address: The Right Reverend the Lord Bishop of ——; *or* The Lord Bishop of ——; *or* (very formal) The Right Reverend Father in God, ——, by Divine Permission Lord Bishop of ——
In formal documents the Bishop of Durham is addressed as The Most Reverend Father in God ——, by Divine Providence Lord Bishop of Durham
begin: My Lord Bishop; *or* My Lord
bishop (Methodist)
address: The Reverend —— ——, D.D.
begin: Reverend Sir; *or* Dear Sir; *or* Dear Bishop ——; *or* My dear Bishop ——
bishop (Protestant Episcopal)
address: To the Right Reverend —— ——, Bishop of ——
begin: Right Reverend and Dear Sir; *or* (informal) Dear Bishop ——; *or* My dear Bishop ——
bishop (Roman Catholic)
In England
address: The Lord Bishop of ——; *or* The Right Reverend —— ——, Bishop of ——
begin: My Lord Bishop; *or* My Lord
In the U.S.
address: The Most Reverend —— ——, Bishop of ——
begin: Your Excellency
In Italy
address: To His Excellency, the Most Illustrious and Most Reverend Monsignor ——, Bishop of ——
begin: Most Illustrious and Most Reverend Lord; *or* Excellency
brother of a religious order
address: Brother ——, (followed by the initials of the order)
begin: Dear Brother ——

cabinet officer (United States)
address: The Honorable the Secretary of State (or Defense, Agriculture, etc.); The Honorable the Secretary of the Treasury; The Honorable the Postmaster General; *or* The Honorable ———, Secretary of State, etc.; *or* The Secretary of State; The Attorney General, etc.
begin: Sir; *or* Dear Sir; *or* My dear Mr. Secretary; *or* My dear Mr. Attorney General

canon
address: The Very Reverend Canon ———; *or* The Very Reverend ———, Canon of ———
begin: Very Reverend Canon; *or* Dear Canon

canon regular see priest regular

cardinal
address: His Eminence John Cardinal Doe
begin: Your Eminence*

cardinal (if also an archbishop)
address: His Eminence ——— Cardinal ———, Archbishop of ———
begin: Your Eminence

Carthusian see priest

chargé d'affaires
address: The Chargé d'Affaires of ———; *or* ——— ———, Esq., Chargé d'Affaires; *or* Mr. ———, Chargé d'Affaires
begin: Dear Sir; *or* Sir; *or* My dear Mr. ——— (use military, naval, or hereditary title, if there is one)†

chief justice of the Supreme Court of Canada
address: The Honourable ———, Chief Justice of Canada
begin: Sir

chief justice of the United States
address: The Chief Justice of the United States; *or* The Chief Justice, The Supreme Court, Washington, D.C.; *or*, if to the chief justice and his wife, The Chief Justice and Mrs. ———
begin: Sir; *or* My dear Mr. Chief Justice

children see baron's daughter, baron's son, duke's eldest son; children of a peeress in her own right married to a commoner receive the same courtesy titles as though their father were a peer of the mother's rank

Cistercian see priest

clergyman
address: The Reverend ——— ——— (Rev. and Mrs. ———); *or* (if a doctor of divinity) The Rev. Dr. ———; *or* The Reverend ———, D.D.
begin: Dear Sir; *or* Reverend Sir; *or* My dear Mr. (or Dr.) ———; *or* Dear Mr. (or Dr.) ———; see also archbishop, bishop, priest (most authorities disapprove the use of *Rev.* with the last name alone)

clerk (Anglican Church)
address: The Reverend ———; *or* (if the son of a duke or marquess) The Reverend Lord ———; *or* (if the son of an earl, viscount, or baron) The Rev. The Hon. ———†
begin: Reverend Sir; *or* Sir

clerk (below the order of priesthood in Roman Catholic Church)
address: The Reverend ———
begin: Reverend Sir; *or* Dear Mr. ———

clerk of the Senate or House
address: The Honorable ———, Clerk of ———
begin: Sir; *or* Dear Sir

commissioner of a bureau (as U.S. Commissioner of Education)
address: The Honorable ———, Commissioner of the Bureau of Education
begin: Sir; *or* Dear Sir

common forms
man
address: Mr. ——— ———
begin: Dear Sir; My dear Sir; My dear Mr. ———; *or* Dear Mr. ———
pl. address: Messrs. ——— and ——— ———
begin: Gentlemen
married woman
address: Mrs. John Doe
begin: Dear Madam; My dear Madam; My dear Mrs. Doe; *or* Dear Mrs. Doe
pl. address: Mmes. ——— and ———
begin: Mesdames; *or* Ladies
unmarried woman
address: Miss Doe (eldest daughter); *or* Miss Jane Doe (younger daughter)
begin: Dear Madam; My dear Miss Doe; etc.
pl. address: The Misses Doe
begin: Ladies; *or* Mesdames

comptroller of Treasury
address: The Honorable ——— ———, Comptroller of the Treasury
begin: Sir; *or* Dear Sir

congressman
address: The Honorable ——— ———, House of Representatives, Washington, D.C.; *or* Honorable John Doe, Representative in Congress, Springfield, Mass.
(some authorities disapprove the use of the prefix Hon. without first name or initials)
begin: Sir; *or* Dear Sir; *or* My dear Mr. ———

consul
address: To the American Consul at ———; *or* ——— ———, Esq., American Consul at ———; *or* Mr. ———, United States Consul at ———; *or* To ——— ———, Esq., Her Majesty's Consul for the United Kingdom
begin: Dear Sir

countess
address: To the Right Honourable The Countess of ———; *or* The Countess ———
begin: Madam

dame
address: Dame ——— ——— (followed with initials of the order, or if the lady has a higher title, with these initials after that title)†
begin: Madam

deacon (Anglican and Protestant Episcopal)
address: The Reverend Deacon ———
begin: Reverend Sir
(for deacons of other churches there is no special form of address)

dean (cathedral)
address: The Very Reverend the Dean of ———
begin: Very Reverend Sir; *or* Sir

dean (Roman Catholic)
address: The Very Reverend ———, V.F.
begin: Very Reverend Father

dean of a college or graduate school
address: Dean ———
begin: Dear Sir (*or* Madam); *or* Dear Dean ———

diplomat see ambassador, chargé d'affaires, minister (diplomatic); for diplomats of lower rank, having no other title, use common forms

divorced woman
(ordinarily *Mrs.* with her maiden name as a prename instead of her ex-husband's prename is preferred; some divorced women prefer to resume the *Miss;* the form of address preferred by the woman herself, if that is known, should be used unless there has been a court decision; divorced peeresses lose officially any title gained by marriage; courtesy use of former title is optional)

doctor of divinity
address: ——— ———, D.D.; *or* Dr. ——— ———; *or* Rev. Dr. ———
begin: Dear Sir; *or* My dear Dr. ———; *or* Dear Dr. ———; *or* Reverend and Dear Sir; *or* Reverend Doctor

doctor of philosophy, laws, medicine, etc.
address: ——— ———, Ph.D. [LL.D.] [M.D.]; *or* Dr. ——— ———; (Dr. and Mrs. ———; etc.)
begin: Dear Sir; *or* My dear Dr. ———; *or* Dear Dr. ———
(if a higher title is applicable, it should be preferred; see professor, president of a college)†

domestic prelate of the pope
address: The Right Reverend Monsignor ———, Domestic Prelate (or D.P.)
begin: Right Reverend Monsignor; *or* Dear Monsignor ———

dowager see widow

duchess
address: Her Grace the Duchess of ———; *or* The Most Noble the Duchess of ———
begin: Madam; *or* Your Grace

duchess of the blood royal
address: Her Royal Highness The Duchess of ———
begin: Madam; *or* May it please your Royal Highness

duke
address: His Grace the Duke of ———; *or* The Most Noble the Duke of ———
begin: My Lord Duke; *or* Your Grace

duke of the blood royal
address: His Royal Highness The Duke of ———
begin: Sir; *or* May it please your Royal Highness

duke's daughter†
address: The Lady Mary ———; *or* The Right Honourable Lady ———
begin: Madam; *or* My Lady
(if her husband holds a title of nobility, either by right or courtesy, the wife is ordinarily addressed according to her husband's title)

duke's eldest son
address: The Most Honourable the Marquess ———; *or* The Marquess of ———
begin: My Lord Marquess; *or* My Lord

duke's eldest son's daughter same as baron's daughter

duke's eldest son's eldest son use grandfather's third title

duke's eldest son's wife
address: The Most Honourable the Marchioness of ———
begin: My Lady Marchioness

duke's wife = duchess

duke's younger son
address: The Right Honourable Lord ———
begin: My Lord

duke's younger son's wife
address: Lady ———
begin: Madam; *or* My Lady; *or* Your Ladyship

earl
address: The Right Honourable The Earl of ———; *or* The Earl of ———
begin: My Lord

earl's daughter like duke's daughter

earl's eldest son
address: The Right Honourable the Viscount ———; *or* The Right Honourable Lord ———
begin: My Lord Viscount ———

earl's wife = countess

earl's younger son same as baron's son

earl's younger son's wife†
address: Honourable Mrs. ———
begin: Madam

envoy same as minister (diplomatic)

esquire
address: ——— ———, Esq.
begin: Sir; *or* Dear Sir; *or* Dear Mr. ———
(*Esq.* is never used if the person is addressed by any other title, even *Mr.*)

French common forms
(these forms are acceptable for nearly all diplomats other than English-speaking)
man
address: M.——— ———
begin: Monsieur
pl. address: Messrs. ——— ———
begin: Messieurs
married woman
address: Mme. ——— ———
begin: Madame
pl. address: Mmes. ——— ——— et ———
begin: Mesdames
unmarried woman
address: Mlle. ——— ———
begin: Madame (formal); *or* Mademoiselle (informal)
pl. address: Mlles. ——— ——— et ———
begin: Mesdames

German common forms
man
address: Herrn ——— ———
begin: Sehr geehrter Herr ———
pl. address: Herren ——— ———
begin: Geehrte Herren
married woman
address: Frau ———
begin: Sehr geehrte Frau ———
unmarried young woman
address: Fräulein ———
begin: Mein liebes Fräulein (cordial)

governor
address (in Massachusetts and in New Hampshire and by courtesy in some other states) His Excellency, The Governor of ———; *or* His Excellency ———; *or* (in other states of the U.S.) The Honorable the Governor of ———; *or* The Honorable ———, Governor of ———
begin: Sir; *or* Dear Sir

governor-general of a commonwealth country
address: His Excellency ——— ——— (personal title and name), Governor-General of ———
begin: Sir (*or* according to rank)

governor-general of Canada†
address: His Excellency The Right Honourable ———, (plus personal rank or title, if any)
begin: My Lord; *or* Sir (according to rank)

governor-general's wife
address: Her Excellency ——— ——— (plus personal rank or title, if any)
begin: Madam

honorary chamberlain to the pope same as papal chamberlain

internuncio see papal nuncio

Italian common forms
man
address: Gentilissimo Signore ———
begin: Gentilissimo Signore ———
pl. address: Spettabile Ditta ———
begin: Spettabile Ditta
married woman
address: Distinta Signora ———
begin: Distinta Signora ———
unmarried woman
address: Esimia Signorina ———
begin: Esimia Signorina ———

judge (in Britain and countries of the British Commonwealth)
address: The Honourable Mr. Justice ——— (if of a superior court); *or* His Honour Judge ——— (if of a lower court)
begin: Sir

judge (in U.S.)
address: The Honorable —— ——, United States District Judge (or Chief Judge of the Court of Appeals, etc.)
begin: Dear Sir; *or* My dear Judge
see also chief justice, associate justice
junior added to a son's name to distinguish him from his father with the same name, —— ——, Jr.; *or* —— ——, Jr., Ph.D.; *or* jr.
justice see associate justice, chief justice, judge

king
address: The King's Most Excellent Majesty; *or* His Most Gracious Majesty, King ——
begin: Sir; *or* May it please your Majesty
king's counsel
address: To —— ——, Esq., K.C.
begin: Sir; *or* Dear Sir
knight
address: Sir —— —— (initials of his order, if any, as K.C.B.)
begin: Sir
knight's wife see lady

lady
address: Lady ——; *or* (if the daughter of a baron or viscount) Hon. Lady ——; *or* (if the daughter of an earl, marquess, or duke) Lady Florence ——
begin: Madam; *or* My Lady; *or* Your Ladyship
lady mayoress see lord mayor's wife
lawyer
address: —— ——, Esq.; *or* Mr. —— ——, Attorney-at-Law
begin: Dear Sir; *or* My dear Mr. ——
(Mr. —— ——, Esq. is incorrect)
lieutenant governor
address: The Honorable —— ——, Lieutenant Governor of ——; (British) His Honour The Lieutenant Governor of ——†
begin: Sir; *or* Dear Sir
lord advocate†
address: To the Right Honourable the Lord Advocate; *or* The Right Honourable —— ——
begin: Sir
lord chancellor†
address: The Right Honourable the Lord High Chancellor; *or* The Right Honourable —— (hereditary title), Lord High Chancellor
begin: My Lord (or according to rank)
lord chief justice of England†
address: To the Lord Chief Justice of England; *or* To the Rt. Hon. Baron ——, Lord Chief Justice of England
begin: My Lord
lord mayor (of London, York, Belfast, Melbourne, Sydney, Brisbane, Hobart, Adelaide, and Perth)
address: The Right Honourable Lord Mayor of ——; *or* The Right Honourable —— ——, Lord Mayor of ——
(all other lord mayors are addressed as The Right Worshipful)
begin: My Lord
lord mayor's wife
address: Mrs. —— ——
begin: Madam
lord of appeal in ordinary same as baron
lord of appeal in ordinary's children same as baron's children
lord of appeal in ordinary's wife same as baroness
lord of council and session
address: Honourable Lord ——
begin: My Lord
lord of council and session's wife
address: Lady ——
begin: Madam
lord provost
address: The Honourable the Lord Provost; *or* The Honourable ——, Lord Provost of ——; *or* (in Edinburgh and Glasgow) The Right Honourable the Lord Provost, etc.
begin: Sir

maid of honor
address: The Honourable Miss ——
begin: Madam
marchioness
address: The Most Honourable the Marchioness of ——
begin: Madam
marquess
address: The Most Honourable the Marquess of ——; *or* The Marquess of ——
begin: My Lord Marquess
marquess's children like duke's children
married woman see common forms
master of the rolls
address: To the Right Honourable the Master of the Rolls
begin: Sir
mayor (in Canadian cities and towns, and English boroughs)
address: His Worship, The Mayor of ——
begin: Sir

mayor (in English cities)
address: The Right Worshipful the Mayor of ——
begin: Sir
(see also lord mayor)
mayor (in the U.S.)
address: The Honorable —— ——, Mayor of ——; *or* The Mayor of the City of ——
begin: Sir; *or* Dear Sir; *or* Dear Mr. Mayor; *or* My dear Mr. Mayor
member of parliament (or of a legislative council) the ordinary form of address followed by M.P. (*or* M.L.C.)
military officers see army officers
minister (diplomatic)
address: The Honorable —— ——, Minister of Costa Rica; *or* Her Majesty's Minister for the United Kingdom
begin: Sir (or with personal title, as My Lord, Your Grace, etc.); *or* My dear Mr. Minister
minister of a provincial cabinet of Canada
address: The Honourable —— ——, Minister of ——
begin: Sir
minister of religion see clergyman, priest, rabbi
moderator (of the General Assembly of the Church of Scotland)
address: The Right Reverend ——
begin: Right Reverend Sir
monk see priest regular, clerk
monsignor see domestic prelate, papal chamberlain, protonotary apostolic, vicar-general
mother superior of a sisterhood
address: The Reverend Mother Superior, Convent of ——; *or* Reverend Mother ——, O.S.F. (or other initials of her order); *or* Mother ——, Superior, Convent of ——
begin: Reverend Mother; *or* Dear Madam; *or* Dear Reverend Mother (informal); *or* My dear Reverend Mother ——

naval officer
address: The Admiral of the Navy of the United States; *or* Admiral ——, Commanding United States Navy; Captain —— ——, U.S.N.
begin: Sir; *or* (informal) My dear Admiral ——; Dear Commander ——; but for officers below the rank of commander, Dear Mr. ——
nun see sister of a religious order
nuncio see papal nuncio

papal ablegate
address: The Right Reverend Monsignor ——, Ablegate of His Holiness the Pope
begin: Right Reverend Monsignor
papal chamberlain
address: The Very Reverend Monsignor ——
begin: Very Reverend and dear Monsignor ——
papal chaplain same as papal chamberlain
papal nuncio or internuncio or apostolic delegate
address: His Excellency, The Papal Nuncio (or Internuncio or Apostolic Delegate) to ——
begin: Your Excellency
parliament, member of see member of parliament
patriarch (Eastern Church)
address: His Beatitude the Patriarch of ——; *or* His Beatitude the Lord ——, Patriarch of ——
begin: Most Reverend Lord; *or* Your Beatitude
patriarch (Roman Catholic Church)
address: His Excellency, the Patriarch (Archbishop) of ——
begin: Your Excellency
peer see duke, marquess, earl, baron
pope
address: To His Holiness Pope ——
begin: Most Holy Father; *or* Your Holiness
postmaster general see cabinet officers
preacher general
address: The Venerable and Very Reverend Father ——, O.P., P.G.
begin: Very Reverend Father
premier of a province of Canada
address: The Honourable ——, Premier of the Province of ——
begin: Sir
president of a Canadian legislative council
address: The Honourable ——, The President of the Legislative Council
begin: Sir
president of a college or university
address: —— ——, LL.D. (or if he is not an LL.D., the initials of his highest degree), President of —— University (or President, —— University); *or* President —— ——
If he is a clergyman, Reverend —— ——, LL.D., President of —— University
begin: Dear Sir; *or* Dear President ——
president of a theological seminary

address: The Reverend President ——
begin: Dear Sir; *or* Dear President ——
president of state senate
address: The Honorable —— ——, President of the Senate of ——
begin: Sir
president of the Senate of the United States
address: The Honorable, The President of the Senate of the United States; *or* The Honorable —— ——, President of the Senate
begin: Sir
president of the United States
address: The President, The White House (*His Excellency* should not be used)
begin: Mr. President; *or* The President; *or* My Dear Mr. President
priest (Roman Catholic Church)
regular (except as noted below)
address: Reverend —— ——, O.S.M. (or other initials of his order)
begin: Dear Father —— (religious name)
Benedictine, Cistercian, or canon regular
address: The Reverend Dom —— ——, C.R.L. (or other initials of his order)
begin: Reverend Father; *or* Dear Father

Carthusian
address: The Venerable Father Dom —— ——, O. Cart.
begin: Venerable Father; *or* Dear Father

secular
address: Reverend —— ——, (followed by the initials of his degree)
begin: Reverend and dear Father ——
prime minister of Canada
address: The Right Honourable —— ——, P.C., Prime Minister of Canada
begin: Sir
prime minister of the United Kingdom
address: The Right Honourable —— ——, P.C., M.P., Prime Minister
begin: Sir
prince of the blood royal
address: His Royal Highness Prince —— (given name)
begin: Sir
see also duke of the blood royal
prince of Wales
address: His Royal Highness The Prince of Wales
begin: Sir; *or* May it please your Royal Highness
princess of the blood royal
address: Her Royal Highness the Princess —— (given name)
begin: Madam
see also duchess of the blood royal
princess of Wales
address: Her Royal Highness The Princess of Wales
begin: Madam
prior, claustral
address: The Very Reverend Dom —— ——, O.C. (or other initials of his order); *or* The Very Reverend Father Prior, —— Abbey
begin: Very Reverend Father; *or* Dear Father Prior
prior, conventual
address: The Very Reverend the Prior of ——; *or* The Very Reverend Father (or Dom) —— ——, O.P. (or other initials of his order), Prior of ——; *or* The Very Reverend Father Guardian, O.F.M.
begin: Very Reverend Father; *or* Dear Father Prior; *or* Very Reverend and Dear Father
prioress
address: The Very Reverend the Prioress of —— *or* The Very Reverend Mother (or Dame) ——, (followed by the initials of her order), Prioress of ——
begin: Very Reverend Mother; *or* Dear Mother Prioress
privy chamberlain to the pope same as papal chamberlain
privy councillor (British imperial)†
address: To the Right Honourable —— ——, P.C.
begin: Sir
If other titles are used, they should come after *The Right Honourable*; as, The Right Honourable Sir John ——; The Right Honourable Lord ——
privy councillor (of Canada)
address: The Honourable ——
begin: Sir
professor in a college or university
address: Professor —— ——; *or* —— ——, Ph.D. (or LL.D., M.D., etc., using only the initials of his highest degree, if the degrees are in the same field), Professor of ——
begin: Dear Sir; *or* My dear Professor ——; *or* Dear Professor ——; *or* My dear Professor; etc.
professor in a theological seminary
address: The Reverend Professor ——; *or* The Reverend —— ——, D.D.; *or* Professor —— ——
begin: Dear Sir; *or* Dear Professor ——

protonotary apostolic
address: The Right Reverend Monsignor —— ——, Protonotary Apostolic (or P.A.).
begin: Right Reverend Monsignor; *or* Dear Monsignor ——

provincial of a religious order
address: The Very Reverend Father Provincial, O.F.M. (*or* other initials of order); *or* The Very Reverend Father ——, Provincial, S.J.
begin: Very Reverend and dear Father

provost see lord provost

provost (Roman Catholic Church)
address: The Very Reverend Provost ——
begin: Very Reverend Provost; *or* Dear Provost ——

puisne judge of the Supreme Court of Canada
address: The Honourable Mr. Justice ——
begin: Sir

queen
address: The Queen's Most Excellent Majesty; *or* Her Gracious Majesty, The Queen
begin: Madam; *or* May it please your Majesty

queen mother
address: Her Gracious Majesty Queen ——
begin: Madam; *or* May it please your Majesty

rabbi
address: Rabbi —— ——; *or* Rev. —— ——
begin: Reverend Sir; *or* Dear Sir; *or* My dear Rabbi ——; *or* Dear Rabbi ——
(if he holds a doctor's degree, Dr. may be substituted for Rabbi)

recorder
address: His Honour Recorder ——
begin: Sir

rector of a religious house *or* **of a seminary**
address: The Very Reverend —— ——, O.S.B. (*or* other initials of his order), Rector, Brothers of St. Francis
begin: Very Reverend and dear Father

representative see congressman

Scottish land court chairman same as lord of council and session

secretary of agriculture, state, defense, etc. see cabinet officer

secretary of state (England)
address: His Majesty's Principal Secretary of State for the —— Department (this may be preceded by hereditary title)
begin: according to rank (Your Grace, My Lord, etc.)

senator (Canadian)
address: The Honourable —— ——
begin: Dear Sir; Dear Senator ——; etc.

senator (U.S.)
address: The Honorable —— ——, The United States Senate, Washington, D.C.
begin: Dear Sir; *or* My dear Senator

senior added to a father's name to distinguish him from a son of the same name; as, ——, Sr.; *or* —— ——, Sr., Ph.D.; *or* sr.

señor see Spanish common forms

serjeant-at-law
address: Serjeant ——; *or* Mr. Serjeant ——
begin: Sir; *or* Dear Sir

sister of a religious order
address: Sister ——, (followed by the initials of the order)
begin: Dear Sister; *or* My dear Sister; *or* Dear Sister ——; *or* My dear Sister ——

solicitor general (Canada)
address: The Honourable ——
begin: Sir

solicitor general (U.S.)
address: The Solicitor General
begin: Sir; *or* Dear Sir; *or* Dear Mr. ——

Spanish common forms

man
address: Señor —— ——
begin: Muy señor mío
pl. address: Señores —— ——
begin: Muy señores nuestros

married woman
address: Señora de ——; *or* Señora Doña —— de ——
begin: Muy estimada señora

unmarried woman
address: Señorita ——; *or* Señorita Doña ——
begin: Muy distinguida señorita

speaker of a provincial legislature of Canada
address: The Honourable ——, The Speaker of (name of legislature)
begin: Dear Mr. Speaker

speaker of the House of Commons (Canada)
address: The Honourable —— ——, The Speaker of the House of Commons
begin: Dear Mr. Speaker

speaker of the House of Representatives of the United States
address: The Honorable —— ——, Speaker of the House of Representatives
begin: Sir; *or* Mr. Speaker; *or* My dear Mr. Speaker

speaker of the Senate (Canada)
address: The Honourable —— ——, Speaker of the Senate
begin: Dear Mr. Speaker

state representative like congressman

state senator like senator (U.S.)

superior general of a religious community of priests
address: The Most Reverend Father —— (followed by the initials of the order), Superior General of the —— Fathers
begin: Most Reverend Father General

superior general of a religious order (female)
address: The Reverend Mother ——, (followed by the initials of the order), Superior General of ——
begin: Reverend Mother

Supreme Court see chief justice, associate justice

undersecretary of state (U.S.)
address: The Undersecretary of State; *or* The Honorable —— ——, Undersecretary of State
begin: Sir; *or* Dear Sir; *or* Dear Mr. ——

unmarried woman see common forms

vicar-general
address: The Right Reverend Monsignor —— ——, V.G.; *or* The Right Reverend the Vicar-General
begin: Right Reverend and dear Monsignor

vice-chancellor (law) same as judge (in England)

vice-consul similar to consul

vice-president
address: The Vice-President; *or* The Honorable, The Vice-President of the United States; *or* The Honorable —— ——, Vice-President of the United States
begin: Mr. Vice-President; *or* Sir; *or* My dear Mr. Vice-President

viceroy
address: His Excellency, The Lord Lieutenant of Ireland (The Viceroy of India)
begin: Excellency

viscount
address: The Right Honourable the Viscount ——; *or* The Viscount ——
begin: My Lord

viscountess
address: The Right Honourable the Viscountess ——; *or* The Viscountess ——
begin: Madam

viscount's children same as baron's children

widow
(ordinarily addressed by her former title: as, Mrs. John Doe, not Mrs. Jane Doe, unless the latter form is preferred by the person herself; but if her married son, stepson, or grandson now holds a title of nobility formerly held by her late husband, the word dowager may be added before (or after) her title to distinguish her from the younger lady of the same title; as, Her Grace the Dowager Duchess of ——; The Dowager Lady ——; when such relationship does not exist, she may be distinguished by using her given name; as, The Right Honourable Jane, Countess of ——; the latter form is now generally preferred by ladies entitled to the distinction *Dowager*; officially a widow who remarries is not recognized as having any claim to bear the title of her deceased husband, but courtesy usually accords her this title)

A PRONOUNCING VOCABULARY OF COMMON ENGLISH GIVEN NAMES

The following vocabulary presents given names that are most frequent in English use. The list is not exhaustive either of the names themselves or of the variant spellings of those names which are entered. Compound or double names and surnames used as given names are not entered except in cases where long-continued or common use gives them an independent character.

Besides the pronunciations of the names, the list usually provides one or more of the following kinds of information at each entry: (1) etymology, indicating the language source but not the original form of the name; (2) meaning where known or ascertainable with reasonable certainty; (3) foreign-language equivalents when frequently used by English-speaking peoples.

I NAMES OF MEN

Aar·on \'ar-ən, 'er-\ [Heb]
Abra·ham \'ā-brə-,ham\ [Heb]
Ad·am \'ad-əm\ [Heb] man
Ad·di·son \'ad-ə-sən\ [fr. a surname]
Adolph \'ad-,älf, 'ā-,dälf\ [Gmc] noble wolf, i.e., noble hero F *Adolphe*, G *Adolf*, It & Sp *Adolfo*
Adri·an \'ā-drē-ən\ [L] of Hadria, ancient town in central Italy
Al \'al\ *dim of* AL-
Al·an \'al-ən\ [Celt]
Al·bert \'al-bərt\ [Gmc] illustrious through nobility F *Albert*, G *Adalbert*, It & Sp *Alberto*
Al·bin \'al-bən\ [L] white
Al·den \'ol-dən\ [OE] old friend
Al·ex \'al-iks, 'el-\ or **Al·ec** \-ik\ *dim of* ALEXANDER
Al·ex·an·der \,al-ig-'zan-dər, ,el-\ [Gk] a defender of men Russ *Aleksandr*, *Alexander*
Al·fred \'al-frəd, -fərd\ [OE] elf counsel, i.e., good counsel
Al·len or **Al·lan** or **Al·lyn** \'al-ən\ *var of* ALAN
Al·ton \'olt-ᵊn, 'alt-\ [prob. fr. a surname]
Al·va or **Al·vah** \'al-və\ [Heb]
Al·vin \'al-vən\ [Gmc] *prob* noble friend
Amos \'ā-məs\ [Heb]
An·dre \'än-(,)drā\ [F] *var of* ANDREW
An·drew \'an-(,)drü\ [Gk] manly F *André*, Sp *Andrés*
An·dy \'an-dē\ *dim of* ANDREW
An·ge·lo \'an-jə-,lō\ [It, fr. Gk] angel, messenger
An·gus \'aŋ-gəs\ [Celt]
An·tho·ny \'an(t)-thə-nē, *chiefly. Brit* 'an-tə-\ [L] F *Antoine*, It & Sp *Antonio*
An·ton \'ant-ᵊn, 'an-,tän\ [G & Slav] *var of* ANTHONY
An·to·nio \an-'tō-nē-,ō\ [It] *var of* ANTHONY
Ar·chie \'är-chē\ *dim of* ARCHIBALD
Ar·den \'ärd-ᵊn\ [prob. fr. a surname]
Ar·len or **Ar·lin** \'är-lən\ [prob. fr. a surname]
Ar·lo \'är-(,)lō\
Ar·mand \'är-,mänd, -mənd\ [F] *var of* HERMAN
Arne \'ärn\ [Scand] eagle
Ar·nold \'ärn-ᵊld\ [Gmc] power of an eagle
Ar·thur \'är-thər\ [prob. L]
Ar·vid \'är-vəd\ [Scand] eagle forest
Au·brey \'o-brē\ [Gmc] elf ruler
Au·gust \'o-gəst\ [L] August, majestic G *August*
Aus·tin \'os-tən, 'äs-\ *alter of* AUGUSTINE

Bai·ley \'bā-lē\ [fr. a surname]
Bar·clay \'bär-klē\ [fr. a surname]
Bar·net or **Bar·nett** \'bär-'net\ [fr. a surname]
Bar·ney \'bär-nē\ *dim of* BERNARD
Bar·rett \'bar-ət\ [fr. a surname]
Bar·ry or **Bar·rie** \'bar-ē\ [Ir]
Bart \'bärt\ *dim of* BARTHOLOMEW
Bar·ton \'bärt-ᵊn\ [fr. a surname]
Ba·sil \'baz-əl, 'bas-, 'bās-, 'bāz-\ [Gk] kingly, royal
Ben \'ben\ or **Ben·nie** or **Ben·ny** \'ben-ē\ *dim of* BENJAMIN
Ben·ja·min \'benj-(ə-)mən\ [Heb] son of the right hand
Ben·nett \'ben-ət\ [OF] *var of* BENEDICT
Ben·ton \'bent-ᵊn\ [fr. a surname]
Ber·nard \'bər-nərd, (,)bər-'närd\ or **Bern·hard** \'bərn-,härd\ [Gmc] bold as a bear G *Bernhard*

Ber·nie \'bər-nē\ *dim of* BERNARD
Bert or **Burt** \'bərt\ *dim of* -BERT *or* BERT-
Ber·tram \'bər-trəm\ [Gmc] bright raven
Bill \'bil\ or **Bil·ly** or **Bil·lie** \'bil-ē\ *dim of* WILLIAM
Blaine \'blān\ [fr. a surname]
Blair \'bla(ə)r, 'ble(ə)r\ [fr. a surname]
Bob·by \'bäb-ē\ or **Bob** \'bäb\ *dim of* ROBERT
Bo·ris \'bōr-əs, 'bor-, 'bär-\ [Russ]
Boyd \'bóid\ [fr. a surname]
Brad·ford \'brad-fərd\ [fr. a surname]
Brad·ley \'brad-lē\ [fr. a surname]
Brent \'brent\ [fr. a surname]
Bri·an or **Bry·an** \'brī-ən\ [Celt]
Brooks \'brüks\ [fr. a surname]
Bruce \'brüs\ [fr. a surname]
Bru·no \'brü-(,)nō\ [It, fr. Gmc] brown
Bryce or **Brice** \'brīs\ [fr. a surname]
Bud·dy \'bəd-ē\ [prob. alter. of *brother*]
Bu·ford \'byü-fərd\ [fr. a surname]
Burke \'bərk\ [fr. a surname]
Bur·ton \'bərt-ᵊn\ [fr. a surname]
By·ron \'bī-rən\ [fr. a surname]

Cal·vin \'kal-vən\ [fr. a surname]
Cam·er·on \'kam-(ə-)rən\ [fr. a surname]
Carl \'kärl\ *var of* KARL
Car·los \'kär-ləs, -,lōs\ [Sp] *var of* CHARLES
Carl·ton or **Carle·ton** \'kär-(ə)l-tən, 'kärlt-ᵊn\ [fr. a surname]
Car·men \'kär-mən\ [Sp, fr. L] song
Car·roll \'kar-əl\ [fr. a surname]
Car·son \'kärs-ᵊn\ [fr. a surname]
Car·ter \'kärt-ər\ [fr. a surname]
Cary or **Car·ey** \'ka(ə)r-ē, 'ke(ə)r-ē\ [fr. a surname]
Ce·cil \'sē-səl, 'ses-əl\ [L]
Charles \'chär(-ə)lz\ [Gmc] man of the common people F *Charles*, It *Carlo*, Sp *Carlos*, G *Carl*, *Karl*
Ches·ter \'ches-tər\ [fr. a surname]
Chris \'kris\ *dim of* CHRISTOPHER
Chris·tian \'kris(h)-chən\ [Gk] Christian (the believer)
Chris·to·pher \'kris-tə-fər\ [Gk] Christ bearer
Clar·ence \'klar-ən(t)s\ [fr. the English dukedom]
Clark or **Clarke** \'klärk\ [fr. a surname]
Claude or **Claud** \'klod\ [L] It & Sp *Claudio*
Clay \'klā\ *dim of* CLAYTON
Clay·ton \'klāt-ᵊn\ [fr. a surname]
Clem \'klem\ *dim of* CLEMENT
Clem·ent \'klem-ənt\ [L] mild, merciful
Clif·ford \'klif-ərd\ [fr. a surname]
Clif·ton \'klif-tən\ [fr. a surname]
Clint \'klint\ *dim of* CLINTON
Clin·ton \'klint-ᵊn\ [fr. a surname]
Clyde \'klīd\ [fr. a surname]
Co·lin \'käl-ən, 'kō-lən\ or **Col·lin** \'käl-ən\ *dim of* NICHOLAS
Con·rad \'kän-,rad, -rəd\ [Gmc] bold counsel G *Konrad*
Con·stan·tine \'kän(t)-stən-,tēn, -,tīn\ [L]
Cor·ne·lius \kor-'nēl-yəs\ [L]
Coy \'koi\ [fr. a surname]
Craig \'krāg\ [fr. a surname]
Cur·tis \'kərt-əs\ [OF] courteous
Cyr·il \'sir-əl\ [Gk] lordly
Cy·rus \'sī-rəs\ [OPer]

Dale \'dā(ə)l\ [fr. a surname]

Dal·las \'dal-əs, -is\ [fr. a surname]
Dal·ton \'dolt-ᵊn\ [fr. a surname]
Dan \'dan\ [Heb] judge
Da·na \'dā-nə\ [fr. a surname]
Dan·iel \'dan-yəl *also* 'dan-ᵊl\ [Heb] God has judged
Dan·ny \'dan-ē\ *dim of* DANIEL
Dar·old \'dar-əld\ *perh alter of* DARRELL
Dar·rell or **Dar·rel** or **Dar·ryl** or **Dar·yl** \'dar-əl\ [fr. a surname]
Dar·win \'där-wən\ [fr. a surname]
Dave \'dāv\ *dim of* DAVID
Da·vid \'dā-vəd\ [Heb] beloved
Da·vis \'dā-vəs\ [fr. a surname]
Dean or **Deane** \'dēn\ [fr. a surname]
Del·a·no \'del-ə-,nō\ [fr. a surname]
Del·bert \'del-bərt\ *dim of* ADALBERT
Del·mar \'del-mər, -,mär\ or **Del·mer** \-mər\ [fr. a surname]
Den·nis or **Den·is** \'den-əs\ [OF, fr. Gk] belonging to Dionysus, god of wine
Den·ny \'den-ē\ *dim of* DENNIS
Den·ton \'dent-ᵊn\ [fr. a surname]
Der·ek \'der-ik\ [MD, fr. Gmc] ruler of the people
Dew·ey \'d(y)ü-ē\ [fr. a surname]
De·witt \di-'wit\ [fr. a surname]
Dex·ter \'dek-stər\ [L] on the right hand, fortunate
Dick \'dik\ *dim of* RICHARD
Die·ter \'dēt-ər\ [G] *var of* DIETRICH
Dirk \'dərk\ [D] *var of* DEREK
Dom·i·nic or **Dom·i·nick** \'däm-ə-(,)nik\ [L] belonging to the Lord
Don or **Donn** \'dän\ *dim of* DONALD
Don·al \'dän-ᵊl\ *var of* DONALD
Don·ald \'dän-ᵊld\ [ScGael] world ruler
Don·nie \'dän-ē\ *dim of* DON
Don·o·van \'dän-ə-vən, 'dən-\ [fr. a surname]
Doug \'dəg\ *dim of* DOUGLAS
Doug·las or **Doug·lass** \'dəg-ləs\ [fr. a surname]
Doyle \'dói(ə)l\ [fr. a surname]
Duane \dù-'ān, 'dwān\ [fr. a surname]
Dud·ley \'dəd-lē\ [fr. a surname]
Dun·can \'dəŋ-kən\ [ScGael] brown head
Dur·ward \'dər-wərd\ [fr. a surname]
Dwayne or **Dwaine** \'dwān\ [fr. a surname]
Dwight \'dwīt\ [fr. a surname]

Earl or **Earle** \'ər(-ə)l\ [OE] warrior, noble
Ed \'ed\ *dim of* ED-
Ed·die or **Ed·dy** \'ed-ē\ *dim of* ED
Ed·gar \'ed-gər\ [OE] spear of wealth
Ed·mund or **Ed·mond** \'ed-mənd\ [OE] protector of wealth F *Edmond*
Ed·son \'ed-sən\ [fr. a surname]
Ed·ward \'ed-wərd\ [OE] guardian of wealth
Ed·win \'ed-wən\ [OE] friend of wealth
El·bert \'el-bərt\ *var of* ALBERT
El·don or **El·den** \'el-dən\ [prob. fr. a surname]
Eli \'ē-,lī\ [Heb] high
Eli·as \i-'lī-əs\ [Gk] *var of* ELIJAH
El·liott or **El·liot** or **El·iot** \'el-ē-ət, 'el-yət\ [fr. a surname]
El·lis \'el-əs\ *var of* ELIAS
Ells·worth \'elz-(,)wərth\ [fr. a surname]
El·mer \'el-mər\ [fr. a surname]
El·mo \'el-(,)mō\ [It, fr. Gk] lovable
El·ton \'elt-ᵊn\ [fr. a surname]
El·vin \'el-vən\ [fr. a surname]

ə abut; ᵊ kitten; ər further; a back; ā bake; ä cot, cart; aù out; ch chin; e less; ē easy; g gift; i trip; ī life
j joke; ŋ sing; ō flow; ò flaw; ói coin; th thin; t̠h this; ü loot; ù foot; y yet; yü few; yù furious; zh vision

El·wood or **Ell·wood** \'el-ˌwu̇d\ [fr. a surname]

El·wyn or **El·win** \'el-wən\ [fr. a surname]

Eman·u·el or **Em·man·u·el** \i-'man-yə(-wə)l\ [Heb] God with us Sp *Manuel*, Pg *Manuel*

Em·er·son \'em-ər-sən\ [fr. a surname]

Emil \'ā-məl\ or **Emile** \ā-'mē(ə)l\ [L] F *Émile*, G *Emil*

Em·mett \'em-ət\ [fr. a surname]

Em·o·ry or **Em·ery** \'em-(ə-)rē\ [Gmc] It *Amerigo*

Er·ic or **Er·ich** or **Er·ik** \'er-ik\ [Scand]

Er·nest or **Ear·nest** \'ər-nəst\ [G] earnestness G *Ernst*

Er·nie \'ər-nē\ dim of ERNEST

Ernst \'ərn(t)st, 'e(ə)rn(t)st\ [G] var of ERNEST

Er·rol \'er-əl\ [prob. fr. a surname]

Er·vin \'ər-vən\ [fr. a surname]

Er·win \'ər-wən\ [fr. a surname]

Ethan \'ē-thən\ [Heb] strength

Eu·gene \yu̇-'jēn, 'yü-\ [Gk] wellborn

Ev·an \'ev-ən\ [W] var of JOHN

Ev·er·ett \'ev-(ə-)rət\ [fr. a surname]

Fe·lix \'fē-liks\ [L] happy, prosperous

Fer·di·nand \'fərd-ᵊn-ˌand\ [Gmc] prob venture of a military expedition Sp *Fernando*

Fer·nan·do \fər-'nan-(ˌ)dō\ [Sp] var of FERDINAND

Fletch·er \'flech-ər\ [fr. a surname]

Floyd \'flȯid\ [fr. a surname]

For·rest or **For·est** \'fȯr-əst, 'fär-\ [fr. a surname]

Fos·ter \'fȯs-tər, 'fäs-\ [fr. a surname]

Fran·cis \'fran(t)-səs\ [OIt & OF] Frenchman F *François*, G *Franz*, Sp *Francisco*

Fran·cis·co \fran-'sis-(ˌ)kō\ [Sp] var of FRANCIS

Frank \'fraŋk\ [Gmc] freeman, Frank

Frank·lin or **Frank·lyn** \'fraŋ-klən\ [fr. a surname]

Fred \'fred\ dim of -FRED or FRED-

Fred·die \'fred-ē\ dim of FREDERICK

Fred·er·ick or **Fred·er·ic** or **Fred·rick** or **Fred·ric** \'fred-(ə-)rik\ [Gmc] peaceful ruler G *Friedrich*, Fritz

Free·man \'frē-mən\ [fr. a surname]

Fritz \'frits\ [G] dim of FRIEDRICH

Ga·bri·el \'gā-brē-əl\ [Heb] man of God

Ga·len \'gā-lən\ [Gk]

Gar·land \'gär-lənd\ [fr. a surname]

Gar·rett \'gar-ət\ [fr. a surname]

Garth \'gärth\ [fr. a surname]

Gary \'ga(ə)r-ē, 'ge(ə)r-ē\ or **Gar·ry** \'gar-\ [prob. fr. a surname]

Gay·lord \'gā-ˌlȯ(ə)rd\ [fr. a surname]

Gene \'jēn\ dim of EUGENE

Geof·frey \'jef-rē\ [OF, fr. Gmc]

George \'jȯ(ə)rj\ [Gk] of or relating to a farmer

Ger·ald \'jer-əld\ [Gmc] spear dominion

Ge·rard \jə-'rärd, chiefly Brit 'jer-ˌärd, -ərd\ or **Ger·hard** \'ge(ə)r-ˌhärd\ [Gmc] strong with the spear

Ger·ry \'jer-ē\ var of JERRY

Gil·bert \'gil-bərt\ [Gmc] prob illustrious through hostages

Giles \'jī(ə)lz\ [OF, fr. LL]

Glenn or **Glen** \'glen\ [fr. a surname]

Gor·don \'gȯrd-ᵊn\ [fr. a surname]

Gra·dy \'grād-ē\ [fr. a surname]

Gra·ham \'grā-əm, 'gra(-ə)m\ [fr. a surname]

Grant \'grant\ [fr. a surname]

Gran·ville \'gran-ˌvil\ [fr. a surname]

Gray \'grā\ [fr. a surname]

Gregg or **Greg** \'greg\ dim of GREGORY

Greg·o·ry \'greg-(ə-)rē\ [LGk] vigilant

Gro·ver \'grō-vər\ [fr. a surname]

Gus \'gəs\ dim of -GUS- or GUS-

Gus·tav or **Gus·tave** \'gəs-təv\ [Gmc] dim of GUSTAVUS

Guy \'gī\ [OF, fr. Gmc] It *Guido*

Hal \'hal\ dim of HENRY

Hall \'hȯl\ [fr. a surname]

Ham·il·ton \'ham-əl-tən, -əlt-ᵊn\ [fr. a surname]

Hans \'hanz, 'hän(t)s\ [G] dim of JOHANNES

Har·lan \'här-lən\ or **Har·land** \-lənd\ [fr. a surname]

Har·ley \'här-lē\ [fr. a surname]

Har·low \'här-ˌlō\ [fr. a surname]

Har·mon \'här-mən\ [fr. a surname]

Har·old \'har-əld\ [OE] army dominion

Har·ris \'har-əs\ [fr. a surname]

Har·ri·son \'har-ə-sən\ [fr. a surname]

Har·ry \'har-ē\ dim of HENRY

Har·vey \'här-vē\ [fr. a surname]

Hayes \'hāz\ [fr. a surname]

Hec·tor \'hek-tər\ [Gk] holding fast

Hel·mut \'hel-mət, -ˌmüt\ [G] helmet courage

Hen·ry \'hen-rē\ [Gmc] ruler of the home

F *Henri*, It *Enrico*, G *Heinrich*, D *Hendrik*

Her·bert \'hər-bərt\ [Gmc] illustrious by reason of an army

Her·man or **Her·mann** \'hər-mən\ [Gmc] warrior G *Hermann*

Her·schel or **Her·shel** \'hər-shəl\ [fr. a surname]

Hi·ram \'hī-rəm\ [Phoenician]

Ho·bart \'hō-bərt, -ˌbärt\ [fr. a surname]

Hol·lis \'häl-əs\ [fr. a surname]

Ho·mer \'hō-mər\ [Gk]

Hor·ace \'hȯr-əs, 'här-\ [L]

How·ard \'hau̇(-ə)rd\ [fr. a surname]

How·ell \'hau̇(-ə)l\ [W]

Hoyt \'hȯit\ [fr. a surname]

Hu·bert \'hyü-bərt\ [Gmc] bright in spirit

Hud·son \'həd-sən\ [fr. a surname]

Hugh \'hyü\ or **Hu·go** \'hyü-(ˌ)gō\ [Gmc] prob mind, spirit

Ian \'ē-ən\ [ScGael] var of JOHN

Ira \'ī-rə\ [Heb] prob watchful

Ir·ving \'ər-viŋ\ or **Ir·vin** \-vən\ [fr. a surname]

Ir·win \'ər-wən\ [fr. a surname]

Isaac \'ī-zik, -zək\ [Heb] he laughs

Ivan \'ī-vən\ [Russ] var of JOHN

Jack \'jak\ dim of JOHN

Jack·son \'jak-sən\ [fr. a surname]

Ja·cob \'jā-kəb, -kəp\ [Heb] supplanter F *Jacques*

Jacques or **Jacque** \'zhäk\ [F] var of JAMES

Jake \'jāk\ dim of JACOB

James \'jāmz\ [OF, fr. LL *Jacobus*] var of JACOB

Jan \'jan\ [D & LG] var of JOHN

Jar·ed \'jar-əd, 'jer-\ [Heb] descent

Ja·son \'jās-ᵊn\ [Gk] prob healer

Jay \'jā\ [prob. fr. a surname]

Jef·frey or **Jeff·ery** or **Jef·fry** \'jef-(ə-)rē\ var of GEOFFREY

Jer·ald or **Jer·old** or **Jer·rold** \'jer-əld\ var of GERALD

Jer·e·my \'jer-ə-mē\ or **Jer·e·mi·ah** \ˌjer-ə-'mī-ə\ [Heb] prob Yahweh exalts

Je·rome \jə-'rōm, Brit also 'jer-əm\ [Gk] bearing a holy name

Jer·ry or **Jere** \'jer-ē\ dim of GER- or JER-

Jes·se \'jes-ē\ [Heb]

Jim \'jim\ or **Jim·my** or **Jim·mie** \'jim-ē\ dim of JAMES

Joe \'jō\ dim of JOSEPH

Jo·el \'jō-əl\ [Heb] Yahweh is God

John \'jän\ [Heb] Yahweh is gracious F *Jean*, It *Giovanni*, Sp *Juan*, G *Johann*, *Johannes*, *Hans*, D *Jan*, Russ *Ivan*

Jon \'jän\ var of JOHN

Jon·a·than \'jän-ə-thən\ [Heb] Yahweh has given

Jo·seph or **Jo·sef** \'jō-zəf also -səf\ [Heb] he shall add It *Giuseppe*, Sp *José*

Josh·u·a \'jäsh-(ə-)wə\ [Heb] Yahweh saves

Jud·son \'jəd-sən\ [fr. a surname]

Jules \'jülz\ [F] var of JULIUS

Ju·lian or **Ju·lien** \'jül-yən\ [L] sprung from or belonging to Julius

Ju·lius \'jül-yəs\ or **Ju·lio** \-(ˌ)yō\ [L]

Jus·tin \'jəs-tən\ or **Jus·tus** \-təs\ [L] just

Karl \'kär(-ə)l\ [G & Scand] var of CHARLES

Keith \'kēth\ [fr. a surname]

Kel·ly \'kel-ē\ [fr. a surname]

Ken \'ken\ dim of KENNETH

Ken·dall \'ken-dᵊl\ [fr. a surname]

Ken·neth \'ken-əth\ [ScGael]

Kent \'kent\ [prob. fr. a surname]

Ken·ton \'kent-ᵊn\ [fr. a surname]

Ker·mit \'kər-mət\ [prob. fr. a surname]

Ker·ry \'ker-ē\ [prob. fr. the county of Ireland]

Kev·in \'kev-ən\ [OIr]

Kir·by \'kər-bē\ [fr. a surname]

Kirk \'kərk\ [fr. a surname]

Klaus \'klau̇s, 'klȯs\ [G] dim of NIKOLAUS

Kurt \'kərt, 'ku̇(ə)rt\ [G] dim of CONRAD

La·mar \lə-'mär\ [fr. a surname]

Lance \'lan(t)s\ dim of LANCELOT

Lane \'lān\ [fr. a surname]

Lan·ny \'lan-ē\ prob dim of LAWRENCE

Lar·ry \'lar-ē\ dim of LAWRENCE

Lars \'lärz\ [Sw] var of LAWRENCE

Lasz·lo \'laz-(ˌ)lō\ [Hung]

Law·rence or **Lau·rence** \'lȯr-ən(t)s, 'lär-\ [L] of Laurentum, ancient city in central Italy F *Laurent*, It *Lorenzo*, G *Lorenz*

Lee or **Leigh** \'lē\ [fr. a surname]

Leigh·ton or **Lay·ton** \'lāt-ᵊn\ [fr. a surname]

Le·land \'lē-lənd\ [fr. a surname]

Leo \'lē-(ˌ)ō\ [L] lion

Le·on \'lē-ˌän, -ən\ [Sp] var of LEO

Leon·ard \'len-ərd\ [Gmc] strong or brave as a lion

Le·roy \li-'rȯi, 'lē-\ [OF] royal

Les·lie \'les-lē also 'lez-\ [fr. a surname]

Les·ter \'les-tər\ [fr. a surname]

Lew·is \'lü-əs\ var of LOUIS

Lin·coln \'liŋ-kən\ [fr. a surname]

Li·o·nel \'lī-ən-ᵊl, -ə-ˌnel\ [OF] young lion

Lloyd or **Loyd** \'lȯid\ [W] gray

Lo·gan \'lō-gən\ [fr. a surname]

Lon \'län\ dim of ALONZO

Lon·nie or **Lon·ny** \'län-ē\ dim of LON

Lo·ren \'lȯr-ən, 'lȯr-\ dim of LORENZO

Lou·ie \'lü-ē\ var of LOUIS

Lou·is or **Lu·is** \'lü-əs, 'lü-ē\ [Gmc] famous warrior Sp *Luis*, G *Ludwig*

Low·ell \'lō-əl\ [fr. a surname]

Lu·cian \'lü-shən\ [Gk] F *Lucien*

Lud·wig \'ləd-(ˌ)wig, 'lüd-\ [G] var of LOUIS

Luke \'lük\ [Gk] prob dim of LUCIUS L *Lucas*

Lu·ther \'lü-thər\ [fr. a surname]

Lyle \'lī(ə)l\ [fr. a surname]

Ly·man \'lī-mən\ [fr. a surname]

Lynn \'lin\ [fr. a surname]

Mack or **Mac** \'mak\ [fr. surnames beginning with Mc or Mac, fr. Gael *mac* son]

Mal·colm \'mal-kəm\ [ScGael] servant of (St.) Columba

Man·fred \'man-frəd\ [Gmc] peace among men

Man·u·el \'man-yə(-wə)l\ [Sp & Pg] var of EMMANUEL

Mar·cus \'mär-kəs\ [L] F *Marc*, It *Marco*

Ma·rio \'mär-ē-ˌō\ [It] var of MARIUS

Mar·i·on \'mer-ē-ən, 'mar-\ [fr. a surname]

Mark or **Marc** \'märk\ var of MARCUS

Mar·lin \'mär-lən\ [prob. fr. a surname]

Mar·shall or **Mar·shal** \'mär-shəl\ [fr. a surname]

Mar·tin \'märt-ᵊn\ [LL] of Mars

Mar·vin \'mär-vən\ [prob. fr. a surname]

Ma·son \'mās-ᵊn\ [fr. a surname]

Mat·thew \'math-(ˌ)yü also 'math-(ˌ)ü\ [Heb] gift of Yahweh

Mau·rice \'mȯr-əs, 'mär-; mȯ-'rēs\ [LL] prob Moorish

Max \'maks\ dim of MAXIMILIAN

Max·well \'mak-ˌswel, -swəl\ [fr. a surname]

May·nard \'mā-nərd\ [Gmc] bold in strength

Mel·ville \'mel-ˌvil\ [fr. a surname]

Mel·vin or **Mel·vyn** \'mel-vən\ [prob. fr. a surname]

Mer·e·dith \'mer-əd-əth\ [W]

Merle \'mər(-ə)l\ [F] blackbird

Mer·lin or **Mer·lyn** \'mər-lən\ [Celt]

Mer·rill \'mer-əl\ [fr. a surname]

Mer·ritt \'mer-ət\ [fr. a surname]

Mer·vin \'mər-vən\ var of MARVIN

Mi·chael \'mī-kəl\ [Heb] who is like God? F *Michel*, Sp & Pg *Miguel*

Mick·ey \'mik-ē\ dim of MICHAEL

Mike \'mīk\ dim of MICHAEL

Mi·lan \'mī-lən\ [prob. fr. the city in Italy]

Miles or **Myles** \'mī(ə)lz\ [Gmc]

Mil·ford \'mil-fərd\ [fr. a surname]

Mil·lard \'mil-ərd, mil-'ärd\ [fr. a surname]

Mi·lo \'mī-(ˌ)lō\ [prob. L]

Mil·ton \'milt-ᵊn\ [fr. a surname]

Mitch·ell \'mich-əl\ [fr. a surname]

Mon·roe \mən-'rō, 'mən-ˌ\ [fr. a surname]

Mon·te or **Mon·ty** \'mänt-ē\ dim of MONTAGUE

Mor·gan \'mȯr-gən\ [W] prob dweller on the sea

Mor·ris \'mȯr-əs, 'mär-\ var of MAURICE

Mor·ton \'mȯrt-ᵊn\ [fr. a surname]

Mur·ray \'mər-ē, 'mə-rē\ [fr. a surname]

My·ron \'mī-rən\ [Gk]

Na·than \'nā-thən\ [Heb] given, gift

Na·than·iel \nə-'than-yəl\ [Heb] gift of God

Ned \'ned\ dim of ED-

Neil or **Neal** \'nē(ə)l\ [Celt]

Nel·son \'nel-sən\ [fr. a surname]

Nev·ille \'nev-əl\ [fr. a surname]

Nev·in \'nev-ən\ [fr. a surname]

New·ell \'n(y)ü-əl\ [fr. a surname]

New·ton \'n(y)üt-ᵊn\ [fr. a surname]

Nich·o·las \'nik-(ə-)ləs\ [Gk] victorious among the people

Nick \'nik\ dim of NICHOLAS

Niles \'nī(ə)lz\ [fr. a surname]

Nils \'nils, 'nē(ə)ls\ [Scand]

No·ah \'nō-ə\ [Heb] rest

No·el \'nō-əl\ [F, fr. L] Christmas F *Noël*

No·lan \'nō-lən\ [fr. a surname]

Nor·bert \'nȯr-bərt\ [Gmc] shining in the north

Nor·man \'nȯr-mən\ [Gmc] Norseman, Norman

Nor·ris \'nȯr-əs, 'när-\ [fr. a surname]

Nor·ton \'nȯrt-ᵊn\ [fr. a surname]

Olin or Olen \'ō-lən\ [fr. a surname]
Ol·i·ver \'äl-ə-vər\ [OF]
Ol·lie \'äl-ē\ dim of OLIVER
Ora \'ōr-ə, 'ór-\
Or·lan·do \ór-'lan-(,)dō\ [It] var of ROLAND
Or·rin \'ör-ən, är-\ or Orin or Oren \'ór-, 'är-, 'ór-\ [prob. fr. a surname]
Or·ville or Or·val \'ór-vəl\ [prob. fr. a surname]
Os·car \'äs-kər\ [OE] spear of a deity
Otis \'ōt-əs\ [fr. a surname]
Ot·to \'ät-(,)ō\ [Gmc] prob properly
Ow·en \'ō-ən\ [OW]

Palm·er \'päm-ər, 'päl-mər\ [fr. a surname]
Par·ker \'pär-kər\ [fr. a surname]
Pat \'pat\ dim of PATRICK
Pat·rick \'pa-trik\ [L] patrician
Paul \'pól\ [L] little It Paolo, Sp Pablo
Pe·dro \'pe-(,)drō, 'pā-\ [Sp] var of PETER
Per·cy \'pər-sē\ [fr. a surname]
Per·ry \'per-ē\ [fr. a surname]
Pete \'pēt\ dim of PETER
Pe·ter \'pēt-ər\ [Gk] rock F Pierre, It Pietro, Sp & Pg Pedro
Phil \'fil\ dim of PHILIP
Phil·ip or Phil·lip \'fil-əp\ [Gk] lover of horses
Pierre \pē-'e(ə)r, 'pi(ə)r\ [F] var of PETER
Por·ter \'pōrt-ər, 'pórt-\ [fr. a surname]
Pres·ton \'pres-tən\ [fr. a surname]

Quen·tin \'kwent-ᵊn\ [LL] of or relating to the fifth

Ra·fa·el or Ra·pha·el \'raf-ē-əl, 'rä-fē-\ [Heb] God has healed
Ra·leigh \'ról-ē, 'räl-\ [fr. a surname]
Ralph \'ralf, Brit also 'rāf\ [Gmc] wolf in counsel F Raoul
Ra·mon \'rə-'mōn, 'rä-mən\ [Sp] var of RAYMOND
Ran·dall or Ran·dal \'ran-dᵊl\ var of RANDOLPH
Ran·dolph \'ran-,dälf\ [Gmc] shield wolf
Ran·dy \'rand-ē\ dim of RANDOLPH
Ray \'rā\ dim of RAYMOND
Ray·mond \'rā-mənd\ [Gmc] wise protection
Reed or Reid \'rēd\ [fr. a surname]
Reg·i·nald \'rej-ən-ᵊld\ [Gmc] wise dominion
Re·gis \'rē-jəs\ [fr. a proper name]
Re·ne \ren-(,)ā, rə-'nā, 'rā-nē, 'rē-nē\ [F, fr. L] reborn
Reu·ben or Ru·ben \'rü-bən\ [Heb]
Rex \'reks\ [L] king
Reyn·old \'ren-ᵊld\ var of REGINALD
Rich·ard \'rich-ərd\ [Gmc] strong in rule
Ri·ley \'rī-lē\ [fr. a surname]
Rob·ert \'räb-ərt\ [Gmc] bright in fame G Ruprecht
Ro·ber·to \rə-'bərt-(,)ō, rō-, -'be(ə)rt-\ [Sp & It] var of ROBERT
Rob·in \'räb-ən\ dim of ROBERT
Rod·er·ick \'räd-(ə-)rik\ [Gmc] famous ruler
Rod·ney \'räd-nē\ [fr. a surname]
Rog·er or Rod·ger \'räj-ər\ [Gmc] famous spear
Rog·ers \'räj-ərz\ [fr. a surname]
Ro·land or Rol·land \'rō-lənd\ or Rol·land \'räl-ənd\ or Row·land \'rō-lənd\ [Gmc] famous land It Orlando
Rolf \'rälf\ var of RUDOLPH

Rol·lin \'räl-ən\ var of ROLAND
Ron \'rän\ dim of RONALD
Ron·al \'rän-ᵊl\ var of RONALD
Ron·ald \'rän-ᵊld\ [ON] var of REGINALD
Ron·nie or Ron·ny \'rän-ē\ dim of RONALD
Ros·coe \'räs-(,)kō, 'rós-\ [fr. a surname]
Ross \'rós\ [fr. a surname]
Roy \'rói\ [ScGael]
Roy·al \'rói(-ə)l\ [prob. fr. a surname]
Royce \'róis\ [fr. a surname]
Ru·dolph or Ru·dolf \'rü-,dälf\ [Gmc] famous wolf F Rodolphe, Raoul, G Rudolf
Ru·dy \'rüd-ē\ dim of RUDOLPH
Ru·fus \'rü-fəs\ [L] red, red-haired
Ru·pert \'rü-pərt\ var of ROBERT
Rus·sell or Rus·sel \'rəs-əl\ [fr. a surname]
Ry·land \'rī-lənd\ [fr. a surname]

Sal·va·tore \'sal-və-,tō(ə)r, -,tó(ə)r; ,sal-və-'tōr-ē, -'tór-\ [It] savior
Sam \'sam\ dim of SAMUEL
Sam·my or Sam·mie \'sam-ē\ dim of SAM
Sam·u·el \'sam-yə(-wə)l\ [Heb] name of God
San·ford \'san-fərd\ [fr. a surname]
Saul \'sól\ [Heb] asked for
Scott \'skät\ [fr. a surname]
Sean \'shón\ [Ir] var of JOHN
Seth \'seth\ [Heb]
Sey·mour \'sē-,mō(ə)r, -,mó(ə)r\ [fr. a surname]
Shel·by \'shel-bē\ [fr. a surname]
Shel·don \'shel-dən\ [fr. a surname]
Sher·i·dan \'sher-əd-ᵊn\ [fr. a surname]
Sher·man \'shər-mən\ [fr. a surname]
Sher·win \'shər-wən\ [fr. a surname]
Sher·wood \'shər-,wùd, 'she(ə)r-\ [fr. a surname]
Sid·ney or Syd·ney \'sid-nē\ [fr. a surname]
Sieg·fried \'sig-,frēd, 'sēg-\ [Gmc] victorious peace
Sig·mund \'sig-mənd\ [Gmc] victorious protection
Si·mon \'sī-mən\ [Heb]
Sol·o·mon \'säl-ə-mən\ [Heb] peaceable
Spen·cer \'spen(t)-sər\ [fr. a surname]
Stan \'stan\ dim of STANLEY
Stan·ford \'stan-fərd\ [fr. a surname]
Stan·ley \'stan-lē\ [fr. a surname]
Stan·ton \'stant-ᵊn\ [fr. a surname]
Ste·fan \'stef-ən, -,än\ [Pol] var of STEPHEN
Ste·phen or Ste·ven or Ste·phan \'stē-vən\ [Gk] crown
Ster·ling \'stər-liŋ\ [fr. a surname]
Steve \'stēv\ dim of STEVEN
Stu·art or Stew·art \'st(y)ü-ərt, 'st(y)ù-(-ə)rt\ [fr. a surname]
Syl·ves·ter \sil-'ves-tər\ [L] woodsy, of the woods

Tay·lor \'tā-lər\ [fr. a surname]
Ted \'ted\ or Ted·dy \'ted-ē\ dim of ED-WARD, THEODORE
Ter·ence or Ter·rance or Ter·rence \'ter-ən(t)s\ [L]
Ter·rell or Ter·rill \'ter-əl\ [fr. a surname]
Ter·ry \'ter-ē\ dim of TERENCE
Thad \'thad\ dim of THADDEUS
Thad·de·us \'thad-ē-əs\ [Gk]
The·o·dore \'thē-ə-,dō(ə)r, -,dó(ə)r, -əd-ər\ [Gk] gift of God
The·ron \'thir-ən\ [Gk]

Thom·as \'täm-əs\ [Aram] twin
Thur·man \'thər-mən\ [fr. a surname]
Thur·ston \'thər-stən\ [Scand] Thor's stone
Tim \'tim\ dim of TIMOTHY
Tim·o·thy \'tim-ə-thē\ [Gk] revering God
To·by \'tō-bē\ dim of TOBIAS
Todd \'täd\ [prob. fr. a surname]
Tom \'täm\ or Tom·my or Tom·mie \'täm-ē\ dim of THOMAS
To·ny \'tō-nē\ dim of ANTHONY
Tra·cy \'trā-sē\ [fr. a surname]
Trav·is \'trav-əs\ [fr. a surname]
Trent \'trent\ [fr. a surname]
Troy \'trói\ [prob. fr. a surname]
Tru·man \'trü-mən\ [fr. a surname]
Ty·rone \'tī-,rōn, tī-'; tir-'ōn\ [prob. fr. the county in Ireland]

Val \'val\ dim of VALENTINE
Van \'van\ [fr. surnames beginning with Van, fr. D van of]
Vance \'van(t)s\ [fr. a surname]
Vaughn \'vón, 'vän\ [fr. a surname]
Verne or Vern \'vərn\ prob alter of VERNON
Ver·non \'vər-nən\ [prob. fr. a surname]
Vic·tor \'vik-tər\ [L] conqueror
Vin·cent \'vin(t)-sənt\ [LL] of or relating to the conquering one
Vir·gil \'vər-jəl\ [L]

Wade \'wād\ [fr. a surname]
Wal·do \'wól-(,)dō, 'wäl-\ [fr. a surname]
Wal·lace or Wal·lis \'wäl-əs\ [fr. a surname]
Wal·ter \'wól-tər\ [Gmc] army of dominion
Wal·ton \'wólt-ᵊn\ [fr. a surname]
Ward \'wó(ə)rd\ [fr. a surname]
War·ner \'wór-nər\ [fr. a surname]
War·ren \'wór-ən, 'wär-\ [fr. a surname]
Wayne \'wān\ [fr. a surname]
Wel·don \'wel-dən\ [fr. a surname]
Wen·dell \'wen-dᵊl\ [fr. a surname]
Wer·ner \'wər-nər, 'we(ə)r-\ [Gmc] army of the Varini, a Germanic people
Wes·ley \'wes-lē also 'wez-\ [fr a surname]
Wil·bert \'wil-bərt\ [fr. a surname]
Wil·bur or Wil·ber \'wil-bər\ [fr. a surname]
Wil·burn \'wil-bərn\ [fr. a surname]
Wi·ley or Wy·lie \'wī-lē\ [fr. a surname]
Wil·ford \'wil-fərd\ [fr. a surname]
Wil·fred \'wil-frəd\ [OE] desired peace
Will \'wil\ or Wil·lie \-ē\ dim of WILLIAM
Wil·lard \'wil-ərd\ [fr. a surname]
Wil·liam \'wil-yəm\ [Gmc] desired helmet G Wilhelm
Wil·lis \'wil-əs\ [fr. a surname]
Wil·mer \'wil-mər\ [fr. a surname]
Wil·son \'wil-sən\ [fr. a surname]
Wil·ton \'wilt-ᵊn\ [fr. a surname]
Win·field \'win-,fēld\ [fr. a surname]
Win·fred \'win-frəd\ [OE] prob joyous peace
Win·ston \'win(t)-stən\ [fr. a surname]
Win·ton \'wint-ᵊn\ [fr. a surname]
Wolf·gang \'wùlf-,gaŋ\ [OHG] path of a wolf
Wood·row \'wùd-(,)rō\ [fr. a surname]
Wy·att \'wī-ət\ [fr. a surname]

Yale \'yā(ə)l\ [fr. a surname]

Zane \'zān\ [fr. a surname]

II NAMES OF WOMEN

Ab·by \'ab-ē\ dim of ABIGAIL
Ab·i·gail \'ab-ə-,gāl\ [Heb] prob source of joy
Ada \'ād-ə\ [Heb] prob ornament
Ad·e·laide \'ad-ᵊl-,ād\ [Gmc] of noble rank
Adele \ə-'del\ [Gmc] noble F Adèle
Adri·enne \,ā-drē-'en, -ən\ [F] fem of ADRIEN
Ag·nes \'ag-nəs\ [LL]
Ai·leen \ī-'lēn\ [IrGael] var of HELEN
Al·ber·ta \al-'bərt-ə\ fem of ALBERT
Al·ex·an·dra \,al-ig-'zan-drə, ,el-\ [Gk] fem of ALEXANDER
Al·ice or Al·yce \'al-əs\ [OF] var of ADELAIDE
Al·i·cia \ə-'lish-ə\ [ML] var of ADELAIDE
Al·i·son or Al·li·son \'al-ə-sən\ [OF] dim of ALICE
Al·ma \'al-mə\ [L] nourishing, cherishing
Al·ta \'al-tə\ [L] high
Al·va \'al-və\ [Sp, fr. L] white

Aman·da \ə-'man-də\ [L] worthy to be loved
Ame·lia \ə-'mēl-yə\ [Gmc] F Amélie
Amy \'ā-mē\ [L] beloved
An·as·ta·sia \,an-ə-'stā-zh(ē-)ə\ [LGk] of the resurrection
An·drea \'an-drē-ə, an-'drā-ə\ fem of AN-DREW
An·ge·la \'an-jə-lə\ [It, fr. Gk] angel
An·ge·line \'an-jə-,līn, -,lēn\ dim of ANGELA
Ani·ta \ə-'nēt-ə\ [Sp] dim of ANN
Ann or Anne \'an\ or An·na \'an-ə\ [Heb] grace
An·na·belle \'an-ə-,bel\ prob var of MABEL
An·nette \a-'net, ə-\ or An·net·ta \-'net-ə\ [F] dim of ANN
An·nie \'an-ē\ dim of ANN
An·toi·nette \,an-t(w)ə-'net\ [F] dim of ANTONIA
April \'ā-prəl\ [E] April (the month)

Ar·dell or Ar·delle \är-'del\ var of ADELE
Ar·dis \'ärd-əs\
Ar·lene or Ar·leen or Ar·line \är-'lēn\
As·trid \'as-trəd\ [Scand] beautiful as a deity
Au·drey \'ó-drē\ [OE] noble strength

Ba·bette \ba-'bet\ [F] dim of ELIZABETH
Bar·ba·ra \'bär-b(ə-)rə\ [Gk] foreign
Be·atrice \'bē-ə-trəs also bē-'a-trəs\ [It, fr. ML] she that makes happy L Beatrix
Becky \'bek-ē\ dim of REBECCA
Ber·na·dette \,bər-nə-'det\ [F] fem of BERNARD
Ber·na·dine \'bər-nə-,dēn\ fem of BERNARD
Ber·nice \(,)bər-'nēs, 'bər-nəs\ [Gk] bringing victory
Ber·tha \'bər-thə\ [Gmc] bright F Berthe
Ber·yl \'ber-əl\ [Gk] beryl (the mineral)
Bes·sie \'bes-ē\ dim of ELIZABETH
Beth \'beth\ dim of ELIZABETH

Bet·sy or Bet·sey \'bet-sē\ dim of ELIZA-BETH

Bet·ty or Bet·te or Bet·tye or Bet·tie \'bet-ē\ dim of ELIZABETH

Beu·lah \'byü-lə\ [Heb] married

Bev·er·ly or Bev·er·ley \'bev-ər-lē\ [prob. fr. a surname]

Bil·lie \'bil-ē\ fem of BILLY

Blanche \'blanch\ [OF, fr. Gmc] white It Bianca

Bob·bie \'bäb-ē\ dim of ROBERTA

Bo·ni·ta \bə-'nēt-ə\ [Sp] pretty

Bon·nie \'bän-ē\ [ME] pretty

Bren·da \'bren-də\ [Scand]

Bri·gitte \'brij-ət, brə-'jit\ [G] var of BRIDGET

Ca·mil·la \kə-'mil-ə\ [L] freeborn girl attendant at a sacrifice

Ca·mille \kə-'mē(ə)l\ [F] var of CAMILLA

Can·da·ce \kan-'dā-sē, 'kan-də-(,)sē, 'kan-dəs\ [Gk]

Car·la \'kär-lə\ [It] fem of CARLO

Car·lene \kär-'lēn\ var of CARLA

Car·lot·ta \kär-'lät-ə\ [It] var of CHAR-LOTTE

Car·men \'kär-mən\ or Car·mine \kär-'mēn, 'kär-mən\ [Sp, fr. L] song

Car·ol or Car·ole or Car·yl \'kar-əl\ dim of CAROLYN

Car·o·lyn \'kar-ə-lən\ or Car·o·line \-lən, -,līn\ [It] fem of CHARLES It & Sp Carolina

Car·rie \'kar-ē\ dim of CAROLINE

Cath·er·ine or Cath·a·rine \'kath-(ə-)rən\ [LGk] G Katharine, Katrina

Cath·leen \kath-'lēn\ [IrGael] var of CATHERINE

Cath·ryn \'kath-rən\ var of CATHERINE

Cathy or Cath·ie \'kath-ē\ dim of CATH-ERINE

Ce·cile \sə-'sē(ə)l\ var of CECILIA

Ce·ci·lia \sə-'sēl-yə, -'sil-\ or Ce·ce·lia \-'sēl-\ [L] fem of CECIL

Ce·leste \sə-'lest\ [L] heavenly

Ce·lia \'sēl-yə\ dim of CECILIA

Char·lene \shär-'lēn\ fem of CHARLES

Char·lotte \'shär-lət\ [F] fem dim of CHARLES It Carlotta

Cher·ie \'sher-ē\ [F] dear

Cher·ry \'cher-ē\ [E] cherry

Cher·yl \'cher-əl, 'sher-\ prob var of CHERRY

Chloe \'klō-ē\ [Gk] young verdure

Chris·tine \kris-'tēn\ or Chris·ti·na \-'tē-nə\ [Gk] Christian

Cin·dy \'sin-dē\ dim of LUCINDA

Claire or Clare \'kla(ə)r, 'kle(ə)r\ var of CLARA

Clara \'klar-ə\ [L] bright

Cla·rice \'klar-əs, klə-'rēs\ dim of CLARA

Clau·dette \klȯ-'det\ [F] fem of CLAUDE

Clau·dia \'klȯd-ē-ə\ [L] fem of CLAUDE

Clau·dine \klȯ-'dēn\ [F] fem of CLAUDE

Cleo \'klē-(,)ō\ dim of CLEOPATRA

Co·lette \kä-'let\ [OF] fem dim of NICHOLAS

Col·leen \kä-'lēn\ [IrGael] girl

Con·nie \'kän-ē\ dim of CONSTANCE

Con·stance \'kän(t)-stən(t)s\ [L] constancy

Co·ra \'kōr-ə, 'kȯr-\ [Gk] maiden

Co·rinne or Cor·rine \kə-'rin, -'rēn\ [Gk] dim of CORA

Cor·ne·lia \kȯr-'nēl-yə\ [L] fem of COR-NELIUS

Cyn·thia \'sin(t)-thē-ə\ [Gk] she of Mount Cynthus on the island of Delos (i.e. the goddess Artemis, supposed to have been born there)

Dai·sy \'dā-zē\ [E] daisy

Dale \'dā(ə)l\ [E] valley

Da·na \'dā-nə\ [fr. a surname]

Daph·ne \'daf-nē\ [Gk] laurel

Dar·la \'där-lə\ [deriv. of darling]

Dar·lene \där-'lēn\ [deriv. of darling]

Dawn \'dȯn, 'dän\ [E] dawn

De·an·na \dē-'an-ə\ or De·anne \-'an\ var of DIANA

Deb·o·rah or Deb·o·ra \'deb-(ə-)rə\ [Heb] bee

Deb·ra \'deb-rə\ var of DEBORAH

Dee \'dē\ prob dim of EDITH

Deir·dre \'di(ə)r-drē, 'de(ə)r-\ [IrGael]

De·lia \'dēl-yə\ [Gk] she of Delos (i.e. the goddess Artemis)

Del·la \'del-ə\ dim of -DEL or -DEL-

De·lo·res \də-'lōr-əs, -'lȯr-\ var of DOLORES

De·na or Dee·na \'dē-nə\ dim of GERALDINE

De·nise \də-'nēz, -'nēs\ [F] fem of DENIS

Di·ana or Di·an·na \dī-'an-ə\ [L]

Di·ane or Di·anne or Di·an or Di·ann \dī-'an\ [F] var of DIANA

Di·na or Di·nah \'dī-nə\ [Heb] judged

Dix·ie \'dik-sē\ [E] prob Dixie (nickname for the southern states of the U.S.)

Do·lo·res \də-'lōr-əs, -'lȯr-\ [Sp, fr. L] sorrows (i.e. those of the Virgin Mary)

Don·na \'dän-ə\ or Do·na \'dän-ə, 'dō-nə\ [It, fr. L] lady

Do·ra \'dōr-ə, 'dȯr-\ dim of -DORA

Dor·cas \'dȯr-kəs\ [Gk] gazelle

Do·reen \dȯ-'rēn, də-\ [IrGael]

Dor·is \'dȯr-əs, 'där-\ [Gk] prob Dorian

Dor·o·thy \'dȯr-ə-thē, 'där-\ or Dor·o·thea \,dȯr-ə-'thē-ə, ,där-\ [LGk] goddess of gifts

Edith or Edythe \'ēd-əth\ [OE] L Editha

Ed·na \'ed-nə\ [Aram] prob var of ANN

Ed·wi·na \e-'dwē-nə, -'dwin-ə\ fem of ED-WIN

Ef·fie \'ef-ē\ dim of EUPHEMIA

Ei·leen \ī-'lēn\ [IrGael]

Elaine \i-'lān\ [OF] var of HELEN

El·ea·nor or El·i·nor or El·ea·nore \'el-ə-nər, -,nȯ(ə)r, -,nō(ə)r\ [OProv] var of HELEN F Eléonore, It Eleonora, G Eleonore

Ele·na \ə-'lā-nə, ə-'lē-nə\ [It] var of HELEN

Elise \ə-'lēz, -'lēs\ [F] var of ELIZABETH

Eliz·a·beth or Elis·a·beth \i-'liz-ə-bəth\ [Heb] God has sworn F Élise, It Elisa

El·la \'el-ə\ [OF]

El·len or El·lyn \'el-ən\ var of HELEN

El·o·ise \'el-ə-,wēz, ,el-ə-'\ [OF, fr. Gmc]

El·sa \'el-sə\ [G] dim of ELIZABETH

El·sie \'el-sē\ dim of ELIZABETH

El·va \'el-və\ [Gmc] elf

Em·i·ly or Em·i·lie \'em-(ə-)lē\ [L] fem of EMIL F Émilie, It & Sp Emilia

Em·ma \'em-ə\ [Gmc] var of ERMA

Enid \'ē-nəd\ [W]

Er·i·ka \'er-i-kə\ fem of ERIC

Er·ma \'ər-mə\ [Gmc] dim of ERM-

Er·na \'ər-nə\ dim of ERNESTINE

Er·nes·tine \'ər-nə-,stēn\ fem of ERNEST

Es·telle \e-'stel\ or Es·tel·la \e-'stel-ə\ [OProv, fr. L] star

Es·ther \'es-tər\ [prob. fr. Per] prob star

Eth·el \'eth-əl\ [OE] noble

Et·ta \'et-ə\ dim of HENRIETTA

Eu·ge·nia \yü-'jēn-yə\ or Eu·ge·nie \-'jē-nē\ fem of EUGENE F Eugénie

Eu·nice \'yü-nəs\ [Gk] having (i.e. bringing) happy victory

Eva \'ē-və\ var of EVE

Evan·ge·line \i-'van-jə-lən, -,lēn, -,līn\ [Gk] bringing good news

Eve \'ēv\ [Heb] life, living

Ev·e·lyn \'ev-(ə-)lən, chiefly Brit 'ēv-\ [OF, fr. Gmc]

Faith \'fāth\ [E] faith

Faye or Fay \'fā\ dim of FAITH

Fe·lice \fə-'lēs\ [L] happiness

Fern or Ferne \'fərn\ [E] fern

Flo·ra \'flōr-ə, 'flȯr-\ [L] goddess of flowers

Flor·ence \'flȯr-ən(t)s, 'flär-\ [L] bloom, prosperity

Fran·ces \'fran(t)-səs, -,səz\ fem of FRANCIS It Francesca

Fran·cine \fran-'sēn\ [F] prob dim of FRANCES

Fre·da or Frie·da \'frēd-ə\ dim of WINIFRED

Fred·er·ic·ka or Fred·er·i·ca \,fred-(ə-)'rē-kə, -'rik-ə\ fem of FREDERICK

Gail or Gayle or Gale \'gā(ə)l\ dim of ABIGAIL

Gay \'gā\ [E] gay

Ge·ne·va \jə-'nē-və\ var of GENEVIEVE

Gen·e·vieve \'jen-ə-,vēv\ [prob. fr. Celt]

George·ann \jȯr-'jan\ [George + Ann]

Geor·gia \'jȯr-jə\ fem of GEORGE

Geor·gi·na \jȯr-'jē-nə\ fem of GEORGE

Ger·al·dine \'jer-əl-,dēn\ fem of GERALD

Ger·trude \'gər-,trüd\ [Gmc] spear strength

Gin·ger \'jin-jər\ [E] ginger

Gi·sela \jə-'sel-ə, -'zel-\ [Gmc] pledge

Glad·ys \'glad-əs\ [W]

Glen·da \'glen-də\ prob var of GLENNA

Glen·na \'glen-ə\ fem of GLENN

Glo·ria \'glōr-ē-ə, 'glȯr-\ [L] glory

Grace \'grās\ [L] favor, grace

Gre·ta \'grēt-ə, 'gret-\ dim of MARGARET

Gretch·en \'grech-ən\ [G] dim of MAR-GARET

Gwen \'gwen\ dim of GWENDOLYN

Gwen·do·lyn \'gwen-də-lən\ [W]

Han·nah \'han-ə\ [Heb] var of ANN

Har·ri·et or Har·ri·ett or Har·ri·ette \'har-ē-ət\ var of HENRIETTA

Hat·tie \'hat-ē\ dim of HARRIET

Ha·zel \'hā-zəl\ [E] hazel

Heath·er \'heth-ər\ [ME] heather (the shrub)

Hei·di \'hīd-ē\ [G] dim of ADELAIDE

He·laine \hə-'lān\ var of HELEN

Hel·en \'hel-ən\ or He·le·na \'hel-ə-nə, hə-'lē-nə\ [Gk] F Hélène, It Elena

He·lene \hə-'lēn\ [F] var of HELEN

Hel·ga \'hel-gə\ [Scand] holy

Hen·ri·et·ta \,hen-rē-'et-ə\ [MF] fem of HENRY F Henriette

Her·mine \'hər-,mēn\ [G] prob fem of HERMAN

Hes·ter \'hes-tər\ var of ESTHER

Hil·da \'hil-də\ [OE] battle

Hil·de·gard or Hil·de·garde \'hil-də-,gärd\ [Gmc] prob battle enclosure

Hol·ly \'häl-ē\ [E] holly

Hope \'hōp\ [E] hope

Ida \'īd-ə\ [Gmc]

Ila \'ī-lə\

Ilene \ī-'lēn\ var of EILEEN

Ilo·na \ī-'lō-nə, il-'ō-\ [Hung] var of HELEN

Imo·gene \'im-ə-,jēn, 'ī-mə-\

Ina \'ī-nə\

Inez \'ī-,nez, 'ī-nəz\ [Sp] var of AGNES

In·grid \'iŋ-grəd\ [Scand] beautiful as Ing (an ancient Germanic god)

Irene \ī-'rēn\ [Gk] peace

Iris \'ī-rəs\ [Gk] rainbow

Ir·ma \'ər-mə\ var of ERMA

Is·a·bel or Is·a·belle \'iz-ə-,bel\ [OProv] var of ELIZABETH

Iva \'ī-və\ perh dim of GODIVA

Jac·que·line or Jac·que·lyn or Jac·que·lin \'jak-(w)ə-lən, -,lēn\ [OF] fem of JACOB

Jan \'jan\ dim of JANET

Jane or Jayne \'jān\ [OF] var of JOAN

Ja·net or Ja·nette \'jan-ət, jə-'net\ dim of JANE

Ja·nice or Jan·is \'jan-əs, jə-'nēs\ prob dim of JANE

Ja·nie \'jā-nē\ dim of JANE

Jean or Jeanne \'jēn\ [OF] var of JOAN

Jea·nette or Jean·nette \jə-'net\ [F] dim of JEANNE

Jean·nie or Jean·ie \'jē-nē\ dim of JEAN

Jean·nine or Jea·nine \jə-'nēn\ [F] dim of JEANNE

Jen·nie or Jen·ny \'jen-ē\ dim of JANE

Jen·ni·fer \'jen-ə-fər\ [Celt]

Jer·al·dine \'jer-əl-,dēn\ var of GERALDINE

Jer·i·lyn \'jer-ə-lən\ var of GERALDINE

Jer·ry or Jeri or Jer·rie \'jer-ē\ dim of GERALDINE

Jes·si·ca \'jes-i-kə\ [prob. Heb]

Jes·sie \'jes-ē\ [Sc] dim of JANET

Jew·el or Jew·ell \'jü-(ə)l, 'jü-(ə)l\ [E] jewel

Jill \'jil\ dim of JULIANA

Jo \'jō\ dim of JOSEPHINE

Joan or Joann or Joanne \'jō-(ə)n, jō-'an\ [Gk] fem of JOHN F Jeanne, It Giovanna

Jo·an·na \jō-'an-ə\ or Jo·han·na \-'(h)an-ə\ var of JOAN

Joc·e·lyn \'jäs-(ə-)lən\ [OF, fr. Gmc]

Jo·lene \jō-'lēn\ prob dim of JO

Jo·se·phine \'jō-zə-,fēn also 'jō-sə-\ fem of JOSEPH

Joy \'jȯi\ [E] joy

Joyce \'jȯis\ [OF]

Jua·ni·ta \wä-'nēt-ə\ [Sp] fem dim of JOHN

Ju·dith \'jüd-əth\ [Heb] Jewess

Ju·dy or Ju·di or Ju·die \'jüd-ē\ dim of JUDITH

Ju·lia \'jül-yə\ [L] fem of JULIUS

Ju·li·ana \,jü-lē-'an-ə\ [LL] fem of JULIAN F Julienne

Ju·li·anne or Ju·li·ann \,jü-lē-'an, jül-'yan\ var of JULIANA

Ju·lie \'jü-lē\ [MF] var of JULIA

Ju·liet \'jü-lē-ət, -ē-,et, -ē-ət; jül-ē-'et, jül-'yet, 'jül-,yet\ [It] dim of JULIA

June \'jün\ [E] June (the month)

Jus·tine \,jəs-'tēn\ [F] fem of JUSTIN

Kar·en or Kar·in or Kaa·ren \'kar-ən, 'kär-\ [Scand] var of CATHERINE

Kar·la \'kär-lə\ var of CARLA

Kar·ol \'kar-əl\ var of CAROL

Kar·o·lyn \'kar-ə-lən\ var of CAROLYN

Kate \'kāt\ dim of CATHERINE

Kath·er·ine or Kath·a·rine or Kath·ryn \'kath-(ə-)rən\ var of CATHERINE

Kath·leen \kath-'lēn\ [IrGael] var of CATHERINE

Kathy \'kath-ē\ dim of CATHERINE

Ka·tie \'kāt-ē\ dim of KATE

Kay or Kaye \'kā\ dim of CATHERINE

Kit·ty \'kit-ē\ dim of CATHERINE

Kris·tin \'kris-tən\ [Scand] var of CHRIS-TINE

Kris·tine \kris-'tēn\ var of CHRISTINE

La·na \'lan-ə, 'län-ə, 'lā-nə\

Lau·ra \'lȯr-ə, 'lär-\ [ML] prob fem dim of LAWRENCE

Lau·rel \'lȯr-əl, 'lär-\ [E] laurel

Lau·rie \'lȯr-ē, 'lär-\ dim of LAURA

La·verne or La·vern \lə-'vərn\

Le·ah \'lē-ə\ [Heb] prob wild cow

Le·anne \lē-'an\ [prob. fr. Lee + Ann]

Lee \'lē\ [fr. a surname]

Lei·la or Le·la \'lē-lə\ [Per] dark as night

Le·lia \'lēl-yə\ [L]

Le·na \'lē-nə\ [G] dim of HELENA & MAGDALENA

Le·nore \lə-'nō(ə)r, -'nȯ(ə)r\ or Le·no·ra \lə-'nōr-ə, -'nȯr-\ var of LEONORA

Le·o·na \lē-'ō-nə\ fem of LEON F Léonie

Le·o·no·ra \,lē-ə-'nōr-ə, -'nȯr-\ var of ELEANOR G Leonore, Lenore

Les·lie or **Les·ley** \'les-lē also 'lez-\ [fr. a surname]
Le·ta \'lēt-ə\
Le·ti·tia \li-'tish-ə, -'tē-shə\ [L] gladness
Lib·by \'lib-ē\ dim of ELIZABETH
Li·la \'lī-lə\ var of LEILA
Lil·lian \'lil-yən, 'lil-ē-ən\ prob dim of ELIZABETH
Lil·lie \'lil-ē\ dim of LILLIAN
Lily \'lil-ē\ [E] lily
Lin·da or **Lyn·da** \'lin-də\ dim of -LINDA
Li·sa \'lī-zə, 'lē-\ dim of ELIZABETH
Lo·is \'lō-əs\ [Gk]
Lo·la \'lō-lə\ [Sp] dim of DOLORES
Lon·na \'län-ə\ fem of LON
Lo·ra \'lōr-ə, 'lòr-\ var of LAURA
Lo·re·lei \'lōr-ə-,lī, 'lòr-\ [G]
Lo·rene \lò-'rēn\ dim of LORA
Lo·ret·ta \lə-'ret-ə, lò-\ [ML] var of LAURETTA
Lor·na \'lòr-nə\
Lor·raine or **Lo·raine** \lə-'rān, lò-\ [prob. fr. Lorraine, region in northeast France]
Lou \'lü\ dim of LOUISE
Lou·ise \lù-'ēz\ or **Lou·i·sa** \-'ē-zə\ fem of LOUIS G Luise
Lu·anne \lü-'an\ [Lu- + Anne]
Lu·cille or **Lu·cile** \lü-'sē(ə)l\ [L] prob dim of LUCIA
Lu·cin·da \lü-'sin-də\ [L] var of LUCY
Lu·cre·tia \lü-'krē-shə\ [L]
Lu·cy \'lü-sē\ or **Lu·cia** \'lü-shə\ [L] fem of LUCIUS F Lucie, It Lucia
Lu·el·la \lü-'el-ə\ [prob. fr. Lou (dim. of Louise) + Ella]
Lyd·ia \'lid-ē-ə\ [Gk] Lydian woman
Ly·nette \lə-'net\ [W]
Lynne or **Lynn** \'lin\ var of -LYN

Ma·bel \'mā-bəl\ [L] lovable
Mad·e·line or **Mad·e·leine** or **Mad·e·lyn** \'mad-ᵊl-ən\ [Gk] woman of Magdala, ancient town in northern Palestine
Madge \'maj\ dim of MARGARET
Ma·mie \'mā-mē\ dim of MARGARET
Ma·ra \'mär-ə\ var of MARY
Mar·cel·la \mär-'sel-ə\ [L] fem of MARCELLUS F Marcelle
Mar·cia \'mär-shə\ [L] fem of MARCUS
Mar·ga·ret \'mär-g(ə-)rət\ [Gk] pearl F Marguerite, It Margherita, Sp Margarita, G Margarete
Mar·gery \'märj-(ə-)rē\ [OF] var of MARGARET
Mar·gie \'mär-jē\ dim of MARGARET
Mar·go \'mär-(,)gō\ var of MARGOT
Mar·got \'mär-(,)gō, -gət\ dim of MARGARET
Mar·gue·rite \,mär-g(y)ə-'rēt\ [OF] var of MARGARET
Ma·ria \mə-'rē-ə also -'rī-\ var of MARY
Mar·i·an \'mer-ē-ən, 'mar-\ var of MARIANNE
Mar·i·anne \,mer-ē-'an, ,mar-\ or **Mar·i·an·na** \-'an-ə\ [fem of MARY]
Ma·rie \mə-'rē\ [OF] var of MARY
Mar·i·et·ta \,mer-ē-'et-ə, ,mar-\ dim of MARY
Mar·i·lee \'mer-ə-(,)lē, 'mar-\ [prob. fr. Mary + Lee]
Mar·i·lyn or **Mar·i·lynn** or **Mar·y·lyn** \'mer-ə-lən, 'mar-\ [prob. fr. Mary + -lyn]
Ma·ri·na \mə-'rē-nə\ [LGk]
Mar·i·on \'mer-ē-ən, 'mar-\ dim of MARY
Mar·jo·rie or **Mar·jo·ry** \'märj-(ə-)rē\ var of MARGERY
Mar·la \'mär-lə\ prob dim of MARLENE
Mar·lene \mär-'lēn(-ə), -'lā-nə\ [G] var of MAGDALENE
Mar·lyn \'mär-lən\ prob var of MARLENE
Mar·lys \'mär-ləs\
Mar·na \'mär-nə\
Mar·sha \'mär-shə\ var of MARCIA
Mar·ta \'märt-ə\ [It] var of MARTHA
Mar·tha \'mär-thə\ [Aram] lady F Marthe, It & Sp Marta
Mar·va \'mär-və\ prob fem of MARVIN
Mary \'me(ə)r-ē, 'ma(ə)r-ē, 'mā-rē\ [Gk, fr. Heb] F Marie, G Maria, Sp María
Mary·ann or **Mary·anne** \,mer-ē-'an, ,mar-ē-, ,mā-rē-\ [Mary + Ann]
Mary·el·len \,mer-ē-'el-ən, ,mar-ē-, ,mā-rē-\ [Mary + Ellen]
Mar·y·lon \'mer-ə-lən, 'mar-\ var of MARILYN
Maude \'mòd\ [OF] var of MATILDA
Mau·reen or **Mau·rine** \mò-'rēn\ dim of MAURA
Max·ine \mak-'sēn\ [F] fem dim of MAXIMILIAN
May or **Mae** \'mā\ dim of MARY

Mel·a·nie \'mel-ə-nē\ [Gk] blackness
Mel·ba \'mel-bə\ [E] woman of Melbourne, Australia
Me·lin·da \mə-'lin-də\ prob alter of BELINDA
Me·lis·sa \mə-'lis-ə\ [Gk] bee
Mel·va \'mel-və\ prob fem of MELVIN
Mer·e·dith \'mer-əd-əth\ [W]
Merle \'mər(-ə)l\ [F] blackbird
Mer·ri·ly \'mer-ə-lē\ alter of MARILEE
Mer·ry \'mer-ē\ [E] merry
Mi·chele or **Mi·chelle** \mi-'shel\ [F] fem of MICHAEL
Mil·dred \'mil-drəd\ [OE] gentle strength
Mil·li·cent \'mil-ə-sənt\ [Gmc]
Mil·lie \'mil-ē\ dim of MILDRED
Min·nie \'min-ē\ [Sc] dim of MARY
Mir·i·am \'mir-ē-əm\ [Heb] var of MARY
Mit·zi \'mit-sē\ prob dim of MARGARET
Mol·ly or **Mol·lie** \'mäl-ē\ dim of MARY
Mo·na \'mō-nə\ [IrGael]
Mon·i·ca \'män-i-kə\ [LL]
Mu·ri·el \'myùr-ē-əl\ [prob. Celt]
My·ra \'mī-rə\
Myr·na \'mər-nə\
Myr·tle \'mərt-ᵊl\ [Gk] myrtle

Na·dine \nā-'dēn, nə-\ [F, fr. Russ] hope
Nan \'nan\ dim of ANN
Nan·cy \'nan(t)-sē\ dim of ANN
Nan·nette or **Na·nette** \na-'net, nə-\ [F] dim of ANN
Na·o·mi \nā-'ō-mē\ [Heb] pleasant
Nat·a·lie \'nat-ᵊl-ē\ [LL] of or relating to Christmas
Ne·dra \'ned-rə, 'nē-drə\
Nel·da \'nel-də\
Nel·lie \'nel-ē\ or **Nell** \'nel\ dim of -EL-
Net·tie \'net-ē\ [Sc] dim of JANET
Ne·va \'nē-və\
Ni·na \'nī-nə, 'nē-\ [Russ] dim of ANN
Ni·ta \'nēt-ə\ [Sp] dim of JUANITA
No·la \'nō-lə\
No·na \'nō-nə\ [L] ninth
No·ra \'nōr-ə, 'nòr-\ dim of -NOR-
No·reen \nò-'rēn\ [IrGael] dim of NORA
Nor·ma \'nòr-mə\ [It]

Ol·ga \'äl-gə, 'òl-\ [Russ] var of HELGA
Ol·ive \'äl-iv, -əv\ or **O·liv·ia** \ə-'liv-ē-ə, ō-\ [L] olive
Opal \'ō-pəl\ [E] opal

Pa·me·la \'pam-ə-lə; pə-'mē-lə, pa-\
Pa·tri·cia \pə-'trish-ə, -'trē-shə\ [L] fem of PATRICK
Pat·sy \'pat-sē\ dim of PATRICIA
Pat·ty or **Pat·ti** or **Pat·tie** \'pat-ē\ dim of PATRICIA
Pau·la \'pò-lə\ [L] fem of PAUL
Pau·lette \pò-'let\ dim of PAUL
Pau·line \pò-'lēn\ fem dim of PAUL
Pearl \'pər(-ə)l\ [E] pearl
Peg·gy \'peg-ē\ dim of MARGARET
Pe·nel·o·pe \pə-'nel-ə-pē\ [Gk]
Pen·ny \'pen-ē\ dim of PENELOPE
Phoe·be \'fē-bē\ [Gk] shining
Phyl·lis \'fil-əs\ [Gk] green leaf
Pol·ly \'päl-ē\ dim of MARY
Por·tia \'pōr-shə, 'pòr-\ [L]
Pris·cil·la \prə-'sil-ə\ [L]
Pru·dence \'prüd-ᵊn(t)s\ [E] prudence

Ra·chel \'rā-chəl\ [Heb] ewe
Rae \'rā\ dim of RACHEL
Ra·mo·na \rə-'mō-nə\ [Sp] fem of RAMON
Re·ba \'rē-bə\ dim of REBECCA
Re·bec·ca \ri-'bek-ə\ [Heb]
Re·gi·na \ri-'jē-nə, -'jī-\ [L] queen
Re·na \'rē-nə\
Re·nee \rə-'nā, 'ren-(,)ā, 'rā-nē, 'rē-nē\ [F, fr. L] reborn
Rhea \'rē-ə\ [Gk]
Rho·da \'rōd-ə\ [Gk] rose
Ri·ta \'rēt-ə\ dim of MARGARET
Ro·ber·ta \rə-'bərt-ə, rō-\ fem of ROBERT
Rob·in or **Rob·yn** \'räb-ən\ [E] robin
Ro·chelle \rō-'shel\ [prob. fr. a surname]
Ro·na or **Rho·na** \'rō-nə\
Ron·da \'rän-də\ var of RHONDA
Ron·nie \'rän-ē\ dim of VERONICA
Ro·sa·lie \'rō-zə-,(,)lē, 'räz-ə-\ [L] festival of roses
Ro·sa·lind \'räz-(ə-)lənd, 'rō-zə-lənd\ [Sp, prob. fr. Gmc]
Rose \'rōz\ or **Ro·sa** \'rō-zə\ [L] rose
Rose·anne \rō-'zan\ [Rose + Anne]

Rose·mary \'rōz-,mer-ē\ or **Rose·ma·rie** \,rōz-mə-'rē\ [E] rosemary
Ro·set·ta \rō-'zet-ə\ dim of ROSE
Ros·lyn \'räz-lən\ or **Ro·sa·lyn** or **Ro·se·lyn** \'räz-(ə-)lən, 'rō-zə-lən\ var of ROSALIND
Ro·we·na \rə-'wē-nə\ [perh. fr. OE]
Rox·ane \räk-'san\ [OPer]
Ru·by \'rü-bē\ [E] ruby
Ruth \'rüth\ [Heb]
Ruth·ann \rü-'than\ [Ruth + Ann]

Sa·bra \'sā-brə\ dim of SABRINA
Sa·die \'sād-ē\ dim of SARA
Sal·ly or **Sal·lie** \'sal-ē\ dim of SARA
San·dra \'san-drə, 'sän-\ dim of ALEXANDRA
Sar·ah or **Sara** \'ser-ə, 'sar-ə, 'sā-rə\ [Heb] princess
Sara·lee \'ser-ə-(,)lē, 'sar-\ [prob. fr. Sara + Lee]
Saun·dra \'sòn-drə, 'sän-\ var of SANDRA
Sel·ma \'sel-mə\ [Sw] fem dim of ANSELM
Shari \'sha(ə)r-ē, 'she(ə)r-\ dim of SHARON
Shar·lene \shär-'lēn\ var of CHARLENE
Shar·on or **Shar·ron** \'shar-ən, 'sher-\ [Heb] prob plain n
Shei·la \'shē-lə\ [IrGael] var of CECILIA
She·lia \'shēl-yə\ var of SHEILA
Shel·ley \'shel-ē\ [fr. a surname]
Sher·rill or **Sher·yl** \'sher-əl\ [prob. fr. a surname]
Sher·ry or **Sher·rie** or **Sheri** \'sher-ē\
Shir·ley \'shər-lē\ [fr. a surname]
Sig·rid \'sig-rəd\ [Scand] beautiful as victory
Son·dra \'sän-drə\ var of SANDRA
So·nia or **So·nya** or **So·nja** \'sō-nyə, 'sò-\ [Russ] dim of SOPHIA
So·phia \sə-'fē-ə, -'fī-\ or **So·phie** \'sō-fē\ [Gk] wisdom F Sophie
Stel·la \'stel-ə\ [L] star F Estelle
Steph·a·nie \'stef-ə-nē\ fem of STEPHEN F Stéphanie
Sue \'sü\ or **Su·sie** \'sü-zē\ dim of SUSAN
Su·el·len \sü-'el-ən\ [Sue + Ellen]
Su·san or **Su·zan** \'süz-ᵊn\ dim of SUSANNA
Su·san·na or **Su·san·nah** \sü-'zan-ə\ [Heb] lily F Suzanne
Su·zanne or **Su·sanne** or **Su·zann** \sü-'zan\ [F] var of SUSAN
Syb·il \'sib-əl\ [Gk] sibyl
Syl·via \'sil-vē-ə\ [L] she of the forest

Ta·mara \tə-'mar-ə\ [prob. fr. Georgian]
Tan·ya \'tan-yə\ [Russ] dim of TATIANA
Te·re·sa \tə-'rē-sə\ var of THERESA
Ter·ry or **Ter·ri** \'ter-ē\ dim of THERESA
Thel·ma \'thel-mə\
The·o·do·ra \,thē-ə-'dōr-ə, -'dòr-\ [LGk] fem of THEODORE
The·re·sa or **Te·re·sa** \tə-'rē-sə\ [LL] F Thérèse, It & Sp Teresa
The·rese \tə-'rēs\ var of THERESA
Ti·na \'tē-nə\ dim of -TINA
To·by \'tō-bē\
To·ni \'tō-nē\ dim of ANTONIA
Tru·dy \'trüd-ē\ dim of GERTRUDE

Ur·su·la \'ər-sə-lə\ [LL] little she-bear

Val·er·ie \'val-ə-rē\ [L] prob strong
Vel·ma \'vel-mə\
Ve·ra \'vir-ə\ [Russ] faith
Ver·na \'vər-nə\ prob fem of VERNON
Ve·ron·i·ca \və-'rän-i-kə\ [LL]
Vicki or **Vicky** or **Vick·ie** \'vik-ē\ dim of VICTORIA
Vic·to·ria \vik-'tōr-ē-ə, -'tòr-\ [L] victory F Victoire
Vi·da \'vēd-ə, 'vīd-\ fem dim of DAVID
Vi·o·la \vī-'ō-lə, vē-'ō-, 'vī-ə-, 'vē-ə-\ [L] violet
Vi·o·let \'vī-ə-lət\ [OF, fr. L] violet
Vir·gin·ia \vər-'jin-yə, -'jin-ē-ə\ [L] F Virginie
Viv·i·an \'viv-ē-ən\ [LL] F Vivienne

Wan·da \'wän-də\ [Pol]
Wen·dy \'wen-dē\
Wil·da \'wil-də\ var of WILLA
Wil·la \'wil-ə\ or **Wil·lie** \'wil-ē\ prob fem dim of WILLIAM
Wil·ma \'wil-mə\ prob fem dim of WILLIAM
Win·i·fred \'win-ə-frəd\ [W]

Yvette \i-'vet\ [F]
Yvonne \i-'vän\ [F]

Zel·da \'zel-də\ dim of GRISELDA

VOCABULARY OF RHYMES

This vocabulary of rhymes lists only words and pronunciations that are in current good use and are in keeping with the practice of poets who observe traditional rules of rhyming. Obsolete and nonstandard words and pronunciations are not recognized. A few foreign words of frequent occurrence in English speech and writing have been entered. As a rule rhymes "to the eye", as *bough* and *though*, are not given.

There are two common forms of rhymes: rhymes of monosyllables or of final accented syllables (called *single* or *masculine* rhymes); rhymes of two syllables the first of which is accented (called *double* or *feminine* rhymes), as *pastor*, *faster*, *aiding*, *fading*. Single or masculine rhymes are the only ones listed in this vocabulary.

The rhymes are listed by their sounds, except that cross-references are given for the terminal spelling of all words rhyming in \ə\. See the Merriam-Webster pronunciation symbols on the inside covers of this book. The entries beginning with \ə\ come first. The primary stress mark before this character is to be understood as indicating also the secondary stress, as \'ət *or* ˌət\. Entries in \au̇\ follow \ä\; \ŋ\ follows \n\, \ȯi\ follows \ȯz\, and \th\ follows \th\.

\'əb\ chub, club, cub, drub, dub, grub, hub, rub, scrub, shrub, snub, stub, tub; hubbub; sillabub

\'əch\ clutch, crutch, hutch, much, smutch, such, touch

\'əd\ blood, bud, cud, dud, flood, mud, scud, spud, stud, thud

\'əf\ bluff, buff, chough, cuff, duff, fluff, gruff, huff, luff, muff, puff, rough, ruff, scruff, scuff, slough, snuff, sough, stuff, tough; enough, rebuff; overstuff

\'əft\ tuft; *also pasts of verbs in* \əf\, *as* bluffed, sloughed

\'əg\ bug, drug, dug, hug, jug, lug, mug, plug, pug, rug, shrug, slug, smug, snug, thug, tug

\'əj\ budge, drudge, fudge, grudge, judge, nudge, sludge, smudge, trudge; adjudge, begrudge, misjudge

\'ək\ buck, chuck, cluck, duck, luck, muck, pluck, puck, ruck, shuck, struck, stuck, suck, truck, tuck; amuck

\'əks\ crux, flux, tux; *also plurals and possessives of nouns and 3d sing presents of verbs in* \ək\, *as* ducks, trucks

\'əkt\ duct; abduct, conduct, construct, deduct, induct, instruct, obstruct; aqueduct, viaduct; *also pasts of verbs in* \ək\, *as* plucked

\'əl\ cull, dull, gull, hull, lull, mull, null, scull, skull, trull; annul, mogul; disannul

\'əlch\ gulch, mulch

\'əlj\ bulge; divulge, effulge, indulge, promulge

\'əlk\ bulk, hulk, skulk, sulk

\'əlp\ gulp, pulp, sculp

\'əls\ pulse; appulse, convulse, repulse

\'əlt\ cult; adult, consult, exult, insult, occult, result; catapult, difficult

\'əm\ chum, come, crumb, drum, dumb, glum, grum, gum, hum, mum, numb, plum, plumb, rum, scum, slum, some, strum, stum, sum, swum, thrum, thumb; become, benumb, succumb; *also antepenult-stressed words having in or as the ultima ordinarily unstressed* \əm\, *as* cumbersome, martyrdom, medium

\'əmp\ bump, chump, clump, dump, hump, jump, lump, plump, pump, rump, slump, stump, thump, trump

\'ən\ bun, done, dun, fun, gun, none, nun, one, pun, run, son, spun, stun, sun, ton, tun, won; begun, outrun, undone

\'ənch\ bunch, crunch, hunch, lunch, munch, punch, scrunch

\'ənd\ bund, fund; obtund, refund, rotund; moribund, orotund, rubicund; *also pasts of verbs in* \ən\, *as* punned

\'ənj\ lunge, plunge, sponge; expunge

\'əns, 'ənts\ dunce, once; *also plurals and possessives of nouns and 3d sing presents of verbs in* \ənt\, *as* hunts

\'ənt\ blunt, brunt, bunt, front, grunt, hunt, runt, shunt, stunt

\'əŋ\ bung, clung, dung, flung, hung, lung, rung, slung, sprung, strung, stung, sung, swung, tongue, wrung, young; among, unstrung, unsung

\'əŋk\ bunk, chunk, drunk, dunk, funk, gunk, hunk, junk, monk, punk, shrunk, skunk, slunk, spunk, sunk, trunk

\'əŋkt, 'əŋt\ defunct, disjunct; *also pasts of verbs in* \əŋk\, *as* funked

\'əp\ cup, pup, scup, sup, up

\'əpt\ cupped, supped, upped; abrupt, corrupt, disrupt, erupt; interrupt

\'ər\ blur, bur, cur, err, fir, fur, her, myrrh, per, purr, shirr, sir, slur, spur, stir, were, whir; aver, bestir, chasseur, chauffeur, concur, confer, defer, demur, deter, hauteur, incur, infer, inter, occur, prefer, recur, refer, transfer; amateur, arbiter, chorister, connoisseur, harbinger, presbyter, sepulcher, voyageur; administer, idolater; *also comparatives of adjectives and agent nouns accented on the antepenult, as* cosier, kindlier, flatterer

\'ərb\ curb, herb, verb; acerb, disturb, perturb, superb

\'ərch\ birch, church, lurch, perch, search, smirch; research

\'ərd\ bird, curd, gird, heard, herd, surd, third, word; *also pasts of many verbs in* \ər\, *as* averred, bestirred, demurred

\'ərf\ scurf, serf, surf, turf

\'ərg\ berg, burgh; exergue, iceberg

\'ərj\ dirge, merge, purge, scourge, serge, spurge, surge, urge, verge; converge, diverge, emerge, immerge, submerge; demiurge

\'ərk\ clerk, dirk, irk, jerk, kirk, lurk, murk, perk, quirk, shirk, smirk, work

\'ərl, 'ər-əl\ burl, churl, curl, earl, furl, girl, hurl, knurl, pearl, purl, squirrel, swirl, twirl, whirl; uncurl, unfurl

\'ərld, 'ər-əld\ curled, furled, hurled, swirled, world

\'ərm\ berm, firm, germ, squirm, term, worm; affirm, confirm, infirm; pachyderm

\'ərn\ burn, churn, earn, fern, kern, learn, spurn, tern, turn, urn, yearn; adjourn, concern, discern, return, sojourn

\'ərnt\ burnt, learnt, weren't

\'ərp\ burp, chirp, slurp; usurp

\'ərs\ burse, curse, hearse, nurse, purse, terse, verse, worse; accurse, adverse, asperse, averse, coerce, converse, disburse, disperse, diverse, imburse, immerse, inverse, perverse, rehearse, reverse, transverse; intersperse, universe

\'ərst\ burst, durst, first, thirst, versed, worst; accurst, athirst; *also pasts of verbs in* \ərs\, *as* coerced, nursed

\'ərt\ blurt, curt, dirt, flirt, girt, hurt, pert, shirt, spurt, squirt; advert, alert, assert, avert, concert, convert, desert, dessert, divert, exert, expert, inert, insert, invert, pervert, revert, subvert

\'ərth\ berth, birth, dearth, earth, firth, girth, mirth, worth

\'ərv\ curve, nerve, serve, swerve, verve; conserve, deserve, observe, preserve, reserve, unnerve

\'əs\ bus, buss, cuss, fuss, muss, plus, pus, truss, us; discuss; blunderbuss, omnibus; *also antepenult-stressed words having in or as the ultima ordinarily unstressed* \əs\, *as* fabulous, impetus

\'əsh\ blush, brush, crush, flush, gush, hush, lush, mush, plush, rush, slush, thrush, tush

\'əsk\ brusque, cusk, dusk, husk, musk, rusk, tusk

\'əst\ bust, crust, dust, gust, joust, just, lust, must, rust, thrust, trust; adjust, adust, august, disgust, distrust, intrust, mistrust, robust, unjust; *also pasts of verbs in* \əs\, *as* discussed, trussed

\'ət\ but, butt, cut, glut, gut, hut, jut, mutt, nut, putt, rut, shut, slut, smut, soot, strut, tut; abut, rebut, uncut

\'əv\ dove, glove, love, shove; above, belove, unglove; turtledove

\'əz\ buzz, does, fuzz

\ā\ aye, bay, bray, clay, day, dray, eh, fay, fey, flay, fray, gay, gray, hay, jay, lay, may, nay, neigh, pay, play, pray, prey, quay, ray, say, slay, sleigh, spay, splay, spray, stay, stray, sway, trait, tray, trey, way, weigh, whey; affray, allay, array, assay, astray, away, belay, betray, bewray, bouquet, convey, croquet, decay, defray, delay, dismay, display, essay, gainsay, inlay, inveigh, mislay, obey, portray, purvey, relay, repay, risqué, sachet, survey, waylay; émigré, matinee, negligee, protégé, roundelay, virelay

\ä\ ah, bah, ha, ma, pa, shah, spa; hurrah

\ab\ blab, cab, crab, dab, drab, gab, grab, jab, lab, nab, scab, slab, stab, tab

\āb\ babe; astrolabe

\äb\ blob, bob, cob, fob, gob, hob, job, knob, lob, mob, rob, snob, sob, squab, swab, throb

\ach\ batch, catch, hatch, latch, match, patch, scratch, snatch, thatch; attach, detach, dispatch

\äch\ blotch, botch, crotch, notch, scotch, splotch, watch

\ad\ add, bad, bade, brad, cad, clad, dad, fad, gad, glad, had, lad, mad, pad, plaid, sad, scad, shad; forbade

\ād\ aid, blade, braid, fade, glade, grade, jade, lade, laid, made, maid, raid, shade, spade, staid, suede, trade, wade; abrade, afraid, arcade, blockade, brigade, brocade, cascade, charade, cockade, crusade, degrade, dissuade, evade, forbade, grenade, invade, parade, persuade, pervade, stockade, tirade, upbraid; ambuscade, balustrade, barricade, cannonade, cavalcade, colonnade, enfilade, escalade, escapade, esplanade, fusillade, lemonade, marmalade, masquerade, palisade, promenade, renegade, retrograde, serenade; harlequinade, rodomontade; *also, pasts of verbs in* \ā\, *as* played, obeyed, weighed

\äd\ clod, cod, god, hod, nod, odd, plod, pod, prod, quad, rod, shod, sod, squad, trod, wad; demigod, goldenrod

\äd, ȧd\ ballade, facade, roulade; accolade, promenade

\af, ȧf\ calf, chaff, gaff, graph, half, laugh, quaff, staff; behalf, carafe, giraffe; autograph, cenotaph, epitaph, lithograph, monograph, paragraph, phonograph, photograph, telegraph

\āf\ chafe, safe, waif; vouchsafe

\äf, ȧf\ see \ȯf\

\aft, ȧft\ aft, craft, daft, draft, draught, graft, haft, raft, shaft, waft; abaft, aircraft, ingraft; handicraft, overdraft; *also, pasts of verbs in* \af, ȧf\, *as* chaffed, quaffed

\ag\ bag, brag, crag, drag, fag, flag, gag, hag, jag, lag, nag, rag, sag, scrag, shag, slag, snag, stag, swag, tag, wag; ragtag, wigwag, zigzag; bullyrag, scalawag

\āg\ egg, leg, plague, vague

\äg\ see \ȯg\

\āj\ badge, cadge

\āj\ age, cage, gauge, page, rage, sage, stage, swage, wage; assuage, engage, enrage, outrage, presage; disengage

\äj\ dodge, lodge, stodge; garage, hodgepodge

\ak\ back, black, clack, claque, crack, hack, jack, knack, lack, pack, plaque, quack, rack, sac, sack, shack, slack, smack, snack, stack, tack, thwack, track, whack, wrack; aback, ack-ack, alack, attack, bivouac, gimcrack, knickknack, ransack, shellac, ticktack; almanac, bric-a-brac, cardiac, cul-de-sac; demoniac, symposiac

\āk\ ache, bake, brake, break, cake, drake, fake, flake, hake, lake, make, quake, rake, sake, shake, slake, snake, spake, stake, steak, strake, take, wake; betake, forsake,

---

1182

mistake, opaque, partake; overtake, undertake

\äk block, clock, cock, crock, dock, flock, frock, hock, knock, lock, mock, pock, rock, shock, smock, sock, stock; unlock

\aks ax, flax, lax, tax, wax; relax; battle-ax, parallax; *also plurals and possessives of nouns and 3d sing presents of verbs in* \ak\, *as* backs, lacks, packs

\äks box, fox, ox, phlox; equinox, orthodox, paradox; heterodox; *also plurals and possessives of nouns and 3d sing presents of verbs in* \äk\, *as* locks, stocks

\akt act, bract, fact, pact, tact, tract; abstract, attract, compact, contract, detract, diffract, distract, enact, entr'acte, exact, extract, impact, infract, intact, protract, react, redact, refract, retract, subtract, transact; cataract, counteract, re-enact, retroact; *also pasts of verbs in* \ak\, *as* backed, hacked

\äkt concoct, decoct; *also pasts of verbs in* \äk\, *as* blocked, locked

\al banal, cabal, canal, corral, locale, morale, timbale; musicale

\āl, āəl ail, ale, bail, bale, dale, fail, flail, frail, gale, grail, hail, hale, jail, kale, mail, male, nail, pail, pale, quail, rail, sail, sale, scale, snail, stale, swale, tail, tale, trail, vale, veil, wail, wale, whale; assail, avail, bewail, curtail, detail, entail, exhale, impale, inhale, prevail, regale, retail, travail, unveil; betrayal, countervail, defrayal, nightingale, portrayal

\äl doll, loll; banal, extol; folderol, protocol

\alp alp, palp, scalp

\älv, ȯlv solve; absolve, convolve, devolve, dissolve, evolve, involve, resolve, revolve

\am am, cam, clam, cram, dam, damn, dram, gram, ham, jam, jamb, lam, lamb, ram, scram, sham, slam, swam, tram, yam; anagram, cablegram, diagram, diaphragm, dithyramb, epigram, monogram, telegram; radiogram

\ām aim, blame, came, claim, dame, fame, flame, frame, game, lame, maim, name, same, shame, tame; acclaim, became, declaim, defame, exclaim, inflame, misname, nickname, proclaim, reclaim, surname; overcame

\äm bomb, from, tom

\äm, ȧm balm, calm, palm, psalm, qualm; embalm, salaam

\amp camp, champ, clamp, cramp, damp, guimpe, lamp, ramp, scamp, stamp, tamp, tramp, vamp; decamp, encamp

\ämp pomp, romp, swamp

\ämpt prompt, romped, swamped

\an ban, bran, can, clan, fan, man, pan, plan, ran, scan, span, tan, van; began, divan, japan, pecan, rattan, sedan, trepan, unman; caravan

\ān bane, brain, cane, chain, crane, deign, drain, feign, gain, grain, lain, lane, main, mane, pain, pane, plain, plane, rain, reign, rein, sane, skein, slain, sprain, stain, strain, swain, thane, train, twain, vain, vane, vein, wane; abstain, airplane, amain, arraign, attain, campaign, champagne, chilblain, complain, constrain, contain, demesne, detain, disdain, distrain, domain, enchain, explain, germane, humane, inane, insane, maintain, obtain, ordain, pertain, profane, refrain, regain, remain, restrain, retain, sustain, urbane; appertain, ascertain, chatelaine, counterpane, entertain, hurricane

\än gone, on, shone, swan, wan; anon, begone, pecan, upon; paragon; phenomenon

\anch, ȧnch blanch, branch, ranch, stanch; avalanche

\änch see \ȯnch\

\and band, bland, brand, gland, grand, hand, land, rand, sand, stand, strand; command, demand, disband, expand, remand, withstand; contraband, countermand, reprimand, saraband, understand; *also pasts of verbs in* \an\, *as* planned

\änd blond, bond, fond, frond, pond, wand, yond; abscond, beyond, despond, respond; correspond, vagabond; *also pasts of verbs in* \än\, *as* conned, donned

\ānj change, grange, mange, range, strange; arrange, derange, estrange, exchange; disarrange, interchange

\ans, ants, ȧns, ȧnts chance, dance, glance, lance, manse, prance, trance; advance, askance, enhance, entrance, expanse, finance, mischance, perchance, romance; circumstance; *also 3d sing presents of verbs in* \ant, ȧnt\, *as* plants

\äns, änts nonce, sconce, ensconce, response; *also plurals and possessives of nouns and 3d sing presents of verbs in* \änt\, *as* wants

\ant, ȧnt ant, aunt, cant, chant, grant, pant, plant, rant, scant, slant; aslant, decant, descant, displant, enchant, gallant, implant, recant, supplant, transplant; commandant

\ānt faint, feint, paint, plaint, quaint, saint, taint; acquaint, attaint, complaint, constraint, distraint, restraint

\änt daunt, flaunt, font, gaunt, haunt, jaunt, taunt, vaunt, want; see also \ȯnt\

\aŋ bang, clang, fang, gang, hang, pang, rang, sang, slang, sprang, tang, whang; harangue, meringue; boomerang

\äŋ gong, prong; sarong; *also words at* \ȯŋ\

\aŋk bank, blank, clank, crank, dank, drank, flank, frank, hank, lank, plank, prank, rank, sank, shank, shrank, spank, stank, swank, tank, thank, yank; disrank, embank, outflank, outrank

\äŋk, ȯŋk conch, honk

\ap cap, chap, clap, flap, gap, hap, lap, map, nap, pap, rap, sap, scrap, slap, snap, strap, tap, trap, wrap; entrap, enwrap, mishap, unwrap

\āp ape, cape, chape, crepe, drape, grape, jape, nape, rape, scrape, shape, tape; agape, escape, shipshape

\äp bop, chop, cop, crop, drop, flop, fop, hop, lop, mop, prop, shop, slop, sop, stop, strop, swap, top; airdrop, eavesdrop; overstop

\aps apse, craps, lapse; collapse, elapse, perhaps, relapse; *also plurals and possessives of nouns and 3d sing presents of verbs in* \ap\, *as* caps, laps, saps

\apt apt, rapt, wrapt; adapt; *also pasts of verbs in* \ap\, *as* slapped, tapped

\äpt adopt; *pasts of verbs in* \äp\, *as* hopped, lopped

\ar, er, a(ə)r, e(ə)r air, bare, bear, blare, care, chair, dare, e'er, ere, fair, fare, flair, flare, glair, glare, hair, hare, heir, lair, mare, ne'er, pair, pare, pear, prayer, rare, scare, share, snare, spare, square, stair, stare, swear, tare, tear, their, there, ware, wear, where; affair, aware, beware, compare, declare, despair, ensnare, forbear, forswear, howe'er, impair, prepare, repair, whate'er, whene'er, where'er; debonair, doctrinaire, millionaire

\är bar, car, char, far, jar, mar, par, scar, spar, star, tar, tsar; afar, bazaar, bizarre, catarrh, debar, devoir, disbar, guitar, hussar, lascar; avatar, caviar, registrar, reservoir, samovar, seminar

\ärb barb, garb

\ärch arch, larch, march, parch, starch

\ärd bard, card, chard, guard, hard, lard, shard, yard; bombard, canard, discard, petard, placard, regard, retard; boulevard, disregard, interlard; *also pasts of verbs in* \är\, *as* barred, scarred

\ärj barge, charge, large; discharge, enlarge, surcharge

\ärk arc, ark, bark, cark, dark, hark, lark, mark, park, shark, spark, stark; debark, embark, remark; hierarch, matriarch, patriarch

\ärl gnarl, quarrel, snarl

\ärm arm, barm, charm, farm, harm; alarm, disarm, gendarme, unarm

\arn, ern, a(ə)rn, e(ə)rn bairn, cairn

\ärn barn, darn, yarn

\ärp carp, harp, scarp, sharp; escarp; counterscarp

\ärs, ȧrs farce, parse, sparse

\ärsh harsh, marsh

\ärt art, cart, chart, dart, heart, mart, part, smart, start, tart; apart, depart, dispart, impart, sweetheart, upstart

\ärv carve, starve

\arz, erz, a(ə)rz, e(ə)rz theirs; unawares; *also plurals and possessives of nouns and 3d sing presents of verbs in* \a(ə)r, e(ə)r\, *as* cares, pairs, bears, heirs

\as, ȧs ass, bass, brass, class, gas, glass, grass, lass, mass, pass; alas, amass, crevasse, cuirass, morass, repass, surpass; sassafras

\ās ace, base, bass, brace, case, chase, dace, face, grace, lace, mace, pace, place, race, space, trace, vase; abase, apace, debase, deface, disgrace, displace, efface, embrace, encase, erase, footpace, grimace, misplace, outface, outpace, replace, retrace, ukase; commonplace, interlace, interspace

\äs see \ȯs\

\ash ash, bash, brash, cache, cash, clash, crash, dash, flash, gash, gnash, hash, lash, mash, plash, rash, sash, slash, smash, thrash, trash; abash, calash; balderdash, calabash

\äsh quash, squash, swash, wash; awash, galosh; mackintosh

\ask, ȧsk ask, bask, cask, flask, mask, masque, task; unmask

\äsk mosque; kiosk

\asp, ȧsp asp, clasp, gasp, grasp, hasp, rasp; enclasp, unclasp

\ast, ȧst bast, blast, cast, caste, fast, last, mast, past, vast; aghast, broadcast, contrast, forecast, outcast, repast; overcast; *also pasts of verbs in* \as, ȧs\, *as* amassed

\āst baste, chaste, haste, paste, taste, waist, waste; distaste; *also pasts of verbs in* \ās\, *as* faced, placed

\äst see \ȯst\

\at at, bat, brat, cat, chat, fat, flat, gnat, hat, mat, pat, plat, rat, sat, slat, spat, sprat, tat, that, vat; cravat, thereat, whereat

\āt bait, bate, crate, date, eight, fate, fete, freight, gait, gate, grate, great, hate, late, mate, pate, plait, plate, prate, quoit, rate, sate, skate, slate, state, straight, strait, trait, wait, weight; abate, await, belate, collate, create, debate, dilate, elate, estate, inflate, ingrate, innate, irate, rebate, relate, sedate, translate; abdicate, advocate, aggravate, agitate, animate, antiquate, arbitrate, calculate, candidate, captivate, celebrate, circulate, congregate, consecrate, cultivate, dedicate, delegate, deprecate, derogate, dissipate, educate, elevate, emulate, estimate, extricate, generate, hesitate, imitate, imprecate, innovate, instigate, intimate, irritate, laureate, liberate, lubricate, magistrate, mediate, mitigate, moderate, nominate, opiate, penetrate, perpetrate, potentate, profligate, propagate, radiate, regulate, reprobate, segregate, separate, simulate, stimulate, stipulate, subjugate, suffocate, supplicate, terminate, tolerate, venerate, vindicate, violate; abominate, accelerate, accommodate, accumulate, adulterate, annihilate, anticipate, articulate, assassinate, capacitate, capitulate, commemorate, commiserate, communicate, compassionate, congratulate, contaminate, degenerate, denominate, desegregate, discriminate, evaporate, exaggerate, exasperate, facilitate, illuminate, intimidate, intoxicate, invalidate, inviolate, matriculate, participate, pontificate, precipitate, predestinate, predominate, premeditate, prevaricate, regenerate, reiterate, rejuvenate

\ät blot, clot, cot, dot, got, hot, jot, knot, lot, not, plot, pot, rot, shot, slot, sot, spot, squat, tot, trot, what, yacht; allot, besot, forgot, gavotte, unknot; polyglot

\ath, ȧth bath, hath, lath, path, snath, wrath; aftermath, allopath

\āth faith, wraith

\äth swath, wrath; see \ath\

\āt͟h bathe, lathe, scathe, swathe; enswathe, unswathe

\au̇ bough, bow, brow, cow, how, mow, now, plow, prow, row, scow, slough, sow, thou, vow; allow, avow, endow, kotow

\au̇ch couch, crouch, grouch, ouch, pouch, slouch, vouch; avouch

\au̇d cloud, crowd, loud, proud, shroud; aloud, becloud, enshroud; *also pasts of verbs in* \au̇\, *as* bowed

\au̇l cowl, foul, fowl, growl, howl, jowl, owl, prowl, scowl, yowl; befoul

\au̇n brown, clown, crown, down, drown, frown, gown, noun, town; embrown, renown

\au̇nd bound, found, ground, hound, mound, pound, round, sound, wound; abound, aground, astound, compound, confound, expound, profound, propound, rebound, redound, resound, surround; *also pasts of verbs in* \au̇n\, *as* frowned

\au̇ns, au̇nts bounce, flounce, ounce, pounce, trounce; announce, denounce, pronounce, renounce; *also plurals and possessives of nouns and 3d sing presents of verbs in* \au̇nt\, *as* counts

\au̇nt count, fount, mount; account, amount, discount, dismount, miscount, recount, remount, surmount; catamount, paramount, tantamount

\au̇r, au̇(ə)r flour, hour, our, scour, sour; devour; *also words ending in* -ower, *as* bower, cower, flower, glower, lower, power, shower, tower

\au̇rz, au̇(ə)rz ours; *also plurals and possessives of nouns, and 3d sing presents of verbs in* \au̇(ə)r, au̇(-ə)r\, *as* hours, scours, bowers, showers

\au̇s blouse, douse, grouse, house, louse, mouse, souse, spouse; espouse

\au̇st oust, joust; *also pasts of verbs in* \au̇s\, *as* loused, soused

\au̇t bout, clout, doubt, drought, flout, gout, grout, knout, lout, out, pout, rout, route, scout, shout, snout, spout, sprout, stout, tout, trout; about, devout, redoubt, without

\au̇th drouth, mouth, south

\au̇t͟h mouth, south

\au̇z blouse, browse, drowse, house, mouse, rouse, spouse; arouse, carouse, espouse; *also plurals and possessives of nouns and 3d sing presents of verbs in* \au̇\, *as* brows, plows

\av, ȧv calve, halve, salve

\āv brave, cave, crave, gave, grave, knave, lave, nave, pave, rave, save, shave, slave, stave, waive, wave; behave, concave, deprave, engrave, enslave, forgave, misgave; architrave

\āz blaze, braise, braze, chaise, craze, daze, faze, gaze, glaze, graze, haze, maze, phrase, praise, raise, raze; ablaze, amaze, dispraise; chrysoprase, paraphrase; *also plurals and possessives of nouns and 3d sing presents of verbs in* \ā\, *as* days, inveighs, obeys

\azəm, azm chasm, spasm; cataplasm, protoplasm; enthusiasm, iconoclasm

\äzh, ȧzh barrage, corsage, garage, menage, mirage; badinage, persiflage

\ē\ be, bee, fee, flea, flee, free, glee, he, key, knee, lea, lee, me, pea, plea, quay, sea, see, she, spree, tea, tee, thee, three, tree, we; agree, debris, decree, degree, foresee; absentee, coterie, jubilee, pedigree, referee, refugee; *also antepenult-stressed words having in* or *as the ultima ordinarily unstressed* \i\, *as* melody
-earch see \erch\
-eard see \ord\
-earl see \orl\
-earn see \orn\
-earnt see \ornt\
-earse see \ors\
-earth see \orth\
\eb\ ebb, web
\ech\ etch, fetch, ketch, retch, sketch, stretch, vetch, wretch
\ēch\ beach, beech, bleach, breach, breech, each, leech, peach, preach, reach, screech, speech, teach; beseech, impeach
\ed\ bed, bled, bread, bred, dead, dread, fed, fled, head, lead, led, read, red, said, shed, shred, sled, sped, spread, stead, ted, thread, tread, wed; abed, behead, inbred, instead, misled
\ēd\ bead, bleed, breed, cede, creed, deed, feed, freed, greed, heed, knead, lead, mead, need, plead, read, reed, seed, speed, steed, tweed, weed; concede, exceed, impede, indeed, precede, proceed, recede, stampede, succeed; intercede, supersede
\ef\ chef, clef, deaf
\ēf\ beef, brief, chief, fief, grief, leaf, lief, reef, sheaf, thief; belief, relief; disbelief, unbelief
\eft\ cleft, deft, heft, left, reft, theft, weft; bereft
\eg\ beg, dreg, egg, keg, leg, peg, skeg; renege
\ēg\ klieg, league; colleague, enleague, fatigue, intrigue
\ej\ dredge, edge, fledge, hedge, ledge, pledge, sedge, sledge, wedge; allege, sacrilege, sortilege
\ēj\ liege, siege; besiege
\ek\ beck, check, deck, fleck, neck, peck, speck, trek, wreck
\ēk\ beak, bleak, cheek, clique, creak, creek, freak, leak, leek, meek, peak, pique, reek, seek, shriek, sleek, sneak, speak, squeak, streak, teak, tweak, weak, week, wreak; antique, critique, oblique, physique, unique
\eks\ flex, sex, vex; annex, complex, convex, perplex; circumflex; *also plurals and possessives of nouns and 3d sing presents of verbs in* \ek\, *as* checks, decks, wrecks
\ekst\ next, text; pretext; *also pasts of verbs in* \eks\, *as* annexed, vexed
\ekt\ sect; abject, affect, collect, connect, correct, defect, deflect, deject, detect, direct, dissect, effect, eject, elect, erect, expect, infect, inject, inspect, neglect, object, project, protect, reflect, reject, respect, select, subject, suspect; architect, circumspect, dialect, intellect, intersect, recollect; *also pasts of verbs in* \ek\, *as* checked, decked
\el\ bell, belle, cell, dell, dwell, ell, fell, hell, knell, quell, sell, shell, smell, spell, swell, tell, well, yell; befell, compel, dispel, excel, expel, foretell, gazelle, impel, rebel, repel; asphodel, bagatelle, citadel, demoiselle, hydromel, parallel, philomel
\ēl\ deal, eel, feel, heal, heel, keel, kneel, meal, peal, peel, reel, seal, squeal, steal, steel, teal, veal, weal, wheel, zeal; anneal, appeal, conceal, congeal, genteel, repeal, reveal
\eld\ geld, held, meld, weld; beheld, upheld, withheld; *also pasts of verbs in* \el\, *as* felled, swelled
\ēld\ field, shield, wield, yield; afield; *also pasts of verbs in* \ēl\, *as* healed, sealed
\elf\ elf, pelf, self, shelf
\elk\ elk, whelk
\elm\ elm, helm, realm, whelm; overwhelm
\elp\ help, kelp, whelp, yelp
\elt\ belt, dealt, dwelt, felt, knelt, melt, pelt, smelt, spelt, svelte, welt
\elth\ health, stealth, wealth; commonwealth
\elv\ delve, helve, shelve, twelve
\elvz\ *plurals and possessives of nouns in* \elf, elv\, *as* shelves, twelves
\em\ em, gem, hem, phlegm, stem, them; begem, condemn, contemn; apothegm, diadem
\ēm\ beam, bream, cream, deem, dream, gleam, ream, scheme, scream, seam, seem, steam, stream, team, teem, theme; blaspheme, esteem, extreme, redeem, supreme
\emt, empt\ dreamt, tempt; attempt, contempt, exempt, preempt, unkempt
\en\ den, fen, glen, hen, ken, men, pen, ten, then, wen, when, wren, yen; again; regimen
\ēn\ bean, clean, dean, glean, green, keen, lean, lien, mean, mien, preen, queen, scene, screen, seen, sheen, spleen, wean; baleen, between, canteen, careen, convene, cuisine, demean, demesne, foreseen, machine, marine, obscene, ravine, routine, sardine, serene, subvene, tontine, unclean; submarine

\ench\ bench, blench, clench, drench, quench, stench, tench, trench, wench, wrench; intrench, retrench
\end\ bend, blend, end, fend, friend, lend, mend, rend, send, spend, tend, trend, vend, wend; amend, ascend, attend, befriend, commend, contend, defend, depend, descend, distend, emend, expend, extend, forefend, impend, intend, offend, portend, pretend, suspend, transcend, unbend; apprehend, comprehend, condescend, dividend, recommend, reprehend; *also pasts of verbs in* \en\, *as* kenned, penned
\ēnd\ fiend; *also pasts of verbs in* \ēn\, *as* gleaned, weaned
\endz, enz\ cleanse, lens; amends; *also plurals and possessives of nouns and 3d sing presents of verbs in* \en\ *and* \end\, *as* friends, pens, sends
\enj\ avenge, revenge
\ens, ents\ dense, fence, hence, pence, sense, tense, thence, whence; commence, condense, defense, dispense, expense, immense, incense, intense, offense, pretense, suspense; abstinence, affluence, confidence, consequence, continence, difference, diffidence, diligence, eloquence, eminence, evidence, excellence, immanence, imminence, impotence, impudence, indigence, indolence, inference, influence, innocence, negligence, penitence, preference, providence, reference, reverence, sapience, violence, virulence; beneficence, benevolence, grandiloquence, inconsequence, intelligence, magnificence, munificence, obedience, omnipotence; *also plurals and possessives of nouns and 3d sing presents of verbs in* \ent\, *as* dents
\enst, entst\ against; *also pasts of verbs in* \en(t)s\, *as* commenced, sensed
\ent\ bent, blent, cent, dent, leant, lent, meant, pent, rent, scent, sent, spent, tent, vent, went; absent, ascent, assent, augment, cement, comment, consent, content, descent, dissent, event, extent, ferment, foment, frequent, indent, intent, invent, lament, misspent, portent, present, prevent, relent, repent, resent, torment, unbent, unspent; abstinent, aliment, argument, banishment, battlement, blandishment, chastisement, competent, complement, compliment, continent, detriment, different, diligent, document, element, eloquent, eminent, excellent, exigent, firmament, fraudulent, government, immanent, imminent, implement, impotent, impudent, indigent, innocent, insolent, instrument, languishment, management, monument, negligent, nourishment, nutriment, opulent, ornament, parliament, penitent, permanent, pertinent, precedent, prevalent, punishment, ravishment, redolent, regiment, reverent, rudiment, sacrament, sentiment, settlement, supplement, tenement, testament, vehement, violent, virulent, wonderment; acknowledgment, astonishment, belligerent, benevolent, impenitent, impertinent, imprisonment, intelligent, irreverent, magnificent
\enz\ see \endz\
\enth, enkth\ length, strength
\ep\ hep, pep, rep, step, steppe; footstep, misstep; demirep
\ēp\ cheap, cheep, creep, deep, heap, keep, leap, neap, peep, reap, seep, sheep, sleep, steep, sweep, weep; asleep
\ept\ crept, kept, slept, stepped, swept, wept; accept, adept, except, inept
-er see \or\
\er\ see \ar\
-erb see \orb\
-erch see \orch\
-erd see \ord\
-erf see \orf\
-erg see \org\
-erge see \orj\
-erk see \ork\
-erm see \orm\
-ern see \orn\
-err see \or\
-erse see \ors\
-ersed see \orst\
-ert see \ort\
-erth see \orth\
-erve see \orv\
\es\ bless, chess, cress, dress, guess, less, mess, press, stress, tress, yes; access, address, assess, caress, compress, confess, depress, digress, distress, egress, excess, express, finesse, impress, ingress, obsess, oppress, possess, profess, progress, recess, redress, repress, success, suppress, transgress, undress, unless; acquiesce, coalesce, convalesce, effervesce; *also many abstract nouns ending in* -ness, *as* sacredness
\ēs\ cease, crease, fleece, geese, grease, lease, niece, peace, piece; decease, decrease, increase, obese, police, release, surcease; frontispiece
\esh\ crèche, flesh, fresh, mesh, thresh; afresh, enmesh, immesh, refresh
\esk\ desk; burlesque, grotesque; arabesque, picaresque, picturesque, statuesque
\est\ best, blest, breast, chest, crest, guest,

jest, lest, nest, pest, quest, rest, test, vest, west, wrest, zest; abreast, attest, behest, bequest, congest, contest, detest, digest, divest, infest, invest, molest, protest, request, suggest, unblest, unrest; anapest, manifest; *also pasts of verbs in* \es\, *as* dressed, expressed
\ēst\ beast, east, feast, least, priest, yeast; artiste; *also pasts of verbs in* \ēs\, *as* ceased, increased
\et\ bet, debt, fret, get, jet, let, met, net, pet, set, stet, sweat, threat, wet, whet, yet; abet, aigrette, beget, beset, cadet, coquette, curvet, duet, forget, gazette, regret, rosette, soubrette, vignette; alphabet, amulet, annulet, bayonet, cigarette, coronet, epaulet, epithet, etiquette, mignonette, minaret, parapet, rivulet, silhouette
\ēt\ beat, bleat, cheat, eat, feat, feet, fleet, greet, heat, meat, meet, neat, peat, pleat, seat, sheet, sleet, street, suite, sweet, teat, treat, wheat; compete, complete, conceit, concrete, deceit, defeat, delete, deplete, discreet, effete, entreat, receipt, replete, retreat, secrete
\eth\ breath, death; *also archaic 3d sing presents of verbs, as* saith
\ēth\ heath, sheath, teeth, wreath; beneath, bequeath; underneath
\ēth\ breathe, seethe, sheathe, teethe, wreathe; bequeath, enwreathe
-eur see \or\
\ev\ breve, rev
\ēv\ breve, cleave, eve, grieve, heave, leave, peeve, sleeve, thieve, weave; achieve, aggrieve, believe, bereave, conceive, deceive, naïve, perceive, receive, relieve, reprieve, retrieve
\ēz\ breeze, cheese, ease, freeze, frieze, grease, lees, please, seize, sneeze, squeeze, tease, these, wheeze; appease, disease, displease; *also plurals and possessives of nouns and 3d sing presents of verbs in* \ē\, *as* frees, tees, teas
\ezh\ barege, cortege, manege
\ī\ aye, buy, by, cry, die, dry, dye, eye, fie, fly, fry, guy, hie, high, lie, lye, my, nigh, pie, ply, pry, rye, shy, sigh, sky, sly, spry, spy, sty, thigh, thy, tie, try, vie, why, wry; ally, apply, awry, belie, comply, decry, defy, deny, imply, outcry, rely, reply, supply, untie; amplify, beautify, butterfly, certify, crucify, dignify, edify, fortify, glorify, gratify, justify, lullaby, magnify, modify, mollify, multiply, occupy, pacify, prophesy, purify, qualify, ratify, rectify, salsify, sanctify, satisfy, signify, terrify, testify, verify
\ib\ bib, crib, fib, glib, jib, nib, rib, sib, squib
\īb\ bribe, gibe, scribe, tribe; ascribe, describe, imbibe, inscribe, prescribe, proscribe, subscribe, transcribe; circumscribe, diatribe
\ich\ bitch, ditch, fitch, flitch, hitch, itch, niche, pitch, rich, stitch, switch, twitch, which, witch; bewitch
\id\ bid, chid, did, grid, hid, kid, lid, mid, quid, rid, skid, slid, squid; amid, forbid, outbid, outdid, undid; pyramid, underbid
\īd\ bide, bride, chide, glide, guide, hide, pied, pride, ride, side, slide, stride, tide, wide; abide, aside, astride, beside, bestride, collide, confide, decide, deride, divide, elide, misguide, noontide, outside, preside, provide, reside, subside; fractricide, genocide, homicide, matricide, parricide, regicide, suicide; *also pasts of verbs in* \ī\, *as* died, sighed, replied
\īdz\ ides; besides; *also plurals and possessives of nouns, and 3d sing presents of verbs in* \īd\, *as* rides
\if\ cliff, if, miff, skiff, sniff, stiff, tiff, whiff; hieroglyph
\īf\ fife, knife, life, rife, strife, wife
\ift\ drift, gift, lift, rift, shift, shrift, sift, swift, thrift; adrift, uplift; *also pasts of verbs in* \if\, *as* whiffed
\ig\ big, brig, dig, fig, gig, jig, pig, prig, rig, sprig, swig, twig, wig; renege; periwig, whirligig
\ij\ bridge, midge, ridge; abridge; anchorage, average, cartilage, equipage, foliage, heritage, hermitage, parentage, parsonage, pasturage, patronage, personage, pilgrimage, privilege, tutelage, vicarage
\ik\ brick, chick, click, clique, creek, crick, flick, kick, lick, nick, pick, prick, quick, rick, sick, snick, thick, tick, trick, wick; bailiwick, catholic, choleric, heretic, politic, rhetoric; arithmetic
\īk\ dike, hike, like, pike, shrike, spike, strike, tyke; alike, dislike, oblique
\iks\ fix, mix, pyx, six; affix, commix, prefix, prolix, transfix; crucifix, intermix, politics; *also plurals and possessives of nouns and 3d sing presents of verbs in* \ik\, *as* licks, picks
\ikst\ betwixt; *pasts of verbs in* \iks\, *as* fixed
\ikt\ strict; addict, afflict, convict, depict, inflict, predict, restrict; benedict, contradict, derelict; *also pasts of verbs in* \ik\, *as* kicked, licked

\il bill, chill, dill, drill, fill, frill, gill, grill, hill, ill, kill, kiln, mill, nil, pill, quill, shrill, sill, skill, spill, squill, still, swill, thill, thrill, till, trill, twill, will; distill, fulfill, instill, quadrille; codicil, daffodil, whippoorwill; *also many words ending with an -ile spelling with primary accent on the antepenult*
\īl, īəl aisle, bile, chyle, faille, file, guile, isle, lisle, mile, pile, rile, smile, spile, stile, style, tile, vile, while, wile; awhile, beguile, compile, defile, erewhile, revile; juvenile, reconcile
\ild build, gild, guild; rebuild, self-willed, unskilled; *also pasts of verbs in* \il\, *as* filled, killed
\īld, īəld aisled, child, mild, wild; *also pasts of monosyllabic or finally accented verbs in* \ī(ə)l\, *as* piled, reviled
\ilk bilk, ilk, milk, silk
\ilt built, gilt, guilt, hilt, jilt, kilt, lilt, milt, quilt, silt, spilt, stilt, tilt, wilt
\ilth filth, spilth, tilth
\im bream, brim, dim, glim, grim, him, hymn, limb, limn, prim, rim, skim, slim, swim, trim, vim, whim; bedim; cherubim, interim, paradigm, seraphim
\īm chime, chyme, climb, crime, cyme, dime, grime, lime, mime, prime, rhyme, slime, thyme, time; begrime, sublime, upclimb; maritime, pantomime, paradigm
\imf, impf lymph, nymph
\imp blimp, crimp, gimp, imp, limp, pimp, primp, scrimp, shrimp, skimp
\imps, ims glimpse; *plurals of nouns and 3d sing presents of verbs in* \imp\, *as* imps, limps
\īmz betimes, ofttimes, sometimes; *also plurals and possessives of nouns, and 3d sing presents of verbs in* \īm\, *as* chimes, rhymes
\in been, bin, chin, din, fin, gin, grin, in, inn, jinn, kin, pin, shin, sin, skin, spin, thin, tin, twin, win; akin, begin, chagrin; discipline, mandolin, paladin, violin
\īn brine, chine, dine, fine, line, mine, nine, pine, shine, shrine, sign, sine, spine, stein, swine, tine, trine, twine, vine, whine, wine; align, assign, benign, combine, condign, confine, consign, decline, define, design, divine, enshrine, entwine, incline, opine, outshine, recline, refine, repine, resign, sunshine, supine; anodyne; *also many adjectives with one pronunciation* \īn\, *as* aquiline
\inch chinch, cinch, clinch, finch, flinch, inch, lynch, pinch, winch
\ind wind; rescind; *also pasts of verbs in* \in\, *as* pinned, tinned
\īnd bind, blind, find, grind, hind, kind, mind, rind, wind; behind, mankind, remind, unkind; *also pasts of verbs in* \īn\, *as* refined
\inj binge, cringe, fringe, hinge, singe, springe, swinge, tinge, twinge; impinge, infringe, syringe
\ins, ints chintz, mince, prince, quince, rinse, since, wince; convince, evince; *also plurals and possessives of nouns and 3d sing presents of verbs in* \int\, *as* prints
\int dint, flint, glint, hint, lint, mint, print, splint, sprint, squint, stint, tint; footprint, imprint
\inth, intth plinth; hyacinth, labyrinth
\iŋ bring, cling, ding, fling, king, ping, ring, sing, sling, spring, sting, string, swing, thing, wing, wring; *also present participles and diminutives in* \liŋ\ *with accent on the antepenult, as* covering, fostering
\iŋk blink, brink, chink, clink, drink, ink, kink, link, pink, shrink, sink, slink, stink, think, wink, zinc; hoodwink; bobolink
\iŋks, iŋs lynx, minx, sphinx; methinks; *also plurals and possessives of nouns and 3d sing presents of verbs in* \iŋk\, *as* drinks, winks
\iŋt, iŋkt tinct; distinct, extinct, instinct, precinct, succinct; *also pasts of verbs in* \iŋk\, *as* linked, pinked
\ip chip, clip, dip, drip, flip, grip, grippe, hip, lip, nip, pip, quip, rip, scrip, ship, sip, skip, slip, snip, strip, tip, trip, whip; equip, transship
\īp gripe, pipe, ripe, snipe, stipe, stripe, swipe, tripe, type, wipe; unripe; archetype, prototype; stereotype
\ips eclipse, ellipse; apocalypse; *also plurals and possessives of nouns and 3d sing presents of verbs in* \ip\, *as* lips, strips
-ir see \ər\
\ir, iər beer, bier, blear, cheer, clear, dear, deer, drear, ear, fear, gear, hear, here, jeer, leer, mere, near, peer, pier, queer, rear, sear, seer, sere, shear, sheer, smear, sneer, spear, sphere, steer, tear, tier, veer, year; appear, austere, career, cohere, compeer, revere, severe, sincere; buccaneer, chanticleer, disappear, domineer, engineer, hemisphere, interfere, mountaineer, mutineer, persevere, pioneer, sonneteer; charioteer
\īr byre, choir, dire, fire, hire, ire, lyre, mire, pyre, quire, shire, sire, spire, squire, tire, wire; acquire, admire, aspire, attire, conspire, desire, entire, expire, inquire, inspire, perspire, require, respire, retire, transpire; *also nouns and possessives formed from verbs ending in* \ī\, *as* buyer, crier, dyer, liar *and such comparatives of adjectives as* nigher, shyer
-irch see \ərch\
-ird see \ərd\
\ird, iərd beard, weird; *also pasts of verbs in* \i(ə)r\, *as* feared, revered
-irge see \ərj\
-irk see \ərk\
-irl see \ərl\
-irled see \ərld\
-irm see \ərm\
-irp see \ərp\
-irr see \ər\
\irs, iərs fierce, pierce, tierce
-irst see \ərst\
-irt see \ərt\
-irth see \ərth\
\is bliss, hiss, kiss, miss, this; abyss, amiss, dismiss, remiss
\īs dice, ice, lice, mice, nice, price, rice, slice, spice, splice, thrice, trice, twice, vice, vise; advice, concise, device, entice, precise; paradise, sacrifice
\ish dish, fish, swish, wish
\isk bisque, brisk, disk, frisk, risk, whisk; basilisk, obelisk, tamarisk
\isp crisp, lisp, wisp
\ist cyst, fist, gist, grist, hist, list, mist, schist, tryst, twist, whist, wrist; assist, consist, desist, exist, insist, persist, resist, subsist; *also pasts of verbs in* \is\, *as* hissed, missed
\īst tryst; *pasts of verbs in* \īs\, *as* spliced
\it bit, chit, fit, flit, grit, hit, kit, knit, lit, pit, quit, sit, slit, smit, spit, split, sprit, tit, twit, whit, wit, writ; acquit, admit, befit, commit, emit, omit, outwit, permit, remit, submit, transmit; benefit; *also many words ending in the spelling -et*
\īt bight, bite, blight, bright, cite, fight, flight, fright, height, kite, knight, light, might, mite, night, plight, quite, right, rite, sight, site, sleight, slight, smite, spite, sprite, tight, trite, white, write; alight, aright, contrite, delight, despite, excite, ignite, incite, indict, indite, invite, polite, recite, requite, tonight, unite; acolyte, aconite, appetite, dynamite, expedite, oversight, parasite, proselyte, satellite, underwrite
\ith kith, myth, pith, smith, with; forthwith, herewith, therewith, wherewith
\it͟h with; forthwith, herewith, therewith, wherewith
\īt͟h blithe, lithe, scythe, tithe, writhe
\iv give, live, sieve; forgive, misgive, outlive; amative, formative, fugitive, negative, positive, primitive, relative, sedative, sensitive, tentative, transitive
\īv dive, drive, five, hive, live, shrive, strive, thrive, wive; arrive, connive, contrive, deprive, derive, revive, survive
\iz fizz, friz, frizz, his, is, quiz, whiz
\īz guise, prize, rise, size, wise; advise, apprise, arise, assize, baptize, chastise, comprise, demise, despise, devise, disguise, emprise, excise, incise, revise, surmise, surprise, uprise; advertise, authorize, canonize, civilize, colonize, criticize, enterprise, equalize, exercise, idolize, lionize, localize, moralize, organize, paradise, patronize, recognize, solemnize, sympathize, temporize, tyrannize, utilize, vitalize; *also plurals and possessives of nouns and 3d sing presents of verbs in* \ī\, *as* lies, pies, flies
\izəm, izm chrism, prism, schism; altruism, barbarism, cataclysm, criticism, egoism, egotism, heroism, mysticism, optimism, organism, realism, solecism, syllogism, witticism
\ō beau, blow, bow, crow, doe, dough, floe, flow, foe, fro, glow, go, grow, hoe, know, lo, low, mot, mow, no, O, oh, owe, roe, row, sew, show, sloe, slow, snow, so, sow, stow, throe, throw, toe, tow, woe; aglow, ago, below, bestow, chapeau, château, foreknow, foreshow, outgrow, rainbow, tableau, trousseau; buffalo, bungalow, calico, overflow, overgrow, overthrow
\ȯ awe, caw, claw, craw, daw, draw, flaw, gnaw, haw, jaw, law, ma, maw, pa, paw, raw, saw, shah, squaw, straw, thaw, yaw; foresaw, macaw, withdraw
\ōb globe, lobe, probe, robe; disrobe, enrobe, unrobe
\ōch broach, brooch, coach, poach, roach; approach, encroach, reproach
\ōd bode, code, goad, load, lode, mode, node, ode, road, rode, strode, toad; abode, commode, corrode, explode, forebode, unload; episode; *also pasts of verbs in* \ō\, *as* owed
\ȯd bawd, broad, fraud, gaud, laud; abroad, applaud, defraud, maraud; *also pasts of verbs in* \ȯ\, *as* gnawed, sawed
-oes see \əz\
\ōf oaf, loaf
\ȯf, äf cough, doff, off, scoff, trough
\ȯft croft, loft, oft, soft; aloft; *also pasts of verbs in* \ȯf\, *as* scoffed
\ōg brogue, rogue, vogue; prorogue; disembogue
\ȯg, äg bog, clog, cog, dog, flog, fog, frog, grog, hog, jog, log, nog, slog; catalog, decalogue, dialogue, epilogue, tog, monologue, pedagogue, synagogue
\ōj doge; gamboge
\ōk broke, choke, cloak, coke, folk, joke, poke, smoke, soak, spoke, stoke, stroke, woke, yoke, yolk; awoke, bespoke, convoke, invoke, provoke, revoke
\ȯk balk, calk, chalk, gawk, hawk, squawk, stalk, talk, walk; tomahawk
\ōks coax, hoax; *also plurals and possessives of nouns and 3d sing presents of verbs in* \ōk\, *as* oaks, smokes
\ōl bole, bowl, coal, dole, droll, foal, goal, hole, jowl, knoll, mole, pole, role, roll, scroll, shoal, sole, soul, stole, stroll, toll, troll, whole; cajole, condole, console, control, enroll, parole
\ȯl all, awl, ball, bawl, brawl, call, crawl, drawl, fall, gall, hall, haul, maul, pall, pawl, scrawl, shawl, small, sprawl, squall, stall, tall, thrall, trawl, wall, yawl; appall, befall, enthrall, forestall, install
\ōld bold, cold, fold, gold, hold, mold, mould, old, scold, sold, told; behold, enfold, foretold, unfold, untold, uphold, withhold; manifold, marigold; *also pasts of verbs in* \ōl\, *as* rolled, cajoled, foaled
\ȯld bald, scald; *also pasts of verbs in* \ȯl\, *as* called, mauled, scrawled
\ōlt bolt, colt, dolt, jolt, molt, poult; revolt; thunderbolt
\ȯlt fault, halt, malt, salt, smalt, vault; assault, basalt, default, exalt
-om see \əm\
\ōm chrome, comb, dome, foam, gnome, home, loam, ohm, roam, tome; aerodrome, catacomb, hippodrome
-ome see \əm\
-on see \ən\
\ōn bone, cone, crone, drone, flown, groan, grown, hone, known, loan, lone, moan, mown, own, phone, prone, roan, shown, sown, stone, throne, thrown, tone, zone; alone, atone, condone, dethrone, enthrone, intone, postpone
\ȯn awn, brawn, dawn, drawn, faun, fawn, gone, lawn, on, pawn, prawn, spawn, yawn
-once see \əns\
\ȯnch, änch craunch, haunch, launch, paunch, staunch
-one see \ən\
-ong see \əŋ\, \äŋ\, \ȯŋ\
-onge see \ənj\
-ongue see \əŋ\
-ont see \ənt\
\ȯnt, änt daunt, flaunt, gaunt, haunt, jaunt, taunt, vaunt, want; avaunt
\ȯŋ long, song, strong, thong, throng, wrong; along, belong, prolong; *also words at* \äŋ\
-ood see \əd\
\ōp cope, grope, hope, mope, pope, rope, scope, slope, soap, tope, trope; elope; antelope, cantaloupe, horoscope, interlope, telescope; heliotrope
\ōr, ȯr boar, bore, core, corps, door, floor, fore, four, gore, lore, moor, more, oar, ore, poor, pore, pour, roar, score, shore, snore, soar, sore, store, swore, tore, wore, yore; adore, ashore, before, deplore, explore, forbore, forswore, galore, ignore, implore, restore; evermore, nevermore, pompadour, sophomore, sycamore; see \ȯr\
\ȯr for, or, nor, war; abhor; *also words ending in the spelling -or, as* bailor, donor, lessor, vendor, *when used in contrast with correlatives in -ee*
\ȯrb orb; absorb
\ȯrch porch, scorch, torch
-ord see \ərd\
\ōrd, ȯrd board, ford, hoard, sword; aboard, afford; *also pasts of verbs in* \ōr\, *as* bored
\ȯrd chord, cord, lord, sward, ward; abhorred, accord, award, record, reward
\ȯrf dwarf, wharf
\ȯrj forge, gorge; disgorge, engorge
-ork see \ərk\
\ȯrk cork, fork, pork, stork, torque
-orld see \ərld\
-orm see \ərm\
\ȯrm form, norm, storm, swarm, warm; conform, deform, inform, perform, reform, transform; chloroform, cruciform, uniform
\ōrn, ȯrn borne, bourn, mourn, shorn, sworn, torn, worn; forsworn
\ȯrn born, borne, bourn, corn, horn, morn, mourn, scorn, shorn, sworn, thorn, torn, warn, worn; adorn, forewarn, forlorn, forsworn, suborn; unicorn
\ōrs coarse, course, force, hoarse, source; discourse, divorce, enforce, perforce, recourse, resource
\ȯrs coarse, course, force, gorse, hoarse, horse, source; discourse, divorce, endorse, enforce, perforce, recourse, remorse, resource, unhorse
-orse see \ərs\
-orst see \ərst\
\ōrt court, fort, port, sport; comport, disport, export, import, report
\ȯrt court, fort, port, short, sort, sport,

thwart, tort, wart; abort, assort, athwart, comport, consort, disport, distort, escort, exhort, export, extort, import, resort, retort

-orth see \ərth\

\òrth\ forth, fourth, north

\ōs\ close, dose, gross; engross, jocose, morose, verbose; bellicose, comatose, grandiose, otiose

\òs\ boss, cross, dross, floss, gloss, joss, loss, moss, sauce, toss; across, emboss, lacrosse

\òsh\ see \äsh\

\ōst\ boast, coast, ghost, host, most, post, roast, toast; *also antepenult-stressed words in* \mōst\, *as* uttermost

\òst\ cost, frost, lost; accost, exhaust; holocaust; *also pasts of verbs in* \òs\, *as* crossed, embossed

\ōt\ bloat, boat, coat, cote, dote, float, gloat, goat, groat, moat, mote, note, oat, quote, rote, shoat, smote, stoat, throat, tote, vote, wrote; afloat, denote, devote, promote, remote; anecdote, antidote, table d'hôte

\òt\ aught, bought, brought, caught, fought, fraught, naught, nought, ought, sought, taught, taut, thought, wrought; distraught, inwrought; aeronaut, astronaut, cosmonaut, overwrought

\ōth\ both, growth, loath, oath, sloth, wroth; betroth

\òth\ broth, cloth, froth, moth, sloth, troth, wroth; betroth; see \äth\

\ōth\ betroth, clothe, loath

-ouch see \ouch\

-ough see \əf\

-oung \see əŋ\

-ourge see \ərj\

-ourn see \ərn\

-oust see \əst\

\ōv\ clove, cove, dove, drove, grove, hove, mauve, rove, shrove, stove, strove, throve, wove; inwove; interwove

-ove see \əv\

\ōz\ chose, close, doze, froze, nose, pose, prose, rose, those; arose, compose, depose, disclose, dispose, enclose, expose, foreclose, impose, oppose, propose, repose, suppose, transpose; *also plurals and possessives of nouns and 3d sing presents of verbs in* \ō\, *as* foes, glows, goes

\òz\ cause, clause, gauze, hawse, pause, was, yaws; applause, because; *also plurals of nouns and 3d sing presents of verbs in* \ò\, *as* laws, saws

\òi\ boy, buoy, cloy, coy, joy, toy, troy; alloy, annoy, convoy, decoy, deploy, destroy, employ, enjoy

\òid\ void; avoid, devoid; aneroid, asteroid; *also pasts of verbs in* \òi\, *as* cloyed, toyed

\òil\ boil, broil, coil, foil, oil, roil, soil, spoil, toil; despoil, embroil, recoil, uncoil

\òin\ coign, coin, groin, join, loin, quoin; adjoin, conjoin, disjoin, enjoin, purloin, rejoin, subjoin

\òint\ joint, point; anoint, appoint, conjoint, disjoint; counterpoint, disappoint

\òis\ choice, voice; rejoice

\òist\ foist, hoist, joist, moist; *also pasts of verbs in* \òis\, *as* rejoiced

\òit\ adroit, exploit

\òiz\ noise, poise; counterpoise, equipoise; avoirdupois; *also plurals of nouns and 3d sing presents of verbs in* \òi\, *as* boys, cloys

\ü, yü\ blew, blue, brew, chew, clue, coo, crew, cue, dew, do, drew, due, few, flew, glue, grew, hew, hue, knew, loo, mew, new, pew, rue, screw, shoe, shrew, skew, slew, sou, stew, strew, sue, threw, through, to, too, true, two, view, who, woo, yew, you; accrue, adieu, ado, askew, bamboo, bedew, canoe, debut, endue, ensue, eschew, halloo,

imbue, outdo, pursue, ragout, renew, review, shampoo, snafu, subdue, taboo, tattoo, undo, withdrew; avenue, ingenue, interview, rendezvous, residue, retinue, revenue

-ub see \əb\

\üb, yüb\ boob, cube, lube, rube, tube

-uch see \əch\

\üch\ brooch, hooch, mooch, pooch

-uck see \ək\

-uct see \əkt\

-ud see \əd\

\üd, yüd\ brood, crude, dude, feud, food, hood, lewd, mood, nude, prude, rood, rude, snood; allude, collude, conclude, delude, denude, elude, exclude, exude, include, obtrude, preclude, protrude, seclude; altitude, aptitude, desuetude, fortitude, gratitude, habitude, interlude, lassitude, latitude, longitude, magnitude, multitude, plenitude, promptitude, quietude, servitude, similitude, solicitude, solitude, turpitude; vicissitude; *also pasts of verbs in* \ü, yü\, *as* cooed, rued, stewed, subdued

\ùd\ could, good, hood, should, stood, wood, would; brotherhood, livelihood, maidenhood, motherhood, neighborhood, sisterhood, understood, womanhood

-udge see \əj\

\üf\ goof, hoof, proof, roof, woof; aloof, behoof, disproof, reproof; see \ùf\

\ùf\ hoof, roof, woof; see \üf\

-uff see \əf\

-uft see \əft\

-ug see \əg\

\üj, yüj\ huge, stooge; centrifuge, febrifuge, subterfuge, vermifuge

\ük, yük\ duke, fluke, puke, snook, spook; peruke, rebuke

\ùk\ book, brook, cook, crook, hook, look, nook, rook, shook, snook, took; caoutchouc, forsook, mistook; overlook

-ul see \əl\

\ül, yül\ cool, drool, fool, mule, pool, pule, rule, school, spool, stool, tool, tulle, yule; molecule, overrule

\ùl\ bull, full, pull, wool

-ulch see \əlch\

-ulge see \əlj\

-ulk see \əlk\

-ull see \əl\

-ulp see \əlp\

-ulse see \əls\

-ult see \əlt\

-um see \əm\

\üm, yüm\ bloom, boom, broom, brume, doom, flume, gloom, glume, groom, loom, plume, rheum, room, spume, tomb, whom, womb; assume, consume, costume, entomb, exhume, legume, perfume, presume, resume

\ùm\ broom, groom, room

-umb see \əm\

-ump see \əmp\

-un see \ən\

\ün, yün\ boon, coon, croon, dune, hewn, loon, moon, noon, prune, rune, soon, spoon, swoon, tune; attune, baboon, balloon, bassoon, buffoon, cartoon, cocoon, commune, dragoon, festoon, galloon, harpoon, impugn, lagoon, lampoon, maroon, monsoon, oppugn, platoon, pontoon, raccoon, typhoon; honeymoon, importune, opportune, picayune

-unce see \əns\

-unch see \ənch\

-unct see \əŋkt\

-und see \ənd\

\ünd, yünd\ wound; *also pasts of verbs in* \ün, yün\, *as* crooned, tuned

-ung see \əŋ\

-unge see \ənj\

-unk see \əŋk\

-unt see \ənt\

-up see \əp\

\üp, yüp\ coop, croup, droop, drupe, dupe, group, hoop, loop, poop, scoop, sloop, soup, stoop, swoop, troop, whoop

\ùp\ coop, hoop, whoop

-upt see \əpt\

-ur see \ər\

\ür, yür\ boor, cure, lure, moor, poor, pure, tour, your; allure, amour, assure, contour, demure, endure, immure, impure, insure, manure, mature, obscure, procure, secure; aperture, cynosure, epicure, forfeiture, furniture, immature, overture, paramour, premature, sinecure; miniature, temperature

-urb see \ərb\

-urch see \ərch\

-urd see \ərd\

-urf see \ərf\

-urge see \ərj\

-urgh see \ərg\

-urk see \ərk\

-url see \ərl\

-urled see \ərld\

-urn see \ərn\

-urnt see \ərnt\

-urp see \ərp\

-urr see \ər\

-urse see \ərs\

-urst see \ərst\

-urt see \ərt\

-urve see \ərv\

\ürz\ yours; *plurals of nouns and 3d sing presents of verbs in* \ür, yür\, *as* tours, cures, endures

-us see \əs\

\üs, yüs\ deuce, goose, juice, loose, moose, mousse, noose, puce, ruse, sluice, spruce, truce, use; abstruse, abuse, adduce, conduce, deduce, diffuse, disuse, excuse, induce, misuse, obtuse, produce, profuse, recluse, reduce, seduce, traduce; introduce

-ush see \əsh\

\üsh\ douche, ruche; barouche, cartouche, debouch

\ùsh\ bush, push

-usk see \əsk\

-usque see \əsk\

-uss see \əs\

-ust see \əst\

\üt, yüt\ boot, brute, butte, chute, coot, cute, flute, fruit, hoot, loot, lute, moot, mute, newt, root, route, shoot, suit, suite, toot; acute, astute, commute, compute, confute, depute, dilute, dispute, impute, minute, pollute, pursuit, recruit, refute, repute, salute, transmute, uproot, volute; absolute, attribute, constitute, destitute, dissolute, execute, institute, parchute, persecute, prosecute, resolute, substitute

\ùt\ foot, put, root, soot; uproot

-utch see \əch\

\üth\ booth, ruth, sleuth, sooth, tooth, truth, youth; forsooth, uncouth

\ùth\ smooth, soothe

-utt see \ət\

\üv\ groove, move, prove; approve, behoove, disprove, improve, reprove; disapprove

-ux see \əks\

\üz, yüz\ booze, bruise, choose, cruise, fuse, lose, muse, news, ooze, ruse, snooze, use, whose; abuse, accuse, amuse, confuse, diffuse, disuse, excuse, infuse, misuse, peruse, refuse, suffuse, transfuse; *also plurals of nouns and 3d sing presents of verbs in* \ü, yü\, *as* dews, imbues

-uzz see \əz\

\yü\ see \ü\

SPELLING

1.1 Words ending in -x are unchanged before any suffix: *coax→ coaxed, coaxing; fix→ fixable, fixer; six→ sixty.*

1.2 Words ending in -c remain unchanged before *a, o, u* or a consonant: *frolic→ frolicsome; sac→ saclike; zinc→ zincate, zincoid, zincous;* but before suffixal *e, i,* and *y* usually add *k* if the pronunciation of the *c* remains hard but add nothing if the pronunciation of the *c* becomes soft: *critic→ criticism, criticize; frolic→ frolicked, frolicking; music→ musician; physic→ physicist; toxic→ toxicity.*

1.3 Words ending in consonant plus -c usually remain unchanged before any suffix, but forms with an inserted *k* occur occasionally: *arc→ arced*/sometimes *arcked, arcing*/sometimes *arcking; disc→ disced, discing; zinc→ zincing/zincking, zincite; talc→ talcky.*

1.4.1 Words ending in a single consonant except x or c immediately preceded by two or more vowels in the same syllable remain unchanged before any suffix: *air→ aired, airing, airy; appeal→ appealed, appealing; brief→ briefed, briefer, briefly; cloud→ clouded, cloudless; cool→ cooled, cooler, coolest, cooling, coolly; suit→ suitable, suitor.*
EXCEPTION: *wool→ wooly*/but *woolly* is more frequent.

1.4.2 Words ending in a single consonant immediately preceded by a single vowel bearing primary stress double the consonant before a suffixal vowel but not before a suffixal consonant: *abet→ abetted, abetting, abettor; bag→ baggage; begin→ beginner; clan→ clannish; drop→ droplet, dropped; fit→ fitness, fitting; glad→ gladden, gladly.*

EXCEPTIONS: *chagrin→ chagrined, chagrining; combat→ combated, combating; prefer→ preferable, preference; gas→ gaseous, gasify* but *gassed, gassing.*

1.4.3 Words ending in a single consonant immediately preceded by a single vowel bearing secondary stress vary greatly in their derivatives: (1) some always double the consonant: *handicap→ handicapped, handicapping; humbug→ humbugged, humbugging;* (2) some have single consonant only: *catalog→ cataloged, cataloging; chaperon→ chaperoned, chaperoning; parallel→ paralleled, paralleling;* (3) some have both forms: *benefit→ benefited/benefitted, benefiting/benefitting; kidnap→ kidnapped/kidnaped, kidnapping/kidnaping; program→ programmed/programed, programming/programing.*

1.4.4 Words ending in a single consonant immediately preceded by one or more vowels without stress remain unchanged before any suffix: *bargain→ bargained, bargaining; credit→ credited, crediting, creditor; gallop→ galloped, galloping; solid→ solider, solidest, solidify, solidly.*

EXCEPTIONS: (1) a large group of words doubles a final consonant immediately preceded by a single unstressed vowel before a suffixal vowel; in British use this is the regular practice; in U.S. use it is usually an accepted alternative to the one-consonant spelling: *apparel, bevel, bias, cancel, chisel, counsel, cudgel, dial, duel, equal, focus, fuel, label, libel, model, panel, quarrel, rival, signal, snivel, spiral, stencil, symbol, total, travel;* (2) two *l*'s are more common in adjectives like *gravelly, tinselly* than in derivatives with other suffixes; (3) for derivatives of *worship* the one-*p* and two-*p* forms are about equally common.

1.5 Words ending in a single consonant that is silent remain unchanged before any suffix: *chamois→ chamoised, chamoising; hurrah→ hurrahed, hurrahing.*

EXCEPTION: *ricochet→ ricocheted/ricochetted.*

1.6 Words ending in two or more consonants the last of which is not c remain unchanged before any suffix: *art→ artistic, artless; attach→ attached, attachment; buzz→ buzzed, buzzer, buzzing; condemn→ condemnatory, condemned, condemning; length→ lengthen, lengthy; odd→ oddity, oddly.*

EXCEPTIONS: (1) words ending in -*ll* often drop one *l: dull→ dulness; skill→ skilful; thrall→ thraldom;* (2) the second *l* of final -*ll* frequently disappears before suffixal *l;* it always disappears before -*ly* (*droll→ drolly; dull→ dully; full→ fully*); before -*less* it may disappear, but hyphened forms retaining all three *l*'s are more frequent (*hull-less*); with -*like* the hyphened form retaining all three *l*'s is usual (*bell-like, scroll-like*).

1.7 Words ending in silent -e drop the vowel before a suffixal vowel but remain unchanged before a suffixal consonant: *bone→ boned, boning,* but *boneless; curve→ curvature, curved, curving,* but *curvesome; imagine→ imaginable, imagining,* but *imagines.*

EXCEPTIONS: (1) proper names ending in single -*e* preceded by one or more consonants usually keep the -*e* before the suffix -*an;* in the derivatives so formed the -*e* is sounded, whether or not it is silent in the base: *Europe→ European; Shakespeare→ Shakespearean* usually preferred to /*Shakespearian;* (2) *mile→ mileage* much more frequent than /*milage; nurse→ nursling;* (3) before the suffix -*ly* words ending in consonantal -*le* usually drop the -*le; gentle→ gently; subtle→ subtly*/but also *subtlely;* (4) some words ending in -*re* retain the -*e* before a suffixal vowel: *acre→ acreage;* (5) words ending in -*ce* or -*ge* usually retain the -*e* before any suffixal letter except *e, i,* or *y,* thus preserving the softness of the *c* or *g: change→ changeable, changeless* (but *changing*); *courage→ courageous, encouragement* (but *encouraged, encouraging*); *grace→ graceful* (but *disgraced, disgracing*); *peace→ peaceable; range→ rangy*/but also *rangey.* A *d* preceding *g*

may in a few cases act as a preserver of the soft sound and permit the dropping of the -*e:* *abridge*→ *abridgment*/but *abridgement* especially in Britain; *judge*→ *judgment*/but *judgement* especially in Britain; (6) although final -*e* regularly drops before the suffix -*able,* some adjectives in -*able* have alternatives retaining the -*e:* *like*→ *likable/likeable;* *love*→ *lovable/loveable;* *size*→ *sizable/sizeable;* (7) usage fluctuates considerably with regard to dropping or retaining final -*e* before derivatives formed with the suffix -*y;* many have both the -*ey* and the -*y* alternative: *home*→ *homey/homy;* *horse*→ *horsey/horsy;* *mouse*→ *mousy/mousey;* *stone*→ *stony/stoney;* and some words have only one form in common usage: *rose*→ *rosy;* *shade*→ *shady;* (8) the silent -*e* remains in some present participles to distinguish them from the corresponding forms of other verbs: *dye*→ *dyeing* (in contrast to *dying*); *singe*→ *singeing* (in contrast to *singing*).

1.8 Words ending in -e preceded by a vowel drop the final -*e* before suffixal -*a*- and -*e*-: *argue*→ *arguable, argued; awe*→ *awed; blue*→ *blued, bluer, bluest; lie*→ *liar.*

EXCEPTIONS: (1) words ending in -*ee* usually retain both *e*'s before *a* and always before suffixal -*i*-: *agree*→ *agreeable, agreeing;* (2) -*ie* in an accented syllable becomes -*y* before suffixal -*i*-: *die*→ *dying;* (3) -*ie* in an unaccented syllable remains unchanged before suffixal -*i*-: *stymie*→ *stymieing;* (4) -*oe* remains unchanged before suffixal -*i*-: *canoe*→ *canoeing; hoe*→ *hoeing;* (5) -*ue* usually drops -*e* before suffixal -*i*-: *argue*→ *arguing; true*→ *truism*/but *trueing/truing;* (6) -*ye* alternatively keeps or drops -*e* before suffixal -*i*-: *eye*→ *eyeing/eying;* (7) adjectives with the suffix -*y* retain -*e: glue*→ *gluey;* (8) the double vowel usually remains unchanged before a suffixal consonant: *agree*→ *agreement; blue*→ *blueness; woe*→ *woeful*/but also *woful;* but: *argue*→ *argument; awe*→ *awful* (but *awesome*); *true*→ *truly.*

1.9 Verbs derived from the French and ending in -é usually form their past and past participle in -*éd,* less often in -*éed;* they form their present participle in -*éing: appliqué*→ *appliquéd, appliquéing; visé*→ *viséd*/also *viséed.*

1.10 Words ending in -y preceded by a consonant usually change the -*y* to -*i*- before any suffixal letter except *i* and the possessive sign '*s: beauty*→ *beautiful, beautify; body*→ *bodily, embodiment; contrary*→ *contrariwise; copy*→ *copyist; defy*→ *defiant, defying; fancy*→ *fanciful, fancying; happy*→ *happiness; likely*→ *likelihood; mercy*→ *merciless; thirty*→ *thirtyish;* but: *everybody*→ *everybody's; Mary*→ *Mary's.*

EXCEPTIONS: (1) one-syllable words usually retain -*y* before -*ly* and -*ness: dry*→ *dryly, dryness;* (2) comparatives and superlatives of one-syllable adjectives alternatively retain -*y* or replace it with -*i*-: *dry*→ *drier, driest*/more common than *dryer, dryest;* (3) *fly*→ *flier/flyer;* (4) -*y* remains unchanged before -*like* and -*ship: lady*→ *ladylike;* in derivatives of *baby* and *lady: baby*→ *babyhood; lady*→ *ladykin;* (5) -*y* may be lost completely before suffixal -*i*-, especially when separated by one or more syllables from the primary stress of the base word: *accompany*→ *accompanist; military*→ *militarism, militarist, militarize.*

1.11 Words ending in -y preceded by a vowel usually remain unchanged before any suffix: *alloy*→ *alloys; attorney*→ *attorneys; enjoy*→ *enjoying, enjoyment; play*→ *played, playing, player, playful, playlet.*

EXCEPTIONS: (1) *day*→ *daily; lay*→ *laid; say*→ *saith; slay*→ *slain;* (2) *gay*→ *gaiety/gayety, gaily/gayly, stay*→ *staid/stayed;* (3) comparatives and superlatives of adjectives ending in -*ey* replace these two letters with -*i*-: *gluey*→ *gluier, gluiest, gluily; phoney*→ *phonier, phoniest, phonily;* (4) adjectives ending in -*wy* change the -*y* to -*i*- before any suffix: *dewy*→ *dewier, dewiest, dewily, dewiness; showy*→ *showier, showiest, showily, showiness.*

1.12 Words ending in a vowel except e or y, when adding a suffix beginning with a consonant, remain unchanged: *China*→ *Chinaman; radio*→ *radiogram.*

1.13.1 Verbs ending in a vowel except e or y, when adding a suffix beginning with a vowel, remain unchanged before their inflectional suffixes: *alibi*→ *alibied, alibiing; boo*→ *booed; radio*→ *radioed, radioing; ski*→ *skied, skiing, skier.*

EXCEPTIONS: verbs ending in single -*o* usually insert *e* before adding -*s* for the third person singular: *echo*→ *echoes; lasso*→ *lassoes.*

1.13.2 Nouns ending in a vowel when adding one of the suffixes -esque, -ism, -ist usually remain unchanged especially if the base word is short and the final vowel is essential to its recognition: *solo*→ *soloist; Tito*→ *Titoism; Zola*→ *Zolaesque.*

EXCEPTIONS: *cello*→ *cellist; Nazi*→ *Nazism*/but also *Naziism; propaganda*→ *propagandist.*

1.13.3 Geographical and personal names ending in -a regularly drop the -*a* before the suffix -*an/-ian: America*→ *American; Canada*→ *Canadian; Victoria*→ *Victorian.*

1.13.4 Some geographical names ending in -o drop the -*o* before -*an/-ian: Mexico*→ *Mexican; Ontario*→ *Ontarian; San Diego*→ *San Diegan.*

1.13.5 Scientific terms of Greek or Latin origin ending in -a regularly drop the -*a* before a suffix beginning with a vowel: *pleura*→ *pleural; urea*→ *urease, ureic.*

1.13.6 Words ending in -o insert *e* before suffixal -*y: goo*→ *gooey; mosquito*→ *mosquitoey.*

1.13.7 Geographical and personal names ending in -o or a combination of vowels pronounced \ō often insert *n* or *v* before -*an/-ian: Buffalo*→ *Buffalonian; Marlow*→ *Marlovian; Thoreau*→ *Thoreauvian,* but some geographical names ending in -*o* remain unchanged before -*an: Chicago*→ *Chicagoan.*

1.14 When adding a prefix that forms a new word, a base word usually remains unchanged: *act*→ *enact; call*→ *recall; change*→ *exchange; prove*→ *disprove; veil*→ *unveil.*

EXCEPTIONS: words ending in -*ll* often drop one *l* when adding a prefix; this practice, common in Britain, is widespread also in the U.S., but the unchanged (-*ll*) forms prevail in this country: *fill*→ *fulfil, fulfilment; roll*→ *enrol.* By analogy even some infinitives which are not derivatives of English base words sometimes drop one *l.* For these words, too, the one -*l* spelling prevails in

Britain, whereas in the U.S. it exists side by side with the -*ll* form: *distil/distill; instal/install.*

1.15 Two or more words joining to form a compound usually retain the full spelling of both component words: *billfold, makeup, sidestep, widespread.*

EXCEPTIONS: many compounds which are long-established in the language and in which the full literal force of one or both elements has been weakened or lost have dropped a letter from one, sometimes both, of the original elements: *almost, alone, already, always; wherewithal; welcome, welfare; artful, hateful; fulfill; pastime; until; wherever.*

2.1 -able/-ible. English has a large group of adjectives in -*able*, another in -*ible;* the force of the suffix in both groups is the same. Many of these adjectives are from Latin adjectives in -*abilis* and -*ibilis;* -*abilis* occurs after first-conjugation stems, -*ibilis* after stems of the other conjugations. With -*abilis* the stem used is the present, with -*ibilis* it is sometimes the present, sometimes the participial. Examples: (first conjugation) *laudabilis;* (second, third, fourth conjugations respectively, present stem) *horribilis, credibilis, audibilis;* (second, third, fourth conjugations respectively, participial stem) *risibilis, defensibilis, sensibilis.* These and many other such Latin adjectives have been borrowed by English, with change of -*ilis* to -*le.* In addition, many others have been analogically formed in English, or in French and borrowed by English. Since Latin provides precedent for either the present or the participial stem with -*ibilis*, two quite or substantially synonymous -*ible* words with different stems have in some cases been introduced into English (*corrodible/corrosible, submergible/submersible*). Further, -*able* has become a productive suffix in English and has been attached to a multitude of English verbs. Many of these that are Latin-derived are (*a*) from second-, third-, and fourth-conjugation stems, or (*b*) from first-conjugation participial stems, with none of which -*abilis* occurs. Hence, English has a few variants of the type *preventible/preventable* (class *a*) and a probably larger number of the type *educable/educatable* (class *b*).

2.2 e/ae, o/oe. The digraphs *ae/æ* and *oe/œ* of Latin and of Greek transliterated into Latin are sometimes retained in English derivatives and borrowings, sometimes reduced to *e.* Sometimes one form strongly prevails throughout English, and variants are infrequent: *economy, enigma, estuary, ether, aer-* words (as *aerial, aeronautics*). When variants are frequent, the one-letter variant is nearly always in greater favor in U.S. use than in British: *anemia/anaemia; anesthetic/anaesthetic; diarrhea/diarrhoea; esophagus/oesophagus; fetus/foetus; hemoglobin/haemoglobin.*

2.3 -ant/-ent. English contains a large group of words ending in -*ant* and another in -*ent*, both pronounced \ənt\. Most of the -*ant* words stem from Latin present participles of the first conjugation (*radiant*, from Latin *radians, -antis*), the -*ent* words from Latin present participles of the other conjugations (*regent*, from Latin *regens, -entis*); but not always (*tenant*, ultimately from a Latin verb of the second conjugation, owes its *a* to Old French). The two endings do not differ in force, and, though usually all English words that derive from the present participle of the same Latin verb have *a* only or *e* only, in some families of such derivatives there is variation: *pendant* noun, *pendency, dependent* adj., *independent, dependent* also *dependant* noun; *propellant, expellant, repellent, impellent.*

2.4 -ction/-xion. Most nouns ending in \kshən\ are spelled -*ction* only; a few are alternatively -*ction/-xion;* a few are -*xion* only. Those that are -*ction* only are ultimately from a Latin verb whose participial stem ends in -*ct: direction*, from *directio* from *direct*(*us*). Those that are alternatively -*ction/-xion* are ultimately from a Latin verb whose participial stem ends in -*x* and whose present stem ends in -*ct;* the participial stem is the source of the -*xion* variant, the present stem is the source, usually via an English verb, of the -*ction* variant: thus *inflexion* is from *inflexio* from *inflex*(*us*); *inflection* is *inflexion* with *x* assimilated to the *ct* of English *inflect*, from *inflect*(*ere*), an assimilation catalyzed by the analogy of nouns like *direction.* Nouns that are -*xion* only are ultimately from Latin verbs of which the present stem does not end in -*ct* and which accordingly have not procreated English verbs in -*ct* (*crucifixion, transfixion,* and *fluxion*): *deflection* U.S., *deflexion* Brit.; *inflection* U.S., *inflexion,* Brit.; *connection* U.S., *connexion,* Brit.

2.5.1 em-/im-, en-/in-. The Latin preposition or adverb *in*, in such English derivatives as *inoculate, intrude, invent*, occurs as a prefix in many Latin verbs and verb derivatives. Sometimes the *in-* is unchanged (*inoculare, intrudere, invenire*). At other times the phonetic influence of an initial consonant of the base that follows the *in-* changes the *n* to a consonant having the same articulation as the base-initial consonant. The change is to *m* before *m, b,* and *p* (*immigrare, imbibere, implorare*), to *l* before *l* (*illuminare*), to *r* before *r* (*irradiare*).

2.5.2 French — Old and Modern — has borrowed many of these compounds and retained the Latin spelling of the prefix (*inoculer, inventer, immigrer, imbiber, implorer, illuminer, irradier*). However, Latin *in* became *en* in French, and when similar compounds were constructed in French on French words as a base the vowel used in the prefix was *e.* The assimilation of the *n* to *m* before *m, b,* and *p* continued (*emmener, embaumer, employer*); the assimilation of the *n* to *l* and *r* before *l* and *r* respectively did not (*enlargier, enrager*).

2.5.3 English, like French, has borrowed many of the Latin compound verbs and retained the Latin spelling of the prefix (*inoculate, invent, immigrate, imbibe, implore, illuminate, irradiate*). English has borrowed also from French many forms in *em-* and *en-* (*embalm, employ, enlarge*). English has taken over also the prefixes *im-, in-, em-, en-* and attached them to English nouns and adjectives to make verbs, or to verbs to make other verbs (*imbed, encage, enkindle*). As in French formations, -*m* is usually used before *m, b, p* (*immarble/emmarble, imbed/embed, impanel/empanel*) but in the compound having *mesh* as base both *m* and *n* are found prefixally.

2.5.4 Of the borrowings from French *em-* and *en-* forms, and of the formations within English, some have now *e* now *i* as the prefixal vowel (*enclose/inclose, embed/imbed, embitter/imbitter*); others, some of which formerly showed the same variation, are found with *e* only or with *i* only (*embalm, encamp, impeach*). *i* is more frequent before *m* than before *n.*

2.5.5 In most of the intra-English formations the prefix adds little or nothing semantically to the base. Before an adjective or noun it serves chiefly as a sign that the adjective or noun has been made a verb. This verb-forming prefix is closest to being completely functionless when it is added to a verb: thus *kindle* and *enkindle* are not easily discriminable. If the prefix makes a substantial semantic contribution, usually the prefixal vowel is *i* and the prefixal consonant is *n* whatever letter follows (*inborn, inbound, inbred/* but *imbred* occasionally).

2.6 -er/-re. Some English words, mostly derived from French words in *-re*, which in turn are mostly derived from Greek or Latin, alternatively end in *-er/-re*. But the *-er*, of different origin, that is a productive suffix freely attachable to English bases (*writer, header, four-poster, New Yorker*) does not have the variant *-re*. Most of the variants are usually *-er* in U.S., *-re* in Britain: *caliber/calibre; center/centre; somber/ sombre.*

EXCEPTIONS: (1) in both U.S. and British use *-re* is usually the form after *c*, the immediately following *r* ensuring the hardness of the *c* (*acre, chancre, involucre, lucre, massacre, mediocre, nacre, wiseacre*). But after *g* (which, like *c*, may be hard or soft) the same is not true (U.S. *meager*/British *meagre;* but both countries prefer *eager, ogre*); (2) U.S. and British usage both prefer *cadre* \'kad-rē\, *macabre, timbre* "tone quality". The latter (often \'tam-bər\) is not to be confused with *timber* "wood" (\'tim-bər\), a different word, which has only *-er* in both countries; (3) although *meter/metre*, the metric system unit of measurement (which is ultimately from Greek *metron*), and its compounds (*centimet-, decimet-, millimet-*) are *-re* in Britain, *meter* (which is *mete + -er*) is universal in both countries for any device for measuring (electric *meter*), as is also *-meter* as the second element of many names for specific measuring devices (*altimeter, barometer, galvanometer, gasometer, ohmmeter, speedometer, thermometer, voltmeter, volumeter*). Some of these compounds are simply a joining or telescoping of an English first element and *meter* "measuring device", but most are not. In a few the quality of the *e* that follows the *m* is the same as in the simplex word; in most this *e* is of a different quality and without stress. In metric-system names the sound values in *-meter/-metre* are the same as in the simplex; (4) although *meter/metre* "rhythm" is *metre* in Britain, for names of individual measures (*trimeter, tetrameter, pentameter, hexameter*) *-meter* is the spelling there as well as in the U.S. In these, too, the *e* following the *m* is without stress; (5) both *theater/theatre* have wide currency in the U.S., only the second in Britain. In New York City, the theatrical center of the U.S., the spelling is usually *theatre*; (6) *neuter* and *sober* are in both countries *-er* only.

2.7.1 -er/-or. These are the most common endings in English for agent nouns. This *-or* does not have a variant *-our* except in *saviour*. A few agent nouns have *a* rather than *e* or *o* before the *r* (*beggar, liar, pedlar* sometimes). Such nouns of this class as are based on a Latin perfect stem, whether the nouns are formed in English from an English verb so based or are taken from the Latin or, with somewhat altered spelling, from French (*author*) usually have *-or*: *actor, collector, conductor, confessor, inspector, operator, supervisor, translator.*

2.7.2 Other agent nouns usually have *-er*, such as nouns based on Latin present stems and nouns based on verbs of Germanic origin: *designer, digger, distiller, invader, producer, subscriber, voyager.*

2.7.3 Occasionally, however, an English agent noun, although its base is from a Latin perfect stem, has *-er* for suffix, as a less frequent variant of *-or*. In such pairs the *-or* form is on the analogy of Latin, the *-er* form is the English suffix added to an English verb that is from the same Latin perfect stem as the *-or* noun (*executor*/archaic *executer*). Conversely, sometimes an agent noun, though its base is from a Latin present stem, has *-or* alone or as a variant of *-er*. Sometimes false analogy may be responsible: some Latin present stems have the same final consonant or consonant cluster as some Latin perfect stems (compare the present participle *reflect*[ere] and the past participle *elect*[us]); the coiner of *reflector* may have used as his model a quite regular formation of the type *elector*. So also *adaptor* and *advisor* are unexpected (compare *adapt*[are], *advis*[are]), *captor* and *supervisor* are regular (compare *capt*[us], *supervis*[us]).

2.7.4 Old French is the source of numerous *-or* agent nouns. Many are law terms or have a legal sense, and of these many have correlatives in *-ee* (*bailor, bailee*). Most of the terms have variants in *-er*, and *-er* is the usual spelling in nonlegal use of such terms as have both legal and nonlegal senses: *abettor, bailor, consignor, mortgagor, vendor.*

2.8 -ph-/-f-. \'səl-fər\ as a chemical term and chemical terms based on it are usually spelled *sulf-* by U.S. scientists, *sulph-* by British scientists. Nonscientists in both countries usually spell *sulph-*.

2.9 -ize/-ise. Ancient Greek has a verb suffix *-izein*, which descended into postclassical Latin as *-izare* and into French as *-iser*. English has borrowed verbs (all of more than one syllable) containing this suffix from all three languages (*ostracize, pulverize, moralize*). In addition, English has isolated the suffix and used it quite freely, attaching it to bases both Greek (*criticize, mechanize*) and non-Greek (to Latin bases, *anglicize;* to English nouns, *victimize, memorize;* to English adjectives, *normalize, victorianize;* to proper names, *londonize, bowdlerize*). In U.S. use the suffix is nearly always spelled *-ize*, even in words from French, in which the spelling is *-iser*. In Britain, however, many not only retain *s* in borrowings from French but use *s* instead of *z* in borrowings from Greek and Latin and in English formations. Many others in Britain, however, including several influential publications, use *-ize* in all words in which \īz\ is descended from Greek *-izein*.

EXCEPTIONS: (1) although \īz\ in *exorci-e* and *chasti-e* derives (in the second somewhat circuitously) from Greek *-izein*, there is a strong preference for *s* over *z* in these words; (2) the ending \īz\ in some English verbs (and a few nouns) not only is from etyma spelled with *s* rather than *z* but has no etymological relationship to the ending discussed in the preceding paragraph. For *adverti-e s* strongly prevails in both the U.S. and Britain. In Britain *z* seems to prevail in *amorti-e, assi-e, recogni-e*, strongly prevails in *aggrandi-e, capsi-e, cogni-e, gormandi-e*; in the U.S. *z* alone occurs

or strongly prevails in all seven words. The verb *merchandi-e* occasionally has *z*, the noun seldom. The following are usually found with *s*: *advise, comprise, compromise, demise, despise, devise, disguise, enterprise, excise, franchise, improvise, revise, supervise, surmise, surprise;* (3) in the small group of words *analy-e, dialy-e, electroly-e, paraly-e,* in which *-ly-e* derives from the Greek noun *lysis, s* seems to be somewhat more common than *z* in Britain but *z* is much more common than *s* in the U.S.

2.10 -ol/-oul. In the words *mold/mould, molder/moulder, molt/moult,* and *smolder/smoulder,* the *u* is likely to be more often dropped than kept in the U.S., is almost always kept in Britain. *Molten* (from *melt*) has no variant with *u*.

2.11 -or/-our. English contains a group of *r*-final nouns that are descended from Latin nouns having nominative *-or,* that are not agent nouns (compare 2.7.1), and that are usually spelled *-or* in the U.S. but *-our* in Britain: *ardor/ardour; color/colour; fervor/fervour; honor/ honour; labor/labour; rigor/rigour; tumor/ tumour.* The first such borrowings into English were from early Old French, and the termination in both lending and borrowing language was *-or* or *-ur.* In French as spoken in Britain after the Norman Conquest the ending became *-our.* English borrowings from this Anglo-French retained the *-our,* and earlier borrowings from continental French became *-our* by assimilation. After the Renaissance made Latin more widely known, words of this category were usually borrowed, in their Latin spelling, with *-or* as the ending. Many words once spelled *-our* in English are in Britain now written *-or,* but others are not. In the U.S. the *-our* spelling is seldom used in these words.

EXCEPTIONS: (1) although the *-our* ending formerly occurred also in agent nouns, *saviour* is the only important survival; (2) *glamour* and *saviour* are the only two *-our* forms that have wide currency in the U.S.; (3) not all *-or/-our* words derive ultimately from Latin *-or* words (*arbor* "latticework", *armor, behavior, harbor, neighbor*). In Britain, *u* is usually retained before suffixes that had their origin within English (*favourer, flavourful, humourless, neighbourhood, neighbourly, vapourish*); before Latin suffixes that are not freely addable to English words *u* usually disappears (*coloration, honorary, honorific, odoriferous, odorous*); before Greek and Latin suffixes that have been naturalized (*-able, -ism, -ist, -ite, -ize*) the spelling varies.

2.12 -ped/-pede (from Latin *pes, pedis,* foot). *-pede* is more common than *-ped* after *milli-* and possibly the only form after *veloci-* and *centi-.* After other elements *-ped* is usual and is probably the only form that is now used after *bi-* and *quadru-.*

2.13 -c-/-s-: *defence/defense; offence/offense; pretence/pretense; vice/vise* "tool". In all four words *c* is the preference in Britain, *s* in the U.S.; *defensive, offensive,* and *pretension,* however, are the usual word forms in both countries; *licence/license; practice/practise:* U.S. usually spells *license* both noun and verb with *s;* Britain almost invariably spells the noun with *c,* usually spells the verb with *s.* U.S. uses *c* more often than *s* in the noun *practice,* uses one letter about as often as the other in the verb *practise;* Britain strongly prefers *c* in the noun (*s* seems nonexistent), *s* in the verb. Although noun and verb were once undifferentiated, on both sides of the Atlantic *prophecy* is more common for the noun, *prophesy* for the verb.

PLURALS

1. The plurals of English nouns are regularly formed in writing by the suffixation of the letter *-s* (*hat→ hats*) or the letters *-es* (*cross→ crosses*) and in speaking by the addition of the sound \s\ (\'hat→ 'hats\), the sound \z\ (\'bói→ 'bóiz\), or the sound \əz\ (\'krós→ 'kró-səz\). Although there are many exceptions to be noted, this regularity is so dominant that in theory all English nouns may be said to be capable of an analogical plural in the letters *-s* or *-es,* and in practice little hesitation in so forming a new or unknown plural should be felt. Native speakers of English have no difficulty in using the sounds of pluralization in accordance with regular patterns. This treatment of plurals will be limited to written words, typically selected, not exhaustive.

2. -s. Most nouns simply add *-s: bag→ bags; violet→ violets.*

3. silent -e. Nouns ending in *-e* that is silent regularly add *-s: college→ colleges; race→ races.*

4. -es. Nouns ending in *-s, -z, -x, -ch,* or *-sh* regularly add *-es: buzz→ buzzes; dash→ dashes; fox→ foxes; gas→ gases; torch→ torches.*

5. consonant + -y. Nouns ending in *-y* preceded by a consonant regularly change *-y* to *-i-* and add *-es: army→ armies; courtesy→ cour-*

tesies; sky→ skies; except proper names: *Germany→ Germanys; Kentucky→ Kentuckys; Mary→ Marys.*

6. -quy. Nouns ending in *-quy* regularly change *-y* to *-i-* and add *-es: colloquy→ colloquies.*

7. vowel + -y. Nouns ending in *-y* preceded by a vowel (except those ending in *-quy*) regularly add *-s: bay→ bays; boy→ boys; guy→ guys; key→ keys.*

8. vowel + -o. Nouns ending in *-o* preceded by a vowel regularly add *-s: duo→ duos; embryo→ embryos; studio→ studios.*

9. consonant + -o. Most nouns ending in *-o* preceded by a consonant add *-s: alto→ altos; ego→ egos; piano→ pianos; two→ twos;* but other nouns ending in *-o* preceded by a consonant add *-es: echo→ echoes; hero→ heroes; potato→ potatoes.* The consonant or cluster preceding the *-o* does not determine whether the plural will add *-s* or *-es.* A few nouns add either: *bravo→ bravos/bravoes; cargo→ cargos/cargoes; domino→ dominos/dominoes; zero→ zeros/zeroes.*

10. -oo. Nouns ending in *-oo* regularly add *-s: coo→ coos; cuckoo→ cuckoos; tattoo→ tattoos.*

11. -i. Most nouns ending in *-i* add *-s: rabbi→ rabbis; ski→ skis;* but a few add either *-s* or *-es: taxi→ taxis/taxies.*

12. -f. A few nouns ending in *-f* change the *-f* to *-v-* and add *-es: leaf→ leaves; self→ selves; thief→ thieves; wolf→ wolves;* but some of these also add *-s* without consonant change: *calf→ calves/calfs; wharf→ wharves/wharfs.*

13. -fe. A few nouns ending in *-fe* change *-f-* to *-v-* and add *-s: knife→ knives; life→ lives.*

14. one-letter words. Single letters, numbers, figures, and signs add either apostrophe and *-s* or just *-s: A→ A's/As; 4→ 4's/4s; 1920→ 1920's/1920s; △→ △'s/△s; #→ #'s/#s.*

15.1 nouns formed from abbreviations. Abbreviations formed by literation and used as nouns add either apostrophe and *-s* or more often just *-s: GI→ GI's/GIs; IQ→ IQ's/IQs; Ph.D.→ Ph.D.'s/Ph.D.s.*

15.2 Abbreviations formed by truncation or contraction usually add *-s* without apostrophe: *apt→ apts; bbl→ bbls; cap→ caps; mt→ mts;* but some become plural without any change: 1 *hr→* 4 *hr;* 1 *mo→* 4 *mo;* 1 *oz→* 4 *oz;* 1 *yd→* 4 *yd.*

15.3 Some single-letter abbreviations double an initial consonant: *c.→ cc.* (chapters); *p.→ pp.* (pages); *v.→ vv.* (verses, violins).

16. -en. One noun usually adds *-en: ox→ oxen;* and another changes the stem and adds *-en: child→ children;* and one sometimes changes the stem and adds *-en: brother→ brethren.*

17. umlaut. Six nouns change the medial vowel: *foot→ feet; goose→ geese; louse→ lice; man→ men; mouse→ mice; tooth→ teeth.* Compounds in which one of these is the final element likewise change: *dormouse→ dormice; Englishman→ Englishmen; eyetooth→ eyeteeth; forefoot→ forefeet; woman→ women.*

18. foreign endings. Many nouns of foreign origin retain the foreign plural; most of them have also a regular English *-s* or *-es* plural, which is often preferred, although sometimes a foreign plural signals a difference in meaning (compare *stadia* and *stadiums*).

18.1 Latin. Most of these common anglicized foreign words come from Latin: *alga→ algae; minutia→ minutiae; alumnus→ alumni; fungus→ fungi; index→ indices; matrix→ matrices; addendum→ addenda; medium→ media; ovum→ ova; genus→ genera; opus→ opera; crux→ cruces; nomen→ nomina; apparatus→ apparatus; series→ series.*

18.2 Greek. The second largest group of anglicized foreign words comes from Greek: *analysis→ analyses; ellipsis→ ellipses; thesis→ theses; criterion→ criteria; phenomenon→ phenomena; carcinoma→ carcinomata; lemma→ lemmata; aphis→ aphides; phalanx→ phalanges.*

18.3 Italian. A comparatively small number of Italian plurals have become anglicized: *bambino→ bambini; dilettante→ dilettanti; libretto→ libretti.*

18.4 French. A small number of French plurals have been anglicized: *adieu→ adieux; beau→ beaux; madame→ mesdames; monsieur→ messieurs.*

18.5 miscellaneous: *cherub→ cherubim* (Hebrew); *fellah→ fellahin* (Arabic); *señor→ señores* (Spanish).

19.1 compounds. Two-word compounds consisting of initial noun plus adjective hyphened or open customarily pluralize the noun: *cousin-german→ cousins-german; heir apparent→ heirs apparent; knight-errant→ knights-errant;* but not invariably; sometimes the adjective is construed as a noun and a regular suffix is alternatively added to it: *attorney general→ attorneys general/attorney generals; court-martial→ courts-martial/court-martials; notary public→ notaries public/notary publics; sergeant major→ sergeants major/sergeant majors.* In similar-appearing compounds in which the second word is a noun a regular suffix is added at the end: *brigadier general→ brigadier generals; judge advocate→ judge advocates.* A few similar compounds have double plurals: *gentleman-usher→ gentlemen-ushers; lord justice→ lords justices; thing-in-itself→ things-in-themselves.*

19.2 Three-word compounds consisting of initial noun plus prepositional phrase hyphened or open customarily pluralize the initial noun: *aide-de-camp→ aides-de-camp; brother-in-law→ brothers-in-law; man-of-war→ men-of-war.*

20. animals. Many names of fishes, birds, and mammals have both a plural with a suffix and a zero plural that is identical with the singular. Some have one or the other. Some present a choice according to meaning or according to a special interest of the user.

20.1 Examples of some that form a plural with a suffix (except occasionally when modified by an adjective like *wild, native, sea, mountain*): *bird, cow, crow, dog, eagle, hen, monkey, rat, shark, swallow.*

20.2 The following have both plurals of which the zero plural is likely to be preferred by those who hunt or fish: *antelope, bear, doe, duck, flounder, hare, quail, rabbit, raccoon, squirrel, tuna.*

20.3 The following have both plurals of which the zero plural is the commoner but the plural with a suffix is used to signify diversity in kind or species (*trouts* of the Rocky mountains; *fishes* of the Atlantic): *bass, cod, elk, pike, pout.*

20.4 The following customarily prefer the zero plural: *cattle, deer, grouse, moose, sheep, swine.*

21. numbers. A small number of general terms for numbers or quantities have both a plural form with suffix and a zero plural used in some constructions: *brace→ brace/braces; dozen→ dozen/dozens; hundred→ hundred/hundreds; score→ score/scores.*

22. peoples. Many names of tribal origin have a zero plural and also an anglicized plural with suffix: *Bantu→ Bantu/Bantus; Choctaw→ Choctaw/Choctaws; Eskimo→ Eskimo/Eskimos.*

23. -ese. Most names derived from a place name and ending in *-ese* have only a zero plural: *Burmese, Cantonese, Chinese, Japanese, Portuguese.*

PUNCTUATION

,	comma
;	semicolon
:	colon
.	period *or* full stop
—	dash *or* em dash
–	dash *or* en dash
∼	swung dash
?	question mark *or* interrogation point
¿ ?	question marks, Spanish
!	exclamation point
( )	parentheses *or* curves
[ ]	brackets, square
⟨ ⟩	brackets, angle
’ *or* '	apostrophe
-	hyphen
⸗ *or* ⸗	double hyphen
´ (é)	acute accent
` (è)	grave accent
ˆ (ô) *or* ⌢ *or* ~	circumflex
~ (ñ)	tilde
¯ (ō)	macron
˘ (ŭ)	breve
¨ (oö)	diaeresis
¸ (ç)	cedilla
∧	caret
“ ” *or* " "	quotation marks
« »	quotation marks, French
» « *or* „ “	quotation marks, German
‘ ’ *or* ' '	quotation marks, single
“ *or* ” *or* "	ditto marks
/	virgule *or* slant
\	reversed virgule
{ *or* } *or* ⏞	brace
. . . *or* * * * *or* ——	ellipsis
. . .	suspension points
*	asterisk
†	dagger
‡	double dagger
§	section *or* numbered clause
‖	parallels
¶ *or* ⁋	paragraph
☞	index *or* fist
⁂ *or* ⁂	asterism

0.1 Speech consists not merely of sounds but of organized sound sequences that follow various structural patterns and are uttered with significant modifications of pitch and stress and significant pauses. Besides representing the basic sounds of speech, the English writing system accordingly utilizes signs called punctuation marks to separate groups of words and to convey some indication of the varying pitch and volume and especially the pauses in the flow of speech sounds.

0.2 A pause in speech is accompanied by a significant adjustment in the pitch of the voice, which may rise, fall, or remain the same. There may also be an increase or decrease in stress with or without actual cessation of sound. Three principal types of pauses are readily perceptible in English speech: (1) The fading pause, a falling into silence with a full stop, is marked by a lowering of pitch and decrease of stress until the production of sound ceases. This pause signifies the termination of an utterance and in writing is usually indicated by the period or the semicolon. (2) The rising pause is characterized by an upturn in pitch often combined with a lengthening of word sounds just before the break. This pause is used to set off word groups within utterances, especially whenever there is anticipation of supplementary or explanatory matter to follow, and is usually indicated in writing by a comma or, at the end of a question, by a question mark. (3) The sustained pause occurs whenever there is a break without any change in the pitch of the voice or when the same pitch is continued across a break. This pause is often indicated in writing by a comma, particularly when a rising pause would also be appropriate. The sustained pause is indicated also by such marks as a dash or ellipsis where a person stops speaking without altering the pitch of his voice, as when he is interrupted.

0.3 Much written expression consists of discourse never actually spoken but formulated in the writer's mind and immediately expressed in writing. Somewhat more formal in its structural patterns than actual speech, such written expression is nevertheless a reflection of the spoken language, is itself capable of being spoken, and is therefore punctuated as the written expression of actual speech.

0.4 As will be indicated, punctuation marks are often used in an arbitrary or mechanical manner not directly related to language structure or to patterns of speech sounds. To a considerable extent, however, punctuation may be explained in terms of the structural divisions of speech — sentences, clauses, phrases, and other word groups — and some of the more obvious elements of pitch, stress, and pause that indicate their separation or their relationship.

1.1 Like a fading pause and full stop in speech, a **period** usually terminates a sentence that is neither interrogative nor exclamatory ⟨The mountain is 5000 feet high. If the climbers have a good day, they will reach the top in a few hours. At the summit they will eat the lunch which has been prepared, and then they will start down early enough to reach the bottom before dark.⟩

1.1.1 Utterances terminated by a fading pause do not always have a complete subject-predicate structure. In the context of consecutive speech, however, the meaning of such utterances is entirely clear, and in writing they are usually terminated with a period ⟨"Tell me when you came in." "Just now."⟩ ⟨"Please close the door." "Certainly."⟩

1.1.2 Structurally incomplete or fragmentary elements terminating in a period occur frequently in modern narrative writing and are usually

terminated with a period ⟨The sound of artillery through the night. The enemy again. Banging away to keep everyone nervous and awake.⟩

1.2 A period often follows an abbreviation ⟨Reedville, Mass., pop. 879⟩ ⟨cap. or l. c.⟩ ⟨7 a. m.⟩ ⟨30 mins.⟩ ⟨lg. pkg.⟩ ⟨no. 72⟩ ⟨5s. 6d.⟩ ⟨bks. marked o. p.⟩ ⟨dept. bulls.⟩ ⟨50 pp.⟩ ⟨U. S. S. *Wyoming*⟩ ⟨Dr. John H. Doe, 7 Pine St., New York, N. Y.⟩ ⟨Dec. 7, 1941⟩ ⟨Lt. Col. John Doe⟩

1.2.1 Periods do not usually follow abbreviations of compound names of international organizations and government agencies, official abbreviations designating equipment, and a large number of similar compound abbreviations usually written without spaces ⟨NATO⟩ ⟨UN⟩ ⟨UNESCO⟩ ⟨TVA⟩ ⟨VT fuze⟩ ⟨pfc⟩ ⟨EST⟩

1.2.2 Periods usually follow common contractions made by omitting medial letters ⟨secy.⟩ ⟨advt.⟩ ⟨mfg.⟩ ⟨recd.⟩

1.2.3 Some publishers, chiefly British, often do not put a period after *Mr, Mrs*, and *Dr* ⟨Dr and Mrs John H. Doe⟩

1.2.4 A period does not follow symbols of chemical elements ⟨*Al*⟩ ⟨*Cu*⟩ ⟨*U 235*⟩

1.2.5 Such terms as 1st, 2d, 3d, 4th, 8vo, and 12mo are not abbreviations and do not require a period.

1.2.6 Isolated letters of the alphabet used as designations do not require a period ⟨T square⟩ ⟨A 1⟩ ⟨I beam⟩

1.2.7 After titles of books and articles, after headings, and in display printing, printers usually omit a period at the ends of lines, as well as other punctuation except an essential question mark or an exclamation point.

1.3 A period is necessary before a decimal and between dollars and cents in figures ⟨16.63 ft.⟩ ⟨.32 cal.⟩ ⟨$12.17⟩

1.4 A period may or may not follow a roman numeral. In particular contexts usage is often quite uniform; thus a period is used after a roman numeral designating a chapter of a book in the Bible ⟨2 Sam. xix. 12⟩ but no period is used after a roman numeral following a personal name ⟨Elizabeth II of England⟩

1.5 Dictionaries use centered periods to indicate division between syllables of words where division is not otherwise indicated by accent marks or hyphens.

2.1 A **question mark** usually indicates in writing the incompleteness or anticipation conveyed in speech by any of various intonation patterns and frequently though not exclusively by a rising pause. The word order may be that of a question or a statement ⟨When did he leave?⟩ ⟨You say he never came back?⟩ ⟨An Oxford degree — or was it foreign travel? — lured him to England.⟩

2.1.1 A question mark does not follow an indirect question, which has the intonation pattern and fading pause of a positive statement ⟨They are asking him where he plans to go.⟩

2.1.2 A request expressed in interrogative form for the sake of courtesy usually ends in a period corresponding to the fading pause of a positive statement ⟨Will you kindly fill out this questionnaire and return it to the personnel office.⟩

2.1.3 When used as the terminal mark of a direct quotation, the question mark, as well as the exclamation point, usually takes the place of a comma or period which would otherwise be used at that point in the sentence ⟨After he had affixed the title "What is Progress?" he folded the manuscript of his speech.⟩

2.2 A question mark, usually enclosed in parentheses, often follows arbitrarily after a word, phrase, or date to indicate uncertainty of its accuracy or to mark a gap in available information ⟨Omar Khayyám, Persian poet (?–1123?)⟩

3.1 An **exclamation point** follows an expression or statement that is an exclamation and corresponds to a heavy, relatively high-pitched terminal stress in speech ⟨Oh no! Not that!⟩ ⟨I wish he would!⟩ ⟨Do you think we will stand for this any longer!⟩ ⟨Hurry! We need help!⟩

4.0 Of all the marks of punctuation the **comma** offers the most difficulty in use and the widest range for individual choice. Though often marking rhetorical or elocutionary pauses, the comma is used primarily to separate or to set off in a group. It sometimes distinguishes nonrestrictive modifiers from restrictive modifiers. Since the genus-terms of definitions in this dictionary are intended to be modified only by differentiae that are restrictive in some degree, the use of commas either to separate or to group is severely limited chiefly to units in apposition or in series.

4.1 Commas That Set Off. A word, phrase, or clause is often inserted in a sentence to supply explanatory or supplementary information. In speech the rising pause or sometimes the sustained pause sets off such material when it is of relatively minor importance and is not essential to the main idea. In writing, commas usually indicate the subordinate status of such matter. These commas always make a pair unless the element set off begins or ends a sentence.

4.1.1 Commas usually set off words, phrases, and other sentence elements that are parenthetical or independent. Items of this sort are contrasting expressions, prefatory exclamations, the names of persons directly addressed, and expressions like *he said* in direct quotations ⟨Work, not words, is what is needed.⟩ ⟨The outcome, though hardly to our liking, is better than expected.⟩ ⟨The animals, nervous and restless, pace interminably in their cages.⟩ ⟨He is often late, to be sure, but we can rely on him in a crisis.⟩ ⟨"Listen, John," he said, "drive carefully."⟩ ⟨Oh bosh, pay no attention to him (the comma that goes with the comma after *bosh* gives way to the capital *O*).⟩

4.1.2 Commas usually set off appositional or modifying words, phrases, or clauses that do not limit or restrict the main idea of a sentence. Such constructions are termed nonrestrictive ⟨George, his own brother, is turning against him.⟩ ⟨John, whom we saw yesterday, is away today.⟩ ⟨His father, dressed in a new gray suit, came early for the ceremony.⟩ The second of the pair of commas in the next three gives way to the period that closes the sentence ⟨There stood John, smiling quietly to himself.⟩ ⟨We leave at 3 o'clock, when the bell rings.⟩ ⟨The formation is of great interest to geologists, although most of us would hardly notice it.⟩

4.1.2.1 When inserted or appended words, phrases, or clauses are restrictive or essential to the main idea of a statement, they are spoken without the pauses or other significant intonation that would indicate matter of minor importance. In writing, commas are likewise unnecessary ⟨His friend George is turning against him.⟩ ⟨The man whom we saw yesterday is not here today.⟩ ⟨The man dressed in the new gray suit is his father.⟩ ⟨John is the boy standing in the rear and smiling to himself.⟩ ⟨We leave when the bell rings.⟩ ⟨He will come if his safe-conduct is guaranteed.⟩

4.1.2.2 Sometimes the presence or absence of commas corresponding to spoken pauses constitutes the sole means of determining whether a phrase or clause is essential or nonessential, restrictive or nonrestrictive ⟨Our friends, who live out of town, do not like the new parking laws/Our friends who live out of town do not like the new parking laws.⟩ ⟨The men, draining the swamp, searched all day for the boy/The men draining the swamp searched all day for the boy.⟩ ⟨We do not visit him, because he always serves liquor/We do not visit him because he always serves liquor.⟩

4.1.3 Commas set off transitional words and expressions (as *on the contrary, on the other hand, consequently, furthermore, moreover, nevertheless, therefore*) whenever they are or would be spoken with the adjacent rising or sustained pauses that indicate subordinate matter ⟨The question, however, remains unsettled.⟩ ⟨Nevertheless, we shall go.⟩ ⟨On the contrary, under the rules a vote is in order.⟩

4.1.3.1 Such expressions may occur in context so as to be spoken without significant pauses and may likewise require no punctuation ⟨We shall therefore proceed with the operation.⟩ ⟨The weaklings will consequently be forced to drop out.⟩ ⟨A clear-cut decision is on the other hand too much to expect.⟩

4.2.1 Commas That Separate. Various expressions are often used in sentences to introduce or qualify something that follows. To separate these elements in speech a rising or sustained pause denotes the end of the introductory information and the beginning of the main part of the statement. In writing, a comma accordingly often separates an introductory word or phrase from the rest of the sentence, particularly when the introductory material is long or when ambiguity might otherwise occur ⟨Unfortunately, we shall have to decline the invitation.⟩ ⟨In the first place, you will get very little information from him.⟩ ⟨To gain popularity, he betrayed his convictions.⟩ ⟨Immediately upon reaching the surface, he swam to shore.⟩ ⟨Seeing the dog approaching, he ran off down the street.⟩

4.2.2 Whenever in spoken English there is an enumeration of items, a rising or sustained pause separates and distinguishes each member of the series. In writing, a comma likewise usually separates words, phrases, or clauses that occur in a series ⟨The estate is to be divided among Robert, John, and William.⟩ ⟨Trees, trees, trees were all we could see.⟩ ⟨He opened the can, removed the contents, and replaced the lid.⟩ ⟨The one who befriended us, watched over us, and gave us help is now no more.⟩ ⟨The prisoner will not talk, he refuses to eat, and he pounds the bars continually.⟩

4.2.2.1 Before *and* or *or* introducing the final term in a closed series, writers usually put a comma ⟨*a, b,* and *c*⟩ ⟨a coat, a hat, and a pair of gloves⟩ ⟨scientific, technical, and learned periodicals⟩ but sometimes omit it in a short series ⟨a coat, a hat and a pair of gloves⟩ ⟨*a, b* and *c*⟩

4.2.2.2 Modifying words in an open series preceding a noun are often separated and distinguished in speech by pauses and in writing by commas ⟨a rural, agricultural, idyllic life⟩ ⟨journalistic, literary, popular publications⟩. Sometimes, however, the pause and hence the comma may be unnecessary when the second modifier relates more closely to the noun than the first, or when the first modifier applies to the second modifier and the noun as a unit ⟨a quiet rural atmosphere⟩ ⟨a vivid red tie⟩ ⟨a brilliant military strategist⟩

4.2.3 Statements or clauses joined by a coordinating conjunction are separated in speech by a sustained or rising pause. In writing, a comma usually effects this separation ⟨He seemed inattentive, but not a word escaped him.⟩ ⟨His face showed his disappointment, for he knew he had failed.⟩ ⟨He did not like intruders of the sort that now confronted him, nor did he see any way of avoiding them.⟩ ⟨She knew very little about him, and he volunteered nothing.⟩

4.2.3.1 When the statements or clauses joined by a coordinating conjunction are brief and unambiguous, and usually when the subject is the same, the comma may be omitted ⟨He will suffer but he will recover.⟩

4.2.3.2 A comma alone without the conjunction sometimes separates brief and closely related statements or clauses. In such instances a sustained or slightly falling pause may occur in speech rather than the fading pause and full stop designated by the period ⟨The boy went to the store, then he went home.⟩ ⟨Don't bother, it doesn't make any difference.⟩ ⟨He would always remember, the experience was now a part of him.⟩ This comma may or may not be permissive in the treatment of the comma fault in various handbooks of composition.

4.2.3.3 When a conjunction joins two predicative constructions that have the same subject, the clarifying pause in speech may be slight or imperceptible. In writing, a comma is likewise not considered necessary except to avoid ambiguity ⟨The car teetered for a moment on the edge of the road and then plunged down the embankment.⟩ ⟨Sailing an iceboat is thrilling sport but requires great skill.⟩

4.2.4 Corresponding to the rising or sustained pause necessary in speech to distinguish items in addresses and dates, a comma usually separates such matter in writing ⟨Born January 1, 1900, in Delhi, India, the university's outstanding student received his college degree in June, 1922.⟩ ⟨Apply for the booklet at the Superintendent of Documents, Washington 25, D. C.⟩

4.2.4.1 Usage is about evenly divided, however, when the day is not given ⟨in June 1922⟩ or ⟨in June, 1922⟩

4.2.4.2 Sometimes writers omit the comma after the year ⟨born January 1, 1900 in India⟩

4.2.5 When such expressions as *namely, that is, i. e., e. g., viz.* introduce an illustration or example, a comma that corresponds in function to

a rising or sustained pause in speech usually separates it from what follows ⟨There are two ways to do the job: namely, a right way and a wrong way.⟩ ⟨He forbade future forays; that is, there were to be no more raids on the neighbors' gardens.⟩

4.2.6 A comma usually indicates the place of an omitted word or word group to achieve a separation like that effected in speech by a sustained or rising pause ⟨The tractor is used for hauling; the bulldozer, for excavating.⟩

4.2.7 Like a sustained or rising pause in speech, a comma usually separates a direct quotation from the rest of a sentence or context ⟨"Make way for liberty," he cried.⟩ ⟨He asked abruptly, "Which way do you vote?"⟩ ⟨As some say, "Virtue is its own reward."⟩

4.3 Commas Used Arbitrarily. The comma often functions in an arbitrary manner as a mechanical device.

4.3.1 In numbers the comma usually separates thousands, millions, and other groups of three digits except in dates, page numbers, and street numbers, and in numbers of four digits ⟨an altitude of 7525 feet⟩ ⟨3600 rpm⟩

4.3.2 A comma usually sets off inverted names in bibliographies and reference lists ⟨Doe, John, Jr.⟩

4.3.3 A comma usually separates a proper name and an academic or honorary title, also two or more such titles in succession ⟨John Doe, M.A., Ph.D., President⟩

4.3.4 A comma is the customary mark after the salutation in personal letters and after the complimentary close in all letters ⟨Dear Jack,⟩ ⟨Sincerely yours,⟩ ⟨Yours very truly,⟩

4.4.1 One may avoid excessive or uncertain use of the comma by eliminating commas, excepting those used arbitrarily, where there are no significant pauses. In terms of structure, a comma does not usually separate closely related grammatical sequences ⟨The advice his father gave him/remained long in his mind.⟩ ⟨The result of the long and detailed planning was / that the forces were well prepared for the battle.⟩ ⟨The flea-bitten, shaggy / dog padded desolately down the alley.⟩ ⟨The long, happy, and successful trip/ was one he will never forget.⟩ ⟨His new car is a fast / and powerful machine.⟩

4.4.2 It is equally important to insert a comma to prevent misreading or ambiguity. The need for a rising or sustained pause in speech usually indicates that a comma is necessary in writing ⟨Inside, the fire was burning brightly.⟩ ⟨Ever since, the little man comes at dark to clean the kitchen.⟩ ⟨Whoever lost it, lost an invaluable treasure.⟩ ⟨To Ruth, John appeared as a mighty warrior on a white horse.⟩ ⟨In 1925, 25 percent of the graduates of the school went on to college.⟩ ⟨The railroad had no resources, but the trains were somehow kept running.⟩ ⟨As the car struck, the utility pole fell with a crash.⟩

5.1 In general the **semicolon** functions as a weak period or as a strong comma. As a weak period the semicolon corresponds to a fading pause and full stop in speech similar to but perhaps not quite as final as that represented by a period. As a strong comma the semicolon cor-

responds to a rising or sustained pause in speech possibly longer or slightly more definitive than that represented by a comma.

5.1.1 As a weak period a semicolon usually separates independent statements or clauses joined together in one sentence without a conjunction. Such statements or clauses are usually closely related ⟨Make no terms; resist until the last breath.⟩ ⟨A fool babbles continuously; a wise man holds his tongue.⟩

5.1.2 As a weak period a semicolon usually separates two statements or clauses when the second begins with a sentence connector or conjunctive adverb, as *accordingly, also, consequently, furthermore, hence, however, indeed, moreover, nevertheless, otherwise, so, still, then, therefore, thus, yet* ⟨You have recommended this man; therefore I will give him a trial.⟩ ⟨His conduct has always been exemplary; nevertheless he will not be permitted to go.⟩

5.1.3 As a strong comma a semicolon usually separates phrases or clauses that are themselves broken up by punctuation ⟨The country's resources consist of large ore deposits; lumber, waterpower, and fertile soils; a favorable climate; and a strong, rugged people.⟩ ⟨When the presently available natural resources are greatly depleted, man will have to develop new sources of food and power; and then will come the real test of his energies, his imagination, and his ingenuity.⟩

5.1.4 A semicolon sometimes separates arbitrarily in lists of names with addresses, titles, or figures where a comma alone would not clearly separate items or references ⟨Genesis 3:1–19; 4:1–16⟩

6.1 The **colon,** corresponding to a fading or sustained pause in speech, is a rhetorical mark of supplementation. It links clauses, phrases, or less often single words; it indicates that what follows it coordinates with some element of what precedes or sometimes with all of what precedes back to the beginning of a sentence. Specific types of supplementation are mentioned in parentheses after the examples ⟨The same forced yes-or-no choice appears on referenda on public questions: the voter cannot express approval of some parts and disapproval of others unless amended. (elaboration)⟩ ⟨It vigorously opposes clandestine marriages: that is, marriages which were made outside the auspices of the Church. (definition)⟩ ⟨His ambition must be stirred: his greed must be played upon. (balance)⟩ ⟨The following items of equipment are necessary: sleeping bag, ground cloth, cooking utensils, and a small axe. (enumeration)⟩ ⟨Representatives of ten countries presented papers at the formal meetings, including: Brazil, England, France, Holland, India, Italy, Japan, the United States, the U. S. S. R., and West Germany —Allen Kent. (enumeration)⟩ ⟨The author never exploits any whimsical or romantic elements in this subject: he maintains throughout the decent, workmanlike attitude he has set himself. (restatement)⟩ ⟨Local currencies, like local laws, were not suppressed: they were encouraged to improve. (antithesis)⟩ ⟨His death raised the possibility that his political heirs might seek the final solution for insolvent, disorganized governments: war. (summation)⟩ ⟨The question is this: will the removal of restrictions lead to freedom or license? (apposition)⟩ Usually what precedes a colon is general and what follows is specific but sometimes the rela-

tion is reversed ⟨Physics and biology, evolution and anthropology, conservation and religion: he discusses them all.⟩

Sometimes paired colons correlate ⟨He has ambition: it must be stirred. He has a belief in fair play: it must be honored.⟩

Frequently the colon is reinforced by anticipatory phrasing (as *thus, namely, for example, as follows*).

6.2 A colon functions as a mechanical device in set formulas involving separation of parts, as when relating the antecedent of a ratio to its consequent ⟨12 : 19⟩ or one ratio to another ⟨12 : 19 : : x : 57⟩ or when relating subdivisional units in a descending series to specify or particularize one member, especially in time-telling by hour, minute, and second ⟨2:31:30⟩, in bibliographical reference by volume and page ⟨*National Geographic* 33:89⟩ or by chapter and verse ⟨Luke 2:12⟩ or by place and publisher ⟨Springfield : G. & C. Merriam Co.⟩, or in accounting by pounds, shillings, and pence ⟨46 : 6 : 11⟩

6.3 A colon symbolizes a conventional separation or emphatic pause after a formal salutation in a letter ⟨Dear Sir:⟩ or an address ⟨Mr. Chairman, Ladies and Gentlemen:⟩ or between a book title and a subtitle not otherwise differentiated ⟨*Victory : A History of the Recent Struggle*⟩

6.4 A colon introduces a quotation especially when quotation marks are omitted and when the quoted matter is indented ⟨We quote from the text: "Greater love hath no man".⟩:

He reads these words from Ruth:
Whither thou goest, I will go.

Mother: Where did you go?
Child: I won't tell.

A colon joins terms that are being contrasted or compared and is sometimes centered or spaced ⟨Seventeenth century rhymes include *prayer: afar* and *brass : was : ass.*⟩ ⟨The stature of the two sexes shows very nearly the same female : male proportions.⟩

7.0 In its function in writing and in the speech intonation to which it corresponds, the **dash** is similar to the comma and the colon, and a pair of dashes is similar to parentheses.

7.1 A dash usually marks an abrupt change or suspension in the thought or structure of a sentence ⟨If you will listen I will explain — but perhaps another time will be better.⟩ ⟨The mountain we climbed is higher than — oh, never mind how high it is.⟩ ⟨He was — how shall I put it — a controversial figure to say the least.⟩ ⟨"Yes, but I — er — I'll have to —" and he stopped hopelessly.⟩

7.2 A dash often makes parenthetic, appositional, or explanatory matter stand out clearly or emphatically ⟨Three of the country's most important products — oil, steel, and wheat — are produced in greater quantities than ever before.⟩ ⟨Two of our group — Eddie and John — came walking down the street.⟩ ⟨He is willing to discuss all problems — those he has solved and those for which there is no immediate solution.⟩

7.3 A dash often occurs before a summarizing statement or clause ⟨Oil, steel, and wheat — these are the sinews of industrialization.⟩

7.4 A dash sometimes sets off appositional or parenthetic matter that is introduced by such expressions as *namely, for example, that is* ⟨Sports develop two valuable traits — namely, self-control and the ability to make quick decisions.⟩

7.5 A dash often mechanically precedes the name of an author or source at the end of a quoted passage ⟨There is a tide in the affairs of men which, taken at the flood, leads on to fortune —William Shakespeare⟩ ⟨"In the beginning God created the heavens and the earth" —Genesis 1:1⟩

7.6 A long dash often functions as a notational device to indicate the omission of a word or of letters in a word ⟨yelling —— loudly⟩ ⟨Mr. M—— of New York⟩ ⟨go to the d———l⟩

7.7 A short dash — slightly larger than a hyphen — often serves as an arbitrary equivalent of *to and including* between numbers or dates and in compounding capitalized two-word names with the hyphen ⟨pages 40–98⟩ ⟨the decade 1951–60⟩ ⟨the New York–Lisbon plane⟩

8.1 Parentheses often set off parenthetic matter when the interruption is more marked than that usually indicated by commas ⟨Three old destroyers (all now out of commission) will be scrapped.⟩ ⟨He is hoping (as we all are) that this time he will succeed.⟩

8.2 Parentheses often set off supplementary or explanatory matter that is not a part of the main statement or not a structural element of the sentence ⟨The more distant mountain (I think you have climbed it before) is our goal.⟩ ⟨The diagram (Fig. 3) illustrates the action of the pump.⟩ ⟨The Springfield (Illinois) stop is the first on the tour.⟩

8.3 Parentheses often mechanically enclose sequential numbers or letters in a series (but do not take the place of required punctuation) ⟨We must clearly set forth (1) our long-term goals, (2) our immediate objectives, and (3) the means at our disposal.⟩

8.4 Parentheses usually arbitrarily enclose an arabic number confirming a number expressed in words ⟨Delivery will be made in thirty (30) days.⟩ ⟨Payment due is twenty dollars ($20.00).⟩

9.1 Brackets usually set off mechanically a word or phrase that is extraneous or incidental to the context, such as editorial interpolations ⟨He wrote, "I am just as cheerful as when you was [sic] here."⟩ ⟨A fly is said to be a two-winged dipterous [does that make four wings?] insect.⟩ ⟨The officer in charge [General Doe] had to countersign the order.⟩

9.2 Brackets often function as parentheses within parentheses ⟨Bowman Act (22 Stat., ch. 4, § [or sec.] 4, p. 50).⟩

10.1 Consisting usually of three spaced periods (**suspension points**) or asterisks and corresponding in effect to a sustained pause in speech, an **ellipsis** often indicates an interrupted or unfinished sentence. Wherever an ellipsis is terminal, a period follows ⟨"I shall . . . that is . . . if we can only. . . ." He faltered and stopped speaking.⟩ ⟨"Cut the line and cast. . . ." His voice was lost in the crash of the next wave.⟩

10.2 An ellipsis often occurs as a notational device to indicate an omission in quoted matter, as a word or a group of consecutive words unessential or undesirable for quotation ⟨"Oh say can you see . . . what so proudly we hailed . . .?"⟩

10.3 An ellipsis on a line by itself in poetry indicates the omission of one or more lines of verse. Sometimes it consists of periods spaced and extended in number to the full measure of the line:

Thus driven

By the bright shadow of that lovely dream,

. . . .

He fled

—P. B. Shelley

11.1 A **centered period** in a dictionary entry indicates syllabic or end-of-line division ⟨dy·nam·ic⟩.

12.1.1 A **hyphen** is a mark of separation or division at the end of a line which terminates with a syllable of a word that is to be carried over to the next line ⟨mill- [end of line] stone⟩ ⟨pas-sion⟩

12.1.2 A hyphen divides letters or syllables to give the effect of stuttering, sobbing, or halting ⟨S-s-sammy⟩ ⟨ah-ah-ah⟩ ⟨y-y-es⟩

12.1.3 A hyphen suspends the second part of a hyphened compound used in combination with another hyphened compound ⟨a six- or eight-cylindered engine⟩ ⟨in ten- and twenty-dollar bills⟩

12.1.4 Hyphens indicate a word spelled out letter by letter ⟨p-r-o-b-a-t-i-o-n⟩

12.2 A hyphen before a word element indicates that it is a suffix or a terminal combining form ⟨-ous⟩ ⟨-ship⟩

12.3 A hyphen after a word element indicates that it is a prefix or initial combining form ⟨anti-⟩ ⟨fore-⟩

12.4 Hyphens before and after a word element indicate that it is a medial word element ⟨-o-⟩

13.1 **Quotation marks** often enclose a direct quotation from a speaker or from a text or other written matter ⟨"When I am dead," said one of the keenest of modern minds, one of the greatest of modern poets, "lay a sword on my coffin, for I was a soldier in the war for the liberation of humanity."⟩
Quotation marks are not used to enclose oft-quoted familiar phrases (as *to err is human*).
Quotation marks are not used to enclose indirect quotations ⟨*direct* — The man said, "I am going home."⟩ ⟨*indirect* — The man said that he was going home.⟩

13.2 In long quotations, excepting extracts from plays, left-hand quotation marks are placed at the beginning of every paragraph included in the quotation in addition to those placed at the beginning and at the end of the selection.

13.3 Quotation marks are usually not used when the quoted matter is set in smaller type or in paragraphs indented on both sides.

13.4 Single quotation marks enclose a quotation within a quotation; or if single quotation marks are used primarily, double quotation marks enclose a quotation within a quotation ⟨The witness said, "I distinctly heard him say, 'Don't be late'; then I heard the door close".⟩

13.5 Quotation marks usually enclose titles of short poems, paintings, lectures, articles, and parts or chapters of books. (Titles of whole books, periodicals, and newspapers are usually italicized in context.)

13.5.1 In American usage printers usually place a period or comma inside closing quotation marks whether it belongs logically to the quoted matter or to the whole sentence or context ⟨The package is labeled "Handle with Care."⟩ ⟨The golden rule, "Do unto others as you would have them do unto you," is easier to remember than to practice.⟩
But when a logical or exact distinction is desired in specialized work in which clarity is more important than usual (as in this dictionary), a period or comma can be placed outside quotation marks when it belongs not to the quoted matter but to a large unit containing the quoted matter ⟨The package is labeled "Handle with Care".⟩ ⟨This act may be cited as the "Army-Navy Medical Services Corps Act of 1947".⟩ ⟨The Prime Minister, after reporting the negotiations, declared resolutely, "Our only course is to resist aggression".⟩ ⟨Replying with the one word "Bunk", he subsided.⟩

13.5.2 Only one other mark accompanies closing quotation marks, whether the quotation and the whole sentence or context call for the same mark or for different marks ⟨Did he keep asking you, "What is your number?"⟩ ⟨We shouted in unison, "Where do you think you're going?"⟩ ⟨Just as he screamed, "I will not!" he slammed the door.⟩ ⟨Is this the gratitude I receive, to have you bellow, "Get out of here and don't come back!"⟩

13.5.3 A colon or semicolon is usually placed outside of quotation marks ⟨"Fame is proof that people are gullible"; with this quotation he retired in silence.⟩

13.5.4 A colon or semicolon is sometimes placed inside the quotation marks when it belongs inseparably to the quotation ⟨"Sirs:" is a salutation used in letters to a newspaper.⟩; however, a terminal colon or semicolon of quoted matter incorporated in a sentence usually gives place to appropriate end punctuation.

13.5.5 A question mark or exclamation point is usually placed inside or outside the quotation marks according to whether it belongs to the quoted matter or to the whole sentence or clause that includes the quotation ⟨Can you forget his angry exit after he shouted "Include me out"?⟩ ⟨"And what do you think of this new novel?" his friend asked.⟩

13.6 Quotation marks, often single quotation marks, sometimes enclose technical terms unfamiliar to the reader; words used in an unusual sense; and coined words, trade or shop jargon, or slang for which the writer implies a slight apology ⟨An "em" is a unit of measure used in printing.⟩ ⟨The plates of copper are hung by "corrosion hooks" in the acid.⟩ ⟨This venture is a "wildcat" invented to prey upon the unwary.⟩ ⟨We've had enough of your "unshrinkable" shirts.⟩ ⟨He is "goofy" according to their lingo.⟩

14.0 An **apostrophe** and *s* are usually added to a noun to indicate ownership or a relation analogous to ownership. This possessive form is a survival of the *es* ending in Old and Middle English, from which the vowel sound has disappeared in Modern English except in nouns ending with the sound \s\, \z\, \sh\, \zh\, \ch\, or \j\. In early Modern English the *s* of the possessive was

often dropped from the possessive of nouns already ending in an *s* or *z* sound, both in speaking and in writing, leaving only the apostrophe in writing, as is evident in various idioms and in poetry. Since the middle of the 19th century, however, the form with the apostrophe and *s* has been generally adopted for the possessives in which the extra syllable is not awkward to pronounce in context.

14.1 An apostrophe and *s* form the possessive case of singular or plural nouns that do not end in an *s* or *z* sound ⟨boy's⟩ ⟨carpenter's⟩ ⟨dog's⟩ ⟨president's⟩ ⟨at his wit's end⟩ ⟨garage's responsibility⟩ ⟨Senator Doe's constituency⟩ ⟨the church's policy⟩ ⟨men's⟩ ⟨Descartes's philosophy⟩ ⟨Delacroix's painting⟩

14.2 An apostrophe either with or without *s* forms the possessive case of singular nouns ending in an *s* or *z* sound.

14.2.1 Singular nouns ending in an *s* or *z* sound that consist of one syllable or have a primary or secondary accent on the last syllable usually add an apostrophe and *s* to form the possessive case ⟨the class's recitation⟩ ⟨the press's description⟩ ⟨the fox's tail⟩ ⟨King James's reign⟩ ⟨Laplace's theories⟩ ⟨the marquise's jewels⟩

14.2.2 Singular nouns ending in an *s* or *z* sound that consist of more than one syllable and have no primary or secondary accent on the last syllable often add the apostrophe and *s* to form the possessive case unless the additional syllable with the *s* or *z* sound would be unpleasant or difficult to pronounce in context. Sometimes such a syllable is necessary to avoid ambiguity in pronunciation. Usage is divided in this matter (1) ⟨an audience's / audience' reaction⟩ ⟨the waitress's / waitress' duties⟩ ⟨the phoenix's/ phoenix' nest⟩ ⟨for appearance's / appearance' sake⟩ (2) ⟨Dr. Adams' / Adams's services⟩ ⟨the octopus' / octopus's snaky appearance⟩ ⟨Dickens'/ Dickens's novels⟩

14.2.3 With some exceptions various classical and biblical names are treated as in 14.2.1 and 14.2.2 ⟨Zeus's son⟩ ⟨Mars's help⟩ ⟨Venus's/ Venus'⟩ ⟨Judas's/Judas'⟩ but ⟨Brutus'/Brutus's⟩ ⟨Odysseus' / Odysseus's⟩, and ⟨Jesus'⟩ ⟨Moses'⟩ ⟨Pythagoras's / Pythagoras'⟩ ⟨Herodotus's/ Herodotus'⟩⟨Oedipus's/Oedipus'⟩,but⟨Aristophanes' / Aristophanes's⟩ ⟨Socrates' / Socrates's⟩ ⟨Thucydides' / Thucydides's⟩

14.3 An apostrophe without *s* usually forms the possessive case of plural nouns ending in an *s* or *z* sound ⟨consumers' protest⟩ ⟨foxes' holes⟩ ⟨the Joneses' invitation⟩ ⟨the two chateaux' occupants⟩ but ⟨geese's⟩ ⟨lice's⟩ ⟨mice's⟩

14.4 An apostrophe and *s* usually form the possessive case of various indefinite pronouns ⟨anybody's⟩ ⟨anyone's⟩ ⟨everybody's⟩ ⟨everyone's⟩ ⟨somebody's⟩ ⟨someone's⟩ but no apostrophe is used in the possessive pronouns *his, hers, its, ours, yours, theirs.*

COMPOUNDS

1.1 A *compound*, as the term is used here, is a word or word group of two or more elements at least one of which is an independent word of the same language. The elements in an English compound are variously written solid, open, or hyphened when they are all English words that can be written independently. When one of the elements in an English compound is not an independent English word, the elements are usually solid (*watery, antiperiodic, predate*) or hyphened (*de-emphasize*).

1.2 To show in a dictionary all of the stylings that are found for English compounds would necessitate excluding other information much more likely to be sought by the dictionary user. This dictionary therefore limits itself almost without exception to a single styling for a compound. When a compound occurs frequently and one styling predominates, this styling is used. When a compound is rare or when the examples indicate that two or three stylings are approximately equal in frequency, the choice is based on the analogy of parallel compounds or is made arbitrarily.

2.1 The dependent element in most compounds formed within English is a prefix or a suffix. It is added to several or many English words and exerts the same modification of sense on all of them.

2.1.1 Prefixes in borrowed compounds. In prefix-containing foreign-language compounds borrowed into English, if the prefix ends and the base word begins with the same vowel letter, a hyphen is often used between the two vowels, or a diaeresis is sometimes placed over the second vowel (*co-operate/coöperate*) but usually the form is solid (*cooperate*). If two vowels that are not identical come together at the point of juncture, usually neither hyphen nor diaeresis is used (*coalesce, coerce*). If the junctural letters are two consonants, or a vowel and a consonant, or a consonant and vowel, neither hyphen nor diaeresis is used (*collect, diagram, anarchy*).

2.1.2 Prefixes in compounds formed within English. In prefix-containing compounds formed in English a prefix and a base word are seldom open-styled. Some combinations are usually close-styled (*in-* and *un-*, as in *inexpressible, untenable*), some are usually hyphened (*ex-* in *ex-president*), some are frequently styled either way (*anti-, co-, extra-, non-, pre-, semi-*). With prefixes of this last class the hyphened styling is usual when the prefix ends with a vowel letter and the base word begins with the same letter (*anti-* + *intellectualism, infra-* + *angelic, semi-* + *independent*); the hyphened styling is less frequent when the junctural letters are two vowels that are not identical (*de-* + *adjectival, fore-* + *oath*); but solid styling is usual when the junctural letters are two consonants, or a vowel and a consonant (*non-* + *metallic, non-* + *alcoholic, extra-* + *legal*).

2.1.3 When the base word begins with a capital, a hyphen is usual (*un-* + *American*).

2.1.4 Some elements sometimes regarded as prefixes function as adjectives when they stand open before a noun (*a pseudo liberal; quasi independence*). But a styling like *a semi annual sale* is seldom seen outside newspaper advertisements.

2.1.5 When a prefix governs two or more words, it is almost invariably followed by a hyphen, and

the styling of the group of words to which the hyphen applies varies: sometimes the members of the group are left spaced, sometimes they are hyphened (*an ex-vice president/an ex-vice-president, pre-World War prices/pre-World-War prices, the ex-Republican majority leader/the ex-Republican-majority-leader*). Although spaced styling in such cases is often ambiguous, mere substitution of hyphens for spaces is not always a solution.

2.1.6 Sometimes the same succession of letters forms two words that contain the same prefix but that are different in sense, pronunciation, and styling, one word being solid and the other hyphened. In such cases the solid compound was formed in and borrowed from another language, the hyphened compound was formed in English; the second element may or may not be ultimately the same word etymologically in both cases (*recover* "to get back", *re-cover* "to cover again"; *recreation* "diversion", *re-creation* "a creating again").

2.2 Suffix–containing compounds. Suffixes are close-styled (*shoeless, meanness, freer*), except that a succession of three identical consonants is hyphened (*hull-less*) if one is not dropped (*hulless*).

2.2.1 Some independent English words (*like, worthy*) which are sometimes regarded as suffixes when they are joined to the word they govern may be joined by a hyphen: *Christlike/ Christ-like, praiseworthy/praise-worthy.*

2.2.2 When a suffix is added to two or more words that are written separate before suffixation, the styling of these words varies (*baby farming/baby-farming, bitter-ender/bitter ender, otherworldly/other-worldly*). The composition of some of these compounds, especially those that end in *-er*, may be ambiguous. Thus *lime-juicer* "a British ship" is *lime juice + -er;* whereas *lime juicer* "a device for squeezing or juicing limes" is *lime + juicer.* Both words might appear in any of three stylings — hyphened, open, or solid.

2.3.1 Other real or apparent compounds of this category. In other compounds in which one element is also an independent English word and the other is not or seems not to be, some are usually solid (*raspberry, bonfire, bookmobile, cheeseburger*), others are usually spaced (*tonka bean, shea tree*).

2.3.2 In some words that appear to be similar compounds the apparent independent English word is an assimilation to an English word (*crayfish, gillyflower, gridiron, andiron*). The solid styling is usual for such apparent compounds.

3.1 Noun + noun, as in *fruit + cake, cherry + pie, ox + bow, shoulder + blade, car + load, calamity + howler, emancipation + proclamation.*

3.1.1 In most noun-plus-noun compounds the first noun is uninflected and singular. Some of these compounds are freely styled in all three ways (*prize fighter/prizefighter/prize-fighter*). Some are rarely seen, at least in American English, other than solid (*newspaper, typewriter, pineapple*). Some are usually open (*gunnery sergeant, secretary bird*). Since there is a long precedent for the purely uniting function of the hyphen, it is not out of place in almost any noun=plus-noun compound where both elements are lowercase (*ox-bow, power-transmission, security=*

regulations), but it seems to be used less often today than it formerly was. The compounds in which it is most likely to be used are those that would be written solid except that they contain at the point of juncture letters in a sequence unusual within an English word so that apprehension of this point may be retarded. Thus the hyphen is often not so much a uniter of words as it is a separator of letters.

3.1.2 Typically, two-noun noun compounds that are often or usually solid are fairly short, are of frequent occurrence, are concrete rather than abstract, and have primary stress on the first element and secondary stress on the second element (*notebook, paperweight, grasshopper, battlewagon, newspaperman*). Five-syllable solid compounds are comparatively rare. Compounds that sometimes have even stress usually solidify only if short and very common (*corn + meal, air + mail, life + blood, arm + chair, eye + tooth, pot + luck, bed + rock, jaw + bone, barb + wire, car + load, bow + knot, death + bed, bell + wether*).

3.1.3 Falling accentuation (primary stress on first element and secondary stress on second element) is almost a prerequisite to solidification. Observation of how compounds in the spoken language are stressed provides information of possibly more value than an examination of how compounds in the written language are styled. A large proportion of the compounds that are written solid may with equal acceptability be open or hyphened (*matchbox / match box/ match-box*); but in the spoken language falling stress may be acceptable whereas even stress may not be, except when one is making a contrast between one compound and another with the same first element (*matchbox, matchstick*); in such contrasts supersession of the "normal" stress is regular. But the accentuation of compounds, like the accentuation of noncompound phrases, is a matter of usage, which does not fall into neat patterns. In some cases the meaning of a compound is a reliable guide to its accentuation, in other cases not. The native speaker knows that if *wood + box* means "a box made of wood" the stress is \ˈ⸚ˌ⸚\ and that if it means "a box in which wood is placed" the stress is \ˈ⸚ˌ⸚\. On the other hand he may be unable to be sure of the stress of another compound even after reading a definition of it. Some speakers stress a compound one way, and other speakers another way. To make rules that would cover the stress of all compounds seems impossible. Certain conditions seem to make for one kind of stress or the other; these conditions leave the stress on many compounds unexplained.

3.1.4 In what follows
A = *1st half of a two-part compound*
B = *2d half of a two-part compound*
C = *3d part of a three-part compound*
The relative specificity of B seems to account for many variations in stress between compounds whose elements stand in the same logical relationship to each other: the more specific, the less general and inclusive B is, the more likely the compound is to have even stress; thus ˈtown + ˈhall but (in the same sense) ˈtown + ˌhouse: hall is a more specific term than *house*, whose wide applicability is shown by the combinations or phrases *doll + house, chicken + house, discount + house, mail + order + house,* the *houses* of Congress or Parliament, the *house* of Rothschild. Other examples: ˈfinger + ˈnail (some-

times) but 'finger + ,tip, 'alligator + 'pear but 'alligator + ,weed, 'timothy + ,grass but 'timothy + 'hay, 'church + ,service but 'church + 'liturgy, 'corner + 'store but 'corner + ,stone, 'key + 'signature but 'key + ,note, 'desk + 'drawer but 'desk + ,leg.

3.1.5 Compounds that name something which requires the synchronous association or combination of what is named by A and what is named by B are usually even-stressed: 'leather + 'shoe but 'shoe + ,leather (shoe + leather can exist even though it may never be made into a shoe, or has ceased to exist in the form of a shoe), 'bottle + 'beer but 'beer + ,bottle, 'paper + 'book but 'book + ,paper, 'beef + 'soup and 'beef + 'stew but 'beef + ,broth (the last is merely a product of beef flesh, which is not present in the broth as it is in the soup and stew). Among the most numerous members of this category are compounds in which A names a thing of a sort that is the sole or an essential ingredient of B: 'cherry + 'pie (cherries or something of the sort — berries, apples, apricots, peaches — are a necessary part of a pie), 'gold + 'cup, 'glass + 'pendant, 'kid + 'gloves, 'rye + 'bread. When A is a thing of a sort that is secondary or incidental to B, falling stress is more likely: 'fruit + ,cake, 'raisin + ,bread (cake and bread can be quite plain, without anything of the order of raisins or other fruit). Compounds of the first category mentioned in this paragraph may have falling stress if B is lacking in specificity: 'glass + ,ware, 'paper + ,goods.

3.1.6 When A and B stand in an appositive relationship to each other, the stress is usually even: 'baby + 'boy, 'woman + 'driver. Boy + friend, however, has falling stress. It differs from the first two compounds in not being literal when it does not mean any friend who is a boy.

3.1.7 Metonymic compounds (compounds that name an entire thing by naming some feature of the thing, the first element sometimes being metaphorical) invariably have falling stress. They rarely have open styling. If they are not long and if there is no troublesome series of letters at the juncture, they are commonly solid: sheath + bill, frog + mouth, paper + back, egg + head, leather + neck, butter + fingers; otherwise they are usually hyphened: violet + ear.

3.1.8 There is a numerous class of words in which the second element is a verb plus -er or -ing and in the definition of which the first element is the object of the verb or the object of a preposition following the verb: orange + sucker, potato + digger, baby + sitter. These nearly always have falling accent, and appear quite freely in all three possible stylings. The hyphen is more often used in this class than it is in most other classes.

3.1.9 The relationship of the three elements in the preceding class of compounds can be represented thus: (A) (B, suffix). There is another class of compounds in which two elements are followed by a suffix (one of which may be -er, as in the preceding class) but in which the relationship of the three elements is different. Such compounds are broad jumper and Bay Stater in which the relationship is (A,B) (suffix), not (A) (B, suffix). Another such compound is gold + medal + -ist. Such compounds follow the accentuation of the two-part compound to which the suffix is added: 'broad + ,jump (er), 'Bay + ,State (r), 'gold + 'medal (ist). Such compounds

exhibit all three stylings. In noun compounds of the class (A,B) (suffix), both of the first two elements need not be nouns: bitter + end + -er, America + first + -er.

3.2 Noun+(')s+**noun,** as in fool(')s + cap, cock(')s + comb, woman(')s + club, women(')s + club, or **noun**+**s**(')+**noun,** as in boys(') + club, ladies(') + room.

3.2.1 When these have a literal meaning, they are often written open, and with an apostrophe before the s if the first element is in the singular (red as a cock's comb, a man's house is his castle) or in the plural but not ending in s (children's clothes). A few literal compounds of this class, however, are solid and without apostrophe, especially by assimilation to a form that is usual or frequent for an extended sense; thus cockscomb occurs for both the comb of a cock and a garden plant; menswear and womenswear occur usually. If the elements are written solid the apostrophe is not used, whether the first element is singular or plural (foolscap/never fool'scap, menswear/probably never men'swear). If the first element is singular and the elements are spaced, the apostrophe is not omitted: a fool's cap, a man's thoughts, a woman's thoughts.

3.2.2 When the compound is literal in meaning and open, and the first element is a plural ending in -s or is the possessive of a collective singular, the apostrophe is often omitted in titles in which the first element means "for the use of" or "operated by": farmers(') cooperative, a students(') dictionary, People(')s Industrial Bank, Ladies(') Aid Society. When the first element is the possessive of a plural that does not end in -s, omission of the apostrophe seems to be less frequent: women's club/womens club.

3.2.3 The first element may in some cases be either singular or plural: woman's club/women's club/womens club.

3.2.4 Compounds in which the first element has a possessive s are very common in an extended or figurative sense, especially in plant names. Use of the apostrophe seems to be usual for such compounds and the hyphen is sometimes used. There is often variation between a singular and a plural first element: baby's breath/babies' breath, ladies' man/lady's man. The solid form without apostrophe also occurs: cockscomb, foolscap, swansdown.

3.3 Adjective + noun, as in blue + bird, black + tern, red + head, blue + blood.

3.3.1 When an adjective and an immediately following noun are used with full literalness of meaning and nonattributively, the two are written with a space between and are spoken with level stress: I saw a 'blue 'bird (a bird that was blue; variety unknown), a doll with a 'red 'head. But when there is some abridgment of full literalness, the adjective and the noun may be written solid or hyphened and be spoken with falling stress: I saw one jay and two 'blue,birds (two 'blue 'birds of the variety known to scientists as Sialia sialis; the jay is also a 'blue 'bird); redheads are proverbially hot-tempered. Here again, however, as in the case of noun + noun compounds, specificity is important: the more specific the second element of the compound, the more likely the compound is to be written spaced and pronounced with even stress. Thus a typical dictionary definition of blue + bird begins "any

of several birds more or less blue above", and a typical definition of *black + tern* begins "any of several small terns with black plumage"; but the first is usually *'blue,bird*, the second is usually *'black 'tern*.

3.3.2 Metonyms with an adjective as the first element, like those with a noun as the first element, have falling stress and are usually solid or hyphened: *'red + ,head*, *'free + ,stone*, *'blue + ,stocking*.

3.3.3 Adjective + noun pairs in which the application of the adjective to the noun is not a literal one commonly have falling stress and may be hyphened or solid; but the solid styling is less frequent than for specifying compounds like *black + bird: cold + chisel, easy + chair*.

3.3.4 A few literal even-stressed adjective + noun compounds are styled in any of the three possible ways: *good + will, long + suffering, loving + kindness*.

3.4 Verb + noun, as in (a) *kill + joy, pick + pocket, cure + all, turn + coat, skin + flint, sling + shot, tattle + tale*, and (b) as in *bake + shop, turn + table, drip + coffee, try + square*.

3.4.1 In the (a) class the second element is the direct object of the verb. Words of this class have falling stress and are not open-styled. They are usually solid if short and if there are no troublesome letter combinations, like *e + a* in *cure + all*, which makes a hyphen usual.

3.4.2 In the compounds in class (b) the second element is not the direct object of the first element. It is impossible to be sure whether the first element of many compounds of this class is to be regarded as a verb or a noun. No practical difficulty arises from this because the styling and stress of these compounds parallels that of noun + noun compounds: all three stylings occur, and the stress is falling in some cases, level in others.

3.5 Particle + noun, as in *down + pour, down + draft, down + card, out + come, out + house, on + rush, on + going, on + position*.

3.5.1 A particle, as used here, is one of a small class of words that have sometimes adverbial, sometimes adjectival, sometimes prepositional force. When a verbal idea is present in the noun that is the second element, as it commonly is when the second element is identical in spelling with a corresponding verb, or when the second element ends in *-ing*, such compounds are rarely open, and the solid styling is more frequent than the hyphened: *down + pour, on + going*. When the second element is a concrete noun without any verbal idea and the first element has adjective force, all three stylings may occur: *down + card, down + pipe, off + horse, out + garrison, through + street, up + train*.

3.6 Noun + adjective, as in *battle + royal, court + martial, cousin + german, letters + patent, postmaster + general, sum + total*. These occur both hyphened and spaced.

3.7 Verb or verb derivative + adverb, as in *write + up, lean + to, pin + up, cut + up, shoo + in, follow + through, grown + up, get + together, shut + in, damping + off, goings + on, passer + by, hanger + on*.

3.7.1 Both the solid and the hyphened stylings are common for such of these nouns as do not have a first element ending in the suffix *-ing* or *-er*. The hyphen prevails when both junctural letters are vowels, as in *write + up, shoo + in*. For compounds whose first element ends in the suffix *-ing*, both the hyphened and the open styling are common. For compounds whose first element ends in the suffix *-er*, the hyphened or solid styling is usual, the open styling occasional.

4.1 Verb compounds. A verb and an adverb that accompanies and follows it usually have a space between them: *to throw out a ball, to throw a ball out, to talk loudly*. An adverb preceding a verb usually has a space following: *he loudly demanded reform, I well remember the day, he soon returned;* but the words considered as particles (in 3.5.) are usually not followed by a space but are close-styled, less often hyphened: *to uproot*/less often *up-root an evil*.

4.2 When a solid or hyphened noun compound is used as a verb by functional change, the styling of the noun compound is generally retained. Thus one who uses the solid or hyphened styling for the nouns *snow + shoe, sand + bag, court + martial* will probably use the same styling in *to snow + shoe across a field, to sand + bag a dike, to court + martial a soldier*.

4.3 For compound verbs that do not belong to any of the categories enumerated in the preceding paragraphs all three stylings are found. The hyphened styling is the most frequent; the open styling seems to be less common in formal than in informal English. Examples: *to double + space a manuscript, to heat + treat a metal, to cold + roll steel*.

4.4 A verb compound that has a verb as its second element and that has the suffix *-ing* at the end of the verb may be hyphened when an object follows but either hyphened or spaced when no object follows. Thus the same writer may write *heat-treating these metals is not recommended* but *for these metals, heat treating is not recommended*. In the latter, *heat + treatment*, whose usual styling is probably open, could be substituted.

5.1 Compound adverbs of the type illustrated by *to run hot + foot to the window, to go bare + foot, recommended sight + unseen, to win hands + down, to dive in head + first* are infrequently found, and at least two stylings can be found for all of these and for some, three. Combinations of adjective + noun are likely to be solid (*hot-foot*), but if the first element is a plural noun or the second a past participle, the form is likely to be open (*arms akimbo, feet first, sight unseen*).

5.2 Compound adverbs like *light + hearted + -ly* usually follow the styling of the corresponding compound adjective. See 6.5.

5.3 Some compounds with adverbial force consist of a preposition followed by a noun, with loss of the commonly preceding article: *down + town, up + stream, below + stairs, between + decks, over + board*. Although each of the three stylings occurs, the solid is probably usual for most.

6.1 Noun or adjective + adjective or participle, as in *snow + white, red + hot, rusty + red, bitter + sweet, acrid + smelling, smoke + filled*. These are usually hyphened, occasionally solid

(when the compound is short and common), or less frequently open (more often in predicative than in attributive position).

6.2 Adverb + adjective or participle, as in *well + known, better + known, widely + acclaimed, very + ignorant, twice + told.* The solid styling sometimes occurs for these compounds when the first element is a word freely usable as an adverb (*straight + forward, plain + spoken*). Most adverb + adjective compounds are either hyphened or open. In attributive position an adverb + adjective compound is most likely to be open if the first element is an adverb ending in *-ly* (*an extremely + important matter*); is most likely to be hyphened if the first element is an adverb that is identical in spelling with an adjective: *a slow + moving van.* Here a hyphen between *slow* and *moving* tells the reader that the writer has in mind a van of no particular variety that is moving slowly; a space between *slow* and *moving* would leave the expression open to the interpretation that the van is a variety known as a moving van and that it is slow; if the latter were the writer's intent, he might very well make it clear by inserting a hyphen between *moving* and *van*, even though he might use the open styling in *the moving + van has arrived.* In predicative position, open styling is more frequent than in attributive position; it is the most frequent styling by far when the first element has only adverbial use (*his hair is now + gray, he was once + wealthy*); it is less frequent when the first element is a form that is used as both adverb and adjective (*the van was large and slow + moving, he is plain + spoken*).

6.3 Particle + participle, as in *out + spoken, up + swept, out + bound.* These are solid or, less often, hyphened, whether attributive or predicative.

6.4 Noun or adjective + noun, as in *seed + case integument, stove + pipe hat, grandfather + clock collector, short + term loan, small + store owner.* Pairs that are consistently solid or hyphened in nonattributive position are usually so in attributive position: *the seedcase/seed-case is tough, the seedcase/seed-case integument, twenty blackbirds, a blackbird hater.* Sometimes a writer who uses the spaced styling nonattributively uses the solid styling attributively: *cut with a jig saw; a jigsaw puzzle.* Ordinarily, however, noun pairs that are open-styled nonattributively are either hyphened or open attributively; the open styling is more common in informal than formal English. Noun + noun + noun groups are probably less often ambiguous than adjective + noun + noun groups and accordingly are probably less often written with a space between A and B. Thus *feed + store owner* presents little or no ambiguity, whereas *small + store owner* written with a space between *small* and *store* is apprehensible, if the context affords no help, either as "owner of a small store" or "store owner who is small". If the first is the meaning intended, many would insert a hyphen between *small* and *store;* if the second many would insert a hyphen between *store* and *owner.*

6.5 Adjective or noun + noun + -ed, as in *red + head + -ed, club + foot + -ed, hot + temper + -ed, cloud + cap + -ped.* In these the middle element and the suffix are always solid. The first and middle elements are seldom spaced, whether in predicative or attributive position; are usually hyphened; are solid in a few short compounds of frequent occurrence.

6.6 Adjective or participle + particle, as in *to be hard + up, to be done + in, to be fed + up, warmed + over cabbage, a turned + down collar.* These are usually spaced in predicative position, hyphened in attributive position. When a prefix is added, the prefix and the middle element are usually written solid; the middle element and the particle are either spaced or hyphened in predicative position, hyphened in attributive position: *an un + heard + of accomplishment, such appliances were un + dreamed + of in those days.*

6.7 Preposition—initial adjective compounds, as in *down + stream, up + hill, over + seas, out + of + date, on + the + house, down + in + the + mouth.* Two-part compounds with no article between are usually solid, less often hyphened or open, in attributive position; in predicative position both solid and open stylings are common. *an up + hill pull, over + seas possessions, the race will be down + stream.* Compounds having three or more parts are open or hyphened in predicative position, usually hyphened in attributive position: *book is out + of + date, an out + of + date book, looked down + in + the + mouth.*

6.8 When something in the typography makes the interrelationship of a multiple-word adjective obvious, the hyphen is usually omitted:

A Jim Crow law   (capital letters)
an *a priori* argument   (italics)
his "big shot" talk   (quotation marks)

In an expression like *April + fool joke, Indian + club enthusiast,* where the typography of one member of the attributive (*April*) does not parallel that of the other (*fool*), the hyphen is frequently or usually present (*April-fool joke*).

6.9 Compound adjectives not covered by any of the categories enumerated above are usually hyphened: *a pop + up toaster, a middle + of + the + road course, his never + the + twain + shall + meet policy.* The solid styling is probably found occasionally for some of the shorter compounds as *pop + up.* The open styling is more common in informal than formal English: *a middle of the road course.*

CAPITALIZATION

1. The essential distinction in the use of capitals and lowercase letters beginning words lies in the particularizing or individualizing significance of capitals as against the generic or generalizing significance of lowercase. A capital is used with proper nouns, that is, nouns that distinguish some individual person, place, or thing from others of the same class, and with proper adjectives, that is, adjectives that take their descriptive meaning from what is characteristic of the person, place, or thing named by the noun. Most proper nouns and proper adjectives used not in the primary signification but in a derived, secondary, or special sense (as *cashmere*, the fabric; *quixotism*, *herculean*) are written usually without capitalization.

2. A capital letter in normal practice in continuous textual matter:

2.1 begins the first word of a sentence or an expression standing for a sentence ⟨You urge in vain.⟩ ⟨Recant my views?⟩ ⟨Never!⟩

2.2 usually begins a direct formal quotation ⟨God said, Let there be light —Gen 1:3⟩

2.3 usually begins a direct question within a sentence even though not quoted ⟨The eighteenth century asked of any action, Is it decorous?⟩

2.4 often and traditionally begins a line of verse:
    Our fears in Banquo
Stick deep; and in his royalty of nature
Reigns that which would be fear'd —Shak.

2.5 usually begins proper nouns, words used as proper nouns, and their derivatives used in the primary sense ⟨George→Georgian⟩ ⟨Spain→Spanish⟩ ⟨Americanism⟩ ⟨New-Yorky⟩ ⟨Roman customs⟩ but verbs are less often capitalized than adjectives or nouns ⟨anglicize⟩

2.6 represents the first person pronoun ⟨he and I disagree⟩

2.7 usually begins the names of peoples, races, tribes, and languages ⟨Phoenician⟩ ⟨Japanese⟩ ⟨Iroquois⟩ ⟨Indo-European⟩ ⟨Latin⟩

2.8 begins titles of honor, academic and religious titles, and professional and business titles used before proper nouns and epithets used in place of proper nouns ⟨Queen Elizabeth I⟩ ⟨His Eminence the Cardinal Archbishop of New York⟩ ⟨Iron Chancellor⟩ ⟨Citizen King⟩ ⟨Old Hickory⟩ ⟨the Hoosier Poet⟩ ⟨All-America team⟩ ⟨Associate Professor John Doe⟩ ⟨Chief Engineer John Doe⟩ ⟨Treasurer John Doe⟩ but not usually when used after ⟨Henry VIII, king of England⟩ ⟨King George V, emperor of India⟩

2.9 begins official and government titles and titles of nobility (as *president, governor, senator, speaker of the House, secretary for defense, postmaster general, prime minister*) when preceding a proper name or used in direct address; as ⟨U.S. Minister John Doe⟩ ⟨Secretary John Doe⟩ ⟨His Honor the Mayor⟩ ⟨Mr. President⟩ ⟨Your Honor⟩ but ⟨John Adams, president of the U.S.⟩

2.10 begins official names of national or international governmental bodies or documents and sometimes short forms of these used specifically or with a capitalized name but not usually any short forms or modified forms of them in general reference ⟨The Constitution of the United States⟩ ⟨the Eightieth Congress⟩ ⟨the Federal Reserve system⟩ ⟨Federal Reserve banks⟩ ⟨the Federal Communications Commission⟩ ⟨Charter of the United Nations (*or* the Charter)⟩ ⟨the Security Council (*or* the Council)⟩ ⟨the International Bank⟩ but ⟨according to the constitution⟩ ⟨administration policies⟩ ⟨federal agency⟩

2.11 usually begins nouns and often also adjectives that refer to the Deity and pronouns and pronominal adjectives referring to the Deity when not closely preceding or following their antecedent naming Deity ⟨God⟩ ⟨the Supreme Being⟩ ⟨the Almighty⟩ ⟨Allah⟩ ⟨Great Manito⟩ ⟨Providence⟩ ⟨Lord⟩ ⟨the Trinity⟩ ⟨Holy Ghost⟩ ⟨trust Him who doeth all things well; take time to think about God and his beneficence⟩ ⟨The Almighty has his own purposes —Abraham Lincoln⟩ ⟨so lonely 'twas, that God himself scarce seemed there to be —S.T.Coleridge⟩ ⟨Lamb of God, who takest away the sins of the world, only in thy grace shall my soul be healed —Katherine Anne Porter⟩

2.11.1 Some writers and a few hymnals capitalize a pronoun or pronominal adjective referring to Deity, even when close to the antecedent naming Deity and thus not requiring a capital for clarity of reference ⟨a personal God, creator and governor of all, Who will bring His children into fellowship with Himself⟩ ⟨Jesus and His disciples⟩ ⟨"My Jesu, as Thou wilt"⟩ ⟨teach me, my God and King, in all things Thee to see —George Herbert⟩ ⟨God's in His heaven — all's right with the world —Robert Browning⟩ ⟨all Thy works, O Lord, shall bless Thee —*Oxford Amer. Hymnal*⟩

2.12 usually begins names for the Bible or parts, versions, or editions of it and names of other sacred books and often derivative adjectives when the adjective refers explicitly to the Bible or Scriptures (otherwise not capitalized) ⟨Bible⟩ ⟨Vedas⟩ ⟨the Scriptures⟩ ⟨Old Testament⟩ ⟨Pentateuch⟩ ⟨Apocrypha⟩ ⟨Gospel of Mark⟩ ⟨Apocalypse⟩

2.13 begins names of creeds and confessions, religious denominations, monastic orders, and *Church* when used to designate a specific body or edifice ⟨Apostles' Creed⟩ ⟨the Thirty-nine Articles of the Church of England⟩ ⟨Hunt Memorial Church⟩

2.14 usually begins holidays and holy days generally, the months of the year, and the days of the week ⟨Fourth of July⟩ ⟨Good Friday⟩ ⟨Holy Week⟩ ⟨Labor Day⟩ ⟨January⟩ ⟨next Tuesday⟩

2.15 begins names of congresses, councils, and expositions, of organizations and institutions, of governmental departments, and of political parties (but not the word *party*) ⟨the Yalta Conference⟩ ⟨the Security Council of the United Nations⟩ ⟨Louisiana Purchase Exposition⟩ ⟨the Progressive party⟩ ⟨the Smithsonian Institution⟩ ⟨Bureau of Engraving and Printing⟩ ⟨Congress of Industrial Organizations⟩

2.16 begins names of specific courts of law ⟨Circuit Court of the United States for the 2d

Circuit (*but* the circuit court)⟩ ⟨the Michigan Court of Appeals (*but* the state court of appeals)⟩

2.17 begins names of treaties, laws, acts, important events, historical epochs, literary periods, wars ⟨Versailles Treaty⟩ ⟨the Crusades⟩ ⟨Middle Ages⟩ ⟨the Enlightenment⟩ ⟨the Civil War⟩ ⟨War of 1812⟩

2.18 usually begins names of geological eras, periods, epochs, strata, and names of prehistoric divisions ⟨Carboniferous⟩ ⟨Upper Jurassic⟩ ⟨Age of Reptiles⟩ ⟨Neolithic age⟩

2.19 begins names of genera but not of species in binomial scientific names in zoology and botany ⟨a marine worm (*Nereis diversicolor*)⟩ ⟨*Spiraea latifolia*⟩

2.20 begins New Latin names of classes, families, and all other groups above genera in zoology and botany but not derivative adjectives or nouns ⟨Gastropoda *but* gastropod⟩ ⟨Thallophyta *but* thallophyte⟩

2.21 usually begins a breed name ⟨Belgian hare⟩ ⟨Airedale terrier⟩ ⟨Guernsey bull⟩

2.22 begins names of planets, constellations, asteroids, stars, and groups of stars but not sun, earth, and moon unless listed with other astronomical names ⟨Mercury⟩ ⟨the planet Venus⟩ ⟨Pleiades⟩ ⟨Big Dipper⟩

2.23 usually begins generic geographical terms that form an integral part of a specific proper name (as *bay, borough, colony, continent, county, district, hemisphere, island, lake, mountain, pass,* and likewise *avenue, boulevard, bridge, park, road, square, street*) ⟨Hudson Bay⟩ ⟨Grand Canyon⟩ ⟨Niagara Falls⟩ ⟨Long Island⟩ ⟨Crater Lake⟩ ⟨Blue Ridge⟩ ⟨Park Drive⟩ but ⟨the Atlantic coast of Labrador⟩ ⟨Pacific islands⟩ ⟨Swiss mountains⟩ ⟨the Ohio river valley⟩ ⟨Indian ocean⟩ ⟨Florida keys⟩ ⟨Sahara desert⟩ ⟨born in Chekiang province⟩ ⟨on the Ohio river⟩ ⟨Oak avenue⟩ ⟨the Leeward and Windward islands⟩ ⟨at the confluence of the Missouri and Platte rivers⟩

2.24 usually begins generic political terms that form an integral part of a specific proper name, denoting a political division (as *colony, department, dominion, empire, kingdom, republic, state, territory*) ⟨the Holy Roman Empire⟩ ⟨the Province of Quebec⟩ ⟨the State of Ohio⟩ ⟨the Third Republic⟩

2.25 usually begins names of definite geographical divisions ⟨the Orient⟩ ⟨the Old World⟩ ⟨the Middle East⟩ ⟨the Middle West⟩

2.26 usually begins points of the compass used to designate geographical portions of a country or divisions of the world and also nouns or adjectives derived therefrom ⟨the South⟩ ⟨the Northwest⟩ ⟨a Northerner⟩ but not when used to denote direction only ⟨due east⟩ ⟨go west⟩

2.27 usually begins abstract ideas or inanimate objects personified and names of seasons only when personified or sometimes when referred to specifically or with special connotations ⟨do the bidding of Nature⟩ ⟨the Winter at Valley Forge⟩ ⟨the Plague Year of 1665⟩ ⟨where Spring her verdant mantle cast⟩

2.28 usually begins all words in titles of books, periodicals, essays, poems except unemphatic prepositions, conjunctions and articles ⟨Shakespeare's *Taming of the Shrew*⟩ ⟨the *Journal of the American Medical Association*⟩ ⟨"Phosphorus: Bearer of Light and Life," *Scientific American* 178:101 *ff.*⟩ and except in cataloging and often in bibliographies when only the first word and proper names are capitalized.

2.29 usually begins the article *the* when part of a proper name or title or when incorporated as part of the legal name but usually not in referring to newspapers and magazines in running text ⟨The Honorable John Doe⟩ but ⟨the *Chicago Daily News*⟩ ⟨the *Saturday Evening Post*⟩

2.30 usually begins particles in American names but in foreign names only when not preceded by a forename, a professional title, or a title of nobility or of courtesy ⟨Reginald De Koven⟩ ⟨Della Crusca⟩ ⟨Von Moltke (Count von Moltke)⟩

2.31 usually begins German common nouns that have not been anglicized, when used in English text ⟨Frau⟩ ⟨Junker⟩ ⟨Luftwaffe⟩ but anglicized German nouns may be written with a small initial letter ⟨blitzkrieg⟩ ⟨gestalt⟩ ⟨leitmotiv⟩ ⟨pumpernickel⟩ ⟨rathskeller⟩ ⟨sauerkraut⟩ ⟨turnverein⟩

2.32 usually represents academic degrees ⟨A.B.⟩ ⟨LL.D.⟩ ⟨Ph.D.⟩

2.33 begins names of registered trademarks.

ITALICIZATION

1. Foreign words and phrases that are not fully naturalized are usually italicized in English context. This is done in manuscript or typescript by single underlining. The choice of roman or italic text properly belongs to the user on the basis of subject matter and expected readers. A dictionary cannot prescribe or even record in a matter so subjective. These examples simply show words and phrases that are often italicized in English context ⟨*ancien régime*⟩ ⟨*cognoscente*⟩ ⟨*de trop*⟩ ⟨*dolce far niente*⟩ ⟨*jeu d'esprit*⟩ ⟨*mañana*⟩ ⟨*noblesse oblige*⟩ ⟨*rapprochement*⟩ ⟨*zeitgeist*⟩

2. Titles of books (not parts of books), plays, works of art, magazines, newspapers are usually italicized but not the Bible or its books ⟨Stevenson's *Treasure Island*⟩ ⟨Verdi's *Il Trovatore*⟩ ⟨Michelangelo's *David*⟩ ⟨the *Christian Science Monitor*⟩ ⟨*Saturday Evening Post*⟩

3. Names of ships and aircraft are usually italicized ⟨Lindbergh's *Spirit of St. Louis*⟩ ⟨the carrier *Lexington*⟩

4. Names of long-range missiles and man-made satellites are often italicized.

5. A word spoken of as a word, a phrase as a phrase, a letter as a letter (except that a letter indicating shape is printed in type most nearly depicting the shape; thus, V-shaped; I beam) are usually italicized.

6. New Latin scientific names of genera, species, subspecies, and varieties (but not groups of higher rank, as phyla, classes, orders) in botanical and zoological names are italicized ⟨a thick-shelled American clam (*Mercenaria mercenaria*)⟩

COLLEGES AND UNIVERSITIES IN THE UNITED STATES AND CANADA

The first list contains collegiate institutions of higher education in the United States, according to information available at the date of compilation. It includes some (but not all) branches which retain by general recognition their individual names, but no attempt is made to indicate relationship of one institution to another or connection with a state university system.

The entry gives pronunciation, location, zip code, and date. Pronunciations not given may be found elsewhere in this dictionary. The location is that of the main administrative center or campus only. The state, or sometimes the city, is omitted when it is part of the title and when no uncertainty is likely. The word *junior*, as used when not a part of the name, indicates a junior college.

The date is intended to be the earliest assignable to the institution's establishment; it is not always the year when the current name was adopted.

The second list, following, contains Canadian institutions.

Recurrent institutional designations are abbreviated as follows:

A. & M.	Agricultural and Mechanical	*Mech.*	Mechanical
Acad.	Academy	*Med.*	Medical
Agric.	Agriculture	*Sch.*	School
C.	College	*Sem.*	Seminary
Ed.	Education	*Tech.*	Technology
Inst.	Institute	*Theol.*	Theological
		U.	University

UNITED STATES COLLEGES AND UNIVERSITIES

Abilene Christian C. Tex. 79601; 1906
Abra·ham Bald·win Agricultural C. \ˌā-brə-ˌham-'bȯl-dwən-\ Tifton, Ga. 31794; junior, 1907
Ad·ams State C. of Colorado \'ad-əmz-\ Alamosa 81101; 1921
Adel·phi U. \ə-'del-ˌfī-\ Garden City, N.Y. 11530; 1896
Ad·i·ron·dack Community C. \ˌad-ə-'rän-ˌdak-\ Glens Falls, N.Y. 12801; junior, 1961
Adri·an C. \'ā-drē-ən-\ Adrian, Mich. 49221; 1845
Aeronautics, Acad. of La Guardia Airport, N.Y. 11371; junior, 1932
Ag·nes Scott C. \ˌag-nə(s)-'skät-\ Decatur, Ga. 30030; 1889
Aims C. \'āmz-\ Greeley, Colo. 80631; junior, 1967
Akron, U. of Ohio 44304; 1870
Alabama, U. of University, 35486; 1831
Alabama A. & M. C. Normal, 35762; 1873
Alabama Christian C. Montgomery, 36109; junior, 1942
Alabama State U. Montgomery, 36101; 1874
Alaska, U. of College, 99701; 1915
Alaska Methodist U. Anchorage, 99504; 1957
Albany Junior C. Albany, Ga. 31705; 1966
Albany State C. Albany, Ga. 31705; 1903
Al·be·marle, C. of the \-'al-bə-ˌmärl\ Elizabeth City, N.C. 27909; junior, 1960
Al·ber·tus Mag·nus C. \al-ˌbərt-ə-'smag-nəs-\ New Haven, Conn. 06511; 1925
Al·bi·on C. \'al-bē-ən-\ Albion, Mich. 49224; 1835
Al·bright C. \'ȯl-ˌbrīt-\ Reading, Pa. 19604; 1856
Albuquerque, U. of N. Mex. 87105; 1940
Al·corn A. & M. C. \'ȯl-ˌkȯ(ə)rn-\ Lorman, Miss. 39096; 1871
Al·der·son–Broad·dus C. \ˌȯl-dər-sən-'brȯd-əs-\ Philippi, W. Va. 26416; 1871
Al·ex·an·der City State Junior C. \ˌal-ig-'zan-dər-, ˌel-\ Alexander City, Ala. 35010; 1965
Al·fred U. \'al-frəd-, -fərd-\ Alfred, N.Y. 14802; 1836
Alice Lloyd C. \-'lȯid-\ Pippa Passes, Ky. 48144; junior, 1923
Al·lan Han·cock C. \ˌal-ən-'han-ˌkäk-\ Santa Maria, Calif. 93454; junior, 1920
Al·le·ga·ny Community C. \ˌal-ə-'gā-nē-\ Cumberland, Md. 21502; junior, 1961
Al·le·ghe·ny C. \ˌal-ə-'gā-nē-\ Meadville, Pa. 16335; 1815
Allegheny County, Community C. of Pittsburgh, Pa. 15219; junior, 1965
Al·len County Community Junior C. \'al-ən-\ Iola, Kans. 66749; 1923
Allen Military Acad. and Junior C. Bryan, Tex. 77801; 1886
Allen U. Columbia, S.C. 29204; 1870
Al·li·ance C. \ə-'lī-ən(t)s-\ Cambridge Springs, Pa. 16403; 1912
Al·ma C. \'al-mə-\ Alma, Mich. 48801; 1886
Alma White C. \ˌal-mə-'(h)wīt\ Zarephath, N.J. 08890; 1921
Al·pe·na Community C. \al-'pē-nə-\ Alpena, Mich. 49707; junior, 1952
Al·phon·sus C. \al-'fän(t)-səs-, -'fän-zəs-\ Woodcliff Lake, N.J. 07675; junior, 1961
Al·tus Junior C. \'al-təs-\ Altus, Okla. 73521; 1926
Al·ver·nia C. \al-'vər-nē-ə-\ Reading, Pa. 19607; 1958
Al·ver·no C. \al-'vər-nō-\ Milwaukee, Wis. 53215; 1887
Al·vin Junior C. \'al-vən-\ Alvin, Tex. 77511; 1949
Amarillo C. Tex. 79105; junior, 1929
American Baptist C. of the Bible Nashville, Tenn. 37207; 1924
American Conservatory of Music Chicago, Ill. 60605; 1886
American International C. Springfield, Mass. 01109; 1885
American River C. Sacramento, Calif. 95841; junior, 1955
American U. Washington, D.C. 20016; 1893
Am·herst C. \'am-(ˌ)ərst-\ Amherst, Mass. 01002; 1821

An·cil·la Do·mi·ni C. \an-ˌshil-ə-'dō-mə-nē-\ Donaldson, Ind 46513; junior, 1937
Anderson C. Anderson, Ind. 46011; 1917
Anderson C. Anderson, S.C. 29621; junior, 1911
An·drew C. \'an-ˌdrü-\ Cuthbert, Ga. 31740; junior, 1854
An·drews U. \'an-ˌdrüz-\ Berrien Springs, Mich. 49104; 1874
An·ge·li·na City Junior C. \ˌan-jə-'lē-nə-\ Lufkin, Tex. 75901; 1968
An·ge·lo State C. \'an-jə-ˌlō-\ San Angelo, Tex. 76901; 1928
An·na Ma·ria C. \ˌan-ə-mə-'rē-ə-\ Paxton, Mass. 01612; 1946
Anne Arun·del Community C. \ˌan-ə-'rən-dᵊl-\ Severna Park, Md. 21012; junior, 1961
Ann·hurst C. \'an-ˌhərst-\ Woodstock, Conn. 06281; 1941
Annunciation C. Victoria, Tex. 77901; junior, 1959
Ano·ka–Ram·sey State Junior C. \ə-ˌnō-kə-'ram-zē-\ Coon Rapids, Minn. 55433; 1965
Antelope Valley C. Lancaster, Calif. 93534; junior, 1929
An·ti·och C. \'ant-ē-ˌäk-\ Yellow Springs, Ohio 45387; 1852
Appalachian Bible Inst. Bradley, W. Va. 25818; 1950
Appalachian State U. Boone, N.C. 28607; 1903
Aqui·nas C. \ə-'kwī-nəs-\ Grand Rapids, Mich. 49506; 1886
Aquinas Inst. of Philosophy and Theology River Forest, Ill. 60305; 1939
Aquinas Junior C. Nashville, Tenn. 37205; 1961
Arapahoe Junior C. Littleton, Colo. 80120; 1965
Area Ten Community C. Cedar Rapids, Iowa 52406; junior, 1965
Arizona, U. of Tucson, 85721; 1885
Arizona State U. Tempe, 85281; 1885
Arizona Western C. Yuma, 85364; junior, 1963
Ar·kan·sas, State C. of \-'är-kən-ˌsȯ\ Conway, 72032; 1907
Arkansas, U. of Fayetteville, 72701; 1871
Arkansas A. & M. C. College Heights, 71655; 1909
Arkansas Agricultural, Mech., and Normal C. Pine Bluff, 71601; 1873
Arkansas at Little Rock, U. of 72204; 1927
Arkansas Baptist C. Little Rock, 72200; 1884
Arkansas C. Batesville, 72501; 1872
Arkansas Polytechnic C. Russellville, 72801; 1909
Arkansas State U. State University, 72467; 1909
Arm·strong C. \'ärm-ˌstrȯŋ-\ Berkeley, Calif. 94704; 1918
Armstrong State C. Savannah, Ga. 31406; 1935
Art Center C. of Design Los Angeles, Calif. 90005; 1930
Ar·te·sia, C. of \-är-'tē-zhə\ N.Mex. 88210; 1966
Art Inst. of Chicago, Sch. of the Ill. 60603; 1866
As·bury C. \'az-ˌber-ē-, -b(ə)rē-\ Wilmore, Ky. 40390; 1890
Ashe·ville–Bilt·more C. \ˌash-ˌvil-'bilt-ˌmō(ə)r-, -vəl-, -ˌmȯ(ə)r-\ Asheville, N.C. 28801; 1927
Ash·land C. \'ash-lənd-\ Ashland, Ohio 44805; 1878
Ashland County Teachers C. Ashland, Wis. 54806; junior, 1914
As·sump·tion C. \ə-'səm(p)-shən-\ Worcester, Mass. 01609; 1904
Assumption C. Richardton, N. Dak. 58652; junior, 1899
Assumption C. for Sisters Mendham, N.J. 07945; junior, 1953
Ath·e·nae·um of Ohio, The \-ˌath-ə-'nē-əm-\ Norwood, 45212; 1829
Ath·ens C. \'ath-ənz-\ Athens, Ala. 35611; 1822
Atlanta Christian C. East Point, Ga. 30344; 1937
Atlanta U. Ga. 30314; 1865
Atlantic Christian C. Wilson, N. C. 27893; 1902
Atlantic Community C. Mays Landing, N.J. 08330; junior, 1964
Atlantic Union C. South Lancaster, Mass. 01561; 1882
Auburn Community C. Auburn, N.Y. 13021; junior, 1953
Auburn Maine Sch. of Commerce Auburn, Me. 04210; junior, 1916
Auburn U. Auburn, Ala. 36830; 1856

Augs·burg C. \'ȯgz-,bȯrg-\ Minneapolis, Minn. 55404; 1869
Augusta C. Ga. 30904; 1925
Au·gus·tana C. \,ȯ-gə-'stan-ə-\ Rock Island, Ill. 61201; 1860
Augustana C. Sioux Falls, S. Dak. 57102; 1860
Aurora C. Aurora, Ill. 60507; 1893
Austin C. Sherman, Tex. 75090; 1849
Austin Peay State U. \-'pē-\ Clarksville, Tenn. 37040; 1927
Austin State Junior C. Austin, Minn. 55912; 1940
Aver·ett C. \'āv-(ə-)rət\ Danville, Va. 24541; junior, 1859
Av·i·la C. \'av-ə-lə-\ Kansas City, Mo. 64145; 1866
Azusa Pacific C. Azusa, Calif. 91702; 1899

Bab·son Inst. of Business Administration \'bab-sən-\ Babson Park, Mass. 02157; 1919
Ba·cone C. \bā-kōn-\ Bacone, Okla. 74420; junior, 1880
Ba·ker C. Baker, Oreg. 97814; junior, 1957
Baker U. Baldwin City, Kans. 66006; 1858
Bakersfield C. Bakersfield, Calif. 93305; junior, 1913
Bal·dwin–Wal·lace C. \,bȯl-dwən-'wȯl-əs-\ Berea, Ohio 44017; 1845
Ball State U. \'bȯl-\ Muncie, Ind. 47306; 1918
Baltimore, Community C. of Md. 21215; junior, 1947
Baltimore, U. of Md. 21201; 1925
Baltimore C. of Commerce Md. 21201; 1909
Baltimore Hebrew C. Md. 21215; 1919
Bangor Theol. Sem. Me. 04401; 1814
Baptist Bible Sem. Clarks Summit, Pa. 18411; 1932
Baptist C. of Charleston S.C. 29411; 1960
Ba·rat C. \bə-'rä\ Lake Forest, Ill. 60045; 1857
Bar·ber–Sco·tia C. \,bär-bər-'skō-shə-\ Concord, N.C. 28025; 1867
Bard C. \'bärd-\ Annandale-on-Hudson, N.Y. 12504; 1860
Bar·nard C. \'bär-nərd-\ New York, N.Y. 10027; 1889
Bar·ring·ton C. \'bar-iŋ-tən-\ Barrington, R.I. 02806; 1900
Bar·ron County Teachers C. \'bar-ən-\ Rice Lake, Wis. 54868; junior, 1907
Bar·ry C. \'bar-ē-\ Miami, Fla. 33161; 1940
Bar·stow C. \'bär-(,)stō-\ Barstow, Calif. 92311; junior, 1960
Bartlesville Wesleyan C. Okla. 74003; 1910
Bar·ton County Community Junior C. \'bärt-ᵊn-\ Great Bend, Kans. 67530; 1965
Bates C. \'bāts-\ Lewiston, Me. 04240; 1864
Bay de Noc Community C. \-də-'näk-\ Escanaba, Mich. 49829; junior, 1963
Bay·lor U. \'bā-lər-\ Waco, Tex. 76703; 1845
Bay Path Junior C. \'bā-,path-\ Longmeadow, Mass. 01106; 1897
Beal Business C. \'bē(ə)l-\ Bangor, Me. 04401; 1891
Bea·ver C. \'bē-vər-\ Glenside, Pa. 19038; 1853
Beaver County, Community C. of Freedom, Pa. 15042; junior, 1966
Beck·er Junior C. \'bek-ər-\ Worcester, Mass. 01609; 1887
Beck·ley C. \'bek-lē-\ Beckley, W. Va. 25801; junior, 1933
Bee County C. \'bē-\ Beeville, Tex. 78102; junior, 1966
Bel·ha·ven C. \'bel-,hā-vən-\ Jackson, Miss. 39202; 1894
Bel·knap C. \'bel-,nap-\ Center Harbor, N.H. 03226; 1963
Bel·lar·mine–Ur·su·line C. \'bel-ər-mən-'ər-sə-lən-, -,līn-, -,lēn-\ Louisville, Ky. 40205; 1950
Belleville Junior C. Belleville, Ill. 62221; 1946
Belle·vue Community C. \'bel-,vyü-\ Bellevue, Wash. 98004; junior, 1966
Bel·mont Abbey C. \'bel-,mänt-\ Belmont, N.C. 28012; 1878
Belmont C. Nashville, Tenn. 37203; 1951
Beloit C. Beloit, Wis. 53511; 1846
Be·mid·ji State C. \bə-'mij-ē-\ Bemidji, Minn. 56601; 1913
Ben·e·dict C. \'ben-ə-,dikt\ Columbia, S.C. 29204; 1870
Benjamin Franklin U. Washington, D.C. 20036; 1925
Ben·nett U. \'ben-ət-\ Millbrook, N.Y. 12545; junior, 1891
Bennett C. Greensboro, N.C. 27420; 1873
Ben·ning·ton C. \'ben-iŋ-tən-\ Bennington, Vt. 05201; 1925
Bent·ley C. of Accounting and Finance \'bent-lē-\ Waltham, Mass. 02154; 1917
Be·rea C. \bə-'rē-ə-\ Berea, Ky. 40403; 1855
Ber·gen Community C. \'bər-gən-\ Paramus, N.J. 07652; junior, 1965
Berkshire Christian C. Lenox, Mass. 01240; 1897
Berkshire Community C. Pittsfield, Mass. 01201; junior, 1960
Ber·ry C. \'ber-ē-\ Mount Berry, Ga. 30149; 1902
Beth·a·ny Bible C. \'beth-ə-nē-\ Santa Cruz, Calif. 95060; 1919
Bethany C. Lindsborg, Kans. 67456; 1881
Bethany C. Bethany, W. Va. 26032; 1840
Bethany Lutheran C. Mankato, Minn. 56001; junior, 1911
Bethany Naz·a·rene C. \-,naz-ə-'rēn-\ Bethany, Okla. 73008; 1899
Beth·el C. \'beth-əl-\ Mishawaka, Ind. 46544; 1947
Bethel C. North Newton, Kans. 67117; 1887
Bethel C. St. Paul, Minn. 55101; 1871
Bethel C. McKenzie, Tenn. 38201; 1842
Be·thune–Cook·man C. \,bā-,th(y)ün-'kùk-mən-\ Daytona Beach, Fla. 32015; 1872
Beu·lah Heights C. \'byü-lə-\ Atlanta, Ga. 30316; 1928
Big Bend Community C. Moses Lake, Wash. 98837; junior, 1962
Bi·o·la C. \bī-'ō-lə-\ La Mirada, Calif. 90638; 1908
Birmingham–Southern C. Birmingham, Ala. 35204; 1856
Biscayne C. Opa-Locka, Fla. 33054; 1962
Bishop C. Dallas, Tex. 75241; 1881
Bismarck Junior C. Bismarck, N. Dak. 58501; 1939
Black·burn C. \'blak-bərn-\ Carlinville, Ill. 62626; 1835
Black Hawk C. Moline, Ill. 61265; junior, 1946
Black Hills State C. Spearfish, S. Dak. 57783; 1883

Blinn C. \'blin-\ Brenham, Tex. 77833; junior, 1883
Bliss C. \'blis-\ Columbus, Ohio 43215; 1899
Bloom Community C. \'blüm-\ Chicago Heights, Ill. 60411; junior, 1958
Bloomfield C. Bloomfield, N.J. 07003; 1868
Blooms·burg State C. \'blümz-,bərg-\ Bloomsburg, Pa. 17815; 1839
Blue·field C. \'blü-,fēld-\ Bluefield, Va. 24605; junior, 1922
Bluefield State C. Bluefield, W. Va. 24701; 1895
Blue Mountain C. Blue Mountain, Miss. 38610; 1873
Blue Mountain Community C. Pendleton, Oreg. 97801; junior, 1962
Blue Ridge Community C. Weyers Cave, Va. 24486; junior, 1967
Bluff·ton C. \'bləf-tən-\ Bluffton, Ohio 45817; 1900
Bob Jones U. \'bäb-'jōnz-\ Greenville, S.C. 29614; 1927
Boise State C. Boise, Idaho 83701; 1932
Boone Junior C. \'bün-\ Boone, Iowa 50036; 1927
Borough of Manhattan Community C. N.Y. 10020; junior, 1963
Bor·ro·meo Sem. of Ohio \,bȯr-ə-'mā(,)ō-, ,bär\ Wickliffe 44092; 1953
Boston C. Chestnut Hill, Mass. 02167; 1863
Boston Conservatory of Music Mass. 02115; 1867
Boston U. Mass. 02215; 1839
Bow·doin C. \'bōd-ᵊn-\ Brunswick, Me. 04011; 1794
Bow·ie State C. \'bü-ē-\ Bowie, Md. 20715; 1867
Bowling Green State U. Bowling Green, Ohio 43402; 1910
Bradford Junior C. Bradford, Mass. 01830; 1803
Brad·ley U. \'brad-lē-\ Peoria, Ill. 61606; 1896
Brai·nerd State Junior C. \'brā-nərd-\ Brainerd, Minn. 56401; 1938
Bran·deis U. \'bran-,dīs-, -,dīz-\ Waltham, Mass. 02154; 1947
Brandywine Junior C. Wilmington, Del. 19803; 1967
Braz·os·port Junior C. \'braz-əs-,pō(ə)rt-, -,pȯərt-\ Freeport, Tex. 77541; 1968
Bre·nau C. \brə-'naù-\ Gainesville, Ga. 30501; 1878
Brent·wood C. \'brent-,wùd-\ Brentwood, N.Y. 11717; 1955
Bres·cia C. \'bresh-ə-\ Owensboro, Ky. 42301; 1874
Bre·vard C. \brə-'värd-\ Brevard, N.C. 28712; junior, 1853
Brevard Junior C. Cocoa, Fla. 32922; 1960
Brew·ton–Par·ker C. \,brüt-ᵊn-'pär-kər-\ Mt. Vernon, Ga. 30445; junior, 1904
Bri·ar Cliff C. \'brī-(ə-)r-,klif-\ Sioux City, Iowa 51104; 1930
Briar·cliff C. \'brī-(-ə)r-,klif-\ Briarcliff Manor, N.Y. 10510; 1904
Bridgeport, U. of Conn. 06602; 1927
Bridgeport Engineering Inst. Conn. 06606; 1924
Bridge·wa·ter C. \'brij-,wȯt-ər-, -,wät-\ Bridgewater, Va. 22812; 1880
Brig·ham Young U. \,brig-əm-'yəŋ-\ Provo, Utah 84601; 1875
Bristol Community C. Fall River, Mass. 02720; junior, 1966
Bronx Community C. Bronx, N.Y. 10468; junior, 1957
Brooklyn C. N.Y. 11210; 1930
Brooks Inst. of Photography \'brùks-\ Santa Barbara, Calif. 93103; 1945
Broome Technical Community C. \'brüm-, 'brùm-\ Binghamton, N.Y. 13902; junior, 1946
Brow·ard Junior C. \'braù(-ə)rd-\ Fort Lauderdale, Fla. 33314; 1960
Brown U. \'braùn-\ Providence, R.I. 02912; 1764
Brunswick Junior C. Brunswick, Ga. 31520; 1964
Bry·ant C. \'brī-ənt-\ Providence, R.I. 02906; 1863
Bryn Mawr C. \brin-'mär-\ Bryn Mawr, Pa. 19010; 1880
Buck·nell U. \,bək-'nel-, 'bək-,nel-\ Lewisburg, Pa. 17837; 1846
Bucks County Community C. \'bəks-\ Newtown, Pa. 18940; junior, 1965
Bue·na Vis·ta C. \,byü-nə-'vis-tə-\ Storm Lake, Iowa 50588; 1891
Buffalo County Teachers C. Alma, Wis. 54610; junior, 1902
Buffalo Diocesan Preparatory Sem. N.Y. 14208; 1925
Bur·dett C. \(,)bər-'det-\ Boston, Mass. 02116; junior, 1879
Burlington County C. Pemberton, N.J. 08068; junior, 1966
But·ler County Community C. \'bət-lər-\ Butler, Pa. 16001; junior, 1965
Butler County Community Junior C. El Dorado, Kans. 67042; 1927
Butler U. Indianapolis, Ind. 46208; 1850
Butte Junior C. \'byüt-\ Durham, Calif. 95938; 1967

Ca·bril·lo C. \kə-'brē-(,)(y)ō-, -'bril-(,)ō-\ Aptos, Calif. 95003; junior, 1959
Ca·bri·ni C. \kə-'brē-nē-\ Radnor, Pa. 19087; 1957
Cald·well C. for Women \'kȯl-,dwel-, -dwəl-, 'käl-\ Caldwell, N.J. 07006; 1939
California, U. of Berkeley, 94720; 1868
California, U. of Davis, 95606; 1908
California, U. of Irvine, 92664; 1965
California, U. of Los Angeles, 90024; 1881
California, U. of Riverside, 92502; 1907
California, U. of San Diego, 92037; 1901
California, U. of San Francisco, 94122; 1864
California, U. of Santa Barbara, 93106; 1891
California, U. of Santa Cruz, 95060; 1965
California Baptist C. Riverside, 92504; 1950
California C. of Arts and Crafts Oakland, 94618; 1907
California Con·cor·dia C. \-kən-'kȯrd-ē-ə-\ Oakland, 94605; junior, 1906
California Inst. of Tech. Pasadena, 91109; 1891
California Inst. of the Arts Los Angeles, 90057; 1883
California Lutheran C. Thousand Oaks, 91360; 1959
California Maritime Acad. Vallejo, 94590; 1929

California Podiatry C. San Francisco, 94115; 1914
California State C. California, Pa. 15419; 1852
California State C., Do·min·guez Hills \-də-'miŋ-gəz-\ 90247; 1965
California State C. at Ful·ler·ton \-'fül-ərt-ᵊn\ 92631; 1957
California State C. at Hay·ward \'hā-wərd\ 94542; 1957
California State C. at Long Beach, 90801; 1949
California State C. at Los Angeles, 90032; 1947
California State C. at San Bernardino, 92499; 1960
California State Polytechnic C. Pomona, 91766; 1956
California State Polytechnic C. San Luis Obispo, 93401; 1901
Cal·va·ry Bible C. \'kalv-(ə-)rē-\ Kansas City, Mo. 64111; 1932
Cal·vin C. \'kal-vən\ Grand Rapids, Mich. 49506; 1876
Cambridge Junior C. Cambridge, Mass. 02140; 1934
Camden County C. Blackwood, N.J. 08012; junior, 1966
Cam·er·on State Agricultural C. \'kam-(ə-)rən\ Lawton, Okla. 73501; 1908
Camp·bell C. \'kam-(b)əl-\ Buies Creek, N.C. 27506; 1887
Camp·bells·ville C. \'kam-(b)əlz-,vil-\ Campbellsville, Ky. 42718; 1906
Canaan C. Canaan, N.H. 03741; 1955
Ca·ña·da C. \kən-'yäd-ə-\ Redwood City, Calif. 94061; junior, 1968
Canal Zone C. Balboa Heights, junior, 1933
Ca·ni·sius C. \kə-'nish-əs-, -'nē-shəs-\ Buffalo, N.Y. 14208; 1870
Cape Cod Community C. Hyannis, Mass. 02601; junior, 1961
Capital U. Columbus, Ohio 43209; 1850
Capitol Inst. of Tech. Washington, D.C. 20010; 1964
Cardinal Cush·ing C. \-'kush-iŋ-\ Brookline, Mass. 02146; 1952
Cardinal Glen·non C. \-'glen-ən\ St. Louis, Mo. 63119; 1900
Cardinal Stritch C. \'strich\ Milwaukee, Wis. 53217; 1932
Car·le·ton C. \'kär(ə)lt-ᵊn\ Northfield, Minn. 55057; 1866
Car·low C. \'kär-(,)lō-\ Pittsburgh, Pa. 15213; 1929
Carl Sand·burg C. \-'san(d)-,bərg-\ Galesburg, Ill. 61401; junior, 1967
Car·ne·gie–Mel·lon U. \,kär-nə-gē-'mel-ən-, kär-'neg-ē-\ Pittsburgh, Pa. 15213; 1900
Car·roll C. \'kar-əl-\ Helena, Mont. 59601; 1909
Carroll C. Waukesha, Wis. 53186; 1840
Car·son–New·man C. \,kärs-ᵊn-'n(y)ü-mən-\ Jefferson City, Tenn. 37760; 1851
Car·thage C. \'kär-thij\ Kenosha, Wis. 53140; 1846
Car·ver Bible Inst. and C. \'kär-vər-\ Atlanta, Ga. 30302; 1943
Case Western Reserve U. \'kās-\ Cleveland, Ohio 44106; 1826
Casper C. Casper, Wyo. 82601; junior, 1945
Cas·tle·ton State C. \'kas-əl-tən-\ Castleton, Vt. 05735; 1787
Ca·taw·ba C. \kə-'tȯ-bə-\ Salisbury, N.C. 28144; 1851
Cathedral C. of the Immaculate Conception Douglaston, N.Y. 11362; 1914
Catherine Spal·ding C. \-'spȯl-diŋ-\ Louisville, Ky. 40203; 1829
Catholic Teachers C. Providence, R.I. 02903; 1929
Catholic U. of America Washington, D.C. 20017; 1887
Catholic U. of Puerto Rico Ponce, 00731; 1948
Catonsville Community C. Catonsville, Md. 21228; junior, 1957
Caz·e·no·via C. \,kaz-ᵊn-'ō-vē-ə-\ Cazenovia, N.Y. 13035; junior, 1824
Cedar Crest C. Allentown, Pa. 18104; 1867
Cen·te·na·ry C. for Women \sen-'tē-nə-rē-\ Hackettstown, N.J. 07840; 1867
Cen·te·nary C. of Louisiana \'sent-ᵊn-,er-ē-\ Shreveport, 71104; 1825
Center for Early Education Los Angeles, Calif. 90048; junior, 1963
Cen·ter·ville Community C. \'sent-ər-,vil-\ Centerville, Iowa 52544; junior, 1930
Central Arizona C. Coolidge, Ariz. 85228; junior, 1969
Central Baptist C. Conway, Ark. 72032; 1950
Central Bible C. Springfield, Mo. 65802; 1922
Central U. of Iowa Pella, 50219; 1853
Central C. McPherson, Kans. 67460; junior, 1914
Central Connecticut State C. New Britain, 06050; 1849
Central Florida Junior C. Ocala, 32670; 1958
Cen·tra·lia C. \sen-'trāl-yə-\ Centralia, Wash. 98531; junior, 1925
Central Methodist C. Fayette, Mo. 65248; 1854
Central Michigan U. Mount Pleasant, 48858; 1892
Central Missouri State C. Warrensburg, 64093; 1870
Central Oregon Community C. Bend, 97701; junior, 1949
Central Pied·mont Community C. \-'pēd-,mänt-\ Charlotte, N.C. 28204; junior, 1963
Central State C. Edmond, Okla. 73034; 1890
Central State U. Wilberforce, Ohio 45384; 1887
Central Technical Inst. Kansas City, Mo. 64108; junior, 1937
Central Texas C. Killeen, 76541; junior, 1967
Central Washington State C. Ellensburg, 98926; 1891
Central Wesleyan C. Central, S.C. 29630; 1906
Central Wyoming C. Riverton, 82501; junior, 1966
Central YMCA Community C. Chicago, Ill. 60606; junior, 1960
Centre C. of Kentucky Danville, 40422; 1819
Cer·ri·tos C. \sə-'rēt-əs-\ Norwalk, Calif. 90650; junior, 1955
Cha·bot C. \sha-'bō-\ Hayward, Calif. 94545; junior, 1961
Chad·ron State C. \'shad-rən-\ Chadron, Nebr. 69337; 1911
Chaf·fey C. \'chā-fē-\ Alta Loma, Calif. 91701; junior, 1883
Cham·ber·layne Junior C. \'chäm-bər-,lān-, -lən-\ Boston, Mass. 02116; 1892
Cham·i·nade C. of Honolulu \,sham-ə-'nad-\ Hawaii 96816; 1955
Cham·plain C. \sham-'plān-\ Burlington, Vt. 05401; junior, 1861
Charles County Community C. \'chär(ə)lz-\ La Plata, Md. 20646; junior, 1958
Charleston, C. of S.C. 29401; 1770
Chat·ham C. \'chat-əm-\ Pittsburgh, Pa. 15232; 1869

Chattanooga, U. of Tennessee at, 37403; 1886
Chattanooga State Technical Inst. Tenn. 37406; junior, 1963
Chesapeake C. Centreville, Md. 21617; junior, 1967
Chestnut Hill C. Philadelphia, Pa. 19118; 1871
Chey·ney State C. \'chā-nē-\ Cheyney, Pa. 19319; 1837
Chicago, U. of Ill. 60637; 1891
Chicago City C. Ill. 60601; junior, 1931
Chicago State C. Ill. 60621; 1869
Chicago Technical C. Ill. 60616; 1904
Chi·co State C. \'chē-(,)kō-\ Chico, Calif. 95926; 1887
Chi·po·la Junior C. \chə-'pō-lə-\ Marianna, Fla. 32446; 1947
Cho·wan C. \chə-'wän\ Murfreesboro, N.C. 27855; junior, 1848
Christian Brothers C. Memphis, Tenn. 38104; 1871
Christian C. of the Southwest Mesquite, Tex. 75149; junior, 1962
Christ the Saviour Sem. of Johnstown, Pa. 15906; 1940
Church C. of Hawaii, The Laie, Oahu, 96762; 1955
Cincinnati, U. of Ohio 45221; 1819
Cincinnati Bible Sem., The Ohio 45204; 1924
Cis·co Junior C. \'sis-(,)kō-\ Cisco, Tex. 76437; 1940
Citadel, The Charleston, S.C. 29409; 1842
Citrus C. Azusa, Calif. 91702; junior, 1915
City C. New York, N.Y. 10033; 1847
City C. of San Francisco Calif. 94112; junior, 1935
City U. of New York 10021; 1961
Claf·lin U. \'klaf-lən-\ Orangeburg, S.C. 29115; 1869
Clare·mont Men's C. \'kla(ə)r-,mänt-, 'kle(ə)r-\ Claremont, Calif. 91711; 1946
Clar·en·don C. \'klar-ən-dən-\ Clarendon, Tex. 79226; junior, 1927
Clar·i·on State C. \'klar-ē-on-\ Clarion, Pa. 16214; 1866
Clark C. \'klärk-\ Atlanta, Ga. 30314; 1869
Clark C. Vancouver, Wash. 98663; junior, 1933
Clarke C. \'klärk-\ Dubuque, Iowa 52001; 1843
Clarke Memorial C. Newton, Miss. 39345; junior, 1908
Clark·son C. of Tech. \'klärk-sən-\ Potsdam, N.Y. 13676; 1896
Clark U. Worcester, Mass. 01610; 1887
Clat·sop Community C. \'klat-səp-\ Astoria, Oreg. 97103; junior, 1958
Clea·ry C. \'kli(ə)r-ē-\ Ypsilanti, Mich. 48197; 1883
Clem·son U. \'klem(p)-sən-\ Clemson, S.C. 29631; 1889
Cleveland Inst. of Music Ohio 44106; 1920
Cleveland State Community C. Cleveland, Tenn. 37311; junior, 1967
Cleveland State U. Ohio 44102; 1923
Clin·ton Community C. \'klint-ᵊn-\ Plattsburgh, N.Y. 12901; junior, 1966
Cloud County Community Junior C. \'klaud-\ Concordia, Kans. 66901; 1965
Coa·ho·ma Junior C. \kō-'hō-mə-\ Clarksdale, Miss. 38614; 1926
Coa·lin·ga C. \kō-'liŋ-gə-\ Coalinga, Calif. 93210; junior, 1932
Co·chise C. \kō-'chēz-, -'chēs-\ Douglas, Ariz. 85607; junior, 1962
Coe C. \'kō-\ Cedar Rapids, Iowa 52402; 1851
Coffeyville C. Coffeyville, Kans. 67337; junior, 1923
Cogs·well Polytechnical C. \'kägz-,wel-, -wəl-\ San Francisco, Calif. 94110; junior, 1930
Co·ker C. \'kō-kər-\ Hartsville, S.C. 29550; 1894
Col·by C. \'kōl-bē-\ Waterville, Me. 04901; 1813
Colby Community Junior C. Colby, Kans. 67701; 1964
Colby Junior C. for Women New London, N.H. 03257; 1837
Colgate U. Hamilton, N.Y. 13346; 1819
Colorado, U. of Boulder, 80302; 1861
Colorado Al·pine C. \-'al-,pīn-\ Steamboat Springs, 80477; 1961
Colorado C. Colorado Springs, 80903; 1874
Colorado Mountain C. Glenwood Springs 81601; junior, 1967
Colorado Sch. of Mines Golden, 80401; 1874
Colorado State C. Greeley, 80631; 1889
Colorado State U. Fort Collins, 80521; 1870
Co·lum·bia Basin C. \kə-'ləm-bē-ə-\ Pasco, Wash. 99301; junior, 1955
Columbia Bible C. Columbia, S.C. 29203; 1923
Columbia Christian C. Portland, Oreg. 97220; junior, 1956
Columbia C. Chicago, Ill. 60611; 1890
Columbia C. Columbia, Mo. 65201; junior, 1851
Columbia C. Columbia, S.C. 29203; 1854
Columbia County Teachers C. Columbus, Wis. 53925; junior, 1908
Columbia–Greene Community C. Athens, N.Y. 12015; junior, 1967
Columbia Junior C. Columbia, Calif. 95310; 1968
Columbia State Community C. Columbia, Tenn. 38401; junior, 1966
Columbia Union C. Takoma Park, Md. 20012; 1904
Columbia U. New York, N.Y. 10027; 1754
Columbus C. Columbus, Ga. 31907; junior, 1958
Combs C. of Music \'kōmz-\ Philadelphia, Pa. 19119; 1885
Compton C. Compton, Calif. 90221; junior, 1927
Con·cord C. \'kän-,kȯ(ə)rd-, 'käŋ-\ Athens, W. Va. 24712; 1872
Con·cor·dia C. \kən-'kȯrd-ē-ə-\ Moorhead, Minn. 56560; 1891
Concordia C. St. Paul, Minn. 55104; 1893
Concordia C. Portland, Oreg. 97211; junior, 1905
Concordia C. Milwaukee, Wis. 53208; junior, 1881
Concordia Junior C. Bronxville, N.Y. 10708; 1881
Concordia Lutheran C. Austin, Tex. 78705; junior, 1926
Concordia Lutheran Junior C. Ann Arbor, Mich. 48105; 1963
Concordia Sem. St. Louis, Mo. 63105; 1839
Concordia Senior C. Fort Wayne, Ind. 46805; 1839
Concordia Teachers C. River Forest, Ill. 60305; 1864
Concordia Teachers C. Seward, Nebr. 68434; 1894
Connecticut, U. of Storrs, 06268; 1881
Connecticut C. New London 06320; 1911

Con·nors State C. \\'kän-ərz-\\ Warner, Okla. 74469; junior, 1908
Con·tra Cos·ta C. \\,kän-trə-'käs-tə-, -'kós-\\ San Pablo, Calif. 94806; junior, 1949
Con·verse C. \\'kän-(,)vərs-\\ Spartanburg, S.C. 29301; 1889
Cooke County Junior C. \\'kúk-\\ Gainesville, Tex. 76240; 1924
Coo·per Union \\,kü-pər-, 'kúp-ər-\\ New York, N.Y. 10003; 1859
Co·pi·ah–Lincoln Junior C. \\kə-,pī-ə-\\ Wesson, Miss. 39191; 1915
Cop·pin State C. \\'käp-ən-\\ Baltimore, Md. 21216; 1900
Cor·bett C. \\'kór-bət-\\ Crookston, Minn. 56716; junior, 1957
Cor·nell C. \\kór-'nel-\\ Mount Vernon, Iowa 52314; 1853
Cornell U. Ithaca, N.Y. 14850; 1865
Cor·ning Community C. \\'kór-niŋ-\\ Corning, N.Y. 14830; junior, 1956
Corpus Christi, U. of Corpus Christi, Tex. 78411; 1947
Cot·tey C. \\'kät-ē-\\ Nevada, Mo. 64772; junior, 1884
County C. of Mor·ris \\-'mór-əs, -'mär-\\ Dover, N.J. 07801; junior, 1968
Covenant C. Lookout Mountain, Tenn. 37350; 1955
Cow·ley County Community Junior C. \\'kaù-lē-\\ Arkansas City, Kans. 67005; 1922
Cran·brook Acad. of Art \\'kran-,brúk-\\ Bloomfield Hills, Mich. 48013; 1927
Creigh·ton U. \\'krāt-ᵊn-\\ Omaha, Nebr. 68131; 1878
Cro·sier Sem. \\'krō-zhər-\\ Onamia, Minn. 56359; junior, 1922
Crow·der C. \\'kraùd-ər-\\ Neosho, Mo. 64850; junior, 1963
Crow·ley's Ridge C. \\'krō-lēz-\\ Paragould, Ark. 72450; junior, 1964
Cues·ta C. \\'kwes-tə-\\ San Luis Obispo, Calif. 93401; junior, 1963
Cul·ver–Stock·ton C. \\,kəl-vər-'stäk-tən-\\ Canton, Mo. 63435; 1853
Cum·ber·land C. \\'kəm-bər-lənd-\\ Williamsburg, Ky. 40769; 1888
Cumberland C. of Tennessee Lebanon, 37087; junior, 1842
Cumberland County C. Vineland, N.J. 08360; junior, 1964
Cur·ry C. \\'kər-ē-, 'kə-rē-\\ Milton, Mass. 02186; 1879
Cur·tis Inst. of Music \\'kərt-əs-\\ Philadelphia, Pa. 19103; 1924
Cuy·a·hoga Community C. \\,kī-(-ə)-'hò-gə-, kə-'hò-, -'hä-, -'hō-\\ Cleveland, Ohio 44115; junior, 1963
Cypress Junior C. Cypress, Calif. 90630; 1966

Dab·ney S. Lancaster Community C. \\,dab-nē-,es-\\ Clifton Forge, Va. 24422; junior, 1964
Da·ko·ta State C. \\də-'kōt-ə-\\ Madison, S. Dak. 57042; 1881
Dakota Wesleyan U. Mitchell, S. Dak. 57301; 1883
Dallas, U. of Irving, Tex. 75060; 1956
Dallas Baptist C. Tex. 75211; junior, 1891
Dallas Bible C. Tex. 75228; 1940
Dalton Junior C. Dalton, Ga. 30720; 1966
Dana C. \\'dan-ə-\\ Blair, Nebr. 68008; 1884
Daniel Payne C. \\-'pān-\\ Birmingham, Ala. 35212; 1889
Danville Junior C. Danville, Ill. 61832; 1946
Dart·mouth C. \\'därt-məth-\\ Hanover, N.H. 03755; 1769
Dav·en·port C. of Business \\'dav-ən-,pō(ə)rt-, -,pò(ə)rt-\\ Grand Rapids, Mich. 49502; junior, 1910
David Lips·comb C. \\-'lip-skəm-\\ Nashville, Tenn. 37203; 1891
Da·vid·son C. \\'dā-vəd-sən-\\ Davidson, N.C. 28036; 1836
Davidson County Community C. Lexington, N.C. 27292; junior, 1961
Da·vis and El·kins C. \\,dā-və-sən-'(d)el-kənz-\\ Elkins, W. Va. 26241; 1903
Daw·son C. \\'dòs-ᵊn-\\ Glendive, Mont. 59330; junior, 1940
Dayton, U. of Ohio 45409; 1850
Daytona Beach Junior C. Fla. 32015; 1958
Dean Junior C. \\'dēn-\\ Franklin, Mass. 02038; 1865
Deep Springs C. Deep Springs, Calif. 89010; junior, 1917
De·fi·ance C. \\di-'fī-ən(t)s-\\ Defiance, Ohio 43512; 1850
De·Kalb C. \\di-'ka(l)b-\\ Clarkston, Ga. 30021; junior, 1963
Delaware, U. of Newark, 19711; 1743
Delaware State C. Dover, 19901; 1891
Delaware Technical and Community C. Dover, 19901; junior, 1967
Delaware Valley C. of Science and Agric. Doylestown, Pa. 18901; 1896
Del·ga·do C. \\del-'gäd-(,)ō-\\ New Orleans, La. 70119; junior, 1921
De Li·ma Junior C. \\də-'lē-mə-\\ Oxford, Mich. 48051; 1958
Del Mar C. \\del-'mär-\\ Corpus Christi, Tex. 78404; junior, 1935
De Lourdes C. \\də-'lü(ə)rd-\\ Des Plaines, Ill. 60016; 1951
Delta C. University Center, Mich. 48710; junior, 1961
Delta State C. Cleveland, Miss. 38732; 1924
Den·i·son U. \\'den-ə-sən-\\ Granville, Ohio 43023; 1831
Denver, U. of Colo. 80210; 1864
De Paul U. \\di-'pòl-\\ Chicago, Ill. 60604; 1898
De·Pauw U. \\di-'pò-\\ Greencastle, Ind. 46135; 1837
De Sales Preparatory Sem. \\di-'sā(ə)lz-\\ Milwaukee, Wis. 53207; junior, 1856
Desert, C. of the Palm Desert, Calif. 92260; junior, 1961
Detroit, U. of Mich. 48221; 1877
Detroit Bible C. Mich. 48235; 1945
Detroit C. of Business Dearborn, Mich. 48126; 1906
Detroit Inst. of Musical Art Mich. 48202; 1914
Detroit Inst. of Tech. Mich. 48201; 1891
Diablo Valley C. Pleasant Hill, Calif. 94523; junior, 1949
Dick·in·son C. \\'dik-ən-sən-\\ Carlisle, Pa. 17013; 1773
Dickinson State C. Dickinson, N. Dak. 58601; 1918
Dil·lard U. \\'dil-ərd-\\ New Orleans, La. 70122; 1869
Diocesan Sisters C. Bloomfield, Conn. 06002; 1949
District of Columbia Teachers C. Washington, 20009; 1851
Divine Word C. Epworth, Iowa 52045; 1913
Divine Word Sem. Techny, Ill. 60082; 1909

Dix·ie C. \\'dik-sē-\\ St. George, Utah 84770; junior, 1911
Doane C. \\'dōn-\\ Crete, Nebr. 68333; 1872
Dodge City Community Junior C. \\'däj-\\ Dodge City, Kans. 67801; 1935
Dodge County Teachers C. Mayville, Wis. 53050; junior, 1925
Dominican C. Houston, Tex. 77021; 1946
Dominican C. Racine, Wis. 53402; 1935
Dominican C. of Blau·velt \\-'blō-,velt\\ Blauvelt, N.Y. 10913; 1952
Dominican C. of San Ra·fael \\-,san-rə-'fel\\ San Rafael, Calif. 94901; 1890
Don Bos·co C. \\'dän-'bäs-(,)kō-\\ Newton, N.J. 07860; 1929
Don·nel·ly C. \\'dän-ᵊl-ē-\\ Kansas City, Kans. 66102; junior, 1949
Door–Ke·wau·nee County Teachers C. \\'dō(ə)r-ki-'wò-nē-, 'dó(ə)r-\\ Algoma, Wis. 54201; junior, 1909
Dordt C. \\'dó(ə)rt-\\ Sioux Center, Iowa 51250; 1955
Dow·ling C. \\'daù-liŋ-\\ Oakdale, N.Y. 11769; 1959
Drake U. Des Moines, Iowa 19104; 1881
Drew U. \\'drü-\\ Madison, N.J. 07940; 1866
Drex·el Inst. of Tech. \\'drek-səl-\\ Philadelphia, Pa. 19104; 1891
Dr. Mar·tin Lu·ther C. \\-,märt-ᵊn-'lü-thər-\\ New Ulm, Minn. 56073; 1884
Dru·ry C. \\'drù(ə)r-ē\\ Springfield, Mo. 65802; 1873
Dubuque, U. of Iowa 52001; 1852
Duke U. \\'d(y)ük-\\ Durham, N.C. 27706; 1838
Dun·bar·ton C. of Holy Cross \\,dən-'bärt-ᵊn-\\ Washington, D.C. 20008; 1935
Duns Sco·tus C. \\,dən(z)-'skōt-əs-\\ Southfield, Mich. 48075; 1930
Du·Page, C. of \\-dù-'päj\\ Naperville, Ill. 60540; junior, 1966
Du·quesne U. \\dü-'kän-\\ Pittsburgh, Pa. 15219; 1878
Dutch·ess Community C. \\'dəch-əs-\\ Poughkeepsie, N.Y. 12601; junior, 1957
Dyke C. \\'dīk-\\ Cleveland, Ohio 44114; 1848
D'You·ville C. \\'dyü-,vil\\ Buffalo, N.Y. 14201; 1908

Earl·ham C. \\'ər-ləm-\\ Richmond, Ind. 47374; 1847
East Carolina U. Greenville, N.C. 27834; 1907
East Central Junior C. Decatur, Miss. 39327; 1914
East Central State C. Ada, Okla. 74820; 1909
East Coast U. Brooksville, Fla. 33519; 1947
Eastern Arizona C. Thatcher, 85552; junior, 1891
Eastern Baptist C. St. Davids, Pa. 19087; 1952
Eastern C. Baltimore, Md. 21201; 1928
Eastern Connecticut State C. Willimantic, 06226; 1889
Eastern Illinois U. Charleston, 61920; 1895
Eastern Iowa Community C. Clinton, 52732; junior, 1929
Eastern Kentucky U. Richmond, 40475; 1906
Eastern Mennonite C. Harrisonburg, Va. 22801; 1917
Eastern Michigan U. Ypsilanti, 48197; 1849
Eastern Montana C. Billings, 59101; 1925
Eastern Naz·a·rene C. \\-,naz-ə-'rēn\\ Wollaston, Mass. 02170; 1900
Eastern New Mexico U. Portales, 88130; 1934
Eastern Oklahoma A. & M. C. Wilburton, 74578; junior, 1909
Eastern Oregon C. La Grande, 97850; 1929
Eastern Pilgrim C. Allentown, Pa. 18103; 1921
Eastern Washington State C. Cheney, 99004; 1890
Eastern Wyoming C. Torrington, 82240; junior, 1948
East Los Angeles C. Los Angeles, Calif. 90022; junior, 1945
East Mississippi Junior C. Scooba, 39358; 1927
East Strouds·burg State C. \\-'straudz-,bərg-\\ East Stroudsburg, Pa. 18301; 1893
East Tennessee State U. Johnson City, 37601; 1909
East Texas Baptist C. Marshall, 75670; 1914
East Texas State U. Commerce, 75428; 1889
Edge·wood C. of the Sacred Heart \\'ej-,wúd-\\ Madison, Wis. 53711; 1927
Ed·in·boro State C. \\'ed-ᵊn-,bər-ə, -,bə-rə-\\ Edinboro, Pa. 16412; 1859
Ed·i·son Junior C. \\'ed-ə-sən-\\ Fort Myers, Fla. 33901; 1962
Ed·monds Community C. \\'ed-mən(d)z-\\ Edmonds, Wash. 98020; junior, 1967
Ed·ward Wa·ters C. \\,ed-wərd-'wòt-ərz-, -'wät-\\ Jacksonville, Fla. 32209; 1866
Ei·sen·how·er C. \\'īz-ᵊn-,haù(-ə)r-\\ Seneca Falls, N.Y. 13148; 1965
El Ca·mi·no C. \\,el-kə-'mē-(,)nō-\\ El Camino College, Calif. 90506; junior, 1946
El Cen·tro C. \\el-'sen-(,)trō-\\ Dallas, Tex. 75202; junior, 1965
Elgin Community C. Elgin, Ill. 60120; junior, 1949
Eliz·a·beth City State C. \\i-'liz-ə-bəth-\\ Elizabeth City, N.C. 27909; 1891
Elizabeth Se·ton C. \\-'sēt-ᵊn-\\ Yonkers, N.Y. 10701; junior, 1961
Eliz·a·beth·town C. \\i-'liz-ə-bəth-,taùn-\\ Elizabethtown, Pa. 17022; 1899
El·len Cush·ing Junior C. \\,el-ən-'kúsh-iŋ-\\ Bryn Mawr, Pa. 19010; 1892
Ells·worth Community C. \\'elz-(,)wərth-\\ Iowa Falls, Iowa 50126; junior, 1890
Elmhurst C. Elmhurst, Ill. 60126; 1871
Elmira C. Elmira, N.Y. 14901; 1853
Elon C. \\'ē-,län-\\ Elon College, N.C. 27244; 1889
El Re·no C. \\el-'rē-(,)nō-\\ El Reno, Okla. 73036; junior, 1938
Ely State Junior C. \\'ē-lē-\\ Ely, Minn. 55731; 1922
Em·bry–Rid·dle Aeronautical Inst. \\,em-brē-'rid-ᵊl-\\ Daytona Beach, Fla. 32015; 1926
Em·er·son C. \\'em-ər-sən-\\ Boston, Mass. 02116; 1880
Em·man·u·el C. \\i-'man-yə-(-wə)l\\ Boston, Mass. 02115; 1919
Em·ma·us Bible Sch. \\e-'mä-əs-\\ Oak Park, Ill. 60301; 1941
Em·mets·burg Community C. \\'em-əts-,bərg-\\ Emmetsburg, Iowa 50536; junior, 1930

Em·o·ry and Henry C. \'em-(ə-)rē-\ Emory, Va. 24327; 1838
Emory U. Atlanta, Ga. 30322; 1836
Em·po·ria, C. of \-'pōr-ē-ə, -'pȯr-\ Kans. 66801; 1882
En·di·cott Junior C. \'en-di-kət, -də-,kät\ Beverly, Mass. 01915; 1939
Englewood Cliffs C. Englewood Cliffs, N.J. 07632; junior, 1962
Enterprise State Junior C. Enterprise, Ala. 36330; 1965
Epiphany Apostolic C. Newburgh, N.Y. 12550; junior, 1888
Erie Community C. Buffalo, N.Y. 14221; junior, 1946
Er·skine C. \'ər-skən-\ Due West, S.C. 29639; 1839
Essex Community C. Baltimore, Md. 21237; junior, 1957
Essex County C. Newark, N.J. 07102; junior, 1968
Eu·re·ka C. \yu̇-'rē-kə-\ Eureka, Ill. 61530; 1848
Evan·gel C. \i-'van-jəl\ Springfield, Mo. 65802; 1955
Evansville, U. of Evansville, Ind. 47704; 1854
Everett Community C. Everett, Wash. 98201; junior, 1941

Fair·bury Junior C. \'fa(ə)r-,ber-ē-, 'fe(ə)r-\ Fairbury, Nebr. 68352; 1941
Fairfield U. Fairfield, Conn. 06430; 1942
Fair·leigh Dick·in·son U. \,fa(ə)r-lē-'dik-ən-sən-, ,fe(ə)r-\ Rutherford, N.J. 07070; 1942
Fairmont State C. Fairmont, W. Va. 26554; 1867
Faith Baptist Bible C. Ankeny, Iowa 50021; 1924
Fashion Inst. of Tech. New York, N.Y. 10001; junior, 1944
Father Judge Mission Sem. \-'jəj-\ Monroe, Va. 24574; junior, 1924
Fayetteville State C. Fayetteville, N.C. 28301; 1867
Fayetteville Technical Inst. Fayetteville, N.C. 28303; junior, 1961
Federal City C. Washington, D.C. 20001; 1966
Fe·li·cian C., The \-fə-'lish-ən-, -'lē-shən-\ Chicago, Ill. 60645; junior, 1926
Fer·gus Falls State Junior C. \,fər-gəs-\ Fergus Falls, Minn. 56537; 1960
Fer·ris State C. \'fer-əs-\ Big Rapids, Mich. 49307; 1884
Fer·rum Junior C. \'fer-əm-\ Ferrum, Va. 24088; 1914
Finch C. \'finch-\ New York, N.Y. 10021; 1900
Findlay C. Findlay, Ohio 45840; 1882
Finger Lakes, Community C. of the Canandaigua, N.Y. 14424; junior, 1965
Fish·er Junior C. \'fish-ər-\ Boston, Mass. 02116; 1903
Fisk U. \'fisk-\ Nashville, Tenn. 37203; 1866
Flag·ler C. \'flag-lər-\ St. Augustine, Fla. 32084; 1963
Flint Community Junior C. Flint, Mich. 48503; 1923
Florence State U. Florence, Ala. 35630; 1830
Florida, U. of Gainesville, 32601; 1853
Florida A. & M. U. Tallahassee, 32307; 1887
Florida Atlantic U. Boca Raton, 33432; 1964
Florida C. Temple Terrace, 33617; junior, 1944
Florida Inst. of Tech. Melbourne, 32901; 1958
Florida Junior C. at Jacksonville, 32207; 1963
Florida Keys Junior C. Key West, 33040; 1965
Florida Memorial C. Miami, 33054; 1879
Florida Presbyterian C. St. Petersburg, 33733; 1960
Florida Southern C. Lakeland, 33802; 1885
Florida State U. Tallahassee, 32306; 1857
Font·bonne C. \'fänt-,bän-\ St. Louis, Mo. 63105; 1923
Foot·hill C. \'fut-,hil-\ Los Altos Hills, Calif. 94022; junior, 1957
Ford·ham U. \'fȯrd-əm-, 'fȯrd-\ New York, N.Y. 10458; 1841
For·syth Technical Inst. \fȯr-'sīth-, fər-\ Winston-Salem, N.C. 27103; junior, 1960
Fort Hays Kansas State C. \-'hāz-\ Hays, Kans. 67601; 1901
Fort Lauderdale U. Fla. 33301; 1940
Fort Lew·is C. \-'lü-əs-\ Durango, Colo. 81301; 1911
Fort Scott Community Junior C. \-'skät-\ Fort Scott, Kans. 66701; 1919
Fort Steil·a·coom Community C. \-'stil-ə-kəm-\ Lakewood Center, Wash. 98499; junior, 1965
Fort Valley State C. \'fȯ(ə)rt-,, 'fȯ(ə)rt-,\ Fort Valley, Ga. 31030; 1895
Fort Wayne Bible C. Fort Wayne, Ind. 46807; 1904
Fort Worth Christian C. Tex. 76118; junior, 1956
Fort Wright C. of the Holy Names Spokane, Wash. 99204; 1907
Franconia C. Franconia, N.H. 03580; junior, 1962
Frank·lin and Mar·shall C. \'fraŋ-klə-nən-'mär-shəl-\ Lancaster, Pa. 17604; 1787
Franklin C. of Indiana Franklin, 46131; 1834
Franklin Inst. of Boston Mass. 02116; junior, 1908
Franklin Pierce C. Rindge, N.H. 03461; 1962
Franklin U. Columbus, Ohio 43215; 1902
Frank Phil·lips C. \-'fil-əps-\ Borger, Tex. 79007; junior, 1946
Fred·er·ick C. \'fred-(ə-)rik-\ Portsmouth, Va. 23703; 1958
Frederick Community C. Frederick, Md. 21701; junior, 1957
Freed–Har·de·man C. \'frēd-'härd-ə-mən-\ Henderson, Tenn. 38340; junior, 1908
Free·man Junior C. \'frē-mən-\ Freeman, S. Dak. 57029; 1900
Free Will Baptist Bible C. Nashville, Tenn. 37205; 1942
Fre·mont–Newark Junior C. \,frē-,mänt-\ Newark, Calif. 94560; 1966
Fresno City C. Fresno, Calif. 93704; junior, 1910
Fresno State C. Fresno, Calif. 93726; 1911
Friends Bible C. Haviland, Kans. 67059; 1917
Friendship Junior C. Rock Hill, S.C. 29730; 1891
Friends U. Wichita, Kans. 67213; 1898
Frost·burg State C. \'frȯs(t)-,bərg-\ Frostburg, Md. 21532; 1898
Ful·ton–Mont·gom·ery Community C. \'fu̇lt-ᵊn-(,)mən(t)-'gəm-(ə-)rē-, -män(t)-, -'gäm-\ Johnstown, N.Y. 12095; junior, 1963
Fur·man U. \'fər-mən-\ Greenville, S.C. 29613; 1825

Gadsden State Junior C. Gadsden, Ala. 35903; 1965
Gainesville Junior C. Gainesville, Ga. 30501; 1965

Gal·lau·det C. \,gal-ə-'det-\ Washington, D.C. 20002; 1864
Galveston Community C. Tex. 77550; junior, 1967
Gan·non C. \'gan-ən-\ Erie, Pa. 16501; 1933
Garden City Community Junior C. Garden City, Kans. 67846; 1919
Gard·ner–Webb C. \,gärd-nər-'web-\ Boiling Springs, N.C. 28017; junior, 1905
Gar·land Junior C. \'gär-lən(d)-\ Boston, Mass. 02215; 1872
Gas·ton C. \'gas-tən-\ Gastonia, N.C. 28052; junior, 1963
Gav·i·lan C. \'gav-ə-,lan-\ Gilroy, Calif. 95020; junior, 1919
General Motors Inst. Flint, Mich. 48502; 1919
Genesee Community C. Batavia, N.Y. 14020; junior, 1966
Ge·ne·va C. \jə-'nē-və-\ Beaver Falls, Pa. 15010; 1848
George C. Wal·lace State Junior C. \-'wäl-əs-\ Dothan, Ala. 36301; 1965
George Fox C. \-'fäks-\ Newberg, Oreg. 97132; 1891
George Pea·body C. for Teachers \-'pē-,bäd-ē-, -bəd-ē-\ Nashville, Tenn. 37203; 1875
Georgetown C. Georgetown, Ky. 40324; 1787
Georgetown U. Washington, D.C. 20007; 1789
George Washington U. Washington, D.C. 20006; 1821
George Wil·liams C. \-'wil-yəmz-\ Downers Grove, Ill. 60515; 1884
Georgia, U. of Athens, 30601; 1785
Georgia C. at Mil·ledge·ville \-'mil-ij-,vil, -vəl\ 31061; 1889
Georgia Inst. of Tech. Atlanta, 30332; 1885
Georgia Military C. Milledgeville, 31061; junior, 1879
Georgia Southern C. Statesboro, 30458; 1908
Georgia Southwestern C. Americus, 31709; 1906
Georgia State C. Atlanta, 30303; 1913
Gettysburg C. Pa. 17325; 1832
Glass·boro State C. \'glas-,bər-ə-, -,bə-rə-\ Glassboro, N.J. 08028; 1923
Glendale C. Glendale, Calif. 91208; junior, 1927
Glendale Community C. Glendale, Ariz. 85301; junior, 1965
Glen Oaks Community C. Centreville, Mich. 49032; junior, 1965
Glen·ville State C. \'glen-,vil-\ Glenville, W. Va. 26351; 1872
Gloucester County C. Sewell, N.J. 08080; junior, 1968
God·dard C. \'gäd-ərd-\ Plainfield, Vt. 05667; 1938
Go·ge·bic Community C. \gō-'gē-bik-\ Ironwood, Mich. 49938; junior, 1932
Golden Gate C. San Francisco, Calif. 94012; 1901
Golden West C. Huntington Beach, Calif. 92647; junior, 1966
Gol·dey Bea·com Junior C. \,gōl-də-'bē-kəm-\ Wilmington, Del. 19899; 1886
Gon·zaga U. \gən-'zag-ə-, -'zäg-\ Spokane, Wash. 99202; 1887
Good Counsel C. White Plains, N.Y. 10603; 1923
Gor·don C. \'gȯrd-ᵊn-\ Wenham, Mass. 01984; 1889
Gordon Military C. Barnesville, Ga. 30204; junior, 1852
Go·shen C. \'gō-shən-\ Goshen, Ind. 46526; 1894
Gou·cher C. \'gau̇-chər-\ Towson, Md. 21204; 1885
Grace Bible C. \'grās-\ Grand Rapids, Mich. 49509; 1946
Grace Bible Inst. Omaha, Nebr. 68108; 1943
Grace C. Winona Lake, Ind. 46590; 1937
Grace·land C. \'grā-slən(d)-\ Lamoni, Iowa 50140; 1895
Grahm Junior C. \'grā-əm-, 'gra(-ə)m-\ Boston, Mass. 02215; 1950
Gram·bling C. \'gram-bliŋ-\ Grambling, La. 71245; 1929
Grand Canyon C. Phoenix, Ariz. 85017; 1949
Grand Rapids Baptist Bible C. and Sem. Mich. 49505; 1941
Grand Rapids Junior C. Mich. 49502; 1914
Grand Valley State C. Allendale, Mich. 49401; 1963
Grand View C. Des Moines, Iowa 50316; junior, 1896
Gratz C. \'gräts-\ Philadelphia, Pa. 19141; 1895
Grays Harbor C. \'grāz-\ Aberdeen, Wash. 98520; junior, 1930
Gray·son County C. \'grās-ᵊn-\ Denison, Tex. 75020; junior, 1964
Greater Hartford Community C. Hartford, Conn. 06106; junior, 1967
Great Falls, C. of Great Falls, Mont. 59401; 1932
Green·bri·er C. \'grēn-,brī(-ə)r-\ Lewisburg, W. Va. 24901; junior, 1808
Green County Teachers C. Monroe, Wis. 53566; junior, 1910
Green·field Community C. \'grēn-,fēld-\ Greenfield, Mass. 01301; junior, 1962
Green Mountain C. Poultney, Vt. 05764; junior, 1834
Green River C. Auburn, Wash. 98002; junior, 1965
Greensboro C. Greensboro, N.C. 27402; 1838
Green·ville C. \'grēn-,vil-\ Greenville, Ill. 62246; 1855
Grin·nell C. \grə-'nel-\ Grinnell, Iowa 50112; 1846
Gross·mont C. \'grȯs-,mänt-\ El Cajon, Calif. 92020; junior, 1961
Grove City C. Grove City, Pa. 16127; 1876
Guam, C. of Agana, 96910; 1952
Guil·ford C. \'gil-fərd-\ Greensboro, N.C. 27410; 1834
Gulf-Coast Bible C. Houston, Tex. 77008; 1953
Gulf Coast Junior C. Panama City, Fla. 32401; 1957
Gulf Park C. Long Beach, Miss. 39560; junior, 1919
Gus·ta·vus Adol·phus C. \(,)gə-,stä-və-sə-'däl-fəs-\ St. Peter, Minn. 56082; 1862
Gwyn·edd–Mercy C. \'gwin-əd-\ Gwynedd Valley, Pa. 19437; 1948

Hagerstown Junior C. Hagerstown, Md. 21740; 1946
Ham·il·ton C. \'ham-əl-tən-, -əlt-ᵊn-\ Clinton, N.Y. 13323; 1793
Ham·line U. \'ham-lən-\ St. Paul, Minn. 55101; 1854
Hamp·den–Syd·ney C. \,ham(p)-dən-'sid-nē-\ Hampden-Sydney, Va. 23943; 1776
Hampton Inst. Hampton, Va. 23368; 1868
Han·o·ver C. \'han-ə-vər-\ Hanover, Ind. 47243; 1827
Har·cum Junior C. \'här-kəm-\ Bryn Mawr, Pa. 19010; 1915
Har·ding C. \'härd-iŋ-\ Searcy, Ark. 72143; 1924
Har·din–Sim·mons U. \,härd-ᵊn-'sim-ənz-\ Abilene, Tex. 79601; 1891

Har·ford Junior C. \'här-fərd-\ Bel Air, Md. 21014; 1957
Har·ri·man C. \'har-ə-mən-\ Harriman, N.Y. 10926; junior, 1956
Harrisburg Area Community C. Harrisburg, Pa. 17110; junior, 1964
Har·ris Teachers C. \'har-əs-\ St. Louis, Mo. 63103; 1857
Hartford, U. of West Hartford, Conn. 06117; 1877
Hartford C. for Women Conn. 06105; junior, 1933
Hartford State Technical C. Conn. 06106; junior, 1946
Hart·nell C. \'härt-,nel-\ Salinas, Calif. 93901; junior, 1920
Hart·wick C. \'härt-,wik-\ Oneonta, N.Y. 13820; 1928
Har·vard C. \'här-vərd-\ Cambridge, Mass. 02138; 1636
Har·vey Mudd C. \,här-vē-'məd-\ Claremont, Calif. 91711; 1955
Has·tings C. \'hā-stiŋz-\ Hastings, Nebr. 68901; 1882
Haverford C. Haverford, Pa. 19041; 1833
Hawaii, U. of Honolulu, 96822; 1907
Hawaii Loa C. \-'lō-ə-\ Honolulu, 96810; 1963
Heald Engineering C. \'hē(ə)ld-\ San Francisco, Calif. 94109; 1863
Hebrew Teachers C. Brookline, Mass. 02146; 1918
Hebrew Theol. C. Skokie, Ill. 60076; 1922
Hebrew Union C.–Jewish Inst. of Religion Cincinnati, Ohio 45220; 1875
Hei·del·berg C. \'hīd-əl-,bərg-\ Tiffin, Ohio 44883; 1850
Hel·len·ic C. \he-'len-ik-, hə-\ Brookline, Mass. 02146; 1937
Hen·der·son County Junior C. \'hen-dər-sən-\ Athens, Tex. 75751; 1946
Henderson State C. Arkadelphia, Ark. 71923; 1929
Hen·drix C. \'hen-driks-\ Conway, Ark. 72032; 1876
Henry Ford Community C. \-'fō(ə)rd-, -'fó(ə)rd-\ Dearborn, Mich. 48126; junior, 1938
Herbert H. Leh·man C. \-'lē-mən-\ Bronx, N.Y. 10468; 1931
Her·ki·mer County Community C. \'hər-kə-mər-\ Ilion, N.Y. 13357; junior, 1966
Her·ron Sch. of Art \'her-ən-\ Indianapolis, Ind. 46202; 1878
Hess·ton C. \'hes-tən-\ Hesston, Kans. 67062; junior, 1909
Hib·bing State Junior C. \'hib-iŋ-\ Hibbing, Minn. 55746; 1916
High·land Community C. \'hī-lən(d)-\ Freeport, Ill. 61032; junior, 1961
Highland Community Junior C. Highland, Kans. 66035; 1858
Highland Park C. Highland Park, Mich. 48203; junior, 1918
High·line C. \'hī-,līn-\ Midway, Wash. 98031; junior, 1961
High Point C. High Point, N.C. 27262; 1924
Hill Junior C. Hillsboro, Tex. 76645; 1962
Hills·bor·ough Junior C. \'hilz-,bər-ə-, -,bə-rə-\ Tampa, Fla. 33699; 1968
Hills·dale C. \'hilz-,dāl-\ Hillsdale, Mich. 49242; 1844
Hinds Junior C. \'hīn(d)z-\ Raymond, Miss. 39154; 1917
Hi·ram C. \'hī-rəm-\ Hiram, Ohio 44234; 1849
Hiram Scott C. \-'skät-\ Scottsbluff, Nebr. 69361; 1965
Hi·was·see C. \hī-'wäs-ē-\ Madisonville, Tenn. 37354; junior, 1849
Ho·bart and William Smith Colleges \'hō-bərt-\ Geneva, N.Y. 14456; 1822
Hof·stra U. \'häf-strə-\ Hempstead, N.Y. 11550; 1935
Hol·lins C. \'häl-ənz-\ Hollins College, Va. 24020; 1842
Holmes Junior C. \'hōmz-, 'hōlmz-\ Goodman, Miss. 39079; 1911
Holy Apostles Sem. Cromwell, Conn. 06416; 1956
Holy Cross, C. of the Worcester, Mass. 01610; 1843
Holy Cross Junior C. Notre Dame, Ind. 46556; 1966
Holy Family C. San Francisco, Calif. 94117; 1945
Holy Family C. Philadelphia, Pa. 19114; 1954
Holy Family C. Manitowoc, Wis. 54220; 1869
Holy Family Junior C. Fremont, Calif. 91738; 1952
Holy Names, C. of the Oakland, Calif. 94619; 1868
Holy Names, C. of the Albany, N.Y. 12208; junior, 1961
Holyoke Community C. Holyoke, Mass. 01040; junior, 1946
Hood C. \'hud-\ Frederick, Md. 21701; 1893
Hope C. \'hōp-\ Holland, Mich. 49423; 1851
Hough·ton C. \'hōt-ᵊn-\ Houghton, N.Y. 14744; 1883
Housatonic Community C. Stratford, Conn. 06497; junior, 1966
Houston, U. of Tex. 77004; 1934
Houston Baptist C. Tex. 77036; 1960
Howard County Junior C. Big Spring, Tex. 79720; 1945
Howard Payne C. \-'pān-\ Brownwood, Tex. 76801; 1889
Howard U. Washington, D.C. 20001; 1867
Hudson Valley Community C. Troy, N.Y. 12180; junior, 1953
Hum·boldt State C. \'həm-,bōlt-\ Arcata, Calif. 95521; 1913
Hum·phreys C. \'həm(p)-frēz-\ Stockton, Calif. 95207; junior, 1896
Hun·ter C. \'hənt-ər-\ New York, N.Y. 10021; 1870
Hun·ting·don C. \'hənt-iŋ-dən-\ Montgomery, Ala. 36106; 1854
Hun·ting·ton C. \'hənt-iŋ-tən-\ Huntington, Ind. 46750; 1897
Hu·ron C. \'hyur-ən-\ Huron, S. Dak. 57350; 1883
Hus·son C. \'həs-ᵊn-\ Bangor, Me. 04401; 1898
Hus·ton–Til·lot·son C. \'(h)yü-stən-'til-ət-sən-\ Austin, Tex. 78702; 1877
Hutchinson Community Junior C. Hutchinson, Kans. 67501· 1928

Idaho, C. of Caldwell, 83605; 1891
Idaho, U. of Moscow, 83843; 1889
Idaho State U. Pocatello, 83201; 1901
Illinois, U. of Urbana, 61801; 1867
Illinois Central C. East Peoria, 61611; junior, 1966
Illinois C. Jacksonville, 62650; 1829
Illinois C. of Optometry Chicago, 60616; 1872
Illinois Inst. of Tech. Chicago, 60616; 1892
Illinois State U. Normal, 61761; 1857
Illinois Valley Community C. La Salle, 61301; junior, 1924

Illinois Wesleyan U. Bloomington, 61701; 1850
Im·mac·u·la·ta C. \im-,ak-yə-'lät-ə-\ Bartlett, Ill. 60103; junior, 1955
Immaculata C. Hamburg, N.Y. 14075; junior, 1928
Immaculata C. Immaculata, Pa. 19345; 1920
Immaculata C. of Washington D.C. 20016; junior, 1905
Immaculate Conception Junior C. Lodi, N.J. 07644; 1923
Immaculate Conception Sem. Conception, Mo. 64433; 1883
Immaculate Conception Sem. Darlington, N.J. 07446; 1856
Immaculate Heart C. Los Angeles, Calif. 90027; 1916
Imperial Valley C. Imperial, Calif. 92251; junior, 1922
Incarnate Word C. San Antonio, Tex. 78209; 1881
Independence Community Junior C. Independence, Kans. 67301; 1925
Indiana Central C. Indianapolis, 46227; 1902
Indiana Inst. of Tech. Fort Wayne, 46803; 1930
Indiana State U. Terre Haute, Ind. 47809; 1865
Indiana U. Bloomington, 47401; 1820
Indiana U. of Pennsylvania Indiana, Pa. 15701; 1875
Indian River Junior C. Fort Pierce, Fla. 33450; 1960
Insurance, C. of New York, N.Y. 10038; 1962
Inter American U. of Puerto Rico San Germán, 00753; 1912
Io·na C. \ī-'ō-nə-\ New Rochelle, N.Y. 10801; 1940
Iowa, U. of Iowa City, 52240; 1847
Iowa Central Community C. Fort Dodge, 50501; junior, 1921
Iowa Lakes Community C. Estherville, Iowa 51334; junior, 1924
Iowa State U. of Science and Tech. Ames, 50010; 1858
Iowa Wesleyan C. Mount Pleasant, 52641; 1842
Iowa Western Community C. Clarinda, 51632; junior, 1923
Isothermal Community C. Spindale, N.C. 28160; junior, 1966
Itas·ca State Junior C. \ī-'tas-kə-\ Grand Rapids, Minn. 55744; 1922
It·a·wam·ba Junior C. \,it-ə-'wäm-bə-\ Fulton, Miss. 38843; 1948
Ithaca C. Ithaca, N.Y. 14850; 1892

Jack·son C. \'jak-sən-\ Honolulu, Hawaii 96822; 1949
Jackson Community C. Jackson, Mich. 49201; junior, 1928
Jackson State C. Jackson, Miss. 39217; 1877
Jackson State Community C. Jackson, Tenn. 38301; junior, 1965
Jack·son·ville C. \'jak-sən-,vil-, -vəl-\ Jacksonville, Tex. 75766; junior, 1899
Jacksonville State U. Jacksonville, Ala. 36265; 1883
Jacksonville U. Jacksonville, Fla. 32211; 1934
James·town C. \'jām-,staun-\ Jamestown, N. Dak. 58401; 1883
Jamestown Community C. Jamestown, N.Y. 14701; junior, 1934
Jar·vis Christian C. \'jär-vəs-\ Hawkins, Tex. 75765; 1912
Jef·fer·son C. \'jef-ər-sən-\ Hillsboro, Mo. 63050; junior, 1963
Jefferson Community C. Louisville, Ky. 40201; junior, 1967
Jefferson Community C. Watertown, N.Y. 13601; junior, 1963
Jefferson State Junior C. Birmingham, Ala. 35215; 1963
Jersey City State C. N.J. 07305; 1921
Jewish Theol. Sem. of America New York, N.Y. 10027; 1886
John A. Lo·gan C. \-'lō-gən-\ Carterville, Ill. 62918; junior, 1967
John Brown U. \-'braun-\ Siloam Springs, Ark. 72761; 1919
John Car·roll U. \-'kar-əl-\ Cleveland, Ohio 44118; 1886
John C. Cal·houn State Technical Junior C. \-kal-hün-\ Decatur, Ala. 35601; 1965
John F. Kennedy C. Wahoo, Nebr. 68006; 1965
John F. Kennedy U. Martinez, Calif. 94553; 1964
John Jay C. of Criminal Justice New York, N.Y. 10003; 1965
Johns Hop·kins U. \'jänz-'häp-kənz-\ Baltimore, Md. 21218; 1876
John·son and Wales Junior C. of Business \,jän(t)-sə-nən-'wā(ə)lz-\ Providence, R.I. 02903; 1914
John·son Bible C. \'jän(t)-sən-\ Kimberlin Heights, Tenn. 37920; 1893
Johnson C. Smith U. \-'smith-\ Charlotte, N.C. 28208; 1867
Johnson State C. Johnson, Vt. 05656; 1867
Johnstown C. Johnstown, Pa. 15902; junior, 1927
John Ty·ler Community C. \-'tī-lər-\ Chester, Va. 23831; junior, 1967
Joliet Junior C. Joliet, Ill. 60432; 1902
Jones C. \'jōnz-\ Jacksonville, Fla. 33211; junior, 1918
Jones County Junior C. Ellisville, Miss. 39437; 1911
Judaism, U. of Los Angeles, Calif. 90028; 1947
Jud·son Baptist C. \'jəd-sən-\ Portland, Oreg. 97220; 1956
Judson C. Marion, Ala. 36756; 1838
Judson C. Elgin, Ill. 60120; 1913
Juil·liard Sch. of Music \'jül-,yärd-\ New York, N.Y. 10027; 1905
Ju·neau County Teachers C. \'jü-,nō-\ New Lisbon, Wis. 53950; junior, 1916
Ju·ni·a·ta C. \,jü-nē-'at-ə-\ Huntingdon, Pa. 16652; 1876

Kalamazoo C. Kalamazoo, Mich. 49001; 1833
Kalamazoo Valley Community C. Kalamazoo, Mich. 49001; junior, 1966
Kankakee Community C. Kankakee, Ill. 60901; junior, 1966
Kansas, U. of Lawrence, 66044; 1863
Kansas City Art Inst. Mo. 64111; 1885
Kansas City Kansas Community Junior C. 66101; 1923
Kansas State C. of Pittsburg Pittsburg, Kans. 66762; 1903
Kansas State Teachers C. Emporia, 66801; 1863
Kansas State U. of Agric. and Applied Science Manhattan, 66502; 1863
Kansas Wesleyan U. Salina, 67401; 1886
Kaskaskia C. Centralia, Ill. 62801; junior, 1940
Kear·ney State C. \'kär-nē-\ Kearney, Nebr. 68847; 1905
Keene State C. Keene, N.H. 03431; 1909

Kel·logg Community C. \'kel-ˌȯg-, -ˌȧg-\ Battle Creek, Mich. 49016; junior, 1956
Kem·per Military Sch. and C. \'kem-pər-\ Boonville, Mo. 65233; junior, 1844
Ken·dall C. \'ken-dᵊl-\ Evanston, Ill. 60204; junior, 1934
Kennesaw Junior C. Marietta, Ga. 30060; 1963
Kent State U. \'kent-\ Kent, Ohio 44240; 1910
Kentucky, U. of Lexington, 40506; 1865
Kentucky Christian C. Grayson, 41143; 1919
Kentucky Southern C. Louisville, 40222; 1960
Kentucky State C. Frankfort, 40601; 1886
Kentucky Wesleyan C. Owensboro, 42301; 1866
Ken·yon C. \'ken-yən\ Gambier, Ohio 43022; 1824
Ket·er·ing C. of Medical Arts \'ket-ə-riŋ\ Kettering, Ohio 45429; junior, 1967
Keu·ka C. \'kyü-kə-, kā-'yü-\ Keuka Park, N.Y. 14478; 1890
Keystone Junior C. La Plume, Pa. 18440; 1868
Kil·gore C. \'kil-ˌgō(ə)r-, -ˌgȯ(ə)r-\ Kilgore, Tex. 75662; junior, 1935
Kil·roe Sem. of the Sacred Heart \'kil-ˌrō-\ Honesdale, Pa. 18431; 1955
King C. Bristol, Tenn. 37620; 1867
Kings·bor·ough Community C. \'kiŋz-ˌbər-ə-, -ˌbə-rə-\ Brooklyn, N.Y. 11235; junior, 1963
King's C., The Briarcliff Manor, N.Y. 10510; 1938
King's C. Charlotte, N.C. 28201; junior, 1901
King's C. Wilkes-Barre, Pa. 18702; 1946
Kirk·land C. \'kər-klənd-\ Clinton, N.Y. 13323; 1965
Kirkland Hall C. Easton, Md. 21601; junior, 1967
Kirt·land Community C. \'kərt-lənd-\ Roscommon, Mich. 48653; junior, 1966
Kish·wau·kee C. \kish-'wȯ-kē-\ Malta, Ill. 60150; junior, 1967
Kit·trell C. \'ki-trəl-\ Kittrell, N.C. 27544; 1886
Knox C. \'näks-\ Galesburg, Ill. 61401; 1837
Knoxville C. Knoxville, Tenn. 37921; 1863
Kutz·town State C. \'kŭt-ˌstaȯn-\ Kutztown, Pa. 19530; 1860

La·bette Community Junior C. \lə-'bet-\ Parsons, Kans. 67357; 1923
Lack·a·wan·na Junior C. \ˌlak-ə-'wän-ə-\ Scranton, Pa. 18503; 1894
La·dy·cliff C. \'lād-ē-ˌklif\ Highland Falls, N.Y. 10928; 1933
La·fay·ette C. \ˌläf-ē-'et-, ˌlaf-\ Easton, Pa. 18042; 1826
La Grange C. \lə-'grānj\ La Grange, Ga. 30240; 1831
Lake City Junior C. and Forest Ranger Sch. Lake City, Fla. 32055; 1947
Lake County, C. of Grayslake, Ill. 60085; junior, 1967
Lake Erie C. Painesville, Ohio 44077; 1856
Lake Forest C. Lake Forest, Ill. 60045; 1857
Lake Land C. \lā-'kland-\ Mattoon, Ill. 61938; junior, 1966
Lake·land C. \'lā-klən(d)-\ Sheboygan, Wis. 53081; 1862
Lakeland Community C. Mentor, Ohio 44060; junior, 1967
Lake Michigan C. Benton Harbor, Mich. 49022; junior, 1946
Lake Region Junior C. Devils Lake, N. Dak. 58301; 1941
Lake-Sum·ter Junior C. \-'səm(p)-tər-\ Leesburg, Fla. 32748; 1962
Lake Superior State C. Sault Ste. Marie, Mich. 49783; 1946
Lake·wood State Junior C. \'lā-ˌkwŭd-\ White Bear Lake, Minn. 55110; 1967
La·mar Junior C. \lə-'mär-\ Lamar, Colo. 81052; 1937
Lamar State C. of Tech. Beaumont, Tex. 77705; 1923
Lam·buth C. \'lam-bəth-\ Jackson, Tenn. 38301; 1924
Lancaster Sch. of the Bible Lancaster, Pa. 17601; 1933
Lan·der C. \'lan-dər-\ Greenwood, S.C. 29646; 1872
Lane C. \'lān-\ Jackson, Tenn. 38301; 1882
Lane Community C. Eugene, Oreg. 97405; junior, 1965
La·ney C. \'lā-nē-\ Oakland, Calif. 94606; junior, 1927
Lang·lade County Teachers C. \'laŋ-ˌlād-\ Antigo, Wis. 54409; junior, 1905
Lang·ston U. \'laŋ-stən-\ Langston, Okla. 73050; 1897
Lansing Community C. Lansing, Mich. 48914; junior, 1957
Laredo Junior C. Laredo, Tex. 78040; 1947
La Roche C. \lə-'rōsh\ Allison Park, Pa. 15101; 1963
La Sa·lette Sem. \ˌläs-ə-'let-\ Altamont, N.Y. 12009; junior, 1924
La Salle C. \lə-'sal-\ Philadelphia, Pa. 19141; 1863
La·sell Junior C. \lə-'sel-\ Auburndale, Mass. 02166; 1851
Las·sen C. \'las-ᵊn-\ Susanville, Calif. 96130; junior, 1925
Latter-day Saints Business C. Salt Lake City, Utah 84111; junior, 1886
La Verne C. \lə-'vərn-\ La Verne, Calif. 91750; 1891
Lawrence Inst. of Tech. Southfield, Mich. 48075; 1932
Lawrence U. Appleton, Wis. 54911; 1847
Lay·ton Sch. of Art \'lāt-ᵊn-\ Milwaukee, Wis. 53202; 1920
Lea C. \'lē-\ Albert Lea, Minn. 56007; 1965
Leb·a·non Valley C. \'leb-(ə-)nən-\ Annville, Pa. 17003; 1866
Lee C. \'lē-\ Cleveland, Tenn. 37311; 1918
Lee C. Baytown, Tex. 77520; junior, 1934
Lees Junior C. \'lēz-\ Jackson, Ky. 41339; 1883
Lees-Mc·Rae C. \-mə-'krā-\ Banner Elk, N.C. 28604; junior, 1900
Le·high County Community C. \'lē-ˌhī-\ Allentown, Pa., 18101; 1966
Lehigh U. Bethlehem, Pa. 18015; 1865
Leices·ter Junior C. \'les-tər-\ Leicester, Mass. 01524; 1784
Le Moyne C. \lə-'mȯin-\ Syracuse, N.Y. 13214; 1946
Le·Moyne-Ow·en C. \lə-'mȯin-'ō-ən\ Memphis, Tenn. 38126; 1870
Le·noir County Community C. \lə-'nō(ə)r-, -'nȯ(ə)r-\ Kinston, N.C. 28501; junior, 1960
Le·noir Rhyne C. \lə-'nōr-'(r)īn-, -'nȯr-, -'nōə(r)-'rīn-, -'nȯə(r)-\ Hickory, N.C. 28601; 1891
Les·ley C. \'les-lē-\ Cambridge, Mass. 02138; 1909
Le·Tour·neau C. \lə-'tər-(ˌ)nō-\ Longview, Tex. 75601; 1946

Lewis and Clark C. Portland, Oreg. 97219; 1867
Lewis-Clark Normal Sch. Lewiston, Idaho 83501; 1955
Lewis C. Lockport, Ill. 60441; 1930
Lime·stone C. \'līm-ˌstōn-\ Gaffney, S.C. 29340; 1845
Lin·coln Christian C. \'liŋ-kən-\ Lincoln, Ill. 62656; 1944
Lincoln C. Lincoln, Ill. 62656; junior, 1865
Lincoln County Teachers C. Merrill, Wis. 54452; junior, 1907
Lincoln Land Community C. Springfield, Ill. 62703; junior, 1967
Lincoln Memorial U. Harrogate, Tenn. 37752; 1897
Lincoln U. Jefferson City, Mo. 65101; 1866
Lincoln U. Lincoln University, Pa. 19352; 1854
Lin·den·wood C. \'lin-dən-ˌwŭd-\ St. Charles, Mo. 63301; 1827
Lind·sey Wil·son C. \ˌlin-zē-'wil-sən-\ Columbia, Ky. 42728; junior, 1903
Lin·field C. \'lin-ˌfēl(d)-\ McMinnville, Oreg. 97128; 1857
Liv·ing·stone C. \'liv-iŋ-stən-\ Salisbury, N.C. 28144; 1879
Liv·ing·ston U. \'liv-iŋ-stən-\ Livingston, Ala. 35470; 1840
Lock Ha·ven State C. \ˌläk-'hā-vən-\ Lock Haven, Pa. 17745; 1870
Lo·ma Lin·da U. \ˌlō-mə-'lin-də-\ Loma Linda, Calif. 92354; 1905
Long Beach City C. Long Beach, Calif. 90808; junior, 1913
Long Island U. Greenvale, N.Y. 11548; 1926
Long·wood C. \'lȯŋ-ˌwŭd-\ Farmville, Va. 23901; 1884
Lon Mor·ris C. \'län-'mȯr-əs-, -'mär-\ Jacksonville, Tex. 75766; junior, 1873
Lo·rain County Community C. \lə-'rān-\ Elyria, Ohio 44035; junior, 1963
Lo·ras C. \'lōr-əs-, 'lȯr-\ Dubuque, Iowa 52001; 1839
Lo·ret·to Heights C. \lə-ˌret-ō-\ Denver, Colo. 80236; 1891
Los Angeles Baptist C. Newhall, Calif. 91321; 1927
Los Angeles City C. Calif. 90029; junior, 1929
Los Angeles C. of Optometry Calif. 90007; 1904
Los Angeles Harbor C. Wilmington, Calif. 90744; junior, 1949
Los Angeles Pierce C. \-'pi(ə)rs-\ Woodland Hills, Calif. 91364; junior, 1947
Los Angeles Trade-Technical C. Calif. 90015; junior, 1949
Los Angeles Valley C. Van Nuys, Calif. 91401; junior, 1949
Lou·is·burg C. \'lü-əs-ˌbərg-\ Louisburg, N.C. 27549; junior, 1787
Louisiana C. Pineville, 71360; 1906
Louisiana Polytechnic Inst. Ruston, 71270; 1894
Louisiana State U. and A. & M. C. Baton Rouge, 70803; 1860
Louisiana State U. in New Orleans 70112; 1958
Louisville, U. of Ky. 40208; 1798
Lourdes Junior C. \'lŭ(ə)rd-\ Sylvania, Ohio 43560; 1957
Lowell State C. Lowell, Mass. 01850; 1894
Lowell Technological Inst. Lowell, Mass. 01854; 1895
Lower Columbia C. Longview, Wash. 98632; junior, 1934
Loy·o·la C. \lȯi-'ō-lə-\ Baltimore, Md. 21210; 1852
Loyola U. Chicago, Ill. 60611; 1869
Loyola U. New Orleans, La. 70118; 1849
Loyola U. of Los Angeles Calif. 90045; 1865
Lub·bock Christian C. \'ləb-ək-\ Lubbock, Tex. 79407; junior, 1957
Lu·ther C. \'lü-thər-\ Decorah, Iowa 52101; 1861
Luther C. of the Bible and Liberal Arts Teaneck, N.J. 07666; junior, 1948
Luther Rice C. \-'rīs-\ Alexandria, Va. 22310; 1967
Lu·zerne County Community C. \-lü-'zərn-\ Wilkes-Barre, Pa. 18700; junior, 1966
Ly·com·ing C. \lī-'kəm-iŋ-, -'kōm-\ Williamsport, Pa. 17701; 1812
Lynchburg C. Lynchburg, Va. 24504; 1903
Lyn·don State C. \'lin-dən-\ Lyndon Center, Vt. 05851; 1911

Mac·al·es·ter C. \mə-'kal-ə-stər-\ St. Paul, Minn. 55101; 1853
Mc·Cook C. \mə-'kŭk-\ McCook, Nebr. 69001; junior, 1926
Mac·Cor·mac C. \mə-'kȯr-mək-, -mik-\ Chicago, Ill. 60604; junior, 1904
Mc·Hen·ry County C. \mə-'ken-rē-\ Crystal Lake, Ill. 60014; junior, 1967
Mc·Ken·dree C. \mə-'ken-drē-\ Lebanon, Ill. 62254; 1828
Mack·i·nac C. \'mak-ə-ˌnȯ-\ Mackinac Island, Mich. 49757; 1965
Mc·Len·nan Community C. \mə-'klen-ən-\ Waco, Tex. 76703; junior, 1966
Mac·Mur·ray C. \mək-'mər-ē-, mək-'mə-rē-\ Jacksonville, Ill. 62650; 1846
Mc·Mur·ry C. \mək-'mər-ē-, -'mə-rē-\ Abilene, Tex. 79605; 1923
Mc·Neese State C. \mək-'nēs-\ Lake Charles, La. 70601; 1939
Ma·comb County Community C. \mə-'kōm-\ Warren, Mich. 48093; junior, 1953
Ma·con Junior C. \'mā-kən-\ Ga. 31201; 1968
Mc·Pher·son C. \mək-'fərs-ᵊn-\ McPherson, Kans. 67460; 1887
Mad·i·son Business C. \'mad-ə-sən-\ Wis. 53703; 1856
Madison C. Harrisonburg, Va. 22802; 1908
Madison Vocational, Technical and Adult Schools Wis. 53703; junior, 1912
Ma·don·na C. \mə-'dän-ə-\ Livonia, Mich. 48150; 1937
Maine, U. of Orono, 04473; 1865
Maine Aroos·took State C., U. of \-ə-'rüs-tək-, -'rus-\ Presque Isle, 04769; 1903
Maine Farm·ing·ton State C., U. of \-'fär-miŋ-tən-\ Farmington, 04938; 1864
Maine Fort Kent State C., U. of \-'kent-\ Fort Kent, 04743; 1878
Maine Gor·ham State C., U. of \-'gȯr-əm-\ Gorham, 04038; 1878
Maine Maritime Acad. Castine, 04421; 1941
Maine Washington State C., U. of Machias, 04654; 1909
Mal·linck·rodt C. \'mal-ən-ˌkrät-\ Wilmette, Ill. 60091; junior, 1918

Ma·lone C. \mə-'lōn-\ Canton, Ohio 44709; 1892
Man·a·tee Junior C. \'man-ə-ˌtē-\ Bradenton, Fla. 33505; 1958
Man·ches·ter C. \'man-ˌches-tər-, -chə-stər-\ North Manchester, Ind. 46962; 1889
Manchester Community C. Conn. 06040; junior, 1963
Manhattan Bible C. Manhattan, Kans. 66502; 1927
Manhattan C. New York, N.Y. 10471; 1853
Manhattan Sch. of Music New York, N.Y., coed., 1917
Man·hat·tan·ville C. \man-'hat-ᵊn-ˌvil-, mən-\ Purchase, N.Y. 10577; 1841
Manitowoc County Teachers C. Manitowoc, Wis. 54220; junior, 1901
Man·ka·to State C. \man-'kāt-ˌō-\ Mankato, Minn. 56001; 1867
Man·nes C. of Music \'man-əs-\ New York, N.Y. 10021; 1916
Manor Junior C. Jenkintown, Pa. 19046; 1947
Mans·field State C. \'manz-ˌfēld-, 'man(t)s-\ Mansfield, Pa. 16933; 1857
Ma·ria C. \mə-'rē-ə-\ Albany, N.Y. 12208; junior, 1958
Maria Junior C. Chicago, Ill. 60629; 1948
Mar·i·an C. \'mer-ē-ən-, 'mar-ē-, 'mä-rē-\ Indianapolis, Ind. 46222; 1937
Marian C. of Fond du Lac Wis. 54935; 1936
Ma·ria Re·gi·na C. \mə-ˌrē-ə-ri-'jē-nə-\ Syracuse, N.Y. 13208; junior, 1934
Mar·i·et·ta C. \ˌmar-ē-'et-ə-, ˌmer-\ Marietta, Ohio 45750; 1797
Mar·il·lac C. \'mar-ē-(ˌ)(y)ak-, 'mer-\ St. Louis, Mo. 63121; 1955
Ma·rin, C. of \-mə-'rin\ Kentfield, Calif. 94904; junior, 1926
Marion C. Marion, Ind. 46952; 1920
Marion C. Marion, Va. 24354; junior, 1873
Marion Inst. Marion, Ala. 36756; junior, 1842
Mar·ist C. \'mar-əst-, 'mer-\ Poughkeepsie, N.Y. 12601; 1946
Marist C. and Sem. Framingham Center, Mass. 01701; 1939
Marjorie Web·ster Junior C. \-'web-stər-\ Washington, D.C. 20012; 1920
Marl·boro C. \'märl-ˌbər-ə-, -ˌbə-rə-\ Marlboro, Vt. 05344; 1946
Mar·quette U. \mär-'ket-\ Milwaukee, Wis. 53233; 1857
Mar·shall·town Community C. \'mär-shəl-ˌtaün-\ Marshalltown, Iowa 50158; junior, 1927
Mar·shall U. \'mär-shəl-\ Huntington, W. Va. 25701; 1837
Mars Hill C. \'märz-\ Mars Hill, N.C. 28754; 1856
Mar·tin C. \'märt-ᵊn-\ Pulaski, Tenn. 38478; junior, 1870
Mary Bal·dwin C. \-'bȯl-dwən-\ Staunton, Va. 24401; 1842
Mary C. Bismarck, N. Dak. 58501; 1959
Mary·crest C. \'mer-ē-ˌkrest-, 'mar-ē-, 'mä-rē-\ Davenport, Iowa 52804; 1939
Mary·glade C. \-ˌglād-\ Memphis, Mich. 48041; 1960
Mary·grove C. \-ˌgrōv-\ Detroit, Mich. 48221; 1906
Mary Har·din-Bay·lor C. \-'härd-ᵊn-'bā-lər-\ Belton, Tex. 76513; 1845
Mary Holmes Junior C. \-'hōmz-, -'hȯlmz-\ West Point, Miss. 39773; 1892
Mary Immaculate Sem. and C. Northampton, Pa. 18067; 1939
Mary·knoll C. \'mer-ē-ˌnōl-, mar-ē-, 'mä-re-\ Glen Ellyn, Ill. 60137; 1949
Maryland, U. of College Park, 20740; 1807
Maryland Inst., C. of Art, The Baltimore, 21217; 1826
Maryland State C. Princess Anne, 21853; 1886
Mar·yl·hurst C. \'mar-əl-ˌhərst-, 'mer-\ Marylhurst, Oreg. 97036; 1893
Mary Manse C. \-'man(t)s-\ Toledo, Ohio 43620; 1873
Marymount C. \'mer-ē-ˌmaünt-, 'mar-ē-, 'mä-rē-\ Boca Raton, Fla. 33432; 1963
Marymount C. Salina, Kans. 67401; 1922
Marymount C. Tarrytown, N.Y. 10591; 1907
Marymount C. Arlington, Va. 22207; junior, 1950
Marymount C. at Loyola U. Los Angeles, Calif. 90045; 1933
Marymount Manhattan C. New York, N.Y. 10021; 1948
Mary Rog·ers C. \-'räj-ərz\ Maryknoll, N.Y. 10545; 1931
Mary·ville C. \'mar-i-vəl-, 'mer-, -ˌvil-\ Maryville, Tenn. 37801; 1819
Mary·ville C. of the Sacred Heart \'mer-ē-ˌvil-, 'mar-e-, 'mä-rē-\ St. Louis, Mo. 63141; 1846
Mary Washington C. of the U. of Virginia Fredericksburg, 22401; 1908
Mary·wood C. \'mer-ē-, wud-, 'mar-ē-, 'mä-rē-\ Scranton, Pa. 18509; 1915
Massachusetts, U. of Amherst, 01002; 1863
Massachusetts Bay Community C. Watertown, Mass. 02172; junior, 1961
Massachusetts C. of Art Boston, 02215; 1873
Massachusetts C. of Optometry Boston, 02116; 1894
Massachusetts C. of Pharmacy Boston, 02115; 1823
Massachusetts Inst. of Tech. Cambridge, 03139; 1859
Massachusetts Maritime Acad. Buzzards Bay, 02532; 1891
Massachusetts State C. at Boston 02115; 1852
Massachusetts State C. at Bridge·wa·ter \'brij-ˌwȯt-ər, -ˌwät-\ 02324; 1840
Massachusetts State C. at Fitchburg 01420; 1894
Massachusetts State C. at Framingham 01701; 1839
Massachusetts State C. at North Adams 01247; 1894
Massachusetts State C. at Salem 01970; 1854
Massachusetts State C. at Westfield 01085; 1839
Massachusetts State C. at Worcester 01620; 1871
Mas·sa·soit Community C. \ˌmas-ə-'sȯit-\ North Abington, Mass. 02351; junior, 1966
Ma·ter Chris·ti Sem. \ˌmät-ər-'kris-tē-\ Albany, N.Y. 12208; junior, 1954
Ma·ter Dei C. \ˌmät-ər-'dā-ˌē-\ Ogdensburg, N.Y. 13369; junior, 1960
Mat·ta·tuck Community C. \'mat-ə-ˌtək-\ Waterbury, Conn. 06702; junior, 1967

Mau·na·olu C. \ˌmaù-nə-'ō-(ˌ)lü-\ Paia, Maui, Hawaii 96779; junior, 1861
Mays·ville Community C. \'māz-ˌvil-\ Maysville, Ky. 41056; junior, 1968
May·ville State C. \'mā-ˌvil-\ Mayville, N. Dak. 58257; 1889
Me·daille C. \mə-'dī-\ Buffalo, N.Y. 14214; 1937
Me·har·ry Med. C. \mə-'har-ē-\ Nashville, Tenn. 37208; 1876
Memphis Acad. of Arts Tenn. 38112; 1936
Memphis State U. Tenn. 38111; 1909
Men·lo C. \'men-(ˌ)lō-\ Menlo Park, Calif. 94025; 1915
Merced C. Merced, Calif. 95340; junior, 1963
Mer·cer County Community C. \'mər-sər-\ Trenton, N.J. 08608; junior, 1947
Mercer U. Macon, Ga. 31207; 1833
Mercy C. Dobbs Ferry, N.Y. 10522; 1950
Mercy C. Cumberland, R.I. 02864; 1957
Mercy C. of Detroit Mich. 48219; 1941
Mer·cy·hurst C. \'mər-sē-ˌhərst-\ Erie, Pa. 16501; 1871
Mercy Inst. Portland, Me. 04103; junior, 1956
Mercy Junior C. St. Louis, Mo. 63131; 1952
Mer·e·dith C. \'mer-əd-əth-\ Raleigh, N.C. 27602; 1891
Meridian Junior C. Meridian, Miss. 39301; 1937
Mer·ri·mack C. \'mer-ə-ˌmak-\ North Andover, Mass. 01845; 1947
Mer·ritt C. \'mer-ət-\ Oakland, Calif. 94609; junior, 1953
Me·sa·bi State Junior C. \mə-'säb-ē-\ Virginia, Minn. 55792; 1918
Me·sa C. \'mä-sə-\ Grand Junction, Colo. 81501; junior, 1925
Mesa Community C. Mesa, Ariz. 85201; junior, 1963
Mes·si·ah C. \mə-'sī-ə-\ Grantham, Pa. 17027; 1909
Methodist C. Fayetteville, N.C. 28301; 1956
Metropolitan Junior C. Kansas City, Mo. 64111; 1915
Metropolitan State Junior C. Minneapolis, Minn. 55403; 1965
Miami, U. of Coral Gables, Fla. 33124; 1925
Miami Christian U. Fla. 33167; 1946
Miami-Dade Junior C. \-'dād-\ Miami, Fla. 33167; 1960
Miami-Ja·cobs Junior C. of Business \-'jā-kəbz-\ Dayton, Ohio 45402; 1860
Miami U. Oxford, Ohio 45056; 1809
Michigan, U. of Ann Arbor, 48104; 1817
Michigan Christian Junior C. Rochester, 48063; 1955
Michigan Lutheran C. Detroit, 48202; 1962
Michigan State U. East Lansing, 48823; 1855
Michigan Technological U. Houghton, 49931; 1885
Mid-America Nazarene C. Olathe, Kans. 66061; 1966
Mid·dle·bury C. \'mid-ᵊl-ˌber-ē-\ Middlebury, Vt. 05753; 1800
Middle Georgia C. Cochran, 31014; junior, 1920
Middlesex Community C. Middletown, Conn. 06457; junior, 1966
Middlesex County C. Edison, N.J. 08817; junior, 1964
Middle Tennessee State U. Murfreesboro, 37130; 1909
Mid·land Lutheran C. \'mid-lən(d)-\ Fremont, Nebr. 68025; 1887
Mid Michigan Community C. Harrison, 48625; junior, 1965
Mid-South Bible C. Memphis, Tenn. 38112; 1944
Mid·way Junior C. \'mid-ˌwā-\ Midway, Ky. 40347; 1847
Midwestern C. Denison, Iowa 51442; 1965
Midwestern U. Wichita Falls, Tex. 76308; 1922
Midwest Inst. of Business Administration Eureka, Kans. 67045; 1946
Miles C. \'mī(ə)lz-\ Birmingham, Ala. 35208; 1907
Miles Community C. Miles City, Mont. 59301; junior, 1939
Mil·lers·ville State C. \'mil-ərz-ˌvil-\ Millersville, Pa. 17551; 1854
Mil·li·gan C. \'mil-i-gən-\ Milligan College, Tenn. 37682; 1882
Mil·li·kin U. \'mil-i-kən-\ Decatur, Ill. 62522; 1901
Mill·saps C. \'mil-ˌsaps-\ Jackson, Miss. 39210; 1890
Mills C. \'milz-\ Oakland, Calif. 94613; 1852
Mills C. of Ed. New York, N.Y. 10011; 1909
Mil·ton C. \'milt-ᵊn-\ Milton, Wis. 53563; 1844
Mil·ton·vale Wesleyan C. \'milt-ᵊn-ˌvāl-\ Miltonvale, Kans. 67466; 1909
Milwaukee Sch. of Engineering Wis. 53201; 1903
Milwaukee Technical C. Wis. 53203; junior, 1923
Mineral Area C. Flat River, Mo. 63601; junior, 1922
Minneapolis Sch. of Art Minn. 55404; 1886
Minnesota, U. of Minneapolis, 55455; 1851
Minnesota Bible C. Minneapolis, 55414; 1913
Minot State C. Minot, N. Dak. 58701; 1913
Mi·ra Cos·ta C. \ˌmir-ə-'kō-stə-\ Oceanside, Calif. 92054; junior, 1934
Mi·seri·cor·dia, C. \-mə-ˌzer-ə-'kȯrd-ē-ə-, -ˌser-\ Dallas, Pa. 18612; 1923
Mississippi, U. of University, 38677; 1844
Mississippi C. Clinton, 39056; 1826
Mississippi Delta Junior C. Moorhead, Miss. 38761; 1911
Mississippi Industrial C. Holly Springs, 38635; 1905
Mississippi State C. for Women Columbus, 39701; 1884
Mississippi State U. State College, 39762; 1878
Mississippi Valley State C. Itta Bena, 38941; 1946
Missouri, U. of Columbia, 65201; 1839
Missouri at Kansas City, U. of 64110; 1929
Missouri at Rol·la, U. of \-'räl-ə-\ 65401; 1870
Missouri at St. Louis, U. of 63121; 1960
Missouri Baptist C.-Hannibal 63401; junior, 1858
Missouri Southern C. Joplin, 64801; 1937
Missouri Valley C. Marshall, Mo. 65340; 1888
Missouri Western C. St. Joseph, 64501; junior, 1915
Mitch·ell C. \'mich-əl-\ New London, Conn. 06320; junior, 1938
Mitchell C. Statesville, N.C. 28677; junior, 1853

M. J. Lewi C. of Podiatry \'lü-ē-\ New York, N.Y. 10035; 1911
Mo·ber·ly Junior C. \'mō-bər-lē-\ Moberly, Mo. 65270; 1927
Mobile C. Ala. 36613; 1961
Mobile State Junior C. Ala. 36603; 1965
Modesto Junior C. Modesto, Calif. 95350; 1921
Mo·hawk Valley Community C. \'mō-,hȯk-\ Utica, N.Y. 13501; junior, 1946
Mol·loy Catholic C. for Women \mə-'lȯi-\ Rockville Centre, N.Y. 11570; 1955
Mon·mouth C. \'män-məth-\ Monmouth, Ill. 61462; 1853
Monmouth C. West Long Branch, N.J. 07764; 1933
Mon·roe Community C. \mən-'rō-\ Rochester, N.Y. 14607; junior, 1962
Monroe County Community C. Monroe, Mich. 48161; junior, 1964
Montana, U. of Missoula, 59801; 1893
Montana C. of Mineral Science and Tech. Butte, 59701; 1893
Montana State U. Bozeman, 59715; 1893
Mont·calm Community C. \mänt-'kä(l)m-\ Sidney, Mich. 48885; junior, 1965
Montclair State C. Upper Montclair, N.J. 07043; 1908
Monterey Inst. of Foreign Studies Monterey, Calif. 93940; 1955
Monterey Peninsula C. Monterey, Calif. 93940; junior, 1947
Mon·te·val·lo, U. of \-,mänt-i-'val-(,)ō\ Ala. 35115; 1896
Mont·gom·ery County Community C. \(,)mən(t)-'gəm-(ə-)rē-, män)-, -'gäm-\ Conshohocken, Pa. 19428; junior, 1964
Montgomery Junior C. Takoma Park, Md. 20012; 1946
Mon·ti·cel·lo C. \,mänt-ə-'sel-(,)ō-\ Godfrey, Ill. 62035; junior, 1835
Mon·treat–An·der·son C. \män-'trēt-'an-dər-sən-\ Montreat, N.C. 28757; junior, 1916
Moo·dy Bible Inst. \'müd-ē-\ Chicago, Ill. 60610; 1886
Moore C. of Art \'mō(ə)r-, 'mȯ(ə)r-, 'mu̇(ə)r-\ Philadelphia, Pa. 19103; 1844
Moorhead State C. Moorhead, Minn. 56560; 1885
Moraine Valley Community C. Palos Hills, Ill. 60465; 1967
Moravian C. Bethlehem, Pa. 18018; 1807
More·head State U. \'mō(ə)r-,hed-, 'mȯ(ə)r-\ Morehead, Ky. 40351; 1922
More·house C. \'mō(ə)r-,hau̇s-, 'mȯ(ə)r-\ Atlanta, Ga. 30314; 1867
Mor·gan State C. \'mȯr-gən-\ Baltimore, Md. 21212; 1867
Morn·ing·side C. \'mȯr-niŋ-,sīd-\ Sioux City, Iowa 51106; 1889
Mor·ris Brown C. \,mȯr-əs-'brau̇n-, ,mär-\ Atlanta, Ga. 30314; 1881
Morris C. Sumter, S.C. 29150; 1908
Morris Har·vey C. \-'här-vē-\ Charleston, W. Va. 25304; 1888
Mor·ris·town C. \'mȯr-ə-,stau̇n-, ,mär-\ Morristown, Tenn. 37814; junior, 1881
Morse C. \'mȯ(ə)rs-\ Hartford, Conn. 06103; junior, 1860
Mor·ton Junior C. \'mȯrt-ᵊn-\ Cicero, Ill. 60650; 1924
Mount Al·oy·sius Junior C. \-,al-ə-'wish-əs-\ Cresson, Pa. 16630; 1848
Mount Al·ver·nia C. \-,al-'vər-nē-ə-\ Newton, Mass. 02158; 1959
Mount An·gel C. \-'än-jəl-\ Mount Angel, Oreg. 97362; 1887
Mount Angel Sem. St. Benedict, Oreg. 97373; 1887
Mount Car·mel Junior C. \-'kär-məl-\ New Orleans, La. 70124; 1924
Mount Hol·yoke C. \-'hōl-,yōk-\ South Hadley, Mass. 01075; 1837
Mount Hood Community C. \-'hu̇d-\ Gresham, Oreg. 97030; junior, 1965
Mount Ida Junior C. Newton Centre, Mass. 02159; 1899
Mount Mar·ty C. \-'märt-ē-\ Yankton, S. Dak. 57078; 1922
Mount Mary C. Milwaukee, Wis. 53222; 1872
Mount Mercy C. Cedar Rapids, Iowa 52402; 1875
Mount Olive Junior C. Mount Olive, N.C. 28365; 1951
Mount Providence Junior C. Baltimore, Md. 21227; 1952
Mount Sacred Heart C. Hamden, Conn. 06514; junior, 1954
Mount Saint Ag·nes C. \-'ag-nəs-\ Baltimore, Md. 21209; 1867
Mount St. Clare C. \-'kla(ə)r-, -'kle(ə)r-\ Clinton, Iowa 52732; junior, 1895
Mount Saint Jo·seph C. \-'jō-zəf- also -səf-\ Wakefield, R.I. 02880; 1953
Mount St. Joseph–on–the–Ohio, C. of Mount St. Joseph, Ohio 45051; 1854
Mount St. Mary C. Hooksett, N.H. 03106; 1934
Mount St. Mary C. North Plainfield, N.J. 07060; junior, 1905
Mount St. Mary C. Newburgh, N.Y. 12550; 1930
Mount St. Mary's C. Los Angeles, Calif. 90049; 1925
Mount St. Mary's C. Emmitsburg, Md. 21227; 1808
Mount St. Paul C. Waukesha, Wis. 53186; 1962
Mount St. Scho·las·ti·ca C. \-skə-'las-ti-kə-\ Atchison, Kans. 66002; 1863
Mount St. Vin·cent, C. of \-'vin(t)-sənt\ Bronx, N.Y. 10471; 1847
Mount San An·to·nio C. \-,san-ən-'tō-nē-,ō-\ Walnut, Calif. 91789; junior, 1945
Mount San Ja·cin·to C. \-,san-jə-'sint-(,)ō-, -'sint-ə-\ Gilman Hot Springs, Calif. 92340; junior, 1963
Mount Se·na·rio C. \-sə-'när-ē-(,)ō-\ Ladysmith, Wis. 54848; 1962
Mount Union C. Alliance, Ohio 44601; 1846
Mount Ver·non Junior C. \-'vər-nən-\ Washington, D.C. 20007; 1875
Mount Vernon Nazarene C. Mount Vernon, Ohio 43050; junior, 1966
Mount Wa·chu·sett Community C. \-wä-'chü-sət-\ Gardner, Mass. 01440; junior, 1963
Muh·len·berg C. \'myü-lən-,bərg-\ Allentown, Pa. 18104; 1848
Multnomah Sch. of the Bible Portland, Oreg. 97220; 1936

Mun·de·lein C. \'mən-də̇l-,īn-\ Chicago, Ill. 60626; 1930
Mur·ray State C. \'mər-ē-, 'mə-rē-\ Tishomingo, Okla. 73460; junior, 1908
Murray State U. Murray, Ky. 42071; 1922
Muskegon Business C. Muskegon, Mich. 49442; junior, 1885
Muskegon County Community C. Muskegon, Mich. 49443; junior, 1926
Mus·kin·gum C. \mə-'skiŋ-(g)əm-\ New Concord, Ohio 43762; 1837

Napa C. \'nap-ə-\ Napa, Calif. 94558; junior, 1941
Nas·sau Community C. \'nas-,ȯ-\ Garden City, N.Y. 11533; junior, 1960
Nas·son C. \nə-'sän-, na-; 'nas-,än-\ Springvale, Me. 04083; 1912
Natch·ez Junior C. \'nach-əz-\ Miss. 39120; 1885
Nathaniel Hawthorne C. Antrim, N.H. 03440; 1962
National Business C. Roanoke, Va. 24009; junior, 1886
National C. of Ed. Evanston, Ill. 60201; 1886
Na·var·ro Junior C. \nə-'var-(,)ō-\ Corsicana, Tex. 75110; 1946
Naz·a·reth C. \'naz-(ə-)rəth-\ Kalamazoo, Mich. 49074; 1897
Nazareth C. of Kentucky Nazareth, 40048; 1814
Nazareth C. of Rochester N.Y. 14610; 1924
Nebraska, U. of Lincoln, 68508; 1869
Nebraska at Omaha, U. of 68101; 1908
Nebraska Wesleyan U. Lincoln, 68504; 1887
Ne·o·sho County Community Junior C. \nē-'ō-(,)shō-, -shə-\ Chanute, Kans. 66720; 1936
Ner Israel Rabbinical C. \'nər-\ Baltimore, Md. 21215; 1933
Nevada, U. of Reno, 89507; 1874
Nevada, Las Vegas, U. of 89109; 1957
Newark C. of Engineering N.J. 07102; 1881
Newark State C. Union, N.J. 07083; 1855
New·ber·ry C. \'n(y)ü-,ber-ē-, -b(ə-)rē-\ Newberry, S.C. 29108; 1856
New Church, Acad. of the Bryn Athyn, Pa. 19009; 1876
New College Sarasota, Fla. 33578; 1960
New·comb C. \'n(y)ü-kəm-\ New Orleans, La. 70118; 1886
New England Aeronautical Inst. Nashua, N.H. 03060; junior, 1965
New England C. Henniker, N.H. 03242; 1946
New England Conservatory of Music Boston, Mass. 02115; 1867
New Hampshire, U. of Durham, 03824; 1866
New Hampshire C. of Accounting and Commerce Manchester, 03101; 1932
New Hampshire Technical Inst. Concord, 03301; junior, 1961
New Haven C. West Haven, Conn. 06516; 1920
New Mexico, U. of Albuquerque, 87106; 1889
New Mexico Highlands U. Las Vegas, 87701; 1893
New Mexico Inst. of Mining and Tech. Socorro, 87801; 1889
New Mexico Junior C. Hobbs, 88240; 1965
New Mexico Military Inst. Roswell, 88201; junior, 1891
New Mexico State U. Las Cruces, 88001; 1888
New Rochelle, C. of New Rochelle, N.Y. 10801; 1904
New Sch. for Social Research New York, N.Y. 10011; 1919
Newton C. of the Sacred Heart Newton, Mass. 02159; 1946
Newton Junior C. Newtonville, Mass. 02160; 1946
New York Agricultural and Technical C., State U. of Canton, 13617; junior, 1907
New York Agricultural and Technical C., State U. of Cobleskill, 12043; junior, 1911
New York Agricultural and Technical C., State U. of Delhi, 13753; junior, 1913
New York Agricultural and Technical C., State U. of Farmingdale, 11735; junior, 1912
New York Agricultural and Technical C., State U. of Morrisville, 13408; junior, 1908
New York Al·fred State C., State U. of \-'al-frəd-, -fərd-\ Alfred, 14802; junior, 1909
New York at Albany, State U. of 12203; 1844
New York at Binghamton, State U. of 13901; 1946
New York at Buffalo, State U. of 14214; 1846
New York at Old West·bury, State U. of \-'west-,ber-ē, -b(ə-)rē\ 11568; 1966
New York at Stony Brook, State U. of 11790; 1957
New York City Community C. of Applied Arts and Sciences Brooklyn, N.Y. 11201; junior, 1946
New York C. at Brock·port, State U. of \-'bräk-,pō(ə)rt, -,pȯ(ə)rt\ 14420; 1841
New York C. at Buffalo, State U. of 14222; 1867
New York C. at Cortland, State U. of 13045; 1863
New York C. at Fre·do·nia, State U. of \-fri-'dō-nē-ə, -nyə\ 14063; 1866
New York C. at Gen·e·seo, State U. of \-,jen-ə-'sē-(,)ō\ 14454; 1867
New York C. at New Paltz, State U. of \-'n(y)ü-,pȯlts\ 12561; 1828
New York C. at One·on·ta, State U. of \-,ō-nē-'änt-ə\ 13820; 1889
New York C. at Oswego, State U. of 13126; 1861
New York C. at Plattsburgh, State U. of 12901; 1889
New York C. at Pots·dam, State U. of \-'päts-,dam\ 13676; 1816
New York C. at Pur·chase, State U. of \-'pər-chəs\ 10577; 1967
New York Downstate Medical Center, State U. of Brooklyn, 11203; 1930
New York Inst. of Tech. Old Westbury, 11568; 1910
New York Maritime C., State U. of Bronx, 10465; 1874
New York U. New York City, 10003; 1831
New York Upstate Medical Center, State U. of Syracuse, 13210; 1834
Niagara County Community C. Niagara Falls, N.Y. 14303; junior, 1963

Niagara U. Niagara University, N.Y. 14109; 1856
Nich·olls State C. \'nik-əlz-\ Thibodaux, La. 70301; 1948
Nich·ols C. of Business Administration \'nik-əlz-\ Dudley, Mass. 01570; 1815
Norfolk Junior C. Norfolk, Nebr. 68701; 1927
Norfolk State C. Va. 23504; 1935
Nor·man C. \'nȯ(ə)r-mən-\ Norman Park, Ga. 31771; junior, 1900
Nor·man·dale State Junior C. \'nȯr-mən-ˌdāl-\ Bloomington, Minn. 55431; 1968
North American Baptist Sem. Sioux Falls, S. Dak. 57105; 1850
Northampton County Area Community C. Bethlehem, Pa. 18017; junior, 1966
Northampton Junior C. Northampton, Mass. 01060; 1896
North Carolina Agricultural and Technical State U. Greensboro, 27411; 1891
North Carolina Central U. Durham, 27707; 1909
North Carolina at Chapel Hill, U. of \-ˌchap-əl-\ 27514; 1789
North Carolina at Charlotte, U. of 28205; 1946
North Carolina at Greensboro, U. of 27412; 1891
North Carolina State U. at Raleigh 27607; 1887
North Carolina Wesleyan C. Rocky Mount, 27801; 1956
North Central Bible C. Minneapolis, Minn. 55404; 1930
North Central C. Naperville, Ill. 60540; 1861
North Central Michigan C. Petoskey, 49770; junior, 1958
North Country Community C. Saranac Lake, N.Y. 12983; junior, 1967
North Dakota, U. of Grand Forks, 58201; 1883
North Dakota Sch. of Forestry Bottineau, 58318; junior, 1889
North Dakota State Sch. of Science Wahpeton, 58075; junior, 1889
North Dakota State U. of Agric. and Applied Science Fargo, 58102; 1890
Northeast Alabama State Junior C. Rainsville, 35986; 1963
Northeast Bible Inst. Green Lane, Pa. 18054; 1938
Northeastern Christian Junior C. Villanova, Pa. 19085; 1956
Northeastern Collegiate Bible Inst. Essex Fells, N.J. 07021; 1950
Northeastern Illinois State C. Chicago, 60625; 1961
Northeastern Junior C. of Colorado Sterling, 80751; 1941
Northeastern Oklahoma A. & M. C. Miami, 74354; junior, 1919
Northeastern State C. Tahlequah, Okla. 74464; 1846
Northeastern U. Boston, Mass. 02115; 1898
Northeast Louisiana State C. Monroe, 71201; 1931
Northeast Mississippi Junior C. Booneville, 38829; 1948
Northeast Missouri State C. Kirksville, 63501; 1867
Northern Arizona U. Flagstaff, 86001; 1899
Northern Conservatory of Music Bangor, Me. 04401; 1929
Northern Essex Community C. Haverhill, Mass. 01830; junior, 1961
Northern Illinois U. De Kalb, 60115; 1895
Northern Iowa, U. of Cedar Falls, 50613; 1876
Northern Michigan U. Marquette, 49855; 1899
Northern Montana C. Havre, 59501; 1913
Northern Oklahoma C. Tonkawa, 74653; junior, 1901
Northern State C. Aberdeen, S. Dak. 57401; 1899
Northern Virginia Community C. Bailey's Crossroads, 22041; junior, 1965
Northern Wyoming Community C. Sheridan, 82801; junior, 1948
North Florida Junior C. Madison, 32340; 1958
North Georgia C. Dahlonega, 30533; 1873
North Greenville Junior C. Tigerville, S.C. 29688; 1892
North Hen·ne·pin State Junior C. \-'hen-ə-pən-\ Osseo, Minn. 55369; 1966
North Idaho Junior C. Coeur d'Alene, 83814; 1939
North Iowa Area Community C. Mason City, 50401; junior, 1918
North·land C. \'nȯrth-lənd-\ Ashland, Wis. 54806; 1892
Northland State Junior C. Thief River Falls, Minn. 56701; 1965
North Park C. Chicago, Ill. 60625; 1891
North Platte Junior C. North Platte, Nebr. 69101; 1964
Nor·throp Inst. of Tech. \'nȯr-thrəp-\ Inglewood, Calif. 90306; 1942
North Shore Community C. Beverly, Mass. 01915; junior, 1965
North Texas State U. Denton, 76203; 1890
Northwest Alabama State Junior C. Phil Campbell, 35581; 1963
Northwest Bible C. Minot, N. Dak. 58701; 1934
Northwest Christian C. Eugene, Oreg. 97401; 1895
Northwest C. Kirkland, Wash. 98033; 1934
Northwest Community C. Powell, Wyo. 82435; junior, 1946
Northwestern C. Orange City, Iowa 51041; 1882
Northwestern C. Watertown, Wis. 53094; 1865
Northwestern Connecticut Community C. Winsted, 06098; junior, 1965
Northwestern Michigan C. Traverse City, 49684; junior, 1951
Northwestern State C. Alva, Okla. 73717; 1897
Northwestern State C. of Louisiana Natchitoches, 71457; 1884
Northwestern U. Evanston, Ill. 60201; 1851
Northwest Mississippi Junior C. Senatobia, 38668; 1915
Northwest Missouri State C. Maryville, 64468; 1905
Northwest Nazarene C. Nampa, Idaho 83651; 1913
North·wood Inst. \'nȯrth-ˌwùd-\ Midland, Mich. 48640; junior, 1959
Norwalk Community C. Norwalk, Conn. 06850; junior, 1961
Norwalk State Technical C. Conn. 06854; junior, 1961
Nor·wich U. \'nȯ(ə)r-(ˌ)wich\ Northfield, Vt. 05663; 1819
No·tre Dame, C. of \-ˌnō-trə-'däm\ Belmont, Calif. 94002; 1851
No·tre Dame, U. of \-ˌnōt-ər-'däm\ Notre Dame, Ind. 46556; 1842
No·tre Dame C. \ˌnȯt-ər-'däm-\ St. Louis, Mo. 63125; 1896
No·tre Dame C. \ˌnō-trə-'däm-\ Manchester, N.H. 03104; 1950

No·tre Dame C. \ˌnō-trə-'däm-\ Cleveland, Ohio 44121; 1922
No·tre Dame C. of Staten Island \ˌnə-trə-'dam-\ N.Y. 10301; 1931
No·tre Dame of Maryland, C. of \-ˌnō-trə-'däm-\ Baltimore, 21210; 1848
No·tre Dame of Wil·ton, C. of \-ˌnō-trə-'däm-; -'wilt-ᵊn\ Wilton, Conn. 06897; 1961
No·tre Dame Sem. \ˌnōt-ər-'däm-\ New Orleans, La. 70118; 1923
Ny·ack Missionary C. \'nī-ˌak-\ Nyack, N.Y. 10960; 1882

Oakland City C. Oakland City, Ind. 47560; 1885
Oakland Community C. Bloomfield Hills, Mich. 48013; junior, 1964
Oakland U. Rochester, Mich. 48063; 1959
Oak·wood C. \'ō-ˌkwùd-\ Huntsville, Ala. 35806; 1896
Ober·lin C. \'ō-bər-lən-\ Oberlin, Ohio 44074; 1832
Ob·late C. \'äb-ˌlāt-\ Washington, D.C. 20017; 1904
Occidental C. Los Angeles, Calif. 90041; 1887
Ocean County C. Toms River, N.J. 08753; junior, 1964
Odessa C. Odessa, Tex. 79760; junior, 1946
Ogle·thorpe C. \'ō-gəl-ˌthȯrp-\ Atlanta, Ga. 30319; 1835
Ohio C. of Applied Science Cincinnati, 45210; junior, 1828
Ohio Dominican C. Columbus, 43219; 1911
Ohio Northern U. Ada, 45810; 1871
Ohio State U. Columbus, 43210; 1870
Ohio Technical C. Columbus, 43219; junior, 1952
Ohio U. Athens, 45701; 1804
Ohio Valley C. Parkersburg, W. Va. 26101; junior, 1960
Ohio Wesleyan U. Delaware, Ohio 43015; 1841
Oh·lo·ne C. \ˌō-lə-'nē\ Fremont, Calif. 94537; junior, 1966
Oka·loo·sa–Wal·ton Junior C. \ˌō-kə-ˌlü-sə-'wȯlt-ᵊn-\ Valparaiso, Fla. 32580; 1963
Oklahoma, U. of Norman, 73069; 1890
Oklahoma Baptist U. Shawnee, 74801; 1906
Oklahoma Christian C. Oklahoma City, 73111; 1950
Oklahoma City Southwestern C. Okla. 73127; junior, 1946
Oklahoma City U. Okla. 73106; 1911
Oklahoma C. of Liberal Arts Chickasha, 73018; 1908
Oklahoma Military Acad. Claremore, 74017; junior, 1910
Oklahoma Panhandle State C. Goodwell, 73939; 1909
Oklahoma Sch. of Business, Accountancy, Law, and Finance Tulsa, 74119; junior, 1919
Oklahoma State U. of Agric. and Applied Science Stillwater, 74074; 1890
Old Dominion U. Norfolk, Va. 23508; 1930
Ol·i·vet C. \ˌäl-ə-'vet\ Olivet, Mich. 49076; 1844
Olivet Naz·a·rene C. \-ˌnaz-ə-'rēn\ Kankakee, Ill. 60901; 1907
Ol·ney Community C. \'äl-nē-\ Olney, Ill. 62450; junior, 1963
Olym·pic C. \ə-'lim-pik-, ō-\ Bremerton, Wash. 98310; junior, 1946
On·on·da·ga Community C. \ˌän-ə(n)-'dȯ-gə-\ Syracuse, N.Y. 13210; junior, 1962
Open Bible C. Des Moines, Iowa 50321; 1932
Oral Rob·erts U. \ˌȯr-əl-'räb-ərts-, ˌȯr-, ˌär-\ Tulsa, Okla. 74105; 1963
Orange Coast C. Costa Mesa, Calif. 92626; junior, 1947
Orange County Community C. Middletown, N.Y. 10940; junior, 1950
Oregon, U. of Eugene, 97403; 1872
Oregon C. of Ed. Monmouth, 97361; 1856
Oregon Polytechnic State C. Klamath Falls, 97601; junior, 1947
Oregon State U. Corvallis, 97331; 1858
Orlando, The C. of Orlando, Fla. 32803; junior, 1941
Otero Junior C. \ō-'te(ə)r-(ˌ)ō-\ La Junta, Colo. 81050; 1941
Ot·ta·wa U. \'ät-ə-wə-, -ˌwä-, -ˌwȯ-\ Ottawa, Kans. 66067; 1865
Ot·ter·bein C. \'ät-ər-ˌbīn-\ Westerville, Ohio 43081; 1847
Ottumwa Heights C. Ottumwa, Iowa 52501; junior, 1925
Ouachita Baptist U. Arkadelphia, Ark. 71923; 1885
Our Lady of Cincinnati C. Cincinnati, Ohio 45206; 1935
Our Lady of Holy Cross C. New Orleans, La. 70114; 1916
Our Lady of Hope Sem. Newburgh, N.Y. 12550; junior, 1900
Our Lady of Providence, Sem. of Warwick, R.I. 02889; 1939
Our Lady of the Angels Junior C. Enfield, Conn. 06030; 1945
Our Lady of the Elms, C. of Chicopee, Mass. 01013; 1928
Our Lady of the Lake C. San Antonio, Tex. 78207; 1896
Out·a·ga·mie County Teachers C. \ˌaùt-ə-'gam-ē-, -'gä-mē-\ Kaukauna, Wis. 54130; junior, 1912
Owosso C. Owosso, Mich. 48867; 1909
Ozark Bible C. \'ō-ˌzärk-\ Joplin, Mo. 64801; 1942
Ozarks, C. of the \-'ō-ˌzärks\ Clarksville, Ark. 72830; 1891
Ozarks, Sch. of the Point Lookout, Mo. 65726; 1906

Pace C. \'pās-\ New York, N.Y. 10038; 1906
Pacific, U. of the Stockton, Calif. 95204; 1851
Pacific Christian C. Long Beach, Calif. 90804; 1928
Pacific C. Fresno, Calif. 93702; 1944
Pacific Lutheran U. Tacoma, Wash. 98447; 1890
Pacific Oaks C. Pasadena, Calif. 91105; 1945
Pacific Union C. Angwin, Calif. 94508; 1882
Pacific U. Forest Grove, Oreg. 97116; 1849
Pacific Western C. Renton, Wash. 98055; 1965
Pack·er Collegiate Inst. \'pak-ər-\ Brooklyn, N.Y. 11201; junior, 1845
Paine C. \'pān-\ Augusta, Ga. 30901; 1882
Palm Beach Junior C. Lake Worth, Fla. 33460; 1933
Palm·er C. \'päm-ər-, 'päl-mər-\ Charleston, S.C. 29401; junior, 1903
Pal·o·mar C. \'pal-ə-ˌmär-\ San Marcos, Calif. 92069; junior, 1946
Palo Ver·de C. \ˌpal-ō-'vərd-ē-\ Blythe, Calif. 92225; junior, 1947

Pan American C. \,pan-\ Edinburg, Tex. 78539; 1927
Pa·no·la C. \pə-'nō-lə-\ Carthage, Tex. 75633; junior, 1947
Par·is Junior C. \'par-əs-\ Paris, Tex. 75460; 1924
Park C. \'pärk-\ Parkville, Mo. 64152; 1875
Par·sons C. \'pärs-ᵊnz-\ Fairfield, Iowa 52556; 1875
Pasadena City C. Pasadena, Calif. 91106; junior, 1924
Pasadena C. Pasadena, Calif. 91104; 1902
Pasadena Playhouse C. of Theatre Arts Calif. 91101; 1920
Passionist Monastic Sem. Jamaica, N.Y. 11432; 1929
Pat·er·son State C. \'pat-ər-sən-\ Wayne, N.J. 07470; 1855
Pat·rick Henry State Junior C. \,pa-trik-\ Monroeville, Ala. 36460; 1965
Paul Quinn C. \'pól-'kwin-\ Waco, Tex. 76703; 1881
Paul Smith's C. Paul Smiths, N.Y. 12970; junior, 1937
Pea·body Conservatory of Music \'pē-,bäd-ē-, -bəd-ē-\ Baltimore, Md. 21202; 1857
Peace C. Raleigh, N.C. 27602; junior, 1857
Pearl River Junior C. \'pər-(ə)l-\ Poplarville, Miss. 39470; 1909
Peirce Junior C. \'pi(ə)rs-\ Philadelphia, Pa. 19102; 1865
Pem·broke C. \'pem-,brōk-\ Providence, R.I. 02912; 1891
Pembroke State C. Pembroke, N.C. 28372; 1887
Peninsula C. Port Angeles, Wash. 98362; junior, 1961
Penn Hall Junior C. \'pen-\ Chambersburg, Pa. 17201; 1906
Pennsylvania, U. of Philadelphia, 19104; 1740
Pennsylvania C. of Optometry Philadelphia, 19141; 1919
Pennsylvania State U. University Park, 16802; 1855
Pensacola Junior C. Pensacola, Fla. 32504; 1948
Pep·per·dine C. \'pep-ər-,dīn-\ Los Angeles, Calif. 90044; 1937
Pe·ral·ta Junior C. \pə-'ral-tə-\ Oakland, Calif. 94606; 1927
Per·kins·ton C. \'pər-kən-stən-\ Perkinston, Miss. 39573; junior, 1911
Per·ry Normal Sch. \'per-ē-\ Boston, Mass. 02116; junior, 1898
Per·shing C. \'pər-shiŋ-, -zhiŋ-\ Beatrice, Nebr. 68310; 1966
Pe·ru State C. \pə-'rü-\ Peru, Nebr. 68421; 1867
Pes·ta·loz·zi Froe·bel Teachers C. \,pes-tə-'lät-sē-'frā-bəl-\ Chicago, Ill. 60601; 1896
Pfeif·fer C. \'fī-fər-\ Misenheimer, N.C. 28109; 1887
Philadelphia, Community C. of Pa. 19107; junior, 1965
Philadelphia C. of Art Pa. 19102; 1876
Philadelphia C. of Bible Pa. 19103; 1913
Philadelphia C. of Pharmacy and Science Pa. 19104; 1821
Philadelphia C. of Textiles and Science Pa. 19144; 1883
Philadelphia Musical Acad. Pa. 19103; 1870
Phi·lan·der Smith C. \fə-,lan-dər-'smith-\ Little Rock, Ark. 72203; 1868
Phil·lips County Community C. \,fil-əps-\ Helena, Ark. 72342; junior, 1965
Phillips U. Enid, Okla. 73701; 1906
Phoenix C. Phoenix, Ariz. 85013; junior, 1920
Piedmont Bible C. Winston-Salem, N.C. 27101; 1945
Piedmont C. Demorest, Ga. 30535; 1897
Pike·ville C. \'pīk-,vil-\ Pikeville, Ky. 41501; 1889
Pine·brook Junior C. \'pīn-,brůk-\ East Stroudsburg, Pa. 18301; 1950
Pine Manor Junior C. Chestnut Hill, Mass. 02167; 1911
Pittsburgh, U. of Pa. 15213; 1787
Pit·zer C. \'pit-sər-\ Claremont, Calif. 91711; 1964
Pla·no, U. of \'plā-(,)nō-\ Plano, Tex. 75074; 1964
Platte Junior C. Columbus, Nebr. 68501; 1967
Plym·outh State C. \'plim-əth-\ Plymouth, N.H. 03264; 1870
PMC Colleges \,pē-,em-'sē-\ Chester, Pa. 19013; 1821
Point Park C. Pittsburgh, Pa. 15222; 1933
Polk County Teachers C. \'pōk-\ Frederic, Wis. 54837; junior, 1905
Polk Junior C. Winter Haven, Fla. 33880; 1964
Polytechnic Inst. of Brooklyn N.Y. 11201; 1854
Po·mo·na C. \pə-'mō-nə-\ Claremont, Calif. 91711; 1887
Pontifical C. Jo·se·phi·num \-,jō-zə-'fī-nəm *also* -sə-\ Worthington, Ohio 43085; 1888
Por·ter·ville C. \'pōrt-ər-,vil-, 'pórt-\ Porterville, Calif. 93257; junior, 1927
Portland, U. of Oreg. 97203; 1901
Portland Community C. Oreg. 97201; junior, 1961
Portland State C. Oreg. 97207; 1946
Post Junior C. Waterbury, Conn. 06708; 1890
Po·teau Community C. \'pōt-(,)ō-\ Poteau, Okla. 74953; junior, 1934
Potomac State C. of West Virginia U. Keyser, 26726; junior, 1901
Prairie State C. Chicago Heights, Ill. 60411; junior, 1958
Prairie View A. & M. C. Prairie View, Tex. 77445; 1876
Pratt Community Junior C. Pratt, Kans. 67124; 1938
Pratt Inst. \'prat-\ Brooklyn, N.Y. 11205; 1887
Pren·tiss Normal and Industrial Inst. \'prent-əs-\ Prentiss, Miss. 39474; junior, 1907
Presbyterian C. Clinton, S.C. 29325; 1880
Presbyterian Sch. of Christian Ed. Richmond, Va. 23227; 1914
Pres·cott C. \'pres-kət-\ Prescott, Ariz. 71857; 1966
Presentation C. Aberdeen, S. Dak. 57401; junior, 1922
Prince George's Community C. Largo, Md. 20870; junior, 1958
Prince·ton U. \'prin(t)-stən-\ Princeton, N.J. 08540; 1746
Prin·cip·ia C., The \'prin-'sip-ē-ə-\ Elsah, Ill. 62028; 1898
Providence C. R.I. 02918; 1917
Puerto Rico, U. of Río Piedras, 00931; 1900
Puerto Rico Junior C. Río Piedras, 00928; 1949
Puget Sound, U. of Tacoma, Wash. 98416; 1888
Pur·due U. \pər-'d(y)ü-\ Lafayette, Ind. 47907; 1865

Queen of Peace Mission Sem. Jaffrey Center, N.H. 03454; 1954
Queens·bor·ough Community C. \'kwēnz-,bər-ə-, -,bə-rə-\ Bayside, N.Y. 11364; junior, 1960
Queens C. Flushing, N.Y. 11367; 1937

Queens C. Charlotte, N.C. 28207; 1857
Quin·cy C. \'kwin(t)-sē-\ Quincy, Ill. 62301; 1860
Quin·cy Junior C. \'kwin-zē-\ Quincy, Mass. 02169; 1958
Quin·ni·pi·ac C. \'kwin-ə-pē-,ak-\ Hamden, Conn. 06518; 1929
Quin·sig·a·mond Community C. \kwin-'sig-ə-mən(d)-\ Worcester, Mass. 01605; junior, 1963

Rabbinical C. of Tel·she \-'tel-(,)shä\ Wickliffe, Ohio 44092; 1876
Ra·cine–Ke·no·sha County Teachers C. \rə-'sēn-kə-,nō-shə-, rä-\ Union Grove, Wis. 53182; junior, 1913
Rad·cliffe C. \'rad-,klif-\ Cambridge, Mass. 02138; 1879
Rad·ford C. \'rad-fərd-\ Radford, Va. 24141; 1910
Ran·dolph–Ma·con C. \,ran-,dälf-'mā-kən-\ Ashland, Va. 23005; 1830
Randolph–Macon Woman's C. Lynchburg, Va. 24504; 1891
Range·ly C. \'ranj-lē-\ Rangely, Colo. 81648; junior, 1962
Rang·er C. \'rān-jər-\ Ranger, Tex. 76470; junior, 1926
Redlands, U. of Redlands, Calif. 92373; 1907
Redwoods, C. of the Eureka, Calif. 95501; junior, 1965
Reed C. \'rēd-\ Portland, Oreg. 97202; 1904
Reed·ley C. \'rēd-lē-\ Reedley, Calif. 93654; junior, 1926
Reformed Bible Inst. Grand Rapids, Mich. 49506; 1940
Re·gis C. \'rē-jəs-\ Denver, Colo. 80221; 1877
Regis C. Weston, Mass. 02193; 1927
Rein·hardt C. \'rīn-,härt-\ Waleska, Ga. 30183; junior, 1883
Rend Lake C. \'ren(d)-\ Mount Vernon, Ill. 62864; junior, 1956
Rens·se·laer Polytechnic Inst. \'ren(t)-s-(ə-)lər-, ,ren(t)-sə-'li(ə)r-\ Troy, N.Y. 12181; 1824
Rhode Island, U. of Kingston, 02881; 1892
Rhode Island C. Providence, 02908; 1854
Rhode Island Junior C. Providence, 02908; junior, 1964
Rhode Island Sch. of Design Providence, 02903; 1877
Rich·land County Teachers C. \'rich-lən(d)-\ Richland Center, Wis. 53581; junior, 1903
Richmond, U. of Va. 23173; 1832
Rick·er C. \'rik-ər-\ Houlton, Me. 04730; 1848
Ricks C. \'riks-\ Rexburg, Idaho 83440; junior, 1888
Ri·der C. \'rīd-ər-\ Trenton, N.J. 08602; 1865
Rio Grande C. \,rī-ō-'gran(d)-\ Rio Grande, Ohio 45674; 1876
Rio Hon·do Junior C. \,rē-ə-'hän-(,)dō-\ Whittier, Calif. 90601; 1963
Rip·on C. \'rip-ən-, -,än-\ Ripon, Wis. 54971; 1850
Riverside City C. Riverside, Calif. 92506; junior, 1916
Ri·vi·er C. \'rē-vē-,ā-, 'riv-ē-\ Nashua, N.H. 03060; 1933
Ro·a·noke C. \'rō-(ə-),nōk-\ Salem, Va. 24153; 1842
Robert Mor·ris Junior C. \-'mór-əs-, -'mär-\ Pittsburgh, Pa. 15219; 1921
Robert Morris C. Carthage, Ill. 62321; 1965
Rob·erts Wesleyan C. \'räb-ərts-\ North Chili, N.Y. 14514; 1866
Rochester, U. of N.Y. 14627; 1850
Rochester Inst. of Tech. N.Y. 14623; 1829
Rochester State Junior C. Rochester, Minn. 55901; 1915
Rockford C. Rockford, Ill. 61101; 1847
Rock·hurst C. \'räk-,hərst-\ Kansas City, Mo. 64110; 1910
Rock·ing·ham Community C. \'räk-iŋ-,ham-\ Wentworth, N.C. 27375; junior, 1964
Rock·land Community C. \'räk-lən(d)-\ Suffern, N.Y. 10901; junior, 1959
Rock·mont C. \'räk-,mänt-\ Denver, Colo. 80226; 1914
Rock Valley C. Rockford, Ill. 61111; junior, 1964
Rocky Mountain C. Billings, Mont. 59102; 1883
Rog·er Wil·liams C. \,räj-ər-'wil-yəmz-\ Bristol, R.I. 02809; 1919
Rol·lins C. \'räl-ənz-\ Winter Park, Fla. 32789; 1885
Roosevelt U. Chicago, Ill. 60605; 1945
Rosary C. River Forest, Ill. 60305; 1848
Rosary Hill C. Buffalo, N.Y. 14226; 1948
Rose·mont C. \'rōz-,mänt-\ Rosemont, Pa. 19010; 1921
Rose Polytechnic Inst. \'rōz-\ Terre Haute, Ind. 47803; 1874
Roy·al·ton C. \'rói-(ə)l-tən-\ South Royalton, Vt. 05068; 1965
Rus·sell C. \'rəs-əl-\ Burlingame, Calif. 94010; 1928
Russell Sage C. \-'sāj-\ Troy, N.Y. 12180; 1916
Rust C. \'rəst-\ Holly Springs, Miss. 38635; 1866
Rut·gers–The State U. \'rət-gərz-\ New Brunswick, N.J. 08903; 1766

Sacramento City C. Sacramento, Calif. 95822; junior, 1916
Sacramento State C. Sacramento, Calif. 95819; 1947
Sacred Heart, C. of the Santurce, Puerto Rico 00914; 1935
Sacred Heart C. Cullman, Ala. 35055; junior, 1940
Sacred Heart C. Wichita, Kans. 67213; 1933
Sacred Heart C. Belmont, N.C. 28012; 1892
Sacred Heart Junior C. Yardley, Pa. 19067; 1958
Sacred Heart Novitiate Monroe, Mich. 48161; 1949
Sacred Hearts, C. of the Fall River, Mass. 02720; 1934
Sacred Heart Sem. Detroit, Mich. 48206; 1921
Sacred Heart U. Bridgeport, Conn. 06604; 1963
Saint Al·phon·sus C. \-al-'fän(t)-səs-\ Suffield, Conn. 06078; 1963
Saint Am·brose C. \-'am-,brōz-\ Davenport, Iowa 52803; 1882
Saint An·drews Presbyterian C. \-'an-,drüz-\ Laurinburg, N.C. 28352; 1857
Saint An·selm's C. \-'an-,selmz-\ Manchester, N.H. 03102; 1889
Saint An·tho·ny Sem. \-'an(t)-thə-nē-\ Hudson, N.H. 03051; 1956
Saint Au·gus·tine's C. \-ó-'gəs-tənz-, -ə-'gəs-\ Raleigh, N.C. 27602; 1867
Saint Bas·il's C. \-'baz-əlz-\ Stamford, Conn. 06902; 1939
Saint Ben·e·dict, C. of \-,dik(t)-\ St. Joseph, Minn. 56374; 1913
Saint Benedict C. \-,dik(t)-\ Ferdinand, Ind. 47532; 1914
Saint Benedict's C. \-,dik(t)s-\ Atchison, Kans. 66002; 1857
Saint Ber·nard C. \-'bər-nərd-\ St. Bernard, Ala. 35138; 1892

Saint Ber·nard's Sem. and C. \-'bər-nərdz-\ Rochester, N.Y. 14612; 1893
Saint Bon·a·ven·ture U. \-,bän-ə-'ven-chər-, -'bän-ə-,ven-chər-\ St. Bonaventure, N.Y. 14778; 1859
Saint Cath·a·rine C. \-'kath-(ə-)rən\ St. Catharine, Ky. 40061; junior, 1932
Saint Cath·er·ine, C. of \-'kath-(ə)rən\ St. Paul, Minn. 55116; 1906
Saint Charles Bor·ro·meo Sem. \-,bȯr-ə-'mā-(,)ō-, -,bär-\ Philadelphia, Pa. 19151; 1832
Saint Clair County Community C. Port Huron, Mich. 48060; junior, 1923
Saint Clare C. \-'kla(ə)r-, -'kle(ə)r-\ Williamsville, N.Y. 14221; junior, 1957
Saint Cloud State C. St. Cloud, Minn. 56301; 1866
Saint Co·lum·ban's C. and Sem. \-kə-'ləm-bənz-\ Milton, Mass. 02186; 1923
Saint Dom·i·nic C. \-'däm-ə-(,)nik-\ St. Charles, Ill. 60174; 1963
Saint Ed·ward's U. \-'ed-wərdz-\ Austin, Tex. 78704; 1876
Saint Eliz·a·beth, C. of \-'l-'iz-ə-bəth, -i'liz-\ Convent Station, N.J. 07961; 1899
Saint Fi·de·lis C. and Sem. \-fə-'del-əs-, -fi-'dā-ləs-\ Herman, Pa. 16039; 1877
Saint Fran·cis, C. of \-'fran(t)-səs\ Joliet, Ill. 60435; 1874
Saint Francis C. Fort Wayne, Ind. 46808; 1890
Saint Francis C. Biddeford, Me. 04005; 1953
Saint Francis C. Brooklyn, N.Y. 11201; 1858
Saint Francis C. Loretto, Pa. 15940; 1847
Saint Francis C. Burlington, Wis. 53105; 1930
Saint Francis Sem. Milwaukee, Wis. 53207; 1856
Saint Ger·trude, C. of \-'gər-,trüd\ Cottonwood, Idaho 83522; junior, 1956
Saint Greg·o·ry's C. \-'greg-(ə-)rēz\ Shawnee, Okla. 74801; junior, 1915
Saint Hy·a·cinth C. and Sem. \-'hī-ə-(,)sin(t)th-\ Granby, Mass. 01033; 1957
Saint John C. of Cleveland \-'jän-\ Ohio 44114; 1928
Saint John Fish·er C. \-,jän-'fish-ər-\ Rochester, N.Y. 14618; 1952
Saint John's C. Camarillo, Calif. 93010; 1939
Saint John's C. Winfield, Kans. 67156; junior, 1893
Saint John's C. Annapolis, Md. 21404; 1696
Saint John's Provincial Sem. Plymouth, Mich. 48170; 1949
Saint Johns River Junior C. \-,jänz-\ Palatka, Fla. 32077; 1958
Saint John's Sem. Brighton, Mass. 02135; 1884
Saint John's U. Collegeville, Minn. 56321; 1857
Saint John's U. Jamaica, N.Y. 14618; 1870
Saint John Vi·an·ney Minor Sem. \-vē-'än-ē-, -'an-\ Miami, Fla. 33165; junior, 1960
Saint John Vianney Sem. East Aurora, N.Y. 14052; 1961
Saint Joseph C. West Hartford, Conn. 06117; 1925
Saint Joseph C. Emmitsburg, Md. 21727; 1809
Saint Joseph C. Old Bennington, Vt. 05201; junior, 1926
Saint Joseph C. of Florida Jensen Beach, 33457; junior, 1957
Saint Joseph C. of Orange Orange, Calif. 92666; 1933
Saint Joseph's C. Rensselaer, Ind. 47978; 1889
Saint Joseph's C. North Windham, Me. 04062; 1915
Saint Joseph's C. Princeton, N.J. 08540; junior, 1938
Saint Joseph's C. Philadelphia, Pa. 19131; 1851
Saint Joseph's C. for Women Brooklyn, N.Y. 11205; 1916
Saint Joseph Sem. St. Benedict, La. 70457; 1891
Saint Joseph's Sem. Washington, D.C. 20017; 1892
Saint Joseph's Sem. and C. Yonkers, N.Y. 10704; 1839
Saint Joseph the Provider, C. of Rutland, Vt. 05701; 1957
Saint Law·rence Sem. \-'lȯr-ən(t)s-, -'lär-\ Mt. Calvary, Wis. 53057; junior, 1860
Saint Lawrence U. Canton, N.Y. 13617; 1856
Saint Leo C. \-lē-(,)ō-\ St. Leo, Fla. 33574; 1959
Saint Louis, Junior C. of Mo. 63105; 1963
Saint Louis C. of Pharmacy Mo. 63110; 1864
Saint Louis Inst. of Music Mo. 63105; 1924
Saint Louis U. Mo. 63103; 1818
Saint Mar·tin's C. \-'märt-ᵊnz-\ Olympia, Wash. 98501; 1895
Saint Mary, C. of \-'me(ə)r-ē, -'ma(ə)r-ē, -'mā-rē\ Omaha, Nebr. 68124; 1923
Saint Mary C. Xavier, Kans. 66098; 1882
Saint Mary of the Plains C. Dodge City, Kans. 67801; 1913
Saint Mary-of-the-Woods C. Saint Mary-of-the-Woods, Ind. 47876; 1840
Saint Mary's C. Notre Dame, Ind. 46556; 1844
Saint Mary's C. St. Mary, Ky. 40063; 1821
Saint Mary's C. Orchard Lake, Mich. 48034; 1885
Saint Mary's C. Winona, Minn. 55987; 1912
Saint Mary's C. of California St. Mary's College 94575; 1863
Saint Mary's C. of Maryland St. Mary's City, 20686; 1839
Saint Mary's C. of O'Fal·lon \-ō-'fal-ən\ O'Fallon, Mo. 63366; junior, 1929
Saint Mary's Dominican C. New Orleans, La. 70118; 1910
Saint Mary's Junior C. Minneapolis, Minn. 55406; 1964
Saint Mary's Junior C. Raleigh, N.C. 27602; 1842
Saint Mary's Sem. Norwalk, Conn. 06850; 1906
Saint Mary's Sem. Perryville, Mo. 63775; 1818
Saint Mary's Sem. Cleveland, Ohio 44108; 1848
Saint Mary's Sem. and U. Baltimore, Md. 21210; 1791
Saint Mary's U. of San Antonio Tex. 78228; 1852
Saint Mein·rad C. \-'mīn-rəd\ St. Meinrad, Ind. 47577; 1854
Saint Mi·chael's C. \-'mī-kəlz-\ Winooski, Vt. 05404; 1904
Saint Nor·bert C. \-'nȯr-bərt\ West De Pere, Wis. 54178; 1893
Saint Olaf C. \-'ō-ləf\ Northfield, Minn. 55057; 1874
Saint Pat·rick's C. \-'pa-trik(s)-\ Mountain View, Calif. 94040; 1898

Saint Paul Bible C. St. Paul, Minn. 55104; 1916
Saint Paul's C. \-'pȯlz-\ Washington, D.C. 20017; 1889
Saint Paul's C. Concordia, Mo. 64020; junior, 1884
Saint Paul's C. Lawrenceville, Va. 23868; 1888
Saint Paul Sem. St. Paul, Minn. 55101; 1895
Saint Petersburg Junior C. St. Petersburg, Fla. 33733; 1927
Saint Pe·ter's C. \-'pēt-ərz-\ Jersey City, N.J. 07306; 1872
Saint Phil·ip's C. \-'fil-əps-\ San Antonio, Tex. 78203; junior, 1898
Saint Pi·us X Sem. \-,pī-əs-the-'ten(t)th-\ Garrison, N.Y. 10524; 1956
Saint Pro·co·pi·us C. \-prə-'kō-pē-əs-\ Lisle, Ill. 60532; 1887
Saint Rose, C. of \-'rōz\ Albany, N.Y. 12203; 1920
Saint Scho·las·ti·ca, C. of \-skə-'las-ti-kə\ Duluth, Minn. 55811; 1912
Saints Junior C. Lexington, Miss. 39095; 1918
Saint Te·re·sa, C. of \-tə-'rē-sə\ Winona, Minn. 55987; 1907
Saint Thomas, C. of \-'täm-əs\ St. Paul, Minn. 55101; 1885
Saint Thomas, U. of Houston, Tex. 77006; 1947
Saint Thomas Aquinas C. Sparkill, N.Y. 10976; 1952
Saint Thomas Sem. Denver, Colo. 80210; 1906
Saint Thomas Sem. Bloomfield, Conn. 06002; junior, 1897
Saint Vin·cent C. \-'vin(t)-sənt-\ Latrobe, Pa. 15650; 1840
Saint Xav·i·er C. \-'zav-ē-ər-\ Chicago, Ill. 60655; 1846
Sa·lem C. \'sā-ləm-\ Winston-Salem, N.C. 27108; 1772
Salem C. Salem, W. Va. 26426; 1888
Salem Technical-Vocational Community C. Salem, Oreg. 97303; junior, 1954
Sa·le·sian C. \sə-'lē-zhən\ North Haledon, N.J. 07508; junior, 1948
Salisbury State C. Salisbury, Md. 21801; 1925
Salm·on P. Chase C., Sch. of Law \,sam-ən-,pē-'chās-\ Cincinnati, Ohio 45210; 1920
Sal·ve Re·gi·na C. \,säl-(,)vä-rā- gē-nə-\ Newport, R.I. 02840; 1934
Sam·ford U. \'sam(p)-fərd\ Birmingham, Ala. 35209; 1842
Sam Hous·ton State C. \sam-'(h)yü-stən-\ Huntsville, Tex. 77340; 1879
San Antonio C. Tex. 78212; junior, 1925
San Bernardino Valley C. San Bernardino, Calif. 92403; junior, 1926
Sand·hills Community C. \'sand-,hilz-\ Southern Pines, N.C. 28387; junior, 1963
San Diego C. for Men, U. of Calif. 92110; 1949
San Diego C. for Women, U. of Calif. 92110; 1952
San Diego City C. Calif. 92101; junior, 1914
San Diego Mesa C. Calif. 92111; junior, 1964
San Diego State C. Calif. 92115; 1897
San Fernando Valley State C. Northridge, Calif. 91324; 1956
San Francisco, U. of Calif. 94117; 1855
San Francisco Art Inst. C. Calif. 94133; 1874
San Francisco C. for Women Calif. 94118; 1930
San Francisco C. of Mortuary Science Calif. 94109; junior, 1930
San Francisco Conservatory of Music Calif. 94122; 1917
San Francisco State C. Calif. 94132; 1899
San Ja·cin·to C. \,san-jə-'sint-ə-\ Pasadena, Tex. 77505; junior, 1961
San Joaquin Delta C. Stockton, Calif. 95204; junior, 1935
San Jose Bible C. San Jose, Calif. 95108; 1939
San Jose City C. San Jose, Calif. 95114; junior, 1921
San Jose State C. San Jose, Calif. 95114; 1857
San Mateo, C. of San Mateo, Calif. 94402; junior, 1922
Santa Ana C. Santa Ana, Calif. 92706; junior, 1915
Santa Barbara City C. Santa Barbara, Calif. 93105; junior, 1946
Santa Clara, U. of Santa Clara, Calif. 95053; 1851
Santa Fe, C. of N. Mex. 87501; 1947
Santa Fe Junior C. Gainesville, Fla. 32601; 1965
Santa Monica City C. Santa Monica, Calif. 90406; junior, 1929
Santa Rosa Junior C. Santa Rosa, Calif. 95401; 1918
Sar·ah Law·rence C. \,ser-ə-'lȯr-ən(t)s-, ,sar-ə-, ,sā-rə-, -'lär-\ Bronxville, N.Y. 10708; 1926
Sauk County Teachers C. \'sȯk-\ Reedsburg, Wis. 53959; junior, 1906
Sauk Valley C. Dixon, Ill. 61021; junior, 1965
Savannah State C. Savannah, Ga. 31404; 1890
Sayre Junior C. \'sa(ə)r-, 'se(ə)r-\ Sayre, Okla. 73662; 1938
Scar·ritt C. for Christian Workers \'skar-ət-\ Nashville, Tenn. 37203; 1924
Schenectady Community C. N.Y. 12305; junior, 1968
School·craft C. \'skül-,kraft-\ Livonia, Mich. 48151; junior, 1961
Schrei·ner Inst. \'shrī-nər-, esp South 'srī-\ Kerrville, Tex. 78028; junior, 1923
Scotts Bluff County Junior C. \'skäts-,bləf-\ Scottsbluff, Nebr. 69361; 1926
Scranton, U. of Scranton, Pa. 18510; 1888
Scripps C. \'skrips-\ Claremont, Calif. 91711; 1926
Seat of Wisdom C. Litchfield, Conn. 06759; 1958
Seattle Community C. Wash. 98122; junior, 1966
Seattle Pacific C. Seattle, Wash. 98119; 1891
Seattle U. Wash. 98122; 1892
Selma U. Selma, Ala. 36701; 1878
Sem·i·nole Junior C. \'sem-ə-,nōl-\ Sanford, Fla. 32771; 1965
Seminole Junior C. Seminole, Okla. 74868; 1931
Se·quoi·as, C. of the \-si-'kwȯi-əz\ Visalia, Calif. 93277; junior, 1926
Se·ton Hall U. \,sēt-ᵊn-\ South Orange, N.J. 07079; 1856
Seton Hill C. Greensburg, Pa. 15601; 1883
Sew·ard County Community Junior C. \'sü-ərd-\ Liberal, Kans. 67901; 1967
Shas·ta C. \'shas-tə-\ Redding, Calif. 96001; junior, 1949
Shaw·nee Community C. \shȯ-'nē-, 'shȯ-(,)nē-\ Ullin, Ill. 62992; junior, 1967

Shaw U. \'shȯ-\ Raleigh, N.C. 27602; 1865
Sheboygan County Teachers C. Sheboygan Falls, Wis. 53085 junior, 1909
Shel·don Jack·son Junior C. \,shel-dən-'jak-sən-\ Sitka, Alaska 99835; 1878
Shel·ton C. \'shelt-ᵊn-\ Cape May, N.J. 08204; 1907
Shen·an·do·ah C. and Shenandoah Conservatory of Music \,shen-ən-'dō-ə-, ,shan-ə-'dō-ə-\ Winchester, Va. 22601; 1875
Shep·herd C. \'shep-ərd-\ Shepherdstown, W. Va. 25443; 1871
Shi·mer C. \'shī-mər-\ Mount Carroll, Ill. 61053; 1853
Ship·pens·burg State C. \'ship-ənz-,bərg-\ Shippensburg, Pa. 17257; 1871
Shore·line Community C. \'shō(ə)r-,līn-, 'shȯ(ə)r-\ Seattle, Wash. 98133; junior, 1964
Shor·ter C. \'shȯrt-ər-\ North Little Rock, Ark. 72114; 1884
Shorter C. Rome, Ga. 30161; 1873
Si·ena C. \sē-'en-ə-\ Loudonville, N.Y. 12211; 1937
Siena C. Memphis, Tenn. 38117; 1921
Siena Heights C. Adrian, Mich. 49221; 1919
Si·er·ra C. \sē-'er-ə-\ Rocklin, Calif. 95677; junior, 1914
Sil·ver·mine C. of Art \'sil-vər-,mīn-\ New Canaan, Conn. 06840; junior, 1924
Sim·mons C. \sim-ənz-\ Boston, Mass. 02115; 1899
Simmons U. Louisville, Ky. 40210; 1879
Simp·son Bible C. \'sim(p)-sən-\ San Francisco, Calif. 94134; 1921
Simpson C. Indianola, Iowa 50125; 1860
Sin·clair Community C. \'sin-,kla(ə)r-, 'siŋ-, -,kle(ə)r-, sin-', siŋ-'\ Dayton, Ohio 45402; junior, 1887
Sioux Empire C. \'sü-\ Hawarden, Iowa 51023; junior, 1967
Sioux Falls C. Sioux Falls, S. Dak. 57101; 1883
Sis·ki·yous, C. of the \-'sis-ki-,yüz\ Weed, Calif. 96094; junior, 1959
Skag·it Valley C. \'skaj-ət-\ Mount Vernon, Wash. 98273; junior, 1926
Skid·more C. \'skid-,mō(ə)r-, -,mȯ(ə)r-\ Saratoga Springs, N.Y. 12866; 1911
Slippery Rock State C. Slippery Rock, Pa. 16057; 1889
Smith C. \'smith-\ Northampton, Mass. 01060; 1871
Snead State Junior C. \'snēd-\ Boaz, Ala. 35957; 1898
So·la·no C. \sə-'län-(,)ō-\ Vallejo, Calif. 94590; junior, 1945
Som·er·set County C. \'səm-ər-,set-, -sət-\ Somerville, N.J. 08876; junior, 1968
So·no·ma State C. \sə-'nō-mə-\ Rohnert Park, Calif. 94928; 1960
South, U. of the Sewanee, Tenn. 37375; 1857
South Alabama, U. of Mobile, 36608; 1963
South Carolina, U. of Columbia, 29208; 1801
South Carolina State C. Orangeburg, 29115; 1896
South Central Community C. Hamden, Conn. 06517; junior, 1967
South Dakota, U. of Vermillion, 57069; 1862
South Dakota Sch. of Mines and Tech. Rapid City, 57701; 1885
South Dakota State U. Brookings, 57006; 1881
Southeastern Baptist C. Laurel, Miss. 39440; junior, 1948
Southeastern Bible C. Birmingham, Ala. 35205; 1934
South–Eastern Bible C. Lakeland, Fla. 33801; 1935
Southeastern Christian C. Winchester, Ky. 40391; junior, 1949
Southeastern Community C. Whiteville, N.C. 28472; junior, 1964
Southeastern Illinois C. Harrisburg, 62946; junior, 1961
Southeastern Iowa Area Community C. Burlington, 52601; junior, 1920
Southeastern Louisiana C. Hammond, 70401; 1925
Southeastern Massachusetts Technological Inst. North Dartmouth, 02747; 1960
Southeastern State C. Durant, Okla. 74701; 1909
Southeastern U. Washington, D.C. 20006; 1879
Southeast Missouri State C. Cape Girardeau, 63701; 1873
Southern Baptist C. Walnut Ridge, Ark. 72476; junior, 1941
Southern California, U. of Los Angeles, 90007; 1879
Southern California C. Costa Mesa, 92626; 1920
Southern C. of Optometry Memphis, Tenn. 38104; 1932
Southern Colorado State C. Pueblo, 81005; 1933
Southern Connecticut State C. New Haven, 06515; 1893
Southern Idaho, C. of Twin Falls, 83301; junior, 1964
Southern Illinois U. Carbondale, 62901; 1874
Southern Methodist U. Dallas, Tex. 75222; 1910
Southern Missionary C. Collegedale, Tenn. 37315; 1893
Southern Mississippi, U. of Hattiesburg, 39401; 1910
Southern Oregon C. Ashland, 97520; 1926
Southern Pilgrim C. Kernersville, N.C. 27284; 1946
Southern Sem. Junior C. Buena Vista, Va. 24416; 1868
Southern State C. Magnolia, Ark. 71753; 1909
Southern State C. Springfield, S. Dak. 57062; 1881
Southern Union State Junior C. Wadley, Ala. 36276; 1934
Southern U. and A. & M. C. Baton Rouge, La. 70813; 1880
Southern Utah State C. Cedar City, 84720; 1897
South Florida, U. of Tampa, 33620; 1956
South Florida Junior C. Avon Park, 33825; 1965
South Georgia C. Douglas, 31533; junior, 1907
South Plains C. Levelland, Tex. 79336; junior, 1958
South Texas Junior C. Houston, 77002; 1948
Southwest, C. of the Hobbs, N. Mex. 88240; 1957
Southwest Baptist C. Bolivar, Mo. 65613; 1878
Southwestern Assemblies of God C. Waxahachie, Tex. 75165; junior, 1927
Southwestern at Memphis Tenn. 38112; 1848
Southwestern Christian C. Terrell, Tex. 75160; junior, 1950
Southwestern C. Chula Vista, Calif. 92010; junior, 1961
Southwestern C. Winfield, Kans. 67156; 1885
Southwestern C. Oklahoma City, Okla. 73127; junior, 1946
Southwestern Community C. Creston, Iowa 50801; junior, 1966
Southwestern Louisiana, The U. of Lafayette, 70501; 1900
Southwestern Michigan C. Dowagiac, 49047; junior, 1964

Southwestern Oregon Community C. Coos Bay, 97420; junior, 1961
Southwestern State C. Weatherford, Okla. 73096; 1901
Southwestern Union C. Keene, Tex. 76059; junior, 1893
Southwestern U. Los Angeles, Calif. 90015; 1911
Southwestern U. Georgetown, Tex. 78626; 1840
Southwest Minnesota State C. Marshall, 56258; 1963
Southwest Mississippi Junior C. Summit, 39666; 1918
Southwest Missouri State C. Springfield, 65802; 1905
Southwest Texas Junior C. Uvalde, 78801; 1946
Southwest Texas State C. San Marcos, 78666; 1899
Southwest Virginia Community C. Richlands, 24641; junior, 1968
South·wood C. \'saüth-,wüd-\ Salemburg, N.C. 28385; junior, 1875
Spartanburg Junior C. Spartanburg, S.C. 29301; 1911
Spel·man C. \'spel-mən-\ Atlanta, Ga. 30314; 1881
Spo·kane Community C. \spō-'kan-\ Wash. 99204; junior, 1963
Spoon River C. \'spün-\ Canton, Ill. 61520; junior, 1959
Spring Arbor C. Spring Arbor, Mich. 49283; 1873
Springfield C. Springfield, Mass. 01109; 1885
Springfield Junior C. Springfield, Ill. 62702; 1929
Springfield Technical Community C. Springfield, Mass. 01105; junior, 1965
Spring Garden C. Philadelphia, Pa. 19123; junior, 1850
Spring Hill C. Mobile, Ala. 36608; 1830
Stan·ford U. \'stan-fərd-\ Palo Alto, Calif. 94305; 1885
Stan·is·laus State C. \'stan-ə-,slȯ(-)s-\ Turlock, Calif. 95380; 1957
State Fair Community C. Sedalia, Mo. 65301; junior, 1966
Staten Island Community C. N.Y. 10301; junior, 1956
Ste·phen F. Aus·tin State C. \,stē-və-,nef-'ȯs-tən-, -'äs-\ Nacogdoches, Tex. 75961; 1917
Ste·phens C. \'stē-vənz-\ Columbia, Mo. 65201; 1833
Ster·ling C. \'stər-liŋ-\ Sterling, Kans. 67579; 1887
Stet·son U. \'stet-sən-\ De Land, Fla. 32720; 1883
Steu·ben·ville, C. of \'st(y)ü-bən-,vil\ Steubenville, Ohio 43952; 1946
Ste·vens C. \'stē-vənz-\ Hubbardston, Mass. 01452; 1895
Ste·vens Hen·a·ger C. \,stē-vənz-'hen-i-gər-\ Salt Lake City, Utah 84102; junior, 1907
Stevens Inst. of Tech. Hoboken, N.J. 07030; 1867
Still·man C. \'stil-mən-\ Tuscaloosa, Ala. 35401; 1876
Stone·hill C. \'stōn-,hil-\ North Easton, Mass. 02356; 1948
Stout State U. \'staüt-\ Menomonie, Wis. 54751; 1893
Strat·ford C. \'strat-fərd-\ Danville, Va. 24541; junior, 1852
Stray·er Junior C. \'strā-ər-, 'stre(-ə)r-\ Washington, D.C. 20005; 1904
Sue Ben·nett C. \sü-'ben-ət-\ London, Ky. 40741; junior, 1896
Suf·folk County Community C. \'səf-ək-, -,ȯk-\ Lake Ronkonkoma, N.Y. 11779; junior, 1960
Suffolk U. Boston, Mass. 02114; 1906
Sul·lins C. \'səl-ənz-\ Bristol, Va. 24201; junior, 1870
Sul·li·van County Community C. \,səl-ə-vən-\ South Fallsburg, N.Y. 12779; junior, 1963
Sul·pi·cian Sem. of the Northwest \,səl-'pish-ən-\ Kenmore, Wash. 98028; 1930
Sul Ross State C. \'səl-'rȯs-\ Alpine, Tex. 79830; 1920
Suo·mi C. \'swȯ-mē-\ Hancock, Mich. 49930; junior, 1896
Sur·ry Community C. \'sər-ē-, 'sə-rē-\ Dobson, N.C. 27017; junior, 1965
Sus·que·han·na U. \,səs-kwə-'han-ə-\ Selinsgrove, Pa. 17870; 1858
Swarth·more C. \'swȯrth-,mō(ə)r-, 'swäth-, -,mȯ(ə)r-\ Swarthmore, Pa. 19081; 1864
Sweet Bri·ar C. \'swēt-,brī(-ə)r-\ Sweet Briar, Va. 24595; 1901
Syracuse U. Syracuse, N.Y. 13210; 1870

Ta·bor C. \'tā-bər-\ Hillsboro, Kans. 67063; 1908
Tacoma Community C. Wash. 98465; junior, 1965
Taft C. \'taf(t)-\ Taft, Calif. 93268; junior, 1922
Talladega C. Talladega, Ala. 35160; 1867
Tallahassee Junior C. Fla. 32303; 1965
Tampa, U. of Fla. 33606; 1931
Tar·kio C. \'tär-kē-,ō-\ Tarkio, Mo. 64491; 1883
Tarle·ton State C. \'tär(ə)lt-ᵊn-\ Stephenville, Tex. 76401; 1899
Tar·rant County Junior C. \'tar-ənt-\ Fort Worth, Tex. 76102; 1965
Tay·lor County Teachers C. \'tā-lər-\ Medford, Wis. 54451; junior, 1912
Taylor U. Upland, Ind. 46989; 1846
Teachers C. New York, N.Y. 10027; 1888
Temple Bu·ell C. \-'byü-əl-\ Denver, Colo. 80220; 1909
Temple Junior C. Temple, Tex. 76501; 1926
Temple U. Philadelphia, Pa. 19122; 1884
Tennessee, U. of Knoxville, 37916; 1794
Tennessee Agricultural and Industrial State U. Nashville, 37203; 1909
Tennessee Technological U. Cookeville, 38501; 1915
Tennessee Temple C. Chattanooga, 37404; 1946
Tennessee Wesleyan C. Athens, 37303; 1866
Texarkana C. Texarkana, Tex. 75501; junior, 1927
Texas, U. of Austin, 78712; 1881
Texas A. & M. U. College Station, 77843; 1876
Texas Arts and Industries U. Kingsville, 78363; 1917
Texas at Arlington, U. of 76010; 1895
Texas at El Paso, U. of 79999; 1913
Texas Christian U. Fort Worth, 76129; 1873
Texas C. Tyler, 75701; 1894
Texas Lutheran C. Seguin, 78155; 1891
Texas Southern U. Houston, 77004; 1927
Texas South·most C. \-'saüth-,mōst-\ Brownsville, 78520; junior, 1926

Texas Technological C. Lubbock, 79409; 1923
Texas Wesleyan C. Fort Worth, 76105; 1890
Texas Woman's U. Denton, 76204; 1901
Thames Valley State Technical C. Norwich, Conn. 06360; junior, 1963
Thiel C. \'tē(ə)l-\ Greenville, Pa. 16125; 1866
Thom·as C. \'täm-əs-\ Waterville, Me. 04901; 1894
Thomas More C. Fort Mitchell, Ky. 41017; 1921
Thorn·ton Junior C. \'thȯrnt-ᵊn-\ Harvey, Ill. 60426; 1927
Three Rivers Junior C. Poplar Bluff, Mo. 63901; 1966
Tif·fin U. \'tif-ən-\ Tiffin, Ohio 44883; 1924
Tift C. \'tif(t)-\ Forsyth, Ga. 31029; 1847
T. J. Har·ris Junior C. \-'har-əs-\ Meridian, Miss. 39301; 1956
Toc·coa Falls Inst. \tə-'kō-ə-\ Toccoa Falls, Ga. 30577; 1911
Toledo, U. of Ohio 43606; 1872
Tol·en·tine C. \'täl-ən-,tīn-\ Olympia Fields, Ill. 60461; 1958
Tom·brock C. \'täm-,bräk-\ West Paterson, N.J. 07424; junior, 1956
Tomlinson C. Cleveland, Tenn. 37311; junior, 1966
Tomp·kins–Cort·land Community C. \,täm(p)-kənz-'kȯrt-lən(d)-\ Groton, N.Y. 13073; junior, 1967
Tou·ga·loo C. \'tü-gə-,lü-\ Tougaloo, Miss. 39174; 1869
Tow·son State C. \'taůs-ᵊn\ Towson, Md. 21204; 1866
Tran·syl·va·nia C. \,tran(t)s-əl-'vā-nyə-, -nē-ə-\ Lexington, Ky. 40508; 1780
Treasure Valley Community C. Ontario, Oreg. 97914; junior, 1962
Tren·ton Junior C. \'trent-ᵊn-\ Trenton, Mo. 64683; 1925
Trenton State C. Trenton, N.J. 08625; 1855
Tre·vec·ca Nazarene C. \tri-'vek-ə-,naz-ə-'rēn-\ Nashville, Tenn. 37210; 1901
Trin·i·dad State Junior C. \'trin-ə-,dad-\ Trinidad, Colo. 81082; 1925
Trinitarian C. Baltimore, Md. 21208; junior, 1956
Trinity Christian C. Palos Heights, Ill. 60463; junior, 1959
Trinity C. Hartford, Conn. 06106; 1823
Trinity C. Washington, D.C. 20017; 1897
Trinity C. Deerfield, Ill. 60015; 1897
Trinity C. Burlington, Vt. 05401; 1925
Trinity U. San Antonio, Tex. 78212; 1869
Tri–State C. \'trī-,stāt-\ Angola, Ind. 46703; 1884
Tri·ton C. \'trī-'tän\ Northlake, Ill. 60164; junior, 1964
Tro·caire C. \'trō-,ka(ə)r-, -,ke(ə)r-\ Buffalo, N.Y. 14220; junior, 1958
Troy State U. \'trȯi-\ Troy, Ala. 36081; 1887
Tru·ett Mc·Con·nell C. \,trü-ət-mə-'kän-ᵊl-\ Cleveland, Ga. 30528; junior, 1947
Tufts U. \'təf(t)s-\ Medford, Mass. 02155; 1852
Tu·lane U. of Louisiana \t(y)ü-'lān-\ New Orleans, 70118; 1834
Tulsa, U. of Okla. 74104; 1894
Tus·cu·lum C. \'təs-k(y)ə-ləm-\ Greeneville, Tenn. 37743; 1794
Tus·ke·gee Inst. \(,)tə-'skē-gē-\ Tuskegee Institute, Ala. 36088; 1881
Tyler Junior C. Tyler, Tex. 75701; 1926

Ul·ster County Community C. \,əl-stər-\ Stone Ridge, N.Y. 12484; junior, 1963
Ump·qua Community C. \'əm(p)-,kwȯ-\ Roseburg, Oreg. 97470; junior, 1964
Union C. Barbourville, Ky. 40906; 1879
Union C. Lincoln, Nebr. 68506; 1891
Union C. and U. Schenectady, N.Y. 12308; 1795
Union Junior C. Cranford, N.J. 07016; 1933
Union U. Jackson, Tenn. 38301; 1834
United States Air Force Acad. Colorado Springs, Colo. 80840; 1954
United States Coast Guard Acad. New London, Conn. 06320; 1876
United States International U. San Diego, Calif. 92106; 1924
United States Merchant Marine Acad. Kings Point, N.Y. 11024; 1938
United States Military Acad. West Point, N.Y. 10996; 1802
United States Naval Acad. Annapolis, Md. 21402; 1845
United States Naval Postgraduate Sch. Monterey, Calif. 93940; 1909
Unity C. Unity, Me. 04988; 1966
Upper Iowa C. Fayette, 52142; 1857
Up·sa·la C. \,əp-'säl-ə-\ East Orange, N.J. 07019; 1893
Ur·bana C. \,ər-\ Urbana, Ohio 43078; 1850
Ur·si·nus C. \,ər-'sī-nəs-\ Collegeville, Pa. 19426; 1869
Ur·su·line C. for Women \'ər-sə-lən-, -,līn-, -,lēn-\ Cleveland, Ohio 44124; 1871
Utah, U. of Salt Lake City, 84112; 1850
Utah State U. of Agric. and Applied Science Logan, 84321; 1888
Utica C. of Syracuse U. Utica, N.Y. 13502; 1946
Utica Junior C. Utica, Miss. 39175; 1903

Valdosta State C. Valdosta, Ga. 31601; 1906
Valley City State C. Valley City, N. Dak. 58072; 1889
Valley Forge Military Junior C. Wayne, Pa. 19087; 1928
Valparaiso Technical Inst. Valparaiso, Ind. 46383; 1934
Valparaiso U. Valparaiso, Ind. 46383; 1859
Van·der·bilt U. \'van-dər-,bilt-\ Nashville, Tenn. 37203; 1872
Vas·sar C. \'vas-ər-\ Poughkeepsie, N.Y. 12601; 1861
Ve·nard C. \və-'närd-\ University Park, Iowa 52595; 1910
Ventura C. Ventura, Calif. 93003; junior, 1925
Vermont, U. of Burlington, 05401; 1791
Vermont C. Montpelier, 05602; 1834
Vermont Technical C. Randolph Center, 05061; junior, 1957

Ver·non County Teachers C. \'vər-nən-\ Viroqua, Wis. 54665; junior, 1909
Vernon Court Junior C. Newport, R.I. 02840; 1963
Victoria C. Victoria, Tex. 77901; junior, 1925
Vic·tor Valley C. \,vik-tər-\ Victorville, Calif. 92392; junior, 1961
Vil·la Ju·lie C. \,vil-ə-'jü-lē-\ Stevenson, Md. 21153; junior, 1947
Villa Ma·ria C. \-mə-'rē-ə-\ Erie, Pa. 16505; 1882
Villa Maria C. of Buffalo N.Y. 14225; junior, 1960
Vil·la·no·va U. \,vil-ə-'nō-və-\ Villanova, Pa. 19085; 1842
Villa Walsh C. \-'wȯlsh-\ Morristown, N.J. 07960; junior, 1928
Vincennes U. Vincennes, Ind. 47591; junior, 1804
Virginia, U. of Charlottesville, 22903; 1819
Virginia Commonwealth U. Richmond, 23220; 1838
Virginia In·ter·mont C. \-'int-ər-,mänt-\ Bristol, 24201; junior, 1884
Virginia Military Inst. Lexington, 24450; 1839
Virginia Polytechnic Inst. Blacksburg, 24061; 1872
Virginia Sem. and C. Lynchburg, 24501; 1888
Virginia Southern C. Roanoke, 24008; junior, 1933
Virginia State C. Petersburg, 23803; 1882
Virginia Union U. Richmond, 23220; 1865
Virginia Wes·ley·an C. \-'wes-lē-ən-\ Norfolk, 23502; 1961
Virginia Western Community C. Roanoke, 24015; junior, 1966
Virgin Islands, C. of the St. Thomas, 00802; 1963
Vi·ter·bo C. \və-'tər-(,)bō-\ La Crosse, Wis. 54601; 1931
Voor·hees C. \'vō(ə)r-,hēz-, 'vȯ(ə)r-; 'vȯr-ēz, 'vȯr-\ Denmark, S.C. 29042; 1897
Voorhees Technical Inst. New York, N.Y. 10036; junior, 1881

Wa·bash \'wȯ-,bash-\ Crawfordsville, Ind. 47933; 1832
Wabash Valley C. Mt. Carmel, Ill. 62863; junior, 1961
Wad·hams Hall \'wäd-əmz-\ Ogdensburg, N.Y. 13669; 1924
Wag·ner C. \'wag-nər-\ Staten Island, N.Y. 10301; 1883
Wake Forest U. \wāk-\ Winston-Salem, N.C. 27109; 1834
Wal·dorf C. \'wȯl-,dȯrf-\ Forest City, Iowa 50436; junior, 1903
Walk·er C. \'wȯ-kər-\ Jasper, Ala. 35501; junior, 1938
Walla Walla C. College Place, Wash. 99324; 1892
Walla Walla Community C. Wash. 99362; junior, 1967
Walsh C. \'wȯlsh-\ Canton, Ohio 44720; 1960
War·ner Pacific C. \'wȯr-nər-\ Portland, Oreg. 97215; 1937
War·ren Wilson C. \,wȯr-ən-'wil-sən-, ,wär-\ Swannanoa, N.C. 28778; junior, 1893
Wart·burg C. \'wȯrt-,bərg-\ Waverly, Iowa 50677; 1852
Wash·burn U. of Topeka \'wȯsh-(,)bərn-, 'wäsh-\ Kans. 66621; 1865
Washington, U. of Seattle, 98105; 1861
Washington and Jefferson C. Washington, Pa. 15301; 1780
Washington and Lee U. \-'lē-\ Lexington, Va. 24450; 1749
Washington Bible C. Lanham, Md. 20801; 1919
Washington C. Chestertown, Md. 21620; 1706
Washington State U. Pullman, 99163; 1890
Washington Technical Inst. D.C. 20008; junior, 1966
Washington U. St. Louis, Mo. 63130; 1853
Wash·te·naw Community C. \'wȯsh-tə-,nȯ-, 'wäsh-\ Ann Arbor, Mich. 48107; junior, 1965
Waterbury State Technical C. Waterbury, Conn. 06708; junior, 1964
Wau·shara County Teachers C. \wȯ-'shar-ə-\ Wautoma, Wis. 54982; junior, 1911
Way·land Baptist C. \'wā-lən(d)-\ Plainview, Tex. 79072; 1909
Wayne Community C. \'wān-\ Goldsboro, N.C. 27530; junior, 1957
Waynes·burg C. \'wānz-,bərg-\ Waynesburg, Pa. 15370; 1850
Wayne State C. \'wān-\ Wayne, Nebr. 68787; 1891
Wayne State U. \'wān-\ Detroit, Mich. 48202; 1868
Weath·er·ford C. \'weth-ə(r)-fərd-\ Weatherford, Tex. 76086; junior, 1869
Web·ber C. \'web-ər-\ Babson Park, Fla. 33827; junior, 1927
Webb Inst. of Naval Architecture \'web-\ Glen Cove, N.Y. 11542; 1889
We·ber State C. \'wē-bər-\ Ogden, Utah 84403; 1889
Web·ster C. \'web-stər-\ Webster Groves, Mo. 63119; 1915
Wellesley C. Wellesley, Mass. 02181; 1870
Wells C. \'welz-\ Aurora, N.Y. 13026; 1868
Wenatchee Valley C. Wenatchee, Wash. 98801; junior, 1939
We·no·nah State Technical Junior C. \wə-'nō-nə-\ Birmingham, Ala. 35211; 1963
Went·worth Inst. \'went-(,)wərth-\ Boston, Mass. 02115; junior, 1904
Wentworth Military Acad. Lexington, Mo. 64067; junior, 1880
Wes·ley·an C. \'wes-lē-ən-\ Macon, Ga. 31201; 1836
Wesleyan U. Middletown, Conn. 06457; 1831
Wes·ley C. \'wes-lē-\ Dover, Del. 19901; junior, 1873
West·ark Junior C. \'wes-,tärk-\ Fort Smith, Ark. 72901; 1928
West·brook Junior C. \'wes(t)-,brük-\ Portland, Me. 04103; 1831
West·ches·ter Community C. \'wes(t)-,ches-tər-\ Valhalla, N.Y. 10595; junior, 1946
West Ches·ter State C. \'wes(t)-,ches-tər-\ West Chester, Pa. 19380; 1812
West Coast U. Los Angeles, Calif. 90005; 1909
Western Baptist Bible C. Salem, Oreg. 97302; 1946
Western Bible Inst. Morrison, Colo. 80465; 1948
Western Carolina U. Cullowhee, N.C. 28723; 1889
Western C. for Women Oxford, Ohio 45056; 1853
Western Connecticut State C. Danbury, 06810; 1903
Western Illinois U. Macomb, 61455; 1899
Western Kentucky U. Bowling Green, 42101; 1906
Western Maryland C. Westminster, 21157; 1867
Western Michigan U. Kalamazoo, 49001; 1903
Western Montana C. Dillon, 59725; 1893

Western New England C. Springfield, Mass. 01119; 1919
Western New Mexico U. Silver City, 88061; 1893
Western Piedmont Community C. Morganton, N.C. 28655; junior, 1964
Western State C. of Colorado Gunnison, 81230; 1901
Western States C. of Engineering Inglewood, Calif. 90301; 1946
Western Washington State C. Bellingham, 98225; 1893
Western Wyoming Community C. Reliance, 82943; junior, 1959
West Florida, U. of Pensacola, 32504; 1967
West Georgia C. Carrollton, 30117; 1933
West Liberty State C. West Liberty, W. Va. 26074; 1837
West·mar C. \'wes(t)-,mär-\ Le Mars, Iowa 51031; 1900
West·min·ster Choir C. \'wes(t)-,min(t)-stər-\ Princeton, N.J. 08540; 1926
Westminster C. Fulton, Mo. 65251; 1851
Westminster C. New Wilmington, Pa. 16142; 1852
Westminster C. Salt Lake City, Utah 84105; 1875
West·mont C. \'wes(t)-,mänt-\ Santa Barbara, Calif. 93103; 1940
West Shore Community C. Scottville, Mich. 49454; junior, 1967
West Texas State U. Canyon, 79015; 1909
West Valley Junior C. Campbell, Calif. 95008; 1963
West Virginia Inst. of Tech. Montgomery, 25136; 1895
West Virginia State C. Institute, 25112; 1891
West Virginia U. Morgantown, 26506; 1867
West Virginia Wesleyan C. Buckhannon, 26201; 1890
Whar·ton County Junior C. \'hwȯrt-ᵊn-, 'wȯrt-\ Wharton, Tex. 77488; 1946
Wheaton C. Wheaton, Ill. 60187; 1853
Wheaton C. Norton, Mass. 02766; 1834
Wheeling C. Wheeling, W. Va. 26003; 1954
Whee·lock C. \'hwē-,läk-, 'wē-\ Boston, Mass. 02215; 1889
White Pines C. Chester, N.H. 03036; junior, 1965
Whit·man C. \'hwit-mən-, 'wit-\ Walla Walla, Wash. 99362; 1859
Whittier C. Whittier, Calif. 90608; 1901
Whit·worth C. \'hwit-(,)wərth-, 'wit-\ Spokane, Wash. 99218; 1890
Wichita State U. Kans. 67208; 1892
Wil·ber·force U. \'wil-bər-,fō(ə)rs-, -,fȯ(ə)rs-\ Wilberforce, Ohio 45384; 1856
Wi·ley C. \'wī-lē-\ Marshall, Tex. 75670; 1873
Wilkes C. \'wilks-\ Wilkes-Barre, Pa. 18703; 1933
Wilkes Community C. Wilkesboro, N.C. 28697; junior, 1965
Wil·lam·ette U. \wə-'lam-ət-\ Salem, Oreg. 97301; 1842
William and Mary, C. of Williamsburg, Va. 23185; 1693
William Car·ey C. \-'kā(ə)r-ē-, -'ke(ə)r-ē-\ Hattiesburg, Miss. 39401; 1911
William Car·ter C. \-'kärt-ər-\ Goldsboro, N.C. 27530; 1952
William Jen·nings Bry·an C. \-,jen-iŋz-'brī-ən-\ Dayton, Tenn. 37321; 1930
William Jew·ell C. \-'jü(-ə)l-, -'jù(-ə)l-\ Liberty, Mo. 64068; 1849
William Marsh Rice U. \-'märsh-'rīs-\ Houston, Tex. 77001; 1891
William Mitch·ell C. of Law \-'mich-əl-\ St. Paul, Minn. 55105; 1900
William Penn C. \-'pen-\ Oskaloosa, Iowa 52577; 1873
William Rai·ney Har·per C. \-,rā-nē-'här-pər-\ Palatine, Ill. 60067; junior, 1965
Wil·liams C. \'wil-yəmz-\ Williamstown, Mass. 01267; 1785

Williamsport Area Community C. Williamsport, Pa. 17701; junior, 1920
William Woods C. \-'wùdz-\ Fulton, Mo. 65251; 1890
Will·mar State Junior C. \'wil-mər-\ Willmar, Minn. 56201; 1961
Wilmington C. Wilmington Manor, Del. 19720; 1967
Wilmington C. Wilmington, N.C. 28401; 1947
Wilmington C. Wilmington, Ohio 45177; 1863
Wil·son C. \'wil-sən-\ Chambersburg, Pa. 17201; 1869
Wind·ham C. \'win-dəm-\ Putney, Vt. 05346; 1951
Win·gate C. \'win-,gāt-\ Wingate, N.C. 28174; junior, 1896
Wi·no·na State C. \wə-'nō-nə-\ Winona, Minn. 55987; 1858
Winston Churchill C. Pontiac, Ill. 61764; junior, 1965
Winston–Salem State C. Winston-Salem, N.C. 27102; 1892
Win·throp C. \'win(t)-thrəp-\ Rock Hill, S.C. 29730; 1886
Wisconsin C. Conservatory Milwaukee, 53202; 1899
Wisconsin—Madison, U. of 53706; 1836
Wisconsin—Milwaukee, U. of 53201; 1908
Wisconsin State U.—Eau Claire 54701; 1916
Wisconsin State U.—La Crosse 54601; 1909
Wisconsin State U.—Oshkosh 54901; 1871
Wisconsin State U.—Platte·ville \-'plat-,vil\ 53818; 1866
Wisconsin State U.—River Falls 54022; 1875
Wisconsin State U.—Ste·vens Point \-,stē-vənz-\ 54481; 1894
Wisconsin State U.—Superior 54880; 1896
Wisconsin State U.—White·wa·ter \-'hwīt-,wȯt-ər, -'wīt-,wät-\ 53190; 1868
Wit·ten·berg U. \'wit-ᵊn-,bərg-\ Springfield, Ohio 45501; 1842
W. L. Yan·cey State Junior C. \-'yan(t)-sē-\ Bay Minette, Ala. 36507; 1965
Wof·ford C. \'wȯf-ərd-, 'wäf-\ Spartanburg, S.C. 29301; 1854
Wood·bury C. \'wùd-,ber-ē-\ Los Angeles, Calif. 90017; 1884
Wood Junior C. Mathiston, Miss. 39752; 1886
Woos·ter, C. of \-'wùs-tər\ Wooster, Ohio 44691; 1866
Worcester Junior C. Mass. 01608; 1905
Worcester Polytechnic Inst. Mass. 01609; 1865
Wor·thing·ton State Junior C. \'wər-thiŋ-tən-\ Worthington, Minn. 56187; 1936
Wright State U. \'rīt-\ Dayton, Ohio 45431; 1964
Wyoming, U. of Laramie, 82070; 1886

Xa·ve·ri·an C. \zā-'vir-ē-ən-\ Silver Spring, Md. 20903; junior, 1931
Xa·vi·er U. \'zā-vē-ər-\ Cincinnati, Ohio 45207; 1831
Xav·i·er U. of Louisiana \'zav-ē-ər-\ New Orleans, 70125; 1915

Yakima Valley C. Yakima, Wash. 98902; junior, 1928
Yale U. \'yā(ə)l-\ New Haven, Conn. 06520; 1701
Yank·ton C. \'yaŋ(k)-tən-\ Yankton, S. Dak. 57078; 1881
Ya·va·pai College \'yäv-ə-,pī-\ Prescott, Ariz. 86301; 1966
Ye·shi·va U. \yə-'shē-və-\ New York, N.Y. 10033; 1886
York C. \'yȯ(ə)rk-\ York, Nebr. 68467; junior, 1890
York C. Flushing, N.Y. 11365; 1967
York C. of Pennsylvania York, 17405; 1941
Young Har·ris C. \,yəŋ-'har-əs-\ Young Harris, Ga. 30582; junior, 1886
Youngstown State U. Youngstown, Ohio 44503; 1908
Yu·ba C. \'yü-bə-\ Marysville, Calif. 95901; junior, 1927

CANADIAN COLLEGES AND UNIVERSITIES

Abbreviations used in the preceding list are used here except that French names require the following spellings: *Acad.* Aca·dé·mie\à·kà·dā·mē\ *C.* Col·lège \kò·lezh\ *Inst.* In·sti·tut \aⁿ·stē·tǖ\ *Sém.* Sé·mi·naire \sā·mē·ner\ and *U.* Uni·ver·si·té \ǖ·nē·ver·sē·tā\. *École* is \ā·kòl\

Acadia U. Wolfville, N.S., 1838
Alberta, U. of Edmonton, 1906
Al·ders·gate C. \'òl·dərz,gāt-\ Moose Jaw, Sask., 1940
Al·go·ma C. \al·'gō·mə-\ Sault Ste. Marie, Ont., 1965
Amos, Sém. d' \-dà·mós\ Amos, P.Q., 1940
An·dré–Gras·set, C. \-äⁿ·drā·grä·sā\ Montreal, P.Q., 1927
An·gèle Mé·ri·ci, C. \-äⁿ·zhel·mà·rē·sē\ Quebec, P.Q., 1936
Anglican Theol. C. of British Columbia Vancouver, 1912
Assumption U. Windsor, Ont., 1857

Ba·sile–Mo·reau, C. \-bà·zil·mó·rō\ St. Laurent, P.Q., 1929
Bath·urst, C. de \-də·'bath·(,)ərst\ N. B., 1899
Bishop's U. Lennoxville, P.Q., 1843
Bon Pas·teur, C. du \-dǖ·bōⁿ·pä·stœr\ Chicoutimi, P.Q., 1947
Bour·get, C. \-bùr·zhā\ Rigaud, P.Q., 1850
Bran·don U. \'bran·dən-\ Brandon, Man., 1899
Bres·cia C. \'bresh·ə-\ London, Ont., 1919
British Columbia, U. of Vancouver, 1890
Brock U. \'bräk-\ St. Catharines, Ont., 1962
Bru·yère, C. \-brǖ·yer\ Ottawa, Ont., 1925

Calgary, U. of Alta., 1945
Cam·pi·on C. \'kam·pē·ən-\ Regina, Sask., 1917
Cam·rose Junior C. \'kam·rōz-\ Camrose, Alta., 1911
Canadian Bible C. Regina, Sask., 1941
Canadian Mennonite Bible C. Winnipeg, Man., 1944
Can·ter·bury C. \'kan·tə(r)-,ber·ē-\ Windsor, Ont., 1957
Car·ey Hall \'ka(ə)r·ē-, 'ke(ə)r-\ Vancouver, B.C., 1960
Carle·ton U. \'kär(ə)lt·ᵊn-\ Ottawa, Ont., 1942
Chi·cou·ti·mi, Sém. de \-də·shē·kü·tē·mē\ Chicoutimi, P.Q., 1873
Christian Training Inst. Edmonton, Alta., 1939
Christ the King, Sem. of Mission City, B.C., 1932
Con·cor·dia C. \kən·'kòrd·ē·ə-\ Edmonton, Alta., junior, 1921
Conrad Greb·el C. \-'greb·əl-\ Waterloo, Ont., 1961
Corn·wall, C. Clas·sique de \-kla·sik·də·kòrn·wòl\ Cornwall, Ont., 1949

Dal·hou·sie U. \dal·'haù·zē-\ Halifax, N.S., 1818

Em·man·u·el and Saint Chad, C. of \-i·'man·yə(·wə)l-, -'chad\ Saskatoon, Sask., 1879

Gardes–Ma·lades, École des \-dā·gàrd·mà·làd\ Edmundston, N.B., 1946
Gas·pé, Sém. de \-də·gàs·pā\ Gaspé, P.Q., 1926
Gra·vel·bourg, C. Ca·tho·lique de \-kà·tò·lik·də·grà·vel·bùr\ Gravelbourg, Sask., 1917
Guelph, U. of Ont., 1964

Hautes Études Com·mer·ciales, École des \-dā·ōt·zā·tǖed·kó·mer·syàl\ Montreal, P.Q., 1907
Hearst, C. de \-də·'hòrst\ Hearst, Ont., 1952
Holy Heart Sem. Halifax, N.S., 1895
Holy Names C. Windsor, Ont., 1934
Holy Redeemer C. Windsor, Ont., 1956
Hun·ting·ton U. \'hənt·iŋ·tən-\ Sudbury, Ont., 1960
Hu·ron C. \'hyùr·ən-\ London, Ont., 1863

Ig·na·tius C. \ig·'nā·sh(ē·)əs-\ Guelph, Ont., 1913
Io·na C. \ī·'ō·nə-\ Windsor, Ont., 1964

Jean–de–Bré·beuf, C. \-zhäⁿ·də·brā·bœf\ Montreal, P.Q., 1928
Jean–Jacques Olier, C. \-zhäⁿ·zhà·kò·lyā\ Verdun, P.Q., 1951
Jé·suites, C. des \-dā·zhā·zw'it\ Quebec, P.Q., 1635
Jé·sus–Ma·rie, C. \-zhā·zǖ·mà·rē\ Shippegan, N.B., 1960
Jésus–Marie de Sil·le·ry, C. \-də·sē·yə·rē\ Quebec, P.Q., 1857
Jésus–Marie d'Ou·tre·mont, C. \-dü·trə·mōⁿ\ Outremont, P.Q., 1933
Jo·liette, Sém. de \-də·zhò·lyet\ Joliette, P.Q., 1846
Journalism, Sch. of Halifax, N.S., 1945

King's C. \'kiŋz-\ London, Ont., 1912
King's C., U. of Halifax, N.S., 1789
Knox C. \'näks-\ Toronto, Ont., 1844

Lake·head U. \'lāk-,hed-\ Port Arthur, Ont., 1946
L'As·somp·tion, C. \-là·sōⁿp·syōⁿ\ Moncton, N.B., 1943
L'Assomption, C. de L'Assomption, P.Q., 1832
Lau·ren·tian U. of Sudbury \lò·'ren·chən-\ Sudbury, Ont., 1960
La·val, U. \-là·vàl\ Quebec, P.Q., 1852
Lethbridge, U. of Lethbridge, Alta., 1967
Lethbridge Junior C. Lethbridge, Alta., 1957
Lé·vis, C. de \-də·lā·vē\ Levis, P.Q., 1853
London C. of Bible and Missions London, Ont., 1935
Lon·gueuil, Ex·ter·nat Clas·sique de \es·ter·nà·klà·sēk·də·lōⁿ·gœi\ Ville Jacques-Cartier, P.Q., 1950
Loy·o·la C. \lòi·'ō·lə-\ Montreal, P.Q., 1896
Lutheran Theol. Sem. Saskatoon, Sask., 1913
Lu·ther C. \'lü·thər-\ Regina, Sask., junior, 1921

Mc·Gill U. \mə·'gil-\ Montreal, P.Q., 1821
Mc·Mas·ter Divinity C. \mək·'mas·tər-\ Hamilton, Ont., 1957
McMaster U. Hamilton, Ont., 1887
Mail·let, C. \-mà·yā\ Saint-Basile, N.B., 1949
Manitoba, U. of Winnipeg, 1877
Manitoba Law Sch. Winnipeg, 1914
Mar·gue·rite–Bour·geoys, C. \-màr·gə·rit·bùr·zhwä\ Montreal, P.Q., 1908
Marguerite d'You·ville, C. \-dyü·vil\ Hull, P.Q., 1945
Marguerite d'Youville, Inst. Montreal, P.Q., 1934

Mar·i·a·nop·o·lis C. \,mer·ē·ə·'näp·(ə·)ləs-, ,mar-\ Montreal, P.Q., 1943
Ma·rie–Anne, C. \-mà·rē·än\ Ahuntsic, Montreal, P.Q., 1932
Marie de France, C. \-də·fräⁿs\ Montreal, P.Q., 1939
Marie–de–la–Pré·sen·ta·tion, C. \-də·là·prā·zäⁿ·tä·syōⁿ\ Drummondville, P.Q., 1955
Marie de l'In·car·na·tion, C. \-də·laⁿ·kàr·nä·syōⁿ\ Trois-Rivières, P.Q., 1697
Ma·rie–Im·ma·cu·lée, Sém. Ob·lat de \-ò·blà·də·mà·rē·ē·mà·kǖ·lā\ Chambly, P.Q., 1926
Marie–Mé·dia·trice, C. \-mā·dyà·tris\ Hull, P.Q., 1938
Maritime C. of Pharmacy Halifax, N.S., 1911
Maritime Sch. of Social Work Halifax, N.S., 1941
Mé·de·cine Vé·té·ri·naire, L'É·cole \lā·kòl·met·sin·vā·tā·rē·ner\ St. Hyacinthe, P.Q., 1886
Medicine Hat Junior C. Medicine Hat, Alta., 1965
Memorial U. of Newfoundland St. John's, 1925
Mennonite Brethren C. of Arts Winnipeg, Man., 1944
Monc·ton, U. de \-də·'məŋ(k)·tən\ N.B., 1864
Mont·ré·al, C. de \-də·mōⁿ·rā·àl\ P.Q., 1767
Montréal, U. de P.Q., 1876
Montreal Diocesan Theol. C. P.Q., 1873
Mont–St.–Lou·is, C. \-mōⁿ·saⁿ·lwē\ Montreal, P.Q., 1888
Mount Al·li·son U. \-'al·ə·sən-\ Sackville, N.B., 1839
Mount Roy·al C. \-'ròi(·ə)l-\ Calgary, Alta., junior, 1910
Mount St. Ber·nard C. \-'bər·nərd-\ Antigonish, N.S., 1883
Mount St. Vin·cent U. \-'vin(t)·sənt-\ Halifax, N.S., 1873
Mu·sique, École de \-də·mǖ·zik\ Edmundston, N.B., 1950

New Brunswick, U. of Fredericton, 1785
Ni·co·let, Sém. de \-də·nē·kò·lā\ Nicolet, P.Q., 1801
Nipissing C. North Bay, Ont., 1967
Nor·male Se·con·daire, École \-nòr·màl·sə·gōⁿ·der\ Montreal, P.Q., 1941
North American Baptist C. South Edmonton, Alta., 1939
No·tre–Dame, C. \-nó·trə·dàm, -nót·dàm\ Prince Albert, Sask., 1958
No·tre Dame C. \,nōt·ər·'dām-\ Wilcox, Sask., 1933
No·tre–Dame d'A·ca·die, C. \-nó·trə·dàm·dà·kà·dē, -nót·dàm-\ Moncton, N.B., 1943
Notre–Dame de Belle·vue, C. \-də·bel·vǖ\ Quebec, P.Q., 1937
Notre–Dame de Grâce, Sco·las·ti·cat \skó·là·stē·kà·nó·trə·dàm·də·gräs, -nót·dàm-\ Hull, P.Q., 1940
Notre–Dame de l'As·somp·tion, C. \-də·là·sōⁿp·syōⁿ\ Nicolet, P.Q., 1937
Notre–Dame du Per·pé·tu·el Se·cours, Sém. \-dǖ·per·pā·tw'el·sə·kùr\ Moncton, N.B., 1956
Notre–Dame du St.–Ro·saire, Sco·las·ti·cat \skó·là·stē·kà·nó·trə·dàm·dǖ·saⁿ·rō·zer, -nót·dàm-\ Rimouski, P.Q., 1957
No·tre Dame U. of Nelson \,nōt·ər·'dàm-\ B.C., 1950
Nova Scotia Agricultural C. Truro, junior, 1905
Nova Scotia C. of Art Halifax, 1887
Nova Scotia Technical C. Halifax, 1907

Oka, Inst. Agri·cole d' \-à·grē·kòl·dò·kà\ La Trappe, P.Q., 1893
Ontario Agricultural C. Guelph, 1874
Ontario Bible C. Toronto, 1935
Ontario Veterinary C. Guelph, 1862
Op·to·mé·trie, École d' \-dòp·tò·mā·trē\ Montreal, P.Q., 1910
Os·goode Hall Law Sch. \'äz·,gùd-\ Toronto, Ont., 1872
Ot·ta·wa, Grand Sém. d' \grän·sā·mē·ner·dò·tà·wà\ Ont., 1847
Ottawa, Pe·tit Sém. d' \pə·tē-\ Ont., 1925
Ottawa, U. d' Ont., 1848

Pé·da·go·gie Fa·mi·liale, Inst. de \-də·pā·dà·gò·zhē·fà·mē·lyàl\ Montreal, P.Q., 1943
Pé·da·go·gique, Inst. \-pā·dà·gò·zhik\ Montreal, P.Q., 1926
Pédagogique St.–Georges, Inst. \-saⁿ·zhòrzh\ Laval des Rapides, P.Q., 1929
Phi·la·thea C. \fə·'lā·thē·ə-\ London, Ont., 1946
Phi·lo·so·phie, Sém. de \-də·fē·lò·zò·fē\ Montreal, P.Q., 1876
Pine Hill Divinity Hall Halifax, N.S., 1820
Po·ly·tech·nique, École \-pò·lē·tek·nik\ Montreal, P.Q., 1873
Pontifical Inst. of Mediaeval Studies Toronto, Ont., 1929
Presbyterian C. of Montreal P.Q., 1865
Prince Edward Island, U. of Charlottetown, 1969
Provincial Inst. of Tech. and Art Calgary, Alta., junior, 1916

Qué·bec, Acad. de \-də·kā·bek\ Quebec, P.Q., 1862
Québec, Sém. de Quebec, P.Q., 1663
Queen's C. \'kwēnz-\ St. John's, Nfld., 1841
Queen's Theol. C. Kingston, Ont., 1912
Queen's U. at Kingston Ont., 1841

Red Deer Junior C. Red Deer, Alta., 1964
Re·gis C. \'rē·jəs-\ Toronto, Ont., 1930
Ren·i·son C. \'ren·ə·sən-\ Waterloo, Ont., 1959
Ri·mous·ki, Sém. de \-də·rē·mü·skē\ Rimouski, P.Q., 1855
Rou·yn, C. Clas·sique de \-klà·sik·də·rwaⁿ\ Rouyn, P.Q., 1948
Royal Military C. of Canada Kingston, Ont., 1876
Royal Roads Victoria, B.C., junior, 1942

Sa·cré–Coeur, C. du \-dǖ·sà·krā·kœr\ Sherbrooke, P.Q., 1945
Sacré–Coeur, Sco·las·ti·cat du \skó·là·stē·kà·dǖ\ Lebret, Sask., 1926
Sacré–Coeur, Sém. du St. Victor, P.Q., 1910
Sacred Heart, Convent of the Halifax, N.S., junior, 1849
Saint–Alex·an·dre, C. \-saⁿ·tà·lek·säⁿdr\ Limbour, P.Q., 1912

Saint-Al·phonse, Sém. \-saⁿ-tȧl-fōⁿs\ Aylmer, P.Q., 1896
Saint An·drew's C. \sänt-'an-ˌdrüz-, sənt-\ Winnipeg, Man., 1946
Saint Andrew's C. Saskatoon, Sask., 1912
Saint Andrew's Hall Vancouver, B.C., 1957
Saint-An·toine, Sém. \-saⁿ-tän-twȧn\ Quebec, P.Q., 1902
Saint-Augustin, Sém \-saⁿ-tȯ-gū̄-staⁿ\ Cap-Rouge, P.Q., 1965
Saint Au·gus·tine's C. \-ȯ-'gəs-tənz-, -ə-'gəs-\ Scarborough, Ont., 1913
Saint-Bo·ni·face, C. de \-də-saⁿ-bȯ-nē-fȧs\ St. Boniface, Man., 1818
Saint Bride's C. \sänt-'brīdz-, sənt\ Littledale, Nfld., 1884
Saint-De·nis, C. \-saⁿ-də-nē\ Montreal, P.Q., 1950
Sainte-Anne, C. \-saⁿ-tän\ Church Point, N.S., 1890
Sainte-Anne-de-la-Po·ca·tière, C. \-də-là-pȯ-kȧ-tyer\ Ste. Anne de la Pocatière, P.Q., 1827
Sainte-Croix, C. \-saⁿ-tə-krwä\ Montreal, P.Q., 1929
Sainte-Croix, Sém. St. Laurent, P.Q., 1899
Sainte-Ma·rie, C. \-saⁿt-má-rē\ Montreal, P.Q., 1848
Sainte-Marie, Sém. Shawinigan, P.Q., 1947
Sainte-Thé·rèse, Sém. de \-də-saⁿt-tā-rez\ Sainte-Thérèse-de-Blainville, P.Q., 1825
Saint Fran·cis Xa·vi·er U. \sänt-ˌfran(t)-sə-'zā-vē-ər-, sənt-\ Antigonish, N.S., 1853
Saint-Georges, Sém. de \-də-saⁿ-zhȯrzh\ Saint-Georges, Beauce, Que., 1946
Saint-Hya·cinthe, Sém. de \-də-saⁿ-tyȧ-saⁿt\ St. Hyacinthe, P.Q., 1811
Saint-Jean, C. \-saⁿ-zhän\ Edmonton, Alta., 1908
Saint-Jean, C. de Saint-Jean, P.Q., 1911
Saint-Jean, C. Mi·li·taire Roy·al de \-mē-lē-ter-rwä-yȧl-də\ Saint Jean, P.Q., 1952
Saint-Jean, Sco·las·ti·cat \skȯ-là-stē-kȧ-\ Ottawa, Ont., 1902
Saint-Jean-Eudes, Ex·ter·nat Clas·sique \es-ter-nȧ-klä-sik-saⁿ-zhäⁿ-nœ̄d\ Quebec, P.Q., 1937
Saint Je·rome's C., U. of \-ˌsänt-jə-'rōmz-, -sənt-\ Waterloo, Ont., 1864
Saint John's C. \-'jänz-\ Winnipeg, Man., 1829
Saint-Jo·seph, Sém. \-saⁿ-zhō-zef\ Mont Laurier, P.Q., 1915
Saint-Joseph, Sém. Trois-Rivières, P.Q., 1663
Saint-Joseph, C. Moncton, N.B., 1864
Saint Jo·seph's C. \sänt-'jō-zəfs-, sənt- *also* -səfs-\ Edmonton, Alta., 1927
Saint Joseph's C. Yorkton, Sask., 1919
Saint-Lau·rent, C. \-saⁿ-lȯ-räⁿ\ St. Laurent, P.Q., 1847
Saint-Louis, C. \-saⁿ-lwē\ Edmundston, N.B., 1946
Saint Mark's C. \sänt-'märks-, sənt-\ Vancouver, B.C., 1956
Saint Mar·tha's Sch. of Nursing \-'där-thəz-\ Antigonish, N.S., 1933
Saint Mary's U. Halifax, N.S., 1802
Saint-Mau·rice, C. \-saⁿ-mȯ-ris\ St. Hyacinthe, P.Q., 1935
Saint Mi·chael's C., U. of \sänt-'mī-kəlz-, sənt-\ Toronto, Ont., 1852
Saint Pat·rick's C. \-'pa-triks-\ Ottawa, Ont., 1932
Saint-Paul, C. \-saⁿ-pȯl\ Montreal, P.Q., 1957
Saint Paul's C. \sänt-'pȯlz-, sənt-\ Winnipeg, Man., 1926
Saint Paul's United C. Waterloo, Ont., 1961
Saint Paul U. Ottawa, Ont., 1848
Saint Pe·ter's C. \-'pēt-ərz-\ Muenster, Sask., junior, 1922
Saint-Sa·cre·ment, Sém. des Pères du \-dā-per-dū̄-saⁿ-sȧ-krə-mäⁿ\.Terrebonne, P.Q., 1902

Saints-Apô·tres, Sém. des \-dā-saⁿ-zȧ-pōtrᵃ\ Côte Sainte Catherine, Comté de Laprairie, P.Q., 1952
Saint Ste·phen's C. \sänt-'stē-vənz-, sənt-\ Edmonton, Alta., 1903
Saint Thom·as C. \-'täm-əs-\ North Battleford, Sask., 1932
Saint Thomas More C. \-ˌtäm-ə-'smō(ə)r-, -'smȯ(ə)r-\ Saskatoon, Sask., 1936
Saint Thomas U. Fredericton, N.B., 1876
Saint-Via·teur, C. \-saⁿ-vyȧ-tœr\ Montreal, P.Q., 1951
Saskatchewan, U. of Saskatoon, 1907
Sciences Do·mes·tiques, École des \-dā-syäⁿs-dȯ-mes-tik\ Sherbrooke, P.Q., 1956
Sherbrooke, Sém. de P.Q., 1875
Sherbrooke, U. de P.Q., 1954
Simon Fra·ser U. \ˌsī-mən-'frā-zər-\ Burnaby, B.C., 1963
Sir George Wil·liams U. \-'jȯrj-'wil-yəmz-\ Montreal, P.Q., 1873
Spi·ri·tain de Sainte-Foy, Sém. \-spē-rē-taⁿ-də-saⁿt-fwä\ Ste. Foy, P.Q., 1940
Sta·nis·las, C. \-stȧ-nis-läs\ Montreal, P.Q., 1938
Sudbury, U. de Ont., 1913

Thom·as More Inst. for Adult Education \ˌtäm-ə-'smō(ə)r-, -'smȯ(ə)r-\ Montreal, P.Q., 1948
Thorne·loe U. \'thȯrn-(ˌ)lō-\ Sudbury, Ont., 1961
Toronto, U. of Ont., 1827
Toronto Bible C. Ont., 1894
Trent U. \'trent-\ Peterborough, Ont., 1960
Trinity C., U. of Toronto, Ont., 1852
Trois-Ri·vières, Sém. de \-də-trwä-rē-vyer\ Trois-Rivières, P.Q., 1860

Union C. of British Columbia Vancouver, 1927
United C. Winnipeg, Man., 1871
United Theol. C. of Montreal P.Q., 1926
Ur·su·lines, C. des \-dā-zür-sū̄-lin\ Rimouski, P.Q., 1906

Val·ley·field, Sém. de \-də-'val-ē-ˌfēld\ Valleyfield, P.Q., 1893
Victoria, U. of Victoria, B.C., 1902
Victoria U. Toronto, Ont., 1836
Vic·to·ria·ville, C. de \-də-ˌvik-'tȯr-ē-ə-ˌvil, -'tȯr-\ Victoriaville, P.Q., 1872
Vo·ca·tions Tar·dives, Sém. des \-dā-vȯ-kä-syōⁿ-tȧr-div\ Nicolet, P.Q., 1956

Waterloo, U. of Waterloo, Ont., 1959
Waterloo Lutheran U. Waterloo, Ont., 1910
Western Ontario, U. of London, 1878
Windsor, U. of Ont., 1963
Winnipeg, U. of Man., 1871
Winnipeg Bible C. Man., 1925
Wyc·liffe C. \'wik-ˌlif-, -ləf-\ Toronto, Ont., 1877

York U. \'yȯ(ə)rk-\ Toronto, Ont., 1959

ə abut; ᵊ kitten; ər further; a back; ā bake; ä cot, cart; aù out; ch chin; e less; ē easy; g gift; i trip; ī life
j joke; ŋ sing; ō flow; ȯ flaw; ȯi coin; th thin; t̲h̲ this; ü loot; ù foot; y yet; yü few; yù furious; zh vision
ᵊ F table; ȧ F bac; ḵ G ich, Buch; ⁿ F vin; œ F bœuf; œ̄ F feu; ᵫ G füllen; ū̄ F rue; ʸ F digne \dēnʸ\, nuit \nwʸē\

INDEX

	PAGE
Abbreviations Used in this Work	22a
Abbreviations, Vocabulary of	1042
Address, Forms of	1173
Alphabet (table)	26
American Colleges and Universities	1206
Apostrophe, Use of	1198
Arbitrary Signs and Symbols	1050
Attributive Nouns	9a
Beaufort Scale (table)	75
Bells, Ship's (table)	78
Bible (table)	82
Biographical Names	1053
Brackets, Use of	1197
Braille Alphabet (table)	101
Canadian Colleges and Universities	1221
Capitalization	9a, 1204
Centered Period, Use of	7a
Chemical Elements (table)	267
Christian Names	1177
Colleges and Universities in the United States and Canada	1206
Colon, Use of	11a, 12a, 1196
Combining Forms	14a
Commas, Use of	1194, 1195, 1196
Common English Given Names	1177
Compounds	1199
Cross-references	13a
Dash, Use of	1197
Divisions in Pronunciations	18a
Easter Dates (table)	261
Ellipsis, Use of	1197
Etymology	10a
Exclamation Point, Use of	1194
Explanatory Notes	7a
Foreign Words	19a, 1205
Forms of Address	1173
Gazetteer, Pronouncing	1092
Given Names	1177
Guide to Pronunciation	15a
Hyphen, Use of	1198
Indo-European Languages (table)	429
Inflectional Forms	8a
Italicization	1205
Labels	8a
Marks of Punctuation (see also *symbols*)	1193
Measures and Weights (table)	525
Men's Names	1177
Metric System (table)	534
Money (table)	546
Months of the Principal Calendars (table)	118
Morse Code (table)	552
Names of Men	1177
Names of Women	1179
Notes, Explanatory	7a
Numbers (table)	579
Parenthesis, Use of	1197
Period, Use of	7a, 1193
Periodic (table)	628
Planets (table)	647
Plurals	1191
Pronouncing Gazetteer	1092
Pronunciation, Guide to	15a
Pronunciation Symbols	15a
Proofreaders' Marks	1051
Proper Names	14a
Punctuation	1193
Question Mark, Use of	1194
Quotation Marks, Use of	1198
Radio Frequencies (table)	705
Rhymes, Vocabulary of	1182
Run-ons	13a
Semicolon, Use of	1196
Sense Division	12a
Ship's Bells (table)	78
Signs and Symbols	1050
Spelling	1187
Standard Time (table)	853
Symbolic Colon	11a
Symbols	15a, 1051
Synonymies	13a
Time, Standard (table)	853
Type (table)	961
Universities in the United States and Canada	1206
Verbal Illustrations	12a
Vocabulary Entry	14a
Volume Formulas (table)	997
Women's Names	1179
Zodiac (table)	1040

OTHER FINE DICTIONARIES

PREPARED BY
The Merriam-Webster Editorial Staff

WEBSTER'S THIRD NEW INTERNATIONAL DICTIONARY
UNABRIDGED

From the first word to the last—in contents, size, shape, and design—this is a completely new unabridged dictionary. It presents the English language in a new modern way to give you the most useful, understandable, and enjoyable fund of word information ever available and covering every area of human thought. A masterpiece of modern defining, every definition is given in a single phrase of precise meaning. Thousands of quotations from well-known writers demonstrate word usage to make meanings clearly understandable. 450,000 entries, including 100,000 new words or meanings never before covered in the unabridged Merriam-Webster. 3,000 terms newly illustrated with twenty true-to-life plates in glorious color. Simplified pronunciation key, clear and informative etymologies, 1,000 synonym articles. This is one of the most remarkable literary achievements of all time. 2,728 pages.

WEBSTER'S NEW DICTIONARY OF SYNONYMS

This completely new word guide is the only thesaurus with words defined, discriminated, and illustrated with thousands of quotations that help you use the right word in the right place. Alphabetically arranged. Quicker to use and easier to understand. When you need a thesaurus, this is the book to ask for.

WEBSTER'S ELEMENTARY DICTIONARY

The only dictionary specifically written for boys and girls in the fourth, fifth, sixth, and seventh grades. 18,000 vocabulary entries selected for elementary-school needs—and to help the child at home. 1,600 pictures to increase understanding and interest. Large, clear, easily readable type with simplified pronunciation. Sturdily bound.

WEBSTER'S NEW PRACTICAL SCHOOL DICTIONARY

Especially designed to meet teen-age needs in junior high school and higher grades. 45,000 entries and 800 illustrations. Sturdily bound.

WEBSTER'S BIOGRAPHICAL DICTIONARY

Concise information about the lives of more than 40,000 men and women from all countries, every period of history. 1,700 pages.

WEBSTER'S GEOGRAPHICAL DICTIONARY

The greatest fund of geographical information obtainable in a single volume. 40,000 of the world's important places. 1,326 pages.

G. & C. MERRIAM COMPANY, Publishers, Springfield, Mass.